KU-997-701

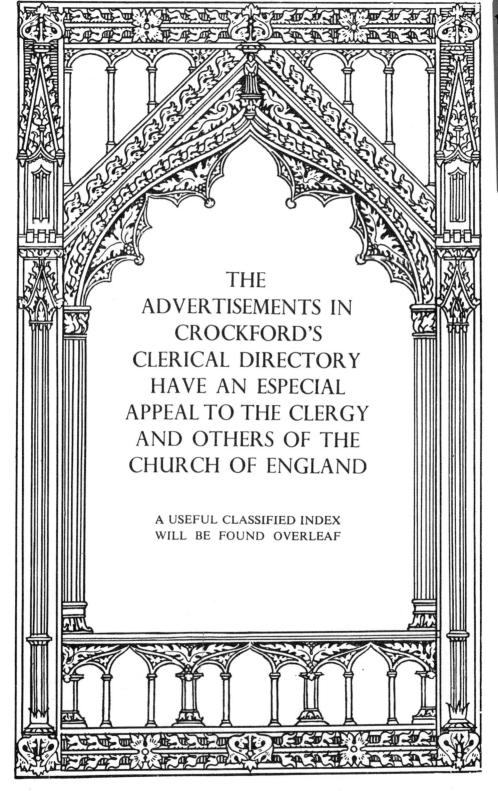

THE ADVERTISEMENTS IN CROCKFORD'S CLERICAL DIRECTORY HAVE AN ESPECIAL APPEAL TO THE CLERGY AND OTHERS OF THE CHURCH OF ENGLAND

A USEFUL CLASSIFIED INDEX
WILL BE FOUND OVERLEAF

CLASSIFIED INDEX TO ADVERTISEMENTS

☞ *The figures at the end of each name denote the page upon which the advertisement may be found*

THE MINISTRY OF THE WORD

through daily readings, guides to new Lectionary, group courses, soundstrips, recorded talks and 'starters', confirmation readings . . . *Send for list of Bible Aids available*

The Bible Reading Fellowship

St. Michael's House 2 Elizabeth Street
London SW1W 9RQ
Telephone: 01-730 9181

THE PRAYER BOOK SOCIETY

40 GREAT SMITH STREET, LONDON SW1P 3BU

President: SIR JOHN COLVILLE, C.B., C.V.O.

Vice-Presidents:
The Rt. Hon. The LORD SUDELEY
The Rev. PREBENDARY R. N. HETHERINGTON
The Rt. Hon. LORD GLENAMARA, P.C., C.H.
Professor DAVID MARTIN   ELDON GRIFFITHS, Esq., M.P.
Immediate Past President: The Rt. Hon. The EARL of ONSLOW

Chairman: R. J. R. TREFUSIS, Esq.

Vice-Chairman: C. A. ANTHONY KILMISTER, Esq.

Joint Hon. Secretaries: Miss E. M. GWYER and Dr. ROGER HOMAN

Hon. Treasurer: Colonel H. D. ROGERS, O.B.E.

Trustees:
Miss K. E. YOUNG, PETER FLEETWOOD-HESKETH, Esq., L. G. PINE, Esq.

Churchmen of widely differing forms of churchmanship united in 1975 to build this nation-wide network of people pledged:

* To uphold the worship and doctrine of the Church of England as enshrined in the Book of Common Prayer

* To encourage the use of the Book of Common Prayer as a major element in the worshipping life of the Church of England

The Prayer Book Society

* does NOT propagate Prayer Book fundamentalism but believes a modest amount of flexibility in usage is both sensible and to be desired

* does NOT seek to suppress the Alternative Services but is, however, concerned at the extent to which the Alternative Services have displaced the Prayer Book and is alarmed by the extensive pastoral problems which often result from an unfeeling implementation of liturgical change

The Prayer Book Society aims

* To encourage the use of the Book of Common Prayer for the training of Ordinands and Confirmands

* To spread knowledge of the Book of Common Prayer and the doctrine contained therein and above all to see it *used*

Please support* THE PRAYER BOOK SOCIETY: *write now to:

40 GREAT SMITH STREET, LONDON SW1P 3BU

i.a.

Formed over 25 years ago by a group of ileostomists and members of the medical profession, the Ileostomy Association was the first ostomy organisation in this country.

An estimated 20,000 people in the UK have had an ileostomy, but because of the psychological barriers that this can present and its 'delicate' nature, public awareness of the subject and the association is still limited.

e.g.

Ileostomy surgery is a complex technique to remove the large intestine and create an artificial outlet – the ileostomy. As a result of such surgery many people have been given the opportunity to continue to lead a full and normal life. Which means that you have probably met an ileostomist at some time, without even realising it.

o.k.

The Ileostomy Association is a mutual-aid group that exists primarily to assist and advise those people who have had, or are about to have the operation; to help them with all aspects of their rehabilitation, including their social activities and various relationships.

We do this in a number of ways that include members meetings, equipment exhibitions and a quarterly journal of news, views, correspondence and information.

n.b.

The Ileostomy Association helps those people who need it most, but in addition, a considerable amount of time and effort is spent on research into the different aspects of living with an ileostomy, and the illnesses that can cause it.

As a registered charity supported by voluntary workers and voluntary funds there is always a limit to our resources. To be able to continue with our work we are always grateful for all forms of assistance.

If you can help, or would like further information, please contact us at the following address:

ia

ILEOSTOMY ASSOCIATION OF GREAT BRITAIN AND IRELAND
Amblehurst House, Chobham, Woking, Surrey. GU24 8PZ.

A. W. ELLIOTT

(Steeplejacks) & Co. Ltd.

Radford Road, New Basford, NOTTINGHAM. NG7 7EB

'Phone: Nottingham 787235

After Hours. 292682

CHURCH RESTORATION

INSPECTIONS of Church Towers and Spires, &c. Reports submitted with Photographic Evidence.

RESTORATION of Masonry and Brickwork.

RESHINGLING, Slating and Tiling.

TREATMENT of Timbers to prevent Ravages of the Death Watch Beetle and Dry Rot.

LIGHTNING CONDUCTORS installed, tested and repaired.

INTERIOR DECORATING and cleansing by Vacuum process.

WIRE GUARDS fitted to Spire and Tower lights to exclude birds and protect Stained Glass windows.

FLAGMASTS—New installations complete. Existing Masts fully maintained.

REGILDING and Repairs to Weathercocks, Vanes, &c. New Vanes supplied to any design.

STAINED GLASS WINDOWS

Memorial Windows in Traditional or Contemporary style individually designed by experienced Artists

Designs and estimates submitted on request

WINDOW GUARDS
We can protect your valuable Stained Glass Windows against vandalism and/or accidental damage.
REPAIRS and RESTORATION
A SPECIALITY

Please write for Illustrated Booklet from

G. MAILE & SON

DAVID G. MAILE, M.A.

10–12 THE BOROUGH, CANTERBURY, KENT

Telephone: Canterbury 61296 *Founded 1785*

CLAYTON & BELL

M. C. FARRAR BELL *Fellow of the British Society of Master Glass Painters*

DESIGNERS

AND MAKERS OF

STAINED
GLASS
WINDOWS

EXPERTS
IN RESTORING
OLD GLASS

HADDENHAM
AYLESBURY
BUCKS

Telephone: Haddenham 271

ARTISTS IN STAINED GLASS

DESIGNERS AND MAKERS OF WINDOWS IN ALL TREATMENTS OF STAINED GLASS

NEW DESIGN REQUIRES BOLDNESS OF VISION AS WELL AS APPRECIATION OF TRADITION. OUR DESIGNERS ARE ALWAYS AVAILABLE FOR CONSULTATION AT THE CHURCH

CELTIC STUDIOS
5 PROSPECT PLACE
SWANSEA SA1 1QP. TEL. 54833

CANADIAN REPRESENTATIVE:
MRS. RONALD MATTHEWS, 54 QUEEN MARY'S DRIVE
TORONTO, ONTARIO. M8X 1S4

Goddard & Gibbs Studios Ltd.

STAINED GLASS ARTISTS & CRAFTSMEN

We are the largest stained glass studios in the United Kingdom specialising in:

Design and making of stained glass windows in traditional or modern designs using the beauty of hand-made glass,

Repair and restoration of all types of stained and leaded glass,
window screens composed of galvanised wire mesh or polycarbonate sheet.

Designs and estimates are without obligation, and help and advice is always available.

41–49 KINGSLAND ROAD,
LONDON E2 8AD
Telephone: 01–739–6563

STAINED GLASS

WINDOWS DESIGNED AND MADE BY EXPERIENCED ARTISTS AND CRAFTSMEN IN TRADITIONAL OR MODERN TECHNIQUES

RESTORATION OF OLD GLASS ALSO A SPECIALITY

Write or telephone:

JOHN HARDMAN STUDIOS

LIGHTWOODS PARK, HAGLEY ROAD WEST, WARLEY, WEST MIDLANDS B67 5DP

TEL. 021 429 7609

RYDER & AMIES

22 Kings Parade
CAMBRIDGE, CB2 1SP
Tele: 0223 350371

Makers of Clerical, Academical, Legal and Municipal Robes.

Clergy Cassocks from stock, or made to measure.

Albs, Surplices, Shirts, Collars, Vestocks, Scarves, etc. all at keenest prices.

Choir robes to order.

Price lists and cloth patterns sent by return post.

WIPPELL'S

J. WIPPELL & COMPANY LIMITED
Head Office: P.O.Box 1, Buller Road,
EXETER EX4 1DE. Tel. 0392–54234
LONDON SW1P 3QB: 11 Tufton Street,
Tel. 01–222 4528
MANCHESTER M2 6AG: 24 King Street
Tel. 061–834 7967

WIPPELL'S ARE MAKERS OF ROBES FOR THE CLERGY AND CHOIR AND CLERICAL OUTFITTERS OF REPUTE

WIPPELL MOWBRAY ARE SPECIALISTS IN CHURCH FURNISHING IN WOODWORK, METALWORK, STAINED GLASS, EMBROIDERIES AND ALSO SUPPLIERS OF SACRISTY NEEDS

WIPPELL MOWBRAY (CHURCH FURNISHING LTD.) services available at the above addresses as well as at Margaret Street, London W1N 7LB, Oxford, Cambridge, Birmingham.

WIPPELL MOWBRAY

Academic Robe and Gown Manufacturers Ltd
62 FITZWILLIAM STREET, HUDDERSFIELD HD1 5BB
Welcome your enquiries for:
Clergy and Choir/Servers Robes, Cassocks, Cottas, Surplices etc.
Applique embroidery on Vestments, Stoles, Frontals and Academic Gowns.
Catalogue on request.
Our showroom is open from 9 am to 4 pm daily.
Please telephone Mrs Dickin at (0484) 45459.

GRAHAM D MARTIN
interior design consultant
...invites enquiries from clergy and church councils requiring professional assistance with the re-planning and re-furnishing of their places of worship
55 UXBRIDGE ROAD · RICKMANSWORTH · HERTS

WATTS & CO.

ESTABLISHED FOR OVER 100 YEARS AND FAMOUS FOR FINE VESTMENTS AND QUALITY FURNISHINGS.

WE CAN GIVE ON-SITE CONSULTATIONS ON ALL ASPECTS OF CHURCH FURNISHING INCLUDING STATUARY AND ORNAMENTAL WORK.

OUR CRAFTSMEN ARE SPECIALISED IN THE DESIGN AND EXECUTION OF SILVERWARE, METALWORK AND WOODWORK AND ALL REPAIRS AND RESTORATION.

ON DISPLAY AT OUR SHOWROOM WE ALSO HAVE A WIDE SELECTION OF FABRICS AND TRIMMINGS BY THE YARD AND A RANGE OF READY-MADE CASSOCKS COTTAS, ALBS, &c.

WATTS & CO.

7 TUFTON STREET, LONDON, SW1P 3QE
TELEPHONE 01-222 7169/2893

THE HOUSE OF VANHEEMS

BROOMFIELD WORKS, 6 BROOMFIELD PLACE, EALING, LONDON W13 9LB

Established 1793

ROBEMAKERS, CLERICAL TAILORS & CHURCH FURNISHERS

Clerical Tailoring
Clergy Cassocks, Surplices,
Cloaks, Hoods, Scarves,
Vestments, etc

Cut and made on the premises; first class materials and workmanship, at keenly competitive prices

Academic Gowns, Preaching Gowns,
Clerical Collars, Stocks and Shirts,
Bespoke Suits and Overcoats.

Choir Robes
Cassocks, Surplices and Gowns

Church Furnishings
Altar Frontals, Linen Cloths,
Pulpit Falls, Hymn Boards,
Hassocks, Flags, etc.

Catalogue and fabric samples upon request

Church Silver and Brassware
Chalices, Ciboria,
Wafer Boxes,
Vases, Candlesticks,
Altar and Processional Crosses, etc.

Please write for details stating your interests

BROOMFIELD WORKS, BROOMFIELD PLACE, EALING, LONDON, W13 9LB. Telephone 567 7885

CHURCH SILVER

CHALICES · CIBORIA · FLAGONS
CRUETS · POCKET PYXES
SICK CALL SETS · VIATICUM
WAFER BOXES · REGILDING

Our 44-page CHURCH SILVER Catalogue available free to the Clergy on request

The Canterbury
Height $6\frac{3}{4}''$ (Design 2344)

The Salisbury
Height $7\frac{5}{8}''$ (Design 2349)

AUMBRY SAFES

CHURCH METALWORK

ALMS DISHES · ALTAR SETS
BRACKET LAMPS · PASCHALS
CROSSES · CANDLESTICKS
FONT EWERS · VASES · BOWLS
SANCTUARY LAMPS · AUMBRY
MEMORIAL TABLETS

Our 40-page Catalogue of Church brasswork and Aumbry safes available free to the Clergy on request

CHURCH CAUSTIN **METALWORK**

CAUSTIN BROS. LIMITED

ACTUAL MANUFACTURERS - DESIGNERS - SUPPLIERS

LONDON SHOWROOM AND WORKS

188a Warham Street (off Camberwell New Road) London SE5 0SX

Telephone: 01-735 8329. Showroom Hours: 10 a.m.—4 p.m. Monday to Friday. Closed Saturday

For Quality at a modest price—

***Choir/Servers' Robes**

* Frontals
* Cassock-albs
* Vestments
* Copes, Stoles
* Cassocks and Shirts
* Fabrics and Trlmmings

ST. MARTIN VESTMENT LTD.

Lutton, Spalding, Lincs. PE12 9LR

Telephone: Holbeach (0406) 362386

THE CHURCH PULPIT YEAR BOOK

A Complete Set of Expository Sermon Outlines for the Sundays of the Year, also for Saints' Days and Special Occasions.

Available from

CHANSITOR PUBLICATIONS LTD.

146 Queen Victoria Street,
London EC4V 4BY
Tel : 01-248 6085

N. P. Mander Ltd.

(incorporating Henry Speechly and Sons, established 1860)

St. Peter's Organ Works,
London E 2.
01 739 4747

A firm entirely owned and run by the family which founded it.

Organ builders to St. Paul's, Canterbury, and other Cathedrals and churches in many parts of the World.

Resident serviceman in NIGERIA.

Tuning, rebuilding and repairs carried out in any part of the United Kingdom.

BISHOP & SON, *Organ Builders*

58 Beethoven Street, London, W10 4LG, and at Ipswich

Telephones: LONDON 01–969 4328, IPSWICH 55165

BUILDERS OF ORGANS IN ALL PARTS OF THE WORLD

ESTABLISHED IN 1794

We shall have pleasure in giving expert advice on all matters connected with organs

CHARLES HIGHAM (SPCK)

Secondhand Theological Bookshop

SPCK HEADQUARTERS
HOLY TRINITY CHURCH, MARYLEBONE ROAD
LONDON NW1 4DU

Telephone: 01–387 5282

SECONDHAND THEOLOGICAL BOOKS BOUGHT AND SOLD

IN ADDITION, SPCK BOOKSHOPS AT BATH, BRADFORD, BRISTOL, CANTERBURY, DURHAM, EXETER, JERSEY, LEICESTER, LINCOLN, NORWICH, WINCHESTER AND YORK NOW HAVE SECONDHAND DEPARTMENTS

J.G.Ford & Son

Altar Wines

J. G. Ford & Son, established in 1838 will supply the needs of your Parish at reasonable prices.

Excellent wines, pure and certificated, supplied in bottles and five-gallon dispensers.

Prompt and free delivery service.

Please ask for our Candle list.

TELEPHONE	OFFICES AND CELLARS	DEPOTS
01–262 6364	16 Paddington Green	Oxford
01–723 2223	London W2 ILJ	Cambridge

WITH AN UNBROKEN HISTORY OF OVER 400 YEARS THE WHITECHAPEL FOUNDRY HAS A WEALTH OF EXPERIENCE TO OFFER THOSE SEEKING THE INSTALLATION OR RESTORATION OF CHURCH BELLS

Whitechapel Bell Foundry Ltd.

32–34 WHITECHAPEL RD., LONDON, E1 1DY

Telephone: 01–247 2599 *Cables:* CHIMINGS, LONDON

THEIR SOUND IS GONE OUT INTO ALL LANDS

John Taylor & Co, (Bellfounders) Ltd.

The Bell Foundry,
Loughborough,
Leics. LE11 1AR

Tel: (0509) 212241

TAYLOR LOUGHBOROUGH

Do not hesitate to call us for the complete service in church bell work.

Non-alcoholic Communion Wines

We have been producers of these and other non-alcoholic beverages since 1858. It was in that year, during the early days of temperance reformation, that Mr. Frank Wright founded this company. Mr. Wright, a teetotaller, was concerned that, in spite of practising abstinence from alcohol, he and other teetotallers were called upon to partake of it during Holy Communion. Having seen in some ancient writings certain references to the preparation of unfermented wine, Mr. Wright, a chemist by profession, spent some years developing a product which was to be the forerunner of our now world-famous Number 1 and Number 5 brands of non-alcoholic wines.

Write or telephone us for details of your local stockists or our direct sales price list

FRANK WRIGHT MUNDY & CO LTD
Business Est. in 1858

Thomas Street House
Cirencester Gloucestershire GL7 2AX
Telephone: Cirencester 67807/8

Raising the Roof

may not be necessary
but YOUR Church needs
REGULAR GIVING
reviewed at least annually
to keep up with inflation

For all schemes contact

Church Finance Supplies Limited

RADLEY ROAD INDUSTRIAL ESTATE
ABINGDON OXON OX14 3SE Telephone 24488

OLD NATIVE CURIOS

Collector wishes to
buy old tribal objects and
old native curios of all kinds,
from Africa, the Pacific,
and the Americas.

Please write or telephone:

MRS L. A. BARNARD FINER
4 Heath Villas,
Vale of Health,
London NW3
Tel: 01-435 4191

Is there a Gay Christian in your congregation ?

Many people are seeking to reconcile
homosexuality with Christian beliefs.

The

GAY CHRISTIAN MOVEMENT

can help.

Experienced, trained counsellors & advisers, both clerical and lay, can assist with consultations and referrals. Publications are available, and there are local groups throughout the UK who would welcome serious enquiry.

interdenominational
women's and evangelical groups

GCM BM Box 6914, London WC1N 3XX
Telephone 01-283 5165

Make extra funds for your church

You can now offer people getting married the convenience of ordering their wedding stationery through your church.

Many churches are finding this an excellent and profitable means of raising money for either their own funds or to support other charities.

If your church is not taking advantage of this opportunity to raise substantial extra funds why not send off today, and without obligation, get the full details?

The range is exclusively available through the churches.

Designed for giving

Designed for Giving Ltd.,
Refuge House,
River Front,
Enfield,
Middx. EN1 3SZ.

PHILLIPS & DREW

STOCKBROKERS

Investment Management
and Advisory Services
for Charitable Funds

H. Harris Hughes
LEE HOUSE, LONDON WALL,
LONDON EC2Y 5AP
01–628 4444

MARLBOROUGH COLLEGE

Assistance with Fees for Children of Clergy

1. Marlborough College was founded as a school 'for the sons of clergy and others'.
2. Today girls are admitted as well as boys (6th Form only).
3. From the "Children of Clergy Fund" grants-in-aid are made to children of clergymen on grounds of need. This means that, while the basic fee for children of clergy is 85% of the full fee, most are admitted on fees substantially below that amount, and where home circumstances make a boarding school especially important, it is occasionally possible for the fee to be very small.
4. In addition, there are three closed competitive ('Foundation') Scholarships (value £500 to £100) for sons of clergymen each year.
5. Sons of clergymen may also enter for Open Scholarships, of which about ten are awarded annually (value full fees to £100).

Particulars from

The Registrar, Marlborough College, Wiltshire.

CRANLEIGH SCHOOL

Entrance Scholarships restricted to sons of Clergymen of the Church of England are offered annually and include one at full fees and Whately-Simmonds Awards of substantial value. Peek Foundation Bursaries of up to £400 p.a. are open to the sons of Clergy in the Dioceses of Winchester, Salisbury, Portsmouth and Guildford and are awarded on a boy's performance in the Common Entrance examination and interview. Apart from these Closed Awards, Open Scholarships are offered; these are one at full fees, one at two-thirds fees, one at half fees. Eight other awards at up to one quarter fees are also offered. All awards are fees-linked, increasing in value at the same percentage as the fees. Full details may be obtained from the Headmaster, Cranleigh School, Surrey.

CHRIST'S HOSPITAL

A competitive examination for boys at Christ's Hospital, Horsham, and for girls at Christ's Hospital, Hertford, is held annually in JANUARY.

Children must be between 10¼ and 12 years of age on 1st September following the examination, though able Candidates may apply for consideration if 10 years or over on that date, provided that they will have completed a full primary course of instruction before entry.

Parents must fulfil the Hospital's requirement of being 'in need of assistance' towards their children's education. As a rough guide, and subject to certain adjustments, it may be taken that, where the gross family income does not exceed £8,500 p.a. with one dependent child (an extra allowance of £500 p.a. is made for each additional dependent child), the candidate may be eligible to compete.

A small number of places will also be available by competition for which there is no restriction in parental income.

Contributions are required towards the cost of clothing, education and maintenance, ranging at admission from nil to £1,251 p.a., according to income. Each case is reviewed annually, and, in the event of improved financial circumstances, an increased contribution, up to as much as full cost (at present about £3,619 p.a.), may be required.

Further particulars and forms of application (available from 1st September to 10th October) may be obtained from: The Clerk of Christ's Hospital, 26 Great Tower Street, London, EC3R 5AL.

Dean Close School
Dean Close Junior School
Cheltenham

Dean Close School is an independent, co-educational day and boarding H.M.C. School of 430 pupils, 130 of them girls.

Dean Close Junior School is a self-contained I.A.P.S. School under its own Headmaster and staff. Of the 270 pupils, just less than half are girls. There is an eight year old and eleven year old entry.

CLERGY SCHOLARSHIPS
AND BURSARIES

Scholarships of 90% of Fees
and
Bursaries
are
available in both Schools

Prospectus and information about further Open, Music, Sixth Form and Day Scholarships from the Headmaster, Dean Close School, Shelburne Road, Cheltenham (Cheltenham 22640) and the Headmaster, Dean Close Junior School, Lansdown Road, Cheltenham (Cheltenham 512217).

HUYTON COLLEGE
LIVERPOOL

Head Mistress: Mrs. E. M. Rees,
B.A., L.R.A.M.

An Independent Day and Boarding School for girls between the ages of 5 and 18.

For both boarders and day girls the following scholarships and exhibitions are available: One scholarship two-thirds of school fees, one of one-third of school fees, one of £100 and some minor scholarships. A special award for music is offered each year. Candidates should be over 10 years 4 months and under 14 years 4 months by January 1st of the year of entry.

There are scholarships and bursaries reserved for daughters of Clergy.

Daughters of Clergy fees: Boarding/Senior £770 per term. Preparatory £679.

Day/Senior £368 per term. Preparatory £342.

HURSTPIERPOINT COLLEGE

There are Bursaries for sons of serving or former regular officers of the Armed Forces, and for sons of the Clergy. All awards are subject to good Common Entrance Examination results and a means test.

Open Scholarships are offered on a percentage of fees basis, the top award being to the value of two-thirds the current fees.

Music Scholarships available, the top award being two-thirds of current fees.

School fees £3,600 per annum.

Particulars from the Headmaster, Hurstpierpoint College, Hassocks, West Sussex.

KING'S SCHOOL
ROCHESTER

SCHOLARSHIPS

King's Scholarships and Minor King's Scholarships are awarded on the basis of an examination in the Lent Term. They have a value of up to half fees; parents' means are taken into consideration. Candidates should be under 14 years of age on June 1st.

Scholarships to the Junior School may be awarded on the Entrance Examination for boys in the 8–10 age group.

SONS OF CLERGY BURSARIES

Bursaries with the value of a one third reduction in fees are available for the sons of clergy.

Further particulars can be obtained from the Headmaster, King's School, Rochester.

MONKTON COMBE SCHOOL

Near BATH, AVON

An Independent, mainly Boys' Boarding School with a strong Christian tradition

JUNIOR SCHOOL
Combe Down (0225) 837912

100 Boarders, 70 Day Boys

Entry to Pre-Preparatory from age 4 and to the Preparatory School from age 8.

SENIOR SCHOOL
Limpley Stoke (022–122) 3523

300 Boarders, 30 Day Pupils – 150 in Sixth Form.

Main Entry for boys at age 13 and for boys and girls to the Sixth Form.

8 Inflation-linked Scholarships (including up to 2 for Music) offered at 13.

Remissions of up to ⅓rd of the fees are granted to the sons of Clergy and Missionaries on proof of need and Government Assisted Places also available to them at age 11, 13 and 16.

For a prospectus write or telephone the Headmaster

ROSSALL SCHOOL

FLEETWOOD LANCASHIRE

Rossall was founded for 'the sons of clergy and others'. Substantial bursaries are offered to the sons of clergy. There are also up to 10 Open Scholarships value 15–75% fees and up to 4 Music Scholarships of 15–50% fees. Examination: March.

Full fees £4,089 p.a.

Full particulars from the Headmaster

ST. JOHN'S SCHOOL

LEATHERHEAD, SURREY

Founded 1851 *Royal Charter 1922*

Patron:
H.R.H. THE DUCHESS OF GLOUCESTER

Visitor:
THE MOST REV. & RT. HON. THE LORD ARCHBISHOP OF CANTERBURY D.D.

Chairman of Council:
A. H. C. GREENWOOD, CBE, JP

Headmaster:
E. J. HARTWELL M.A. (Oxon.)

St. John's School was founded for the assisted education of sons of the clergy, on Public School lines. There are 50 sons of the clergy on the Foundation drawn from all parts of England and Wales and some whose fathers are serving the Church abroad.

Help is needed by donation, annual subscription, legacy or church collections.

Cheques should be made payable to 'St. John's School'.

Bursar and Secretary to the Council:
M. J. M. ALBROW

SCHOOL OF ST. CLARE, PENZANCE

A Girls' School of the Woodard Corporation.
Member of G.B.G.S.A

Girls aged 5–18 (boarders accepted from 8).
Courses lead to 'O' and 'A' level G.C.E. and University.
Provision for Drama, Music and Dancing.

Sixth form courses for which new entrants at 16 are considered, include 'A' levels, and also Secretarial, Pre-Nursing, Domestic Science and Art.

The School is set in beautiful grounds and provides opportunity for games, swimming, riding and athletics.

Special Terms for Clergy Daughters where need is shown.

Prospectus from the Headmistress,
Miss M. M. Coney, B.D.

ST. ELPHIN'S SCHOOL

DARLEY DALE MATLOCK

Church of England Independent School for Girls, founded in 1844. Pupils receive preparation for public examinations and University Entrance.

Reduced fees and scholarships available for clergy daughters.

Applications to Secretary.

Headmaster

A. P. C. POLLARD ESQ.

B.A., Cert.Ed.

TRENT COLLEGE

Long Eaton, Nottingham

Scholarships for sons of clergy are worth half the current school fees. There are also smaller Bursaries for sons of clergy. Both can be augmented in cases of need. The Scholarship Examination is held annually in May.

The school fees 1981/2 are £3462 p.a. for boarders over the age of 13 and £3237 p.a. for boarders of 11–13. Music Scholarships up to 3/5 of school fees are offered annually.

Further particulars may be obtained from the Headmaster. (06076–2737).

WESTONBIRT SCHOOL

SCHOLARSHIPS. Scholarships and Exhibitions, including awards for Music, are offered annually. The examination is held in January/February and is open to girls under 14 on September 1st in the year of entry, and girls entering the SIXTH FORM to follow Advanced Level courses. All awards will be determined according to financial need and for a girl of outstanding academic or musical ability a free place may be available.

Further particulars from the Headmaster, Westonbirt School, Near Tetbury, Glos. GL8 8QG

INTER-CHURCH TRAVEL

First in the Field of Ecumenical Pilgrimages and Tours

TRAVEL, THE PATH TO UNITY
TO:
HOLY LAND: ASIA:
THE FAR EAST:
EUROPE
GREAT BRITAIN,
A PARADISE FOR PILGRIMS!

Send Yearly For Your Free Coloured Brochure

Inter-Church Travel Ltd.
13–17 New Burlington Place,
London, W1X 2LB.
Tel: (01) 734 0942

A member of the
Thomas Cook Group of Companies
ABTA

"How about a little Peace and Quiet!"

A little peace and quiet towards the end of the day is what most people want. Most clergymen would like this sort of opportunity to relax when the time comes to retire, but it is not always so easy. When a clergyman retires he has to give up his home, and home-hunting on a pension is not a relaxing activity!

The Church of England Pensions Board administers nine homes including a nursing home, which are scattered around the country. A place in any one of these nine will mean a real home offering security, friends and privacy, as in most cases the residents have their own rooms or flatlets, but also the comfort of knowing that if there is an accident the matron is near at hand.

The Church of England Pensions Board also administers over 600 flats, bungalows and houses, most of which have been given or bequeathed or bought out of funds given to the Board to help those people who have given up their lives for the benefit of others for occupation under licences, and the occupants pay a maintenance charge.

Your donation or bequest could mean a home for someone in need.

For further information write to:

The Secretary,
The Church of England Pensions Board,
Department CD, 53 Tufton Street, London SW1P 3QP.

Our Country for Christ

The Society provides financial support for a biblical and pastoral ministry in the parishes of England and Wales by giving grants of over £50,000 a year.

CPAS also helps by stimulating evangelism, encouraging those considering parish ministry, as well as through camps, literature, women's work, lay training, and youth work through CYFA, Pathfinders, Explorers, and Climbers.

cpas

Church Pastoral Aid Society

Falcon Court, 32 Fleet Street,
London, EC4Y 1DB
Tel: 01–353 0751

UNITED SOCIETY FOR THE PROPAGATION OF THE GOSPEL

(*Society for the Propagation of the Gospel in Foreign parts, founded by Royal Charter in 1701; and the Universities' Mission to Central Africa, founded 1860, joined to form USPG in 1965. The Cambridge Mission to Delhi merged with the Society in 1968.*)

President: The Archbishop of Canterbury

USPG supports the work of the Anglican Churches in 50 countries in 21 Provinces overseas and four Provinces in Britain.

More than 300 men and women, including priests, doctors, teachers and farmers, from Great Britain and Ireland, are on its list of missionaries. Financial support is given to many more people of other nationalities who are serving the Church in their own country or in another place.

USPG provides training in mission for priests and lay workers whether they go overseas from here or come here from their own country, or are preparing to work at home—wherever home is.

The Society plays a particular role, under Partners in Mission, alerting people to partnership possibilities and helping the world Church, through the movement of people and also through funding, to be transformed from dependence to partnership.

USPG works ecumenically with other Societies, especially in support of the United Churches of the Indian sub-continent.

The Society spends more than £2,500,000 a year. Would you be prepared to help?

UNITED SOCIETY FOR THE PROPAGATION OF THE GOSPEL

15 Tufton Street, London, SW1P 3QQ. *Telephone:* 01-222 4222

(*Registered Charity No. 234518*)

ROYAL AGRICULTURAL BENEVOLENT INSTITUTION

Patron: H.M. The Queen

Founded 1860 *Incorporated by Royal Charter 1935*

Reg. No. 208858

The only charity which for over 122 years has existed solely for the relief of elderly or disabled farmers or their dependants who are in need. Over four million pounds have been distributed in Pensions and many other forms of relief to those who suffered loss of health and wealth in their efforts to maintain the productivity of the land on which our national security and well-being so largely depend. Today, the R.A.B.I. is supporting nearly 700 of them.

LEGACIES, DONATIONS and SUBSCRIPTIONS

are most urgently needed

PLEASE REMEMBER THE PLOUGH
and inaugurate an offertory at
HARVEST FESTIVAL TIME

For further information on our work, kindly address.

The Secretary,

ROYAL AGRICULTURAL BENEVOLENT INSTITUTION,
SHAW HOUSE, 27 WEST WAY, OXFORD, OX2 0QH

Telephone: Oxford (0865) 724931

SONS OF THE CLERGY

Founded A.D. 1655

CORPORATION

Incorporated by Royal Charter A.D. 1678

For assisting Clergymen of the Anglican Church and their Widows and Dependants, and for providing Grants for Education, Maintenance or Apprenticeship of Children of the Clergy of the Dioceses of the United Kingdom, Ireland and the Mission Field

Office: 1 DEAN TRENCH STREET, WESTMINSTER, LONDON, SW1P 3HB

Telephone: 01–799 3696 & 01–222 5887

President:

The LORD ARCHBISHOP OF CANTERBURY

The Most R verend and Right Honourable Robert Alexander Kennedy Runcie, M.C., D.D.

Vice-President:

The Right Honourable LORD JUSTICE TEMPLEMAN, M.B.E.

Treasurers:

JOHN S. KEITH, Esq.

The Venerable J. R. YOUENS, C.B., O.B.E., M.C. PAUL GRIFFIN, Esq., M.B.E., M.A.

THE ARCHBISHOP OF ARMAGH AND PRIMATE OF ALL IRELAND, The Most Rev. J. W. ARMSTRONG, D.D.
COLIN F. BADCOCK, Esq., M.A.
THOMAS D. BAXENDALE, Esq.
Sir THOMAS GORE BROWNE
Sir DENYS BUCKLEY, M.B.E.
C. B. BYFORD, Esq., A.T.I.
THE VISCOUNT CHURCHILL
R. H. N. DASHWOOD, Esq.
JOHN C. DAUKES, Esq.
THE BISHOP OF EDINBURGH AND PRIMUS IN SCOTLAND, The Most Rev. ALISTAIR I. M. HAGGART
Sir DAVID FLOYD EWIN, M.V.O., O.B.E., M.A., C.C.
The Hon. F. F. FISHER, C.B.E., M.C., M.A.
Alderman Sir MURRAY FOX, G.B.E., D.Litt., M.A.
Alderman Sir PETER GADSDEN, G.B.E., M.A., D.Sc., F.Eng.
ALLAN W. GRANT, Esq., O.B.E., M.C., T.D., LL.B., F.C.I.I.
ARTHUR E. C. GREEN, Esq., M.B.E., T.D., D.L., F.R.I.C.S., C.C.
Sir RONALD HARRIS, K.C.V.O., C.B.
The Ven. J. D. R. HAYWARD, M.A.
S. K. HODSON, Esq., F.C.A.
N. J. R. JAMES, Esq., M.A., J.P.
The Rev. DENNIS LANE, B.D., A.K.C.
Colonel R. S. LANGTON, M.V.O., M.C.
The Hon. ARTHUR LAWSON JOHNSTON
IAN S. LOCKHART, Esq., M.A.
THE LORD BISHOP OF LONDON, The Rt. Rev. and Rt. Hon. GRAHAM D. LEONARD, D.D.
M. L. J. MARSHALL, Esq., F.R.I.C.S.
Major-General J. I. H. OWEN, O.B.E.
The Rev. CYRIL G. H. RODGERS
The Rev. Preb. A. R. ROYALL
Colonel W. A. SALMON, O.B.E.
Sir JAMES STUBBS, K.C.V.O.
Sir ANTHONY WAGNER, K.C.B., K.C.V.O., D.Litt., F.S.A.
THE ARCHBISHOP OF WALES, The Most Rev. GWILYM O. WILLIAMS, D.D.
IRVINE WATSON, Esq., O.B.E., M.A.
Dr. ELIZABETH M. WEBB, M.B., B.S. M.R.C.G.P.
ANTONY E. WOODALL, Esq.
A. R. D. WRIGHT, Esq., M.A.
THE LORD ARCHBISHOP OF YORK, The Most Rev. and Rt. Hon. STUART Y. BLANCH, D.D.

The Corporation now distributes approximately £630,000 annually in benefactions and owns 49 houses for retired clergymen. Those assisted with grants or pensions include about 560 Clergymen, 900 Widows and over 300 other dependants; in addition educational and maintenance help is given to about 70 Ordinands during their training, and to about 1,276 boys and girls.

The ANNUAL FESTIVAL in St. Paul's Cathedral is normally held in the month of May and anyone wishing to obtain tickets should apply to the Registrar at the address shown above.

Donors of £31·50 and upwards are elected Governors of the Corporation.

LEGACIES are a most important feature in our receipts, and it is hoped that this Corporation, the oldest and most comprehensive Society of its kind, will not be overlooked in these inflationary times.

SUBSCRIPTIONS, DONATIONS, CHURCH and SCHOOL COLLECTIONS, and LEGACIES, in aid of funds or towards the extension of any of the above branches of work, are requested, and will be gratefully acknowledged by the Registrar, who will provide any information required.

1 DEAN TRENCH STREET, WESTMINSTER, LONDON, SW1P 3HB

Major-General M. CALLAN, C.B., Registrar

The College of
St. BARNABAS

for RETIRED CLERGY
(independent Regd. Charity)
Library, Common Room, Refectory,
Chapel, nursing for those who fall ill.

PLEASE HELP US MEET EVER RISING COSTS by legacies, covenants, donations . . . .

Particulars: The Warden
College of St. Barnabas,
Lingfield, Surrey RH7 6NJ

concerned with people . . . .

The Society was founded in 1835 and exists for the spiritual and social uplift of the people of London, mainly by house to house visitation and evangelism in industry. It depends on voluntary contributions, subscriptions and legacies to maintain this vital work.
Testamentary Bequests earnestly solicited
Latest report gladly sent on request.

Chairman: D. H. Thornton, Esq.
Treasurer: O. B. Gilbart-Smith, Esq.
Secretary: The Rev. D. M. Whyte, M.A.
Bankers: Barclays Bank Ltd.,
54 Lombard Street, E.C.3.

London City Mission
175 Tower Bridge Road,
SE1 2AH

Christian Witness to Israel

is a missionary society working in most major denominations throughout the world, including the Anglican Communion, helping and encouraging Christians to testify to Jewish people that Messiah has come "to save his people from their sins."

Its missionary staff are supported by the prayers and gifts of Churches and Christian individuals. Deputation speakers are available on request.

Please write to:—
The Director, CWI(CC), 44 Lubbock Road, Chislehurst, Kent BR7 5JX

The Leprosy Mission

Reaching out in the Name of Christ to more and more of the world's 15,000,000 untreated leprosy victims

ROOM 41, 50 PORTLAND PLACE, LONDON W1N 3DG

SIGHT . . .
YOUR CHRISTIAN
GIFT

to the Royal Commonwealth Society for the Blind.

Over six million people in the Commonwealth countries in which we work are needlessly blind for lack of simple surgery.

£3 will restore sight to a blind villager;
£130 will give sight to a whole village.

During the past 12 years, in Asian village eye camps, over one million blind people had sight restored and over 6½ million villagers were treated for conditions that could have led to blindness.

Please help us to continue and increase this work by sending your gift to

The Royal Commonwealth
Society for the Blind

Commonwealth House
Haywards Heath, West Sussex RH16 3AZ.
Tel. (0444) 412424
Patron: H.M. The Queen

CHURCH SOCIETY

Church Society aims to educate and encourage members of the Church of England in an up-to-date understanding of the centrality of the Gospel and Lordship of Jesus Christ in church life and individual commitment.

Church Society seeks to expound the teaching of the Bible as the authoritative Word of God, and affirms the teaching of the Anglican Reformation foundations (the Thirty-nine Articles and the Book of Common Prayer) as the right resources for building up the life of the Church of England as the national church.

serving the church in. . .

partnership

- ☐prayer bulletins uniting a nationwide fellowship of praying parishes and individuals
- ☐direct help to parishes with advice and literature
- ☐service to individual members of General Synod
- ☐back-up for Diocesan Evangelical Unions
- ☐national, area and parochial conferences

public statements

and exposition of classical Anglican doctrine

Church Society Trust

- ☐patrons of 120 benefices
- ☐trustees of charitable funds

publishing

- ☐CHURCHMAN—the only Anglican evangelical journal of theology
- ☐CROSS + WAY—a practical magazine for local church leaders, synod and PCC members
- ☐evangelical classics, theological works, booklets and aids to worship and pastoring
- ☐copyright of the ANGLICAN HYMN BOOK
- ☐audio-visual aids—tapes, cassettes and film strips—available for purchase or hire
- ☐church-centred educational and teaching programmes

Whitefield House, 186 Kennington Park Road, London SE11 4BT
01-582 0132

THE CHURCH UNION

PRESIDENT: The Rt Revd Dr Eric Kemp, Bishop of Chichester
GENERAL SECRETARY: The Revd Peter Geldard

The CHURCH UNION was founded in 1859 as a result of the great renewal which began in Oxford in 1833, to recall the Church of England to her true Catholic identity, and to ensure that the great truths of the faith are defended and shared with others.

In the 1980s we must not only defend our heritage but make sure that we take the initiative to go forward and bring the faith to others. The Church Union is fully committed to the Catholic Renewal movement, and the aims of both bodies can only be achieved if we have one single united and representative voice speaking on behalf of as many parishes and individuals as possible. The CHURCH UNION *is the only organisation* with the staff, the premises, and the experience that, with your support, can do this.

Join the Church Union, as an individual or by parish membership, and you will be forwarding the work of Catholic Renewal, qualify for the advice and assistance that the Union can give, and assist the work of THE CHURCH LITERATURE ASSOCIATION, the only independent publishing house committed to the Catholic movement.

Write or telephone for membership details:

THE CHURCH UNION

Faith House 7 Tufton Street London SW1P 3QN. Telephone 01-222 6952

THE CHURCH LADS' AND CHURCH GIRLS' BRIGADE

The Church Lads' Brigade and the Church Girls' Brigade, two organisations serving exclusively within the Anglican Communion, have now amalgamated to form one uniformed Anglican Brigade.

This new Brigade combines the gathered experience and expertise of the two partners into a modern, active and effective organisation for young people firmly rooted within the Church of England.

The Incumbent of a parish appoints leaders to work with the young people of the parish and is himself responsible for the Christian Education Programme.

Why not have a Company in your Parish?

Write to the General Secretary, The Reverend Charles Grice at

CLAUDE HARDY HOUSE, 15 ETCHINGHAM PARK ROAD,
FINCHLEY, LONDON N3 2DU
Telephone 01-349 2616/7

A LEGACY MEANS A LOT TO THE LIMBLESS

10,500 limbless Ex-Servicemen depend on the British Limbless Ex-Service Men's Association.

BLESMA is not aided by the State. But we urgently need money to help these brave men conquer their handicap. And to equip and maintain homes in which they convalesce and are given care and comfort in their old age.

Help the disabled by helping BLESMA. A donation from you will give hope and encouragement to those who gave so much for their country. A legacy would mean a lot to them.

Donations and information:
Major The Earl of Ancaster, KCVO, TD
Midland Bank Ltd., 60 West Smithfield,
London EC1A 9DX

50 years in the service of Disabled Ex-Service Men

BLESMA

BRITISH LIMBLESS
EX-SERVICE MEN'S ASSOCIATION

MAGAZINE COVERS—
FOLDERS for Order of Service—
NOTELETS for Invitations to Services—

over 100 designs

also Publishers of

The Bethlehem Carol Sheet
and Bethlehem Series Greeting Cards

THE BIBLE LANDS SOCIETY
(Est. 1854)

Mail Orders:
POST OFFICE BOX 50,
HIGH WYCOMBE, BUCKS.
Tel: (0494) 21351

The Young Men's Christian Association

offers young men and women challenging opportunities of full-time Christian service and also a two-year Training Course giving a recognized qualification in Youth and Community work.

Apply to the Secretary for Personnel and Training, National Council of YMCAs, 640 Forest Road, London, E17 3DZ

C E M S

THE CHURCH OF ENGLAND MEN'S SOCIETY
Central Office, 18, Hertford Street, Coventry CV1 1LF.
Telephone: Coventry (0203) 22053

PRESIDENTS: The Archbishops of Canterbury, York and Wales
Chairman: The Bishop of Grantham
General Secretary: The Reverend David Murfet, M.A.

Cassettes, written material, programme suggestions for men's groups.

What do you want as you grow older?

Security, comfort,
a helping hand (not too obtrusive)
above all, your independence
and self-respect.

This is what we aim to provide
in our sheltered flats.

We have 1,000 such flats
throughout the country,
and would like to build many more.
The Government pays for basic building
but we depend on your help to turn
what we build into the homes
our tenants deserve.

CHURCH ARMY HOUSING LTD.
112a Shirland Road
London W9 2EL

SOCIETY FOR THE ASSISTANCE OF LADIES IN REDUCED CIRCUMSTANCES

(Founded by the late Miss Smallwood)

Patron: Her Majesty The Queen

This Society is entirely supported by Voluntary Contributions

Please Remember our Numerous Poor Ladies in Need

Many elderly and invalid can no longer cope with the problems of living in these difficult days, and the anxiety that inflation brings. Without the continued support of Donations or Legacies their needs could not be met.

Please make cheques payable to:

S.A.L.R.C.

Lancaster House (c), 25 Hornyold Rd.
MALVERN, Worcs. WR14 1QQ
Charity Registration No. 205798

CORRYMEELA
Working for Peace in Northern Ireland

The CORRYMEELA COMMUNITY is a ministry of Reconciliation in Northern Ireland. It is dedicated to bringing Peace through understanding and tolerance.

It is demanding in TIME, PRAYER and FINANCE.

"WAGE PEACE" IN NORTHERN IRELAND BY SUPPORTING CORRYMEELA

Information and Donations
CORRYMEELA LINK (C)
P.O. Box 118, Reading RG1 1CL.

Patrons of Corrymeela Link:
Adam Curle, Representing the Religious Society of Friends, His Grace the Archbishop of Canterbury, The Chief Rabbi, The Moderator of the Free Church Federal Council, The Moderator of the General Assembly of the Church of Scotland, His Grace the Archbishop of Liverpool, His Lordship the Roman Catholic Bishop of Portsmouth, His Lordship the Bishop of Reading, His Eminence the Cardinal Archbishop of St Andrews and Edinburgh, His Eminence the Cardinal Archbishop of Westminster.

HISTORIC CHURCHES PRESERVATION TRUST

Patron: HER MAJESTY THE QUEEN

Chairman: THE ARCHBISHOP OF CANTERBURY

Chairman, Executive Committee: THE DUKE OF GRAFTON

Secretary: MAJOR I. R. RADFORD, M.B.E.

Will you help to preserve England's heritage of ancient and beautiful churches? Over 4,000 churches and chapels have already been helped, but hundreds still urgently need repair. Many of the finest serve small parishes where their upkeep has always been a difficult problem. Funds must be raised to augment local efforts. Grants from the Trust are a valuable stimulus to parishes striving to preserve for posterity the buildings which collectively reflect the history of a thousand years.

LEGACIES, DONATIONS, AND SUBSCRIPTIONS
will be gratefully received by the Secretary
who will be glad to provide further information and literature

HISTORIC CHURCHES PRESERVATION TRUST
FULHAM PALACE, LONDON, SW6 6EA
Telephone: 01-736 3054

Loneliness is just one problem

And it is a fairly common problem for seamen – away from home for months at a time – but it is only one of the many different troubles that people bring to us. And we are there, ready to give all the help we can, in all parts of the world. Over the years, since our foundation in 1856, seafarers have come to depend on us. They know we care. Our care is an expression of our Christian faith.
Do you care enough to help us?

The Missions to Seamen
St. Michael Paternoster Royal,
College Hill, London EC4R 2RL.

CLERGY ORPHAN CORPORATION

Fatherless Children of the Clergy are educated, maintained, and clothed by the CORPORATION

PLEASE SUPPORT US

We have at the present time 300 children in our care and we DESPERATELY need more money to meet their needs.

Patron: HER MAJESTY THE QUEEN

President: THE ARCHBISHOP OF CANTERBURY *Treasurer*: MAJOR-GENERAL J. I. H. OWEN, O.B.E.
Secretary: MISS V. B. WARTERS, O.B.E.

Please send contributions to the Secretary at:
57B TUFTON STREET, WESTMINSTER, LONDON SW1P 3QL

ST. LUKE'S HOSPITAL FOR THE CLERGY

(FORMERLY ST. LUKE'S NURSING HOME FOR THE CLERGY)
Registered Charity No. 209236

President: HIS GRACE THE ARCHBISHOP OF CANTERBURY

St. Luke's was founded in 1892 as a gift from the laity to the clergy to provide free medical and surgical treatment for the clergy, their wives, widows, dependent children, lay Church workers licensed by a Bishop, members of recognised monastic and conventual orders, missionaries and ordinands.

Please help St. Luke's to help the clergy

Donations or requests for covenant forms to:

REV. P. NICHOLSON, GENERAL SECRETARY, ST. LUKE'S HOSPITAL FOR THE CLERGY, 14 FITZROY SQUARE, LONDON, W1P 6AH Tel. 01-388 4954

No future with no one to care
Family tragedies can shatter a childs life leaving misery and neglect for those innocent of all blame. Church Army helps with comfort and practical help. We confidently ask you to show your concern for those who have little or nothing in life. Send your donation today–and help make their tomorrows brighter.
Christian action for a world in need
Please send something now.
I enclose a donation of (tick box) £1☐ £2☐ £5☐ £10☐ £25☐ £______
I would like to know more about Wills/Covenants ☐
I would like to know how I can help Church Army ☐
Please make cheque/PO payable to Church Army.
Name
Address
Church Army
Jesus loves you
Post to Room CC, Church Army Headquarters,
Independents Road, Blackheath, London SE3.

Jerusalem and the Middle East Church Association

(lately the Jerusalem and the East Mission)

The Old Gatehouse, Castle Hill, Farnham, Surrey, GU9 0AE

Gen. Sec.: The VENERABLE R. A. LINDLEY, C.B.E.

J. & M. E. C. A. is the channel through which your parish can help the work of the Episcopal Church in Jerusalem and the Middle East, in the dioceses of Jerusalem, Iran, Egypt, and Cyprus and the Gulf, and assist in the maintenance of Cathedral worship in Jerusalem.

GFS

GIRLS FRIENDLY SOCIETY AND TOWNSEND FELLOWSHIP

A Society of the Church for girls and women meeting contemporary needs by varied activities, including branch work in parishes, hostels, holiday houses and courses for girls at work and school leavers

The Society co-operates with industrial chaplaincies and diocesan educational teams.

Further information from The General Secretary:

GFS, 126 Queen's Gate, London SW7 5LQ

Telephone 01–589–9628

A SERVICE WE CAN SHARE

Church support strengthens immeasurably the Scouts' aim of developing young people physically, mentally and spiritually so that they may take a constructive place in society; and sponsoring a Scout Group can strengthen the links between church and young people and their families.

There are over 640,000 Scouts in the country. There would be many more if there were Groups to accept them. To find out how sponsoring a Group could help your church to extend its work and service and help us to help more boys, write to:

The Relationships Secretary,
The Scout Association,
Baden-Powell House, Queen's Gate, London, SW7 5JS.

Scouts

THE FRIENDS OF THE CLERGY CORPORATION

(INCORPORATING THE POOR CLERGY RELIEF CORPORATION AND THE FRIEND OF THE CLERGY CORPORATION)

Last year we gave help in time of need to clergy and to clergy widows and orphan daughters in over 1,550 cases.

To give relief to those who have served—or who are serving—the Church and who are in distress is surely a cause to touch the heart of everyone.

We are entirely dependent upon voluntary contributions.

We ask your help—by donation—by covenanted subscription—by legacy, or the gift of property we can adapt for use as retirement homes for the Clergy.

Please send now to the Chairman:

THE REVD. CANON C. E. V. BOWKETT,

THE FRIENDS OF THE CLERGY CORPORATION

27 MEDWAY STREET, WESTMINSTER, LONDON, SW1P 2BD

ADDITIONAL CURATES SOCIETY

A.C.S. IS A MISSIONARY SOCIETY

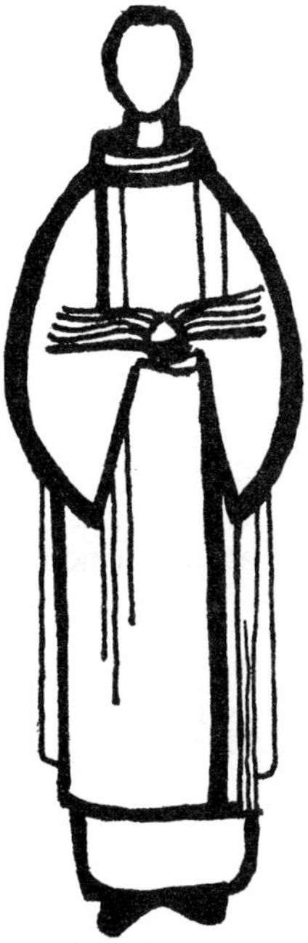

A.C.S. HELPS THE CHURCH PROCLAIM THE GOOD NEWS OF JESUS TO THE PEOPLE OF ENGLAND AND WALES.

£140,000 each year towards the cost of stipends, housing and expenses of Assistant Priests in 480 parishes.

£10,000 each year on various activities to encourage young men aged 16–25 to think about vocation to the Priesthood.

£5,000 each year to help students qualify for entry to a theological college.

Enquiries about speakers, preachers, and ways of helping . . . . . and enquiries about grants and vocational activities:

The General Secretary: A.C.S.
264a Washwood Heath Road, Birmingham, B8 2XS

EVERY PENNY GIVEN TO THE A.C.S. IS USED TO PROVIDE MORE PRIESTS!

Oxford University Press

The Alternative Service Book 1980

Oxford/Mowbray Editions.

Printed with the rubrics to the services in second colour blue.

Pew Editions Bound in durable cloth on boards. With or without the Liturgical Psalter.

Fine Bindings A complete range bound in imitation leather, French morocco leather, and best Calfskin. All printed on fine paper and with ribbon markers.

The Ministry of the Word
Edited G. Cuming

Handbook to the Alternative Service Book Lectionary.

A commentary on The Holy Communion lessons, written by a team of biblical scholars and parish priests of different denominations. Published in co-operation with the Bible Reading Fellowship.

The New English Bible

Still acknowledged leader among scholarly modern translations.

Lectern Editions Bound in moroccoette or hand grained morocco leather. With or without Apocrypha.

Pew Editions Stoutly bound in green linson on boards, with jacket. Grant terms available for initial purchase.

Personal and gift editions in three sizes and a variety of bindings.

The Oxford Study Edition with Apocrypha

This Study Edition contains the complete text of The New English Bible with the Apocrypha. There are Introductions to the Testaments and the Apocrypha, as well as to each of the separate books, giving general background and setting as well as information on the author.

On every page of this edition there are annotations which will help the student and layman understand the various literary, historical, geographical, and archaeological aspects of the text and which give cross-references from one passage to another. Special articles also serve to highlight certain areas of general interest in order to enhance the reader's understanding of the Bible.

CROCKFORD'S CLERICAL DIRECTORY

1980–82

A REFERENCE BOOK OF THE CLERGY OF THE PROVINCES OF CANTERBURY AND YORK AND OF OTHER ANGLICAN PROVINCES AND DIOCESES

EIGHTY-EIGHTH ISSUE

(*First Issue 1858*)

OXFORD NEW YORK TORONTO MELBOURNE

OXFORD UNIVERSITY PRESS

© *Oxford University Press 1983*

ISBN 0 19 200010 1

[*Printed in Great Britain*]

"Where there is no vision, the people will die."
Proverbs 29, v. 18

Your Church <u>needs</u> a Good Magazine

With 111 years'
experience and work in this field

"HOME WORDS"
can help you with
Illustrated Picture Covers in Full Colour &
the 16 page **Home Words** &
Church News Insets.

A specialised complete Magazine Printing &
Duplicating Service.

Also: Freewill Offering Booklets, Christian Stewardship
Cartons, Gift Day Envelopes, Publicity Leaflets,
Collecting Boxes etc.

0192 000 101 7246

Write or Phone

HOME WORDS & CHURCH NEWS

P.O. Box 44, Guildford, Surrey GU1 1XL

Telephone 0483 33944

203

MR 4092

PREFACE

It is a relief to know that *Crockford's Clerical Directory*, first published in 1858 and the responsibility of the Oxford University Press since 1921, is assured of a future under the care of the Church of England. It ought to be a useful future. In view of this development a Preface-writer, customarily independent and anonymous, may be permitted to add a few words to the tribute to the present publishers which he paid in the last issue, when readers around the world were celebrating five hundred years of scholarly printing and publishing in Oxford. Now it may be added that an enormous amount of trouble has been taken by the staff of the Press, both in the offices at Neasden and in the Printing Division at Oxford, to bring this Directory's store of information about the Anglican clergy in many nations to perfection — or as near to perfection as was possible for humanity assisted in recent years by a computer. Substantial financial losses have been accepted. The OUP's treatment of Crockford over sixty years has been an example of devotion to duty, of craftsmanship, and of generosity.

Crockford's own problems

However, Crockford has never given much space to eulogies and we take this opportunity to reassert the tradition of Anglican self-criticism, giving truthfulness a higher priority than tactfulness and honesty a higher moral value than optimism. This tradition has had noted expressions in the prefaces written by our predecessors, and although our successors may face the problem of official air being breathed down their necks we should like to give them a sword which has not been blunted. We therefore begin this year's meditation on trends in the Church of England with some thoughts about the reasons why *Crockford's Clerical Directory* in its old shape became too expensive for its market. These reasons are, we believe, relevant to the problems now being acknowledged increasingly by many other British institutions, including the Church of England.

In order to be comprehensive, Crockford has expensively compiled and printed information some of which in recent years has also been available either in private lists such as the Clerical Register maintained by the Church Commissioners for England or in national, provincial, or diocesan publications such as *The Church of England Yearbook*. The assembly of such information in one public place was convenient, but it was convenience bought at a price which can no longer be accepted. In future the chief foundation of the Directory will be the Commissioners' Register, and the overlap with other publications will be reduced. The need to economize is familiar to all who struggle with the finances of institutions, and the problem is well known that for a corporate body as for an individual slimming is never so simple to carry out as it is to desire.

Crockford has devoted two-fifths of its space to clergy outside the United Kingdom although less than a tenth of its sales was overseas. Clergymen working outside Europe will very probably not be listed in future issues. We are consoled by the thought that over many years no great disaster struck the clergy of the Episcopal Church in the USA because their names did not appear in this Directory. We offer, too, the reflection that this lessening of the scope of Crockford is a minor illustration of the process in which Britain is being compelled to let go of its imperial past.

Crockford has until now included a variety of pleasant features such as lists of bishops tracing the succession back to the origin of each see, pages naming the rural deans of England, and maps displaying the geography of the dioceses. These features have had to be sacrificed to the need to provide facts at a tolerable price. The sacrifice will disappoint some readers; but here again we have found some consolation. The end of affluence in Britain is not the end of the world. While the need to economize cannot be welcome to a country which until recently was the centre of an empire including a quarter of mankind, and which is still the admired birthplace of the world's leading language and literature, other peoples are flourishing.

Partners in Mission

Because the danger of a post-imperial island becoming exclusively insular is so real, we gladly respond at some length to a bold and unique example of commentary on the Church of England from outside. Sharp comment by outsiders should always be welcomed by an institution; it shows an interest and it makes insiders think. (The debate which the new General Synod held in November 1980 on 'What is the Church for?' had its uses but would have been more valuable if there had been a ruder introduction than the Bishop of Guildford's excellent piece of devotional theology.) To respond with bland platitudes after such provocation would not be a sign of true thankfulness for what we have received.

In June 1981 a National Partners in Mission Consultation provided an occasion when visitors drawn from nine other parts of the Anglican Communion and from eight non-Anglican Churches could say what they thought about the Church of England. It was an inescapable exercise, for since the process was launched by the Anglican Consultative Council in 1973 twenty-eight of the thirty Churches in the Anglican Communion had held PIM Consultations and in a considerable number of these meetings representatives of the Church of England had been eloquent. Since England is well known to have become one of the most secular countries in the world, no one could plausibly deny that the Church of England needed advice about its missionary responsibilities. Nor could anyone argue that it would be courteous or ethical for English Anglicans to distribute advice far and wide without being prepared to take the medicine themselves. But the English Consultation was an inevitably difficult exercise, which is why gratitude is due to visitors prepared to stick their necks into the mouth of a lion of advanced age and uncertain temper. Not only was there no real prospect of other Churches giving much help in manpower or money as well as in exhortations or rebukes — a prospect which must have encouraged other Churches to preserve their courtesy when receiving advice from English visitors. There was also little likelihood that visitors from other Churches would rapidly unravel the complexities of life in the Church of England. Thus the delay in holding the National Consultation in England is excusable. So, too, is the effort to make the discussion precise and useful by confining it to the work of the synods and their boards or committees and of the national voluntary agencies, leaving wider problems to consultations at the diocesan level. There are many problems — the relationship of the Church Commissioners and the General Synod, for example — which are important in ecclesiastical administration and which outsiders equipped with relevant experience and prepared to take time could explore with a stimulating freshness. In the end, though, a National Consultation was inescapable — and it is also understandable that the visitors (who, it must be confessed, were not for the most part people entrusted with leadership in their own Churches) brushed aside any suggestion that the talk should be confined to dry subjects in ecclesiastical administration. An opportunity had come to review the Church of England in the light of their own experience; and they were going to seize it. In the end their report *To a Rebellious House?* was edited by Canon John Kingsnorth. It was a mixture of unpalatable but nutritious home truths with some suggestions which were stale because the Church of England had already quite often considered and rejected them for good reasons — and with some slogans which, although well intentioned, were less than perfectly baked.

The fresh home truths included criticisms of the Church's central boards and national voluntary agencies. Answers to a questionnaire had 'raised some doubt as to whether the national bodies were facing up to the world in which we live'. While there was 'a growing professionalism and reliance on full-time staff', the staff themselves complained that they were 'in the last resort only advisory, with little initiatory power'. Since the impression left was as vague as that, and was an impression which would have been given by bureaucracies in many of the world's Churches, visitors in a hurry must have found it hard to say exactly what was wrong. Their report shed little light. The visitors were attracted by the idea of merging some voluntary agencies — missionary societies for example, or the societies for helping clergy widows and families (a better example); but since they had no time in which to produce any detailed consideration of the arguments for the existing situation of independence tempered by collaboration, they were unable to produce reasons likely to be accepted by the voluntary agencies as decisive. A request to Bishops' Councils to discuss 'what contribution official and voluntary bodies made to mission in the diocese' elicited little useful response. It probably seemed too reminiscent of an alarming question in an examination, and a quarter of the councils sent in no reply.

One idea which secured a mention in the final report was that there might be an annual meeting of the staffs and key board members of Church's central boards and national voluntary agencies. It would be a gentle piece of training or horizon-widening growing out of the present modest exercise immodestly called Partnership for World Mission. Such a gathering might profitably replace one of the three annual meetings of the General Synod. It might stimulate the pooling of resources and assist the learning of two linked lessons which Mr Giles Ecclestone, the outstandingly able Secretary of the Board for Social Responsibility, said the consultation had helped him to learn — the need to check the 'increasing professionalization and centralization' and the need 'to see things through the eyes of those at the bottom of the heap'.

In their initial assessment of the Church of England as a whole, bravely reproduced in their final report, the 'external partners' lamented the absence of a 'clear vision'. This led to some sensible suggestions for the improvement of the work of the clergy — ecumenical training wherever possible; compilation of a job description to accompany each new appointment; more teamwork and in-service training; training to cope with the stresses and strains to which clergy families are subject; more serious attention to the non-stipendiary ministry and to the permanent diaconate; more sharing of the work (including decision making) with the laity. But other suggestions revealed how little the external partners had been able to study the peculiar opportunities of the Church of England, despite a belated recognition in the last paragraph of this initial assessment. It was claimed that the clergy's 'statutory roles as state baptizers, marriers and buriers' left 'little time for the proclamation of the Gospel' — as if in a secularized society anyone could invent a better opportunity to proclaim salvation to individuals than an interview asked for by people facing marriage, birth, or bereavement. A 'slow separation — step by step — of Church and State' was recommended — as if anyone could ask for a greater chance to proclaim salvation to a society than an act of worship, or a chaplain's or bishop's quiet ministry of influence, which is made possible on the present scale only because the Church of England is recognized as the National Church. The freehold tenure of their offices by the clergy was alleged to prevent 'any accountability of clergy to people, to those granting the benefices, or even to God' — as if the experience of bishops and ecclesiastical courts seeking to terminate the rare cases of a breakdown in a pastoral relationship had not included a stout defence of the local man by parishioners who resented any outside interference.

Obviously some parish priests do spend too much time baptizing, marrying, or consoling people who thereafter never come to church; obviously some aspects of the Church-State connection do need reform; and obviously the present provisions for ending a pastoral relationship would need strengthening were it ever to be felt that many unsatisfactory pastors deserved ejection. But it is no use having a vision which is 'clear' if the eye is not directed to the actual scene in England, where on the whole the hard-pressed clergy are known to labour devotedly in the service both of their congregations and of the wider community.

Parts of the initial assessment of the Church of England by these external partners reminded us how wounding partnership can be (however unintentionally) when to be external is to be aloof, not condescending to make detailed criticisms or constructive suggestions. 'The Church is failing in its ministry to youth. . . . As we have gone round the dioceses our overwhelming impression has been of near empty churches. The liturgy does not speak to the people. . . .' These were the impressions left by two Sundays in seventeen dioceses. There is a tragic truth in them, but it is not the whole truth. Other parts of the initial assessment displayed a sad insensitivity to the reasons why some recent proposals for change have been resisted in the Church of England.

Two examples may be cited. To the 'external partners' the old system of the private patronage of parishes seemed an abuse which ought simply to be abolished. The calling of a pastor by the diocese and the Parochial Church Council acting together is a tendency which we applaud, but it is insensitive not to notice that under the current, far more cautious, Benefices Measure a good many Parochial Church Councils seem likely to want to keep their private patrons (with reduced powers) for many years yet. Again: the ordination of women to the priesthood is said to be 'inevitable' because it 'witnesses to the world that men and women are equal in the sight of God'. That is a conclusion with which we agree, but it is insensitive to omit even to consider the objections which are made with passion on theological or ecumenical (or even biblical) grounds. The Church of England seeks to include conservatives as well as radicals happily in its ranks and to reach out in mutual understanding to fellow Catholics as well as to fellow Protestants in other Churches. That noble tradition accounts for the acceptability of so many checks and balances in the present system of ecclesiastical government, including the need to secure large majorities in all three Houses of the General Synod after consultation with the Diocesan Synods. The Church is right to be tender to the consciences of its own conservatives, who feel themselves to be allied with large numbers who are even more conservative in other Churches. The model of Parliamentary democracy, where a majority of one is enough, is not to be copied within a Church ready to pay the price of Christian charity and comprehensiveness.

By the time that the final report of the Consultation was drafted some of the initial reactions by the external partners had been toned down in discussion. For example, the final version tells us that 'we do not propose any effort to restructure the Establishment'. What was proposed instead was a change in attitude and atmosphere, making the Church of England more clearly a home for all age groups and all classes. Such a change is obviously desirable but is specially difficult for a body so long identified with the State, with the mature, and with the privileged. No attempt was made to explore sociological realities, but had such an attempt been made the sensible conclusion might have been reached that the Church of England's biggest opportunity to become less hoity-toity lies in reunion with Methodism and Roman Catholicism. The 'difficulty experienced in reaching mutual understanding and agreement about evangelism' was confessed — and was illustrated by the inclusion of two rival statements, equally forgettable. Other difficult problems were shirked. The section on the work of the General Synod failed to work out the implications of a comment reported from an Australian partner, deploring 'the enormous loss of time for mission by your leading people attending meetings'. The same visitor's comment on 'the general lack of obvious prayerfulness, or at least spontaneity in prayer' was met only by the recommendation that people 'need more teaching about prayer'.

Two themes not prominent in the initial assessment were at this final stage developed into recommendations which we believe to be profoundly mistaken. Church schools were discouraged; 'only those which can be seen to have a particular mission in the community as a whole' should be retained. Yet almost all of these schools have waiting lists of parents anxious to use them, and to throw them away when there is no financial need to do so would be to abandon the chief mission which they already discharge acceptably. It is not nearly so certain that sixth form colleges and institutions of further education would be willing to welcome 'new patterns of ministry' as recommended.

Secondly, it was urged that the Church Commissioners should cease to fulfil the main purpose for which they were set up in 1836 since 'by 1995 the costs of parochial ministerial stipends should cease to be a charge on the Commissioners' funds'. The external partners added that 'the Commissioners should immediately be put under the authority of the General Synod' and should change their investment policy since 'the present income seems inadequate'. With or without changes in investments (left conveniently unspecified), the Commissioners' assets would be inadequate for all the 'wider purposes' to which the income would be applied if these visitors had their way. We can, however, be certain that there would be a drastic reduction of the full-time parochial ministry, particularly in inner-city and rural areas. More than half the cost of the stipends of the parochial clergy is still met by the Commissioners, although the proportion has been falling. Plainly there is room for improvement in giving by the Anglican laity in England; the contrast with North American standards is great. But it should be remembered that it is very difficult to change a reliance on endowments, an attitude inherited in England as it is not in North America; and that the (allegedly priest-ridden) Roman Catholic communicants in England, who seem to be about equal in numbers to the regular Anglican communicants, support about half the number of clergy, all of whom are celibates.

Anyway, how much freedom do we have? The Commissioners already enjoy and exercise some elasticity in the making of grants (for example, to church buildings in new housing areas), and the General Synod might well request them to subsidize some other good causes, but the large-scale diversion of funds to 'wider purposes' would be a clear breach of trust, since the endowments held by the Commissioners were in every case given for the support of the clergy. On this ground Parliament would be almost certain to veto it, and would be almost universally praised for doing so. It is not as if Anglican churchgoers need to raid the Commissioners' funds in order to fulfil their duties to the poor; for churchgoers, in addition to their voluntary giving which is very considerable, pay taxes in order to sustain a still-elaborate Welfare State. Nor is it as if the Commissioners had money to spare. They reported that in 1980 18p in every £1 of their income went to clergy pensions or retirement lump sums and that this proportion is bound to increase. Recently the conditions of the retired clergy, particularly in housing, have been improved and great credit is due to the Pensions Board; it would be tragic if this act of justice were to be undone or if those of the clergy who will retire in the next ten years (an alarming number) were to be faced by poverty for themselves and their widows. Almost seventy per cent of the Commissioners' income now goes to the pay and housing of the working clergy, yet since only a third of the total pay of the clergy comes from giving, the national minimum for incumbents from 1 April 1982 is just over £100 a week before tax. Curates have to make do on less. Poverty can be known by priests whose children are at school and whose wives do not work outside the home and parish.

'I look for a revived Church of England in a revived England — nothing less.' So the Archbishop of York, who had acted as chairman, summed up the impact made on his mind by the Partners in Mission at a great Eucharist for the General Synod in York Minster. We have no wish to dispute that revival is both needed and possible; but surely for this purpose what most needs to be revived is the conviction of the English that what Christianity says about God and man is true. Yet the question of religious belief was mentioned during the Consultation only in an oblique manner. The failure to regard popular scepticism about religious claims as the chief problem provides an astonishing example of how absorbed the Church, in England or overseas, can be in issues which are trivial in comparison with the 'death of God' experienced by so many of the twentieth-century English and other Europeans. All the committees in the Church, however radically reorganized, cannot by themselves produce one commitment to believe and trust in God through Christ in the power of the Holy Spirit. The clergy know better than anyone else the main reason why the Church's liturgy (Tudor or neo-Elizabethan) does not speak to the people: it is that the people see no need to assemble in order to worship God. The same simple explanation accounts for much of the moral anarchy: the people see no need to obey the commandments of God. It is undeniable that more teaching about prayer is needed. The crucial question is what that teaching is to be. What, for example, is the Christian doing when he intercedes? There are hints given in Bishop Michael Ramsey's *Be Still and Know*, his 1982 gift to the Church, which deserve to be developed and popularized.

To acknowledge the seriousness of the rejection of Christian belief and behaviour in so much of English life is of great importance in the pastoral care of the faithful; for while it is no doubt true that many churches could be fuller if their local leaders thoroughly accepted the principles advocated by the PIM external partners (and by many others who write or speak about evangelism and Church growth), it is also true that in many areas the most dedicated clergy or laity would be foolish to expect a large harvest of recruits. Some areas may be more favourable ground than others, for reasons which can be analysed sociologically — the family-conscious outer suburb, for example, or the proudly historic country town. Some churches are more favourably placed than others; for example, a definitely Evangelical pulpit can attract adherents from many other parishes. But thanks to urbanization and the media the English culture is remarkably unified, and its unity has grown remote from organized religion — whatever the organization may be. The evangelist who ignores this is risking a broken heart.

It is understandable that the external partners failed to address themselves to the present English inability to believe strongly in God. Many Christians, particularly in Africa, Latin America, or India, belong to cultures where the presence of God is still usually taken for granted and the most urgent task confronting the Church is to identify it more with the people, destroying the image of Christianity as the white colonialist's religion. In the USA the habit of churchgoing is still widespread and piety commends a politician. It is natural that partners coming from such religious backgrounds should fail to notice the extent to which the tide of faith has withdrawn from the shores of England, but should instead concentrate on removing sociological barriers to church membership. Thus the General Synod was criticized in the PIM report not because it is usually too gentlemanly to mention God, or to examine its neighbours' reasons for ignoring God more systematically, but because it is too gentlemanly to include enough women, workers, or young people. Miss Jenny Bond, a young Roman Catholic, was right to assure the General Synod that it was 'utterly crazy' to meet midweek; but more weekend synods would not automatically fill churches. She made the mistake in drawing from the interest in 'transcendental meditation and all that sort of thing' the conclusion that 'there is in this country a real hunger for spiritual renewal and prayer'. Alas, that is not true on any large scale about non-churchgoers. There is much emptiness — but, as parish priests who visit widely know, not much hunger. A General Synod meeting at weekends and fully feminine, proletarian, and young would still not seem relevant to many women, workers, or young people, because religion does not seem relevant. While indifference to God marks so much of English life (although the English, disliking all theories, do not care to say outright that there is no God), many ecclesiastical documents and consultations on 'mission' are defective because they suggest that the Church's reorganization in order to be more inclusive is what matters most.

A Diocesan Consultation

Several dioceses in the Church of England have derived great benefit from being hosts to Partners in Mission Consultations. A report to the Oxford Diocesan Synod in October 1981 may be taken as an example. More modest than the national report, it is also more useful, partly because external partners are more likely to feel at home with the problems and joys of congregations and counties than with unique national structures; and partly because the quality of a report must depend on the quality of its authors, curiously higher in the visitation of the Oxford diocese than in the visitation of the Church of England. Another reason seems to be that the Church is itself at its best in parish and diocese rather than in the national committee. In some ways it is a pity that the Church of England still has the resources to attempt so much at the national level. The General Synod and its committees and central services now cost more than £2,250,000 a year. Although this sum is too little to meet all the demands made on the dedicated staff of these central bodies (and Sir Ronald Harris has pointed out that the amount spent on central purposes other than training 'has been nearly halved in real terms during the last decade'), in relation to the financial problems of parishes and parishioners £2,250,000 feels like too much.

The analysis in this report to a diocese took the same line as the national report but went deeper. 'We have met a great many able and dedicated people and seen much excellent work. Yet behind all the ability, sophistication, and material wealth we have detected a spiritual hunger and a longing for something that will give meaning to life.

Many people, both clergy and laity, feel a deep loneliness and isolation leading to a loss of direction and sense of failure which is only deepened by the contemplation of the apparently "successful" efforts of others.' It was recognized that 'in most places evangelism sprang from a powerful experience of God'. The line of argument was then somewhat deflected from the central problem of England's spiritual vacuum, largely perhaps because 'partnership' was felt to be the necessary theme. The theme lured the partners into stating 'the truth that we can only survive if we minister to one another at all levels' — a proposition which, if left standing by itself, is godless.

The more detailed recommendations were more worthy of Christianity as a religion of partnership with God. Among them we noted pleas for more, and more biblical, preaching; more contemporary prayer; more lay participation in worship ('some services give the impression of a show going on independently of the people's presence' and 'we were sorry to have left our binoculars at home because without them we could hardly see where the priest had gone'); more effective training for children and adolescents ('family services are "nice" but cannot be a substitute for educational effort' and 'the main loss of the young takes place at the age of 12+'); more house groups ('in many places the tools for the renewal of Christian life'); and more contact between the chaplains in industry, hospitals, prisons, colleges, etc. and parish priests. The concentration on making prayer more real did not prevent some down-to-earth comments on the administration of the diocese, including a suggestion that it was time that an Evangelical was appointed as an area bishop or archdeacon. Nor did the recognition of a certain spiritual hunger within the Church prevent the acknowledgment of strong points: 'This diocese is rich in resources, in theological learning, in people of experience and influence in public life, in economic prosperity, in growing points of technological advance, in churches of beauty and sanctity, in religious communities with an inheritance of devotion and entailed wealth.' Always when commenting on the Church of England it is fatal to forget either its present lack of spiritual power or the abundance of its inherited glory.

Anglican–Roman Catholic agreement?

The final report of the Anglican/Roman Catholic International Commission, published in March 1982 after work which began in 1967, was so concise, so careful, and so deliberately couched in terminology familiar only to theologians that many laymen have wondered what all the fuss has been about; and it is indeed important not to exaggerate the significance of the consensus which has been achieved by a commission composed of scholarly men who are courteous and (more or less) liberal in their temper of mind. What needs to take place is nothing less than the healing of the wounds inflicted on the Body of Christ by the Reformation and the Counter-Reformation. In that crisis in the sixteenth century a number of scholarly and eirenic attempts to combine the best of Catholicism and Protestantism in a revival of the simplicities of the religion of the gospels came to nothing because on each side the emotional, sociological, and political drives towards separation were too strong for the peacemakers. In the twentieth century a great deal more than an accord between selected theologians will be necessary before the two streams of the Anglican Communion and the Roman Catholic Church can flow on to a visible reunion.

On the Anglican side the psychological change which is necessary is the confession that it is no longer appropriate to be an Anglican in any exclusive sense. When the Church of England was established under the Tudors the claim was made that it was the only valid Christian and Catholic Church in the land; the claim, celebrated in theology by Richard Hooker, was enforced by executions. Not until a century and a half ago was it thought safe to allow Roman Catholics to sit in Parliament, so bitter was the 'No Popery' cry in response to various seventeenth-century provocations from the Gunpowder Plot to the follies of James II. Still in the 1980s it is constitutionally necessary for the monarch to be a Protestant. The overseas expansion of the work of the clergy of the Church of England in the eighteenth and nineteenth centuries was often in rivalry with Roman Catholic missions and an appeal was often made to the protection of this Protestant Crown. During the first sixty years or so of our own century the emphasis was all on the growth of the Anglican Communion in extent and in depth of churchmanship, and one reason was that the spiritual link with the Church of England continued to be part of a strong colonial, or at least cultural, link between peoples. Still in the 1980s Anglican gatherings seldom act (although they sometimes talk) as if awaiting the merging of the thirty Anglican Churches into wider fellowships. The Church of England in particular is still full of people who value their heritage so highly that in their hearts they find no real wish to see it changed.

The ARCIC report is, however, a challenge to Anglicans to acknowledge some growing spiritual realities. The nation fashioned by the Tudors is gradually moving back into the European community which has a strong Catholic element — as the Church of England has been reminded by the inauguration of the diocese of Gibraltar-in-Europe. Already England contains a large, thoroughly settled, Roman Catholic community, thanks mainly to Irish immigration — as the Pope's Pastoral visit in 1982 must remind the world. The Papal visit is also to be understood as a reminder to England that the world exists — that Christianity is international, although not now in a Victorian style. The British Empire has been dissolved and it can only be a matter of time before the Anglican Communion, which was in many ways its ecclesiastical counterpart, is also dissolved. Above all, Anglicans and Roman Catholics know that they share important convictions as minorities in various non-Christian cultures, and as traditional Churches surrounded by sectarian forms of Christianity, and they find themselves co-operating in order to reaffirm a heritage which they believe to be greater than any national glory. These realities are beginning to inspire a longing for a truly international embodiment of the Catholic tradition with its capacity to breed saints.

On the Roman Catholic side the psychological change which is necessary is a confession that it is no longer appropriate to be Roman in Church government. The response to the Reformation was to centralize authority and to standardize doctrine and devotion. That far more definite and militant variety of Catholicism sustained a remarkably effective mission in many unfavourable territories, including Protestant England and the British colonies. It reached its peak at the First Vatican Council in 1870, at the very time when the Papacy lost the remnants of its temporal power. But the Counter-Reformation has been visibly collapsing ever since the death of Pius XII. Many of the demands of the sixteenth-century Reformers are being accepted in essence although the circumstances are so different that the lack of acknowledgement is excusable. The basic change is to bring a more educated laity fully into the worship of the Church — a move which must have consequences in the whole of the Church's life. One of the consequences is far more emphasis on the Bible, which the laity can read as well as the clergy. Another is the admission that centralization and standardization have become unrealistic, despite the love which still surrounds the Holy Father. Another is a welcome to the demand for a restatement of Catholicism coming from Roman Catholics who, while devout, are also citizens of the age of democracy and science. These trends were all to be observed in the National Pastoral Congress at Liverpool in May 1980.

When ARCIC tackled the apparently technical subjects of the Eucharist, the Ministry, and Authority, these were the spiritual realities in the background. This joint commission moved away from a view of the priesthood which the popular preaching of the Counter-Reformation developed from popular medieval piety: a view of the priest that saw a man apart and above, given by the bishop the power to make bread and wine into the Body and Blood of Christ, to make a fresh sacrifice of Christ in the Mass, and to make this fresh sacrifice efficacious as an intercession on behalf of the living and the dead. With this view of the priesthood went (in piety if not in strict logic) the exaltation of the Blessed Virgin Mary and of the Pope as being in their different ways indispensable channels in the distribution of Christ's grace. In the thinking of ARCIC the Mass has been set firmly in the context of the community, the Church. The Eucharist is seen as the making effective in the present of the one sacrifice of himself offered by Christ — not a repetition of that sacrifice but a special kind of memorial in which Christ is present and active, offering himself to faithful Christians in communion. It is also seen as an intercessory act by and on behalf of the whole Church, militant and departed, in which the faithful plead before the Father the merits of Christ's life, death, and resurrection — the sole ground on which sinful humanity is entitled to stand. The bread and wine do not change physically but their significance is altered, and the faithful receive them as much more than bread and wine. Talk about their 'substance' is outmoded, but what is believed about this sacrament is no mere Zwinglian memorialism. The weary old controversies are thus transcended, and those who were present at the Windsor meeting in 1971 still remember the almost terrified silence, lasting some minutes, which followed the realization that substantial agreement about the Eucharist had been reached — an agreement holding out hope of a common understanding of priesthood.

The ordained ministry is also set within the Christian community. It is an expression of the eternal Christ's own work in that community, and those ministers of Christ who exercise oversight (*episcope*) do so in order to enable all the people to use the gifts of the Holy Spirit which they have received. Authority in the Church is now understood as a service for the sake of its fellowship, not as a lordship to be justified legally. The primacy of the Bishop of Rome is valued as a focus of the world-wide unity of Christians, and although normally the Church's decisions are taken in parish, diocese, or council, it is said to be right for the Pope to express the whole Church's faith in emergencies. The Church is preserved by Christ from falling into serious and permanent error; thus it is maintained in the truth which is pre-eminently set forth in the Bible. It is claimed that the dogmas that the Blessed Virgin Mary was 'kept free from all stain of original sin' and was 'in body and soul assumed into heavenly glory' — dogmas proclaimed by Popes as binding on all the faithful in 1854 and 1950 — are to be understood as expressions of truths which all the faithful do believe: that the salvation won by Christ was operative among all mankind before his birth, and that his mother's glory in heaven involves full participation in the fruits of that salvation. The term 'infallibility' is applicable unconditionally only to God, and the teaching ministry of the Pope can be understood better in less dangerous terms.

The first Anglican responses to these agreements have already shown that some questions remain. Is it possible that Roman Catholicism is really prepared to meet the protests of the Churches of the Reformation and the probings of the children of a science-based society? As the Anglican Consultative Council noted, many of these suspicions can be allayed if attention is also given to the agreements resulting from regional and international discussions between Lutherans and Roman Catholics. There 'justifying faith', or trust in God the Father through Christ in the power of the Holy Spirit, is distinguished both from the performance of ecclesiastical duties and from the acceptance of propositions taught by ecclesiastical authority. Luther's central point is thus met — but without lapsing into the individualism and emotionalism which have sometimes disfigured Protestantism. As for the interpretation of the Marian dogmas offered by ARCIC, we are assured that it is the kind of interpretation which is often offered to students in the Roman Catholic seminaries of Europe and North America. It is an interpretation likely to encourage increasing numbers of Anglicans to pay more attention to Mary's place in the story of our salvation.

The largest theological change now in mind is, it is clear, a growth away from Counter-Reformation categories of thought in the Roman Catholic Church. At least in Europe and North America the theology of ARCIC represents what many educated Roman Catholic laymen and intellectual priests believe nowadays. Roman Catholic bishops are, however, famous for being more sensitive to the pastoral needs of simple believers than to the discontents of the educated. In Germany their conflicts with academic theologians commanding large student followings, including Hans Küng, have recently been notorious. Elsewhere — extensively in the USA, for example — they have found themselves unable to communicate with some of their ablest priests, who have requested laicization in a mood of despair. Students, with their questioning but idealistic minds, have felt fewer vocations to serve such an authoritarian Church;

the French statistics of decline are startling. Yet the ecclesiastical authorities have not read these signs of the times as any kind of instruction to alter traditions which they believe to have been entrusted to them. On the contrary, the prevailing tendency is to reaffirm traditions. In the Netherlands, for example, conservatism has been reimposed thanks to the power of Rome in episcopal appointments, while in Africa the rule of priestly celibacy has been maintained (at least in theory) despite its result, a disastrous shortage of priests. The Jesuits have been disciplined for 'progressivism'. It therefore remains to be seen how far the Vatican will bless the agreements reached by ARCIC. The final report was subjected to an ominous delay before publication was authorized. The wars waged by recent Popes against modernism, and against any existential or demythologized emphasis in theology, are too recent for the new liberal tendency to be expected to gain much official ground rapidly. The probability is that years will pass before the theological revolution can be seen to have reached the Sacred Congregation for the Doctrine of the Faith — and even then there will be a great reluctance to admit that anything essential has altered.

Parallel with this development within Roman Catholicism there must be an increasing willingness among Anglicans to think in terms wider than Anglicanism and to hope for reunion with Rome as the fulfilment of the Reformation. This willingness will, we believe, be voiced with varying degrees of clarity as the different Anglican provinces respond to the work of ARCIC: the response in Sydney will be more hesitant than the response in Accra. For the time being each development, Roman Catholic or Anglican, must be allowed its own integrity, which might be compromised were there to be premature attempts at any merger of the two Communions. Canterbury to Rome and back is a long journey, allowing no short cuts.

Three practical problems

While these parallel developments take their time, three practical problems must arouse the concern of all who seek the reconciliation of the Anglican Communion with the Roman Catholic Church.

The recognition of Anglican Orders is already an accomplished fact in the shape of acts of courtesy to visiting clergy in some areas of the world, but it seldom occurs in England and the outright condemnation by Pope Leo XIII in 1896 (*Apostolicae Curae)* presents a major problem at the official and international level. It is most unlikely that any Pope will simply tear that bull up. It was essentially an assessment of the history of the sixteenth century, and it cannot be faulted for its assertion that the English Ordinal of 1552 was, and was intended to be, firmly on the Protestant side as the Catholic-Protestant division was then understood. What it said then was no more than had already been said by the bishops appointed under Mary I and by generations of Recusants who also rejected the Elizabethan 'settlement' of religion. Moreover, since the age of the Reformation the difficulty of recognizing Anglican clergymen as Catholic bishops, priests, or deacons has been exacerbated by their frequently obvious dependence on the patronage of the Crown, a dependence particularly noticed by Irish Catholics.

The work of ARCIC, however, leads naturally to the conclusion that the Anglican clergy have exercised a valid ministry of the Word and sacraments within the Anglican Communion, preserving at least in name the scriptures, the ecumenical creeds, and the threefold Catholic ministry (much to the indignation of many other Protestants). That is now seen to matter more than the precise words or actions employed in their ordinations. The crucial questions are whether the Anglican Communion is a part of the Church of Christ, and whether the Anglican intention when ordaining priests is compatible with the Roman Catholic Church's intention. The work of ARCIC suggests clearly that the answer to both questions is yes, so that the question of Anglican Orders has been put in a new context. Hopes of Pope John Paul II making a dramatic concession in return for English hospitality are naïve, but it will be surprising if *Apostolicae Curae* has not been supplemented, and in effect replaced, by a fresh declaration before 1996.

Already invitations to Anglicans to communion at Roman Catholic altars are issued, but these invitations are unofficial except where there is 'serious spiritual need' such as a lack of access to Anglican sacraments. When Lord Coggan, then Archbishop of Canterbury, praised the practice and asked for its extension during sermons in Rome and in Westminster Cathedral the effect was, we understand, to cause great offence and to harden the official teaching that communion must follow, not precede, agreement in doctrine. However, here again the work of ARCIC has put an old question into a new context. As agreement about the Eucharist and the Ministry is more and more widely recognized, it seems likely that the obligation to offer hospitality at the Lord's table will be accepted at the official level as well as privately. Gradually the feeling may increase that it would be right for the Roman Catholic Church to covenant for unity by the recognition and reconciliation of the ministries of Churches now divided. When they grow impatient, Anglicans do well to remember that until recently it was in many provinces the standard Anglican teaching that there was insufficient agreement with other Churches of the Reformation to warrant official 'intercommunion'; the report which marked the change of conviction in the Church of England was published as recently as 1968. It would be a sign that Anglicans have taken the Roman Catholic position seriously were the Lambeth Conference of 1988 to express a strong hope (stronger than was possible in 1978) for the restoration of communion with the Bishop of Rome.

Already many 'mixed marriages' are celebrated in Anglican churches and the children of them receive a religious education which is Roman Catholic or Anglican or both according to their parents' conscientious wishes. The requirements that the Roman Catholic partner in such a marriage should insist on his or her church as the setting and sign an undertaking to secure the baptism and education of any children in his or her faith are no longer invariable (*Matrimonia Mixta,* 1970). A dispensation for a mixed marriage can be granted after only a verbal promise to do all in the partner's power in this direction, and the 1976 joint report on *Anglican-Roman Catholic Marriage* suggested as an alternative that it should be deemed sufficient for the Roman Catholic parish priest to certify that he had reminded the partner concerned of his or her obligations. While it would greatly improve the ecumenical situation if this alternative were to become standard practice, it seems unlikely that the Roman Catholic Church will in the near future formally recognize the rights of both parents to determine their children's education by agreement. That must wait upon a more extensive recognition of the limitations of the disciplinary rights of the clergy. The timing of the formal acceptance of artificial contraception seems to involve similar considerations and expectations. However, all the evidence suggests that in many countries (including Britain) most Roman Catholic married couples have already decided to ignore the Papal teaching both in bed and in the confessional, whereas in mixed marriages the common practice appears to favour the stronger, Roman Catholic, position where there is any real religious education at all. The results can arouse great resentment, particularly in the Republic of Ireland where the numbers of Anglicans have diminished.

To sum up: the recognition of Anglican Orders, official intercommunion, and equality in mixed marriages all depend on the growing acceptance on both sides of the doctrinal agreements which ARCIC has now outlined prophetically.

Covenanting with Free Churches

If we comment more narrowly on *Towards Visible Unity*, the 1980 report proposing a covenant between the Church of England, the Methodists, the Moravians, and the United Reformed Church, the reason is not that we think it insignificant in comparison with the work of ARCIC. It seems right to pursue negotiations with the Roman Catholic Church and with the Free Churches with equal determination, since it is the Anglican vocation to preserve both the Catholic vision and the Reformation insights in order to prepare the way for a truly international and renewed Catholicism. The explanation of the narrower range of our comment is simply that we write before the 1982 votes in the highest courts of the participating Churches. At the moment it seems likely that the Methodist Conference will repeat the almost unanimous acceptance of the proposals registered as its preliminary response in 1981; that the United Reformed Church, which contains elements strongly anti-episcopalian because of Presbyterian or Congregationalist traditions, will ask for a clarification of the proposed role of bishops; and that the voting in the General Synod of the Church of England will, mainly as a result of continuing hesitations in the House of Clergy, end up somewhere between the decisive yes and the decisive no. With such a prospect in view it seems sensible to add to the general support for 'covenanting' offered in previous Prefaces some thoughts about the Anglican opposition.

This has been less substantial than at the time of the Anglican-Methodist reunion scheme because then the opposition included some (not all) Evangelicals who objected to the proposed rite which could be interpreted as the episcopal ordination of individual Methodist ministers. No such rite is included in the present plan. The opposition then included also many eloquent conservatives, headed by Lord Fisher of Lambeth, who feared the unsettling effects of moving by definite stages towards union. The present plan is not a union scheme and after the proposed covenant the Church of England would still be free to retain its Establishment and other oddities which it is said to hold dear. Another factor is that since Lord Fisher's day the pace of change has accelerated in the Church and although churchgoers are often conservatives they less often have the energy left to be militants, except when fearing for the future of the Book of Common Prayer in view of the widespread use of the Alternative Service Book. The Prayer Book (Protection) Bill introduced into Parliament did represent a substantial body of opinion, particularly among those who without going to church regularly like to think that the 'language of Shakespeare' is still in use outside the theatre; but that manifesto by alarmed peers and MPs never became an Established Church (Protection) Act.

Vocal opposition to the covenanting plan has, in fact, been largely confined to the Catholic movement in the Church of England. Although this may seem curious when we note the protests within the Free Churches (for example, in 95 Theses affixed to Canterbury Cathedral) that the plan is a sell-out to Catholicism, such opposition may well be decisive in the terms of ecclesiastical politics. Not all Anglicans who greatly value Catholicism oppose the plan, but the present officers of the English Church Union, allied with other 'Catholic societies', have thrown themselves into the battle and some 'Catholic spokesmen' have been implacably opposed. Their hostility has alarmed some, perhaps many, who are reluctant to risk sacrificing the unity of the Church of England to the cause of unity with Churches which in England are much smaller and are believed to be declining. The main arguments deployed by Anglican 'Catholic' spokesmen therefore deserve examination.

By far the strongest argument is that the plan would move the Church of England further from the possibility of reconciliation with the Roman Catholic Church on the basis of agreement about Catholic 'faith and order'. It would mean that ministers or presbyters who had not been episcopally ordained would be recognized as able to preside at Eucharists in Anglican churches if invited. In an article in *The Times* in 1978 Bishop Christopher Butler, a distinguished Roman Catholic scholar and ecumenist, warned that such a recognition 'would cast doubt on the acceptance by the Church of England of the doctrine of the ordained ministry agreed by ARCIC'. In a letter to *The Times* in 1982 Bishop Alan Clark, Co-Chairman of ARCIC and Chairman of the Roman Catholic Ecumenical Commission for England and Wales, stated: 'I fail to see how certain constituent elements in Anglicanism are adequately safeguarded' if the covenant proposals 'are accepted as they stand'. Bishop Clark instanced the failure of the plan to confer ministry by episcopal ordination; 'we do not find that the selective ordination or ordination by proxy conforms to the accepted tradition of the Church'.

There has been concern among Catholic-minded Anglicans at the prospect of the Church of England recognizing women ministers as true presbyters of the Catholic Church, since it is believed that no one branch of the Catholic Church has the right to alter the priesthood unilaterally. Although bishops would be consecrated from among the Methodist or URC ministers, there has also been concern at the danger of confusion about the bishop's role. Bishops of the Church of England would, it is feared, not be able to follow their consciences by forbidding women to preside at the Eucharist — and by being compelled to engage in 'common decision making' with Free Church leaders they might find themselves and their flocks trapped in a bureaucratic jungle. The erosion of the episcopal office also seemed to be implied in the decision to allow some URC moderators to continue to function without being made bishops and in the lack of insistence on a record of ministers who had participated personally in the services held to recognize and accept them. These points, together with concern that the diaconate would be absent from the ministry of one of the covenanting Churches and that the lay celebration of Holy Communion might continue, were the grounds of the disquiet expressed in the Memorandum of Dissent added to the 1980 report. The dissentients were Dr Graham Leonard (now Bishop of London), Canon Peter Boulton (now Prolocutor of the Convocation of Canterbury), and Mr O.W.H. Clarke (now Chairman of the House of Laity) — a formidable trio. Their points reappeared in later opposition to the scheme, together with others of less substance.

A debate in the General Synod during 1981 ended with majorities in favour, but in the House of Clergy these majorities were at two points less than the two-thirds majority which will be required before an effective yes can be delivered in 1982. The subsequent debates in the Diocesan Synods showed a roughly similar pattern. This element of disquiet added weight to the Archbishop of Canterbury's plea for changes, although plainly no changes can be made in the plan while the Churches concerned are still voting on it. Writing as we do before the 1982 vote in the General Synod, it seems possible that some changes might be made after that vote which might in due course secure overwhelming Anglican support for a covenant. These changes are, we think, desirable however the vote goes.

The developments we should like to see include a much clearer statement of the Roman Catholic position or positions. As things are, some confusion has been left by the fact that the Episcopal Conference of England and Wales has never been pressed to make any solid response. While declining to 'covenant' (for reasons which have always been obvious), the bishops have declared that they would 'continue and increase collaboration in the search for unity with Churches able to covenant in terms of the Ten Propositions' and that they welcomed the prospect of a Common Ordinal with a 'common doctrine of ministry incorporating episcopal, presbyteral, and lay roles'. One of the two official observers on the Churches' Council for Covenanting, Father John Coventry, S.J., has been eloquent in his defence of the 1980 plan and of the theology behind it. In his 1982 *Times* letter Bishop Clark wrote that 'a Roman Catholic should be grateful for an initiative which has a certain greatness in its vision' and he cited the Episcopal Conference's recent public assurance of 'close and sympathetic attention'. Is it too much to hope that the authorities of the Roman Catholic Church will be challenged to say constructively how they think the plan should be improved, and that a brief renegotiation of the covenant will attach great importance to this brotherly contribution? If the answer is that the Roman Catholic Church cannot make an agreed, official comment because opinion is divided, it would be valuable to have that situation acknowledged and registered.

We do not suggest the introduction of a rite which could be interpreted as acknowledging the necessity of episcopal ordination for Methodist or URC ministers. Such a rite would not command adequate support in Methodism, the URC, or the Church of England. In the Memorandum of Dissent, as in much other recent thought in the Anglican Communion, we find a 'whole-hearted' statement that 'it is not for any covenanting Church to affirm or deny anything about the sufficiency of the ministry of its own Church prior to the point of covenanting'. We find also 'real thanksgiving' that 'from the time of covenanting onwards all our Churches shall have bishops and shall be pledged for the future to episcopal ordering'. Here is, we believe, that basic sympathy with the plan to be expected from men of integrity willing to serve actively on the Churches' Council for Covenanting, which used their talents for drafting at several key points where Anglo-Catholic criticism was expected (although Mr Clarke resigned in 1982). It is not a plan which involves 'selective ordination' or 'ordination by proxy'; in the proposed service no one is ordained except those who have not already been ordained anywhere — and they are ordained episcopally. Yet surely the proposed act of recognition and reconciliation in the setting of the Eucharist can be further improved in wording, so as to make yet clearer the incorporation of ordained Methodist (or other) ministers into the Catholic ministry as retained by the Church of England? Surely, too, records can be kept by bishops of which ministers took the trouble to be present at a national or regional service, and only those ministers could be licensed to take services in the Church of England? And surely the alarm about a 'bureaucratic jungle' can be answered by a plea for time in which sensible bishops sharing a common consecration can find how to work together — and by a reminder of the great damage to the Christian mission inflicted by the present disunity? The parallel existence of Uniate Churches has for long been accepted as a necessity when thinking in terms of a reconciliation to Rome.

The question of women presbyters is often thought to be the real stumbling block in securing 'Catholic' consent to the plan. It needs to be seen, we suggest, in the global context of the Anglican Communion. There are now several hundred canonically ordained Anglican priests who are women; that is a fact with which the Roman Catholic Church has already come to terms as it has continued to converse and to collaborate with the Anglican Communion. It is amazing and saddening that the General Synod of the Church of England has not yet allowed such priests to celebrate the Eucharist at its altars when invited to do so by the incumbent with the approval of the bishop and of the Parochial Church Council. This needs to be put right rapidly. To deny parishes this freedom seems a denial of the unity of the Anglican Communion — and of the right of the Anglican majority (supported in this instance by some well-known Roman Catholic theologians) to follow its conscience. When this anomaly is corrected, it ought to be easier to allow English women ordained within Methodism or the URC to minister to Anglicans if invited after their incorporation into the priesthood as known in the Church of England. And the recognition of the Church of England's own deaconesses as being in Holy Orders ought also to ease the situation. Women are not admitted to the priesthood in the Church of England, and probably will not be for another ten years or so, but a psychological barrier will be broken when deaconesses are entitled to wear clerical dress, to be called 'the Reverend', and to appear in *Crockford's Clerical Directory*. But it would still be vital to protect the rights of a bishop to veto such invitations in his diocese (preferably with the agreement of his synod) and of an incumbent or church council to refuse to bow to pressure to issue an invitation. Every troubled conscience deserves respect.

However, the conscience of the majority which thinks reunion a part of Christian obedience also deserves respect. With some such improvements and reassurances, the plan to covenant ought to commend itself as the vital move in the healing of divisions which ought never to have been allowed to afflict the Body of Christ and which have in fact poisoned English history. It ought also to lead into a process of reunion which other Churches, including the Roman Catholic Church, could join in their own ways and in the growing light of their own consciences. If 1982 sees an inconclusive verdict in the General Synod, it will be tempting to abandon all efforts of this sort (referred to pejoratively as 'schemes') in despair. After the failure of the Anglican-Methodist plan many felt that they were in darkness and some have never come out of it. But it seems likely that this time the obstacles to unity will be comparatively trivial. If this were to be generally felt, it would be tragically wrong for the Church of England to ignore two major facts. According to the New Testament, Christ commands visible unity; and according to repeated, overwhelming votes in the Methodist Conference, reunion is possible in England now while safeguarding the Catholic heritage on which Anglicans have traditionally insisted. In the light of these two facts, it does not seem to be open to Anglicans to abandon the quest for the visible unity of Christ's people in England. Covenanting ought to be renegotiated with determination.

The Archbishop of Canterbury

The personality of the Archbishop of Canterbury is always important to many Anglicans and that is our excuse for including a comment which slightly overlaps with the Preface to *The Church of England Yearbook* for 1982. The choice of Robert Runcie aroused unusual interest both because it was the first time that elected representatives of the Church of England had been officially consulted by the agents of the Crown and also because it was the first appointment of a man born after the First World War. The media quickly took the new archbishop to their hearts as a wartime hero, as a part-time pig-keeper, and as a former chairman of the committee which advises the BBC and IBA about their religious programmes; and additionally several television interviews have shown him to be a well-informed, thoughtful, and gently humorous man, more diffident than would generally be expected of holders of the Military Cross. There has also been a general welcome among the clergy, many of whom know of his excellent work as the chief pastor of the diocese of St Albans. In churchmanship he combines a firm hold of the tradition of Catholic spirituality with an open attitude to many modern realities. One of his chief interests has been in theological conversations with the Orthodox Churches, yet he has also been bold in applying pressure on the General Synod to provide a warmer pastoral care for people remarried after divorce and for homosexuals; he has surprised conservatives by publicly arguing that homosexuality is a handicap rather than a sin or a sickness (although he also annoyed 'gay' propagandists by his caution). On the issue of women priests he has annoyed enthusiasts, and American women in particular have been irritated by the impression that he takes Orthodox bishops more seriously than he takes them; but he has given a few signs of being open to conversion. The only clerical element tempted to be disgruntled about the promotion of this liberal Catholic has been the conservative Evangelical movement, which perhaps had been inclined to the illusion that everything was going its way; but any such critics would have been unable to produce a plausible alternative candidate. The Archbishop of York, whose background is Evangelical although he is no fundamentalist, is widely liked and greatly valued as a pastor and expositor of the Bible, but is known to find high office a strain. His sensitivity is deeper than is indicated by the easy charm of his social manner, his often topical or humorous sermons, and his felicitous public addresses.

During his enthronement in Canterbury Dr Runcie (as Oxford University has enabled us to call him) revealed his character. His realism is well suited to a period when the Church of England, far from triumphant in spiritual reality, is tempted to exaggerate the stories which it can tell of success, and when the Anglican Communion, unsure about its theological foundations and its future, is tempted merely to stress its present fellowship. 'The temptation to gain the Church's end by using the world's means is still with us', he declared. 'We are tempted to organize ourselves like any other party or pressure group, to establish sharper dividing lines between those who are members and those who are not, to compete more aggressively for attention from the public, to recruit new members with a strident self-confidence which suggests that we have nothing to learn, to persuade with a loud voice rather than with the quiet reasons of the heart.' Rejecting what he frankly called 'salesmanship', he turned instead to the examples of Mother Teresa of Calcutta and of Archbishop Romero of San Salvador (whose murder dominated the news on that very day, 25 March 1980) and to the simplicity of African Christianity. 'Our lives must be full of longing as we struggle to become more Christ-like', he said; and that involved 'a firm lead against rigid thinking, a judging temper of mind, the disposition to over-simplify the difficult and complex problems'. This enthronement sermon included a memorable act of self-denial by a man who is the centre of much affection and has about him the aura of success: 'if the Church gives Jesus Christ's sort of lead it will not be popular.'

Since his enthronement Dr Runcie has made no dramatic calls to the nation and has seldom said anything very original in his teaching within the Church. Historians may not find much to write about as they ponder these two years. It has nevertheless been instructive to observe how decisive his interventions have become in General Synod debates (all the more genuinely influential now that the Archbishop of Canterbury is seldom in the chair) and how on a very public and very glamorous occasion such as the wedding of the Prince of Wales he struck millions as a man who could talk sense. Wisely he delegates; he has surrounded himself with an able staff at Lambeth (headed by Bishop Ross Hook, who sacrificed the status of a diocesan bishop in order to be this kind of a servant) and by an energetic team in the leadership of the diocese of Canterbury. He has made a point of consulting his brother bishops and also has a wider circle of counsellors. It is surprising to think of such moves as innovations, but such they were to a large extent. Thus sheltered from some of the administrative pressures and spared the risks of a solo performance, he has had some time to be available as a pastor to troubled souls and to talk with people outside the English ecclesiastical machine. He has begun to gather knowledge, to win friends, and to develop a personal authority by international journeys, rightly believing that committees such as the Anglican Consultative Council can be no substitute for the person-to-person contacts made by a travelling pilgrim from Canterbury. He always strikes foreigners as being very much an English gentleman, but fortunately he is seldom called upon to move outside those circles where such an assessment is, on the whole, a compliment. The miracle wrought by his assistant and representative, Mr Terry Waite, in rescuing missionaries from an Iranian prison after trumped up charges of espionage is only one example of the influence which an Archbishop of Canterbury can still wield if he takes the trouble to study and prepare the ground. Another example is the respectful attention given to his addresses about world problems in the USA, where he attracted audiences wider than would normally be expected by the Episcopal Church, a comparatively small denomination.

This may be the beginning of a Primacy as effective as, say, Randall Davidson's (1903-28), although in tune with an almost totally different age. Lord Davidson was no theologian and Dr Runcie has not been granted all the personal gifts which his five most recent predecessors exercised, but the more 'ordinary' man may well turn out to be better than any of the eccentric giants at the work of the primate of All England and the president of the Anglican Communion. Robert Runcie is splendidly gifted as a co-ordinating manager, and as a charming communicator. In this hope many pray for him.

Catholic leadership

We should be less than honest if we did not confess that behind that tribute to Dr Runcie's style lies a concern about the narrow-mindedness of some other leaders of contemporary Catholicism.

In the Church of England there is a movement for 'Catholic Renewal' which deserves the support it has received — and more support. But the leadership of the Anglican societies bearing the name Catholic often seems to be preoccupied by narrow and negative causes such as the resistance to women priests and to any conceivable terms of reunion which might be acceptable in the Free Churches. The contrast with the willingness of many Evangelicals to be somewhat flexible for the sake of evangelism is glaring. The Fountain Trust, for some years the successful focus of the Charismatic movement in the British Churches, has felt guided to sacrifice its own existence; but no such guidance appears to have been heard by the quite numerous Anglican Catholic societies. These 'Catholic leaders' seem to be skilled in the tactics of ecclesiastical politics, but to lack any greatness of strategic vision. If, as we believe, the Anglican Consultative Council has been right to call for a coherent ecumenical strategy, we also believe that some Anglican Catholic leaders bear the heaviest responsibility because they have failed to see that the first step is the sharing of Catholic order with non-episcopal Churches in a way which does not insult those Churches' existing ministries. If we are being unfair to Anglican Catholic leaders, we are not alone in hoping to see them prove their greatness. Many Anglicans want a Catholicism which is certainly the foundation of order in the Church — but is gloriously large and positive, as is the Gospel of the world's salvation, entrusted to the Catholic Church.

The personality of Pope John Paul II is often admired as being large and positive.

The last Preface to Crockford welcomed his election — and was rebuked by the religious correspondent of *The Times* for being naïve in its welcome. Clearly he is a big man as well as the holder of a big office, and on the eve of his visit to Britain we still share much of the hero-worship which usually surrounds him. There is no need to repeat here the personal tributes paid to him by, for example, the Archbishop of Canterbury. If his visit strengthens his own dawning interest in Anglicanism, that will be one of the ecumenical gains. As many commentators have noted, however, so far in his pontificate he has disappointingly displayed the limitations as well as the strengths of the character of the 'Pope from Poland'. The extent of his travels shows how unjust it would be to call him an isolationist, but every now and then a rigid conservatism in his religion obtrudes itself and distresses the flocks to whom he is trying to minister at great personal cost. He has been to Latin America, but the question remains whether he has really understood the economic and social situation which by its stinking injustice has persuaded many of the bishops and priests to be, as he thinks, too political. He has been to the USA, but has he been able to absorb the challenge of that still rumbustious democracy including its 'women's movement'? He has been to Africa, but it is doubtful whether he has really felt the power of the African traditions which are expressed in the pleas that priests should be allowed to have wives and children and that congregations should be allowed to use many ancestral customs which still make the supernatural vividly present. He has been to France and Germany, but has he listened to their laity in a Europe which seems very remote from any supernatural world? He has read many books and has met scientists, but does he understand personally and profoundly why in a science-based, freely democratic, and largely secular culture, Christianity needs to be restated in its faith and morals? He has revealed some distaste for the *dolce vita* pursued in the more secular quarters of Rome, but has he fully grasped why most of Rome's churches are poorly attended? In brief, has he ever really left Poland? It is reported that even bishops or cardinals or Vatican officials find it difficult to gain access to him for genuine discussions about tough problems. To be the Church of the people, the Church has only to stand firm, proclaiming the people's dignity along with its own: that is the Polish faith, arising out of the Polish experience, and it is noble. All who love freedom and courage admire the Poles and their strongly Christian leaders for being inflexibly themselves under a dehumanizing brand of Marxism imposed on them by foreign conquerors. But the situation in many other parts of the world including England is very different and far more complicated. In such places Catholicism needs a largeness which includes a discriminatingly affirmative attitude to a strange new world. There Catholic leadership needs to be positive but also open, for God is at work creatively in this world; new life is springing up, the wheat along with the weeds.

The comparison of personalities always tends to be odious, but when the Pope meets Dr Runcie the Anglican leader need not feel completely dwarfed; far more than John Paul II he embodies the Catholicism of the future.

The work of a bishop

Few complaints are heard these days about the appointment of bishops. Instead there seems to be a general acceptance of the system by which since 1977 the Prime Minister has had names fed to him or her by the Crown Appointments Commission (or, in the case of suffragans, by the diocesan bishop) — names which, it can be guessed, have been gathered by the Appointments Secretaries of the Prime Minister and the Archbishops. Apart from a few grumbles about the appointment of an outspoken theologian to Birmingham, the only controversy surrounded the translation of Dr Graham Leonard — a man equally outspoken because brave — from Truro to London announced in March 1981. It was a controversy marred by indiscretions about the confidential proceedings of the Crown Appointments Commission and by some surprisingly crude statements to the press. But those who regretted Dr Leonard's promotion because they disagreed with his ecclesiastical politics could not say that he lacked either the pastoral or the intellectual equipment for his new position. Many hopes surround him as he undertakes his heavy new responsibilities in the nation's largely unchurched capital while continuing to be a hard-working and shrewd chairman of the Board for Social Responsibility. Nor could critics say that the Prime Minister had failed to nominate the man whom the diocesan Vacancy in See Committee would have elected if left to itself. Empty ceremonies to elect and 'confirm' the new bishop, which have strangely persisted since 1533, need reform in accordance with a sensible report welcomed by the General Synod in 1982; but the only valid and crucial objection to the present procedures is theological. The system still gives the Prime Minister, who unlike the Queen need not be a member of the Church of England, the possibility of deciding which of two men should be the chief pastor of a diocese. This intrusion of the State into the proper sphere of the Church has many precedents, including medieval and Roman Catholic ones; but it will have to be abandoned before the Church of England can proceed from covenanting and co-operation to a full union with any of the Free Churches. It seems to most non-Anglicans as serious a matter as any of the problems noted in the three Anglicans' Memorandum of Dissent, and it is generous of the non-Anglicans not to have dissented from covenanting on this ground.

There is no room for complacency about the work which bishops do when appointed. Recent debates in the United Reformed Church have included many passionate refusals to accept bishops — and the evidence cited is evidence about the present practice of episcopacy in England. The Methodists have been considering whether the superintendents of circuits ought not to be made bishops instead of the chairmen of the larger districts. The National Pastoral Congress made a clear request for smaller dioceses in the Roman Catholic Church. Anglicans, too, have complained. Most of the complaints are about bishops being remote. In the description of a bishop's work in the proposed service of reconciliation inaugurating the covenant it is said: 'He is to know his people and be known by them.' Yet it is absurdly impossible for any diocesan bishop to know his whole diocese at any depth, and if he tries to do so he either overworks or, failing in the work, overtalks. The Bishop of Hereford explained the situation when he obtained the General Synod's support for the creation of a suffragan see: 'A parish priest feels a greater need for accountability to, and support from, the bishop. . . . Parishes are no longer content with a short episcopal visit for confirmation.' He also pointed out that the supply of assistant bishops from overseas has dried up.

So suffragans there must be — but of what kind? There can be frustration for them and for others when they are regarded as episcopal curates and not entrusted with a definite area in which they are for most purposes 'the' bishop. The practice now adopted by dioceses such as urban London and rural Salisbury seems an obvious improvement which ought to be copied everywhere with the appropriate changes: a diocesan bishop who is preferably something of a scholar and a statesman (a category which definitely includes the new Bishop of Salisbury) delegates most of the pastoral care to area bishops, although he is ready to handle exceptionally difficult problems and although for his own soul's health he knows that he ought never to be so grand as to be aloof. The most effective decision-making body in the diocese then becomes the diocesan bishop's Staff Meeting, although many decisions which remain the responsibility of the diocese as a whole are rightly reserved to more democratic bodies such as the Bishop's Council, the Board of Finance, and the Pastoral Committee. This pattern seems more desirable than the creation of a very large number of dioceses without much distinction to, or co-ordination between, them. The number of area bishops ought, we believe, to be increased substantially; but in the present administration of the Church of England the work of an archdeacon overlaps with that of an area or suffragan bishop, and provided that a workable area was given to the one bishop-archdeacon probably the number of clergy not in the parochial front line need not be much increased.

How to make effective the bishop's own claim to have the 'cure of souls' is the question most thoughtful churchmen ask as they experience the present system or non-system. The proposed service of reconciliation rightly stresses the bishop's teaching office. 'He shares with his fellow bishops a special responsibility to maintain and further unity of the Church, to uphold its discipline, and to guard its faith. . . . He is to teach and govern them after the example of the Apostles, speaking to them in the name of God and interpreting the Gospel of Christ'. The reality, however, is that not all of the present diocesan or area or suffragan bishops teach their own dioceses or the wider Church systematically. With many other pressures eating into their time, it is too easy for them to fall into thinking that their responsibility is discharged by pastorally informal confirmation and institution addresses, by brief remarks to synods, and by jolly after-dinner speeches. It is also too easy for them to seek exemption from the study of less familiar subjects by developing the habit of talking about themselves. Conspicuous exceptions include the Bishop of Chichester and, from a different school in churchmanship, the Bishop of Birmingham, whose Advent 1981 Pastoral Letter on *The Kingdom of God in Our Land* was a model of its kind.

Nowadays the House of Bishops does not corporately utter on doctrinal questions, however fundamental. There is a great contrast between the 1911–14 discussion which led up to a two-day debate in the Upper House of the Convocation of Canterbury and very carefully prepared resolutions carried *nem. con.* (as summarized in G. K. A. Bell's *Randall Davidson,* chapter xli) and the deafening silence in all official Church circles which greeted the publication by the SCM Press in 1980 of the Rev. Don Cupitt's *Taking Leave of God,* an essay far more hostile to the Christian faith in God the Creator through Christ the Saviour than any of the publications which stirred up such anger and evoked such cautious wisdom in the 1910s. Its publisher summed up the message of Mr Cupitt's 'painfully explicit' book thus: 'We need to abandon theological realism, to part company with the thought of an objective God, some kind of immense cosmic or supracosmic Creator-Mind, and struggle to realize religious values in this life, in relation to social and economic conditions objectively and presently prevailing, for that is all that we have.' Of course we recognize and welcome the pluralism in Anglican theology, now eloquently stated and blessed by the Church of England Doctrine Commission's 1981 report, *Believing in the Church.* There are nevertheless limits to pluralism if the Church is to be the Church. There is much to be said for the Anglican practice of waiting to see whether an ultra-radical theologian will find himself compelled by his own conscience to withdraw from any responsibility as one of the Church's accredited teachers (as Dr Michael Goulder of Birmingham University did when he resigned his orders in 1982, announcing that he could no longer believe in God). But there is nothing to be said for the abdication of responsibility implied in the failure to make any corporate comment on a total and public rejection of the heart of the Church's faith by a well-known priest rightly honoured for his intellectual eminence.

No man can be sufficient for all the tasks expected of a bishop nowadays. Since we have repeated and supported the common charge that bishops are not effective enough as pastors and teachers, we feel obliged to suggest one negative step which could be taken in order to save a bishop's time and one positive step which could increase his spiritual and intellectual impact. Negatively, we advocate the drastic reduction in the number of Anglican bishops with seats in the House of Lords. The House holds debates which are intrinsically valuable but not widely reported, and the ratio between the time spent by bishops in the House (or travelling to it) and the effect of their contributions is distressing to those who know or imagine how many opportunities await their attention in their dioceses. Bishops with a special gift for this work — Dr Gerald Ellison, Bishop of London 1973–81, was one such, and the present Bishop of Durham is, like his predecessor, another — are rare. The withdrawal of most of the bishops from the Lords would release them for their proper duties and would help to release the Church from an image which, as the Partners in Mission pointed out, damages evangelism. Positively, we advocate a firm plan of biblical and other spiritual studies for the clerical chapters and for the synods of deaneries, a plan in which bishops should take the lead as lecturers. At present too many deanery chapters feel most purposeful at breakfast, and too many deanery synods think that their only really serious business is the allocation to the parishes of the financial 'quota' decreed by the diocese.

The work of presbyter

The ordinal which is proposed for common use from the date of the covenant between the Church of England and others is practically identical with the provision made in the Alternative Service Book of 1980. It is in no way incompatible with the agreement reached by ARCIC. A statement about baptism, the Eucharist and the Ministry has come from Faith and Order meetings of the World Council of Churches — meetings which included representatives of an even wider range of Churches, from Charismatic or modernist Protestants to Eastern Orthodox and Roman Catholics. The latest meeting of this kind was at Lima in 1982. It can be said truthfully — and, in the context of past controversies, remarkably — that there is now a very large measure of agreement about the ideals. The theoretical agreement, however, does not mean that in practice Christians are clear about what a 'presbyter' (the title that commands the widest acceptance) ought to be doing in his or her parish or special ministry; and the lack of a practical agreement is accompanied by a crisis of confidence in the hearts of many ordained ministers, who work hard but are not sure that it is work which they ought to be doing. The time has come for radical thoughts and experiments.

One problem which is important for the Church of England concerns the relationship between the professional and the honorary. The last Preface to Crockford was taken to task for questioning whether it really was absolutely essential to recruit 400–450 full-time clergymen each year in order to maintain the Church of England. We admit that our questioning of the target was in poor taste, since the House of Bishops' ambitious figures were acclaimed by the General Synod and since no one would wish to argue that the Church be worse off if 400–450 acceptable candidates did present themselves each year, could be trained, and could be financed until their deaths. We can see why the tone of the references to the 'non-stipendiary' ministry in the official 1980 survey of *The Church's Ministry* was dismissive. Nevertheless we continue to ask whether the shortfall in the recruitment of paid full-timers (about a hundred a year too few despite recent improvements) must do quite the damage that the bishops anticipated in 1978.

Cannot more emphasis be put on honorary presbyters? Since the last Preface both the discussion and the action in this field have made progress, and the change is indeed remarkable since the cautious Bishops' Regulations of 1970; but we continue to ask the question. And the question will not go away even if the full-time ministry of the Church of England is enriched by the greater availability of Methodist or URC ministers. As we persist in this tactless question, our motive is not to impugn the value in English history or in the present day of the full-time priest utterly dedicated to the welfare of his parishioners. Our one wish is to see the whole Church escaping from the habit of seeing the laity as a silent society which keeps church buildings open and clergy families fed. Many lay people give of their time and money in the belief that all their present giving is their Christian duty — and in the belief that, as they are often told, they ought to be giving much more. So far the membership of the Church has accepted this burden with a generosity which, considering how materialistic our age is, we reckon heroic. As the burden grows with inflation, however, it becomes necessary to say out loud that in the New Testament the laity do not support the clergy (apart from the support of a few full-timers such as apostles). The clergy support the laity who are the Church witnessing in the world.

In November 1980 the Bishop of Winchester told the General Synod: 'It seems to me that we are faced with two traditions in our Church which are contradictory. . . . There is the tradition of a local parochial community, with a fully sacramental congregation served by its own ordained minister as one focal point of its identity, and there is the tradition of a fully professional clergy, professional as to the standard of their specialist training, professional as to the parity of their common discourse so that they can talk their own "in" language like any other profession, and professional rather than amateur as to their financial status.' The contrast was well drawn, and it was a valid point to say that the idea that a fully professional ministry can be or ought to be chiefly responsible for the pastoral care of all the parishes in England is not two centuries old; the history was set out in Anthony Russell's *The Clerical Profession* (SPCK, 1980). Is it not an exaggeration, though, to call the two traditions 'contradictory'? The local community needs to have its own leader and pastor. It needs to know its own, partly because it needs to know itself as a community by having its own. (That was the virtue in the medieval system of the resident parish priest who was often not easily distinguishable from the villagers whose confessions he heard and understood and could probably have extended out of his own information. The priest who ministered to the parish might enjoy at least a part of the tithes, but his hands were likely to be dirty with the work of the countryside and that was no bad thing for a pastor's heart.) However, there is also a place for the professional, since the local pastor needs to be supported, guided, and supplemented and the work involved in that wider — it should never be said, higher — ministry demands a minister's full-time dedication. (That was true of the medieval graduate priest or monk or friar.) Indeed, the Bishop of Winchester himself went on to speak sensitively about this full-time ministry of service and oversight, which he rightly linked with the responsibility of a bishop. Dr Taylor might equally well have described the full-time ministry in terms of the missionary's traditional role in Africa or Asia, being himself a former General Secretary of the CMS.

At present the decline in the number of clergy in the Church of England (from just over 13,000 in 1973 to just under 11,000 in 1981) is officially regarded as a disaster which must be reversed. The Ministry Co-ordinating Group under that exceptionally skilled administrator and pastor the Bishop of Rochester periodically reminds the Church of how the needs of the dioceses are greater than the supply, so that priests and deacons must be dealt out like rationed goods in wartime, the formula being a triumph of mathematics. In a sense the group is not mistaken. Both rural and urban dioceses feel themselves morally obliged to maintain networks of churches with small congregations but expensively professional pastors, and the assets of the Church Commissioners still encourage them to think in these conservative terms. When a church can be declared redundant, an elaborate process must be gone through, for the building is sacred; and when parishes must be combined in united benefices or groups or teams, the emphasis is very much on the full-time clergy, a sacred caste doing all that they can to replace 'our own vicar'. It is rightly stressed by bishops that four non-stipendiary ministers are needed to do the work which can be done by one full-time priest; so that there is no 'bargain' way of getting the present service. But slowly attitudes are changing. All the time the emphasis is moving away from dependence on buildings and on professionals — and economics is not the only influence at work, for the Church which is slowly emerging more closely resembles the Spirit-filled Body of Christ in the New Testament. We hope that in years to come this Directory will include more and more names of honorary presbyters, and that the difference between their ministry and that of the professionals will never be thought of in terms of contradiction or subordination. It is in this sense we believe that it is possible and right to respond to the challenge put by Bishop Din Dayal from North India to the General Synod: 'If the mission of the Church is to be carried out, the ministry of the Church will have to be expanded many times over.'

The revival of the diaconate as an honourable and permanent order of ordained servants continues to attract discussion. The reasons why the idea is attractive are obvious: deacons are important in the New Testament, yet their importance is as servants and 'service' is very much the key-word for those who have the renewal of the twentieth-century Church at heart. We see clearly that there ought to be room in the Church of England for men and women with the vocation to give their lives as deacons. Reducing the diaconate to an apprenticeship for the priesthood, while talking loudly to other Churches about the 'historic threefold ministry', has become intolerable. But we remain unconvinced that the numbers of such vocations are likely to be large. We also remain unconvinced that here is an alternative to large numbers of honorary presbyters. The centrality of Holy Communion in the parochial life of the Church of England is one of its strongest points and it is to be hoped that the presidency at the Eucharist will always be confined to priests or presbyters. The idea, sometimes canvassed, of 'lay celebration' is theological, and particularly ecumenical, dynamite. One need not be a deacon in order to take other services or preach; more than six thousand 'Readers' in the Church of England disprove that. Nor is it necessary to make people deacons in order to persuade them to accept training for their mission. All that is really needed for 'adult education' or 'lay training' to take off in the Church of England is for the Church at every level to take it seriously — as the Church has not yet done.

A strategy for the Church

It cannot escape notice how often criticism or questioning of the Church of England — from the Partners in Mission, for example, or from the Anglican Consultative Council — is based on the belief that there is too little vision or sense of strategy. That is a fair criticism. The most powerful answer to it is provided by the Evangelical insistence on the conversion of the individual, and that explains why the Evangelical movement continues to have such an impact. Almost half the men now being trained for full-time ministry in the Church of England are at definitely Evangelical colleges. Yet the traditional Evangelical answer is not wide enough. It is not for us to produce a detailed plan for the Church of England, which in any case does not take kindly to national or international plans or calls; but we accept the implied challenge. The highest service to be rendered to the Church at this moment is to sum up clearly a hope for it and for the society around it. We too look for a revived Church of England in a revived England.

As the inspiration of any real hope for the future of the Christian Church, a restatement of Christian belief is of the highest importance. Fortunately in the Church of England there are many signs that the mood of destructive radicalism whose symbols were *Honest to God* and *The Myth of God Incarnate* has matured into a desire to restate in the light of modern knowledge and experience something recognizable by Evangelicals as the everlasting Gospel. Since this is no place to attempt a theological essay, we content ourselves with welcoming the intention of the Doctrine Commission to progress beyond its studies of *Christian Belief* and *Believing in the Church* to a more positive, perhaps even systematic, attempt to say what should nowadays be believed; and we mention only a few representative publications. Recent books by Bishop John Robinson and Professor Maurice Wiles, often regarded as the heresiarchs of Cambridge and Oxford, have shown that those theologians include conservative streaks in their complex personalities. It so happened that the Oxford University Press was the publisher of two books which superbly summed up the present tendencies of a devout but intelligent middle-of-the-road Anglicanism: *Reasonable Belief* by the twin brothers Professor Anthony Hanson and Bishop Richard Hanson and the slightly more idiosyncratic *God as Spirit* by the late Geoffrey Lampe, whose death was a loss to true religion as well as to sound learning. The Collins Religious Book Award has deservedly gone to two Anglican parish priests for their spiritual writings: *Yes to God* by Alan Ecclestone and *Love's Endeavour, Love's Expense* by W.H. Vanstone. Another Anglican layman, Professor Ninian Smart, has contributed perceptively to the new dialogue between mankind's great faiths; and a priest-scientist, A.R. Peacocke, has looked down the telescope or microscope into marvels which evoke faith. What is now needed is a determined effort to popularize excitingly the conclusions reached in such books, as an alternative to the conservative Catholicism and Evangelicalism which have, and will continue to have, many sincere adherents because the presence of the holy God is to be found within the discipline of those venerable systems.

When outlining hopes for the deeper and wider revival of English Church life, anyone writing in 1982 must be conscious of the widespread feeling that there is no reason to hope — that what can be expected is a declining Church in a declining and increasingly secular nation, until a bloody rebirth comes amid persecution or until the victory of Antichrist is seen to be a prelude to the final Apocalypse. We believe that other, slightly less alarming, developments are also possible, and can be made to happen if the present generation co-operates with good purposes greater than its own.

Our hope is that an agreement to move forward into visible unity with Methodism, and with the United Reformed Church when possible, will gradually result in a movement of renewal where one vital stage will be a reconciliation with Rome. The Papacy is the providential centre of the 'blessed company' of all Christian people on this planet, but much of its history has been deeply tragic; the full recognition of the Church of England as a Uniate Church in communion with the Bishop of Rome would help to show that the Papacy is no longer the ghost of the empire of the Caesars. It would be good for England if this rebirth of the English Churches could take place in the setting of a renewal of politics including a position of much greater influence for the reconciling moderates given new teeth by the SDP/Liberal Alliance; and it would be good for England if the fulfilment of this process could be in the United States of Europe. Although these moderate and unitive political movements do not nowadays enjoy the blessing of the World Council of Churches, they are for England the wisest form of the social involvement which the WCC rightly advocates. Such movements could recover for Church and people the thrill of dynamic crusading; but this time the thrill would come in the cause of a greater unity — not a cause stressed by most crusades in the past. They could also free the Church of England of much of its stuffily middle-class lifestyle, for with the aid of Christians who have long known themselves to belong to minorities many pieces of luggage acquired during a history now becoming remote could with advantage be lost. These disposable items include many features of the present Establishment of the Church of England, but nothing would be gained by losing our Church's essential character as a thoughtful, comprehensive body patient with minorities and honouring truth, beauty, and love wherever they are to be found. The mission of the English Church or Churches will almost always be the quiet meeting of people, and it is in order to make friendly conversations about religion more constructive that more adult education is needed. The mission deserves the consecration of a very wide variety of talents, including the talents given to those prepared to dedicate and sacrifice their whole lives as bishops, presbyters, or deacons. Part-time, honorary leadership is also needed on a massive scale. That ought to come more easily as the society upon which the Church draws becomes more educated and more leisured. What counts, whether the Christian is ordained or lay, paid or honorary, is being able to say from the heart, with the full assent of the intelligence, to another human heart: 'I believe and I trust, because I have met God in the living Christ.'

Lent 1982

How to keep well-informed . . .

on the Church

at work in the world

It is more than ever essential that Churchpeople should keep themselves fully informed about the important discussions and developments that are taking place in the Church of England today.

The Church newspaper with universal appeal that gives the widest coverage of Church news, both home and overseas, is the *Church Times*. Its responsible editorials, stimulating articles, special features, and book reviews are read by scores of thousands of active and thoughtful people of all shades of churchmanship and political following.

The *Church Times* plays an indispensable part in the life of the Church of England; it has maintained the highest standards of journalism throughout its 119 years of life.

In order to introduce the *Church Times* to potential new readers we shall be very pleased to supply free specimen copies to any parish willing to promote the sale of the paper.

CHURCH TIMES

Free specimen copy from the publishers:

G. J. Palmer & Sons, Ltd., 7 Portugal Street, London, WC2A 2HP

CONTENTS

PUBLISHER'S NOTE

The Publisher gratefully acknowledges financial assistance from the Central Board of Finance of the Church of England and the Church Commissioners for England in preparing for publication this eighty-eighth issue of *Crockford's Clerical Directory*.

ABBREVIATIONS USED IN CROCKFORD'S CLERICAL DIRECTORY

A

A	Associate
AA	All Angels
AAF	Auxiliary Air Force
A & N	Andaman and Nicobar Islands
ABM	Australian Board of Missions
ACA	Associate (of the Institute of) Chartered Accountants
ACCM	Advisory Council for the Church's Ministry
ACG	Assistant Chaplain-General
ACII	Associate of the Chartered Insurance Institute
ACIS	Associate of the Chartered Institute of Secretaries
ACS	Additional Curates Society
ACT	Australian College of Theology, Australian Capital Territory
ACIS	Additional Clergy Society
AEGM	Anglican Evangelical Group Movement
AIF	Australian Imperial Forces
AIM	Africa Inland Mission
AIQS	Associate of the Institute of Quantity Surveyors
AKC	Associate of King's College, London
ALCD	Associate of London College of Divinity
APM	Auxiliary Pastoral Ministry
ARA	Associate of the Royal Academy
ARCS	Associate of the Royal College of Science
ATCL	Associate of Trinity College of Music, London
Aber	Aberdeen
Abp	Archbishop
Abth	Aberystwyth
Acad	Academy Academical
Achon	Achonry
Actg	Acting
Addl	Additional
Adel	Adelaide
ad eund	*Ad eundem gradum*
Adm	Admiral
Admin	Administrator Administrative
Adv	Adviser
Ægr	Ægrotat
Afr	Africa African
Agr	Agriculture Agricultural
Alex	Alexander
Alg	Algoma
All H	All Hallows
All S	All Souls
All SS	All Saints
alt	alternate
Alta	Alberta
Ambat	Ambato-haranana
Amer	America American
Amrit	Amritsar
Andr	Andrew
Angl	Anglican
Ank	Ankole
Ankole-K	Ankole-Kigezi
Annunc	Annunciation
Antan	Antananarivo
Anthrop	Anthropological
Antig	Antigua
Antiq	Antiquary Antiquarian Antiquaries
Antr	Antrim
Ap	Apostle
apptd	appointed
Archaeol	Archaeologist Archaeology Archaeological
Archd	Archdeacon Archdeaconry
Archit	Architect Architecture
Ard	Ardagh
Ardf and Agh	Ardfert and Aghadoe
Arg Is	Argyll and the Isles
Argent	Argentina
Arm	Armagh
Armid	Armidale
Ascen	Ascension
Ashton L	Ashton-under-Lyne
Assoc	Association Associate
Asst	Assistance Assistant
Asyl	Asylum
Athab	Athabasca
Auckld	Auckland
Aug	Augustine
Austr	Australia
Austrn	Australian
Auth	Authorized
Aux	Auxiliary

B

b	born
B & W	Bath and Wells
BA	Bachelor of Arts British Academy
BASc	Bachelor of Applied Science
BArch	Bachelor of Architecture
BC	British Columbia
BCC	British Council of Churches
BC Coll Bris	Bible Churchmen's College, Bristol
BCL	Bachelor of Civil Law
BChir	Bachelor of Surgery
BCom	Bachelor of Commerce
BCMS	Bible Churchmen's Missionary Society
BD	Bachelor of Divinity
BEM	British Empire Medal
BEng	Bachelor of Engineering
BFBS	British and Foreign Bible Society
BH Cross	Brotherhood of the Holy Cross
BLitt	Bachelor of Letters
BNC	Brasenose College
BPaed	Bachelor of Paediatrics
BS	Bachelor of Surgery
BSA	Bachelor of Science in Agriculture
BSW	Bachelor of Social Work
BSc	Bachelor of Science
BT	Bachelor of Teaching
BTh	Bachelor of Theology
BVM	Blessed Virgin Mary
Bal	Ballarat
Ball	Balliol
Ban	Bangor
Bapt	Baptist
Barb	Barbados
Barn	Barnabas
Barrow-F	Barrow-in-Furness
Bart	Bartholomew
Basuto	Basutoland
Bath	Bathurst
Bd	Board
Bd of Patr	Board of Patronage
Beds	Bedfordshire
Bel	Belize
Belf	Belfast
Bend	Bendigo
Benef	Benefice
Benev	Benevolent
Berks	Berkshire
Berm	Bermuda
Bhag	Bhagalpur
Bibl	Biblical
Biol	Biological
Birm	Birmingham
Blackb	Blackburn
Bloemf	Bloemfontein
Boga-Z	Boga-Zaire
Bom	Bombay
Bonif	Boniface
Bp	Bishop
B'pore	Barrackpore
Br	British
Bradf	Bradford
Bran	Brandon
Brech	Brechin
Brecons	Brecknockshire
Bris	Bristol
Brisb	Brisbane
Bro	Brotherhood
Brunsw	Brunswick
Bt	Baronet
Bucks	Buckinghamshire
Bunb	Bunbury
Bur	Burundi
But	Butare

C

C	Curate Curacy
c	charge circiter
CA	Church Army
CAF	Curates' Augmentation Fund
C & Goulb	Canberra and Goulburn
CB	Companion of the Bath
CCA	Association of Certified Accountants
CCC	Corpus Christi College
CCCS	Commonwealth and Continental Church Society
CD	Canadian Forces Decoration
CE	Civil Engineer
CECS	Church of England Children's Society
CETS	Church of England Temperance Society
CF	Chaplain to the Forces
CF (EC)	Chaplain to the Forces—Emergency Commission
CF (R of O)	Chaplain to the Forces—Reserve of Officers
CF (TA)	Chaplain to the Forces—Territorial Army
CF (TA—R of O)	Chaplain to the Forces—Territorial Army—Reserve of Officers
CGA	Community of the Glorious Ascension
CH	Companion of Honour
CIE	Companion of the Order of the Indian Empire
C-in-c	Curate-in-charge
CIS	Chartered Institute of Secretaries
CLB	Church Lads' Brigade
CM Coll	Church Missionary College
CMF	Commonwealth Military Forces
CMJ	Church's Ministry among Jews
CMS	Church Missionary Society
C of E	Church of England
C of I	Church of Ireland
CORAT	Christian Organisations Research and Advisory Trust
CP	Cape Province College of Preceptors
CPAS	Church Pastoral-Aid Society
CPS	Church Patronage Society
CR	Community of the Resurrection
CS	Civil Service Chemical Society
CSI	Companion of the Order of the Star of India
CSSM	Children's Special Service Mission
CSWG	Community of the Servants of the Will of God
CUM	Cambridge University Mission
Caerns	Caernarvonshire
Cal	Calendar
Calc	Calcutta
Caled	Caledonia
Calg	Calgary
Cam	Cambridge
Cambs	Cambridgeshire
Can	Canon Canonically Canonry
Canad	Canadian

Cand	Candidate
Cant	Canterbury
Capetn	Cape Town
Capt	Captain
Cards	Cardiganshire
Carib	Cariboo
Carl	Carlisle
Carms	Carmarthenshire
Carp	Carpentaria
Cash	Cashel
Cath	Catharine
Cathl	Cathedral
Cem	Cemetery
Centr	Central
Centr Afr	Central Africa
Certif	Certificate
	Certificated
Ch	Christ
	Christ's
	Church
Ch Ch	Christ Church
	Christchurch
Ch Coll	Christ's College
Ch K	Christ the King
Chan	Chancellor
	Chancery
Chan Scho	Chancellor's Scholar
Chap	Chaplain
	Chaplaincy
	Chapel
	Chapelry
Charl	Charlotte
Chas	Charles
Chelmsf	Chelmsford
Cheltm	Cheltenham
Chem	Chemistry
Ches	Chester
Chesh	Cheshire
Chich	Chichester
Chile	Chile, Bolivia, and Peru
Cho	Choral
Chota N	Chota Nagpur
Chr	Christian
Chris	Christopher
Chrys	Chrysostom
Chy	Charity
Civ	Civil
cl	class
Cl	Classics
	Classical
	Clergy
Clem	Clement
Cler	Clerical
Cleve	Cleveland
Clk	Clerk
Clk O	Clerk in Orders
Clogh	Clogher
Clonf	Clonfert
Co	Company
	County
Coadj	Coadjutor
Codr Coll	Codrington College
Col	Colonel
	Colony
	Colonial
Coll	College
Colleg	Collegiate
Colom	Colombo
Columb	Columbia
Com	Commerce
	Commodore
Comm	Commission
	Commissioner
Commd	Command
Commdr	Commander
Commiss	Commissary
Commun	Community
Comp	Composition
Cond	Conduct
Conf	Conference
Cons	Consecrated
Cont	Continental
Conv	Conventional
	Convocation
	Convent
Convalesc	Convalescent
Cornw	Cornwall
Corp	Corporation
Coun	Council
Cov	Coventry
cr	created
Crem	Crematorium
Crisp	Crispin
C'tte	Committee
Cudd	Cuddesdon
Cumb	Cumbria
	Cumberland
Cuthb	Cuthbert
Cypr	Cyprian

D

d	Deacon (ordination)
d	Deacon
D	Doctor
D and C	Dean and Chapter
	Dean and Canons
DACG	Deputy Assistant Chaplain-General
DCG	Deputy Chaplain-General
DCL	Doctor of Civil Law
DCnL	Doctor of Canon Law
DCM	Distinguished Conduct Medal
DD	Doctor of Divinity
DFC	Distinguished Flying Cross
DHM	Diocesan Home Missioner
DLitt	Doctor of Letters/Literature
DPH	Diploma in Public Health
DSc	Doctor of Science
DSC	Distinguished Service Cross
DSM	Distinguished Service Medal
DSO	Distinguished Service Order
DTh	Doctor of Theology
DUM	Dublin University Mission
Damar	Damaraland
Dar-S	Dar-es-Salaam
Dedic	Dedication
Denbighs	Denbighshire
Dep	Deputy
	Dependent
Dept	Department
Deputn	Deputation
Derbys	Derbyshire
desig	designate
Diego S	Diego Suarez
dim	dimissory
Dio	Diocese
Dioc	Diocesan
Dioc Conf	Diocesan Conference
Dioc Syn	Diocesan Synod
Dios	Dioceses
Dipl	Diploma
Dir	Director
Distinc	Distinction
Distr	District
Div	Divine
	Divinity
	Division
Div Test	Divinity Testimonium
Dk	Dock
Dom	Domestic
Doneg	Donegal
Dorch	Dorchester
Dorn	Dornakal
Down	Downing
Drom	Dromore
dss	deaconess
Dub	Dublin
Dun	Dunedin
Dunbl	Dunblane
Dunk	Dunkeld
Dur	Durham
Dyd	Dockyard

E

E	East
	Eastern
ED	Efficiency Decoration
ERD	Emergency Reserve Decoration
Eccles	Ecclesiastical
Econ	Economy
	Economics
Ecumen	Ecumenical
Ed	Editor
	Edition
	Editorial
Edin	Edinburgh
Edm	Edmund
Edmon	Edmonton
Educl	Educational
Educn	Education
Edw	Edward
Eliz	Elizabeth
Elph	Elphin
Em	Emmanuel
Emer	Emeritus
Endow	Endowment
Eng	Engineer
	Engineering
Engl	England
	English
Epiph	Epiphany
Episc	Episcopal
Est	Establishment
	Estimated
Eth	Ethics
Evang	Evangelist
	Evangelical
	Evangelism
Ex	Exeter
	Extension
Exam	Examiner
	Examining
Examn	Examination
Exhib	Exhibition
	Exhibitioner
Exor	Executor
Exors	Executors
Exper	Experimental
Extr	Extraordinary

F

F	Fellow of a Society
f	Formerly
FBA	Fellow of the British Academy
FCII	Fellow of the Chartered Insurance Institute
FPS	Fellow of the Pharmaceutical Society
Fr	Father
FTCL	Fellow of Trinity College of Music, London
Falkld Is	Falkland Isles
Fell	Fellow of a College
Ferman	Fermanagh
Fitzw	Fitzwilliam
Flints	Flintshire
Found	Foundation
Fred	Fredericton
Ft Hall	Fort Hall

G

G and C	Gonville and Caius
GBRE	General Board of Religious Education
GC	George Cross
GCB	Grand Commander of the Bath
GCSI	Grand Commander of the Star of India
GM	George Medal
GRSM	Graduate of the Royal Schools of Music
GSM	Guildhall School of Music
Gabr	Gabriel
Gall	Galloway
Galw	Galway
Gen	General
Gen L	General Licence
Geo	George
Geog	Geography
Geol	Geology
Georgetn	Georgetown
Gibr	Gibraltar
Gippsld	Gippsland
Glam	Glamorganshire
Glas	Glasgow
Glendal	Glendalough
Glos	Gloucestershire
Glouc	Gloucester
Goulb	Goulburn
Gov	Governor
Govt	Government
Gr	Greek
Gr Sch	Grammar School
Graft	Grafton
Grahmstn	Grahamstown
Greg	Gregory
Gt	Great
Gtr	Greater
Gui	Guiana
Guildf	Guildford
Guy	Guyana
Gwyn	Gwynedd

H

H	Holy
HBM	Her Britannic Majesty
HE	His Excellency
HM	Her Majesty
	Her Majesty's
HMAS	Her Majesty's Australian Ship
HMS	Her Majesty's Ship
HQ	Headquarters
H Trin	Holy Trinity
Hants	Hampshire
Hatf	Hatfield
Hd	Head
Hebr	Hebrew
	Hebrides
Heref	Hereford
Herefs	Herefordshire
Hertf	Hertford
Herts	Hertfordshire
Hib	Hibernian
Hist	History
	Historical
Ho	House
Hon	Honorary
	Honourable
Hond	Honduras
Hong	Victoria, Hong Kong
Hons	Honours
Hosp	Hospital
	Hospitaller
Humb	Humberside
Hunts.	Huntingdonshire
Hur	Huron

I

I	Incumbent
	Isle
	Island
IA	Institute of Actuaries
	Indian Army
ICF	Industrial Christian Fellowship
ICM	Irish Church Missions
IM	Isle of Man
ISO	Companion of the Imperial Service Order
IW	Isle of Wight
Ibad	Ibadan
Im	Immanuel
Incorp	Incorporated
	Incorporation
Ind	Independent
	Indian
Industr	Industrial
Inf	Infantry
Infirm	Infirmary
Innoc	Innocents
Insp	Inspector
Inst	Institute
	Instituted
	Institution
Inst MM	Institute of Mining and Metallurgy
Internat	International
Is	Isles
	Islands
Isl	Islington
Itin	Itinerating

J

JEM	Jerusalem and the East Mission
Ja	Jamaica
Jas	James
Jer	Jerusalem
Jes Coll	Jesus College
Jess	Jesselton

Jo Bapt	John the Baptist
Jo Div	John the Divine
Jo Evang	John the Evangelist
Johann	Johannesburg
Jos	Joseph
Jt	Joint
Jun	Junior
jure dig	*Jure dignitatis*
Jurisd	Jurisdiction
Jurispr	Jurisprudence

K

K	King King's
KCVO	Knight Commander of the Victorian Order
KS	King's School
Kalg	Kalgoorlie
Kamp	Kampala
Kar	Karachi
Kara	Karamoja
Kath	Katharine
Keew	Keewatin
Kens	Kensington
Kig	Kigezi
Kiga	Kigali
Kild	Kildare
Kilfen	Kilfenora
Kilk	Kilkenny
Kilm	Kilmore
Kilmac	Kilmacduagh
Kimb	Kimberley
Kimb K	Kimberley and Kuruman
Kingston T	Kingston-upon-Thames
Koot	Kootenay
Kuch	Kuching
Kum	Kumasi
Kurun	Kurunagala
Kwangsi-H	Kwangsi-Hunan

L

L	Less Licence Licentiate Literate Little
LCM	London College of Music
LCP	Licentiate of the College of Preceptors
LDHM	London Diocesan Home Missioner
LDiv	Licentiate in Divinity
LJS	London Jews Society
LLB	Bachelor of Laws
LLD	Doctor of Laws
LLM	Master of Laws
LMSSA	Licentiate in Medicine and Surgery of the Society of Apothecaries
LPr	Licensed Preacher
LS	Linnean Society
LST	Licentiate in Sacred Theology
LT	Licentiate in Teaching
LTh	Licentiate in Theology
LTCL	Licentiate of Trinity College of Music, London
LTSC	Licentiate Tonic Sol-fa College
Lah	Lahore
Lamp	Lampeter
Lanc	Lancaster
Lancs	Lancashire
Lang	Language Languages
Lat	Latin Latitude
Laur	Laurence
Lawr	Lawrence
Ld	Lord
Lebom	Lebombo
Lect	Lecturer Lectureship
Legisln	Legislation
Leic	Leicester
Leics	Leicestershire
Leigh	Leighlin
Leitr	Leitrim
Lennox	Lennoxville
Leon	Leonard
Les	Lesotho
Libr	Library Librarian
Lich	Lichfield
Lik	Likoma
Lim	Limerick
Linc	Lincoln
Lincs	Lincolnshire
Lism	Lismore
Lit	Literary Literature
LitHum	Literae Humaniores
Liv	Liverpool
Llan	Llandaff
Lon	London
Longf	Longford
Lt	Lieutenant
Luckn	Lucknow

M

M	Member
MA	Master of Arts
M & W Nile	Madi and West Nile
MB	Bachelor of Medicine
MC	Military Cross
MCE	Master of Civil Engineering
MCR	Member of the Community of the Resurrection
MD	Doctor of Medicine
MDiv	Master of Divinity
MDTC	Montreal Diocesan Theological College
MEducn	Master of Education
ML	Licentiate in Medicines
MM	Military Medal
MMT	Martyrs Memorial Trust
MP	Member of Parliament
MPS	Member of Pharmaceutical Society
MRSL	Member Royal Society of Literature
MRST	Member Royal Society of Teachers
MS	Missionary Society
MSCC	Missionary Society of the Canadian Church
MSc	Master of Science
MVO	Member of the Royal Victorian Order
Mack	MacKenzie
Madag	Madagascar
Madr	Madras
Magd	Magdalene
Maint	Maintenance
Maj	Major
Mal	Malaysia
Man	Manchester
Mand	Mandalay
Manit	Manitoba
Marg	Margaret
Marg Prof	Lady Margaret's Professor
Marlb	Marlborough
Marq	Marquis
Marshl	Marischal
Mart	Martyr
Mashon	Mashonaland
Matab	Matabeleland
Math	Mathematics Mathematical
Matt	Matthew
Maur	Mauritius
Mech	Mechanical
Med	Medal Medallist Medical Mediterranean
Melan	Melanesia
Melb	Melbourne
Mem	Memorial
Men in Disp	Mentioned in Dispatches
Ment	Mental
Mer	Merseyside
Merions	Merionethshire
Mert	Merton
Met	Metaphysics Meteorological
Metrop	Metropolis Metropolitan Metropolitical
Mich	Michael
Middx	Middlesex
Midl	Midland Midlands
Mil	Military
Min	Minister Ministry
Min Can	Minor Canon
Miss	Mission Missionary
Missr	Missioner
Mkt	Market
Mod	Moderator
Mods	Moderations, or 1st Public Examination at Oxford
Momb	Mombasa
Mon	Monmouth Monmouthshire
Monagh	Monaghan
Montr	Montreal
Monts	Montgomeryshire
Moos	Moosonee
Mor	Moral
Moro	Morogoro
Mt	Mount
Mus	Music Musical
MusBac	Bachelor of Music
MusDoc	Doctor of Music

N

N	North Northern
NAC	Native Anglican Church of Uganda
NB	New Brunswick
NIH	New Inn Hall
NMS	National Missionary Society
NS	National Society, Nova Scotia
NSW	New South Wales
NT	New Testament
N Terr	Northern Territory (Diocese)
NUI	National University of Ireland
NWT	North West Territory
NY	New York
NZ	New Zealand
N and C Eur	North and Central Europe
N Nig	Northern Nigeria
N Queensld	North Queensland
Nagp	Nagpur
Nai	Nairobi
Nak	Nakuru
Nam	Namirembe
Nand	Nandyal
Nass	Nassau and the Bahamas
Nat	National Natural
Nath	Nathaniel
Nativ	Nativity
Nel	Nelson
Newc	Newcastle (Australia)
Newc L	Newcastle-under-Lyme
Newc T	Dio. Newc. in Prov. of York and Newcastle upon Tyne
Newfld	Newfoundland
New Westmr	New Westminster
Niag	Niagara
Nich	Nicholas
Nig Delta	Niger Delta
Nig Ter	Niger Territory
Nomn	Nomination
Non-res	Non-resident
Nor	Norwich
Norf	Norfolk
Northants	Northamptonshire
Northn	Northampton
Northumb	Northumberland
Nottm	Nottingham
Notts	Nottinghamshire
Nyasa	Nyasaland

O

O	Order
OFS	Orange Free State
OGS	Oratory of the Good Shepherd
OMC	Oxford Mission to Calcutta
OSB	Order of St. Benedict
OSP	Order of St. Paul
OT	Old Testament
OUM	Oxford University Mission
Offg	Officiating
Offic	Officiate
Ondo-B	Ondo-Benin
Ont	Ontario
Ophth	Ophthalmic
Opt	Optime
Or	Oriel Oriental
Ord	Ordinary
Ordin	Ordination
Org	Organizer Organizing
Ork	Orkney
Orph	Orphan Orphanage
Oss	Ossory
Osw	Oswald
Ott	Ottawa
Ow	Owerri
Ox	Oxford
Oxon	Oxfordshire

P

P	Pastor Priest
p	Priest (ordination)
PC	Perpetual Curate
PCC	Parochial Church Council
PEI	Prince Edward Island
P-in-c	Priest in charge
PQ	Province of Quebec
Papua	Papua–New Guinea
Par	Parish Parochial
Parag	Paraguay
Past	Pastorate
Patr	Patrick Patristic Patronage
Pemb	Pembroke
Pembs	Pembrokeshire
Penit	Penitentiary
Perm	Permission
Pet	Peter Peterborough
Peterho	Peterhouse
PhD	Doctor of Philosophy
Phil	Philip Philosophy
Phys	Physics
Physiol	Physiology
Pk	Park
Pmbg	Pietermaritzburg
Pol	Political

Poly ...... Polytechnic
Polyn ..... Polynesia
Pop ...... Population
Portsm .... Portsmouth
Pr .... Preacher
Preb ...... Prebend
Prebendary
Prec ...... Precentor
Prem ..... Premium
Prep ...... Preparatory
Pres....... President
Pret ...... Pretoria
Pri .... Prize
Prizeman
Prin ...... Principal
Pris ...... Prison
Priv ...... Private
Proc ...... Proctor
Prof ...... Profession
Professor
Professorship
Prot ...... Protestant
Prov ...... Province
Provinces
Provincial
Psychol ... Psychology
Publ ...... Public
publd ..... published

Q

QC .... Queen's Counsel
QUB ..... Queen's University, Belfast
QUI ...... Queen's University in Ireland
Qu .... Queen
Queen's
Queens'
Qu'App ... Qu'Appelle
Queb...... Quebec
Queensld .. Queensland

R

R .... Rector
Rectory
Rectorial
Royal
RA .... Royal Academician, Royal Artillery
RAAF..... Royal Australian Air Force
RADD .... Royal Association in Aid of the Deaf and Dumb
RAF ...... Royal Air Force
RAI ...... Royal Anthropological Institute
RAM ..... Royal Academy of Music
RAN ..... Royal Australian Navy
RAS ...... Royal Academy of Science
Royal Astronomical Society
RC .... Roman Catholic
RCA...... Royal College of Arts
RCAF .... Royal Canadian Air Force
RCB ...... Representative Church Body (Ireland)
RCC ..... Representative Church Council (Scotland)
RCM ..... Royal College of Music
RCO ..... Royal College of Organists
RCP ...... Royal College of Physicians
RCS ...... Royal College of Science
Royal College of Surgeons
RD .... Rural Dean
Rural Deanery
Royal Navy Reserve Decoration
RIA ...... Royal Irish Academy

RIBA ..... Royal Institute of British Architects
RIC ...... Royal Institute of Chemistry
RICS ..... Royal Institute of Chartered Surveyors
RM ...... Royal Marines
RMA ..... Royal Marine Artillery
RMC ..... Royal Military College
RMS ..... Royal Military School
RN .... Royal Navy
RNR ..... Royal Naval Reserve
RS .... Royal Society
RSAI ..... Royal Society of Antiquaries for Ireland
RSCM .... Royal School of Church Music
RSL ...... Royal Society of Literature
RSM ..... Royal Society Medicine
RUI ...... Royal University of Ireland
Radnors ... Radnorshire
Rang ..... Rangoon
Raph ..... Raphael
Raphoe
rec .... received
Reform ... Reformatory
Regmtl .... Regimental
Reg ...... Regional
Regis...... Registry
Regr ...... Registrar
Relig ..... Religion
Religious
Relns ..... Relations
Rep ...... Representative
Res .... Resident
Residentiary
res .... resigned
resignation
Resp ...... Respondent
Resurr .... Resurrection
Rev ...... Reverend
Rhod ..... Rhodesia
River ..... Riverina
Rly .... Railway
Roch ..... Rochester
Rockptn ... Rockhampton
Rosc ...... Roscommon
Rt Hon ... Right Honourable
Rt Rev .... Right Reverend
Ruanda-U . Ruanda-Urundi
Rupld .... Rupert's Land
Ruv ...... Ruvuma
Ruw ...... Ruwenzori
Rwa ...... Rwanda
Rwanda B . Rwanda and Burundi

S

S .... Society
South
Southern
SA .... Society of Apothecaries
SA Ch .... South African Church
SAMS .... South American Missionary Society
S & M .... Sodor and Man
s .... super
SB .... Serving Brother
sc .... Shortened Honours Course
SCF ...... Senior Chaplain to the Forces
SCM ..... Student Christian Movement
SG .... Society of Genealogists
SGM ..... Sea Gallantry Medal
SOC ...... Southwark Ordination Course
SPCK .... Society for Promoting Christian Knowledge

SPG ...... Society for the Propagation of the Gospel
SRC ...... Society of Retreat Conductors
SRN ..... State Registered Nurse
SS .... Saints
Sidney Sussex
SSC ...... Special Service Clergyman
SSF ...... Society of St. Francis
SSJD ..... Sisterhood of St. John the Divine
SSJE ..... Society of St. John the Evangelist
SSM ..... Society of the Sacred Mission
STh ...... Scholar/Student in Theology
STB ...... *Sacrae Theologiae Baccalaureus* (Bachelor of Theology)
STD ..... (Doctor of Theology)
STM ..... (Master of Theology)
SUM ..... Sudan United Mission
SW Tang . South-West Tanganyika
St .... Saint
St A ...... St. Asaph
St Aid .... St. Aidan
St. Aidan's
St Aid Coll St. Aidan's College, Birkenhead
St. Alb .... St. Albans
St Alb Hall St. Alban Hall
St Andr ... St. Andrew's
St Ant .... St. Antony's
St Arn .... St. Arnaud
St Cath Coll St. Catharine's College
St D ...... St. David's
St E ...... St. Edmundsbury and Ipswich
St Edm Hall St. Edmund Hall
St Hel .... St. Helena
St Mary Virg..... St. Mary the Virgin
St Mich AA St. Michael and All Angels
Sacr ...... Sacrist
Salop ..... Shropshire
Salv ...... Salvador
Sanat ..... Sanatorium
Sarum .... Salisbury
Sask ...... Saskatchewan
Sav .... Saviour
Sc .... Science
Sch .... School
Scho ...... Scholar
Scholarship
Scholastic
Scot ...... Scottish
Scotld .... Scotland
Script ..... Scripture
Sec .... Secretary
Selk ...... Selkirk
Selw ...... Selwyn
Sem ...... Seminary
Sen .... Senior
Seq .... Sequestrator
Sey....... Seychelles
Sheff ..... Sheffield
Sier L .... Sierra Leone
Sin .... Sinecure
Sing ...... Singapore
Singapore and Malaya (Diocese)
Sktn ...... Saskatoon
Soc .... Sociology
Sociologist
Somt ..... Somerset
Southn .... Southampton
Southw ... Southwell
Staffs ..... Staffordshire
Ste .... Sainte
Steph ..... Stephen
Stud ...... Student
Studies
Succr ..... Succentor
Suff ...... Suffolk

Suffr ..... Suffragan
Super ..... Supernumerary
Supr ...... Superior
Supt ...... Superintendent
Surr ...... Surrogate
Swan B ... Swansea and Brecon
S'wark .... Southwark
Swaz ..... Swaziland
Swith ..... Swithin
Swithun
Syd ...... Sydney
Syn ...... Synod
Szech ..... Szechwan

T

TA .... Territorial Army
TAVR .... Territorial and Army Volunteer Reserve
TCF ..... Temporary Chaplain to the Forces
TCD ..... Trinity College, Dublin
TD ..... Territorial Decoration
TE .... Theological Examination
Tam ...... Tamatave
Tang ..... Tanganyika
Tas .... Tasmania
Tech...... Technical
Technology
temp ..... temporary
temporarily
Test ...... Testament
Testimonium
Th .... Theology
Theological
Theologian
ThD....... Doctorate in Theology
ThL ...... Theological Licentiate
Thos ..... Thomas
Tinn ..... Tinnevelly
Tip .... Tipperary
tn .... town
township
Tor ...... Toronto
Toxt ...... Toxteth
Tr .... Training
Trans ..... Translator
Transfig ... Transfiguration
Transv .... Transvaal
Trav ...... Travancore
Travelling
Treas ..... Treasurer
Trin ...... Trinity
Trinid .... Trinidad
Trip ...... Tripos
Trld ...... Translated
Tyr ...... Tyrone

U

U .... Union
Upper
UB .... United Benefice
UMCA ... Universities' Mission to Central Africa
USA ..... United States of America
USPG .... United Society for the Propagation of the Gospel
Ugan ..... Uganda
Univ ..... University

V

V .... Vicar
Vicarage
V Cho .... Vicar Choral
VC .... Victoria Cross
VG .... Vicar-General
VRD ..... Volunteer Reserve Officers' Decoration
Vanc...... Vancouver
Ven ...... Venerable
Venez..... Venezuela
Vic .... Victoria
Victorian
Vic Nyan .. Victoria Nyanza
Vinc ...... Vincent

Visc....... Viscount
Vol....... Voluntary

W

W........ West
Western
w........ with
W Bugan .. West Buganda
WCC..... World Council of Churches
WI....... West Indies

Wadh..... Wadham
Wai...... Waiapu
Waik..... Waikato
Wakef.... Wakefield
Wang..... Wangaratta
Warm.... Warminster
Warw..... Warwick
Warws.... Warwickshire
Waterf.... Waterford
Wel...... Wellington
Westmd... Westmorland
Westmr... Westminster

Wexf..... Wexford
Wickl..... Wicklow
Willoch... Willochra
Wilts..... Wiltshire
Win...... Winchester
Windw Is . Windward Islands
Wor...... Worshipful
Worc..... Worcester
Worcs.... Worcestershire
Wrang.... Wrangler
Wycl..... Wycliffe

Y

Yorks..... Yorkshire

Z

Zam...... Zambia
Zanz T ... Zanzibar and Tanga
Zulu...... Zululand

HOW TO ADDRESS THE CLERGY

As a guide to laymen, who may have difficulty in knowing how to address the various grades of the clergy, we give below the forms in common usage today, (a) *on the envelope of a letter, and* (b) *in a letter or in speech. The alternative form, given in brackets, is more formal and seldom used nowadays save at official functions and formal gatherings.*

ARCHBISHOPS

(*a*) The Most Reverend The Lord Archbishop of. . . .
(*b*) 'Archbishop' ('Your Grace').

Note: (i) ENGLAND. The full style of the two English Primates, being Privy Councillors, is 'The Most Reverend and Right Honourable The Lord Archbishop of Canterbury' or 'of York'.

(ii) SCOTLAND. The Presiding Bishop of the Episcopal Church is called the Primus. He is addressed as:
(*a*) The Most Reverend The Primus.
(*b*) 'Primus'.

(iii) U.S.A. The Head of the Episcopal Church in the U.S.A. is called the Presiding Bishop. He is addressed as:
(*a*) The Most Reverend The Presiding Bishop or The Right Reverend A. B. Smith.
(*b*) 'Bishop' or 'Bishop Smith'.

(iv) JAPAN. The Presiding Bishop of the Nippon Sei Ko Kwai (Japan) is addressed as:
(*a*) The Most Reverend the Bishop of . . . (his diocese).
(*b*) 'Bishop'.

(v) METROPOLITANS
AUSTRALIA AND CANADA have Primates as well as Metropolitans of Provinces.
SOUTH AFRICA. The Metropolitan of the Church in South Africa is always the Archbishop of Cape Town.
WEST INDIES, NEW ZEALAND, and WEST AFRICA. The Metropolitans can be appointed from any Diocese within the Provinces.

vi) RETIRED ARCHBISHOPS. Upon retirement an Archbishop properly goes back to the status of a Bishop but he is given as a courtesy the style and address of an Archbishop. If an Archbishop is appointed to a Bishopric or some other office he is addressed as a Bishop.

BISHOPS

(*a*) The Right Reverend The Lord Bishop of. . . .
or The Right Reverend A. B. Smith.
(*b*) 'Bishop' ('My Lord')

Note: (i) Bishops of the Episcopal Church in the U.S.A. are addressed as:
(*a*) The Right Reverend A. B. Smith.
(*b*) 'Bishop' or 'Bishop Smith'.

(ii) The Bishop of London, being a Privy Councillor, is addressed on the envelope as 'The Right Reverend and Right Honourable The Lord Bishop of London'.

(iii) The Bishop of Meath in Ireland, by tradition, is always addressed on the envelope as 'The Most Reverend The Bishop of Meath'.

DEANS AND PROVOSTS

(*a*) The Very Reverend The Dean (The Provost) of . . . (name of the Cathedral City).
(*b*) 'Dean' ('Mr. Dean') or 'Provost' ('Mr. Provost').

ARCHDEACONS

(*a*) The Venerable The Archdeacon of . . . (name of the Archdeaconry).
(*b*) 'Archdeacon' ('Mr. Archdeacon').

Note: A Bishop who holds office as Dean or Archdeacon may be addressed by the title of his office, e.g. The Dean of . . . or the Archdeacon of . . ., but even so the title is prefixed by the words 'The Right Reverend' in the address and in public announcements.

CANONS

Both Residentiary Canons (who live in the Cathedral precincts and have Cathedral duties) and Honorary Canons (who are usually holders of benefices within the Diocese to whom this title is given as a mark of appreciation of their work) are addressed as:

(*a*) The Reverend Canon A. B. Smith.
(*b*) 'Canon Smith'.

Note: Minor Canons are appointed to assist in the conduct of the services in Cathedrals. They are addressed as:
(*a*) The Reverend A. B. Smith.
(*b*) 'Mr. Smith'.

PREBENDARIES

(*a*) The Reverend Prebendary A. B. Smith.
(*b*) 'Prebendary Smith'.

RURAL DEANS

This is a title of office and conveys no special designation.

OTHER CLERGY

All other clergy, whether beneficed or unbeneficed, are addressed as follows:

(*a*) The Reverend A. B. Smith.
(*b*) 'Mr. Smith'.

Note: (i) In speaking to or about these clergymen it should always be 'Mr. Smith' (or on some formal occasions 'The Reverend Mr. Smith'), but never 'The Reverend Smith'.
(ii) Married clergy and their wives should be addressed jointly as 'The Reverend A. B. and Mrs. Smith'.
(iii) It is customary for parishioners to address their incumbent as 'Rector' or 'Vicar', as the case may be.

CHAPLAINS TO THE ARMED FORCES

SENIOR CHAPLAINS

The senior chaplain in each of the three Services has the status of Archdeacon. The correct title of each is:

Royal Navy	The Ven. The Chaplain of the Fleet and Archdeacon for the Royal Navy.
Army	The Ven. The Chaplain General to the Forces.
Royal Air Force	The Ven. The Chaplain in Chief, RAF.

They are addressed as 'Archdeacon' or 'Padre' (or their formal title).

OTHER CHAPLAINS

a) The Reverend A. B. Smith, RN (or CF or RAF, etc.)
(*b*) 'Padre' or 'Padre Smith'.

Note: In no circumstances should military titles be used.

Ordained members of religious orders are normally addressed as Father, and lay members as Brother, except that all members of the Society of St. Francis are addressed as Brother. Father may also be used for addressing any priest if that is his personal preference.

BY APPOINTMENT
TO H.M. QUEEN ELIZABETH
THE QUEEN MOTHER
SUPPLIERS OF FINE BINDINGS
A. R. MOWBRAY & CO LTD.

Mowbrays bookshops for choice

BIBLES, PRAYER & HYMN BOOKS
BOOKS OF REMEMBRANCE
FINE BINDINGS, CALLIGRAPHY
CHRISTIAN PAPERBACKS
—wide range for the bookstall
THEOLOGY & REFERENCE BOOKS
CHURCH REGISTERS & FORMS
CHURCH REQUISITES, including
Candles, Wafers & Communion Wine

Mowbrays London shop has large general books departments, where any book in print in UK may be obtained, either from stock, or to order. There is an efficient mail order service. Also a well-stocked Religious Records dept.

ASK TO BE PUT ON OUR MAILING LIST FOR MOWBRAYS JOURNAL OF NEW AND RECENT RELIGIOUS BOOKS

MOWBRAYS
BOOKSHOP

28 Margaret Street, Oxford Circus
London, W1N 7LB — Tel: 01-580 2812

Branches at 14 Kings Parade, Cambridge St. Martins, Bull Ring, Birmingham 5
and associated with The Newman-Mowbray Bookshop, 87 St. Aldates, Oxford

CROCKFORD'S CLERICAL DIRECTORY
1980–82

BIOGRAPHIES

The biographies record changes notified to us by 28 February 1982.

Complete your parish magazine with Mowbray's full-colour picture covers and The Sign inset

Available in both A4 and A5 format

Attractive, economical, and full of positive Christian teaching material

Ideal monthly supplement for your local editorial

Samples and prices from

MOWBRAY'S PUBLISHING DIVISION

Saint Thomas House, Becket Street
Oxford OX1 1SJ

Telephone: Oxford (0865) 242507

A

AAMA, Drummond. St Pet Coll Siota. **d** 53 Melan. d Dio Melan from 53. *Pawa, British Solomon Islands.*

AARON, Canon Silas Chukwunyere. b 24. Trin Coll Umuahia 59. **d** 60 **p** 61 Ow. P Dio Ow 60-70; Dio Ibad from 70; Can of Ibad from 75. *St Paul's Anglican Church, SW7/150A Oke-Bola, Ibadan, Nigeria.*

ABA, Lord Bishop of. *See* Afonya, Right Rev Hubert Alafuro Ibibama.

ABA, Provost of. *See* Akoma, Very Rev Israel Enyinna.

ABAJINGIN, Daniel Olasupo. Melville Hall, Ibad 54. **d** 55 **p** 56 Lagos. P Dio Lagos from 54. *St Paul's Vicarage, Ago-Iwoye, Ijebu-Igbo, Nigeria.*

ABALA, Canon Saulo. **d** 59 Momb **p** 62 Maseno. P Dio Momb 59-61; Dio Maseno 61-70; Dio Maseno N from 70; Hon Can of Maseno N from 72. *Lubinu, Box 11, Mumias, Kenya.*

ABANGITE, Noa. **d** 70 Ugan. d Dio Ugan from 70. *c/o PO Box 190, Nyangilia Koboko, Via Arua, West Nile, Uganda.*

ABANI, Christopher Chimezie Onuoha. Trin Coll Umuahia, 58. **d** 60 Niger. d Dio Niger 60-69; Dio Enugu 69-81. *c/o St Matthew's Church, Umuaga, Nigeria.*

ABARA, Herbert Smart. Trin Th Coll Umuahia 66. **d** 66 Niger **p** 68 Bp Uzodike. P Dio Ow from 68. *Parsonage, Umuduru-Mbano, Okigwa, Nigeria.*

ABAYEH, Matthew Henry Dumotayo. Awka Coll. **d** 29 **p** 31 Niger. P Dio Niger 29-52; Dio Nig Delta 52-60; Can of Nig Delta 53-60. *c/o Anglican Church, Okpo, Brass, Nigeria.*

ABAZIE, Amaefule Okom. b 38. Trin Coll Umuahia 75. **d** 78 Aba. d Dio Aba. *All Saints Parsonage, Abayi Umuocham, Nigeria.*

ABBEY, Anthony James. b 36. Selw Coll Cam 2nd cl Th Trip pt i 57, BA (2nd cl Th Trip pt ii) 59, MA 63. ARCO 61. Ely Th Coll 59. **d** 61 **p** 62 Chelmsf. C of Wanstead 61-63; Laindon w Basildon 63-67; R of Sandon 67-76; V of Epping Dio Chelmsf from 76; Surr from 78. *Vicarage, Hartland Road, Epping, Essex, CM16 4PD.* (Epping 72906)

ABBOTT, Barry Ingle. b 31. Sarum Th Coll 65. **d** 67 **p** 68 Sarum. C of Wootton Bassett and of Broad Town 67-69; Wilton w Netherhampton 69-70; V of Ch Ch Warm 71-76; Publ Pr Dio Sarum 76-77; P-in-c of Figheldean w Milston 77-79; Bulford 77-79; L to Offic Dio B & W from 79; Dio Ex from 80. *The Mount, Cottage Lane, Dulverton, Somt, TA22 9HR.*

ABBOTT, Charles Leo. Hur Coll 12. **d** 14 **p** 15 Hur. I of Dundalk 14-16; C-in-c of Pine River 17-21; in Amer Ch 21-56; P-in-c of Fishing Lake Ind Reserve 56-59; Gainsborough Oxbow 59-60; Golden 60-65; Westwold Miss 65-67. *RR 1, Fulford Harbour, Salt Spring Island, BC, Canada.*

ABBOTT, Charles Peter. b 25. Univ of Maryland 60. **d** and **p** 62 Kansas. [f in Amer Ch] C of Oxhey 66-70; St Barn Dulwich and Asst Chap Alleyn's Coll Dulwich 70-72; V of H Spirit Southway Plymouth 72-78; Whitgift w Adlingfleet and Eastoft 78-79. *Address temp unknown.*

ABBOTT, Christopher Ralph. b 38. St D Coll Lamp BA 59. Wells Th Coll 59. **d** 61 **p** 62 S'wark. C of Camberwell 61-67; St Mary Portsea 67-70; V of St Cuthb Copnor Dio Portsm from 70. *St Cuthbert's Vicarage, Lichfield Road, Copnor, Portsmouth, PO3 6DE.* (Portsm 27071)

ABBOTT, David. **d** 30 Perth **p** 31 W Austr. C of Palmyra 30-33; R of Gingin 33-36; Meckering 36-40; R of Swan and Chap of Swan Boys' Orphanage 40-42; Chap AIF 42-46; R of Mundaring 46; Carlisle 46-48; St Matt Guildford 48-53; Min of W Preston 53-55; Hastings 55-57; I of H Trin E Melb 57-60; St Mary E Preston 60-65; Perm to Offic Dio Melb from 65. *Unit 4, 8 Jika Street, Heidelberg, Vic. 3084, Australia.*

ABBOTT, David Robert. b 49. Univ of Edin BD 72. Qu Coll Birm 72. **d** 74 Warrington for Liv **p** 75 Liv. C of Kirkby 74-78; St Mich Ditton 78-80; R of Ashton-in-Makerfield Dio Liv from 80. *Rectory, North Ashton, Wigan, Lancs, WN4 0QF.* (Ashton-in-Makerfield 727241)

ABBOTT, Douglas Charles. Moore Th Coll Syd ACT ThL 52, Th Scho (2nd cl) 62. **d** 52 **p** 53 Syd. C of Ryde 52-55; CF (Austr) from 55. *5 Hudson Close, Turramurra, NSW, Australia 2074.* (449-6684)

ABBOTT, Eric Symes. b 06. KCVO 66. Late Scho of Jes Coll Cam 1st cl Cl Trip Pt i 27, BA (2nd cl Cl Trip pt ii) 28, MA 32, Hon Fell 65. Fell K Coll Lon 46. Univ of Ox MA (by incorp) 55. DD (Lambeth) 59. Hon Fell Keble Coll Ox 60. Univ of Lon Hon DD 66. Westcott Ho Cam 28. **d** 30 **p** 31 Lon. C of St Jo Evang Westmr 30-32; Chap of K Coll Lon 32-36; K Coll Th Hostel 34-36; Exam Chap to Bp of Ripon 35-45; Chap Lincoln's Inn 35-36; Warden Linc Th Coll 36-45; Exam Chap to Bp of Linc 36-60; Can and Preb of Sanctae Crucis in Linc Cathl 40-60; Commiss Kimb K 45-60; Bom 50-60 and from 63; Johann 50-60 and 61-75; Gui 52-60 and 62-74; Dean of K Coll Lon 45-55; Exam Chap to Bps of S'wark and B & W 46-59; to Bp of Truro 51-59; to Bp of Ox 56-60; Select Pr Univ of Cam 39, 53 and 61; Univ of Ox 46-47, 57 and 59; Chap to HM the King 48-52; to HM the Queen 52-59; Warden of Keble Coll Ox 56-60; Dean of Westmr 59-74; Extra-Chap to HM the Queen from 74. *17 Vincent Square, SW1.*

ABBOTT, Eugene Pearce. Mem Univ Newfld. **d** 65 Bp Seaborn for Newfld **p** 66 Newfld. C of St Jo Bapt Cathl St John's 65-67; R of Pushthrough 67-69; White Bay 70-73; Harbour Breton Dio Newfld (Centr Newfld from 76) from 73. *PO Drawer 100, Harbour Breton, Newfoundland, Canada.* (709-885-2225)

ABBOTT, John Phillip. b 48. St Barn Coll Belair 73. **d** 75 **p** 76 River. C of Leeton 75-78; Griffith 78-79; P-in-c of Balranald Dio River from 79. *St Barnabas Rectory, Balranald, NSW, Australia 2715.*

ABBOTT, John Williamson. b 16. Selw Coll Cam BA 38, MA 44. Qu Coll Birm 38. **d** 39 **p** 40 Man. C of St Marg Prestwich 39-43; St Mary Oldham 43-50; R of St Pet Stretford 50-65; Healing Dio Linc from 65; V of Stallingbrough Dio Linc from 65. *7 The Avenue, Healing, Grimsby, S Humberside, DN37 7NA.* (0472-883481)

ABBOTT, Kenneth Batten. Qu Coll St John's Newfld BA 56. **d** 59 Bp Davis for NS **p** 61 NS. I of Petite Rivière 59-64; on leave 64-66 and 70-76; C of Foxtrap 66-70; L to Offic Dio E Newfld from 76. *c/o Smallwood Collegiate, Wabush, Labrador, Canada.*

ABBOTT, Leonard Mackay. Univ of Adel BEng 43. BD Lon 60. Univ of New Engl Dipl Educn 64. Moore Th Coll Syd ACT ThL (1st cl) 59. **d** 60 **p** 61 Adel. C of St Matt Kens 60-61; Chap C of E Gr Sch Syd 61-73; R of Peakhurst (w Lugarno 74-77) 74-80; St Matt Windsor Dio Syd from 80. *Rectory, Moses Street, Windsor, NSW, Australia 2756.* (77-3193)

ABBOTT, Leslie Leonard. b 24. ARICS 47. Wycl Hall, Ox 55. **d** and **p** 56 Southw. C of Attenborough w Bramcote 56-58; R of Trowell 58-62; CF (TA) 59-67; V of Lenton 62-67; Attenborough (w Bramcote to 67) w Chilwell 67-73; Surr 72-73; Perm to Offic Dio Chich from 73. *20 Winfield Avenue, Patcham, Brighton, E Sussex, BN1 8QH.* (Brighton 553684)

ABBOTT, Michael Reginald. Univ of Hull BSc 64. Cudd Coll 64. **d** 66 Penrith for Carl **p** 67 Carl. C of Workington 66-68; Ambleside w Rydal and Brathay 68-70; Chap of St Paul's Boys Coll Hong Kong 70-71; Chap RN 71-72; C of Dalton-in-Furness 72-73; V of Stanbridge w Tilsworth 73-78; Team V of Dunstable Dio St Alb from 78. *St Fremund's Vicarage, 22 Princes Street, Dunstable, Beds, LU7 3AX.* (Dunstable 68996)

ABBOTT, Very Rev Nigel Douglas Blayney. b 37. Bp's Coll Cheshunt 58. **d** 61 **p** 62 Pet. C of St Mich AA Northn 61-64; Wanstead 64-66; Chap and Ho Master St John's Approved Sch Tiffield 66-69; V of Earl's Barton 69-73; H Trin Cov 73-80; Surr 73-80; M Gen Syn Cov 78-80; Provost and R of St Jo Div Cathl Oban Dio Arg Is from 80. *Rectory, Oban, Argyll, PA34 5DJ.* (0631 62323)

ABBOTT, Stephen Anthony. b 43. K Coll Cam BA 65, MA 69. Univ of Edin BD 68. Univ of Harvard ThM 69. Edin Th

Coll 65-68. **d** 69 Dover for Cant **p** 70 Cant. C of Deal 69-72; Chap K Coll Cam 72-75; C of St Matt Cam 75-77; Asst Chap Bris Univ from 77; Hon C of St Paul Clifton 77-80; Perm to Offic Dio Bris from 81. *2 Leighton Road, Knowle, Bristol, BS4 2LL.* (0272-779270)

ABBOTT, Stephen William. Moore Th Coll Syd BTh 77. **d** 78 Syd **p** 78 Bp Short for Syd. C of Miranda 78-79; St John Parramatta Dio Syd from 80. *21 Campbell Street, Parramatta, NSW, Australia 2150.*

ABBOTTSMITH, Alexander Charles. Moore Th Coll Syd 62. ACT ThL 62. Mona Vale 62-63; Turramurra 63-65; **d** 62 **p** 63 Syd. C of Gladesville 65-66; I of Winchelsea 66-69; Asst Master St Andr Cathl Sch Syd 70; Chap from 71; C of Summer Hill 70. *51 Talara Road, Gymea, NSW, Australia 2227.* (524-5451)

ABDEL MALIK, Ghais. St Geo Coll Jer 61. **d** 62 Jer for Egypt. C of Old Cairo Dio Egypt from 62. *c/o All Saints' Cathedral, Cairo, Egypt.*

✠ ABDULAH, Right Rev Clive. Univ of Pennsylvania, BA 50. Trin Coll Tor LTh 54, STB 55. U Th Sem NY STM 65. **d** 53 Tor for Ja **p** 54 Ja. C of Kingston 54-57; R of Highgate and of Belfield 57-66; Stony Hill 66-70; Cons Ld Bp of Trinid in H Trin Cathl Port of Spain 29 Sept 70 by Abp of WI; Bps of Barb; Ja; Br Hond; Nass; Windw Is; Antig; and Berm; Bps Suffr of Guy; Trinid; and Ja; and Bp Howe. *Hayes Court, 21 Maraval Road, Port of Spain, Trinidad, WI.* (62-27387)

ABDY, Ven James Ivan. Bro of St Paul, Barton, Yorks 48. **d** 50 **p** 51 Kimb K. C of St John's Miss Motito 50-51; St Matt Miss Kimb 51-53; Dir of Upington Miss and R of Upington w Kenhardt 53-59; Dir of Ovamboland Miss 59-62; Archd of Ovamboland 59-62; Keetmanshoop 62-67; R of Keetmanshoop 62-67; Walvis Bay Dio Damar (Namibia from 80) from 67; Archd of Walvis Bay from 70. *PO Box 58, Walvis Bay, SW Africa.* (0642 2109)

ABDY, John Channing. b 38. Univ of Nottm BA (2nd cl Th) 63. Cudd Coll 63. **d** 65 **p** 66 St Alb. C of Leagrave 65-69; N Mymms 69-72; V of King's Walden 72-79; S Woodham Ferrers Dio Chelmsf from 79. *Vicarage, Cornwallis Drive, South Woodham Ferrers, Essex, CM3 5YE.* (0245-320201)

ABE, Canon Appolos Lekagha. St Paul's Coll Awka. Trin Th Coll Umuahia 60. **d** 62 **p** 63 Nig Delta. P Dio Nig Delta 62-68 and from 69; C of St Cuthb Everton 68-69; Can of Nig Delta from 72. *PO Box 74, Calabar, Nigeria.* (Calabar 2415)

ABE, Ezekiel Akinsola. Melv Hall Ibad. **d** 56 **p** 57 Ibad. P Dio Ibad 56-72; Dio Ekiti from 72. *Holy Trinity Vicarage, Odo-Oja, Ikere, Nigeria.*

ABE, Gabriel Oyedele. Im Coll Ibad 67. **d** 69 Ekiti. d Dio Ekiti. *St Paul's Vicarage, Ijan, Ekiti, Nigeria.*

ABE, Samuel Adedayo. b 44. Im Coll Ibad Dipl Th 70. **d** 70 **p** 71 Ondo. P Dio Ondo. *University of Ife, Ile-Ife, Oyo, Nigeria.*

ABE, Stephen Olanipekun. b 28. **d** 72 **p** 73 Ekiti. P Dio Ekiti. *St John's Vicarage, Ilasa, Ekiti, Nigeria.*

ABEBE, Patrick Aluge. Im Coll Ibad 79. **d** 81 Benin. d Dio Benin. *c/o Registrar, PO Box 82, Benin City, Nigeria.*

ABEL, David John. b 31. SOC 71. **d** 74 **p** 75 S'wark. Hon C of Crowhurst Dio S'wark from 74. *Arden Green, Bowerland Lane, Lingfield, Surrey.*

ABELL, Brian. b 37. Univ of Nottm BA (2nd cl Th) 61. Cudd Coll 61. **d** 63 **p** 64 Wakef. C of Lightcliffe 63-66; C-in-c of H Nativ Conv Distr Mixenden Halifax 66-68; Lect Linc Coll Tech 68-69; Chap Trent Coll Derbys 70-74; V of Thorner Dio Ripon from 74; Warden of Readers Dio Ripon from 78. *Thorner Vicarage, Leeds, Yorks, LS14 3EG.* (Leeds 892437)

ABELL, George Derek. b 31. Selw Coll Cam BA (2nd cl Th Trip pt ii) 54, MA 68. Qu Coll Birm 54. **d** 56 **p** 57 Lich. C of Stoke-on-Trent 56-60; Wolverhampton 60-64; R of St Mary Magd Bridgnorth and C-in-c of Oldbury 64-70; Atherton N Queensld 70-73; R of Withington w Westhide and Weston Beggard Dio Heref from 73; C-in-c of Sutton Dio Heref 76-81; R from 81. *Rectory, Sutton, Hereford, HR1 3BA.*

ABELL, James Thornton. b 04. Univ of Liv BA (Span) 25. Kelham Th Coll 25. **d** 29 **p** 30 Linc. C of St Andr Linc 29-34; Hawarden 34-38; Gainsborough 38-39; PC of St Mich Castleford 39-55; Sub-Warden of Commun of St Jo Bapt Clewer 55-59; Warden 59-63; L to Offic Dio Ox 55-63; V of Lower Whitley 63-72. *129 Melton Road, West Bridgford, Nottingham, NG2 6FG.*

ABELL, Peter John. b 45. Chich Th Coll 67. **d** 70 **p** 71 Glouc. C of St Jo Evang Churchdown 70-74; Chap RAF from 74. *c/o Ministry of Defence, Adastral House, WC1.*

ABERCROMBIE, Lionel Hugh Lindsay. Trin Coll Dub BA 28, Div Test 29, MA 31. **d** 29 **p** 30 Down. C of Ballywillan Portrush 29-33; C-in-c of All SS w Burt 33-39; R 39-42; I of Donagh w Clonmany and Cloncha 42-50; Chap Distr Hosp Carndonagh 42-50. *21 Wistaria House, Restmore Gardens, Redhill Drive, Bournemouth, Hants.*

ABERDEEN, Provost of. *See* Howard, Very Rev Donald.

ABERDEEN and ORKNEY, Lord Bishop of. *See* Darwent, Right Rev Frederick Charles.

ABERDEEN and ORKNEY, Dean of. *See* Adamson, Very Rev Alexander Campbell.

ABERNETHY, Alan Francis. b 57. Qu Univ Belf BA 78. Ch of Ireland Th Coll Dipl Th 81. **d** 81 Down. C of Dundonald Dio Down from 81. *6 Mount Regan Avenue, Ballyregan Road, Dundonald, Co Down, N Ireland.*

ABERNETHY, David Terence Phillips. b 42. St D Coll Lamp 61, **d** 65 Swan B for St A **p** 66 St A. C of Abergele 65-72; Pembroke, Berm 72-79; V of St Mark I and Dio Berm from 79. *St Mark's Vicarage, Bermuda.*

ABERNETHY, Walter Mervyn. b 12. Trin Coll Dub BA 33, Div Test 34, MA 45. **d** 36 **p** 37 Newc T. C of Tweedmouth 36-38; St Ambrose Bris 38-39; I of Achill 39-42; CF (EC) 42-44; R of Castlemagner 44; Kirby Cane 45-53; Chap Heckingham Inst 48-53; V of Briston w Burgh Parva R 53-57; CF (TA) 53-62; CF (TA-R of O) 62-67; Hon CF from 67; V of Snettisham 57-64; Sproxton w Saltby and Coston 64-68; R of Tibberton 68-72; R of Kynnersley 68-72; V of Llanyblodwell 72-77; Perm to Offic Dio Nor 78-80; Dio Lich from 80. *Dovaston Manse, Kinnerley, Oswestry, Shropshire, SY10 8DS.* (Knockin 320)

ABEYESINGHE, Felix Abraham Dias. b 10. Div Sch Colom. **d** 34 **p** 37 Colom. C of St Luke Borella 34-37; Kandyan Centr Itin 37-39; Baddegama Miss 39; All SS Galle 39-43 and 66-74; Talampitiya Distr 43-45; P-in-c of St Luke Ratnapura 45-47; I of St Mark Badulla w Passara 42-57; Dehiwela 57-66; C of St Mark w St Bart Dalston 76-81. *68a Sandringham Road, E8.* (01-254 2971)

ABEYWARDENA, Patrick Cyril de Silva. b 19. Bp's Coll Calc. **d** 43 **p** 45 Colom. P Dio Colom 43-73; C of Ch Ch Luton 73-74; All SS w St Pet Luton 74-78; Welwyn Dio St Alb from 78. *St Michael's House, Woolmer Green, Knebworth, Herts.* (Stevenage 813043)

ABIALA, Ebenezer Babatunde. b 45. Im Coll Ibad 79. **d** 80 **p** 81 Ijebu. P Dio Ijebu. *Christ Church Porogun, PO Box 23, Ijebu-Ode, Nigeria.*

ABIGO, Martin Chetem Isaian. b 46. Trin Coll Umuahia 75. **d** 76 Nig Delta. d Dio Nig Delta. *St Matthias Parsonage, Emelogo Odual, Abua/Odual, Rivers State, Nigeria.*

ABIODUN, Hezekaih Oludotun. b 24. **d** 72 **p** 74 Lagos. P Dio Lagos 72-76; Dio Egba from 76. *St James's Church, Orile-Ilugun, Abeokuta, Nigeria.*

ABLETT, Edwin John. b 37. Clifton Th Coll 64. **d** 67 **p** 68 Southw. C of St Chris Sneinton 67-70; R of Good Easter and High Easter w Margaret Roding 70-73; SAMS Miss Dio Chile 73-75; C of Gt Baddow (in c of St Paul's) 75-78; V of Newchapel Dio Lich from 78. *Vicarage, Pennyfields Road, Newchapel, Stoke-on-Trent, ST7 4PN.* (Kidsgrove 2837)

ABLEWHITE, Stanley Edward. b 30. Univ of Birm BSocSc 59. Wycl Hall Ox 73. **d** 73 Warrington for Liv **p** 74 Liv. C of Much Woolton 73-77; V of Brough w Stainmore Dio Carl from 77. *Church Brough Vicarage, Kirkby Stephen, Cumbria, CA17 4EJ.* (Brough 238)

ABODE, Paul Uanzeki. b 16. **d** 74 **p** 75 Benin. P Dio Benin. *St Michael's Vicarage, Uzebba, Iuleha, via Benin City, Nigeria.*

ABODUNRIN, Amos Adeniji. b 28. **d** 74 **p** 76 Ibad. P Dio Ibad. *St Stephen's Vicarage, Jago, Ibadan, Nigeria.*

ABOLARINWA, Samuel Oyeniyi. b 32. **d** 75 **p** 76 Kwara. P Dio Kwara. *Omupo Grammar School, via Ilorin, Kwara State, Nigeria.*

ABONGI, Kithoy. b 36. **d** 76 **p** 77 Boga-Z. P Dio Boga-Z. *BP 154, Bunia, Zaire.*

ABONYO, Elijah. St Phil Coll Kongwa 64. **d** 66 Vic Nyan **p** 67 Bp Madinda for Vic Nyan. P Dio Vic Nyan. *Box 278, Mwanza, Tanzania, E Africa.*

ABORISADE, Nathaniel Olukoya. Melville Hall Ibad. **d** 52 Bp Phillips for Lagos **p** 53 Lagos. P Dio Lagos 52-58; Dio Niger 58-62; Dio Lagos from 62. *Magbon Alade, PA Ibeju, via Epe, Nigeria.*

ABOTIMAE, Luke. St Pet Coll Siota. **d** 69 **p** 71 Melan. P Dio Melan 69-75; Dio Centr Melan from 75. *Bia, Haununu, Solomon Islands.*

ABRAHAM, Ven Alfred. Em Coll Sktn. Huron Coll Ont LTh 41. **d** 33 Sask for Caled **p** 34 Caled. Miss at Anyox 33-35; Qu Charlotte Is 35-42; R of St Andr Lon Ont 42-60; Can of St Paul's Cathl Lon Ont 49-60; Archd of Lambton 60-71; Middx 71-74; Archd (Emer) from 74; R of St Geo Sarnia 60-71; Hyde Park 71-74. *728 Hillcrest Drive, London, Ont., Canada.*

ABRAHAM, Charles John. Bp's Univ Lennox BA 53. **d** 51 Queb for Newfld **p** 52 Newfld. Miss of Labrador Miss 51-52; C of Trin Mem Ch Montr 52-54; I of Cow Head 54-58; C of St Jo Bapt Cathl St John's 58-63; I of St Aug St John's 63-69; R of Burgeo 69-71; Corner Brook Dio Newfld (W Newfld from 76) from 71; Commiss to Bp of W Newfld from 76.

Rectory, Main Street, Corner Brook, Newfoundland, Canada. (709-634-2373)

ABRAHAM, David Alexander. b 37. K Coll Lon and Warm AKC 61. **d** 62 **p** 63 Lich. C of Oswestry 62-63; Gt Wyrley 63-65; Sprowston 65-67; V of Ormesby St Marg w Scratby and Ormesby St Mich 67-81; R of Hilborough Group (Cockley Cley w Gooderstone, Oxburgh w Foulden, Hilborough w Bodney, Gt w L Cressingham and Threxton, and Didlington) Dio Nor from 81. *Cockley Cley Rectory, Swaffham, Norf, PE37 8AN.* (Swaffham 21297)

ABRAHAM, Canon John Callis Harford. Univ of W Austr BA 52, 2nd cl Engl 53. Westcott Ho Cam 53. **d** 55 **p** 56 Liv. C of St Anne Wigan 55-57; Northam W Austr 57-60; R of Wongan Hills 60-63; Vice-Warden Wollaston Th Coll Claremont 63-67; R of Graylands Mt Claremont 63-67; L to Offic Dio Birm 67-68; R of Applecross 68-76; Exam Chap to Abp of Perth from 69; Can of Perth from 71; R of Leeming w S Willetton Chap Home Miss Dio Perth from 79. *104 Woolwich Street, Leederville, W Australia 6007.* (381-1652)

ABRAHAM, Richard James. b 42. Univ of Liv BA 63. Ridley Hall Cam 64. **d** 66 Warrington for Liv **p** 67 Liv. C of St Ann Warrington 66-70; Golborne 70-72; V of Bickershaw 73-78; R of Kirkby Laythorpe w Asgarby Dio Linc from 78. *Kirkby Laythorpe Rectory, Sleaford, Lincs.* (Sleaford 2257)

ABRAHAM, Canon Sheldon Duncan. Univ of Tor BA 52. Trin Coll Tor LTh and STB 55. **d** 54 **p** 55 Tor. C of St Mich AA Tor 54 57; R of St Andr Scarborough Tor 57-65; Cobourg 65-70; St Clem Eglington Tor 70-81; Can of Tor from 72; Dir of Ch Development Dio Tor from 81. *135 Adelaide Street East, Toronto, Ont., Canada.*

ABRAHAMS, Edward Victor. b 36. **d** 73 **p** 76 Kimb K. P Dio Kimb K. *St Barnabas Vicarage, Community Road, Kimberley, S Africa.*

ABRAHAMS, Peter William. b 42. Univ of Southn BA 77. Sarum Wells Th Coll 77. **d** 78 **p** 79 Win. C of Bitterne Park 78-82; Team V of Old Brumby Dio Linc from 82. *Vicarage, Dorchester Road, Westcliff, Scunthorpe, S Humberside.*

ABRAHAMS, Stuart Noel. Moore Th Coll Syd 61. ACT ThL 62. **d** 62 **p** 63 Syd. C of St Mich Wollongong 62-63; Home Sec CMS NSW 64-66; R of Northbridge 66-73; St Andr Wahroonga 73-76; All SS Howra Dio Syd from 76. *66 Plunkett Street, Nowra, NSW, Australia 2540.* (044-22018)

ABRAM, Norman. b 09. Men in Disp 44. St Aid Coll 28. Univ of Dur Lth 33. **d** 35 **p** 36 York. C of St Thos York 35-37; Acomb 37-39; Fulford York 39-40; CF 40-55; R of Templeton w Loxbeare 55-66; V of Studham w Whipsnade 66-76. *2 Suffolk Close, Holland-on-Sea, Essex.* (Clacton 812591)

ABRAM, Paul Robert Carrington. b 36. Keble Coll Ox BA (3rd cl Geog) 62, MA 65. Chich Th Coll 60. **d** 62 **p** 63 York. C of Redcar 62-65; CF from 65. *c/o Lloyds Bank, 115 Victoria Road, Aldershot, Hants.*

ABRAM, Steven James. b 50. Univ of Lon Dipl Th (Extra-Mural Stud) 74. BD (Lon) 76. Oak Hill Coll 71. **d** 76 **p** 77 Lich. C of Biddulph 76-79; St John Heatherlands Parkstone Dio Sarum from 78. *35 Stanfield Road, Parkstone, Poole, BH12 3HR.* (Parkstone 746744)

ABSALOM, Hugh Pryse. Fitzw Ho Cam BA (2nd cl Engl Trip pt ii) 31, MA 36. BD (Lon) 56. **d** 36 **p** 37 Mon. C of H Trin Abergavenny 36-39; St Luke (in c of St Mich AA) Torquay 39-43; Chap RAFVR 43-49; V of Compton Queb 49-52; Lect in Div Bp's Univ Lennox 51-52; C of Brixham 52-53; V of Friday Bridge 53-57; Coldham 53-57; Lucton w Eyton 57-61; C-in-c of Croft w Yarpole 57-61; Chap and Master Lucton Sch 57-61; Chap and Sen Lect St Hild's Tr Coll Durham 61-73; R of Walton w Talbenny and Haroldston W 73-77. *34 Ruther Park, Haverfordwest, Dyfed.*

ABSOLON, Canon Peter Chambers. b 27. St Jo Coll Cam BA 50, MA 55. Linc Th Coll 50. **d** 53 Glouc **p** 54 Bp Barkway for Cant. C of Yate 53-56; Belvedere 56-60; Erith 60-61; V 61-67; Bp's Industr Chap in Erith and Belvedere 60-67; Min of St Nich Strood 67-72; Member of Strood Team Min 72-79; Hon Can of Roch Cathl from 79; C of Strood 80-81; V of H Trin Twydall Gillingham Dio Roch from 81. *2 Waltham Road, Gillingham, Kent.* (Medway 31690)

ABU-DIGIN, Ismail Gabriel. b 52. **d** 81 Omdurman. d Dio Omdurman. *PO Box 65, Omdurman, Sudan.*

ABUBAKAR, Adamu. d 64 N Nig. d Dio N Nig from 64. *St Bartholomew's Church, Wusasa PA, Zaria, Nigeria.*

ABUKAYA, Yonasani. d 62 N Ugan. d Dio N Ugan 62-69; Dio M & W Nile from 69. *P.O. Koboko, Uganda.*

ABURASU, Enosa. d 60 **p** 61 Sudan. P Dio Sudan 60-76; Dio Yambio from 76. *ECS, Maridi, Sudan.*

ACCRA, Lord Bishop of. *See* Lemaire, Most Rev Ishmael Samuel Mills.

ACCRA, Assistant Bishop of. *See* Nelson, Right Rev Aruna Kodjo.

ACCRA, Provost of. *See* Ashiety, Very Rev Robert Emmanuel.

ACHAGBUE, Joseph Wosu. b 36. St Paul's Coll Awka 76. **d** 77 Aba. d Dio Aba. *St Andrew's Parsonage, Ohuru, Asa via Aba, Nigeria.*

ACHALLA, Simeon. d and **p** 75 Bunyoro. P Dio Bunyoro. *PO Kagadi, Hoima, Uganda.*

ACHESON, Canon Russell Robert. b 16. Late Scho of Univ Coll Ox (2nd cl Lit Hum) BA 39, MA 45, Dipl Th 47. Wells Th Coll 45. **d** 47 **p** 48 Bris. C of Bedminster Down 47-49; Youth Chap Dio Bris 49-54; Angl Chap to Univ of Bris 55-66; V of St Paul Clifton 57-66; Hon Can of Bris 64-66; V of Much Wenlock w Bourton 66-79; Exam Chap to Bp of Heref from 66; P-in-c of Church Preen (w Hughley from 73) 69-79; RD of Condover 72-78; C-in-c of Harley 73-75; Kenley 73-79; Preb of Heref Cathl from 74; P-in-c of Easthope w Long Stanton 76-79; Shipton 76-79; Can Res of Heref Cathl from 79; Warden of Readers Dio Heref from 78. *Cathedral Close, Hereford, HR1 2NG.* (Heref 266193)

ACHONRY, Archdeacon of. *See* Killala.

ACHONRY, Bishop of. *See* Tuam.

ACHONRY, Dean of. *See* Tuam.

ACKERLEY, Herbert. b 20. **d** 61 **p** 63 Man. C of Atherton 61-64; R of St Matt Ardwick Man 64-68; C-in-c of St Clem Longsight 67-68; R of St Matt w St Clem Longsight 68-71; St Luke Longsight Dio Man from 71. *St Luke's Rectory, Stockport Road, Manchester, M13 9AB.* (061-273 6662)

ACKLAM, Leslie Charles. b 46. Univ of Birm BEducn 71. Ripon Coll Cudd 78. **d** 80 Chelmsf **p** 81 Barking for Chelmsf. C of St Anne Chingford Dio Chelmsf from 80. *49 Wyemead Crescent, Chingford, E4.*

✠ **ACKON, Right Rev John Alexander.** b 37. Univ of Nottm BTh 72. STh (Lambeth) 77. Kelham Th Coll 63. **d** and **p** 68 Accra. C of H Trin Cathl Accra 68-69; Chap Adisadel Coll Cape Coast 73-77; Can and Prec of H Trin Cathl Accra 77-80; R of St Nich Cape Coast 80-81; Cons Ld Bp of Cape Coast 18 Oct 81 in H Trin Cathl Accra by Abps of W Afr and Nigeria; Bps of Kum, Gambia, Sierr L and Bo; Abps Ramsey and Scott; and Bps Howe and Daly. *Bishop's Lodge, Box 38, Cape Coast, Ghana.*

ACKROYD, Christopher. b 05. CCC Ox BA (3rd cl Hist) 27, 3rd cl Th 28, MA 32. **d** 54 **p** 55 Bradf. C of Gargrave 54-56; C-in-c of Carleton-in-Craven 56-57; R 57-63; V of Fridaythorpe w Fimber and Thixendale 63-75; Perm to Offic Dio York from 76. *46 Fellbrook Avenue, York, YO2 5PS.* (York 791074)

ACKROYD, Dennis. b 36. Cranmer Hall Dur 67. **d** 70 **p** 71 Lich. C of St Giles Newc L 70-73; Horsell 74-77; P-in-c of Moreton and Woodsford w Tincleton Dio Sarum from 77; RD of Dorch from 79. *Moreton Rectory, Dorchester, Dorset, DT2 8RH.* (0929-462466)

ACKROYD, Eric. b 29. Univ of Leeds BA 51. Univ of Liv MA 71. St Jo Coll Dur 53. **d** 55 Whitby for York **p** 56 York. C of St John Newland York 55-58; Succr of Birm Cathl 58-61; Chap K Sch Bruton 61-67; Lect Kirkby Fields Tr Coll Liv 67-72; Sen Lect Northn Coll of Educn 72-73; Nene Coll of Higher Educn Northn from 73. *49a Landcross Drive, Northampton, NN3 3LN.*

ACKROYD, John Michael Calvert. b 32. BSc (Lon) 53. Ripon Hall Ox 71. **d** 73 **p** 74 Bradf. C of Keighley (in c of All SS from 76) 73-81; V of All SS Keighley 81; St Mary Virg and All SS Whalley Dio Blackb from 81. *Vicarage, The Sands, Whalley, Blackburn, Lancs, BB6 9TL.* (Whalley 3249)

ACKROYD, Peter Runham. b 17. Down Coll Cam BA 38; Trin Coll Cam MA 42, PhD 45. Univ of Lon MTh 42, DD 70. Univ of St Andr Hon DD 70. Westcott Ho Cam 57. **d** 57 **p** 58 Ely. Hon C of H Trin, Cam 57-61; Lect in Div Univ of Cam 57-61; Prof OT Stud Univ of Lon 61-82; Fell K Coll Lon from 69. *19 Gayfere Street, SW1P 3HP.*

ACKROYD, William Lancelot. b 1900. Egerton Hall Man 31. **d** 33 **p** 34 Man. C of Ch Ch Salford 33-35; St John Pendlebury 35-37; R of St Thos Ardwick 37-42; V of St Simon and St Jude Bolton 42-45; Org Sec BFBS for Staffs and Salop 45-47; R of St Jo Evang Old Trafford 47-53; V of St Petherwyn w Trewen 53-60; St Germans 60-64; R of Eastleach Martin w Eastleach Turville and Southrop 64-68; C of Stokenham w Sherford 69-71; Perm to Offic Dio Truro from 72. *2 Trelawney Road, Callington, Cornw.*

ACLAND, Simon Henry Harper. b 41. Westcott Ho Cam 65. **d** 67 **p** 68 Man. C of St Marg Prestwich 67-69; C of Papanui 69; C of Belfast-Redwood 69-71; V of St Paul Sing 71-74; Chap of Ch Coll Ch Ch 75-78; V of St Luke City and Dio Ch Ch from 78. *185 Kilmore Street, Christchurch 1, NZ.* (62-253)

ACOSTA, Jose Daniel. d 75 Bp Leake for N Argent. d Dio N Argent. *The Parsonage, Pozo Algarrobo, N Argentina.*

ACOTT, David. b 32. Clifton Th Coll 54. **d** 58 **p** 59 S'wark. C of Streatham Pk 58-60; St Faith Maidstone 60-64; R of Pettaugh w Winston (and Framsden from 76) 64-77; Area Sec CMS Dios Cant and Roch from 77. *473 Tonbridge Road, Maidstone, Kent, ME16 9LH.* (Maidstone 26666)

ACWORTH, Oswald Roney. b 10. SS Coll Cam BA 33, MA 37. Westcott Ho Cam. **d** 46 **p** 47 St E. C of St Aug Ipswich 46-48; V of Chobham (w Valley End from 56) 48-79. *c/o Vicarage, Chobham, Surrey.* (Chobham 8197)

ACWORTH, Richard Foote. b 36. SS Coll Cam BA 62, MA 65. Cudd Coll 61. **d** 63 Lon **p** 64 Man. C of St Etheldreda Fulham 63; All SS and Marts Langley 64-66; Bridgwater 66-69; V of Yatton 69-81; Yatton Moor 81; M Gen Syn from 80; P-in-c of Taunton Dio B & W from 81; P-in-c of St Jo Evang Taunton Dio B & W from 81. *St Mary's Vicarage, Taunton, Somt.* (Taunton 72441)

ACWORTH, Richard John Philip. b 30. Ch Ch Ox BA 52, MA 56. **d** and **p** 63 RC Bp of Limburg. Rec into C of E by Bp of Chelmsf 68. C of Walthamstow 68-70; C-in-c of L Sampford 70-76; Gt Sampford 74-76; Lect Bath Coll of Higher Educn 76-77; Derby Lonsdale Coll of Higher Educn from 77; L to Offic Dio Derby from 78. *9 The Wharf, Shardlow, Derby.*

ADAIR, Raymond. b 33. Ripon Hall Ox 70. **d** 72 Wakef **p** 73 Pontefract for Wakef. C of Knottingley 72-74; Sandal Magna 74-77; V of St Cath Sandal Dio Wakef from 77. *218 Doncaster Road, Wakefield, WF1 5HG.* (Wakef 74120)

ADAIR, William Matthew. b 52. TCD Div Test 77. **d** 77 **p** 78 Arm. C of Portadown 77-78; Asst Chap Miss to Seamen Belf 78-80; C of Ch Ch Cathl Lisburn Dio Connor from 80. *24a Castle Street, Lisburn, Co Antrim, N Ireland.*

ADAM, Andrew John. St Jo Coll Morpeth ACT ThL 57. **d** 56 **p** 57 Newc. C of Cessnock 56-60; Singleton 60-62; R of Clarencetown 62-66; Nabiac 66-72; Wyong Dio Newc from 72. *27 Byron Street, Wyong, NSW, Australia 2259.* (043-5 1474)

ADAM, David. b 36. Kelham Th Coll 54. **d** 59 **p** 60 Dur. C of St Helen Bp Auckland 59-63; St Jas Conv Distr Owton Manor W Hartlepool 63-67; V of Danby w Castleton Dio York from 67. *Danby Vicarage, Whitby, York.* (Castleton 388)

ADAM, Jack Emmanuel. McGill Univ BA 48, BD 52. Montr Dioc Th Coll. **d** 52 **p** 53 Montr. C of St Bart Tor 56-60; R of Cookstown 60-63; St Geo Pet 63-72; St Geo Willowdale City and Dio Tor from 72. *77 Canterbury Place, Willowvale, Ont., Canada.* (416-225 1922)

ADAM, James Douglas Campbell. b 13. Qu Univ Belf BSc 34. **d** 81 Heref (NSM). L to Offic Dio Heref from 81. *Windsor House, Lea Cross, Shrewsbury, SY5 8JE.*

ADAM, Canon John Marshall William. b 09. Late Scho of Or Coll Ox BA (2nd cl Mod Hist) 31, 2nd cl Th 33, MA 36. Wycl Hall Ox 31. **d** 33 **p** 34 Sheff. C of St Aug Sheff 33-35; Cathl Ch Sheff 35-36; Chap St Steph Coll Delhi (CMD) 36-39; Jun Chap and Succr of Sheff Cathl 39; Sen Chap and Prec 39-42; V of Paddock 42-46; Proc Conv Wakef 45-46; Home Sec Overseas Coun Ch Assembly 46-55; Actg Gen Sec 54-55; R of Friern Barnet 55-63; V of Preston 63-69; Broughton Blackb 69-74; Hon Can of Blackb 64-74; Can (Emer) from 74; RD of Preston 67-70; M Gen Syn 70-75; M C of E Pensions Bd 71-79. *7 Caton Green Road, Brookhouse, Nr Lancaster, LA2 9JL.* (0524 770030)

ADAM, Peter James Hedderwick. b 46. Univ of Lon BD 73, MTh 76. Ridley Coll Melb ACT ThL 69. **d** 70 **p** 71 Melb. C of St Jas, Ivanhoe 70-72; Rosanna 72; on leave 72-73; C of St Thos Essendon and Tutor Ridley Coll 73-74; L to Offic Dio Dur 75-81; Tutor St Jo Coll Dur 75-81; P-in-c of St Jude Carlton Dio Melb from 82. *St Jude's Vicarage, 235 Palmerston Street, Carlton, Vic, Australia 3053.*

✠ **ADAMS, Right Rev Albert James.** b 15. King's Coll Lon 39. St Andr Coll Whittlesford 41. **d** 42 **p** 43 Sheff. C of Walkley 42; Succr of Sheff Cathl 44; Prec 45-47; R of Bermondsey and Chap Bermondsey Med Miss 47-55; C-in-c of Ch Ch Parkers Row Bermondsey 47-51; RD of Bermondsey 55; R of Stoke Damerel Devonport 55-63; Surr 56-63; R of Wanstead 63-71; Surr 66-75; Archd of W Ham 70-75; Cons Ld Bp Suffr of Barking in St Paul's Cathl 24 June 75 by Abp of Cant; Bps of Lon, Chelmsf, Birm, Derby, Lich and Nor; Bps Suffr of Stepney, Kens, Willesden, Fulham & Gibr, Colchester, Bradwell, Shrewsbury, Warrington and Dudley, Bp Stannard and others. *670 High Road, Buckhurst Hill, Essex, IG9 5HN.* (01-505 1372)

ADAMS, Albert Leslie. b 17. Linc Th Coll 56. **d** 56 **p** 57 Linc. C of Bourne 56-58; PC of Belton in I-of-Axholme Dio Linc 58-68; V from 68; RD of I-of-Axholme from 80. *Belton Rectory, Doncaster, Yorks.* (Epworth 872207)

ADAMS, Aldred Samuel. b 32. St Deiniol's Libr Hawarden 72. **d** 73 **p** 74 St D. C of Milford Haven 73-74; C-in-c of Walwyn's Castle w Robeston W Dio St D 74-76; R from 76. *Walwyn's Castle Rectory, Haverfordwest, Dyfed, SA62 3ED.* (Broad Haven 257)

ADAMS, Alexander Geoffrey. Ch Coll Hobart ACT ThL 49. **d** 47 **p** 48 Tas. R of Woodbridge 48-49; Cullenswood 49-54; Queenstown 54-58; Hamilton 58-63; Latrobe 63-72; H Trin Launceston 72-76. *55 Norwood Avenue, Launceston, Tasmania 7250.* (003-446980)

ADAMS, Canon Alfred John. b 15. Univ of Wales BA (French) 36. St Mich Coll Llan 41. **d** 42 **p** 43 Llan. C of Cadoxton juxta Barry 42-46; St Sav Roath 46-54; C-in-c of U Grangetown Cardiff 54-63; V of St Julian, Newport 63-69; Llanddewi-Rhydderch w Llafapley Llanfihangel Gobion and Llangattock-juxta-Usk 69-75; Risca 75-80; Pontypool Dio Mon from 80; Can of Mon in St Woolos Cathl from 77. *Vicarage, Pontypool, Gwent.* (Pontypool 3066)

ADAMS, Ambrose Douglas. Trin Coll Dub BA 11, MA 16. St Aid Coll. **d** 12 **p** 13 Liv. C of Rainford 12-16; Mariners' Ch Kingstown 16-17; Delgany 17-18; Bitterne 18-22; Hampreston 22-23; V of St John Wimborne 23-27; St Geo Leeds 27-30; Chap of Chateau d'Oex 30-34; H Trin, Cannes 34-42; V of St Jude Southsea 42-46; Chap H Trin Cannes 46-49; Ch Ch Montreux Chateau d'Oex and Les Avants 49-66; Chap Chateau d'Oex Dio Lon (N & C Eur) from 68. *La Charmille, 1801 Fenil-sur-Vevey, Switzerland.*

ADAMS, Arthur White. b 12. Univ of Sheff BA (1st cl Engl Lang and Lit) 35, MA 36. Ch Ch Ox and Magd Coll Ox MA (by decree) 49, BD 50, Sen Denyer and Johnson Scho 57, DD 67. Ripon Hall, Ox 35. **d** 36 **p** 37 Sheff. C of St Jo Evang Ranmoor Sheff 36-38; Chap and Tutor Ripon Hall Ox 38-40; L to Offic Dio Ox 38-40; Chap R Hosp and Infirm Sheff 40-44; V of Wribbenhall 44-49; Lect in Th Qu Coll Birm 48-49; Dean of Div 49-75; Fell of Magd Coll Ox 49-79; Fell (Emer) from 79; Chap 49-65; Vice-Pres 65-66; Univ Lect in Th 50-79; Grinfield Lect on the Septuagint 53-59; Select Pr Univ of Ox 58-60; Lect St Anne's Coll Ox 74-79; St Hugh's Coll Ox 74-77; Jt-Ed 'Modern Churchman' 57-65. *30 Frenchay Road, Oxford, OX2 6TG.* (Oxford 55029)

ADAMS, Basil David. b 44. Federal Th Sem Pmbg Dipl Th 77. **d** 77 **p** 78 Capetn. C of Bonteheuwel 77-80; R of Calvinia Dio Capetn from 80. *Box 65, Klawer 8145, CP, S Africa.*

ADAMS, Brian Hugh. b 32. Pemb Coll Ox BA 54, MA 57. Dipl Th (Lon) 56. Sarum Wells Th Coll 77. **d** 79 **p** 80 Ex. C of Crediton 79-81; Chap to St Brandon's Sch Clevedon Avon from 81. *The Anchorage, 254 Old Church Road, Clevedon, Avon.*

ADAMS, Ven Charles Alexander. MBE 73. CBE 82. K Coll Lon and Warm AKC 59. **d** 60 **p** 61 Dur. C of Bp Wearmouth 60-63; St Phil and St Jas Ox 63-66; St Barn Tunbridge Wells 66-68; R of N Grenadines Dio Windw Is from 68; Can of St Geo Cathl Kingstown St Vincent from 73; Archd of St Vincent from 76. *St Mary's Rectory, Bequia, Northern Grenadines, Windward Islands, W Indies.* (83234)

ADAMS, David Cameron. Wycl Coll Tor LTh 65. **d** 64 **p** 65 Bp Snell for Tor. C-in-c of St Andr-by-the-Lake Tor 64-65; C of St Columba Tor 65-66; R of Elmvale 66-71; Streetsville 71-76; C of St Clem Riverdale Tor 76-77; R of St D Prince Albert Dio Sask from 77. *518 24th Street East, Prince Albert, Sask, Canada.*

ADAMS, Denis Leslie. St Steph Ho Ox 78. **d** 81 Buckingham for Ox (NSM). C of All SS Reading Dio Ox from 81. *32 Josephine Court, Southcote Road, Reading, Berks, RG3 2DQ.*

ADAMS, Canon Douglass Arthur. b 04. Univ of Dur LTh 33. Bp Wilson Th Coll IM 29. **d** 32 **p** 33 Liv. C of St Pet Aintree 32-34; Ch Ch Sparkbrook 34-36; V of Thorpe Satchville w Twyford 36-46 (and Ashby Folville from 41); St Mich and AA, Belgrave 46-54; Market Harborough 54-73; Hon Can of Leic 59-73; Can (Emer) from 73; RD of Gartree I 69-76; L to Offic Dio Leic from 73. *1 Chestnut Avenue, Lutterworth, Leics, LE17 4TJ.*

ADAMS, Frederick George. b 18. TD 66. Qu Coll Birm 47. **d** 50 **p** 51 Lich. C of St Andr Wolverhampton 50-54; Shirley Birm 54-56; Forest Row (in c of St Dunstan) 57-59; R of E Carlton 59-63; C-in-c of Cottingham w Middleton 61-63; R of Cottingham w Middleton and E Carlton 63-72; V of King's Heath Northants 72-78. *56 Carr's Way, Harpole, Northampton, NN7 4DA.* (0604-830541)

ADAMS, Geoffrey Owen. Univ of NZ BA 31, LLB 37, LTh 41. **d** 40 **p** 41 Auckld. C of St Andr Epsom 40-44; C-in-c of Kaitaia 44-46; V of Warkworth 46-51; Papatoetoe 51-66; St Chad, Sandringham 66-70; Paparoa 70-75; P-in-c of Blockhouse Bay 75; P-in-c of Port Chevalier Dio Auckld from 78. *111 St John's Road, Auckland 5, NZ.* (586-824)

ADAMS, George Ernest. Sarum Th Coll 37. **d** 39 **p** 40 Sarum. C of Fordington St Geo 39-42; C-in-c of H Trin Stevenage 42-43; St Phil Reigate 43-44; V of Gestingthorpe 44-47; R of Belchamp-Otten 47-56; V of Bulmer w Belchamp Walter 47-56; Chap RAF 56-59; R of Wreslingworth 59-66; V of Dunton 59-66; C-in-c of Eyeworth 63-66; V of Arlesey w Astwick 66-70; R of Gillingham w Geldeston and Stockton 70-80. *4 The Street, Alburgh, IP20 0DF,*

ADAMS, George Henry. b 10. Univ of Sask BA 35. Em Coll Sktn LTh 35. **d** 35 **p** 36 Bran. C of Pilot Mound 35-36; R 36-39; R of Holland 39-41; Chap CASF 41-46; R of Russell

46-49; Neepawa Dio Bran 49-51; C of Ch Ch Milton-next-Gravesend 51-54; V of Halling 54-75; Perm to Offic Dio Cant from 76. *47 Ragstone Road, Bearsted, Maidstone, Kent.*

ADAMS, John. b 38. Dipl Educn (Lon) 66. Open Univ BA 79. Linc Th Coll 68. **d** 70 **p** 71 Bradf. C of Skipton-in-Craven 70-72; Bassingham 72-73; Chap Lingfield Hosp Sch 73-74; Hon C of Keighley 76-79; P-in-c of Bredenbury w Grendon Bp and Wacton Dio Heref from 79; Edvin Ralph w Collington and Thornbury Dio Heref from 79; Pencome w Marston Stannett and L Cowarne Dio Heref from 79. *Bredenbury Rectory, Bromyard, Herefs.* (Bromyard 2236)

ADAMS, John Christopher Ronald. St Paul's Coll Grahmstn LTh 55. **d** 55 **p** 56 Matab. C of St Marg Bulawayo 55-61; R of Shabani 61-66; C of St Barn Northolt Pk 67-68; St Mary The Boltons Kens 68-69; Umtali 69-71; R of Melfort & P-in-c of Cranborne Mashon 71-75; R of Greendale Dio Mashon from 75. *St Luke's Rectory, PO Highlands, Salisbury, Zimbabwe.*

ADAMS, John David Andrew. b 37. TCD BA 60, MA 64, BD 69. Univ of Reading MEducn 74. **d** 62 **p** 63 Connor. C of St Steph Belf 62-65; Asst Master Tower Ramparts Sch Ipswich 67-70; Counsellor at Robert Haining Sch Mytchett 70-73; Hd Master St Paul's Sch Addlestone from 74. *Brookside Farmhouse, Oast House Crescent, Farnham, Surrey.*

ADAMS, Canon John Herbert. b 1897. Ex Coll Ox BA (2nd cl Th) 21, MA 25. Cudd Coll 21. **d** 22 **p** 23 Glouc. C of Minchinhampton 22-26; Kidderminster 26-30; R of Landulph 30-61; RD of E Wivelshire 52-57; Hon Can of Truro 55-67; Can (Emer) from 67; V of Gorran w Caerhays 61-67. *Grove Cottage, Town Hill, St Agnes, Cornw.* (St Agnes 644)

ADAMS, John Peregrine. b 25. Magd Coll Ox BA 46, MA 50. Wells Th Coll. **d** 49 **p** 50 Linc. C of Boston 49-54; PC of H Trin Skirbeck 54-57; V of Stapleford w Berwick St Jas Dio Sarum from 57; RD of Wylye and Wilton from 77. *Stapleford Vicarage, Salisbury, Wilts.* (0722-79 261)

ADAMS, John Peter. b 42. BD (Lon) 69. Oak Hill Th Coll 65. **d** 70 Bp McKie for Cov **p** 71 Cov. C of St Marg Whitnash Leamington Spa 70-73; Chap at Davos 74-75; Dusseldorf 75-76; C of Gt Baddow 77-80; Perm to Offic Dio Chelmsf from 80. *Sandgasse 44a, A-6850 Dornbirn, Austria.*

ADAMS, John Richard. b 38. St D Coll Lamp BA (Th) 62. Lich Th Coll 62. **d** 64 **p** 65 Truro. C of Falmouth 64-68; Twerton-on-Avon 68-72: Milton Win 72-79; P-in-c of St Edm Weymouth Dio Sarum from 79. *St Edmund's Vicarage, Lynch Road, Weymouth, Dorset.* (Weymouth 782408)

ADAMS, Canon John Wrigley. b 07. St Chad's Coll Dur BA 31, Dipl Th 32, MA 34. **d** 32 **p** 33 Wakef. C of St Mich AA Wakef 32-36; Hermanus 36-39; Asst P Ovamboland Dio Damar 39-42; CF (S Afr) 42-46; C of Hermanus 46-47; Sedbergh 47-49; V of St Mark Low Moor 49-64; RD of Bowling 60-64; Ewecross from 64; V of St Marg Bentham 64-72; Hon Can of Bradf 64-72; Can (Emer) from 72. *46 Wollaston Road, Cleethorpes, S Humb, DN35 8DX.*

ADAMS, Jonathan Henry. b 48. Univ of St Andr MA 73. Cranmer Hall Dur 73. **d** 76 Penrith for Carl **p** 77 Carl. C of St Jo Bapt Upperby Carl 76-78; St Chad E Herrington Sunderland Dio Dur from 78. *86 Aberdare Road, Sunderland, SR3 3EG.* (Sunderland 288568)

ADAMS, Keith Edward Douglas. Trin Coll Tor LTh 66. **d** 65 Moos for Tor **p** 66 Tor. C of St Chris Downsview Tor 65-66; St Jo Bapt Norway Tor 66-68; I of Manvers 68-72; Campbellford 72-75; St Alb Pet 76-77; St Geo Pet Dio Tor from 77. *272 Braidwood Avenue, Peterborough, Ont, Canada.* (705-745 7271)

ADAMS, Michael John. b 48. St Jo Coll Dur BA 77. Ripon Coll Cudd 77. **d** 79 **p** 80 Truro. C of K Chas Mart Falmouth 79-81; St Buryan, St Levan & Sennen Dio Truro from 81. *26 Mayon Green Crescent, Sennen, Penzance, Cornwall, TR19 7BS.* (Sennen 475)

ADAMS, Peter. b 37. K Coll Lon and Warm AKC 65. Trin Coll Cam MA (by incorp) 70. **d** 66 **p** 67 S'wark. C of Clapham 66-70; Chap Trin Coll Cam 70-75; V of St Geo Camberwell and Warden Trin Coll Cam Miss Dio S'wark from 75; RD of Camberwell from 81. *113 Wells Way, SE5 7SZ.* (01-703 2895)

ADAMS, Peter Anthony. b 48. AKC and BD 70. Univ of Lon MTh 72. St Aug Coll Cant 70. **d** 72 Cant **p** 74 Maidstone for Cant. L to Offic Dio Gibr 72-73; C of Ashford Cant 73-78; P-in-c of H Trin Ramsgate Dio Cant from 78. *Rectory, Winterstoke Way, Ramsgate, Kent.* (Thanet 53593)

ADAMS, Peter Harrison. b 41. Tyndale Hall Bris 63. **d** 68 Penrith for Carl **p** 69 Carl. C of St Thos Kendal 68-71; Good Shepherd W Bromwich 71-75; R of Marks Tey Dio Chelmsf from 75; Aldham Dio Chelmsf from 75. *Marks Tey Rectory, Colchester, Essex.* (Colchester 210396)

ADAMS, Raymond Michael. b 41. ALCD 66. BD (Lon) 67. **d** 67 **p** 68 Worc. C of Old Hill 67-73; R of Ipsley Dio Worc from 73. *Ipsley Rectory, Redditch, Worcs, B98 0AN.* (Redditch 23307)

ADAMS, Richard. b 10. Sen Exhib of Trin Coll Dub 30, Scho and Jun Hebr Pri (1st) 31, Wray Pri BA (1st cl Mod and Large Gold Med) and Mod Research Pri 32, Div Test (1st) 33, MA 35, BD 44, PhD 46. **d** 33 **p** 34 Down. C of St Donard Belf 33-36; Shankill Lurgan 36-40; I of Magheralin or Maralin 40-43; All SS Bel 43-60; RD of S Belf 55-60; Can and Preb of Maynooth in St Patr Cathl Dub 59-63; R of Ch Ch Cathl Lisburn 60-75; Preb of Rasharkin in Connor Cathl 61-63; Dean of Connor 63-75. *100 Newtown Breda Road, Belfast 8, N Ireland.*

ADAMS, Robert Elliott. Hur Coll LTh 53. **d** 53 Hur for Moos **p** 53 Moos. I of Centr Patricia 53-54; Hornepayne 54-56; Cochrane 56-64; St Monica Niagara Falls 64-70; R of St Jas Hamilton Dio Niag from 70. *227 Grosvenor Avenue South, Hamilton, Ont., Canada.* (416-549 8424)

ADAMS, Robin. b 54. Qu Univ Belf BSc 76. Oak Hill Coll BA 79. **d** 79 **p** 80 Down. C of Magheralin Dio Down from 79. *67 Belfast Road, Dollingstown, Craigavon, BT67 0QJ, N Ireland.*

ADAMS, Roger Charles. Em Coll Cam 2nd cl Cl Trip pt i 59, BA (2nd cl Th Trip pt ia) 60, MA 64. Tyndale Hall Bris 60. **d** 62 **p** 63 Sarum. C of Longfleet 62-65; Uphill (in c of St Barn) 66-71; R of Ramsden Crays 71-78; Area Sec BFBS SW Engl from 78; Perm to Offic Dio Ex from 78. *207 Elburton Road, Elburton, Plymouth, Devon, PL9 8HX.* (Plymouth 43145)

ADAMS, Ronald Foye Glynn. b 10. AKC 39. **d** 39 Willesden for Lon **p** 40 Lon. C of St Gabr Pimlico 39-43; Chap RAFVR 43-46; C of St Mary Finchley 46-48; V of Portslade (w Hangleton to 55) 48-62; Findon 62-76. *9 Link Hill, Storrington, Sussex, RH20 4LS.*

ADAMS, Ronald Frederick. St Aid Th Coll Bal ACT ThL 23. **d** 23 **p** 24 Bal. C of Ch Ch Warrnambool 23-24; P-in-c of Tresco 24-26; V of Sea Lake 26-29; RD and V of Swan Hill 29-35; V of Avoca and RD of Maryborough 35-37; R of Donald 37-41; RD of St Arn 40-41; Min of Hastings 41-43; St Mark Sunshine 43-50; St Matthias N Richmond 50-52; Newport 52-56; Ringwood 56-60; V of Queenscliff 60-66; Perm to Offic Dio Melb from 66. *18 Darling Avenue, Upwey, Vic, Australia 3158.* (03-754 3013)

ADAMS, Susan. b 47. **d** 78 **p** 79 Auckld. Hon C of Glenfield Dio Auckld from 78. *57 Ayton Drive, Glenfield, Auckland 10, NZ.*

ADAMS, Thomas. Jes Coll Ox BA (2nd cl Hist) 37, MA 41. Ely Th Coll 37. **d** 38 Swan B **p** 40 Llan. C of Ch Ch Swansea 38-39; St Aug Penarth w Lavernock 39-43; Perm to Offic at Burnham Dio Ox 44-45; Asst Master Denstone Coll Staffs 45-48; Chap and Tutor of Victoria Coll Jersey 48-50. *Shady Side Academy, 423 Fox Chapel Road, Pittsburgh, Penn., USA.*

ADAMS, Trevor Bruce. b 51. St Paul's Coll Grahmstn Dipl Th 80. **d** 80 Port Eliz. C of Ch the King Gelvandale Dio Port Eliz from 80. *PO Box 16083, Gelvandale, Port Elizabeth, CP 6016, S Africa.*

ADAMS, William. St Jo Coll Morpeth ACT ThL 58. **d** 57 **p** 58 Perth. C of St Mary W Perth 57-59; R of Morawa (in c of Mingenew) 59-64; Gosnells 64-73; N Beach Dio Perth from 73. *22 James Street, North Beach, W Australia 6020.* (447 1843)

ADAMSON, Very Rev Alexander Campbell. b 21. Lich Th Coll 57. **d** 59 Wakef **p** 60 Pontefract for Wakef. C of Pontefract 59-62; V of Honley w Brockholes 62-69; CF (TA) 62-67; CF (TAVR) 67-69; R of St Jo Evang Aber 69-79; Can of Aber Cathl from 73; Synod Clk 76-78; Dean of Aber and Ork from 78; R of Aboyne Dio Aber from 79; Ballater Dio Aber from 79; Braemar Dio Aber from 80. *Glenmoriston, Invercauld Road, Ballater, Aberdeenshire.* (Ballater 55726)

ADAMSON, Anthony Scott. b 49. Univ of Newc T BA 70. St Jo Coll Dur 75. **d** 78 **p** 79 Newc T. C of St Paul Elswick City and Dio Newc T from 78. *28 Victoria Street, Elswick, Newcastle-upon-Tyne 4.*

ADAMSON, Arthur John. b 38. Keble Coll Ox BA (2nd cl Nat Sc) 61, MA 65. Tyndale Hall Bris. **d** 63 **p** 64 S'wark. C of H Trin Redhill 63-66; Cockfosters 66-70; Chap Trent Park Coll of Educn 66-69; V of St Geo w St Andr Battersea 70-74; R of Reedham 74-80; Offg Min Beighton w Moulton 75-77; Asst Min 77-79; P-in-c of Cantley w Limpenhoe & Southwood 77-80; R of St Mich Oulton Dio Nor from 80. *St Michael's Rectory, Christmas Lane, Oulton Broad, Lowestoft, NR32 3JX.* (Lowestoft 65722)

ADAMSON, Frederick. b 16. Univ Coll Dur 34. AKC 39. **d** 39 **p** 40 Derby. C of Heanor 39-42; Whitfield (in c of St Luke) 42-47; PC of Totley 47-62; R of Hemsworth 62-76; Surr 62-76; Chap Southmoor Hosp 62-76; RD of Pontefract 71-74; R of W Tanfield and Well w Snape 76-81. *8 Jackson Croft, Morland, Nr Penrith, Cumb, CA10 3AU.*

ADAMSON, Paul. b 35. Univ of Leeds, BA 58. Coll of Resurr Mirfield. **d** 60 **p** 61 Dur. C of St Columba Southwick 60-63; St Phil Georgetn 63-65; V of St Barn Georgetn 65-69;

Yupukari w Rupununi Distr Miss 69-75; C of Benwell (in c of Ven Bede) 75-77; V of St Pet Cowgate City and Dio Newc T from 77. *Vicarage, Druridge Drive, Cowgate, Newcastle-upon-Tyne, NE5 3LP.* (Newc T 869913)

ADAMSON, Rodney John. Univ of Sask BA 59. Em Coll Sktn LTh 59. **d** 59 **p** 60 Sask. I of Kinistino 59-63; R of H Trin and of St D Prince Albert 63-69; I of All SS Regina 69-73; on leave 73-74; I of Elnora 74-76; All SS Medicine Hat Dio Calg from 76. *1135 Bullivant Crescent, Medicine Hat, Alta., T1A 5G8, Canada.* (526-8541)

ADAMSON, William Paul. St Paul's Coll Grahmstn 45. **d** 47 **p** 48 Bloemf. C of Leribe Miss 47-48; St Sav E London 48-51; R of St Sav Port Eliz 60-63; Chap UDF Camp Wynberg from 64; R of Voortrekkerhoogte 67; L to Offic Dio Capetn 74-75; C of Bellville 76-77; R of Devil's Peak Dio Capetn from 77. *Rectory, Pypies Plein, Devil's Peak, Capetown, S Africa.* (45-6485)

ADAMU, Tomaso. b 38. St Cypr Coll Rondo 69. **d** 72 **p** 73 Abp Sepeku for Masasi. P Dio Masasi. *PB Masasi, Mtwara Region, Tanzania.*

ADANO, Andrew. b 48. **d** 74 Mt Kenya **p** 76 Mt Kenya E. d Dio Mt Kenya 74-75; Mt Kenya S 75-76; V of Moyale 76-78; Bubisa Dio Mt Kenya E from 78. *Box 71, Marsabit, Kenya.*

ADARA, Samson Adeyinka. Melville Hall Ibad 50. **d** 52 **p** 53 Lagos. P Dio Lagos. *All Saints' Vicarage, Owode, Abeokuta, Nigeria.*

ADARAMOLA, Daniel Oyewole. **d** 52 **p** 53 Ibad. P Dio Ibad 52-64; Dio Ondo from 64. *Omuo, Akoko North, Nigeria.*

ADCOCK, Arthur Clement. Late Scho of K Coll Cam 2nd Cl Hist Trip pt i 33, BA (1st cl Hist Trip pt ii) 34, 2nd cl Th Trip pt ii and Burney Pri 35, Burney Stud 37, MA 38. Ridley Hall Cam 35. New Coll Ox MA (by incorp) 57. **d** 39 **p** 40 Birm. C of Northfield 39-41; Wolvercote 41-43; V of Dorney 43-60; Yarnton Dio Ox from 60. *Yarnton Vicarage, Oxford.* (Kidlington 3215)

ADDENBROOKE, Frank Gordon. b 06. Late Sen Scho of Trin Coll Cam 1st cl Cl Trip pt i 25, BA (2nd cl Cl Trip pt ii) 27, MA 31. Westcott Ho Cam 28. **d** 29 **p** 31 Lich. C of St Mary Shrewsbury 29-36; V of St Chad Stafford 36-40; Rushall 40-46; R of Lympstone 46-63; Exam Chap to Bp of Ex 50-60; R of E Hendred 63-74; V of W Hendred 63-74; Perm to Offic Dio Ox 74-76; Dio Chich from 76. *44 Gaisford Road, Worthing, W Sussex, BN14 7HW.* (Worthing 33646)

ADDENBROOKE, Peter Homfray. b 38. Trin Coll Cam BA 59. Lich Th Coll 61. **d** 63 **p** 64 Derby. C of Bakewell 63-67; Horsham (in c of St Leon) 67-73; C-in-c and Seq of Colgate Dio Chich from 73; Adv for Pastoral Care and Counselling Dio Chich from 73. *Colgate Vicarage, Horsham, W Sussex, RH12 4SZ.* (Faygate 362)

ADDERLEY, Patrick Livingstone. b 48. Univ of Nottm BTh 74. Kelham Th Coll 70. **d** 74 **p** 75 Nass. C of St John Abaco 74-78; Good Shepherd Grand Bahama Dio Nass from 78. *Box F-2115, Freeport, Grand Bahama, Bahamas.*

ADDIE, Canon Gordon Rennie. McGill Univ BA 30. Montr Dioc Coll LTh 30. **d** 30 Montr **p** 30 Queb for Montr. I of Rouyn W Noranda 30-32; R of Rawdon 32-37; Cowansville 37-39; Chap CASF 39-45; R of St John's (P-in-c of Iberville Sabrevois L'Acadie and St Luc) 45-48; R of Ch of the Ascen Montr 48-64; Trin Mem Ch, Montreal 64-71; Hon Can of Montr 60-71; Can (Emer) from 72. *124 Village Road, St Catherine's, Ont, Canada L2T 3C1.*

ADDINGTON HALL, Gerald Richard. b 38. Qu Coll Ox BA 62, MA 67. Univ of Birm MA 69. Qu Coll Birm 62. **d** 65 Knaresborough for Ripon **p** 66 Ripon. C of St Sav Leeds 65-69; Korogwe 69-70; P-in-c of St Andr New Korogwe 71-75; V of St Francis Ipswich 75-81; Pakenham w Norton and Tostock Dio St E from 81. *Vicarage, Church Hill, Pakenham, Bury St Edmunds, Suff, IP31 2LN.* (Pakenham 30287)

ADDINGTON HALL, Gerald Richard. Qu Coll Ox BA 62, MA 67. Univ of Birm MA 69. Qu Coll Birm 62. **d** 65 Knaresborough for Ripon **p** 66 Ripon. C of St Sav Leeds 65-69; Korogwe 69-70; Youth Chap Dio Zanz T from 69; P-in-c of St Andr New Korogwe Dio Zanz T from 71; Chap St Andr Teachers' Tr Coll Korogwe from 71. *CPEA, PO Box 35, Korogwe, Tanga, Tanzania.*

ADDIS, Arthur Lewis. b 11. TD. Worc Ordin Coll 62. **d** 64 **p** 65 Win. C of Highcliffe w Hinton Admiral 64-66; R of W Dean w E Grimstead 66-70; V of Stratford-sub-Castle 70-79; Perm to Offic Dio Sarum from 79. *78 Park Street, Salisbury, SP1 3AU.*

ADDIS, (Alban) Graham George Brisland. b 24. Cudd Coll 63. M SSF 55. **d** 64 **p** 65 Sarum. Publ Pr Dio Sarum 64-66; Dio Chelmsf 64-69; Dio Worc from 69. *St Mary at the Cross, Glasshampton, Shrawley, Worcester.* (Gt Witley 345)

ADDISON, Bernard Michael Bruce. b 31. Univ of Cam MA 73. St Steph Ho Ox 58. **d** 61 **p** 62 Lon. C of St Sav Paddington 61-64; St Mary Virg Primrose Hill 64-66; St Sav Claremont CP 66-69; St Jas Syd 70-72; St Andr Catford 72-73; Chap Ch Coll Cam 73-78; at Bonn and Cologne Dio (Gibr in Eur from 80) Lon (N and C Eur) 79-81. *c/o British Embassy, Bonn, W Germany.*

ADDISON, David John Frederick. b 37. Univ of Dur BA 60, Univ of Birm MA 79. Wells Th Coll 64. **d** 66 Wakef **p** 71 Bradf. C of St Matt Rastrick Wakef 66-67; Perm to Offic Dio Bradf 67-71; C of St Luke Manningham 71-73; Perm to Offic Dio Glouc 77-79; C of Bisley 79-81; P-in-c of Newland w Redbrook Dio Glouc from 81; Clearwell Dio Glouc from 81. *Newland Vicarage, Coleford, Glos.* (Dean 33777)

ADDISON, Philip Ives. b 29. Univ of Dur 49. Ely Th Coll 59. **d** 61 **p** 62 St Alb. C of Waltham Cross 61-64; St Paul Bedford 64-66; Chap RN 66-70; V of Foleshill 70-74; Owthorne and Rimswell w Withersea Dio York from 74; C-in-c of Halsham 74-78; Surr from 75. *Vicarage, Park Avenue, Withernsea, N Humb, HU19 2JU.* (Withernsea 3598)

ADDLESHAW, Very Rev George William Outram. b 06. Trin Coll Ox 2nd Cl Mod Hist 28, BA 29, MA 32, BD 35. FRHistS 49. Cudd Coll 29. **d** 30 Win **p** 31 Southampton for Win. C of Ch Ch Portswood 30-37; Basingstoke 37-39; Vice-Prin of St Chad's Coll Dur 39-46; Exam Chap to Abp of York 42-63; to Bp of Ches from 55; Proc Conv Dur 45-50; York 50-62; Can and Treas of York and Preb of Tockerington in York Minster 46-62; Lect Leeds Par Ch 47-54; C-in-c of St Mich le Belfrey York 49-55 and 56-62; Select Pr Univ of Ox 54-56; Univ of Cam 55; Chap to HM Queen 57-64; Dep Prolocutor Lower Ho of Conv York 57-66; Prolocutor from 66-75; Dean of Ches 63-77; Dean (Emer) from 77; Hon CF 69-78. *Flat 3, 37 Station Road, Thames Ditton, Surrey.*

ADEAGBO, Joseph Afolabi. Im Coll Ibad 62. **d** 64 **p** 65 Ibad. P Dio Ibad 64-75; Dio Ilesha from 75. *PO Box 45, Ilesha, Nigeria.*

ADEBAMIWA, Joshua Alakinde Adediran. Dipl Th (Lon) 66. Im Coll Ibad 64. **d** 66 Bp Jadesimi for Ibad **p** 66 Ibad. P Dio Ibad; Exam Chap to Bp of Ibad from 79. *PO Box 182, Ibadan, Nigeria.* (Ibadan 61888)

ADEBAYO, Samuel Afolabi. Im Coll Ibad 55. **d** 57 **p** 58 Ibad. P Dio Ibad 57-63 and from 64; C of Sparkhill Birm 63-64. *Holy Trinity, Omofe, Ilesha, Ibadan, Nigeria.*

ADEBESO, Samuel Olusesan. b 38. **d** 72 **p** 74 Lagos. P Dio Lagos 72-79; Dio Egba from 79. *27 Sokenu Road, Oke-Ijeun, Abeokuta, Nigeria.*

ADEBIYI, Gabriel Aina Asaolu. **d** 58 **p** 59 Ondo-B. P Dio Ekiti. *St Paul's Vicarage, Osi, via Ido, Nigeria.*

ADEBIYI, Peter Awelewa. b 43. Im Coll Ibad 67. **d** 70 Ondo. d Dio Ekiti from 70. *Holy Trinity Vicarage, Ilawe-Ekiti, Nigeria.*

ADEBOLA, Barnabas. b 45. Im Coll Ibad. **d** 80 Kano. d Dio Kano. *St Paul's Church, PO Box 18, Bauchi, Nigeria.*

ADEBOLA, Simeon Oluwemimo Monday. b 44. Univ of Ibad BA 64. Mansfield Coll Ox BLitt 71. Univ of Ibad BA 64. **d** 71 **p** 72 Lagos. P Dio Lagos. *Bishopscourt, 29 Marina, Box 13, Lagos, Nigeria.* (25648)

ADEBONA, Abiodun Craig. b 37. Univ of Nottm BSc 64. Univ of Lon PhD 67. **d** 81 Ilesha. d Dio Ilesha. *Faculty of Biological Sciences, University of Ife, Ile-Ife, Nigeria.*

ADEBUSOYE, Ven Folayemi Adedapo. Melville Hall Ibad 53. **d** 55 **p** 56 Lagos. P Dio Lagos 55-62; L to Offic Dio Ibad 62-77; Can of Ibad 71-76; Archd Dio Ilesha from 77; Dioc Sec from 77; Exam Chap to Bp of Ilesha from 77. *Box 33, Omofe, Ilesha, Nigeria.*

ADEBUSUYI, Samuel Adesanmi. Melville Hall Ibad 51. **d** 53 **p** 54 Ibad. P Dio Ibad 54-66; Dio Ekiti 66-70 and from 71; C of St Clem w St Cypr Ordshall Salford 70; St Matt Crumpsall 71; Youth Chap Dio Ekiti from 71. *St Paul's Vicarage, Box 100, Ado-Ekiti, Western State, Nigeria.*

ADEDAPO, Timothy Ademola. Im Coll Ibad 66. **d** 69 **p** 70 Ibad. P Dio Ibad. *PO Box 125, Ibadan, Nigeria.*

ADEDAYO, Nathaniel Adedotun. Univ of Dur (Fourah Bay Coll) BA 50. **d** 59 Ibad **p** 61 Ondo-B. Prin Obokun High Sch Ilesha 60-68; Ijesha Comprehensive High Sch Ilesha Dio Ibad from 68. *PO Box 35, Ede, Nigeria.*

ADEDIPE, Julius Oluwadare Arifalo. Im Coll Ibad 58. **d** 60 Ondo-B for Ibad **p** 61 Ibad. P Dio Ibad. *Omupo, Ibadan, Nigeria.*

ADEDIRAN, Joseph Olokuntuyi. St Andr Coll Oyo 27. **d** 28 **p** 30 Bp Oluwole for Lagos. P Dio Lagos 45-52; Dio Ibad 52-56; Dio Lagos 56-63. *c/o Emmanuel Church, Ado-Ekiti, Nigeria.*

ADEGBITE, Titus Adewole. b 27. **d** 73 Ekiti. d Dio Ekiti. *St Peter's Vicarage, Iropora, Ekiti, Nigeria.*

ADEGOROYE, Jacob Peter. Melville Hall Ibad. **d** 52 Bp Phillips for Lagos **p** 53 W Afr. P Dio Lagos 52-76. *Iyin-Ekiti, Nigeria.*

ADEJIMI, Samuel Adegoke. Im Coll Ibad 59. **d** 61 Ibad **p** 62 Lagos. P Dio Lagos. *PO Box 8, Aiyetoro-Egbado, via Abeokuta, Nigeria.*

ADEJIMI, Canon Samuel Adewole. Melville Hall Ibad. **d** 55 **p** 56 Ibad. P Dio Ibad 56-74; Dio Kwara 75-76; Dio Egba from 76; Can of Ibad 71-74; Egba from 76. *Fry Memorial Church, Isaga-Orile, Egbado, Nigeria.*

ADEJUGBE, Lawrence Ayodele. d 77 Ondo. d Dio Ondo. *Vicarage, Emure-Ile, Ondo, Nigeria.*

ADEJUMO, Moses Oluyemi. Im Coll Ibad 58. **d** 60 **p** 61 N Nig. P Dio N Nig 60-65; Dio Ibad from 65. *PO Box 41, Ile-Ife, Nigeria.* (Ile-Ife 2023)

ADEKOLA, Canon Daniel Adeagbo. Univ of Dur (Fourah Bay Coll) BA 58, MA 61. **d** 59 Ibad **p** 61 Ondo-B. Prin Esie-Iludun Gr Sch 60-67; Esa-Oke Gr Sch Ibad 67-78; Prec of Ibad Cathl 66-78; Hon Can of Ibad 74-75; Can 75-78; Can Res from 78. *St James's Cathedral, Okebola, Ibadan, Nigeria.*

ADELAIDE, Lord Archbishop of, and Metropolitan of Province of S Australia.. *See* Rayner, Most Rev Keith.

ADELAIDE, Assistant Bishop of. *See* Renfrey, Right Rev Lionel Edward William.

ADELAIDE, Dean of. *See* Renfrey, Right Rev Lionel Edward William.

ADELAJA, Ven Beniah Adeleke. Fourah Bay Coll BA 39, Dipl in Th 40, MA 44. **d** 41 **p** 43 Lagos. P Dio Lagos; Vice-Prin Ijebu-Ode Grammar Sch 42-49; Prin CMS Gr Sch Lagos 49-72; Hon Chap Cathl Ch Lagos 49-55; Succr 55-61; Hon Can 54-72; Archd of Ijebu 72-74; Lagos from 75; Exam Chap to Bp of Lagos from 72. *Box 1262, Lagos, Nigeria.* (25336)

ADELEYE, Ezekiel Akinlolu. Im Coll Ibad Dipl Th 77. **d** 77 **p** 78 Ondo. P Dio Ondo. *Vicarage, Imoru, Ondo State, Nigeria.*

ADELORE, Julius Kolawole. b 46. Im Coll Ibad 73. **d** 75 **p** 76 Ibad. P Dio Ibad. *St Peter's Church, Iba, via Ikirun, Nigeria.*

ADELOYE, David Oyebiyi. d and **p** 56 Accra. P Dio Accra 56-72; Dio Ekiti from 72. *St John's Vicarage, Ido-Ajinare, Nigeria.*

ADELUGBA, Olugbemiga. b 52. Im Coll Ibad 74. **d** 77 **p** 78 Ilesha. P Dio Ilesha. *University of Ife, Ile-Ife, Nigeria.*

ADEMOWO, Canon Ephraim Adebola. b 48. Im Coll Ibad Dipl Th 72. **d** 72 **p** 73 Ibad. P Dio Ibad 72-77; Dio Ilesha from 77; Hon Can from 80. *Box 118, Isona, Ilesha, Nigeria.*

ADENEY, Arthur Webster. b 06. Late Scho of Clare Coll Cam 24, Bell Scho and 1st cl Cl Trip pt i 25, BA (1st cl Cl Trip pt ii) and Wordsworth Exhib 27, Beck Exhib 28, MA 32. Ridley Hall Cam 27. **d** 29 **p** 31 Portsm. C of St Mary Portsea 29-32; Asst Chap of Ch of Epiph Port Said 32-35; Exam Chap to Bp in Egypt 34-35; Perm to Offic at Ch Ch Woburn Sq 35-36; L to Offic Dio Jer 36-41; Asst Master Scots Coll Safad 36-37; St Luke's Sch Haifa 37-38; Chap Basrah and Persian Gulf 38-41; Chap at Port Said 41-45; C-in-c of St Patr Milton Portsm 46; V of St Edm Tyseley Birm 46-49; St Mark Southampton 49-55; Archd of Cyprus and Chap at Nicosia 55-58; R of Witney 59-67; Surr from 59; Exam Chap to Bp of Jer 56-58; V of Foxton w Gumley (and Laughton 74) 67-74; Perm to Offic Dio Win from 75. *Apple Tree Cottage, Burford Lane, Brockenhurst, Hants.*

ADENEY, Bernard Frederick. b 17. Qu Coll Cam BA 38, MA 47. Ridley Hall Cam 38. **d** 40 S'wark for E Szech **p** 42 E Szech. C of Morden 40-41; CIM Miss Dio E Szech 41-49; C of High Ongar 49-51; V of N Weald 51-56; Highbury 56-65; Sec CPAS Metrop Area 65-72; Dep Gen Sec CMJ from 72; Cand's Sec from 77. *8 Ashdown Close, Beckenham, Kent, BR3 2TJ.* (01-658 0724)

ADENEY, Halord. d 75 **p** 76 Buye. P Dio Buye. *Buhiga, D/S 127, Bujumbura, Burundi.*

ADENEY, Harold Walter. OBE 76. b 14. Qu Coll Cam BA 35, MB., B.Chir 38, MA 53. Trin Coll Bris 76. **d** 75 Bur **p** 76 Nor for Bur. Past Miss Dir Bur from 75. *c/o BP 1300, Bujumbura, Burundi.*

ADENEY, Canon Ronald Edward. b 19. Qu Coll Cam 2nd Cl Geog Trip pt i BA 40 (3rd Cl Th Trip pt i 41), MA 44. Ridley Hall Cam 41. **d** 42 **p** 43 Lon. C of St Matt Fulham 42-46; CMJ Youth Sec 46-47; CMJ Miss Dio Jer 47-73 and 75-80; Warden Stella Carmel Isfiya 61-70; Asst Master Holte Sch Birm 73-75; Perm to Offic Dio Birm 73-75; R of Ch Ch Jer 75-80; Hon Can of Jer 77-80; Can (Emer) from 80; P-in-c of Fulmer Dio Ox from 81. *Fulmer Rectory, Slough, Bucks.* (Fulmer 2110)

ADENIBUYAN, Abraham Akinsola. Im Coll Ibad 59. **d** 62 **p** 64 Ibad. P Dio Ibad 62-74; Dio Ilesha from 74. *St Stephen's Vicarage, Ifewara, via Ilesha, Nigeria.*

ADENIJI, David Olatunji. Melville Hall Ibad 50. **d** 52 **p** 53 Lagos. P Dio Lagos 52-57; Dio Ibad from 58. *Ogunjana, Ibadan, Nigeria.*

ADENIYI, Ven Andrew Oluwole. Melville Hall Ibad. **d** 56 **p** 57 Lagos. P Dio Lagos 56-80; Dio Kaduna from 80; Archd of Zaria from 80; Exam Chap to Bp of Kaduna from 80. *Box 28, Zaria, Nigeria.*

ADENIYI, James Akinwale. b 36. **d** 72 **p** 74 Lagos. P Dio Lagos 72-76; Dio Ijebu 76-80; Dio Kano from 80. *Holy Trinity Cathedral, Kano, Nigeria.*

✠ **ADENIYI, Right Rev Jonathan Soremi.** Fourah Bay Coll BA 43. **d** 46 **p** 47 Lagos. Tutor Abeokuta Gr Sch 47-48; Prin 55-67; Sabongidda Gr Sch 48-55; V of Ebute Metta 67-70; Can of Lagos from 67-70; Cons Asst Bp of Lagos in Ch Ch Cathl Lagos 9 Aug 70 by Abp of W Afr; Bps of Lagos; Ondo; Benin; N Nig; Gambia; and Bp Jadesimi; Archd of Abeokuta 70-76; Exam Chap to Bp of Lagos 70-76; Apptd Bp of Egba-Egbado 76; res 79. *Grace Villa, PO Box 5067, Abeokuta, Nigeria.* (Abeokuta 2453)

ADENIYI, Joseph Olorundare. d 77 Ondo. d Dio Ondo. *St John's Vicarage, Ayila, Ondo, Nigeria.*

ADENUBA, Victor Sunday Olusola. b 36. BA (Lon) 61. **d** 70 **p** 71 Lagos. C of All SS, Yaba Dio Lagos from 70. *Apostolic Church Grammar School, P.O. Box 299, Yaba, Lagos, Nigeria.*

ADENUGA, Ezekiel Adewumi Bolaji. b 22. Im Coll Ibad 72. **d** 73 **p** 74 Ibad. P Dio Ibad. *St Paul's Church, Yemetu, Ibadan, Nigeria.*

ADENUGA, Joel Af'olorunso. b 29. Im Coll Ibad. **d** 73 **p** 74 Lagos. P Dio Lagos. *Premier Grammar School, Abeokuta, Nigeria.*

ADEOBA, Joshua Iluyomade. Im Coll Ibad Dipl Th 68. **d** 68 **p** 69 Ondo. P Dio Ondo. *St Luke's Vicarage, Odo Irun, Akoko, Nigeria.*

ADEODU, Canon Shadrach Adesanmi. Melville Hall Ibad. **d** 50 **p** 51 Lagos. P Dio Lagos 50-52; Dio Ondo-B 52-56 and 59-62; Dio Ondo 62-66; Dio Ekiti from 66; C of St Geo Ovenden Halifax 56-59; Can of Ekiti from 66. *St John's Vicarage, Ido-Ekiti, Nigeria.*

ADEOGUN, Samuel Ogudu. Melville Hall Ibad. **d** 48 **p** 49 Lagos. P Dio Lagos 48-68; Dio Ondo from 68. *Okeluse, Ifon, Nigeria.*

ADEOSUN, James Oluwole. b 24. **d** 73 Ekiti. d Dio ekiti. *St Andrew's Anglican Church, Ake, Ekiti, Nigeria.*

ADEOSUN, Samuel Afolarin. Im Coll Ibad 59. **d** 61 Ibad **p** 62 Lagos. P Dio Lagos 61-76; Dio Egba from 76. *St Paul's Church, Sojuolu, Nigeria.*

ADEOSUN, Solomon Albert. Melville Hall Ibad 47. **d** 49, **p** 50 Lagos. P Dio Lagos 49-52; Dio Ondo-B 52-62; Dio Ondo 62-74; Hon Can of Ondo 67-68; Archd of Lokoja 69-74. *Holy Trinity Vicarage, Lokoja, Nigeria.*

ADEOYE, Canon Jacob Adepoju. Melville Hall Ibad. **d** 54 **p** 55 Ibad. P Dio Ibad; Can of Ibad from 71. *St Michael's Vicarage, P.O. Box 23, Oyo, Nigeria.*

ADEPETU, Samuel Adewunmi Fakanle. d 63 **p** 65 Ondo. P Dio Ondo. *St Luke's Vicarage, Igboegunrin, Ondo, Nigeria.*

ADEREMI, Ven Albert Akindoyin. Melville Hall Ibad. **d** 48 **p** 49 Lagos. P Dio Lagos 48-52; Dio Ondo-B 52-62; Dio Ondo 62-66; Dio Ekiti from 66; Hon Can of Ondo 62-66; Ekiti 66-69; Archd of E Ekiti from 69. *St Paul's Vicarage, Ikole-Ekiti, Nigeria.*

ADERIBIGBE, Canon Erastus Adepoju. Im Coll Ibad 55. **d** 57 **p** 59 Ibad. P Dio Ibad 57-76; Dio Kwara from 76; Can of Kwara from 76. *St Andrew's Church, Okere, Kwara, Nigeria.*

ADERIBIGBE, Canon Frederick Olakanmi. Im Coll Ibad 59. **d** 62 **p** 63 Ibad. P Dio Ibad 62-77; Dio Ijebu from 77; Hon Can from 79. *St Paul's Church, Ago-Iwoye, Nigeria.*

ADERIBOLE, Adetomisoye Moses. b 38. **d** 72 Ibad. d Dio Ibad. *Box 10, Oro, via Ilorin, Nigeria.*

ADERIN, Samuel Olufunmulade. Melville Hall Ibad 55. **d** 56 **p** 57 Ibad. P Dio Ibad; Can of Ibad 71-73; Exam Chap to Bp of Ibad 71-80; Archd of Oshogbo 73-76; Ibad S 76-80. *c/o Box 3075, Ibadan, Nigeria.*

ADEROSIN, Michael. b 34. **d** 73 Ekiti. d Dio Ekiti. *St John's Vicarage, Ilogbo, Ekiti, Nigeria.*

ADESEGUN, Johnson Oludotun. b 27. **d** 79 **p** 81 Egba. d Dio Egba. *9 Lasotu Street, Igbein Abeokuta, Ogun State, Nigeria.*

ADESEKO, Joseph Oni. d and **p** 41 Accra. P Dio Accra 41-51; Dio Lagos 51-53; Dio Ondo-B 53-62; Dio Ondo 62-65. *62 Dallimore Street, Ado-Ekiti, Nigeria.*

ADESIMBO, Ephraim Olusola. b 32. **d** 72 **p** 74 Lagos. P Dio Lagos. *St Andrew's Anglican Church, Ipaja via Agege, Lagos, Nigeria.*

ADESINA, David Ogunleye. Melville Hall Ibad 52. **d** 53 **p** 54 W Afr. P Dio Lagos; Hon Can of Lagos 65-74. *Holy Trinity Church, PO Box 208, Abeokuta, Nigeria.*

ADESINA, Oluwole. b 27. Univ of Dur BA. Im Coll of Th Ibad 78. **d** 79 **p** 81 Egba. P Dio Egba. *Emmanuel Anglican Church, Keesi, Abeokuta, Ogun State, Nigeria.*

ADESIPE, Felix Adedoyin. b 49. Im Coll Ibad 72. **d** 75 **p** 76 Ibad. P Dio Ibad. *St Stephen's Church, Atala, Ogbomosho, Nigeria.*

ADESOGAN, Joel Adetiba. d 63 **p** 65 Ondo. P Dio Ondo

63-66; Dio Ekiti from 66. *St Andrew's Vicarage, Isinbode, Ekiti, Nigeria.*

ADESOLA, Canon Timothy Ebun Idowu. Melville Hall Ibad 54. **d** 55 **p** 56 N Nig. P Dio N Nig; Can of N Nig from 69. *Box 180, Kano, Nigeria.*

ADESOTE, Israel Olaniyan. b 29. **d** 72 **p** 74 Lagos. P Dio Lagos. *St Luke's Vicarage, Oru Ijebu, PA Oru, via Ijebu-Igbo, Nigeria.*

ADESUYAN, Joel Olawumi. b 42. Im Coll Ibad 71. **d** 74 **p** 75 Lagos. P Dio Lagos. *St Paul's Church, Breadfruit, Box 1262, Lagos, Nigeria.*

✠ **ADETILOYE, Right Rev Joseph Abiodun.** Univ of Lon BD 61. Melville Hall Ibad Dipl Th 54. **d** and **p** 54 Lagos. P Dio Lagos 54-62; Tutor Im Coll Ibad 62-66; Provost of Ibad 66-70; Exam Chap to Bp of Ibad 66-70; to Bp of Ekiti 67-70; Cons Ld Bp of Ekiti in St Jas Cathl Ibad on 4 Oct 70 by Abp of W Africa; Bps of Lagos; The Niger; Ondo; Asst Bps of Lagos; Ibad. *Bishopscourt, Box 12, Ado-Ekiti, Nigeria.*

ADETULA, Clement Olusegun Oluwole. Im Coll Ibad 64. **d** 66 **p** 67 Ondo. P Dio Ondo 66-67; Dio Gambia 67-69; Dio Ondo from 69. *Vicarage, Akungba-Akoko, Ondo, Nigeria.*

ADEWALE, Samuel Adebola. b 28. Im Coll Ibad 58. **d** 60 **p** 61 Lagos. P Dio Lagos; Hon Can of Lagos from 76. *St John's Vicarage, PO Box 4194, Aroloya, Nigeria.*

ADEWOYE, Albert Noel Adebayo. Univ of Dur (Fourah Bay Coll) BA 57. **d** 59 Ibad **p** 61 Ondo-B for Ibad. Prin Angl Gr Sch Otan-Aiyegbaju 59-73; L to Offic Dio Ondo from 73. *Epinmi Training College, Epinmi-Akoko, Nigeria.*

ADEWOYE, Daniel Towoju. Melville Hall Ibad 48. **d** 50 Bp Phillips for Lagos **p** 51 Lagos. P Dio Lagos 50-51; Dio Ibad 52-74. *Ada, Nigeria.*

ADEY, Albert Ernest. b 06. Dorch Miss Coll. **d** 31 **p** 32 Dur. C of H Trin Darlington 31-33; St Sav Cathl Maritz 33-39; Wednesbury 39-41; V of St Mary Sedgley 41-47; R of Kingsley Staffs 47-54; V of L Drayton 54-69. *19 Victoria Road, Fallings Park, Wolverhampton, Staffs, WV10 0NG.* (Wolverhampton 735-204)

ADEY, John Douglas. b 33. Univ of Man BSc 54. Coll of Resurr Mirfield 56. **d** 58 **p** 59 Porstm. C of Forton 58-64; Northolt 64-67; V of Snibston 67-72; Outwood 72-78; Clifton 78; V of Upton Priory, Macclesfield 80-81; St Thos Hyde Dio Ches from 81. *St Thomas' Vicarage, Walker Lane, Hyde, Chesh, SK14 5PL.* (061-368 1406)

ADEYANJU, Michael Kolawole. b 25. **d** 71 **p** 73 Lagos. P Dio Lagos 71-76; Dio Egba from 76. *St Paul's Vicarage, Kajola-Iboro, Via Otta, Nigeria.*

ADEYEFA, Samuel Adedoja. Fourah Bay Coll BA 40, Dipl Th 41, MA 43, BCL 49. **d** 43 Lagos **p** 44 Bp Akinyele for Lagos. Prin Oduduwa Coll Ile Ife 42-60; Sen Lect Univ of Nigeria Nsukka 61-68; L to Offic Dio Niger 61-68; Dio Ibad from 68. *School Board, Ilesha, Nigeria.*

ADEYELU, Emmanuel Ogundeji. Im Coll Ibad Dipl Th 68. **d** 68 **p** 69 Ondo. P Dio Ondo. *Box 3, Akure, Nigeria.*

ADEYEYE, Daniel Adewale. b 16. **d** 73 **p** 74 Ibad. P Dio Ibad. *St Peter's Church, Ife-Odan, Oyo, Nigeria.*

ADFIELD, Richard Ernest. b 31. Oak Hill Th Coll 62. **d** 64 Bp McKie for Cov **p** 65 Cov. C of Bedworth 64-67; V of St Andr Whitehall Pk U Holloway 67-77; St Helen w H Trin N Kens Dio Lon from 77. *Vicarage, St Helen's Gardens, W10 6LP.* (01-969 1520)

ADIE, Ven Michael Edgar. b 29. St Jo Coll Ox BA 52, MA 56. Westcott Ho Cam 52. **d** 54 **p** 55 Dur. C of St Luke Pallion 54-57; Res Chap to Abp of Cant 57-60; V of St Mark Sheff 60-69; RD of Hallam 66-69; Proc Conv Sheff 67-69; R of Louth (w Welton-le-Wold to 75) 69-76; C-in-c of N and S Elkington 70-75; M Gen Syn from 75; Can of Linc Cathl from 77; V of Morton w Hacconby Dio Linc from 76; Archd of Linc from 77. *Morton Vicarage, Bourne, Lincs, PE10 0NR.* (Morton 239)

ADIELE, Albert Ubochioma. b 30. St Paul's Coll Awka 75. **d** 76 **p** 77 Aba. P Dio Aba. *Holy Trinity Parsonage, Ubakala, via Umuahia, Nigeria.*

ADIGUN, Emmanuel Adeleke. St Andr Coll Oyo 27. **d** 28 **p** 29 Bp Oluwole for Lagos. P Dio Lagos 28-52; Dio Ibad 52-54; Can of Ibad 54-64. *Box 21, Ibadan, Nigeria.*

ADIGUN, Samuel Adebayo. b 33. Im Coll Ibad Dipl Th 72. **d** 72 **p** 73 Ondo. P Dio Ondo. *Vicarage, Ajowa-Akoko, Ondo, Nigeria.*

ADINYA, Canon Edwin. Th Coll Limuru 54. **d** 55 **p** 57 Momb. P Dio Momb 55-63; Archd of Nairobi 63-66; V of St Steph Nairobi Dio Momb 61-64; Dio Nai 64-70; P Dio Maseno S from 70; Hon Can of Maseno S from 72. *Box 121, Kisii, Kenya.*

ADJAAYI, Canon Richard Jonathan Adjetey. Univ of Ghana, LTh 61. **d** 61 Accra. d Dio Accra; Hon Can of Accra from 78. *PO Box 83, Cape Coast, Ghana.*

ADKINS, Canon George William Pemberton. St Aid Coll 24. **d** 27 **p** 28 Liv. C of St Andr Litherland 27-30; Skelton-in-Cleveland (in c of St Pet N Skelton) 30; C-in-c of Dunscroft Conv Distr 30-33; V of St Polycarp Malin Bridge 34-39; Stocksbridge 39-46; Surr 39-66; C-in-c of Attercliffe Parishes 46-49; V of Attercliffe w Carbrook Sheff 49-53; Hon Can of Sheff 50-66; Can (Emer) from 67; R of Wombwell 53-61; RD of Wath 55-61; Snaith 61-66; V of Goole 61-66. *6 Hawthorne Terrace, Goole, Yorks.* (Goole 2591)

ADKINS, Canon Harold. b 20. Univ of Lon BA (Latin) 41. Wycl Hall Ox. **d** 43 **p** 44 Leic. C of Hugglesote 43-45; All SS Loughborough 45-47; Chap at Beirut 47-48; Chap HM Legation Beirut 48-54; Beirut w Damascus 50-54; Sub-Dean St Geo Colleg Ch Jer 54-67; Exam Chap to Abp in Jer 51-73; to Bp in Jordan 58-73; Hd Master St Geo Sch Jer 63-73; Hon Can of St Geo Colleg Ch Jer 63-65; Can Res 65-70; Can (Emer) from 73; Dean 70-73; Chap and Sub-Prelate O of St John of Jer from 72; V of Barkby Dio Leic from 74. *Vicarage, Barkby, Leics, LE7 8QD.*

ADKINS, Peter Vincent Alexander. b 44. Univ of Lancaster BA 71. Kelham Th Coll 63. M SSM 67. **d** Lanc for Blackb **p** 70 Blackb. Tutor Kelham Th Coll 71-73; Perm to Offic Dio Jer 74-75; Dio Ely 76; Hon C of St Giles Cam 76-78; Perm to Offic Dio Lon 81; Hon C of Northolt Dio Lon from 81. *135 Hazelmere Road, Northolt, Middx, UB5 6UW.*

ADKINS, Phillip John. Ridley Coll Melb ACT ThL 53. **d** 54 **p** 55 Melb. C of Heidelberg 54-56; Min of Whittlesea 56-61; I of Collingwood 61-63; V of Bacchus Marsh 63-67; St Thos Essendon 67-70; Perm to Offic Dio Melb 77-79; I of St Mary Preston Dio Melb from 79. *233 Tyler Street, Preston, Vic, Australia 3072.* (470-1127)

ADKINS, Robin Frank. b 42. St Barn Coll Adel 76. **d** 78 **p** 79 Melb. C of St Barn Barlwyn 78-80; R of Corryong Dio Wang from 80. *Box 31, Corryong, Vic, Australia 3707.*

ADKINS, Ronald Charles Rutherford. b 14. St Cath Coll Cam 3rd cl Engl Trip pt i 34, BA (2nd cl Hist Trip pt ii) 35, MA 47. Chich Th Coll 37. **d** 38 Lon **p** 39 Ex. C of St Mary Hornsey Rise 38-39; Black Torrington 39-41; Asst Master Mount Ho Sch Tavistock 41-43; C of Lydney w Aylburton and Primrose Hill 43-44; R of Cherington 44-48; South Pool w Chivelstone 48-74. *c/o South Pool Rectory, Kingsbridge, Devon.* (Frogmore 252)

ADKINS, Stephen Benjamin. Qu Coll St John's, Newfld LTh 69. **d** 69 **p** 70 Newfld. C of St Mich AA, St John's Newfld 69-72; R of Fogo I 72-77; Whitbourne Dio E Newfld from 77. *Box 9, Whitbourne, Newfoundland, Canada.* (709-759 2870)

ADLER, Thomas Payne. b 07. Selw Coll Cam BA 29, MA 36. Wells Th Coll 29. **d** 30 **p** 31 Leic. C of St Barn Leic 30-34; Hinckley 34-36; V of Rothwell w Orton (and Glendon to 40) 36-47; CF (R of O) 39-45; R of Castor w Ailsworth 47-74; R of Marholm 47-74. *Hill Cottage, Cottons Lane, Ashton-under-Hill, Evesham, WR11 6SS.* (Evesham 881431)

ADLEY, Ernest George. b 38. Univ of Leeds BA (2nd cl Gen) 61. Wells Th Coll 62. **d** 64 **p** 65 Ex. C of Bideford 64-67; St Mich AA Yeovil 67-70; V of St Pet Lyngford Taunton 70-79; R of Skegness w Winthorpe Dio Linc from 79. *Rectory, Lumley Avenue, Skegness, Lincs.* (Skegness 3875)

ADLINGTON, David John. b 51. AKC 73. St Aug Coll Cant 73. **d** 74 **p** 75 S'wark. C of St Paul Clapham 74-77; Bethnal Green 77-80; P-in-c of St Pet w St Benet Mile End, Stepney Dio Lon from 80. *95 Cephas Street, E1 4AU.* (01-790 7077)

ADLINGTON, Kenneth Leonard. b 27. **d** 74 **p** 75 Leic. C of Braunstone 74-76; St Hugh Eyres Monsell Leic 76-78; V of Whetstone Dio Leic from 78. *Vicarage, Church Lane, Whetstone, Leicester.* (Leicester 848713)

ADNETT, Roy Gumley. b 14. Tyndale Hall Bris. **d** 42 **p** 43 Blackb. C of Ch Ch Blackb 42-44; St Jas Carl 44-46; V of Constable Lee 46-49; R of Peldon 49-55; V of Chilcompton (w Downside and Stratton-on-the-Fosse from 80) 55-81; RD of Midsomer Norton 78-81. *129 Harrowgate Drive, Birstall, Leicester.* (Leic 675815)

ADOKOTHO, Efraim. **d** 62 **p** 63 N Ugan. P Dio N Ugan 62-69; Dio M & W Nile from 69. *Okoro P.O. Box 37, Arua, Uganda.*

ADOKU, Yosam. **d** 63 **p** 64 Soroti. P Dio Soroti. *Kalaki, Teso, Uganda.*

ADONIS, Ven Douglas Nkosinathi. St Bede's Coll Umtata 57. **d** 58 **p** 59 St Jo Kaffr. P Dio St John's; Archd of St Mark's 69-76; Pondoland from 76. *PO Holy Cross, CP, S Africa.* (Holy Cross 1)

ADOYO, Ven Julius. Th Coll Limuru. **d** 55 **p** 57 Momb. P Dio Momb 55-61; Dio Maseno 61-62 and 63-70; C of Rugby and Chap Cov Cathl 62-63; Exam Chap to Bp of Maseno 64-70; P Dio Nak from 70; Exam Chap to Bp of Nak from 70; Archd of Eldoret from 70; Can of Nak from 73. *Box 245, Kitale, Kenya.*

ADRALE, Ephraim. Univ of Makerere Kamp Dipl Th 74. Bp Tucker Coll Mukono 71. **d** 75 M & W Nile. d Dio M & W Nile. *Box 63, Arua, Uganda.*

ADROA, Ven Sira. Buwalasi Th Coll. **d** 54 U Nile **p** 56 Bp

Russell for U Nile. P Dio U Nile 54-61; Dio N Ugan 61-69; Dio M & W Nile from 69; Archd of Maracha from 77. *PO Koboko, Uganda.*

ADSETTS, Clifford Rowland. b 50. Univ of the Witwatersrand BA 77. St Paul's Coll Grahmstn 78. **d** 80 Bp Stanage for Johann. C of Vereeniging Dio Johann from 80. *PO Box 3167, Three Rivers, S Africa 1935.*

ADU, Thomas Idowu Olaitan. Im Coll Ibad. **d** and **p** 64 Benin. P Dio Benin 64-74; Dio Ibad from 74. *St James's Cathedral, Okeaola, Ibadan, Nigeria.*

ADU-ANDOH, Samuel. b 48. Trin Coll Legon 71. **d** 74 **p** 75 Kum. P Dio Kum. *Box 17, Mampong, Ashanti, Ghana.*

ADUBE, Daniel O. U.. b 41. Im Coll Ibad 71. **d** 74 **p** 75 Benin. P Dio Benin. *St John's Parsonage, Owodokpokpo, c/o Box 14, Oleh, M-W Nigeria.*

ADUOGO, Hezron Blastus. St Paul's Th Coll Limuru. **d** 64 **p** 65 Maseno. P Dio Maseno 65-70; Dio Maseno S 70-77; Dio Nai from 77. *PO Box 41573, Nairobi, Kenya.* (501123)

ADYA, Yakoba Soma. Bp Gwynne Coll Mundri 61. **d** 65 Bp Dotiro for Sudan. d Dio Sudan. *E.C.S. Kajo Kaji, Equatoria Province, Sudan.*

ADYE, Canon Edwin Ralph George. Wycl Coll Tor LTh 25. **d** 25 **p** 26 Tor. C of St Jas Kinmount w Burnt River 25-28; Cobourg 28-30; R of Whitby 30-40; RD of E York 40-41; Chap CASF 41-46; C of St Olave Tor 46-49; R of Collingwood 48-55; Distr Sec BFBS Dios Queb and Montr 55-58; Can of Tor from 58; Sen Sec U Canad Bible S from 58; Hon C of Annunc Tor 58-63; St John Weston Tor 63-65. *434 Melrose Avenue, Toronto 12, Canada.*

AEDEKE, Joseph. Buwalasi Th Coll. **d** 57 **p** 59 U Nile. P Dio U Nile 57-60; Dio Soroti from 60; Dioc Treas Dio Soroti 63-64. *PO Box 3001, Ngoro, Mbale, Uganda.*

AEGEAN, Archdeacon of the. *See* Evans, Ven Geoffrey Bainbridge.

AFERE, Joel Adejumo. d 77 Ondo. d Dio Ondo. *Vicarage, Isua-Ile, via Ikare-Akoko, Ondo, Nigeria.*

AFFLECK, John. b 20. Univ of Liv LLB 48. St Aug Coll Cant 71. **d** 71 Chelmsf **p** 72 Bradwell for Chelmsf. C of Hutton 71-74; P-in-c of Hawkchurch w Fishpond, Bettiscombe w Marshwood and Pilsdon Dio Sarum from 74; Whitchurch Canonicorum w Stanton, Wootton Fitzpaine and Monkton Wyld Dio Sarum from 81. *Vicarage, Whitchurch Canonicorum, Bridport, Dorset, DT6 6RQ.* (Chideock 223)

AFFLECK, Stuart John. b 47. AKC 69. St Aug Coll Cant 69. **d** 70 Bp Bradwell for Chelmsf. C of St Mary Prittlewell 70-75; Asst Chap of Charterhouse Sch 75-78; Chap 78-80; Warden Pilsdon Commun Dio Sarum from 80. *Pilsdon Community, Pilsdon by Bridport, Dorset.*

AFOLABI, Samuel Oluwafemi. b 34. Im Th Coll Ibad 67. **d** 70 Bp Jadesimi for Ibad **p** 71 Gambia. P Dio Ibad from 71. *St Paul's Vicarage, PO Box 2, Oyan-Oshogbo, Nigeria.*

✠ **AFONYA, Right Rev Hubert Alafuro Ibibama.** St Paul's Coll Awka 47. **d** 47 Bp Onyeabo for Niger **p** 49 Niger. P Dio Niger 47-52; P Niger Delta 52-57; Synod Sec from 56; Cons Asst Bp on the Niger Delta in St Steph Cathl Bonny 10 Nov 57 by Abp of W Afr; Bp on The Niger; Bps of Nig Delta; Ondo-B; Lagos; Accra; and Bps Nkemena, P J Jones, Awosika and Martinson; Apptd Ld Bp of Aba 71; R of Port Harcourt 57-71; Archd of Bonny 62-71; Prov Dean of Nigeria from 79. *Bishop's House, Box 212, Aba, Nigeria.*

AFRICA, Cyril Francis. d 71 **p** 72 Pret. C of All SS Barberton 71-80; St Matthias Barberton Dio Pret from 80. *PO Box 140, Barberton 1300, Pretoria, S Africa.* (373)

AFRICA, CENTRAL, Metropolitan of Province of. *See* Makhulu, Most Rev Walter Paul.

AFRICA, WEST, Metropolitan of Province of. *See* Lemaire, Most Rev Ishmael Samuel Mills.

AFRICANDER, Victor Vivian Sipho. Coll of Resurr Mirfield and St Pet Rosettenville. **d** 56 **p** 57 Zulu. P Dio Zulu 56-73; Dio Swaz 73-75; Dio Natal from 75. *Box 45, Imbali, Natal, S Africa.*

AGAR, Edward Walter Finlay. b 37. Univ of Lon BD and AKC 68. Ripon Hall Ox 68. **d** 70 **p** 71 S'wark. C of St Mary Putney 70-73; Asst Sec C of E Coun for Social Aid 73-75; Gen Sec from 76. *38 Ebury Street, SW1 0LU.* (01-730 6175)

AGAR-HAMILTON, John Augustus Ion. Univ of S Afr BA 14, MA 18. Keble Coll Ox BA (2nd cl Hist) 22, BLitt 22, MA 29. **d** 55 Pret **p** 60 Grahmstn. C of Pret Cathl 55-60; L to Offic Dio Grahmstn 60-67; Ed S Afr Ch Directory and Year Book 67-69; I of Ch Ch Grahmstn 69-79; L to Offic Dio Grahmstn from 80. *7 Somerset Lodge, Somerset Street, Grahamstown, C.P., S Africa.*

AGARD, Ven William Oscar. b 24. Univ of the WI BA 77. Codr Coll Barb 74. **d** 77 Barb for Guy **p** 77 Bp George for Guy. C of St Geo Cathl Georgetn 77-79; Dioc Sec from 79; C of Ch Ch Georgetn 79-80; Hon Can of St Geo Cathl and Archd Dio Guy from 80. *22k Camperville, Georgetown, Guyana.*

AGASSIZ, David John Lawrence. b 42. St Pet Coll Ox BA (3rd cl Math) 64, MA 68. Ripon Hall Ox 64. **d** 66 Win **p** 67. Bp Cornwall for Win. C of St Mary w H Trin Southn Dio Win 66-71; V of St Jas Enfield Highway 71-80; P-in-c of Grays Dio Chelmsf from 80; All SS Grays Dio Chelmsf from 81; L Thurrock Dio Chelmsf from 81. *Vicarage, High View Avenue, Grays, Essex.* (Grays Thurrock 73215)

AGBAIM, Very Rev Isaiah Chukwuesoghimem. b 27. BD (Lon) 62. Univ of Calif MA 65. Trin Coll Umuahia 67. **d** 68 Bp Uzodike **p** 68 Niger. P Dio Niger from 68; Can of Niger 71-74; Provost of All SS Cathl Onitsha from 74. *All Saints' Cathedral, P.O. Box 361, Onitsha, Nigeria.*

AGBAJE, Albert Aduloju. b 37. Univ of Nigeria BA 66. Im Coll Ibad 60. **d** 62 **p** 73 Benin. P Dio Benin. *Ministry of Education, Afuze, Mid West State, Nigeria.*

AGBAJE, Samuel Olufunminiyi. Im Coll Ibad Dipl Th 77. **d** 77 **p** 78 Ondo. P Dio Ondo. *St James Vicarage, Oda, Ondo, Nigeria.*

AGBASIMALO, Gabriel Usokanandu. St Paul's Coll Awka. **d** 60 **p** 61 Ow. P Dio Ow 60-73. *Parsonage, Awo-Idemili, Orlu, Nigeria.*

AGBONZE, John Otasowie. Im Coll Ibad. **d** 61 **p** 62 Benin. P Dio Benin. *St Peter's Vicarage, Uhomora, Benin, Nigeria.*

AGBOOLA, Michael Ayodele. b 47. Im Coll Ibad 77. **d** 80 **p** 81 Ijebu. P Dio Ijebu. *PO Box 16, Ijebu-Ode, Nigeria.*

AGGREY, Daniel Ewusi. b 28. **d** 77 **p** 78 Kum. P Dio Kum. *St Cyprian's Anglican Cathedral, PO Box 33, Nkawie Ashanti, Kumasi, Ghana.*

AGGREY, Philip Dawson. Univ of Ghana 58. BD (Lon) 62. **d** 62 **p** 63 Accra. P Dio Accra 62-73; Dio Kum from 73; Exam Chap to Bp of Kum from 73. *Anglican Training College, Box 292, Kumasi, Ghana.*

AGHADOE, Bishop of. *See* Limerick.

AGHADOE, Archdeacon of. *See* Ardfert.

AGNEW, Kenneth David. b 33. Jes Coll Cam BA (3rd cl Law Trip pt i) 58, MA 62. Clifton Th Coll 58. **d** 60 Birm **p** 61 Aston for Birm. C of St Silas Lozells 60-63; Skellingthorpe 63-68; C-in-c of Birchwood 68-72; R of Willand Dio Ex from 72. *Willand Rectory, Cullompton, Devon, EX15 2RH.* (Cullompton 2247)

AGNEW, Stephen Mark. b 54. Univ of Wales (Bangor) BSc 76. Univ of Southn BTh 81. Sarum Wells Th Coll 76. **d** 79 **p** 80 Ches. C of Wilmslow Dio Ches from 79. *1 Orchard Close, Wilmslow, Cheshire, SK9 6AU.*

AGOI, Joseph Taiwo Twin. Univ of Ibad BEducn 69. **d** 76 Ondo. d Dio Ondo. *Adeyemi College, Ondo, Nigeria.*

✠ **AGOLA, Right Rev Evan.** St Paul's Div Sch Limuru 42. **d** 43 **p** 45 Momb. I of Ng'iya and Akoka 44-46; Kitale 47-48; Maseno Bible Sch and Kisumu 49-50; Nairobi 50-52; Nakuru 52-53; Ramba 53-57; Can of Momb 58-61; Maseno 61-65; Exam Chap to Bp of Maseno 64-65; Cons Asst Bp of Maseno in St Steph Pro-Cathl Kisumu 21 Dec 65 By Abp of E Afr; Bps of Mt Kenya; Maseno; and Vic Nyan; Apptd Ld Bp of Maseno S 70; res 73. *c/o PO Box 91, Siaya, Kenya.*

AGOMO, James Bernard Onwugbufo. b 29. Episc Th Sem of SW, Texas MDiv 71. Trin Coll Umuahia. **d** 59 **p** 60 Nig Delta. P Dio Nig Delta. *Etche Girls' School, Umuola, Nigeria.*

AGORDEKPE, Canon Amos Roger. St Aug Th Coll Kumasi. **d** 51 **p** 52 Accra. P Dio Accra; Hon Can of Accra from 73. *Box 1238, Accra, Ghana.*

AGUNBIADE, Joseph Adebayo. b 13. **d** 72 **p** 73 Ekiti. P Dio Ekiti. *St James's Church, Ipole Iloro, Ekiti, Nigeria.*

AGWUOCHA, Eleazer Ononiwu. Trin Coll Legon 69. **d** 72 **p** 73 Owerri. P Dio Owerri. *St Andrew's Parsonage, Obizi, Owerri, Nigeria.*

AGYEMAN-DUA, Joseph. b 25. **d** 77. d Dio Kum. *St Cyprian's Cathedral, PO Box 144, Kumasi, Ghana.*

AGYEMANG, Andrew Christian. d and **p** 41 Accra. P Dio Accra 41-79; Archd of Sunyani-Tamale 75-79. *Box 23, Sunyani, Brong-Ahafo, Ghana.* (Sunyani 213)

AH-LEUNG, Paul. b 38. BA (Lon) 66. St Paul's Coll Maur 66. **d** 71 **p** 72 Maur. C of Vacoas 71-73; H Trin Rose Hill 73-76; St Andr Quatre-Bornes Dio Maur from 76. *Avenue Beau-Sejour, Belle Rose-Quatre Bornes, Mauritius.*

AHENAKEW, Gordon. d 67 **p** 68 Sask. Miss Big Whitefish Reserve 67-71; Montr Lake 71-75; Big Whitefish 75-77; Fort La Corne 77-78; P-in-c of Hines Miss and Big Whitefish 78-80. *Box 115, Canwood, Sask, Canada.*

AHIM, Augustine. b 15. Ho of Epiph Kuch 70. **d** 71 Kuch. C of St Thos Cathl, Kuch 71-75; St Francis Lundu Dio Kuch from 75. *St Francis Church, Lundu, Sarawak, Malaysia.*

AHIMBISIBWE, Duncan. Bp Tucker Coll Mukono 78. **d** 80 E Ank. d Dio E Ank. *Naama COU, PO Kiruhura, Uganda.*

AHMOAH, Augustine Dawson. St Aug Th Coll Kumasi

45. **d** and **p** 48 Accra. P Dio Accra from 48; Can of Accra 68-75; Archd of Koforidua 75-80. *Box 166, Koforidua, Ghana.* (Koforidua 2329)

✠ **AH MYA, Most Rev Francis.** Bp's Coll Calc 27. **d** 31 **p** 33 Rang. Tutor Div Sch Rang 31-33; P Dio Rang 33-40; St Matt Moulmein 46-47; Cons Asst Bp of Rang in Calc Cathl 5 June 49 by Bp of Calc (Metrop); Bps of Chota N; Bom; Bhag; and Bps Banerjee and Tarafdar; Warden of H Cross Coll 52-55; Archd of Moulmein 56-66; P-in-c of Pa'an 57-66; Apptd Ld Bp of Rang 66; res 72; Elected Abp and Metrop of Prov of Burma 70; res 72; Dir Prov Project from 73. *Bishop's Lodge, Institute Village, East Bank, Toungoo, Burma.*

AH MYA, Harold. H Cross Coll Rang BA 65. **d** 68 **p** 69 Rang. C of All SS Rang 68-72; Prin Em Div Sch 73-76; H Cross Th Coll Rang from 76. *104 Inya Road, Rangoon, Burma.*

AHN, Francis. d 73 **p** 75 Taejon. P Dio Taejon. *493 Namsandong, Chong Eup, Chunbuk, Korea.*

AHN, Paul. St Mich Sem Oryudong 66. **d** and **p** 67 Seoul. P Dio Seoul 67-78; Archd P of Seoul 77-78. *58-76, 3 Ka Munraedong, Yongdungp'o, Seoul 150, Korea.* (Seoul 63-6290)

AHOKAVA, Mataiasi. b 31. St Jo Bapt Coll Suva 62. **d** 65 **p** 67 Polyn. P Dio Polyn. *PO Box 120, Neiafu, Vavau, Tonga.*

AHUMBYA, Philemon. b 39. Bp Tucker Coll Mukono 71. **d** 73 Ruw. d Dio Ruw. *Box 12, Fort Portal, Uganda.*

AIBE, Philemon Boko. d 75 Kwara. d Dio Kwara. *St Paul's Church, Oguma P.A., Via Lokoja, Nigeria.*

AIKEN, Colin Gordon. Ridley Coll Melb ACT ThL 66. NZ Bd of Th Stud LTh 68. **d** 66 **p** 67 Bath. C of Northmead 66-67; Gordon 67-68; E Orange 68-69; Parkes 69-71. *43 Currajong Street, Parkes, NSW, Australia.*

AIKEN, David Leslie. BA Univ NZ 43. **d** 43 **p** 44 Ch Ch. C of Sumner NZ 43-47; V of Chatham Is 47-50; C of Merrivale 50; CMS (NZ) Miss in Karachi 51; Sukkur 52-55; Khairpur 56-59; V of Ch Ch Karachi 61-65; C of All SS Palmerston N 66-67; Tutor NZ Bible Tr Inst from 68; Perm to Offic Dio Auckld 68-70; Hon C of Henderson 71-77; Glen Eden Dio Auckld from 77. *Bible Training Institute, Lincoln Road, Henderson, Auckland 8, NZ.* (83-66 924)

AILWOOD, Frederick Charles. St Francis Coll Brisb. **d** 63 Bp Hudson for Brisb **p** 63 Brisb. C of St Alb Auchenflower Brisb 63-65; St Andr Lutwyche Brisb 65-68; V of Caboolture 68-74; R of Goondiwindi 74-80; St Andr Pittsworth Dio Brisb from 80. *Rectory, Murray Street, Pittsworth, Queensland, Australia 4356.* (076-931029)

✠ **AINANI, Right Rev Dunstan.** St Andr Coll Mponda's 64. **d** 66 **p** 67 Bp Mtekateka for Malawi. P Dio Malawi 66-71; Dio Lake Malawi 71-73; Dio S Malawi 73-79; Cons Bp Suffr of S Malawi at Chilema, Zomba 17 June 79 by Abp of Centr Afr; Bp of Lake Malawi; Bps Suffr of Aston and Texas (USA); and Bp Mtekateka; Apptd Bp of S Malawi 81. *P/A Chilema, PO Zomba, Malawi.* (Domasi 240)

AINGE, David Stanley. b 47. Univ of Lon Dipl Th (Extra-Mural Stud) 74. Oak Hill Coll 70. **d** 73 **p** 74 Win. C of Bitterne 73-77; Castlechurch 77-79; P-in-c of St Alb Becontree Dio Chelmsf from 79. *St Alban's Vicarage, Vincent Road, Becontree, Essex, RM9 6AL.* (01-592 5410)

AINGER, John Allen. b 18. St Chad's Coll Dur BA 39, MA 42. Ripon Hall Ox 39. **d** 41 **p** 42 St E. C of St Greg w St Pet Sudbury 41-43; All H Ipswich 43-44; St Jo Bapt Ches 44-47; Chap RNVR 47-49; C of Hampstead 49-51; R of Melmerby w Ousby 52-56; V of Langford 56-61; Asst Master Bedford High Sch for Girls 62-79; Publ Pr Dio St Alb from 62. *80 Falcon Avenue, Bedford.* (Bedford 54683)

AINGER, John Dawson. b 02. Bp's Coll Cheshunt 33. **d** 35 **p** 36 Lon. C of St Mary Twickenham 35-37; Chap Nat Nautical Sch Portishead 37-38; C of St Mary Virg Yatton 38-39; Serving in RN 39-46; R of Farleigh-Hungerford w Tellisford 46-48; PC of Cleeve 48-52; Chap at Oslo 52-54; V of E Harptree 54-68. *Filey House, Landemann Circus, Weston-super-Mare, Avon, BS23 2QF.*

AINSCOW, Harold Mason. b 1893. St Edm Hall Ox BA 14, MA 18. Ridley Hall Cam 19. **d** 19 Rip **p** 20 York for Rip. C of St Mary Beeston Leeds 19-22; St Cypr Edge Hill Liv 22-23; Surr 23-27; V of St Jas Wigan 23-27; Raughton Head w Gatesgill 27-30; St Mich AA Blackb 30-33; R of Ousby 33-37; Lowther w Askham 37-47; RD of Lowther 45-47; V of Bourton 47-49; Abbot's Kerswell 49-59; Perm to Offic Dio Ex from 59. *Crag Lodge, Higher Downs Road, Babbacombe, Torquay, Devon.* (Torquay 37593)

AINSLEY, Canon Anthony Dixon. b 29. Or Coll Ox BA (2nd cl Mod Lang) 52, MA 57. Univ of S Africa BA 74. St Steph Ho Ox 53. **d** 55 **p** 56 Blackb. C of St Cath Burnley 55-60; All Saints CP 60-62; P-in-c of Nqamakwe 62-68; Idutywa 69-80; Can of St Jo Cathl Umtata 73-80; Hon Can from 81; Archd of All SS 73-80; Chap SW France Dio Gibr in Eur 81; V of St Steph Blackpool Dio Blackb from 81. *St Stephens Vicarage, Blackpool, Lancs.* (0253 51484)

AINSLEY, Peter Dixon. b 32. St Steph Ho Ox 58. **d** 60 **p** 61 Man. C of St Thos Bury 60-62; Chap RN from 62. *c/o Ministry of Defence, Lacon House, Theobalds Road, WC1X 8RY.*

AINSWORTH, Arthur Nicholls. b 06. Univ of Lon BSc (2nd cl Chem) 30. St Aug Coll Cant 58. **d** 59 Thetford for Nor **p** 60 Nor. C of Fakenham (in c of Kettlestone) 59-62; R of Foulsham 62-76; Perm to Offic Dio Lon from 76. *99 Shaftesbury Avenue, South Harrow, HA2 0PP.*

AINSWORTH, Clifford Charles. b 49. Moore Th Coll Syd BTh, BD. **d** 79 **p** 80 Armid. V of Boggabri Dio Armid from 79. *88 Laidlaw Street, Boggabri, NSW, Australia 2382.*

AINSWORTH, David Lawrence. b 28. K Coll Lon and Warm AKC 54. **d** 55 **p** 56 Lon. C of St Jas and St John Friern Barnet 55-58; All SS Harrow Weald (in c of St Barn) 58-63; R of Northrepps Dio Nor from 63; R of Sidestrand Dio Nor from 63; C-in-c of Roughton 75-79. *Northrepps Rectory, Cromer, Norf, NR27 0LH.* (Overstrand 444)

AINSWORTH, Howard Charles. St Jo Coll Morpeth ACT ThL 62. **d** 62 **p** 63 C & Goulb. C of St Sav Cathl Goulb 62-65; St Jo Bapt Canberra 65-66; R of Delegate 66-68; Dept of Chaps Melb 69-72; Chap Preston and Northcote Hosps and Perm to Offic Dio Melb from 73. *184 Hawdon Street, Heidelberg, Vic, Australia 3084.*

AINSWORTH, Michael Ronald. b 50. K Coll Lon LLB 71, LLM 72. Trin Hall Cam BA 74, MA 79. Westcott Ho Cam 73. **d** 75 Burnley for Blackb **p** 76 Blackb. C of Scotforth 75-78; Chap St Martin's Coll Lanc 78-82. *c/o St Martin's College, Lancaster, LA1 3JD.* (0524 63446)

AINSWORTH, Peter. b 34. Univ of Lon BD 57. Coll Resurr Mirfield 69. **d** 70 **p** 71 Ripon. C of St Wilfrid Harehills 70-74; Team V of Tong 74-77; V of Fairweather Green Dio Bradf from 77. *Vicarage, Ings Way, Fairweather Green, Bradford 8, Yorks.* (Bradford 44807)

AINSWORTH-SMITH, Ian Martin. b 41. Selw Coll Cam 2nd cl Th Trip pt i 62, BA (2nd cl Th Trip pt ii) 64, 2nd cl Th Trip pt iii 66, MA 68. Westcott Ho Cam 64. **d** 66 **p** 67 Lon. C of John Keble Ch Mill Hill 66-69; in Amer Ch 69-71; C of St Mark Woodcote, Purley 71-73; Chap St Geo Hosp Lon from 73. *107 West Side, SW4 9AZ.* (01-223 5302)

AIPA, Ven Benson Nathanael. St Jo Sem Lusaka 62. **d** 63 Nyasa **p** 65 Bp Mtekateka for Malawi. P Dio Malawi 63-71; Dio S Malawi from 71; Archd of Mangochi W from 78. *Box 54, Mangochi, Malawi.*

AIPO RONGO, Lord Bishop of. *See* Ashton, Right Rev Jeremy Claude.

AIPO RONGO, Assistant Bishop of. *See* Kerina, Right Rev Blake Tawaru.

AIRD, Arthur Rickerby. b 35. Univ of Bris BA (2nd cl Th) 61. Tyndale Hall Bris 57. **d** 62 Penrith for Carl **p** 63 Carl. C of St Andr Mirehouse Whitehaven 62-66; Gt Sankey 67-70; V of Tebay 70-77; V of St Phil Southport Dio Liv from 77. *St Philip's Vicarage, Scarisbrick New Road, Southport, Mer, PR8 6QF.* (Southport 32886)

AIRD, Donald Allan Ross. b 33. K Coll Lon and Warm AKC 55. **d** 56 **p** 57 Lon. C of St Cuthb N Wembley 56-59; Sidmouth (in c of St Francis Woolbrook) 59-62; Dioc Youth Chap Dio Ely 62-68; V of Swaffham Bulbeck 62-69; Ascen Wembley 69-79; St Mark Hamilton Terrace St John's Wood Dio Lon from 79. *St Mark's Vicarage, Hamilton Terrace, NW8 9UT.* (01-328 4373)

AIRD, Robert Malcolm. b 31. BSc (Lon) 54. Westcott Ho Cam 75. **d** 77 Taunton for B & W **p** 78 B & W. C of Burnham-on-Sea 77-79; C-in-c of St Pet Lyngford Taunton Dio B & W from 79. *St Peter's Vicarage, Eastwick Road, Taunton, TA2 7HD.* (0823 75085)

AIRES, Raymond Charles. Univ of NZ BA 33, MA (2nd cl Hist) 35. NZ Bd of Th Stud LTh 37. St Jo Coll Auckld 29. **d** and **p** 33 Waik. C of St Pet Hamilton 33; Te Awamutu 33-34; Gisborne 35-38; V of Waerenga-a-hika 38-42; CF (NZ) 42-46; V of Waipawa 46-50; Porangahau 50-56; Taradale 56-57; L to Offic Dio Wai 57-64; V of Mt Herbert 64-69; Rakaia 69-73; C of Spreydon 73-74; L to Offic Dio Ch Ch from 74. *7 Purau Avenue, Diamond Harbour, NZ.* (Diamond Harbour 875)

AIRNE, Canon Charles Clement Wallace. Selw Coll Cam BA (2nd cl Hist pt i) 47, MA 52. Qu Coll Birm 47. **d** 49 **p** 50 Liv. C of St Thos Eccleston St Helens 49-51; Roby (in c of St Andr) 51-53; V of Bacup 53-58; Lydgate Dio Man from 58; Hon Can of Man Cathl from 80. *Lydgate Vicarage, Oldham, OL4 4JJ.* (Saddleworth 2117)

AIRTON, James Boyd. b 1894. Wycl Hall Ox 51. **d** 51 **p** 52 Linc. C of Asterby w Goulceby 51-53; V of Witherslack 53-55; R of Horton w L Sodbury 55-64; Perm to Offic Dio

Sarum from 64; Dio Guildf from 77. *Manormead, Tilford Road, Hindhead, Surrey.* (Hindhead 5188)

AISBITT, Osmond John. b 35. St Chad's Coll Dur BA (2nd cl Mod Hist) 57, Dipl Th (w distinc) 61. **d** 61 **p** 62 Newc T. C of Ashington 61-64; St Mary Blyth 64-68; V of St Jo Evang Cleckheaton 68-75; Horbury (w Horbury Bridge from 78) Dio Wakef from 75; M Gen Syn from 80. *St Peter's Vicarage, Northgate, Horbury, Wakefield, WF4 6AS.* (Horbury 27-3477)

AISH, Norman Cyril Roslyn. b 20. St Steph Ho Ox 52. **d** 54 **p** 55 Cov. C of Wyken 54-57; St Kath Southbourne 57-59; Dioc Adv for Chr Stewardship Dio Win 59-62; V of H Ascen Hyde Win 62-73; Dir Bournemouth Distr Samaritans from 70; Publ Pr Dio Win from 73; Adv for Social Responsibility Dio Win from 73. *Church House, 9 The Close, Winchester, Hants.* (Winchester 62507)

AISIRA, Virgil. Newton Coll Dogura 68. **d** 72 Papua **p** 72 Bp Meredith for Papua. P Dio Papua 72-77; Dio Aipo from 77. *Box 355, Goroka, Papua New Guinea.*

AISU, Geresom. **d** 63 **p** 64 Soroti. P Dio Soroti. *Kanyum, Soroti, Uganda.*

AISUM, Cornel. b 43. **d** 78 **p** 79 New Guinea Is. P Dio New Guinea Is 78-81. *PO Box 159, Rabaul, ENBP, Papua New Guinea.*

AITCHISON, John Frederick. Ripon Hall Ox 66. **d** 67 Birm **p** 68 Aston for Birm. C of Boldmere 67-70; Pembury and Asst Chap Pembury Hosp 70-73; V of Bassingbourn Dio Ely from 73; Whaddon Dio Ely from 74. *Bassingbourn Vicarage, Royston, Herts.* (Royston 43119)

AITCHISON, John Jacques William. b 44. Univ of Natal BA 65. **d** 76 Natal. C of Cathl Ch of St Sav Pietermaritzburg Dio Natal from 76. *PO Box 1329, Pietermaritzburg, S Africa.*

AITKEN, Christopher William Mark. b 53. Grey Coll Dur BA 75. Westcott Ho Cam 76. **d** 79 Edm for Lon **p** 80 Lon. C of St Mary Finchley Dio Lon from 79. *28 Hendon Lane, Finchley, N3.* (01-346 7573)

AITKEN, Leslie Robert. b 20. MBE 76. St Aid Coll Dur. **d** 46 **p** 47 Wakef. C of St Andr Wakef 46-48; C of H Trin Hull 48-52; V of Burley Yorks 52-56; R of S Normanton 56-58; V of Audenshaw 58-63; Stamber Mill 63-68; R of Alvechurch Dio Worc from 68. *Alvechurch Rectory, Birmingham, B48 7SB.* (021-445 1087)

AITKEN, Leslie St John Robert. b 41. Open Univ BA 75. Cranmer Hall Dur 62. **d** 65 **p** 66 Worc. C of St Barn Worc 65-69; Halesowen w Hasbury and Lapal 69-73; C-in-c of All SS Wyche 73-80; R of St Pet Blackley Dio Man from 80. *1161 Rochdale Road, Manchester, M9 2FP.* (061-740 2124)

✠ **AITKEN, Right Rev William Aubrey.** b 11. Trin Coll Ox BA (2nd cl Mod Hist) 33, MA 37. Wells Th Coll 34. **d** 34 **p** 35 Newc T. C of Ch Ch Tynemouth 34-37; St Geo Kingston Ja 37-40; R of Kessingland 40-43; V of Sprowston 43-53; R of St Andr Beeston 43-53; RD of Taverham 45-53; V of St Marg w St Nich King's Lynn 53-61; Proc Conv Nor 44-62; Hon Can of Nor 58-73; Archd of Nor 61-73; Lynn 73-80; Commiss New Guinea 68-71; Papua from 71; Cons Ld Bp Suffr of Lynn in St Paul's Cathl 2 Feb 73 by Abp of Cant; Bps of Win, Linc, Glouc, Ely, Nor; Bps Suffr of Grantham, Huntingdon, Maidstone, Thetford and Willesden and others. *Broad House, Ranworth, Norwich.* (South Walsham 248)

AITON, Robert Neilson. b 36. Univ Coll of S Wales & Mon BA 59. Chich Th Coll 74. **d** 76 Chich **p** 77 Horsham for Chich. C of E Grinstead (in c of St Luke from 78) Dio Chich from 76. *St Luke's House, Holtye Avenue, East Grinstead, RH19 3EG.* (E Grinstead 23800)

AIYEBOLA, Stephen Adeyeye. **d** 70 **p** 71 Lagos. P Dio Lagos. *PO Box 61, Ikoto, Ijebu-Ode, Nigeria.*

AIYEDUN, William Omotunji. Fourah Bay Coll BA 19, MA 39. **d** 20 Bp Oluwole for Lagos **p** 22 Lagos. P Dio Lagos 20-60. *86 Wakeman Street, Yaba, Lagos, Nigeria.*

AIYEJOTO, Canon Rufus Ibikunle. Melville Hall Ibad 50. **d** 51 Lagos **p** 52 Ondo-B. d Dio Lagos 51; P Dio Ondo-B 52-62; Dio Ondo from 62; Hon Can of Ondo from 72. *Holy Trinity Vicarage, Idoani, Nigeria.*

AIZLEWOOD, Geoffrey Rymer. b 27. St Aid Coll. **d** 61 **p** 62 Liv. C of St Luke W Derby 61-65; St Thos Ashton-in-Makerfield (in c of St Luke Stubshaw Cross) 65-69; V of St Mark Liv 69-75. *21 Statton Road, Broadgreen, Liverpool, L13 4BE.* (051-228 5728)

AJAELO, Canon Vincent Nwokeabia. Trin Coll Umuahia 56. **d** 58 Niger **p** 59 Ow. P Dio Ow; Hon Can of Ow from 73. *Parsonage, Mbieri, Owerri, Nigeria.*

AJAERO, Anthony Rapuruchukwu Okonkwo. b 40. Trin Coll Umuahia 72. **d** 74 Enugu. d Dio Enugu. *St Stephen's Parsonage, Akiyi Umulokpa, via Naukka, Nigeria.*

AJAKEMO, Festus Nwokenyinnwa. Trin Coll Umuahia 49. **d** 51 **p** 53 Niger. P Dio Niger 53-59; Dio Ow 59-74; Can of Ow 66-74. *St Peter's Church, Ubonukam, Onicha, Nigeria.*

AJAKOR, Jonah Eziorachukwu. b 52. Trin Coll Umuahia 74. **d** 76 Niger. d Dio Niger. *St Gabriel's, Umuleri, Anambra, Nigeria.*

AJALA, Joseph Oladele. b 36. Bowling Green State Univ Ohio BSc 72, MEducn 73, PhD 76. **d** 79 **p** 81 Egba. P Dio Egba. *PMB 2210, Abeokuta, Ogun State, Nigeria.*

AJAYI, Bukola Adebiyi. b 21. Im Coll Ibad 70. **d** 72 **p** 73 Lagos. P Dio Lagos. *Shrict Church, Porogun, Box 23, Ijebu-Ode, Nigeria.*

AJAYI, Cornelius Olanrewaju. **d** 72 Ibad. d Dio Ibad. *Anglican Church, Jebba, Basita, Nigeria.*

AJAYI, Edward Ebilola Oladipo. Im Coll Ibad 65. **d** 67 **p** 68 Lagos. P Dio Lagos. *PO Box 68, Ijebu-Igbo, Nigeria.*

AJAYI, Emanuel Odukoya. Univ of Lon BA 27. **d** 29 **p** 30 Bp Oluwole for Lagos. Tutor St Andr Tr Coll Oyo 29-33; P Dio Lagos 33-52; Dio Ondo-B 52-57; Dio Lagos 57-59. *c/o St Andrew's Vicarage, Ijebu-Ode, Nigeria.*

AJAYI, Emanuel Okunola. b 29. **d** 76 Ijebu. d Dio Ijebu 76-79; Dio Egba from 79. *St Michael's Church, Ago-Oba, Abeokuta, Nigeria.*

AJAYI, Francis George. Im Coll Ibad 70. **d** 73 Ekiti. d Dio Ekiti. *St Peter's Vicarage, Iro, Ekiti, Nigeria.*

AJAYI, Issac Oluwemimo. Im Coll Ibad 62. **d** 64 Ondo **p** 69 Ekiti. d Dio Ondo 64-69; P Dio Ekiti 69-75; Dio Ondo from 76. *Vicarage, Ifira-Akoko, Ondo, Nigeria,*

AJAYI, James Emila. Im Coll Ibad 59. **d** 61 **p** 62 Ondo-B. P Dio Ondo-B 61-62; Dio Ondo 62-66; Dio Ekiti from 66. *St Paul's Vicarage, Odo Owa, Ijero, Ekiti, Nigeria.*

AJAYI, John Bamidele. Im Coll Ibad 61. **d** 63 **p** 65 Ibad. P Dio Ibad 63-76. *St Peter's Church, Orile-Owu, Ibadan, Nigeria.*

AJAYI, Joseph Adesuyi. **d** 41 **p** 43 Lagos. P Dio Lagos 41-52; Dio Ondo-B 52-62; Dio Ondo 62-66; Hon Can of Ondo 56-66. *c/o P.O. Box 12, Ado-Ekiti, Nigeria.*

AJAYI, Ven Joseph Olamide Abiodun. b 29. **d** 58 **p** 59 Lagos. P Dio Lagos 58-76; Dio Ijebu from 76; Hon Can of Lagos 74-76; Archd Dio Ijebu from 77. *Box 23, Ijebu-Ode, Nigeria.* (Ijebu-Ode 65)

AJAYI, Joseph Seyindemi. b 19. **d** 58 **p** 59 Lagos. P Dio Lagos. *St John's Vicarage, Ode-Lemo, via Shagamu, Nigeria.*

AJAYI, Josiah Olawale. **d** 77 Ondo. d Dio Ondo. *Vicarage, Aiyesan, via Okitipupa, Ondo, Nigeria.*

AJAYI, Olorunfemi Paul. b 40. **d** 75 **p** 76 Ibad. P Dio Ibad. *St Mary's Church, Osogun, via Iseyin, Nigeria.*

AJAYI, Samuel Akinlabi. b 35. Im Coll Ibad Dipl Th 73. **d** 73 Ondo. d Dio Ondo. *St Paul's Church, Okengwen, via Okene & Owo, Nigeria.*

AJAYI, Samuel Babadayisi. Im Coll Ibad 62. **d** 64 **p** 65 Ibad. P Dio Ibad 64-79; Dio Ilesha from 79. *St Peter's Vicarage, Erinmo, Nigeria.*

AJAYI, Canon William Olaseinde. Melville Hall Ibad 50. ALCD (1st cl) 57. **d** and **p** 52 Ondo-B. P Dio Ondo-B 52-57 and 60-62; Dio Ondo 62-65; C of St Ambrose Bris 57-60; P Dio Ibad from 65; Exam Chap to Bp of Gambia 67-73; to Bp of Ibad 69-70; Can of Ibad from 69. *c/o University of Ife, Ibadan, Nigeria.*

AJEPE, Christopher Adeyemi. b 36. Univ of Ibad BA 64. **d** 70 **p** 72 Ondo. P Dio Ondo; Prin Akure Gr Sch from 75. *CAC Grammar School, Akure, Nigeria.*

AJEWOLE, Samson Adebayo. Im Coll Ibad 59. **d** 61 **p** 62 Ondo-B. P Dio Ondo-B 61-62; Dio Ondo from 62. *St Paul's Vicarage, Okeluse, Nigeria.*

AJIBOLA, Emmanuel Olajuyite. **d** 20 **p** 23 Bp Oluwole for Lagos. P Dio Lagos; Hon Can of Lagos 44-57; V of St Pet Ife 41-58. *Iremo, Ile-ife, Nigeria.*

AJIBOLA, Jacob Olorunsuyi. **d** 73 **p** 74 Kware. P Dio Kwara 73-78; Dio Ondo from 78. *Box 23, Ikare-Akoko, Ondo, Nigeria.*

AJIERE, Christopher Marcus. St Paul's Coll Awka. **d** 62 **p** 63 Nig Delta. P Dio Nig Delta. *St Peter's Parsonage, Orika, Nigeria.*

AJOMO, Gabriel Kayode. **d** 41 **p** 43 Lagos. P Dio Lagos 41-52; Dio Ondo-B 52-62; Dio Benin from 62; Can of Benin 62-67; Archd 67-78. *Vicarage, P.O. Box 11, Auchi, Nigeria.*

AJULE, Ven Hezekiah. Buwalasi Coll. **d** 49 **p** 51 U Nile. P Dio U Nile 49-61; Dio N Ugan 61-64; Dio M & W Nile from 64; Archd of W Nile 64-70; Arua from 70; Can of M & W Nile from 72. *Box 370, Arua, Uganda.*

AJUMOBI, Canon Joseph Dada. Melville Hall Ibad 53. **d** 54 **p** 55 Ibad. P Dio Ibad; Can of Ibad 76-78; Hon Can from 78. *St Paul's Vicarage, Iseyia, Nigeria.*

AK ENGKUANG, Lipson Timbang. St Andr Th Sem Manila BTh 80. **d** 80 Kuch. d Dio Kuch. *St Columba's Church, PO Box 233, Miri, Sarawak, E Malaysia.*

AKALIMA, Anton. St Cypr Coll Lindi 71. **d** 74 **p** 75 Masasi. P Dio Masasi. *Box 16, Masasi, Tanzania.*

AKANBI, Hezekiah Folugbayimu. Melville Hall Ibad 47. **d** 49 Bp Phillips for Lagos **p** 51 Lagos. P Dio Lagos 51-52; Dio

Ondo-B 52-59. *P.O. Box 1, Ipetu-Ijesa, Nigeria.*

AKANBI, Joseph. b 35. Im Coll Ibad Dipl Th 72. **d** 72 **p** 73 Ekiti. P Dio Ekiti. *Emmanuel Anglican Church, Awo, Akiti, Nigeria.*

AKANDE, Joseph Kolawole. b 40. Im Coll Ibad 69. **d** 72 **p** 73 Lagos. P Dio Lagos. *St Matthew's Church, Imodi Box 12, Ijebu-Ode, Nigeria.*

AKANDU, Ven Albert Otimgba. b 19. Trin Coll Umuahia 54. **d** 56 **p** 57 Nig Delta. P Dio Nig Delta 56-72; Dio Aba from 72; Archd of Aba from 72. *Archdeaconry House, Abayi Umuocham, Box 43, Aba, Nigeria.*

AKANYA, Cornelius Alaiki. Im Coll Ibad 61. **d** 63 **p** 64 Ondo. P Dio Ondo. *Iyara, Kabba, Nigeria.*

AKAO, John Osemeikhian. b 43. Univ of Ibad BA 77. Im Coll Ibad 70. **d** 73 **p** 74 Ibad. P Dio Ibad. *c/o Ikereku P.A, via Ibadan, Nigeria.*

AKE, Godwin Abraham. Trin Coll Umuahia 60. **d** 62 **p** 63 Nig Delta. P Dio Nig Delta. *Parsonage, Okomoko-Egwi-Umuanyagwu, Egwi, Nigeria.*

AKECH, John Philip. d 65 **p** 67 Maseno. P Dio Maseno 65-70; Dio Maseno S from 70. *Box 135, Sare, Kenya.*

AKEHURST, Peter Russell. b 16. Univ of Reading BSc (Agric) 38. Trin Hall Cam. Wycl Hall Ox. **d** 48 **p** 49 Roch. C of Tonbridge 48-51; St Mark Kennington 51; St John Wynberg 51-62; Commiss in S Afr for Centr Tang 63-70; P-in-c of Bergvliet 62-66; Dir of Ch Expansion Dio Bloemf 66-69; Chap to Bp of Bloemf 69-70; R of Didsbury 70-74; Commiss Bloemf 72-81; C-in-c of Totland Bay Portsm 75; V 75-81. *14 Market Street, Abbotsbury, Weymouth, Dorset, DT3 4JR.*

AKELEY, Tom Cox. Johns Hopkins Univ BA 60. Seabury-W Th Sem BD 61. Pemb Coll Cam PhD 64. **d** 57 **p** 58 Maryland. [f in Amer Ch] C of St Luke Chesterton 60-61; Asst Prof Cant Coll Windsor Dio Huron from 64. *c/o Canterbury College, Windsor, Ont., Canada.*

AKEREDOLU, Ven Jeremiah Olatusi. St Andr Coll Oyo. **d** 46 **p** 47 Lagos. P Dio Lagos 46-56; Dio N Nig 56-64; Dio Ondo from 64; Hon Can of Ondo 66-68; Archd of Owo 69-78; Akoko from 78. *Box 23, Ikare-Akoko, Nigeria.*

AKERELE, Ven Ezekiel Sakede. Im Coll Ibad 58. **d** 60 **p** 61 N Nig. P Dio N Nig 60-80; Can of N Nig 75-80; Exam Chap and Archd Dio Kano from 80. *Box 170, Maiduguri, Nigeria.*

AKERLEY, George Charles. K Coll NS. **d** 53 **p** 54 Fred. R of Simonds 53-57; St Jas St John 57-63; Hampton 63-66; St Clem, Millidgeville, St John 66-75; Ketepec St John 74-75; St Phil Moncton Dio Fred from 75. *30 Lynch Street, Moncton, NB, Canada.*

AKERMAN, Roy. b 37. ALCD (1st cl) 63. **d** 63 **p** 64 Chelmsf. C of St Paul E Ham 63-67; Hornchurch 67-69; Area Sec CMS Dios Ox and Win 69-75; V of Ollerton 75-79; Boughton 75-79; N and S Leverton Dio Southw from 79. *North Leverton Vicarage, Retford, Notts.* (Gainsborough 880882)

AKI, Jackson O Brume. b 27. Im Coll Ibad 70. **d** and **p** 73 Benin. P Dio Benin. *St Matthew's Cathedral, Benin City, Nigeria.*

AKINBAMIJO, Ven Joseph Foluso. b 27. Melville Hall Ibad 55. **d** and **p** 56 Ondo-B. P Dio Ondo-B 56-62; Dio Ondo 62-68; Dio Lagos 68-76; Dio Ibad from 76; Hon Can of Lagos 71-75; Archd of Otan-Aiyegbaju from 76. *Rectory, Otan-Aiyegbaju, Nigeria.*

AKINBIYI, Gabriel Akinbolarin. b 49. Im Coll Ibad 78. **d** 81 Kaduna. d Dio Kaduna. *PO Box 64, Gusau, Sokoto State, Nigeria.*

AKINBOLA, Canon Clement Agboole. Melville Hall Ibad 55. **d** 57 **p** 58 Lagos. P Dio Lagos; Hon Can of Lagos from 72. *Vining Memorial Church, Ikeja, Lagos, Nigeria.*

AKINBOLA, Festus. b 25. **d** 71 **p** 73 Lagos. P Dio Lagos. *St Paul's Vicarage, Sojuolu, Box 98, Ifo, Nigeria.*

AKINBORO, Ezekiel Opeolu. Im Coll Ibad 59. **d** 61 Ibad **p** 62 Lagos. P Dio Lagos. *PO Box 10, Otta, Nigeria.*

AKINBOSEDE, Philip Olaolu. Im Coll Ibad. **d** 71 **p** 72 Ibad. P Dio Ibad. *PO Box 182, Ibadan, Nigeria.* (Ibad 61888)

AKINDUKO, Canon Moses Akintade. St Jo Coll Owo 46. **d** 55 **p** 56 Ondo-B. P Dio Ondo-B 55-62; Dio Ondo from 62; Hon Can of Ondo from 74. *Vicarage, Ijare, Ondo State, Nigeria.*

AKINGBESOTE, Gabriel Afolabi. b 36. Univ of Ibad BA 66. Im Coll Ibad 70. **d** 70 **p** 72 Ondo. P Dio Ondo; Prin Ekimogum Gr Sch from 76. *Ekimogum Grammar School, B'Olorunduro, Nigeria.*

AKINLADE, Timothy Adedokun Akinloye. Im Coll Ibad Dipl Th 67. **d** 67 **p** 68 Ibad. P Dio Ibad. *Pierre Benignus Study Centre, Box 4045, Ibadan, Nigeria.* (61784)

AKINLALU, Abraham Olaoluwa. Im Coll Ibad Dipl Th 77. **d** 77 **p** 78 Ondo. P Dio Ondo. *Box 4, Ondo, Nigeria.*

AKINLAWON, Moses Akinyele. b 46. Im Coll Ibad. **d** 76 **p** 77 Ibad. P Dio Ibad. *St Barnabas Anglican Church, Ogunrana, c/o Apatere PA, via Ibadan, Nigeria.*

AKINOLA, Daniel Alao. Im Coll Ibad 60. **d** 63 **p** 64 Ibad. P Dio Ibad 63-74. *St Paul's Church, Odo-Ona, PMB 5058, Ibadan, Nigeria.*

AKINOLA, Emmanuel Ladipo Abiodun. b 46. Univ of Ife BA 77. Im Coll Ibad 71. **d** 76 **p** 79 Ibad. P Dio Ibad. *University of Ife, Dept of Religious Studies, Ile-Ife, Nigeria.*

AKINOLA, Festus Akinyele. b 20. **d** 78 **p** 79 Ilesha. P Dio Ilesha. *Emmanuel Church, Oke-Ola, Ilesha, Nigeria.*

AKINREMI, Christopher Adebayo. Melville Hall Ibad 53. **d** 54 **p** 55 Ondo-B. P Dio Ondo-B 54-62; Dio Ondo 62-65; CF (Nigeria) from 66. *PMB 2022, Kaduna, Nigeria.*

AKINRINSOLA, Joshua Olatunji. b 13. **d** 73 Ekiti. d Dio Ekiti. *St Stephen's Vicarage, Ora, Ekiti, Nigeria.*

AKINSANPE, Canon Theophilus Peter Olasoji. Bp Phillips Hall Owo 56. **d** 56 **p** 57 Ondo-B. P Dio Ondo-B 56-62; Dio Ondo 62-66; Dio Ekiti from 66; Can of Ekiti from 66. *St Paul's Vicarge, Effon-Alaye, Ekiti, Nigeria.*

AKINSEYE, Joseph Edward Ibitayo. b 14. **d** 77 **p** 79 Ijebu. P Dio Ijebu. *Holy Trinity Church, Idomila, via Ijebu-Ode, Nigeria.*

AKINSOLA, David Babawale. Dipl Th (Lon) 59. Im Coll Ibad 56. **d** 59 Ibad **p** 60 Ondo-B for Ibad. P Dio Ibad. *Kutayi, Ibadan, Nigeria.*

AKINTADE, Olamide. d 77 Ondo. d Dio Ondo. *Box 20, Ile-Oluji, via Ondo, Nigeria.*

✠ **AKINTAYO, Right Rev Titus Ilori.** Melville Hall Ibad 50. **d** 52 **p** 53 Lagos. P Dio Lagos 52-71; Hon Can of Lagos 68-71; Provost of Ibad 71-77; Exam Chap to Bp of Ibad 71-77; Synod Sec Dio Ibad 72-77; Cons Ld Bp of Warri in St Matt Cathl Benin City 6 Aug 77 by Abp of w Afr; Bps of Lagos, Niger, Gambia, Nig Delta, Ibad, Ondo, N Nig, Ow, Ekiti, Enugu, Aba, Kum, Kwara. Ilesha, Egba-Egbado and Ijebu; res 79; Bp of Egba-Egbado 80. *Bishopscourt, Box 267, Ibara Abeokuta, Ogun State, Nigeria.* (039-230933)

AKINTEMI, Akinwunmi Abayomi. b 40. Univ of Ibad MB, BS 66. **d** 81 Ilesha. d Dio Ilesha. *St Peter's Vicarage, Isona, PO Box 118, Ilesha, Nigeria.*

✠ **AKINTEMI, Right Rev Isaac Bamidele Omowaiye.** Melville Hall Ibad 53. **d** and **p** 55 Ondo-B. Lect Bp Phillips Hall 55-76; Exam Chap to Bp of Ondo 63-76; Hon Can of Ondo 63-65; Provost 65-76; Synod Sec Dio Ondo 68-76; VG 71-72; Cons Ld Bp of Ijebu in Cathl Ch of St Steph Ondo 6 Aug 76 by Abp of W Africa; Bps of Aba, Gambia, Lagos, Ekiti, Kumasi, Ow, Ondo, Enugu, Kwara, Ilesha, Nig Delta, Niger and N Nig; and others. *Bishop's House, Box 112, Ijebu-Ode, Nigeria.*

AKINTOLA, Moses Olorundahunsi. b 12. **d** 74 **p** 76 Ondo. P Dio Ondo. *St Michael's Vicarage, Ero, Igbara Oke, via Akure, Nigeria.*

AKINWALE, Joseph Ifelodun. b 36. **d** 81 Ijebu. d Dio Ijebu. *St Thomas Church, Abigi, Ijebu Water-side, Nigeria.*

AKINWALE, Rufus Ayoade. Im Coll Ibad 70. **d** 71 **p** 72 Lagos. P Dio Lagos. *Holy Trinity Church, Ikate, Box 245, Surulere, Lagos, Nigeria.*

AKINWALE, Canon Wilfred Adebayo Titilayo. Im Coll Ibad 64. **d** 66 Bp Jadesimi for Ibad **p** 67 Ibad. P Dio Ibad 66-74; Dio Egba from 79; C of St Etheldreda w St Clem Fulham 74-75; Can of Egba from 79. *Christ Church, Iporo-Ake, Abeokuta, Nigeria.*

AKINWUNMI, Akinlabi Ademola. b 33. Lagos Univ BSc 68. **d** 79 **p** 81 Egba. P Dio Egba. *West African Breweries, PO Box 2246, Lagos, Nigeria.*

AKINYELE, Ven Gaddiel Olusegun. Dipl Th (Lon) 55. Im Coll Ibad 53. **d** Ondo-B for N Nig **p** N Nig 55. P Dio N Nig 55-56; Dio Ibad 57-76; Dio Egba from 76; Asst Master Oshogbo Gr Sch 57-66; Exam Chap to Bp of Egba from 76; Archd of Egba from 76; Syn Sec Dio Egba from 81. *Box 129, Abeokuta, Nigeria.*

AKINYELE, Jacob Ilesanmi. d 63 Ondo **p** 67 Ekiti. d Dio Ondo 63-67; P Dio Ekiti from 67. *St Mary's Girls' Secondary School, Ikole, Nigeria.*

AKINYELE, Olusegun Akinlolu. Im Coll Ibad 63. **d** 65 **p** 66 Ibad. P Dio Ibad 65-74. *St James's Vicarage, Box 324, Ibadan, Nigeria.*

AKINYEMI, Gabriel Eni-Olorunda. d 77 Ondo. d Dio Ondo. *Vicarage, Idogun, via Owo, Ondo, Nigeria.*

AKINYEMI, Canon Jude Oyeleye. Im Coll Ibad 62. **d** 64 **p** 65 Lagos. P Dio Lagos 64-77; Dio Ijebu from 77; Can from 79. *St John's Church, Okesopen, Nigeria.*

AKINYEMI, Michael Oluwakayode. b 47. Im Coll Ibad 73. **d** 76 **p** 77 Ibad. P Dio Ibad. *St James Anglican Church, Tonkere, via Edunabon, Ile-Ife, Nigeria.*

AKIRU, Christopher. d 74 **p** 76 Maseno N. P Dio Maseno N. *Box 185, Webuya, Kenya.*

AKIYAMA, John Yoshitaka. Coll Ho Ch Ch. **d** 54 Ch Ch.

C of Ashburton 54-55; in Ch of Japan from 55. *Immanuel Church, Tokushima, Japan.*

AKOL, Washington. **d** 76 **p** 77 Soroti. P Dio Soroti. *Nyero, Kumi County, South Teso, Soroti, Uganda.*

AKOMA, Very Rev Israel Enyinna. b 34. Univ of Nigeria BA 67. **d** 74 **p** 76 Aba. P Dio Aba; Provost of St Mich Cathl Aba from 80. *St Michael's Cathedral, Aba, Nigeria.*

AKOMOLEHIN, Raphael Aladejoye. b 42. Im Coll Ibad 74. **d** 77 **p** 78 Ibad. P Dio Ibad. *c/o Box 3075, Ibadan, Nigeria.*

AKOSILE, Benjamin Olayinka. Univ of Nigeria BSc 64. **d** 68 **p** 69 Ondo. P Dio Ondo; Prin Jubilee Gr Sch Ondo from 76. *Jubilee Grammar School, Ondo, Nigeria.*

AKPAIDA, Canon Paul Osikhokha. Melville Hall Ibad. **d** 57 **p** 58 Lagos. P Dio Lagos 57-76; Dio Egba from 76; Hon Can of Egba from 76. *Christ Church, Ajebo, Abeokuta, Nigeria.*

AKROFI, John Ofori. St Aug Coll Kumasi. **d** 52 **p** 53. P Dio Accra. *PO Box 1588, Accra, Ghana.*

AKUCHIGOMBO, Eriko. St Athan Th Coll Hegongo 24. **d** 25 **p** 26 Zanz. UMCA Miss Dio Zanz 25-26; Dio Masasi 26-55. *Nanyindwa, Masasi, Lindi, Tanzania.*

AKUM, Felix Nwachuku. Trin Coll Umuahia 54. **d** 56 **p** 57 Niger. P Dio Niger 56-59; Dio Ow 59-72. *St Matthew's Church, Nguru, Mbaise, Nigeria.*

AKUMIA, Samuel Osei Kodwo. b 22. **d** and **p** 74 Kum. P Dio Kum. *Box 1, Jachie, Ashanti, Ghana.*

AKUTU, Yolamu. **d** 46 **p** 48 U Nile. P Dio U Nile 46-60; Dio Soroti 60-76. *Odudui, Soroti, Uganda, E Africa .*

AKUWA, Canon Samuel Nwadiuku. Trin Coll Umuahia 59. **d** 61 **p** 62 Nig Delta. P Dio Nig Delta 61-68; Dio Niger from 69; Hon Can of Niger from 80. *St Peter's Church, Agulu, via Awka, Nigeria.*

AKYAB, Lord Bishop of. *See* Theaung Hawi, Right Rev Barnabas.

ALABI, David Adebayo. Im Coll Ibad 65. **d** 68 Bp Jadesimi for Ibad **p** 69 Ibad. P Dio Ibad. *St Mary's Vicarage, Igbaye, via Oshogbo, Nigeria.*

ALABI, John Oduola Mosobalaje. Im Coll Ibad 62. **d** 65 **p** 69 Lagos. P Dio Lagos 65-76; Dio Egba from 76. *Box 80, Ilaro, Nigeria.*

ALABI, Moses Rotimi. b 32. Im Coll Ibad 61. **d** 63 **p** 64 Lagos. P Dio Lagos. *St Peter's Church, Isara, Ijebu-Remo, Nigeria.*

ALABI, Samuel Ajayi. Im Coll Ibad 72. **d** 75 **p** 76 Ondo. P Dio Ondo. *Box 7, Akure, Nigeria.*

ALABI, Zaccheus Ola. b 51. Melville Hall Ibad 48. **d** 50 **p** 51 Lagos. P Dio Lagos 50-52 and from 55; Dio Ibad 52-55. *St Peter's Church, Magbon Alade, via Epe, Nigeria.*

ALAIS, Gerald. Moore Th Coll Syd 61, ACT ThL (2nd cl) 62. **d** 62 **p** 63 Syd. C of Randwick 62-64; C-in-c of Fairy Meadow 64-69; CF(Austr) from 69; R of St Pet Campbelltown Dio Syd from 78. *Rectory, Cordeaux Street, Campbelltown, NSW, Australia 2560.* (25-1041)

ALAMU, Joseph Olatunde. b 36. Univ of Ife BA 69. Im Coll Ibad 74. **d** 76 **p** 77 Ibad. P Dio Ibad. *St Luke's* (T.T.C) *Church, Molete, Ibadan, Nigeria.*

ALANYA, Canon John Sospeter. **d** 59 Momb **p** 61 Maseno. d Dio Momb 59-61; P Dio Maseno 61-70; Dio Maseno S from 70; Hon Can of Maseno S from 72. *Box 25, Songhor, Kenya.*

ALAO, David Adebayo. BD (Lon) 62. **d** 62 **p** 65 Ondo-B. P Dio Ondo-B 62-66; Dio Ibad from 66. *Grammar School, P.O. Box 21, Ibadan, Nigeria.*

ALAO, Raphael Sunday Oluwole. Im Coll Ibad 57. **d** 60 **p** 61 Ondo-B for Ibad. P Dio Ibad 60-67 and 69-76; Dio N Nig 67-69; C of St Nich Blundellsands 76-77. *Address temp unknown.*

ALASOMUKA, Canon Nicholas Adikitoruweri. b 15. Cranmer Hall Dur. **d** 55 **p** 57 Nig Delta. P Dio Nig Delta from 55; Can of Nig Delta from 72. *PO Box 4, Ahoada, Nigeria.*

ALAYANDE, Emmanuel Oladipo. MBE 62. Univ of Dur (Fourah Bay Coll) BA 46. **d** 50 **p** 51 Lagos. Prin of Ibad Gr Sch 50-68; Exam Chap to Bp of Ibad 54-59; Hon Can of Ibad 60-64; Can 64-76; Archd of Ibad 76-80. *Box 1903, Ibadan, Nigeria.*

ALBAN, Anthony Julian. St D Coll Lamp BA 34. **d** 34 **p** 35 S'wark. C of St John Battersea 34-39; Hemel Hempstead 39-45; CF 45-65; V of Endon w Stanley Dio Lich from 66. *Endon Vicarage, Stoke-on-Trent, Staffs.* (Stoke-on-Trent 502166)

ALBANY, Christopher. b 48. Univ of W Austr BSc 70. Trin Coll Melb BD 74. **d** and **p** 75 Perth. C of Wanneroo w Greenwood 75-76; Fremantle w Beaconsfield 77-78; R of Morawa-Perenjori Dio Perth from 78. *Rectory, Prater Street, Morawa, W Australia 6623.* (099-71 1190)

ALBANY, Edric George. **d** 39 **p** 41 St E. C of St Mary Virg Stoke Ipswich 39-42; CF (EC) 42-45; PC of Wareside 45-50; C of St Jo Bapt Felixstowe 50-51; R of Holton St Pet w Blyford R 51-56; PC of St Jas Goff's Oak Cheshunt 56-59; R of Merredin 59-61; Rosalie 61-63; Collie 63-66; Boyanup 66-68; C of Albany 68-69; P-in-c of St Bonif Cathl Bunb 69-71; R of Donnybrook 71-72; L to Offic Dio Bunb from 73. *7 Leslie Street, Mandurah, W Australia 6210.* (095-35 2923)

ALBANY, Jeremiah. b 04. **d** and **p** 74 Keew. C of Fort Severn Dio Keew from 74. *St Peter's Church, Fort Severn, via Central Patricia, Ont, Canada.*

ALBANY, John Brian. ALCD 40. **d** 40 **p** 41 Chelmsf. C of St Jas Forest Gate 40-44 (in c from 42); R of Farnham 44-49; Dioc Insp of Relig Educn Chelmsf 47-49; R of Morawa 49-58; P-in-c of Mingenew 53-58; Narrogin 58-63; Archd of Albany 60-64; Bunb 64-66; Dioc Missr Bunb 63-66; R of Mingenew 66-67; Moora 67-70; Kalamunda 70-77; Hon Can of Perth 76-78; Chap Parkerville Home 76-78; Perm to Offic Dio Perth from 77. *Parry House, Lesmurdie, W Australia 6076.* (291 6505)

ALBERTYN, Ven Charles Henry. Capetn Dioc Cl Sch 53. LTh 56. **d** 55 **p** 56 Capetn. C of Matroosfontein 55-60; P-in-c of St Helena Bay 60-64; C of Silvertown 64-71; P-in-c of Heideveld 71-76; Kraaifontein 76-78; Can of Capetn from 72; R of Bonteheuwel Dio Capetn from 78; Archd of Bellville from 81. *Priest's House, David Profit Street, Bonteheuwel, CP, S Africa.* (67-2215)

ALBERTYN, John Richard. b 08. **d** 73 **p** 76 Kimb K. P Dio Kimb K 73-81. *34 Carnation Avenue, Kimberley, CP, S Africa.* (Kimberley 41336)

ALBIN, Hugh Oliver. b 21. Late Scho and Sen Exhib Trin Coll Dub, 1st Cl Mod and Gold Medal in Ment and Mor Sc, Mod Ancient Hist and Pol Sc, BA 41; Mod Research Pri 41; Bp Forster and Downes Div Prems Div Test 43; MA 44; BD 46. **d** 44 **p** 45 Connor. C of Templecorran w Islandmagee 44-47; St Columba Knock Belf 47-52; Lect in Chr Eth QUB 50-52; R of Moston 52-57; V of Bethersden 57-69; St Dunstan w H Cross City and Dio Cant from 69. *St Dunstan's Vicarage, St Dunstan's Street, Canterbury, Kent.* (Canterbury 63654)

ALBISTON, Robert Graham. Montr Dioc Th Coll LTh 65. **d** 64 Montr. C-in-c of Mansonville 64-68; R of St Steph Lachine Montr 68-80. *145-45th Avenue, Apt 1, Lachine, PQ., Canada.* (514-637 7398)

ALBUTT, Alfred Victor. b 22. Cudd Coll Ox 70. **d** 71 Aston for Birm **p** 72 Birm. C of St Francis Bournville 71-74; Tettenhall Regis 74-77; R of Ashley Dio Lich from 77. *Ashley Rectory, Market Drayton, Salop, TF9 4LQ.* (063-087 2210)

ALBY, Harold Oriel. b 45. Univ of the Witwatersrand BA 68. **d** 71 **p** 72 Bp Carter for Johann. C of St Mary's Cathl Johann 71-75; R of Ermelo 75-78; Potchefstroom Dio Johann from 78. *Box 444 Potchefstroom 2520, Transvaal, S Africa.*

ALCOCK, Allan Reginald. Moore Th Coll Syd ACT ThL 64. **d** 64 **p** 65 Syd. C of St Andr Summer Hill 64-66; R of Clovelly Dio Syd from 67. *20 Arden Street, Waverley, NSW, Australia 2024.* (665-6535)

ALCOCK, Edwin James. b 31. K Coll Lon and Warm AKC 57. **d** 58 **p** 59 Lon. C of Old St Pancras w St Matt Oakley Square 58-62; St Andr Uxbridge 62-81; V of St Gabr N Acton Dio Lon from 81. *Vicarage, Balfour Road, W3 0DG.* (01-992 5938)

ALCOCK, Canon Reginald Noel. St Jo Coll Winnipeg. **d** 51 **p** 52 Edmon. I of St D Edmon 51-53; Mannville 53-55; P-in-c of Mayo 55-59; Elsa and Keno City 57-59; I of Winfield 59-61; St Barn Edmon 61-66; Grand Centre Dio Edmon from 66; Can of Edmon from 69. *Box 240, Grand Centre, Alta., Canada.* (403-594 3871)

ALCOCK, Richard. b 1899. OBE (Mil) 51. Wells Th Coll. **d** 63 **p** 64 Glouc. C of St Osw Coney Hill Glouc 63-67; St Phil and St Jas Leckhampton 67-69; Blockley w Aston Magna 69-73; Hon C 73-78. *Paxton House, Blockley, Moreton-in-the-Marsh, Glos.* (Blockley 213)

ALDER, Allen Edward. b 20. Univ of Wales BA 47. Coll of Resurr Mirfield 46. **d** 48 **p** 49 Llan. C of St Martin Roath 48-56; St Sav Roath 56-59; V of Abercwmboi 59-66; Trealaw 66-77; St Andr and St Teilo Cardiff Dio Llan from 77. *St Teilo's Vicarage, Flora Street, Cathays, Cardiff, CF2 4EP.* (Cardiff 32407)

ALDER, Eric Reginald Alfred. b 23. BA (Lon) 55. Chich Th Coll 70. **d** 71 **p** 72 Cant. C of Deal 71-80; P-in-c of Woodnesborough Dio Cant from 80; Staple Dio Cant from 80; Worth Dio Cant from 80. *Woodnesborough Vicarage, Sandwich, Kent, CT13 0HF.* (Sandwich 3056)

ALDER, Richard Aubrey. Fitzw Ho Cam BA 33, MA 44. Coll of Resurr Mirfield 34. **d** 37 **p** 38 Ches. C of Nantwich 37-40; St Paul Coppenhall Crewe 40-50; V of Appleton Thorn 50-75; L to Offic Dio Ches from 77. *48 Booth's Lane, Lymm, Chesh.*

ALDER, William. b 09. Ripon Hall Ox. **d** 55, **p** 56 Portsm. C of H Trin Fareham 55-59; R of Silchester 59-81; L to Offic

Dio Ox from 81. *17 Isis Close, Long Hanborough, Oxon, OX7 2JN.* (Freeland 882198)

ALDERMAN, John David. b 49. Univ of Man BA 71. Selw Coll Cam BA (Th) 79. Ridley Hall Cam 77. **d** 80 **p** 81 Win. C of Hartley Wintney Dio Win from 80. *40 Pool Road, Hartley Wintney, Basingstoke, Hants, RG27 8RD.*

ALDERSON, Albert George. b 22. K Coll Lon 46; St Bonif Coll Warm. **d** 50 **p** 51 Dur. C of Whitworth w Spennymoor 50-54; Min of Eccles Distr of St Francis S Shields 54-69; C-in-c 69-72; V of St Jude S Shields 69-72; R of Penshaw 72-79; P-in-c of Hawnby w Old Byland 79-80; Scawton w Cold Kirby 79-80; Bilsdale Midcable 79-80; R of U Ryedale Dio York from 80. *Scawton Rectory, Thirsk, N Yorks.*

ALDERSON, Christopher Derek. b 21. K Coll Lon and Warm AKC (2nd cl) 55. **d** 55 **p** 56 Chich. C of Goring 55-59; V of Gt Bentley 59-67; R of L Bentley 60-67; V of Dunster Dio B & W from 67. *The Priory, Dunster, Minehead, Somt.* (Dunster 265)

ALDERSON, Richard. b 1877. St Paul's Coll Burgh 06. Em Coll Sktn Div Test 12. Angl Th Coll BC LTh 24. **d** 10 **p** 12 Sask. R of St Pet Okotoks and RD of High River 13-16; I of St Agnes N Vanc 16-17; R of Armstrong BC 19-25; V of W Vale 25-30; Pickhill 30-35; R of Sawley Yorks 36; PC of Arkengarthdale 36-43; V of North Stainley 43-50; R of Wycliffe w Hutton Magna 50-54; L to Offic Dio Ripon from 54. *16 Birch Road, Barnard Castle, Co Durham.*

ALDERSON, Roger James. b 47. Univ of Lon BD 70, AKC 71. St Aug Coll Cant 70. **d** 71 Man **p** 72 Hulme for Man. C of St Mich AA Lawton Moor 71-74; Peel Green w Barton-on-Irwell 74-76; R of St Thos Heaton Norris Dio Man from 76. *6 Heaton Moor Road, Heaton Chapel, Stockport, SK4 4NS.* (061-432 1912)

ALDIS, Canon Brian Cyril. b 14. St Pet Hall Ox BA 36, MSc 38. Lon Coll of Div 39. **d** 40 **p** 41 Lon. C of St John Ealing Dean 40-43; St Mary Magd Addiscombe 43-46; V of St Sav Forest Gate 46-51; R of Hamworthy Dio Sarum from 51; Can and Preb of Sarum Cathl from 68; RD of Poole 68-75. *Hamworthy Rectory, Poole, Dorset.*

ALDIS, Gordon Hudson. b 05. St Edm Hall Ox BA 27, MA 54. **d** 31 **p** 33 W China. Miss (CIM) at Nanchung 31-36; Lanchung E Szech 36-42; Chap of Holy Light School Chunking (Soochow from 46) 43-50; Miss Hong Kong 51-52; Taiwan 52-76; Perm to Offic Dio St Alb from 77. *17 Byron Crescent, Bedford.*

ALDIS, John Arnold. b 43. Univ of Wales BA 65. BD (Lon) 67. Clifton Th Coll 68. **d** 69 **p** 70 Roch. C of Tonbridge 69-72; All S Langham Place Lon 72-77; Overseas Service Adv and Under Sec CMS 77-80; V of H Trin w St Jo Div City and Dio Leic from 80. *16 Shirley Avenue, Stoneygate, Leicester, LE2 3NA.* (Leic 704986)

ALDIS, Preb John Steadman. b 07. Magd Coll Cam BA (3rd cl Th Trip) 28, MA 42. Cudd Coll 42. **d** 43 **p** 44 Ox. C of Newport Pagnell 43-47; Aylesbury (in c of St Jo Evang) 47-49; V of St Mich Wood Green 49-68; RD of Tottenham 62-67; E Haringey 67-68; Preb of St Paul's Cathl Lon 63-75; Preb (Emer) from 75; Chap to Br Embassies Vienna Budapest and Prague 68-71; Bp's Chap Edmon 71-75; Commiss N and C Eur and Gibr 71-78; Hon Can of Gibr from 75; Hon C of All SS Edmonton 76-80; St Mary w St Jo Evang U Edmonton Dio Lon from 76. *12 Freshfield Drive, Southgate, N14 4QW.* (01-440 5893)

ALDRED, Donald Bottomley. b 30. K Coll Lon and Warm AKC 55. **d** 56 **p** 57 Wakef. C of Cudworth 56-59; Heckmondwike 59-62; V of Gomersal 62-69; Burley-in-Wharfedale Dio Bradf from 69; Chap Scalebor Pk Hosp from 69. *Burley-in-Wharfedale Vicarage, Ilkley, W Yorks., LS29 7DR.* (Burley-in-Wharfedale 863216)

ALDRIDGE, Christopher John. b 35. Trin Hall Cam 1st cl Cl Trip pt i 56, BA (2nd cl Cl Trip pt ii) 57, 3rd cl. Th Trip pt ii 59. MA 61. Ripon Hall Ox 59. **d** 60 Bp Maxwell for Leic **p** 61 Leic. C of Coalville 60-64; C-in-c of St Francis Clifton 64-72; V of Gospel Lane Dio Birm from 72. *237 Lakey Lane, Birmingham, B28 8QT.* (021-777 6132)

ALDRIDGE, Harold. b 35. Keble Coll Ox BA (3rd cl Mod Hist) 61, MA 71. Chich Th Coll 60. **d** 62 **p** 63 Lon. C of All SS w St Columb Notting Hill Kens 62-65; St Mary Abbots Kens 65-69; Asst Master Beech Hall Sch Macclesfield from 69; Perm to Offic Dio Ches from 69. *Beech Hall School, Macclesfield, Chesh.*

ALDRIDGE, Harold John. b 42. Dipl Th (Lon) 67. Oak Hill Th Coll 65. **d** 69 Hulme for Man **p** 70 Man. C of Rawtenstall 69-72; CMJ Ethiopia 72-76; C of Woodford Wells 76-79; Team V of Morebath, Oakford, Rackenford and Stoodleigh (Exe Valley Team Min) Dio Ex from 79. *Castleland, Oakfordbridge, Tiverton, Devon.* (Oakford 373)

ALDRIDGE, Canon Noel Mestaer. St Paul's Coll Grahmstn 41. **d** 43 **p** 44 Johann. C of Yeoville Johann 43-47; Krugersdorp 47-48; R of Standerton 48-51; Potchefstroom 51-56; Belgravia Johann 56-58; Robertsham Johann 58-65; St Kath Uitenhage 65-73; Boksburg Dio Johann from 73; Hon Can of Johann from 81. *Box 300, Boksburg, Transvaal, S Africa.* (011-52 1480)

ALDWORTH, Alexander William. d and **p** 55 Waik. P-in-c of Mokau 55-57; V of Ngaruawahia 57-59; Waitara 59-66; Okato 66-71; Perm to Offic Dio Waik from 71. *92 Taylor Street, Cambridge, NZ.* (Cam 7594)

ALEDARE, Jonathan. b 31. **d** 73 Ekiti. d Dio Ekiti. *St David's Vicarage, Afao, Ekiti, Nigeria.*

ALEGBELEYE, Canon Gabriel Oloruntola. d 42 **p** 43 Lagos. P Dio Lagos 42-52: Dio Ondo-B 52-62; Dio Ondo 62-64; Hon Can of Ondo from 64. *Holy Trinity Church, Odo Iwaro, Oka, Nigeria.*

ALEGBELEYE, Ven Isaiah Egbe Oluwafemi. Melville Hall Ibad 49. **d** 50 **p** 51 Lagos. P Dio Lagos 50-52; Dio Ondo-B 52-62; Dio Ondo 62-66; Dio Ekiti from 66; Can of Ekiti 66-69; Archd of Ekiti W from 69. *Christ Church Vicarage, Ijero-Ekiti, Nigeria.*

ALEKU, Misaki. Mukono Coll. **d** 58 **p** 60 U Nile. P Dio U Nile 58-60; Dio Soroti from 60. *Kyere, Uganda.*

ALEXANDER, Charles. Em Coll Sktn LTh 67. Univ of Winnipeg BTh 71. **d** 65 **p** 66 Bran. C of Snow Lake 65-67; R of Neepawa 67-71; C of St Steph, Calgary 71-74; R of St Jas City and Dio Calg from 74; Exam Chap to Bp of Calg from 78. *6351 Ranchview Drive NW, Calgary, Alta, Canada.*

ALEXANDER, Ernest William. b 08. AKC 34. **d** 34 **p** 36 Bp Golding-Bird for Guildf. C of Headley 34-37; Lakenham 37-38; St John Felixstowe 38-40; Gt Yarmouth (in c of St Paul) 40-42; R of Swanton Abbot w Skeyton 42-48; Chap RAFVR 44-46; R of Burgh Castle and of Belton 48-57; Acle 57-75; C-in-c of Beighton w Moulton 57-59; R 60-75; Perm to Offic Dio Guildf from 75. *1 Glebe Cottage, Newdigate, Dorking, Surrey, RH5 5AA.* (Newdigate 587)

ALEXANDER, Francis Robert. b 10. Trin Coll Dub BA 32, Div Test 33, MA and BD 38. **d** 33 **p** 34 Dub. C of St Geo Dub 33-36; St Cath Dub 36-40; H Trin Rathmines 40-43; I of Athy w Kilberry 43-48; Clondalkin w Tallaght (and Rathcoole from 63) 48-80; RD of Taney 65-76; Can of Ch Ch Cathl Dub 70-80; Preb 78-80. *1 Rostrevor Road, Rathgar, Dublin 6, Irish Republic.*

ALEXANDER, Fraser Roland. Rhodes Univ S Afr BA 49, LTh 51. St Paul's Coll Grahmstn 50. **d** 51 **p** 52 Johann. C of Malvern Johann 51-53; Rosettenville 53-54; R of Bloemhof and P-in-c of Bloemhof Miss 54-59; Vanderbijl Pk 59-65; Kens Johann 65-77; R of Robertsham Dio Johann from 77. *38 Frimley Road, Robertsham, Johannesburg, S Africa.* (011-830 3611)

ALEXANDER, Graham Brian. b 47. Univ of the Witwatersrand BSc 68. **d** 80 Bp Ndwandwe for Johann (NSM). C of Benoni Dio Johann from 80. *88 Edward Street, Benoni, S Africa 1500.*

ALEXANDER, Hugh Crighton. b 03. Qu Coll Cam BA 24, MA 30. Ridley Hall Cam 29. **d** 30 **p** 31 Birm. C of St John Sparkhill 30-33; Henbury (in c of Aust and Northwick) 33-37; V of St Aug Plymouth 37-46; Uffculme 46-58; RD of Cullompton 51-54; PC of St Francis Sarum 58-64; R of Hazelbury Bryan w Stoke Wake 64-71; Fifehead Neville w Fifehead St Quintin 64-71; Mappowder 67-71. *The Corner House, Keinton Mandeville, Somerton, Somt.*

ALEXANDER, James Crighton. b 43. Qu Coll Cam 2nd cl Th Trip pt i 63, BA (2nd cl Th Trip pt ii) 65, MA 69. Cudd Coll 68. **d** 68 **p** 69 Heref. C of Much Wenlock w Bourton 68-72; V of Oakington Dio Ely from 72. *Oakington Vicarage, Cambridge, CB4 5AL.* (Histon 2396)

ALEXANDER, Canon James Douglas. b 27. Linc Th Coll 57. **d** 58 **p** 59 Linc. C of Frodingham 58-61; V of Alvingham w N and S Cockerington 61-65; V of Keddington 61-65; R of Gunhouse w Burringham 65-69; Peterhead 69-76; St Mary City and Dio Aber from 76; Can of Aber Cathl from 79. *28 Stanley Street, Aberdeen.* (0224-25491)

ALEXANDER, Ven John James. K Coll NS BA 24, Hon DCnL 54. **d** and **p** 27 Fred. Asst Chap Rothesay Colleg Sch Fred 27-28; C of Moncton 28-32; R 32-66; Archd of Chatham 57-67; Archd (Emer) from 67. *141 Cameron Street, Moncton, NB, Canada.*

ALEXANDER, Kelsick Ernest. b 1897. G and C Coll Cam 19. Knutsford Test Sch 23. Sarum Th Coll 25. **d** 34 **p** 35 Sarum. C of Wyke Regis 34-39; V of Kenton 39-66; L to Offic Dio Ex from 66. *10 Portland Avenue, Higher Woodway, Teignmouth, Devon.*

ALEXANDER, Ven Leopold Douglas. St Paul's Th Coll Grahmstn. **d** 48 **p** 49 Johann. C of Boksburg 48-50; Germiston w Primrose 50-52; R of Primrose Dio Johann 52-56; C of Gt Greenford 57-59; R of Klerksdorp 59-64; St Alb Johann 64-67; Regent Hill Johann 68-70; Randfontein Dio Johann from 78; Archd of W Transv 71-75; Archd of W Rand 71-75; Klerksdorp 75-78; Vereeniging from 75. *5 Benson Avenue, Randfontein 2520, S Africa.*

ALEXANDER, Michael George. b 47. Sarum Wells Th

Coll 74. **d** 77 **p** 78 Lich. C of St Thos Wednesfield 77-80; Tettenhall Wood Dio Lich from 80. *12 Windmill Lane, Castlecroft, Wolverhampton, WV3 8HJ.* (Wolv 761170)

ALEXANDER, Norman William. b 27. Chich Th Coll 54. **d** 56 **p** 57 S'wark. C of St Cath Hatcham Pk 56-59; Horley 59-61; V of Markington w S Stainley 61-69; R of Mutford w Rushmere (w Gisleham and N Cove w Barnby from 72) 69-74; C-in-c of Gisleham 69-72; C-in-c of N Cove w Barnby 69-72; R of W Winch 74-81; V of Frensham Dio Guildf from 81. *Frensham Vicarage, Farnham, Surrey.* (025-125 2137)

ALEXANDER, Oswald Carlton. b 25. **d** 80 Trin. C of St Faith Rio Claro Dio Trin from 80. *St Faith's Rectory, Rio Claro, Trinidad, WI.*

ALEXANDER, Reginald Claude. b 34. St Pet Th Coll Alice CP 67. **d** 69 Capetn. C of Resurr Bonteheuwel 69-73; R of St Mich AA Port Eliz 74-76; P-in-c of Heideveld Dio Capetn from 76. *Priest's House, Bailey Crescent, Heideveld, CP, S Africa.* (67-5426)

ALEXANDER, Robert. b 37. Univ of Lon LLB (2nd cl) 60. St Cath Coll Ox BA (2nd cl Th) 62. St Steph Ho Ox 60. **d** 63 **p** 64 Lon. C of St Mary Abbots, Kens 63-68; St Jo Notting Hill Kens Dio Lon 71-74; Team V 75-79; St Jas City and Dio Syd from 79. *5/31 Alexandra Street, Drummoyne, NSW, Australia 2047.* (232-3592)

ALEXANDER, Wilfred Robert Donald. b 35. TCD BA (2nd cl Mod) 58, MA 80. **d** and **p** 63 Dub. C of Raheny w Coolock 63-67; Min Can of St Patr Cathl Dub 65-67; Hon C of Herne Hill 68-70; Asst Master Gosforth Grammar Sch 71-76; Chap St Mary and St Anne Sch Abbots Bromley 76-80; V of Cauldon Dio Lich from 80; Waterfall Dio Lich from 80; P-in-c of Calton Dio Lich from 80; Grindon Dio Lich from 80. *Vicarage, Waterfall Lane, Waterhouses, Stoke-on-Trent, Staffs, ST10 3HT.*

ALEXANDER-SMITH (formerly SMITH), Peter Donald. **d** 64 **p** 65 Adel. C of St John Salisbury 64-66; Glandore 66-67; Supt St Mary's Miss Alice Springs 66-70; V of Miles 70-73; C of Toowoomba 73-75; P-in-c of Northfield 75-76. *c/o 10 Stewart Avenue, Northfield, S Australia 5085.*

ALFLATT, Malcolm. b 35. Late Pri of Bp's Univ Lennox BA 64. BD (Lon) 69. Univ of New Brunsw MA 74. FCA 68. Wells Th Coll 64. **d** 66 Ripon **p** 68 Fred. C of St Marg Leeds 66-67; I of Ludlow w Blissfield 68-70; Bright 70-77; New Carl Queb 77-81; C of St Osw Millhouses Abbeydale City and Dio Sheff from 81. *64 Glenorchy Road, Sheffield, S7 2EN.* (Sheff 581871)

ALFORD, John. b 35. Univ of Nottm BSc 58. Qu Coll Birm 75. **d** 77 **p** 78 Lich (APM). C of Edgmond Dio Lich from 77. *23 Shrewsbury Road, Edgmond, Newport, Salop.*

ALFORD, Ven John Richard. b 19. Fitzw Ho Cam 2nd cl Hist Trip pt i 40, BA (2nd cl Hist Trip pt ii) 41, MA 47. Cudd Coll 41. **d** 43 **p** 44 Wakef. C of St Paul King Cross Halifax 43-47; Wakef Cathl 47-50; Tutor Wells Th Coll and PV of Wells Cathl 50-55; Publ Pr Dio B and W 51-55; LPr and Vice-Prin of Qu Coll Birm 55-67; Exam Chap to Bp of Kimb K 61-65; V of Shotwick 67-72; Dom Chap to Bp of Ches 67-72; Exam Chap to Bp of Ches 67-72; to Bp of Wakef from 72; Dir of Ordinands Dio Ches 67-72; Hon Can of Ches 69-72; Can (Emer) from 72; Archd of Halifax from 72; Can Res of Wakef from 73. *5 South Parade, Wakefield, Yorks, WF1 1LR.* (Wakefield 378532)

ALFORD, Sidney Edward. b 06. AKC 33. **d** 33 **p** 34 Lon. C of St Barn Homerton 33-38; St John Whetstone 38-43; V of St Barn Homerton 43-81; Chap Hackney Hosp 43-48; Hon Sec Chr Evidence S 70-81. *The Cottage, Dunton Hills Farm, E Horndon, Essex, CM13 3LY.* (Brentwood 811731)

ALGAR, John Herbert. b 29. Tyndale Hall Bris 54. **d** 57 **p** 58 Derby. C of Stapenhill 57-61; Willesborough 61-69; V of Tipton Dio Lich from 69. *Tipton Vicarage, Dudley Port, Tipton, W Midl.* (021-557 1902)

ALGOMA, Lord Bishop of. *See* Nock, Right Rev Frank Foley.

ALGOMA, Dean of. (Vacant)

ALGREEN-USSING, Allen. St Barn Coll Adel. **d** 75 **p** 76 St Arn. C of Mildura 75-77; R of Avoca Dio Bend from 77. *Rectory, Rutherford Street, Avoca, Vic, Australia 3467.*

ALIGAWESA, Canon Voeri. **d** 39 **p** 40 Ugan. P Dio Ugan 39-60; Dio W Bugan from 60; Can of W Bugan from 63. *Church of Uganda, Kagulwe, Box 101, Mpigi, Uganda.*

ALIGO, Martin Wani. Bp Gwynne Coll Mundri. **d** and **p** 63 Sudan. P Dio Sudan. *ECS, Yei, Sudan.*

ALIMWIKE, Frank David. St Cypr Th Coll Tunduru 57. **d** 59 **p** 62 Masasi. P Dio Masasi. *PB Masasi, Mtwara Region, Tanzania.*

ALIU, Luke Ayo. Trin Coll Umuahia. **d** 63 **p** 64 Benin. P Dio Benin 63-72. *c/o St John's Church, Ora, Nigeria.*

ALKER, Adrian. b 49. Wadh Coll Ox BA 70. Univ of Lanc MA 71. Ripon Coll Cudd 77. **d** 79 **p** 80 Liv. C of W Derby Dio Liv from 79. *2 The Village, West Derby, Liverpool 12.*

ALLAN, Andrew John. b 47. Westcott Ho Cam 76. **d** 79 **p** 80 Cant. C of All SS Whitstable Dio Cant from 79. *St Andrew's Church House, Saddleton Road, Whitstable, Kent.*

ALLAN, Archibald Blackie. b 35. Edin Th Coll 57. **d** 60 **p** 61 Aber. C of St John Aber 60-63; St Paul's Cathl Dundee 63-68; P-in-c of St Clem, Aber 68-76; Vice-Provost of Aber Cathl from 76. *10 Louiseville Avenue, Aberdeen, AB1 6TX.* (Aberdeen 36984)

ALLAN, Arthur Ashford. b 18. Kelham Th Coll 39. **d** 44 **p** 45 S'wark. C of Ch Ch Streatham 44-48; St Mich AA S Beddington 48-51; Min of St Barn Conv Distr Coulsdon 51-57; V of St Pet Penhill 57-67; Brislington 67-76; P-in-c of Coalpit Heath 76-80. *4 Homer Close, Bratton Fleming, Barnstaple, Devon.* (Brayford 556)

ALLAN, Arthur Murray. Oak Hill Th Coll 62. **d** 63 **p** 64 Lon. C of St Paul Portman Square 63-67; I of Holland Manit 67-68. *4109 Louisiana Street, San Diego, Calif. 92104, USA.*

ALLAN, Brian Douglas. b 51. Carleton Univ Ott BA 71. Montr Dioc Coll BTh 80. **d** and **p** 80 Ott. C of Clarendon Dio Ott 80; I from 80. *Box 278, Shawville, Quebec, Canada, J0X 2Y0.*

ALLAN, Donald. Moore Th Coll Syd ACT ThL (2nd cl) 57. **d** and **p** 59 N Queensld. C of Atherton 59-60; Mayfield 61-63; Adamstown 63-64; P-in-c of Dora Creek 64-70; Swansea 70-74. *c/o 28 Josephson Street, Swansea, NSW 2281, Australia.*

ALLAN, Donald James. b 35. Sarum Th Coll 63. **d** 65 **p** 66 Man. C of St Paul Royton 65-71; V of Middleton Junction 71-78; R-desig of Gtr Shelswell Group. *Finmere Rectory, Valley Road, Finmere, Nr Buckingham, MK18 4AS.* (028-04 7184)

ALLAN, Douglas John. Ridley Coll Melb 60. ACT ThL 63. **d** 63 Bp Sambell for Melb **p** 64 Melb. C of Mornington 63-65; Melb Dioc Task Force 65-66; Min of Lorne 66-68; I of Sunbury 68-72; Perm to Offic Dio Melb from 76. *8-43 Armadale Street, Armadale, Vic, Australia 3143.*

✠ **ALLAN, Right Rev Hugh James Pearson.** Univ of Manit BA 57. St Jo Th Coll Winnipeg LTh 56, Hon DD 74. **d** 54 **p** 55 Rupld. C of St Aidan Winnipeg 54-55; All SS Winnipeg 55-56; I of Peguis Ind Reserve 56-60; R of St Mark St Vital Winnipeg 60-68; Hon Can of St Jo Cathl Winnipeg 66-68; R of Swift Current Dio Qu'App 68-70; Dean and R of St Paul's Pro-Cathl Regina 70-74; Cons Ld Bp of Keew in St Alb Cathl Kenora 7 May 74 by Abp of Rupld; Bps of Athab, Bran and Rupld. *Bishopstowe, Box 118, Kenora, Ont., Canada.* (807-468 5655)

ALLAN, Peter George. b 50. Wadham Coll Ox BA 72, MA 76. Univ of Leeds Dipl Th 74. Coll of Resurr Mirfield 72. **d** 75 **p** 76 St Alb. C of Stevenage 75-78; St Mary Virg City and Dio Ox from 78; Chap Wadh Coll Ox from 78. *22 Stratford Street, Oxford, OX4 1SW.* (Ox 47592)

ALLAN, Peter William. St Mich Ho Crafers 71. **d** and **p** 73 N Terr. C of Alice Springs 73-76; St Jas Toowoomba 76-77; Ch Ch St Lucia Brisb 77-78; P-in-c of Kangaroo Point 78-80; Ecumen Chap to Tertiary Insts Dio Brisb from 80. *455 Main Street, Kangaroo Point, Queensland, Australia 4169.*

ALLAN, Preb Philip Andrew. b 10. Late Rustat Exhib of Jes Coll Cam 3rd cl Cl Trip pt i 31, BA (2nd cl Anthrop and Archaeol Trip pt i) 32, MA 51. Wells Th Coll 32. **d** 34 **p** 35 B and W. C of Hendford 34-42; V of S Petherton 42-51; PC of Lopen 42-51; RD of Crewkerne 50-51; PC of Wincanton 51-62; Surr from 52; RD of Bruton 53-62; Preb of Wells Cathl from 57; V of Ilminster w Whitelackington 62-75. *Red Cottage, Fore Street, Milverton, Taunton, Somt.* (Milverton 400460)

ALLAN, Robert Clifford. **d** 41 **p** 42 Bradf. L to Offic Dio Bradf and Dioc Youth Chap 41-46; V of Thornton-in-Lonsdale 46-54; Tosside 57-67. *Lower Pythorns, Wigglesworth, Skipton, Yorks.* (Long Preston 315)

ALLAN, Stuart Wayne. b 46. Univ of NB. BA 69. Univ of K Coll Halifax MDiv 72. **d** 72 **p** 73 Fred. C of Cam w Waterborough 72-73; R 73-75; Hammond River Dio Fred from 75. *RR 309-20, Rothesay, NB, Canada.*

ALLAN, Ysbrand Gadsonides. b 09. Codr Coll Barb. **d** and **p** 49 Antig. R of Anguilla 49-52; P-in-c of St Martin 49-52; Aruba 52-54; Saba 54-60; P-in-c of St Bart and of St Eustatius WI 59-60; C of St Barn Pimlico Westmr 62; Blakenall Heath 62-66; C-in-c of St Chad's Conv Distr Tunstall Staffs 66-72; Chap All SS Conv Lon Colney 72-73; Birm 73-77. *681 Alum Rock Road, Birmingham, B8 3JA.*

ALLANDER, William Edward Morgell Kidd. b 15. TCD BA and Div Test 37, MA 40. **d** 38 Down **p** 39 Bp Kennedy for Down. C of St Columba Knock Belf 38-43; Hd of Trin Coll Miss Belf 43-46; L to Offic Dio Lon 46-51; C of Foleshill 53-55; P-in-c of St Chad Cov 55-57; V 57-64; Atherstone 64-73; I of Rathcooney Dio Cork from 73. *Glanmire Rectory, Cork, Irish Republic.* (Cork 821098)

ALLARD, John Ambrose. b 30. Bps' Coll Cheshunt 63. **d** 65 Barking for Chelmsf **p** 66 Chelmsf. C of St Marg Leigh

65-69; C-in-c of Rawreth 69-70; R 70-72; R of Rettendon 71-72; V of St Francis of Assisi Barkingside Dio Chelmsf from 72. *Vicarage, Fencepiece Road, Barkingside, Ilford, Essex.* (01-500 2970)

ALLARD, Victor James. b 13. SOC 65. **d** 68 Kens for Lon **p** 69 Lon. Hdmaster of Isleworth C of E Primary Sch 59-73; C of Isleworth 68-73; Stansted Mountfitchet 73-80; Mayfield Dio Chich from 80. *Holmstall Oast Cottage, Five Ashes, Mayfield, TN20 6NG.* (Mayfield 3430)

ALLARDICE, Alexander Edwin. b 49. Chich Th Coll 73. **d** 76 Lich **p** 77 Stafford for Lich. C of Rugeley 76-79; St Jo Bapt Felixstowe 79-81; Team V of St Francis Ipswich Dio St E from 81. *29 Belmont Road, Ipswich, Suffolk.*

ALLASSEH, Canon Mercy Dokubo Samuel. Trin Coll Umuahia 56. **d** 58 **p** 59 Nig Delta. P Dio Nig Delta; Can of Nig Delta from 77. *Box 54, Port Harcourt, Nigeria.*

ALLCHIN, Canon Arthur Macdonald. b 30. Ch Ch Ox BA (2nd cl Mod Hist) 51, MA 55, BLitt 56. Th Inst Bucharest Hon DD 77. Cudd Coll 54. **d** 56 **p** 57 Lon. C of St Mary Abbots Kens 56-60; Ed 'Sobornost' 60-77; Jt Ed 'Chr' from 76; Libr Pusey Ho Ox 60-69; Exam Chap to Bp of Pet 66-73; Lect Gen Th Sem NY 67-68; Warden Commun of Sisters of the Love of God, Ox from 68; Can Res of Cant from 73; Exam Chap to Abp of Cant from 73. *12 The Precincts, Canterbury, Kent, CT1 2EH.* (Canterbury 63060)

ALLCHIN, Maurice Usmar. b 05. St Jo Coll Dur. **d** 50 **p** 51 Worc. C of St Jas Dudley 50-51; H Trin Worc 51-53; V of Himbleton and PC of Huddington 53-57; V of Castle Donington 57-73. *7 Elmpark Gardens, Selsdon, Surrey, CR2 8RW.*

ALLCHIN, Norman Edward. Univ of Melb BA 66, MA 73. Ridley Coll Melb ACT ThL 56. **d** 59 **p** 60 Adel. C of H Trin Adel 59-63; Perm to Offic Dio Melb 64-73; Chap Macleod High Sch 64-69; Lect Ridley Coll Melb from 69-73; Dioc Consultant Dept of Chr Educn and L to Offic Dio Melb 73-76; I of Ch Ch Hawthorn 76-78; Forest Hill Dio Melb from 78. *321 Canterbury Road, Forest Hill, Vic, Australia 3131.* (878 1831)

ALLCOCK, Arthur Charles Horace. b 12. AKC 36. **d** 36 **p** 37 Lich. C of Darlaston 36-39; Stockport 39-40; CF (EC) 40-46; V of Water Orton 46-49; CF 49-66; Perm to Offic Dio Ex 66-68; and from 79; R of E Bickleigh 68-76; R of Cadeleigh 68-76. *Mount Pleasant, Poughill, Crediton, Devon.*

ALLCOCK, David. b 28. Coll of Resurr Mirfield. **d** 66 **p** 67 Lich. C of St Chad Shrewsbury 66-70; Asst Chap K Coll Taunton 70-71; Chap 71-78; Shrewsbury Sch from 78. *The Schools, Shrewsbury, SY3 7AP.* (Shrewsbury 3203)

ALLCOCK, Peter Michael. b 37. Oak Hill Th Coll 65. **d** 68 **p** 69 S'wark. C of St Matthias U Tulse Hill 68-71; Dunkeswell 71-72; P-in-c of Luppitt 72-75; Monkton 72-75; V of Okehampton w Inwardleigh 75-80; Surr 76-80; Team V of Solihull Dio Birm from 80. *c/o Rectory, Church Hill Road, Solihull, W Midl.*

ALLDRIT, Nicolas Sebastian Fitz-Ansculf. b 41. St Edm Hall Ox BA 63, MA 69, DPhil 69. Cudd Coll 72. **d** 72 **p** 73 S'wark. C of Limpsfield w Titsey 72-81; Tutor and NT Lect Linc Th Coll from 81. *1 Greestone Terrace, Lincoln.* (Linc 37339)

ALLEN, Andrew Stephen. b 55. Univ of Nottm BPharm 77. MPS. St Steph Ho Ox 78. **d** 81 Barking for Chelmsf. C of St Mary Gt Ilford Dio Chelmsf from 81. *2 Elizabeth Avenue, Great Ilford, Essex, IG1 1TU.*

ALLEN, Anthony Stuart. Kelham Th Coll. **d** 62 S'wark. C of Old Charlton 62. *89 Cheviot Gardens, NW2.*

ALLEN, Brian Stanley. b 24. Roch Th Coll 65. **d** 67 **p** 68 Roch. C of St Pet w St Marg (w St Nich and St Clem from 72) Roch 67-74; C-in-c of St John Drypool 74-80; Team V 80; V of Marlpool Dio Derby from 80. *Marlpool Vicarage, Heanor, Derbys, DE7 7BP.* (Langley Mill 2097)

ALLEN, Canon Bruce Horwood. St Paul's Th Coll Grahmstn 60. **d** 63 **p** 64 Grahmstn. C of St Sav E London 63-64; St Mich AA Queenstn 64-67; R of Barkly E 67-72; All SS Orange Grove E Lon 72-78; Sub-Dean of Cathl Ch of St Mich and St Geo Grahmstn from 78; Can of Grahmstn from 81. *Box 102, Grahamstown 6140, S Africa.*

ALLEN, Bruce Owen. b 14. Univ of Lon BA 37. Clifton Th Coll. **d** 39 **p** 40 Chelmsf. C of Leyton 39-42; St Mary Deane 42-46; C-in-c of Lostock Conv Distr 46-51; V of Hopwood 51-65; Topcliffe w Dalton and Dishforth 65-81. *Minerva, Bormans Lane, North Thoresby, Grimsby.* (N Thoresby 425)

ALLEN, Byron Cecil. **d** 75 Ja (APM). C of Mona Heights Dio Ja from 75. *4 Erin Avenue, Boulevard PA, St Andrew, Jamaica, WI.*

ALLEN, Christopher Dennis. b 50. Fitzw Coll Cam BA 73, MA 77. Ripon Coll Cudd 76. **d** 76 **p** 77 Pet. C of St Andr Kettering 76-79; H Spirit Bretton Dio Pet from 79. *98 Benland, Bretton, Peterborough.* (Pet 269196)

ALLEN, Christopher Leslie. b 56. Univ of Leeds BA 78. St Jo Coll Nottm 79. **d** 80 **p** 81 Birm. C of St Martin City and Dio Birm from 80. *3 Ashdown Close, Moseley, Birmingham, B13 9ST.* (021-449 5906)

ALLEN, David. b 38. **d** 76 **p** 77 Llan. C of Fairwater Dio Llan from 76. *16 Restways Close, Llandaff, Cardiff, CF5 2SB.*

ALLEN, David Newall. **d** 65 Bradf. C of Allerton 65; L to Offic Dio Newfld 74-75; Hon d of Vic Pk Dio Man from 75. *St John Chrysostom's Rectory, Daisy Bank Road, Victoria Park, Manchester 14.*

ALLEN, Derek Milton. b 45. Univ of Bradf BTech 67. Univ of Man BD 80. Oak Hill Coll 80. **d** 81 Man. C of Ch Ch Chadderton Dio Man from 81. *23 Lindale Avenue, Chadderton, Oldham, Lancs, OL9 9DW.*

ALLEN, Derek William. b 25. Or Coll Ox BA (2nd cl Phil Pol and Econ) 49 (1st cl Th 51) MA 54. St Steph Ho Ox 50. **d** 52 **p** 53 Lon. C of Ch the Sav Ealing 52-54; Tutor of St Steph Ho Ox 54-56; Chap 56-60; L to Office Dio ox 55-60 and from 62; Asst Chap Pemb Coll Ox 55-60; Lect in Th K Coll Lon and Sub-Warden K Coll Hostel 60-62; Prin St Steph Ho Ox 62-74; Warden Commun of St Mary Virg Wantage 66-80; Commiss Accra from 68; Damar from 70; Exam Chap to Bp of Accra 68-73; to Bp of Nor 71-76; Chap and Sub-Warden of Congregation of the Servants of Christ Burnham 75-81; V of St Sav w St Pet Eastbourne Dio Chich from 76; Exam Chap to Bp of Chich from 80; Warden of Conv of the H Rood Lindfield from 81. *Vicarage, Spencer Road, Eastbourne, Sussex, BN21 4PA.* (Eastbourne 22317)

ALLEN, Preb Donovan Bawden. b 14. Keble Coll Ox BA 36, MA 40. Westcott Ho Cam 36. **d** 38 **p** 39 Lich. C of Whitchurch w Dodington 38-42; Chap RNVR 42-46; Men in Disp 45; C of H Trin South Shore Blackpool 47-49; R of Mucklestone 49-57; Bridgnorth w Tasley 57-68; C-in-c of Astley Abbots 61-68; Surr 64-68; R of Berrington w Betton Strange 68-80; Chap Cross Ho Hosp 68-80; Preb of Heref 73-80; Preb (Emer) from 80. *13 Claremont Hill, Shrewsbury, Salop.*

ALLEN, Douglas Geoffrey. **d** 58 **p** 73 St Arn. Hon C of Mildura Dio St Arn (Dio Bend from 77) from 58. *1a Cedar Avenue, Mildura, Vic, Australia 3500.* (050-23 2481)

ALLEN, Edward Charles. b 22. Bps' Coll Cheshunt. **d** 50 **p** 51 Ex. C of St Andr w St Cath Plymouth 50-52; Epsom 52-57; Burgh Heath 57-60; V of E Molesey Dio Guildf from 60. *Vicarage, St Mary's Road, East Molesey, Surrey, KT8 0ST.* (01-979 1441)

ALLEN, Canon Eric. b 1898. AKC (2nd cl) 23. **d** 23 **p** 24 Bradf. C of St Paul Manningham 23-27; on staff of Bp in Kobe 27-30; P-in-c of St Pet Kobe 30-40; SPG Treas Dio Kobe 35-42; Exam Chap to Bp of Kobe 37-40; V of St Osw Bradf 43-51; Langcliffe w Stainforth 51-76; Hon Can of Bradf 74-76; Can (Emer) from 76; Perm to Offic Dio Bradf from 76. *9 Town Head, Settle, N Yorks.*

ALLEN, Eric Thomas. b 12. Qu Coll Cam 2nd cl Geog Trip pt i 38. BA (3rd cl Geog Trip pt ii) 39, MA 43. Lon Coll of Div 39. **d** 40 **p** 41 Liv. C of Sutton Dio Liv 40-43; Normanton-by-Derby 43-46; Org Sec SE Distr CMJ 46-47; Youth Sec CMJ 47-52; Educn Sec 52-54; Actg Chap St Luke Haifa 51-52; V of Stoughton 54-60; R of Radipole 60-76; C-in-c of Buckland Ripers 68-70; R 70-74. *435 Dorchester Road, Weymouth, Dorset, DT3 5BN.*

ALLEN, Ernest. b 1889. Univ of Alberta 21. **d** 28. **p** 29 Chelmsf. C of St Mary Plaistow 28-33; V of Hatfield Heath 33-36; Milnrow Dio Man 36-44; Area Sec CMS Dios Chich, Guildf and Portsm 44-49; Perm to Offic Dio Guildf 44-49; V of H Trin Sheerness 49-58; River 58-63. *20 Oakmount Avenue, Highfield, Southampton.*

ALLEN, Ernest Tarrant. b 1897. Jes Coll Cam BA 21, Mus Bac 24, MA 25. Westcott Ho Cam 23. **d** 27 **p** 28 S'wark. C of Clapham 27-29; St John (in c of St Edm) Felixstowe 29-30; V of King's Bromley 30-43; Chan V of Lich Cathl 30-40; Dean's V 41-43; V of St Aug Vic Pk 43-45; W Wycombe 45-53; R of St Bride Glas 53-64; PC of Nordelph 64-75; Perm to Offic Dio Ely from 75. *18 The Lane, Hauxton, Cambridge, CB2 5HP.* (Cam 871210)

ALLEN, Canon Francis Arthur Patrick. Em Coll Sktn Div Test 52. **d** 51 **p** 52 Sask. C-in-c of Nipawin 51-52; Miss at Meadow Lake 52-54; Medstead 54-57; C of St Nich Bp Wearmouth 57-59; Chap Miss to Seamen Kobe 59-63; V of St Matt Hull 63-67; Commiss and Can of Kobe from 63; P-in-c of Oberon 67-73; R of Cobar 73-76; Chap to Bp of Carp 77-78; P-in-c of St Paul Miss Carp 77-78; R of Waikerie Dio Murray from 78. *Rectory, O'Loughlin Street, Waikerie, S Australia 5330.* (085-412947)

ALLEN, Francis Coombe Stafford. b 14. Pemb Coll Cam BA 35, MA 57. Westcott Ho Cam 56. **d** 57 Sherborne for Sarum **p** 58 Sarum. C of Pewsey 57-60; R of Baconsthorpe w Plumstead 60-78; V of Hempstead-by-Holt 60-78; Perm to Offic Dio Nor from 78. *53 Norwich Road, Horsham St Faith, Norwich, NR10 3HH.* (Nor 897263)

ALLEN, Francis le Champion. St Jo Coll Auckld 41, LTh 47. **d** 41 **p** 43 Auckld. C of St Aid Remuera 41-44; V of Bay of Is 44-46; Te Ngawai 46-52; Akaroa 52-55; St Jas Riccarton 55-60; Amberley 60-63; Mt Somers 63-67; P-in-c of Tinwald 67-70; L to Offic Dio Ch Ch 70 and from 72; P-in-c of Highfield 70-71; Linwood 70-71; Hon C of Timaru 71-72. *56A Burnett Street, Ashburton, NZ.* (89-351)

ALLEN, Frank Brian. b 47. K Coll Lon BD AKC 71. St Aug Coll Cant 71. **d** 71 **p** 72 Dur. C of St Andr Leam Lane Heworth 71-74; Tynemouth 74-78; Chap Newc T Poly from 78. *9 Chester Crescent, Sandyford, Newcastle-upon-Tyne, NE2 1DH.*

ALLEN, Frank Hartley. Late Scho of Qu Coll Ox 1st cl Cl Mods 34, BA (2nd cl Lit Hum) 36, MA 39, BD 44. Wycl Hall Ox 37; Liddon Stud 37. **d** 38 **p** 39 Liv. C of St Matt and St Jas Mossley Hill 38-42; St Pet Belgrave 42-48; V of Dunton Bassett 48-54; Quorn (or Quorndon) 54-57; Lect Hur Coll 57-60; Prof 60-79. *165 Regent Street, London, Ont, Canada.*

ALLEN, Frank John. b 17. CCHem, FRIC 58. Univ of Aston in Birm BSc 66. Univ of Birm Dipl Th 75. Qu Coll Birm 75. **d** and **p** 76 Birm (APM). Hon C of Hob's Moat 76-79; Perm to Offic Dio Heref from 79. *Haresfield, Luston, Nr Leominster, Herefs, HR6 0EB.*

ALLEN, Canon Frederick Wayne. Bp's Univ Lennox BA 64, STB 65. **d** 65 **p** 67 Ott. C of Smith's Falls 66-67; on leave 68-72; I of Ashton 72-75; Episc Sec Dio Ott 75-78; Chap to Bp of Ott 77-78, Hon Can of Ott from 77; R of Smith's Falls Dio Ott from 78. *6 Pearl Street, Townhouse 6D, Smith's Falls, Ont., Canada.*

ALLEN, Geoffrey. Univ of Dur BA 60. Univ of Birm Dipl Th 62. Qu Coll Birm 60. **d** 62 **p** 63 Man. C of Fallowfield 62-65; Chap St Anselm Hall Univ of Man 63-65; Tutor St Aid Coll Birkenhead and L to Offic Dio Ches 65-69; R of St Thos Ardwick Man and Asst Dir Relig Educn Dio Man 69-73; Asst Chap HM Pris Wandsworth 73-74; Chap HM Pris Leeds 74-76; Asst Master Eccles CE High Sch 76-80; C of Peel Green w Barton 78-80; St Jo Evang Broughton, Salford Dio Man from 80. *237 Great Clowes Street, Salford, Lancs, M7 9EU.* (061-792 9161)

✠ **ALLEN, Right Rev Geoffrey Francis.** b 02. Late Scho of Univ Coll Ox 1st cl Phil Pol and Econ 24, BA 25, 2nd cl Th 26, MA 28. Ripon Hall Ox 24. **d** 27 **p** 28 Liv. C of St Sav Liv 27-28; Chap Ripon Hall Ox 28-30; L to Offic Dio Ox 28-35; Fell Chap and Tutor Linc Coll Ox 30-35; CMS Miss Dio Vic 35-44; Union Th Coll Canton 35-40; Dep Provost and Hon Can of Birm 41; Can (Emer) from 42; Sec Nat Chr Coun of China 42-44; Archd of Birm 44-47; Exam Chap to Bp of Birm 45-47; Cons Ld Bp in Egypt in S'wark Cathl 25 Jan 47 by Abp of Cant; Abp of Thyateira; Bps of Lon; Birm; Heref; S'wark; Worc; Bps Suffr of Kingston T; Woolwich; Willesden; Bps Van de Oord Gwynne Linton Roberts and Neill; res 52; Prin of Ripon Hall Ox 52-59; Exam Chap to Bp of St E 57-59; Apptd Ld Bp of Derby 59; res 69. *The Knowle, Deddington, Oxford, OX5 4TB.* (Deddington 38225)

ALLEN, Geoffrey Gordon. Sarum Th Coll 64. **d** 66 Buckingham for Ox **p** 67 Ox. C of Langley Marish 66-70; Chap Miss to Seamen Tilbury 70-72; Schiedam 72-75; Antwerp 75-78; Rotterdam Dio (Gibr in Eur from 80) Lon (N and C Eur) from 78; Chap of St Mary Rotterdam Dio (Gibr in Eur from 80) Lon (N and C Eur) from 78. *Pieter de Hoochweg 133, Rotterdam, Holland.* (764043)

ALLEN, George William. b 14. St Aid Coll 47. **d** 50 **p** 51 Bradf. C of Ingrow 50-53; H Trin Bingley 53-54; R of Caundle Bishop w Caundle Marsh 54-66; C-in-c of Holwell 56-63; R 63-66; Maiden Newton w Frome Vauchurch 66-80; R of Compton Abbas W w Wynford Eagle and Toller Fratrum 66-80. *22 Ashley Road, Marnhull, Sturminster Newton, Dorset, DT10 1LQ.*

ALLEN, Gordon Richard. St Jo Coll Dur BA (2nd cl Th) 54, Dipl Th 55, MA 58. **d** 55 **p** 56 Liv. C of Southport 55-58; Educn Officer and Chap Teso Coll Ugan 58-63; C-in-c of St Bride Liv 64; V of Lathom 64-68. *Virginia Episcopal School, Lynchburg, Virginia, USA.*

ALLEN, Hugh Edward. b 47. Sarum Wells Th Coll 79. **d** 81 Taunton for B & W. C of St Jo Bapt and of Ch Ch Frome Dio B & W from 81; Woodlands Dio B & W from 81. *19 Westover, Frome, Somerset, BA11 4ET.* (Frome 62951)

ALLEN, Canon James David. b 09. Univ of Wales BA 35, 2nd cl Engl Hons 36. St Mich Coll Llan 36. **d** 37 **p** 38 Mon. C of St Geo Tredegar 37-40; CF (EC) 40-46; Men in Disp 46; Hon CF 46; C of Oxted (in c of Hurst Green) 46; St Jas Clacton-on-Sea 46-47; R of Beaumont w Moze 47-60; Chap Butlin's Holiday Camp Clacton 53-60; V of Layer de la Haye 60-76; Surr 63-76; Asst RD of Colchester 65-69; RD 69-75; Hon Can of Chelmsf 71-76; Can (Emer) from 76. *35 Tenterfields, Dunmow, Essex, CM6 1HJ.* (Great Dunmow 3116)

ALLEN, Canon John Austin. b 02. Linc Coll Ox BA 25, MA 29. Ely Th Coll 26. **d** 26 **p** 27 Ox. C of All SS Boyne Hill 26-30; St Mark Walworth and Asst Missr Wel Coll Miss 30-34; C of St Mary Magd Munster Sq 34-36; Carshalton (in c of Good Shepherd) 36-43; V of The Ascen Lavender Hill 43-58; Proc Conv S'wark 55-60; V of St Luke Kingston T 58-67; Hon Can of S'wark 67; Can (Emer) from 67; Chap Commun of Jes the Good Shepherd 67-68; L to Offic Dio Worc 68-72; Perm to Offic Dio Worc 72-74. *College of St Barnabas, Lingfield, Surrey, RH7 6NJ.*

ALLEN, John Blandford. Seager Hall Ont 63. **d** 64 Hur for Qu'App **p** 65 Qu'App. I of Saltcoats 64-67; Rosetown 67-81. *Box 1116, Rosetown, Sask., Canada.* (882-2202)

ALLEN, John Catling. b 25. Univ of Leeds BA 50. Coll of Resurr Mirfield 50. **d** 52 **p** 53 Bris. C of H Nativ Knowle 52-54; St Pet De Beauvoir Square Hackney 54-57; St Barn Beckenham 57-60; V of St Andr Orpington 60-66; V of St Jo Bapt Ermine City and Dio Linc from 66. *St John's Vicarage, Sudbrooke Drive, Ermine, Lincoln, LN2 2EF.*

ALLEN, John Clement. b 32. K Coll Lon and Warm 54. **d** 58 **p** 59 York. C of St Martin Middlesbrough 58-60; Northallerton 60-64; V of Larkfield 64-70; R of Ash w Ridley 70-79; Chislehurst Dio Roch from 79; RD of Cobham 76-79. *Rectory, Chislehurst, Kent.* (01-467 0196)

ALLEN, John Edward. b 32. Univ Coll Ox BA (2nd cl Phil Pol Econ) 56, MA 63. Fitzw Coll Cam BA (2nd cl Th Trip pt iii) 68. Westcott Ho Cam 66. **d** 68 **p** 69 Cant. C of Deal 68-71; P-in-c of St Paul Ap Clifton 71-78; Chap Univ of Bris 71-78; P-in-c of Chippenham w Tytherton Lucas Dio Bris from 78. *Vicarage, St Mary Street, Chippenham, Wilts, SN15 3JW.* (Chippenham 2439)

ALLEN, John Maurice. b 17. Selw Coll Cam BA 39, MA 46. Bps' Coll Cheshunt. **d** 50 **p** 51 Carl. C of St Paul Barrow-in-Furness 50-54; St Jo Bapt Upperby Carl 54-56; C-in-c of St Elisabeth Conv Distr Harraby Carl 56-59; Min 59-61; R of Bowness-on-Solway 61-72; V of Kirkoswald w Renwick (and Ainstable from 76) Dio Carl from 72. *Kirkoswald Vicarage, Penrith, Cumb, CA10 1DH.* (Lazonby 206)

ALLEN, John Michael. b 27. Cudd Coll 71. **d** 72 **p** 73 Lich. C of St Giles Shrewsbury 72-75; V of Hengoed w Gobowen Dio Lich from 75; Surr from 76. *Gobowen Vicarage, Oswestry, Salop.* (Gobowen 226)

ALLEN, John Ord. b 29. Wells Th Coll 64. **d** 66 **p** 67 Ex. C of Honiton 66-71; V of Sidbury w Sidford Dio Ex from 71. *Sidbury Vicarage, Sidmouth, Devon.* (Sidbury 318)

ALLEN, Kenneth Percival. b 43. Moore Coll Syd ACT ThL 71. **d** 71 Armid. C of W Tamworth 71-72; V of Baradine 72-74; Walgett 74-77; Gunnedah Dio Armid from 77. *Vicarage, Gunnedah, NSW, Australia 2380.* (42 0038)

ALLEN, Michael Edward Gerald. b 26. Selw Coll Cam BA (2nd cl Hist Trip) 50, MA 53. Chich Th Coll 50. **d** 52 **p** 53 Guildf. C of Farncombe 52-56; R of Bentley Hants 56-60; V of Berkswich w Walton 60-75; W Hoathly (and Highbrook from 75) Dio Chich from 75; RD of Cuckfield from 77. *West Hoathly Vicarage, East Grinstead, W Sussex.* (Sharpthorne 810494)

ALLEN, Michael Stephen. b 37. Univ of Nottm BA (Econ) 60. Cranmer Hall Dur 60. **d** 62 **p** 63 Wakef. C of Sandal Magna w Newmillerdam 62-66; St Pet Tile Cross Yardley 66-70; Bletchley 70-72; V of St Pet Tile Cross Dio Birm from 72. *Vicarage, Haywood Road, Tile Cross, Birmingham 33.* (021-779 2739)

ALLEN, Michael Tarrant. b 30. St Cath Coll Cam BA 56. MA 61. Ely Th Coll 56. **d** 58 **p** 59 Chich. C of Portslade 58-64; St Sav Folkestone 64-65; V of Harston w Hauxton Dio Ely from 65. *Harston Vicarage, Cambridge, CB2 5NP.* (Cambridge 870201)

ALLEN, Noel Stephen. Kelham Th Coll. **d** 63 **p** 64 Cov. C of St Mary Nuneaton 63-67; Bro of Good Shepherd Dio Bath 67-68; P-in-c of Tennant Creek 68-75; C of Ch Ch Cathl Darwin 75-81; R of Alice Springs Dio N Terr from 81. *Box 51, Alice Springs, NT, Australia 5750.* (52-1056)

ALLEN, Peter Henry. b 34. Univ of Nottm BA (2nd cl Th) 66. Kelham Th Coll 58. **d** 66 **p** 67 Sarum. C of St Martin Sarum 66-70; Melksham 70-73; Paignton 73-76; P-in-c of St D W Holloway 76-77; V of Barnsbury Dio Lon from 77. *43 Eden Grove, N7 8EE.* (01-607 3980)

ALLEN, Peter John Douglas. b 35. Jes Coll Cam BA 61, MA 64. Westcott Ho Cam 60. **d** 62 Bp McKie for Cov **p** 63 Cov. C of Wyken 62-65; Ch of the Advent Boston Mass USA 65-66; Chap Jes Coll Cam 66-72; Chap, Asst Master, and Ho Master K Sch Cant from 72; Hon Min Can of Cant Cathl from 73. *Linacre House, King's School, Canterbury, Kent.* (Canterbury 65219)

ALLEN, Philip Gerald. b 48. Univ of Lon Dipl Th (Extra-Mural Stud) 71. Trin Coll Bris 71. **d** 73 **p** 74 Portsm. C of St Luke Portsea 73-79; St Jude Portsea 75-79; P-in-c of St Paul Gatten Shanklin Dio Portsm from 79. *St Paul's Vicarage, Shanklin, IW.* (Shanklin 2027)

ALLEN, Philip Vernon Moor. b 08. Keble Coll Ox BA (2nd cl Th) 34, MA 75. Coll of Resurr Mirfield 34. **d** 36 **p** 37 Roch.

C of St Aug Gillingham Kent 36-40; W w E Rounton 40-44; South Bank Middlesbrough Yorks 44-51; Chap of All S Sch Charters Towers Dio N Queensld 51-53; C of Gt Greenford (in c of St Edw Perivale Pk) 54-57; R of Tunstall Kent 57-77. *Kingsfield House, Briton Road, Faversham, Kent.* (Faversham 2388)

ALLEN, Richard James. b 46. Wells Th Coll 69. **d** 71 Warrington for Liv **p** 72 Liv. C of St Thos Martyr Up Holland 71-75; Team V of Up Holland (in c of Ch the Servant Digmoor) 76-79. *c/o 206 Birkrig, Skelmersdale, WN8 9HW.* (Skelmersdale 20527)

ALLEN, Richard Walter Hugh. b 48. Linc Th Coll 75. **d** 77 **p** 78 Ex. C of Plymstock 77-80; Leckhampton 80-81; Shepton Mallet Dio B & W from 81. *142 Whitstone Road, Shepton Mallet, Somt, BA4 5PY.*

ALLEN, Canon Ronald Edward Taylor. b 1897. Univ Coll Ox BA 21, MA 24. Ripon Hall Ox 26. MC 19. **d** 27 **p** 28 Man. C of St Jas Birch-in-Rusholme 27-31; R of St Chris Withington 32-38; Northenden 38-44; Gen Sec C'tte for Chr Reconstruction in Eur 44-46; Hon Chap to Abp of Cant 44; Sec Eur Chs Comm 45-46; LPr Dio Man 46-49; V of Edgbaston 49-65; Surr 52-65; Hon Can of Birm 50-65; Can (Emer) from 65; Proc Conv Birm 58-59; Hon Chap Univ of Birm 58-65; RD of Edgbaston 60-65; Perm to Offic Dio Heref 65-68; L to Offic 68-69; P-in-c of Ashford Bowdler w Ashford Carbonell 69-73; L to Offic Dio Heref 73-82. *22 Park Street, Kingscliffe, Near Stamford, Lincs.* (Kingscliffe 502)

ALLEN, Ronald Royston. b 26. St Paul's Coll Grahmstn 73. **d** 75 **p** 76 Grahmstn. C of St Mark Amalinda and St Mark Cam 75-78; St Mich and St Geo Cathl Grahmstn 78-80; R of St Pet E Lon Dio Grahmstn from 80; Chap Miss to Seamen E Lon from 80. *2 Buffalo Street, East London, CP, S Africa.*

ALLEN, Ross Beresford. Univ of NZ BSc 58. NZ Bd of Th Stud LTh 66. Ch Ch Coll 60. **d** and **p** 63 Ch Ch. C of Timaru 63-65; Geraldine 65-66; Papanui 66-69; V of Ascen Sing 69-75; Amberley 76-78; Shirley Dio Ch Ch from 78. *6 Emmett Street, Christchurch I, NZ.* (852-027)

ALLEN, Roy Vernon. b 43. Open Univ BA 81. Sarum Th Coll 67. **d** 70 **p** 71 Birm. C of Ascen Hall Green 70-74; V of Temple Balsall 74-78; P-in-c of St Mich AA Smethwick 78-81; St Steph Smethwick Dio Birm 78-81; V (w St Mich) from 81. *94 Regent Street, Smethwick, Warley, W Midl, B66 3BH.* (021-558 3583)

ALLEN, Samuel Joseph. b 25. TCD **d** 65 **p** 66 Dub. C of Bray 65-75; C-in-c of Carbury Dio Kild from 75. *Rectory, Carbury, Co Kildare, Irish Republic.* (Carbury 42)

ALLEN, Sinclair Stormont. Worc OTC 56. **d** 57 **p** 58 Worc. C of St Jo Bapt Claines Worc 57-64. *20 Farnham Road, Bangor, Co. Down, N Ireland.*

ALLEN, Canon Stanley Leonard Sidney. b 26. K Coll Lon and Warm BD and AKC (2nd cl) 52. **d** 53 **p** 54 Lon. C of Friern Barnet 53-55; Tutor Qu Coll St John's Newfld 55-57; Vice-Prin 57-58; Asst Chap K Coll Newc T 58-61; C-in-c of Ch Ch Woburn Square 61-66; Chap Hosp for Sick Children Gt Ormond Str Lon 61-66; Can of Roch 66-70; Warden Roch Th Coll from 66; V of St Jo Evang Sidcup Dio Roch from 70; Chap Qu Mary Hosp Sidcup from 70; Hon Can of Roch from 70; Surr from 70; RD of Sidcup from 75. *Vicarage, 13 Church Avenue, Sidcup, Kent. DA14 6BU.* (01-300 0383)

ALLEN, Steven. b 49. Univ of Nottm BA 73. St Jo Coll Nottm 73. **d** 75 **p** 76 Bradf. C of St Jo Evang Gt Horton Bradf 75-80; V of Ch Ch U Armley Dio Ripon from 80. *Christ Church Vicarage, Armley Ridge Road, Leeds, LS12 3LE.* (Leeds 638788)

ALLEN, Sydney James. b 04. **d** 66 Bp Horstead for Leic **p** 67 Leic. C of Scraptoft 66-70; V of Tugby w E Norton and Skeffington 70-76. *Address temp unknown.*

ALLEN, Terence Meredith. Univ of BC BASc 54, Angl Th Coll Vanc STB 65. **d** 65 Koot **p** 65 Carib for Koot. C-in-c of Shuswap Lakes 65-68; R of Castlegar 68-74; St Helen Vanc 74-79; on leave. *206-1770 West 12th Avenue, Vancouver, BC, Canada.*

ALLEN, Thomas Delemere Rex. St Chad's Coll Regina. **d** 45 **p** 46 Qu'App. I of Wadena 45-49; St Mich Moose Jaw 49-51; Prince George 51-66; Can of Carib 58-66; R of H Trin, New Westmr 66-78. *706-841 McBride Boulevard, New Westminster, BC, Canada.*

ALLEN, Tom Gladstone. b 03. **d** 61 **p** 62 Cov. C of St Marg Cov 61-65; R of Whitchurch w Preston-on-Stour 65-68; C-in-c of Atherstone-on-Stour 65-68; Perm to Offic Dio Ches 69-79. *16 Bankfield Avenue, Wistaston, Crewe, Chesh.*

ALLEN, William Benjamin. **d** 76 Ja. C of Porus Dio Ja from 76. *PO Williamsfield, Jamaica, W Indies.*

ALLEN, William Charles Ralph. b 09. Clifton Th Coll 46. **d** 47 **p** 48 Bris. C of St Mich Arch Bris 47-51; Bishopston 51-53; V of St Leon Redfield 53-74; Perm to Offic Dio Bris from 74. *17 Creswicke Avenue, Hanham, Bristol, BS15 4D.*

ALLEN, William Percy. b 1894. **d** 52 **p** 53 S & M. C of Lezayre and Chap of Sulby 52-57; V of Foxdale 57-61. *Southlands, Port Erin, IM.*

ALLEN, Zachary Edward. b 52. Warwick Univ BA 74. Ripon Coll Cudd 78. **d** 81 Chich. C of Bognor Dio Chich from 81. *44 Southdown Road, Bognor Regis, PO21 2JP.* (Bognor R 825400)

✠ **ALLENBY, Right Rev David Howard Nicholas.** b 09. MA (Lambeth) 57. MSSM 33. Kelham Th Coll 28. **d** 34 **p** 35 Liv. C of St Jude Liv 34-36; Tutor Kelham Th Coll and Publ Pr Dio Southw 36-44; R of Averham w Kelham 44-57; Proc Conv Southw 50-57; Ed Dioc News and Southw Review 50-55; Hon Can of Southw 53-57; Can (Emer) 57-62; Personal Chap to Bp of Southw 54-57; RD of Newark 55-57; Prov of SSM in Austr 57-62; Commiss Melan 58-62; Warden Commun of H Name Melb 61-62; Cons Ld Bp of Kuch in S'wark Cathl 30 November 62 by Abp of Cant; Bps of Southw; Lon; Ely; and Worc; Bp Suffr of Taunton and Bps Cornwall Trapp Way Clarkson and others; res 68; Asst Bp of Worc from 68; Commiss Kuch from 69; Dir of Min Dio Worc 71-74; Chap St Osw Hosp Worc from 73. *Chaplain's House, St Oswald's Close, The Tything, Worcester, WR1 1HR.* (Worc 22922)

ALLERTON, Arthur Sydney. Wycl Coll Tor. **d** 66 Tor. I of Manvers 66-67; Lloydtown Dio Tor from 67. *Schomberg, Ont., Canada.* (416-939 2314)

ALLEY, Elspeth. b 24. Mills Coll Calif BA 46. Vanc Sch of Th MDiv 72. **d** 72 **p** 76 New Westmr. C of St Cath Capilano 72-74; St Faith Vanc 74-76; P-in-c of St Edw Richmond 76-79; H Trin Vanc Dio New Westmr from 79. *4006 Yew Street, Vancouver, BC., Canada.*

ALLEY, Leonard Norman. b 1899. Ely Th Coll. **d** 58 **p** 59 Linc. C of Grimsby 58-60; R of Gt Coates 60-63; PC of Aylesby 60-63; L Pr Dio Linc 63-66; C-in-c of Goxhill 66-67. *8 Frinton Court, Frinton-on-Sea, Essex, CO13 9DW.*

ALLEYNE, John Olpherts Campbell. b 28. Jes Coll Cam BA 50, MA 55. **d** 55 **p** 56 Win. C of Southn 55-58; Chap Cov Cathl 58-62; Clare Coll Cam 62-66; Cathl Chap to Bp of Bris from 66; Toc H Area Sec SW Engl 68-71; V of Speke 71-73; R 73-75; Weeke Dio Win from 75. *44 Cheriton Road, Winchester.* (Win 4849)

ALLIN, Philip Ronald. b 43. Lich Th Coll 71. **d** 71 **p** 72 Southw. C of St Mary Magd Sutton-in-Ashfield 71-74; Publ Pr Dio Southw 74-76; R of Ordsall 76-80; C-in-c of Grove 76-77; Sec Dioc BD for Social Responsibility Dio Southw 80-81; V of St Mark Mansfield Dio Southw from 81. *St Mark's Vicarage, Mansfield, Notts.* (Mansfield 22894)

ALLINGHAM, Canon Charles. b 1900. AKC 33. St Steph Ho Ox 33. **d** 33 **p** 34 Lon. C of St Leon Heston 33-36; St Jo Evang Farncombe 36-43; V of Cove w S Hawley 43-46; R of Farncombe 46-67; RD of Godalming 62-67; Surr 62-67; Hon Can of Guildf 66-67; Can (Emer) from 67; Perm to Offic Dio Ex from 67; Dio Guildf from 73. *21 Parsonage Lane, Windsor, Berks.* (Windsor 57904)

ALLINGTON-SMITH (formerly SMITH), Richard. b 28. Univ of Lon BA (2nd cl Hist) 49, MA 52. Wells Th Coll 54. **d** 56 **p** 57 Roch. C of Ch Ch Milton-next-Gravesend 56-61; R of Cuxton 61-67; V of Rainham 67-79; Surr 67-79; V of Gt Yarmouth Dio Nor from 79; Surr from 79. *Vicarage, Barnard Avenue, Gt Yarmouth, Norfolk, NR30 4DS.* (0493 50666)

ALLISON, Dennis Cecil. b 29. Chich Th Coll 74. **d** 76 **p** 77 Portsm. C of St Sav Shanklin 76-79; V of Wymering w Widley Dio Portsm from 79. *Wymering Vicarage, Cosham, Hants, PO6 3NH.* (Cosham 76307)

ALLISON, Elliott Desmond. b 36. Univ of S Afr BA 64. K Coll Lon MTh 74. St Pet Coll Alice 67. **d** 69 **p** 70 Grahmstn. C of Grahmstn Cathl 70-72; Lewisham 73-76; V of St Edw Mottingham 76-80; Ferry Fryston Dio Wakef from 80. *Vicarage, Ferrybridge, W Yorks, WF11 8PN.* (Knottingley 82772)

ALLISON, Keith. b 34. Univ of Dur BA 59. Ely Th Coll 59. **d** 61 **p** 62 York. C of Sculcoates 61-64; Stainton-in-Cleveland 64-65; Leeds 65-70; V of Micklefield 70-74; Appleton-le-Street w Amotherby 74-78; P-in-c of Barton-le-Street 77-78; Salton 77-80; R of Amotherby w Appleton-le-Street and Barton-le-Street 78-82; P-in-c of St Ippolyts Dio St Alb from 82. *Vicarage, Sperberry Hill, St Ippolyts, Hitchin, Herts SG4 7NZ.* (Hitchin 2935)

ALLISON, Lester Frederic. **d** 45 Dun **p** 47 Waik. C of Oamaru 45-47; P-in-c of Pio Pio 47-50; All SS Palmerston North 50-51; V of Mangaweka 51-53; Patea 53-57; CF (NZ) 57-61; Chap Rolleston Prison 58-61; L to Offic Dio Ch Ch 59-61; C of Sydenham 61-63; New Brighton 63-65; Sumner-Heathcote 65-69; V of Leeston 69-73; Tinwald-Hinds 73-78; C of St Pet Riccarton Dio Ch Ch from 78. *29 Yaldhurst Road, Christchurch 4, NZ.* (41-991)

ALLISON, Michael John. St Mich Coll Crafers 75. **d** and **p** 77 River. Perm to Offic Dio Adel 77; C of Leeton 77-79;

Deniliruin 79-80; P-in-c of Ivanhoe and Menindee Dio River from 80. *Box 99, Leeton, NSW, Australia 2878.*

✠ **ALLISON, Right Rev Oliver Claude.** b 08. CBE 71. Qu Coll Cam 3rd cl Cl Trip pt i 29, BA (3rd cl Th Trip pt i) 30, MA 34. Ridley Hall Cam 31. **d** 32 **p** 33 Sheff. C of Fulwood 32-36; C of St John Boscombe and Jt Sec Win Dioc Coun of Youth 36-38; CMS Miss at Juba 38-48; Cons Asst Bp in the Sudan in St Alb Abbey 25 April 48 by Abp of Cant; Bps of Chich; Ely; St Alb; St Andr; and Worc; Bps Suffr of Kingston T; Kens; and Croydon; and Bps Gwynne; Furse; Heywood; Gerard; Skelton; and Ridsdale; Apptd Ld Bp in the Sudan 53; res 74; Commiss Sudan 74-81; Trav Sec Sudan Ch Assoc from 75. *1 Gloucester Avenue, Bexhill-on-Sea, E Sussex, TN40 2LA.*

ALLISON, Canon Roger Grant. b 10. MBE 54. Jes Coll Cam 3rd cl Cl Trip pt i 31, BA (2nd cl Th Trip pt i) 33, MA 36. Ridley Hall Cam 32. **d** 34 **p** 35 Ripon. C of St Jo New Wortley 34-37; St Matthias U Tulse Hill 37-39; CMJ Miss in Poland 39; Bucharest 39-40; Jerusalem 41; Chap at Haifa 42-45; CMJ Miss Jaffa 46-48; Tel Aviv 48-67; Jer 67-69; I of Ch Ch Jer 69-75; Hon Can of Tiberias in St Geo Colleg Ch Jer 63-75; Can (Emer) from 75. *11 Gloucester Avenue, Bexhill-on-Sea, Sussex, TN40 2LA.* (0424-218786)

✠ **ALLISON, Right Rev Sherard Falkner.** b 07. Late Rustat Scho of Jes Coll Cam 1st cl Cl Trip pt i 28, BA (1st cl Cl Trip pt ii) and Wordsworth Stud 29, 2nd cl Th Trip pt i and Jeremie LXX Pri 30, MA 33, Hon Fell 63. DD (Lambeth) 51. Occidental Coll Calif Hon DD 59. Wycl Coll Tor Hon DD 59. Ch Div Sch Calif Hon STD 59. Univ of Sheff Hon LLD 60. Univ of Southn Hon LLD 74. Ridley Hall Cam 29. **d** 31 **p** 32 Roch. C of St Jas Tunbridge Wells 31-34; Chap Ridley Hall Cam and C of St Mark Cam 34-36; Exam Chap to Bp of Bradf and L to Offic Dio Bradf 34-36; V of Rodbourne Cheney 36-40; Erith 40-45; Exam Chap to Bp of Roch 44-51; to Bp of Ely 47-51; Prin Ridley Hall Cam 45-51; Commiss Sudan 45-51; Select Pr Univ of Cam 46, 55, and 62; Univ of Ox 53-55 and 62-63; Proc Conv Ely 49-51; Cons Ld Bp of Chelmsf in Westmr Abbey 2 Feb 51 by Abp of Cant; Bps of Lon; Nor; Sarum; Ely; Roch; Derby; St E; Portsm; S & M; and Liv; Bps Suffr of Colchester; Kens; and Bps Walsh and Ridsdale; Trld to Win 61; res 74; Prelate of Most Noble Order of Garter and Prov Chan of Cant 61-74. *Winton Lodge, Alde Lane, Aldeburgh, Suff.*

ALLISON, Wallace Corsbie. Wycl Coll Tor 06. **d** 09 **p** 10 Keew. C of Lac du Bonnet Manit 09-10; I 10-11; I of Dryden 11-16; Dungannon w Port Albert Ont 17-19; Eastwood 21-23; Granton 23-26; R of Hanover w Allan Park 26-42; RD of Bruce 33-42; I of Delaware w Mt Brydges 42-55. *Apt 304, 16 Tremont Drive, St Catherines, Ont., Canada.*

ALLISON, William Gordon. b 12. Qu Coll Cam MA 31. Ridley Hall Cam 34. **d** 38 **p** 39 Chich. C of St Matt St Leonards-on-Sea 38-41; St Clem Ox 41-43; V of Willesley 43-47; Measham 43-47; R of Springfield 47-59; Hollington 59-67; Inkpen (w Combe from 74) 67-78; C-in-c of Combe 67-68; V 68-74. *1 Gloucester Avenue, Bexhill-on-Sea, E Sussex, TN40 2LA.* (Bexhill 217462)

ALLISON, William Osborne. b 09. ALCD 32 (LTh from 74). **d** 33 **p** 34 S and M. C of Kirk Braddan and Chap of St Luke Baldwin IM 33-35; C of St Jo Evang Bromley 35-40; R of Castle Rising w Roydon 41-45; V of Marham 45-53; R of Brampton 53-74. *5 Girton Crescent, Hartford, Huntingdon, Cambs, PE18 7QH.* (Huntingdon 52048)

ALLISTER, Donald Spargo. b 52. Peterho Cam BA 74, MA 77. Trin Coll Bris 74. **d** 76 **p** 77 Ches. C of St Geo Hyde 76-79; Sevenoaks Dio Roch from 79. *21 Valley Drive, Sevenoaks, Kent.* (0732-454221)

ALLISTER, Preb Wilfred Thompson. b 25. Trin Coll Dub BA 47, MA 49. **d** 47 **p** 48 Connor. C of St Andr Belf 47-49; C-in-c of Pettigo 49-50; St Mark Newtownsaville 50-63; R of Devenish w Bohoe Dio Clogh from 63; Preb of St Patr Cathl Dub from 79. *Devenish Rectory, Monea, Enniskillen, Co. Fermanagh, N. Ireland.* (Springfield 228)

ALLISTON, Cyril John. Fitzw Ho Cam 3rd cl Hist Trip pt i 31, BA (3rd cl Th Trip pt i) 33, MA 37, Cudd Coll 34. **d** 35 **p** 36 Ox. C of All SS Boyne Hill 35-37; Hessle 37-40; Chap S Afr Ch Rly Miss 40-45; R of Douglas w Cambell Griquatown and Hopetown (also Dir of Miss) Dio Kimb K 45-50; C-in-c of St Columba Miri and Sarawak Oil Field 50-52; Archd of N Borneo and R of Jesselton Dio Borneo 52-59; Can of St Thos Cathl Kuching 55-59; R of Somersham w Pidley-cum-Fenton and Colne 60-63; V of Penponds 63-70; R of Hermanus 71-76. *c/o St Peter's Rectory, Hermanus, CP, S Africa.* (101)

ALLMARK, Harold. Univ of Dur LTh 15. St Aid Coll 13. **d** 15 **p** 16 Man. C of St Steph Audenshaw 15-17; Leyland 18-21; Fernworth w Kearsley 21-22; V of St Steph Kearsley Moor 22-29; St John Bury 29-54; Buckland-Brewer 54-62; R of Alwington 55-62; L to Offic Dio Ex from 62. *Northesk, Avon Lane, Westward Ho, Bideford, Devon.*

ALLOM, Barrie Haldane. St Jo Coll Auckld LTh (1st cl) 63. **d** 63 **p** 64 Auckld. C of Whangarei 63-66; Henderson 67-68; St Aug Napier 68-71; V of Waikoku 71-73; Waipukurau 73-78; St Aug Napier 78-80; Can of Wai 79-80. *46 Riverbend Road, Napier, NZ.* (437-823)

ALLOOLOO, Jonas. b 47. Arthur Turner Tr Sch Pangnirtung 72. **d** 75 **p** 76 Arctic. I of Broughton I Dio Arctic from 75. *St Michael & All Angels Mission, Broughton Island, NWT, Canada.*

ALLOTT, Laurence Henry. St Columb's Hall Wang 60. **d** 62 **p** 63 Wang. C of Milawa 62-64; Shepparton 64-65; R of Yackandandah 59-69; Cobram 69-76; Tallangatta Dio Wang from 76. *Rectory, Talangatta, Vic, Australia 3700.*

ALLPORT, David Jack. **d** 80 Dorchester for Ox **p** 81 Ox. C of Abingdon Dio Ox from 80. *9 Preston Road, Abingdon, Oxon.* (Abingdon 22684)

ALLRED, Frank. b 23. Tyndale Hall Bris 62. **d** 64 Middleton for Man **p** 65 Man. C of St Pet Halliwell 64-67; V of Ravenhead 67-75; R of St Mary Chadwell Dio Chelmsf from 75. *Chadwell St Mary Rectory, Grays, Essex.* (Tilbury 2176)

ALLSO, Sydney Ernest. b 10. Qu Coll Birm 32. **d** 34 **p** 35 Ches. C of St John Dukinfield 34-36; H Trin Stroud Green 36-38; St Ninian's Cathl Perth (in c of St Finnian Lochgelly) 39-40; CF (EC) 40-45; Hon CF 45; Perm to Offic Dio Win 45-46; V of E Halton 46-50; Killinghome 46-50; PC of Tattershall w Thorpe 50-53; V of All SS E Finchley 53-66; Radley 66-71; Commiss Windw Is from 60; Perm to Offic Dio Sarum 71-73; C of Bawtry w Austerfield 73-75; V of Kirkby Woodhouse 75-79; Perm to Offic Dio Linc from 79. *27 Witham Place, Boston, Lincs, PE21 6LG.* (Boston 66425)

ALLSOP, Anthony James. b 37. K Coll Lon and Warm AKC 62. **d** 63 **p** 64 Chelmsf. C of St Marg w St Columba Leytonstone 63-68; V of St Alb Gt Ilford 68-80; St Jo Div Gainsborough Dio Linc from 80. *St John's Vicarage, Sandsfield Lane, Gainsborough, Lincs, DN21 1DA.* (Gainsborough 2847)

ALLSOP, Patrick Leslie Fewtrell. b 52. Fitzw Coll Cam BA 74, MA 78. Ripon Coll Cudd BA (Th) 78. **d** 79 **p** 80 Penrith for Carl. C of St Matt Barrow-F Dio Carl from 79. *St Francis House, Schneider Road, Barrow-in-Furness, Cumbria.* (Barrow 23155)

ALLSOP, Peter William. b 33. Kelham Th Coll. **d** 58 **p** 59 Chelmsf. C of St Barn Woodford Green 58-61; Upholland 61-64; V of St Geo Wigan 64-71; C-in-c Marham 71-72; Team V in Priory Cross Group (Fincham from 74) 72-76; V of Trawden Dio Blackb from 76. *Trawden Vicarage, Colne, Lancs, BB8 8PN.* (Colne 864046)

ALLSOPP, Edmund Gibson. b 16. St Pet Coll Ja 37. Univ of Dur LTh 41. **d** 41 **p** 42 Ja. C of St Luke Cross Roads Ja 41-43; R of Vere 43-44; P-in-c of Montego Bay 44-45; R of Balaclava w Keynsham and Siloah 45-47; St Ann's Bay w Ocho Rios and Lime Hall 48-51; Retreat 51-56; Claremont w Blackstonedge and Guy's Hill 56-58; St Marg Liguanea 58-62; Par Ch Kingston and of The Grove 63-70; Ascen Mona 71-73; Commiss Br Hond (Bel from 73) 69-73; V of Talland 73-80; St Neot Dio Truro from 80; R of Lansallos 73-80; RD of W Wivelshire from 81. *Vicarage, St Neot, Liskeard, Cornw, PL14 6NG.* (Dobwalls 20472)

ALLSOPP, John Edwin. Angl Th Coll BC. **d** 39 **p** 41 New Westmr. C-in-c of St Matt Barnaby w St Marg Lochdale 39-40; C of St Marg Cedar Cottage S Vanc 40-42; P-in-c St Paul's Pro-Cathl Dawson 42-44; R of Ashton 44-48; Prin St Mich Sch Alert Bay 48-51; R of Clayton 51-56; St Steph Ott 56-62; Ch of Ascen Ott 62-72. *3100 Carling Avenue, Ottawa, Ont., Canada.*

ALLSOPP, Robert Edward. b 23. Edin Th Coll 54. **d** 56 **p** 57 Glas. C of St Ninian Pollokshields Glas 56-59; P-in-c of St Serf Shettleston Glas (w St Andr Gartcosh from 61) 59-65; R of St Andr Wishaw 65-75; St Jas City and Dio Aber from 75. *31 Gladstone Place, Aberdeen, AB1 6UX.* (Aberdeen 322631)

ALLTON, Derek Roland. St Mich Ho Crafers ACT Th L 56. **d** 54 **p** 55 Perth. C of Northam 56-58; R of St Mary-in-the-Valley 58-60; N Midlands 60-65; Proserpine 65-66; V of St Paul Aspley City and Dio Brisb 66-68; R from 68. *4 Luckins Street, Aspley, Queensland, Australia 4034.* (263 3518)

ALLTON, Paul Irving. b 38. Univ of Man BA (2nd cl Engl) 60. Univ of Dur Dipl Th (w distinc) 62. **d** 63 **p** 64 Leic. C of Kibworth Beauchamp 63-66; St Mary Virg w All SS St Sav and St Mark Reading (in c of St Matt) 66-70; R of Caston and V of Griston 70-75; C-in-c of Tottington w Tompson and Sturston 70-75; V of Hunstanton w Ringstead Parva 75-80; Holme-next-the-Sea 75-80; C-in-c of Thornham 75-80; V of Hunstanton St Mary w Ringstead Parva, Holme-next-the-Sea and Thornham Dio Nor from 80; RD of Heacham and

Rising from 81. *Vicarage, Old Hunstanton, Norf.* (Hunstanton 2169)

ALLUM, Jeremy Warner. b 32. Wycl Hall Ox 60. **d** 62 **p** 63 Chelmsf. C of Hornchurch 62-67; PC of St Luke, W Derby 67-69; V 69-75; C-in-c of Boulton Dio Derby from 75. *1 St Mary's Close, Boulton Lane, Alvaston, Derby, DE2 0GF.* (Derby 71296)

ALLUM, Peter Drage. b 11. Univ Coll Dur Th Exhib and LTh 35, BA 36, MA 42. Sarum Th Coll 32. **d** 36 **p** 37 Chich. C of Moulescoomb 36-41; Fort William (in c of Lochaber) 41-43; Annan (in c of All SS Gretna and St John Eastriggs) 43-46; C-in-c of Clonfadforan w Castletown 46-48; R 48-51; PC (V from 68) of Sheepscombe 51-77. *Rose Cottage, Kempley, Dymock, Glos.*

ALLY, Yohana. St Phil Coll Kongwa. **d** 68 Bp Madinda for Centr Tang **p** 68 Centr Tang. P Dio Centr Tang. *Box 264, Dodoma, Tanzania.*

ALMOND, Kenneth Alfred. b 36. Linc Th Coll 78. **d** 79 Grantham for Linc **p** 80 Linc. C of Boston Dio Linc from 79. *2 Tower Street, Boston, Lincs, PE21 8RX.* (0205-65556)

ALONGE, Canon Joseph George. Im Coll Ibad 57. **d** 58 **p** 60 Ibad. P Dio Ibad 58-74; Dio Ilesha from 74; Hon Can of Ilesha from 77. *Vicarage, Ifewara, via Ilesha, Nigeria.*

ALSBURY, Colin. b 56. Ch Ch Ox BA 77, MA 81. Ripon Coll Cudd 77. **d** 80 **p** 81 Ches. C of Oxton Dio Ches from 80. *36 Noctorum Dell, Birkenhead, Mer.*

ALSOP, Eric George. b 12. Dorch Miss Coll 34. Men in Disp 43. **d** 37 Linc **p** 38 Grimsby for Linc. C of All SS Grimsby 37-39; Chap RAF 39-50; Sen Chap Cosford 50-53; Staff Chap BAOR 53-55; Chap Gaydon 55-58; Christmas I 58; Wyton Huntingdon 59-60; Asst Chap-in-Chief MEAF 60-62; Bomber and Transport Commds 62-65; Germany 65-66; Hon Chap to HM the Queen 65-66; V of Over 67-69; C of Bodiam and of Salehurst 69-72; V of Burwash Weald 72-77; Perm to Offic Dio Chich from 77. *125 London Road, Hurst Green, Etchingham, Sussex.* (Hurst Green 591)

ALSTIN, Phillip John. b 51. St Barn Coll Adel 75. **d** and **p** 77 River. C of Deniliquin 77-79; Culcairn-Henty 79; R of Macarthur Dio Bal from 79. *Rectory, Macarthur, Vic, Australia 3286.*

ALSTON, Graham Ernest. b 47. St Paul's Coll Grahmstn. **d** 75 **p** 76 Natal. C of Kloof 75-78; Mooi River Dio Natal 78-80; R from 80. *Box 55, Mooi River, Natal, S Africa.*

ALTAMIRANO, Colin. b 39. **d** and **p** 66 Argent. P Dio Argent 66-73; N Argent from 73. *Parsonage, Alto de la Sierrz, N Argentina.*

ALTON, Bruce Scott. Univ of W Ont BA 59, MA 61. Montr Dioc Th Coll BD and LTh 63. **d** 62 **p** 63 Hur. Hon C of All S City and Dio Tor 69; on leave. *202 York Mills Road, Willowdale, Ont., Canada.*

✠ **ALUFURAI, Right Rev Leonard.** OBE 64. NZ Bd of Th Stud LTh 64. St Jo Coll Auckld 48. **d** 52 Auckld for Melan **p** 56 Melan. P Dio Melan 52-63. Cons Asst Bp of Melan in All SS Cathl Honiara 30 Nov 63 by Abp of NZ; Bps of Melan; Nel; Polyn; New Guinea; and Carp; Bp Suffr of Aotearoa; Bp Coadj of Brisb; and Asst Bp of New Guinea; Apptd Bp Suffr 68; Bp of Malaita 75; res 81; Archd of E Solomons 68-75. *c/o Bishop's House, Auki, Malaita, Solomon Islands.*

ALUKO, Michael Akinola. b 24. Im Coll Ibad. **d** 60 **p** 61 Lagos. P Dio Lagos. *Box 45, Ebute-Metta, Nigeria.*

ALWAY, Cecil William. b 24. **d** 69 **p** 70 Glouc. C of Wotton-under-Edge 69-73; C-in-c of Upleadon w Pauntley 73-76; V of Quinton (w Marston Sicca) Dio Glouc from 76. *Vicarage, Lower Quinton, Stratford-on-Avon, Warws, CV37 8SG.* (Stratford-on-Avon 720707)

AMA, Drummond. St Pet Coll Siota. **d** 53 **p** 57 Melan. P Dio Melan 53-75; Dio Ysabel from 75. *Samasodu, Katova District, Solomon Islands.*

AMABEBE, Adolphus. b 42. Trin Coll Umuahia. **d** 75 **p** 76 Nig Delta. P Dio Nig Delta. *St Cyprian's Parsonage, Box 15, Port Harcourt, Nigeria.*

AMADI, Emmanuel Sunday Onyegorom. b 36. Trin Coll Legon LTh 71. **d** and **p** 73 Nig Delta. P Dio Nig Delta. *Parsonage, Nonwa, Tai-Eleme, Nigeria.*

AMADI, Gilbert Wamadi Otuonye. b 23. **d** 74 **p** 76 Nig Delta. P Dio Nig Delta. *Holy Trinity Parsonage, c/o IBAA PA, via Port Harcourt, Nigeria.*

AMADI, Noel Onukwuforobi Justin. Im Coll Ibad 62. **d** 64 Ow. d Dio Ow. *St Paul's Parsonage, Nkwerre, Orlu, Nigeria.*

AMADI, Silas Chikwendu. Trin Coll Umuahia 62. **d** 64 Ow. d Dio Ow. *Parsonage, Nekede, Nigeria.*

AMAH, Jeremia Wenike. b 33. Im Coll Ibad. **d** 73 **p** 74 Nig Delta. P Dio Nig Delta. *St John's Parsonage, Ndele, via Ahoada, Nigeria.*

AMAIYO, Jonathan Enekorue Oforofuo. b 34. Im Coll Ibad 72. **d** 74 **p** 75 Benin. P Dio Benin. *St Paul's Parsonage, Ikpidiama PA, via Oleh, M-W Nigeria.*

AMALEMA, Tomaso. St Cypr Th Coll Tunduru. **d** 59 **p** 62 Masasi. P Dio Masasi. *PO Chuingutwa, Mtwara Region, Tanzania.*

AMANGALA, George Igabo. **d** 31 **p** 33 Bp Howells for Niger. P Dio Niger 31-52; Dio Nig Delta from 52. *St Mark's, Kaiama, Nigeria.*

AMANZE, James. b 45. **d** 73 **p** 74 S Malawi. P Dio S Malawi. *Box 175, Zomba, Malawi.*

AMBALI, Canon George Herbert. St Andr Coll Likoma 50. **d** 52 SW Tang **p** 55 Nyasa. P Dio SW Tang 52-55; Dio Nyasa 55-64; Dio Malawi 64-71; Dio Lake Malawi 71-74; Hon Can of Lake Malawi from 73. *Mbamba, PO Likoma, Malawi.*

AMBAR, Canon Sagi. St Paul Th Coll Thursday I. **d** 49 **p** 51 Carp. C of Murray I 49-50; Torres Strait Miss 50-52; Miss Darnley I 52-56; Boigu 56-60; Yam I 60-66; Boigu I 66-74; Hon Can of Carp from 71; Mabuiag I Dio Carp from 74. *Mabuiag Island, via Thursday Island, Queensland, Australia.*

✠ **AMBO, Right Rev George.** OBE 78. Newton Th Coll Dogura 52. **d** 55 **p** 58 New Guinea. C of Menapi 55-57; Dogura 57-58; P-in-c of Boianai 58-63; Cons Asst Bp of New Guinea in St Jo Cathl Brisb 28 Oct 60 by Abp of Brisb; Abp of Syd; Bps of New Guinea; N Queensld; Rockptn; Carp; Polyn; Melan; and Newc; and Bps Hand Hudson and Dixon; Apptd Bp of Popondota 77; Miss at Wamira 63-69. *PO Box 26, Popondota, Papua New Guinea.* (29-7194)

AMBROSE, Edgar. b 22. NOC 80. **d** 81 Blackb. C of Broughton Dio Blackb from 81. *76 Conway Drive, Fulwood, Preston, PR2 3EQ.*

AMBROSE, Frederick Lee Giles. Kelham Th Coll 28. MSSM 35. **d** 36 **p** 37 Southw. C of St Geo Nottm 36-39; St Patr Miss Bloemf 39-47; Modderpoort 47-52; Miss P at St Patr Miss Bloemf 53-54; R of Teyateyaneng Miss 55-60; Dir of Bloemf Miss Distr 60-63; L to Offic Dio Southw 63-70; C of St Patr Miss Bloemf 70-72; Bp's Missr Dio Pret from 72; R of H Trin Rustenburg Dio Pret from 72. *PO Box 64, Rustenburg, Transvaal, S Africa.* (Rustenburg 22681)

AMBROSE, James Field. b 51. Univ of Newc T BA 73. St Jo Coll Dur 77. **d** 80 **p** 81 Penrith for Carl. C of Barrow-in-Furness Dio Carl from 80. *100 Roose Road, Barrow-in-Furness, Cumbria, LA13 9RL.* (Barrow 22792)

AMBROSE, John George. b 30. **d** 74 Bradwell for Chelmsf **p** 75 Chelmsf. [f Bapt Min] C of Rayleigh 74-79; V of St Barn Hadleigh Dio Chelmsf from 79. *St Barnabas Vicarage, Hadleigh, Benfleet, Essex.* (Southend-on-Sea 558591)

AMBROSE, Thomas. b 47. Univ of Sheff BSc 69. PhD 73. Em Coll Cam BA 77. Westcott Ho Cam 75. **d** 78 **p** 79 Newc T. C of Morpeth Dio Newc T from 78. *5 Spelvit Lane, Morpeth, NE61 2QU.*

AMECHI, Innocent Chukuma. b 35. Trin Coll Umuahia. **d** 75 **p** 76 Nig Delta. P Dio Nig Delta. *Holy Trinity Parsonage, Box 213, Port Harcourt, Nigeria.*

AMECHI, Mark Oba. Trin Coll Umuahia 56. **d** 58 Niger. d Dio Niger 58-63; Dio Ow from 63. *St Matthew's Parsonage, Ata PA, Owerri, Nigeria.*

AMECU, John Robert. Buwalasi Th Coll 60. **d** 61 **p** 62 Soroti. P Dio Soroti. *PO Box 107, Soroti, Uganda.*

AMENT, Robert Francis. Melb Coll of Div LTh 62. St Francis Th Coll Brisb. **d** 60 **p** 61 Brisb. C of St Pet Wynnum Brisb 60-63; V of Mt Gravatt, Brisb 63-67; R 67-72; Perm to Offic Dio Brisb from 72. *103 Phillips Street, Coochie Mudlo, Queensland, Australia 4163.*

AMES, Edward Francis Welldon. b 1886 Pemb Coll Cam BA (3rd cl Cl Trip) 08, MA 12. TD 34. **d** 09 Lon **p** 10 Kens for Lon. C of St Marg Uxbridge 09-12; H Trin Latimer Road Kens 12-14; V of St Mary Stoke-by-Nayland 14-20; Theydon Bois Essex 20-46; CF (TA) 14-46; RD of Chigwell 40-46; R of Cawston 46-63; C-in-c of Haveringland 57-63; RD of Ingworth 60-63. *81 Hales Road, Cheltenham, Glos.* (Cheltenham 55418)

AMES, Henry George. b 33. Em Coll Cam BA 56, MA 60. BD (Lon) 58. Tyndale Hall Bris 56. **d** 59 **p** 60 Portsm. C of St Jude Southsea Portsea 59-62; Morden (in c of Em) 62-66; Chap Highbury Technical Coll Portsm from 66. *49 Carmarthen Avenue, Cosham, Portsmouth, Hants.*

AMES, Jeremy Peter. b 49. BD (Lon) and AKC 71. St Aug Coll Cant 71. **d** 72 **p** 73 S'wark. C of St Jo Div Kennington 72-75; Chap RN from 75. *c/o Ministry of Defence, Lacon House, Theobald's Road, WC2.*

AMES, Murray Wallace. Univ of Sask BA 53. Em Coll Sktn LTh (w distinc) 53. **d** 53 **p** 54 Bran. R of Gilbert Plains 53-56; St Pet Flin Flon 56-59; St Geo Bran 59-64; Hon Can of Bran 61-66; Sec and Treas Dio Bran 65-69; Archd of Bran 66-73; R of Minnedosa 69-73; on leave 74-75; I of Boissevain 76-79; St Paul Vic Dio BC from 80. *1379 Esquimalt Road, Victoria, BC, Canada.*

AMES, Reginald John. b 27. Bps' Coll Cheshunt 51. **d** 54 Kens for Lon **p** 55 Lon. C of St Alphege Edmon 54-58; John

Keble Ch Mill Hill 58-60; C-in-c of St Edm Eccles Distr Northwood Hills Pinner Dio Lon 61-64; V from 64. *41 Pinner Hill Road, Pinner, HA5 3SD.* (01-866 9230)

AMES, Stephen Allan Henry. b 44. Univ of Melb BSc 65, PhD 71. Trin Coll Melb 62. **d** 69 Bp Arnott for Melb **p** 70 Melb. C of W Coburg 69-70; on leave 70-73; P-in-c of Deepdene Dio Melb 73-76; V from 76. *47 Naroo Street, Balwyn, Vic, Australia 3103.* (03-85 6625)

AMES-LEWIS, Richard. b 45. Em Coll Cam BA 66, MA 70. Westcott Ho Cam 76. **d** 78 **p** 79 Roch. C of St Mark Bromley 78-81; Edenbridge Dio Roch from 81. *Vicarage, Mill Hill, Edenbridge, Kent, TN8 5DA.*

AMEY, Graham George. b 44. BD 70 (Lon). Tyndale Hall Bris 67. **d** 71 **p** 72 Stepney for Lon. C of St Mary Hornsey Rise 71-74; St Helens 74-79; V of All SS Springwood City and Dio Liv from 79. *Springwood Vicarage, Mather Avenue, Liverpool, L19 4TF.* (051-427 5699)

AMEY, Harry. Bp's Univ Lennox BA 40. **d** 40 **p** 41 Ott. C of Beachburg 40-43; P-in-c 41-43; R of S March 43-53; Bearbrook Dio Ott 53-55; I of St Geo Scarborough 55-58; Hon C of St Barn Danforth Avenue Tor 58-75; Publ Inst Chap 60-75; P-in-c of St Edm-the-Mart Tor 75-76. *47 Broadlands Boulevard, Don Mills, Ont., Canada.*

AMEY, Lindsay Gordon. Ridley Coll Melb 32. ACT ThL 34. **d** 34 Melb for U Nile **p** 35 U Nile. Miss at Lira 34-38; furlough 38-39; CMS Miss at Kitgum 39-40; Gulu 40-41 and 53-65, Lira 41-52, RD of Tororo 48-52, Archd of E Nile 53-61; Can of N Ugan 62-64; Chap Oenpelli Miss 65-69; Perm to Offic Dio Melb from 69. *3 Nutter Crescent, St John's Park, Mooroolbark, Vic., Australia 3138.* (723-2720)

AMIMO, Gilbert. b 27. St Paul's Th Coll Limuru 67. **d** 69 Maseno **p** 70 Maseno N. P Dio Maseno N 70-77; Dio Nai from 77. *PO Box 40539, Nairobi, Kenya.* (20715)

AMIS, Ronald. b 37. Linc Th Coll 74. **d** 76 **p** 77 Linc. C of Grantham 76-79; P-in-c of Holbeach Hurn 79-81; Holbeach Bank 79-81; V of Long Bennington w Foston Dio Linc from 81. *Long Bennington Vicarage, Newark-on-Trent, Notts.* (Loveden 81237)

AMOLO, Samson. **d** 65 **p** 66 Maseno. P Dio Maseno 65-70; Dio Maseno S from 70; Exam Chap to Bp of Maseno S from 77. *PO Box 16, Homa Bay, Kenya.*

✠ **AMOORE, Right Rev Frederick Andrew.** Univ of Leeds BA (2nd cl Hist) 34. Coll of Resurr Mirfield 34. **d** 36 **p** 37 S'wark. C of Clapham 36-39; St Mary Port Eliz 39-45; R of St Sav East London 44-50; RD of East London 45-50; Dean of Pret and R of St Alb Cathl Pret 50-61; P-in-c of Premier Mine 56-61; R of W Suburbs 57-60; Archd of Pret 60-61; Can of Pret 62-67; Hon Can 67-75; Can (Emer) from 75; Prov Executive Officer in S Afr 62-67; Cons Ld Bp of Bloemf in St Andr and St Mich Cathl Bloemf 9 July 67 by Abp of Capetn; Bps of Pret; Grahmstn; Natal; Johann; Les; St John's; Geo; and Bp Suffr of Les. *Bishop's House, 16 York Road, Bloemfontein, OFS, S Africa.* (051-73861)

AMOORE, Thomas Frederck. b 51. Univ of Capetn BA 73, BSc 74. Rhodes Univ Grahmstn BA 77. St Paul's Coll Grahmstn 75. **d** 76 Bp Carter for Johann **p** 77 Johann. C of Germiston Dio Johann from 76. *Box 624, Germiston 1400, S Africa.* (011-51 2851)

AMOR, Peter David Card. b 28. K Coll Lon and Warm AKC 53. **d** 54 Lon **p** 55 St Alb. C of St Margaret's-on-Thames 54; Leighton Buzzard 54-58; St Agnes Toxt Pk 58-62; Aldershot (in c of Ch of Ascen) 62-65; V of H Trin Bingley 65-72; R of Collingbourne Ducis 72-75; V of Collingbourne Kingston 72-75; R of The Collingbournes and Everleigh 75-77; V of Thorpe Dio Guildf from 77. *Vicarage, Thorpe, Egham, Surrey, TW20 8TQ.* (Chertsey 65986)

AMORY, Edward Henry. b 17. **d** 80 Pret. C of H Trin Rustenburg Dio Pret from 80. *PO Box 144, Rustenburg 0300, S Africa.*

AMOS, Alan John. b 44. OBE 79. Univ of Lon BD (2nd cl) 66, MTh and AKC 67. St Steph Ho Ox 68. **d** 69 Lon **p** 70 Stepney for Lon. C of H Trin w St Mary Hoxton 69-72; CMS Miss Beirut Dio Jordan from 73. *c/o All Saints' Church, PO Box 2211, Beirut, Lebanon.*

AMOS, Gerald. b 31. Univ of Wales. St Mich Coll Llan. **d** 58 St A **p** 62 S'wark. C of Rhos-y-Medre 58-59; St Andr w All SS Peckham 62-65; All SS and St Steph Walworth 65-72; H Trin (w St Pet from 74) S Wimbledon 72-75; Warlingham w Chelsham 75-78; Team V of Speke Dio Liv from 78. *All Saints Vicarage, Speke Church Road, Liverpool, L24 3TA.* (051-486 2922)

AMOS, Patrick Henry. b 31. Roch Th Coll 63. **d** 65 **p** 66 Roch. C of St Nich Strood 65-68; Polegate 68-71; V of Horam Dio Chich from 71. *Vicarage, Horam, Heathfield, Sussex.* (Horam Road 2563)

AMPAH, Gabriel-Marie Sam. St Steph Ho Ox 60. **d** 61 **p** 62 Accra. P Dio Accra. *All Saint's Church, Takoradi, Ghana.*

AMUAH, Samuel. b 36. Trin Coll Legon 68. **d** 71 **p** 72 Accra. P Dio Accra 71-74; Kum from 75. *Box 9, Mampong, Ashanti, Ghana.*

AMUCA, David. **d** 61 **p** 62 N Ugan. P Dio N Ugan 61-76; Dio Lango from 76. *PO Aloi, Lira, Uganda.*

AMULI, Yonathan. St Cypr Th Coll Tunduru 64. **d** Bp Soseleje for Masasi **p** 68 Masasi. P Dio Masasi. *Mumbaka, Tanzania.*

AN, Aidan Kwisop. b 43. St Mich Sem Seoul 71. **d** 74 **p** 75 Seoul. P Dio Seoul. *79 Onsuri, Kilsang Myon, Kanghwa 150-23, Korea.*

AN, Francis Yongwon. b 31. **d** 73 Taejon. d Dio Taejon. *Anglican Church, 493 Namsan-dong, Chongup, Chonbuk 560, Korea.*

ANAMINYI, Joash. St Paul's Th Coll Limuru. **d** 52 **p** 55 Momb. P Dio Momb 52-61; Dio Maseno 61-70; Dio N Maseno from 70. *Anglican Church, Shiamboho, Kenya.*

ANCRUM, John. b 28. Clifton Th Coll 55. **d** 58 Bris for Sarum **p** 59 Sarum. C of St Clem Branksome 58-61; Sparkhill 61-63; V of Tibshelf Derby 63-70; Lintlaw Sktn 70-74; C-in-c of Salwarpe 74-75; Tibberton w Bredicot 75-76; Hadzor w Oddingley (and Tibberton w Bredicot from 76) 75-77; Asst Dioc Chr Stewardship Adv Dio Chelmsf 78-81; Asst Chap HM Pris Stafford from 81. *c/o HM Prison, 54 Gaol Road, Stafford.*

ANDA, Athanasius. **d** 64 New Guinea. d Dio New Guinea 64-70; Dio Papua from 71. *Anglican Church, Sag Sag, via Kimbe, Papua New Guinea.*

ANDA, Augustus. b 46. **d** 81 Aipo Rongo. d Dio Aipo Rongo. *Anglican Church, Keinambe PMB, via Mount Hagen, Papua New Guinea.*

ANDAMA, Isaac. Bp Tucker Coll Mukono. **d** 78 M & W Nile. d Dio M & W Nile. *PO Box 370, Arua, Uganda.*

ANDEMBE, Hudson. St Paul's U Th Coll Limuru. **d** 61 **p** 62 Maseno. P Dio Maseno 62-70; Dio Maseno N from 70. *Bungoma, Kenya.*

ANDERS, Jonathan Cyril. b 36. Wycl Hall Ox 69. **d** 71 Warrington for Liv **p** 72 Liv. C of St Mary Prescot (in c of St Paul Bryer Estate from 74) 71-76; R of St Mary Wavertree 76-81; V of Aigburth Dio Liv from 81. *389 Aigburth Road, Liverpool, L17 6BH.* (051-727 1101)

ANDERS-RICHARDS, Donald. Univ of Dur BA (Th) 60, MA 62. Univ of Leic MEducn 72. Univ of Sheff PhD 76. Coll of Resurr Mirfield 60. **d** 62 **p** 63 Win. C of St Francis Bournemouth 62-64; Asst Chap and Master Quainton Hall Sch Harrow and C of St Mary Virg Kenton 63-68; Lect Totley-Thornbridge Coll of Educn Sheff 68-75; City of Sheff Poly from 75; L to Offic Dio Derby from 68. *4 Catcliff Close, Woodside Park, Bakewell, Derbys., DE4 1AZ.*

ANDERSEN, Francis Ian. b 25. Univ of Qld BSc 47. Univ of Melb MSc 51, BA 55. BD (Lon) 56. Johns Hopkins Univ USA MA 58, PhD 60. Ch Div Sch of Pacific DD 72. **d** 58 Maryland USA **p** 60 Melb. Asst Chap Ridley Coll Melb 60-62; in USA 63-72; Warden of St Jo Coll Auckld 71-73; 71-73; Can of Auckld 73-74; L to Offic Dios Wai and Auckld 73-74; Perm to Offic Dio Melb 74-75; Dio Syd 75-81; Dio Brisb from 81. *86 Pullenvale Road, Pullenvale, Queensld, Australia 4069.* (378 5104)

ANDERSEN, John Charles Victor. St John's Th Coll Morpeth ACT ThL 42. **d** 43 **p** 44 Newc. C of Cessnock 43-44; Ch Ch Cathl Newc 44-46; P-in-c of Boianai New Guinea 46-57. *162 Alt Street, Haberfield, NSW, Australia.*

ANDERSON, Albert Geoffrey. b 42. Univ of Ex BA 65, MA 67. Univ of Birm Dipl Th 75. Qu Coll Birm 73. **d** 75 **p** 76 Ches. C of Helsby and of Ince and of Dunham-on-the-Hill 75-78; Team V of Gleadless Dio Sheff from 78. *51 White Lane, Sheffield, S12 3GD.* (Sheff 396132)

ANDERSON, Ven Alfred Reid. Univ of NZ MSc 33. St Jo Coll Auckld. **d** 37 **p** 38 Auckld. C of St Mark Remuera 37-40; Chap King's Coll Middlemore Auckld 40-41; CF (NZ) 41-43; Chap RNZAF 43-46; V of Helensville 46-49; Onehunga 49-65; Pukekohe 65-73; Archd of Waitemata 63-65; Manukau 65-73; Archd (Emer) from 73; Hon C of Pukekohe Dio Auckld from 73. *9 Bledisloe Court, Pukekohe, NZ.* (87-367)

ANDERSON, Allan James. Bp's Univ Lennox BA 32. **d** 32 **p** 33 Ont. C of St Geo Cathl Kingston 32-35; I of Marysburg 35-40; Actg Chap Kingston Penit 40-43; Chap CASF 43-46; Chap of Kingston Penit 46-48; R of Stirling w Frankford 48-51; I of St Thos Rawdon 48-51; R of Barriefield w Pittsburg 51-55; Dom Chap to Bp of Ont from 49-69; Sec Dio Ont 55-76; Can of Ont 56-69; Archd (without territorial jurisd) 69-70; Archd of Kingston 70-77; Bp's Commiss Dio Ont 76-80. *175 Union Street, Kingston, Ont, Canada.* (613-546 6007)

ANDERSON, Brian Arthur. b 42. Sarum Wells Th Coll 75. **d** 78 **p** 79 Ex. C of St Jas L Plymouth 78-80; Cler Org Sec CECS Dios B & W, Ex and Truro from 80. *26 Ayreville Road, Beacon Park, Plymouth, PL2 2RA.* (0752 53944)

ANDERSON, (Jeremy) Brian Glaister. b 35. K Coll Lon 57. **d** and **p** 79 Heref. M SSF 75-79; Chap St Francis Sch

Hooke 79; C of Croydon Dio Cant from 79. *37 Alton Road, Waddon, Croydon, CR0 4LZ.* (01-686 1636)

ANDERSON, David. b 19. Selw Coll Cam (2nd cl Engl Trip pt i) 40, BA 41, 2nd cl Th Trip pt i 47, MA 45. Wycl Hall Ox 47. **d** 49 **p** 50 Dur . C of St Gabr Bp Wearmouth 49-52; Tutor St Aid Coll 52-56; Chap Heswall Nautical Tr Coll 52-53; Warden Melville Hall Ibad 56-58; Prin Im Coll Ibad 58-62; Can of Ibad 59-62; Prin Wycl Hall Ox 62-69; Exam Chap to Bp of Liv 69-74; Sen Lect Relig Educn Wall Hall Coll Aldenham Herts 70-74; Prin Lect from 74; Exam Chap to Bp of St Alb 72-80. *1 Woodwaye, Watford, WD1 4NN.* (Watford 24117)

ANDERSON, Donald Craig. Univ of BC BA 54. Angl Th Coll of BC LTh 57. **d** 56 **p** 57 Calg. I of Rimbey 56-59; Strathmore 59-62; C of Trail 62-67; R of Cranbrook 67-71; St Timothy Edmon 71-73; Chap Misericordia Hosp Edmon from 73; Hon C of St Aug City and Dio Edmon from 74. *8010 154th Street, Edmonton, Alta., Canada.*

ANDERSON, Donald George. b 38. Moore Th Coll Syd ACT ThL 62, Th Scho 68. **d** 62 **p** 63 Syd. C of Austinmer 62-63; Liv 64-65; Enfield 65-66; C-in-c of Jamberoo 66-69; C of Alperton 69-72; C-in-c of Matraville 72-76; St Matt Botany 73-76; Ruse, Airds and Kentlyn Dio Syd from 76. *1 Riverside Drive, Airds, NSW, Australia 2560.* (046-25 8828)

ANDERSON, Donald Whimbey. Univ of Tor BA 54, MA 59, LTh and STB 57. Trin Coll Tor 54. **d** 56 **p** 57 Tor. C of H Trin Tor 56-57; St Jas Cathl Tor 57-59; on leave 59-75; Gen Sec Gnod Coun of Chs from 76. *Church House, 600 Jarvis Street, Toronto, Ont, Canada.*

ANDERSON, Francis Hindley. Ch Coll Cam 2nd cl Cl Trip pt i 41, BA (2nd cl Th Trip pt i) 43, MA 47. Wycl Hall Ox. **d** 44 **p** 45 S'wark. C of St Matt Surbiton 44-48; Loughborough 48-50; St Pet Eaton Square Lon 50-59; V of St Sav Chelsea Dio Lon from 59. *71 Cadogan Place, SW1X 9RP.* (01-235 3468)

ANDERSON, George Alexander. Seager Hall Ont. **d** 62 Bp Appleyard for Hur **p** 63 Hur. I of Gorrie 62-66; St Paul Chatham 66-69; Exeter Dio Hur from 69. *267 Andrew Street, Exeter, Ont., Canada.* (519-235 2335)

ANDERSON, Canon Gordon Fleming. b 19. TCD BA 41, MA 46. **d** 42 **p** 43 Derry. C of Drumholm Union 42-46; All SS Clooney 46-47; I of Termonamongan 47-57; C-in-c of Lower Cumber Dio Derry 57-61; I from 61; Banagher Dio Derry from 72; Can of Derry from 76. *291 Glenshane Road, Killaloo, Londonderry, BT47 3SW, N Ireland.*

ANDERSON, Hector David. b 06. TCD Hist and Polit Sc Scho 28, BA (3rd cl Mod) 29, Div Test 30, Downes Pri 29 and 30, MA 32, BD 49. MVO (4th Class) 51. **d** 30 Dover for Cant **p** 31 Cant. C of Shirley Surrey 30-33; St Mich Chester Square Lon 33-39; CF (TA) 39-42; R of Sandringham w W Newton and Appleton 42-55; Dom Chap to HM the King 42-52; to HM the Queen 52-55; R of Lutterworth w Cotesbach 55-61; Chap to HM the Queen 55-76; Surr 56-61; RD of Guthlaxton ii 58-61; Hon Can of Leic 59-61; R of Swanage w Herston 61-69. *Adare, The Hyde, Langton Matravers, Dorset.* (Swanage 3206)

ANDERSON, Henry Irvine Keys. b 09. TCD BA 33, Div Test 34, MA 40. **d** 34 Arm for Down **p** 35 Down. C of Carrickfergus 34-39; C-in-c of Gowna w Columbkille 39-43; I of Billis U 43-54; Killesher 54-79; Surr 54-79; Can of Annagh in Kilm Cathl 64-72; Dioc Regr Dio Kilm 65-79; Can and Preb of St Patr Cathl Dub 72-79; RD of Drumlease 72-79. *70 Windsor Avenue, Whitehead, Carrickfergus, Co Antrim, N Ireland.*

ANDERSON, Hugh Richard Oswald. b 35. Roch Th Coll 68. **d** 70 Bp Wilson for B & W **p** 71 B & W. C of St Mich AA Minehead 70-76; Darley w S Darley 76-80; R of Hasland Dio Derby from 80; V of Temple-Normanton Dio Derby from 80. *Hasland Rectory, Chesterfield, Derbys, S41 0JX.* (Chesterfield 32486)

ANDERSON, Ian Roy. b 34. St Paul's Coll Grahmstn 71. **d** 73 **p** 74 Johann. C of Springs 73-77; R of Bedfordview Dio Johann from 77. *Box 620, Bedfordview, Transvaal, S Africa.* (011-53 4979)

ANDERSON, James Boyd. b 14. Univ of Glas MA 40. Edin Th Coll 39. **d** 41 **p** 42 Edin. C of Old St Paul Edin 41-45; St Salvador Edin 45-48; R of Coatbridge 48-53; CF 53-58; C of St Alb Teddington 58-59; P-in-c of Kirkcudbright w Gatehouse 59-62; R of Ch Ch Glas 62-67; Dioc Super and Hosp Chap Dio Glas 67-75; R of Clydebank 75-80; Chap H Trin Madeira Dio Gibr from 80. *Rua do Quebra Costas 20, Funchal, Madeira.*

ANDERSON, James Frederick Wale. b 34. G and C Coll Cam BA 58, MA 62. Cudd Coll 60. **d** 62 **p** 63 St Alb. C of St Luke Leagrave Luton 62-65; Eastleigh 65-70; R of Sherfield-on-Loddon Dio Win from 70; C-in-c of Stratfield Saye w Hartley Wespall Dio Win from 75. *Rectory, Breach Lane, Sherfield-on-Loddon, Basingstoke, Hants.*

ANDERSON, James Raffan. b 33. Univ of Edin MA 54. Edin Th Coll 56. **d** 58 **p** 59 Aber. Chap St Andr Cathl Aber 58-59; Prec 59-62; CF (TA) 59-67; Chap Univ of Aber 60-62; Univ of Glas 62-69; Lect Jordanhill Coll of Educn 63-69; Chap Lucton Sch 69-71; Barnard Castle Sch 71-74; P-in-c of Whitechapel Lancs 74-78; Asst Dir of Educn Dio Blackb 74-78; Bp's Officer for Min Dio Cov from 78. *Shilton Vicarage, Coventry, CV7 9LA.* (0203-617512)

ANDERSON, James William. K Coll NS BA 63, LTh 65. **d** 64 **p** 65 Ont. C of St Geo Trenton 64-66; R of Barriefield 67-71; on leave 71-80; Hon C of St Pet Winnipeg Dio Rupld from 80. *556 Ash Street, Winnipeg, Canada.*

ANDERSON, Jeremy Dudgeon. b 41. Univ of Edin BSc 63. Trin Coll Bris 75. **d** 77 **p** 78 Win. C of Bitterne 77-81; Team V of Wexcombe Dio Sarum from 81. *Vicarage, Eastcourt, Burbage, Wilts, SN8 3AG.*

ANDERSON, John. Trin Coll Dub. **d** 28 **p** 30 Kilm. L to Offic Dio Kilm from 28; Dom Chap to Bp of Kilm from 44. *Royal School, Cavan, Irish Republic.*

ANDERSON, John Clement. Ch Ch Coll. NZ Bd of Th Stud LTh 69. **d** 67 **p** 68 Bp McKenzie for Wel. C of All SS Palmerston N 67-69; Chap Massey Univ Palmerston N 70-73; V of Eketahuna 73-80; Waikanae Dio Wel from 80. *499 Te Moana Road, Waikanae, NZ.* (6210)

ANDERSON, John Edward. b 03. Univ Coll Ox 2nd cl Mod Hist 24, BA 25. Westcott Ho Cam 35. **d** 36 **p** 37 Guildf. Asst Master Charterho Sch 25-45; Asst Chap 36-45; R of Lamport w Faxton 45-53; Chap and Asst Master Giggleswick Sch 53-54; W Buckland Sch 55; Aldenham Sch 55-59; Chap St John Angl Ch Menton 72-75. *Kingsfold, Chepbourne Road, Bexhill-on-Sea, Sussex.* (B-on-Sea 211980)

ANDERSON, John Lanoseh Taiwo. Fourah Bay Coll Univ of Dur BA 26. **d** 36 **p** 41 Sier L. Tutor CMS Gr Sch from 36; C of H Trin Freetown 43-47; St Phil Freetown 47-48; St Geo Cathl Freetown 48-59; V of Bp Crowther Mem Ch Freetown 59-65; Wilberforce 65-67; St John Freetown 67-75; Can of St Geo Cathl Freetown 65-75. *10 Bombay Lane, Freetown, Sierra Leone, W Africa.*

ANDERSON, John Laurence. Trin Coll Cam BA 21, MA 26. Ridley Hall Cam. **d** 23 Bradf **p** 25 Nel. C of Farsley 23-24; Perm to Offic Dio Nel 24-25; V of Suburban N 25-27; Perm to Offic Dio Dun 28-61. *17 Woodford Terrace, Fendalton, Christchurch 5, NZ.*

ANDERSON, John Michael. b 17. Univ of Madras BA 38. St Aug Coll Cant 59. **d** 60 **p** 61 Birm. C of St Alb Smethwick 60-62; Stockland Green 62-65; Braunstone 65-69; R of Pleasantville Trinid 69-73; V of St Sav City and Dio Leic from 73. *St Saviour's Vicarage, Wood Hill, Leicester, LE5 3JB.* (0533 57636)

ANDERSON, Keith Bernard. Qu Coll Cam BA 60, MA 64. Tyndale Hall Bris 60. **d** 62 Warrington for Liv **p** 63 Liv. C of St Leon Bootle 62-65; Lect Can Warner Mem Coll Buye 66-73; Mweya United Th Sem Bur 74; Dir of Stud Dio Nak 74-77; Relig Educn Dio Mt Kenya E from 78. *PO Box 369, Kerugoya, Kenya.*

ANDERSON, Keith Edward. b 42. Fitzw Coll Cam BA 77. Ridley Hall Cam 74. **d** 77 Chelmsf **p** 78 Barking for Chelmsf. C of Goodmayes 77-80; Chap Coll of St Mark & St John Plymouth from 80. *Staff House 4, College of St Mark & St John, Derriford Road, Ext 248)*

ANDERSON, Kenneth. G and C Coll Cam BA 62, MA 66. Westcott Ho Cam 63. **d** 65 **p** 66 Nor. C of St Steph Nor 65-68; Wareham 68-71; Chap Sherborne Sch Dorset from 71. *Sherborne School, Dorset.*

ANDERSON, Kenneth. b 47. Univ of W Ont BA 68. Univ of Windsor Ont MA 70. Hur Coll Lon Ont MDiv 73. **d** 73 **p** 74 Hur. C of St Jas Lon Ont 73-77; Tutor Codr Coll Barb 77-79; I of Lambeth w Delaware Dio Hur from 79. *Box 882, Lambeth, Ont, Canada.*

ANDERSON, Canon Leslie William Shallad. **d** 54 **p** 55 Waik. C of Tokoroa 54-55; P-in-c 55; V 55-61; Te Kuiti 61-64; Stratford 64-70; Can of St Pet Cathl Hamilton from 69; V of Te Aroha 70-72; C of Hillcrest Dio Waik from 72. *131 Silverdale Road, Hamilton, NZ.* (64-544)

ANDERSON, Mark Thornton Reid. b 44. St Jo Coll Auckld. **d** 78 Bp Spence for Auckld **p** 79 Auckld. C of Kohimarama Dio Auckld from 78. *49 Te Arawa Street, Kohimarama, Auckland, NZ.* (584-400)

ANDERSON, Marlowe Dean. Univ of Missouri BA 61, MA 67, PhD 69. Kenyon Coll Ohio BD 64. **d** 64 **p** 65 Missouri. In Amer Ch 64-72; V of Port Hardy BC 72-73; Chap Univ of Vic BC 73-76; C of St Mary's Oak Bay Vic 77-80; Chap Univ of Vic from 80. *2594 Beach Drive, Victoria, BC, Canada.*

ANDERSON, Michael Garland. b 42. Clifton Th Coll 62. **d** 66 **p** 67 Portsm. C of St Jo Evang Fareham 66-69; Worting 69-74; V of Hordle Dio Win from 74. *Hordle Vicarage, Lymington, Hants.* (New Milton 614428)

ANDERSON, Michael John Austen. b 35. K Coll Lon and Warm AKC 60. **d** 66 **p** 67 Lon. C of Ch the Redeemer

Southall 66-69; St Jude-on-the-Hill Hampstead Garden Suburb 69-73; V of S Mymms 73-80; The Brents and Davington w Oare and Luddenham Dio Cant from 80. *Vicarage, Brent Hill, Faversham, Kent.* (Faversham 3272)

ANDERSON, Canon Percy. b 1894. Linc Th Coll 26. **d** 27 **p** 28 Linc. C of St Jas Louth 27-31; V of Baildon 31-38; RD of Calverley 36-38; V of Ch Ch Lanc 38-46; Surr 39-46; Chap RAFVR 41-46; V of Chisledon w Draycott Foliat 46-53; RD of Marlborough 53; Dorchester 53-67; V of Charminster and Chap Herrison Hosp 53-69; Surr 56-69; Can and Preb of Sarum Cathl 59-74; Can (Emer) from 74; Perm to Offic Dio Ely from 75. *18 High Street, Linton, Cambs.*

ANDERSON, Peter John. b 44. Univ of Nottm BA 65, BA (Th) 73. St Jo Coll Nottm 71. **d** 74 **p** 75 Bradf. C of Otley 74-77; Team V of Marfleet Dio York from 77. *St Philip's House, Amethyst Road, Bilton Grange, Hull, HU9 4JG.* (Hull 76208)

ANDERSON, Peter Scott. b 49. Univ of Nottm BTh 72. Kelham Th Coll 68. **d** 74 Doncaster for Sheff **p** 75 Sheff. C of St Cecilia Parson Cross Sheff 74-77; St Marg w St Columba Leytonstone 77-81; P-in-c of St Edm Forest Gate Dio Chelmsf from 81. *Vicarage, Katherine Road, E7 8NP.* (01-472 1866)

ANDERSON, Phillip John. b 40. United Th Coll Syd 77. **d** 81 River. C of Griffith Dio River from 81. *PO Box 31, Griffith, NSW, Australia 2680.* (069-62 3204)

ANDERSON, Robert Edwin. b 42. Univ of Leeds Dipl Th 68. Coll of the Resurr Mirfield 68. **d** 70 **p** 71 Barking for Chelmsf. C of St Edm Forest Gate 70-73; Chap RN 73-78; Chap at Belgrade 78-80; Bucharest and Sofia 78-81; V of St Alb Romford Dio Chelmsf from 81. *7 King's Road, Romford, Essex, RM1 2ST.* (Romford 45157)

ANDERSON, Robert James. b 46. St Jo Coll Morpeth NSW 71. **d** 71 Kalg **p** 73 Perth. d Dio Kalg 71-73; C of Kalamunda w Forrestfield 73-76; R of Wongan Hills w Dalwallinu 76-80; Innaloo w Karrinyup Dio Perth from 80. *53 Burroughs Road, Karrinyup, W Australia 6018.*

ANDERSON, Roderick Stephen. b 43. Univ of Cant NZ BSc 63, PhD 67. New Coll Ox BA 72. Wycl Hall Ox 70. **d** 73 **p** 74 Bradf. C of St Pet Cathl Bradf 73-75; Allerton 75-78; V of Cottingley Dio Bradf from 78. *Cottingley Vicarage, Littlelands, Bingley, Yorks, BD16 1RR.* (Bradford 562278)

ANDERSON, Rua. b 14. **d** 76 **p** 77 Waik. Hon C of Waitomo Past Dio Waik from 76. *46 Turongo Street, Otorohanga, NZ.* (7234)

ANDERSON, Russell Edward. b 27. Coll of Em & St Chad Sktn 78. **d** 80 **p** 81 Sktn for NS. C of Canso Dio NS from 80. *Box 59, Canso, NS, Canada, B0H 1H0.*

ANDERSON, Canon Stuart. Univ of Dur BA 52. Linc Th Coll 52. **d** 54 **p** 55 Dur. C of Billingham 54-57; St Etheldreda Fulham 57-61; V of Port Chalmers 61-64; Wakatipu 64-67; Mornington 67-70; Can of Nel 71-76; V of Blenheim 71-76; Hastings Dio Wai from 76; Can of Wai from 80. *Vicarage, King Street South, Hastings, NZ.* (89-274)

ANDERSON, Thomas. b 07. Dorch Miss Coll 32. **d** 36 **p** 37 York. C of St Paul Middlesbrough 36-39; Bolton Percy 39-43; V of Bubwith 43-49; St Luke York 49-57; Appleton-le-Street w Amotherby 57-70. *Hillside Cottage, Appleton-le-Street, Malton, Yorks.*

ANDERSON, William Bruce. b 34. G and C Coll Cam BA 57, MA 61. Westcott Ho Cam 58. **d** 60 **p** 61 Nor. C of Lowestoft 60-64; C-in-c of St Steph Preston 64-66; V of St Steph Elton 66-75; St Jas New Bury Farnworth Dio Man from 75. *New Bury Vicarage, Highfield Road, Farnworth, Bolton, BL4 0AJ.* (Farnworth 72334)

ANDERSON, William David. b 39. St Jo Coll Auckld LTh 69. **d** 69 **p** 70 Bp McKenzie for Wel. Chap Huntley Sch Marton 69-77; V of Featherston 77-80; Bulls-Rangotea Dio Wel from 80. *203 Bridge Street, Bulls, NZ.*

ANDERSON, William Gloster. b 1892. Ord Test Sch Knutsford 22. Linc Th Coll 23. **d** 26 **p** 27 Linc. C of Grantham 26-28; St Alb Sneinton Nottm 28-30; Perm to Offic at St Bart Nottm 30-31; C of Warsop (in c of Welbeck) 31-36; Min of St Andr E Kirkby 36-39; V of Annesley 39-60; Perm to Offic Dio Lon from 60. *84 Halstead Road, N 21.*

ANDERSON, William John. b 33. Hur Coll Ont MDiv 72. **d** 72 **p** 73 Hur. C of Ox Centre Beachville & Eastwood 72-75; I of Mitchell 75-81; St Andr La Salle Dio Hur from 81. *220 Lafferty Avenue, Windsor, Ont., Canada.*

ANDERSON, William John. b 50. Univ of Windsor Ont BA 72. McGill Univ Montr MA 75. Montr Dioc Th Coll. **d** 75 Carib. C of St Paul's Cathl Carib 75-77; on leave 77-81; Perm to Offic Dio Caled from 81. *2288 Hemlock Street, Terrace, BC, Canada.*

ANDERSSON, Mervyn Ian. b 27. **d** 79 Bp Stanage for Johann **p** 80 Johann (NSM). C of Auckland Park Dio Johann from 79. *PO Box 73, Fontainebleau, S Africa 2032.*

ANDERTON, Frederic Michael. b 31. Pemb Coll Cam BA 58, MA 60. Westcott Ho Cam 65. **d** 66 **p** 67 Lon. C of St John's Wood Ch 66-71; All H Barking-by-the-Tower 71-77; St Giles Cripplegate City and Dio Lon from 77. *St Luke's House, Roscoe Street, EC1.* (01-253 4720)

ANDEWEG, Arie Jozinus. **d** 63 **p** 66 Jordan. P Dio Jordan 63-75; Dio Jer from 76. *c/o Christian Deaf Community, Box 2211, Beirut, Lebanon.*

ANDRE, John Frederick William. b 32. Univ of Dur BSc 59. Bps' Coll Cheshunt 59. **d** 61 Kens for Lon **p** 62 Lon. C of Ickenham 61-66; Chipping Barnet (in c of St Steph) 66-71; V of Arlesey w Astwick Dio St Alb from 71. *The Vicarage, Church Lane, Arlesey, Beds, SG15 6UX.* (Hitchin 731227)

ANDRESS, James Russell. Univ of Man BSc 25, MA 27. Cudd Coll 27. **d** 29 **p** 30 Wakef. C of Paddock 29-31; SPG Miss Kolhapur 31-37; Kolhapur 38; SPG Sec Dio Bom 38-50; Chap at Kurduwadi and at Sholapur 50-52; at Hubli Dio Bom 52-57; C of St Paul Crewe 57-61; V of St Thos Liscard Wallasey 61-67; RD of Wallasey 64-67; Hosp Chap I and Dio Nass from 67. *Box N-107, Nassau, Bahamas, W Indies.* (23299)

ANDREW, Brian. b 31. Oak Hill Coll 75. **d** 77 **p** 78 Chich. C of Broadwater 77-81; R of Nettlebed w Bix, Pishill and Highmoor Dio Ox from 81. *Rectory, Nettlebed, Henley-on-Thames, Oxon.*

ANDREW, Donald. Tyndale Hall Bris 63. **d** 66 Dover for Cant **p** 67 Cant. C of Ch Ch Croydon 66-69; Ravenhead 69-72; with Script U 72-77; V of Rushen Dio S & M from 77. *Rushen Vicarage, Port St Mary, IM.* (Port St Mary 2275)

ANDREW, Frank. b 17. St D Coll Lamp BA 49. Ely Th Coll 50. **d** 51 Whitby for York **p** 52 York. C of Howden 51-55; PC of Mosbrough 55-59; Min of St Pet Eccles Distr Greenhill Derbys 59-65; V 65-69; R of St John March 69-77; St Mary March 71-77; RD of March 73-77; Surr from 75; R of Tilbrook w Covington and Gt Catworth Dio Ely from 77. *Tilbrook Rectory, Huntingdon, Cambs, PE18 0JS.* (Tilbrook 329)

ANDREW, George Allen. Dalhousie Coll NS BA 04. Wycl Coll Tor 07. DD (*hon causa*). O of Excellent Crop (6th cl) 22. **d** 07 NS for Hur **p** 08 Hur. C of Mem Ch London Ont 07-09; R of Sebringville Hur 09-11; C of St Geo Winnipeg 11-13; R of Arichat Cape Breton 13-19; MSCC Miss at Kaifeng 19-25; Dioc Miss Dio Honan 25-40; Archd of W Honan 40-48; L to Offic at St Mich AA Tor 48-57. *89 Ellsworth Avenue, Toronto, Ont., Canada.*

ANDREW, George Herbert. b 10. KCMG 63. CB 56. CCC Ox BA 30, MA 34. St Deiniol's Libr Hawarden 71. **d** 71 **p** 72 York. C of Kirkbymoorside w Gillamoor, Bransdale & Farndale 71-76; Edenbridge Dio Roch from 77. *18 Stangrove Road, Edenbridge, Kent.* (Edenbridge 862569)

ANDREW, John. b 07. Univ of Lon 35. AKC 38. **d** 38 **p** 39 Man. C of H Trin Shaw 38-40; All SS Hindley 40-43; H Trin (in c of St Luke) Warrington 43-47; R of St Andr-by-the-Green Glas 47-51; Gourock 51-54; Lockerbie 54-59; V of Wrightington 59-69; Hognaston w Kniveton 69-73. *White House, Scredington, Sleaford, Lincs, NG34 0AB.*

ANDREW, John Gerald Barton. b 31. Late Squire Scho of Keble Coll Ox BA 55, MA 58. Nashotah Ho Sem Wisc Hon DD 77. Cudd Coll 54. **d** 56 **p** 57 York. C of Redcar 56-59; in Amer Ch 59-60; Dom Chap to Abp of York 60-61; Chap to Abp of Cant 61-69; Six Pr in Cant Cathl 67-72; V of Preston 69-72; RD of Preston 70-72; in Amer Ch from 72. *St Thomas Church, 5th Avenue & 53rd Street, New York, NY 10019, USA.*

ANDREW, Richard Lachlan. Moore Th Coll Syd. BD (Lon) 70; **d** 69 **p** 70 Syd. C of H Trin Miller's Point 69; H Trin Peakhurst 69-72; SAMS Miss 72-79; Exam Chap to Bp of Parag 76-79. *21 Lewis Street, Balgowlah, NSW, Australia.*

ANDREW, Richard Paul. b 53. Keble Coll Ox BA 75. St Steph Ho Ox 75. **d** 77 **p** 78 S'wark. C of St Pet Streatham 77-80; St Mary Kenton Dio Lon from 80. *660 Kenton Road, Kenton, HA3 9QN.* (01-204 1446)

ANDREW, Ronald Arthur. b 27. Sarum Th Coll 64. **d** 65 **p** 66 Blackb. C of St Cuthb Darwen 65-69; Padiham 69-71; V of H Trin Colne 71-76; Adlington Dio Blackb from 76. *35 Grove Crescent, Adlington, Chorley, Lancs.* (Adlington 480253)

ANDREW, Canon William Hugh. b 32. Selw Coll Cam 2nd cl Geog Trip pt i 55, BA 56, 2nd cl Th Trip pt ii 57, MA 60. Ridley Hall Cam 56. **d** 58 Kingston T for Guildf **p** 59 Guildf. C of St Mary of Bethany Woking 58-61; Farnborough (in c of Ch of Good Shepherd) 61-64; V of St Paul Gatten Shanklin 64-71; R of St Mary Weymouth 71-76; M Gen Syn from 75; V of St Jo Evang Heatherlands Parkstone Dio Sarum from 76; Can and Preb of Sarum Cathl from 81. *St John's Vicarage, Alexandra Road, Parkstone, Poole, Dorset, BH14 9EW.* (Parkstone 741276)

ANDREWES UTHWATT, Henry. b 25. Jes Coll Cam BA 49, MA 51. Wells Th Coll 49. **d** 51 **p** 52 Portsm. C of H Trin Fareham 51-55; Haslemere 55-59; Wimbledon (in c of Ch Ch) 59-61; V of Ch Ch W Wimbledon 61-73; Yeovil w Preston

Plucknett and Kingston Pitney 73-76; Team R of Yeovil Dio B & W from 76. *Rectory, West Park, Yeovil, Somt, BA20 1DE.* (Yeovil 5396)

ANDREWS, Thomas George Desmond. TCD **d** 63 Down **p** 64 Tuam for Down. C of Ballymacarrett 63-66; Ballynafeigh 66-70; I of Scarva 70-81; V of Newry Dio Drom from 81. *Vicarage, Windsor Avenue, Newry, Co Down.*

ANDREWS, Canon Alan Robert Williams. b 14. AKC 37. **d** 37 **p** 38 Roch. C of Ch Ch Milton-next-Gravesend 37-40; Stratfield-Mortimer (in c of St John) 40-45; Heanor (in c of All SS Marlpool) 45-47; R of Whittington Derbys 47-58; PC of Quarndon 58-68; V 68-79; Dir of Ordinands 58-78; Hon Can of Derby Cathl 77-79; Can (Emer) from 79. *12 Blenheim Drive, Allestree, Derby, DE3 2LB.*

ANDREWS, Alfred John. d 78 **p** 79 N Queensld. C of H Trin Ingham Dio N Queensld from 78. *c/o PO Box 58, Ingham, Qld, Australia 4850.*

ANDREWS, Alfred Vincent. St D Coll Lamp 54. **d** 56 **p** 57 St A. C of Rhosllanerchrugog 56-58; St Sav Pimlico 58-78. *Address temp unknown.*

ANDREWS, Anthony Brian. b 33. Univ of Lon BA (3rd cl Engl) 54, AKC 58. Coll of Resurr Mirfield 56. **d** 58 **p** 59 Lon. C of St Columba Haggerston 58-60; St Kath Hammersmith 60-63; V of Goldthorpe 63-74; St Mich AA Ladbroke Grove w Ch Ch Notting Hill Kens Dio Lon from 74. *35 St Lawrence Terrace, Ladbroke Grove, W10 5SR.* (01-969 0776)

ANDREWS, Anthony Bryan de Tabley. b 20. K Coll Lon BA 42. Linc Th Coll 42. **d** 44 **p** 45 Chelmsf. C of All SS, Hutton 44-48; All SS Marg Street St Marylebone 48-57; Chap to Ho of SS Mary and John Holyrood Witney 57-59; C of St Barn Ox 57-59; PC (V from 68) of Babbacombe 59-75; R of Worth Dio Chich from 75; RD of E Grinstead from 77. *Worth Rectory, Crawley, E Sussex, RH10 4RT.* (Crawley 882229)

ANDREWS, Anthony Frederick. b 25. K Coll Lon and Warm 54. **d** 55 **p** 56 Lon. C of Kentish Town 55-58; Belmont 58-60; R of Evershot w Frome St Quintin and Melbury Bubb 60-66; CF 66-69; C of St Mary Bridgwater 69-70; R of Cossington 70-73; C of Highworth w Sevenhampton, Inglesham & Hannington Dio Bris from 75. *Burford House, Highworth, SN6 7AD.* (Highworth 762796)

ANDREWS, Anthony John. b 35. SOC 75. **d** 80 **p** 81 S'wark. C of Cheam Dio S'wark from 80. *22 Priory Road, Cheam, Surrey, SM3 8LN.*

ANDREWS, Brian Keith. b 39. Keble Coll Ox BA 62, MA 69. Coll of Resurr Mirfield 62. **d** 64 **p** 65 Lon. C of Ch of Ch and St John w St Luke Isle of Dogs Poplar 64-68; Hemel Hempstead 68-71; Team V 71-79; V of Abbots Langley Dio St Alb from 79. *Vicarage, Abbots Langley, Watford, Herts, WD5 0AS.* (Kings Langley 63013)

ANDREWS, Christopher Paul. b 47. Fitzw Coll Cam BA 70, MA 73. Westcott Ho Cam 69. **d** 71 **p** 73 Cant. C of Croydon 72-75; All SS Gosforth (in c of Kingston Pk from 78) 75-80; Team V of The Epiph City and Dio Newc T from 80. *c/o 12 Shannon Court, Kingston Park, Newcastle upon Tyne, NE3 2XF.* (0632-864050)

ANDREWS, Clive Francis. b 50. AKC and BD 72. St Aug Coll Cant 72. **d** 73 **p** 74 S'wark. C of H Trin Clapham 73-75; Kidbrooke (in c of St Nich) 75-78; Dioc Youth Adv and Publ Pr Dio S'wark from 79. *48 Union Street, SE1 1TD.* (01-407 7911)

ANDREWS, Dennis Arthur. FCA (Engl) 62. Wycl Coll Tor Dipl Th 59. **d** 59 **p** 60 Fred. C of Portland 59-61; St John Deptford Lon 61-63; I of Prince William 63-67; H Trin Halifax Dio NS from 68. *6297 Jennings Street, Halifax, NS, Canada.* (422-9484)

ANDREWS, Derek George Hindmarsh. Trin Coll Dub (3rd cl Ment and Mor Sc) 51. MC 55. Cudd Coll 57. **d** 59 **p** 60 Ex. C of Paignton 59-62; St Mary Church 62-63; Chap Ch Coll Brecon 63-65; R of Syresham w Whitfield 65-68; Asst Hosp St Thos Hosp Lon 68-70; Chap Middx Hosp 70-72; V of St Luke Gt Ilford 72-76; Chap Gordon Sch Woking from 76. *The Gordon School, West End, Woking, Surrey.* (Chobham 8576)

ANDREWS, Donald. Montr Dioc Th Coll LTh 34. **d** 32 **p** 34 Montr. C of N Clarendon 32-34; I 34-38; I of Campbell's Bay 38-42; R of St Armand W 42-50; P-in-c of Hemmingford 50-56; R of St Alb Montr 56-62; P-in-c of St Hilda Montr 62-69. *3020 Glencrest Road, Apt 405, Burlington, Ont, L7N 2H2, Canada.*

ANDREWS, Canon Donald Finch. b 04. Univ of Lon BSc 25. Westcott Ho Cam 27. **d** 28 **p** 29 Win. C of St Mary Sholing 28-32; Ch Ch Luton (in c of St Pet) 32-35; V of Desborough 35-46; CF (R of O) 39-45; RD of Rothwell ii 45-46; V of Kingsthorpe 46-65; RD of Northn and Surr 55-65; Can (Non-res) of Pet 56-65; Proc Conv Pet 59-70; V of All SS Fulham 65-72; L to Offic Dio Pet from 72; Can (Emer) Dio Pet from 72. *11 Astrop Road, Kings Sutton, Banbury, Oxon.* (Banbury 811321)

ANDREWS, Donald Howes. St Francis Coll Brisb 75. **d** 77 **p** 78 Brisb. C of Southport 77-78; Perm to Offic Dio Brisb from 78. *10 Warwick Street, Toowoomba, Queensland, Australia 4350.*

ANDREWS, Edward Robert. b 33. St Mich Coll Llan 62. **d** 64 **p** 65 Lich. C of St Mary Kingswinford 64-70; Chap RAF from 70. *c/o Ministry of Defence, Adastral House, WC1.*

ANDREWS, Eric Charles. AKC 41. **d** 41 **p** 42 Liv. C of St Jo Bapt Tuebrook 41-44; All SS Kettering 44-46; Letchworth 46-54; V of All S Clive Vale Hastings 54-63; St Andr Eastbourne 63-73; R of E Blatchington Dio Chich from 73. *East Blatchington Rectory, Blatchington Hill, Seaford, Sussex.* (Seaford 892964)

ANDREWS, Eric Keith. b 11. Tyndale Hall Bris 36. **d** 38 Lon **p** 39 Willesden for Lon. C of St Mary North End Fulham 38-40; P-in-c of St Thos Kensal Town Lon 40-42; C of H Trin Worthing (in c of St Matt) 42-47; R of Newick 47-56; Pembridge w Moorcourt 56-66; V of Kiambu and Limuru Kenya 66-70; R of Stanton 70-76; Perm to Offic Dio Heref from 76. *Old Post House, Hope-under-Dinmore, Leominster, Herefs, HR6 0PJ.* (Bodenham 631)

ANDREWS, Herbert Frederick Richard. Roch Th Coll. **d** 64 **p** 65 Ex. C of Tipton St John w Venn Ottery 64-66; Sidbury w Sidford 66-76. *14 Parkside, Belmont Park, Bedhampton, Havant, Hants.*

ANDREWS, John. b 25. Bps' Coll Cheshunt 67. **d** 68 **p** 69 Hertf for Cant for St Alb. C of All SS, Hockerill 68-73; V of Rye Pk 73-80; R of L Berkhamsted w Bayford, Essendon and Ponsbourne Dio St Alb from 80. *Rectory, Little Berkhamsted, Hertford.* (Cuffley 5940)

ANDREWS, John Colin. b 47. Sarum Wells Th Coll 78. **d** 80 B & W **p** 81 Taunton for B & W. C of Burnham-on-Sea Dio B & W from 80. *6 Jaycroft Road, Burnham-on-Sea, Somerset, TA8 1LE.*

ANDREWS, Preb John Douglas. b 19. Keble Coll Ox BA 39, MA 44. Chich Th Coll 40. **d** 42 **p** 43 S'wark. C of St Aug S Bermondsey 42-44; St Jo Evang w All SS Waterloo Road Lon 44-46; Towcester 46-50; H Cross Shrewsbury 50-52; V of Ettingshall 52-59; St Andr Walsall 59-68; Penkhull 68-80; P-in-c of Chebsey Dio Lich from 80; Ellenhall Dio Lich from 80; Preb at Lich Cathl from 81. *Chebsey Vicarage, Stafford, ST21 6JU. Stafford 760271)*

ANDREWS, John Elfric. b 35. Ex Coll Ox BA (3rd cl Th) 59, MA 63. Wycl Hall Ox. **d** 61 Glouc **p** 62 Tewkesbury for Glouc. C of Cheltm 61-66; Cands' Sec Lon City Miss from 66. *27 Woodbourne Avenue, Streatham, SW16 1UP.* (01-769 7569)

ANDREWS, John Francis. b 34. Jes Coll Cam BA 58, MA 61. SOC 78. **d** 81 Cant. Hon C of All SS w St Marg U Norwood Dio Cant from 81. *46 Cypress Road, SE25 4AU.*

ANDREWS, John George William. b 42. Qu Coll Birm 65. **d** 68 Aston for Birm **p** 69 Birm. C of St Matt Smethwick 68-71; CF from 71. *RAChD, Bagshot Park, Bagshot, Surrey.*

ANDREWS, Preb John Hugh Barker. MBE 64. Worc Coll Ox BA (1st cl Th) 28, MA 32. **d** 29 **p** 30 Ex. Asst Chap and Master Blundell's Sch 29-33; C and Lect of Leeds 33-35; C of Filleigh w E Buckland and Offg Chap and Asst Master W Buckland Sch 35-37; Perm to Offic at Leeds 37-39; Offg Chap and Asst Master Leeds Gr Sch 38-39; Chap RNVR 40-46; V of Chittlehampton w Umberleigh Dio Ex from 46; Proc Conv Ex 59-80; RD of S Molton 60-65; Preb of Ex from 61; Sub-Dean of Ex Cathl from 71. *Chittlehampton Vicarage, Umberleigh, Devon.* (Chittlehamholt 201)

ANDREWS, John Viccars. b 31. St Edm Hall Ox BA (3rd cl Phys) 55. St Steph Ho Ox 55. **d** 58 **p** 59 Lon. C of H Redeemer Clerkenwell 58-63; Tilehurst 63-69; Abingdon w Shippon 69-76; R of Mundford w Lynford Dio Nor from 76; Ickburgh w Langford Dio Nor from 76; Cranwich Dio Nor from 76. *Mundford Rectory, Thetford, Norf, IP26 5DS.* (Mundford 220)

ANDREWS, Joseph William. b 38. **d** 76 Les. d Dio Les. *St Joseph's Mission, Mohloka, PO Lebihan Falls, via Masau, Lesotho, S Africa.*

ANDREWS, Keith. b 47. St Mich AA Coll Llan 79. **d** 81 Llan. C of Penarth w Lavernock Dio Llan from 81. *153 Windsor Road, Penarth, S Glam.*

ANDREWS, Canon Leonard Martin. b 1886. MC 17, MBE 44, CVO 46. Qu Coll Cam BA 09, MA 21. **d** 09 **p** 10 Lon. C of St Paul Winchmore Hill 09-12; R of Brewarrina NSW 13-14; Vice-Prin Bro of Good Shepherd NSW 14-15; TCF 14-19; Hon CF 21; Chap at Khartoum 20-22; RD of Trigg Major 29-32; R of Stoke Climsland 22-68; Hon Can of St Carantoc in Truro Cathl from 32; Chap to HM the King 36-52; to HM the Queen 52-69; Proc Conv Truro 47-50 and 51-60. *Climsland, Downderry, Torpoint, Cornw.* (Downderry 261)

ANDREWS, Moses R. b 36. Trin Coll Legon 71. **d** 74 **p** 75 Kum. P Dio Kum. *Box 144, Kumasi, Ghana.*

ANDREWS, Neville John William. **d** 62 **p** 63 C & Goulb. C of Yass 62-64; Wagga Wagga 64-70; St Laur Barkingside 70-73; P-in-c of Belconnen *B* Canberra 73-76; Perm to Offic Dio C & Goulb from 76. *5 Toomey Place, Spence, ACT, Australia 2615.*

ANDREWS, Paul Rodney Gwyther. b 16. **d** 77 **p** 78 Mon (NSM). C of Geotre 77-80; L to Offic Dio Swan B from 81. *Bromelys, Llangorse, Brecon, Powys, LD3 7UG.* (0874-84296)

ANDREWS, Peter Alwyne. b 44. Univ of Lon BSc 67. Westcott Ho Cam 70. **d** 73 **p** 74 Bradf. C of Barnoldswick 73-76; Maltby 77-78; V of St Osw Little Horton City and Dio Bradf from 78. *St Oswald's Vicarage, Christopher Street, Bradford, BD5 9DH.* (Bradf 71748)

ANDREWS, Robert Ernest. Moore Th Coll Syd THl 56. **d** and **p** 57 Syd. C of Mosman 57-59; CMS Miss Dio Centr Tang 59-65; Dio Moro 65-71; P-in-c of Milton 72; Assoc R of Kangaroo Valley 72-73; CMS Miss Dio Nak 73-78; R of Regents Pk w Birrong Dio Syd from 78. *128 Kingsland Road, Regents Park, NSW, Australia 2143.* (64-2500)

ANDREWS, Rodney Osborne. Univ of Sask BA 63. Em Coll Sktn BTh 65. **d** 64 **p** 65 Calg. C of Red Deer 64; Lethbridge 65; R of Okotoks 66-73; St Leon-on-the-Hill Red Deer 73-76; I of Blood Miss 76-79; Coaldale Dio Calg from 79. *Box 1093, Coaldale, Alta, Canada, T0K 0L0.* (345 5918)

ANDREWS, Ronald Sidney. b 29. St Alb Ministerial Tr Scheme 77. **d** 80 **p** 81 St Alb. C of Hitchin Dio St Alb from 80. *96 Old Hale Way, Hitchin, Herts, SG5 1XS.*

ANDREWS, Canon Roydon Percival. Univ of NZ BA 63. Coll Ho Ch Ch NZ Bd of Th Stud LTh 39. **d** 38 **p** 39 Ch Ch. C of Fendalton 38-41; P-in-c of Akaroa 41-43; CF (NZ) 43-46; V of Akaroa 46-48; RD of Banks Peninsula 46; V of Addington 48-51; Highfield 51-57; Linwood-Aranui 57-60; Hosp Chap Ch Ch 60-65; Hon Can of Ch Ch 61-75; Can (Emer) from 75; V of Cashmere Hills 65-70; Prec of Ch Ch Cathl 71-75; Chap St Geo Hosp Ch Ch 72-75; P-in-c of Ngalo 75-76; Chap Wel Hosps 76-77; Perm to Offic Dio Wel from 77. *21 Oriwa Street, Waikanae, NZ.* (3208)

ANDREWS, Canon Stanley. Montr Dioc Th Coll. **d** 27 Queb for Montr **p** 27 Montr. C of Charteris 27-29; R of All SS Montr 29-38; Chap of St Andr Home Montr 38-41 and from 45; Chap NPAM 41-45; Dom Chap to Bp of Montr 40-41 and 52-55; Hon Can of Montr 53-54 and 65-69; Can (Emer) from 69; Sec Ont Dioc Synod 54-55; Hon Can of Ch Ch Cathl Kingston Ont 55; R of St Matt Montr 55-68; L to Offic Dio BC from 71. *Apt 301, 1555 Richmond Avenue, Victoria, BC, Canada.*

ANDREWS, Walford Brian. b 34. St D Coll Lamp BA 54. St Mich Coll Llan. **d** 57 **p** 58 Llan. C of Canton 57-62; Port Chap Miss to Seamen Madras 62-65; Rotterdam 65-66; Bunbury 66-69; Port Chap Miss to Seamen Rotterdam 70-77; RD of The Netherlands 75-77; Chap Miss to Seamen Kingston-upon-Hull from 77. *900 Hedon Road, Hull.* (Hull 76322)

ANDREWS, Wilfrid Seymour. Trin Coll Ox BA (2nd cl Hist) 34, MA 38. PhD (Lon) 53. Ely Th Coll 34. **d** 35 **p** 36 S'wark. C of St Sav Brockley Hill 35-36; St Jas New Malden 36-40; Asst Master and Chap of Aldenham Sch 40-45; R of Gt Warley 45-50; Asst Master Brentwood Sch 47-50; Gresham's Sch Holt 50-72; Chap 50-60; Dioc Insp of Schs Dio Chelmsf 46-50; LPr Dio Nor from 50. *Hill House, Cley-next-the-Sea, Holt, Norfolk.* (Cley 740 737)

ANDRIAMAROMANANA, Rivosoa Alphonse. **d** 75 **p** 77 Antan. P Dio Antan. *Ambanitsena, Sadabe, Manjakandriana, Malagasy Republic.*

ANDRIAMIHARISOA, Lala. K Coll Lon and Warm 61. **d** 65 **p** 66 Madag. P Dio Madag 65-68; Dio Antan from 68; Vice-Prin of St Paul's Th Coll Antan 70-75; Sub-Dean of Antan Cathl from 75. *BP 3715, Antananarivo, Malagasy Republic.*

ANDRIES, William Lloyd Lisle. Codr Coll Barb 57. **d** 61 Barb for Gui **p** 61 Gui. C of Bartica 61-65; V of Morawhanna 65-68; CF (Guy) 68-69; V of Leguam 69-74; St Barn Georgetn 74-76. *c/o Vicarage, Bourda, Georgetown, Guyana.* (02-61728)

ANENE, Daniel Ebozinem. b 35. Trin Coll Umuahia 71. **d** 73 **p** 74 Niger. P Dio Niger. *Ebenezer Parsonage, Box 40, Afoigwe, Ogida, ECS, Nigeria.*

ANGA, Vincent Kalaru Kulo. **d** 47 Bp Onyeabo for Niger. d Dio Niger 47-52; Dio Nig Delta 52-70. *c/o St Martin's Church, Ogu, Via Okrika, Nigeria.*

ANG'ANG'O, Richard. St Paul's Th Coll Limuru 66. **d** 68 **p** 69 Maseno. P Dio Maseno 68-69; Dio Maseno N from 70; Exam Chap to Bp of Maseno N from 76. *PO Box 1, Maseno, Kenya.*

ANGEES, Moses. b 36. **d** 77 **p** 78 Keew. C of St Jas Wunnumin Lake Dio Keew from 77. *St James Church, Wunnumin Lake, Ont, P0V 2Z0, Canada.*

ANGEL, Gervais Thomas David. b 36. Ch Ch Ox 2nd cl Cl Mods 57, BA (2nd cl Lit Hum) 59, 2nd cl Th 61, MA 62. Univ of Bris MEducn 78. **d** 61 **p** 62 St D. C of Abth 61-65; Tutor Clifton Th Coll from 65; L to Offic Dio Bris from 65; Dean of Stud Trin Coll Bris 72-81; Dir of Stud from 81. *24 Stoke Hill, Stoke Bishop, Bristol 9.* (Bristol 683996)

ANGELA, Johannes Otieno. **d** 76 **p** 77 Maseno S. P Dio Maseno S. *Box 11, Maseno, Kenya.*

ANG'IELA, Hezron. St Phil Sch. **d** 67 **p** 68 Maseno. P Dio Maseno S from 68. *AC Manyatta, PO Papondìti, Kisumu, Kenya.*

ANGOLIBO, Ven Eriya. **d** 50 U Nile **p** 53 Bp Tomusange for U Nile. P Dio U Nile 50-61; Dio N Ugan 61-69; Dio M & W Nile from 69; Archd of Oyibu from 74. *PO Box 37, Arua, Uganda.*

ANGULU, John Ndace. **d** and **p** 55 N Nig. P Dio N Nig 55-80; Can of N Nig 72-80. *Box 14, Bida, Nigeria.*

ANGUS, Brian. Univ of Natal BA 64. Westcott Ho Cam 67. **d** 68 **p** 69 Natal. C of St Pet, Pietermaritzburg 68-73; L to Offic Dio Natal 73-80; Dio Johann from 80. *31 Urania Street, Observatory 2198, S Africa.*

ANGUS, Edward. b 39. Univ of Man BA 60. Univ of Birm Dipl Th 61. Qu Coll Birm 60. **d** 62 **p** 63 Blackb. C of St Geo Chorley 62-65; H Trin S Shore Blackpool 65-68; R of Bretherton 68-76; V of Altham w Clayton-le-Moors Dio Blackb from 76. *Vicarage, Church Street, Clayton-le-Moors, Accrington, Lancs BB5 5HT.* (Accrington 384321)

ANGUS, Francis James Glendenning. b 12. Univ of Lon BD and AKC 35. QUB PhD 59. **d** 35 **p** 36 Pet. C of Finedon 35-38; The Quinton 38-39; Boxmoor 39-44; Chap Abbot's Hill Sch 42-44; CF (EC) 44-47; Asst Dir of Relig Educn Dio Cov 47-50; Dir 50-54; Sen Script Master R Belf Acad Inst 54-77. *2 Sarum Way, Calne, Wilts, SN11 0EZ.*

ANGWIN, Richard Paul. b 25. K Coll Lon and Warm AKC 56. ACA 49, FCA 60. **d** 56 **p** 57 Chelmsf. C of St Jas Clacton-on-Sea 56-59; V of Brightlingsea 59-69; Surr from 65; V of S Woodford 69-75; Chap Wanstead Hosp 69-75; V of Halstead (w Greenstead Green from 79) Dio Chelmsf from 75; C-in-c of Greenstead Green 75-79. *Vicarage, Parsonage Street, Halstead, Essex, CO9 2LD.* (Halstead 472171)

ANIAGO, Moses Chukuemeka. **d** 53 **p** 55 Niger. P Dio Niger 53-71. *c/o St Philip's Parsonage, Ogidi, Nigeria.*

ANIDO, John David Forsdyke. b 16. Mert Coll Ox 2nd cl Cl Mods 36, BA (3rd cl Lit Hum) 38, 2nd cl Th 39, MA 41. McGill Univ Montr PhD 75. Westcott Ho Cam 39. **d** 40 **p** 41 Lon. C of St Mary Stoke Newington 40-45; Cobham (in c of St John's Miss Ch) 45-47; P-in-c Labrador Miss Dio Queb 47-51; R of Harbledown 52-57; Hon Sec Cant Dioc Conf 54-57; Prof and Warden of Div Ho at Bp's Univ Lennoxville 57-76; V of Bp Auckland Dio Dur from 76. *St Andrew's Vicarage, Park Street, Bishop Auckland, Co Durham, DL14*

ANIKWENWA, Canon Maxwell Samuel Chukwunweike. b 40. Trin Coll Umuahia 64. **d** 66 **p** 68 Niger. P Dio Niger from 68; Hon Can of Niger and Synod Sec from 76. *St Andrew's Church, Onitsha, Nigeria.*

ANIONS, Richard Henzell. Hur Th Coll. **d** 55 **p** 58 Hur. I of Lion's Head 55-57; Ailsa Craig 57-62; Wiarton 62-68; R of Glencoe 68-70; Southn 70-75; Woodhouse 75-80; Listowel and Palmerston 80-81; Miss at St John Ft Smith Dio Arctic from 81. *Box 64, Fort Smith, NWT, Canada.*

ANJULU, Barnaba. **d** 74 Sudan. d Dio Sudan 74-76; Dio Omdurman from 76. *Box 8, Kadugli, Sudan.*

ANKER, George William. b 10. K Coll Lon and Warm AKC (2nd cl) 51. **d** 51 **p** 52 S'wark. C of Richmond Surrey 51-54; St Pet Battersea 54-57; Shere 57-62; Leatherhead (in c of All SS) 62-68; V of Brockley Hill 68-72; C of Sanderstead 72-76; Perm to Offic Dio S'wark from 76. *11 Hamsey Green Gardens, Warlingham, Surrey, CR3 9RS.* (01-820 2636)

ANKER, Malcolm. b 39. St D Coll Lamp BA (2nd cl Mod Hist) 61. Bps' Coll Cheshunt 61. **d** 63 **p** 64 York. C of Marfleet 63-66; Cottingham 66-69; V of Skirlaugh w Long Riston 69-74; Elloughton and Brough w Brantingham Dio York from 74. *Elloughton Vicarage, Brough, N Humb, HU15 1HT.* (Hull 667431)

ANKETELL, Jeyarajan. b 41. Univ of Lon BSc 62, PhD 67. Coll of Resurr Mirfield 69. **d** 73 **p** 74 Newc T. Asst Chap Univ of Newc T 73-75; Univ of Lon (W) 75-77; Asst Master ILEA from 78; L to Offic Dio S'wark from 81. *5 Norman Court, 296 Leigham Court Road, SW16 2QP.*

ANKOLE, EAST, Lord Bishop of. *See* Betungura, Right Rev Amos.

ANKOLE, WEST, Lord Bishop of. *See* Bamunoba, Right Rev Yoramu.

ANKOR, Robert William. ACT ThL 75. St Barn Coll Adel. **d** 74 **p** 75 Murray. C of Naracoorte 74-75; Mt Gambier 76-78; P-in-c of Pinnaroo 78-81; R of Mannum w Mt Pleasant Dio Murray from 81. *6 Adelaide Road, Mannum, S Australia 5238.* (085-69 1130)

ANKRAH, Canon Leopold. BSc (Econ) Lon 55. Hur Coll Dipl Th 67. **d** 67 **p** 68 Accra. P Dio Accra; Hon Can of Accra and Exam Chap to Bp of Accra from 75. *PO Box 8, Accra, Ghana.* (Accra 63853)

ANKRAH, Robert Amoo Aflah Cofie. St Aug Coll Kumasi. **d** and **p** 32 Accra. P Dio Accra 32-68. *P.O. Box 36, Kaneshi, Accra, Ghana.*

ANNAKIN, William. b 15. Worc Ordin Coll 63. **d** 65 **p** 66 Linc. C of Barton-on-Humber 65-69; P-in-c of Wigtoft 69-72; V 72-77; P-in-c of Kirton Holme 75-76; Langrick w Wildmore Dio Linc from 76; V of Brothertoft (w Kirton Holme 76-79) Dio Linc from 76. *Brothertoft Vicarage, Boston, Lincs, PE20 3SW.* (Langrick 267)

ANNEAR, Francis William John. Univ of Lon BA (3rd cl Hist) and AKC 33. **d** 65 **p** 66 Perth. C of Scarborough 65-67; P-in-c of Margaret River 72-74; R of Donnybrook 74-76; Perm to Offic Dio Perth from 80. *48 Leach Highway, Melville, W Australia 6156.*

ANNEAR, Hubert Tours. b 24. Bede Coll Dur BA 49. Univ of Leeds MA (Th) 58. Linc Th Coll 49. **d** 51 **p** 52 Ripon. C of Holbeck 51-55; Adel 55-57; V of Middleton 57-64; Miss UMCA 64-65; USPG 65-71; V of Bierley 71-76; St Paul Morley Dio Wakef from 76. *St Paul's Vicarage, Morley, Leeds, LS27 9ER.* (Morley 534530)

ANNELY, Maurice James Leonard. b 22 Qu Coll Birm 77. **d** 80 Shrewsbury for Lich (NSM). C of Tettenhall Regis Dio Lich from 80. *177 Tettenhall Road, Wolverhampton, WV6 0BZ.*

ANNESLEY, William Gerald. K Coll Lon BD 72. St Aug Coll Cant 72. **d** 73 Kens for Lon **p** 74 Lon. C of St Steph w St Thos Hammersmith 73-76; Team V of Fincham 77-81; Lowestoft Group Dio Nor from 81. *St Peter's Rectory, Kirkley, Lowestoft, Suffolk.* (Lowestoft 5391)

ANNET, John Thomas. b 20. TD 66. Selw Coll Cam BA (3rd cl Th Trip Pt i) 49, MA 53. Westcott Ho Cam 49. **d** 51 **p** 52 Man. C of Chorlton-cum-Hardy 51-54; Ch Ch Ashton L 54-56; CF (TA) 54-67; V of Hindsford 56-66; R of Ch Ch W Didsbury 66-75; V of Gt Budworth Dio Ches from 75. *Great Budworth Vicarage, Northwich, Chesh.* (Comberbach 891324)

ANNIS, Herman North. Lich Th Coll 62. **d** 64 **p** 65 Lon. C of St Aug Kilburn 64-67; St Agnes Toxt Pk Dio Liv 67-70; V from 70. *The Vicarage, 1 Buckingham Avenue, Liverpool, L17 3BA.* (051-733 1742)

ANNIS, Rodney James. b 43. Univ of Ex BA (Th) 75, MA (Moral & Soc Phil) 79. Ripon Coll Cudd 75. **d** 76 **p** 77 Ex. C of Brixham 76-77; Asst Chap Univ of Ex and Chap Ex Sch 77-80; Lect St Botolph Boston from 80. *Ashby Lodge, 22 South Parade, Boston, Lincs, PE21 7PN.*

ANNOBIL, Theophilus Amos. St Aug Coll Kumasi. **d** and **p** 48 Accra. P Dio Accra. *P.O. Box 25, Saltpond, Nigeria.*

✠ **ANNOBIL, Right Rev Theophilus Samuel Anyanya.** Univ of Ghana LTh 65. **d** 65 **p** 66 Accra. P Dio Accra 65-81; Can of Accra 68-81; Cons Ld Bp of Sekondi 18 Oct 81. *PO Box 14, Takoradi, Ghana.* (Takoradi 3647)

ANOKWUO, Aaron Nna. b 34. Trin Coll Umuahia 62. **d** 64 **p** 65 Nig Delta. P Dio Nig Delta 65-72; Dio Aba 72-78. *c/o St Stephen's Church, Umuobasi, Amavo, Nigeria.*

ANONBY, Daniel Erling. b 38. Univ of BC BA 64. **d** and **p** 80 Caled. Assoc P of St Matt Terrace Dio Caled from 80. *4011 N Eby Street, Terrace, BC, Canada, V8G 2Z9.*

ANOSIKE, Stephen Oparaocha. St Paul's Coll Awka 63. **d** 63 **p** 64 Ow. P Dio Ow. *Parsonage, Iheteoha, Box 64, Owerri, Nigeria.*

ANOZIE, Philip Obiagwu. Trin Coll Umuahia. **d** 53 **p** 57 Nig Delta. P Dio Nig Delta 53-69; Dio Ow 70-76. *St Stephen's Church, Ogberuru, Nigeria.*

ANSCOMBE, John Thomas. b 51. Univ of Ex BA 72. Cranmer Hall Dur Dipl Th 73. **d** 74 **p** 75 Ripon. C of Ch Ch U Armley 74-77; St Geo Leeds 78-81; Executive Producer Script U Sound & Vision Unit from 81. *78 The Drive, Beckenham, Kent, BR3 1EG.* (01-650 7669)

ANSCOMBE, Canon Thomas. b 15. Qu Coll Cam 2nd cl Cl Trip pt i 36, BA 37, MA 41. Ridley Hall Cam 37. **d** 39 **p** 40 Southw. C of Lenton 39-45; V of St Mary Becontree 45-52; R of St Nich Nottm 52-57; Prin Clifton Th Coll Bris 57-64; R of Kirkheaton 64-80; Hon Can of Wakef Cathl 77-80; Can (Emer) from 80; L to Offic Dio Bradf from 80. *51 Long Meadow, Skipton, N Yorks, BD23 1BP.*

ANSELL, Antony Michael. b 40. St Jo Coll Nottm 78. **d** 80 **p** 81 Willesden for Lon. C of St Mich AA Harrow Weald Dio Lon from 80. *74 Bishop Ken Road, Harrow, Middx, HA3 7HR.* (01-861 1710)

ANSELL, Howard. b 36. St Jo Coll Cam BA 59, MA 62. N-W Ordin Course 73. **d** 76 **p** 77 Doncaster for Sheff. C of Chapeltown 76-79; V of St Thos w St Jas Worsbrough Dio Sheff from 79. *13 Bank End Road, Worsbrough Dale, Barnsley, Yorks, S70 4AF.* (Barnsley 203426)

ANSELL, John Christopher. b 49. Sarum & Wells Th Coll 79. **d** 81 Roch. C of St Alb Dartford Dio Roch from 81. *11 Teesdale Road, Dartford, Kent, DA2 6LJ.* (Dartford 70444)

ANSELL, Kenneth Frank. St Jo Coll Morpeth ACT ThL 63. **d** 64 **p** 65 Graft. C of Port Macquarie 64-66; St Thos N Syd 66-68; P-in-c of Howrah Par Distr 68-69; R 69-77; Chap Avalon Commun Lara 77-78; I of H Trin Coburg Dio Melb from 78. *520 Sydney Road, Coburg, Vic, Australia 3058.* (35 1439)

ANSON, Peter George. b 35. ACT ThL 69. St Barn Coll Adel 67. **d** 70 **p** 71 Adel. C of St D Burnside 70-72; P-in-c of Kidman Pk w Flinders Pk 72-76; R of Loxton 76-80; Perm to Offic Dio Adel from 80. *115 Swaine Avenue, Toorak Gardens, S Australia 5065.*

ANSTEY, Christopher Robin Paul. b 25. Late Scho of Trin Coll Ox 1st cl Cl Mods 42, BA (2nd cl Lit Hum) and Liddon Stud 49, 2nd cl Th 50, MA 50. St Steph Ho Ox 49. **d** 51 **p** 52 Lon. C of St Nich Chiswick 51-57; PV of Chich Cathl and Vice-Prin Chich Th Coll 57-64; V of St Andr Headington Ox 64-71; L to Offic Dio Ches 72-75; Dio Worc 75-79; Chap Westwood Ho Sch Pet from 79; Hon Min Can of Pet Cathl from 79. *164 Welland Road, Peterborough, Cambs.*

ANSTICE, John Neville. b 39. Univ of Lon BSc (Math) 63. Cudd Coll 69. **d** 71 **p** 72 Stepney for Lon. C of St Mich AA, Stoke Newington 71-74; Chap Woodbridge Sch 74-76; Team V of Droitwich (in c of St Mich Salwarpe) Dio Worc from 76. *Salwarpe Rectory, Droitwich, Worcs, WR6 0AH.* (Droitwich 3011)

ANTANANARIVO, Lord Bishop of. *See* Randrianovona, Right Rev Ephraim.

ANTHONISZ, Matthew Wilfred. b 30. Univ of Adel BA 55. **d** 74 **p** 75 Sing (APM). P Dio Sing. *41 Ceylon Road, Singapore 15.*

ANTHONY, Charles William. b 15. St Cath Coll Cam 2nd cl Hist Trip Pt i 37, BA (2nd cl Hist Trip pt ii) 38, MA 42. Ely Th Coll 38. **d** 39 **p** 40 Wakef. C of Battyeford 39-41; St Mich AA Conv Distr Hull 42-43; St Lawr w St Nich and New Fulford York 43-45; Asst Master Barnsley Gr Sch 45-52; Boys' County Sec Sch Barnsley 52-55; C of Stocksbridge 55-59; V of Hook (w Airmyn from 78) Dio Sheff from 59; C-in-c of Airmyn 59-78. *Hook Vicarage, Goole, N Humb, DN14 5PN.* (Goole 3654)

ANTHONY, David. St Francis Th Coll Brisb. ACT ThL 59. **d** 58 **p** 59 Brisb. C of Ch Ch Bundaberg 58-59; All SS Chermside 59-61; V of All SS Texas 61-65; P-in-c of Beenleigh 65-77; Kingston-Woodridge Dio Brisb from 77. *Redford Street, Kingston, Queensland, Australia 4114.* (208 9869)

ANTHONY, Canon David Ivor Morgan. St Aug Coll Cant 26. Univ of Dur LTh 32. **d** 31 **p** 32 Leic. C of St Matt Leic 31-34; M of St Steph Bush Bro and R of Quorn 34-37; P-in-c of St Luke Bal 37-42; Jamestown 42-44; V and Sub-Dean of Ch Ch Cathl Bal 44-51; Can 47-57; Chap C of E Girls' Gr Sch Bal 48-51; V of St John Horsham Vic 51-57; R of St Paul Bend 57-74; Can of Bend 58-74; Hon Can 74-75; Can (Emer) from 75; Perm to Offic Dio Bend from 74. *222 Neale Street, Bendigo, Vic, Australia.* (054-43 0641)

ANTHONY, Gerald Caldecott. b 18. Down Coll Cam BA 41, MA 44. Wycl Hall OX 41. **d** 43 **p** 44 Lon. C of Ch Ch Roxeth 43-47; Harlington (in c of Ch Ch Miss) 47-49; V of St Bart Gray's Inn Road Lon 49-51; C of St Budeaux Devonport (in c of Ernesettle) 51-55; V of All SS w St Barn S Lambeth 55-58; Chap Parkstone Sea Tr Sch Poole 58-64; Chap RN 64-65; C-in-c of Bulmer w Welburn and Castle Howard Dio York 65-66; R 66-72; V of Broughton-in-Furness w Woodland 72-75; C-in-c of Ulpha w Seathwaite 73-75; V of Broughton and Duddon Dio Carl from 75. *Vicarage, Broughton-in-Furness, Cumb, LA20 6HS.* (Broughton-in-Furness 305)

ANTHONY, Hugh George Barnabas. b 09. Selw Coll Cam BA 31, MA 40. Wells Th Coll 32. **d** 32 **p** 33 S'wark. C of St Aug S Bermonsey 32-35; Limpsfield (in c of St Andr) 35-40; CF 40-50; C of St Mary Wimbledon 50-53; V of Wonersh 53-80; RD of Guildf 63-68. *3 Southbury, Lawn Road, Guildford, Surrey, GU2 5DD.* (Guildford 34172)

ANTHONY, Ian Charles. b 47. N-W Ordin Course 76. **d** 79 **p** 80 Man. Hon C of L Lever Dio Man from 79; Dep Hd St Matt's Sch L Lever from 79. *36 Meadow Close, Little Lever, Bolton, Lancs.* (Farnworth 791437)

ANTHONY, Isaac. **d** 48 **p** 49 Natal. C of St Paul's Miss Pietermaritzburg 48-54; P-in-c 54-60; C of St Aid Durban 60-62; P-in-c of Ch Ch Overport Durban 62-65; R 65-67; St Paul Pietermaritzburg 67-68. *3 George Street, Pietermaritzburg, Natal, S Africa.*

ANTHONY, Thomas Murray. b 35. Univ of BC BA 58. Gen Th Sem NY STB 61. **d** 61 New Westmr **p** 62 Puerto Rico. In Amer Ch 62-72; Dir Nat & World Programme Angl Ch of Canada from 72. *c/o 600 Jarvis Street, Toronto, Ont, Canada.*

ANTHONÝ, William Robert. K Coll NS. **d** 46 **p** 47 NS. R of Falmouth 46-49; St Clements 49-54; Parrsboro 54-58;

Jordan 58-61; St Aid Oakville 61-69; Thorold 69-74; Hon Can of Niag 70-80; R of Fort Erie 74-80. *493 Patricia Drive, Oakville, Ont., Canada.*

ANTIGUA, Lord Bishop of. *See* Lindsay, Right Rev Orland Ugham.

ANTIGUA, Dean of. *See* Carty, Very Rev Hilton Manasseh.

ANTSIRANANA, Lord Bishop of. *See* Josoa, Right Rev Gabriel.

ANUSIEM, Goodwill Uzuebo Andrew. Melville Hall Ibad. **d** 54 Nig Delta **p** 55 N Nig. P Dio N Nig 55-59; Dio Ow from 59. *Parsonage, Ehime, Owerri, Nigeria.*

ANYANGO, Harrison. b 44. St Paul's Coll Limuru 70. **d** 72 **p** 73 Maseno S. P Dio Maseno S. *Box 1710, Ngere, Kisumu, Kenya.*

ANYANWU, Jeremiah Nnadozie. Trin Coll Umuahia 60. **d** 62 **p** 63 Ow. P Dio Ow. *Parsonage, Oguta, Owerri, Nigeria.* (Oguta 32)

ANYEKO, Nikolasi. **d** 77 Lango. d Dio Lango. *PO Orum, Olilum, Lira, Uganda.*

ANYIAM, Nathan Alwadibenma. Im Coll Ibad 55. **d** 58 **p** 59 N Nig. P Dio N Nig 59-66; Dio Nig from 67. *Parsonage, Ojoto, Nigeria.*

ANYIWO, Jeremiah Ude. St Paul's Coll Awka. **d** 45 **p** 47 Niger. P Dio Lagos 45-50; Dio Niger 50-59; Dio Ow 59-68; Can of All SS Cathl Egbu 59-64; Archd of Ow 64-68. *c/o St Mary's Parsonage, PO Box 36, Oguta, Nigeria.*

AOTEAROA, Bishop of. *See* Vercoe, Right Rev Whakahuihui.

APATA, Gabriel Adepoju. Im Coll Ibad. **d** 65 **p** 66 Ibad. P Dio Ibad 65-74; Dio Ilesha from 74. *Vicarage, Esa-Oke, via Ilesha, Nigeria.*

APENA, Benjamin Paul. **d** 39 **p** 41 Niger. P Dio Niger 41-62; Dio Benin from 62; Can of Benin 62-67; Archd 67-77. *Parsonage, P.O. Box 3, Oleh, Ughelli, Nigeria.*

ap IORWERTH, Geraint. b 50. St D Coll Lamp Dipl Th 72. Open Univ BA 78. St Mich Coll Llan 73. **d** 74 **p** 75 Ban. C of Holyhead 74-78; R of Pennal and Corris Dio Ban from 78. *Rectory, Pennal, Near Machynlleth, Gwyn, SY20 9JS.* (Pennal 216)

AP IVOR, Cyril Bernard Gwynne. b 17. St Chad's Coll Dur BA 38, MA 44. Bp's Coll Cheshunt 39. **d** 40 Llan for Mon **p** 41 Mon. C of Usk w Glascoed Monkswood and Gwehelog 40-43; CF (EC) 43-47; V of Much Dewchurch 47-56; R of Mohales Hoek 56-59; St Thos Stockport 59-75; V of St Jo Evang Macclesfield Dio Ches from 75; RD of Macclesfield from 80. *47 Ivy Lane, Macclesfield, Chesh.* (Macclesfield 24185)

AP IVOR, Ven David Llewelyn Sculthorpe. St Paul's Th Coll Grahmstn LTh (S Afr) 51. **d** 51 **p** 52 S Rhod. C of Hillside Bulawayo 51-54; Chap St Andr Sch Bloemf 54-58; C of Gwelo 58-60; P-in-c of Madinare 60-65; PC of Pencoys 66-68; C-in-c of Carnmenellis 66-68; R of St Mich Regina 68-72; Hosp Chap Regina 72-76; I of Kamsack Dio Qu'App from 76; Hon Can of Qu'App 79-80; Archd of Moose Mountain from 80. *Box 1686, Kamsack, Sask, Canada.* (542-2178)

APPIAH, Augustus Wilfred Ebeau. Livingstone Coll USA BA 49. **d** 66 **p** 67 Accra. P Dio Accra. *c/o Christ Church, P.O. Box 38, Cape Coast, Ghana.*

APPLEBY, Alan Neil. ACT ThL 52. **d** 53 **p** 54 Melb. C of Essendon 53-55; Min of Romsey w Lancefield 55-57; Greensborough 57-64; Dept of Chap Melb 64-73; C of St Jas w St John Miss Melb 73-80; I of St Luke S Melb Dio Melb from 80. *210 Dorcas Street, South Melbourne, Vic, Australia 3205.*

APPLEBY, Anthony Robert Nightingale. b 40. K Coll Lon and Warm AKC 62. **d** 63 Bp McKie for Cov **p** 64 Cov. C of St Mark Cov 63-67; CF from 67. *c/o Ministry of Defence, Bagshot Park, Bagshot, Surrey.*

APPLEBY, Dale Bruce. b 45. ACT ThL 71. BD (Lon) 73. Moore Coll Syd 69. **d** 73 Bp Holland for Perth **p** 73 Perth. C of St John Fremantle 73-76; R of Whitford Dio Perth from 76. *210 Bridgewater Drive, Kallaroo, W Australia 6025.* (401 6007)

APPLEBY, Richard Franklin. Univ of Melb BSc 65. St Jo Coll Morpeth ACT ThL (2nd cl) 66. **d** 67 **p** 68 Melb. C of Glenroy 67-69; St Silas N Balwyn 69-70; Chap to Abp of Perth and to Ch Ch Gr Sch Claremont 70-71; Exam and Dom Chap to Abp of Perth 72-75; R of Belmont Dio Perth from 75. *123 Arlunya Avenue, Cloverdale, W Australia 6105.* (277 4338)

APPLEBY, William Arnold. b 12 ALCD 37. **d** 37 Wakef **p** 38 Pontefract for Wakef. C of Rashcliffe 37-40; Hoole 41-43; H Trin Darlington 43-45; Audlem 45-48; V of Acton Trussell w Bednall 48-80. *22 Greenway, Littleworth, Stafford, ST16 2TS.*

APPLEFORD, Canon Patrick Robert Norman. b 25. Trin Coll Cam BA (2nd cl Hist Trip pt i) 49, 2nd cl Engl Trip pt ii 50, MA 54. Chich Th Coll 50. **d** 52 **p** 53 Lon. C of Poplar 52-58; Chap Bps' Coll Cheshunt 58-61; Educn Sec USPG 61-66; Publ Pr Dio S'wark 61-66; Dean and R of H Cross Cathl Lusaka Dio Zam 66-71; Dio Lusaka 71-72; C-in-c of Sutton 73-75; Dioc Dir of Educn Dio Chelmsf from 75; Hon Can of Chelmsf from 78. *6 Chestnut Walk, Chelmsford, Essex.* (Chelmsford 65907)

✠ **APPLETON, Most Rev George.** b 02. CMG 72. Late Scho of Selw Coll Cam 2nd cl Math Trip pt i 22, BA (1st cl Th Trip pt i) 24, MA 29. St Aug Coll Cant 21. **d** 25 Lon **p** 26 Willesden for Lon. C of St Dunstan Stepney 25-27; SPG Miss Kemmendine 27-33; Exam Chap to Bp of Rang 30-35; Prin Div Sch Rang 33-36; Warden Coll of H Cross (Div Sch) Rangoon 36-41; Archd of Rang 43-46; Dir of Publ Relations Govt of Burma 45-46; P-in-c of H Cross Kokine Rang 46-47; Commiss Rang 47-63; V of Headstone 47-50; C-in-c of St Mich Cricklewood 50-57; Sec Conf of British Miss S Edin Ho 50-57; V of St Botolph Aldgate w H Trin Minories Lon 57-62; Ed Quarterly Intercession Paper for the Church's Work Abroad 60-62; Archd of Lon 62-63; Exam Chap to Bp of Lon 62-63; Can Res of St Paul's Cathl Lon 62-63; Cons Ld Abp of Perth in St Paul's Cathl Lon 24 June 63 by Abp of Cant; Abp of Melb; Bps of Lon; St E; Adel; Rockptn; and Gippsld; Asst Bp of Rang (Aung Hla); Bps Suffr of Willesden; Fulham; Dunwich; Kens; and Stepney; and Bps Fyffe; Tubbs; Simpson; Wand; West; Montgomery Campbell; Craske; and McKie; Trld to Jer 89; res 74; C of St Mich Cornhill Lon 74-80; Perm to Offic Dio Ox from 81. *112a St Mary's Road, Oxford, OX4 1QF* (0865-48272)

APPLETON, John Bearby. b 42. Linc Th Coll 74. **d** 76 **p** 77 York. C of Selby Abbey 76-79; St Barn Epsom Dio Guildf from 79. *St Barnabas House, 63 Temple Road, Epsom, KT19 8EY* (Epsom 40546)

APPLETON, Canon Leonard George. b 1900. SS Coll Cam 3rd cl Math Trip pt i 20, BA (2nd cl Hist Trip pt II) 22, MA 26. Univ of Kent Hon DCL 81. Westcott Ho Cam 22. **d** 24 **p** 25 Southw. C of St John Derby 24-26; Chap Toc H for W Lon 26-33; C of All H Barking Lon 29-33; St Martin-in-the-Fields Lon 33-36; V of St Paul Harringay 36-40; Escot 40-44; H Trin Barnstaple 44-45; Asst Dir of Relig Educn Dio Ex 43-45; Dir of Relig Educn Dio Cant 45-69; Six Pr Cant Cathl 50-57; L to Offic Dio Cant from 45; C-in-c of Bekesbourne 50-56; Hon Can of Cant Cathl 57-80; Can (Emer) from 80. *20 Whitehall Bridge Road, Canterbury, Kent.* (Canterbury 63792)

APPLETON, Canon Paul Valentine. b 19. Late Choral Scho of K Coll Cam BA 42, MA 46. Lich Th Coll 42. **d** 44 **p** 45 Lich. C of St Chad Shrewsbury 44-46; Sub-R of St Mary Stafford 46-48; V of Rangemore 48-60; Dunstall 52-60; Succr of Linc Cathl from 60; Hd Master Cathl Sch 60-70; R of Owmby w Normanby and Glentham w Caenby Dio Linc from 70; P-in-c of Spridlington w Saxby Dio Linc from 73; Hon Can of Linc Cathl from 77. *Rectory, Owmby, Lincoln.* (Normanby-by-Spital 275)

APPLETON, Raymond Kendrew. St Jo Coll Winnipeg. **d** 56 **p** 58 Rupld. C of St Jas Winnipeg 56-57; R of Woodlands 58-61; St Anne Winnipeg 61-66; P-in-c of St Cuthb Winnipeg 66-68; L to Offic Dio Rupld 68-71; P-in-c of St Barn Winnipeg 71-73; Hon C of St Bart Winnipeg 73-77. *11 Falk Avenue, Ottowa, Ont., Canada.*

APPLETON, Canon Ronald Percival. b 15. St Pet Hall Ox BA (2nd cl Th) 36, MA 40. Ridley Hall Cam 36. **d** 38 **p** 39 Ripon. C of Hunsingore w Cowthorpe 38-39; Ch Ch Harrogate 39-42; Bromley 42-44; R of Knockholt 44-53; V of St Luke Bromley Common 53-62; Winchcombe w Gretton and Sudeley Manor (and Stanley Pontlarge from 79) Dio Glouc from 62; RD of Winchcombe from 63; Hon Can of Glouc Cathl from 80. *Winchcombe Vicarage, Cheltenham, Glos.* (Winchcombe 602368)

APPLETON, Stanley Basil. b 04. Wycl Hall Ox 66. **d** and **p** 66 Ox. L to Offic Dio Ox from 66. *Leigh Cottage, Wickham, Newbury, Berks, RG16 8HD.* (Boxford 239)

APPLETON, Thomas McCullough. **d** and **p** 56 Niag. C of Guelph 56-58; R of Good Shepherd (w St Andr from 60) Hamilton 58-65; St Jas, Guelph 65-73; Aldershot Dio Niag from 73. *116 Plains Road East, Aldershot, Ont., Canada.* (416-632 2546)

APPLETON, Timothy Charles. b 36. Selw Coll Cam BA (Nat Sc) 60, MA 65. K Coll Lon PhD (Zoology) 67. Univ of Cam DSc 81. SOC 69. **d** 72 Ely **p** 73 Huntingdon for Ely. Hon C of Harston W Hauxton 72-79; Lect Univ of Cam from 73; Hon P-in-c of Gt Eversden w L Eversden Dio Ely from 79. *Little Eversden Rectory, Cambridge.* (Comberton 2251)

APPLETON, Timothy Miles. b 47. Univ of Windsor Ont BA 69. Univ of Chicago MA 71, DMin 74. **d** and **p** 79 Rupld. Hosp Chap Health Sc Centre Winnipeg from 79; Hon C of All SS Winnipeg 79-81; P-in-c of St Thos Winnipeg Dio Rupld from 81. *1549 William Avenue, Winnipeg, Manit, Canada, R3E 1A7.*

APPLEYARD, Edward. b 19. OBE 75. RD (RNR) 68. Kelham Th Coll 37. **d** 43 Hull for York **p** 44 York. C of St Aid Middlesbrough 43-46; Horton Bank Top Conv Distr 46-47; Chap RN HMS *Ajax* 47-48; Chap RN Barracks Chatham 48-49; Chap RAF 49-53; V of Swine 53-56; Chap of Wm Baker Technical Sch Dr Barnardo's Homes 56-58; V of Flamborough 60-68; V of Gt Ayton w Easby and Newton-in-Cleveland 68-78; RD of Stokesley 70-77; P-in-c of St Columba w St Paul Middlesbrough Dio York from 78. *St Columba's Vicarage, Cambridge Road, Middlesbrough, Cleve, TS5 5HF.* (Middlesbrough 824779)

✠ **APPLEYARD, Right Rev Harold Frederick Gaviller.** Univ of W Ont BA 27. Hur Coll LTh 29, DD (*hon causa*) 59. MC 45. **d** 29 **p** 30 Hur. C of Bervie w Kingarf and Kinlough 29-30; R 30-32; R of Kerrwood w Adel and Warw 32-38; Ch Ch Meaford 38-49; Dom Chap to Bp of Hur 48-50; Exam Chap 50-51; R of Grace Ch Brantford 49-61; Can of Hur 51-54; CF (Canad) 42-46; Archd of Brant 54-61; Cons Ld Bp Suffr of Hur (Bp of Georgian Bay) in St Paul's Cathl Lon Ont 6 Jan 61 by Abp of Alg; Abp of Edmon; Bps of Hur; Niag; Ont; Ott; The Arctic; Michigan (USA); Bp Zielinski; and others; res 73. *720 Springbank Drive, London, Ont., Canada.*

APPLEYARD, Canon Reginald Thomas Peel. Univ of W Ont BA 26, BD 32, MA 37. Hur Coll LTh 27. **d** 28 **p** 29 Hur. C of Florence 28-30; I of Kerrwood Adel and Warw 30-32; Lect and Asst Dean Hur Coll 33-38; Amer Ch 38-43; I of [illegible] 303 *Central Avenue, London 14, Ont., Canada.*

APPLIN, David Edward. b 39. Oak Hill Th Coll 63. **d** 65 **p** 66 Ox. C of St Clem Ox 65-69; Felixstowe 69-71; Trav Sec Ruanda Miss of CMS 71-74; Home Sec 74-77; Gen Sec 77-81; Publ Pr Dio Win from 71; Dir of Tear Fund's Overseas Personnel Dept from 82. *c/o 11 Station Road, Teddington, Middx.*

APPS, Anthony Howard. b 22. Ch Coll Cam BA 47, MA 51. **d** 49 **p** 50 Lon. C of Poplar 49-55; V of H Trin Stepney 55-66; St Mark Myddelton Square Clerkenwell Dio Lon from 66. *15 Wilmington Square, WC1X 0ER.* (01-837 1782)

APPS, Bryan Gerald. St D Coll Lamp BA (2nd cl Hist) 59. St Cath S Ox BA (3rd cl Th) 61, MA 65. Wycl Hall Ox 59. **d** 61 Southn for Cant **p** 62 Win. C of St Alb Southn 61-65; Andover w Foxcote 65-69; C-in-c of Freemantle 69-72; R 73-78; V of All SS Southbourne Dio Win from 78. *14 Stourwood Road, Bournemouth, Dorset.* (Bournemouth 43747)

APPS, David Ronald. b 34. St D Coll Lamp BA 57. Sarum Th Coll 57. **d** 59 **p** 60 Win. C of St Chris Southbourne Bournemouth 59-62; Weeke 62-67; V of All SS Alton 67-80; Charlestown Dio Truro from 80. *Charlestown Vicarage, St Austell, Cornw.* (Par 2824)

APPS, Canon (Bernard) Michael John. b 28. Pemb Coll Cam BA 52, 2nd cl Th Trip pt ii 53, MA 56. Cudd Coll 53. **d** 55 **p** 56 Linc. C of Spalding 55-58; M SSF 58; Perm to Offic Dio Chelmsf 59-69; P-in-c of St Phil, Plaistow 63-67; Perm to Offic Dio Brisb 69-75; Exam Chap to Abp of Brisb 71-75; M Gen Syn Cant from 77; Guardian St Nich Friary Harbledown 77-78; Hilfield Friary Dorch from 78; Can (Non-res) Sarum Cathl from 81. *Hilfield Friary, Dorchester, Dorset, DT2 7BE.* (Cerne Abbas 345)

APPS, Peter Alfred. b 17. Ch Coll Cam BA 39, 2nd cl Th Trip pt i 40, MA 46. Westcott Ho Cam 39. **d** 41 Win **p** 42 Southn for Win. C of Eastleigh 41-45; Chap St Paul's Cathl Ranchi 45-47; Exam Chap to Bp of Chota N 49-60; Dioc Treas 57-60; Miss Manoharpur 47-56; Murhu 56-58; Ranchi 58-60; V of S Tawton w S Zeal 61-78; RD of Okehampton 72-77; R of Lydford w Bridestowe and Sourton w Brent Tor Dio Ex from 78; P-in-c of Lamerton w Sydenham Dameral Dio Ex from 79. *Rectory, Lydford, Okehampton, Devon, EX20 4BH.* (Lydford 306)

APSEY, Gordon John. St Aid Th Coll Bal ACT ThL (2nd cl) 31. **d** 31 **p** 32 Bal. C of St Matt Wendouree 31-33; P-in-c of Hopetoun 33; Minyip 33-35; Hopetoun w Beulah 35-38; V of Murtoa 38-40; St John Bal 40-51; Chap RAAF 40-46; Bal Dioc Gr Sch 48-51; I of St Paul Geelong 51-68; St Paul E Kew 68-76; Perm to Offic Dio Melb from 76. *38 Cole Avenue, East Kew, Vic, Australia 3102.* (85-2226)

APTHORP, Canon Arthur Norman. Pemb Coll Cam BA 47, MA 50. Chich Th Coll. **d** 50 Guildf for Chich **p** 51 Chich. C of Henfield 50-52; Hove 52-56; R of Narembeen 56-60; Boulder 60-66; Northam 66-72; Kalgoorlie 73-77; Dianella Dio Perth from 78; Hon Can of Perth 73-77 and from 79. *14 Ashington Street, Dianella, W Australia 6062.* (276 5521)

APTHORP, Christopher John. b 52. Univ of Auckld BA 74. St Jo Coll Auckld 74. **d** 76 **p** 77 Auckld. C of St Luke Mt Albert 76-78; Kaitaia 78-80; V of N Hokianga Dio Auckld from 80. *Box 7, Broadwood, Northland, NZ.*

APUULI-KINOBE, Meshach. b 45. Bp Tucker Coll 68. **d** 71 Ruw. C of Kabarole Dio Ruw from 71. *St John's Cathedral, PO Box 37, Fort Portal, Uganda.*

ARAGU, Wellington. **d** 75 **p** 78 Carp. C of Dauan I Dio Carp 75-78; P-in-c from 78. *PO Box 79, Thursday Island, Queensland, Australia 4875.*

ARANNILEWA, Isaac Ale Adetayo. **d** 63 **p** 65 Ondo. P Dio Ondo 63-66; Dio Ekiti from 66. *Vicarage, Igogo, Ekiti, Nigeria.*

ARAP MUGE, Alexander. b 48. **d** 75 **p** 76 Nai. P Dio Nai. *PO Box 29190, Kabete, Nairobi, Kenya.*

ARATUNDE, Samuel Adegboyega. Im Coll Ibad 58. **d** 61 **p** 63 Ibad. P Dio Ibad 61-67; Dio Lagos from 67. *St James's Church, Oke-Odan, Ilaro, Egbado District, Nigeria.*

ARAWORE, Samson Enajero. Trin Coll Umuahia 55. **d** 57 **p** 58 Niger. P Dio Niger 57-62; Dio Benin 62-77; Can of Benin 69-75; Archd Dio Benin 75-77; Dio Warri 77-80. *c/o St Andrew's Parsonage, Box 52, Warri, Nigeria.*

ARBERY, Canon Richard Neil. b 25. K Coll Lon and Warm AKC 49. **d** 50 **p** 51 Liv. C of Pemberton 50-55; V of Roundthorn 55-59; Hindley 59-78; RD of Wigan from 75; V of St Andr Wigan Dio Liv from 78; Hon Can of Liv from 77. *St Andrew's Vicarage, Wigan, Lancs, WN6 7NA.* (Wigan 43514)

ARBLASTER, Edmund Hyde. Univ of W Austr BA 40. Ridley Coll Melb ACT ThL 41. **d** and **p** 42 Perth. C of Ch Ch Claremont 42-44; St Geo Cathl Perth 44-46; R of Trayning 46-47; C of St Pet Cathl 47-49; CMS Miss Dio Centr Tang 49; [illegible] Chap at Mvumi 55-57; Morogoro 57-59; Tabora 61-62; Archd of W Tang 61-62; Arusha 63-64; V of Arusha 63-64; Prov Can of Nai and Chap to Abp 64-66; R of Nedlands and Commiss Nak 66-68; Dir Inter-Ch Aid Austr Coun of Chs and L to Offic Dios Syd and C and Goulb 68-74; Dir Bible Reading Fellowship Austr and Bible Stud Tr Officer Dio C & Goulb 74-77; R of St Luke Isfahan 77; Dom Chap to Bp of Iran 77; Perm to Offic Dios Syd and C & Goulb from 77. *4/41 Gottenham Street, Glebe, NSW, Australia 2037.*

ARBUCKLE, Canon James Hugh. b 19. K Coll Lon and Warm AKC 49. **d** 49 Lewes for Chich **p** 50 Chich. C of Seaford 49-52; Crosby 52-54; V of Barnetby-le-Wold 54-76; C-in-c of Bigby 64-76; Somerby 74-76; Sec Linc Dioc Conf 63-70; Can and Preb of Linc Cathl from 70; RD of Yarborough 70-76; Proc Conv Linc from 70; Surr 71-76; Sec Linc Dioc Syn and Pastoral C'tte from 76. *The Burghersh Chantry, 17 James Street, Lincoln, LN2 1QE.* (Lincoln 29666)

ARBUTHNOT, Andrew Robert Coghill. b 26. SOC 71. **d** 74 **p** 75 S'wark. C of Mortlake w E Sheen 74-77; L to Offic Dio Guildf from 78. *Monksfield House, Tilford, Nr Farnham, Surrey, GU10 2AL.* (Runfold 2233)

ARBUTHNOT, James. b 19. QUB BA 42; TCD Div Test 44. **d** 44 **p** 45 Connor. C of St Aid Belf 44-47; St Simon Belf 47-51; I of Ardglass w Dunsford 51-60; St Phil Belf 60-70; St Paul Belf Dio Connor from 70. *50 Sunningdale Park, Belfast, BT14 6RW, N Ireland.* (Belfast 776979)

ARCH, Peter Arthur John. Selw Coll Cam BA 46, MA 48. Ely Th Coll 46. **d** 48 **p** 49 Linc. C of St Aug Grimsby 48-52; CF 52-55; PC of St Andr Grimsby 55-58; R of Hughenden 58-62; V of Kaniva 62-65; P-in-c of Churchill 65-73; L to Offic Dio Gippsld 73-74; Perm to Offic Dio Melb 74-79; I of Myrtleford Dio Wang from 79. *Church Street, Bright, Vic, Australia 3741.*

ARCH, Richard. b 05. Late Sen Scho and Pri of St D Coll Lamp BA (1st cl Hist) 27, BD 69. Jes Coll Ox 2nd cl Th 29, BA and MA 34. **d** 29 **p** 30 St D. C of St Mich Aberystwyth 29-31; H Trin Felinfoel 31-36; V of Cilycwm 36-44; Potterspury w Furtho and Yardley Gobion 44-49; R of Scartho and Chap Springfield Hosp 49-58; R of Rotherfield Peppard 58-71. *Adress temp unknown.*

ARCHER, Alan Robert. b 38. K Coll Lon 56. Lich Th Coll 65. **d** 68 **p** 69 Worc. C of Stourport 68-71; Foley Park Kidderminster 71-74; V of Warndon 74-79; P-in-c of Clifton-on-Teme 79-81; The Shelsleys 79-81; Lower Sapey 79-81; Malvern Wells and Wyche Dio Worc from 81. *Vicarage, Malvern Wells, Worc.* (Malvern 5123)

ARCHER, Arthur William. **d** 67 Bunb. Hon C of Ravensthorpe Dio Bunb from 67. *Box 5, Ravensthorpe, W Australia.*

ARCHER, Delano Kelvin Luther. b 43. Sarum Wells Th Coll 70. **d** 72 **p** 73 Nass. C of St Anne Nass 72-74; R of St Jo Bapt Marsh Harbour 75-76; St Sav Cat I 75-76; Exuma Dio Nass from 76. *Box 93, George Town, Exuma, Bahamas.* (336-2633)

ARCHER, Frederick John. b 06. Clifton Th Coll 29. **d** 33 Trinid **p** 38 Lich. Chap HM Prisons and Publ Insts Port of Spain 33-35; Perm to Offic (Col Cl Act) at Burslem 35-38; C of Aldridge 38-39; Bucknall w Bagnall (in c of St John Abbey Hulton) 39-40; Bedworth 40-44; V of St Jo Evang Kenilworth 44-53; Surr from 45; Dioc Sec CETS and Police Court and Pris Gate Miss 47-53; V of Dunton 53-58; R of Wrestlingworth 53-58; Woolstone w Oxenton and Gotherington 58-61; Corse w Staunton 61-73. *The School House, Staunton, Gloucester, GL19 3QF.* (Staunton Court 259)

ARCHER, Geoffrey Balfour. Angl Th Coll BC Lth 62. **d** 53 **p** 54 New Westmr. V of St Luke (w St Timothy 56-59) Vanc 54-61; R of St Geo Vanc 62; on leave 62-72; Perm to Offic Dio New Westmr 73-74; R of St Geo Vanc 74-78; St Chad Vanc Dio New Westmr from 78. *3874 Trafalgar Street, Vancouver, BC, Canada.*

ARCHER, George Selbourne Adoltron. Univ of Sask BA 72. Em & St Chad's Coll Sktn 67. **d** 73 Sktn for Venez **p** 73 Venez. R of All SS Curacao Dio Venez from 73. *Heelsumstraat 29, Curacao, Dutch Antilles, W Indies.*

ARCHER, John Thomas. b 28. E Midl Jt Ordin Tr Scheme 79. **d** 80 Repton for Derby **p** 81 Derby (NSM). C of St Thos City and Dio Derby from 80. *The Smithy, Kedleston, Derby, DE6 4JL.*

ARCHER, Keith Malcolm. b 40. Univ of Man BA (Engl) 61, MA (Th) 80. Magd Coll Cam BA (Th) 67, MA 72. **d** 68 **p** 69 York. C of Newland 68-72; Industr Chap Dio Man from 72; Hon C of St Paul Kersal Salford 72-79. *67 Woodward Road, Prestwich, Manchester, M28 8TX.* (061-773 2249)

ARCHER, Kenneth Daniel. b 23. Edin Th Coll 50. **d** 53 **p** 54 Glas. C of St Ninian Glas 53-55; R of Woodhead 55-59; P-in-c of Cuminestown 57-59; R of Girvan 59-62; Inverurie 62-72; R of Monymusk w Kemnay 63-72; Cranham Dio Chelmsf from 72. *Rectory, Cranham, Upminster, Essex.* (Upminster 20130)

ARCHER, Michael John. b 37. Trin Coll Bris 76. **d** 78 Sarum **p** 79 Bp D J Wilson for Sarum. C of Kinson Dio Sarum from 78. *10 Castleton Avenue, Kinson, Bournemouth, BH10 7HP.*

ARCHER, Robert Kenneth. St Mich Ho Crafers ThL 71. **d** and **p** 71 Bath. C of Good Shepherd Bourke 71-72; Longreach 72-73; Baewarrina 74; Warrnambool 75-77; Perm to Offic Dio Bal 78; C of Warrnambool and Hon Chap to Bp of Bal from 80. *Box 259, Warrnambol, Vic, Australia 3280.* (055-62 5198)

ARCHER, Samuel John. b 03. ALCD 30. **d** 30 **p** 31 Lich. C of St Paul Burslem 30-33; V of St Paul Withnell 33-39; Org Sec BCMS for N Prov 39-42; V of St Pet U Holloway 42-58. Chap Whittington Hosp 51-58; V of Ch Ch, Dover 58-73; Chap R Vic Hosp Dover 58-73; Perm to Offic Dios Lon and St Alb from 74. *18 Gallants Farm Road, East Barnet, Herts.* (01-361 1701)

ARCHER, Stanley Edwin. b 21. St Jo Coll Dur 80. **d** 81 Knaresborough for Ripon. C of U Nidderdale Dio Ripon from 81. *Bewerley Grange, Bewerley, Harrogate, HG3 5HX.*

ARCHER, Wilfred Lawson. b 08. Ripon Hall Ox. **d** 61 **p** 62 Southw. C of E Retford 61-63; V of Awsworth w Cossall 63-65; Caunton 65-73; V of Maplebeck 65-73; Perm to Offic Dio Southw from 73. *2 The Flats, Upton Fields, Southwell, Notts, NG25 0QA.* (Southwell 812831)

ARCHIBALD, George Stirling. Kelham Th Coll 30. **d** 36 **p** 37 Guildf. C of St Mark S Farnborough 36-43; Woodham 43-44. CF (EC) 44-47; C of All SS Onslow Village Conv Distr Guildf 47-48; C-in-c of New Cathl Conv Distr Guildf 48-50; V of Chertsey Dio Guildf from 50. *Vicarage, Chertsey, Surrey.* (Chertsey 3141)

ARCTIC, THE, Lord Bishop of. *See* Sperry, Right Rev John Reginald.

ARCTIC, THE, Bishop Suffragan of. *See* Clarke, Right Rev James Charles MacLeod.

ARCUS, Jeffrey. b 40. N-W Ordin Course 72. **d** 75 Man **p** 76 Hulme for Man. C of St Thos Halliwell 75-78; Walmsley 78-81; C-in-c of Ch K Bury Dio Man from 81. *St Thomas's Vicarage, Pimhole Road, Bury, Lancs, BL9 7EY.* (061-764 1157)

ARDAGH, Bishop of. *See* Moore, Right Rev Edward Francis Butler.

ARDAGH, Archdeacon of. *See* Elphin.

ARDAGH, Dean of. *See* Elphin.

ARDAGH-WALTER, Christopher Richard. b 35. St D Coll Lamp BA (2nd cl Th) 58. Chich Th Coll 58. **d** 60 **p** 61 Ex. C of Heavitree 60-64; Redcar 64-67; Kings Worthy Dio Win 67-69; Min of Four Marks Conv Distr (V from 73) Alton 69-75; Team R of Eling, Testwood and Marchwood 76-78; Totton Dio Win from 78. *Testwood Vicarage, Salisbury Road, Totton, Southampton.* (Totton 865103)

✠ **ARDEN, Right Rev Donald Seymour.** Univ of Leeds BA (1st cl Gen) 37. Coll of Resurr Mirfield 37. **d** 39 **p** 40 S'wark. C of St Cath Hatcham 39-40; Nettleden w Potten End 41-43; Asst P Pret Native Miss Dio Pret 44-51; Dir of Usuthu Miss 51-61; Can of Zulu 59-61; Cons Ld Bp of Nyasa (Malawi from 64) in Ch of Ascen Likwenu 30 Nov 61 by Abp of Centr Afr; and Bps of Mashon; N Rhod; Zulu and Ft Hall; Apptd Bp of Southern Malawi 71; Elected Abp and Metrop of Prov of Centr Afr 71; res 80; Asst Bp in Dio Lon from 81; P-in-c of St Marg Uxbridge Dio Lon from 81. *Uxbridge Vicarage, Harefield Road, Uxbridge, Middx.* (Uxbridge 39055)

ARDEN, Edward. b 01. St Paul's Th Coll Grahmstn 24. S Afr LTh 26. **d** 26 **p** 27 Kimb. K Warden of Bp's Hostel and C of St Alb Kimb 26- 27; Perm to Offic at Wylde Green Birm 28-30; R of Barkly E CGH 30-33; C of St Jo Bapt Kidderminster (in c of H Innoc Foley Pk) 33-36; Min of H Innoc Foley Pk 37-38; V 38-41; R of Croyland 41-46; Chap RAFVR 42-46; R of Gautby w Waddingworth 46-50; V of Minting 46-50; Dir Kwa-Magwaza Miss 50-60; Dir St Aug Miss 60-63; R of Manzini 63; Usuthu 64-69; Archd of E Zulu 53-60; W Zulu 60-63; Swaz 63-69; VG of Zulu 60-61, 63, 64, 65-66 and 68-69. *c/o Barclays National Bank Ltd, PO Box 923, Durban 4000, S Africa.*

ARDFERT, Bishop of. *See* Limerick.

ARDFERT and AGHADOE, Archdeacon of. *See* Doherty, Ven Raymond William Patrick.

ARDFERT and AGHADOE, Dean of. *See* Thompson, Very Rev Robert Henry.

ARDIS, Edward George. b 54. Univ of Dur BA 76. **d** 78 **p** 79 Dub. C of Drumcondra w N Strand and St Barn Dub 78-81; St Bart Clyde Road w Ch Ch Leeson Park City and Dio Dub from 81. *28A Clyde Lane, Dublin 4, Irish Republic.* (Dublin 685520)

ARDLEY, Evan Lloyd. b 46. Ch Ch Coll NZ Bd of Th Stud LTh 69. **d** 69 **p** 71 Ch Ch. C of Rangiora 69-72; Paraparamu 72-73; V of Ruapehu 73-74; on leave 75-79; Chap Huntley and Nga Tawa Schs Dio Wel 79-80. *c/o Huntley School, Wanganui Road, Marton, NZ.*

ARDLEY, John Owen. b 39. BD (Lon) 70. SOC 70. **d** 72 **p** 73 S'wark. C of Caterham Valley 72-76; V of St Mich AA Abbey Wood Plumstead Dio S'wark from 76; Sub-Dean of Woolwich 77-82. *1 Conference Road, SE2 0YH.* (01-311 0377)

AREGBESOLA, Theophilus Adeusi Adeyemo. Im Coll Ibad. **d** 59 Ibad **p** 61 Ondo-B for Ibad. Prin Bp Smith Mem Coll Offa 59-69; Amoye Gr Sch Ikere from 70. *Amoye Grammar School, Ikere-Ekiti, Nigeria.*

AREMU, Samuel Olalekan. b 38. **d** 73 **p** 74 Ibad. P Dio Ibad. *St Paul's Vicarage, Gbongan, Nigeria.*

ARENDSE, Joseph Peter. b 18. **d** and **p** 77 Capetn (APM). C of St Marg Parow 77-80; Ravensmead Dio Capetn from 80. *16th Avenue, Elsies River 7460, CP, S Africa.* (98-0872)

ARENDSE, Rhodes Eugene Lyle. b 50. St Bede's Coll Umtata 75. **d** 75 **p** 76 Capetn. C of St Nich Matroosfontein 75-78; Namaqualand 78-80; St Alb Pacaltsdorp Dio Geo from 80. *Box 61, George, CP, S Africa.*

AREVALOS, Jorge. b 50. **d** 76 **p** 77 Parag. P Dio Parag. *a/c Casilla 1124, Asuncion, Paraguay.*

ARGENTINA and EASTERN SOUTH AMERICA, Lord Bishop in. *See* Cutts, Right Rev Richard Stanley.

ARGUILE, Roger Henry William. b 43. Univ of Dur LLB 64. Keble Coll Ox BA 70, MA 75. Ripon Hall Ox 70. **d** 71 **p** 72 Lich. C of St Matt Walsall 71-76; Team V of Blakenall Heath Dio Lich from 76. *St Chad's Vicarage, Edison Road, Beechdale, Walsall, W Midl.* (Walsall 612081)

ARGYLE, Douglas Causer. b 17. St Jo Coll Cam Sizarship 36, 3rd cl Cl Trip pt i 38, BA 39, MA 43. Ridley Hall Cam 39. **d** 41 **p** 42 Derby. C of Somercotes 41-44; CF (EC) 44-47; Asst Chap and Asst Master Repton Sch 47-59; LPr Dio Derby 47-59; Chap and Asst Master Gresham's Sch 59-74; LPr Dio Nor 59-74; C-in-c of Eastleach Martin w Eastleach Turville and Southrop 74-82. *East Lynn, Fairford, Glos.*

ARGYLE, Frank Martin. b 12. Clare Coll Cam BA (2nd cl Cl Trip pt i) 33, 2nd cl Th Trip pt i 34, MA 38. Bp's Coll Cheshunt 38. **d** 38 St Alb **p** 39 Bedford for St Alb. Asst Master Haileybury and Imperial Service Coll 38-49; Warden of St Columba's Coll Dub 49-74; V of Newbottle w Charlton 74-77; C-in-c of Aynho 74-77; R of Aynho w Newbottle and Charlton 77-81; Perm to Offic Dio Ex from 81. *11 Cedar Road, Preston, Paignton, Devon, TQ3 2DB.*

ARGYLL and THE ISLES, Lord Bishop of. *See* Henderson, Right Rev George Kennedy Buchanan.

ARGYLL and THE ISLES, Dean of. *See* Wilson, Very Rev Ian George MacQueen.

ARHIN, Ven Emmanuel Kofi Tawiah. Kelham Th Coll 59. **d** 65 **p** 66 Accra. P Dio Accra; Archd of Sunyani from 79. *Box 23, Sunyani, Brong-Ahafo, Ghana.*

ARIAKA, Caleb. Bp Tucker Coll Mukono 72. **d** 75 **p** 76 M & W Nile. P Dio M & W Nile. *Nyapea College, PO Paidha, Arua, Uganda.*

ARIBANUSI, Solomon Oluwayomi. **d** 77 Ondo. d Dio Ondo from 77. *Box 20, Ile-Oluji, Ondo, Nigeria.*

ARIES, William Albert. b 28. Bps' Coll Cheshunt. ACT ThL 61. **d** 60 **p** 61 Cov. C of St Mary Nuneaton 60-63; Chandler's Ford 63-66; C-in-c of St Ives and St Leon Conv Distr Ringwood 66-70; V 70-75; St Clem w St Mary Bournemouth Dio Win from 75. *Vicarage, St Clement's Road, Bournemouth, Dorset.* (Bournemouth 33151)

ARIJE, Joseph Ajayi. Melville Hall Ibad 51. **d** and **p** 53 Ondo-B. P Dio Ondo-B 53-62; Dio Ondo 62-66; Dio Ekiti from 66. *Holy Trinity Vicarage, Ijesha-Isu, Ekiti, Nigeria.*

ARIMANA, Charles. **d** 79 **p** 80 Centr Melan. P Dio Centr Melan. *Bunana Training Centre, Gela Region, Solomon Islands.*

ARINAITWE, Ephraim. Buwalasi Th Coll 65. **d** 66 Ankole-K. d Dio Ankole-K 66-67; Dio Kig from 67. *Kinyasaano, PO Rukungiri, Uganda.*

ARIROOBWE, Samwiri. **d** and **p** 75 Bunyoro. P Dio Bunyoro. *Box 544, Kakumiro-Mubende, Kyabasaija, Uganda.*

ARIYO, Rufus Eniola. b 28. Fourah Bay Coll BA (Dur) 54. Im Coll Ibad 70. **d** 70 **p** 72 Ondo. P Dio Ondo 70-72 and from 76; Dio Lagos 73-75; Prin Angl Gr Sch Ijebu-Ode 73-75; Ondo High Sch from 76. *Box 31, Ondo, Nigeria.* (Ondo 2033)

ARKELL, Colin Robert. St Francis Th Coll Brisb. **d** 58 **p** 59 Brisb. C of Redcliffe 58-61; St Mark Warwick 61-63; P-in-c of Mundubbera w Eidsvold 63-66; R 66-67; Nambour 67-73; Org Sec Home Miss Fund Dio Brisb 73-76; Social Welfare Dept Dio Brisb from 76. *46 Garozza Street, Boondall, Queensland, Australia 4034.* (265 1346)

ARKELL, Richard Gordon. b 10. Coll of Resurr Mirfield 40. MCR 42. **d** 42 **p** 43 Wakef. L to Offic Dio Wakef 42-45; Asst P Sekhukhuniland Miss 45-52; Miss P St Aug Miss Penhalonga 52-56; Perm to Offic Dio Llan 56-60; Dio Wakef from 60. *House of the Resurrection, Mirfield, Yorks.*

ARKELL, Warren John. St Jo Coll Morpeth ACT ThL 53. **d** 53 **p** 54 Graft. C of Lismore 53-56; Port Macquarie 56-60; R of Aber 60-64; Belmont 64-72; Perm to Offic Dio Newc from 72. *Ocean Beach Road, Woy Woy, NSW, Australia 2256.*

ARKORFUL, Kwamina Ephraim Yanyi. Bp's Ho Accra 56. **d** and **p** 58 Accra. P Dio Accra 58-72; Dio Kum from 73. *PO Box 4, Kumawu, Ashanti, Ghana.*

ARLIDGE, John Brett. Univ of NZ BA 39. St Jo Coll Auckld 37. St Edm Hall Ox BA 49, MA 56. **d** 45 **p** 46 Wel. C of Masterton 45-47; St Luke Benchill Dio Man 49-50; V of Johnsonville 50-54; Taita 54-57; Opunake 57-66; Aramoho 66-72; Pohangina 72-76; Perm to Offic Dio Ch Ch from 78. *31 Yaldhurst Road, Upper Riccarton, Christchurch, NZ.*

ARLOW, Canon William James. b 26. Edin Th Coll 59. **d** 59 **p** 60 Down. C of Ballymacarrett 59-61; Centr Adv on Chr Stewardship to Ch of Ireland 61-66; I of St Patr Newry 66-70; St Donard Belf 70-74; Dep Sec Irish Coun of Chs 74-75; Sec 75-79; Can of Belfast Cathl from 79. *4 Craigdarragh Park, Craigavad, Holywood, Co Down, BT18 0EA.* (Holywood 5301)

ARMAGH, Lord Archbishop of, Primate of All Ireland, and Metropolitan. *See* Armstrong, Most Rev John Ward.

ARMAGH, Archdeacon of. *See* Gowing, Ven Frederick William.

ARMAGH, Dean of. *See* Crooks, Very Rev John Robert Megaw.

ARMAH, Canon John Ntaku. St Aug Coll Kumasi. **d** and **p** 31 Accra. P Dio Accra 31-75; Can of Accra 56-75; Can (Emer) from 75. *Old Palace, Beyin, Ghana.*

ARMAN, Brian Robert. b 54. St Jo Coll Dur BA 77, Dipl Th 78. Cranmer Hall Dur 74. **d** 78 **p** 79 Bris. C of Lawrence Weston Dio Bris from 78. *186 Broadlands Drive, Lawrence Weston, Bristol.*

ARMES, John Andrew. b 55. SS Coll Cam BA 77, MA 81. Sarum Wells Th Coll 77. **d** 79 Penrith for Carl **p** 80 Carl. C of St Mary Walney Dio Carl from 79. *10 Roding Green, Walney, Barrow-in-Furness, Cumbria, LA14 3XL.*

ARMFELT, Julian Roger. b 31. K Coll Cam 3rd cl Hist Trip pt i 52, BA (3rd cl Th Trip pt i) 53. Wells Th Coll 54. **d** 56 **p** 58 Sheff. C of Stocksbridge 56-57; Cantley 57-59; C-in-c of Frickley w Clayton 59-61; C of Eglingham 61-63; V of Aukborough w Whitton 63-64; in RC Ch 64-68; Re-rec into Angl Commun by R of Falstone 68; C of Corringham 69-72; Team V in Priory Cross Group (Fincham from 74) 72-75; V of Freckleton 75-79; P-in-c of Sherburn Dio York 79-80; V (w W and E Heslerton and Yedingham) from 80; P-in-c of W & E Heslerton w Knapton and Yedingham 79-81. *Sherburn Vicarage, Malton, N Yorks, YO17 8PL.* (Sherburn 524)

ARMIDALE, Lord Bishop of. *See* Chiswell, Right Rev Peter.

ARMIDALE, Dean of. *See* Holbeck, Very Rev James Evans.

ARMITAGE, Bryan Ambrose. b 28. K Coll Lon and Warm AKC 55, BD 58. **d** 56 **p** 57 Ripon. C of St Pet Harrogate 56-59; Chap St Andr Coll Grahmstn 59-61; Chap Sir Samuel Baker Sch Gulu 61-65; Hd Master Mengo Sen Sec Sch Nam 65-74; Chap of Sutton Valence Sch 74-75; Chap and Asst Master Qu Ethelburga's Sch Harrogate from 76. *5 York Road, Harrogate, N Yorks, HG1 2QA.* (Harrogate 504410)

ARMITAGE, Michael Stanley. b 45. Jes Coll Cam BA 67, MA 71. Cudd Coll 67. **d** 69 **p** 70 S'wark. C of Sanderstead 69-70; St Mary Battersea 70-71; Chap Kingston Poly and Hon C St Jo Evang Kingston T 72-73; V of St Jo Evang Angell Town Brixton Dio S'wark from 73. *St John's Vicarage, Wiltshire Road, SW9 7NF.* (01-733 0585)

ARMITAGE, Richard Norris. b 51. AKC 72. St Aug Coll Cant 73. **d** 74 Pontefract for Wakef **p** 75 Wakef. C of Chapelthorpe 74-77; W Bromwich Dio Lich from 77. *67 Charlemont Avenue, West Bromwich, B71 3BZ.* (021-588 2739)

ARMITAGE, Canon William Robert Ramsay. MC 19. Univ of Dalhousie BA 09. Univ of Tor MA 13. McMaster Univ Ont LLD 52. Wycl Coll Tor BD 25, Hon DD 36. Trin Coll Tor Hon DD 48. K Coll Halifax, NS Hon DD 48. Em Coll Sktn Hon DD 59. Hur Coll Hon DD 61. St Jo Coll Manit Hon DD 62. Angl Th Coll Vanc Hon DD 63. **d** 13 **p** 14 Tor. TCF 16-19; Chap NPAM 20-39; CASF 39-40; C of Ch of The Messiah Tor 13-21; V 21-29; R 29-36; Dean and R of Ch Ch Cathl Vanc and Exam Chap to Abp of New Westmr 36-40; Prin of Wycl Coll Tor 40-59; R of Maple 59-81; Can of Tor from 76. *c/o 16 The Links, Willowdale, Ont., Canada, M2P 1T5.*

ARMITSTEAD, Geoffrey Arthur Dymoke. b 02. Keble Coll Ox BA (2nd cl Th) 24, MA 34; Cudd Coll 26. **d** 26 Southw **p** 27 Guildf. C of St Mark Mansfield 26-27; Hindhead 27-30; All SS Margate 30-34; Horsham (in c of H Trin) 34-39; Chap O of H Paraclete and St Hilda's Sch Whitby 39-60; V of Flimwell 60-63; All S, Clive Vale, Hastings 63-78. *43 First Avenue, Bexhill-on-Sea, E. Sussex.* (Bexhill 215566)

ARMSON, Canon Eric Briggs. b 21. Pemb Coll Ox (2nd cl Mod Hist 41; 2nd cl Th 43) BA 41, MA 45. Ripon Hall Ox 41-43. **d** 44 **p** 45 Wakef. C of H Trin Huddersfield 44-47; St Mich Stoke Cov 47-51; St Mary Stoke Ipswich 51-54; C-in-c of St Andr Conv Distr Ipswich 54-58; Min 58-69; V 69-80; Chap St Clem Hosp Ipswich 57-80; V of Bentley w Tattingstone Dio St E from 80; Hon Can of St E from 80. *Bentley Vicarage, Ipswich, Suff, IP9 2BL.* (Gt Wenham 311495)

ARMSON, John Moss. b 39. Selw Coll Cam BA 61, MA 65. Univ of St Andr PhD 65. Coll of Resurr Mirfield 64. **d** 66 Kens for Lon **p** 67 Lon. C of St Jo Evang Notting Hill Kens 66-69; Fell and Chap Down Coll Cam 69-73; Chap Westcott Ho Cam 73-76; Vice-Prin 77-81; Prin Edin Th Coll from 82. *The Theological College, Roseberry Crescent, Edinburgh, EH12 5JT.* (031-337 3838)

ARMSTEAD, Geoffrey Malcolm. K Coll Lon and Warm BD 63, AKC 56. **d** 57 Sherborne for Sarum **p** 58 Sarum. C of H Trin Weymouth 57-60; Mortlake w E Sheen 60-63; Chap Em Sch Wandsworth and Publ Pr Dio S'wark 63-74. *Polecat Cottage, Polecat Corner, Tunworth, Basingstoke, Hants.*

ARMSTEAD, Gordon. b 33. Oak Hill Coll 73. **d** 74 **p** 75 Knaresborough for Ripon. C of Woodside 74-76; Ch Ch Heaton 76-79; R of Toora w Welshpool and Hedley 79-81; St Mark Levenshulme Dio Man from 81. *St Mark's Rectory, Levenshulme, Manchester, M19 3HW.* (061-224 9551)

ARMSTEAD, Canon William Thomas. **d** and **p** 55 Bath. C of Dubbo 55-57; R of Peak Hill 57-61; Warren 61-65; W Wyalong 65-77; Narromine Dio Bath from 77; Can of All SS Cathl Bath from 76. *Rectory, Narromine, NSW, Australia 2821.* (068-89 1046)

ARMSTRONG, Arthur Francis Ffolliott. b 03. Sarum Th Coll 24. **d** 27 **p** 28 Man. C of St Luke Weaste 27-30; Castleford (in c of St John Lock Lane) 30-33; V of Gawber 33-41; R of Ackworth 41-71; V of E Hardwick 45-71; RD of Pontefract 66-71; Hon Can of Wakef 67-71. *Tilford, Mount Pleasant North, Robin Hood's Bay, N Yorks, YO22 4RE.*

ARMSTRONG, Arthur Patrick. b 1898. TCD BA 20, Div Test (2nd cl) 22, MA 42. **d** 22 Clogh **p** 23 Down for Arm. C of Enniskillen 22-23; Miss (DUM) at Hazaribagh 23-27; C of St Pet and St Audoen Dib 28-29; Chap and Regr Kirwan Ho Dub 29-42; I of Cahir w Clogheen U 42-68; RD of Cahir 45-67; Lism Cahir 55-68; Preb of Kilrosanty and Treas of Lism Cathl 56-60; Preb of St Patr and Treas of Waterf Cathl 56-60; Prec 58-60; Preb of Rossduff and Chan of Waterf Cathl 60-681 Archd of Waterf and Lism 61-68. *Glenhilton, Herbert Road, Bray, Co Wicklow.*

ARMSTRONG, Bruce Leo. b 29. **d** 80 Auckld. C of Titirangi Dio Auckld from 80. *239 Golf Road, Titirangi, Auckland, NZ.*

ARMSTRONG, Christopher John. b 47. Univ of Nottm BTh 75. Kelham Coll Dur 72. **d** 75 **p** 76 Cant. C of Maidstone 75-79; Chap of St Hild & St Bede Coll Dur from 79. *St Hild & St Bede College, University of Durham, DH1 1SZ.* (Dur 63741)

ARMSTRONG, Christopher John Richard. b 35. Univ of Cam BA 64, MA 68, PhD 80. Univ of Fribough LTh 61. Edin Th Coll. **d** 59 RC Bp of Burgos **p** 59 RC Bp of Apamea. In RC Ch 59-71; Rec into Angl Commun 71 by Bp of Aber & Ork; Lect Univ of Aber 68-74; C of Ledbury 74-76; P-in-c of Bredenbury w Grendon Bp and Wacton 76-79; Edvin Ralph w Collington and Thornbury 76-79; Pencombe w Marston Stannett and L Cowarne 76-79; R of Cherry Burton 79-80; Dir of Stud and Tutor Westcott Ho Cam from 80. *Westcott House, Cambridge.*

ARMSTRONG, Canon Claude Blakeley. b 1889. Late Scho of Trin Coll Dub BA (Sen Mod Cl and Phil) 11, Fellowship Pri 12 and 13, MA 14, BD 20. **d** 15 **p** 19 Cork. Hd Master Gr Sch Cork and C of St Anne Shandon 15-20; Warden of St Columba's Coll Rathfarnham 20-34; Hd Master of St Andr Coll Grahmstn 34-38; R of Clannaborough 40-43; Clyst St Geo 43- 47; Can of Worc 48-70; Exam Chap to Bp of Worc 48-70; Warden Worc Ordin Coll 52-64; Treas Worc Cathl 64-70; Can (Emer) of Worc Cathl from 70. *12A College Green, Worcester.*

ARMSTRONG, Colin John. St Cath S Ox BA 59, MA 65. Wells Th Coll 59. **d** 61 **p** 62 York. C of St Steph Acomb York 61-64; Newland 64-67; Chap and Tutor Coll of All SS Tottenham (W Middx Poly from 78) from 67. *c/o All Saints' College, Tottenham, N17.*

ARMSTRONG, Edwin. b 23. Trin Coll Dub BA 45, MA 69. **d** 46 **p** 47 Connor. C of Trin Coll Miss Belf 46-49; Donaghadee (in c of Millisle) 49-57; I of Gilford Dio Drom from 57. *Vicarage, Stranore Road, Gilford, Co Down, N Ireland.* (Gilford 272)

ARMSTRONG, Fred Carlisle. St Jo Coll Morpeth 50. **d** 52 **p** 53 Perth. C of St Hilda Perth 52-54; R of N Midlands 54-60; Gosnells 60-63; Como 63 67; Albany 67-72; Hon Can of Bunb 67-72; Can Res 72-75; CF (Austr) from 75. *AMF, Broadmeadows, Vic., Australia.*

ARMSTRONG, Geoffrey William Harry. b 16. **d** 49 B & W for Col Bp **p** 49 Trinid. C of St Crispin Port of Spain and Chap to HM Publ Insts 49-53; P-in-c of Pembroke Tobago 53-54; C of H Trin Bridgwater 54-57; C-in-c 57-58; R of Aller 58-61; R of Pitney-Lortie 58-61; V of W Wratting 61-64; V of W Wickham 61-64; R of Montrose w Inverbervie 64-79; C of the Howden Dio York from 81. *35/b Pinfold Street, Howden, Near Goole, N Humberside, DN14 7DE.* (Howden 30703)

ARMSTRONG, Canon George. b 09. Clifton Th Coll. **d** 32 **p** 33 Liv. C of Em Fazakerley 32-37; St Osw Winwick 37-40; CF (EC) 40-46; Hon CF 46; R of Layer-Marney Dio Chelmsf from 46; R of Gt w L Birch and Layer-Breton Dio Chelmsf from 47; RD of Coggeshall and Tey 68-79; Hon Can of Chelmsf from 77. *Birch Rectory, Colchester, Essex.* (Colchester 330241)

ARMSTRONG, George Aubrey Whitcombe. Univ of NZ BA 53, MA 55, BD 58. Princeton Th Sem NJ PhD 73. Selw Coll Dun 57. **d** 58 **p** 59 Dun. C of Roslyn 58-60; V of Green I 60-62; Cashmere Hills 62-65; Lect St Jo Th Coll Auckld 65-70 and from 73; Perm to Offic Dio Auckld 65-70; in Amer Ch 71-73; Hon C of Meadowbank 73-76; Mangere Miss Distr Dio Auckld from 76. *c/o St John's College, Auckland 5, NZ.* (581-693)

ARMSTRONG, Guy Lionel Walter. b 18. Wycl Hall Ox 60. **d** 61 **p** 62 Ox. C of Caversham 61-65; V of Bagshot 65-73; Ripley 73-77; Chap of HM Detention Centre Send 73-77; RD of Woking 73-77; Exam Chap to Bp of Guildf 74-77. *Kyngsmead, Station Road, Brading, Sandown, IW, PO36 0DY.* (Brading 610)

ARMSTRONG, Henry Denis. b 12. Lich Th Coll 58. **d** 59 **p** 60 Lich. C of Tamworth 59-62; V of Betley 62-81. *Brook Cottage, Main Road, Betley, Crewe, CW3 9BH.* (Crewe 820016)

ARMSTRONG, James Irwin. St Aid Coll 57. **d** 59 **p** 60 Kilm. C of St Mary Virg and St Jo Bapt Sligo 59-61; I of Stradbally 61-65; Badoney U 65-75; Camus-juxta-Bann Dio Derry from 75. *19 Dundarg Road, Macosquin, Coleraine, Co Derry, BT51 4PN, N Ireland.* (Coleraine 3918)

✠ **ARMSTRONG, Right Rev John.** b 05. CB (Mil) 62. OBE (Mil) 42. St Francis Coll Nundah ACT ThL 32. **d** 32 Goulb **p** 33 Newc for Goulb. M of Commun of Ascen Goulb 32-33; C of St Martin Scarborough 33-35; Chap RN 35-63; Men in Disp 40. Hon Chap to HM the Queen 58-63; Chap of the Fleet and Archd of the RN 60-63; Commiss St Hel 60-63; Cons Ld Bp of Berm in Westmr Abbey Lon 25 March 63 by Abp of Cant; Bps of Lon; Cov; St E; and Roch; Bp Suffr of Dunwich; and Bps Boys Craske Williams and Chamberlain; res 68; V of Yarcombe 69-73; Asst Bp of Ex from 69. *Foundry Farm, Yarcombe, Honiton, Devon, EX14 9AZ.* (Chard 3332)

ARMSTRONG, Preb John Arthur Lloyd. b 1900. Or Coll Ox 19. Bps' Coll Cheshunt 20. **d** 23 **p** 24 Lon. C of St Simon Zelotes Bethnal Green 23-28; V of Gilgandra NSW 28-32; C of Minehead 32-35; V of H Trin Hendford Yeovil 35-44; R of Street 44-56; Ditcheat 56-65; RD of Glastonbury 55-56; Preb of Wells Cathl from 49. *Old Hinges, Coxley, Wells, Somt.* (Wells 73367)

ARMSTRONG, Canon John Hammond. b 24. St Jo Coll Dur BA 47, Dipl in Th 49. **d** 49 **p** 50 Dur. C of St Gabr Bp Wearmouth 49-52; Staindrop w Cockfield (in c of Cockfield) 52-54; V of Skipwith 54-59; V of Thorganby 54-59; N Ferriby 59-63; R of Sutton-on-Derwent 63-71; Dioc Adv on Chr Stewardship Dio York 63-75; C-in-c of All SS Pavement w St Pet and St Crux w St Sav and St Sampson w H Trin K Court York 71-72; R (w St Denys) 72-77; Team R of All SS, Pavement w St Crux and St Martin w St Helen and St Denys City and Dio York from 77; Can and Preb of York Minster from 72; C-in-c of St Denys w St Geo St Marg and St Pet-le-Willows 74-76; RD of York from 76. *Rectory, St Andrewgate, York, YO1 2BZ.* (York 31116)

✠ **ARMSTRONG, Most Rev John Ward.** b 15. Trin Coll Dub Abp King Pri (2nd) 37, BA (Resp) Bibl Gr Pri, Downes Pri (1st) and Div Test (1st cl) 38, BD 45, MA 57, Hon DD 81. **d** 38 **p** 39 Dub. C of All SS Grangegorman Dub 38-44; Hon Cler V of Ch Ch Cathl Dub 40-44; Dean's V in St Patr Cathl Dub 44-51; Chapter Clerk St Patr Cathl Dub 49-51; Can and Preb of Tassagard in St Patr Cathl Dub 50-58; R of Ch Ch Leeson Pk Dub 51-58; Dean of Residence Nat Univ of Dub 51-63; Wallace Lect Trin Coll Dub 54-63; Dean of St Patr Cathl Dub 58-68; Cons Ld Bp of Cash, Emly, Waterf and Lism in St Patr Cathl Dub 21 Sep 68 by Abp of Dub; Abp of Arm; Bps of Meath; Cork; Connor; Killaloe; Lim; and Bps Hodges and Willis; Bp of United Dios of Cash, Waterf and Lism w Oss, Ferns and Leigh 77; Trld to Arm 80 (Primate of All Ireland). *The See House, Cathedral Close, Armagh, BT61 7EE, N Ireland.*

ARMSTRONG, Llewellyn. Codr Coll Barb 59. **d** 62 **p** 63 Barb. C of St Mich Cathl Barb 62-66; R of St Aug Barb 68-75. *c/o St Augustine's Rectory, St George, Barbados, W Indies.*

✠ **ARMSTRONG, Right Rev Mervyn.** b 06. OBE 46. Ball Coll Ox BA and Herbert Pri 28, MA 33. Westcott Ho Cam 38. **d** 38 Southn for Win **p** 39 Win. C of Milford-on-Sea 38-40; Chap RNVR 40-43; Chap Miss to Seamen Vic Dk Road and Tilbury 43-44; Hon Chap to Abp of Cant 44; Adv on Seamen's Welfare to Min of War Transpt and Dir of Seamen's Welfare Govt of India 44-45; L to Offic Dio Lah 45; V of Margate 46-49; Chap to Abp of Cant 49-51; Archd of Stow 51-54; Preb of Leic St Marg in Linc Cathl 51-54; R of Epworth 51-54; R of Wroot 51-54; Provost of Leic and V of St Martin, Leic 54-58; Proc Conv Leic 54-59; Cons Ld Bp Suffr of Jarrow in York Minster 29 Sept 58 by Abp of York; Bps of Dur; Leic; Southw; and Wakef; Bps Suffr of Selby; Stockport; Burnley; and Hull; and Bp Gerard; res 64; Industr Adv to Abp of York 64-70; Asst Bp in Dio York 64-70. *Glen Brathay, Skelwith Fold, Ambleside, Cumbria, LA22 0HT.* (Ambleside 3249)

ARMSTRONG, Peter James Sagar. **d** 66 Zam **p** 67 Bp Mataka for Zam. P Dio Zam 67-71; Dio N Zam 71-75; Dom Chap to Bp of N Zam 73-75; Chap at Istanbul Dio Gibr (Gibr in Eur from 80) from 75. *c/o British Embassy, Istanbul.*

ARMSTRONG, Philip Halford. **d** and **p** 51 Brisb. C of St Matt Sherwood Brisb 51-53; M of Bush Bro of St Paul Charleville 53-56; CF (Austr) and LPr Dio Brisb 56-60; V of Palmwoods 60-61; Mareeba 61-63; Ch Ch St Geo 63-71; R of St Paul E Brisb 71-74; Perm to Offic Dio Brisb from 74; Hosp Chap Dio Brisb from 80. *104 Lister Street, Sunnybank, Brisbane, Australia 4109.* (345 2722)

ARMSTRONG, Canon Richard Gregg. McGill Univ BCom 51, BD 55. Montr Th Coll 52. **d** 55 **p** 56 Keew. I of Pine Falls 55-56; Miss at Atikokan 56-60; I of Rainy River 60-62; V of St Barn Winnipeg 62-65; L to Offic Dio Rupld 65-70; Hon C of St Jas Winnipeg 71-78; St Bede Winnipeg Dio Rupld from 78; Hon Can of Rupld from 79. *138 Roseberry Street, Winnipeg, Manit., R3J IS9, Canada.*

ARMSTRONG, Robert Charles. b 24. Trin Coll Dub BA 46, Div Test (2nd cl) 47, Higher Dipl in Educn 52, MA 57. **d** 47 **p** 48 Connor. C of St Luke Belf 48-50; Succr of St Patr Cathl Dub and Warden of Gr Sch Dub 50-59; Min Can 59-62; R of Finglas 59-67; Dun Laoghaire Dio Dub from 67; Mariners Dun Laoghaire Dio Dub from 67; Treas V of St Patr Cathl Dub from 62; Dom Chap to Abp of Dub from 64; RD of Newcastle 71-76; Monkstown from 76; Dir Ordinands Dio Dub from 74. *Dun Laoghaire Rectory, Dublin, Irish Republic.* (Dublin 809537)

ARMSTRONG, Ronald. b 09. St Jo Coll Dur BA 38, MA 42. **d** 38 **p** 39 Bradf. C of St Lawr Pudsey 38-41; Chester-le-Street 41-43; Dom Chap to Bp of Lagos 43-45; Tutor at Melville Hall Ibad 45-52; C of Bridport 53-54; C-in-c 54; C-in-c of Hartcliffe Conv Distr Bris 54-59; V of Beckermet 59-60; Ch Ch Penrith 60-63; Em Leyton 63-65; Chap Whipps Cross Hosp Leytonstone 65-79; Publ Pr Dio Chelmsf 74-80. *7 Mason Road, Woodford Green, Essex.*

ARMSTRONG, Ronald Edward. Univ of Tor BA 50. Wycl Coll Tor 52. **d** 53 **p** 54 Tor. C of Ap Ch Tor 53-54; St Jas Pro-Cathl Tor 54-56; R of Ajax 56-59; St Eliz Queensway Tor 59-67; on leave 68-75; P-in-c of Richvale Dio Tor from 75.

15 Mackay Drive, Thornhill, Ont., Canada.

ARMSTRONG, Thomas Ernest. b 44. Coll of Em & St Chad Sask 74. **d** and **p** 74 Caled. I of Stewart 74-76; Burns Lake 76-81. *Box 190, Rose Blanche, Newfoundland, Canada.*

ARMSTRONG, Wilfrid Theodore. b 17. OBE (Mil) 67. TD 66. Men in Disp 45. Keble Coll Ox BA (Th) 39, MA 45. Westcott Ho Cam and Ely Th Coll. **d** 46 Lon **p** 47 Willesden for Lon. C of Ch Ch Hampstead 46-49; V of Whaplode 49-53; PC of Holbeach Fen 52-53; Surr 53-63; CF (TA) 54-67; DACG 65-67; V of St Nich w St John Newport Linc 53-63; R of Riseholme w Grange-de-Lings 53-63; Flixborough w Burton-on-Stather 63-73; RD of Manlake 66-69; V of Eridge Green 73-78; Lower Beeding Dio Chich from 78. *Vicarage, Lower Beeding, Horsham, W Sussex, RH13 6NU.* (L Beeding 367)

ARMSTRONG, William. Sarum Th Coll 52. **p** 55 Dur. C of Hebburn-on-Tyne 54-55; Ferryhill 55-57; Gateshead (in c of H Trin) 57-60; PC of Cassop w Quarrington 60-66; M Bush Bro of St Barn Ravenshoe 66-68; Liv and Dioc Schs Adv from 81. Perm to Offic Dio Brisb 68-69; R of S Gladstone w Miriam Vale 69-71; Perm to Offic Dio Melb 71-81; V of Aintree Dio Liv from 81; Dioc Schs Adv from 81. *St Peter's Vicarage, Church Avenue, Aintree, Liverpool, L9 4SG.* (051-525 2489)

ARMSTRONG, William Gerald. b 30. Univ of Nottm BA (2nd cl Th) 58. St Cath S Ox Dipl Soc 59. Ripon Hall Ox 58. **d** 60 **p** 61 York. C of Beverley Minster 60-62; St Jas Sutton-in Holderness 62-64; V of Charlesworth 64-70; R of Ashbourne w Mapleton (w Clifton 70-73) 70-75; Surr 70-75; V of Broughton Dio Blackb from 75. *Broughton Vicarage, Garstang Road, Preston, Lancs, PR3 5JB.* (0772 862330)

ARNAUD, John Charles Stanley. b 23. Univ of Aber MA 48. **d** 78 **p** 79 Moray. Hon C of H Trin Keith Dio Moray from 78. *10 Kynoch Terrace, Keith, Banffshire, AB5 3EX.*

ARNESEN, Christopher Paul. b 48. Univ of Lon BA 70. Sarum Wells Th Coll 78. **d** 80 Carl **p** 81 Penrith for Carl. C of Dalton-in-Furness Dio Carl from 80. *Vicarage Cottage, Market Place, Dalton-in-Furness, Cumbria, LA15 8AZ.*

ARNESEN, Raymond Halfdan. b 25. Qu Coll Cam BA 49, MA 54. M SSF 55. Linc Th Coll 50. **d** 52 **p** 53 Newc T. C of St Francis High Heaton 52-55. *Ewell Monastery, West Malling, Kent.*

ARNOLD, Alan Roy. b 33. Univ of Lon Bd 79. SOC 75. **d** 78 **p** 79 Guildf. C of Fleet 78-81; V of Hinchley Wood Dio Guildf from 81. *98 Manor Road North, Hinchley Wood, Esher, Surrey.* (01-398 4443)

ARNOLD, Arthur Philip. b 46. Em Coll Cam BA (2nd cl Th) 67, MA 71. Qu Coll Birm Dipl Th 69. **d** 70 Hulme for York **p** 71 Man. C of H Family Conv Distr Failsworth 70-74; Asst Chap Hurstpierpoint Coll 74-77; Chap K Coll Cam 77-80; St Chad's Coll Dur from 80. *21 North Bailey, Durham, DH1 2EW* (Durham 48088)

ARNOLD, Craig Jerome. b 49. ACA 76. Ridley Coll Melb BTh 80. **d** 81 Tas. C of Glenorchy Dio Tas from 81. *482 Main Road, Glenorchy, Tasmania, 7010.*

ARNOLD, Donald Feversham. K Coll NS. **d** 68 Bp Arnold for NS **p** 70 NS. C-in-c of Falkland 68-70; C of St Paul Halifax 70-74; St Paul Charlottetown Dio NS from 74. *101 Prince Street, Charlottetown, PEI, Canada.* (892-8058)

ARNOLD, Ernest Stephen. b 27. **d** 64 Bp T M Hughes for Llan **p** 65 Llan. C of Aberavon 64-68; V of Ferndale 68-74; L to Offic Dio Cyprus from 81. *Box 4503, Dubai, Arabian Gulf.*

✠ **ARNOLD, Right Rev George Feversham.** KCNS LTh 37, BD 44. Dalhousie Univ BA 35, MA 38, Hon DD 68. **d** 37 **p** 39 NS. C of Louisburg 37-41; R of St Jas Mahone Bay 41-50; St John Fairview Halifax 50-52; Windsor 52-58; Cler Sec and NS Dioc Regr 58-67; Exam Chap to Bp of NS 47-70; Chap 58-67; Hon Can of All SS Cathl Halifax 59-63; Can 63-67; Cons Bp Suffr of NS in All SS Cathl Halifax 21 Sept 67 by Abp of Fred; Bps of Alg; Athab; NS; Newfld; and Montr; Bp Suffr of Hur (Appleyard); and Bp Waterman; Apptd Ld Bp of NS 75; res 79. *56 Holmes Hill Road, Hantsport, NS, BOP 1PO, Canada.*

ARNOLD, George Innes. b 22. Roch Th Coll. **d** 61 **p** 62 Newc T. C of St Geo Cullercoats 61-64; St Jas Benwell Newc T 64-68; Chap at Benghazi Dio Egypt 68-70; V of St Jas Croydon 71-80; P-in-c of Dullingham Dio Ely from 80; Stetchworth Dio Ely from 80. *Dullingham Vicarage, Newmarket, CB8 9UZ.* (Stetchworth 225)

ARNOLD, John Frederic. Univ of Syd BA 60. BD (Lon) 61. ACT ThL (2nd cl) 61. Moore Th Coll Syd 61. **d** 61 Bp Kerle for Syd **p** 62 Syd. C of St Clem Mosman 61-65; Asst Chap for Youth Dio Syd 65-67; R of Blacktown 67-75; Gen Sec CMS Queensld and Northern NSW 75-79; Perm to Offic Dio Brisb 78-79. *87 Gloucester Street, Brisbane, Queensland, Australia 4101.* (44 5497)

ARNOLD, Very Rev John Robert. b 33. Late Exhib and Scho of SS Coll Cam BA (1st cl Mod and Med Lang Trip pt ii) 57, 2nd cl Th Trip pt ii 59. Westcott Ho Cam 58. **d** 60 **p** 61 Sheff. C of H Trin Millhouses 60-63; Sir Henry Stephenson Fell Univ of Sheff 62-63; Chap and Lect Univ of Southn 63-72; Sec Bd for Miss and Unity of Gen Syn 72-78; Hon Can of Win Cathl 74-78; Dean of Roch from 78. *Deanery, Rochester, Kent.* (Medway 44023)

✠ **ARNOLD, Right Rev Keith Appleby.** b 26. Trin Coll Cam BA 50, MA 55. Westcott Ho Cam 50. **d** 52 **p** 53 Newc T. C of Haltwhistle 52-55; St Jo Evang Edin 55-61; R 61-69; CF (TA) 58-62; V of Kirkby Lonsdale w Mansergh 69-73; R of Hemel Hempstead 73-80; RD of Berkhamsted 73-80; Cons Ld Bp Suffr of Warwick in St Paul's Cathl Lon 30 Sept 80 by Abp of Cant; Bps of Lon, Cov, Birm, Chelmsf, Derby, Ex, Leic, Ox, St E and Worc; Bps Suffr of Edmon, Stafford and Thetford; and Bps Allenby, Bulley, Franklin, Porter, Daly and Riches. *Warwick House, 9 Armorial Road, Coventry, CV3 6GH.* (0203-416200)

ARNOLD, Richard Nicholas. b 54. AKC 76. SOC 76. **d** 77 **p** 78 S'wark. C of Nunhead 77-80; St Pet Walworth Dio S'wark from 80. *45 Aldbridge Street, SE17.* (01-703 2893)

ARNOLD, Robert Horace. b 22. Univ Coll Dur (Coll Organist 41) BA 47. Cudd Coll 47. **d** 49 **p** 50 Win. C of Basingstoke 49-55; R of Hook Norton 55-59; Asst Hosp St Bart's Hosp 59-63; Hosp from 63; C of St Bart L City and Dio Lon 59-63; V from 63. *22 Charterhouse Square, EC1M 6EU.* (01-600 9000)

ARNOLD, Roy. b 38. St D Coll Lamp BA 62, Dipl Th (w distinc) 63. **d** 63 **p** 64 Bris. C of St Luke Brislington 63-66; St Mary-without-the-Walls Ches 67-70; V of Brinnington (w Portwood from 71) 70-75; St Paul Sale Dio Ches from 75; Ed Ches Dioc Leaflet from 76; Dioc Information Officer from 79. *St Paul's Vicarage, Sale, Chesh, M33 1XG.* (061-973 1042)

ARNOLD, Canon Walter Charles. OBE 77. Univ of NZ BA 42. **d** 43 **p** 44 Ch Ch. C of Hokitika 43-45; Ashburton-Tinwald 45-47; V of Mt Somers 47-51; C of Shirley Surrey 51-54; V of Phillipstown 54-60; Kaiapoi 60-64; City Missr Dio Wel from 64; Hon Can of Wel from 70. *City Mission, Taranaki Street, Wellington, NZ.* (555-979)

ARNOLD, William Charles. St Jo Coll Morpeth ACT ThL 28. **d** 28 **p** 29 Bath. C of Cowra 28-31; R of Hill End 31-32; Condobolin 32-37; W Wyalong 37-40; O'Connell 40-46; Kelso 46-49; Parkes 49-60; Can of Bath 44-52; Archd of Marsden 52-54, 60-65, and 68-72; without territorial jurisd 72-74; Camidge 54-60; Barker 67-68; R of E Orange 60-64; Oberon 64-67; Dioc Centenery Comm Bath 67-74; Chap Marsden Girls Sch Bath 70-74; Perm to Offic Dio Syd from 74. *1-4 Broughton Avenue, Mowll Memorial Village, Castle Hill, NSW, Australia 2154.* (634-6328)

ARNOTT, Arthur Frederick. b 14. SOC 66. **d** 70 **p** 71 S'wark. C of Reigate 70-74; Hon C of Ch Ch Chislehurst Dio Roch from 74. *17 Hatton Court, Lubbock Road, Chislehurst, Kent.* (01-467 4835)

ARNOTT, David. b 44. Em Coll Cam BA (Hons Th) 66. Qu Coll Birm 68. **d** 69 Woolwich for S'wark **p** 70 S'wark. C of Old Charlton 69-73; St Mich AA S Beddington 73-78; (in c of Roundshaw Ecumen Exp 73-78; Chap Liv Poly from 78. *94 Fulwood Road, Aigburth, Liverpool, L17 9QA.* (051-727 2150)

ARNOTT, Eric William. b 12. Cranmer Hall Dur 67. **d** 68 Bp Ramsbotham for Newc T **p** 69 Newc T. C of Gosforth 68-71; Wooler 71-74; C-in-c of Kirknewton 71-74; Team V 74-78; Perm to Offic Dio Sarum from 78. *Forge Cottage, Hoopers Lane, Puncknowle, Dorchester, Dorset DT2 9BE.* (Long Bredy 311)

✠ **ARNOTT, Most Rev Felix Raymond.** CMG 81. Keble Coll Ox Squire Scho 29, 3rd cl Cl Mods 31, BA (1st cl Th) 33. ACT ThD 50. Cudd Coll 33. **d** 34 **p** 35 Wakef. C of Elland 34-38; Exam Chap to Bp of Wakef 36-39; Vice-Prin Bps' Coll Cheshunt 38-39; Warden St Jo Coll Brisb and Exam Chap to Abp of Brisb 39-46; I of St Mary Kangaroo Point 42-46; Warden St Paul's Coll Syd 46-63; Cons Bp Coadj of Melb in St Andr Cathl Syd 29 June 63 by Abp of Syd; Bps of St Arn; Newc; and Bath; and Bps Sambell and A W G Hudson; apptd Abp of Brisb (Metrop of Prov of Queensld) 70; res 80; Chap at Venice Dio Gibr from 80. *Dorsoduro 870, 30123 Venice, Italy.* (29195)

ARNOTT, Michael Arthur Farre. b 43. St Bede's Coll Umtata 77. **d** 79 Bp Ndwandwe for Johann **p** 80 Johann. C of Germiston Dio Johann from 79. *PO Box 624, Germiston, S Africa 1400.*

ARNOTT, Thomas Grenfell. b 11. Cranmer Hall Dur. **d** 68 **p** 69 Dur. [f Solicitor] C of Ryton-on-Tyne 68-71; V of Em, Weston-s-Mare 71-73; R of Brandesburton 73-78; RD of N Holderness 76-78; Perm to Offic Dio York from 78. *Hall Barn, Levisham, Nr Pickering, N Yorks, YO18 7NL.*

ARONSOHN, Gustav. b 1898. **d** 57 Bp Maxwell for Leic **p**

58 Leic. C of St Pet w St Hilda Leic 57-59; R of Ravenstone 59-66; Hon C of East Dean w Friston & Jevington Dio Chich from 66. *1 The Dentons, Meads, Eastbourne, Sussex, BN20 7SW.* (Eastbourne 37966)

AROSO, Ven David Obafemi. Melville Hall Ibad 50. **d** 51 Lagos **p** 52 Ondo-B. d Dio Lagos 51-52; P Dio Ondo-B 52-55 and 57-62; C of St Mich AA Blackb 55-57; P Dio Ondo 62-80; Dio Ilesha from 80; Hon Can of Ondo 67-80; Archd Dio Ilesha from 81. *Box 2, Ipetu-Ijesa, Nigeria.*

AROTIBA, Moses Ogunbodede. b 41. Im Coll Ibad. **d** 72 **p** 73 Ibad. P Dio Ibad; Dom Chap to Bp of Ibad 74-75. *PO Box 3075, Ibadan, Nigeria.*

AROWOLO, Canon Michael Ladapo. Melville Hall Ibad 50. **d** 52 **p** 53 Lagos. P Dio Lagos 52-66; Dio Ibad from 66; Can of Ibad from 76. *St Paul's Vicarage, Ipetu-Ijesha, Nigeria.*

ARPEE, Stephen Trowbridge. Wooster Coll Ohio BA 57. Gen Th Sem NY STB 65. **d** 65 Newark USA **p** 66 Iran. P Dio Iran 66-78. *c/o 383 Washington Road, Lake Forest, IL 60045, USA.*

ARRAND, Geoffrey William. b 44. K Coll Lon and Warm BD and AKC 66. **d** 67 **p** 68 Dur. C of Washington 67-70; S Ormsby 70-73; Team V of Gt Grimsby 73-79; R of Halesworth and Linstead w Chediston Dio St E 79-80; Team R (w Holton, Blyford, Spexhall and Wissett) from 80; P-in-c of Holton, Blyford, Spexhall and Wissett 80. *Rectory, Highfield Road, Halesworth, Suff* (Halesworth 2602)

ARRANTASH, Canon Reginald Thomas. Linc Th Coll 33. **d** 30 S'wark **p** 37 S'wark for Col Bp. C of St Jo Div Kennington 36-37; Cathl Ch Perth 37-40; R of Wyalkatchem 40-45; Katanning W Austr 45-48; Bishopstone Herefs 48-52; Kenchester w Bridge Sollers 48-52; Midl Junction W Austr 52-59; Albany 59-67; Busselton 67-76; Kojonup 76-79; Can of Bunb 67-79; Can (Emer) from 79; P-in-c of Manning Dio Perth from 79. *14 Gunbar Way, Kalamunda, W Australia 6076.* (293 3659)

ARREAK, Benjamin Tatigat. b 47. Arthur Turner Tr Sch Pangnirtung 72. **d** 75 **p** 76 Arctic. C of Sugluk Dio Arctic from 75. *St James' Mission Sugluk, Que, Canada.*

ARRIDGE, Leonard Owen. b 22. Univ of Wales BA 51. **d** 67 Swan B for St A **p** 68 St A. Hon C of Hope 67-69; Wrexham 69-79; Min Can of Ban Cathl from 79. *Y Canondy, Bangor, Gwyn.* (Bangor 2840)

ARRIL, Robert John. b 47. Univ of Alta BA 72. Huron Coll Lon MDiv 75. **d** 75 **p** 76 Edmon. C of Ch Ch Edmon 75-79; R of Cooksville S Dio Tor from 79. *2055 Hurantario Street, Mississauga, Ont., Canada.*

ARROWSMITH, Alan Winston. St Jo Coll Auckld. **d** 64 **p** 65 Wai. C of Dannevirke 64-67; P-in-c of Turangi Miss Distr 67-71; V of Takapau 71-74; Otumoetai Par Distr 74-80; Taupo Dio Wai from 80. *Vicarage, Taupo, NZ.* (86059)

ARROWSMITH, Frederick John. b 39. Late Exhib of Pemb Coll Ox Liddon Stud and BA (2nd cl Engl Lit) 61, 2nd cl Th 63, MA 66. St Steph Ho Ox 61. **d** 64 **p** 65 Heref. C of St Martin Heref 64-68; St Paul Knightsbridge 68-73; P-in-c of H Trin Kingsway w St Jo Evang Drury Lane Dio Lon from 73; St Paul Covent Gdn Westmr Dio Lon from 75; M Gen Syn from 75. *14 Burleigh Street, WC2E 7PX.*

ARROWSMITH, Harry. b 1895. St Aid Coll 27. **d** 28 **p** 29 Liv. C of St Benedict Everton 28-31; St Mich AA Claughton 31-32; Chap of Dudley Rd Hosp Summerfield Hosp and Summer Hill Homes Birm 32-60; L to Offic Dio St E 60-80; Dio Blackb from 80. *Fosbrooke House, Lytham St Annes, Lancs.*

ARROWSMITH, Canon Herbert Maxwell. MBE 55. Moore Th Coll 38, ACT ThL 39. **d** 40 **p** 41 Syd. Actg Gen Sec CMS for NSW 40-45; V of Toorak 45-49; BFBS Commonwealth Sec for Austr 49-68; C of St Andr Cathl Syd 51-67; Perm to Offic Dio Melb 51-60; Hon Can of Syd 55-60 and from 62; Archd of Syd City 60-62; C of St Phil Syd 69-72; L to Offic Dio Syd from 72. *28 Western Road, Mowll Memorial Village, Castle Hill, NSW, Australia 2154.* (634-4782)

ARSCOTT, Barry James. b 36. K Coll Lon and Warm AKC 59. **d** 60 **p** 61 Chelmsf. C of St Andr Walthamstow 60-65; P-in-c of St Luke Leyton 65-67; V 67-77; P-in-c of St Barn L Ilford Dio Chelmsf from 77. *St Barnabas Vicarage, Browning Road, Manor Park, E12.* (01-472 2777)

ARTER, David John William Lloyd. Keble Coll Ox 33. BA 43, MA 43. Wells Th Coll 36. **d** 39 Swan B for St D **p** 40 St D. C of Llanstadwell 39-41; Lamphey w Hodgeston 41-42; Tenby 42-44; Chap RNVR 44-46; Chap RN 46-67. *Manor House, Medmenham, Bucks.* (Hambleden 441)

ARTHUR, Charles Williams. b 12. St Chad's Coll Dur BA (3rd cl Cl and Gen Lit) 33, MA 36, Dipl Th 34. Univ of Wales BD 47. **d** 35 Bp Wentworth-Sheilds for Ban **p** 36 Ban. C of Llandudno 35-43; R of Llanfair-Pwll-Gwyngyll 43-50; Dioc Insp of Schs 45-57; Dir of Relig Educn Dio Ban 50-57; Lect in Div St Mary's Tr Coll Ban 54-57; Succr of Ban Cathl 55-57; V of Aberdare (w Cwmbach to 60) 57-81; RD of Aberdare 65-81; Exam Chap to Bp of Llan 65-81; Surr 66-81; Can of Llan Cathl 71-81; Prec 75-81. *Graif Wen, 17 Elm Grove, Gadlys, Aberdare, Mid Glam.* (Aberdare 873058)

ARTHUR, Edgar Kenneth Thornton. b 16. Ely Th Coll. **d** 50 **p** 51 Sheff. C of St Paul Arbourthorne Sheff 50-53; C-in-c of Bramley Hellaby and Sunnyside Conv Distr 53-56; Chap HM Pris Wandsworth 56-57; Holloway 57-59; V of Fishlake 59-62; St Hilda Halifax 62-67; R of Shobrooke 67-81; R of Stockleigh Pomeroy 67-76; RD of Cadbury 71-76. *17 Park Road, Crediton, Devon, EX17 3ES.* (Crediton 2076)

ARTHUR, Ian Willoughby. b 40. Univ of Lon BA (Gen) 63, BA 66. Ripon Coll Cudd 78. **d** 80 **p** 81 St Alb. C of Transfig Kempston Dio St Alb from 80. *16 Rosedale Way, Kempston, Bedford, MK42 8JE.*

✠ **ARTHUR, Right Rev John Benjamin. d** and **p** 42 Accra. P Dio Accra 42-63; Hon Can of Accra 63-65; Archd of Kumasi from 65; Cons Asst Bp of Accra in Cathl Ch of Most H Trin Accra 11 Dec 66 by Abp of W Afr; Apptd Ld Bp of Kumasi 73. *PO Box 114, Kumasi, Ghana.* (Kumasi 4117)

✠ **ARTHUR, Right Rev Robert Gordon.** b 09. Univ of Melb BA 30, MA 34. **d** and **p** 49 Goulb. C of St Sav Cathl Goulb 49-50; R of Berridale 50-53; R and Archd of Canberra 53-60; R and Archd of Wagga Wagga 60-61; Cons Bp Coadj of C & Goulb 1 May 56 in St Andr Cathl Syd by Abp of Syd; Abp of Brisb; Bps of Newc; C & Goulb; River; Graft; Kurun; Bps Collins; Barrett; Pilcher; Hilliard; and Storrs; Trld to Graft 61; res 73; R of St Phil O'Connor, Canberra 73-74; P-in-c of Bratton 75-78; RD of Heytesbury 76-77; Perm to Offic Dio C & Goulb from 81. *4 Berry Street, Downer, ACT, Australia 2602.*

ARTHURSON, Charles John. b 37. **d** and **p** 72 Keew. I of St Pet Big Trout Lake Ont 72-74; Split Lake 74-81; Sioux Lookout Dio Keew from 81. *Box 626, Sioux Lookout, Ont, Canada.*

ARTISS, Joseph Sturge. b 28. Univ of Dur BSc (Botany) 52, Dipl Th 67. Cranmer Hall Dur 65. **d** 67 **p** 68 Dur. C of St Cuthb Dur 67-68; Chester-le-Street 68-70; V of St Pet Walsall Dio Lich from 70. *St Peter's Vicarage, Walsall, Staffs.*

ARTLEY, Clive Mansell. b 30. St Jo Coll Dur BA 56, Dipl Th 58. **d** 58 **p** 59 York. C of Eston w Normanby 58-61; R of Burythorpe w E Acklam and Leavening 61-64; V of Westow 61-64; CF 64-73; Perm to Offic Dio York from 73. *42 Marwood Drive, Great Ayton, Middlesbrough, TS9 6PE.*

ARULEFELA, Canon Joseph Oluwafemi. Melville Hall Ibad 55. Dipl Th 57. **d** and **p** 57 Ondo-B. P Dio Ondo-B 57-62; Dio Ondo 62-67; Dio Ibad from 67; Exam Chap to Bp of Ibad from 71; Hon Can of Ondo from 72. *Immanuel College, Ibadan, Nigeria.* (22441)

ARULPRAGASM, Lemuel Balasingham. d 57 **p** 59 Colom. P Dio Colom 57-67 and 71-72; Dio W Mal from 72; Chap St Jo Coll Jaffna 68-71. *243 Jalan Ipoh, Kuala Lumpur, Malaysia.*

ARUNDEL, Michael. b 36. Qu Coll Ox BA (2nd cl Mod Hist) 60, MA 64. Linc Th Coll 60. **d** 62 **p** 63 Man. C of Hollinwood 62-65; Leesfield 65-69; R of Newton Heath 69-80; RD of N Man 75-80; P-in-c of Eccles 80-81; Team R of St Mary w St Andr Eccles Dio Man from 81. *Eccles Vicarage, Westminster Road, Eccles, M30 9EB.* (061-789 1034)

ARUOREN, James Onakorieru. b 36. Im Coll Ibad 70. **d** and **p** 73 Benin. P Dio Benin 73-77; Dio Warri from 77. *Box 18, Ughelli, Nigeria.*

ASABA, Bishop of. *See* Nwosu, Right Rev Rowland Nwafo Chukwunweike.

ASANI, Patrick. d 74 **p** 75 S Malawi. P Dio S Malawi. *Queen Elizabeth Hospital, Box 95, Blantyre, Malawi.* (30333)

ASAOLU, John Ibikunle. Im Coll Ibad 65. **d** 68 **p** 69 Ekiti. P Dio Ekiti. *St John's Vicarage, Iye, via Ido, Nigeria.*

ASAOLU, Zaccheus Orire. Im Coll Ibad 62. **d** 65 N Nig. d Dio N Nig 65-68; Dio Ekiti from 68. *St Michael's Vicarage, Ifaki-Ekiti, Nigeria.*

ASBIL, Peter George Frederick. Sir Geo Williams Univ Montr. Montr Dioc Th Coll LTh 67. **d** 67 Montr. I of Clarenceville 67-69; Carmacks 69-73; Arundel 73-75; Chomedey-Bordeaux 75-77: Grenville Dio Montr from 77. *Box 239, Grenville, PQ, Canada.* (819-242 3278)

ASBIL, Canon Walter Gordon. Sir Geo Williams Univ Montr BA 54. McGill Univ BD 57, STM 67. Montr Dioc Coll. **d** and **p** 57 Montr. P-in-c of Aylwin and of River Desert 57-60; I of S Shore 60-65; R of St Steph Westmount Montr 65-67; Ste Anne de Bellevue 67-70; R of St Geo, St Catherine's Dio Niag from 70; Hon Can of Niag from 73. *PO Box 893, St Catharines, Ont., Canada.* (416-682 0382)

ASBRIDGE, John Hawell. St Chad's Coll Dur BA 47. Bps' Coll Cheshunt 47. **d** 49 **p** 50 Carl. C of St Geo Barrow-F 49-52; Fort William 52-54; London Docks 54-55; St Aug Kilburn 55-59; V of St Barn Northolt Pk 59-66; St Steph w St

Thos Shepherd's Bush Dio Lon from 66. *St Stephen's Vicarage, Coverdale Road, W12 8JJ.* (01-743 4515)

ASEKA, Joash. d 72 p 73 Bunyoro. P Dio Bunyoro. *Box 20, Hoima, Uganda.*

ASH, Brian John. b 32. ALCD 62. **d** 62 **p** 63 Ex. C of St Andr Plymouth 62-66; CMS Area Sec Dios Cant and Roch 66-73; V of St Aug Bromley Common Dio Roch from 73. *St Augustine's Vicarage, Southborough Lane, Bromley, Kent, BR2 8AT.* (01-467 1351)

ASH, Charles Ferris. b 07. AKC (1st cl) 37. **d** 37 **p** 38 Roch. C of Chislehurst 37-39; Chap Lawr Mem Sch Lovedale 39-45; Prin of St Geo's Homes Ketti 45-57; Ch of S India 47-61; C of Wooburn (in c of St Mark Bourne End) 61-66; Hambleden 66-73; C-in-c of Turville 73-76; Perm to Offic Dio Ox from 76. *66 Parsonage Close, High Wycombe, Bucks.*

ASH, Daniel Gordon. Univ of Manit BA 69. Hur Coll Ont MDiv 72. **d** and **p** 72 Rupld. C of St Matt Winnipeg 72-74; Dioc Dir of Min to Youth 72-74; P Assoc of Selkirk 75-79; R of St Geo Transcona Winnipeg Dio Rupld from 79. *425 Rosseau Avenue, E Winnipeg, Manit, Canada.*

ASH, Glenn Huntington. Em Th Coll Sktn LTh 56, BA 57, BD 66. **d** and **p** 56 Athab. I of Colinton 56-59; Beaver Lodge 59-63; Athab 64-70; Hon Can of St Jas Cathl Peace River 65-70; R of St Jas Sktn 70-81; Hon Can of Sktn 70-81. *38-330 Haight Crescent, Saskatoon, Canada.*

ASH, Joseph Raymond. b 17. Tyndale Hall Bris. **d** 47 **p** 48 Chelmsf. C of Dagenham 47-50; Chap RAF 50-72. *c/o Lloyds Bank, Romford, Essex.*

ASH, Ronald Victor. Moore Th Coll Syd. **d** 47 **p** 48 Syd. C of Kingsford 47-48; Wollongong 48-49; P-in-c of Groote Eylandt and Roper River Miss 50-52; Supr Oenpelli Miss 53-59; R of Kurrajong 59-62; C-in-c of Abbotsford w Russell Lea 62-70; w Home Miss S Dio Syd 70-73; R of H Trin Miller's Point Sydney 74-76; Asquith 76-81; St Hilda Katoomba Dio Syd from 81. *68 Kattoomba Street, Katoomba, NSW, Australia 2780.* (82-1608)

ASHBURNER, David Barrington. b 26. Ch Coll Cam 2nd cl Hist Trip pt i 50, BA (3rd cl Th Trip pt ia) 51, MA 55. Wycl Hall Ox 51. **d** 53 **p** 54 Leic. C of Coalville 53-56; H Ap Leic 56-58; V of Bucklebury w Marlston 58-70; Belton (w Osgathorpe from 75) 70-79; C-in-c of Osgathorpe 73-75; V of Frisby-on-the-Wreake w Kirkby Bellars 79-82; Uffington w Woolstone and Baulking Dio Ox from 82. *Vicarage, Broad Street, Uffington, Near Faringdon, SN7 7RH, Oxon.* (Uffington 663)

ASHBY, Eric. b 37. E Midl Min Tr Course. **d** 81 Sherwood for Southw. C of Hucknall Torkard Dio Southw from 81. *25 St Patrick's Road, Hucknall, Notts, NG15 6LU.*

ASHBY, Eric. b 28. St Jo Coll Dur BA 52, MA 58. **d** 53 **p** 54 Bradf. C of Ilkley 53-55; Heanor (in c of Marlpool) 55-58; V of Settle Dio Bradf from 58. *Vicarage, Settle, N Yorks, BD24 9JB.* (Settle 2288)

ASHBY, George Winston. Univ of WI LTh 71. Codr Coll Barb 68. **d** 73 Trinid. C of St Marg Port of Spain 73-80. *c/o St Margaret's Church, Port of Spain, Trinidad.*

✠ **ASHBY, Right Rev Godfrey William Ernest Candler.** Univ of Lon BD (2nd cl) 54, PhD 69. K Coll Lon and Warm AKC (1st cl) 54. **d** 55 **p** 56 S'wark. C of St Helier Surrey 55-58; P-in-c of St Mark's Miss CP 58-60; Sub-Warden of St Paul's Coll Grahmstn 60-66; R of Alice 66-68; Sen Lect OT Rhodes Univ Grahmstn 68-75; Can of Grahmstn Cathl 69-75; L to Offic Dio Grahmstn 76; Archd of Grahmstn 76-80; Dean 76-80; Cons Ld Bp of St John's in St John's Cathl Umtata 24 Feb 80 by Abp of Capetn; Bps of Natal, Bloemf, Grahmstn and Zulu; Bps Suffr of Ramsbury and Capetn; and Bps Zulu and Sobokwe. *Bishopsmead, Box 163, Umtata, Transkei, S Africa.*

ASHBY, Howard Hauangiangi. b 41. **d** 81 Auckld. C of Waimate North Dio Auckld from 81. *7 Taraire Street, Kaikohe, NZ.*

ASHBY, John Robert Patrick. b 36. Univ of Lon BSc (Eng) 57. Coll of Resurr Mirfield. **d** 60 Lon **p** 61 Kens for Lon. C of Northolt 60-64; Chap and Asst Master St Andr Coll Minaki 64-66; C of St Mary The Boltons Kens 66-68; V of St Gabr N Acton 68-80; Arlington Dio Chich from 80; Wilmington Dio Chich from 80; R of Folkington Dio Chich from 80. *Wilmington Vicarage, Polegate, E Sussex, BN26 5SL.* (Alfriston 870324)

ASHBY, Kevin Patrick. b 53. Jes Coll Ox BA 76, MA 80. Wycl Hall Ox 76. **d** 78 **p** 79 Leic. C of Market Harborough Dio Leic from 78. *11 Lincoln Court, Market Harborough, Leics.*

ASHBY, Norman. b 18. Egerton Hall Man. **d** 39 **p** 40 Man. C of St John Farnworth 39-41; Ross-on-Wye 41-43; Hove 43-44; CF (EC) 44-47; C of Portsm Cathl 47-48; Cler Org Sec Dr Barnardo's Homes 49; CF (TA) from 49; Chap of St Pet Basra w Shaibah and Port Chap Miss to Seamen Basra 50-52; Warden Ripon Dioc Ho 62-70; C-in-c of Pickhill Dio Ripon 70-72; V from 72; R of Kirkby Wiske w Maunby Dio Ripon from 77. *Kirkby Wiske Rectory, Thirsk, Yorks, YO7 4ER.* (Kirkby Wiske 392)

ASHBY, Peter George. b 49. Univ of Wales (Cardiff) BSc (Econ) 70. Univ of Nottm Dipl Th 71. Linc Th Coll 70. **d** 73 **p** 74 St Alb. C of Bengeo 73-75; Apsley End 80-81; Chap Hatfield Poly 76-79; Team V of Chabersbury, Hemel Hempstead Dio St Alb from 81. *65 Peascroft Road, Bennetts End, Hemel Hempstead, Herts.* (Hemel Hempstead 55052)

ASHBY, Thomas Alexander. b 10. Wells Th Coll 69. **d** 70 **p** 71 Linc. C of N Hykeham 70-73; Dioc Chap to the Deaf 71-74; P-in-c of E Kirkby w Miningsby 73-77; Hagnaby 73-77; Bolingbroke w Hareby 73-77; Perm to Offic Dio Linc 77-80; C of Steeton Dio Bradf from 80. *12 Parkway, Steeton, Keighley, BD20 6SX.* (Steeton 54270)

ASHBY, William Thomas David. Hur Th Coll STh 57. **d** 57 **p** 58 Hur. I of St Mich AA Lon Ont 57-68; R of Amherstburg Dio Hur from 68. *Box 24, Amherstburg, Ont., Canada.* (519-736 5110)

ASHCROFT, Ernest. b 45. Univ of Leeds BSc 67, PhD 70. St Jo Coll Nottm 72. **d** 75 **p** 76 Capetn. C of St Jo Wynberg Dio Capetn from 75. *Christ Church House, Richmond Road, Kenilworth 7700, CP, S Africa.* (77-6332)

ASHCROFT, Ven Lawrence. b 01. Univ Coll Dur 22. Lich Th Coll 24. **d** 26 **p** 27 Carl. C of Ulverston 26-29; Egremont (in c of Bigrigg) 29-30; Distr Sec BFBS for N Midlds 30-33; Min of St Sav Distr Chap Retford 34-40; CF (EC) 40-43; R of St Mich Stoke Cov 43-54; Surr 44-54; RD of Cov 49-54; Hon Can of Cov 52-54; Can of Leic St Marg in Linc Cathl Archd of Stow and R of Flixborough w Burton-on-Stather 54-62; Proc Conv Linc 55-62. *c/o Lloyds Bank, St Helier, CI.*

ASHDOWN, Anthony Hughes. K Coll Lon and Warm AKC 63. **d** 64 **p** 65 Lich. C of Tettenhall Regis 64-67; Bassaleg (in c of St Anne High Cross) 67-70; P-in-c of Gatooma 70-77; R of Longton (w St Jo Bapt from 78) 77-80; Cove Dio Guildf from 80; St Jo Bapt Longton 77-78. *Cove Vicarage, Farnborough, Hants.* (Farnborough 44544)

ASHDOWN, Barry Frederick. b 42. St Pet Coll Ox BA (2nd cl Th) 65, MA 69. Ridley Hall Cam 66. **d** 68 **p** 69 Bradf. C of St Pet Shipley 68-71; St Mary Rushden 71-74; R of Haworth Dio Bradf from 74. *Haworth Rectory, Keighley, W Yorks, BD22 8EN.* (Haworth 42169)

ASHDOWN, David Norman. Coll of Em & St Chad Sask. **d** 77 Sask **p** 78 Qu'App. On leave 77-78; C of Pipestone 78-80; I of Prairie Cross Dio Qu'App from 80. *Box 401, Gull Lake, Sask, Canada.*

ASHE, Francis John. b 53. Univ of Sheff BMet 74. Ridley Hall Cam 77. **d** 79 **p** 80 Guildf. C of Ashtead Dio Guildf from 79. *17 Loraine Gardens, Ashtead, Surrey, KT21 1PD.* (Ashtead 73819)

ASHE, Francis Patrick Bellesme. b 15. MBE 80. St Jo Coll Cam BA 37, MA 41. Westcott Ho Cam 37. **d** 40 **p** 41 S'wark. C of Woolwich 40-44; Relief work in Greece 44-46; Bp of S'wark's Chap to Youth 46-50; V of Blindley Heath 50-56; Commiss Egypt 50-60; V of Otley 56-64; St Mary Leamington 64-72; R of Ch Stretton 72-74; Chairman-Admin of Project Vietnam Orph 75-81. *62 Busbridge Lane, Godalming, Surrey.*

ASHENDEN, Gavin Roy Pelham. b 54. Univ of Bris LLB 76, BA 80. Oak Hill Coll 77. **d** 80 **p** 81 S'wark. C of St Jas Bermondsey Dio S'wark from 80. *2a Thurland Road, Bermondsey, SE16 4AA.*

ASHENDEN, Norman Edward. b 1892. St Edm Hall Ox BA 16, MA 19. Ridley Hall Cam 19. **d** 20 **p** 21 Win. C of St Simon Southsea 20-24; H Trin Cam 24-26; St Mary Magd (in c of St Paul) Peckham 26-27; V of St Barn Hull 27-32; Metrop Sec CMS 32-41; V of Studley 41-48; R of St Paul Fisherton Anger 48-55; V of Mark Cross 55-58; R of Horsington 58-60. *24 Queen Mary Road, Salisbury, Wilts.*

ASHER, David Blake. b 51. Univ of Alta BSc 73. Coll of Em & St Chad 77. **d** 78 **p** 79 Calg. P-in-c of Cochrane 78-81; I of St Aug City and Dio Calg from 81. *2404 Olympia Drive SE, Calgary, Alta, T2C 1H5, Canada.*

ASHER-RELF, Charles William. b 08. St Mich Coll Llan. **d** 56 **p** 57 Swan B. C of Llanguicke (Pontardawe) 56-58; V of Llanstephan w Boughrood (w All SS Glasbury from 60) 58-63; Trelystan w Leighton 63-66; R of Bix (with Pishill from 73) 66-77; C-in-c of Pishill 66-73; Perm to Offic Dio Ox from 77. *28 Blacklands Road, Benson, Oxon, OX9 6NW.* (Wallingford 38755)

ASHFOLD, Sidney Sayer. b 10. St Jo Coll Morpeth. **d** 42 **p** 43 Bath. M of Bro of Good Shepherd Nyngan 42-49; Jt Metrop Sec SPG 49-53; Perm to Offic at St Barn Southfields 49-50; at All SS W Dulwich 50-53; at All SS Sydenham 53-58; C of St Paul Deptford 58-61; Commiss Bath 59-80; Min of St Hugh's Conv Distr S'wark (Charterho Miss) 62-68; V of Henlow 68-77; Perm to Offic Dios Sarum and Win 77-80. *c/o 4 Karinga Avenue, Killara, NSW, Australia 2071.*

ASHFORD, Geoffrey. b 34. Kelham Th Coll 54. **d** 58 **p** 59 Newc T. C of Wallsend 58-63; St Jas Bolton 63-66; P-in-c of St Paul Manningham 66-69; V of Cowling Dio Bradf 69-71; Asst Chap HM Pris Pentonville 71; Chap HM Pris Exeter 71-75; Leeds from 75. *Chaplain's Office, HM Prison, Armley, Leeds.* (Leeds 636411)

ASHFORD, Percival Leonard. b 27. Univ of Bris 50. Tyndale Hall Bris 49. **d** 54 Ex **p** 55 Truro for Ex. C of St Phil and St Jas Ilfracombe 54-56; H Trin Aylesbury 56-59; V of Poughill 59-65; Chap HM Pris Wormwood Scrubs 65-66; HM Remand Centre Risley Warrington 66-69; HM Pris Dur 69-71; Wandsworth 71-75; Win 75-77; SW Reg Chap of Prisons and Borstals 77-81; Chap Gen of Prisons from 81; Chap to HM the Queen from 82. *Portland House, Stag Place, SW1E 5BX.*

ASHFORTH, David Edward. b 37. Univ of Lon BSc (2nd cl Chem) and ARCS 59. Univ of Birm Dipl Th 61. Qu Coll Birm. **d** 61 **p** 62 York. C of St Columba Scarborough 61-65; Northallerton w Kirby Sigston and Romanby 65-67; V of Keyingham 67-73; Chap Univ of Lon from 73. *1 Porchester Gardens, W2 3LA.* (01-229 5089)

ASHIETEY, Very Rev Robert Emmanuel. St Aug Th Coll Kumasi. **d** and **p** 47 Accra. P Dio Accra; Prec of Accra Cathl 58-64; Archd of Accra 68-77; Provost of Accra Cathl from 78. *PO Box 8, Accra, Ghana.* (Accra 66103)

ASHIMALA, Enos Zablon. St Paul's Th Coll Limuru 65. **d** 67 **p** 68 Maseno. P Dio Maseno 68-70, Dio Nak from 71. *Box 18, Kapsabet, Kenya.*

ASHLEY, Brian. SOC 75. **d** 77 **p** 78 Guildf. C of Horsell Dio Guildf from 77. *Starston, Church Hill, Horsell, Woking, Surrey.*

ASHLEY, Brian Christenson. b 33. Roch Th Coll 68. **d** 70 Grantham for Linc **p** 71 Linc. C of New Sleaford 70-72; Ridgeway (in c of St Pet Basegreen) 72-74; Team V of Gleadless 74-77; R of Dinnington Dio Sheff from 77. *217 Nursery Road, Dinnington, Sheffield, S31 7QU.* (Dinnington 562335)

ASHLEY, John Michael. b 28. Worc Coll Ox BA 51, MA 54. Linc Th Coll 50. **d** and **p** 55 N Queensld. C of Cairns 55-58; Miss Chap Dio N Queensld 58-60; R of Anderby w Cumberworth 60-66; C-in-c of Huttoft 60-61; V 61-66; Sec Linc Dioc Miss Coun 61-68; R of W w E Allington and Sedgebrook Dio Linc from 66; R of Woolsthorpe w Stainwith Dio Linc from 66; CF (TAVR) from 79. *Woolsthorpe Rectory, Grantham, Lincs.* (Knipton 206)

ASHLEY, Reginald Clifford. b 16. Kelham Th Coll 34. BD (Lon) 63. MSSM 39. **d** 39 **p** 40 Sheff. C of St Cecilia Parson Cross 39-42 and 44-53; Averham w Kelham 42-44; St Geo w St Jo Bapt Nottm 53-56; Chap and Tutor Ho of the Sacred Miss Kelham from 56; Publ Pr Dio Southw 57-71; C of Ratby w Groby 71-78; St Pet Braunstone City and Dio Leic 78-81; Team V from 81. *3 Ashurst Road, Leicester, LE3 2UA.* (Leic 895609)

ASHLEY-BROWN, Peter William. ACT ThL 59. **d** 59 **p** 60 Newc. C of Mayfield 59-61; Gosford 62-64; Singleton 64; on leave 65-67; R of Cardiff Newc 67-75; Muswellbrook Dio Newc from 75. *Rectory, Brook Street, Muswellbrook, NSW, Australia 2333.* (Muswellbrook 34)

ASHLEY-ROBERTS, James. b 53. BD (Lon) 77. Wycl Hall Ox 79. **d** 80 Chelmsf **p** 81 Bradwell for Chelmsf. C of Ch Ch Gt Warley Dio Chelmsf from 80. *Church House, Junction Road, Warley, Brentwood, Essex.*

ASHLING, Raymond Charles. b 32. Univ of Dur BA 58. Linc Th Coll 58. **d** 60 **p** 61 Wakef. C of St Aug Halifax 60-63; Farlington Hants 63-65; Chap St Steph Coll Balla Balla 65-68; P-in-c of Filabusi Conv Distr Matab 69-71; Chap Rishworth Sch 71-75; Hd Master St Steph Sch Mohales Hoek Dio Les from 76. *Box 73, Mohales Hoek, Lesotho.* (245)

ASHMAN, John Edmund George. b 47. Chich Th Coll 79. **d** 81 Ex. C of St Francis Honicknowle Devonport Dio Ex from 81. *36 Hirmandale Road, West Park, Plymouth, Devon, PL5 2JZ.*

ASHTON, Anthony Joseph. b 37. Oak Hill Th Coll 62. **d** 65 **p** 66 Sheff. C of St Thos Crookes Sheff 65-68; Heeley, Sheff 68-73; V of St Steph Bowling 73-78; R of H Trin Chesterfield Dio Derby from 78. *31 Newbold Road, Chesterfield, Derbys.* (Chesterfield 32048)

ASHTON, Cyril Guy. b 42. Oak Hill Th Coll 64. **d** 67 **p** 68 Blackb. C of St Thos Blackpool 67-70; Voc Sec CPAS 70-74; V of St Thos Lanc Dio Blackb from 74. *33 Belle Vue Terrace, Lancaster.* (Lanc 32134

✠ **ASHTON, Right Rev Jeremy Claude.** Trin Coll Cam BA 53, MA 57. Westcott Ho Cam. **d** 55 **p** 56 Man. C of Bury 55-60; CF (TA) 57-60; CF (TA - R of O) from 60; Miss P Dio New Guinea 60-61; R of Eroro New Guinea 61-70; Dioc Regr New Guinea 70-71; Dio Papua 71-75; C of Lae 70-75; Port Moresby and Bp's Chap Dio Papua 75-76; Cons Asst Bp of Papua in Univ of Tech Lae 2 May 76 by Abp of Brisb; Bp of Papua; and Bps Ambo, Meredith and Uka; Apptd Bp of Aipo Rongo 77. *PO Box 1767, Lae, Papua New Guinea.* (42-2667)

ASHTON, John. b 03. St Bonif Coll Warm 25. Univ of Dur 28. TD 58. **d** 31 **p** 32 Wakef. C of St Paul Morley 31-33; St Faith Linc 33-36; V of E Halton 36-37; Wellingore w Temple Bruer 37-46; CF (TA) from 38; PC of All SS Grimsby 46-53; V of Alberbury w Cardeston 53-60; RD of Pontesbury 56-60; V of Cleobury Mortimer w Hopton Wafers 60-66; C-in-c of Doddington 62-66; Neen Sollars w Milson 62-66; R of Ashcombe 66-70; Ideford 66-70; PC of Luton Devon 66-70. *Westerton Cottage, Dalcross, Inverness, IV1 2JL.* (Ardersier 62588)

ASHTON, Joseph Patrick Bankes. b 27. Jes Coll Cam BA 49, MA 52. Wells Th Coll 53. **d** 55 **p** 56 Lich. C of Cheadle 55-59; Caverswall 59-61; C-in-c of St Phil Conv Distr Werrington 61-64; V 64-66; R of Eyke w Bromeswell and Rendlesham (w Wantisden from 76 and Tunstall from 78) Dio St E from 66; C-in-c of Wantisden 75-76. *Eyke Rectory, Woodbridge, Suff.* (Eyke 289)

✠ **ASHTON, Right Rev Leonard James.** b 15. Tyndale Hall Bris 40. CB 70. **d** 42 **p** 43 Ches. C of Cheadle 42-45; Chap RAF 45-73; Asst Chap-in-Chief 62-65; Res Chap St Clem Danes Westmr 65-69; Chap-in-Chief and Archd 69-73; Hon Chap to HM the Queen from 67; Can & Preb of Linc Cathl 69-73; Can (Emer) from 73; Cons Asst Bp in Jer Abpric in Ch of St Clem Danes Westmr 22 Jan 74 by Abps of Cant and Jer; Bps of Lon, Roch, Nor and Guildf; Bps Suffr of Croydon, Shrewsbury, Buckingham, Grantham and Maidstone; and others; Apptd Bp in Cyprus and the Gulf 76; Episc Can of St Geo Jer from 76; Chap O of St John of Jer from 76. *c/o 60 Lowndes Avenue, Chesham, Bucks; and 5a John Clerides Street, Box 2075, Nicosia, Cyprus.*

ASHTON, Mark Hewett. b 48. Ch Ch Ox BA 70, MA 74. Trin Coll Cam 2nd cl Th Trip pt ii BA 72. Ridley Hall Cam 71. **d** 73 **p** 74 Roch. C of Ch Ch Beckenham 73-77; Asst Chap Win Coll 78-81; Sec of Ch Youth Fellowship Assoc (CPAS) from 81. *4 Thornton Road, SW12.*

ASHTON, Neville Anthony. b 45. Sarum Wells Th Coll 78. **d** 80 **p** 81 Ches. C of Hattersley Dio Ches from 80. *58 Callington Drive, Hattersley, Hyde, Cheshire.*

ASHTON, Nigel Charles. b 49. **d** 78 **p** 79 Truro. C of St Steph-by-Saltash Dio Truro from 78. *1 Summerfields, Saltash, Cornwall, PL12 4AB.*

ASHTON, Canon Patrick Thomas. b 16. MVO 63. Ch Ch Ox BA and MA 46. Westcott Ho Cam 46. **d** 47 **p** 48 Lon. C of St Martin-in-the-Fields Westmr 47-51; R of Clifton Beds 51-55; Sandringham w W Newton and Appleton 55-63; Dom Chap to HM the Queen 55-70; C-in-c of Flitcham 63-70; Hillington 63-70; Castle Rising 63-70; Wolferton w Babingley 63-70; Team R of Swanborough (in c of Wilcot Oare and Huish) 70-73; C-in-c of Avebury w Winterbourne Monkton and Berwick Bassett 74-75; Team R of Upper Kennet 75-77; Can of Sarum Cathl from 75; RD of Marlb 76-77. *Field Cottage, Bottlesford, Pewsey, Wilts, SN9 6LU.* (Woodborough 340)

ASHTON, Peter Donald. b 34. ALCD 61. BD Lon 62. **d** 62 **p** 63 Chelmsf. C of Walthamstow 62-68; V of Girlington 68-73; Dir of Past Tr St Jo Coll Nottm 73-80; Publ Pr Dio Southw 74-80; Team R of Billericay w L Burstead Dio Chelmsf from 80. *Rectory, Billericay, Essex, CM12 9LD.* (Billericay 22837)

ASHTON, Thomas. b 1887. Lon Coll of Div 24. **d** 26 **p** 27 Man. C of St Paul Withington 26-28; V of St Thos Preston 28-34; Gen Sec National Ch League 34-42; LPr Dio Lon 34-53; C-in-c of Standon 41-45; Sec Friend of the Cl Corp 42-58; Commiss Bhag 45-54; V of Ponsbourne 54-56; Perm to Offic Dio Guildf from 56. *c/o Barry Lodge, Pond Road, Woking, Surrey.* (Woking 63420)

ASHTON, Thomas Eyre Maunsell. b 13. St Edm Hall Ox BA 36, MA 39. Wycl Hall Ox 36. **d** 38 **p** 39 Win. C of Shirley 38-41; Chap RAFVR 41-46 (Men in Disp 44); PC of Derringham Bank 46-47; V of St Martin Hull 47-54; Crewkerne 54-67; R of St Marg, Lee 67-75; RD of E Lewisham 73-75; Chap of Morden Coll Blackheath from 75. *Chaplain's Flat, Morden College, Blackheath, SE3 0PW.* (01-853 1576)

ASHTON, Thomas Richard. b 22. Ch Coll Cam BA 48, MA 51. Wycl Hall Ox 51. **d** 52 Leic **p** 53 Bp Hollis for Cant. C of The Martyrs Leic 52-55; Chap Kuwait Oil Co Kuwait 55-62; Deputn Sec JEM 62-63; Home Sec 63-65 Perm to Offic Dio Lon 63-65; Ed Bible Lands 63-67; V of St Dionis Parson's Green Fulham Dio Lon from 65; Commiss Iran from 68; RD of Hammersmith from 75; Surr from 75. *St Dionis's Vicarage, Parson's Green, SW6 4UH.* (01-736 2585)

ASHWIN, Vincent George. b 42. Worc Coll Ox BA 66. Coll of Resurr Mirfield. **d** 67 **p** 68 Dur. C of Shildon 67-70; St Francis High Heaton Newc T 70-72; R of Mhlosheni Swaz 72-75; Manzini Swaz 75-79; V of Shildon Dio Dur from 79.

Vicarage, Shildon, Co Durham, DL4 1DW. (Shildon 2122)

ASHWORTH, Brian. Ridley Coll Melb 57. ACT ThL 59. **d** 58 **p** 59 Melb. C of Drysdale 58; St Mark Camberwell 58-60; Dandenong 60-61; I of St Jas E Thornbury 61-64; CF (Austr) 64-71; R of Penola 71-74; Mt Gambier Dio Murray from 74. *27 Power Street, Mount Gambier, S Australia 5290.* (Mt Gambier 25 2537)

ASHWORTH, David. b 40. Univ of Nottm BPharm 62. Linc Th Coll 63. **d** 65 **p** 66 Man. C of St Thos Halliwell 65-69; St Jas Heywood Man 69-72; P-in-c of St Marg Conv Distr Heywood 72-78; V of Hale Chesh Dio Ches from 78. *Vicarage, Harrop Road, Hale, Altrincham, Gtr Man.* (061-928 4182)

ASHWORTH, Edward James. Clifton Th Coll 60. **d** 63 **p** 64 Lon. C of Ch Ch w All SS Spitalfields 63-65; St Pancras Pennycross 65-69; Ch Ch Blackb 69-72; V of W Seaton 72-79; Tunstead Dio Man from 79. *Tunstead Vicarage, Stacksteads, Bacup, Lancs.* (Bacup 4508)

ASHWORTH, Canon James George Brooks. b 10. Edin Th Coll 30. Late Th Exhib of Hatf Coll Dur LTh 33, BA 34. **d** 34 **p** 35 Glas. C of St Ninian Glas 34-37; St Luke W Norwood 37-41; Chap and Succr of Edin Cathl 41-42; C of St Martin-in-the-Fields Westmr 42-44; V of St Mich Wood Green 44-49; R of Abington Northants 49-57; V of Ilkeston 57-62; RD of Ilkeston 57-62; Chap Commun of St Mary Virg Wantage 62-66; Can Res of Ripon Cathl 66-79; Can (Emer) from 79. *391a Wellingborough Road, Northampton, NN1 4EQ.*

ASHWORTH, John Russell. b 33. Lich Th Coll 57. **d** 60 **p** 61 Wakef. C of Castleford 60-62; St Sav Luton 63-67; V of Clipstone 67-70; Bolton-upon-Dearne Dio Sheff from 70. *Bolton-upon-Dearne Vicarage, Rotherham, S Yorks, S63 8AA.* (Rotherham 893163)

ASHWORTH, Keith Benjamin. b 33. N-W Ordin Course 76. **d** 79 **p** 80 Man. C of Pennington Dio Man from 79. *9 Brooklands Avenue, Leigh, Lancs, WN7 3HJ.*

ASHWORTH, Kenneth. b 13. Univ of Birm BA. (3rd cl Hist) 34. Lich Th Coll 34. **d** 36 **p** 37 Ches. C of St Mark Bredbury 36-38; Over w Winsford 38-40; Offg C-in-c of Wharton 40-43; V of Tushingham 43-45; Wharton 45-47; Hulme Walfield 47-49; Org Sec SAMS 49-50; V of Rainow w Saltersford 50-52; R of Yelden w Melchbourne 52-57; C-in-c of Dean w Shelton 54-55; V 55-57; RD of Riseley 56-57; V of Woodside 57-66; Southill 66-69; L to Offic Dio Nor 69-71; Hon C of Elsing w Bylaugh and Lyng w Sparham 71-74; N Pickenham w Houghton-on-the-Hill 74-80; S Pickenham 74-80; Perm to Offic Dio Heref from 80. *17 Little Paradise, Marden, Hereford, HR1 3DR.*

ASHWORTH, Martin. b 41. K Coll Lon and Warm AKC 63. **d** 64 Hulme for Man **p** 65 Man. C of Wm Temple Conv Distr Woodhouse Pk 64-71; C-in-c of St Anne Haughton Dio Man 71; R from 71. *St Anne's Rectory, Denton, Manchester, M34 3EB.* (061-336 2374)

ASIEGBU, Canon George Chukuma. Trin Coll Umuahia 54. **d** 56 **p** 57 Niger. P Dio Niger 56-61; Dio Nig Delta 61-69; Dio Ow from 69; Hon Can of Ow from 75. *Parsonage, Ndizuogu, Nigeria.* (Ndizuogu 12)

ASIEKWU, Andrew Nwanze. **d** 20 **p** 23 Niger. P Dio Niger 20-46. *Asaba, S Nigeria.*

ASIEKWU, Agustus Nwabata. b 46. Trin Coll Umuahia 78. **d** 81 Asaba. d Dio Asaba. *St John's Parsonage, PO Box 5, Agbor, Bendel State, Nigeria.*

ASKE, Sir Conan, Bt. b 12. Ball Coll Ox BA (4th cl Jurispr) 33, MA 39. Wycl Hall Ox 69. **d** 70 **p** 71 Worc. C of Hagley 70-72; St Jo Bapt-in-Bedwardine Worc 72-80. *167 Malvern Road, Worcester, WR2 4NN.* (Worc 422817)

ASKEW, Dennis. b 30. Open Univ BA 76. Lich Th Coll 55. **d** 58 Ripon **p** 59 Knaresborough for York. C of Garforth 58-61; Seacroft (in c of Ascen from 62) 61-64; PC of Holland Fen w Amber Hill and Chap Hill 64-69; R of Folkingham w Laughton 69-77; V of Threckingham 69-77; R of Pickworth w Walcot 69-77; V of Osbournby w Scott Willoughby 69-77; R of Aswarby w Swarby 69-77; C-in-c of Newton w Haceby 72-77; Aunsby w Dembleby 72-77; R of S Lafford Dio Linc from 77. *Folkingham Rectory, Sleaford, Lincs, NG34 0SN.* (Folkingham 391)

ASKEW, Canon Reginald James Albert. b 28. CCC Cam BA 51, MA 55. Linc Th Coll 55. **d** 57 **p** 58 Lon. C of Highgate 57-61; Tutor Wells Th Coll 61-63; Chap 63-65; Vice-Prin 66-69; PV of Wells Cathl 61-69; V of Ch Ch Lanc Gate 69-73; Prin Sarum Wells Th Coll from 74; Can of Sarum Cathl from 75. *19a The Close, Salisbury, Wilts, SP1 2EE.* (Sarum 4856)

ASKEW, Richard George. b 35. BNC Ox BA 59, MA 63. Ridley Hall Cam 62. **d** 64 **p** 65 Ox. C of Chesham 64-66; Mossley Hill 66-67; Chap Ox Past 67-72; Asst Chap BNC Ox 67-71; R of Ashtead Dio Guildf from 72; RD of Leatherhead from 80. *Rectory, Ashtead, Surrey.* (Ashtead 72135)

ASKEW, Sydney Derek. b 29. Roch Th Coll 66. **d** 68 Ripon **p** 69 Knaresborough for Ripon. C of Kirkstall 68-73; V of Markington w S Stainley and Bp Thornton Dio Ripon from 73. *Markington Vicarage, Harrogate, N Yorks., HG3 3PB.* (Ripon 87282)

ASKEW, William Edward. Univ of BC BA 42. Angl Th Coll BC LTh 43, BD 49. **d** 43 **p** 44 BC. C of Ch Ch Cathl Victoria BC 43-45; I of Ogden w Killarney 45-47; V of St Martin w St Mark Calg 47-53; C of St Clem Eglinton Tor 53-56; R of Thornhill 56-60; St Barn Danforth Avenue Tor 60-65; Asst Dir Dioc Services Tor 65-68; Dir 68-72; Can of Tor 69-72; R of St Thos, St John's 72-80; Can of E Newfld 79-80; I of St Anselm Vanc Dio New Westmr from 80. *4739 Chancellor Boulevard, Vancouver, BC, Canada.*

ASKEY, John Stuart. b 39. Chich Th Coll 63. **d** 66 **p** 67 Lon. C of St Dunstan Feltham 66-69; Ch Ch Epsom 69-72; Good Shepherd Chesterton 72-74; R of Stretham w L Thetford Dio Ely from 74; Youth Officer Dio Ely from 80. *Stretham Rectory, Ely, Cambs.* (Stretham 233)

ASKHAM, Leonard Charles. b 1898. Keble Coll Ox BA 25. Ely Th Coll 25. **d** 26 **p** 28 Chelmsf. C of Ascen Vic Dks 26-27; E Ham 28-29; Saffron Walden 29-31; Lowestoft 31-33; Ramsey 34-37; V of Godmanchester 37-42; R of Ashover 42-46; V of Harston w Hauxton 46-54; Barton 54-68. *11 Roman Hill, Barton, Cambridge, CB3 7AX.* (Comberton 2831)

ASLACHSEN, Grosvenor Trevelyan. b 03. Lich Th Coll 24. Univ of Dur 25. **d** 28 Roch **p** 29 Bp King for Roch. C of St Marg Roch 28-35; Speldhurst w Groombridge 35-40; R of Halstead Kent 40-67. *4 Manor Park, Tunbridge Wells, Kent.* (Tunbridge Wells 31535)

ASOKO, Samuel Foladinran Agbadu. Im Coll Ibad 56. **d** 58 Ibad **p** 60 Ondo-B for Ibad. P Dio Ibad. *St James's Vicarage, Oke Bola, Ibadan, Nigeria.*

ASOR, Mackenzie. Newton Coll Dogura 67. **d** 69 **p** 70 New Guinea. P Dio New Guinea 69-70; Dio Papua 71-76; Dio Port Moresby from 77. *Box 213, Port Moresby, Papua New Guinea.*

ASORONYE, Sidney Philip Obiechefu. Trin Coll Umuahia 57. **d** 60 Niger. d Dio Niger 60-69; Dio Ow from 70. *Parsonage, Ihiagwa, Owerri, Nigeria.*

ASPDEN, Peter George. b 28. St D Coll Lamp BA 50. Ely Th Coll 52. **d** 53 **p** 54 Blackb. C of St Barn Morecambe 53-55; Marton 55-58; V of Tockholes 58-63; C of St Annes-on-Sea (in c of St Marg) 63-66; V of St Marg, St Annes-on-Sea 66-75; Ch Ch Lanc 75-79; R of Eccleston Dio Blackb from 79. *Eccleston Rectory, Chorley, Lancs, PR7 6NA.* (Eccleston 451206)

ASPDEN, Richard William. b 49. Chich Th Coll 75. **d** 78 Bp Hulme for Man **p** 79 Man. C of St Thos Bedford Leigh 78-81; All Souls Leeds Dio Ripon from 81. *All Souls Vicarage, Blackman Lane, Leeds, LS2 9EY.* (Leeds 453078)

ASPELL, Colin Paxton. b 34. K Coll Lon and Warm AKC 60. **d** 61 Bp McKie for Cov for Tor **p** 62 Tor. C of St Aid Tor 61-63; R of Brighton 63-67; St Jude, Wexford Tor 67-73; V of Old Windsor 73-81; R of Ewhurst Dio Guildf from 81. *Ewhurst Rectory, Cranleigh, Surrey, GU6 7PX.* (Ewhurst 584)

ASPINALL, David George. Univ of W Ont BA 63. Trin Coll Tor STB 66. **d** 66 **p** 67 Sask. C of All SS Peterborough 66-67; I of Fort Pitt and of Turtleford 68-71; R of St Geo, Prince Albert E 71-75; Exam Chap to Bp of Sask 71-75; I of Harrow Dio Hur from 75. *Box 293, Harrow, Ont, Canada.*

ASPINALL, John Robert. b 1900. Bp Wilson Th Coll IM 24. **d** 26 **p** 27 Liv. C of St Clem Toxteth Park 26-29; Wootton Bassett 29-30; Longfleet 30-33; R of Albert Mem Ch Man 33-36; V of Daubhill 36-44; Kinson 44-54; Fowey 54-56; St Pet Rushden 56-58; S Malling 58-66. *Address temp unknown.*

ASQUITH, Eric Lees. St Aid Coll 55. **d** 56 **p** 57 Wakef. C of Hanging Heaton 56-59; V of Netherthong 59-68. *15 Heycroft Way, Nayland, Colchester, Essex, CO6 4LN.* (Nayland 262593)

ASSAL, Riah. Serampore Coll BD 64. Bp's Coll Calc. **d** 65 **p** 66 Jer. P Dio Jer from 65. *Christ Church, Nazareth, Israel.* (065-54017)

ASSON, Geoffrey Ormrod. b 34. Univ Coll of N Wales BA (Engl and Educn) 54. St Cath S Ox BA (Th) 56, MA 61. St Steph Ho Ox 54. **d** 57 Swan B for Wales **p** 58 Llan. C of Aberdare w Cwmbach 57-59; Roath 59-61; R of Hagworthingham w Lusby and Asgarby 61-65; C-in-c of Mavis-Enderby w Raithby 62-65; V of Friskney 65-69; R of S Ormsby w Ketsby, Calceby and Driby 69-74; R of Harrington w Brinkhill 69-74; R of Oxcombe 69-74; R of Ruckland W Farforth and Maidenwell 69-74; R of Somersby w Bag Enderby 69-74; R of Tetford w Salmonby 69-74; C-in-c of Belchford 71-74; W Ashby 71-74; V of Riverhead (w Dunton Green from 75) 74-80; Kington w Huntington Dio Heref from 80; C-in-c of Dunton Green 74-75; RD of Kington and Weobley from 80. *Vicarage, Kington, Herefs.* (Kington 230525)

ASTETE, Marcos. b 50. **d** 80 Skinner for Chile. d Dio

Chile. *Casilla 861, Vina del Mar, Chile.*

ASTILL, Cyril John. b 33. Oak Hill Th Coll 62. Dipl Th (Lon) 64. **d** 65 Penrith for Carl **p** 66 Carl. C of St Jo Evang Carl 65-68; St Helens 68-71; V of Ch of the Sav, City and Dio Blackb from 71; P-in-c of Ch Ch w St Matt City and Dio Blackb from 81. *Vicarage, Onchan Road, Blackburn, Lancs.* (Blackb 55344)

ASTILL, Edward George Richard. b 13. SOC. **d** 67 **p** 68 S'wark. C of St Jo Bapt Southend Lewisham 67-73; St John Southend Catford and Downham Dio S'wark from 73, Lewisham Dio S'wark from 78. *90 Passfields, Bromley Road, SE6 2RF.* (01-698 6584)

ASTIN, Alfred Ronald. b 18. St Pet Hall Ox BA 43, MA 45. Ridley Hall Cam. **d** 47 **p** 48 Man. C of St Luke Weaste 47-50; Ch Ch Harpurhey 50-51; V of Leesfield 51-57; PC of St Anne Earlham 57-70; Asst RD of Nor 67-70; V of Sheringham Dio Nor from 70. *10 North Street, Sheringham, Norf, NR26 8LW.* (Sheringham 822089)

ASTLEY, Gordon. b 03. St D Coll Lamp BA 27. **d** 27 St A **p** 28 Maenan for St A. C of Flint 27-32; Newtown 32-35; Jun V Cho and V of St A Cathl 35-39; Sen V Cho and C 39-41; R of Llandegla 41-48; Llandysilio (w Penrhos from 55) 48-59; Cefn 59-63; Llansantfraid-Glan-Conway 63-73; RD of Llanrwst 71-73. *Roe Parc, St Asaph, Clwyd.* (St Asaph 583728)

ASTLEY, Jeffrey. b 47. Down Coll Cam 1st cl Nat Sc Trip pt ia 66, 1st cl Nat Sc Trip pt ib 67, BA (1st cl Th Trip pt ia) 68, MA 72. Univ of Birm Dipl Th 69. Univ of Dur PhD 79. Qu Coll Birm 68. **d** 70 **p** 71 Lich. C of Cannock 70-73; Chap and Lect St Hild's Coll Dur 73-75; Chap and Sen Lect Coll of St Hild and St Bede Dur 75-77; Hon Lect from 81; Prin Lect and Hd of Relig Stud at Bp Grosseteste Coll Linc 77-81; Dir N of Engl Inst for Chr Educn from 81. *Leazes House, Leazes Place, Durham, DH1 1RE.* (Durham 41034)

ASTON, Lord Bishop Suffragen of. (Vacant).

ASTON, Archdeacon of. (Vacant)

ASTON, Glyn. b 29. Univ of Wales (Abth) BA 54. **d** 79 **p** 80 Mon. L to Offic Dio Mon from 79. *2 Vale View, Newport, Gwent.*

ASTON, John Bernard. b 34. Univ of Leeds BA 55. Qu Coll Birm 72. **d** 75 **p** 76 Lich (APM). Hon C of Shenstone Dio Lich from 75. *21 Wordsworth Close, Lichfield, Staffs, WS14 9BY.*

ASTON, John Leslie. b 47. Oak Hill Coll 77. **d** 80 **p** 81 Lich. C of Trentham Dio Lich from 80. *47 Pacific Road, Trentham, Stoke-on-Trent, Staffs.*

ASVAT, David Malcolm. b 32. Wycl Hall Ox 62. **d** 64 **p** 65 S'wark. C of St Pet Brockley 64-67; Brockley Hill 67-70; Hon C of Perry Hill 70-74; Perm to Offic Dio Chich from 74. *25 Station Road, Crawley, W Sussex, RH10 1HY.* (Crawley 21058)

ATAEMBO, Walter. b 40. Newton Th Coll Papua 64. **d** 66 **p** 67 New Guinea. P Dio Papua 67-77; Dio Port Moresby from 77. *Department of Health, Port Moresby, Papua, New Guinea.*

ATAGOTALUK, Andrew Philip. b 50. Arthur Turner Tr Sch Pangnirtung 72. **d** 75 **p** 76 Arctic. C of Frobisher Bay 75-77; I of Spence Bay Dio Arctic from 77. *Spence Bay, NWT, Canada.*

ATCHESON, David Andrew Gregory. Trin Coll Dub BA 36, Div Test (2nd cl) 37. **d** 37 **p** 38 Cant. C of St Sav Croydon 37-38; St Pet in I of Thanet 38-40; Kenilworth 41-43; CF (EC) 43-46; V of Harbury 47-54; Studley w Mappleborough Green Dio Cov from 65. *Studley Vicarage, Warws.*

ATEEK, Canon Na'im. Ch Div Sch of the Pacific USA BD 66. **d** 66 **p** 67 Jer. P Dio Jer from 67; Can Res of Bethlehem in St Geo Colleg Ch Jer 70-75; Hon Can from 76. *Box 1796, Haifa, Israel.*

ATHABASCA, Lord Bishop of. *See* Crabb, Most Rev Frederick Hugh Wright.

ATHABASCA, Dean of. *See* Hugh, Very Rev Fabian Woolcott.

ATHERLEY, Cecil Atherley. b 01. Univ of Dur LTh 28. St Aug Coll Cant. **d** 28 **p** 29 Lon. C of St Matt W Kens 28-33; TCF Aldershot 33-35; Egypt and Palestine 36; Catterick Camp 35-36 and 37; R of Middleham 37-45; V of H Trin Knaresborough 45-57; Aldborough w Dunsforth 57-72. *Ivy House, Aldborough, Boroughbridge, Yorks.* (Boro'bridge 2439)

ATHERLEY, Keith Philip. b 56. St Steph Ho Ox 77. **d** 80 **p** 81 Knaresborough for Ripon. C of St Bart Armley Dio Ripon from 80. *19 Cedar Close, Armley, Leeds.* (Leeds 792498)

ATHERSTONE, Castell Hugh. b 45. Univ of Natal BA 67. St Chad's Coll Dur Dip Th 69. **d** 70 Dur for Natal **p** 70 Bp Hallowes. C of St Alphege, Pietermaritzburg 70-72; St Thos Berea, Durban 72-74; Kloor 74-77; R of Hillcrest 77-80; Newcastle Dio Natal from 80. *Box 33, Newcastle, Natal, S Africa.*

ATHERSTONE, Ivor Leslie Hyde. St Paul's Coll Grahmstn LTh 64. **d** 64 **p** 65 Zulu. C of Empangeni 64-66; R 66-70; Dioc Sec Zulu 70-74; L to Offic Dio Zulu 70-76; I of St Aug Bethlehem 76-81; P-in-c of All SS Ficksburg Dio Bloemf from 81. *PO Box 54, Ficksburg, OFS, S Africa.*

ATHERSTONE, Walter Eustace Castell. b 12. **d** 71 **p** 72 Johann. C of Rosebank 71-79; St Paul's Durban Dio Natal from 79. *Box 878, Hillcrest, Natal, S Africa.* (011-47 3211)

ATHERTON, Albert. b 26. St Aid Coll 60. **d** 62 **p** 63 Man. C of Northenden 62-64; St Francis' Conv Distr Newall Green Wythenshawe 64-66; V of Patricroft 66-70; L to Offic Dio Man 71-72; V of Mossley Dio Man from 77. *Vicarage, Stamford Street, Mossley, Ashton-under-Lyne, OL5 0LP.* (Mossley 2219)

ATHERTON, Graham Bryson. b 47. GRSM, FTCL 69. Episc Th Coll of Edin 77. **d** 79 **p** 80 Liv. C of St Marg and All H Orford Dio Liv from 79. *Orford Vicarage, Orford Green, Warrington, Cheshire, WA2 8PH.*

ATHERTON, Henry Anthony. b 44. Univ of Wales (Swansea) BSc 67. Fitzw Coll Cam BA (3rd cl Th Trip pt ii) 72, MA 75. Westcott Ho Cam 70. **d** 72 **p** 73 Cov. C of Leamington Priors 72-75; Orpington 75-78; V of St Mary Gravesend Dio Roch from 78. *57 New House Lane, Gravesend, Kent, DA11 7HJ.* (Gravesend 52162)

ATHERTON, John Edward. b 27. **d** 75 Bp Carter of Johann **p** 76 Johann. C of Springs Dio Johann from 75. *22 Waiha Road, Selcourt 1560, S Africa.*

ATHERTON, John Robert. b 39. Univ of Lon BA (2nd cl Hist) 60. Coll of Resurr Mirfield 60. **d** 62 **p** 63 Aber. C of St Marg Aber 62-64; St Mark Bury 64-67; R of St Geo Hulme, Man 68-74; Industr Chap Dio Man 68-74; Asst Dir William Temple Found Man 74-79; Dir from 79; LPr Dio Man from 74; Chairman of the Bd for Social Responsibility Dio Man from 80. *William Temple College, Manchester Business School, Manchester, M15 6PB.*

ATHERTON, Lionel Thomas. b 45. Univ of N Wales (Bangor) BA 74. S Steph Ho Ox 74. **d** 76 Dorchester for Ox **p** 77 Ox. C of Chenies w L Chalfont 76-79; C of Fleet (in c of St Phil and St Jas) Dio Guildf from 79. *91 Kings Road, Fleet, Hants.*

ATHERTON, Percy Francis. b 22. Univ of Man BA 47. Univ of Minnesota MA 56. Seabury-Western Th Sem Ill 52. **d** 52 Minn **p** 53 Coadj Bp of Minn. In Amer Ch 52-57; Asst Chap and Ho Master Rushworth Sch Halifax 57-61; Sen Lect and Chap Bretton Hall Coll of Educn 62-66; L to Offic Dio Wakef 62-66; Dio Ex from 66; Hd Master Macon Internat Sch Arequipa Peru 75-76; Prin Dov Court Sch Sing and Hon C of St Andr Cathl Sing 76-77; R of Bow w Colebrook 78-79; P-in-c of Zeal Monachorum 78-79; Prin Pullman-Kellogg Sch Skikda Algeria 80-81. *The Old Dame's Cottage, Cove, Nr Tiverton, Devon, EX16 7RX.* (Bampton 489)

ATHERTON, Peter. ACT ThL 63. St Mich Th Coll Crafers 58. **d** 63 **p** 64 Adel. C of Mt Gambier 63-65; Chap Seacliff Miss (w Darlington to 66; w Marino from 66) 65-69; R of Strathalbyn 69-72; P-in-c of Glenelg N 72-79; R of Mt Barker Dio Murray from 79. *44 Hutchinson Street, Mount Barker, S Australia 5251.* (388 1142)

ATIBA, Joseph Ade. Im Coll Ibad. **d** 76 **p** 77 Ondo. P Dio Ondo. *Vicarage, Akunu-Akoko, Ondo State, Nigeria.*

ATIKPE, John Weotsukome Oberuomo. b 18. St Paul's Coll Awka 50. **d** and **p** 73 Benin. P Dio Benin. *St Luke's Vicarage, Box 52, Sapele, Nigeria.*

ATIM, Paul. b 52. **d** 78 Lango. d Dio Lango. *PO Akokoro, Lira, Uganda.*

ATIMOYOO, Smith. Em Coll Sktn. **d** 42 **p** 52 Sask. C of Shoal Lake 42-48; Big Whitefish Reserve 48-55; Sturgeon Lake 55-59; I of Fort à la Corne 60-61; Pelican Narrows 61-64. *c/o Synod Office, Box 1088, Prince Albert, Sask., Canada.*

ATKIN, Arthur Courtney Qu'appelle. b 19. Univ of Dur BA 44. Lich Th Coll 59. **d** 59 **p** 60 Worc. C of St Geo Kidderminster 59-60; Chap Bromsgrove Jun Sch 59-64; C of All SS Bromsgrove 60-64; Chap RNR 61-64; RN 64-69; Chap and Asst Master R Hosp Sch Holbrook 69-72; Asst Master Churston Ferrers Gr Sch Brixham 72-74; P-in-c of St Pet Brixham 72-74; Chap and Asst Master Colston's Sch Bris 74-79; P-in-c of Pitcombe w Shepton Montague and Bratton St Maur Dio B & W from 79. *Pitcombe Rectory, Pitcombe, Bruton, Somt, BA10 0PE.* (Bruton 2579)

ATKIN, John Anthony. b 33. Glouc Th Course 70. **d** 72 **p** 73 Cov (APM). C of Leamington Priors 72-77; Barford w Wasperton and Sherbourne 77-80; C-in-c of Exford w Exmoor Dio B & W from 80; Hawkridge w Withypool Dio B & W from 80. *Rectory, Exford, Minehead, Somt.* (Exford 388)

ATKIN, Richard Henry. b 1889. St Jo Th Coll Perth. **d** 29 Kalg for Perth **p** 30 Perth. C of Victoria Pk 29-31; V of Wyalkatchem 31-33; Perm to Offic (Col Cl Act) at Wath on Dearne 33; C 34-35; V of Sykehouse 35-50; Barnby Dun

50-62; Perm to Offic Dio Perth from 74. *Parry House, Grove Road, Lesmurdie, W Australia 6076.*

ATKINS, Alfred Edwin. b 04. Tyndale Hall Bris 56. **d** 57 **p** 58 Chelmsf. C of St Pet Harold Wood 57-59; V of Wicken 59-65; Terrington St Clem 65-73. *51 Caves Close, Terrington St Clement, King's Lynn, Norf.*

ATKINS, Christopher Leigh. b 33. Keble Coll Ox BA (2nd cl Lit Hum) 55, MA 58, Wells Th Coll 57. **d** 59 **p** 60 Worc. C of H Innoc Kidderminster 59-62; Eastleigh 62-69; Min in Ecum Team at Lord's Hill Southn 69-81; M Gen Syn Win 70-75; V of Lord's Hill Southn Dio Win from 81. *1 Tangmere Drive, Lords Hill, Southampton.* (0703-731182)

ATKINS, David John. b 43. Dipl Th (Lon) 68. Kelham Th Coll 64. **d** 68 **p** 69 S'wark. C of Lewisham 68-72; Min of H Cross Conv Distr Motspur Pk Raynes Pk 72-77; V of Ascen Mitcham Dio S'wark from 77. *Vicarage, Sherwood Park Road, Mitcham, Surrey.* (01-764 1258)

ATKINS, Eric Charles. Late Exhib of Univ of Birm BSc (2nd cl Chem) 28, Wycl Hall Ox 37. **d** 38 **p** 39 S'wark. C of H Trin Tulse Hill 38-43; Chap RAFVR 43-47; V of H Redeemer Streatham Vale 47-59; V of Harwell 59-76; R of Chilton 59-76. *22 Butler's Drive, Carterton, Oxon, OX8 3QU.*

ATKINS, Graham Anthony Hazlewood. b 28. Selw Coll Cam BA 52, MA 57. Coll of Resurr Mirfield 52. **d** 54 B & W for Ex **p** 55 Ex. C of St Mary Church 54-57; Chap of Prestfelde Sch 58-76; Ho Master 62-76; L to Offic Dio Lich 59-76; C-in-c of Ash 76-77; Chap St Mich Coll and P-in-c of Tenbury Dio Heref from 77. *St Michael's College, Tenbury Worcs.* (Tenbury Wells 810073)

ATKINS, Canon Herbert Francis. b 01. Late Scho of Univ of Birm. BCom 20. Late Exhib of St Chad's Coll Dur LTh and BA 27. St Bonif Coll Warm 25. **d** 27 **p** 28 Birm. C of Sutton Coldfield 27-31; Hay Mill 31-34; V of St Paul W Brixton 34-44; R of All SS Church Lench w Ab Lench (and Abbots Morton from 54; Rous Lench from 57) 44-70; Priv Chap to Bp of Worc 47; RD of Feckenham 50-65; Hon Can of Worc from 61; P-in-c of Madresfield 70-80. *29 The Avenue, Marlbank, Welland, Malvern.* (Hanley Swan 531)

ATKINS, Canon John Hamilton. b 15. AKC 42. **d** 42 **p** 43 S'wark. C of St John Southend Lewisham 42-46; Hayes (in c of St Nich) 46-51; C-in-c of St Geo Conv Distr Badshot Lea 51-55; V of Addlestone 55-63; Cuddington 63-72; RD of Epsom 70-75; Hon Can of Guildf Cathl 71-80; Can (Emer) from 80; R of Walton-on-the-Hill 72-80. *2 Thames Close, Warminster, Wilts, BA12 9QB.* (Warminster 213035)

ATKINS, Paul Hardy. Late Scho of K Coll Cam 2nd cl Hist Trip pt i 30, BA (2nd cl Hist Trip pt ii) 31, MA 35. Ely Th Coll 35. **d** 35 S'wark **p** 37 Cant. C of St Jo Evang E Dulwich 35-37; All SS Lydd 37-41; V of Chart Sutton 41-46; Chap of HM Pris Maidstone 46-51; V of Headcorn 51-57; R of Beverley w Brookton W Austr 57-62; St Mary W Perth 62-64; Toodyay w Goomalling 64-71; Broughton Valley w Crystal Brook 71-76; Perm to Offic Dio Perth from 76. *280b St George's Road, Bakers Hill, W Australia 6562.*

ATKINS, Paul Henry. b 38. Dipl Th (Wales) 65. St Mich Coll Llan 62. **d** 65 **p** 66 Nor. C of Sheringham 65-68; V of Southtown Dio Nor from 68; RD of Flegg from 78. *Southtown Vicarage, Great Yarmouth, Norf.* (Great Yarmouth 55048)

ATKINS, Peter. b 29. Univ of Edin MA 52. Edin Th Coll 52. **d** 54 **p** 55 Edin. C of Old St Paul Edin 54-59; P-in-c of St D of Scotld Edin 59-64; Chap Fulbourn Hosp Cam 64-66; R of Galashiels 66-69; Perm to Offic Dio Edin 69-72; Div Dir of Social Services Brighton from 72. *Signpost House, Barcombe Cross, Lewes, Sussex.*

ATKINS, Ven Peter Geoffrey. SS Coll Cam 3rd cl Cl Trip pt i 59, BA (2nd cl Th Trip pt ia) 60, MA 64. Univ of Otago BD 64. NZ Bd of Th Stud LTh 65. St Jo Coll Auckld. **d** 62 Bp McKenzie for Wel. **p** 63 Wel. C of Karori w Makara 62-64; Karori 64-65; Tutor St Pet Coll Siota 66-67; C of Dannevirke 68-70; V of Waipukurau 70-73; Dioc Sec and Regr Dio Wai 73-79; Can of Wai 74-79; V of Havelock N Dio Wai from 79; Archd of Hawkes Bay from 79; VG Dio Wai from 80. *61 Te Mata Road, Havelock North, Hawkes Bay, NZ.* (778-775)

ATKINS, Peter Ronald. Ridley Coll ACT ThL 63. **d** 62 **p** 63 Tas. C of Burnie 62-64; Teluk Anson 64-67; P-in-c of S Perak Miss Distr 67-69; V of Lower Perak 69-74; All SS Taiping 75-76; R of Ulverstone Dio Tas from 76. *Rectory, Ulverstone, Tasmania 7315.* (004-251003)

ATKINS, Reginald Arthur. b 02. Dorch Miss Coll 26. **d** 28 Zanz (in Abbey Ch Dorchester Oxon) **p** 29 Zanz. Miss Dio Zanz 29-31; C of St Aug Kilburn 32; Miss Dio Zanz 32-33; P-in-c of Tanga 33-36; C of Thorpe St Andr 37-38; St Marg w St Nich King's Lynn 38-39; R of St Bart Heigham 39-42; Thornage w Brinton 42-49; Burgh St Marg and St Mary w Billockby 49-53; Haynford 53-70; R of Stratton Strawless 53-70; RD of Taverham 59-70; L to Offic Dio Nor from 70. *43 Cromer Road, Hellesdon, Norwich, NR6 6LX.* (Norwich 46705)

ATKINS, Roger Francis. b 30. K Coll Lon and Warm AKC 54. **d** 55 **p** 56 Lon. C of All H Bromley-by-Bow 55-58; Eastleigh Hants 58-62; Miss at Murray I 62-65; R of Mossman 65-69; Archd of Carp 69-71; Exam Chap to Bp of Carp 69-71; Dioc Regr Dio Carp 69-71; Hon Sec English Carp Assoc 78-81; Chairman from 81; V of Wolverley 71-76; St Mich AA Lon Fields Hackney Dio Lon from 76. *Vicarage, Lamb Lane, E8 3PJ.* (01-254 3483)

ATKINS, Timothy David. b 45. Ridley Hall Cam 71. **d** 74 **p** 75 Guildf. C of Em Stoughton 74-78; Chilwell w Inham Nook Dio Southw from 78. *Church House, Inham Nook, Chilwell, Nottingham.* (Nottingham 221879)

ATKINS, Timothy James. b 38. Worc Coll Ox BA (2nd cl Th) 62. Cudd Coll 62. **d** 64 **p** 65 Lich. C of Stafford 64-67; St Pet Loughborough 67-69; Usworth 69-71; Communicare Team Min Killingworth Newc T 71-76; P-in-c of Slaley Dio Newc T from 76. *Slaley Vicarage, Hexham, Northumb.* (Slaley 212)

ATKINS, Timothy Samuel. b 22. DSC 44. Em Coll Cam BA 46, MA 52. Ridley Hall Cam 47. **d** 49 **p** 50 Leic. C of Melton Mowbray 49-51; Preston Lancs 51-54; V of Baxenden Accrington 54-58; Mildenhall 58-63; V of Bunbury Dio Ches from 63; Surr from 71. *Bunbury Vicarage, Tarporley, Chesh, CW6 9PE.* (Bunbury 260283)

ATKINS, William Maynard. b 11. Trin Coll Dub BA 33, MA 41. **d** 35 **p** 36 Arm. C of Dundalk 35-40; I of Clonfeacle 40-46; Dep Min Can St Paul's Cathl Lon 46-49; Asst Master Cathl Choir Sch 46-49; C of St Sepulchre Holborn 49-55; Min Can St Paul's Cathl Lon 49-55; Hon Min Can from 55; Jun Cardinal 52-54; Sen Cardinal 54-55; Libr 52-60; R of St Geo Hanover Square (w St Mark from 74) Westmr Dio Lon from 55; Chap Mercers' Sch Holborn 54-59; City of Lon Sch 62-67; C-in-c of St Mark N Audley Street Westmr 68-74. *2a Mill Street, W1R 9LB.* (01-629 0874)

ATKINSON, Albert Edward. b 35. St Deiniol's Libr Hawarden 79. **d** 79 **p** 80 Ches. C of Ellesmere Port Dio Ches 79-81; Team V from 81. *Vicarage, Seymour Drive, Ellesmere Port, S Wirral, Chesh, L66 1LZ.* (051-355 3988)

ATKINSON, Christopher Lionel Varley. b 39. K Coll Lon 60. Chich Th Coll 65. **d** 67 Pontefract for Wakef **p** 68 Wakef. C of Sowerby Bridge w Norland 67-70; P-in-c of Flushing and Dioc Adv in Relig Educn 70-73; Perm to Offic Dio Worc 74-78; R of Halesowen w Hasbury and Lapal Dio Worc 78-79; Team R from 79; RD of Dudley from 79. *Rectory, Bundle Hill, Halesowen, W Midl, B63 4AR.* (021-550 1158)

ATKINSON, David George. b 50. Univ of W Austr BEcon 71. Univ of Melb BD 73. Wollaston Coll Perth. **d** and **p** 74 Perth. C of Esperance 74-76; H Cross Cathl Geraldton 76-77; Assoc P of Whitford 77-80; R of N Midlands Dio Perth from 80. *Box 64, Carnamah, W Australia 6517.* (099-511140)

ATKINSON, Preb David James. b 41. Univ of Lon BD and AKC 63. Selw Coll Cam BA 65, MA 72. Linc Th Coll 65. **d** 66 **p** 67 Linc. C of St Giles Lincoln 66-70; Asst Chap Univ of Newc T 70-73; P-in-c of Adbaston 73-80; Adult Educn Officer Lich 73-75; Dioc Dir of Relig Educn Dio Lich from 75; Preb of Lich Cathl from 79. *Adbaston Vicarage, Stafford, ST20 0QG.* (Adbaston 237)

ATKINSON, David John. b 43. K Coll Lon BSc 65, PhD 69. Univ of Bris Dipl Th 70, MLitt 73. Trin Coll Bris 69. **d** 72 Man **p** 73 Middleton for Man. C of St Pet Halliwell 72-74; St Jo Bapt Harborne 74-77; Actg Chap CCC Ox and Assoc Libr Latimer Ho Ox 77-80; Chap from 80; Th Consultant to Care and Counsel from 80. *87 Harefields, Oxford, OX2 8NR.* (Ox 53720)

ATKINSON, Derek Arthur. b 31. K Coll Lon and Warm BD and AKC 59. **d** 60 Maidstone for Cant **p** 61 Cant. C of St Mary Virg Ashford 60-64; Deal 64-68; R of E w W Ogwell 68-81; Ogwell and Denbury Dio Ex from 81; Asst Dir of Relig Educn Dio Ex 68-78; Dep Dir from 78. *Ogwell Rectory, Newton Abbot, Devon, TQ12 6AH.* (Newton Abbot 4330)

ATKINSON, Eric Harry. b 36. Dipl Th (Lon) 63. Tyndale Hall Bris 61. **d** 64 Hulme for Man **p** 65 Man. C of St Marg Whalley Range 64-65; Horwich 65-69; St Jo Bapt Woking 69-71; V of Cadishead 71-74; P-in-c of Gwennap w Carharrack 74-79; Lannarth 75-79; V of Constantine Dio Truro from 79. *Constantine Vicarage, Falmouth, Cornw.* (Constantine 259)

ATKINSON, Hubert Veysey. b 01. St Aid Coll 26. **d** 28 **p** 29 Liv. [f CA] C of Em Ch Southport 28-31; Aston Warws 31-32; V of H Trin Parr Mt 33-36; Orrell 36-45; All S Springwood Liv 45-63; Claybrooke w Wibtoft 63-71; L to Offic Dio Carl from 74. *Flat 8, Ellergreen, Burneside, Kendal, Cumb, LA9 5SD.* (Kendal 20561)

ATKINSON, Ian. b 33. BNC Ox BA 58, MA 63. Coll of Resurr Mirfield. **d** 58 **p** 59 S'wark. C of Welling 58-62; Camberwell 62-63; V of St Mary Magd Wandsworth Common 63-67; C of St Alb Cathl Pret 67-68; Oxted 68-69; Asst Chap Ch Hosp Horsham from 70. *Middleton B, Christ's Hospital, Horsham, Sussex.* (Horsham 63356)

ATKINSON, Canon James. b 14. St Jo Coll Dur BA 36, MA 39, MLitt 50. DTh Univ of Münster 55. **d** 37 **p** 38 Newc T. C of H Cross Fenham Newc T 37-41; Jun Chap and Succr of Sheff Cathl 41-42; Sen Chap and Prec 42-44; V of St Jas and St Chris Lower Shiregreen 44-51; Fell of Sheff Univ from 51; Can Th of Leic 54-70; Lect in Th Univ of Hull 56-66; Reader 66-67; Prof of Bibl Studies Univ of Sheff 67-79; L to Offic Dio Sheff 68-81; Exam Chap to Bp of Leic from 70; Bp of Derby from 75; Can Th of Sheff from 70; on Staff of Evang Angl Research Centre Latimer Ho Ox from 81. *131 Banbury Road, Oxford, OX2 7AJ.* (Oxford 59522)

ATKINSON, John Dudley. b 38. ACA 60. FCA 71. Qu Coll Birm 63. **d** 66 **p** 67 St Alb. C of Bp's Stortford 66-70; Norton (in c of St Thos) 70-73; V of Markyate 73-80; R of Baldock w Bygrave Dio St Alb from 80. *Rectory, Pond Lane, Baldock, Herts, SG7 5AS.* (Baldock 894398)

ATKINSON, Kenneth. b 16. BA (Lon) 37. **d** 77 Ox **p** 78 Reading for Ox (NSM). C of Steventon Dio Ox from 77. *21 Tatlings Road, Steventon, Abingdon, Oxon. OX13 6AT.*

ATKINSON, Kenneth. b 24. Qu Coll Birm 74. **d** and **p** 77 Birm (NSM). C of Olton Dio Birm from 77. *33 New Coventry Road, Sheldon, Birmingham, B26 3BA.*

ATKINSON, Michael Hubert. b 33. Qu Coll Ox BA (2nd cl Th) 58, MA 60. Ripon Hall Ox 56. **d** 58 **p** 59 Sheff. C of Attercliffe w Carbrook 58-60; Asst Missr Sheff Industr Miss 60-66; C of St Andr Sharrow Sheff 61-66; Industr Chap to Bp of Pet 66-71; Sen Chap Croydon Industr Chap 71-79, Research Officer Gen Syn Bd for Social Responsibility from 79; Chap to Ch Ho from 80. *Church House, Dean's Yard, Westminster, SW1P 3NZ.* (01-222 9011)

ATKINSON, Michael James. b 38. K Coll Lon and Warm AKC 62. **d** 63 **p** 64 Ripon. C of Halton 63-65; Lewsey Conv Distr Luton 65-71; Caversham 71-73; C-in-c of N Woolwich 73-74; V (w Silvertown) 74-77; C-in-c of St Barn Silvertown Vic Dks 73-74; V of Clavering w Langley and Arkesden Dio Chelmsf from 77. *Clavering Vicarage, Saffron Walden, Essex, CB11 4PQ.* (Clavering 256)

ATKINSON, Canon Nelson Horace. Univ of Sask. Em Coll Sktn LTh 41. **d** 40 **p** 42 Sktn. C of Kerrobert 40-42; C-in-c of Smithers 42-45; R of Belmont and Ninette 45-49; I of Southminster 49-54; Vanderhoof 54-56; R of Merritt 56-60; N Kamloops 60-76; Hon Can of St Paul's Cathl Ch Kamloops from 62; Dioc Chap Dio Carib 76-80; Perm to Offic Dio Carib from 80. *10-460 Dalgleish Drive, Kamloops, BC, Canada.* (374-7680)

ATKINSON, Patrick Victor. **d** 61 Hur for Moos. I of Hornepayne 61-65; Port Hardy 65-66; St Sav Dio Vic 66-73; Val D'Or 73-74; Atitkokan 74-79; Gravenhurst Dio Alg from 79. *Box 909, Gravenhurst, Ont., Canada.*

ATKINSON, Peter Duncan. b 41. Univ of Dur. Linc Th Coll 63. **d** 65 **p** 66 Roch. C of St Geo Beckenham 65-69; Caversham (in c of St Jo Bapt) 69-75; C-in-c of St Mark Millfield Bp Wearmouth Dio Dur from 75. *5 Valebrooke, Tunstall Road, Sunderland, T & W.* (Sunderland 56372)

ATKINSON, Peter Gordon. b 52. St Jo Coll Ox BA 74, MA 78. Westcott Ho Cam 77. **d** 79 **p** 80 S'wark. C in Clapham Old Town Team Min Dio S'wark from 79. *The Glebe House, 6 Rectory Grove, Clapham, SW4.* (01-720 3370)

ATKINSON, Preb Samuel Charles Donald. b 30. Univ of Dub BA 54. **d** 55 Connor **p** 56 Down. C of St Simon Belf 55-62; I of Ballinaclough 62-68; Cloughjordan Dio Killaloe from 68; Preb of Killaloe Cathl from 76. *Modreeny Rectory, Cloughjordan, Co Tipperary, Irish Republic.* (Cloughjordan 17)

ATKINSON, William John Stanley. **d** 60 **p** 62 C & Goulb. C of St Jo Bapt Canberra 60-62; St Phil Canberra 62-64; R of Delegate 64-66; P-in-c of Pearce-Torrens Provisional Distr 67-73; St Geo Canberra 73-76; Perm to Offic Dio C & Goulb from 76. *152 Beasley Street, Torrens, ACT, Australia 2607.*

ATTERBURY, Ernest Harold. b 17. Oak Hill Th Coll. **d** 61 **p** 62 Roch. C of St Jo Bapt Beckenham 61-64; Broadwater 64-72; V of Hemswell w Harpswell 72-80; Glentworth 72-80. *Address temp unknown.*

ATTFIELD, David George. b 31. Magd Coll Ox BA 54, MA 58, BD 61. K Coll Lon MPhil 72. Univ of Dur MA 81. Westcott Ho Cam 57. **d** 58 Birm **p** 59 Aston for Birm. C of St Aug Edgbaston 58-61; Ward End 61-62; Lect in Div St Kath Coll Tottenham 62-64; Coll of All SS Tottenham 64-68; Lect in Educn Bede Coll (Coll of St Hild and St Bede from 75) 68-80; Team V of Drypool Dio York from 80. *St John's Vicarage, Southcoates Lane, Hull, HU9 3UN.* (Hull 781090)

ATTFIELD, James Andrew. b 07. Codr Coll Barb. **d** 55 **p** 56 Barb. C of St Mary Barb 55-56; V of St Marg Barb 56-57; St Martin Barb 57-61; C of Sunderland 61-62; Chap Newington Lodge 62-72; Perm to Offic Dio S'wark from 72. *17 Bushey Hill Road, Camberwell, SE5 8QF.* (01-703 8725)

ATTLEY, Ronald. b 46. Chich Th Coll 68. **d** 70 Jarrow for Dur **p** 71 Dur. C of Heworth 70-73; The Ascen Hulme Man 73-75; R of Corozal and Orange Walk Bel 76-79; V of Leadgate Dio Dur from 79. *Leadgate Vicarage, Consett, Co Durham.* (Consett 503918)

ATTOE, Walter Thomas Davenport. b 16. St Aid Coll 41. **d** 43 **p** 44 Lich. C of H Trin Shrewsbury 43-45; St Paul Walsall 45-48; Cannock (in c of Chadsmoor) 48-50; V of Brown Edge 50-56; St Paul Wolverhampton Dio Lich from 56; St Jo Evang Wolverhampton Dio Lich from 62. *169 Penn Road, Wolverhampton, Staffs, WV3 0EQ.* (Wolverhampton 35049)

ATTRILL, Norman Edmund Charles. b 16. K Coll Lon BA (1st cl Geog) 37. Ripon Hall Ox 67. **d** 68 **p** 69 Portsm. C of Portsea 68-72; V of St Pet Seaview 72-80. *27 Church Street, Henley-on-Thames, Oxon, RG9 1SE.*

ATTWATER, Charles Henry. b 30. Kelham Th Coll 54. **d** 59 **p** 60 Sheff. C of Lower Shiregreen Sheff 59-61; Stirling 61-63; R of Wick 63-67; C-in-c of Thurso 63-67; R of Narborough w Narford 67-74; V of Pentney w W Bilney 67-74; Org E Area Leprosy Miss 74-77; Communications Dir for Leprosy Miss Engl and Wales from 77; Perm to Offic Dios Ox and Nor from 77. *50 Portland Place, W1N 3DG.*

ATTWELL, Ven Arthur Henry. b 20. Univ of Leeds BA 41. Univ of Lon BD 47, MTh 58. MA (Lon) 72. Coll of Resurr Mirfield 41. **d** 43 **p** 44 Ox. C of St Geo Wolverton 43-45; Wigan 45-51; Sub-Warden of St Paul's Coll Grahmstn 51-52; Dean of Kimb 52-59; VG 54-59; Chap of Bp's Hostel Kimb 56-59; R of Workington 60-72; Surr 60-72; Commiss Kimb K 61-65; Hon Can of Carl 64-72; Proc Conv Carl from 65; RD of Cockermouth and Workington 66-70, Can Res of Carl Cathl 72-78; Hon Can from 78; Exam Chap to Bp of Carl from 73; Archd of Westmorland and Furness from 78; V of St Jo Evang Windermere Dio Carl from 78; Dir of Carl Dioc Tr Inst from 78. *St John's Vicarage, Windermere, Cumb.* (Windermere 3447)

ATTWELL, Edward Charles. Hur Coll LTh 54. **d** 54 **p** 55 Hur. C of Kitchener 55; Sarnia 55-57; I of Gorrie 57-62; Chap Ashbury Coll Ott 62-65; R of S March Dio Ott from 65. *Rectory, RR1, South March, Ont., Canada.* (1-613-592-4747)

ATTWOOD, Anthony Norman. b 47. Univ of Wales (Abth) BSc (Econ) 69. Univ of Birm Dipl Th 71. Qu Coll Birm 69. **d** 72 Repton for Derby **p** 73 Sheff for Derby. C of St Pet Greenhill Sheff 72-75; V of Elsecar 76-81; Team V of Maltby Dio Sheff from 81. *Maltby Team Vicarage, Haids Road, Maltby, Rotherham, Yorks S66 8BH.* (Rotherham 814951)

ATTWOOD, Carl Norman Harry. b 53. Univ of Bris BA 74. Univ of Ox BA (Th) 76, MA 80. Cudd Coll 74. **d** 77 **p** 78 Heref. C of Tupsley Dio Heref from 77. *34 Church Road, Tupsley, Hereford, HR1 1RR.*

ATTWOOD, David John Edwin. b 51. Univ of Dur BA 76. Em Coll Cam MA 77. Cranmer Hall Dur 74. **d** 77 **p** 78 Bris. C of Rodbourne-Cheney 77-79; Lydiard Millicent w Lydiard Tregoz Dio Bris from 79. *63 Oakham Close, Toothill, Swindon, Wilts.* (Swindon 30896)

ATTY, Canon Norman Hughes. b 40. Univ of Dur BA 62. Cranmer Hall Dur 62. **d** 65 Burnley for Blackb **p** 66 Blackb. C of St Gabr Blackb 65-67; Asst Master Billinge Sch Blackb 67-71; City of Leic Boys' Sch 71-73; Asst Youth Officer Dio Worc 73-74; Youth Chap 74-78; C-in-c of Elmley w Hampton Lovett Dio Worc 73-78; R (w Elmbridge and Rushock) from 78; Elmbridge w Rushock 74-78; Hon Can of Worc Cathl from 81. *Rectory, Elmley Lovett, Droitwich, Worc.* (Hartlebury 250255)

ATWELL, James Edgar. b 46. Ex Coll Ox BA (2nd cl Th) 68, MA 73. Harvard Univ ThM 70. Cudd Coll 68. **d** 70 **p** 71 S'wark. C of St Jo Evang, East Dulwich 70-74; St Mary Gt w St Mich AA Cam 74-77; Chap of Jes Coll Cam 77-81; V of Towcester w Easton Neston Dio Pet from 81. *Vicarage, Towcester, Northants, NN12 7AB.* (Towcester 50459)

ATWELL, Robert Ronald. b 54. St Jo Coll Dur BA 75. Univ of Dur MLitt 79. Westcott Ho Cam 76. **d** 78 Lon **p** 79 Edmon for Lon. C of John Keble Ch Mill Hill 78-81; Chap Trin Coll Cam from 81. *Trinity College, Cambridge, CB2 1TQ.* (0223-358201)

AU, Derek. St Pet Coll Siota 66. **d** 68 Bp Alufurai for Melan **p** 70 Melan. P Dio Melan 68-75; Dio Ysabel from 75. *Tasia Training Centre, Santa Ysabel, Solomon Islands.*

AU, Mary. b 45. SE Asia Sch of Th Hong BD 74. Chung Chi Coll Hong 73. **d** 75 **p** 77 Hong. C of H Trin Kowloon 75-76; P-in-c of Kindly Light Ch Kowloon Dio Hong from 76. *Sheng Kung Hui Kindly Light Church, c/o York Wing Primary School, 61 West, Tsz Wan Shan Estates, Kowloon, Hong Kong.*

AU, William. **d** 34 **p** 38 Melan. P Dio Melan 34-75; Dio Malaita 75-77. *Walande, S Malaita, Solomon Islands.*

AUBREY, Canon John Watkin. b 17. Late Tancred Stud of Ch Coll Cam (2nd cl Th Trip pt i) BA 39, MA 43. Westcott Ho Cam 39. **d** 40 **p** 41 Win. C of Romsey 40-43; Chap RNVR 43-48; Prec of St Geo Cathl Capetn 48-51; R of St Sav Claremont 51-64; Can of Capetn 58-64; Hon Can 64-66; Can (Emer) from 66; Commiss Damar 62-70; St Paul's Coll

Grahmstn 64-65; Hd Master St Andr Coll Grahmstn 65-72; R of Fish Hoek 72-76; Collyweston w Duddington w Tixover Dio Pet from 76. *Collyweston Rectory, Stamford, Lincs.* (Duddington 238)

AUBREY, Joseph Thomas. b 05. Bps' Coll Cheshunt 35. **d** 35 **p** 36 Lon. C of St Geo Enfield 35-38; Standish (in c of Hardwicke) 38-43; V of Church Honeybourne w Cow Honeybourne 43-48; Hawkesbury 48-52; Coaley 52-58; Bp's Castle w Mainstone 58-70; RD of Stokesay 64-70. *14 Linden Road, Clevedon, Avon, BS21 7SN.* (Clevedon 878145)

AUCKLAND, Lord Bishop of. *See* Reeves, Most Rev Paul Alfred.

AUCKLAND, Assistant Bishops of. *See* Wilson, Right Rev Godfrey Edward Armstrong; and Buckle, Right Rev Edward Gilbert.

AUCKLAND (Dio Dur), Archdeacon of. *See* Marchant, Ven George John Charles

AUCKLAND, Dean of. *See* Rymer, Very Rev John Oliver

AUCKLAND, Canon Allan Frank. b 13. K Coll Lon. **d** 49 **p** 50 S'wark. C of St Anselm Kennington Cross 49-52; St Chrys Peckham 52-56; V of St Cath Hatcham 56-74; RD of Greenwich and Deptford 61-65; Lewisham 65-70; Hon Can of S'wark from 67; R of Burstow 74-81. *14 The Pavement, Front Road, Woodchurch, Ashford, Kent, TN26 2QE.* (Shirley Moor 231)

AUCKLAND, Canon Clifford Aubrey. b 14. Late Exhib of Univ of Lon BD (2nd cl) 41. ALCD (1st cl w distinc) 41. **d** 41 **p** 42 Sheff. C of St Geo Sheff 41-43; Rotherham 43-46; C-in-c of Marr 46-50; Sheff Dioc Youth Work Org 46-50; V of Maltby 50-80; Hon Can of Sheff from 80; Sheff Industr Missr from 80. *141 Trap Lane, Bents Green, Sheffield, S11 7RF.* (Sheff 308120)

AUDEN, Lawson Philip. b 45. Qu Coll Birm 73. **d** 78 Grantham for Linc **p** 81 Linc. C of Spalding 78-81; Team V of Wordsley Dio Lich from 81. *25 Middleway Avenue, Wordsley, Stourbridge, W Midl, DY8 5NB.* (Kingswinford 293350)

AUDSLEY, Peter Clement. b 42. Univ of Nottm BSc (2nd cl Chem) 63. Fitzw Coll Cam BA (3rd cl Th Trip pt ii) 69. Ridley Hall Cam 67. **d** 70 **p** 71 Ches. C of Hale 70-73; Industr Chap Kidderminster 73-77; V of Lindridge Dio Worc from 77; Knighton-on-Teme Dio Worc from 78; R of Stanford-on-Teme w Orleton and Stockton-on-Teme Dio Worc from 78. *Lindridge Vicarage, Tenbury Wells, Worcs, WR15 8JQ.* (Eardiston 331)

AUDSLEY, Ronald Brian. b 34. ACT ThDip 71. Ridley Coll Melb 71. **d** 71 Melb **p** 72 Bp Muston for Melb. C of St Andr Brighton 71-73; P-in-c of St John Frankston w Carrum Downs 73-75; Ch of Ascen Burwood E 75-76; I 76-78; Geelong W Dio Melb from 78. *Vicarage, Albert Street, Geelong West, Vic, Australia 3218.* (052-92477)

AULT, Harold Frank. Univ of NZ BA 23, MA 24. ACT ThL 26, Th Scho 53. Univ of Melb BD 44. **d** 24 **p** 26 Ch Ch. C of Rangiora 24-26; St Alb NZ 26-27; Perm to Offic at St Mary Magd Holloway 28; CMS Miss Karachi 28-31; Prin CMS High Sch and Miss-in-c Karachi 31-33; Furlough 33-34; V of Oxford NZ 34-38; Org Sec NZ Angl Bd of Miss 38-44; V of Southbridge-Leeston 44-48; Akaroa 48-52; All SS Nelson 52-66; Hinds 66-68; Exam Chap to Bp of Nel 54-66; Archd of Waimea 56-66; L to Offic Dio Ch Ch from 68. *43 Kirkwood Avenue, Christchurch 4, NZ.* (489-910)

AULT, Olive Beatrice. Univ of NZ BA 30. **d** 41 **p** 78 Ch Ch. Youth Officer Dio Ch Ch 41-48; C of Merivale 48-67; Perm to Offic Dio Ch Ch 67-77; Hon C of Merivale Dio Ch Ch from 78. *43 Kirkwood Avenue, Christchurch 4, NZ.* (489-910)

✠ **AUNG HLA, Most Rev John. d** 38 **p** 39 Rang. P Dio Rang 38-45; Archd of Mandalay 45-66; Cons Asst Bp of Rang in Calc Cathl 5 June 49 by Bp of Calc; Bps of Chota N; Bom; Bhag; Bps Banjerjee and Tarafdar; res 66; P-in-c of Maymyo 54-70; Chap Miss to Seamen, Rang 70-73; Apptd Ld Bp of Rang and Elected Abp and Metrop of Prov of Burma 73; res 79. *Yadana Aung Yeik, 152 Circular Road, Maymyo, Burma.*

AUNG KHUNG, d 71 **p** 74 Akyab. P Dio Akyab. *St Matthew's Church, Pa Vum, Burma.*

AUNG LONE, d 77 **p** 79 Akyab. P Dio Akyab. *St Thomas' Church, Sima Vum, Burma.*

AUNG MIN, Eliya. H Cross Coll Rang. **d** 59 **p** 60 Rang. P Dio Rang 59-70; Dio Pa-an from 70. *Church of the Resurrection, Mawchi, Kayah State, Burma.*

AUNG MYINT, Ambrose. d 70 **p** 71 Rang. P Dio Rang. *Bishopscourt, 140 Pyidaungsu Yeiktha Road, Rangoon, Burma.*

AUNG SEIN, John. d 66 **p** 67 Rang. P Dio Rang 66-75. *St Mathias Church, Okshitpin Village, Padaung, Burma.*

AUNG THA TUN, d 69 **p** 72 Rang. P Dio Rang 69-70; Dio Akyab from 70. *St John's Church, Paletwa, Burma.*

AUNG THANG, d 78 **p** 79 Akyab. P Dio Akyab. *Calvary Church, Kanaung, Burma.*

AUNG TIN NYUNT, Peter. d 76 **p** 77 Rang. P Dio Rang. *St Paul's Church, Yelegyi, Shwedaungmaw PO, Maubin District, Burma.*

AURET, Daniel Alfred Thomas. St Paul's Coll Grahmstn Dipl Th 67. **d** 66 **p** 67 Capetn. C of Milnerton 66-69; Bredasdorp 69-71; R 71-76; St John Mafeking 77-80; Robertson Dio Capetn from 80. *Rectory, White Street, Robertson 6705, CP, S Africa.*

AURET, Maynard Peter. b 22. **d** 76 **p** 77 Pret. C of Gezina Dio Pret from 76. *207 Dunstan Road, Queenswood 0186, S Africa.*

AURICHT, Canon Ernst Oswald. St Barn Coll Adel 23. ACT ThL 25. **d** 25 **p** 26 Adel. C of All SS Hindmarsh 25-28; P-in-c of Robe Miss w Kingston 28-33; Angaston Miss 33-39; R of Balaklava 39-40; Croydon w Kilkenny 40-67; RD of W Suburbs 49-67; Hon Can of Adel from 65; C of Mitcham 67-68; L to Offic Dio Adel from 69. *5 Laurence Street, Lower Mitcham, S Australia 5062.* (276-9151)

AUST, Arthur John. b 14. St Aug Coll Cant 62. **d** 63 **p** 64 Chelmsf. C of Dagenham 63-65; CMS Miss Dio Momb 65-67; R of Theddlethorpe w Mablethorpe 67-71; C-in-c of Skidbrook w Saltfleet Haven 67-69; V of St Geo Kano 71-74; R of Ixopo 74-77; Team V of Clyst Valley 79-81. *Overhill, Upper Street, Kingsdown, Deal, Kent, CT14 8DR.*

AUSTEN, John. b 46. St Cath Coll Cam BA 69, MA 72. Univ of Birm Dipl Th 70. Qu Coll Birm 69. **d** 71 **p** 72 York. C of Thornaby-on-Tees 71-74; St Jas Aston Dio Birm from 74. *245 Albert Road, Aston, Birmingham, B6 4LX.* (021-327 3451)

AUSTER, Neville Walter Lucas. b 12. Or Coll Ox BA 34, MA 38. Wells Th Coll 36. **d** 37 **p** 38 Bris. C of St Paul Swindon 37-39; St Jo Bapt Moordown Bournemouth 39-41; Chap RNVR 41-46; Chap St Geo Coll Quilmes Dio Argent 47-50; C of Ch Ch Southgate 50-51; R of Riddlesworth w Gasthorpe and Knettishall 51-69; C-in-c of Brettenham w Rushford and Shadwell 51-52; R 52-69; V of Dullingham 69-79; C-in-c of Stetchworth 75-79; Perm to Offic Dio Ex from 79. *9 Land Park, Chulmleigh, Devon.*

AUSTERBERRY, David Naylor. b 35. Univ of Birm BA (2nd cl Th) 58. Wells Th Coll 58. **d** 60 **p** 61 Lich. C of Leek 60-63; V of Isfahan 65-66; Yazd 65-70; Shiraz 66-67; Exam Chap to Bp of Iran 65-70; Chap CMS Foxbury 70-73; V of St John The Pleck and Bescot Walsall 73-82; R of Brierley Hill Dio Lich from 82. *Rectory, Church Hill, Brierley Hill, Dudley, W Midl, DY5 3PX.* (Brierley Hill 78146)

AUSTERBERRY, Ven Sidney Denham. b 08. Univ of Man 27, Egerton Hall Man 30. **d** 31 **p** 33 Lich. C of St Giles Newc L 31-38; V of St Alkmund Shrewsbury 38-52; Chap of L Berwick 42-52; Surr from 42; V of Brewood 52-59; V of Bishop's Wood 52-59; Hon Sec Lich Dioc Conf 54-70; RD of Penkridge 58-59; Archd of Salop 59-79; V Archd (Emer) from 80; of Gt Ness 59-77; P-in-c of L Ness 64-67; V 67-77; Hon Can of Lich from 67. *6 Honeysuckle Drive, Sutton Park, Shrewsbury, SY3 7TW.* (Shrewsbury 68080)

AUSTIN, Alfred George. Ridley Th Coll Melb 59. **d** 61 **p** 62 Bend. C of Tatura 61-62; All SS Cathl Bend 62-64; R of Woodend 64-70; Eaglehawk 70-77; Dom Chap to Bp of Bend 69-77; C of St Alb Dartford 77-79. *Address temp unknown.*

AUSTIN, David Jesse James. b 38. Oak Hill Coll 77. **d** 80 Chelmsf **p** 81 Colchester for Chelmsf (NSM). C of Bocking Dio Chelmsf from 80. *17 Devonshire Gardens, Braintree, Essex.*

AUSTIN, Ven Frederick Charles. Univ of BC BA 50. Vanc Th Coll LTh 49. **d** 49 New Westmr **p** 50 Calg. R of Mirror 50-56; I of Rocky Mountain House 56-58; Hon Can of Calg 55-58; I of Port Alberni 58-71; Port Alice 71-73; Port Hardy 73-77; Archd of Quatsino 71-77; Archd (Emer) from 77; Perm to Offic Dio BC from 78. *6189 River Road, Port Alberni, BC, Canada.* (724-2458)

AUSTIN, Canon George Bernard. b 31. St D Coll Lamp BA 53. Chich Th Coll 53. **d** 55 **p** 56 Blackb. C of St Pet Chorley 55-57; St Clem Notting Dale 57-60; Asst Chap Univ of Lon 60-61; C of Dunstable 61-64; V of Eaton Bray 64-70; Bushey Heath Dio St Alb from 70; M Gen Syn from 70; Hon Can of St Alb from 78; Ch Comm from 78. *19 High Road, Bushey Heath, Watford, Herts, WD2 1EA* (01-950 1424)

AUSTIN, Hugh Warren. Qu Coll Cam BA 13, MA 17. Ridley Hall Cam 13. **d** 14 **p** 15 B & W. C of Walcot 14-19; TCF 15-19; C of Ch Ch Cathl Nelson NZ 19-21; Chap Colleg Sch Wanganui 21-55; LPr Dio Wel from 56. *89 Karaka Street, Castlecliff, Wanganui, NZ.*

AUSTIN, John Michael. b 39. St Edm Hall Ox BA (3rd cl Phil Pol and Econ) 63. St Steph Ho Ox 62. **d** 64 **p** 65 S'wark. C of St Jo Evang E Dulwich 64-68; St Jas Cathl Chicago USA 68-69; Warden Pembroke Ho & Missr St Chris Conv Distr Walworth 69-76; Team V of St Pet Walworth 75-76; Adv for

Social Responsibility Dio St Alb from 76. *8 Wordsworth Road, Harpenden, Herts.* (Harpenden 60965)

AUSTIN, Leslie Ernest. b 46. Trin Coll Bris 72. **d** 74 **p** 75 Roch. C of Paddock Wood 74-79; Ch Ch U Armley 79-81; V of All SS Horton City and Dio Bradf from 81. *Vicarage, Little Horton Green, Bradford, W Yorks, BD5 0NG.* (Bradf 27976)

AUSTIN, Canon Michael Ridgwell. b 33. ALCD 56. BD (Lon) 57, PhD (Lon) 69. Univ of Birm MA 66. **d** 57 Birm **p** 58 Aston for Birm. C of Ward End 57-60; PC of St Andr Derby 60-66; Lect in Th Bp Lonsdale Coll Derby 66-73; Prin Lect from 73; Chap Derby Cathl and L to Offic Dio Derby 66-81; Can Res of Derby Cathl from 81. *2a Louvain Road, Derby, DE3 6BZ.*

AUSTIN, Raymond Charles. b 23. St Edm Hall Ox BA 48, MA 53. BD (Lon) 70. Linc Th Coll. **d** 50 **p** 51 Dur. C of St Mich AA Norton Dur 50-53; Wolverhampton 53-56; V of Chapel-en-le-Frith 57-66; RD of Buxton 64-66; Perm to Offic Dio Mon from 66. *Wenallt House, Pont-y-Saison, Tintern, Chepstow, Gwent NP6 6TP.* (029-18 309)

AUSTIN, Trevor Albert. Moore Th Coll Syd 55. **d** 56 Gippsld **p** 57 Graft. C of Bairnsdale 56-57; Casino 57-59; Murwillumbah 59-60; V of U Macleay 60-62; R of Nimbin 62-66; Wauchope Dio Graft from 66. *Rectory, Wauchope, NSW, Australia.* (065 881119)

AUSTIN, William Bouldin. b 49. Univ of the S Tenn BA 71. Seabury-Western Th Sem Ill MDiv 75. **d** 75 **p** 76 Nass. P-in-c of St Pet Long I 75-78; R of St Mich and St Nich Grand Bahama 78-80. *c/o Box F-2703. Freeport, Grand Bahama, Bahamas.*

AUSTRALIA, Primate of. (Vacant)

AUSTRALIA, NORTH-WEST, Lord Bishop of. *See* Muston, Right Rev Gerald Bruce.

AUSTRALIA, NORTH-WEST, Dean of. *See* Kerr, Very Rev Eric John.

AUSTRALIA, SOUTH, Metropolitan of. *See* Rayner, Most Rev Keith.

AUSTRALIA, WESTERN, Metropolitan of. *See* Sambell, Most Rev Geoffrey Tremayne.

AUTTON, Canon Norman William James. b 20. Selw Coll Cam BA 42, MA 46. St Mich Coll Llan 42. **d** 44 **p** 45 Llan. C of Merthyr Tydfil 44-50; Newcastle (Bridgend) 50-52; Hillingdon 52-54; Asst Chap Guild of Health 54-56; Chap Deva Hosp Ches 56-61; St Geo Hosp Lon 61-67; Dir of Tr Hosp Chaps Coun of Gen Syn 67-72; Chap Univ Hosp of Wales from 72; Can of Llan from 77. *Chaplain, University Hospital of Wales, Heath Park, Cardiff, CF4 4XW.* (0222-755944)

AVENDANO, Ernesto. b 36. **d** 68 **p** 69 Argent. P Dio Argent 68-73; N Argent from 73. *Parsonage, Saucelito, N Argentina.*

AVENDANO, Samuel. **d** 66 **p** 67 Chile. P Dio Chile. *Casilla 4, Cholchol, Chile, S America.*

AVENT, Raymond John. b 28. St D Coll Lamp BA 55. Coll of Resurr Mirfield. **d** 57 **p** 58 Man. C of H Trin Bury 57-60; St Alb Holborn 60-66; St Mary Magd Munster Square St Pancras 66-67; V of St Paul Tottenham 67-77; RD of E Haringey 76-77; V of St Aug w St John Kilburn Dio Lon from 77; Area Dean of Westmr (Paddington) from 79. *St Augustine's House, Kilburn Park Road, NW6 5XB.* (01-624 1637)

AVERY, Gordon Bruce. **d** 63 **p** 64 Melb. C of St Oswald Glen Iris 63-65; Miss ABM New Guinea 65-67; P-in-c of Mooroolbark 68-71; ABM Papua 71-74; I of Warrandyte w Pk Orchards 74-79; Perm to Offic Dio Melb from 79. *Scotchman's Road, Bellingham, NSW, Australia 2454.*

AVERY, Richard Julian. b 52. Keble Coll Ox BA 73. St Jo Coll Nottm 74. **d** 77 **p** 78 Ches. C of St Mich Macclesfield Dio Ches from 77. *57 Beech Farm Drive, Macclesfield, Cheshire, SK10 2ER.*

AVERY, Russel Harrold. b 46. Moore Coll Syd ACT ThDip 75. **d** and **p** 77 C & Goulb. Hon C of Good Shepherd Canberra 77; S Queanbeyan 77-78; C of St Steph Prenton 78-79; Chap St Geo Tunis Dio Egypt from 79. *5 rue des Protestants, 1006 Bab Souika, Tunis, Tunisia.*

AVERY, Canon William Ewart. St Jo Coll Morpeth 24. **d** 26 **p** 28 Graft. M of Bush Bro of Our Sav Bellbrook 26-28; Grevillia 29-32; V of Burringbar w U Tweed 32-35; Perm to Offic (Col Cl Act) at Silverdale Lancs 35-36; St Steph Walworth 36-37; V of Bowraville 37; Lower Macleay 37-38; Coraki 38-39; L to Offic Dio Graft 39-41; C-in-c of U Clarence 41-42; R of Mid Clarence 42-43; I of Ulmarra 43-52; Eureka 52-55; Bangalow 55-76; Can of Graft 64-76; Can (Emer) from 76; Perm to Offic Dio Graft from 76. *Pacific Lea, Bangalow, NSW, Australia 2479.*

AVERYT, Michael Edwin. b 50. Concordia Univ Montr BA 72, MDiv 77. **d** and **p** 79 Ott. C of Carleton Place Dio Ott from 79. *c/o 225 Edmund Street, Carleton Place, Ont, Canada. K0A 1J0.*

AVES, John Albert. b 51. AKC 73, BD 74. St Aug Coll Cant 73. **d** 75 **p** 76 Chelmsf. C of St Andr (w St Phil and St Jas from 77) Plaistow 75-77; Perm to Offic Dio Lon 77-78; Asst Chap HM Pris Brixton 78-79; C of St Pet Mancroft City and Dio Nor from 79. *52 Whitehall Road, Norwich, NR2 3EW.* (0603-610258)

AVEYARD, Ian. b 46. Univ of Liv BSc 68. St Jo Coll Nottm ALCD 72. **d** 71 **p** 72 Wakef. C of Bradley 71-74; Knowle 74-79; P-in-c of Barnt Green and Cofton Hackett Dio Birm from 79. *24 Blackwell Road, Barnt Green, Birmingham, B45 8BU.* (021-445 1835)

AVEZO, Canon Obadiya. Bp Tucker Coll Mukono. **d** 63 **p** 66 Ruw. P Dio Ruw 63-72; Dio Boga-Z from 72; Can of Boga-Z from 79. *BP 154, Bunia, Zaire.*

AVIS, Paul David Loup. b 47. BD (Lon) 70, PhD (Lon) 76. Westcott Ho Cam 73. **d** 75 **p** 76 Ex. C of S Molton 75-80; V of Stoke Canon, Poltimore w Huxham and Rewe w Netherexe Dio Ex from 80. *Stoke Canon Vicarage, Exeter, Devon, EX5 4AS.* (Stoke Canon 583)

AVU'BU, Bullen Doli. St Paul's Th Coll Limuru 66. **d** 67 N Ugan. **p** 69 M & W Nile. P Dio Sudan from 69. *c/o Clergy House, P.O. Box 153, Khartoum, Sudan.*

AWANI, Owuhi Gray. b 22. **d** 73 **p** 74 Benin. P Dio Benin. *St Peter's Church, Igbudu, c/o Box 52, Warri, Nigeria.*

AWCOCK, Canon Alec Mervyn. Bp's Univ Lennox BA (Th) 54. **d** 54 **p** 55 Queb. C of Queb Cathl 54-55; Miss in Labrador 55-60; C of Goldington Beds 60-62; R of La Tuque 62-67; Shawinigan and Grand'mere 67-77; Can of Queb from 75; I of St Geo Lennoxville Dio Queb from 77. *86 Queen Street, Lennoxville, PQ, Canada.*

AWDRY, Wilbert Vere. b 11. St Pet Hall Ox BA 32, MA 36. Wycl Hall OX 32. **d** 36 **p** 37 Win. C of Odiham 36-39; Bp's Lavington w L Cheverell and Gt Cheverell 39-40; Kings Norton 40-46; R of Elsworth w Knapwell 46-53: RD of Bourn 50-53; V of Emneth 53-65; Perm to Offic Dio Glouc from 65. *Sodor, Rodborough Avenue, Stroud, Glos, GL5 3RS.*

AWE, Jacob Sunday. b 38. Im Coll Ibad 72. **d** 75 **p** 76 Lagos. P Dio Lagos 76; Dio Ijebu from 76. *Christ Church Vicarage, Odosenlu Olaro, via Ijebu-ode, Nigeria.*

AWE, Matthew Babafemi. Im Coll Ibad 61. **d** 63 **p** 64 Ondo. P Dio Ondo 63-66; Dio Ekiti 66-68 and from 69; C of Andover Hants 68-69. *St Michael's Vicarage, Okemesi, Ekiti, Nigeria.*

AWE, Simeon Olaniran. Im Coll Ibad 63. **d** 65 **p** 66 Ondo. P Dio Ondo 65-67; Dio Ekiti from 67. *St Andrew's Vicarage, Ikole, Ekiti, Nigeria.*

AWINO, Zadok. b 28. **d** and **p** 74 Vic Nyan. P Dio Vic Nyan. *Box 1026, Bunda, Tanzania.*

AWODA, Simon Peter. Newton Th Coll Dogura. **d** 55 **p** 58 New Guinea. P Dio New Guinea 55-71; Dio Papua from 71. *Anglican Church, Gona, via Popondetta, Papua.*

AWOFADEJI, Isaac Adegbola. b 30. Im Coll Ibad 66. **d** 69 Ibad **p** 70 Bp Jadesimi for Ibad. P Dio Ibad. *All Saints' Vicarage, Oke-Onigbin, Ilorin, Nigeria.*

AWOLALU, Canon Joseph Omosade. b 29. BD (Lon) 62. Union Th Sem NY STM 63. Univ of Ibad PhD 71. **d** 70 Bp Jadesimi **p** 71 Ibad. P Dio Ibad; Lect in Relig Stud Univ of Ibad from 64; Hon Can of Ibad from 80. *Dept of Religious Studies, University of Ibadan, Ibadan, Nigeria.* (62550)

AWOPETU, Timothy Olatunji. b 42. Im Coll Ibad 74. **d** 77 **p** 78 Ibad. P Dio Ibad. *St Paul's Anglican Church, Kuffi II, Nigeria.*

AWOSAN, Ven Abraham Oluyemi. Im Coll Ibad 56. **d** 56 **p** 57 Ibad. P Dio Ibad 56-77; Exam Chap to Bp of Ibad 72-76; to Bp of Ilesha 74-77; Hon Can of Ibad 74-77; Provost of N Nig 78-80; Kaduna from 80; Exam Chap to Bp of Kaduna from 80. *Box 16, Kaduna, Nigeria.*

AWOSANMI, Samuel Abiola. BA (Lon) 62. **d** 65 **p** 66 Ondo. P Dio Ondo 65-72; L to Offic Dio Ibad from 72. *Kiriji Memorial College, Igbajo, Nigeria.*

AWOSIKA, Samuel Festus Ojo. Melville Hall Ibad 48. **d** 50 **p** 51 Lagos. P Dio Lagos 50-52; Dio Ondo-B 52-62; Dio Ondo 62-76. *c/o Box 4, Ondo, Nigeria.*

AWOSOGA, Ezekiel Ayodele. b 50. Univ of Ife BPharm 75. Im Coll of Th Dipl Th 81. **d** 81 Ilesha. d Dio Ilesha. *Bishopscourt, Oke-Oyi, PO Box 237, Ilesha, Nigeria.*

AWOSUSI, Israel Olatunji. b 42. Im Coll Ibad 66. **d** 69 **p** 70 Ondo. P Dio Ondo. *St John's Vicarage, Oba-Ile, Akure, Nigeria.*

AWOSUSI, Canon Nathanial Babaoloa. Melville Hall Ibad 50. **d** 52 Bp Phillips for Lagos **p** 53 Lagos. P Dio Lagos 52-65; Dio Ondo 65-66; Dio Ekiti from 66; Can of Lagos 59-65; Ekiti from 66. *St James's Vicarage, Igbara-Odo, Ekiti, Nigeria.*

AWOT, Fenekasi. **d** 77 Lango. d Dio Lango. *PO Anyeke, Minakulo, Lira, Uganda.*

AWRE, Edward Francis Wintour. b 11. St Jo Coll Dur BA 37, Dipl Th 38, MA 40. **d** 38 **p** 39 Bris. C of St Barn Knowle 38-41; Chippenham 41-43; Henbury (in c of Aust and

Northwick) 43-47; V of Merriott 47-56; Nether Stowey 56-70; C-in-c of Over Stowey 69-70; Hon C of Burnham-on-Sea Dio B & W from 72. *3 Seaview Road, Burnham-on-Sea, Somt.* (Burnham-on-Sea 782493)

AWRE, Richard William Esgar. b 56. Univ of Wales BA 78. Wycl Hall Ox 78. **d** 81 Burnley for Blackb **p** 82 Blackb. C of St Jo Evang Blackpool Dio Blackb from 81. *2a Lincoln Road, Blackpool, FY1 4HB.* (Blackpool 24036)

AWUMA, Gerald Otto. d 66 Accra. d Dio Accra. *P.O. Box 144, Kumasi, Ghana.*

AWUMA, William Senyo. d 62 **p** 63 Accra. P Dio Accra. *Box 85, Sekondi, Ghana.*

AWUONDA, Joseph. Maseno Bible Sch. **d** 62 **p** 65 Maseno. P Dio Maseno 62-70; Dio Maseno S from 70. *Box 66, Maseno, Kenya.*

AXCELL, Peter. St Jo Coll Auckld LTh 67. **d** 67 **p** 68 Nel. C of Blenheim 67-71; Ch Ch Cathl Nel 71-73; V of Reefton 73-77; Spreydon Dio Ch Ch from 77. *15 Dundee Place, Christchurch, NZ.* (384-062)

AXFORD, Donald Gordon. b 37. Univ of Manit BA 62. Hur Coll Ont MDiv 77. **d** 77 **p** 78 Hur. C-in-c of St D & St Luke Windsor Dio Hur from 77. *3411 Byng Road, Windsor, Ont, Canada, N8W 3H6.*

AXON, Ven Robert. Angl Th Coll BC LTh 17. Trin Coll Tor BD 19. St Jo Coll Winnipeg DD 50. **d** 16 Columb for New Westmr **p** 17 New Westmr. C of St John N Vanc and St Clem Lynn Valley BC 16-17; on leave 17-19; R of Marpole 19-27; St John Shaughnessy Heights 27-28; R of Kamloops 28-31; Exam Chap to Bp of Carib 28-34; to Bp of Calg 34-64; I of Drumheller 32-34; R of St Mark and St Martin Calg 34-36; I and RD of MacLeod 36-45; Hon Can of Calg 43-45; Can (Emer) from 64; Archd of Calg 45-64; Archd (Emer) from 64; Sec-Treas and Dioc Miss Dio Calg 45-64; Regr 64-68. *2127 90th Avenue SW, Calgary, Alta, Canada.* (281 5572)

AXT, Humberto Edmundo. b 46. **d** 79 **p** 80 N Argent. P-in-c of Salta Dio N Argent from 79. *Casilla 187, 4400 Salta, Argentina.*

AXTELL, Ronald Arthur John. BSc (Lon) 54. St Cath S Ox BA 58, MA 62. Wycl Hall Ox 56. **d** 58 Liv **p** 59 Warrington for Liv. C of Walton Breck 58-61; Chap at Tehran 63-67; Kerman 67-68; Shiraz Iran 69-78; Exam Chap to Bp of Iran 77-78; Chr Witness to Israel Miss from 79; Perm to Offic Dio Man, Ches, Liv & Blackb from 79. *94 Clyde Road, West Didsbury, Manchester m20 8WN.*

AYAD, Karl. b 25. Univ of Lon MSc 53, PhD 55. St Steph Ho Ox 80. **d** 81 Warrington for Liv. C of Allerton Dio Liv from 81. *7 Wyndcote Road, Allerton, Liverpool, L18 2EB.*

✠ **AYAM, Right Rev Baima Bertram.** Melville Hall Ibad 48. **d** 50 **p** 51 Lagos. P Dio Lagos 50-52; Dio N Nig 52-80; Can of N Nig 65-69; Exam Chap to Bp of N Nig 65-80; Archd of Kano 69-80; Cons Ld Bp of Kano in St Mich Cathl Kaduna 6 Jan 80 by Abp of Nigeria; Bps of Aba, Asaba, Benin, Ow, Egba-Egbado, Enugu, Ijebu, Ilesha, Kwara, Lagos, Niger, Nig Delta and Ondo. *Bishopscourt, Box 362, Kano, Nigeria.* (7816)

AYANGA, John Robert. b 23. **d** 74 **p** 75 Maseno N. P Dio Maseno N. *c/o PO Box 120, Butere, Kenya.*

AYEBIOWEI, Nestor Schulle Wilkinson. b 19. **d** 74 Lagos. d Dio Lagos. *St Jude's Vicarage, Box 45, Ebbute-Metta, Nigeria.*

AYE MAUNG, Paul. d 31 **p** 34 Rang. P Dio Rang 45-68. *c/o St Paul's Church, Yelegyi, Maubin, Burma.*

AYENI, David Ojo. Im Coll Ibad 68. **d** 71 **p** 72 Ondo. P Dio Ondo. *Vicarage, Alade, via Akure, Nigeria.*

AYENI, Canon Uanbahoro Ohiomoba. b 23. Univ of Hull BSc (Econ) 57. **d** 68 **p** 69 Benin. P Dio Benin from 69; Can of Benin from 69. *PO Box 6, Ubulu-Uku, Mid-West Nigeria.*

AYERS, John. b 40. Univ of Bris BEducn 75. **d** 77 **p** 78 Bris. C of Gtr Corsham Dio Bris from 77. *Toad Hall, Middlehill, Box, Corsham, Wilts SN14 9QP.*

AYERS, John Ronald. b 32. Univ of Otago MB, ChB 60. Univ of Auckld BA 73. **d** 77 Bp Spence for Auckld **p** 78 Auckld (APM). Hon C of Manurewa 77-79; Balmoral 79-81; Bucklands Beach Dio Auckld from 81. *Box 452, Manurewa, Auckland, NZ.*

AYERS, Canon William John Clinton. Univ of Manit BA 42. St Jo Coll Winnipeg BA 42, LTh 47. **d** 47 **p** 48 Keew. Miss at Atikokan and Steep Rock Mines 47-56; C of Cathl Ch Calg 56-59; R of Ch Ch Winnipeg 59-79; Can of St John's Cathl Winnipeg 66-77; Hon Can from 77; Hon C of St Geo Winnipeg Dio Rupld from 81. *400 Carpathia Road, Winnipeg, Manit, Canada.*

AYERST, Edward Richard. b 25. Univ of Leeds BA 51. Coll of Resurr Mirfield 51. **d** 53 Lon **p** 54 Kens for Lon. C of St John Bethnal Green 53-57; Hayes 58-60; V of St Mary w St Jo Evang U Edmon 60-66; R of Whippingham w E Cowes 66-77; V of Bridgwater w Chilton Trinity Dio B & W from 77; Durleigh Dio B & W from 77. *7 Durleigh Road, Bridgwater, Somt.* (Bridgwater 2437)

AYINLA, Samuel Oyewale Dadepo. b 34. **d** 76 **p** 78 Ibad. P Dio Ibad. *Holy Trinity Church, Igbajo, via Ikirun, Nigeria.*

AYITA, Samuel Folorunso. b 39. Im Coll Ibad Dipl Th 70. **d** 70 **p** 71 Ondo. P Dio Ondo. *Vicarage, Odigbo, Ondo, Nigeria.*

AYKROYD, Harold Allan. b 22. Univ of Man BA 48. Qu Coll Birm 73. **d** and **p** 76 Birm (APM). C of St Agnes Moseley Dio Birm from 76; Springfield Dio Birm from 79. *14 Astor Drive, Wake Green Road, Moseley, Birmingham, b13 9QR.* (021- 778 1017)

AYLARD, Bruce Leslie. b 29. Univ of BC BA 51. Angl Th Coll BC LTh 64. **d** 64 **p** 65 New Westmr. C of Burnaby 64-65; I of Castor 65-69; R of Hanna 70-75; Athab Dio Athab from 75. *PO Box 30, Athabasca, Alta, TOG 0B0, Canada.*

AYLEN, George Richard. Chich Th Coll 48. **d** 52 Croydon for Cant **p** 53 Cant. C of St Greg Gt Cant 52-55; All SS Westbrook Margate 55-58; V of All SS Spring Pk Croydon 58-61; Newington 61-67; St Pet Whitstable 67-75; R of Petham w Waltham and Lower Hardres w Nackington 75-78. *20 Seymour Place, Canterbury, Kent.*

AYLES, Raymond Frederick. St Mich Ho Crafers 63. ACT ThL 67. **d** 68 **p** 69 Adel. C of Glenelg 68-71; C of Salisbury 71-73; P-in-c of Para Hills Miss Distr 73-75; Cloncurry Dio N Queensld from 75. *Box 54, Cloncurry, Queensland, Australia 4824.*

AYLESWORTH, Samuel William. Univ of Alta BSc 61. Angl Th Coll BC LTh 64. **d** and **p** 64 Koot. V of Lumby 64-65; on leave. *71 Gloucester Crescent, Calgary, Alta, Canada.*

AYLING, Arnold Paul. b 38. Late Exhib of Ball Coll Ox BA 61. Wells Th Coll. **d** 67 **p** 68 Sarum. C of H Trin Weymouth 67-70; Chap K Alfred's Coll of Educn Win 70-73; Asst Chap Miss to Seamen Lon 73-74; Chap Miss to Seamen Lagos from 74. *c/o Missions to Seamen, Lagos, Nigeria.*

AYLING, Preb John Charles. b 02. St Jo Coll Dur Capel Cure Pri and BA 29. **d** 29 Roch **p** 30 Bp King for Roch. C of St Jas Gravesend 29-32; St Thos Heigham 32-35; V of St Paul Walsall 35-43; Chap of Manor Hosp and Beacon Lodge 35-43; V of Bilston 43-59; Broughton 59-70; R of Myddle 59-70; C-in-c of Grinshill 59-65; Dir of Relig Educn Dio Lich 59-75; Preb of Lich Cathl 61-75; Preb (Emer) from 75. *10 Church Close, Bicton, Shrewsbury, Salop.* (Shrewsbury 850491)

AYLING, John Michael. b 37. St Cath Coll Cam BA 60, MA 64. Linc Th Coll 60. **d** 62 **p** 63 Lich. C of Stoke-on-Trent 62-66; Codsall 66-67; P-in-c of Findon w Seaton Dio Adel 67-71; Tutor Patteson Th Centre, Kohimarama Melan 71-72; Asst Master Adeyfield Sch Hemel Hempstead 72-77; Bushey Hall Sch from 78; L to Offic Dio St Alb from 72. *58 Slimmons Drive, St Albans, Herts, AL4 9AP.* (St Albans 62935)

AYNSLEY, Ernest Edgar. b 02. K Coll Univ of Dur BSc (1st cl Chem) 23, MSc 24, PhD 34, DSc 62. Westcott Ho Cam 42. **d** 42 **p** 43 Newc T. C of Long Benton 42-54; Asst Master Rutherford Gr Sch Newc T 25-47; Sen Lect K Coll Univ of Dur from 47; C-in-c of St Jude Newc T 53-57; C of Gosforth 57-62; Prof of Chem Univ of Newc T 63-67; Prof (Emer) from 67; Perm to Offic Dio Newc T from 63. *6 Mayfair Gardens, Ponteland, Newcastle upon Tyne.* (Ponteland 3274)

AYNSLEY, John Swinburn. b 11. Univ of Man BA 32. Lich Th Coll 33. **d** 34 **p** 35 Carl. C of Dalston 34-37; St Geo Barrow-F 37-40; R of Crosby Garrett 40-46; V of Soulby 40-46; Dearham 46-53; Preston Patrick 53-56; Arnside 56-71; Troutbeck 71-77; RD of Kirkby Lonsdale 69-70; Windermere 70-76. *Two Views, Bridge Lane, Troutbeck, Windermere, LA23 1LA.* (Windermere 5662)

AYODELE, Abraham Orunkiya. Melville Hall Ibad. **d** 48 **p** 49 Lagos. P Dio Lagos 48-52 and from 62; Dio Ondo-B 52-62. *c/o Bishopscourt, PO Box 13, Lagos, Nigeria.*

AYODELE, Gabriel Adebayo. d 75 **p** 76 Ibad. P Dio Ibad. *1 Infantry Brigade, Nigerian Army, Minna, Nigeria.*

AYODELE, Robert Stephen Adebayo. Im Coll Ibad. **d** 61 **p** 62 Ondo-B. P Dio Ondo-B 62; Dio Benin 62-65; Dio Ondo from 74. *Box 3, Akure, Nigeria.*

AYOLI NGAJI, Samuel. b 39. **d** 77 Rumbek. d Dio Rumbek. *ECS, Momuolo, Sudan.*

AYOUNGMAN, Arthur. d 78 **p** 79 Calg. C of Blackfoot Miss Gleichen Dio Calg from 78. *Box 122, Gleichen, Alta, Canada, T0H 1N0.*

AYRE, George. b 09. AKC 31. **d** 32 **p** 33 Ex. C of Ottery St Mary 32-38; V of Payhembury 38-52; R of Wembworthy w Eggesford 52-60; V of Stoke Canon 60-73; C-in-c of Rewe w Netherexe Dio Ex 62-63; R 63-73; Perm to Offic Dio Ex from 73. *Ridgway, Fore Street, North Molton, South Molton, Devon.*

AYRE, Henry George. AKC 38. **d** 38 **p** 39 Southw. C of Bestwood Pk 38-40; St Matt Ex 40-43; Bideford 43; C-in-c of

E Downe w Arlington 44-46; R of Kentisbury (w Trentishoe, E Downe and Arlington from 72) Dio Ex from 46; R of Trentishoe 60-72; C-in-c of East Downe w Arlington 70-72. *Kentisbury Rectory, Barnstaple, Devon, EX31 4NH.* (Combe Martin 2487)

AYRE, Canon James. Tyndale Hall Bris 46. Clifton Th Coll 48. **d** and **p** 49 Ches. C of Cheadle 49-54; Chap at Tel Aviv 54-56; Jer 56-59; Haifa Dio Jer 59-60; R of Cheadle Dio Ches from 61; Hon Can of Ches Cathl from 74. *Rectory, Cheadle, Chesh.* (Gatley 34400

AYRES, Anthony Lawrence. b 47. Trin Coll Bris 69. **d** 73 **p** 74 S'wark. C of All SS Shooter's Hill, Plumstead Dio S'wark from 73. *43 Mereworth Drive, Shooters Hill, SE18 3ED.* (01-855 5527)

AYRIS, Joseph Frederick. Qu Coll Newfld. **d** 32 **p** 33 Newfld. C-in-c of Rose Blanche 32-33; P-in-c 33-38; C of Corner Brook 38-42; R of Joe Batt's Arm 42-52; Smith's Sound 52-55; Hosp Chap St John's Newfld 55-77. *23 Symond Place, St John's, Newfoundland, Canada.*

AYUNG, Julius. d 49 Melan **p** 50 Papua. P Dio New Guinea 49-71; Dio Papua 71-77; Dio New Guinea Is from 77; Vice-Prin St Aid Coll Dogura 55-56. *St Boniface Mission, Kumbun, via Kandrian, WNBP, Papua New Guinea.*

AZAR, Musa Abdu. d 43 **p** 45 Jer. P-in-c El Husn 43-47; Shefa 'Amr 47-50; Ramleh 50-54; Husn 54-60; Salt 60-66; Nablus 66-69. *Evangelical Church, El Husn, Jordan.*

AZIBAKANYE, Constant Kienworio. b 30. **d** 77 Nig Delta. d Dio Nig Delta. *St John's Church, Onuebum, Ogbia District, Rivers State, Nigeria.*

AZINGE, Canon Nicholas Olisajindu. b 30. Nat Univ of Ireland MB, BCh 57. MRCP (Ireland) 64. **d** 73 **p** 74 Benin. P Dio Benin; Hon Can of Benin from 75. *Specialist Hospital, Benin City, Nigeria.*

AZU, Hart Amuchionu Stephen. b 37. St Paul's Coll Awka 76. **d** 77 Aba. d Dio Aba. *St Michael's Cathedral, PO Box 818, Aba, Nigeria.*

AZUBUIKE, Joshua Ojimadu Echemanti. b 34. Trin Coll Umuahia 65. **d** 67 **p** 68 Nig Delta. P Dio Nig Delta 68-72; Dio Aba from 72. *St Peter's Parsonage, Amizi Olokoro, Box 29, Umuahia, Nigeria.*

AZUBUIKE, Canon Vincent Nwaeze. Trin Coll Umuahia 54. **d** 56 **p** 57 N Nig. P Dio N Nig 56-59; Dio Ow from 70; Hon Can of Ow from 75. *Parsonage, Orodo, via Owerri, Nigeria.*

B

BAALE, Yairo Kiseke. Bp Tucker Coll Mukono. **d** 50 **p** 52 Ugan. P Dio Ugan 50-58; Dio Sudan 58-63; Dio Nam from 63; Can of Nam from 72; Archd of Ndejje 74-77. *Box 20183, Namugongo, Uganda.*

BABA, James. d 65 **p** 66 N Ugan. P Dio N Ugan 65-69; Dio M & W Nile from 69. *c/o PO Box 370, Arua, Uganda.*

BABALOLA, Ezekiel Adeleke. Melville Hall Ibad. **d** 48 **p** 49 Lagos. P Dio Lagos from 48. *6 Igbo Juwo Street, Box 4143, Lagos, Nigeria.*

BABALOLA, John Akinola. b 38. Univ of Ibad BEducn 68. Im Coll Ibad 75. **d** 76 **p** 77 Ibad. P Dio Ibad. *Box 166, Ibadan, Nigeria.*

BABALOLA, Canon Jonathan Adepoju. d 61 **p** 62 Ondo-B. P Dio Ondo-B 61-62; Dio Ondo 62-66; Dio Ekiti from 66; Can of Ekiti from 69. *PO Box 12, Ado-Ekiti, Nigeria.*

BABALOLA, Samson Oladokun. b 40. Im Th Coll Ibad 67. **d** 70 Bp Jadesimi for Ibad **p** 71 Gambia. P Dio Ibad from 70. *Box 21, Offa, Kwara State, Nigeria.*

BABARINSA, Michael Oluwole. Im Coll Ibad 64. **d** 66 **p** 67 Lagos. P Dio Lagos. *Ake, Abeokuta, Lagos, Nigeria.*

BABATAYO, Titus Olatunde. b 35. Im Coll Ibad 62. **d** 65 **p** 66 Lagos. P Dio Lagos. *Vicarage, Ososa, via Ijeb-Ode, Nigeria.*

BABATUNDE, Emmanuel Taiwo. Melville Hall Oyo 27. **d** 28 **p** 29 Bp Oluwole for Lagos. P Dio Lagos 28-51; Dio Ibad 52-66; Hon Can of Ibad 62-64; Can 64-66; (retired). *St Phillip's Rectory, Otan-Aiyegbaju, Oshogbo, Lagos, Nigeria.*

BABB, Charles Thomas. b 47. Mem Univ of Newfld BA 70. Qu Coll Newfld. **d** 70 **p** 72 Newfld. I of King's Cove 72-74; Churchill Falls 74-76; Bay L'Argent 76-80; Chap Miss to Seamen Antwerp Dio Gibr in Eur from 80. *Seafarers' Centre, Italielei 72, Antwerp, Belgium.* (031-333475)

BABB, Geoffrey. b 42. Univ of Man BSc (2nd cl Math and Phil) 64. Linacre Coll Ox BA (2nd cl Th) 67. Univ of Man MA (Th) 74. Ripon Hall Ox 65. **d** 68 **p** 69 Man. C of St Luke Heywood 68-71; C-in-c of Ascen Loundsley Green Conv Distr 71-76; Team V of Old Brampton and Loundsley Green 76-77; Stafford Dio Lich from 79; Social Responsibility Officer Dio Lich from 77. *9 Brunswick Terrace, Stafford, ST16 1BB.* (Stafford 46838)

BABB, Henry Cecil. b 06. Univ of Lon BSc 28. Peterho Cam BA 37. Westcott Ho Cam 34. **d** 35 **p** 36 Ely. C of St Andr Chesterton 35-37; CF Woolwich; Lydd; Middle E; Sing; Thailand 37-46; Chap Culham Coll 46-64; Lect 64-75. *c/o 80 Appleton Road, Cumnor, Oxford.*

BABB, Canon Randall Richard. Qu Coll Newfld. Trin Coll Tor. **d** 40 **p** 41 Newfld. C of Bay St Geo 40-42; St Geo Mart Tor 42-43; R of Burin 43-54; St Mary St John's 54-81; Can of St Jo Bapt Cathl Newfld from 65. *c/o The Rectory, Cornwall Crescent, St John's, Newfoundland, Canada.* (709-579-3361)

BABBAGE, Malcolm Stuart. b 46. Moore Th Coll Syd ThL 72. **d** and **p** 73 Syd. C of St Thos N Syd 73-74; Chatswood 74-76; Weipa 77-79; Perm to Offic Dio Newc from 79; Youth Sec NSW 80; State Sec from 81. *135 Bathurst Street, Sydney, NSW, Australia 2000.* (264-3164)

BABBAGE, Stuart Barton. Univ of NZ BA 35, MA 36. K Coll Lon PhD 42. ACT ThD 50. St Jo Coll Auckld 35. Tyndale Hall Bris 37. **d** 39 **p** 40 Chelmsf. C of Havering-atte-Bower 39-41; Asst Chap TCG 41; Sen Chap RAF 42-46; Dioc Miss Dio Syd 46; Lect Moore Th Coll Syd 46; RD of Cook's River 51-53; Dean of Syd 47-53; R of H Trin Miller's Point Syd 50-52; Prin Ridley Coll Melb 53-63; Dean of Melb 53-62; in Amer Ch 63-73; Master New Coll Univ NSW from 73; Actg Dean of Syd 73. *New College, Anzac Parade, Kensington, NSW, Australia 2033.* (663-6066)

BABCOCK, Clarence Edward. b 28. Em Coll Sktn 63. **d** 63 **p** 64 Athab. I of Atikameg 63-66; Crow's Nest Pass Dio Calg 66-69; V in The Winfarthing Par Group 69-73; I of Kitley and N Augusta 73-80; Bath w Amherst Dio Ont from 80. *Box 283, Bath, Ont., Canada.* (613-352 7529)

BABER, Leslie Civil. b 02. ACII 25. St Edm Hall Ox BA (2nd cl Th) 29, MA 33. Westcott Ho Cam 29. **d** 30 **p** 31 S'wark. C of St Sav Brockley Hill 30-35; Sutton Coldfield 35-37; R of Broughton w N Newington 37-45; Asst Sec Ely Dioc Bd of Finance 45-46; Sec 46-55; Perm to Offic Dio Win 67-72; Dio Portsm from 71; C of Brockenhurst Dio Win from 72. *Bonham, Church Lane, Sway, Lymington, Hants. SO4 0AD.* (0590-682776)

BABIA, Eric. St Columb's Hall Wang 66. **d** and **p** 67 Carp. C of All S Cathl Thursday I 67-70; L to Offic Dio Carp 70; Miss Dio Papua 70-72; St Paul Miss Moa I 73; C of Carp Cathl 74; P-in-c of Murray I 75-76. *c/o Box 79, Thursday Island, Queensland, Australia 4875.*

BABINGTON, Canon Gervase Hamilton. b 30. Keble Coll Ox BA and MA 57. Wells Th Coll 1955. **d** 57 **p** 58 Sheff. C of St Geo Sheff 57-60; C-in-c of Manor Pk Conv Distr Sheff 60-65; R of Waddington 65-81; RD of Graffoe 74-81; Hon Can of Linc Cathl from 77; V of Gainsborough Dio Linc from 81. *Vicarage, Gainsborough, Lincs.* (Gainsborough 2965)

BABINGTON, Richard Andrew. b 27. Keble Coll Ox BA 49. **d** 51 **p** 52 St E. C of All SS Newmarket 51-54; V of All SS Elton Bury 54-63; R of Honiton w Gittisham 63-72; Combe Raleigh 66-72; R of Blandford Forum (and Langton Long w Blandford St Mary from 73) Dio Sarum from 72; R of Langton Long 72-73. *Rectory, Blandford Forum, Dorset.* (Blandford 53294)

BABINGTON, Ven Richard Hamilton. b 01. Keble Coll Ox BA (2nd cl Mod Hist) 23, MA 47. Wells Th Coll 24. **d** 25 **p** 26 Win. C of Banstead 25-29; V of Westend 29-42; St Mary-le-Tower Ipswich 42-58; Hon Can of St E 47-58; Preb of Ex Cathl 58-76; Archd of Ex 58-70; Archd (Emer) from 70; Can (Res) of Ex 58-70; Exam Chap to Bp of Ex 59-70; Treas of Ex Cathl 62-70. *2 Beauvale Close, Ottery St Mary, EX11 1AA.* (Ottery St Mary 2431)

BABOO, Canon Paramanatham Israel Samuel. Univ of Madr BA 28; Serampore Coll BD 34; Bp's Coll Calc Dipl Th 34. **d** 34 Bp Walsh for Tinn **p** 35 Tinn. P Dio Tinn 34-39; L to Offic Dio Sing 39-41; V of Ch Ch, Sing 41-72; Actg Commiss for Tamil Work Dio Sing 43-45; Hon Can of Sing 50-72; Can (Emer) from 72. *Address temp unknown.*

BABURU, Enosa. d 72 **p** 73 Sudan. P Dio Sudan 72-76; Dio Yambio from 76. *ECS, Ezo, Sudan.*

BACH, John Edward Goulden. b 40. Univ of Dur BA 66, Dipl Th 69. Cranmer Hall Dur 66. **d** 69 **p** 70 Bradf. C of St Pet Cathl Bradf 69-72; Chap and Lect New Univ of Ulster from 73. *c/o New University of Ulster, Coleraine, BT52 1SA, N Ireland.*

BACH, Neil Sebastian. b 50. ACT ThL 78. Ridley Coll Melb 75. **d** 78 **p** 79 Melb. C of St Mark Camberwell 78-80; H Trin Doncaster Dio Melb from 80. *104 Church Road, Doncaster, Vic, Australia 3108.*

BACHE, Edward Cyril Forbes. b 07. Univ of Dur BA 33, MA 56. **d** 34 **p** 35 Lon. C of St Barn Temple Fortune 34-35; St Hilda Tottenham 35-36; Chap of Momb 36-39; Chap RAF

39-46; C of St Paul St Alb 46-48; Chap K Alfred Sch BAOR 48-53; R of Ufton and Dir of Relig Educn Dio Cov 53-57; V of Husborne Crawley (w Ridgmont from 66) 57-71; C-in-c of Ridgmont 61-66; Chap St Felix Sch Southwold 71-74; L to Offic Dio St E 71-75; Team V of Linstead w Chediston and Halesworth 75-77; C of Hardwick w Tusmore and of Cottisford 77-80; L to Offic Dio St E from 81. *Brook Cottage, Newbourne, Woodbridge, suff.*

BACHELL, Kenneth George. b 22. Univ of Lon BD (2nd cl Hons) 49. St Bonif Coll Warm 55. **d** 56 **p** 57 Win. C of Ascen Bitterne Pk 56-60; Min of St Mich AA Eccles Distr Andover 60-64; V 64-68; St Alb Southn 68-76; Warden Man Dioc Conf Ho and C-in-c of Crawshawbooth 76-79; V of Holdenhurst w Throop Dio Win from 79. *6 Broad Avenue, Queen's Park, Bournemouth, Hants, BH8 9HG.* (Bournemouth 33438)

BACHMANN, Paul Douglas. b 45. **d** 79 **p** 80 Arctic. C of Cam Bay Dio Arctic from 79. *St George's Anglican Mission, Cambridge Bay, NWT, Canada X0E 0C0.*

BACK, Christopher George. b 46. St Chad's Coll Dur BA (2nd cl Engl) 69. Linacre Coll Ox BA 71. St Steph Ho 69. **d** 72 **p** 73 Stepney for Lon. C of H Trin Hoxton 72-75; Kenton Dio Lon from 75. *75 Kenton Gardens, Kenton, Middx.* (01-907 9717)

BACK, Edward James. b 24. BSc (Eng) Lon 49. ALCD 65. **d** 65 **p** 66 Lon. C of Em Northwood 65-69. *8 Wolsey Road, Moor Park, Northwood, Middx, HA6 2HW.* (Northwood 25332)

BACK, Peter Robert. b 44. Moore Th Coll Syd 76. **d** 77 Bp Dain for Syd **p** 77 Syd. C of St Bede Beverly Hills 77-78; Sans Souci 79-80; Brighton-le-Sands 80; Assoc R Botany Mascot 80; on leave 81. *Box 209, Sanar, Yemen.*

BACKHOUSE, Alan Eric. b 37. Late Exhib of Keble Coll Ox BA 61, MA 67. Tyndale Hall, Bris 61. **d** 64 Middleton for Man **p** 65 Man. C of Burnage 64-67; St Andr Cheadle Hulme 67-70; V of Buglawton 70-80; New Ferry Dio Ches from 80. *New Ferry Vicarage, Bebington, Wirral, Chesh.* (051-645 2638)

BACKHOUSE, John. b 30. Univ Coll Southn BA (2nd cl Hist) Lon 50. Wycl Hall Ox 51. **d** 53 **p** 54 Liv. C of St Luke Eccleston 53-55; Maghull 56-58; V of Lathom 58-64; CMS Area Sec Dios Linc and Ely 64-71; Dios Leic and Pet 72-75; Dios Leic and Cov 75-78; L to Offic Dio Linc 64-71; Dio Leic 72-78; V of Thorpe Acre w Dishley Dio Leic from 78. *Thorpe Acre Vicarage, Thorpe Acre Road, Loughborough, Leics, LE11 0LF.* (Loughborough 214553)

BACKHOUSE, Robert. b 45. ALCD 70. **d** 70 **p** 71 Bradwell for Chelmsf. C of St Pet Harold Wood Hornchurch 70-74; Publications Sec CPAS from 74. *Church Pastoral Aid Society, Falcon Court, 32 Fleet Street, EC4.*

BACKHOUSE, Walter Gilbert. Ridley Coll Melb ACT ThL (2nd cl) 16. **d** 16 **p** 17 Gippsld. C of St Geo Wonthaggi Vic 16-17; St Paul Bendigo 17; Chap AIF 18-19; V of Bruthen Vic 19-22; R of Orbost 22-26; Min of Barrabool and Modewarre 26-28; W Geelong 28-32; W Footscray 32-38; E Brighton 38-45; I of Clifton Hill 45-58. *8 Horsley Court, 45 Wilson Street, Brighton, Vic. 3186, Australia.*

BACON, Derek Robert Alexander. b 44. Div Hostel Dub 69. **d** 71 **p** 72 Derry. C of Templemore 71-73; V Cho of St Columb Cathl Derry 72-73; C of Heeley (in c of St Leon) Sheff 74-76; V of St Pet Abbeydale City and Dio Sheff from 76. *21 Ashland Road, Sheffield, S7 1RH.* (Sheffield 50719)

BACON, Eric Arthur. b 23. Qu Coll Birm 68. **d** 69 **p** 70 Linc. C of St Pet-at-Gowts w St Andr Lincoln 69-71; C in Asterby Group 71-74; V of Anwick 74-78; S w N Kyme 74-78; C-in-c of Kirby Laythorpe w Asgarby 76-78; Ewerby w Evedon 76-78; V of Messingham w E Butterwick Dio Linc from 78. *Messingham Vicarage, Scunthorpe, S Humb, DN17 3SG.* (Scunthorpe 762823)

BACON, Frederick John. b 13. Chich Th Coll 49. **d** 50 **p** 51 Chich. C of Aldrington 50-53; S w N Bersted 53-57; V of St Mary w St Jas Brighton 57-67; St Mary Kemptown Brighton Dio Chich from 67. *Vicarage, 11 West Drive, Brighton 7, Sussex.* (Brighton 682451)

BACON, Geoffrey Harold Walker. Univ of Witwatersrand BSc 24. LTh (S Afr) 34. St Paul's Coll Grahamstn 36. **d** 37 **p** 38 St Jo Kaffr. C of H Cross 37-38; Matatiele 38-41; P-in-c of Mqanduli 41; CF (S Afr) 41-45; P-in-c of St Mark's 46-50; R of Maclear 50-58; P-in-c of Mqanduli Dio St Jo Kaffr 58-60; Dio St John's 60-69; C of St John's Cathl, Umtata 70-72; R of Port St John's Dio St John's from 72. *Rectory, Church Street, Port St John's, CP, S Africa.* (Port St John's 55)

BACON, Geoffrey William Anthony. b 28. K Coll Lon and Warm AKC 54. **d** 56 **p** 61 Lon. C of Ch Ch W Green Tottenham 56-57; St Mary Finchley 61-64; Haywards Heath (in c of St Edm) 64-66; R of Snailwell 66-69; V of Chippenham Cambs 67-69; L to Offic Dio Lon 69-75; Team V of Thornaby-on-Tees Dio York from 81. *St Peter's Vicarage, Whitehouse Road, Thornaby Green, Stockton-on-Tees, 1)*

BACON, Harold. b 17. Kelham Th Coll 35. **d** and **p** 41 York. C of N Ormesby 41-43; St Mary w Ch Ch and St Paul Scarborough 43-44; St Geo Cathl Georgetown 44-45; V of St Joseph Port Mourant w St Barn Gibr and St Mark Alness 45-46; St Hilda Crofton Park 46-47; St Werburgh Derby 47-49; PC of St Jas Moulton Linc 49-50; C of Uitenhage 50; R of Molteno 50-51; Curate of Rosettenville 51-53; R of Turffontein 53-56; PC of Cross Stone 56-61; Chap Springfield Psychiatric Hosp Man 61-66; L to Offic Dio Man 61-66; V of Hubberholme 66-73; Commiss Windw Is from 68; Maur from 73; V of St Pet Accrington 73-81. *Address temp unknown.*

BACON, John Martindale. b 22. St Aid Coll. **d** 57 **p** 58 Man. C of St Paul Bury 57-59; C-in-c of St Thos Conv Distr Clifton Green 59-71; V of Astley Bridge Dio Man from 71. *Vicarage, Sweetloves Lane, Astley Bridge, Bolton, BL1 7ET.* (Bolton 54119)

BACON, Lionel William Rupert. b 06. Univ Coll Dur LTh 31, BA 32, MA 40. St Paul's Coll Burgh 27. **d** 33 **p** 34 Dur. C of St Pet Bp Auckland 33-35; Chap at Morro Velho 35-39; Perm to Offic at St Martin Gospel Oak 39-40; Castle Bromwich 40-41; Org Sec CCCS for SW Area 41-47; L to Offic Dio Momb and Supervisor of Schs Nyanza 47-52; R of Whitfield 53-55; V of Ninebanks 53-55; PC of Carshield (or W Allen) 53-55; Dioc Insp of Schs 53-55; R of Laceby 55-59; R of Irby upon Humber 55-59; V of Ancaster 59-73; Honington 59-73. *12 West Avenue, West Worthing, Sussex.* (Worthing 48930)

BADDELEY, Canon Martin James. b 36. Keble Coll Ox BA (2nd cl Th) 60, Hall-Houghton Jun Septuagint Pri 61, MA 64. Linc Th Coll 60. **d** 62 **p** 63 Man. C of St Matt Stretford 62-64; Lect Linc Th Coll 65-66; Tutor 66-69; Chap 68-69; L to Offic Dio Linc 65-69; Chap Fitzw Coll and New Hall Cam 69-74; Exam Chap to Bp of Man 71-74; to Bp of St E 73-75; to Bp of Roch from 77; Can Res of Roch Cathl 74-80; Hon Can from 80; Prin SOC from 80. *27 Blackfriars Road, SE1 8NY.* (01-928 4793)

BADDELEY, Very Rev William Pye. b 14. St Chad's Coll Dur BA 40. Cudd Coll 40. **d** 41 Kingston T for S'wark **p** 42 S'wark. C of St Luke Camberwell 41-44; St Anne Wandsworth 44-46; St Steph Bournemouth 46-49; V of St Pancras (w St Jas and Ch Ch from 54) and Chap of Elizabeth Garret Anderson Hosp 49-58; C-in-c of St Jo Evang Fitzroy Square w St Sav 1949-52; Chap St Luke's Hostel 52-54; Dean of Brisb 58-67; Dean (Emer) from 81; Sub-Chap O of St John of Jer 60-70; Chap from 70; Hon Chap to Abp of Brisb 63-67; Commiss Brisb from 67; Wang and Papua 70-80; Newc from 76; R of St Jas Piccadilly 67-80; RD of Westmr (St Marg) 74-79. *Cumberland House, Woodbridge, Suff, IP12 4AH.* (Woodbridge 4104)

BADDOKWAYO, Ven Yakobo. b 16. Bp Tucker Coll Mukono 67. **d** 68 **p** 70 Nam. P Dio Nam; Archd of Ndejje Dio Nam from 77. *Ndejje Archdeaconry, PO Ndejje, Bbombo, Uganda*

BADEJO, Erasmus Victor. b 21. BSc (Lon) 54. Im Coll Ibad 70. **d** 71 Lagos **p** 73 Bp Cragg for Jer for Lagos. Hon Chap St Sav Lagos 71-72; St Matt Addis Ababa Dio Egypt 72-75; Hon C of Ascen Wembley 75-76; All SS W Dulwich 76-78; Commiss Ondo from 77; C of Cheam (in c of St Osw) Dio S'wark from 79. *49 Brock's Drive, N Cheam, Surrey.* (01-644 7042)

BADEN, Peter Michael. b 35. CCC Cam BA 59, MA 62. Cudd Coll 58. **d** 60 **p** 61 Ripon. C of Hunslet 60-63; L to Offic Dio Wakef 63-64; C of E Grinstead 65-68; V of St Martin Brighton 68-74; R of The Resurr Brighton 74-76; Westbourne Dio Chich from 76; V of Forest Side Dio Chich from 76. *Westbourne Rectory, Emsworth, Hants.* (Emsworth 2867)

BADGER, Canon Bernard. b 16. Jes Coll Ox BA 39, MA 46. Cudd Coll 46. **d** 48 **p** 49 Leic. C of St Mark Leic 48-51; H Spirit w St Bart Southsea 51-53; V of St Andr City and Dio Leic from 53; Hon Can of Leic from 76; P-in-c of All S City and Dio Leic from 79. *St Andrew's Vicarage, Jarrom Street, Leicester, LE2 7DH.* (Leicester 549658)

BADGER, Canon Edwin. Univ of Bris BA 32. BD (Lon) 57. St Bonif Coll Warm 28. **d** 34 **p** 35 Worc. C of St John Kidderminster 34-36; SPG Miss Dio Kobe 36-41; Min of Mordialloc 41-42; Perm to Offic Dio Melb 42; War Service 42-46; Min of Merlynston 46-51; Nathalia 51-56; Avoca 56-59; R of Euroa 59-61; Exam Chap to Bp of Wang 60-76; Warden of St Columb's Hall Wang and R of Milawa 61-64; P-in-c of Moyhu 65-76; Hon Can of Wang 69-76; Can (Emer) from 76; Perm to Offic Dio Melb from 76. *5 Malcolm Street, Bacchus Marsh, Vic, Australia 3340.* (053-67 2316)

BADGER, Canon John Lee. b 13. LTh (S Afr) 44. Linc Th Coll 46. **d** 47 **p** 48 York. C of Bridlington and Bessingby 47-49; St Andr Drypool 49-51; V of Ledsham w Fairburn 51-55; W Acklam 55-58; Em Bridlington Dio York from 58; RD of Bridlington from 69; Surr from 69; Can and Preb of

York Minster from 78. *Vicarage, 68 Cardigan Road, Bridlington, Yorks, YO15 3JT.* (Bridlington 73748)

BADGER, Mervyn Hector. b 03. Jes Coll Ox. St D Coll Lamp. **d** 39 **p** 40 St D. C of Llanrhian 39-42; C-in-c of Llangorwen 42-45; C of Eglwys Newydd 45-46; I of Walton East w Llysyfran 46-56; R of St Florence w Redberth 56-61; V of Penrhyncoch w Elerch 61-71. *35 St Margaret's Close, Merlins Bridge, Haverfordwest, Dyfed.*

BADHAM, Canon Herbert William. b 09. Late Exhib of Hatf Coll Dur LTh 30, BA 31. St Bonif Coll Warm 27. **d** 32 **p** 33 S'wark. C of St Cath Hatcham 32-35; SPG Miss Lourenço Marques 35-40; C of St Sav Raynes Park 40-42; CF (EC) 42-46; Supr Native Miss Pietermaritzburg and Can of Natal 46-54; Metrop Sec SPG and Publ Pr Dio S'wark 54-59; Commiss Natal from 1954; Chap at Oslo 59-62; SPG Area Sec for Dios Chich Portsm and Win 62-64; USPG Area Sec for Dios Portsm and Win 65-66; Hon Can of Natal from 1967; L to Offic Dio Johann 66-68; Dir S Miss Churchmen (S Afr) 66-68; V of St Clem w St Mary Bournemouth 68-75. *3 Halton Close, Burley Road, Bransgore, Christchurch, Dorset BH23 8HZ.*

BADHAM, Paul Brian Leslie. b 42. Jes Coll Ox BA (2nd cl Th) 65, MA 69. Late Scho of Jes Coll Cam BA (1st cl Th Trip pt iii) 68, MA 72. Univ of Birm PhD 73. Westcott Ho Cam 66. **d** 68 Bp Sinker for Birm **p** 69 Aston for Birm. C of Edgbaston 68-69; Rubery 69-73; Lect St D Coll Lamp from 73; Publ Pr Dio St D from 73. *Godre'r, Coed, Lampeter, Dyfed.* (Lampeter 422241)

BADIREGA, Mark. d 74 Papua. d Dio Papua. *Anglican Church, Agaun, via Alotau, Papua New Guinea.*

BADUZA, Obed Solomon Samuel. b 14. St Bede's Coll Umtata 80. **d** 79 **p** 80 Grahmstn (APM). C of Aliwal N Dio Grahmstn from 79. *548 Block C, Aliwal North 5530, CP, S Africa.*

BAELZ, Very Rev Peter Richard. b 23. Ch Coll Cam BA 44, MA 48, BD 71, DD 79. Westcott Ho Cam 44. **d** 47 Birm **p** 50 Sarum. C of Bournville 47-50; Sherborne 50-52; Asst Chap of Ripon Hall Ox 52-54; R of Wishaw 54-56; V of Bournville 56-60; Dean of Jes Coll Cam 60-72; L to Office Dio Ely from 61; Exam Chap to Bp of Birm 62-70; to Bp of St E 67-78; Select Pr Univ of Cam 63; Hulsean Lect 64-66; Lect in Div 66-72; Can of Ch Ch Ox 72-79; Hulsean Pr 78; Regius Prof of Moral and Past Th Univ of Ox 72-79; Bampton Lect 74; Dean of Dur from 80. *Deanery, Durham, DH1 3EQ.* (Durham 47500)

BAFANA, Andrew. d 77 **p** 78 Matab. P Dio Matab. *Box 17, Victoria Falls, Zimbabwe.*

BAGANIZI, Canon Wilson. d 66 Ank. d Dio Ank 66-76; Dio E Ank from 76; Dioc Regr and Treas Dio Ank 72-73; Can of Ank 74-76; E Ank from 76. *Church of Uganda, P.O. Box 14, Mbarara, Uganda.*

BAGARUKAYO, Francis. d and **p** 79 W Ank. P Dio W Ank. *Box 140, Bushenyi, Uganda.*

BAGGALEY, Canon Dennis. b 31. St Jo Coll Dur BA 53, Dipl Th 56, Long Pri 52. Univ of Liv MA 79. **d** 56 **p** 57 Man. C of Ch Ch Pennington 56-59; N Meols 59-60; V of Ch Ch Bacup 60-65; R of St Nich Burnage 65-71; V of Kirk Onchan Dio S & M from 71; Surr from 71; Can of St German Cathl Peel from 80. *Kirk Onchan Vicarage, Onchan, Isle of Man.* (Douglas 5797)

BAGGALEY, John Roger Pocklington. b 14. MC 45. Keble Coll Ox BA 36, MA 45. Westcott Ho Cam. **d** 47 **p** 48 Dur. C of Bishopwearmouth 47-50; CF 50-69; R of Badger Dio Lich from 69; Beckbury Dio Lich from 69; Ryton Dio Lich from 69. *Beckbury Rectory, Shifnal, Salop, TF11 9DG.* (Ryton 241)

BAGGLEY, John Samuel. b 40. Univ of Dur BA (2nd cl Hist) 62. Kelham Th Coll 62. **d** 66 **p** 67 Lon. C of Poplar 66-71; Team V of Poplar 71-72; V of St Pet De Beauvoir Town Dio Lon from 72. *St Peter's Vicarage, De Beauvoir Road, N1.* (01-254 5670)

BAGGS, John Randall. *See* Randall, John Randall.

BAGIWI, Zeburuna. b 24. Bp Gwynne Coll Mundri. **d** 65 Bp Dotiro for Sudan **p** 69 Sudan. P Dio Sudan 65-76; Dio Yambio from 76. *ECS, Yamio, Sudan.*

BAGLEY, Canon Edward Ronald. St Pet Hall Ox BA (2nd cl Hist) 35, MA 40. Ridley Hall Cam 35. **d** 37 **p** 38 Liv. C of All S Springwood 37-38; Lect St Jo Coll Winnipeg 38-44; PV of St Jo Cathl 40-42; Chap St John's Coll Sch Winnipeg 42-44; Chap Trin Coll Sch Port Hope Ont 44-50; P-in-c of Annunc Tor 50-53; R of St Jo Bapt Norway Tor 5365; Exam Chap to Bp of Tor 56-59; Can of Tor 58-59 and from 65; Archd of Tor E 59-65; Chap Bp Strachan Sch Dio Tor 65-78. *12 Bloomsgrove Avenue, Port Hope, Ont, Canada.*

BAGLEY, Canon John Marmaduke Erskine. b 08. G and C Coll Cam 3rd cl Hist Trip pt i 29, BA 30, MA 36. Ely Th Coll 30. **p** 32 Malmesbury for Bris **p** 33 Bris. C of St Mark, Swindon 32-36; St Mary L, Cam 36-38; Chap at Ch Ch, Jubbulpore 38-44; C of Littleham w Exmouth 45-46; R of Huntingdon 46-63; V of Gt Stukeley 52-63; Chap to HM Borstal Inst Gaynes Hall 52-55; V of H Trin w St Mary, Ely 63-74; Chap Ely Cathl 63-74; Surr 63-74; RD of Ely 66-71; Hon Can of Ely 68-74; Can (Emer) from 74 C-in-c of Chettisham 68-74; Perm to Offic Dio St E 74-77; Dio Ely from 77. *14 Dendys, Hemingford Grey, Huntingdon, Cambs.* (St Ives 69279)

BAGLEY, Richard Alexander. New Coll Ox BA (2nd cl Engl Lang and Lit) 51, MA 55. K Coll Cam MA (*ad eund*) 57. Cudd Coll 51. **d** 53 **p** 54 Ely. C of St Mary L Cam 53-58; Perm to Offic Dios Ely and Lon 59-66. *75 Marina Street, Senglea, Malta.*

BAGNALL, Ven Harold Robert. d 47 **p** 48 Niag. R of St Martin Niag 47-52; Welland 52-60; Can of Niag 59-63; R of St Catharines 60-63; Dean and R of Ch Ch Cathl, Hamilton 63-73; Archd of Niag from 73; R of Beamsville Dio Niag from 73. *Box 280, Beamsville, Ont., Canada.* (416-563 7338)

BAGNALL, Harry. SOC 64. **d** 67 **p** 68 Sheff. C of Goole 67-70; St Leon and St Jude Doncaster 70-72; C-in-c of New Cantley Conv Distr Doncaster 72-79; Chap in the Falkland Is from 79. *Deanery, Port Stanley, Falkland Islands.*

BAGNALL, James Newton. Univ of Queensld LTh 1938. **d** and **p** 50 Armid. C of St Pet Cathl Armid 50-54; V of Quirindi 54-60; I of Ch Ch, Geelong 60-64; Home Sec ABM Syd 64-71; L to Offic Dio Syd 66-71; R of Cremorne 71-79; Sen Field Officer Dept of Chr Educn and L to Offic Dio Melb from 79. *24 Kendall Street, Preston, Vic, Australia 3072.*

BAGNALL, Canon John Thomas. b 12. Univ of Leeds BA 34. Coll of Resurr Mirfield 34. **d** 36 **p** 37 S'wark. C of All H S'wark 36-38; St Mary de Castro Leic 38-46; CF (EC) 43-46; CF 46-49; SPG Miss Maur 49-64; Can of Maur 56-64; Hon Can from 64; USPG Area Sec Dios Derby Leic and Southw 65-66; Dios Portsm and Win 66-71; V of St Luke Bournemouth 71-79. *57a Wentworth Avenue, Boscombe, Bournemouth, BH5 2EH.* (Bournemouth 422356)

BAGNALL, Roger. b 15. St Edm Hall Ox BA (3rd cl Hist) 37, MA 41. Linc Th Coll 37. **d** 39 **p** 40 St Alb. C of Hitchin 39-44; Chap RNVR 44-47; C of Kempston 47-51; V of Blackfordby 51-55; V of Smisby 52-55; Elvaston w Thurlaston and Ambaston 55-66; R of Shardlow w Gt Wilne 56-66; V of Ticknal w Calke Dio Derby from 66; RD of Melb 68-78; V of Smisby Dio Derby from 69; P-in-c of Stanton-by-Bridge Dio Derby from 80. *Ticknall Vicarage, Derby, DE7 1JU.* (Melbourne 2549)

✠ **BAGNALL, Right Rev Walter Edward.** Univ of W Ont BA 27. Bp's Univ DCL 56. McMaster Univ LLD 59. Hur Coll LTh 27. Trin Coll Tor DD 54. **d** 27 **p** 28 Hur. C of All SS Windsor 27-28; I of St Mark Lon 28-30; R of St John Preston 30-36; RD of Waterloo 32-36; R of All SS Hamilton 36-40; St Geo St Cath 40-47; Can of Niag 44-48; Dean 48-49; Cons Ld Bp of Niag in Ch Ch Cathl Hamilton 21 Sept 49 by Abp of Ont; Bps of Moos; Ott; Koot; Alg; Caled; Hur; and Tor; Bps Broughall; White; and Jabinski; res 73. *3 St James Place, Hamilton 10, Ont., Canada.*

BAGOT, Harold Duncan. b 02. Univ of Syd BA 26. Moore Th Coll Syd 25. **d** 26 **p** 27 Syd. C of St John Darlinghurst NSW 27-28; Chap Toc H Man 28-30; Publ Pr Dio Man 29-30; Perm to Offic at St Dionis Fulham 30; C of St Geo Cathl Perth W Austr 30-33; St Matt Oxhey (in c of St Francis Broadfield) 33-39; Min of St Francis Conv Distr Broadfield 39-40; PC of H Trin Bedford 40-70; Surr from 47; Commiss Gippsld 55-73; RD of Bedford 62-69. *La Petite Blaye, Alderney, CI.*

BAGOTT, Robert Blakeway. b 25. St Aid Coll 51. **d** 54 Bp Stuart for Worc **p** 55 Worc. C of Gt Malvern 54-56; Bexleyheath 56-59; V of Paddock Wood 59-66; R of Luton Kent 66-77; Chap All SS Hosp Chatham 70-77; R of Dowlishwake w W Dowlish, Chaffcombe, Knowle St Giles w Cricket Malherbie and Kingstone Dio B & W from 77. *Dowlishwake Rectory, Ilminster, Somt.* (Ilminster 3374)

BAGSHAWE, John Allen. b 45. Univ of Dur BA 70, Dipl Th 71. Cranmer Hall Dur 67. **d** 71 York **p** 72 Hull for York. C of Bridlington 71-75; N Ferriby Dio York 75-79; V of St Matt w St Barn Hull Dio York from 79. *St Matthew's Vicarage, Boulevard, Hull, HU3 2TA.* (Hull 26573)

BAGULEY, Henry. b 23. Qu Coll Birm 55. **d** 58 **p** 59 Ches. C of Wilmslow 58-61; V of Kelsall 61-75; St Jas New Brighton Dio Ches from 75. *St James' Vicarage, Victoria Road, New Brighton, Wallasey, Merseyside.* (051-639 5844)

BAGUMA, Agabus. d 78 **p** 79 Ruw. P Dio Ruw. *Box 37, Fort Portal, Uganda.*

BAGUMA, Samuel. Bp Usher-Wilson Coll Buwalasi 64. **d** 66 **p** 67 Ruw. P Dio Ruw; Dioc Regr and Sec from 79. *Box 37, Fort Portal, Uganda.*

BAGUMA, Yustasi. d 78 **p** 79 Ruw. P Dio Ruw. *c/o Box 227, Fort Portal, Uganda.*

BAGYENDERA, Ven Musa. b 16. Can Barham Sch 63. **d** 64 **p** 66 Kig. P Dio Kig 64-81; Dio Kig N from 81; Archd Dio

Kig N from 81. *PO Box 23, Rukungiri, Uganda.*

BAHAGAMYI, Yohana. b 38. **d** 80 Bujumbura. d Dio Bujumbura. *E.P.E.B., B.P. 1300, Bujumbura, Burundi, Africa.*

BAHEMUKA, Ndahura. b 39. Bp Tucker Coll Mukono 72. **d** 74 **p** 75 Boga-Z. P Dio Boga-Z. *BP 154, Bunia, Zaire.*

BAHNAN, Fu'ad Judeh. Near E Sch of Th 49-52. **d** 52 **p** 53 Jer. P Dio Jer. *c/o Dr. Izal Tarmous, Palestine Arab Refugee Office, 801 2nd Avenue, New York 17, N.Y., U.S.A.*

BA HTET, Henry. d 33 **p** 35 Rang. P Dio Rang 33-72. *c/o Cathedral Parsonage, Rangoon, Burma.*

BAI, Canon Jerome Johnson Bede. St Jo Coll Lusaka. **d** 55 **p** 57 Nyasa. P Dio Nyasa 55-64; Dio Malawi 64-71; Dio Lake Malawi from 71; Can of Lake Malawi from 74. *St Mark's Church, PO Likoma, Malawi.*

BAI-MARRO, Samuel. d 66 **p** 67 Sier L. P Dio Sier L. *St James's Church, Port Loko, Sierra Leone.*

BAIGENT, Kempster William. St Jo Coll Auckld LTh (2nd cl) 59. **d** 59 **p** 60 Waik. C of St Geo Frankton 59-62; V of Mangakino 62-65; Paeroa 65-70; Huntly 70-80; Melville Dio Waik from 80. *6 St Luke's Place, Melville, Hamilton, NZ.* (436 332)

BAILES, Kenneth. b 35. Univ of Dur BA 69, Dipl Th 71. **d** 71 York. C of Redcar w Kirkleatham 71-72; Team V 72-74; C-in-c of Appleton Roebuck w Acaster Selby 74-80; P-in-c of Sutton-on-the-Forest Dio York from 80. *Vicarage, Sutton-on-the-Forest, York, YO6 1DW.* (Easingwold 810251)

BAILEY, Alan George. b 10. Qu Coll Cam BA 39, MA 43. Linc Th Coll 39. **d** 40 **p** 41 Bradf. C of Ch Ch Skipton 40-43; St Jo Bapt Croydon 43-48; PC of Selsdon 48-55; R of Gt Mongeham 55-60; R of Ripple 56-60; Hon C of Walmer 61-68; St Clem I and Dio Barb 73-78. *15 Mullings Court, Dollar Street, Cirencester, Glos, G17 2AW.*

BAILEY, Alan George. b 40. Ripon Hall Ox 62. **d** 64 Warrington for Liv **p** 65 Liv. C of H Trin Formby 64-67; Up Holland 67-70; C-in-c of St Dunstan, Edge Hill 70-74; V 74-81; RD of Toxteth 78-81. *Address temp unknown.*

BAILEY, Andrew Henley. b 57. AKC 78. Sarum Wells Th Coll 79. **d** 80 **p** 81 Win. C of Romsey Abbey Dio Win from 80. *7 Queen's Close, Romsey, Hants, SO5 8EG.*

BAILEY, Andrew John. b 37. Trin Coll Cam 3rd cl Cl Trip pt i 59, BA (3rd cl Th Trip pt ii) 61. Ridley Hall Cam 60. **d** 63 **p** 64 York. C of Drypool 63-66; Melton Mowbray 66-69; M Skelmersdale Ecumen Centre 69-79; V of Langley Mill Dio Derby from 79. *214 Cromford Road, Langley Mill, Nottingham, NG16 4HB.* (Langley Mill 2441)

BAILEY, Anthony. b 27. St D Coll Lamp BA (2nd cl Hist) 51. Ely Th Coll 51. **d** 53 **p** 54 Chelmsf. C of Barkingside 53-55; Chap W Buckland Sch 55-59; R of Machen w Rudry 59-66; Chap Bris Cathl Sch and Min Can of Bris Cathl from 66; Succr from 68. *18 Codrington Road, Bristol, BS7 8ET.* (Bristol 44253)

BAILEY, Anthony Deans. b 09. St Edm Hall Ox BA 33. Linc Th Coll 33. **d** 34 **p** 35 Linc. C of Frodingham 34-37; All SS Cathl Salisbury S Rhod 37-39; Daramombe w Enkeldoorn and Umvuma 39-47; V of St Pet Battersea 47-53; Bellingham 53-60; St Mich AA Abbey Wood Dio S'wark 60-70; V of Barrington 70-74; Hon C of Northrepps, Sidestrand and Roughton 75-78; Perm to Offic Dio Nor from 78. *5 Cliff Drive, Cromer, Norf, NR27 0AW.* (Cromer 513908)

BAILEY, Bertram Arthur. Tyndale Hall Bris 65. **d** 67 **p** 68 B & W. C of St Luke Bath 67-72; Bickenhill w Elmdon 72-73; R of N Tawton (w Bondleigh from 79) Dio Ex from 73; P-in-c of Bondleigh 79. *Rectory, North Tawton, Devon, EX20 2EX.* (N Tawton 270)

BAILEY, Brian Constable. b 36. K Coll Lon and Warm AKC 62. **d** 63 **p** 64 Lon. C of John Keble Ch Mill Hill 63-66; Gt Stanmore 66-69; Gt Marlow (in c of St Mary, Marlow Bottom) 69-72; R of Burghfield 72-81; R of Wokingham Dio Ox from 81. *All Saints' Rectory, Wiltshire Road, Wokingham, Berks, RG11 1TP.* (Wokingham 792797)

BAILEY, Charles Marshal. ACT ThL 56. **d** 55 **p** 56 Bend. C of All SS Cathl Bendigo 55-56; V of Pyramid Hill 57-62; R of Echuca 62-69; Asst C in Dept of Chaplaincies Melb 69-72 and from 74; Chap to Pentridge Gaol Melb 69-72 and from 74; on leave 73-74. *56 Quinn Street, Heidelberg, Vic, Australia 3084.* (03-45 4923)

BAILEY, Clarence Eric Stanley. b 1896. OBE 69. Univ of Edin MB, ChB 31. **d** 74 **p** 80 Antig. C of St John's Cathl Antig from 74. *Nevis Street, Box 70, St John's Antigua, WI.*

BAILEY, Colin Norman. b 47. Sarum Wells Th Coll 71. **d** 74 **p** 75 Bris. C of Filton 74-78; P-in-c of Avonmouth Dio Bris 78-80; V from 80. *St Andrew's Vicarage, Avonmouth, Bristol, BS11 9ES.* (Bristol 822302)

BAILEY, Canon David. b 27. Jes Coll Cam BA 50, MA 55. Westcott Ho Cam 56. **d** 57 **p** 58 Ely. C of Shelford Magna 57-60; Christchurch (in c of St Geo) 60-62; V of Bothenhampton w Walditch 62-69; R of Swanage w Herston Dio Sarum from 69; Can and Preb of Sarum Cathl from 80. *Rectory, Swanage, Dorset.* (Swanage 2916)

BAILEY, David Charles. b 52. Linc Coll Ox BA 75, MA 78, MSc 77. St Jo Coll Nottm BA (Th) 79. **d** 80 **p** 81 Southw. C of St Jo Worksop Dio Southw from 80. *5 Overend Road, Worksop, Notts, S80 1QG.* (0909 485903)

BAILEY, Dennis. b 53. Univ of Nottm BTh 79. St Jo Coll Nottm 77. **d** 79 **p** 80 Liv. C of Netherley Dio Liv from 79. *49 Middlemass Hey, Netherley, Liverpool, L27 7AP.*

BAILEY, Derek Gilbert. b 42. Div Hostel Dub 65. **d** 68 **p** 69 Cork. C of St Luke w St Ann Shandon Cork 68-72; CF from 72. *Ministry of Defence, Bagshot Park, Bagshot, Surrey, GU19 5PL.*

BAILEY, Derek William. b 39. Dipl Th (Lon) 71. Cranmer Hall Dur 64. **d** 67 Warrington for Liv **p** 68 Liv. C of Sutton Lancs 67-69; Chapel-en-le-Frith 69-73; V of Hadfield Dio Derby from 73. *122 Hadfield Road, Hadfield, Hyde, Chesh, SK14 8DR.* (Glossop 2431)

BAILEY, Preb Derrick Sherwin. b 10. ACII 34. Linc Th Coll 40. Univ of Edin PhD 47, DLitt 62. **d** 42 Grimsby for Linc **p** 43 Linc. C of St Mary Mablethorpe and Theddlethorpe St Helen w Theddlethorpe All SS 42-44; St Jo Evang Edin and Angl Chap Edin Univ and Colls 44-51; Angl Lect in Div Moray House Tr Coll Edin 48-51; Centr Lect to C of E Moral Welfare Counc 51-55; Actg Educn Sec 54-55; Study Sec 55-59; Perm to Offic Dio Birm 51-59; R of Lyndon w Manton Martinsthorpe and Gunthorpe 59-62; Preb of Wells Cathl from 62; Can Res 62-74; Chan 62-71; Prec 68-74; Select Pr Univ Cam 63; Exam Chap to Bp of B & W 63-74. *23 Kippax Avenue, Wells, Somt, BA5 2TT.* (Wells 75061)

BAILEY, Douglas Allen. d 71 **p** 73 Pret. C of Potgietersrus 71-80; H Trin Middelburg Dio Pret from 80. *Box 699, Middelburg, Transvaal, S Africa.*

BAILEY, Edward Charles George. b 31. SOC 75. **d** 78 **p** 79 S'wark. C of St John (Southend) Catford Dio S'wark from 78. *69 Coniston Road, Bromley, BR1 4JG.*

BAILEY, Edward Ian. b 35. CCC Cam BA 59, MA 63. Univ of Bris MA 69, PhD 77. Westcott Ho Cam 61. **d** 63 **p** 64 Newc T. C of St Jo Bapt Newc T 63-65; Asst Chap Marlborough Coll 65-68; Perm to Offic Dio Bris 69-70; R of Winterbourne Dio Bris from 70; P-in-c of Winterbourne Down 75-81; RD of Stapleton from 77. *58 High Street, Winterbourne, Bristol, BS17 1JQ.* (Winterbourne 772131)

BAILEY, Edward Peter. b 35. Qu Coll Birm. **d** 62 Southw **p** 63 Bp Gelsthorpe for Southw. C of Ordsall 62-66; Clifton w Glapton (in c of H Trin Clifton) 66-71; V of All H Lady Bay w Bridgford Dio Southw from 71. *Vicarage, 121 Holme Road, West Bridgford, Nottingham.* (Nottm 864817)

BAILEY, Eric Arthur. b 14. AKC 37. **d** 37 **p** 38 S'wark. C of St Geo Mart S'wark 37-39; H Trin Waltham Cross 39-41; St Mary Virg Diss 41-42; CF (EC) 42-43; C of Kingsbury (in c of Hurley and Wood End) 44-45; V of Dordon St Leonards w St Mary Freasley 45-52; R of Londesborough 52-60; C-in-c of Nunburnholme 53-54; R 54-60; C-in-c of Burnby 53-54; R 54-60; V of Gt w L Ouseburn 60-65; V of Marton w Grafton 60-65; Stonegate Dio Chich 65-79; Perm to Offic Dio St E from 79. *Hill End, Sapiston, Bury St Edmunds, Suffolk, IP31 1RR.*

BAILEY, Ernest. b 07. Univ Coll Dur BA 48. St Aid Coll. **d** 49 **p** 50 Dur. C of St Andr w St Anne Auckland 49-53; R of W Rainton 53-59; V of Satley 59-61; Lamesley 61-71. *25 Laburnum Grove, Cleadon, Sunderland, Durham.*

BAILEY, Ernest Athol. St Jo Coll Morpeth. **d** 54 Bp Ash for Newc **p** 56 Newc. C of Largs 54-55; E Maitland 55-56; Taree 56-59; R of Cardiff 59-67; Wallsend 67-74; Aberdeen 74-81; Cessnock w Wollombi Dio Newc from 81. *Rectory, Westcott Street, Cessnock, NSW, Australia.*

BAILEY, Frederick Hugh. b 18. Keble Coll Ox BA 40. Linc Th Coll 40. **d** 42 Grimsby for Linc **p** 43 Linc. C of Boultham 42-49; R of Quarrington w Old Sleaford Dio Linc from 49; Chap of Rauceby Ment Hosp from 49; R of Silk Willoughby Dio Linc from 57. *Quarrington Rectory, Sleaford, Lincs.*

BAILEY, Graham William Francis. St Francis Coll Brisb 77. **d** 79 **p** 80 Brisb. C of St Paul Ipswich Dio Brisb from 79. *56a Thorn Street, Ipswich, Queensland, Australia 4305.* (281 0455)

BAILEY, Harold Edward. b 07. ARICS 29, FRICS 43. Bps' Coll Cheshunt 65. **d** 66 **p** 67 Willesden for Lon. C of Hornsey 66-67; Hazlemere 67-71; Hon C of Friern Barnet 71-74; Perm to Offic Dio Win from 75. *11 Seaway, Milford Road, New Milton, Hants.* (N Milton 617015)

BAILEY, Harry Roberts Lewis. ACT ThL 61. **d** 56 **p** 57 Melb. C of Barrabool 56-59; V of Ivanhoe E 59-61; C of St Jas and St John Melb 61-64; V of Northcote 64-76. *14 Rosamond Crescent, Doncaster, Vic, Australia 3109.* (842-1443)

BAILEY, Ivan John. b 33. Keble Coll Ox BA (2nd cl Engl) 57, MA 65, Dipl Th 58. St Steph Ho Ox. **d** 59 **p** 60 St E. C of All H Ipswich 59-62; Cler Sec CEMS 62-66; V of Cringleford 66-81; Colney 80-81; RD of Humbleyard 73-81; Relig Adv Anglia TV and Bp's Chap for TV and Broadcasting Dio Nor from 81; P-in-c of Kirby Bedon w Bixley Dio Nor from 81. *21 Cranleigh Rise, Eaton, Norwich, NR4 6PQ.* (Nor 53565)

BAILEY, John Ernest. b 32. Univ of Leeds BA (3rd cl Gen) 57. Coll of Resurr Mirfield. **d** 59 **p** 60 Ox. C of Newbury 59-62; P-in-c Bamaga Qnsld 62-63; V of Uffington w Woolstone and Baulking 63-70; C-in-c of Gt w L Oakley 70-72; Chap Centr Hosp Warw Dio Cov from 72. *22 Hill Wootton Road, Leek Wootton, Warwick, Warws. CV35 7QL.*

BAILEY, John Robert. b 40. St Jo Coll Cam BA 62, MA 66. Univ of Nottm MEducn 77. SOC 68. **d** 69 S'wark **p** 70 St Alb. Lon Sec Chr Educn Movement 69-71; Hon C of Wm Temple Ch Abbey Wood 69-70; Markyate 70-71; Relig Educn Adv Lincs 72-80; Publ Pr Dio Linc 73-80. *Address temp unknown.*

BAILEY, Ven Jonathan Sansbury. b 40. Trin Coll Cam 2nd cl Hist Trip pt i 60, BA 2nd cl Hist Trip pt ii 61, 2nd cl Th Trip pt ii 63, MA 65. Ridley Hall, Cam 62. **d** 65 Warrington for Liv **p** 66 Liv. C of Sutton 65-68; St Paul Warrington 68-71; Warden of Marrick Priory Youth Centre Dio Ripon 71-76; V of Wetherby 76-82; Archd of Southend from 82. *144 Alexandra Road, Southend-on-Sea, Essex.* (Southend 45175)

BAILEY, Kenneth Albert. b 25. Chich Th Coll 63. **d** 65 **p** 66 Roch. C of St Aug Gillingham 65-68; St Alb Copnor 68-71; V of St Sav-on-the-Cliff Shanklin 71-78; C-in-c of Lake 76-78; V of St Pet Southsea Dio Portsm from 78. *St Peter's Vicarage, Southsea, Hants.* (Portsm 822786)

BAILEY, Lionel Herman. Selw Coll Cam BA 34, MA 37. Ridley Hall, Cam 34. **d** 36 **p** 37 Sheff. C of Wadsley 36-40; St Marg Ward End 40-45; Dioc Chap and Offg C-in-c of St Nich w St Edw Birm 45-47; St Phil Conv Distr Dorridge 47-67; R of W Coker 67-82. *c/o West Coker Rectory, Yeovil, Somt.*

BAILEY, Peter Robin. b 43. St Jo Coll Dur BA 64. Trin Coll Bris 72. **d** 74 **p** 75 Pet. C of St Columba Corby 74-77; Bishopsworth Dio Bris from 77. *63 Turtlegate Avenue, Withywood, Bristol, BS13 8NN.* (Bristol 641263)

BAILEY, Reginald James. b 04. Worc Ordin Coll 58. **d** 58 **p** 59 B & W. C of Keynsham 58-61; PC of E Hunstspill 61-64; R of Radstock 64-69; C-in-c of Writhlington 64-69. *St Anne's, Brinsea Road, Congresbury, Bristol.* (Yatton 838938)

BAILEY, Richard William. b 38. Univ of Man BSc 59. Ripon Hall Ox 63. **d** 65 Hulme for Man **p** 66 Man. C of Tonge w Breightmet 65-68; Stretford 68-71; R of St Geo Abbey Hey Gorton 71-80; V of E Crompton Dio Man from 80. *St James's Vicarage, East Crompton, Shaw, Oldham, Lancs, OL2 7TE.* (Shaw 847454)

BAILEY, Robert William. b 49. Lich Th Coll 69. **d** 72 **p** 73 Cov. C of Stoke St Mich Cov 72-75; Chap RAF from 75. *c/o Ministry of Defence, Adastral House, WC1.*

BAILEY, Canon Ronald George Bainton. b 07. Late Sizar of Trin Coll Cam BA (Math Trip Sen Opt) 28, MA 37. Wycl Hall Ox 30. **d** 32 **p** 33 Cant. C of Ch Ch Croydon (in c of St Chris from 33) 32-36; Ch Ch Folkestone 36-38; V of Claygate 38-44; Dir and Hon Sec Guildf Dioc Miss Coun 43-44; V of St Helens Lancs 44-60; Proc Conv Liv 50-70; Can of Liv 52-69; Can *Emer* from 74; V and RD of Ormskirk 60-69; V of Wray w Tatham Fells 69-73. *6 Ashbrook Crescent, Church Stretton, Shropshire, SY6 6ER.* (Church Stretton 722974)

BAILEY, Ronald William. b 12. Linc Coll Ox BA (1st cl Chem) 35, BSc 36, MA 45. Ripon Hall Ox 57. **d** 58 **p** 59 Win. C of N Stoneham w Bassett 58-61; V of Lamberhurst 61-77. *Tamarisk, Wagg Drove, Huish Episcopi, Langport, Somt TA10 9ER.* (0458-250103)

BAILEY, Simon Paul. b 55. Univ of Ox BA 77, MA 81. Em Coll Cam BA 80. Westcott Ho Cam 78. **d** 81 Sheff. C of Norton Dio Sheff from 81. *44 Bowshaw View, Batemoor, Sheffield, S8 8FE.* (Sheff 376263)

BAILEY, Stephen. b 39. Univ of Leic BA 61. Clifton Th Coll 61. **d** 62 Stafford for Lich **p** 63 Shrewsbury for Lich. C of All SS Wel 62-66; Rainham Essex 66-69; V of High Ercall 69-75; V of Rowton 69-75; RD of Wrockwardine from 72; V of Good Shepherd w St Jo Evang W Bromwich Dio Lich from 75; P-in-c of St Phil W Bromwich Dio Lich from 80. *4 Bromford Lane, West Bromwich, W Midl, B70 7HP.* (021-553 1140)

BAILEY, Canon Thomas. Angl Th Coll BC LTh 38, BD 52. Univ of BC BA 39. Keble Coll Ox BA (2nd cl Th) 48, MA 52. **d** 38 **p** 39 New Westmr. C of St Sav Vanc 38-39; I of Gibson's Landing w Robert's Creek and Sechelt 39-41; V of St Matt Vanc w St Marg Lochdale and St Andr Broadview 41-42; St Pet w St Matt Vanc 42-44; Chap RCN 44-45; Dean of Residence and Lect in NT at Angl Th Coll of BC 48-51; Prof 51-52; R of Beamsville 52-55; St Barn Vic 55-62; Exam Chap to Bp of BC 58-79; Hon Can of BC 59-79; Regr and Prof Angl Th Coll of BC 62-71; Vanc Sch of Th 71-72; John Albert Hall Lect BC 72-79; Perm to Offic Dio BC from 79. *1770 Keith Place, Victoria, BC, Canada.* (604-598 2758)

BAILEY, Victor Joseph. b 19. K Coll Lon BA and AKC 49. Univ of Lon BMus 50. Cudd Coll 55. **d** 56 **p** 57 Ox. C of Chalfont St Pet 56-59; Perm to Offic Dio Ox from 59; Asst Master and Chap Westmr City Sch 59-68; St Mary's Sch Gerrards Cross 68-69; Hd Master 69-72; Asst Master R Gr Sch High Wycombe 73-78. *St Peter's Lodge, Chalfont St Peter, Gerrards Cross, Bucks.*

BAILEY, William John. b 52. Univ of BC BA 74. Univ of Ox MA 81. Trin Coll Tor 76. **d** 77 **p** 78 Tor. C of St Timothy Scarborough Tor 77-79; I of Salt Spring I Dio BC from 79. *Box 214, Ganges, BC, Canada.*

BAILEY, William Thomas Law. Wycl Coll Tor LTh 69. **d** 69 **p** 70 Tor. I of MacGregor 69-72; R of Glenboro 72-74; Rivers 74-78. *348 Sunset Avenue, Windsor, Ont, Canada.*

BAILIE, James Gibson. b 22. LRCP I 58. St Barn Coll Adel 76. **d** 78 **p** 79 Adel. C of St Chad Fullarton Dio Adel from 78. *9 Fitzroy Terrace, Fitzroy, S Australia 5082.*

BAILLIE, Alistair Hope Pattison. b 50. Loughborough Univ BSc 73. Ripon Coll Cudd 73. **d** 76 **p** 77 Leic. C of St Andr Aylestone 76-79; All SS Leic 79-82; H Spirit City and Dio Leic from 82. *2 Sawday Street, Leicester, LE2 7JW.* (Leic 548710)

BAILLIE, Frederick Alexander. b 21. Open Univ BA 75. Trin Coll Dub and QUB. **d** 55 **p** 56 Connor. C of St Paul Belf 55-59; Dunmurry 59-61; V of All SS Eglantine 61-69; Whiterock 69-74; Hd of S Ch Miss Ballymacarrett 74-79; I of Magheraculmoney Dio Clogh from 79; Dioc Information Officer Dio Clogh from 80. *Rectory, Kesh, Co Fermanagh, N Ireland.* (Kesh 31210)

BAILLIE, John Launcelot. AKC 47. **d** 47 **p** 48 Pontefract for Wakef. C of Elland 47-49; Illingworth 49-52; V of Hightown 52-59; Milborne St Andrew w Dewlish 59-70; Chap at Lima Peru Dio Chile 70-74; V of Felkirk w Brierley 75-80; R of Sudbourne w Orford, Chillesford and Butley 80-82; Iken 80-82. *99 Abbey Road, Leiston, Suff.* (Leiston 830365)

BAILLIE, Terence John. b 46. New Coll Ox BA 69, MA 78. Univ of Man MSc 72. St Jo Coll Nottm 74. **d** 77 Chelmsf **p** 78 Barking for Chelmsf. C of Chadwell Heath 77-80; Bickenhill w Elmdon Dio Birm from 80. *15 Coppice Road, Solihull, W Midl.* (021-704 9461)

BAILY, Canon Robert Spencer Canning. b 21. Late Scho of G and C Coll Cam BA 42, MA 46. Westcott Ho Cam 42. **d** 44 **p** 45 Sarum. C of Sherborne w Castleton and Lillington 44-46; Heacham 46-47; Perm to Offic St Geo Worc 47-48; C of All SS Bedford 48-50; C-in-c of St Edm Yeading Hayes 50-56; R of Blofield w Hemblington 56-69; P-in-c of Perlethorpe Dio Southw from 69; Dir of Educn Dio Southw from 69; Hon Can of Southw Minster from 80. *Chaplain's House, Perlethorpe, Newark, Notts, NG22 9EF.* (Mansfield 822106)

BAILY, Rodney Alexander. b 39. Univ of Bris LLB 61. Westcott Ho Cam 76. **d** 78 **p** 79 Newc T. C of Monkseaton 78-81; Hexham Dio Newc T from 81. *2 Woodside, Hexham, Northumb, NE46 1HU.* (Hexham 605344)

BAILY, Canon Thomas Emmanuel Herbert. b 14. Late Exhib of Or Coll Ox BA (2nd cl Th) 36, MA 40. Qu Coll Birm 37. **d** 37 **p** 38 Derby. C of Norton 37-42; V of Shap w Swindale 42-79; Hon Can of Carl 66-79; Can (Emer) from 79. *58 Stricklandgate, Penrith, Cumbria, CA11 7NJ.*

BAIN, Alan. b 48. Thames Poly BSc 72. St Jo Coll Nottm Dipl Th 75. **d** 77 **p** 78 Wakef. C of St Andr w St Mary 77-81; V of Odd Down Dio B & W from 81. *39 Frome Road, Odd Down, Bath, BA2 2QF.* (Combe Down 832838)

BAIN, David Roualeyn Findlater. b 54. Univ of Bris BA 75. Ripon Coll Cudd 76. **d** 78 **p** 79 S'wark. C of Perry Hill 78-81; Succr of S'wark Cathl from 81. *St Paul's Vicarage, Kipling Street, SE1.* (01-407 8290)

BAIN, Harry. b 55. Univ of W Indies LTh 77. Codr Coll Barb 74. **d** 78 **p** 79 Nass. L to Offic Dio Nass 78-80; R of St Patr Eleuthera Dio Nass from 81. *PO Box 27, Governor's Harbour, Eleuthera, Bahamas, W Indies.*

BAIN, John Stuart. b 55. Van Mildert Coll Dur BA 77. Westcott Ho Cam 78. **d** 80 **p** 81 Dur. C of H Trin Washington Dio Dur from 80. *101 Roche Court, Glebe, Washington, T & W.* (Washington 473887)

BAIN, Michael Chamberlin Learmonth. b 44. St Jo Coll Morpeth. **d** and **p** 70 Bath. C of H Trin Orange 70-73; R of W Dubbo Dio Bath from 74. *Rectory, Dubbo, NSW, Australia.* (068-82 1978)

BAINBRIDGE, John Richard. b 35. Pemb Coll Cam BA 59, MA 63. Clifton Th Coll 65. **d** 67 Crediton for Ex **p** 68 Ex. C of St Leon Ex 67-70; C-in-c of St Paul, Penge 70-73; Chap Uppingham Sch from 73. *48 High Street West, Uppingham, Rutland, LE15 9QD.* (Uppingham 3243)

BAINBRIDGE, Norman Harold. b 15. St Jo Coll Dur LTh 38. ALCD 38. **d** 38 **p** 39 S'wark. C of Morden 38-46; CF (EC) 43-46; Men in Disp 43; V of St Matt Bayswater 46-58; St Jas Muswell Hill 58-66; St Jo Evang Boscombe 66-80. *18 Stileham Bank, Milborne St Andrew, Blandford Forum, Dorset, DT11 32)*

BAINES, John Edmund. b 22. Down Coll Cam 2nd cl Engl Trip pt i 47, BA 47, 2nd cl Hist Trip pt ii 48, MA 50. Univ of Lon BD (2nd cl) 51. **d** 58 Pontefract for Wakef **p** 59 Wakef.

C of Penistone 58-60; V of St Thos Batley 60-69; Cawthorne Dio Wakef from 69. *Vicarage, Cawthorne, Barnsley, S Yorks, S75 4HP.* (Barnsley 8235)

BAINES, Noel Edward. b 29. St Jo Coll Dur BSc 52, Dipl Th 54, MA 62. **d** 54 **p** 55 Chelmsf. C of Rainham 54-58; Ch Ch Surbiton Hill (in c of Em Tolworth) 58-61; V of St Matt Southborough 61-67; St Jo Bapt Beckenham 67-74; Asst Master Taunton Manor High Sch Coulsdon from 74; L to Offic Dio Roch from 78. *10 Bromley Avenue, Bromley, Kent.* (01-460 8256)

BAINES, Canon Roger Holford. b 07. St Jo Coll Cam 2nd cl Hist Trip pt i 27, BA (3rd cl Th Trip pt i) 29, MA 32. Westcott Ho Cam 29. **d** 30 **p** 31 Cov. C of Chilvers Coton 30-33; Rugby (in c of St John) 33-35; CMS Miss Nyakasura 35-37; Masindi 37-39; C-in-c of Epiph Gipton Leeds 39-43; PC of St Mary Beeston 43-47; V of St Pet Harrogate 47-66; RD of Knaresborough 54-66; Hon Can of Ripon 55-66; Can (Emer) from 66; L to Offic Dio Heref from 68. *Barn House, Ashford Bowdler, Ludlow, Shropshire, SY8 4DJ.* (Richard's Castle 602)

BAINTON, Alex Peter. b 49. St Barn Coll Adel ACT ThDip 77. **d** 76 Bp Renfrey for Adel **p** 77 Adel. C of Toorak Gardens 76-78; Edwardstown 78; R of Kangaroo I Dio Adel from 79. *Box 87, Kingscote, S Australia 5223.* (2 2065)

BAIRD, Canon Duncan. b 05. Univ of Dur 28. St Aid Coll 28. **d** 31 **p** 32 Ches. C of St Pet Birkenhead 31-34; Bollington (in c of St Osw) 34-38; V of Wharton 38-45; CF (EC) 40-45; Hon CF 45; V of Werneth (or Compstall) 45-56; Hyde Chesh 56-67; Alvanley 67-71; Hon Can of Ches 62-71; Can (Emer) from 71; RD of Mottram 63-67. *76 Manley Road, Sale, Cheshire.*

BAIRD, Edward Simpson. b 17. BD (Lon) 58. Sarum Th Coll. **d** 55 **p** 56 Dur. C of S Westoe S Shields 55-58; V of Swalwell 58-66; R of Harrington 66-75; V of Peel Green w Barton 75-80; R of Ch Ch Jarrow Grange Dio Dur from 80. *Christ Church Rectory, Clayton Street, Jarrow, T & W.* (Jarrow 897227)

BAIRD, Iain Peter. Sir Geo Williams Univ Montr BA 60. McGill Univ Montr BD 63. Montr Dioc Th Coll LTh 63. **d** 63 New Westmr. Miss Columb Coast Miss 63-65. C of St Phil Vanc 65-66; Chap Miss to Seamen Vanc Dio New Westmr 66-69; on study leave. *6050 Chancellor Boulevard, Vancouver 8, BC, Canada.*

BAIRD, Canon Leonard Johnston. Bp's Univ Lennox BA 46. **d** 46 Ott. PC of St John Smith Falls 46-48; I of Mattawa 48-50; C of St Matt Ott 50-54; R of Port Hope 54-57; St Geo Ott 57-61; I of St Pet Carlington Ott 61-67; R of St Thos, City and Dio Ott from 67; Exam Chap to Bp of Ott from 72; Can of Ott from 72. *2345 Alta Vista Drive, Ottawa 8, Ont., Canada.* (1-613-731-9249)

BAIRD, William Stanley. b 33. Trin Coll Dub BA (2nd cl Mod in Mental and Moral Sc) 54. **d** 56 **p** 57 Leigh. C of Carlow 56-59; I of Dunganstown 59-64; C of St Columba Knock Belf 64-69; C-in-c of Kilwarlin 69-71; R 71-72; Warden Ch Ministry of Healing, Ireland 72-79; R of Drumcondra w N Strand and St Barn City and Dio Dub from 79. *74 Grace Park Road, Drumcondra, Dublin 9, Irish Republic.* (Dublin 372505)

BAISLEY, George. b 45. Sarum Wells Th Coll 78. **d** 80 **p** 81 Glouc. C of St Geo Lower Tuffley City and Dio Glouc from 80. *3 Rylands, Tuffley, Gloucester, GL4 0QA.*

BAITWA, Yosamu. **d** 64 Ankole-K. d dio Ankole-K 64-67; Dio Ank from 67. *Church of Uganda, Rukoni, Ankole, Uganda, E Africa.*

BAJI, Dunstan. b 45. St Mark's Coll Dar-S 77. **d** 79 Zanz T **p** 80 Bp Russell for Zanz T. P Dio Zanz T. *PO Box 57, Muheza, Tanga Region, Tanzania.*

BAKAITWAKO, Edward. b 46. Bp Tucker Coll Mukono Dipl Th 72. **d** 72 **p** 73 Kig. P Dio Kig. *Kigizi College Butobere, Box 90, Kabale, Kigezi, Uganda.*

BAKAJWARA, Yonasani. Bp Tucker Coll Mukono. **d** 53 **p** 56 Ugan. P Dio Ugan 53-60; Dio Ruw 60-79. *PO Kyegegwa, Uganda.*

BAKAMWANGA, Kesi. Bp Tucker Coll Mukono 60. **d** 60 **p** 62 Ankole-K. P Dio Ankole-K 60-67; Dio Ank 67-76; Dio W Ank 77-80. *PO Rubaare, Ankole, Uganda.*

BAKARE, Ven Samuel Omokehinde. **d** 44 **p** 45 Lagos. P Dio Lagos 44-53; Dio Ibad from 53; Hon Can of Ibad 62-65; Can 65-76; Archd of Oyo from 76. *PO Box 23, Oyo, Nigeria.*

BAKARE, Sebastian. **d** 61 **p** 63 N Rhod. P Dio N Rhod 61-63; Dio Zam 63-70; Dio N Zam 71-76. *St Michael's Church, Kitwe, Zambia.*

BAKARE, Canon Solomon Taiwo Asani. **d** 52 **p** 53 Ondo-B. P Dio Ondo-B 52-62; Dio Ondo 62-66; P Dio Ekiti from 66; Can of Ekiti from 73. *St John's Vicarage, Ilupeju-Ekiti, Nigeria.*

BAKARI, Aidano. St Cypr Th Coll Tunduru. **d** 57 **p** 61 Masasi. P Dio Masasi. *USPG, Lindi, Tanzania.*

BAKENGA, Yona. Bp Tucker Coll Mukono 59. **d** 61 **p** 63 W Bugan. P Dio W Bugan from 61. *Church of Uganda, Bukwiri, P.O. Kiboga, Uganda.*

BAKER, Alan Ormond. Ridley Coll Melb 59. ACT ThL 62. **d** 62 Melb **p** 63 Bp Sambell for Melb. C of Ivanhoe 62-64; P-in-c of Timboon 64-67; V 67-69; R of Nightcliff 69-71; I of Lilydale 71-75; St Mark E Brighton Dio Melb from 75. *721 Hawthorn Road, East Brighton, Vic, Australia 3187.* (03-92 1450)

BAKER, Albert George. b 30. Qu Coll Birm. **d** 61 **p** 62 S'wark. C of Merton 61-64; Limpsfield 64-65; Chapel-en-le-Frith (in c of St Paul Dove Holes) 65-68; R of Odd Rode 68-76; V of Holme Cultram 76-78; R of Blofield w Hemblington Dio Nor from 78. *Blofield Rectory, Stocks Lane, Norwich, NR13 4JZ.* (Norwich 713160)

BAKER, Alfred gordon. Univ of Tor Mus Bac 54. Wycl Coll Tor LTh 54, BD 58. Hur Coll Hon DD 66. **d** 54 Tor for NS **p** 54 NS. C of Ch of Transfig Tor 54-56; R of Uxbridge 56-58; Ed 'Canadian Churchman' 58-67; P-in-c of H Trin Oshawa 58-63; St Chad Tor 63-66; R of Bp Cronyn Mem Ch Lon 67; Can of Hur 70-76; Archd of Middx 76-78; Archd Without Jurisd 78-80; Prin Coll of Em and St Chad Sktn 78-80; R of Grace Ch-on-the-Hill City and Dio Tor from 80. *300 Lonsdale Road, Toronto, Ont, Canada, M4V 1X4.* (416-488 7884)

BAKER, Alfred Searcy Kendall. b 04. St Barn Coll Adel 26. ACT ThL 29. **d** 29 Adel for Willoch **p** 30 Willoch. C of Port Linc 29-31; P-in-c of Franklin Harbour Miss 31-32; Solomontown 33-34; Perm to Offic (Col Cl Act) at Our Lady of Mercy and St Thos of Cant Gorton 34-35; C of St Mary Usk 35-37; C of St Mark Noel Pk 37-40; CF (EC) 40-45; Hon CF 46; V of St Geo 45-49; Asst Hosp St Bart Hosp Lon 49-53; V of Wotton Underwood w Ashendon 53-56; R of Bradenham 56-71; Perm to Offic Dio Mon 71-79. *Inglenook, Abergavenny Road, Usk, Gwent, NP5 1SB.* (Usk 2569)

BAKER, Anthony Peter. b 38. Late Scho of Hertf Coll Ox BA (2nd cl Mod Hist) 59, MA 63. Clifton Th Coll 60. **d** 63 **p** 64 Ox. C of St Ebbe Ox 63-66; St Jo Evang Welling (in c of Bp Ridley Ch) 66-70; V of Redland 70-79; Ch Ch Beckenham Dio Roch from 79; Lect Tyndale Hall Bris 70-71; Trin Coll Bris 71-77. *Christ Church Vicarage, 18 Court Downs Road, Beckenham, Kent, BR3 2LR.* (01-650 3847)

BAKER, Arthur Alan. b 20. Univ of Edin MA 42, BD 47. Edin Th Coll 42. **d** 44 **p** 45. St Andr Chap of St Ninian's Cath Perth 44-48. C of St Pet Eaton Square Lon 48-50; Taunton 50-52; Newc L 52-55; Min of Conv Distr of St Andr Westlands 55-59; R of St Andr Kelso 59-72; Hd of RE Dept Magdalen Coll Sch Brackley 72-80; L to Offic Dio Pet 72-80; Chap Heathfield Sch Ascot from 80. *Heathfield School, Ascot, Berks.*

BAKER, Barry John. Trin Coll Tor BA 55, LTh and STB 58. **d** 57 **p** 58 Niag. R of Grimsby Beach 57-61; Ch Ch St Catharines 61-64; Chap Trin Coll Sch Port Hope 64-69. *PO Box 60, Sault Ste Marie, Ont., Canada.* (705-253-4620)

BAKER, Canon Bernard George Coleman. BD (Lon) 61. Oak Hill Th Coll 61. **d** 63 **p** 64 Chich. C of Broadwater 63-66; BCMS Miss P Dio Moro 66-79; Hon Can of Moro from 77; V of St Marg Moshi Dio Centr Tang from 79. *Box 306, Moshi, Tanzania.*

BAKER, Brian Ernest Harry. b 38. Sarum Wells Th Coll 74. **d** 76 **p** 77 Lich. C of Cannock 76-79; Penkridge w Stretton 79; Dunston w Coppenhall 79-80; P-in-c of Earl Stonham w Stonham Parva and Creeting Dio St E from 80. *Earl Stonham Rectory, Stowmarket, Suff.* (Stonham 347)

BAKER, Cherie Violet Dorothy. b 28. **d** 74 **p** 77 Wai. Hon C of Gisborne 74-77; C 77-80; V of Riverslea Dio Wai from 80. *703 Windsor Avenue, Hastings, NZ.* (85-889)

BAKER, David Clive. b 47. Sarum Wells Th Coll 76. **d** 78 **p** 79 Birm. C of Shirley 78-82; R of Wainfleet Dio Linc from 82; P-in-c of St Mary Wainfleet Dio Linc from 82; Croft Dio Linc from 82. *St Mary's Vicarage, Vicarage Lane, Wainfleet St Mary's, Skegness, Lincs.* (0754-880401)

BAKER, David Frederick. b 32. Clifton Th Coll 67. **d** 69 Knaresborough for Ripon **p** 70 Ripon. C of Bilton 69-71; H Trin Heworth w St Cuthb Peaseholme, York 71-75; V of Sand Hutton w Gate and U Helmsley (w Bossall and Buttercrambe from 77) 75-79; C-in-c of Bossall w Buttercrambe 75-77; R of Preston-in-Holderness (w Sproatley from 80) Dio York from 79; P-in-c of Sproatley 79-80. *Preston Rectory, Hull, HU12 8TB.* (Hull 898375)

BAKER, David James. St D Coll Lamp BA 62. Linacre Ho Ox BA 64, MA 68. St Steph Ho Ox 62. **d** 65 **p** 66 Newc T. C of St Jo Bapt Newc T 65-69; Leigh-on-Sea 69-73; L to Offic Dio Nor 73-78; V of St Alb Hull Dio York from 78. *264 Cottingham Road, Hull, HU6 8QA.* (0482-42391)

BAKER, David John. b 27. LRAM 50. GRSM 51. Ely Th Coll 53. **d** 55 **p** 56 Roch. C of St Mary Virg Swanley 55-58; St Nich Guildf 58-63; Prec of St Alb Cathl 63-67; PC of St Pet-le-Poer Muswell Hill Dio Lon 67-68; V 68-73; Tattenham

Corner and Burgh Heath Dio Guildf from 73. *Vicarage, St Mark's Road, Tattenham Corner, Epsom, Surrey.* (Burgh Heath 53011)

BAKER, David Jordan. b 35. St D Coll Lamp BA 59. Ely Th Coll 59. **d** 61 **p** 62 Linc. C of Spalding 61-66; Gainsborough 66-69; V of Wrawby 69-78; V of Melton Ross w New Barnetby 69-78; St Pet-at-Gowts & St Andr City and Dio Linc from 78. *St Peter's Vicarage, Sibthorp Street, Lincoln.* (Linc 30256)

BAKER, Donald Alex. b 08. K Coll Lon and Warm 54. **d** and **p** 59 S'wark. C of Beddington 59-62; R of Burstow 62-74; Chap Beechfield Remand Home Copthorne 74-77. *1 Westview, Peeks Lane, Fernhill, Horley, Surrey, RH6 9ST.*

BAKER, Donald Shearsmith. b 09. TD 46. St Aug Coll Cant. **d** 59 Dover for Cant **p** 60 Cant. C of Margate 59-63; R of Emley 63-75; Perm to Offic Dio Cant 75-78; Dio Chich from 79; Chap Shoreham Coll from 80. *8 Montague Court, Rectory Road, Shoreham-on-Sea, BN4 6EL.* (Brighton 595979)

BAKER, Douglas Arthur. b 17. Dipl Th (Lon) 42. St Andr Coll Pampisford 49. **d** 49 Kens for Lon **p** 50 Lon. [f Bapt Min] C of Harlesden 49-51; Palmers Green 51-54; R of Empangeni 54-57; Bremersdorp 57-60; V of St Aug Brinksway w Cheadle Heath 60-67; Hooton Pagnell Doncaster 67-72; C-in-c of Hickleton 71-72; R of Kirby Underdale w Bugthorpe 72-80; RD of Pocklington 76-80; R of Normanby w Edston and Salton Dio York from 80. *Normanby Rectory, Sinnington, York, YO6 6RH.* (Kirkbymoorside 31288)

BAKER, Edward Alfred. b 1900. Chich Th Coll 26. **d** 28 **p** 29 Sheff. C of Rawmarsh 28-32; St Mich AA Yeovil 32-42; PC of Tuckhill Dio Heref 42-69; V 69-76; w Pastoral Care from 76. *c/o Tuckhill Vicarage, Bridgnorth, Salop.* (Quatt 297)

BAKER, Eric Paul. New Coll Ox BA (2nd cl Mod Hist) 28, MA 32. Westcott Ho Cam 31. **d** 33 **p** 34 Portsm. C of Fareham 33-37; Hon Chap to Bp of Portsm 34-36; C of Cathl Ch Portsm 37-39; St Jude Birm 40; St Jas Shirley 41-44; R of Heyford Warren 44-54; V of Gt Milton Dio Ox from 54; C-in-c of L Milton 61-81. *Great Milton Vicarage, Oxford, OX9 7BP.* (Gt Milton 221)

BAKER, Frank Thomas. b 36. Selw Coll Cam BA 61. Coll of Resurr, Mirfield. **d** 63 **p** 64 Derby. C of St Francis Mackworth 63-66; C and Prec of Leeds 66-73; R of Crook 73-74; C-in-c of Stanley 73-74; Chap at Bucharest 74-75; C of Tewkesbury 75-81; Min Can of Coll of St Geo Windsor Castle from 81. *College of St George, Windsor Castle, Berks.*

BAKER, Frederick Leonard. b 06. K Coll Lon and Warm 58. **d** 59 **p** 60 Ex. C of Brixham 59-61; V of Coleford 61-69; R of Heyford Warren w Lower Heyford and Rousham 69-75; Perm to Offic Dio Ex from 76. *42 Ridgeway Road, Aller Park, Newton Abbot, Devon, TQ12 4LS.* (Newton Abbot 5444)

BAKER, Frederick Peter. b 24. Bps' Coll Cheshunt 58. **d** 60 **p** 61 S'wark. C of St Chrys Peckham 60-63; St Mark Mitcham 63-66; St Pet Northn 66-69; C-in-c of St Lawr Northn 69-71; V of St Edm Northn 71-78; Spratton Dio Pet from 78. *Spratton Vicarage, Northampton, NN6 8HR.* (Northn 847212)

BAKER, Geoffrey Gorton. b 26. Chich Th Coll 63. **d** 65 **p** 66 Win. C of St Mark Evang Jersey Dio Win 65-66; V 66-73; Tutor Vic Coll Jersey 73-80; Chap HM Pris Jersey from 80. *La Rousse, Le Bourg, St Clement, Jersey, CI.*

BAKER, Canon George Arden. b 10. St Jo Coll Dur LTh 33, BA 34. ALCD 32. **d** 33 **p** 34 S'wark. C of St Mich AA Southfields 33-36; St John Tunbridge Wells 36-38; C-in-c of Conv Distr Ch Ch Orpington 38-40; V 40-42; V of St Mary Ide Hill 42-46; Org Sec for Metrop Distr of CPAS 46-48; V of Ch Ch Barnet 48-57; Reigate 57-77; Surr 58-77; RD of Reigate 62-71; Hon Can of S'wark 66-77; Can (Emer) from 77; Perm to Offic Dio Roch from 77. *Finches, Ide Hill, Sevenoaks, Kent.* (Ide Hill 470)

BAKER, George Stanley. OBE 71. Codr Coll Barb BA 26, MA 31. **d** 25 **p** 26 Antig. C of St Jo Cathl Antig 25-30; R of Anguilla 30-36; St Thos St Kitts 36-37; St John's Cathl I and Dio Antig from 37; Exam Chap to Bp of Antig 37-44; Can of St John's Cathl Antig 37-43; Sub-Dean 39-43; Dean 43-70; Dioc Regr 54-57; Exam Chap to Bp of Antig 71-74. *St Michael's School, Redcliffe Street, St John's, Antigua, W Indies.*

BAKER, Canon Gerald Stothert. b 30. Univ of NZ MA 54. St Jo Coll Auckld LTh 56. **d** 56 **p** 57 Waik. C of Morrinsville 56-59; V of Mokau 59-61; Paeroa 61-65; Huntly 65-70; Stratford Dio Waik from Paeroa 61-65; Huntly 65-70; Stratford 70-73; Exam Chap to Bp of Waik 70-73; V of Karori City and Dio Wel from 73; Hon Can of Wel from 80. *8 Fancourt Street, Karori, Wellington, NZ.* (767-492)

BAKER, Canon Gerrard Andrewes. St Jo Coll Armid ACT ThL 21. **d** 24 **p** 25 Armid. C of Bukkulla 24; Glen Innes 24-28; Armidale 28-30; V of W Tamworth 30-69; RD of Tamworth 47-69; Hon Can of Armid 54-66; Can (Emer) from 66; L to Offic Dio Armid from 69. *PO Box 109, Tamworth, NSW, Australia 2340.*

BAKER, Very Rev Grahame Brinkworth. K Coll Lon and Warm AKC 54. ARCanadCO 59. **d** 55 **p** 56 S'wark. C of St Anne Wandsworth 55-58; Ch Ch Cathl Vanc 58-65; R of St John Vic 65-77; Hon Can of New Westmr 64-65; Ch Ch Cathl Vic 71-77; Dean and R of St Geo Cathl Kingston Dio Ont from 77; Admin and Bp's Commiss Dio Ont from 80. *Box 475, Kingston, Ont, Canada.* (613-548 4808)

BAKER, Harry Hallas. b 16. FPS 54. Bps' Coll Cheshunt 51. **d** 53 **p** 54 Newc T. C of Killingworth 53-58; V of Mickley 58-63; Howdon Panns 63-73; Asst P of Alnwick Dio Newc T from 73. *Clergy House, Canongate, Alnwick, Northumb, NE66 1ND.* (Alnwick 602411)

BAKER, Henry Edward. b 09. Univ of Bris BA 31. Sarum Th Coll 31. **d** 32 Malmesbury for Bris **p** 33 Bris. C of St Aug Swindon 32-35; St Osw Bedminster Down 35-38; V of Hullavington 38-51; Norton 48-51; All SS Fishponds 51-59; Neston 59-66; Bitton 66-69; C of Kingswood 69-74; Perm to Offic Dio Bris from 75. *The Curatage, 285 North Street, Bristol, BS3 1JP.* (Bristol 634110)

BAKER, Hugh John. b 46. Univ of Birm BSocSc 68. Univ of Nottm Dipl Th 69. Cudd Coll 69. **d** 71 **p** 72 Cov. C of St Bart, Binley w Coombe Fields, Cov 71-74; St Mark Newtown Pemberton 74-77; Team V of Sutton Dio Liv from 78. *St Michaels Vicarage, Gartons Lane, Sutton Manor, St Helens, Mer 13738)*

BAKER, Ivon Robert. b 28. St Aug Coll Cant 59. **d** 60 **p** 61 Southw. C of Sutton-in-Ashfield 60-62; V of Gringley-on-the-Hill Dio Southw from 62; Chap HM Detention Centre Gringley from 62. *Gringley-on-the-Hill Vicarage, Doncaster, S Yorks, DN10 4QP.* (0777-817237)

BAKER, James Henry. b 39. b 39. Kelham Th Coll 62. Dipl Th (Lon) 66. **d** 67 **p** 68 Sheff. C of St Paul Arbourthorne Sheff 67-70; St John Pemberton w St Francis, Kitt Green 70-71; Chap and Prec Edin Cathl 71-74; R of Lochgelly w Ballingry Dio St Andr from 74; P-in-c of Rosyth Dio St Andr from 76; Inverkeithing Dio St Andr from 76. *St Finnian's Rectory, Foulford Road, Cowdenbeath, Fife.* (Cowdenbeath 510002)

BAKER, John Albert. b 29. St Edm Hall Ox BA (2nd cl Engl Lit) 52, MA 56. BSc (2nd cl Sociology) Lon 68, Council for Nat Acad Awards MSc 76. Cudd Coll 52. **d** 54 **p** 55 S'wark. C of St Luke Battersea 54-58; Richmond 58-62; V of All SS Battersea Pk Dio S'wark from 62. *Vicarage, Prince of Wales Drive, SW11 4BD.* (01-622 3809)

✠ **BAKER, Right Rev John Austin.** b 28. Oriel Coll Ox 3rd cl Cl Mods 50, BA (1st Cl Th) 52, Bp Fraser Scho 52-53, MA 55, BLitt 55. Cudd Coll 52. **d** 54 Buckingham for Cant **p** 55 Ox. C of Cuddesdon and Tutor Cudd Coll 54-57; C of Hatch End and Lect in Th K Coll Lon 57-59; Fell, Chap and Lect in Div CCC Ox 59-73; Lect in Th BNC and Linc Coll Ox 59-73; Exam Chap to Bp of Ox 60-78; to Bp of S'wark 73-78; M Abp's Comm on Christian Doctrine 67-81: Lect in Hebr Ex Coll Ox 68-73; Can of Westmr 73-82; Sub-Dean 78-82; R of St Marg Westmr 78-82; Chap to Speaker of Ho of Commons 78-82; Cons Ld Bp of Salisbury in Westmr Abbey 2 Feb 82 by Abp of Cant; Bps of Lon, Win, Portsm, Birm, Bris, Derby, Ely, Ex, Chelmsf, Glouc, Lich, Ox, St Alb, Southw and Truro; Bps Suffr of Barking, Basingstoke, Bedford, Crediton, Bradwell, Croydon, Colchester, Edmon, Grantham, Hull, Maidstone, Ramsbury, Sherborne, Sherwood, Shrewsbury, Southn, Stockport and Willesden; and Bps Coggan, Knapp-Fisher, Hodson, Patterson, Woollcombe, Claxton and others. *South Canonry, The Close, Salisbury, Wilts, SP1 2ER.* (Salisbury 4031)

BAKER, John Carl. b 55. Chich Th Coll 77. **d** 80 **p** 81 Liv. C of St Andr Wigan Dio Liv from 80. *55 Dumbarton Green, Beech Hill, Wigan, WN6 7NY.*

BAKER, Canon John Charles Theodore. b 02 Ex Coll Ox BA 25, MA 46. Ridley Hall Cam 25. **d** 26 **p** 27 Bradf. C of Cathl Ch Bradf 26-30; Bingley 30-32; V of Morton Yorks 32-36; Ingrow w Hainworth 36-42; RD of S Craven 41-42; V of All SS Little Horton Bradf 42-49; R of Linton-in-Craven w Hebden 49-62; Chap Grassington Sanat 49-62; Hon Can of Bradf from 56; Dioc Insp of Schs 56-71; V of Waddington 62-67; RD of Bolland 62-67; R of Leathley w Farnley 67-71; Dir of Relig Educn Dio Bradf 67-73. *20 Grassington Road, Skipton, N Yorks, BD23 1LL.* (Skipton 4496)

✠ **BAKER, Right Rev John Gilbert Hindley.** Late Exhib of Ch Ch Ox BA (2nd cl Hist) 32, MA 46. Westcott Ho Cam 34. **d** 35 **p** 36 Vic. C of Ch of Our Sav Canton 35-39; St John Kunming Dio Vic 39-45; Perm to Offic at St Martin-in-the-Fields Lon 46; Chap of St John's Univ and Tutor Centr Th Coll Shanghai 47-49; Tutor Union Th Coll Canton 49-51; in Amer Ch 52-55; Gen Sec Overseas Coun of Ch Assembly 55-63; V of St Nich Cole Abbey Lon 55-66; Commiss Kuch and Jess 63-66; Cons Ld Bp of Hong Kong in St John's Cathl Hong Kong 6 Dec 66 by Bps of Jess; Kuch; Taejon; Taiwan (USA); Bp Cabanban (Philippine Episc Ch); and Bp de Los Reyes (Philippine Ind Ch); res 81. *Orchard End, Nower Road, Dorking, Surrey.*

BAKER, John Martin Luther. b 36. E Centr State Coll Okla BA 64. Phillips Univ Okla MDiv 68. **d** and **p** 75 BC. C of Nanaimo 75-76; R of View R 76-79; Transfig St Catherines Dio Niag from 79. *84 Masterton Drive, St Catherines, Ont, Canada L2T 3P9.*

BAKER, John Patrick. b 36. St Jo Coll Ox BA 59, MA 63. BD (1st cl) Lon 61. Tyndale Hall Bris 59. **d** and **p** 63 Glouc. C of St Mark Cheltm 63-69; St Mark, Gillingham 69-73; R of Newick Dio Chich from 73. *Rectory, Church Road, Newick, Nr Lewes, E Sussex, BN8 4JX.*

BAKER, Kenneth Francis. Moore Th Coll Syd ACT ThL 57. **d** and **p** 58 Bp Hilliard for Syd. C of Carlingford 58-60; R of Blacktown 60-67; Earlwood 67-72; Mittagong 72-77; St Steph Coorparoo City and Dio Brisb from 77. *349 Cavendish Road, Coorparoo, Queensland, Australia 4151.* (397 0555)

BAKER, Lancelot Fagge. b 05. AKC 29. **d** 29 **p** 30 Lon. C of St Simon Bethnal Green 29-30; St Paul Bow Common 31-32; R of Ch Ch Rawdon Montr 32; I of St Pet Hemaruka Qu'App 33-36; Asst Master Ravensfield Coll Hendon 38-43; Hdmaster Cannock Sch 44-73; Actg Chap Huggens Coll 75-78; Hon C of Chelsfield Dio Roch from 79. *Fairview, Chelsfield Lane, Orpington, Kent.* (Orpington 27568)

BAKER, Michael Robert Henry. b 39. Lich Th Coll 63. **d** 66 **p** 67 Pet. C of All SS Wellingborough 66-68; All SS (in c of Dogsthorpe), Pet 68-73; V of Earls Barton Dio Pet from 73; RD of Wellingborough from 76; P-in-c of Gt Doddington 77-82; Surr from 78. *Earl's Barton Vicarage, Northampton, NN6 0JG.* (Northampton 810447)

BAKER, Michael William. b 38. Roch Th Coll 68. **d** 70 **p** 71 S'wark. C of Woodmansterne 70-75; Chap Chelmsf and Essex Hosp 75-78; C of Danbury 75-78; P-in-c of Shepreth Dio Ely from 78; Barrington Dio Ely from 78. *4 Church Road, Shepreth, Royston, Herts, SG8 6RG.* (Royston 60172)

BAKER, Neville Duff. b 35. St Aid Coll 60. **d** 63 Jarrow for Dur **p** 64 Dur. C of Stranton 63-66; Houghton-le-Spring 66-68; V of Tudhoe Grange Dio Dur from 68. *Vicarage, Barnfield Road, Spennymoor, Co Durham.* (Spennymoor 814817)

BAKER, Noel Edward Lloyd. b 37. Sarum Wells Th Coll 73. **d** 75 Tewkesbury for Glouc **p** 76 Glouc. C of St Mary Charlton Kings 75-79; P-in-c of Clearwell 79-81; R of Eastington w Frocester Dio Glouc from 81. *Eastington Rectory, Stonehouse, Glos, GL10 3SG.* (Stonehouse 2437)

BAKER, Peter Malcolm. b 21. Lich Th Coll 40. **d** 43 **p** 45 Bris. C of St Aldhelm Bedminster 43-47; H Ap Charlton Kings 47-49; Halesowen 49-53; V of St Luke Dudley 53-59; CF(TA) 53-75; R of Hindlip w Martin Hussingtree 59-67; Warden of Readers Dio Worc 59-78; Chap from 78; V of Inkberrow w Cookhill (and Kington w Dormston from 75) 67-77; P-in-c of Kingston w Dormston 74-75; Wilden 77-80; R of Mamble w Bayton Dio Worc from 80; RD of Stourport from 79. *Bayton Vicarage, Kidderminster, Worcs, DY14 9LP.* (Clows Top 257)

BAKER, Canon Philip Bartrum. Univ of NZ BA 45. NZ Bd of Th Stud LTh (1st cl) 48. St Jo Coll Auckld. **d** 48 **p** 49 Auckld. C of Whangeri 48-49; St Mark Remuera Auckld 49-51; Miss P Melan 51-56; on leave 57; Warden Siota Th Coll Melan 58-63; Can of All SS Cathl Honiara 61-63; V of Hinds 63-65; St Mich AA City and Dio Ch Ch from 65; Hon Can of Ch Ch from 76. *St Michael's Vicarage, Oxford Terrace, Christchurch 1, NZ.* (74-835)

BAKER, Ransford Ansell. St Pet Coll Ja. **d** 59 Ja **p** 60 Kingston for Ja. C of Spanish Town Cathl 59-62; R of Highgate 62-63; Golden Grove 63-69; on leave. *5 Rose Terrace, May Pen, Clarendon, Jamaica.*

BAKER, Robert Bruce. McMaster Univ Ont BA 56. Trin Coll Tor STB 60. **d** and **p** 60 Montr. C of St Jo Div Montr 60-64; R of Farnham 64-69; St Jo Div Verdun City and Dio Montr from 69; Sec of Syn Dio Montr from 78. *440 Beatty Avenue, Verdun, Montreal, PQ, Canada.* (514-768 0895)

BAKER, Robert Mark. b 50. Univ of Bris BA 73. St Jo Coll Nottm 74. **d** 76 **p** 77 Southn for Win. C of Ch Ch Portswood (or Highfield) Southn 76-80; R of Witton w Brundall and Bradeston Dio Nor from 80. *73 The Street, Brundall, Norwich, NR13 5LZ.* (Nor 713089)

BAKER, Robin Henry. b 31. Univ of Man BA 52. Cudd Coll 54. **d** 56 **p** 57 Man. C of St Pet Swinton 56-59; Birch-in-Rusholme 59-61; R of All SS Stretford 61-66; Chap High Royds Hosp Menston 66-72; P Missr of Simpson w Woughton-on-the-Green 72-74; R of Woughton 74-79; V of Ch the Corner Stone Milton Keynes Dio Ox from 80; RD of Milton Keynes from 78. *21 Kindleton, Great Linford, Milton Keynes, MK14 5EA.* (Milton Keynes 605957)

BAKER, Ronald Duncan. TCD BA 58, Dipl Bibl Stud 58, Downes Liturgy Pri and Div Test 59, Higher Dipl Educn 60, MA and Elrington Th Pri 61, BD 62. Ch Ch Ox MA 66. **d** 59 **p** 60 Down. C of Knockbreda 59-61; Zion Ch Rathgar Dub 61-63; Asst Master K Hosp Dub 63-64; Min Can of St Patr Cathl Dub 62-64; Ho Master Harcourt Sch Weyhill 64-65; Hd Master 65-67; Lect in Th Rolle Coll Exmouth 67-71; Ex Coll 72-73; CF (TA) 65-67; CF (TA-R of O) from 67. *Haldon House, Dunchideock, Exeter, EX6 7YF.* (Exeter 832600)

BAKER, Ronald Harry. b 21. Ely Th Coll 62. **d** 64 **p** 65 Ex. C of Crediton 64-66; R of Thornbury 66-73; R of Bradford, Devon 67-73; Black Torrington Bradford and Thornbury 73-77; P-in-c of Berry Pomeroy, Littlehempston, Broadhempston w Woodland Dio Ex 77-78; V from 78. *Broadhempston Vicarage, Totnes, Devon.* (Ipplepen 812232)

BAKER, Roy David. b 36. Dipl Th (Lon) 61. St Aid Coll 59. **d** 62 Warrington for Liv **p** 63 Liv. C of Garston 62-64; N Meols 64-68; V of All SS, Newton-in-Makerfield 68-73; St John Crossens Dio Liv from 73. *Vicarage, Rufford Road, Crossens, Southport, Lancs, PR9 8JH.* (Southport 27662)

BAKER, Very Rev Thomas George Adames. b 20 Ex Coll Ox BA (2nd cl Mods, 1st cl Th) 43, MA 50. Linc Th Coll 43. **d** 44 **p** 45 Birm. C of All SS King's Heath 44-47; V of St Jas Edgbaston 47-54; Sub-Warden Linc Th Coll and LPr Dio Linc 54-60; Can Th of Leic 59-66; Prin Wells Th Coll 60-71; Preb of Wells Cathl 60-75; Select Pr Univ of Cam 63; Ox 74; Archd of Bath 71-75; Dean of Worc from 75. *Deanery, College Green, Worcester, WR1 2LH.* (Worcester 23501)

BAKER, Thomas James William. b 35. St Edm Hall Ox BA (3rd cl Th) 59, MA 64. St Steph Ho Ox 59. **d** 61 **p** 62 Win. C of Bitterne Pk 61-64; All SS Southbourne Bournemouth 64-68; Asst Chap and Master Lancing Coll 68-69; Chap 70-79; V of Thatcham Dio Ox from 79. *Thatcham Vicarage, Newbury, Berks, RG13 4PJ.* (Thatcham 62616)

BAKER, Walter Donald. St Aid Coll 42. **d** 44 **p** 45 Blackb. C of St Thos Preston 44-46; R of Elsing w Bylaugh 46-50; Scottow w Lammas and L Hautbois 50-54; Blankney 54-58; V of St Paul Old Ford 58-64; R of Hanwell 64-68; V of St Steph U Holloway 68-81. *8 St James's Close, Bishop Street, N1 8PH.* (01-359 3498)

BAKER, William Alfred Douglas. b 21. Univ of Lon BSc 52, MSc 56. Qu Coll Birm 72. **d** 75 **p** 76 Heref. Hon C of St Leon Bridgnorth Dio Heref from 75. *Oaklea, Astley Abbotts, Bridgnorth, Salop.*

BAKER, William Douglas Willson. b 19. Linc Th Coll 79. **d** 80 Grimsby for Linc **p** 81 Linc (NSM). C of Mablethorpe w Trusthorpe Dio Linc from 80. *7 Grove Road, Sutton-on-Sea, Mablethorpe, Lincs, LN12 2LP.*

BAKER, William George Kenneth. b 20. DFM 43. Bps' Coll Cheshunt 59. **d** 60 Win **p** 61 Southn for Cant. C of St Andr Boscombe 60-65; R of Hinton Parva 65-71; PC of St Jas Holt 65-71; C-in-c of St Francis City and Dio Sarum 71-72; V from 72; P-in-c of Stratford-sub-Castle Dio Sarum from 79. *52 Park Lane, Salisbury, Wilts.*

BAKER, William Henry Cecil. b 04. ALCD 34. **d** 34 **p** 35 Lon. C of St Luke W Kilburn 34-37; Longfleet 37-41; Org Sec CCCS for NW Distr 41-45; V of Cheadle Hulme 45-49; Surr from 47; N Cler Sec CEZMS 49-51; R of St Grade w Ruan Minor 51-58; V of St Merryn 58-74. *17 Fernside Park, Tremar Coombe, Liskeard, Cornw, PL14 5HY.*

✠ **BAKER, Right Rev William Scott.** b 02. K Coll Cam 3rd cl Cl Trip pt i 23, BA (3rd cl Cl Trip pt ii) 24, MA 28. Cudd Coll 25. **d** 25 **p** 27 Ely. C of St Giles w St Pet Cam and Chap K Coll Cam 25-32; Exam Chap to Bp of Wakef 28-32; V of St John Newc T 32-43; Exam Chap to Bp of Newc T 41-43; Proc Conv Newc T 43; Cons Ld Bp of Zanz (Zanz T from 65) in Westmr Abbey 21 Sept 43 by Abp of Cant; Bps of Lon; Win; Glouc; and Newc T; and Bp Birley; Res 68; Asst Bp of Liv from 68. *11 Woolacombe Road, Liverpool L16 9JG.* (051-722 5035)

BAKEWELL, Canon Lionel John. Trin Coll Melb BA (2nd cl Hons) 25, MA 27. ACT ThL (1st cl) 26. **d** and **p** 27 Melb. C of St Steph Richmond Melb 27-28; Trav Sec Austr SCM 28-29; Chap Bukoba 29-40; Kasulu 40-43; Berega 43-45; Murgwanza 45-47; Dodoma 48; furlough 48-49; Chan Dio Centr Tang 48-63; Miss at Katoke 49-50; Gihwahuru 50-55; Exam Chap to Bp of Centr Tang 50-63; Archd of Western 49-58; without Territorial jurisd Dio Centr Tang 58-63; Miss at Kigoma 55-57; Kasulu 57-63; Hon Can Centr Tang from 63; Prin CMS Lang Sch Nairobi 63-71; L to Offic Dio Nai 64-71; C of St Hilary, Kew 72-73; Commiss Nak from 72; Perm to Offic Dio Melb from 73. *Bobinvale, Deddick, via Bonang, Vic, Australia 3888.*

BAKO, John Patteson. **d** 76 **p** 77 Ysabel. P Dio Ysabel. *Sepi, Bugotu District, Santa Ysabel, Solomon Islands.*

BAKO, Jonathan Albert. **d** 23 **p** 25 Bp Oluwole for Lagos.

P Dio Lagos (retired). *c/o St Jude's Vicarage, Ebute Metta, Lagos, Nigeria.*

BAKULUBOMBE, Lusenge. b 34. Bp Tucker Coll Mukono 73. **d** 74 **p** 75 Boga-Z. P Dio Boga-Z 74-76; Dio Bukavu from 76. *BP 145, Beni, Nord-Kivu, Zaire.*

BA KYAW, Paul. H Cross Coll Rang. **d** 66 **p** 67 Rang. P Dio Rang. *St Mathias Church, Oskhitpin, Padaung P.O., Prome District, Burma.*

BALCH, John Robin. b 37. BSc (2nd cl Chem) Lon 61. ALCD 68. **d** 68 **p** 69 B & W. C of Walcot 68-71; Fulwood (in c of St Luke Lodge Moor) Sheff 71-76; V of St Paul Erith Dio Roch from 76. *44 Colyers Lane, Erith, Kent, DA8 3NP.* (Erith 32809)

BALCHIN, Arthur Richard. St Jo Coll Morpeth ACT ThL 33. **d** 33 **p** 34 Bath. C of Mudgee 33-37; R of Rockley 38-44; Millthorpe 44-48; Cudal 47-63; Carcoar 63-72; Rockley 72-74. *284 Katoomba Street, Katoomba, NSW, Australia 2780.*

BALCHIN, Michael John. b 38. Selw Coll Cam BA 60, MA 64. Wells Th Coll 60. **d** 62 **p** 63 Win. C of H Epiph Bournemouth 62-65; St Mary Redcliffe Bedminster 65-69; R of Norton-sub-Hamdon (w Chiselborough from 70) 69-77; C-in-c of Chiselborough 69-70; Chipstable w Raddington and Huish Champflower w Clatworthy Dio B & W from 77. *Rectory, Chipstable, Taunton, Somt, TA4 2PZ.* (Wiveliscombe 23619)

BALDOCK, Norman. b 29. K Coll Lon and Warm AKC and BD (2nd cl) 52. **d** 53 Dover for Cant **p** 54 Cant. C of St Pet Cant 53-54; St Jude Thornton Heath 54-58; V of Ash-next-Sandwich w W Marsh 58-67; H Trin w St Paul, Sheerness 67-75; Margate Dio Cant from 75; RD of Thanet from 80. *Vicarage, Margate, Kent, CT9 1TH.* (Thanet 21300)

BALDOCK, Reginald David. b 48. Oak Hill Coll 72. **d** 75 **p** 76 Ex. C of St Jude Plymouth 75-78; Ardsley Dio Sheff from 79. *Church Flat, Gerald Walk, Kendray, Barnsley, S70 3BJ.* (Barnsley 203906)

BALDRY, John Netherway. b 19. BA (Lon) 53. **d** 79 **p** 80 Chich. C of St Paul Brighton Dio Chich from 79. *26 Braybon Avenue, Brighton, BN1 8HG.*

BALDRY, Ralph Yorke. b 18. St Jo Coll Ox BA (2nd cl Th) 40, MA 44. Wycl Hall, Ox 40. **d** 41 **p** 42 Lon. C of H Trin Southall 41-45; Oakwood Middx 45-47; V of Clay Hill Enfield 47-52; V of Stonebridge Willesden 52-58; Chap Ch Army Tr Coll St Marylebone 58-64; V of St Luke Finchley 64-72; St Alb Golders Green 72-80; C-in-c of St Mich Golders Green 76-80; V of Golders Green Dio Lon from 80. *3 St Alban's Close, North End Road, NW11 7RA.* (01-455 4525)

BALDWICK, Frank Eric. b 24. Ripon Hall Ox 54. **d** 55 **p** 56 Southw. C of Ch Ch Newark and of Hawton 55-58; W Bridgford 58-60; V of St Barn Oldham 60-65; R of St Mich w St Bart Gt Lever 65-78; V of Hindsford 78-81; Team V of Clifton w Glapton Dio Southw from 81. *St Francis Vicarage, Southchurch Drive, Clifton, Nottingham, NG11 8AQ.* (Nottm 212446)

BALDWIN, David Boyd. McMaster Univ BA 54. Waterloo Univ MA 69. Trin Coll Tor LTh 57. **d** 56 **p** 57 Niag. C of Oakville 56-58; St Jo Evang Montr 58-59; I of St Columba Waterloo 59-67. *7 Spring Street East, Waterloo, Ont., Canada.*

BALDWIN, Derek Wilfred Walter. b 23. ALCD 56 (LTh from 74). **d** 52 **p** 53 Sheff. C of St Andr Sharrow Sheff 52-54; Woodlands 54-56; V of Shepley 56-59; Earls Heaton 59-66; Cler Org Sec CECS Dios B & W, Ex and Truro 66-72; L to Offic Dio Ex 67-73; R of Morchard Bp 72-73; Org Sec CECS Dios St Alb and Ox 73-77; C of Portishead 77-79; R of Wymondham w Edmondthorpe 79-80; P-in-c of St Mewan Dio Truro from 80. *St Mewan Rectory, St Austell, Cornw.* (St Austell 2679)

BALDWIN, Eric Royston. Ridley Coll Melb ACT ThL 45. **d** 46 **p** 47 Melb. C of St Mary Caulfield 46-48; Min of Drysdale and Portarlington 48-51; Chelsea 51-55; R of St Silas N Balwyn 55-59; Chap Lockhart River Miss 59-60; R of Woodburn 60-62; I of Port Melb 62-65; Surrey Hills Melb 65-70; P-in-c of Wilcannia 70-73; I of Sunbury 73-75; W Brunswick Dio Melb from 75. *494A Victoria Street, West Brunswick, Vic, Australia 3055.* (03-38 1465)

BALDWIN, Peter Alan. b 48. Bede Coll Dur BA 70. Qu Coll Birm Dipl Th 72. **d** 73 **p** 74 Dur. C of St Osw W Hartlepool 73-75; H Trin Darlington 75-78; P-in-c Woodhouse Close Area of Ecumen Experiment Bp Auckld 78-82; V of Ferryhill Dio Dur from 82. *Vicarage, Ferryhill, Co Durham.* (Ferryhill 438)

BALDWIN, Peter Cecil. b 39. Univ of W Ont BA 76. Hur Coll Lon Ont MDiv 80. **d** 80 Hur **p** Bp Parke-Taylor for Hur. I of Milverton Dio Hur from 80. *Box 378, Milverton, Ont, Canada, N0K 1M0.*

BALDWIN, William. b 48. N-W Ordin Course 75. **d** 78 Hulme for Man **p** 79 Man. C of St Anne Longsight Royton 78-81; V of St Thos Halliwell Dio Man from 81. *Vicarage, Eskrick Street, Halliwell, Bolton, Gtr Man.* (Bolton 41731)

BALDWIN, William Warren. Univ of Tor BA 53, MA 56, LTh 56. Wycl Coll Tor. **d** 55 **p** 56 Tor. C of St Barn Danforth Avenue Tor 56-58; I of S Porcupine 58-60; on leave 60-79. *Address temp unknown.*

BALE, Aubrey Alfred. Kelham Th Coll. **d** 33 **p** 34 Portsm. C of All SS Portsea 33-35; M of Bush Bro Dio N Queensld 35-42 and 48-51; Chap AIF 42-46; V of Wymynswold and Min of St Pet Aylesham Conv Distr Dio Cant 51-54; R of Blackall 54-59; Brisb Valley 59-64; Gympie 64-76. *2220 Gympie Road, Bald Hills, Queensland, Australia 4036.*

BALE, Edward William Carr-e. b 22. K Coll Lon and Warm AKC 55. **d** 55 **p** 56 Southw. C of St Pet and St Paul Mansfield 55-59; Corby 59-61; Min of St Pet and St Andr Eccles Distr Corby 61-69; V of Wollaston w Strixton Dio Pet from 69. *Wollaston Vicarage, Wellingborough, Northants.* (0933-664256)

BALE, James Henry. St Pet Hall Ox BA (2nd cl Eng Lang and Lit) 53, MA 57. Oak Hill Th Coll 56. **d** 58 **p** 59 B & W. C of Walcot 58-61; Kinson (in c of St Phil) 61-64; Miss Middle E Gen Miss Asmara Dio Sudan from 64. *P.O. Box 1042, Asmara, Ethiopia.*

BALE, John. b 45. Bp Patteson Th Coll Kohimarama 74. **d** 77 Ysabel. d Dio Ysabel. *Tasia Training Centre, Maringe Lagoon, Santa Ysabel, Solomon Islands.*

BALE, Kenneth John. b 34. St D Coll Lamp BA 58. Univ of Birm Dipl Th 60. Qu Coll Birm 58. **d** 60 **p** 61 S'wark. C of St Olave Mitcham 60-63; Warlingham w Chelsham and Farleigh 63-67; V of St Mark Battersea Dio S'wark from 67. *7 Elsynge Road, SW18.* (01-874 6022)

BALENI, Ernest. b 15. **d** 68 **p** 70 Matab. P Dio Matab 68-81; Dio Lundi from 81. *Box 978, Gwelo, Zimbabwe.*

BALES, Charles Noel. b 07. Dorch Miss Coll 31. **d** 35 **p** 36 Pet. C of All SS Kettering 35-38; Perm to Offic at St Pet Folkestone 38-40; Dio Nor 40-42; V of Marshland St Jas Dio Ely from 42. *Vicarage, Marshland St James, Middle Drove, Wisbech, Cambs.* (Marshland Smeeth 240)

BALES, John Lampier. Monash Univ BSc 75, MSc 79. Ridley Coll Melb BTh 78. **d** and **p** 80 Syd. C of St Thos N Syd Dio Syd from 80. *45 Pitt Street, Redfern, NSW, Australia 2016.*

BALFOUR, Alfred Clive. b 26. **d** and **p** 71 Rupld. Hon C of All SS Winnipeg Dio Rupld from 71. *505 Beresford Avenue, Winnipeg, Manit., Canada.*

BALFOUR, Charles Edward. b 50. Univ of Guelph Ont BA 72. Wycl Coll Tor MDiv 75. **d** 75 Bp Read for Tor **p** 76 Tor. C of St Andr Scarborough Tor 75-78; I of Hastings Dio Tor from 78. *Box 218, Hastings, Ont, Canada.* (705-696 2832)

BALFOUR, David Ian Bailey Balfour. Ch Ch Coll 60. **d** and **p** 63 Ch Ch. C of St Steph Ashburton 63-66; V of Aranui Miss Distr 66-71; Lyttleton 71-75; St Paul City and Dio Auckld from 75. *33 Symonds Street, Auckland, NZ.* (372-485)

BALFOUR, Hugh Rowlatt. b 54 SS Coll Cam BA 76. Ridley Hall Cam 78. **d** 81 Hertf for St Alb. C of Ch Ch Bedford Dio St Alb from 81. *142 George Street, Bedford, MK40 3SH.* (Bedford 216203)

BALIBWEGULE, Duncan Geoffrey Ilakola. b 47. St Phil Coll Kongwa 70. **d** 72 **p** 73 Vic Nyan. P Dio Vic Nyan. *PO Box 278, Mwanza, Tanzania.*

BALINDA, Ven Kandole. Bp Tucker Coll Mukono 64. **d** 64 **p** 68 Ruw. P Dio Ruw 63-72; Dio Boga-Z 72-76; Dio Bukavu from 76; Archd of Beni from 75. *BP 145, Beni, Zaire.*

BALIYEGUJE, Justin. **d** 78 W Tang. d Dio W Tang. *DWT Bukuba, c/o PO Box 86, Kasulu, Tanzania.*

BALKWILL, Roger Bruce. b 41. Dipl Th (Wales) 64. St Mich Coll Llan 61. **d** 64 Bp T M Hughes for Llan **p** 65 Llan. C of Llantrisant 64-68; Caerphilly 68-73; Youth Chap Dio Matab 73-74; C of Ascen Hillside Bulawayo 74-76; P-in-c of Ilam w Blore-Ray and Okeover 76-81; Albrighton Dio Lich from 81; Warden Dovedale Ho Lich 76-81. *Vicarage, High Street, Albrighton, Wolverhampton, Staffs, WV7 3EQ.* (Albrighton 2701)

BALL, Alan. b 26. Qu Coll Birm 72. **d** and **p** 75 Birm (APM). C of St Paul Hampstead Dio Birm from 75. *4 Kingshayes Road, Aldridge, Staffs, WS9 8RU.*

BALL, Albert Bernard. b 15. Coll of Resurr Mirfield. **d** 62 **p** 63 Man. C of Ch Ch Moss Side 62-65; R of St Clem Greenheys 65-71; V of St John Werneth Oldham 71-80. *4 Holly Mount, Seymour Grove, Stretford, Manchester, M16 0ET.* (061-860 7289)

BALL, Andrew Thomas. b 54. AKC and BD 75. Sarum Wells Th Coll 76. **d** 77 Lanc for Blackb **p** 78 Blackb. C of Ribbleton 77-80; All SS Sedgley Dio Lich from 80. *16 Browning Road, The Straits, Lower Gornal, Dudley, W Midl.* (Sedgley 77451)

BALL, Anthony Charles. b 46. Univ of Lon BD 71. Chich Th Coll 72. **d** 73 Bp Partridge for Heref **p** 74 Heref. C of St

Martin Heref 73-76; St Pet Ealing Dio Lon from 76. *Vicarage Flat, St Peter's Vicarage, Mount Park Road, W5 2RU.*

BALL, Anthony Michael. b 46. Kelham Th Coll 65. **d** 70 **p** 71 Lich. C of St Mary Kingswinford 70-74; W Brom 74-76; P-in-c of Priors Lee Dio Lich 76-81; V from 81. *St Peter's Vicarage, Snedshill, Telford, Shropshire, TF2 9EA.* (Telford 612923)

BALL, Ernest Robert. b 05. Kelham Th Coll 24. M SSM 28. **d** 29 **p** 30 Man. C of St Jas New Bury 29-33; St Nich Liv 33-38; St Cecilia Parson Cross 38-40; war service 40-43; L to Offic Dio Southw 46-57; R of Averham w Kelham 57-60; Perm to Offic Dio Lon 61-62; Tutor Melan Bro Honiara Melan 62-68; L to Offic Dio Southw 70-72; Dio Blackb from 74. *Society of the Sacred Mission, Quernmore, Lancaster.*

BALL, Frank. Univ of Leeds BA 47. Coll of Resurr, Mirfield 46. **d** 48 **p** 49 Sheff. C of St Hilda Shiregreen Sheff 48-50; Attercliffe (in c of St Alb Darnall) 50-53; V of Handsworth-Woodhouse 53-61; St Leon Norwood City and Dio Sheff from 61; RD of Ecclesfield from 80. *Vicarage, Everingham Road, Sheffield 5, Yorks.* (Sheffield 386689)

BALL, George Raymond. b 15. St D Coll Lamp BA 40. St Mich Coll Llan 40. **d** 42 **p** 43 Swan B. C of Llansamlet 42-46; St Nich-on-the-Hill Swansea 46-50; R of Bosherston w St Twynnell Dio St D from 50. *Bosherston Rectory, Pembroke, Dyfed.* (Castlemartin 231)

BALL, Harold Francis Noel. b 19. Univ of Leeds BA (2nd Cl Hist) 41. Coll of Resurr Mirfield, 41. **d** 43 **p** 44 Chelmsf. C of St Mich AA Walthamstow 43-45; St Mark Gillingham, Kent 45-46; CF 46-74; R of W Grinstead w Partridge Green Dio Chich from 74; Hon Chap to HM Queen 74. *West Grinstead Rectory, Horsham, Sussex.* (Partridge Green 710339)

BALL, John Kenneth. b 42. AKC 64. Univ of Lon BSc 64. Linc Th Coll 69. **d** 71 Warrington for Liv **p** 72 Liv. C of Garston 71-74; Eastham 74-75; Barnston 75-77; V of St Jo Evang Over Dio Ches from 77. *St John's Vicarage, Over, Winsford, Chesh.* (Winsford 4651)

BALL, John Leslie. Univ of Sask BA and LTh 32. **d** 31 Sask **p** 32 Southw for Lon for Col. Miss at Fort a la Corne 32-33; Thunderchild's Reserve 33-34; Spruce Lake 34-37; C of Lenton (in c of Priory Ch) 37-39; I of Gorrie Fordwich and Wroxeter 39-42; Chap CASF 42-46; R of St Paul Kerrwood 46-47; I of Kincardine and Pine River 47-52; in Amer Ch 52-61; R of Unionville 62-67; on leave 67-68; I of Kinmount 69-71. *197 Elmore Drive, Acton, Ont., Canada.*

BALL, John Martin. b 34. Univ of Wales BA 55. Tyndale Hall Bris. **d** 59 Lanc for Blackb **p** 60 Burnley for York. C of St Jude Blackb 59-63; Eldoret Kenya 63-71; Good Shepherd Cathl Nak 71-75; V of St Francis Nai 75-80; Perm to Offic Dio Roch from 80; Dep Gen Sec BCMS 80-81; Gen Sec from 81. *Bible Churchmen's Missionary Society, 251 Lewisham Way, SE4 1XF.* (01-691 6111)

BALL, Kenneth Vernon James. b 06. Jes Coll Ox BA (2nd cl Hist) 27, 3rd cl Th 29, MA 38. Wycl Hall Ox 27. **d** 32 **p** 33 Bris. C of St Paul Bedminster 32-35; Temple (or Holy Cross) Bris 35-38; V of St Barn Bris 38-42; St Leon Redfield Bris 42-47; Bp of Liv's Special Service Staff 47-50; V of St Nich w St Clem Roch 50-59; Can of Roch 53-59; V of Leatherhead 59-70; RD of Leatherhead 64-67; R of Piddlehinton 70-72. *Manormead, Tilford Road, Hindhead, Surrey, GU26 6RA.*

BALL, Leslie Prideaux. B 36. St Mary's Univ Halifax NS BA. Atlantic Sch of Th Halifax NS MDiv 80. **d** 79 NS. On leave. *PO Box 1313* (North), *Halifax, NS, Canada.*

BALL, Leopold George. Trin Coll Melb BA 27, MA 29. ACT ThL 23. **d** 26 **p** 27 Wang. Tutor St Columb's Hall Wang and C of Milawa 26-28; Tutor Codr Coll Barb 30; R of Alexandra 31-35; C of St Anne Eastbourne 36-37; V of Cohuna 37-42; C of Kyabram Dio Bend 42-46; Sec Bush Ch Aid S Dio Melb 46-51; C of St Steph Richmond 50-51; Min of Greensborough 51-54; Perm to Offic Dio Melb from 60. *13-261 Glenlyon Road, North Fitzroy, Vic., Australia 3068.* (489-7471)

BALL, Michael Gordon. St Aid Coll 45. **d** 48 **p** 49 Ex. C of Bideford 48-52; V of H Trin Barnstaple (w St Pet from 63) 52-64; R of Wexham 64-70; R of Newington Bagpath w Kingscote and Ozleworth 70-74; C-in-c of Boxwell w Leighterton 71-72; R of Withington w Compton Abdale (and Haselton from 75) 74-77. *5 Instow House, Marine Parade, Instow, Bideford, Devon EX39 4JJ.*

✠ **BALL, Right Rev Michael Thomas.** b 32. Qu Coll Cam BA 55, MA 59. **d** and **p** 71 Glouc. M CGA. C of Whiteshill Stroud 71-76; P-in-c of Stanmer w Falmer 76-80; Sen Chap Sussex Univ 76-80; Cons Ld Bp Suffr of Jarrow in York Minster 10 Oct 80 by Abp of York; Bps of Dur, Chich, Liv, Southw, Blackb and Sheff; Bps Suffr of Pontefract, Whitby, Selby, Sherwood, Penrith, Lewes, Horsham and Knaresborough. *Melkridge House, Gilesgate, Durham, DH1 1JB.* (Durham 43797)

BALL, Nicholas Edward. b 54. Univ of Man BA 75. Ripon Coll Cudd BA (Th) 79. **d** 80 **p** 81 Birm. C of Yardley Wood Dio Birm from 80. *60 Willson Croft, Hall Green, Birmingham, B28 9SS.* (021-430 3393)

BALL, Norman. Univ of Liv BA (2nd cl Hist) 63. Cudd Coll 67. **d** 68 **p** 69 Heref. C of Broseley w Benthall 68-72; Asst Master Christleton High Sch and L to Offic Dio Ches 72-75; V of Plemstall w Guilden Sutton 75-79; Perm to Offic Dio Ches from 79; Asst Master Neston Co Comprehensive Sch Neston from 79. *19 Weaver Grove, Mickle Trafford, Ches.*

BALL, Peter Bradshaw. Moore Th Coll Syd ACT ThL 59. BD (Lon) 75. **d** 59 Bp Hilliard for Syd **p** 59 Syd. Chap Gr Sch Syd 59-64; C-in-c of Keiraville Distr 64-66; Chap RAN 66-73; Asst Master Barker Coll and Perm to Offic Dio Syd from 77. *Barker College, Pacific Highway, Hornsby, NSW, Australia 2077.* (47-1456)

BALL, Peter Edwin. b 44. BD (Lon) 65. Wycl Hall Ox 75. **d** 77 **p** 78 Liv. C of Prescot 77-80; R of Lawford Dio Chelmsf from 80. *Lawford Rectory, Manningtree, Essex.* (Manningtree 2659)

✠ **BALL, Right Rev Peter John.** b 32. Qu Coll Cam 3rd cl Nat Sc Trip pt i 53, BA 54, MA 58. Wells Th Coll 54. **d** 56 **p** 57 Chich. M CGA. C of Rottingdean 56-58; Prior CGA 60-77; Publ Pr Dio Birm 65-66; C-in-c of Hoar Cross 66-69; L to Offic Dio B & W 69-77; Cons Bp Suffr of Lewes in St Paul's Cathl Lon 18 Oct 77 by Abp of Cant; Bps of Lon, Chich, Linc, Lich and Nor; Bps Suffr of Fulham & Gibr, Stepney, Buckingham, Horsham, Pontefract, Sherborne and Tonbridge; and Bps M Hodson, E Trapp and E Henderson; and others; Can and Preb of Chich Cathl from 78. *Litlington Rectory, Polegate, E Sussex, BN26 5RB.* (0323-870387)

BALL, Peter Prior. b 25. St Jo Coll Ox BA (3rd cl Agric) 50, MA 55. Ridley Hall Cam 51. **d** 53 **p** 54 Chelmsf. C of Gt Baddow 53-56; Farnborough Hants 56-60; Chap RN 60-76; H Trin Cannes Dio Gibr (Gibr in Eur from 80) from 76. *1 Rue Général, Ferrié, Cannes, France.* (93-385461)

BALL, Peter Royston. b 38. St Mich Coll Llan 61. **d** 65 **p** 66 Roch. C of St Alb Dartford 65-67; Annunc Chislehurst 67-71; Ch Ch and St Paul Marylebone 71-75. *11 Cupar Road, Battersea Park, SW11.*

BALL, Preb Peter William. b 30. Worc Coll Ox 2nd cl Cl Mods 51, BA (2nd cl Lit Hum) 53, MA 57. Cudd Coll 53. **d** 55 **p** 56 Lon. C of All SS Poplar 55-61; PC of Ch of Ascen Wembley 61-68; R of Shepperton Dio Lon from 68; RD of Staines 72-74; Spelthorne from 74; Preb of St Paul's Cathl Lon from 76. Preb of St Paul's Cathl Lon from 76. *Rectory, Shepperton, Middx, TW17 9JY.* (Walton-on-Thames 20511)

BALL, Richard. b 10. Univ of Dur 32. St Paul's Coll Burgh. **d** 36 **p** 37 Wakef. C of Southowram 36-37; All SS Banstead 37-39; Walton-on-Thames 39-40; Hatfield Herts 40-45; Bp's Stortford 45-47; V of Flitwick 47-78; RD of Ampthill 63-68. *108 College Lane, Roe Green, Hatfield, Herts.* (Hatfield 69162)

BALL, Canon Robert George. b 14. Pemb Coll Cam 3rd cl Engl Trip pt i 35, BA (3rd cl Th Trip pt i) 36, MA 40. Ely Th Coll 36. **d** 37 **p** 38 Lon. C of St Barn Wood End Northolt 37-38; St Etheldreda Fulham 38-40; C-in-c of St Chad Conv Distr Devonport (w St Steph Devonport 42-44) 40-44; PC of Plymstock 44-53; Surr 45-53; Chap RAF 53-59; R of Gt Livermere w Troston 59-63; PC (V from 68) of St Thos, Ipswich 63-81; Hon Can of St E from 70; RD of Ipswich 72-78. *c/o St Thomas's Vicarage, Ipswich, Suff.* (Ipswich 41215)

BALL, Ross Barrington. St Barn Coll Adel 39. ACT ThL 43. **d** 43 Adel for Bunb **p** 44 Adel. C of St Cuthb Prospect 43-44; St Aug Renmark 44-46; R of Margaret River 46-51; Mt Barker 51-55; Mundaring 55-59; on leave 60-62; P-in-c of Osborne Pk 62-66; Warden Le Fanu House 66-70; L to Offic Dio Perth from 66. *58 Davies Crescent, Gooseberry Hill, W Australia 6076.*

BALL, Sydney Thomas. Ridley Coll Melb ACT ThL (1st cl) 21. Th Scho 34. **d** 21 **p** 22 Gippsld. C of Sale Vic 21-23; V of Omeo 23-29; R of Warragul 29-35; Traralgon 35-44; Exam Chap to Bp of Gippsld 43-52; V of Heidelberg 44-49; Sandringham 49-54; S Yarra 54-65; Perm to Offic Dio Melb from 66. *Canterbury Hostel, Chatham Road, Camberwell, Vic. 3124, Australia.*

BALLANCE, Hedley Tabor. b 1892. St Chad's Hall Dur BA 14. St Chad's Hostel, Hooton Pagnell 11. **d** 15 **p** 16 Newc T. C of Hexham Abbey 15-17; Long Benton 17-19; C of St Agnes Toxt Pk and Sen Master Liv Coll Sch 19-37; V of St Luke Liv 37-46; Chap R Infirm Liv 37-46; CF (EC) 40-46; Hon CF 52; V of Heytesbury w Tytherington and Knook 46-53; St Feock 53-58. *3 Cauleston Close, Exmouth, Devon.*

BALLANTINE, Peter Sinclair. b 46. AKC and BA 68.

ALCD 71 (LTh from 74), BD 73. St Jo Coll Nottm 70. **d** 73 Chelmsf **p** 74 Barking for Chelmsf. C of Rainham and of Wennington 73-77; Team V of Barton-Mills, Beck Row w Kenny Hill, Freckenham, Mildenhall w Red Lodge, W Row and Worlington Dio St E from 77. *1 Martin Close, Mildenhall, Bury St Edmunds, Suffolk, IP28 7LQ.* (Mildenhall 715647)

BALLANTINE, Roderic Keith. b 44. Chich Th Coll 66. **d** 69 **p** 70 S'wark. C of St Antony Nunhead 69-72; St John of Jer w Ch Ch S Hackney 72-75; P-in-c of St Thos Kensal Town 75-79; V of St Andr Stoke Newington Dio Lon from 79. *Flat C, 144 Bethune Road, N16 5DS.*

BALLANTINE-JONES, Bruce Albert. BD (Lon) 70. Moore Coll Syd ThL 69. **d** 71 **p** 72 Syd. C of Caringbah 71-74; R of Concord N 75-78; St Clem Jannali Dio Syd from 78. *83 Wattle Road, Jannali, NSW, Australia 2226.* (528-9130)

BALLANTYNE, John Ivan Terence. SS Coll Cam BA (2nd cl Cl Trip pt ii) 54. Ely Th Coll 55. **d** 57 **p** 58 Lon. C of All SS w St Frideswide Poplar 57-61; Asst Chap Univ of Lon 61-63; C of Ch Ch w St John and St Luke Isle of Dogs Poplar 63-64; Youth Chap Dio Kimb K 64-66; P-in-c of St Alb Kimb 64-66; P-in-c of Barkly W 64-66. (Address temp. unknown)

BALLANTYNE, Simon Thorne. Univ of Cant BA 64. NZ Bd of Th Stud LTh 65. Ch Ch Coll 61. **d** 65 **p** 66 Ch Ch. C of Cashmere Hills 65-67; Ashburton 67-71; V of Ross w S Westland 70-72; Methven 72-77, Kens-Otipua Dio Ch Ch from 77. *135A Otipua Road, Timaru, NZ.* (88-463)

BALLARAT, Lord Bishop of. *See* Hazlewood, Right Rev John.

BALLARAT, Assistant Bishop of. *See* Walden, Right Rev Graham Howard.

BALLARAT, Dean of. *See* Beer, Very Rev Kenneth Gordon.

BALLARD, Andrew Edgar. b 44. Univ of Dur BA (2nd cl Th) 66. Westcott Ho Cam 66. **d** 68 Willesden for Lon. **p** 69 Lon. C of St Mary Bryanston Square, St Marylebone 68-72; St Mary Portsea 72-76; V of Haslingden w Haslingden Grane 76-81; Walkden Dio Man from 81. *Vicarage, Manchester Road, Walkden, Manchester, M28 5LN.* (061-790 2483)

BALLARD, Arthur Henry. b 12. St Jo Coll Dur BA (w Distinc) and Van Mildert Scho 38, Dipl Th 39, MA 41. **d** 39 **p** 40 Chelmsf. C of Walthamstow 39-43; R of St Jo Evang Higher Broughton 43-46; All SS Stand 46-72; RD of Radcliffe and Prestwich 52-66; Hon Can of Man 58-66; Archd of Rochdale 66-72; Man 72-80; Can Res of Man 72-80; M Gen Syn 72-80. *30 Rathen Road, Withington, Manchester, M20 9GH.* (061-445 4703)

BALLARD, George Douglas. b 20. Worc Ordin Coll 62. **d** 64 **p** 65 Chich. C of All SS w St Thos and St Jo-sub-Castro Lewes 64-65; Seaford 65-69; R of Jevington 69-73; Thakeham w Warminghurst (w Sullington from 77) 73-80; C of Hambleden Valley Dio Ox from 80. *c/o Turville Vicarage, Henley-on-Thames, Oxon, RG9 6QU.*

BALLARD, Michael Arthur. b 44. BA (Lon) 66. Westcott Ho Cam 68. **d** 70 **p** 71 Willesden for Lon. C of All SS Harrow Weald 70-73; Aylesbury 73-77; V of Eastwood Dio Chelmsf from 77. *Vicarage, Eastwoodbury Lane, Southend-on-Sea, Essex, SS2 6UH.* (Southend-on-Sea 525272)

BALLARD, Richard Ernest. b 37. Linc Coll Ox BA (2nd cl Mod Hist) 60, MA 66. BD Lon 68. Wells Th Coll 60. **d** 62 **p** 63 Guildf. C of Farnham Surrey 62-67; Chap Pierrepont Sch Frensham 67-69; Asst Chap Eton Coll Windsor 69-74; C-in-c of Fiddington 74-76; Stoke Courcy (or Stogursey) 74-76; R (w Fiddington) 76-78; V of Trull w Angersleigh 78-81; Chap Wells Cathl Sch from 81. *18 Vicars Close, Wells, Somt, BA5 2UJ.*

BALLARD, Steven Peter. b 52. Univ of Man BA 73, MA 74. S Steph Ho Ox 76. **d** 78 Blackb **p** 79 Lanc for Blackb. C of Lancaster 78-81; St Mich AA Blackpool Dio Blackb from 81. *59 Dinmore Avenue, Grange Park, Blackpool, Lancs.* (Blackpool 301196)

BALLARD, William David. St Jo Coll Morpeth ACT ThL 62. **d** 63 **p** 63 C & Goulb. C of All SS Canberra 62-63; P-in-c of Downer Provisional Distr 63-65; R of Cobargo 65-72. *PO Box 21, Cobargo, NSW, Australia 2547.*

BALLEY, John Frederick. b 05. ALCD (1st cl) 41. **d** 41 **p** 42 Truro. C of Illogan 41-44; V of L Abington 44-47; V of Gt Abington (w L Abington from 47) 44-49; C-in-c of Hildersham 47-48; R 48-49; V of St Sav Brixton Hill 49-56; H Trin Richmond 56-65; Chap Torbay Hosp Torquay 65-70; L to Offic Dio Ex 65-70; Perm to Offic 70-73; Dio Ox 73-78. *1 Datchet Green, Brightwell-cum-Sotwell, Wallingford, Oxon, OX10 0QB.*

BALLINGER, Francis James. b 43. AKC 70. St Aug Coll Cant 70. **d** 71 Taunton for B & W. C of St Sav Weston-super-Mare 71-72. *c/o 17a Stafford Road, Weston-super-Mare, Somt.*

BALLONZI, Denys. Kongwa Coll 46. **d** and **p** 48 Centr Tang. P Dio Centr Tang 48-63; Dio Vic Nyan 63-75. *Box 278, Mwanza, Tanzania.*

BALMFORTH, Ven Anthony James. b 26. BNC Ox BA 50, MA 51. Linc Th Coll 50. **d** 52 Bp Weller for Southw **p** 53 Southw. C of Mansfield 52-55; V of Skegby 55-61; St Jo Bapt Kidderminster 61-65; King's Norton (w W Heath 65-66) 65-72; R 72-79; RD of King's Norton 73-79; Hon Can of Birm 75-79; Bris from 79; Exam Chap to Bp of Birm 78-79; Archd of Bris from 79; Exam Chap to Bp of Bris from 81. *10 Great Brockeridge, Westbury-on-Trym, Bristol, BS9 3TY.* (Bristol 622438)

BALUBULIZA, Saulo. Bp Tucker Mem Coll. **d** 24 **p** 26 Ugan. P Dio Ugan 24-26; Dio U Nile 26-46. *Mubende, Uganda.*

BALUNGUZA, Amos. **d** 67 **p** 68 W Tang. P Dio W Tang. *Munyegera, Kasulu, Tanzania.*

BAMAI, Sulaimanu Likita. Im Coll Ibad. **d** 66 **p** 67 N Nig. P Dio N Nig. *P.O Wusasa, Zaria, Nigeria.*

✠ **BA MAW, Right Rev Peter.** H Cross Coll Rang 35. **d** 40 **p** 47 Rang. P Dio Rang: Chap to Bp of Rang from 56; Hon Can of Rang 66-70; Cons Asst Bp of Rang in H Trin Cathl Rang on 24 Aug 69 by Bp of Rang; Apptd Ld Bp of Mandalay 70. *Christ Church Cathedral, 22nd Street, Mandalay, Burma.*

BAMBER, David Beverley. b 51. St D Coll Lamp BA 75. St Steph Ho Ox 75. **d** 77 **p** 78 Ches. C of St Geo Altrincham 77-80; Oxton Dio Ches from 80. *36 Noctorum Dell, Noctorum, Birkenhead. L43 9UL.* (051-652 8050)

BAMBER, Harry. b 30. Univ of Leeds BA 54. Coll of Resurr Mirfield 54. **d** 56 **p** 57 St Alb. C of Dunstable 56-59; St Anselm Hatch End 59-61; R of Yardley Hastings 61-66; V of Denton 64-66; Chap Miss to Seamen Fremantle Dio Perth 66-71; V of Swavesey Dio Ely from 71; P-in-c of Fen-Drayton Dio Ely from 79. *Vicarage, Swavesey, Cambridge.* (Swavesey 30250)

BAMBURY, Canon Owen Ronald. St Jo Coll Auckld. **d** 47 **p** 48 Ch Ch. C of Fendalton 47-50; Chap Medbury Sch 50-52; V of Hororata 52-54; Cashmere Hills 54-62; Te Awamutu 62-67; Mt Albert 67-73; Dir Selwyn Found City and Dio Auckld from 73; Hon Can of Auckld from 78. *Box 44106, Auckland, NZ.* (860-119)

BAMFORD, Alfred James. ACT ThL 19. **d** 19 **p** 20 Bend. C of White Hills 19-20; Regr Dio Bend 18-21; V of Mooroopna 21-24; R and RD of Kerang 24-28; Kyneton w Barfold 28-37; RD of S Chapter 36-37; Min of Diamond Creek and Greensborough 37-45; V of N Carlton 45-53; St Luke S Melb 53-64 (retired). *13 John Street, Beaumaris, Vic, Australia 3193.* (03-99 1635)

BAMFORTH, Marvin John. b 48. NOC 78. **d** 81 Bradf. C of Barnoldswick w Bracewell Dio Bradf from 81. *6 Park Avenue, Barnoldswick, Colne, Lancs.*

BAMFORTH, Stuart Michael. b 35. Late Scho of Hertf Coll Ox BA (3rd cl Lit Hum) 58, MA 61. Sarum Th Coll 60. **d** 62 **p** 63 Ripon. C of Adel 62-67; V of Hempton w Pudding Norton 67-71; V of Toftrees w Shereford 67-71; C-in-c of Pensthorpe 67-71; C-in-c of Colkirk w Oxwick 69-70; Publ Pr Dio Derby 72-76; Dio Ripon from 77; Asst Master Long Eaton Gr Sch 72-78; Ralph Thoresby High School from 76. *36 Gainsborough Avenue, Adel, Leeds, LS16 7PQ.*

BAMGBOSE, John Olaniyi. b 35. Im Coll Ibadan 67. **d** 70 **p** 71 Lagos. P Dio Lagos 70-76; Dio Ijebu from 76. *Box 16, Ijebu-Igbo, Nigeria.*

BAMIGBOJE, Oyewole Zacchaeus. b 30. **d** 78 Kwara. d Dio Kwara. *Lennon Memorial College, Ohene, Kwara State, Nigeria.*

BAMISEBI, Canon Joseph. Univ of Ibad BA 71. Melville Hall Ibad. **d** 58 Liv for Lagos **p** 59 Lagos. P Dio Lagos; Can of Lagos from 77. *Holy Trinity Vicarage, Ebute-Ero, Lagos, Nigeria.* (23108)

BAMUCWANIRA, Edward. b 53. Bp Tucker Coll Mukono 79. **d** 80 Ruw. d Dio Ruw. *PO Box 368, Fort Portal, Uganda.*

✠ **BAMUNOBA, Right Rev Yoramu.** b 31. **d** 66 **p** 67 Ankole-K. P Dio Ankole-K 66-72; Kamp 72-76; Cons Ld Bp of W Ank in St Pet Ch Bweranyangi 30 Jan 77 by Abp of Ugan; Bps of E Ank, Bukedi, Kara, Busoga, Kiga, Soroti, Bunyoro, W Buganda, Mbale, Ruw, Bujumbura, Buye, But, N Ugan, Kig and Lango. *Box 140, Bushenyi, Uganda.* (Bushenyi 80)

BAMUTENDE, George. **d** and **p** 79 W Ank. P Dio W Ank. *Box 54, Bushenyi, Uganda.*

BAMUTUNGIRE, Very Rev William. Bp Tucker Coll Mukono 56. **d** 57 Ugan **p** 60 Ankole-K. P Dio Ugan 57-60; Dio Ankole-K 60-67; P Dio Ank 67-76; Dio E Ank from 76; Treas Ank 67-71; Dean of St Jas Cathl Mbarara from 71; Archd of Ank 74-76; E Ank from 76. *Deanery, St James's Cathedral, Mbarara, Ankole, Uganda.*

BAMWANGA, Wilson. Bp Tucker Coll 68. **d** 70 **p** 71 Kig. P Dio Kig from 71. *PO Box 59, Kabale, Uganda.*

BAMWESIGYE, John. d 79 W Ank. d Dio W Ank. *Box 25, Bushenyi, Uganda.*

BAMWITE, Tomasi. d 65 **p** 66 Ruw. P Dio Ruw. *Anglican Church, Kyabenda, Uganda.*

✠ **BAMWOZE, Right Rev Cyprian Kikunyi.** Bp Tucker Mem Coll Mukono 60. **d** 60 Nam **p** 63 Linc for Nam. P Dio Nam 60-72; Cons Ld Bp of Busoga in St Paul's Cathl Kampala 6 Aug 72 by Abp of Ugan; Bps of W Bugan; Nam; Ank; Kig; M & W Nile; Mbale; Soroti; Ruw; N Ugan; Boga-Z; and others. *Box 1658, Jinja, Uganda.* (Jinja 20617)

BANA, Johnson Naban. b 49. Bp Patteson Th Coll Kohimarama 70. **d** 77 Ysabel. d Dio Ysabel. *Tasia Training Centre, Ysabel, Solomon Islands.*

BANCE, Walter Thomas. b 44. Lon Coll of Div 65. **d** 69 Willesden for Lon **p** 70 Lon. C of St Edm Northwood Hills 69-72; St Mary Virg (in c of H Spirit) Kenton 72-74; Chap RN 74-78; P-in-c of Wendron 78-80; H Trin Ryde Dio Portsm from 80. *Vicarage, Belvedere Street, Ryde, IW, PO33 2JW.* (Ryde 62351)

BANDA, Constantino. d 72 **p** 73 Lusaka. P Dio Lusaka. *Box 46, Msoro, Chipata, Zambia.*

BANDA, Martin. St Pet Coll Rosettenville 48. **d** 50 **p** 51 S Rhod. P Dio S Rhod 51-52; Dio Mashon from 52. *P.O. Box 15, Gatooma, Rhodesia.*

BANDIYOMUHITO, Gerison. b 31. **d** and **p** 76 Vic Nyan. P Dio Vic Nyan. *PO Box 24, Biharomulo, Tanzania.*

BANDS, Leonard Michael. b 40. Rhodes Univ BA 68. St Paul's Coll Grahmstn Dip Th 69. **d** 69 Grahmstn **p** 70 Port Eliz. C of St Kath, Uitenhage 70-72; R of Alexandria 72-74; Chap Rhodes Univ Grahmstn 75-80; Dioc Sch for Girls Grahmstn from 80. *16 Worcester Street, Grahamstown, CP, S Africa.*

BANFIELD, Andrew Henry. b 48. AKC 71. St Aug Coll Cant 72. **d** 73 **p** 74 Roch. C of Crayford 73-76; Youth Officer Dio Glouc from 76. *Vicarage, Sandhurst, Gloucester, GL2 9NP.*

BANFIELD, Colin Clement. St Jo Coll Auckld NZ Bd of Th Stud LTh 64. **d** 62 Bp McKenzie for Wel **p** 63 Wel. C of Masterton 62-66; Epsom Surrey 66-67; V of St Cuthb Berhampore Wel 68-70; C of Palmerston N 70-72; V of I Bay 72-76; Offg Min Dio Auckld from 76; Hon P-in-c of The Is Auckld 78-80. *8 Thorp Street, St Johns, Auckland 5, NZ.*

BANFIELD, David John. b 33. ALCD 56. **d** 57 **p** 58 Man. C of Middleton 57-62; Chap Scargill Conf House Kettlewell 62-65; Asst Warden 65-67; V of Addiscombe 67-80; Luton Dio St Alb from 80. *48 Crawley Green Road, Luton, Beds, LU2 0QX.* (Luton 28925)

BANFIELD, Thomas Harrie. ACT ThL 57. **d** 56 Geelong for Wang **p** 57 Wang. C of H Trin Cathl Wang 56-59; R of Murchison 60-61; C of St Wilfrid Halton Yorks 61-62; Bp's Youth Chap and L to Offic Dio Derby 62-66; V of E Doncaster 67-76; Cobram 76-80. *c/o Rectory, High Street, Cobram, Vic, Australia 3644.* (058-72 1211)

BANGAFU, William. d 75 Sudan **p** 77 Yambio. d Dio Sudan 75-76; P Dio Yambio 77; Dio Juba from 77. *Box 110, Juba, Sudan.*

BANGBERE, Firipo. d 72 **p** 73 Sudan. P Dio Sudan 72-76; Dio Yambio from 76. *ECS, Maridi, Sudan.*

BANGERT, Harry Alfred. b 07. ALCD 33. **d** 33 **p** 34 Cant. C of Ch Ch Ramsgate 33-35; Harlington 35-37; Sprowston (in c of Beeston St Andr) 37-39; R of Gimingham 39-43; V of Bamford 43-50; Chap Bromsgrove Group Hosps 50-67; Knowle Hosp Fareham 67-75; Hon C of E Preston w Kingston 75-80. *7 Long Meadow, Findon Valley, Worthing, BN14 0HU.* (Findon 2649)

BANGOR, Lord Bishop of. *See* Williams, Most Rev Gwilym Owen.

BANGOR, Archdeacon of. *See* Evans, Ven Hugh Arfon.

BANGOR, Dean of. *See* Rees, Very Rev John Ivor.

BANHAM, Peter George. b 18. Bps' Coll Cheshunt. **d** 63 **p** 64 St Alb. C of Leighton Buzzard 63-66; V of Rye Pk 66-73; C of Digswell 73; V of Offley w Lilley 74-77; C of Hatfield Hyde Dio St Alb from 78. *Church House, Hollybush Lane, Welwyn Garden City, Herts.* (W G C 23214)

BANHAM, Harry Eustace Lorrane. b 04. **d** 75 **p** 76 Moray. C of St Columba Nairn 75-80; Hon Chap St Andr Cathl Inverness from 80. *Dellachaple, Lochloy Road, Nairn, Scotland, IV12 5AF.* (Nairn 52763)

BANI, Barnabas. d 79 New Hebr **p** 81 Vanuatu. P Dio New Hebr 79-80; Dio Vanuatu from 80. *Navonda, Longana, Aoba, Vanuatu.*

BANI, Benjamin. d 34 **p** 38 Melan. P Dio Melan 34-74. *South Maewo, New Hebrides.*

BANI, John Bennett. St Jo Coll Auckld 66. NZ Bd of Th Stud LTh 69. **d** 69 **p** 70 Melan. P Dio Melan 70-75; Dio New Hebr 75-80; Dio Vanuatu from 80. *Box 238, Santo, Vanuatu.*

BANI, Ven Michael. St Paul's Th Coll Moa I 56. **d** 56 **p** 63 Carp. I of Murray I 67-69; Badu I 70-74; Thursday I 74-79; Archd of Torres Strait from 76; P-in-c of Bamaga Dio Carp from 79. *c/o Box 79, Thursday Island, Queensland, Australia 4875.*

BANISTER, Martin John. b 39. Worc Coll Ox BA (2nd cl Th) 62, MA 68. Chich Th Coll 62. **d** 64 **p** 65 Pet. C of Wellingborough 64-67; Heene 67-70; V of Denford w Ringstead 70-78; P-in-c of Houghton Conquest 78-80; Wilshamstead Dio St Alb 78-80; V (w Houghton Conquest) from 80. *15 Vicarage Lane, Wilshamstead, Bedford, MK45 3EU.* (0234 740423)

BANISTER, Michael Brett. b 07. Late Scho of Worc Coll Ox BA (2nd cl Mod Hist) 29, 2nd cl Th 31, MA 34. St Steph Ho, Ox 29. **d** 31 **p** 32 Derby. C of St Anne Derby 31-35; St Jo Bapt Cov 35-39; V of Seaforth 39-45; Flockton w Denby Grange 45-51; Long Eaton 51-62; Surr 57-62; V of King's Sutton 62-74; Perm to Offic Dio Derby from 74. *32 Brookfields Drive, Breadsall, Derby.* (0332-831 958)

BANJO, Samuel Ayodele. MBE 62. Univ of Lon BA 33. Univ of Dur (Fourah Bay Coll) DTh OT 36. **d** 39 **p** 40 Lagos. Tutor Dio Lagos 39-45; P-in-c St John Aroloya 45-48; Prin Ibad Elem Tr Centre Ibad 48-63; Synod Sec Dio Ibad 52-72; Exam Chap to Bp of Ibad 54-71; Can of Ibad 54-65; Chairman Ibad Centr Distr Ch Coun 64-72; Archd of Ibad 65-72. *Immanuel College, PO Box 15, Ibadan, Nigeria.*

BANK, Ven Louis. Univ of Stellenbosch BSc 51. Rhodes Univ Gramstn BA 56, BD (2nd cl) 61. St Paul's Th Coll Grahmstn 57. **d** 58 **p** 59 Geo. C of Knysna 58-62; Prittlewell Essex 62-64; St Andr Riversdale 64-70; P-in-c of Manenberg Township 70-73; Dioc Dir of Educn and Miss Dio Capetn 73-76; R of St Paul Rondebosch Dio Capetn from 76; Archd of The Cape from 80. *Rectory, Roslyn Road, Rondebosch, CP, S Africa.* (6-3512)

BANKES, William John Hawtrey. b 08. St Bonif Coll Warm 28. **d** 31 Southampton for Win **p** 33 Win. C of St Pet Bournemouth 31-33; Andover 33-35; Chap Miss to Seamen and Sub Dean of St Jas Cathl Port Louis 36-39; Chap RNVR 39-47; RN 47-60; R of St Mary Pembroke Tobago 60-62; PC of Burcombe 62-66; R of Shotley w Erwarton 66-74. *College of St Barnabas, Blackberry Lane, Lingfield, Surrey, RH7 6NJ.*

BANKS, Aleck George. b 18. Univ of Lon BD 42, AKC 42. **d** 42 **p** 43 Chelmsf. C of St Jas Colchester 42-45; Leigh-on-Sea 45-51; V of Bradfield 51-56; St Geo Becontree 56-61; S Benfleet Dio Chelmsf from 61. *Vicarage, South Benfleet, Essex.* (South Benfleet 2294)

BANKS, Brian William Eric. b 35. Dipl Th (Lon) 65, BD (Lon) 69. Wycl Hall Ox 63. **d** 65 Malmesbury for Bris **p** 66 Bris. C of Ch Ch Swindon 65-68; Halesowen w Hasbury 68-71; V of Wychbold w Upton Warren 71-77; Ed Worc Dioc News 71-76; V of Bengeworth Dio Worc from 77; RD of Evesham from 81. *1 Broadway Road, Evesham, Worcs.* (Evesham 6164)

BANKS, Ernest Leslie. b 10. Men in Disp 45. Oak Hill Th Coll. **d** 55 **p** 56 St Alb. C of Ch Ch St Alb 55-58; Attenborough 58-60; R of Kimberley Dio Southw from 60; Surr from 72. *Kimberley Rectory, Nottingham, NG16 2LL.* (Nottm 383565)

BANKS, Ven George Frederick. Wycl Coll Tor LTh 29. **d** 29 **p** 30 Tor. C of St John W Tor 29-31; R of Erindale 31-64; RD of Peel 42-60; Can of St Jas Pro-Cathl Tor 52-60; Archd of Etobicoke 60-64; Archd (Emer) from 65. *2579 Proudfoot Street, Erindale, Cooksville, Ont., Canada.*

BANKS, John Alan. b 32. Late Exhib of Hertf Coll Ox BA (2nd cl Mod Hist) 54, MA 58. Westcott Ho Cam 56. **d** 58 **p** 59 Southw. C of Warsop 58-61; St Aldate w H Trin Ox 61-64; V of Ollerton 64-75; Boughton 64-75; Surr from 69; M Gen Syn Southw from 73; R of Wollaton Dio Southw from 75; RD of Beeston 77-81. *Rectory, Russell Drive, Wollaton, Nottingham.* (Nottm 281798)

BANKS, Joseph. b 23. CEng MIMechE 65. **d** 80 Ches **p** 81 Stockport for Ches (NSM). C of St Jo Bapt Bollington Dio Ches from 80. *28 Packsaddle Park, Prestbury, Macclesfield, SK10 4PT.*

BANKS, Michael Thomas Harvey. b 35. Open Univ BA 75. St Cuthb Coll Dur 58. **d** 63 **p** 64 RC Bp of Hexham and Newc T. Rec into C of E by Bp of Dur 69. Perm to Offic St Pet Stockton 69; C of St Paul Winlaton 69-71; C-in-c of Good Shepherd Bp Wearmouth 71-75; Team V of Melton Mowbray 75-80; R of Em Ch Loughborough Dio Leic from 80. *Emmanuel Rectory, Loughborough, Leics, LE11 3NW.* (Loughboro 63264)

BANKS, Robert John. Univ of Syd BA 59. BD (1st cl) Lon 62. ACT ThL (1st cl) 62. Moore Th Coll Syd 59. **d** 63 **p** 64 Adel. C of H Trin Adel 63-64; on leave from 64. *c/o 3 Darling Street, Menindie, S. Australia.*

BANNER, John William. b 36. Open Univ BA 78. Tyndale

Hall Bris 61. **d** 64 Warrington for Liv **p** 65 Liv. C of St Leon Bootle 64-66; St Jas Wigan 66-69; H Trin Stapleton 69-70; Gen Sec Script U (Queensld) w Perm to Offic Dio Brisb 70-72; V of Ch Ch (Bp Chavasse Mem Ch) Norris Green Dio Liv from 72. *Christ Church Vicarage, Sedgemoor Road, Liverpool 11.* (051-226 1774)

BANNERMAN, David Douglas. b 38. Canberra Coll of Min 75. **d** and **p** 78 C & Goulb. C of S Monaro 78-80; R of Gunning Dio C & Goulb from 80. *Rectory, Biala Street, Gunning, NSW, Australia 2581.*

BANNERMAN, David Hugh. b 48. St Paul's Coll Grahmstn 69. **d** 72 **p** 73 Matab. C of St John's Cathl Bulawayo 72-75; St Cuthb Gwelo 75-76; R of St Jo Bapt Harrismith Dio Bloemf from 77. *Box 421, Harrismith, OFS, S Africa.*

BANNISTER, Anthony Peter. b 40. Univ of Ex BA (2nd cl Econ) 62. Clifton Th Coll 63. **d** 65 Taunton for B & W **p** 66 B & W. C of Uphill 65-69; C of Bp Hannington Mem Ch w H Cross, Hove 69-74; V of Wembdon Dio B & W from 74; RD of Bridgwater from 80. *12 Greenacre, Wembdon, Bridgwater, Somt, TA6 7RD.*

BANNISTER, Edward. b 06. Lich Th Coll 27. **d** 29 **p** 30 Man. C of Patricroft 29-32; Dom Chap to Bp of Bom 32-35; C of Ch Ch Moss Side 35-37; Min Can and Sacr of Win Cathl 37-38 and 51-56; C of Rickmansworth 38-43; PC of St Jas High Wych 43-51; V of Sparsholt w Lainston 56-73; Hon Min Can of Win Cathl 60; Warden Morley Coll Win from 76. *8 Morley College, Winchester.*

BANNISTER, Grattan Eric McGillycuddy Colm Brendon. Trin Coll Dub BA 50, MA 53. **d** 52 Clogh **p** 57 Worc. C of St Barn Rainbow Hill Worc 57-58; St Luke Cork 61-63; R of Schull Dio Cork from 63. *Rectory, Schull, Co Cork, Irish Republic.*

BANNISTER, John. b 24. Westcott Ho Cam 68. **d** 69 Chich **p** 70 Lewes for Chich. C of Rye and Playden (w Guldeford 69-73) and Hd Master St Mich Sch Playden Dio Chich from 69. *Wynfields, Grove Lane, Iden, Rye, Sussex.* (Iden 229)

BANNISTER, Kenneth William. b 06. **d** 61 **p** 62 Truro. C of Bodmin 61-65; Chap at St Endellion 65-69; V of Wendron 69-77. *St Gwendron, Rock, Wadebridge, Cornw.*

BANNISTER, Michael Barnabas St Leger Hurst. *See* Hurst-Bannister, Michael Barnabas St Leger.

BANNISTER, Peter Edward. b 38. Univ of Leeds BSc 60. Linc Th Coll 72. **d** 74 **p** 75 Cant. C of Norbury 74-77; Allington w St Pet Maidstone 77-80; R of Temple Ewell w Lydden Dio Cant from 80. *Rectory, Green Lane, Temple Ewell, Dover, Kent.* (Kearnsey 2865)

BANNISTER, Canon Simon Monro. b 38. St Jo Coll Ox BA 62, MA 69. Linc Th Coll 61. **d** 63 Hulme for Man **p** 64 Man. C of St Marg Prestwich 63-66; Farnborough Kent 66-70; V of St Mark Bury 70-78; Oldham Dio Man 78; R from 78; Hon Can of Man Cathl from 80. *Rectory, Egerton Street, Oldham, Gtr Man, OL1 3SE.* (061-624 4866)

BANNON, Richard Babington. b 20. Trin Coll Dub BA 42. MA 47. Div Test 48. **d** 48 Bp Hind for Down **p** 49 Down. C of Bangor Abbey 48-51; St Luke Belfast 51-55; I of Ardclinis w Tickmacrevan Dio Connor from 55. *Rectory, Carnlough, Ballymena, Co Antrim, N Ireland.* (Carnlough 85618)

BANOBERE, Azaliya. **d** 45 **p** 46 Ugan. P Dio Ugan 45-60; Dio Ruw 60-80. *PO Kyegegwa, Uganda.*

BANTING, David Percy. b 51. Magd Coll Cam MA 74. Wycl Hall Ox BA (Th) 80. **d** 80 **p** 81 Ox. C of St Ebbe City and Dio Ox from 80. *St Ebbe's Flat, 1 Roger Bacon Lane, Oxford, OX1 1QE.* (Ox 48365)

BANTING, Canon Harry Maurice James. b 05. Late Scho of Selw Coll Cam, 1st cl Hist Trip pt i 26, BA (1st cl Th Trip pt i) 27, 1st cl Th Trip pt ii 28, MA 31. Westcott Ho Cam 28. **d** 29 **p** 30 Ely. Chap Pemb Coll Cam 29-33; Exam Chap to Bp of Roch 30-39; C of New Mills 33-36; Perm to Offic at St Mary Selly Oak 36-37; V of Studley 37-42; Lode 42-49; Madingley 49-56; Kimbolton 56-58; RD of Kimbolton 57-58; Exam Chap to Bp of Ely from 46; Select Pr Univ of Cam 54; R of Teversham 58-74; Hon Can of Ely 65-79; Can (Emer) from 79; Perm to Offic Dio Ely from 79. *Countryman, Cardinal's Green, Horseheath, Cambridge, CB1 6QX.* (Cambridge 891661)

BANTING, Kenneth Mervyn Lancelot Hadfield. b 37. Pemb Coll Cam BA 61, MA 65. Cudd Coll 64. **d** 65 **p** 66 Win. Asst Chap Win Coll 65-70; C of Leigh Park 70-73; Team V of Hemel Hempstead 73-79; V of Goldington Dio St Alb from 79; P-in-c of Renhold Dio St Alb from 80. *Goldington Vicarage, Turnpike Way, Bedford, MK41 0EX.* (Bedford 55024)

BANTING, Warren Charles Snowden. Hur Coll Ont. St Chad's Coll Regina 51. **d** 53 **p** 54 Qu'App. C of Moose Jaw 53-54; I of Murillo 54-56; Miss at West Thunder Bay 56-58; R of Espanola 58-59; I of All SS, Sault Ste Marie 59-70; Temiscaming 70-72; P-in-c of Apsley 72-73; I of Bay Ridges 73-77; St Agnes City and Dio Tor from 77. *69 Long Branch Avenue, Islington, Ont, Canada.*

BANTONG, Emmanuel Adamu. b 52. Im Coll Ibad 78. **d** 81 Kaduna. d Dio Kaduna. *PO Box 125, Kafanchan, Kaduna State, Nigeria.*

BANU, Masepah Samuel. St Paul's Coll Moa I. **d** 55 **p** 56 Carp. C of Thursday I 56; Yam I 56-58; P-in-c 58-60; Murray I 60; Saibai and Dauan Is 60-63; Edw River Miss 63-65; Chap Mitchell River Miss 66-69; Prec Carp Cathl 69; P-in-c of Darnley I 69-73; Boigu I 74-76. *Boigu Island, via Thursday Island, Queensland, Australia.*

BANWO, Ven Zaccheus Omatayo. **d** 51 **p** 52 Lagos. P Dio Lagos 52-56 and from 59; Dio Ibad 56-59; Can of Lagos 71-77; Archd of the Mainland and Exam Chap to Bp of Lagos from 77. *St Jude's Vicarage, Box 45, Ebute Metta, Lagos, Nigeria.* (Lagos 44221)

BANYAGA, Simon. b 19. **d** 76 **p** 77 Kiga. P Dio Kiga. *c/o BP, 19 Rwamagana, Rwanda.*

BANYARD, Douglas. b 20. Univ of Edin MA (3rd cl Mental Phil) 42. Westcott Ho Cam 42. Edin Th Coll 43. **d** 45 **p** 46 Aber. Chap St Andr Cathl Aber 45-46; Asst Dioc Chap and C of St Mark's Miss Aber 46-47; St Jo Evang Aber 47-50; Abington (in c of St Alb Mart) 50-52; CF (TA) 49-52; CF 52-70; R of St Mary-in-the-Castle Dover 60; St Thos Aboyne 70-78; P-in-c of Cattistock w Chilfrome and Rampisham w Wraxall 78-79; Team V of Melbury Dio Sarum from 79. *Cattistock Rectory, Dorchester, Dorset.* (Maiden Newton 245)

BANYARD, Peter Vernon. b 35. Sarum Th Coll 57. **d** 59 **p** 60 Win. C of St Pet Maybush 59-63; Tilbury Docks 63-65; Chap Miss to Seamen Tilbury 63-65; Walvis Bay, SW Afr 65-68; V of SS Aug, Chesterfield 68-73; Team V of Grantham (in c of Harrowby) 73-79; Chap Warm Sch Wilts from 79; Commiss Namibia from 80. *c/o Warminster School, Wilts.*

BANYENKAZI, Ven Yosia. **d** 64 Ankole-K. d Dio Ankole-K 64-71; Dio Ank 67-71; Dio Kig (N Kig from 81) from 71; Archd and Can of Kig (N Kig from 81) from 76. *Box 23, Rukungiri, Uganda.*

BANYENZAKI, Ven Yokana. Bp Tucker Coll Mukono. **d** 51 **p** 53 Ugan. P Dio Ugan 51-60; Dio Ankole-K 60-67; Dio Ank 67-76; Dio W Ank from 77; Can of Ank 70-76; W Ank from 77. *Box 140, Bushenyi, Ankole, Uganda.*

BANYENZAKI, Yosia. **d** 64 Ankole-K. d Dio Ankole-K 64-67; Dio Ank from 67. *Private Bag, Mbarara, Uganda, E Africa.*

BANYIRI, Paulo Banga. **d** 60 **p** 61 Sudan. P Dio Sudan. *C.M.S., Panyana, Sudan.*

BARAMANA, Moses. Warner Th Coll Buye 67. **d** 69 Bur. d Dio Bur. *Buye, P.O. Box 58, Ngozi, Burundi, Centr Africa.*

BARARUKIZE, G Wilson. **d** and **p** 79 W Ank. P Dio W Ank. *Box 94, Bushenyi, Uganda.*

BARASA, Ven Zefania. Buwalasi Th Coll 60. **d** 62 **p** 63 Mbale. P Dio Mbale 62-72; Dio Bukedi from 72; Archd of Tororo from 81. *Box 170, Tororo, Uganda.*

BARBADOS, Lord Bishop of. *See* Gomez, Right Rev Drexel Wellington.

BARBADOS, Dean of. *See* Crichlow, Very Rev Harold Edmund.

BARBARA, Michael Geoffrey. St Jo Coll Morpeth 62. **d** 65 **p** 66 C & Goulb. C of St Sav Cathl Goulburn 65-66; Young 66-67; Queanbeyan 67-69; R of Adaminaby 69-71. *Rectory, Adaminaby, N.S.W., Australia.*

BARBER, Charles Clyde. b 05. Qu Coll Ox Heath Harrison Scho 25, BA (1st cl Mod Lang) 26, MA 30. BD 72. Univ of Giessen D Phil 32. Wells Th Coll 32. **d** 32 Malmesbury for Bris **p** 33 Bris. C of St Jo Evang Clifton Bris 32-41; Asst Lect in German Univ of Bris 30-35; Lect 35-41; R of Upton Scudamore 41-46; Lect Univ of Aber 46-56; Sen Lect 56-75; Perm to Offic Dio Aber from 48. *503 King Street, Aberdeen, AB2 3BT.* (Aberdeen 44326)

BARBER, Christopher Albert. b 33. Late Tancred Stud of Ch Coll Cam 1st cl Cl Trip pt i 52, BA (2nd cl Cl Trip pt ii) 53, 2nd cl Th Trip pt ia 54, MA 57. Coll of Resurr Mirfield 56. **d** 58 **p** 59 Cov. C of St Pet Cov 58-61; Stokenchurch w Cadmore End 61-64; V of St Paul Royton 64-70; Stapleford 70-80; Cherry Hinton Dio Ely from 80; RD of Shelford 76-80. *Cherry Hinton Vicarage, Fulbourn, Old Drift, Cambridge, CB1 4LR.* (Cam 247740)

BARBER, David. b 45. **d** 72 **p** 73 Edmon for Lon. C of St Matt Muswell Hill 72-75; St Pancras 75-77; Chap Brook Gen Hosp Woolwich and Greenwich Distr Hosp 77-80. *Address temp unknown.*

BARBER, Eric Skottowe. b 11. Late Exhib of TCD BA (2nd cl Mod) 33, MA 42, 1st Downes Oratory Pri, 1st Abp King Div Pri, and 1st Bp Forster Pri 34, 1st Downes Comp Pri and Div Test (1st cl) 35. **d** 35 **p** 36 Down. C of St Mary Magd Belf 35-37; Bangor 37-40; C-in-c of St Brendan Belf 40-41; I of St Jas Belf 41-45; Holywood Dio Down from 45; RD of Holywood 51-59; Can and Preb of St Patr Cathl Dub from 59; Hon Sec Down Dioc Synod and Coun from 70; Chan of Down 74; Archd of Down 74-78. *Holywood Vicarage, Belfast, N Ireland.* (Holywood 2069)

BARBER, Frank Thomas. b 13. St Chad's Coll Dur LTh 42, BA 43. St Aid Coll 39. **d** 43 **p** 44 St A. C of Hawarden 43-53; V of S Moor 53-58; Micklefield 58-69; Glaisdale 69-78; Perm to Offic Dio Cant from 78. *2 Warden Road, Eastchurch, Isle of Sheppey, Kent, ME12 4EJ.* (Eastchurch 407)

BARBER, Canon Frederick Hugh. b 15. Univ of Birm Dipl Th 46. Univ of Bris MA 64. Tyndale Hall Bris 38. **d** 42 **p** 43 Lich. C of Aldridge 42-47; V of Shenstone 47-56; Min of St Paul's Conv Distr Hainault 56-58; Eccles Distr 58-60; Perm to Offic Dio S'wark 60-63; R of Fordham 63-81; RD of Dedham 74-79; Dedham & Tey 79-81; Hon Can of Chelmsf Cathl 79-81; Can (Emer) from 81. *Myholm, Chappel Road, Great Tey, Colchester, Essex.* (Colchester 211334)

BARBER, Garth Antony. b 48. Univ of Southn BSc 69. St Jo Coll Nottm LTh 76. **d** 76 Lon **p** 77 Kens for Lon. C of H Trin Hounslow Dio Lon from 76; Chap City of Lon Poly from 79. *16 Balfour Road, Hounslow, Middx, TW3 1JX.*

BARBER, Geoffrey Thomas. b 23. St D Coll Lamp BA 51. Ridley Hall Cam 51. **d** 53 **p** 54 Chelmsf. C of Walthamstow 53-55; Woking 56-57; V of St Jo Evang Chelsea 57-66; St Pet Rushden 66-75; Em Leyton 75-81. *8 Minster View, Wimborne Minster, Dorset, BH21 1BA.* (Wimborne 885268)

BARBER, John Eric Michael. b 30. Wycl Hall Ox 63. **d** 65 **p** 66 Wakef. C of Lupset 65-68; Halifax 68-70; V of St Matt West Town w St Jo Bapt Dewsbury 70-80; Perry Common Dio Birm from 80. *148 Witton Lodge Road, Perry Common, Birmingham, B23 5AP.* (021-382 7666)

BARBER, Martin John. b 35. Univ of Lon BA (3rd cl Hist) 61. Linc Th Coll 61. **d** 63 **p** 64 Lon. C of Stepney 63-67; Chap K Sch Bruton and L to Offic Dio B & W from 67. *Hugh Sexey's Hospital, Bruton, Somt, BA10 0AS.* (Bruton 2290)

BARBER, Michael. b 40. Oak Hill Coll 69. **d** 71 **p** 72 Leic. C of Rothley 71-74; The Martyrs Leic 74-76; V of Queniborough 76-82; All SS Monk Wearmouth Dio Dur from 82. *All Saints Vicarage, Fulwell Road, Sunderland, T & W.* (0783 56606)

BARBER, Ven Paul Everard. b 35. St Jo Coll Cam BA 58 MA 66. Wells Th Coll 58. **d** 60 **p** 61 Guildf. C of St Francis Westborough 60-66; V of Camberley w Yorktown 66-73; St Thos-on-the Bourne 73-80; RD of Farnham 74-79; Archd of Surrey and Hon Can of Guildford Cathl from 80. *71 Boundstone Road, Rowledge, Farnham, Surrey, GU10 4AT.* (Frensham 3987)

BARBER, Philip Kenneth. b 43. St Jo Coll Dur BA (Th) 65. N-W Ordin Course 74. **d** 76 **p** 77 Liv. Asst Master Ormskirk Gr Sch and C of Burscough Bridge Dio Liv from 76. *28 Abbey Dale, Briars Park, Lathom, Nr Ormskirk, Lancs L40 5SU.*

BARBER, Thomas Edward Morton. b 07. Ch Coll Cam BA 32, MA 36. Linc Th Coll 32. **d** 33 **p** 34 Linc. C of St Nich w St John Newport (in c of St Matthias from 36) 33-39; V of Spondon Dio Derby from 39. *Spondon Vicarage, Derby.* (Derby 61573)

BARBER, William Ewart Worsley. b 15. Univ of Leeds BA 38. Coll of Resurr Mirfield 38. **d** 40 **p** 41 Dur. C of St Helen Auckland 40-41; Heworth 41-44; Winlaton (in c of St Patr High Spen) 44-47; H Trin (in c of Abbey Ch Whitley) Cov 47-53; V of H Trin Drybrook 53-59; Sandhurst 59-64; Asst Youth Chap Dio Glouc 60-64; C-in-c of St Geo Conv Distr Lower Tuffey Glouc 64-67; V 67-74; R of Huntley w May Hill 74-79. *The Old Rectory, Bromsberrow, Ledbury, Herefs.*

BARBOUR, Walter Iain. b 28. Pemb Coll Cam BA 48, MA 53. FICE 65. **d** 81 Buckingham for Ox (NSM). C of Bray w Braywood Dio Ox from 81. *St Michael's House, Bray, by Maidenhead, Berks.*

BARCLAY, Albert John Howard. Univ of Tor BA 49 Wycl Coll Tor LTh 52. **d** 52 Tor **p** 52 Bp Wells for Tor. I of Cardiff and Monmouth 52-54; R of Bobcaygeon 54-59; I of Penetanguishene 59-73; St D Donlands City and Dio Tor from 73. *83 Strathmore Boulevard, Toronto 6, Ont., Canada.* (416-465 4940)

BARCLAY, David Norman. Wycl Coll Tor. **d** and **p** 55 Niag. I of Harriston 55-58; C of All SS Pet 58-60; St Cuthb Church-on-Wheels 61-67; I of Grand Marais 67-70; Portage la Prairie 70-71; on leave 71-72; C of Selkirk 72-77; H Trin Winnipeg 77-80; P-in-c of St Thos Winnipeg Dio Rupld from 80; St Anne Winnipeg Dio Rupld from 81. *95 Gull Lake Road, Winnipeg, Manit, Canada.*

BARCLAY, Ian Newton. b 33. Clifton Th Coll 58. **d** 61 **p** 62 Ex. C of Cullompton 61-63; Ashill 63-66; V of St Phil and St Jas Chatham 66-69; Assoc R of St Helen, Bishopsgate w St Martin, Outwich 70-73; V of Prestonville 73-81; in Amer Ch. *Address temp unknown.*

BARCLAY, Nigel Ernest William. Univ of NZ BA 27, MA 28. **d** 39 **p** 40 Waik. Dioc Chap Dio Waik 39-43; Offg Min Dio Ch Ch 43-53; Dio Wel 53-56. *c/o Ruapehu College, Ohakune, N.Z.*

BARCROFT, Ambrose William Edgar. b 17. Trin Coll Dub BA 40, Div Test 41, MA 46. **d** 41 **p** 42 Derry. C of Drumachose 41-46; Chap RN 46-70; R of Pitlochry 70-82. *Old School House, Struan, Calvine, Perthshire.* (Calvine 224)

BARD, Christopher Frederick Jesse. b 52. AKC 75. St Aug Coll Cant 73. **d** 76 **p** 77 Dur. C of St Cuthb Billingham 76-79; Egglescliffe 79-81 Chap to Arts & Recreation in NE Engl 79-81; P-in-c of Epping Upland Dio Chelmsf from 81; Dioc Communications Officer Dio Chelmsf from 81. *Vicarage, Epping Green, Epping, Essex.* (Epping 72949).

BARDELL, Frank Stanley. b 04. Univ of Lon BA (1st cl Archit) 24. ARIBA 38. Oak Hill Th Coll 54. **d** 55 **p** 56 Lon. C of Ch Ch Barnet 55-59; R of Maresfield 59-73. *13 Orchard Way, Dibden Purlieu, Southampton, SO4 5AP.*

✠ **BARDSLEY, Right Rev Cuthbert Killick Norman.** b 07. CBE 52. New Coll Ox BA 29, MA 34, DD 56. Univ of Warw Hon DLitt 76. Westcott Ho Cam 31. **d** 32 **p** 33 Lon. C of All H Barking-by-the-Tower Lon 32-34; R of Woolwich 40-44; Provost of S'wark Cathl 44-48; R of St Pet w St Sav S'wark 44-48; Proc Conv S'wark 45-47; Hon Can of Cant 47-56; Cons Ld Bp Suffr of Croydon in S'wark Cathl 1 Nov 47 by Abp of Cant; Bps of Lon; Southw; S'wark; and Roch; Bps Suffr of Kingston T; Woolwich; and Dover; Bps Sherwood-Jones; Linton; and Gwynne; Trld to Cov 56; res 76; Abp's Episc Repres with the Services from 47; Commiss Gambia 48-56; Ja 50-56; Chairman CEMS 56-74; Select Pr Univ of Cam 59-60; Sub-Prelate O of St John of Jer from 76. *Grey Walls, Berkeley Road, Cirencester, Glos, GL7 1TY.* (Cirencester 3520)

BARDSLEY, Cyril Booth. b 08. Univ of Dur LTh 32. St Aid Coll 30. **d** 32 **p** 33 Southw. C of Lenton (in c of St Barn 37-39) 32-43; PC of Ch Ch Newark 43-65; Surr 47-65; R of Hawton 53-65; V of Muker w Melbecks 65-73. *Abbotside, Burtersett Road, Hawes, N Yorks, DL8 3NT.* (Hawes 417)

BARDSLEY, Edwin Roy. b 24. St Jo Coll Cam BA 47, MA 52. Wells Th Coll 48. **d** 49 **p** 50 Man. C of Oldham 49-53; Min of St Geo Conv Distr Romford 53-58; V of Moulsham 58-74; Chap to Chelmsf and Essex Hosp 58-74; R of Bittadon 74-77; Marwood 74-77; P-in-c of Weare Giffard w Landcross 77-80; Littleham 77-80; Monkleigh 77-80; RD of Hartland 79-80; V of St Andr Tiverton Dio Ex from 80. *49 Tidcombe Lane, Tiverton, Devon.* (Tiverton 2210)

BARDSLEY, Canon John. b 04. Worc Coll Ox BA 26, Dipl Th 27. Wycl Hall Ox 26. **d** 27 Liv **p** 28 Leic for Liv. C of St Mary Wavertree 27-28; Tutor and Chap Prince of Wales Coll Achimota 28-49; Sec Christian Counc and P-in-c of Ridge Ch Accra 49-52; C of St Mary Virg Loughton 52-53; V of Bedfont 53-62; RD of Staines 55-57; R of Odell 62-73; V of Pavenham 62-73; Hon Can of St Alb Cathl 72-73; Can (Emer) from 73. *93 Spenser Road, Bedford, MK40 2BE.* (Bedford 52557)

BARDSLEY, Warren Nigel Antony. b 52. AKC 74. St Aug Coll Cant 74. **d** 75 **p** 76 Ripon. C of St Aidan Leeds 75-78; St Jo Bapt Cov 78-80; P-in-c of Stoke Golding w Dadlington Dio Leic from 80. *Stoke Golding Vicarage, Nuneaton, Warws, CV13 6HN.* (Hinckley 212317)

BARDWELL, Edward Mercer. b 12. Univ of Lon 28. ALCD 41 (LTh from 74). **d** 41 **p** 43 Leic. C of H Ap Leic 41-46; St Francis Dudley 46-49; St Simon Southsea 49-51; V of St Sav Battersea 51-59; R of Cranworth w Letton and Southbergh 59-79; Perm to Offic Dios Ely and Nor from 79. *6 Cromwell Road, Weeting, Brandon, Suffolk.*

BARENDSEN, Peter Martin. Univ of Natal 54. St Paul's Coll Grahmstn 58. **d** and **p** 61 Natal. C of St Pet Pietermaritzburg 61-64; R of Umhlatuzaua 64-66; St Barn Bluff, Durban 73-78; Greytown Dio Natal from 78. *Box 112, Greytown, Natal, S Africa.*

BARFETT, Ven Thomas. b 16. Keble Coll Ox BA (3rd cl Th) 38, MA 42. Wells Th Coll 38. **d** 39 **p** 40 Portsm. C of Ch Ch Gosport 39-44; St Francis of Assisi, Gladstone Park 44-47; St Andr Undershaft w St Mary Axe Lon 47-49; Asst Sec Lon Dioc Council for Youth 44-49; PC of Penzance 49-55; Sec Truro Dioc Conf 52-67; R of Falmouth 55-77; Chap Falmouth and Distr Hosp 55-77; Surr 55-77; Proc Conv Truro 58-77; M Gen Syn from 77; Asst Chap O of St John of Jer 63-71; Sub-Chap from 71; Hon Can of Truro 64-77; Chap to HM the Queen from 75; Archd of Heref from 77; Can Res and Preb of Heref Cathl from 77. *Archdeacon's House, The Close, Hereford, HR1 2NG.* (0432-2873)

BARFF, John Robert. b 43. Ch Coll Cam BA 66, MA 70. ALCD 68. MTh (Lon) 69. **d** 69 **p** 70 Kens for Lon. C of St Mary Hammersmith Road Fulham 69-73; CMS Tr 73-74; CMS Miss at Omdurman Dio Sudan (Dio Omdurman from 76) from 75. *PO Box 65, Omdurman, Sudan.*

BARFORD, John Crawford. b 08. Em Coll Sktn 69. **d** and

p 70 Edmon. I of Ch of Good Shepherd Edmon 70-80. *705, 10011-116 Street, Edmonton, Alta., Canada.*

BARHAM, Ian Harold. b 40. Clifton Th Coll 64. **d** 66 **p** 67 Chich. C of Broadwater 66-69; Miss in Burundi 71-72; C of Broadwater 72-76; R of Beyton w Hessett 76-79; Perm to Offic Dio St E 80-81; Hon C of St Mary Bury St Edms Dio St E from 81. *19 Hickling Drive, Bury St Edmunds, Suff.*

BARHAM, Kenneth Lawrence. b 36. Clifton Th Coll. **d** 63 **p** 64 Chich. C of St Geo Worthing 63-65; St Nich Sevenoaks 65-67; St Mark Cheltm 67-70; V of St Luke Maidstone 70-79; S Area Sec Ruanda Miss from 79. *Rosewood, Canadia Road, Battle, E Sussex, TN33 0LR.* (Battle 3073)

BARHAM, Raymond James. OBE (Mil) 43. DSO 45. Moore Th Coll Syd 60. **d** 61 **p** 62 Syd. C of St Phil Eastwood 61-63; R of Narellan w Cobbitty 63-69; Longford w Perth 70-78. *85 Wellington Street, Longford, Tasmania 7301.* (003-91 1164)

BARHAM, William Allan Berridge. b 11. Univ of Lon BD 36. St Aug Coll Cant 35. **d** 37 **p** 38 Lich. C of All SS Darlaston 37-38; Bedworth 38-40; Asst Chap Lawr R Mil Sch Sanawar 40-43; CMS Miss Taljhari 43-46; C of Stratford on Avon 46-47; R of Lighthorne 47-51; V of Chesterton 48-51; Clifton-upon-Dunsmore w Brownsover and Newton 51-57; Grandborough w Willoughby 57-73. *22 Rushmead Close, Whitstable Road, Canterbury, CT2 7RP.* (0227 52825)

BARIBUGANDA, Eliasafu. b 34. **d** E Ank. d Dio E Ank. *PO Box 4049, Ntungamo, Mbarara, Uganda.*

BARIDAU, Sebastian. b 54. **d** 76 Papua **p** 78 Aipo. d Dio Papua 76-77; New Guinea Is 77-78; Dio Aipo 78-79. *St Michael's Church, Sag Sag Private Bag, Kimbe WNBP, Papua New Guinea.*

BARKER, Alan Gilbert. b 06. Univ Coll Ox BA (3rd cl Hist) 28. 2nd cl Th 30. Wycl Hall Ox 28. **d** 30 **p** 31 Edin. Chap St Mary's Cathl Edin 30-34; C of St Andr Kingswood (in c of Ch of the Good Shepherd Tadworth) 34-41; V of Kilndown 41-45; CF (R of O) 39-45; Chap Dioc Tr Coll for Teachers Dio Sarum 45-50; V of Laverstock 50-55; St Anne Kemnay w Monymusk 55-59; R of All SS Lockerbie 59-62. *1 Church Road, Kington, Herefs.*

BARKER, Allan Jones. Univ of W Ont BA (Econ and Pol Sc) 47. Univ of Wisconsin MA 53. Hur Coll BTh 59. **d** 57 **p** 58 Hur. I of Lion's Head 57; C of H Sav Waterloo 58-59; P-in-c of All SS Waterloo 59-64; Chap Renison Coll Waterloo 58-60; Dir of Social Service Dio Rupld 64-67; Angl Centre Sec 67-68; C of Kelowna 68-73; I of Chase 74; Beaver Valley 74-75; Whitewood 76-79; Dir of Indian and Metis Min Dio Qu'App from 79. *1501 College Avenue, Regina, Sask, Canada.*

BARKER, Arthur John Willoughby. b 10. LCD 46. **d** 48 Dover for Cant **p** 49 Cant. C of Addiscombe 48-53; V of Westgate-on-Sea 53-58; Warden of Scargill Ho Kettlewell 58-61; V of Dent (w Cowgill from 74) 61-76; V of Cowgill 61-76; Perm to Offic Dio Bradf from 76. *West Banks, Dent, Sedbergh, Cumb.*

BARKER, Arundel Charles. b 24. Qu Coll Cam. Tyndale Hall Bris 54. **d** 56 **p** 57 Bris. C of Rodbourne Cheney 56-58; V of St Steph w St Bart and St Matt Islington 58-65; R of Passenham w Deanshanger Dio Pet from 65; C-in-c of Cosgrove 65-66. *Deanshanger Rectory, Milton Keynes, MK19 6JP.* (Milton Keynes 562442)

BARKER, Bertie. **d** 64 Guy **p** 74 Starbroek for Guy. C of Ruimveldt 64-75; R of Ft Wel Dio Guy from 75. *Rectory, Fort Wellington, West Coast, Berbice, Guyana.*

BARKER, Brian Wallwork. b 26. G and C Coll Cam, Mod and Med Lang Trip pt i 49, BA (3rd cl Th Trip pt ia) 50, MA 55. Wells Th Coll 51. **d** 52 **p** 53 Man. C of Bradford 52-58; Chap St Andr Cathl Sing 55-58; P-in-c of Ch of Ascen Sing 58-61; V of St John Ipoh Perak 62-64; V of St Jas Ashton L 65-71; R of St Nich Burnage Dio Man from 71. *Rectory, Fog Lane, Burnage, Manchester, M19 1PL.* (061-432 3384)

BARKER, Charles Gordon. b 19. St Aug Coll Cant 60. **d** 61 **p** 62 Heref. C of Bridgnorth 61-64; R of Hope w Shelve Dio Heref 64-68; C-in-c 68-69; C-in-c of Middleton-in-Chirbury 64-69; V of Chirbury 68-69; V of Marton-in-Chirbury 68-69; C-in-c of Trelystan w Leighton 68-69; L to Offic Dio Heref 70-78; P-in-c of Lydbury N 78-80; Hopesay w Edgton 78-80. *Little Argoed, Clun, Craven Arms, Salop, SY7 8NW.* (Clun 427)

BARKER, Christopher Henry Binks. b 04. Late Holroyd Mus Scho of Keble Coll Ox Ba 26. MA 33. Ely Th Coll 28. **d** 29 **p** 30 Newc T. C of St Gabr Heaton 29-33; St Jo Bapt Stockton-on-Tees 34-42; All SS Middlesbrough 42-43; R of Yarm 43-74. *39 Farmanby Close, Thornton-Dale, Pickering, Yorks, YO18 7TD.* (Pickering 74547)

✠ **BARKER, Right Rev Clifford Conder.** b 26. TD 71. Or Coll Ox BA 50, MA 55. St Chad's Coll Dur Dipl Th 52. **d** 52 **p** 53 York. C of All SS Scarborough 52-55; Redcar 55-57; V of Sculcoates 57-63; CF (TA) 58-74; C-in-c of St Silas Sculcoates 59-61; V of Rudby-in-Cleveland w Middleton 63-70; St Olave w St Giles York 70-76; RD of Stokesley 65-70; of York 71-75; Can of York Minster 73-76; Cons Ld Bp Suffr of Whitby in York Minster 27 Jan 76 by Abp of York; Bps of Southw, Blackb, Ches, Liv and Moray; Bps Suffr of Jarrow, Hull, Stockport, Burnley, Penrith, Pontefract, Selby, Knaresborough, Doncaster, Birkenhead, Sherwood and Hulme; and others. *60 West Green, Stokesley, Middlesbrough, Cleve, TS9 5BD.* (Stokesley 710390)

BARKER, David George. b 51. Univ of Tor BA 72. Trin Coll Tor MDiv 75. **d** 75 Bp Read for Tor **p** 76 Tor. C of St Wilfrid Islington 75-78; I of Minden 78-80; St Paul Washago Dio Tor from 80. *Box 3, Washago, Ont, Canada.*

BARKER, David Robert. b 45. Worc Coll Ox BA 67, MA 70. Virginia Th Sem BD 72. **d** 72 **p** 73 S'wark. C of Roehampton 72-75; Chap Goldsmiths' Coll Lon 75-79; Tr Officer for Min Dio Cov from 79. *367 Dunchurch Road, Bilton, Rugby, CV22 6HU.*

BARKER, Donald Charles. St Edm Hall Ox BA 29, MA 67. Ely Th Coll 27. **d** 28 **p** 29 Lon. C of St Jas Gt Bethnal Green 28-33; St Mich Bromley-by-Bow 33-39; Littleham (in c of St Andr Exmouth) 39-42; Min of St Christopher Conv Distr Hanwell 42-44; R of Horsmonden 44-60; V of St Paul Haggerston 60-67; Master Hugh Sexey's Hosp Bruton from 67. *Hugh Sexey's Hospital, Bruton, Somt, BA10 0AS.* (Bruton 3369)

BARKER, Donald Charles. b 49. Moore Coll Syd 72. **d** 74 **p** 75 Armid. C of Gunnedah 74-77; V of Baradine 77-78; Assoc R of Concord N Dio Syd from 79. *62 Brays Road, Concord, NSW, Australia 2137.* (73-1185)

BARKER, Canon Eric Arthur Joseph. St Jo Coll Morpeth ACT ThL 52. **d** and **p** 52 Newc. C of Waratah 52-54; Ch Ch Newc 54-57; LPr Dio Newc 57-60; R of Bath 60-74; Can of Bath 60-71; Dean 71-74; Dioc Can Missr Dio Newc from 74; Dom Chap to Bp of Newc 74-79; Can Res of Bris Cathl 79; R of St John City and Dio Newc from 80. *St John's Rectory, Parry Street, Newcastle, NSW, Australia 2300.* (2-2691)

BARKER, Frank. b 50. Univ of Nottm BTh 77. Linc Th Coll 73. **d** 77 **p** 78 Win. C of Chandler's Ford Dio Win from 77. *50 Randall Road, Chandler's Ford, Hants.*

BARKER, Harold Sidney Michael. b 16. St Chad's Coll Dur BA 39. **d** 39 **p** 40 Linc. C of St Andr Grimsby 39-42; St Andr Walsall 42-45; St Sav Pimlico 45-51; PC of St Pet-le-Poer Muswell Hill 51-61; V of St Mary Brookfield Dio Lon from 61. *Vicarage, Dartmouth Park Road, NW5 1SL.* (01-267 5941)

BARKER, Canon Hugh Remington. b 19. Pemb Coll Cam BA 41, MA 45. Chich Th Coll 41. **d** 43 **p** 44 Lon. C of St Mich AA Mill Hill 43-48; Legal Distr of St Mary the Virgin Welling 48-51; V of St Steph Walworth Common 51-56; C-in-c of All SS Newington 51-56; V of All SS and St Steph Walworth 56-62; Chap Newington Lodge 51-62; V of Wisbech St Mary 62-75; RD of Wisbech 72-75; P-in-c of Walpole St Pet Dio Ely 75-77; R from 77; P-in-c of Walpole St Andr Dio Ely 75-77; V from 77; RD of Lynn Marshland from 76; Surr from 76; Hon Can of Ely Cathl from 81. *Rectory, Walpole St Peter, Wisbech, Cambs, PE14 7NX.* (0945-780252)

BARKER, James Gavin. b 33. Kelham Th Coll. **d** 58 **p** 59 Lon. C of H Cross Greenford 58-61; St Mary Virg Bournemouth 61-66; St Jas Pokesdown Bournemouth 66-70; V of St Luke Stanmore Win 70-77; Chap and Ho Master Bessels Leigh Sch from 77; Hon C of S Hinksey 77-79; Wootton Dio Ox from 79. *c/o Bessels Leigh School, Abingdon, Oxon.*

BARKER, John Frederic Waller. b 18. MBE (Mil) 45. Selw Coll Cam BA 49, MA 53. Linc Th Coll 49. **d** 51 **p** 52 Ripon. C and Succr of Leeds 51-54; C of St D Ex 54-56; Chap Univ Coll Hosp Lon from 56. *Chaplain's Office, University College Hospital, Gower Street, WC1.* (01-387 9300)

BARKER, Very Rev John Kidman Stuart Ridley. b 12. Univ of Lon 30. Univ Coll Dur 31. Lich Th Coll 32. **d** 35 **p** 36 Dur. C of St Paul Stockton-on-Tees 35-39; Barnard Castle 39-42; C-in-c of Castleside 42; V 42-50; V of Cornforth 50-54; Warter w Huggate 54-60; R of Over Whitacre (w Shustoke from 61) 60-73; Chap to the High Sheriff of Warws 71-72; Dean and R of Cloyne Dio Cloyne from 73; Prec and Can of Cork from 73; R of Corkbeg w Inch and Aghada Dio Cloyne from 73; Midleton Dio Cloyne from 78. *Deanery, Midleton, Co Cork, Irish Republic.* (Cork 631449)

BARKER, Ven John Llewellyn. Ch Ch Coll 62. **d** and **p** 63 Ch Ch. C of Merivale 63-65; V of Hororata 65-69; New Brighton 69-74; Avonside 74-77; Waimate Dio Ch Ch from 77; Archd of Timaru from 77. *Box 10, Waimate, NZ.* (8389)

BARKER, John Stuart. b 30. Univ Coll of N Staffs BA 55. Wells Th Coll 55. **d** 57 **p** 58 Lich. C of St Osw Oswestry 57-60; Portishead 60-63; R of Priston and V of Englishcombe 63-69; V of Chew Magna (w Dundry from 75) Dio B & W from 69. *Vicarage, Chew Magna, Bristol.* (Chew Magna 2472)

BARKER, Julian Roland Palgrave. b 37. Magd Coll Cam BA 61, MA 65. Westcott Ho Cam 61. **d** 63 **p** 64 Lich. C of

Stafford 63-66; Chap Clare Coll Cam 66-70; L to Offic Dio Cant 70-71; Tutor St Aug Coll Cant 70-71; V in Raveningham Group Dio Nor 71-76; R from 76. *Thurlton Rectory, Norwich, NR14 6RN.* (Raveningham 285)

BARKER, Leonard Ralph. b 11. ALCD 39. **d** 39 Bp Willis for Leic **p** 40 Leic. C of H Ap Leic 39-41; Chap RNVR 41-46; R of Nether Broughton 46-48; Nuthall 48-63; Lynby w Papplewick 63-78. *53 Lancaster Drive, Long Sutton, Spalding, Lincs, PE12 9BD.*

BARKER, Canon Leonard Roy. b 24. Selw Coll Cam BA 49, MA 53. Ridley Hall Cam 49. **d** 51 **p** 52 Ripon. C of St Luke Harrogate 51-53; Succr of Bradf Cathl 53-55; V of St Luke Eccleston 55-62; Overchurch (or Upton) 62-80; M Gen Syn 70; Hon Can of Ches Cathl 78-80; Can (Emer) from 80; Dir of Pastoral Stud Ridley Hall Cam from 80. *Ridley Hall, Cambridge, CB3 9HG.*

BARKER, Leslie Cameron. b 48. Univ of Tor BA 76. Wycl Coll Tor MDiv 79. **d** 79 Bp Read for Tor **p** 80 Tor. C of Mississauga 79-80; I of Stayner and Wasaga Beach Dio Tor from 81. *Box 295, Stayner, Ont, Canada, L0M 1S0.*

BARKER, Neil Anthony. b 52. Univ of St Andr BSc 73. Ridley Hall Cam 74. **d** 77 Bp Mort for Leic **p** 78 Leic. C of H Ap City and Dio Leic from 77. *23 Meredith Road, Leicester.* (Leic 824137)

BARKER, Nicholas John Willoughby. b 49. Oriel Coll Ox BA 73, BA (Th) 75, MA 77. Trin Coll Bris 75. **d** 77 **p** 78 St Alb. C of St Mary Watford 77-80; Team V of St Jas and Em Didsbury Dio Man from 80. *6 Barlow Moor Road, Didsbury, Manchester, M20 0TR.*

BARKER, Peter Martin. Ch Coll Hobart. **d** 64 **p** 65 Tas. P-in-c of Risdon Vale 64-67; Asst Chap Hutchins Sch Hobart Dio Tas from 67. *c/o Hutchins School, Nelson Road, Sandy Bay, Tasmania.*

BARKER, Reginald Stanley. Moore Th Coll Syd ACT ThL 58. **d** 59 Bp Hilliard for Syd **p** 59 Syd. C of Bulli 59-60; R of Riverstone 60-64; Chap CMS Miss Angurugu 64-69; C-in-c of Keiraville 69-74; R 74-75; Moorebank Dio Syd from 75. *68 Lucas Avenue, Moorebank, NSW, Australia 2170.* (602-8836)

BARKER, Very Rev Roy Thomas. K Coll Lon and Warm BD and AKC 57. **d** 58 Ripon **p** 59 Knaresborough for York. C of Headingley 58-62; St Mary Virg Hawksworth Wood Leeds (in c of St Andr) 62-66; Chap Univ of Capetn 66-72; Exam Chap to Abp of Capetn from 66; Sub-Dean of St Geo Cathl Capetn 73-80; Can 75-80; Dean of Grahmstn from 80. *Deanery, Box 102, Grahamstown, S Africa.* (2445)

BARKER, Sidney. Lich Th Coll. **d** 23 **p** 25 Lich. C of Hodnet 23-27; Gt w L Driffield 27-29; V of Brafferton w Pilmoor 29-36; All SS Middlesbrough 36-55; Surr 42-65; V of Saltburn-by-the-Sea 55-58; Stainton-in-Cleveland 58-65. *24 Eden Street, Saltburn, Yorks.*

BARKER, Timothy Reed. b 56. Qu Coll Cam BA 79, MA 82. Westcott Ho Cam 78. **d** 80 **p** 81 Ches. C of Nantwich Dio Ches from 80. *41 Highfield Drive, Nantwich, Cheshire, CW5 6EY.* (Nantwich 624939)

BARKER, Wallace Hamilton. b 08. Cudd Coll 56. **d** 57 **p** 58 Birm. C of Northfield 58-59; C-in-c of Balsall Common Eccles Distr 59-67; V of Arreton 67-70; V of Newchurch 67-70. *Coachman's Bathwick Hill, Bath, BA2 6EP.* (Bath 62160)

BARKER, Walter Frederick. b 25. Univ of Lon BD 48. ALCD 48. **d** 51 **p** 52 Chich. C of St Geo Worthing 51-53; St Geo Leeds (in c of St Andr) 53-56; V of St Mark Holloway 56-63; V of St Anne Holloway 56-63; Org Sec CMJ Midl Area and Perm to Offic Dios Pet and Worc 63-66; Home Sec CMJ 66-72; Gen Sec from 72. *Vincent House, Vincent Square, SW1P 2PX.* (01-834 4527)

BARKER, William Edward. b 28. Kelham Th Coll 49. **d** 54 Southw. C of Warsop w Sookholme 54-55; Bawtry w Austerfield 55-57; V of Frizington 57-64; St Jas Barrow-F 64-70; St Mary Windermere Dio Carl from 70. *St Mary's Vicarage, Windermere, Cumb, LA23 1BA.* (Windermere 3032)

BARKING, Lord Bishop Suffragan of. *See* Adams, Right Rev Albert James.

BARKMAN, Alex. b 02. **d** and **p** 74 Keew. C of Sachigo Lake Dio Keew from 74. *St Clement's Church, Sachigo Lake, via Central Patricia, Ont, Canada.*

BARKS, Jeffrey Stephen. b 45. Cranmer Hall Dur 66. **d** 71 **p** 72 St Alb. C of St Mary Wootton 71-74; St Jo Evang Boscombe 74-76; Ringwood 76-80; Spaxton w Charlynch, Enmore and Goathurst Dio B & W from 80. *c/o Spaxton Rectory, Bridgwater, Somt.* (Spaxton 265)

BARKWAY, Peter. Qu Univ Ont BA 61. Trin Coll Tor STB (2nd cl) 63. **d** 63 **p** 64 Ott. C of Trin Ch Cornwall Ont 63-66; on leave. *Box 633, Cornwall, Ont., Canada.*

BARKWELL, Canon William Henry. b 1893. St Chad's Coll Regina LTh 31. **d** 28 **p** 29 Qu'App. C of St Geo Moose Jaw 28-30; St Mary Walkley 30-32; Perm to Offic at Eston 32-33; C-in-c of New Bentley Conv Distr 33-35; R of Hardenhuish w Woodlands 35-39; V of St Osw Bedminster Down 39-45; R of Christian Malford 45-60; RD of Chippenham 51-60; Hon Can of Bris 55-60; Can (Emer) from 61; V of Wigtoft 61-68. *Manormead, Hindhead, Surrey.* (Hindhead 5766)

BARLEY, Leslie Roy. b 42. Moore Coll Syd LTh 72. **d** and **p** 79 C & Goulb. C of Gunning 79-80; R of Binda Dio C & Goulb from 81. *St James' Rectory, Binda, NSW, Australia 2625.*

BARLING, Michael Keith. b 38. Oak Hill Th Coll 63. **d** 66 **p** 67 Lon. C of St Paul Portman Square 66-70; Ch Ch Cockfosters 70-74; V of St Andr Sidcup 74-78; L to Offic Dio Guildf 78-81; Dio Chich from 81; Dir Fountain Trust 79-81; Chap Bethany Commun from 81. *The Hyde, Handcross, Haywards Heath, Sussex, RH17 6EZ.* (Handcross 400231)

BARLOW, Alan David. b 36. Worc Coll Ox BA (2nd cl Lit Hum) 59, 2nd cl Th 61, MA 65. Wycl Hall Ox 59. **d** 61 **p** 62 Lon. C of Wealdstone 61-67; V of Neasden 67-74; Chap Cranleigh Sch Surrey from 74. *Cranleigh School, Surrey.*

BARLOW, Arthur Stanley. Bp Wilson Th Coll IM 39. **d** 39 **p** 41 Ches. C of St Mark Dukinfield 39-47; V of H Trin Stalybridge 47-58; St Mich AA Runcorn 58-77; Perm to Offic Dio Ches from 78. *26 Hallastone Road, Helsby, Warrington, Chesh.* (Helsby 3115)

BARLOW, Charles William Moore. b 32. Univ of Man BA 57. ALCM 50. Cudd Coll 56. **d** 58 **p** 59 Man. C of Atherton 58-61; St Pet Swinton 61-64; V of Dobcross (w Scouthead from 76) Dio Man from 64. *Dobcross Vicarage, Oldham, Lancs.* (Saddleworth 2342)

BARLOW, Clive Christopher. b 42. Linc Th Coll 67. **d** 70 **p** 71 S'wark. C of St Mark Surbiton 70-74; All SS Spring Pk Croydon 74-77; V of Ash w Westmarsh Dio Cant from 77. *Vicarage, Chequer Lane, Ash, Canterbury, Kent, CT3 2ET.* (Ash 812296)

BARLOW, David. b 50. Univ of Leeds BA 71. Wycl Hall Ox 71. **d** 73 **p** 74 Lich. C of Horninglow 73-75; Wednesfield 75-77; Bloxwich 77-78. *Address temp unknown.*

BARLOW, Edward Burnley. b 29. St Aid Coll 56. **d** 58 **p** 59 Southw. C of St Barn Lenton Abbey 58-61; All SS Ipswich 61-63; R of Fishtoft 63-76; V of St Giles City and Dio Linc from 76. *St Giles Vicarage, Shelley Drive, Lincoln, LN2 4BY.* (Lincoln 27655)

BARLOW, Ven Ian Fleming. **d** 61 **p** 62 Willoch. C of Gladstone 61-63; P-in-c 63-66; R of Pet w Terowie and Yongala 66-71; Clare Dio Willoch from 71; Can of Willoch 76-78; Archd of Yorke Peninsula and The Broughton from 78. *PO Box 34, Clare, S Australia 5453.* (088-422835)

BARLOW, Canon Montague Michael. b 1898. BNC Ox BA 21, MA 25. Westcott Ho Cam 24. **d** 24 Southw for Carl **p** 25 Carl. C of Stanwix 24-28; Penrith 28-31; V of Millom w Kirksanton and Hill Chap 31-35; Corbridge-on-Tyne w Halton 35-47; Proc Conv Newc T 44-47; V of Richmond 47-59; Surr 47-59; R of Buckland 59-67; Hon Can of S'wark 67-68; Can (Emer) from 68; Perm to Offic Dio St E from 67. *97 Bures Road, Great Cornard, Sudbury, Suff.* (Sudbury 72023)

BARLOW, Norman Edward. b 09. St Jo Coll Dur LTh 36, BA 37, MA 42. ALCD 36. **d** 37 **p** 38 Roch. C of H Trin Beckenham 37-41; Frindsbury 41-42; Kippington 42-45; V of Stechford 45-56; R of Tydd St Mary 56-63; Windlesham 63-76; Perm to Offic Dio Guildf from 77. *Holly Bank, Horseshoe Lane, Cranleigh, Surrey.* (Cranleigh 2839)

BARLOW, Paul Benson. Fitzw Coll Cam BA 73, MA 77. **d** 64 B & W **p** 65 Taunton for B & W. C of Bath Abbey w St Jas Bath 64-74; Perm to Offic Dio Bris 64-70; Dio Worc 76-81; Dep Hd Leys High Sch Redditch 74-81; Hd Master John Kyrle High Sch Ross-on-Wye from 82. *John Kyrle High School, Ross-on-Wye, Herefs.*

BARLOW, Robert. MBE 62. St Aug Coll Cant. **d** 38 Sarum for Col Bp **p** 40 Cant for Col Bp. L to Offic Dio Argent 38-40; Perm to Offic (Col Cl Act) at Cranbrook 40; CF (EC) 40-42; served w army 42-53; Chap R Bom Seamen's S 53-63. *10 Alexandra Avenue, Great Yarmouth, Norf.*

BARLOW, Rodney Hugh. Wycl Coll Tor LTh 68. **d** 68 Bp H R Hunt **p** 69 Tor. C of St Anne Tor 68-70; St Paul Bloor St Tor 70-72; R of Midl Dio tor from 72. *303 Third Street, Midland, Ont., Canada.* (705-526 6562)

BARLOW, Timothy David. b 46. Univ Coll Ox BA 67, MA 71. BD (Lon) 71. Oak Hill Coll 71. **d** 71 **p** 72 Ches. C of All SS, Marple 71-74; Em Northwood 74-78; Chap at Vevey and Chateau D'Oex Dio (Gibr in Eur from 80) Lon (N and C Eur) from 78. *1807 Blonay, Switzerland.* (021-532239)

BARLOW, William George. b 40. Univ of Liv BSc 62. Univ of Wales BD 65. St Mich AA Coll Llan 76. **d** 76 **p** 77 Llan. C of Roath 76-80. *c/o 18 Sandringham Road, Roath, Cardiff.*

BARNACLE, Ronald William. b 20. Wells Th Coll 64. **d** 66 Bp McKie for Cov **p** 67 Cov. C of All SS Warwick 66-67; Nuneaton 67-69; Camp Hill w Galley Common 69-70; R of

Etton w Dalton Holme 70-76; Hinderwell w Roxby 76-78; P-in-c of Buckland Newton 78-81; Wootton-Glanville w Holnest 78-81; Pulham 78-81; R of Radwinter w Hempstead Dio Chelmsf from 81. *Rectory, Radwinter, Saffron Walden, Essex.* (Radwinter 332)

BARNARD, Canon Anthony Nevin. b 36. St Jo Coll Cam BA 60, MA 64. Wells Th Coll 61. **d** 63 **p** 64 St Alb. C of Cheshunt 63-65; Tutor Wells Th Coll 65-66; Chap 66-69; Vice-Prin 69-71; Dep-Prin Sarum and Wells Th Coll 71-77; Dir S Dios Ministerial Tr Scheme 74-77; Can Res and Chan of Lich Cathl from 77. *13 The Close, Lichfield, Staffs, WS13 7LD.* (Lichfield 55168)

BARNARD, Anthony Rosenhagen. b 14. St Cath Coll Cam 2nd cl Math Trip pt i 34. 2nd cl Geog Trip pt i 35. BA 36. Linc Th Coll 36. **d** 37 **p** 38 Man. C of St Mary Prestwich 37-40; Fenton (in c of St Mich) 40-43; St Mary Market Drayton 43-46; V of Newborough w Needwood 46-48; PC of Lawton Moor 48-55; V of Osbaldwick w Murton 55-61; Asst Master Pocklington Sch 62-81. *7 Aireside Terrace, Cononley, Keighley, BD20 8LY.* (Cross Hills 35964)

BARNARD, Canon George Patrick. b 01. OBE 61. Bps' Coll Cheshunt 32. **d** 34 **p** 35 Lon. C of St Anne Limehouse 34-39; P-in-c of Enugu Nig 39-41; P-in-c of Nsukka Distr 41-44 and 48-50; CF 44-46; P-in-c of Enugu Distr 46-48; Nsukka 49-50; Oleh 50-61; Hon Can of Niger from 59; Archd of Warri 62-64. *Davenham, Graham Road, Malvern, Worcs.*

BARNARD, Canon Harold Reginald. b 07. AKC 35. **d** 35 **p** 36 Roch. C of Orpington 35-37; Burnham 36-41; V of Langley Marish 41-44; Org Sec (SW Area) ICF 44-46; C of Fishponds Dio Bris 46-49; V 49-75; Surr from 52; Proc Conv Bris 59-64; RD of Stapleton 65-76; Hon Can of Bris 67-81; Can (Emer) from 81. *68 Oldbury Court Road, Fishponds, Bristol.* (Bris 65 9105)

BARNARD, Canon John Stuart. b 19. Em Coll Cam BA (2nd cl Nat Sc Trip pt i) 41. MA 45. Ridley Hall Cam 41. **d** 43 **p** 44 Roch. C of Erith 43-46; Tonbridge 46-49; St Aldate Ox 49-53; Min of St Aug Bromley 53-58; V 58-73; RD of Bromley 66-73; Hon Can of Roch from 70; V of Seal Dio Roch from 73. *Seal Vicarage, Sevenoaks, Kent.* (Sevenoaks 61153)

BARNARD, Jonathan Dixon. b 46. St Cath Coll Cam BA 68. Cudd Coll 69. **d** 71 Dur. C of St Matt, New Silksworth 71-74; Hatfield Hyde 74-78; Team V of Hitchin (in c of St Mark) Dio St Alb from 78. *54 Lancaster Avenue, Hitchin, Herts.* (Hitchin 4686)

BARNARD, Kevin James. b 52. Keble Coll Ox BA 77, MA 79. Cranmer Hall Dur 77. **d** 79 **p** 80 Sheff. C of Swinton Dio Sheff from 79. *34 Church Street, Swinton, Mexborough, S Yorks, S64 8QA.*

BARNARD, Leslie William. b 24. St Cath S Ox BA (2nd cl Th) 50, MA 55. Univ of Southn PhD 70. Cudd Coll 51. **d** 51 **p** 52 Win. C of Ch Ch Southn 51-55; V of Shaw 55-61; R of All SS w St Andr Chilcomb and St Pet Chesil Win 61-68; Exam Chap to Bp of Win 67-69; Lect in Th Univ of Leeds 69-73; Sen Lect from 73; Dir of Post-Ordin Tr Dio Ripon 70-76. *3 Carlton Road, Harrogate, Yorks, HG2 8DD.* (Harrogate 871289)

BARNARD, Philip Michael George. b 34. Selw Coll Cam 2nd cl Th Trip pt i 56, BA (3rd cl Th Trip pt ii) 58, MA 62. Linc Th Coll. **d** 60 **p** 61 S'wark. C of St Barn Southfields 60-62; St John's Conv Distr Churchdown 62-65; R of Matson 65-78; St Paul City and Dio Glouc from 78. *2 King Edward's Avenue, Gloucester.* (Gloucester 23732)

BARNARD, Robert James. b 15. Lich Th Coll 54. **d** 55 Ely **p** 56 Bp Walsh for Cant. C of Wisbech 55-58; PC of Holbrooke 58-65; R of Clenchwarton 65-77; P-in-c of Hinxton 77-80. *Flat 23, Bromley College, London Road, Bromley, Kent.*

BARNARD, Canon William Henry. b 09. Dorch Miss Coll 37. **d** 39 Bp Willis for Leic. **p** 40 Leic. C of St Paul Leic 39-43; All S Brighton 43-51; Barrow Hill (in c of St Francis Hollingwood) 51-52; Newbold 52-53; R of Hinton-Martel Dio Sarum from 53; RD of Wimborne 75-79; Can and Preb of Sarum Cathl from 79. *Hinton Martel Rectory, Wimborne, Dorset, BH21 7HD.* (Witchampton 840256)

BARNBY, Canon Bertram Louis. b 13. Late Exhib of Ch Coll Cam BA 35, MA 39. Ridley Hall Cam 36. **d** 38 **p** 39 Man. C of St John Pendlebury 38-42; Middleton (in c of All SS Rhodes) 42-44; Min Can of Man Cathl 44-50; V of St Aid Sudden Rochdale 50-56; Chap Springfield Sanat and Marland Hosp 50-56; V of Bramhall 56-69; C-in-c of Wilmslow 69-72; R 72-76; Hon Can of Ches from 74; V of St Andr W Kirby Dio Ches from 76. *2 Lingdale Road, West Kirby, Wirral, Chesh.* (051-632 4728)

BARNES, Alan Duff. b 42. St Steph Ho Ox 75. **d** 77 Barking for Chelmsf **p** 78 Chelmsf. C of H Trin Hermon Hill S Woodford 77-80; St Jas Clacton-on-Sea Dio Chelmsf from 80. *8 Trafalgar Road, Clacton-on-Sea, CO15 1LR.*

BARNES, Arthur Percy Abbott. b 19. St Pet Hall Ox BA 41, MA 44. Linc Th Coll 41. **d** 43 Sherborne for Sarum **p** 44 Sarum. C of Bradford-on-Avon 43-46; Maidstone 46-50; V of Chislet 50-58; C-in-c of Hoath 52-58; V of Winslow Dio Ox from 58; R of Addington Dio Ox from 58; Surr from 68. *Winslow Vicarage, Bletchley, Bucks.* (Winslow 2564)

BARNES, Bertram. b 1898. Late Exhib of Magd Coll Ox, Heath Harrison Trav Scho and BA 21, MA 24, B Litt 26, M Litt. Egerton Hall Man 40. **d** 41 **p** 42 Man. C of Atherton 41-44; Walkden 44; V of Peel 48-65. *6 Rutland Road, Walkden, Manchester.* (061-790 2728)

BARNES, Bruce Roy. b 52. St Steph Ho Ox 73. **d** 76 **p** 77 Birm. C of St Pet Birm 76-81; St Mary Portsea Dio Portsm from 81. *2 Glebe Flats, Nutfield Place, Fratton, Portsmouth, Hants.* (Portsm 830154)

BARNES, Bryan Peter. b 24 Univ of Leeds BA 50. Coll of Resurr Mirfield 50. **d** 52 **p** 53 Bris. C of St Mark Swindon 52-59; St Mary and All SS Cathl Salisbury S Rhod 59-63; R of Belvedere S Rhod 63-66; V of St Matt Moorfields Bris 66-71; C-in-c of Winterbourne Down 71-75; V of Fishponds Dio Bris from 75. *Vicarage, Vicars Close, Fishponds, Bristol, BS16 3TH.* (Bristol 654462)

BARNES, Canon Charles Peter Kentish. b 19. Ch Coll Cam BA 40, MA 44. Ridley Hall Cam 40. **d** 42 **p** 43 Ox. C of St John Reading 42-45; Sutton Coldfield (in c of St Chad) 45-49; Sub-Dean of All SS Cathl Cairo 49-52; R of St Mary Wavertree 52-56; V of Maghull 56-69; Stratford-on-Avon 69-75; R 75-81; Dir Post Ordin Tr Dio Cov 73-78; Hon Can of Cov from 75; V of Priors Hardwick w Priors Marston and Wormleighton Dio Cov from 81. *Vicarage, Priors Marston, Rugby, Warws, CV23 8AT.* (Byfield 60053)

BARNES, Colin. b 33. St Aid Coll 61. **d** 64 Middleton for Man **p** 65 Man. C of Eccles 64-66; St Geo w St Luke Barrow-F 66-68; V of Goodshaw 68-80; P-in-c of St Martin Wythenshawe Dio Man from 80. *2 Blackcarr Road, Wythenshawe, Manchester, M23 8LX.* (061-998 3408)

BARNES, Very Rev Cyril Arthur. b 26. Edin Th Coll 47. **d** 50 **p** 51 Aber. C of St Jo Evang Aber 50-53; R of Forres 53-55; C of Darrington w Wentbridge 55-58; V of Ripponden w Rishworth 58-67; V of Thorpe Yorks 66-67; R of Huntly Dio Moray from 67; R of Aberchirder Dio Moray from 67; Can of St Andr Cathl Inverness from 71; Dioc Sec and M Cathl Chapter from 71; R of Keith Dio Moray from 74; Syn Clk Dio Moray 77-80; Dean of Moray, Ross and Caithness from 77. *Rectory, Huntly, Aberdeens.* (Huntly 2667)

BARNES, David John. b 37. Chich Th Coll 65. **d** 68 **p** 69 Roch. C of Crayford 68-71; Chap RAF 71-75; Wroughton Hosp 74-75; Chap & Asst Master Sutton Valence Sch from 75. *Aylmer House, Sutton Valence, Maidstone, Kent, ME17 3AD.* (Sutton Valence 842147)

BARNES, Derek Ian. b 44. Univ of Leeds BA (2nd cl French) 66. Westcott Ho Cam 66. **d** 68 Ripon **p** 69 Knaresborough for Ripon. C of Far Headingley 68-71; Chap to Univs in Lon 72-77; Warden Lee Abbey Internat Students Club Lon 77-81; further Educn Project Officer and Hon C of St Gabr Willesden Dio Lon from 81. *St Anne's Vicarage, Salusbury Road, NW6 6RG.* (01-625 6182)

BARNES, Donald. b 44. St Barn Coll Adel. **d** 70 Adel. C of Tea Tree Gully 70; Broadview 70-71; Perm to Offic Dio Adel from 70. *31 Tidworth Crescent, Colonel Light Gardens, S Australia 5041.*

BARNES, Donald Edward. b 26. K Coll Lon and Warm BD (1st cl) and AKC 51. **d** 52 **p** 53 Lon. C of St Matt Willesden 52-59; V of Cricklewood 59-79; St Pet Belsize Pk Dio Lon from 79; Lect Bps' Coll Cheshunt 63-68; Exam Chap to Bp of Edmon 71-76. *Vicarage, Belsize Square, NW3 4HY.* (01-794 4020)

BARNES, Canon Edward Hartley. Late Exhib of St D Coll Lamp BA 39. Sarum Th Coll 31. **d** 39 **p** 40 Ches. C of Ch Ch Ellesmere Port (in c of St Thos Whitby) 39-40; Offg C-in-c of L Budworth 40-41; V of Ashton Hayes 41-79; CF (R of O) 48-79; Hon Can of Ches 68-79; Can (Emer) from 79. *Canon's Corner, Springside, Smithy Lane, Mouldsworth, Nr Chester.*

BARNES, Edwin George. b 11. St Aid Coll 45. **d** 47 Warrington for Liv **p** 48 Liv. C of St Luke Eccleston 47-51; Org Sec CPAS Lon Area 51-55; R of St Mich Oulton 55-80; Chap Lothingland Hosp from 55. *35 St James Crescent, Belton, Gt Yarmouth, NR31 9JN.* (Gt Yarmouth 781964)

BARNES, Edwin Ronald. b 35. Late Scho of Pemb Coll Ox BA 58, MA 62. Cudd Coll 58. **d** 60 **p** 61 Portsm. C of St Mark Portsea 60-64; Woodham 64-67; R of Farncombe 67-78; M Gen Syn 75-78; V of Hessle Dio York from 78. *Vicarage, Hessle, HU13 9LQ.* (Hull 648555)

BARNES, Esdaile Lenox. b 13. ALCD 40. **d** 40 **p** 41 B & W. C of Street 40-43; R of Priston 43-45; V of St Matthias Upper Tulse Hill 45-52; PC of St Andr w St Mary Maidenhead 52-60; V of Uralla 61-65; Moree 65-69; C of Tamworth (in c of St Jas) 69-70; St Pet Cathl Armid 70-72; H Trin w Ch Ch Folkestone 72-74; R of Grimston w Congham (and Roydon to 75) 74-75; Roydon 75; Perm to Offic Dio Syd from 77. *36 Shorter Avenue, Beverly Hills North, NSW, Australia 2209.*

BARNES, Harold Leslie. b 02. ARCO 29. LTCL 57. **d** 62 **p** 63 Leic. Hon C of Melton Mowbray 62-66; V of Tugby w E Norton and Skeffington 66-70; Sulgrave w Thorpe Mandeville 70-76. *Castle Cottage, The Green, Sulgrave, Banbury, Oxon.*

BARNES, James. b 10. Lon Coll Div. **d** 53 **p** 54 S & M. C of Malew and Chap of St Mark 53-55; R of St Phil Bradford Road Man (w St Mark from 58) 55-60; V of St Luke Blackb 60-66; St Lawr Barton 66-68; St Osw Preston 68-75; Chap Deepdale Hosp Blackb 71-75; L to Offic Dio Blackb from 79. *7 Caton Green Road, Brook House, Lancaster.*

BARNES, James Barrie. b 27. Bps' Coll Cheshunt 51. **d** 53 Bp Hollis for Leic **p** 54 Leic. C of St Phil Leic 53-59; V of Blackfordby 59-76; V of Smisby 59-69; RD of Akeley W 69-76; V of Broom Leys Dio Leic from 76. *7 Greenhill Road, Coalville, Leicester, LE6 3RL.* (Coalville 36262)

BARNES, John Barwick. b 32. K Coll Lon and Warm AKC 58. **d** 59 **p** 60 Chelmsf. C of Brentwood 59-65; V of Arkesden w Wicken Bonhunt 65-71; St Mary Virg Gt Ilford Dio Chelmsf from 71. *St Mary's Vicarage, South Park Road, Ilford, Essex.* (01-478 0546)

BARNES, John Christopher. b 43. Linc Th Coll 78. **d** 80 **p** 81 Bradf. C of Guiseley Dio Bradf from 80. *5 Ashtofts Mount, Guiseley, LS20 9BZ.*

BARNES, John Durham. b 21. Sarum Wells Th Coll 77. **d** 80 Sarum **p** 81 Bp Tiarks for Sarum (NSM). C of H Angels Lilliput Dio Sarum from 80. *27 Blake Hill Crescent, Parkstone, Poole, Dorset.*

BARNES, John Edgar. b 45. Late Scho of St D Coll Lamp BA 66. St Chad Coll Univ of Dur MA 67. St Steph Ho Ox 68. **d** 70 Bp Ramsbotham for Newc T **p** 71 Newc T. C of St Jo Bapt Newc T 70-73; C & V Cho of St A Cathl 73-77; V of Walsingham w Houghton-in-the-Dale Dio Nor from 77. *Vicarage, Walsingham, Norf, NR22 6BL.* (Walsingham 345)

BARNES, John Kenneth. b 04. Late Scho of Jes Coll Ox 3rd cl Cl Mods 25, BA (3rd cl Lit Hum) 27, MA 35. Univ of Lon 30. Ripon Hall Ox 34. **d** 36 **p** 37 S'wark. C of H Trin S Wimbledon 36-38; All SS Wandsworth 38-42; Perm to Offic at St Francis W Wickham 42-43; C of Ch Ch Croydon 43-44; All SS Sedgley 44-46; Handsworth (in c of St Matthias) 46-48; V of Brilley w Michaelchurch (R) 48-57; R of Kinnersley w Norton Canon V 57-74. *12 Falstaff Road, Hereford, HR2 7QF.*

BARNES, John Seymour. b 30. Qu Coll Birm 58. **d** 61 **p** 62 Worc. C of Bromsgrove 61-64; Kingsthorpe 64-66; Styvechale 66-69; P-in-c of Farnborough w Avon Dassett 69-75; St Alb Stoke Heath Dio Cov from 75. *St Alban's Vicarage, Mercer Avenue, Coventry, CV2 4PQ.* (Cov 452493)

BARNES, Lewis Agassiz. St Jo Coll Auckld Univ of NZ BA 26, MA 29. Univ of Otago BD 80. NZ BD of Th Stud LTh 26. **d** 25 **p** 26 Wel. C of Hawera 25-28; St Mark Wel 28-29; V of Raetihi w Ohakune 30-34; Kiwitea 34-36; Temuka 36-42; St John Highfield Timaru 42-51; Fendalton 51-61; Chap at Thika Kenya 61-65; C-in-c of Malvern NZ 65-66; L to Offic Dio Ch Ch 66-78; Commiss Dio Mt Kenya 70-75; Mt Kenya S from 75; Perm to Offic Dio Waik from 78. *52 Kowhai Street, Hamilton, NZ.* (395-208)

BARNES, Neil. b 42 Bps' Coll Cheshunt 65. **d** 68 Blackb **p** 69 Burnley for Blackb. C of Poulton-le-Fylde 68-72; Ribbleton (in c of The Ascen) 72-75; V of Knuzden 75-81; Chap Prestwich Hosp Dio Man from 81. *Prestwich Hospital, Bury New Road, Manchester, M25 7BL.* (061-773 2236)

BARNES, Peter Frank. b 52. St Jo Coll Nottm L Th 81. **d** 81 Blackb. C of St Bart Colne Dio Blackb from 81. *41 Birtwistle Avenue, Colne, Lancs, BB8 9RS.*

BARNES, Peter John. b 49. Mem Univ Newfld BSc 71. Trin Coll Tor MDiv 74. **d** 74 **p** 75 Newfld. C of Channel 74-75; Assoc P 75-77; R of White Bay Dio W Newfld from 77. *Rectory, Jackson's Arm, White Bay, Newfoundland, Canada.* (709-3111)

BARNES, Robert James. Trin Coll Dub BA 39. **d** 39 Bp Kennedy for Down **p** 40 Down. C of Donaghcloney 39-41; C-in-c of Newtonsaville 41-51; RD of Kilskeely 48-51; Chap Miss to Seamen Hull 51-59 and from 64; Beira 59-60; Dub 60-62; Ho Master Malone Tr Sch Belf 62-64. *3 Malone Avenue, Belfast 9, Northern Ireland.*

BARNES, Robert Varley. St Francis Coll Brisb 53. **d** and **p** 56 56 Brisb. C of St Jas Toowoomba 56-57; V of Caboolture 57-62; on leave 62-63; Vice-Warden Newton Th Coll Dogura New Guinea 63-67; Chap St Aid Teacher's Tr Coll Dogura 64-66; P-in-c of Taupota 67-73; Warden Bible Centre Awaiama Dio Papua from 75. *Anglican Church, Awaiama, via Dogura, Papua New Guinea.*

BARNES, Ronald Leslie. Univ of Tor BA 56. Trin Coll Tor STB. **d** 60 **p** 61 Alg. C of St John N Bay 60-62; I of Blind River 62-69; R of St Barn New Westmr 69-75; St Clem Vanc N Dio New Westmr from 75. *3401 Church Street, N Vancouver, BC, V7K 2L3, Canada.*

BARNES, Stanley John. b 09. St D Coll Lamp BA 38. **d** 39 Stafford for Lich **p** 40 Lich. C of St Paul Stafford 39-43; Ellesmere Port 42-48; V of St Matt Stockport Dio Ches from 48. *St Matthew's Vicarage, Stockport, Chesh.* (Stockport 480-5515)

BARNES, Stephen. b 46. Univ of Hull BA (Geog and Soc) 69. Univ of Bris Dipl Th 71. Clifton Coll Bris 69. **d** 72 Ripon **p** 73 Bradf. C of Girlington 72-74; V in R Benef of Glyncorrwg w Afan Vale and Cymer Afan Dio Llan 74-79; R from 79. *Rectory, Church Street, Glyncorrwg, Port Talbot, W Glam, SA13 3BW.* (Cymer 850423)

BARNES, Walter Cameron Graham. Hur Coll 59. **d** 59 **p** 60 Hur. C of St Jo Evang Lon 59-62; R of Essex 62-64 and 66-68; River John 64-66; Pugwash 64-66; L to Offic Dio Calg 68-74; P-in-c of New Hamburg 74-76; I of Trin Sarnia Dio Hur from 76. *1186 Murphy Road, Sarnia, Ont., Canada.* (519-542 9261)

BARNES, William Arthur Cyril. b 28. ALCD 56 (LTh from 74). **d** 56 **p** 57 Man. C of St Pet Blackley 56-59; C-in-c of St Mark's Conv Distr Blackley 59-66; V of Aldborough Hatch Dio Chelmsf from 66. *Vicarage, Oaks Lane, Ilford, Essex, IG2 7QN.* (01-599 0524)

BARNES, William Richard. b 15. Down Coll Cam BA 39, MA 42. Ridley Hall Cam 39. **d** 41 **p** 42 St E. C of Beccles 41-45; Halifax 45-52; V of Mytholmroyd 52-67; Belvedere 67-81. *Great Stubb, Mytholmroyd, Halifax, W Yorks.*

BARNES, William Thomas. b 39. Univ of Dur BA 60. Wycl Hall Ox 60. **d** 62 **p** 63 Blackb. C of Scotforth 62-66; Cleveleys 66-67; V of Ch Ch Colne 67-74; V of Bamber Bridge Dio Blackb from 74. *St Saviour's Vicarage, Bamber Bridge, Preston, Lancs, PR5 6AJ.* (Preston 35374)

BARNES-CEENEY, Brian. b 35. St Aid Coll 59. **d** 62 **p** 63 Chelmsf. C of St Andr Plaistow 62-64; Waltham Abbey 64-66; PC of Falfield 66-71; R of Rockptn 66-71; Chap HM Detention Centre Eastwood Pk 68-71; Chap HM Borstal Everthorpe 71-76; HM Pris Coldingley 76-79; Horfield from 79. *c/o Horfield Prison, Bristol, BS7 8PS.*

BARNES-CLAY, Peter John Granger. b 43. Chich Th Coll 72. **d** 75 Thetford for Nor. C of St Anne Earlham 75-76; Asst Master Hewett Sch Nor from 76. *20 Amderley Drive, Eaton Village, Norwich, NR4 6HZ.* (Nor 51705)

BARNETT, Alec James Leon. b 44. Em Coll Cam BA 66, MA 70. Cudd Coll. **d** 69 **p** 70 Blackb. C of Preston 69-72; Asst Master Hutton Gr Sch 70-72; Asst Chap (Hd of Relig Stud from 73) Uppingham Sch 72-80; Research Assoc Farmington Inst for Chr Stud from 79; C of Witney w Curbridge & Wood Green Dio Ox from 80. *Batt School House, Marlborough Lane, Witney, Oxon, OX8 7EB.* (Witney 72191)

BARNETT, David John. b 33. Magd Coll Ox BA (2nd cl Mod Lang) 56, 2nd cl Th 58, MA 61. St Steph Ho Ox 56. **d** 59 **p** 60 Cov. C of Styvechale 59-62; Chap Rhodes Univ and P-in-c of St Bart Grahmstn 62-68; Lic to Offic in Dio Capetn 68-69; Chap and Lect Univ of Rhod 70-76; V of St Matthias Colindale Hendon Dio Lon from 77. *Vicarage, Rushgrove Avenue, NW9 6QY.* (01-205 8783)

BARNETT, Dudley Graham. b 36. Ch Ch Ox BA (3rd cl Th) 62, MA 65. St Steph Ho Ox 62. **d** 64 **p** 65 Man. C of St Geo Abbey Hey Gorton 64-68; V of H Rood Swinton Dio Man from 68. *Vicarage, 33 Moorside Road, Swinton, Manchester M27 3EL.* (061-794 2464)

BARNETT, Frederick Gavin. Sir Geo Williams Univ Montr BA 55. McGill Univ BD 58, MA 75. Montr Dioc Th Coll LTh 58. **d** 58 Montr for Athab **p** 58 Athab. I of Fort Vermilion 58-61; C of Ch Ch Calg 61-63; I of Mascouche 63-65; Chateauguay 65-69; R of Pointe Claire 69-73; on leave 73-79; V of Chap of St Francis Cant Hills Conf Centre Dio Niag from 80. *Box 7068, Ancaster, Ont, Canada.*

BARNETT, Herbert Arthur. b 1893. Vic Univ of Man BA 19, BD 21. Egerton Hall Man 19. **d** 21 **p** 22 Man. C of St Jas Birch-in-Rusholme 21-28; Sen Lect in Egerton Hall Man 21-31; I of St Nich Burnage 29-32; R 32-38; Exam Chap to Bp of Man 30-47; to Bp of B & W 40-75; V of Twerton-on-Avon 38-47; RD of Keynsham 41-47; Preb of Wells Cathl 44-76; Cler Sec Dioc Committee of Tr for the Ministry 44-54; V of Wells 47-63; RD of Shepton Mallet 54-57. *3 Portway Avenue, Wells, Somt, BA5 2QF.*

BARNETT, James. Bp's Univ Lennox. **d** 29 **p** 30 Queb. C of All SS Winnipeg 29-30; Miss St Clem Miss Labrador 30-34; C of Cathl Ch Queb 34-37; R of Ireland Queb 37-42; CF (Canad) 40-60; R of Ch Ch Sorel 60-62; St Bart Ott 62-72. *325 Cooper Street, Ottawa, Ont., Canada.*

BARNETT, John Raymond. b 51. Univ of Lon LLB (external) 74. Westcott Ho Cam 74. **d** 77 **p** 78 Birm. C of Northfield 77-81; V of St Bernard Hamstead Dio Birm from 81. *147 Hamstead Road, Great Barr, Birmingham, B43 5BB.* (021-358 1286)

BARNETT, Kevin Percy. Univ of NZ BA 56. St Jo Coll

Auckld LTh 58. **d** 58 **p** 59 Auckld. C of Kohimarama Distr Auckld 58-61; E Coast Bays 61-64; V of Helensville 64-67; V of Kaitaia 67-70; Frankton 70-80; Otumoetai Dio Wai from 80. *163 Pillans Road, Otumoetai, NZ.* (Tauranga) *66617)*

BARNETT, Canon Norman. b 19. Univ of Wales BA 41. St Mich Coll Llan 41. **d** 43 **p** 44 Llan. C of St German Roath 43-49; Chap Llan Cathl 49-53; R of Liss Dio Portsm from 53; RD of Petersfield 70-75; Hon Can of Portsm from 76. *Rectory, Liss, Hants.* (Liss 3175)

BARNETT, Paul William. BD Lon 63. Univ of Syd MA 74. PhD (Lon) 78. ACT ThL 63. Moore Th Coll Syd. **d** 63 **p** 64 Syd. Lect Moore Th Coll Syd 63-73; C of Ashbury 63-64; St Barn Broadway 64-67; Chap Syd Univ 67-73; R of Broadway 67-73; H Trin Adel 73-79; Master Robert Menzies Coll from 80. *Box 145, North Ryde, NSW, Australia 2116.* (888-7133)

BARNETT, Peter Geoffrey. b 46. AKC 71. St Aug Coll Cant 71. **d** 72 **p** 73 Lich. C of Wolverhampton 72-77; P-in-c of St Mich AA Caldmore, Walsall Dio Lich from 77. *St Michael's Vicarage, Caldmore, Walsall, Staffs, WS1 3RQ.* (Walsall 23445)

BARNETT, Phillip Charles. b 43. Univ of Lon BA 65. St Jo Coll Winnipeg MDiv 80. **d** 80 Rupld. C of St Mary Winnipeg Dio Rupld from 80. *3820 Roblin Boulevard, Winnipeg, Manit, Canada, R3R 0E4.*

BARNETT, Raymond Michael. b 31. Univ of Man BA (3rd cl French) 54. Wells Th Coll 54. **d** 56 **p** 57 Man. C of Fallowfield 56-59; Miss in Madag 59-60; V of Blackrod 60-67; Woolavington 67-76; RD of Bridgwater 72-76; Quantock from 78; V of St Decuman's Dio B & W from 76. *Vicarage, Watchet, Somt, TA23 0HU.* (Watchet 31228)

BARNETT, Canon Robert Theodore. b 15. Ch Coll Cam 3rd cl Hist Trip pt i 36, BA (3rd cl Hist Trip pt ii) 37, MA 41. Chich Th Coll 38. **d** 40 **p** 41 Glouc. C of Batsford w Moreton-in-Marsh 40-42; Chap RNVR 42-48; C of Parkend (in c of St Luke Yorkley) 48-49; V of Horsley 49-52; Highcliffe (w Hinton Admiral from 54) 52-78; Ed 'Win Churchman' 63-77; Hon Can of Win from 71-78; Can (Emer) from 78; Perm to Offic Dio Ban from 78. *Berwyn, Newborough, Llanfairpwllgwyngyll, Anglesey, Gwynedd LL61 6SG.* (Newborough 603)

BARNETT, Russell Scott. b 20. Oak Hill Th Coll 56. **d** 58 Penrith for Carl. **p** 59 Carl. C of Ulverston 58-61; V of St Paul Kirkdale 61-67; All SS Salterhebble, Halifax 67-77; R of Aikton Dio Carl from 77; Gt Orton Dio Carl from 77. *Aikton Rectory, Wigton, Cumbria, CA7 0HP.* (Wigton 2229)

BARNETT, Stanley. b 02. Linc Th Coll 41. **d** and **p** 41 Sheff. C of All SS Owston 41-43; Doncaster 43-45; V of Wortley Sheff 45-54; Chap St John of Beverley Stoke Newington (for Deaf and Dumb) 54-67. *9 Stone Terrace, Five Roads, Llanelli, Dyfed.*

BARNETT, Star Epiphany. St Pet Coll Alice 64. **d** 66 **p** 67 Kimb K. C of St Luke Prieska Dio Kimb K from 66. *P.O. Box 100, Prieska, CP, S Africa.* (Prieska 3)

BARNETT, Thomas Albert Macaulay. Univ of Tor BA 41, MA 42. Wycl Coll Tor. **d** 43 Tor **p** 46 Bp of Connecticut for Tor. C of St Clem Tor 43-45; in Amer Ch 45-51; Prof Wycl Coll Tor 51-60; Regr and Prof Angl Th Coll of BC Vancouver 60-64; Gen Sec SCM Canada 65-67; Prof of OT Knox Coll Tor 67-68; on leave. *Apt 106a, 2055 Carling Avenue, Ottawa 13, Canada.*

BARNEY, Michael Frank. b 29. New Coll Ox BA 53, MA 58. Chich Th Coll 53. **d** 55 **p** 56 Lon. C of Hampstead 55-59; St Paul Knightsbridge 59-68; St Mary Abbots Kens (in c of St Geo Campden Hill) 68-75; V of St Mich Sutton Court Chiswick Dio Lon from 75. *59 Sutton Lane South, W4 3JR.* (01-994 3173)

BARNIER, Gordon William. b 44. St Mich Ho Crafers 65. **d** 69 **p** 70 Newc. C of Merewether 69-70; Wallsend 70-71; Taree 71-74; Charlestown 74; Prec of Carp Cathl 75-76; Can Res 76-78; Dean 78-80; Supt Cathl Coll Thursday I from 80. *Cathedral College, Thursday Island, Queensland, Australia 4875.*

BARNISH, Canon John Geoffrey. b 24. Wadh Coll Ox BA (2nd cl Th) 55, MA 59, BD 66. RD 65. Linc Th Coll 55. **d** 56 **p** 57 Portsm. C of Farlington 56-59; Chap RNR 58-75; V of Cleeve Prior 59-64; R of All SS w St Andr St Helen St Alb and St Mich Worc 64-67; Shrawley (w The Witleys and Hillhampton from 78) Dio Worc from 67; Dir Relig Educn Dio Worc 65-76; Hon Can of Worc from 70; P-in-c of Gt w L Witley and Hillhampton 77-78; Astley Dio Worc from 81. *Shrawley Rectory, Worcester, WR6 6TS.* (Worcester 620489)

BARNSLEY, John Warren. b 04. Lich Th Coll 25. **d** 28 **p** 29 Lich. C of St Paul Forebridge 28-30; St Chad Stafford 30-31; All SS W Bromwich 31-35; C-in-c of St Martin Conv Distr Rough Hills 35-38; V 38-48; R of St Andr Guernsey 48-57; Chap K Edw Sanat 52-57; Chap Torquay Sanat and Convalesc Home 57-59; C of Farnham Surrey 59-60; V of Bledlow 60-64; R of Churchstanton 64-68; C-in-c of Otterford 66-68; R of Compton Martin 68-71; R of Ubley 68-71; R of Compton Martin w Ubley 71-73; Perm to Offic Dio B & W 73-79; Dio Leic from 80. *37 Donnington Drive, Ashby de la Zouch, Leics.*

BARNSLEY, Melvyn. b 46. Univ of Dur BA 67, Dipl Th 69. St Chad's Coll Dur 64. **d** 71 **p** 72 Cov. C of St Jo Bapt and of St Thos Cov 71-75; V of New Bilton Dio Cov from 75. *New Bilton Vicarage, Lawford Road, Rugby, Warws.* (Rugby 4011)

BARNSLEY, Michael. b 10. St Jo Coll Ox BA 41, MA 47. St Andr Coll Pampisford 40. **d** 41 **p** 42 Sheff. C of Mexborough 41-44; Ranmoor 44-47; Cathl Salisbury S Rhod 47-50; R of St Martin Salisbury S Rhod 50-53; C of Wimborne Minster 53-54; R of Fontmell Magna 54-58; C-in-c of Melbury Abbas 54-58; R of Tackley 58-75; Chap HM Detention Centre Campsfield House 71-75. *12 Beaufort West, Bath, Avon, BA1 6QB.*

BARNSTAPLE, Archdeacon of. *See* Herniman, Ven Ronald George.

BARON, Noel Spencer Peter. b 15. K Coll Cam BA 39, MA 42. Linc Th Coll 40. **d** 41 **p** 42 St Alb. C of Welwyn Garden City 41-43; Welwyn 43-48; V of Holcombe Rogus w Hockworthy 48-52; West Malvern Dio Worc from 52. *230 West Malvern Road, Malvern, Worcs, WR14 4BD.* (Malvern 3593)

BARR, Alaister McDougall. b 05. Bp Wilson Th Coll IM 37. **d** 39 **p** 40 S & M. C of St Thos Douglas 39-43; St Pet Harrogate 43-45; V of St Andr Wakef 45-55; R of St Paul Kersal 55-67; Bride I.M. 67-70. *16 Emscote Road, Warwick.*

BARR, David James Osborne. b 23. Trin Coll Dub BA (2nd cl Mod Ment and Mor Sc) 45. Div Test 46. **d** 46 **p** 47 Connor. C of Derriaghy 46-48; St Mary Donnybrook Dub 48-51; St Ann Dub 51-57; I of St Mark Dub 57-65; R of Booterstown w Carysfort Dio Dub from 65. *Rectory, Cross Avenue, Blackrock, Co Dublin, Irish Republic.* (Dublin 887118)

BARR, Peter Hugh Dickson. b 41. Univ of Tas BSc 65. Ridley Coll Melb 75. **d** 76 **p** 77 Melb. C of H Trin Kew 76-78; St John Camberwell 78-79; P-in-c of St Mark Reservoir Dio Melb from 79. *19 Beatty Street, Reservoir West, Vic, Australia 3073.* (470-1956)

BARR, Terence David. b 45. **d** 74 Bris **p** 75 Malmesbury for Bris. C of Patchway 74-76; Youth Chap Swindon 76-79; Chap of Bris Cathl 76-79; P-in-c of Lockleaze Dio Bris 79-80; V from 80. *Parsonage, Copley Gardens, Lockleaze, Bristol, BS7 9YE.* (Bris 512516)

BARR, Very Rev William Norman Cochran. b 20. Trin Coll Dub BA (1st cl Ment and Mor Sc) 44, Div Test (1st cl) 45, MA 50, BD 50. **d** and **p** 46 Connor. C of Ballymena 46-52; St Anne's Cathl Belf 52-54; I of Duneane w Ballyscullion 54-58; Dom Chap to Bp of Connor 56-71; C-in-c of Whiterock 58-61; I of Derriaghy 61-82; Exam Chap to Bp of Connor from 71; RD of Derriaghy 72-82; Can of Connor Cathl 80-82; Dean of Connor from 82; R of Ch Ch Cathl Lisburn Dio Connor from 82. *Cathedral Rectory, 2 Clonevin Park, Lisburn, N Ireland.* (Lisburn 2855)

BARRACLOUGH, Dennis. b 35. LCP 62. STh (Lambeth) 68. FCP 74. Ripon Hall Ox 66. **d** 68 Wakef **p** 69 Pontefract for Wakef. C of Woodhouse 68-71; V of Gildersome Dio Wakef from 71. *Vicarage, Street Lane, Gildersome, Leeds, LS27 7HR.* (Leeds 533339)

BARRACLOUGH, Owen Conrad. b 32. Pemb Coll Cam 3rd cl Math Trip pt 1 53, BA (2nd cl Econ Trip pt ii) 55, MA 59. Westcott Ho Cam 56. **d** 57 Bris **p** 58 Malmesbury for Bris. C of Chippenham 57-62; V of Harringay 62-70; Bp of Cov Chap for Commun Rels 70-77; C-in-c of Baginton 72-77; V of Swindon Dio Bris from 77. *Christ Church Vicarage, Bath Road, Swindon, Wilts.* (Swindon 22832)

BARRACLOUGH, Raymond George. b 41. Univ of Queensld BA 62. BD (Lon) 69. Moore Coll Syd 66. **d** 74 **p** 75 Brisb. C of St Jas Toowoomba 74-77; R of St John U Mt Gravatt Brisb 77-79; Chap Univ of Qld and P-in-c of St Pet West End City and Dio Brisb from 79. *14 Mitchell Street, West End, Queensland, Australia 4101.* (44-5115)

BARRALL, John Henry. b 31. Bps' Coll Cheshunt. **d** 61 **p** 62 St Alb. C of Digswell 61-65; Aldershot (in c of Ch of Ascen) 65-70; Team V of Hemel Hempstead Dio St A from 70. *St Albans Vicarage, Warners End Road, Hemel Hempstead, HP1 3QF.*

BARRAND, George William. Lon Coll of Div 59. **d** 62 **p** 63 Lich. C of Bucknall w Bagnall 62-65; Parr 65-70; R of Berrima w Moss Vale 70-79; Warburton Dio Melb from 79. *Box 222, Warburton, Vic, Australia 3799.*

BARRATT, Ven Anthony John. BC Coll Bris. **d** 49 Ox **p** 50 Warrington for Ox. C of Slough 49-52; SAMS Miss at Cholchol 52-64; Hon Can of Ch Ch Cathl Port Stanley, Falkd Is 57-64; SAMS Miss at Asuncion 64-70; Tucuman Dio Parag 70-73; Dio N Argent from 73; Archd of Paraguay 64-70; Archd in N Argent from 70. *Misión Anglicana, Tucuman, Argentina, S America.*

BARRATT, Peter. b 29. Down Coll Cam BA 53, MA 57. Ridley Hall Cam 53. **d** 55 **p** 56 Ches. C of Bebington 55-58; C-in-c of St Martin's Conv Distr Cam 58-61; PC 61-68; V of Rawtenstall Dio Man from 68; RD of Rossendale from 81. *Rawtenstall Vicarage, Rossendale, Lancs, BB4 6RX.* (Rossendale 215585)

BARRATT, Peter. Linc Coll Ox BA (2nd cl Mod Lang) 59. Cudd Coll 66. **d** 68 Mashon. C of St Mary and All SS Cathl Salisbury Mashon from 68. *PO Box 981, Salisbury, Rhodesia.*

BARRATT, Sydney. Dorch Miss Coll 05. **d** 06 Lon for Col Bp **p** 07 St Jo Kaffr. C of Matatiele Cape Col 06-09; P-in-c of Mt Fletcher 09-17; Idutywa 17-54; Archd of St Mark's and Can of St Jo Kaffr 44-54. *P.O. Box 771, Johannesburg, S Africa.*

BARRATT, Terrick. d and **p** 71 Parag. P Dio Parag 71-73; Dio N Argent 73-80; Dio Chile from 80. *Casilla 561, Vina Del Mar, Chile.*

BARRELL, Adrian Edward. b 36. Keble Coll Ox BA (4th cl Mod Hist) 59. Ely Th Coll 59. **d** 62 **p** 63 Ex. C of St Jas L Ham Plymouth 62-66; Bideford 66-70; V of Walkhampton 70-80. *3 Oakery Crescent, Princetown, Yelverton, Devon, PL20 6QE.*

BARRET-LENNARD, Richard John Sterling. b 51. Univ of W Austr BA 74. Univ of Ox BA (Th) 76. Wycl Hall Ox 74. **d** 78 Perth. On study leave. *Wollaston College, Wollaston Road, Mount Claremont, W Australia 6010.*

BARRETT, Alan. b 48. Univ of Southn BA 69. Wycl Hall Ox 74. **d** 77 **p** 78 Doncaster for Sheff. C of Conisbrough 77-80; St Paul Homerton 80-81; P-in-c of Good Shepherd Conv Distr Hounslow Dio Lon from 81. *360 Beavers Lane, Hounslow, TW4 6HJ.* (01-570 4035)

BARRETT, Brian William. b 28. BA (Lon) 60. **d** 75 Ox **p** 76 Buckingham for Ox (NSM). Hdmaster St Edw Sch Reading from 73; Hon C of Goring Dio Ox from 75. *3 Chestnut Cottages, Wallingford Road, Streatley, Reading, RG8 9JQ.*

BARRETT, Christopher Paul. b 49. AKC 71. St Aug Coll Cant 71. **d** 72 **p** 73 Heref. C of Tupsley 72-75; St Thos Ex 75-78; C-in-c 78-79; R of Atherington w High Bickington Dio Ex from 79; V of Burrington Dio Ex from 79. *Rectory, High Bickington, Umberleigh, Devon.* (High Bickington 283)

BARRETT, David Brian. Late Scho of Clare Coll Cam BA (2nd cl Mech Sc) 48, MA 52, BD 69. Union Th Sem NY STM (*magna cum laude*) 63. Columb Univ NY PhD 65. Ridley Hall Cam 52. **d** 54 **p** 55 Bradf. C of Bradf Cathl 54-57; CMS Miss at Kisii 57-62; Research Sec Prov of E Afr 65-68; Hon C of All SS Cathl City and Dio Nai from 66. *Unit of Research, PO Box 40230, Nairobi, Kenya.* (Nairobi 23649)

BARRETT, David Douglas. b 50. Atlantic Sch of Th Halifax NS BTh 79. **d** 79 E Newfld. C of Random Dio E Newfld from 79. *Hodges Cove, Newfoundland, Canada, A0E 2B0.*

BARRETT, Ven Denis. MBE 43. **d** 59 **p** 60 Nel. Dom Chap to Bp of Nel 59-60; V of Waimea 60-66; Wairau Valley 66-70; Can of Nel 69-70; V of Westport 70-75; Archd of Mawhera 70-75; Archd (Emer) from 75; VG Nel 71-75; L to Offic Dio Nel from 75. *99 Alfred Street, Blenheim, NZ.*

BARRETT, Derek Leonard. b 25. St Francis Coll Brisb ACT ThL (2nd cl) 57. **d** 57 **p** 58 Brisb. C of Maryborough 57-58; P-in-c of Kilkivan 58-59; C of Toowoomba 59-60; P-in-c of Biggenden 60-62; R 62-63; C of St Geo Ramsgate 64-65; Putney 65-67; V of St Jo Bapt Kidderminster 67-77; Hon Chap Miss to Seamen from 70; V of St Thos Stourbridge Dio Worc from 77. *34 South Road, Stourbridge, W Midl, DY8 3TB.* (Stourbridge 2401)

BARRETT, Edmund. Bp Wilson Th Coll IM 35. **d** 38 Pontefract for Wakef **p** 39 Wakef. C of Ossett 38-40; Mold Green 40-42; Armley 42-44; Dep Chap HM Pris Leeds 43-44; Chap HM Pris Feltham 44-46; R of Long Riston w Catwick 46-51; C-in-c of New Edlington 51-54; V 54-56; Chap of Crookhill Hall Sanat Conisborough 51-56; V of Bentley 56-61; R of Kirk Smeaton 61-65; Chap RADD Essex Area and L to Offic Dio Chelmsf 65-69; C of Aveley 69-74; Gt Warley Dio Chelmsf from 74. *Church House, Junction Road, Warley, Brentwood, Essex.*

BARRETT, Harry Bernard. Univ of BC BA 51. Angl Th Coll of BC LTh 53, BD 55. **d** 53 **p** 54 New Westmr. I of Steveston 53-56; Dean of Res and NT Lect at Angl Th Coll Vanc 56-58; Asst Prof of NT 58-59; Assoc Sec Dept of Relig Educn Angl Ch of Canada 59-62; R of Trail 62-67; Koot Boundary Reg Par Dio Koot from 67-69; Can of Pro-Cathl of St Sav, Nelson BC 64-69; R of St Geo Edmon 69-72; St Mary Richmond Hill 72-79; All SS Westboro City and Dio Ott from 79. *519 Denbury Avenue, Ottawa, K2A 2N8, Ont, Canada.* (613-722 2805)

BARRETT, James Stanley. St Francis Th Coll Brisb. **d** and **p** 65 Brisb. L to Offic Dio Brisb 65-66; C of St Steph Coorparoo Brisb 66-68; P-in-c of Laidley 68-70; R 70-77; Childers Dio Brisb from 77. *Rectory, Macrossan Street, Childers, Queensland, Australia 4660.* (Childers 126)

BARRETT, Canon John Alan Gardiner. b 29. Trin Coll Dub 57. **d** 59 **p** 60 Dub. C of Bray 59-63; I of Enniskeen 63-69; Navan Dio Meath from 69; Can of Meath from 81; RD of Ardnurcher and Clonmacnoise from 78. *Rectory, Trim Road, Navan, Irish Republic.* (046 21172)

BARRETT, John Edward. b 40. E Anglian Min Tr Scheme 78. **d** 81 Ely (APM). C of Everton w Tetworth Dio Ely from 81; Perm to Offic Dio St Alb from 81. *17 The Lawns, Everton, Sandy, Beds, SG19 2LB.* (0767-80618)

BARRETT, John Joseph James. b 38. BD (Lon) 65. **d** 78 Bradwell for Chelmsf **p** 78 Colchester for Chelmsf. C of Danbury 78-80; Dovercourt Dio Chelmsf from 80. *3 Elmhurst Road, Dovercourt, Harwich, CO12 3SA.*

BARRETT, Kenneth. b 42. St D Coll Lamp BA 64. St Steph Ho Ox 65. **d** 67 **p** 68 Blackb. C of Poulton-le-Fylde 67-69; C of H Trin S Shore Blackpool 69-72; V of Brierfield Dio Blackb from 72. *Vicarage, 22 Reedley Road, Reedley, Burnley, Lancs.* (Nelson 63235)

BARRETT, Canon Kenneth Sydney. Roch Th Coll. **d** 62 **p** 63 Southw. C of Wollaton 62-65; Hucknall Torkard (in c of St John) 65-67; R of Collie 67-73; Mandurah Dio Bunb from 73; Can of Bunb from 76. *Rectory, Leslie Street, Mandurah, W Australia 6210.* (095-35 1308)

BARRETT, Peter Francis. b 56. TCD BA 78, MA 81. Ch of Ireland Th Coll Dipl Th 81. **d** 81 **p** 82 Derry. C of Drumachose w Limavady Dio Derry from 81. *17 Castle Gardens, Limavady, Co Derry, N Ireland.* (Limavady 6341)

BARRETT, Philip Leslie Sibborn. b 47. Ex Coll Ox BA (2nd cl Th) 68, MA 72. Cudd Coll 68. **d** 70 **p** 71 Worc. C of Pershore w Pinvin, Wick and Birlingham 70-73; Bournemouth 74-76; V Chor of Heref Cathl from 76; M Gen Syn from 80. *7 The Cloisters, Cathedral Close, Hereford, HR1 2NG.* (0432-273400)

BARRETT, Raymond William. b 23. St Mich AA Coll Llan 72. **d** 73 **p** 74 Glouc. C of St Luke w St John Cheltm 73-75; P-in-c of Holbeach Bank 75-78; Holbeach Hurn 75-78; V of Baston (w Langtoft 78, Braceborough and Wilsthorpe from 80) Dio Linc from 75; Langtoft 78. *Baston Vicarage, Peterborough.* (Greatford 287)

BARRETT, Robert Edwin. b 46. Univ of Cant BSc 69. St Jo Coll Auckld 70. **d** 70 **p** 71 Ch Ch. C of Cashmere Hills 70-72; Hornby 72; Chap Dilworth Sch Auckld 73-75; Hon C of St Mark Remuera Auckld 73-75; V of Blockhouse Bay Dio Auckld from 76. *Box 48-020, Blockhouse Bay, Auckland 7, NZ.* (678-779)

BARRETT, Ronald Reginald. b 30. Roch Th Coll 61. **d** 64 **p** 65 Cant. C of All SS Spring Park Croydon 64-66; St Jude Thornton Heath 66-68; V of Greengates 68-73; Shelf 73-79; Embsay w Eastby Dio Bradf from 79. *Embsay Vicarage, Skipton, Yorks.* (Skipton 2755)

BARRETT, Stephen David Norman. b 54. Univ of Aber BSc 75. Univ of Edin BD 78. Edin Th Coll 75. **d** 78 **p** 79 Glas. C of Ardrossan and of Irvine 78-80; R of Peterhead 80-81; Renfrew Dio Glas from 81. *2 Oxford Road, Renfrew.*

BARRETT, Stephen Graham. Moore Th Coll Syd 69. **d** 71 Bp Begbie for Syd **p** 72 Syd. C of St Alb Epping 71-74; w SAMS Dio N Argent from 75; Exam Chap to Bp of N Argent from 80. *Casilla 17, Embarcacion, Salta, Argentina.*

BARRETT, Theodore Louis Joseph. b 10. Lich Th Coll 55. **d** 56 **p** 57 Southw. C of Bingham 56-59; V of St Mary Ladybrook Mansfield 59-62; Crosthwaite 62-75; PC of Cartmel Fell 62-73; V 73-75. *11 Vicarage Road, Levens, Kendal, Cumb.*

BARRETT, Tufnell Sealy Douglas. b 01. Trin Coll Ox 20. St Steph Ho Ox. **d** 24 **p** 25 Lon. C of St Etheldreda Fulham 24-25; St Matt Westmr 25-26; St Mark Swindon (in c of St John from 28) 26-38; R of Kirkby-Thore (w Temple Sowerby V from 41) 38-46; CF (R of O) 39-46; V of Goldthorpe 46-53; R of Hopesay w Edgton 53-61; Ch Ch Lochgilphead 61-69; Can of St Jo Cathl Oban 65-79; Perm to Offic Dio Ox from 80. *The Old Vicarage, Moulsford, Wallingford, Oxon.*

BARRETT, Wesley Litton. B 27. **d** 73 Rupld. Hon C in the Hodgson-Peguis Area Dio Rupld from 73. *Box 219, Fisher Branch, Manitoba, Canada.*

BARRETT-LENNARD, Richard. Univ of W Austr BA 74. Univ of Ox BA 76. **d** and **p** 78 Perth. C of Fremantle w Beaconsfield 78-80; R of Bruce Rock w Narembeen Dio Perth from 80. *62 Butcher Street, Bruce Rock, W Australia 6410.* (090-611334)

BARRIBAL, Richard James Pitt. b 45. Trin Coll Bris Dipl Higher Educn (Th) 80. **d** 80 **p** 81 Pet. C of St Giles Northn Dio Pet from 80. *6 York Road, Northampton, NN1 5QG.* (Northn 39410)

BARRIE, Canon Alexander Stewart Whyte. b 23. Univ of Glas MA 44. Edin Th Coll 44. **d** 46 **p** 47 Glas. C of St Mary's Cathl Glas 46-49; Chap Angl Students Univ of Glas 46-49; C of St John Bridgwater 49-55; St Thos w St Mich Win 55-56; V of St Just-in-Penwith 56-72; V of Sancreed 62-72; RD of Penwith 70-72; V of Bodmin Dio Truro from 72; Hon Can of

Truro from 79. *Vicarage, Bodmin, Cornwall, PL31 2AB.* (Bodmin 3867)

BARRIE, John Arthur. b 38. Bps' Coll Cheshunt. **d** 63 **p** 64 Lon. C of St Mich-at-Bowes Bowes Pk 63-66; CF from 66. *c/o Williams and Glyns Bank Ltd., Kirkland House, Whitehall, SW1.*

BARRIE, Robert Chadwick. b 45. Moore Th Coll Syd ACT ThL 76. **d** 77 Bp Dain for Syd **p** 77 Syd. C of St Mark W Wollongong 77-78; St Paul Castle Hill Dio Syd from 79. *30 Showground Road, Castle Hill, NSW, Australia 2154.* (634-1035)

BARRINGTON-WARD, Canon Simon. b 30. Magd Coll Cam BA 53, MA 57. Westcott Ho Cam 54. **d** 56 Bp Walsh for Cant **p** 57 Ely. Chap Magd Coll Cam 56-60; Select Pr Univ of Cam 59; Lect Relig Stud Univ Coll of Ibad 60-63; Fell and Dean of Chapel Magd Coll Cam 63-69; Prin CMS Miss Tr Coll Selly Oak 69-74; Gen Sec CMS from 75; Hon Can of Derby Cathl from 75. *c/o CMS, 157 Waterloo Road, SE1 8UU.*

BARRODALE, George Bryan. b 44. St Mich Coll Llan 67. **d** 69 **p** 70 Mon. C of Maindee 69-72; V in R Benef of Merthyr Tydfil and Cyfarthfa 72-76; R of Cotgrave Dio Southw from 76; CF (TAVR) from 76. *Rectory, Cotgrave, Nottingham, NG12 3HT.* (Nottm 892223)

BARRON, Charles Leslie. b 20. AKC 49. St Steph Ho Ox 49. **d** 50 **p** 51 Dur. C of Esh w Langley Park 50-52; Winlaton (in c of St Barn Rowlands Gill) 52-55; PC (V from 68) of St Mary Magd Millfield Dio Dur from 55; Div Master Argyle House Sch Sunderland 58-65; Prin 65-71; Chap Havelock Hosp Sunderland 75-76; P-in-c of Good Shepherd Ford Estate 76-79. *St Mary Magdalene's Vicarage, Millfield, Sunderland, Tyne & Wear, SR4 6HJ.* (Sunderland 56318)

BARRON, Leslie Gill. b 44. ACII 69. Lich Th Coll 67. **d** 70 **p** 71 Dur. C of Ch Ch Bp Wearmouth 70-72; St Mary w St Pet Conv Distr Bp Wearmouth 72-75; Harton 75-77; V of Lumley Dio Dur from 77. *Christ Church Vicarage, Great Lumley, Chester-le-Street, Co Durham.* (Chester-le-St 882228)

✠ **BARRON, Right Rev Patrick Harold Falkiner.** Univ of Leeds BA 35. Coll of Resurr Mirfield 32. **d** 38 **p** 39 Lon. C of H Redeemer w St Phil Clerkenwell 38-40; Boksburg 40-41; CF (S Afr) 41-45; R of Zeerust and P-in-c of Zeerust Miss Distr 45-50; R of Potchefstroom 50-51; Blyvooruitzicht 51-55; P-in-c of St Cypr Miss Johann 55-59; Chap Johann Pris 56-59; Archd of Germiston 57-59; Dean of St Mary's Cathl Johann and Archd of Cathl 59-64; Cons Ld Bp Suffr of Capetn in St Mary's Cathl Johann 15 Nov 64 by Abp of Capetn; Bps of Geo; Johann; Basuto; Natal; Kimb K; St John's; Bloemf; Lebom; Pret; Damar; and Grahmstn; Asst Bps of St John's; and Natal (Paget); and Bp Fosseus; Archd of Caledon 65-66; Trld to George 66; res 77; R of Camps Bay 78-80; L to Offic Dio Capetn from 80. *E37 Edingight Flats, Queen Road, Rondebosch 7700, Cape Town, S Africa.* (69-1820)

BARRON, Richard Davidson. b 51. BSc (Lon) 74. Trin Coll Bris 75. **d** 78 **p** 79 Wakef. C of Bradley 78-81; H Trin Heworth City and Dio York from 81. *30 Muncaster Gate, Heworth, York, YO3 9LA.* (Heworth 425188)

BARRON, Victor Robert. b 45. Trin Coll Bris 76. **d** 78 Chelmsf **p** 79 Barking for Chelmsf. C of Rainham 78-81; V of H Trin w St Gabr and St Lawr Easton City and Dio Bris from 81. *69 Stapleton Road, Bristol, BS5 0PQ.* (Bris 554255)

BARRON, Canon William Basil Mansergh. Em Coll Cam 3rd cl Hist Trip pt i 33, BA (3rd cl Hist Trip pt ii) 34, MA 38. **d** 35 **p** 36 Lon. C of Hillingdon 35-38; Krugersdorp 38-41; CF (S Afr) 41-45; Men in Disp (twice) 44; R of Orange Grove Johann 46-48; C of Germiston 48-51; Woodstock 51-52; R of Observatory 52-62; Chap Groote Schuur Hosp City and Dio Capetn from 62; Hon Can of Capetn from 70. *6 Banksia Road, Rosebank, CP, S Africa.* (66-8437)

BARROSSO, Juan. d 68 **p** 69 Argent. P Dio Argent 68-73; N Argent from 73. *Parsonage, Carboncito, N Argentina.*

BARROW, Colin Vere. Codr Coll 49. **d** and **p** 55 Barb. C of St Geo Cathl Gui 55-58; V of Belladrum w Lich 58-61; Belladrum 62-75. *c/o St Patrick's Vicarage, Barbados, W Indies.*

BARROW, John Michael Gordon. b 14. Late Found Scho of St Jo Coll Dur, Lightfoot Scho 36, BA (2nd cl Cl) 36, Dipl Th 37, MA 39. **d** 37 Warrington for Liv **p** 38 Liv. C of Fazakerley 37-43; R of St Matthias w St Simon Salford 43-46; Sec of Liv Dioc Branch of CETS 46-50; V of St Cleopas Toxteth Pk 50-57; Earlestown 57-64; St Mich-in-the-Hamlet Toxteth Pk 64-75; P-in-c of St Nath Fazakerley Walton-on-the-Hill 75-78; V 78-79. *19 Fford Tanrallt, Meliden, Nr Prestatyn, Clwyd.*

BARROW, Michael David Johnstone. b 36. Dipl Th (Wales) 64. St Mich Coll Llan 61. **d** 64 **p** 65 S'wark. C of Old Charlton 64-70; Wadhurst and of Tidebrook 70-71; Minster-in-Sheppey (in c of St Pet Halfway) 72-79; V of St Mich AA Tenterden Dio Cant from 79. *Vicarage, St Michael's, Tenterden, Kent, TN30 6PY.* (Tenterden 4670)

BARROW, Norman Beynon. St Jo Coll Dur BA 36, Dipl in Th 37, MA 39. **d** 37 **p** 38 Liv. C of St Jo Bapt Burscough Bridge 37-40; CF (EC) 40-46; Men in Disp 45; Chap Belmont Road Hosp and Olive Mt Children's Hosp 47-51; V of St Athanasius Kirkdale 51-64; C-in-c of St Aid Liv 51-58; Chap Stanley Hosp Liv 51-64; Chap to Bp of Liv 57-61; V of All S Springwood Liv 64-74. *2 Cottage Road, Westminster Park, Chester, CH4 7QB.*

BARROW, Owen Gore. Trin Coll Tor LTh 34. **d** 34 Niag **p** 35 Tor. C of Grand Valley w Colbeck 34-35; Trin Tor 35-36; St Steph Walworth Common 37-39; Corby 39-40; Min of St Columba Corby 40-41; Offg C-in-c of Rothwell w Orton 41-44; Miss at Teulon 44-45; R of Schreiber 45-47; Marathon w Heron Bay 47-54; Campbellford 55-67; Ch of Nativity Tor 67-76; Hon C of Grace Ch Markham 76-78. *Apt 502, 65 Park Street East, Mississauga, Ont, Canada.*

BARROW, Wilfrid Edward. b 10. Worc Ordin Coll 60. **d** 62 **p** 63 St Alb. C of Boreham Wood 62-66; V of Heath w Reach Dio St Alb from 66. *Vicarage, Shenley Hill Road, Leighton Buzzard, Beds, LU7 8BY.* (Leighton Buzzard 377122)

BARRY, Herbert Brian. b 25. QUB 43. Edin Th Coll 46. **d** 48 **p** 49 Edin. C of Old St Paul Edin 48-52; R of Burntisland w Aberdour and Kinghorn 52-56; C of Hayes (in c of St Nich) 56-63; R of St Salvador Edin 63-69; C of St Barn, Northolt Pk Lon 69-72; C-in-c of All SS S Acton Dio Lon from 72; V of St Alb Acton Green Dio Lon from 75. *41 South Parade, W4 1JS.* (01-994 5328)

BARRY, Canon John. b 15. Late Scho of TCD BA (1st cl Ment and Mor Sc Mod) Downes Pri (1st) and Div Test 38, MA 41. **d** 38 Down **p** 39 Bp Kennedy for Down. C of St Matt Belf 38-41; St Mark Dundela 41-45; R of Dunluce 45-49; Hillsborough Dio Down from 49; Surr from 52; Can of St Anne's Cathl Belf from 56; Exam Chap to Bp of Down from 57; Chan of Down Cathl 64-73; Preb and Can of St Patr Cathl Dub from 73. *Rectory, Hillsborough, Co Down, N Ireland.* (Hillsborough 366)

BARRY, Jonathan Peter Oulton. b 47. TCD BA 70, MA 73. Univ of Hull BA (Th) 73. Ripon Hall Ox 73. **d** 74 **p** 75 Down. C of Dundela 74-79; R of Ballyphilip w Ardquin Dio Down from 79. *Rectory, Cloughey Road, Portaferry, N Ireland.* (Portaferry 233)

BARRY, Lewis Lindon. b 24. St Paul Th Coll Maur 64. **d** 71 **p** 72 Maur. C of Curepipe Dio Maur from 71. *Prison Road, Beau-Bassin, Mauritius.*

BARRY, Milton James. Univ of Sask BA 67. Trin Coll Tor STB 69. **d** 68 **p** 69 Qu'App. C of Pipestone 68-69; Whitewood 69-73; St Thos Tor 74-76; R of Lorne Pk Dio Tor from 76. *1190 Lorne Park Avenue, Mississauga, Ont., Canada* (416-278 4765)

BARRY, Philip Maurice. b 07. Late Choral Exhib of G and C Coll Cam 3rd cl Cl Trip 28, BA (3rd cl Th Trip) 29, Exhib 30, MA 33. Univ of Ox MA (by incorp) 44. Westcott Ho Cam 29. **d** 31 **p** 32 Chich. C of W Tarring 31-34; Melksham 34-37; V of Bradford-on-Avon 37-44; Chap Ch Ch Ox 44-45; LPr Dio Ox 45; Asst R of St Botolph Bishopsgate Lon 45-46; V of H Trin Leamington 46-48; Henfield 48-55; Littlehampton 56-64; R of Sedlescombe w Whatlington 64-72; P-in-c of Heyshott 73-78; Birdham w Itchenor W 78-80. *85 Broyle Road, Chichester, Sussex PO19 4BE.* (Chich 776545)

BARRY, Robert. King's Coll NS 45. **d** 50 **p** 51 Moos. C of Nakina 50-59; R of St Martin's 59-63; Richibucto 63-64; I of Hardwicke 64-74; McAdam Dio Fred from 74. *Rectory, McAdam, NB, Canada.*

BARRY-JUPP, Laurence Richard David. *See* Jupp, Laurence Richard David Barry.

BARRYMORE, Arthur Norman. Kelham Th Coll 61. Dipl Th (Lon) 67. **d** 67 **p** 68 Guildf. C of St Nich 67-69; P-in-c of St Edw Burgess Hill 66-74; Good Shepherd Conv Distr Mile Oak, Portslade 74-80; Chap Supt Sussex Dioc Assoc for the Deaf from 80. *32 York Avenue, Hove, Sussex, BN3 1PH.* (Brighton 23076)

BARSLEY, Anthony Noel. b 11. St Aid Coll 46. **d** 47 **p** 48 Liv. C of Hindley 47-50; Penn 50-53; V of Gailey w Hatherton 53-59; Lower Gornal 59-61; Chebsey 61-76. *5 Brookside Close, Bedale, N Yorks, DL8 2Dr.*

BARSLEY, Robin Cairns. b 23. Wadh Coll Ox BA and MA 48. Westcott Ho Cam 48. **d** 49 **p** 50 Man. C of Heywood 49-53; Oldham 53-54; V of St Pet Ashton L 54-60; Hadlow 60-66; R of St Mary Hulme 68-75; Bp's Chap for Social Work Dio Birm 75-77; C-in-c of St Paul Ramsbottom 77-81; V of St John and St Paul Ramsbottom Dio Man from 81. *St Paul's Vicarage, Ramsbottom, Bury, Lancs, BL0 0AN.* (Ramsbottom 3387)

BARTER, Ven Donald. b 34. St Francis Coll Brisb ACT ThL 69. **d** 69 N Queensld **p** 70 Bp Miles for N Queensld. C of Heatley 70-72; R of Mareeba 71-81; Mt Isa Dio N Queensld from 81; Archd of the West from 81. *Rectory, Mount Isa, Queensland, Australia 4825.*

BARTER, Geoffrey Roger. b 41. Univ of Bris BSc (2nd cl Elec Eng) 63. Clifton Th Coll 65. **d** 67 Repton for Derby **p** 68 Derby. C of Normanton-by-Derby 67-70; C of Rainham 70-75; V of St Jo Bapt w St Jas and St Paul Plumstead Dio S'wark from 75. *176 Griffin Road, Plumstead, SE18 7QA.* (01-854 1552)

BARTER, John Herbert. b 30 K Coll Lon and Warm AKC 56. **d** 57 **p** 58 Chich. C of Horsham 57-62; V of Desborough 62-71; C-in-c of Braybrooke 67-71; C-in-c of Brampton Ash w Dingley 70-72; V of H Trin Hounslow Dio Lon from 72. *Vicarage, 66 Lampton Road, Hounslow, Middx.* (01-570 3066)

BARTHOLOMEUSZ, Douglas Brian. Div Sch Colom 50. **d** 52 **p** 53 Colom. P Dio Colom 53-59; P-in-c of Beenleigh Queensld 59-62; V 62-63; R of Crow's Nest 63-70; R of Rosewood 70-74; St Mark The Gap City and Dio Brisb from 74. *1073 Waterworks Road, The Gap, Brisbane, Australia 4061.* (30 1502)

BARTHOLOMEUSZ, Samuel Douglas. Div Sch Colom. **d** 40 **p** 43 Colom. C of Kandy 40-44; Perm to Offic at St Andr Hertford 44-49; I of Mount Lavinia 50-56; C of Acock's Green 57-58; R of Broadford 59-62; I of Ch Ch Brunswick 62-67; Dean of Bal 67-71; I of Middle Park 72-81; L to Offic Dio Melb from 81. *177 Springvale Road, Glen Waverley, Vic, Australia 3150.*

BARTHOLOMEUSZ, Teddy Cecil Lorensz. d 59 **p** 60 Colom. C of St Paul Milagiriya 59-63; Dagenham 66-68; St Cuthb Eccles Distr Castle Vale 68-71; I of Foleyet 71-74. *1513 Dixie Road, Mississauga, Ont., Canada.*

BARTLAM, Graham Frederick. b 37. BA (Lon) 63. Oak Hill Th Coll 59. **d** 64 **p** 65 Chelmsf. C of Hawkwell 64-68; Ch Ch Gt Warley Dio Chelmsf 68-74; R of Good Easter and High Easter w Margaret Roding Dio Chelmsf from 74. *Rectory, Good Easter, Chelmsford, Essex.* (Good Easter 429)

BARTLE, David Colin. b 29. Em Coll Cam BA 53, MA 57. Ridley Hall Cam 53. **d** 55 **p** 56 Birm. C of St Martin Birm 55-57; St Jo Evang Boscombe 57-60; V of St Jo Evang Lowestoft 60-70; Team R of Thetford 70-75; Surr 70-75; C-in-c of Croxton and Kilverstone 70-75; Asst Master Bournemouth Sch from 75. *37 Fenton Road, Bournemouth, BH6 5EY.* (Bournemouth 426339)

BARTLE, George Clement. b 1898. **d** 30 Stepney for Lon **p** 31 Lon. C of Spitalfields 30-33; Reigate 33-35; R of Spitalfields 35-46; Surr 37-46; R of Bidborough 46-50; V of Ch Ch Tunbridge Wells 50-54; Ch Ch Chislehurst 54-61; R of Woodham Mortimer w Hazeleigh 61-67; R of Woodham Walter 61-67; Perm to Offic Dio St E from 67; Dio Chelmsf from 67; Dio Ely 75-80; C of Saffron Walden 69-75. *Flat 8, Manormead, Tilford Road, Hindhead, Surrey GU26 6RA.*

BARTLE, Reginald Stephen. b 24. K Coll Lon and Warm AKC 51, BD 52. **d** 52 **p** 53 Roch. C of Penge 52-55; SAMS Miss at Quepe 55-58; Cholchol 58-62; Temuco Dio Chile from 63; Hon Can of St Andr Cathl Santiago 64-70; Archd of S Chile 64-69; of N Chile 69-70; NW Area Sec SAMS 70-73; Home Sec from 73; L to Offic Dio Chelmsf from 73; Hon C of Southborough 76-78; St Jas Tunbridge Wells Dio Roch 78-80; C from 80. *The Curatage, Birken Road, Tunbridge Wells, Kent.* (Tun Wells 30131)

BARTLE-JENKINS, Canon Leonard Christmas. b 13. St D Coll Lamp BA 35; Lich Th Coll 35. **d** 38 Mon **p** 39 Llan for Mon. C of Fleur-de-Lys 38-41; Trevethin 41-48; V of Llangattock-vibon-Avel w Llanfaenor Chapel w St Maughans 48-55; Bassaleg 55-73; Can of Mon from 64; RD of Bassaleg from 67; R of Michaelston-y-Fedw (w Rudry from 75) Dio Mon from 74. *Michaelston-y-Fedw Rectory, Cardiff, CF3 9XS.* (Castleton 680414)

BARTLEET, Bryan Neville. St Paul's Coll Grahmstn 58. **d** 60 Capetn for St Hel **p** 61 St Hel. P-in-c of St Matt St Hel 60-64; C of St Mary's Colleg Ch Port Eliz 64-69; P-in-c of St Pet Port Eliz 69-72; St Mary Magd Salt Lake 72-81; Swartkops River Valley Dio Port Eliz from 81. *Box 45, Swartkops 6210, CP, S Africa.*

BARTLEET, Canon David Henry. b 29. St Pet Hall Ox BA (3rd cl Th) 55, MA 61. Westcott Ho Cam 55. **d** 57 St E **p** 58 Dunwich for St E. C of St Mary-le-Tower Ipswich 57-60; Doncaster 60-64; V of Edenbridge 64-73; Bromley Dio Roch from 73; Hon Can of Roch from 79. *Vicarage, St Paul's Square, Bromley, Kent.* (01-460 6275)

BARTLES-SMITH, Douglas Leslie. b 37. St Edm Hall Ox BA 61, MA 75. Wells Th Coll 61. **d** 63 **p** 64 Lon. C of St Steph Roch Row w St Jo Evang Westmr 63-68; C-in-c of St Mich AA w All S and Em Ch Camberwell 68-72; V 72-75; St Luke Battersea Dio S'wark from 75; RD of Battersea from 81. *192 Ramsden Road, SW12 8RQ.* (01-673 6049)

BARTLETT, Alan. b 38. Qu Coll Birm. **d** 79 **p** 80 Birm. C of Perry Beeches Dio Birm from 79. *43 Delhurst Road, Great Barr, Birmingham, B44 9HT.*

BARTLETT, Alban Denys. b 26. St D Coll Lamp St Jo Coll Ox BA 50, MA 55. St Mich Coll Llan 50. **d** 52 **p** 53 Llan. C of Neath 52-54; St Mark Newport 54-57; CF 57-81; Chap R Hosp Chelsea from 81. *Royal Hospital, Chelsea, SW3.*

BARTLETT, Anthony Martin. b 43. St Jo Coll Dur 76. **d** 77 **p** 78 Dur. C of Heworth 77-80; V of Cleadon Dio Dur from 80; CF (TA) from 81. *Cleadon Vicarage, Sunderland, Co Durham, SR6 7UR.* (Boldon 367147)

BARTLETT, Canon Archibald Thomas. b 15. Kelham Th Coll 31. **d** 38 **p** 39 Carl. C of St Luke Barrow-F 38-42; Chap RAFVR 42-47; C of St Marg Leigh-on-Sea 47-51; V of Offenham 51-59; St Edm Dudley 59-76; Proc Conv Worc 63-70 and 75-80; Hon Can of Worc Cathl from 74; P-in-c of Wichenford 76-79; Martley (and Wichenford from 79) Dio Worc from 77. *Wichenford Vicarage, Worcester, WR6 6XY.*

BARTLETT, Basil Gordon. b 11. Selw Coll Cam BA 34, MA 38. Men in Disp 42. Wells Th Coll 34. **d** 36 **p** 37 Swan B. C of Llansamlet 36-39; Chap RAF 39-46; V of St Swithun Sheff 46-51; Prin and Chap of R Sch for Blind Leatherhead 50-76; Perm to Offic Dios B & W and Ex from 76. *Jasmine Cottage, Winsford, Nr Minehead, Somt, TA24 7JE.* (Winsford 317)

BARTLETT, Clifford William Tudor. b 15. ALCD 38. **d** 38 Lon **p** 39 Willesden for Lon. C of Em Hornsey Road 38-41; Haveringatte-Bower 41-44; CF (EC) 44-47; C of Rothbury (in c of Hepple and Thropton) 47-49; V of Otterburn 49-60; V of Horsley w Byrness 53-60; Ovingham 60-80; Perm to Offic Dio Newc T from 80. *69 Rectory Lane, Winlaton, Blaydon, T & W, NE21 6PJ.* (Blaydon 444236)

BARTLETT, Canon David Blandford. Selw Coll Cam BA 49. Sarum Th Coll 49. **d** 51 **p** 52 Wakef. C of Brighouse 51-54; Warden of Kalole Th Coll Minaki 54-56; Sub-Warden of Namasakata Th Coll 56-58; Chap St Andr Coll Minaki 58-65; Asst P at Korogwe 60-61; Warden St Cypr Th Coll Masasi 65-66; C of Lulindi 66-67; P-in-c of St Alb, Dar-S 68-71; Miss Dio Zanz T from 71; Can of Zanz T from 72; Dir of Relig Educn Dio Zanz T from 77; Exam Chap to Bp of Zanz T from 78. *c/o PO Box 57, Muheza, Tanzania.* (Muheza 38)

BARTLETT, David John. b 36. Pemb Coll Ox BA 61. Linc Th Coll 63. **d** 65 **p** 66 Southw. C of Wollaton 65-70; V of St Mark Woodthorpe Nottm Dio Southw from 70. *37a Melbury Road, Woodthorpe, Nottingham. NG5 4PG.* (Nottm 267859)

BARTLETT, Douglas William Guest. b 03. St Cath S Ox BA 40, MA 46. MRCS 47. LRCP 47. Sarum Th Coll 28. **d** 29 **p** 31 Swan B. C of Llanthetty w Llansantffraed Usk and Glyncollwng 29-33; Publ Pr Dio Swan B 34-36; C-in-c of Llanwenarth Citra 36-38; R of Mkt Overton w Thistleton 38-40; Perm to Offic Dio Ox 40-48; R of N w S Wootton 48-63; V of Charlbury w Chadlington and Shorthampton 63-71. *The Old Tavern, Leafield, Oxon.* (Asthall Leigh 632)

BARTLETT, George. b 32. Oak Hill Th Coll 58. **d** 60 **p** 61 Lon. C of St Mark Tollington Pk 60-63; Dagenham 63-64; PC of Samlesbury 64-67; V of St Matt Blackb 67-71; P-in-c of W Thurrock w Purfleet 71-78; Fobbing Dio Chelmsf from 78; Industr Chap Dio Chelmsf from 71. *Fobbing Rectory, Stanford-le-Hope, Essex.* (Stanford-le-Hope 2002)

BARTLETT, James Roger. AKC 71. St Aug Coll Cant 71. **d** 72 Bp Skelton for Dur **p** 73 Dur. C of Whickham 72-74; W Harton 74-75; Beckenham 76-81; R of Gravesend w Ifield Dio Roch from 81. *2 Wilberforce Way, Gravesend, Kent, DA12 5DQ.* (Gravesend 63038)

BARTLETT, John Raymond. b 37. Late Exhib of BNC Ox BA 59, MA 62, B Litt 62. TCD MA 70. Linc Th Coll. **d** 63 Bp Gelsthorpe for Southw **p** 64 Southw. C of W Bridgford 63-66; Lect in Div TCD from 66; Fell of TCD from 75. *School of Hebrew, Biblical & Theological Studies, Trinity College, Dublin, Irish Republic.*

BARTLETT, Kenneth Vincent John. b 36. Late Scho of Or Coll Ox 2nd cl Cl Mods 59. BA (2nd cl Lit Hum) 61, 2nd cl Th 63. Ripon Hall Ox. **d** 63 **p** 64 Lon. Dir Paddington Ch Housing Assoc and C of St Jas Paddington 63-67; L to Offic Dio Lon from 67. *4 Barlby Road, W10.* (01-459 8622)

BARTLETT, Canon Lawrence Francis. ACT ThL 63. Ridley Coll Melb 58. **d** 61 Syd for Melb **p** 61 Syd. C of H Trin Williamstn 61-62; Willoughby 62; Prec of St Andr Cathl Syd 62-68; R of Enfield 68-75; St Mich Vaucluse Dio Syd from 75; Can of Syd from 75. *2 New South Head Road, Vaucluse, NSW, Australia 2030.* (371-4338)

BARTLETT, Leslie Guest. b 05. Chich Th Coll 29. **d** 33 **p** 35 Swan B. C of St Mark Swansea 33-37; Chipping Campden 37-40; CF (EC) 40-42; V of Exton w Whitwell Horn 42-72. *Wold's End, Chipping Campden, Glos.*

BARTLETT, Maurice Edward. b 33. G and C Coll Cam BA 59, MA 63. Wells Th Coll 59. **d** 60 **p** 61 Wakef. C of Batley 60-64; Dom Chap to Bp of Wakef 64-66; Asst Chap HM Pris Wakef 64-66; Dir of Ordinands Dio Wakef 64-66; V of Allerton 66-81; Asst Sec Dioc Syn 72-77; Sec 77-81; V of Lanc

Dio Blackb from 81; Chap HM Pris Lanc from 81. *Vicarage, Priory Close, Lancaster, LA1 1AZ.* (Lanc 63200)

BARTLETT, Michael Frederick. b 52. Univ of Ex BA 74. Univ of Liv BPhil 75. Univ of Ox BA 79. Ripon Coll Cudd 76. **d** 79 **p** 80 Liv. C of Kirkby Dio Liv from 79. *148 Quarry Green, Northwood, Kirkby, L33 8YA.*

BARTLETT, Ronald James. b 02. Lon Coll of Div 21. **d** 25 **p** 26 Liv. C of St Paul Kirkdale 25-27; St Barn Clapham Common 28-30; St Matt Ox 30-31; Surr from 31; V of St Pet Clerkenwell 31-39; St Jas Bethnal Green 39-44; V of Alperton 44-60; R of Harlington 60-73; Perm to Offic Dio Guildf from 74. *104 Palace Road, East Molesey, Surrey, KT8 9DU.* (01-979 4798)

BARTLETT, Stephen Giles Howard. b 39. Lich Th Coll 65. **d** 67 **p** 68 Linc. C of Old Brumby 67-70; Cleobury Mortimer w Hopton Wafers 70-72; Caversham 72-77; V of Chalgrove w Berrick Salome Dio Ox from 77. *Chalgrove Vicarage, Oxford, OX9 7SS.* (Stadhampton 890392)

BARTLEY, Francis William. b 14. **d** 72 **p** 73 Newc T (APM). C of Burradon 72-77; Killingworth Dio Newc T from 77. *19 Weetslade Road, Dudley, Cramlington, Northumberland.*

BARTON, Albert Eaton. Univ of Man 22. **d** 45 Adel **p** 57 Hong. Perm to Offic Dio Melb 45-55 and 64-69; LPr Dio Hong 55-64 and 69-73; Perm to Offic Dio Perth from 73. *2 Humphrey Street, St James, W Australia 6102.*

BARTON, Alfred Ernest. b 19. Univ of Man BA (Th) 52. Qu Coll Birm 50. **d** 52 **p** 53 Man. C of Rochdale 52-54; V of The Sav Bolton 54-57; Sen Chap United Sheff Hosps 57-63; Sec Chap King Edw Hosp Fund 62-65; C-in-c of Cottisford 63-65; R 65-67; C-in-c of Hardwick w Tusmore 63-65; R 65-67; V of Benson Dio Ox from 67; RD of Cuddesdon from 73. *Benson Vicarage, Oxford.* (Wallingford 38254)

BARTON, Allen Francis. b 42. Wollaston Th Coll 70. **d** 71 **p** 72 Perth. C of Claremont 71-72; R of Wyalkatchem 72-76; Moora 76-79; E Fremantle w Palmyra Dio Perth from 79. *2 Hammad Street, Palmyra, W Australia 6157.* (339 2603)

BARTON, Arthur Michael. b 33. CCC Cam 2nd cl Hist Trip pt i 56, BA (3rd cl Th Trip pt ia) 57, MA 61. Wycl Hall Ox 57. **d** 59 **p** 60 Bradf. C of Bradf Cathl 59-61; Maltby (in c of Bede Ch Centre) 61-63; V of Silsden 63-70; Moor Allerton Dio Ripon 70-81; Team R from 81; Surr from 75. *St John's Vicarage, Fir Tree Lane, Leeds, LS17 7BZ.* (684598)

BARTON, Charles Denis Hampden. BD (Lon) 63. Moore Th Coll Syd ACT ThL (2nd cl) 63. **d** 64 **p** 65 Adel. C of H Trin Adel 64-68. *c/o Church Office, 18 King William Road, North Adelaide, S Australia.*

BARTON, Charles John Greenwood. b 36. ALCD 63. **d** 63 **p** 64 Cant. C of St Mary Bredin Cant 63-66; V of Whitfield w W Langdon 66-75; C-in-c of Guston 74; V of St Luke S Kens Dio Lon from 75; Area Dean of Chelsea from 80. *1 Cathcart Road, SW10 9NL.* (01-352 7553)

BARTON, Cyril Albert. b 28. St Pet Hall Ox BA 50, MA 54. Ridley Hall Cam. **d** 52 **p** 53 Liv. C of Maghull 52-55; Bradf Cathl (in c of St John L Horton) 55-58; V of St Paul Oldham 58-68; Norbury Dio Ches from 68. *Vicarage, 75 Chester Road, Hazel Grove, Stockport, Chesh.* (061-483 8640)

BARTON, David Gerald Story. b 38. Selw Coll Cam BA 62, MA 66. Cudd Coll 63. **d** 65 **p** 66 Ox. C of Cowley 65-68; Hambleden 68-72; Hon C of St Jo Evang Hammersmith 73-77; C of St Jas Paddington Dio Lon from 77. *60 Hiley Road, NW10.* (01-960-2958)

BARTON, Edward. b 23. **d** 75 **p** 76 St Germans for Truro. C of St Budock 75-79; P-in-c of St Stythians w St Perranar-Worthal Dio Truro 79-80; V (w Gwennap) from 80. *Vicarage, Old Vicarage Close, Stithians, Truro.* (Stithians 860123)

BARTON, Eric Alfred. b 13. Clifton Th Coll 38. **d** 40 **p** 41 Chelmsf. C of St Paul Stratford 40-42; Ch Ch Barnet 42-44; V of St Barn Holloway 44-45; St Mary Magd Islington Lon 45-48; H Trin Ripon 48-53; St Phil and St Jas Clifton York 53-59; R of Haworth 59-61; V of Buttershaw 61-70; Ch Ch Nailsea 70-82. *Hen House, Hen Street, Bradninch, Devon.* (0392-88529)

BARTON, Geoffrey. b 27. Or Coll Ox BA (2nd cl Th) 48, MA 52. Chich Th Coll 49. **d** 51 **p** 52 Southw. C of Arnold 51-53; E Retford 53-54; V of St Paul Mirfield 54-60; Boroughbridge w Roecliffe (and Aldborough 73) 60-73; C-in-c of Farnham w Scotton 73-74; R (w Staveley and Copgrove) 74-77; C-in-c of Staveley w Copgrove 73-74; Chap Roundway & Devizes Hosps from 77. *Chaplain's Office, Roundway Hospital, Devizes, Wilts., SN10 5DS.* (0380 3592)

BARTON, Henry Herbert Redvers. b 1900. AKC 29. Bps' Coll Cheshunt 29. **d** 29 **p** 30 Lon. C of St Faith Stepney 29-33; All SS Woodham 33-36; W Molesey 36-38; All SS Pokesdown 38-42; R of Studland 42-49; Lowestoft 49-57; Banham 57-70; Surr 50-70; Perm to Offic Dio Nor from 70. *27 Breydon Road, Sprowston, Norwich, NR7 8EF.*

BARTON, Herbert. b 06. St Andr Coll Pampisford. **d** 46 **p** 47 Lich. C of Swynnerton 46-48; Cheadle 48-50; PC of Longsdon 50-68; V 69-78. *College of St Barnabas, Blackberry Lane, Lingfield, Surrey, RH7 6NJ.*

BARTON, Canon John. b 25. Keble Coll Ox BA 2nd cl Th 48, MA 50. Ely Th Coll 48. **d** 50 **p** 51 Southw. C of St Anne Worksop 50-53; St Wilfrid Harrogate 53-56; PC of H Spirit Beeston Hill 56-60; Chap Pinderfields and Stanley Royd Hosps Wakef 60-72; Asst RD of Wakef 67-68; RD of Wakef 68-72; Chap to United Ox Hosps 72-74; Ox Area Health Authority from 74; Hon Can of Ch Ch Cathl Ox from 77. *11 Frenchay Road, Oxford, OX2 6TG.* (Oxford 58817)

BARTON, John. b 48. Keble Coll Ox BA 1st cl Th 69, MA 73, DPhil 74. **d** and **p** 73 Ox. Research F Merton Coll Ox 73-74; Lect and Fell St Cross Coll Ox from 74; Chap from 79. *11 Withington Court, Abingdon, Oxon.*

BARTON, John Christopher Peter. b 28. Trin Hall Cam BA 51, MA 56. Ridley Hall Cam 51. **d** 53 **p** 54 Roch. C of Northumberland Heath 53-56; Cockfosters 56-64; V of Welling 64-75; P-in-c of Malmesbury w Westport Dio Bris from 75. *Abbey Vicarage, Malmesbury, Wilts, SN16 9BA.* (Malmesbury 3126)

BARTON, John Michael. b 40. Trin Coll Dub BA 62. **d** 63 **p** 64 Connor. C of Coleraine 63-68; Portadown 68-71; R of Carnteel and Crilly Dio Arm from 71. *The Rectory, Aughnacloy, Co Tyrone, N Ireland.* (Aughnacloy 682)

BARTON, John Stafford. Univ of Tor BA 52. St Jo Coll Cam BA 54, MA 58. McGill Univ Montr BD 57. Montr Dioc Th Coll. **d** and **p** 57 Montr. Sec of SCM 57-61; Miss Dio Nam 62-68; Vice-Prin Bp Tucker Coll Mukono 64-68; V of St Jas Cathl Tor 68-71; R of Fraser-Cheam Dio New Westmr from 71. *6330 Edson Drive, RR3, Sardis, BC, Canada.*

BARTON, Peter Dennys. b 15. Univ of Lon 33, AKC 38. **d** 38 **p** 39 Guildf. C of Ch Ch Epsom 38-40; Walton-on-Thames 40-44; CF (EC) 44-47; CF (TA) 53-70; C of Godalming 47-52; St Jo Bapt Ches 52-54; V of Northwood 54-61; Battlefield w Albrighton 61-81; Uffington 61-80. *58 Gardens Walk, Upton-upon-Severn, Worcs, WR8 0JE.* (U-o-S 3734)

BARTON, Stanley William John. b 24. Lich Th Coll 58. **d** 60 **p** 61 Worc. C of St Geo Redditch 60-62; Min of St Pet Conv Distr Kidderminster 62-66; V of Elmbridge w Rushock 66-74; C-in-c of St Paul Worc 74-80; St Mark-in-the-Cherry-Orchard Worc 76-80; V of St Phil Hove Dio Chich from 80. *77 New Church Road, Hove, BN3 4BB.* (Brighton 737915)

BARTON, Stephen William. b 50. St Jo Coll Cam BA 73, MA 76. Coll of Resurr Mirfield 75. **d** 77 **p** 78 Bradf. C of All SS L Horton Bradf 77-80. *c/o 15 Little Horton Green, Bradford, BD5 0NG.*

BARTON, Canon Sydney Gerald. b 1900. St Jo Coll Dur LTh 29, BA 33. St Aid Coll 26. **d** 30 **p** 31 Ches. C of H Trin Birkenhead 30-33; Wallasey 33-37; V of St Barn Crewe 37-43; Prenton 43-53; R of W Kirby 53-70; Surr from 39; Chap Caldy Manor Hosp from 59; Hon Can of Ches 61-70; Hon Can (Emer) from 70. *6 Hydro Avenue, West Kirby, Wirral.* (051-625 1545)

BARTON, Canon Terence Moore. Univ of Auckld BCom 35, MCom 37, St Jo Coll Auckld 61. **d** 61 **p** 62 Auckld. C of St Helier's Bay 61-66; Chap to Bp of Auckld 67-72; Auckld Dioc Sec 70-72; P Asst to Bp of Auckld 72-79; Asst to Commiss Dio Auckld from 79; Can of Auckld 78-79; Can (Emer) from 79. *344 Kohimarama Road, Auckland 5, NZ.* (589-030)

BARTON, Timothy Charles. b 47. Sarum Wells Th Coll 73. **d** 76 **p** 77 Liv. C of Up Holland 76-80; V of St Mich AA Dalton 80-81. *Address temp unknown.*

BARTON, William Howard. b 47. Chich Th Coll 78. **d** 79 Ex. C of Barnstaple Dio Ex from 79. *15 Britten Drive, Barnstaple, N Devon.*

BARUGAHARA, Wilson. **d** and **p** 75 Bunyoro. P Dio Bunyoro. *Box 105, Kakindo, Hoima, Uganda.*

BARUNA, Asai. St Paul's Th Coll Moa I 55. **d** 60 **p** 75 Carp. C of St Jas Murray I 60-73; Bamaga 73-75; P-in-c of Warraber I Dio Carp from 75. *Warraber Island, via Thursday Island, Queensland, Australia 4875.*

BARUTI, Ven Idumbilwa. b 15. Trin Coll Nai 74. **d** 75 Boga-Z **p** 75 Bp Bezaleri for Boga-Z. P Dio Boga-Z 75-76; Dio Bukavu from 76; Archd of Maniema from 76. *BP 220, Kindu, Zaire.*

BARWELL, Brian Bernard Beale. b 30. K Coll Lon and Warm AKC 59. **d** 60 **p** 61 Man. C of St Jas Heywood 60-63; V of Smallbridge 63-69; Farington 69-72; C of St Phil w St Luke Blackb 73-76; L to Offic Dio Blackb from 76. *70 Claytongate, Coppull, Chorley, Lancs.*

BARWOOD, Frederick James. b 05. Selw Coll Cam 3rd cl Hist Trip pt i 29, BA (3rd cl Th Trip pt i) 30, MA 34. Ely Th Coll 33. **d** 34 **p** 35 S'wark. C of St Matt Redhill 34-37; Mortlake w E Sheen 37-39; V of Cornard Magna 39-49; Offg C-in-c of L Cornard 44-49; V of St Luke w All SS Weaste

49-51; Surr 50; R of Odell 51-61; V of Pavenham 54-61; RD of Felmersham 54-61; C-in-c of Felmersham 60-61; V of Hordle 61-74. *94 Manor Road, New Milton, Hants, BH25 5EJ.* (New Milton 616150)

BARYAGWISA, Phenehas. b 39. Bp Tucker Coll Mukono 75. **d** 77 **p** 78 W Ank. P Dio W Ank. *Bikungu Parish, PO Mitooma, Uganda.*

BARYARUHA, Erimoth. **d** and **p** 75 Bunyoro. P Dio Bunyoro 75-80; Dio W Ank from 80. *Box 140, Bushenyi, Uganda.*

BASADA, Benson. **d** 73 **p** 74 Papua. C of Sakarina 73-76; P-in-c 76-78; Perm to Offic Dio Adel from 79. *St Barnabas College, Gloucester Avenue, Belair, S Australia 5052.*

BASAKO, Thomas. b 50. Bp Patteson Th Coll Kohimarama 72. **d** 75 **p** 76 Ysabel. P Dio Ysabel. *St Paul's Church, Buala, West Maringe District, Santa Ysabel, Solomon Islands.*

BASDEN, Canon Maurice Edward. Linc Coll Ox 2nd cl Lit Hum BA 49, MA 55. Westcott Ho Cam. **d** 51 **p** 52 Win. C of St Mark Southampton 51-54; Christchurch Hants 54-57; Suva 57-61; V of Vanua Levu S 61-62; Cakaudrove Dio Polyn 62-68; C from 68-76; Hon Can of H Trin Cathl, Suva 67-73 (and from 76); Can 73-76; Perm to Offic Dio Lon from 76. *Harescombe, Watford Road, Northwood, Middx.*

BASHE, Very Rev Gideon Velile. St Bede's Coll Umtata 49. **d** 50 **p** 52 St Jo Kaffr. P Dio St John's from 50; Archd of Centr Transkei 67-81; Dean of St John's Cathl Umtata from 81. *Box 25, Umtata, Transkei, S Africa.*

BA[illegible], Erasmus Kalolo. Bp Tucker Coll Mukono 64. **d** 67 Nam **p** 69 N Ugan. P Dio N Ugan 69-71; Dio Kig from 71. *Box 1201, Mparo, Kigezi, Uganda.*

BASHFORD, Richard Frederick. b 36. Dipl Th (Lon) 68. Clifton Th Coll. **d** 68 Cov **p** 69 Bp Daly for Cov. C of Bedworth 68-71; St Paul L Homerton 71-75; V of St Paul Bordesley Green 75-81; Bp Latimer Mem Ch w All SS City and Dio Birm from 81. *Vicarage, Handsworth New Road, Birmingham, B18 4PT.* (021-554 2221)

BASILE, George. **d** 42 **p** 47 Melan. P Dio Melan 42-74. *Melanesian Mission, British Solomon Islands.*

BASINGSTOKE, Lord Bishop Suffragan of. *See* Manktelow, Right Rev Michael Richard John.

BASINGSTOKE, Archdeacon of. *See* Finch, Ven Geoffrey Grenville.

BASIRE, Ian James. Univ of NZ B Eng 61. NZ Bd of Th Stud LTh 64. St Jo Coll Auckld. **d** 62 Bp McKenzie for Wel **p** 63 Wel. C of St Pet Palmerston N 62-67; V of Pongaroa 67-71; Brooklyn Wel 71-77; Perm to Offic Dio Wel from 77. *8 Anthony Grove, Paraparaumu Beach, NZ.* (6127)

BASON, Brian. b 27. Univ of Leeds BA 49. BD (Lon) 69. Coll of the Resurr Mirfield 49. **d** 51 **p** 52 Lon. C of St Aug Haggerston 51-55; St Mary Bow 55-56; V of St Hilda Audenshaw Dio Man from 56. *St Hilda's Vicarage, Denton, Manchester, M34 3LG.* (061-336 2310)

BASS, George Michael. b 39. Ely Th Coll 62. **d** 65 **p** 66 Ripon. C of Romaldkirk 65-68; Kenton Newc T 68-71; CF from 71. *c/o Ministry of Defence, Bagshot Park, Bagshot, Surrey, GU19 5PL.*

BASSETT, Abner Gerwyn. St D Coll Lamp BA 48, LTh 50. **d** 50 St D **p** 51 Bp RW Jones for Llan. C of Henfynyw w Aberayron 50-53; Bettws w Ammanford 53-58; C-in-c of Llanfair-ar-y-Bryn 58-73; V of Llandyssilio w Egremont and Llanglydwen w Cilymaenllwyd Dio St D from 73. *Vicarage, Llandyssilio, Clynderwen, Dyfed.*

BASSETT, John Edmund. b 33. St Aid Coll 63. **d** 66 **p** 67 Bradf. C of Guiseley 66-67; Stechford 67-71; Ross-on-Wye 71-72; P-in-c of Brampton Abbotts 73-75; Weston-under-Penyard 73-75; Hope Mansel 73-75; R of Halesworth and Linstead w Chediston 75-78; Laceby w Irby-upon-Humber Dio Linc from 78. *Laceby Rectory, Grimsby, Humb.* (Grimsby 71285)

BASSETT, Philip Albert. Univ of NSW BSc 66. Moore Th Coll Syd ThL 79. **d** and **p** 80 Syd. C of St Pet Hornsby Dio Syd from 80. *157 Galston Road, Hornsby Heights, NSW, Australia 2077.*

BASSETT, Canon Ralph Harry. b 09. Late Exhib of Keble Coll Ox 2nd cl Cl Mods 30, BA (3rd cl Lit Hum) 32, MA 35. Dorch Miss Coll 34. **d** 36 **p** 37 S'wark. C of St John Southend Lewisham 36-38; Chap Dorch Miss Coll Burcote and L to Offic Dio Ox 38-41; CF (EC) 41-47; C of St Pet Southsea 47-49; V of Sea View 49-52; Exam Chap to Bp of Portsm 51-59; RD of E Wight 52-56 and 60-62; V of Ryde 53-62; Hon Can of Portsm 61-77; Can (Emer) from 77; R of Havant 62-68; V of Hambledon 68-77; Perm to Offic Dio Portsm from 77. *17 Frensham Road, Southsea, Hants, PO4 8AD.* (Portsm 738571)

BASTEDO, Canon Ralph Crosby. **d** 59 **p** 60 Qu'app. P Dio Qu'app 60-72; I of Oyama 73-75; Dom Chap to Bp of Koot and Hon Can of Koot from 75; Hon C of Vernon 76-78; Kelowna Dio Koot from 78. *331 Lake Avenue, Kelowna, BC, Canada.*

BASTEN, Richard Henry. b 40. Codr Coll Barb 60. **d** 63 Barb for Br Hon **p** 64 Br Hond. C of St Jo Bapt Cathl Belize 63-64; L to Offic Dio Br Hond 64-65; Chap HM Pris Belize City 64-65; P-in-c of N Distr Miss Br Hond 65-67; C of St Geo Barb 68-70; R of St Matt Barb 70-72; C of H Trin Hartlepool 72-73; Clun 73-77; P-in-c of Clungunford 77-78; R of Clungunford w Clunbury & Clunton, Bedstone w Hopton Castle Dio Heref from 79. *Clungunford Rectory, Craven Arms, Salop, SY7 0PN.* (Little Brampton 342)

BASTIAN, Ven Frederick Charles. Ridley Coll Melb ACT ThL 47. **d** 47 **p** 48 Bend. V of H Trin Bend 47-50; Tonga-Nukualofa 50-53; Levuka 53-56; R of Kangaroo Flat 56-62; P-in-c of Taupota 62-63; R of Maitland 63-74; Archd of Yorke Peninsula 68-74; Eyre Peninsula 74-80; Willoch (Inner) from 80; R of Cummins-Tumby Bay 74-78; Dioc Regr Dio Willoch from 78. *Box 96, Gladstone, S Australia 5473.* (086-622249)

BASTIDE, Derek. b 44. Univ of Dur BA 65. Univ of Sussex MA (Educn) 77. Chich Th Coll 76. **d** 77 Chich **p** 78 Lewes for Chich. C of Lewes Dio Chich from 77. *4 Harvard Road, Ringmer, Lewes, E Sussex, BN8 5HJ.* (Ringmer 812139)

BASTIN, Edward James. b 06. Univ of Lon BSc 28. Ridley Hall Cam 28. **d** 30 Dover for Cant **p** 31 Cant. C of H Trin Maidstone 30-32; Nuneaton 32-36; V of Keresley w Coundon 36-71; Proc Conv Cov 48-50; Perm to Offic Dio Cov from 76. *9 Margetts Close, Kenilworth, CV8 1EN.* (Kenilworth 59855)

BASTOCK, Kenneth William. b 22. Launde Abbey [illegible] 7[illegible] **d** 76 **p** 77 Leic. C of Glen Parva w S Wigston 76-80; V of Orton-on-the-Hill w Twycross and Norton-by-Twycross Dio Leic from 80. *Twycross Vicarage, Atherstone, Warws.* (Tamworth 880295)

BASTOCK, Peter Leslie. b 26. MBE 75. N Ordin Course 77. **d** 80 York **p** 81 Selby for York. C of St Mary Bishophill Jun w All SS N Street City and Dio York from 80. *61 Lamplugh Crescent, Bishopthorpe, York, YO2 1SR.*

BATAAGA, Benjamin. b 44. Mukono Th Coll 69. **d** 70 Ruw. D Dio Ruw 70-73; Dio Boga-Z from 73. *BP 154, Bunia, Zaire.*

BATCHELOR, John Millar. b 35. Div Hostel Dub 76. **d** 78 **p** 79 Connor. C of All SS Belf 78-80; R of Eglish Dio Arm from 80; Killylea Dio Arm from 80. *149 Killylea Road, Armagh, BT60 4LN, N Ireland.* (Caledon 320)

BATCUP, John Aubrey. b 08. Univ of Dur 30. Lich Th Coll 29. Univ of Lon BD 54. **d** 32 **p** 33 Man. C of St Geo Tyldesley 32-35; St Cath Hatcham 35-36; W Cheam 36-42; Raynes Park (in c of H Cross) 42-45; R of Cucklington w Stoke Trister 45-51; PC of St Benedict Glastonbury 51-59; V of Bounds Green 59-77; Chap St Kath Coll Tottenham 62-63; Ed 'Lon Churchman' 64-67. *16 Green Close, Mayals, Swansea, W Glam, SA3 5DW.* (0792 402564)

BATE, Ven Alban Frederick. KCWNS BA 14, MA 18. **d** 16 **p** 17 Fred. C of Ch Ch Cathl Fred 16-20; R 20-32; Archd of Fred 32-36; R of St Paul St John 36-63; Can of Ch Ch Cathl Fred 46-63; Archd of St John 49-64; Archd (Emer) from 64. *361 Charlotte Street, Saint John West, NB, Canada.*

BATE, Bernard Percival. b 12. Selw Coll Cam BA 37, MA 41. Wells Th Coll 37. **d** 38 **p** 39 Blackb. C of Cathl Ch Blackb 38-41; Adlington 41-42; CF (EC) 42-46; Chap and Asst Master Malvern Coll and L to Offic Dio Worc 46-50; Chap Cho Ches Cathl and Hd Master Choir Sch 50-55; Prec of Nor Cathl and Asst Master K Edw VI Sch Nor 55-58; Hd Master Preb Sch Chich 58-68; R of Lurgashall w Roundhurst 68-78; Perm to Offic Dio Bradf from 79. *Beech Cottage, Grindleton, Clitheroe, Lancs.*

BATE, Canon Herbert Roland. b 1895. MC 18. Leeds Univ BA 20. Coll of Resurr Mirfield 13. **d** 22 St Alb for Johann **p** 23 Johann. C of St Mary's Pro-Cathl Johann 22-25; V of Booysens Johann 25-27; C of St Paul Bedford 27-31; R of Welwyn 31-63; SCF (EC) 40-42; RD of Welwyn 43-50; Hon Can of St Alb 53-63; Can (Emer) from 63. *Church Cottage, Waldron, Heathfield, Sussex, TN21 0QS.* (Horam Rd 2379)

BATE, Lawrence Mark. b 40. Univ Coll Ox. Coll of Resurr Mirfield 65. **d** 67 **p** 68 Newc T. C of St Jas Benwell 67-69; St Pet Monkseaton 69-72; Team V of Withycombe Raleigh w Exmouth Dio Ex from 72; RD of Aylesbeare from 81. *Dormers, St John's Road, Withycombe Raleigh, Exmouth.* (Exmouth 3342)

BATE, Maurice William. b 31. Montr Dioc Th Coll 74. **d** 76 **p** 77 Montr. C of Greenfield Pk 76-80; I of Rosemere Dio Montr from 80. *333 Pine Street, Rosemere, Quebec, Canada, J7A 1T7.* (514-621 6198)

BATE, Michael Keith. b 42. Lich Th Coll 67. **d** 69 **p** 70 Shrewsbury for Lich. C of St Jas West Bromwich 69-73; Thornhill 73-76; V of Wrenthorpe Dio Wakef from 76. *121 Wrenthorpe Road, Wrenthorpe, Wakefield, W Yorks, WF2 0JS.* (Wakef 373758)

BATE, Ronald Arthur Hodgson. b 04. Dorch Miss Coll 25.

d 30 p 31 Ex. C of Tavistock 30-32; St Mary Church Torquay 32-34; V of St Mary Magd Barnstaple 34-46; Chap RAFVR 41-46; R of St Jas w St Ann's Chapel Ex 46-49; PC of Babbacombe 49-59; Proc Conv Ex 59-72; R of Kenn 59-72; R of Mamhead 63-72; RD of Kenn 63-68; L to Offic Dio Ex from 79. *Chappell Court, Kenn, Exeter, EX6 7UR.* (Kenn-ford 832555)

BATEMAN, Alexander Wesley. St Barn Coll Adel Th L 43. **d** 43 **p** 44 Perth. C of Morawa 43-44; P-in-c 44-45; C of St Luke Cottesloe 45-47; Chap Toc H Dio Perth from 45; P-in-c of St Bart Perth and Chap R Perth Hosp 48-58; P-in-c of Gingin 58-65; R of Swan 58-65; C of St Patr Perth 65-71; L to Offic Dio Perth 71-76; Chap Fremantle Hosp 76-79; Perm to Offic Dio Perth from 80. *37 Eighth Avenue, Maylands, W Australia 6051.* (271 8019)

BATEMAN, (Clement) David Daubeny. Univ of Queensld BA 54. Em Coll Cam BA 56, MA 60. ACT ThL 48. M SSF 59. St Jo Coll Morpeth. **d** and **p** 50 Newc. C of Mayfield 50-51; Bellbird 51-54; C (Col Cl Act) of St Andr Chesterton 54-56; LPr Dio Sarum 57-60; Miss P St Francis Friary Jegarata 60-72; Perm to Offic Dio Papua from 73. *Amonpon Farm, Agaun, via Alotau, Papua New Guinea.*

BATEMAN, Preb Gilbert Herschell Alun. b 13. Bp Wilson Th Coll IM. **d** 36 **p** 37 Lich. C of Chasetown 36-39; Perm to Offic at Sedgley 39-41; C of Tamworth 41-42; C-in-c of Rough Close Conv Distr 42-48; PC of St Francis Meir Heath 48-68; V 68-77; Preb of Lich Cathl 72-80; Preb (Emer) from 80; RD of Stoke-on-Trent 74-77; P-in-c of Draycott-le-Moors 77-81. *Address temp unknown.*

BATEMAN, James Edward. b 44. Univ of Lon BSc (Eng) 65. Univ of Bris Dipl Th 74. Trin Coll Bris 71. **d** 74 Doncaster for Sheff **p** 75 Sheff. C of Woodlands 74-77; C (in c of St Pet) of Rushden Dio Pet from 77. *45 Pytchley Road, Rushden, Northants.* (Rushden 56398)

BATEMAN, Canon John de Beverley. b 17. Keble Coll Ox BA (3rd cl Th) 39, MA 46. Cudd Coll 40. **d** 41 **p** 42 York. C of Hornsea 41-46; Vice-Prin Bro of Good Shepherd Dubbo 48-52; R of Bourke NSW 46-52; V of Thornton-le-Street w N Otterington Thornton-le-Moor and Thornton-le-Beans 52-58; Chap HM Pris Northallerton 52-58; Surr 58-78; V of New Malton 58-62; Hornsea (w Goxhill 62-72; w Atwick from 72) 62-78; V of Atwick w Nunkeeling and Bewholme 62-72; C-in-c of Mappleton 65-73; RD of N Holderness 69-76; V of Harome, Pockley and Stonegrave w Nunnington Dio York from 78; Can and Preb of Riccall in York Minster from 77. *Harome Vicarage, York, YO6 5JE.* (Helmsley 70394)

BATEMAN, John Reinhardt. Magd Coll Cam 2nd cl Hist Trip pt i 26, BA (2nd cl Engl Trip) 27, MA 31. Ripon Hall Ox 31. **d** 33 **p** 34 St E. C of St Marg Ipswich 33-36; Chap of Ripon Hall Ox and L to Offic Dio Ox 36-37; Chap of Cathl Ch Cov 37-39; CF (EC) 39-45; Control Comm Germany 46-47; Asst Master Sir William Turner's Sch Coatham 48-49; Chap and Asst Master Worc Coll for the Blind 49-52; Perm to Offic Dio Ox and Lect Newlands Park Tr Coll 52-53; Dept of Educn Cam 53-54; Lect Kesteven Tr Coll Grantham 54-56; Lect and Tutor Saltley Tr Coll and L to Offic Dio Birm from 56. *16 Coleshill Street, Sutton Coldfield, W Midl, B72 1SH.*

BATEMAN, Canon Martyn Henry. b 31. Jes Coll Cam 54, MA 58. Clifton Th Coll 54. **d** 56 **p** 57 Sarum. C of St John Heatherlands Parkstone 56-59; New Malden w Coombe 59-60; Chap at Khuzistan Oilfields 60-62; PC of Charsfield 62-69; R of Monewden w Hoo 62-69; V of Wickham Mkt 69-82; Felixstowe Dio St E from 82; Hon Can of St E from 81. *Vicarage, Felixstowe, Suffolk.*

BATEMAN, Richard William. b 36. K Coll Lon & Warm AKC 61. **d** 62 **p** 63 Dur. C of St Thos Conv Distr Pennywell Bp Wearmouth 62-66; R of Siparia Trinid 66-70; Etherley 70-77; Industr Chap Medway Tns Dio Roch from 77. *55 Pattens Lane, Chatham, Kent.* (Medway 47389)

BATEMAN, Thomas Norman. Trin Coll Dub BA (Resp) 32. **d** 32 **p** 33 Oss. C of Kilnamanagh 32-34; C-in-c of Templeshambo 34-35; I of Mulrankin 35-38; C-in-c of Crosspatrick w Kilcommon 38-42; Asst Chap Miss to Seamen Belf 42-43; Chap Miss to Seamen Swansea 43-46; C-in-c of Ardcarneand Kilbryan 46-50; I of Kiltoghart w Annandaff 50-55; RD of Edgeworthstown 53-55; V of St Phil, Dewsbury 55-58; Landrake w St Erny 58-70; Perm to Offic Dio Wakef from 71. *11 Wauchope Street, Wakefield, Yorks.*

BATEMAN, William Henry. b 17. St D Coll Lamp BA 39. **d** 41 **p** 42 Dur. C of Herrington 41-43; St Nich-on-the-Hill Swansea 43-46; St Mary Swansea 46-47; Cler Deputn Sec Dr Barnardo's Homes for Wales and Herefs 48-55; V of Crickadarn and Gwenddwr (and Alltmawr from 62) 55-65; Llanrhidian (and Llanmadoc w Cheriton from 72) 65-81. *9 Westbourne Place, Mumbles, Swansea, W Glam.*

BATES, David William. b 25. Cranmer Hall Dur 59. **d** 61 **p** 62 Linc. C of L Coates 61-63; V of Wrawby 63-68; V of Melton Ross w New Barnetby 65-68; St Pet-at-Gowts w St Andr, Linc 68-77; Metheringham Dio Linc from 77. *Metheringham Vicarage, Lincoln, LN4 3EZ.* (Metheringham 20204)

BATES, Derek Alvin. b 27. St Mich Coll Llan 57. **d** 59 **p** 60 Glouc. C of Bp's Cleeve 59-63; V of Shebbear 67-71; R of Buckland Filleigh 67-71; Highampton w Sheepwash 71; Coates 72-80; Clovelly Dio Ex from 80; V of W Woolfardisworthy and Bucks Mills Dio Ex from 80. *Clovelly Rectory, Bideford, Devon.* (Clovelly 571)

BATES, Canon Gordon. b 34. Kelham Th Coll 54. **d** 58 Woolwich for Cant **p** 59 S'wark. C of All SS New Eltham 58-62; Asst Youth Chap Dio Glouc 62-64; Youth Chap Dio Liv and Chap Ch Ch Cathl Liv 65-69; V of Huyton 69-73; Can Res and Prec of Liv and Dioc Dir of Ordinands from 73. *The Cathedral, Liverpool, L1 7AZ.* (051-709 6271)

BATES, Harry. Univ of Sheff BSc 32. BC Coll Bris 39. **d** 40 Bris for Col Bp **p** 41 Syd. C of Sans Souci 40-43; R of St Phil Eastwood NSW 43-45; R of Barnwell 46-52; C-in-c of Stoke Doyle 50-52; Lect at Moore Th Coll Syd 52-59; L to Offic Dio Syd 60-68; Dio C & Goulb 69-74; R of Yass 74-76; L to Offic Dio C & Goulb 76-79; Dio Syd from 79. *34 Pindari Avenue, Camden, NSW, Australia 2570.* (046-667920)

BATES, James. b 46. Linc Th Coll 73. **d** 75 **p** 76 Guildf. C of Ewell 75-77; Farncombe 77-79; V of St Mary City and Dio Pet from 79. *214 Eastfield Road, Peterborough, PE1 4BD.* (Pet 43418)

BATES, Canon John Gwilym. b 15. St Jo Coll Dur BA (2nd cl Hist) 37, Dipl in Th 38, MA 40. **d** 38 **p** 39 Dur. C of St Pet Sacriston 38-39; C-in-c 39-43; V of St Paul Darlington 43-55; Dioc Adult Educn Sec 54-69; V of Frosterley 55-61; C-in-c of Eastgate 58-61; V of H Trin Stockton-on-Tees 61-68; C-in-c of St Mark's Cov Distr Stockton-on-Tees 62-65; V of St Andr Roker Monk Wearmouth 68-80; N Prov Chairman CEMS 68-78; Gov SPCK from 75; Hon Can of Dur from 78; R of Wolsingham w Thornley Dio Dur from 80. *Wolsingham Rectory, Bishop Auckland, Co Durham.* (Wolsingham 7340)

BATES, Michael. b 33. Univ of Dur BSc (2nd cl Physics) 57. Clifton Th Coll. **d** 59 **p** 60 York. C of Drypool Hull 59-62; Cheadle (in c of St Phil) 62-67; V of Newbottle 67-75; Dioc Chap GFS 69-75; Asst Master Bilton Grange Sen High Sch Hull from 76; Hon C of H Trin Hull Dio York from 81. *68 Davenport Avenue, Hessle, N Humb, HU13 0RW.* (Hull 646392)

BATES, Paul Spencer. b 40. CCC Cam BA 62, MA 66. Linc Th Coll 63. **d** 65 **p** 66 Bris. C of Hartcliffe 65-69; Chap Win Coll 70-80; Dioc Dir of Tr Dio Win from 80. *28 Lark Hill Rise, Winchester, SO22 4LX.*

BATES, Sidney. b 02. Worc Ordin Coll 58. **d** 60 **p** 61 Linc. C of Lenton w Ingoldsby 60-63; R of Saxby 63-71; V of Bonby 63-71. *3 Princess Royal Close, Sewell Road, Lincoln, LN2 5RX.* (Lincoln 30072)

BATES, Stanley. b 1899. AKC 30. Cudd Coll 30. **d** 30 **p** 31 S'wark. L to Offic in St Barn Ch for Deaf and Dumb Deptford 30-33; C of Bocking 33-34; V of Pontesbright (or Chappel) (w Wakes Colne R from 38) 34-41; Chap RAFVR 41-46; V of Alconbury w Weston 46-52; C-in-c of Woolley 46-50; R of Buckworth 50-52; V of Diddington and R of Southoe w Hail Weston 52-60; R of Slindom w Eartham 60-70. *Flat 5, Manormead, Tilford Road, Hindhead, Surrey, GU26 6RA.* (042 873)

BATES, Vincent. b 24. **d** and **p** 65 Momb. Supt Dr Barnardo's Homes Nai and C of All SS Cathl Nai 65-66; Perm to Offic Dio Bris 66-67; Dio Ox 68-72; C of Yarlington 72-76; L to Offic Dio Ox from 76. *Home Farm, Rousham, Oxford.*

BATES, Wilfred Abel. b 11. AKC (2nd cl) and Relton Pri 33. Bps' Coll Cheshunt 33. **d** 34 **p** 36 Derby. C of Whittington 34-36; Heanor 36-38; Westwood 38-44; Netherton (in c of St Pet Darby End) 44-47; V of Catshill 47-53; R of St Nich w St Pet Droitwich 53-63; V of St John, Dudley 63-73; Offenham 73-79; C-in-c of Bretforton 76-79; V of Offenham and Bretforton Dio Worc from 79. *Offenham Vicarage, Evesham, Worcs, WR11 5RW.* (Evesham 2096)

BATES, William Dawson. Univ of Manit BA 52. Wycl Coll Tor. **d** 54 **p** 55 Calg. C of St Mich AA Calg 54-55; I of Bowness 55-62; Hosp Chap Dio Calg 60-67; on leave 67-73; Hon C of St Marg Winnipeg Dio Rupld from 73. *35 Loyola Bay, Winnipeg, Manit., Canada.*

BATES, William Edward. b 1884. Univ of Leeds BA 07. Coll of Resurr Mirfield 03. **d** 09 **p** 10 Man. C of Ch Ch Heaton Norris 09-11; Pickering 11-13; Dinnington 13-19; TCF 16-19; C-in-c of New Bentley Conv Distr 19-23; V of Newbottle w Charlton 23-32; Greetham 32-45; Lockerley w East Dean 45-55; Perm to Offic Dios Portsm and Win from 55. *15 Carlton Avenue, Barton on Sea, Hants.*

BATES, William Frederic. b 49. St Jo Coll Dur BSc 72, BA 74. Cranmer Hall Dur Dipl Th 75. **d** 75 **p** 76 Ches. C of Knutsford 75-78; Ripley 78-80; R of Nether Seale w Over Seale Dio Derby from 81; V of Lullington Dio Derby from 81. *Nether Seale Rectory, Burton-on-Trent, Staffs, DE12 2BQ.* (B-on-T 761174)

BATES, William Hugh. b 33. Late Scho of Keble Coll Ox 1st cl Cl Mods 54, BA (2nd cl Lit Hum) 56, Liddon Stud and 2nd cl Th 58, MA 59. Westcott Ho Cam 59. **d** 60 **p** 61 Ripon. C of Horsforth 60-63; Tutor and Libr St Chad's Coll Dur 63-70; Exam Chap to Bp of Carl 67-70; V of Bp Wilton 70-75; Pickering Dio York from 76; RD of Pocklington 74-76. *Vicarage, Whitby Road, Pickering, N Yorks.* (Pickering 72983)

BATESON, Bernard Lionel. b 07. Clifton Th Coll 58. **d** 59 **p** 60 Chelmsf. C of Woodford Wells 59-61; R of Holton w Bratton St Maur 61-69; V of Winsham w Cricket 69-80. *26 Summershard, South Petherton, Somt, TA13 5DP.* (S Petherton 41489)

BATESON, Canon Geoffrey Frederick. b 27. K Coll Lon and Warm BD and AKC (2nd cl) 51. **d** 52 **p** 53 Newc T. C of St Paul Cullercoats 52-56; All SS Gosforth (in c of Ascen Kenton) 56-60; V of St Pet Monkseaton 60-68; St Geo Jesmond Newc T 68-77; Proc Conv Newc T 67-80; RD of Newc Centr 75-77; R of Morpeth Dio Newc T from 77; Hon Can of Newc T from 80. *Rectory, Morpeth, Northumb, NE61 2SS.* (Morpeth 3517)

BATEY, George Thomas. b 16. Late Exhib of St Chad's Coll Dur BA 38, Dipl Th 39, MA 42. **d** 39 **p** 40 Dur. C of Easington Colliery 39-44; St Hilda, S Shields 44-45; CF (EC) 45-48; C of St Aid W Hartlepool 48; PC of St Simon S Shields 48-53; V of All S Castleton and Hon Chap St Anne's Dioc Maternity Home Heywood 53-62; Milnrow 62-79. *The Cottage, Old Wall, Irthington, Cumb, CA6 4PP.*

BATEY, Herbert Taylor. b 22. Late Scho of Qu Coll Ox BA 46, 2nd cl Th 47, MA 48. Linc Th Coll. **d** 48 **p** 49 Carl. C of Dalton-in-Furness 48-50; Egremont 50-52; V of Cleator Moor 52-59; Chap and Master St Bees Sch 59-64; LPr Dio Carl 59-64; Chap and Lect Culham Coll 64-75; LPr Dio Ox 64-68; C-in-c of Culham 69-75; Select Pr Univ of Ox 75; Vice-Prin Coll of Ripon & York St Jo from 75; L to Offic Dio Ripon from 75. *St Margaret's Lodge, The College, Ripon, N Yorks.* (Ripon 3654)

BATEY, William Abbott. b 20. Cranmer Hall Dur 62. **d** 63 **p** 64 Carl. C of Appleby w Murton and Hilton 63-66; R of Moresby 66-77; P-in-c of Arnside Dio Carl from 77. *Vicarage, Church Hill, Arnside, Cumb.* (Arnside 761319)

BATH AND WELLS, Lord Bishop of. *See* Bickersteth, Right Rev John Monier.

BATH AND WELLS, Assistant Bishop of. (Vacant).

BATH, Archdeacon of. *See* Burgess, Ven John Edward.

BATH, Edward Nelson. b 16. Bps' Coll Cheshunt. **d** 57 Dover for Cant **p** 58 Cant. C of All SS U Norwood 57-60; R of St Laur Allington w St Nich Maidstone 60-67; V of Charing Heath w Egerton Dio Cant from 67; P-in-c of Pluckley Dio Cant from 78. *Egerton Vicarage, Ashford, Kent.* (Egerton 224)

BATHGATE, Neville Cyril. Moore Th Coll Syd ACT ThL 50. **d** and **p** 50 Syd. C of Lithgow 50-51; W Manly 51-52; on leave 53-54; Chap Children's Court Syd 55-56; Youth Chap Syd 56-60; R of Watson's Bay 60-75. *c/o 70 Bathurst Street, Sydney, Australia 2000.*

BATHGATE, Ronald Norman. b 03. Wells Th Coll 46. **d** 48 **p** 49 B & W. C of Ilchester 48-50; R of Puckington w Stocklynch 50-56; R of N w S Bradon 50-56; V of Merriott 56-63; R of Compton Martin 63-68; R of Ubley 63-68; C-in-c of Ch Ch Walcot 69-71; Perm to Offic Dio B & W from 71; Asst Youth Chap Dio B & W 71-75; C of St Barn Twerton Hill Bath 72-75. *Seven Crosses, Stogumber, Taunton, TA4 3TA.*

BATHIE, Gordon Kenneth. b 24. Oak Hill Th Coll 54. **d** 56 **p** 57 Bradf. C of Clayton 56-59; St Steph Bowling 59-61; V of Crich Dio Derby from 61. *Crich Vicarage, Matlock, Derbys.* (Ambergate 2449)

BATHURST, Lord Bishop of. *See* Witt, Right Rev Howell Arthur John.

BATHURST, Bishop Coadjutor of. (Vacant.)

BATHURST, Dean of. (Vacant)

BATHURST, Keith Orton. Univ of NZ MA 41, LTh 42. **d** 41 **p** 42 Ch Ch. C of Merivale 41-43; Kensington w Otipua 43-45; V of Ross and S Westland 45-52; Leeston 52-58; Rangiora 58-62; St Alb Ch Ch 62-76; Hon Can of Ch Ch Cathl 69-71; Archd of Akaroa and Ashburton 71-74; Sumner 74-76; L to Offic Dio Auckld 77-78; C of Bay of Is 78; Hon C of Waimate N 79-80; Perm to Offic Dio Auckld from 80. *Causeway Road, Haruru Falls, RD1, Paihia, NZ.*

BATHURST, Paul Douglas. b 51. Univ of Cant BSc 73. St Jo Coll Auckld 73. **d** 75 **p** 76 Ch Ch. C of Avonhead 75-76; P-in-c of Twizel 76-77; C of Shirley Dio Ch Ch from 77. *32 Hope Street, Christchurch 6, NZ.* (858-808)

BATLEY, Alfred William. St Jo Coll Morpeth. **d** 53 **p** 54 Newc. Federal Sec CA in Austr 53-68; C of Cardiff 53-56; LPr Dio Syd 56-63; C-in-c of St Mich w St D Surry Hills Syd 63-69; C of St Paul Canberra 69-70; Port Macquarie 71-77. *44 Georgia Avenue, Wyoming, NSW, Australia 2251.*

BATLEY, Philip Yorke. b 12. Westcott Ho Cam 66. **d** 68 **p** 69 Ches. C of Bramhall 68-78. *53 Lowndes Park, Driffield, N Humberside, YO25 7BE.* (0377-43781)

BATONDAINE, John Wilson. d and **p** 79 W Ank. P Dio W Ank. *Box 24, Bushenyi, Uganda.*

BATSLEER, Canon Albert. b 21. Selw Coll Cam BA 46, MA 54. Cudd Coll 46. **d** 48 **p** 49 Leic. C of St Phil Leic 48-50; St Jas Hope Salford 50-52; V of Heap Bridge 52-56; Glossop 56-65; R of Staveley 65-72; Surr from 66; V of Riddings 72-81; RD of Alfreton 76-81; V of New Mills Dio Derby from 81; RD of Glossop from 81; Hon Can of Derby from 81. *New Mills Vicarage, Stockport, Chesh.* (New Mills 43225)

BATSON, David Frederick. b 38. K Coll Lon and Warm AKC 61. **d** 62 Warrington for Liv **p** 63 Liv. C of H Trin Southport 62-64; Asst Chap Hurstpierpoint Coll 64-65; C of Cleator Moor 65-66; Asst Master K Geo V Sch Southport 66-67; L to Offic Dio Worc from 68; Hon Asst Chap Commun of H Name Malvern Link 68-73. *Crowcroft Cottage, Leigh Sinton, Worcs.* (Leigh Sinton 32986)

BATSON, John Gordon Kemp. b 38. SSM Kelham 60-63; Bps' Coll Cheshunt 64. **d** 65 **p** 66 Roch. C of Holy Redeemer Lamorbey 65-69; H Trin Cathl Port of Spain 69-71; R of St Clem Naparima Trinid 71-74; V of Borough Green Dio Roch from 74. *Vicarage, Borough Green, Sevenoaks, Kent, TN15 8BD.* (0732-882447)

BATSON, Paul Leonard. b 47. Univ of Southn BTh 79. Sarum Wells Th Coll 73. **d** 75 Buckingham for Ox **p** 76 Ox. C of Chesham 75-79; Dioc Youth Adv Dio Newc T from 79. *c/o Church House, Grainger Park Road, Newcastle upon Tyne.*

BATSON, William Francis Robert. b 43. Univ of Dur BA 72. St Jo Coll Dur 69. **d** 73 **p** 74 Southw. C of Eastwood 73-77; R of Long Marton w Dufton and Milburn 77-79; V of Flimby Dio Carl from 79. *Flimby Vicarage, Maryport, Cumb.* (Maryport 2386)

BATT, Allan Keith. Ridley Coll Melb ACT ThL 51. **d** 52 **p** 53 Melb. C of Balaclava 52-53; Min of Warburton 53-56; C (Col Cl Act) of Faversham 56-57; in Amer Ch 57-58; Min of N Geelong 58-63; Chap RAN from 63; L to Offic Dio Syd from 64. *47 Woonana Avenue, Wahroonga, NSW, Australia 2076.* (48-0433)

BATT, Joseph William. b 39. Univ of Keele BA (2nd cl Pol Insts and Soc Stud) 62, Dipl Soc Stud 62. Ripon Hall Ox 63. **d** 64 Stafford for Lich **p** 65 Lich. C of Bushbury 64-68; Walsall 68-71; Tr Officer & Youth Chap Dio Ibad 71-75; Area Sec CMS Dios Guildf and Chich from 75. *72 Bedford Road, Horsham, Sussex, RH13 5BH.*

BATT, Kenneth Victor. b 41. Wycl Hall Ox 68. **d** 71 Southn for Win **p** 72 Win. C of Yateley 71-76; V of The Candover Valley Dio Win from 76. *Preston Candover Vicarage, Basingstoke, Hants.* (Preston Candover 245)

BATTELL, Colin Frank. b 44. Keble Coll Ox BA (Th) 66, MA 71. St Steph Ho Ox 66. **d** 68 **p** 69 Pet. C of St Mary Wellingborough 68-71; L to Offic Dio Gibr 70-71; C of Wanstead 71-76; Chap in Addis Ababa Dio Egypt from 76. *PO Box 109, Addis Ababa, Ethiopia.*

BATTEN, George William John. b 34. Bris & Glouc Sch for Min 76. **d** 80 Tewkesbury for Glouc **p** 81 Glouc. C of Parkend Dio Glouc from 80. *2 Crown Cottage, Parkend, Lydney, Glos, GL15 4JE.*

BATTEN, Graham John. b 39. Open Univ BA 81. Dipl Th (Wales) 66. St D Coll Lamp. **d** 66 **p** 67 Llan. C of Llangynwyd w Maesteg 66-70; St Andrew's Major 70-72; Chap RN from 72. *c/o Ministry of Defence, Lacon House, Theobalds Road, WC1X 8RY.*

BATTEN, Stanley Trevor. St Francis Coll Brisb 53. **d** and **p** 57 Brisb. C of Redcliffe 57-59; M Bush Bro St Paul Quilpie 59-65; V of St Hugh Inala 65-72; Perm to Offic Dio Brisb 72-79. *c/o PO Box 101, Inala, Queensland, Australia 4077.*

BATTEN, Thomas Cyril. St Jo Coll Dur BA 37, MA 40; Dipl in Th 38. **d** 38 **p** 39 Blackb. C of Ch Ch (in c of St John) Thornton-le-Fylde 38-40; Marton 40-42; V of St Osw Preston and Chap Deepdale Hosp 42-59; Mellor 59-70; L to Offic Dio Blackb from 70. *40 Belgrave Avenue, Penwortham, Preston, Lancs, PR1 0BH.* (Preston 746473)

BATTERBURY, Charles. b 46. St Jo Coll Auckld 67. **d** 72 **p** 73 Ch Ch. C of Highfield 72-74; Sydenham-Beckenham 74-78; Chap at Twizel Dio Ch Ch from 78. *43 Jollie Road, Twizel, NZ.*

BATTERSBY, David George Sellers. b 32. K Coll Lon and Warm AKC 57. STh 81. **d** 58 **p** 59 Glas. C of St Marg Newlands Glas 58-60; Burnley 60-62; V of St Paul Warton 62-71; Chap King Wm Coll Dio S & M from 71. *Clybane Cottage, Phildraw Road, Ballasalla, IM.*

BATTERSBY, Harold. b 16. **d** 79 **p** 80 Ches. C of St Paul Werneth (or Compstall) Dio Ches from 79. *2 Belmont Drive, Marple Bridge, Stockport, SK6 5EA.* (061-427 3981)

BATTERSBY, Paul Clifford. b 49. St Jo Coll Dur BA 74. Cranmer Hall Dur Dipl Th 75. **d** 75 **p** 76 Dur. C of St Chad E Herrington Sunderland 75-78; Chap St Geo Coll Buenos

Aires Argent 78-81; Dioc Youth Officer and P-in-c of Holme Dio carl from 81. *Holme Vicarage, Carnforth, Lancs.* (Burton 781372)

BATTLEY, Donald Hollingworth. Univ of Auckld BCom 61. NZ Bd of Th Stud LTh (1st cl) 67. St Jo Coll Auckld 62. **d** 63 **p** 64 Auckld. C of Takapuna 63-65; All SS Ponsonby Auckld 65-68; V of Ruawai 69-71; Pakuranga Dio Auckld from 71. *Vicarage, Reeves Road, Pakuranga, Auckland, NZ.* (566-325)

BATTMAN, John Brian. b 37. ALCD 61. **d** 61 Kens for Lon **p** 62 Lon. C of Ch Ch Fulham 61-64; SAMS Miss at Asuncion Dio Argent 64-69; Dio Parag 69-76; Archd of Paraguay 70-76; Extension Sec to SAMS 77-80; V of Ch of Good Shepherd Romford Dio Chelmsf from 80. *Good Shepherd Vicarage, Collier Row Lane, Romford, Essex, RM5 3BA.* (Romford 45626)

BATTY, John Ivan. b 35. Clifton Th Coll 59. **d** 62 **p** 63 Bradf. C of Clayton Yorks 62-67; V of St Clem, Toxt Pk 67-73; R of Darfield Dio Sheff from 73. *Darfield Rectory, Barnsley, S Yorks.* (0226 752236)

BATTY, Canon William Alan. b 27. Pemb Coll Cam 2nd cl Hist Trip pt i 47, BA (2nd cl Th Trip pt i) 49, MA 53. Ely Th Coll 51. **d** 53 **p** 54 Carl. C of St Matt Barrow-F 53-59; V of Cleator Moor 59-63; Warden Rydal Hall Ambleside 63-68; L to Offic Dio Carl 63-68; Proc Conv Carl from 65; Can Res of Carl 68-72; Hon Can from 72; Dir Relig Educn Dio Carl 68-72. V of Penrith 72-79; R of Newton Reigny 72-79; RD of Penrith 73-78; Ch Comm from 78; Team R of Penrith w Newton Reigny and Plumpton Wall Dio Carl from 79. *Vicarage, Penrith, Cumb.* (Penrith 63000)

BATTYE, John Noel. b 42. Trin Coll Dub BA (Resp) 64, Bp Forster Pri & Abp K Div Prem 65, Div Test (1st cl) 66, MA 73. Pembroke Coll Cam MA (by incorp) 73. **d** 66 **p** 67 Arm. C of Drumglass 66-69; Ballynafeigh 70-73; Chap Pemb Coll Cam 73-78; Bp's C of Knocknagoney 78-80; R of Cregagh 80-82; Chap Cheltm Ladies Coll from 82. *22 Moorend Road, Leckhampton, Cheltenham, GL53 0GU.* (Cheltm 584668)

BATUMALAI, Sadayandy. b 46. Trin Th Coll Sing 70. **d** and **p** 73 W Mal. V of H Spirit Ipoh Perak Dio W Mal from 73. *Rumah Padri, 159-A Jalan Spooner, Ipoh, Perak, W Malaysia.*

BATY, Edward. b 30. ARICS 59. Open Univ BA 77. St Aid Coll 60. **d** 62 **p** 63 York. C of St Steph Acomb York 62-64; C and Succr of St Mary Virg Cathl Chelmsf 64-67; V of St Cedd Becontree 67-71; R of Hope Bowdler w Eaton-under-Heywood 71-79; Rushbury 71-79; C-in-c of Cardington 71-79; Team R of Fincham Dio Ely from 79. *Fincham Rectory, King's Lynn, Norf, PE33 9EL.* (Fincham 340)

BATY, Ernest John. b 20. Univ of Wales BA 42. St Mich Coll Llan 42. **d** 44 **p** 45 Swan B. C of Kilvey 44-47; Devynock w Rhydybriw 47-49; Caerphilly 49-52; St Cath Wigan 53; V of St Geo Huyton 53-56; St Mark Newtown Pemberton 56-62; Lydiate 62-67; L to Offic Dio Liv from 67; Hon C of Sephton Dio Liv from 69. *7 Delph Park Avenue, Aughton, Ormskirk.* (Aughton Green 423711)

BAUGH, Canon Horace. **d** 43 **p** 44 Fred. Miss at Ludlow w Bissfield 43-49; R of Grand Manan 49-50; Mille Is w Morin Heights and St Sauveur Dio Montr from 50; Hon Can of Montr from 76. *PO Box 114, Morin Heights, PQ, Canada.* (514-226 2508)

✠**BAUGHEN, Right Rev Michael Alfred.** b 30. Univ of Lon BD 55. Oak Hill Th Coll 51. **d** 56 **p** 57 Southw. C of St Paul Hyson Green Nottm 56-59; Reigate 59-61; Ord Cands Sec CPAS 61-64; R of H Trin Rusholme 64-70; Team V of All S Langham Place St Marylebone 70-75; R (w St Pet and St Jo Evang) 75-82; Area Dean of St Marylebone 78-82; Preb of St Paul's Cathl Lon from 79; M Gen Syn 75-82; Cons Ld Bp of Ches 29 June 82 in York Minster by Abp of York. *Bishop's House, Abbey Square, Chester, CH1 2JD.* (0244-20864)

BAULCH, Preb John Francis. b 28. Bps' Coll Cheshunt. **d** 59 **p** 60 Lon. C of John Keble Ch Mill Hill 59-64; V of All SS Hillingdon 64-70; St Martin City and Dio Heref from 71; Bullinghope w Grafton Dio Heref from 71; R of Dewsall w Callow Dio Heref from 71; P-in-c of Holme Lacy w Dyndor Dio Heref from 73; L Dewchurch w Aconbury, Ballingham and Bolstone Dio Heref from 78; RD of Heref City from 75; Preb of Heref Cathl from 80. *St Martin's Vicarage, Hereford.* (Hereford 2792)

BAULCOMB, Geoffrey Gordon. b 46. K Coll Lon and Warm AKC 68. **d** 69 **p** 70 S'wark. C of Crofton Pk w Brockley 69-74; Team V of Padgate (in c of Woolston) 74-79; R of Whitton and Thurleston w Akenham Dio St E from 79. *Whitton Rectory, Ipswich, Suffolk.* (0473 41389)

BAVERSTOCK, Gordon Henry. Peterho Cam BA 62 MA 65. Ridley Hall Cam 61. **d** 63 **p** 64 Sarum. C of St Paul Fisherton Anger Sarum 63-66; Tutor and Chap Sarum Coll of Techn 66-80. *Address temp unknown.*

✠ **BAVIN, Right Rev Timothy John.** b 35. Worc Coll Ox BA 59, MA 61. Cudd Coll 59. **d** 61 St Alb for Cant for Col Bp **p** 62 Pret. C of St Alb Cathl Pret 61-64; Chap St Alb Coll Pret and L to Offic Dio Pret 65-69; C of Uckfield Horsted Parva and Isfield 69-71; V of Good Shepherd Preston 71-73; Dean and R of St Mary Virg Cathl Johann 73-74; Archd of Johann Centr 73-74; Cons Ld Bp of Johann in St Thos Ch Durban 8 Nov 74 by Abp of Capetn; Bps of Les, Pret, Kimb K, St John's, Zulu, Geo, Port Eliz, Lebom, Bloemf and Swaz; and others. *PO Box 1131, Johannesburg, S Africa.* (011-834 5181)

BAWTREE, Ernest Anderson. b 06. **d** 32 **p** 37 Ugan. Miss Dio Ugan 32-50; Tutor Bp Tucker Coll 34-53; Archd of Toro-Bunyoro-Mboga (ex W Prov) 50-60; Ruwenzori 60-61; R of Hemingford Abbots 61-76; Perm to Offic Dio Ely from 77. *1 Bishop Wynn Close, Ely, Cambs.*

BAWTREE, Robert John. b 39. Oak Hill Th Coll 62. **d** 67 **p** 68 Cant. C of St Jo Bapt Folkestone 67-70; St Jo Evang Boscombe Bournemouth 70-73; Kinson in c of St Philip) 73-75; Team V in Bramerton Group Dio Nor from 75. *Rectory, Rockland St Mary, Norfolk.* (Surlingham 619)

BAWTREE-WILLIAMS, Hubert Garth. b 01. Wells Th Coll 47. **d** 47 **p** 48 B & W. C of St Cuthb Wells 47-49; PC of Witham Friary 49-59; R of L Berkhamsted 59-66; Chap Burrswood Home of Healing Groombridge 66-69; C of St Jo Evang Meads Eastbourne Dio Chich from 70. *Flat 1, Buxton Lodge, Buxton Road, Eastbourne, Sussex.* (Eastbourne 25570)

BAXANDALL, Peter. b 45. Tyndale Hall Bris 67. **d** 70 Shrewsbury for Lich **p** 72 Liv. C of St Thos, Kidsgrove 70-71; St Mark St Helens 71-75; Ardsley 75-77; Rep Leprosy Miss E Anglia from 77; Perm to Offic Dios St E, Ely, Nor, Pet and St Alb from 77. *58 Lantree Crescent, Trumpington, Cambs, CB2 2NJ.*

BAXENDALE, Rodney Douglas. b 45. Univ of Ex BA 66. Univ of Nottm Dipl Th 79. Linc Th Coll 78. **d** 80 **p** 81 Cant. C of All SS Maidstone Dio Cant from 80. *13 Meadow Walk, Maidstone, Kent, ME15 7RY.*

BAXTER, Alan John. Univ of Melb BA 70. Trin Coll Melb St Francis Coll Brisb ACT ThL 57. **d** 54 **p** 55 St Arn. C-in-c of Wedderburn 54-55; V 55-58; In Amer Ch 58-62; Dir of Relig Educn Dio Adel 62-65; R of Clare 65-68; C of St Luke N Altona 68-70; Perm to Offic Dio Melb 70-71; Assoc Dir Gen Bd of Relig Educn Melb 70-73; Dir Gen 73-77; I of St John Croydon Dio Melb from 77. *6 Ellesmere Avenue, Croydon, Vic, Australia 3136.* (03-723 2137)

BAXTER, Brian Raymond. b 31. Tyndale Hall Bris. **d** 58 **p** 59 York. C of H Trin Heworth 58-61; Belper (in c of St Swith Cow Hill) 61-65; R of Leverton 65-67; C of St Cath Nor 74-76; Farnborough Guildf 76-79; Leader of Southgate Chr Project Bury St E from 79; Chap W Suff Hosp 79-81; R of Ringsfield w Redisham, Barsham, Shipmeadow and Mettingham Dio St E from 82. *Rectory, Ringsfield, Suff.*

BAXTER, Christopher David. b 48. St Jo Coll Morpeth BTh 78. **d** and **p** 78 Bp Parker for Newc. C of Waratah 78-80; Taree Dio Newc from 80. *91 Main Road, Cundletown, NSW, Australia 2430.* (065-53 9249)

BAXTER, David Norman. b 39. Kelham Th Coll 59. **d** 64 **p** 65 Man. C of Tonge Moor 64-68; Chap RN from 69. *c/o Ministry of Defence, Lacon House, Theobalds Road, WC1X 8RY.*

BAXTER, George John. ACT ThL 22. **d** 22 **p** 23 Gippsld. Min of Meeniyan 22-23; V of Foster 23-26; Drouin 26-34; C of St John Toorak Melb 34; R of Geeveston 34-38; Stanley 38-42; Actg R of St Steph Hobart 42-43; Kingston 43-45; R of St Mich AA Hobart 45-51; Chap to HM Gaol Hobart 48-50; Perm to Offic Dio Tas 50-57; C of St Jo Evang Newtown 57-62. *6 Ruthwell Avenue, Montrose, Tasmania.*

BAXTER, Harold Leslie. b 11. Roch Th Coll 62. **d** 64 **p** 65 Bris. C of Corsham 64-67; Lyncombe 67-69; V of Shapwick w Ashcott Dio B & W from 70; C-in-c of Burtle Dio B & W from 75. *Shapwick Vicarage, Bridgwater, Somt.* (Ashcott 260)

BAXTER, John. Moore Th Coll Syd ACT ThL 63. **d** 63 **p** 64 Syd. C of St Mary's w Rooty Hill 63-65; C-in-c of Rooty Hill w Mt Druitt Provisional Distr 65-68; Chap Bd of Educn Dio Syd 68-70; R of Glenbrook Dio Syd from 70. *3 Ross Crescent, Blaxland, NSW, Australia 2774.* (047-39-1324)

BAXTER, Peter James. b 29. St Chad's Coll Dur BA 53, Dipl Th 55. **d** 55 Ely **p** 56 Bp Walsh for Cant. C of Stanground 55-58; St Mich AA w All SS Paddington 58-59; Woodston 59-62; R of Eynesbury Dio Ely from 62. *Eynesbury Rectory, St Neots, Huntingdon, Cambs, PE19 2JA.* (0480 72174)

BAXTER, Ven Ralph Esdale. b 32. Bps' Coll Cheshunt 61. **d** 62 **p** 63 Down. C of Orangefield 62-64; Donaghcloney 64-66; I of Kilnasoolagh U 66-72; Sec Irish Coun of Chs 72-75; P Assoc River N Pars 75-76; P Supervisor 76-80; Archd of Winnipeg 77-80; Dioc Archd from 80; Dir of Min Project and Hon C of St Steph Winnipeg Dio Rupld from 80.

Box 114, GP2, Winnipeg, Manit, Canada.

BAXTER, Richard David. b 33. Kelham Th Coll 53. **d** 57 **p** 58 Carl. C of St Barn Carl 57-59; St Matt Barrow-F (in c of St Francis) 59-64; V of Drighlington 64-73; Penistone (w Midhope to 76) 73-80; St Aid w Ch Ch City and Dio Carl from 80; Surr 73-80. *167 Warwick Road, Carlisle, Cumb.* (Carl 22942)

BAXTER, Robert David. b 02. St Cath Coll Cam 3rd cl Math Trip pt i 21, BA (Jun Opt) 23, MA 72. Coll of Resurr Mirfield 25. **d** 27 **p** 28 Dur. C of St Cuthb Hebburn 27-31; Skerton 31-33; St Thos Derby (in c of St Chris) 33-36; Pleasley (in c of Ch Ch New Houghton) 36-43; CF (EC) 43-46; R of Stanton-by-Dale w Dale Abbey 46-53; V of Woodville 53-67; C of St Luke Pallion Bp Wearmouth 67-70; Perm to Offic Dio Dur 71-72. *College of St Barnabas, Blackberry Lane, Lingfield, Surrey, RH7 6NJ.*

BAXTER, Ross Charles. b 16. Roch Th Coll 62. **d** 64 **p** 65 Chich. C of Aldrington 64-67; Pembroke Berm 67-68; Old w New Shoreham 68-69; V of St Jo Div W Worthing 69-77. *Terry's Cross, Bungalow No 2, Brighton Road, Henfield, West Sussex, BN5 9SX.*

BAXTER, Stanley Robert. b 31. Chich Th Coll 79. **d** 80 **p** 81 Ripon. [f Lutheran Min] C of Far Headingley (in c of St Osw) Dio Ripon from 80. *64 Becketts Park Crescent, Far Headingley, Leeds 6.* (Leeds 743636)

BAXTER, Stuart. b 43. Univ of Liv BA 65. Cudd Coll 66. **d** 70 **p** 71 Liv. C of St Martin Southdene Kirkby 70-73; Ainsdale 73-76; Chap to St Aug Hill Station Freetown Dio Sier L from 77; Hon Chap for Miss to Seamen Freetown from 77. *11 Lower Savage Square, PO Box 719, Freetown, Sierra Leone.* (Freetown 50255)

BAYCOCK, Philip Louis. b 33. Wells Th Coll 64. **d** 66 **p** 67 Pet. C of Kettering 66-68; St Pet-in-I-of-Thanet 68-72; V of Bobbing w Iwade 72-73; Perm to Offic Dio Cant 73-76; V of Thanington w Milton Dio Cant from 77. *Thanington Vicarage, 70 Ashford Road, Canterbury, Kent, CT1 3XE.* (Cant 64516)

BAYCROFT, Canon John Arthur. Ch Coll Cam BA 54 MA 58. Trin Coll Tor BD 59. Ripon Hall Ox 54. **d** 55 **p** 56 Ont. R of Loughboro Ont 55-57; C of St Matt Ott 57-62; R of Perth Ott 62-67; St Matthias City and Dio Ott from 67; Exam Chap to Bp of Ott 72-79; Hon Can of Ott 77-79 and from 80; Archd of Ott W 79-80. *555 Parkdale Avenue, Ottawa, Ont., Canada.* (1-613-729-1912)

BAYELO, Likunde. b 27. Trin Coll Nai 74. **d** 75 **p** 76 Boga-Z. P Dio Boga-Z. *BP 861, Kisangani, Zaire.*

BAYES, Canon Charles Sidney. b 14. Univ of Lon BA 47. Cudd Coll 52. **d** 53 **p** 54 Southw. C of St Mary Nottm 53-57; Chief Insp of Schs and Dir of Ch Day Schs Dio Southw 54-57; V of St Mark Mansfield 57-67; Proc Conv Southw 66-70; R of Lambley 67-71; Exam Chap to Bp of Southw 67-81; Dir of Ords 67-81; Hon Can of Southw 68-71; Chairman Dioc Syn 70-76; Can Res 71-81; Can (Emer) from 81; Dir of Post-Ordin Tr 71-80. *Chesterfield House, Aldborough, Norwich, NR11 7AA.* (0263-768063)

BAYES, Paul. b 53. Univ of Birm BA 75, Dipl Th 78. Qu Coll Birm 76. **d** 79 **p** 80 Newc T. C of St Paul Whitley Bay Dio Newc T from 79. *5 Chollerford Avenue, Whitley Bay, T & W, NE25 8QD.*

BAYLEY, Albert William David. b 15. Lon Coll of Div 66. **d** 68 **p** 69 Ox. C of Denham 68-71; St Giles-in-the-Fields Lon 71-78. *30 Braithwaite Court, Malzeard Road, Luton, Beds.*

BAYLEY, Frederick Ernest. b 06. AKC 29. **d** 29 **p** 30 Chelmsf. C of St Martin's Distr Ch Dagenham 29-31; Upminster 31-35; C-in-c of St Martin Plaistow 35-38; V of St Jas Gt Walthamstow 38-44; H Trin Halstead 44-58; PC of H Trin Hermon Hill Wanstead 58-69; Chap Wanstead Hosp 58-69; Surr from 61; V of Broxted w Chickney and Tilty 69-75; RD of Dunmow 70-75; C-in-c of L Easton 74-75. *3 High Street, Great Bradfield, Braintree, Essex.* (Gt Dunmow 810653)

BAYLEY, Canon John Benson. b 39. K Coll Cam 2nd cl Cl Trip pt i 59, BA (2nd cl Cl Trip pt ii) 60, MA 64. Qu Coll Birm 61. **d** 63 Linc **p** 64 Bp Dunlop for Linc. C of Clee 63-68; V of H Trin w St Geo, Gainsborough 68-73; C-in-c of St Pet-in-Eastgate Linc 73-74; St Mary Magd w St Paul-in-the-Bail Linc 73-74; St Mich-on-the-Mt Linc 73-74; R of Minster City and Dio Linc from 74; Can and Preb of Linc Cathl from 74. *St Peter-in-Eastgate Vicarage, Lee Road, Lincoln, LN2 4BH.* (Lincoln 25741)

BAYLEY, Michael John. b 36. CCC Cam 2nd cl Th Trip pt i 58, BA (2nd cl Th Trip pt ii) 60. Univ of Sheff PhD 72. Linc Th Coll 60. **d** 62 **p** 63 Ripon. C of Epiph Gipton Leeds 62-66; L to Offic Dio Sheff from 67. *27 Thornsett Road, Sheffield, S7 1NB.* (Sheff 585248)

BAYLEY, Raymond. b 46. Keble Coll Ox BA (2nd cl Th) 68, MA 72. Univ of Dur Dipl Th 69. St Chad's Coll Dur 68. **d** 69 **p** 70 St A. C of Mold 69-74; Llan Cathl 74; PV of Llan 74-77; V of Cwmbach 77-80; Dir of Pastoral Stud St Mich Coll Llan from 80. *St Michael's College, Llandaff, Cardiff, CF5 2YJ.* (Cardiff 566374)

BAYLEY, Walter George. Angl Th Coll BC 66. **d** 69 New Westmr for Carib. C of St Paul Vanc 69-71; Miss Centr Carib Miss 71-74; I of Quesnel 74-76; St Mich Vanc Dio New Westmr from 77. *2475 Guelph Street, Vancouver, BC, V5T 2S6, Canada.*

BAYLISS, Douglas Claude. St Chad's Coll Regina S Th 64. **d** 63 **p** 64 Qu'App. I of Balgonie 63-64; Cupar 64-68; Assiniboia 68-74; Sask-Gateway 74-79; Chap Correctional Centre Sask from 79. *Box 88, Dysart, Sask, Canada.*

BAYLISS, Maurice Selwyn. b 13. Univ of Wales BA 36. St Mich Coll Llan 36. **d** 37 **p** 38 Birm. C of Castle Bromwich 37-40; Witham 40-41; Ch Ch Southgate 41-47; V of St Aldhelm Edmonton 47-57; St Steph Bush Hill Pk 57-80. *Seven Temple House, Bulls Cross Ride, Theobalds Park, Waltham Cross, s 24463)*

BAYLISS, Paul Harley. Univ of Syd BA 61. Melb Coll of Div BD 73. Ridley Coll Melb 72. **d** and **p** 74 Syd. C of French's Forest 74-76; Redfern 76-78; St Sav S Syd 78-80; R of St Paul Harris Pk Dio Syd from 81. *13 Crown Street, Harris Park, NSW, Australia 2150.* (637-1430)

BAYLY, Samuel Niall Maurice. TCD BA 64, Div Test 65. **d** 65 **p** 66 Connor. C of St Matt Shankill Belf 65-68; Chap Miss to Seamen 68-69; C of St Pet Belf 69-74; R of Ch Ch Belf Dio Connor from 74. *25 Beechlands, Malone Road, Belfast 9, N Ireland.* (Belfast 668732)

BAYLY JONES, Gilbert Denham. b 26. Or Coll Ox BA (3rd cl Th) 50, MA 54. Univ of Cam MA (by incorp) 59. Sarum Th Coll 50. **d** 52 **p** 53 Leic. C of St Andr Aylestone Leic 52-56; Libr Pusey Ho Ox 56-59; Chap Trin Coll Cam 59-65; Chap RNR 61-72; R of Pointe-à-Pierre Trinid 66-73; P-in-c of Hitcham 73-81; Chalfont St Giles Dio Ox from 81. *Rectory, Chalfont St Giles, Bucks.* (Chalfont St Giles 2097)

BAYNES, Leopold. Codr Coll Barb 69. **d** 71 **p** 73 Windw Is. C of The Grenadines 71-73; H Trin St Lucia 73-77; R of Rivière Dorèe 77-78; St Andr Grenada Dio Windw Is from 78. *St Andrew's Rectory, St Andrew's, Grenada, W Indies.* (7222)

BAYNES, Simon Hamilton. b 33. New Coll Ox BA 57, Dipl Th 58, MA 62. Wycl Hall Ox. **d** 59 **p** 60 Bris. C of Rodbourne Cheney 59-62; CMS Miss Japan 63-80; C of Keynsham Dio B & W from 80. *88 Chandag Road, Keynsham, BS18 1QE.*

BAYNES, Timothy Francis De Brissac. b 29. Ely Th Coll 59. **d** 61 **p** 62 St Alb. C of Hockerill 61-65; Mansfield Woodhouse 65-67; Industr Chap SE Lancs Industr Miss and C-in-c of St Jo Evang Miles Platting 67-72; LPr Dio Man from 73; Industr Chap Dio Man from 73. *2 The Thorns, Chorltonville, Manchester, M21 2DX.* (061-881 2081)

BAYNES, William Hendrie. b 39. Univ of Adel BA 60, BA (Mod Hist) 61. SOC 77. **d** 79 Kens for Lon **p** 80 Lon. C of Notting Hill Dio Lon from 79. *92b Oxford Gardens, W10 5UW.* (01-969 3715)

BAYNES CLARKE, Godfrey. b 25. CEng FIStructE 60. Oak Hill Coll 71. **d** 73 Kens for Lon **p** 74 Lon. C of St Mich Ches Sq Lon 73-75; R of Beeston Regis 76-80; Chap at Santiago Dio Chile from 80. *Santiago Community Church, Casilla 16144/9 Santiago, Chile.*

BAYNHAM, Canon Albert John. b 23. St Aid Coll 49. **d** 52 **p** 53 Aber. Asst Super Dio Aber 52-53; R of Portsoy 53-56; Burntisland w Aberdour (and Kinghorn to 81) Dio St Andr from 56; Can of St Ninian's Cathl Perth from 79. *Rectory, Cromwell Road, Burntisland, Fife, KY3 9EH.* (0592 873762)

BAYNHAM, Canon George Thorp. b 19. Trin Coll Dub BA (3rd cl Mod) 41. **d** 42 **p** 43 Meath. C of Dunboyne w Moyglare Kilcock and Maynooth 42-44; St Cath Dub 44-52; I of Castlemacadam Dio Glendal from 52; Kilbride 64-73; Ballinaclash Dio Glendal from 73; Can of Ch Ch Cathl Dio Dub from 70. *Rectory, Avoca, Arklow, Co Wicklow, Irish Republic.* (0402 5127)

BAYNHAM, Verner Beresford Henry. b 30. Ridley Hall Cam 62. **d** 64 **p** 65 Chelmsf. C of Barking 64-66; Chap Reed's Sch Cobham 66-67; Ho Master and Asst Chap Bearwood Coll Wokingham and Perm to Offic Dio Ox from 67. *Hawkins House, Bearwood College, Wokingham, Berks, RG11 5BG.*

BAYNHAM, William Benjamin. Fitzw Ho Cam 3rd cl Hist Trip pt i 32, BA (2nd cl Th Trip pt i) 34, MA 37, MCR 44. Cudd Coll 34. **d** 35 **p** 36 Cant. C of All SS Maidstone 35-37; Asst P St Aug Miss Penhalonga 38-42; L to Offic Dio Johann 42-43 and 46-51; Dio Wakef 44-46 and 68-69; Warden St Pet Hostel Rosettenville 46-51; P-in-c of St Aug Miss Penhalonga 51-68; Prov of CR in S Afr and of Ch the K Alice Dio Grahmstn from 69; C of Stellenbosch Dio Capetn from 75. *8 Helderberg Street, Stellenbosch, CP, S Africa.* (3215)

BAYNTON, Geoffrey Cecil. b 30. Selw Coll Cam 3rd cl Th Trip pt i 52, BA (2nd cl Th Trip pt ii) 54, MA 58. Cudd Coll 54. **d** 56 **p** 57 Bris. C of St Greg Horfield 56-60; Pattoki W Pakistan 60-66; Ludlow 66-67; V of Awre w Blakeney 67-72;

P-in-c of Minsterworth 72-80; Standish w Haresfield and Moreton Valence Dio Glouc 80-82; V from 82. *Vicarage, Moreton Valence, Gloucester, GL2 7NB.* (Gloucester 720258)

BAYODE, Daniel Folarim. b 07. **d** 72 **p** 73 Ekiti. P Dio Ekiti. *St Michael's Vicarage, Ikoro, Ekiti, Nigeria.*

BAYS, Canon Eric. Univ of Manit BSc 55. Univ of Sask BA 59. Em Coll Sktn LTh (w distinc) 59. **d** 59 **p** 60 Rupld. C of All SS Winnipeg 59-61; Lect Em Coll Sktn 61-62; I of Burn's Lake 62-63; Masset Inlet Miss 63-65; St Sav Winnipeg 65-67; St Cath Winnipeg 67-68; R of All SS Winnipeg 68-76; Can of St Jo Cathl Winnipeg 71-76; Hon Can from 76; on leave. *1015 13th Street East, Saskatoon, Sask., Canada.*

BAYS, John Gerald. Univ of Manit BSc 55. Univ of Sask BA 62. Em Coll Sktn LTh 60. **d** 60 **p** 61 Rupld. C of St Luke Winnipeg 60-62; R of Carman 62-68; St Andr, Winnipeg 66-70; on leave 70-71; L to Offic Dio Bran 71-75; on leave 75-76; Hon C of All SS Winnipeg Dio Rupld from 76. *14 Granada Crescent, Winnipeg, Manit., Canada.*

BAYTON, John. St Francis Coll Brisb ACT ThL (2nd cl) 56. **d** 56 New Guinea for Rockptn **p** 57 Rockptn. C of St Paul's Cathl Rockptn 56-59; R of Longreach 59-63; Sub-Dean and R of All S Cath Thursday I 63-65; Can of Carp 63-65; R of St Alb Auchenflower Brisb 65-68; Dean and R of St Paul's Cathl Rockptn 68-80; Bp's Commiss Dio Rockptn 72-80; I of St Pet City and Dio Melb from 80. *St Peter's Vicarage, Eastern Hill, Melbourne, Vic, Australia 3002.*

BAYUK, Bayuk Saleem. St Aug Coll Cant 62. **d** 65 **p** 66 Jer. P Dio Jer. *45 Golom Street, Lod, Israel.*

BAZAALE, Seremosi. b 23. Bp Tucker Coll Mukono 68. **d** 68 Ruw **p** 69 Bp Rwakaikara. P Dio Ruw. *Box 170, Hoima, Uganda.*

BAZELL, Mervyn Basil. b 1895. Or Coll Ox BA (3rd cl Th) 23, MA 46. Sarum Th Coll 24. **d** 25 **p** 26 B and W. C of St Andr Taunton 25-29; Knowle (in c of St Kath Pylle Hill) 29-33; R of Ansford 33-47; PC of St Mich AA Penn Mill Yeovil 47-55; V of Fenton 55-58; Surr 55-58; R of Chedzoy 58-68. *29 Parkway, Midsomer Norton, Bath, Avon, BA3 2HD.* (Midsomer Norton 418129)

BAZELY, Dennis Rupert. Bp's Coll Calc. **d** 27 Bp Walsh for Madr **p** 28 Madr. Asst Chap of St John Trichinopoly 27-29; Nellore and Bitragunta 29-30; furlough 35; Chap St Mattias Vepery 30-44; St John Trichinopoly 44-45; St Mark Bangalore 45-48; C-in-c of Kensington W Aus 48-49; R of Merredin 49-54; Toodyay 54-57; Kens 57-59; L to Offic Dios Bunb Perth and Kalg 59-64; Org Sec Angl Miss Coun W Austr 59-64; Commiss Polyn 59-66; R of Kalamunda 64-66; Chap Marjorie Appleton Ho Dio Perth from 67; Perm to Offic Dio Perth from 67. *12/11 Freedman Road, Mount Lawley, W Australia 6050.* (271 6241)

BAZELY, Frank Dennis Martin. **d** and **p** 59 Perth. C of Cottesloe 59-62; P-in-c of W Northam 62-65; R of N Midlands 65-70; C of Mosman Pk 70-74; P-in-c of Swan Dio Perth from 74. *Chaplain's Cottage, Swanleigh, Midland, W Australia 6056.* (74 2661)

BAZELY, William Francis. b 53. Univ of Sheff BEng 75. Univ of Nottm Dipl Th 79. St Jo Coll Nottm 78. **d** 81 Warrington for Liv. C of St Geo Huyton Dio Liv from 81. *31 Endmoor Road, Huyton, Liverpool, L36 3UH.*

BAZEN, David Peter. b 44. St Chad's Coll Dur BA 65, Dipl Th 69. Univ of Birm BPhil 78. **d** 69 Kens for Lon **p** 71 Birm. C of St Pet Acton Green 69-70; Hon C of Wylde Green 70-78; St Benedict Bordesley Dio Birm from 78. *82 Redacre Road, Sutton Coldfield, W Midl, B73 5EE.*

BAZIN, Jean Jacques Emmanuel Fritz. b 41. **d** 66 **p** 67 Bp Voegeli (USA). In Amer Ch 66-74; P-in-c of St Jude I and Dio Barb from 75. *St Jude's Rectory, St George, Barbados, WI.*

BAZIN, Lewis Charles John Wadsworth. b 09. ALCD 43. **d** 43 **p** 44 Roch. C of St Paul Chatham 43-47; Gt Clacton (in c of St Bart Holland-on-Sea) 47-49; Rainham 49-50; Min of Conv Distr of Wigmore w All SS Hempstead 50-53; R of Southfleet 53-70; V of Underriver 70-80. *Address temp unknown.*

BAZIRE, Canon Reginald Victor. b 1900. **d** 27 **p** 29 W China. Miss Dio E Szech 27-36; CIM Schs for Missionaries' Children Chefoo 36-45; C of Tooting Graveney 46-49; V of St Barn Clapham Common 49-67; RD of Battersea 53-66; Hon Can of S'wark 59-67; Proc Conv S'wark 59-64 and 67-75; Archd of S'wark 67-73; Wandsworth 73-75; Hon Can of S'wark Cathl from 75. *7 Grosvenor Park, Bath, Avon, BA1 6BL.* (Bath 64100)

✠ **BAZLEY, Right Rev Colin Frederick.** St Pet Hall Ox BA 57 MA 61. Tyndale Hall Bris. **d** 59 **p** 60 Liv. C of St Leon Bootle 59-62; SAMS Miss at Cholchol 62-69; Cons Ld Bp Suffr of Cautin and Malleco (Santiago from 75) in H Trin Ch Temuco 25 May 69 by Bps of Chile; Columbia (PECUSA); and Bp Krischke (Episc Ch of Brazil); Apptd Bp in Chile 77; Elected Presiding Bp Angl Coun of S Amer 77. *Casilla 675, Santiago, Chile.*

BEACH, Canon Arthur James. b 04. Univ of Leeds BA (3rd cl Hist) 28. Coll of Resurr Mirfield 25. **d** 30 **p** 31 Birm. C of St Barn Balsall Heath 30-32; St Wulstan Bournbrook 32-35; Org Sec SPG Dios Win Sarum and Portsm 36-42; L to Offic Dio Win 37-42; V of Hound w Netley Abbey 42-72; Hon Can of Win 64-72; Can (Emer) from 72; Perm to Offic Dio Worc from 73. *Whistlewood, Sinton Green, Hallow, Worcester, WR2 6NW.* (Worcester 640048)

BEACH, George. Montr Dioc Th Coll LTh 65. **d** 65 **p** 66 Montr. C-in-c of Pincourt Miss 65-66; I of Bondville w Foster 66-69; R of All SS Verdun Montr 69-72; Canso w Queensport 72-75; Blandford Dio NS from 75. *Blandford, Lunen Co, NS, Canada.* (228-8012)

BEACHAM, Frederick George. b 39. Vanc Sch of Th BTh 73. **d** 74 **p** 75 Yukon. C of Watson Lake 74-77; I of Cassiar 77-79. *Box 306, Cassiar, BC, Canada.*

BEACHAM, Ian William Henry. b 17. Univ of Dur LTh 41. ALCD (1st cl) 41. **d** 41 **p** 42 B and W. C of Twerton-on-Avon 41-48; C-in-c of Westfield 48-53; V 53-58; Asst Master Wells Cathl Sch 52-58; Chap 54-58; V of Kidlington 58-70; R of Hampton Poyle 58-70; Surr from 67; V of Banbury Dio Ox 70-73; R from 74; Chap Horton Gen Hosp from 70. *89 Oxford Road, Banbury, Oxon.* (Banbury 62370)

BEACHAM, Peter Martyn. b 44. Ex Coll Ox BA 65, MA 70. Univ of Lon MPhil 67. Sarum Wells Th Coll 70. **d** 73 **p** 74 Ex. C of St Martin, St Steph, St Lawr w All H (Goldsmith St) & St Paul Ex 73-74; Ex Centr Dio Ex from 74. *Bellever, Barrack Road, Exeter, Devon.* (Ex 35074)

BEACOM, Canon Thomas Ernest. Trin Coll Dub BA 33, MA 40, BD 40. **d** and **p** 36 Lim. C of St Laur w St John and H Trin Lim 36-38; Seapatrick 38-44; C-in-c of St Kath Belf Dio Connor 44-58; R from 58; RD of N Belfast 54-65; Dioc Regr Dio Connor from 63; Can of St Anne's Cathl Belf from 66. *Rectory, 24 Lansdown Road, Belfast, N Ireland.* (Belfast 77647)

BEACON, Ralph Anthony. b 44. Univ of Wales (Ban) Dipl Th 70. St Mich Th Coll Llan 70. **d** 71 **p** 72 Llan. C of Neath 71-74; Team V of Holyhead 74-78; R of Llanenddwyn w Llanddwywe Dio Ban from 78. *Rectory, Dyffryn Ardudwy, Gwyn, LL44 2EY.* (Dyffryn Ardudwy 207)

BEAIRSTO, Andrew. Trin Coll Tor BA 52, LTh and STB 55. **d** 54 **p** 55 Edmon. C of Wetaskiwin 54-55; I of Ponoka 55-60; R of Lloydminster 60-71; I of Big Country 71-78; Lumsden Dio Qu'App from 78. *Box 96, Lumsden, Sask, Canada.* (485-2516)

BEAK, Richard John. b 34. Open Univ BA 75. St Aid Coll 59. **d** 62 **p** 63 Leic. C of St Pet w St Hilda Leic 62-64; Glen Parva w S Wigston 64-66; R of Grange Hill Ja 66-69; V of Ch Ch Thurnby Lodge Leic 69-74; Perm to Offic Dio Leic from 80. *8 Freer Close, Houghton-on-the-Hill, Leicester, LE7 9HU.*

BEAK, Robert Michael Cawthorn. b 25. Wycl Hall Ox. **d** 53 **p** 54 Roch. C of St John Tunbridge Wells 53-55; Miss BCMS Dio U Nile 56-58; Dio Nak 58-69; R of Heanton Punchardon (w Marwood from 77) Dio Ex from 70; RD of Barnstaple 77-81. *Heanton Punchardon Rectory, Barnstaple, Devon.* (0271-812249)

BEAKE, Christopher Martyn Grandfield. K Coll Lon and Warm AKC 60. **d** 61 **p** 62 Newc T. C of Berwick-on-Tweed 61-66; V of H Trin N Shields 66-78; Hanslope w Castlethorpe Dio Ox from 78. *Vicarage, Park Road, Milton Keynes, Bucks, MK19 7LT.* (Milton Keynes 510542)

BEAKE, Kenneth George. b 37. Ripon Coll Cudd 75. **d** 77 **p** 78 York. C of Guisborough 77-80; V of St Martin Hull Dio York from 80. *942 Anlaby Road, Hull, HU4 6AH.* (Hull 52995)

BEAKE, Stuart Alexander. b 49. Em Coll Cam BA 72, MA 76. Cudd Coll 72. **d** 74 Bedford for St Alb **p** 75 St Alb. C of Hitchin 74-79; Team V of Hemel Hempstead Dio St Alb from 79; M Gen Syn from 80. *St Mary's Vicarage, Midland Road, Hemel Hempstead, HP2 5BH.* (Hemel Hempstead 56708)

BEAL, Malcolm. b 31. Univ of Bris BA (2nd cl Lat) 52. Ridley Hall Cam. **d** 59 **p** 60 B & W. C of Keynsham 59-62; Speke 62-65; Chap Nyakasura Sch Fort Portal 65-74; V of Salford Priors Dio Cov from 74. *Salford Priors Vicarage, Evesham, Worcs, WR11 5UX.* (Bidford-on-Avon 772445)

BEAL, Very Rev Robert George. St Francis Coll Brisb ACT ThL (2nd cl) 52. **d** and **p** 53 Brisb. C of St Francis Nundah Brisb 53-55; R of St John S Townsville 55-59; St Alb Auchenflower Brisb 59-65; Dean of H Trin Cathl, Wang 65-72; R of St Paul Ipswich 72-75; Can Res of Brisb 74-75; Dean on Newc from 75; Exam Chap to Bp of Newc from 79. *Deanery, Newcomen Street, Newcastle, NSW, Australia 2300.* (2-2052)

BEAL, Royston David. b 35. K Coll Lon and Warm BD and AKC 60. **d** 61 **p** 62 Derby. C of Chesterfield 61-64; Chiswick 64-70; V of St Jo Evang Kensal Green Dio Lon from 70. *St John's Vicarage, Kensal Green, W10 4AA.* (01-969-2615)

BEALE, Mark Thomas. b 50. St Jo Coll Auckld 77. **d** 79 **p** 80 Auckld. C of St Paul Mt Eden Auckld from 79. *21 Dexter Avenue, Mount Eden, Auckland 3, NZ.*

BEALE, Wilfred Henry Ellson. b 11. FCCA 38. FCIS. **d** 69 Lon **p** 71 Willesden for Lon. Hon C of H Trin Northwood Dio Lon from 69. *43 Moor Park Road, Northwood, HA6 2DH.* (Northwood 26301)

BEALE, William Edgar. b 11. K Coll Lon 37. Bps' Coll Cheshunt 40. **d** 42 **p** 43 St Alb. C of Sawbridgeworth 42-45; Chap Pishiobury Sch Sawbridgeworth 45-48; LCC Resid Sch Hutton 48-51; Chap and Asst Supt LCC Resid Sch Banstead 51-52; C of St Jo Bapt Felixstowe 52-53; V of Lakenheath 53-56; St Mich Colom 56-60; H Trin Nuwara Eliya 60-64; R of Kedington 64-72; C of St Paul's Brighton 72-73; Bingley 73-77. *Jersey House, Bishop's Avenue, N2 0BE.* (01-455 6443)

BEALES, Christopher Leader Day. b 51. Univ of Dur BA 72. St Jo Coll Dur 72. **d** 76 **p** 77 Ripon. C of Ch Ch U Armley 76-79; Chap Leeds Industr Miss 76-79; Teesside Industr Miss from 79. *15 Westbrooke Avenue, Hartlepool, Cleve, TS25 5HS.* (Hartlepool 78892)

BEALING, Andrew John. b 42. Sarum Th Coll 67. **d** 69 **p** 70 Dur. C of Bp Auckland 69-73; C-in-c of Eastgate Dio Dur from 73; Rookhope Dio Dur from 73; V of Frosterley Dio Dur from 76. *Vicarage, Frosterley, Bishop Auckland, Co Durham.* (Wolsingham 320)

BEALL, James Herbert Forke. b 45. Qu Univ Kingston Ont BA 67. Trin Coll Tor MDiv 79. **d** and **p** 80 Ott. C of St Matthias City and Dio Ott from 80. *c/o 555 Parkdale Avenue, Ottawa, Ont, Canada, K1Y 1H9.*

BEALL, John. b 19. Clare Coll Cam 2nd cl Econ Trip pt I 39, BA (3rd cl Th Trip pt i) 41, MA 45. Westcott Ho Cam 41. **d** 42 **p** 43 Bris. C of St Matt Moorfields Bris 42-44; CF (EC) 44-47; Ch of S India 48-54; Chap and Lect St Jo Coll Agra 54-55; V of St Matt Moorfields Bris. 55-61; Oswaldtwistle Dio Blackb from 61. *Oswaldtwistle Vicarage, Accrington, Lancs.* (Accrington 33962)

BEAMENT, Owen John. b 41. Bps' Coll Cheshunt 61. **d** 64 **p** 65 S'wark. C of St Paul w St Mark Deptford 64-68; St John Peckham 69-73; St Pet Vauxhall 73-74; V of Hatcham Pk Dio S'wark from 74. *56 Kender Street, SE14.* (01-639 3497)

BEAMER, Neville David. b 40. Late Exhib of St D Coll Lamp BA (2nd cl Th) 62. Jes Coll Ox BA (3rd cl Th) 65. Wycl Hall Ox 66, MA 70. **d** 65 **p** 66 Chelmsf. C of Hornchurch 65-68; Warwick 68-72; Chap of Sherbourne 68-72; V of Holton-le-Clay 72-75; P-in-c of Stoneleigh w Ashow 75-79; Baginton 77-79; V of Fletchamstead Dio Cov from 79. *St James's Vicarage, Tile Hill Lane, Coventry, W Midl, CV4 9DP.* (Cov 466262)

BEAMES, William Stanley. Angl Th Coll BC LTh 25. **d** 25 **p** 26 Athab. C of Peace River 25; P-in-c 26; I of East Trail (or Fruitvale) and Distr 27-28; R of Revelstoke 28-33; Penticton 33-51; V of Kaslo and Kokanee 51-56; L to Offic Dio Koot 56-64; P-in-c of Naramata 64-66. *102-495 Winnipeg Street, Penticton, BC, Canada.*

BEAMISH, Francis Edward. Trin Coll Dub BA 49. **d** 50 **p** 52 Connor. C of Templecorran 49-53; Drumglass 53-61; R of Caledon w Brantry Dio Arm from 61. *Rectory, Caledon, Co Tyrone, N Ireland.* (Caledon 205)

BEAMISH, John William. b 25. Trin Coll Dub BA 47, MA 81. **d** 49 **p** 50 Connor. C of St Aid Belfast 49-51; Derriaghy 51-53; I of Brackaville Dio Arm from 53. *Rectory, Derry Road, Coalisland, Co Tyrone, N Ireland.* (Coalisland 40424)

BEAN, Alan Evison. b 13. Late Exhib of Ch Coll Cam 2nd cl Hist Trip pt i 34, BA (2nd cl Hist Trip pt ii) 35, MA 39. Ely Th Coll 35. M SSJE 47. **d** 36 **p** 37 Dur. C of St Ignatius Hendon Dur 36-40; CF (EC) 42-46; Perm to Offic Dio Ox 41-50; Chap at H Name Poona 50-52; St Pet Mazagon Bom 52-55; Miss at Lonavla 57-64; L to Offic Dio Ox from 65. *228 Iffley Road, Oxford, OX4 1SE.* (Oxford 48116)

BEAN, Basil Thomas. b 15. Late Exhib of Ch Coll Cam 1st cl Hist Trip pt i and Hist Scho 36, BA (2nd cl Hist Trip pt ii) 37, MA 41. Ely Th Coll 37. **d** 38 **p** 39 Lon. C of St Mich Camden Town 38-45; Chap to Schs R Assoc for Deaf and Dumb 45-55; Perm to Offic Dio Lon 53-55; Publ Pr Dio S'wark 53-55; Chap and Supt Sussex Dioc Assoc for Deaf and Dumb 55-80; Perm to Offic Dio Chich from 80. *19 Aston Rise, Pulborough, Sussex.* (Pulborough 2835)

BEAN, Bernard Willoughby. b 1889. Pemb Coll Ox BA 12. Westcott Ho Cam. **d** 32 **p** 34 Calc. Prin CMS Boys' Sch Krishnagar 32-43; War work with YMCA 43-46; Miss at Ratnapur Nadia Distr 46-50; Bollobhpur 50-53; R of Somerleyton w Ashby 53-69; C-in-c of Herringfleet 64-69; Commiss B'pore from 60; Perm to Offic Dio Nor from 78. *92 Links Road, Gorleston-on-Sea, Great Yarmouth, Norf.*

BEAN, Douglas Jeyes Lendrum. b 25. Worc Coll Ox BA (3rd cl Th) 50, MA 53. Ely Th Coll 50. **d** 51 Dover for Cant **p** 52 Cant. C of St Luke Woodside Croydon 51-54; Min Can of St Geo Chap Windsor 54-59; L to Offic at Windsor 56-59; V of St Laur Reading 59-68; Chap HM Borstal Inst Reading 61-68; RD of Reading 65-68; Min Can of St Paul's Cathl 68-72; Hon Min Can from 72; L to Offic Dio Lon 69-72; V of St Pancras w St Jas and Ch Ch Dio Lon from 72. *Vicarage, 12 Fitzroy Square, W1.* (01-387 6460)

BEAN, Canon John Victor. b 25. Down Coll Cam BA 47, MA 51. Sarum Th Coll 48. **d** 50 **p** 51 Portsm. C of St Jas Milton 50-55; Fareham 55-59; V of St Helens IW 59-66; St Mary Cowes Dio Portsm from 66; RD of W Wight 68-72; Hon Can of Portsm from 70; M Gen Syn 74-80; P-in-c of St Faith Cowes 77-80; Gurnard Dio Portsm from 78; Chap to HM the Queen from 80. *Vicarage, Church Road, Cowes, PO31 8HA, IW.* (Cowes 292509)

BEAN, Peter Douglas. Ch Ch Coll LTh 67. **d** 66 **p** 67 Ch Ch. C of Avonside 66-68; Timaru 68-71; P-in-c of Marchwiel 71; N Brighton 71-74; Chap RNZN from 74; Hon C of Takapuna 74-76; Devonport 76-80; Perm to Offic Dio Auckld from 80. *36 Montgomery Avenue, Bayswater, Auckland 9, NZ.*

BEANEY, John. b 47. Trin Coll Bris 77. **d** 79 **p** 80 Roch. C of Ch Ch Bromley Dio Roch from 79. *68 Warren Avenue, Bromley, Kent, BR1 4BS.*

BEAR, Canon Harold Gatehouse. b 10. Kelham Th Coll 28. **d** 34 **p** 35 S'wark. C of St Paul Deptford (in c of St Mark from 37) 34-45; Chap RAFVR 41-45; V of St Anne Wandsworth 45-53; Surr from 50; R of Old Charlton 53-66; V of Lewisham 66-77; Hon Can of S'wark from 67; Can (Emer) from 77; Commiss Seoul from 68. *28a Belmont Park, SE13 5BJ.* (01-318 6113)

BEAR, William. b 1892. **d** 57 **p** 58 Cant. C of Milton Regis 57-71; Perm to Offic Dio Cant from 71. *32 Wyllie Court, Milton Regis, Sittingbourne, Kent.*

BEARANCE, William Robert. b 45. Qu Univ Kingston Ont BA 74. McGill Univ Montr BTh 75. **d** 76 Ont **p** 77 Bp Creeggan for Ont. On leave 76-77; C of St Barn St Lambert 77-78; R of Lansdowne Rear 78-79; Parham and Sharbot Lake Dio Ont from 80. *Box 26, Sharbot Lake, Ont, Canada.* (613-279 2192)

BEARD, Douglas. b 03. Late Exhib of Fitzw Hall Cam BA (3rd cl Th Trip pt i) 25, MA 29. Wycl Hall Ox 25. **d** 26 **p** 27 Chelmsf. C of St Jo Bapt Leytonstone 26-28; Saffron Walden 28-29; St Jo Bapt Leytonstone 29-34; V of St Mary Magd, The Tything, Worc 34-75; Perm to Offic Dio Worc from 77. *9 Sunnyside Road, Worcester, WR1 1RL.* (Worcester 29278)

BEARD, Graham. Moore Th Coll Syd. **d** and **p** 57 Syd. C of Liv 57-58; Port Kembla 58-62; C-in-c of Merrylands W 62-66; R of Concord N 66-74; Chap RAAF from 75. *RAAF Base, East Sale, Vic., Australia 3852.*

BEARD, Peter Harley. b 39. Coll of Resurr Mirfield 60. **d** 71 **p** 72 Damar. C of Tsumeb 71-73; Fish Hoek Capetn 73-75; Asst Chap Miss to Seamen Mersey 75-76; Chap Supt 76-81; Chap Miss to Seamen Tilbury 81-82; V of St Osyth Dio Chelmsf from 82. *St Osyth Vicarage, Clacton-on-sea, Essex.* (St Osyth 820348)

BEARD, Ronald Noble. Moore Th Coll Syd 58. ACT ThL 60. **d** 61 Syd **p** 61 Bp Kerle for Syd. C of St Nich Coogee 61-62; C-in-c of St Paul S Coogee 62-64; All SS Provisional Distr Albion Park 64-70; w Bush Ch Aid S 70-73; R of Gascoyne-Ashburton 70-72; Bulli Dio Syd from 74. *66 Park Road, Bulli, NSW, Australia 2516.* (042-84 3021)

BEARDALL, Frank Leslie. Univ Coll Dur LTh 28, BA 29. Edin Th Coll 29. **d** 31 **p** 32 Glas. C of St Mary Cathl, Glas 31-34; St Alb Mart Cheetwood 34-35; R of St Martin, Polmadie, Glas 35-41; CF (EC) 40-45; PC of St Andr, Linc 45-49; R of All SS, Edin 49-56; V of St Cuthb w All SS Newc T 56-60; R of Kokstad 60-68; Archd of Kokstad 65-68; C of St Jas Miss Nyamandhlovu Dio Matab 69-75; P-in-c from 76. *Box 638, Bulawayo, Zimbabwe.* (64208)

BEARDALL, Raymond. b 32. St Jo Coll Nottm 70. **d** 72 **p** 73 Bradf. C of Ilkley 72-74; Seasalter 74-79; V of Farndon Dio Southw from 79; R of Thorpe-by-Newark Dio Southw from 79. *Vicarage, 3 Marsh Lane, Farndon, Newark, Notts.* (Newark 705048)

BEARDMORE, John Keith. b 42. Univ of Bris BEducn 74. **d** 77 **p** 78 Mon (APM). C of Maindee Dio Mon from 77. *16 Hove Avenue, Newport, Gwent, NPT 7QP.*

BEARDSHAW, David. b 37. Wells Th Coll 65. **d** 67 Bp McKie for Cov **p** 68 Cov. C of St Chad Cov 67-69; St Mich Stoke 70-73; V of Whitley 73-77; Youth Officer Dio Cov from 77. *Rectory, Bubbenhall, Coventry, Warws, CV8 3BD.*

BEARDSLEY, Christopher. b 51. Univ of Sussex BA 73. Westcott Ho Cam 76. **d** 78 **p** 79 Portsm. C of St Mark North End Portsea (in c of St Francis from 81) Dio Portsm from 78. *St Francis House, Northern Parade, Hilsea, Portsmouth, PO2 9LU.* (Portsm 662467)

BEARDSMORE, Alan. b 45. Wycl Hall Ox 67. **d** 70 **p** 71 Chelmsf. C of Annunc, Prittlewell, Southend 70-72; Epsom 72-78; P-in-c of Burbage 78-79; E Grafton w Tidcombe and Fosbury 78-79; Team V of Wexcombe Dio Sarum from 79.

Vicarage, Eastcourt, Burbage, Marlborough, Wilts, SN8 3AG. (Burbage 810258)

BEARDSMORE, John. b 19. Kelham Th Coll 46. **d** 51 **p** 51 Lich. C of St Mich AA Caldmore Walsall 51-53; Otley Yorks 53-55; V of Burley-in-Wharfedale 55-69; H Trin Bromley Common 69-70; Chap Scalebor Pk Hosp 55-69; V of Buttershaw Dio Bradf from 70. *St Paul's Vicarage, Wibsey Park Avenue, Bradford, BD6 3QA.*

BEARDY, Eleazer. b 09. **d** and **p** 74 Keew. C of Muskrat Dam Lake Dio Keew from 74. *Muskrat Dam Lake, via Central Patricia, Ont, Canada.*

BEARDY, Steven. d 63 **p** 66 Keew. I of Split Lake 63-65; Bearskin 65-70; Keewatin Dio Keew from 70. *Box 398, Keewatin, Ont, Canada.*

BEARE, Francis Wright. Trin Coll Tor BA 25. Univ of Chicago PhD 45. **d** and **p** 47 Tor. Prof of NT Trin Coll Tor 47-68; Exam Chap to Bp of Tor 64-73. *2116, Hobbs Road, Nashville, Tenn, USA.*

BEARE, William. Trin Coll Dub BA 58. **d** 59 **p** 60 Cash. C of Waterford 59-62; H Trin w St Mary Shandon Cork 62-64; I of Rathcormac 64-68; Marmullane w Monkstown 68-76; Dioc C Dio Ross from 76. *c/o The Palace, Bishop Street, Cork, Irish Republic.*

BEARMAN, Henry Kenneth Gordon. b 07. **d** 51 **p** 62 Chich. C of Bosham 51-68; P-in-c of St Wilfrid Conv Distr Parklands Chich 68-78. *7 Sherborne Road, Chichester, Sussex, PO19 3AB.*

BEARMAN, Leslie Raymond Livingstone. b 09. ALCD 35. **d** 35 **p** 36 Chelmsf. C of St Luke Walthamstow 35-38; St Cuthb w Ch Ch Bedford 38-40; Publ Pr Dio St Alb 40-43; Chap HM Pris Bedford 43-45; R of Clophill 45-51; Chap Bedford Modern Sch and Publ Pr Dio St Alb 51-61; R of Sherington w Chicheley 61-75; RD of Newport 70-73; C-in-c of N Crawley w Astwood and Hardmead 73-74; R 74-75. *Highcroft, Ashley Lane, Moulton, Northampton, NN3 1TH.* (Northampton 42326)

BEARPARK, John Michael. b 36. Late Exhib of Ex Coll Ox BA (2nd cl Th) 59, MA 63. Linc Th Coll 59. **d** 61 York for Bradf **p** 62 Bradf. C of H Trin Bingley 61-64; Baildon 64-67; V of Fairweather Green 67-77; Steeton w Eastburn Dio Bradf from 77. *Vicarage, 2 Halsteads Way, Steeton, Keighley, W Yorks, BD20 6SN.* (Steeton 52004)

BEASLEY, Canon Arthur James. b 12. Hertf Coll Ox BA (3rd cl Mod Hist) 33, MA 38. Ridley Hall Cam 34. **d** 36 **p** 37 Man. C of Ch Ch Harpurhey 36-39; St Mich Flixton 39-42; Actg C-in-c of All SS Stand 42-43; R of Ch Ch Moss Side 43-48; Chap R Infirm Man 43-48; V of Ch Ch Heaton 48-81; Hon Can of Man 72-81; Can (Emer) from 81. *40 Chorley New Road, Lostock, Bolton, Lancs, BL 6 4AL.* (Bolton 494450)

BEASLEY, Bernard Robinson. b 07. OBE (Mil) 56. Univ of Leeds BA 30, MA 45. Coll of Resurr Mirfield 25. **d** 31 **p** 32 S'wark. C of St Pet Vauxhall 31-34; Chap RN 34-62; Hon Chap to HM the Queen 60; V of Easebourne 62-72; RD of Midhurst 64-72. *Agra Cottage, Worton, Devizes, Wilts, SN10 5SE.* (Devizes 3383)

BEASLEY, James Samuel. d 15 **p** 16 Gippsld. C of Morwell Vic 15-16; V of Loch 16-17; C of St Luke Concord w Burwood 17-19; Mudgee 20-21; Rylstone NSW 21-22; R of Warren NSW 22-25; Chap Govt Schs 25-28; St Andr Home Kurseong 29-33; Planter's Chap at Kurseong 25-33; Jamalpur 33-34; Cuttack 34-46; Perm to Offic Dio Wang 48-51. *Glenburn, via Yea, Victoria, Australia.*

BEASLEY, Michael John. b 41. Univ of Dur BA (2nd cl Th) 63. Sarum Th Coll 63. **d** 65 **p** 66 B & W. C of St Jo Evang Weston Somt 65-67; Pinner 67-69; E Grinstead 69-72; Chap of Mayday, Queens and St Mary's Hosps Croydon 72-77; Team V of Swanborough Dio Sarum from 77. *Wilcot Vicarage, Pewsey, Wilts, SN9 5NS.* (06726 2282)

BEASLEY, Walter Sydney. b 33. Univ of Nottm BA 57. Linc Th Coll 57. **d** 59 Bp Gelsthorpe for Southw **p** 60 Southw. C of Harworth 59-64; V of Forest Town 64-70; R of Bulwell Dio Southw from 70; Surr from 72. *Bulwell Rectory, Nottingham.* (Nottm 278468)

BEASLEY, (Hilary) William Isaac. b 23. Univ of Leeds BA (2nd cl Mod Hist) 47. MCR 56. Coll of Resurr Mirfield 47. **d** 49 **p** 50 Cov. C of St Mark Cov 49-53; Warden and Prior Hostel of Resurr Leeds and L to Offic Dio Ripon 61-64. *House of the Resurrection, Mirfield, Yorks.* (Mirfield 494318)

BEATER, David MacPherson. b 41. Univ of Leeds. Chich Th Coll 66. **d** 69 **p** 70 Middleton for Man. C of St Crispin, Withington 69-72; Lightbowne 72-74; V of St Hilda Prestwich 74-81; Northfleet Dio Roch from 81. *Vicarage, The Hill, Northfleet, Kent, DA11 9EU.* (Gravesend 66400)

BEATON, Victor Henry. b 10. Univ of Lon 32. AKC 38, BD 44. **d** 38 **p** 39 Chich. C of St John Hollington (in c of St Jas Silverdale) 38-42; V of Willoughby-on-the-Wolds w Wysall and Thorpe-in-the-Glebe 42-47; R of Rougham 47-59; St E Dioc Insp of Schs 48-59; V of Broadwater Down 59-76; Perm to Offic Dio St E from 76; Dio Ely from 77; Dio Nor from 78. *10 The Street, Barton Mills, Bury St Edmunds, Suff, IP28 6AW.* (0638 714979)

BEATTIE, Ian David. Univ of NZ BA 58. NZ Bd of Th Stud LTh (1st cl) 60. St Jo Coll Auckld 58. **d** 60 **p** 61 Auckld. C of St Andr Epsom NZ 60-64; Perm to Offic at St Jo Evang Shirley Surrey 64-65; V of St Andr Wimbledon 65-71; C of St Aug Napier 71-73; V of St Pet Onehunga City and Dio Auckld from 73. *57 Grey Street, Onehunga, Auckland 6, NZ.* (666-368)

BEATTIE, Canon James Dunn Fleming. Univ of Sask BA (Hons Phil and Engl) 35, MA 46. Em Coll Sktn LTh 35, BD 41, Hon DD 72. Wycl Coll Tor Hon DD 68. **d** 35 **p** 36 Sktn. C of Kerrobert 35-38; I of Melfort 38-45; Exam Chap to Bp of Sask 43-73; Prof of Ch Hist Em Coll Sktn 45-64; Prof of Phil of Relig from 65; Hon Can of Sktn 55-73; Can (Emer) from 73; R of H Trin Sktn 55-67; Vice-Prin Em Coll Sktn 59-68; Prin 68-73; Hon Fell from 73. *200 Poplar Crescent, Saskatoon, Sask, Canada.*

BEATTIE, James Walker. Chich Th Coll 52. **d** 52 **p** 53 Dur. C of W Harton 52-56; V of S Hylton Bp Wearmouth 56-59; PC of Hedworth 59-70; R of Hawthorn Dio Dur from 70. *Hawthorn Rectory, Seaham, Co Durham.* (Easington 215)

BEATTIE, John Carson. d 23 **p** 24 Derry. C of All SS Clooney 23-28; C-in-c of Ballynascreen 28-43; Dioc C of Clogh 43-44; C-in-c of Templecarne 44-49; Donaghmoyne 49-50. *Highclere House, High Road, Portstewart, Co Derry, N Ireland.*

BEATTIE, Noel Christopher. b 41. Dub Th Coll 65. **d** 68 **p** 69 Connor. C of H Trin Belf 68-70; S Bart Belf 70-73; St Mary Doncaster (in c of St Paul) 73-77; Team V of Em Northn Dio Pet from 77. *4 Booth Lane North, Boothville, Northampton, NN3 1JG.* (Northampton 402150)

BEATTIE, Ronald Charles. St Columb's Hall Wang 67. **d** 69 Wang for Carp **p** 69 Brisb for Carp. C of Milawa 69; All S Cathl Thursday I 70; St Paul Ipswich 71-72; V of Mid-Clarence 73-74; R of Woodenbong 74-76; C of Lismore 77-78; P-in-c of Broadmeadows Dio Melb from 78. *15 Jenson Road, Broadmeadows, Vic, Australia 3047.*

BEATTIE, Thomas Low Forbes. Edin Th Coll 35. **d** 38 **p** 39 St Andr. C of St Serf Burntisland 38-40; Bucksburn (in c of Hilton) 40-42; Chap RNVR 42-46; R of Aldborough (w Thurgarton from 47) 46-49; I of Durham and Melbourne 49-52; R of Chambly 52-59; St Thos Aboyne 59-70; Asst Master Hampton Sch Ja from 70. *Hampton School, Malvern, St Elizabeth, Jamaica.*

BEATTIE, William Bruce. d 48 **p** 49 Nel. C of Blenheim 48-49; Greymouth 49; C-in-c of Brightwater 49-50; Murchison 50; V of Havelock and of The Sounds 50-57; Awatere 57-64; Master Whakarewa Home Hon C of Motueka 64-67; C of Feilding 67-69; Naenae-Epuni 69-74; L to Offic Dio Wel from 74. *31 Molesworth Street, Taita, Wellington, NZ.* (672-021)

BEATTIE, William Gilmour. Wycl Coll Tor BA 45, LTh 48. **d** 45 Tor **p** 46 Sask. I of Hudson Bay Junction 45-50; Shellbrook 50-53; R of E Passage 53-58; C of St Brice N Bay 58-60; Distr Sec Canad Bible S 60-71; I of Manitowaning 71-76. *RR4, Meaford, Ont, Canada.*

BEATTY, Ven Clive Ernest Kingsley. ACT Dipl Th 69. **d** 56 **p** 58 St Arn. C of Dunolly 56-58; Mildura 58-60; V of Manangatang 60-61; R 61-63; Inglewood 63-69; Red Cliffs 69-74; Chap to Bp of St Arn 69-74; Can of St Arn 73-74; Archd of St Arn from 74; R of Maryborough Dio St Arn (Dio Bend from 77) from 74; VG Dio St Arn 76. *Rectory, Clarendon Street, Maryborough, Vic, Australia 3465.* (054-61 1061)

BEATTY, Gordon Rupert. Moore Th Coll Syd 31. ACT ThL 34. **d** 33 Bp Kirkby for Syd **p** 35 Syd. C of Castle Hill 33-34; Wahroonga 34-35; St John Ashfield 35-38; P-in-c of Heytesbury Bal 38-41; Actg I of St Martin Kens 41-42; Hon C of St John Ashfield 42-47; Chap AIF 42-47; NSW Repat Comm Med Instits 47-51; Chap RAN 51-59; RAN (EL) from 59; Dir Pastoral Counselling Centre Dio Syd and C of St Andr Cathl City and Dio Syd from 59. *134 George Street, Homebush, NSW, Australia 2140.* (73-1685)

BEATTY, Canon John Donald. Univ of W Ont BA 60. Hur Coll BTh 63. **d** 62 **p** 63 Tor. C of St Matt Islington Tor 62-66; R of Calvary Ch (w St Mark W Tor from 71) Tor 67-75; Ch Mem Ch Oshawa Dio Tor from 75; Can of Tor from 78. *965 Oshawa Boulevard North, Ont., Canada.* (416-728 8251)

BEATTY, Robert Harold. b 27. Univ of W Ont BA 48. Trin Coll Tor LTh and BD 51. Keble Coll Ox BA (2nd cl Or Stud) 55, MA 58. McGill Univ PhD 62. **d** 51 **p** 52 Hur. C of Woodstock Ont (in c of Ch of Good Shepherd) 51; Perm to Offic (Col Cl Act) Dio Ox 52-55; Dean of Residence St Chad's Coll Regina 55-57; Tutor Bp's Coll Cheshunt 57-58; Fell of McGill Univ 58-60; Prof at Hur Coll 60-63; R of All SS Woodstock 63-67; C of W Byfleet Dio Guildf 67-71; St Luke Oseney Cresc w St Paul Camden Sq St Pancras 71-72;

R of Cosgrove Dio Pet from 72. *Rectory, Cosgrove, Milton Keynes, MK19 7JA, Bucks.* (Milton Keynes 56 3336)

BEAU, Brown. St Pet Coll Melan. **d** 46 **p** 51 Melan. P Dio Melan. *Melanesian Mission, British Solomon Islands.*

BEAUCHAMP, Anthony Hazlerigg Proctor. b 40. Trin Coll Cam BA 62, MA 66. St Jo Coll Nottm 73. **d** 75 **p** 76 Leic. C of St Barn Leic 75-77; C of Polegate (in c of Lower Willingdon) 77-80; Chap of Bethany Sch Goudhurst from 80. *Providence Cottage, Curtisden Green, Goudhurst, Kent.*

BEAUCHAMP, Donald Charles. St Jo Coll Auckld 54. LTh 64. **d** 57 **p** 58 Waik. C of Hamilton Cathl 57-59; V of Ohura 59-61; Waihi 61-63; C of New Plymouth 63-66; V of Brooklands 66-71; Otorohanga 71-76; I of Bay City and Dio Wel from 77. *13 Humber Street, Wellington 2, NZ.* (838 547)

BEAUCHAMP, Gerald Charles. b 55. Univ of Hull BA 78. Coll of Resurr Mirfield 78. **d** 80 **p** 81 S'wark. C of St Cath Hatcham Dio S'wark from 80. *61 Erlanger Road, New Cross, SE14 5TQ.*

BEAUFORT-JONES, Michael. b 37. Trin Coll Bris 76. **d** 78 **p** 79 Wakef. C of Normanton Dio Wakef from 78. *109 Church Lane, Normanton, W Yorks.*

BEAUFOY, Canon Mark Raymond. Wadh Coll Ox BA (2nd cl Mod Hist) 34, MA 38. Montr Dioc Th Coll Hon DD 73. Ridley Hall Cam 34. **d** 36 **p** 37 Cant. C of Ch Ch Croydon 36-38; Temple Ewell and River w Guston 38-40; C of St Geo Altrincham 40-42; V of Littlebourne 42-48; I of Waterville 48-52; Lect in Ch Hist at Bp's Univ Lennox 51-52; I of Montebello 52-61; Warden Montr Dioc Th Coll 61-64; Vice-Prin 64-70; R of Grenville 70-77; Hon Can of Montr 74-77; Can (Emer) from 78. *384 Bedard Boulevard, Lachute, PQ, Canada.*

BEAUMONT, Albert Edward. b 10. Kelham Th Coll 31. **d** 37 **p** 38 Ripon. C of Leeds 37-39; CF (EC) 39-46; Hon CF 46; V of St Luke Beeston Hill 46-54; Knottingley 54-70; L to Offic Dio Gibr (Gibr in Eur from 80) from 70. *68 Siren Street, Senglea, Malta GC.*

BEAUMONT, Arthur. b 1898. Em Coll Cam BA 22, MA 26. Wycl Hall Ox. **d** 29 **p** 30 Blackb. C of St Silas Blackb 29-32; Polesworth 32-37; PC of St Edm Tyseley 37-46; R of Sheldon 46-52; Newton Regis w Seckington 52-60; V of Marbury 60-69; C-in-c of Burleydam 64-67. *32 School Lane, Brereton, Sandbach, Chesh, CW11 9RN.*

BEAUMONT, Arthur. b 29. Late Exhib of BNC Ox BA (2nd cl Th) 52, MA 57. Cudd Coll 52. **d** 54 York **p** 55 Whitby for York. C of St Osw Middlesbrough 54-57; St Martin Scarborough 57-60; C and Prec of All SS Cathl Wakef 60-63; V of Shelley Dio Wakef from 63. *Shelley Vicarage, Huddersfield, W Yorks, HD8 8LH.* (Huddersfield 602205)

BEAUMONT, Canon Brian Maxwell. b 34. Univ of Nottm BA 56. Wells Th Coll 58. **d** 59 **p** 60 Southw. C of H Trin Clifton 59-62; E Stoke w Syerstone 62; St Geo Edgbaston 62-65; V of St Alb Smethwick 65-70; H Trin Blackb 70-77; Asst Dioc Dir of Educn Dio Blackb 70-73; Dir from 73; Hon Can of Blackb Cathl 73-77; Leasehold Can Res from 77. *St John's House, Clarence Street, Blackburn, Lancs.* (Blackb 57088)

BEAUMONT, Christopher John. b 16. **d** 74 **p** 75 Kimb K. C of St John Mafeking 74-78; K William's Town 78-79; R of Ch Ch adel and St Andr Bedford Dio Grahmstn from 79. *Box 95, Adelaide, CP, S Africa.*

BEAUMONT, Gerald Edward. St Mich Crafers ACT ThL 68. **d** 68 **p** 69 Melb. C of St Andr Brighton 68-70; St Jo W Geelong 70-71; P-in-c of Mooroolbark 71-72; I 72-74; on leave 74-75; I of Armadale w Hawksburn Dio Melb from 75. *27 Cromwell Road, South Yarra, Vic, Australia 3141.* (24-3324)

BEAUMONT, Canon John Philip. b 32. Univ of Leeds BA 55. Coll of Resurr Mirfield 55. **d** 57 **p** 58 Ripon. C of St Marg of Antioch Leeds 57-60; Wellingborough 60-64; Min of St Andr Eccles Distr Wellingborough 64-67; V 67-70; Chap HM Borstal Wellingborough 64-70; V of Finedon Dio Pet from 70; Can of Pet from 80. *Finedon Vicarage, Wellingborough, Northants, NN9 5NR.* (Wellingborough 680285)

BEAUMONT, John William. b 19. MBE (Mil) 48. R Mil Coll Sandhurst 38. Qu Coll Birm 48. **d** 51 **p** 52 Portsm. C of St Mark Portsea 51-54: C-in-c of Leigh Pk Conv Distr Portsm 54-59; V of S w N Hayling 59-74; R of Droxford Dio Portsm from 74; Meonstoke w Corhampton and Exton Dio Portsm from 78. *Rectory, Droxford, Southampton.* (Droxford 512)

BEAUMONT, Stephen Martin. b 51. K Coll Lon BD 73. AKC 74. St Aug Coll Cant 73. **d** 74 **p** 75 Newc T. C of St Jas Benwell Newc T 74-77; Asst Chap Marlborough Coll 77-81; R of Ideford, Luton & Ashcombe Dio Ex from 81; Dom Chap to Bp of Ex from 81. *Ideford Rectory, Newton Abbot, Devon, TQ13 0BA.* (Chudleigh 852192)

BEAUMONT, Terence Mayes. b 41. Univ of Lon BA (2nd cl Spanish) 63. Univ of Nottm Dipl Th (w distinc) 69. Linc Th Coll. **d** 71 **p** 72 St Alb. C of Hitchin 71-74; Harpenden 74-79; V of St Pet Broadwater Stevenage Dio St Alb from 79. *1 The Willows, Broadwater, Stevenage, Herts, SG2 8AN.* (Stevenage 52447)

BEAUMONT, Victor George. b 30. St Jo Coll Auckld LTh 66. **d** and **p** 73 Dun. C of St John Roslyn 73-75; Hon C of Green I Dio Dun from 75. *312 Main South Road, Green Island, Dunedin, NZ.* (Dunedin 882-399)

BEAVAN, Charles Kenneth. b 15. BA (2nd cl Hist) Lon 49. **d** 67 **p** 68 Lich. Hd Master Meole-Brace Sch 53-76; Hon C of Meole-Brace 67-71; C-in-c of St Alkmund Shrewsbury Dio Lich from 71. *School House, Meole-Brace, Shrewsbury, Salop, SY3 9EZ.* (Shrewsbury 4172)

BEAVAN, Edward Hugh. b 43. Ex Coll Ox BA (2nd cl Th) 70, MA 74. Cudd Coll 69. **d** 71 **p** 72 Kens for Lon. C of St Hilda, Ashford Lon 71-74; St Mary Newington 74-76; R of Sandon Dio Chelmsf from 76. *Sandon Rectory, Chelmsford, Essex, CM2 7SQ.* (Chelmsford 72262)

BEAVAN, Ernest George. St Pet Hall Ox BA 32, MA 40. Qu Coll Newfld 34. **d** 35 **p** 36 Newfld. C-in-c of Botwood 35-36; C of Corner Brook 36-37; in CE in S Afr 37-40; YMCA (S Afr) 40-41; S Afr AF 42-45; Org Sec CCCS for NW Distr 45-48; P-in-c of Timboon 48-52; L to Offic Dio Melb 52-61; I of Ch of Epiph Northcote 61-65; R of Hamilton 65-71; St Geo Hobart Dio Tas from 71. *28 Cromwell Street, Hobart, Tasmania 7000.* (002-23 7476)

BEAVER, Christopher Martin. b 31. K Coll Lon and Warm AKC 56. **d** 60 **p** 61 Lich. C of All SS Leek 60-64; Uttoxeter w Bramshall 64-67; V of Normacot 67-77; Pheasey Dio Lich from 77. *St Chad's Vicarage, Hillingford Ave, Pheasey, Birmingham, B43 7HN.* (021-360 7556)

BEAVER, Dawson George. b 27. Em Coll Sktn 58. **d** 58 Sask **p** 58 Athab. I of N Star 58-62; Slave Lake 62-67; Fort McMurray 67-71; R of Fairview 71-76; Hon Can of St Jas Cathl Peace River 71-76; L to Offic Dio Athab from 77. *Box 151, Fairview, Alta., Canada.*

BEAVER, Frederick William. b 1900. Worc Ordin Coll 60. **d** 61 Lich for Pet **p** 62 Pet. C of Holcot 61-66; V of Gretton 66-73. *26 Bayley Close, Uppingham, Rutland.* (Uppingham 3481)

BEAVER, Maurice John. b 15. Qu Coll Birm 77. **d** 77 **p** 78 Worc (NSM). C of Hagley Dio Worc from 77. *37 Park Road, Hagley, Stourbridge, W Midl, DY9 0NS.* (Hagley 883566)

BEAVERSTOCK, John Spencer. ACT ThL 56. **d** 55 **p** 56 Tas. C of Moonah 55-56; Burnie 56-57; R of Avoca 57-60; C-in-c of St Alb w St Paul Conv Distr Burnley 61-63; R of St Paul Launceston 63-65; Winton 65-67; Smithton 67-71; New Norfolk 71-73; Chap Lakeside Hosp Bal from 73. *Chaplain's Office, Lakeside Hospital, Ballarat, Vic., Australia 3350.* (053-34 1204)

BEAVIS, David Norman. b 14. Tyndale Hall Bris 40. **d** 43 **p** 45 Man. C of St Paul Halliwell 43-45; Daubhill 45-48; Cheadle 48-50; R of Burlingham St Edm (w St Andr and St Pet from 56) w Lingwood V 50-57; C-in-c of Burlingham St Andr w St Pet 53-56; Chap Homelea County Home 53-57; PC of St Barn Blackb 57-67; V of Heapey 67-80. *Low Beck, South Nutfield, Redhill, Surrey, RH1 5NJ.* (Nutfield Ridge 3206)

BEBB, John. b 08. St Chad's Coll Dur BA and Van Mildert Exhib 34, Dipl in Th w distinc 35, MA 37. **d** 35 **p** 36 Liv. C of St Thos Seaforth 35-37; St Pet Wolverhampton 37-42; V of St Marg, Ladywood, Birm 42-50; St Edm, Dudley 50-59; Offenham 59-72. *33 Leslie Close, Littleover Derby.*

BEBB, John Edwin. b 13. Late Found Scho of St Jo Coll Dur BA (2nd cl Th) 35, MA 38. Wycl Hall Ox 35. **d** 36 Warrington for Liv **p** 37 Liv. C of St John and St Jas Litherland 36-40; H Trin Wavertree 40-44; V of St Mary Lower Ince 45-52; R and V of Silloth 52-62; V of Hengrove 62-67; Asst Master Blackpool Grammar Sch 67-72; V of Sandown 72-80. *c/o Vicarage, Sandown, IW.* (Sandown 2548)

BEBBINGTON, Myles. b 35. Kelham Th Coll 56. **d** 61 **p** 62 Wakef. C of Horbury 61-64; St Benedict Ardwick Man 64-66; V of Cudworth 66-73; P-in-c of St Jo Bapt Holland Road Kens 73-78; St Mich AA Walthamstow Dio Chelmsf 78-80; V from 80. *Vicarage, Palmerston Road, E17 6PQ.* (01-520 6328)

BEBEE, Morgan David. **d** 53 **p** 55 Moos. I of Mattagami 53-55; Centr Patricia 55-58; Pickle Crow 58-62; Iroquois Falls 62-69; R of Rivière Dorée 69-71; P-in-c of Eastmain 71-74; Kashechewan 71-74; R of N Addington and N Frontenac 74-76; on leave. *Plevna, Ont, Canada.* (613-479 2432)

BECK, Alan. b 28. K Coll Lon and Warm AKC 50. **d** 53 **p** 54 Lon. C of St Alb N Harrow 53-56; Northolt 56-59; Loughborough 59-61; V of Crookham 61-69; Puriton (w Pawlett from 78) 69-79; C-in-c of Pawlett 74-78; P-in-c of Staplegrove Dio B & W from 80. *Staplegrove Rectory, Taunton, Somt.* (0823-72787)

BECK, Arthur Alan Wilfrid. **d** 77 Qu'App. C of St Mary

Regina Dio Qu'App from 77. *112 Riddell Crescent, Regina, Sask, Canada.*

BECK, Ernest Edward. b 05. St Aid Coll 40. **d** 42 Hull for York **p** 43 York. C of H Trin Hull 42-44; Halesowen w Hasbury 44-45; Hagley (in c of St Sav w Hagley) 45-48; V of St Francis Dudley 48-50; R of Salwarpe 50-52; V of Stramshall 52-55; Tilstock 55-67; V of Ruyton-XI-Towns 67-70. *8 Newport Road, Whitchurch, Salop, SY13 1QE.* (Whitchurch 4298)

BECK, Preb Henry Wolferstan. AKC (1st cl) 28. Bps' Coll Cheshunt. **d** 28 **p** 29 Lon. C of St Phil Earl's Court 28-33; V of St Jo Bapt Harrow-on-the-Hill 33-44; Hessle 44-45; St Jude S Kens. 45-61; Preb of Oxgate in St Paul's Cathl 60-61; Preb (Emer) from 61; R of Wotton 61-65. *Wotton Rectory, Dorking, Surrey.*

BECK, John Edward. b 28. St Jo Coll Ox BA (2nd cl Mus) 56, MA 59. ARCM 52. FRCO 59. Wells Th Coll 56. **d** 58 Glouc **p** 59 Tewkesbury for Glouc. C of Dursley 58-61; St Paul, Glouc 61-63; St Mary and All SS Cathl, Salisbury Rhod 63-70; Ch Ch Cheltm 70-77; Pr-Organist and C of Cirencester Dio Glouc from 77. *38 Cecily Hill, Cirencester, GL7 2EF.* (Cirencester 3778)

BECK, Michael Leonard. b 50. AKC and BD 77. Linc Th Coll 77. **d** 78 **p** 79 Linc. C of Gt Grimsby Dio Linc from 78. *7 Manor Avenue, Grimsby, S Humb, DN32 0QR.* (Grimsby 56385)

BECK, Peter George Cornford. b 36. Univ of Dur BA 61. Ridley Hall Cam 61. **d** 63 **p** 64 Roch. C of Slade Green 63-65; Aylesford 65-68; Min of St Mark's Eccles Distr Brampton 68-71; V of St Mark Brampton 71-75; P-in-c of Alvaston Dio Derby from 75. *Alvaston Vicarage, Derby, DE2 0PR.* (Derby 71143)

BECK, Peter John. b 48. Merton Coll Ox BA (2nd cl Mod Hist) 69, MA 75. Sarum Wells Th Coll 70. **d** 72 Dorch for Ox **p** 73 Reading for Ox. C of Banbury w Neithrop 72-76; Team V 76-78; P-in-c of St Mary le Wigford w St Mark Linc 78-81; V of Glenfield Dio Auckld from 81. *470 Glenfield Road, Auckland 10, NZ.* (449477)

BECK, Raymond Morris. b 13. Magd Coll Ox 2nd cl Th 35, BA 36, MA 40. Cudd Coll 37. **d** 38 **p** 39 Ex. C of Crediton 38-41; St Matt Southsea 41-48; Chap RNVR 43-47; C of St Cuthb Kens 47-49; V of St Jo Ap Whetstone 49-56; St Jo Evang Taunton 56-80; Proc Conv B & W 65-80; Preb of Wells Cathl 76-80; C of Hedworth Dio Dur from 80. *2 Hendon Gardens, Jarrow, T & W.* (Boldon 368779)

BECK, Roger William. b 48. Chich Th Coll 79. **d** 81 Ex. C of St Marychurch Dio Ex from 81. *9 Hilly Gardens Road, Torquay, TQ1 4QL.*

BECK, Canon Stephen. b 16. St Pet Hall Ox BA 44, MA 45. Westcott Ho Cam 45. **d** 47 **p** 48 Portsm. C of St Mark Portsea 47-56; CF 56-59; V of St Agnes Moseley Dio Birm from 59; RD of Moseley 71-81; Hon Can of Birm from 76. *St Agnes' Vicarage, Moseley, Birmingham 13.* (021-449 0368)

BECKE, Justice. b 05. MBE (Mil) 43, TD 50. ACA 29, FCA 60. K Coll Lon. **d** 58 **p** 59 S'wark. C of Ch Ch Sutton 58-60; Chap HM Pris Wandsworth 60-62; V of All SS S Merstham 62-66; Chap St Jas Hosp Balham 66-73; St Benedict's Hosp Tooting 66-78; Perm to Offic Dio Chich from 80. *51 St Pancras, Chichester, PO19 4LT.* (Chich 784295)

BECKERLEG, Barzillai. b 20. Selw Coll Cam 2nd cl Hist Trip pt i 42, BA (3rd cl Th Trip pt i) 43, MA 46. Westcott Ho Cam 42. **d** 44 Lon **p** 45 Stepney for Lon. C of St Alb Golders Green 44-48; Chap St Jo Coll Dur 48-52; L to Offic Dio Dur 49-52; V of Battersea 52-58; Surr from 53; V of Wentworth 58-59; Hd Master Newc T Cathl Choir Sch 59-62; Prec of Newc T Cathl 59-62; R of Duncton 62-64; R of Burton w Coates 62-64; Seq of Up-Waltham 62-64; V of Kippington 64-75; R of E Bergholt 75-79; Chap St Mary's Sch Wantage from 79. *c/o St Mary's School, Wantage, Oxon.*

BECKETT, Canon Bruce Arthur Westenra. St Jo Coll Auckld LTh 54. **d** 54 **p** 55 Ch Ch. C of Highfield 54-58; V of Banks Peninsula 58-62; Burwood 62-71; Chap Burwood Hosp 62-71; V of Sydenham-Beckenham Dio Ch Ch from 71; Hon Can of Ch Ch from 77. *8 Roxburgh Street, Christchurch 2, NZ.* (35-921)

BECKETT, Gerald. b 42. Univ of Lon BD 73. Macquarie Univ MA 78. Moore Coll Syd ThL 72. **d** and **p** 73 Syd. C of Narrabeen 73-76; R of Belmore Dio Syd from 76. *2a Victory Street, Belmore, NSW, Australia 2192.* (759-2086)

BECKETT, Stanley. b 20. Linc Th Coll. **d** 64 **p** 65 Ches. C of Barnston 64-71; V of Daresbury Dio Ches from 71. *Daresbury Vicarage, Warrington, Lancs.* (Moore 348)

BECKETT, William Vincent. ALCD 50. **d** 50 **p** 51 Ex. C of St Phil and St Jas Ilfracombe 50-53; V of St D Holloway 53-57; St Steph Hyson Green Nottm Dio Southw from 57. *St Stephen's Vicarage, Hyson Green, Nottingham.*

BECKHAM, John Francis. b 25. Bps' Coll Cheshunt 65. **d** 67 Barking for Chelmsf **p** 68 Chelmsf. C of St Jo Bapt Leytonstone 67-70; St Mary-at-the-Walls Colchester 70-73; R of Lawford 73-80; V of Gt w L Chesterford Dio Chelmsf from 80. *Vicarage, Great Chesterford, Saffron Walden, Essex.* (S Walden 30317)

BECKLEY, Peter William. b 52. Univ of Lon BSc 73. Trin Coll Bris 76. **d** 79 **p** 80 Ex. C of St Jude Plymouth Dio Ex from 79. *75 Knighton Road, Plymouth, PL4 9BZ.* (Plymouth 266130)

BECKLEY, Simon Richard. b 38. BA (Lon) 61. Oak Hill Th Coll 58. **d** 63 **p** 64 St Alb C of St Luke Watford 63-67; New Ferry 67-70; Ch Ch Chadderton 70-73; V of Friar Mere 73-80; St Cath Higher Tranmere Dio Ches from 80. *9 The Wiend, Birkenhead, Mer, L42 6RY.* (051-645 4533)

BECKWITH, Canon George. b 12. Hatf Coll Dur BA and Hatfield Exhib 32, Dipl in Th 33, MA 35. St Steph Ho Ox 34. **d** 35 Dur **p** 36 Jarrow for Dur. C of St Aid Annfield Plain 35-38; H Trin Stockton-on-Tees 38-39; P-in-c of Staindrop 39-42; V of Shotton 42-55; R of Jarrow 55-64; V of Lanchester 64-77; Hon Can of Dur from 65; RD of Lanchester 66-74. *15 The Rise, Darlington, Co Durham.*

BECKWITH, Ian Stanley. b 36. Univ of Nottm BA 58. Linc Th Coll 78. **d** 80 **p** 81 Linc. Sen Lect Bp Grosseteste Coll from 80; Hon C of Linc Cathl from 80. *20 Curle Avenue, Lincoln, LN2 4AN.*

BECKWITH, John Douglas. b 33. K Coll Lon and Warm Plumptre Pri 56, AKC 57. **d** 58 **p** 65 S'wark. C of Streatham 58-59; L to Offic Dio Ripon 59-60; Dio Lagos 60-62; Sen Tutor Ijebu-Igbo Gr Sch and Molusi Coll 60-62; C of Bedale 62-63; Mottingham 65-69; Ho Tutor Eltham Coll 64-69; Chap at Gothenburg Dio Lon (N & C Eur) 69-70; Chap to Bp Suffr of Edmonton 70-77; Hon Chap from 77; Dir Ordin Tr and L to Offic Dio Lon 70-77; V of St Anne Brookfield Dio Lon from 77. *106 Highgate West Hill, N6 6AP.* (01-340 5190)

BECKWITH, Roger Thomas. b 29. St Edm Hall Ox BA (3rd cl Engl) 52, MA 56. Ripon Hall Ox 51. Tyndale Hall Bris 52. Cudd Coll 54. **d** 54 **p** 55 Chelmsf. C of Harold Wood 54-57; Bursar Tyndale Hall Bris 57-59; Tutor 59-63; C of St Luke w St Silas Bedminster 57-59; Libr Latimer Ho Ox 63-73; Warden from 73; Lect Wycl Hall Ox from 71. *Latimer House, 131 Banbury Road, Oxford, OX2 7AJ.* (Oxford 57340)

BEDBROOK, Frederick Ernest. b 21. Univ of Melb BCom 51. ACT ThA 52. AASA (Sen) 47. **d** 69 Centr Afr for Melb **p** 70 Melb. Vic Sec Austr Bd of Miss Dio Melb 70-72; Dioc Sec Papua 72-76; Perm to Offic Dio Melb 76; P-in-c of St Mary Camberwell 76-79; Gen Sec SPCK Austr from 76. *Cathedral Buildings, Flinders Lane, Melbourne, Vic, Australia 3000.* (63-9101)

BEDDER, William Lewis Johnson. **d** 44 **p** 45 Win. C of St Thos w St Mich and St Swithun Win 44-51; Bp's Messenger for Youth and Sec SPG in Win Deanery 47-51; V of St Mary Extra (Pear Tree) Southn 51-58; PC of St Jo Bapt Portland 58-68; V 68-74; Chap Portland Hosp 58-74. *107 Chafeys Avenue, Weymouth, Dorset.* (Weymouth 4361)

BEDDINGTON, Peter Jon. b 36. ACP 68. N-W Ordin Course 71. **d** 74 Man **p** 75 Middleton for Man. C of St Pet Bury 74-77; Ch K Bury Dio Man from 77. *18 Throstle Grove, Brandlesholme, Bury, Lancs, BL8 1EB.* (061-764 3292)

BEDDOES, Ronald Alfred. b 12. St Chad Coll Dur Long Pri 34, BA 35, MA 50. **d** 36 **p** 37 Dur. C of Dawdon 36-39; Offg C-in-c of Grindon 39-40; V of Greatham 40-44; Easington Colliery 44-53; Sec Dur Dioc Conf 51-53; Provost of Derby and V of All SS Cathl Ch Derby 53-80; P-in-c of Beeley w Edensor Dio Derby from 80. *Edensor Vicarage, Bakewell, Derbys.* (Baslow 2130)

BEDDOW, Arthur Josiah Comyns. b 13. Ch Coll Cam BA 35, MA 41. Linc Th Coll 38. **d** 40 **p** 41 Sarum. C of Sherborne w Castleton and Lillington 40-46; Bideford 46-54; R of Nymet Rowland w Coleridge 54-63; Insp of Ch Schs 55-78; Asst Dir of Relig Educn and Dioc Youth Officer Dio Ex 56-62; R of Bere Ferrers w Bere Alston 63-78. *Flat 6, Hillside, South Street, Sherborne, Dorset, DT9 3NH.*

BEDDOW, Leslie Philip. b 1900. Dorch Miss Coll 31. **d** 34 **p** 35 Lon. C of Bethnal Green 34-39; All SS Plymouth 39-41; St Mich Croydon 41-44; Cowley 44-47; working with YMCA Germany 47-49; C of St Aug Croydon 49-51; V of St Bart Herne Bay 51-70; Vice Master Eastbridge Hosp Cant from 71. *Flat 4, Eastbridge Hospital, St Peter's Street, Canterbury, Kent CT1 2BD.*

BEDDOW, Nicholas Mark Johnstone-Wallace. b 47. Univ of Birm BA (2nd cl Geo and Th) 69. Qu Coll Birm 69. **d** 71 Aston for Birm **p** 72 Birm. C of St Paul, Blackheath 71-75; P Theologian Dios Lusaka Centr and N Zambia 75-80; V of Escomb Dio Dur from 80; Witton-Pk Dio Dur from 80; Dom Chap to Bp of Dur from 80. *Escomb Vicarage, Bishop Auckland, Co Durham.* (Bp Auckland 602861)

BEDDY, Ven Arthur James Rex. St Paul's Th Coll Grahmstn 48. **d** 52 **p** 53 Kimb K. C of St Cypr Cathl Kimberley 52-53; Mafeking 53-56; R and Dir of Prieska Miss 56-60; Vryburg 61-62; C of St Jas Durban 62-66; R of Jansenville and of Uniondale 66-69; Oudtshoorn Dio Geo from 69; Archd of Karoo from 78. *Rectory, Oudtshoorn, CP, S Africa.* (2486)

BEDFORD, Lord Bishop Suffragan of. *See* Farmbrough, Right Rev David John.

BEDFORD, Archdeacon of. *See* Mayfield, Ven Christopher John

BEDFORD, Christopher John Charles. b 46. Univ of Lon BD (2nd cl) 69. AKC 69. St Aug Coll Cant 69. **d** 70 Bp Gerard for Sheff. C of Ch Ch Doncaster 70-73; H Cross w St Jude and St Pet St Pancras 73-76; C-in-c of Old St Pancras w St Matt Oakley Square 76-81; Selection Sec ACCM 76-81; P-in-c of Bethnal Green Dio Lon from 81. *St. Matthew's Rectory, Hereford Street, E2 6EX.* (01-739 7586)

BEDFORD, Colin Michael. b 35. ALCD 60. **d** 61 **p** 62 Guildf. C of St Mary-of-Bethany Woking 61-63; St Sav Guildf 63-65; Morden (in c of St Geo from 66) 65-69; V of St Philemon Toxt Pk 69-75; C-in-c of St Gabr Toxt Pk 69-75; St Jas w St Matt and H Trin Toxt Pk 69-75; St Paul Princes Pk Toxt Pk 70-75; R of Toxteth Team Min (V of St Philemon Toxteth Pk) Dio Liv from 75; C-in-c of St Cleopas Toxteth Pk 73-78. *40 Devonshire Road, Liverpool, L8 3TZ.* (051-727 1248)

BEDFORD, George. b 15. Linc Th Coll. **d** 60 Maidstone for Cant **p** 61 Cant. C of St Pet-in-I of Thanet 60-64; V of The Brents w Davington (w Oare w Luddenham from 66) 64-71; C-in-c of Oare w Luddenham and Stone 64-66; V of Minster-in-Thanet (w Monkton from 74) Dio Cant from 71; C-in-c of Monkton 72-74. *Minster-in-Thanet Vicarage, Ramsgate, Kent.* (Minster 250)

BEDFORD, Canon John Plasket. **d** 60 St Arn for Bal **p** 61 Bal. C of Colac 60-63; P-in-c of Rupanyup w Murtoa 63-67; R 67-69; Portland 69-79; Horsham, Dio Bal from 79; Hon Can of Bal 78-80; Can from 80. *Rectory, Horsham, Vic, Australia 3400.*

BEDFORD, Norman Stuart. b 28. Oak Hill Th Coll 66. **d** 68 **p** 69 Ox. C of Iver 68-71; V of Warfield 71-75; Southwold Dio St E from 75. *Vicarage, Southwold, Suff.* (Southwold 2397)

BEDFORD, Richard Derek Warner. b 27. Clare Coll Cam BA 52. ALCD 54. **d** 54 **p** 55 S'wark. C of Wallington 54-56; Sanderstead 56-57; Weybridge 57-59; Addlestone (in c of All SS New Haw) 59-62; C-in-c of New Haw Conv Distr 62-66; V of Ch Ch Epsom 66-81; R of Walton-on-the-Hill Dio Guildf from 81. *Rectory, Walton-on-the-Hill, Tadworth, Surrey.* (Tadworth 2105)

BEDFORD-JONES, Canon Hugh Macaulay. Univ of Tor BA 35. Trin Coll Tor LTh 37. **d** 37 Bp Beverley for Tor **p** 38 Tor. C of St Simon Tor 37-43; R of St Matthias Tor 43-48; Cobourg 48-58; Can of Tor from 56; R of St Simon 58-72; on leave 72-73. *Box 69, Maitland, Ont, Canada.*

BEDFORD-JONES, Michael Hugh Harold. b 42. Univ of Tor BA 65. Trin Coll Tor STB 68. **d** 67 Bp Hunt for Tor **p** 68 Tor. C of St Jas Cathl Tor 68-75; I of Epiph Scarborough Dio Tor from 76. *700 Kennedy Road, Scarborough, Ont., Canada.*

BEDLOE, Horace Walter. b 11. Sarum Th Coll 34. **d** 37 **p** 38 Roch. C of St Barn Gillingham 37-41; C-in-c of St Steph Conv Distr Chatham 41-45; V of Kingsclere 45-49; R of Brown's Town Ja 49-56; C-in-c of Stewart Town & Gibraltar Ja 50-56; V of All SS Perry Street Kent 56-60; R of Retreat Ja 60-62; St Ann's Bay Ja 62-69; Can Res of Bradf 70-71; V of H Trin Queensbury 71-72; R of Marley 72-74; Blackstonedge 74-76; C of St Jo Evang Brighton 76-78; Perm to Offic Dio Antig 78; Dio Ox 81; Chap at Malaga Dio Gibr in Eur from 81. *Las Yucas 1, Calle Republica Argentin, Limonar Alto, Malaga, Spain.*

BEDNALL, Ian William Gordon. b 35. Univ of Adel BE. St Barn Coll Belair 78. **d** 80 Willoch. C of Clare Dio Willoch from 80. *PO Box 410, Clare 5453, S Australia.*

BEDWELL, Stanley Frederick. b 20. MPS 42. St Steph Ho Ox (NSM) 77. **d** 80 **p** 81 Ox. C of Farnham R and Hedgerley Dio Ox from 80. *Southwood, Green Lane, Farnham Common, Slough, SL2 3SR.*

BEEBEE, Joseph Thevarajah. b 20. **d** 74 **p** 75 Sing (APM). P Dio Sing. *4a Chancery Hill Road, Singapore 11.*

BEEBEE, Preb Stephen James Shelton. b 17. Univ Coll Ox BA 40, MA 43. Cudd Coll 40. **d** 41 **p** 42 Lon. C of All SS S Acton 41-46; St Paul Ruislip Manor (in c of St Mary S Ruislip) 46-51; C-in-c of St Mary's Conv Distr S Ruislip 51-53; V of St Mich AA Bedford Park 53-65; Commiss Carp 58-73; R of Cranford Dio Lon from 65; Preb of St Paul's Cathl Lon from 72; C-in-c of H Angels Cranford Dio Lon from 71; RD of Hounslow from 75. *34 High Street, Cranford, Hounslow, Middx, TW5 9RG.* (01-897 8836)

BEEBY, Lawrence Clifford. b 28. SOC 70. **d** 73 Kens for Lon **p** 74 Lon. C of St Jo Notting Hill 73-74; Sunbury-on-Thames 74-76; P-in-c of Good Shepherd Conv Distr Hounslow 76-80; Chap Botleys Pk Hosp Chertsey from 80. *Chaplain's Office, Botleys Park Hospital, Chertsey, Surrey.*

BEECH, Albert Edward. b 06. St Aid Coll 48. **d** 50 **p** 51 Bradf. C of St Jas Bolton 50-51; Queensbury 51-52; Stone Staffs 52-54; V of Marston w Whitgreave 54-56; St Paul Burslem 56-63; R of Swynnerton 63-67. *101 Oxford Gardens, Stafford, ST16 3JD.* (Stafford 53558)

BEECH, Frank Thomas. b 36. Tyndale Hall Bris 64. **d** 66 **p** 67 Lich. C of Penn Fields 66-70; Attenborough (w Chilwell to 74) Dio Southw 71-74; C-in-c (w Toton) 74-76; V from 76. *4 St Mary's Close, Close, Attenborough, Beeston, Nottingham.* (Nottm 250405)

BEECH, Canon Harold. b 17. Univ of Wales BA 39. Chich Th Coll 39. **d** 41 **p** 42 Mon. C of Abertillery 41-51; C-in-c of Abercwmboi 51-56; V 56-59; Chap of Hill End and Cell Barnes Hosp St Alb from 59; Hon Can of St Alb Cathl from 77. *14 Wellington Road, St Albans, Herts, AL1 5NL.* (St Alb 31996)

BEECH, John Thomas. b 38. St Aid Coll 64. **d** 67 **p** 68 Lich. C of St Paul Burton-on-Trent 67-70; Chap RN from 70. *c/o Ministry of Defence, Lacon House, Theobalds Road, WC1X 8RY.*

BEECH, Matthew James. b 44. St Jo Coll Auckld. **d** 78 Nel. C of All SS City and Dio Nel from 78. *123 Waimea Road, Nelson, NZ.* (89-840)

BEECH, Michael John. b 48. Jes Coll Cam BA 70. Westcott Ho Cam 72. **d** 75 **p** 76 S'wark. C of St Andr Catford 75-81; All H City and Dio Lon from 81. *42 Crutched Friars, EC3N 2AP.* (01-488 4854)

BEECH, Peter John. b 34. Bps' Coll Cheshunt 58. **d** 61 **p** 62 Lon. C of All SS Fulham 61-64; St John Mafeking 64-65; Prec of St Cypr Cathl Kimberley and Dom Chap to Bp of Kimb K 65-67; V of St Mich AA Lon Fields Hackney 68-75; C-in-c of St Paul Haggerston 68-71; V 71-75; V of H Trin Hermon Hill S Woodford Dio Chelmsf from 75. *Holy Trinity Vicarage, Hermon Hill, South Woodford, E18 1QQ.* (01-989 0912)

BEECH, Walter Herbert. St Jo Coll Auckld LTh 36. **d** 37 **p** 38 Auckld. C of Ellerslie Auckld 37-38; Tamaki W 38-39; V of Bay of Is 40-44; Papakura 44-48; Chap RNZN 48-50; V of Taieri 50-52; Hampden w Maheno 52-59; Asst Miss City Miss Wel 59-66; Perm to Offic Dio Auckld from 67. *1 Ravenwood Drive, Forrest Hill, Takapuna, Auckland 9, NZ.*

✠ **BEECHER, Most Rev Leonard James.** CMG 61. Univ of Lon BSc 27, MA 37. ARCS 26. DD (Lambeth) 62. **d** 29 **p** 31 Momb. Asst Master Alliance High Sch Kikuyu 27-30; CMS Miss Kahuhia 30-36; C of St Nich Sevenoaks 33; CMS Miss at Kabare and Mutira 37-39; Lit Sec Dio Momb 39-43; Exam Chap to Bp of Momb 41-53; CMS Miss Nakuru 44-45; Actg Sec CMS Kenya Miss 43; Cler Sec of Synod and Ed of Kenya Ch Review 42-53; Archd Dio Momb 45-53; Can of Momb 45-53; Actg Sub-Dean of Momb Cathl 46-48; Bp's Commiss Momb 48-59; Cons Asst Bp of Momb in St Paul's Cathl Lon 25 July 50 by Abp of Cant; Bps of Lon; Lich; Roch; S'wark; and Ban; Bps Suffr of Barking; and Fulham; and Bps Heywood; Willis; Wright; Stanton-Jones; and Mann; Apptd Bp of Momb 53; Trld to Nai 64; Elected Abp and Metrop of E Afr 60; res 70; Abp (Emer) and Hon Can of Nai from 70. *8 Naivasha Road, PO Box 21066, Nairobi, Kenya.* (Nairobi 67485)

BEECHEY, Preb George Alfred. b 1890. Univ of Dur LTh 14. Sarum Th Coll 14. **d** 15 **p** 16 Sarum. C of Wilsford w Woodford and Lake 15-19; Donyatt 19-22; St Jo Bapt Weston-s-Mare 22-27; R of Shipham w Rowberrow 27-45; Yatton 45-62; Preb of Wells Cathl from 47. *Acorns, Higher Horton, Ilminster, Somt.*

BEECHEY, Canon George Emyr. b 16. Univ of Wales BA 40. St D Coll Lamp 41. **d** 43 **p** 44 Llan. C of Aberdare 43-46; Ch Ch Win 46-49; Min of St Luke's Conv Distr Win 49-54; V of St Pet (w St Paul w All SS from 56) Southn 54-70; Chap R S Hants Hosp 54-70; R of New Alresford (w Ovington and Itchen Stoke from 73) Dio Win from 70; RD of Alresford 70-80; Hon Can of Win Cathl from 74. *Rectory, New Alresford, Hants.* (Alresford 2105)

BEEDELL, Trevor Francis. b 31. ALCD (2nd cl) 65. **d** 65 Dunwich for St E **p** 66 St E. C of Walton 65-68; R of Hartshorne 68-79; RD of Repton 74-79; Surr from 78; V of Doveridge Dio Derby from 79; Chap HM Detention Centre Foston Hall Derby 79-80; Dir of Chr Stewardship Dio Derby from 79. *Vicarage, Church Lane, Doveridge, Derby, DE6 5NN.* (Uttoxeter 3420)

BEEK, Canon Michael Peter. b 27. Em Coll Cam BA 50, MA 55. Linc Th Coll 50. **d** 52 **p** 53 S'wark. C of St Barn Mitcham 52-55; Talbot Village 55-58; V of Higham w Merston 58-66; R of Gravesend 66-74; Surr from 67; RD of Gravesend 70-74; Tunbridge Wells from 74; Hon Can of Roch from 73; R of Speldhurst w Groombridge (and Ashurst from 77) Dio Roch from 74; C-in-c of Ashurst 76-77. *Speldhurst Rectory, Tunbridge Wells, Kent.* (Langton 2821)

BEEN, Lamuel Wellington. b 39. Codr Coll Barb 79. **d** 81

Nass. C of St Geo Dio Nass from 81. *PO Box N-1103, Nassau, Bahamas.*

BEENY, Canon Reginald Charles Morris. b 10. OBE 75. Univ of Leeds BA (3rd cl Hist) 32. Coll of Resurr Mirfield 32. **d** 34 **p** 35 S'wark. C of St Laur Catford 34-36; Ch Ch Streatham 36-40; Cler Org Sec C of E Children's S 40-44; Executive Officer 44-49; Asst Sec 49-64; Dir from 64; LPr Dio S'wark from 41; Can (Emer) of S'wark from 75. *28 Woodbourne Avenue, Streatham, SW16 1UU.* (01-769 5718)

BEEPUT, Clifford James. Codr Coll Barb 63. **d** and **p** 65 Trinid. C of Belmont 65-67; R of Chaguanas 67-81. *c/o St Thomas's Rectory, Chaguanas, Trinidad, W Indies.*

BEER, John Geoffrey. b 31. Univ of Syd BA 71, MA 79. St Jo Coll Morpeth 58. **d** 58 **p** 59 Armid. C of Tamworth 58-60; St Pet Cathl Armid 61; V of Emmaville 61-65; Dir Dept of Miss Dio N Queensld 65; C of Mundingburra 66; Chap Stuart Pris Townsville 66; Perm to Offic Dio Syd 67-81; Asst Master Syd Gr Sch from 71; Fell of St Paul's Coll Univ of Syd from 80; Hon C of St Jas City and Dio Syd from 81. *13 Edward Street, Marrickville, NSW, Australia 2204.* (569-3189)

BEER, John Stuart. b 44. Pemb Coll Ox BA (Th) 65, Wakef Pri 65, MA 70. Fitzw Coll Cam MA 78. Westcott Ho Cam 69. **d** 71 **p** 72 Ripon. C of St Jo Bapt, Knaresborough 71-74; Chap Fitzw Coll and New Hall Cam 74-80; Fell 78-80; L to Offic Dio Ely 74-80; P-in-c of Toft w Caldecote and Childerley Dio Ely 80-82; R from 82; P in c of Hardwick Dio Ely 80-81; R from 82. *Hardwick Rectory, Cambridge.*

BEER, Very Rev Kenneth Gordon. St Francis Th Coll Brisb 62. **d** 63 Bp Hudson for Brisb **p** 63 Brisb. C of St Barn Sunnybank Brisb 63-64; Sandgate 64-67; R of Winton 67-69; Keppel 69-70; C of St Clem Stafford, Brisb 71-73; Katherine 73-75; Perm to Offic Dio Bal 75-78; Dean of Bal from 79. *Box 89, Ballarat, Vic, Australia 3350.*

BEER, Michael Trevor. b 44. Chich Th Coll 66. **d** 69 **p** 70 St Alb. C of St Luke Leagrave 69-73; St Geo Cathl Kingstown St Vincent Dio Windw Is 73-74; C of Thorley w H Trin Bp's Stortford 74-80; V of Colney St Pet Dio St Alb from 80. *Colney St Peter Vicarage, St Albans, Herts.* (Bowmans Green 2122)

BEER, William Barclay. b 43. St Steph Ho Ox. **d** 71 **p** 72 Ex. C of St Marychurch, Torquay 71-75; V of Pattishall w Cold Higham 76-82; Northn St Benedict Dio Pet from 82. *c/o Registrar, 37 Priestgate, Peterborough, PE1 1JS.*

BEESLEY, Dennis Arthur. b 26. Ripon Hall Ox 69. **d** 70 **p** 71 Cov. C of Exhall Cov 70-72; Wyken 72-76; Team V of Caludon 76-81; V of Bp's Tachbrook Dio Cov from 81. *Vicarage, Mallory Road, Bishop's Tachbrook, Leamington Spa, Warws.* (Leamington Spa 26922)

BEESLEY, Ramon John. b 27. Magd Coll Ox BA 51, MA 55. Wycl Hall Ox 51. **d** 53 Ox **p** 56 Win. C of Gerrards Cross 53-54; Asst Chap Embley Sch Romsey 54-58; Perm to Offic Dio Win 54-58 and from 63; Dio Guildf 59-63; Asst Master Farnham Gr Sch 58-62; Gore Sch New Milton 63-69; Dep Hd Master Dibden Purlieu Sch 69-74; Hd Master Bellemoor Sch Southn from 74. *Wayfarers, Burley, Ringwood, Hants, BH24 4HW.* (Burley 2284)

BEESLEY, Symon Richard. b 27. Univ of Bris BA 53. Tyndale Hall Bris 47. **d** 53 **p** 54 Nor. C of Mile Cross 53-55; CCCS Chap at Kongwa Tang 55-58; Iringa Sch Tang 59-60; Sutton Valence Sch and L to Offic Dio Cant 60-64; V of H Trin Leic 64-72; Chap HM Pris Leic 64-69; Jt Gen Sec of CCCS 72-76; L to Offic Dio Lon 73-76; P-in-c of St Leonards-on-Sea Dio Chich 76-77; R 77-81; Dir of Th Educn by Ex Dio Mt Kenya E from 82. *Box 189, Embu, Kenya.*

BEESON, Christopher George. b 48. Univ of Man BSc 70. Qu Coll Birm 72. **d** 75 **p** 76 Man. C of Flixton 75-78; Newton Heath 78-80; R of St Jas Gorton Dio Man from 80. *St James's Rectory, Wellington Street, Gorton, Manchester, M18 8LJ.* (061-223 0708)

BEESON, Canon Trevor Randall. b 26. MA (Lambeth) 76. K Coll Lon and Warm AKC 50. **d** 51 Dur **p** 52 Jarrow for Dur. C of Leadgate 51-54; Norton 54-56; C-in-c of St Chad's Conv Distr Roseworth Stockton-on-Tees 56-59; Min 59-60; PC 60-65; Ed *Parish and People* 64-67; *New Christian* 65-70; C of St Martin-in-the-Fields Westmr 65-71; Hon Chap of St Bride Fleet Street Lon from 67; Eur Ed *The Christian Century* from 70; V of Ware 71-76; Can of Westmr from 76; Treas from 78; Select Pr Univ of Ox 78; R of St Marg Westmr from 81. *2 Little Cloister, Westminster Abbey, SW1P 3PL.*

BEETGE, David Albert. b48. St Paul's Th Coll Grahmstn 80. **d** 80 Bp Stanage for Johann. C of Germiston Dio Johann from 80. *PO Box 624, Germiston, S Africa 1400.*

BEETHAM, Anthony. b 32. Univ of Lon BSc 53. **d** 75 Ox **p** 76 Dorchester for Ox (APM). C of St Clem City and Dio Ox from 75. *44 Rose Hill, Oxford.* (Ox 770923)

BEETON, David Moore. b 39. St D Coll Lamp 58. Chich Th Coll 62. **d** 65 Barking for Chelmsf **p** 66 Chelmsf. C of St Edm K and Mart Forest Gate 65-71; V of St Aug Rush Green, Romford 71-81; Coggeshall w Markshall Dio Chelmsf from 81. *4 Church Green, Coggeshall, Colchester, Essex, CO6 1TU.* (Coggeshall 61234)

BEEVERS, Reginald. b 22. Univ of Dur BA 48. Qu Coll Birm 48. **d** 50 **p** 51 Dur. C of H Trin Stockton-on-Tees 50-52; Esh (in c of Langley Pk) 52-53; C-in-c of Conv Distr of Peterlee 53-57; V 57-60; Chap Worc R Infirm 60-63; Chap and Div Master Hulme Gr Sch Oldham 63-65; LPr Dio Man 63-65; Chap Guy's Hosp Lon 65-70; Liv Coll 70-81; C-in-c of Curry Mallet Dio B & W 81-82; R from 82; Hatch-Beauchamp w Beercrocombe Dio B & W 81-82; R from 82; West Hatch Dio B & W 81-82; R from 82. *Rectory, Hatch Beauchamp, Taunton, Somt.* (Hatch Beauchamp 220)

BEEVOR, Michael Branthwayt. b 24. Sarum Th Coll 64. **d** 66 Croydon for Cant **p** 66 Cant. C of Ramsgate 66-68; Alton 68-70; Christchurch w Mudeford 70-73; St Mary w St Clem Bournemouth 73-75; Hayling Dio Portsm from 75. *5 Culver Drive, Hayling Island, PO11 9LX.* (Hayling Is 2906)

BEGBIE, Graeme Ridley. b 46. Univ of Syd BA 74. Moore Coll Syd ThL 72. **d** and **p** 73 Syd. C of St Paul Wahroonga 73; Blacktown 74-77; R of Ashbury Dio Syd from 77. *44 Goodlet Street, Ashbury, NSW, Australia 2193.* (798-4019)

BEGBIE, Hugh McKay. b 49. Moore Coll Syd 74. **d** 76 **p** 77 Armid. C of Narrabri 76-79; V of Collarenebri Dio Armid from 79. *Vicarage, Collarenebri, NSW, Australia 2383.*

BEGBIE, Richard Alan. Moore Th Coll Syd ACT ThL 67. **d** 68 **p** 69 Syd. C of St Ives 68-71; C-in-c of Centennial Pk 71-72. *440 Moore Park Road, Centennial Park, NSW, Australia.*

✠ **BEGG, Right Rev Ian Forbes.** b 10. Univ of Aber MA 31, Hon DD 71. Westcott Ho Cam 32. **d** 33 **p** 34 Liv. C of St Paul Princes Pk 33-35; P-in-c of St Ninian, Seaton Aber 35-73; Can of Aber 65-73; Dean of Aber and Ork 69-73; Cons Ld Bp of Aber and Ork in St Andr Cathl Aber 1 Mar 73 by Bp of Glas (Primus); Bps of Brech, Arg Is, St Andr, Moray, Chich and Swan B; and Bps R N Russell and Easson; res 77. *430 King Street, Aberdeen, AB2 3BS.* (Aberdeen 632169)

BEGLEY, Frank William. b 18. St D Coll Lamp BA 48. **d** 49 **p** 50 Mon. C of Ch Ch Ebbw Vale 49-55; St Jo Div Richmond 55-57; Lulindi 57-58; P-in-c of Lindi 58-61; Chap at Lushoto Zanz 61-63; C-in-c of St Francis's Conv Distr Hammerfield 64-66; V of Enmore Dio Guy 66-70; C of Roath 70-74; V of St Dyfrig w St Samson Cardiff Dio Llan from 74. *48 Merches Gardens, Cardiff, CF1 7RE.* (Cardiff 23417)

BEGUMISA, Sitafano. Bp Tucker Coll Mukono. **d** 53 **p** 56 Ugan. P Dio Ugan 53-60; Dio Ankole-K 60-67; Dio Ank from 67. *Box 14, Mbarara, Ankole, Uganda.*

BEHRENS, Andrew James. b 50. AKC 73. St Aug Coll Cant 73. **d** 74 Roch **p** 75 Tonbridge for Roch. C of St Mary Swanley 74-76; Crayford 76-79; St Leon & St Jude Doncaster Dio Sheff from 79. *65a Norman Crescent, Sunnyfields, Doncaster, DN5 8RX.* (Doncaster 781013)

BEIAWA, Philip. b 35. St Aid Coll Dogura. **d** 65 **p** 67 New Guinea. P Dio Papua. *Box 213, Port Moresby, New Guinea.*

BEIERS, John Leonard. b 37. Univ of Queensld BEng 60, PhD 66. St Francis Coll Brisb ACT ThL 69. **d** 69 **p** 70 Brisb. C of Auchenflower 69-70; Ch Ch Bundaberg 70-72; V of Ch Ch St Geo 72-75; P-in-c of Cunnamulla 77-78; Perm to Offic Dio Brisb 78-81; R of Port Adel Dio Adel from 81. *1 Greenfield Avenue, West Lakes, Shores, S Australia 5020.*

BEKUNDA, Solomon. Bp Tucker Coll Mukono 62. **d** 62 **p** 63 Ankole-K. P Dio Ankole-K 62-67; Dio Kig from 67. *PO Box 3, Kabale, Uganda.*

BELBEN, Kenneth Frank. b 30. TD 77. St Jo Coll Dur 51. **d** 55 **p** 56 Chelmsf. C of Plaistow 55-58; C of Chadwell Heath 58-60; Min of St Mark's Eccles Distr Marks Gate Chadwell Heath 60-64; V of Gt and L Maplestead (w Gestingthorpe from 76) Dio Chelmsf 64-76; R (w Gestingthorpe) from 76; CF (TA) from 65; C-in-c of Gestingthorpe 75-76; Chap O of St John of Jer from 77. *Great Maplestead Vicarage, Halstead, Essex, CO9 2RG.* (Hedingham 60294)

BELCHER, David John. b 44. Ch Ch Ox BA 65, MA 69. Cudd Coll 68. **d** 70 **p** 71 Dur. C of St Mary Gateshead 70-73; St Pet Stockton 73-76; L to Offic Dio Lich 76-81; Warden of St George's Ho Wolverhampton 78-81; P-in-c of Ch Ch W Bromwich Dio Lich from 81. *Christ Church Vicarage, West Bromwich, W Midl, B70 8QP.* (021-553 3538)

BELCHER, Derek George. b 50. Chich Th Coll 74. **d** 77 **p** 78 Llan. C of Newton Nottage 77-81; St Pet and St Paul Llandaff Dio Llan from 81. *2 White House, The Cathedral Green, Llandaff, Cardiff, CF5 2EB.* (Cardiff 552313)

BELCHER, Frederick William. b 30. Kelham Th Coll 45. Chich Th Coll 53. **d** 54 **p** 55 S'wark. C of Catford 54-58; St Mich AA Plumstead 58-59; Min of Conv Distr of William Temple Ch Abbey Wood 59-62; V of St Luke Eltham 62-64; Publ Pr Dio S'wark 65-81. *52 Long Street, Cerne Abbas, Dorset.* (Cerne Abbas 555)

BELDEN, David Leon. Bp's Univ Lennox LST 67. **d** 68 **p**

69 Queb. I of Malbay 68-72; Magdalen Is 72-73; I in Team Ministry of Gtr Coaticook 73-74; in Amer Ch 75-78; C of St Jo Evang City and Dio Montr from 78. *137 President Kennedy Avenue, Montreal, PQ, Canada.* (514-288 4428)

BELFAST, Dean of. *See* Crooks, Very Rev Samuel Bennett.

BELFORD, Canon William James. Bp's Univ Lennox BA 36. **d** 36 **p** 37 Queb. C of Magdalen I 36-37; Grindstone 38-41; Miss at Hatley 41-46; I of Peninsula PQ 46; Chap Ashbury Coll Ott 46-52; R of Fitzroy Harbour 52-58; Bell's Corners 58-66; Temiskaming 66-68; Hull Ott 68-76; Can of Ott Cathl 70-77; Hon Can from 77. *Fitzroy Harbour, Ont., Canada.*

BELHAM, John Edward. b 42. AKC and BSc 65. PhD (Lon) 70. Oak Hill Th Coll 69. **d** 72 Ches **p** 73 Stockport for Ches. C of St Andr Cheadle Hulme 72-75; Cheadle Dio Ches from 75. *6 Carrs Road, Cheadle, Chesh, SK8 2EE.*

BELHAM, Michael. b 23. BSc(Eng) Lon 50. **d** 67 **p** 68 Willesden for Lon. C of St Edm Northwood Hills Pinner 67-69; Hendon 69-73; V of H Trin Tottenham 73-78; Hillingdon Dio Lon from 78. *Hillingdon Vicarage, Royal Lane, Uxbridge, Middx, UB8 3QR.* (Uxbridge 33932)

BELIMBI, Likuta. b 31. **d** 80 Boga-Z. d Dio Boga-Z. *E.A.Z. Longba, BP 154, Bunia, Zaire.*

BELING, David Gibson. b 30. Fitzw Ho Cam BA 54, MA 58. **d** 56 **p** 57 Sarum. C of Radipole 56-59; Broadwater (in c of St Steph) 59-61; R of W Knighton w Broadmayne 61-73; V of St Paul Preston Dio Ex from 73. *St Paul's Vicarage, Preston, Paignton, Devon.* (Paignton 522872)

BELIQA, Harry Palmer. St Pet Coll Siota. **d** 56 **p** 61 Melan. P Dio Melan 56-74. *Toga, Torres Islands, New Hebrides.*

BELIZE, Lord Bishop of. *See* McMillan, Right Rev Keith Alphonso.

BELIZE, Dean of. (Vacant)

BELL, Adrian Christopher. b 48. AKC 70. St Aug Coll Cant 70. **d** 71 **p** 72 Sheff. C of St Aidan w St Luke Sheff 71-74; Willesborough w Hinxhill 74-78; P-in-c of Hollingbourne Dio Cant from 78; Wormshill 78; Leeds w Broomfield Dio Cant from 79. *Hollingbourne Vicarage, Maidstone, Kent.* (Hollingbourne 243)

BELL, Alan John. b 47. Univ of Liv BA (2nd cl Econ) 68. Ridley Hall Cam 69. **d** 72 Warrington for Liv **p** 73 Liv. C of Speke 72-77; P-in-c of St Mary Halewood 77-81; R of St Mary Wavertree Dio Liv from 81. *1 South Drive, Wavertree, Liverpool, L15 8JJ.* (051-722 1253)

BELL, Alfred. St Jo Coll Manit STh 56. **d** 50 **p** 52 Rupld. I of Emerson 51-56; R of Innisfail 56-63; St Andr Calg 63-72; Sec and Treas Dio Calg 72-74; Hon Can of Calg 73-75; R of Quamichan 74-79; Perm to Offic Dio BC from 79. *10383 Island Highway, RR1, Chemainus, BC, Canada.*

BELL, Andrew John. Univ of NSW BEng 54. St Francis Th Coll Brisb ACT ThL 57. **d** 58 **p** 59 N Queensld. C of Cairns 58-62; Chap CMF from 59; I of Gulliver Townsville 62-73; C in Dept of Chaps Dio Melb from 73; Chap R Melb Hosp from 80. *6 Clota Avenue, Box Hill, Vic, Australia 3128.* (03-88 4336)

BELL, Anthony Lawson. b 47. AKC 72. St Aug Coll Cant 71. **d** 72 **p** 73 Dur. C of Peterlee Dio Dur from 72. *c/o The Vicarage, Manor Way, Peterlee, Co Durham.*

BELL, Antony Fancourt. b 28. Magd Coll Ox 3rd cl Cl Mods 49, BA (2nd cl Lit Hum) 51, MA 58. Wells Th Coll 54. **d** 56 **p** 57 S'wark. C of Clapham 56-59; Gillingham Dorset 59-61; R of Stanway Dio Chelmsf from 61; RD of Dedham and Tey from 81. *Stanway Rectory, Colchester, Essex.* (Colchester 210407)

BELL, Arthur Francis. Univ of Leeds BA 39. Bps' Coll Cheshunt 40. **d** 41 **p** 42 St Alb. C of H Trin Bedford 41-43; Chesterfield 43-45; Barrow Hill (in c of St Francis Hollingwood) 45-46; Westbury-on-Trym 46-48; H Nativity Knowle 48-50; R of Priston 50-61; V of Englishcombe 55-61; R of Charlcombe Dio B & W from 61. *Charlcombe Rectory, Bath, Avon, BA1 8DR.* (Bath 310870)

BELL, Arthur James. b 33. Ch Coll Cam BA (3rd cl Archaeol and Anthrop Trip pt i) 55, 3rd cl Th Trip pt ii 57, MA 60. Coll of Resurr Mirfield 57. **d** 59 Bp Dunlop for Linc **p** 60 Linc. C of New Cleethorpes 59-63; Upperby Carl 63-66; I of Wabasca Dio Athab 67-72 and from 77; Perm to Offic Dio Ely 73-75; L to Offic Dio Carl 75-76. *Rectory, Wabasca, Alta, TOG 2KO, Canada.* (403-891 3853)

BELL, Aubrey Wilbur. Univ of BC BA 51. Angl Th Coll BC 67. **d** 67 **p** 68 New Westmr. C-in-c of Squamish w Woodfibre 67-69; I of Pemberton 69-71; R of Mission 71-75; Thedford 75-79; St John Leamington Dio Hur from 79. *Box 142, Leamington, Ont, Canada.*

BELL, Bryan Bland. b 07. Wadh Coll Ox BA 30. Tyndale Hall Bris 38. **d** 40 **p** 41 Chelmsf. C of Braintree 40-42; St Mark New Milverton 42-44; CF (EC) 44-46; R of Wickhambreaux w Stodmarsh 46-50; PC of Mile Cross 50-54; R of Barnwell and of Stoke-Doyle 54-60; Poole 60-68; Nedging w Naughton 68-72; Perm to Offic Dio Ex 73-78; and from 81; P-in-c of Chawleigh w Cheldon 78-81. *32 South Street, Hatherleigh, Devon.*

BELL, Charles Melvyn Guy. Hur Coll STh 59. **d** 59 **p** 60 Edmon. I of Hardisty 59-61; R of Jasper 61-65; L to Offic Dio Carib 77-78; I of Watson Lake Dio Yukon from 78. *Box 15, Watson Lake, Yukon, Canada Y0A 1C0.*

BELL, Charles William. b 43. Trin Coll Dub BA 66, MA 69. **d** 67 **p** 68 Down. C of Newtownards 67-70; Larne and Inver 70-74; Ballymena w Ballyclug Dio Connor from 74. *34 Dunvale, Dunclug, Ballymena, Co Antrim, BT43 6NX, N Ireland.* (Ballymena 3543)

BELL, Cyril John. b 22. Univ Coll Hull BA (Lon) 48. Wycl Hall Ox 52. **d** 53 **p** 54 Dur. C of St Pet w St Cuthb Monkwearmouth 53-56; Ch of S India 56-60; L to Offic at Westlands Dio Lich 66-71; L to Offic Dio Ches from 71; Asst Master Marple Hall Sch from 71. *1 Churchill Crescent, Marple, Stockport, Chesh, SK6 6HL.*

BELL, David Owain. b 49. Univ of Dur BA (Hist) 69. Univ of Nott Dipl Th 70. Fitzw Coll Cam BA 2nd cl Th Trip pt iii 72, MA 80. Westcott Ho Cam 70. **d** 72 **p** 73 Dur. C of Houghton-le-Spring 72-76; St Mary Virg Norton 76-78; P-in-c of St Clem City and Dio Worc from 78. *St Clement's Rectory, Laugherne Road, Worcester.* (Worcester 422675)

BELL, Derek Arthur. b 35. K Coll Lon and Warm BD and AKC 61. **d** 62 **p** 63 Blackb. C of H Trin S Shore Blackpool 62-66; Asst Master Arnold Sch Blackpool from 66. *427 Lytham Road, South Shore, Blackpool, Lancs.* (Blackpool 43616)

BELL, Donald John. b 50. Sarum Wells Th Coll 73. **d** 76 **p** 77 Dur. C of Jarrow 76-80; St Cuthb Darlington Dio Dur from 80. *65 Carmel Road South, Darlington.* (Darlington 62568)

BELL, Edwin Lucius Wyndham. b 19. Worc Coll Ox BA (3rd cl Mod Hist) 41, MA 45. Westcott Ho Cam 41. **d** 43 **p** 44 Cant. C of St Jo Bapt Croydon (in c of St Geo Waddon from 47) 43-50; CF 50-54; V of Bapchild w Tonge (and Rodmersham from 57) 54-63; C-in-c of Murston 54-57; V of St Paul Maidstone 63-78; P-in-c of Nonington w Barfreystone Dio Cant from 78; Wymonswold Dio Cant from 78. *Nonington Vicarage, Dover, Kent, CT15 4JT.* (Nonington 840271)

BELL, Edwin Ray. b 23. Clifton Th Coll 60. **d** 62 **p** 63 Heref. C of Madely 62-65; V of Rashcliffe 65-76; Holmbridge Dio Wakef from 76. *Holmbridge Vicarage, Huddersfield, W Yorks, HD7 1NH.* (Holmfirth 3559)

BELL, Francis William Albert. b 28. Trin Coll Dub BA 52, MA and BD 57. **d** 53 **p** 54 Connor. C of St Mich Belf 53-55; All SS Belf 55-61; St Jude Ballynafeigh 61-63; C-in-c of Ballyhalbert 63-71; C-in-c of Ardkeen 67-71; I of Ballyhalbert w Ardkeen Dio Down from 71; RD of Ards from 73. *187 Main Road, Portavogie, Co Down, N Ireland.*

BELL, Frank Cecil. **d** and **p** 61 Ont. I of Wolfe I 61-63; Marysburg w Milford 63-65; Rideau 65-71; R of Deseronto (Quinte from 72) 71-75; Barriefield w Pittsburgh 75-77; Hosp Chap Kingston Dio Ont from 77. *227 Victoria Street, Kingston, Ont, Canada.*

BELL, Godfrey Bryan. b 44. Oak Hill Coll 72. **d** 75 **p** 76 Lich. C of Penn Fields 75-79; R of Dolton and of Iddesleigh w Dowland and of Monkokehampton Dio Ex from 79. *Dolton Rectory, Winkleigh, Devon.* (Dolton 264)

BELL, Graham Dennis Robert. b 42. Univ of Lon BSc (2nd cl) and AKC 63. Univ of Nottm MTh 73. Tyndale Hall Bris 65. **d** 68 **p** 69 Southw. C of Stapleford 68-71; Barton Seagrave w Warkton 71-76; Asst Master Redenhall C of E Sch Harleston 76-78; Perm to Offic Dio Nor from 76; Asst Master Abp Sancroft High Sch from 78. *10 Willow Walk, Harleston, Norf.* (Harleston 853257)

BELL, Grant Melville. b 53. Moore Th Coll Syd BTh 80. **d** 80 Armid. C of S Tamworth Dio Armid from 80. *48 Vera Street, South Tamworth, NSW, Australia 2340.*

BELL, Jack Gorman. b 23. BSc (Lon) 48. Oak Hill Th Coll 51. **d** 53 Lancaster for Blackb **p** 54 Blackb. C of Ch Ch Blackpool 53-55; Ch Ch Chadderton 55-59; R of St Jerome w St Silas Ardwick Man 59-69; V of Mosley Common Dio Man from 69. *St John's Vicarage, Mosley Common Road, Worsley, Manchester, M28 4AN.* (061-790 2957)

BELL, James. b 50. Wycl Coll Tor 79. **d** 80 Bp JCM Clarke for Arctic **p** 81 Arctic. P-in-c of Pond Inlet Dio Arctic from 80. *St Timothy's Anglican Mission, Pond Inlet, NWT X0A 0S0. Canada.*

BELL, James Arthur Herbert. b 1889. MC 19. Ch Coll Cam BA (2nd cl Th Trip pts i and ii) 11, MA 15. **d** 13 **p** 14 Linc. C of Boston 13-17; Mkt Deeping 17-18; TCF 18-19; C of St Pet-in-Eastgate Linc 19-24; Ed Linc Dio Cal 19-21; Vice-Prin Wells Th Coll 24-31; R of Gumley 31-33; V of Thriplow 33-36; Babraham 37-40; R of Goathurst 40-45; C of All SS Weston-super-Mare 45-47; V of Nempnett Thrubwell 47-50; R of Butcombe 47-50; V of Matterdale 50-55; L to

Offic Dio Carl from 55. *St John's Home, St Mary's Road, Oxford, OX4 1QE.* (OX 48208)

BELL, James Harold. b 50. St Jo Coll Dur BA (Mod Hist) 72. St Pet Coll Ox BA (Th) 74, MA 78. Wycl Hall Ox 72. **d** 75 Ox **p** 76 Buckingham for Ox. C of St Mich Ox 75-76; Chap and Lect Brasenose Coll Ox from 76; Fell from 79. *Brasenose College, Oxford.* (Oxford 48641)

BELL, James Henry Boyd. *See* Boyd-Bell, Henry James.

BELL, James Samuel. b 40. MBE (Civil) 71. St Chad's Coll Dur BA Th) 69. Coll of Resurr Mirfield 71. **d** 72 **p** 73 S'wark. C of St Phil Lambeth 72-74; North Lambeth 74; P-in-c of St Ninian Invergordon 74-77; Brora 74-77; Dornoch 74-77; V of H Spirit Bretton City and Dio Pet from 77; P-in-c of Marholm Dio Pet from 82. *Vicarage, Westhawe, Bretton, Peterborough, PE3 8BA.* (0733 264418)

BELL, Jeffrey William. b 37. Sarum Th Coll 60. **d** 63 **p** 64 Pet. C of St Matt Northn 63-66; Portishead 66-68; Digswell 68-72; V of St Jude Pet 72-79; Buckingham Dio Ox from 79. *Vicarage, Church Street, Buckingham, MK18 1BY.* (Buckingham 3178)

BELL, Very Rev John. MM 17. St Jo Th Coll Perth. **d** 26 **p** 28 Perth. C of Ch Ch Claremont 26-29; R of S Perth 29-32; Claremont 33-34; Can of St Geo Cathl Perth 38-44; Org Sec (for NSW) ABM 43-48; Dean of Armid 46-48; Exam Chap to Bp of Armid 46-48; R of Oddington w Adlestrop 48-52; Dean and R of St Geo Cathl Perth 53-59; Dean (Emer) from 59; L to Offic Dio Perth 59-73. *182 Great Eastern Highway, Greenmount, W Australia.*

BELL, Canon John Alexander Monteith. Trin Coll Tor BA 24. **d** 26 **p** 27 Niag. C of Guelph 26-29; Hd Master Appleby Coll Oakville Ont 29-69; Hon Can of Niag 55-72; Can (Emer) from 72. *302 Trafalgar Road, Oakville, Ont., Canada.*

BELL, John Alfred Collingwood. Fitzw Coll Cam BA 47, MA 52. St Jo Coll Dur 49. **d** 51 Dur **p** 52 Jarrow for Dur. C of Norton Co Dur 51-55; Chap Warlingham Pk Hosp 55-58; Chap and Asst Master Sutton Valence Sch 59-61; L to Offic Dio Cant 59-61; Perm to Offic Dio Roch 67-74; CF (TA) from 71; C of Beverley Minster 74-77; Team V of Thornaby-on-Tees 77-78; C of Scalby w Ravenscar 78-79; All SS w St Pet Luton 79-80; Perm to Offic Dio York 80-81; C of N & S Hykeham (in c of St Hugh) Dio Linc from 81. *45 Harewood Crescent, North Hykeham, Lincoln, LN6 8JG.* (0522 681480)

BELL, John Christopher. b 33. Trin Coll Dub BA 56. **d** 56 Down. C of Newtownards 56-59; Willowfield 59-62; I of Carrowdore 62-70; Drumbo Dio Down from 70; RD of Hillsborough from 81. *Drumbo Rectory, Ballylesson, Belfast.* (Drumbo 225)

BELL, John Edward. b 34. Cranmer Hall Dur. **d** 67 **p** 68 Carl. C of St Elisabeth Harraby Carl 67-70; C of Dalton-in-Furness 70-72; V of Pennington 72-75; St Herbert Currock w St Steph Carl Dio Carl from 75. *St Herbert's Vicarage, Blackwell Road, Currock, Carlisle, CA2 4RA.* (Carl 23375)

BELL, John Holmes. b 50. Counc for Nat Acad Awards BA 80. Oak Hill Coll 77. **d** 80 **p** 81 Leic. C of St Phil City and Dio Leic from 80. *22 Trueway Road, Leicester, LE5 5UF.*

BELL, Joseph William. b 30. Pemb Coll Cam 2nd cl Engl Trip pt i 52, BA (2nd cl Engl Trip pt ii) 53, MA 57. St Cath S Ox BA (by incorp) 53. Wycl Hall Ox 53. **d** 55 **p** 56 Liv. C of Blundellsands 55-58; CF 58-68 and from 70; V of Roby 68-70. *c/o Ministry of Defence, Bagshot Park, Bagshot, Surrey, GU19 5PL.*

BELL, Karl Edwin. b 33. Univ of Minnesota BA 56. Seabury W Th Sem 61. **d** 61 Bp HH Kellogg **p** 62 Bp MacNairy. [f in Amer Ch] R of Caracas 71-75. *Apartado 61, 116 del Este, Caracas, Venezuela.*

BELL, Kenneth Murray. b 30. Sarum Wells Th Coll 75. **d** 74 S Malawi **p** 76 Basingstoke for Win. Perm to Offic Dio Guildf 74-76; C of Hartley Wintney 76-80; V of Fair Oak Dio Win from 80. *Fair Oak Vicarage, Eastleigh, Hants.* (Southampton 692238)

BELL, Lendon. b 02. Pemb Coll Cam 2nd cl Hist Trip pt i 23, BA (2nd cl Hist Trip pt ii) 24, MA 28, Linc Th Coll 31. **d** 32 **p** 33 Ox. C of Farnham Royal 32-35; Perm to Offic at St Cuthb Portsm 35-36; Hendon (in c of Holders Hill) 36-40; C 37-40; V of Bitton 40-47; Box (w Hazlebury from 48) 47-54; Rogate 54-62; R of Terwick 54-62. *2 Russell Way, Petersfield, Hants.*

BELL, Lionel Borradaile. Late Jun Patteson Stud of Selw Coll Cam BA 20, MA 23. Cudd Coll. **d** 22 **p** 23 Ox. C of High Wycombe 22-25; V of Plumtree S Rhod 25-30; R of Gwelo 30-34; Chap of Sherborne Sch 34-46; PC of Derry Hill Wilts 46-49; R of Marandellas 50-54; Chap Ruzawi Sch and LPr Dio Mashon 54-57. *Westways, Marandellas, Rhodesia.*

BELL, Malcolm Francis. St Francis Coll Brisb 65. **d** 68 Brisb. C of St Luke Toowoomba 68-69; Perm to Offic Dio Brisb 69-70; C of St Pet W End City and Dio Brisb from 71. *c/o St Peter's Vicarage, West End, Brisbane, Australia.*

BELL, Nicholas Philip Johnson. b 46. St Jo Coll Dur BSc 69. Univ of Nottm Dipl Th 72. St Jo Coll Nottm 70. **d** 73 Man **p** 74 Hulme for Man. C of Chadderton 73-77; H Trin Frogmore (in c of St Luke Bricket Wood) 77-81; V of Bricket Wood Dio St Alb from 81. *20 West Riding, Bricket Wood, St Albans, Herts, AL2 3QP.* (Garston 76401)

BELL, Philip Harold. b 19. Univ of Leeds BA 45. Coll of Resurr Mirfield 38. **d** 44 Carl. **p** 45 Penrith for Carl. C of St Matt Barrow-F 44-49; St John Southend Lewisham (in c of St Barn Downham) 50-56; Chap Tristan da Cunha 56-61; R of Crawley w Littleton 61-72; V of Holdenhurst w Throop 72-78; P-in-c of Hilperton w Whaddon Dio Sarum from 78; Staverton Dio Sarum from 78. *Hilperton Rectory, Trowbridge, Wilts, BA14 7RL.* (Trowbridge 2804)

BELL, Reginald Leslie. b 13. Trin Coll Bris 72. **d** 74 **p** 75 Bris. C of Stoke Bishop 74-75; Horfield 75-77; Stoke Bishop Dio Bris from 78. *14 Pitch and Pay Lane, Sneyd Park, Avon.* (Bristol 681510)

BELL, Richard Alexander. b 14. St Pet Hall Ox BA 37, MA 42. Westcott Ho Cam 37. **d** and **p** 39 Lon. C of Ch Ch Hampstead 39-42; Bp Wearmouth 42-49; R of Middleton St Geo 49-58; Clayton w Keymer 58-70; V of Amberley w N Stoke 70-75; CMS Chap Tel Aviv 76-79; Herzliya Dio Jer from 79. *15 Hacongress Street, Herzliyya Pituach, Israel.* (052-70530)

BELL, Robert Clarke. b 30. Roch Th Coll 63. **d** 65 **p** 66 Ripon. C of All SS w St Alb Leeds 65-67; Claxby w Normanby-le-Wold Linc 67-69; V of St Leon Newark 69-71; Gosberton Clough 71-74; C-in-c of Quadring 73-74; Dioc Chap to the Deaf Dio Linc from 75. *2 Pottergate, Lincoln, LN2 1PH.*

BELL, Robert Mason. b 35. Lon Coll of Div 66. **d** 68 **p** 69 Chich. C of St Andr Burgess Hill 68-78; R of St Jo Bapt-sub-Castro Lewes Dio Chich from 78. *1 The Avenue, Lewes, East Sussex, BN7 1BA.* (Lewes 3080)

BELL, Robert William. b 1899. Univ of Dur 29. Lich Th Coll 28. **d** 31 **p** 33 Lich. C of St Paul Newc L 31-33; Stoke-on-Trent (in c of St Paul Mt Pleasant) 33-36; V of Meir 36-46; Chap RAFVR 41-46; V of Ocker Hill 46-57; R of Lyons 57-72. *1 Woodside Court, Forest Hall, Newcastle-upon-Tyne 12.*

BELL, Samuel James. Univ of Sask BA 45. Em Coll Sktn. LTh (w distinc) 45. **d** 36 Sask for Athab **p** 37 Athab. Miss at Hines Creek 36-41; V of Manville 41-46; Wetaskiwin 46-48; Miss at Fort Simpson 48-53; C-in-c of Derrylane 53-54; R of Hanover 54-57; Timmins 57-61; Dean of Moos 57-61; Exam Chap to Bp of Moos 60-61; Miss at Hay River 61-63; I of Walter's Falls 63-66; R of Kirkton 66-69; Chesley 69-75; P-in-c of Wheatley 76-78; R of St Patr Mt Pleasant Dio Trinid from 81. *Rectory, Mt Pleasant, Tobago, W Indies.*

BELL, Stuart Rodney. b 46. Univ of Ex BA (2nd cl Th) 67. Tyndale Hall Bris 69. **d** 71 **p** 72 St D. C of Henfynyw 71-74; V of Llangeler 74-80; V of Henfynyw w Aberaeron and Llanddewi Aberarth Dio St D from 81. *Vicarage, Aberaeron, Dyfed.* (Aberaeron 570433)

BELL, Canon Thomas Donald. b 15. St Jo Coll Dur BA (3rd cl Th) 42. **d** 42 **p** 43 Dur. C of St Andr Bp Auckland 42-50; V of St Luke Hartlepool 50-80; Hon Can of Dur from 78. *49 Westlands Road, Darlington, Co Durham, DL3 9JH.* (Darlington 51556)

BELL, Thomas Ronald. **d** 66 **p** 67 Leic. C of Ratby w Groby 66-70; V of St Pet Mountsorrel Dio Leic from 70. *St Peter's Vicarage, Mountsorrel, Loughborough, Leics.*

BELL, Vernon Schuster. St Jo Coll Manit 12. **d** 15 **p** 16 Rupld. C of Moore Park 15-16; I of Glenboro w Stockton 16-17; Elkhorn 17-20; C of St Paul Preston Lancs 21-24; Thorney 24-26; Skegness 29; R of Salmonby 29-35; PC of Chapel St Leon 35-58. *Norwood Road, Skegness, Lincs.*

BELL, Vicars Walker. b 04. MBE 64. Ho of Resurr Mirfield 63. **d** and **p** 64 Ex. C of Tavistock w Gulworthy 64-66; V of Clawton 66-77; R of Tetcott w Luffincott 66-77; Perm to Offic Dio Ex from 77. *20 Watts Road, Tavistock, Devon.* (Tavistock 4820)

BELL-BOOTH, William Louis. St Jo Coll Auckld LTh 43. **d** 42 **p** 43 Wel. C of Ch Ch Wanganui 42-47; V of Raetihi 47-51; Lyall Bay Wel 51-63; Taihape 63-75; L to Offic Dio Waik from 76. *9 Waitahanui Avenue, Taupo, NZ.*

BELL-RICHARDS, Douglas Maurice. b 23. St Steph Ho Ox 59. **d** 61 Glouc **p** 62 Tewkesbury for Glouc. C of Chipping Campden 61-62; Thornbury Glos 62-67; R of Dymock w Donnington 67-75; V of Fairford Dio Glouc from 75. *Vicarage, Fairford, Glos, GL7 4BB.* (Fairford 712467)

BELLAMY, Charles Gordon. b 15. Late Scho of St Chad's Coll Dur Bp Robertson Div Pri 41. BA 42. Knutsford Ordin Test Sch Hawarden 36. **d** 42 **p** 43 Newc T. C of Howdon Panns 42-44; St Anthony Newc T 44-46; Horton 45-50; Seghill 50-56; V of St Matt Habergham Eaves Burnley 56-67; Surr 65-67; V of Overton 67-80; Hon C of St Mary Monkseaton Dio Newc T from 80. *60 Davison Avenue, Whitley Bay, T & W, NE26 1SH.* (0632-513355)

BELLAMY, Mervyn Roger Hunter. St Mich AA Llan Dipl Th 81. **d** 81 Doncaster for Sheff. C of Frecheville w Hackenthorpe Dio Sheff from 81. *46 Smalldale Road, Sheffield, S12 47B.*

BELLAMY, Peter Charles William. b 38. K Coll Lon and Warm AKC 61. Birm Univ MA 70, PhD 79. **d** 62 **p** 63 Derby. C of Allestree 62-65; Chap All SS Hosp Birm 65-73; Lect and Chap St Pet Coll Birm 73-78; Qu Eliz Med Centre Birm from 78. *Queen Elizabeth Medical Centre, Birmingham, B15 2TH.*

BELLAMY, William John. Mem Univ Newfld BA 63. Qu Coll Newfld LTh 64. **d** 64 **p** 65 Newfld. C of Channel 64-68; I of Labrador Newfld 68-73; Perm to Offic Dio Newfld 73-78; I of Portugal Cove Dio E Newfld from 78. *Box 100, Portugal Cove, Newfoundland, Canada.*

BELLE, Coswyn Vincent Selwyn. b 15. ACP 46. **d** 75 **p** 76 Barb. C of St Mary I and Dio Barb from 75; Dioc Sec Dio Barb from 76. *The Palms, Cheapside, Bridgetown, Barbados, WI.*

BELLENES, Peter Charles. b 49. Linc Th Coll 79. **d** 81 Wakef. C of Penistone Dio Wakef from 81. *38 Park Avenue, Penistone, S Yorks, S30 6DN*

BELLINGER, Denys Gordon. b 29. Univ of Sheff BA 49. Westcott Ho Cam 51. **d** 53 **p** 54 Blackb. C of Ribbleton 53-56; Lancaster 56-58; V of H Trin Colne 58-68; Scotforth Dio Blackb from 68. *St Paul's Vicarage, Scotforth Road, Lancaster.* (Lancaster 32106)

BELLINGHAM, Charles Eric William. Univ of Syd BA (3rd cl Gk) 26, MA (1st cl Psychol) 28. Ridley Hall Cam. **d** 30 **p** 31 Chelmsf. C of W Ham 30-32; Gordon NSW 32-33; CMS Miss Hyderabad 33-42; Chap RAF 42-46; Chap St Geo Sch Hyderabad 46-60; Prin 53-60; Ch of S India 47-61; L to Offic Dio Syd 61-62 and from 74; C-in-c of St Pet E Lindfield 62-64; R of Greenwich 64-74; Perm to Offic Dio Newc from 74. *24 Shelley Beach Road, Empire Bay, NSW, Australia 2256.*

BELLINGHAM, John Kingston. b 23. **d** 62 Bp McKenzie for Wel **p** 63 Wel. C of Wainuiomata 62-63; St Mark Wel 64-65; V of Opotiki 65-70; Chap Tongariro Pris and Perm to Offic Dio Wai 70-72; V of Foxton 72-74; Chap Miss to Seamen Port of Lon 74-76; V of NE Valley Dio Dun from 76. *15 Gillespie Street, Dunedin, NZ.* (Dunedin 738-027)

BELLO, Gabriel Esezobo. **d** 58 **p** 59 Lagos. P Dio Lagos. *St Jude's, Odi-Olowo, Nigeria.*

BELMER, Frederick Roy. b 13. Univ of Cant NZ MA 40. **d** 78 **p** 79 Dun. Hon C of St Paul's Cathl Ch Dun 78-80; Offg Min Dio Wai from 80. *39 College Road, Edgecumbe, NZ.*

BELMONTES, Mervyn Lancelot. Codr Coll Barb Dipl Th 74. **d** 74 **p** 75 Trinid. C of H Trin Cathl Port of Spain Dio Trinid from 74. *30a Abercromby Street, Port of Spain, Trinidad.*

BELO, Michael Adebayo. Im Coll Ibad. **d** 69 Ekiti. d Dio Ekiti from 69. *St Paul's Vicarage, Oraye, Ise-Ekiti, Nigeria.*

BELOE, Archibald John Martin. b 15. Qu Coll Cam BA 37, MA 41. Egerton Hall Man 37. **d** 39 **p** 40 Man. C of St Clem Spotland 39-42; St Jas Gorton 42-45; R of St Mary Beswick 45-49; V of Oakington 49-61; R of Hilgay 61-79; V of St Mary Fordham 71-79; *c/o Hilgay Rectory, Downham Market, Norf, PE38 0JL.* (036 66293)

BELOE, Robert Francis. b 39. Trin Coll Dub. Sarum Th Coll. **d** 65 Nor **p** 71 Lon. C of St Francis Conv Distr Heartsease Sprowston 65-66; St Mary w St Jo Evang Edmonton 68-70; Ch Ch w St Paul St Marylebone Lon 70-74; C-in-c of Wicken Dio Ely 74-76; V from 76. *Wicken Vicarage, Ely, Cambs.* (Ely 243)

BELU, Collin Colben Kolisile. b 37. St Bede's Coll Umtata 78. **d** 80 **p** 81 Grahmstn. C of St Matt Keiskammahoek Dio Grahmstn from 80. *St Matthew's Mission, PO Matthews 5680, CP, S Africa.*

BELWAY, Donald Franklyn. Trin Coll Tor BA 49, LTh 52, STB 53. **d** 52 Ont **p** 53 New Westmr. C of St Jas Vanc 53-55; I of Agassiz 55-59; R of St Bart Tor 59-77; on leave 77-78; Hon C of Markham 78-79; R of Colborne and Grafton Dio Tor from 79. *Trinity Church, King Street, Colborne, Ont, Canada.*

BEMAN, Donald Oliver. b 37. Univ of Southn BA 58. Coll of Resurr Mirfield 58. **d** 60 Portsm **p** 65 Win. C of Forton 60-61; Hon C of Hound w Netley Abbey 64-68; LPr Dio Win from 69. *Flat 28, 11 Denzil Avenue, Southampton.*

BEMBRIDGE, Harold. b 18. **d** 56 **p** 57 Brech. C of St Paul's Cathl Dundee 56-58; Prec 58-59; R of St Ternan Banchory 59-64; St Luke Miles Platting Man 64-72; C of Newchurch-in-Rossendale 72-78; C-in-c of Ringley 78-80; C of Reddish Dio Man from 80. *109 Blackbrook Road, Heaton Chapel, Stockport, SK4 5PB.* (061-442 8432)

BENCE, Canon Graham Edwin. b 16. BA (3rd cl Hist) (Lon) 54. Sarum Th Coll 64. **d** 65 Barking for Chelmsf **p** 66 Chelmsf. C of St Jas Clacton-on-Sea 65-68; R of Barlborough Dio Derby from 68; RD of Bolsover (and Staveley from 73) 70-78; Hon Can of Derby from 78. *Barlborough Rectory, Chesterfield, Derbys.* (Chesterfield 810401)

BENCE, Norman Murray. b 34. **d** 63 Win **p** 64 Southn for Win. C of Eling 63-65; Hampton Melb 66; Publ Pr Dio Win 67-74; Chap Melb C of E Gr Sch 75-77; Publ Pr Dio Win from 77. *72 Corhampton Road, Bournemouth, Dorset, B46 5PG.*

BENCE, Roy. Chich Th Coll 55. **d** 57 **p** 58 Lon. C of St Dunstan and All SS Stepney 57-60; V of St Mark Notting Hill 61-66; Chap at Zurich 66-69; V of St Jas w St Jude Bethnal Green 69-72; St Mark Bush Hill Pk 72-79; St Aug of Cant Highgate Dio Lon from 79. *St Augustine's Vicarage, Langdon Park Road, N6 5BH.* (01-340 3567)

BENDALL, Kenneth Albert. **d** 62 Bp McKenzie for Wel **p** 64 Wel. C of Johnsonville 62-65; Marton 65-66; P-in-c of Waiwheto 66-67; V of Hunterville 67-69; C of Paraparaumu 69; Petone 69-71; V of Opunake 71-75; Chap Lower Hutt Hosps 75-78; Offg Min Dio Wai from 79. *301 Clifford Street, Gisborne, NZ.*

BENDELOW, Thomas Arthur. b 11. Univ of Dur BA 37. Westcott Ho Cam 37. **d** 38 **p** 39 Newc T. C of Sugley 38-41; St Mary Virg and Univ SCM Sec Ox 41-44; Chap Oriel Coll Ox 42-44; w YMCA 44-45; Field Sec C'tte for Chr Reconstr in Eur 45-46; R of Southwick 47-54; V of Ch Ch Harrogate 54-70; C of Friern Barnet 70-72; V of Warter w Huggate Dio York from 72. *Warter Vicarage, York.* (Pocklington 3159)

BENDIGO, Lord Bishop of. *See* Heyward, Right Rev Oliver Spencer.

BENDIGO, Dean of. *See* McKenzie, Very Rev Alexander George.

BENFIELD, Desmond Ernest. St Mich Th Coll Crafers ACT ThL 67. **d** 66 **p** 67 St Arn. C of Swan Hill 67-70; V of Robinvale (w Manangatang from 71) 70-73; R 73-77; Exam Chap to Bp of St Arn and Dir of Relig Educn 71-76; R of Eaglehawk Dio Bend from 77. *St Peter's Rectory, Eaglehawk, Vic, Australia 3556.*

BENFIELD, Gordon. b 29. BD (Lon) 60. STh (Lambeth) 78. Univ of Birm MA 81. **d** 80 McKie for Cov **p** Cov. Hon C of St Mary w St Nich Warwick Dio Cov from 80. *Station House, Hatton, Nr Warwick, CV35 7LE.* (Claverdon 2031)

BENGE, Charles David. b 40. Cranmer Hall Dur 63. **d** 68 **p** 69 Dur. C of St Mark Millfield Sunderland 68-72; Hensingham 72-75; Team V of Maghull Dio Liv from 75. *1 St Peter's Row, Moorhey Road, Maghull, Lancs.* (051-526 3434)

BENHAM, Noel Francis. Univ of Dur LTh 25. St Aug Coll Cant 24. **d** 25 **p** 26 S'wark. C of St Jo Bapt Plumstead 25-27; V of Hampden w Maheno 27-30; Opotiki 30-33; Org Sec Gen Dioc Fund Dio Wai and Chap to Bp of Wai 33-36; V of Tolaga Bay 36-40; Waikouaiti 40-50; Port Chalmers w Warrington 50-58; Chap Tokanui Hosp Te Awamutu 58-64; V of Te Kauwhata 64-68; C of Opawa 68-69; P-in-c of Barrington Ch Ch 69-70; Tinwald 70; L to Offic Dio Auckld 70-72; Hon C of Halswell Dio Ch Ch from 72. *303 Hoon Hay Road, Christchurch 2, NZ.* (383-305)

BENIAMS, Alec Charles. b 28. K Coll Lon and Warm AKC 52. **d** 53 **p** 54 Newc T. C of All SS Gosforth 53-56; Cullercoats 56-58; Eltham (in c of St Francis Horne Pk) 58-59; Min of Lynemouth Conv Distr 59-61; V 61-63; CF (TA) 60-67; CF (TA - R of O) from 67; V of Whittingham 63-67; Willington-on-Tyne 67-71; V of Haydon Bridge Dio Newc T from 71. *Haydon Bridge Vicarage, Hexham, Northumb.* (Haydon Bridge 307)

BENIANS, Martin Ackland. b 19. St Jo Coll Cam BA 41, MA 45. Ridley Hall Cam 59. **d** 59 **p** 60 Lon. C of St Geo Headstone Hatch End 59-62; R of Rackheath Dio Nor from 62; V of Salhouse Dio Nor from 62. *Rackheath Rectory, Norwich, NR13 6NG.* (Norwich 720097)

BENIN, Lord Bishop of. *See* Idahosa, Right Rev John Wilfred Izeobokun.

BENISON, Brian. b 41. K Coll Lon 61. Bps' Coll Cheshunt 63. **d** 66 **p** 67 Newc T. C of Tynemouth 66-70; All SS Gosforth (in c of St Hugh Regent Farm Estate) Newc T 70-72; Team V of Cullercoats 73-81; V of Denton City and Dio Newc T from 81. *Denton Vicarage, Dunblane Crescent, Newcastle-upon-Tyne, NE5 2BE.* (Newcastle 674376)

BENJAFIELD, Lancelot Frederic. Ch Coll Hobert. ACT ThL 34. **d** 34 **p** 36 Tas. C of St John Launceston 34-36; St Geo Hobart 36-38; R of Channel 38-40; C-in-c of St Steph Sandy Bay Hobart 40-42; R of Ulverstone 42-49; St Paul Glenorchy 49-58; St Jo Bapt Hobart Dio Tas 60-69; L to Offic Dio Tas from 70. *27 Proctor's Road, Dynnyrne, Tasmania 7005.* (002-23 6195)

BENJAMIN, Adrian Victor. b 42. Wadh Coll Ox 3rd cl Engl 64, BA (2nd cl Th) 66, MA 68. Cudd Coll 66. **d** 68 Bp Ramsbotham for Newc T **p** 69 Newc T. C of All SS Gosforth 68-71; St Dunstan & All SS Stepney 71-75; V of All SS Friern Barnet Dio Lon from 75. *14 Oakleigh Park South, N20 9JU.* (01-445 4654)

BENJAMIN, David Stephen. b 42. Univ of WI LTh 70.

Codr Coll Barb 66. **d** 70 Bp Marshall for Trinid **p** 71 Trinid. C of Woodbrook 70-72; R of St David's Toco 72-78; St Mary's Tacarigua Dio Trinid from 78. *St Mary's Rectory, Eastern Main Road, Tacarigua, Trinidad.*

BENJAMIN, Canon Neil Sigismund Parkinson. **d** 64 Gui **p** 69 Guy. C of Lodge 64-69; CF (Guy) from 69; L to Offic Dio Guy 69-74; V of St Sav Georgetn Dio Guy from 74; Hon Can of Guy from 80. *Chaplain's Office, Camp Ayanganna, Thomas Lands, Georgetown, Guyana.*

BENJAMIN, Stanley Max. b 04. St Cath S Ox BA and MA 35. St Mich Coll Llan 34. **d** 36 **p** 37 Mon. C of Christchurch 36-39; Chap of Mon Cathl 39-44; R of Kenchester w Bridge Sollers 44-48; Bishopstone 44-48; St Jas Tredegar 48-51; Chap of St Jas Hosp Tredegar 48-51; V of Canon Frome 51-57; V of Stretton Grandison w Ashperton and Eggleton 51-57; Buckland Dinham w Elm 57-70; Perm to Offic Dio B & W from 70. *104 Broadway, Frome, Somt, BA11 3HG.*

BENN, Wallace Parke. b 47. Univ Coll Dub BA (Gen) 69. Univ of Lon Dipl Th 71. Trin Coll Bris 69. **d** 72 **p** 73 Ches. C of New Ferry Dio Ches from 72. *1 Kempton Road, New Ferry, Wirral, Mer, L62 1DL.*

BENNELL, Canon Richard. b 25. Univ of Leeds BA 45. Coll of Resurr Mirfield 46. **d** 48 **p** 49 Bris. C of Bedminster 48-51; St Anne Brislington 51-56; V of St Jo Div Fishponds 56-68; St Martin Knowle 68-73; R of Knowle 73-80; Proc Conv Bris 64-80; RD of Brislington 73-79; Hon Can of Bris from 76; Chap St Monica's Home of Rest Bris from 80; Publ Pr Dio Bris from 80; M Gen Syn Bris from 81. *St Augustine, Cote Lane, Bristol, BS9 3UL.* (Bris 623310)

BENNET, The Hon George Arthur Grey. b 25. CCC Cam BA 46, MA 51. Clifton Th Coll 68. **d** 69 Bp MacInnes for Sarum **p** 70 Sarum. C of Radipole 69-71; C-in-c of Motcombe w Enmore Green 71-73; Team V of Shaston 73-80; R of Redenhall w Harleston and Wortwell Dio Nor from 80; P-in-c of Needham Dio Nor from 80. *Redenhall Rectory, Swan Lane, Harleston, Norf.* (Harleston 852068)

BENNET, Gordon Duncan Affleck. b 31. Univ of Lon BSc (Econ) 55. Clifton Th Coll 55. **d** 57 **p** 58 Carl. C of St Jo Evang Carl 57-60; St Luke w St Simon and St Jude W Kilburn 60-63; P-in-c of St Mark Dallam Warrington 63-69; NW Area Sec CPAS 69-75; L to Offic Dio Man 69-75; R of Edgware Dio Lon from 75. *Rectory, Station Road, Edgware, Middx, HA8 7LG.* (01-952 1081)

BENNETT, Alan Robert. b 31. Roch Th Coll 62. **d** 64 **p** 65 Linc. C of Asterby w Goulceby 64-67; St Pet St Alb 67-70; R of Banham 70-72; CF 72-77; Team V of St Leon and St Mary Magd w St Steph Colchester 77-81; R of Colne Engaine Dio Chelmsf from 81. *Colne Engaine Rectory, Colchester, Essex.* (Earls Colne 2279)

BENNETT, Alan William. b 42. Sarum Th Coll 65. **d** 68 **p** 69 Portsm. C of H Trin Fareham 68-71; St Matthias Preston Chich 71-73; Stanmer w Falmer and Moulescomb (in c of H Nativ Lower Bevendean) 73-76; V of St Jo Evang Sandown 76-80; Soberton w Newtown Dio Portsm from 80. *Soberton Vicarage, Southampton, SO3 1PF.* (Droxford 400)

BENNETT, Anthony. b 31. Qu Coll Birm 72. **d** and **p** 74 Birm. C of Hob's Moat 74-76; St Jas Hill Birm 76-79; R of Grendon Dio Birm from 79. *Rectory, Grendon, Atherstone, Warws. CV9 3DP.* (Atherstone 2154)

BENNETT, Arnold Ernest. b 29. K Coll Lon and Warm AKC 53, BD 59. **d** 54 **p** 55 Portsm. C of Hayling I 54-59; Stevenage 59-64; R of N w S Wootton 64-73; V of N w S Hykeham Dio Linc from 74. *Hykeham Vicarage, Lincoln, LN6 9PA.* (Linc 681168)

BENNETT, Canon Arthur. b 15. Dipl Th (Lon) 68. Lambeth STh 77. Clifton Th Coll 40. **d** 42 **p** 43 Wakef. C of Ch Ch Woodhouse 42-44; Chesham 44-46; R of Gunton St Pet 46-49; V of Ch Ch Ware 49-56; St Paul St Alb 56-64; Proc Conv St Alb 59-80; R of L Munden 64-81; R of Sacombe 64-81; Hon Can of St Alb 70-81; Can (Emer) from 81. *5 Green Lane, Clapham, Bedford, MK41 6EP.* (0234-54462)

BENNETT, Arthur Vincent. b 49. Lawrence Univ Wisc BA 73. Trin Coll Tor MDiv 79. **d** 79 **p** 80 Alg. C of St Luke's Cathl Dio Alg from 79. *94 Lucy Terrace, Saulte Ste Marie, Ont, Canada, P6A 3V3.*

BENNETT, Arthur Harling. b 22. Ripon Hall Ox 70. **d** 71 **p** 72 Blackb. C of Standish 71-74; Team V of Darwen 75-79; V of Whitechapel Lancs Dio Blackb from 79. *Vicarage, Whitechapel, Preston, Lancs, PR3 2EP.* (Brock 40282)

BENNETT, Arthur William Edwin. Trin Coll Melb BA 27. St Aid Coll Bal ACT ThL 28. **d** 30 Bal **p** 31 Lon for Col Bp. C of St John Bethnal Green 30-32; P-in-c of Apollo Bay 33-36; V of Birregurra 36-41; CF 41-44; V of Terang 44-67; R 67-70; L to Offic Dio Bal from 70. *Rannoch Flats, Apollo Bay, Vic., Australia 3233.* (052-37 6624)

BENNETT, Basil Edward. b 02. St Aug Coll Cant 21. **d** 25 **p** 26 Chelmsf. C of St Paul Goodmayes 25-28; St Mary Jeppestown (in c of St Andr Kens) Johann 28-29; Cathl Ch Johann 29-31; R of Modderfontein 31-33; Chap Tr Ship *General Botha* Simonstown 33; C of St Mark (in c of H Innoc) S Norwood 33-34; Battle (in c of Ascen Telham) 35-38; St Jo Evang Newbury (in c of St Geo Wash Common) 38-40; V of Leckhampstead 40-48; Dioc Insp of Schs Dio Ox 41-48; Asst Chap O of St Jo of Jer from 42; Asst Master Healm Wic Sch 46-48; C-in-c of St Alb Cheam 48-49; C of Richmond (in c of St Matthias) 49-52; Stansted Mountfitchet 52-55; R of Downham 55-65; V of Stoke-by-Clare w Wixoe (R) Dio St E from 65. *Vicarage, Stoke-by-Clare, Sudbury, Suff.* (Clare 277367)

BENNETT, Bernard Michael. b 27. St Aid Coll 55. **d** 58 Pontefract for Wakef **p** 59 Wakef. C of Hemsworth 58-60; Chapelthorpe 60-62; V of All SS w St Bede Birkenhead 62-71; St Jas Latchford 71-75; Appleton Thorn w Antrobus Dio Ches from 75; Chap HM Pris Appleton Thorn from 75; HM Remand Centre Risley from 81. *Appleton Thorn Vicarage, Warrington, Ches.* (Warrington 63434)

BENNETT, Bryan James. b 39. Tyndale Hall Bris 64. **d** 67 **p** 68 Dur. C of Consett 67-70; CF from 70. *c/o Midland Bank Ltd., Felpham, Bognor Regis, Sussex.*

BENNETT, Preb Cecil William Frederick. b 1895. Em Coll Cam BA (2nd cl Th Trip) 20, MA 24. St Aug Coll Cant. **d** 21 Win **p** 22 Southampton for Win. C of St Steph Portsmouth 21-25; SPG Miss Dio Tinn 25-37; Lect St Jo Coll Palamcottah 25-37; Actg Prin 32-33 and 36-37; Chap Ch Ch Palamcottah 34-37; Furlough 30-31 and 37; Org Sec SPG Dios Cant Roch Chich and Guildf and L to Offic Dio Chich 37-43; R of Uckfield 43-56; RD of Uckfield 45-56; Surr 46-74; R of Horsted Parva 51-56; R of Isfield 51-56; V of St Pet Gt Chich 56-74; RD of Chich 56-70; Preb of Chich Cathl from 70. *c/o Old School House, Fletching, Uckfield, Sussex.* (Newick 2533)

BENNETT, Charles William. NZ Bd of Th Stud LTh (2nd cl) 65. St Jo Coll Auckld. **d** 63 **p** 64 Wai. C of Tauranga 63-68; V of Clive Par Distr 68-71; C of St Jo Cathl Napier 71-73; Prec 73-74; V of Waerenga-a-Hika 74-80; Waipaoa 74-80; P-in-c of Patutahi 74-80; C of N Walsham 80-81. *Address temp unknown.*

BENNETT, Canon Christopher Cayley Oliver. b 16. Selw Coll Cam BA 37, MA 41. Westcott Ho Cam 39. **d** 40 **p** 41 Bris. C of St Cuthb Brislington 40-42; Perm to Offic at Ellesmere Port 42; St Leon Streatham 43; St Mary Woolwich 44-45; C of St Mary Woolwich 45-49; R of L Berkhamsted 49-57; Stockton 57-61; V of Finham 61-72; Perm to Offic Dio Sarum from 72; V of Wellesbourne Dio Cov from 72; RD of Cov S 63-72; Stratford-on-Avon 73-77; C-in-c of Walton D'Eivile Dio Cov 72-74; R from 74; Hon Can of Cov from 73. *Wellesbourne Vicarage, Warwick, CV35 9LS.* (Stratford-on-Avon 840262)

BENNETT, Clifford Orford. b 32. St Mich Coll Llan 73. **d** 75 **p** 76 St A. C of Holywell 75-79; V of Pontblyddyn Dio St A from 79. *Vicarage, Pontblyddyn, Mold, Clwyd, CH7 4HG.* (Pontybodkin 771489)

BENNETT, Cuthbert Nigel. **d** 77 **p** 78 N Queensld. C of St John Cairns Dio N Queensld from 77. *c/o PO Box 52, Cairns, Qld, Australia 4870.*

BENNETT, Cyril Fortescue Price. St Chad's Coll Dur BA 28, Dipl in Th 29, MA 31. **d** 29 **p** 31 Ripon. C of St Wilfrid Harehills Leeds 29-32; St Nich w St John Newport and Chap of St Matthias Linc 32-34; C of Hagley (in c of W Hagley) 34-37; St Botolph (in c of St Steph) Colchester 37-39; R of E Mersea Dio Chelmsf 39-51; I of Dutton 51-53; Medicine Hat w Redcliffe 53-71. *503D Allowance Avenue, Medicine Hat, Alta., Canada.*

BENNETT, David Edward. b 35. Fitzw Ho Cam BA 56, MA 60. Wells Th Coll 58. **d** 60 **p** 61 Wakef. C of Lightcliffe 60-62; Sec Chr Educn Movement NE Region 62-68; L to Offic Dio Southw 68-80. *Address temp unknown.*

BENNETT, David Lawrence. Univ of Liv. BA (2nd cl French) 61. Ripon Hall Ox 61. **d** 63 **p** 64 Lon. C of Harlington 63-66. *c/o University of Zambia, P.O. Box 2379, Lusaka, Zambia, Centr Africa.*

BENNETT, Dennis Stanley. b 13. Chich Th Coll 37. **d** 39 **p** 40 York. C of St Martin of Tours Linthorpe Middlesbrough 39-41; St Sav Ealing 42-47; Chap RNVR 47; RN 47-59; C of Fenny Stratford 59-60; C-in-c of St Pet Stockport 60-63; PC 63-65; R of Frampton Cotterell 65-72; C of Wrington and Redhill (w Butcombe from 73) 72-78; C-in-c of Butcombe 73. *Ashcombe, West Hay Road, Wrington, Bristol, BS18 7NN.* (Wrington 862529)

BENNETT, Edwin James. b 23. St Barn Coll Adel ACT ThL 47, STh 52. **d** 47 **p** 48 Perth. C of St Mary Perth 47-48; St John Northam 48-50; R of W Northam 50-52; CF (Austr) 52-59 and from 62; R of Bruce Rock 59-62; L to Offic Dio C & Goulb 64-66; Dio Syd 66-74; Dio N Queensld 69-74; V of St Barn Oldham 74-79; St Anne Alderney Dio Win from 79. *St Anne's Vicarage, Alderney, CI.* (Alderney 2335)

BENNETT, Eugene Raymond John. b 45. ACT ThL 74. St Mich Ho Crafers 69. **d** 73 **p** 75 Murray. C of Murray Bridge

73-74; Perm to Offic Dio Adel 75; C of Christies Beach 76-77; P-in-c of Tailem Bend 77-80; R of Loxton Dio Murray from 80. *William Street, Loxton, S Australia 5333.* (085-84 7491)

BENNETT, Canon Gareth Vaughan. b 29. Late Scho of Ch Coll Cam 1st cl Hist Trip and Lloyd Stud BA 51, Allen Scho 53, PhD 54, MA and Thirlwall Pri 55. New Coll Ox MA and DPhil (by incorp) 59. FRHistS 58. Westcott Ho Cam 55. **d** 56 **p** 57 Chelmsf. Lect in Hist K Coll Lon 54-59; C of Prittlewell 56-59; Fell and Tutor New Coll Ox from 59; Dean of Div 59-79; Libr from 64; Lect in Hist Univ of Ox from 60; L to Offic Dio Ox from 60; Wiccamical Preb of Exceit in Chich Cathl from 61; Visiting Prof Univ of S Carolina 75; M Gen Syn from 75; Exam Chap to Bp of Lon from 76. *New College, Oxford.* (Ox 48451)

BENNETT, Garry Raymond. b 46. K Coll Lon 66. St Aug Coll Cant 69. **d** 70 **p** 71 S'wark. C of St Mark, Mitcham 70-73; Mortlake w E Sheen 73-75; Team V 76-78; V of Herne Hill Dio S'wark from 78. *Vicarage, Herne Hill, SE24 9LY.* (01-274 6336)

BENNETT, Geoffrey Samuel. b 02. **d** 61 Penrith for Carl **p** 62 Carl. C of Penrith 61-62; V of Rockcliffe w Cargo 62-66; C-in-c of St Mary w St Paul Carl 66-72; L to Offic Dio Carl from 72. *414 London Road, Carlisle, CA1 3ER.* (Carl 22472)

BENNETT, George Darley. b 21. ACIS 47. **d** 66 Zam **p** 67 Bp Mataka for Zam. P Dio Zam 66-76; R of Hulland w Atlow and Bradley (and Hognaston from 78) Dio Derby from 76; P-in-c of Hognaston 76-78; RD of Ashbourne from 81. *Vicarage, Eaton Close, Hulland Ward, Derby, DE6 3EX.* (Ashbourne 70605)

BENNETT, George Edward. b 51. Univ of Wales (Abth) BA 72. St Steph Ho Ox 73. **d** 76 **p** 77 Bris. C of All SS Clifton 76-82; Team V of Newbury Dio Ox from 82. *St John's Vicarage, Link Road, Newbury, Berks, RG14 7LU.* (0635-40387)

BENNETT, George Ronald Dampier. b 03. AKC 34. **d** 34 **p** 35 St E. C of Woodbridge 34-43; LPr Dio Heref 43-53; Chap St Mich Coll Tenbury 43-52; Hd Master of Hillbrow Prep Sch Featherstone Castle 52-54; R of Halwill w Beaworthy 54-57; Lowther w Askham 57-60; Simonburn 60-69; Warkleigh w Satterleigh and Chittlehamholt 69-73; Perm to Offic Dio Ex from 73; P-in-c of Zeal Monachorum 79-80. *Rectory, Zeal Monachorum, Crediton, Devon, EX17 6DG.* (Bow 342)

BENNETT, Gordon Herbert. Codr Coll Barb. **d** 53 Nass **p** 55 Antig. C of St Barn Nass 53-55; St Ant Montserrat 55-56; P-in-c of St Mary Cayon St Kitts 56-57; C of St Paul Leic 57-59; Clearwell 59-60; Perivale 60-61; R of St Paul w St Barn Antig 61; P-in-c of St Jas Nevis 62-64; R of Aruba 64-68; P-in-c of Murchison w Rushworth Dio Wang 68-69. *c/o Diocesan Council, Antigua, W Indies.*

BENNETT, Guy. b 33. St Edm Hall Ox BA (3rd cl Hist) 56. Wells Th Coll 56. **d** 58 Croydon for Cant **p** 59 Cant. C of St Phil Norbury 58-61; Minehead 61-63; Raynes Park 63-66; Chap Butlin's Holiday Camp Clacton 63; Min of H Cross Conv Distr Motspur Pk Raynes Pk 66-72; R of Oxted Dio S'wark from 72. *29 Chichele Road, Oxted, Surrey.* (Oxted 2955)

BENNETT, Harold Archibald Timson. b 11. Keble Coll Ox BA (2nd cl Phil Pol and Econ) 33, MA 45. St Steph Ho Ox 34. **d** 35 **p** 36 Roch. C of St Jas Elmers End 35-38; St Greg Gt Small Heath 38-39; C-in-c 39-45; R of Wootton 45-52; V of Cropredy (w Gt Bourton from 56) 52-65; Gt Bourton 52-56; Kennington 65-79; Proc Conv Ox 59-70; Asst Synod Sec Conv of Cant 69-70; Synod Sec 70-79 and from 80; M Gen Syn 75; C of St Mary Magd City and Dio Ox from 79. *94 Sunningwell Road, Oxford, OX1 4SY.* (Oxford 46937)

BENNETT, Harold Thomas. b 1896. Univ of Dur LTh 26. St Bonif Coll Warm 23. **d** 26 **p** 27 Win. C of Eastleigh (in c of All SS from 28) 26-31; V of St Alb Southampton 32-46; C of Shepton Mallet 52-54; R of Chew-Stoke 54-63. *33 Castle Road, Flat 4, Clevedon, Avon.*

BENNETT, Ian Frederick. b 30. Ch Coll Cam. BA 54, MA 62. Westcott Ho Cam 61. **d** 63 **p** 64 St Alb. C of Hemel Hempstead 63-68; St Ambrose Chorlton-on-Medlock 69-73; C-in-c 73-79; R 79; Asst Chap Univ of Man 69-73; Sen Chap 73-79; Dioc Tr Officer Dio Birm from 79. *1 Cartland Road, Kings Heath, Birmingham B14 7NS,* (021-444 4064)

BENNETT, James Edward William. Angl Th Coll BC Dipl Th 66. **d** and **p** 66 Bp Greenwood for Carib. C of Lytton 66-71; I of Mannville 71; Viking Dio Edmon from 71. *Box 778, Viking, Alta., Canada.* (403-336 3100)

BENNETT, James Kenneth Bretherton. b 11. St Jo Coll Ox BA and Casberd Exhib 33, Dipl in Th 34, MA 37. Wycl Hall Ox 33. **d** 35 **p** 36 Leic. C of H Ap Leic 35-38; Selston (in c of St Mary Westwood) 38-46; CF (EC) 40-46; V of Lythe 46-49; R of Bainton 49-57; C-in-c of N Dalton 50-54; V 54-57; Chap Glebe Ho Sch Hunstanton 57-59; Hd Master 59-67; L to Offic Dio Nor 57-67; Perm to Offic Dio Edin from 67; Dio Arg Is from 76; Asst Master Loretto Jun Sch Musselburgh 67-73; Chap Caldicott Sch Farnham Royal 73-76. *Address temp unknown.*

BENNETT, James Winston. Codr Coll Barb 62. **d** 65 Barb for Gui **p** 66 Guy. C of Bartica 65-69; Dir Dioc Youth Centre from 69; R of Plaisance Dio Guy from 76. *Diocesan Youth Centre, Third Avenue, Subryanville, E.C.D. Guyana, S America.* (02-66208)

BENNETT, Canon John Peter. Codr Coll Barb 49. **d** and **p** 49 Gui. C of All SS New Amsterdam 49-53; P-in-c of Bartica and of Yuparki 53-56; Waramuri 57-60; V 60-65; Kabakaburi Dio Guy from 65; Can of Guy from 77. *Vicarage, Kabakaburi, Pomeroon, Guyana.*

BENNETT, John Walker. b 09. Hatf Coll Dur BA and LTh 39, MA 41. St Aug Coll Cant 35. **d** 39 Colchester for Chelmsf **p** 40 Chelmsf. C of Buckhurst Hill 39-42; Seaham 42-44; PC of St Geo Gateshead 44-48; R of Barcaldine Queensld 48-53; V of Kingsbury (w Dosthill and Wood End to 59) w Hurley 53-64; R of Bradfield St Geo w Rushbrooke 64-77; R of Bradfield St Clare 64-77; Perm to Offic Dio St E from 77. *5 Orchard Way, Barrow, Bury St Edmunds, Suffolk.* (Bury St E 810617)

BENNETT, Joyce Mary. b 23. OBE 79. Univ of Lon BA 44. K Coll Lon Dipl Th 61. **d** 62 **p** 71 Hong [CMS Miss and Teacher from 49] C of St Thos Kowloon 62-66; Crown of Thorns Hong 67-68; St Barn Macao Dio Hong from 68; Lect U Th Sem Hong 63-66; Prin St Cath Girls' Sch Macao from 68. *St Catharine's School, Hong Lee Road, Kwun Tong, Kowloon, Hong Kong.* (3-428292)

BENNETT, Kenneth Leigh. b 18. Jesus Coll Ox BA 42, MA 46. **d** 44 **p** 45 Linc. C of St John Spitalgate 44-46; St Andr Grimsby 46-47; Hucknall Torkard 47-55; V of St Matthias Sneinton Dio Southw from 55. *St Matthias's Vicarage, Sneinton, Nottingham, NG3 2FB.* (Nottingham 52750)

BENNETT, Lloyd Kenneth. b 32. Moore Th Coll Syd ACT ThL 64. **d** 64 **p** 65 Syd. NSW Youth Sec CMS Austr 64-66; L to Offic Dio Syd 65-66; C of Bondi 66-67; R of Mulgoa 67-72; Avalon w Palm Beach 72-77; Chap Trin Gr Sch and L to Offic Dio Syd from 78. *22 Henson Street, Summer Hill, NSW, Australia 2130.* (797-0689)

BENNETT, Lyle Albert. Seager Hall Ont. **d** 60 Hur **p** 61 Bp Luxton for Hur. I of Bervie 61-62; Kirkton 62-66; St Luke St Thomas 66-69; on leave. *Apt 502, 1639, Bloor Street West, Toronto 165, Ont., Canada.*

✠ **BENNETT, Right Rev Manu Augustus.** CMG 81. Univ of Hawaii BSc 54, Hon DD 64. Te Aute Coll. **d** 39 **p** 40 Wai. C Dio Wai 39; V of Tauranga Maori Distr 40-44; CF (NZ) 44-46; Maori Miss at Rangitikei-Manawatu 46-52; Maori Pastor Wel 52 and 54-57; in Amer Ch 53-54; V of Ohinemutu Past 57-64; L to Offic Dio Wai 64-68; Chap HM Pris Te Awamutu 64-68; Cons Ld Bp Suffr of Aotearoa in St Jo Evang Cathl Napier 18 Oct 68 by Abp of NZ; Bps of Waik; Wel; Dun; Nel; Ch Ch; and Honolulu (USA); Asst Bps of Polyn; Wel; and Auckld; and Bp Panapa; Bp for the Maori People 78; res 81; Perm to Offic Dio Wai from 81. *PO Box 115, Te Puke, NZ.* (37-380)

BENNETT, Michael Edgar. Keble Coll Ox BA 53, MA 58. Wells Th Coll 59. **d** 61 **p** 62 Sarum. C of Calne 61-64; Tewkesbury 64-69; R of Swindon w Uckington and Elmstone Hardwicke Dio Glouc from 69; Ed Glouc Dioc Gazette from 71. *Swindon Rectory, Cheltenham, Glos.* (Cheltenham 22786)

BENNETT, Michael John. b 43. K Coll Lon and Warm AKC (2nd cl) 66. **d** 67 **p** 68 Dur. C of Chester-le-Street 67-71; Portland 71-74; V of St Jo Bapt Portland Dio Sarum from 74. *St John the Baptist Vicarage, Portland, Dorset, DT5 1JE.* (Portland 820103)

BENNETT, Michael Lindsay. b 39. Moore Coll Syd ACT ThL 68. **d** 69 **p** 70 Brisb. C of St Steph Coorparoo 69-71; Ch Ch St Ives 73-75; R of Yagoona 75-78; Perm to Offic Dio Syd from 79. *32 Oleander Parade, Caringbah, NSW, Australia 2999.* (523-9024)

BENNETT, Nigel John. b 47. Dipl Th (Lon) 69. Oak Hill Coll 66. **d** 71 **p** 72 Roch. C of St Steph Tonbridge 71-75; St John Heatherlands Parkstone 75-79; P-in-c of Kingham w Daylesford 79-80; Sarsden w Churchill 79-80; R of Kingham w Churchill, Daylesford and Sarsden from 80. *Rectory, Kingham, Oxon, OX7 6YT.* (Kingham 230)

BENNETT, Osmond Shirley. b 36. Oriel Coll Ox BA 67. Ripon Hall Ox 64. **d** 68 Bp Horstead for Leic **p** 69 Leic. C of St Luke Leic 68-71; Thurcaston 71-72; V of St Marg City and Dio Leic from 72. *St Margaret's Vicarage, Brading Road, Leicester, LE3 9BG.* (Leic 27362)

BENNETT, Paul Rider. b 41. Univ of Man BMus 64. ARMCM and GRMCM 64. ARCO 64. Chich Th Coll 64. **d** 66 Huntingdon for Ely **p** 67 Ely. C of Stanground 66-69; Hon C of Ramsey Dio Ely from 74. *11 Bentley Close, Upwood, Huntingdon, PE17 1QW.* (Ramsey 812682)

BENNETT, Peter Harry Edward. b 19. Chich Th Coll 53.

d 55 **p** 56 Chich. C of E Grinstead 55-58; Heathfield 58-61; V of St Richard Heathfield 61-71; RD of Dallington 66-71; V of Goring Dio Chich from 71. *Vicarage, Compton Avenue, Goring-by-Sea, Sussex, BN12 4UJ.* (Worthing 42525)

BENNETT, Peter Hugh. b 22. K Coll Lon and Warm 46. **d** 50 **p** 51 York. C of Ch of Transfig Newington 50-53; Bottesford w Ashby 53-57; C-in-c of Tile Hill 57-58; V 58-64; Hillmorton 64-75; R of Beaudesert w Henley-in-Arden (and Ullenhall from 81) Dio Cov from 75; C-in-c of Ullenhall w Apsley 75-81. *Henley-in-Arden Rectory, Solihull, W Midl.* (Henley-in-Arden 2570)

BENNETT, Reginald George. b 11. King's Coll Lon 31. **d** 35 **p** 36 Ox. C of St Leon Grimsbury 35-37; Batsford w Moreton-in-Marsh 37-40; CF (EC) 40-46; V of Aldsworth 46-52; PC of Morville w Aston Eyre 52-57; PC of Acton Round 52-57; R of Todenham w Lemington 57-61; V of Kirtlington Dio Ox from 61; P-in-c of Weston-on-the-Green Dio Ox from 76. *Kirtlington Vicarage, Oxford, OX5 3HA.* (Bletchington 224)

BENNETT, Reginald Marchmont. Moore Th Coll Syd. **d** 55 **p** 56 Nel. C of Greymouth 55-56; Stoke 56; Hanmer 56-58; V 58-64; Granity w Waimangaroa 64-66; Murchison 66-74; L to Offic Dio Ch Ch from 74. *5 Hilltop Lane, St Andrew's Hill, Christchurch 8, NZ.*

BENNETT, Richard Edward Stuart. b 24. St Jo Coll Ox BA (3rd cl Th) 49, MA 55. Wells Th Coll 50. **d** 51 **p** 52 B & W. C of Twerton-on-Avon 51-56; V of Gt Staughton 56-63, Chap HM Borstal Inst Gaynes Hall 56-63; R of Camerton (w Dunkerton, Foxcote and Shoscombe from 80) Dio B & W from 63; Dunkerton 63-80. *Camerton Rectory, Bath, Avon, BA3 1PU.* (Timsbury 70249)

BENNETT, Robert Francis Henry. b 12. TCD BA 40, MA 47. NW Ordin Course 73. **d** 73 **p** 74 Blackb. C of Feniscliffe 73-78; L to Offic Dio Blackb from 78. *28 Tower Road, Blackburn, BB2 5LE.* (Blackburn 21815)

BENNETT, Robert Franklin. b 49. Univ of W Ont BA 71. Hur Coll Ont MDiv 74. **d** 74 **p** 75 Hur. C of Chesley Tara & Paisley 74-80; I of St Geo Kitchener Dio Hur from 80. *311 Fischer Road, Kitchener, Ont, Canada, N2M 4X9.*

BENNETT, Robin. b 34. Univ of Dur BA (2nd cl Pol and Econ) 58. Univ of Birm Dipl Th 60. Qu Coll Birm 58. **d** 60 **p** 61 Chelmsf. C of Prittlewell 60-63; St Andr Plaistow (in c of St Martin) 63-65; V of St Cedd Canning Town 65-71; R of Loughton 71-75; Dep Dir Urban Min Project and Dir Ox Inst for Ch and S 75-78; Prin The Aston Tr Scheme from 77; P-in-c of Bletchingdon 78-81; St Pet City and Dio Birm from 81. *32 George Street West, Birmingham, B18 7HF.* (021-236 2165)

BENNETT, Roger Sherwood. b 35. Univ of Nottm BA (Th) 56. Wells Th Coll 58. **d** 59 Southw **p** 60 Grantham for Linc. C of Mansfield Woodhouse 59-60; Spalding 60-63; V of Gedney 63-69; Chap RNR 65-69; RN from 69. *c/o Ministry of Defence, Lacon House, Theobald's Road, WC1X 8RY.*

BENNETT, Roy Donald. b 40. St Jo Coll Nottm. 78. **d** 80 **p** 81 Cov. C of Fletchamstead Dio Cov from 80. *2a Beech Tree Avenue, Coventry, CV4 9FG.*

BENNETT, Sidney Ernest. Ely Th Coll 30. **d** 32 **p** 33 Lon. C of St Matt Westmr 32-34; St Mich AA Woolwich 34-37; R of Sabie 37-39; PC of Barrow Hill 40-45; Org Sec E Counties UMCA 45-48; R of Bremersdorp 48-51; Warden of St Mich Sch 48-53; R of Klerksdorp 53-59; Archd of Potchefstroom 57-66; R of Lichtenburg w Zeerust 59-66; Potchefstroom 66-70; Can of Johann 66-74; C of Rosebank 70-74. *c/o 36 Eastwood Road, Dunkeld, Johannesburg, S Africa.*

BENNETT, Stanley Gilbert. b 08. Univ of Bonn PhD 35. Ridley Hall Cam 36. **d** 37 Bp Mounsey for Bradf **p** 38 Bradf. C of H Trin Idle 37-40; Chap RAFVR 40-46; C of Barnoldswick (in c of Bracewell) 46-47; V of Dent 47-61; Cowgill 47-61; Harden w Wilsden 61-70; Lothersdale 70-76; Perm to Offic Dio Bradf from 77. *34 Rombalds Crescent, Keighley, Yorks.* (0535-54225)

BENNETT, Victor John. b 1897. Qu Coll Birm 48. **d** 50 **p** 51 Sheff. C of Carlton-juxta-Snaith 50-54; V of Ansty w Shilton 54-71. *St Michael's, Waltham-on-the-Wolds, Melton Mowbray, Leics.* (Waltham 816)

BENNETT, Wilfrid John. b 01. Down Coll Cam 3rd cl Geog Trip pt i 23, BA (3rd cl Geog. Trip pt ii) 25. **d** 27 **p** 28 St A. C of Connah's Quay 27-30; Widcombe 30-34; V of Otterford 34-38; Evercreech w Chesterblade 38-52; Chilton-super-Polden w Edington 52-58; Chap of St Bernard's Hosp Southall 58-59; R of Byton 59-62; V of Kinsham 59-62; C-in-c of Staunton-on-Arrow 60-62; R of Staunton-on-Arrow w Byton and Kinsham 62-67. *13 Buckingham Road, Town Moor, Doncaster, DN2 5DD, Yorks.* (Doncaster 62828)

BENNETT, William McNeil. Seager Hall Ont. **d** 64 **p** 65 Hur. C of Bp Cronyn Mem Ch Lon 64-65; I of Port Burwell 65-67; C of St Paul's Cathl Lon 67-70; R of Ridgetown 70-76; I of Bayfield Dio Hur from 76. *Box 241, Bayfield, Ont., Canada.*

BENNETTS, Colin James. b 40. Late Exhib of Jes Coll Cam BA 63, 2nd cl Th Trip Pt ii 64, MA 67. Ridley Hall Cam 63. **d** 65 **p** 66 Roch. C of St Steph Tonbridge 65-69; Chap Ox Past and C of St Aldate Ox 69-73; Asst Chap Jes Coll Ox 73-75; Chap from 75; P-in-c of St Andr City and Dio Ox 78-79; V from 79. *13 Northmoor Road, Oxford.* (Oxford 58756)

BENNETTS, Gordon Vivian. B 15. TD 62. Open Univ BA 78. **d** 77 **p** 78 Truro (APM). C of Phillack 77-79; Redruth Dio Truro from 79. *Petroc's Cross, South Drive, Tehidy, Camborne, Cornwall, TR14 0EZ.*

BENNETTS, William Rawling. Univ of W Austr BSc 49, BA 54. Cudd Coll 56. **d** 58 **p** 59 Portsm. C of Portsea 58-60; Nedlands W Austr 60-63; R of Bruce Rock 63-67; Kilburn 67-70; Coromandel Valley Dio Adel from 70. *35 Coromandel Parade, Blackwood, S Australia 5051.* (08-278 1693)

BENNIE, Alexander Peter Bruce. Univ of Melb BA 36, MA 38. ACT ThL 37. **d** 38 Melb for Brisb **p** 39 Brisb. C of All SS Brisb 38-42; V of Mary Valley 42-45; Sub-Dean of Quetta Mem Cathl and Admin Dio Carp 45-52; Exam Chap to Bp of Carp and Archd of Carp 49-52; R of All SS Brisb 53-63; Lect St Francis Coll Brisb 53-63; in Div Univ of Queensld 61-63; Can Res of Brisb 61-63; Warden St Paul's Coll Syd and L to Offic Dio Syd from 63; Commiss N Queensld from 66. *St Paul's College, University of Sydney, Newtown, NSW, Australia 2042.* (51-1447)

BENNIE, Stanley James Gordon. b 43. Univ of Edin MA 65. Coll of Resurr Mirfield 66. **d** 68 Bp Ramsbotham for Newc T **p** 69 Newc T. C of Ashington 68-70; Prec St Andr Cathl Inverness 70-74; Itin P Dio Moray 74-81; R of Portsoy Dio Aber from 81; All SS Buckie Dio Aber from 81. *All Saints Rectory, Buckie, Banff, AB5 1HA.* (Buckie 32312)

BENNION, John Richard. b 15. Univ of Leeds BA 36. Coll of Resurr Mirfield 36. **d** 38 **p** 39 Lich. C of Wolstanton 38-41; Tamworth 41-43; Chap RAF 43-48; Tamworth (in c of St Chad Hopwas) 48-54; V of Pelsall 54-55; R of Harlaston 55-63; V of Edingale 57-63; PC of Ashley Green 63-80. *c/o Ashley Green Vicarage, Chesham, Bucks.* (Berkhamsted 3764)

BENNISON, Philip Owen. b 42. Univ of Dur BA 64. Coll of Resurr Mirfield. **d** 66 **p** 67 York. C of Guisborough 66-67; S Bank 67-71; Team V of Thornaby 71-74; R of Skelton-in-Cleveland 74-78; V of Upleatham 74-78. *c/o Rectory, Skelton-in-Cleveland, Saltburn, Yorks.* (Skelton 50329)

BENNITT, Albert John. b 07. Late Scho of Clare Coll Cam 1st cl Math Trip pt i 27, BA (1st cl Math Trip pt ii) and Wordsworth Stud 49, 2nd cl Th Trip pt i 30, MA 39. Westcott Ho Cam 29. **d** 30 **p** 31 Newc T. C of St Luke Newc T 30-33; Chap St Paul's Coll Hong Kong 33-38; Supt Chinese Miss Dio Sing 38-46; Miss Sec SCM 46-48; Master of St Thos Mart Newc T 48-69; Master of St Mary Magd Hosp Chap of Hunter's Moor Hosp and Hon Chap K Coll Newc T 48-69; Hon Sec Hong Dioc Assoc 49-58; Commiss Sing 49-72; Select Pr Univ of Dur 58; Hon Can of Newc T 62-69; R of Risby 69-79; P-in-c of Lackford 69-79; Chap St Mary's Hosp Bury St Edm 71-79; Perm to Offic Dio St E from 79. *4 Kytson Cottages, Bury Road, Hengrave, Bury St Edmunds, Suffolk.*

BENSLEY, Ross Everard. Moore Coll Syd ThL 71. **d** and **p** 72 Syd. C of Lalor Pk 72-74; Andes Evang Miss 74-79; in Amer Ch. *135 North Oakland Avenue, Pasadena, CA 91101, USA.*

BENSLEY, Thomas William Dorward. Lich Th Coll 24. Univ of Dur 25. **d** 26 **p** 27 Lich. C of Heath Town 26-35; V of Ch of the Good Shepherd W Bromwich 35-42; Horton 42-68. *32 Emily Street, West Bromwich, Staffs.*

BENSON, Christopher Hewetson. b 04. Late Scho of Jes Coll Cam 23, Bell Scho 24, 1st cl Cl Trip pt i 25, BA (1st cl Cl Trip pt ii w Distinc) 26, 2nd cl Th Trip pt ii 27, MA 32. Bps' Coll Cheshunt 28. **d** 28 **p** 29 Lon. Chap and Asst Master Highgate Sch 28-66; L to Offic Dio Ex from 67. *7 Longfield, Pitt Hill, Appledore, Bideford, Devon.*

BENSON, Christopher Hugh. b 53. Bath Acad of Art BA 75. Keble Coll Ox BA (Th) 78. Chich Th Coll 78. **d** 80 **p** 81 Ex. C of St Mich AA Heavitree City and Dio Ex from 80. *2 Sherwood Close, Heavitree, Exeter, Devon.* (Ex 78591)

BENSON, Donald. b 26. N-W Ordin Course 75. **d** 78 **p** 79 Liv. C of St Dunstan Edge Hill Dio Liv from 78. *82 Ramilies Road, Liverpool, L18 2EF.*

BENSON, Douglas Arthur Terrell. b 08. St Jo Coll Dur BA 36. Lon Coll of Div 32. **d** 36 **p** 37 Lich. C of St Luke Wolverhampton 36-39; Cheadle 39-42 and 43-44; Perm to Offic as C of New Ferry 42-43; PC of St Jas Stockton-on-Tees 44-48; V of Clapham, Bedford 48-76. *3 Gayhurst Close, Caversham Park, Reading, RG4 0QW.*

BENSON, James Christopher Reginald. Trin Coll Dub BA 35, MA 60. **d** 37 **p** 38 Down. C of St Andr Belf 37-48; Ballinderry 38-39; Dioc C Dio Clogh 40-41; C-in-c of Inishmacsaint 41-44; Tempo 44-47; Lack (or Colaghty) 47-51; Derrybrusk 51-53; R of Trillick 53-57; I of Mullaghdun 57-61. *81 Sicily Park, Belfast 10, N Ireland.*

BENSON, John. b 02. **d** 38 **p** 39 Ripon. C of All H Leeds 38-41; C-in-c of Kirkby Ravensworth 41-42; V of St Clem Sheepscar Leeds 42-49; Aysgarth 49-65; Felixkirk w Boltby 65-71; C-in-c of Kirkby Knowle 65-66; R 66-71. *Oldstead, Coxwold, York, YO6 4BL.* (Coxwold 463)

BENSON, John David. b 36. Dipl Th (Lon) 61. St Aid Coll 58. **d** 61 **p** 62 York. C of St Martin Hull 61-65; Marfleet 65-68; V of Ingleby Greenhow 68-72; C-in-c of Kildale 68-72; Asst Youth Chap Dio York 68-72; Dioc Youth Chap Sheff 72-78; V of Thorne Dio Sheff from 78. *Thorne Vicarage, Doncaster, DN8 4AZ.* (Thorne 814055)

BENSON, John Godwin. Trin Coll Dub BA 37, Div Test (2nd cl) 37, MA 53. **d** 38 **p** 39 Lim. C of St Mary's Cathl Lim 38-40; I of Ballymackey U 40-41; CF (EC) 41-46; I of Bourney w Dunkerrin 46-48; Monasteroris Union 48-49; S Sec Hib Miss S 49; L to Offic Dio Dub 49-50; I of Dunlavin 50-52; Home Sec CMS and L to Offic Dio Melb 52-53; Dio Bal 54-64. *c/o ANZ Bank, 161 Flinders Lane, Melbourne, C 1. Australia.*

BENSON, John Patrick. b 52. Ch Coll Cam BA 73, MA 76, PhD 76. Trin Coll Bris 78. **d** 81 Birm. C of Walmley Dio Birm from 81. *90 Walmley Ash Road, Walmley, Sutton Coldfield, W Midl, B76 8JB.*

BENSON, John Simmonds. b 06. Tyndale Hall Bris 36. **d** 39 Willesden for Lon **p** 40 Lon. C of H Trin Barnsbury 39-41; H Trin Rusholme Dio Man 41-42; All S Leichardt Dio Syd 42-43; Actg R of St Alb Corrimal 43-45; Chap AMF 45-46; R of Passenham w Old Stratford Deanshanger and Puxley 47-59; R of Cosgrove 47-59; V of H Trin Cloudesley Square Isl 59-69; Bucknell w Buckton 69-76. *5 Brock Hollands, Lydney, Glos, GL15 4PP.*

BENSON, Reginald James. b 1889. Pemb Coll Ox BA 13, MA 17. Ridley Hall Cam 13. **d** 14 **p** 15 Ox. C of Thame 14-18; Nechells Birm 18-19; Aston 19-24; Org Sec LJS for S Midl Distr 24-26; V of St Luke Barton Hill Bris 26-32; St Nath Liv 32-45; St Ninian Douglas 45-55; R of Pulverbatch 55-64; C-in-c of Smethcote 55-64. *3 Ringer's Way, Admaston, Telford, Salop, TF5 0BD.* (Telford 3356)

BENSON, Richard Edmund Miller. b 12. Trin Coll Dub BA 35, MA 50. **d** 36 **p** 37 Lim. C of Tralee and Dioc C of Ardf and Aghadoe 36-39; C-in-c of Garvary 39-44; R of Donagh 44-47; I of Dromore 47-51; C of Portadown 51-52; I of Sixmilecross (w Dunmoyle 52-69 and Termonmaguirke from 69) 52-76. *14 Dellmount Park, Bangor, Co Down, N Ireland.*

BENSON, Riou George. b 14. Univ Coll Ox 34. Linc Th Coll 38. **d** 39 **p** 40 Wakef. C of Penistone w Midhope 39-44; PC of Goff's Oak 44-50; Burghill and Chap of Burghill Hosp 50-61; V of Clun w Chapel Lawn 61-79; Chap St Cath Hosp Clun 61-75; P-in-c of Bettws-y-Crwyn w Newc 61-63; V 63-79; P-in-c of Clungunford 63-77; Bedstone w Hopton Castle 65-79; P-in-c of Llanfair-Waterpine w Stowe 73-79; Clunbury w Clunton 75-79; Preb of Heref Cathl 65-79; RD of Clun 68-72. *Maiden Hill Wood, All Stretton, Church Stretton, Shropshire, SY6 6LA.*

BENSON, Roy William. b 32. Coll of Em & St Chad Sktn LTh 76, MDiv 76. **d** 76 **p** 77 Qu'App. C of Pipestone 76-78; R of Craik Qu'App 78-80; C of St Mich E Wickham 80; I of Kinistino Dio Sask from 80. *176, Kinistino, Sask, Canada.*

BENSON, Stuart Lawrence. **d** 67 **p** 68 Newc. C of New Lambton 67-69; Singleton 69-72; R of Terrigal Dio Newc from 72. *Rectory, Church Street, Terrigal, NSW, Australia 2260.* (043-84 1053)

BENSON, Terence Edward Benjamin. b 17. Trin Coll Dub BA 37. **d** 41 **p** 42 Cork. Dioc C Dio Cork 41-42; C-in-c of Corbally 42-44 and 49-52; I of Templecharry 44-46; Hd Master of Killaloe Dioc Sch 46-52; I of Brinny U 52-56; Asst Master Portora R Sch Enniskillen 56-79. *Portora Royal School, Enniskillen, Co Fermanagh, N Ireland.*

BENSON, Preb William Fitzgerald. b 13. Trin Coll Dub BA 35, MA 38, Div Test 35. **d** 53 **p** 54 Oss. C of Maryborough 53-56; I of Clonegal Dio Ferns from 56; Preb of Ferns Cathl from 80. *Clonegal Rectory, Enniscorthy, Co Wexford, Irish Republic.*

BENSON, William George. b 26. BA (Lon) 51. Univ of Ex BA 56. Sarum Wells Th Coll 76. **d** 79 **p** 80 Ex. C of Heanton-Punchardon w Marwood Dio Ex from 79. *1 Goodgates Park, Braunton, N Devon.*

BENSON, Preb William John Robinson. b 02. QUB BA 25. **d** 26 **p** 27 Down. C of St Mich Belf 26-31; R 31-40; C of St Mary Magd Belf 31; R 40-56; I of St Donard Belf 56-62; Coleraine 62-76; Preb of St Patr Cathl Dub from 63. *16 Ratheane Avenue, Mountsandel Road, Coleraine, Co Derry, N Ireland.* (Coleraine 51922)

BENSTED, James de Carl Sowerby. b 11. Ex Coll Ox BA (4th cl Mod Hist) 34, MA 46. Ripon Hall Ox 34. **d** 36 **p** 37 Birm. C of St Gabr Weoley Castle w St Mich AA Bartley Green 36-38; St Jas Handsworth 38-46; Chap RNVR 40-46; V of Sparkbrook 46-49; Peterchurch 49-56; Vowchurch w Turnastone 53-56; R of Ewhurst 56-76. *15 Madeline Road, Petersfield, Hants.* (Petersfield 2455)

BENT, James. b 31. St Deiniol's Libr Hawarden 79. **d** 81 Birkenhead for Ches. C of Prenton Dio Ches from 81. *83 Bramwell Avenue, Prenton, Birkenhead, Mer, L43 0RQ.*

BENT, Ven Michael Charles. Kelham Th Coll 51. **d** 55 Bp Vernon for Pet **p** 56 Pet. C of St Mary Wellingborough 55-60; Suva 60-64; Cakaudrove 64-66; L to Offic Dio Polyn 66-76; Wel 66-70; Waik 70-76; Dun 71-76; Ch Ch 70-76; Asst Sec NZ Angl Bd of Miss 66-70; Gen Sec 70-76; Hon C of St Mark Wel 70-76; L to Offic Dio Auckld 70-76; V of New Plymouth Dio Waik from 76; Archd of Taranaki from 76; Commiss Polyn from 77; Dep VG Dio Waik from 78. *37 Vivian Street, New Plymouth, NZ.* (83-111)

BENTALL, Arthur. b 1895. Clifton Th Coll 51. **d** 52 **p** 53 Chich. C of Prestonville 52-54; C of Em and in c of St Mary-in-the-Castle Hastings 54-56; R of Langley 56-60. *60 Cissbury Gardens, Findon Valley, Worthing, Sussex.* (Findon 3166)

BENTINCK, Richard. b 13. Univ of Madras BA 35. Madras Chr Coll. **d** 43 **p** 44 Lah. Asst Master Bp Cotton Sch Simla 43-54; Sherwood Coll Naini Tal 54-65; C of St Steph Acomb York 65-67; V of Kirkby-in-Cleveland 67-74; St Martin Middlesbrough Dio York from 75; P-in-c of St Cuthb Middlesbrough 79-81. *St Martin's Vicarage, Kirby Avenue, Middlesbrough, Cleve, TS5 4LA.* (Middlesbrough 89634)

BENTLEY, Canon David Edward. b 35. Univ of Leeds BA (2nd cl Engl) 56. Westcott Ho Cam 58. **d** 60 **p** 61 Bris. C of St Ambrose Bris 60-62; H Trin Guildf 62-66; R of All SS Headley 66-73; Esher Dio Guildf from 73; RD of Emly from 73; Chairman Guildf Dioc Coun for Social Responsibility from 80; Hon Can of Guildf from 80. *12 Esher Park Avenue, Esher, Surrey.* (Esher 62611)

BENTLEY, Edward John. b 35. Univ of Bris BA (3rd cl Th) 61. Tyndale Hall Bris 58. **d** 63 **p** 64 Lich. C of St Luke Wolverhampton 63-66; Miss BCMS 66-72; C of St Mark Cheltm 72-78; V of St Nich Wallasey Dio Ches from 78. *St Nicholas's Vicarage, 22 Groveland Road, Wallasey, Chesh.* (051-639 3589)

BENTLEY, Frank Richard. b 41. K Coll Lon and Warm BD and AKC (2nd cl) 67. **d** 68 Kens for Lon **p** 69 Lon. C of Feltham 68-72; C-in-c of St Bart Bethnal Green 72-77; R of Bow w Bromley St Leon Dio Lon from 77; All H Bromley Dio Lon from 77; H Trin Mile End Old Town Stepney Dio Lon from 77. *63 Coborn Road, E3 2DB.* (01-980 2074)

BENTLEY, Frank William Henry. b 34. AKC 57. **d** 58 B & W **p** 59 Taunton for B & W. C of Shepton Mallet 58-62; R of Kingsdon w Podymore Milton 62-66; C-in-c of Yeovilton 62-66; Babcary 64-66; V of Wiveliscombe 66-76; RD of Tone 73-76; V of St Jo Bapt-in-Bedwardine City and Dio Worc from 76; RD of Martley and Worc W from 79. *143 Malvern Road, St John's, Worcester, WR2 4LN.*

BENTLEY, Frederick Alexander. **d** 55 **p** 57 Bal. C-in-c of Alvie w Beeac 55-57; P-in-c 57-67; V 67-73; Perm to Offic Dio Bal from 73. *Dreeite, Vic., Australia.* (052-34 8373)

BENTLEY, Canon Geoffrey Bryan. b 09. Late Cl Scho of King's Coll Cam, 1st cl Cl Trip pt i 30, BA (1st cl Th Trip pt ii) and Carus Gk Test Pri 32, MA 35. Cudd Coll 32. **d** 33 **p** 34 Portsm. C of St Cuthb Copnor 33-35; Tutor Bp's Hostel Linc 35-38; Lect 38-52; L to Offic Dio Linc 35-52; Chap Linc County Hosp 38-52; PV Linc Cathl 38-52; Proc Conv Linc 45-55; R of Milton Abbot w Dunterton 52-57; Exam Chap to Bp of Ex 52-73; Commiss to Bp of SW Tang 52-62; Can of Windsor from 57. *5 The Cloisters, Windsor Castle, Berks, SL4 1NJ.* (Windsor 63001)

BENTLEY, Graham John. b 29. SOC 77. **d** 80 **p** 81 S'wark. Hon C of St Mary Merton Dio S'wark from 80. *67 Grand Drive, Raynes Park, SW20 9DG.*

BENTLEY, Ian Ronald. b 51. Coun for Nat Acad Awards BA 79. Oak Hill Coll 76. **d** 79 Willesden for Lon **p** 80 Lon. C of Em Northwood Dio Lon from 79. *64 Chester Road, Northwood, Middx.* (Northwood 25019)

BENTLEY, James. b 37. TD 78. Late Postmaster of Mert Coll Ox BA (2nd cl Mod Hist) 59, 2nd cl Th 61, MA 63. Univ of Ox BD 75. Univ of Sussex D Phil 80. St Steph Ho Ox 59. **d** 62 Hulme for Man **p** 63 Man. C of St Steph Elton 62-64; Swinton (in c of All SS) 64-66; CF (TAVR) from 65; R of All SS Stretford 66-72; V of Oldham 73-77; Maurice Reckitt Research Fell Univ of Sussex 77-79; Conduct and Sen Chap Eton Coll 79-81. *37 Montagu Road, Datchet, Slough, Berks, SL3 9DT.* (Slough 45627)

BENTLEY, Robert George. St Jo Coll Morpeth 66. **d** 67 **p** 68 Melb. C of Bentleigh 67-68; St Geo Footscray W 68-70; P-in-c of Kenwick w Thornlie 70-71; R of Wanneroo w Yanchep 77; Perm to Offic Dio Perth from 77. *14 Starrs Road, Quinns Rocks, W Australia 6030.*

BENTLEY, William. Univ Coll Dur BA 39, Dipl in Th 40, MA 42. St Andr Coll Whittlesford 40. **d** 41 **p** 42 Dur. C of Chester-le-Street 41-46; Bishopwearmouth 46-49; PC of St

Pet Bp Auckland 49-59; R of Hartlepool Dio Dur from 59. *Rectory, Church Close, Hartlepool, Cleveland, TS24 0PW.* (Hartlepool 67030)

BENTON, John Anthony. b 27. Ex Coll Ox BA (Th) 48, MA 52. Sarum Th Coll 49. **d** 50 **p** 51 Ex. C of St Thos Devonport 50-52; Tavistock 52-55; St Mich AA Heavitree Ex 55-56; V of Silsoe 56-61; R of Lower Gravenhurst 56-61; V of U Gravenhurst 56-61; C of St Cuthb Port Eliz 61-63; R of St Sav Port Eliz 64-68; Moretonhampstead 68-74; RD of Moreton 73-74; R of Holsworthy w Hollacombe and Cookbury 74-80; Surr from 75; Team R of Withycombe Raleigh w Exmouth Dio Ex from 80. *Rectory, Withycombe Village Road, Exmouth, Devon, EX8 3AE.* (Exmouth 4182)

BENTON, Kerry William. b 48. St Jo Coll Auckld LTh 75. **d** 75 **p** 76 Auckld. C of St Heliers Bay 75-78; Henderson 78-80; V of Thames 80-81; Perm to Offic Dio Auckld from 81. *347 Triangle Road, Henderson, Auckland, NZ.*

BENTON, Michael John. b 38. Univ of Lon BSc 60. Sarum Wells Th Coll 72. **d** and **p** 74 Win. C of Weeke 74-76; Bursledon 76-78; Lect K Alfred's Coll Win 74-76; R of Over Wallop and Nether Wallop Dio Win from 78; Dir of Educn Dio Win from 79. *Over Wallop Rectory, Stockbridge, Hants.* (Wallop 345)

BENWELL, Rosemary Anne. b 15. Wycl Coll Tor 40. **d** 77 Bp Read for Tor **p** 77 Tor. Hon C of St Jo Div Scarborough Tor 77-81. *St John's Convent, 1 Botham Road, Willowdale, Ont, Canada M2N 2J5.*

BENZIES, Keith John. Univ of Glas MA 59. Sarum Th Coll 60. **d** 62 **p** 63 York. C of St Nich Hull 62-66; Vice-Prin St Paul's Th Coll Ambat 66-69; Prin from 69; C of Ambat 68-75; Dioc Sec Dio Antan 68-79; Chan 70-75; P-in-c of Ambatoharanana 75-79; Antsir from 79; Bp's Sec Dio Antsir from 79. *18 Rue de la Prison, Antsiranana, Malagasy.*

BERDINNER, Clifford. b 24. **d** 64 **p** 65 Leic. C of St Pet w St Hilda Leic 64-67; R of Heather 67-72. *Hilltop, Asharington, Totnes, Devon.*

BERDOE, Bertram Walter Manby. b 08. St Cath Coll Cam BA 31, MA 35. Ridley Hall Cam 31. **d** 33 **p** 34 Lon. C of Ch Ch Spitalfields 33-35; Chap of Dohnavur Fellowship Dio Tinn 35-42; w Indian Army 42-45; CMS Miss at Palamcottah Dio Tinn 46-53; R of Ch Ch w All SS Spitalfields 53-60; V of Cullompton 60-66; Chap Nai Hosps 66-72. *102,Southover, Burton Bradstock, Bridport, Dorset DT6 4RD.*

BEREGHA, Davidson Inifuroboemi. CMS Coll Awka Nigeria 32. **d** 33 **p** 35 Niger. Hd Master St Paul's Sch Opobo 33-35; P Dio Niger 35-52; Dio Nig Delta 52-72; Archd of Delta W 60-66. *c/o St Luke's Parsonage, Box 8, Nembe, Nigeria.*

BERESFORD, Ven Alfred de la Poer. St Paul's Coll Grahmstn 58. **d** 59 **p** 60 St John's. C of Clydesdale 59-62; All Saints 62-64; P-in-c 64-74; St Mary and St Matt Ugie 74-81; Hon Can of St John's 76-81; Archd of Centr Transkei from 81; P-in-c of St Cuthb and St Paul U Mjika Dio St John's from 81. *PO St Cuthbert's 5171, TranskEi, S Africa.*

BERESFORD, John Claudius William. MC 45. Trin Coll Dub BA 35, MA 50. **d** 36 **p** 37 Oss. C of Rathdowney 36-39; Dioc C Dios Kilm Elph and Ard 39-40; CF (EC) 40-46; I of Loughrea w Tynagh and Killinane 46-50; Carbury 50-54; Naas Dio Kild from 54; Treas and Can of Kild Cathl 61-64; Chan 64-72 and from 77; Prec 72-76 and from 79; Archd of Kild 76-79. *St David's Castle, Naas, Co Kildare, Irish Republic.* (Naas 7206)

BERESFORD, Peter Marcus de la Poer. b 49. St Jo Coll Dur 74. **d** 77 Penrith for Carl **p** 78 Carl. C of Walney Is 77-80; Netherton Dio Carl from 80. *20 Galloway Close, Maryport, Cumbria, CA15 7QR,* (Maryport 4870)

BERESFORD-DAVIES, Thomas. St D Coll Lamp BD 67. **d** 42 **p** 43 Glouc. C of St Mary de Lode Glouc 42-46; Langley-Marish (in c of St John Langley) 46; St Jas Glouc 46-48; V of Church Honeybourne w Cow Honeybourne 48-51; R of Rudford 51-56; PC of Upleadon (w Pauntley from 55) 51-62; V of Down-Hatherley w Twigworth Dio Glouc from 62. *Twigworth Rectory, Gloucester, GL2 4PQ.* (Gloucester 730362)

BERESFORD-PEIRSE, Mark de la Poer. b 45. Qu Coll Birm 73. **d** 76 Knaresborough for Ripon **p** 77 Ripon. C of Garforth 76-79; Beeston Dio Ripon from 79. *St David's House, Waincliffe Drive, Leeds, LS11 8ET.* (Leeds 702829)

BERESFORD-PEIRSE, Peter de la Poer. b 07. Magd Coll Ox BA 29, MA 54. Cudd Coll 30. **d** 31 **p** 32 Lon. C of St Mary of Eton Hackney Wick 31-35; Farnham Royal 35-42; C-in-c of St Mich Newland Hull 42-45; V of St Aug Newland Hull 45-48; Overbury w Teddington 48-54; R of Richmond Yorks 54-62; Tilehurst 62-70; RD of Reading from 68; V of Warborough 70-75. *Sandwith Lodge, Bedale, N Yorks, DL8 1HB.*

BERG, John Russell. MBE 78. Sarum Th Coll 57. **d** 60 **p** 61 St E. C of St Aug of Hippo Ipswich 60-64; Whitton 64-65; Chap Miss to Seamen Hong Kong 65-68; Yokohama from 68. *The Missions to Seamen, Port P.O. Box 139, Yokohama, Japan.*

BERG, Paul Michael. b 31. Univ of Lon BA 53. Oak Hill Th Coll 54. **d** 56 **p** 57 Chelmsf. C of Woodford Wells 56-60; V of Tittensor 60-65; Rainham 65-74; R of Wennington 65-74; V of Ch Ch (w Em to 74) Clifton Dio Bris from 74. *16 Mortimer Road, Clifton, Bristol, BS8 4EY.* (Bris 736524)

BERGER, Jeffrey Alan. b 47. ACT BTh 77. St Jo Coll Morpeth 75. **d** and **p** 78 Melb. C of St Bart Ferntree Gully 78-80; I of Warrandyte w Pk Orchard Dio Melb from 80. *St Stephen's Vicarage, Warrandyte, Vic, Australia 3113.*

BERKSHIRE, Archdeacon of. *See* Brown, Ven John Edward.

BERLIN, George Albert. Episc Th Sem Kentucky LTh 73. **d** 73 Kentucky **p** 73 Athab. I of Fort Chipewyan Dio Athab from 73. *Box 18, Fort Chipewyan, Alta., Canada.* (835-2363)

BERMUDA, Lord Bishop of. *See* Genders, Right Rev (Anselm) Roger Alban Marson.

BERNARDI, Frederick John. b 33. Chich Th Coll 55. **d** 58 **p** 59 Blackb. C of St Luke Blackb 58-60; Ribbleton 60-63; V of Brinsley w Underwood 63-66; St Leon Barb 67-71; Chap HM Pris Barb 68-71; V of St Agatha Sparkbrook 71-77; C-in-c of Ch Ch Sparkbrook 73-75; V of Haywards Heath Dio Chich 77-80; Team R from 80; Surr from 78. *Rectory, St Wilfrid's Way, Haywards Heath, W Sussex, RH16 3QH.* (0444-413300)

BERNERS-WILSON, Daniel Downing. b 10. ALCD 37. **d** 36 **p** 37 Portsm. C of St Jude Southsea 36-38; H Trin Cambridge 38-39; Perm to Offic Dio Portsm 39-44; LPr Dio Lon 44-53; Chap RAFVR 41-44; Officer for Relig Training Nat Assoc of Boys' Clubs 45-46; Warden of Ford Castle Nat Assoc of Boys' Clubs 45-48; Chap Eton Coll 49-53; R of Frant 53-72. *The Hop House, Cousley Wood, Wadhurst, E Sussex.*

BEROBERO, Alban. **d** 78 Aipo. d Dio Aipo. *Koinambe P.M.B, via Mount Hagen, Papua New Guinea.*

BEROBERO, Malchus Euri. St Aidan's Coll Dogura. **d** 68 Bp Kendall for New Guinea **p** 72 Papua. D Dio New Guinea 68-71; P Dio Papua 71-77; Dio Aipo 77-79. *Movi, via Goroka, Papua New Guinea.*

BERRETT, Paul Graham. b 49. St Chad's Coll Dur BA 70. St Steph Ho Ox 71. **d** 74 **p** 75 St Alb. C of Hockerill 74-77; Leighton Buzzard Dio St Alb from 77. *St Andrew's House, Beaudesert, Leighton Buzzard, Beds.* (0525-372163)

BERRIDGE, Grahame Richard. b 38. St Jo Coll Dur 62. SOC 71. **d** 72 **p** 73 S'wark. C of St Mich and AA S Beddington 72-75; St Jas Merton Dio S'wark from 75. *186 Wandle Road, Morden, Surrey.* (01-640 7568)

BERRIMAN, Colin George Frederick. Moore Coll Syd ThL 70. **d** and **p** 71 Syd. C of N Syd 71-72; Port Kembla 72-75; Chap Norf I 75-77; C-in-c of Kangaroo Valley 77-79; R of St Luke Berry w Kangaroo Valley Dio Syd from 79. *66 Princess Street, Berry, NSW, Australia 2535.* (64-1058)

BERRIMAN, Walter. b 11. Worc Ordin Coll 61. **d** 63 **p** 64 Ripon. C of St Mary Beeston 63-68; V of Ottringham w Sunk Is Dio York from 68; P-in-c of Halsham Dio York from 78; RD of S Holderness from 81. *Ottringham Vicarage, Hull, Yorks, HU12 0AL.* (Keyingham 2007)

BERROW, Philip Rees. b 36. St D Coll Lamp 59. **d** 62 Bp T M Hughes for Llan **p** 63 Llan. C of Neath w Llantwit 62-66; CF from 67. *c/o Ministry of Defence, Bagshot Park, Bagshot, Surrey.*

BERRY, Adrian Charles. b 50. Merton Coll Ox BA 71. Cudd Coll 72. **d** 75 Tewkesbury for Glouc **p** 76 Glouc. C of St Mary Prestbury 75-81; Cirencester w Watermoor Dio Glouc from 81. *Watermoor Parsonage, Cirencester, Glos.* (Cirencester 2299)

BERRY, Alan Peter. b 36. N-W Ordin Course 74. **d** 77 **p** 78 Ripon (APM). C of Headingley 77-78; Chapel Allerton Dio Ripon from 78. *4 Carr Manor Garth, Leeds, LS17 5AS.*

BERRY, Brian. b 10. St Mich Coll Llan 42. **d** 44 **p** 45 Mon. C of Christchurch 44-47; St Aug Haggerston 47-50; Lynton 50-51; St Mich Golders Green 51-55; All SS Twickenham 55-57; V of St Phil Tottenham 57-64; R of Bridford 64-66; V of Colaton Raleigh 66-81. *63 Polsloe Road, Exeter, EX1 2EA.* (Exeter 55234)

BERRY, David Llewellyn Edward. b 39. St Jo Coll Cam 2nd cl Law Trip pt i 60, BA (3rd cl Law Trip pt ii) 61, MA 65. Wells Th Coll 64. **d** 66 **p** 67 Lon. C of All SS w St Frideswide Poplar 66-69; Ellesmere Port 69-73; V of Brafferton w Pilmoor and Myton-on-Swale 73-79; P-in-c of Thormanby 78-79; R of Skelton-in-Cleveland w Upleatham Dio York from 79. *Rectory, Skelton-in-Cleveland, Saltburn, Cleve, TS12 2ES.* (Guisborough 50329)

BERRY, Geoffrey Wilbur Ronald. b 22. Ridley Hall Cam 54. **d** 56 **p** 57 Lon. C of Em Northwood 56-59; V of St Matthias Poplar 59-70; Westacre 70-79; R of Gayton-Thorpe w E Walton 70-79; V of Nutley Dio Chich from 79; R of

Maresfield Dio Chich from 79. *Vicarage, Nutley, Uckfield, E Sussex, TN22 3NH.*

BERRY, (Silvanus) Graham Renwick. b 24. Univ of NZ BA 54. Coll of Resurr Mirfield. M CR 64. **d** 57 **p** 58 Lon. C of St Cuthb w St Matthias Earls Court 57-61; Warden and Prior Ho of Resurr Leeds and L to Offic Dio Ripon 68-75; Prior Ho of Resurr Mirfield from 75. *House of the Resurrection, Mirfield, W Yorks.* (Mirfield 493272)

BERRY, John. b 41. Univ of Dur BA (2nd cl Psychology) 62. Oak Hill Th Coll 63. **d** 65 **p** 66 Man. C of Burnage 65-68; Middleton Lancs 68-70; Perm to Offic Dio Liv and Man 70-73; Trav Sec Inter-Varsity Fellowship 70-73; V of St Pet (and Ch Ch w H Trin from 76) Derby 73-81; C-in-c of Ch Ch w H Trin Derby 73-76; Bp's Officer for Evang and P-in-c of Bampton w Mardale Dio Carl from 81. *Vicarage, Bampton Grange, Penrith, Cumb.* (Bampton 239)

BERRY, Kenneth Percy John. b 33. Sussex Coll of Tech BSc 76. Sarum Wells Th Coll 79. **d** 75 **p** 77 Botswana. d Dio Botswana 75-77; P Dio Matab from 78. *12 Bredon Road, Tegela, North End, Bulawayo, Zimbabwe.*

BERRY, Michael. b 22. Ex Coll Ox BA 49, MA 54, Westcott Ho Cam 69. **d** 71 Reading for Ox **p** 72 Ox. C of All SS Didcot 71-75; R of Farthinghoe and Hinton-in-the-Hedges w Steane Dio Pet from 75. *Farthinghoe Rectory, Brackley, Northants, NN13 5NY.* (0295-710946)

BERRY, Canon Peter Austin. b 35. Keble Coll Ox BA (3rd cl Engl) 59, 3rd cl Th 61, MA 63. St Steph Ho Ox 59. **d** 62 Bp McKie for Cov **p** 63 Cov. C of St Mark Cov 62-66; St Mich Cathl Cov 66-73; Dioc Commun Relns Chap 64-70; Midl Regional Officer Commun Relns Comm 70-73; Can Res of Cov from 73; Vice-Provost from 77; Adv to Bp of Cov on Commun Relns from 77. *20 Styvechale Avenue, Coventry.* (0203 73704)

BERRY, Richard. b 21. St Deiniol's Libr Hawarden. **d** 62 **p** 63 Ely. C of St Luke Chesterton 62-65; V of E w S Cowton (and Birkby 65-73) 65-78; Barkston w Syston Dio Linc from 78; Belton Dio Linc from 78; Honington Dio Linc from 78. *Parsonage, Syston, Grantham, Lincs, NG32 2BY.* (Honington 381)

✠ **BERRY, Right Rev Robert Edward Fraser.** Sir Geo Williams Coll Montr BA 50. Montr Dioc Th Coll LTh and BD (McGill) 53, Hon DD 73. **d** 53 Montr for Br Columb **p** 54 Br Columb. C of Ch Ch Cathl Vic 53-55; I of St Marg Hamilton Ont 55-61; R of Orangeville 61-63; St Luke Winnipeg 63-67; Kelowna 67-71; Cons Ld Bp of Kootenay in Ch of St Mich AA Kelowna on 24 June 71 by Abp Scott (Primate); Abp of New Westmr; Bps of BC; Caled; Calg; Carib; Rupld; Yukon; and Bp Somerville. *1857 Maple Street, Kelowna, BC, Canada.* (604-762 3306)

BERRY, Samuel John. b 09. Ch Coll Cam 2nd cl Hist Trip pt i 29, BA (3rd cl Th Trip pt i) 31, MA 34. Ridley Hall Cam 31. **d** 32 **p** 33 S'wark. C of H Trin Richmond 32-35; CMS Miss at Buwalasi Tr Coll 35-47; Prin 35-47; Exam Chap to Bp on U Nile 42-47; V of Pampisford 48-50; Warden of St Andr Coll Pampisford 48-49; V of Babraham 48-50; St Mark Wolverhampton 50-54; Ropley (w W Tisted from 56) 54-61; R of L Hallingbury 61-69; LPr Dio S'wark from 69; Perm to Offic Dio Roch from 69; Asst Chap S Lon Crem and Streatham Pk Cem 69-74. *29 Woodside Road, Bickley, Bromley, Kent, BR1 2ES.* (01-467 1528)

BERRY, Walter Richard. b 13. St Andr Coll Pampisford. **d** 47 **p** 48 Nor. C of Gt Yarmouth 47-51; V of Steeple Claydon 51-54; R of St Werburgh Bris 54-58; L Pr Dio Bris from 58. *11 Anne Close, Thorpe St Andrew, Norwich, NR7 0PH.* (0603-35196)

BERRY, William James. b 25. Bps' Coll Cheshunt 62. **d** 63 **p** 64 St Alb. C of Redbourn 63-65; Hatfield Hyde 65-67; V of Lidlington 67-72; Dunton w Wrestlingworth and Eyeworth Dio St Alb from 72. *Dunton Vicarage, Biggleswade, Beds.* (Biggleswade 313744)

BERRYMAN, Canon Carl. b 39. Late Exhib of Ex Coll Ox BA (2nd cl Th) 61, MA 65. Univ of Birm Dipl Th 62. Qu Coll Birm 61. **d** 63 **p** 64 Blackb. C of Penwortham 63-66; Altham w Clayton-le-Moors 66-68; V of St Pet Chorley Dio Blackb from 68; Chap Eaves Lane Hosp Chorley 68; RD of Chorley from 73; Hon Canon of Blackb Cathl from 80. *St Peter's Vicarage, Harpers Lane, Chorley, Lancs.* (Chorley 63423)

BERRYMAN, Richard James. b 32. Bp's Univ Lennox BA 55, LST 57. Univ of W Ont MA 71. **d** 56 **p** 57 Niag. C of Stoney Creek and P-in-c of Fruitland 57-60; I of Ch of Transfig Lon 60-62; R 63-65; on leave 65-69; R of Tillsonburg 69-71; Assoc P Ch Ch Cathl Hamilton Dio Nag 74-79; Hon C from 79; Consultant Dio Niag and Gen Syn Angl Ch of Canada 74-79; Media Officer Angl Ch of Canada from 79. *600 Jarvis Street, Toronto, Ont, Canada.* (416-924 9191)

BERRYMAN, William Arthur David. b 47. Univ of Lon BD 69. Sarum Wells Th Coll 75. **d** 76 Taunton for B & W **p** 77 B & W. Asst Master Preston Sch Yeovil and C of St Mich AA Yeovil 76-80; C of St D City and Dio Ex from 80; Chap Ex Coll from 80. *58 Velwell Road, Exeter, Devon.*

BERSON, Alan Charles. b 31. Univ of Michigan BA 52, MA 53. Univ of Lon PhD 62. St Steph Ho Ox 63. **d** 65 **p** 66 Ripon. C of Leeds 65-68; St Giles-in-the-Fields 68; L to Offic Dio Lon from 69. *74 Ridgmount Gardens, WC 1.* (01-636 1990)

BERTHOLD, Basil Stanley. St Paul's Coll Grahmstn LTh 48. **d** 48 **p** 49 Johann. C of Orange Grove Johann 49-51; R of Standerton 51-52; C of Mossel Bay 52-55; Knysna 55-56; R of Formosa 56-59; Oudtshoorn 59-69; P-in-c of Milnerton 69-78; R of Ch K Claremont Dio Capetn from 78. *Garfield Road, Claremont 7700, CP, S Africa.* (61-3431)

BERTRAM, Peter William. ACT ThL 61. **d** 61 **p** 62 C & Goulb. C of St Jo Bapt Canberra 61-62; St Paul Canberra 62-66; R of Bribbaree 66-69; Binda 69-73; Bombala 73-81; Moruya Dio C & Goulb from 81. *Box 58, Moruya, NSW, Australia 2537.*

BERTRAM, Richard Henry. b 27. Trin Coll Dub BA and Div Test 50, MA 64. **d** 53 Elph **p** 54 Kilm. C of Sligo 53-56; Booterstown 56-58; I of Stranorla w Kilteevogue and Meenglass 58-65; St Cath w St Jas Dub 65-73; RD of Raph 65-66; R of St Matt Irishtown City and Dio Dub from 73; St Mary Donnybrook City and Dio Dub from 74. *4 Ailesbury Grove, Dublin 4.*

BERUGARI, Ananias. St Aid Coll Dogura. **d** 57 New Guinea. d Dio New Guinea 57-71; Dio Papua from 71. *Gona Anglican Mission, via Popondota, Papua New Guinea.*

BESS, Calvin Wendell. Codr Coll Barb 62. **d** 65 **p** 66 Trinid. C of Scarboro' Tobago 65-68; H Trin Cathl Port of Spain 68-69; St Patr, Tobago 69-79; H Cross Marabella Dio Trinid from 79. *Rectory, Plaisance Park, Marabella Trinidad, W Indies.*

BESS, Canon Cyril Henry George. b 20. AKC 50. **d** 50 **p** 51 Roch. C of St Alb Dartford 50-53; Moulsecoomb 53-60; V of St Mary Virg E Grinstead 60-75; RD of E Grinstead 70-75; Eastbourne from 75; V of Eastbourne Dio Chich from 75; Can and Preb of Chich Cathl from 75. *28 Vicarage Drive, Eastbourne, BN20 8AP.* (Eastbourne 20420)

BESSANT, Brian Keith. b 32. Roch Th Coll 65. **d** 67 **p** 68 Roch. C of St William's Eccles Distr Chatham 67-71; Cove 71-74; V of Frimley Green Dio Guildf from 74. *Vicarage, Sturt Road, Frimley Green, Camberley, Surrey, GU16 6HY.* (Deepcut 5179)

BESSANT, Idwal Brian. b 39. Univ of Wales Dipl Th 68. St Mich Coll Llan 65. **d** 68 Bp T M Hughes for Llan **p** 69 Llan. C of Llantwit Major w St Donat 68-73; R of Llangammarch w Garth Llanfechan and Llanlleonfel 73-77; Crickhowell 77-78; St Hel Larnaca 79-80: St Andr Larnaca Dio Cyprus from 80; Chap to Bp of Cyprus 79-80. *Box 500, Larnaca, Cyprus.*

BESSANT, Simon David. b 56. Univ of Sheff BMus 77. St Jo Coll Nottm Dipl Th 79. **d** 81 Warrington for Liv. C of St John & St Jas Litherland Dio Liv from 81. *86 Monfa Road, Bootle, Liverpool, L20 6BG.*

BESSENT, Stephen Lyn. b 53. Univ of Bris BA 75. Wycl Hall Ox 75. **d** 77 **p** 78 Bris. C of Patchway 77-80; Team V of St Jo Bapt and St Andr Swindon Dio Bris from 80. *Church House, Raleigh Avenue, Walcot, Swindon, SN3 3DZ.* (Swindon 36505)

BEST, David Christopher. b 45. St Jo Coll Auckld 70. **d** 70 **p** 71 Ch Ch. C of St Alb Ch Ch 70-72; Timaru 72-74; V of Glenmark-Waikari 74-78; Tinwald-Hinds Dio Ch Ch from 78. *Vicarage, Jane Street, Tinwald, NZ.* (Ash 83575)

BEST, Frank Milner. b 21. Linc Coll Ox BA and MA 49. Bps' Coll Cheshunt 49. **d** 50 **p** 51 Leic. C of St Phil Leic 50-53; SPG Miss P Dio Chota N 53-56; C of Goring-by-Sea 56-58; Min of Ch Ch Conv Distr Horam 58-63; R of Sibson w Upton 63-75; P-in-c of Quendon w Rickling Dio Chelmsf 75-78; R (w Wicken Bonhunt) from 78. *Quendon Rectory, Saffron Walden, Essex, CB11 3XJ.* (Rickling 238)

BEST, Harold Arthur Frank. b 15. Cudd Coll. **d** 47 **p** 48 Bris. C of St Andr Chippenham 47-50; V of Chislehampton w Stadhampton 50-57; R of Drayton St Leon 50-57; V of Dorchester-on-Thames (w Burcote 57-63; w Berinsfield 63-74) 57-74; RD of Cudd 66-73; C-in-c of Leigh w Batcombe and Chetnole 74-76; R of High Stoy 76-80. *14 Acreman Street, Cerne Abbas, Dorchester, Dorset, DT2 7JX.* (Cerne Abbas 413)

BEST, Canon Harold James. KCNS BA 22, MA 23. **d** 23 **p** 24 Fred. Min of Burton w Maugerville 23-27; C of H Trin St John 27-32; Miss in Salisbury and Havelock 32-39; R of Woodstock 39-51; V of French Creek 51-52; R of Qualicum Beach 52-56; Hon Can of BC from 56; LPr Dio BC from 56. *1368 West 21st Street, North Vancouver, BC, Canada.*

BEST, Howard Clifford. **d** 65 Bp Snell for Tor **p** 66 Tor. C of St Steph Tor 65-68; Minden 68-71; R of St John Weston Tor 71-80; St Paul Runnymede City and Dio Tor from 80. *404 Willard Avenue, Toronto, M6S 3R5, Ont, Canada.*

BEST, John William. b 02. Bps' Coll Cheshunt 37. **d** 37 **p** 38 Lon. C of St Paul Tottenham 37-40; St Paul Hasland 40-45; St Mary Wirksworth 45-47; St Geo Barkingside 47-53; R of E Donyland 53-65; C-in-c of Fingringhoe 60-62; V of Em Leyton 65-74; Perm to Offic Dio Chelmsf from 74. *110a Orford Road, E17.*

BEST, Raymond. b 42. Sarum and Wells Th Coll 71. **d** 74 **p** 75 Newc T. C of Whorlton 74-78; Seaton Hirst (in c of St Andr) Dio Newc T from 78. *St Andrew's House, Hawthorn Road, Ashington, Northumb.* (Ashington 818691)

BEST, Sydney Harold John. St Barn Coll N Adel ThL 39. **d** 39 **p** 40 Perth. C of St Andr Subiaco 39-41; R of Meckering and Quairading 41-42; Chap and Supt Forrest River Miss 42-47; C of Ch Ch Claremont 47-48; R of Moora 48-54; Nedlands 54-66; Can of Perth 64-66; Perm to Offic Dio Perth from 67; Dio NW Austr 70-78; C of Port Hedland 78-79; P-in-c of Ravensthorpe Dio Bunb from 79. *Rectory, Ravensthorpe, W Australia 6346.*

BESTELINK, William Meindert Croft. b 48. Univ of Hull BA 70. Cudd Coll 71. **d** 73 **p** 74 Nor. C of Holt Nor 73-74; E Dereham 74-76; Thorpe-Episcopi 76-80; R of Felmingham Dio Nor from 80; Suffield Dio Nor from 80; Colby w Banningham and Tuttington Dio Nor from 80. *Felmingham Rectory, North Walsham, Norf.* (N Walsham 402382)

BESTER, Michael Nicholas. b 15. **d** 74 **p** 75 Capetn (APM). C of Bellville S Dio Capetn from 74. *72 Brand Street, Bellville South, CP, S Africa.*

BESWICK, Canon Colin Edward. b 28. Univ of Leeds BA 51. Univ of Ex MA 75. Sarum Th Coll 58. **d** 60 **p** 61 Lich. C of Shrewsbury 60-63; Min Can, Prec and Sacr of Worc Cathl 63-73; R of Bredon w Bredon's Norton 73-79; RD of Pershore 76-79; Hon Can of Worc Cathl from 78; Dir of Min Dio Worc from 79; M Advisory Bd for Redundant Chs from 79. *Vicarage, Overbury, Tewkesbury, Glos, GL20 7NT.* (Overbury 231)

BESWICK, Gary Lancelot. b 38. ALCD 63. **d** 63 **p** 64 Chelmsf. C of Walthamstow 63-67; Laisterdyke 67-70; V of Idle 70-78; N W Area Sec SAMS from 78; Publ Pr Dio Man from 78. *1 Abercorn Road, Smithills, Bolton, BL1 6LF.* (0204-43565)

BESWICK, Joseph Hubert. b 25. Univ of Birm MB ChB 48. Dipl Th (Lon) 58. **d** 59 **p** 60 Southw. LPr Dio Southw from 59. *19 Chilwell Road, Beeston, Notts.*

BESWICK, Canon Walter. b 13. St Aid Coll 46. **d** 48 **p** 49 York. C of St Steph Acomb York 48-52; R of Bulmer w Welburn and Castle Howard 52-64; Terrington Dio York from 64; R of Dalby w Whenby Dio York from 64; RD of Malton from 75; Can and Preb of York Minster from 79. *Terrington Rectory, York.* (Coneysthorpe 226)

BETEBOYE, Alowiye Green. **d** 76 Nig Delta. d Dio Nig Delta. *St Mark's Parsonage, Kaiama P.A., via Ahoada, Rivers State, Nigeria.*

BETETSE, David. b 41. St Phil Th Coll Kongwa 67. **d** 69 **p** 70 W Tang. P Dio W Tang from 70. *PO Box 44, Urambo, Tanzania.*

BETHEL, John Elvin. Univ of Manit BA 42. Trin Coll Tor LTh 44. **d** 44 **p** 45 Rupld. C of Snowflake 44-45; I 45-46; C of All SS Winnipeg 46-48; R of Maniton 48-52; St Phil Norwood Winnipeg 52-61; St Jo Evang Edmon 61-74; Can of Edmon 67-74; R of St Mary Kerrisdale Vanc Dio New Westmr from 74. *2490 West 37th Avenue, Vancouver, BC, Canada.*

BETSIMBIRE, Ven Yeremiya. Bp Tucker Coll Mukono 60. **d** 60 **p** 62 Ankole-K. P Dio Ankole-K 60-67; Dio Kig (N Kig from 81) from 67; Can of Kig 75-81; Archd Dio N Kig from 81. *Box 23, Rukungiri, Uganda.*

BETTERIDGE, Maurice Stanley. Univ of NZ BA 47, MA 49, BD and Fulbright Scho 55. Gen Th Sem NY STM 59. NZ Bd of Th Stud LTh 53. **d** 51 **p** 52 Nel. C of Nel Cathl 51-54; Papanui 54-55; V of Lincoln 55-59; St Matt Dun 59-65; Chap Univ of New Engl Armid 65-72; Archd of Armid 70-72; Exam Chap to Bp of Armid 66-72; Federal Sec CMS Syd 73-79; Perm to Offic Dio C & Goulb 77-79; Prin Ridley Coll Melb and L to Offic Dio Melb from 79. *Ridley College, Walker Street, Parkville, Vic, Australia 3052.* (380 1396)

BETTON, Very Rev John Richard. b 25. Pemb Coll Ox BA (2nd cl Mod Hist) 48, Dipl Th 49, MA 53. Cudd Coll 49. **d** 51 **p** 52 Dur. C of H Trin Southwick 51-55; Cowley (in c of St Luke) 55-59; V 59-66; Surr 60-66; Proc Conv Ox 64-70; C-in-c of Swaby w S Thoresby and Belleau 66-73; St Hugh's Missr Linc 66-73; Can and Preb of Linc Cathl 73-77; Can (Emer) from 77; R of Hadleigh w Layham and Shelley Dio St E from 73; Dean of Bocking from 73; RD of Hadleigh from 76; Surr from 80; Hon Can of St E from 81. *Deanery, Hadleigh, Ipswich, Suff, IP7 5DT.* (Hadleigh 822218)

BETTRIDGE, Winston Graham. b 39. Kelham Th Coll 60. **d** 65 **p** 66 Bradf. C of Burley-in-Wharfedale 65-67; Baildon 67-70; V of St Sav Harden w St Matt Wilsden Bingley 70-81; M Gen Syn 80-81; Team R of Kirkby Lonsdale Dio Carl from 81. *Rectory, Vicarage Lane, Kirkby Lonsdale, Carnforth, Lancs LA6 2BA.* (Kirkby Lonsdale 71320)

BETTS, Anthony Clive. b 40. Wells Th Coll 63. **d** 65 **p** 66 Ripon. C of All H w St Simon Leeds 65-67; Wetherby 67-70; Adel 70-73; V of All SS Leeds 73-79; C-in-c of St Sav w St Hilda Cross Green 75-79; V of All SS and St Hilda w St Sav Cross Green, Richmond Hill Leeds Dio Ripon from 79. *All Saints Vicarage, Pontefract Lane, Leeds, LS9 9AE.* (Leeds 480971)

BETTS, Anthony Percy. b 26. BD (Lon) 52. ALCD 52. **d** 52 **p** 53 Guildf. C of St Sav Stoke Guildf 52-56; Hanworth 56-59; PC of St Aug Derby 59-68; V 68-74; RD of Derby 71-74; Surr 72-74; V of Bracebridge Dio Linc from 74. *60 Chiltern Road, Bracebridge, Lincoln, LN5 8SE.* (Lincoln 32636)

BETTS, Cyril James. Hur Coll 56. **d** 59 **p** 60 Ont. I of Newboyne 58-59; Madoc 59-63; R of N Augusta 63-68; P-in-c of Oxford Ont 68-69; I of Tyendinaga 69-75; Kemptville Dio Ont from 75. *103 Oxford Street, Kemptville, Ont, Canada.* (613-258 3012)

BETTS, David John. b 38. Univ of Lon BSc 61. Oak Hill Th Coll 63. **d** 65 **p** 66 Ox. C of St Paul Slough 65-70; Welling (in c of Bp Ridley Ch) 70-75; V of St Paul Swanley Dio Roch from 75. *Vicarage, Hextable, Swanley, Kent, BR8 7RL.* (Swanley 62320)

BETTS, Edmund John. b 51. St Chad's Coll Dur BA 72. Univ of Birm Dipl Th 75. Univ of Lanc MA 81. Qu Coll Birm 73. **d** 76 St Alb **p** 77 Hertford for St Alb. C of St Luke Leagrave Luton 76-79; Asst Chap R Albert Hosp Lanc 79-81; Chap of Kidderminster Gen & Lea Castle Hosps from 81. *29 Humphries Drive, Worcester Rise, Kidderminster, Worcs.* (0562-745531)

BETTS, George William John. Univ Coll Ex BA (Lon) 51. Westcott Ho Cam 51. **d** 53 **p** 54 Newc T. C of St Luke Wallsend 53-54; St Jas Benwell Newc T 54-56; Plumstead 56; St Andr Peckham 56-57; Eltham 57-60; Findon 60-67; St Jo Bapt Cathl Bulawayo 67-68; Sherborne w Castleton and Lillington 68-69; St Mary The Boltons Kens 75-76. *Flat 2, 13a Cranley Gardens, SW7.*

BETTS, Ivan Ringland. b 38. Trin Coll Dub BA 61, MA 67. **d** 62 **p** 63 Down. C of Ballyholme 62-65; Dundela 65-69; Chap Miss to Seamen Wilton, Yorks 69; Port Sudan 69-71; Port of Spain Dio Trinid 71-73; C of Drumglass 73-81; R of Augher w Newtownsaville Dio Clogh from 81. *Rectory, Augher, Co Tyrone, N Ireland.*

BETTS, Paul Robert. b 31. Univ of Lon BSc (Eng) 51. Oak Hill Th Coll 53. **d** 56 **p** 57 Ex. C of St Jude Plymouth 56-59; St Mark Cheltm 59-63; V of St Paul Finchley 63-76; Perm to Offic Dio Ely 76-79; Warden St Columba Centre Cam 76-79; R of Datchworth w Tewin Dio St Alb from 79. *Rectory, Brookbridge Lane, Datchworth, Herts, SG3 6SU.* (Stevenage 813067)

✠ **BETTS, Right Rev Stanley Woodley.** b 12. CBE 67. Jes Coll Cam 2nd cl Hist Trip pt i 32, BA (3rd cl Law Trip pt ii) 33, MA 37. Ridley Hall Cam 33. **d** 35 **p** 36 Glouc. C of St Paul Cheltm 35-38; Chap RAF 38-47; Men in Disp 44; Chap Clare Coll Cam 47-49; Chap Cam Past 47-56; Exam Chap to Bp of Southw 47-56; V of H Trin Cam 49-57; Proc Conv Ely 52-59; Select Pr Univ of Cam 55; Cons Ld Bp Suffr of Maidstone in S'wark Cathl 1 Nov 56 by Abp of Cant; Bps of Lon; S'wark; Cov; Chelmsf; Portsm; and St E; Bps Suffr of Dover; Woolwich; Kingston T; and Croydon; and Bps Walsh and Mann; Res 66; Abp's Repr w HM Forces 57-66; Dean of Roch 66-77. *2 Kings Houses, Old Pevensey, E Sussex.* (Eastbourne 762421)

✠ **BETUNGURA, Right Rev Amos.** Bp Tucker Coll Mukono 56. **d** 57 **p** 60 Ugan. Tutor Bp Tucker Coll Mukono 57-65; Prin 65-70; Cons Ld Bp of Ankole in St James Cathl Ruharo 6 Dec 70 by Abps of Ugan and Cant; and Bps of Prov of Ugan; Apptd Bp of E Ank 76. *Box 14, Mbarara, Uganda.* (Mbarara 2119)

BEUKES, Douglas. Oak Hill Th Coll 46. **d** 51 **p** 52 Chelmsf. C of Walthamstow 51-53; E Barnet 53-55; Chap RAF 55-58; Chap at Utrecht Dio (Gibr in Eur from 80) Lon (N & C Eur) from 59. *Van Hogendorpstraat 26, Utrecht, Holland.* (513424)

BEUKES, Peter Edwin. St Jo Vianney RC Sem Pret 62. **d** 66 RC Abp of Pret **p** 67 RC Bp of Johann. In RC Ch 66-70; Rec into Angl Commun 70 by Bp Suffr of Johann; L to Offic Dio Natal 70-72; P-in-c of Mooi River 72-73; St John Mtubatuba 73-78; Utrecht Dio Zulu from 78. *Box 347, Utrecht, Zululand, S Africa.*

BEVAN, Alan John. b 29. Univ of Bris BA 54. Oak Hill Th Coll 54. **d** 56 **p** 59 Lich. C of Penn Fields 56-57; Corsham 58-61; Wath-upon-Dearne 61-68; Darfield 68-71; Drypool (in c of St Andr) 71-79; Chap HM Pris Wandsworth from 79. *123 Magdalene Road, Wandsworth, SW18.* (01-874 3190)

BEVAN, Bryan David. Univ of Lon BD 60, MA 70. S Th

(Lambeth) 62. St Aug Coll Cant 62. **d** 64 Nor **p** 66 Chich. C of E Dereham 64-65; Hove 65-67; Lect St Mich Coll Sarum 67-70; The Coll Bedford from 70. *Old Barn Farm, Broad Oak Lane, Bexhill-on-Sea, Sussex.*

BEVAN, Charles Joseph Godfrey. b 22. Trin Coll Dub BA 44, MA 52. **d** 45 **p** 46 Dub. C of St Geo Dub 45-49; I of Rathvilly 49-59; Carbury 59-64; R of Drogheda Dio Arm from 64. *St Peter's Rectory, Drogheda, Co Louth, Irish Republic.* (Drogheda 8441)

BEVAN, David Graham. b 34. St D Coll Lamp BA 54, LTh 56. Gen Th Sem NY MDiv 57. **d** 57 **p** 58 St D. C of Llanelly 57-60; CF 60-76. *148 Bromley Heath Road, Downend, Bristol.*

BEVAN, David John. St D Coll Lamp BA 32. **d** 30 **p** 31 St A. C of Wrexham 30-38; R of Ysceifiog 38-53; Chap to Walton Hosp Liv 53-63; R of Llansantffraid-Glyn-Dyfrdwy 63-77. *Erw Dalar, Carrog, Corwen, Clwyd.*

BEVAN, Dennis Butler. b 24. Univ of Bris BA 51. St Mich Coll Llan 53. **d** 54 **p** 55 Llan. C of St Cath Canton 54-56; Llangynwyd w Maesteg 56-59; Porthkerry w Barry 59-67; V of Cymmer w Porth 67-79; St Bride's Major Dio Llan from 79. *Vicarage, St Bride's Major, Bridgend, Mid-Glam CF32 0SE.* (Southerndown 880108)

BEVAN, Donald Keith. b 16. Univ of Lon BD 40. ALCD 40. **d** 40 **p** 41 Liv. C of Ch Ch Kens 40-44; St Luke Farnworth 44-48; St Luke Walton-on-the-Hill Liv 48-51; Gt Sankey 51-52; Dioc C Liv 52-53; C of Litherland 53-56; Huyton 56-59. *9b Hoscote Park, West Kirby, Chesh.*

BEVAN, Edward Geoffrey. b 02. St Jo Coll Dur LTh 26, BA 44. Lon Coll of Div 20. **d** 25 **p** 26 St E. C of Southwold 25-27; St Luke Harrogate 27-29; St Paul Margate 29-31; PC of Cringleford 31-35; V of Loddon w Sisland 35-44; St Mary Low Harrogate w Harlow Hill 44-52; Hall Green 52-60; Abbotsham 60-70. *1 Essex Court, Essex Drive, Taunton, Somt.* (Taunton 82941)

BEVAN, Canon Ernest Guy. b 1896. Lon Coll of Div 19. Univ of Lon BD 22. **d** 22 **p** 23 S'wark. C of St Paul Plumstead 22-25; Perm to Offic at St Geo Tufnell Pk 25-26; Tutor Lon Coll Div 26-33; Vice-Prin 33-36; Lect 36-40; Exam Chap to Bp of W China 34-37; E Szech 37-51; V of St Paul Leyton 36-44; Harlow 44-60; Chap Leytonstone Ho 37-44; Hillingdon Hosp 48-60; Exam Chap to Bp of Chelmsf 39-60; RD of Harlow 52-60; Surr 52-60; Hon Can of Chelmsf 55-60; Can (Emer) from 60; V of Tetsworth 60-67. *The Laurels, Bowerchalke, Salisbury, Wilts, SP5 5AY.* (Broadchalke 375)

BEVAN, Gordon Richard. b 26. N-W Ordin Course. **d** 75 Repton for Derby **p** 76 Derby. C of Spondon 75-81; R of U Langwith w Whaley Thorns Dio Derby from 81. *Upper Langwith Rectory, Mansfield, Notts.* (Shirebrook 2413)

BEVAN, Herbert Richard. b 28. Univ of Birm Dipl Th 56, MA 67. **d** 57 Birm **p** 58 Aston for Birm. C of Sutton Coldfield 57-60; All SS Chelsea 60-62; R of Abberley Dio Worc from 62; Chap Abberley Hall Sch from 62; RD of Mitton from 72; P-in-c of Pensax Dio Worc from 80. *Abberley Rectory, Worcester, WR6 6BN.* (Great Witley 248)

BEVAN, Hubert Basil Henry. b 24. St D Coll Lamp BA 52, LTh 54. Univ of Wales MTh 77, PhD 78. **d** 54 **p** 55 Swan B. C of Knighton w Heyhope 54-60; St Marg Toxt Pk 60-61; V of St Mary w All SS Palfrey Walsall 61-64; R of Sunderland 64-66; R of St Paul Hendon Bp Wearmouth 64-66; V of Gilfach Goch w Llandyfodwg 66-73; Llansantffraed-in-Elwel w Bettws-Disserth and Cregina 73-78; Glascwm and Rhulen 76-78; R of Llanferres w Nercwys and Erryrys 78-80; V of Treuddyn w Nercwys and Erryrys Dio St A from 80. *Vicarage, Treuddyn, clwyd.*

BEVAN, John Vernon. b 16. Univ of Wales BA (3rd cl Latin) 38. St Mich Coll Llan 38. **d** 39 Ban for Llan **p** 40 Llan. C of Llangeinor 39-43; St Jo Bapt Cardiff 43-50; V of Newton 50-57; R of Enmore w Goathurst 57-71; V of Carhampton 71-81. *c/o Carhampton Vicarage, Minehead, Somt.* (Dunster 376)

✠ **BEVAN, Right Rev Kenneth Graham.** b 1898. Lon Coll of Div 20. **d** 23 **p** 24 Roch. C of H Trin Tunbridge Wells 23-25; Miss Dio W China 25-36; Dio E Szech 36-40; Cons Ld Bp of E Szech in Shanghai Cathl 18 Oct 40 by Bp of N China; Bps of Chek and Shantung and Bp Norris; res 50; Commiss E Szech 50-53; V of Woolhope 51-66; R of Putley 53-66; RD of Heref S 55-66; Preb de Moreton et Whaddon in Heref Cathl 56-66; Master Abp Holgate's Hosp Hemsworth 66-77; Asst Bp in Dio Wakef 68-77. *12 Howard Link, Shipton Road, York, YO3 6UU.* (York 51895)

BEVAN, Lewis George. Chich Th Coll. **d** 31 Llan **p** 38 Sheff. C of St Paul Grangetown 31-33; Perm to Offic at Treharris 34-37; C of Brodsworth 37-38; St Chad Norton Woodseats 38-39; C-in-c of St Wilfrith's Conv Distr Moor Ends 39-44; V of St Hilda Thurnscoe E 44-52; Blacktoft 52-58; V of Laxton 52-58; R of Hawnby w Old Byland 58-61; Scawton w Cold Kirby 58-61; V of Ebberston w Allerston 61-74; C-in-c of Yedingham 64-74. *Thistleboot, West Burton, Leyburn, Yorks.* (Aysgarth 445)

BEVAN, Noel Haden. b 34. St Aid Coll 61. **d** 63 **p** 64 Bradf. C of Girlington 63-66; St Jo Evang Worksop 66-68; V of Everton w Mattersey (and Clayworth from 70) 68-77; Team V of Barton-Mills, Beck Row w Kenny Hill, Freckenham, Mildenhall w Red Lodge, W Row and Worlington Dio St E from 77. *Vicarage, Worlington, Bury St Edmunds, Suff, IP28 8RU.* (Mildenhall 713877)

BEVAN, Peter John. b 54. AKC and BA 76. St Steph Ho Ox BA (Th) 79. **d** 80 **p** 81 Wakef. C of St Martin Brighouse Dio Wakef from 80. *5 East Mount, Brighouse, W Yorks, HD6 2BP.* (Brighouse 718919)

BEVAN, Philip Frank. Chich Th Coll 65. **d** 67 Warrington for Liv **p** 68 Liv. C of Walton-on-the-Hill 67-71; P-in-c of Turks & Caicos Is 71; St Paul Long Is 71-74; R of St Matt I Nass 74-78. *c/o N-963, Nassau, Bahamas.* (52191)

BEVAN, Reginald Morgan. b 10. St D Coll Lamp BA (1st cl Hist Hons) 31. Keble Coll Ox BA (2nd cl Hist) 33, MA 37. St Mich Coll Llan 33. **d** 34 **p** 35 Llan. C of Roath 34-41; Llanishen w Lisvane 41-45; St Mary Bridgwater 45-49; PC of Walton 49-54; Whitchurch Somt 54-67; R of Norton-Malreward 54-67; V of Montacute 67-77. *1 Northfield Close, Caerleon, Newport, Gwent, NP6 1EZ.*

BEVAN, Richard Justin William. b 22. St Chad's Coll Dur LTh 42, BA (3rd cl Th) 45, Bp Robertson Div Pri 44, Capel Cure Pri 45. St Aug Coll Cant 39. **d** 45 **p** 46 Lich. C of St Pet Stoke-on-Trent 45-49; Asst Master and Chap Aberlour Orph and L to Offic Dio Moray 49-51; Asst Master at Towneley Technical High Sch Burnley 51-61; Publ Pr Dio Blackb 51-52; C of Church Kirk 52-56; Whalley 56-61; R of St Mary-le-Bow w St Mary L Dur 61-64; C-in-c 64-67; Chap Univ of Dur 61-74; V of St Osw (w St Mary-le-Bow & St Mary L from 67) Dur 64-74; Exam Chap to Bp of Carl from 71; R of Grasmere Dio Carl from 74. *Rectory, Grasmere, Cumbria.* (Grasmere 326)

BEVAN, Trevor. b 07. St D Coll Lamp BA 28. St Mich Coll Llan 29. **d** 30 **p** 31 Llan. C of Aberdare 30-34; Pencoed 34-37; Gawr Valley 37-43; Roath 43-50; R of St Nicholas (w Bonvilston from 53 and St Geo-super-Ely from 70) 50-76; Perm to Offic Dio Llan from 78. *Hawthorns, The Drope, St George-super-Ely, Cardiff, S Glam.*

BEVER, Michael Charles Stephen. b 44. Selw Coll Cam BA 66, MA 70. **d** 69 **p** 70 Bradf. C of Steeton w Eastburn 69-72; St Mary Northn 72-74; Dioc Missr Dio Niger 75-79; P-in-c of Elmstead Dio Chelmsf from 80. *Elmstead Vicarage, Colchester, Essex, CO7 7AW.* (Wivenhoe 2431)

BEVERIDGE, Bryan Merrill. b 49. Univ of Guelph Ont BSc 73. Trin Coll Tor MDiv 76. **d** and **p** 76 Ott. I of Pakenham 76-81; Ingleside and Long Sault Dio Ott from 81. *Box 239, Ingleside, Ont, Canada.*

BEVERIDGE, Wilbert Esler. b 16. Trin Coll Dub BA (1st cl Mod) and Scho 38, 1st cl Div Test 40, MA 48, BLitt 52, MLitt 60. Univ of Lon MA 64. **d** 40 **p** 41 Down. C of St Mary Belf 40-42; CF (EC) 43-47; St Paul St Alb 47-48; St Jo Bapt Harrow 48-50; Min Eccles Distr Ascen Wembley 51-57; V 57-61; Sen Industr Chap Dio Lon 61-69; Prin Lect Middx Poly 69-81. *55 Hiliary Gardens, Stanmore, HA7 2NH.* (01-907 6838)

BEVERLEY, Canon Arthur Leslie. b 14. Univ Coll Dur BA 37. Ely Th Coll 37. **d** 39 **p** 40 Wakef. C of Featherstone 39-43; PC of Brothertoft 43-48; V of Skirbeck Quarter 48-59; R of Ruskington 59-78; V of Dorrington 59-78; Can and Preb of Linc Cathl 72-79; Can (Emer) from 79; RD of Lafford 73-78; C of St Nich w St John Linc 78-79. *3 Middleton's Field, Lincoln.* (Linc 23637)

BEVERLEY, David. b 46. St D Coll Lamp BA 68. Linc Th Coll 71. **d** 73 Bp McKie for Cov **p** 74 Cov. C of Cov E Team Min 73-76; Immingham Dio Linc from 77. *St John's House, Pilgrim Avenue, Immingham, S Humb.*

BEVERN, Glen Charles. b 46. ACT ThDip 77. Canberra Coll of Min 75. **d** and **p** 78 C & Goulb. C of Bega 78-80; R of Kameruka 80-81. *c/o 80 Auckland Street, Bega, NSW, Australia 2550.*

BEVINGTON, Colin Reginald. b 36. ALCD 63. **d** 63 **p** 64 Ex. C of St Budeaux 63-65; Attenborough (w Bramcote to 67) and Chilwell 65-68; R of Benhall w Sternfield 68-74; V of Selly Hill 74-81; Exam Chap to Bp of Birm from 78; P-in-c of St Wulstan Selly Oak 80-81; V of St Steph and St Wulstan Selly Pk Dio Birm from 81. *20 Elmdon Road, Birmingham, B29 7LF.* (021-472 0050)

BEVINGTON, David John. b 51. Ch Coll Cam BA 72, MA 76. Trin Coll Bris 73. **d** 76 **p** 77 S'wark. C of H Trin Tulse Hill 76-79; Galleywood Dio Chelmsf from 79. *13 Roughtons, Galleywood, Chelmsford, CM2 8PE.*

BEVINGTON, Preb George Herbert Woodyear. b 18. Ch Coll Cam BA 39, MA 43. Ridley Hall Cam 39. **d** 41 **p** 42 Lon. C of St Jas Alperton 41-44; C of St Pet Cathl Bradf 44-49; Asst Chap and Prec of All SS Cathl Nairobi 49-54; PC of

Poole (w St Paul from 58) 54-60; R of St Leon w H Trin City and Dio Ex from 60; Preb of Ex Cathl from 70; RD of Christianity from 81. *10 Matford Lane, Exeter, EX2 4PS.* (Ex 55681)

BEVIS, Barry Johnson. Univ of S Afr BA 76. Moore Th Coll Syd ACT ThL 65. **d** 66 Bp Loane for Syd **p** 67 Syd. C of Kingsford 66-70; C-in-c of Canley Vale 70-73; R of Oatley W 73-80; St Pet Hornsby Dio Syd from 80. *207 Pacific Highway, Hornsby, NSW, Australia 2077.* (477-1025)

BEVIS, William Albert. b 13. Univ of Lon BSc (Eng) 35. Bps' Coll Cheshunt. **d** 56 **p** 57 Lon. C of St Andr Kingsbury 56-59; Hemel Hempstead 59-64; R of Toddington 64-79. *2 Lea Villas, Brendon, Lynton, N Devon.*

BEWAJI, Ven Benjamin Bolavinwa Oludikun. Bp's Ho Accra 56. **d** and **p** 58 Accra. P Dio Accra 58-72; Dio Kum from 73; Archd of Kum from 77. *Box 2093, Kumasi, Ghana.*

BEWES, Emmanuel John. b 21. Edin Th Coll 49. **d** 52 **p** 53 Carl. C of Walney I 52-55; St John Workington 55-60; V of Hesket-in-the-Forest w Calthwaite (and Armathwaite from 76) Dio Carl from 60. *Hesket-in-the-Forest Vicarage, High Hesket, Carlisle, Cumb, CA4 0HU.* (Southwaite 320)

BEWES, Richard Thomas. b 34. Em Coll Cam 3rd cl Geog Trip pt i 56, BA (2nd cl Th Trip pt II) 58, MA 61. Ridley Hall Cam. **d** 59 Roch **p** 60 Tonbridge for Cant. C of Ch Ch Beckenham 59-65; V of St Pet Harold Wood Hornchurch 65-74; Em Northwood Dio Lon from 74. *3 Gatehill Road, Northwood, HA6 3QB.* (Northwood 21598)

BEWES, Canon Thomas Francis Cecil. b 02. Late Choral Exhib of Em Coll Cam BA 23, MA 27. Ridley Hall Cam 23. **d** 25 **p** 26 Ex. C of St Leon Ex 25-29; furlough 33-34 38-39 and 48-49; CMS Miss Kabete 29-34; Kabare 34-37; Weithaga 37-43; Gen Sec Afr Ch Coun 43-48; Exam Chap to Bp of Momb 44-48; Archd Dio Momb 45-49; Actg Sec CMS Kenya Miss 45-47; Commiss Momb 48-61; Can (Emer) of Momb 49-61; Africa Sec CMS and Publ Pr Dio S'wark 49-59; V and RD of Tonbridge 59-70; Can (Emer) of Ft Hall 61-65; Mt Kenya from 65; Commiss Ft Hall 61-65; Maseno 67-72; Mt Kenya 65-75; Mt Kenya S from 75. *53 Kewhurst Avenue, Cooden, Bexhill-on-Sea.* (Cooden 3630)

BEWICK, Charles Graham. b 46. Coll of the Resurr Mirfield 77. **d** 79 **p** 80 S'wark. C of St Mary Magd Richmond Dio S'wark from 79. *8 Church Walk, Richmond, Surrey, TW9 1SN.* (01-940 4102)

BEWLEY, Albert Latham. Univ of Leeds BA (2nd cl Gen) 61. Ely Th Coll 61. **d** 63 Warrington for Liv **p** 64 Liv. C of St Mich Wigan 63-65; Caistor 65-69; R of St Pet W Lynn King's Lynn 69-76; V of Lakenham Dio Nor from 76. *Lakenham Vicarage, Harwood Road, Norwich, NR1 2NG.* (Norwich 25678)

BEWLEY, Graham Vincent. b 37. Dipl Th (Lon) 66. Oak Hill Th Coll. **d** 67 **p** 68 S'wark. C of All SS Wandsworth 67-70; C of Drypool (in c of St John) 71-74; Area Sec CMS Dios Southw and Sheff 74-78; V of St Jo Evang Pk City and Dio Sheff from 78. *91 Manor Oaks Road, Sheffield, S2 5EA.* (Sheffield 22833)

BEWLEY, Guy Patrick. b 16. Ripon Hall Ox. **d** 58 **p** 59 Roch. C of Aylesford 58-59; V of Preston Candover w Nutley and Bradley 59-65; Christian Aid Area Sec Glos Herefs Warws and Worcs 65-74; L to Offic Dio Carl from 75. *Town Head, Dean, Workington, Cumb, CA14 4TJ.*

BEYER, Andrew Phillip. b 49. St Jo Coll Auckld LTh 72. **d** 72 **p** 73 Auckld. C of St Helier's Bay 72-75; Assoc Dir Bd of Chr Educn Dio Auckld 76-79; Dir from 79; C of St Matt City and Dio Auckld from 80. *187 Federal Street, Auckland, NZ.*

BEYER, Thomas David. MBE (Mil) 50. Ridley Coll Melb 31. ACT ThL 32. **d** 32 **p** 33 Gippsld. C of Paynesville Paroch Distr 33-34; P-in-c of Drouin 34-35; R of Morwell 35-49; Chap RAAF 40-52; Perm to Offic Dio Melb from 51. *224 Whitehorse Road, Croydon, Vic., Australia.* (723-2197)

BEYNON, David Griffith. St D Coll Lamp BA 34. **d** 41 **p** 42 St D. C of Llanlwchaiarn 41-44; C-in-c of Bosherston w St Twynnell 44-46; Llandilo Fawr (in c of Maesteilo) 46-50; V of Llanwinio w Eglwys-Fair-a-Churig (w Llanfyrnach from 64) Dio St D from 50. *Vicarage, Llanwinio, Dyfed.*

BEYNON, Edward Leslie. St D Coll Lamp BA 34. **d** 34 **p** 35 Llan. C of Llantwit Fardre 34-37; Whitchurch 37-40; L to Offic Dio Guildf 40-45; V of Valley End 45-48; Addlestone Surrey 48-55; R of Gnowangerup 55-58; Bicton-Attadale 58-79; Perm to Offic Dio Perth from 79. *13 Groves Avenue, Alfred Cove, W Australia 6154.* (330 3670)

BEYNON, Ven James Royston. Univ of Dur LTh 31. St Aug Coll Cant 27. **d** 31 **p** 32 Lon. C of St Barn Homerton 31-33; Chap (ACS) Saugor 33-37; Chap (Eccles Est) Lebong 37; Fort William 37-40; Kasauli 40-41; Peshawar 41-43; Quetta 43-46 (including E Persia 43-46); Hon CF 47; Archd of Lah 47-48; V of Twyford 48-73; Commiss Lah 52-68; RD of Win 59-62; Archd of Win 62-73; Archd (Emer) from 73; Hon Can of Win 62-73. *1511 Geary Avenue, London, Ont, Canada.*

BEYNON, Malcolm. b 36. St D Coll Lamp BA 56. Univ Coll of Swansea Dipl Soc Sc 60. St Mich Coll Llan. **d** 59 **p** 60 Llan. C of Aberavon 59-63; Whitchurch 63-68; V of Llanwonno 68-74; Relig Educn Adv and Inspector of Ch Schs 72-74; Chap Old Hall Sch Wellington Salop 74-75; Perm to Offic Dio Leic 75-77; L to Offic 77-82; Asst Master Nevill Holt Sch Mkt Harborough 75-82; Chap 77-82; Smallwood Manor, Uttoxeter Staffs from 82. *The Forge, Smallwood Manor, Uttoxeter, Staffs, ST14 8NS.* (Uttoxeter 2014)

BEYNON, Sidney James. b 09. St D Coll Lamp BA 34. **d** 35 **p** 36 Llan. C of Ystradyfodwg 35-37; St Mary Llansawel 37-43; Fochriw and Deri 43-46; V of Bedlinog 47-59; Llanddewi Rhondda 59-65; St Andr w St Phil Liswerry Newport 65-76; L to Offic Dio Mon from 76. *37 Fairfield Road, Caerleon, Gwent.*

BEYNON, Vincent Wyn. b 54. Univ of Wales Dipl Th 81. St Mich AA Llan 78. **d** 81 Llan. C of Llantrisant Dio Llan from 81. *17 Parkdale View, Southgate, Llantrisant, Mid Glam, CF7 8DT.*

BEYNON, William Arthur Edmund. St D Coll Lamp BA 39. **d** 41 **p** 42 St D. C of St Paul Llanelly 41-44; Cwmamman 44-59; V of Capel Coelbren Dio Swan B from 59. *Coelbren Vicarage, Neath, W Glam.* (Seven Sisters 273)

BHENGU, Hamilton Richard Ndabezinhle. St Bede Coll Umtata. **d** 57 **p** 58 Zulu. P Dio Zulu 57-66; Dio Natal 66-77. *c/o Bhengu's Store, Wessels Nek, Natal, S Africa.* (3000)

BHENGU, Lancelot Harold Sipho. b 42. Univ of S Afr BA 63. Univ of Lon BD 80. St Pet Coll Alice 70. **d** 72 **p** 73 Zulu. P Dio Zulu 72-77; Dio St John's from 80. *PO Box 328, Umtata, Transkei.*

BHOLA, Herman. b 29. **d** 71 **p** 76 Windw Is. C of St Andr Grenada 71-73; St Patr Grenada Dio Windw Is from 73. *c/o St Patrick's Rectory, Grenada, W Indies.*

BIANCHI, Frederick Joseph. b 20. Bp's Coll Cheshunt 66. **d** Bp Cornwall for Win **p** 68 Win. C of St Luke Stanmore Win 67-71; C-in-c of St Aug of Cant Northam Southn 71-73; Team V of Southn (City Centre) 73-76; V of Otterbourne Dio Win from 76. *Vicarage, Kiln Lane, Otterbourne, Winchester, SO21 2EJ.* (Twyford 713400)

BIANCHI, Robert Frederick. b 56. St Jo Coll Dur BA 77. Cranmer Hall Dur 78. **d** 80 Dur **p** 81 Jarrow for Dur. C of Chester-le-Street Dio Dur from 80. *24 Hilda Park, Chester-le-Street, Co Durham.*

BIBBS, Herbert John. Angl Th Coll BC. **d** 58 **p** 60 BC. C of H Trin Cumberland 58-61; R of Alert Bay 61-64; I of Notukeu 64-67; Perm to Offic Dio BC from 72. *Pylades Road, RR1, Ladysmith, BC, Canada.*

BIBBY, Frank. b 37. K Coll Lon and Warm BD (2nd cl) and AKC (2nd cl) 64. ACP 60. **d** 65 Warrington for Liv **p** 66 Liv. C of Upholland 65-67; Lect Birm Coll of Educn 67-72; V of St Gabr Prestwich 72-76; Bp of Man Chap for Ordins 72-76; V of St Jas Hope Salford Dio Man from 76. *Hope Vicarage, Vicarage Close, Salford 6, Gtr Man, M6 8EJ.* (061-789 3303)

BIBBY, Paul Benington. b 27. Magd Coll Cam BA 51, MA 56. Westcott Ho Cam 55. **d** 57 **p** 58 Man. C of Flixton 57-60; Woolwich 60-62; V of Hurst 62-69; Hd of Cam Ho Camberwell 69-76; R of Shepton Mallet (w Doulting from 81) Dio B & W from 76; P-in-c of Doulting w W Cranmore 78-81. *Rectory, Shepton Mallet, Somt, BA4 5BL.* (Shepton Mallet 2163)

BICE, Michael Kenneth. b 38. Univ of Syd MB BS 63. Gen Th Sem NY STB 67. **d** 67 Vermont **p** 67 NY. In Amer Ch 67-71; C of St Jas-the-Less w H Trin Westmr 71-72; Chap Univ of Lon 72-75; Lect St Luke's Medical Centre Chicago from 75. *Rush Presbyterian, St Luke's Medical Centre, Chicago, USA.*

BICK, David Jim. b 33. ALCD 59 (LTh from 74). **d** 59 **p** 60 Glouc. C of St Cath Glouc 59-61; Coleford 61-63; R of Blaisdon w Flaxley 63-72; V of Coaley Dio Glouc from 72; P-in-c of Frampton-on-Severn w Whitminster Dio Glouc from 80; Arlingham Dio Glouc from 80. *Coaley Vicarage, Dursley, Glos.*

BICKERDYKE, James Clifford. b 17. St Jo Coll Dur LTh 41, BA 42, MA 45. Oak Hill Th Coll 38. **d** 42 Ches **p** 43 Lich. C of St Geo Stockport 42-43; Cannock 43-45; Asst Master at Normanton Sch Buxton 45-47; Chadderton Gr Sch 47-50; CF 51-67; Asst Master Launceston Coll 67-75; The Grove Sch Hindhead 75-81. *Lonningarth, Hawkshead, Cumb.* (Hawkshead 264)

BICKERSTAFF, Edgar Radcliffe. b 07. Selw Coll Cam BA 29, MA 35. Ridley Hall Cam 30. **d** 31 Warrington for Liv **p** 32 Liv. C of St John Waterloo 31-35; Perm to Offic at St Sav (in c of St Marg) Nottm 35-36; Org Sec CPAS for Midl and Publ Pr Dio Birm 36-39; C of St Anne Duddeston (in c of St Cath Nechells) 39-44; V of Horsley Derbys 44-53; Littleover 53-73; Proc Conv Derby 59-69. *15 Onslow Road, Mickleover, Derby, DE3 5JH.* (Derby 512532)

BICKERSTAFF, John Austin Isaac. b 10. Univ of Birm BA

(3rd cl Hist) 34. Qu Coll Birm 31. **d** 36 **p** 37 Lon. C of St Gabr N Acton 36-39; St Andr Eastbourne 39-41; Haywards Heath 41-61; V of Ch Ch Brighton 61-80. *16 Reigate Road, Brighton, BN1 5AJ.* (Brighton 556879)

BICKERSTETH, Anthony Cyril. b 33. K Coll Lon 54. Bps' Coll Cheshunt 55. **d** 58 **p** 59 York. C of St Osw Middlesbrough 58-61; Dom Chap to Bp of Kimb K 61-64; Hon Chap from 64; P-in-c of All SS Beaconsfield CP 62-64; V of Stillington w Marton and Farlington 64-68; St Mich AA Stoke Newington Common 68-74; Nayland w Wissington 74-82; Commiss Kimb K 64-66; R of Tolleshunt Knights w Tiptree Dio Chelmsf from 82. *Rectory, Tiptree, Colchester, Essex.* (Tiptree 815260)

BICKERSTETH, Craufurd Wilfrid. b 1891. St Jo Coll Ox BA 14, MA 47. Linc Th Coll 52. **d** 52 **p** 53 Ripon. C of Moor Allerton 52-56; R of Ripley w Burnt Yates 56-61; L to Offic Dio Ripon from 62; Hon C of St Pet Harrogate 62-74; Knaresborough Dio Ripon from 74. *1 Church View Terrace, Knaresborough, Yorks.*

BICKERSTETH, David Craufurd. b 50. Wycl Hall Ox 71. **d** 75 **p** 76 York. C of Beverley Minster 75-79; Farnborough Hants 79-81; P-in-c of Dearham Dio Carl from 81. *Dearham Vicarage, Maryport, Cumb, CA15 7HX.* (Maryport 2320)

BICKERSTETH, John David. b 26. Ch Ch Ox BA 50, MA 53. Oak Hill Th Coll 52. **d** 54 Dover for Cant **p** 55 Cant. C of Em S Croydon 54-58; C-in-c of Ashburnham w Penhurst Dio Chich 58-62; V from 62. *Ashburnham Place, Battle, E Sussex, TN33 9NF.* (0424 892244)

✠ **BICKERSTETH, Right Rev John Monier.** b 21. Ch Ch Ox BA 49, MA 53. Wells Th Coll 48. **d** 50 **p** 51 Bris. C of St Matt Moorfields Bris 50-54; Min of Conv Distr of St Jo Evang Hurst Green Oxted 54-62; V of St Steph Chatham 62-70; Hon Can of Roch 68-70; Cons Ld Bp Suffr of Warrington in Liv Cathl on 7 April 70 by Abp of York; Bps of Blackb, Ches, Liv, Roch and Wakef; Bps Suffr of Barking, Birkenhead, Grantham, Lancaster, Pontefract, and Tonbridge; Bps Gerard, Robinson, Russell, Sansbury and White; Trld to B & W 75; Chap and Sub-Prelate O of St John from 77; Clerk of the Closet to HM the Queen from 79. *The Palace, Wells, Somt, BA5 2PD.* (Wells 72341)

BICKERTON, David John Theodore. b 09. Univ of Lon BA 30. Coll of Resurr Mirfield 31. **d** 33 **p** 34 St Alb. C of St Andr Hertford 33-35; Abbey Ch St Alb 35-38; Thaxted 38-42; V of Redbourn 42-53; Sandon 53-59; R of Wallington w Rushden 53-59; L Gaddesden 59-61; Hon Can of St Alb 61; R of Sampford Courtenay w Honeychurch Dio Ex from 61; RD of Okehampton 66-72; P-in-c of Exbourne w Jacobstowe Dio Ex from 77. *Sampford Courtenay Rectory, Okehampton, Devon.* (North Tawton 251)

BICKERTON, Frank. b 17. Tyndale Hall Bris 64. **d** 64 **p** 65 Blackb. C of St Thos Blackpool 64-67; Chipping Barnet 67-70; V of Kilnhurst 70-72; St Paul Oswaldtwistle 72-80; Fishlake Dio Sheff from 80; P-in-c of Sykehouse Dio Sheff from 80. *Fishlake Vicarage, Doncaster, S Yorks, DN7 5JW.* (Doncaster 841396)

BICKLEY, John. Late Exhib of Magd Coll Ox BA (2nd cl Mod Hist) 34, 3rd cl Th 35, MA 38. Sarum Th Coll 35. **d** 36 **p** 37 Lich. C of Ch Ch Tunstall 36-40; Tettenhall Regis 40-45 (in c 43-45) V of Golden Hill 45-52; Newborough w Needwood 52-53; Mossley 53-61; Preston 61-63; Ch Ch Colne 63-67; R of Slimbridge 67-70; Huntingfield w Cookley 70-77; Perm to Offic Dio St E from 77. *Breckland Cottage, Santon Downham, Brandon, Suff.* (0842-810497)

BICKLEY, Maurice Lincoln. b 21. Dipl Th (Lon) 44. **d** 49 **p** 50 Bris. C of Fishponds 49-54; V of St Thos Ap Eastville Bris 54-62; Ascen Crownhill Devonport 62-73. *Address temp unknown.*

BIDDELL, Canon Christopher David. b 27. Ch Coll Cam 2nd cl Mod and Med Lang Trip pt i 47, BA 48, 2nd cl Th 49, MA 52. Ridley Hall Cam 51. **d** 51 **p** 52 Chelmsf. C of Hornchurch 51-54; PV and Succr of S'wark Cathl 54-56; PC of Wroxall 56-62; Dioc Insp Schs Portsm 61-72; R of Bp's Waltham 62-75; RD of Bp's Waltham 69-74; V of St Geo Stockport Dio Ches from 75; Hon Can of Ches from 81. *25 Bramhall Lane, Stockport, Chesh, SK2 6HT.* (061-480 2453)

BIDDELL, John Herman. b 15. Worc Coll Ox BA 38, MA 45. Wells Th Coll 38. **d** 47 **p** 48 Win. C of St Mich Basingstoke 47-51; V of Pennington 51-58; R of Merstham w Gatton 58-65; V of Milverton 65-80; C-in-c of Fitzhead 65-77; R 77-80; RD of Wellington 68-73. *c/o Milverton Vicarage, Taunton, Somt.* (Milverton 305)

BIDDER, John. b 19. Cudd Coll. **d** 62 **p** 63 Leic. [f CMS Lay Miss] C of Birstall 62-65; R of Croft 65-71; V of Witcham w Mepal 71-80; R of Coates Dio Ely from 80. *Coates Rectory, Peterborough, Cambs.* (Turves 254)

BIDDICK, John Edgar Peter. b 15. Univ of Leeds BA 36. Coll of Resurr Mirfield 36. **d** 38 Grantham for Linc **p** 39 Linc. C of St Aid New Cleethorpes 38-40; Mells w Vobster 40-43; C-in-c of Westfield Conv Distr 43-48; Asst Master at Frome Gr Sch 48-76. *Springside, Maperton, Wincanton, Somt.* (Wincanton 32524)

BIDDLE, Netane James. b 49. **d** 80 Wai. Hon C of Waipatu-Moteo Dio Wai from 80. *606 Gordon Road, Hastings, NZ.*

BIDDLECOMBE, Francis William. b 30. St Mich Coll Llan. **d** 59 **p** 60 Llan. C of Llangynwyd w Maesteg 59-62; Roath 62-65; V of Llanddewi Rhondda 65-71; Berse w Southsea 71-79; P-in-c of Teme Valley S Dio Worc from 79. *Hanley Rectory, Broadheath, Tenbury Wells, Worcs, WR15 8QW.*

BIDDLECOMBE, Paul Holman. b 11. Late Exhib of St Jo Coll Ox BA (2nd cl Th) 34, MA 43. Wycl Hall Ox 34. **d** 36 **p** 37 S'wark. C of Lee 36-39; H Trin Fareham 39-44; R of Greatham 44-47; Rowner 47-52; Polstead 52-60; C-in-c of Boxford w Hadleigh Hamlet 56-60; V of Playford w Culpho and Tuddenham 60-65; Chap Felixstowe Coll 65-79. *43 Brook Lane, Felixstowe, Suff.*

BIDDLESTONE, Joseph. b 15. Wycl Hall Ox 67. **d** and **p** 68 Ox. C of Woodley 68-71; P-in-c of Dunsden 71-77; Wootton Dio Ox from 77; Kiddington Dio Ox from 77. *Wootton Rectory, Woodstock, Oxford, OX7 1HA.* (Woodstock 811521)

BIDE, Peter William. b 12. St Cath S Ox BA (2nd cl Engl Lang and Lit) 39, MA 45. Wells Th Coll 48. **d** 49 **p** 50 Chich. C of Portslade w Hangleton 49-55; PC of Hangleton 55-57; V of Goring-by-Sea 57-59; Asst Gen Sec Br Coun of Chs 59-61; R of L Hadham 61-64; V of St Luke Battersea 64-68; Chap Lady Marg Hall Ox 68-80; Fell 78-80; Prec Ch Ch Cathl Ox from 80. *Christ Church, Oxford.* (Oxford 40118)

BIDEN, Neville Douglas. b 31. SOC 76. **d** 79 **p** 80 Guildf. C of Ash Dio Guildf from 79. *19 Grange Farm Road, Ash, Nr Aldershot, Hants.*

BIDGOOD, Kevin Patrick. b 46. Chich Th Coll 78. **d** 80 **p** 81 Portsm. C of Leigh Pk Dio Portsm from 80. *32 Hursley Road, Leigh Park, Havant, Hants.*

BIELBY, John Hamilton. Univ of W Ont BA 54. Hur Coll LTh 55. **d** 54 Hur **p** 55 Niag. C of St Jas Lon 54-55; St Geo St Catherines 55-58; R of Palermo 58-64; St Phil, Burlington 64-74; St Hilda Oakville Dio Niag from 75. *166 Westminster Drive, Oakville, Ont., Canada.* (416-827 1927)

BIERLEY, George Leslie. b 11. Worc Ordin Coll 58. **d** 60 **p** 61 Linc. C of Clee w Cleethorpes 60-63; R of Gt Coates and PC of Aylesby 63-70; R of N Thoresby Dio Linc from 70; R of Grainsby and V of Waythe Dio Linc from 71. *North Thoresby Rectory, Grimsby, Lincs.* (N Thoresby 228)

BIGARUKA, Ezrah. Bp Tucker Coll Mukono 64. **d** 66 Ankole-K. d Dio Kig. *Box 1012, Kisoro, Kigezi, Uganda.*

BIGBY, Preb John Harman. b 18. Sarum Th Coll. **d** 48 **p** 49 Lich. C of Brierley Hill 48-50; W Bromwich 50-52; C-in-c of Conv Distr of St Chad Tunstall 52-54; Porthill St Andr 54-59; V of Ettingshall 59-79; R of Moreton Saye Dio Lich from 79; Preb of Lich Cathl from 80. *Moreton Saye Rectory, Market Drayton, Salop.* (Teon Hill 219)

BIGENI, Yakobo. Msalato Bible Sch 69. **d** 69 **p** 70 W Tang. P Dio W Tang from 70. *Musagala, PO Munanira, Kigoma, Tanzania.*

BIGG, Howard Clive. b 40. Jes Coll Cam BA 68, MA 72. Ridley Hall Cam 73. **d** 74 **p** 75 Southw. C of St Jo Evang Worksop 74-76; Prec of Cathl and Abbey Ch St Alb 76-77; Perm to Offic Dio Ches from 78. *c/o Rectory, Thurstaston, Wirral, Chesh.* (051-648 1816)

BIGGAR, Dennis Alfred. b 21. Ripon Hall Ox 55. **d** 57 **p** 58 Bris. C of Ch Ch Swindon (in c of St Andr from 59) 57-61; All SS Boyne Hill, Maidenhead 61-64; V of Skegby 64-72; The Brents and Davington w Oare and Luddenham 72-80; All S Cheriton w Newington Dio Cant from 80. *1 Ashley Avenue, Cheriton, Folkestone, CT19 4PX.* (Folkestone 75483)

BIGGERS, Jackson Cunningham. Univ of Mississippi BA 60. Univ of S Th Sch USA 63. **d** 63 Bp Allin for Mississippi **p** 64 Mississippi. L to Offic Dio Malawi 65-68; P-in-c of Kasamba 68-69; in Amer Ch 69-72 and from 76; P-in-c of Lilongwe 72-75; Archd of Lilongwe 73-75. *Box 633, Biloxi, Mississippi, 39533, USA.*

BIGGIN, Ronald. b 20. N-W Ordin Course. **d** 73 Stockport for Ches **p** 74 Ches. C of Thelwall Dio Ches 73-78; V from 78. *Thelwall Vicarage, Warrington, Chesh.* (Warrington 61531)

BIGGINS, Cyril Leslie. **d** 24 **p** 25 Brisb. C of St Colomb Clayfield 24-27; Bundaberg 27-28; V of Zillmere w Chermside 28-30; Mary Valley 30-32; Nanango 32-35; Palmwoods 35-39; R of Laidley 39-42; Killarney 42-46; Pittsworth 47-56; St Colomb Clayfield Brisb 56-65; Perm to Offic Dio Brisb from 65. *24 Deloraine Street, Wavell Heights, Queensland, Australia 4012.* (266 8006)

BIGGINS, Edward Charles. St Jo Coll Dur LTh 30, BA 31, ALCD 30. **d** 31 Wakef for Bradf **p** 32 Bradf. C of Eccleshill 31-33; Hornsea 33-35; Chap RN 35-37; C of Filey 37-39; LPr

Dio York 39-42; C-in-c of Keighley 42-44; C of Good Shepherd Lee 54-59; St Geo Hanover Square Lon 59-61. *24 Bloomsbury Street, WC1.*

BIGGS, Alfred Edwin. ACT ThL 15. **d** 16 **p** 17 Tas. C of Forth and Leven Tas 16-17; St Jo Bapt Hobart 17-19; R of Zeekan 19-22; Kempton 22-28; Derby 28-34; Kingston 34-36; Clarence 36-44; Chap AIF 44-46; R of Longford 46-48; Chap Lockhart River 48-52. *c/o Vicarage, Edenhope, Vic., Australia.*

BIGGS, Allan Basil. Univ of W Austr BA 60. **d** 65 Perth. C of St Geo Cathl Perth 65-79; Perm to Offic Dio Adel from 79. *19 Emu Avenue, Glenalta, S Australia 5052.*

BIGGS, George Ramsay. b 45. Univ of Liv BA 67. Qu Coll Cam BA 73. Westcott Ho 72. **d** 74 **p** 75 S'wark. C of St Aug Grove Park Lee 74-78; Team V of Totton Dio Win from 78. *Netley Marsh Vicarage, Totton, Southampton, Hants.*

BIGGS, Harold Guy. Ch Coll Hobart ACT ThL 45. **d** 41 Tas **p** 43 Gippsld for Tas. C of Burnie 41-45; R of Furneaux Is 45-48; Lilydale 48-53; Hamilton 53-58; Brighton 58-64; Franklin 64-67; C of All SS Hobart 67-71; Richmond Tas 71-72. *20 East Derwent Highway, Rose Bay, Tasmania 7015.* (002-43 6726)

BIGGS, Laurence Walter. Roch Th Coll 64. **d** 66 **p** 67 Linc. C of Cleethorpes 66-69; St Germans Dio Truro 69-71; V of Poowong w Loch 71-76; R of Drouin Dio Gippsld from 76. *Rectory, Francis Street, Vic., Australia 3818.* (056-25 1623)

BIGGS, Philip John. b 51. Ripon Coll Cudd 75. **d** 77 **p** 78 Cant. C of Maidstone 77-80; Dioc Youth Officer Truro from 80. *Diocesan Youth Office, Alverton Terrace, Mitchell Hill, Truro, Cornw TR1 1JQ.* (Truro 74352)

BIGNELL, David Charles. b 41. E Midl Jt Ordin Tr Scheme 76. **d** 79 Sherwood for Southw **p** 80 Southw. C of St Jas Porchester Dio Southw from 79. *127a Digby Avenue, Mapperley, Nottingham, NG3 6DT.* (Nottm 877553)

BIGNELL, Alan Guy. b 39. Univ of Lon BA (Gen) 64, BA (Engl) 69. **d** 81 Buckingham for Ox (NSM). C of Upton w Chalvey Dio Ox from 81. *c/o The Rectory, 18 Albert Street, Slough, SL1 2BU.*

BIGNOUX, Paul Allan. b 45. Ridley Coll Melb ACT ThL 70. **d** 70 Melb for Maur **p** 71 Maur. C of Ringwood Melb 70-71; Rose-Hill 72-74; Vacoas 74-77; V of Pyramid Hill Dio Bend from 77. *Vicarage, Durham Ox Road, Pyramid Hill, Vic, Australia 3575.*

BIGRIGG, Roland. **d** 52 Lon for Col Bp **p** 53 Graft. C of Lismore 53-55; R of Coramba 55-59; on leave 59-62; Youth Chap Dio Graft 62-64; C of Wagga Wagga 64-65; P-in-c of Adaminaby 65-66; L to Offic Dio Brisb 67-68; C of St Nich Sandgate 68-71; Perm to Offic Dio Brisb 71-72; and 79; Chap R Brisb Hosp 72-79; C of Maryborough Dio Brisb from 79. *204 Fort Street, Maryborough, Queensland, Australia 4650.*

BIIMO, Tito Do'bo. Bp Gwynne Coll Mundri 61. **d** 64 Bp Dotiro for Sudan **p** 66 Mbale. P Dio Sudan 64-66; Dio Mbale 66-68; Dio Soroti 68-76; Dio Yambio from 76. *ECS, Maridi, Sudan.*

BILES, David George. b 35. Open Univ BA 75. K Coll Lon and Warm AKC 58. **d** 59 **p** 60 Dur. C of Cockerton 59-62; Winlaton (in c of St Barn Rowlands Gill) 62-67; PC of Dipton 67-74; R of Wolviston Dio Dur from 74. *1 Clifton Avenue, Billingham, Cleveland, TS22 5DE.* (Stockton 551666)

BILES, Timothy Mark Frowde. b 35. Dipl Th (Wales) 64. St Mich Coll Llan 60. **d** 64 Ripon **p** 66 Sarum. C of St Cross Middleton 64-66; Chap and Asst Master St Francis's Sch Hooke 66-72; P-in-c of Toller Porcorum w Hooke 72-79; Mapperton w Melpash 74-79; Beaminster 77-79; Team R of Beaminster Area Dio Sarum from 79. *Rectory, Beaminster, Dorset.* (Beaminster 862150)

BILL, Alan. b 29. K Coll Lon and Warm BD (2nd cl) and AKC 66. **d** 67 Barking for Chelmsf **p** 68 Chelmsf. C of Gt Burstead 67-70; Thornaby-on-Tees 70-71; Team V Thornaby-on-Tees 71-76; R of E Gilling 76-81; Dioc Stewardship Adv Dio York 76-81; V of Ormesby Dio York from 81. *54 Church Lane, Ormesby, Middlesbrough, Cleve, TS7 9AU.* (Middlesbrough 314445)

BILL, Denis Aubrey. b 20. Univ of Leeds 45. Coll of Resurr Mirfield 48. **d** 50 **p** 51 Newc T. C of Ch Ch Shieldfield Newc T 50-59; V of Cambois 59-64; H Island Dio Newc T from 64. *Lindisfarne Vicarage, Holy Island, Berwick-on-Tweed, TD15 2RX.* (Holy Island 89216)

BILL, Herbert Sydney. b 12. Keble Coll Ox BA (4th cl Mod Hist) 34, Dipl Th 35. Wells Th Coll 35. **d** 36 **p** 37 Lon. C of St Sav Chelsea 36-39; St Pet Acton Green 39-41; Actg C of St Jude-on-the-Hill Hampstead Garden Suburb 41-43; Min of Wood End Conv Distr Northolt 43-45; V of Washwood Heath 45-52; St Aug Dudley 52-60; Worc Dioc Miss from 54; R of Feckenham w Bradley Dio Worc from 60; RD of Feckenham 65-73. *Feckenham Vicarage, Redditch, Worcs.* (Astwood Bank 2420)

BILL, Thomas Andrew Graham. b 47. Univ of Dur BA 76. St Jo Coll Dur Dipl Th 78. **d** 77 Lanc for Blackb **p** 78 Blackb. C of St Mary Penwortham 77-80; Torrisholme 80-82; P-in-c of St Pet Accrington Dio Blackb from 82; Stonefold Dio Blackb from 82. *Vicarage, Roundhill Lane, Haslingden, Rossendale, Lancs BB4 5BJ.* (0706-215819)

BILLARD, Ralph Archibald. b 36. Mem Univ of Newfld LTh 67. Qu Th Coll. **d** 67 **p** 68 Newfld. C of Gambo 67-70; I of Burin 70-76; Pouch Cove Dio E Newfld from 76. *Box 29, Pouch Cove, Newfoundland, Canada.* (709-335 2363)

BILLCLIFF, Ian. b 43. Univ of Lon BSc 66. Linc Th Coll 66. **d** 68 **p** 69 Newc T. C of St Paul Cullercoats 68-71; St Sav Walthamstow 71-72; H Cross Fenham 72-74; Perm to Offic Dio York from 74. *45 Cambridge Road, Middlesbrough, Cleve.*

BILLINGHAM, Peter Charles Geoffrey. b 34. Univ of Leeds BA (2nd cl Th) 56. Westcott Ho Cam 61. **d** 62 **p** 63 Worc. C of Halesowen w Hasbury 62-66; R of Addingham 66-70; Droitwich St Andr and St Nich w St Pet Dio Worc from 70; Surr from 74; P-in-c of Salwarpe 76-80; RD of Droitwich from 78. *Rectory, Droitwich, Worcs, WR9 7AA.* (Droitwich 773134)

BILLINGHAM, Sidney. b 1898. Tyndale Hall Bris 29. **d** 32 **p** 33 Man. C of St Marg Burnage 32-34; St Mich Braintree 34-35; R of Bedingfield 35-36; V of St Mark Haydock 36-48; CF (EC) 40-43; V of All SS Salterhebble 48-53; H Trin Heworth York 53-58; Rufforth 58-65. *32 Stuart Avenue, Bare, Morecambe, Lancs.*

BILLINGHURST, Peter John. b 30. St Deiniol's Libr Hawarden 77. **d** 79 **p** 80 St A (APM). C of Hawarden Dio St A from 79. *14 Manor Park, Great Barrow, Chester.* (Tarvin 40537)

BILLINGHURST, Richard George. b 48. St Jo Coll Cam BA 70, MA 74. Ridley Hall Cam 76. **d** 79 **p** 80 Lich. C of Caverswall 79-81; Cullompton Dio Ex from 81. *81 Bilbie Close, Cullompton, Exeter, EX15 1LG.* (0884-33494)

BILLINGS, Alan Roy. b 42. Em Coll Cam 2nd cl Th Trip pt i 63, BA (2nd cl Th Trip pt ii) 65, MA 69. Univ of Leic MEducn 75. Linc Th Coll 66. **d** 68 **p** 69 Leic. C of Knighton 68-72; C-in-c of St Silas Sheff 72-76; V of Beighton 76-78; Perm to Offic Dio Sheff 78-81; Asst Master Broadway Sch Barnsley 78-81; V of Walkley Dio Sheff from 81. *150 Walkley Road, Sheffield, S6 2XQ.* (Sheff 345029)

BILLINGS, Derek Donald. b 30. Fitzw Ho Cam BA 54, MA 59. Tyndale Hall Bris 55. **d** 56 **p** 57 Southw. C of Attenborough w Bramcote and Chilwell 56-59; R of Ashley w Silverley 59-66; V of Bottisham 66-80; R of Houghton w Wyton Dio Ely from 80. *Rectory, Rectory Lane, Wyton, Huntingdon, Cambs, PE17 2AQ.* (St Ives 62499)

BILLINGS, Canon Joseph Sidney. b 11. Late Scho of Selw Coll Cam 1st cl Cl Trip pt i 32, BA (1st cl Cl Trip pt ii) 33, MA 37. Cudd Coll 36. **d** 36 **p** 37 Birm. C of Solihull 36-39; Chap RNVR 39-46; V of Shirley 42-51; Stourport 51-59; Dodderhill 59-68; Stoulton w Drakes Broughton (and Pirton from 74) 68-77; Dir of Tr Dio Worc from 59-71; Exam Chap to Bp of Worc from 59-71; Hon Can of Worc from 66; C-in-c of Pirton 71-74. *Old School House, Great Comberton, Pershore, Worcs, WR10 3DP.* (Elmley Castle 246)

BILLINGS, Roger Key. b 41. AIB 54. Counc for Nat Acad Awards BA 80. Oak Hill Coll 77. **d** 80 **p** 81 Roch. C of St Jas Tunbridge Wells Dio Roch from 80. *3 Andrews Close, Tunbridge Wells, Kent, TN2 3PA.* (0892-31297)

BILLINGSLEY, Jeffrey. Univ of N Ont BA 32. Hur Coll Ont LTh 32. **d** 32 **p** 33 Hur. C-in-c of Trin Ch Dur 32-34; C of All SS Windsor 34-38; I of Ch of Resurr Lon Ont 38-40; C of St Paul's Cathl Lon Ont 40-42; C-in-c of H Trin Chatham 42-43; R 43-53; Distr Sec of U Canada Bible Soc 53-54; I of Dixie 54-74. *1047 Henley Road, Mississauga, Ont., Canada.*

BILLINGTON, Charles Alfred. b 30. Univ of Leeds BA 53. Coll of Resurr Mirfield 53. **d** 55 **p** 56 Carl. C of H Trin Carl 55-59; L to Offic Dio Wakef 60-64; R of St Aid Man 64-66; V of St Faith Gt Crosby 66-72; Harrold w Carlton and Chellington 72-80; Tintinhull, Chilthorne Domer w Yeovil Marsh & Thorne Coffin Dio B & W from 80. *Tintinhull Rectory, Yeovil, Somt.* (Martock 2655)

BILLINGTON, Eric. b 17. St Aid Coll LTh 45. St Jo Coll Dur BA 46. **d** 46 **p** 47 Blackb. C of Ashton-on-Ribble 46-50; Habergham 50-52; Thornton-le-Fylde 52-54; V of Newton-Moor 54-63; Wyresdale 63-81. *16 Station Road, Hest Bank, Lancs, LA2 6HP.*

BILLINGTON, John Keith. b 16. **d** 61 **p** 62 Wakef. C of St Geo Ovenden Halifax 61-63; Pontefract 63-64; V of Shepley 64-68; Parish Admin Seacroft Dio Ripon 68-73. *Walker Acre, School Lane, Addingham, Ilkley, Yorks.* (Addingham 830093)

BILLINGTON, Thomas. b 06. Univ of Man BA (3rd cl Phil) 30. Egerton Hall Man 30. **d** 32 **p** 33 Man. C of St Jas Heywood 32-36; St Paul Kersal 36-38; R of St Jas Higher Broughton 38-43; V of Dixon Green 43-53; Worsley w Ellenbrook 53-72. *Ashley Cottage, Seaton Ross, York.*

BILLOWES, David. b 20. **d** 76 **p** 77 Portsm (APM). C of St

Mary W Cowes Dio Portsm from 76. *45 Fernbank, Solent View Road, Gurnard, Cowes, IoW PO31 8JZ.*

BILLS, Reginald. b 18. Lich Th Coll 69. **d** 70 **p** 71 Lich. C of St Thos, Wednesfield 70-74; St Pet Wolverhampton 74-79; St Andr Wolverhampton 79-81; P-in-c of Brockmoor Dio Lich from 81. *Brockmoor Vicarage, Brierley Hill, W Midl, DY5 3UR.* (B Hill 78375)

BILNEY, Kenneth Henry. b 25. St Deiniol's Libr Hawarden 75. **d** 75 **p** 76 Leic. Hon C of St Mary Magd Knighton Leic 75-78; St Jas Gtr Leic 78-80; R of Leire w Ashby Parva and Dunton Bassett Dio Leic from 80. *Leire Rectory, Lutterworth, Leics.* (Leire 209421)

BILSBORROW, John William. Ridley Th Coll Melb ACT ThL 54. **d** and **p** 64 Melb. C of Toorak 64-65; Min of Emerald 65-68; Home Sec CMS Dio Melb 68-70; Hon C of St Paul's Cathl Melb 68-70; V of Glen Waverley 70-76; Perm to Offic Dio Melb 79. *Kallista-Emerald Road, The Patch, Vic, Australia 3792.* (756 7025)

BILTON, Paul Michael. b 52. AKC 74. St Aug Coll Cant 74. **d** 75 **p** 76 Bradf. C of Ch Ch Skipton-in-Craven 75-79; Industr Chap Bromsgrove & Redditch 79-80. *Address temp unknown.*

BINA, Ven Yakana. Bp Tucker Mem Coll. **d** 25 **p** 28 Ugan. Asst Tutor Bp Tucker Mem Coll 25-34; P Dio Ugan from 34; RD of Singo 35-38; Engo from 38; Can of Ugan 39-49; Archd Dio Ugan 49-59; Archd (Emer) from 59. *P.O. Box 56, Kampala, Uganda.*

BINAISA, Ananiya. Bp Tucker Mem Coll. **d** 24 **p** 26 Ugan. P Dio Ugan. Hd Master Centr Sch Natete 26-30; Can of Ugan 59-60; Nam 60-64; Hon Can of Nam 64-73; P Dio Kamp from 74. *Box 335, Kampala, Uganda.*

BINDEEBA, Joseph. **d** and **p** 79 W Ank. P Dio Ank. *Box 4, Rubirizi, Uganda.*

BINDER, Charles Louis Laurence. b 23. St Pet Hall Ox BA 46, MA 48. [f Free Ch Min] Wycl Hall Ox. **d** 58 **p** 59 Ox. C of Maidenhead 58-61; V of St John Southall 61-67; St Barn Clapham Common 67-73; St Mary Hammersmith Road, Fulham 73-79; St Simon Hammersmith 76-79; Surr 75-79; V of St Matt Millbrook Jersey Dio Win from 79; R of St Lawr Jersey Dio Win from 80. *St Matthew's Vicarage, Milbrook, Jersey, CI.* (20934)

BINDON, David Charles. b 33. Univ of Lon BSc 58. Sarum Wells Th Coll 77. **d** 79 **p** 80 B & W. C of Yeovil Dio B & W from 79. *68 Preston Road, Yeovil, Somt, BA20 2DL.* (0935-6540)

BINDON, David Howard Vereker. St Jo Coll Auckld LTh 66. **d** 66 **p** 67 Auckld. C of E Coast Bays 66-69; M SSF from 70; Perm to Offic Dio Auckld 69-70; Dio Brisb 70-72 and 73-75; Dio Melan 72-73; V of Glen Innes 75-80; Kohimarama Dio Auckld from 80. *116 Selwyn Avenue, Mission Bay, Auckland, NZ.* (585-166)

BINES, Harry Frederick. b 09. Worc Ordin Coll 63. **d** 65 **p** 66 Ex. C of Ch Ch Paignton 65-69; Bratton Fleming 69-74; P-in-c of High Bickington w Atherington 74-79. *23 White House Close, Instow, Devon.*

BINGHAM, Geoffrey Cyril. Moore Th Coll Syd ACT ThL 52. **d** and **p** 53 Syd. R of H Trin Miller's Point Syd 53-57; P-in-c of Bible Tr Inst (Austr CMS) Dio Lah 57-63; Dio Kar 63-66; Perm to Offic Dio Adel 69; Dio Murray 70-77; Dio Adel from 75. *Box 403, Blackwood, S Australia 5051.*

BINGHAM, Montague Marshall. Univ of BC BA 50. Angl Th Coll Vanc 50-52. **d** 51 New Westmr **p** 52 Carib. V of Quesnel 52-55; Chap RCAF 55-63; Angl Th Coll Vanc 63-67; on leave. *2956 Pt Grey Road, Vancouver 8, BC, Canada.*

BINGHAM, Norman James Frederick. b 26. Univ of Lon BSc (Eng) 51. Tyndale Hall Bris 61. **d** 63 **p** 64 Lich. C of Chell 63-67; Macclesfield 67-71; P-in-c of St Pet Macclesfield 71-73; V of St Mary w St Edw Leyton Dio Chelmsf from 73; RD of Waltham Forest from 81. *4 Vicarage Road, E10 5EA.* (01-539 7882)

BINITIE, John Omateye. **d** 69 Benin. d Dio Benin. *P.O. Box 12, Warrie, Midwestern, Nigeria.*

BINKS, Edmund Vardy. K Coll Lon and Warm BD and AKC 61. **d** 62 **p** 63 York. C of Selby 62-65; Asst Chap and Lect Coll of Ripon and York St John from 65. *College of Ripon and York St John, Lord Mayor's Walk, York, YO3 7EX.*

BINKS, Thomas Arthur. b 29. **d** and **p** 79 Gippsld. Educn Officer Dio Gippsld from 79. *PO Box 28, Sale, Vic, Australia 3850.*

BINNEY, Hibbert Donald. b 21. **d** 77 **p** 78 Calg. Sec-Treas Dio Calg from 78. *3015 Glencoe Road S.W, Calgary, Alta, Canada, T2S 2Lp.*

BINNIE, Alexander David. b 22. Ripon Hall Ox 67. **d** 68 Birm **p** 69 Aston for Birm. C of Sutton Coldfield 68-72; V of Dosthill and Wood End Dio Birm from 72. *Dosthill Vicarage, Tamworth, Staffs, B77 1LU.* (Tamworth 281349)

BINNIE, Graham Alfred. AKC 37. **d** 37 **p** 38 Lon. C of St Aid Belmont 37-38; Gt Stanmore and Chap to RNO Hosp 38-44; V of H Trin Tottenham and Chap to Prince of Wales Hosp 44-47; R of Stisted 47-53; Dioc Insp of Schs 49-74; V of Hatfield Peverel (w Ulting 74) 53-74; Surr 53-74; C-in-c of Ulting 56-74; RD of Witham 61-74; Actg RD 75-76; Chap Bridge Hosp Witham 64-74; Chap High Sheriff Essex 70-74. *Silvermere, Llandygwydd, Cardigan, Dyfed.* (Llechryd 271)

BINNS, Alwyne Alfred Edwin. b 04. Univ of the Punjab BA 27. Ripon Hall Ox 28. **d** 29 **p** 30 S'wark. C of Ch Ch E Greenwich 29-32; Prin Sherwood Coll Naini Tal 32-48; Guildf Gr Sch Perth W Austr 48-49; Chap to Lucton Sch and V of Lucton Eyton 49-50; Chap to Bancroft's Sch Woodford Green 51-65; R of St Phil de Torteval Guernsey 66-79. *Brookland, Lamare Road, Vazon, Guernsey, CI.*

BINNS, Arthur Watson. b 09. Bp Wilson Coll IM 41. **d** 43 **p** 44 Carl. C of H Trin w Ch Ch Whitehaven 43-46; R of Lamplugh 46-54; V of Cleator 54-58; Crosby-on-Eden 58-77; Perm to Offic Dio Carl from 77. *Moor Cottage, Crosby Moor, Crosby-on-Eden, Carlisle, Cumb.* (Crosby-on-Eden 228)

BINNS, David Alan. b 42. St Francis Coll Brisb. **d** and **p** 72 Brisb. C of St Matt Holland Pk 72; St Mark Warwick 73-75; Chap Writtle Hylands Sch Essex 76-78; Prec St John's Cathl City and Dio Brisb from 78. *Precentor's House, St John's Cathedral, Ann Street, Brisbane, Australia 4000.* (221 2420)

BINNS, David John. Moore Th Coll Syd ACT ThL 64. **d** 64 **p** 65 Adel. C of Mt Gambier 64-66; Port Adel 66-67; St Pet Norbiton 67-70; C-in-c of St Jude Carlton 70-75; I of Vermont 75-80; R of St Luke City and Dio Adel from 80. *18 Burke Street, Tusmore, S Australia 5065.*

BINNS, David William. St Paul's Coll Grahmstn LTh 66. **d** 66 **p** 67 Capetn. C of Stellenbosch 66-67; St Phil Capetn 67-70; Namaqualand 70-71; Somerset W 71-73; R of Faure 74-80; St Mich AA Observatory Dio Capetn from 80. *Rectory, 8 Howe Street, Observatory, CP, S Africa.*

BINNS, John Richard. b 51. Coll of Resurr Mirfield 74. **d** 76 **p** 77 S'wark. C of H Trin Clapham 76-80; Mortlake Dio S'wark from 80. *17 Sheen Gate Gardens, SW14.* (01-876 5002)

BINNS, Laughton O'Connel. Hur Coll Ont. **d** and **p** 64 Niag. C of St Chris Burlington 64-67; R of Geraldton 67-69; on leave 69-72; I of Cochrane 72-75; R of Good Shepherd St Catharines Dio Niag from 75. *6 Brentwood Drive, St Catharines, Ont, Canada.* (416-934 5271)

BINNS, Peter Rodney. b 44. Univ of St Andr MA 66. **d** 75 Ox **p** 76 Buckingham for Ox (NSM). C of St Mich AA Amersham-on-the-Hill Dio Ox from 75. *8 Quickberry Place, Station Road, Amersham, Bucks HP7 0BA.* (Amersham 6034)

BINNY, John Wallace. b 46. St D Coll Lamp BA 70. St Mich Coll Llan. **d** 71 **p** 72 Llan. C of Llantrisant 71-77; V of Troedyrhiw 77-82; R of Eglwysbrewis w St Athan and Flemington w Gileston Dio Llan from 82. *Rectory, St Athan, S Glam.* (St Athan 540)

BINYOMO, Ezekyeri. Bp Tucker Coll Ugan **d** 33 **p** 34 Ugan. P Dio Ugan. *c/o PO Box 37, Fort Portal, Uganda.*

BIRAMAHIRE, Ezira. **d** 76 **p** 77 Ruw. P Dio Ruw. *Box 150, Kasese, Uganda.*

BIRBECK, Anthony Leng. b 33. Linc Coll Ox BA (3rd cl Th) 59, MA 61. Linc Th Coll 58. **d** 60 **p** 61 York. C of Redcar (w Kirkleatham 73) 60-74; Chap Teesside Industr Miss 62-74; Can Res and Treas of Wells Cathl 74-78; L to Offic Dio B & W from 78. *4 Mount Pleasant Avenue, Wells, Som, BA5 2JQ.* (Wells 73246)

BIRCH, Arthur Clarkson. b 1889. King's Coll Cam BA (2nd cl Hist Trip) 11, MA 15. Cudd Coll 12. **d** 12 **p** 13 York. C of St Mary Virg Cottingham 12-15; UMCA Miss at Msoro 15-18; C of Hessle 18-22; V of Rosedale 22-24; Middleton w Cropton 24-32; Cloughton 32-55. *8 Orchard Way, Strensall, York.* (Strensall 478)

BIRCH, Arthur James Fleet. b 14. Univ Coll Dur BA (3rd cl Th Hons) 36, MA 39. **d** 37 Lich **p** 38 Stafford for Lich. C of Ch Ch W Bromwich 37-41; Wroxeter (in c of Easton Constantine 42-43) 41-43; St Jo Bapt Crewe 43-46; V of Lostock Gralam 46-55; Guilden Sutton w Plemstall 55-59; Hooton 59-70; R of Lymm 70-79. *21 Arran Drive, Frodsham, Chesh, WA6 6AL.*

BIRCH, Arthur Kenneth. b 15. Qu Coll Birm 46. **d** 48 **p** 49 St Alb. [f CMS Miss Nigeria] C of St Paul St Alb 48-50; CMS Area Sec for Dios Ely Nor and St E 50-55; V of Ch Ch New Catton Nor 55-60; Buxton w Oxnead 60-71; R of Lammas w Hautbois 60-71; CMS Miss N Ugan 72-75; V of Fence-in-Pendle 75-76; C of St Jo Bapt Bollington 76-79; R of Church Lawton 79-81. *Address temp unknown.*

BIRCH, Derek. b 31. St D Coll Lamp BA 58. Coll of Resurr Mirfield 58. **d** 60 **p** 61 Wakef. C of S Elmsall 60-62; Penistone w Midhope 62-66; V of Silkstone Dio Wakef from 66; Chap of Stainborough from 76. *12 High Street, Silkstone, Barnsley, Yorks, S75 4JN.* (Barnsley 790232)

BIRCH, Gordon Clifford. b 20. Dur Univ BA 45, MA 66.

RD 66. Oak Hill Th Coll 39. **d** 43 **p** 44 York. C of St Barn Linthorpe Middlesbrough 43-46; Chap RNVR 46-47; RNR 51-75; C of St Geo Leeds (in c of St Andr) 47-49; R of St Paul Bradf 49-52; V of St Mich AA Sutton-in-Holderness 52-59; Chap HM Borstal Inst Hull 52-57; Asst Master Technical Sch for Boys Middlesbrough 59-60; Div Master Acklam Hall Gr Sch Middlesbrough 60-64; Grangefield Gr Sch Stockton-on-Tees 64-68; V of St Osw Middlesbrough 68-74; R of Yarm Dio York from 74. *Rectory, Yarm-on-Tees, Cleve, TS15 9BU.* (Eaglescliffe 781115)

BIRCH, Henry Arthur. St Jo Coll Dur BA 48. Tyndale Hall Bris 48. **d** 49 **p** 50 Edin. C of St Thos Edin 49-51; Ch Ch Surbiton Hill (in c of Em Tolworth) 51-54; R of Uphill 54-69; Surr 61-69; Proc Conv B & W 64-69; C-in-c of Sylvania Heights 69-77; R 77-81; St Pet Mowbray Dio Capetn from 81. *5 Vredenburg Circus, Rosebank 7700, CP, S Africa.* (Cape Town 66 4732)

BIRCH, Hugh. b 06. Keble Coll Ox BA (2nd cl Th) 28, MA 35. Ridley Hall Cam 29. **d** 30 **p** 31 Chelmsf. C of Ch Ch Stratford 30-33; Lindley 33-37; C and Lect of Halifax 37-40; Chap Waterhouse Chy 38-40; V of Gomersal 40-49; Rastrick 49-60; Coley 60-71. *12 Greenacres, Skipton, Yorks.* (Skipton 4543)

BIRCH, Leonard James. b 07. Univ of Dur LTh 47. Lich Th Coll 26. **d** 31 **p** 32 Lich. C of Ch Ch Tunstall 31-33; Perm to Offic at St Paul Burton-on-Trent 33-34; C of St Paul Wood Green Wednesbury 34-37; St Nich Arundel w S Stoke and Tortington 37-39; Malvern Link 39-46; CF (EC) 40-46; Hon CF 46; V of Beoley 46-49; R of Hanbury 49-63; CF (TA) 54-57; CF (TA - R of O) 57-62; R of Bredon w Bredon's Norton 63-73; RD of Bredon 71-73; Hon C of Clifton-on-Teme and of Lower Sapey and of The Shelsleys Dio Worc from 73. *Shelsley Beauchamp Rectory, Worcester, WR6 6RA.* (Shelsley Beauchamp 691)

BIRCH, Thomas Reginald. b 33. AKC 57. St Bonif Coll Warm 67. **d** 68 Colchester for Chelmsf. C of St Andr Eccles Distr Basildon 68-69; Chap Basildon Industr Chap from 69. *165 Church Road, Basildon, Essex.* (Basildon 22523)

BIRCH, William Michael. b 40. Univ of BC BA 67. Angl Th Coll Vanc STB 70. **d** 70 BC. C of St Mary Virg Vic 70-72; I of Oyen 72-74; R of St Jo Evang City and Dio Calg from 74. *1419-8th Avenue SE, Calgary, Alta., Canada.* (265-5283)

BIRCHALL, Maurice Molyneux. Univ of Dur LTh 41, BA 45. Edin Th Coll 36. **d** 39 **p** 40 St Andr. C of St Serf Burntisland 39-42; Ch Ch Falkirk (in c of St Mary Grangemouth) 42-44; Chap of St Chad's Coll Dur 44-45; C of St Geo Cullercoats 45-46; St Andr Penrith 46-48; V of Castle Sowerby 48-56; Sowerby 56-65; V of Thorpe 56-65; Cler Org Sec CECS 65-73; C of H Trin (in c of St Osw) (in c of St Osw) Habergham Eaves Burnley Dio Blackb from 73. *117 Wellfield Drive, Burnley, Lancs.*

BIRCHAM, Canon Ronald George. b 12. AKC 40. Ely Th Coll 40. **d** 40 Bp Price for Ely **p** 41 Ely. C of Downham 40-45; St Luke Chesterton 45-47; V of Sawston 48-78; RD of Camps 58-69; Surr 59-78; Hon Can of Ely from 69; Perm to Offic Dio Ely from 79. *70 London Road, Stapleford, Cambridge, CB2 5DR.* (Cam 843387)

BIRCHARD, Thaddeus Jude. b 45. Louisiana State Univ BA 66. Univ of Nottm Dipl Th 68. Kelham Th Coll 66. **d** 70 **p** 71 Ex. C of St Mark Ford Devonport 70-73; All SS Southend-on-Sea 73-75; Team V of Poplar 76-80; V of St Jo Evang w St Mich AA Paddington Dio Lon from 80. *18 Somers Crescent, W2 2PN.* (01-262 1732)

BIRCHBY, Martin Cecil. b 17. Worc Ordin Coll 66. **d** 68 **p** 69 Heref. C of Bromyard 68-70; C-in-c of Bredenbury w Grendon Bp and Wacton 70-75; P-in-c of Edvin Ralph w Collington and Thornbury 71-75; Pembridge w Moorcourt Dio Heref 75-80; R (w Shobdon) from 80; Shobdon 79-80; P-in-c of Staunton-on-Arrow w Byton Dio Heref from 81. *Pembridge Rectory, Leominster, Herefs.* (Pembridge 439)

BIRCHETT, Canon Ronald John. b 15. Univ of Lon AKC 38, BD (2nd cl) 38. TD 65. Ely Th Coll 38. **d** 38 Lon **p** 39 Willesden for Lon. C of Hayes Middx 38-43; Offg C-in-c of St Edm Yeading 40-43; St Mich York Town 43-47; CF (EC) 47-50; Min of Peel Distr of St Ambrose Oldham 50-55; CF (TA) 52-65; R of St Werburgh Chorlton-cum-Hardy Dio Man from 55; Proc Conv Man 63-64; RD of Stretford 67-77; Hon Can of Man from 76. *St Werburgh's Rectory, Chorlton-cum-Hardy, Manchester 21.* (061-881 1642)

BIRCHMORE, Brian Leonard. b 35. ALCD (2nd cl) 59. **d** 59 Roch **p** 60 Tonbridge for Cant. C of Rusthall 59-62; Rainham Kent 62-64; Belvedere (in c of St Andr Bostall Heath) 64-66; V of Meopham 66-74; R of Chatham 74-75; Commun Officer Basildon Distr Coun 75-78; Sen Commun Officer from 78; Perm to Offic Dio Chelmsf from 81. *7 Kennel Lane, Billericay, Essex, CM12 9RU.* (Billericay 56660)

BIRCHNALL, Canon Simeon Robert. b 18. St Jo Coll Dur BA 42, MA 45, Dipl in Th 43. **d** 43 **p** 44 Sheff. C of H Trin Wicker Sheff 43-46; Conisborough 46-47; St Jas Clifton 47-50; Chingford (in c of St Anne) 50-53; Min of St Anne's Conv Distr Chingford 53-56; V 56-64; R of St Mary Woodford (w St Phil & St Jas from 70) Dio Chelmsf from 64; Hon Can of Chelmsf from 76; RD of Redbridge from 76. *Rectory, Buckingham Road, E 18.* (01-504 3472)

BIRD, Preb Albert Harry. b 1896. Lich Th Coll 15. Late Exhib of St Chad's Coll Dur LTh 18. **d** 19 **p** 20 Lich. C of Fenton 19-23; All SS Sedgley 23-26; St Geo Wolverhampton 26-31; V of All SS Shrewsbury 31-61; Chap HM Pris Shrewsbury 34-58; Preb of Pipa Min in Lich Cathl 51-65; Preb (Emer) from 65; RD of Shrewsbury 56-62. *25 Monkmoor Avenue, Shrewsbury, SY2 5ED.* (Shrewsbury 57546)

BIRD, Alfred. Late Exhib of Keble Coll Ox BA (1st cl Mod Hist) 32, MA 39. Melb Coll of Div MTh 75. Bps' Coll Cheshunt 33. **d** 34 Barrow-F for Carl **p** 35 Carl. C of St Aid w Ch Ch Carl 34-38; LPr Dio S'wark and Asst Chap St Thos Hosp 38-41; C of Cockington 41-42; Chap RNVR 42-46; L to Offic Dio Armid 46-48; Exam Chap to Bp of Armid 46-48; Chap and Asst Master Eastbourne Coll 48-51; Chap Trin Coll Melb 51-61; V of Aberfeldie 62-66; Regr Melb Coll of Div 66-75; Perm to Offic Dio Melb 66-74; L to Offic 74-75. *523 Lygon Street, Carlton North, Vic, Australia 3054.* (03-387 3162)

BIRD, Anthony Peter. b 31. Late Sch of St Jo Coll Ox 2nd cl Cl Mods 52, BA (2nd cl Lit Hum) 54, 2nd cl Th 55, Liddon Stud 55, MA 57. Univ of Birm MB ChB 70. Cudd Coll 55. **d** 57 **p** 58 Lich. C of Stafford 57-60; Chap Cudd Coll 60-61; Vice-Prin 61-64; C of St Wulstan Selly Oak 64-68; L to Offic Dio Birm from 68; Prin Qu Coll Birm 74-79. *Queen's College, Somerset Road, Birmingham, B15 2QH.* (021-454 1527)

BIRD, Archibald Brian. b 02. AKC 28. **d** 28 Dover for Cant **p** 31 Chelmsf. C of St Luke Woodside 28-29; St Matt W Ham 31-33; Romford 33-34; Shenfield 34-35; Chap RN 35-39; V of Edwardstone (w Groton from 46) 40-71; Perm to Offic Dio St E and Chelmsf from 72. *38 Maidenburgh Street, Colchester, Essex, CO1 1UB.* (Colchester 44757)

BIRD, Canon Arthur Leyland. b 02. Qu Coll Ox 20. Can Scho Linc 23. **d** 25 **p** 26 York. C of N Ormesby 25-31; M of Bro of Good Shepherd Dubbo 31-37; R of Brewarrina NSW 34-37; V of St Mary Virg Burgh Heath 37-62; CF (R of O) 39-43; Commiss Bath from 50; Hon CF 57; RD of Epsom 60-65 and 68-69; R of Walton-on-the-Hill 62-71; Hon Can of Guildf 62-71; Can (Emer) from 71; Hon C of St Martin Dorking 72-81. *3 Queens Close, Walton-on-the-Hill, Tadworth, Surrey, KT20 7SU.* (Tadworth 3733)

BIRD, Christopher Charles. b 48. St Jo Coll Morpeth ThDip 78. **d** 78 **p** 79 Newc. C of Woy Woy 78-81; Wallsend Dio Newc from 81. *24 Metcalfe Street, Wallsend, NSW, Australia 2287.*

BIRD, Colin Richard Bateman. b 33. Selw Coll Cam BA 56, MA 61. Cudd Coll 56. **d** 58 Kingston T for Lon for Geo **p** 59 Geo. C of St Mark's Cathl Geo 58-61; St Sav Claremont Cape Town 61-64; R of N Suburbs Pret 64-66; Tzaneen w Duiwelskloof and Phalaborwa 66-70; C of Limpsfield (in c of St Andr Limpsfield Chart) 70-74; V of St Cath Hatcham Dio S'wark from 75; Exam Chap to Bp of S'wark from 78; RD of Deptford from 80. *102 Pepys Road, SE14 5SG.* (01-639 1050)

BIRD, David John. b 46. St D Coll Lamp BA (2nd cl Th) 70. Gen Th Sem NY STM 74. **d** 70 **p** 71 Worc. C of St Geo Kidderminster 70-72; in Amer Ch from 72. *Trinity School, 139 West 91 Street, New York City, NY 10024, USA.*

BIRD, Donald Wilfred Ray. b 27. Univ of Dur BA 52. Linc Th Coll 61. **d** 63 **p** 64 Linc. C of W Barkwith 63-66; Chap and Asst Master Cyrene Sch Bulawayo 66-67; Chap St Pet Dioc Sch Bulawayo 67-68; Chap Llewellin Barracks, Bulawayo 68-74; R of Marlborough 74-80; Scotter w East Ferry Dio Linc from 80. *Scotter Rectory, Gainsborough, Lincs.* (Scunthorpe 762662)

BIRD, Edward Herbert John Richards. b 14. St Deiniol's Libr Hawarden 77. **d** 77 **p** 78 Ches. (NSM) C of Partington w Carrington Dio Ches from 77. *1 Westbrook Cottages, Manchester Road, Carrington, Manchester, M31 4BD.*

BIRD, Eric Robert. Moore Coll Syd ThL 71. **d** and **p** 72 Syd. C of St Sav Punchbowl 72-73; Wollongong 74-75; R of Keiraville Dio Syd from 76. *4 Moore Street, Gwynneville, NSW, Australia 2500.* (042-29 5561)

BIRD, Frederick Hinton. b 38. Late Scho of St Edm Hall Ox BA 62, MA 66. St D Coll Lamp BD 72. Univ of Wales MEducn 81. **d** 65 **p** 66 Mon. C of Mynyddyslwyn 65-67; Min Can of St Woolos Cathl, Newport 67-70; Chap Anglo-Amer Coll Faringdon 70-71; Perm to Offic Dio Ox 70; Dio Cant from 72; Dio Mon from 76. *2 Delius Close, Rogerstone, Gwent.*

BIRD, Geoffrey Neville. b 22. AKC 48. St Bonif Coll Warm 48. **d** 49 **p** 50 Glouc. C of Berkeley 49-53; Malden 53-54; St Aldate Glouc 54-56; R of The Edge w Pitchcombe Dio Glouc from 56; P-in-c of Harescombe Dio Glouc from

76. *Edge Rectory, Stroud, Glos, GL6 6PF* (Painswick 812319)

BIRD, Gilbert Warren. b 16. **d** 77 Sask. C of Montr Lake Dio Sask from 77. *Montreal Lake, Sask, Canada.*

BIRD, Canon Harold Wallace. b 1893. Univ Coll Lon 13. Bp's Coll Calc 19. Hon CF (India) 22. **d** 22 **p** 23 Lah. Chap of St Andr Lah 22-25; Exam Univ of Punjab 24; Org Sec SPG Dios York and Sheff 25-27; C of Scarborough 26-27; Chap AMF 27-33; R of Subiaco and Sec ABM Perth 27-29; Commiss Centr Tang 28-33; R of St Aug Unley w St Chad Fullarton and Em Ch Wayville S Austr 29-33; C-in-c of St Elis Distr Ch Eastbourne 33-36; V 36-41; Commiss Bal from 37; V of St Mary Brighton 41-44; St Jas Brighton 41-44; L to Offic Dio Chich 44-46; C of St Luke W Norwood 46-47; V of St Mark Kennington 47-63; Surr from 50; Hon Can of S'wark 60-67; Can (Emer) from 67; Warden Homes of St Barn Dormans 63-65; L to Offic Dio Guildf from 70; Publ Pr Dio Berm 73-75. *2 Portsmouth Road, Liphook, GU 30 7AA.* (Liphook 723344)

BIRD, Henry John Joseph. b 37. Qu Coll Cam BA 59, MA 63. Linc Th Coll 62. **d** 64 **p** 65 Cant. C of St Mich AA Harbledown 64-68; Skipton-in-Craven 68-70; V of Oakworth 70-81; Chap Abingdon Sch from 81. *15 Meadowside, Abingdon, OX14 5DU.* (Abingdon 29085)

BIRD, Hugh Chapman. b 13. **d** 73 **p** 74 Perth. C of Applecross 73-79; P-in-c of Leeming 79-80; C of Applecross Dio Perth from 80. *29 Cunningham Street, Applecross, W Australia 6153.* (364-1292)

BIRD, Jeremy Paul. b 56. Univ of Ex BSc 77, Dipl Th 78. Sarum Wells Th Coll 78. **d** 80 **p** 81 Ex. C of Tavistock Dio Ex from 80. *81 Westmoor Park, Tavistock, Devon, PL19 9AB.*

BIRD, Maurice Pidding. b 19. Linc Coll Ox BA 40, MA 44. Cudd Coll 40. **d** 42 S'wark **p** 43 Ox. C of Malden 42-43; Headington 43-46; Eastney 47-55; Chap to Hostel of God Clapham 55-59; R of Winterton w E Somerton 59-71; V of St Barn (w St Bart from 75), Heigham Dio Nor from 71. *St Barnabas Vicarage, Russell Street, Norwich, NR2 4QT.* (Norwich 27859)

BIRD, Peter Andrew. b 40. Wadh Coll Ox BA (2nd cl Physics) 62, MA 68. Ridley Hall Cam 63. **d** 65 Taunton for B & W **p** 66 B & W. C of Keynsham 65-68; St Nich Strood 68-72; Team V 72-79; V of S Gillingham Dio Roch from 79. *4 Drewery Drive, Gillingham, Kent, ME8 ONX.* (Medway 31071)

BIRD, Very Rev Rex Alan. b 30. Clifton Th Coll 54. **d** 57 **p** 58 Lich. C of Wel 57-59; St Paul St Alb 59-61; V of Rainham Essex 61-65; R of Wennington 61-65; CF (TA) from 65; Lavenham 65-75; M Gen Syn 70-75; RD of Lavenham 72-75; Dean and V of Battle Dio Chich from 75. *Deanery, Battle, Sussex, TN33 0AQ.* (Battle 2693)

BIRD, Roger Alfred. b 49. AKC 72. St Aug Coll Cant 72. **d** 73 **p** 74 St A. C of Prestatyn 73-78; R of Llandysilio, Penrhos, Llandrinio and Criggion Dio St A from 78. *Llandysilio Rectory, Llanymynech, Powys, SY22 6QZ.* (Llanymynech 533)

BIRDSALL, Richard Alan. Hertf Coll Ox BA (2nd cl Th) 59, MA 63. Chich Th Coll 60. **d** 62 Warrington for Liv **p** 63 Liv. C of Up Holland 62-65; Perm to Offic Dio Ex 65-71. *c/o Phillips, Woodleigh, Freshford, Bath, Somt.*

BIRDWOOD, William Halhed. b 51. St Jo Coll Dur BA 73. Sarum Wells Th Coll 76. **d** 78 **p** 79 St Alb. C of Royston Dio St Alb from 78. *12 Prince Andrews Close, Royston, Herts.* (Royston 43265)

BIREA, Ilford Newman. d 64 New Guinea **p** 79 Popondota. P Dio New Guinea 64-71; Dio Papua 71-77; Dio Popondota 77-80; Dio Port Moresby from 81. *PO Box 7, Kupiano, Papua New Guinea.*

BIREMA, Abel. d 80 Kiga. d Dio Kiga. *BP 166, Gisenyi, Rwanda.*

BIRIBWOHA, James. d 74 **p** 75 Ank. P Dio Ank 74-76; Dio E Ank from 76. *PO Box 606, Mbarara, Uganda.*

BIRKENHEAD, Lord Bishop Suffragan of. *See* Brown, Right Rev Ronald.

BIRKET, Cyril. b 28. ACIS 70. N-W Ordin Course 71. **d** 74 Lanc for Blackb **p** 75 Blackb. C of Broughton 74-79; V of Wesham Dio Blackb from 79. *Vicarage, Wesham, Kirkham, Preston, Lancs PR4 3HA.* (Kirkham 682206)

BIRKETT, Neil Warren. b 45. Univ of Lanc BEducn 74. Kelham Coll Nottm 65. **d** 77 Southn for Win **p** Basingstoke for Win (APM). C of Weeke Dio Win from 7. *18 Grovelands Road, Teg Down, Winchester, Hants.*

BIRKETT, Peter. b 13. Univ Coll Dur BA 35, MA 39. **d** 36 **p** 37 Cant. C of Boxley 36-38; Birchington 38-40; Chap RAFVR 40-46; V of Charing 46-51; R of Little Chart 46-51; Crowcombe 51-64; C-in-c of Bicknoller 60-62; V of Castle Cary w Ansford 64-69; R of Holford w Dodington 69-77. *Tee Slash Dee Ranch, Anahim Lake, BC, Canada.*

BIRKS, Cyril Edmund. Selw Coll Cam BA 23, MA 27. Westcott Ho Cam 24. **d** 24 **p** 25 Swan B. Asst Chap of Ch Coll Brecon 24-28; Chap Kelly Coll Tavistock 28-35; Chap Michaelhouse Sch Natal 35-46; Hd Master Kenton Coll Nai 47-67; L to Offic Dio Momb 47-66; R of Mooi River Natal 66-67; L to Offic Dio Grahmstn 67-71; Dio Capetn 71-80; Perm to Offic from 80. *Bahati, Winkle Way, Clovelly, Fish Hoek, CP, S Africa.* (82-5270)

BIRLEY, John Lindsay. b 19. Kelham Th Coll 37. **d** 43 **p** 44 S'wark. C of St Andr Coulsdon 43-46; Asst Chap Wellingborough School 46-48; Sub-organist Ex Cathl and Asst Master Choristers' Sch 48-50; Chap and Asst Master Reed's Sch for Boys Cobham 50-54; Asst Chap and Asst Master St Jo Sch Leatherhead 54-64; L to Offic Dio Guildf 50-64; Asst Master Wel Coll and Perm to Offic Dio Ox 64-76. *5567 Grosslittgen Abtei, Himmerod, W Germany.*

BIRMINGHAM, Lord Bishop of. *See* Montefiore, Right Rev Hugh William.

BIRMINGHAM, Assistant Bishop of. *See* Sinker, Right Rev George.

BIRMINGHAM, Archdeacon of. *See* Hollis, Ven Gerald.

BIRMINGHAM, Provost of. *See* Moss, Very Rev Basil Stanley.

BIRT, Malcolm Douglas. b 33. Trin Coll Cam BA 56, MA 60. Ridley Hall Cam 56. **d** 58 **p** 59 Carl. C of St Mark Barrow-F 58-60; St John Tunbridge Wells 60-63; V of Constable Lee 63-72; R of Rolleston Dio Lich from 72; V of Anslow Dio Lich from 72. *Rolleston Rectory, Burton-on-Trent, Staffs.*

BIRT, Patrick. b 34. Glouc Ordin Course 71. **d** and **p** 75 Tewkesbury for Glouc. Hon C of Bisley 75-76; Whiteshill 76-81; P-in-c of Ruardean Dio Glouc from 81. *Ruardean Rectory, Gloucester, GL17 9US.* (Dean 542214)

BIRT, Richard Arthur. b 43. Late Choral Exhib of Ch Ch, Ox BA (Lit Hum) 66, MA 69. Cudd Coll 67. **d** 69 **p** 70 York. C of Sutton-in-Holderness 69-71; Wollaton 71-75; R of Kirkby-in-Ashfield 75-80; P-in-c of Duxford Dio Ely from 80; Ickleton Dio Ely from 80; Hinxton Dio Ely from 80; Ed Ely Dioc Gazette from 81. *Rectory, St Johns Street, Duxford; Cambridge, CB2 4RA.* (Cam 832137)

BIRT, Canon William Raymond. b 11. Ely Th Coll 55. **d** 56 **p** 57 Ox. C of Caversham 56-59; St Jo Evang Newbury (in c of St Geo Wash Common) 59-63; PC of St Geo Wash Common 63-71; P-in-c of Enborne w Hamstead Marshall 68-70; RD of Newbury 70-73; R of W Woodhay 71-81; Archd of Berks 73-77; C of W Woodhay, Enborne w Hamstead Marshall, Inkpen and Combe; Dio Ox from 81; Hon Can of Ch Ch Ox from 79. *West Woodhay Rectory, Newbury, Berks, RG15 0BL.* (Inkpen 359)

BIRTCH, John Edward McKay. Univ of W Ont BA 51, Hur Coll LTh 52, BD 61. **d** 52 **p** 53 Hur. I of St Barn Lon Ont 52-54; on leave 54-55; R of St Andr Sarnia 55-59; St Bart, Sarnia 59-68; Preston Hur 68-71; in Amer Ch from 71. *2644 65th Avenue, St Petersburg, Fla 33712, USA.*

BIRTCH, Robert William Arnold. Univ of W Ont BA 66. Hur Coll BTh 69. **d** 69 **p** 70 Hur. I of Princeton 69-72; St Timothy Lon 72-77; St Jas St Mary's Dio Hur from 77. *Box 1238, St Marys, Ont., Canada.* (519 284 1053)

BIRTWELL, Stanley. b 15. St Jo Coll Ox BA 37, Dipl in Th 38, MA 41. Wycl Hall Ox 37. **d** 39 **p** 40 Blackb. C of St Luke Brierfield 39-42; V 44-50; C of St Bart Colne 42-44; V of St Mary Magd Clitheroe 50-61; RD of Whalley 60-61; V of St Giles Ox 61-72; RD of Ox 68-70. *38 Park Avenue, Clitheroe, BB7 2HW.* (Clitheroe 25903)

BIRTWISTLE, James. b 33. FCA 66. Ely Th Coll 57. **d** 59 **p** 60 Liv. C of St Luke Southport 59-63; V of Cleator Moor (w Cleator from 68) 63-70; C-in-c of Cleator 65-68; R of Letchworth 70-73; Schools Officer Dio St Alb 73; Dep Dir Educn 77-79; Dir from 79; C-in-c of Wareside 73-80. *c/o 66 Fordwich Rise, Hertford, Herts.* (Hertf 59718)

BISBROWN, Alan Kay. b 16. Univ of Man BA 40. Lich Th Coll 40. **d** 42 **p** 43 Blackb. C of H Trin Darwen 42-46; CF 46-49; C of Chapel-Allerton 49-51; V of Tockholes 51-55; Weeton 55-59; St Paul Low Moor Clitheroe 59-72; Ch Ch Glasson Dio Blackb from 72. *Glasson Vicarage, Lancaster.* (Galgate 751366)

BISEREKO, Canon Erasto. d 42 **p** 43 Ugan. P Dio Ugan 42-60; Dio Ruw 60-72; Dio Bunyoro from 72; Can of St John's Cathl Fort Portal from 68. *Box 105, Hoima, Bunyoro, Uganda, E Africa.*

BISH, Donald. b 26. Ripon Hall Ox 74. **d** and **p** 75 Roch. C of S Gillingham 75-79; R of Wateringbury w Teston and W Farleigh Dio Roch from 79. *Rectory, Teston, Nr Maidstone, Kent, ME18 5AJ.* (Maidstone 812494)

BISHOP, Alfred Graham. d and **p** 57 Bal. C-in-c of Swan Marsh 57-58; Hopetoun 58-60; L to Offic Dio Carp 60-68; Dio N Terr 68-75; Hon C of Ch Ch Cathl Darwin 72-75; Perm to Offic Dio Perth 75-77; Dio C & Goulb from 77. *54 Caley Crescent, Narrabundah, ACt, Australia 2604.*

BISHOP, Anthony John. b 43. G and C Coll Cam BA 66, MA 69. Univ of Lon MTh 69. Lon Coll of Div 67. **d** 69

Warrington for Liv **p** 70 Liv. C of St Luke Eccleston 69-73; Gt Baddow 73-76; CMS Miss in Nigeria from 77. *Box 64, Bukuru, Plateau State, Nigeria.*

BISHOP, Anthony Peter. b 46. ALCD 71 (LTh from 74). **d** 71 **p** 72 Roch. C of Beckenham 71-75; Chap RAF from 75; Perm to Offic Dio Moray 80-81. *c/o Ministry of Defence, Adastral House, WC1.*

BISHOP, Arthur Jack. b 07. St Jo Coll Dur BA (2nd cl Th) and Lightfoot Sch 28, Jenkyns Scho 29, MA 31. **d** 30 Barking for Chelmsf **p** 31 Colchester for Chelmsf. C of Em Forest Gate 30-33; Succr of Leic Cathl 33-35; CF 36-45; V of Mexborough 45-55; RD of Wath 50-55; R of Harthill 55-59; V of N w S Hykeham 59-66; R of Scotter w E Ferry 66-72; Lympsham 72-75; Perm to Offic Dio Melb from 77. *6 Wattle Valley Road, Mitcham, Vic, Australia 3132.*

BISHOP, Bryan Hope. b 07. Univ of Leeds BA (3rd cl Hist) 28. Coll of Resurr Mirfield 25. **d** 30 **p** 31 Lich. C of Penn 30-35; St Luke Hanley 35-38; V of Holmebridge 38-51; CF (EC) 40-45; V of St Andr Huddersfield 51-55; R of Cholderton 55-70; R of Newton Tony 55-70; V of W Alvington 70-77; Perm to Offic Dio Ex from 77. *9 Venn Lane, Stoke Fleming, Dartmouth, S Devon.*

BISHOP, Canon Charles Peyton. St Jo Coll Manit LTh 36. Univ of Manit BA 37. **d** 36 **p** 37 Calg. Miss at Foremost 36-37; C of St Steph Calg 37-39; I of Canmore w Exhaw 39-42; Chap CASF 42-46; R of Okotoks 46-49; St Jo Evang N Vanc 49-60; Can of New Westmr 59 60; R of Ch Ch Edmon 60-65, Hon Can of Edmon 65-69; R of Cadboro Bay 68-74. *24042-80 Avenue, RR6, Langley, BC, Canada.*

BISHOP, Christopher. b 48. St Aug Coll Cant 71. **d** 72 **p** 73 Barking for Chelmsf. C of St Mary Virg Gt Ilford 72-75; Upminster 75-80; Dioc Youth Officer and Publ Pr Dio Chelmsf from 80. *85 St Lawrence Road, Upminster, Essex, RM14 2UN.*

✠ **BISHOP, Right Rev Clifford Leofric Purdy.** b 08. Ch Coll Cam 2nd cl Hist Trip pt i 29, BA (3rd cl Th Trip pt i) 31. Linc Th Coll 31. **d** 32 **p** 33 S'wark. C of St John Walworth 32-38; St John Middlesbrough (in c of St Mich AA) 38-41; V of St Geo Camberwell 41-49; RD of Camberwell 43-49; C-in-c of All S Grosvenor Park Newington 44-47; R of Blakeney w Langham Parva 49-53; RD of Walsingham 51-53; R of Bp Wearmouth 53-62; RD of Wearmouth and Surr 53-62; Hon Can of Dur 58-62; Cons Ld Bp Suffr of Malmesbury in S'wark Cathl 1 May 62 by Abp of Cant; Bps of Bris; and Wakef; Bps Suffr of Kens; Dover; and Kingston T; and Bp Herbert; res 73; Can of Bris 62-73; Exam Chap to Bp of Bris from 62; P-in-c of Cley-next-Sea w Wiveton 76-78. *Rectory Cottage, Cley-next-Sea, Holt, Norf.* (Cley 250)

BISHOP, Canon David Harold. b 28. ARIBA 53. Westcott Ho Cam 55. **d** 57 **p** 58 Lich. C of Cannock 57-61; Gt Barr (in c of St Chad's Gt Barr) 61-67; V of All H Lon Wall Lon 67-80; Architectural Adv to Coun for Places of Worship 67-80; Perm to Offic Dio Roch 68-80; Actg P-in-c of Lamberhurst 77-78; Can Res of Nor Cathl from 80. *26 The Close, Norwich, Norf, NR1 4DZ.* (Norwich 24825)

BISHOP, David Henry Ryder. b 27. Tyndale Hall Bris. Dipl Th (Lon) 57. **d** 57 **p** 58 Roch. C of Sevenoaks 57-59; St Clem Parkstone Dorset 59-64; Chap at Jinja 64-67; Deputn Sec CCCS 68; R of St Clem City and Dio Ox from 69. *St Clement's Rectory, Oxford, OX4 1AW.* (Ox 48735)

BISHOP, Donald. b 22. Univ of Lon BSc (Econ) 48. Qu Coll Birm 56. **d** 57 **p** 58 Sarum. C of H Trin Trowbridge 57-60; CF (TA) 58-67; CF (TAVR) 67-68; PC of Bodicote Dio Ox 60-68; V from 68; P-in-c of Broughton w N Newington Dio Ox from 71. *Bodicote Vicarage, Banbury, Oxon, OX15 4BN.* (Banbury 3944)

BISHOP, Edward Forbes. b 02. Selw Coll Cam BA 25. Ely Th Coll 25. M SSJE 35. **d** 26 **p** 27 Nor. C of St Mark Lakenham 26-34; SSJE Miss P Panch Howd Poona 35-57; Can of Bom 52-67; Miss at Lonavla 55-57; I of St Pet Mazagon Bom 57-67; SSJE Miss St Crispin Yerandavna 63-67; Lonavla 64-67; L to Offic Dio Ox 68-80; Perm to Offic Dio Leic from 80. *St Johns House, 2 Woodland Avenue, Leicester.*

BISHOP, Ernest Arthur. b 08. AKC 34. **d** 34 **p** 35 Chelmsf. C of St Matthias Canning Town 34-38; Chingford 38-41; C-in-c of St Paul Walthamstow 41-47; V of St Alb Upton Pk 47-53; Holme 53-63; R of Conington 53-63; RD of Leightonstone 57-63; R of Stilton w Denton and Caldecote 63-73; C-in-c of Folksworth 64-69; Morborne 64-73; L to Offic Dio St A from 73. *8 Clifton Drive, Lytham St Annes, Lancs.*

BISHOP, Hilary Alfred Warner. Trin Coll Melb ACT. **d** 49 **p** 50 Melb. Chap of St John's Boys' Home Cant Melb 49-50; Min of Warburton 50-53; Ringwood 53-56; I of Aberfeldie 56-61; V of Menton (w Parkdale to 64) 61-66; Perm to Offic Dio Melb 67-73; Dio Wang 73-77; R of Yea 77-80. *13 Hoadley Avenue, Frankston, Vic, Australia 3139.*

BISHOP, Huw Daniel. b 49. St D Coll Lamp BA 71, Powys Exhib Dipl Th 73. Bp Burgess Hall Lamp 71. 1 73 **p** 74 St D. C of Carmarthen 73-78; V of Llanybydder 79-80; CF 80. *Address temp unknown.*

BISHOP, James William Frier. b 49. St Barn Coll Adel Th Dip 72. **d** and **p** 73 Bal. C of H Trin Ararat 73-75; Hon Chap to Bp of Bal from 76; V of Natimuk 76-79. *Hill End, via Moe, Vic, Australia 3825.*

BISHOP, John Albert. b 11. Lon Coll of Div 39. **d** 41 **p** 42 Liv. C of St Lawe Kirkdale 41-44; Bispham Blackpool 44-46; V of Ch Ch Blackb 46-53; St Mark St Helens 53-59; R of Carlton-in-the-Willows 59-73; Gamston w Eaton and W Drayton 73-78; R of Ft Simpson 78-81. *c/o Box 7, Fort Simpson, NWT, Canada.*

BISHOP, John Baylis. b 32. Selw Coll Cam 2nd cl Th Trip pt i 52, BA (3rd cl Th Trip pt ii) 54, MA 58. Cudd Coll 54. **d** 56 **p** 57 York. C of St Osw Middlesbrough 56-59; Romsey 59-62; Chap RN 62-66; C-in-c of St Mary le Wigford Linc 66-67; V of St Faith (w St Martin from 69) Linc 66-71; Publ Pr Dio Bris from 72. *16 Chesterfield Road, St Andrew's Park, Bristol, BS6 5DL.*

BISHOP, (Simeon) John Charles. b 46. Chich Th Coll 77. **d** 79 **p** 79 Lon for Heref. M SSF from 66. *Friary, 135 Boswall Parkway, Edinburgh, EH5 2LY.* (031-552 4452)

BISHOP, John Graham. Univ of Bris BA (1st cl Hist) 52, BD (1st cl) (Lon) 59. PhD (Lon) 73. Chich Th Coll 54. **d** 56 **p** 57 Ex. C of St Thos Ex 56-59; E Wickham 59-61; Tutor and Libr Chich Th Coll 61-70; C of Tamerton Foliot 70-71; R of Dartington Dio Ex from 71; RD of Totnes from 75; M Gen Syn Ex from 75; V of Rattery Dio Ex from 79. *Parsonage, Dartington, Totnes, Devon, TQ9 6NS.* (Totnes 863206)

BISHOP, John Harold. b 09. Univ Coll Dur BA 31, MA 45. Cudd Coll 34. **d** 35 **p** 36 Glouc. C of St Steph Glouc 35-37; Miss P CMD and SPG Delhi 37-42; Miss at Moradabad 42-45; Warden of St Paul's Hostel Delhi 46-51; V of Hugglescote w Donington 51-60; Commiss Delhi 52-79; R of Singleton 60-79; V of E Dean 60-79; W Dean 75-79. *6 Tregarth Road, Chichester, PO19 4QU.* (Chich 527612)

BISHOP, Canon Kenneth Mackay. b 08. St Edm Hall Ox BA (2nd cl Th) 29, MA 33. Wycl Hall Ox 29. **d** 31 **p** 32 Portsm. C of St Jude Southsea 31-33; Cathl Ch Bradf 33-37; R of St Mary Droylsden 37-46; St Paul Kersal 46-50; V of Deane 50-74; Surr 45-74; Proc Conv Man 51-70; Hon Can of Man 64-74; Can (Emer) from 74; RD of Deane 66-74; perm to Offic Dio Carl from 74. *8 The Hawthorns, Penrith Road, Keswick, Cumbria, CA12 4LL.* (0596 72441)

BISHOP, Malcolm Geoffrey. b 33. Univ of Leeds BA (3rd cl Gen) 59. Coll of Resurr Mirfield 59. **d** 61 **p** 62 Lich. C of St Mary Kingswinford 61-67; V of Birches Head 67-72; C-in-c of Oakamoor w Cotton 72-78; Team V of St Aid Billingham Dio Dur from 78. *17 Shadforth Drive, Billingham, Cleve, TS23 3PW.*

BISHOP, Mark Wreford. b 20. Ex Coll Ox Hasker Scho 3rd cl Mod 40, BA (2nd cl Th) 42, MA 45. Wycl Hall Ox 42. **d** 43 Plymouth for Ex **p** 44 Ex. C of Chas Ch Plymouth 43-47; CMS Miss Chap and Th Tutor Buwalasi Coll 48-56; Exam Chap to Bp on U Nile 53-56; V of Riddlesden 56-61; Girlington 61-67; Dioc Insp of Schs Dio Bradf 57-64; Sec Bradf Dioc Miss & Ecumen Coun 62-67; Bradf Coun of Chs 67-71; L to Offic Dio Bradf 67-71; V of Helme 71-77; Ecumen Officer in Dio Wakef 71-77; P-in-c of Graveley w Yelling and Papworth St Agnes 77-78; R (w Toseland) from 78. *Rectory, Graveley, Cambs, PE18 9PW.* (Huntingdon 830222)

BISHOP, Michael George. b 27. Wycl Hall Ox 63. **d** 65 **p** 66 Glouc. C of St Mary Virg w St Matt Cheltm 65-68; C-in-c of Edale 68-71; Warden Derby Dioc Youth Centre Edale 68-71; V of Doveridge 71-79; Cotmanhay and Shipley 79-81; Chap HM Detention Centre Foston Hall Derby 73-79; in Amer Ch from 81. *Box 38, Claremont, CA 91711, USA.* (714-626 7170)

BISHOP, Neville Edwin. Univ of W Ont BA 55. Trin Coll Tor LTh 58. **d** 57 **p** 58 Tor. C of St John Weston 57-58; St Hilda Tor 58-60; R of St Marg New Tor 60-69; R of King 69-77; St Chad City and Dio Tor from 77. *1695 Dufferin Street, Toronto, Ont, Canada.* (416-652 1794)

BISHOP, Paul George.. b 47. Mem Univ of Newfld BA 70. Qu Th Coll LTh 69. **d** 70 **p** 71 Newfld. C of St Thos, St John's Newfld 70-72; R of Belleoram 72-76; I of Botwood Dio Centr Newfld from 76. *Box 419, Botwood, Newfoundland, Canada.* (709-257 2393)

BISHOP, Canon Peter Charles. Univ of Leic BSc 64. Em Coll Sktn 64. **d** 68 **p** 69 Arctic. P-in-c of Coppermine 68-81; Hon Can of St Jude's Cathl Frobisher Bay from 78; Exam Chap to Bp of the Arctic from 81; Prin Arthur Turner Tr Sch Pangnirtung from 81. *Arthur Turner School, Pangnirtung, NWT, Canada.*

BISHOP, Philip Michael. b 47. Univ of Lon BD and AKC 69. St Aug Coll Cant 70. **d** 71 **p** 72 Southw. C of Mansfield Woodhouse 71-76; Liscard 76-78; V of Thornton-le-Moors w

Ince and Elton Dio Ches from 78. *Vicarage, Ince Lane, Elton, Chester.*

BISHOP, Phillip Leslie. b 44. K Coll Lon and Warm BD and AKC 66. **d** 67 **p** 68 Lich. C of Albrighton 67-70; St Geo-in-the-E Stepney 70-71; Ascen Berwick Hill Middlesbrough 71-73; C-in-c of Withernwick 73-76; Industr Chap Dio York from 73. *1023 Anlaby High Road, Hull, HU4 7PN.* (Hull 52212)

BISHOP, Thomas Harold. b 21. Ridley Hall Cam 60. **d** 61 Warrington for Liv **p** 62 Liv. C of Wavertree 61-64; V of St Bridget Wavertree 64-69; Rainford Dio Liv from 69. *Rainford Vicarage, Rainford, St Helens, WA11 8HD.* (Rainford 2200)

BISHOP, Thomas Harveyson. Coll of Resurr Mirfield. **d** 56 **p** 57 Johann. C of Malvern Johann 56-57; Germiston 57-61; R of Westonaria 61-63; Parkhurst Johann 63-64; C of Rosebank 64-72; R of Melmouth 72-74; Sea Point 75-79; Commiss Geo from 79. *91 Park Avenue North, NW10 1JU.*

BISHOP, Victor. d and **p** 76 E Newfld (APM). C of Port de Grave 76-79; Brigus Dio E Newfld from 79. *Box 6, Clarke's Beach, Newfoundland, Canada.*

BISHOP, Walter John. Montr Dioc Th Coll LTh 43. **d** 43 **p** 44 Montr. C of St Luke Montr 43-44; Regional Sec SCM 44-53; R of Sapperton 53; St Mary New Westmr 53-58; Chap Univ of BC Vanc 58-63; R of St Jo Div Burnaby Dio New Westmr from 63. *5238 Oakland Street, South Burnaby, BC, Canada.*

BISHOP, (Hugh) William Fletcher. b 07. Keble Coll Ox BA 29, MA 38. Cudd Coll 32. M CR 40-74; **d** 33 **p** 34 Carl. C of Workington 33-35; C of Cuddesdon and Lect Cudd Coll 35-37; CF (EC) 40-45; Commiss Borneo 49-62; Zam 60-70; Masasi 60-69; Les 60-75; Nass 60-70; Kimb K 68-74; Lusaka 71-74; N Zam and Centr Zam 71-74; Prin Coll of Resurr Mirfield 56-66; Supr 66-74; Exam Chap to Bp of Wakef 59-74; Proc Conv Wakef 66-70; Proc Conv Relig Communs Prov York 70-74; L to Offic Dio Wakef from 74. *19 St John's Terrace, Leeds, LS3 1DY.* (Leeds 459180)

BISHOP, William Marshall. Dalhousie Univ NS BA 51. K Coll NS LTh 49. **d** 45 **p** 46 NS. C of Dartmouth 45-46; All SS Cathl Halifax NS 46-47; M SSJE Dio Alg 47-52; R of Port Dufferin 52-57; Hd Master St Jo Coll Nassau 57-67; P-in-c of Lyford Cay 62-64; Exam Chap to Bp of Nass 58-62; C of Southgate 67; R of New Ross 68-70; on leave. *c/o High School, Freeport, Grand Bahama.*

BISHTON, Gerald Arthur. b 32. St Pet Hall Ox BA 59, MA 63. Ruskin Coll Ox. Qu Coll Birm. **d** 61 **p** 62 Chelmsf. C of St Edm Forest Gate 61-64; Asst Chap Univ of Lon 64-67; Chap NE Lon Poly 68-74; Co-ordinator for Handicapped Studs 74-80; Hosp Chap Ilford 68-80; P-in-c of Sutton w Shopland Dio Chelmsf from 80. *Sutton Rectory, Rochford, Essex.* (Southend 544587)

BISIWEI, John Ralph. St Pet Coll Siota 64. **d** 69 **p** 70 Melan. P Dio Melan 69-75; Dio New Hebr from 75. *Motolava, Banks Islands, New Hebrides.*

BISSELL, George Edward Kitchener. Wycl Coll Tor. **d** 45 Bp White for Keew **p** 45 Keew. C of St John Lac du Bonnet w Pointe du Bois and Great Falls 45-48; I of Wiarton 48-52; Brantford 52-62; R of Corunna 62-76; Markdale Dio Hur from 76. *Box 238, Markdale, Ont., Canada.* (519-672 8306)

BISSET, Canon John Davidson. b 1896. Univ of Aber MA 19. Edin Th Coll 19. **d** 20 **p** 21 Edin. C of H Trin Stirling 20-22; All SS Bearsden w St Andr Milngavie 22-23; Miss at Chanda 23-25; Nagpur 25-27; Chap at Bandikui 27-32; P-in-c of H Trin Monifieth 32-46; R of Drumtochty w Drumlithie 46-53; Fasque w Lochlee 46-53; Doune 53-66; Aberfoyle 53-66; Can of St Ninian's Cathl Perth 65-66; Hon Can from 67. *Westgarth, Kirkmay Road, Crail, Fife, Scotland.* (Crail 289)

BISSET, Robert MacBain. b 05. Univ of Glas MA 30. Edin Th Coll 30. **d** 32 **p** 33 Glas. C of Ch Ch Glas 32-37; R of St Luke Glas 37-41; Ch Ch Lanark 41-47; All SS Bearsden 47-73; St Andr Milngavie 54-73; Can of Glas 62-73. *32 Andrew Avenue, Lenzie, Dunb.*

BISSETT, Norman Arthur Richard. Moore Th Coll Syd 59. **d** 63 Syd. C of Summer Hill 63-64; L to Offic Dio Syd 64-65; CMS 65-67; Chap at Devoto w Hurlingham 67-69; L to Offic Dio Argent 70-76; C-in-c of Flemington Dio Syd from 76. *13 Hornsey Road, Homebush West, NSW, Australia 2140.* (76-7672)

BITABABAJE, Wilson. d 78 **p** 79 Vic Nyan. P Dio Vic Nyan. *Box 185, Magu, Tanzania.*

BITAMAZIRE, Nathan. b 48. Bp Tucker Coll Mukono 71. **d** 73 Ruw. d Dio Ruw. *Box 524, Bwera, Katwe, Uganda.*

BITASHOBOROKIRE, Canon Yekoniya. Bp Tucker Coll 68. **d** 71 **p** 72 Ank. P Dio Ank 71-76; Dio E Ank from 76; Can from 79. *Bishop Stuart College, Box 152, Mbarara, Uganda.*

BITOROTOORWA, Eliasaph. d 74 **p** 75 Ank. P Dio Ank 74-76; Dio E Ank from 76. *Box 132, Mbarara, Uganda.*

BIVAS, Laurence. b 32. **d** 78 **p** 81 Aipo. P Dio Aipo. *Movi PMB, via Goroka, Papua New Guinea.*

BIY, Stephen. d 78 Nak. d Dio Nak. *c/o Box 244, Nakuru, Kenya.*

BIYELA, Canon Peter. St Pet Coll Rosettenville LTh 42. **d** 42 Zulu **p** 43 Natal for Zulu. C of Etaleneni 42-44; Empangeni 44-45; Kwamagwaza 45-52; R of Nkonjeni 52-67; Can of Zulu 59-67 and from 74; R of Etalaneni 67-73; Archd of W Zulu 67-73; Dir of Chr Educn Dio Zulu from 74. *P/Bag 802, Melmoth, Zululand, S Africa.* (Melmoth 1203)

BJERRING, Bryan Davis. b 42. Lakehead Univ BA 68. St Jo Coll Winnipeg MDiv 77. **d** 76 **p** 77 Rupld. C of St Matt Winnipeg 76-78; R of St Pet Winnipeg Dio Rupld from 78. *Box 367, Winnipeg, manit, R3M 3V3, Canada.*

BLABER, Kenneth James Robert. Univ of W Ont Dipl Th 66. Hur Coll. **d** 66 Hur for Moos **p** 67 Moos. I of Mistassini 66-70; Chapais and Chibougamau 70-74; Val D'or 74-76; C of N Bay and P-in-c of Sturgeon Falls Dio Alg from 76. *19 Van Horne Crescent, North Bay, Ont., Canada.*

BLACHFORD, Canon Kenneth Frederick. Trin Coll Tor BA 34, LTh 36. **d** 36 **p** 37 Tor. C of St Jo Evang Tor 36-38; St Geo St Cath 38-41; St Geo Cathl Kingston 41-44; V of St Geo Trenton 44-45; Actg Missr at Pittsburg 45-51; R of Deseronton 51-55; Trenton 55-70; Dom Chap to Bp of Ont 53-70; Can of Ont from 61; R of Gananoque 70-80; Exam Chap to Bp of Ont 76-80. *171 King Street West, Ont, Canada.*

BLACK, Alexander Stevenson. b 28. Univ of Glas MA 53. **d** 55 **p** 56 Glas. C of St Jo Evang Dumfries 55-58; St Mary's Cathl Glas 58-61; Chap Univ of Glas 58-61; C-in-c of St Mark E Kilbride 61-69; R of St Columba Edin 69-79; Team V of St Jo Evang City and Dio Edin from 79. *3 Randolph Place, Edinburgh, EH3 7TQ.* (031-2265111)

BLACK, Arthur Bryden Sims. d 79 **p** 80 Mashon. P Dio Mashon. *c/o Anglican Diocesan Offices, PO Box UA7, Salisbury, Zimbabwe.*

BLACK, Brian Colin. Moore Th Coll ACT ThL 56. **d** and **p** 57 Syd. C of Toongabbie 57-59; C-in-c of Yagoona 59-64; R of Westmead 66-67; L to Offic Dio Syd 67-75; C of Carlingford 75-76; R of Blackheath Dio Syd from 77. *Rectory, Hat Hill Road, Blackheath, NSW, Australia 2785.* (047-878127)

BLACK, Charles Sidney. Univ of Tor BA 58. Hur Coll BTh 61. Trin Coll Tor BD 68. **d** 60 **p** 61 Hur. R of Ilderton 61-64; Listowel 64-66; Chap R Canad N from 66; Perm to Offic Dio Calg from 80. *14 Arras Drive SW, Calgary, Alta, Canada. T2T 5L6.*

BLACK, David William. St Jo Coll Morpeth ACT ThL 50. **d** 50 **p** 51 C and Goulb. C of Cooma 50-52; Albury 52-56; R of Pambula 56-60; Braidwood 60-64; P-in-c of St Geo Provisional Distr Canberra 65-66. *34 Inverness Avenue, Penhurst, NSW, Australia.*

BLACK, George Moffatt. b 1893. AKC 24. Bps' Coll Cheshunt 24. **d** 24 Lon **p** 26 Willesden for Lon. C of St Jas Ealing 24-39; Perm to Offic Dio Lon 40-63; CF (EC) 42-44; Hon CF 44; Chap Nunhead Cem 50-63. *Ballyholme Hotel, Ballyholme, Bangor, Co Down, N Ireland.*

BLACK, Gordon McCully. Mt Allison Univ NB BA 34, Mus Bac 35. ARCO 40. Bp's Univ Lennox LST 51, BD 58. **d** 50 **p** 51 Fred. C of St Marg Fred 50-54; R of Gladstone 54-57; Bracebridge 57-58; Asst Libr St Mich Coll Tor 59-60; P-in-c of Roslin 61-65; I of Ludlow and Blissfield 65-67; R of Dominion and New Waterford Dio NS from 73. *3430 Ellsworth Avenue, New Waterford, NS, Canada.* (862-2383)

BLACK, Henry. b 40. Edin Th Coll 64. **d** 67 **p** 68 Dur. C of Horden 67-69; Cleadon Pk 69-73; Winlaton (in c of St Patr High Spen) 73-78; R of S Ockendon Dio Chelmsf from 78. *Rectory, North Road, South Ockendon, Essex.* (S Ockendon 3349)

BLACK, Ian Forbes. b 29. St Aid Coll 55. **d** 58 **p** 59 Ches. C of Bramhall 58-61; Witton 61-63; P-in-c of St Andr Prestonpans 63-68; R of Ch Ch Leith 68-71; Asst Chap HM Pris Walton, Liv 71-72; Chap HM Pris Haverigg 72-73; R of Bootle w Corney (and Whicham w Whitbeck from 75) Dio Carl from 73; C-in-c of Whicham w Whitbeck 73-75. *Rectory, Bootle Millom, Cumb, LA19 5TH.* (Bootle 223)

BLACK, Jay Theodore. Harvard Coll BA 30. Gen Th Sem STB. **d** 33 **p** 34 Oregon. P-in-c of St Agnes Nass 44-45; St Steph Grand Bahama Nass 53-55; Asst Master St Jo Coll Nass 56-59; P-in-c of Abaco Dio Nass from 63. *St Peter's Rectory, Green Turtle Bay, Abaco, W Indies.*

BLACK, Leonard Albert. b 49. Edin Th Coll 69. **d** 72 **p** 73 Aber. C of St Marg of Scotld Gallowgate Aber 72-75; Chap of St Paul's Cathl Dundee 75-77; P-in-c of St Martin Dundee 75-77; St Ninian Seaton Aber 77-80; R of St Jo Evang w St Mich AA Inverness Dio Moray from 80. *St Michael's Rectory, Abban Street, Inverness, IV3 6HH.* (Inverness 33797)

BLACK, Malcolm Bruce. Bp's Univ Lennox BA (Th) 54. **d** 54 Queb **p** 55 Ott. C of St Matt Ott 54-58; R of Kars 58-63; St

Jo Div Nepean Ott 63-68; Hon C of St D and St Patr Guelph Dio Niag from 69. *587 Woodlawn Road, East Guelph, Ont., Canada.*

BLACK, Montague John. b 47. Univ of Cant NZ BA 70. St Jo Coll Auckld 69. **d** 71 **p** 72 Bp McKenzie for Wel. C of Hawera 71-74; St Paul's Cathl Wel 74-76; V of Kiwitea 76-78; Taihape 78-81; Stratford Dio Waik from 81. *32 Orlando Street, Stratford, NZ.* (6369)

BLACK, Neville. b 36. Oak Hill Th Coll 61. **d** 64 Warrington for Liv **p** 65 Liv. C of St Ambrose w St Timothy Everton 64-69; C-in-c of St Geo Everton 69-71; V 71-80; C-in-c of St Benedict Everton 70-72; St Chad w Ch Ch Everton 70-72; P-in-c of St Nath Windsor, Edge Hill Dio Liv from 80. *Windsor Vicarage, Queens Drive, Mossley Hill, Liverpool, L18 2DT.* (051-722 1625)

BLACK, Robert John Edward Francis Butler. b 41. Trin Coll Dub BA 65, Div Test 66. **d** 66 **p** 67 Connor. C of Jordanstown 66-71; St Steph and St Ann Dub 71-73; Stillorgan Dio Dub from 73. *19 Weirview Drive, Stillorgan, Co Dublin, Irish Republic.* (887178)

BLACK, Robert Merrill. b 53. Univ of Sktn BA 74. McGill Univ Montr BTh 76, STM 78. Montr Dioc Th Coll 75. **d** 79 **p** 80 Montr. C of Vaudreuil 79-81; on leave. *Trinity College, Toronto, Ont, Canada.*

BLACK, Samuel James. b 38. TCD 65. **d** 68 **p** 69 Connor. C of Cloughfern 68-72; St Paul Lisburn 72-78; I of Rasharkin w Finvoy Dio Connor from 78. *153 Finvoy Road, Ballymoney, Co Antrim, N Ireland.* (Rasharkin 262)

BLACKALL, Robin Jeremy McRae. b 35. Ridley Hall Cam 67. **d** 69 **p** 70 St E. C of Stowmarket 69-72; R of Stanstead w Shimplingthorne and Alpheton 72-76; Bradwell-justa-Mare 76-79; St Lawr Chelmsf 76-79; Warden Bede Ho Staplehurst 80-81; Chap HM Detention Centre Blantyre Ho Tonbridge from 81. *Blantyre House, Goudhurst, Tonbridge, Kent.* (0580 211367)

BLACKBURN, Lord Bishop of. *See* Cross, Right Rev David Stewart.

BLACKBURN, Archdeacon of. *See* Carroll, Ven Charles William Desmond.

BLACKBURN, Provost of. *See* Jackson, Very Rev Lawrence.

BLACKBURN, Canon Alan Hopton. Selw Coll Dun NZ Bd of Th Stud LTh 39. **d** 38 **p** 39 Dun. C of St Luke Oamaru 38-42; V of Maniototo w Naseby 42-48; Winton 48-51; Waikouaiti 51-56; NE Valley 56-65; Roslyn (w Flagstaff 73-75) 65-79; Hon Can of Dun 66-79; Can (Emer) from 79; L to Offic Dio Dun from 79. *34 Collins Street, Waikouaiti, NZ.*

BLACKBURN, Canon Donald. b 02. OBE 56. St Jo Coll Dur BA (2nd cl Th) 30, MA 33. Wycl Hall Ox 30. **d** 31 **p** 32 Liv. C of St Cath Edge Hill 31-33; St Mary Battersea 34; CMS Miss Jer 34-36; Es-Salt 36-45; Chap St Mich Sch Limpsfield 45-46; Nablus 46-48; Jer 50-51; Amman Jordan and Sec Jordan Miss 51-56; Exam Chap to Bp in Jer 52-56; R of Beer Hackett w Thornford 56-60; V of Bradf Abbas w Clifton Maybank 56-60; Provost of All SS Cathl Cairo 60-67; C-in-c of Steventon Ox 68-71; Commiss Egypt from 68; Hon Can of All SS Cathl Cairo from 74. *The Cottage, Weston Lane, Oswestry, Salop, SY11 2BG.* (Oswestry 59136)

BLACKBURN, Frederick John Barrie. TD 73. Lich Th Coll 52. **d** 55 **p** 56 Dur. C of Hebburn 55-58; St Mary Virg w St Pet Conv Distr Bp Wearmouth 58-61; V of Hunwick 61-64; CF (TA) from 61; V of Eighton Banks 64-75; R of Stella Dio Dur from 75. *Rectory, Blaydon-on-Tyne, Tyne & Wear.* (Blaydon 442720)

BLACKBURN, John. b 47. Univ of Wales (Cardiff) Dipl Th 69. St Mich Coll Llan 66. **d** 71 Llan for Mon **p** 72 Mon. C of Risca 71-76; Chap TAVR 73-76; CF from 76. *c/o Ministry of Defence, Bagshot Park, Bagshot, Surrey.*

BLACKBURN, Keith Christopher. b 39. K Coll Lon and Warm BD and AKC 63. **d** 64 **p** 65 S'wark. C of St Andr Surbiton 64-66; Asst Master Sir Walter St John's Sch Battersea 67-70; Crown Woods Sch Eltham 70-76; Dep Hd Master Altwood Sch Maidenhead from 76. *9 Turpins Green, Maidenhead, Berks.* (Maidenhead 30143)

BLACKBURN, Peter James Whittaker. b 47. Univ of Syd BA 69. Univ of Leeds Dipl Th 71. Coll of Resurr Mirfield 70. **d** 72 **p** 73 St E. C of St Jo Bapt Felixstowe 72-77; Bournemouth 77-79; R of Burythorpe, Acklam and Leavening w Weston Dio York from 79. *Rectory, Burythorpe, Malton, N Yorks.* (Burythorpe 220)

BLACKBURN, Canon William Kenneth. b 20. BNC Ox BA (3rd cl Mod Hist) 42, MA 46. Westcott Ho Cam 42. **d** and **p** 44 Win. C of Basingstoke 44-46; Radlett 46-48; V 48-58; Chap Edge Grove Sch Aldenham 47-58; Archd in Cyprus and Chap at Nicosia w Skouriotissa and Kyrenia 58-60; V of Far Headingley 60-70; R of Halesowen w Hasbury and Lapal 70-77; Hon Can of Worc from 75; V of Broadway Dio Worc from 77; RD of Evesham from 79. *4 Lifford Gardens, Broadway, Worcs, WR12 7DA.* (Broadway 2352)

✠ **BLACKBURNE, Right Rev Hugh Charles.** b 12. Clare Coll Cam BA 34, MA 39. Westcott Ho Cam 36. **d** 37 Wakef **p** 38 Pontefract for Wakef. C of Almondbury 37-39; Chap Clare Coll Cam 39-46; CF (R of O) 39-77; Chap R Mil Coll 46-47; R of Milton 47-53; V of Harrow 53-61; Commiss Ja 59-70; R of Hilborough Group (Cockley Cley w Gooderstone, Hilborough w Bodney, Oxburgh w Foulden and Caldecot, Gt Cressingham w L Cressingham and Threxton) 61-72; C-in-c of Didlington 64-72; Chap to HM the Queen 61-77; RD of Swaffham 64-69; Hon Can of Nor from 65; Chap Norf Broads 72-77; V of Ranworth 72-77; Cons Ld Bp Suffr of Thetford in S'wark Cathl 6 Jan 77 by Abp of Cant; Bps of Nor, S'wark, Pet, Ox, Ely, St E, Bradf and S & M; Bps Suffr of Edmonton, Huntingdon, Jarrow, Knaresborough, Lynn, Shrewsbury and Tonbridge; and others; res 80. *39 Northgate, Beccles, Suff, NR34 9AU.*

BLACKDUKE, Alfred Wari. **d** 29 **p** 32 Bp Howell for Niger. P Dio Niger. *c/o St Augustine's Parsonage, Abonnema, Nigeria.*

BLACKER, Herbert John. b 36. Univ of Bris BSc (2nd cl Chem) 59. Univ of Dur Dipl Th 61. Cranmer Hall Dur 59. **d** 61 **p** 62 Lich. C of Wednesbury 61-63; Chasetown 63-65; Chigwell 65-69; V in Barnham Broom Group 69-76; Briston w Burgh Parva Dio Nor from 76. *Briston Vicarage, Melton Constable, Norf, NR24 2HD.* (Melton Constable 860280)

BLACKETT, James Gilbert. b 27. Tyndale Hall Bris 52. **d** 55 Selby for York **p** 56 York. C of Heworth York 55-57; Newburn 57-58; St Barn w St Jude Newc T 58-61; V of Broomfleet w Faxfleet 61-67; Ledsham w Fairburn 67-74; All SS (w Ch Ch from 82) Burton-on-Trent Dio Lich from 74. *242 Blackpool Street, Burton-on-Trent, DE14 3AU.* (Burton 65134)

BLACKFORD, David Walker. b 25. **d** 70 **p** 71 Ban. C of Holyhead 70-72; L to Offic Dio Blackb 72-80. *Address temp unknown*

BLACKFORD, Donald Francis. Roch Th Coll 65. **d** 67 Barking for Chelmsf **p** 68 Chelmsf. C of Moulsham 67-69; P-in-c of Williams 69-71; R of Mt Barker 71-73; Collie 73-76; C of Timboon 76-79; R of Rupanyup Dio Bal from 79. *Rectory, Rupanyup, Vic, Australia 3383.*

BLACKFORD, Eric Donald Hill. b 09. Sarum Th Coll 68. **d** 69 Bp A C MacInnes for Sarum **p** 70 Sarum. C of Gillingham w E Stower W Stower and Milton 69-72; V in Bishopstone Group (C-in-c of Ebbesbourne Wake w Fifield Bavant and Alvediston) 72-75; C of Bearsted 76-79; Hon Chap Guild of St Barn Sarum from 81. *Flat 10, Thaxted, Campbell Road, Salisbury, Wilts.*

BLACKIE, (Edmund) Richard Footner. b 37. St Cath Coll Cam BA 59, MA 63. Worc Coll Ox BA (by incorp) 59, BSc 61. Ely Th Coll 60. **d** 62 **p** 63 Chelmsf. C of Saffron Walden 62-65; M SSF 69. *Friary, Alnmouth, Alnwick, Northumb, NE66 3NJ.* (066-573 213)

BLACKLEDGE, Robert Dallas. b 1891. MC 17. Ch Coll Cam BA (2nd cl Cl Trip pt i) 13, 2nd cl Cl Trip pt ii 14, MA 46. **d** 19 Burnley for Man **p** 20 Man. C of Ch Ch Denton 19-27; Min of Roundthorn 27-29; R of Anstey Herts 29-36; V of Bourn 36-44; R of Burnham Westgate w Burnham Norton 44-49; Studham w Whipsnade 49-57. *12 The Crescent, Felpham, Bognor Regis, Sussex.*

BLACKLER, Stuart Edward. Univ of Melb BA 57, BEducn 72. **d** 65 St Arn for Melb **p** 67 Bp Arnott for Melb. C of St Paul's Cathl Melb 65-66; S Yarra 67-69; St John, W Geelong 69-70; Min of Nunawading 70-71; Chap C of E Gr Sch Melb from 71; Dir of Stud from 76. *10 Radnor Street, Camberwell, Vic, Australia 3124.* (29-5797)

BLACKMAN, Clive John. b 51. Univ of Hull BSc 73, MSc 74. Univ of Birm Dipl Th 77. Qu Coll Birm 75. **d** 78 **p** 79 Cant. C of St Sav Folkestone 78-81; Chap Univ of Birm from 81. *St Francis' Hall, Edgbaston Park Road, Birmingham, B15 2TU.* (021-472 1841)

BLACKMAN, John Franklyn. b 34. SOC 72. **d** 75 Bp Barker for Cov **p** 76 Bp McKie for Cov (APM). C of H Trin Cov 75-81. *43 Rochester Road, Coventry, CV5 6AF.* (Cov 73522)

BLACKMAN, Michael Orville. b 46. Univ of WI LTh 70. **d** 71 Barb. C of St John's Cathl Antig 71-72; R of H Innoc w St Sav I and Dio Barb from 72. *Holy Innocents' Rectory, St Thomas, Barbados, WI.*

BLACKMAN, Peter Richard. b 28. Sarum Th Coll 52. **d** 55 **p** 56 Leic. C of Aylestone 55-60; V of Ratby w Groby Dio Leic from 60. *Ratby Vicarage, Leicester, LE6 0LJ.* (Leic 393009)

BLACKMORE, Cuthbert. b 17. Qu Coll Birm 57. **d** 59 **p** 60 York. C of St Steph Acomb York 59-62; V of Hackness w Harwood Dale 62-66; Seamer w E Ayton Dio York from 66; RD of Scarborough 72-76. *Seamer Vicarage, Scarborough, Yorks.* (West Ayton 3102)

BLACKMORE, Frank Ellis. St D Coll Lamp BA 66, Wells Th Coll 65. **d** 67 **p** 68 S'wark. C of St Geo Mart S'wark 67-72.

91 Mint Street, SE1.

BLACKMORE, Robert Ivor. b 37. Open Univ BA 76. St D Coll Lamp. **d** 62 **p** 63 Llan. C of Llangynwyd w Maesteg 62-65; Dowlais 65-67; Neath w Llantwit 67-71; V of Fochriw and Deri 71-73; Troedrhiw Garth 73-80; Seven Sisters Dio Llan from 80. *Vicarage, Seven Sisters, Neath, W Glam, SA10 9DT.* (Seven Sisters 286)

BLACKSHAW, Alfred. b 14. St Jo Coll Dur BA 39, Dipl in Th 40, MA 42. **d** 40 **p** 41 Blackb. C of St Barn Darwen 40-3; St Thos Crookes 43-44; R of St Cath Collyhurst 44-48; V of St Mark Haydock 48-55; Ch Ch Blackpool 55-66; Chesham 66-72; Copp (or Gt Eccleston) 72-79. *Address temp unknown.*

BLACKSHAW, Trevor Roland. b 36. Lon Coll of Div 67. **d** 69 Nor **p** 70 Lynn for Nor. C of St Luke New Catton 69-73; St Hugh Lewsey, Luton 73-78; V of Llandinam w Trefeglwys and Penstrowed Dio Ban from 78. *Vicarage, Llandinam, Powys, SY17 5BS.* (Caersws 341)

BLACKSTOCK, Eric. d and **p** 56 Athab. I of Fort Vermilion 56-58; Slave Lake 58-62; Westlock 62-64; French Creek 64-68; W Coast Miss 68-74; on leave 75-76; I of Fort Nel, Yukon 76-80; Prince Geo Dio Caled from 81. *4409, West Austin Road, Prince George, BC, Canada.*

BLACKSTOCK, William Henry. Bp's Univ Montr BA 46. Em Coll Sask BD 65. **d** 46 **p** 47 Montr. C of St Luke Montr 46-47; St Jo Evang Montr 47-49; Miss at Fort St John 49-52; I of Oxbow 52-56; St Pet Regina 56-61; Raymore 61-66; I of Indian Head Dio Qu'App 66-73; Exam Chap to Bp of Qu'App 62-66; I of Touchwood Hills 73-76; Cupar Dio Qu'App from 76. *Box 417, Cupar, Sask, Canada.* (723-4206)

BLACKWALL, David d'Arcy Russell. b 35. Univ of Southn BSc (3rd cl Eng) 60. Wycl Hall Ox. **d** 65 Southn for Win **p** 66 Win. C of St Chris Conv Distr Thornhill Southn 65-69; V of Long Sutton 69-72; Chap Ld Wandsworth Coll Dio Win from 69; Hon C of Odiham 72-75; Chap St Lawr Coll Ramsgate from 75. *St Lawrence College, Ramsgate, Kent.*

BLACKWALL, John George Russell. b 03. Bp's Coll Cheshunt 38. **d** 38 **p** 39 Lon. C of St Alb Golder's Green 38-41; R of Madresfield 41-47; V of King's Somborne w Ashley 47-62; Burley 62-71. *24 Old Green Road, Broadstairs, Kent, CT10 3BP.* (0843-602076)

BLACKWELL, Canon Douglas Charles. Wycl Coll Tor Dipl Th 64, LTh 68. **d** 63 **p** 64 Calg. C of St Steph Calg 63-66; I of Cochrane 66-68; R of N Battleford 68-74; Archd of Sktn 73-74; Hon C of Newmarket 75-77; Executive Asst to Bp of Tor from 77; Can of Tor from 78. *135 Adelaide Street East, Toronto, Ont., Canada.* (416-363 6021)

BLACKWELL, Ven Ernest Edward. St Chad's Coll Regina LTh 44, Hon DD 63. **d** 34 **p** 35 Qu'App. C of Climax 34-35; I 35-36; I of Milden 36-42; Kamsack 42-46; I and RD of Assiniboia 46-52; I of Balcarres 52-61; Hon Can of Qu'App 56-58; Exam Chap to Bp of Qu'App 44-74; Archd of Qu'App 58-68; Moose Mountain 68-74; Archd (Emer) from 75; I of Moosomin 61-74. *Box 144, Moosomin, Sask, Canada.*

BLACKWELL, Geoffrey Albert. b 27. Lon Coll of Div 62. **d** 65 **p** 66 York. C of St Phil and St Jas Clifton York 65-69; Chap RN 69-73; Warden St Mich Home of Healing Dur 73-75; V of S Hetton Dio Dur from 75. *Vicarage, South Hetton, Co Durham, DH6 2SW.* (Haswell 273)

BLACKWELL, Geoffrey David. b 34. Jes Coll Ox BA (2nd cl Th) 57, MA 61. Chich Th Coll. **d** 59 **p** 60 Chelmsf. C of Romford 59-62; Chap St Paul's Coll Grahmstn 62-68; Westcott Ho Cam 68-73; P-in-c of St Edm Forest Gate 73-74; V 74-81. *2 Woodland Avenue, Leicester, LE2 3HG.*

BLACKWELL, Harold Donald Gordon. Macquarie Univ BA 78. Moore Th Coll Syd 56. ACT ThL 58. Melb Coll of Div Dipl Relig Educn 61. **d** and **p** 59 Syd. C of Corrimal 59-60; W Manly 60-62; C-in-c of Oaks w Burragorang 62-64; St Paul S Coogee 64-69; R of Punchbowl 69-74; Chap Gladesville Hosp Dio Syd 75-81; Rozelle Hosp Dio Syd from 81. *17 Chesterfield Road, Epping, NSW, Australia 2121.* (86-2919)

BLACKWELL, Joseph. b 1899. TCD BA 23, MA 30. **d** 25 **p** 26 Dub. C of St Kevin Dub 25-29; St Matt Irishtown 29-30; I of Ballinaclash 30-36; St Luke Dub 36-44; Blessington w Kilbride 44-51; RD of Ballymore 44-59; Wicklow 59-71; I of Newcastle Wicklow (w Newtownmount Kennedy from 59) 51-70; Can of Ch Ch Cathl Dub 57-70. *Kiltennel Lodge, Gorey, Co Wexford, Irish Republic.*

BLACKWELL, Canon Robert John. Trin Coll Tor BA 49, LTh 52. **d** and **p** 52 Niag. C of Guelph 52-54; R of St D Welland 54-59; Stamford 59-67; Burlington Dio Niag from 67; Dom Chap to Bp of Niag 64-74; Hon Can of Niag 70-74 and from 79; Archd of Trafalgar 74-79. *1382 Ontario Street, Burlington, Ont., Canada.* (416-634 4605)

BLACKWELL-SMYTH, Charles Peter Bernard. b 42. TCD BA 64, Div Test (1st cl) Abp King and Bp Forster Pri 64. Univ of Dub MA 71, MB 73, BChir 73. Gen Th Sem NY MDiv 65. **d** 65 Montana for Down **p** 66 Down. C of Bangor Abbey 65-67; Ch Ch Leeson Pk Dur 67-69; C-in-c of Carbury 73-75. *Parc Gwyn, St Stephen, St Austell, Cornw.*

BLACKWOOD, Canon David Vincent. Montr Dioc Th Coll LTh 52. **d** 52 **p** 53 Niag. C-in-c of Wainfleet w Welland Junction 52-56; C of Welland 56-59; R of Mount Forest 59-65; I of St Luke Hamilton Dio Niag from 65; Hon Can of Niag from 76. *454 John Street North, Hamilton, Ont., Canada.* (416-529 1244)

BLACKWOOD, Gary Dean. b 50. St Jo Coll Auckld 71. **d** 73 Bp Monteith for Auckld **p** 74 Auckld. C of Henderson Auckld 73-76; St Barn Erdington 77-78; St Jas Somt Berm 78; P-in-c of Hoon Hay 79; V of Fairlie Dio Ch Ch from 79. *Vicarage, Fairlie, NZ.* (8389)

BLACOE, Brian Thomas. b 36. Oak Hill Th Coll 63. **d** 66 **p** 67 Down. C of Dundonald 66-69; Drumcree 69-74; I of Ardtrea w Desertcreat 74-78; R of Annalong Dio Drom from 78. *Rectory, Annalong, Newry, Co Down, N Ireland.*

BLADE, Alfred John. Kelham Th Coll 28. **d** 34 **p** 35 Sheff. C of Darnall 34-42; CF (EC) 42-46; C of St Phil and St Anne Sheff 46-50; V of St Nath Sheff 50-55; C-in-c of Conv Distr of Cantley Estate Doncaster 55-63; V of Swinton 63-65; Miss Dio Kuch 65-69; Can of Kuch 68-69; Dean of St Thos Cathl Kuch 69-75; V of St Marg Seria Kuch 75-79; Perm to Offic Dio Glouc from 80. *The Almshouses, Newland, Glos.*

BLADE, Brian Alan. b 24. Roch Th Coll 67. **d** 69 **p** 70 Roch. C of Barnehurst 69-71; Crayford 71-76; V of St Aid Buttershaw 76-80; R of Etton w Helpston Dio Pet from 80. *Parsonage, Golden Drop, Helpston, Peterborough, PE6 7DW.*

BLADES, James Frederick. Univ of Adel BA 47. St Barn Coll ACT ThL 49. Keble Coll Ox BA (3rd cl Th) 55, MA 62. **d** 49 **p** 50 Adel. C of Ch Ch N Adel 49-50; Mt Gambier 50-51; Miss Chap at Penola 51-53; on leave 53-56; C (Col Cl Act) of St Anne Stanley Liv 55-56; R of Maitland S Austr 56-63; Riverton 63-68; Chap St Mary's Sch Maravovo 68-71; Tutor Patteson Th Centre Kohimarama 71-72; L to Offic Dio Adel 73; P-in-c of Seacliff Dio Adel from 74. *2 Seawynd Court, Seacliff Park, S Australia 5049.* (08-296 9616)

BLADES, Canon Joseph Henry. b 13. St Chad's Coll Dur BA 34, Dipl Th (w distinc) 35, MA 37. **d** 36 **p** 37 Derby. C of New Mills 36-39; C-in-c of Bamford 39-43; Chap RAFVR 43-47; PC of St Mark Derby 47-68; Surr from 67; Darley Abbey Dio Derby from 68; RD of Derby 62-71; Hon Can of Derby from 67. *Darley Abbey Vicarage, Derby, DE3 1EX.* (Derby 57406)

BLADON, Ernest Albert. b 19. Univ of Ex Dipl Educn 58. **d** and **p** 78 Glouc. Hon C of St John Cinderford Dio Glouc from 78. *Highfields, Grange Road, Littledean, Cinderford, Glos.*

BLADON, Horace Wilkins. b 04. Lich Th Coll 52. **d** 53 Ches **p** 54 Stockport for Ches. C of Timperley 53-56; V of Millbrook w Micklehurst 56-59; Barton-on-Irwell 59-69. *4 Dover Park, Urmston, Manchester, M31 1SX.*

BLAGDON-GAMLEN, Peter Eugène. AKC 48. St Bonif Coll Warm 48. **d** 49 **p** 50 B & W. C of Wellington w W Buckland and Nynehead 49-51; St Martin Conv Distr Barton 51-52; Evesham 52-53; V of Swinefleet 53-56; PC of St Bart Derby 56-64; CF (R of O) 59-75; R of Harrold w Carlton and Chellington 64-68; R & V of Eastchurch (w Leysdown and Harty from 71) Dio Cant from 68; P-in-c of Leysdown w Harty 68-71; Perm to Offic Dio Edin from 72; CF (TA) from 78. *Eastchurch Rectory, Isle of Sheppey, Kent, ME12 4DF.* (Eastchurch 205)

BLAGG, Colin. b 31. Univ of Leeds BA (3rd cl Gen Stud) 57. Coll of Resurr Mirfield. **d** 59 **p** 60 Edin. C of Old St Paul Edin 59-63; R of Gourock 63-68; Chap RADD Lon 68-74; C of Woodberry Down Lon 73-74; Chap Sussex Dioc Assoc for the Deaf 74-80; V of Shoreham Beach Dio Chich from 80. *Vicarage, West Beach Road, Shoreham-by-Sea, Sussex, BN4 5LF.* (Shoreham 3768)

BLAGRAVE, Charles Nisbet Patrick. Trin Coll Tor. **d** and **p** 48 Niag. C of St Geo St Catharines 48-50; I of Fonthill 50-54; R of Niag-on-Lake 54-59; Oakville Dio Niag from 59; Can of Niag 61-72; R of Rothesay Dio Fred from 72. *Rectory, Rothesay, NB, Canada.*

BLAIN, Alexander Francis John. Univ of W Austr BA 33. Cudd Coll 33. **d** 34 **p** 35 Wakef. C of Birstall Yorks 34-37; R of Mt Marshall and Nungarin 37-40; Chap St Geo Coll Perth 40-43; Chap RAN 43-46; R of E Claremont 46-55; Dalkeith 55-68; P-in-c of Wau 67-68; Perm to Offic Dios Bunb and Perth from 68; Chap Kobeelya Girls Sch Katanning 70-71. *Riversbend, Rosa Brook, W. Australia.* (57 4518)

BLAIN, Michael Winston. Univ of Cant NZ BA 65, MA (2nd cl Lat) 66. Coll of Resurr Mirfield 66. **d** 67 **p** 68 Sheff. C of Goldthorpe 67-70; Avonside 70-72; P-in-c of Bishopdale-Harewood 72-77; V of Ross w Westland 77-78; Roseneath Dio Wel from 78; Chap Cathl Gr Sch Ch Ch 73-76. *20 Lindum Terrace, Wellington, NZ.* (848 985)

BLAIR, Canon Harold Arthur. b 02. Late Exhib of St Edm

Hall Ox BA (2nd cl Th) 25, MA 37, BD 45. Sarum Th Coll 39. **d** 39 **p** 40 Sarum. C of Sherborne w Castleton and Lillington 39-41; V of Horningsham 41-45; Winterbourne Earls w Dauntsey and Winterbourne Gunner 45-54; Exam Chap to Bp of Sarum 50-60; Can of Alton Australis in Sarum Cathl 53-60; PC of Southbroom 54-60; Can Res and Chan of Truro Cathl 60-75; Can (Emer) from 75; Commiss Dacca 60-75; Exam Chap to Bp of Truro 60-81; Dioc Dir of Ordins 60-75. *Beech Cottage, Acreman Street, Sherborne, Dorset.*

BLAIR, Harriet Ruth. b 47. Univ of Cant NZ MA 70, BD 77. St Jo Coll Auckld BD 77. **d** 77 **p** 78 Ch Ch. C of St Alb 77-79; Hon Assoc Chap St Hilda's Colleg Sch Dun and Offg Min Dio Dun from 79. *54 Orbell Street, Dunedin, NZ.* (730 177)

BLAIR, James William. b 04. St Edm Hall Ox BA 26, MA 32. Wells Th Coll 26. **d** 28 **p** 29 Carl. C of Cleator Moor 28-35; Seaton Hirst 35-38; R of Ousby (w Melmerby from 49) 38-51; V of Pennington 51-72; L to Offic Dio Carl from 72. *Park House Cottage, Bigrigg, Egremont, Cumb, CA22 2TL.* (Cleator Moor 810059)

BLAIR, John Wallace. b 48. BSc (Eng) Lon 76. Qu Coll Birm 79. **d** 81 Man. C of St Werburgh Chorlton-cum-Hardy Dio Man from 81. *72 Egerton Road, Chorlton-cum-Hardy, Manchester, M21 1ZH.* (061-881-4902)

BLAIR, John William Harold. McMaster Univ Ont BA 62. Trin Coll Tor STB 65. **d** 65 Niag for Rupld **p** 65 Bp Anderson for Rupld. I of Oakville 65-68; R of St Andrews 68-70; R of St Paul Middlechurch Winnipeg 68-70; C of Grace Church Tor 70-75; on leave 75-79; R of St Martin Niagara Falls Dio Niag from 79. *5952 Brookfield Avenue, Niagara Falls, Ont, Canada.*

BLAIR, Leonard John. d 64 **p** 65 Melb. C of Dandenong 64-68; Dept of Evang and Ex Dio Melb 68-69; Min of Thomastown w Epping 69-73; C in Dept of Chaps Dio Melb from 73. *295 Waiora Road, Macleod, Vic, Australia 3085.* (03-45 0211)

BLAIR, Patrick Allen. b 31. Trin Coll Cam 2nd cl Nat Sc Trip pt i 53, BA 54, 2nd cl th Trip pt ii 55, 2nd cl Th Trip pt iii 56. Ridley Hall Cam 54. **d** 56 **p** 57 Ox. C of Harwell 56-59; Chap and Asst Master Oundle Sch Pet 59-64; Tutor St Geo Coll Jer and Chap to Abp in Jer 64-66; Provost of All SS Cathl Khartoum 67-71; Exam Chap to Bp in Sudan 67-71; R of Chester-le-Street 71-77; Barking Dio Chelmsf from 77. *Rectory, Ripple Road, Barking, IG11 7NR.* (01-594 2932)

BLAIR, Philip Hugh. St Edm Hall Ox BA (2nd cl Th) 62, MA 67. Ridley Hall Cam 62. **d** 64 **p** 65 Truro. C of Camborne 64-68; St Kenwyn w Tregavethan 68-70; CMS P at Omduran 70-73; C-in-c of St Enoder 73-76; Res Tutor Univ of Ex 76-77; Lect Univ of Khartoum from 78. *Box 322, Khartoum, Sudan.*

BLAIR, Riga Wells. MBE 45. Coll Ho Ch Ch LTh 67. **d** 46 **p** 47 Ch Ch. C of St Pet Riccarton 46-48; V of Leeston 48-51; CF (NZ) and L to Offic Dio Ch Ch 52-56; V of Halswell-Prebbleton Dio Ch Ch from 57. *329 Halswell Road, Christchurch 3, NZ.* (228-723)

BLAIR-BROWN, Dennis. b 17: Em Coll Sktn 52. **d** and **p** 56 Athab. I of Cherry Point 56; White Fish Lake Indian Miss Athab 56-63; C of Lymington 63-70; V of E and W Wellow Dio Win from 70. *Wellow Vicarage, Romsey, Hants.* (Wellow 22295)

BLAIR-FISH, Canon John Christopher. b 20. Late Scho of Linc Coll Ox BA 46 (2nd cl Th), MA 47. Cudd Coll 48. **d** 49 **p** 50 S'wark. C of St Andr Mottingham 49-51; Warlingham w Chelsham 51-55; V of Surbiton 55-72; R of Chipstead Dio S'wark from 73; Hon Can of S'wark Cathl from 79. *Rectory, Elmore Road, Chipstead, Coulsdon, Surrey, CR3 3SG.* (Downland 53527)

BLAKE, Canon Arthur Vernon. b 17. St D Coll Lamp BA (3rd cl Mod Hist) 39. St Mich Coll Llan 39. **d** 40 **p** 41 Llan. C of Ystrad Mynach 40-44; St Jo Evang Newport 44-50; V of Penalt w Pentwyn 50-58; Raglan w Llandenny (w Llansoy from 72) 58-75; Ed Mon Dioc Year Book 66-76; Can of Mon from 72; Sec Mon Dioc Conf and Patr Bd 76-81; V of Llanfrechfa Dio Mon from 75. *Vicarage, Llanfrechfa, Cwmbran, Gwent, NP4 2DQ.* (Newport 211244)

BLAKE, Derek Gordon. b 10. St Jo Coll Dur 32. **d** 36 **p** 37 S'wark. C of St Crispin Bermondsey 36-39; Plumstead 39-42; V of St Mary w Ch Ch Maryport 42-57; Surr from 45; V of St Aid w Ch Ch Carl 57-69; St Cuthb Holme Cultram Dio Carl from 69; P-in-c of Allonby 76-81. *Holme Saint Cuthbert Vicarage, Mawbray, Maryport, Cumb, CA15 6QZ.* (Allonby 303)

BLAKE, Ven Douglas. OBE 69. St Columb's Hall Wang ACT ThL 29, Th Scho 32. **d** 29 **p** 30 Wang. C of Seymour 29-31; R of Cobram 31-32; Kiewa 32-35; Alexandra 35-39; Min of Lorne 39-40; Chap AIF 40-44; I of Ch Ch Essendon 44-48; All SS St Kilda 48-61; St John W Geelong 61-71; Archd of Geelong 61-71; Archd (Emer) from 71; Perm to Offic Dio Melb 71-79; Dio Syd from 79. *5 Buchan Court, Buchan Street, Mollymook, NSW, Australia 2539.*

BLAKE, Canon Edward Cyril. b 12. Linc Th Coll 45. MRST 38. **d** 46 **p** 47 Ches. C of Ch Ch Latchford 46-49; V of Gosberton Clough 49-52; Cherry Willingham w Greetwelll 52-54; Welton St Mary 54-56; Dir of Educn Dio Linc 56-68; Can and Preb of Linc Cathl from 60; V of Morton w Hacconby 68-76; C of Bourne 76-77. *3 Beech Avenue, Bourne, Lincs, PE10 9RN.*

BLAKE, Francis Richard Arthur. Univ of Lon BSc (2nd cl Econ) 33. Bps' Coll Cheshunt 33. M CR 46. **d** 35 **p** 36 S'wark. C of St Andr Coulsdon 35-39; Perm to Offic as C-in-c of Em Lambeth 39-42; C-in-c 42-44; L to Offic Dio Wakef 45-49; P-in-c of Sekhukuniland Miss and Chap Jane Furse Hosp 49-58; R of Sophiatown 58-62; L to Offic Dio Johann 62-71; Chap Coronation Hosp Johan 62-66; St Joseph's Home Johann 66-71; Sub-Prior St Pet Priory Johann 68-71; R of Stellenbosch 71-76; Miss P at St Aug Penhalonga from 80; Actg R of Makoni w Headlands Dio Mutare from 81. *Rectory, Makoni, Zimbabwe.*

BLAKE, Harold Gordon. Wycl Coll Tor LTh 33. **d** 33 **p** 34 Tor. C of King 33-34; Fenelon Fall 34-35; I of N Essa 35-40; Beeton 41-42; R of Bradford 42-52; St Barn, Tor 52-59; Ch Ch Mimico 59-72. *Apt 302, 810 Royal York Road, Toronto 18, Ont., Canada.*

BLAKE, Ian Martyn. b 57. Coun for Nat Acad Awards BA 79. Oak Hill Coll 76. **d** 80 Chelmsf **p** 81 Bradwell for Chelmsf. C of St Mary Widford Dio Chelmsf from 80. *16 Wood Street, Chelmsford, Essex, CM2 9AS.* (Chelmsf 56377)

BLAKE, Jonathan Clive. b 56. St Jo Coll Dur BA 77. St Jo Coll Nottm 79. **d** 81 Bradf. C of St Pet Allerton Dio Bradf from 81. *2 Brander House, Ayresome Oval, Alllerton, Bradford, BD15 7UX.*

BLAKE, Preb Patrick John. b 30. Univ of Wales BA (2nd cl Hist) 51. St Edm Hall Ox 2nd cl Hons Th 54, MA 58. St Mich Coll Llan 54. **d** 55 **p** 56 St A. C of Buckley 55-59; Oystermouth 59-63; V of Cleeve-in-Yatton 63-71; Bruton w Wyke and Redlynch 71; C-in-c of Lamyatt 71; R of Bruton w Wyke, Redlynch & Lamyatt Dio B & W from 71; Dioc Ecumen Officer Dio B & W from 79; Preb of Wells Cathl from 79. *Rectory, Bruton, Somt, BA10 0EF.* (Bruton 2372)

BLAKE, Peter Douglas Stuart. b 27. BNC Ox BA 52, MA 57. Westcott Ho Cam 52. **d** 54 **p** 55 Ripon. C of Armley 54-58; R of Mufulira 58-65; V of Cropthorne w Charlton 65-69; St Edw the Confessor Leek 69-76; Surr 70-76; P-in-c of Hartfield Dio Chich 76-78; R (w Coleman's Hatch) from 78. *Hartfield Rectory, Tunbridge Wells, TN7 4AG.* (Hartfield 259)

BLAKE, Philip Charles. Dipl Th (Lon) 57. Oak Hill Th Coll 54. **d** 57 **p** 58 Ox. C of Slough 57-60; Uphill (in c of St Barn Old Mixon) 60-62; V of Branston 62-69; C-in-c of Marsfield w Denistone E 69-72; R 72-75; Chap Long Bay Pris Dio Syd 75-80; W Metrop Pris Dio Syd from 81. *37 Finch Avenue, East Ryde, NSW, Australia 2113.* (88-1781)

BLAKE, Canon Roy Harold David. b 25. Chich Th Coll 54. **d** 57 Malmesbury for Bris **p** 58 Bris. C of Westbury-on-Trym 57-61; Bishopston 61-65; V of St Agnes w St Simon Bris 65-72; R (w St Werburgh) 72-74; RD of Bris City 73-74; Cricklade from 76; V of Purton Dio Bris from 74; Hon Can of Bris from 77; Mityana from 81. *Vicarage, Purton, Wilts.* (0793 770210)

BLAKE, Thomas Herbert. b 11. Worc Ordin Coll 65. **d** 67 **p** 68 Worc. C of St Barn Rainbow Hill 67-70; R of Church Lench w Ab Lench, Abbots Morton and Rous Lench 70-77; Perm to Offic Dio Worc from 78. *130 Astwood Road, Worcester, WR3 8EZ.* (Worc 26837)

BLAKE, Canon Victor Kenneth. Trin Coll Tor BA 47, LTh 50. **d** 50 Tor for Newfld **p** 51 Newfld. C of Bell Isle 50-54; R of Waterford 54-57; I of St Pet Windsor 57-71; Can of Huron 70-79; Can Res from 79; Chap Hur Coll and Univ of W Ont 71-79. *472 Richmond Street, London, Ont, Canada.*

BLAKE, William Cornford. b 18. Ripon Hall Ox. **d** 67 **p** 68 S'wark. C of Putney 67-73; Diss w St Remigius Roydon Dio Nor 73-76; P-in-c 76-79; R from 79. *Rectory, Roydon, via Diss, Norfolk.* (Diss 2180)

BLAKE, Winston. d and **p** 77 Ja. C of Siloah Dio Ja from 77. *Carron Hall, Maggotty PO, Jamaica, W Indies.*

BLAKELEY, Robert Daniel. b 29. Univ of Sask BA 63. St Pet Coll Ox BA 67, MA 70. Em Coll Sask LTh 56. **d** 56 **p** 57 Sktn. I of Radisson 56-59; in Amer Ch 59-68; C of High Wycombe 68-70; in Amer Ch 71-75; St Mary Bryanston Sq St Marylebone Dio Lon from 75. *7 Wyndham Place, W1H 1PR.* (01-723 0466)

BLAKEMAN, Walter John. b 37. Qu Coll Birm 74. **d** 76 **p** 77 Lich. C of Gnosall Dio Lich from 76. *Keswick, Cross Street, Gnosall, Stafford.* (Stafford 822305)

BLAKENEY, Ivan Gordon. b 20. Late Scho Trin Coll Dub BA (Mod) 41, MA 50. **d** 43 **p** 44 Down. C of Coleraine 43-46; Chap Miss to Seamen Belf 46-47; Japan 47-52; Santos Brazil

52-56; R of High Easter w Margaret Roding and V of Good Easter 56-61; R of Wrabness 61-69; Asst Master Headington Co Sec Sch Ox 69-71; Lect Bp Grosseteste Coll Linc 71-73; Sen Lect 73-80. *40 Lee Road, Lincoln, LN2 4BQ.*

BLAKESLEY, John. b 50. Late Exhib of Keble Coll Ox BA 72, MA 76. St Steph Ho Ox 72. **d** 74 **p** 75 Carl. C of Egremont 74-77; Ch Ch Doncaster 77-79; V of St Helen Bp Auckland Dio Dur from 79. *St Helen's Vicarage, St Helen's Auckland, Bishop Auckland, Co Durham, 604152)*

BLAKEWAY, Lionel Norman. St Barn Coll Adel 34. ACT ThL 36. **d** 36 **p** 38 Adel. C of Ch Ch N Adel 36-39; P-in-c of Pinnaroo w Lameroo 39-40; Chap AIF 40-46; Chap of St Mark's Coll Adel 46-48; St Pet Coll Sch 48-50; L to Offic Dio Adel 50-70; Dio Murray from 70. *16 Aldinga Beach, S Australia 5173.* (Aldinga 56 5196)

BLAKEWAY, Roger Lett. St Jo Coll Morpeth. ACT Dipl Th 72. **d** and **p** 73 Perth. C of Kalg w Boulder 73-75; R of Kellerberrin w Tammin 75-80; Swanbourne Dio Perth from 80. *105 Shenton Road, Swanbourne, W Australia 6010.* (384 2958)

BLAKEWAY-PHILLIPS, Richard John. b 19. St Chad's Coll Dur BA (3rd cl Th) 43. **d** 43 **p** 44 Heref. C of Ledbury 43-45; St Jo Bapt Cirencester 45-50; Lydney w Aylburton 50-52; R of Dumbleton w Wormington 52-58; V of Crawley Down 58-69; R of Orwell 69-77; Wimpole 69-77; V of Arrington 69-77; P-in-c of Gt w L Abington Dio Ely from 77; Hildersham Dio Ely from 77. *Little Abington Vicarage, Cambridge.* (Cam 891350)

BLAKEY, Cedric Lambert. b 54. Fitzw Coll Cam BA 76, MA 80. St Jo Coll Nottm 77. **d** 79 **p** 80 Derby. C of Cotmanhay & Shipley Dio Derby from 79. *12 Windley Drive, Ilkeston, Derbyshire, DE7 8UY.*

BLAKIE, Cecil Douglas. Ch Ch Coll 56. **d** 58 **p** 59 Ch Ch. C of Linwood-Aranui 58-62; V of Banks Peninsula 62-66; Temuka 66-70; Hokitika 70-74; Burwood Dio Ch Ch from 74. *307 New Brighton Road, Christchurch 6, NZ.* (81-766)

BLAKISTON, Patrick. b 14. Magd Coll Cam BA 36, MA 42. Linc Th Coll 36. **d** 39 **p** 40 Linc. C of All SS Gainsborough 39-42; St Andr Corbridge 42-45; V of Cambo 45-50; R of Middle w E Claydon 50-52; Halesowen w Hasbury 52-59; Surr 52-59; R of Alvechurch 59-68; V of Whittingham 68-79. *97 Monkton Deverill, Warminster, Wilts.* (Maiden Braley 282)

BLAKISTON, Canon Peter Henley. **d** 40 Ch Ch for Wai **p** 41 Auckld for Wai. C of Hastings Hawkes Bay 41-43; V of Te Karaka 43-50; CF 45-50; V of Waipukurau 50-60; Mt Maunganui 60-75; Hon Can of Wai 66-75; Can (Emer) from 75; L to Offic Dio Wai from 75. *17 Rawhiti Street, Greerton, Tauranga, NZ.*

BLAKISTON, Robert Ralph Christian. b 1890. St Aid Coll 10. Univ Coll Dur LTh 12, BA 14, MA 17. **d** 14 **p** 16 Liv. C of St Andr Liv 14-15; Walton Breck Liv 15-19; Succr Liv Cathl 20-24; C of Childwall 20-26; St Luke Farnworth 26-28; V of All SS Newton-le-Willows 28-47; R of Willian 47-71. *4 Bungalow, Terry's Cross, Brighton Road, Woodmancote, W Sussex, BN5 9SX.* (Henfield 2907)

BLAKLEY, Raymond Leonard. Univ of NZ MSc 48, PhD 51. Austr Nat Univ DSc 66. **d** 57 **p** 59 C & Goulb. C of N Canberra 57-60; All SS Canberra 60-66; St Jo Bapt Canberra 66-69. *9 Patey Street, Campbell, ACT, Australia.*

BLAMIRE-BROWN, Charles Richard. b 21. St Cath S Ox BA (3rd cl Th) 49, MA 53. Cudd Coll 49. **d** 51 **p** 52 Ripon. C of Bedale 51-53; Welwyn 53-58; C-in-c of Tewin 58-67; R 67-75; RD of Hatfield 71-75; V of Chipperfield Dio St Alb from 75. *Chipperfield Vicarage, King's Langley, Herts, WD4 9BJ.* (King's Langley 63054)

BLAMIRES, Canon Norman. b 11. Linc Coll Ox BA (2nd cl Th) 34, MA 37. M CR 66. Ely Th Coll 34. **d** 35 **p** 36 York. C of St Osw Middlesbrough 35-40; Thornaby-on-Tees 41-47; Sub-Warden St Paul's Coll Grahmstn 47-50; Warden 54-63; St Matt Coll Grahmstn 50-54; Can and Chan of Grahmstn Cathl 57-63; Hon Can from 64; Exam Chap to Bp of Geo 59-64; Vice-Prin Codr Coll Barb 66-69. *House of the Resurrection, Mirfield, Yorks.*

BLANCH, Allan Morrison. BD (2nd cl) Lon 65. Moore Th Coll Syd ACT ThL 64. **d** 55 Bp Loane for Syd **p** 67 Syd. C of Gladesville 66-70; C-in-c of Prov Distr St Phil Turramurra S 70-74; R of St Barn City and Dio Syd from 74. *35 Arundel Street, Forest Lodge, Sydney, NSW, Australia 2037.* (660-2161)

✠ **BLANCH, Most Rev and Right Hon Stuart Yarworth.** b 18. PC 75. St Cath S Ox BA (1st cl Th) 48, MA 52. Univ of Liv Hon LLD 75. Univ of Hull Hon DD 77. Univ of York Hon D 79. Wycl Coll Tor Hon DD 79. Wycl Hall Ox 46. **d** 49 **p** 50 Ox. C of Highfield 49-52; V of Eynsham 52-57; Tutor and Vice-Prin of Wycl Hall Ox 57-60; Oriel Can of Roch 60-66; Warden of Roch Th Coll 60-66; Hon Fell of St Pet Coll Ox from 66; Cons Ld Bp of Liv in York Minster 25 March 66 by Abp of York; Bps of Dur; Carl; Man; Newc T; Wakef; Blackb; Bradf; Sheff; Southw; Roch; and Linc; Bps Suffr of Burnley; Penrith; Warrington; Whitby; Pontefract; Selby; Jarrow; Hull; Sherwood; Stockport; Tonbridge; Huntingdon; and Grantham; and Bps Gerard; Townley; de Candole; West; and Stannard; Trld to York (Abp, Primate of England and Metrop) 75; Chairman Wycl Hall Coun from 67; Chap and Sub-Prelate O of St John of Jer from 74; Pro-Chan Hull Univ from 75; York Univ from 77. *Bishopthorpe, York, YO2 1QE.* (York 707021)

BLANCHARD, Christopher John. b 46. St D Coll Lamp BA. **d** 79 **p** 80 Mon (APM). C of Chepstow Dio Mon from 79. *Appletree Cottage, Llandogo, Monmouth, Gwent.*

BLANCHARD, Canon Ernest Desmond. b 26. Late Scho of St Jo Coll Dur BA (2nd cl Th) and De Bury Exhib 55, Dipl Th 56. **d** 56 **p** 57 Newc T. C of St Cuthb Bedlington 56-60; R of St Bart Salford 60-66; V of Ch Ch Ashton L Dio Man from 66; RD of Ashton L from 74; Hon Can of Man from 78. *Christ Church Vicarage, Ashton-under-Lyne, Gtr Man, OL7 9QY.* (061-330 1601)

BLANCHARD, Frank Hugh. b 30. St Jo Coll Dur BA (3rd cl Th) 54, Dipl Th 55, MA 62. **d** 55 Linc **p** 56 Grimsby for Cant. C of Bottesford w Ashby 55-58; CMS 58-65; C of Kirby Grindalythe Dio York 65-67; V 67-71; C of N Grimston w Wharram Percy and Wharram-le-Street Dio York 65-67; V 67-71; C-in-c of Settrington 67-68; C-in-c of Thorpe Bassett 67-71; V of St Jas Scarborough (and H Trin from 79) Dio York from 71; P-in-c of H Trin Scarborough 78-79. *St James' Vicarage, Scarborough, Yorks.* (Scarborough 61469)

BLANCHARD, Lawrence Gordon. Univ of Edin MA (2nd cl Ment Phil) 60. Linc Th Coll 63. **d** 65 **p** 66 Wakef. C of Woodhouse 65-67; Cannock 67-70; Chap of Waterford Sch Mbabane 70-72; L to Offic Dio Swaz 70-72; R of All SS Mbabane 73-75; L to Offic Dio Swaz 75-76; Team V of Raveningham 76-80; V of Ancaster Dio Linc from 80. *Vicarage, Ancaster, Grantham, Lincs.*

BLANCHETT, Arthur William. Lich Th Coll 33. **d** 35 **p** 36 Ox. C of Headington Quarry 35-40; Charlbury w Chadlington and Shorthampton 40-46; V of Steeple Barton 46-51; R of Islip 51-69; R of Noke 51-69; RD of Islip 55-57; C-in-c of Woodeaton 56-69. *49 Grove Walk, Norwich, NR1 2QQ.* (Nor 26150)

BLANCHETT, John Eric. b 08. Qu Coll Cam BA 31, MA 38. Ridley Hall Cam 31. **d** 32 **p** 33 Leic. C of H Trin Leic 32-35; Ch Ch Barnet 35-38; PC of St Cuthb Chitts Hill Lon 38-44; V of St Luke Ramsgate 44-55; R of Wickhambreaux w Stodmarsh 55-58; Fovant 58-71; Sutton Mandeville 58-71; V of Compton Chamberlayne 58-71; R of Fovant w Compton Chamberlayne and Sutton Mandeville 72-74; RD of Chalke 69-74. *40 Station Approach Road, Ramsgate, Kent, CT11 7RJ.* (Thanet 581064)

BLAND, Albert Edward. b 14. St Mich Coll Llan. **d** 62 Blackb **p** 63 Burnley for Blackb. C of St Cuthb Darwen 62-65; C-in-c of St Jo Evang Darwen 65-66; V 66-67; Feniscowles Dio Blackb from 67. *Feniscowles Vicarage, Preston Old Road, Blackburn, Lancs, BB2 5EN.* (Blackburn 21236)

BLAND, Graham William. b 53. Univ of Leeds BA 74. Wycl Coll Tor MDiv 80. **d** 80 Niag **p** 81 Bp CM Mitchell for Niag. V of St Alb Glen Williams and C of St Geo Georgetown Ont Dio Niag from 80. *537 Main Street, Georgetown, Ont, Canada, L7G 3T1.*

BLAND, Michael. St Pet Hall Ox BA (3rd cl Mod Hist) 49, 3rd cl Th 51, MA 54. Wycl Hall Ox. **d** 52 **p** 53 Win. C of St Mary Southampton 52-54; Milford Hants 54-55; Newbury Berks 55-58; R of Stanton w Snowshill Dio Glouc from 58; R of Buckland w Laverton Dio Glouc from 58. *Buckland Rectory, Broadway, Worcs.* (Broadway 852479)

BLAND, Thomas. b 12. Clifton Th Coll 39. **d** 42 **p** 43 Bris. C of Bishopston 42-44; Styvechale 44-45; V 45-61; Stratford-on-Avon 61-69; Hon Can of Cov 67-69. *1 Chillingham Green, Bedford.*

BLANDFORD, Robert Holmes. b 07. ALCD 38. **d** 38 Lon **p** 39 Willesden for Lon. C of St John Southall 38-46; C-in-c of Elburton Conv Distr 46-51; V of Ch Ch Cov 51-64; Budbrooke w Hampton-on-the-Hill 64-73; Perm to Offic Dio Ex from 74. *19 Kingsdown Crescent, Dawlish, Devon.*

BLANEY, Laurence. b 41. Dipl Th (Lon) 69. Oak Hill Th Coll 66. **d** 69 Barking for Chelmsf **p** 70 Chelmsf. C of St Mary and of St Edw, Leyton 69-73; C-in-c of Wimbish w Thunderley 73-77; Mayland Dio Chelmsf from 77; Steeple Dio Chelmsf from 77. *Mayland Vicarage, Chelmsford, Essex, CM3 6DZ.* (Maldon 740943)

BLANKENSHIP, Charles Everett. b 42. Univ of Santa Clara Calif BA 64. Cudd Coll 71. **d** 74 **p** 75 S'wark. C of St Jo Bapt Southend Lewisham 74-78; V of St Phil w St Bart Battersea Dio S'wark from 78. *Vicarage, Queenstown Road, SW8.* (01-622 1929)

BLANKET, Edmund. St Paul's Th Coll Moa I. **d** 69 **p** 72 Carp. C of All SS Cathl, Thursday I 69-70; Boigu I 70-72;

Badu I 72-74; Bamaga 74-76; P-in-c of Badu I Dio Carp from 76; Western Is Dio Carp from 78. *c/o Box 79, Thursday Island, Queensland, Australia 4875.*

BLANKLEY, Roger Henry. b 32. ARICS 60. Clifton Th Coll. **d** 66 **p** 67 S'wark. C of Peckham 66-69; SAMS Miss 70-80; R of Gillingham w Geldeston, Stockton, Ellingham and Kirby Cane Dio Nor from 80. *Geldeston Rectory, Beccles, Suff.* (Beccles 712255)

BLANT, Ven Edgar. St Chad's Coll Dur BA 47, Dipl Th 48. **d** 48 **p** 49 Lich. C of Meir 48-54; P-in-c of St Pet Montserrat 54-60; Nevis Dio Antig from 60; Hon Can of Antig from 68; Archd of St Kitts from 78. *St George's Rectory, Gingerland, Nevis, W Indies.* (Nevis 441)

BLAS, Raymond Henry. b 30. Univ of Tor LTh 70. Wycl Coll Tor 66. **d** 70 Rupld **p** 71 Calg. C of Calg Cathl 70-73; L to Offic Dio Calg 73-74; I of All SS Calg 74-81; Midnapore Dio Calg from 81. *207 Midridge Crescent SE, Calgary, Alta, Canada, T2X 1C7.* (271-8243)

BLASE, Hendrik Willem. McGill Univ BD 57. Montr Dioc Th Coll. **d** and **p** 57 Montr. P-in-c of Wakefield 57-63; R of Grace Ch Montr 63-68; Chap St Vinc de Paul Penit Montr 68-72. *2798 Laurnell Crescent, Abbotsford, BC, Canada.*

BLATCHLY, Owen Ronald Maxwell. b 30. Bps' Coll Cheshunt 62. **d** 64 **p** 65 St Alb. C of Boxmoor 64-67; Boreham Wood 67-69; Frimley (in c of St Francis) 69-77; V of Manaccan w St Anthony-in-Meneage Dio Truro from 77. *Vicarage, Manaccan, Helston, Cornw, TR12 6HA.* (Manaccan 261)

BLATHWAYT, Canon Linley Dennys. b 16. Qu Coll Cam BA 38, MA 44. Wells Th Coll 38, **d** 40 **p** 41 Wakef. C of Halifax 40-45; Ch Ch North Shields 45-48; V of Bywell St Pet 48-56; St Pet Monkseaton 56-59; Shalbourne w Bagshot Ham and Buttermere 59-66; R of Ballachulish 66-69; R of Glencoe 66-69; St Mich w All SS Gussage 69-71; Corscombe 71-75; C-in-c of Evershot w Frome St Quintin w Melbury Bubb 71-75; R (w Melbury Osmund w Melbury Sampford) 75-79; Team R of Melbury 79-81; RD of Beaminster 75-81; Can and Preb of Sarum Cathl from 79. *c/o Rectory, Evershot, Dorchester, Dorset.*

BLATHWAYT, Canon Wynter. b 18. St Pet Hall Ox BA Engl) 40, MA 44. Ripon Hall Ox 40. **d** 41 **p** 42 Cant. C of Herne Bay 41-46; Earlham 46-48; R of Chedgrave w Hardley and Langley V 48-56; V of St Andr Nor 56-66; R of St Mich-at-Pleas w St Pet Hungate Nor 56-66; V of Horning Dio Nor from 66; CF (TA) 60-67; P-in-c of Beeston w Ashmanhaugh Dio Nor from 78; Hon Can of Nor Cathl from 81. *Horning Vicarage, Norwich, Norf, NOR 39Z.* (Horning 216)

BLAXELL, Alwyn. St Jo Coll Morpeth ACT ThL 37, Th Scho 49. **d** 45 **p** 46 River. C of St Alb Griffith 45-48; R of Ganmain 48-50; Tumby Bay 50-51; Port Lincoln 51-56; Can of Willoch 54-59; R of Port Pirie 56-59; Belmont 59-64; Waratah 64-75; Perm to Offic Dio Newc from 75. *2 Nevill Street, Mayfield, NSW, Australia 2304.*

BLAXLAND, Gregory Montgomery Alfred. Moore Th Coll Syd. ACT ThL 58. **d** 59 Bp Hilliard for Syd **p** 59 Syd. C of Manly 59-60; C-in-c of The Oaks 60-62; SAMS Chap at Valparaiso Chile 62-65 and 69-72; C-in-c of Keiraville 66-69; Hon Can of Chile 72-74; Commiss Chile from 72; Gen Sec SAMS Syd from 73. *25 Alexander Parade, Roseville, NSW, Australia 2069.* (419-2471)

BLEAKLEY, John Donald. St Jo Coll Morpeth 55. **d** 58 **p** 59 Newc. C of New Lambton 59-60; Cessnock 60-62; Ch Ch Cathl Newc 62-68; Prec of St Jo Evang Cathl, Brisb 68-72; Perm to Offic Dio Brisb 73-74 and from 76; C of Wandal Rockptn 74-75; Hosp Chap Dio Brisb from 77. *1-7 Butterfield Street, Herston, Queensland, Australia.* (52-7603)

BLEAKLEY, Melvyn Thomas. b 43. K Coll Lon and Warm BD and AKC 66. **d** 67 **p** 68 Lich. C of Cross Heath 67-70; High Wycombe (in c of St Anne Wycombe Marsh and St Pet Micklefield) 70-77; Perm to Offic Dio Ox from 77. *17 Wendover Street, High Wycombe, Bucks.*

BLEASE, Anthony. b 28. Wells Th Coll 67. **d** 68 **p** 69 Chich (APM). C of Bognor 68-71; Perm to Offic Dio Chich 71-75; C of Felpham 75-80; Coun for Social Responsibility Dio Win from 80. *1 Durrant Road, Bournemouth, Dorset, BH2 6LE.* (Bournemouth 22066)

BLEASE, John Thomas. b 19. Edin Th Coll 41. **d** 43 **p** 44 Edin. C of St Paul and St Geo Edin 43-45; Actg C of St John Greenock 45-46; Perm to Offic at St Aidan w Ch Ch Carl 46-47; Chap RN 47-74; Perm to Offic Dios Lon and Guildf from 74. *180 Manor Road North, Thames Ditton, Surrey, KT7 0BQ.* (01-398 5117)

BLEBY, Canon John Raymond. Univ of Adel BA 33. St Barn Coll Adel 36. ACT ThL 37. **d** 38 **p** 39 Adel. C of St Pet Glenelg 38-40; P-in-c of Millicent 40-44; R of Ch Ch Strathalbyn 44-51; Gawler 51-57; Burnside and Exam Chap to Bp of Adel 57-70; Archd of The Broughton 57-66; SE 66-69; Hon Can of Adel 62-70; Commiss Polyn 65-69. R of St Thomas, Balhannah 70-73; Exam Chap to Bp of The Murray 71-78; Hon Can of The Murray 73-78; Can (Emer) from 78; R of Renmark 73-78; L to Offic Dio Adel from 78. *554 Glynburn Road, Burnside, S Australia 5066.*

BLEBY, Martin Edward. b 46. Univ of Adel BA (Hist) 67. ACT ThL 69. St Barn Th Coll Belair 69. **d** and **p** 71 Adel for The Murray. C of Mt Gambier 71-72; P-in-c of Tailem Bend 72-77; R of Kapunda Dio Adel from 77. *Christ Church Rectory, Kapunda, S Australia 5373.* (085-66 2030)

BLEH HTOO, H Cross Th Coll. **d** and **p** 51 Rang. P Dio Rang 51-70; Dio Pa-an from 70. *Klewa Hochi, Toungoo, Burma.*

BLENCOE, Charles Dennis. Univ of Lon BA 38. Bps' Coll Cheshunt 38. **d** 41 **p** 42 Southw. C of Sutton-in-Ashfield 41-43; Chap RAF 43-61; Chap Univ Sch Vic BC 61-64; C of Oak Bay 64-69; I of Fort Vermilion 70; Chap St Mich Univ Sch Vic BC from 71; Perm to Offic Dio BC from 72. *3400 Richmond Avenue, Victoria, BC, Canada.*

BLENKIN, Hugh Linton. b 16. Trin Coll Cam 2nd cl Mor Sc Trip pt i 37, BA (3rd cl Th Trip pt i) 39, MA 43, STh (2nd cl) Lambeth 56. Westcott Ho Cam 39. **d** 40 **p** 41 St Alb. C of Hitchin 40-43; Prec and C of St Albans Abbey 43-48; Chap and Lect Hockerill Tr Coll 48-66; Lect in Relig Studs Coll of Sarum St Mich Sarum 66-78. *Hill Brow, The Green, Pitton, Salisbury, Wilts.* (Farley 318)

BLENNERHASSETT, Richard Noel Rowland. b 09. Trin Coll Dub BA 33, MA 52. **d** 33 **p** 34 Cork. C of Queenstown (Clonmel) 33-37; I of Kilrosanty (w Stradbally and Monksland 39-45; I of Knappagh 45-47; Aughavale w Burrishoole (w Achill w Dugort from 68) 47-69; RD of Cong 47-49; Omey 49-53; Dom Chap to Bp of Tuam 51-57; Can and Preb of Kilmoylan and Taghsaxon in Tuam Cathl 52-56; Can and Preb of Kilmainmore and Kilmeen 56-69; RD of Tuam 54-56; Ballinrobe 56-63; Archd of Tuam 56-69; Can and Preb of Kilmactalway in St Patr Cathl Dub 60-67; I of Timoleague 69-73. *The Moorings, Fenit, Co Kerry, Irish Republic.*

BLENNERHASSETT, Canon Thomas Francis. TCD Bedell Scho 36, BA (1st cl Mod) 37, 1st Abp King's and 2nd Bp Forster's Prizes 38, 2nd cl Div Test and Comp Pri 39, BD 43, MA 68. **d** 39 **p** 40 Dub. C of St Geo Dub 39-43; Booterstown w Carysfoot 43-47; I of Balbriggan w Balrothery 47-58; Howth Dio Dub from 58; Can of Ch Ch Cathl Dub from 76; Commiss Geo from 78. *Rectory, Howth, Co Dublin, Irish Republic.* (Dublin 323019)

BLEWETT, Philip Richard Walton. b 23. Univ of Wales BSc 43. MInstP 45. Sarum Th Coll 50. **d** 52 **p** 53 Guildf. C of Chertsey w Eastworth 52-54; Weybridge (in c of St Mich AA) 54-62; Chap Red Rose Hosp Weybridge 54-62; Publ Pr Dio S'wark from 62; Asst Master Kidbrooke Sch 62-67; Sir John Cass and Red Coat Sch 67-71; St Paul's Way Sch Lon from 71; Perm to Offic Dio Lon from 67; Colleg P All H Barking-by-the-Tower City and Dio Lon from 73; Chap from 75. *22 Edgar Road, Sanderstead, South Croydon, Surrey, CR2 0NG.* (01-660 6867)

BLICK, John Harold Leslie. b 36. St D Coll Lamp BA 61, Bps' Coll Cheshunt 61. **d** 63 **p** 64 St Alb. C of Radlett 63-66; P-in-c of St Clem Miss Labrador 66-71; Min of H Cross Conv Distr Marsh Farm Luton 71-76; R of Shaw-cum-Donnington Dio Ox from 76. *Rectory, Love Lane, Donnington, Newbury, RG13 2JG.* (Newbury 40450)

BLIGH, Peter Alan. b 27. N-E Ordin Course 78. **d** 81 York (NSM). C of Thornaby-on-Tees Dio York from 81. *52 Cambridge Road, Thornaby, Stockton-on-Tees, Cleveland, TS17 6LR.*

BLIGHT, Ralph Ernest. Univ of W Ont BA 47, LTh 49. **d** 49 **p** 49 Hur. I of Bervie w Kingarf and Linlough 49-51; R of Morpeth 51-56; Blenheim 56-61; on leave from 61. *1579 Applewood Road, Port Credit, Ont, Canada.*

BLINSTON, John. b 29. St Aid Coll 56. **d** 56 **p** 57 Blackb. C of St Steph Burnley 56-59; Wilmslow 59-61; V of St Barn Warrington 61-64; C of Mackay Queensld 64-65; R of Violet Tn w Dookie Wang 65-69; V of St Luke Harrogate 69-75; L to Offic Dio Ripon from 77. *55 Wedderburn Road, Harrogate, N Yorks.* (Harrogate 884747)

BLISS, Alfred Charles. b 02. Bps' Coll Cheshunt 45. **d** 46 **p** 47 Chelmsf. C of St Barn Woodford Green 46-48; Chingford 48-54; R of Maids Moreton w Foscott 54-56; V of St Steph Battersea 57-67; Perm to Offic Dios S'wark and Lon 67-72; Dio Chich from 72. *Ramsay Hall, Byron Road, Worthing, BN11 3HW.*

BLISS, Allan Ernest Newport. b 29. K Coll Lon and Warm. **d** 54 Reading for Cant **p** 57 Ox. C of Wooburn 54-56; Ch Ch Reading 56-58; Hatcham Pk 63-68; Sundon w Streatley 68-74; P-in-c of Caldecote Dio St Alb 74-78; V from 78; Old Warden Dio St Alb from 81. *Vicarage, Upper Caldecote, Biggleswade, Beds.* (Biggleswade 315578)

BLISS, John Derek Clegg. Sarum Th Coll 65. **d** 68 Nor **p** 69 Thetford for Nor. C of Wymondham 68-73; R of Colton 73-80; V of Easton 73-80; in Amer Ch. *c/o 504 Barsotti, Madera, CA 93637, USA.*

BLISS, Canon Leslie John. b 12. K Coll Lon 48. **d** 49 **p** 50 S'wark. C of The Ascen Balham Hill 49-51; V of St Crispin w Ch Ch Bermondsey 51-59; R of Mottingham 59-65; RD of Eltham 64-65; R of Hagworthingham w Asgarby and Lusby 65-70; R of Mavis-Enderby w Raithby 67-70; V of Sutton-le-Marsh 70-79; RD of Calcewaith and Candleshoe 71-77; Can and Preb of Linc Cathl 74-79; Can (Emer) from 80. *15 Mattock Crescent, Torrisholme, Morecambe, Lancs.* (Morecambe 419688)

BLISS, Neil Humberstone. b 29. Late Found Scho of Trin Coll Dub BA (2nd cl Exper Sc Mod) 54, MA 59. Coll of Resurr Mirfield 55. **d** 57 **p** 58 Ex. C of St Thos Keyham Devonport 57-60; Usuthu 61-65; P-in-c of Piet Retief 65-66; R 66-67; Chap St Chris Sch Swaziland 68-73; Waterford Kamhlaba Sch Mbabane 73-78; L to Offic Dio Swaz 68-78; R of Piggs Peak 78-80; P-in-c of Osmington 80-81; Team V of Preston w Sutton Poyntz and Osmington w Poxwell Dio Sarum from 81. *30 Culliford Way, Littlemore, Weymouth, DT3 6AW.* (Preston 832691)

BLISS, Rupert Geoffrey. b 05. K Coll Cam BA 31, MA 45. Ridley Hall Cam 31. **d** and **p** 50 Roch. [f Lay Miss] C of Bromley 50-55; Sec S Metrop Area CMS 52-55; Prin Dunford Coll Midhurst 55-65; C-in-c of Heyshott 65-66; Perm to Offic Dio Sarum 67-68; C-in-c of Melbury Abbas 68-73; Perm to Offic Dio Sarum from 73. *67 Bimport, Shaftesbury, Dorset, SP7 8BA.* (Shaftesbury 2365)

BLISSARD-BARNES, Christopher John. b 36. Late Scho of Linc Coll Ox BA 61, MA 64. ARCO 55. Ridley Hall Cam 61. **d** 63 **p** 64 Guildf. C of St Paul Woking 63-67; Ch Ch Orpington 67-71; P-in-c of St Jas Heref 71-78; Chap Hereford Gen Hosp 71-78; R of Hampreston Dio Sarum from 78; RD of Wimborne from 80. *Rectory, Pinewood Road, Ferndown, Wimborne, Dorset, BH22 9RW.* (0202-872084)

BLISSETT, Walter Francis. b 09. St Jo Coll Morpeth ACT ThL 40. **d** 41 **p** 44 Armid. C of Gunnedah 41-42; Chap AIF 42-45; C of Horfield (Col Clergy Act) 47-53; V of St Barn Swindon 53-58; St Dunstan Bedminster 58-72; Perm to Offic Dio St D 72-73; Dio B & W from 73. *6 Garstons, Wrington, Bristol.*

BLIZZARD, William Terry. b 48. Trin Coll Tor 74. **d** 75 **p** 77 Queb. C of Eaton-Dudswell 75-78; R 78-79; St Pet Queb 79-81; New Carl Dio Queb from 81. *CP 128, New Carlisle, PQ, Canada.*

BLOEMFONTEIN, Lord Bishop of. *See* Amoore, Right Rev Frederick Andrew.

BLOEMFONTEIN, Dean of. *See* Cross, Very Rev Aidan Harrison.

BLOFELD, Thomas Guest. St D Coll Lamp BA 59. Cranmer Hall Dur 59. **d** 62 Bp Gerard for Sheff. C of Maltby 62-63; Goole 63-66; Pocklington 67-68; H Trin w St Mary Ely 68-70; St Jo Div Pemberton Dio Liv 70-72; V of St Jo Evang Walton-on-the-Hill 72-74; Barkisland w W Scammonden 74-80; V of Smallbridge Dio Man from 80. *Smallbridge Vicarage, Rochdale, Lancs.* (Rochdale 47512)

BLOOD, David John. b 36. G and C Coll Cam BA 60, MA 64. Westcott Ho Cam 62. **d** 62 **p** 63 St E. C of Rushmere 62-66; Harringay 66-71; L to Offic Dio Lon from 71. *33 Rosebery Gardens, N 8.* (01-340 3312)

BLOOD, Michael William. b 44. K Coll Lon and Warm AKC 67. **d** 69 **p** 70 Birm. C of St Agnes Moseley 69-75; V of The Cotteridge Dio Birm from 75. *27 Middleton Hall Road, Kings Norton, Birmingham, B30 1AB.* (021-458 2815)

BLOOD, Stephen John. Keble Coll Ox BA 53, MA 58. Coll of Resurr Mirfield 53. **d** 55 **p** 56 Lon. C of Gt Greenford 55-58; St Edm Forest Gate 58-61; Min of St Hilda's Conv Distr Ashford Middx 61-73; V of St Hilda Ashford Middx Dio Lon from 73. *8 Station Crescent, Ashford, Middx.* (Ashford 54237)

BLOOM, David Vine. b 35. Wycl Coll Tor LTh 68. **d** 68 **p** 69 Edmon. I of Viking 68-71; St Paul City and Dio Edmon from 71. *16033-95 Avenue, Edmonton, Alta, Canada.*

BLOOM, James Herbert. b 14. Trin Coll Dub BA 37, MA 40, Downes Liturgy Pri (2nd) 38. **d** 38 Down **p** 39 Tuam for Down. C of St John Malone Belf and Asst Chap of Malone Tr Sch 38-43; Chap RNVR 43-65; RNR 65-69; P-in-c of Ascen Mosspark Glas 46-52; R of E Allington 52-56; V of Castle Acre w Newton 56-71; R of Southacre 56-71; RD of Swaffham 69-70; R of Aylmerton w Runton Dio Nor from 71. *Rectory, West Runton, Cromer, Norf, NR27 9QT.* (West Runton 279)

BLOOMER, Noah Reginald. b 08. Univ of Leeds BA 33. Coll of Resurr Mirfield 28. **d** 33 **p** 34 Lich. C of St Mich AA Walsall 33-36; Tettenhall 36-39; All SS Cheltm 39-43; Hanley w Hope (in c of St Matt Birches Head) 43-44; C-in-c of Birches Head Conv Distr 44-47; V of Rushall Staffs 47-55. *Pendle, Old Cleeve, Minehead, Somt, TA24 6HN.* (Washford 350)

✠ **BLOOMER, Right Rev Thomas.** b 1894. TCD BA 16, Bibl Gr Pri and Hebr Pri 17, Downes Pri and Div Test (2nd cl) 18, MA 23, DD (*jure dig*) 46. Freeman City of Carl 66. **d** 18 **p** 19 Down. C of Carrickfergus 18-22; St Martin Castleton 22-23; Cheltenham 23-27; V of Lyncombe 27-35; Chap of St Mary Magd Holloway Bath 28-35; V of Barking 35-46; RD of Barking 43-46; Hon Can of Samuel Harsnett (Abp) in Chelmsf Cathl 43-46; Chap to HM the King 44-46; Cons Ld Bp of Carl in York Minster 18 Oct 46 by Abp of York; Bps of Dur; Man; Chelmsf; Newc T; Southw; S & M; and Liv; Bps Suffr of Barking; Hull; Burnley; Lanc; Knaresborough; Penrith; Pontefract; Jarrow; Selby; and Warrington; and Bps Mounsey; Gerard; and Powell; res 66; Assisting Bp of Johann 68; P-in-c of Monkton-Combe 70-72. *33 Greengate, Levens, Nr Kendal, Cumb.* (0448-60771)

BLOOMFIELD, Harry. Chich Th Coll 57. **d** 60 **p** 61 Chich C of St Mich AA Brighton 60-64; Wantage w Charlton Dio Ox from 64. *Vicarage, Wantage, Oxon, OX12 8AQ.* (Wantage 2214)

BLOOMFIELD, Harry Hildyard. b 1900. Qu Coll Cam BA 25, MA 29. Ripon Hall Ox 25. **d** 27 **p** 28 Ripon. C of St Mary Hunslet 27-30; All SS Leamington 30-33; V Cho in Sarum Cathl 33-39; R of St Martin Salisbury 39-45; Perm to Offic Dio Roch 45-47; L to Offic Dio Lon 46-48 and 56-57; Dioc Missr and Archd of St Kitts 47-52; V of St Marg Barb 52-56; C of Lamorbey 57-60; C-in-c of St Francis of Assisi Conv Distr Hammerfield Hemel Hempstead 60-63; R of Holwell 63-67. *Cullum Welch Court, Morden College, SE3 0PW.* (01-858 7676)

BLOOMFIELD, John Michael. b 35. St D Coll Lamp BA 57. Sarum Th Coll 59. **d** 61 **p** 62 Sarum. C of Fordington 61-64; Branksome 64-66; Bp's Youth Chap Dio Win 66-69; R of All SS w St Andr Chilcomb and St Pet Chesil Win 71-79; P-in-c of Corsley w Chapmanslade 79-81. *Address temp unknown.*

BLOOMFIELD, Canon Peter Grayson. b 19. K Coll Lon and Warm BD 60, AKC 61. **d** 61 Guildf for Matab **p** Matab. C of St Marg of Scotld Bulawayo 61-63; R of Francistown 63-70; St Francis w St Mark Bulawayo 70-78; Dioc Sec Dio Matab 71-77; Can of Matab 75-78; Hon Can from 78; P-in-c of Symondsbury w Eype and Broadoak Dio Sarum from 78; Chideock Dio Sarum from 78. *Symondsbury Rectory, Bridport, Dorset DT6 6HF.* (0308-22145)

BLORE, John Francis. b 49. Jes Coll Ox BA 72, MA 76. Wycl Hall Ox 73. **d** 75 **p** 76 Chelmsf. C of Waltham Abbey 75-78; St Geo East Ham 78-81; R of St Mich Myland Dio Chelmsf from 81. *Myland Rectory, Rectory Close, Mile End Road, Colchester, Essex CO4 5BX.* (Colchester 73076)

BLORE, Robert William. b 12. AKC 39. **d** 39 **p** 40 S'wark. C of St Barn Sutton New Town 39-42; CF (EC) 42-46; Hon CF 46; L to Offic Dio St Alb 46-47; C of St Matt Oxhey 47-48; Tring 48-49; R of Woodham Ferrers 49-56; V of Thorpe Bay 56-79. *10 Victoria Close, Wivenhoe, Colchester, Essex.* (Wivenhoe 4550)

BLOTT, William Richard. McMaster Univ BA 53, Trin Coll Tor. **d** 55 **p** 56 Niag. C of Grace Ch Hamilton 55-56; St Mary Hamilton 56-59; R of Port Dalhousie 59-63; St John St Catharines 63-66; Chap Appleby Coll Oakville 66-69. *311 Glasgow Street, Kitchener, Ont., Canada.*

BLOUNT, Robin George. b 38. Dipl Th (Lon) 68. Wycl Hall Ox 67. **d** 68 **p** 69 Ox. C of Bletchley 68-71; Washington 71-74; Team V of Chelmsley Wood 74-76; C of St John Dudley and Industr Chap Dio Worc from 78. *9 Tansley Hill Road, Dudley, W Midl DY2 7ER.* (Dudley 53084)

BLOUNT, Ronald Bernard. b 26. Oak Hill Th Coll 50. **d** 54 **p** 55 Ches. C of Higher Tranmere 54-56; CF 57-60; V of E Boldre w S Baddesley 60-63; Chap at Duesseldorf 63-69; R of Arthingworth w Kelmarsh and Harrington 69-78; Chap at Dhahran Dio Cyprus from 78. *Box 2506, Dhahran, Saudi Arabia.*

BLOW, Colin Joseph. St Francis Th Coll Brisb 51. **d** and **p** 54 Rockptn. C of N Rockptn 54-58; P-in-c of Dawson Valley Distr 58-61; V of Emerald 61-65; C of Warwick 65-66; Perm to Offic Dio Brisb from 66. *PO Box 103, Stones Corner, Queensland, Australia 4120.* (397 8437)

BLOWERS, Ralph Barrie. b 28. Fitzw Ho Cam BA 50, MA 61. Ridley Hall Cam 51. **d** 53 **p** 54 Man. C of St Clem Higher Openshaw 53-56; R of Albert Mem Ch Man 56-69; RD of Cheetham 63-69; Proc Conv Man 64-69; V of Normanton-by-Derby, Dio Derby from 69; RD of Derby 74-79; Derby S from 79. *Normanton Vicarage, Browning Street, Derby DE3 8DN.* (Derby 767483)

BLOWS, Canon Derek Reeve. b 26. Linc Coll Ox BA 50, MA 52, Cudd Coll 50. **d** 52 **p** 53 Cov. C of St Mark Cov 52-56; LPr Dio Sarum 57-58; Chap Warlingham Pk Hosp 58-65; V of St Mark Woodcote Purley 65-70; Dir of Past Care and Counselling Dio S'wark 70-80; Westmr Past Found from 81; Hon Can of S'wark from 72. *14 Woodcote Valley Road, Purley, Surrey.* (01-660 5788)

BLOXHAM, Ernest John. b 06. ALCD 36. **d** 36 **p** 37

Chelmsf. C of St Mary Magd Colchester 36-39; St Jas Clapham Pk 39-41; C-in-c 41-44; V 44-60; H Redeemer Streatham Vale 60-72; Publ Pr Dio S'wark from 72. *42 Wide Way, Mitcham, Surrey.* (01-679 2454)

BLOXHAM, Oliver. b 27. Ely Th Coll 60. **d** 62 **p** 63 Newc T. C of H Cross Fenham Newc T 62-65; Ponteland 65-69; V of Dudley 69-79; P-in-c of St Pet Balkwell Tynemouth Dio Newc T from 79. *St Peter's Vicarage, The Quadrant, North Shields, Northumb.* (N Shields 70952)

BLOXHAM, William. Moore Th Coll Syd 61. **d** 61 Bp Kerle for Syd **p** 62 Syd. C of Wahroonga 61-62; R of Emu Plains w Castlereagh 63-68; Naremburn 68-72; L to Offic Dio Syd from 72. *46 Bayswater Road, Kings Cross, NSW, Australia 2011.* (33-4320)

BLOY, Philip Penrose. b 19. St Edm Hall Ox MA (Mod Hist) 49. Univ of Lanc MA (Relig Stud) 71. Wells Th Coll 49. **d** 51 **p** 53 Sheff. Asst Industr Missr Dio Sheff 51-60; Industr Adv Mindolo Ecumen Found Dio N Rhod 60-62; Urban and Industr Sec All Afr Conf of Chs 62-69; C-in-c of St Geo E Bris 72-73; Chap Gatwick Airport Dio Chich from 73. *Chaplaincy, London-Gatwick Airport, Gatwick, W Sussex, RH6 0NP.* (0293 503857)

BLUCK, John Elder. b 16. St D Coll Lamp BA 49. **d** 50 Ban for St A **p** 51 St A. C of Rhosymedre 50-53; Hawarden 53-57; V of Newbold Pacey w Moreton Morrell 57-75; P-in-c of Alderminster Dio Cov from 75, Halford Dio Cov from 75; RD of Shipston-on-Stour from 78. *Alderminster Vicarage, Stratford-on-Avon.* (Alderminster 208)

BLUCK, John William. b 43. Univ of Cant NZ BA 66, MA 67. Episc Th Sch, Cam, USA BD (*cum laude*) 70. **d** 70 **p** 71 Wai. C of Gisborne 70-72; St Pet Wel 72-73; Hon C of St Matt Auckld 73-77; Dir Dept of Communications WCC from 80. *150 Route de Ferney, 1211 Geneva 20, Switzerland.*

BLUNDELL, Derek George. b 32. Tyndale Hall Bris. **d** 61 **p** 62 Liv. C of Em Fazakerley 61-64; Min of St Phil and St Jas Eccles Distr Odd Down S Lyncombe 64-69; V of Odd Down Bath 69-74; Tulse Hill 74-81; Org Afr P Fund from 81. *17 West Avenue, Stoke Park, Coventry, CV2 4DG.* (0203-448068)

BLUNDELL, Gary James. b 49. St Jo Coll Auckld LTh 73. **d** 73 Bp Monteith for Auckld **p** 74 Auckld. C of Kaitaia 73-76; St Mark Remuera City and Dio Auckld 76-78; P-in-c from 78; V of Te Atatu Dio Auckld from 78. *32 Taikata Road, Te Atatu, Auckland 8, NZ.*

BLUNSUM, Charles Michael. b 28. AIB 51. **d** 74 **p** 75 Malmesbury for Bris (APM). C of Stoke Bp 74-78; Perm to Offic Dio Ex 78-82; Chap Brunel Manor Chr Centre Torquay from 79. *Brunel Manor, Watcombe Park, Torquay, Devon.* (Torquay 37421)

BLUNT, Paul David. b 44. Univ of Lon BSc 65. Univ of Leeds Dipl Th 70. Coll of Resurr Mirfield 67. **d** 70 **p** 71 Cant. C of Norbury Cant 70-73; St Matt Ott 73-75; I of Ashton 75-81; R of Trin Ch City and Dio Ott from 81. *53 Sunnyside Avenue, Ottawa, Ont, Canada, K1S 0P9.* (613-236 3529)

BLUNT, Peter Walton Rexford. b 37. McGill Univ BSc 60, BD 70. Montr Dioc Th Coll LTh 70. **d** and **p** 70 Montr. C of Greenfield Park 70-73; R of Iberville 73-77; Two Mountains Dio Montr from 77. *1806 Normandie Street, City of Two Mountains, PQ, Canada.* (514-473 6119)

BLYDE, Ian Hay. b 52. Univ of Liv BSc 74. Univ of Edin BD 80. Edin Th Coll 77. **d** 80 Liv **p** 81 Warrington for Liv. C of Ainsdale Dio Liv from 80. *25 Pinfold Lane, Ainsdale, Merseyside.*

BLYTH, Bryan Edward Perceval. b 22. Linc Coll Ox BA 49, MA 52. Wells Th Coll 48. **d** 50 Ches **p** 51 Stockport for Ches. C of Timperley 50-52; Talbot Village 52-55; Min of St Edm Conv Distr Weymouth 55-56; PC 56-64; Asst Dir Relig Educn for Youth Dio Chelmsf 64-67; Publ Pr Dio Chelmsf from 64. *4 Downer Road North, Thundersley, Benfleet, Essex, SS7 3EG.* (S Benfleet 54287)

BLYTH, Drummond Gwyn. b 26. Ch Coll Cam 43. St Bonif Coll Warm 53. **d** 54 **p** 55 Nor. C of King's Lynn 54-59; Parson Cross Sheff 59-62; R of Carlton Colville 62-70; V of Stalham w Brunstead (and E Ruston from 77) Dio Nor from 70; P-in-c of E Ruston 76-77; RD of Waxham from 77. *Stalham Vicarage, Norwich, NR12 9DT.* (Stalham 80250)

BLYTH, Very Rev John Carter. Univ of Tor BA 61. Trin Coll Tor STB 63. **d** 63 **p** 64 Caled. C of Port Edward 63-67; I of Aiyansh 67-79; Archd of Caled 76-80; Dean and R of Cathl Ch of Redeemer City and Dio Calg from 80. *2nd Floor, 602-First Street SE, Calgary, Alta, Canada.*

BLYTH, John Reddie. b 25. Wadh Coll Ox BA 48, MA 50. Ridley Hall Cam 48. **d** 50 **p** 51 Liv. C of Ch Ch Southport 50-52; Cockfosters in c of Hadley Wood 52-55; PC of St Jude Plymouth 55-63; Area Sec CPAS in E Midl 63-70; Perm to Offic Dios Chelmsf Ely Nor Pet St Alb and St E 63-70; Dios Leic Linc and Southw 63-67; V of St Luke Parkstone Dio Sarum from 70; Chap Uplands Sch Parkstone 70-73. *2 Birchwood Road, Parkstone, Poole, Dorset, BH14 9NP.* (Parkstone 741030)

BLYTH, John Stuart. b 36. Univ of Lon BD 64. Lich Th Coll 63. **d** 65 **p** 66 Bris. C of St Barn Knowle 65-68; Whitchurch Somt 68-70; P-in-c of Sutton Heref 70-73; Adv Relig Educn Dio Heref 70-73; Chap RAF 73-77; P-in-c of Launton 77-79; Team V of Bicester w Bucknell, Caversfield and Launton Dio Ox from 79. *Launton Rectory, Bicester, Oxon, OX6 0DP.* (Bicester 2377)

BLYTH, Kenneth Henry. b 35. Dipl Th (Lon) 60. Oak Hill Th Coll 58. **d** 61 **p** 62 St Alb. C of St Paul St Alb 61-65; C-in-c of Aspenden w Layston and Buntingford Dio St Alb 65-66; R 66-72; R of Exe Valley Team Min Dio Ex from 72; C-in-c of Cruwys-Morchard 72-74; RD of Tiverton from 76. *Rectory, Washfield, Tiverton, Devon, EX16 9QY.* (Tiverton 255006)

BLYTH, Ven Richard John. LTh (S Afr) 59. St Paul's Th Coll Grahmstn 57. **d** 59 Johann **p** 60 Bp Paget for Capetn. C of Randfontein 60-61; St Mary Virg Cathl Johann 61-64; P-in-c of Jeppe 64-65; R of Turffontein 67-69; I of Magdalen Is 69-72; R of St Matt and St Mich Sillery City and Dio Queb from 72; Dom Chap to Bp of Queb 75-78; Archd of Queb from 78; Exam Chap to Bp of Queb from 80. *1841 St Michael's Street, Sillery, PQ, Canada.*

BLYTON, Geoffrey Richard. b 23. **d** 70 **p** 71 C & Goulb. Hon C of Cooma 70-73; R of Bribbaree 73-74; Temora 74-80; Crookwell Dio C & Goulb from 80. *Box 44, Crookwell, NSW, Australia 2625.*

BO, Lord Bishop of. *See* Keili, Right Rev Michael.

BOADEN, John Edward. b 15. Down Coll Cam 2nd cl Hist Trip pt i 40, BA 41, 3rd cl Th Trip pt i 42, MA 45. Ridley Hall Cam 41. **d** 43 **p** 44 Lon. C of H Trin Southall 43-47; St Steph E Twickenham 47-50; R of Openshaw 50-56; V of Bitterne 56-67; R of Blackley 67-77; C-in-c of Parkfield 77-81; Hon C of Constable Lee Dio Man from 81. *11 Horncliffe Close, Rossendale, Lancs, BB4 6EE.* (Rossendale 223696)

BOAG, David. b 46. Edin Th Coll 69. **d** 72 **p** 73 Edin. C of Old St Paul City Edin 72-74; P-in-c of St Aid Miss Niddrie Mains City and Dio Edin from 74. *House of St Aidan, Duddingston Park South, Edinburgh, EH15 3EH.* (031-669 4756)

BOAKE, Henry Vaux. b 16. TCD BA 38, Div Test 38, MA 62. **d** 39 **p** 40 Lim. Dioc C Dios Ardf and Agh and C of Tralee 39-43; C of Wexford 43-44; C-in-c of Kilscoran 44-46; I of Crosspatrick 46-79; RD of Crosspatrick 59-65; Gorey 65-79; Can of Clone and Crosspatrick in Ferns Cathl 62-69; Treas 69-71; Chan 71-79. *Little Orton, Rutland, Palatine, Carlow, Irish Republic.*

BOAKES, Norman. b 50. Univ of Wales (Swansea) BA (Hist) 71. St D Coll Lamp LTh 73. Bp Burgess Hall Lamp 71. **d** 73 **p** 74 Swan B. C of Swansea 73-76; Chap Univ Coll Swansea 76-78; K Alfred's Coll Win 82; V of Colbury Dio Win from 82. *The Hawthorns, Woodlands Road, Ashurst, Southampton, SO4 2AD.* (Ashurst 2862)

BOAN, David Thomas Clifford. Ridley Coll Melb 64. ACT ThL 67. **d** 68 **p** 69 Melb. C of St Mark Camberwell 68-69; Caulfield 69-70; Chap Caulfield Gr Sch Melb 70-73; Perm to Offic Dio Melb 73; C of Rosanna 73-75; C-in-c of St Jude Carlton 75-81. *c/o 235 Palmerston Street, Carlton, Vic, Australia 3053.* (03-347 5152)

BOAN, Stewart Fraser. ACT ThL 69. **d** 69 Melb. C of St Mary Caulfield Dio Melb from 69 *c/o Church Office, 2 Hood Crescent, Caulfield, Vic. 3161, Australia.*

BOAR, Alan Bennett. b 23. Sarum Th Coll 56. **d** 58 Nor **p** 59 Thetford for Cant. C of Dereham 58-60; Gorleston 60-63; V of Tibenham 63-67; C-in-c of Tivetshall 64-67; R of Beeston w Ashmanhaugh and Hoveton 67-78; P-in-c of Tunstead w Sco Ruston 67-78; Marsham Dio Nor from 78; Burgh next Aylsham Dio Nor from 78. *Marsham Rectory, Norwich, Norf, NR10 5PP.* (Aylsham 3249)

BOARDMAN, Frederick Henry. b 35. Univ of Liv BSc 46. St Cath S Ox BA 49, MA 54. Univ of Birm MEducn 71, PhD 77. Wycl Hall Ox 47. **d** 50 **p** 51 Liv. C of Ch Ch Bootle 50-52; C-in-c of St Osw Conv Distr Netherton 52-57; V of Stechford 57-63; Publ Pr Dio Birm 63-69; Asst Master Bierton Sch 63-65; K Edw VI Sch Camp Hill Birm 65-69; Lect Padgate Coll of Educn from 70; L to Offic Dio Liv from 71. *Beecholme, Grosvenor Road, St Helens, Mersey, WA10 3HX.*

BOARDMAN, John Frederick. b 37. K Coll Lon and Warm AKC (2nd cl) 64. **d** 65 **p** 66 Ripon. C of St Wilfrid, Harrogate 65-68; Fleetwood (in c of St Nich) 68-71; Centr Torquay 71-77; Chap and Lect S Devon Coll of Tech Torquay 71-76; P-in-c of Ch Ch Torquay 76-77; V of Milber Dio Ex from 77. *Milber Vicarage, Newton Abbot, Devon, TQ12 4LQ.* (Newton Abbot 65837)

BOARDMAN, William. b 21. K Coll Lon and Warm AKC 52. **d** 53 Dover for Cant **p** 54 Cant. C of All SS Spring Pk Croydon 53-57; Chap Holloway Sanat 57-58; C of Portchester 60-63; C-in-c of Barton IW Dio Portsm 63-67; V from 67; RD of W Wight from 78. *Barton Vicarage, Newport, IW.* (Newport 522075)

BOASE, David John. b 49. St Jo Coll Dur BA 71. Cudd Coll 71. **d** 73 Penrith for Carl **p** 74 Carl. C of Penrith 73-76; Chap and Tutor Greystoke Th Coll 76-78; Prec of Gibr Cathl 78-81; Chap Mediterranean Miss to Seamen 78-81; Chap St Andr Gothenburg Dio Gibr in Eur from 81. *Norra Liden 15, S 411 18 Gothenburg, Sweden.* (031-111915)

BOATRIGHT, Vivian John Ernest. b 18. St Pet Hall Ox 38. Oak Hill Th Coll 45. **d** 48 **p** 49 Pet. C of Rushden 48-50; Gaywood w Bawsey and Mintlyn 50-52; Chap RAF 52-74; V of Werrington and St Giles in the Heath w Virginstowe Dio Truro from 74. *Werrington Vicarage, Launceston, Cornw.*

BOAZ, Richard James. Hur Coll L.Th 66. **d** 66 Bp Appleyard for Hur **p** 67 Hur. I of Paisley 66-69; Markdale 69-73; St Clair Beach Dio Hur from 73. *390 Grace Road, Windsor, Ont., Canada.* (519-735 4921)

BOB, Scotty. b 29. **d** 80 Carp. C of Warraber I Dio Carp from 80. *Warraber Island, Queensland, Australia.*

BOCKUS, Canon Walter Alfred. d 43 **p** 44 Montr. C of St Clem Montr 43-47; I of Bondville 47-50; Redeemer Montr 50-56; Greenfield Pk 56-64; Andover 64-66; R of St Geo St John, Fred 66-79; Can of Ch Ch Cathl Fred from 71. *186 Lancaster Street West, St John, NB, Canada.*

BODDINGTON, Alan Charles Peter. b 37. Dipl Th (Lon) 65. Oak Hill Th Coll 63. **d** 66 **p** 67 Cov. C of Bedworth 66-69; Bp of Cov Chap for Miss 69-75; C-in-c of Honiley and of Wroxall 72-75; V of Westwood Dio Cov from 75; Asst Chap Univ of Warw from 78. *St John's Vicarage, Westwood Heath Road, Coventry, CV4 7DD.* (Cov 466227)

BODDINGTON, Benjamin. St Jo Coll Morpeth ACT ThL 37, Th Scho 43. **d** and **p** 38 Goulb. C of Ch Ch W Goulb 38; Albury 39-42; R of Temora 42-46; Bodalla 46-50; Gunning 51-56; Cootamundra 56-70; Can of St Sav Cathl Goulburn 63-74; R of Tarcutta 70-74; Perm to Offic Dio C & Goulb 74-79; Dio Syd From 79. *49 Werri Street, Werri Beach, NSW, Australia 2534.*

BODDINGTON, Clive Frederick Malcolm. Qu Coll Cam BA 59, MA 63. Ridley Hall Cam 59. **d** 61 **p** 62 Roch. C of Tonbridge 61-64; St Leonards-on-Sea 64-66; BCMS Miss P at Nyandarau 67-68; Chap Univ Coll Nai 69-73. *P.O. Box 8802, Nairobi, Kenya.*

BODDINGTON, John Slater. b 17. Wells Th Coll 63. **d** 64 Lon **p** 65 Willesden for Lon. C of St Pet Harrow 64-68; St Andr Harrow 68-71; V of St Martin W Acton Dio Lon from 71. *25 Birch Grove, W3.* (01-992 2333)

BODDY, Canon William Kenneth. b 16. St Jo Coll Dur BA 39. TD 63. Dipl in Th 40, Westcott Ho Cam 40. **d** 40 **p** 41 Ripon. C of Hunslet 40-43; Benwell 43-49; CF (TA) from 49; V of Tynemouth Priory 49-65; Wylam-on-Tyne Dio Newc T from 65; RD of Corbridge from 71; Hon Can of Newc T from 74. *Vicarage, Wylam-on-Tyne, Northumb.* (Wylam 3254)

BODEN, Canon John Posnett. b 1894. Late Found Scho of St Chad's Coll Dur Maltby Pri 19, Lightfoot Scho and BA (1st cl Cl) 20, 1st cl Th 21, MA 23. **d** 21 **p** 22 Dur. Fell and Tutor of St Chad's Coll Dur 21-37; Lect in Univ of Dur 27-37; L to Offic Dio Dur 22-37; C of St Wilfrid Harrogate 37-39; L Pr Dio Win from 39; Min Can and Prec of Win Cathl 39-65; Libr 54-65; Hon Can 57-65; Can (Emer) from 65. *Ramsay Hall, Byron Road, Worthing, W Sussex, BN11 3HW.* (Worthing 36880)

BODGER, Roland. Montr Th Coll LTh 35. **d** 34 **p** 35 Montr. C of St Jas Ap Montr 34-37; R of St Cuthb Montr 37-59; Beaurepaire 59-64; St Cypr Montr 65-70; P-in-c of St Chad Montr 65-70; C of Trin Mem Ch Montr 70-71. *1 Philie Crescent, Chateauguay, PQ, Canada.* (514-691 9794)

BODMIN, Archdeacon of. *See* Temple, Ven George Frederick.

BODY, Andrew. b 46. Pemb Coll Cam BA 68, MA 71. Ridley Hall Cam 68. **d** 70 **p** 71 Man. C of New Bury Farnworth 70; Team V of Droylsden 73-78; V of St Mary Low Harrogate w Harlow Hill Dio Ripon from 78. *22 Harlow Oval, Harrogate, HG2 0DS.* (Harrogate 502614)

BODYCOMB, Peter Lionel. b 28. Roch Th Coll 65. **d** 67 **p** 68 Roch. C of Gravesend 67-70; Hawley 70-75; V of St Paul Egham Hythe 75-78. *12 Willow Lodge, Grangewood Drive, Sunbury on Thames, TW16 7DL.* (Sunbury 80761)

BODYCOMBE, David Parry. b 14. CCC Cam 2nd cl Th Trip pt i 35, BA (2nd cl Th Trip pt ii) 36, MA 40. Linc Th Coll 36. **d** 37 **p** 38 York. C of St Barn Linthorpe 37-46; Chap RAFVR 43-46; PC of St Chad York 46-54; Min of Legal Distr of St Luke Scarborough 54-56; V 56-59; Chap Scarborough Hosp 54-59; V of W Acklam Dio York from 59; Chap Carter Bequest Hosp from 62. *Vicarage, Church Lane, Acklam, Middlesbrough, Teesside TS5 7EB.* (Middlesbrough 87150)

BOE, Hugh Blessing. Pacific Th Coll BD 74. **d** 75 New Hebr **p** 76 Melan for New Hebr. P Dio New Hebr 75-80; Dio Vanuatu from 80. *Kerepei, Maewo, Vanuatu.*

BOESIRO, Samuel. St Pet Coll Siota. **d** 70 **p** 71 Melan. P Dio Melan 70-75; Dio New Hebr 75-80; Dio Vanuatu from 80. *Gaua, Banks Islands, Vanuatu.*

BOFF, Charles Roy. b 31. Pemb Coll Ox BA (4th cl Engl) 57, MA 60. Clifton Th Coll 55. **d** 57 **p** 58 S'wark. C of All SS Plumstead 57-61; V of Ch Ch Gipsy Hill 61-68; Felbridge 68-79; R of Ashurst Dio Chich from 79; V of Steyning Dio Chich from 79. *Vicarage, Steyning, Sussex, BN4 3YL.* (Steyning 813256)

BOFFEY, Ian. b 40. Univ of Glas MA 63. **d** 75 **p** 78 Glas. C of Dalry Dio Glas from 75. *2 Kinloch Avenue, Stewarton, Kilmarnock, Ayrshire, KA3 3HF.*

BOGA-ZAIRE, Lord Bishop of. *See* NJOJO, Right Rev Patrice Byankya.

BOGA-ZAIRE, Assistant Bishop of. (Vacant)

BOGAR, John William. Newton Coll Dogura 59. **d** 61 **p** 63 New Guinea. P Dio New Guinea 63-71; Dio Papua from 71. *Gadovisu, PO Dogura, via Boroko, New Guinea.*

BOGGIS, Canon Augustine Thomas Isaac. b 08. Ex Coll Ox BA (2nd cl Th) 30, MA 45. Sarum Th Coll 34. **d** 34 **p** 35 Chich. C of St Paul Chich 34-38; Chap and Asst Master Sedbergh Sch 38-74; L to Offic Dio Bradf from 39; Hon Can of Bradf from 68. *8 Main Street, Sedbergh, Cumb, LA10 5BN.* (0587-20481)

BOGLE, James Main Lindam Linton. b 33. Peterho Cam BA 56, MA 60. Wells Th Coll 59. **d** 61 **p** 62 S'wark. C of St Anne Bermondsey 61-65; Chap Univ of York 65-72; V of Brayton w Barlow 72-76; Honor Oak Pk Dio S'wark from 76. *8 Hengrave Road, SE23.* (01-699 1535)

BOHUN, (Hugh) Roger Alexander. b 32. Univ of Lon BSc (Agr) 58. Cudd Coll 65. **d** 68 Bp McKie for Cov. **p** 69 Cov. C of Rugby Cov 68-74; M SSF from 74; L to Offic Dio Sarum 74-76; Dio Newc T 76-78; Dio Dar-S from 78. *Box 2227, Dar-Es-Salaam, Tanzania.*

BOIT, Mervyn Hayes. St Mich Coll Llan. **d** 61 **p** 62 Llan. C of St German Roath 61-63; Skewen 63-69; V of Pontycymmer w Blaengarw Dio Llan from 69. *Vicarage, Pontycymmer, Mid Glam.* (Pontycymmer 280)

BOKABA, Joshua Duke. St Pet Coll Rosettenville 59. **d** 62 **p** 63 Johann. P Dio Johann. *St Andrew's, Payneville, Transvaal, S Africa.* (011-56 9666)

BOLAJI, Ebenezer Olaniyi. b 42. Im Th Coll Ibad 67. **d** 70 **p** 71 Ibad. P Dio Ibad 71-74; Dio Ilesha from 74. *Vicarage, Erin-Ijesha, via Ilesha, Nigeria.*

BOLAJI, Timothy Ipadeola Olaniyi. Dipl Th (Lon) 64. Im Coll Ibad 62. **d** 64 Ibad. d Dio Ibad 64-74. *St Paul's Church, Yemetu, Ibadan, Nigeria.*

BOLAMBA, Baombolia. b 44. **d** 78 Boga-Z. d Dio Boga-Z. *Boga, BP 154, Bunia, Zaire.*

BOLARINWA-BEWAJI, Benjamin. St Aug Th Coll Accra 56. **d** 58 Accra. d Dio Accra. *Bishop's House, P.O. Box 8, Accra, Ghana.*

BOLD, Thomas Arthur. b 1894. CCC Cam BA 20, MA 23. **d** 22 **p** 23 S'wark. C of St Pet Greenwich 22-24; St John Southend Lewisham 24-26; Offg CF Trowbridge 26-38; PC of H Trin Trowbridge 26-38; V of Grantchester 38-54; Sec Cam YMCA 41-45; Select Pr Univ of Cam 52; V of Over 54-59; Perm to Offic Dio Win 59-69; Dio Portsm 60-65; Dio Chich 67-77. *22 Manormead, Tilford Road, Hindhead, Surrey.*

BOLE, Malcolm Dennis. b 30. Oak Hill Th Coll 65. **d** 67 **p** 68 York. C of Bridlington Priory 67-70; Lect Stanley Smith Th Coll Gahini, Ruanda 71; Prin 71-72; Lect Ecole de Theologie Butare 72-73; V of Odd Down 74-81; C-in-c of Combe Hay 74-81; P-in-c of St Jas Taunton Dio B & W from 81. *St James's Vicarage, Richmond Road, Taunton, Somt.* (Taunton 3194)

BOLLARD, Richard George. b 39. Fitzw Ho Cam 2nd cl Mod Lang Trip Pt i 59, BA (2nd cl Mod Lang Trip pt ii) 61, MA 65. K Coll Lon and Warm BD (2nd cl) and AKC 63. **d** 64 **p** 65 Win. C of Maybush 64-68; Chap Univ of Aston in Birm 68-74; R of Chelmsley Wood Dio Birm from 74; M Gen Syn from 80; M ACCM from 81. *The Rectory, Pike Drive, Chelmsley Wood, Birmingham, B37 7US.* (021-770 4444)

BOLLE, Victor E. d 43 **p** 45 Milwaukee. In Amer Ch 43-70; R of Blackstonedge Ja 70-72; C of Mandeville Ja 73-76; Brown's Town Dio Ja from 76. *Brown's Town P.O, Jamaica, W Indies.*

BOLLEN, Brian Hayward. b 26. **d** 77 **p** 78 Bris (APM). Hon C of St Pet Chippenham Dio Bris from 77. *27 The Tinings, Chippenham, Wilts, SN15 3LY.*

BOLLOM, Canon David. b 23. Wycl Hall Ox 72. **d** 74 **p** 75 S'wark. C of Norbiton 74-77; Dioc Sec Dio S'wark from 77; Can (Emer) of S'wark Cathl from 78. *14 Cupar Road, SW11 4JW.* (01-720 3787)

BOLSIN, Canon Cyril Edward. b 10. AKC 41. **d** 41 **p** 42 Chelmsf. C of St Jo Bapt Tilbury Docks 41-43; Hornchurch (in c of St Geo from 45) 43-47; SPG Miss Dio Delhi 47-56; V of Heybridge w Langford 56-62; Chap Heybridge Hosp 56-

62; R of Myland 62-80; Chap Myland Hosp 63-80; Surr 64-80; Hon Can of Chelmsf from 76. *Myland, Ford Street, Fordham, Colchester, Essex, CO6 3LL.* (Colchester 240553)

BOLT, Anthony Laurence. Univ of W Austr BA 48. Crafers Th Coll 48. **d** 52 Adel **p** 55 Dun. M SSM 52-55; Tutor SSM Th Coll Crafers and L to Offic Dio Adel 52-55; C-in-c of Wakatipu 55; C of Invercargill 55-57; V of Maniototo 57; L to Offic Dio Perth 58-60; Vice-Warden of John Wollaston Th Coll 58-60; R of Armadale 60-70; Chap St Hilda's Sch Mosman Pk 70-79; Dir Dept of Educn and Tr Dio Perth from 79. *5 Pitt Street, St James, Mosman Park, W Australia 6102.* (458 1103)

BOLT, David Dingley. b 18. Called to Bar Gray's Inn 53. St Jo Coll Cam LLB 58. Westcott Ho Cam 66. **d** 68 **p** 69 Malawi. C of St Paul Blantyre 68-70; Good Shep Chesterton 70-71; C-in-c of Gt Wilbraham Dio Ely 71-74; V from 74; C-in-c of L Wilbraham w Six Mile Bottom Dio Ely 71-74; R from 74; RD of Quy 75-80. *Vicarage, Great Wilbraham, Cambridge, CB1 5JF.* (Cambridge 880332)

BOLT, Philip John Mitchell. b 15. Bps' Coll Cheshunt 49. **d** 52 **p** 53 Blackb. C of Carnforth 52-56; C-in-c of St Mark's Conv Distr Burnley 56-59; Min 59-65; R of Nunney (w Wanstrow and Cloford from 74) 65-79; C-in-c of Wanstrow w Cloford 72-74; V of St Paul w St Mich and St John Ferham Pk, Rotherham 79-81. *Address temp unknown.*

BOLT, Reginald Victor. **d** 59 **p** 60 Melb. C of St Barn Balwyn 59-60; V of Cranbourne 60-73; Chap Miss to Seamen Melb from 73. *Mission to Seamen, Flinders Street, Melbourne, Vic, Australia 3000.* (03-62 7083)

BOLT, William John. b 03. Univ of Leeds BA (2nd cl Engl Lang and Lit) 26, Univ of Lon LLB 47, LLM 54, PhD 58, Coll of Resurr Mirfield 26. **d** 28 Aber for Lon **p** 29 Lon. C of St Columb Notting Hill 28-31; St Thos w St Mich and St Swith Win 31-32; St Jas Milton (in c of St Cross Eastney) 32-35; Alverstoke (in c of St Faith Gosport) 35-37; St Mary Pet 39-42; C-in-c of Bondleigh w Brushford 42-43; Atherington 43-45; R of Highampton w Sheepwash 45-52; Org Sec CETS SW Engl 45-52; C of St Martin Kentish Town 52-56; V of St Paul Lisson Grove w St Matt and Em St Marylebone 56-70; Chap Tottenham Tech Coll 70-72; Perm to Offic Dio Llan from 72. *21 Vincent Court, Ely, Cardiff.* (Cardiff 568342)

BOLTON, Archdeacon of. *See* Hoyle, Ven Frederick James.

BOLTON, Brian Geoffrey. b 54. St Pet Coll Natal Dipl Th 78. **d** 78 **p** 79 Capetn. C of Malmesbury Dio Capetn from 78. *PO Box 100, Malmesbury, CP 7300, S Africa.*

BOLTON, David Charles. Trin Coll Tor BA 60. Gen Th Sem NY 61. **d** 63 **p** 64 Ott. C of All SS Westboro Ott 63-66; Campbell's Bay 66-71; I of St Mark Ott 71-77; Assoc P of Grace Ch on-the-Hill Tor 77-80; I of St Richard of Chich City and Dio Tor from 80. *240 The Westway, Weston, Toronto, Ont, Canada.*

BOLTON, Very Rev Frederick Rothwell. b 08. Fitzw Ho Cam 3rd cl Hist Trip pt i 29, BA (3rd cl Engl Trip pt ii) 30, MA 35, BD 60. Linc Th Coll 31. **d** 33 **p** 34 Derby. C of Beighton 33-35; Chesterfield 35-36; St Jo Bapt Frome 36-38; Chesterfield 38-43 (Perm to Offic at Whitwell 41-43); V of E Markham w W Drayton 43-55; I of Kilscoran 55-60; R of Ardara 60-63; Chap St Columba's Hosp Killybegs 60-63; I of Leigh w Shankill Grange Sylvae Wells and Graigue (w Clonagoose from 75) Dio Leigh from 63; Dean of Leigh from 63; Preb of Ascoffin in Kilkenny Cathl from 63. *St Laserian's Deanery, Old Leighlin, Carlow, Irish Republic.* (Carlow 21411)

BOLTON, George Henry Denne. b 16. Trin Coll Dub BA 39, MA 50. **d** 39 **p** 40 Arm. C of Arm 39-42; CF 42-67; Asst Chap HM Pris Wandsworth 67; Chap HM Pris Birm 67-69; Chap at Algarve Portugal 71-74. *70 West Street, Minehead, Somt.* (Minehead 5365)

BOLTON, Ven Kenneth Charles. St John's Coll Manit LTh and BA 32, BD 53. **d** 32 **p** 33 Bran. C of Glenboro w Stockton 32-33; of Shoal Lake 36-38; P-in-c of N Clarendon 39-41; R of Shawville 41-44; Knowlton 44-46; St Jo Div Verdun 46-50; Walkerton 50-52; St Andr Windsor 52-56; Exam Chap to Bp of Hur 54-58; Archd of Essex 55-58; Lambton 58-60; Archd without territorial jurisd 60-73; Archd (Emer) from 74; R of St Geo Sarnia 58-60; Chap Hur Coll 60-70; Assoc Prof of Pastoral Th 62-73; Hon C of St Matt Lon Hur 70-73; Dioc Missr Dio Windw Is 73-76. *589 Piccadilly Street, London, Ont, Canada.*

BOLTON, Richard David Edward. b 52. St Steph Ho Ox 79. **d** 81 Sheff. C of Rawmarsh Dio Sheff from 81. *St Nicholas House, Kilnhurst Road, Rawmarsh, S Yorks.*

BOLTON, Robert. b 28. ALCD 58. **d** 58 Warrington for Liv **p** 59 Liv. C of St Phil Litherland 58-60; St Mary Wavertree 60-63; V of St Aug Bradf 63-67; C of Llangywyd w Maesteg Dio Llan from 77. *Ysgol Cefn Glas, Llangewydd Road, Bridgend, Mid Glam, CF31 4JP.* (Bridgend 4826)

BOLTON, Sidney Robert. b 15. Univ of Dur 41. Edin Th Coll 42. **d** 44 **p** 45 Ox. C of St James w St Luke Cowley 44-47; St Geo the Martyr Wolverton 47-50; P-in-c of Ermington 51-53; Area Padre for Toc H in SW Engl 50-53; Lincs 53-58; R of Nettleton 53-58; V of Stainton-by-Langworth w Newball Coldstead and Reasby 58-59; Barlings w Langworth 58-59; Bloxham w Milcolmbe (and S Newington from 81) Dio Ox from 59; P-in-c of S Newington 80-81. *Bloxham Vicarage, Banbury, Oxon, OX15 4ES.* (Banbury 720252)

BOLTON, William. Tyndale Hall Bris 31. **d** 33 **p** 34 Blackb. C of St Barn Blackb 33-36; St Jas Chorley 36-39; V of St Paul Withnell 39-51; Higher Tranmere 51-65; Chap of St Cath Hosp Annex and Birkenhead Ment Hosp 51-65; V of St Ninian Douglas 65-74. *Arrandale, The Avenue, Ellenbrook, Braddan, IM.*

BOMA, Eliyo Sadala. **d** 35 **p** 36 Centr Tang. P Dio Centr Tang from 35; CF (E Afr) 43-46; Can of Centr Tang 65-73; *Box 26, Kongwa, Tanzania.*

BOMFORD, Canon Raymond Joseph. Moore Th Coll Syd ACT ThL 51. **d** and **p** 52 Syd. C-in-c of Toongabbie 52-55; R of Nowra 55-59; St Clem Mosman 59-71; Org Sec Bd of Educn Syd 71-74; R of Springwood Dio Syd from 74; Can of St John's Prov Cathl Parramatta from 77. *14 Charles Street, Springwood, NSW, Australia 2777.* (047-51 1065)

BOMFORD, Rodney William George. b 43. BNC Ox BA 64, Dipl Th 66, MA 68. Union Th Sem NY STM 69. Coll of Resurr Mirfield 67. **d** 69 **p** 70 S'wark. C of St Paul w St Mark Deptford 69-77; V of Camberwell Dio S'wark from 77. *St Giles's Vicarage, Benhill Road, SE5.* (01-703 4504)

BOMYER, Julian Richard. b 55. AKC 78. Sarum Wells Th Coll 78. **d** 79 McKie for Cov **p** 80 Cov. C of St Andr Rugby Dio Cov from 79. *27 Arnold Street, Rugby, Warws, CV21 3HD.*

BON, Lui Dalton. b 38. St Barn Coll Adel 79. **d** 81 Carp. C of Cathl Ch of Thursday I Dio Carp from 81. *Box 79, Thursday Island, Australia 4875.*

BONABY, Ven Murillo Abraham. Codr Coll Barb 57. **d** 60 Barb **p** 61 Nass. P-in-c of St Sav Cat I Nass 61-63; C of Shelf 63-65; Popular 65-66; St Agnes Nass 66-68; St Barn Nass 68; P-in-c of Ch K Nass 69-73; R 73-75; Archd of S Bahamas from 75. *PO Box N-9721, Nassau, Bahamas, WI.*

BONATHAN, Canon John Bertram. Trin Coll Tor LTh 27. **d** 26 **p** 27 Tor. C of St Mich AA Tor 26-29; St Jo Evang Montr 29-35; R of St Mark Longueiul 35-70; Hon Can of Montr 65-70; Can (Emer) from 71. *460 Pine Avenue, St Lambert, PQ, Canada.* (514-672 4573)

BOND, Preb Alan Gilman. b 09. Univ of Birm BSc 31. Lich Th Coll 33. **d** 35 **p** 36 Lich. C of Ch Ch Fenton 35-38; Stoke-on-Trent 38-43; PC of St Werburgh Burslem 43-50; V of St Paul Newc L 50-56; Chap Univ Coll of N Staffs 53-56; V of Willenhall 56-65; Surr from 43; R of Hanley w Hope 65-74; RD of N Stoke 65-75; Preb of Lich Cathl 67-75; Preb (Emer) from 75. *35 Queen's Park South Drive, Bournemouth, Dorset, BH8 9BH.*

BOND, Allan. McGill Univ BA 53, BD 57. Trin Coll Tor STB 59. Montr Dioc Th Coll. **d** 58 **p** 59 Montr. C of St Matt Hampstead 58-60; on leave 60-73; R of Quyon 74-77; Ingleside 77-81. *Box 239, Ingleside, Ont, Canada.* (613-537 2184)

BOND, Arthur Edward (Stephen). b 44. St Steph Ho Ox 66. **d** and **p** St John's 69. C of Clydesdale Transkei 69-70; St Alphage Hendon 70-73; OGS 70-73; OSP from 74; Asst Sec ACS from 75. *264a Washwood Heath Road, Birmingham, B8 2XS.* (021-328 0749)

✠ **BOND, Right Rev Charles Derek.** b 27. K Coll Lon and Warm AKC (2nd cl) 51. **d** 52 **p** 53 Lon. C of Friern Barnet 52-56; Midl Area Sec SCM in Schs and Publ Pr Dio Birm 56-58; V of Harringay 58-62; Harrow Weald 62-71; M Gen Syn Lon 70-71; Archd of Colchester 72-76; C-in-c of Pebmarsh 72-73; M Gen Syn Chelmsf 75-76; Cons Ld Bp Suffr of Bradwell in Chelmsf Cathl 29 Sept 76 by Abp of Cant; Bp of Chelmsf; Bps Suffr of Barking and Colchester; and Bps Chadwick and Welch. *188 New London Road, Chelmsford, Essex, CM2 0AR.* (Chelmsf 84235)

BOND, Charles Robert. b 25. Trin Coll Bris 78. **d** 80 **p** 81 Man. C of Woodhouse Park Dio Man from 80. *76 Portway, Woodhouse Park, Manchester, M22 6SH.*

BOND, Clifford Frank. b 24. St Aid Coll 60. **d** 62 **p** 63 Blackb. C of Kirkham 62-64; Wallingford 64-69; Missr of St Barn Conv Distr Reading 69-73; R of St Barn Reading Dio Ox from 73. *St Barnabas Rectory, 14 Elm Road, Reading, Berks.* (Reading 81718)

BOND, David. b 36. Oak Hill Coll 72. **d** 74 **p** 75 Chelmsf. C of Leyton 74-78; Slough 78-80; V of St Jas Ap Selby Dio York from 80; P-in-c of Wistow Dio York from 80. *St James's Vicarage, Selby, Yorks.* (Selby 2861)

BOND, David Matthew. b 38. Univ of Leic BA (2nd cl Hist) 59. Sarum Th Coll 59. **d** 61 **p** 62 Leic. C of St Anne Leic 61-64; E Engl Sec SCM from 64; Hon C of St Pet Mancroft

Nor 64-67; Perm to Offic Dio Linc 67-74; Hon C of All SS Stamford Dio Linc from 74; Lect Pet Tech Coll from 67. *2 The Courtyard, Cotterstock, Peterborough, PE8 5HD.*

BOND, Douglas Gregory. b 39. **d** 76 **p** 77 Edin (APM). C of St Paul w St Geo City and Dio Edin from 76. *5 Steel's Place, Edinburgh, EH10 4QR.* (031-447 5801)

BOND, Elton Howard. b 31. McGill Univ Montr BA (1st cl Mod Lang) 54. Harvard Univ MA 55. BA (2nd cl German) (Lon) 57, BD (Lon) 60. Univ of Birm Dipl Th 61, PhD 64. Univ of Bris MEducn 75. Qu Coll Birm 60. **d** 62 **p** 63 Lich. C of Walsall 62-65; Chap R Wolverhampton Sch 65-68; Lect in Div Weymouth Coll of Educn 68-71; Sen Lect 71-74; L to Offic Dio Sarum 68-74; Dio Newc T 74-78; Prin Lect in Relig Stud Northumb Coll of Educn 74-78; Chap Blue Coat Comprehensive Sch Walsall 78-81. *Address temp unknown.*

BOND, Gordon. b 44. Chich Th Coll 68. **d** 71 Huntingdon for Ely **p** 72 Ely. C of St Aug Wisbech 71-74; Wembley Pk 74-77; St Mich Camberley 77-80; Team V of Haywards Heath Dio Chich from 80. *Ascension Vicarage, Sandy Vale, Haywards Heath, W. Sussex, RH16 4JH.* (H Heath 50173)

BOND, Jack Cyril. b 05. St Andr Coll Whittlesford 42. **d** 43 **p** 45 Wakef. C of Kirkburton 43-47; Kirkheaton 47-49; V of Mold Green 49-53; Coverham w Horsehouse 53-57; Burton-in-Lonsdale 57-58; PC of Bolton w Redmire 58-68; V 68-70; Perm to Offic Dios Wakef and Sheff 70-76; Dio York from 77. *7 Burn Hall Crescent, Burn, Selby, YO8 8LT.* (Burn 686)

BOND, John Albert. b 33. St Cath Coll Ox BA (2nd cl Th) 61, MA 65, MPhil 77. Seabury-Western Th Sem BD 62. LRAM 55. GGSM 56. Wycl Hall Ox. **d** 62 **p** 63 Chelmsf. C of St Mary Virg Cathl Chelmsf 62-63; Succr 63-64; Prec 64-66; Lect in Div St Osyth Coll Clacton 66-69; Sen Lect in Relig Stud Ch Ch Coll Cant and L to Offic Dio Cant from 69; Hon Min Can Cant Cathl from 70; Abp's Adv for Ch Schs from 71. *St Lawrence Priory, Old Dover Road, Canterbury, Kent.*

BOND, John Frederick Augustus. b 45. Open Univ BA 75. Trin Coll Dub 64. **d** 67 **p** 69 Connor. C of St Paul Lisburn 67-70; C of Finaghy 70-77; Dom Chap to Bp of Connor 71-77; R of Ballynure w Ballyeaston Dio Connor from 77. *Rectory, Ballynure, Ballyclare, Co Antrim, BT39 9UF, N Ireland.* (Ballyclare 22350)

BOND, Leslie George. **d** 61 **p** 62 Melb. C of Mentone 61-62; St Geo Malvern 62-64; V of Inverleigh 64-68; I of Sunshine 68-74; P-in-c of N Brighton Dio Melb from 74. *394 Bay Street, Brighton, Vic, Australia 3186.* (03-596 4270)

BOND, Lindsay Francis. **d** and **p** 79 N Queensld. C of Mt Isa Min Centre Dio N Queensld from 79. *PO Box 1849, Mount Isa, Qld, Australia 4825.*

BOND, Norman. b 23. Wycl Hall Ox. **d** 70 **p** 71 Warrington for Liv. C of St Ann, Warrington 70-73; C-in-c 73-77; St Pet Warrington 73-77; V of St Cath Wigan Dio Liv from 77. *St Catherine's Vicarage, Wigan, Lancs, WN1 3JW.* (Wigan 42536)

BOND, Paul Maxwell. b 36. TD 70. AIB 58. b 36. Oak Hill Coll 76. **d** 79 **p** 80 Guildf. C of Wisley w Pyrford Dio Guildf from 79. *Fosters, Wood End Close, Pyrford, Woking, Surrey.*

BOND, Richard Jack. Lich Th Coll 38. **d** 41 **p** 42 Bris. C of Filton 41-44; Chippenham 44-46; Chap and Asst Master St Mich Coll Bexley and Lon Choir Sch 46-47; Chap RAF 47-50; C of St Mary Redcliffe 50-53; St Andr Newc T 64-66; C-in-c of St Pet Conv Distr Balkwell Tynemouth 66-68; V 68-78; R of Allendale (w Whitfield from 79) Dio Newc T from 78. *Allendale Rectory, Hexham, Northumb.* (Allendale 336)

BOND, Ven Thomas James. b 18. TCD BA 41, MA 68, Div Test 41. **d** 42 **p** 43 Kilm. C of Annagh (Belturbet) 42-44; Sligo 44-47; I of Kilgobbin 47-49; Bourney w Dunkerrin 49-52; Kilkeevin w Kiltullagh 52-55; Surr from 54; I of Bailieborough 55-60; Templemichael Longford Dio Ard from 60; Preb of Elph Cathl from 67; Archd of Elph and Ard from 78. *Rectory, Battery Road, Longford, Irish Republic.* (Longford 6442)

BONE, Donald Robert Ernest. Univ of W Ont BA 60. Hur Coll LTh 63, BTh 64. **d** 63 Bp Snell for Tor **p** 64 Tor. C of St Mary Richmond Hill Tor 63-66; R of Roche's Point 67-70; St Paul L'Amoureux Tor 70-81; Aurora Dio Tor from 81. *Box 42, Aurora, Ont, Canada.*

BONE, Ven John Frank Ewan. b 30. St Pet Coll Ox BA (2nd cl Pol Phil and Econ) 54, MA 59. Ely Th Coll 54. **d** 56 **p** 57 Lon. C of St Gabr Westmr 56-60; Henley-on-Thames 60-63; V of Datchet 63-76; RD of Burnham 74-77; R of St Mary Upton w Chalvey, Slough 76-78; Archd of Buckingham from 78. *60 Wendover Road, Aylesbury, Bucks, HP21 7LW.* (Aylesbury 23269)

BONE, Noel Francis. Clifton Th Coll. **d** 59 **p** 60 Lon. TD 64. C of St Cuthb Hampstead 59-61; CF (TA) 60-67; V of Ryarsh 61-69; Supt Chap Br Sailors' S 69-71; L to Offic Dio Lon 69-71; C of Boxmoor 71-72; R of Aston w Benington Dio St Alb from 72. *Rectory, Benington, Stevenage, Herts.* (Benington 409)

BONE, Trevor Hubert. b 25. Ch Ch Ox BA (3rd cl Mod Lang) 49, MA 50. Qu Coll Birm. **d** 51 **p** 52 Ripon. C of St Pet Harrogate 51-54; Leeds 55-61; V of Hebden Bridge 61-69; St Edw Barnsley Dio Wakef from 69. *St Edward's Vicarage, Racecommon Road, Barnsley, Yorks, S70 6JY.* (Barnsley 203919)

BONHAM, Frederick Thomas. b 37. St Deiniol's Libr Hawarden 70. **d** 72 **p** 73 Willesden for Lon. C of St Edm Northwood Hills Pinner 72-75; Clewer Dio Ox from 75. *St Agnes Presbytery, St Leonard's Road, Windsor, Berks.* (Windsor 61508)

BONIFACE, Aram. **d** 41 **p** 43 Centr Tang. P Dio Centr Tang. *Kibondo, Kigoma, Tanzania.*

BONIFACE, Lionel Ernest George. b 36. BD (Lon) 64. ALCD 63. **d** 64 **p** 65 Southw. C of Attenborough w Bramcote and Chilwell 64-69; Farndon 69-71; Thorpe-by-Newark 69-71; P-in-c of St Aug, Mansfield 71-77; V of Oughtibridge Dio Sheff from 77. *Oughtibridge Vicarage, Sheffield, S30 3FU.* (Oughtibridge 2317)

BONIS, Robert Raynes. Wycl Coll Tor LTh 32. Univ of Tor BA 28. **d** 31 Tor **p** 32 Niag for Tor. C of Minden 31-38; I of Scarborough Tor 38-48; West Hill 48-58; C of St Timothy Agincourt City and Dio Tor from 58. *151 Colonel Danforth Trail, RR 1, West Hill, Ont., Canada.*

BONIWELL, Timothy Richard. b 51. AKC 73. St Aug Coll Cant 74. **d** 75 **p** 76 Chelmsf. C of St Mich AA Walthamstow 75-78; Wigmore Abbey Dio Heref from 78. *St Mary's House, Tipton Lane, Leintwardine, Craven Arms, Salop, SY7 0LN.* (Leintwardine 607)

BONNARD, Canon John Maurice. Hur Coll BTh 56. **d** 56 **p** 57 Keew. I of Big Beaver Ho 56-64; Norway Ho 64-68; Can of St Alb Pro-Cathl Kenora 64-68; Hon Can from 68; Prin of La Tuque Res Sch 69-78. *Institution de Montmirail, Montmirail 2075, Switzerland.*

BONNE, Jeremiah Manyie. b 21. Im Coll Ibad 72. **d** 72 Nig Delta. d Dio Nig Delta. *Holy Trinity Church, Nchia Eleme, via Port Harcourt, Nigeria.*

BONNER, David Robert. b 28. FCIS 72. SOC 74. **d** 77 Kens for Lon **p** 78 Lon. C of All SS Hampton Dio Lon from 77. *17 St James's Road, Hampton Hill, Middx, TW12 1DH.*

BONNER, Frederick Charles. b 10. Worc Ordin Coll 63. **d** 65 **p** 66 Ox. C of Hungerford w Denford 65-69; R of Farnborough w W Ilsley 69-75; C-in-c of E Ilsley 70-74. *Beechwood, Leeds Road, Collingham, Wetherby, W Yorks, LS22 5AA.* (Collbridge 72825)

BONNER, George Llewelyn. b 47. Univ of WI BA (Th) 77. Codr Coll Barb 73. **d** 77 Barb. C of St Mary City and Dio Bel from 77. *c/o Diocesan Office, PO Box 535, Belize City, Belize.*

BONNER, James Maxwell Campbell. Univ of Syd BSc 48, BD (Lon) 59. Oak Hill Th Coll. **d** 60 **p** 61 Chelmsf. C of Walthamstow 60-63; Morden 63-65; L to Offic Dio Syd 66-67; C of Manly 67; C-in-c of St Nich Provisional Distr Croydon Pk Dio Syd from 67. *13 Waratah Street, Croydon Park, NSW, Australia 2133.* (74-9832)

BONSALL, Charles Henry Brash. b 42. Univ of Ex BA (2nd cl Th) 66. Ridley Hall Cam 66. **d** 68 **p** 69 Glouc. C of Cheltm 68-72; Chap at Khartoum Dio Sudan 72-76; Dio Omdurman 76-78; Perm to Offic Dio Nor from 78. *85 Grove Road, Norwich, NR1 3RT.*

BONSER, Canon David. b 34. Univ of Man MA (Th) 75. K Coll Lon and Warm AKC 61. **d** 62 **p** 63 Wakef. C of Heckmondwike 62-65; St Geo Sheff 65-68; R of Chorlton-cum-Hardy Dio Man from 68; Hon Can of Man Cathl from 80; M Gen Syn from 81; RD of Hulme from 81. *Rectory, 6 Edge Lane, Chorlton-cum-Hardy, Manchester M21 1JF.* (061-881 3063)

BONSEY, Hugh Lowry. b 15. Bps' Coll Cheshunt 39. **d** 40 **p** 41 Lon. C of St Jo Bapt Tottenham 40-42; All SS Friern Barnet 42-44; Brixham w Churston Ferrers 44-46; PC of L Wymondley 46-52; V of Breage w Germoe 52-59; Cutcombe w Luxborough 59-69; R of Lydeard St Lawr w Combe Florey and Tolland 69-78; C-in-c of Luccombe 78-80; Perm to Offic Dio Ex from 81. *11 Barton Orchard, Tipton St John, Sidmouth, Devon.*

BONSEY, Hugh Richmond Lowry. b 49. Sarum Wells Th Coll 74. **d** 76 **p** 77 Bris. C of St Mary Redcliffe w Temple Bris and St Jo Bapt Bedminster Dio Bris from 76. *1c Colston Parade, Redcliffe, Bristol, BS1 6RA.*

BONSEY, Ven Thory Richmond. b 18. St Chad's Coll Dur 37. Cudd Coll 46. **d** 47 **p** 48 Sarum. C of St Martin Sarum 47-50; Kingsthorpe (in c of St David) 50-53; V of Ashwick w Oakhill 53-57; Desborough 57-61; R of Teigh w Whissendine 61-67; Ecton 67-73; Warden of Ecton Ho 67-73; Can (Non-res) of Pet 73-77; V of Ketton 73-77; RD of Barnack 76-77; R of Tarcutta 77-81; Cobargo Dio C & Goulb from 81; Archd

Dio C & Goulb from 81. *Box 78, Bermagui South, NSW, Australia 2547.*

BONTOFT de St-QUENTIN (formerly BONTOFT), Reginald Arthur. b 01. Ch Coll Cam Tancred Stud 19, 3rd cl Cl Trip pt i 21, BA (3rd cl Th Trip pt i) 22, MA 26. Wycl Hall Ox 22. **d** 24 **p** 25 Southw. C of St Anne Worksop 24-27; PC of Scofton w Osberton 27-30; Chap (Eccles Est) Peshawar and Quetta 30-32; Lah Cathl 32-34; Dagshai 34; Karachi 34-35; Nyanza Province E Afr 35; Org Sec SPCK NW Distr 36-38; R of Offord d'Arcy w Offord Cluny 38-45; CF (TA - R of O) from 37; TD 50; PC of Kingston Lacy 48-57; V of Shapwick 48-57; Cholsey 57-68. *10 The Crescent, Frinton-on-Sea, Essex.*

BOOCOCK, John Walter. b 31. Wells Th Coll 63. **d** 65 **p** 66 York. C of Guisborough 65-67; Bottesford w Ashby 67-73; Team V 73-74; V of Riddlesden Dio Bradf from 74. *St Mary's Vicarage, Keighley, W Yorks, BD20 5PA.* (Keighley 603419)

BOOKER, Gerald Dennis. b 30. St Pet Coll Ox BA 52, MA 56. Oak Hill Th Coll 80. **d** 81 St Alb. Hon C of All SS Hertford Dio St Alb from 81. *5 The Chestnuts, Hertford, Herts, SG13 8AQ.*

BOOKER, Michael Charles. b 36. LLCM 57. ARCO 58. LTh (1st cl) 63. **d** 63 **p** 64 St Alb. C of Royston 63-66; Mildenhall 66-68; Min Can (Sacr from 68, Prec from 70) of St Jas Cathl Bury St Edm Dio St E from 68. *152 Southgate Street, Bury St Edmunds, Suff.* (Bury St Edmunds 5868)

BOOKLESS, John Guy. b 19. Late Scho of Clare Coll Cam 1st cl Cl Trip pt i 39, pt ii 40 BA, (1st cl Th Trip pt i) 48, MA 46. Serampore Univ MTh 72. Ridley Hall, Cam 47. **d** 49 **p** 50 Liv. C of Ch Ch Toxteth Pk 49-50; Em Fazackerley 50-51; Tutor Ridley Hall Cam 51-52; Miss Dio Bhag 53-60; Tutor Bp's Coll Calc 61-65; Lect United Th Coll Bangalore 66-72; C of St Mich St Alb 73-76; Team V of Harlow New Town 76-79; V of Willoughby-on-the-Wolds w Wysall Dio Southw from 79; P-in-c of Widmerpool Dio Southw from 79. *Vicarage, Keyworth Road, Wysall, Nottingham,* (Wymeswold 880269)

BOOL, Wilfrid Arthur. St Jo Coll Auckld LTh 32. **d** 32 Wai **p** 33 Wel. C of Hawera 32-34; P-in-c of Ngaruawahia 34-35; V 35-37; C of Wanganui 37-38; Addington 38-39; Kens w Otipua 40-43; CF (NZ) 43-45; C of Sydenham Ch Ch 45-48; V of Otaio w Bluecliffs 48-55; Akaroa 55-61; Woodend 61-70; Glenmark 70-72; Dom Chap to Bp of Ch Ch 72-75; Perm to Offic Dio Nel from 75. *145 South Bay Parade, Kaikoura, NZ.*

BOOLE, Charles Anthony Macdonald. b 15. **d** 64 **p** 65 Ott. C of Smiths Falls 64-65; R of Mattawa 66-67; C of Earley 68-69; R of Wallingford 69-74; V of Cranbourne 74-81. *4 The Cloister, Ewelme, Oxford.*

BOOLE, Charles Julius. b 43. Carleton Univ Ott BA 67. Univ of Leeds Dipl Th 70. **d** 70 Ox for Ott **p** 70 Ott. C of St Jo Evang Ott 70; R of Campbell's Bay 71-75; St Chris City and Dio Ott from 75. *29 Mowat Street, Ottawa, Ont., Canada.* (1-613-741-1418)

BOOLE, Robert Hugh Philip. b 12. Linc Th Coll 46. **d** 47 **p** 48 Linc. C of Gt Grimsby (in c of St Barn from 50) 47-53; CF (TA) 50-55; PC of All SS Gt Grimsby 53-66; V of Metheringham 66-77. *5 Lon y Gaer, Deganwy, Conwy, Gwyn, LL31 9RG.* (Deganwy 81856)

BOOTES, Michael Charles Edward. b 35. ACP 70. M OGS 68. Sarum Th Coll 58. **d** 61 **p** 62 Lon. C of Winchmore Hill 61-64; Chap and Hd Master Rosenberg Coll St Gallen 64-65; Chap Aiglon Coll and Villars Switzerland 65-67; Hd Master Choir Sch and C of All SS Margaret Street Marylebone 67-68; Asst Master Geo Green's Sch Poplar 68-69; Chap Kingsley St Mich Sch and St Marg Conv E Grinstead 69-75; V of Brandon 75-78; Chap Shoreham Gr Sch 78-79; C of Clayton w Keymer (in c of St Francis) Dio Chich from 79. *11 The Spinney, Hassocks, W sussex, BN6 8EJ.* (Hassocks 2399)

BOOTH, Alexander John. b 23. Ripon Hall Ox. **d** 66 **p** 67 Man. C of Walkden 66-69; V of St Andr, Oldham 69-75; Cadishead Dio Man from 75; Cler Warden CEMS Dio Man from 80. *St Mary's Vicarage, Penry Avenue, Cadishead, Manchester, M30 5AF.* (061-775 2171)

BOOTH, Brian. b 39. SOC 77. **d** 80 **p** 81 S'wark. C of Catford Dio S'wark from 80. *35 Bromley Road, Catford, SE6 2TS.*

BOOTH, Cecil. b 1896. Trin Hall Cam BA (3rd cl Hist Trip pt ii) 21, MA 26. Westcott Ho 22. **d** 23 **p** 24 Dur. C of Houghton-le-Spring 23-25; C-in-c of Cleadon Pk Conv Distr 25-29; V of H Trin S Shields 29-31; Hall Green 31-38; R of Farlington 38-65; V of Gayton 65-73; L to Offic Dio Pet from 73. *9 Benefield Road, Oundle, Peterborough.* (Oundle 3660)

BOOTH, David. b 44. Coll of Resurr Mirfield 72. **d** 74 **p** 75 Ripon. C of St Phil Osmondthorpe Leeds 74-77; Armley 77-79; V of St Wilfrid Leeds Dio Ripon from 79. *St Wilfrid's Vicarage, Chatsworth Road, Leeds, LS8 3RS.* (Leeds 497724)

BOOTH, Canon David Herbert. b 07. MBE 44. Pemb Coll Cam BA 31, MA 36. Ely Th Coll 31. **d** 32 **p** 33 Lon. C of All SS Hampton 32-34; Chap of Tonbridge Sch 35-40; Chap RNVR 40-45; R of Stepney 45-53; Select Pr Univ of Cam 47; Chap Lon Hosp 51-53; V of Brighton 53-59; Can and Preb of Waltham in Chich Cathl 53-59; Seq of St Mary Magd Brighton and Surr 53-59; RD of Brighton 53-59; Chap to HM the Queen from 57; Archd of Lewes 59-72; Hd Master Shoreham Gr Sch 72-77; Can & Preb of Chich Cathl 72-77; Can (Emer) from 77. *Hurst Mill Cottage, Hothfield, Ashford, Kent.* (Puckley 549)

BOOTH, Derek. K Coll Lon and Warm AKC 61. **d** 62 **p** 63 Ches. C of Woodchurch 62-65; Penrith 65-67: St Paul S Tranmere 67-69; Wilmslow 69-73; V of Micklehurst Dio Ches from 73. *Vicarage, Church Lane, Mossley, Ashton-under-Lyne.* (Mossley 2393)

BOOTH, George Kenneth. Late Scho of Pemb Coll Ox BA 37, MA 40. Wells Th Coll 37. **d** 39 Portsm **p** 50 Edin. C of St Sav Portsea 39-40; St Mary Portchester 40-41; Asst Master Epsom Coll 41-46; Felsted Sch Essex 46; Ho Master Fettes Coll Edin 47-59; C of St Ninian Edin 50-55; Chap and Prin Lect St Luke's Coll Ex 59-79; L to Offic Dio Ex 59-79. *Furcroft, Rock, Wadebridge, Cornwall.*

BOOTH, Harold Eldon. St Jo Coll Morpeth 75. **d** and **p** 77 River. C of Corowa 77-79; Moama Dio River from 79. *Rectory, Moama, NSW, Australia 2739.* (82 1014)

BOOTH, Harry James. Univ of Rang BSc 35. U Th Sem New York 55. **d** 62 **p** 63 Rang. Prin St John's Dioc Sch Rang 62-64; C of Northam 64-66; Perm to Offic Dio Perth from 67; Asst Chap Ch Ch Gr Sch Perth 71-76. *Unit 42, 11 Freedman Road, Mount Lawley, W Australia 6050.*

BOOTH, Ven Herbert Charles Spencer. St Francis Coll Brisb ACT ThL 52. **d** 53 **p** 54 Brisb. C of Gympie 53-54; M Bush Bro of St Paul 54-60; R of Cleveland 60-66; Charleville 66-69; Roma 69-75; Warwick Dio Brisb from 75; Archd of The Downs from 76. *Rectory, Albion Street, Warwick, Queensland, Australia 4370.* (Warwick 61-1043)

BOOTH, Ven Ian Edgar Arthur. Moore Th Coll Syd ACT ThL 50. **d** 51 **p** 52 Syd. C of Wollongong 51-52; C-in-c of The Oaks w Burragorang 52-53; C of Ceduna 53-55; P-in-c of Orroroo 55-59; Peterborough S Austr 59-62; R of Oatlands 62-65; St Paul Launceston 65-68; Vic Sec Bush Ch Aid S 68-71; R of Devonport 71-74; St Jo Launceston 74-81; Evandale Dio Tas from 81; Can of Tas from 77; Archd of Launceston from 79. *Rectory, Evandale, Tasmania 7212.* (003 91 8112)

BOOTH, James Roger. b 46. Keble Coll Ox BA (LitHum) 71, MA 74, BA (Th) 77. Wycl Hall Ox 75. **d** 78 **p** 79 York. C of St Mary Bridlington Dio York from 78. *25 St Oswald Road, Bridlington, N Humb, YO16 5SD.* (0262 78138)

BOOTH, John Bowmar. St Francis Th Coll Brisb ACT ThL (2nd cl) 61. **d** and **p** 64 Brisb. C of St Jas Toowomba 64-65; Dalby 65-68; R of Wau New Guinea 68-71; Papua 71-72; W Cairns 72-74; Perm to Offic Dio Newc from 74. *9 Nickson Street, Bar Reach, Newcastle, NSW, Australia 2300.*

BOOTH, Jon Alfred. b 42. Univ of Nottm BA 64. Univ of Lon MPhil 72. Coll of the Resurr Mirfield 78. **d** 80 **p** 81 Wakef. C of Elland Dio Wakef from 80. *15 Ravenstone Drive, Greetland, Halifax, W Yorks.*

BOOTH, Joseph Arthur Paul. b 31. Dipl Th (Lon) 59. St Aid Coll. **d** 60 **p** 61 Man. C of Blackley 60-63; Wickford 63-65; V of St Geo Thundersley 65-72; R of Gorton 72-80; Bradwell-Juxta-Mare Dio Chelmsf from 80; St Lawr Dio Chelmsf from 80. *Rectory, East End Road, Bradwell-on-Sea, Essex, CM0 7PX.* (Maldon 76203)

BOOTH, Kenneth Neville. Univ of Otago BA 62, MA 63, BD 66, MTh 69. Univ of St Andr PhD 74. **d** 65 **p** 66 Dun. C of St Paul's Cathl Dun 65-69; Perm to Offic Dio St Andr, Dunk and Dunbl 70-71; Lect in Ch Hist St Jo Th Coll Auckld from 72; Hon C of Glen Innes 72; Tamaki 73-80; Perm to Offic Dio Ox 80-81; Warden and Chap Selwyn Coll and Exam Chap to Bp of Dun from 81. *560 Castle Street, Dunedin, NZ.* (773-326)

BOOTH, Leonard Francis. b 09. St Andr Coll Whittlesford. **d** 43 Shrewsbury for Lich **p** 44 Lich. C of Wem 43-45; R of Swynnerton 45-55; CF 55-68; R of W Grinstead w Partridge Green 68-74; Chap Eastbourne Coll 74-79. *4 Kings Houses, High Street, Pevensey, E Sussex.* (Eastbourne 762435)

BOOTH, Leonard William. b 46. AKC & BD 70. St Aug Coll Cant. **d** 71 Dur. C of St Mary Cockerton 71-73; St Barn Hove 73-76; Team V of the Resurr Brighton 76-78; C of St Mary Virg E Grinstead 78-81; in Amer Ch. *c/o 5306 Arbor Road, Long Beach, CA 90808, USA.*

BOOTH, Leonard Wright. b 05. Qu Coll Birm MBE (Mil) and Men in Disp 45. **d** 49 **p** 50 Wakef. C of Hemsworth 49-52;

C-in-c of Wrangbrook Conv Distr 52-55; CF 55-59; R of Gt w L Whelnetham 59-61; Chap Miss to Seamen Antwerp 61-68; V of St Bede Nelson-in-Marsden 68-70. *9 Hill Place, Oxenholme, Kendal, Cumb, LA9 7HB.* (Kendal 26794)

BOOTH, Paul Harris. b 49. St Jo Coll Nottm LTh 79. **d** 79 **p** 80 Bradf. C of Thorpe Edge Dio Bradf from 79. *6 Rowantree Drive, Thorpe Edge, Bradford, BD10 8ES.* (0274 611791)

BOOTH, Percy Elliott. b 26. Lich Th Coll 55. **d** 58 **p** 59 Lich. C of St Gabr Walsall 58-61; Whitchurch Salop 61-64; V of St Martin 64-66; Silverdale Staffs Dio Lich from 66. *21 Pepper Street, Silverdale, Newcastle, Staffs ST5 6QJ.* (Newcastle 624293)

BOOTH, Raymond Lister. b 15. Univ of Leeds BA (2nd cl German) 37, MA (Engl) 43. Lich Th Coll 37. **d** 39 **p** 40 Southw. C of Newark-on-Trent 39-42; St Aug Sheff 42-46; Holmfirth (in c of Thongsbridge) 46-48; V of St John Bradshaw Halifax 48-53; St Jo Bapt Dawgreen Dewsbury 53-63; Teacher 64-68; P-in-c of St Phil Whitwood 69-74; All SS Whitwood 74-81. *Address temp unknown.*

BOOTH, Stephen Paul. b 43. Amherst Coll USA BA 65. Episc Th Sem of the SW USA MDiv 71. **d** 71 Texas for W Mass and **p** Bp Garnsworthy for Tor. C of Caledon East 71-73; R 73-77; P-in-c of Ch of Ap Tor 77-79; C of St Clem Eglinton Tor 79-81; Chap Hart Ho Tor from 81. *7 Hart House, Circle, Toronto, M5S 1A1, Ont, Canada.*

BOOTH, Terrence Richard. St Jo Coll Morpeth 66. **d** 69 **p** 70 River. C of Corowa 69-71; Broken Hill 71-74; P-in-c of Urana-Jerilderie 74-79. *c/o PO Box 6, Urana, NSW, Australia 2645.*

BOOTH, Wallace. b 14. **d** 62 **p** 63 Cant. C of St Luke Woodside Croydon 62-66; V of Woodnesborough 66-80; C-in-c of Staple 76-80. *c/o Woodnesborough Vicarage, Sandwich, Kent, CT13 0HF.* (Sandwich 3056)

BOOTH, William James. b 39. TCD BA 60, Div Test 62, MA 75. **d** 62 **p** 63 Connor. C of St Luke Belf 62-64; Chap Cranleigh Sch 65-74; Westmr Sch from 74; P-in-Ord to HM the Queen from 76. *14 Barton Street, SW1.* (01-222 3707)

✠ **BOOTH-CLIBBORN, Right Rev Stanley Eric Francis.** b 24. Or Coll Ox BA 51, MA 56. Westcott Ho Cam 50. **d** 52 **p** 53 Sheff. C of Heeley 52-54; Attercliffe w Carbrook Sheff 54-56; L to Offic Dio Momb 56-61; Dio Ft Hall 61-64; Dio Mt Kenya 64-67; C of St Steph Nai 64-67; C-in-c of St Mary-le-Wigford 67-70; St Mark Linc 67-70; V of St Mary Gt w St Mich AA Cam 70-78; Hon Can of Ely from 76; Cons Ld Bp of Man in York Minster 2 Feb 79 by Abp of York; Bps of Dur, Southw, Sheff, Birm, Blackb, Bradf, Carl, Newc T, Chester, S & M, Liv, Lich, Wakef and Ripon; Bps Suffr of Middleton, Jarrow, Stockport, Pontefract, Selby, Knaresborough, Birkenhead, Sherwood, Hulme, Huntingdon, Whitby, Warrington, Doncaster and Hull; and others. *Bishopscourt, Bury New Road, Manchester, M7 0LE.* (061-792 2096)

BOOTHBY, Frank. St D Coll Lamp 56. **d** 58 Liv **p** 59 Warrington for Liv. C of St Andr Maghull 58-61; N Meols 61-64. *17 Ashton Road, Hillside, Southport, Lancs.*

BOOTHMAN, Canon Samuel. b 09. TCD BA 34, Div Test 35, MA 37. **d** and **p** 35 Clogh. C of Enniskillen w Trory 35-37; St Thos and St Mich Win 37-40; CF (EC) 40-46; Men in Disp 45; Hon CF 46; R of Farley-Chamberlayne w Braishfield 46-81; RD of Romsey 71-79; Hon Can of Win 73-81; Can (Emer) from 81; P-in-c of Michelmersh w Timsbury and Eldon 80-81; R of Michelmersh and Timsbury w Farley Chamberlayne and Braishfield 81. *Boldbrook Lodge, Pound Lane, Ampfield, Romsey, Hants SO5 9BP.* (Braishfield 68143)

BOOTHROYD, John Hubert. b 14. St Edm Hall Ox BA 36, MA 43. Wycl Hall Ox 36. **d** 38 **p** 39 Chelmsf. C of St Mich AA Gidea Pk 38-40; Sholing Southn 40-43; St Paul Worthing 43-48; R of Addington 48-53; Trottiscliffe 48-53; Asst Master Furzedown Sch Littlehampton 53-58; Brighton Coll Jun Sch 58-65; Chap 69-79; Perm to Offic Dio Chich from 53. *Fair Havens, Fletching Street, Mayfield, E Sussex, TN20 6TH.* (Mayfield 873080)

BOOTLE, John Stewart Hamilton. Moore Th Coll ACT ThL 49. **d** and **p** 50 Syd. C of St Anne Strathfield 50-53; H Trin Northwood (Col Cl Act) Middx 53-54; C of Crundle NSW 59-62; R of Rylestone 62-66; Chap Shepparton High Sch and L to Offic Dio Wang 66-69; Perm to Offic Dio Syd from 70. *10 Mona Street, Wahroonga, NSW, Australia 2076.*

BOOTS, Claude Donald Roy. b 26. Roch Th Coll 67. **d** 69 **p** 70 B & W. C of Midsomer Norton 69-73; V of Westfield 73-80; P-in-c of Ilton 80; Ile Abbots 80; Hambridge w Earnshill and Ile Brewers 80; R of Ilton w Hambridge, Earnshill, Ile Brewers and Ile Abbots Dio B & W from 80. *Ilton Vicarage, Ilminster, Somt, TA19 9ET.* (Ilminster 2860)

BOOTY, Jack Grattan. **d** 43 **p** 44 Perth. L to Offic Dio Perth 43-44 and from 46; C of Claremont 44-46. *365 Cambridge Street, Wembley, W Australia 6014.* (299 6458)

BOOTY, John Robert. AKC (2nd cl) 31. **d** 31 **p** 32 Chelmsf. C of St Luke Walthamstow 31-33; St Mary Magd Colchester 33-36; Houghton Regis 36-49; V of Colney St Pet 49-79. *18 Larch Avenue, Bricket Wood, St Albans, Herts.* (St Alb 61602)

BORA, Cuthbert Matthew. St Cypr Coll Lindi 74. **d** 74 **p** 75 Masasi. P Dio Masasi. *PO Chinngutwa, Mtwara Region, Tanzania.*

BORAI, Richmond. b 50. **d** 77 **p** 78 Papua. P Dio Papua 77-78; Dio Port Moresby from 78. *Box 191, Daru, Papua New Guinea.*

BORDEN, Matthew Suydam. b 36. Cornell Univ NY BA 58. Nashotah Ho Wisc 66. **d** 75 Tor for Bran **p** 76 Bran. C of St Andr Miss Wabowden 75-79; I of Cupar Dio Qu'App from 79. *Box 417, Cupar, Sask, Canada.*

BOREHAM, Harold Leslie. b 37. SOC. **d** 72 **p** 73 St E. C of Whitton and Thurleston w Akenham 72-77; R of Saxmundham Dio St E from 77. *Rectory, Saxmundham, Suff.* (Saxmundham 2179)

BORERWE, Jonah Gilbert. St John's Sem Lusaka 64. **d** 66 **p** 68 Mashon. P Dio Mashon 66-81; Dio Mutare from 81. *Rectory, Marange, Zimbabwe.*

BORERWE, Canon Noel. St Pet Coll Rosettenville 54. **d** 56 **p** 57 Mashon. P Dio Mashon; Hon Can of Mashon from 76. *Church House, Rugare Township, Lochinvar, Zimbabwe.*

BORISAMBI, Stephen Akintunde. Im Coll Ibad 73. **d** 76 **p** 77 Ondo. P Dio Ondo. *St Mark's Church, Ore, via Ondo, Nigeria.*

BORLAND, Robert Ralph. b 16. Late Scho Trin Coll Dub BA (2nd cl Math Mod) and Brooke Pri 39, Div Test (1st cl) 40, MA 46. **d** 40 **p** 41 Lon. C of St Mary Spring Grove 40-42; Gt Yarmouth (in c of St Paul) 42-45; V of Ch Ch Ramsgate 45-56; Surr from 45; R of Ch Ch Brondesbury 56-60; V of Leiston w Sizewell 60-67; Min Can of Glouc Cathl and Asst Master KS Glouc 67-81. *7 Osborne Lodge, The Park, Cheltenham, Glos.*

BORNE, John Frederick Eric. b 17. Ely Th Coll 52. **d** 54 York **p** 55 Selby for York. C of Thornaby-on-Tees 54-56; C-in-c of St Paul Sculcoates 57-59; CF (TA) 58-67; V of St Mich AA Sutton-in-Holderness Dio York from 59. *751 Marfleet Lane, Hull, Yorks.* (Hull 74509)

BOROKINI, Ven Jacob Kayode. Melville Hall Ibad 49. **d** 54 **p** 55 Lagos. P Dio Lagos 54-59 and 62-76; Dio Ijebu from 76; Dio Ondo-B 59-62; Hon Can of Lagos 74-76; Archd Dio Ijebu from 77; Exam Chap to Bp of Ijebu from 77. *St Matthew's Vicarage, Ijebu-Igbo, Nigeria.* (Ijebu-Igbo 20)

BOROKINI, Joseph Oluwafemi. b 33. Im Coll Ibad 78. **d** 81 Ijebu. d Dio Ijebu. *Emmanuel Church, Isonyin, via Ijebu-Ode, Nigeria.*

BORRETT, Canon Charles Walter. b 16. Em Coll Cam BA 39, MA 43. Ridley Hall Cam 39. **d** 41 **p** 43 St E. C of All SS Newmarket 41-45; St Paul Wolverhampton 45-48; Tettenhall Regis Dio Lich 48-49; V 49-70; RD of Trysull 58-70; Preb of Flixton in Lich Cathl 64-71; Hon Can from 71; Archd of Stoke-on-Trent 71-82; C-in-c of Sandon 76-82; Chap to HM the Queen from 80. *c/o Sandon Vicarage, Stafford, ST18 0DB.* (Sandon 261)

BORRILL, John. b 19. Univ of Lon BD 41. AKC 41. Westcott Ho Cam 41. **d** 42 **p** 43 Lon. C of St Thos Hanwell 42-45; St Pet Ealing 45-48; P-in-c of Gore Curacy Dio Dun 48-49; LDHM at St Aug of Cant Dist Whitton 49-51; Min 51-58; V 58-59; V of St Pancras w St Jas and Ch Ch Dio Lon 59-71; Chap Elizabeth Garrett Anderson Hosp and Nat Temperance Hosp 62-71; London Ho Mecklenburgh Sq 62-63; V of Hendon Dio Lon from 71. *Vicarage, Parson Street, NW4 1QR* (01-203 2884)

BORSBEY, Alan. b 38. Linc Th Coll 71. **d** and **p** 73 Man. C of Bardsley 73-75; All SS Elton Bury 75-78; V of St Paul Bury Dio Man from 78. *St Paul's Vicarage, Parsonage Street, Bury, BL9 6BG.* (061-761 6991)

BORTHWICK, Alexander Heywood. b 36. Open Univ BA 80. Lich Th Coll 57. **d** 60 **p** 61 Glas. C of Ch Ch Glas 60-62; St Paul Landore 62-64; St Thos Swansea 64-65; C of Lodge Guy 65-67; P-in-c of NE La Penitence Guy 67-69; C of Oystermouth Dio Swan B 70-71; USPG Area Sec for Dios Man & Liv 71-76; Dios Blackb & S & M 73-76; LPr Dio Man 71-76; USPG Sch and Children's Work Sec from 76; Publ Pr Dio S'wark from 79. *USPG, 15 Tufton Street, SW1P 3QQ.* (01-222 4222)

BORTHWICK, Richard Graham. St Mich Coll Crafers 58. **d** and **p** 63 Perth. C of Bayswater 63-65; M SSM 65-74; Perm to Offic Dio Perth 73-74; on leave. *c/o St John's College, Cambridge.*

BOSAMATA, Artaban. b 40. Bp Patteson Th Coll Kohimarama 71. **d** 73 Melan **p** 74 Bp Dudley for Melan. P Dio Melan 73-74; Dio Ysabel 75-76; Dio Centr Melan from 76. *Maravovo Training Centre, Guadalcanal, Solomon Islands.*

BOSAMATA, Jimmy. b 46. Bp Patteson Th Coll Kohimarama 71. **d** 73 Melan **p** 74 Bp Dudley for Melan. P Dio Melan 73-75; Dio Ysabel from 76. *Susubona, Hograno, Ysabel, Solomon Islands.*

BOSAMATA, John Pengoni. St Pet Coll Siota 54. **d** 56 **p** 59 Melan. P Dio Melan 56-75; Dio Ysabel 75-76. *Dede, Gela, British Solomon Islands.*

BOSANQUET, Richard Frederick. Moore Th Coll ACT ThL 48. **d** and **p** 49 Syd. C of Marrickville 49-50; R of S Kogarah 51-53; Asst Master C of E Gr Sch N Syd 53-58 and from 65; Hd Master Illawarra Gr Sch Wollongong 58-65; L to Offic Dio Syd from 62. *C of E Grammar School, Blue Street, Sydney, NSW, Australia 2060.* (92-1757)

BOSLEY, Canon Clarence Frank George. b 06. Lon Coll of Div 40. **d** 41 **p** 42 Lon. C of St John Highbury Vale 41-44; V of Ch Ch N Brixton 44-49; St Matt Southborough 49-53; Chap HM Pris Brixton 46-49; R of Rishangles w Thorndon 53-63; Chap Kerrison Approved Sch Thorndon 53-63; RD of S Hartismere 60-63; V of Mildenhall 63-76; Surr 64-76; Hon Can of St E Cathl 75-76; Can (Emer) from 76; Perm to Offic Dios St E and Ely from 76. *The New Bungalow, Bargate Lane, West Row, Bury St Edmunds, Suff.*

BOSLEY, Frederick Thomas. b 06. BA (Lon) 28. **d** 74 Maseno N **p** 75 Bradf. d Dio Maseno N 74; Commiss Maseno N from 74; Hon C of Keighley 75-80; Perm to Offic Dio Bradf from 80. *5 Iron Row, Burley in Wharfedale, LS29 7BZ.*

BOSLEY, Leonard Ernest William. b 1899. New Coll Ox BA 22, MA 27. Egerton Hall. Man. **d** 23 **p** 24 Man. C of Ch Ch Heaton Norris 23-26; St Pet Swinton 26-27; Succr St Mich Cathl Ch Cov 27-29; V of St Nich Radford Cov 29-38; St Jo Bapt Pet 38-70; RD of Pet i 38-52; Surr 40-70; Proc Conv Pet 45-55; Non-Res Can of Pet 45-70; Chap Pet Group of Hosps 50-70; Sub-Chap O of St John of Jer from 61; Perm to Offic Dio Roch from 71. *Coach House, Ferndale Road, Tunbridge Wells, Kent.* (Tunbridge Wells 45387)

BOSMAN, Michael John. St Paul's Coll Grahmstn 55. **d** 57 **p** 58 Johann. C of N Rand 57-63; R of Kempton Pk Dio Johann from 63. *Box 480, Kempton Park, Transvaal, S Africa.* (011-975 5359)

BOSSCHAERT, Anthony John. ACT ThL 69. St Francis Coll Brisb 65. **d** 68 **p** 69 Brisb. C of Maryborough 68-72; Roath 72-73; St Phil & St Jas Leckhampton w St Jas Cheltm 73-76; R of Skipton, Vic 76-80; C of St Steph w St Jo Westmr Dio Lon from 80. *Flat A, Napier Hall, Hide Place, SW1P 4NJ.* (01-821 6656)

BOSSER, Allan William. ACT ThL 49. **d** 50 **p** 51 Bal. V of Koroit 50-55; Buninyong 55-59; C of St Jas Syd 59-63; R of Batlow 63-67; Braidwood 67-73; L to Offic Dio C & Goulb 73-76; Perm to Offic Dio Syd from 76. *32 Rose Avenue, Wheeler Heights, NSW, Australia 2098.* (98-1300)

BOSTOCK, Canon Charles Howard. b 08. Selw Coll Cam BA 30, MA 34. Westcott Ho Cam 32. **d** 34 **p** 35 S'wark. C of St Paul Newington Surrey 34-38; Res Chap K Coll Hosp and C of St Jo Div Kennington 38-42; V of St Paul Newington 42-47; Surr 45-47 and 48-74; Commiss Masasi 45-52; V of Lymington 47-74; Commiss SW Tang 52-62; RD of Lyndhurst 69-74; Hon Can of Win 71-74; Can (Emer) from 74. *6 South View Road, Winchester, Hants, SO22 4HD.*

BOSTOCK, Ernest. b 10. St Aid Coll 47. **d** 49 **p** 50 Man. C of Horwich 49-51; Westhoughton 51-53; V of Kearsley Moor 53-65; Middlesmoor w Ramsgill 65-76. *9 Lyndon Close, Tottington, Nr Bury, Lancs.*

BOSTOCK, Canon Geoffrey Kentigern. b 30. Sarum Th Coll 66. **d** 68 **p** 69 Lich. C of St Chad Shrewsbury 68-72; Team V of Hanley 72-74; P-in-c of St Jo Evang Wednesbury 74-79; V of St Aug Holly Hall Dudley 79-80; St Cecilia Parson Cross City and Dio Sheff from 80; Hon Can of St Mary Cathl Banjul from 81. *St Cecilia's Priory, Chaucer Close, Sheffield, S5 9QE.* (Sheff 321084)

BOSTOCK, Canon Peter Geoffrey. b 11. Qu Coll Ox BA 33, MA 37. Wycl Hall Ox 33. **d** 35 Leic for Lon for Col Bp **p** 37 Momb. CMS Miss Dio Momb 35-58; Kaloleni 35-37; Wusi 37-44; Sub-Dean Momb Cathl 46-48; Hon Can 52-59; Can (Emer) from 59; RD of Coast 46-48; Prin St Paul's Dioc Div Sch Limuru 49-50; Sec Afr Coun 50-53; Exam Chap to Bp of Momb 50-59; Archd and VG Dio Momb 55-59; Archd of Doncaster 59-67; V of Melton-on-the-Hill 59-67; Exam Chap to Bp of Sheff 62-67; Asst Sec Miss and Ecumen Coun of Ch Assembly 67-70; Dep Sec Bd Miss and Unity Gen Syn 71-73; Clergy Appts Adv 74-76; Perm to Offic Dio Ox from 77. *6 Moreton Road, Oxford.*

BOSTON, David Mack. K Coll NS. **d** 66 **p** 67 NS. L to Offic Dio NS 66-67; I of Tangier 67-74; Timberlea w Lakeside Dio NS from 74; Terence Bay Dio NS from 76. *Box 8053a, Halifax, NS, Canada.* (876-7551)

BOSTON, Edwin Richard. b 24. Jes Coll Cam BA 46, MA 49. Linc Th Coll 49. **d** 50 **p** 51 Ely. C of Wisbech 50-55; St Neots 55-56; Gt w L Paxton and Toseland 55-56; St Mary de Castro Leic 56-57; C-in-c of Cadeby w Sutton Cheney Dio Leic 57-60; R from 60; P-in-c of Congerstone Dio Leic from 79. *Cadeby Rectory, Nuneaton, Warws.* (Market Bosworth 290462)

BOSTON, Jonathan Bertram. b 40. Ely Th Coll 61. **d** 64 **p** 65 Nor. C of Eaton 64-69; V of Horsford Dio Nor from 70; Horsham St Faith Dio Nor from 70; Sen Chap Army Cadet Force Norfolk from 70. *Horsford Vicarage, Norwich, NR10 3DB.* (Nor 898266)

BOSTWICK, Brian Douglas. b 41. Em & St Chad Coll Sktn 76. **d** 76 **p** 77 Alg. w SSJE Dio Alg from 76. *Box 660, Bracebridge, Ont P0B 1C0, Canada.*

BOSWELL, Colin John. b 47. Sarum Wells Th Coll 72. **d** 74 **p** 75 S'wark. C of H Trin U Tooting 74-78; St Phil Sydenham 78-80; St Pet St Helier Morden Dio S'wark from 80. *Bishop Andrew's House, Wigmore Road, Carshalton, Surrey.* (01-644 9203)

BOTHA, Canon Benjamin Oswell. Bp Gray Th Coll Capetn 59. **d** 61 **p** 63 Geo. C of Swellendam 61-64; St Paul Geo 64-66; St Andr Riversdale 66-72; P-in-c of St Matt Miss Beaufort W 72-74; C of St Silas Nunhead 74-76; R of St Mich City and Dio Port Eliz from 77; Can of Port Eliz from 79. *Box 8009, Schauderville, Port Elizabeth, S Africa.*

BOTHAM, Norman. b 29. Univ of Nottm MPhil. SOC 63. **d** 66 **p** 67 Guildf. C of Englefield Green 66-69; Bagshot 69-73; Lect Coll of St Mark and St John Chelsea 66-69; Sen Lect Shoreditch Coll Egham 69-74; C-in-c of H Trin Bath 74; Asst Dir of Educn B & W 74; Sen Lect Doncaster Coll of Educn from 74; Publ Pr Dio Southw from 75. *Rufford, Mattersey Road, Ranskill, Retford, Notts DN22 8NF.* (Retford 818234)

BOTHAMLEY, Ven Leonard. Univ of Dur LTh 33. St Aug Coll Cant 29. **d** 33 **p** 34 Perth. C of St John Fremantle 33-35; R of Wyalkatchem 35-39; Kellerberrin 39-43; AMF 39-41; RAAF 41-44; R of Northam 44-55 (w W Northam 55-61) 43-66; Can of Perth 50-76; Archd of Northam 54-66; Archd (Emer) from 66; Chap Repatriation Gen Hosp Hollywood 66-72; Fremantle Hosp 73-76; Perm to Offic Dio Perth from 76. *93 Barker Road, Subiaco, W Australia 6008.* (81 8515)

BOTHWELL, David George. b 16. Trin Coll Dub BA 39, Div Test 41. **d** 41 Bp Hind for Down **p** 42 Down. C of St Mary Newry w Donaghmore 41-45; St Mark Portadown 45-47; R of Donaghendry w Ballyclog Dio Arm from 47. *Rectory, Stewartstown, Dungannon, Co Tyrone, N Ireland.* (Stewartstown 494)

✠ **BOTHWELL, Right Rev John Charles.** Trin Coll Tor BA 48, LTh 51, BD 52. **d** 51 **p** 52 Tor. C of St Jas Cathl Tor 51-53; Ch Ch Cathl Vanc 53-56; R of St Aid Oakville 56-60; Dundas 60-65; Hon Can of Niag from 64; Can Missr Dio Niag 65-69; Exec Dir of Planning Angl Ch Canada 69-71; Cons Bp Coadj of Niag 11 June 71 in Ch Ch Cathl Hamilton by Abp of Alg; Bps of Tor, Moos, Ont, Niag, and W NY; Apptd Bp of Niag 73. *838 Glenwood Avenue, Burlington, Ont., Canada.*

BOTO, Gilbert. St Paul's Coll Ambat 61. **d** 60 **p** 61 Madag. P Dio Madag 60-69; Dio Antan from 69. *Antanetibe-Zazamanga, Ambohidratrimo, Madagascar.*

BOTOBE, Paul. b 03. **d** 70 Tam. d Dio Tam from 70. *Mission Anglicane, Tamatave, Madagascar.*

BOTOHAZA, Benjamin. St Paul's Coll Ambat. **d** 32 **p** 33 Madag. P Dio Madag 32-69. *c/o Eklesia Episkopaly Malagasy, Tamatave, Madagascar.*

BOTOMWITO, Asoyo. b 20. Trin Coll Nai 74. **d** 74 **p** 75 Boga-Z. P Dio Boga-Z. *BP 861, Kisangani, Zaire.*

BOTOSERA, Vincent. Mahanoro Past Coll 71. **d** 71 **p** 72 Tam. C-in-c of Ampasimanjeva 71-74. *Ampasimanjeva, Sahasinaka, FCE, Malagasy Republic.*

BOTSWANA, Lord Bishop of. *See* Makhulu, Most Rev Walter Paul

BOTT, Alfred Henry. Bro of St Paul, Bardfield 33. ACT ThL 50. **d** 35 **p** 36 Waik. C of St Pet Cathl Hamilton 35-37; P-in-c of Ngaruawahia 37-38; Asst Missr Auckld City Miss 39-44; V of Emerald 45-48; Springsure 47-48; R of Miriam Vale 49-52; St Matt Townsville 52-54; Org Sec ABM and LPr Dio Adel 54-59; R of Alice Springs 59-62; Archd of N Territory 59-66; Carp 66-69; Supt St Mary's Miss Alice Springs 62-66; Sub-Dean of All S Cathl, Thursday I 66-69; Chap of St Geo Miss Palm I 72-78. *34 Macrossan Street, Townsville, Queensland, Australia.*

BOTT, Canon Frederick Trevor. b 03. Bp's Hostel Trinid 28. **d** 29 **p** 30 Trinid. C of St Paul San Fernando 29-34; V of St Clem Naparima 34-38; C of St Thos Stourbridge 38-44; Priv Chap to Bp of Worc 43; V of St Paul-in-the-Blockhouse Worc 44-52; Surr 46-52; PC of St Swith Linc 52-59; Chap Linc County Hosp 52-57; Commis N Nig from 53-70; V of Norton w Lenchwick 59-63; Newland Worcs and Warden Beauchamp Charities 63-66; Stoulton w Drakes Broughton 66-68; Perm to Offic Dio Chich 68-70; Guildf from 70; Hon Can of N Nig 69-70; Can (Emer) from 70. *Terry's Cross, Brighton Road, Henfield, W Sussex, NB5 95X.*

BOTTERILL, Canon Charles Wilfred. b 1898. Sarum Th Coll 20. Univ of Dur LTh 26. **d** 23 **p** 25 Pet. C of St Mary Hinckley 23-26; St Barn Leic 26-30; V of Thurmaston 30-70; RD of Goscote II 55-69; Hon Can of Leic 68-73; Can (Emer) from 73; L to Offic Dio Leic from 69. *17 Brailsford Road, Wigston, LE8 IBG.* (Leic 885824)

BOTTING, Michael Hugh. b 25. K Coll Lon BSc 51. AKC 52. Ridley Hall Cam. **d** 56 **p** 57 Lon. C of St Paul Kens 56-61; V of St Matt Fulham 61-72; RD of Hammersmith 67; Surr 68-72; M Gen Syn from 70; V of St Geo Leeds Dio Ripon from 72; RD of Headingley from 81. *208 Kirkstall Lane, Leeds, LS5 2AB.* (Leeds 756556)

BOTTING, Paul Lloyd. b 43. St Mich Coll Llan 69. **d** 71 **p** 72 Southw. C of Hucknall Torkard 71-74; Torquay Centr 74-76; C-in-c of St Mich AA Sutton-in-Ashfield Dio Southw 76-77; V from 77. *Vicarage, Northern View, Sutton-in-Ashfield, Notts, NG17 2AQ.* (Mansfield 555031)

BOTTLEY, David Thomas. b 39. Clifton Th Coll 64. **d** 67 **p** 68 Ripon. C of Burley 67-75; V of Owlerton City and Dio Sheff from 75. *Owlerton Vicarage, Forbes Road, Sheffield, S6 2NW.* (Sheffield 343560)

BOTTOMLEY, Canon Arthur Philip. b 04. OBE 60. Armstrong Coll Dur BA 25. Wycl Hall Ox 28. **d** 29 **p** 30 Newc T. C of St Paul Newc T 29-33; Hd Master Nabumali High Sch 33-64; Hon Can of U Nile 50-61; Mbale 61-64; Can (Emer) from 64; Chap St Brandon's Sch Clevedon 64-71. *12a Beechwood Court, Queen's Road, Harrogate, N Yorks, HG2 0HD.*

BOTTOMLEY, George Edward. b 06. St Jo Coll Dur LTh 34. BC Coll Bris 30. **d** 35 **p** 36 Lon. C of St John U Holloway 35-37; All SS Marple 37-40; Jt Org Sec ICM 40-42; R of Bucknall w Bagnall 42-50; Surr from 42; V of St Luke Wolverhampton 50-54; L to Offic as R of St Silas English Episcopal Ch Glas 54-61; V of St Mark Cheltm 61-76; Hon C of Camborne Dio Truro from 77. *Salem, Reskadinnick Road, Camborne, Cornw.* (Camborne 713028)

BOTTOMLEY, Gordon. b 31. Oak Hill Th Coll 51. **d** 55 **p** 56 Sarum. C of Kinson 55-58; N Area Sec BCMS and Perm to Offic Dios Sheff; York; Ches; Blackb; Bradf; Carl; Dur; Liv; Newc; Ripon; and S & M 58-63; LPr Dio Man 58-63; V of Hemswell w Harpswell 63-71; Glentworth 63-71; Chap RAF Hemswell 63-71; R of Bucknall w Bagnall Dio Lich 72-80; Team R from 80. *Rectory, Werrington Road, Bucknall, Stoke-on-Trent, Staffs, ST2 9AQ.* (S-on-T 24455)

BOTTOMLEY, Philip. b 45. Univ of Dur BA 67, Dipl Th 69. Cranmer Hall Dur 66. **d** 70 **p** 71 Barking for Chelmsf. C of St Paul Harlow 70-74; St Luke w St Simon & St Jude W Kilburn 74-78; Midl Sec Ch Min among the Jews from 78; Perm to Offic Dio Birm from 78. *92 Durley Dean Road, Selly Oak, Birmingham, B29 6RX.* (021-472 4788)

BOTTOMS, Geoffrey Dennis. b 45. Linc Th Coll 71. **d** 73 **p** 74 Blackb. C of St Matt Preston 73-76; Fleetwood (in c of St Nich) 76-79; H Cross Woodchurch Dio Ches from 80. *School House, Church Lane, Woodchurch, Mer, L49 7LS.* (051-678 3395)

BOUCHER, Brian Albert. b 39. Late Exhib of St D Coll Lamp BA (2nd cl Hist) 61. Chich Th Coll 61. **d** 63 **p** 64 Lon. C of H Trin w St Mary Hoxton 63-67; Chap Tr Ship *Mercury* Hamble 67-68; Asst Chap (Chap from 73) and Master Harrow Sch from 68. *16 Crown Street, Harrow-on-the-Hill, Middx.* (01-422 0522)

BOUGHEY, Richard Keith. b 26. Univ of Man MEducn 71. Qu Coll Birm 77. **d** 80 Lich (APM). C of Stoke-on-Trent and of U Tean 80-81; St Mary Uttoxeter Dio Lich from 81. *Kontokali, Old Lane, Checkley, Stoke-on-Trent, Staffs.*

BOUGHTON, Gordon Charles Matheson. Moore Coll Syd ACT ThL 74. BD (Lon) 76. **d** and **p** 76 Syd. C of H Trin Peakhurst 76-77; St Alb Epping 77; CMS Miss Dio Sabah from 78. *Box 1397, Kota Kinabalu, Sabah, Malaysia.*

BOUGHTON, Michael John. b 37. Kelham Th Coll 57. **d** 62 **p** 63 Linc. C of Grantham 62-66; Kingsthorpe 66-68; St Nich w St John Newport 68-72; V of All SS Scunthorpe 72-79; Crowle Dio Linc from 79. *Crowle Vicarage, Scunthorpe, S Humb.* (0724-710268)

BOULCOTT, Thomas William. b 16. Bps' Coll Cheshunt 47. **d** 49 St Alb **p** 50 Bedford for Cant. C of Hitchin 49-51; Kempston Beds 51-54; Chap Bedford Hosp 52-54; V of St Aug Leic 54-61; Chap Leic Isolation Hosp 58-61; V of St Steph N Evington 61-73; Chap Leic Gen Hosp 62-73; V of Loppington w Newtown Dio Lich from 73. *Loppington Vicarage, Salop.* (Wem 33388)

BOULD, Arthur Roger. b 32. Selw Coll Cam BA 54, MA 58. Wadh Coll Ox BA (by incorp) 55, Dipl Th 56, MA 58. St Steph Ho Ox 54. **d** 57 **p** 58 Lich. C of Wednesfield 57-64; V of Ch Ch Wellington 64-71; Surr from 70; R of Cheadle Dio Lich from 71; RD of Cheadle from 72. *Cheadle Rectory, Stoke-on-Trent, Staffs, ST10 1HU* (Cheadle 3337)

BOULD, Stephen Frederick. b 49. AKC and BD 78. Sarum Wells Th Coll 78. **d** 79 **p** 80 Liv. C of St Jude Cantril Farm City and Dio Liv from 79. *58 Firscraig, Cantril Farm, Liverpool, L28 5RT.* (051-480 7847)

BOULSOVER, Philip John. Kelham Th Coll 34. ACT ThL 55. **d** 40 **p** 41 York. C of St Cuthb Middlesbrough 40-41; Northallerton 41-43; Bexhill (in C of St Mich E Bexhill) 43-51; R of Atherton N Queensld 51-56; St Luke Wandal Rockptn 56-67; Hon Can of Rockptn 65-67; R of St Luke Canberra 67-81; Perm to Offic Dio C & Goulb from 81. *21 Chillagoe Street, Fisher, ACT, Australia 2611.*

BOULT, Canon Anthony Christopher. b 22. Ch Ch Ox BA 43, MA 47. Coll of Resurr Mirfield 44. **d** 45 **p** 46 Ox. C of Aylesbury 45-50; Upton w Chalvey (in c of St Pet Chalvey) 50-58; PC of Grimsbury 58-66; V of St Giles Reading Dio Ox from 66; M Gen Syn 70-80; RD of Reading from 74; Hon Can of Ch Ch Cathl Ox from 75. *St Giles' Vicarage, Reading, Berks.* (Reading 52831)

BOULT, Geoffrey Michael. b 56. Sarum Wells Th Coll 77. **d** 80 **p** 81 Southw. C of St Mary Newark-on-Trent Dio Southw from 80. *14 Winchilsea Avenue, Newark-upon-Trent, Notts.*

BOULTBEE, James. b 1895. St Edm Hall Ox BA 19, MA 22. Wycl Hall Ox 19. **d** 20 **p** 21 Liv. C of St Clem Toxteth Pk 20-25; St Mary Cheadle 25-27; V of St Luke Wolverhampton 27-38; New Ferry 38-54; Tolleshunt Major 54-73. *14 Valley Road, Bothenhampton, Bridport, Dorset, DT6 4JR.* (Bridport 4680)

BOULTBEE, John Michael Godolphin. b 22. Oak Hill Th Coll 66. **d** 68 Bradwell for Chelmsf **p** 69 Chelmsf. C of Hawkwell 68-71; C of St Keverne 71-73; V of Constantine 73-79; P-in-c of St Merryn Dio Truro 79-81; V from 81. *Vicarage, St Merryn, Padstow, Cornw.* (St Merryn 520379)

BOULTBEE, Thomas Milner. b 10. St D Coll Lamp BA 32. Egerton Hall Man 35. **d** 35 **p** 37 Man. C of St Bart Salford 35-38; St Jas w St Luke Hull 38-42; LPr Dio Win 42-43; Dio Man 43-44; R of St Geo Oldham Road Man 44-53; V of Roughtown 53-59; Tintwistle 59-76. *21 Mallory Avenue, Waterloo, Ashton-under-Lyne, Gtr Man.*

BOULTBY, Albert Eric. b 06. Late Scho of Univ Coll Dur BA 32, MA 47. Bps' Coll Cheshunt 38. **d** 39 **p** 40 Blackb. C of St Pet Fleetwood 39-45; St Sav Scarborough 45-46; Radcliffe-on-Trent (in c of Shelford) 46-48; Basford 48-50; Burbage w Harpur Hill (in c of St Jas) 50-56; Seal Nether w Over 56-58; Kirk Ireton 58-68; Ilkeston 68-70; C-in-c Radbourne Derby 70-71. *Lower Flat, 3 Lime Avenue, Burton Road, Derby, DE1 1TU.*

BOULTER, Michael Geoffrey. b 32. BD (Lon) 56. Tyndale Hall Bris 53. **d** 57 **p** 58 Ches. C of St Cath Higher Tranmere 57-60; R of St Luke Cheetham Man 60-65; Tollard Royal w Farnham 65-66; V of St Clem Branksome Dio Sarum from 66. *7 Parkstone Heights, Parkstone, Poole, Dorset, BH14 0QE.* (0202-748058)

BOULTER, Robert. St Aug Coll Cant 72. **d** 75 Man **p** 76 Hulme for Man. C of All SS & Marts Langley 75-80; V of St Aid Kersal, Salford Dio Man from 80. *Vicarage, Littleton Road, Salford, Lancs. M7 0TN.* (061-792 3072)

BOULTON, Christopher David. b 50. Keble Coll Ox BA 71, MA 80. Cudd Coll 71. **d** 74 **p** 75 Chelmsf. C of Latton 74-77; Shrub End 77-79; P-in-c of Gt Bentley Dio Chelmsf from 80. *Great Bentley Rectory, Colchester, Essex, CO7 8PG.* (Gt Bentley 250476)

BOULTON, Canon Peter Henry. b 25. St Chad's Coll Dur BA 2nd cl Th 49. Ely Th Coll 49. **d** 50 **p** 51 Ches. C of St Mich Coppenhall 50-54; St Mark Mansfield 54-55; V of Clipstone 55-60; St Jo Bapt Carlton 60-67; Worksop Priory Dio Southw from 67; Proc Conv Southw from 59; Hon Can of Southw Cathl from 75; Prolocutor of Conv of York from 80. *Vicarage, Worksop, Notts, S80 2HX.* (Worksop 2180)

BOULTON, Preb Thomas Oswald. b 10. Keble Coll Ox BA 35, MA 39. Wycl Hall Ox 35. **d** 36 **p** 37 Lich. C of Oswestry 36-39; St Mich Garston 39; CF 39-44; Hon CF 44; V of St Aid Shobnall 45-48; Penn 48-60; Oswestry 60-76; RD of Oswestry 60-76; Surr 60-76; Preb of Lich Cathl 67-76; Preb (Emer) from 76. *21 Rayleigh Road, Harrogate, N Yorks, HG2 8QR.* (Harrogate 871753)

BOULTON, Wallace Dawson. b 31. Lon Coll of Div 65. **d** 67 **p** 68 Southw. C of Bramcote 67-71; St Bride Fleet Street Dio Lon from 71; PRO Dio Southw 69-71; Publicity Sec CMS 71-82. *19 St Dominic Close, St Leonards, E Sussex, TN38 0PH.* (0424-713743)

BOULTON, Walter. b 01. Late Exhib of Ball Coll Ox 2nd cl Mod Hist 22, BA 23, MA 30. Cudd Coll 23. **d** 24 **p** 25 Ripon. C of St Mark Woodhouse Leeds 24-27; Asst Chap of Cathl Ch Calc 27-34; Chap of Lebong 34-35; Shillong 35-39 and 45-48; St Paul's Cathl Calc 39-45; Can of Calc 40-48; V of Fleet 48-52; Provost of Guildf and R of H Trin w St Mary Guildf 52-61; Proc Conv Guildf 53-61; R of Market Overton w Thistleton 61-72. *Milton House, Lindfield, Haywards Heath, Sussex.* (Lindfield 2416)

BOULTON-LEA, Peter John. b 46. St Jo Coll Dur BA

(2nd cl Gen) 68. Westcott Ho Cam 69. **d** 71 **p** 72 Portsm. C of Farlington 72-75; St John (in c of St Herbert) Darlington 75-77; R of E w W Horndon and L Warley Dio Chelmsf from 77. *Rectory, Thorndon Avenue, West Horndon, Brentwood, Essex.* (Brentwood 811223)

BOULTON JONES, John Kenneth. b 09. OBE (Mil) 64. Univ of Leeds BA 36, BD 46, PhD 68. Florida Southern Coll (USA) Hon LLD 45. Ripon Hall Ox 33. **d** 34 Knaresborough for Ripon **p** 35 Ripon. C of St Matt Leeds 34-37; Burley 37-38; Ch Ch Harrogate 38-40; V of Hovingham 40-45; Chap RNVR 42-46; Chap RN 46-63; Chap St Gabr Tr Coll Camberwell 64-73; Lect from 64; L to Offic Dio S'wark 64-78; Perm to Offic Dio Chich from 76; Dio Portsm from 77. *Pointers, Rogate, Petersfield, Hants, GU31 5DD.* (Rogate 750)

BOUMA, Gary Donald. b 42. Calvin Coll Mich BA 63. Cornell Univ NY MA 68, PhD 70. Princeton Th Sem BD 66. **d** 81 Melb. Perm to Offic Dio Melb from 81. *40 Lambeth Avenue, Armadale, Vic, Australia 3143.*

BOUNDS, John Henry. Clifton Th Coll 36. **d** 40 **p** 41 Bris. C of St Ambrose Whitehall Park Bris 40-42; Radipole 42-47; R of L Munden 47-57; R of Sacombe 54-57; V of Leigh Roch 57-80; Hon C of Uckfield Dio Chich from 81. *39 Manor End, Uckfield, E Sussex, TN22 1DN.*

BOUNDS, Stanley Frederick. St D Coll Lamp BA 49. **d** 50 **p** 51 Chelmsf. C of Dovercourt 50-53; St Laurence-in-Thanet 53-56; S Ashford Kent 56-59; R of H Trin Ramsgate 59-69; V of Clearwell 69-73; R of Hasfield w Tirley and Ashleworth 73-81; RD of Glouc N from 78. *c/o Hasfield Rectory, Gloucester, GL19 4LQ.* (Tirley 360)

BOUNDY, David. b 34. Kelham Th Coll 55. **d** 59 Aston for Birm **p** 60 Birm. C of Stirchley 59-64; V of St Osw Bordesley 64-70; St Mich AA S Yardley 70-74; R of Bideford Dio Ex from 74; M Gen Syn 75-80; RD of Hartland from 80. *Rectory, Bideford, Devon.* (Bideford 3769)

BOUNDY, Gerald Neville. b 36. Univ of Bris Linc Th Coll. **d** 65 **p** 66 Bris. C of St Mary Redcliffe w Temple Bedminster 65-70; C-in-c of St Steph Southmead 70-72; V 72-81; St Mary w St Sav Cotham Dio Bris from 81. *160 Redland Road, Bristol, BS6 6YG.* (Bris 732909)

BOUNDY, Canon Harold Dixon. Wycl Coll Tor STh 64. **d** 58 **p** 59 Tor. I of Vespra 58-61; P-in-c of St Paul L'Amoureux 61-70; R of Sharon 71-78; Can of Tor from 75. *147 Wellington Street West, Aurora, Ont, Canada.*

BOUNDY, Stewart Fraser. ACT ThL 67. Ridley Coll Melb 65. **d** 68 **p** 69 Melb. C of Surrey Hills 68-69; St Mark Camberwell 69-71; C-in-c of St Mary Warburton 71-72; I 72-73; Perm to Offic Dio Melb from 73. *16 Gallus Close, Vermont, Vic, Australia 3133.*

BOURDEAUX, Michael Alan. b 34. St Edm Hall Ox BA (2nd cl Mod Lang) 57, 2nd cl Th 59, MA 61, BD 68. Wycl Hall Ox 57. **d** 60 **p** 61 Lon. C of Enfield 60-64; St Luke Charlton 65-66; L to Offic Dio Roch from 66; Dir Keston Coll from 70; Research F RInst Internat Affairs 71-73. *34 Lubbock Road, Chislehurst, Kent, BR7 5JJ.* (01-467 3550)

BOURKE, Very Rev Francis Robert. b 16. Trin Coll Dub BA (Resp) 40, Div Test (1st cl) 41, BD 46, PhD 61. **d** 42 Lim for Killaloe **p** 42 Killaloe. C of Killaloe 42-43; I of Kilbarron 43-57; Birr 57-72; RD of U Ormond from 51; Chap to Bp of Killaloe 57-63; Preb of Inniscattery in Killaloe Cathl 61-63; Regr Dio Killaloe from 62; Treas and Preb of Tulloh 63-65; Chan and Preb of Clondegad 65-67; Prec and Preb of Tuamgravey 67-72; Dean of Killaloe and Kilfenora from 72; R of Killaloe Dio Killaloe from 72; Stradbally Dio Killaloe from 76; Preb of Dysart from 72; Clonfert Cathl from 72; Exam Chap to Bp of Killaloe from 78. *Deanery, Killaloe, Co Clare, Irish Republic* (Killaloe 76245)

BOURKE, Kerry Edmund. K Coll NS BA 59, BST 62. **d** 61 **p** 62 Bp W W Davis for NS. R of Blandford 62-67; Chester 67-72; New Glasgow 72-74; Trenton 72-74; C of All SS Cathl Halifax Dio NS from 74. *5732 College Street, Halifax, NS, Canada.* (429-0907)

BOURKE, Michael Gay. b 41. CCC Cam BA 63, MA 67. Cudd Coll 65. **d** 67 Grantham for Linc. **p** 68 Linc. C of Gt Grimsby 67-71; Digswell 71-73; C-in-c of Panshanger Conv Distr Digswell 73-78; M Gen Syn 75-80; V of Southill Dio St Alb from 78. *Vicarage, Southill, Biggleswade, Beds, SG18 9LH.* (Hitchin 813331)

BOURKE, Stanley Gordon. b 48. TCD Div Test 78. **d** 78 **p** 79 Down. C of Dundonald 78-80; Shankill Lurgan Dio Drom from 81. *136 Lough Road, Lurgan, Craigavon, BT66 6JL, N Ireland.* (Lurgan 5962)

BOURNE, Charles Wittwer Wilfrid. b 02. AKC 30. **d** 30 **p** 31 Chelmsf. C of Gt Ilford 30-33; St Mary Harrow 33-36; V of Grove 36-71; V of Denchworth 40-71; RD of Wantage 54-66; Surr 56-71; Hon Can of Ch Ch Ox 64-71. *4 Thoroughgood Road, Clacton-on-Sea, Essex, CO15 6AN.* (Clacton-on-Sea 21827)

BOURNE, David James. b 54. Univ of Reading BA 76. Trin Coll Bris 77. **d** 79 Wolverhampton for Lich **p** 80 Lich. C of Ch of Good Shepherd w Bromwich 79-81. *Address temp unknown.*

BOURNE, Dennis John. b 32. Ridley Hall Cam. **d** 60 **p** 61 Nor. C of Gorleston 60-64; P-in-c of St Mary Magd Conv Distr Gorleston 64-79; V of Costessey Dio Nor from 79. *Costessey Vicarage, Norwich, NR8 5DP.* (Nor 742818)

BOURNE, Francis Frederick. b 16. ACT ThDip 73. St Barn Coll Adel. **d** 71 **p** 72 Adel. C of St Columba, Hawthorn 71-72; Mt Gambier 73; P-in-c of Keith 73-77; R of Naracoorte 77-81. *11 Wattle Grove, Belair, S Australia 5052.* (08-278 1550)

BOURNE, Henry. b 34. Spurgeon's Coll 55. **d** 64 Birm **p** 65 Aston for Birm. [f Baptist Min] C of Handsworth 64-67; Chap RAF from 67. *c/o Ministry of Defence, Adastral House, WC 1.*

BOURNE, Ven Ian Grant. Univ of NZ BA 55. NZ Bd of Th Stud LTh 61. Coll Ho Ch Ch 51. **d** 56 Wel **p** 57 Bp Rich for Wel. C of Lower Hutt 56-58; V of Eketahuna 58-65; C of Epsom Surrey 65-67; V of Otaki 67-71; Haitaitai-Kilbirnie City and Dio Wel from 71; Archd of Wel from 78. *All Saint's Vicarage, Hamilton Road, Wellington, NZ.* (862-140)

BOURNE, Michael. b 30. K Coll Lon and Warm AKC 58. **d** 59 **p** 60 Bris. C of Southmead 59-62; C-in-c of St Alb W Leigh Conv Distr Havant 62-67; V of Wroxall 67-73; R of Poplar Dio Lon from 73. *Rectory, Newby Place, E14 0EY.* (01-987 3133)

BOURNE, Peter Maxwell. b 52. ACT Th Dip 78. St Barn Coll Adel 76. **d** 78 **p** 79 The Murray. C of Willunga 78-80; P-in-c of Tailem Bend Dio Murray from 80. *Rectory, Allen Street, Meningie, S Aystralia 5264.*

BOURNE, William Temple. b 09. Hertf Coll Ox 3rd cl Mod Hist 31. BA 32, MA 35. Wells Th Coll 34. **d** 36 **p** 37 Bris. C of Corsham 36-38; Kettering 38-40; CF (EC) 40-45; CF 45-55; C of Prescot 55-58; R of Melton Constable w Swanton Novers 58-65; PC of Briningham 58-65; V of Swardeston 65-75; R of E Carleton 65-75. *35 Rothbury Road, Wymondham, Norf, NR18 0PD.* (Wymondham 604289)

BOURNES, Fraser James. Univ of Tor BA 48. Wycl Coll Tor LTh 49. **d** 48 Calg for NS **p** 49 Tor for NS. R of Guysboro and Halfway Cove 49-52; Markham 52-54; Chap RCN 54-57; R of St Jas Humber Bay 57-61; Ch Ch Brampton 61-66; Ch Ch Deer Pk Tor 66-74; H Trin Scarborough Tor 74-78. *1548 Tangerine Street, Clearwater, Florida, USA.*

BOURNON, Dennis Harry. b 20. St Cuthb S Dur LTh 48, BA 49. Oak Hill Th Coll 46. **d** 49 Whitby for York **p** 50 York. C of H Trin Heworth York 49-51; Bebington 51-54; V of St Jo Evang Everton 54-58; Gunton Suff 58-65; R of Eastrop 65-80; Surr 77-80; V of Nursling w Rownhams Dio Win from 80. *Vicarage, Horns Drove, Rownhams, Southampton, SO1 8AH.* (Rownsham 738293)

BOURNON, Canon John Raymond. b 18. St Cath S Ox BA (3rd cl Phil, Pol and Econ) 48, MA 52. Oak Hill Th Coll 48. **d** 50 **p** 51 Lich. C of Wellington w Eyton 50-53; V of Wombridge 53-60; Ch Ch Ware Dio St Alb from 60; RD of Hertford 71-77; Hon Can of St Alb Cathl from 80. *Christ Church Vicarage, Ware, Herts, SG12 7BZ.* (Ware 3165)

BOUSFIELD, David Frederick. Univ of Tor BA 61. Trin Coll Tor STB 64. **d** 64 Bp Snell for Tor **p** 65 Tor. C of Ch Ch Brampton 64-67; R of Brighton 67-69; on leave 70-78; R of Bramalea Dio Tor from 78. *102 Addington Crescent, Brampton, Ont., Canada.*

BOUTCHER, Morley Josiah Ewan. Mem Univ of Newfld 54. **d** 59 **p** 60 Newfld. I of Smith's Sound Miss 59; Whitbourne 60-61; Seal Cove 61-67; Random 67-72; on leave 72-73; C of St Aug St John's 73-76; I of Bell Island Dio E Newfld from 76. *Wabana, Bell Island, Newfoundland, Canada.* (709-579-3426)

BOUTFLOWER, David Curtis. b 45. Univ of Man BSc 67. Linacre Coll Ox BA (3rd cl Th) 70. Ripon Hall Ox 67. **d** 70 **p** 71 Birm. C of All SS Shard End 70-73; Mortlake w E Sheen Dio S'wark from 73. *5 Vernon Road, SW14.* (01-876 9696)

BOUTLE, David Francis. b 44. Univ of Leeds BSc 67. Univ of Lon Dipl Th 72. Cudd Coll 69. **d** 72 **p** 73 Linc. C of Boston 72-77; Waltham (in c of St Matt) 77-80; P-in-c of St Paul Morton Dio Linc 80-81; V from 81. *Vicarage, Morton Front, Gainsborough, Lincs, DN21 3AD.* (Gainsborough 2654)

BOVEY, Canon Denis Philip. b 29. Ely Th Coll 50. **d** 53 **p** 54 Dur. C of St Columba Southwick 53-57; Perm to Offic Dio Ox 57-59; L to Offic Dio Chich 62-64; C of St Aid W Hartlepool 64-66; R of St Jas Aber 66-74; St Drostan Old Deer Dio Aber from 74; St John Longside Dio Aber from 74; Strichen Dio Aber from 74; Can of Aber from 75; Synod Clk from 78. *Old Deer Rectory, Peterhead, Aberdeen, AB4 8LN.*

BOVEY, Canon Philip Sidney John. b 1898. Univ Coll Lon BSc (1st cl Eng) 19. **d** 55 **p** 56 Glas. C of H Trin Paisley (in c of St Marg Renfrew) 55-63; R of Renfrew 63-65; P-in-c of St

Pet Stornoway 65-72 Hon Can of Oban Cathl from 79. *4 Lever Terrace, Leverburgh, Isle of Harris.*

BOVI, Very Rev Alfred Wodeha. Legon Univ Ghana BA 54. **d** 68 **p** 79 Benin. P Dio Benin 68-77; Dio Warri from 77; Dean of St Andr Cathl Warri from 80. *Box 52, Warri, Bedel State, Nigeria.*

BOVILL, Francis William. b 34. Dipl Th (Lon) 58. St Aid Coll 55. **d** 58 Blackb **p** 59 Lanc for Blackb. C of Bispham 58-61; Crosthwaite Cumb 61-64; V of St Andr Radcliffe 64-68; PC (V from 69) of St Steph Cinderford 68-73; Scotby Dio Carl from 73. *Scotby Vicarage, Carlisle, Cumb.* (Scotby 205)

BOVINGTON, Ven James Gordon. Montr Dioc Th Coll. **d** 49 **p** 50 Montr. C of Ch of Ascen Montr 49-51; R of Aylmer 51-67; P-in-c of Gatineau 60-67; R of Perth Dio Ott from 67; Can of Ott 65-73; Archd of Lanark from 73. *12 Harvey Street, Perth, Ont., Canada.* (1-613-267-1301)

BOVIS, Bert Lindsay. Moore Th Coll Syd ACT ThL 63. **d** 63 **p** 64 Syd. C of Gymea w Gymea Bay 63-64; Liverpool 64-66; C-in-c of Hurstville Grove 66-70; R of Harris Pk 70-76; L to Offic Dio Syd from 77. *46 Riverview Road, Nowra, NSW, Australia 2540.* (044-22659)

BOWAJE, Joshua Adedayo. Im Coll Ibad 63. **d** 65 Ondo. d Dio Ondo. *Royal Orthopaedic Hospital, Lagos, Nigeria.*

BOWAK, Donald Charles Erith. Ridley Coll Melb ACT ThL 59. **d** 60 **p** 61 Melb. C of Trin Cathl Wang 60-61; C of St Phil W Heidelberg 61-63; Pascoe Vale 62-63; Wembley-Floreat 63-64; R of Kensington 64-67; L to Offic Dio Perth from 67. *8 Peplar Avenue, Manning, W Australia 6152.*

BOWAK, Wenman Allison. St Aid Th Coll Bal 24. ACT ThL 29, Th Scho 50. **d** 26 **p** 27 Bal. C of St Pet Bal 26-28; St Steph E Bal 28-29; Colac 29-30; P-in-c of Jeparit 30-32; Skipton 32-35; C of St Olave Woodberry Down Middx 35-40; CF (EC) 40-46; Hon CF from 46; Perm to Offic Dios Nasik, Chota N and Calc 42-46; Chap at Lakhimpur and Chap to Bp of Assam 46-50; Metrop's Commis 48-49; Min of Kalista Vic 50-52; I of Brunswick 52-61; RD of Brunswick 60-61; Commiss River 61-65; I of All SS E St Kilda 61-72; RD of St Kilda 68-72; Perm to Offic Dio Melb from 73. *Unit 2, 12 Chanak Street, East Malvern, Vic, Australia 3145.* (03-211 4975)

BOWDEN, Frank James. b 12. Univ of Lon BA (1st cl Cl) 35. **d** 38 **p** 40 Nor. Publ Pr Dio Nor from 38. *52 Heigham Road, Norwich, NR2 3AU.* (Nor 24481)

BOWDEN, Frederick Sidney Ralph. b 32. St D Coll Lamp BA 52. Coll of Resurr Mirfield. **d** 56 **p** 57 Mon. C of Abertillery 56-59; Machen w Rudry 59-62; V of Cwmtillery 62-71; RD of Blaenau Gwent 68-71; Pontypool from 77; V of Trevethin Dio Mon from 71; Surr from 77. *Vicarage, Trevethin, Pontypool, Gwent, NP4 8JF.*

BOWDEN, John Stephen. b 35. Late Scho of CCC Ox 1st cl Cl Mods 57, BA (2nd cl Th) 59, Hall-Houghton Sen Septuagint Pri 60, Hall Sen Gr Test Pri 61, MA 62. Univ of Edin Hon DD 81. Linc Th Coll 59. **d** 61 **p** 62 Southw. C of Nottm 61-64; Lect Univ of Nottm 64-66; Ed and Managing Dir SCM Press from 66; Hon C of All SS Highgate Dio Lon from 66; St Faith Brentford Dio Lon from 80; Visiting Prof K Coll Lon from 80. *20 Southwood Avenue, N6 5RZ.* (01-340 7548)

BOWDEN, Raymond David. St Jo Coll Morpeth. ACT ThL 60. **d** 60 **p** 61 Armid. C of St Pet Cathl Armid 60-64; W Tamworth 64-65; V of Warialda 65-69; on leave 69-72; Chap Armid Sch 73-74; V of Glen Innes Dio Armid from 74. *Vicarage, Glen Innes, NSW, Australia 2370.* (Glen Innes 143)

BOWDEN, Robert Andrew. b 38. Late Scho of Worc Coll Ox BA (2nd cl Hist) 62, Dipl Th 63, MA 67, BD 68. Cudd Coll 63. **d** 65 **p** 66 Lich. C of St Geo Wolverhampton 65-69; Duston 69-71; R of Byfield 72-78; Coates, Rodmarton and Sapperton w Frampton Mansell Dio Glouc from 79; Bp's Adv on Rural S from 81. *Coates Rectory, Cirencester, Glos, GL7 6NR.* (Kemble 235)

BOWDER, Reginald William Maxwell. b 46. TCD BA 68, MA 81. SOC 78. **d** 80 Edmon for Lon. C of St Steph Bush Hill Park Dio Lon from 81. *57 Uvedale Road, Bush Hill Park, Enfield, Middx.*

BOWDITCH, Noel James. b 53. Univ of Newc BA 74, BD 81. St Jo Coll Morpeth 78. **d** and **p** 81 Newc. C of Muswellbrook Dio Newc from 81. *38 Carl Street, Muswellbrook 2333, NSW, Australia.*

BOWDLER, Denis Harper. b 01. Univ of Dur LTh 25. Lich Th Coll 22. **d** 25 **p** 26 Lich. C of Brierley Hill 25-28; St Luke Hanley 28-32; Wednesbury (in c of St Andr King's Hill) 32-36; V of Alsagers Bank 36-53; Surr from 39; V of Goldenhill 53-60; St Jude Hanley 60-69. *14 Avenue Road, Shelton, Stoke-on-Trent, Staffs, ST4 2DT.* (Stoke-on-Trent 45514)

BOWDLER, Ernest Roy. b 10. Lich Th Coll 32. **d** 34 **p** 36 Lich. C of St Mary Sedgley 34-38; Goldenhill 38-40; V of Smallthorne 40-50; Chap RNVR 43-46; V of St Chad Coseley 50-57; Ch Ch Wolverhampton 57-71; Chap to the Commun W Ogwell 71-73; C of Langley Marish 73-75. *5 St Barnabas, Newland, Malvern, Worcs, WR13 5AX.* (Malvern 61044)

BOWDLER, Richard Edward Hope. b 22. Trin Coll Ox BA 43, MA 48. Ridley Hall Cam 46. **d** 49 **p** 50 S'wark. C of Morden 49-53; All S Langham Place Lon 53-58; Youth Sec of Ch S 58-75; CPAS from 75. *10 Marston Ferry Road, Oxford.* (Oxford 55532)

BOWEN, Cyril. b 13. MPS 35. Roch Th Coll 62. **d** 63 Bp McKie for Cov **p** 64 Cov. C of St Nich Warw 63-66; V of Bp's Itchington 66-72; R of Stockton 72-75; Exhall w Wixford Dio Cov from 75; V of Temple Grafton w Binton Dio Cov from 75. *Temple Grafton Vicarage, Alcester, Warws.* (Bidford-on-Avon 972314)

BOWEN, Daniel Austin. b 11. St D Coll Lamp Welsh Ch and Philip's Scho 32, BA (2nd cl Hist) 33. St Steph Ho Ox 33. **d** 35 St D **p** 36 Swan B for St D. C of Llanelly 35-41; R of Puncheston w L Newcastle 41-48; V of Llandyfriog w Llanfair-Trelygen 48-58; Llanfihangel Aberbythick 58-67; St Nich Monkton Pembroke 67-78; Perm to Offic Dio Chich from 79. *Greenbanks, Mill Lane, High Salvington, Worthing, BN13 3DE.* (Worthing 63813)

BOWEN, David Gregory. b 47. Lanchester Poly Cov BSc 69. Cudd Coll 70. **d** 74 **p** 75 Bp McKie for Cov. C of Rugby 74-78; Hon C of Charlton 78-80; Asst Master Blackheath Bluecoat Sch 78-80; Team V of Stantonbury Dio Ox from 80. *c/o Rectory, Great Linford, Milton Keynes, Bucks, MK14 5BD,*

BOWEN, Desmond Gordon. Carleton Coll Ott BA (Hons Hist) 50. Qu Univ Kingston Ont MA 54, PhD 63. Ripon Hall Ox 54. **d** and **p** 56 Ont. I of Sharbot Lake 56-58; R of St Chris Ott 59-62; Assoc Prof of Hist Carleton Univ Ott 65-68; Prof from 68; Lect in Ecclesiology Univ of Ott from 69. *28 Melgund Avenue, Ottawa, Ont., Canada.*

BOWEN, Euros. b 04. OBE 71. Univ of Wales BA (2nd cl Phil) 28. BD 31. Mansfield Coll and St Cath S Ox (Aegr] Th 33, MA 43, St D Coll Lamp 33. **d** 34 **p** 35 St A. C of Wrexham 34-39; C-in-c of Llangywair (Llangower) 39-58; V of Llanuwchllyn w Llangywair (Llangower) 58-73. *4 Ffordd Cynan, Wrexham, Clwyd.*

BOWEN, Glyn. b 18. Univ of Wales BA 40. St Steph Ho Ox 40. **d** 42 **p** 43 Llan. C of U Grangetown 42-44; St Theodore Port Talbot 44-55; V of Oakwood 55-64; Ton Pentre 64-71; Port Talbot Dio Llan from 71. *St Theodore's Vicarage, Port Talbot, W Glam., SA13 1LB.* (Port T 883935)

BOWEN, Gwyn Humphrey. b 21. St D Coll Lamp BA 54. **d** 56 Llan **p** 57 Mon for Llan. C of Penarth w Lavernock 56-63; Garw Valley 63-65; V of Cwmaman Dio Llan from 65. *27 Byron Street, Cwmaman, Aberdare, Mid Glam, CF44 6HP.* (Aberdare 872902)

BOWEN, Howard Charles Campbell. b 13. St D Coll Lamp BA 36. **d** 36 **p** 37 St D. C of Tenby 36-39; Llanelly 39-44; CF 41-63; V of N Newton w St Michaelchurch 63-74; C-in-c of Thurloxton 63-64; Langford Budville w Runnington 74-79. *c/o Langford Budville Vicarage, Wellington, Somt.* (Milverton 339)

BOWEN, John. b 39. Dipl Th (Wales) 63. St Mich Coll Llan 60. **d** 68 Bp T M Hughes for Llan **p** 69 Llan. C of Aberavon 68-73; St Paul Canberra 73; R of Binda 73-76; Tumbarumba 76-81; Deakin Dio C & Goulb from 81. *44 Newdegate Street, Deakin, ACT, Australia 2600.*

BOWEN, John Francis William Minett. b 11. Univ of Wales BA 34. TD 57. St Mich Coll Llan 35. **d** 35 **p** 36 St A. C of Gresford 35-40; CF (TA) 40-46; R of Welsh Newton w Llanrothal 46-52; CF 52-67; R of Selworthy 67-78. *Badger House, Merrivale Lane, Ross-on-Wye, Herefs.* (Ross-on-Wye 4925)

BOWEN, John Roger. b 34. St Jo Coll Ox BA 59, MA 62. Tyndale Hall Bris 59. **d** 61 **p** 62 Ely. C of St Paul Cam 61-65; Chap at Moshi 65-67; Tutor St Phil Th Coll Kongwa and L to Offic Dio Centr Tang 67-76; Actg Provost of All SS Cathl Nai 76; Tutor St Paul's Th Coll Limuru 78-80; Dir of Pastoral Stud St Jo Coll Nottm from 80. *St John's College, Bramcote, Nottingham, NG9 3DS.*

BOWEN, Very Rev Lawrence. b 14. Univ of Wales BA 36. St Mich Coll Llan 37. **d** 38 **p** 39 St D. C of Pembrey 38-40; C and PV of St D Cathl 40-46; V of St Clears w Llanginning 46-63; R of Tenby w Gumfreston (w Penally from 70) 63-72; Can of St D Cathl 72; Dean and Prec from 72. *Deanery, St David's, Dyfed.* (St David's 202)

BOWEN, Lionel James. b 16. SOC 63. **d** 64 **p** 65 S'wark. C of St Pet Vauxhall 64-67; All SS Sanderstead (in c of Hamsey Green) 67-74; V of Pill 74-79. *43 Sussex Court, Eaton Road, Hove, Sussex.*

BOWEN, Ven Peter Desmond Akeroyd. St Paul's Coll Grahmstn LTh **d** 60 **p** 61 Grahmstn. C of St Sav E Lon 60-63; H Trin K William's Tn 63-64; R of Humansdorp 64-68; Can of Grahmstn 69-71; R of Somerset E 70-71; Archd of Uitenhage 71-79; Port Eliz from 79; R of St Kath Uitenhage 71-79;

St Paul Parsons Hill Dio Port Eliz from 79. *16 Tucker Street, Parsons Hill, Port Elizabeth 6001, S Africa.*

BOWEN, Philip Jackson. b 10. St D Coll Lamp BA 33. St Steph Ho Ox 33. **d** 35 St D **p** 36 Swan B for St D. C of Pontyberem 35-37; Llandilo Vawr (in c of St John Maesteilo) 37-40; Chap RAF 40-64; Asst Chap-in-Chief 60-64; V of Llandeilo Fawr w Llandefeisant 64-72. *Brodawel, Llanegwad, Dyfed.* (026-788418)

BOWEN, Roger William. b 47. Magd Coll Cam 3rd cl Econ Trip pt i 67, BA (2nd cl Archaeol & Anthrop Trip pt ii) 69, MA 73. St Jo Coll Nottm 69. **d** 72 Man **p** 73 Middleton for Man. C of Rusholme 72-75; Ruanda Miss (CMS) Burundi from 75. *BP 1300, Bujumbura, Burundi.*

BOWEN, Stephen Guy. b 47. Qu Coll Cam BA 68, MA 72. Univ of Bris MA 72. Clifton Th Coll 69. **d** 71 **p** 72 Kens for Lon. C of St Jo Evang Chelsea 71-73; St Sav Guildf 73-77; H Trin Wallington (in c of St Patr) 77-79; V of Felbridge Dio S'wark from 79. *Felbridge Vicarage, East Grinstead, Sussex.* (E Grinstead 21524)

BOWEN, Sydney. Univ of Wales BA (3rd cl Econ and Pol Sc) 37. St D Coll Lamp 36. **d** 37 **p** 38 Llan. C of Dowlais 37-39; St Theodore, Port Talbot 39-44; Neath w Llantwit 44-53; C-in-c of Cymmer w Abercregan Conv Distr 53-59; V of Ystradyfodwg 59-73. *19 Queen's Drive, Crown Hill, Llantwit Fardre, Mid Glam.*

BOWEN, Thomas Raymond. b 20. St D Coll Lamp BA 42. **d** 48 **p** 49 St D. C of Monkton 48-52; Haverfordwest 52-53; Chap RAF (Asst Chap-in-Chief Near East Air Forces from 71) 53-75; Chap Gresham Sch Holt from 75. *c/o Gresham's School, Holt, Norf.* (Holt 3529)

BOWEN, Thomas Reginald Fraser. St Aug Coll Cant 39. **d** 39 **p** 40 Southw. C of St Mary Bulwell 39-41; C and PV of Southw Cathl 41-45; R of Hannington 45-52; R of Ramsdale 48-52; Minstead 52-62; L Dewchurch w Aconbury Ballingham and Bolstone 62-78. *The Court Cottage, Hope under Dinmore, Hereford.*

BOWEN, Vincent Paul. b 26. Qu Coll Cam BA 50, MA 55. Ely Th Coll 51. **d** 53 Ox **p** 54 Reading for Cant. C of Cowley St John Ox 53-56; Brentwood 56-61; R of Cranham 61-71; Commiss Dio Kurun from 70; R of Wanstead Dio Chelmsf from 71. *Wanstead Rectory, E11 2SW.* (01-989 9101)

BOWEN, Wynford Colin. b 48. Bp Burgess Th Coll 67. **d** 71 **p** 72 St D. C of Hubberston 71-75; R of Cosheston w Nash and Upton Dio St D from 75; Carew Dio St D from 77. *Cosheston Rectory, Pembroke Dock, Dyfed, SA72 4UJ.* (Pembroke 682477)

BOWER, Godfrey. b 08. Peterho Cam BA 31, MA 42. St Steph Ho Ox 32. **d** 32 **p** 33 Roch. C of St Luke Bromley Common 32-35; St Andr Ham 35-38; Chap RN 38-63; R of Englefield 63-67; C of Bushey 67-70; Chipping Barnet 70-74. *69 Eastgate Street, Bury St Edmunds, Suff, IP33 1YR.* (0284 64678)

BOWER, James Hugh Marsh. b 17. St Chad's Coll Dur BA 39, Dipl in Th 40, MA 43. **d** 40 **p** 41 Lich. C of St Mary Shrewsbury 40-41; Rugeley 41-42; St Pet Wolverhampton 42-48; V of Northwood Staffs 48-54; St Mich AA Walsall 54-58; St Andr Wolverhampton 58-74; R of Cavendish Dio St E from 74; P-in-c of Stansfield Dio St E from 78. *Cavendish Rectory, Sudbury, Suff.* (Glemsford 280330)

BOWERING, John Anthony. b 34. SS Coll Cam 3rd cl Econ Trip pt i 55, BA (3rd cl Econ Trip pt ii) 57. Wycl Hall Ox 57. **d** 59 **p** 60 Chelmsf. C of Hornchurch 59-62; Succr of Chelmsf Cathl 62; Prec 63; V of Brampton Bierlow 64-69; Norton Lees Sheff 70-80; Tickhill w Stainton Dio Sheff from 80. *Tickhill Vicarage, Doncaster, Yorks.* (Doncaster 742224)

BOWERING, Michael Ernest. b 35. Kelham Th Coll 55. **d** 59 **p** 60 York. C of St Osw Middlesbrough 59-62; All SS Huntington York 62-64; V of Brayton w Barlow 64-72; Saltburn-by-the-Sea 72-81; RD of Selby 71-72; Sec of Miss & Evang Dio York from 81; Can Res of York Minster from 81. *9 Precentor's Court, York, YO1 2JN.* (York 27625)

BOWERS, Arnold Raymond. St Barn Coll Adel 40. Melb Coll of Div LTh 41. ACT ThL 41, Th Scho 47. **d** 41 **p** 42 Adel. C of St Paul Adel 41-42; Chap of Enfield w Broadview 42-44; R of H Trin Riverton 44-50; Asst Tutor St Barn Coll Adel 49-50; R of Whyalla 50-75; L to Offic Dio Willoch from 75. *187 McBryde Terrace, Whyalla, S Australia 5600.* (45-7496)

BOWERS, Canon Dermot Nichols. b 13. TCD BA and BCom 36, MA 63. **d** and **p** 41 Clogh. C of Monaghan w Tyholland 41-42; Chap RAF 42-46; R of Lissadell 46-48; Asst Sec CCCS (Irish Aux) 48-53; I of Baltinglass 53-57; Surr 53-66; I of Enniscorthy 57-66; Preb of Kilrane and Taghmon in St Edan's Cathl Ferns 63-66; V of Bangkok w Vientiane 66-72; St Thomas Ap Douglas 72-79; Can of St German Cathl Peel 78-79; Can (Emer) from 80. *21 Birch Crescent, Wickersley, Rotherham, S Yorks, S66 0NG.* (0709-547870)

BOWERS, Canon John Edward. b 23. AKC 50. St Bonif Coll Warm 50. TD 68. **d** 51 **p** 52 Leic. C of St Pet Leic 51-55; CF (TA) 56-67; CF (R of O) 67-78; Sacr of S'wark Cathl 55-57; V of St Pet Loughborough 57-63; Ashby-de-la-Zouch Dio Leic from 63; Surr from 64; RD of Akeley W from 76; Hon Can of Leic Cathl from 78. *Vicarage, Ashby-de-la-Zouch, Leics, LE6 5BX.* (Ashby 412180)

BOWERS, Canon John Edward William. b 32. St Aid Coll 60. **d** 63 **p** 64 Ches. C of Bromborough 63-68; Crewe Industr Chap 68-73; C-in-c of St Pet Crewe 69-71; V of Crewe Green 71-74; R of Ellesmere Port 74-79; Surr from 74; V of Hattersley Dio Ches from 79; Hon Can of Ches Cathl from 80. *Vicarage, Hattersley Road East, Hyde, Chesh.* (061-368 2795)

BOWERS, John Keith. b 25. BSc (Lon) 45. **d** 66 **p** 67 Glouc. C of Wotton-under-Edge 66-69; L to Offic Dio Glouc 69-70; C of Wotton-under-Edge (w Ozleworth and N Nibley from 77) Dio Glouc from 70. *Coombe Vale, Coombe, Wotton-under-Edge, Glos.* (W-u-E 2147)

BOWERS, Julian Michael. b 48. Edin Th Coll 69. **d** 72 **p** 73 Bris. C of Chippenham 72-74; Henbury 74-77; Chap H Trin Coll Kandy from 77. *c/o CMS, 157 Waterloo Road, SE1 8UU.*

BOWERS, Maxwell John Douglas. b 42. St Barn Th Coll Belair. **d** 70 **p** 72 Bend. C of St Paul Bend 70-73; V of Pyramid Hill 73-76; Perm to Offic Dio Melb 76-79; C of Shepparton 79-81; R of Cobram Dio Wang from 81. *4 High Street, Cobram, Vic, Australia 3644.*

BOWERS, Peter. b 47. Linc Th Coll 72. **d** 76 Repton for Derby **p** 77 Derby. C of St Francis Mackworth 76-78; C of St Martin Maidstone Dio Cant from 78. *Church House, Wallis Avenue, Park Wood, Maidstone, Kent.* (Maidstone 64170)

BOWERS, Peter William Albert. b 36. K Coll Lon and Warm BD and AKC 61. **d** 62 **p** 63 Blackb. C of St Pet Chorley 62-64; Sleaford 64-67; H Trin Folkestone 67-72; V of St Geo Mart Deal 72-80; Dir Galilee Commun from 80. *The Elms, Hacklinge, Deal, Kent, CT14 0AT.* (Sandwich 617900)

BOWERS, Raymond Franklin. b 16. Univ of Lon BD 40. ALCD 40. **d** 40 **p** 41 Lon. C of St Cath Neasden w Kingsbury 40-43; CF (EC) 43-47; C of St Mich AA Willesden Lon 47; CMS Miss Dio Ugan 47-60; Home Educn Sec CMS 61-66; V of St Steph Bath 66-76; RD of Bath 71-76; P-in-c of Gosforth 76-78; R 78-80. *Brow House, Blackbeck, Egremont, Cumb, CA22 2NY.* (Beckermet 345)

BOWERS, Stanley Percival. b 20. BD (Lon) 45. Wells Th Coll. **d** and **p** 66 Bris. [f Methodist Min] C of St Pet Lawrence Weston 66-69; V of Two Mile Hill Dio Bris from 69. *St Michael's Vicarage, Two Mile Hill, Bristol, BS15 1BE.* (Bristol 671371)

BOWES, Ernest Ward. b 04. Trin Coll Cam BA 27, MA 30. Ridley Hall Cam 27. **d** 29 **p** 30 Bradf. C of St Steph Bowling 29-33; Em W Hampstead 34-41; Area Sec CMS 41-49; CMS Publicity Field Org and L to Offic Dio Lon 49-52; V of Em Weston-s-Mare 52-70. *40 Exmoor Drive, Worthing, W Sussex, BN13 2PH.* (Worthing 60741)

BOWES, John Anthony Hugh. b 39. Ch Ch Ox 3rd cl Cl Mods 60, BA (3rd cl Lit Hum) 62, Dipl Th 63, MA 65. Westcott Ho Cam 63. **d** 65. Hulme for Man **p** 66 Man. C of All SS and Marts, Langley 65-68; Asst Chap Univ of Bris 68-73; Team V of Cramlington 73-76; P-in-c of Oldland Dio Bris 76-80; Team R from 80. *Vicarage, Oldland Common, Bristol, BS15 6PN.* (Bitton 2143)

BOWIE, Richard John. b 45. St Mich Ho Crafers 73. **d** 78 **p** 80 Graft. Hon C of Bonalbo 78-80; P-in-c of Moa I Dio Carp from 80. *St Paul's Mission, Moa Island, Queensld, Australia.*

BOWIE, Richard William. Bp's Coll Calc 55. Serampore Coll BD 64. **d** 58 **p** 59 Calc. C of The Old Miss Calc 58-64; St Paul's Cathl Calc 65-68; Lect Bp's Coll Calc 68-70; Prin 70-74; V of St Bart Bardon City and Dio Brisb from 74. *9 Bardon Esplanade, Bardon, Brisbane, Queensland, Australia 4065.* (36 3301)

BOWIE, Roderick William. Univ of Syd BA (1st cl Educn) 64. Moore Th Coll Syd. **d** 45 **p** 46 Syd. C of St Clem Mosman 45-46; Miss at Chengtu 46-51; L to Offic Dio Syd 51-52; Asst Master St Steph Boys' Coll Hong Kong 52-56; C-in-c of St Barn Syd 57-59; Croydon Pk 59-61; R of Turramurra 62-66; Dean and R of Ch Ch Cathl Graft 66-68; Asst Master Barker Coll Hornsby 69-74; L to Offic Dio Syd from 69. *8 Park Crescent, Pymble, NSW, Australia 2073.* (44-6021)

BOWKER, Archibald Edward. Univ of Manit BA 52. St Jo Coll Winnipeg, LTh 51. **d** 51 Edmon **p** 52 Athab. C of Windsor 52-55; St Paul's Cathl Lon Ont 55-57; R of Thedford Ont 57-59; C of All SS Monk Wearmouth 59-61; PC of Blackhill 61-68; V 68-79. *19 Greenside, Greatham, Hartlepool, Cleve, TS25 2HS.*

BOWKER, John Westerdale. b 35. Worc Coll Ox BA (1st cl Th) and Liddon Stud 58. Ripon Hall Ox. **d** 61 Sheff **p** 62 Ely. C of St Aug Sheff 61-62; Fell Lect and Dir of Studies (Th) CCC Cam from 62; Hulsean Pr 64-65; Lect in Div Univ of Cam 70-74; Wilde Lect Ox 72-75; Prof of Relig Studs Lanc from 74; M Doctrine Comm from 77. *The Cottage, Bailrigg, Lancaster.*

BOWKETT, Canon Cyril Edward Vivian. St Jo Coll Dur LTh 38, BA 39, MA 68. Clifton Th Coll 35. **d** 39 **p** 40 Bris. C of St Mich Bris 39-42; St Barnabas Knowle 42-47; R of St Geo Mart (w St Mich AA from 56; w St Steph from 64) Borough and Dio S'wark from 47; C-in-c of St Mich AA S'wark 47-56; St Steph S'wark 61-64; Hon Can of S'wark from 66; C-in-c of St Jude Borough and Dio S'wark from 75. *St George the Martyr Rectory, Tabard Gardens, SE1 1JP.* (01-407 2796)

BOWKETT, Henry Thomas. b 14. **d** 73 Bp Greenwood for Ott **p** 75 Ott. On leave 73; I of Centr Dundas 74-77; Clarendon 77-80. *211 Castlefrank Drive, Kanata, Ont, Canada.*

BOWKETT, William Roy. Univ of Manit BA 66. St Jo Coll Winnipeg BTh 67. **d** 66 **p** 67 Bp J O Anderson for Rupld. C of St Matt Winnipeg 66-69; L to Offic Dio Rupld 69-70; Dio Bran 70-72; Hon C of St Pet Winnipeg Dio Rupld from 73. *550 Elm Street, Winnipeg, Manit, Canada.*

BOWLAND, John Michael. b 44. Ch Coll Cam 2nd cl Hist pt i 64, BA (1st cl Th pt ii) 66. Keble Coll Ox DPhil 70. St Steph Ho Ox 66. **d** 68 S'wark **p** 72 Edmon for Lon. C of St Steph Lewisham 68-69; St Jas Friern Barnet 72-75; St Pet Ealing 75-76; St Andr Willesden and of St Francis Gladstone Pk 76-79. *c/o 11 Ellesmere Road, NW10 1JS.* (01-452 7939)

✠ **BOWLBY, Right Rev Ronald Oliver.** b 26. Trin Coll Ox BA (2nd cl Mod Hist) 50, MA 54. Westcott Ho Cam 50. **d** 52 Jarrow for Dur **p** 53 Dur. C of St Luke Pallion 52-56; St Cuthb Billingham 56-57; C-in-c St Aidan Billingham 57-59; Min 59-60; PC 60-66; V of Croydon 66-73; Hon Can of Cant 70-73; Cons Ld Bp of Newc T in Dur Cathl 6 Jan 73 by Abp of York; Bps of Ches, Ripon, Man, Southw, Sheff, Bradf, Carl, and Roch; Bps Suffr of Jarrow, Burnley, Pontefract, Whitby, Selby, Knaresborough, Doncaster, Croydon and others; Trld to S'wark 80; Chairman of Hosp Chaps Coun 74-80; M Angl Consultative Coun from 77. *38 Tooting Bec Gardens, SW16 1QZ.* (01-769 3256)

BOWLES, Etienne Everette Edison. b 39. Hur Coll DMin 70. McGill Univ MA 72. **d** 69 **p** 70 Nass. C of St Marg Andros 70-71; Sec and Treas Dio Nass 72-77; on leave. *Apt 6, 34811 University Street, Montreal, Canada.*

BOWLER, David Henderson. b 54. Univ of Kent at Cant BA 75. St Jo Coll Nottm 75. **d** 78 **p** 79 Southw. C of Bramcote Dio Southw from 78. *50 Bankfield Drive, Beeston, Nottingham, NG9 3EG.*

BOWLER, Denis Charles Stanley. b 16. **d** 66 **p** 67 Glouc. C of Bp's Cleeve 66-69; C of Coleford 69-72; V of St Osw Coney Hill Glouc 72-77; Lydbrook Dio Glouc from 77. *Vicarage, Church Hill, Lydbrook, Glos.* (Lydbrook 976225)

BOWLER, Frederick Wallace. b 11. AKC 34. MBE 46. **d** 34 **p** 35 S'wark. C of St John Walworth 34-37; Scarborough 37-39; CF (EC) 40-46 (Men in Disp 46); Hon CF from 51; V of Woburn Sands 46-50; P-in-c of Jesselton 51-52; St Columba Miri 52-55; V of Marston Magna 55-58; Westfield 58-66; PC of Alcombe 66-68; V 68-72; Perm to Offic Dio Ex from 73. *11 Capper Close, Newton Poppleford, Sidmouth, Devon.*

BOWLER, Kenneth Neville. b 37. K Coll Lon and Warm 57. **d** 61 **p** 62 Derby. C of Buxton 61-67; R of Sandiacre 67-75; V of Bedfont Dio Lon from 75. *Vicarage, Hatton Road, Bedfont, Middx, TW14 8JR.* (01-751 0088)

BOWLER, Reginald James. b 13. Keble Coll Ox BA 33, MA 64. St Steph Ho Ox 33. **d** 36 **p** 37 Lich. C of Blakenall Heath 36-40; Goldenhill 40-43; Northaw (in c of St Andr Cuffley) 43-44; H Cross Shrewsbury 44-47; Asst Master Prestelde Sch Shrewsbury and L to Offic Dio Lich 47-48; C of Newbold w Dunstan 48-50; Elland (in c of All SS) 50-52; L to Offic Dio Lich 52-54; C-in-c of St Greg Conv Distr Blackhalve Wednesfield 54-58; V of Cantley 58-62; Chap St Geo's Sch Harpenden 62-64; L to Offic Dio St Alb 64-71; R of Kirkmanshulme 71-75; C of Hollinwood 75-78; Perm to Offic Dio Lich from 78. *45 Woodland Avenue, Norton-le-Moors, Stoke-on-Trent, ST6 8NE.* (S-o-T 544458)

BOWLER, Roy Harold. Late Scho of Wadh Coll Ox BA (2nd Cl Nat Sci) 48, MA 57. Wells Th Coll 52. **d** 53 **p** 54 Lon. C of H Redeemer Clerkenwell 53-55; Tottenham 55-57; L to Offic Dio Cant and Asst Master St Edm Sch Cant 57-61; Bernard Mizeki Coll Marandellas 62-67; St Paul's Colleg Sch Hamilton 67-71; Hon C of St Pet Cathl Hamilton Dio Waik 68-70; Chap St D Miss Bonda Dio Mashon (Dio Mutare from 80) from 71. *St David's Mission, Bonda, Umtali, Zimbabwe.*

✠ **BOWLES, Right Rev Cyril William Johnston.** b 16. Em Coll Cam 2nd cl Mor Sc Trip pt i 36, Lady Kay Scho of Jes Coll Cam BA (1st cl Th Trip pt i) 38, 2nd cl Th Trip pt ii 39, MA 41. Ridley Hall Cam 37. **d** 39 **p** 40 Chelmsf. C of Barking 39-41; Chap Ridley Hall Cam 42-44; Vice-Prin 44-51; Prin 51-63; Select Pr Univ of Cam 45 53 58 and 63; Univs of Ox and Dub 61; L to Offic Dio Ely 45-63; Exam Chap to Bp of Carl 50-63; to Bps of Roch; Ely; and Chelmsf 51-63; Bradf 56-61; Bris 63-69; Hon Can of Ely 59-63; Bris 63-69; Archd of Swindon 63-69; Surr 63-69; Commiss Argent 63-69; Cons Ld Bp of Derby in Westmr Abbey 1 Nov 69 by Abp of Cant; Bps of Lon; Win; Ox; Portsm; Guildf; Chelmsf; Bris and others. *Bishop's House, 6 King Street, Duffield, Derby, DE6 4EU.* (Derby 46744)

BOWLES, David Anthony. b 44. Kelham Th Coll 63. **d** 68 **p** 69 Southw. C of Bilborough w Strelley 68-72; Beeston 72-75; Chap of Ascen I 75-77; V of St Mark Wellingborough Dio Pet from 77; P-in-c of Wilby Dio Pet from 78. *Vicarage, Queensway, Wellingborough, Northants.* (Wellingborough 673893)

BOWLES, John Ernest. St Jo Coll Auckld. **d** 77 **p** 78 Wel. Hon C of St Pet City and Dio Wel from 77. *11 Park Mews, Moxham Avenue, Wellington 3, NZ.* (861-990)

BOWLES, John Robin. Magd Coll Cam BA 52. Clifton Th Coll 60. **d** 62 **p** 63 Nak. Miss Dio Nak 63-65; P-in-c of Thomson's Falls 65-68; C of Nakuru 68-72; P-in-c of Lavington Dio Nai from 72. *Box 25030, Nairobi, Kenya.* (Nairobi 48352)

BOWLES, Michael Hubert Venn. b 36. Selwyn Coll Cam 1st cl Th Trip pt i 57, BA (2nd cl Th Trip pt ii) 59, 2nd cl Th Trip pt iii 60, MA 63. Ridley Hall Cam 59. **d** 61 **p** 62 Lon. C of St Barn Woodside Pk Finchley 61-64; Swanage 64-67; Lect St Mich Coll Llan 67-72; Chap 67-70; Libr 70-72; Lect in Th Univ of Wales (Cardiff) 67-72; Perm to Offic Dio Llan 68-71; L to Offic Dio Llan 71-72; R of Gt Stanmore Dio Lon from 72. *Rectory, Great Stanmore, Middx.* (01-954 0276)

BOWLES, Peter John. b 39. Univ of Lon BA 60. Linc Th Coll 71. **d** 73 **p** 74 Derby. C of Clay Cross 73-76; Boulton 76-79; R of Brailsford w Shirley Dio Derby from 79; P-in-c of Edlaston and Osmaston 81. *Rectory, Brailsford, Derby.* (Brailsford 362)

BOWLES, Ralph Gordon. Univ of Syd BA 75. Moore Th Coll ThL 78, BD 79. **d** 80 Syd **p** 80 Bp Robinson for Syd. C of St Clem Lalor Pk Dio Syd from 80. *18 First Avenue, Seven Hills, NSW, Australia 2147.* (671-1869)

BOWLES, Ronald Leonard. b 24. K Coll Lon and Warm BD 52. AKC 52. **d** 53 **p** 54 Newc T. C of Berwick-on-Tweed 53-56; Christchurch 56-60; R of Nursling w Rownhams 60-66; V of Woolston 66-75; St Jo Bapt Moordown Bournemouth Dio Win from 75. *St John's Vicarage, Moordown, Bournemouth, Dorset.* (Bournemouth 528612)

BOWLEY, John Richard Lyon. b 46. Univ of Dur BA 68. Qu Univ Belf MSc 72. M RTPI 76. Div Hostel Dub 78. **d** 79 **p** 80 Down. C of St Columba Knock Belf 79-81; Bp's C of Knocknagoney Dio Down from 81. *11 Glenmillan Park, Belfast, BT4 2JE, N Ireland.* (Belfast 63795)

BOWMAN, Canon Andrew Michael. Hertf Coll Ox BA 55, MA 57. Oak Hill Th Coll 55. **d** 57 **p** 58 Chelmsf. C of Walthamstow 57-61; CMS Miss 61-68; C of Mile Cross 68-71; CMS Miss Bukuku 70-77; Dioc Treas Dio Ruw 72-77; Can of Ruw from 76; C of Ch Ch Purley 77-79; P-in-c of Worstead w Westwick and Sloley Dio Nor from 79; Tunstead w Sco Ruston Dio Nor from 79. *Worstead Vicarage, North Walsham, Norf.* (Smallburgh 800)

BOWMAN, George Henry Lindsay. b 15. Linc Th Coll 45. **d** 47 **p** 48 Ches. C of Ashton-on-Mersey 47-51; Newark-on-Trent w Codington 51-54; Chap HM Borstal Inst Borstal 54-63; Min Can of Roch Cathl 56-63; Chap HM Pris Wakef 63-66; V of Steeton w Eastburn 66-76; C of Cleethorpes 76-80. *14 Broadway, Lincoln, LN2 1SH.* (Linc 26579)

BOWMAN, Ian Hinchcliffe. b 33. Tyndale Hall Bris 53. BD (Lon) 57. **d** 57 Warrington for Liv **p** 58 Liv. C of St Simon and St Jude Southport 57-61; St Pet Halliwell 61-63; R of Asby w Ormside 63-68; Bootle w Corney 68-72; V of Camerton w Seaton Dio Carl from 72. *Camerton Vicarage, Workington, Cumb, CA14 1LP.* (Workington 2162)

BOWMAN, John. Univ of Glas MA (1st cl) 38, BD (w distinc in Systematic Th) 41. Ch Ch Ox DPhil 45. **d** 50 **p** 54 Ripon. Hd of Dept of Semitic Lang and Lit Univ of Leeds 48-59; Hon C of Leeds 51-53; Kirkstall 53-54; Perm to Offic at Hinderwell 54-59; Prof of Middle E Stud Univ of Melb from 59; Hon C of H Trin Surrey Hills 59-72; Perm to Offic Dio Melb from 73. *140 Arden Street, North Melbourne, Vic., Australia.* (03-329 0072)

BOWMAN-EADIE, Russell Ian. b 45. ACP 68. AKC and BD 71. St Aug Coll Cant 71. **d** 72 **p** 73 Kens for Lon. C of St Pet Hammersmith 72-74; V of St Nich Leic 74-81; Chap to Univ of Leic 74-81; Dioc Adult Educn Officer Dio Dur from 81. *1 Broadoaks, Bishop Middleham, Ferryhill, Co Durham.* (Ferryhill 55315)

BOWN, Francis Adrian Charles Simon. b 48. Late Exhib Jes Coll Cam BA 72, MA 74. Jes Coll Ox BA (Th) 75, MA 78. Linc Th Coll 76. **d** 77 **p** 78 York. C of Howden 77-80; P-in-c of St Steph Sculcoates Hull Dio York from 80. *29 Westbourne Avenue, Hull, HU5 3HN.* (Hull 46075)

BOWN, Canon John Frederick Olney. b 13. Late Exhib of K Coll Cam 2nd cl Hist Trip pt i 35, BA (3rd cl Hist Trip pt ii) 36, MA 70. TD 50. Cudd Coll 36. **d** 37 **p** 38 Chelmsf. C of Prittlewell 37-39; CF (TA) 39-44; CF 44-70; R of St Mary-in-the-Castle 44-45; Can of Momb 56-58; Prov Can of Nai 61-77; Hon Can from 78; Commiss Nai from 64; Hon Chap to HM the Queen from 67; V of Fordingbridge w Ibsley 70-79; RD of Christchurch 74-78; P-in-c of Longstock and Leckford Dio Win from 79. *7 Trafalgar Way, Stockbridge, Hants.* (Stockbridge 672)

BOWRING, David Michael. b 43. Univ of Tor BA 64. Knox Coll Tor BD 67, MTh 76. **d** and **p** 76 Alg. On leave. *95 Burnside Drive, Toronto, Ont, Canada M6S 2M9.*

BOWRON, Hugh Mark. b 52. Univ of Cant NZ BA 74, MA 76. Dipl Th (Leeds) 78. Coll of the Resurr Mirfield 76. **d** 79 **p** 80 Pet. C of St Mary Virg Northn Dio Pet from 79. *10 Winchester Road, Far Cotton, Northampton, NN4 9AY.* (Northn 61883)

BOWRON, Norman Cecil. St Jo Coll Ox 2nd cl Math Mods 35, BA (3rd cl Nat Sc) 37, Dipl Th 38. **d** 39 B & W **p** 40 Cant. C of Weston-s-Mare 39; St Andr Deal 39-40; St Alb S Norwood 40-42; CF (EC) 42-48; P-in-c of Sandakan 48-50; Chap St Mark's Coll Mapanza 64-67; L to Offic Dio Barb 67-68; C of Kenora Dio Keew from 73. *St Mary's Church, Whitedog, Ont., Canada.*

BOWSER, Alan. b 35. St D Coll Lamp BA 60, Dipl Th 63. **d** 63 **p** 64 Dur. C of St Chad Bensham Gateshead 63-67; St Jas Conv Distr Owton Manor, Hartlepool 67-72; V of Horden Dio Dur from 72. *Horden Vicarage, Peterlee, Co Durham.* (Horden 4423)

BOWSER, Lawrence Charles. b 41. Barrington Coll RI USA BA 65. Westcott Ho Cam 76. **d** 78 **p** 79 Ripon. Succr and Min Can Ripon Cathl 78-81; Chap Ch Ch Coll Cant from 81. *Christ Church College, Canterbury, CT1 1QU.* (0227-65548)

BOWYER, David George. Waterloo Univ Ont BA 74. Hur Coll Lon Ont MDiv 77. **d** 77 Bp Parke-Taylor for Hur **p** 78 Hur. C of St Jo Evang Kitchener 77-79; R of Dover Dio Hur from 79. *RR1, Paincourt, Ont, Canada.*

BOWYER, Edwin Cyril. Trin Coll Tor STh 43. **d** and **p** 44 Alg. C of Englehart 44-46; I of Elmsdale 46-47; in Amer Ch 47-62; R of Consort 62-67; St Alb, Regina 67-77; St Mich Regina 72-76. *2144 Edward Street, Regina, Sask, Canada.*

BOWYER, Frank. b 28. Univ of Man BA (Th) 49, BD 56. Oak Hill Th Coll 53. **d** 55 **p** 56 Man. C of St Paul Halliwell 55-57; St Kentigern Crosthwaite 57-59; V of Thornham 59-63; R of Burnage 63-81; Gosforth w Nether Wasdale & Wasdale Head Dio Carl from 81. *Rectory, Gosforth, Seascale, Cumb, CA20 1AZ.* (Gosforth 251)

BOWYER, Henry George. Univ of NZ BSc 40, BD 54. Selw Coll Dun LTh 47. **d** and **p** 42 Wel. C of Petone 42-46; CF (NZ) 44-46; C of Masterton 46-48; V of Aramoho 48-53; Petone 53-61; Hawera 61-69; Whangarei Dio Auckld from 69; Archd of Waimate 69-76. *51a Kamo Road, Whangarei, Auckland, NZ.* (84-745)

BOWYER, John Breedon. St Jo Coll Morpeth 55. **d** 57 **p** 58 Perth. C of Scarborough 57-60; Wembley w Floreat 60-63; R of Bellevue w Darlington 64-71; Kwinana 70-75; Canning Dio Perth from 75. *Box 67, Cannington, W Australia 6107.* (458 1348)

BOWYER, Robert Joscelyn. b 13. St Jo Coll Dur LTh 36, BA 37. St Aid Coll 33. **d** 37 **p** 38 Derby. C of Normanton-by-Derby 37-40; St Werburgh Derby 40-44; PC of Somercotes 44-48; St Luke Derby 48-53; R of Brooke w Mottistone 53-78. *Southbrook, Brook, IW, PO30 4EJ.* (0983 740482)

BOX, David Norman. b 28. Univ of Lon BD and AKC 48. St Bonif Coll Warm 50. **d** 51 **p** 52 Chelmsf. C of Grays 51-53; Asst Master St Benedict's Sch Aldershot and Perm to Offic at Ascen Ch Aldershot 53-55; C of All SS Weston Thames Ditton 55-58; Camberley 58-61; V of Blackheath w Chilworth 61-69; Allerton Bradf 69-75; R of Exford w Exmoor 75-80; V of Castle Cary w Ansford Dio B & W from 80. *Vicarage, Castle Cary, Somt.* (Castle Cary 332)

BOX, Harry Charles Edmond. b 23. Wells Th Coll 64. **d** 65 **p** 66 Wakef. C of Hanging Heaton 65-68; V of Northowram 68-76; Kirkburton Dio Wakef from 76. *Kirkburton Vicarage, Huddersfield, Yorks, HD8 0SJ.* (Kirkburton 2188)

BOX, Canon Hubert Stanley. b 04. K Coll Lon Relton Prize and AKC (1st cl) 26. Univ of Lon BD 26, 2nd cl Hons in Bibl and Hist Th 27, PhD 33. **d** 27 **p** 28 Glouc. C of Westbury-on-Severn 27-29; St Barn Bexhill-on-Sea 29-30; St John (in c of All SS) Eastover Bridgwater 30-31; Perm to Offic Dio Lon 31-34; Asst Master and Asst Chap Hurstpierpoint Coll 33-34; L to Offic Dio Chich 35-36; C of Heene 36-40; V of Scaynes Hill 40-55; Proc Conv Chich 45-70; RD of Cuckfield 46-55; V of St Barn Bexhill 55-74; Surr 65-74; Can and Preb of Chich Cathl 66-77; Can (Emer) from 77; Perm to Offic Dio Chich from 74. *Bungalow 3, Terry's Cross, Woodmancote, Henfield, Sussex.* (Henfield 493335)

BOX, Kenneth John. b 45. St Jo Coll Morpeth ThDip 79. **d** 80 **p** 81 Tas. C of Burnie 80-81; St Jas New Tn Dio Tas from 81. *13 Sharp's Road, Lenah Valley, Tasmania 7008.*

BOX, Reginald Gilbert. b 20. AKC (2nd cl) 41. Univ of Lon BD (2nd cl) 41. Em Coll Cam BA (2nd cl Th Trip pt iii) 52, MA 57. Westcott Ho Cam 41. **d** 43 **p** 44 Chelmsf. M SSF 56. C of Chingford 43-47; Chap Bps' Coll Cheshunt 47-50; L to Offic Dio Ely 51-57; Dio Sarum 57-61; C of St Benedict Cam 61-67; Chap Coll of St Mark and St John Chelsea 67-69; L to Offic Dio Auckld 69; Min of Pacific Prov of SSF from 70; Perm to Offic Dio Melan from 73; Dio Brisb 75-77; Hon C of Glen Innes 77-79; Perm to Offic Dio Auckld from 79. *132 Taniwha Street, Glen Innes, Auckland, NZ.*

BOX, Thomas Allen. Bp's Univ Lennox BA 64. Trin Coll Tor STB 67. **d** and **p** 67 Ott. C of St Mark Ott 67-68; I of Petawawa 68-72; Deep River 72-78; Arnprior Dio Ott from 78. *99 Ottawa Street, Arnprior, Ont, Canada.* (613-623 2663)

BOXALL, David John. b 41 Univ of Dur BA (2nd cl Geog) 63, Dipl Th 65. Sarum Th Coll 65. **d** 66 **p** 67 St E. C of St Aug of Hippo Ipswich 66-69; Bourne 69-71; St Barn Woodside Pk Finchley 71-72; Thundersley 72-76; Team V of Stanground and Farcet Dio Ely from 76. *2 Peterborough Road, Farcet, Peterborough, PE7 3BH.* (Peterborough 240286)

BOXALL, Martin Alleyne. b 37. Wells Th Coll 65. **d** 67 Dorch for Ox **p** 68 Ox. C of Crowthorne 68-70; St Mich (in c of St Cath of Sienna) Tilehurst 70-76; V of St Cath of Sienna Tilehurst 76-78; Padstow Dio Truro from 78. *Vicarage, Padstow, Cornw.* (Padstow 532224)

BOXALL, Norman Alan. Montr Th Coll LTh 64. **d** 63 **p** 64 Calg. I of Elnora 63-67; Bowness 67-75; Stettler 75-79. *c/o Box 549, Kelowna, BC, Canada.*

BOXALL, Simon Roger. b 55. St Jo Coll Cam BA 76. Ridley Hall cam 77. **d** 79 **p** 80 Nor. C of Eaton Dio Nor from 79. *14 Merrow Gardens, Eaton, Norwich, Norfolk, NR4 6HH.*

BOXLEY, Christopher. b 45. K Coll Lon and Warm BD and AKC 68. **d** 69 **p** 70 Win. C of Ascen Bitterne Pk 69-73; Perm to Offic Dio Chich 73-78; Asst Master Midhurst Gr Sch from 73; P-in-c of Heyshott Dio Chich from 78. *Rectory, Heyshott, Midhurst, W Sussex, GU29 0DL.* (Midhurst 4405)

BOXLEY, John Edwin. b 15. Ch Coll Cam BA 38, MA 41. Ridley Hall Cam 37. **d** 39 **p** 40 Man. C of Rochdale 39-44; Ch Ch and H Trin Folkestone 44-46; Chap Nzoia Dio Momb 47-49; Trans-Nzoia 49-54; V of Seasalter 54-57; Chap and Asst Master Sir Roger Manwood's Sch Sandwich 57-62; Dulwich Coll 62-76; R of W Mersea w E Mersea 76-80. *45 Mount Pleasant Avenue, Wells, Somt.* (0749-75073)

BOYCE, Ven Brian David Michael. Fitzw Ho Cam BA 55, MA 62. Wells Th Coll 55. **d** 57 **p** 58 Ex. C of Tavistock 57-60; Paignton 60-62; Germiston 62-64; R of Ermelo 64-67; Primrose 67-75; Springs Dio Johann from 75; Archd of SE Transv 75; Springs from 75. *PO Box 949, Springs, Transvaal, S Africa.* (011-56 1602)

BOYCE, John Frederick. b 33. ALCD 57. **d** 57 **p** 58 S'wark. C of St Andr Earlsfield 57-60; Westerham 60-63; Farnborough Kent 63-66; V of Sutton-at-Hone 66-73; P in c of Chiddingstone 73-74; R of Chiddingstone w Chiddingstone Causeway Dio Roch from 74. *Chiddingstone Rectory, Edenbridge, Kent.* (Penshurst 870478)

BOYCE, Kenneth. St Aid Coll 59. **d** 60 **p** 61 Man. C of Pendleton and of St Anne Brindle Heath 60-63; R of St Jas Collyhurst Man 63-65; N Reddish Dio Man from 65. *551 Gorton Road, North Reddish, Stockport, SK5 6NF.* (061-223 0692)

BOYCE, Kenneth Albert. b 51. St Edm Hall Ox BA 72, MA 76. Selw Coll Cam BA 75. Westcott Ho Cam 73. **d** 75 **p** 76 Leic. C of St Denys Evington Leic 75-78; P-in-c of Gt Bowden w Welham and Dioc Stewardship Adv 78-81; Chap Leic Poly from 81; Team V of H Spirit City and Dio Leic from 82. *2 Sawday Street, Leicester, LE2 7JW.* (Leic 552540)

BOYCE, Noel James. b 40. Moore Th Coll Syd ACT ThL 68. **d** 69 **p** 70 Armid. C of Moree 69-71; V of Mungindi 71-75; V of Ashford w Delungra and Tinga 75-81; CF (Austr) from 81. *c/o Box 198, Armidale, NSW, Australia.*

BOYD, Alan McLean. b 50. St Jo Coll Nottm BTh 79. **d** 79 **p** 80 Portsm. C of Bp's Waltham Dio Portsm from 79. *11 Churchill Avenue, Bishops Waltham, Southampton.*

BOYD, Alexander Jamieson. b 46. St Chad's Coll Dur BSc 68. Coll of the Resurr Mirfield 69. **d** 79 **p** 80 Edin. Asst Master Loretto Sch Musselburgh; Hon C of Musselburgh Dio Edin from 79. *2 Albert Terrace, Musselburgh, Midlothian.* (031-665 2393)

BOYD, David Anthony. b 42. Sarum Wells Th Coll 72. **d** 75 **p** 76 Ches. C of H Trin Ches 75-79; V of St Jas Congleton Dio Ches from 79. *116 Holmes Chapel Road, Congleton, Ches.* (Congleton 3722)

BOYD, Kevin Henry. St Jo Coll Morpeth. **d** 50 **p** 51 Bath.

C of Gilgandra 49; C-in-c of Brewarrina 49-55; C of Cowra 55-56; Narrendera 59-62. *c/o 67 Brunswick Street, Fitzroy, Vic., Australia.*

BOYD, Leonard Douglas Peter. b 47. Kelham Th Coll 65. **d** 70 Grimsby for Linc **p** 71 Linc. C of St Aug Grimsby Linc 70-73; C of St Alb Mart Holborn 73-78; P-in-c of St Agatha Sparkbrook Dio Birm from 78; St Barn Balsall Heath Dio Birm from 81. *St Agatha's Presbytery, 25 Merton Road, Moseley, Birmingham, B13 9BX.* (021-449 2790)

BOYD, Michael Stephen. b 51. Acadia Univ Wolfville NS BSc 73. Trin Coll Tor MDiv 77. **d** 75 NS **p** 77 Bp Hatfield for NS. R of Digby Dio NS from 76; Weymouth Dio NS from 76. *PO Box 1307, Digby, NS, Canada, BOV 1AO.*

BOYD, Michael Victor. b 33. Univ of Dur BA (2nd cl Th) 57, MEducn 77. Coll of Resurr Mirfield. **d** 59 **p** 60 Southw. C of Warsop w Sookholm 59-62; Chap St Geo Coll Quilmes Argent 62-63; Asst Master Wolsingham Secondary Sch 63-67; Lect in Div St Hild's Coll Dur 67-75; Prin Lect Relig Stud Coll of St Hild and St Bede Dur 75-81. *Address temp unknown.*

BOYD, Robert Henry. b 36. **d** 66 **p** 67 Arm. C of Drumcree 66-69; I of Annaghmore Dio Arm from 69. *54 Moss Road, Annaghmore, Portadown, Armagh, N Ireland.*

BOYD, Canon Robert Shields. Wycl Coll Tor BA 17. **d** 21 Hur **p** 22 Niag. C of Otterville 21-22; St Geo St Catharines 22-24; I of Fonthill w Port Robinson 24-27; Hornby w Stewarttown and Norval 27-35; on leave 35-38; Mayo 38-41; Chap CASF 41-46; Miss at Mayo Yukon 46; C of St Trin Tor 46-48; Ch of Epiph Tor 48-52; I of Keewatin 52-55; Dom Chap to Bp of Keew 53-65; R of Sioux Lookout 55-60; I of Thompson 60-62; Ignace 62-65; Hon Can of St Alb Cathl Kenora from 59; Hon C of St Pet Tor 65-68. *3-2155 Dewdney Trunk Road, Maple Ridge, BC, Canada.*

BOYD, Roland Philip. b 46. AKC 75. St Aug Coll Cant 75. **d** 76 **p** 77 Glouc. C of Dursley 76-77. *Address temp unknown.*

BOYD, William Green. b 07. AKC and BA 29. Oak Hill Coll 74. **d** 75 **p** 76 Chelmsf. C of Chingford 75-81; Hon C of Buckhurst Hill Dio Chelmsf from 81. *2 Leyland Gardens, Woodford Green, Essex, IG8 7QT.* (01-505 5752)

BOYD, Preb William John Peter. b 28. BA (Lon) 48, BD (Lon) 53, PhD (Lon) 77. Univ of Birm MA 60. **d** 57 **p** 58 Birm. C of St Pet and St Paul Aston 57-60; V of St Paul W Smethwick 60-63; St Breward 63-68; R of St Ewe 68-73; Preb of Trehaverock in Preb Ch of St Endellion from 73; V of St Kew 73-77; M Gen Syn from 75; R of Falmouth Dio Truro from 77. *Rectory, Albany Road, Falmouth, Cornw, TR11 3RP.* (Falmouth 314176)

BOYD, William Thomas. b 15. TCD BA 38, MA 43. **d** 39 Bp Kennedy for Down **p** 40 Down. C of Carrickfergus 39-42; Chap RAFVR 42-46; I of Mullavilly 46-51; Chap RAF 51-70; Asst Chap-in-Chief 65-70; Hon Chap to HM the Queen 68-70; R of W Parley 70-76. *4 Heath Farm Close, Ferndown, Wimborne, Dorset, BH22 8JP.* (Ferndown 892055)

BOYDEN, Peter Frederick. b 41. Univ of Lon BSc (1st cl) and AKC 62. Em Coll Cam BA (2nd cl Th Trip pt ii) 64, MA 68, MLitt 69. Ridley Hall Cam. **d** 66 **p** 67 Ely. C of Chesterton 66-68; Wimbledon 68-72; Chap and Asst Master K Sch Cant from 72. *Flat 2, 58 London Road, Canterbury, CT2 8JY.* (Cant 62287)

BOYE, Samuel Hunu. **d** 67 Accra. d Dio Accra. *Box 491, Accra, Ghana.*

BOYES, David Arthur Stiles. b 30. Lon Coll of Div 62. **d** 63 **p** 64 Lon. C of St Mary Islington 63-71; V of St Steph Canonbury Road Lon 71-75; St Barn Cray Dio Roch from 75. *St Barnabas Vicarage, Rushet Road, St Paul's Cray, Orpington, Kent BR5 2PU.* (Orpington 21353)

BOYES, John Cecil. b 14. Bps' Coll Cheshunt 47. **d** 50 **p** 51 Ex. C of St Pet Plymouth 50-52; St Ives Cornw 52-57; V of Saltash 57-81. *19 Westover Road, Callington, Cornw.*

BOYES, Jonathan Richard. b 46. Vic Univ of Wel BA 69. St Jo Coll Auckld 70. **d** 72 **p** 73 Wel. C of St Pet Palmerston North 72-76; V of Shannon 76-81; Porirua Dio Wel from 81. *1 Derby Place, Porirua, NZ.* (75-800)

BOYES, Michael Charles. b 27. Univ of Lon BA 53. BD (Lon) 58. Wells Th Coll 53. **d** 55 **p** 56 Ex. C of Heavitree Ex 55-61; V of Exwick Ex 61-68; Broad Clyst w Westwood Dio Ex from 68; RD of Aylesbeare 77-81. *Prior's Court, Broad Clyst, Exeter, Devon.* (Broad Clyst 280)

BOYI, Nason Mika. b 45. St Phil Coll Kongwa 74. **d** and **p** 76 Centr Tang. P Dio Centr Tang. *Box 27, Kongwa, Tanzania.*

BOYLE, Christopher John. b 51. AKC 75. St Aug Coll Cant 75. **d** 76 **p** 77 Birm. C of Wylde Green 76-80; Dom Chap to Bp of Birm from 80. *Chaplain's Lodge, Bishop's Croft, Harborne, Birmingham, B17 0BG.* (021-427 1163)

BOYLE, Noel Stuart Stirling. b 1888. Ex Coll Ox BA (3rd cl Th) 12, MA 51. Wells Th Coll 13. **d** 13 **p** 14 Win. C of St Steph Portsm 13-20; TCF 18-20; C of Christchurch 20-23; St Mary Bournemouth 23-31; V of St Benedict Bordesley 31-39; Upton w Skilgate R 39-44; R of Ruishton w Thornfalcon 44-52; L to Offic Dio B & W 52-60; Perm to Offic Dio Ex from 60. *Greystones, Noss Mayo, Plymouth, Devon, PL8 1ED.* (0752 872321)

BOYLE, Canon Richard Henry. b 08. TCD BA 30, LLB 37, MA 47. **d** 45 **p** 46 Oss. C of Killermogh 45-47; C-in-c of Kilmacshalgan 47-50; I of Skreen w Dromard and Kilmacshalgan 50-60; Rynagh (w Kinnitty from 70) Dio Meath from 60; Ballyboy w Killoughley Dio Meath from 70; Can of Meath from 69. *Rectory, Banagher, Offaly, Irish Republic.* (Banagher 39)

BOYLE, Terence Robert. b 26. **d** 77 Ox **p** 78 Buckingham for Ox (APM). C of Wexham Dio Ox from 77. *1 Wexham Springs Cottages, Framewood Road, Wexham, Bucks.*

BOYLES, Harry Cecil. b 15. AKC 38. **d** 38 **p** 39 Pet. C of All SS City and Dio Pet 38-42; All SS Boyne Hill 42-44; St Pet and St Paul Teddington 44-47; St Andr w H Innoc Grenada 47; St Geo Cathl St Vincent 47-49; St Pet Acton Green Lon 49-51; St Pet Folkestone 52-53; St Steph Clewer 53-57; V of H Trin Reading 57-63; C of St Pet Folkestone 63-68; P-in-c of St Pet Maidstone 68-73. *4 Barn Meadow Cottages, Boxley, Maidstone.*

BOYLES, James Bruce. Yale Univ BD 68. **d** 68 **p** 69 Ott. I of Mablerly-Lanark 68-72; Asst to Gen Sec Gen Synod of Canada 72-76; Ecumen Officer 76-81; R of St Geo Georgetown Dio Niag from 81. *7 Edith Street, Georgetown, Ont, Canada.* (416-877 8044)

BOYLES, Sara Leuna. b 40. Carleton Univ Ott BA 65. Trin Coll Tor MDiv 80. **d** and **p** 80 Ott. on leave. *c/o The Registrar, 200 University Avenue, Toronto, Ont, Canada, M5H 3E1.*

BOYLING, Denis Hudson. b 16. Keble Coll Ox 2nd cl Math Mods 36, BA (2nd cl Math) 38, Dipl in Th 39, MA 42. Cudd Coll 39. **d** 40 **p** 41 Sheff. C of St Cuthb Fir Vale Sheff. 40-46; Chap King's Coll Hosp 46-49; United Sheff Hosps 49-57; V of St Aug Sheff 57-68; Hon Can of Sheff 58-68; V of Almondbury 68-75; RD of Almondbury 68-75; Hon Can of Wakef 72-75; Can Res of Wakef 75-82. *Brendon, Berrington Road, Tenbury Wells.*

BOYLING, Mark Christopher. b 52. Keble Coll Ox BA (Hist) 74, BA (Th) 76, MA 78. Cudd Coll 74. **d** 77 **p** 78 Liv. C of St Mark Northwood Kirkby Dio Liv 77-79; P-in-c 79-80; Team V from 80. *St Mark's House, Brook Hey Drive, Northwood, Kirkby, Liverpool L33 9TE.* (051-546 2645)

BOYNS, Martin Laurence Harley. b 26. St Jo Coll Cam BA 49, MA 51. Ridley Hall Cam 50. **d** 52 **p** 53 S'wark. C of Woodmansterne 52-55; H Trin w Ch Ch Folkestone 55-58; V of Duffield 58-71; Rawdon 71-76; R of Melton Dio St E from 76. *Melton Rectory, Woodbridge, Suff.* (Woodbridge 2492)

BOYS SMITH, Canon John Sandwith. b 01. Late Found Scho of St Jo Coll Cam 2nd cl Econ Trip 21, BA (1st cl Th Trip pt i) 22, Naden Div Stud 22, Burney Stud and 1st cl Th Trip pt ii 24, MA 26, Hon LLD 70. Westcott Ho Cam 22 **d** 26 Birm **p** 27 Ely. C of Sutton Coldfield 26-27; Exam Chap to Bp of Ripon 27-34 and 35-40; to Bp of Birm 35-53; to Bp of Truro 40-51; Select Pr Univ of Cam 30 and 59-60; Ox 36-37 and 73; Hulsean Pri Univ of Cam 33-34; Chap St Jo Coll Cam 27-34; Dir of Th Stud 27-40 and 44-52; Asst Tutor 31-34; Tutor 34-39; Junior Bursar 39-40; Fell 27-59 and from 69; Sen Bursar 44-59; Master 59-69; Univ Lect in Div 31-40; Stanton Lect in Phil of Relig Univ of Cam 34-37; Ely Prof of Div Univ of Cam and Can of Ely Cathl 40-43; Sec Ely Dioc Conf 42-56; LPR Dio Ely from 44; Can (Emer) of Ely from 48; Vice-Chan Univ of Cam 63-65. *Trinity House, Castle Street, Saffron Walden, Essex, CB10 1BP.* (S Walden 23692)

BOYSE, Felix Vivian Allan. b 17. MVO 78. Late Found Scho of CCC Cam 1st cl Cl Trip pt i 37, BA (1st cl Th Trip pt i) 39, MA 42. Cudd Coll 39. **d** 40 **p** 41 Derby. C of New Mills 40-43; C-in-c 43-45; Vice-Prin Cudd Coll 45-51; L to Offic Dio Ox 46-51; V of St Andr Kingswood 51-58; Exam Chap to Bp of S'wark 53-59; V of St Mary Abchurch Lon 58-61; Select Pr Univ of Cam 60 and 67; Prin St Geo Coll Jer and Can of St Geo Colleg Ch Jer 61-64; Chap to HM the Queen from 65; Chap Hampton Court Palace 65-81; Pr Lincoln's Inn from 81. *2 Elsworthy, Thames Ditton, Surrey.* (01-398 1258)

BOZON, David Hamish. b 28. Fitzw Ho Cam BA 52, MA 56. Linc Th Coll 53. **d** 55 **p** 56 Lich. C of Berkswich w Walton 55-58; St Mary's Cathl Salisbury S Rhod 58-59; R of Mazoe S Rhod 59-64; C of Westbury-on-Trym 64-65; Chap to Deaf Dio Bris 65-68; Publ Pr Dio Bris 66-68; Information Officer RADD from 68; Perm to Offic Dios Cant, Lon, Guildf, S'wark and Roch from 68; Publ Pr Dio Chelmsf from 74. *101 Horn Lane, Woodford Green, Essex.* (01-504 8159)

BOZONGWANA, Wallace. b 28. **d** 72 **p** 73 Matab. P Dio Matab. *PB Q5285, Bulawayo, Zimbabwe.*

BRABY, Franklin George. St Chad's Coll Regina 53. **d** 55 **p** 56 Qu'app. I of Stoughton 55-58; Raymore 58-61; Chatsworth 61-64; C of H Trin Galt 64-66; I of Brussels 66-69; St

Steph Stratford 69-71. *164 Cobourg Street, Stratford, Ont., Canada.*

BRABY, Peter. b 11. Ch Ch Ox BA (2nd cl Mod Hist) 32, MA 37. Wells Th Coll 37. **d** 38 **p** 39 Lon. C of St Jas Friern Barnet 38-43; V of All SS Twickenham 43-47; St Alb N Harrow 47-58; Badsey 58-73; Wickhamford 58-73; RD of Evesham 68-72; Temple Guiting w Cutsdean 73-76; C-in-c of Guiting Power 74-76; V of The Guitings, Cutsdean and Farmcote 76. *3 Farriers Road, Middle Barton, Oxford.*

BRABYN, Frederick James. b 1897. Bps' Coll Cheshunt 29. **d** 29 **p** 30 Chelmsf. C of St John Stratford 29-32; Chap Port of Man and Org Sec (Miss to Seamen) for NW Distr 32-35; V of St Thos Bury Lancs 35-43; CF (TA-R of O) from 39; CF (EC) 43-51; Men in Disp 45; TD 50; R of Clowne 51-58; Whitwell Derbys 58-67. *107 Gilbert Road, Cambridge.*

BRACE, Stuart. b 49. St D Coll Lamp Dipl Th 74. Bp Burgess Hall Lamp 71. **d** 74 **p** 75 St D. C of Ch Ch Llanelly 74-76; Tenby 76-77; V of Strata Florida and Ystradmeurig 77-81. *Address temp unknown.*

BRACE, Thomas Harry. b 17. St D Coll Lamp BA 41. **d** 43 **p** 44 St D. C of Cwmamman 43-47; Llangathen w Llanfihangel Cilfargen 47-53; V of Llawhaden w Bletherston 53-61; Llansadwrn w Llandwrda (and Manordeilo from 78) Dio St D from 61; RD of Llangadog and Llandeilo from 75. *Vicarage, Llanwrda, Dyfed.* (Llangadog 343)

BRACEGIRDLE, Robert Kevin Stewart. b 47. Univ Coll Ox BA 69, MA 73. St Steph Ho Ox 70. **d** 73 **p** 74 Sarum. C of Dorchester Team Ministry 73-75; Woodchurch 75-78; V of Bidston Dio Ches from 78. *St Oswald's Vicarage, School Lane, Bidston, Birkenhead, Mer L43 7RD.* (051-652 4852)

BRACEWELL, David John. b 44. Univ of Leeds BA (Engl and Th) 66. Tyndale Hall, Bris 67. **d** 69 **p** 70 Roch. C of St Steph Tonbridge 69-72; St Pet Shipley 72-75; V of Halliwell Dio Man from 75. *St Paul's Vicarage, Halliwell, Bolton, BL1 8BP.* (Bolton 43456)

BRACEWELL, Howard Waring. b 35. Tyndale Hall Bris. **d** 63 Warrington for Liv for Arctic **p** 63 Arctic. I of Pond Inlet 63-72; C-in-c of Ashill 72-74; Trav Miss World Radio Miss Fellowship from 74; Perm to Offic Dio Bris from 77. *58 Rossall Avenue, Little Stoke, Bristol, BS12 6JU.* (Bristol 696892)

BRACEY, David Harold. b 36. K Coll Lon and Warm AKC 63. **d** 64 **p** 65 Man. C of St Pet Westleigh 64-67; Dunstable 67-70; V of Benchill 70-76; St Steph Elton Dio Man from 76. *St Stephen's Vicarage, Elton, Bury, BL8 2NR.* (061-764 1775)

BRACHER, John Noel. Angl Th Coll BC LTh 42. **d** 42 **p** 43 New Westmr. C of St Helen Vanc 42-44; Youth Work Sec for Dio New Westmr 44-49; Chap RCAF 50-72; Perm to Offic Dio BC 72; C of St Helen Vanc 72-74; Perm to Offic Dio BC from 75. *RR2, Ganges, BC, Canada.*

BRACK, Christopher Francis. b 07. Em Coll Cam BA 30, MA 34. Westcott Ho Cam. **d** 66 **p** 67 Glouc. C of St Luke Cheltenham 66-72; Perm to Offic Dio Chich from 74. *c/o Cottesmore School, Buchan Hill, Crawley, W Sussex.*

BRACK, Edward James. b 37. Sarum Th Coll 67. **d** 69 Tonbridge for Roch. C of St Aidan Gravesend 70-73; St Barn Woodside Park Finchley 73-77; St Mich-at-Bowes Bowes Pk 77-80; V of Whitton Dio Lon from 80. *Vicarage, Kneller Road, Whitton, Twickenham, Middx.* (01-894 1932)

BRACKEN, Canon Henry Newman Wooding. Trin Coll Tor BA 39, BD 45. **d** 41 **p** 42 Tor. C of St John Peterborough 41-42; I of Mono E 42-47; St Aug Dio Tor from 47; Can of Tor from 69. *38 Donlea Drive, Toronto, Ont., Canada.* (416-485 2656)

BRACKENBURY, Canon Michael Palmer. b 30. Linc Th Coll 64. **d** 66 **p** 67 Linc. C of S Ormsby 66-69; R of Sudbrooke w Scothern 69-77; RD of Lawres 73-78; Dioc Dir of Ordinands from 77; Personal Asst to Bp of Linc from 77; Can and Preb of Linc Cathl from 79. *Felbrigg, Sudbrooke Road, Scothern, Lincoln, LN2 2UZ.* (Scothern 256)

BRACKLEY, Franklin Osmond. b 13. Sarum Th Coll 54. **d** 55 **p** 56 Win. C of Fordingbridge 55-59; PC of Breamore 59-61; R of St Martin Jersey 61-81; Vice-Dean of Jersey 77-81. *23 Boyatt Crescent, Otterbourne, Hants.*

BRACKLEY, Ian James. b 47. Keble Coll Ox BA (2nd cl Th) 69, MA 73. Cudd Coll 69. **d** 71 **p** 72 Bris. C of Lockleaze 71-74; Asst Chap Bryanston Sch Blandford 74-77; Chap 77-80; V of E Preston w Kingston Dio Chich from 80. *Vicarage, Vicarage Lane, East Preston, Littlehampton, BN16 2SP.* (Rustington 3318)

BRADBERRY, John. b 20. Clifton Th Coll 46. **d** 47 **p** 48 Leic. C of H Trin Hinckley 47-50; St Anne Earlham 50-51; V of Ch Ch Leyton 51-55; SAMS Miss Dio Argent 55-61; V of St Mark, Siddal, Halifax 61-72; R of Bentham Dio Bradf from 72. *Rectory, Low Bentham, Lancaster.* (Bentham 61422)

BRADBERRY, John Stephen. b 47. Univ of Hull BSc 70. N-W Ordin Course 76. **d** 79 **p** 80 Wakef (APM). Hon C of St Jo Evang Warley Halifax Dio Wakef from 79. *129 Paddock Lane, Norton Tower, Halifax, W Yorks, HX2 0NT.*

BRADBROOK, Peter David. b 33. Kelham Th Coll 54. **d** 60 **p** 61 Ches. C of St Osw Ches 60-64; St Etheldreda Fulham 64-65; V of St Jas Congleton 65-79; Wheelock Dio Ches from 79. *Wheelock Vicarage, Sandbach, Chesh, CW11 0RE.* (Sandbach 2377)

BRADBROOK, Sydney Morgan. d and **p** 37 Newfld. C of Lamaline 37-38; R 38-43; R of Greenspond 43-47; P-in-c of Bellcoram 47-54; R of Burin 54-64; Topsail 64-77. *Cottage 50, Topsail Road, St John's, Newfoundland, Canada.*

BRADBROOKE, Canon Edward. b 06. Qu Coll Ox 3rd cl Mod Lang 28, BA and MA 32. Bps' Coll Cheshunt 36. **d** 37 Lewes for Chich **p** 38 Chich. C of Petworth 37-39; CF (R of O) from 39; V of St Paul Chich 45-51; R of Slaugham w Handcross 51-66; Graffham w Woolavington 66-74; RD of Cuckfield 58-66; Can and Preb of Chich Cathl 65-74; Can (Emer) from 74. *68 Moorlands Park, Martock, Somt, TA12 6DY.*

BRADBURY, Alan Harry. b 32. K Coll Lon and Warm BD and AKC 56. **d** 57 **p** 58 Chelmsf. C of St Jo Bapt Leytonstone 57-60; Prec of Chelmsf Cathl 60-63; V of St Jo Evang Seven Kings 63-68; C-in-c of Abbey Wood Conv Distr 68-70; Chap and Lect St Pet Coll of Educn Saltley 70-73; Asst Master Milton Secondary Sch Southsea 73-74; Publ Pr Dio Win from 73; Warden Brighton Hill Commun Sch and Centre Basingstoke 74-76; Commun Educn Warden Harrow Way Sch Andover from 76. *25 Millway Road, Andover, Hants, SP10 2AS.* (0264 2275)

BRADBURY, Herbert Cedric. b 30. Linc Th Coll 64. **d** 66 Lanc for Blackb **p** 67 Blackb. C of St Steph Blackpool 66-71; V in Hempnall Group 71-74; R 74-77; Team R of Hempnall 77-81; Morningthorpe w Fritton 74-77; Shelton w Hardwick 74-77; RD of Depwade 77-81; V of Wroxham w Hoveton and Belaugh Dio Nor from 81. *Vicarage, Wroxham, NR12 8JH.* (Wroxham 2678)

BRADBURY, Julian Nicholas Anstey. b 49. BNC Ox BA 71, MA 75. Cudd Coll 71. **d** 73 **p** 74 S'wark. C of H Trin S'wark 73-76; in Amer Ch 76-79; V of H Trin Tottenham Dio Lon from 80. *Holy Trinity Vicarage, Philip Lane, High Cross, N15 4HZ.* (01-801 3021)

BRADBURY, Kenneth James Frank. b 23. Qu Coll Birm 72. **d** 75 Lich **p** 76 Hereford for Lich (APM). C of Central Telford 75-80; V of Chirbury Dio Heref from 80; Marton-in-Chirbury Dio Heref from 80; Trelystan w Leighton Dio Heref from 80. *Chirbury Vicarage, Montgomery, Powys.*

BRADBURY, Norman Lunn. b 15. Univ of Lon BA 36, AKC 36. N Ordin Course 76. **d** 77 Pontefract for Wakef **p** 78 Wakef. (NSM). C of All SS Paddock 77-81; Lockwood and of Rashcliffe Dio Wakef from 81. *23 Springwood Hall Gardens, Huddersfield, HD1 4HA.*

BRADBURY, Robert Douglas. b 50. Ripon Coll Cudd 75. **d** 76 **p** 77 Lich. C of Harlescott 76-81; V of Ruyton-XI-Towns Dio Lich from 81. *Ruyton-XI-Towns Vicarage, Shrewsbury, Salop.* (Baschurch 254)

BRADBURY, Roy Albert. b 30. Chich Th Coll 72. **d** 74 **p** 75 Cov. C of St Barbara Earlsdon Cov 74-76; Caludon Team Min Cov 76-78; P-in-c of Calow Dio Derby from 78. *Calow Vicarage, Chesterfield, Derbys, S44 5AF.* (Chesterfield 73486)

BRADDOCK, Arthur Derek. b 25. Lich Th Coll 56. **d** 59 **p** 60 Man. C of Droylsden 59-61; St Jas Farnworth 61-65; V of Kearsley Moor 65-79; C of Ellesmere Port Dio Ches from 79. *500 Overpool Road, Ellesmere Port, Chesh.* (051-355 4571)

BRADDOCK, David Alwyn. St Jo Coll Auckld LTh 54. **d** 53 **p** 54 Auckld. C of St Aid Remuera 53-56; CF (NZ) 56; V of Waiuku 56-62; Point Chevalier 62-66; Glenfield 66-70; One Tree Hill 70-77; Stoke Dio Nel from 77. *523 Main Road, Stoke, Nelson, NZ.*

BRADDON, Russell Leslie. Ridley Coll Melb ACT ThL 63. **d** 63 Bp Sambell for Melb **p** 64 Melb. C of St Mary Caulfield 63-64; Blackburn 64-66; C-in-c of N Springvale 66-70; I of Newport 71-75; C of St Jas w St John Miss Distr Melb 75-78; P-in-c of St Mark Leopold Dio Melb from 78. *Vicarage, Leopold, Vic, Australia 3221.* (052-50 1401)

BRADFORD, Lord Bishop of. *See* Paul, Right Rev Geoffrey John.

BRADFORD, Assistant Bishop of. *See* Robinson, Right Rev John Arthur Thomas.

BRADFORD, Archdeacon of. *See* Sargeant, Ven Frank Pilkington.

BRADFORD, Provost of. *See* Jackson, Very Rev Brandon Donald.

BRADFORD, DAvid. b 16. **d** 80 Alg. Chap Miss to Seamen Thunder Bay Dio Alg from 80. *83 Windermere Avenue North, Thunder Bay, Ont, Canada P7A 6B3.*

BRADFORD, John. b 34. Univ of Lon BA 60. Univ of Birm MEducn 81. Oak Hill Th Coll 55. **d** 60 **p** 61 B & W. C of Walcot 60-64; Asst Master Wendover C of E Primary Sch

64-65; Dr Challoner's High Sch L Chalfont 65-69; Perm to Offic Dio Ox 66-70; Dio Birm 70-71; Lect St Pet Coll of Educn Saltley Birm 70-77; LPr Dio Birm from 71; Nat Chap-Missr CECS from 77; Perm to Offic Dio Cov from 81. *27 Marsh Lane, Solihull, W Midl, B91 2PG.* (021-704 9895)

BRADFORD, Kenneth. b 13. St Chad's Coll Dur Capel Cure Pri 41, Barry Scho 42, BA (1st cl Th) 43, MA 46. **d** 43 **p** 44 Dur. C of St Luke Pallion Bp Wearmouth 43-49; Ludlow 49-51; V of Castletown 51-56; Shildon 56-65; Proc Conv Dur 61-65; R of Ratcliffe-on-the-Wreake w Rearsby 65-68; V of Wyken 68-73; Bidford-on-Avon 74-80. *44 Kingsmead Road, Knighton, Leicester, LE2 3YB.*

BRADFORD, Murray Edward. Montr Dioc Th Coll LTh 66. **d** 66 **p** 67 Alg. C of Epiph Sudbury 66-69; R of Gore Bay 69-73; C of St Luke's Cathl Sault Ste Marie 73-75; I of Lake of Bays Dio Alg from 75. *Anglican Rectory, Dorset, Ont., Canada.* (705-766-2206)

BRADFORD, Peter. b 38. Sarum Th Coll 69. **d** 70 **p** 71 Bp Cornw for Win. C of St John, Holdenhurst 70-73; St Luke Stanmore Win 73-77; Team V of Eling, Testwood and Marchwood 77-78; R of Marchwood Dio Win from 78. *Marchwood Vicarage, Marchwood, Nr Southampton.* (Totton 861496)

BRADLEY, Brian Hugh Granville. b 32. Univ Coll Ox 51. Lon Coll of Div 58. **d** 62 **p** 63 Lon. C of St Steph E Twickenham 62-65; Herne Bay 65-69; Chap Miss to Seamen 69-71; in Ch of Eng Lonkn 71-75; Chap at Amsterdam 75-79; Lyon and Grenoble Dio (Gibr in Eur from 80) Lon (N and C Eur) from 79. *38 Le Coteau, Chemin de Taffignon, 69110 Ste Foy-les-Lyon, France.* (596706)

BRADLEY, Preb Cecil Robert Jones. b 23. Trin Coll Dub BA 47, Div Test (2nd cl) 48, Downes Pri 48, MA 50. **d** 48 **p** 49 Derry. C of Clooney 48-50; St Columb's Cathl Derry 50-67; Dean's V of St Patr Cathl City and Dio Dub from 67; Preb of St Patr Cathl Dub from 81. *Vicarage, St Patrick's Close, Dublin 8, Irish Republic.* (Dublin 754817)

BRADLEY, Charles John Andrew. MBE (Mil) 51. OBE (Mil) 60. Kelham Th Coll 30. **d** 37 **p** 38 Sheff. C of Ecclesfield 37-39; St Cecilia Parson Cross 39-43; CF (EC) 43-47; Men in Disp 45; CF 47-62; V of St Pet, St Alb 62-71; Surr 65-75; Asst RD of St Alb 66-71; RD 71; V of Woburn and Battlesden w Pottesgrove 71-75; Chap and Dioc Liaison Officer CA Housing 75-78; Perm to Offic Dio Lon 75-78; Dio Roch from 75. *20 Hawes Road, Bromley, Kent, BR1 3JR.* (01-464 0841)

BRADLEY, Clifford David. b 36. Univ of Lon BA 60. St Aid Coll 60. **d** 62 Warrington for Liv **p** 63 Liv. C of Stoneycroft 62-65; Chipping Sodbury w Old Sodbury 65-68; R of Pomona Br Hond 68-70; C of St Phil & St Jas Leckhampton 70-71; V of Badgeworth w Shurdington 71-79; Braddan Dio S & M from 79; Santan Dio S & M from 79; Dioc Missr Dio S & M from 79; Exam Chap to Bp of S & M from 80; Dom Chap from 81. *Braddan Vicarage, Douglas, IM.* (Douglas 5523)

BRADLEY, Colin John. b 46. Univ of Edin MA 69. Sarum Wells Th Coll 72. **d** 75 Buckingham for Ox **p** 76 Ox. C of Easthampstead 75-79; V of Shawbury Dio Lich from 79; R of Moreton Corbet Dio Lich from 80; P-in-c of Stanton-upon-Hine Heath Dio Lich from 81. *Shawbury Vicarage, Shrewsbury, Salop.* (Shawbury 250419)

BRADLEY, Connla John Osman. BC Coll Bris. **d** and **p** 47 Roch. C of H Trin Tunbridge Wells 47-49; V of Ch Ch Camberwell 49-55; Frogmore 55-68; Havering-atte-Bower 68-76. *53 Marine Drive, Bishopstone, E Sussex.*

BRADLEY, Canon Donald John Walter. b 19. Late Exhib of Em Coll Cam BA 40, MA 44. Westcott Ho Cam 40. **d** 42 **p** 43 S'wark. C of St Mark Woodcote 42-44; St Sav w St Pet S'wark and Succr and Sacr of S'wark Cathl 44-48; Chap and Tutor Saltley Tr Coll Birm 48-49; LPr Dio Birm 48-49; Chap Cudd Coll 49; Vice-Prin 51-53; Chap Ch Ch Ox 51-53; V of St Luke Battersea 53-63; Hon Chap to Bp of S'wark 60-63; Dir of Relig Educn Dio Birm 63-72; Publ Pr Dio Birm 63-71; Hon Can of Birm from 70; V of St Geo Edgbaston Dio Birm from 71; RD of Edgbaston from 77; Surr from 77; Exam Chap to Bp of Birm from 78. *3 Westbourne Road, Edgbaston, Birmingham, B15 3TH.* (021-454 2303)

BRADLEY, Canon Edward Athelstan. St Francis Coll Brisb ACT ThL 46. **d** 46 **p** 47 Brisb. C of St Paul Ipswich 46-51; M of Bush Bro of St Paul Charleville 51-55; Asst Chap R Melb Hosp 55-56; Chap of Austin Hosp Melb 56-58; Brisb Ment Hosp 58-62; Miss Dio Polyn 62-66; V of Samabula 66; R of St Jas Kelvin Grove Brisb 67-80; St Osw Banyo City and Dio Brisb from 80; Hon Can of Brisb from 78. *9 Froude Street, Banyo, Queensland, Australia 4014.* (267-5329)

BRADLEY, Gary Scott. b 53. Univ of Lon LLB 75. Ripon Coll Cudd 75. **d** 78 Lon **p** 79 Bp Woollcombe for Lon. C of St John's Wood Ch Dio Lon from 78. *3 St John's Hall, St John's Wood High Street, NW8.* (01-722 9188)

BRADLEY, George Herbert. b 1899. Univ of Liv BCom 25. Bps' Coll Cheshunt 27. **d** 28 **p** 29 Lon. C of St Mary Twickenham 28-32; Ashford Middx 32-35; V of Bedfont 35-37; Gt Sutton Ches 37-73. *14 Park Mount Drive, Macclesfield, Chesh, SK11 8NS.*

BRADLEY, John Elliott. b 40. McGill Univ BA 63. Trin Coll Tor STB 70. **d** and **p** 70 Montr. C of St Barn, St Lambert 70-71; Chap St Vinc de Paul Penitentiary Montr 73-75; I of St Marg Montr 75-80; R of Chateauguay Dio Montr from 80. *94 Vanier Street, Chateauguay, PQ, Canada.* (514-691 7451)

BRADLEY, Canon John Lloyd. Univ of Tor BA 38. Trin Coll Tor LTh 40. **d** 40 **p** 41 Ott. C of Russell 40-44; I of Stafford 44-51; R of Richmond 51-55; Renfrew 55-67; St Pet Carlington Ott 67-72; Smiths Falls 72-79; Can of Ott 72-79; Hon Can from 79. *102 Fenton Street, Kemptville, Ont, Canada.*

BRADLEY, John Owen. b 30. Jes Coll Ox BA (Th) 55, Ma 56. St Mich Coll Llan 52. **d** 56 Llan **p** 57 Swan B for Wales. C of St Mary Virg Cardiff 56-60; Lect St Mich Coll Llan 59-71; C of Caerau w Ely 60-61; Newton Nottage 61-65; V of H Trin Aberavon 65-69; Exam Chap to Bp of Llan 65-69; Publ Pr Dio Cov 70-76; C of St Bridget W Kirby 76-79; Team V of Knowle Dio Bris 79-80; Team R from 80. *41 Lilymead Avenue, Knowle, Bristol, BS4 2BY.* (Bris 774260)

BRADLEY, Kenneth Sutton. b 08. ALCD 39. **d** 38 **p** 39 Sarum. C of St Luke Parkstone 38-41; All SS and St Pet Portland 41-43; Chap RAFVR 43-47; R of Ellisfield 47-53; Bradley 47-53; Dogmersfield w Winchfield 53-72; Chap to Winchfield Hosp 53-73. *Sangford, Ewshott Lane, Ewshott, Farnham, Surrey.* (Aldershot 850666)

BRADLEY, Michael Frederick John. b 44. Qu Coll Birm 76. **d** 77 **p** 78 Doncaster for Sheff. C of St Cuthb Firvale Sheff 77-78; Missr in Alford Group Dio Linc from 78. *Bilsby Vicarage, Alford, Lincs, LN13 9PY.*

BRADLEY, Peter David Douglas. b 49. Univ of Nottm BTh 79. Linc Th Coll 75. **d** 79 **p** 80 Liv. C of Up Holland Dio Liv from 79. *8 Beacon View Drive, Up Holland, Skelmersdale, Lancs, WN8 0LH.* (Up H 622181)

BRADLEY, Canon Roy Algernon. Trin Coll Melb BA 50, LTh 51. **d** and **p** 52 Bal. C of Horsham 52-53; R in c of Natimuk 53-57; R of Kyabram 57-59; C in Dept of Chaps Melb 59-63; on leave 63-66; Chap Austin Hosp Dio Melb 66-74; Dir Pastoral Care and Chap R Perth Hosp from 75; Hon Can of Perth from 80. *36 St Leonards Avenue, West Leederville, W Australia 6006.* (381-3873)

BRADLEY, Wilfred Hankin. Univ of Tor BA 33. Trin Coll Tor BD 38. **d** 35 **p** 36 Ott. C of St Geo Ott 35-36; St Matt Ott 36-43; R of N Gower 43-50; H Trin Ott 50-67; Trin Ch Cornw 67-73; Exam Chap to Bp of Ott 54-73; Hon Can of Ott 58-67; Archd of Cornw 67-72; Regr Dio Ott from 73. *610-457 Cambridge Street, Ottawa, Ont., Canada.*

BRADLEY, Wilfred John. b 03. MBE 72. **d** 73 **p** 75 Ch Ch. Hon C of Highfield Dio Ch Ch 73-76; C from 76. *220 Otipua Road, Timaru, NZ.* (88-361)

BRADLEY, William John. b 49. Univ of Tor BA 73. Trin Coll Tor MDiv 79. **d** and **p** 79 Ott. C of Smith's Falls Dio Ott from 79. *c/o 2 George Street S, Smith's Falls, Ont, Canada, K7A 1X4.*

BRADNUM, Richard James. b 39. Pemb Coll Ox BA (1st cl Th) 62, MA 67. Ridley Hall, Cam 62. **d** 64 Aston for Birm **p** 65 Birm. C of St Martin Birm 64-68; St Jas Sutton-in-Holderness 68-69; Perm to Offic Dio Wakef 71-72; C of Batley 72-74; V of Gawthorpe and Chickenley Heath Dio Wakef from 74. *Vicarage, Chickenley Lane, Dewsbury, W Yorks, WF12 8QD.* (Wakef 273287)

BRADSHAW, Charles Anthony. b 44. Univ of Birm MA 76. Qu Coll Birm Dipl Th 74. **d** 75 **p** 76 Dur. C of Whickham 75-78; Bilton 78-81; Team V of Caludon Team Min Dio Cov from 81. *Wyken Vicarage, Wyken Croft, Coventry, CV2 3AD.* (Cov 612547)

BRADSHAW, Ven Charles Herbert Reginald. Trin Coll Cam BA 21, MA 25. Em Coll Sktn LTh 25. **d** 25 **p** 26 Sask. C of Maymont 25-26; R 26-28; L to Offic (under Col Cl Act) as C of Woking 29; LPr Dio Sktn 30-35; Dio Carib 35-37; Dom Chap to Bp of Carib 35-41; I of N Kamloops 41-55; P-in-c of Thompson River Miss 41-58; Cler Sec Dio Carib 44-58; Archd of Carib 45-58; Archd (Emer) from 58; Treas 52-58; L to Offic Dio BC from 58; Hon C of Ch Ch Cathl Vic from 60. *2985 Uplands Road, Victoria, BC, Canada.*

BRADSHAW, Denis Matthew. b 52. Chich Th Coll 77. **d** 80 **p** 81 Willesden for Lon. C of St Martin Ruislip Dio Lon from 80. *34 Midcroft, Ruislip, Middx.* (Ruislip 32605)

BRADSHAW, George Henry. b 28. Wycl Hall Ox **d** 62 **p** 63 Ox. C of Thame 62-65; R of Wittering w Thornhaugh and Wansford Dio Pet from 65; Surr from 73. *Wittering Rectory, Peterborough, PE8 6AQ.* (Stamford 782428)

BRADSHAW, Gordon George. b 31. St Pet Coll Ox BA (Th) 56. MA 59. Wycl Hall Ox 56. **d** 58 Lich **p** 59 Stafford for Lich. C of Newc L 58-61; Mossley Hill 61-63; V of St Geo Kano Nigeria 63-65; Bp's Chap Univ of Liv and Chap Liv Cathl 65-68; PC of St Jas W Derby 68-75; R of Keynsham

Dio B & W from 75. *1 The Park, Keynsham, Bristol, BS18 2BL.* (Keynsham 3554)

BRADSHAW, Howard Roger Christopher. b 50. St Paul's Coll Grahmstn 73. **d** 75 **p** 76 Grahmstn. C of St Sav E Lon 75-78; R of Barkly E w Dordrecht and Indwe Dio Grahmstn from 78. *Box 139, Barkly East, CP, S Africa.*

BRADSHAW, Jolyon Anthony. b 51. St Jo Coll Dur BA 73. Trin Coll Bris 73. **d** 76 **p** 77 Wakef. C of Normanton Dio Wakef from 76. *252 Queen Elizabeth Drive, Normanton, Yorks.*

BRADSHAW, Kenneth Allan. Roch Th Coll 60. **d** 62 **p** 63 S'wark. C of St Phil Cheam Common 62-65; Portslade 65-67; St Matthias Preston 67-71; Hayward's Heath Dio Chich from 71. *87 New England Road, Hayward's Heath, W Sussex, RH16 3LE.* (Hayward's Heath 454417)

BRADSHAW, Malcolm McNeille. b 45. Kelham Th Coll 65. Dipl Th (Lon) 69. **d** 70 **p** 71 Cant. C of New Addington, Croydon 70-76; Chap All SS Milan Dio Gibr (Gibr in Eur from 80) from 77. *All Saints' English Church, Via Solferino 17, Milan, Italy.* (662258)

BRADSHAW, Maurice Wadham. b 03. St Aug Coll Cant 24. Univ of Dur LTh 28. M CR 37. **d** 28 Lon for St Alb **p** 29 St Alb. C of St Mich AA Watford 28-31; Miss St Aug Miss Betong 31-32; P-in-c 32-34; L to Offic Dio Wakef 35-38; Miss P St Aug Penhalonga 38-45; P-in-c of Sekhukhuniland Miss 45-50; Miss P Penhalonga Dio S Rhod 50-52; Dio Mashon 52-71; C of Stellenbosch 71-75. *Emmaus, Prospect Row, Sunderland, T & W, SR1 2BP.*

BRADSHAW, Paul Frederick. b 45. Late Beck Exhib Clare Coll Cam, 1st cl Th Trip pt i 64, BA (2nd cl Th Trip pt ii) 66, MA 70. George Williams Pri 68. PhD (Lon) 71. Westcott Ho Cam 67. **d** 69 **p** 70 Cant. C of W Wickham 69-71; C of St Martin w St Paul Cant 71-73; Lect and Tutor Chich Th Coll 73-78; V of Flamstead Dio St Alb from 78; M C of E Liturgical Comm from 81. *Flamstead Vicarage, St Albans, Herts.* (Luton 840271)

BRADSHAW, Canon Peter. b 15. Fitzw Ho Cam BA 48, MA 53. Westcott Ho Cam. **d** 48 **p** 49 Lon. C of St Steph St John's Wood Lon 48-52; R of Colkirk w Oxwick 52-57; Harpenden 57-64; Surr 59-64; R of Hempnall Group (R of Morningthorpe w Fritton 64-74; C-in-c of Shelton w Hardwick 64-67; R 67-74; RD of Depwade 68-74; Hon Can of Nor 70-74; Can Res from 74; Vice Dean 79. *52 The Close, Norwich, NR1 4EG.*

BRADSHAW, Canon Reginald Sydney George. b 06. St Aid Coll 27. **d** 30 **p** 31 S'wark. C of St Luke W Norwood 30-33; Woolwich 33-37; Merton (in C of St Jas) 37-38; Missr of St Jas Conv Distr Merton 38-43; V of Ch Ch Battersea 43-45; Sec of Cant Dioc Miss Coun 45-47; V of Cranbrook 47-71; RD of W Charing 59-71; Hon Can of Cant from 62; Warden, Clk and Chap Jesus Hosp Cant from 71. *Petham Lodge, Petham, Canterbury, CT4 5RX.* (Petham 214)

BRADSHAW, Richard Graham Alfred. b 24. Univ of BC BSA 55. Univ of Tor LTh 70. Wycl Coll Tor 70. **d** 71 BC for Bran **p** 72 Bran. R of Neepawa 71-79; Port Edw 79-81; Port Hardy Dio BC from 81. *Port Hardy, BC, Canada.*

BRADSHAW, Timothy. b 50. Keble Coll Ox BA 72, MA 78. Univ of Nottm BA (Th) 75. St Jo Coll Nottm 73. **d** 76 Lon **p** 77 Stepney for Lon. C of All S Clapton 76-80; Perm to Offic Dio Bris from 80. *Trinity College, Stoke Hill, Bristol, BS9 1JP.*

BRADWELL, Lord Bishop Suffragan of. *See* Bond, Right Rev Charles Derek.

BRADY, Very Rev Ernest William. b 17. Univ of Dur LTh 42. Edin Th Coll 39. **d** 42 **p** 43 Glas. C of Ch Ch Glas 42-46; St Alphage Hendon 46-48; R of All SS Buckie 48-57; All SS (w St Mich from 65) Edin 57-71; Can of St Mary's Cathl Edin from 67; Syn Clk Dio Edin 69-77; Hosp Chap and Edin Dioc Super 72-74; P-in-c of St Mary S Queensferry Dio Edin from 74; Dean of Edin from 76. *St Mary's House, South Queensferry, West Lothian.* (031-331 1055)

BRADY, Frederick Herbert James. Univ of Syd BSc 55, BD (Lon) 65. Moore Th Coll Syd ACT ThL 59. **d** and **p** 60 Syd. C of St Paul Burwood 60-61; Asst Chap Trin Coll Univ of Melb 62-63; L to Offic Dio Lon 63-69; Chap Univ of Melb 69-78; C of St Mary N Melb Dio Melb from 78. *163 Howard Street, N Melbourne, Vic, Australia 3051.* (28 2028)

BRADY, Graeme Alan. NZ Bd of Th Stud LTh 65. St Jo Coll Auckld 63. **d** 65 **p** 66 Ch Ch. C of Ashburton 65-67; CF (NZ) 67; C of Papanui 68; Assoc Dir Chr Educn Dio Wel 68-71; V of Aranui Miss Distr 71-74; Adv in Chr Educn Dio Wai 74-77; V of Kaiapoi Dio Ch Ch from 77. *Vicarage, Cass Street, Kaiapoi, Canterbury, NZ.* (277-084)

BRAGG, Randolph Merritt. b 47. Virginia Commonwealth Univ BA 70. Virginia Th Coll MDiv 73. **d** 73 S Virginia for Zulu **p** 73 Zulu. C of Empangeni 73-78; R of All SS Gingindlovu Dio Zulu from 78. *Box 170, Gingindlovu, Zululand.*

BRAHAM, Renaldo Oswald. Univ Th Coll of WI 74. **d** and **p** 74 Ja. C-in-c of Retreat Dio Ja 74; R from 75. *Rectory, PO Retreat, Jamaica, WI.*

BRAIN, Donald Harry. b 08. Qu Coll Birm 46. **d** 48 **p** 49 Bris. C of Corsham 48-50; Bedminster (in c of St Hugh) 50-53; Chippenham (in c of Lowden) 53-55; Min of Conv Distr of St Pet Lowden Chippenham 55-61; P-in-c of St Chad's Conv Distr Patchway 61-64; V 64-65; Hullavington 65-73; Norton 65-73. *1 St Andrew's Drive, Clevedon, Avon, BS21 7UG.* (Clevedon 872797)

BRAIN, George. St Chad's Coll Dur BA (Math) 41, Dipl Th 43, MA 44. **d** 43 **p** 44 Liv. C of St Jas the Gt Haydock 43-44; St Anne Beech Hill Wigan 44-47; St Pet Leic (in c of St Hilda from 49) 47-50; St Jo Bapt Whitwick (in c of St D Broom Leys) 50-54; V of St Leon Leic 54-81. *1 Steyning Crescent, Glenfield, Leicester, LE3 8PL.*

BRAIN, John William Alfred. St Jo Coll Morpeth 49. **d** 50 C & Goulb **p** 51 Bp Clements for C & Goulb. C of Albury 50-52; C-in-c of Taralga 52-54; Snowy Mountains 54-57; LPr Dio C & Goulb 57-62 and from 63; R of Tumut 62-63; LPr Dio Syd from 64. *1 Cammeray Road, Cammeray, NSW, Australia 2062.* (90-2091)

BRAIN, Michael Charles. b 39. ACP 65. Lich Th Coll 68. **d** 70 **p** 71 Lich. Hon C of St Mich Stone Lich 70-73; Asst Master Alleyne's Sch Stone 69-73; C of Harlescott 73-76; Min of Longton 76-77; V of St Edm Dudley Dio Worc from 77. *St Edmund's Vicarage, Ednam Road, Dudley, W Midl, DY1 1JX.* (Dudley 52532)

BRAIN, Peter Robert. Moore Th Coll Syd. **d** 74 **p** 75 Syd. C of St Andr Sans Souci 76; H Trin Adel 77-80; R of Maddington Dio Perth from 80. *79 Pitchford Avenue, Maddington, W Australia 6109.* (459-5169)

BRAIN, Robert Theodore Francis. MC 44. Trin Coll Tor LTh 34. **d** 34 **p** 35 Tor. C-in-c of St Nich Lakeview 34-36; C of St John Pet 36-40; Chap CASF 40-46; R of St Mary Magd Tor 46-52; I of Norwich Ont 60-64; R of St Barn Lon 64-69; I of Port Rowan 70-75. *1580 Adelaide Street North, Ont., Canada.*

BRAIN, Vernon Roy. b 15. St D Coll Lamp BA 38. Ripon Hall Ox 41. **d** 42 **p** 43 St A. C of Bistre 42-45; Almondbury 45-50; V of Gomersal 50-53; CMS Area Sec Dios Dur and Newc T 53-61; V of Seaham w Seaham Harbour 61-80. *61 Vicarage Close, Silksworth, Sunderland, T & W, SR3 1JL.* (Sunderland 210847)

BRAINERD, Winthrop John. b 39. Ripon Hall Ox 68. **d** 69 Bp Carrington for Newfld **p** 70 Newfld. Chap Kirkland Ho Harvard Univ 69-71; R of Battle Harbour 71-73; in Amer Ch from 73. *1208 St Paul Street, Baltimore, Maryland 21202, USA.* (301-837 6491)

BRAITHWAITE, Albert Alfred. b 24. Clifton Th Coll. **d** 59 Bp Gelsthorpe for Southw **p** 60 Southw. C of St Matt Bestwood 59-62; Chap RN 62-81; Hon Chap to HM the Queen from 77; C of St Jude Southsea Dio Portsm from 81. *3 Lorne Road, Southsea, PO5 1RR.* (Portsm 738753)

BRAITHWAITE, de Courcey Bindley. Codr Coll Barb L.Th 50. **d** 43 **p** 44 Barb. C of St Jos Barb 43-44; Chap Westbury Cem 44-47; V of St Jude Barb 44-75. *Coffee Gully, St Joseph, Barbados, W Indies.*

BRAITHWAITE, Michael Royce. b 34. Linc Th Coll 71. **d** 73 Penrith for Carl **p** 74 Carl. C of Barrow-F 73-77; V of St Pet Kells Whitehaven Dio Carl from 77. *St Peter's Vicarage, Kells, Whitehaven, Cumb, CA28 9ET.* (Whitehaven 2496)

BRAITHWAITE, Richard Herbert Bevan. b 1900. Pemb Coll Ox BA 22, MA 45. Wycl Hall Ox 23. **d** 24 **p** 25 Man. C of Ch Ch Walmersley 24-28; St Clem Ordsall 28-31; Bexley 31-33; St Mary Bury St Edms 33-35; H Trin Stroud 35-37; Ilminster w Whitelackington 37-38; Tidenham w Beachley and Lancaut 39-45; PC of Elmore 45-48; C of Winchcombe w Gretton and Sudeley Manor 48-55; Hon Asst Chap Chich Dioc Conf and Retreat Ho Haywards Heath 58-63. *Loo Water Nursing Home, Heacham, King's Lynn, Norf.*

BRAITHWAITE, Roy. b 34. Univ of Dur BA 56. Ridley Hall Cam 58. **d** 60 Lanc for York **p** 61 Blackb. C of St Gabr Blackb 60-63; Burnley 63-66; V of St Andr Accrington 66-74; St Jas Borough and Dio Blackb from 74. *St James' Vicarage, Cromer Place, Blackburn, Lancs, BB1 8EL.* (Blackburn 56465)

BRAITHWAITE, Wilfrid. b 14. St Chad's Coll Dur BA and Van Mildert Exhib 41, MA 44. **d** 42 **p** 43 Carl. C of Harrington 42-45; Kendal 45-46; V of Soulby 46-51; R of Crosby Garrett 46-51; V of Ireleth w Askam 51-62; Lanercost w Kirkcambeck 62-79. *Brougham Lodge, Eamont Bridge, Penrith, Cumb.*

BRAITHWAITE, William Beresford. St Aug Coll Cant 32. Univ of Dur LTh 35. **d** 36 **p** 38 Antig. C of St Geo St Kitts 36-38; R of St Mary Antig 38-40; St Mary w St Aug Anguilla 40-45; P-in-c of St Martins 45-50; V of St Mark Barb 50-70; St Luke I & Dio Barb from 70. *St Luke's Vicarage, St George, Barbados, W Indies.*

BRAKE, Allen Edgar. b 41. Mem Univ Newfld BA 68, LTh 69. Trin Coll Tor STB 70. Qu Coll Newfld. **d** 69 **p** 70 Newfld. P-in-c of Forteau 70-73; R of Bonne Bay Dio Newfld (W Newfld from 76) from 73. *PO Box 40, Woody Point, Bonne Bay, Newfoundland, Canada.* (709-453-2204)

BRAKE, James North. **d** 62 **p** 64 Bend. C of Raywood 62-63; V 63-67; R of Elmore 67-68; Perm to Offic Dio Brisb 69-79. *c/o 47 Manstead Street, Wellers Hill, Queensland, Australia 4121.* (397 4321)

BRALANT, Louis Arthur. ALCD 34 (LTh from 74). **d** 34 **p** 35 Lon. C of St Pet Clerkenwell 34-37; Ch Ch Camberwell 37-39; V of Mannville Alta 39-41; I of Cadomin 41-42; St Thos Wainwright 42-46; CF (Canad) 43-46; C of Em Ch Hastings 46-48; R of N Waltham w Steventon 48-50; V of St Matt Muswell Hill 50-63; St Helen w H Trin Kens Lon 63-76. *456 Buckfield Road, Leominster, Herefs, HR6 8SD.* (Leominster 4489)

BRALESFORD, Nicholas Robert. b 53. St Jo Coll Nottm LTh, BTh 79. **d** 79 Bp Mort for Leic **p** 80 Leic. C of St Chris City and Dio Leic from 79. *29 Elston Fields, Leicester, LE2 6NH.* (Leic 835439)

BRAMBLE, Peter Wilkin Duke. b 45. Yale Univ USA MA 72. Codr Coll Barb 66. **d** and **p** 72 Antig. on leave. *c/o Yale University, Conn, USA.*

BRAMHALL, Eric. St Cath Coll Cam BA 61, MA 65. Tyndale Hall Bris 61. **d** 63 Warrington for Liv **p** 64 Liv. C of St Luke Eccleston 63-66; Em Bolton 66-69; Asst Master Wallasey Gr Sch 70-74; Perm to Offic Dio Ches 70-74; V of Ch Ch Aughton Dio Liv from 75. *Christ Church Vicarage, Aughton, Ormskirk, Lancs, L39 5AT.* (Aughton Green 422175)

BRAMLEY, Canon Charles Edward. b 14. Keble Coll Ox 2nd Cl Hist 35, BA 37, MA 50. Lich Th Coll 36. **d** and **p** 38 Blackb. C of H Trin S Shore Blackpool 38-42; St Pet Haslingden 42-43; Chap RAFVR 43-47; V of St Geo Chorley 47-56; R of Standish 56-80; RD of Leyland 63; Chorley 64-72; Hon Can of Blackb 66-80; Can (Emer) from 80. *2 Primrose Cottages, Dawbers Lane, Euxton, Chorley, Lancs.*

BRAMLEY-MOORE, Michael. b 16. **d** 67 **p** 68 Glouc. C of Lydney w Aylburton Glouc 67-73; P-in-c of Saintbridge Exper Area 73-78; Littledean Dio Glouc from 78. *Littledean Rectory, Cinderford, Glos.* (Cinderford 22236)

BRAMMER, Charles Harold. b 08. Ripon Hall Ox 54. **d** 54 **p** 55 Man. C of St Martin Conv Distr Wythenshawe 54-56; V of Smallbridge 56-63; Hindley Green 63-65; St Cleer 65-75. *97 Shellfield Road, Churchtown, Southport, PR9 9UL.* (Southport 211589)

BRAMSEN, Septimus Mervyn. St Barn Coll Adel. ACT ThL 40. **d** 39 **p** 41 Armid. C of Armid Cathl 39-40; Narrabri 40-42; V of Ashford 42-49; Narrabri 49-53; Bingara 53-56; Bellingen 56-58; Casterton 58-62; R of Henley Beach 62-68; Mt Barker 68-71; Perm to Offic Dio Murray 71-77; L to Offic Dio Adel 71-72; and from 73; C of Brighton 72-73. *21 Crown Street, Dover Gardens, S Australia 5048.* (08-296 3811)

BRANCH, Clarence Henry. b 09. **d** and **p** 42 York. C of Gt w L Driffield 42-45; St Lawrence York 45-49; V of Ferry Fryston 49-78. *46 Pontefract Road, Knottingley, Yorks.* (Knottingley 82030)

BRANCH, Claude Frederick. b 04. ACP 65. **d** and **p** 66 B & W. C of St Sav Bath 66-75; Perm to Offic Dio Ox from 76. *12 Middle Way, Summertown, Oxford.*

BRANCH, Jack Archibald. b 25. ACIS 66. ACP 70. Bp's Coll Cheshunt 49. **d** 71 **p** 72 Croydon for Cant. C of Croydon and of St Andr Croydon 71-73; Selsdon 73-75; St Jas and St Aug Beckenham 75-78; R of E and W Tilbury and Linford Dio Chelmsf from 78. *East Tilbury Rectory, Nr Grays, Essex.* (Tilbury 2809)

BRANCHE, Brian Maurice. b 37. Chich Th Coll 73. **d** 75 **p** 76 Chich. C of The Resurr Brighton 75-78; All SS w St Marg U Norwood 78-80; V of St Martin Croydon Dio Cant from 80. *97 Stretton Road, Croydon, CR0 6ET.* (01-654 4938)

BRAND, Frank Ronald Walter. b 25. ALCD 56 (LTh from 74). **d** 56 **p** 57 Lon. C of St Anne Brondesbury w H Trin Kilburn 56-58; V of Port Mourant 58-61; Enmore Guy 61-67; V of All H N Greenford Dio Lon from 67. *Vicarage, Horsenden Lane North, Greenford, Middx.* (01-422 3183)

BRAND, Stuart William. b 30. Univ of Leeds BSc 53. Coll of Resurr Mirfield. **d** 55 **p** 56 Lon. C of Stepney 55-59; St Pet Acton Green 59-60; C-in-c of St Alb Godshill 60-64; R of Blantyre Malawi 64-67; V of Wymering w Widley 67-72; Sen Chap of Fieldhead Pinderfields and Stanley Royd Hosps Wakef 72-80; Chap Brook Gen Hosp Woolwich and Greenwich Distr Hosp from 80. *Chaplain's Office, Greenwich Hospital, Vanbrugh Hill, SE10.* (01-858 8141)

BRANDIE, Beaumont Lauder. b 40. K Coll Lon and Warm AKC 64, BD 66. **d** 65 Lon **p** 66 Kens for Lon. C of St Aug of Cant Whitton Middx 65-71; Portsea (in c of St Wilfrid) 71-77; R of The Resurr Brighton Dio Chich from 77. *St Martin's Vicarage, Upper Wellington Road, Brighton, BN2 3AN.* (Brighton 604687)

BRANDON, Lord Bishop of. *See* Conlin, Right Rev John Fletcher Stout.

BRANDON, Alan Norman. **d** 48 **p** 49 Ont. R of Pleyna w Ardoch and Ompah 48-50; Maynooth and N Frontenac 50-52; Adolphustown 52-58; Ox 58-59; Tamworth 59-69; Newboro 67-78. *Box 441, Westport, Ont, Canada.*

BRANDON, Dennis Ralph. b 24. Univ of Leeds BA 50. Linc Th Coll 53. **d** 55 Whitby for York **p** 56 York. C of St Steph Acomb York 55-59; R of Thwing 59-63; V of Wold Newton 59-63; Kirby Moorside w Gillamoor 63-68; V of Bransdale w Farndale 63-68; C of Pickering York 68-71; C-in-c of Newton-on-Rawcliffe 71-74; C-in-c of Newton Kyme Dio York from 74. *Newton Kyme Rectory, Tadcaster, Yorks, LS24 9LR.* (Tadcaster 833431)

BRANDON, Preb Ernest Arthur. b 19. TCD BA (3rd cl Mod) 42, Div Test 43. MA 45. **d** 43 **p** 44 Oss. C of Kilkenny 43-46; St Donard Belf 46-47; St Clem Belf 47-49; Booterstown and Carysfort 49-51; I of Celbridge w Straffan 51-63; R of Horetown w Taghmon Dio Ferns from 63; Preb of Ferns Cathl from 81. *Horetown Rectory, Foulksmills, Co Wexford, Irish Republic.* (051 63688)

BRANDON, Michael Charles. b 56. Em Coll Cam BA 78. Coll of Resurr Mirfield 78. **d** 80 **p** 81 Willesden for Lon. C of St Jo Bapt Pinner Dio Lon from 80. *16 Barrow Point Avenue, Pinner, Middx.*

BRANDON, Owen Rupert. b 08. ALCD 34. Univ of Bris MA 51. Univ of Dur MLitt 62. **d** 34 **p** 35 Ches. C of St Mark Evang New Ferry 34-37; St Jo Evang Boscombe 37-41; R of St Nich Worc 41-47; Wingfield 47-49; Tutor St Andr Hall Surbiton 49-50; Prin 50-51; Hon C of Ch Ch Surbiton Hill 49-51; R of Hawkwell 51-53; Tutor Lon Coll of Div 53-64; Fell St Aug Coll Cant 65-73; L to Offic Dio Cant 65-66; R of Fordwich 66-73; L to Offic Dio Chich from 73. *51 Lower Park Road, Hastings, E Sussex, TN34 2LA.*

BRANDRETH, Henry Renaud Turner. b 14. Linc Th Coll 40. **d** 42 **p** 43 Ely. C of St Ives w Oldhurst and Woodhurst 42-45; St Barn Wood End Conv Distr Northolt Park Lon 45-49; Chap St Geo Paris 49-65; V of St Sav Aberdeen Pk Highbury 65-82; Guild V of St Dunstan-in-the-West Lon 70-76; P-in-c 76-78; Assoc Sec of C of E Coun on Foreign Relns 70-74. *c/o 43 Aberdeen Park, N5 2AR.*

BRANDRETH, Roderick Gary. **d** 68 Perth. C of Quairading 68-71; Perm to Offic Dio Perth from 71. *19 Austin Way, Padbury, W Australia 6025.* (92 6317)

BRANDRICK, Ven Horace William. Univ of Sask 48. Em Coll Sktn 49. **d** and **p** 51 Keew. I of Sioux Lookout 51-54; R of St Geo Sktn 54-74; Can of St John's Cathl, Sktn from 65; Archd of Sktn from 67; Exam Chap to Bp of Sktn from 74. *63 Baldwin Crescent, Saskatoon, Sask., Canada.*

BRANDWOOD, Herbert. b 05. Late Exhib of Wadh Coll Ox BA (2nd cl Lit Hum) 27, 2nd cl Hist 29. St Aid Coll 38. **d** 39 **p** 40 Blackb. C of Ch Ch Accrington 39-42; St Marg Aberlour and Sub-Warden Aberlour Orph 42-45; C of Nether Seale (in c of St Matt Overseal) 45-46; V of Halvergate w Tunstall 46-49; Strumpshaw w Bradeston 49-51; R of Buckenham w Hassingham and Strumpshaw 51-54; L to Offic Dio Accra 54-60; Chap Bp's Coll Sch Lennoxville 60-61; L to Offic Dio Queb 60-62; Chap Colston's Sch Bris 62-63; R of Knipton w Harston 63-73; L to Offic 73-75; P-in-c of Bodham 75-79; W Beckham 75-78. *37 Nelson Road, Sheringham, Norfolk, NR26 8BX.* (Sheringham 3514)

BRANNAGAN, Alan McKenzie. b 34. Chich Th Coll 66. **d** 68 **p** 69 York. C of St Mich AA Hull 68-70; Dunstable 70-75; V of E w W Rudham 75-81; Houghton-next-Harpley 75-81; Team V of Wolverhampton Dio Lich from 81. *All Saints Vicarage, Vicarage Road, Wolverhampton, WV2 1DT.* (Wolverhampton 51997)

BRANSBY, Albert Edgar. b 17. Tyndale Hall Bris 46. **d** 49 **p** 50 Man. C of St Pet Halliwell 49-51; Chorley Wood 51-53; R of Stokesby w Herringby 53-55 V of St Geo w St Andr Battersea 55-60; R of Cosgrove 60-65; R of Passenham w Deanshanger 60-65; RD of Preston 62-65; Surr from 63; V of St Giles Northn 65-75; R of Buckenham w Hassingham and Strumpshaw Dio Nor from 75. *Strumpshaw Rectory, Norwich, Norf, NR13 4NT.* (Norwich 712181)

BRANSGROVE, Geoffrey Kench. b 42. Ridley Coll Melb BTh 77. **d** 79 **p** 80 Graft. C of Lismore Dio Graft from 79. *PO Box 378, Lismore, NSW, Australia 2480.*

BRANSON, Canon Charles Stanley. b 07. Univ of Lon 32. St Aug Coll Cant 34. **d** 37 **p** 38 Derby. C of Whitwell 37-40; C-in-c of Pilsley 40-43; V of Elmton w Creswell 43-53; R of Eckington w Renishaw 53-69; Surr from 53; RD of Staveley 66-69; V of Old Brampton (w Loundsley Green R from 76) 69-78; Hon Can of Derby Cathl 74-78; Can (Emer) from 78. *5 Westbourne Grove, Chesterfield, Derby.*

BRANSON, James Watson. b 1894. MIEE 36. Edin Th

Coll 54. **d** and **p** 55 Edin. C of St Cuthb Colinton (in c of St Mungo Balerno) 55-61; Perm to Offic Dio Guildf from 61. *15 Upper St Michael's Road, Aldershot, Hants.* (Aldershot 24342)

BRANSON, Robert David. b 46. Linc Th Coll 74. **d** 77 **p** 78 St Alb. C of Ch of Transfig Kempston 77-80; Goldington Dio St Alb from 80. *46 Church End, Renhold, Bedford, MK1 0LU.* (Bedf 771317)

BRANT, Anthony William. b 31. TD 67. Linc Th Coll 73. **d** 75 Guildf **p** 76 Guildf. C of Cove 75-79; P-in-c of Puttenham w Wanborough Dio Guildf from 79. *Puttenham Rectory, Guildford, Surrey, GU3 1AH.* (0483-810338)

BRANT, Leslie Harold. b 11. **d** 71 **p** 72 Portsm. C of St Jo Evang, Sandown 71-74; C-in-c of Newchurch IW 75-81. *Glebe Cottage, Swanmore, Ryde, PO33 3ED.* (Ryde 67071)

BRANT, Robert Glendon. Bp's Univ Lennox LTS 59. **d** 59 Ont **p** 62 Nass. C of Trenton, Ont 59-62; St Mary, Nass 62-66; R of Exuma 66-73; St Mary I and Dio Nass from 73. *PO Box N-8753, Nassau, Bahamas, W Indies.* (36591)

BRANTHWAITE, Ven John Walter. Univ of NZ BA 49. Selw Coll Dun 49. NZ Bd of Th Stud LTh 65. **d** 51 Dun **p** 52 Ch Ch for Dun. C of Invercargill 51-54; V of Waitaki 54-55; Wakatipu 55-58; C of Opawa 57-60; V of Kens-Otipua 60-67; Ashburton Dio Ch Ch from 67; Archd of Timaru 75-77; Akaroa and Ashburton from 77; Exam Chap to Bp of Ch Ch from 75. *16 Cameron Street, Ashburton, NZ.* (Ashburton 5618)

BRANWELL, Edward Bruce. b 20. St Cath Coll Cam BA 42, MA 46. Linc Th Coll 42. **d** 44 Lon **p** 45 Stepney for Lon. C of St Sav Hampstead Lon 44-46; H Trin Cathl Port of Spain 46-47; St Paul San Fernando Trinidad 47-49; C of Rugby (in c of H Trin) 49-51; V of Glossop 51-56; Area Sec UMCA for SE Engl 56-58; V of Lavender Hill 58-64; Chap Aldenham Sch 64-70; Asst Master Burlington Sch Lon 70-77; Queenswood Sch Hatfield from 77. *9 The Grey House, Alexandra Road, Watford, Herts.* (Watford 22505)

BRASINGTON, Keith Andrew. St Jo Coll Morpeth 53. **d** 54 **p** 55 Armid. C of Moree 54-56; Armid Cathl 56-59; V of Warialda 59-65; Gunnedah 65-69; C of Warrnambool 69; R of Edenhope 69-71; Wendouree Dio Bal from 71. *Rectory, Forest Street, Wendouree, Vic., Australia 3355.* (053-39 1657)

BRASNETT, Bertrand Rippington. b 1893. Late Squire Scho of Keble Coll Ox 2nd cl Cl Mods 13, BA (2nd cl Lit Hum) 15, MA 18, Dipl Th (w distinc) 20, BD 24, DD 35, Cudd Coll 16. **d** 16 **p** 18 Ox. Chap and Asst Master Bradfield Coll 16-18; C of Amersham (in c of Coleshill) 18-22; Chap Bps' Coll Cheshunt 22-25; Hon Chap of St Mary's Cathl Edin 26-29; Vice-Prin of Edin Th Coll 25-29; Pantonian Prof of Th and Prin 30-42; Exam Chap to Bp of Edin 30-42; Can of Edin Cathl 30-42; Chan 40-42; Select Pr Univ of Ox 41-43. *15 Jack Straw's Lane, Headington, Oxford, OX3 0DL.*

BRASNETT, Canon Leslie Stanley. b 1897. Late Scho of Ch Ch, Ox BA (1st cl Th) 21, MA 24. Cudd Coll 21. **d** 21 **p** 22 Ches. C of St Chad Over 21-24; Vice-Prin of Edin Th Coll 24-25; R of Fringford w Hethe 25-31; V of Gt Budworth 31-47; Runcorn 47-55; RD of Gt Budworth 44-47; Frodsham 47-55; Surr from 45; Exam Chap to Bp of Ches 46-55; Hon Can of Ches 50-55; Can (Emer) from 55; Proc Conv Ches 50-55; Perm to Offic Dios Win, Sarum and Portsm 55-78. *Devoncourt Hotel, Douglas Avenue, Exmouth, Devon, EX8 2EX.* (Exmouth 72277)

BRASS, Victor Miller. b 23. Em & St Chad Coll Sktn 79. **d** 80 **p** 81 Sktn. I of Meridian Dio Sktn from 80. *PO Box 86, Macklin, Sask, Canada, S0l 2C0.*

BRASSEL, Raymond Ernest. Hur Coll LTh 67. **d** 66 **p** 67 Hur. I of Tyrconnell Dutton and W Lorne 66-70; Listowel 70-77; H Trin Lon Hur 77-81; Good Shepherd City and Dio Calg from 81. *407-37th Street SW, Calgary, Alta, Canada.*

BRASSELL, Kenneth William. Kelham Th Coll 46. **d** 50 **p** 51 St E. C of Woodbridge 40-53; C-in-c of All SS Conv Distr Bury St Edms 53-57; PC of St Thos Ipswich 57-63; V of St Jas Elmers End Beckenham Dio Roch from 63; C-in-c of St Aug (w St Mich AA from 77), Beckenham 66-78. *15 St James's Avenue, Elmers End, Beckenham, Kent.* (Beckenham 0420)

BRASSINGTON, Leonard Roy. ACT ThL 56. **d** and **p** 57 C & Goulb. C of Queanbeyan 57-59; R of Cobargo 59-61; W Goulb 61-64; Asst Chap R Melb Hosp 64-65; Chap R Pk Psychiatric Hosp Melb 65-80; Willesmere Hosp Melb from 80. *10 Wills Street, Kew, Vic, Australia 3101.*

BRATHWAITE, Eglon Leslie. b 24. **d** 74 Windw Is. C of H Trin Castries St Lucia Dio Windw Is from 74. *La Clery, Castries, St Lucia, Windward Islands.* (St Lucia 4027)

BRAUN, Robert Roy. St Francis Coll Brisb ACT ThL 71. **d** and **p** 72 Brisb. C of St Clem Stafford Brisb 72-74; Bundaberg 74-76; Miss Chap Dio Brisb 76-77; P-in-c of St Alb Cunnamulla Dio Brisb from 78. *Rectory, Jane Street, Cunnamulla, Queensland, Australia 4490.* (Cunnamulla 110)

BRAUND, George Basil. b 26. SS Coll Cam 2nd cl Hist Trip pt i, 49, BA (2nd Hist Trip pt ii) 50, MA 54. Ely Th Coll 51. **d** 53 **p** 54 Ely. C of St Luke Chesterton 53-60; Chap SS Coll Cam and L to Offic Dio Ely 60-68; Trav Missr USPG 68-73; Sec 73-79; L to Offic Dio Lon 68-69; Supr OGS 69-75. L to Offic Dio Ox from 69; Commiss Newc 73-77; N Terr from 74; S Malawi 75-80; Assoc Sec for Miss Angl Consultative Coun from 79; Sec Internat Angl Th and Doctrinal Comm from 80. *14 Great Peter Street, SW1P 3NQ.* (01-222 2851)

BRAVINGTON, Timothy Frederick Desmond. Trin Coll Cam BA 56, MA 70. Cudd Coll 56. **d** 58 **p** 59 Capetn. C of Caldedon 58-61; Asst Chap St Andr Coll Grahmstn 61-64; R of Namaqualand 64-71; Bellville 71-75; St Martin Durban N Dio Natal from 76. *12 Chelsea Drive, N Durban, Natal, S Africa.* (Durban 832564)

BRAY, Anthony Markham. b 16. Magd Coll Cam 2nd cl Hist Trip pt i 36, BA (2nd cl Hist Trip pt ii) 37, MA 43. Cudd Coll 38. **d** 39 **p** 40 Dur. C of St Osw Dur 39-42; St Jo Evang E Dulwich 42-46; St Andr Kingswood (in c of Ch of Wisdom of God Lower Kingswood) 46-53; V of Crediton 53-75; PC (V from 69) of Posbury Chap 53-75; C-in-c of Colebrooke 65-68; Hittesleigh 65-68; RD of Cadbury 56-65; P-in-c of Otterton 75-80. *Quince, King Street, Colyton, Devon, EX13 6LA.*

BRAY, Christopher Laurence. b 53. Univ of Leeds BSc 74. Qu Univ Kingston Ont MSc 76. Univ of Nottm Dipl Th 79. St Jo Coll Nottm 78. **d** 81 Liv. C of Ch Ch Aughton Dio Liv from 81. *25 Peet Avenue, Ormskirk, Lancs, L39 4SH.*

BRAY, Gerald Lewis. b 48. McGill Univ Montr BA 69. Ridley Hall Cam 76. **d** 78 Barking for Chelmsf **p** 79 Chelmsf. C of St Cedd Canning Town 78-80; Tutor Oak Hill Coll from 80. *Oak Hill Theological College, N14 4PS.* (01-449 3162)

BRAY, Jeremy Grainger. b 40. Univ of Man BA (2nd cl Engl) 62. Wells Th Coll 62. **d** 64 **p** 65 Bris. C of St Andr w St Bart Bris 64-67; H Cross Inns Court Bris 67-71; C-in-c of Stockwood Conv Distr Brislington 71-73; V of Stockwood Dio Bris from 73; RD of Brislington from 79. *Vicarage, Goslet Road, Stockwood, Bristol, BS14 8SP.* (Whitchurch (832633)

BRAY, John Eric. St Jo Coll Auckld 54. NZ Bd of Th Stud LTh 57. **d** 56 **p** 58 Dun. C of Invercargill 56-58; All SS Dun 58-59; Oamaru 59-60. *48 Elgin Road, Dunedin, NZ.*

BRAY, Kenneth Frank. b 08. AKC 30. Wells Th Coll 30. **d** 31 **p** 32 Pet. C of St Sepulchre Northn 31-34; All SS Leamington Spa 34-39; Gatton 39-42; St Mich AA Camberwell 42-45; St Pet Limpsfield 45-47; V of Davidstow w Otterham (R) 47-48; St Teath w Delabole and Michaelstow (R) 48-53; Winchcombe w Gretton and Sudeley Manor 53-59; RD of Winchcombe 56-59; Chap St Jas, Oporto 59-70; Hon C of St Ambrose Bournemouth 71-81. *Address temp unknown.*

BRAY, Kenneth John. b 31. **d** 67 Swan B **p** 72 Willesden for Lon. C of Killay 67-68; St Paul S Harrow 71-73; Hillingdon 73-76; Chipping Sodbury w Old Sodbury 76-79; Min in Ecumen Par of Worle 79-80. *c/o 2a St Mark's Road, Worle, Weston-super-Mare, Avon, BS22 0PW.* (W-s-M 512093)

BRAY, Canon Raymond Gordon. Sir Geo Williams Univ Montr BA 57. Hur Coll LTh 60. **d** 60 **p** 61 Tor. C of St Matt Islington 60-63; I of Chase 63-65; R of Fernie 65-72; P-in-c of Westbank Dio Koot from 72; Hon Can of Koot from 75; Bp's Commiss Dio Koot from 78. *Box 257, Westbank, BC, Canada.* (768-5723)

BRAY, Richard. b 29. Linc Th Coll 55. **d** 57 **p** 58 Chelmsf. C of St Barn L Ilford 57-62; R of Tye Green w Netteswell Dio Chelmsf from 62; Surr from 67. *Tye Green Rectory, Harlow, Essex.* (Harlow 25138)

BRAY, Thomas Chadwick. b 08. Qu Coll Birm 46. **d** 48 **p** 49 Lich. C of Gnosall w Knightley 48-51; Shifnal 51-55; R of Ryton 55-69; C-in-c of Badger 55-56; R 56-69; C-in-c of Beckbury 55-56; R 56-69; RD of Shifnal 65-69; V of Bolam 69-74. *2 Walnut Close, Newport, Shropshire.*

BRAYBROOK, Ian James. St Jo Coll Morpeth ThL 68. **d** 69 **p** 70 Melb. C of St Geo Malvern 69-71; C of All SS Geelong 71; Werribee 71-74; P-in-c of Hopper's Crossing 74-77; I of Croydon S Dio Melb from 77. *199 Bayswater Road, Bayswater, Vic, Australia 3153.* (03-729 2692)

BRAYBROOKE, Marcus Christopher Rossi. b 38. Magd Coll Cam 1st cl Hist Trip pt i 60, BA (2nd cl Th Trip pt ii) 62, MA 65. MPhil (Lon) 68. Wells Th Coll 63. **d** 64 **p** 65 Lon. C of St Mich Highgate 64-67; Frindsbury 67-72; Team V of Strood 72-73; C-in-c of Swainswick w Langridge (and Woolley from 75) 73-76; R 76-79; Chairman World Congress of Faiths from 78; Dioc Dir of Tr Dio B & W from 79. *Old Deanery, Wells, Somt.* (Wells 73308)

BRAYBROOKE, Oliver Henry. b 08. Pemb Coll Cam BA 30, MA 58. Wells Th Coll 58. **d** 58 **p** 59 St E. C of Wrentham 58-61; R of Bredfield w Boulge 61-73; Debach 61-73; Perm to Offic Dio St E from 73. *Regency House, Great Bealings, Woodbridge, Suff.* (Grundisburgh 325)

BRAZEL, Harold James. Wycl Coll Tor LTh 70. **d** and **p** 70 Queb. I of Murdochville 70-72; Valcartier 72-75; W Sherbrooke 75-79; Thetford Mines Dio Queb from 79. *Box 742, Thetford Mines, PQ, Canada.*

BRAZELL, Denis Illtyd Anthony. b 42. Trin Coll Cam BA 64, MA 68. Wycl Hall Ox 78. **d** 80 **p** 81 Glouc. C of Ch Ch Cheltm Dio Glouc from 80. *224 Gloucester Road, Cheltenham, Glos.* (Cheltenham 515915)

BRAZIER, Kenneth Samuel. b 14. Tyndale Hall Bris 57. **d** 58 Lich **p** 59 Stafford for Lich. C of Bucknall 58-60; V of Knypersley 60-63; R of Hawkwell 63-67; V of Over Kellett 67-75; Willoughby-on-the-Wolds w Wysall 75-79; P-in-c of Widmerpool 75-79. *7a Shrubbery Walk West, Weston-super-Mare, Avon.* (W-s-M 22700)

✠ **BRAZIER, Right Rev Percy James.** b 03. Em Coll Cam 2nd cl Hist Trip pt 1 24, BA (2nd cl Hist Trip pt ii) 25, MA 39. Ridley Hall Cam 25. **d** 27 **p** 28 S'wark. C of St Jo Evang Blackheath 27-29; CMS Miss Kabale 29-34; Kigeme 34-51; Archd of Ruanda 46-51; Cons Asst Bp of Ugan in Westmr Abbey 2 Feb 51 by Abp of Cant; Bps of Nor; Lich; Heref; B & W; St Alb; and Barb; Bps Suffr of Barking; and Warrington; and Bp Mann; Trld to Rwanda and Burundi 60; Res 64; R of Padworth and PC of Mortimer West End 64-70. *Lark Rise, Peasemore, Newbury, Berks.*

BRAZIER, Raymond Venner. b 40. Wells Th Coll 68. **d** 71 **p** 72 Bris. C of St Gregory Horfield 71-75; P-in-c of St Nath w St Kath City and Dio Bris 75-79; V from 79; P-in-c of St Matt Kingsdown City and Dio Bris from 80. *11 Glentworth Road, Bristol, BS6 7EG.* (Bris 44186)

BRAZILL, Brock Rodney. Sir Geo Williams Univ Tor BA 60. Wycl Coll Tor LTh and BTh 64. **d** 64 **p** 65 Alg. C of St Luke's Cathl Sault Ste Marie 64-66; Burwash 66-71; R of Resurr Sudbury Alg 70-74; New Liskeard 74-78; on leave 79-80; I of Emsdale Miss Dio Alg from 81. *Kearney, Ont, Canada.*

BRAZILL, Cyril Clyde. Univ of Tor BA 52. Trin Coll Tor LTh 33. CD 63. **d** 32 **p** 33 Ont. C of Bannockburn 33-35; I 35-36; R of Adolphustown 36-43; Stirling and Frankford 43-48; St Edm Mart Tor 48-75. *Box 66, Brighton, Ont., Canada.*

BRAZINGTON, David Albert. b 36. **d** 78 Tewkesbury for Glouc **p** 79 Glouc. C of H Trin Longlevens Dio Glouc from 78. *50 Oxstalls Way, Longlevens, Gloucester, GL2 9HU.*

BREADEN, Canon Robert William. b 37. Edin Th Coll 58. **d** 61 **p** 62 Brech. C of Broughty Ferry 61-64; R of H Rood Carnoustie 65-71; Broughty Ferry Dio Brech from 71; Can of St Paul's Cathl Brechin from 77. *46 Seafield Road, Broughty Ferry, Dundee, DD5 3AN.* (Dundee 77477)

BREAY, John. b 19. Selw Coll Cam BA 41, MA 45. St Chad's Coll Dur Dipl Th 42. **d** 42 **p** 43 Carl. C of Lowther w Askham 42-44; Kendal 44-48; C-in-c of Kirkandrews-on-Esk 48-49; R 49-52; V of Soulby (w Crosby-Garrett from 54) 52-55; Seq of Crosby-Garrett 52-54; V of Warcop w Musgrave 55-59; Shepreth 59-77; Surr 67-71; RD of Barton 67-72; V of Barrington 77; Gt w L Chesterford 77-79; Perm to Offic Dio Ely from 79. *66 Montague Road, Cambridge, CB4 1BX.* (Cambridge 358448)

BRECHIN, Lord Bishop of. *See* Luscombe, Right Rev Lawrence Edward.

BRECHIN, Dean of. *See* Hayes, Very Rev Ernest.

BRECKLES, Robert Wynford. b 48. St Edm Hall Ox BA 72, MA 74. St John's Coll Dur 77. **d** Sherwood for Southw **p** 80 Southw. C of St Mary Bulwell Dio Southw from 79. *1 Millbank Court, Crabtree Farm Estate, Bulwell, Nottingham.*

BRECKNELL, David Jackson. b 32. Keble Coll Ox BA 53, MA 57. St Steph Ho Ox 56. **d** 58 **p** 59 S'wark. C of St Pet Streatham 58-62; C of Sneinton (in c of St Alb) 62-64; Solihull 64-68; V of St Paul Furzedown Streatham 68-75; R of Rumboldswyke Chich 75-81; P-in-c of Portfield 79-81; R of Whyke w Rumboldswyke and Portfield Dio Chich from 81. *200 Whyke Road, Chichester, W Sussex, PO19 2HQ.* (0243 782535)

BRECON, Archdeacon of. *See* Jones, Ven Owain William.

BRECON, Dean of. *See* Jones, Very Rev Alwyn Rice.

BREDIN, Very Rev Thomas Andrew Noble. b 27. TCD BA 50, MA 56. **d** 51 **p** 52 Waterf. C of Waterford 51-53; Dean's V of Kilkenny Cathl 53-55; R of Moynalty w Moybologue 55-62; Roscrea 62-79; Preb of Lockeen Killaloe 72-79; Kilteskill and Kinvara Clonfert 72-79; Hon Sec Dioc Board of Educn 73-79; Archd of Killaloe and Clonfert 74-79; Exam Chap to Bp of Killaloe 74-79; I of Trim Dio Meath and Dean of Clonmacnoise from 79. *St Patrick's Deanery, Trim, Co Meath, Irish Republic.* (Trim 31254)

BREE, Reginald Hooper. b 13. **d** 61 **p** 62 Worc. Westcott Ho Cam. C of Astwood Bank w Crabbs Cross 61-66; V of Broadwaters 66-78. *c/o 29 Batham Road, Kidderminster, Worcs.* (Kidderminster 2874)

BREED, Kenneth Wilfred. b 11. Univ of Leeds BA (2nd cl Hist) 33. Coll of Resurr Mirfield 33. **d** 35 **p** 36 Cov. C of H Trin Cov 35-37; St Pet Parkstone w Branksea 37-43; Chap RNVR 43-46; C of Eastleigh 46-49; Cheam (in c of St Alb) 49-51; V of Shirley 51-77; Hon C of St Andr Holborn City and Dio Lon from 77. *5 St Andrew's Street, EC4A 3AB.* (01-353 4114)

BREESE, Kenneth Edmund. Qu Coll Birm 46. **d** 49 Cov. C of Radford Warws 49-51. *129 Carlingford Drive, Westcliff-on-Sea, Essex.*

BREHAUT, Austin Philip. Ridley Coll Melb 65. **d** 65 **p** 66 Bal. C of Kaniva 65-66; Heywood 66-69; R 69-70; Otway 70-74; Dimboola 74-80; Edenhope Dio Bal from 80. *Rectory, Edenhope, Vic, Australia 3318.*

BRENCHLEY, Canon Frederick George. b 05. BC Coll Bris. **d** 28 Lon for Col Bp **p** 29 Persia. BCMS Miss at Duzdab 28-31; Seistan 31-33; C of H Trin Wallington Surrey 33-35; St Pet (in c of St John) St Alb 35-38; V of St Paul St Alb 38-56; RD of St Alb 46-53; Hon Can of St Alb 50-71; Can (Emer) from 71; C-in-c of Colney Heath 52-54; R of Baldock w Bygrave and Clothall 56-67; V of Dunton w Wrestlingworth and Eyeworth 67-71; RD of Baldock 58-65; L to Offic Dio St Alb from 75. *9 Roundwood Close, Hitchin, Herts.* (Hitchin 51880)

BRENNAN, John Lester. b 20. Univ of Lon MB and BS 44, MD 52, Dipl Th 47. MRCP 51. FRCPath 77. Called to Bar Middle Temple 71. **d** 55 **p** 56 Amrit. Prof of Pathology and Chap Chr Med Coll Ludhiana 55-65; P-in-c of Ch Ch Ludhiana 56-65; Hon C of St Barn Woodside Pk Finchley 65-69; L to Offic Dio Lich from 69. *18 Ardmillan Lane, Oswestry, Salop, SY11 2JY.* (Oswestry 4593)

BRENNAN, Samuel James. St Aid Coll. **d** 57 **p** 58 Down. C of Maralin 57-60; Down and Min Can of Down Cathl 60-63; I of Scarva 63-69; Aghalee Dio Drom from 69; RD of Shankill from 77. *39 Soldierstown Road, Aghalee, Craigavon, Co Armagh, N Ireland.* (Aghalee 233)

BRENNAN, William Joseph. b 24. **d** 81 Glas (NSM). C of Challoch w Newton Stewart Dio Glas from 81. *4 Philip Avenue, Newton Stewart, Wigtownshire, DG8 6HF.*

BRENNEN, Canon Colin. b 15. Univ of Lon BA (Hons Hist) 47, BD 56. Linc Th Coll 46. **d** 48 **p** 49 Newc T. C of Seaton Hirst 48-50; Bp Wearmouth 50-52; PC of Grangetown 52-58; V of Whitworth w Spennymoor 58-78; RD of Auckland from 74; P-in-c of Byers Green 76-78; Hamsterley Dio Dur from 78; Hon Can of Dur Cathl from 78. *Hamsterley Vicarage, Bishop Auckland, Co Durham.*

BRENTON, Basil. b 28. Sarum Th Coll. **d** 55 **p** 56 Lon. C of St Mary Abbots Kens 55-59; CF 59-62; Chap H Trin Sliema Malta 62-65; C-in-c of St Edm Conv Distr Yeading Hayes 65-68; V of Cowfold Dio Chich from 68. *Cowfold Vicarage, Horsham, Sussex.* (Cowfold 296)

BRESEE, Canon Glendon Clark. b 28. Trin Coll Tor BA 50, LTh 53, BD 55. Univ of Alta MEducn 75. **d** 52 **p** 53 Niag. R of Palmerston 53-55; C of St Jas Ap Hamilton 55-58; St Jas Edmon 58-63; R of St Aug City and Dio Edmon from 63; Can of Edmon from 72. *4704 109th Avenue, Edmonton 80, Alta., Canada.* (403-466 6540)

BRETEL, Keith Michael. St Mich AA Th Coll Llan 79. **d** 81 Bradwell for Chelmsf. C of Thundersley Dio Chelmsf from 81. *45 Grandview Road, Thundersley, S Benfleet, Essex, SS7 3JZ.*

BRETHERTON, Anthony Atkinson. b 51. Univ of Cant NZ BA 74. St Jo Coll Auckld LTh 74, STh 76. **d** 75 **p** 76 Ch Ch. C of Ashburton 75-78; on leave 78-81; V of Te Kauwhata Dio Waik from 81. *Vicarage, Te Kauwhata, NZ.*

BRETHERTON, Donald John. b 18. BD (Lon) 57. St Aug Coll Cant. **d** 60 Maidstone for Cant **p** 61 Cant. C of St Martin and St Paul Cant 60-62; V of St Jude Thornton Heath 62-70; Herne Dio Cant from 70; RD of Reculver from 74. *Herne Vicarage, Herne Bay, Kent, CT6 7HE.* (Herne Bay 4328)

BRETHERTON, Humphrey. b 1889. Trin Coll Cam BA (3rd cl Th Trip) 11, MA 23. Ely Th Coll 11. **d** 12 **p** 13 Man. C of St Aug Pendlebury 12-18; R of Eccleston 19-58; RD of Leyland 30-35; Hon C of Eccleston 58-63. *Springkell, Wood Road, Hindhead, Surrey.*

BRETHERTON, Canon William Alan. b 22. St Cath Coll Cam BA 43, MA 47. ALCD 49. Univ of Lon BD 49. **d** 49 **p** 50 Liv. C of Em Fazakerley Liv 49-52; V of St Chrys Everton 52-65; Ince-in-Makerfield 65-72; Proc Conv Liv from 61; V of St Mary Kirkdale (and St Athanasius from 73) Dio Liv from 72; Hon Can of Liv Cathl from 81; RD of Liverpool from 81. *54 Fonthill Road, Liverpool, L4 1QQ.* (051-933 6860)

BRETHERTON-HAWKSHEAD-TALBOT, Richard Dolben. b 11. Trin Coll Cam 2nd cl Hist Trip pt i 31, BA (2nd cl Hist Trip pt ii) and Hist Exhib 32. Ely Th Coll 32. **d** 34 **p** 35 Dur. C of Ryhope 34-38; Whitby (in c of St Jo Evang) 39-40; PC of St Geo E Bolden 40-47; Actg C of Eccleston 47-58; R 58-78; Sec ACS Dio Blackb from 69. *45 South Road, Bretherton, Nr Preston, Lancs, PR5 7AJ.*

BRETT, Aaron Raymond. **d** 55 Newfld **p** 56 NS for Newfld. C of Grand Falls 55-56; I of Battle Harbour 57-59; Twillingate 59-64; R of Canso w Queensport 64-68; on leave. *Box 367, Springdale, Newfoundland, Canada.*

BRETT, Donald Angus Adair. b 17. Chich Th Coll 52. **d** 55 **p** 56 Chich. C of W Tarring 55-60; Seaford w Sutton (in c of St Luke) 60-65; Findon (in c of All SS from 78) 65-81; Perm to Offic Dio Chich from 81. *19 Loxwood Avenue, Worthing, Sussex.* (Worthing 201910)

BRETT, Canon George Thomas. b 12. St Edm Hall Ox BA 34, MA 39. Wycl Hall Ox 34. **d** 36 Bradf **p** 37 Bp Mounsey for Bradf. C of St Clem Bradf 36-39; St John Meads Eastbourne 39-40; CF (EC) 40-46; V of H Trin Beckenham 46-53; St Pet (w St Marg from 54) Roch 53-61; R of Trowbridge 61-73; RD of Bradf 69-73; Can and Preb of Sarum from 72; V of Potterne 73-77; Worton 73-77. *7 The Stocks, Seend Cleeve, Near Melksham, Wilts, SN12 6PH.* (Seend 259)

BRETT, Canon John Henry Macklem. Bp's Univ Lennox BA 29, LST 31. **d** 31 **p** 32 Niag. C of W Flamboro w Rockston 32-33; I of Jarvis and Nanticoke 33-38; Malbay 38-41; Valcartier 41-46; in c of Rimouski Miss 43-46; I of Hatley 46-49; Abbotsford w Rougemont 49-53; P-in-c of W Shefford 52-53; R of Sutton Montr 53-73; Hon Can of Ch Ch Cathl Montr 70-73; Can (Emer) from 74. *Box 337, Sutton, PQ, Canada.* (514-538 3839)

BRETT, Canon Kenneth Keith. Seager Hall Ont STh 62. **d** 59 **p** 60 Hur. C of St John Windsor 59-62; Merlin w Erieau and Ouvry 62-65; I of Ch of Good Shepherd Woodstock (w Huntingford from 68) 65-72; St Steph and St Paul Brantford Dio Hur from 72; Can of Hur from 80. *50 Admiral Road, Brantford, Ont., Canada.* (519-753 1729)

BRETT, Leslie James Arthur. b 1900. Wycl Hall Ox. **d** 45 **p** 46 Chelmsf. C of Gt Baddow 45-48; R of Cranworth w Letton and Southburgh 48-52; V of Wisbey 52-66; L to Offic Dio Bradf from 67. *656 Bradford Road, Oakenshaw, Bradford, Yorks.*

BRETT, Paul Gadsby. b 41. St Edm Hall Ox BA (2nd cl Th) 62, MA 66. Wycl Hall Ox 64. **d** 65 **p** 66 Man. C of St Pet Bury 65-68; Asst Industr Chap and L to Offic Dio Man 68-72; Sen Industr Chap Kidderminster 72-76; Asst Sec (Industr and Econ Affairs) Gen Syn Bd for Social Responsibility from 76; Perm to Offic Dio S'wark from 76. *7 Keswick Heights, Keswick Road, SW15 2JR.* (01-870 8912)

BRETT, Peter Graham Cecil. b 35. Em Coll Cam BA 59, MA 63. Cudd Coll 59. **d** 61 Glouc **p** 62 Tewkesbury for Glouc. C of Tewkesbury 61-64; Bournemouth 64-66; Chap Univ and Hatf Colls Univ of Dur and L to Offic Dio Dur 66-72; R of Houghton-le-Spring Dio Dur from 72; M Gen Syn from 75; RD of Houghton-le-Spring from 80. *Rectory, Houghton-le-Spring, T & W, DH4 5PR.* (H-le-Spring 842198)

BRETT-PERRING, Claude Shays. Bp's Univ Lennox STh 53. **d** 41 **p** 42 Queb. Miss at Sandy Beach 41-42; Peninsula 42-44; Saguenay 44-45; Labrador Miss 45-47; P-in-c of Peninsula 47-52; I of Chandler 52-58; E Angus 58-59; St D Galt Dio Hur from 59. *20 Elgin Street North, Cambridge, Ont., Canada.* (519-621 8113)

BRETTELL, Robert Michael. St Cath S Ox BA (2nd cl Th) 49, MA 54. Wycl Hall Ox 47. LCD 46. **d** 49 **p** 50 S'wark. C of St Jo Evang Blackheath 49-51; Norbiton 51-53; V of St Mary-of-Bethany Woking 53-62; Ch Ch Clifton (w Em Ch from 63) 62-73; H Trin Eastbourne Dio Chich from 73. *Holy Trinity Vicarage, Eastbourne, Sussex.* (Eastbourne 29046)

BREW, Robert Sidney. b 02. Univ of Liv BSc (2nd cl Hons Physics) 24. Bp Wilson Th Coll IM 36. **d** 38 **p** 39 Liv. C of Earlestown 38-41; St Anne Aigburth 41-44; Bp of Liv's Special Service Staff 44-58; C-in-c of St Mich-in-the-City Liv 45-51; Sen Chap Liv R Inf 46-51; Chap Newsham Gen Hosp Liv 51-58; C of Berry Pomeroy w Bridgetown 58-62; Braunton w Saunton and Knowle 62-64; C-in-c of Black Torrington Dio Ex 64-73; Perm to Offic Dio Truro from 76. *Wentworth Rest Home, St Austell, Cornw.*

BREWER, Arthur George. Univ of W Ont BA 59, LTh 61. Hur Coll 59. **d** 61 Hur for Ott **p** 62 Ott. D Dio Ott 61-62; C of St Jo Beachburg 68-73; R of Richmond Dio Ott from 73. *Rectory, Richmond, Ont., Canada.* (1-613-838-2451)

BREWER, Barry James. b 44. Oak Hill Coll 72. **d** 75 **p** 76 Chich. C of Bp Hannington Mem Ch Hove 75-78; Church Stretton 78-81; Team V of Oakmoor Dio Ex from 81. *c/o Molland Vicarage, South Molton, N Devon.*

BREWER, Canon Douglas Charles. **d** 56 **p** 59 Qu'App. I of Saltcoats 56-62; Canora 62-70; Melville (now Parkland) 70-77; R of St Mich AA Moose Jaw 77-80; Swift Cirrent Dio Qu'App from 80; Hon Can of Qu'App from 79. *108-2nd Avenue North East, Swift Current, Sask, Canada.*

BREWER, John Herbert. b 13. St Steph Ho Ox 37. **d** 39 Willesden for Lon **p** 40 Lon. C of St Clem City Road 39-40; St Jas Gt Bethnal Green 40-42; Ch Ch Ealing 42-48; CF (EC) 44-47; Hon CF 47; V of Kumasi 48-52; Archd of Kumasi 51-56; Can of Accra 56-60; Bp's Miss to N Territory 56-60; Commiss Accra from 61; V of All SS w St Columb Notting Hill Kens 61-66; St Francis Isleworth 66-78; Perm to Offic Dio Nor from 78. *36 Cleave's Drive, Walsingham, Norf, NR 22 6EQ.*

BREWER, Peter Macdonald. St Francis Coll Brisb. **d** 60 **p** 61 Brisb. C of Toowong 61; Camp Hill 61-63; P-in-c of Mitchell 63-66; C of Warwick 66-68; Southport 68; R of Cleveland 68-73; Grovely 73-80; Ch Ch Yeronga City and Dio Brisb from 80. *21 Dublin Street, Yeronga, Queensland, Australia 4014.* (48 1638)

BREWIN, David Frederick. b 39. Lich Th Coll 63. **d** 66 **p** 67 Lich. C of H Cross Shrewsbury 66-69; Birstall, Leics 69-73; V of St Hugh, Eyres Monsell Leic 73-79; E Goscote Dio Leic from 79. *25 Ling Dale, East Goscote, Leicester.* (Leic 605938)

BREWIN, Donald Stewart. b 41. Ch Coll Cam BA 62, MA 66. Ridley Hall 68. **d** 71 **p** 72 Sheff. C of Ecclesall 71-75; V of Anston 75-81; H Trin Aylesbury Dio Ox from 81. *Holy Trinity Vicarage, Wendover Road, Aylesbury, Bucks, HP21 7NL.* (Aylesbury 82068)

BREWIN, Canon Eric Walter. b 16. Hertf Coll Ox BA (3rd cl Phil, Pol and Econ) 38, 2nd cl Th 40, MA 42. Ripon Hall Ox 38. **d** 40 **p** 41 Leic. C of St Marg Leic 40-42; Industr Sec SCM 42-46; LPr Dio Lon 43; C of St Mary Virg Ox 46-48; V of Coleford w Staunton (R) 48-70; RD of S Forest 57-81; Hon Can of Glouc from 65; R of Leckhampton 70-81. *The Pleck, Llangrove, Ross-on-Wye, Heref.* (Llang 487)

BREWIN, Wilfred Michael. b 45. Nottm Univ BA (1st cl Th and Phil) 69. Cudd Coll 69. **d** 70 **p** 71 Bp Ramsbotham for Newc T. C of Ch Ch, Walker 70-73; Alnwick w Edlingham and Bolton 73-76; Sir Henry Stephenson Fell Univ of Sheff 77-79; P-in-c of Egglestone 79-80; V of St Mich AA Norton Dio Dur from 80. *Vicarage, Imperial Avenue, Norton, Stockton-on-Tees, TS20 2EW.* (Stockton 553984)

BREWIS, Charles Gent. Edin Th Coll 38. **d** 41 **p** 42 Glas. C of St John Greenock 41-45; Eglingham 45-48; CF 48-70; V of Chevington 48-75; Surr 50-79; V of St Aug Newc T 75-79. *16 Burswell Avenue, Hexham, Northumb, NE46 3JL.* (Hexham 605133)

BREWSTER, David Pearson. b 30. Clare Coll Cam BA 54, MA 58. BA (2nd cl Arabic) Lon 65. Or Coll Ox MA (by incorp) 66, DPhil 76. Ridley Hall Cam. **d** 58 **p** 59 Win. C of St Mary w H Trin Southn 58-61; St Mark N Audley Str Lon 61-62 and 63-65; St Geo Tunis 62-63; Home Sec JEM 65-66; C of St Mary Virg Ox 66-68; Lect Lady Spencer-Churchill Coll Ox 68-71; Univ of Cant Ch Ch 71-76; Sen Lect 76-78; Offg Min Dio Ch Ch 74-78; V of Brockenhurst Dio Win from 78. *Vicarage, Brockenhurst, Hants, SO4 7SP.* (Lymington 22150)

BREWSTER, Lester Arnold. b 27. Fitzw Ho Cam BA 3rd cl (Hist) 51, MA 55. Wycl Hall Ox 51. **d** 53 **p** 54 Roch. C of Swanley 53-55; High Wycombe 55-57; Cler Deputn Sec for Dr Barnardo's Homes Dios Cant, Chich, Guildf, Roch and S'wark 57-60; Org Sec Ox Miss to Calc 60-67; Hon C of Carshalton Dio S'wark from 60; Commiss Dacca from 63; A & N from 69. *155 Demesne Road, Wallington, Surrey, SM6 8EW.* (01-647 4174)

BREWSTER, Noel Theodore. b 16. CCC Cam BA (1st cl Th Trip pt i) 38, MA 42. Qu Coll Birm 38. **d** 39 **p** 40 Win. C of Ch Ch Portswood 39-42; All SS W Southbourne 42-46; St Mark Portsm (in c of St Francis) 46-49; Vice-Prin Qu Coll Newfld 49-52; V of St Mary Bourne w Litchfield 52-61; R of Fawley 61-69; All SS w St Andr Chilcomb and St Pet Chesil Win 69-70; V of Grantchester Dio Ely from 71. *Grantchester Vicarage, Cambridge, CB3 9NG.* (Cam 841110)

BREWSTER, Theodore Frederick. b 1893. **d** 46 Sherborne for Sarum **p** 47 Sarum. C of St Luke Parkstone w Branksea 46-48; V of Horton 48-61; R of Chalbury 48-61; RD of Wimborne 56-68; LPr Dio Sarum from 62; L to Offic Dio Win from 68. *Olinda, Dudsbury Avenue, Ferndown, Wimborne, Dorset.* (Ferndown 3884)

BREWSTER, William Taylor. b 26. Bps' Coll Cheshunt 58. **d** 59 **p** 60 Ex. C of Bideford 59-61; R of E Woolfardisworthy w Kennerleigh 61-71; R of Washford Pyne w Puddington 61-71; RD of Cadbury 68-71 C-in-c of Cruwys Morchard 68-71; Poughill w Stockleigh English 71; Asst Chap HM Pris Man 71; Chap HM Pris Maidstone 72-77; Blundeston from 77. *Chaplain's Office, HM Prison, Blundeston, Lowestoft, Suff, NR32 5BG.*

BRIANT, Virginia Woods. b 26. Univ of Oregon BA 50. Vanc Sch of Th MDiv 73. **d** 73 **p** 76 New Westmr. C of Ch Ch Cathl New Westmr 73-81; St Richared Vanc Dio New Westmr from 81. *501-6060 Balsam, Vancouver, BC, Canada.*

BRICE, Keith Patrick. b 55. SSM Th Coll Adel 76. **d** 80 **p** 81 Adel. C of St Marg Woodville Dio Adel from 80. *37 Danvers Grove, Woodville Gardens, S Australia 5012.*

BRIDCUT, William John. b 38. Div Hostel Dub 68. **d** 70 **p** 71 Connor. C of Ch Ch Cathl Lisburn 71-74; Supt ICM from 74. *Irish Church Missions, 28 Bachelors Walk, Dublin 1, Irish Republic.*

BRIDE, Graham Lindsay. Univ of Melb BCom 56. Trin Coll Melb ACT ThL 58. **d** 59 **p** 60 Melb. C of Hampton 59-61; Chap Sheff Industr Miss and C of Thrybergh 62-64; Industr Chap Dio Melb 64-68; Perm to Offic Dio Melb from 69. *8 Coventry Street, Montmorency, Vic, Australia 3094.* (03-439 7573)

BRIDGE, Very Rev Antony Cyprian. b 14. Linc Th Coll 53. **d** 55 Croydon for Cant. **p** 56 Cant. C of Hythe 55-58; V of Ch Ch Lanc Gate Lon 58-68; Exam Chap to Bp of Nor from 65; Dean of Guildf from 68. *Deanery, Cathedral Close, Ridgemount, Guildford, GU2 5TL.* (Guildford 60328)

BRIDGE, Arthur Ernest. b 52. STh (Lambeth) 77. St Steph Ho Ox 73. **d** 79 **p** 80 Birm. C of St Sav Saltley 79-81. *Walsh Arms Hotel, Llanddewi, Powys.*

BRIDGE, Martin. b 45. Univ of Lon BA (Slav Stud) 66. Linacre Coll Ox BA 71. St Steph Ho Ox 69. **d** 72 **p** 73 Cant. C of St Pet-in-I of Thanet 72-77; Henderson 77-78; Team V of Mangere Dio Auckld from 78. *32 Church Road, Mangere Bridge, NZ.* (663 009)

BRIDGE, Stanley. b 16. Univ of Leeds BA 38. Coll of Resurr Mirfield 38. **d** 40 **p** 41 Derby. C of Brimington 40-43; H Trin Ilkeston 43-47; C-in-c of Hallam Fields Ilkeston 47-54; PC of Riddings 54-59; R of Tilbrook 59-74; Covington 59-74; Gt Catworth 68-74; P-in-c of Shingay Group Dio Ely from 74; RD of Shingay from 74. *Guilden Morden Vicarage, Royston, Herts, SG8 0JD.* (0763 852285)

BRIDGE, Walter George. b 10. Kelham Th Coll 26. **d** 33 **p** 34 Lon. C of St Pet Mile End Stepney 33-35; St Barn Heigham 35-44; V of Wighton 44-51; R of All SS King's Lynn Dio Nor from 51; RD of Walsingham 48-51. *33 Goodwin's Road, King's Lynn, Norf.* (King's Lynn 2738)

BRIDGE-COLLYNS, Douglas Herbert. b 26. Univ of Nottm BSc (Econ) 48, MPhil 71. St Steph Ho Ox 51. **d** 53 **p** 54 Leic. C of St Pet Leic 53-57; Chap Cyrene Miss Sch Westacre S Rhod 58-60; Hd Master 60-65; Asst Master Hucknall Ch Sch and C of St Pet Nottm 65-68; Lect and Warden Linden Lodge Bp Lonsdale Coll Derby 68-71; Sen Lect and Asst Dean of Studs from 71; Prin Lect from 72; L to Offic Dio Derby from 68; Perm to Offic Dio Southw from 76. *48 Russell Crescent, Wollaton, Nottingham.* (Nottm 282441)

BRIDGEN, John William. b 40. K Coll Cam 2nd cl Engl Trip pt i 61, BA (2nd cl Engl Trip pt ii) 62, MA 66. Ripon Hall Ox 66. **d** 70 **p** 72 Willesden for Lon. C of St Geo Headstone Harrow 70-71; St Mary Hanwell 71-75; Team V of Ch Ch Tolladine Worc 75-76; R of Barrow Dio St E from 76; V of St Mary Denham Dio St E from 76. *Barrow Rectory, Bury St Edmunds, Suff.* (Barrow 810279)

BRIDGER, Edward Basil. b 01. Keble Coll Ox BA 24, MA 35. Cudd Coll 24. **d** 25 **p** 26 Win. C of Lymington 25-36; V of Hooe 36-44; Northam w Westward Ho 44-62; RD of Hartland 59-62; V of Strete 62-68; V of Slapton 62-68; L to Offic Dio Ex from 68. *7 West View Close, Whimple, Exeter, Devon.*

BRIDGER, Francis William. b 51. Pemb Coll Ox BA 73, MA 78. Univ of Bris PhD 80. Trin Coll Bris Dipl Th 75. **d** 78 Bp Howell for Lon **p** 79 Lon. C of St Jude Mildmay Park Isl Dio Lon from 78. *71 Marquess Road, Canonbury, N1 2PT.* (01-226 5924)

BRIDGER, Gordon Frederick. b 32. Selw Coll Cam BA (2nd cl Th Trip pt ii) 53. Ridley Hall Cam 54. **d** 56 **p** 57 Lon. C of Islington 56-60; H Sepulchre Cam 60-62; V of St Mary Hammersmith Road Fulham 62-69; Chap St Thos Edin 69-75; R of Most H Trin Heigham Dio Nor from 76; RD of Norwich S from 79; Exam Chap to Bp of Nor from 81. *Holy Trinity Rectory, Essex Street, Norwich, NR2 2BL.* (Norwich 21120)

BRIDGER, John Richard. Clare Coll Cam 1st cl Mod Lang Trip pt i 41, BA (1st cl Th Trip pt i) 42. Ridley Hall Cam 43. **d** 44 **p** 45 Lon. C of St Paul Portman Square 44-46; Asst Master Marlborough Coll 46-58; Asst Chap 52-58; Warden Tyndale Ho Libr Cam 58-60; Asst Master Uppingham Sch 60-68; St Lawr Coll Ramsgate from 68. *St Lawrence College, Ramsgate, Kent.*

BRIDGER, Malcolm John. b 36. K Coll Lon and Warm AKC (2nd cl) 62. **d** 63 **p** 64 Sheff. C of St Cuthb Firvale Sheff 63-66; Wm Temple Woodhouse Pk 66-67; C-in-c of St Aid Conv Distr Lower Kersal, salford Man 67-72; V of St Aid Lower Kersal Salford 72-74; C of Ifield 75-78; Team V (in c of Gossops Green) Dio Chich from 78. *St Alban's Vicarage, Gossops Drive, Gossops Green, Crawley, W Sussex, RH11 8LD.*

BRIDGER, Nigel Egerton. RN Coll Dartmouth 40. Wells Th Coll 59. **d** 61 **p** 62 Ches. C of Neston 61-64; St Mary Port Eliz 64-67; Chap Miss to Seamen Port Eliz 64-67; C of St Sav E Lon 67-76; St Paul Aliwal N 76-81; St D Queenstn Dio Grahmstn from 81. *Box 119, Queenstown, CP, S Africa.*

BRIDGES, Dewi Morris. b 33. Late Scho of St D Coll Lamp BA (1st cl Hist) 54. Late Purvis Exhib and Pri of CCC Cam BA (2nd cl Th Trip pt ii) 56, MA 61. Westcott Ho Cam 57. **d** 57 **p** 58 Mon. C of Rhymney 57-60; Chepstow 60-63; V of St Jas Tredegar 63-65; Lect in Relig Educn Summerfield Coll Kidderminster and L to Offic Dio Worc 65-69; V of Kempsey 69-79; RD of Upton 74-78; Narberth from 80; R of Tenby w Gumfreston Dio St D from 79. *Rectory, Church Park, Tenby, Dyfed.* (Tenby 2068)

BRIDGES, Harold Eugene. b 21. **d** and **p** 75 Ott. C of St Steph Ott 75-76; St Geo City and Dio Ott from 76. *Box 509, Manotick, Ont, Canada.* (613-692 4844)

BRIDGES, Harry. b 05. Lon Coll of Div 27. **d** 31 **p** 32 Lon. C of St Paul Ball's Pond Canonbury 31-35; St Andr Gt Ilford 35-37; V of Mutford w Rushmere 37-44; St Paul, Sheerness 44-48; R of Gt w L Moulton and Aslacton 48-54; Wackton Magna w Wacton Parva 50-54; C-in-c of Scottow 54-56; V 56-62; R of Swanton Abbot w Skeyton 54-62; V of Kenninghall 62-71; C-in-c of Quidenham 65-67; R of Saxlingham-Nethergate 71-76. *1 Broadcote Close, High Green, Brooke, NR15 1HZ.*

BRIDGES, Ven Peter Sydney Godfrey. b 25. ARIBA 51. Linc Th Coll 56. **d** 58 **p** 59 St Alb. C of Hemel Hempstead 58-64; Research Fell Inst for Study of Worship and Relig Architecture Univ of Birm 64-67; Warden Angl Chap Univ of Birm 65-68; Perm to Offic Dio Birm 65-72; Archd of Southend 72-77; C-in-c of St John w St Mark Southend-on-Sea 72-74; Archd of Cov from 77; Can Th of Cov Cathl from 77. *Archdeacon's House, Baginton, Coventry, CV8 3AR.* (Coventry 302508)

BRIDGEWOOD, Bruce William. St Paul's Coll Grahmstn Dipl Th 67. **d** 67 **p** 68 Capetn. C of Plumstead 67-71; Namaqualand Dio Capetn from 71. *Box 12, O'Okiep, CP, S Africa.*

BRIDGLAND, Cyril John Edwin. b 21. Tyndale Hall Bris 42. **d** 45 **p** 46 Truro. C of Illogan 45-48; Em Ch Northwood 48-50; V of H Trin Cloudesley Square Islington 50-58; H Trin Redhill Dio S'wark from 58. *Holy Trinity Vicarage, Redhill, Surrey, RH1 2BX.* (Redhill 66604)

BRIDGMAN, Gerald Bernard. b 22. St Cath Coll Cam BA 50, MA 55. Wycl Hall Ox 50. **d** 51 **p** 52 Chich. C of Broadwater 51-54; St Aldate Ox 54-56; C-in-c of Southgate Conv Distr Crawley 56-59; V 59-67; Proc Conv Chich 64-67; V of H Trin Hull Dio York from 67; M Gen Syn York 75-80; Area Dean of Centr & N Hull from 81. *Holy Trinity Vicarage, Pearson Park, Hull, HU5 2TQ.* (Hull 42292)

BRIDGWATER, Edward Roden Gresham. b 1898. K Coll NS Bp Binney Pri 21, Crawford Mem Pri and BA 22, MA 23. Union Th Sem NY MDiv 28. **d** 24 **p** 25 Fred. Min of Wilmot w Wicklow 24-26; R of Grand Manan 26-28; in Amer Ch 28; R of Crapaud w Springfield PEI 28-38; C of St Andr Kingsbury 38-42; V of St Martin Kensal Rise 42-51; St Steph Hounslow 51-62; Chilworth 62-72; Perm to Offic Dio Llan from 76. *79 Minehead Avenue, Sully, S Glam.* (Sully 530569)

BRIDLE, Reginald. b 05. Univ of Lon BA 30, BD (2nd cl Hons) 50. Ripon Hall Ox 34. **d** 34 **p** 35 Bradf. C of St Steph Bowling Bradf 34-37; Ch Ch Hampstead 37-39; St Mary Finchley 39-41; V of Caddington 41-46; CF (EC) 43-48; C-in-c of U Clatford 49-54; Warden ICF Tr Coll Selly Oak Birm 54-55; Chap at Valparaiso Chile 55-66; V of St Chris Kaduna 67-69; Chap St Paul's Coll Zaria 69-71. *65 Barlows Lane, Andover, Hants, SP10 2HB.* (Andover 52666)

BRIDLE, Thomas Henry. Wycl Coll Tor. **d** 44 Tor **p** 47 Moos. I of Coboconk 44-47; Centr Patricia 47-55; R of Alliston 55-62; Distr Sec Canad Bible S Regina 62-70; on leave 70-73; R of Mulmur 73-78. *47 McDonald Street, Alliston, Ont., Canada.*

BRIENT, Canon Edward Ampah. St Aug Coll Kumasi. **d** 51 **p** 52 Accra. P Dio Accra; Hon Can of Accra from 73. *Box 157, Essikadu, Sekondi, Ghana.* (Sekondi 6428)

BRIENT, Thomas Ampah. Edin Th Coll 65. **d** 67 Accra. d Dio Accra. *Wiawso Anglican Training College, Sefwi-Wiawso, Ghana.* (Sefwi-Wiawso 34)

BRIERLEY, David James. b 53. Univ of Bris BA (Th) 75. Oak Hill Coll 75. **d** 77 Middleton for Man **p** 78 Man. C of St Mary Balderstone Rochdale 77-80; P-in-c of St Andr Eccles 80-81; Ecumen Officer Dio Man from 81; Team V of St Mary w St Andr Eccles Dio Man from 81. *St Andrew's Vicarage, Abbey Grove, Eccles, Manchester, M30 9QN.* (061-707 1742)

BRIERLEY, Eric. b 21. St Aid Coll 47. **d** 50 **p** 51 Man. C of St Paul Oldham 50-53; Stand 53-54; R of St Jas Moss Side 54-57; V of St Andr Ramsbottom 57-66; St Cath Horwich 66-74; Irlam 74-81; Farndon and Coddington Dio Ches from 81. *Farndon Vicarage, Chester.* (Farndon 270270)

BRIERLEY, John Michael. b 32. BD (Lon) 71. Lich Th Coll 57. **d** 60 **p** 61 Worc. C of Stourport 60-62; C-in-c of Dines Green Conv Distr 62-67; Eccles Distr 67-69; V of Dines Green 69-71; R of Eastham w Rochford 71-78; C-in-c of Knighton-on-Teme 76-78; R of Churchill-in-Halfshire w Blakedown 78-79; P-in-c of Reddal Hill Dio Worc 79-81; V from 81. *Cradley Vicarage, Colley Gate, Halesowen, W Midl, B63 2BU.* (Cradley Heath 69865)

BRIERLEY, William Peter. b 13. Univ of Dur BSc 38. Cranmer Hall Dur 65. **d** 66 **p** 67 Newc T. C of Haltwhistle 66-69; Otterburn (in c of Kirkwhelpington w Kirkheaton) 69-75; V of Greenhead 75-78. *8 Hadrian Crescent, Gilsland, Carlisle, Cumb, CA6 7BP.*

BRIERLY, Henry Barnard Lancelot. b 30. Or Coll Ox BA 55, MA 63. Clifton Th Coll 55. **d** 58 **p** 59 Derby. C of Normanton-by-Derby 58-61; St Helens (in c of St Mary) 61-63; V of Tebay 63-69; R of Ashwellthorpe w Wreningham 69-74; C-in-c of Fundenhall and of Tacolneston 70-74; Team R of Wreningham Dio Nor from 74; P-in-c of Hapton 79-81. *Wreningham Rectory, Norwich, NOR 90W.* (Fundenhall 237)

BRIERTY, Kenneth John. Ridley Coll Melb. **d** 60 **p** 61 Melb. C of Ch of Epiph Northcote 60-61; Blackburn 61-62; Melb Dioc Task Force 62-66; V of St Pet Fawkner 66-69; Eltham 69-72; C in Dept of Evang and Ex Dio Melb 72-78; I of Preston Dio Melb from 78. *105 Locksley Road, Ivanhoe, Vic, Australia 3079.* (03-497 2706)

BRIFFETT, Edward Alan. b 38. Huron Coll Ont. **d** 69 Huron for Moos. Hon C of St Geo Willowdale Tor 69-72; I of Prairie Cross 72-79; Last Mountain Dio Qu'App from 79. *Box 70, Nokomis, Sask, Canada.*

BRIGGS, Ven Archie. b 17. Univ of Dur BA 39, Dipl Th 40, MA 42. **d** 41 **p** 42 Wakef. C of Outwood 41-47; SPG Miss Dio N China 47-52; M Bush Bro of St Barn and Min of Mt Isa 53-58; Perm to Offic Dio Ely 58-59; SPG Miss Dio Borneo 59-60; Hon Can and Archd of Jess 63-68; Sabah 68-71; Archd (Emer) from 75; Dean and R of All SS Cathl Kota Kinabalu Sabah 70-74. *c/o Episcopal Church, 1-105-7 Hangchow South Road, Taipei, Taiwan.*

BRIGGS, Bernard William. b 06. OBE (Mil) 55. Univ of Lon BD 52. Tyndale Hall Bris 29. **d** 31 **p** 32 Lon. C of St Mark Vic Pk 31-34; Chap Miss to Seamen Yokohama 34-37; Chap RN 37-61; C-in-c of N Wraxall 61-64; R of Teffont-Ewyas w Teffont-Magna 64-70; V of Dinton 64-70; Perm to Offic Dio Sarum from 70. *16 Constable Way, Harnham, Salisbury, Wilts.*

BRIGGS, Derek. b 26. St Aid Coll 52. Dipl Th (Lon) 55. **d** 55 **p** 56 Wakef. C of Brownhill 55-57; St Jas Trowbridge 57-60; R of Levenshulme 60-67; V of Farsley Dio Bradf from 67. *9 St John's Avenue, Farsley, Pudsey, W Yorks, LS28 5DN.* (Pudsey 574009)

BRIGGS, Garry LeRoy. b 34. Univ of Utah PhD 69. Texas Chr Univ BD 64, MA 66. **d** 74 **p** 75 Edmon. C of All SS Cathl Edmon 74-75; Hon C of St D City and Dio Edmon from 75. *7903 Saskatchewan Drive, Edmonton, Alta., Canada.* (403-436 3913)

✠ **BRIGGS, Right Rev George Cardell.** CMG 80. SS Coll Cam BA 33, MA 37. Cudd Coll 33. **d** 34 **p** 35 Ches. C of St Alb Stockport 34-37; UMCA Miss Dio Masasi 37-40; Mikindani 40-43; Newala 43-62; Archd of Newala and Can of Masasi 55-64; R of St Alb Dar-S 64-68; Can of Zanz 64-65; Dar-S 65-69; Masasi 69-73; L to Offic Dio Dar-S 68-69; Warden St Cypr Coll Tunduru 69-73; Cons Ld Bp of Seychelles in St Jas Cathl Port Louis 25 March 73 by Bp of Maur, Abps of Capetn and Tanzania; Bps of Antan, Tam and Diego S; res 79; Asst Bp of Derby 79-80; C of Matlock w Tansley 79-80. *c/o Bishop's House, Phoenix, Mauritius.*

BRIGGS, Harry. b 03. Bp Wilson Th Coll IM 31. **d** 34 **p** 35 S & M. C of Kirk Andreas 34-38; All SS Little Horton 38-39; C-in-c of St Pet Toftshaw Conv Distr 39-43; V of Cross Roads w Lees 43-55; St Andr Huddersfield 55-61; Sharlston 61-68; L to Offic Dio Blackb from 68. *37 South Avenue, Morecambe, Lancs.* (Morecambe 5347)

BRIGGS, Harry Fitzherbert. b 02. Bps' Coll Cheshunt 54. **d** 55 **p** 56 Nor. C of Gt Yarmouth 55-57; V of Hemsby 57-72. *Primrose Cottage, Smallhythe, Tenterden, Kent.* (Tenterden 2477)

BRIGGS, Herbert. b 15. Linc Th Coll **d** 45 **p** 46 Grimsby for Linc. C of Burton-on-Stather w Flixborough 45-49; Skegness 49-52; V of Winthorpe 52-57; Billinghay w Walcot 57-68; R of Gt Ponton Dio Linc from 68; N and S Stoke w Easton Dio Linc from 68; P-in-c of L Ponton Dio Linc from 73; Skillington Dio Linc from 76. *Great Ponton Rectory, Grantham, Lincs.* (Great Ponton 251)

BRIGGS, John. b 39. Univ of Edin MA (2nd cl Hist) 61. Ridley Hall Cam 61. **d** 63 **p** 64 Newc T. C of Jesmond Newc T 63-66; Schs Sec for Script U 66-79; Asst Tutor St Jo Coll Dur 67-74; L to Offic Dio Dur 67-74; Dio Edin 74-79; V of Chadkirk (or Romiley) Dio Ches from 79. *St Chad's Vicarage, Chadkirk Road, Romiley, Chesh.* (061-430 4652)

BRIGGS, Canon John Arthur. b 12. St Jo Coll Dur BA 34, MA 38. Univ of Lon BD 43. Wycl Hall Ox 34. **d** 35 **p** 36 Liv. C of Em Fazakerley 35-37; Ch Ch Norris Green 37-42; V of Em Everton 42-45; H Trin Ulverston 45-48; St Paul Newbarns w Hawcoat Barrow-F 48-53; Ed *Carl Dioc Gazette* 51-53; V of St Mich Garston 53-60; Ed *Liv Dioc Leaflet* 56-60; Proc Conv Liv 59-60; V of Broughton-in-Furness w Woodland 60-62; H Trin Formby 62-78; Dioc Warden of Readers 65-74; Hon Can of Liv 69-78; Can (Emer) from 78. *26 Oakfield Drive, Formby, Liverpool, L37 1NR.* (Formby 77739)

BRIGGS, Michael Weston. b 40. Edin Th Coll 61. **d** 64 **p** 65 Southw. C of Sneinton 64-67; Beeston 67-70; C-in-c of Kirkby Woodhouse 70-74; V of Harworth w Bircotes 74-81; Harby w Thorney and N & S Clifton Dio Southw from 81. *Vicarage, Front Street, South Clifton, Newark, Notts, NG23 7AA.* (052-277258)

BRIGGS, Ralph Irvin. b 27. BD (Lon) 66. Westcott Ho Cam 66. **d** 68 Bradwell for Chelmsf **p** 69 Chelmsf. C of Chadwell Heath Chelmsf 68-73; Canning Town Dio Chelmsf 73-76; C-in-c from 76. *230B Grange Road, E13 0HG.* (01-476 9318)

BRIGGS, Canon Robin Campbell Rawdon. Univ of Capetn BA 60. St Paul's Coll Grahmstn LTh 63. **d** 63 **p** 64 Grahmstn. C of St Mich Miss Queenstn 63-67; St Matt Miss 67-68; Warden of St Matt Coll Dio Grahmstn 68-69; Vice-Prin St Bede's Coll Umtata Dio St John's 70-72; Prin 72-76; Can of St John's 73-76; Exam chap to Bp of Pret from 77; Sub-Dean of St Alb Cathl Pret 77-79; Can from 78; R of Waterkloof Dio Pret from 79. *573 Milner Street, Waterkloof, Pretoria, S Africa.*

BRIGGS, Roger Edward. ALCD 61. **d** 61 Bradf for Arctic **p** 61 Arctic. Miss Gt Whale River 61-67; Churchill 67-71; C of Ch Ch U Armley 71-72; Miss at Povungnituk 72-74; Yellowknife 75-78; Hon Can of St Jude's Cathl Frobisher Bay 75-78; Chap to Native People Dio Ott from 78. *390 First Avenue, Ottawa, Ont, Canada.* (613-235 5267)

BRIGGS, Canon Thomas Vickers. b 11. St Bonif Coll Warm 34. **d** 37 Wakef **p** 38 Pontefract for Wakef. C of Brownhill 37-40; Cumberworth (in c of Denby Dale) 40-48; CF (EC) 44-47; V of Staincross 48-53; Airedale 53-59; Harley Wood 59-68; V of Cornholme 59-68; Holmfirth w Thongsbridge 68-77; Hon Can of Wakef Cathl from 75; Hon Chap from 77. *4 South Parade, Wakefield, W Yorks, WF1 1LP.* (Wakefield 376835)

BRIGGS, Canon William Sorby. b 01. Univ of Sheff BSc (Hons in Chem) 24. Bp's Coll Cheshunt 24. **d** 26 **p** 27 Sheff. C of St Geo Sheff 26-33; V of Walkley 33-43; Asst RD of Sheff 41-42; RD of Hallam 42-43; Sec Sheff Dioc Bd of Finance 43-47; R of Wickersley 47-70; Hon Can of Sheff 50-70; Can (Emer) from 70; Chapter Clk Dio Sheff 52-65. *19 Avonhurst, Tiddington, Stratford-on-Avon, Warws, CV37 7AH.* (Stratford 66153)

BRIGHAM, John Keith. b 48. St Steph Ho Ox 71. **d** 74 **p** 75 Ches. C of H Trin Ches 74-77; Ch The Sav Ealing Dio Lon from 77. *Clergy House, The Grove, Ealing, W5 5DX.* (01-567 9299)

BRIGHT, George Frank. b 50. Peterho Cam BA 71, MA 75. Univ of Leeds Dipl Th 73. Coll of Resurr Mirfield 71. **d** 74 **p** 75 Kens for Lon. C of St Clem w St Mark Notting Hill 74-77; Child Care Officer Heath Pk Children's Home Hampstead 77-80; Perm to Offic Dio Lon from 80. *4 Parsifal Road, NW6.* (01-794 6564)

BRIGHT, Jonathan Irwin. b 52. Ridley Coll Melb BTh 79. **d** and **p** 80 Wang. C of Wang Dio Wang from 80. *7 The Close, Wangaratta, Victoria, Australia 3677.*

BRIGHT, Patrick Edmund. b 53. Univ of K Coll Halifax NS BA 77. Trin Coll Tor MDiv 80. **d** 80 NS. C of Sandy Cove Dio NS from 80. *Sandy Cove, NS, B0V 1E0, Canada.*

BRIGHT, Patrick John Michael. b 36. Keble Coll Ox BA 59, MA 64. Chich Th Coll 59. **d** 61 **p** 62 Ox. C of Bracknell 61-68; V of H Sav Hitchin 68-75; Royston Dio St Alb from 76. *31 Baldock Road, Royston, Herts.* (Royston 43145)

BRIGHT, Reginald. b 26. Tyndale Hall Bris 57. **d** 60 **p** 61 Liv. C of St Philemon w St Silas Toxt Pk 60-63; C-in-c of St Polycarp Everton 63-65; R of Gt Orton 65-72; V of Holme 72-79; Bromfield w Waverton 79-81; P-in-c of Westnewton 79-81; R of Bowness-on-Solway Dio Carl from 81. *Rectory, Bowness-on-Solway, Carlisle, Cumb, CA5 5AF.* (Kirkbride 328)

BRIGHT, Winston Spencer George. b 40. **d** 80 Port Eliz (APM). C of St Kath Uitenhage Dio Port Eliz from 80. *10 Phillpot Street, Uitenhage 6230, S Africa.*

BRIGHTLING, Canon Beverley George. Univ Coll Tor BA 51. Wycl Coll Tor LTh 52. **d** 53 Bp Coadj for Tor **p** 54 Tor. I of Cannington, Beaverton and Sunderland 53-55; Penetanguishene 55-59; R of Resurr Tor 59-70; Dioc Sec of Synod Tor 67-74; R of Ch of Ascen City and Dio Tor from 70; Can of Tor from 75. *33 Overland Drive, Box 25, Don Mills, Ont., Canada.* (416-444 8881)

BRIGHTMAN, Peter Arthur. b 30. ALCD 61 (LTh from 74). **d** 64 **p** 65 Cant. C of Westgate-on-Sea 64-67; Lydd 67-70; L Coates Dio Linc 70; Ch Ch, Heaton 71-72; V of St Simon and St Jude, Bolton-le-Moors 72-77; R of St Sav Bath Dio B

& W from 77. *Rectory, Claremont Road, Bath, Avon.* (Bath 311637)

BRIGHTON, Herbert Ernest. b 1896. Univ of Bris BA 22. St Aid Coll 23. **d** 24 **p** 25 Bris. C of St Aldhelm Bedminster 24-27; Ch Ch Mitcham 27-30; V of Baddesley Ensor 30-39; R of Barton Mills 39-47; Burnsall 47-57. *Lamorna, Grateley, Andover, Hants, SP11 8LG.*

BRIGHTON, Terry Alan. b 49. Univ of Lanc BA 71. Qu Coll Birm 71. **d** 74 **p** 75 Heref. C of St Martin Heref 74-77; St Jo Bapt Spalding 77-79; Team V of Grantham Dio Linc from 79. *Earlesfield Vicarage, Grantham, Lincs, NG31 7PU.* (Grantham 1869)

BRILLINGER, Paul Edward Frederick. Univ of Tor MEducn 75. **d** and **p** 60 Niag. C of Ancaster 60-63; Ch Ch Cathl Hamilton 63-65; R of Bronte 65-70; on leave 71-74; R of Organville 75-81; St Geo Niag Falls Dio Niag from 81. *3428 Portage Road North, Niagara Falls, Ont, Canada.* (416-354 1227)

BRINCKLOW, John Hugh. b 08. Clifton Th Coll 51. **d** 52 **p** 53 Chelmsf. C of St Jo Bapt Southend-on-Sea 52-55; V of Knypersley 55-60; St Chris Sneinton 60-68; St Jude Mapperley Nottm 68-75. *2 Coningsby Road, Woodthorpe, Nottingham.* (Nottingham 268480)

BRINDLE, John Harold. St Jo Coll Dur LTh 42, BA 43, MA 46. St Aid Coll 39. **d** 44 **p** 45 Blackb. C of St Mich AA Ashton-on-Ribble 44-47; St John Sandylands 47-51; V of Grimsargh Dio Blackb from 51. *Grimsargh Vicarage, Preston, Lancs.* (Longridge 3283)

BRINDLE, Peter John. b 47. MIStructE 72. NOC 78. **d** 81 Bradf. Hon C of Bingley Dio Bradf from 81. *24 Heaton Crescent, Eldwick, Bingley, W Yorks.*

BRINDLEY, Brian Dominick Frederick Titus. Late Scho of Ex Coll Ox BA 54, MA 59. **d** 62 **p** 63 Ox. C of Clewer 62-67; PC (V from 68) of H Trin Reading Dio Ox from 67; M Gen Syn from 75. *Presbytery, Baker Street, Reading, Berks.* (Reading 52650)

BRINDLEY, David Charles. b 53. AKC and BD 75, MTh 76, MPhil 81. St Aug Coll Cant 75. **d** 76 Chelmsf **p** 77 Barking for Chelmsf. C of Epping 76-79; Lect Coll of St Paul and St Mary Cheltm from 79; L to Offic Dio Glouc from 79. *1 Rosehill Gardens, New Barn Lane, Cheltenham, Glos.* (Cheltenham 39320)

BRINDLEY, Stuart Geoffrey Noel. b 30. St Jo Coll Dur BA (3rd cl German) 53, Dipl Th 55. **d** 55 **p** 56 Newc T. C of St Ann Newc T 55-58; St Paul Cullercoats 58-60; Killingworth (in c of St Paul Dudley) 60-63; V of St Bede Newsham Blyth 63-69; Chap Windsor Boys' Sch Hamm 69-76; Asst Master Wyvern Sch Weston-s-Mare 76-80; V of Stocksbridge Dio Sheff from 80. *Vicarage, Victoria Road, Stocksbridge, Sheffield, S30 5FX.* (Sheff 886964)

BRINGLOE, Canon Denis Noel Edward. b 06. St Aug Coll Cant 32. Univ of Dur LTh 34. Men in Disp 46. **d** 34 **p** 35 Sheff. C of Ecclesall Bierlow 34-37; C-in-c of St Cuthb Conv Distr Herringthorpe 37-39; CF (R of O) 39-61; R of Gaywood w Bawsey and Mintlyn 45-63; RD of Lynn 53-62; Hon Can of Nor from 60; R of Pakefield 63-81. *7 Bek Close, Eaton, Norwich, Norf, NR4 7NT.* (Norwich 504545)

BRINKMAN, Stanley Ernest. b 24. St Aug Coll Cant. **d** 60 Chelmsf **p** 61 Colchester for Chelmsf. C of Gt Clacton w L Holland 60-62; Chap RAF 62-78; R of Tankersley Dio Sheff from 78. *Tankersley Rectory, Hoyland Common, Barnsley, S Yorks, S74 0DT.* (Barnsley 743246)

BRINKWORTH, Christopher Michael Gibbs. b 41. Univ of Lanc BA (Relig Studs) 70. Kelham Th Coll 62. M SSM 67-70. **d** 67 **p** 68 Blackb. C of Lanc 67-70; Milton 70-74; V of Ault Hucknall Dio Derby from 74. *Ault Hucknall Vicarage, Glapwell Hill, Chesterfield, Derbys, S44 5LX.* (Chesterfield 850371)

BRINSMEAD, Keith. b 06. DSO 44. **d** and **p** 78 Sarum. Pastoral Care of Ebbesbourne Wake w Fifield Bavant and Alvediston Dio Sarum from 78. *Wheelwright Cottage, Flamstone Street, Bishopstone, Salisbury, Wilts SP5 4BZ.*

BRINSON, David Wayne Evans. b 32. St D Coll Lamp BA 53, LTh 55. **d** 55 **p** 56 Llan. C of Tylorstown 55-58; Skewen 58-63; C-in-c of St Jo Bapt Hafod Swansea Dio Swan B from 63. *St John's Vicarage, Bowen Street, Hafod, Swansea, SA1 2NA.* (Swansea 54040)

BRION, Martin Philip. b 33. Univ of Ex BA (Lon) (2nd cl Hist) 55. Ridley Hall Cam 57. **d** 59 **p** 60 Man. C of Balderstone 59-62; Morden 62-66; V of St Steph, Low Elswick Newc T 66-73; P-in-c of Giggleswick 73-77; V 77-80; W Seaton Dio Carl from 80. *Vicarage, Northside Road, Northside, Workington, Cumb CA14 1BD.* (Workington 2982)

BRISBANE, Lord Archbishop of, and Metropolitan of Province of Queensland. *See* Grindrod, Most Rev John Basil Rowland.

BRISBANE, Assistant Bishop of. *See* Wicks, Right Rev Edwin Ralph.

BRISBANE, Dean of. (Vacant)

BRISCOE, Gordon. b 24. Ely Th Coll 51. **d** 53 **p** 54 Lon. C of St Francis Isleworth 53-54; Ch the Sav Ealing 54-57; Chap Prince Rupert Sch Wilhelmshaven 57-62; Fortescue Ho Sch Twickenham 62-65; C of Twickenham 62-65; Perm to Offic Dio Lon 65-66 and from 67; Hon C of St Francis Isleworth 66-67; St Anne Brookfield 67-77; C of St Steph w St Luke Paddington 77-80; Ch of Annunc Bryanston Street St Marylebone Dio Lon from 81. *5 Croftdown, 25 Shepherds Hill, Highgate, N6 5QJ.* (01-348 4205)

BRISCOE, Henry Ellis. b 15. QUB BA 44. TCD MA 49. Div Test 46. **d** 46 **p** 47 Lon. C of St Mary Spring Grove 46-48; Gt Yarmouth (in c of St Luke) 48-52; R of St Bride Stretford Man 52-58; Perm to Offic Dio Birm 58-62; V of Sneyd 62-77; Llanyblodwell Dio Lich from 77. *Llanyblodwell Vicarage, Oswestry, Salop, SY10 8ND.* (Llansantffraid 448)

BRISON, William Stanly. b 29. Alfred Univ NY BSc 51. Berkeley Div Sch Conn MDiv 57, STM 71. **d** and **p** 57 W Mass. In Amer Ch 57-72; V of Ch Ch Davyhulme 72-81; R of Newton Heath Dio Man from 81; RD of N Man from 81. *Rectory, Culcheth Lane, Newton Heath, Manchester, M10 6LR.* (061-681 3102)

BRISTOL, Lord Bishop of. *See* Tinsley, Right Rev Ernest John.

BRISTOL, Archdeacon of. *See* Balmforth, Ven Anthony James.

BRISTOL, Dean of. *See* Dammers, Very Rev Alfred Hounsell.

BRISTOW, Arthur George Raymond. b 09. Lich Th Coll 32. **d** 35 **p** 36 Lich. C of St Mary and St Chad Longton 35-38; Perm to Offic Dio Roch 38; Perm to Offic at St Mich and AA Ox 38-39; at St Mary and St Chad Longton Dio Lich 39-40; Dio Ox 41; C of St Matt Sheffield 41-43; V of St Sav Saltley 43-52; R of St Jo Wednesbury 52-57; V of St Steph Willenhall 57-75; C of All SS Emscote Warwick Dio Cov from 75. *1 All Saints Road, Warwick, CV34 5NL.* (Warwick 41450)

BRISTOW, Kenneth Alfred. b 24. Univ of Lon BSc (Eng) 45. Ripon Hall Ox 55. **d** 57 **p** 58 S'wark. C of St Paul Herne Hill 57-60; Cheam 60-63; V of St Andr Wimbledon 63-65; Henderson Auckld 65-68; St Osw Coney Hill Glouc 68-71; C-in-c of Selsley 73-75; Asst Master Highwood Sch Nailsworth 72-81; Perm to Offic Dio Glouc 72-81; V of Kemble, Poole Keynes, Somerford Keynes and Sharncote Dio Glouc from 81. *Kemble Vicarage, Cirencester, Glos, GL7 6AD.* (Kemble 240)

BRISTOW, Philip Robert. b 45. Sir Geo Wms Univ Montr BComm 69. McGill Univ Tor BTh 71. Montr Dioc Th Coll 70. **d** and **p** 72 Montr. C of St Paul Lachine Montr 72; Ste Anne de Bellevue Montr 73-76; R of Lachute 76-79; St Mark, St Laurent Dio Montr from 79. *1650 Decelles Street, St Laurent, PQ, Canada.* (514-747 4566)

BRITISH COLUMBIA, Metropolitan of Province of. *See* Hambidge, Most Rev Douglas Walter.

BRITISH COLUMBIA, Lord Bishop of. *See* Jones, Right Rev Hywel James.

BRITISH COLUMBIA, Dean of. *See* Frame, Right Rev John Timothy.

BRITISH HONDURAS, Diocese of. *See* Belize.

BRITT, Eric Stanley. b 47. Univ of Nottm BTh 75. St Jo Coll Nottm LTh 74. **d** 74 **p** 75 St Alb. C of Chorleywood 74-77; Frimley 77-80; P-in-c of Alresford Dio Chelmsf from 80. *Alresford Rectory, Colchester, Essex.* (Wivenhoe 2088)

BRITTAIN, John. b 23. St Aug Coll Cant 59. **d** 60 **p** 61 Heref. C of St Martin Heref 60-62; V of Highley Dio Heref from 62. *Highley Vicarage, Bridgnorth, Salop.* (Highley 861612)

BRITTENDEN, Christopher Ronald Scott. b 44. St Jo Coll Auckld LTh 72. **d** 72 **p** 73 Auckld. C of St Aid Remuera 72-76; Whangarei 76-78; V of Tuakau Dio Auckld from 78. *1 St Johns Avenue, Tuakau, NZ.*

BRITTENDEN, Gerald James Scott. b 40. Ch Ch Coll 66. **d** 68 Bp Warren for Ch Ch **p** 69 Ch Ch. C of Fendalton 68-71; Bishopworth 72-73; Chap H Trin Algiers Dio Egypt from 74. *6 Avenue Souidani, Boudjemma, Algiers, Algeria.*

BRITTON, Basil. b 29. Univ of Bris BA 50. SOC 66-69. **d** 69 **p** 70 S'wark. C of Roehampton 69-73; L to Offic Dio Ox from 77. *5 Coach Ride, Marlow, Bucks.* (Marlow 4339)

BRITTON, Cyril Edward. Kelham Th Coll 26. **d** 31 **p** 32 Lon. C of St Simon Zelotes Bethnal Green 31-34; M of Bush Bros of St Barn N Queensld 34-39; C Stoke-on-Trent (in c of St Andr) 39-42; C-in-c of St Chad's Conv Distr Tunstall 42-47; C of Benoni 47-48; R of Brakpan 48-57; Yeoville Johann 57-71; Chap St Mary's Sch Johann 71-74. *4 Boundary Road, Silvamonte, Johannesburg, S Africa.* (011-45 6753)

BRITTON, John Anthony. b 39. Univ of Dur BA 60. Wycl Hall Ox 61. **d** 63 **p** 64 Sheff. C of St Swith Sheff 63-64; St Aid w St Luke Sheff 64-66; Doncaster 66-68; Grantham (in C of Epiph Earlesfield) 68-72; V of Surfleet 72-76; Bolsover Dio Derby from 76. *Bolsover Vicarage, Chesterfield, Derbys.* (Chesterfield 824888)

BRITTON, John Timothy Hugh. b 50. Univ of Dundee BSc 73. Trin Coll Bris 73. **d** 76 Lynn for Nor **p** 77 Nor. C of Cromer 76-79; P-in-c of Freethorpe w Wickhampton Dio Nor from 79; Halvergate w Tunstall Dio Nor from 79; Beighton w Moulton Dio Nor from 79. *Freethorpe Vicarage, Norwich, NR13 3AH.* (Gt Yarmouth 700322)

BRITTON, Neil Bryan. b 35. Em Coll Cam BA 59, MA 63. Clifton Th Coll 61. **d** 63 **p** 64 Chich. C of All SS Eastbourne 63-67; Ashtead 67-70; Chap Scargill Ho Skipton Yorks 70-74; Aiglon Coll and Villars Dio Lon (N and C Eur) from 74. *Aiglon College, 1885 Chesières-Villars, Switzerland.* (025-32727)

BRITTON, Canon Paul Anthony. b 29. SS Coll Cam 2nd cl Hist Trip pt i 51, BA (2nd cl Hist Trip pt ii) 52, MA 57. Linc Th Coll 52. **d** 54 Croydon for Cant **p** 55 Cant. C of St Jo Evang U Norwood 54-57; Wantage 57-61; PC of St Luke Stanmore Win 61-70; V of Bitterne Pk 70-80; Can Res of Win Cathl from 80. *11 The Close, Winchester, Hants, SO23 9LS.* (Win 68580)

BRITTON, Robert. b 40. Univ of Wales Dipl Th 64. St Mich Coll Llan 61. **d** 64 Bp T M Hughes for Llan **p** 65 Llan. C of Aberdare 64-67; Coity w Nolton 67-71; V of Abercynon 71-75; Tycoch Dio Swan B from 75. *26 Hendrefoilan Road, Tycoch, Swansea, W Glam.*

BRITTON, Robert. b 37. Oak Hill Coll 78. **d** 79 **p** 80 Liv. C of St Helens Dio Liv from 79. *136 Greenfield Road, Dentons Green, St Helens, Mer, WA10 6SH.*

BROACKES, Ronald Reginald. b 17. Wells Th Coll. **d** 72 **p** 73 B & W (NSM). C of St Steph Lansdown Bath 72-78; Min of Ch Ch Bath Dio B & W from 78. *5 Cambridge Place, Widcombe Hill, Bath, Avon, BA2 6AB.* (Bath 317713)

BROAD, Hugh Duncan. b 37. Lich Th Coll 64. **d** 67 **p** 68 Heref. C of H Trin Heref 67-72; Asst Master Bp's Sch Heref 72-73; C of Fareham 74-76; V of All SS (w St Barn from 81) City and Dio Heref from 76. *All Saints Vicarage, Southbank Road, Hereford.* (Hereford 272715)

BROAD, Hugh Robert. b 49. St Mich Coll Llan 71. **d** 72 **p** 73 St D. C of Tenby 72-75; Caerau w Ely 75-79; V of Llanharan w Peterston-super-Montem Dio Llan from 79. *Vicarage, Brynna Road, Llanharan, Pontyclun, Mid Glam.* (Llantrisant 226307)

BROAD, Paul Martin. b 56. St Jo Coll Dur BA 79. Coll of the Resurr Mirfield 79. **d** 81 Carl. C of St Pet Kells Whitehaven Dio Carl from 81. *65 Basket Road, Kells, Whitehaven, Cumbria, CA28 9AH.*

BROAD, William Ernest Lionel. b 40. Ridley Hall Cam 64. **d** 66 **p** 67 Sheff. C of Ecclesfield 66-69; Chap HM Pris Wormwood Scrubs 69; Albany IW 70-74; Remand Centre Risley 74-76; V of Ditton Dio Liv from 76. *Ditton Vicarage, Hough Green, Widnes, Chesh, WA8 8XR.* (051-424 2502)

BROADBENT, Edward Ronald. b 23. Univ of Man BSc 44. Westcott Ho Cam 53. **d** 55 **p** 56 Ches. C of St Mich AA Runcorn 55-59; St Pet and St Mich Ches 59-62; Dio Youth Chap Dio Ches 59-62; V of Bredbury 62; on Staff of SPCK from 63; P-in-c of S Newton Dio Sarum from 80. *2 Marlborough Road, Salisbury, Wilts, SP1 3TH.* (Salisbury 24038)

BROADBENT, Gerald. b 44. LRAM 64. Westcott Ho Cam 66. **d** 68 Bradwell for Chelmsf **p** 69 Chelmsf. C of Tilbury Dks 68-71; St Mary w St Phil & St Jas Woodford 71-74; Asst Master Ongar Comprehensive Sch from 74. *39 Carnarvon Road, South Woodford, E18.* (01-505 4265)

BROADBENT, Hugh Patrick Colin. b 53. Selw Coll Cam BA (Th) 75. Univ of Ox Dipl Th 78. Wycl Hall Ox 76. **d** 78 **p** 79 Roch. C of St Steph Chatham Dio Roch from 78. *59 Greenway, The Davies Estate, Chatham, Kent, ME5 9UX.*

BROADBENT, Kenneth Edward. Wollaston Th Coll Perth. **d** 61 **p** 62 Perth. C of Dalkeith 62; Scarborough 63-64; R of Nollamara 64-71; L to Offic Dio Perth 71-72; R of Kenwick-Thornlie 72-80; Mt Pleasant Dio Perth from 80. *53 St Michael's Terrace, Karrinyup, Pleasant, W Australia 6153.* (364 3037)

BROADBENT, Michael Tom. b 45. Down Coll Cam 2nd cl Law Trip pt i 65, BA (2nd cl Th Trip pt ia) 66, MA 70. Cudd Coll 67. **d** 68 Knaresborough for Ripon **p** 69 Ripon. C of St Aidan Leeds 68-71; St Cypr Kimberley 72-73; P-in-c of St Barn Kimberley 73-77; V of Luddenden 77-79; P-in-c of Luddendenfoot 77-79; Commiss Kimb K 77-79; R of Mazini Dio Swaz from 79. *Box 68, Mazini, Swaziland.*

BROADBENT, Neil Seton. b 53. Qu Coll Birm Dipl Th 80. **d** 81 Ripon. C of Knaresborough Dio Ripon from 81. *9 Castle Yard, Knaresborough, N Yorks, HG5 8AS.*

BROADBENT, Peter Alan. b 52. Jes Coll Cam BA 74, MA 78. St Jo Coll Nottm Dipl Th 75. **d** 77 **p** 78 Dur. C of St Nich Dur 77-80; Em w St Barn Holloway Dio Lon from 80. *Flat 2, St Luke's Vicarage, Penn Road, N7 9RE.* (01-607 6086)

BROADBENT, Peter George Clarke. Ridley Coll Melb ACT ThL 60. **d** 60 **p** 61 Melb. C of St Columb Hawthorn 60-62; Miss CMS (Austr) 62-63; Miss P at Sungai Patani Malaya 63-69; R of Woodlands w Wembley Downs 70-74; Surfers Paradise Dio Brisb from 74. *Rectory, Cambridge Road, Surfers Paradise, Queensland, Australia 4217.* (Gold Coast 31 5338)

BROADBENT, Ralph Andrew. b 55. AKC and BD 76. Chich Th Coll 77. **d** 78 **p** 79 Man. C of St Mary Prestwich Dio Man from 78. *25 Rectory Lane, Prestwich, Manchester, M25 5BP.* (061-773 8934)

BROADBENT, Thomas David Stuart. b 08. Univ of Lon BA 36. Wycl Hall Ox 41. **d** 42 Ripon for Col Bp **p** 43 Lagos. CMS Miss at Lokoja 42-44; Wusasa 44-48; Fagge Kano 49-52; Bida and Kaduna and Exam Chap to Bp of N Nig 52-55; V of Temple Grafton w Binton 55-70; C-in-c of Exhall w Wixford 55-59; R 59-70; V of Priors Hardwick w Priors Marston (w Wormleighton from 77) 70-78. *Redcote, Bussage, Stroud, Glos, GL6 8AT.* (Brimscombe 2414)

BROADBENT, Thomas William. b 45. Churchill Coll Cam BA 66, MA 70. PhD 70. Ridley Hall Cam 75. **d** 78 **p** 79 Cant. C of Allington Dio Cant from 78. *30 Poplar Grove, Maidstone, Kent, ME16 0AE.*

BROADBERRY, Richard St Lawrence. b 31. Trin Coll Dub BA (2nd cl Mod) 53, BD 59, MLitt 66. **d** 54 **p** 55 Dub. C of St Thos Dub 54-56; All SS Grangegorman 56-62; Min Can St Patr Cathl Dub 58-62; C of Clontarf 62-64; Hon Cler V of Ch Ch Cathl Dub 62-64; C of St Jude Thornton Heath 64-66; V of All SS w St Marg U Norwood 66-81; RD of Croydon N from 81. *217 Church Road, SE19 2QQ.* (01-653 2820)

BROADFOOT, James Robert. b 39. Wilfrid Laurier Univ Ont BA 75. Hur Coll Lon MDiv 78. **d** 78 **p** 79 Hur. C-in-c of Clinton and Seaforth Dio Hur from 78. *79 Rattenbury Street, Clinton, Ont, Canada, N0M 1L0.*

BROADHEAD, Malcolm Keith. b 33. Univ of Nottm BA (2nd cl Th) 63. Kelham Th Coll 54. M SSM 59. **d** 62 **p** 63 Southw. Chap and Tutor Kelham Th Coll from 63-70; SSM St Paul's Priory Quernmore Pk Lanc 70-73; C of St Jo Evang Huddersfield 73-75; P-in-c of St Pet March Dio Ely 75-76; R from 76; St Mary March Dio Ely from 78. *St Peter's Rectory, March, Cambs, PE15 9JR.* (March 2297)

BROADHURST, John Charles. b 42. K Coll Lon and Warm AKC 65. STh (Lambeth) 82. **d** 66 Lon **p** 67 Willesden for Lon. C of St Mich-at-Bowes Bowes Pk 66-70; Wembley Park Dio Lon 70-73; C-in-c 73-75; V from 75; M Gen Syn from 73. *St Augustine's Vicarage, Forty Avenue, Wembley Park, Middx.* (01-904 4089)

BROADHURST, John James. b 08. Univ of Birm BA 31. **d** 32 **p** 33 Wakef. C of Heckmondwike 32-37; V of Shelley 37-42; St Pet Newton-in-Makerfield 42-59; Chap Red Bank Approved Sch 43-59; R of Callington w S Hill 59-73. *123 Main Road, Bolton-le-Sands, Carnforth, Lancs.*

BROADHURST, Kenneth. b 33. Lon Coll of Div. **d** 59 **p** 60 Lich. C of Bucknall w Bagnall 59-63; R of Rodington 63-67; V of Longdon-on-Tern 63-67; R of St Jas Clitheroe 67-82; V of St Andr Leyland Dio Blackb from 82. *St Andrews Vicarage, Crocus Field, Leyland, Lancs, PR5 2DY.*

BROCK, Canon Daniel Victor Gordon. TD 56. Bps' Coll Cheshunt 54. **d** 56 **p** 57 Ex. C of St Mark Ford Devonport 56-59; V of Princetown w Postbridge and Huccaby 59-62; Chap Dartmoor Pris 59-62; P Dio Melan 62-68; Hon Can of All SS Cathl Honiara 67-70; Hd Master All H Sch Pawa Ugi 69-70; Archd of Outer Eastern Is 70-74; Hon Can of St Barn Cathl Honiara from 74. *Lueselaba, Santa Cruz, Solomon Islands.*

BROCK, Michael John. b 52. Univ of Birm BSc 74. Univ of Nottm BA (Th) 77. St Jo Coll Nottm 75. **d** 78 **p** 79 Southw. C of Stapleford Dio Southw from 78. *3 Ash Grove, Stapleford, Nottingham, NG9 7GL.*

BROCK, Preb Patrick Laurence. b 18. MBE 45. Trin Coll Ox BA 46, MA 48. Ripon Hall Ox 55. **d** 57 **p** 58 Worc. C of Gt Malvern 57-59; St Martin-in-the-Fields Lon 59-62; V of St Pet Belsize Pk Dio Lon 62-72; R of St Mary Finchley Dio Lon from 72; Preb of St Paul's Cathl Lon from 80; Area Dean of Centr Barnet from 80. *St Mary's Rectory, Rectory Close, Finchley, N3 1TS.* (01-346 4600)

BROCKBANK, Donald Philip. b 56. Univ of Wales (Bangor) BD 78. Sarum Wells Th Coll 79. **d** 81 Ches. C of Prenton Dio Ches from 81. *91 Woodchurch Lane, Prenton, Birkenhead, Merseyside, L42 9PL.*

BROCKBANK, John Keith. b 44. Univ of Dur BA 65. Wells Th Coll 66. **d** 68 **p** 69 Blackb. C of St Matt, Preston 68-71; Lancaster (in c of St George's Marsh) 71-73; V of Habergham Dio Blackb from 73; P-in-c of St Jo Bapt Gannow Dio Blackb from 81. *All Saints Vicarage, Habergham, Burnley, Lancs, BB12 6LH.* (Padiham 72413)

BROCKBANK, Leslie David. St Aid Coll 60. **d** 63 **p** 64 Pet. C of St Pet and St Andr Corby 63-66; Darley w S Darley 66-72; Chap Miss to Seamen Auckld 72-81; V of Paparoa Dio Auckld from 81. *Vicarage, Maungaturoto, Northland, NZ.*

BROCKHOFF, Desmoine Wayne. ACT ThL 50. **d** and **p** 51 Adel. C of Rose Park 51-53; Miss Chap Plympton 53-55; P-in-c 55-56; Miss Chap Pinnaroo 56-59; R of Angaston

59-67; Glandore Dio Adel from 67; Dioc Sec SPCK Dio Adel from 78. *9 Eurilpa Avenue, Everard Park, Adelaide, S Australia 5035.* (08-293 1371)

BROCKHOUSE, Grant Lindley. b 47. Univ of Adel BA 71. Univ of Ex MA 71. ACT ThL 72. St Barn Coll Adel 70. **d** 73 **p** 74 Adel. C of Edwardstown w Ascot Pk 73-74; Res Tutor St Barn Coll Belair 74-78; C of St Jas Ex 79-80; Asst Chap Univ of Ex from 80; Dep PV of Ex Cathl from 81. *Exeter Hall, Pennsylvania Road, Exeter, EX4 6DG.*

BROCKIE, William James Thomson. b 36. Pemb Coll Ox BA (3rd cl Phil Pol and Econ) 58, MA 62. Linc Th Coll. **d** 60 **p** 61 Linc. C of St Jo Bapt Conv Distr Ermine Estate Linc 60-63; V of Gt Staughton 63-68; Chap Gaynes Hall Borstal Inst 63-68; C of St Jo Evang Edin 68-76; Angl Chap to Studs in Edin 71-76; R of St Martin City and Dio Edin from 76; P-in-c of Wester Hailes & Baberton Dio Edin from 79. *28 Palmerston Place, Edinburgh, EH12 5AL.* (031-225 3766)

BROCKLEHURST, John Richard. b 51. Univ Coll Ox BA 72. Oak Hill Coll 78. **d** 81 Man. C of Harwood Dio Man from 81. *89 New Lane, Bolton, BL2 5BY.*

BRODIE, Hugh Malcolm. b 1899. Peterho Cam BA 27, MA 31. St Steph Ho Ox 27. **d** 28 **p** 29 Lon. C of St Mary Somers Town and Magd Coll (Ox) Missr 28-30; Chap and Asst Master Radley Coll Abingdon 30-40; L to Offic Dio Ox 31-40; Chap RNVR 40-45; HD Master Boys' Prep Sch and Perm to Offic Dio Dub 46-63; Dio Chich 61-63; v of Milland 63-72; Perm to Offic Dio Chich from 72. *Fern Hill, Hollist Lane, Midhurst, Sussex.* (Midhurst 2833)

BRODIE, James. Em Coll Sktn. **d** 31 **p** 32 Athab. C of Spirit River 31-32; I 32-35; R of St Pet St Kitts 35-38; St Geo Dominica 38-39; V of St Aug Barb 39-41; P-in-c of Louisburg 42-43; R of Weymouth 43-47; Aultsville 47-50; Campbell River 50-53; Salmon Arm 53-61. *2271, 152a Street, RR 2, White Rock, BC, Canada.*

BRODIE, Keith. Moore Th Coll Syd ACT ThL 30, Th Scho 45. **d** 29 **p** 30 Syd. C of St Mich Syd 29-31; St John Camden NSW 31-33; Chap of Asansol 33-39; R of Richmond Tas 39-43; Exam Chap to Bp of Gippsld 46-55; V of Delegate w Croajingolong 43-46; R of Bairnsdale 46-50; GBRE Tutor in NT and Greek 50-53; P-in-c of Weston 53-56; Distr of Beresfield 56-59; Brisbane Water Par Distr 59-64; Perm to Offic Dio Newc from 73. *16 Batley Street, Gosford, NSW, Australia 2250.*

BRODIE, Robert Gerald Alexander. b 49. Univ of Tor BA 71. Wycl Coll Tor LTh 75. **d** 75 Bp Read for Tor **p** 76 Tor. C of Ch of the Messiah Tor 75-77; I of Alliston Dio Tor from 77. *Box 429, Alliston, Ont, Canada.* (705-435 7220)

BROKENSHIRE, Ven John Joseph. St Jo Coll Auckld LTh 50. **d** 50 **p** 51 Auckld. C of All SS Ponsonby Auckld 50-53; P-in-c of Orewa 53-56; C of St Silas Pentonville 56-58; St Giles Reading 58-60; V of Mt Roskill 61-66; Kohimarama 66-80; P-in-c of Massey E Dio Auckld from 80; Archd of Waitemata from 80. *23 Moire Road, Massey, Auckland 5, NZ.*

BROMBY, Reginald George. b 18. Ex Coll Ox BA 42, MA 45. Coll of Resurr Mirfield 41. **d** 43 **p** 44 Win. C of St Lawr Alton 43-45; All SS Portsea 45-47; St Edm Sarum 47-50; V of St Mary Virg Newc T 50-57; Choppington 57-61; C of St Matt Over Seal 61-66; V of New Whittington 66-78; Team V of Southend-on-Sea 78-81; P-in-c of Goldhanger w L Totham Dio Chelmsf from 81. *Goldhanger Rectory, Maldon, Essex.* (Maldon 88235)

BROME, Henderson La Vere. Codr Coll Barb LTh 69. **d** 69 **p** 70 Barb. C of St Mich Cathl Barb 69-75. *c/o Panama, Bank Hall Road, St Michael, Barbados, W Indies.*

BROME, Rufus Theophilus. Stud Th (Lambeth) 62. Codr Coll Barb. **d** 61 Barb for Antig **p** 62 Antig. C of St Geo St Kitts 61-66; R of St Bart Antig 66-68; St Martin Antig 66-68; H Trin Barb 68-71; St Pet I & Dio Barb from 71. *St Peter's Rectory, Barbados, WI.*

BROMFIELD, Michael. b 32. Lich Th Coll 59. **d** 62 **p** 63 Lich. C of Sedgley 62-64; Tunstall 64-67; C-in-c of Grindon 67-70; R 70-80; C-in-c of Butterton 67-70; V 70-80; R of Hope Bowdler w Eaton-under-Heywood Dio Heref from 80; Rushbury Dio Heref from 80; V of Cardington Dio Heref from 80. *Rectory, Hope Bowdler, Church Stretton, Shropshire, SY6 7DD.* (Ch Stretton 722918)

BROMHAM, Arthur. b 01. Lon Coll of Div 27. **d** 30 **p** 31 Llan. C of St Donat Abercynon 30-32; H Trin w St Mark Nottm 32-35; V of St Ann Nottm 35-46; CF (EC) 40-45; Sen CF 45-46; Hon Sen CF from 46) V of All SS Leyton 46-53; R of Tunstall w Dunningworth 53-60; R of Iken 53-60; V of Wembury 60-67; Shalbourne w Bagshot Ham and Buttermere 67-70; Hon C of Burnham Dio B & W from 80. *19 St Paul's Road, Burnham-on-Sea, Somt.*

BROMHAM, Ivor John. b 18. Univ of Wales BA 40. Clifton Th Coll 40. **d** 42 **p** 43 Swan B. C of St Matt w Greenhill Swansea Dio Swan B 42-43; C-in-c 43-49; V from 49. *Vicarage, Sea View Terrace, Swansea, SA1 6FE, W Glam.* (Swansea 53409)

BROMHAM, William. b 09. Chich Th Coll 30. **d** 33 Bp de Salis for B & W **p** 34 B & W. C of Street 33-39; St Mary Virg Redcliffe (in c of St Mary Barnard's Place) 39-41; Burnham-on-Sea 41-57; V of Churchill w Langford 57-64; Chap of S of Sacred Cross Tymawr 64-70. *The Lodge, Tymawr Convent, Monmouth, Gwent.* (Trellech 860330)

BROMIDGE, Robert Harold. b 28. K Coll Lon and Warm BD and AKC (2nd cl) 52. **d** 53 **p** 54 Sheff. C of St Cuthb Firvale 53-56; Mexborough 56-59, V of Dalton 59-61; St Paul Arbourthorne Sheff 61-70; Sen Tutor Carter Lodge Sch Sheff from 71; L to Offic Dio Sheff from 71. *4 Barnfield Close, Sheffield 10.*

BROMILEY, Geoffrey William. Em Coll Cam 2nd cl Mod and Med Lang Trip pt i 34, Scho 35, BA (1st cl Mod and Med Lang Trip pt ii) 36, MA 40. Univ of Edin PhD 43, DLitt 48, Hon DD 61. Ridley Hall Cam 36. Tyndale Hall Bris 37. **d** 38 **p** 39 Carl. C of St Geo Millom 38-41; St Thos Edin 41-43; St Jo Evang Carl 43-44; V of Haile 44-46; Lect Tyndale Hall Bris 46-51; Vice-Prin 47-51; Chap of St Thos Edin 51-58; Prof of Ch Hist and Hist Th Fuller Th Sem Pasadena from 58. *135 North Oakland Avenue, Pasadena, Calif., USA.*

BROMILOW, John Joseph Maurice. St Barn Coll Adel ThL 41. **d** 41 **p** 42 Bunb. C of Cathl Ch Bunb 41-42; R of Donnybrook 42-47; Wagin 47-52; Manjimup 52-58; Can of Bunb 58-65; C of St Paul's Cathl Bunb 58-60; Archd of Bunb 60-64; R of Pinjarra 60-65; Bayswater 66-78; Perm to Offic Dio Perth from 79. *Unit 51, Moline House, Karrinyup, W Australia 6018.* (341 5235)

BROMLEY, Archdeacon of. *See* Francis, Ven Edward Reginald.

BROMLEY, Arthur Albert. Wycl Coll Tor Dipl Th 61, LTh 67. **d** 61 **p** 62 Tor. C of Ch of Messiah Tor 61-63; Asuncion Paraguay 63-64; R of Chapelton 64-67; C of Ch Ch St Anne Fred 67-69; R of Morant Bay Ja 69-74; Ch Ch St Steph Dio Fred from 74. *Christchurch Rectory, St Stephen, NB, Canada.*

BROMLEY, Ernest John. b 11. Univ of Man BA 33. **d** 40 **p** 41 York. C of N Ormesby 40-41; Perm to Offic as C-in-c of St Jas Scarborough 41-45; C of Newby 45-46; Thornaby-on-Tees 46-49; V of Kilburn Yorks 49-55; Healaugh w Wighill and Bilbrough 55-58; Cawood 58-72; R of Ryther 58-72; RD of Selby 58-64; R of Lockington w Lund 72-78. *40 East Witton, Leyburn, N Yorks, DL8 4SL.*

BROMLEY, James Edward. b 39. ACP 66. Univ of Newc BA, ThL 81. St Jo Coll Morpeth 77. **d** 80 Newc. C of Merewether 80-81; Hon C of Hamilton and Asst Chap Univ of Newc from 81. *10-18 Selwyn Street, Merewether, NSW, Australia 2291.*

BROMLEY, William James. b 44. Univ of Edin BD 74. Edin Th Coll 70. **d** 74 Argyll for Glas **p** 75 Glas. C of St Mary's Cathl Glas 74-77; in Ch of Bangladesh 77-80; R of H Cross Knightswood City and Dio Glas from 80. *64 Cowdenhill Road, Glasgow, G13 2HE.* (041-954 6078)

BROMWICH, Edmund Eustace. b 15. Univ of Bris BA 35. St Cath S Ox BA (3rd cl Th) 39, MA 43. Trin Coll Dub MA (*by incorp*) 50. Ripon Hall Ox 37. **d** 40 **p** 41 Roch. C of St Martin Barnehurst 40-41; Bexleyheath 41-43; LPr Dio Ox and Perm to Offic Dio Bris 43-45; Asst Chap St John's Pro-Cathl Buenos Aires 45-49; Res Chap Toc H Centre Buenos Aires 45-49; V of St Pet Flores 47-49; R of Wanstrow w Cloford 49-57; Asst Master Brighton Coll 57-61; L to Offic Dio Chich 57-61; Dio Ex 61-64; Chap and Asst Master Chilton Cantelo Ho 64-67; Asst Master St Hilary Sch Alderley 67-80; L to Offic Dio Ches from 67. *56 London Road, Alderley Edge, Chesh.*

BROMWICH, John. b 09. Late Scho of K Coll Lon Sen Wordsworth Pri 37, AKC 39. **d** 39 **p** 40 Bris. C of H Trin w St Pet and St Andr Clifton 39-43; CF (EC) 43-47; C of St Andr Chippenham 47-49; V of Banwell 49-76; Perm to Offic Dio B & W 76-81. *The Pound, Christon, Axbridge, Somt.*

BRONNERT, David Llewellyn Edward. b 36. Ch Coll Cam BA 57, MA and PhD 61. BD (Lon) 62. Tyndale Hall Bris 60. **d** 63 **p** 64 Ches. C of St Andr Cheadle Hulme 63-67; St Mary Islington 67-69; Chap N Lon Poly 69-75; V of St John Southall Dio Lon from 75. *St John's Vicarage, Church Avenue, Southall, Middx.* (01-574 2055)

BRONNERT, John. b 33. FCA 57. Dipl Th (Lon) 68. Tyndale Hall Bris 65. **d** 68 **p** 69 Ches. C of All SS, Hoole 68-71; C-in-c of Parr Dio Liv 71-73; Team V from 73. *75 Chain Lane, Blackbrook, St Helens, Mer, WA11 9QF.* (St Helens 35655)

BROOK, Clive Edward. St Mich Ho Crafers ACT ThL 64. **d** 64 **p** 65 Wang for Brisb. C of Gympie 65-67; Roma 67-69; V of Wondai 69-72; R of Noosa Dio Brisb from 72. *PO Box 28, Pomona, Queensland, Australia 4568.* (071-85 1218)

BROOK, James Albert Gregory. b 24. **d** 76 **p** 77 Dun. Hon

C of Ormaru Dio Dun from 76. *17 Wye Street, Oamaru, NZ.* (37-227)

BROOK, John Alexander. Moore Th Coll Syd 54. **d** 56 Geelong for Adel **p** 57 Adel. C of H Trin Adel 56-59; R of Rozelle 59-62; R of Balmain 59-62; C-in-c of Ultimo 59-62; R of St Bart Pyrmont Syd 59-62; L to Offic Dio Adel 62-64; Dio Syd 64-65; Perm to Offic Dio Adel 65-67; R of Normanhurst 67-70; All SS Djakarta 70-74; St Geo Hurstville 74-78; St Paul's Castle Hill Dio Syd from 78; Exam Chap to Abp of Syd from 77. *221 Old Northern Road, Castle Hill, NSW, Australia 2154.* (634-2412)

BROOK, John Llewellyn. b 11. St Aid Coll 47. **d** 49 **p** 50 Blackb. C of Skerton 49-52; St Paul Blackb and Sacr of Blackb Cathl 52-53; PC of Walton-le-Dale 53-63; V of Allonby w Westnewton 63-76. *Home Farm, West Newton, Carlisle, Cumb, CA5 3NX.* (0965-20885)

BROOK, Peter Watts Pitt. b 06. Em Coll Cam BA and Steele Stud 31, MA 36. Ridley Hall Cam 31. **d** 33 **p** 35 Sarum. Asst Chap Canford Sch 33-35; C of St Paul Fisherton Anger Sarum 35-36; Chap Clifton Coll Bris 36-72; CF (EC) 44-46; Perm to Offic Dio Bris from 72. *65 Clifton Park Road, Bristol, BS8 3HN.* (Bristol 39948)

BROOK, Stephen Edward. b 44. Univ of Wales (Abth) BSc 65. Wycl Hall Ox 71. **d** 74 **p** 75 York. C of H Trin Heworth York 74-77; St Barn Linthorpe 77-80; Team V of St Andr Deane Dio Man from 80. *St Andrew's Vicarage, Crescent Avenue, Over Hulton, Bolton, Gtr Man.*

BROOK, Timothy Cyril Pitt. b 06. St Cath Coll Cam 2nd cl Geog Trip 27, BA (3rd cl Hist Trip pt ii) 28, 3rd cl Th Trip pt i 29, MA 32. Ridley Hall Cam 28. **d** 31 **p** 32 Roch. C of Sevenoaks 31-33; Asst Master Stowe Sch and L to Offic Dio Ox 33-41; Hd Master R Merchant N Sch Wokingham 41-45; Asst Master Uppingham Sch 45-46; Asst Master Sherborne Sch 46-65; Ho Master 55-65; Chap 51-58 and 62-64; R of Over Compton w Nether Compton 65-73; C-in-c of Trent 65-66; R 66-73; RD of Sherborne 68-73. *3 Newland Garden, Sherborne, Dorset.* (Sherborne 3152)

BROOK, William Neville. b 31. SOC 66. **d** 69 Maidstone for Cant **p** 70 Cant. C of St Martin Maidstone 69-75; V of Hartlip w Stockbury 75-80; R of Willesborough w Hinxhill Dio Cant from 80. *Rectory, Church Road, Willesborough, Kent, TN24 0JG.* (Ashford 24064)

BROOKE, David Richard. ALCD 58. **d** 58 **p** 59 Lon. C of St Pet Islington 58-60; R of Reston 60-64; Souris 60-64; St Geo Bran 64-66; Killarney 66-69; Fort Simpson Dio Athab from 70. *St David's Mission, Fort Simpson, NWT, Canada.*

BROOKE, Peter Miles. Oak Hill Th Coll 61. **d** 64 **p** 65 Roch. C of St Jo Evang Penge 64-66; I of Belmont 66-68; Swan River Bran 68-71; C of Iver 71-72; V of Gt and L Badminton w Acton Turville 72-74. *Address temp unknown.*

BROOKE, Robert. b 44. Qu Coll Birm 70. **d** 73 Man **p** 74 Hulme for Man. C of The Resurr Man 73-76; Bournville 76-77; Chap Qu Eliz Coll Lon from 77; Team V desig of Bramley. *25a Campden Hill Square, w8 7JY.* (01-727 3804)

BROOKE, Ronald Percival Max. b 23. Wells Th Coll 61. **d** 62 **p** 63 B & W. C of Glastonbury 62-65; R of Longsight 65-67; Batcombe w Upton Noble 67-75; C-in-c of S w N Brewham 67-75; Team V of Basildon w Laindon (and Nevendon from 78) 76-79; P-in-c of Bowers Gifford w N Benfleet Dio Chelmsf from 79. *Bowers Gifford Rectory, Basildon, Essex.* (Basildon 552209)

BROOKE, Vernon. b 41. St Aid Coll 62. **d** 65 **p** 66 S'wark. C of Crofton Pk 65-68; Eccleshill 68-70; Chap Scunthorpe Industr Miss Dio Linc from 70; LPr Dio Linc from 70. *198 Frodingham Road, Scunthorpe, S Humb, DN15 7NN.*

BROOKE, Canon William Edward. b 13. Univ of Birm BA (2nd cl Engl) 34, MA 35. Westcott Ho Cam 35. **d** 37 **p** 38 Birm. C of Em Wylde Green 37-40; St Agatha Sparkbrook 40-44; C-in-c of St Jude Birm 44-50; V 50-60; R of Castle Bromwich 60-78; Hon Can of Birm from 61; Can (Emer) from 78. *Ivy Cottage, Tarrington, Herefs.* (Tarrington 357)

BROOKER, Burne Whittaker. St Barn Th Coll Adel 45. ACT ThL 47. **d** and **p** 48 Adel. C of Glenelg 48-50; Miss Chap at Kilburn w Prospect 51; L to Offic Dio Melb 51-52; P-in-c of Koolunga 52-56; Min of Warburton 56-60; I of St Pet and St Andr Braybrook 60-65; E Bentleigh 65-73; Moorabbin Dio Melb from 73. *4 Redholme Street, Moorabbin, Vic, Australia 3189.* (03-95 1037)

BROOKER, David George. b 34. Ely Th Coll 56. **d** 58 **p** 59 Lon. C of St Pet Ealing 58-60; St Alb Holborn 60-66; W Wycombe (in c of St Mary and St Geo) 67-68; C of Winchmore Hill 68; V of St Mary Virg, Somers Town St Pancras 68-79; St Mark Bush Hill Pk Dio Lon from 79. *St Mark's Vicarage, Bush Hill Park, Enfield, Middx, EN1 1BE.* (01-363 2780)

BROOKER, Stephen John. St Jo Coll Auckld NZ Bd of Th Stud LTh 65. **d** 65 Bp McKenzie for Wel **p** 66 Wel. C of Lower Hutt 65-69; V of St Matt Palmerston N 69-73; Porirua 73-76; Commiss Prov of Melan from 75; Perm to Offic Dios Auckld, Waik, Ch Ch and Dun from 76; Gen Sec NZ Bd of Miss from 76; Hon C of Wel S from 76. *Box 12-012 Wellington, NZ.* (735-172)

BROOKES, Albert. b 06. K Coll Lon and Warm 51. **d** 53 **p** 54 Ches. C of Davenham 53-55; V of Wharton 55-62; Chap Alb Infirm Winsford 59-62; R of Thornton-in-the-Moors 62-68; V of Ince 62-68; Barnton 68-76; Perm to Offic Dio Ches from 76. *The Gables, West Road, Bowdon, Altrincham, Chesh, WA14 2LD.* (061-928 1238)

BROOKES, Arthur George. b 21. AIB 52. Worc Ordin Coll 64. **d** 66 **p** 67 Worc. C of Stourport 66-67; Fladbury w Throckmorton, Wyre Piddle and Moor 67-70; Abberton w Bishampton 67-70; V 70-73; Cradley 73-78; P-in-c of Castle Morton (w Holly Bush and Birtsmorton from 79) 78-80; Holly Bush w Birtsmorton 78-79; Norton w Whittington 80-81; Team V of St Martin w St Pet, St Mark and Norton w Whittington City and Dio Worc from 81. *Vicarage, Walkers Lane, Whittington, Worcester, WR5 2RE.* (Worc 355989)

BROOKES, Charles Harry. Univ of Natal BA 49. **d** 68 Perth. L to Offic Dio Perth from 68. *11 High Street, South Perth, W Australia 6151.* (67 3829)

BROOKES, Derrick Meridyth. b 17. Trin Hall Cam BA 38, MA 42. Westcott Ho Cam 39. **d** 40 **p** 41 Ches. C of St Mich Macclesfield 40-44; Chap RAFVR 44-47; C of Wilmslow 47-49; V of Chipping Sodbury 49-53; Youth Chap Dio Glouc 51-53; Chap RAF 53-72; Asst Master Bris Cathl Sch 72-73; XIV Sch Bris 73-77. *Woodpeckers, Brent Knoll, Somerset.*

BROOKES, Jean. b 37. St Jo Coll Auckld LTh 69. **d** 69 **p** 77 Auckld. C of E Coast Bays 69-71; Glenfield 71-74; Shenley Green Birm 74-76; Howick Dio Auckld from 76; Exam Chap to Bp of Auckld from 78. *Flat 1, 47 Sale Street, Howick, Auckland, NZ.*

BROOKES, Robin Keenan. b 47. Trin Coll Bris 72. **d** 75 **p** 76 Blackb. C of St Andr Livesey 75-78; Burnley 78-80; P-in-c of Bawdeswell w Foxley Dio Nor from 80. *Rectory, Foxley, Dereham, Norf.* (Bawdeswell 397)

BROOKHOUSE, Leslie. b 28. Ridley Hall Cam 69. **d** 70 Hulme for York. C of St Jas Tong-cum-Breightmet 70-72; Ch Ch W Didsbury 72-74; V of Newall Green 74-80; High Crompton Dio Man from 80. *Vicarage, Rushcroft Road, High Crompton, Shaw, Lancs, OL2 7PP.* (Shaw 847455)

BROOKS, Canon Edward Arnold. Univ of Tor BA 30, MA 32. **d** 31 **p** 32 Niag. C of St Steph Tor 32; St Geo Guelph 32-34; St Jo Evang Hamilton 34-38; I of Acton w Rockwood 38-44; R of Grimsby 44-65; Jarvis 65-72; Exam Chap to Bp of Niag 50-56; Hon Can of Niag 54-72; Can (Emer) from 72. *121 St Joseph's Drive, Apt 201, Hamilton, Ont., Canada.*

BROOKS, Canon Edward Brewer. b 13. Keble Coll Ox BA 35, MA 40. Sarum Th Coll 35. **d** 37 **p** 38 Sarum. C of Southbroom 37-40; St John w St Mary Devizes 40-44; Kidderminster 44-45; St Mary Warwick 45-46; V of Rowde 46-56; Fordington St Geo 56-70; Ed *Sarum Gazette* 52-73; Can and Preb of Beaminster Secunda in Sarum Cathl from 61; V of St Thos Sarum 70-74; R of St Thos & St Edm Sarum 74-78. *3 Trinity Cottages, Grey School Passage, High West Street, Dorchester, Dorset.* (Dorchester 68275)

BROOKS, Edward Charles. b 18. Univ of Leeds BA (2nd cl Hist) 42, MA 57, PhD 71. Univ of Lon BD 50. Coll of Resurr Mirfield 42. **d** 44 **p** 45 St Alb. C of Bushey 44-46; St Barn Hove 46-48; St Barn Epsom 48-52; R of Elsing w Bylaugh 52-57; PC of St Cuthb Thetford 57-69; RD of Thetford 58-68; R of Somerleyton w Ashby Dio Nor from 69; C-in-c of Herringfleet Dio Nor from 69. *Somerleyton Rectory, Lowestoft, Suff, NR32 5PT.* (Lowestoft 730221)

BROOKS, Francis Leslie. b 35. Kelham Th Coll. **d** 59 **p** 60 Sheff. C of Woodlands 59-61; Industr Miss S Yorks Coalfields 61-66; V of Moor Ends 66-72; Chap HM Borstal Inst Hatfield 67-72; HM Pris Acklington 72-75; HM Borstal Wellingborough 75-79; HM Pris Wakefield from 79. *c/o HM Prison, Love Lane, Wakefield, Yorks.*

BROOKS, George Edward Thomas. St Aug Coll Cant. **d** 37 Chelmsf for Col Bp **p** 39 Barb. C of St Matthias w St Laur Barb 38-42; V of St Marg Barb 42-45; Actg C of St Mary Thatcham 45-47; Bakewell 47-49; R of Kirriemuir 50-55; Leven 55-69. *1 Juniper Close, Stuppington Lane, Canterbury, Kent, CT1 3LL.*

BROOKS, Henry Craven. b 12. Trin Coll Dub 62. **d** 64 **p** 65 Dub. C of St Michan w St Paul and St Mary Dub 64-67; I of Dunlavin w Hollywood U Dio Glendal from 67. *Rectory, Dunlavin, Co Wicklow, Irish Republic.* (Dunlavin 51218)

BROOKS, Ian George. b 47. Selw Coll Cam BA (2nd cl Th) 68, MA 72. Chich Th Coll 68. **d** 70 **p** 71 Stepney for Lon. C of St Mary Stoke Newington 70-74; H Trin w St Mary Hoxton (in c of St Anne) 74-75; St Anne w St Columba Hoxton 75-80; Min of St Paul's Conv Distr Croxteth, W Derby Dio Liv from 80. *St Paul's Vicarage, Delabole Road, Liverpool, L11 6LG.* (051-548 9009)

BROOKS, John Cowell. b 09. St Jo Coll Cam 2nd cl Cl Trip pt i 30, BA (2nd cl Engl Trip pt ii) 31, MA 35. Coll of

Resurr Mirfield 46. **d** 47 **p** 48 Lon. C of St Barn Conv Distr Northolt 47-54; Vice-Prin Cudd Coll 54-61; R of Ndola Dio N Rhod 61-64; Dio Zam 64-70; Dio Centr Zam 71; Exam Chap to Bp of Zam 67-70; Chap Dover Coll and L to Offic Dio Cant 71-74; R of Northbourne and Tilmanstone w Bettshanger and Ham Dio Cant from 74. *Northbourne Rectory, Deal, Kent.* (Deal 4967)

BROOKS, Joseph. b 27. Univ Coll Dur BA 53. St Aid Coll 52. **d** 54 **p** 55 Man. C of St Agnes Birch-in-Rusholme 54-57; Davyhulme 57-59; V of St Andr Oldham 59-65; St Francis Ipswich 65-75; R of Freston w Woolverstone 75-76; P-in-c of Holbrook 75-76; R of Holbrook w Freston and Woolverstone from 76. *Rectory, Fishpond Lane, Holbrook, Ipswich, IP9 2QZ.* (Holbrook 328900)

BROOKS, Leroy Errol. b 51. Univ of WI BA 75. Codr Coll Barb 72. **d** and **p** 75 Antig. C of St John's Cathl Antig 75-78; R of St Maarten Dio Antig from 78. *Clergy House, Carnation Road, Cul-de-Sac, St Maarten, Netherland Antilles.*

BROOKS, Leslie Frederick. b 08. Wells Th Coll 68. **d** 69 **p** 70 Pet. C of St Sepulchre w St Andr, Northn Pet 69-73; C of Desborough 73-77; Perm to Offic Dio Ches from 78. *93 Weston Grove, Upton-by-Chester.* (Chester 27691)

BROOKS, Neville Charles Wood. b 16. Bps' Coll Cheshunt 50. **d** 53 **p** 54 Dur. C of Whitburn 53-56; Min of Kimblesworth Eccles Distr 56-61; V of St John Rastrick 61-63; C of S Kirkby 63-66; R of Gilmorton w Peatling Parva Dio Leic from 66. *Gilmorton Rectory, Lutterworth, Leics, LE17 5LU.* (Lutterworth 2119)

BROOKS, Patrick John. b 27. Univ of Man BA 49. Oak Hill Coll 78. **d** 77 Buj **p** 79 Bp Mumford for Buj. Dioc Adv Dio Buj 77-80; Perm to Offic Dio Ex from 80. *Morsdon Cottage, Blundell's School, Tiverton, Devon, EX16 4DT.*

BROOKS, Peter Newman. b 31. Late Exhib of Trin Coll Cam BA 54, Lightfoot Scho 55, Crosse Stud 58, MA 58, PhD 60. Cudd Coll 67. **d** 67 Cant **p** 68 Dover for Cant. C of St Steph Hackington Cant 67-70; Lect in Div Univ of Cam from 70; Fell Down Coll Cam from 70; Prec from 78; Select Pr Univ of Cam 81. *Downing College, Cambridge.* (Cambridge 59491)

BROOKS, Raymond Charles. BD (Lon) 63. Ridley Coll Melb ACT ThL 54. **d** 55 **p** 56 Melb. C of Bentleigh 55-56; Ceduna 57-58; R of Menindee 59-62; C-in-c of Beverley Hills, St Luke Regent Pk Syd 62-64; I of Fairfields 64-70; Blackburn Dio Melb from 70. *St John's Vicarage, Queen Street, Blackburn, Vic, Australia 3130.* (03-878 8536)

BROOKS, Raymond Samuel. b 11. ARIBA 39. Clifton Th Coll 63. **d** 65 **p** 66 Chich. C of St Geo Worthing 65-69; P-in-c and Seq of Em and St Mary-in-the-Castle Hastings Dio Chich 69-71; V from 71. *Emmanuel Vicarage, Hastings.* (Hastings 421543)

BROOKS, Reginald George. d 63 Bp Snell for Tor **p** 64 Tor. C of St Geo Oshawa 63-70; on leave 70-73; I of St Edw and St Marg Tor 73-76; Kinmount City and Dio Tor from 76. *Box 44, Kinmount, Ont., Canada.* (705-488 2995)

BROOKS, Richard Sibbald. b 48. Selw Coll Cam 1st cl Th Trip pt i 68, 2nd cl Th Trip pt ii BA 70, MA 74. Trin Coll Bris 71. **d** 73 **p** 74 Worc. C of Old Hill 73-76; Fulwood (in c of St Luke Lodge Moor) City and Dio Sheff from 76. *18 Blackbrook Road, Sheffield, S10 4LP.*

BROOKS, Stephen. b 54. Univ of Wales BEducn 76. St Steph Ho Ox BA 78. **d** 79 **p** 80 Swan B. C of Oystermouth 79-81; Min Can of Brecon Cathl from 81. *The Deanery Flat, Cathedral Close, Brecon, Powys.*

BROOKSBANK, Alan Watson. b 43. St D Coll Lamp BA 64. Univ of Edin MEducn 76. Edin Th Coll 64. **d** 66 **p** 67 Carl. C of Cleator Moor 66-70; V of Dalston w Cumdivock 70-80; R of Greystoke, Matterdale and Mungrisdale Dio Carl from 80; R of Watermillock Dio Carl from 80. *Greystoke Rectory, Penrith, Cumb.* (Greystoke 293)

BROOKSTEIN, Royston. b 29. Qu Coll Birm 60. **d** 62 **p** 63 Birm. C of Rubery 62-66; V of The Cotteridge 66-75; St Pet Hall Green Dio Birm from 75. *St Peter's Vicarage, Paradise Lane, Hall Green, Birmingham, B28 0DY.* (021-777 1935)

BROOM, Bernard William. b 21. Roch Th Coll 64. **d** 66 **p** 67 Nor. C of Diss 66-67; Witton w Brundall and Bradeston 67-69; R of Swannington and of Alderford w Attlebridge 69-75; Chap Hellesdon Hosp 69-75; RD of Sparham 73-75; R of Drayton (w Felthorpe from 80) 75-81; P-in-c of Felthorpe 77-80. *c/o Drayton Rectory, Norwich, NR8 6EF.*

BROOM, Donald Rees. b 14. Late Scho of St D Coll Lamp BA (2nd cl Hist) 36, BD 45. St Cath S Ox BA (3rd cl Th) 38, MA 42. Wycl Hall Ox 36. **d** 38 **p** 39 York. C of Heworth and St Mary Castlegate w St Mich Spurrier Gate York 38-41; Perm to Offic as C of Whitby 41-42; Chap RAFVR 42-46; V of St Steph Hull 47-52; St Pet Hunslet Moor (w St Cuthb from 56) 52-62; Middleton Tyas w Barton 62-75; Barton and Manfield w Cleasby Dio Ripon from 75; Surr from 62. *Barton Vicarage, Richmond, N Yorks, DL10 6LD.* (Barton 274)

BROOMAN, David John. Wycl Coll Tor LTh 69. **d** 69 **p** 69 Qu'App. I of Wawota 68-70; on leave 70-74; and 79-80; L to Offic Dio Calg 74-79; Hon C of St Hilda Oakville 80-81. *14 Parkwood Road, Grimsby, Ont, Canada L3N 4K8.*

BROOME, David Curtis. b 36. Univ of Leeds BA (3rd cl Phil) 63. Coll of Resurr Mirfield. **d** 65 **p** 66 Derby. C of Winshill 65-69; St Marg Leigh 69-73; V of St Marg Leeds 74-81; Stoke H Cross w Dunstan Dio Nor from 81. *Church House, Mill Road, Stoke Holy Cross, Norwich.* (Framlingham Earl 2305)

BROOME, Francis Walter. Kelham Th Coll 32. **d** 36 **p** 37 Ox. C of Cowley St John 36-38; Summertown Ox 39; CF (EC) 39-45; R of Fifield w Idbury 45-51; V of Bracknell (w Chavey Down to 55) 51-66; C-in-c of Easthampstead 54-57; V of Watlington 66-80. *15 Walker Grove, Heysham, Morecambe, Lancs, LA3 2BX.*

BROOME, Gordon Alty. b 13. Ripon Hall Ox 65. **d** 65 **p** 66 Portsm. C of Portchester 65-72; R of Brighstone (w Brooke and Mottistone from 79) 72-80. *St Saviour's Vicarage, Shanklin, IW.* (Shanklin 2786)

BROOME, William Harold. b 09 Egerton Hall Man 32. **d** 34 **p** 35 Lich. C of Ch Ch Coseley 34-37; Ch Ch Tynemouth 38-41; V of St Hilda Jesmond Newc T 41-48; R of St Andr Fort William 48-50; V of Holy I 50-53; St Jude Hanley 53-55; R of St John Forres 55-61; V of Lode 61-64; R of Nairn 64-73; Selkirk 73-75; Can of St Andr Cathl Inverness 66-73; L to Offic Dio Newc T from 75; Hon C of St Mary Morpeth 77-80; Perm to Offic Dio St Andr from 80. *17 Priory Court, Pittenweem, Anstruther, Fife, KY10 2LJ.*

BROOMFIELD, David John. b 37. Univ of Reading BA 59. Oak Hill Th Coll 64. **d** 66 **p** 67 Derby. C of Ch Gresley w Linton 66-71; Rainham (in c of St John St Matt S Hornchurch) 71-77; R of High Ongar w Norton Mandeville Dio Chelmsf from 77. *High Ongar Rectory, Ongar, Essex.* (Ongar 362593)

BROOMFIELD, Canon Frederick Harry. b 08. Univ of Lon BA 29, BD 39. Sarum Th Coll 39. **d** 40 **p** 41 Win. C of St Jo Bapt Moordown 40-45; Christchurch w Mudeford (in c of St Geo) 45-51; V of St Chris Southbourne 51-75; M Gen Syn Win 70-75; Hon Can of Win Cathl 74-75; Can (Emer) from 75. *31 Cowper Road, Moordown, Bournemouth, Dorset.* (Bournemouth 521380)

BROSTER, Godfrey David. b 52. Ealing Tech Coll BA 75. Ripon Coll Cudd 78. **d** 81 Roch. C of Crayford Dio Roch from 81. *1 Kings Close, Crayford, Kent, DA1 4EU.* (Crayford 524790)

BROTHERTON, John Michael. b 35. St Jo Coll Cam BA 59, MA 63. Cudd Coll 59. **d** 61 **p** 62 Lon. C of Chiswick 61-65; Chap Trin Coll Port of Spain 65-69; R of Diego Martin Trinid 69-75; V of Cowley St John City Ox 76-81; Chap St Hilda's Coll Ox 76-81; RD of Cowley 78-81; V of Portsea Dio Portsm from 81. *St Mary's Vicarage, Fratton Road, Portsmouth, PO1 5PA.* (Portsm 822687)

BROTHERTON, Leslie Charles. b 22. St Steph Ho Ox 66. **d** 68 **p** 69 Ox. C of Fenny Stratford 68-71; Solihull 71-76; V of St Anne Moseley Dio Birm from 76. *St Anne's Vicarage, Moseley, Birmingham, B13 8DU.* (021-449 1071)

BROTHERTON, Michael. b 56. Univ of Wales (Abth) BD 80. Wycl Hall Ox 80. **d** 81 St D. C of Pembroke Dock Dio St D from 81. *Church House, Cross Park, Pennar, Pembroke Dock, SA72 65N.* (Pembroke Dock 683679)

BROTHWELL, Paul David. b 37. Lich Th Coll 62. **d** 65 **p** 66 Wakef. C of Honley w Brockholes 65-68; C and Sacr of Wakef Cathl 68-71; V of Whittington Dio Lich from 71; Chap HM Prison Swinfen Hall from 74; P-in-c of Weeford Dio Lich from 78. *Whittington Vicarage, Lichfield, Staffs, WS14 9LH.* (Whittington 432233)

BROUGH, Arthur. b 1896. St Aug Coll Cant Abp's Dipl Th 53. **d** 57 **p** 58 Cant. C of St Mildred Addiscombe 57-59; V of Woodnesborough 59-65; C-in-c of E Bilney w Beetley 66-68; Perm to Offic Dio Cant from 68. *Macknada, Canterbury Road, Lyminge, Folkestone, Kent.* (Lyminge 862683)

BROUGH, Gerald William. b 32. Trin Coll Cam 3rd cl Hist Trip 54, BA (3rd cl Th Trip pt ii) 55, MA 59. Ridley Hall Cam 55. **d** 57 **p** 58 Cant. C of St Jas Westgate 57-60; New Addington 60-62; V of Mancetter 62-73; P-in-c of Stretton-on-Dunsmore w Princethorpe 73-74; V 74-81; P-in-c of Bourton-on-Dunsmore w Frankton Dio Cov 73; R (w Stretton-on-Dunsmore w Princethorpe from 81) from 74. *Rectory, Frankton, Rugby, Warws, CV23 9PB.* (Marton 632805)

BROUGHALL, Canon John. b 25. Pemb Coll Cam BA 46, MA 50. Ely Th Coll 47. **d** 49 **p** 50 Ex. C of St Pet Plymouth 49-53; Missr at Pemb Coll Cam Miss Walworth 53-58; R of Scarborough Tobago 58-63; V of St Mary Welling 63-73; Sub-Dean of Woolwich 66-71; Dir Guildf Dioc Coun for Social Responsibility 73-80; L to Offic Dio Guildf from 73; Hon Can of Guildf from 78. *Diocesan House, Quarry Street, Guildford, Surrey.* (Guildf 71826)

BROUGHAM, Frank. b 17. **d** 67 **p** 68 Portsm. C of Paulsgrove 67-69; St Francis Ipswich 69-72; V of Wymering w Widley 72-79. *5 Knowsley Crescent, Cosham, Portsmouth, Hants.*

BROUGHTON, Alan Rangihuta Herewini. **d** 64 Bp McKenzie for Wel **p** 66 Wel. C of Feilding 64-66; Wairarapa Maori Past 66-67; Wainuiaru Maori Past 67-68; V of Ruapehu 69-73; P-in-c of Aotea-Kurahaupo Past 73-76. *Maxwell, Nukumaru, Waitotara, NZ.*

BROUGHTON, Canon Harry. b 09. Univ of Dur LTh 32. Lich Th Coll 29. **d** 32 **p** 33 York. C of Haxby w Wigginton 32-35; Helmsley 35-37; V of Bransdale w Farndale 37-43; Thirsk (w S Kilvington from 48) 43-56; RD of Thirsk 44-56; V of Coxwold (w Yearsley 56-60) 56-69; RD of Easingwold 62-69; Helmsley 74-75; Can and Preb of Weighton in York Minster from 66. *Charters Garth, Hutton le Hole, York, YO6 6UD.* (Lastingham 288)

BROUGHTON, Stuart Roger. b 36. Univ of Wales Dipl Th 65. St Mich Coll Llan 61. **d** 64 **p** 65 Roch. C of Ch Ch Bromley 64-67; SAMS Miss 67-79; V of Stoke-sub-Hamdon Dio B & W from 79. *Vicarage, Stoke-sub-Hamdon, Somt.* (Martock 2529)

BROUN, Claud Michael. b 30. BNC Ox BA (2nd cl Lit Hum) 55. Edin Th Coll 56. **d** 58 **p** 59 Edin. C of St Mary's Cathl Edin 58-62; C-in-c of Cambuslang w Newton 62-69; R 70-75, St Mary Virg Hamilton Dio Glas from 75. *13 Auchingramont Road, Hamilton, Lanarks, ML3 6JP.* (0698 423725)

BROW, Robert Charles Douglas. Trin Coll Cam BA 50. Univ of Lon BD 52. Tyndale Hall Bris 50. **d** and **p** 54 Luckn. C of St Pet Allahabad 54-71; R of Cavan 71-75; Manvers 74-75; C of Trin E Tor 76-78; R of St Jas Kingston Dio Ont from 78. *156 Barrie Street, Kingston, Ont, Canada.* (613-544 4755)

BROWN, Alan. Tyndale Hall Bris 59. **d** 63 **p** 64 Chelmsf. C of Braintree 63-66; Tooting 66-68; Chesham 68-70; V of Hornsey Rise 70-75; Ch Ch Sidcup Dio Roch from 75. *16 Christchurch Road, Sidcup, Kent.* (01-300 2442)

BROWN, Albert. b 25. Sarum Th Coll 49. **d** 50 **p** 51 Wakef. C of St Mich Wakef 50-53; Almondbury 53-56; V of St John Rastrick 56-60; C of Sowerby Bridge 60-63; V of Walsden 63-72; R of Averham w Kelham 72-79; C-in-c of Rolleston w Fiskerton 76-80; Upton 76-80. *Address temp unknown.*

BROWN, Alec Charles. K Coll Lon and Warm AKC 58. **d** 59 **p** 60 Lon. C of Potters Bar 59-63; Ch Ch Ashford Kent 63-66; P-in-c of Harbour I 66-70; C of Ch Ch Cathl Nass 70-71; V of Richmond 71-76; L to Offic Dio Nel from 76. *24 Examiner Street, Nelson, NZ.* (83-644)

BROWN, Alexander Thomas. b 21. **d** 79 **p** 80 Glas. Hon C of Irvine New Town Dio Glas from 79. *44 Ravenscroft, Irvine, Ayr, KA12 9DE.*

BROWN, Alfred. **d** and **p** 47 Connor. C of St Steph Belf 47-48; St Thos Belf 48-51; DUM to Chota N 51-59; Hd of Miss 55-59; C of St Luke w St Sav and St Matthias Belf 59-60; I 60-67; Rathgraffe 67-76; Delvin 67-76. *113 Bay Road, Carnlough, Ballymena, Co Antrim, N Ireland.*

BROWN, Allan James. b 47. AKC and BD 69, MTh 70. St Aug Coll Cant 69. **d** 73 **p** 74 Jer. Chap St Geo Sch Jer 73-75; C of Clifton 75-77; CF from 77. *c/o Ministry of Defence, Bagshot Park, Bagshot, Surrey.*

BROWN, Andrew. b 55. Univ of Ox BA (Th) 79. Ridley Hall Cam 79. **d** 80 Burnley for Blackb **p** 81 Blackb. C of St Pet Burnley Dio Blackb from 80. *27 Aylesbury Walk, Kibble Bank, Burnley, Lancs.*

BROWN, Anthony Frank Palmer. b 31. Fitzw Ho Cam 3rd cl Th Trip pt i 54, BA 56. Cudd Coll 56. **d** 58 Kingston T for Guildf **p** 59 Guildf. C of St Mich Aldershot 58-61; Chiswick 61-66; Asst Chap Univ of Lon 65-70; L to Offic Dio Lon 68-72; C-in-c of St Mich and St Geo Conv Distr White City Hammersmith 72-74; St Sav U Sunbury Dio Lon 74-80; V from 80. *205 Vicarage Road, Sunbury-on-Thames, Surrey, TW16 7TP.* (Sunbury-on-Thames 82800)

BROWN, Anthony Garnet. b 25. SOC 68. **d** 71 **p** 72 S'wark. C of St Helier, Morden Dio S'wark from 71. *197 Bishopsford Road, Morden, Surrey.* (01-648 2704)

BROWN, Anthony Paul. b 55. Univ of Reading BSc 75. Qu Coll Birm 77. **d** 80 **p** 81 Lich. C of Pelsall Dio Lich from 80. *21 Dovedale Avenue, Walsall, W Midl.*

BROWN, Anthony Storey. b 34. Open Univ BA 73. N-W Ordin Course 75. **d** 78 **p** 79 Ripon (APM). C of Leyburn w Bellerby Dio Ripon from 78; Asst Master Risedale Sch Hipswell from 78. *2 St Matthew's Terrace, Leyburn, N Yorks, DL8 5EL.*

BROWN, Arthur Basil Etheredge. b 17. Univ of Reading BA (Hons French) 39. Wycl Hall Ox 46. **d** 47 Chich for Truro **p** 48 Truro. C of Camborne 47-50; Org Sec for Midl Distr CPAS 50-53; PC of H Trin Scarborough 53-58; V of H Trin Heworth York 58-66; C-in-c of St Cuthb w All SS Peasholm and St Helen on the Walls York 64-66; R of Camborne Dio Truro from 66. *Rectory, Camborne, Cornw.* (Camborne 713340)

✠ **BROWN, Right Rev Arthur Durrant.** Univ of W Ont BA and LTh 49. Hur Coll Hon DD 79. Wycl Coll Hon DD 81. **d** 49 **p** 50 Hur. C of Paisley w Cargill and Pinkerton 49-51; I of St Steph Lon (w Glanworth to 53) 51-55; R of St John, Sandwich, Windsor 55-64; St Mich AA, Tor 64-81; Can of Tor 72-74; Archd of York 74-81; Commiss Bel from 77; Cons Ld Bp Suffr of Tor in St Paul's Ch Bloor Street E, Tor By Abp of Tor; Bps of Alg, Carib, Hur, Moos, Ott and W New York (USA); Bps Suffr of Tor, Niag, Hur and The Arctic; and others. *135 Adelade Street East, Toronto, Ont, M5C 1L8, Canada.* (416-363 6021)

BROWN, Canon Arthur Henry. b 18. St Pet Hall Ox BA (2nd cl Mod Lang) 39, 2nd cl Th 41, MA 43. Wycl Hall Ox 39. **d** 41 **p** 42 Ripon. C of Farnley 41-46; CF 46-50; Hon CF 49; V of Em Nottm 50-56; St Anne Worksop Dio Southw from 56; P-in-c of Scofton w Osberton Dio Southw from 66; RD of Worksop from 72; Hon Can of Southw from 77. *St Anne's Vicarage, Worksop, Notts.* (Worksop 2069)

BROWN, Arthur William Neville. b 08. Kelham Th Coll 30. **d** 36 Bloemf **p** 38 Lich. Asst Chap Modderpoort Schs 36-37; C of Cathl Ch Bloemf 37-38; St Luke Hanley 38; Stoke-on-Trent 38-40; CF (EC) 40-44; V of Pelsall 44-50; R of Moreton-Saye 50-54; C-in-c of Conv Distr of Rickerscote Stafford 54-57; R of Abbots Ripton w L Stukeley 57-66; C-in-c of Wood Alton 62-66; V of Ellington 66-74; R of Grafham 66-74. *Treig, Kendoon, Dalry, Castle Douglas, Kirkcudbright, DG7 3UB.*

BROWN, Arthur William Stawell. b 26. St Jo Coll Ox BA (3rd cl Th) 50, MA 51. Cudd Coll 63. **d** 65 **p** 66 Edin. C of St Jo Evang Edin 65-67; Petersfield w Sheet 67-75; V of St Alb Copnor, Portsea 75-79; R of St Bart Gt City and Dio Lon from 79; St Sepulchre without Newgate City and Dio Lon from 81. *The Watch House, Giltspur Street, EC1A 9DE.* (01-606 5171)

BROWN, Barry Ronald. Ridley Coll Melb ACT ThL 72. **d** 73 **p** 74 Melb. C of Frankston 73-74; H Trin Cathl Wang 74-77; St Jo Div Richmond 77-79; Old St Paul Edin 79-81; Chap at Belgrade Dio Gibr in Eur from 81. *British Embassy, Hadzi Melentijeva, MP 1000, Belgrade, Yugoslavia.* (640 186)

BROWN, Bernard Edwin. b 27. Univ of Bris BA 54. Univ of Ex MA 73. Qu Coll Birm 54. **d** 56 **p** 57 Ex. C of Sutton-on-Plym 56-58; Littleham w Exmouth 58-64; R of Whitestone 64-70; PC of Oldridge 64-70; V of Beckwithshaw 70-79; P-in-c of Stainburn w N Rigton 75-79; Dir of Educn Dio Ripon 70-79; Sec Ox Dioc Pastoral C'tte from 79. *Diocesan Church House, North Hinksey, Oxford, OX2 0NB.* (Ox 44566)

BROWN, Bernard Herbert Vincent. b 26 Mert Coll Ox BA 50, MA 52. Westcott Ho Cam 50. **d** 52 **p** 53 Cov. C of Rugby 52-56; Stoke Bishop 56-59; Dioc Youth Chap Dio Bris 56-62; LPr Dio Bris 59-62; Industr Chap Dio Roch 62-73; Chap to Bp of Roch 66-73; R of Crawley Dio Chich 73-79; Team R from 79. *Rectory, High Street, Crawley, Sussex, RH10 1BQ.* (Crawley 22692)

BROWN, Bernard Maurice Newall. b 26. Oak Hill Th Coll 47. **d** 51 **p** 52 Lich. C of Penn Fields 51-53; BCMS Sec S Area 53-55; BCMS Miss at Marsabit 55-62; R of Hartshorne 62-68; V of Stapenhill w Caldwell 68-72; C of Ch Ch Weston-s-Mare 72-74; R of Spaxton w Charlynch 74-80. *12 Ewart Road, Weston-s-Mare, Somt.* (W-s-M 412170)

BROWN, Canon Brian Llewellyn. Trin Coll Tor STh 56. **d** 55 **p** 56 Edmon. V of Clandonald 55-57; Tofield 57-59; R of Wainwright 59-64; St Mary Edmon 64-73; Can of Edmon from 72; Chap Edmon Univ Hosp from 73. *5648-148th Street, Edmonton, Alta., Canada.* (403-434 7931)

BROWN, Campbell William. St Jo Coll Morpeth 56. ACT ThL 59. **d** 59 **p** 61 Graft. C of Ch Ch Cathl Graft 59-61; Lismore 61-62; Kempsey 62-63; V of Wyan w Rappville 63-64; P-in-c of Nambucca Heads 64-66; C of Waratah 66; Cardiff 66-69; R of Aberdeen 69-73; Hon C of Merewether 73-74; R of Kincumber Dio Newc from 75. *Rectory, Avoca Drive, Kincumber, NSW, Australia 2251.* (043-69 1204)

BROWN, Charles Keith. **d** 64 **p** 65 Fred. C of Petersville w Greenwich 64-65; Grand Manan 65; I of Cambridge w Waterborough 65-72; Coverdale w Hillsborough Dio Fred from 72. *409 Cleveland Avenue, Riverview Heights, NB, Canada.*

BROWN, Charles Rippin. MM 18. Mert Coll Ox BA 21, MA 26. Bps' Coll Cheshunt 21. **d** 23 **p** 24 S'wark. C of St Andr Stockwell 23-27; Chap S Afr Ch Rly Miss Dio Bloemf 27-30; C of St Jo Evang E Dulwich 30-31; Feltham 31-34; V of St Barn Shacklewell 34-36; Cranbourne 36-45; Whalley 45-51; Leafield w Wychwood 51-55; V of Ramsden 53-55; C-in-c of Wilcote 53-55; V of Warfield Berks 55-59; Bardon Brisb 59-61; R of Drayton 61-64; C of Ch Ch Berwick 64-65; R of Laidley 65-68; Perm to Offic Dio Brisb 68-72; Dio Melb from

72. *34 Westerfield Drive, Clayton North, Vic, Australia 3168.*

BROWN, Christopher. b 43. Linc Th Coll 79. **d** 81 Lich. C of St Jo Bapt Stafford Dio Lich from 81. *42 Longhurst Drive, Stafford, ST16 3RG.*

BROWN, Christopher. b 38. K Coll Lon and Warm AKC (2nd cl) 62. **d** 63 **p** 64 S'wark. C of Crofton Pk 63-64; St Mich AA S Beddington 64-67; Hon C of Herne Hill 67-68; L to Offic Dio Southw 68-72; Dio Lich from 72. *58 Mount Road, Penn, Wolverhampton.*

BROWN, Christopher Francis. b 44. Sarum Th Coll 68. **d** 71 Buckingham for Ox **p** 72 Reading for Ox. C of All SS High Wycombe 71-74; Sherborne 74-76; R of Wylye w Fisherton Delamere and The Langfords 79-81; R of Yarnbury 79-81; Portland w Southw Dio Sarum from 82. *Portland Rectory Easton, Portland, Dorset, DT5 1HG.* (Portland 820177)

BROWN, Clifford John. St Francis Th Coll Brisb ACT ThL 55. **d** and **p** 54 Rockptn. C of Rockptn Cathl 54-58; Perm to Offic Dio Rockptn 58-61; V of Miriam Vale 61-62; Keppel 62-65; R of Clermont 65-67; Murchison w Rushworth 67-69; C of St Barn Ithaca 69-70; V of St Mark The Gap Brisb 70-72; R 72-74; Perm to Offic Dio Melb 74-76; P-in-c of Miss Distr Pine Rivers S Brisb 76-78; R of Zillmere Dio Brisb from 78. *Rectory, Bulwer Street, Geebung, Queensland, Australia 4034.* (263 1602)

BROWN, Clive Lindsey. Univ of Southn BA 55. Oak Hill Th Coll 57. **d** 59 **p** 60 Chelmsf. C of St Mary Becontree 59-62; C-in-c of Balgowlah w Manly Vale 62-69; R 69-72; Roseville E Dio Syd from 72. *30 William Street, Roseville, NSW, Australia 2069.* (407-2377)

BROWN, Colin. b 32. Univ of Liv BA (2nd cl German) 53, BD (2nd cl) Lon 58. Univ of Nottm MA 61. Univ of Bris PhD 70. Tyndale Hall Bris 55. **d** 58 **p** 59 Southw. C of Chilwell 58-61; Lect Tyndale Hall (part of Trin Coll from 72) Bris from 61; Vice-Prin 67-70; Dean of Studies 70-71; L to Offic Dio Bris from 61. *Flat 9, Bartlett Court, Clifton Down, Bristol, BS8 3ET.*

BROWN, Colin Greville. Univ of NZ BA 50. St Jo Coll Auckld LTh (1st cl) 53. Gen Th Sem NY STB 63. Union Th Sem NY STM 64. **d** 54 **p** 55 Auckld. C of St Mark Remuera 54-56; LPr Dio Auckld 56-64; Tutor St Jo Coll Auckld 56-64; Lect 64-66; Vice-Prin of Ch Ch Coll Ch Ch 66-67; Lect Univ of Cant and Perm to Offic Dio Ch Ch from 67. *3 Kingsgate Place, Christchurch 5, NZ.* (583-329)

BROWN, Creighton Roy. K Coll NS BA 63, LTh 65. **d** 64 **p** 65 NS. C of St Paul Halifax 64-68; R of Lakeside w Timberlea 68-70; on leave. *22 Westwood Drive, Truro, NS, Canada.* (893-2538)

BROWN, Ven Cyril Graham. Univ of Leeds BA 13. Coll of Resurr Mirfield 09. **d** 15 **p** 16 Man. C of St Jo Bapt Hulme 15-17; TCF 17-19; C of Mirfield 17-19; CF 19; P-in-c of Conv Distr of St Jo Evang Leigh Lancs 20-24; M of Bro of St Barn Dio N Queensld 24-49; Warden 28-41; Archd of N Queensld 29-39; Chap of Yarrabah Miss 39-49; Edward River Miss 49-53; Sub-Dean of All SS Cathl Thursday I 53; Prin of St Paul's Th Coll 53-59; Archd of Carp 53-61; Archd (Emer) from 61; Supt of St Paul's Miss Moa I 54-61; Exam Chap to Bp of Carp 59-69; Chap Edward River Miss 61-66; C of St Jas Cathl Townsville 66-68; Chap Yarrabah Settlement Dio N Queensld from 68. *Yarrabah Settlement, Cairns, Queensland, Australia.*

BROWN, Cyril James. b 04. Keble Coll Ox BA (3rd cl Hist) 26, MA 39. OBE 56. St Steph Ho Ox 26. **d** 27 **p** 28 Lon. C of St Gabr Pimlico 27-31; Chap (Miss to Seamen) Sing 31-34; Hong Kong 34-41; Chap RNVR 41-46; Youth Sec Miss to Seamen 46-47; Supt 47-51; Gen Supt 51-58; Gen Sec 58-69; Chap to HM the Queen 56-74; Preb of Portpool in St Paul's Cathl 58-69; R of Warbleton 70-77. *16 Merlynn, Devonshire Place, Eastbourne, E Sussex, BN21 4AQ.*

✠ **BROWN, Right Rev David Alan.** b 22. Univ of Lon BD (1st cl) 46, MTh 47, BA (1st cl Arabic) 51. ALCD 48. **d** 48 **p** 49 S'wark. C of Im Streatham 48-51; CMS Miss Yambio Dio Sudan 52-54; Prin Bp Gwynne Coll Mundri 55-61; Can Miss Khartoum Cathl 61-63; Miss Amman 63-66; C of St Jo Evang Bromley 66-67; V of Herne Bay 67-73; RD Reculver 72-73; Cons Ld Bp of Guildf in St Paul's Cathl 1 Nov 73 by Abp of Cant; Bps of Lon, Birm, Chich, Derby, Linc, Nor, Ox, Portsm and St E; Bps Suffr of Dover, Dorking, Dorch, Doncaster, Huntingdon, Taunton and Croydon; and others; Warden St Aug Coll Cant 75-79; Chairman Bd for Miss & Unity from 77; C'ttee on Islam in Eur from 80. *Willow Grange, Woking Road, Guildford, Surrey, GU4 7QS.* (Guildford 73922)

BROWN, David Edward Boyce. b 26. Em Th Coll Sktn. **d** 69 **p** 70 Sktn. I of Macklin 69-72; R of Lacombe 72-76; St Edm City and Dio Calg from 76. *8340-34th Avenue NW, Calgary, Alta, Canada.* (288-6330)

BROWN, David Hugh Plunkett. Angl Th Coll BC 67. **d** 67 **p** 68 New Westmr. C of St Timothy Vanc 67-71; I of Gibsons 71-80. *7-19032 Advent Road, Pitt Meadows, BC, Canada.*

BROWN, David Victor Arthur. b 44. Em Coll Cam BA 66, MA 70. Linc Th Coll 72. **d** 74 **p** 75 Linc. C of Bourne 74-77; Chap St Steph Coll Broadstairs 77-79; Team V of Grantham 79-81; C of St Cuthb City and Dio Sheff from 81. *Flat 3, 282 Herries Road, Sheffield, S5 7HA.* (0742-387253)

BROWN, David William. b 48. Univ of Edin MA 70. Oriel Coll Ox BA 72. Clare Coll Cam PhD 76. Westcott Ho Cam 75. **d** 76 Reading for Ox **p** 77 Dorchester for Ox. Chap, Fell and Tutor in Phil and Th Oriel Coll Ox from 76. *Oriel College, Oxford, OX1 4EW.* (Ox 40026)

BROWN, Canon Denis Arthur Whitlock. b 10. Hatf Coll Dur LTh 35, BA 36, MA 47, BCL 55. Univ of Lon BD 50. LCP 63. St Bonif Coll Warm 32. **d** 36 **p** 37 Newc T. C of All SS Gosforth 36-39; CF (TA - R of O) 39-75; Hd Master St Mich Sch Sandakan and Miss P Dio Lab and Sarawak 39-45; Perm to Offic Dio Win 45-46; C-in-c of Farley Chamberlayne w Braishfield 46; V of Weston 46-52; Chap R Vic Mil Hosp Netley 49-52; R of Stanwick 52-57; C-in-c of Hargrave 52-57; V of St Jas Northn 57-70; R of Gayton w Tiffield Dio Pet from 70; Can of Pet from 79. *Gayton Rectory, Northampton, NN7 3EY.* (Blisworth 858250)

BROWN, Canon Dennis Stanley Raymond. b 13. Univ of Wales BA (2nd cl Mus) 34. St Steph Ho Ox 34. **d** 36 **p** 37 Llan. C of St Martin Roath Cardiff 36-42; Chap RAFVR 42-46; V of St Martin Roath Dio Llan from 47; Can of Llan Cathl from 77; RD of Cardiff from 78. *St Martin's Vicarage, Strathnairn Street, Cardiff.* (Cardiff 482295)

BROWN, Canon Derek Frederick. b 27. St Francis Coll Brisb ACT ThL 52. **d** 52 **p** 54 Rockptn. C of Rockptn Cathl 52-54; P-in-c of Winton 54-55; V 55-57; Dioc Comm Rockptn 57-58; Chap All S Sch Charters Towers 58-59; C of Merstham (in c of Epiph) 59-61; R of St Paul w St Mark Deptford 61-69; Havant Dio Portsm from 69; Surr from 61; Chap RNR from 62; Commiss St Hel from 69; Hon Can of St Hel from 75. *2 Emsworth Road, Havant, Hants.* (Havant 483485)

BROWN, Donald Carlyle. McMaster Univ, Hamilton, Ont BA 48. Univ of Alta MA 72. Trin Coll Tor LTh 51. **d** 50 **p** 51 Niag. C of St Geo St Cath 50-53; R of Fergus 53-54; Elora w Drayton 54-58; St Mark Hamilton 58-60; V of Merrit 60-65; R of St Luke Edmon 65-68; Hon C of St Aug Edmon 68-70; Ch Ch Cathl Hamilton Dio Niag from 78; on staff of Gen Syn Canada from 70. *Box 82, Millgrove, Ont, Canada.*

BROWN, Donald Evans. b 10. Ch Coll Cam BA 34, MA 38. Lon Coll of Div 34. **d** 37 **p** 38 Roch. C of Ch Ch Luton Kent 37-39; St Cath Mile Cross 39-41; PC of St Anne Earlham 41-48; R of Wells-next-the-Sea 48-55; Surr 51-55; V of Hemingford Grey 55-77. *21 Manor Drive, Fenstanton, Huntingdon, Cambs, PE18 9QZ.*

BROWN, Donald Fryer. b 31. Univ of Dur BA (2nd cl Th) 56, Dipl Th 61. Cranmer Hall Dur 60. **d** 61 York for Bradf **p** 62 Bradf. C of Bradf Cathl 61-64; Bingley 64-66; V of H Trin Low Moor Dio Bradf from 66. *Holy Trinity Vicarage, Low Moor Bradford, BD12 0HR.* (Bradford 678859)

BROWN, Douglas Adrian Spencer. Univ of W Austr BA 50. St Mich Coll Crafers ACT ThL 50. M SSM 54. **d** 53 **p** 54 Adel. L to Offic Dio Adel 53-60; Tutor and Chap St Mich Coll Crafers 54-60; L to Offic (Col Cler Act) Dio Southw 60-67; Tutor and Chap Kelham Th Coll 60-67; Chap Univ of W Austr and L to Offic Dio Perth 67-71; P-in-c of Lyons w Chifley Prov Distr 71-73; St Alb Canberra 73-75; Perm to Offic Dio Adel 75-78; P-in-c of St John City and Dio Adel from 78. *14 St John's Street, Adelaide, S Australia 5000.* (223 2348)

BROWN, Douglas Charles. b 44. Univ of Tor BA 67, MA 68. Trin Coll Tor 68. **d** 71 Bp Garnsworthy for Tor **p** 72 Tor. C of St Jas Cathl Tor 71-74; R of Minden 74-77; on leave. *Order of the Holy Cross, West Park, NY 12493, USA.*

BROWN, Eric. b 28. N-W Ordin Course 73. **d** 76 **p** 77 Wakef. C of S Kirkby Dio Wakef from 76. *2 Orchard View, White Apron Street, S Kirkby, Pontefract, W Yorks WF9 3LE.*

BROWN, Eric Donald. **d** 60 **p** 61 Waik. C of Te Awamutu 60-63; V of Orakau 63-66; Inglewood 66-70; Perm to Offic Dio Waik 70-81; Dio Wai from 81. *26 Tarata Street, Matua, Tauranga, NZ.*

BROWN, Ernest Frederick Leonard. b 15. Edin Th Coll 46. **d** 49 **p** 50 Moray. Prec of St Andr Cathl Inverness 49-51; C of St Edm S Chingford 51-53; Brentwood (in c of St Geo Mart) 53-59; R of S Ockendon 59-77; Chap S Ockendon Hosp 61-73; R of Foxearth w Pentlow, Liston and Borley Dio Chelmsf from 77. *Foxearth Rectory, Sudbury, Suff, CO10 7JG.* (Sudbury 75697)

BROWN, Ernest George. b 23. Em Coll Cam BA (2nd cl Hist Trip pt i) 51, 3rd cl Th Trip pt i 52, MA 56. Oak Hill Th Coll 52. **d** 53 **p** 54 Sheff. C of Darfield 53-56; V of Ardsley 56-66; Thurnby w Stoughton Dio Leic from 66; RD of

Gartree II from 78. *Thurnby Vicarage, Leicester LE7 9PN.* (Leic 412263)

BROWN, Ernest Harry. b 32. **d** 59 **p** 60 Swan B. C of St Pet Cockett Swansea 59-62; Gowerton 62-68; Chap Deaf and Dumb Miss Swansea from 68. *20 Bryn-y-Mor Crescent, Swansea, W Glam.*

BROWN, Francis Palgrave. b 23. Fitzw Ho Cam cl Hist Trip pt i 49, BA (2nd cl Th Trip pt iii) 51, MA 54. **d** 53 **p** 54 Cov. C of Warw 53-55; St Paul w St Mark Birm 55-60; V of Temple Balsall 60-66; Master of Lady Katherine Leveson's Hosp 60-66; V of St Kath Cree Lon 66-71; Gen Sec ICF 66-76; V of Cropthorne w Charlton Dio Worc from 76; Chap and Dir of Stud Holland Ho 76-80; Adult Educn Officer from 80. *Cropthorne Vicarage, Pershore, Worcs.* (Evesham 86 0279)

BROWN, Frank Edward. b 02. Roch Th Coll 62. **d** 63 **p** 64 Chesh. C of Sale 63-66; St Luke w All SS Weaste Salford 66-68; V of St Aug Pendlebury Dio Man from 68. *St Augustine's Vicarage, Pendlebury, Manchester, M27 1EY.* (061-794 1808)

BROWN, Frank Seymour. b 10. St Aug Coll Cant 65. **d** 65 **p** 66 Roch. C of Bexleyheath 65-70; V of Cratfield w Heveningham and Ubbeston 70-76; Perm to Offic Dio St E from 76; Actg P-in-c of Ixworth w Ixworth Thorpe 78; Barnham w Euston and Fakenham 80. *6 St Edmund Close, Ixworth, Bury St Edmunds, Suff, IP31 2HP.* (Pakenham 30103)

BROWN, Geoffrey Gilbert. b 38. Univ of Dur BA 62. Fitzw Coll Cam BA 69, MA 73. Westcott Ho Cam 69. **d** 70 Bp Ramsbotham for Newc T **p** 71 Newc T. C of All SS Gosforth Newc T 70-73; Chap Dauntsey's Sch W Lavington 73-76; Chap St Paul's Colleg Sch Hamilton NZ 76-78; Chap and Tutor Greystoke Coll 79; V of St Aid Barrow-F Dio Carl from 79. *Vicarage, Middle Hill, Barrow-in-Furness, Cumb, LA13 9HD.* (B-in-F 21912)

BROWN, Canon Geoffrey Harold. b 30. Trin Hall Cam 3rd cl Engl Trip pt i 53, BA (2nd cl Hist Trip pt ii) 54, MA 58. Cudd Coll 54. **d** 56 **p** 57 Chelmsf. C of St Andr Plaistow 56-60; St Pet Birm 60-63; R of St Geo Birm 63-73; Gt Grimsby Dio Linc from 73; Can and Preb of Linc Cathl from 79. *Rectory, Bargate, Grimsby, S Humb.* (Grimsby 41331)

BROWN, Geoffrey Peter. b 44. Univ of Lon BD 69, AKC 69, MTh (distinc) 70. Shelford First Prize Phil of Relig 69. St Aug Coll Cant 69. **d** 71 Barking for Cant **p** 72 Barking for Chelmsf. C of St Mary Woodford (w St Phil & St Jas) 71-74; Chap Westfield & Bedford Colls Lon 74-80; V of St Steph Bush Hill Pk Dio Lon from 80. *Vicarage, Village Road, Bush Hill Park, Enfield, EN1 2ET.* (01-360 1407)

BROWN, George Kenneth. b 08. Fitzw Ho Cam BA 29, MA 33, BD 35. Univ of Edin PhD 31, DLitt 34. Ripon Hall Ox 34. **d** 49 **p** 50 Birm. C of Erdington 49-51; Exam in Div Univ of Lon 49-51; Prof of Phil Mitchell Coll Connecticut 51-54; Dean of Malayan Govt Coll Sing 55; Prof Hist of Relig Univ of Manit 56-59; Lect in Div Univ of Lon 59-60; Prin St Pet Coll Ja 61-64; Exam Chap to Bp of Ja 61-64; Adv to Non-Res Studs Univ of WI 61-67; V of Hursley w Pitt Dio Win from 67. *Hursley Vicarage, Winchester, Hants.* (Hursley 75216)

BROWN, Gerald Arthur Charles. b 35. Late Exhib of CCC Cam 2nd cl Hist Trip pt i 55, BA (2nd cl Th Trip pt ia) 56, MA 60. CCC Ox BA (by incorp) 58, Dipl Th 59. St Steph Ho Ox 58. **d** 60 **p** 61 Lich. C of Wolverhampton 60-66; V of Trent Vale 66-74; St Andr Wolverhampton Dio Lich from 74. *1 Lowe Street, WV6 0QL.* (Wolverhampton 21300)

BROWN, Ven Gordon Allan. Trin Coll Melb BA (Hons) 47. ACT ThL 49. **d** 50 **p** 51 Melb. C of Middle Brighton 50-51; Dir of Youth and Educn Dio Melb 51-54; Min of Burwood 54-59; R of Warrnambool 59-68; Exam Chap to Bp of Bal 61-68; Hon Can of Bal 64-68; I of H Trin Kew 68-78; Archd of Box Hill from 78; Abp's Chap and Exam Chap to Abp of Melb from 78. *205 Gipps Street, E Melbourne, Vic, Australia 3002.* (41-4338)

BROWN, Graeme Eric. b 37. Univ of NZ 56. NZ Bd of Th Stud LTh 62. St Jo Coll Auckld 58. **d** 62 **p** 63 Waik. C of Tokoroa 62-64; Taumarunui 64-66; V of Mokau 66-68; Mangakino 68-71; C of Hastings Wai 71-74; St Francis Heartsease Nor 74-75; V of Gate Pa Tauranga 76-81; Paeroa Dio Waik from 81. *Box 169, Paeroa, NZ.* (7192)

BROWN, Harold George. Mem Univ of Newfld BA 63. Qu Coll Newfld LTh 62. **d** and **p** 62 Newfld. R of Belleoram 62-70; I of Cow Head 69-73; Port de Grave and Brigus w Salmon Cove Dio Newfld (E Newfld from 76) from 73. *PO Box 22, Port de Grave, Conception Bay, Newfoundland, Canada.* (709-786-6581)

BROWN, Harry Hamilton. Montr Dioc Th Coll. **d** 67 Ott. I of Hemmingford 67-70; I of Matawa 70-71; Clayton 71-77; Almonte Dio Ott from 77. *Box 490, Almonte, Ont, Canada.*

BROWN, Hartley. b 15. Selw Coll Cam 2nd cl Hist Trip pt i 35, BA (2nd cl Hist Trip pt ii) 36, 1st cl Th Trip pt i 37, MA 40. Wells Th Coll 37. **d** 38 Pontefract for Wakef **p** 39 Wakef. C of St Mich Wakef 38-41; Elland 41-44; St Matthias at the Link Malvern 44-49; V of St Steph Barbourne Worc 49-65; R of Guarlford 65-80; Chap Beauchamp Trust Almshouse, Newland from 80. *Chaplain's House, Newland, Malvern, Worcs.*

BROWN, Henry. b 27. BSc (Lon) 51. BSc Lon (Special) 52. N-W Ordin Course 72. **d** 75 Lanc for Blackb **p** 76 Blackb. C of Padiham 75-80; V of St Paul Warton Dio Blackb from 80. *Vicarage, Warton, Nr Preston, PR4 1BD.* (Freckleton 632227)

BROWN, Howard Etheredge. b 20. Univ of Reading BA (Hons Hist) 47. Wycl Hall Ox 47. **d** 49 **p** 50 S'wark. C of Gipsy Hill 49-51; Belper 51-53; PC of H Trin Derby 53-56; C of Chapel-en-le-Frith (in c of St Paul Dove Holes) 56-58; PC of Matlock Bath 58-66; R of Norton-in-Hales 66-81. *c/o Norton-in-Hales Rectory, Market Drayton, Salop.* (Market Drayton 3013)

BROWN, Canon Howard Miles. b 11 Univ of Lon BSc 35, BD (2nd cl) 42, PhD 47. Egerton Hall Man 39. **d** and **p** 40 Man. C of St Pet Swinton 40-42; Calstock 42-45; St Gluvias 45-46; PC of Torpoint 46-52; Proc Conv Truro 55-75; V of St Paul Truro 52-62; St Winnow w St Nectan Dio Truro from 62; V of St Veep Dio Truro from 62; Hon Can of Truro from 64; Preb of Bodmin (or Kings) in Preb Ch of St Endellion from 73; RD of Bodmin 71-76. *St Winnow Vicarage, Lostwithiel, Cornw.* (Bodmin 872395)

BROWN, Hugh John Agnew. b 26. Rhodes Univ BA 48. **d** 74 Bloemf **p** 75 Pret. Chap & Hd Master of St Mary's Sch Dio Pret from 74. *PO Box 11379, Brooklyn 0011, S Africa.*

BROWN, Ian David. Univ of E Anglia BA 76. Wycl Hall Ox BA 80. **d** 81 Portsm. C of St Jude Portsea Dio Portsm from 81. *44 Green Road, Southsea, Portsmouth, Hants.* (0705 820080)

BROWN, Ian Frederic. St Jo Coll Morpeth ACT ThL 62. **d** 62 Melb **p** 63 Bp Sambell for Melb. C of Glenroy 62-63; Balwyn 64; Perm to Offic Dio Melb 64-65; C of Croydon 65-68; St Jas Syd 68-69; St Pet Melb 69-70; on leave 70-71; I of Eltham 72-79; St Osw Glen Iris Dio Melb from 79. *96 High Street, Glen Iris, Vic, Australia 3146.*

BROWN, Ivan Ranfurly. b 54. Codr Coll Barb LTh 77. **d** 77 Nass. Perm to Offic Dio Nass 77-80; P-in-c of Our Lady and St Steph Bimini Dio Nass from 80. *PO Box 666, Bimini, Bahamas.*

BROWN, Jack Robin. b 44. Linc Th Coll 67. **d** 69 Barking for Chelmsf **p** 70 Chelmsf. C of St Cedd Canning Town Chelmsf 69-72; Dunstable 72-78; V of St Andr Luton Dio St Alb from 78. *St Andrew's Vicarage, Blenheim Crescent, Luton, Beds.* (Luton 32380)

BROWN, Canon James. b 03. Kelham Th Coll 26. **d** 31 **p** 32 Sheff. C of St Pet Sheff 31-35; C-in-c of New Rossington Conv Distr 35-40; V of St Jo Evang Masbrough 40-49; R of Thurnscoe 49-75; RD of Wath 67-75; Surr 68-75; Hon Can of Sheff 70-75; Can (Emer) from 75. *Ground Floor Flat, Hooton Pagnell Hall, Doncaster, S Yorks.*

BROWN, James Herbert. b 53. Univ of Tor BA 76. Trin Coll Tor MDiv 80. **d** 80 Bp Read for Tor **p** 81 Bp Brown for Tor. C of Grace Ch Markham Dio Tor from 80. *125 Wellington Street W, RR 701, Markham, Ont, Canada, L3P 1B3.*

BROWN, Canon James Lynwood. St Barn Coll Adel. **d** 31 **p** 32 Perth. C of Moora 31-33; Perth Cathl 33-34; R of Morawa 34-38; Beverley 38-44; Chap AIF 42-43; R of W Northam 44-49; Dongarra 49-50; Gosnells 50-56; Chap to Abp of Perth 51-62; R of E Claremont 56-69; Can of St Geo Cathl Perth 57-69; Can (Emer) from 69; Hon C of Kalamunda Dio Perth from 70. *Flat 46, Parry House, Lesmurdie, W Australia 6076.* (93 6324)

BROWN, James Michael. b 49. St Jo Coll Morpeth 74. **d** 77 Bp Parker for Newc. **p** 78 Newc. C of Gosford 77-79; Cessnock 79-82; C of St Hugh Eyres Monsell City and Dio Leic from 82. *c/o St Hugh's Vicarage, Pasley Road, Eyres Monsell, Leicester.*

BROWN, James Philip. b 30. Ex Coll Ox BA 54, MA 55. Westcott Ho Cam 54. **d** 56 **p** 57 St Alb. C of Hemel Hempstead 56-63; PC of Hellesdon 63-71; V in Lowestoft Group (P-in-c of Kirkley) 71-79; Team V 79-80; P-in-c of Northleach and Eastington w Hampnett and Farmington Dio Glouc from 81. *Northleach Vicarage, Cheltenham, Glos.* (Northleach 293)

BROWN, James Roy. Ch Coll Hobart 47 ACT ThL 49. **d** 50 **p** 51 Tas. C of Devonport 50-52; R of Bothwell 52-57; St Osw Launceston Dio Tas from 57. *39 Bain Terrace, Launceston, Tasmania.* (003-31-5845)

BROWN, Canon James Russell. Qu Coll Ox BA 52, MA 56. Nashotah House Wisconsin Hon DD 70. Univ of Winnipeg Hon LLD 77. Seabury-W Th Sem Illinois Hon DD 70. Kelham Th Coll 37. **d** 43 **p** 44 Bris. C of St Jude w St Matthias Bris 43-45; Ch of Good Shepherd Preston 45-47; Portishead 47-49; in USA 52-55; C of Abbots Langley 55-56; R of

Drummondville PQ 56-61; Prof of Old Test and Hebr Nashotah House Wisconsin 61-70; Warden and Vice-Chan of St John's Coll Winnipeg 70-80; Canon of St John's Cathl Winnipeg 70-80; Hon Can from 80; Exam Chap to Abp of Rupld 71-80; Lect Univ of Manit from 80. *96 Kingsway Avenue, Winnipeg, Manit, Canada.*

BROWN, James Russell. Em Coll Sktn LTh 59. **d** 59 **p** 60 Edmon. C of St Paul Edmon 59; St Timothy Edmon 59-60; R of Drayton Valley 60-62; St Timothy Edmon 62-66; St Aid Winnipeg 66-74; Can of St Jo Cathl, Winnipeg 71-74; Dean and R of All SS Cathl Edmon 74-81; Exam Chap to Bp of Edmon 75-76; on leave. *10023-103rd Street, Edmonton, Alta, T5J OX5, Canada.* (403-422 4234)

BROWN, James William Sidney. b 47. Univ of Manit BA 69. Huron Coll Lon MDiv 72. **d** 72 Rupld **p** 72 Bran. R of Swan River 72-74; P Assoc of St Paul Winnipeg 74-77; I of St Phil Winnipeg Dio Rupld from 77. *248 Tache Avenue, Winnipeg, Manit., Canada.*

BROWN, John. **d** 50 **p** 51 Clogh. C of Tydavnet 50-51; C-in-c of Drum 51-58; R of Clontibret w Tullycorbet 58-62; I of Clabby 62-75; R of Fledborough Dio Southw from 75; V of Dunham-on-Trent w Darlton and Ragnall Dio Southw from 75. *Dunham-on-Trent Vicarage, Newark, Notts.* (Dunham-on-Trent 320)

BROWN, John. **d** 72 **p** 73 Gippsld. C of Toora 72-76; R of Mirboo N Dio Gippsld from 76. *Rectory, Mirboo North, Vic, Australia 3871.* (056-68 1346)

BROWN, John. b 24. Oak Hill Th Coll. **d** 53 Stafford for Cant **p** 54 Lich. C of Tipton 53-56; Ch Ch U Armley 56-58; V of Daubhill Bolton-le-Moors 58-65; Regr Midl Bible Tr Coll Birm 65-67; St Paul's Coll of Educn Cheltm 67-69; Middlecroft Sch Staveley 69-75; Silverdale Sch Sheff from 75. *17 Avondale Road, The Green, Inkersall, Chesterfield, Derbyshire, S43 3EQ.*

BROWN, John Bruce. b 42. Univ of Nottm BA (2nd cl Th) 64, MA 68. Cudd Coll 64. **d** 66 Bp McKie for Cov **p** 67 Cov. C of St Nich Warwick Cov 66-71; Bp's Hatfield (in c of St Mich) 71-78; V of St Mich AA Watford Dio St Alb from 78. *St Michael's Vicarage, Mildred Avenue, Watford, Herts.* (Watford 32460)

BROWN, John Charles Westlock. Trin Coll Melb, Rupertswood Th Stud 25, BA (1st cl Lat and Engl) 28, MA 30. ACT ThL 29. New Coll Ox BA 32, MA 42. Wells Th Coll 31. **d** 29 Bp Stephen for Melb **p** 31 Ox. C of St Geo Malvern 29-30 and 32-34; St Barn Ox 31-32; Asst Chap Melb Gr Sch 34-42; Chap 42-72. *93 Station Street, Malvern, Vic, Australia 3144.* (50-4035)

BROWN, John Derek. b 41. Linc Th Coll 71. **d** 73 Doncaster for Sheff **p** 74 Sheff. C of Rotherham 73-76; V of Surfleet (and W Pinchbeck from 78) Dio Linc from 76; P-in-c of W Pinchbeck 76-78. *Surfleet Vicarage, Station Road, Spalding, Lincs.* (Surfleet 230)

BROWN, John Dixon. b 28. Pemb Coll Cam BA (2nd cl Hist Pts i and ii) 52. Oak Hill Th Coll 52. **d** 54 **p** 55 Chich. C of St Geo Worthing 54-57; S w N Bersted 57-63; V of Westhampnett Dio Chich from 63. *Westhampnett Vicarage, Chichester, W Sussex.* (Chichester 782704)

BROWN, John Duncan. b 43. St Pet Coll Ox BA (Geog) 64, (Th) 66, MA 68. Univ of Lon BSc 74. Wycl Hall Ox 65. **d** 67 **p** 68 York. C of Hull 67-69; St Leonards-on-Sea 69-72; C of Norbiton 72-74; Kirkcaldy 75-78; Chap of Chelmsf Cathl from 78. *1b Rainsford Avenue, Chelmsford, Essex, CM1 2PJ.*

BROWN, Ven John Edward. b 30. BD (Lon) 68. Kelham Th Coll 50. **d** 55 **p** 56 Jer. Chap St Geo Colleg Ch Jer 55-57; C of St Mary Virg Reading (in c of All SS) Dio Ox 57-60; Chap of Omdurman and of All SS Cathl Khartoum 60-64; V of Stewkley 64-69; St Luke Maidenhead 69-73; Bracknell 73-77; RD of Sonning 74-77; Commiss Sudan from 74; Archd of Berks from 78; Warden Ascot Priory from 80. *Beech Hill Vicarage, Reading, Berks.* (Reading 882569)

BROWN, Ven John Harvey. Late Scho of Jes Coll Cam (2nd cl Hist Trip pt i) 27, BA (2nd cl Th Trip pt i) 28, MA 32. Westcott Ho Cam 28. **d** 29 **p** 30 Bris. C of St Paul Bedminster 29-33; R of St John Maffra 33-36; Bairnsdale 36-45; Dom Chap to Bp of Gippsld 36-52; Exam Chap 39-55; Chap CMF 41; RAAF 42-45; R of Yallourn 45-55; Hon Can of St Paul's Cathl Sale 49-52; Archd of Latrobe Valley 52-55; V of Kingsville w Spotswood 55-58; I of Surrey Hills 58-65; Archd of Kew 63-66; Brighton 66-72; Archd (Emer) from 72; V of St Marg Caulfield 65-74; on leave 74-76; Perm to Offic Dio Melb from 76. *PO Box 44, Dromana, Vic, Australia 3936.* (059-87 1425)

BROWN, John Henry. Qu Coll Newfld LTh 56. **d** 55 Newfld **p** 56 NS for Newfld. I of Change I 55-57; R of White Bay 57-62; I of Brooklyn 62-65; R of Lamaline 65-70; I of Seal Cove 70-72; L to Offic Dio Newfld 72-76; W Newfld from 76. *Box 366, Baie Verte, White Bay, Newfoundland, Canada.*

BROWN, Canon John Lawley. MBE 63. St Jo Coll Dur LTh 30, BA 31. **d** 31 **p** 33 Lich. C of Cannock 31-34; Asst Chap of H Trin Cathl Shanghai 34-37; C of St Leon Bilston 37-40; V of Wilnecote 40-46; Basford 46-48; Chap Miss to Seamen Port of Lon 48; Auckld 49-72; L to Offic Dio Auckld 49-72; Perm to Offic from 72; Hon Can of Auckld 66-78; Can (Emer) from 78. *34 Duncansby Road, Whangaparaoa, NZ.* (502-258)

BROWN, John Roger. b 37. K Coll Lon and Warm AKC 60. **d** 61 **p** 62 S'wark. C of All SS New Eltham 61-64; Bexhill 64-68; V of St Elis, Eastbourne 68-75; E Grinstead Dio Chich from 75. *Vicarage, East Grinstead, W Sussex, RH19 3BB.* (E Grinstead 23307)

BROWN, John Simpson. b 10. TCD BA 46, MA 49, BD 54. Forster and Downes Pris 46. Ch Coll Cam MA 49 (by incorp). **d** 47 **p** 48 Connor. C of Coleraine 47-50; Chap Ch Coll Cam 50-57; Select Pr Univ of Cam 55; Dir of Educn Ch of Ireland 57-61; Warden of Div Hostel Dub 61-80; L to Offic Dio Dub from 61; Exam Chap to Abp of Dub from 61; to Bp of Connor and L to Offic Dio Connor from 61; Dir of Ordinands Dio Dub 62-67; Prof of Pastoral Th Trin Coll Dub 64-80; Can and Preb of St Patr Cathl Dub 65-73; Treas 73-75; Prec 75-80; Exam Chap to Abp of Arm 69-80. *25 Pasadena Gardens, Belfast, BT5 6HU, N Ireland.*

BROWN, John William. b 05. Tyndale Hall Bris 34. **d** 37 **p** 38 Bris. C of St Luke Barton Hill Bris 37-42; R of Burslem 42-47; Whitewell 47-49; V of St Polycarp Everton 49-53; CF 53-57; R of Cranfield 57-77; C-in-c of Hulcote w Salford 61-77. *c/o Cranfield Rectory, Bedford, MK43 0DR.* (Bedford 750214)

BROWN, John William Etheredge. b 13. St Pet Hall Ox BA (3rd cl Mod Hist) 35, MA 39. Wycl Hall Ox 35. **d** 37 **p** 38 Chelmsf. C of St Paul Stratford 37-40; Rawtenstall 40-42; Thame (in c of Towersey w Aston Sandford) 42-45; V of St Keverne w St Pet 45-51; Hoo All Hallows w Stoke 51-55; Crich 55-61; Widecombe-in-the-Moor Dio Ex 61-79; Team R (w Leusden, Princeton, Postbridge and Huccaby Chap) from 80; Leusden 61-79; C-in-c of Holne 70-75; RD of Moreton 74-80; P-in-c of Princetown w Postbridge and Huccaby Chap 75-79; Dep Chap HM Pris Dartmoor from 75. *Widecombe-in-the-Moor Rectory, Newton Abbot, Devon, TQ13 7TB.* (Widecombe 231)

BROWN, Kenneth Douglas. b 26. St Jo Coll Winnipeg. **d** 81 Rupld. Hon C of St Mary Winnipeg Dio Rupld from 81. *47 Dellwood Crescent, Winnipeg, Manit, Canada, R3R 1S6.*

BROWN, Canon Kenneth Edward. b 22. Qu Coll Cam BA 43, MA 47. Ridley Hall Cam 46. **d** 47 **p** 48 Portsm. C of Farlington 47-51; Attercliffe w Carbrooke Sheff 51-52; V of Rounds Green 52-58; Greenwood Pk Natal 58-63; Seend 63-69; PC of Southbroom Dio Sarum from 69; Can and Preb of Sarum Cathl from 77; RD of Devizes from 77; M Gen Syn from 80. *Southbroom Vicarage, Devizes, Wilts.* (Devizes 3891)

BROWN, Kenneth Hepburn. Fitzw Hall Cam BA 21. St Bonif Coll Warm 21. **d** 22 **p** 23 Capetn. C of St Barn Capetn 23-27; St Barn Temple Fortune 28-30; R of Bellville 30-36; Bredasdorp 36-40; Stellenbosch 40-52; C of Capetn Cathl (in c of Ch of Ascen) 53-57; L to Offic Dio Capetn 57-80; Perm to Offic from 80. *c/o 24 Union Avenue, Pinelands, CP, S Africa.* (53-3567)

BROWN, Kenneth Roger. b 48. Univ of Dur BA 69, Dipl Th 72. St Chad's Coll Dur 70. **d** 73 **p** 74 Bris. C of Patchway 73-77; All SS Fishponds Dio Bris from 77; St Jo Div Fishponds Dio Bris from 77. *c/o All Saints' Vicarage, Fishponds, Bristol, BS16 2BW.*

✠ **BROWN, Right Rev Laurence Ambrose.** b 07. Qu Coll Cam 2nd cl Hist Trip pt i 30, BA (2nd cl Th Trip pt i) 31, MA 46. Cudd Coll 31. **d** 32 **p** 33 S'wark. C of St Jo Div Kennington 32-35; Ch Ch Luton (in c of St Pet) 35-40; V of Hatfield Hyde 40-46; Asst Sec S Lon Ch Fund and S'wark Dioc Bd of Finance 46-52; Sec 52-60; Can Res and Prec of S'wark Cathl 50-56; Archd of Lewisham 55-60; Vice-Provost of S'wark Cathl 56-60; Cons Ld Bp Suffr of Warrington in York Minster 30 Nov 60 by Abp of York; Bps of Dur; Southw; Liv; Newc T; Blackb; and S'wark; Bps Suffr of Selby; Stockport; Pontefract; Whitby; Burnley; Hull; Woolwich; and Kens; and Bps Simpson; Way; Gerard; Graham; and Stannard; Can Dioc of Liv 60-69; Proc Conv Liv 61-69; Trld to Birm 69; res 77; P-in-c of Odstock w Nunton and Bodenham Dio Sarum from 78. *7 St Nicholas Road, Salisbury, SP1 2SN.* (0722 3138)

BROWN, Lawrence Richard. b 08. SOC 63. **d** 66 **p** 67 S'wark. Hon C of Good Shepherd w St Pet Lee 66-78; Perm to Offic Dio S'wark from 78. *30 Scotsdale Road, SE12 8BP.* (01-852 1527)

BROWN, Leslie Maurice. b 04. Univ of Bris BSc 24, MSc 25. Univ of St Andr PhD 38. Edin Th Coll 74. **d** 74 Bp Russell for Edin **p** 74 Edin. Hon C of St Jo Evang City and Dio Edin from 74. *26 Falcon Court, Edinburgh, EH10 4AE.*

✠ **BROWN, Right Rev Leslie Wilfrid.** b 12. CBE 65. Univ of Lon BD 36, MTh 44, DD 57. Univ of Cam MA (*hon causa*) 53. Trin Coll Tor Hon DD 63. ALCD 35. **d** 35 S'wark for Portsm **p** 36 Portsm. C of St Jas Milton 35-38; CMS Miss Kottayam and Exam Chap to Bp of Trav 38-43; Vice-Prin Cam Nicholson Inst Kottayam 38-42; Chap Down Coll Cam and C of H Trin Cam 43-44; Prin Kerala United Th Sem Trivandrum 44-52; Ch of S India 47-52; Select Pr Univ of Cam 50-51 and 67-68 and 79-80; Univ of Ox 67; Chap Jes Coll Cam 50-51; Cons Ld Bp of Ugan in S'wark Cathl 6 Jan 53 by Abp of Cant; Bps of S'wark; Derby; Ely; St Alb; Nyasa; and U Nile; Bps Suffr of Woolwich; Kingston T; and Stepney; and Bps Willis; Kitching; Stuart Mann; and Corfield; Trld to Nam and elected Metrop of Prov of Ugan and Rwanda-B 60; Trld to St E 66; res 78; Hon Fell Down Coll Cam from 66; Chap and Sub-Prelate O of St John of Jer from 68. *47 New Square, Cambridge, CB1 1EZ.* (Cam 352465)

BROWN, Malcolm Arthur. b 54. Oriel Coll Ox BA 76. Westcott Ho Cam 77. **d** 79 **p** 80 Roch. C of Riverhead w Dunton Green Dio Roch from 79. *178 London Road, Dunton Green, Sevenoaks, Kent, TN13 2PB.*

BROWN, Martin Douglas. b 53. Oakhill Coll 78. **d** 81 S'wark. C of Ch Ch New Malden Dio S'wark from 81. *12 Rosebery Avenue, New Malden, Surrey.*

BROWN, Martin Easdale. b 27. Ely Th Coll 53. **d** 55 **p** 56 S'wark. C of St Andr Surbiton 55-59; Blandford Forum 59-62; V of France Lynch 62-75; P-in-c of Aysgarth Dio Ripon 75-77; V (w Bolton and Redmire from 81) from 77; P-in-c of Bolton w Redmire 78-81. *Aysgarth Vicarage, Leyburn, N Yorks.* (Aysgarth 235)

BROWN, Canon Merton Carlyle. Univ of Syd BA 11. **d** 11 **p** 12 Newc. C of Bulahdelah 11-12; Muswell Brook 12-13; Waratah 13-14; Merriwa 14-15; P-in-c of Camden Haven 15-18; W Wallsend w Minmi 18-22; R of Aberdeen 22-28; Wallsend 28-34; Merriwa 34-40; W Maitland 40-50; Murrurundi 50-55; Can of Newc 50-55; Can (Emer) from 55; LPr Dio Newc 55-61. *1 Ledsam Street, Maitland, NSW, Australia.*

BROWN, Michael Cedric. St Jo Coll Dur BA (2nd cl Hist) 54, MA 57, BD 60. Sarum Th Coll 54. **d** 56 Win for Cant for Col Bp **p** 57 N Queensld. C of Townsville Cathl 56-63; Dioc Missr Dio N Queensld 63-64; Sec Austr SCM in Schs 64-68; Perm to Offic Dio Melb 64-69; Chap Bp Luffa Sch Chich 70-72; Perm to Offic Dio Newc T from 72. *7 glencoe, Highfields, Killingworth, Newcastle-on-Tyne, NE12 0QB.*

BROWN, Michael Coningsby. St Jo Coll Ox BA 47, MA 49. Linc Th Coll 47. **d** 49 **p** 50 Lon. C of St Mich AA Mill Hill 49-53; St Paul Knightsbridge 53-56; V of Bures 56-62; C-in-c of Mount Bures 58-62; V of Godalming Dio Guildf from 62; RD of Godalming 74-78 *Vicarage, Godalming, Surrey.* (Godalming 21057)

BROWN, Michael Henry. Univ of Cant BCom 63. Ch Ch Coll 59. NZ Bd of Th Stud LTh 67. **d** 63 **p** 64 Ch Ch. C of Linwood-Aranui 63-66; Ashburton 66-67; V of Marchwiel 67-71; Burwood 71-74; Merivale Dio Ch Ch from 74. *24 Church Lane, Christchurch 1, NZ.* (559-735)

BROWN, Ven Michael Rene Warneford. b 15. Late Squire Scho of St Pet Coll Ox BA (2nd cl Mod Hist) 37, 2nd cl Th 39, MA 41. **d** 41 Chich **p** 42 Lewes for Chich. C of W Grinstead 41-43; Asst Master Ch Hosp 39-43; Chap RNVR 43-46; Chap and Dean St Pet Coll Ox 46; C of St Mary Virg Ox 46; Lect RN Coll Greenwich 46-47; Fell of St Aug Coll Cant 48-52 Libr 48-50; L to Offic Dio Cant 48-60; C-in-c of Bekesbourne 49-50; Asst Sec CACTM 50-60; Exam Chap to Bp of Southw 54-77; to Abp of Cant 59-60; Chap of Ch Ho Westmr 55-60; Commiss Waik 58-69; Archd of Nottm 60-77; Archd (Emer) from 77; M C of E Pensions Bd from 65; Ch Comm 68-78; M Ch Comm Redundant Chs C'ttee 78-80; Chairman from 80; Perm to Offic Dio Cant from 79. *Faygate, Liverpool Road, Walmer, Deal, Kent, CT14 7LR.* (030-45 61326)

BROWN, Mount Stewart Drummond. b 12. **d** 77 Glas (APM). Hon C of St Bride City and Dio Glas from 77. *67 Gardner Street, Glasgow, G11 5BZ.* (041-334 4476)

BROWN, Norman Charles Harry. b 27. Univ of S Wales BSc 46. St Mich Coll Llan 48. **d** 50 **p** 51 Llan. C of St Jo Evang Canton 50-58; Llanishen w Lisvane 58-63; V of Miskin Dio Llan from 63. *Miskin Vicarage, Mountain Ash, Mid Glam.* (0443 473247)

BROWN, Norman John. b 34. Ripon Hall Ox 72. **d** 74 Dorchester for Ox **p** 75 Ox. C of High Wycombe 74-78; V of St Cath Tilehurst Dio Ox from 78. *Vicarage, Wittenham Avenue, Tilehurst, Reading, Berks.* (Reading 27786)

BROWN, Ven Obadiah Datubo Cockeye. d 40 Bp Onyeabo for Niger **p** 41 Niger. P Dio Niger 40-52; Dio Nig Delta 52-61 and from 67; Dio N Nig 61-66; Archd of Jos 61-66; Aba 67-71; Bonny from 72. *PO Box 15, Port Harcourt, Nigeria.* (Port Harcourt 782)

BROWN, Peter. b 47. Kelham Th Coll 69. **d** 74 **p** 75 Dur. C of St Ignatius Hendon Bp Wearmouth 74-80; St Anthony Byker City and Dio Newc T from 80. *Vicarage, Enslin Gardens, Newcastle-upon-Tyne, NE6 3ST.* (Newc T 651605)

BROWN, Peter. b 53. St Chad's Coll Dur BA 75. Sarum Wells Th Coll 75. **d** 77 **p** 78 Lich. C of Tunstall 77-80; Short Heath Dio Lich from 80. *66 Magness Crescent, Short Heath, Willenhall, W Midl.*

BROWN, Peter Francis. b 40. K Coll Lon and Warm AKC 65. **d** 66 **p** 67 Lich. C of Sneyd Green 66-68; Harlescott 68-69; Tamworth w Glascote and Hopwas 69-72; Perm to Offic Dio Lich from 73. *81 Wigginton Road, Tamworth, Staffs.* (Tamworth 62219)

BROWN, Peter John. St Jo Coll Morpeth. **d** 68 **p** 69 C & Goulb. C of Bega 68-70; St Sav Cathl, Goulb 70-73; R of Bungendore Dio C & Goulb from 73. *Rectory, Bungendore, NSW, Australia.*

BROWN, Canon Peter Kimpton. ALCD 58. **d** 60 Maidstone for Cant **p** 61 Cant. C of H Trin Folkestone 60-63; Swanage 63-67; R of Lake Grace 67-70; Harvey 70-74; Chap Bunb Cathl Gr Sch 72-78; Can of Bunb Cathl from 74; Prec from 78. *43 Hamersely Drive, Bunbury, W Australia 6230.* (21 6441)

BROWN, Peter Russell. b 43. Oak Hill Th Coll. **d** 71 Buckingham for Ox **p** 72 Ox. C of Faringdon Ox 71-73; Greyfriars Reading 73-74; V of Jes Ch Forty Hill Enfield 74-81; Laleham Dio Lon from 81. *Laleham Vicarage, Staines, Tw18 1SB.* (Staines 57330)

BROWN, Philip Roy. b 41. St Steph Ho Ox 78. **d** 80 **p** 81 Birm. C of Highters Heath Dio Birm from 80. *28 Maypole Lane, Maypole, Birmingham, B14 5JG.*

BROWN, Raymond Isaac Harry. b 14. Kelham Th Coll 36. **d** 42 **p** 43 Chelmsf. C of St Andr Romford 42-48; Org Sec UMCA for Metrop Area 48-52; V of St Mary Wellingborough 52-66; PC of Tintinhull 66-68; V 68-74; RD of Martock 70-75; R of St Agnes Teyateyaneng Dio Les from 76. *PO Box 22, Teyateyaneng, Lesotho.* (Teyateyaneng 252)

BROWN, Raymond John. b 49. Univ of Ox BEducn 71. Wycl Hall Ox 72. **d** 75 **p** 76 Chelmsf. C of Barking 75-78; H Trin Aylesbury (in c of Good Shepherd) 78-82; V of St Mich AA Enfield Dio Lon from 82. *Vicarage, Gordon Hill, Enfield, EN2 0QP.* (01-363 2483)

BROWN, Reginald. b 16. St Jo Coll Dur BA (2nd cl Hist) 38. Dipl Th 40. MA 41. **d** 39 **p** 40 Dur. C of Stranton 39-45; Actg C-in-c St Paul Hendon Bp Wearmouth 45-46; V of St Barn Bp Wearmouth 46-53; St Jo Evang Darlington 53-63; Ch Ch Bp Wearmouth 63-77; R of Shincliffe Dio Dur from 77. *Shincliffe Rectory, Durham, DH21 2NJ.* (Durham 62142)

BROWN, Richard. b 47. St Steph Ho Ox 71. **d** 74 Warrington for Liv **p** 75 Liv. C of St Marg Toxteth Pk 74-78; St Giles Reading 78-80; V of St Nicolas Earley Dio Ox from 80. *St Nicolas Vicarage, Sutcliffe Avenue, Earley, Reading, Berks, RG6 2JN.* (Reading 663563)

BROWN, Canon Richard Charles. McGill Univ MA 27. Montr Th Coll LTh 28. Univ of W Ont DD 49. **d** 29 **p** 30 Hur. I of Sarnia 29-31; R of St Mark w St Martin Calg 31-34; C of Sarnia 34-37; I 37; in Amer Ch 38-41; R of All SS Windsor 41-49; Dean of Hur and R of St Paul's Cathl Lon Ont 49-61; R of St Mary Walkerville 61-69; St Mary, Windsor 69-72; Can of Hur 61-72; Can (Emer) from 73. *47 Finsbury Crescent, London, Ont., Canada.*

BROWN, Richard George. Univ of Dur BSc (2nd cl Botany) 63. Wells Th Coll 63. **d** 65 **p** 66 Dur. C of Norton 65-69; N Gosforth (in c of St Aidan's Brunton Park) 69-71; Chap Wells Cathl Sch 71-81; C-in-c of Dulverton and Brushford Dio B & W from 81. *Vicarage, Dulverton, Somt, TA22 9DW.* (Dulverton 23425)

BROWN, Richard George Holden. b 28. Univ of Nottm BA 53. Ely Th Coll 53. **d** 55 **p** 56 Lich. C of St Andr W Bromwich 55-58; Caversham (in c of St Barn Emmer Green) 58-63; V of St Swith Purley 63-77; C of St Sav Croydon Dio Cant from 77. *96a Lodge Road, Croydon, Surrey, CR0 2PF.* (01-684 8017)

BROWN, Richard Lessey. b 27. Keble Coll Ox BA (2nd cl Mod Hist) 51, MA 55. Qu Coll Birm 51. **d** 53 **p** 54 York. C of St Lawr York 53-55; St Osw Fulford York 55-57; V of Fridaythorpe w Fimber and Thixendale 57-61; St Luke York 61-75; Barlby Dio York from 75. *Vicarage, Barlby, Selby, N Yorks, YO8 7JP.* (Selby 2384)

BROWN, Robert Frederick. d 51 **p** 52 Rupld. I of Morden 51-56; C of St Jas Winnipeg 57-58; on leave 58-61; Vice-Prin Old Sun Sch Blackfoot Miss and L to Offic Dio Calg 61-64; I of Blackfoot Miss 64-68; on leave. *2601 Arthur Street East, Apt 1, Thunder Bay, Ont., Canada.* (807-623-2978)

BROWN, Ven Robert Saville. b 14. Selw Coll Cam 2nd cl Econ Trip pt i 37, BA (2nd cl Th Trip pt i) 39 MA 43. Linc Th

Coll 39. **d** 40 **p** 41 St Alb. C of Gt Berkhamsted 40-44; Hitchin 44-47; V of Wonersh 47-53; R of Gt Berkhamsted 53-69; Surr from 54; C-in-c of Bourne End 56-65; RD of Berkhamsted 60-67; Hon Can of St Alb 65-74; V of St Paul Bedford 69-74; P-in-c of Old Warden 74-79; M Gen Syn 69-79; Chap HM Pris Bedford 69-74; Archd of Bedford 74-79; Archd (Emer) from 79. *9 Treachers Close, Chesham, Bucks, HP5 2HD.*

BROWN, Robert Walter. Qu Univ Ont BA 58. Wycl Coll Tor LTh 61. **d** 60 Bp Hunt for Tor **p** 61 Bp Snell for Tor. C of Grace Ch Tor 60-63; Ch Ch Cathl Montr 63-65; R of Rawdon 65-66; Chap R Vic Hosp Montr 66-69; Dioc Chap and C of St Jo Cathl Belize Dio Br Hond 69-70; on leave. *436 Castlefield Avenue, Toronto, Ont., Canada.*

BROWN, Robert William Spoor. St Jo Coll Winnipeg. **d** 49 **p** 50 Koot. C of Kelowna 49-54; V of Woodsdale 54-58; Exam Chap to Bp of Koot 58-72; R of Cranbrook 58-64; Dean and R of St Sav Pro-Cathl Nelson 64-67; Can 63-73; Dir Of Program Dio Koot 67-73; R of Kelowna 71-72. *228 Lake Avenue, Kelowna, BC, Canada.*

BROWN, Roger Lee. b 42. St D Coll Lamp BA (2nd cl Hist) 63. Univ of Lon MA 73. Wycl Hall Ox 66. **d** 68 Bp T M Hughes for Llan **p** 69 Llan. C of Dinas w Penygraig 68-70; Bargoed w Brithdir 70-72; Team V in Rectorial Benef of Glyncorrwg w Afan Vale and Cymer Afan 72-74; R 74-79; V of Tongwynlais Dio Llan from 79. *Tongwynlais Vicarage, Merthyr Road, Tongwynlais, Cardiff CF4 7LE.* (Taffs Wel 810437)

✠ **BROWN, Right Rev Ronald.** b 26. St Jo Coll Dur BA 50, Dipl Th 52. **d** 52 Burnley for Blackb **p** 53 Blackb. C of Chorley 52-56; V of Whittle-le-Woods 56-61; St Thos Halliwell 61-69; R of Ashton-under-Lyne 69-74; RD of Ashton-under-Lyne 69-74; Cons Ld Bp Suffr of Birkenhead in York Minster 1 May 74 by Abp of York; Bps of Ches, Man, Ripon, Southw, Blackb, Bradf and Carl; Bps Suffr of Hulme, Stockport, Penrith, Pontefract, Knaresborough, Doncaster and Whitby. *Trafford House, Victoria Crescent, Queen's Park, Chester.* (Chester 675895)

BROWN, Ronald Glyn. b 34. Lich Th Coll 70. **d** 73 **p** 74 Sarum. C of St Paul Weymouth 73-78; Swanage w Herston (in c of St Mark) 78-79; P-in-c of Bromham Dio Sarum 79-80; R (w Chittoe and Sand Lane) from 80; P-in-c of Chittoe 79-80. *Bromham Rectory, Chippenham, Wilts.* (Bromham 850322)

BROWN, Ronald Murray. b 39. St Barn Coll Adel 75. **d** and **p** 77 Perth. C of Subiaco 77-79; R of Moora Dio Perth from 79. *Box 166, Moora, W Australia 6510.* (095-41 1154)

✠ **BROWN, Right Rev Russel Featherstone.** Bp's Univ Lennox BA 33, DCL 61. McGill Univ Montr DD 68. **d** 33 **p** 34 Montr. C of Ch Ch Cathl Montr 33-36; Miss at Fort St John 36-40; R of Sherbrooke 40-54; Can of Queb 48-54; Archd of Queb and R of St Matt Queb 54-60; R of Levis 55-60; Cons Ld Bp of Queb in H Trin Cathl Queb 30 Nov 60 by Abp of Montr; Bps of NS; Ott; Fred; Bp Coadj of NS; and Asst Bp of Newfld; res 71; L to Offic Dio Papua 71-75; Asst Bp of Montr from 76. *3473 University Street, Montreal, Quebec, Canada.*

BROWN, Canon Samuel. b 12. St Jo Coll Dur BA 37, MA 40. **d** 38 Pontefract for Wakef **p** 39 Wakef. C of Mt Pellon 38-41; Ackworth 41-44; CF (EC) 44-47; Hon CF 47; C of Leeds 47-49; Lect of H Trin Leeds 48-49; V of Osmondthorpe Leeds 49-55; Meanwood 55-64; R of Culworth (w Sulgrave and Thorpe Mandeville from 78) Dio Pet from 64; Eydon 64-78; RD of Brackley from 70; Can (non-res) of Pet from 73. *Culworth Rectory, Banbury, Oxon.* (Sulgrave 383)

BROWN, Simon Nicolas Danton. b 37. Clare Coll Cam BA 61, MA 65. Linc Th Coll 63. **d** 64 **p** 65 S'wark. C of Lambeth 64-66; Chap and Warden Lady Margaret Hall Settlement Lambeth 66-72; C-in-c of St Mary w H Trin Southn 72-73; Team V of Southn (City Centre) 73-79; R of Bow Brickhill w Gt and L Brickhill 79-81. *Address temp unknown.*

BROWN, Stanley Frederick. **d** 63 Bp Sambell for Melb **p** 64 Melb. C of Hawthorn 63-64; Surrey Hills 64-65; Brighton 66-68; Dept of Evang and Extens Dio Melb 69-71; Perm to Offic Dio Melb from 71. *20 Rose Street, Bentleigh, Vic, Australia 3204.* (03-97 5273)

BROWN, Stanley George. b 19. Bp's Coll Cheshunt 66. **d** 67 Barking for Chelmsf **p** 68 Chelmsf. C of All SS Shrub End 67-71; R of Dengie w Asheldham Dio Chelmsf from 71; V of Tillingham Dio Chelmsf from 71. *Tillingham Vicarage, Southminster, Essex, CMO 7TW.* (Tillingham 203)

BROWN, Stephen James. b 44. Univ of Bradf BSc (Soc Sc) 69. Westcott Ho Cam 71. **d** 72 **p** 73 Newc T. C of Seaton Hirst 72-75; Marton-in-Cleveland 75-77; Dioc Youth Officer Dio Dur from 77. *24 Monks Crescent, Durham* (Durham 61691)

BROWN, Sunday Iwo Anyim. b 30. Trin Coll Umuahia 76. **d** 76 Nig Delta. d Dio Nig Delta. *St Andrew's Parsonage, PMB 5559, Diobu, Port Harcourt, Rivers State, Nigeria.*

BROWN, Terry Michael. b 44. Univ of Kalamazoo BA 66. Trin Coll Tor MDiv 74. **d** 74 **p** 75 Fred. C of Moncton 74-75; Lect Bp Patteson Th Centre Honiara and L to Offic Dio Centr Melan from 75. *c/o Bishop Patteson Theological College, Honiara, Guadalcanal, Solomon Islands.*

BROWN, Thomas John. b 43. St Jo Coll Auckld LTh 72, STh 76. **d** 72 **p** 73 Ch Ch. C of St Alb Ch Ch 72-74; St Jas Gtr Leic 74-76; V of U Clutha 76-79; Roslyn Dio Dun from 79. *373 High Gate, Roslyn, Dunedin, NZ.* (740-240)

BROWN, Thomas William Griffith. Univ of Queensld BE 58, MEngSc 60. St Mich Coll Crafers 60. ACT ThL 63. M SSM 63. **d** 64 **p** 65 Adel. L to Offic Dio Adel 64-65 and 67-72; Dio Perth 65-66; Warden St Mich Coll Crafers 69-72; L to Offic Dio C & Goulb 73-75; Vice-Prin St Francis Th Coll Milton 75-76; P-in-c of St Alb Canberra Dio C & Goulb from 76. *Box 421, Woden, ACT, Australia 2606.*

BROWN, Victor Charles. b 31. SOC 67. **d** 71 **p** 72 Ex. C of Pinhoe 71-73; Egg Buckland 73-74; Oakdale 74-77; R of Old Trafford Dio Man from 77. *St Hilda's Rectory, Kings Road, Firswood, Manchester, M16 0JD.* (061-881 9332)

BROWN, Victor Frederick George. Sarum Th Coll 64. **d** 66 **p** 67 Win. C of St Pet and St Paul w All SS Southn 66-67; Mackay 67-68; P-in-c of Tully 69-72. *c/o PO Box 7, Salisbury, Rhodesia.*

BROWN, Wallace. b 44. Oakhill Th Coll 77. **d** 79 **p** 80 Leic. C of Oadby Dio Leic from 79. *9 Malton Drive, Oadby, Leicester.*

BROWN, Walter Bertram John. b 09. K Coll Lon 43. **d** 43 **p** 44 Glouc. C of St Mark Glouc 43-47; Chap Glouc Dioc Assoc for Deaf and Dumb 43-47; Chap Sussex Deaf and Dumb Assoc 47-50; Chap in N Lon to R Assoc in Aid of Deaf and Dumb 50-53; Ex and Devon Miss to Adult Deaf and Dumb 53-73; E Sussex Branch for the Deaf and Dumb 73-75. *31 Knowle Road, Fairlight, Hastings, Sussex, TN35 4AT.* (Pett 3347)

BROWN, Warren Wafforn. See Bryden-Brown, Warren.

BROWN, Wilfrid George. **d** 53 **p** 54 Athab. Miss at Fort Chipewyan 53-56; Pouce Coupe 59-61; Kitwanga 61-67; Fort St John 67-70; I of Ocean Falls 71-72; on leave 73-75; R of Telegraph Creek 75-79; Old Crow Dio Yukon from 79. *Rectory, Old Crow, Yukon Y0B 1N0, Canada.*

BROWN, William Arthur James. ACT ThL 41. **d** 41 **p** 42 Newc. C of Islington NSW 41-43; R of Adaminaby 43-45. C of Albury 45-47; Chap RAAF 47-52; R of Murrumburrah 52-54; St D Brisb 54-59; Casino 59-66; Lambton 66-82. *18 Morehead Street, Lambton, NSW, Australia 2299.*

BROWN, William Martyn. b 14. Pemb Coll Cam BA 36, MA 47. Nor Ordin Course 74. **d** 76 **p** 77 Nor (APM). C of Thornage 76-77; P-in-c of Field Dalling w Saxlingham Dio Nor from 77. *Lodge Cottage, Field Dalling, Holt, Norf.* (Binham 403)

BROWN, William Stewart. b 48. Oregon State Univ BA 71. Ch Div Sch of Pacific Calif 76. **d** 76 Calif **p** 78 Bran. In Amer Ch 76-77; C of Cathl Ch of St Matt Bran 78-79; I of Vegreville Dio Edmon from 79. *Box 1086, Vegreville, Alta, Canada.*

BROWN-BERESFORD, Thomas Savin Stuart. Ridley Coll Melb ACT ThL 40. **d** 40 **p** 43 Melb. C of St Cuthb E Brunswick 40-43; Lutwyche Brisb 43-47; R of Nanango 47-51; Hon Miss Chap 51-59; R of St D Chelmer and Graceville Brisb 59-62; Warwick 62-68; St Matt Holland Pk Brisb 68-73; Perm to Offic Dio Brisb 73-79; Dio Graft from 76. *c/o Carramar, College Road, Stanthorpe, Qld., Australia 4380.*

BROWNBRIDGE, Bernard Alan. b 19. N-W Ordin Course 74. **d** 77 **p** 78 York (APM). C of All SS Huntington York 77-80; V of Sand Hutton Dio York from 80. *Vicarage, Sand Hutton, York, YO4 1LB.* (Flaxton Moor 289)

BROWNE, Amos Albert. b 21. Stout State Univ of Wisc USA MSc 73. **d** 80 Trin. C of H Sav Curepe Dio Trin from 80. *67 Maloney Street, San Juan, Trinidad, WI.*

BROWNE, Archie Lynn. **d** 61 **p** 62 Melb. Asst Chap St John's Home Cant 61-62; C of St Columb Hawthorn 62-63; V of Leopold 63-68; St Mark Reservoir 68-72; Chap and Supt Youth Hostels for Boys and Girls Melb from 72-77; I of Mt Duneed Dio Melb from 77. *20 Munday Street, Torquay, Vic, Australia 3228.* (052-61 2329)

BROWNE, Arnold Samuel. b 52. St Jo Coll Ox BA 73, MA 77. Westcott Ho Cam 76. **d** 78 **p** 79 Guildf. C of Esher 78-81; Worplesdon Dio Guildf from 81. *St Alban's House, Wood Street Village, Nr Guildford, Surrey.* (Worplesdon 235136)

BROWNE, Arthur Donal. b 11. MC 44. St Edm Hall Ox BA 34, MA 54, Dipl Th 35. Wycl Hall Ox 34. **d** 35 **p** 36 Lon. C of St Mary Bryanston Square 35-40; CF (EC) 40-45; R of St Mary Bryanston Square 46-62; Chap Samaritan Hosp Marylebone Road 49-62; V of St Jude S Kens 62-78; P-in-c of Lydgate w Ousden and Cowlinge 80-81. *Yew Tree Cottage, Bury Lane, Lydgate, Newmarket, Suffolk.*

BROWNE, Aubrey Robert Caulfeild. b 31. Moore Th Coll Syd 54. **d** 55 **p** 56 Syd. C of St Thos N Syd 55-59; R of N

Balmain 59-65; C of Benalla 65-66; R of S Townsville 67-71; on staff of USPG from 72; Hon C of St Steph Gloucester Road Kens Dio Lon from 79. *c/o USPG, 15 Tufton Street, SW1.*

BROWNE, Very Rev Cecil Charles Wyndham. b 16. TCD BA (1st cl Ment and Mor Phil Mod) 38, Abp King Pri 39, Downes Pri 40, Div Test (1st cl) 40, BD 44. **d** 40 **p** 41 Arm. C of Portadown 40-42; St Ann Dub 42-47; R of St John Sligo w Knockarea Dio Elph from 47; RD of N Elphin from 53; Can and Exam Chap to Bp of Kilm from 61; Dean of Elph and Ard from 67; Regr from 78. *Rectory, Strandhill Road, Sligo, Irish Republic.* (071 2263)

BROWNE, Cecil Harold Bruce. Trin Coll Dub BA 36, MA 63. **d** 36 Lim for Arm **p** 37 Derry for Arm. C of Arm 36-38; St Nich Galway 38-39; I of Knappagh U 39-45; Newtowngore w Corrawallen and Drumreilly 45-51; Collon w Tullyallen 51-64; R of Aghabog U (w Ematris and Rockcomy from 67) 64-79. *c/o Dartrey Rectory, Cootehill, Cavan, Irish Republic.*

BROWNE, Charles. b 1895. Edin Th Coll 45. **d** 46 **p** 47 Glas. [f Presbyterian Min] C of St Marg Glas 46-48; R of Shirland 48-52; V of Apethorpe w Woodnewton 52-54; R of Watlington 54-57; R of Runcton S w Holme and Wallington 54-57; Perm to Offic Dio Ox 57-70 and from 73; C of Shirley 70-73. *2 Crouch Street, Banbury, Oxon.* (Banbury 56170)

BROWNE, Clifford Jesse. b 24. Selw Coll Cam BA 48, MA 51. Chich Th Coll. **d** 50 **p** 51 Portsm. C of St Pet Southsea 50-54; CF 54-79; DACG 69; ACG 75-79; Hon Chap to HM the Queen from 78; P-in-c of Bickleigh W Dio Ex 79-80; V from 80. *Vicarage, Leat Walk, Bickleigh, Roborough, Plymouth, Devon.* (Plymouth 775903)

BROWNE, Cyril Franklin. Coll Ho Ch Ch. **d** 57 **p** 59 Wel. C of All SS Palmerston N 57-60; V of Hunterville 60-63; Ohakune w Wainuiarua 63-67; V of Ruapehu Par Distr 64-67; U Hutt 67-73; St Matt Palmerston N 73-81; Naenae-Epuni Dio Wel from 81. *32 Gibson Crescent, Lower Hutt, NZ.*

BROWNE, Cyril Theodore Martin. b 12. Tyndale Hall Bris 30. **d** 35 **p** 36 Lon. C of Em Holloway 35-38; Ch Ch Finchley 38-41; Broadwater Worthing 41-43; PC of St Matt Muswell Hill 43-50; V of Clerkenwell 50-62; H Trin w St Paul Greenwich 62-74; R of Tilston 74-78; V of Shocklach 74-78; Min of St Mary Chap Castle Street Reading Dio Ox from 78. *151 St Saviours Road, Reading, Berks, R61 6EP.* (Reading 57364)

BROWNE, Donovan Vincent. b 38. Huron Coll Ont BMin 71. **d** 70 Hur for Rupld **p** 71 Tor. I of Fort George 71-74; Walkerton 74-76; Blackfoot Miss 76-80; Sarcee 79-80; Blairmore Dio Calg from 80. *Box 1044, Blairmore, Calgary, Alta, Canada.*

BROWNE, Edwin Stafford. ALCD 33. **d** 33 **p** 34 St E. C of St Jo Bapt Ipswich 33-37; St Luke Maidenhead 37-39; V of Tetney 39-53; Holton-le-Clay 49-53; R of Blaxhall w Stratford St Andr and Farnham 53-73. *The Chymes, Kettleby Lane, Wrawby, Lincs.*

BROWNE, Geoffrey Morrison. Ridley Coll Melb ACT ThL 45. **d** 46 **p** 47 Melb. C of St John E Malvern and Chap Malvern Gr Sch Dio Melb 46-50; C of Wang Cathl and Asst Master of H Trin Hostel for Boys Wang 50; Chap Launceston Gr Sch 51-52; R of Wodonga and P-in-c of Bethanga 52-62; Dom Chap to Bp of Wang 59-63; I of Coburg 62-72; H Advent Malvern Dio Melb from 72. *27 Wattletree Road, Malvern, Vic, Australia 3143.* (03-50 1523)

BROWNE, George Barry. Ridley Coll Melb ACT ThL 69. **d** and **p** 68 St Arn. C of Mildura 68-71; R of Sea Lake 71-73; V of Tyrrell 73; R of Broadford 73-77; R of Myrtleford 77-81; Chap in Dept of Industr Miss Melb from 81. *4 Fosters Road, Keilor Park, Vic, Australia 3036.*

BROWNE, Herbert Keith. St Jo Coll Morpeth 58. ACT ThL 59. **d** 60 **p** 61 Graft. C of Port Macquarie 60-62; Casino 62-63; Youth Sec Austr Bd of Miss 63-66; State Sec NSW 67-70; L to Offic Dio Syd 64-70; C-in-c of St Pet Bundoora 71-72; I 72-75; Bennettswood Dio Melb from 75. *44 Station Street, Burwood, Vic, Australia 3125.* (03-288 1029)

BROWNE, Ian Cameron. b 51. St Cath Coll Ox BA 74, MA 79. Fitzwm Coll Cam BA (Th) 76, MA 80. Ridley Hall Cam 76. **d** 77 **p** 78 Glouc. C of Ch Ch Cheltenham 77-80; St Chad Shrewsbury and Asst Chap Shrewsbury Sch Dio Lich from 80. *17 Crescent Place, Town Walls, Shrewsbury, SY1 1TQ.* (Shrewsbury 55564)

BROWNE, Ian James Langlands. b 11. MBE 72. Worc Ordin Coll 58. **d** 59 Worc **p** 75 St A. C of St Geo Kidderminster 58-61; L to Offic Dio Bradf 61-72; C of Ruthin w Llanrhydd 72-80; Perm to Offic Dio St A from 81. *4 Dyffryn, Pwll-Glas, Ruthin, Clwyd.* (Ruthin 3188)

BROWNE, John Burnell. b 15. MC 45. Qu Coll Cam 2nd cl Eng Trip pt i 35, BA (2nd cl Hist Trip pt ii) 36 MA 40. Westcott Ho Cam 46. **d** 47 **p** 48 Ripon. C of Leeds 47-52; V of St Jo Evang Wortley 52-59; Barnard Castle 59-71; RD of Barnard Castle 59-71; V of Billingham 71-80. *40 Slack top, Heptonstall, Hebden Bridge, W Yorks, HX7 7HA.*

BROWNE, Laurence Edward. b 1887. Late Scho of SS Coll Cam 1st cl Nat Sc Trip pt i 08, BA 09, 1st cl Th Trip pt i 10, pt ii 11 Scholefield Pri and Carus Gr Test Pri 11. Hulsean Pri 12, MA 13, BD 20, DD 34. Univ of Man MA 45. **d** 11 **p** 12 Pet. C of St Matt Leic 11-13; Lect St Aug Coll Cant 13-14; Fell 14-20; Lect Bp's Coll Calc 21-25; Exam Chap to Bp of Calc 24-25; furlough 25-26 and 34-35; Spec Miss SPG 26-29; Lect Henry Martyn Sch Lah 30-34; Select Pr Univ of Ox 35 and 47; Cam 36; R of Gayton 35-46; Exam Chap to Bp of Pet 37-51; Prof of Comp Relig Univ of Man 41-46; Exam Chap to Bp of Ripon 46-57; Prof of Th Univ of Leeds 46-52; Prof (Emer) from 52; V of Shadwell 52-57; Hulsean Lect Univ of Cam from 54; V of Highbrook 57-64. *5 Chichester Drive West, Saltdean, Brighton, Sussex BN2 8SH.* (Brighton 34315)

BROWNE, Norman Desmond. b 21. Trin Coll Dub BA (2nd cl Ment and Mor Sc Mod) 42, Div Test (2nd cl) 43, BD 46, MA 61. **d** 44 **p** 45 Dub. C of Grangegorman 44-47; Ch Ch Leeson Pk Dub 47-59; Upton w Chalvey Slough 59-61; R of Hedgerley 61-80. *24 Glenageary Woods, Dun Laoghaire, Co Dublin, Irish Republic.* (Dub 804061)

BROWNE, Ross Douglas. b 48. Univ of Auckld BA 71. St Jo Coll Auckld 71. **d** 72 **p** 73 Auckld. C of Kohimarama 72-77; P-in-c of Ranui Distr 77-78; C of St Matt Auckld 78-80; Chap Dilworth Sch Auckld from 80. *32 Mount St John Avenue, Epsom, Auckland 2, NZ.*

BROWNE, William Eric. b 34. Trin Coll Dub BA (2nd cl Hebr and Or Lang Mod) 60, MA 75. Edin Th Coll 61. **d** 62 **p** 63 Drom. C of Shankill Lurgan 62-64; St Donard Belf 64-66; Donaghcloney w Waringstown 66-68; Dep Sec Leprosy Miss Belf 68-71; Sec Leprosy Miss Engl and Wales 71-75; P-in-c of Fulmer 75-80; Tutor Div Hostel Dub from 80. *Divinity Hostel, Braemor Park, Rathgar, Dublin, Irish Republic.* (Dublin 975506)

BROWNE, William Harkness. b 06. Jes Coll Ox 2nd cl Cl Mods 27, BA (2nd cl Engl) 28, MA 36. KCL 37. **d** 38 **p** 39 Lon. C of St Mary Woolnoth w St Mary Woolchurch Lon 38-39; Chap RNVR 39-45; Chap RN 46-61; Sen Chap Miss to Seamen Port of Lon 61-64; V of Stalisfield w Otterden 64-73. *7 Champs Beulai, Alderney, CI.* (Alderney 2403)

BROWNELL, Edward. Trin Coll Dub BA and Abp King Pri 15, Div Test (1st cl) 16. **d** 16 **p** 17 Arm. C of Dundalk 16-20; Armagh 20-24; C-in-c of Ballymoyer 24-27; I of Woods Chapel 27-39; R of Carnteel 39-71; RD of Tynan 50-60; Preb of Ballymore in Arm Cathl 60-71. *The Hill, Stackallen, Navan, Co Meath, Irish Republic.*

BROWNHILL, John George. b 46. Wilfred Laurier Univ Ont BA 77. Trin Coll Tor MDiv 79. **d** 79 Bp Read for Tor **p** 80 Tor. C of All SS Peterboro Dio Tor from 79. *235 Rubidge & Sherbrook Sts, Peterboro, Ont, Canada, K9J 3N9.*

BROWNING, Canon Denys James. Keble Coll Ox BA 29, MA 59. Coll of Resurr Mirfield 38. **d** 40 **p** 41 Lich. C of Oxley 40-42; CF (EC) 42-47; (Men in Disp 43); Hon CF from 47; C of St Aid Leeds 48-50; CF (TA) 49-50; Hd of Bush Bro of St Paul Charleville Queensld 50-55; Area Sec SPG Dios Ox and Cov 55-59; Commiss Brisb from 55; Chap Mart Mem Sch Agenehambo Dio New Guinea 59-70; P-in-c of Sefoa 70-72; Wanigela 72-78; Hon Prov Can of Papua from 78, L to Offic Dio New Guinea Is 80-81; Dio Waik from 81. *RD9, Frankton, NZ.*

BROWNING, Canon George Henry. b 06. OBE 46. St Aug Coll Cant 28. Univ of Dur LTh 32. **d** 32 Bp Palmer for Glouc **p** 33 Glouc. C of Dursley 32-34; All SS Cheltm 34-38; PC of St Paul Penzance 38-45; CF 39-45 (Men in Disp 45); R of Wyck Rissington 45-46; L Rissington 45-46; Benington 46-53; Turvey 53-56; V of St Geo Edgbaston 56-71; Hon Can of Birm 69-71; Can (Emer) from 71; L to Offic Dio Worc from 71; Chap of Laslett's Almshouses Worc 74-80. *43 Camp Hill Road, Battenhall, Worcester, WR5 2HE.* (Worc 355947)

BROWNING, George Victor. St Jo Coll Morpeth 63. ACT ThL (1st cl) 66. **d** 66 **p** 67 Armid. C of Inverell 66-68; St Pet Cathl, Armid 68-69; V of Warialda 69-73; Vice-Warden St Jo Coll Morpeth 73-74; Actg Warden 74-75; R of Singleton Dio Newc 76-80 and from 81; on leave 80-81. *Rectory, High Street, Singleton, NSW, Australia 2330.*

BROWNING, John Russell. **d** and **p** 74 Armid. P-in-c of Nundle 74-77; L to Offic Dio Newc from 77. *37 Irawan Crescent, Nelson Bay, NSW, Australia 2315.*

BROWNING, John William. b 36. Univ of Keele BA 61. Ripon Hall Ox 61. **d** 63 **p** 64 Lich. C of Berkswich w Walton 63-66; Chap Monyhull Hosp Birm 67-71; Wharncliffe Hosp Sheff 71-78; Middlewood Hosp Sheff from 71. *8 Rippon Road, Sheffield, S6 4ND.* (Sheff 343740)

BROWNING, Julian. b 51. St Jo Coll Cam BA 72, MA 76. Ripon Coll Cudd 77. **d** 80 **p** 81 Kens for Lon. C of St John Notting Hill 80-81; St Mary w St Pet The Boltons Kens Dio Lon from 81. *13A Cranley Gardens, SW7.* (01-370 2270)

BROWNING, Lionel Beaver. ACT ThL 38. Ch Coll Hobart 36. **d** 39 Tas **p** 43 Gippsld for Tas. C of Burnie 39-40; on leave with AIF 39-43; R of Lilydale 43-44; Buckland 44-48;

Sheffield Tas 48-52; P-in-c of St Leonards 56-59; R of Cressy 59-64; Brighton 64-69; RD Central Deanery 65-69; L to Offic Dio Tas from 70. *17 Roslyn Avenue, Kingston Beach 7151, Tasmania.* (002-29 6820)

BROWNING, Martin Charles. b 06. Keble Coll Ox BA 30. Cudd Coll 31. **d** 31 **p** 32 Wakef. C of Penistone 31-36; Almondbury 36-40; R of Kingsdon (w Podymore-Milton from 43) 40-48; V of N Curry 48-55; Sampford Arundel 55-67. *4 Orchard Close, Woodbury, Exeter, Devon, EX5 1ND.* (Woodbury 32615)

BROWNING, Michael Charles. b 06. Keble Coll Ox BA 33, MA 47. St Steph Ho Ox 46. **d** 48 **p** 49 Truro. C of Redruth 48-50; Perranzabuloe 50-52; V of Gwennap 52-58; R of St Ervan w St Eval 58-68; C-in-c of St Breward 68-74; Perm to Offic Dio Truro from 74. *Riverside, St Breward, Bodmin, Cornw, PL30 4LY.* (Bodmin 850410)

BROWNING, Canon Richard Geoffrey Claude. b 25. Selw Coll Cam BA 50, MA 55. Univ of Lon BD and ALCD 53. **d** 53 **p** 54 Chelmsf. C of Walthamstow 53-56; V of St Paul E Ham 56-65; Old Hill Dio Worc from 65; Hon Can of Worc from 77. *35 Beeches Road, Rowley Regis, Warley, W Midl.* (021-559 7407)

BROWNING, Robert Frank. b 11. K Coll Warm. **d** 57 Guildf **p** 58 Kingston T for Guildf. C of All SS, Headley, Bordon 57-59; C-in-c of Lightwater Conv Distr Guildf 59-63; V 63-76; Perm to Offic Dio Guildf from 76. *Braeholme, Rectory Lane, Windlesham, Surrey.*

BROWNING, Ronald Mark. b 45. Austrn Nat Univ Canberra BA 68. Univ of Edin BD 72. Yale Univ Conn STM 73. Edin Th Coll 69. **d** 74 **p** 75 Melb. C of St Steph Mt Waverley 74-76; Glenroy 76-77; H Trin Kens Dio Melb from 77. *21 Wight Street, Kensington, Vic, Australia 3031.* (376 1084)

BROWNING, Thomas Clive. b 35. Dipl Th (Lon) 65, BD (Lon) 67. Wycl Hall Ox 63. **d** 67 Dunwich for St E **p** 68 St E. C of St Jo Bapt Ipswich 67-69; Chap Scargill Ho Kettlewell 69-70; C of Downend 70-73; Hagley 73-76; Asst Master Bay House Sch Gosport from 77. *81 Oval Gardens, Alverstoke, Gosport, Hants.* (Gosport 84738)

BROWNING, Canon Wilfrid Robert Francis. b 18. Late Squire Scho at Ch Ch Ox BA (2nd cl Th) 40, MA 44, BD 49. Cudd Coll 40. **d** 41 **p** 42 Pet. C of Towcester w Easton Neston 41-44; Ch Ch Woburn Square Lon 44-46; Chap of Heswall Nautical School 46-48; St Deiniol's Libr Hawarden 46-48; Min of St Richard Conv Distr Hove 48-51; R of Gt Haseley 51-59; Lect at Cudd Coll 51-59; and 65-70; Ed *Bulletin Anglican* 55-60; Can Res of Blackb 59-65; Warden of Whalley Abbey 59-63; Exam Chap to Bp of Blackb 60-71; Dir of Post-Ordin Tr Dio Blackb 62-65; Dir of Ordins and Post-Ordin Tr Dio Ox from 65; Res Can of Ch Ch Cathl Ox from 65; Exam Chap to Bp of Ox from 65; Lect Wycliffe Hall Ox 67-69; Exam Chap to Bp of Man 70-78; Select Pr Univ of Ox 72 and 81; Univ of Ex 73; Dir of Ox Tr Course for NSM from 72; M Gen Syn from 73. *70 Yarnells Hill, Oxford, OX2 9BG.* (Oxford 721330)

BROWNING, William Frank. b 1889. Late Exhib of Selw Coll Cam BA 11, MA 34. Leeds Cl Scho 11. **d** 12 Carl **p** 19 St Alb. C of St John Keswick 12-14; served RAMC 14-19; C of Kempston 19-20; Miss at Banks I 21-22; Dio Bath 22-24; Siota 25-33; C of Andover 33-34; V of W Hyde Herts 34-37; Worth Matravers 37-43; R of Lichborough 43-50; St Thos St Kitts 50-51; St Pet St Kitts 51-56; C-in-c of Tysoe w Compton Wynyates 56-64; Perm to Offic Dio Pet from 65. *Parish House, Greatworth, Banbury, Oxon, OX17 2DX.* (Banbury 711532)

BROWNLESS, Brian Paish. b 25. TD 72. Keble Coll Ox BA and MA 50. Wells Th Coll 50. **d** 52 **p** 53 Man. C of St Aid Man 52-54; Chorlton-cum-Hardy 54-56; Swinton 56-58; V of St Steph Elton 58-66; CF (TA) 60-66; CF (TAVR) 66-72; USPG Area Sec Dio Lich and L to Offic Dio Lich 66-77; R of Yoxall Dio Lich from 77. *Yoxall Rectory, Burton-on-Trent, DE13 8PD.* (Yoxall 472528)

BROWNLESS, Philip Paul Stanley. b 19. Selw Coll Cam BA 41, MA 45. Ridley Hall Cam. **d** 47 **p** 48 Chelmsf. C of Prittlewell 47-50; CF (TA) 50-62; Min of Distr Ch of St Luke Prittlewell 50-54; Chap and Asst Master Lambrook Sch 54-56; Hd Master 56-71; V of Heckfield w Mattingley Dio Win 71-74; R (w Rotherwick) from 74. *Rectory, Mattingley, Basingstoke, Hants, RG27 8LF.* (Heckfield 385)

BROWNLIE, Robert Lloyd. b 47. Univ of Manit BA 73. Trin Coll Tor MDiv 77. **d** 76 **p** 77 Rupld. C of Selkirk Area in c of St Andr Group 76-78; R of St Andr, Lockport and Cloverdale, Selkirk Dio Rupld from 78. *St Thomas Rectory, Lockport, Manit, R0C 1W0. Canada.*

BROWNRIGG, Robert Graham. b 09. Tyndale Hall Bris and Th Coll Clifton 34. **d** 38 Ches **p** 40 Dur. C of Bebington 38; Shildon 39-43; V of E Harsley 46-55; Ingleby Arncliffe 46-55; V of White Notley 55-66; R of Faulkbourne 55-66; V of Greenstead Green Dio 66-74. *Sunnyholme, Great Bentley, Colchester, Essex.* (Colchester 250316)

BROWNRIGG, Canon Ronald Allen. b 19. Em Coll Cam BA 47, MA 50. Westcott Ho Cam 47. **d** 49 **p** 50 York. C of Beverley Minster 49-51; Chap and Sub-Dean of Colleg Ch of St Geo Mart Jer 51-54; Min of St Luke Stanmore Win 54-60; R of Bletchingley 60-74; Surr from 63; V of Petersham Dio S'wark from 74; Hon Can of S'wark Cathl from 78. *Vicarage, Sudbrook Lane, Petersham, Surrey, TW10 7AT.* (01-940 2488)

BROWNSELL, John Kenneth. b 48. Hertford Coll Ox BA (Jurispr) 69 (Th) 72. Cudd Coll 70. **d** 73 Kens for Lon **p** 74 Lon. C of All SS Notting Hill Dio Lon 73-76; Team V from 76. *Vicarage, Powis Gardens, W11.* (01-727 5919)

BRUCE, David Allison. b 48. Univ of Mass Amherst BA 71. Univ of Edin BD 77. **d** 77 NS **p** 77 Bp Hatfield for NS. C of Port Hill 77; R 78-80; L to Offic Dio Edmon from 80. *1804, 11135-83rd Avenue, Edmonton, Alta, Canada.*

BRUCE, David Ian. b 47. Univ of Wales (Cardiff) Dipl Th 73. St Mich AA Coll Llan 70. **d** 73 **p** 74 Birm. C of St Benedict Bordesley 73-74; Llanishen and Lisvane 74-80; V of St Steph Canley Dio Cov from 80. *St Stephen's Vicarage, Glebe Close, Canley, Warws.* (Cov 469016)

BRUCE, Francis Bernard. Trin Coll Ox BA (3rd cl Mod Hist) 52, MA 56. Westcott Ho Cam 52. **d** 54 **p** 55 Man. C of Bury 54-59; Sherborne Abbey (in c of St Paul Sherborne) 59-61; R of Croston Dio Blackb from 61. *Croston Rectory, Preston, Lancs.* (Coston 228)

BRUCE, Henry Douglas. b 1900. Keble Coll Ox Squire Scho 20, BA (3rd cl Th) 22. St Steph Ho Ox 22. M SSJE 40. **d** 23 **p** 24 Ox. C of All SS Boyne Hill 23-26; Andros Nass 26-31; P-in-c 31-34; C of St Marg Aber 35-37; Perm to Offic Dio Ox 37-42; L to Offic from 42; Perm to Offic Dio Edin 46-47 and 51-54. *32 Marston Street, Oxford.*

BRUCE, Ian Frederick Percival. b 43. ACT Th Dip 80. St Barn Coll Adel 78. **d** 80 **p** 81 The Murray. C of Christies Beach Dio The Murray from 80. *41 William Road, Christies Beach, S Australia 5165.* (08-382 2556)

BRUCE, John. b 26. **d** 50 Dur for Fred **p** 51 Fred. C of St Luke St John 50-52; R of Coverdale w Hillsborough 52-58; Hampton NB 58-63; V of Broughton Moor 63-66; St Herbert, Currock w St Steph, Carl 66-74; P-in-c of St Geo Kendal Dio Carl 74-76; V from 76. *St George's Vicarage, Kendal, Cumbria, LA9 7AN.* (Kendal 23039)

BRUCE, Leslie Barton. b 23. Univ of Liv MB, ChB 48. **d** 71 Warrington for Liv **p** 72 Liv (APM). C of H Trin Wavertree Dio Liv from 71. *3 Childwall Park Avenue, Liverpool, L16 0JE.* (051-722 2905)

BRUCE, Lewis Stewart. b 07. Knutsford Test Sch 33. Sarum Th Coll 34. **d** 37 **p** 38 Blackb. C of St Paul Adlington 37-40; CF (R of O) from 39; CF (EC) 40-47; Hon CF from 47; Min of Conv Distr of Ascen Torrisholme 47-54; V of Brockworth 54-76; P-in-c of Bourton-on-the-Hill 76-78; Elmore w Longney Dio Glouc from 78. *Sarum House, 1 Rylands, Tuffley, Glos, GL4 0QA.* (Gloucester 414292)

BRUCE, Randolph Frederick. b 47. Univ of Manit BA 70. Trin Coll Tor MDiv 73. **d** 73 **p** 74 Rupld. C of St Phil Montr 73-75; I of Chateauguay 76-79; R of Bedford Dio Montr from 79. *Box 1251, Bedford, PQ, Canada.* (514-248 3923)

BRUERE, Robert Arthur. b 51. Univ of Cant NZ BEng 73. Univ of Otago BD 79. St Jo Coll Auckld 76. **d** 78 **p** 79 Waik. C of St Mary New Plymouth Dio Waik from 78. *43b Fulford Street, New Plymouth, NZ.* (87-338)

BRUMPTON, Canon John Charles Kenyon. b 16. Selw Coll Cam BA 38, MA 42. Linc Th Coll 38. **d** 40 **p** 41 Linc. C of All SS Grimsby 40-44; Rashcliffe 44-47; V of Hepworth 47-52; Cudworth 52-65; Surr from 53; R of Barnsley Dio Wakef from 65; RD of Barnsley from 65; Hon Can of Wakef from 67. *30 Victoria Road, Barnsley, Yorks, S70 2BU.* (Barnsley 2270)

BRUMWELL, Francis John Thomas. b 33. Lich Th Coll 57. **d** 61 **p** 62 Birm. C of St Geo Birm 61-63; St Mark W Gorton 63-65; V of Calderbrook 65-73; Bradley, Staffs Dio Lich from 73; P-in-c of St Mary Bilston 75-78. *Vicarage, King Street, Bradley, Bilston, W Midl.* (Bilston 42160)

BRUNDLE, David Henry. b 14. **d** 77 Tas. C of St John New Town Dio Tas from 77. *30 Highfield Street, Moonah 7009, Tasmania.* (002-28 4311)

BRUNDRITT, Cyril. b 1897. AKC 34. **d** 34 **p** 35 S'wark. C of St Andr Catford 34-38; Perm to Offic at St Andr Mottingham 38-39; C of Clapham 39-44; V of St Aug S Bermondsey 44-59; Surr 56-59; R of Grateley w Quarley 59-66. *The Old Malthouse, Middle Wallop, Stockbridge, Hants.* (Wallop 353)

BRUNING, Arthur Frederick. b 17. ALCD 54. **d** 54 **p** 55 Bradf. C of Ingrow w Hainworth 54-57; St Andr w St Thos Lambeth 57-59; Hatcham 59-62; V of Chalk 62-66; St Luke Deptford 66-72; Sporle w Gt and L Palgrave 72-81; Perm to Offic Dio Nor from 81. *3 Adams Road, Sprowston, Norwich, Norf.*

BRUNNING, David George. b 32. St D Coll Lamp BA 53.

St Mich Coll Llan. **d** 55 **p** 56 Llan. C of Llantwit Major w St Donat 55-59; Usk 59-62; V of Abercarn 62-71; V of H Trin Pontnewydd Dio Mon from 71. *Holy Trinity Vicarage, Pontnewydd, Cwmbran, Gwent, NP4 1AT.* (Cwmbran 2300)

BRUNNING, Neil. b 29. N-W Ordin Course 73. **d** 76 **p** 77 Ches. C of Cheadle Hulme Dio Ches 76-79; V from 79. *Vicarage, Church Road, Cheadle Hulme, Cheadle, Chesh, SK8 7JL.* (061-485 3455)

BRUNNING, Sidney John George. b 13. Ely Th Coll 46. **d** 49 **p** 50 Guildf. C of Aldershot 49-51; St Jas Clacton-on-Sea 51-55; R of Sunningwell 55-81. *Woodlands, Church Close, West Runton, Cromer, Norf NR27 9QY.* (W Runton 495)

BRUNO, Very Rev Allan David. b 34. K Coll Lon and Warm AKC 59. **d** 60 **p** 61 Dur. C of H Trin Darlington 60-64; St Cypr Cathl Kimb 64-65; Chap Bp's Hostel Kimb 64-65; Asst Chap Peterho Dioc Boys' Sch Rhodesia 65-70; Overseas Chap Scot Episc Ch 70-75; C of Old St Paul Edin 75-76; Dir of Miss Prov of S Africa 76-80; L to Offic Dio Johann 76-80; Dean and R of St Geo Cathl Windhoek Dio Damar from 81. *Box 65, Windhoek, SW Africa.* (061 23607)

BRUNSDEN, Maurice Calthorpe. St Paul's Coll Grahmstn. **d** 49 **p** 50 Capetn. C of St Paul Capetn 49-52; R of Calvinia 52-54; Heidelberg 54-77; V of Earley St Bart Reading Dio Ox from 78. *St Bartholomew's Vicarage, Reading, Berks, RG1 3QB.* (Reading 666064)

BRUNSDON, Thomas Kenneth. b 08. Univ of Wales BA (2nd cl Phil) 33. St Mich Coll Llan 33. **d** 34 **p** 35 Swan B. C of Knighton 34-40; V of Llandegley 40-47; Builth w Alltmawr and Llanynis 47-61; Surr 47-76; RD of Builth 55-61; Can of Hay in Brecon Cathl 58-72; Treas 72-76; V of Newton St Pet 61-76. *14 Pantygwydr Road, Uplands, Swansea, SA2 0JB.* (0792-298254)

BRUNSWICK, Robert John. b 38. St Aid Coll 60. **d** 63 **p** 64 Ches. C of Neston 63-66; St Paul Warrington 66-68; CF (TA - R of O) from 65; V of St Paul Stoneycroft 68-78; St Luke Southport Dio Liv from 78. *71 Hawkshead Street, Southport, Mer, PR9 9BT.* (Southport 38703)

BRUNT, Rupert Hoyle. b 10. Univ of Lon BA (2nd cl Hist) 31. AKC 34. **d** 34 **p** 35 Southw. C of Lowdham w Gunthorpe and Caythorpe 34-37; Mansfield 37-46 (in c 40-45); PC of St Faith N Wilford 46-51; V of Hampton Hill 51-80; Perm to Offic Dio Chich from 80. *Flat 2, Richmond Court, Richmond Road, Seaford, E Sussex, BN25 1DR.* (Seaford 894003)

BRUNTON, Heather Jacqueline. b 25. St Jo Coll Auckld LTh 67, STh 74. **d** 67 **p** 77 Auckld. C of Howick 67-72; Exam Chap to Bp of Auckld from 72; C of St Thos Tamaki 73; Grey Lynn 74-81; V of Clevedon Dio Auckld from 81. *Box 21, Clevedon, Auckland, NZ.*

BRUSSELS, Dean of Holy Trinity Cathedral. *See* Weekes, Right Rev Ambrose Walter Marcus.

BRUTTON, Robert Springett. b 14. Trin Coll Cam 2nd cl Hist Trip pt i 33, BA 34, 2nd cl Law Trip pt i 35, MA 55. Cudd Coll 54. **d** 55 **p** 56 Ox. C of Wendover 55-57; V of Radley 57-65; Sonning 65-74; Perm to Offic Dio Sarum from 80. *9 North Street, Langton Matravers, Swanage, Dorset, BH19 3HL.*

BRYAN, Cecil William. b 43. Univ of Dub BA 66, MA 73. Trin Coll Dub 66. **d** 68 **p** 69 Dub. C of Zion Ch Rathgar Dub 68-72; Chap RAF 72-75; I of Castleknock w Mulhuddart and Clonsilla Dio Dub from 75. *Rectory, Castleknock, Co Dublin, Irish Republic.* (Dublin 383083)

BRYAN, Charles Rigney. b 10. Trin Coll Dub BA 47, MA 50. Univ of Leeds MA 60. Bps' Coll Cheshunt 36. **d** 37 **p** 38 York. C of St Hilda w St Pet Middlesbrough 37-39; Helmsley (in c of Rievaulx) 39-40; CF (EC) 40-46; V of Alne w Aldwark 45-57; Cler Sec Chr Ev S in N Prov 50-58; CF (R of O) 52-65; V of Bolton-upon-Dearne 57-65; St Nath Crookesmoor Sheff 65-77; L to Offic Dio Sheff 77-78. *c/o 6 Park Place, St Leonard's, Exeter, Devon.*

BRYAN, Christopher Pavier. b 1897. AKC 36. **d** 36 **p** 37 Portsm. C of H Trin Ryde 36-39; St Barn Hove 39-40; Offg C-in-c of St Cuthman Whitehawk 40-41; V 41-48; R of Etchingham 48-51; V of St Thos Finsbury Pk 51-67; L to Offic Dio Portsm from 67. *35 Green Street, Ryde, IOW.* (Ryde 62200)

BRYAN, Leslie Harold. b 48. Div Hostel Dub 70. **d** 73 **p** 74 Cork. C of St Fin Barre Cathl Cork 73-75; Min Can from 74; R of Templebreedy w Tracton and Nohoval 75-79; CF from 79. *c/o Ministry of Defence, Bagshot Park, Bagshot, Surrey, GU19 5PL.*

BRYAN, Michael John Christopher. b 37. Late Scho of Wadh Coll Ox BA (2nd cl Engl) 58, 2nd cl Th 59, MA 63. Ripon Hall Ox 59. **d** 60 **p** 61 S'wark. C of St Mark Reigate 60-64; Tutor of Sarum Th Coll 64-69; Vice-Prin 69-71; Prof of NT Virginia Th Sem 71-74; Sen Officer Educn and Commun Dept Lon Dioc Bd of Educn 74-79; Chap and Lect Univ of Ex from 79. *School of Educn, St Luke's, Exeter, EX1 2LU.* (Ex 52221)

BRYAN, Nigel Arthur. b 39. St D Coll Lamp BA 61. **d** 63 **p** 64 St D. C of Llanstadwell 63-69; CF from 69. *c/o Ministry of Defence, Adastral House, WC 1.*

BRYAN, Patrick Joseph. b 41. St Jo Coll Cam BA 63, MA 67. St Steph Ho Ox 73. **d** 75 **p** 76 Lich. C of Rushall 75-78; Brierley Hill 78-80; P-in-c of St Mary and All SS Palfrey, Walsall Dio Lich from 80. *Palfrey Vicarage, Walsall, Staffs, WS1 4AN.*

BRYAN, Canon Percival John Milward. St Pet Coll Ox BA 3rd cl Hist 40, 2nd cl Th 47, MA 46. Wycl Hall Ox 46. **d** 48 **p** 49 Roch. C of All SS Belvedere 48-51; St Geo Hobart Dio Tas 51-52; Blindley Heath 53-54; C-in-c of Warkton w Weekley 54-55; R of King's Cliffe Dio Pet from 55; Proc Conv Pet 67-76; Can (Non-res) of Pet from 73; Ch Comm from 73. *King's Cliffe Rectory, Peterborough.* (King's Cliffe 314)

BRYAN, Philip Richard. b 40. Univ of Dur BA 61. Wycl Hall Ox 72. **d** 74 **p** 75 Ches. C of Macclesfield 74-77; V of St Bees Dio Carl from 77; Chap St Bees Sch from 77. *The Priory, St Bees, Cumb, CA27 0DR.* (St Bees 279)

BRYAN, Thomas John. b 06. St D Coll Lamp BA 48. **d** 49 St A **p** 50 Ban for St A. C of Llanrhaiadr-yn-Mochnant w Llanarmon 49-52; Hope 53-53; V of Llawr-y-Bettws w Bettws Gwerfil Goch and Dinmael 53-59; Holt w Isycoed 59-68; Tremeirchion 68-76. *Bryn Haf, Cae Glas, Trefnant, Denbigh, Clwyd.* (Trefnant 279)

BRYAN, William Terence. b 38. Chich Th Coll 73. **d** 75 Shrewsbury for Lich **p** 76 Lich. C of St Giles Shrewsbury 75-79; V of Churchstoke w Hyssington and Sarn Dio Heref from 79. *Vicarage, Churchstoke, Montgomery, Powys, SY15 6AF.* (Churchstoke 228)

BRYANS, Joseph. b 15. Trin Coll Dub BA 39, Div Test 40, MA 43. **d** 42 Hull for York **p** 43 York. C of Kirbymoorside 42-45; St Luke Thornaby 45-47; Seapatrick 47-54; I of Gleneely w Culdaff 54-60; Tamlaghtard w Aghanloo Dio Derry from 60. *4 Duncrun Road, Limavady, Co Londonderry, N Ireland, BT49 0JD.* (Bellarena 239)

BRYANT, Christopher. b 32. K Coll Lon and Warm AKC 60. **d** 61 **p** 62 Portsm. C of H Trin Fareham 61-65; Yatton Keynell Castle Combe and Biddestone w Slaughterford 65-71; V of Chirton w Marden and R of Patney 71-76; V of Chirton Marden Patney Wilsford & Charlton 76-78; P-in-c of Devizes Dio Sarum 78-79; R from 79. *Rectory, Devizes, Wilts.* (Devizes 3705)

BRYANT, Christopher Rex. b 05. Pemb Coll Cam 3rd cl Cl Trip pt i 26, BA (3rd cl Th Trip pt i) 27. St Aug Coll Cant 24. M SSJE 35. **d** 29 **p** 30 S'wark. C of St Paul Clapham 29-32; L to Offic Dio Ox 36-55 and from 68; Dio Lon from 55; Perm to Offic Dio St Andr 45-46; L to Offic in Scotld 46-49; Chap St Aug Coll Cant 69-71; L to Offic Dio Cant 69-80; M Gen Syn Cant 70-75; Perm to Offic Dio Lon from 79. *22 Great College Street, SW1P 3QA.*

BRYANT, David Charles. b 48. Univ of St Andr BSc 72. St Mich Coll Llan 71. **d** 74 **p** 75 Llan. C of Llanilid w Pencoed 74-78; Caerphilly 78-79; V of Crynant Dio Llan from 79. *35 Main Road, Crynant, Neath, W Glam, SA10 8NT.* (Crynant 226)

BRYANT, David Henderson. b 37. K Coll Lon and Warm BD and AKC 60. **d** 61 **p** 62 Sarum. C of H Trin Trowbridge 61-63; Ewell 63-67; V of Leiston w Sizewell 67-73; Chap RN 73-74; C of Northam 74-75; P-in-c of Clavering w Langley and Arkesden 75-77. *Address temp unknown.*

✠ **BRYANT, Right Rev Denis William.** DFC 42. Qu Coll Birm. **d** 58 Kingston T for Guildf **p** 59 Guildf. C of St Thos-on-the-Bourne 58-60; Cuddington 60-61; R of Esperance 61-67; Archd of the Goldfields 66-67; Cons Ld Bp of Kalg in St Geo Cathl Perth 30 Nov 67 by Abp of Perth; Bps of Bunb; and NW Austr; and Bps Frewer; Riley; Macdonald; and Rosier, res 72; R of Northam 72-76; Archd of Northam 72-76; Asst Bp of Perth 73-76; R of Dalkeith Dio Perth from 76. *42 Alexander Road, Dalkeith, W Australia 6009.* (386-3675)

BRYANT, Canon Douglas William. b 18. St Bonif Coll Warm 38. **d** 41 **p** 42 Bris. C of St Mich Two Mile Hill Bris 41-44; Branksome St Adhelm 44-45; St Mark Sarum 45-50; PC of St Pet Devizes 50-57; V of Burpham 57-70; Ed of Guildf Dioc Leaflet from 63; V of St Paul Egham Hythe 70-75; Hon Can of Guildf from 70; R of Fetcham Dio Guildf from 75. *12 The Ridgway, Leatherhead, Surrey.* (Leatherhead 72598)

BRYANT, Edgar James. b 28. Univ of Wales (Swansea) BA 49. St Mich Coll Llan 49. **d** 51 **p** 52 Swan B. C of Brynmawr 51-55; Llandrindod w Cefnllys 55-59; V of Llansantffraed-in-Elwel w Bettws-Disserth (w Disserth to 68) 59-73; C of Wigmore Dio Heref from 73. *c/o Vicarage, Wigmore, Leominster, Herefs.* (Wigmore 272)

BRYANT, Edward Francis Paterson. b 43. Univ of Man BA 64. SOC 75. **d** 78 **p** 79 Roch. C of Hadlow Dio Roch from 78. *18 Appletons, Hadlow, Tonbridge, Kent, TN11 0DT.*

BRYANT, Eric Peter. b 34. Rhodes Univ Grahmstn BA

53, PhD 71. Univ of Capetn BA 57. Pret Univ MA 65. Trin Coll Bris 80. **d** 81 Port Eliz (APM). C of St Paul City and Dio Port Eliz from 81. *c/o 16 Tucker Street, Parsons' Hill, Port Elizabeth 6001, S Africa.*

BRYANT, Graham Trevor. b 41. Keble Coll Ox BA 63, Dipl Th 64, MA 67. Chich Th Coll 64. **d** 66 **p** 67 Ripon. C of St Wilfrid Harehills Leeds 66-69; St Wilfrid Haywards Heath 69-74; V of Crawley Down 74-79; St Aug Bexhill Dio Chich from 79. *St Augustine Vicarage, Bexhill, E Sussex, TN39 3AZ.* (Bexhill 210785)

BRYANT, Mark Watts. b 49. St Jo Coll Dur Ba 72. Cudd Coll 72. **d** 75 **p** 76 Guildf. C of Addlestone 75-79; Chap Trowbridge Tech Coll from 79. *18 Balmoral Road, Trowbridge, Wilts, BA14 0JS.* (Trowbridge 2166)

BRYANT, Max Gordon. b 09. Univ of NZ BA 30, MA 31. Univ of Lon BD 34, 1st cl Th 35. **d** 32 Nel **p** 33 Cant. C of Tenterden w Smallhythe 33-35; Hythe 35-40; V of Headcorn 40-51; Northaw 51-78. *Llanina Aberporth, Dyfed, Cardigan.*

BRYANT, Richard Kirk. b 47. Ch Coll Cam BA 68, MA 72. Univ of Nottm Dipl Th 70. Cudd Coll 70. **d** 72 **p** 73 Newc T. C of St Gabr Heaton 72-75; Morpeth 75-78; Benwell (in c of Ven Bede) Dio Newc T from 78. *23 Benwell Grove, Newcastle-upon-Tyne, NE4 8AN.* (Newc T 735356)

BRYANT, Royston George. b 09. St Aid Coll 54. **d** 56 **p** 57 Bris. C of Ch Ch Clifton 56-59; Swindon 59-61; V of Stratton St Marg 61-69; All SS, Fishponds 69-76; Perm to Offic Dio Bris from 76. *30 Friary Grange Park, Winterbourne, Bristol, BS17 1NA.* (Winterbourne 778334)

BRYANT, Sidney John. b 29. Linc Coll Ox BA (3rd cl Th) 52, MA 56. St Steph Ho Ox 52. **d** 54 Kens for Lon **p** 55 Lon. C of St Andr Southgate 54-58; Ch Ch W Green Tottenham 58-60; V of St Paul New Southgate 60-71; R of Gt Leighs Dio Chelmsf from 71; P-in-c of L Leighs Dio Chelmsf from 71. *Great Leighs Rectory, Boreham Road, Chelmsford, Essex, CM3 1PP.* (Great Leighs 218)

BRYANT, Canon Wilfred Thomas. b 02. St Jo Coll Dur LTh 29. BA 30, MA 38. St Aid Coll 26. **d** 30 **p** 31 Ripon. C of St Mary Low Harrogate 30-33; Wortley de Leeds (in c of Ascen Ch) 33-36; Org Sec CMS Dio Bradf 36-38; Dios Sheff Southw and Wakef and LPr Dio Sheff 36-39; V of St Mary Doncaster 39-60; Asst RD of Doncaster 44-52; Surr from 45; Hon Can of Sheff from 51; R of Harthill 60-71; RD of Laughton 60-71; Ed Sheff Dioc Yr Book 60-71; Proc Conv Sheff 64-70; Chap Shrewsbury Hosp Sheff from 71. *Chaplain's House, Shrewsbury Hospital, Norfolk Road, Sheffield, S2 2SU.* (Sheff 20574)

BRYANT, William George. b 22. Selw Coll Cam MA 58. St Alb Min Tr Scheme 78. **d** 81 St Alb (NSM). C of St Mary Welwyn Dio St Alb from 81. *6 Cylers Thicket, Welwyn, Herts, AL6 9RS.*

BRYCE, Charles William. Angl Th Coll BC LTh 42. **d** 42 **p** 43 New Westmr. C of Abbotsford 42-44; V of Settler 44-48; in USA 48-50; R of Drumheller 50-52; I of St Thos Vancouver 52-56; Chap RCAF 56-67; R of St Jo Evang N Vanc 67-72; I of Abbotsford 72-79. *21-3015 Tretheway Street, Clearbrook, BC, Canada.*

✠ **BRYCE, Right Rev Jabez Leslie.** St Jo Coll Auckld LTh 62. St Andr Sem Phillipines BTh 67. **d** 60 **p** 62 Polyn. C of Suva 60-65; L to Offic Dio Polyn 65-66; Archd of Suva from 67-69; Dep VG of H Trin Cathl Suva 67-72; Lect St Jo Bapt Th Coll Suva 67-69; Archd in Polyn 69-75; V of Viti Levu W 69-75; Exam Chap to Bp of Polyn 69-75; VG of Polyn 72-75; Cons Ld Bp of Polyn in H Trin Cathl Suva II May 75 by Abps of NZ and Melan; Bps of Papua and Ysabel; and Bps G Ambo, M Bennett and Halapua. *Bishop's House, Box 35, Suva, Fiji Islands.*

BRYCE, Robert Richard. Wycl Coll Tor BTh 67. **d** and **p** 67 Keew. I of Wunnumin Lake 67-72; Perm to Offic Dio Keew 74-76; I of Norway Ho 76-81; Indian Par Dio Sktn from 81. *891-112th Street, N Battleford, Sask, Canada.*

BRYDEN, Harry. b 11. St Paul's Coll Burgh 34. St Aid Coll 36. **d** 36 Wakef **p** 37 Pontefract for Wakef. C of St Mich Arch Wakef 36-38; St Thos Bedford 38-42; V of Windhill 42-51; C of Westgate-on-Sea 51-52; V of Ch Ch Forest of Dean Coleford 52-59; Mutford w Rushmere 59-63; R of Gisleham 59-63; V of Eastrington 63-77; L to Offic Dio Nor from 77. *479 London Road South, Lowestoft, Suff, NR33 0PD.*

BRYDEN-BROWN, (formerly BROWN, Warren Wafforn), Canon Warren. Moore Th Coll Syd 42. ACT ThL 42. **d** and **p** 43 Syd. C of Willoughby 43-45; C of E in S Africa 45-49; R of Pitt Town 49-52; Cook's River 52-55; Kiama 55-67; Penrith Dio Syd from 67; Can of St John's Prov Cathl Parramatta from 74. *Rectory, High Street, Penrith, NSW, Australia 2750.* (Penrith 21-2124)

BRYDON, Harry Andrew. Univ of Windsor Ont BA 73. Hur Coll Lon MDiv 76. **d** 76 Hur **p** 77 Bp Parke-Taylor for Hur. I of Lion's Head 76-78; Thamesford and Lakeside Bay Dio Hur from 78. *Thamesford, Ont, Canada N0M 2M0.*

BRYER, Anthony Colin. b 51. Univ of Lon BSc 72. Univ of Bris Dipl Th 75. Trin Coll Bris 72. **d** 75 Burnley for Blackb **p** 76 Blackb. C of St Cuthb Fulwood Preston 75-78; St Mary Becontree 78-81; Team V of St Mary Virg Loughton Dio Chelmsf from 81. *St Michael's House, Roding Road, Loughton, Essex, IG10 3EJ.* (01-508 1489)

BUBBERS, David Bramwell. b 23. Oak Hill Th Coll 51. **d** 54 **p** 55 Roch. C of St Jo Bapt Beckenham 54-58; V of St Mich AA Southfields 58-65; Em Northwood 65-74; Commiss Ank 72-76; E Ank from 76; Gen Sec CPAS from 74. *Church Pastoral Aid Society, Falcon Court, 32 Fleet Street, EC4Y 1DB.* (01-353 0751)

BUBBINGS, Charles Gardam. b 26. Qu Th Coll Birm 68. **d** 69 **p** 70 York. C of St Mary Scarborough 69-72; Fulford York 72-74; V of St Osw Middlesbrough 74-81; Ringley Dio Man from 81. *Ringley Vicarage, Fold Road, Stoneclough, Radcliffe, Gtr Man, M26 9EU.* (Farnworth 73742)

BUBI, Sospateri. d 80 Kiga. d Dio Kiga. *Bp 18, Gatsibo, Rwanda.*

BUCHAN, Ven Eric Ancrum. b 07. St Chad's Coll Dur BA 32. **d** 33 Malmesbury for Bris **p** 34 Bris. C of H Nativ Knowle 33-40; Chap RAFVR 40-45; V of St Mark w St Barn Cov 45-59; Chap Cov and Warws Hosp 46-59; Proc Conv Cov 53-65 and 70-75; Hon Can of Cov 53-65; RD of Cov 54-63; Dir of Chr Stewardship Dio Cov 59-77; Dom Chap to Bp of Cov 61-65; R of Baginton 63-69; Ch Comm 64-77; Archd of Cov 65-77; [illegible] *Cathedral, Gloucester, GL1 2BN.* (0452-415944)

BUCHAN, Kenneth George. b 37. **d** 74 **p** 75 Rupld. P Dio Rupld 74-75; R of Fort Alexander 75-78; Sioux Lookout 78-80. *Box 626, Sioux Lookout, Ont, Canada.* (807-737 2541)

✠ **BUCHANAN, Most Rev Alan Alexander.** b 07. Late Exhib of Trin Coll Dub BA (2nd cl Mod) 28, Hon DD 59. **d** 30 **p** 31 Down. Asst Missr Ch of I Miss Belf 30-33; Hd 33-37; I of Inver (Larne) 37-45; CF (EC) 42-45; I of St Mary Belf 45-55; RD of Mid-Belfast 51-55; R of Bangor 55-58; Can of St Patr Cathl Dub 57-58; Cons Ld Bp of Clogh in St Patr Cathl Armagh 29 Sept 58 by Abp of Armagh; Bps of Meath, Down, Connor, Kilm, and Tuam; Trld to Dub (Abp of Dub, Bp of Glendal [and Kild 69-76], Primate of Ireland, and Metrop) 69; res 77. *Kilbride, Castleknock, Co Dublin, Irish Republic.*

BUCHANAN, Basil Roberts. b 1895. Trin Coll Cam BA 18, MA 21. Ripon Hall Ox 20. **d** 20 Knaresborough for Ripon **p** 21 Ripon. C of Ch Ch Harrogate 20-21; St Mich Headingley 21-24; St Anne Brighton 24-25; High Wycombe 25-28; St Anne Eastbourne 28-31; V of Burlescombe 31-35; R of Broughton w N Newington Oxon 35-37; V of Bloxham w Milcombe 37-49; St Andr Chesterton Cam 49-65; Perm to Offic Dio Ely from 66. *3 Wort's Causeway, Cambridge, CB1 4RJ.* (Cam 248704)

BUCHANAN, Canon Colin Ogilvie. b 34. Linc Coll Ox. Tyndale Hall Bris. **d** 61 **p** 62 Ches. C of Cheadle 61-64; Tutor St Jo Coll Nottm (f Lon Coll Div) from 64; Regr from 69; Dir of Stud from 74; Vice-Prin 75-78; Prin from 79; L to Offic Dio Southw from 70; Proc Conv Southw from 70; Hon Can of Southw Minster from 81. *St John's College, Chilwell Lane, Bramcote, Nottingham, NG9 3DS.* (Nottm 251114)

BUCHANAN, Canon Eric. b 32. Univ of Leeds BA 54. Coll of Resurr Mirfield 54. **d** 56 **p** 57 Cov. C of St Mark Cov 56-59; Asst Chap Univ of Lon 59-64; C of Bloomsbury 59-64; V of Duston 64-79; Wellingborough Dio Pet from 79; RD of Wootton 74-79; Can of Pet Cathl from 77. *Vicarage, Wellingborough, Northants.* (Wellingborough 222002)

BUCHANAN, Canon Frank. b 03. St Edm Hall Ox BA 25, MA 29. Cudd Coll 25. **d** 26 **p** 27 Worc. C of Kidderminster 26-30; Brighouse 30-34; V of Greetland 34-42; Penistone w Midhope 42-53; Polesworth w Birchmoor 53-54; RD of Polesworth 53-65; Hon Can of Birm 57-71; Can (Emer) from 71; PC of St Columba Sutton Coldfield 65-71. *Greenwood, Oakdene Road, Godalming, Surrey.*

BUCHANAN, Frederick Donald. Moore Th Coll Syd ACT ThL 54. **d** and **p** 55 Syd. C of Lithgow 55-56; Asst Chap Miss to Seamen Syd 56-60; C-in-c of Toongabbie w Girraween 60-64; Engadine w Heathcote 64-67; R of Kensington 67-76; Armadale Dio Perth from 76. *Rectory, Jull Street, Armadale, W Australia.* (399 2130)

BUCHANAN, Ven George Duncan. Rhodes Univ Grahmstn BA 57. Gen Th Sem NY STB 60. Ripon Hall Ox 57. **d** 59 Dover for Cant for Natal **p** 60 NY for Natal. C of St Paul Durban 59 and 61-62; Fell and Tutor Gen Th Sem NY 60-61; V of Kingsway 62-66; Exam Chap to Bp of Natal 64-66; Sub-Warden St Paul's Coll City and Dio Grahmstn from 66; Archd of Albany from 75. *7 Durban Street, Grahamstown, CP, S Africa.* (2402)

BUCHANAN, George Rowland. b 15. St Aug Coll Cant. **d**

59 **p** 60 Sarum. C of Sherborne w Castleton and Lillington 59-63; V of Bradford Abbas w Clifton Maybank 63-67; R of Wishford Magna 67-73; L Langford 67-73; RD of Wylye and Wilton 69-73; Proc Conv Sarum 70-73; Cler Org Sec CECS Dios Ex and B & W 73-77; Perm to Offic Dio Sarum 77. *Cobblers, Greenhill, Sherborne, Dorset.* (Sherborne 2263)

BUCHANAN, John Dermot. NZ BD of Th Stud LTh 66. St Jo Coll Auckld 63. **d** 65 **p** 66 Waik. C of Te Aroha 65-66; Matamata 66-67; St Pet Cathl, Hamilton 67-69; Min Can of Waik 68-69; C of Lower Hutt 69-71; Chap Wel Hosps 71-76; on leave 76-78; Adv Advisory Coun on Hosp Chap NZ and Hon C of St Paul's Cathl City and Dio Wel from 79. *6 Brora Crescent, Papakowhai, Plimmerton, NZ.* (31-429)

BUCHANAN, Oswald John. b 48. Moore Th Coll Syd BTh. **d** 81 Syd. C of St Anne Ryde Dio Syd from 81. *5 Woodbine Crescent, Ryde, NSW, Australia 2112.*

BUCHANAN, Stephen Daniel. **d** 70 **p** 73 Ja. C of Pedro Plains Dio Ja from 70. *PO Mountainside, Jamaica, WI.*

BUCHANAN, Theron Brock. Univ of Tor BA 50. Wycl Coll Tor LTh 53. **d** 52 Bp G A Wells for Calg **p** 53 Calg. I of Stettler 53-55; V of Taber 55-57; I of St Richard, N Vanc 59-63. *23 Balaclava Street, Amherstburg, Ont, Canada.*

BUCHNER, Canon Howard Wendel. Univ of Alta BA 43. Trin Coll Tor LTh 47. Berkeley Div Sch USA STM 59 Hon DD 65. **d** and **p** 47 Edmon. C of All SS Cathl Edmon 47-49; P-in-c of Edson 49-58; Hon Can of Edmon from 55; on leave from 58 *c/o Trinity College, Toronto 5, Ont., Canada.*

BUCK, Charles Kemp. b 16. Keble Coll Ox BA 38, MA 42. Chich Th Coll 38. **d** 40 **p** 41 Lon. C of St Dunstan Stepney 40-43; St Dunstan Feltham 43-44; PV of Truro Cathl 44-46; Cler Org Sec C of E Children's S Dios Lon and S'wark 46-47; Dio Ox 48; Dio St Alb 49-53; C of Hambleden (in c of Frieth) 47-49; Asst Master and Chap Bedford Sch 49-50; V of Wilshamstead 50-53; Chap Bedford Gen Hosp 50-53; V of St Bart Dover 53-55; Chap Portsm Cathl 55-57; Prec and Min Can of Ripon Cathl 57-60; Asst Master Ripon Gr Sch 57-60; V of Norbury 60-67; Hindon w Chichlade and Pertwood 67-70; Tutor Sarum Th Coll 68-73; V of Parkstone w Branksea I 70-74; Chap and Lect St Mary Sch Wantage 74-78; V of N and S Muskham Dio Southw from 78; P-in-c of Caunton Dio Southw from 78; Cromwell Dio Southw from 78; RD of Tuxford and Norwell from 80. *South Muskham Vicarage, Newark, Notts, NG23 6EQ.* (Newark 702655)

BUCK, Eric Joseph. b 14. BA (Lon) 35, Dipl Educn (Lon) 54. Ridley Hall Cam. **d** 61 **p** 62 Nor. C of Wymondham 61-62; V of Wicklewood w Crownthorpe (and Deopham w Hackford from 79) 62-80; P-in-c of Hackford (w Deopham from 75) 66-79. *40 Chapel Lane, Wymondham, NR18 0DL.*

BUCK, James Marsden. St Chad's Coll Regina 38. **d** 38 **p** 39 Qu'App. C-in-c of Togo 38-39; I 39-40; Miss at Keyes Ind Reserve 40-43; Chap of Gordon's Ind Reserve 43-44; on active service 44-46; I of Imperal 46-56; Birtle 56-62; Swan River 62-68; Oak Lake 68-74. *Oak Lake, Manit., Canada.*

BUCK, James Stephen Frederick. **d** and **p** 79 Wang. Perm to Offic Dio Wang from 79. *3 St Matthew's Village, Broadford, Victoria, Australia 3658.*

BUCK, John Martin. McGill Univ Montr BEng 49, BD 53, STM 61. Montr Dioc Tr Coll. **d** 53 **p** 54 Montr. C of Rosemount 53-54; P-in-c of Aylwin W River Desert 54-57; I of Beauharnois 57-60; I of Chateauguay 60-65; C of Ch Ch Calg 65-67; L to Offic Dio Calg from 68. *3831 8th Street SW, Calgary 6, Alta., Canada.* (243-2803)

BUCK, John Robert. b 18. **d** 76 **p** 78 Bran. C of The Pas Dio Bran from 76. *Devon Mission, The Pas, Manitoba, R9A 1M2, Canada.*

BUCK, Richard Peter Holdron. b 37. K Coll Lon and Warm AKC 64. **d** 65 **p** 66 Lon. C of John Keble Ch Mill Hill 65-68; All SS Margaret Street St Marylebone 68-74; Can Res and Treas of Truro Cathl 74-76; V of St Mary Virg Primrose Hill w St Paul Hampstead Dio Lon from 76. *7 Elsworthy Road, NW3 3DS.* (01-722 3062)

BUCKETT, Canon James Frederick. b 27. Roch Th Coll 60. **d** 62 **p** 63 Portsm. C of Rowner 62-64; Chap and Lect Highbury Technical Coll Portsm 64-66; L to Offic Dio Portsm 64-66; V of St Helens, IW 66-72; Newport IW Dio Portsm from 72; Dioc Insp of Schools 67-73; Surr from 72; CF (TAVR) from 72; Hon Can of Portsm Cathl from 81. *Newport Vicarage, Mt Pleasant Road, Newport, IW.* (Newport, IW 522733)

BUCKINGHAM, Lord Bishop Suffragan of. *See* Burrows, Right Rev Simon Hedley.

BUCKINGHAM, Archdeacon of. *See* Bone, Ven John Frank Ewan.

BUCKINGHAM, Cecil Harry. b 1898. Univ of Dur LTh 22. Edin Th Coll 20. **d** 22 **p** 23 Edin. C of Ch Ch Falkirk 22-25; Gillingham w Upberry 25-30; R of Snodland 30-39; V of Easton 39-52; CF (EC) 41-48; Hon CF 48; Perm to Offic at St Chrys Peckham 55-57; C of St Jo Bapt Southend Lewisham (in c of St Barn) 57-63; V of Duddington w Tixover 63-68; L to Offic Dio Pet from 68; Perm to Offic Dios Linc and Ely from 68. *177 Broadway, Peterborough, PE1 4DS.* (Peterborough 60970)

BUCKINGHAM, Hugh Fletcher. b 32. Hertf Coll Ox BA 57, MA 60. Westcott Ho Cam 55. **d** 57 **p** 58 Man. C of St Thos Halliwell 57-60; St Silas Sheff 60-65; V of Hindolveston 65-70; V of Guestwick 65-70; R of Fakenham Dio Nor from 70; Chairman Dioc Bd for Social Responsibility Dio Nor from 81; RD of Burnham and Walsingham from 81. *Rectory, Fakenham, Norf.* (Fakenham 2268)

BUCKINGHAM, Keith William. b 45. Em & St Chad's Coll Sktn BTh 79. **d** and **p** 79 Qu'App. I of Notukeu Dio Qu'App from 79. *Box 374, Hodgeville, Sask, Canada, S0H 2B0.*

BUCKINGHAM, Patrick Anthony. b 34. St Steph Ho Ox. **d** 62 Wakef. C of Elland 62-66; M CSWG 66-69; Hon C of St Mary Magd Nor 69-73; St Faith Wandsworth 73-77; M CSWG from 78. *Monastery of CSWG, Crawley Down, Crawley, Sussex.*

BUCKINGHAM, Richard Arthur John. b 49. Univ of Wales (Cardiff) BA 71. Chich Th Coll 73. **d** 76 **p** 77 Llan. C of Llantwit Major 76-80; St Marg Leigh Dio Chelmsf from 80. *38 Fleming Avenue, Leigh-on-Sea, SS9 3AW.*

BUCKINGHAM, Roy Muir. **d** 63 **p** 64 Syd. C of St Mich Syd 63-64; C-in-c of St Paul Syd 64-70; R 70-73; Lithgow 73-80; R of W Pilbara Dio NW Austr from 80. *Samson Way, Karratha, W Australia.*

BUCKLAND, Canon Basil. KCNS BA 36. **d** 38 **p** 39 Fred. Miss at Westmoreland 38-40; R of Cambridge and Waterloo 40-52; Peterville w Greenwich 52-56; Bathurst 56-58; Gagetown 58-70; I of Waterford w St Mark 70-79; Can of Ch Ch Cathl Fred from 71. *RR1, Gagetown, NB, Canada.*

BUCKLAND, Canon Bernard Russell. Moore Th Coll Syd ACT ThL 56. **d** 56 **p** 57 Syd. C of Lithgow 56-58; P-in-c of Franklin Harbour Miss 58-61; Ceduna Miss 62-63; R of Mt Magnet w Murchison Distr 63-68; Derby w Broome 69-75; Hon Can of H Cross Cathl Geraldton from 74; R of Northn-Mullewa Dio NW Austr from 75. *PO Box 157, Northampton, W Australia 6530.* (Northampton 13)

BUCKLAND, Geoffrey Douglas. b 36. Dipl Th (Lon) 61. Clifton Th Coll 59. **d** 62 **p** 63 Lon. C of Ch Ch w All SS Spitalfields 62-68; Good Shepherd Romford 68-71; V of St Lawr Kirkdale Dio Liv from 71. *8 Harrison Drive, Bootle, Mer, L20 9JL.* (051-525 8765)

BUCKLAND, Walter Basil. b 09. St Pet Hall Ox BA (4th cl Engl Lit) 31, Dipl Th 32, MA 36. Wycl Hall Ox 31. **d** 33 Ripon **p** 34 Knaresborough for Ripon. C of St Clem Leeds 33-36; Ch Ch Penge 36-37; V of St Pet Battersea 37-47; Sandon Staffs 47-55; R of Longton 55-69; Surr 60-69; V of Ardington w Lockinge 70-75. *10 Tudor Road, Newbury, Berks.*

✠ **BUCKLE, Right Rev Edward Gilbert.** Moore Th Coll Syd 48. **d** 49 **p** 50 C & Goulb. R of Koorawatha 49-51; C of Berridale 51-53; P-in-c of Adaminaby 53-54; R of Adelong 54-55; Canberra N 55-60; Canberra 60-63; Can of St Sav Cathl Goulb 61-63; Bd of Relig Educn 63-64; V of St Matt Auckld 64-66; Bp of Auckld Commiss for Cathl 66-68; Exec Officer 68-71; Archd of Auckld 71-81; Ecumen Development Officer Dio Auckld 71-81; Cons Asst Bp of Auckld in Cathl Ch of H Trin Auckld 15 Feb 81 by Abp of NZ; Bps of Nel, Ch Ch, Wel, Dun, Wai, Waik and Aotearoa; and Abp Johnston and Bps Wiggins, Wilson, Wiggins, Montieth, Spence and Gowing. *20 Tainui Street, Torbay, Auckland, NZ.*

BUCKLE, Francis George. Mem Univ Newfld BA 62. Qu Coll Newfld LTh 62. **d** and **p** 62 Newfld. I of Cartwright 62-67; R of Bell I 67-69; C of St Jo Bapt Cathl St John's 70-73; R of Happy Valley Dio Newfld (E Newfld from 76) from 73. *PO Box 130, Happy Valley, Labrador, Canada.* (709-896-3350)

BUCKLE, Terrence Owen. b 40. **d** 73 Mack. C of Fort Simpson 73-75; Miss at Inuvik 75-81; Hon Can of St Jude's Cathl Frobisher Bay 78-81. *c/o Box 1040, Inuvik, NWT, Canada.*

BUCKLER, George Anthony. b 35. Open Univ BA 74. Lich Th Coll 58. **d** 61 **p** 62 Worc. C of St Mary Old Swinford 61-65; St Andr w St Mary and St Nich w St Pet Droitwich 65-67; Chap Claybury Hosp 67-78; Linc Hosps from 78. *Lincoln County Hospital, Sewell Road, Lincoln, LN2 5QY.* (Linc 29921)

BUCKLER, Guy Ernest Warr. b 46. ACA 69, FCA 79. Bp's Hostel Linc 71. **d** 74 Bedford for St Alb **p** 75 St Alb. C of Dunstable 74-77; Houghton Regis Dio St Alb from 77. *7 Enfield Close, Houghton Regis, Dunstable, Beds, LU5 5BJ.* (Luton 863292)

BUCKLER, Canon Peter. b 17. OBE 79. BSc (Lon) 38. Linc Th Coll. **d** 66 **p** 67 Birm. C of Baddesley Ensor 66-67; C-in-c of Grendon 67-68; R 68-71; Chap to Colleg Ch of St Mary Warwick 71; Bps' Chap to the N Agr Centre Stoneleigh

Warws from 71; C-in-c of Burton Dasset w North End 71-74; Warden Arthur Rank Centre Dio Cov from 74; Hon Can of Cov from 76. *National Agricultural Centre, Stoneleigh, Kenilworth, Warws.* (Coventry 56151)

BUCKLER, Philip John Warr. b 49. St Pet Coll Ox BA 70, MA 74. Cudd Coll 70. **d** 72 **p** 73 St Alb. C of Bushey Heath 72-75; Chap Trin Coll Cam 75-81; Min Can of St Paul's Cathl Lon from 81; Sacr and Sen Cardinal Coll of Min Can from 81. *7 Amen Court, EC4M 7BU.* (01-248 2531)

BUCKLEY, Alan. b 40. Tyndale Hall Bris. **d** 67 **p** 68 Sheff. C of Owlerton Sheff 67-70; Mansfield 70-73; Charlesworth 73-75; P-in-c of Whitfield Dio Derby from 76. *116 Charlestown Road, Lee Mount, Glossop, Derbys.* (Glossop 64938)

BUCKLEY, Alfred John. b 07. St Pet Coll Ja 37. **d** 37 Ja **p** 38 Bp Sara for Ja. C of Retreat 37-38; Belfield w Bromley and Woodside 38-40; R of Snowdon w Providence Ja 40-45; V of St Paul (w H Trin from 51) Greenwich 45-55; C-in-c of St Pet Greenwich 45-51; C-in-c of H Trin W Greenwich 50-51; Chap Miller Gen Hosp 47-55; R of Booysens Johann 55-56; Min of St Edw Eccles Distr Mottingham 56-58; V 58-73; Publ Pr Dio Truro from 73. *2 Kenwyn Road, Truro, Cornwall.*

BUCKLEY, Basil Foster. b 11 Dorch Miss Coll 35. **d** 38 **p** 39 Man. C of St Ignatius Salford 38-42; R 42-81; Hon C of St Paul w Ch Ch Dio Salford from 82. *22 Alresford Road, Salford 6.*

BUCKLEY, David Rex. b 47. Ripon Coll Cudd 75. **d** 77 **p** 78 Ches. C of St Helen Witton 77-81; V of Backford and Dioc Youth Officer Dio Ches from 81. *Vicarage, Gordon Lane, Backford, Chester, CH2 4DG.* (Gt Mollington 851237)

BUCKLEY, Canon Derek Haslam. b 17. Bps' Coll Cheshunt 52. **d** 54 **p** 55 Wakef. C of Chapelthorpe 54-57; Bakewell 57-59; R of Fenny Bentley w Thorpe and Tissington 59-67; V of Scropton 67-73; R of Boylestone Dio Derby 67-73; C-in-c 73-76; Chap HM Detention Centre Foston Hall 67-73; RD of Longford 71-81; C-in-c of Ch Broughton and Sutton-on-the-Hill Dio Derby 73-76; V (w Boylestone) from 76; P-in-c of Trusley Dio Derby from 77; Hon Can of Derby Cathl from 79. *Vicarage, Chapel Lane, Church Broughton, Derby, DE6 5BB.* (Sudbury 296)

BUCKLEY, Ernest Fairbank. b 25. Jes Coll Cam BA 49, MA 50. Jes Coll Ox BLitt 53. Westcott Ho Cam 55. **d** 55 **p** 56 Man. C of St Chad Rochdale 55-58; V of Hey 58-64; Brooklands 64-79; Clun w Chapel Lawn, Bettws-y-Crwyn and Newc Dio Heref from 79. *Clun Vicarage, Craven Arms, Salop.* (Clun 270)

BUCKLEY, Geoffrey Lloyd. b 32. M Inst Mech Eng 64. CEng 64. Chich Th Coll 73. **d** 73 Buckingham for Ox **p** 73 Ox (APM). Hon C of Sandhurst 73-76; Burley-in-Wharfedale 76-77; St Marg Ilkley Dio Bradf from 77. *Micklefield, Queens Drive Lane, Ilkley, W Yorks, LS29 9QS.* (Ilkley 600827)

BUCKLEY, Harold. b 12. Worc Ordin Coll 68. **d** 69 Middleton for Man **p** 69 Man. C of Atherton Man 69-74; Chap and Asst Master St Mich Sch Sevenoaks from 74; Hon C of St Luke Southport 78; St Thos Bedford Leigh 78-80; Perm to Offic Dio Man from 80. *122 Spring Street, Bury, Lancs.*

BUCKLEY, Michael. b 49. St Jo Coll Dur 77. **d** 79 **p** 80 Liv. C of St John Birkdale Dio Liv from 79. *59 Bedford Road, Birkdale, Southport, Merseyside, PR8 4HU.*

BUCKLEY, Canon Michael Richard. b 20. AKC (2nd cl) 42. Univ of Lon BD (2nd cl) 42. Cudd Coll 42. **d** 43 Kens for Lon **p** 44 Lon. C of St Aug Whitton 43-45; Hatfield (in c of St Mark) 45-48; Leatherhead 48-52; V of Stoneleigh 52-67; R of Weybridge Dio Guildf from 67; Hon Can of Guildf from 75. *Rectory, Weybridge, Surrey.* (Weybridge 42566)

BUCKLEY, Richard Francis. b 44. Ripon Hall Ox 69. **d** 72 **p** 73 Portsm. C of St Cuthb Copnor Portsm 72-75; All SS and St John Portsea 75-79; Chap RN from 79. *c/o Ministry of Defence, Lacon House, Theobald's Road, WC1X 8RY.*

BUCKLEY, Richard John. b 43. Univ of Hull BSc (Econ) 64. Univ of Strathclyde MSc 69. Sarum Th Coll 64. **d** 66 **p** 67 Wakef. C of St Jo Evang Huddersfield 66-68; St Jas Sutton-in-Holderness 69-71; Team V 71-75; V of Handsworth Woodhouse Dio Sheff from 75. *Vicarage, Tithe Barn Lane, Woodhouse, Sheffield, S13 7LL.* (Sheffield 692380)

BUCKLEY, Wyndham Awdry. b 13. St Bonif Coll Warm 32. **d** 37 **p** 38 Man. C of St Jas E Crompton 37-39; St Marg Bloemf 39-40; St Thos Durban 40-43; CF (Ind) 43-45; CF (S Afr) 45-56; R of Ch K Pret 50-56; CF (Cent Afr Fed) and Hon Chap Heany Teachers' Tr Coll S Rhod 56-63; R of Sennen 63-67; V of Langham 67-79; Chap HM Pris Ashwell from 67. *8 Uppingham Road, Oakham, Leics.* (Oakham 56844)

BUCKMAN, Leo Richard. Moore Th Coll Syd ACT ThL 46. **d** and **p** 47 Syd. C of St John Parramatta 47-51; R of Earlwood 51-54; Sec BFBS for S Austr 54-58; for Dio New Guinea 58-68; Commonwealth Liaison Officer in Austr from 68; LPr Dio Adel 54-58; Dio New Guinea 58-68; Dio C & Goulb 69-72; L to Offic Dio Tas 69-72; R of St Andr Strathfield 72-74; Perm to Offic Dio Perth 74-78. *c/o St Andrew's House, Sydney Square, Sydney, Australia 2000.*

BUCKMAN, Rossly David. b 36. Late Found Scho and Pri of TCD BA 64, MA 67. St Pet Coll Ox BA (by incorp) 65, MA 68. Moore Th Coll Syd ACT ThL 59. **d** 59 **p** 60 Syd. C of Eastwood 59-60; Port Kembla 60-61; Harold's Cross Dub 61-64; St Mich Ox 64-65; Lect in Th Bris Univ 65-69; Publ Pr Dio Bris 65-69; CF 69-76; C of St Paul Manuka 76-80; Tutor Canberra Coll 77-80; Lect Austr Nat Univ 79-80; R of Mid Marsh Group Dio Linc from 81. *c/o Grimoldby Rectory, Louth, Lincs LN11 8SW.* (Cockerington 298)

BUCKMASTER, Charles. b 20. St Jo Coll Dur BA 50. Wells Th Coll 50. **d** 51 **p** 52 S'wark. C of St Luke Battersea 51-53; Chap and Lect Ripon Dioc Tr Coll 53-60; L to Offic Dio Derby and Dep-Prin and Div Lect Derby Dioc Tr Coll 60-68; Prin St Pet Coll Birm 68-78; Chap at Limassol and Paphos Dio Cyprus from 78. *Box 1494, Limassol, Cyprus.*

BUCKMASTER, Cuthbert Harold Septimus. b 03. Cudd Coll 25. **d** 26 **p** 27 York. C of St Martin Scarborough and Asst Master of Orleton Sch 26-27; C of St Jo Evang Middlesbrough 27-30; Wigan 30-33; Chap of Denstone Coll 33-36; V of St Mich AA and Warden of St Mich Coll Tenbury 36-46; Chap RNVR 40-47; Chap RN 48-57; R of Ashprington 57-59; V of Cornworthy 57-59; R of Chagford 59-71. *21 Marquis Street, Ashburton, Melbourne, Vic 3147, Australia.*

BUCKMASTER, Edward Arthur Cyprian. b 01. New Coll Ox BA (4th cl Th) 22, MA 26. Ely Th Coll. **d** 33 **p** 34 York. C of St Martin Scarborough 33-37; Perm to Offic at St Mich AA Wigan 38-39; V of St Dunstan Edge Hill 39-47; RD of Liv S 45-47; R of Worthen 47-75. *7 Old Mill Close, The Brook, Worthen, Salop.*

BUCKNALL, Allan. b 35. ALCD 62. **d** 62 **p** 63 Chelmsf. C of Harlow New Town w L Parndon 62-69; Chap W Somt Miss to Deaf 69-71; Perm to Offic Dio Bris from 71; Dio Chich from 73; Asst Master Midhurst Intermediate Sch 73-77; P-in-c of Wisborough Green 77-79; R of Tillington Dio Chich from 79. *Tillington Rectory, Petworth, Sussex.* (Petworth 42117)

BUCKNALL, Samuel Watkin. b 1881. **d** and **p** 44 Roch. C of H Trin, Brompton Chatham 44-46; C-in-c of Grayne 46; V 46-57; Perm to Offic Dio Roch 57-67; Dio Cant from 67. *22 Hastings Road, Rolvenden, Cranbrook, Kent.* (Rolvenden 439)

BUCKNALL, William John. b 44. Dipl Th (Lon) 67. Kelham Th Coll 63. **d** 68 **p** 69 Carl. C of H Trin City and Dio Carl 68-71; C of Berkswich w Walton 71-73; C-in-c of Ilam w Blore-Ray 73-76; Warden Dovedale Ho Lich 73-76; V of St Paul Wednesbury Dio Lich from 76; RD of Wednesbury from 78. *St Paul's Vicarage, Wood Green, Wednesbury, W Midl, WS10 9QT.* (021-556 0687)

BUCKNER, Richard Pentland. b 37. Keble Coll Ox BA 61, MA 64. Wells Th Coll 60. **d** 62 **p** 63 Ex. C of Crediton 62-65; St Matt Ex 65-66; Chap Grenville Coll Bideford 66-74; L to Offic Dio Ex 66-74; Dio Southw from 74; Chap Worksop Coll from 74. *Worksop College, Notts.*

BUCKROYD, Leslie. b 16. St Jo Coll Dur BA 48, Dipl Th 50. **d** 50 **p** 51 Lich. C of Tamworth 50-53; V of Dordon 53-61; St Barn Leic 61-70; Surr from 67; R of Ravenstone Dio Leic from 70. *Ravenstone Rectory, Ravenstone, Leics, LE6 2AS.* (Coalville 32702)

BUCKS, Michael William. b 40. K Coll Lon and Warm BD and AKC 63. **d** 64 Penrith for Carl **p** 65 Carl. C of Workington 64-69; Chap RN from 69. *Tamarin, Brodick, Isle of Arran.*

BUCKWELL, Charles Cecil Leighton. b 05. Late Organ Scho of Or Coll Ox 3rd cl Th 27, BA 28, MA 34. Ely Th Coll 27. **d** 28 Dover for Cant **p** 29 Cant. C of St Mich AA Maidstone 28-31; All SS Clifton 31-35; V of St Agnes Exning 35-38; Littlemore 38-51; St Mich AA Croydon 51-70. *19 St Mary's Street, Ely, Cambs.* (Ely 3866)

BUCUMI, Augustin. d 74 Bur **p** 75 Buye. P Dio Buye. *Buye B.P. 58, Ngozi, Burundi.*

BUCUMI, Nicodeme. d 72 **p** 73 Bur. P Dio Bur 72-75; Dio Buye from 75. *Buye B.P. 58 Ngozi, Burundi.*

BUDD, Gordon. b 08. Linc Th Coll. **d** 53 **p** 54 Lon. C of Whitechapel 53-56; St Faith w St Matthias Stoke Newington 56-58; R of Bacton w Wyverstone 58-61; H Trin Stirling 61-73; P-in-c of St Ninian Seaton Aber 73-76. *St Michael's Parsonage, Dufftown, Banffshire.* (Dufftown 20621)

BUDD, John Victor. b 31. CCC Ox BA 55, MA 58. Bps' Coll Cheshunt 57. **d** 59 **p** 60 Lon. C of Friern Barnet 59-64; Harrow Weald 64-70; L to Offic Dio St Alb 70-73; V of L Amwell Dio St Alb from 73. *Little Amwell Vicarage, Hertford Heath, Hertford, SG13 7RW.* (Hertford 59140)

BUDD, Philip John. b 40. Univ of Dur BA (2nd cl Th) 63, Dipl Th (w Distinc) 65, MLitt 71. Univ of Bris PhD 78. Cranmer Hall Dur. **d** 66 **p** 67 Southw. C of Attenborough w Chilwell 66-69; Lect Clifton Th Coll 69-71; Trin Coll Bris 72-80; Tutor Ripon Coll Cudd amd Westmr Coll Ox from 80.

Westminster College, N Hinksey,Oxford, OX2 9AT.

BUDERUS, John Karl William. b 44. St Mich Ho Crafers 70. **d** and **p** 72 Bal. C of St John Bal 72-73; Warrnambool 74-75; Colac 75-76; Brunswick Dio Melb from 76. *6 Glenlyon Road, Brunswick, Vic, Australia 3056.* (38-1064)

BUDGE, Leonard Percival. b 11. Univ of Dur LTh 40, St Aug Coll Cant 37. **d** 40 **p** 41 York. C of Easington w Skeffling and Kilnsea and Welwick w Holmpton 40-43; St Andr Hertford 43-45; Lukwika 45-46; Masasi 46-48; St Thos Stourbridge 48-51; V of Castle Morton 51-58; Amblecote 58-64; Frithelstock 64-76; Monkleigh 64-76; C-in-c of Littleham 64-70; R 70-76; Perm to Offic Dio Ex from 76. *2 Chestnut Close, Braunton, Devon, EX33 2EH.* (Braunton 814313)

BUDGE, Martin. b 49. Chich Th Coll 70. **d** 73 **p** 74 Heref. C of Leintwardine w Adforton 73-76; Wigmore Abbey 76-77; H Trin Heref 77-78; V of Gt Wollaston Dio Heref from 78; R of Yockleton and Westbury Dio Heref from 78. *Rectory, Westbury, Shrewsbury, Salop.* (Halfway House 216)

BUDGEN, Harold Walter. b 1891. Keble Coll Ox BA 22, MA 26. Ely Th Coll 22. **d** 23 **p** 24 Roch. C of St Luke New Brompton 23-27; Chap LCC Home Leyonstone 27-33; C of Coggeshall 33-34; V of Hyde 34-37; Cler Org Sec C of E Children's S Dios Lon S'wark and St Alb 37-40; R of Charlton-in-Dover 40-61; Perm to Offic Dio Portsm from 78. *21 South Lodge, Fareham, Hants, PO15 5NQ.* (Titchfield 43414)

BUDGETT, Anthony Thomas. b 26. Late Scho of Or Coll Ox BA 50, MA 57. Wells Th Coll 57. **d** 59 Taunton for B & W **p** 60 Taunton for Cant. C of H Trin Hendford Yeovil 59-63; R of Seavington 63-68; PC of Lopen 63-68; V of Somerton (w Compton Dundon from 80 and Charlton Adam, Charlton Mackrell and Kingsdown from 81) Dio B & W from 68; RD of Ilchester 72-81; C-in-c of Compton Dundon 76-80. *Vicarage, Somerton, Somt.* (Somerton 72216)

BUDGETT, Robert Brackenbury. b 08. Ch Coll Cam BA (3rd cl Mech Sc Trip) 30, MA 34. DIC in Chem Eng 31. Ridley Hall Cam 34. **d** 36 **p** 37 Birm. C of Aston-juxta-Birm 36-37; CMS Miss at Bezwada 37-39; Vidyanagar 39-44; Bezwada 44-47; Ch of S India 47-50; V of Hopton 50-53; C-in-c of Conv Distr of St Matt Bestwood 53-61; V 61; R of Overstrand 61-73; P-in-c of Salle 74-78; Perm to Offic Dio Nor from 79. *1 Mill Yard, Burnham Market, King's Lynn, Norf, PE31 8H.* (B Market 342)

BUDHU, Esar. b 47. Univ of WI LTh 75. Codr Coll Barb 72. **d** 75 Barb for Guy **p** 75 Guy. C of St Phil Georgetn 75-76; St Matt Providence 76-77; L to Offic Dio Guy from 77. *National Service Secretariat, Regent & Bourda Streets, Georgetown, Guyana.*

BUFFEE, Canon Leslie John. b 30. K Coll Lon and Warm AKC 53. **d** 54 **p** 55 S'wark. C of Hither Green 54-57; M St Barn Bush Bro 57-62; Warden of St Barn Bush Bro 59-61; Chap St Barn Sch Ravenshoe 61; C of Cheam 63-65; C-in-c of St Pet Becontree 65-67; V 67-72; Min of St Paul's Conv Distr Parkeston Dio Chelmsf from 72; Commiss and Hon Can of N Queensld from 80. *St Paul's Parsonage, Parkeston, Harwich, Essex.* (Harwich 2633)

BUFFETT, Frederick. Keble Coll Ox BA (3rd cl Th) 34, MA 39. St Steph Ho Ox 34. **d** 35 Bp Crick for Derby **p** 36 Derby. C of Chesterfield 35-37; Bell I 38-39; Chap Bp Feild Coll 39-40; Chap Qu Coll St John's Newfld 40-42; CF (EC) 42-46; C of Cowley St John Ox 46-47; V of Whitworth 47-53; Kirton-in-Holland 53-64; Commiss Bunb from 58; V of Ipplepen w Torbryan Dio Ex from 64. *Ipplepen Vicarage, Newton Abbot, Devon.* (Ipplepen 215)

BUFFREY, Samuel John Thomas. b 28. Keble Coll Ox BA 52, MA 57. Cudd Coll 52. **d** 54 Bp Barkway for Cant **p** 55 Glouc. C of St Geo Conv Distr Lower Tuffley Glouc 54-56; St Aldhelm Branksome 56-61; R of St Mich w All SS Gussage 61-69; V of Amesbury 69-80; RD of Avon 77-80; P-in-c of Broadstone Dio Sarum from 80. *Vicarage, Macaulay Road, Broadstone, Dorset.* (Broadstone 694109)

BUGAIGA, John. b 32. Bp Tucker Coll Mbarara 65. **d** 67 **p** 68 Kig. P Dio Kig from 68; Dioc Treas from 74. *Nyakaina Primary School, PO Rukungiri, Kigezi, Uganda.*

BUGALIKA, William. **d** 57 Bp Omari for Centr Tang **p** 57 Centr Tang. P Dio Centr Tang 57-63; Dio Vic Nyan 63-79. *PO Box 12, Muleba, Tanzania.*

BUGBY, Timothy. b 53. AKC 75. Chich Th Coll 76. **d** 77 **p** 78 St Alb. C of Hockerill 77-81; St Mary Bourne Street Pimlico Dio Lon from 81. *St Mary's Presbytery, Graham Terrace, Sloane Square, SW1W 8JJ.* (01-730 2423)

BUGDEN, Ernest William. b 17. Lich Th Coll 56. **d** 58 **p** 59 Guild. C of Esher Dio Guildf 58-68; Hon C from 68. *Traddles, Dawes Court, Esher, Surrey.*

BUGG, Peter Richard. b 33. Univ of BC BA 62. **d** 64 Reading for Ox **p** 64 Ox. C of Ch Ch Reading 64-67; Ludlow 67-69; L to Offic Dio Zam 69-72; C-in-c Kalulushi Zam 71-72; P-in-c of Brill w Boarstall 73-78; C of Chilton w Dorton 75-77; P-in-c 77-78; V of Brill, Boarstall, Chilton and Dorton Dio Ox from 78. *Brill Vicarage, Aylesbury, Bucks, HP18 9ST.* (Brill 238325)

BUGIMBI, Methusera. b 30. Bp Tucker Coll Mukono 74. **d** 74 **p** 75 P Dio Kamp. *c/o Box 703, Kampala, Uganda.*

BUGLER, David Richard. b 38. Amer Univ Washington DC BA 60. **d** 75 Niag for Ont **p** 76 Ont. C of Leeds Rear 75-79; R 79-80; Edwardsburg Dio Ont from 80. *Box 29, Cardinal, Ont, Canada.* (613-657 3161)

BUGORO, Hugo. **d** 40 **p** 50 Melan. P Dio Melan 40-74. *Poro, Gao, Santa Ysabel, Solomon Islands.*

BUHLER, Walter Dennis. Univ of Natal BA 64. Dipl Th (S Afr) 67. St Paul's Coll Grahmstn 65. **d** 66 **p** 67 Natal. C of St Pet Pietermaritzburg 66-70; Kloof 70-75; R of St Luke Pmbg 75-80; L to Offic Dio Capetn from 80. *Box 1, Simonstown 7995, CP, S Africa.* (86-1183)

BUIK, Allan David. b 39. Univ of St Andr BSc 61. Coll of Resurr Mirfield 66. **d** 68 Win **p** 69 Southn for Win. Perm to Offic Dio Win 68-69; C of Eastleigh 69-72; St Bart Brighton 72-74; Lavender Hill 74-78; V of St Mark Kingstanding Dio Birm from 78. *St Mark's Clergy House, Bandywood Crescent, Birmingham B44 9JX,* (021-360 7288)

BUIKE, Desmond Mainwaring. b 32. Ex Coll Ox BA (3rd cl Th) 55, MA 69. Univ of Birm Dipl Th 57. Qu Coll Birm 55. **d** 57 **p** 58 Man. C of St Aid Man 57-60; St Phil and St Jas Ox 60-63; V of Queensbury Yorks 63-71; Perm to Offic Dio Brudf from 71. *10 Ascot Parade, Bradford, BD7 4NJ.*

BUIN, Arthur Lambert. b 09. Worc Ordin Coll. **d** 59 Wakef **p** 60 Pontefract for Wakef. C of St Jo Evang Huddersfield 59-61; V of Middlestown w Netherton 61-67; C of Burnham Sutton w Burnham Ulph Burnham Westgate and Burnham Norton 67-72; St Pet Cleethorpes 72-74; Perm to Offic Dio Linc 74-76; Dio Ex from 76. *87 Barrington Street, Tiverton, Devon.* (0884-255242)

BUJINDIRI, Yona. Stanley-Smith Th Coll Gahini. **d** 64 **p** 65 Rwa. P Dio Rwa 64-75; Dio Kiga from 75. *BP 61, Kigali, Rwanda.*

BUJUMBURA, Lord Bishop of. *See* Sindamuka, Right Rev Samuel.

BUKA, Benjamin. St Pet Coll Siota. **d** 64 **p** 65 P Dio Melan 64-75; Dio Centr Melan from 75. *Gorabau, Guadalcanal, Solomon Islands.*

BUKAVU, Assistant Bishop of. *See* Mbona, Right Rev Kolin.

BUKAVU, Lord Bishop of. (Vacant)

BUKEDI, Lord Bishop of. *See* Okoth, Right Rev Yona.

BUKENYA, Dunstan Kopoliano. b 43. Bp Tucker Coll Mukono 64. **d** 69 **p** 70 W Bugan. Prin Mityana Th Coll from 70. *Mityana Theological College, Box 102, Mityana, Uganda.*

BUKINDURA, Yoramu. Dioc Sch Kabale 63. **d** 64 Ankole-K. d Dio Ankole-K 64-67; Dio Ank 67-76; Dio W Ank from 77. *Box 4, Rubirizi, Uganda.*

BUKO, Benjamin. St Pet Coll Siota 62. **d** 64 **p** 65 Melan. P Dio Melan 64-75; Dio Centr Melan from 75. *Melanesian Mission, Honiara, British Solomon Islands.*

BULALI, Peter. b 50. **d** 81 Centr Tang. d Dio Centr Tang. *Box 35 PO, Mpwapwa, Tanzania.*

BULAWAYO, Dean of. *See* Siyachitema, Very Rev Jonathan.

BULE, Noel. **d** and **p** 77 New Hebr. P Dio New Hebr 77-80; Dio Vanuatu from 80. *Atabulu, Pentecost, Vanuatu.*

BULEGA, Matiya. Bp Tucker Coll Mukono 56. **d** 56 Ugan **p** 58 Bp Balya for Ugan. P Dio Momb 56-61. Dio Nam from 61. *PO Box 6125, Kampala, Uganda.*

BULELIN, Daniel. St Pet Coll Siota 63. **d** 65 **p** 67 Melan. P Dio Melan 65-75; Dio New Hebr from 75. *Lobaha, Aoba, New Hebrides.*

BULETA, Katara. b 49. St Phil Coll Kongwa 77. **d** 80 Boga-Z. d Dio Boga-Z. *E.A.Z. Boga, Bp 154, Bunia, Zaire.*

BULETWENDA, Eryeza. **d** 75 **p** 77 Ruw. P Dio Ruw. *Box 37, Fort Portal, Uganda.*

BULIHAIHI, George. **d** 52 **p** 55 Ugan. P Dio Ugan 52-60; Dio W Bugan 60-67; Dio Ruw from 67. *PO Sunga, Mubende, Uganda.*

BULL, Albert Henry. b 12. Univ of Lond BD (2nd cl Hons) 39. ALCD 39. **d** 39 **p** 40 S'wark. C of St Matthias U Tulse Hill 39-41; CF (EC) 41-44; Asst Exam Relig Kno Univ of Lon 45-50; Univ of Cam 46-50; Chap Thos Coram Sch Berkhamsted 50-53; Perm to Offic Dio S'wark from 57; Dio Guildf from 75; Asst Master Coombe Girls' Sch 60-73; *40 The Warren, Worcester Park, Surrey.* (01-337 2265)

BULL, Cecil Stanley. St Aid Th Coll Bal ACT ThL 25. **d** 25 **p** 27 Bal. C of Marnoo 25-27; P-in-c 27-28; C of Warrnambool 28-29; P-in-c of Cobden 29-31; Murtoa 31-36; V of Viti Levu W 36-39; Prec of H Trin Pro-Cathl Suva and Supt Melan Miss 40-46; VG of Polyn 45-46; Sub-Dean St Luke's Cathl Siota 46-49; V of Beaufort 49-51; N Waimate 50-54; C of Whitby Yorks 54-56; V of Warenga-a-hika 56-62; C of Tauranga 62-64; V of Gate Pa 65-70; Offg Min Dio Wai from

70. *222 Maungatapu Road, Tauranga, NZ.*

BULL, Charles Jack Mark. St Chad's Coll Regina. **d** 62 **p** 63 Qu'App. I of Rockglen 62-64; V of Cabri 64-68; R of Cupar 68-74; Indian Head Dio Qu'App from 74. *Box 1091, Indian Head, Sask., Canada.* (695-3403)

BULL, Canon Edgar Samuel. Univ of Tor BA 40, LTh 48, BD 50. **d** and **p** 48 Calg. C of Pro-Cathl Calg 48-50; St Geo Walkerville 53-55; Chap Trin Coll Tor 55-58; I of St Pet Cobourg 58-65; R of St Thos Tor 65-79; St Nich Birch Cliff City and Dio Tor from 79; Commiss Nass from 72; Can of Tor from 77. *1 Woodland Park Road, Scarborough, Ont, M1N 2X5, Canada.*

BULL, Edward Benjamin. b 1900. Qu Coll Cam 3rd cl Hist Trip pt i 26, BA (3rd cl Th Trip pt i) 28, MA 31. Ridley Hall Cam 27. **d** 29 **p** 30 S'wark. C of New Malden w Coombe 29-31; CMS Prin Nabumali High Sch 31-33; Chap Buwalasi Coll 34-35; V of Ch Ch Ince-in-Makerfield 35-38; H Trin Bris 38-43; St Giles Normanton-by-Derby 43-49; CF 43-68; R of Sudbury (w Somersal-Herbert Boylestone and Scropton 53-56) 49-58; Somersal-Herbert 49-58; RD of Longford 49-58; Chap HM Pris Sudbury Pk 49-58; C-in-c of Scropton 51-53; Boylestone 51-53; V of Beverley Minster 58-68; Dunton Bassett 68-78; RD of Guthlaxton II from 78; L to Offic Dio Leic from 78. *23 Elmhirst Road, Lutterworth, Leics, LE17 4QB.* (Lutterworth 3204)

BULL, Canon Frank Spencer. b 19. ALCD 43. Univ of Lon BD (2nd cl) 43. **d** 43 **p** 44 S'wark. C of St Jas Hatcham 43-46; St Mary Lambeth 46-49; V of All SS (w St Barn from 50) Lambeth 49-55; Herne Hill 55-66; Kenilworth Dio Cov from 66; RD of Kenilworth from 73; Hon Can of Cov from 74. *Vicarage, High Street, Kenilworth, Warws.* (Kenilworth 54367)

BULL, Herbert Frederick. Univ of Tor BA 51. Trin Coll Tor STB 62. **d** 60 **p** 61 Hur. I of Ayr 60-62; H Trin Kitchener 60-67; on leave 67-69; R of St Giles Barrie 69-70; I of Tecumseth Dio Tor from 70. *Box 55, Bondhead, Ont., Canada.* (416-775 6098)

BULL, Ian Henry. b 35. Dipl Th (Lon) 60. Oak Hill Th Coll 60. **d** 62 **p** 63 York. C of H Trin Heworth York 62-64; CF 64-77; R of Arborfield w Barkham Dio Ox from 77. *Arborfield Rectory, Reading, Berks, RG2 9HZ.* (Arborfield Cross 760285)

BULL, Leslie Wallace. ACT ThL 24. **d** and **p** 24 Willoch. C of St Paul Port Pirie 24-26; P-in-c of Kimba w Whyalla 26-27; Kimba Miss 27-28; C of Port Lincoln 28-29; R of Nathalia 29-33; Beechworth 33-40; Perm to Offic Dio Melb 40-41 and from 70; Min of Mt Dandenong w Olinda 41-49; Mordialloc 49-69; P-in-c of Lorne 69. *79 Fairview Avenue, Newtown, Vic, Australia, 3220.* (052-9 7793)

BULL, Martin Wells. b 37. Worc Coll Ox 2nd cl Cl Mods 59, BA (2nd cl Lit Hum) 61, 2nd cl Th 63, MA 68. Ripon Hall Ox 61. **d** 63 Middleton for Man **p** 64 Man. C of Blackley 63-67; All SS L Horton Bradf 67-68; V of Ingrow 68-78; Bingley Dio Bradf 78-80; Team R from 80; RD of S Craven 74-77. *Vicarage, Hall Bank Drive, Bingley, W Yorks, BD16 4BZ.* (Bradf 563113)

BULL, Ven Maxwell Lovelace Arthur. St Jo Coll Auckld. **d** 32 **p** 33 Auckld. C of Whangarei 32-37; V of Paparoa 37-44; Chap Kingseat Hosp 44; V of Waiuku 44-56; Thames 56-65; Archd of Manukau 56-65; Archd (Emer) from 65; L to Offic Dio Auckld 66-72; C of Paparoa Dio Auckld from 72. *Molesworth, RD, Mangawhai, Northland, NZ.* (Mangawhai 664)

BULL, Michael John. b 35. Roch Th Coll 65. **d** 67 Repton for Derby **p** 68 Derby. C of N Wingfield 67-69; Skegness (in c of St Clem) 69-72; R of Ingoldmells w Addlethorpe 72-79; USPG Area Sec Dio S'wark from 79. *c/o 15 Tufton Street, SW1P 3QQ.*

BULL, Norman John. b 16. Trin Coll Ox Ford Student 2nd cl Th 38, BA 39, MA 48. Univ of Reading PhD 67. Linc Th Coll 38. **d** 39 **p** 40 Chelmsf. C of St Botolph Colchester 39-41; St Mary Loughton 41-43; Offg C-in-c of Sheet Petersfield 44-45; C of Croydon 45-46; Youth Chap Dio Cant 46-48; Chap and Lect St Luke's Tr Coll Ex 49-60; Sen Lect Relig Educn 60-63; Prin Lect 63-75. *21 Wonford Road, Exeter, Devon.* (Exeter 55806)

BULL, Robert David. b 51. Ripon Coll Cudd 74. **d** 77 Bp Ramsey for Man **p** 78 Man. C of Worsley 77-80; Peel Dio Man 80; Team V from 81. *4 Greencourt Drive, Little Hulton, Worsley, Manchester, M28 6BZ.* (061-790 7024)

BULL, Robert Humphrey. b 06. FIMarE CEng 73. **d** 74 Dorchester for Ox **p** 74 Reading for Ox (NSM). C of St Jo w St Steph Reading Dio Ox from 74. *1 Tamarisk Avenue, Reading, Berks, RG2 8JB.* (Reading 81441)

BULL, William. b 05. St Aug Coll Cant 57. **d** 57 Guildf **p** 58 Kingston T for Guildf. C of St Pet Hersham 57-58; Merrow 58-60; R of St Cross Clayton 60-65; V of Swallowfield 65-70. *27 Bromley College, London Road, Bromley, Kent, BR1 1PE.*

BULL, William George. b 28. Sarum Th Coll 65. **d** 66 **p** 67 Sarum. C of St Mich AA Sarum 66-69; V of Swallowcliffe w Ansty 69-75; Youth Officer Dio Sarum 69-71; C-in-c of Laverstock Dio Sarum 75-81; V from 81. *14 Church Road, Laverstock, Salisbury, Wilts.* (Salisbury 4036)

BULLED, Trevor John. b 49. ACT ThL 73. Ridley Coll Melb 71. **d** 74 **p** 75 Bend. C of St Paul Ben 74-75; Swan Hill 75-77; M Bush Bro of St Paul Dio Brisb 77-80; R of Camp Hill City and Dio Brisb from 80. *101 Watson Street, Camp Hill, Queensland, Australia 4152.* (398 2106)

BULLEN, George William. St Jo Coll Winnipeg. **d** 54 **p** 55 Keew. I of Jack River 55-59; Prin Chooutla Ind Sch Carcross 59-62; I of Massett Inlet Miss 63-74; Pouce Coupe Dio Caled from 74. *Box 249, Pouce Coupe, BC, Canada.* (604-786 5615)

BULLEN, Grantley Kenneth. Univ of Adel BA 75. St Barn Coll Adel. **d** 79 **p** 80 Adel. C of Edwardstow w Ascot Pk 79-80; on leave from 80. *c/o 58 Marlborough Road, Westbourne Park, S Australia 5041.* (272 4032)

BULLEN, Harvey. b 42. Mem Univ Newfld BA 68, LTh 69. Qu Coll Newfld 68. **d** 68 **p** 69 Newfld. C of Flowers Cove 68-69; Dir Relig Educn Dio Newfld 70-76; C of Gander Dio Centr Newfld from 76. *55a Edinburgh Avenue, Gander, Newfoundland, Canada.*

BULLEN, Richard David Guy. b 43. Ripon Hall Ox 73. **d** 75 **p** 76 York. C of Pocklington 75-78; Team V of Thornaby-on-Tees Dio York from 78. *Vicarage, Acklam Road, Thornaby-on-Tees, Cleve, TS17 7HD.*

BULLEN, Trevor Henry. b 31. Sarum Th Coll 53. **d** 56 **p** 57 St E. C of Rushmere 56-58; St Mark Leic 58-60; V of Wismar w Lower Demerara River 60-64; R of Nedging w Naughton 64-67; V of Gt Bricett 64-67; Chap RN 67-70; R of Freston w Woolverstone 70-75; Cler Org Sec C of E Children's S in NE 75-79; C of Gilling Dio Ripon from 79. *Hill House, Whashton, Richmond, N Yorks, DL11 7JP.* (Richmond 4522)

BULLEY, Roger Charles. b 12. Univ of Lon BCom 34, BA 37. Wells Th Coll 38. **d** 40 **p** 41 Lon. C of St Matt Stepney 40-42; St Pet London Docks 42-48; Perm to Offic Dio Ox 48-50; C of All SS Clifton 50-53; V of St Silas Islington and Chap R Nthn Hosp 53-58; Winterbourne Down 58-71; Chap Frenchay Hosp 65-70; Chap Commun of St Jo Bapt Clewer 71-79; Conv of Sisters of Charity Knowle from 79. *St John's Cottage, Tennis Road, Knowle, Bristol, BS4 2HG.* (Bris 777738)

✠ **BULLEY, Right Rev Sydney Cyril.** b 07. Van Mildert Scho St Chad's Coll Dur BA 32, Dipl Th 33, MA 36. Hon DD 72. **d** 33 **p** 34 Southw. C of Newark w Coddington 33-42; Dir of Relig Educn and Dioc Insp of Schs Dio Southw 36-42; PC of St Anne Worksop 42-46; V of Mansfield 46-51; Org Insp of Schs Dio Southw 41-47; Can of Oxton Prima Pars in Southw Minster and Proc Conv Southw 45-51; RD of Mansfield 46-51; Surr 47-58; Hon Can of Carl 51-58; Archd of Westmorland and Dir of Relig Educn Dio Carl 51-58; V of Ambleside w Rydal 51-59; Exam Chap to Bp of Carl 51-66; Chap to HM the Queen from 56; Archd of Westmorland and Furness 59-65; Cons Ld Bp Suffr of Penrith 24 Feb 59 in York Minster by Abp of York; Bps of Dur; Liv; Carl; Blackb; and Wakef; Bps Suffr of Pontefract; Whitby; Burnley; and Hull; and Bps Gerard and Graham; Trld to Carl 66; Res 72; Chap & Tutor All SS Coll Bathurst 73-74; Hon Asst Bp of Ox from 75. *The Manor, Longcot, Faringdon, Oxon.*

BULLEY, William Joseph. b 28. Chich Th Coll 65. **d** 67 **p** 68 Ex. C of Littleham w Exmouth 67-72; V of Harberton w Harbertonford 72-77; R of Chagford (w Gidleigh and Throwleigh from 79) Dio Ex from 77. *Rectory, Chagford, Devon.* (Chagford 2265)

BULLIMAN, Jack Francis. Worc Ordin Coll 56. **d** 57 **p** 58 Birm. C of Langley 57-60; C-in-c of Conv Distr of Ch Ch Davyhulme 60-63; V of Fishlake 63-66; C-in-c of Sykehouse 63-66; R of Armthorpe 66-69; V of Bramley 69-72; Perm to Offic Dio Sheff from 77. *5 Willow Road, Armthorpe, Doncaster, Yorks.*

BULLIVANT, Canon Ronald. b 13. **d** and **p** 43 Ox. C of Aylesbury 43-45; St Alphege S'wark 45-53; V of Annunc Brighton Dio Chich from 53; Can and Preb of Chich Cathl from 78. *89 Washington Street, Brighton, Sussex BN2 2SR.* (Brighton 681341)

BULLIVANT, Ronald. b 32. St Mich Coll Llan. **d** 59 **p** 60 Llan. C of St German Roath 59-61; C-in-c of H Trin Bradf 61-66; V of Horbury 66-69; L to Offic Dio Ripon from 70; Dio Nor from 81; Lect Bradf Coll 70-73; Peterborough Tech Coll from 74. *22 Cleaves Drive, Walsingham, Norf, NR22 6EQ.* (032-872 526)

BULLMAN, Anthony Horsley. Em Coll Sktn 64. **d** 66 **p** 67 Sktn. I of Lintlaw 66-70; R of Endeavour 69-70; Strathmore 70-72; St Jo Evang Calg 72-73; on leave 74-77; R of Blairmore 77-80; Rocky Mountain Ho Dio Calg from 80. *Box 328, Rocky Mountain House, Alta, Canada.* (845-3592)

BULLOCK, Christopher Lloyd. **d** 78 **p** 79 N Queensld. Prin & Chap All S & St Gabriel's Sch Charters Towers Dio N Queensld from 78. *All Souls' and St Gabriel's School, PO Box 235, Charters Towers, Qld, Australia 4820.*

BULLOCK, Grover Cleveland. St Pet Coll Ja. Univ of Dur LTh 37. **d** 36 **p** 37 Ja. C of All SS Kingston 36-38; R of Pratville 38-43; Grange Hill 43-56; Black River (w Lacovia from 62) 56-67. *4 Sullivan Way, Kingston 8, Jamaica, W Indies.*

BULLOCK, Canon John Raymond. b 16. Ch Ch Ox BA 37, MA 46. Westcott Ho Cam. **d** 48 **p** 49 Dur. C of St Mich AA S Westoe S Shields 48-50; St Martin-in-the-Fields Lon 50-54; PC of Easington Colliery 54-62; Chap Easington Hosps 54-62; RD of Easington 58-62; Hartlepool 62-78; V of St Paul Hartlepool Dio Dur from 62; C-in-c of Ch Ch Hartlepool Dio Dur 65-73; Proc Conv Dur 67-75; Hon Can of Dur Cathl from 70. *6 Hutton Avenue, Hartlepool, Cleve, TS26 9PN.* (Hartlepool 72934)

BULLOCK, Kenneth Poyser. b 27. Down Coll Cam BA 50, MA 55. Ridley Hall Cam 50. **d** 52 Birm **p** 53 Bp Linton for Cant. C of Aston Birm 52-56; R of Openshaw 56-63; V of Ainsworth Dio Man from 63. *Ainsworth Vicarage, Bolton, Lancs, BL2 5RU.* (Bolton 22662)

BULLOCK, Michael. b 49. Hatf Coll Dur BA 71. Univ of Leeds Dipl Th 74. Coll of Resurr Mirfield 73. **d** 75 **p** 76 Pet. C of St Jo Bapt Pet 75-80; Miss at Fiwila Dio Centr Zam from 81. *P Bag 52XK, Kabwe, Zambia.*

BULLOCK-FLINT, Peter. b 22. Kelham Th Coll 39. **d** 45 **p** 46 S'wark. C of St Paul w St Mark Deptford 45-48; Ch Ch Streatham Hill 48-50; Boyne Hill Maidenhead 50-56; C-in-c of St Mary Magd Conv Distr Tilehurst 56-72; V of Hughenden Dio Ox from 72. *Hughenden Vicarage, High Wycombe, Bucks, HP14 4PF.* (Naphil 3439)

BULLOUGH, Canon Walter Herbert. b 15. AKC 39. **d** 39 **p** 40 Liv. C of St Mary Widnes 39-41; Perm to Offic at Much Woolton (in c of St Hilda) 41-44; V of St Matt Highfield 44-59; RD of Wigan 58-59; Ormskirk 69-78; R of Halsall Dio Liv from 59; Hon Can of Liv Cathl from 71. *Halsall Rectory, Ormskirk, Lancs.* (Halsall 840321)

BULMAN, David John. b 22. Univ of Bris BA 49. Tyndale Hall Bris 46. **d** 50 **p** 51 S'wark. C of St John Deptford 50-52; Edgware 52-56; V of St Silas Lozells 56-64; N Ferriby Dio York from 64; Area Dean of W Hull from 79. *Vicarage, North Ferriby, N Humb.* (Hull 631306)

BULMAN, Harold Gordon. b 08. Em Coll Cam BA 32, MA 46. Ridley Hall Cam 32. **d** 34 **p** 35 Sarum. C of St John Heatherlands Parkstone 34-37; CMS Miss Gahini Ruanda 37-46; on furlough 46-48; V of St Gabr (w St Lawr from 54) Easton, Bris 48-72; C-in-c of St Lawr Bris 50-54; H Trin Bris 66-72; C-in-c of Littleton-on-Severn w Elberton 72-74; Perm to Offic Dio Bris from 75. *54 Alma Vale Road, Clifton, Bristol, BS8 2HR.* (Bristol 32925)

BULMAN, Michael Thomas Andrew. b 34. Jes Coll Cam BA 59, MA 62. Ridley Hall Cam 58. **d** 60 Lanc for York **p** 61 Blackb. C of St Mark Layton Blackpool 60-63; St Clem Parkstone 63-67; V of St Barn City and Dio York from 67. *St Barnabas's Vicarage, Leeman Road, York.* (York 54214)

BULMAN, William Irving. b 02. Edin Th Coll 28. **d** 30 **p** 31 Lon. C of St Steph Ealing 30-32; St Gabr Cricklewood 32-37; V 37-71. *Address temp unknown*

BULMER, Alan David. St Francis Coll Brisb ThDip 79. **d** 79 **p** 80 Brisb. C of St Aug Hamilton Dio Brisb from 79. *Flat 3, 18 Ruper Terrace, Ascot, Queensland, Australia 4007.*

BULMER, Garth Elliott. b 45. McGill Univ Montr BD 70. Montr Dioc Th Coll LTh 70. **d** 70 **p** 71 Montr. C of St Phil Montr 70-73; R of All SS Verdun Montr 73-75; Ste Agathe w Ste Marguerite 75-78; Co-Dir of Tyndale St Geo Project Montr from 78. *2270 St Antoine Street West, Montreal, PQ, Canada.*

BULU, Roy. **d** 77 **p** 79 New Hebr. P Dio New Hebr 77-80; Dio Vanuatu from 80. *Aute, N Pentecost, Vanuatu.*

BUNBURY, Lord Bishop of. *See* Goldsworthy, Right Rev Arthur Stanley.

BUNBURY, Coadjutor Bishop of. (Vacant)

BUNBURY, Dean of. *See* Taylor, Very Rev Anthony James.

BUNCE, Michael John. b 49. St Andr Univ MTh 79. Westcott Ho Cam 78. **d** 80 Grantham for Linc **p** 81 Linc. C of Grantham Dio Linc from 80. *26 Castlegate, Grantham, Lincs, NG31 6SW.* (Grantham 4351)

BUNCE, Raymond Frederick. b 28. Ely Th Coll 54. **d** 57 **p** 58 Lon. C of St Andr Uxbridge 57-62; Gt Greenford (in c of St Edw Perivale Pk) 62-67; V of All SS Ealing Dio Lon from 67. *Vicarage, Elm Grove Road, W5 3JH.* (01-567 8166)

BUNCE, Wilfred Lawrence. b 1898. St Edm Hall Ox BA (3rd cl Mod Hist) 23, Dipl in Th 24, MA 28. Ripon Hall Ox 24. **d** 25 **p** 26 S'wark. C of H Trin S Wimbledon 25-28; Caversham (in c of St John) 28-34; Amersham (in c of All SS Coleshill) 34-47; PC of L Faringdon 47-61; V of Langford 47-61; PC of Warborough 61-67; Perm to Offic Dio Ox from 67. *The Close, Burlot, Abingdon, Oxford, OX14 3DP.*

BUNCH, Francis Christopher. b 14. St Pet Hall Ox BA (3rd cl Geog) 36, Dipl in Th 37, MA 40. Wycl Hall Ox 36. **d** 38 **p** 39 S'wark. C of Lambeth 38-41; St John Southend Village Catford (in c of St Barn Downham) 41-43; Chap RNVR 43-46; V of H Trin Bromley Common 46-56; Otford Dio Roch from 56. *Otford Vicarage, Sevenoaks, Kent, TN14 5PD.* (Otford 3185)

BUNDAY, Paul. b 30. Wadh Coll Ox BA 54. MA 58. ALCD 56. **d** 56 **p** 57 Guildf. C of St Jo Bapt Woking 56-60; Chap Reed's Sch Cobham 60-66; R of Landford w Plaitford 66-76; Radipole and Melcombe Regis Dio Sarum 77-79; Team R from 79; RD of Alderbury 73-76. *42 Melcombe Avenue, Weymouth, Dorset, DT4 7TF.* (Wey 785553)

BUNDOCK, Edward Leigh. b 52. Keble Coll Ox BA 73. St Steph Ho Ox 74. **d** 76 **p** 77 Worc. C of Malvern Link w Cowleigh 76-80; P-in-c of Good Shepherd Conv Distr Mile Oak Portslade Dio Chich from 80. *35 Stanley Road, Mile Oak, Portslade, Brighton, BN4 2WH.* (Brighton 419518)

BUNDOCK, Canon John Frederick. b 05. Univ of Lon BSc 25. Univ of Reading BSc 31. St Steph Ho Ox 30. **d** 31 **p** 32 Worc. C of St Paul Worc 31-35; St Steph Lewisham 35-40; Perm to Offic at Malvern Link 40-42; C of Upminster 42-45; V of Highwood 45-52; St Marg Leigh 52-75; Ed *Essex Churchman* 61-63; Asst RD of Canewdon and Southend 65-75; M Gen Syn Chelmsf 70-75; Hon Can of Chelmsf Cathl 74-75; Can (Emer) from 75. *Domus, The Street, Feering, Colchester, Essex CO5 9QQ.* (Kelvedon 71135)

BUNDOCK, John Nicholas Edward. b 45. Wells Th Coll 66. **d** 70 **p** 71 Barking for Chelmsf. C of St Pet and St Paul Chingford 70-74; Scartho Dio Linc from 74; P-in-c of St Matt Fairfield Conv Distr Scartho 74-81; V of Hindhead Dio Guildf from 81. *Vicarage, Wood Road, Hindhead, Surrey, GU26 6PX.* (Hindhead 5305)

BUNDU, George King. Newton Coll Dogura 59. **d** 61 **p** 64 New Guinea. P Dio New Guinea 64-71; Dio Papua from 71. *Anglican Church, Eiwo, via Popondota, Papua New Guinea.*

BUNINGWIRE, Yoeri. MBE 56. Bp Tucker Mem Coll Mukono. **d** 16 **p** 18 Ugan. P Dio Ugan 18-61; Can of Ugan 43-61. *Church of Uganda, Lutoma, PO Box 14, Mbarara, Uganda.*

BUNKER, Harry. b 28. Oak Hill Th Coll. **d** 59 Sherborne for Sarum **p** 60 Sarum. C of Longfleet 59-63; R of Blisworth Dio Pet from 63. *Blisworth Rectory, Northampton.* (Blisworth 858412)

BUNKER, John Herbert George. b 31. K Coll Lon and Warm. AKC 56. **d** 57 **p** 58 Newc T. C of St Jo Bapt Newc T 57-60; St Geo Cullercoats (in c of St Hilda Marden) 60-65; V of St Mich Byker Newc T 65-74; Ashington Dio Newc T from 74. *Vicarage, Ashington, Northumb, NG63 8HZ.* (Ashington 813358)

BUNKER, Michael. b 37. Oak Hill Th Coll 59. **d** 63 **p** 64 Lon. C of Alperton 63-66; St Helens 66-70; V of St Matt Muswell Hill 70-78; St Jas (w St Matt from 79) Muswell Hill Dio Lon from 78. *St James's Vicarage, Muswell Hill, N10 3DB.* (01-883 6277)

BUNNELL, Adrian. b 49. Univ of Wales (Abth) BSc 72. St Mich AA Coll Llan 74. **d** 75 **p** 76 St A. C of Wrexham 75-78; Rhyl 78-79; CF from 79. *c/o Ministry of Defence, Bagshot Park, Bagshot, Surrey.*

BUNSIE, Chimbie. b 53. St Andr Th Sem Manila 76. **d** 80 **p** 81 Kuch. P Dio Kuch. *St Thomas Cathedral, PO Box 347, Kuching, E Malaysia.*

BUNT, Brian William. b 34. Univ of Bris BA 63. BD (Lon) 67. Tyndale Hall Bris. **d** 68 **p** 69 Chich. C of St Pancras w St Jo Evang Chich 68-72; Camborne 72-75; P-in-c of St John City and Dio Truro from 75. *St John's Vicarage, Daniell Road, Truro, Cornw.* (Truro 79873)

BUNTING, Ian David. b 33. Late Exhib of Ex Coll Ox BA 58, MA 61. Tyndale Hall Bris 57. Princeton Th Sem USA ThM 60. **d** 60 **p** 61 Liv. C of St Leon Bootle 60-63; V of St Jo Div Waterloo 64-71; Dir of Past Stud St Jo Coll Dur 71-78; R of Chester-le-Street Dio Dur from 78; RD of Chester-le-Street from 79. *Rectory, Chester-le-Street, Durham, DH3 3PU.* (Chester-le-Street 883295)

BUNTING, Jeremy John. b 34. St Cath Coll Cam BA 56, MA 60. Worc Coll Ox BA 58, MA 60. St Steph Ho Ox 57. **d** 59 **p** 60 Roch. C of Bickley 59-62; St Mary L Cam 62-66; Fell and Tutor Gen Th Sem NY 66-68; R of Stock Harvard Dio Chelmsf from 68; RD of Wickford 73-79; M Gen Syn 75-80. *Stock Rectory, Ingatestone, Essex, CM4 9BN.* (0277 840453)

BUNYAN, John Reynolds. Univ of Syd BA 57. STh (Lambeth) 80. **d** 59 **p** 60 C & Goulb. Asst Master Canberra Gr Sch 59-62; C of Wagga Wagga 63; C of St Paul, Canberra 66-67; Tutor St Mark's Libr Canberra and Perm to Offic Dio C & Goulb 67-68; C of Shirley, Hants 69; Vice-Warden St Jo Coll Morpeth 70-72; Lect 72-75; Prec and Min Can of Ch Ch

Cathl Newc 73-75; C of St Jas Syd 76-78; R of Chester Hill w Sefton Dio Syd from 78. *Box 9, Chester Hill, NSW, Australia 2162.* (644-4196)

BUNYAN, Richard Charles. b 43. Oak Hill Th Coll 63. Ridley Hall Cam 69. **d** 71 **p** 72 Roch. C of Luton Roch 71-74; Bexleyheath 74-76; St Jo Evang Bexley (in c of Blendon) 76-79; Team V of Em Northn 79-81; V of Erith Dio Roch from 81. *100 Park Crescent, Erith, Kent.* (Erith 32555)

BUNYAN, Walter Frederick. b 17. K Coll Lon AKC 41. **d** 41 Bp Mann for Roch **p** 42 Roch. C of St Barn Gillingham 41-44; St Jo Bapt w St Edm Miss Ch Felixstowe 44-46; R of Komgha 46-49; Uitenhage Dio Grahamstn 49-54; V of St Luke Woodside Croydon 54-58; Commiss Grahmstn 57-58; Vice-Provost and R of St Mary's Colleg Ch Port Eliz 58-68; Can of Grahmstn 64-68; Archd of Port Eliz 64-68; R of St Pet Port Eliz 64-68; Metrop Sec USPG 68-69; V of St Andr Kingsbury 69-74; Archd and R of Kroonstad 74-80; Can of Bloemf 74-80; P-in-c of Carbis Bay Dio Truro 80-81; V from 82. *Carbis Bay Vicarage, St Ives, Cornw.* (St Ives 6206)

BUNYORO, Lord Bishop of. *See* Rwakaikara, Right Rev Yonasani.

BUQUE, Naftali. d 47 **p** 48 Lebom. P Dio Lebom; Distr Supt of Maxixe from 75. *Caixa Postal 56, Maxixe, Mozambique.*

BURARINDIMA, Yohana. d 60 **p** 61 Rwanda B. P Dio Rwanda B 60-66; Dio Bur 66-75; Dio Buye from 75; Archd of N Bur 68-75. *P.O. Box 58, Ngozi, Burundi, Centr. Africa.*

BURBERY, Ian Edward. b 37. St D Coll Lamp BA 59. Coll of Resurr Mirfield 59. **d** 61 Llan **p** 62 Bp T M Hughes for Llan. C of Penarth w Lavernock 61-68; V of Porth 68-77; Cainscross w Selsley Dio Glouc from 77. *58 Cashes Green Road, Stroud, Glos, GL5 4RA.* (Stroud 4848)

BURBIDGE, Canon Edward Humphrey. Qu Coll Cam 3rd cl Hist Trip pt i 29, BA (3rd cl Th Trip pt i) 30, MA 34. St Aug Coll Cant 30. **d** 31 **p** 32 Wakef. C of All SS Castleford 31-34; R of Esperance W Austr 34-37; V of Arreton 37-43; St Jo Bapt Purbrook 43-47; Can and R of Pro-Cathl Bunb 47-54; Can (Emer) from 58; R of Wagin 54-58; Mandurah 58-65; on leave 65-66; L to Offic Dio Perth from 66. *48 Ullapool Road, Mount Pleasant, W Australia 6153.* (364 1019)

BURBRIDGE, Ven John Paul. b 32. K Coll Cam BA 54, MA 58. New Coll Ox BA 54, MA 58. Wells Th Coll 58. **d** 59 **p** 60 Chich. C of Eastbourne 59-62; V Cho and Chamberlain of York Minster 62-66; Can Res Succr and Preb 66-76; Prec 69-76; Can Res of Ripon Cathl from 76; Archd of Richmond from 76. *The Old Vicarage, Sharow, Ripon, HG4 5BN.* (Ripon 5771)

BURBRIDGE, Richard James. b 47. Univ of Wales (Bangor) BSc 68. Oak Hill Th Coll 68. **d** 72 **p** 73 Bris. C of Rodbourne-Cheney 72-75; Downend 75-78; P-in-c of H Cross Inns Court Green City and Dio Bris from 78. *Holy Cross Vicarage, Inns Court Green, Bristol, BS4 1TF.* (Bristol 664123)

BURCH, Cyril John. b 18. K Coll Lon and Warm AKC 49. **d** 49 **p** 50 Cant. C of Milton Regis 49-51; St Mich AA Croydon 51-52; PV of Wells Cathl and Asst Master Jun Sch 52-57; Chap Prestfelde Sch Shrewsbury 57-58; Chap Cathl Sch Llan 58-63; V of Stoke Mandeville Dio Ox from 63. *Stoke Mandeville Vicarage, Aylesbury, Bucks.* (Stoke Mandeville 2236)

BURCH, John Anthony. b 37. Open Univ BA 75. Wycl Hall Ox 67. **d** 69 Dorking for Guildf **p** 70 Guildf. C of Ch Ch Guildf 69-72; Cove w S Hawley 72-75; Team V of Fincham 75-79; V of St Barn Huntingdon 79-81. *c/o New Rectory, Oxmoor, Huntingdon.* (Huntingdon 53717)

BURCH, John Christopher. b 50. Trin Coll Cam BA 71, MA 76. St Jo Coll Nottm 73. **d** 76 **p** 77 Sheff. C of St Jo Evang Park Sheff 76-79; Holbeck 79-82; V of Burmantofts Dio Ripon from 82. *Vicarage, Shakespeare Close, Leeds, LS17 9DG.* (Leeds 482648)

BURCH, Peter John. b 36. ACA 60, FCA 71. Ripon Hall Ox 62. **d** 64 **p** 65 S'wark. C of St Matt Brixton 64-67; CMS Miss Dio Sier L 67-72; P-in-c of St Pet Gt Chich 72-76; V of Broadwater Down Dio Chich from 76. *1 St Mark's Road, Tunbridge Wells, Kent, TN2 5LT.* (Tunbridge Wells 26069)

BURCH, Sidney Aldred Richard. Bps' Coll Cheshunt 63. **d** 65 **p** 66 Lon. C of Whitton 65-68; St Sav Westcliff-on-Sea Dio Chelmsf from 68. *107a Crowstone Road, Westcliff-on-Sea, Essex.* (Southend-on-Sea 47460)

BURCH, Victor Ernest Charles. b 18. Nor Ordin Course 73. **d** 76 **p** 77 Nor (APM). C of St Barn w St Bart Heigham 76-80; St Jo Bapt & All SS Lakenham Dio Nor from 80. *35 Oaklands, Framingham Earl, Norwich, NR14 7QS.*

✠ **BURCH, Right Rev William Gerald.** Univ of Tor BA 38. Wycl Coll Tor Hon DD 57. Em Coll Sktn Hon DD 62. **d** 36 **p** 38 Tor. C of Ch Ch Tor 36-40; I of Scarborough Junction w Sandown Pk 40-42; R of St Luke Winnipeg 42-52; All SS Windsor 52-56; Exam Chap to Bp of Hur 55-56; Can of Hur 56; Dean and R of All SS Pro-Cathl Edmon 56-60; Cons Ld Bp Suffr of Edmon in All SS Cathl Edmon 26 Apr 60 by Abp of Rupld; Abp of Edmon (Primate); Bps of Qu'App; Athab; Calg; Sask; and Montana (USA); Elected Bp of Edmon 61; res 76; Asst Bp of BC from 79. *901 Richmond Avenue, Victoria, BC, Canada.*

BURCHILL, William Ian. ACT ThL 66. **d** 54 **p** 55 Nel. C-in-c of Granity 54-57; V of Ahaura w Brunnerton 57-59; R of Milloo w Mitiamo 59-64; Koorawatha 64-67; Bodalla w Narooma 67-71; Warragul Dio Gippsld from 71. *104 Victoria Street, Warragul, Vic., Australia 3820.* (056-23 1655)

BURDEN, Arthur Theodore. b 11. St Pet Hall Ox BA 35, MA 42. Wycl Hall Ox 35. **d** 37 **p** 38 Chelmsf. C of Em, Forest Gate 37-38; Dagenham 38-41; Sidbury 41-42; Chap RAFVR 42-46; V of St Paul, Finchley 46-63; St Paul Dorking 63-73; Defford w Besford 73-78; Eckington 73-78. *7 Golden Valley, Castlemorton, Malvern, Worcs, WR13 6AA,*

BURDEN, Derek. b 29. St Edm Hall Ox BA (2nd cl Mod Lang) 52, MA 56. Wells Th Coll 56. **d** 58 **p** 59 S'wark. C of St Mark Mitcham 58-61; Chap Sarum Tr Coll 61-68; V of Coombe Bissett w Homington 61-69; N Bradley w Southwick (and Brokerswood to 73) 69-79; Steeple Ashton w Semington Dio Sarum from 79; Keevil Dio Sarum from 79. *Steeple Ashton Vicarage, Trowbridge, Wilts.* (Keevil 870236)

BURDEN, Derek Ronald. b 37. Sarum Th Coll 59. **d** 62 **p** 63 Guildf. C of Cuddington 62-64; Leamington 64-67; All SS Stamford (in c of St Mich) 66-74; C-in-c of Ch Ch Stamford 71-74; Ashbury w Compton Beauchamp Dio Ox 74-77; V (w Longcot and Fernham from 81) from 77. *Ashbury Vicarage, Swindon, Wilts.* (Ashbury 231)

BURDEN, Michael Henry. b 36. Selw Coll Cam BA 59, MA 63. Univ of Hull MEducn 81. Ridley Hall Cam 60. **d** 62 **p** 63 Ches. C of St Mary Magd Ashton-on-Mersey 62-65; Chap St Pet Jun Sch York 65-70; Asst Master Beverley Gr Sch 70-74; R of Walkington 74-77; Hd of Commun Stud Sir Leo Schultz High Sch Hull from 77. *Westwood Mill, Beverley, N Humb.* (Beverley 862252)

BURDETT, John Fergusson. b 25. Pemb Coll Cam BA 47, MA 79. **d** 79 **p** 80 Edin. C of St Jo Evang City and Dio Edin from 79. *5 Wardie Avenue, Edinburgh, EH5 2AB.*

BURDETT, Stephen Martin. b 49. AKC 72. St Aug Coll Cant 73. **d** 74 **p** 75 S'wark. C of St Pet Walworth 74-77; All SS Benhilton 77-80; P-in-c of St Jo Div Earlsfield Dio S'wark from 80. *St John's Vicarage, Atheldene Road, SW18 3BW.* (01-874 2837)

BURDON, Anthony James. b 46. Univ of Ex LLB 67. BD (Lon) 73. Oak Hill Coll 71. **d** 73 **p** 74 Ox. C of St Ebbe Ox 73-76; Ch Stretton 76-78; Cand Sec CPAS 78-81; Hon C of Ch Ch Bromley 78-81; Perm to Offic Dio Nor 79-81; V of Filkins w Broadwell, Broughton, Kelmscott & Kencot Dio Ox from 81. *Filkins Vicarage, Lechlade, Glos, GL7 3JQ.* (Filkins 460)

BURDON, Christopher John. b 48. Jes Coll Cam BA 70, MA 74. Univ of Leeds Dipl Th 73. Coll of Resurr Mirfield 71. **d** 74 **p** 75 Chelmsf. C of All SS Chelmsf 74-78; Team V of High Wycombe Dio Ox from 78. *St James's Vicarage, Plomer Hill, High Wycombe, Bucks.* (H Wycombe 25346)

BURDON, Edward Arthur. b 11. Linc Th Coll 44. **d** 46 **p** 47 B & W. C of H Trin Taunton 46-48; Mayfield Sussex 48-54; V of Gosfield 54-72; V of Coggeshall w Markshall 72-80. *20 Naverne Meadow, Woodbridge, Suff.* (Woodbridge 4787)

BURDON, John Edmund. b 08. Chich Th Coll 39. **d** 42 **p** 43 Newc T. C of Prudhoe 42-44; Delaval 44-49; N Gosforth (in c of St Aid Brunton Pk) 49-52;m R of Falstone 52-59; V of Whorlton 59-68; Long Framlington w Brinkburn 68-76. *2 Whitegates, Aydon Road, Corbridge, Northumb, NE45 7DF.* (Corbridge 2563)

BURDON, Roger Allen. Univ of Tor BA 49. Wycl Coll Tor LTh 52. **d** 52 Bran **p** 52 Edmon. C of Ch Ch Edmon 52-55; I of Edgerton 55-56; Pincher Creek (Foothills Miss) 56-63; R of St Phil Edmon 63-70; on leave 71-76; Chap Nanaimo Gen Hosp BC from 76. *Nanaimo Hospital, Nanaimo, BC, Canada.*

BURDON, William. b 23. Univ of Leeds BA 51. Coll of Resurr Mirfield 51. **d** 53 **p** 54 Derby. C of St Anne Derby 53-57; All SS Weston-s-Mare 57-62; All SS Clifton w St Mary Tyndall's Pk 63-64; V of Skirwith (w Ousby & Melmerby from 73) Dio Carl from 64. *Skirwith Vicarage, Penrith, Cumb.* (Culgaith 663)

BURENGERO, Yasoni. d 80 Kiga. d Dio Kiga. *BP 26, Ruhengeri, Rwanda.*

BURFORD, Alfred Graham. b 10. St D Coll Lamp BA 50. Univ of Leic Dipl Educn 51. **d** 58 **p** 59 Leic. C of St Jo Bapt Knighton 58-60; R of Cole Orton 60-65; V of St Paul Leic 65-74; Long Clawson w Hose 74-80. *West End Cottage, The West End, Long Clawson, Melton Mowbray, Leicester, LE14 4PG.*

BURFORD, Jack William. b 03. Univ of Leeds BA (2nd cl Cl) 27. Linc Th Coll 27. **d** 28 **p** 29 S'wark. C of St Luke

Richmond 28-31; St Jas Camberwell 31-33; Tarrant Gunville w Tarrant Rushton Tarrant Rawston and Tarrant Keynston 33-36; R of Stoney Stanton 36-42; V of St Matt Leic 42-52; Brixworth 52-68; L to Offic Dio St A from 71. *Copyhold, Llandyssil, Powys.* (Montg 264)

BURGE, Anthony Ernest Robert. b 41. Univ of Tas BA 70. St Columb's Hall Wang Th Dipl 70. **d** 67 **p** 68 Wang. C of H Trin Cathl Wang 67; Perm to Offic Dios Wang and Tas 67-70; C of Wodonga 70-71; St Mary S Ruislip 71-75; V of St Anselm Hayes 75-79; R of Lake Grace Dio Bunb from 79. *Rectory, Lake Grace, W Australia 6353.*

BURGE, Evan Laurie. Ball Coll Ox BA (1st cl Lit Hum) 58, MA 62. Univ of Queensld BA (1st cl Cl) 56. Princeton Univ MA and PhD 69. **d** 60 **p** 71 C & Goulb. C of St Phil, Canberra 60-74; Warden Trin Coll Melb from 74. *Trinity College, Royal Parade, Parkville, Vic, Australia 3052.* (03-347 1044)

BURGESS, Alfred George. b 18. Univ of Wales BA 39. St Mich Coll Llan 39. **d** 41 **p** 42 Swan B. C of Ch Ch Swansea 41-44; Cefnllys w H Trin Llandrindod 44-47; Stratford-on-Avon 47-49; V of Longford w Hawkesbury 49-58; Alveston 58-81; RD of Stratford-on-Avon 69-73; R of Ilmington w Stretton-on-Fosse Dio Cov from 81. *Ilmington Rectory, Shipston-on-Stour, Warws.* (Ilmington 210)

BURGESS, Christopher Raymond. Univ of Syd BSc 72. Moore Coll Syd ACT ThL 74. BD (Lon) 76. **d** and **p** 76 Syd. C of St David Forestville 76-77; St Steph Penrith 77-80; C-in-c of Cam Pk Dio Syd from 80. *Oxford Street, Cambridge Park, NSW, Australia 2750.* (047-31 6060)

BURGESS, Colin. b 38. St Aid Coll 63. **d** 65 Burnley for Blackb **p** 66 Blackb. C of St Steph Blackb 65-68; Chap Miss to Seamen Trinid 68-71; Hull 71-74; Dar-es-Salaam 74-76. *c/o Box 1179, Dar-es-Salaam, Tanzania.* (051-20887)

BURGESS, Colin Ernest Bryce Hawthorne. Moore Th Coll Syd ACT ThL 31. **d** 31 **p** 32 Syd. C of St John Parramatta 32-36; C-in-c of Dee Why w Brookvale 36-37; R of Hornsby 37-44; Leura 44-56; Haberfield 56-61; L to Offic Dio C & Goulb 61-64. *c/o Parks and Gardens Section, Herbarium, Department of Interior, Canberra, ACT, Australia.*

BURGESS, Colin Gordon. St Columb's Hall Wang ACT ThL 43. **d** 43 Bp Hart for Wang **p** 44 Wang. C of St Columb Distr Wang 43-45; R of Bethanga 45-48; Nathalie 48-51; Cobram 51-58; Miss Dio Polyn 58-62; R of Bright 62-66; Nagambie 66-76; Perm to Offic Dio Wang from 76. *PO Swanpool, Vic, Australia.*

BURGESS, Canon David John. b 39. Trin Hall Cam BA 62, MA 66. Univ Coll Ox MA (by incorp) 66. Cudd Coll 62. **d** 65 **p** 66 Cant. C of All SS Maidstone 65; Asst Chap Univ Coll Ox 66-70; Fellow from 69; Chap 70-78; Dom Bursar 71-78; Can and Treas of Windsor from 78. *6 The Cloisters, Windsor Castle, Windsor, Berks.* (Windsor 66313)

BURGESS, Edwin Michael. b 47. Ch Coll Cam BA 69, MA 73. Coll of Resurr Mirfield 70. **d** 72 **p** 73 Dur. C of Beamish 72-77; Par 77-80; P-in-c of Duloe w Herodsfoot Dio Truro from 80. *Duloe Rectory, Liskeard, Cornw.* (Looe 2846)

BURGESS, Frank Graham. Sir Geo Williams Univ Montr BA 64. Montr Dioc Th Coll LTh 67. **d** 67 Montr. C of Chateauguay 67-68; St Jo Evang, Montr 68-69; R of Farnham 69-74; St Steph, St Hubert Dio Montr from 74. *5345 Hubert Guertin, St Hubert, PQ, Canada.* (514-656 5558)

BURGESS, Frederick William. b 12. Late Scho of St Jo Coll Cam 1st cl Math Trip pt i 31, BA (Wrangler) 33, 2nd cl Th Trip 35, MA 37. FRCO 39. Ridley Hall Cam 34. **d** 36 Chelmsf **p** 39 Ely. C of St Mary Walthamstow 36; Asst Master KS Ely 38-47; Abingdon Sch 47-57; Chap 50-57; R of N w S Lopham 57-59; Asst Master R Masonic Sch Bushey 59-77; L to Offic Dio St Alb 59-77; R of Gt Oakley Dio Chelmsf from 77. *Great Oakley Rectory, Harwich, Essex.* (Ramsey 880230)

BURGESS, Canon Henry James. b 08. Univ of Lon BA (2nd cl Hist) 31, MA (Educn) 49, PhD 54. Wycl Hall Ox 35. **d** 36 **p** 37 B & W. C of St Paul Bath 36-38; St John Tunbridge Wells 38-39; Offg Chap and Asst Master Weymouth Coll 39-40; V of Poughill 40-44; Ch Ch Sidcup 44-50; Cudham w Aperfield 50-61; Dioc Schs Adv Dio Roch 55-61; V of Lucton w Eyton 61-66; R of Hooton Roberts 66-70; Hon Can of Sheff 66-70; Can Res 70-75; Can Emer from 75; Exam Chap to Bp of Sheff 66-75; Dir Ch Schs Dio Sheff 66-70; Dioc Dir of Educn Sheff 70-75; Perm to Offic Dio Truro from 75. *29 Orchard Close, Poughill, Bude, Cornw, EX23 9ES.* (Bude 3261)

BURGESS, Canon Henry Percival. b 21. Univ of Leeds BA 48. Coll of Resurr Mirfield 48. **d** 50 **p** 51 Birm. C of St Laur Northfield Birm 50-54; V of St Mary and St John Saltley 54-62; Wylde Green Dio Birm from 62; Proc Conv Birm 59-64; Hon Can of Birm Cathl from 75; RD of Sutton Coldfield from 76; M Gen Syn 76-80. *17 Greenhill Road, Wylde Green, Sutton Coldfield, Warws.* (021-373 1224)

BURGESS, James Barry. Moore Th Coll Syd ACT ThL 52. **d** 52 Syd for Gippsld **p** 53 Gippsld. C of Moe 52-53; Morwell 53-54; R of Wonthaggi 54-55; C-in-c of The Oaks 55-57; R of Dapto w Albion Pk 58-61; Dapto 61-68; Camden 68-75; Watson's Bay Dio Syd from 75. *Rectory, Old South Head Road, Watson's Bay, NSW, Australia 2030.* (337-1629)

BURGESS, James Graham. b 30. BA (Lon, 2nd cl Hist) 51. Univ of Ox Dipl Th 55. Ripon Hall Ox 53. **d** 55 **p** 56 Pet. C of St Jas Dallington Northn 55-58; Mortlake (in c of All SS E Sheen) 58-60; R of Morley 60-63; L to Offic Dio Leic from 64; Perm to Offic Dio Southw from 75. *26 Chapel Lane, Costock, Loughborough, Leics, LE12 6UY.* (East Leake 2023)

BURGESS, Ven John Edward. b 30. Univ of Lon BD (2nd cl) 57. ALCD (1st cl) 56. **d** 57 **p** 58 S'wark. C of Bermondsey 57-60; Southn 60-62; V of Dunston w Coppenhall 62-67; Chap Staffs Coll of Tech 63-67; V of Keynsham w Qu Charlton 67-75; R of Burnett 67-75; RD of Keynsham 72-75; Surr from 72; Archd of Bath and Preb of Wells Cathl from 75. *The Archdeaconry, Corston, Bath, Avon, BA2 9AP.* (022-17 3609)

BURGESS, John Henry William. b 35. Wells Th Coll 65. **d** 67 Lon **p** 68 Kens for Lon. C of Teddington 67-72; Northolt 72-73. *43 Park Road, Godalming, Surrey, GU7 1SQ.*

BURGESS, John Michael. b 36. ALCD 61. **d** 61 Warrington for Liv **p** 62 Liv. C of St Luke Eccleston 61-64; St Mary Magd Avondale Rhod 64-68; R of Marlborough, Rhod 68-74; V of St Andr Nottm 75-79; Commun Relns Adv to Bp of Southw 77-79; V of Earlestown Dio Liv from 79. *Earlestown Vicarage, Newton-le-Willows, Lancs.* (Newton-le-Willows 4771)

BURGESS, John Mulholland. b 32. Cranmer Hall Dur. **d** 61 **p** 62 Guildf. C of Frimley 61-67; St Luke Chelt̶m 67-69; C-in-c of Withington w Compton Abdale 69-74; R of Woolstone w Oxenton and Gotherington 74-75; Chap Miss to Seamen Rotterdam and Asst Chap St Mary Rotterdam 75-78; Sliema, Malta 78-79; C of All SS Nottm 80-81; Rolleston w Fiskerton and Morton Dio Southw from 81. *c/o Rolleston Vicarage, Newark, Notts.*

BURGESS, Leonard Arthur. St Wilfrid's Coll Tas ACT ThL 24. **d** 24 **p** 25 Tas. C of Forth and Leven Tas 24-26; P-in-c of Castra Miss Tas 26-28; R of The Channel 28-31; Oatlands 31-36; Glenorchy 36-48; Actg R of St Jo Bapt Hobart 48-49; R 49-59; Geeveston w Dover 59-61; on leave 61-63; R of Hamilton Tas 63-65; L to Offic Dio Tas from 69. *229 Acton Road, Lauderdale, Tasmania 7021.*

BURGESS, Leslie. St Aid Th Coll Bal 19. ACT ThL 23. **d** 23 **p** 25 Bal. C of Linton 23-25; P-in-c of Skipton 25-27; V of Alvie 27-31; Willaura 31-38; Casterton 38-40; St Paul Bal 40-50; RD of Bal 44-50; V and Rd of Camperdown and Can of Bal 50-56; Chap to Bp of Bal 51-56; V of Reservoir 56-60; I of St Alb W Coburg 60-67; Queenscliff 67-70; Perm to Offic Dio Melb from 70. *10 Flinders Street, Queenscliff, Vic, Australia 3225.* (052-52 1532)

BURGESS, Michael James. b 42. Coll of the Resurr Mirfield 74. **d** 76 Chelmsf **p** 77 Bradwell for Chelmsf. C of St Marg Leigh 76-79; St Pet-in-Thanet 79-81; Chap St Geo Coll Tor and Hon C of St Jas Cathl City and Dio Tor from 82. *120 Howland Avenue, Toronto, Ont, Canada.* (416-533 7681)

BURGESS, Michael Walter. Bps' Coll Cheshunt 66. **d** 68 Lon **p** 70 St Alb. C of St Matt Hammersmith 68-70; Boreham Wood 70-73; V of Flamstead 74-77; Ch of Annunc Bryanston Street St Marylebone Dio Lon from 77. *4 Wyndham Place, W1H 1AP.* (01-262 4329)

BURGESS, Neil. b 53. St D Coll Lamp BA 75. St Mich AA Llan 75. **d** 77 **p** 78 Lich. C of Cheadle 77-79; Longton Dio Lich from 79. *7 Smith Street, Longton, Stoke-on-Trent, ST3 1DR.* (S-o-T 332756)

BURGESS, Paul Christopher James. b 41. Qu Coll Cam BA 63, MA 67, Lon Coll of Div 66. **d** 68 **p** 69 Lon. C of Islington 68-72; Ch Stretton 73-74; CMS Miss in Pakistan from 74. *c/o CMS, 157 Waterloo Road, SE1 8UU.*

BURGESS, Philip Linton. St Jo Coll Morpeth ACT ThL 54. **d** 54 **p** 55 Bal. C of Willaura 54-58; R of Tallangatta 58-61; V of Mt Duneed 61-64; R of Mansfield 64-69; Wodonga w Bethanga 69-76; Archd of Wang 71-76; I of St Steph Belmont 76-80; R of St Pet City and Dio Bal from 80. *St Peter's Rectory, Sturt Street, Ballarat, Vic, Australia 3350.*

BURGESS, William Edgerton. b 05. Jes Coll Cam BA 27. **d** 70 St John's **p** 70 Bp Sobukwe for St John's. C of H Trin Kokstad Dio St John's from 70. *Box 214, Kokstad, Transkei, S Africa.* (Kokstad 398)

BURGHALL, Kenneth Miles. b 34. Selw Coll Cam BA 57, MA 61. Qu Coll Birm 57. **d** 59 **p** 60 Ches. C of Macclesfield 59-63; CF 63-67; C-in-c of St Mark Birkenhead 67-71; V of St Paul Macclesfield Dio Ches from 71. *St Paul's Vicarage, Swallow Close, Macclesfield, Chesh.* (Macclesfield 22910)

BURGIN, Eric Woollcombe. St Jo Coll Auckld. Univ of NZ BA 22. Bd of Th Stud NZ LTh 23. **d** 22 **p** 23 Wel. C of St Thos Wel 22-26; V of Mangatainoka and Pongaroa 26-32; Mangaweka 32-36; Foxton w Shannon 36-40; Wanganui 40-55; Brooklyn 55-62; Asst Chap Wel Hosp 62-67; Perm to

Offic Dio Auckld 67-71; Dio Waik 71-78; Dio Wai from 78. *c/o Box 227, Napier, NZ.*

BURGIN, Henry Kenneth. b 36. SOC 70. **d** 71 **p** 72 S'wark. C of Caterham Valley 71-73; Benhilton 73-76; V of St Phil Cheam Common Dio S'wark from 76. *St Philip's Vicarage, Nonsuch Walk, Cheam, Surrey, SM2 7LF.* (01-393 9154)

BURGOMASTER, Glen Raymond. b 50. Univ of Guelph BA 73. Trin Coll Tor MDiv 76. **d** 75 NS **p** 76 Qu'App. C of St Luke Regina 75-77; R of Wadena 77-79; Ch Ch Grande Prairie Dio Athab from 79. *9252 106th Avenue, Grande Prairie, Alta T8V 4L3, Canada.*

BURGON, George Irvine. b 41. Edin Th Coll **d** 65 **p** 66 Brech. C of St Mary Magd Dundee 65-68; Wellingborough 68-71; C-in-c of Norton 71-73; Team V of Daventry w Norton 73-75; V of St Mary Virg Northn Dio Pet from 75. *St Mary's Vicarage, Towcester Road, Northampton, NN4 9EZ.* (Northn 61104)

BURGOYNE, Edward Geoffrey. b 27. Univ of Wales (Abth) BA 49. St Mich Coll Llan 49. **d** 51 **p** 52 Llan. C of St Mary Aberavon 51-55; Ynyshir 55-63; V of Bockleton w Leysters 63-70; C-in-c of Hatfield 63-70; Asst Master Bp's Sch Heref 70-72; Ho Master Bp of Heref Bluecoat Sch from 72; L to Offic Dio Heref from 70. *Lawnswood, Tupsley Pitch, Hereford, HR1 1UT.* (Heref 68860)

BURGOYNE, Percy John. b 19. OBE 74. Univ of Wales (Cardiff) BSc 41. St Mich Coll Llan. **d** 43 **p** 44 Llan. C of St Dyfrig Cardiff 43-47; St Marg Roath 47-52; Chap RN 52-78; Hon Chap to HM the Queen 72-75; P-in-c of Kelsale w Carlton Dio St E from 78. *Kelsale Rectory, Saxmundham, Suff.* (Saxmundham 3358)

BURKE, Earl James. b 40. **d** 80 **p** 81 Alg. [f CA in Canada]. C of St Geo Thunder Bay 80-81; Ch Ch Sault Ste Marie Dio Alg from 81. *585 Allan Road, RR 6, Sault Ste Marie, Ont, Canada, P6A 6K4.*

BURKE, Edmund. **d** 70 **p** 71 Ja. C-in-c of Santa Cruz and Gilnock Dio Ja from 70. *Rectory, Santa Cruz, Jamaica, W Indies.*

BURKE, John Elson. McGill Univ BSc 54, BD 57. Montr Dioc Th Coll. **d** 57 Montr **p** 58 Queb. Miss in Labrador 59-65; C of St Jo Evang, Montr 65-68; on leave 68-74; Dir Coun of Angl Commun and Social Services Dio Tor 74-77; Executive Dir Ch Workers Assoc Dio Tor 77-81. *Mimosa Farm, RR5, Belwood, N0B 1J0, Canada.*

BURKE, Lionel de Courcy. Codr Coll Barb. **d** 55 Barb for Antig **p** 56 Antig. C of St Geo St Kitts 55-58; P-in-c of St Mary Cayon St Kitts 58-60; V of St Sav Barb 60-63; All SS Barb 63-69; St Ambrose Barb 69-73; R of St Geo I and Dio Barb from 73. *Rectory, St George, Barbados, W Indies.*

BURKETT, Christopher Paul. b 52. Univ of Warwick BA 75. Qu Coll Birm 75. **d** 78 **p** 79 Lich. C of Streetly 78-81; Harlescott Dio Lich from 81. *324 York Road, Harlescott Grange, Shrewsbury, SY1 3QA.* (Shrewsbury 245548)

BURLEIGH, Leonard Tekenika William Gilbert. b 1891. Qu Coll Cam BA 13, MA 16. Ridley Hall Cam 14. **d** 14 **p** 15 S'wark. C of St Jas Clapham 14-18; St Jo Evang Stratford Essex 18-20; H Trin Tulse Hill 20-25; Gt Yarmouth 25-26; V of Lakenham 26-48; R of Shipdham 48-58. *The Chestnuts, Westbury Terrace, Westerham, Kent, TN16 1RP.* (0959 63295)

BURLES, Albert Edward. b 20. Worc Ordin Coll. **d** 68 **p** 69 Man. [f in CA] C of Newton Heath 68-71; V of Patricroft Dio Man from 71; Chap Bridgewater Hosp from 71. *Vicarage, Cromwell Road, Patricroft, Eccles, Lancs M30 0GT.* (061-789 1234)

BURLEY, Canon John Anderson. b 11. Selw Coll Cam 2nd cl Hist Trip pt i 32, BA (3rd cl Th Trip pt i) 33, MA 37. Ely Th Coll 33. **d** 34 **p** 35 Chelmsf. C of St John Buckhurst Hill 34-39; V of St Pet-in-the-Forest Walthamstow 39-59; CF (EC) 40-46; Hon CF from 46; M C of E Coun on Foreign Relns from 47; Gen Sec S St Willibrord from 50; Hon Chap to Abp of Utrecht from 54; Proc Conv Chelmsf from 52; V of St Jas Clacton-on-Sea 59-70; Surr from 59; Hon Can of Utrecht from 69; R of Gt and of L Braxted Dio Chelmsf from 70. *Little Braxted Rectory, Witham, Essex, CM8 3LD.* (Maldon 891248)

BURLING, Canon Sidney John. b 07. AKC 31. **d** 31 **p** 32 Chelmsf. C of St John Moulsham 31-35; C-in-c of St Barn Conv Distr Hadleigh 35-46; V of H Trin Hermon Hill 46-57; V of Broxted w Chickney (and Tilty from 61) 57-63; RD of Dunmow 61-63; R of Bradwell-juxta-Mare 63-76; St Lawr 63-76; RD of Dengie 66-74; Surr 67-76; Hon Chap to Bp Suffr of Bradwell from 68; Hon Can of Chelmsf 71-76; Can (Emer) from 76. *120 School Road, Copford, Colchester, Essex.* (Colchester 210421)

BURLS, Robert Bruce Vivian. St Jo Coll Morpeth ACT ThL 42. **d** 43 **p** 44 Armid. C of St Pet Cathl Armid 43-44; Inverell 44-45; Actg C-in-c of Cassop w Quarrington 45-46; C of S Moor 46-47; R of Wollombi 47-50; Bullahdelah 50-53; Wingham 53-65; Stockton Dio Newc from 65. *Rectory, Maitland Street, Stockton, NSW, Australia 2295.* (28-1514)

BURLTON, Aelred Harry. b 49. Sarum Wells Th Coll 75. **d** 78 Kens for Lon **p** 79 Lon. C of Feltham Dio Lon from 78. *67 Southville Road, Bedfont, Feltham, Middx.*

BURLTON, Robert Michael. b 18. Ely Th Coll 40. Chich Th Coll 41. **d** 42 **p** 43 Lich. C of St Francis W Bromwich 42-45; Godalming 45-47; Southbourne 47-48; St Teath w Michaelstow 48-50; V of St Gennys 50-52; Penponds 52-63; R of Lound 65-76; C-in-c of St Edm Fritton Dio Nor from 65; R of Blundeston w Flixton (and Lound from 76) Dio Nor from 65. *Rectory, Market Lane, Blundeston, Lowestoft, Suff.* (Lowestoft 730638)

BURLTON, William Frank. b 12. King's Coll Lon. **d** 43 **p** 44. C of St Mark Glouc 43-46; Northleach and Hampnett w Stowell 46-48; C-in-c of Hewelsfield and C of St Briavels 48-51; R of Cromhall (w Tortworth from 78) Dio Glouc from 51; C-in-c of Tortworth 65-78; Chap HM Pris Falfield 54-59; Asst Chap Leyhill 59-77; RD of Hawkesbury 65-77. *Cromhall Rectory, Wotton-under-Edge, Glos.* (Wickwar 336)

BURMA, Metropolitan of Province of. *See* Hla Gyaw, Most Rev Gregory.

BURMAN, Patrick Richard Breach. St Bonif Coll Warm 33. **d** 36 **p** 37 Leic. C of St Pet Leic 36-38; Old St Paul Edin 38-40; CF (EC) 40-46; C of Old St Paul Edin 46; V of All S Leeds 46-53; CF 53-62; V of St Dunstan E Acton 62-67; C-in-c of St Cypr Clarence Gate 67-70; V 70-79; RD of Westmr St Marylebone 67-74. *c/o 146 Ivor Court, Gloucester Place, NW 1.* (01-402 6979)

BURMAN, Philip Harvey. b 47. Kelham Th Coll 66. **d** 70 **p** 71 Warrington for Liv. C of Huyton 70-75; Farnworth 75-77; Team V of Kirkby Dio Liv from 77. *St Martin's House, Peatwood Avenue, Southdene, Kirkby, L32 7PR.* (051-546 2387)

BURN, Alan Edward. b 24. St Chad's Coll Dur BA 49, Dipl Th 51. **d** 51 Dur **p** 52 Jarrow for Dur. C of St Jas W Hartlepool 51-53; Donnington Wood 53-55; Min of St Mark's Eccles Distr Darlington 55-58; V 58-61; P-in-c of Jesselton (Kota Kinabalu Sabah) 61-62; R of All SS Cathl Kota Kinabalu 62-67; Dean 64-67; PC of Binley w Coombe Fields 67-73; Commiss Sabah from 67; RD of Cov E 71-73; Cov N from 79; R of Allesley Dio Cov from 73. *Allesley Rectory, Coventry, W Midl, CV5 9EQ.* (Cov 402006)

BURN, Leonard Louis. b 44. K Coll Lon and Warm BD and AKC 67. **d** 68 **p** 69 Lich. C of Kingswinford 68-70; S Ascot 70-72; Caversham 72-76; Chap Selly Oak Hosp 76-81; Bris City Hosps and P-in-c of St Mich-on-the-Mount Without City and Dio Bris from 81. *13 Fremantle Square, Bristol, BS6 5TL.* (Bris 421039)

BURN, Richard James Southerden. b 34. Pemb Coll Cam 2nd cl Econ Trip pt i 54, BA (2nd cl Hist Trip pt ii) 56. Wells Th Coll 56. **d** 58 **p** 59 St Alb. C of Cheshunt 58-62; Leighton Buzzard 65-66; Glastonbury 66-68; P-in-c of Prestonpans 68-71; Team V of Stokesay 71-75; P-in-c of Leebotwood w Longnor 75-81; Dorrington 75-81; Stapleton 75-81; Smethcote and Woolstaston 81; Team R of Melbury Dio Sarum from 81. *Rectory, Summerlane, Evershot, Dorchester, Dorset.* (Evershot 238)

BURN, Robert. Wollaston Th Coll Perth 60. **d** and **p** 64 Perth. C of Subiaco 64-66; R of Boulder 66-69; Warden St Andr Hostel Esperance 69-71; R of Bruce Rock and of Narembeen 71-75; Mundaring 75-80; Greenwood Dio Perth from 80. *17 Calectasia Street, Greenwood, W Australia 6024.* (447 9243)

BURN, Robert Pemberton. b 34. Peterho Cam BA 56, MA 60. Univ of Lon PhD 68. CMS Miss Tr Coll 60. **d** 63 Bp A.G. Jebaraj (CSI) **p** 81 Huntingdon for Ely (NSM). In Ch of S India 63-71; P-in-c of Foxton Dio Ely from 81. *6 Beaumont Crescent, Cambridge, CB1 4QA.*

BURN-MURDOCH, Aidan Michael. b 35. Trin Coll Cam 2nd cl Hist Trip pt i 58, BA (1st cl Th Trip pt ii) 60, MA 63. Ridley Hall Cam. **d** 61 **p** 62 Dur. C of St Gabr Bp Wearmouth 61-63; Tutor Ridley Hall Cam 63-67; CMS Miss 67-70; R of Hawick 70-77; V of Llangennith Dio Swan B from 77; R of Reynoldston w Penrice Dio Swan B from 77. *Reynoldston Rectory, Swansea, SA3 1AA.* (Reynoldston 303)

BURNAND, Robin Graham. b 35. Wollaston Coll Perth 69. **d** and **p** 72 Perth. C of St Jo Bapt Cathl Kalg 72-73; Kalg w Boulder 73-76. *c/o 30 Moran Street, Boulder, W Australia 6432.* (090-21 3126)

BURNE, Christopher John Sambrooke. b 16. DSO 45. Linc Th Coll 58. **d** 59 **p** 60 Portsm. C of S w N Hayling 59-63; V of N Leigh 63-81. *Beam Ends, Middle Road, Tiptoe, Lymington, Hants SO4 0FX.* (0590-682898)

BURNE, George. Lich Th Coll 28. **d** 32 Bp Hine for Linc **p** 33 Linc. C of Habrough w Immingham (in c of St Andr Immingham) 32-35; Christchurch (in c of St Geo) 35-45; Perm to Offic Dio Win 45-48; C of St D of Scotld Edin 48-49; C-in-c of St Barn Edin 49-51; C of St Steph (in c of St Julian)

St Alb 51-52; C-in-c of L Wymondley 52-58; C of St Ippolyts w Gt Wymondley 52-58; V of Gt w L Wymondley 58-60; Perm to Offic Dio St Alb 60-62; C of St Pet St Alb 62-65; Deputn Sec BFBS 60-66; C of Faversham 66-69; Budleigh Salterton 69-76; Perm to Offic Dio Ex from 76. *27 Victoria Place, Budleigh Salterton, Devon.* (Budleigh Salterton 2875)

BURNE, Canon Wilfrid Durnford Elvis. b 07. OBE 65. Keble Coll Ox BA 29, MA 57. Bps' Coll Cheshunt 30. **d** 31 Bp de Salis for B & W **p** 32 B & W. C of Em Ch Weston-s-Mare 31-35; CMS Miss Isoko Distr Dio Niger 35-43; C of St Pet St Alb 43-45; Gen Manager of Schs Dio Niger 45-54; Archd of Warri 49-53; Onitsha 53-54; Hon Can of All SS Cathl Onitsha from 55; CMS Rep Dio Niger 54-67; Synod Sec 54-59; V of Manea 67-72. *1 Waterloo Road, Salisbury, Wilts, SP1 2JR.*

BURNESS, John Alfred. b 1891. Qu Coll Cam BA 14. Ridley Hall Cam 13. **d** 14 **p** 15 Liv. C of St Luke Walton-on-the-Hill Liv 14-18; All SS Derby 18-20; I of St Andr Miss Lake Saskatoon 20-24; PC of Linstead Magna w Linstead Parva (w Chediston from 26) 25-27; V of St Paul Derby 27-29; R of Helmingham 29-60; V of Framsden 53-60; RD of Claydon 56-60. *Five Gables, Witnesham, Ipswich, Suff.* (Witnesham 243)

BURNET, Norman Andrew Gray. b 32. Univ of Aber BEducn 77. Edin Th Coll 53. **d** 55 **p** 56 Glas. C of H Trin Ayr 55-58; C of St John's Cathl Umtata 58-63; P-in-c of Mount Frere CP 63-69; R of Leven 69-72; Perm to Offic Dios Brech, Aber and Ork 73-81; Dio Ely from 81. *Peterhouse, Cambridge, CB2 1RD.*

BURNETT, Canon Anthony Robin. Univ Coll Ox BA (3rd cl Th) 58, MA 67. Cudd Coll Ox 58. **d** 60 Chich for Capetn **p** 61 Capetn. C of St Paul Rondebosch 60-62; Ch of Good Shepherd Maitland 63-65; R of Hopefield 65-72; P-in-c of Bellville South Dio Capetn 72-78; R from 78; Can of Capetn from 76. *39 Fourie Street, Belville South, CP, S Africa.*

BURNETT, Bernard. b 11. St Chad's Coll Dur BA 33, MA 36. Dipl in Th 34. **d** 34 **p** 35 Man. C of St Luke Weaste 34-36; Ascen Broughton 36-38; SPG Miss at Giddalur 38-46; furlough 46; V of Roundthorn 47-54; St Matt Douglas 54-76; Hon Chap Miss to Seamen Douglas 55-76; Sec of Manx Ch Conv 63-76; Dir of Ordins Dio S & M 67-76; Exam Chap to Bp of S & M 74-76. *41 Wybourn Grove, Onchan, Douglas, IM.* (Douglas 5652)

✠ **BURNETT, Most Rev Bill Bendyshe.** Rhodes Univ Coll BA 40. Univ of S Afr MA 47. St Paul's Coll Grahmstn LTh 46. **d** 46 **p** 47 Natal. C of St Thos Durban 46-50; Chap of Dioc Sch Michaelhouse 50-54; V of Ladysmith 54-57; Cons Ld Bp of Bloemf in St Geo Cathl Capetn 17 Nov 57 by Abp of Capetn; Bps of Grahmstn; Pret; Geo; Kimb K; Johann; Basuto; Natal; Damar; and St Jo Kaffr; and Bps Lavis; Fisher; Parker; Browne; and Stainton; res 67; Asst Bp of Johann 67-69; Apptd Ld Bp of Grahmstn 69; Trld to Capetn 74; res 81. *6 Allenby Road, Selborne, East London 52, S Africa.*

BURNETT, Donald. b 19. Univ of Man Dipl in Th 43. St Aid Coll 46. **d** 46 **p** 47 Bradf. C of Shipley 46-49; Holmfirth (in c of St Andr Thongsbridge) 49-50; V of Greengates 50-55; R of Everingham w Seaton Ross and Harswell 55-60; C-in-c of Bielby 55-60; York Dioc Youth Officer 59-64; V of Tadcaster Dio York from 60; Chap HM Remand Centre Thorp Arch 65-81. *Vicarage, Tadcaster, N Yorks, LS24 9JR.* (Tadcaster 833394)

BURNETT, Douglas. b 26. Ridley Hall Cam 67. **d** 69 **p** 70 Middleton for Man. C of Flixton 69-72; Downend 72-76; Chapel-en-le-Frith (in c of Dove Holes) Dio Derby from 76. *Parsonage, Dove Holes, Buxton, Derbys.*

BURNETT, Canon John. **d** 53 **p** 54 Melb. C of St Jas Thornbury 53; Dioc C Dio Melb 53-57; I of Ch of Epiph Northcote 57-60; R of Swan Hill Dio St Arn from 60; Can of St Arn 64-65; Chap to Bp of St Arn 64-65; Archd of St Arn 65-68; The Murray 68-69; Mallee 69-70; St Arn 70-72; Hon Can of Ch Ch Cathl St Arn 72-76; Ch Ch Old Cathl St Arn from 77; Perm to Offic Dio C & Goulb from 72; Dio St Arn 72-76; Dio Bend from 77. *Box 21, Cobargo, NSW, Australia 2547.*

BURNETT, Canon John Capenhurst. b 19. AKC 49. **d** 49 **p** 50 Bris. C of Shirehampton 49-53; Stoke Bishop 53-56; R and V of Wroughton 56-76; RD of Cricklade 70-76; Hon Can of Bris from 74; V of St Andr w St Bart City and Dio Bris from 76. *Vicarage, Walsingham Road, Bristol, BS6 5BT.* (Bristol 48683)

BURNETT, Llewellyn John. b 36. Univ of Dur BA (3rd cl Th) 61, Dipl Th 62. Cranmer Hall Dur 60. **d** 62 **p** 63 Man. C of Bolton-le-Moors 62-65; St Martin Wythenshawe 65-66; R of St Pet Stretford 66-70; Chap Redhill Gen Hosp from 70. *Mercer House, Redhill General Hospital, Earlswood Common, Redhill, Surrey, RH1 6LA.*

BURNETT, Canon Philip Stephen. b 14. Univ of Lon BA 34. Ball Coll Ox BA (2nd cl Phil Pol and Econ 39) 45, MA 46. Westcott Ho Cam. **d** 47 **p** 48 Ely. [f Solicitor] C of Chesterton 47-49; Asst Gen Sec SCM 49-52; V of St Mary w St Simon and St Matthias Sheff 52-61; RD of Ecclesall 59-65; Can of Sheff 61-70; Can (Emer) from 70; Educn Sec Dio Sheff 61-70; Hon Sec Fell of the Maple Leaf from 65; C of E Bd of Educn 70-80; C of St Botolph City and Dio Lon from 81. *91 Chelverton Road, SW15 1RW.* (01-789 9934)

BURNETT, Ross Ridley. St Francis Coll Brisb ACT ThL 63. **d** and **p** 64 Brisb. C of St Luke Toowoomba 64-66; Chap Southport Sch 66-72; R of Gatton w Ma Ma Creek 72-75; Roma Dio Brisb from 75. *Rectory, Arthur Street, Roma, Queensland, Australia 4455.* (074-29 1199)

BURNHAM, Cecil Champneys. AKC 39. Jun Wordsworth Pri 37, **d** 39 **p** 40 Roch. C of St John Sidcup 39-41; Perm to Offic at H Trin Lamorbey 41-43; C of Pembury 43-45; Gt Driffield w L Driffield 45-47; V of Watton w Beswick 47-49; St Pet Anlaby 50-55; C of Heathfield 55-58; R of Hastings 58-66; V of Westham 66-74; R of Harting 74-79. *c/o Harting Rectory, Petersfield, Hants.* (Harting 234)

BURNHAM, Frank Leslie. b 23. Edin Th Coll 52. **d** 55 Whitby for York **p** 56 York. C of St Mary Bishophill Sen w St Clem York 55-58; Marfleet 58-62; V 62-72; R 72-74; V of St Steph Acomb City and Dio York from 74. *32 Carr Lane, York, YO2 5HX.* (York 798106)

BURNINGHAM, Frederick George. b 34. ALCD 60. **d** 60 Tonbridge for Cant **p** 61 Roch. C of St Paul Beckenham 60-63; Fort Chimo 63-64; C-in-c of Southn I 64-67; C of Wisley w Pyrford 68-69; C-in-c of H Trin Sydenham 69-71; C of Broadwater 72-77; R of Sotterley w Willingham, Shadingfield, Ellough, Weston and Henstead 77-82; St Clem w H Trin Ipswich Dio St E from 82. *Rectory, Rosehill Road, Ipswich, Suff IP3 8ES.* (Ipswich 216606)

BURNINGHAM, George Walter. b 13. Univ of Leeds BA (1st cl Phil) 34, MA w distinc 35. Coll of Resurr Mirfield 34. **d** 36 **p** 37 St A. C of Hawarden 36-38; Fishponds 38-43; Chap and Lect in Coll of St Matthias Fishponds Bris [f Dios Glouc and Bris Dioc Tr Coll] 43-57; Chap to C of E Studs Univ of Leeds from 57; C-in-c of Em Ch Leeds 57-67; R of Morley 67-72; Warden Ch Ho Morley 67-72; Exam Chap to Bp of Derby from 67; V of St Jo Evang City and Dio Derby from 72; St Anne City and Dio Derby from 72; Surr from 77. *St John's Vicarage, Ashbourne Road, Derby.* (Derby 48341)

BURNINGHAM, Kenneth Willis. b 34. Em Coll Sask *Testamur* 70. **d** 70 **p** 71 Sask. C of Arborfield Dio Sask from 70. *PO Box 238, Arborfield, Sask., Canada.*

BURNLEY, Lord Bishop Suffragan of. Watson, Right Rev Richard Charles Challinor.

BURNLEY, William Francis Edward. b 06. BD (2nd cl) Lon 40. Sarum Th Coll 32. **d** 35 **p** 36 Bris. C of Shirehampton 35-38; Stapleton 38-40; CF (EC) 40-45; V of Bowden Hill 45-54; Corston w Rodbourne 54-62; R of Foxley w Bremilham 54-62; V of Highworth w Sevenhampton Hannington and Inglesham 62-68; PC of Westwood 68-74; Perm to Offic Dio Sarum from 74. *2a Perry's Lane, Seend Cleeve, Melksham, Wilts, SN12 6QA.*

BURNS, Clifford John Sexstone. b 10. **d** 71 **p** 72 Llan. Hon C of St Cath Cardiff 71-77; Perm to Offic Dio Roch from 77. *24 Broke Farm Drive, Pratts Bottom, BR6 7SH.* (Farnborough 56358)

BURNS, Ven Douglas Perry. Qu Univ Kingston BA 49. Trin Coll Tor STB 52. **d** and **p** 52 Ont. C of St Geo Cathl Kingston Ont 52-55; R of Winona 55-59; Bath 59-65; Picton 65-67; Trin Ch, Brockville Dio Ont from 67; Can of Ont 74-79; Archd of St Lawr from 79. *126 George Street, Brockville, Ont., Canada.* (613-342 2631)

BURNS, Edward Joseph. b 38. Univ of Liv BSc (2nd cl Chem) 58. St Cath S Ox BA (2nd cl Th) 61, MA 64. Wycl Hall Ox 58. **d** 61 **p** 62 Blackb. C of St Andr Leyland 61-64; Burnley 64-67; V of St Jas Chorley 67-75; M Gen Syn Blackb from 70; V of Fulwood Dio Blackb from 75; RD of Preston from 79. *6 Watling Street Road, Fulwood, Preston, Lancs, PR2 4DY.* (Preston 719210)

BURNS, James Denis. b 43. Lich Th Coll 69. **d** 72 **p** 73 Lich. C of Gt Wyrley 72-75; Atherton 75-76; C-in-c of St Paul w St John Masbrough and St Mich AA Northfield 76-78; V of St Paul w St Mich and St John Ferham Pk, Rotherham (f Masbrough & Northfield) 78-79; Ch Ch (w St Jo Evang and St Anne from 81) Lanc Dio Blackb from 79. *Christ Church Vicarage, East Road, Lancaster.* (Lanc 34430)

BURNS, Michael John. b 53. AKC 76. Chich Th Coll 76. **d** 77 **p** 78 Heref. C of Broseley 77-81; All SS Stevenage Dio St Alb from 81. *8A The Oval, Pin Green, Stevenage, Herts.* (Stevenage 4773)

BURNS, Norman Wesley. b 03. McGill Univ Montr 24. St Aid Coll 28. **d** 32 **p** 34 Carl. C of St Jas Carl 32-35; St Geo Millom 35-37; V of Blackford 37-51; Cotehill w Cumwhinton 51-71; Chap Cumb and Westmd Hosp 51-71. *16 Eden Park Crescent, Botcherby, Carlisle, Cumb.* (Carlisle 31301)

BURNS, Percy. NZ BD of Th Stud LTh 64. St Jo Coll Auckld. **d** 55 **p** 56 Waik. C of New Plymouth 55-57; V of Mokau 57-59; Mangakino 59-60; Miss P Dio Polyn 60-62; V of Labasa 62-64; L to Offic Dio Lon 64-65; Dio Waik 66-68; C of Te Awamutu 65-66; Frankton and of Forest Lake 68-70; L to Offic Dio Waik 70-74; Hon C of Ch Ch Wanganui Dio Wel 70-74; Org Sec in NZ Bible Soc 70-74; V of Te Kaha 74-78; P-in-c of Turangi Miss Distr 78-81. *22 Casper Road, Papatoetoe, Auckland, NZ.*

BURNS, Robert Joseph. b 34. Wycl Hall Ox 66. **d** 71 **p** 72 Win. C of Highfield Southampton 71-73; St Jo Bapt Woking 73-77; St Mary's Cathl Glas 77; Chap to Bp of Glas and Gall 77-78; R of Ch of Good Shepherd Hillington City and Dio Glas from 78; Ascen Mosspark City and Dio Glas from 78. *31 Westfield Drive, Glasgow, G52 2SG.*

BURNS, Sherwood John. b 23. Laurentian Univ of Sudbury Ont BA 61. Hur Coll Ont MDiv 77. **d** 77 **p** 78 Hur. C-in-c of St Matt London Dio Hur from 77. *190 Cherryhill Circle, Apt 304, London, Ont, Canada, N6H 2M3.*

BURNS, Stuart Maitland. b 46. Univ of Leeds BA (Engl and Th) 67. Coll of Resurr Mirfield 67. **d** 69 Knaresborough for Ripon **p** 70 Ripon. C of Ven Bede, Wyther, Leeds 69-73; Asst Chap Leeds Univ and Poly 73-77; P-in-c of Thornthwaite w Darley and Thruscross Dio Ripon from 77. *Christ Church Vicarage, Main Street, Darley, Harrogate, Yorks, HG3 2QF.* (Harrogate 780771)

BUROROSI, Simeon. St Aid Coll Dogura. **d** 35 **p** 39 New Guinea. P Dio New Guinea 39-71; Dio Papua 71-72. *PO Dogura, via Boroko, New Guinea.*

BURR, Brian Gilbert. b 23. K Coll Lon and Warm AKC 49. **d** 50 **p** 51 Ex. C of Babbacombe 50-52; All SS Brixham 52-55; Area Sec UMCA for SW Engl 55-56; Publ Pr Dio Ex 55-56; PC of Tideford 56-58; V of Kingswear 58-63; Churston Ferrers w Goodrington 63-75; RD of Ipplepen 69-77; V of Brixham 75-77; C-in-c of Churston Ferrers 76-77; R of Centr Torquay Dio Ex from 77. *Montpellier House, Montpellier Road, Torquay, Devon.* (Torquay 23926)

BURRELL, Arthur Lewis. b 12. Qu Coll Ox BA 34, MA 39. Westcott Ho Cam 35. **d** 36 **p** 37 Ripon. C of Wrangthorn 36-39; Chap to Bp in Egypt and Asst Chap of All SS Cathl Cairo 39-43; CF (EC) 43-46; V of Langham w Barleythorpe 46-49; Can Res Berm 49-53; Exam Chap to Bp of Berm 51-53; V of St Geo Edgbaston 53-55; Prov of All SS Cathl Cairo 55-57; C of E Cowes (in c of Whippingham) 57-58; V of St Cath Ventnor 58-66; H Trin Ventnor 58-66; R of Sulhampstead-Abbots and Sulhampstead-Bannister w Ufton Nervet 66-80; Chap Allnut's Hosp Goring Heath from 80. *Allnut's Hospital, Goring Heath, Oxon, RG8 7RR.*

BURRELL, Canon Maurice Claude. b 30. Univ of Bris BA 54, MA 63. Univ of Lanc PhD 78. Tyndale Hall Bris. **d** 55 **p** 56 S'wark. C of St Steph Wandsworth 55-57; St Andr Whitehall Pk U Holloway 57-59; R of Kirby Cane 59-63; R of Ellingham 61-63; Chap Hales Hosp 59-63; Chap K Sch Gutersloh Germany 63-67; R of Widford 67-71; Chap and Lect St Mary's Coll Cheltm 71-75; Dir of Educn Dio Nor from 75; Hon Can of Nor from 77. *8 Old Grove Court, Norwich, NR23 3NL.* (Nor 402122)

BURRELL, Timothy Graham. b 43. St Steph Ho Ox 69. **d** 72 Newc T. C of Haltwhistle 72-73. *c/o Midland Bank Ltd., 7 Prospect Crescent, Harrogate, N Yorks, HG1 1RN.*

✠ **BURROUGH, Right Rev John Paul.** b 10. MBE (Mil) 46. St Edm Hall Ox BA 37, MA 45. Ely Th Coll. **d** 46 **p** 47 Guildf. C of St Mich Aldershot 46-51; P-in-c of Chung-chu Korea 51-58; Dioc Missr Dio Korea 58-59; Chap to Overseas Peoples Dio Birm 59-67; Hon Can of Birm 65-67; Can Res 67-68; Cons Ld Bp of Mashon in St Phil Cathl Birm 29 June 68 by Abp of Centr Afr; Bps of Matab; Carib; Malawi; and Birm; Bps Suffr of Lanc; and Buckingham; res 81; Asst Bp of Pet from 81; R of Empingham Dio Pet from 81. *Empingham Rectory, Oakham, Leics, LE15 8PT.* (Empingham 215)

BURROUGHS, Edward Graham. K Coll Lon and Warm BD (2nd cl) and AKC 59. **d** 60 **p** 61 Liv. C of St Mary Walton-on-the-Hill 60-63; Bulawayo Cathl 63-68; Dom Chap to Bp of Matab 69-75; P-in-c of St Columba Miss Bulawayo 75-76; L to Offic Dio Matab from 76. *Box 8045, Belmont, Bulawayo, Zimbabwe.* (19-66679)

BURROWES, Thomas Cecil. b 13. Trin Coll Dub BA 36, MA 43. **d** 37 **p** 38 Down. C of Whitehouse 37-41; All SS Belfast 41-44; C-in-c of Killough 44-50; I of Killinchy 50-78; RD of Bangor 68-71; Killinchy 71-78. *5 Kilmood Church Road, Killinchy, Newtownards, Co Down, BT23 6SA, N Ireland.* (Killinchy 541942)

BURROWS, Brian Albert. b 34. Dipl Th (Lon) 59. St Aid Coll. **d** 59 **p** 60 Ches. C of Sutton 59-62; Miss at Povungnituk 62-67; Frobisher Bay 67-69; V of Stratton St Marg 70-74; R of St Jude's Cathl Frobisher Bay 75-80; Hon Can of St Jude's Cathl Frobisher Bay 78-80. *c/o Box 57, Frobisher Bay, NWT, Canada.*

BURROWS, Cecil James. b 02. Trin Coll Dub BA 24, Div Test 26, MA 33. **d** 26 **p** 27 Dub. C of St Pet U Dub 26-28; Succr of St Patr Cathl and Warden of Cathl Gr Sch Dub 28-32; R of Clonfert 32-70; Can of Kilquane in Clonf Cathl 40-47; Archd of Clonf and Kilmac 47-70; Exam Chap to Bp of Killaloe 51-70; Can and Preb of Tipperkevin in St Patr Cathl Dub 57-70; RD of Aughrim and Loughrea 65-70. *New Prospect, Portland Hill, Lorrha, Nenagh, Co Tipperary, Irish Republic.*

BURROWS, Clifford Robert. b 37. Univ of Wales BSc 62. Univ of Lon PhD 69. M IMechE 68. Chich Th Coll 75. **d** 76 **p** 77 Chich (APM). C of St Pet Brighton Dio Chich from 76. *151 Surrenden Road, Brighton, Sussex, BN1 6ZA.*

BURROWS, Dunstan Noel Augustine. b 42. Coll of Resurr Mirfield 69. **d** 70 Warrington for Liv. C of St Paul Stanley Liv 70-71; P-in-c of Good Shepherd w St Jude and Transfig Grand Bahama 72-77; H Spirit I and Dio Nass from 77. *Box N-8753, Nassau, Bahamas.* (36591)

BURROWS, George Henry Jerram. b 10. Late Sen Exhib of TCD BA (Mod) and Ment and Mor Sc Scho 31, Div Test 33, MA 37. **d** 33 Oss **p** 38 Lim. Dioc C Dio Leigh and Hd Master D'Israeli Sch 33-34; Villiers Endowed Sch Lim 34-47; Dioc C 41-47; Exam Chap to Bp of Lim 46-47; to Bp of Cork from 60; Hd Master Gr High Sch Cork from 47; L to Offic Dio Cork 47-67; Min Can of St Fin Barre's Cathl Cork 67-69; Can and Preb of Dromdaleague in Cork Cathl and of I in Ross Cathl 69-71; C-in-c of St Luke City and Dio Dub from 71; Succr of St Patr Cathl Dub 71-77; Chan V from 77; Sec to Dioc Bd of Educn Dio Dub Glendal and Kild 73-75 and 78-80; Cler V and Hon Sec Ch Ch Cathl Dub from 81. *22 Longwood Avenue, Dublin 8, Irish Republic.* (Dub 755125)

BURROWS, Very Rev Hedley Robert. b 1887. New Coll Ox BA (2nd cl Mod Hist) 09, MA 13. Wells Th Coll 10. Hon CF 18. **d** 11 **p** 12 Win. C of Petersfield 11-14; TCF 14-16; P-in-c of St Columba Kilmartin 17-18; Res Chap to Abp of York 18-19; C of St Mary (in c of Dock St Miss) Southampton 19-21; R of Stoke Abbott 21-25; Hon Chap to Bp of Portsm 27-28; V of St Steph Portsea 25-28; Gt Grimsby 28-36; RD of Grimsby and Cleethorpes 28-36; Can of Linc Cathl 33-43; V of St Pet w St Swith Bournemouth 36-43; Surr Dio Win 36-43; RD of Bournemouth 40-43; Can and Archd of Win 43-47; Dean of Heref 47-61; Dean (Emer) from 61; V of St Jo Bapt Heref 47-61; Master of St Ethelbert's Hosp Heref 47-61; Sub-Chap O of St John of Jer from 48; Perm to Offic Dios Portsm and Win from 62. *Chilland Rise, Itchen Abbas, Winchester, Hants.*

BURROWS, John Edward. b 36. Univ of Leeds BA (2nd cl Hist) 60. Coll of Resurr Mirfield. **d** 63 St Alb **p** 65 Lon. C of Much Hadham 63-65; Hon C of St Mary w St Chad, Haggerston 65-73; C-in-c of St Clem w St Barn and St Matt Finsbury 73-76; Chap Woodbridge Sch and L to Offic Dio St E from 76. *c/o Woodbridge School, Woodbridge, Suff.*

BURROWS, Joseph Atkinson. b 32. St Aid Coll 57. **d** 61 **p** 62 Ches. C of All SS Hoole 61-67; R of Linstead w Bogwalk Ja 67-68; C of H Trin Ayr (in c of St Ninian Prestwick) 68-74; R of St Ninian Prestwick 74-78; C of Cronulla 78-81; R of Naremburn w Cammeray Dio Syd from 81. *28 Rhodes Avenue, Naremburn, NSW, Australia 2065.* (43-1828)

BURROWS, Leonard Ernest. b 14. Roch Th Coll. **d** 62 **p** 63 Roch. C of Gravesend 62-64; St Steph Holloway 64-69; V of Thurmaston 70-79; St Eliz Nether Hall 79-81; L to Offic Dio Ely from 81. *44 Humberley Close, Eynesbury, St Neots, Cambs.*

BURROWS, Leslie Hamilton. Univ of Queensld BA 65. St Francis Th Coll Brisb ACT ThL 51. **d** and **p** 51 Brisb. C of St Francis Nundah Brisb 51-53; Miss Chap Dio Brisb 53-55; C of St Andr Lutwyche 55-56; Bundaberg 56-57; Chermside Brisb 57-58; St Matt Sherwood Brisb 58-66; R of St Paul Taringa Brisb 66-75; Kilcoy Dio Brisb from 76. *37 Ethel Street, Kilcoy, Queensland, Australia 4515.* (Kilcoy 97 1015)

BURROWS, Ven Mathew Brinsmead. Moore Th Coll Syd 56. **d** 56 **p** 57 Armid. C of Glen Innes 56-59; St Pet Cathl Armid 59-60; V of Wee Waa 60-69; Barraba Dio Armid from 70; Archd of Gwydir from 77. *Vicarage, Barraba, NSW, Australia 2347.* (82-1037)

BURROWS, Paul Anthony. b 55. Univ of Nottm BA 77. St Steph Ho Ox 77. **d** 79 **p** 80 S'wark. C of St Giles Camberwell 79-81; St Pet St Helier Dio S'wark from 81. *189 Bishopsford Road, Morden, Surrey.* (01-648 3792)

BURROWS, Reginald Wilfred. b 36. Qu Coll Cam BA 57, MA 62. Clifton Th Coll 61. **d** 63 **p** 64 Lon. C of St Jas Muswell Hill 63-65; St Leon (in c of St Mary w St John 66-69) Bootle 65-69; R of Albert Mem Ch w St Aug Newton Heath Man 69-72; V of St Barn and St Jude City and Dio Newc T from 72. *Vicarage, Springbank Road, Newcastle-on-Tyne, NE2 1PD.* (Newc T 327837)

BURROWS, Samuel Reginald. b 30. K Coll Lon and Warm AKC 57. **d** 58 **p** 59 Dur. C of Shildon 58-62; Heworth (in c of St Andr) 62-67; P-in-c of St Andr Conv Distr Leam

Lane 67-73; St Mary Virg w St Pet Conv Distr Bp Wearmouth 73-77; R of Bewcastle w Stapleton Dio Carl from 77. *Rectory, Stapleton, Carlisle, Cumb, CA6 6LD.* (Roadhead 660)

✠ **BURROWS, Right Rev Simon Hedley.** b 28. K Coll Cam 3rd cl Cl Trip pt i 51, BA 2nd cl Th Trip pt ia 52, MA 56. Westcott Ho Cam 52. **d** 54 Kens for Lon **p** 55 Lon. C of St John's Wood Ch 54-57; Chap Jes Coll Cam 57-60; V of Wyken 60-67; H Trin Fareham 67-71; Team R 71-74; Cons Ld Bp Suffr of Buckingham in Westmr Abbey 18 Oct 74 by Abp of Cant; Bps of Nor, Southw, Cov, Portsm and Ox; Bps Suffr of Basingstoke, Bedford, Dover, Hertf, Kingston T, Maidstone, Plymouth, Dorch, Reading, Tonbridge, and Willesden; and others. *Sheridan, Grimms Hill, Great Missenden, Bucks, HP16 9BD.* (Great Missenden 2173)

BURROWS, Chan Walter Joseph Mayes. b 08. Trin Coll Dub BA 28, Div Test 30, MA 31. **d** 31 **p** 32 Dub. C of Portarlington 31-33; Rathfarnham 33-37; C-in-c of Crumlin 37-59; I of Taney Dio Dub from 59; Hon Cler V of Ch Ch Cathl Dub 35-63; Can 63-70; Chan from 70. *Taney Rectory, Dundrum, Dublin, Irish Republic.* (Dublin 984497)

BURRY, Benjamin Charles. b 42. Mem Univ Newfld BA, LTh 67. Qu Coll Newfld. **d** 67 **p** 68 Newfld. C of Foxtrap 67-69; R of Rose Blanche 69-73; Labrador W 73-79; C of St Aug St John's Dio Newfld from 79. *157 University Avenue, St John's, Newfoundland, Canada.*

BURSELL, Henry. b 07. Montr Dioc Coll. **d** 31 Ont **p** 32 Niag. C of St Geo St Cath 31-33; I of W Flamboro w Rockton 33-34; C of Ecclesfield 34-36; R of Pitsea 36-39; V of St Paul Wood Green Wednesbury 39-42; Chap RAFVR 41-47; Chap RAF 47-50; R of Berkswell 50-59; Tawstock 59-72. *12 St James's Place, Ilfracombe, N Devon, EX34 9BH.*

BURSELL, Rupert David Hingston. b 42. Univ of Ex LLB 63. St Edm Hall Ox BA (2nd cl Th) 67, MA DPhil 72. St Steph Ho Ox. **d** 68 Willesden for Lon **p** 69 Bris (APM). C of St Marylebone 68-69; Almondsbury 69-71; Hon C of St Francis Ashton Gate, Bedminster Dio Bris from 71; L to Offic Dio B & W from 72. *74 Church Road, Winscombe, Avon, BS25 1BP.* (Winscombe 3246)

BURSLEM, Christopher David Jeremy Grant. b 35. K Coll Lon and Warm. **d** 59 **p** 60 Chelmsf. C of Bocking 59-63; All SS Glouc 64-67; R of Amberley Dio Glouc from 67. *Amberley Rectory, Stroud, Glos.* (Amberley 2523)

BURSTON, John Joseph. b 14. **d** 79 **p** 80 Bal. Hon C of Ararat Dio Bal from 79. *Picnic Road, Ararat, Vic, Australia 3377.*

BURSTON, Robert Benjamin Stuart. b 45. Univ of Dur BA 68, Dip Th 70. St Chad's Coll Dur. **d** 70 **p** 71 Bp Ramsbotham for Newc T. C of Whorlton 70-77; V of Alwinton w Holystone, Kidland and Alnham Dio Newc T from 77. *Alwinton Vicarage, Harbottle, Morpeth, Northumb, NE65 7BE.*

BURT, Eric John. b 03. Univ of Dur 26. Edin Th Coll 27. **d** 29 **p** 30 Ex. C of Churchstow w Kingsbridge and Duncombe Lect 29-32; St Budeaux (in c of H Trin Crownhill) 32-36; V of St Mich Stoke Devonport 36-46; Ivybridge 46-62; R of Harford 46-62; RD of Plympton 49-52; V of Curry Rivel 62-71. *63 Seymour Road, Ringwood, Hants.*

BURT, Frederick Owen. b 1896. Kings Coll Lon 19. **d** 22 **p** 23 Newc T. C of St Cuthb Blyth 22-26; All SS Tooting 26-35; V of St Phil Battersea 35-42; St Aug Grove Park 42-56; R of Long Ditton 65-67. *117 Furze Croft, Hove, Sussex, BN3 1PF.*

BURT, Leslie Reginald. b 22. ACIS 49. St Aug Coll Cant 65. **d** 66 **p** 67 Portsm. C of Petersfield 66-70. *44b Victoria Road South, Southsea, Hants, PO5 2BT.* (Portsm 730989)

BURT, Michael John. b 47. Trin Coll Bris 76. **d** 79 **p** 80 Capetn. C of H Trin Paarl Dio Capetn from 79. *Flat 220, Main Street, Paarl, CP 7646, S Africa.*

BURT, Noël Bryce. b 21. Clare Coll Cam BA 49 MA 53. Cudd Coll 49. **d** 51 **p** 52 York. C of St Olave York 51-54; St Martin Scarborough 54-56; V of St Sav Scarborough 56-61; Sledmere 61-67; C-in-c of Cowlam 61-67; R of Invergowrie 67-76; Glencarse 71-76; V of Denton w Ingleton Dio Dur from 76. *Ingleton Vicarage, Darlington, Co Durham, DL2 3HS.* (0325-730382)

BURT, Robert. b 08. Lich Th Coll 31. **d** 34 **p** 35 Dur. C of Ferryhill 34-40; Ch Ch W Hartlepool 40-45; V of Newbottle 45-61; St Matt Darlington 61-77; Perm to Offic Dio Dur from 77. *13 Acacia Street, Darlington.*

BURT, Roger Malcolm. b 45. St Jo Coll Auckld LTh 74. **d** 73 **p** 74 Wel. C of All SS Palmerston N 73-76; V of Tinui 76-80; P-in-c of Easton 80-81; Colton 80-81; V of Easton w Colton and Harlingford Dio Nor from 81. *Easton Vicarage, Norwich, Norf, NR9 5ES.* (Nor 880-235)

BURT, William Henry John. b 14. Univ of Leeds BA 36. Coll of Resurr Mirfield 36. **d** 38 Southn for Win **p** 39 Win. C of St Luke Southn 38-51; Chap to St Mary's Portsm 51-76; P-in-c of Crundale w Godmersham 77-78; Elmsted w Hastingleigh 77-78; U Hardres w Stelling Dio Cant from 79. *Three Elms, Bossingham, Canterbury, CT4 6DX.* (Stelling Minnis 374)

BURTON, Antony William James. b 29. Late Exhib Ch Coll Cam 1st cl Math Trip pt i 50, BA (Sen Opt Math Trip pt ii) 52, MA 56. Cudd Coll 52. **d** 54 **p** 55 Linc. C of St Nich Linc 54-57; St Jo Bapt Croydon 57-62; V of Winterton Dio Linc from 62; Roxby w Risby Dio Linc from 70; RD of Manlake from 76. *Winterton Vicarage, Scunthorpe, S Humb, DN15 9PU.* (Scunthorpe 732262)

BURTON, Cecil John. b 17. Tyndale Hall Bris 39. **d** 43 **p** 44 Liv. C of St Chrys Everton Dio Liv 43-46; Edgware (in c of St Andr Broadfields) 46-48; V of St Jo Evang Everton 48-54; R of Hawkwell 54-63; PC of St Matt Muswell Hill 63-70; Perm to Offic Dio S'wark 70-81; Dio Ches 71-78. *6 Lawman Court, Kew Gardens, Surrey.* (01-940 1578)

BURTON, Christopher Paul. b 38. FCA 75. Clifton Th Coll 67. **d** 69 **p** 70 S'wark. C of Wandsworth 69-72; St Paul York 72-75; V of Castle Vale Dio Birm from 75. *Vicarage, Reed Square, Tangmere Drive, Castle Vale, Birmingham B35 7PS.* (021-747 4041)

BURTON, Desmond Jack. b 49. Sarum Wells Th Coll 70. **d** 73 **p** 74 Nor. C of Lakenham 73-77; St John Gt Yarmouth 77-80; R of Tidworth Dio Sarum from 80. *Tidworth Rectory, St Georges Road, Tidworth, Hants.* (Tidworth 3889)

BURTON, Ven Douglas Harry. OBE 67. Univ Coll Dur LTh 37, BA 38. St Aug Coll Cant. **d** 39 Cant for Col Bp **p** 40 Argent. Asst Chap St Sav Belgrano Buenos Aires Dio Argent 40-45; V from 48; Chap of H Trin Lomas de Zamora 45-48; St Paul's Miss Palermo Buenos Aires 48-59; Hon Can of St John's Pro-Cathl Buenos Aires from 62; Archd of River Plate from 71. *Calle Cramer 1816, Buenos Aires, Argentina.*

BURTON, Edward Arthur. b 15. Tyndale Hall Bris 39. **d** 42 **p** 43 Lich. C of St Martin Tipton 42-45; Offic C-in-c of St Nath Windsor Liv 45-46; C of Morden (in c of St Geo) 46-49; V of Bp Ryder Ch Birm 49-51; St Paul Tipton 51-55; Tibshelf 55-63; Beckford w Ashton-under-Hill 63-78. *7 Loxwood Avenue, Church Crookham, Aldershot, Hants, GU13 0NS.* (Fleet 23286)

BURTON, Edward Arthur. b 40. K Coll Lon and Warm AKC 63. **d** 64 **p** 65 Lon. C of St Pet and St Paul Teddington 64-69; C-in-c of St Mich and St Geo Conv Distr White City Hammersmith 69-71; C of Addlestone 71-74; V of All S Harlesden Dio Lon from 75. *3 Station Road, NW10 4UJ.* (01-965 4988)

BURTON, Eric. b 51. Canberra Coll of Min ACT ThDip 76. **d** and **p** 77 C & Goulb. C of S Wagga Wagga 77-79; Temora 79-81; R of Bribbaree Dio C & Goulb from 81. *Rectory, Bribbaree, NSW, Australia 2724.*

BURTON, Frank George. b 19. AKC 42. **d** 42 **p** 43 Lon. C of St Mark Harlesden 42-45; St Mich Highgate Lon 45-48; Ch Ch Southgate 48-50; V of St Mich AA Enfield 50-66; Edmonton 66-77; Chap Enfield War Mem Hosp and St Mich Hosp 50-66; RD of Enfield 70-75. *15 Lincoln Crescent, Enfield, Middx, EN1 1JY.* (01-366 3620)

BURTON, Frank Victor. b 10. Linc Th Coll 76. **d** 76 **p** 77 Linc. C of Folkingham (S Lafford from 77) 76-78; Helpringham 78-79; Hon C of New Sleaford 79-80; Perm to Offic Dio Linc from 80. *181 Grantham Road, Sleaford, NG34 7NY.*

BURTON, Geoffrey Robert William. b 20. Ridley Hall Cam. **d** 63 Syd **p** 64 Chelmsf. L to Offic Dio Syd 63-64; C of Stanford-le-Hope 64-66; R of Scarning w Wendling 66-71; V of Bacton w Edingthorpe (w Witton and Ridlington from 80) Dio Nor from 71; C-in-c of Witton w Ridlington 75-80. *Vicarage, Bacton, Norwich, NR12 0JP.*

BURTON, Graham John. b 45. Univ of Bris BA 69. Tyndale Hall Bris 69. **d** 71 **p** 72 Leic. C of St Chris Leic 71-75; St John Southall 75-79. *Address temp unknown.*

BURTON, Harold Alban. b 10. **d** 53 **p** 54 Worc. C of Alvechurch 53-56; V of Salford Priors 56-69; C of St Paul Worthing 69-74. *Pitchill Lodge, Salford Priors, Evesham, Worcs, WR11 5SN.*

BURTON, John Harold Stanley. b 13. Univ Coll Ox 3rd cl Cl Mods 33, BA (2nd cl Th) 35, MA 38. Westcott Ho Cam 36. **d** 36 **p** 38 Lon. C of Ch Ch Woburn Sq 36-39; Cranleigh (in c of St Andr) 39-40; Hd of Cam Ho Camberwell 40-43; Chap RAFVR 43-46; Chap Middx Hosp Lon 46-50; R Free Hosp Lon 50-54; Gen Sec CLB 54-64 and 73-76. *Millrace House, Durrus, Nr Bantry, Co Cork, Irish Republic.* (Durrus 18)

BURTON, John Richard. b 22. Em Coll Cam 2nd cl Hist Trip pt i 46, BA (3rd cl Th Trip pt i) 47, MA 51. Wycl Hall Ox 49. **d** 50 **p** 51 Ox. C of St Jo Evang w St Steph Reading 50-52; Plymouth 52-56; PC of Ch Ch Plymouth 56-59; V of Ellacombe 59-74; Team V of Centr Torquay 74-76; C of Centr Torquay Dio Ex from 76. *Manor House, Coffinswell, Newton Abbot, TQ12 4SW.*

BURTON, Leonard Barcham. b 13. St Deiniol's Libr Hawarden 60. **d** 60 **p** 61 Liv. C of St Thos Eccleston 60-64; V of Musbury 64-69; Lower Darwen 69-75; Stalmine 75-81. *6 Harwood Close, Stalmine, Blackpool, FY6.*

BURTON, Lewin Noel. b 15. **d** and **p** 75 Ch Ch. C of St Alb City and Dio Ch Ch from 75. *58 Kensington Avenue, Christchurch 1, NZ.* (83-481)

BURTON, Nicholas John. b 52. St Steph Ho Ox 77. **d** 80 **p** 81 Leic. C of St Matt w St Geo City and Dio Leic from 80. *St Alban's Vicarage, Weymouth Street, Leicester, LE4 6FN.*

BURTON, Philip. b 04. Or Coll Ox 3rd cl Math Mods 24, BA (3rd cl Hist) 26, 3rd cl Th 27. MA 31. Sarum Th Coll 31. **d** 31 **p** 32 Wakef. C of Mirfield 31-35; Pontefract 35-39; V of Marton 39-47; CF (EC) 43-46; V of St Paul Easthorpe Mirfield 47-54; Southowram 54-59; Aberford and Lotherton (w Saxton and Towton from 77) 59-78; Saxton w Towton and Lead 59-77; w Pastoral Care of Ryther 80-81. *De Brome cottage, Lotherton-cum-Aberford, Leeds, W Yorks, LS25 3DA.* (Aberford 267)

BURTON, Theodore Kingwell. K Coll NS LTh 69. **d** 68 **p** 69 NS. I of Melford and Guysborough Dio NS from 68. *PO Box 51, Mulgrave, NS, Canada.* (538-9371)

BURTON-DURHAM, Conway Milton. St Pet Coll Rosettenville 67. **d** 69 Bp Carter for Johann **p** 70 Johann. C of St Pet Krugersdorp Dio Johann from 69. *43 Corlett Avenue, Princess, Roodepoort, Transvaal, S Africa.* (011-763 2561)

BURTWELL, Stanley Peter. b 32. Univ of Leeds BA 55. Coll of Resurr Mirfield 55. **d** 57 **p** 58 Ripon. C of St Hilda Leeds 57-61; Miss Dio Zulu 61-63; R of St Aug Zulu 63-70; Melmoth 70-72; C-in-c of Gt Hanwood Dio Heref 72-78; R from 78; RD of Pontesbury from 80. *Great Hanwood Rectory, Shrewsbury, Shropshire.* (Shrewsbury 860273)

BURUNDI, Diocese of. *See* Buye.

BURUNDI, Isaac Gervase. b 53. St Phil Coll Kongwa 74. **d** 76 **p** 77 Vic Nyan. P Dio Vic Nyan. *PO Box 160, Musoma, Tanzania.*

BURWELL, Peter William Gale. b 45. Edin Th Coll 72. **d** 75 **p** 76 Edin. C of St Jo Evang Edin 75-79; R of Lasswade Dio Edin from 79; Dalkeith Dio Edin from 81. *Rectory, Dobbie's Road, Lasswade, Midlothian.* (031-663 7000)

BURY, Dennis Richard. b 43. Univ of Man BA 66. Andover Newton Th Sch USA MA 71. Sarum Th Coll 66. **d** 69 **p** 71 Liv. C of H Trin Southport 69-71; St Faith Great Crosby 71-72. *262 Hawthorn Road, Rochester, Kent, ME2 2HU.*

BURY, Herbert John Malcolm. b 28. Linc Coll Ox BA (3rd cl Engl) 52, MA 58. Roch Th Coll 68. **d** 69 **p** 70 Roch. C of Bexleyheath 69-72; V of Ryarsh w Birling Dio Roch from 72; C-in-c of Addington w Trottiscliffe Dio Roch from 76. *Vicarage, Ryarsh, West Malling, Kent.* (West Malling 842249)

BURY, Nicholas Ayles Stillingfleet. b 43. Qu Coll Cam BA 65, MA 69. Ch Ch Ox (by incorp) 71. Cudd Coll. **d** 68 Warrington for Liv **p** 69 Liv. C of Our Lady and St Nich Liv 68-71; Chap Ch Ch Ox 71-75; V of St Mary Stevenage Dio St Alb from 75. *148 Hydean Way, Stevenage, Herts.* (Stevenage 51963)

BURY, Phineas. b 02. Ch Coll Cam BA 28, MA 32. St Aug Coll Cant 24. **d** 30 **p** 31 Rip. C of Far Headingley 30-32; Chap of Flores Mendoza and Western Camps 32-35; Asst Chap St John's Pro-Cathl Buenos Aires 35-36; Chap Shawnigan Lake Sch 36-38; Chap (Eccles Est) at Kamptee 39-47; Chap Nagp 43-47; Chap Mhow 47-49; Perm to Offic Dio B & W 49-50; R of Castletownroche w Ballyhooley 50-52; Cloyne w Ballycotton 52-57; Can of Kilbrittain in Cork Cathl and Can of Donaughmore in Cloyne Cathl 53-55; Treas of Cloyne Cathl and Can of Cahirlag in Cork Cathl 55-57; Dean and R of Cloyne and Can of Kilbrogan in Cork Cathl 57-73; Can and Preb of St Patr Cathl, Dub 68-73. *43 Alma Road, Monkstown, Co Dublin, Irish Republic.*

BUSABUSA, Samusoni. **d** 64 **p** 65 Mbale. P Dio Mbale 64-72; Dio Bukedi from 72. *Kamonkoli, Uganda.*

BUSAN, Diocese of. *See* Pusan.

BUSBY, Edward David. **d** 54 Tor **p** 54 Coadj Bp for Tor. C of Ch Ch Tor 54-59; Dir of Angl Conf Centre 59-64; R of Streetsville 64-71; Dir of Leadership Tr Dio Tor from 73. *135 Adelaide Street East, Toronto, Ont., Canada.* (416-363 6021)

BUSBY, Canon Geoffrey. b 10. Lich Th Coll 30. **d** 33 **p** 34 Derby. C of Elmton w Creswell 33-35; St Mary Ilkeston 35-38; V of Charlesworth 38-46; Denby 46-51; Wirksworth w Carsington R Dio Derby from 51; C-in-c of Idridgehay 51-55; V 55-79; V of Middleton-by-Wirksworth Dio Derby from 55; RD of Wirksworth 55-73; Surr from 51; Hon Can of Derby from 57; R of Kirk Ireton 57-79. *Wirksworth Vicarage, Derby.* (Wirksworth 2567)

BUSBY, Ian Frederick Newman. b 32. Roch Th Coll 61. **d** 64 **p** 65 Ripon. C of Bedale 64-67; Stevenage 67-71; V of St Mary Stevenage 71-75; Kildwick Dio Bradf from 75. *Kildwick Vicarage, Keighley, Yorks.*

BUSBY, Jack Wright. b 12. Univ of Leeds BA 35. Coll of Resurr Mirfield 35. **d** 37 **p** 38 Southw. C of St Alb Sneinton 37-41; Hucknall Torkard (in c of St Pet) 41-47; Chap of Newstead Abbey and Colliery 47-56; V of Blidworth 56-66; Goxhill 66-70; Barkestone w Plungar and Redmile 70-77. *39 Apeldoorn Gardens, St John's Road, Spalding, Lincs.*

BUSCH, Henry. b 32. **d** 76 **p** 77 Capetn. C of St Mary Stellenbosch Dio Capetn from 76. *PO Box 213, Stellenbosch 7600, CP, S Africa.*

BUSERI, Job Oweiebigha. Awka Tr Coll. **d** 45 Bp Patterson for Niger **p** 47 Niger. P Dio Niger 45-52; Dio Niger Delta 52-72. *c/o Nigerian Army, Lagos, Nigeria.*

BUSH, Alan Frederick. Bp's Univ Lennox BA 53. Hur Coll LTh 55. **d** 55 Montr **p** 56 New Westmr. C of St Phil Vanc 55-57; I of Wembley 57-59; Grande Prairie and Wembley 59-65. *5402 Trafalgar Street, Vancouver, BC, Canada.*

BUSH, Alfred Edward Leonard. b 09. ALCD 39. **d** 39 **p** 40 Chelmsf. C of St Mary Becontree 39-42; C-in-c of St Alb Becontree 42-43; V of Kentish Town 43-58; Oakwood 58-75; Perm to Offic Dio Chich 75-78; Dio St E from 78. *1 Queen's Road, Bury St Edmunds, Suff.* (Bury St E 3094)

BUSH, David. b 25. Univ of Liv BArchit 47. SOC 73. **d** and **p** 77 S & M. C of St Geo Douglas 77-80; V of Marown Dio S & M from 80. *Marown Vicarage, Crosby, IM.* (Marown 378)

BUSH, Percy Edward. b 20. Sarum Th Coll 57. **d** 59 **p** 60 St Alb. C of Radlett 59-61; Biscot 61-65; V of Castle Bytham 65-71; R of Bytham Parva 65-71; C-in-c of Careby w Holywell and Aunby 65-66; R 66-71; V of Ingham w Cammeringham 71-75; Fillingham 71-75; P-in-c of Scampton Aisthorpe and Brattleby 75; Hubberholme 75-78; Burnsall Dio Bradf from 78. *Burnsall Rectory, Skipton, Yorks, BD23 6BP.* (Burnsall 238)

BUSH, Trevor Noel Wood. Rhodes Univ Grahmstn BA 47. St Paul's Coll Grahmstn LTh 49. **d** and **p** 50 Johann. C of St Patr Malvern Johann 50-51; R of Bremersdorp and Dir of Bremersdorp Miss 51-54; Asst Chap of Michaelhouse Sch Balgowan 54-56; Chap Peterho Sch Marandellas 56-58; St Andr Sch Bloemf 58-60; R of All SS Beaconsfield and Warden Bp's Hostel Kimberley 60-62; Chap Cathl Sch Llan 62-69; Ch Sch Ado-Ekiti Dio Ekiti from 69. *Christ's School, Ado-Ekiti, Nigeria.*

BUSHAU, Reginald Francis. b 49. St Steph Ho Ox BA 73. **d** 74 **p** 75 S'wark. C of Deptford 74-77; St Andr Willesden Green and of St Francis Gladstone Pk Dio Lon from 78. *Vicarage, St Andrew's Road, NW10 2QT.* (01-459 2670)

BUSHELL, Roy. N-W Ordin Course 75. **d** 79 **p** 80 Liv. C of Croft Dio Liv from 79. *24 Eaves Brow Road, Croft, Warrington, Cheshire, WA3 7LQ.*

BUSHIRI, Edgar Raphael. St Cypr Th Coll Tunduru. **d** 47 **p** 50 Masasi. P Dio Masasi. *USPG, Mtwara, Tanzania.*

BUSING, Paul Frederic Wolfgang. Univ of Berlin Univ of Lon BD 45. **d** and **p** 51 Montr. I of Arundel 51-53; Supt Jewish Miss Montr from 53; R of Waterloo and P-in-c of Stukeley S 55-59; R of St Cuthb Montr 59-61; Dioc Miss and Cler V of Ch Ch Cathl Montr 61-63; R of St Jo Evang Montr 63-70; St Andr and St Mark Dorval 70-76. *557 Roosevelt Avenue, Ottawa, Ont, Canada.*

BUSINGYE, John. b 41. Bp Tucker Coll 61. **d** 65 Ank **p** 67 Kig. P Dio Kig 67-71; Chap Ugan Army from 71. *School of Infantry, Uganda Armed Forces, Private Bag, Jinga-Kampala, Uganda.*

BUSK, Horace. b 34. Clifton Th Coll 56. **d** 60 **p** 61 Lich. C of All SS Burton-on-Trent 60-63; Paraguay 63-66; St Matt St Leonard-on-Sea 66-67; L to Offic Dio Sarum 68-69; C of W Kilburn 69-74; Team V of Wreningham 74-81; P-in-c of Meysey Hampton w Marston Meysey and Castle Eaton Dio Glouc from 81. *Meysey Hampton Rectory, Cirencester, Glos, GL7 5JX.* (Poulton 249)

BUSO, Gerald Leonard Msutu. b 47. St Bede's Coll Umtata 75. **d** 76 St John's. d Dio St John's. *Box 192, Nqamakwe, Republic of Transkei, S Africa.*

BUSOGA, Lord Bishop of. *See* Bamwoze, Right Rev Cyprian Kikunyi.

BUSS, Gerald Vere Austen. b 36. St Steph Ho Ox 59. **d** 63 **p** 64 S'wark. C of Petersham 63-66; H Trin Brompton Kens 66-69; Asst Chap Hurstpierpoint Coll 70-73; Chap from 74. *Hurstpierpoint College, Hassocks, Sussex.* (0273 833636)

BUSS, Philip Hodnett. b 37. Ch Coll Cam 1st cl Th Trip pt i 57, BA (1st cl Th Trip pt ii) 59, 2nd cl Th Trip pt iii 61, MA 63. Tyndale Hall Bris 61. **d** 63 **p** 64 Lon. Hon C of Em Northwood 63-70; Tutor Lon Coll of Div 62-66; Chap 66-70; V of Handsworth-Woodhouse 70-74; Ch Ch Fulham Dio Lon from 74. *40 Clancarty Road, SW6 3AA.* (01-736 4261)

BUSSA, Barnabas. b 43. St Phil Coll Kongwa 77. **d** 79 **p** 80 W Tang. P Dio W Tang. *Nyumbigwa, PO Box 74, Kasulu, Tanzania, E Africa.*

BUSSELL, Greader Edmund. b 02. AKC (1st cl) and Barry Pri 34. **d** 34 Bp Palmer for Glouc **p** 35 Glouc. C of Northleach w Hampnett and Stowell 34-35; P-in-c of St Alb Miss Glendale S Rhod 35-39; St Faith Miss Rusapi 39-41; R of Plumtree w Francistown 41-43; Gatooma 43-46; V of Ardington w Lockinge R 46-53; R of Didcot 53-61; RD of Wantage 52-53; Wallingford 55-61; Ottery 67-71; R of Buckerell 61-68; R of Feniton 61-68; L to Offic Dio Ex 69-70; C of Ottery St Mary Dio Ex from 70; Sw Area Sec Melan Miss 70-77. *42 Raleigh Road, Ottery St Mary, Devon.* (Ottery St Mary 3770)

BUSSEY, Norman. b 22. Clifton Th Coll 63. **d** 65 **p** 66 Ches. C of St Mary Upton 65-69; V of Bradley Dio Wakef from 69. *87 Bradley Road, Huddersfield, W Yorks, HD2 1RA.*

BUSTARD, Guy Nicholas. b 51. AKC and BD 77. St Steph Ho Ox 77. **d** 78 **p** 79 Cant. C of Hythe 78-81; Chap RN from 81. *Waylands, Shipbourne, Nr Tonbridge, Kent.*

BUSTIN, Peter Ernest. b 32. Qu Coll Cam BA 56, MA 60. Tyndale Hall Bris 56. **d** 57 **p** 58 Roch. C of Welling 57-60; Farnborough 60-62; V of Hornsey Rise 62-69; R of Barnwell (w Thurning and Luddington from 78) Dio Pet from 70; RD of Oundle from 76; P-in-c of Luddington and Thurning 77-78. *Barnwell Rectory, Peterborough, PE8 5PG.* (Oundle 72374)

BUSTON, Dudley Graham. b 06. Late Scho of Trin Coll Cam 1st cl Math Trip pt i 26, BA (2nd cl Math Trip pt ii) 28, MA 32. Univ of Ox Dipl Th 33. Wycl Hall Ox 32. **d** 34 **p** 35 Portsm. C of St Jas Milton Portsmouth 34-36; Battersea 36-39; V of Cumnor 39-49; R of Ascot Heath and Chap of Heatherwood Hosp 49-55; V of Enfield 55-65; RD of Enfield 58-65; Perm to Offic Dios Lon Win and Ox 65-66; C of Finchampstead 66-69; Wokingham 69-70; C-in-c of Enborne w Hamstead Marshall 70-74; Perm to Offic Dios Lon and Ox 74-80; LPr Dio Lon from 80. *40 Cadogan Place, SW1.* (01-245 9763)

BUSTOS, Julio. d 76 Bp Bazley for Chile. d Dio Chile. *Casilla 561, Vina del Mar, Chile.*

BUSWELL, Edward Wilkinson. b 1899. Qu Coll Cam BA 23, MA 26. Ridley Hall Cam 23. **d** 25 **p** 26 Chelmsf. C of St Andr Walthamstow 25-28; Gt Clacton w L Holland 28-29; St Thos Becontree 29-31; V of Comberton 31-44; C of H Trin (in c of Ch Ch) Chesterfield 44-45; St Chad Derby 45-47; Chapel-en-le-Frith (in c of Dove Holes) 47-49; R of Lockerbie 49-54; P-in-c of Dalry 54-57; C of H Trin Ayr (in c of Prestwick) 57-64; Perm to Offic Dios Arg Is and Glas 64-68; Dio Ex from 68. *3 Dolphin Court, Riverside, Shaldon, Devon, TQ14 ODA.* (Shaldon 2459)

BUSYANYA, Edward. Univ of Dur BA 73. St Paul's Th Coll Limuru 61. **d** 63 Vic Nyan for Centr Tang **p** 64 Centr Tang. P Dio Centr Tang 63-66; Dio W Tang 66-74. *Box 13, Kasulu, Tanzania.*

BUTARE, Lord Bishop of. *See* Ndandali, Right Rev Justin.

BUTCHER, Allan Sydney Tyndale. b 12. St Cath S Ox Abbott Scho 32. Worc Coll Ox 2nd cl Cl Mods 33, BA (3rd cl Th) 35, MA 38. Wycl Hall Ox 35. **d** 36 **p** 37 S'wark. C of H Trin Tulse Hill 36-41; Coulsdon 41-44; Bisley (in c of St Aug Eastcombe) 44-47; R of Edge w Pitchcombe 47-55; V of Kemble w Poole Keynes 55-60; France Lynch 60-62. *Terling, Grove Road, Bladon, Oxford.* (Woodstock 254)

BUTCHER, Andrew John. b 43. Trin Coll Cam BA 66, MA 69. Cudd Coll 66. **d** 68 **p** 69 Sheff. C of St Mark Sheff 68-70; C-in-c of H Trin w St Marg Keddington Louth 70-72; Chap RAF from 72. *c/o Ministry of Defence, Adastral House, Theobalds Road, WC1X 8RU.*

BUTCHER, Canon Douglas Claude. b 08. Ch Coll Cam BA 29, MA 44. Oak Hill Th Coll 50. **d** 51 **p** 52 Egypt. Prin of Engl Miss Coll and C-in-c of Em Ch Cairo 51-56; Hon Can of All SS Cathl Cairo from 55; Chap at Tunis 57; Min of St John Downshire Hill Hampstead and Hd of Lon Miss of CMJ 57-60; Chap at Alexandria 60-72; Actg Provost of All SS Cathl Cairo 67-72; C of Swanage (in c of All SS) 72-78; Commiss Egypt from 75. *7 Brookside, Shreen Way, Gillingham, Dorset, SP8 4HR.* (Gillingham 3865)

BUTCHER, Francis Walter Lowndes. b 17. Bps' Coll Cheshunt 49. **d** 52 **p** 53 Guildf. C of Cuddington 52-55; Putney 55-58; V of Ardleigh 58-63; St Jas Malden 63-80. *12 Glenavon Close, Claygate, Surrey, KT10 0HP.* (Esher 64597)

BUTCHER, Hubert Maxwell. Ch Coll Cam BA 48, MA 53. Trin Coll Tor BD 68. Wycl Hall Ox. **d** 51 **p** 52 Roch. C of St Jo Div Tunbridge Wells 51-53; CMS Miss Dio Luckn 54-58; C-in-c of St John L Horton Bradf 58-63; I of Fort Vermilion 63-67; R of Cloverdale Dio New Westmr from 69; V of Port Kells Dio New Westmr from 69. *6250 180th Street, RR4, Surrey, BC, Canada.*

BUTCHER, Norman. b 13. Wycl Hall Ox 40. **d** 42 **p** 43 Bradf. C of St John Clayton 42-46; Cler Deputn Sec for N Distr to Dr Barnardo's Homes 46-49; V of Kirkby Ravensworth w Dalton 49-59; R of Barwick-in-Elmet 59-79; P-in-c of Middleton w Cropton Dio York from 80. *4 Pippin Road, Mount Park, Malton, N Yorks.* (Malton 5707)

BUTCHER, Philip Warren. b 46. Trin Coll Cam BA 68, MA 70. Cudd Coll 68. **d** 70 **p** 71 Bris. C of Redcliffe 70-73; Asst Master Whitgift Sch and Hon C of St Francis w Wickham 73-78; Asst Master and Chap Abingdon Sch from 78. *c/o Abingdon School, Oxon.*

BUTCHER, Richard Peter. b 50. St Chad's Coll Dur BA (Th) 71. Chich Th Coll 73. **d** 74 Taunton for B & W **p** 75 B & W. C of St Mich AA Penn Mill Yeovil 74-77; Chap Wellingborough Sch from 77. *c/o Wellingborough School, Northants.* (Wellingborough 223878)

BUTCHER, William Maxwell. b 41. St Jo Coll Morpeth ACT ThL 69. **d** 70 Graft **p** 75 Armid. C of Kyogle 70; Graft Cathl 71; Hon C of Tamworth 73-74; C of Inverell 75-77; P-in-c of Surat 77-80; C of St Pet Wynnum City and Dio Brisb from 80. *34 Byrneside Terrace, Wynnum, Queensland, Australia 4178.* (396 8421)

BUTELEZI, Alford. d 23 **p** 28 Zulu. C of St Aug 23-29; Swaziland 29-34; Ingwavuma 34-40; Inhlwati 40-47; Nongoma 47-56. *c/o Lansdowne Mission, Via Mtubatuba, Zululand.*

BUTHELEZI, Lawrence Duma. b 48. **d** 77 **p** 78 Zulu. C of H Name Mvulazi Dio Zulu from 77. *Holy Name Parish, Mvulazi BC School, PO Buxedeni 3938, Zululand, S Africa.*

BUTLAND, Godfrey John. b 51. Grey Coll Dur BA 72. Wycl Hall Ox 73. **d** 75 Warrington for Liv **p** 76 Liv. C of Much Woolton 75-78; Dom Chap to Bp of Liv 78-81; V of St Geo Everton Dio Liv from 81. *Vicarage, Northumberland Terrace, Liverpool 5.* (051-263 1945)

BUTLAND, William Edwin. Lon Coll Div 49. **d** 51 **p** 52 Lon. C of Kentish Town 51-54; Chorley Wood 54-58; C-in-c of Colney Heath 58-59; V 59-80. *9 Studley Road, Wootton, Bedford, MK43 9DL.* (Bedford 767620)

BUTLER, Ven Alan John. b 30. Kelham Th Coll 51. **d** 56 Southw for Bloemf **p** 57 Bloemf. MSSM 56-59; C of St Cypr Cathl Kimberley 60-61; R and Dir of St Paul's Miss Kuruman 61-65; Dir of Bothithong Miss 63-65; Hon Chap to Bp of Kimb K 63-65; R of Gaborone Dio Kimb K 65-66; Dio Matab 66-70; V of St Jas Fletchamstead 70-79; Archd of Griqualand W from 79; R of Postmasburg 79-81; St Mary-le-Bourne Kuruman Dio Kimb K from 81. *Box 34, Kuruman, CP, S Africa.*

✠ **BUTLER, Right Rev Arthur Hamilton.** b 12. MBE (Mil) 44. Trin Coll Dub BA 34, Div Test (2nd cl) 35, MA 37, DD (*jure dig*) 59. **d** 35 **p** 36 Dub. C of Monkstown 35-38; Hon Min Can of St Patr Cathl Dub 37-38; C of Ch Ch Crouch End 38; H Trin Brompton Lon 38-39; CF (R of O) 39-45; I of Monkstown 45-58; Cons Ld Bp of Tuam Killala and Achonry in Arm Cathl 27 May 58 by Apb of Arm; Bps of Meath; Connor; Kilm; Killaloe; Lich; and Kurun; Dean of Achonry 58-69; Trld to Connor 79; res 81. *1 Spa Grange, Ballynahinch, Co Down, N Ireland.* (Ballynahinch 562966)

BUTLER, Cecil Anthony. b 37. Sarum Th Coll 65. **d** 68 Sherborne for Sarum **p** 69 Sarum. C of Gillingham 68-70; CF 70-74; R of St Jo Bapt Whittington Dio Lich from 74. *Whittington Rectory, Oswestry, Shropshire, SY11 4DF.* (Oswestry 62338)

BUTLER, Cecil James. b 1892. RMS Sandhurst 16. KCL Knowling Pri and AKC 38. **d** 38 **p** 39 S'wark. C of St Jo Evang Redhill 38-42; Chap RNVR 42-45; C-in-c of Laverstoke w Freefolk 46-47; R 47-51; V of Huntington York 51-53; SPG Chap at Addis Ababa 53-56; V of Aston Abbots w Cublington 57-59. *84 Chart Lane, Reigate, Surrey.* (Reigate 46243)

BUTLER, Charles David Victor. b 51. ACT BTh 78. Ridley Coll Melb 76. **d** 79 **p** 80 Melb. C of Ch Ch S Yarra Dio Melb from 79. *63 Clowes Street, South Yarra, Vic, Australia 3144.*

BUTLER, Christopher John. b 25. Univ of Leeds BA 50. Chich Th Coll 50. **d** 52 **p** 53 Lon. C of Kens 52-57; M St Barn Bush Bro N Queensld 57-59; V of Blackmoor 60-70; St Andr Wellingborough 70-79; P-in-c of Garsington Dio Ox from 79; Horspath Dio Ox from 80. *Garsington Rectory, Oxford, OX9 9HD.* (Garsington 381)

BUTLER, Ven Cuthbert Hilary. St Jo Coll Cam 2nd cl Hist Trip pt i 34, BA (2nd cl Hist Trip pt ii) 35, Burney Pri 36, 2nd cl Th Trip pt ii and Naden Stud 37, Burney Stud 38, MA 39. **d** 40 **p** 41 Chich. C of Preston 40-42; Chap RAFVR 42-46; C-in-c of St Matthias Preston 46-47; V 47-51; R of Crawley w W Crawley 51-55; Crawley Dio Chich 55-58; R of Oliver 58-61; Lect and Can of Ch Ch Cathl Vic 61-77; Exam Chap to Abp of BC 66-68; Archd of Columb 77-79; Archd (Emer) from 79; Perm to Offic Dio BC from 79. *936 Klahanie Drive, RR1, Victoria, BC, Canada.*

BUTLER, Derek Ralph. b 28. **d** 71 **p** 72 Geo (APM). C of Oudtshoorn Dio Geo from 71. *173 Church Street, Oudtshoorn, CP, S Africa.* (3474)

BUTLER, Donald Arthur. b 31. **d** 79 St Alb **p** 80 Hertf for St Alb. C of Apsley End Dio St Alb from 79. *143 Belswains Lane, Hemel Hempstead, Herts, HP3 9UZ.*

BUTLER, Edward Daniel. b 42. Rhodes Univ BA 65, MA 70. Qu Coll Birm. **d** 68 Birm for Bloemf **p** 69 Birm. C of

Edgbaston 68-72; Perm to Offic Dio Birm 70-73; Dio Chich from 74. *43 Princes Terrace, Brighton, Sussex, BN2 5JS.*

BUTLER, Everett Vincent Thomas. Codr Coll Barb. **d** 50 **p** 51 Nass. C of St Agnes Nass 50-53; P-in-c of All SS Andros 53-58; C of St Barn Nass 58-60; C of St Jos w San Juan Port of Spain 60-62; Chap HM Public Inst and Dioc Chap Dio Trinid 62-64; R of Faust 65-70; I of Canora Dio Qu'App from 70. *Canora, Sask., Canada.*

BUTLER, Frederick Walter. b 28. Chich Th Coll 67. **d** 69 **p** 70 Chich. C of Seaford 69-73; V of Peacehaven 73-75; P-in-c of Copthorne Dio Chich 75-81; V from 81. *Vicarage, Church Road, Copthorne, W Sussex.* (Copthorne 712063)

BUTLER, George James. b 53. AKC 74. St Aug Coll Cant 75. **d** 76 **p** 77 Ches. C of Ellesmere Port 76-79; Eastham Dio Ches 79-80; Chap RAF from 81. *c/o Ministry of Defence, Adastral House, WC1.*

BUTLER, Harold Henry. St Jo Coll Morpeth ACT ThL 47. **d** 39 **p** 40 River. C of St Paul's Pro-Cathl Hay 39-43; P-in-c of Whitton w Hillston 43-44; Ariah Park 44-47; R 47-50; Zeehan 50-52; Deloraine 52-54; Chap at Java 54-56; R of Oatlands Tas 56-62; V of Lautoka 62-69; Can and Chan of H Trin Pro-Cathl Suva 63-73; V of Apia 69-73; R of Cressy 73-80; Bothwell Dio Tas from 80. *Rectory, Bothwell, Tasmania 7212.* (003 91 8112)

BUTLER, Henry. b 25. Ridley Hall Cam 73. **d** 75 Huntingdon for Ely **p** 76 Ely. C of St Paul Cam 75-77; P-in-c of Stilton w Denton and Caldecote Dio Ely from 77; Folkesworth w Morborne Dio Ely from 77. *Stilton Rectory, Peterborough, Cambs, PE7 3RF.* (Pet 240282)

BUTLER, Hugh David. St Jo Coll Morpeth ACT ThL 38. **d** 38 **p** 39 River. C of Broken Hill 38-44; P-in-c of Lake Cargelligo 44-50; R of Wentworth 50-52; Smithton 52-57; ABM Japan 57-64; R of Balhannah 64-69; Naracoorte Dio Adel 69-70; Dio Murray 70-73; R of Wynyard 73-78; Evandale 78-81; Campbell Town & Ross Dio Tas from 81. *Rectory, Campbell Town, Tasmania 7210.* (003 81 1284)

BUTLER, Ian Malcolm. b 39. Univ of Bris BA (2nd cl Th) 67. Clifton Th Coll 67. **d** 69 Stepney for S'wark **p** 70 S'wark. C of St Barn Clapham Common 69-73; Reigate 73-78; V of Sissinghurst w Frittenden Dio Cant from 78. *Vicarage, Frittenden, Cranbrook, Kent, TN17 2DD.* (Frittenden 275)

BUTLER, Isaac. Qu Coll Newfld. Univ of Dur LTh 36. BA 37. **d** 33 **p** 34 Newfld. I of Twillingate 34-36; on leave 36-37; P-in-c of Fogo 37-38; R 38-44; I of Brigus and Salmon Cove 46-47; C of Bay St Geo 47-48; I 48-55; Bay Roberts 55-65; Melford 65-68; R of Londonderry w Bass 69-70; Digby 70-75; Weymouth 70-75. *Marshalltown, Digby, NS, Canada.*

BUTLER, Ivor John. b 36. Univ of Dur BA 58 Ely Th Coll 58. **d** 60 **p** 61 Lich. C of W Bromwich 60-64; V of U Gornal 64-72; St Mich Tividale 72-79; Townstal w Dartmouth Dio Ex from 79. *Mount Boone House, Dartmouth, Devon, TQ6 9PB.* (Dartmouth 2415)

BUTLER, John. b 08. **d** 60 **p** 61 S'wark. [f CA] C of St Barn Sutton New Town 60-63; Horley (in c of St Francis) 63-64; R of Oake w Hill Farrance and Heathfield 64-73; Hon C of Kirkham 73-75; L to Offic Dio Blackb from 75. *Fosbrooke House, 8 Clifton Drive, Lytham, Lancs.*

BUTLER, John. b 38. Dipl Th (Wales) 67. St Mich Coll Llan. **d** 68 **p** 69 Mon. C of Ebbw Vale 68-70; Team V 70-75; Perm to Offic Dio Mon 76-77; P-in-c of Crumlin 77-78; Perm to Offic Dio Mon from 79. *30 Monmouth House, The Mall, Cwmbran, Gwent.*

BUTLER, John Albert. Moore Th Coll Syd ACt ThL 69. **d** 69 **p** 70 Syd. C of St Clem Mosman 69-73; C-in-c of S Coogee Dio Syd 73-77; R 77-79; St Luke Thornleigh w Pennant Hills Dio Syd from 79. *323 Pennant Hills Road, Thornleigh, NSW, Australia 2120.* (84-1887)

BUTLER, John Charles. Trin Coll Dub BA (1st Resp) and Div Test (2nd cl) 31, MA 34. **d** 31 **p** 32 Connor. C of St Jas Belf 31-36; C-in-c of Finaghy 36-45; 1st R 45-66; Dean of Residence QUB 36-45; RD of S Belfast 50-55; Can of St Anne's Cathl Belf 51-67; Exam Chap to Bp of Connor 53-56. *Cloughfin, Bayview Road, Ballyholme, Bangor Co Down, N Ireland.* (Belfast 611050)

BUTLER, John David. St Francis Coll Brisb. **d** 62 **p** 63 Bath. P-in-c of Tottenham 62-66; R of Katherine 66-67; C of St Nich Sandgate Brisb 67-68; H Trin Dubbo Dio Bath from 68. *c/o Holy Trinity Rectory, Dubbo, NSW, Australia.*

BUTLER, John Kenneth. b 27. Keele Univ Dipl in Advanced Stud of Educn 75. St Aid Coll 56. **d** 58 **p** 59 Man. C of Lawton Moor 58-61; V of Unsworth 61-64; C of Knutsford 64-69; Perm to Offic Dio Ches from 69; C of Witton Ches 70-72; Assoc P of St Cross Knutsford 73-75. *4 School Close, Knutsford, Chesh, WA16 OBJ.* (Knutsford 4949)

BUTLER, John Philip. b 47. Univ of Leeds BA 70. Coll of Resurr Mirfield 70. **d** 72 Man **p** 73 Middleton for Man. C of All SS Elton Bury 73-75; Bolton-le-Moors 75-78; Chap Bolton Colls of Further Educn 75-78; Asst Chap Univ of Bris 78-81; V of Llansawel w Briton Ferry Dio Llan from 81. *251 Neath Road, Briton Ferry, W Glam, SA11 2SL.* (B Ferry 812200)

BUTLER, Malcolm. b 40. Linc Th Coll 76. **d** 78 **p** 79 Dur. C of Wickham Dio Dur from 78. *29 Duckpool Lane, Whickham, Newcastle-on-Tyne.*

BUTLER, Michael. b 41. Univ of Wales Dipl Th 63. St Mich Coll Llan 62. **d** 64 **p** 65 St A. C of Welshpool 64-73; Team V of Abth 73-80; Chap Univ Coll of Wales Abth 73-80; V of St Issell Dio St D from 80. *St Issell's Vicarage, Saundersfoot, Dyfed.* (Saundersfoot 812375)

BUTLER, Michael. b 44. Dipl Th (Lon) 68. Kelham Th Coll. **d** 68 **p** 70 Chelmsf. C of All SS Eccles Distr Chelmsf 68-71; Keymer 72-74; Team V of Ovingdean Dio Chich from 74. *43 Ainsworth Avenue, Ovingdean, Brighton, BN2 7BQ.* (Brighton 33633)

BUTLER, Michael John. b 32. Keble Coll Ox BA 58. Coll of Resurr Mirfield. **d** 59 **p** 60 Lon. C of Poplar 59-68; St Steph Walbrook Lon and Dep Dir The Samaritans 68-73; C of Godalming 73-76; C-in-c of St Anne Brighton 77-79; Communications Officer and Dir for Social Responsibility Dio Chich from 77. *30 Bigwood Avenue, Hove, BN3 6FG.*

BUTLER, Michael Weeden. b 38. Clare Coll Cam BA 60, MA 65. Westcott Ho Cam 63. **d** 65 **p** 66 S'wark. C of Bermondsey 65-68; Industr Chap S Lon Miss 68-72; Miss Dio Sier L 73-77; R of Gt Chart Dio Cant from 77; RD of E Charing from 80. *Great Chart Rectory, Ashford, Kent.* (Ashford 20371)

BUTLER, Canon Norman Barry. Moore Th Coll Syd ACT ThL 50, Th Scho 55. **d** 51 **p** 52 Syd. C of Lithgow 51-52; C-in-c of Granville 52-53; CMS Miss from 53; Groote Eylandt 53-55; P-in-c of Provisional Distr of Girraween 64-65; Can of Carp 65-68; N Terr from 68; Miss at Darwin Dio Carp 66-68; Dio N Terr from 68; Dioc Regr Dio N Terr from 70; Hon C of Nightcliff Dio N Terr from 72. *Box 39352, Winnelli, NT, Australia 5789.*

BUTLER, Perry Andrew. b 49. Univ of York BA 70. Jes Coll Ox DPhil 78. Univ of Nottm Dipl Th 79. Linc Th Coll 78. **d** 80 **p** 81 Kens for Lon. C of St Nich w St Mary Magd Chiswick Dio Lon from 80. *St Denys Cottage, Church Street, Chiswick, W4.* (01-995 2019)

BUTLER, Peter Ronald. b 47. St Jo Coll Auckld LTh 76. **d** 76 Bp McKenzie for Wel **p** 77 Wel. C of Feilding 76-78; V of Kiwitea Dio Wel from 78. *Vicarage, Kimbolton, NZ.* (838)

BUTLER, Philip Owen. St D Coll Lamp 49. **d** 53 Ban **p** 54 St A for Ban. C of Amlwch 53-55; Llanbeblig w Caernarvon 55-57; R of Llanymawddwy 57-63; V of Pentir w Glasinfryn and Rhiwlas Dio Ban from 63. *Pentir Vicarage, Bangor, Gwyn, LL57 4YB.* (Bangor 2016)

BUTLER, Richard Charles Burr. b 34. St Pet Hall Ox BA (2nd cl Th) 59, MA 62. Linc Th Coll 58. **d** 60 **p** 61 Kens for Lon. C of St John's Wood Ch 60-63; V of Kingstanding 63-75; R of St Marg Lee Dio S'wark from 75. *Rectory, Brandram Road, Lewisham, SE13 5EA.* (01-852 0633)

BUTLER, Robert Clifford. b 25. K Coll Lon and Warm AKC 54. **d** 55 **p** 56 St Alb. C of Gt Berkhamsted 55-59; Dunstable 59-63; V of Stanbridge w Tilsworth 63-73; R of Maulden 73-80; Oldbury Dio Sarum from 80. *Rectory, Heddington, Calne, Wilts.* (Bromham 850411)

BUTLER, Robert Edwin. b 37. Ely Th Coll 60. **d** 62 **p** 63 S'wark. C of St Jo Bapt Southend Lewisham 62-65; St Eliz Eastbourne 65-69; V of St Richard Langney Eastbourne Dio Chich from 69. *St Richard's Vicarage, Langney, Eastbourne, Sussex, BN23 7AX.* (Eastbourne 761158)

BUTLER, Robert George. b 13. ACIS 35. Oak Hill Coll 74. **d** 76 Colchester for Chelmsf **p** 77 Chelmsf. C of St Mary Saffron Walden Dio Chelmsf from 76. *Grianan, Debden, Saffron Walden, Essex, CB11 3LE.*

BUTLER, Ronald Gerrad. Moore Th Coll Syd 61. **d** 61 **p** 62 Armid. C of Armid 61-63; P-in-c of Baradine 63-64; C of Neutral Bay 67-68; SAMS Miss 68-72; P-in-c of Belconnen C Canberra 72-74; Numbulwar 75-78; Innisfail Dio N Queensld from 78. *Box 184, Innisfail, Queensland, Australia 4860.*

BUTLER, Sidney. b 07. Univ of Dur LTh 35. St Aid Coll 33 **d** 35 **p** 36 Southw. C of St Giles W Bridgford 35-39; Skegby (in c of Stanton Hill) 39-41; St Mary Magd Sutton-in-Ashfield 41-44; PC of St Bart Nottm 44-49; V of E Kirkby 49-69; C-in-c of St Andr E Kirkby 49-62; Surr from 51; R of Bilsthorpe 69-73; R of Eakring 71-73; Perm to Offic Dio Southw from 73. *17 Chestnut Avenue, Mapperley, Nottingham.*

BUTLER, Thomas Bertram. Wycl Coll Tor 19. **d** 20 Yukon for Rupld **p** 21 Rupld. C of Miniota Manit 20-21; Wawanesa 21-24; I of Hamiota 24-27; Miss-in-c of Haliburton Moons and Donald 27-30; R of Etobicoke w Westmount (and Thistletown 30-53) 30-55; Publ Inst Chap Dio Tor from 55. *39 Riverview Heights Drive, Weston, Ont., Canada.*

BUTLER, Ven Thomas Frederick. b 40. Univ of Leeds BSc

(1st cl Eng) 61, MSc 62, PhD 72. Coll of Resurr Mirfield 62. **d** 64 **p** 65 Ely. C of St Aug Wisbech 64-66; St Sav Folkstone 66-67; Lect Univ of Zam 68-73; Chap Univ of Kent Cant 73-80; Six Pr Cathl from 79; Archd of Northolt from 80. *71 Gayton Road, Harrow, Middx, HA1 2LY.*

BUTLER, Ven William Edgar. St Jo Coll Armid ACT ThL 19. **d** 19 **p** 20 Bath. C of Rylestone 19-21; R of Cumnock 21-23; C of Gilgandra 24-27; P-in-c of Stuart Town 27-31; R of Coonabarabran 31-40; W Wyalong 40-65; Can of Bath 47-60; Archd of Camidge 60-65; Archd (Emer) from 65. *7 Martin Street, Katoomba, NSW, Australia.*

BUTLER, Canon William Hamilton Arthur. b 14. **d** 40 Ugan **p** 47 Liv for Ugan. Asst Master Bp Tucker Mem Coll Mukono 40-41; Chap of Nyakasura Sch Fort Portal Toro 41-46; Youth Adv CMS Kako 48-51; Miss at Jinja 51-56; Archd of Busoga 56-63; Hon Can of Nam from 56; R of L Shelford w Newton 63-69; V of St Mary W Kensington 69-72; Gen Sec Rwa (CMS) Miss 72-77; V of Laleham 77-81. *21 Bromley College, Bromley, Kent, BR1 1GP.* (01-250 1362)

BUTLER-SMITH, Basil George. b 30. Bp's Coll Cheshunt 66. **d** 67 **p** 68 Ox. C of Bray 67-71; R of Norton 71-74; C-in-c of Tostock 71-74; R of Rotherfield Peppard Dio Ox from 76; P-in-c of Rotherfield Greys Dio Ox from 79. *Rectory, Rotherfield Peppard, Henley-on-Thames, RG9 5JN.* (Rotherfield Greys 603)

BUTLIN, Canon Cecil Roger. b 17. Em Coll Cam 3rd cl Georg Trip pt i 37, BA (2nd cl Archaeol and Anthrop Trip pt i) 38. Lon Coll of Div 38. **d** 40 **p** 41 Liv. C of St Luke Eccleston 40-44; St John and St Jas Litherland 44-46; R of St Matthias w St Simon Salford 46-52; CF (TA) 50-53; St Clem Higher Openshaw 52-63: Proc Conv Man 59-64; V of St Pet Halliwell 63-79; Hon Can of Man Cathl from 74; V of Chatburn Dio Blackb from 79. *Chatburn Vicarage, Clitheroe, Lancs.* (Clitheroe 41317)

BUTLIN, Claude Charles Jack. **d** 36 **p** 37 Lon. C of St Pet Isl 36-38; Ch Ch Ware 38-40; St Cuthb w Ch Ch Bedford 40-42; C-in-c of St Andr Broadfields Edgware 42-45; Cler Org Sec Ch Assoc 45-47; V of St Silas Toxteth Park 47-52; Surr 48-52; R of Holton w Bratton St Maurice 52-57; V of St Thos Crookes Sheff 57-64; R of Gt Horkesley 64-74. *12 Rustlings Court, Graham Road, Sheffield, S10 3HQ.* (Sheff 307033)

BUTT, Adrian. b 37. **d** 71 **p** 72 St John's. C of Umtata Cathl 71-76; Ilkeston 76-79; R of N and S Wheatley w W Burton Dio Southw from 79; P-in-c of Sturton-le-Steeple w Littleborough Dio Southw from 79; Bole w Saundby Dio Southw from 79. *North Wheatley Rectory, Retford, Notts, DN22 9DA.* (Sturton-le-Steeple 293)

BUTT, Christopher Martin. b 52. St Pet Coll Ox BA 74, MA 78. Fitzw Coll Cam BA 77, MA 81. Ridley Hall Cam 75. **d** 79 Huntingdon for Ely **p** 80 Ely. C of St Barn Cam Dio Ely from 79. *63 Kingston Street, Cambridge, CB1 2NU.*

BUTT, Ven Gordon Alexander. St Jo Coll Auckld LTh (2nd cl) 50. **d** 51 **p** 52 Waik. C of New Plymouth 51-54; V of Putaruru 54-60; Morrinsville 60-63; Can of Waik 61-63; V of Whangarei 64-69; New Plymouth 69-76; Archd of Waimate 64-69; Taranaki 69-76; Belmont from 78; V of Lower Hutt Dio Wel from 76. *132a Woburn Road, Lower Hutt, Wellington, NZ.* (663-005)

BUTT, Martin James. b 52. Univ of Sheff LLB 75. Trin Coll Bris 75. **d** 78 **p** 79 Lich. C of Aldridge Dio Lich from 78. *29 Anchor Road, Aldridge, Walsall, WS9 8PT.*

BUTT, Rowland Donald. b 31. Oak Hill Th Coll 70. **d** 72 **p** 73 Chich. C of Hailsham 72-74; St Paul Worthing 74-77; V of Lynesack Dio Dur from 77. *Lynesack Vicarage, Butterknowle, Bishop Auckland, Co Durham.* (Bp Auckland 718291)

BUTT, William Arthur. b 44. Linc Th Coll 71. **d** 71 Repton for Derby **p** 72 Derby. C of St Francis, Mackworth 71-75; Aston w Aughton 75-79; V of Dalton Dio Sheff from 79. *Dalton Vicarage, Rotherham, S Yorks, S65 3QL.* (Rotherham 850377)

BUTTER, Archibald Charles. **d** 42 Bloemf **p** 43 Bp Stainton for Bloemf. C of Cathl Ch Bloemf 42-46; Minehead 47-48; Maitland Capetn 48-51; Cathl Salisbury 51-53; LPr Dio Johann 33-55; L to Offic Dio Johann 56-59; Dio Mashon 60-66; Dio Johann 68-76 and from 80; C of Vereeniging 76-80. *23 Homestead Villas, Cambridge Street, Farramere, Benoni 1500, S Africa.*

BUTTERFIELD, David John. b 52. Univ of Lon BMus 73. Nottm Univ Dipl Th 75. St Jo Coll Nottm 74. **d** 77 **p** 78 Liv. C of Ch Ch Southport 77-81; Aldridge (in c of St Thos) Dio Lich from 81. *14 St Thomas Close, Aldridge, Walsall, W Midl, WS9 8SC.* (0922-53942)

BUTTERLEY, Harlin John Lascelles. Univ of Syd BA 51. Moore Th Coll Syd ACT ThL (1st cl) 50. **d** and **p** 51 Syd. C of Narabeen w Pittwater 51-52; C-in-c of Mascot 52-54; Gen Sec CMS in Tas 54-57; Chap St Steph Coll Hong Kong 57-67; CF 67-71; Dean and R of St D Cathl Hobart 72-80; I of St Andr Brighton Dio Melb from 80. *230 New Street, Brighton, Vic, Australia 3186.*

BUTTERSS, Canon Robert Leopold. Ridley Coll Melb ACT ThL 54. **d** 55 **p** 56 Melb . C of St Andr Brighton 55-56; V of Lara 56-60; P-in-c of Popondetta 60-64; L to Offic Dio Syd 60-64; V of Pascoe Vale 64-66; Sec Austrn Bd of Miss Vic 66-70; I of Mt Waverley 70-76; Perm to Offic Dios Melb and C & Goulb from 76; Hon Can of St Pet and St Paul Cathl Dogura 76; Chairman ABM Syd from 76; Hon Prov Can of Papua from 78. *164 Beecroft Road, Cheltenham, NSW, Australia.* (02-86 5380)

BUTTERWORTH, Antony James. b 51. Univ of Hull BSc 73. Trin Coll Bris 73. **d** 76 **p** 77 Man. C of St Pet Halliwell 76-81; V of St Thos Werneth Dio Man from 81. *St Thomas Vicarage, Werneth, Oldham, Lancs.* (061-678 8926)

BUTTERWORTH, Derek. b 27. Wells Th Coll 63. **d** 65 Linc **p** 65 Grimsby for Linc. C of Bottesford W Ashby Dio Linc 65-73; Team V from 73. *St Peter's Vicarage, Bottesford, Scunthorpe, S Humb, DN16 3RD.* (Scunthorpe 67256)

BUTTERWORTH, George Michael. Univ of Man BSc (2nd cl Math and Phil) 63. BD (2nd cl) (Lon) 67. Univ of Nottm MPhil (Th) 71. Tyndale Hall Bris. **d** 67 Repton for Derby **p** 68 Derby. C of S Normanton 67-71; in Ch of S India 72-79; Lect United Th Coll Bangalore 72-77; Oak Hill Th Coll from 80; Perm to Offic Dio St Alb from 80. *Oak Hill Theological College, 6 Farm Lane, N14 4PP.*

BUTTERWORTH, Gerald Ernest. St Pet Coll Ja. **d** 60 **p** 61 Ja. C of St Geo Kingston 60-64; P-in-c of Santa Cruz 64-69; R of Claremont 69-71; C of Liguanea 71-76. *11a Hopeview Avenue, Kingston 6, Jamaica.* (092-78696)

BUTTERWORTH, Ian Eric. b 44. Univ of Aber MA 67, MTh 79. Edin Th Coll 67. **d** 69 Hulme for Man **p** 70 Middleton for York. C of All SS and Marts Langley 69-71; Prec of St Andr Cathl Aber 72-75; V of St Matt w St Barn Bolton-le-Moors Dio Man from 75. *St Matthew's Vicarage, Stowell Street, Bolton, BL1 3RQ.* (Bolton 22810)

BUTTERWORTH, James Frederick. b 49. St Chad's Coll Dur BA (Gen) 70. Cudd Coll 70. **d** 72 **p** 73 Worc. C of Kidderminster 72-76; P-in-c of St Barn Dudley 76-79; V 79-82; Prec and Min Can of Worc Cathl from 82. *10A College Green, Worcester, WR1 2CH.* (Worc 24110)

BUTTERWORTH, James Kent. b 49. Univ of Southn BTh 79. Chich Th Coll 75. **d** 79 **p** 80 Wakef. C of Heckmondwike Dio Wakef from 79. *Curacy House, Horton Street, Heckmondwike, W Yorks, WF16 0LL.* (Heckmondwike 409400)

BUTTERWORTH, John David Lawrence. **d** 74 Bath. Hon C of Bath Dio Bath from 74. *Abercrombie House, Bathurst, NSW, Australia 2795.* (31-4037)

BUTTERWORTH, John Walton. b 49. St Jo Coll Dur BSc 70, Dipl Th 73. **d** 74 **p** 75 Wakef. C of Todmorden 74-77; All SS Cathl Wakef 77-78; V of Outwood Dio Wakef from 78. *Outwood Vicarage, Leeds Road, Newton Hill, Wakefield, W Yorks.* (Wakef 823150)

BUTTERWORTH, Keith. b 45. **d** 72 Man **p** 73 Middleton for Man. C of Hollinwood 72-75; H Family Failsworth 75-76; R of Clayton Dio Man from 76. *St Cross Rectory, Clayton Hall Road, Manchester, M11 4WH.* (061-223 0766)

BUTTERWORTH, Robert Andrew. b 44. St Paul's Coll Grahmstn 69. **d** 71 **p** 72 Johann. P Dio Johann 71-74; R of Lichtenburg 74-79; CF (S Afr) from 80. *26 Simpson Crescent, Bloemfontein, S Africa.*

BUTTERWORTH, Roy. b 31. Selw Coll Cam 3rd cl Th Trip pt i 53, BA (3rd cl Th Trip pt ii) 55, MA 59. Wells Th Coll 55. **d** 57 Taunton for B & W **p** 58 B & W. C of St Mary Bathwick 57-61; Prec of St Paul's Cathl Dundee 61-63; V of Dearnley 63-81; Tyldesley Dio Man from 81. *Tyldesley Vicarage, Manchester.* (Atherton 882914)

BUTTIMORE, John Charles. b 27. St Mich Coll Llan. **d** 57 **p** 58 Llan. C of Treherbert 57-60; St Fagan Aberdare 60-64; V of Williamstown 64-71; Caerau w Ely Dio Llan from 71. *Vicarage, Cowbridge Road West, Ely, Cardiff, CF5 5BQ.* (Cardiff 563254)

BUTTLE, Leslie Albert. b 32. Edin Th Coll 61. **d** 64 **p** 65 Wakef. C of Sowerby Bridge w Norland 64-66; Plymstock 66-69; Ilfracombe 69-71; V of Woolfardisworthy W Bucks Mills 71-76; C of St Paul Sticklepath Barnstaple 76-77; Asst Chap HM Pris Leeds and L to Offic Dio Ripon 77-80; Chap HM Borstal Hindley from 80. *Chaplain's Office, HM Borstal, Hindley, Wigan, Lancs, WN2 5TH.* (0942-866255)

BUTTLE, Leslie Ronald Frank. b 07. Univ of Lon Engl Hist Scho 27, BA (1st cl Hist) 28. **d** 34 **p** 35 Chelmsf. C of Wanstead 34-36; Asst Master R Wanstead Sch 31-36; Asst Chap 34-36; Chap KC Otahuhu 36-38; R of Water Stratford 38-39; Asst Chap of Felsted Sch 40; Chap RNVR 41-47; R of Goldhanger w L Totham 47-50; Purleigh 50-55; Gt w L Packington 55-58; V of Maxstoke 55-58; R of Fordham 58-63; V of Hatfield Broad Oak 63-66; V of Bush End 63-66; R of Lowick w Sudborough (w Slipton from 67) 66-73; C-in-c of Slipton 66-67; Perm to Offic Dios Ex and Truro from 74. *5 Castle Street, Launceston, Cornw, PL15 8BA.* (Launceston 2052)

BUTTLE, Richard Newman. Univ of NZ BA 57. St Jo Coll Auckld LTh (1st cl) 59. **d** 59 **p** 60 Auckld. C of St Mary's Cathl Auckld 59-63; Warkworth 63-64; V of Wellsford 64-67; Chap Ch Ch Pris 67-68; Hon C of Riccarton 67-68; Chap K Coll Auckld from 69; C of Otahuhu Dio Auckld 69-70; Hon C from 71. *King's College, Otahuhu, Auckland, NZ.* (27-65 364)

BUTTOLPH, Robert Henry. b 16. Codr Coll Barb 55. **d** 57 **p** 58 Antig. C of St Jo Cathl Antig 57-59; R of St Pet, St Kitts 59-75; Perm to Offic Dio Nor 75-76; V of St Thos Huddersfield Dio Wakef from 76. *78 Bankfield Road, Huddersfield, HD1 3HR.* (Huddersfield 20660)

BUTTON, David Frederick. b 27. St Chad's Coll Dur BA (2nd cl Th) 53, Dipl Th (w distinc) 54. **d** 54 **p** 55 Dur. C of Tyne Dock 54-58; Seacroft 58-60; PC of Holland Fen w Chapel Hill 60-64; Surfleet 64-71; V of Barkston w Syston 71-78; R of Belton 71-78; C-in-c of Honington 73-78; R of Gunness w Burringham Dio Linc from 78. *Gunness Rectory, Scunthorpe, Humb.* (Scunthorpe 782349)

BUTTON, Graham John. b 42. Univ of Cant NZ BA 66. St Jo Coll Auckld 71. **d** 72 **p** 73 Nel. C of All SS Nel 72-76; V of Cobden-Runanga 76-78; Atawhai-Hira Dio Nel from 78. *746 Atawhai Drive, Nelson, NZ.* (521-185)

BUTU, Thomas Henry. St Pet Coll Siota 66. **d** 69 **p** 70 Melan. P Dio Melan 69-75; Dio New Hebr 75-80; Dom Chap to Bp of New Hebr 78-80. *5 Church Walk, Bideford, Devon, EX39 3AB.*

BUTWILL, Norman Michael. b 46. State Univ of San Francisco BA 70. Nashotah Ho Wisc 72. **d** 73 **p** 74 Calif (USA). C of St Paul Lachine Montr 75-77; I of St Aid City and Dio Montr from 77. *6232 Hamilton Street, Montreal, Que, H4E 3C4, Canada.* (514-766 9902)

BUXO, Davidov Carlysle. b 39. Gen Th Sem NY MDiv 81. **d** 80 Trinid. on leave. *General Theological Seminary, 175 Ninth Avenue, New York, NY 10011, USA.*

BUXO, Edward O'Hanley. Codr Coll Barb LTh 35. **d** 34 **p** 36 Windw Is. C of Calliaqua 34-35; Barrouallie 36-37; P-in-c 37-40; C of St Paul San Fernando 40-45; V of St Andr Scarborough Tobago 45-46; R of St Agnes Port of Spain 46-67; Dioc Sec Dio Trinid 56-60; Sec of Trinid Dioc Synod 57-60; R of H Cross Marabella 69-73. *Rectory, Plaisance Park, Pointe-à-Pierre, Trinidad, WI.*

BUXTON, Derek Major. BD (Lon) 63. Ripon Hall Ox 58. **d** 60 **p** 61 Leic. C of St Nich Leic 60-64; Chap Univ of Leic 60-64; Coll of Art & Tech Leic 61-65; C of St Martin's Cathl Leic 64-69; Succr 64-67; Prec 67-69; R of Ibstock (w Heather from 76) Dio Leic from 69. *Ibstock Rectory, Leicester.* (Ibstock 60246)

BUXTON, Digby Hugh. b 16. Trin Coll Cam BA 38, MA 41. Wycl Hall Ox 39. **d** 41 **p** 42 Guildf. C of Stoke-next-Guildf 41-43; St Jas Less Bethnal Green 43-46; All SS Queensbury Lon 46-50; St Mary St John's Newfld 50-52; R of Hantsport 52-54; P-in-c of Saguenay 54-62; Lake St John Miss 62-64; R of N Hatley w Waterville 64-74; Valcartier 74-77; Can of Queb 76-77; C of St Mary Magd Gt Burstead 77-78; Sandhurst 78-81; Hon C of Barkway Dio St Alb from 81. *Vicarage Flat, Barkway, Royston, Herts, SE8 8EJ.* (Barkway 805)

BUXTON, Edmund Digby. b 08. Trin Coll Cam BA 29, MA 33. Ridley Hall Cam 29. **d** 33 Liv **p** 34 Warrington for Liv. C of St Helens 33-37; St Steph Twickenham 37-39; V of St Mary Magd w St Paul Peckham 39-44; St Jo Evang Wembley 44-54; Milborne Port (w Goathill from 65) 54-74; R of Goathill 54-65; RD of Merston 57-68; Preb of Wells Cathl 64-74; Chap Tristan da Cunha 75-78. *Farm Cottage, Winchester Road, Alresford, Hants.*

BUXTON, Edmund Francis. Trin Coll Cam BA 65, MA 68. Linc Th Coll 65. **d** 67 Barking for Chelmsf **p** 68 Chelmsf. C of St Mary Wanstead 67-70; St Mary Gt Cam 70-73; St Marg Barking 74-75; in Ch of S India 75-79; Chap at Bath Univ from 79. *Chaplain's House, The Avenue, Claverton Down, Bath, BA2 7AX.*

BUXTON, Edward Brian. b 41. K Coll Lon and Warm AKC 65. BEducn 79. **d** 66 Colchester for Chelmsf **p** 67 Chelmsf. C of Laindon w Basildon 66-73; C-in-c of All SS Grays 73-76; Perm to Offic Dio Chelmsf from 76. *2 Fieldway, Pitsea, Basildon, Essex, SS13 3DB.*

BUXTON, Richard Fowler. b 40. Univ of Lon BSc (1st cl Eng) 62. Linacre Coll Ox BA (2nd cl Th) 67, MA 71. Univ of Ex PhD 73. St Steph Ho Ox 65. **d** 68 **p** 69 Ox. C of Ch Ch Reading 68-70; Pinhoe 70-71; Asst Chap Univ of Ex 71-73; Tutor Sarum Wells Th Coll 73-77; Vice-Prin 77; Perm to Offic Dio Ches from 77; Dio Man from 81. *221 Dane Road, Sale, Cheshire, M33 2LZ.* (061-973 4727)

BUXTON, Canon William Walter. Em Coll Sktn LTh Univ of Sask BA 45. **d** 43 **p** 44 Edmon. C of All SS Edmon 43-45; R of Fort-Saskatchewan 45-50; St Pet Edmon 50-52; CF (Canad) 52-75; R of Clarksburg Dio Hur from 75; Can of Hur from 80. *Box 105, Clarksburg, Ont., Canada.* (519-599 3423)

BUYE, Lord Bishop of. (Vacant)

BUZIBONA, Nahashon. St Phil Coll Kongwa 76. **d** 78 Bp Mohamed for Centr Tang. d Dio Vic Nyan. *PO Box 93, Ngara, West Lake, Tanzania.*

BUZOYA, Samuel. **d** 74 Bur **p** 75 Buye. P Dio Buye. *Buhiga D/S 127, Bujumbura, Burundi.*

BVUMA, Temai. **d** 76 Mashon. d Dio Mashon 76-81; Dio Mutare from 81. *St Joseph's School, Murehwa, PB P 7036, Umtali, Zimbabwe.*

BWABYE, Yokana. Bp Tucker Coll Mukono. **d** 56 Ugan **p** 58 Bp Balya for Ugan. P Dio Ugan 56-60; Dio W Bugan 60-65; Dio Nam 65-72. *PO Box 39, Mukono, Uganda.*

BWAMBALE, Andrew. **d** 75 **p** 77 Ruw. P Dio Ruw. *Box 21, Kasese, Uganda.*

BWAMBALE, Zadeki. **d** 74 **p** 76 Ruw. P Dio Ruw. *Box 37, Fort Portal, Uganda.*

BWAMBARA, Canon Petro. **d** and **p** 18 Zanz. P-in-c Dio Zanz from 18; Can of Zanz Cathl 52-62; Hon Can from 62. *PO Box 45, Tanga, Tanzania.*

BWANIRAMO, Victor. St Pet Coll Melan **d** 46 **p** 54 Melan. P Dio Melan 46-75. *Melanesian Mission, British Solomon Islands.*

BWAYO, Yoshua Leweri Mutinyu. Bp Tucker Coll Mukono 63. **d** and **p** 66 Mbale. P Dio Mbale; Sub-Dean of Mbale Cathl from 78. *PO Box 473, Mbale, Uganda.*

BWESIGYE, Trajan. **d** 75 **p** 76 Ruw. P Dio Ruw. *Box 37, Fort Portal, Uganda.*

BWETABURE, Kezekia. **d** 76 **p** 77 Ank. P Dio Ank 76-77; Dio W Ank from 77. *PO Rubaare, Rwashamaire, Uganda.*

BYAKISAKA, Chan Festo Bomera. Bp Tucker Coll Mukono. **d** 50 **p** 52 Ugan. P Dio Ugan 50-60; Dio Ruw 60-72; Dio Boga-Z from 72; Archd of Mboga 67-72; Boga 72-80; Chan Dio Boga-Z from 80. *BP 154, Bunia, Zaire.*

BYAMANYWOHA, Eridaadi. Bp Tucker Coll Mukono 69. **d** 71 **p** 72 Ank. d Dio Ank 71-72; P Dio Ank 72-76; Dio E Ank from 76. *PO Box 14, Mbarara, Ankole, Uganda.*

BYANGWENYIMA, Isiraeri. Bp Tucker Coll Mukono 56. **d** 56 Ugan **p** 58 Bp Balya for Ugan. P Dio Ugan 56-60; Dio Ankole-K 60-67; Dio Ank from 67. *PO Box 462, Mbarara, Uganda.*

BYARD, Donald. b 05. **d** 69 **p** 70 Birm. C of St Pet Maney 69-77; P-in-c of Langton w Birdsall 77-81. *33 Huntsman Lane, Stamford Bridge, York, YO4 1ES.* (Stamford Bridge 72229)

BYARD, Canon Henry Adeane. b 04. Keble Coll Ox BA (3rd cl Mod Hist) 26, MA 30. Cudd Coll 26. **d** 27 Ox **p** 28 Bp Shaw for Ox. C of St Mary Virg Reading (in c of St Mark from 31) 27-33; V of Newport Pagnell 33-46; Chap of Newport Pagnell U 33-46; Surr 37-72; R of Lathbury 38-46; V of Aylesbury 46-72; Chap HM Borstal Inst Aylesbury 46-50; R Bucks Hosp, Tindal Gen Hosp 46-75; Manor Ho Hosp Aylesbury 46-72; Stoke Mandeville Hosp from 75; RD of Aylesbury 51-67 and 69-72; Hon Can of Ch Ch Ox from 58. *29 Brudenell Drive, Stoke Mandeville, Bucks.* (Stoke Mandeville 2429)

BYCE, Richard Gordon. Univ of Sask BA 46. Em Coll Sask LTh 46, BD 50. **d** 47 **p** 48 Sask. I of Spiritwood 47-51; Nipawin 51-58; Exam Chap to Bp of Sask 56-58; R of St Mary Regina 58-63; Dom Chap to Bp of Qu'App 61-63; on leave. *51 Ravencliffe, Agincourt, Ont., Canada.*

BYE, Peter John. b 39. BD (Lon) 65. Clifton Th Coll 62. **d** 67 **p** 68 Southw. C of Hyson Green, Nottm 67-70; St Nich Dur 70-73; V of Ch Ch Lowestoft 73-80; St Jo Evang City and Dio Carl from 80. *Vicarage, London Road, Carlisle, CA1 2QQ.* (Carl 21601)

BYERS, Christopher Martin. b 33. Jes Coll Ox BA (4th cl Th) 59, MA 62. Wycl Hall Ox 59. **d** 60 **p** 61 S'wark. C of Bermondsey 60-66; R of Mottingham Dio S'wark from 66. *Rectory, 233 Court Road, SE 9.* (01-857 1691)

BYFIELD, Bruce William. b 50. St Jo Coll Morpeth 71. **d** and **p** 74 Perth. P Dio Perth 74; C of Ch Ch Cathl Darwin 75-76; Assoc R of Spearwood-Willagee 77-78; P-in-c of Beverley w Brookton Dio Perth 78-79; R from 79. *64 John Street, Beverley, W Australia 6304.* (096-46 1112)

BYFIELD, Francis Reginald Stoneman. b 1900. St Cath Coll Cam BA 27, MA 31. Wells Th Coll 27. **d** 29 Ex **p** 33 Bris. C of St Thos Ex 29-31; St Mich Bris 31-33; St Werburgh's Bris 33-34; St Pet Caversham 34-37; Calstock 37-39; V of Zennor 39-50; PC of Towednack 47-50; CF (EC) 42-46; Hon CF 46; V of Bramfield 50-56; Copt Oak 56-61; R of Haughton 61-71; Perm to Offic Dio Sarum from 72. *7 Sandford Road, Wareham, Dorset, BH20 4DG.*

BYFORD, David Charles. b 30. Bps' Coll Cheshunt 58. **d** 61 Aston for Birm **p** 62 Birm. C of Short Heath 61-63; Londonderry Staffs 63-65; Chap Selly Oak Hosp 65-70; V of Rowley Regis 70-78; Polesworth w Birchmoor Dio Birm from 78. *Polesworth Vicarage, Tamworth, Staffs. B78 iDU.* (Tamworth 892340)

BYFORD, Edwin Charles. b 47. Aus Nat Univ BSc 70. Univ of Melb BD 73. Trin Coll Melb 70. **d** and **p** 73 C & Goulb. C of Queanbeyan 73-77; C of St Werburgh Chorlton-cum-Hardy 77-79; Holbrook 79-80; St Paul's Manuka Dio C & Goulb from 80. *6 Boolimba Crescent, Narrabundah, ACT, Australia 2604.*

BYLES, Alfred Thomas Plested. b 02. Univ of Lon George Smith Stud 22, BA (1st cl Engl) 23, MA 25, PhD 33. AKC and Inglis Stud 23. Westcott Ho Cam 37. **d** 37 **p** 38 Ex. Asst Chap of St Luke's Coll Ex 37-38; Lect 25-40; C of St Mark Ex 38-40; CF (EC) 40-46; Hon CF from 46; V of Yealmpton 46-50; St Matt Hammersmith 50-58; R of Brampton Abbotts 58-67; Exam Chap to Bp of Heref 62-73; Dep PV of Ex Cathl and Perm to Offic Dio Ex from 67; Chap of Livery Dole Ex 72-75. *22 Spicer Road, Exeter, EX1 1SY.* (Exeter 71732)

BYLES, Ernest William. b 09. Univ of Lon BA (2nd cl Engl) 31, BD 39. Bps' Coll Cheshunt 34. **d** 36 **p** 37 Chelmsf. C of Brentwood 36-49; CF (EC) 40-45; V of St Geo Becontree 49-56; St Edm Chingford 56-71; Coleford Somt 72-74; Perm to Offic Dio Ex 74-77; B & W from 78. *3 Station Road, Congresbury, Bristol.*

BYLES, Raymond Vincent. b 30 St D Coll Lamp BA 52. St Mich Coll Llan 52. **d** 54 St A for Ban **p** 55 Ban. C of Llanfairisgaer 54-57; Llandudno 57-59; V of Carno 59-64; R of Trelawnyd w Gwaenysgor 64-71; Llysfaen 71-79; St Geo or Kegidog Dio St A from 79; V of Bodelwyddan Dio St A from 79. *Bodelwyddan Vicarage, Abergele, Clwyd.* (St Asaph 583034)

BYNON, William. b 43. St Aid Coll 63. **d** 66 Warrington for Liv **p** 67 Liv. C of Huyton 66-69; Maghull (in c of St Pet; Team V from 72) 69-75; V of Highfield Dio Liv from 75. *St Matthew's Vicarage, Highfield, Pemberton, Wigan WN3 6BL.* (Wigan 222121)

BYRNE, David Patrick. b 48. St Jo Coll Nottm 74. **d** 77 **p** 78 Birm. C of Bordesley Green 77-79; Weoley Castle Dio Birm from 79. *34 Shenley Lane, Weoley Castle, Birmingham, B29 5PL.* (021-476 3990)

BYRNE, David Rodney. b 47. St Jo Coll Cam 2nd cl Cl Trip pt i 68, BA (2nd cl Th Trip pt ii) 70, MA 73. Cranmer Hall Dur Dipl Th 72. **d** 73 Cant **p** 74 Maidstone for Cant. C of St Luke Maidstone 73-77; All SS Patcham Dio Chich from 77. *66 Eldred Avenue, Brighton, E Sussex, BN1 5EG.* (Brighton 503926)

BYRNE, John Victor. b 47. ACA 70, FCA 79. ALCD 73 (LTh from 74). **d** 73 **p** 74 Roch. C of St Mark Gillingham 73-76; St Luke Cranham Pk 76-80; V of Balderstone, Rochdale Dio Man from 80. *Balderstone Vicarage, Oldham Road, Rochdale, Lancs, OL11 2HB.* (Rochdale 49886)

BYRNE, Matthew. b 27. Univ of Man MA (Th) 69. Tyndale Hall Bris 47. **d** 51 **p** 52 Man. C of Rawtenstall 51-54; CF 54-57; R of St Jas Moss Side 57-62; St Marg, Whalley Range 62-80; Chap K Hosp Sch and C-in-c of St Jude Chapelizod City and Dio Dub from 80. *St Jude's Rectory, Kilmainham, Dublin, Irish Republic.* (Dub 51880)

BYRNE, Peter Gordon. Moore Th Coll Syd 61. **d** 62 **p** 63 Syd. C of Port Kembla 62-64; C-in-c of Provisional Distr of Berowra 64-70; Granville S 70-74; R of Lawson Dio Syd from 74. *Honour Avenue, Lawson, NSW, Australia 2783.* (047-59 1024)

BYRNE, Canon Thomas William. b 06. Univ of Man BA 27, MA 32. Wells Th Coll 29. **d** 30 **p** 31 Newc T. C of Jesmond 30-33; C-in-c of St Osw Walker Gate Newc T 33-44; Insp of Schs Dio Newc T from 38; V of Humshaugh 44-75; Ed Newc T Dioc Year Book 52-56; RD of Bellingham 56-75; Hon Can of Newc 69-75; Can (Emer) from 75. *2 Fairsnape Road, Lytham, Lancs, FY8 4HG.* (Lytham 738691)

BYRNES, Stephen Charles. St Francis Coll Brisb ACT ThL 74. **d** 75 **p** 76 Brisb. C of St Pet Southport 75-77; St Barn Sunnybank Brisb 77-78; V of H Trin Taroom Dio Brisb from 78. *Vicarage, Miller Street, Taroom, Queensland, Australia 4420.* (Taroom 58)

BYROM, Canon John Kenneth. b 20. Selw Coll Cam 3rd cl Cl Trip 40, BA 41, MA 45. Westcott Ho Cam 41. **d** 43 Ches **p** 44 Bp Tubbs for Ches. C of Neston 43-48; St Matt Edgeley Stockport 48-50; V of All SS Cheadle Hulme 50-63; Warden Brasted Place Tr Coll 64-74; V of Swaffham Prior w Reach Dio Ely from 74; Exam Chap to Bp of Ely from 74; Dioc Dir of Ordins & Warden of Post Ordin Tr from 75; Hon Can of Ely from 78; RD of Fordham from 78. *Swaffham Prior Vicarage, Cambridge, CB5 0JT.* (Newmarket 741409)

BYROM, Malcolm Senior. b 37. Edin Th Coll 65. **d** 67 **p** 68 Bradf. C of Allerton 67-69; Padstow 69-72; V of Hessenford 72-77; Kenwyn w Tregavethan Dio Truro from 77; C-in-c of St Martin-by-Looe 72-77. *Kenwyn Vicarage, Truro, Cornw, TR1 3DX.* (Truro 2664)

BYROM, Thomas Jackson. b 01. St Bonif Coll Warm 23. Hatf Coll Dur 26. **d** 30 Trinid (in Liv Cathl) **p** 31 Trinid. C of St Paul San Fernando 30-33; R of St Andr Scarboro' 33-44; St Jude Barbados 44-46; V of Hurst Green 46-55; Halvergate w Tunstall 55-61; Bubwith 61-71; C of Porlock w Stoke Pero 71-78; Perm to Offic Dio B & W from 79. *Hayes Cottage, Porlock, Minehead, Somt.* (Porlock 862480)

BYRON, Frederic Thomas Christopher. b 16. Mert Coll Ox BA (2nd cl Mod Hist) 39, MA 43. St Steph Ho Ox 39. **d** 40 **p** 41 Llan. C of St German Roath 40-43; Penmaen (in c of St D Oakdale) 43-46; West Wycombe (in c of Sands) 46-50; R of Cranford 50-57; Hosp of St Thos Hosp Lon 57-62; V of Ruislip 62-70; St Jas Norlands Kens Dio Lon from 70; Chap St Chas Hosp N Kens 70-75. *12 St Ann's Villas, W11 4RS.* (01-603 7149)

BYRON, Frederick. b 14. Univ of Dur BA 38. St Jo Coll Dur 38. **d** 39 **p** 40 Man. C of St Barn Openshaw 39-43; St Paul Oldham 43-46; St Mary Moston 46-50; R of St Cuthb Trafford Pk 50-56; V of St Barn Bolton-le-Moors 56-68; Out Rawcliffe 68-78; C of Standish 78-79. *18 Scott Avenue, Hindley, Wigan, Lancs, WN2 4DG.* (Wigan 53807)

BYRON, Norman. St Jo Coll Morpeth 53. **d** 54 **p** 55 Bath. C of Nyngan 54-56; R 60-63; P-in-c of Tottenham 56-60; R of Dunedoo 63-71; S Bath Dio Bath from 71. *Rectory, South Bathurst, NSW, Australia 2795.* (31-3685)

BYRON, Terence Sherwood. b 26. Keble Coll Ox BA (2nd cl Mod Hist) 50, MA 54. Linc Th Coll 50. **d** 52 Leic **p** 53 Bp Hollis for Cant. C of Melton Mowbray 52-55; Whitwick 55-60, Cathl Ch of Redemption New Delhi 60 65; V of All SS Jaipur w Bandikui, Bharatpur, Gangapur City and Phulera 66-70; In Ch of N India 70-76; C-in-c of Extra-Par Distr of Beaumont Leys Dio Leic from 76. *67 Rannoch Close, Beaumont Leys, Leicester.*

BYRON-DAVIES, Peter. b 49. AKC and BD 75. Aug Coll Cant 75. **d** 76 Sarum **p** 77 Ramsbury for Sarum. C of Wootton Bassett 76-79; Chap Charterhouse Sch 79-80; R of Bassingham Dio Linc from 80; Aubourn w Haddington Dio Linc from 80; Carlton-le-Moorland w Stapleford Dio Linc from 80; Thurlby w Norton Disney Dio Linc from 80. *Rectory, Torgate Lane, Bassingham, Lincoln, LN5 9HF.* (Bassingham 383)

BYRT, Donald Stanley. b 46. Em & St Chad Coll Sktn BTh. **d** 80 **p** 81 Sktn. I of Radisson Dio Sktn from 80. *PO Box 158, Radisson, Sask, Canada, S0K 3L0.*

BYTHELL, Noel John. Univ of NZ MSc (1st cl Chemistry) 37. Ridley Coll Melb 54. ACT ThL 56. **d** 53 **p** 54 Centr Tang. Asst Master Alliance Secondary Sch Dodoma 53-55; Hd Master 55-59. C of Dodoma 55-59; V of Picton 60-69; L to Offic Dio Nel from 69. *19 Hunt Street, Richmond, Nelson, NZ.* (4-7514)

BYWATER, Hector William Robinson. b 10. Univ of Lon 28. ALCD 32. **d** 33 **p** 34 Lich. C of All SS Darlaston 33-36; Brierley Hill 36-40; V of St Alkmund City and Dio Derby from 40. *25 Highfeld Road, Derby, DE3 1GX.* (Derby 32681)

BYWORTH, Christopher Henry Briault. b 39. Or Coll Ox BA 61, MA 65. Univ of Bris BA (2nd cl Th) 63. Lon Coll of Div 64. **d** 65 Barking for Chelmsf **p** 66 Chelmsf. C of Leyton 65-68; Rusholme 68-70; Lect Oak Hill Th Coll 70-75; L to Offic Dio Lon 71-75; Team R of Thetford 75-79; Warden Cranmer Hall Dur from 79. *Cranmer Hall, Durham, DH1 3RJ.*

C

CABEL, Victor William. Em and St Chad Coll Regina. **d** 66 **p** 67 Edmon. I of Onoway 66-68; C of St Timothy, Edmon 68-70; I of Sherwood Pk Dio Edmon from 70. *Box 3024, Sherwood Park, Alta., Canada.* (403-467 8086)

CABEZAS, José Angel. d 64 **p** 65 Chile. P Dio Chile. *Mission Anglicana, Casilla 4, Cholchol, Chile.*

CABLE, John Alfred. Moore Th Coll Syd ACT ThL 34. **d** 35 **p** 36 Syd. C of St Mary Waverley 35-37; SPG Miss Itki Dio Chota N 37-45 and from 53; on leave 45-50; L to Offic Dio Syd 50-52; Dioc Treas Chota N 52-54; Archd of Chota N and Dioc Regr 54-76; L to Offic Dio Syd from 76. *47 Thomas Street, Picnic Point, NSW, Australia.*

CABLE, John Henry. Qu Coll Melb 13. **d** 15 **p** 16 Auckld. C-in-c of St Columba Grey Lynn 15-16; V 16-22; V of St Geo Kingsland 22-27; Henderson 27-38; P-in-c of Hokianga 38-40; Avondale 40-42; Perm to Offic Dio Ch Ch 44-46; Dio Dun from 46. *12 Ings Avenue, St Clair, Dunedin, NZ.*

CABLE, Patrick John. b 50. AKC 72. St Aug Coll Cant 73. **d** 74 Dover for Cant **p** 75 Cant. C of Herne Bay Dio Cant from 74. *14 Blenheim Close, Herne Bay, Kent, CT6 7NB.*

CADDICK, Lloyd Reginald. b 31. Univ of Bris BA (2nd cl Gen) 56. St Cath Coll Ox BA (2nd cl Th) 58, MA 62. Univ Nottm MPhil 73. K Coll Lon PhD 78. Open Univ Hon MA 79. St Steph Ho Ox. **d** 59 Nor **p** 59 Thetford for Cant. C of St Marg King's Lynn 59-62; Chap Oakham Sch 62-66; C-in-c of Bulwick w Harringworth Blatherwycke and Laxton 66-67; R 67-77; V of Oundle Dio Pet from 77; Surr from 78; P-in-c of Cotterstock Dio Pet from 81. *Oundle Vicarage, Peterborough, PE8 4EA.* (0832-73593)

CADDY, Dennis Gordon James. b 27. Bp's Coll Cheshunt 62. **d** 64 **p** 65 Lon. C of St Jo Bapt Greenhill Harrow 64-67; Harlington (in c of Ch Ch) 67-69; C-in-c of Ch Ch Conv Distr Harlington 69-72; V of St Alb N Harrow Dio Lon from 72. *Vicarage, Church Drive, North Harrow, Middx.* (01-868 6567)

CADDY, Michael George Bruce Courtenay. b 45. K Coll Lon and St Aug Coll Cant. **d** 71 Warrington for Liv **p** 72 Liv. C of Walton-on-the-Hill 71-76; Solihull 77-81; V of Shard End Dio Birm from 81. *Shard End Vicarage, Shustoke Road, Birmingham, B34 7BA.* (021-747 3299)

CADE, Canon Ronald William. b 19. Wells Th Coll 48. **d** 48 **p** 49 S'wark. Chap to St Bede's Ch for Deaf and Dumb Clapham 48-59; Abp's Chap to Deaf Croydon 52-72; Chap to Deaf and Dumb Dio Roch from 60; Hon C of St Barn Gillingham Dio Roch from 73; Hon Can of Roch Cathl from 81. *81 Rolvenden Road, Wainscott, Strood, Kent.* (Medway 77900)

CADE, Sydney George. b 02. St Steph Ho Ox 56. **d** 58 **p** 59 Cov. C of St Jo Bapt Leamington Priors 58-60; Oxhey (in c of St Francis Broadfield) 60-65; V of St Matt Littleport 65-74; P-in-c of Keyston w Bythorn 74-78; Perm to Offic Dio Auckld from 78. *c/o 429 Parnell Road, Auckland 1, NZ.*

CADLE, Henry Edward. b 04. **d** 59 **p** 60 Leic. C of Market Bosworth 59-63; R of Stoney Stanton 63-74; L to Offic Dio Leic from 74. *6 Lovelace Crescent, Elmesthorpe, Leicester.*

CADMAN, Kenneth Claude. b 14. St Jo Coll Dur BA 40. **d** 40 **p** 41 Man. C of Ch Ch Harpurhey 40-44; St Chad Rochdale 44-45; St Mark Worsley (in c of Ellenbrook and Boothstown) 45-47; R of All SS Heaton Norris 47-52; V of Rainow w Saltersford 52-54; CF (TA) from 49; R of St Jas Broughton Salford 54-59; St Michel du Valle Guernsey 59-65; V of Alderney 65-69; R of St Pierre du Bois Guernsey 69-80; St Phil de Torteval Guernsey Dio Win from 80. *St Pierre Rectory, Du Bois, Guernsey, CI.* (Guernsey 63544)

CADMAN, Reginald Hugh. b 09. Univ of Man LLB (2nd cl) 30, LLM 52. Wycl Hall Ox 32. **d** 34 **p** 35 Man. C of St Marg Whalley Range (in c of St Geo from 36) 34-38; V of Old St Geo Stalybridge 38-46; Surr 38-56; V of St Mark Glodwick 46-53; Padiham w Higham 53-56; R of Denton 56-66; V of Paul Dio Truro from 66; CF (TA) 49-65; RD of Penwith from 76. *Paul Vicarage, Penzance, Cornw.* (Mousehole 261)

CADMAN, Robert Hugh. b 49. Univ of Nottm Dipl Th 76. St Jo Coll Nottm 77. **d** 78 Doncaster for Sheff **p** 79 Sheff. C of All SS Ecclesall Dio Sheff from 78. *11 Mylor Road, Ecclesall, Sheffield 11, S Yorks.*

CADOGAN, Paul Anthony Cleveland. b 47. AKC 74. St Aug Coll Cant 74. **d** 75 **p** 76 Bris. C of St Jo Div Fishponds 75-79; Swindon New Town (in c of St Luke) 79-81; P-in-c of All SS Swindon Dio Bris from 81. *Vicarage, Southbrook Street, Swindon, Wilts, SN2 1HF.* (Swindon 23572)

CADWALLADER, Alan Harold. b 53. Monash Univ Vic BA 73, LLB 75. ACT BTh 80. Ridley Coll Melb 78. **d** 81 Bp Grant for Melb. C of H Trin Kens Dio Melb from 81. *7 Bangalore Street, Kensington, Vic, Australia 3031.*

CAESAR, Canon Anthony Douglass. b 24. Late Mus Scho of Magd Coll Cam BA 47, MusB (1st cl pt i) 47, 3rd cl Hist Trip pt ii 48, Stewart of Rannoch Scho in Sacred Mus 43, Abbott Exhib 43, MA 49. FRCO 47, St Steph Ho Ox 59. **d** 61 **p** 62 Lon. C of St Mary Abbots Kens 61-65; Asst Sec CACTM 65-66; ACCM 66-70; Chap RSCM Addington 65-70; Dep P-in-Ord to HM the Queen 67-68; P-in-Ord 68-70; C of St Pet (in c of St Steph) Bournemouth 70-73; Prec and Sacr of Win Cathl 74-79; Hon Can of Win Cathl 75-76 and from 79; Can Res 76-79; Sub-Dean of HM Chapels R from 79; Dep Clk of the Closet and Sub-Almoner from 79; Dom Chap to HM the Queen from 79. *Marlborough Gate, St James's Palace, SW1.* (01-930 6609)

CAESAR, Francis Anthony. Em Coll Sktn. **d** 67 **p** 68 Trinid. C of Diego Martin 67-70; R of Siparia 71-73; Tanapuna Dio Trinid from 73. *Good Shepherd Rectory, Tanapuna, Trinidad, WI.*

CAESAR, Marese. b 25. **d** 73 **p** 76 Windw Is. C of St Paul Grenada Dio Windw Is from 73. *St Paul's Rectory, Grenada, W Indies.* (5325)

CAHILL, Kenneth John. b 52. Ridley Coll Melb 75. **d** 78 **p** 79 Melb. C of St Jas Ivanhoe 78-80; St Mark E Brighton Dio Melb from 80. *1 Beddoe Avenue, East Brighton, Vic, Australia 3187.*

CAIGER, Canon Douglas George Colley. b 23. Kelham Th Coll 39. **d** 46 **p** 48 S'wark. C of St Andr Coulsdon 46-48; Kingswood 48-49; Havant 49-54; V of St Helen's IW 54-58; Dio Insp Schs Dio Portsm 55-69; R of Warblington w Emsworth 58-69; R of Lowestoft Group (R of St Marg) 69-78; Proc Conv Portsm 62-70; Hon Can of Nor 73-78; Can (Emer) from 78; R of Shaston Dio Sarum from 78. *St Peter's Rectory, Bimport, Shaftesbury, Dorset, SP7 8AT.* (Shaftesbury 2547)

CAIN, Albert Paul. b 37. Qu Coll Ox BA (2nd cl Mod Lang) 60, 2nd cl Th 62. Ripon Hall Ox 60. **d** 62 **p** 63 Lon. C of Harlington 62-67. *18 Raggleswood Close, Earley, Reading, Berks.*

CAIN, Richard Douglas. b 20. Univ of Edin MA 51. Univ of Cam MA 73. Edin Th Coll 51. **d** 53 **p** 54 Newc T. C of Tynemouth 53-58; R of St Patr Tobago 58-64; V of Westwood 64-67; Chap Univ of Warw 67-73; Churchill Coll Cam 73-81. *Rajneesh Medina Meditation Centre, Herringswell, Suffolk.*

CAINK, Richard David Somerville. b 37. Lich Th Coll 68. **d** 71 Bradwell for Cant for Chelmsf **p** 72 Chelmsf. C of St Mary Virg Prittlewell 71-74; Gt Yarmouth 74-76; P-in-c of Saxthorpe w Corpusty 76-80; Oulton 76-80; Blickling w Ingworth 76-80; R of Cheddington w Mentmore and Marsworth Dio Ox from 80. *Rectory, Mentmore Road, Cheddington, Leighton Buzzard, LU7 0SD.* (Cheddington 661358)

✠ **CAIRD, Most Rev Donald Arthur Richard.** b 25. Late Scho and Sen Exhib of Trin Coll Dub BA (1st cl Mod Phil) 49, Div Test 49, MA and BD 55. **d** 50 **p** 51 Down. C of Dundela 50-54; Asst Master and Chap Portora R Sch 54-57; Lect in Phil St D Coll Lamp 57-58; I of Rathmichael 60-69; Dep Lect in Phil Trin Coll Dub 62-63; Lect in Phil of Relig Div Hostel Dub 65-69; Dean of Ossory Can of Aghold in Leighlin Cathl and I of Kilkenny 69-70; Cons Ld Bp of Lim Ardf and Aghadoe in Ch Ch Cathl Dublin on 29 Sept 70 by Abp of Dub; Bps of Ossory; Cashel; Tuam; and Killaloe; Bps Wyse; Jackson; and Hodges; Trld to Meath and Kildare 76. *The See House, Leixlip, Co Kildare, Irish Republic.*

CAIRD, John Doran. b 39. St Jo Coll Winnipeg, **d** 77 **p** 78 Rupld. C of St Mary Winnipeg 77-80; R of Stonewall Area Dio Rupld from 80. *Box 550, Stonewall, Manit, Canada.*

CAIRNS, Henry Alfred. Univ of Melb BA 49. Ridley Coll Melb ACT ThL 43. **d** 42 **p** 43 Gippsld. C of Bass 42; C-in-c of Blackwood Forest w Bass Par Distr 43-44; Moe 44-47; R of Heyfield 47-52; Leongatha 52-60; Can of Gippsld 59-60; Chap Sunbury Ment Hosp 60-62; Kew Ment Hosp Dio Melb 62-80; Perm to Offic Dio Melb from 80. *32 Tallis Drive, Mornington, Vic, Australia 3931.*

CAIRNS, John Cameron. Sir George Williams Univ Montr BA 55. Trin Coll Tor BD 59. McGill Univ MA 71. Cudd Coll 55. **d** 57 **p** 58 Ott. C of Trin Cornwall 55-59; I of Petawawa 59-64; R of Hawkesbury 64-71; R of St Mich AA City and Dio Ott from 71. *1124 Field Street, Ottawa, Ont., K2C 2P7, Canada.* (1-613-224-1202)

CAIRO, Provost of. *See* Eaton, Very Rev Derek Lionel.

CAITHNESS, *See* Moray.

CALAMINUS, Peter Andrew Franz. b 14. BA (Lon) 44. Cudd Th Coll 69. **d** and **p** 71 Sarum. C of Westbury Sarum 71-73; C-in-c of Pitcombe w Shepton Montague (and Bratton St Maur from 76) 73-76; R 76-78; Chap Capricornia Inst for Further Educn and C of N Rockptn Dio Rockptn from 78. *Capricornia Institute, Rockhampton, Queensland, Australia 4700.*

CALATA, Canon James Arthur. d 21 **p** 26 Grahmstn. Miss of St Steph Port Eliz 21-26; St Ninian Somt E 26-28; St Jas Miss Cradock Dio Grahmstn 28-36 and from 38; L to Offic Dio Grahmstn 36-38; Hon Can of Grahmstn Cathl 59-61 and from 70; Can 61-70; L to Offic Dio Port Eliz from 70. *26 Mongo Street, PO Lingelhle, Cradock, CP, S Africa.* (1256)

CALCOTT-JAMES, Colin Wilfrid. b 25. Univ of Bris BSc 48. SOC 77. **d** 80 **p** 81 S'wark. C of H Trin Barnes Dio S'wark from 80. *23 Gwendolen Avenue, Putney, SW15 6ET.*

CALDER, Canon Ian Keith. McMaster Univ Ont BA 57. Bp's Univ Lennox LST 59. Yale Univ M Relig Educn 61. **d** and **p** 60 Niag. C of St Chris Burlington 60-63; P-in-c of Bronte 63-65; C of Chap of H Spriit Hamilton 65-69; on leave (Niag) 69-73; R of St Matt City and Dio Ott from 73; Can of Ott from 80. *217 First Avenue, Ottawa, Ont., Canada.* (1-613-232-4980)

CALDER, John Wallace. b 35. McMaster Univ Hamilton BA 58. Wycl Coll Tor MDiv 77. **d** 77 **p** 78 Bp Clarke for Niag. C of Welland w Port Colborne 77-78; I Woodburn Dio Niag from 78; P Assoc of Stoney Creek Dio Niag from 78. *72 St Andrew's Drive, Hamilton, Ont, Canada.*

CALDER, Matthew Lewis. Moore Th Coll Syd ACT ThL 40. **d** 41 Waik **p** 43 Aotearoa for Wai. C of St John Te Awamutu 41; on leave 42; C of St John's Cathl Napier 43-44; V of Taradale 44-49; Waipawa 49-60; St Mark City and Dio

Wel from 60. *Vicarage, Dufferin Street, Wellington, NZ.* (858-536)

CALDER, Roger Paul. b 53. Hatf Coll Dur BA 75. Chich Th Coll 76. **d** 79 **p** 80 Guildf. C of Addlestone Dio Guildf from 79. *140a Church Road, Addlestone, Surrey.* (Weybridge 44752)

CALDERLEY, Canon John. Egerton Hall Man **d** 31 **p** 32 Man. C of St Paul Oldham 31-35; V of St Thos Moorside 35-61; St Matt Chadderton 61-75; RD of Middleton 61-75; Surr 62-75; Hon Can of Man Cathl 71-76; Can (Emer) from 76. *6 Clive Avenue, Whitefield, Manchester, M25 7WN.* (061-766 5763)

CALDERWOOD, Robert Henry. Bp's Univ Lennox BA 56, LST 58. **d** 58 Ott **p** 58 Niag. C of St Geo St Catharines 58-60; R of Sedgewick 60 62; Good Shepherd (w St Chad from 67) Edmon 62-68; St Martin-in-the-Fields Winnipeg 68-71; I of St Alb Winnipeg 71-73; Asst to Bp of Rupld 73-75; Dioc Admin Dio Bran 75-79; Admin Archd Dio Bran 77-79; Dioc Sec and Treas Dio Bran 77-79; Executive Asst to Bp of Koot from 79. *Box 549, Kelowna, BC, Canada.*

CALDICOTT, Anthony. b 31. St Jo Coll Dur BA (3rd cl Mus) 53. ARCO 52 FRCO 62. Ripon Hall Ox. **d** 57 **p** 58 Cov. C of Finham 57-61; St Andr Bedford 61-64; Chap Lindisfarne Coll and L to Offic Dio St A 64-67; C of W Bromwich 67-69; Publ Pr Dio Cov 69-75; C of St Mary Virg Twickenham Dio Lon from 75. *St Mary's Flat, 8 Riverside, Twickenham, Middx.* (01-892 6012)

CALDICOTT, John Michael Parlane. b 46. Selw Coll Cam BA (Th Trip) 69. St Steph Ho Ox 69. **d** 71 Lewes for Chich **p** 72 Chich. C of St Dunstans, Mayfield 71-74; Hon C of St Paul Deptford 74-77; V of St Phil Sydenham Dio S'wark from 77; P-in-c of H Trin Sydenham Dio S'wark from 81; All SS Sydenham Dio S'wark from 81. *122 Wells Park Road, SE26 6AS.* (01-699 4930)

CALDWELL, Alan. Oak Hill Th Coll. **d** 67 **p** 68 Guildf. C of H Trin Aldershot 67-69; New Malden w Coombe 69-73; Edgware (in c of St Andr) 73-78; R of Helmingham w Framsden and Pettaugh w Winston Dio St E from 78. *Helmingham Rectory, Stowmarket, Suff.* (Helmingham 226)

CALDWELL, Alan Alfred. b 48. Loughborough Univ of Tech BSc 70. Univ of Nottm Dipl Th 71. Linc Th Coll 70. **d** 73 **p** 74 Southw. C of Bulwell 73-80; Chap Univ of Nottm from 80. *Lenton Lodge, Derby Road, Nottingham, NG7 2QA.* (Nottm 255143)

CALDWELL, Coilpillai Abraham. St Pet Hall and Trin Th Coll Sing 60. **d** 60 **p** 61 Sing. C of Ascen Sing 60-61; Kuala Lumpur 61-62; P-in-c of Ch of Our Sav Sing 63-64; V of St Barn Klang 64-67; St Jas Sentul 67-70; Johore Bahru 70-73; Ch Ch Sing 73-79. *88J, Block 100, Commonwealth Crescent, Singapore 0314.*

CALDWELL, David Denzil. TD 70. Bps' Coll Cheshunt 53. **d** 55 Connor **p** 56 Down for Arm. C of Carnmoney 55-59; CF (TA) 57-67; CF (TAVR) from 67; C of Antrim w Muckamore 59-61; I of Kilwaughter w Cairncastle Dio Connor from 61; RD of Carrickfergus from 70; CF (RARO) 70. *Cairncastle Rectory, Ballygally, Larne, Co Antrim BT40 2RB, N Ireland.* (Ballygally 220)

CALDWELL, Eric Ernest. b 28. **d** 81 Fred (APM). Perm to Offic Dio Fred from 81. *5 Maplewood Court, St Stephen, NB, Canada, E3L 2V3.*

CALDWELL, Gary Edward. Iowa Wesleyan Coll BA 53. Gen Th Sem NY STB 60. **d** and **p** Iowa. [f in Amer Ch.] R of Aruba 68-77. *Rectory, PO Box 159, San Nicholas, Aruba, Netherlands Antilles.* (5142)

CALDWELL, George. b 05. Lich Th Coll 26. Univ of Dur 27. **d** 29 **p** 30 Liv. C of St Martin-in-the-Fields Liv 29-30; St Thos Seaforth 30-34; Eyam (in c of St Helen Grindleford) 34-36; PC of Stony Middleton 36-42; R of H Trin Tansley 42-52; V of Barrow-on-Trent w Twyford 52-55; Ch Ch Latchford 55-68; St Aug Brinksway w Cheadle Heath 68-71; Surr from 58. *88 Fairfield Rd, Stockton Heath, Warrington, WA4 2UX.* (Warrington 61722)

CALDWELL, Ian Charles Reynolds. b 43. St Mich Coll Llan 68. **d** 70 **p** 71 Pet. C and Prec of Oakham 70-74; Swindon New Town (in c of St Luke) 74-78; P-in-c of St Francis Honicknowle Dio Ex 78-80; V from 80. *St Francis Vicarage, Little Dock Lane, Honicknowle, Plymouth, Devon, PL5 2NA.* (0752 773874)

CALDWELL, John Donaldson. b 19. TCD BA 41. **d** 42 Tuam for Down **p** 43 Down. C of St Aid Belfast 42-47; Maralin 47-50; I of Drumgath U 50-55; R Kilmegan w Maghera Dio Drom from 55; RD of Kilmegan from 62. *Rectory, Dundrum, Co Down, N Ireland.* (Dundrum 225)

CALDWELL, Roger Fripp. b 31. Cranmer Hall Dur. **d** 64 **p** 65 Newc T. C of Gosforth 64-67; Sugley 67-74; R of Helmdon w Stuchbury and Radstone Dio Pet from 74; Greatworth Dio Pet from 74. *Helmdon Rectory, Brackley, Northants.* (Sulgrave 513)

CALE, Clifford Roy Fenton. b 38. St Mich Coll Llan 65. **d** 67 **p** 68 Mon. C of Griffithstown 67; V of Cwm 72-73; Abersychan (w Gardiffaith from 79) Dio Mon from 73. *Vicarage, Abersychan, Gwent, Pontypool, NP4 8PL.* (0495 772213)

CALEDONIA, Lord Bishop of. *See* Hannen, Right Rev John Edward.

CALEDONIA, Dean of. *See* Flagg, Very Rev Ernest Geoffrey.

CALEY, Charles Joseph. b 16. Bp Wilson Th Coll IM 35. **d** 39 **p** 40 Chelmsf. C of St Alb Becontree 39-42; CF (EC) 42-46; Hon CF from 46; C of St Pet Paddington 46-47; Stoke Poges 47-54; V of Sturminster Marshall 54-58; C of Stoke Poges (in c of St John) 58-62; V of E Farleigh (and Coxheath from 78) Dio Roch from 62; Chap Linton Hosp from 66. *East Farleigh Vicarage, Maidstone, Kent, ME15 0LX.* (Maidstone 26169)

CALEY, Vincent Harold James. b 1891. Univ of NZ BSc (Agr) 54. ACT ThL (2nd cl) 60. Ridley Coll Melb 59. **d** and **p** 61 Syd. C of Austinmer 61; Summer Hill 61-63; Wentworthville 63-65; Asst Master C of E Sch N Syd 65-67; L to Offic Dio Syd 65-67; Perm to Offic Dio Brisb from 70. *5 Stubbersfield Street, Gatton, Queensland 4343, Australia.*

CALGARY, Bishop of. *See* Goodman, Right Rev Morse Lamb.

CALGARY, Dean of. *See* Blyth, Very Rev John Carter.

33 Whitbarrow Road, lymm, ches. (lymm 3805)

CALLAGHAN, George. b 07. **d** 58 **p** 59 Pontefract for Wakef. C of Kirkheaton 58-61; V of St Cath Sandal 61-70; V of Barkisland w W Scammonden 70-74. *42 Crossley Houses, Arden Road, Almshouse, Halifax, Yorks.*

CALLAGHAN, Harry. b 34. K Coll Lon and Warm AKC 59. **d** 60 **p** 61 Sheff. C of St Cecilia Parson Cross Sheff 60-63; V of Metenmeer-Zorg 63-66; St Sav Georgetn Guy 66-70; Information Officer Caribbean Conf of Chs and L to Offic Dio Barb 70-74; L to Offic Dio Man from 74; Chap Miss to Seamen Man 74-76; USPG Area Sec for Dios Man, Blackb and S & M from 76. *113 Church Road, Urmston, Manchester, M31 1FJ.* (061-748 3086)

CALLAN, Terence Frederick. b 26. Trin Coll Dub 55. **d** 57 Clogh **p** 58 Meath. C of Monaghan 57-58; I of Clogh 58-64; C of Derriaghy 64-66; C-in-c of Ballymacash 67-70; R of St Aid Belf 70-79; Agherton Dio Connor from 79. *Agherton Rectory, Strand Road, Portstewart, Co Derry BT55 7LU.* (Portstewart 2538)

CALLANDER, Nevil John. b 32. St Paul's Coll Grahmstn 69. **d** 72 **p** 73 Capetn. C of Somerset W 72-75; R of Newlands Dio Capetn from 76. *St Andrew's Rectory, Kildare Road, Newlands, Capetown, S Africa.* (6-4497)

CALLARD, David Kingsley. b 37. St Pet Coll Ox BA (3rd cl Th) 61 MA 65. Westcott Ho Cam 61. **d** 63 Bp McKie for Cov **p** 64 Cov. C of H Trin Leamington 63-66; Wyken (in c of H Cross) 66-68; Bp's Hatfield (in c of St John's) 68-73; R of Bilton, Warws Dio Cov from 73. *Bilton Rectory, Rugby, Warws, CV22 7LX.* (Rugby 812613)

CALLENDER, Francis Charles. b 48. TCD BA 70, MA 73. Div Hostel Dub 77. **d** 79 **p** 80 Cork. C of Bandon Dio Cork from 79. *Trinity Cottage, Rice's Road, Bandon, Co Cork, Irish Republic.* (023 41053)

CALLENDER, Thomas Henry. b 13. SS Coll Cam BA 35, MA 39. Sarum Th Coll 35. **d** 37 **p** 38 Worc. C of St John Kidderminster 37-41; Pershore w H Cross Pinvin and Wick 41-46; V of Powick 46-51; St Barn Tuffley Glouc 51-55; St Pet Cranley Gardens Kens 55-57; R of L Stanmore 57-66; Ovington 66-78; V of Carbrooke (w Ovington, Woodrising and Scoulton from 76) 66-78; C-in-c of Scoulton w Wood Rising 70-78; Perm to Offic Dio Nor from 78. *Marloes, Morley St Botolph, Wymondham, Norf.* (Wymondham 603285)

CALLIS, Montagu Clare. b 1893. Peterho Cam BA 15. Linc Th Coll 34. **d** 35 Whitby for York **p** 36 York. C of St Jo Evang Middlesbrough 35-40; C-in-c of Ormesby 40-41; V of Totteridge 41-46; St Hilda w St Pet Middlesbrough 46-52; R of Ibberton w Belchalwell and Woolland 52-59; V of Alderholt 59-65; Perm to Offic Dio Ox from 66; Dio Ex from 69. *c/o The Small Barn, Nunnery Lane, Penshurst, Kent.* (Penshurst 870401)

CALLON, Andrew McMillan. b 56. Chich Th Coll 77. **d** 80 **p** 81 Liv. C of Wigan Dio Liv from 80. *Glebe House, The Hall, New Market Street, Wigan, WN1 1HH.*

CALLOW, Dennis. Moore Th Coll Syd. **d** 56 **p** 57 Syd. C of St Columb w Ryde w Ermington and Rydalmere 56-59; C-in-c of Jannali Provisional Distr 59-65; St Mark's Provisional Distr Revesby Dio Syd from 65. *5 Haddon Crescent, Revesby, NSW, Australia 2212.* (77-8721)

CALLUM, David Theodore. St Cath Coll Cam 2nd cl Engl Trip 31, BA (2nd cl Archaeol and Anthrop) 32, MA 36. Ridley Hall Cam 32. **d** 34 **p** 35 S'wark. C of All SS S Lambeth 34-37; St Mary Southampton 37-40; Org Sec Miss to Seamen S for E Distr 40-48; Ed 'The Church and the Sailor' 45-48; V of Gt Dunmow 48-61; C-in-c of L Canfield 53-61; RD of Dunmow 59-61; Surr from 58; V of Becontree 61-74; R of Stanford Rivers Dio Chelmsf from 74. *Stanford Rivers Rectory, Ongar, Essex, CM5 9PW.* (Ongar 2310)

CALTHROP-OWEN, William Gordon. b 35. Chich Th Coll 62. **d** 63 **p** 64 Ches. C of Egremont 63-68; Bawtry w Austerfield 68-69; C-in-c of St Mich AA Radford 69-73; All S w Ch Ch Radford 69-73; R of Bilsthorpe Dio Southw from 73; R of Eakring Dio Southw from 73; P-in-c of Winkburn and of Maplebeck Dio Southw from 77. *Bilsthorpe Rectory, Newark, Notts, NG22 8RU.* (Mansfield 870256)

CALVER, Sydney Bertram. b 10. Keble Coll Ox 3rd cl Jurispr 32, BA 33. Chich Th Coll 33. **d** 35 **p** 36 Ox. C of Thatcham 35-38; St Pet Walworth 38-42; Chap RAFVR 42-46; Toc H 46-49; Asst Educn Officer Ch Assembly Adult Educn Coun 49-56; R of Stonesfield 56-75; Perm to Offic Dio Ox 75-77; Dio B & W from 77. *8 Parkfield Drive, Taunton, Somt.*

CALVERT, Donald. Wycl Coll Tor LTh 65. **d** 64 Bp Snell for Tor **p** 65 Tor for Fred. R of Waterford w St Mark Fred 65-70; Madawaska Dio Fred from 70. *74 Church Street, Edmundston, NB, Canada.*

CALVERT, Preb Ian Matheson. b 23. Keble Coll Ox BA 49, MA 53. Wells Th Coll. **d** 50 **p** 51 Derby. C of St Giles Matlock 50-53; Stoke-on-Trent 53-55; V of Ault Hucknall 55-58; Ch of S India 58-62; V of St Mary Sedgley 62-71; R of Forton 71-79; C-in-c of Norbury 71-79; Preb of Lich Cathl 76-79; Preb (Emer) from 79; Adv in Miss and Unity Dio Dur from 79; Ecumen Officer Dio Dur from 79. *Satley House, Satley, Bishop Auckland, Co Durham. DL13 4HU.* (Tow Law 730042)

CALVERT, John Raymond. b 42. Lon Coll of Div 64. **d** 67 **p** 68 S'wark. C of St Mark Kennington 67-70; St Pet Southborough 70-72; St Botolph Barton Seagrave 72-75; Asst Master Shaftesbury High Sch 78-79; Children's Officer Dio from 79. *16 Derby Road, Gloucester, GL1 4AE.* (Glouc 20299)

CALVERT, Peter Noel. b 41. Ch Coll Cam 2nd cl Engl Trip pt i 62, BA (2nd cl Th Trip pt ia) 63, MA 67. Cudd Coll 64. **d** 66 **p** 67 Wakef. C of Brighouse 66-71; V of Heptonstall Dio Wakef from 71. *Heptonstall Vicarage, Hebden Bridge, W Yorks, HX7 7NT.* (Hebden Bridge 842004)

CALVERT, Richard Winter. b 16. Univ of Dur LTh 42. Edin Th Coll 39. **d** 42 **p** 43 Brech. C of St Marg Lochee 42-44; C-in-c of St D of Scotld Pilton 44-49; R of St Anne Dunbar w Biel Chap 49-52; CF 52-59; V of N Ormesby 59-72; Boosbeck w Moorsholm 72-74; S Bank Dio York from 74. *259 Normanby Road, South Bank, Middlesbrough, Cleveland TS6 6TB.* (Eston Grange 453679)

CALVIN-THOMAS, David Nigel. b 43. Univ of Wales (Cardiff) BSc 64. BD (Lon) 77. St Mich AA Llan 77. **d** 78 Bp Reece for Llan **p** 79 Llan. C of St Cath Pontypridd 78-80. *c/o 2 Nuns Crescent, Graigwen, Pontypridd, CF37 2EN.*

CAM, Julian Howard. b 48. Univ of York BA 69. Univ of Birm Dipl Th 74. **d** 75 Truro **p** 76 St Germans for Truro. C of St Ives 75-80; St Uny Lelant 78-80; V of Flookburgh Dio Carl from 80. *Flookburgh Vicarage, Grange-over-Sands, Cumb, LA11 7JY.* (Flookburgh 245)

CAMARA, Jean-Baptiste. b 52. Im Coll Ibad 74. **d** 77 **p** 78 Gambia. P Dio Gambia. *c/o Mission Anglicane, BP 105, Conakry, Republic of Guinea.*

CAMENISCH, Richard Frank. b 12. Univ Coll Dur BA 34. Wells Th Coll 34. **d** 35 **p** 36 Sheff. C of St Cuthb Sheff 35-37; Burghwallis w Skelbrooke 39-41; serving w Army 40-45; C of St John Staveley 47-50; R of Treswell w Cottam 50-59; V of Laxton w Moorhouse 59-68; V of Egmanton 59-68; Bicker 68-77; Perm to Offic Dio Southw from 77. *The Whipping Post, Norwell Lane, Newark, Notts, NG23 6JE.* (Newark 821423)

CAMERON, Alan Lindsay. Sir Geo Williams Univ Montr BA 60. McGill Univ BD 63. Montr Dioc Th Coll LTh 63. **d** 62 **p** 63 Montr. I of Clarenceville and P-in-c of Lacolle 62-66; I of Chomedey and P-in-c of Bordeau 66-75; R of Lakeside Heights Dio Montr from 75 *178 Westcliffe Avenue, Pointe Claire, PQ, Canada.* (514-697 8148)

CAMERON, Alexander Russell. St Mich Th Coll Crafers 50. **d** 53 **p** 54 St Arn. d Dio St Arn 53-54; V of Manangatang 54-59; Wedderburn 59-60; R of Victor Harbour 60-65; Fullarton 65-73; Ch Ch N Adel Dio Adel from 73. *35 Palmer Place, North Adelaide, S Australia 5006.* (08-267 2673)

CAMERON, Andrew Bruce. b 41. Edin Th Coll. **d** 64 **p** 65 Glas. C of St Mich AA Helensburgh 64-67; H Cross David-son's Mains 67-70; Youth Chap Dio Edin 69-75; Chap St Mary's Cathl Edin 71-75; R of St Mary Dalmahoy Dio Edin from 75; Chap Heriot-Watt Univ from 75. *Dalmahoy Rectory, Kirknewton, Midlothian, EH27 8EB.* (031-333 1683)

CAMERON, Angus Ewen Hamilton. *See* Cameron of Lundavra, Angus Ewen Hamilton.

CAMERON, Aylmer Peter. b 08. Wells Th Coll 37. **d** 38 **p** 39 Chich. C of St Jo Bapt Bognor Regis 38-40; CF (EC) 40-46; R of Slaugham w Handcross 46-52; V of Kirdford w Plaistow 52-54; R of All SS w St Thos Lewes 54-58; R of St Jo Bapt-sub-Castro Lewes 55-57; Boxgrove 57-64; R of Tangmere 58-64; Steeple Langford 64-73. *27 Montague Road, Salisbury, Wilts, SP2 8NL.* (Salisbury 28844)

CAMERON, Derek Cedric Graham. St Jo Coll Auckld 48, LTh 64. **d** 51 **p** 52 Wai. C of Rotorua 51-54; V of Edgecombe 54; C of Whakatane 54-56; CF (NZ) from 56; L to Offic Dio Wel 64-78; Hon C of U Hutt Dio Wel from 78. *600 Ferguson Drive, Upper Hutt, NZ.* (87-841)

CAMERON, Donald Eric Nelson. b 29. St Jo Coll Dur 68. **d** 70 **p** 71 York. C of H Trin, Hull 70-73; V of Eston w Normanby Dio York from 73. *116 High Street, Eston, Middlesbrough, Teesside.* (0642 453343)

CAMERON, Douglas Maclean. b 35. Edin Th Coll 59. **d** 62 **p** 63 Edin. C of Ch Ch Falkirk 62-65; Miss P at Eiwo 66-67; Movi New Guinea 67-72; R of Goroka 72-74; Archd of New Guinea Mainland 72-74; P-in-c of St Fillan City and Dio Edin 74-78; R from 78; R of St Hilda Colinton Mains City and Dio Edin from 77. *Rectory, Buckstone Drive, Edinburgh, EH10 6PD.*

CAMERON, Canon Ernest. MBE 72. Moore Th Coll Syd 19. **d** 19 **p** 20 Syd. C of H Trin. Wentworth Falls w Em Ch Lawson 19-21; Penrith 21-23; St Steph Willoughby 23-25; P-in-c of Northbridge 25-29; R of 29-30; St Pet Hornsby 30-37; St Luke Mosman 37-63; Hon Can of Syd from 49; Fell St Paul's Coll Univ of Syd from 49; L to Offic Dio Syd from 63. *231 Donnington Court, Flinders Village, Castle Hill, NSW, Australia 2154.* (680-2387)

✠ **CAMERON, Right Rev Ewen Donald.** BD (Lon) 59. Moore Th Coll Syd ACT ThL 58, Th Scho 61. **d** 59 Bp Hilliard for Syd **p** 59 Syd. C of Chatswood 59-63; Lect Moore Th Coll Syd 60-63; R of Bellevue Hill 63-65; Federal Sec CMS of Austr and L to Offic Dio Syd 65-72; Exam Chap to Abp of Syd from 68; Archd of Cumb (w Syd from 73) 72-75; Strathfield from 75; Cons Asst Bp of Syd in St Andr Cathl Syd 24 June 75 by Abps of Syd and Melb, Bps of Armid, Bath, Graft and N Terr; and others. *St Andrew's House, Sydney Square, Sydney, NSW, Australia 2000.* (269-0642)

CAMERON, Canon George Ernest Agar. d 64 **p** 65 Adel. C of Ch of Epiph Crafers 64-65; Miss Chap O'Halloran Hill Miss 66-68; R of Willunga Dio Murray from 69; Hon Can of The Murray from 73. *Rectory, St Andrew's Terrace, Willunga, S Australia 5172.* (085 56 2036)

CAMERON, Ian Alexander. b 43. Ridley Coll Melb ThL 70. **d** 70 **p** 71 Melb. C of St Columb, Hawthorn 70-72; Blackburn 72-73; P-in-c of Winchelsea 73-76; V 76-79; I of Rosanna Dio Melb from 79. *30 Invermay Grove, Rosanna, Vic, Australia 3084.* (45 1535)

CAMERON, John Stansfield. Em and St Chad Coll Sktn. **d** 67 Bp Anderson for Rupld **p** 68 Rupld. C of St Aid Winnipeg 67-70; I of Gimli 70-71; St Pet Winnipeg 71-76; St Timothy City and Dio Sktn from 76. *735 Taylor Street East, Saskatoon, Sask, Canada.*

CAMERON, Canon John Steven Graham. Univ of NZ BA 61. NZ Bd of Th Stud LTh (1st cl) 59. St Jo Coll Auckld 57. **d** 58 **p** 59 Auckld. C of St Aid Remuera 58-59; St Mark Remuera 59-62; Hon C from 62; Chap Dilworth Sch 62-68; Dioc High Sch Dio Auckld from 69; Can of Auckld from 78. *33 Fancourt Street, Meadowbank, Auckland, NZ.* (584-728)

CAMERON, Peter Samuel Griswold. b 30. TD 76. Late Exhib of New Coll Ox 3rd cl Cl Mods 51, BA (2nd cl Lit Hum) 53, MA 56. K Coll Cam MA (by incorp) 60. Wells Th Coll 53. **d** 55 **p** 56 Bris. C of St Alb Westbury Pk 55-58; Henbury w Hallen 58-60; Perm to Offic Dio Ely and Chap K Coll Cam 60-63; CF (TA) 59-67; CF (TAVR) 67-70 and 72-78; C-in-c of Ch Ch Conv Distr Davyhulme 63-67; Min 67-69; V 69-72; Worsley w Ellenbrook 72-79; R of Landbeach Dio Ely from 79; V of Waterbeach Dio Ely from 79; RD of Quy from 81; CF (TA) from 81. *Vicarage, Chapel Street, Waterbeach, Cambridge, CB5 9HR.* (0223-860353)

CAMERON, Ross Donald. b 40. Univ of Queensld BAgrSc 62, BD 69. St Francis Th Coll Brisb 66. **d** 69 **p** 70 Rockptn. C of Park Avenue Rockptn 69-72; Barcaldine 72-73; St Paul's Cathl Rockptn 73-75; R of Longreach Dio Rockptn from 75. *Box 52, Longreach, Queensland, Australia 4730.* (Longreach 116)

CAMERON, Samuel William. Selw Coll Cm BA 48, MA 54. St Chad's Coll Dur Dipl Th 51. **d** 51 **p** 52 Dur. C of St Mary Heworth 51-52; Stockton-on-Tees 52-53; Jarrow 54-59; P-in-c of Beyers Green 59-60; L to Offic Dio Dur from 77. *18 Alwyn Road, Darlington, Co Durham, DL3 0AJ.*

CAMERON, William James. b 35. St Aid Coll 62. **d** 64 Warrington for Liv **p** 65 Liv. C of Halewood 64-66; P-in-c of St Mary Halewood 66-68; Asst Chap Univ of Leeds 68-71; Industr Chap Speke 71-77; Team V of Speke 73-77; Tr Officer

Gen Syn Bd of Educn from 78. *General Synod Board of Education, Church House, Dean's Yard, Westminster, SW1P 3NZ.*

CAMERON, William Steven Graham. d 22 **p** 24 Wai. C of Rotorua 22-26; V of Te Karaka 26-30; Porangahau 30-37; St Andr Napier 37-53; CF (NZ) 42-45; Chap Miss to Seamen Port Ahuriri 49-53; L to Offic Dio Wai from 53. *c/o Diocesan Office, P.O. Box 227, Napier, NZ.*

CAMERON OF LUNDAVRA, (formerly CAMERON) Angus Ewen Hamilton. Univ of BC BA 48. BC Th Coll. **d** and **p** 48 BC. I of W Coast Miss Tofino 48-49; C of Oak Bay 49-51; R of St Faith Vanc 51-53; C of Wimbledon 53-55; Sub Chap of O of St Jo of Jer from 54; R of Como w Denman and Hornby Is 55-58; R of St Matthias Vic 58-65; Cler Sec of Syn Dio BC 59-67; Chap to Abp of BC from 62-71; Hosp Chap Dio BC 65-72. *404-1653 Oak Bay Avenue, Victoria, BC, Canada.*

CAMIER, James. Trin Coll Dub BA 33, MA 67. **d** 35 **p** 36 Cork. C of Kinsale w Rincurran 35-37; I of Drimoleague 37-40; Moyrus (Roundstone) 40-45; Kiltullagh 45-51; Kilnaboy w Kilkreedy 51-61; Borrisokane U Dio Killaloe from 61; Kilbarron w Finnoe Dio Killaloe from 61; RD of Ely O'Carroll from 62; Can of Rath 62-65; Treas of Killaloe Cathl 65-67; Chan 67-72; Preb of Killaloe Cathl from 65; Prec from 72. *Rectory, Borrisokane, Co Tipperary, Irish Republic.*

CAMM, Joseph Arnold. b 12. Worc Ordin Coll 68. Ridley Hall Cam 69. **d** 69 **p** 70 York. C of Gt w L Driffield 69-72; V of Stillingfleet w Naburn 72-78. *8 Barratts Close, Langworth Gate, Lincoln, LN2 4AF.*

CAMP, Frederick Walter. b 19. Sarum Th Coll 47. **d** 49 **p** 50 Lon. C of St Mary Brookfield 49-54; CF 54-58; V of Brigham 58-80; Whittingham Dio Newc T from 80. *Whittingham Vicarage, Alnwick, Northumb.* (Whittingham 224)

CAMP, Michael Maurice. b 52. Sarum Wells Th Coll 78. **d** 81 Barking for Chelmsf. C of St Jo Bapt Loughton Dio Chelmsf from 81. *68 Grosvenor Drive, Loughton, Essex, IG10 2LG.*

CAMPBELL, Alfred Clive. St Pet Th Coll Ja. **d** 52 **p** 53 Ja. C-in-c of Montpelier 52-57; Porus 57-59; Trin Ville and Woburn Lawn 59-63; R of Retreat Ja 63-73; St Alb-the-Mart City and Dio Tor from 76; Commiss Ja from 78. *180 Simcoe Street, Toronto 2, Ont, Canada.*

CAMPBELL, Allan. b 14. Selw Coll Cam 3rd cl Hist Trip pt i 35, BA 36, MA 40. Westcott Ho Cam 36. **d** 38 Carl **p** 39 Penrith for Carl. C of Crosthwaite Cumb 38-39; Chap RNVR 39-46; R of Bletchley 46-63; Proc Conv Ox 55-59; RD of Bletchley 56-63; R of Amersham Dio Ox from 63. *Rectory, Hervines Road, Amersham, Bucks.* (Amersham 7135)

CAMPBELL, Andrew Victor. b 20. St Chad's Coll Dur 39. Linc Th Coll 46. **d** 49 Kens for Lon **p** 50 Lon. C of All SS Poplar 49-52; Native Miss Pret 52-59; P-in-c of Good Shepherd Miss Pret 59-63; Mamelodi and Silverton 63-66; R of Potgietersrus 66-71; Archd of N Transv 67-72; R of Pietersburg Pret 71-72; V of St Edm Hunstanton 72-74; Chap Coll of Ascen Selly Oak 74-75; Team V of St Aubyn Devonport 75-76; P-in-c of Whitleigh Dio Ex 76-80; V from 80; RD of Plymouth from 79. *St Chad's Vicarage, Whitleigh Green, Plymouth, Devon, PL5 4DD.* (Plymouth 773547)

CAMPBELL, Arthur John Ernest. b 10 Trin Coll Dub BA 33, MA 38. **d** 34 **p** 35 Down. C of St Matt Belf 34-42; I of Drumgath w Drumballyroney (w Clonduff from 36) 42-50; I of Glenavy 50-61; R of St Matt Shankill Belf 61-74; RD of Mid-Belf 63-70; Can of St Anne's Cathl Belf 66-78; C of Dunseverick 74-78. *11 Lissanduff Avenue, Portballintrae, Bushmills, Co Antrim, N Ireland.*

CAMPBELL, Colin Alexander. Ch Div Sch Calif 57. **d** 61 Los Angeles **p** 62 BC. C of St Jo Div Vic BC 61-65; CF (Canad) 65-68; RNZN 68-69; C of Hunters Hill 69-71; R of Petersham Dio Syd from 71. *325 Stanmore Road, Petersham, NSW 2049, Australia.*

CAMPBELL, Colin Douglas. b 48. Brock Univ Ont BA 72. Trin Coll Tor MDiv 75. **d** 75 **p** 76 Niag. C of St Jude Oakville 75-78; R of St Monica Niag Falls 78-81; Queenston 78-81; Mt Forest Dio Niag from 81. *124 Fergus Street South, Mount Forest, Ont, Canada.* (519-323 1063)

CAMPBELL, Donald. b 02. Wycl Hall Ox 51. **d** 51 **p** 52 Roch. C of Tonbridge 51-53; V of Burham 53-57; Farningham 57-73; Chap Parkwood Conv Home 57-60. *11 Inverleith Terrace, Edinburgh, EH3 5NS.*

CAMPBELL, Donald Keith. Moore Th Coll Syd ACT ThL (2nd cl) 67. **d** 68 Brisb. C of St Steph Coorparoo 68-70; Booval 70-73; R of Kilkivan 73-79; Sec CMS Dio Brisb from 79. *468 Ann Street, Brisbane, Queensland, Australia 4000.* (221 2459)

CAMPBELL, Frederick David Gordon. b 15. Ex Coll Ox BA (3rd cl Th) 39. Wells Th Coll 39. M SSJE 57. **d** 40 Portsm **p** 41 Bp Kitching for Portsm. C of St Mary Portsea 40-45; Chap RNVR 45-48; C of Fareham 48-49; LDHM of St Mary the Virgin E Hounslow 49-51; V 51-54; LPr Dio Ox from 55; Dio Lon from 69; Supr Gen SSJE from 76. *St Edward's House, 22 Great College Street, Westmnster, SW1P 3QA.* (01-222 9234)

CAMPBELL, George Latimer. b 24. Rutgers Univ NB PhD 63. Montr Th Coll 75. **d** 76 **p** 77 Montr. C of St Matthias Westmount 76-78; R of St Luke Rosemount City and Dio Montr from 78. *3001 Holt Street, Montreal, PQ, Canada.* (514-722 4231)

CAMPBELL, George Latimer III. b 50. Concordia Univ Montr BA 76. Montr Dioc Th Coll 76. **d** 79 **p** 80 Montr. C of Knowlton-Mansonville Dio Montr from 79. *RR1, Mansonville, Que, Canada, JOE 1X0.*

CAMPBELL, George St Clair. b 32. Univ of Lon BSc (2nd cl Econ) 53. Clifton Th Coll 58. **d** 60 Tonbridge for Cant. **p** 61 Roch. C of St Pet Tunbridge Wells 60-64; St Jas Clitheroe 64-70; V of Tibshelf Dio Derby from 70. *Vicarage, Tibshelf, Derbys.* (Riley 872243)

CAMPBELL, George Stuart. b 43. Edin Th Coll 63. **d** 66 **p** 68 Edin. C of Falkirk 66-69; Glenrothes 69-73; R of St Andr and St Geo Rosyth 73-75; Inverkeithing 73-75; St Mark E Kilbride Dio Glas from 75. *2 Platthorn Road, East Kilbride, Glasgow, G74 1NW.* (E Kilbride 22595)

CAMPBELL, Ian David. b 33. K Coll Lon and Warm AKC 57. **d** 58 **p** 59 Liv. C of Our Lady and St Nich Liv 58-62; V of Dunstan Edge Hill 62-69; R of Em Ch Loughborough 70-80; Surr 74-80; V of Leamington Priors Dio Cov from 80. *Vicarage, Leam Terrace, Leamington Spa, CV31 1BQ.* (Leamington 25083)

CAMPBELL, John Eric. b 34. Moore Th Coll ThDip 72. **d** and **p** 73 Syd. C of Sans Souci 73-75; Nowra 75-76; R of All SS Austinmer Dio Syd from 76. *Rectory, Roxborough Avenue, Thirroul, NSW, Australia 2515.* (042-67 1079)

CAMPBELL, John Frederick Stuart. b 25. Moore Th Coll 47. ACT ThL 50. Open Univ BA 80. Oak Hill Th Coll 51. **d** 52 **p** 53 Lon. C of Em Northwood 52-55; Chap RAF 56-59; P-in-c of Mulgoa and R of Emu Plains w Castlereagh 59-60; C-in-c of Miranda 60-61; V of St Paul Camelsdale 62-64; CF (Austr) 65-68; R of Leura 68-74; St Jo Evang Weston, Bath (w Kelston from 81) Dio B & W from 74; P-in-c of Kelston 76-81. *St John's Rectory, Combe Park, Bath, BA1 3NE.* (Bath 27206)

CAMPBELL, Canon John Norman. b 16. Ch Coll Cam BA (2nd cl Nat Sc Trip pt i) 38, MA 42 Ridley Hall Cam 38. **d** 40 **p** 41 Roch. C of Tonbridge 40-43; Ch Ch Crouch End 43-45; LDHM of St Alphege Edmonton Lon 45-49; Miss P at Gulu 49-58; Chap Can Lawrence TTC Lira 58-63; L to Offic Dio Nam 63-70; Hon Can of Nam from 71; R of Stapleton Dio Bris from 70. *Rectory, Park Road, Stapleton, Bristol, BS16 1AZ.* (Bris 653977)

CAMPBELL, Canon Kenneth Walter McVinish. Moore Th Coll Syd ACT ThL 49. ARACI 68. **d** and **p** 50 Syd. C of St Steph Kembla 50-52; C-in-c of W Kembla 52-54; R of St Thos Auburn 54-59; Pitt Town 60-66; L to Offic Dio Syd 67-70; C-in-c of Albion Pk 70-74; R 74-75; Bruthen Dio Gippsld from 75; Can of Gippsld from 81. *Rectory, Bruthen, Vic, Australia 3885.* (051-57 5463)

CAMPBELL, Lawrence Henry. b 41. TCD BA and Div Test (2nd cl) 63, MA 66. **d** 63 **p** 65 Connor. C of Larne (Inver) 63-66; Finaghy 66-67; Chap RN from 67. *c/o Ministry of Defence, Lacon House, Theobalds Road, WC1X 8RY.*

CAMPBELL, Milton Hope. St Jo Coll Auckld 51. NZ Bd of Th Stud LTh (2nd cl) 60. **d** 55 **p** 56 Auckld. C of Whangarei 55-56; Takapuna 56-58; V of Clevedon 58-64; Manurewa 64-78; One Tree Hill Dio Auckld from 78. *251 Campbell Road, Auckland 5, NZ.* (594-678)

CAMPBELL, Nelson James. b 10. AKC (2nd cl) 33. **d** 33 **p** 34 Leic. C of Wigston Magna 33-38; Croxley Green 38-43; H Trin Eltham 44-49; V of St Matt Vic Docks 49-52; Chap of Brentwood Mental Hosp 52-53; K Coll Hosp Denmark Hill 53-58; R of Tunapuna Trinid 58-67; V of Whitton 67-79; Perm to Offic Dio St E from 79. *21 Manderville Road, Bury St Edmunds, Suff.* (0284-62086)

CAMPBELL, Neville Russell. St Paul's Th Coll Grahmstn LTh 60. **d** 61 **p** 63 Johann. C of St Alb Johann 61-63; L to Offic Dio Johann 63-76; R of Turffontein 76-80; L to Offic Dio Johann from 80. *Box 281, Westonaria 1780, S Africa.*

CAMPBELL, Patrick Alistair. b 36. Qu Coll Birm 64. **d** 67 **p** 68 Pet. C of Paston 67-71; Stockton Heath 71-73; V of St John Egremont, Wallasey 73-78; Bredbury Dio Ches from 78. *Vicarage, George Lane, Bredbury, Stockport, SK6 1AT.* (061-430 2311)

CAMPBELL, Peter. LTh (S Afr) 58. St Paul's Th Coll Grahmstn 57. **d** 58 Bp Fisher for Grahmstn **p** 58 Grahmstn. C of St Hugh Port Eliz 59-60; R of St Pet E Lon 60-65; St Mich AA, Queenstn 65-74; R of Tarkastad 65-74; Archd of Queenstn 71-74; R of St Alb E Lon Dio Grahmstn from 74. *5 Durham Road, Vincent, East London, CP, S Africa.* (8-1441)

CAMPBELL, Peter Duncan Arthur. b 28. St Chad's Coll Dur BA 51, Dipl Th 53, MA 59. **d** 53 **p** 54 Guildf. C of Chobham 53-56; St Barn Hove 56-60; V of St Jo Evang Brighton 60-69; C-in-c of All S Brighton 64-67; V of Portslade 69-81; Willingdon Dio Chich from 81. *Vicarage, Church Street, Eastbourne, BN20 9HR.* (Eastbourne 52079)

CAMPBELL, Raoul John. d 63 **p** 64 Bend. P-in-c of Heathcote 63-67; R of H Trin Bend 67-77; Perm to Offic Dio Melb from 77. *14 Donald Street, Belmont, Vic, Australia 3126.* (43 1847)

CAMPBELL, Robert Dean. b 36. Univ of N Colorado BA 63. Nashotah Ho Wisconsin MDiv 66. **d** 66 Fond du Lac **p** 67 Utah. In Amer Ch 66-70; C of Invercargill 70-71; V of Maniototo 71-73; I of Fort Vermilion 73-80; Whitewood Dio Qu'App from 80. *Box 625, Whitewood, Sask, Canada.*

CAMPBELL, Robin William. b 41. Trin Coll Dub BA (2nd cl Hebr and Or Lang Mod) 63, MA 67. Ridley Hall Cam 63. **d** 65 Warrington for Liv **p** 66 Liv. C of St Osw Netherton 65-68; Our Lady and St Nich Liv 68-70; V of Hooton Dio Ches from 70. *Hooton Vicarage, Little Sutton, Wirral, Ches. L66 1QH.* (051-339 2020)

CAMPBELL, Roger Stewart. b 40. Univ of Birm BSc 61, PhD 65. St Jo Coll Dur BA (2nd cl Th) 71. Cranmer Hall Dur 68. **d** 71 **p** 72 Newc T. C of Clayton Mem Ch Jesmond 71-77; V of St John and St Marg City and Dio Sing from 78. *4 Wilton Close, Singapore 5.*

CAMPBELL, Canon Ronald Richmond Mitchell. d 50 **p** 51 Ja. C-in-c of Montpelier 50-52; C of St Mich Kingston (in c of Ch Ch) 52-58 and 59-62; Chap to WI Immigrants in Engl 58-59; R of Ch Ch Vineyard Tn Kingston Dio Ja from 62; Exam Chap to Bp of Ja from 76; Can of Ja from 77. *3 Saumarez Avenue, Vineyard Town, Kingston, Jamaica, W Indies.* (092-60668)

CAMPBELL, Walter John Fletcher. b 12. Magd Coll Ox BA 33, BSc 38, MA 44. Wells Th Coll 37. **d** 38 **p** 39 Portsm. C of St Mary Portsea 38-45; V of Sarisbury w Swanwick 45-47; St Jas Milton 47-60; RD of Portsm 55-60; Commiss Ugan 59-60; L to Offic Dio Lon from 60; Metrop Sec USPG for Lon and Chelmsf 60-66; Promotion and Tr Sec 66-68; Dep Home Sec 68-70; V of Stanton Harcourt w Northmoor 70-75; RD of Witney 71-76; Abingdon from 80; C-in-c of Bampton Proper w Lew 75-76; Bampton Aston w Shifford 75-76. *153 Upper Road, Kennington, Oxford.* (Ox 730467)

CAMPBELL, Canon William George. Trin Coll Tor BA 54, MA 57. Wycl Coll Tor LTh & BTh 57. Gen Syn Tor BD 73. **d** 57 **p** 58 Niag. C of St Geo Hamilton 57-59; R of Fergus 59-64; St Pet Hamilton 64-73; H Trin Prince Albert 73-81; Exam Chap to Bp of Sask 75-81; Hon Can of Sask from 77; I of Drumheller Dio Calg from 81. *Box 593, Drumheller, Alta, Canada.*

CAMPBELL-SMITH, Robert Campbell. b 38. CCC Cam BA 61, MA 66. Linc Th Coll 61. **d** 63 **p** 64 Cant. C of Norbury 63-66; St Mary of Nazareth W Wickham 66-71; V of St Aug Croydon 71-81; Goudhurst Dio Cant from 81. *Vicarage, Goudhurst, Kent, TN17 1AN.* (Goudhurst 211332)

CAMPEN, William Geoffrey. b 50. Univ of Southn BTh 81. Sarum Wells Th Coll 76. **d** 79 **p** 80 S'wark. C of St John Peckham Dio S'wark from 79. *10 Buller Close, SE15.*

CAMPION, Brian Haddon. Trin Coll Dub BA 47, MA 47. **d** 47 **p** 49 Connor. C of St Luke Belfast 47-51; I of Preban w Moyne 51-55; C of Taney 55-59; R of Gordon 59-60; St Mary York Co 60-64; Rothesay 65-72; Can of Ch Ch Cathl Fred 71-72; R of Trin Mem Ch City and Dio Montr from 72. *5220 Sherbrooke Street West, Montreal 260, PQ, Canada.* (514-484 3102)

CAMPION, Jasper Thomas. b 1896. Hertf Coll Ox BA 19, MA 21. Ridley Hall Cam 20. **d** 22 **p** 23 Win. C of St Andr Bournemouth 22-25; St Jas Pokesdown (in c of St Andr Boscombe) 25-29; V of St Andr Boscombe 29-47; R of Kingsworthy 47-52; Asst Chap O of St John of Jer from 46; Chap Blue Nile Prov 52-55; R of Teffont Ewyas w Teffont Magna and V of Dinton 56-59; Cler Sec Sarum Dioc Conf 57-64; R of Odstock w Nunton and Bodenham 59-64; C of Shirley Southn 64-66; Chap St John's Hosp Win 66-70. *19 St Cross Road, Winchester, Hants.* (Win 4130)

CAMPLING, Ven Christopher Russell. b 25. St Edm Hall Ox BA (2nd cl Th) 50, MA 54. Cudd Coll 50. **d** 51 **p** 52 Win. C of Basingstoke 51-55; Min Can of Ely Cathl and Chap K Sch Ely 55-60; Chap Lancing Coll 60-68; V of Pershore w Pinvin, Wick (and Birlingham from 75) 68-76; P-in-c of Birlingham w Nafford 68-75; RD of Pershore 70-76; M Gen Syn Hon Can of Worc Cathl from 74; Dir of Educn Dio Worc from 76; Archd of Dudley from 76; P-in-c of Dodderhill Dio Worc from 76. *Dodderhill Vicarage, Droitwich, Worcs, WR9 8LW.* (Droitwich 773301)

CAMPLING, Michael. b 27. Trin Coll Cam BA 50, MA 61. Wells Th Coll 51. **d** 53 **p** 54 Sarum. C of Calne 53-57; Roehampton 57-61; PC of Crowthorne 61-68; V 68-75; P-in-c of Foleshill D10 Cov 75-81; V from 81. *St Laurence's Vicarage, Old Church Road, Coventry, CV6 7ED.* (COV 88271)

CAMROUX, Frederick John. Moore Th Coll Syd ACT ThL 36. **d** 37 **p** 38 Syd. C of St Steph Willoughby 37-39; Chap AIF 40-46; R of Cronulla 46-72; RD of Sutherland 55-72; Can of Pro-Cathl St Mich Wollongong 69-73; L to Offic Dio Syd from 72. *31 Oatley Park Road, Oatley, NSW, Australia 2223.* (57-4768)

CANADA, Primate of the Anglican Church of. *See* Scott, Most Rev Edward Walter.

CANADA, Metropolitan of Province of. *See* Nutter, Most Rev Harold Lee.

CANBERRA and GOULBURN, Lord Bishop of. *See* Warren, Right Rev Cecil Allan.

CANBERRA and GOULBURN, Assistant Bishop of. *See* Dowling, Right Rev Owen Douglas.

CANDLER, David Cecil. Univ of Capetn BSc 47. Keble Coll Ox BA 50, MA 55. St Paul's Th Coll Grahmstn. **d** 56 **p** 57 Matab. C of Essexvale 57-58; Hd Master St Steph Coll Balla Balla 58-59; Sch Chap and P-in-c of Plumtree Dio Matab from 60. *Plumtree School, Plumtree, Zimbabwe.* (Plumtree 8)

CANDY, Canon Douglas Cleeve. Univ of Tor BA 38. Trin Coll Tor LTh 40. **d** 40 **p** 41 Tor. C of St Andr Centr I Tor 40-43; Chap CASE 43-45; Chap SCM UNiv of Tor 45-48; R of St Cypr Tor 48-57; I of Dixie S 57-81; Can of Tor from 77. *1624 Bloor Street East, Townhouse 43, Mississauga, Ont., Canada.* (416-278 1811)

CANE, Geoffrey Brett. McGill Univ BSc 70. Wycl Hall Ox. **d** 73 Queb **p** 80 Montr. Hon C of H Trin Queb 74-75; St Pet Mt Royal 75-77; on leave 77-80; C of St Pet Mt Royal 80-81; R of St Steph Chambly Dio Montr from 81. *1984 Bourgogne Street, Chambly, PQ, Canada J3L 1Z4.* (514-658 1362)

CANE, Harold Lee. b 06. Cranmer Hall Dur 61. **d** 62 Penrith for Carl **p** 63 Carl. C of Stanwix 62-65; V of Preston Patr 65-72; Perm to Offic Dio Carl 72-78. *70 Rusland Park, Kendal, Cumbria.* (Kendal 23900)

CANE, Peter Geoffrey. b 14. MC 44. Ridley Hall Cam 62. **d** 63 **p** 64 Nor. C of Gt Bircham and of Docking 63-65; V of Comberton 65-74; Hyde Hants Dio Win from 74. *Hyde Vicarage, Fordingbridge, Hants, SP6 2QH.* (Fordingbridge 53216)

CANE, Reginald Albert. b 12. Lich Th Coll 60. **d** 61 Sheff **p** 62 Bp Gerrard for Sheff. C of Goole 61-63; C-in-c of Hensall w Heck 63-67; V of Shrewton w Maddington and Rollestone 67-72; V of Winterbourne Stoke 67-72; Aldbrough w Colden Parva 72-75; Team V of Thirsk 75-76; Perm to Offic Dio Truro from 77. *14 Trelawney Avenue, Poughill, Bude, Cornw, EX23 9HB.*

CANEY, Robert Swinbank. b 37. St Jo Coll Cam 57. Lich Th Coll 58. **d** 61 **p** 62 Lich. C of Kingswinford 61-64; Castlechurch 64-67; V of Bradwell 67-73; Fairfield Dio Derby from 73; RD of Buxton from 78; P-in-c of Wormhill w Peak Dale Dio Derby from 79. *Fairfield Vicarage, Buxton, Derbys.* (Buxton 3629)

CANHAM, John Graham. b 33. St D Coll Lamp BA 55. Chich Th Coll 55. **d** 57 **p** 58 St A. C of Hawarden 57-64; Asst Chap Ellesmere Coll 64-66; Chap Cho of Ches Cathl from 66; Chap and Asst Master Ches Cathl Choir Sch and Perm to Offic Dio Ches 66-73; Asst Chap of Rossall Sch Fleetwood 73-76; Chap from 76; L to Offic Dio Blackb from 73. *c/o Naworth, Rossall School, Fleetwood, Lancs.* (03917-2739)

CANHAM, John Rowland Brindley. St Steph Ho Ox 56. **d** 58 Lich **p** 59 Stafford for Lich. C of Horninglow 58-60; St Aid Burton-on-Trent 60-61; R of Whitwood Mere 61-67; V of Raunds Dio Pet from 67. *Raunds Vicarage, Wellingborough, Northants.* (Raunds 2082)

CANHAM, Philip Edward. b 15. Univ of Man. St Aid Coll 46. **d** 46 **p** 47 Man. C of St Paul Bury 46-49; Miss Ranchi Dio Chota N 49-52; C-in-c of St Herbert Distr Carl 52-56; R of Clayhidon 56-58; P-in-c of Rosyth 58-60; Inverkeithing 58-60; R of Aikton 60-65; V of Dalston w Cumdivock 65-70; Irthington 70-75; P-in-c of Edenhall w Langwathby and Culgaith 75-79; Addingham 75-79; Greenhead 79-81; Lambley 79-81. *The Hillus, Newcastleton, Roxburgh, TD9 0TE.*

CANHAM, Robert Edwin Francis. b 24. FRCO 59. **d** 74 **p** 75 Truro (APM). Hon C of Newlyn 74-75; C of Phillack w St Gwithian and Gwinear Dio Truro 75-79; P-in-c from 79. *Rectory, Phillack, Hayle, TR27 5AW.* (Hayle 753541)

CANHAM, William Alexander. b 26. Clare Coll Cam BA 47, MA 56. Roch Th Coll 65. **d** 67 **p** 68 Roch. C of St Andr Orpington 67-70; St Steph Guernsey 70-75; Hon Chap Eliz Coll Guernsey 72-75; R of Tadley Dio Win from 75. *Rectory, The Green, Tadley, Basingstoke, Hants, RG26 6PB.* (Tadley 4860)

CANN, Arthur. b 01. Worc Ordin Coll 56. **d** 57 **p** 58 Birm. C of Sparkhill 57-58; Yardley (in c of Lea Hall) 58-62; V of

Stoke Prior 62-70. *16 Helmeth Road, Church Stretton, Salop, SY6 7AS.*

CANN, Stanley George. b 16. St Bonif Coll. **d** 43 **p** 44 Cov. C of St Alb Stoke Heath 43-45; UMCA Miss Dio Nyasa 45-52; Dio SW Tang 52-62; P-in-c of Milo 46-48; Manda 49-52; Mbeya 52-62; UMCA Area Sec SE Engl 63-64; USPG Area Sec Dio Chich 65-66; V of All SS Sidley Bexhill Dio Chich from 66; RD of Battle and Bexhill from 77. *Sidley Vicarage, Bexhill-on-Sea, Sussex, TN39 5HA.* (Bexhill 211426)

CANN, Tom. b 1898. **d** 30 **p** 32 Keew. C of Eagle River w Minnitaki 30-32; I 32-34; I of Ignace 34-38; Nipigon 38-43; R of St Geo w St Steph Port Arthur 43-50; RCN Chap *Vindictive* 43-48; PC of Llanveyno w Crasswall 50-56; V of Yarkhill w Weston Beggard 56-64; Perm to Offic Dio Ex 64-70 and 75-76. *37 Devon Square, Newton Abbot, Devon.*

✠ **CANNAN, Right Rev Edward Alexander Capparis.** b 20. K Coll Lon and Warm AKC 49, BD 49. **d** 50 **p** 51 Sarum. C of Blandford Forum 50-53; Chap RAF 53-74; Vice-Prin RAF Chaps' Sch 66-69; Prin 73-74; Asst Chap-in-Chief 69-74; Hon Chap to HM the Queen 71-74; Chap St Marg Sch Bushey 74-79; Cons Ld Bp of St Helena in St Geo Cathl Capetn 14 Oct 79 by Abp of Capetn; Bps of Port Eliz, Geo, Natal, Johann, Grahmstn and Lesotho; Bps Suffr of Capetn; and Bps Stradling, Burron and Nye. *Bishopholme, Island of St Helena, S Atlantic Ocean.*

CANNELL, Philip Gatley Floyd. b 37. Qu Coll Birm 78. **d** 81 Lich (APM). C of St Mich AA Colwich Dio Lich from 81. *Beaumont, Penn Croft, Little Haywood, Stafford, ST18 0UY.*

CANNER, Canon Arthur Cuthbert. b 10. Keble Coll Ox BA 33, MA 38. Ely Th Coll 34. **d** 34 **p** 35 Lon. C of Potters Bar 34-35; St Matt Westmr 35-37; Bodmin 37-41; Tintagel 41-45; PC of Pencoys 45-50; Carnmenellis 45-50; V of Tintagel 50-76; RD of Trigg Minor 55-59; Hon Can of Truro 70-76; Can (Emer) from 76. *3 Daw's Meadow, Camelford, Cornw.*

CANNER, Canon Peter George. b 24. St Chad's Coll Dur BA 49, Dipl Th 51, MA 55. **d** 51 **p** 52 Cov. C of Stoke St Mich Cov 51-53; R of Piet Retief 53-56; Eshowe 56-63; Can of Eshowe Pro-Cathl Zulu 62-63; V of Tynemouth 63-77; Ponteland Dio Newc T from 77; Hon Can of Newc T from 80. *Vicarage, Ponteland, Newcastle upon Tyne, NE20 9PZ.* (Ponteland 22140)

CANNING, Arthur Brian. b 12. Late Scho of St Jo Coll Dur BA 37, MA 40. **d** 37 **p** 38 Dur. C of St Cuthb Darlington 37-42; V of Sellack w King's Capel 42-50; Lugwardine w Bartestree 50-66; Dom Chap to Bp of Heref 54-65; V of New Romney w Hope and St Mary's Bay 66-71; Boughton Monchelsea 71-79. *Harp Cottage, Old Radnor, Presteigne, Powys, LD8 2RH.*

CANNING, Arthur James. b 45. St Jo Coll Dur BA 66. Linacre Coll Ox BA (Th) 70, MA 74. Ripon Hall Ox 67. **d** 71 Aston for Birm **p** 72 Birm. C of St Pet and St Paul Coleshill 71-74; Frome Selwood 74-76; V of Frizington W Arlecdon 76-80; P-in-c of St Paul Foleshill Dio Cov 80-81; V from 81. *Vicarage, St Paul's Road, Coventry, CV6 5DE.* (Cov 88283)

CANNING, Graham Gordon Blakeman. b 33. SOC 73. **d** 76 Edmon for Lon **p** 77 Lon. C of John Keble Ch Mill Hill 76-78; Team V of Dorch Dio Ox from 78. *Vicarage, The Green, Warborough, Oxford, OX9 8DW.* (Warborough 8381)

CANNING, John Graham. b 21. Edin Th Coll 47. **d** 49 **p** 50 Lon. C of St Silas Pentonville 49-54; Ch Ch Poplar 54-55; R of Chingola 55-62; V of St Jo Evang Hammersmith Dio Lon from 62. *St John's Vicarage, Iffley Road, W6 OLS.* (01-748 3928)

CANNING, Richard Dandridge. St Chad's Coll Dur BA 41, Dipl in Th 42, MA 44. **d** 42 Ripon **p** 43 Knaresborough for Ripon. C of St Wilfrid Halton 4-46; St Geo Basseterre St Kitts 46-48; P-in-c of St Paul St Kitts 48-52; Anguilla 52-59; St Bart 55-59; St Martin 52-59; St Geo Antig 59-68; R of St Mary, St Kitts 68-76; Can of Antig 64-76; R of St John w St Mark Grenada 76-81. *c/o St John's Rectory, Grenada, W Indies.* (8212)

CANNING, Robert Kingswood. b 03. St Bonif Coll Warm 51. **d** 52 **p** 53 Worc. C of Kidderminster 52-55; R of Bredenbury w Grendon Bp and Wacton 55-65; C-in-c of Docklow 57-60; V 60-65; Marden 65-72; Perm to Offic Dio C & Goulb from 81. *6 Flower Place, Melba, ACT, Australia 2615.*

CANNON, Alan George. b 35. Univ of Lon BA 57, MA 63, PhD 71. Sarum Wells Th Coll 76. **d** 80 **p** 81 Ex. Hon C of Whipton Dio Ex from 80. *6 Devonshire Place, Exeter, Devon.*

CANSDALE, George Graham. b 38. Mert Coll Ox BA (Th) 60, MA 64. Clifton Th Coll 62. **d** 64 **p** 65 Sarum. C of St Jo Evang Heatherlands Parkstone 64-67; W Pokot 68-70; Warden Ch Tr Centre Kapsabet Dio Nak 70-71; Perm to Offic Dio Nak 71-76; Tutor St Pauls Th Coll Limuru 71-75; P-in-c of Clapham Dio St Alb 76-80; V from 80. *Vicarage, Clapham, Bedford, MK41 6ER.* (Bedford 52814)

CANT, Canon Reginald Edward. b 14. Late Scho of CCC Cam 1st cl Hist Trip pt i 34, BA 35, 1st cl Th Trip pt i 36, MA 39. Cudd Coll 37. **d** 38 **p** 39 Portsm. C of St Mary Portsea 38-41; Vice-Prin of Edin Th Coll 41-46; Exam Chap to Bp of Glas and Gall 44-72; to Abp of York from 57; to Bp of Arg Is from 78; Lect in Th Univ of Dur 46-49; Vice-Prin St Chad's Coll Dur 49-52; V of St Mary L Cam 52-57; Select Pr Univ of Cam 55 and 64; Can and Chan of York Minster 57-81; Can (Emer) from 81; Commiss Kimb K 61-65; Nass 62-81. *7 Sykes Close, St Olave's Road, York, YO3 6HZ.*

CANTERBURY, Lord Archbishop of, Primate of All England, and Metropolitan. *See* Runcie, Most Rev and Right Hon Robert Alexander Kennedy,

CANTERBURY, Assistant Bishop in Diocese of. *See* Warner, Right Rev Kenneth Charles Harman.

CANTERBURY, Archdeacon of. *See* Simpson, Ven John Arthur.

CANTERBURY, Dean of. *See* De Waal, Very Rev Victor Alexander.

CAPE, Edward Arthur Munro. b 04. Fitzw Ho Cam BA 25, MA 29. St Mich Th Coll Llan 25. **d** 27 **p** 28 Llan. C of St John Canton 27-31; Trevethin 31-36; V of Avan Vale 36-54; Margam 54-73; Perm to Offic Dio Llan from 73. *23 Spoonbill Close, Rest Bay, Porthcawl, Mid Glam.*

CAPE, Peter Irwin. Univ of NZ BA 50. Selw Coll Dun 52. **d** 53 Ch Ch for Kalg **p** 54 Kalg. Perm to Offic Dio Dun 52-55; Dir Relig Broadcasts NZ Broadcasting Corp 59-63; Hon C of Trentham 56-62; Producer NZBC Television 63-66; L to Offic Dio Wel 64-70; Hon C of Stokes Valley Dio Wel from 70. *c/o Diocesan Office, Box 12046, Wellington, NZ.*

CAPE COAST, Lord Bishop of. *See* Ackon, Right Rev John Alexander.

CAPE TOWN, Lord Archbishop of, and Metropolitan of Province of South Africa. *See* Russell, Most Rev Philip Welsford Richmond.

CAPE TOWN, Bishops Suffragan of. *See* Swartz, Right Rev George Alfred; and Matolengwe, Right Rev Patrick Monwabisi.

CAPE TOWN, Dean of. *See* King, Very Rev Edward Laurie.

CAPELL, Canon Arthur. Univ of Syd BA 22, MA 31. Univ of Lon PhD 38. **d** 25 **p** 26 Newc. C of St Pet Hamilton 26-28; P-in-c of Belmont 28-29; Asst Master Broughton Sch for Boys Newc 29-32; C of Taree 32; Morpeth 32-35; on leave 36-39; Perm to Offic Dio Syd 40-42; C-in-c of St Paul Cant 42-45; Reader in Oceanic Langs at Syd Univ 45-67; LPr Dio Syd from 45; Hon Can of New Guinea 56-71; Papua from 71. *5-276 Pacific Highway, Lindfield, NSW, Australia 2070.* (46-2157)

CAPENER, Herbert Francis. Jes Coll Ox BA 53, MA 58. Cudd Coll 53. **d** 55 **p** 56 Lon. C of St Aug Highgate 55-60; Ashford Kent 60-63; V of St Geo Shirley Dio 63-70; V of St Pet Folkestone Dio Cant from 70. *St Peter's Vicarage, Folkestone, Kent.* (Folkestone 54472)

CAPES, Arthur Geoffrey. b 33. Bps' Coll Cheshunt 58. **d** 61 **p** 62 Ripon. C of Seacroft 61-66; St Geo Cathl Georgetn Dio Guy 66-68; Prec 68-80; V of H Angels Claremont, Pendleton Dio Man from 80. *Vicarage, Moorfield Road, Salford, Gtr Man, M6 7EY.*

CAPES, Dennis Robert. b 34. **d** 64 **p** 65 Linc. [f Methodist Min] C of L Coates 64-66; R of Miri 66-69; V of Gosberton Clough 69-71; V of Kirton-in-Holland 71-80; Area Sec USPG Dios Cov, Heref and Worc from 80. *70 Kidderminster Road, Bromsgrove, Wrcs, B61 7LD.*

CAPEY, Richard Cyril Neil. b 28. K Coll Lon and Warm AKC 52. **d** 53 **p** 54 Man. C of Littleborough 53-55; Davenham 55-58; Warden Farm of Good Shepherd 55-58; V of St Jas Sutton 58-63; Dioc Youth Chap Dio York 63-72; V of Cawood 72-81; Unsworth Dio Man from 81. *Unsworth Vicarage, Bury, Lancs, BL9 8JJ.* (061-766 2429)

CAPIE, Fergus Bernard. b 49. Univ of Auckld BA 68, MA 71. Wycl Hall Ox BA 77. **d** 77 **p** 78 Ox. C of St Mich Ox 77-80; Chap Summer Fields Sch Ox from 80. *c/o Summer Fields School, Oxford.*

CAPON, Canon Anthony Charles. Trin Coll Cam 1st cl Mod Lang Trip pt i 49, BA (1st cl Mod Lang Trip pt ii) 51, MA 55. Wycl Coll Tor BD 65. Oak Hill Th Coll 51. **d** 53 **p** 54 Willesden for Lon. C of St Paul Portman Square Lon 53-56; on staff of CSSM and Script U Dio Tor 56-75; Dir of Development Wycl Coll Tor 75-78; Hon C of St Pet Tor 56-78; Prin Montr Dioc Th Coll from 78; Hon Can of Montr from 78. *3473 University Street, Montreal, Quebec, Canada.* (514-849 3004)

CAPON, Martin Gedge. b 09. Late Scho of Magd Coll Cam 1st cl Cl Trip pt i, 30, BA (2nd cl Hist Trip pt ii) 31, MA 36. Wycl Hall Ox 34. **d** 35 Lon for Col Bp **p** 36 Crediton for Ex. C of St Leon Ex 35-36; CMS Miss Dio Momb from 36

(Kahuhia Sch 36-38); Exam Chap to Bp of Momb 37-64; to Bp of Nai 64-68; Prin of Div Sch Limuru 38-46; Can of Momb 49-64; Nai 64-68; Chap and Asst Master Prince of Wales Sch Nai 52-65; Vice-Prin 65-66; Chap and Tutor Kenyatta Coll Nai 67-68; C of Sparkhill 68-70; V of Breage w Germoe 70-74; Perm to Offic Dio Ex from 74. *Crossways, Diptford, Totnes, Devon, TQ9 7NZ.* (Gara Bridge 337)

✠ **CAPPER, Right Rev Edmund Michael Hubert.** b 08. OBE 61. Univ of Dur LTh 32. St Aug Coll Cant 28. **d** 32 **p** 33 Roch. C of St Mary Strood 32-36; UMCA Miss Dio Masasi 36-38; P-in-c of Mindu 38-42; TCF (E Afr) 42-46; Hon CF 46; P-in-c Lindi 46-47; Archd and P-in-c of Lindi 48-54; Can of Masasi 49-54; Zanz 54-62; Archd and R of Dar-es-Salaam 54-57; Provost of Colleg Ch of St Alb Dar-es-Salaam 58-62; Chap at Palma 62-67; Cons Ld Bp of St Helena in St Geo Cathl Capetn 13 Aug 67 by Abp of Capetn; Bps of Natal; Johann; Damar; Bloemf and Bp Suffr of Capetn; res 73; Asst Bp of Gibr (Gibr in Eur from 80) from 73; S'wark from 81; Chap at Malaga 73-76. *Morden College, Blackheath, SE3 0PW.* (01-858 9169)

CAPPER, Ian Parode. b 05. Sarum Th Coll. **d** 47 Dover for Cant **p** 48 Cant. C of All SS Maidstone 47-51; V of St Martin Maidstone 51-60; V of St Mark S Norwood 60-71; R of High Halden 71-75. *26 Swalecliffe Road, Tankerton, Whitstable, Kent.* (Whitstable 272800)

CAPPER, Canon James Frank. b 18. Late Scho of Qu Coll Ox BA (1st cl Physics) 40, MA 44, 2nd cl Th 47. Westcott Ho Cam 48. **d** 48 **p** 49 Birm. C of Selly Oak 48-52; Keighley (in c of St Mark) 52-54; C-in-c of St Columba Eccles Distr Sutton Coldfield 54-60; PC 60-64; V of Erdington 64-75; Surr from 65; V of Coleshill Dio Birm from 75; Maxstoke Dio Birm from 75; RD of Coleshill from 77; Hon Can of Birm Cathl from 80. *Coleshill Vicarage, Birmingham.* (Coleshill 62188)

CAPPER, John Raymond. b 29. Univ of Liv BA (2nd cl Hist) 53. Coll of Resurr Mirfield 53. **d** 55 **p** 56 Birm. C of St Aid Small Heath 55-58; Wymering 60-63; St Sav Portsea 63-68; V of H Trin Gosport Dio Portsm from 68. *Vicarage, Trinity Green, Gosport, Hants.* (Gosport 80173)

CAPPER, Michael Arthur. b 21. **d** 70 Bp Wilkinson for Niag. C of St Jas Dundas Dio Niag from 70. *20 Lynndale Drive, Dundas, Ont, Canada.*

CAPPER, Richard. b 49. Univ of Leeds BSc 70. Fitzw Coll Cam 3rd cl Th Trip pt ii BA 72. Westcott Ho Cam 70. **d** 73 Warrington for Liv **p** 74 Liv. C of Wavertree 73-76; P-in-c of St Mary Ince-in-Makerfield Dio Liv 76-79; V from 79. *St Mary's Vicarage, Warrington Road, Ince, Wigan, Lancs.* (Wigan 43176)

CAPPER, Robert Melville. b 52. Churchill Coll Cam BA 74. Wycl Coll Ox 74. **d** 77 **p** 78 Mon. C of Maindee 77-80; Team V of Abth Dio St D from 80. *Vicarage, Buarth Road, Aberystwyth, Dyfed.* (Abth 617125)

CAPRON, David Cooper. b 45. Sarum Wells Th Coll 71. **d** 75 Bp Parker for Cov **p** 76 Bp McKie for Cov. C of St Mary Magd Cov 75-79; Team V of Stratford-on-Avon Dio Cov from 79. *210 Evesham Road, Stratford-on-Avon, Warws.* (Stratford 3381)

CAPRON, James Septimus. b 1891. Linc Th Coll 38. **d** 38 Grimsby for Linc **p** 39 Linc. C of Waltham 38-40; PC of Barlings w Langworth 40-44; V of Stainton-by-Langworth w Newball and Reasby 40-44; Barnetby-le-Wold 44-54; Wellingore w Temple Bruer 54-59; Chap HM Pris Wellingore 55; V of Stainton by Langworth w Newball Colstead and Reasby 59-61; PC of Barlings w Langworth 59-61; LPr Dio Linc from 63. *St Hugh's, Great Coates Road, Healing, Grimsby, Lincs.*

CAPRON, Ronald Beresford. b 35. Clifton Th Coll. **d** 62 Leic for Lon for Arctic **p** 63 Arctic. C of St Andr Miss Coppermine 62-63; Holman Is 63-65; Evington 65-67; R of S Croton w Gaddesby 67-71; V of Beeby 67-71; Chap RAF from 71. *c/o Ministry of Defence, Adastral House, WC 1.*

CAPRON, Canon Ronald Shukburgh. b 1900. Trin Coll Cam BA (2nd cl Hist Trip) 21, MA 27. Westcott Ho Cam 31. **d** 32 **p** 33 Newc T. C of Ch Ch Tynemouth (in c of St Faith's Miss N Shields) 32-34; PC of Shaw Hill 34-35; V 35-41; V of St Barn Balsall Heath 41-45; St Jo Evang Perry Barr 45-50; Hon Chap to Bp of Birm 44-50; RD of Handsworth 46-50; Hon Can of Birm 47-50; Can (Emer) from 50; Lect St Steph Coll Delhi 50-55; V of Blakesley w Adstone 56-70; L to Offic Dio Pet 71-79. *Mandall House, Minster Precincts, Peterborough, PE1 1XX.* (Pet'boro 61807)

CAPSTICK, John Nowell. b 30. K Coll Lon and Warm AKC 54. **d** 55 **p** 56 Bradf. C of Ch Ch Skipton 55-57; Buxton 57-61; V of Codnor 61-63; C-in-c of St Jas Conv Distr Rawthorpe Huddersfield Dio Wakef 63-64; V 64-70; V of Netherthong Dio Wakef from 70. *Netherthong Vicarage, Huddersfield, Yorks.* (Holmfirth 2430)

CAPSTICK, William Richard Dacre. b 32. Pemb Coll Ox. Chich Th Coll 61. **d** 64 **p** 65 Ripon. C of Hunslet w Stourton 64-67; Knaresborough 67-71; V of Stratfield-Mortimer 71-76; P-in-c of Ch Ch w St Paul St Marylebone 76-78; Team V of Ch Ch St Marylebone 78-79; Team R of Newbury Dio Ox from 79. *Rectory, Northcroft Lane, Newbury, Berks, RG13 1BN.* (Newbury 40326)

CARADUS, Selwyn Ross. b 45. Univ of Auckld MSc 58. Univ of S Calif MA 62. Univ of Calif LA PhD 65. Qu Th Coll Kingston Ont MTS 80. **d** 79 **p** 80 Ont. Angl Chap Qu Univ Kingston Dio Ont from 79. *148 Earl Street, Kingston, Ont, Canada, K7L 2H2.* (613-544 6437)

CARBERRY, Robin Linton. b 28. Chich Th Coll 51. **d** 53 **p** 54 Pet. C of St Mich AA Northampton 53-57; St Jo Bapt Pet 57-58; Kibworth Beauchamp 58-61; Cler Org Sec CECS and Perm to Offic Dios Blackb Carl and Man 61-65; Bradf 62-65; R of St Mary Bishophill Sen w St Clem City and Dio York from 65. *13 Nunthorpe Avenue, Scarcroft Road, York.* (24425)

CARBUTT, George Maurice. b 06. M OSP 25-69. **d** 44 **p** 45 Win. C of All SS Alton 44-48; L to Offic Dio Win 49-69; Perm to Offic Dio Wakef from 71. *865 Bradford Road, Batley, W Yorks, WF17 8NN.*

CARD, Terence Leslie. b 37. K Coll Lon and Warm BD (2nd Cl) and AKC 68. **d** 69 Colchester for Chelmsf **p** 70 Chelmsf. C of Thundersley 69-72; Chap of Scargill Ho Skipton Yorks 72-75; L to Offic Dio Bradf 72-75; V of St Anne Chingford 75-81; RD of Waltham Forest 78-81; R of All SS Springfield Dio Chelmsf from 81. *Rectory, Mulberry Way, Springfield, Chelmsford, Essex.* (Chelmsford 356720)

CARDALE, Arthur Mudge. b 17. Westcott Ho Cam 62. **d** 63 **p** 64 Guildf. C of Thames Ditton 63-67; R of Abinger w Coldharbour Dio Guildf from 67. *Rectory, Abinger Common, Dorking, Surrey.* (Dorking 730746)

CARDALE, Charles Anthony. St D Coll Lamp BA 47. Lich Th Coll 55. **d** 56 **p** 57 Ex. C of Honicknowle Conv Distr 56-58; Bideford 58-60; R of Wembworthy w Eggesford 60-69; V of Brushford 63-69; Staverton w Landscove Dio Ex from 69. *Staverton Vicarage, Totnes, Devon, TQ9 6NZ.* (Staverton 277)

CARDALE, Edward Charles. b 50. CCC Ox BA (Th) 72. U Th Sem NY STM 74. Cudd Coll 72. **d** 74 **p** 75 S'wark. C of St Jo Evang E Dulwich 74-77; in Amer Ch 77-80; V of Ponders End Dio Lon from 80. *Vicarage, Church Road, Ponders End, Middx, EN3 4NT.* (01-804 1192)

CARDELL-OLIVER, Ivan Alexander. Jes Coll Cam BA (2nd cl Hist Trip pt i and 3rd cl Law Trip pt ii) 33, LLB 35, MA 37. **d** and **p** 41 Perth. C of St Luke Cottesloe 41-42; R of Bridgetown 42-45; Chap of Guildf Gr Sch Perth 45-50 and 52-54; Chap Trin Coll Glenalmond Dio Dunk 50-52; C of Eastbourne (in c of St Geo) 54-55; Chap at Copenhagen 55-62; RD of Scandinavia 60-62; R of Chalfont St Giles 62-68; Asst Master Canberra Gr Sch 68-78; Chap 69-78; L to Offic Dio C and Goulb 68-78; Perm to Offic Dio Ox 78; Dio C & Goulb from 78. *Dominion Circuit, Deakin, ACT, Australia 2600.*

CARDEN, John Brumfitt. b 24. Lon Coll of Div 48. **d** 52 Liv for York for Lah **p** 53 Lah. Chap at Murree 52-53; U Chr Hosp Lah 53-55; St John Peshawar 55; C of Halton Dio Ripon 56-57; V of St John Peshawar 57-60; CMS Lit Sec 60-65; Regional Sec Lah and Dacca 65-69; Asia Sec from 70; Hon C of St Sav Croydon 75-76; C-in-c of St Steph Bath Dio B & W from 76. *St Stephen's Vicarage, Lansdown, Bath, Avon.* (Bath 317535)

CARDER, Raymond James. Univ of Tor BA 57. Wycl Coll Tor BTh 60. **d** 60 **p** 61 Tor. C of St Jas Kingston 60-62; R of Haliburton 62-69; St John Whitby 69-79; Erindale Dio Tor from 79. *2523 Vineland Road, Mississauga, Ont, Canada.*

CARDEW, Paul Seton. b 47. TCD BA 69, Div Test 70. **d** 70 **p** 71 Dub. C of Rathfarnham 70-74; I of Clane w Donadea 75-79; Perm to Offic Dio Glouc from 80. *Thrift Cottage, High Street, South Cerney, Cirencester, Glos.*

CARDIGAN, Archdeacon of. *See* Jones, Ven John Samuel.

CARDNO, James Alexander. b 15. Univ of Aber MA 38. **d** and **p** 73 Tas. C of Lindisfarne Dio Tas from 73. *29 Derwent Avenue, Lindisfarne, Tasmania 7015.* (002-43 9268)

CARDWELL, Albert. b 04. Linc Th Coll 66. **d** 67 **p** 68 Linc. C of Flixborough w Burton-on-Stather 67-70; St Lawr Frodingham 70-73; Hon C 73-76; Perm to Offic Dio Linc from 77. *31 Brumby Wood Lane, Scunthorpe, S Humb, DN17 1AA.* (Scunthorpe 61676)

CARDWELL, Edward Anthony Colin. b 42. Trin Coll Cam BA 63, MA 68. St Jo Coll Nottm 73. **d** 75 Repton for Derby **p** 76 Derby. C of Stapenhill 75-78; Bramcote 78-81; V of H Trin Southw Dio Southw from 81. *Holy Trinity Vicarage, Southwell, Notts, NG25 0NB.* (Southwell 813243)

CARDWELL, Joseph Robin. b 47. Qu Coll Cam BA 68, MA 77. Trin Coll Bris 73. **d** 76 **p** 77 Roch. C of Ch Ch Bromley 76-79; Shirley Dio Win from 79. *18 Twyford Avenue, Shirley, Southampton, SO1 5NP.* (Southn 773994)

CARDWELL, Kenneth John. McMaster Univ BA 65. Hur Coll BTh 68. **d** 68 Niag **p** 68 Bp M E Coleman for Niag. C of

Ascen Hamilton 68-70; R of Erin 70-72; C of St Alb Cathl Kenora 72-75; R of Mt Forest w Harriston 75-80; Dom Chap to Bp of Niag 79-80. *124 Fergus Street North, Mount Forest, Ont, Canada.* (519-323 1063)

CARDY, Roy Thomas. b 23. **d** 79 **p** 80 Athab. P-in-c of St Bart Grimshaw Dio Athab from 79. *PO Box 557, Grimshaw, Alta, Canada, T0H 1W0.*

CARE, Charles Richard. Late Scho of St D Coll Lamp BA 42. St Mich Th Coll 42. **d** 44 **p** 45 Llan. C of St Paul Cardiff 44-57; R of St Bride's Minor Dio Llan from 57; RD of Bridgend from 76. *St Bride's Minor Rectory, Aberkenfig, Mid-Glam, CF32 9RH.* (Aberkenfig 720274)

CARE, Stephen. St Mich Coll Llan 67. **d** 69 Ex **p** 70 Ex. C of Churston Ferrers 69-70; Ashburton 70-72; Paignton 72-75; C-in-c of Whitleigh 75-76. *Address temp unknown.*

CAREFULL, Alan Vincent. b 24. Late Exhib of Magd Coll Ox BA 50, Dipl Th 51, MA 60. St Steph Ho Ox 49. **d** 52 **p** 53 Man. C of Tonge Moor 52-56; Tue Brook 56-60; Vice-Prin of St Steph Ho Ox 60-65; V of St Jo Bapt Newc T 65-73; L to Offic Dio Nor 73; C-in-c of N W and E Barsham 73-80; Admin of Shrine of Our Lady of Walsingham 73-81. *30 Park Lane, Helhoughton, Fakenham, Norfolk, NR21 7BE.* (E Rudham 680)

CAREW, Bryan Andrew. b 38. AIB 63. St D Coll Lamp Dipl Th 69. **d** 67 **p** 68 St D. C of Pemb Dk 67-70; CF 70-74; P-in-c of Gt Henny w L Henny and Middleton (and Wickham St Paul w Twinstead from 75) Dio Chelmsf 74-76; R from 76. *Great Henny Rectory, Sudbury, Suff.* (Twinstead 336)

CAREY, Charles John. b 29. K Coll Lon AKC and BD 53. St Aug Coll Cant 71. **d** 72 **p** 73 Cant. C of All SS Spring Park Croydon 72-74; Ifield Chich 74-78; St Jo Evang Burgess Hill 78-80; Chap Oldchurch & Rush Green Hosps from 80. *121 Suttons Lane, Hornchurch, Essex, RM12 4LZ.*

CAREY, Christopher Lawrence John. Univ of St Andr BSc (Botany) 61. BD (Lon) 64. Clifton Th Coll 61. **d** 64 **p** 65 S'wark. C of St Sav Battersea Pk 64-67; CMS Miss Kenya from 68; P-in-c of Ukia 68-73; Warden Trin Coll Nai from 73; Exam Chap to Abp of Nai from 73; CMS Reg Sec for Kenya, Uganda and Zaire from 79. *PO Box 40360, Nairobi, Kenya.* (Nairobi 558655)

CAREY, Edward Vincent. Univ of Capetn BSc 60. St Paul's Coll Grahmstn. **d** 63 Capetn **p** 64 Bp Cowdry for Capetn. C of Stellenbosch 63-64; Bellville 64-67; Asst Chap Miss to Seamen Capetn 67-69; L to Offic Dio Capetn 69-75; Dio Grahmstn from 75. *3 Tranmere Road, Vincent, East London, CP, S Africa.*

CAREY, George Leonard. b 35. ALCD (1st cl) 61. BD (Lon) 62, MTh (Lon) 65; PhD (Lon) 71. **d** 62 **p** 63 Lon. C of Islington 62-66; Lect Oak Hill Th Coll 66-70; Lect St Jo Coll Nottm 70-75; V of St Nich Dur 75-82; Chap HM Remand Centre Low Newton 77-81; Prin Trin Th Coll Bris from 82. *Trinity College, Stoke Hill, Bristol, BS9 1JP.* (Bris 684472)

CAREY, Graham Charles. b 33. Kelham Th Coll 53. **d** 57 **p** 58 Dur. C of St Mary Magd Millfield Bp Wearmouth 57-66; V of St Mich AA Northfield 66-76; Team V of Jarrow Dio Dur from 76. *56 Salem Street, Jarrow, T & W, NE32 3AG.* (Jarrow 897071)

CAREY, Very Rev James Maurice George. b 26. TCD BA (2nd cl Mod) 49. Downes Pri (2nd) 50, (1st) 51, Abp King's Div Pri 50. Div Test (1st cl) 51, Th Exhib (1st cl) MA and BD 52. **d** 52 Kilm for Connor **p** 53 Connor. C of Larne w Inver 52-55; Ecumenical Fell of U Th Sem NY 55-56; C of St Ann Dub 57-58; Hon Cler V of Ch Ch Cathl Dub 58; Dean of Residences QUB 58-64; I of St Bart Dub 64-71; S Fin Barre's Cathl (w St Nich and H Trin to 75) Dio Cork from 71; Dean of Cork from 71; Exam Chap to Bp of Cork from 72. *9 Dean Street, Cork, Irish Republic.* (Cork 021-964742)

CAREY, Lennox Noel. Moore Coll Syd ThL 74. **d** 75 **p** 76 Brisb. C of St Steph Coorparoo Brisb 75-77; P-in-c of Par Distr of Mary Valley 77-80; Weipa Dio Carp from 80. *12 Hibiscus Avenue, Weipa, Australia 4874.*

CAREY, Leonard Allan. b 12. Men in Disp 46. FCII 38, Ridley Hall Cam 46. **d** 47 **p** 48 Nor. C of Gaywood 47-49; Min of St Mary and St Paul Conv Distr Hellesdon 49-55; V 55-56; Chap HM Pris Nor 50-56; Min of Nork Eccles Distr 56-59; V of Nork Park 59-77; Hon C of Cheam Dio S'wark from 78. *10 Cooke's Lane, Cheam Village, Surrey, SM3 8QG.* (01-641 4252)

CAREY, Michael Sausmarez. b 13. Keble Coll Ox 2nd cl Mod Hist 35, BA 36, MA 41. Selw Coll Cam MA 67 (by incorp). Cudd Coll 38. **d** 39 **p** 40 S'wark. C of St Jo Evang w All SS Waterloo Road 39-41; Chap Cudd Coll and Exam Chap to Bp of Ches 41-43; Miss at Kristi Kunda Basse Gambia 43-44; R of Hunsdon 45-51; Botley 51-62; Exam Chap to Bp of Portsm 54-62; to Bp of Ely from 64; RD of Bp's Waltham 55-62; Proc Conv Portsm 59-62; Hon Can of Portsm 60-62; Ely 68-70; Archd of Ely 62-70; R of St Botolph Cam 65-70; Dean of Ely 70-82. *23 Kingsway, Blakeney, Norf, NR25 7PL.* (Cley 740730)

CAREY, Canon Ronald Clive Adrian. b 21. Late Scho of K Coll Cam 1st cl Cl Trip pt i 41, BA 46 (2nd cl Th Trip pt ii) MA 48. Chich Th Coll 47. **d** 48 **p** 49 Birm. C of Harborne 48-50; Dom Chap to Bp of Chich 50-52; C of Keighley 52-55; V of Illingworth Halifax 55-59; Asst Relig Broadcasting Dept BBC 59-68; Perm to Offic Dio S'wark 59-68; V of Claygate 68-78; RD of Emly 72-77; Exam Chap to Bp of Guildf from 75; R of H Trin w St Mary City and Dio Guildf from 78; Hon Can of Guildf from 78. *Castle Gate, Guildford, Surrey, GU1 3SX.* (Guildf 575489)

CARHART, John Richards. b 29. Univ of Bris BA (2nd cl Geog) 50. Univ of Salford MSc 77. **d** 65 **p** 66 Ches. C of St Osw (in Ches Team from 72) Ches and Asst Lect Ches Coll of Educn 65-72; Prin Lect from 72; L to Offic Dio Ches from 73. *29 Abbot's Grange, Chester.* (Chester 25487)

CARIBOO, Lord Bishop of. *See* Snowden, Right Rev John Samuel Philip.

CARIBOO, Dean of. *See* Lee, Very Rev Patrick Vaughan.

CARLESS, Andrew Gordon Maxwell. b 35. Trin Hall Cam BA 56, MA 60, BChir 67, MB 68. Ridley Hall Cam 59. **d** and **p** 61 Bradf. C of Keighley 61-63; Perm to Offic Dio Ely 63. *124 Pennsylvania Road, Exeter, EX4 6DW.*

CARLESS, Frank. b 22. Univ of Lon BD 56. St Aid Coll 53. **d** 56 **p** 57 Wakef. C of Normanton 56-59; V of Rashcliffe 59-64; Warley Dio Wakef from 64; RD of Halifax from 81. *455 Burnley Road, Halifax, W Yorks, HX2 7LW.* (Halifax 63623)

CARLETTI, Giacomo Giuseppe. LTh (S Afr) 58. St Paul's Th Coll Grahmstn 55. **d** 57 **p** 58 Grahmstn. C of Vincent 57-60; K William's Tn 60-63; St Marg Parow 63-68; R of Lansdowne 68-79; Perm to Offic Dio Capetn from 79. *71 Fourth Avenue, Rondebosch East, CP, S Africa.* (65-1835)

CARLILE, Edward Wilson. b 15. K Coll Lon AKC 43, BD 46. ACA 39, FCA 59. **d** 43 **p** 44 Lon. C of All SS Queensbury 43-46; Asst Sec Ch Army 46-49; Chief Sec 49-60; V of St Pet w St Hilda Leic 60-73; R of Swithland 73-76; P-in-c of St Mich AA Belgrave 76-81. *Church Cottage, Chadwell, Melton Mowbray, Leics.* (Scalford 347)

CARLILL, Richard Edward. b 38. Westcott Ho Cam 77. **d** 79 Bradwell for Chelmsf **p** 80 Chelmsf. C of St Mary Prittlewell Dio Chelmsf from 79. *27 Tickfield Avenue, Southend-on-Sea, Essex, SS2 6LL.*

CARLIN, William Patrick Bruce. b 53. St Steph Ho Ox 75. **d** 78 **p** 79 Wakef. C of Penistone 78-81; St Mary Barnsley Dio Wakef from 81. *73 Barnsley Road, Dodworth, Barnsley, S Yorks, S75 3JS.*

CARLING, Albert. CCC Cam BA 21, MA 27. Wells Th Coll 21. **d** 23 **p** 24 Lon. C of St Mark Marylebone Road 23-25; St Pet Fulham 26-28; Perm to Offic at St Bart Bethnal Green 25-26 and 28-32; C of St Mary Rotherhithe (in c of St Paul) 32-33; St John Brighton 34-36; St Paul Goodmaye 36-38; R of Thurning w Wood Dalling V 39-53; V of Horsham St Faith 53-56; R of Belaugh 56-76. *The Fairstead, Crown Road, St Faiths, Norwich, Norf.*

CARLISLE, Lord Bishop of. *See* Halsey, Right Rev Henry David.

CARLISLE, Archdeacon of. *See* Ewbank, Ven Walter Frederick.

CARLISLE, Dean of. *See* Churchill, Very Rev John Howard.

CARLISLE, Christopher John. b 39. Univ of Sheff BEng 62. N-W Ordin Course 72. **d** 75 Man **p** 76 Hulme for Man. C of St Paul Bury 75-80; Walkden 80-81; V of St Jo Div Lytham Dio Blackb from 81. *St John's Vicarage, East Beach, Lytham, Lancs, FY8 5EX.* (Lytham 734396)

CARLISLE, Geoffrey Townshend. b 1899. Late Scho of CCC Cam BA (2nd cl Cl Trip pt i) 21, 2nd cl Th Trip pt i 22, MA 25. Cudd Coll. **d** 23 **p** 24 Lon. C of St Mellitus Hanwell 23-26; St Alb Cathl Pret 26; V of St Sav Pret 26-32; R of Barberton 32-38; V of Buxton 38-53; Master of St Cross Hosp and Min of St Faith 53-70. *42 Pilgrims Way, Canterbury, Kent, CT1 1XU.*

CARLOS, Francis John. b 29. Jes Coll Cam BA 54, MA 57. Wells Th Coll 52. **d** 55 **p** 56 Chelmsf. C of St Matthias Canning Town 55-57; Min of St Geo Conv Distr New Thundersley 57-64; V 64-65; R of Wentnor and Ratlinghope w Myndtown and Norbury Dio Heref from 65. *Wentnor Rectory, Bishop's Castle, Salop, SY9 5EE.* (Linley 244)

CARLTON, Roger John. b 51. **d** 80 Malmesbury for Bris **p** 81 Bris (NSM). C of Downend Dio Bris from 80. *1 Fouracre Crescent, Downend, Bristol, BS16 6PR.*

CARMAN, Peter George. Moore Th Coll Syd ACT ThL 59. **d** and **p** 60 Syd. C of Corrimal 60-64; C-in-c of Riverwood 64-70; McCallum's Hill 70-74; Youth Chap Dio Syd from 74. *92 Cabarita Road, Concord, NSW, Australia 2137.* (736-2163)

CARMAN, Thomas Joseph. Univ of Tor BA 76. Wycl Coll

Tor MDiv 79. **d** 79 Tor for Calg **p** 80 Calg. I of Foothills Miss Dio Calg from 79. *Box 157, Pincher Creek, Alberta, Canada, T0K 1W0.*

CARMARTHEN, Archdeacon of. *See* Evans, Ven Thomas John.

CARMICHAEL, Harvey Armstrong. Angl Th Coll BC 41. **d** and **p** 71 Rupld. Hon C of Portage la Prairie 71-77; Assoc P of St Paul's Cathl Kamloops Dio Carib from 77. *747 Chapparel Drive, Kamloops, BC, Canada.*

CARMICHAEL, Canon Michael Jukes Dalziel. St Edm Hall Ox BA (2nd cl Lit Hum) 37, 2nd cl Th 39, MA 43. St Steph Ho Ox 37. **d** 40 **p** 41 Ripon. C of St Aid Leeds 40-43; Perm to Offic Dio Bloemf 43; C of Kimb Cathl 43-44; P-in-c All SS Beaconsfield Kimberley 44-45; C of All SS Engcobo 45-49; Vice-Prin of St Steph Ho Ox 49-54; St Bede's Th Coll Umtata 54-56; Prin 57-72; Can of St John's 58-72; Can (Emer) from 72; Prov Exec Officer S Afr from 72; L to Offic Dio Johann from 72. *Box 31792, Braamfontein, Johannesburg, S Africa.* (725-4515)

CARMICHAEL, Peter Iain. b 28. Chich Th Coll 75. **d** 75 Chich **p** 76 Lewes for Chich. C of Rye 75-80; R of Earnley w E Wittering and Almodington Dio Chich from 80. *East Wittering Rectory, Chichester, W Sussex.* (W Wittering 2260)

CARMODY, Dermot Patrick Roy. b 41. TCD Div Test 77. **d** 77 **p** 78 Dub. C of Zion Ch Rathgar Dub 77-79; R of Dunganstown w Redcross Dio Glendal from 79. *Rectory, Redcross, Wicklow, Irish Republic.* (Wicklow 8637)

CARMYLLIE, Robert Royston. b 23. St Aid Coll 56. **d** 59 **p** 60 Man. C of St Clem Chorlton-cum-Hardy 59-62; R of St Osw Collyhurst Man 62-67; V of St Andr Ramsbottom Dio Man from 67. *St Andrew's Vicarage, Ramsbottom, Bury, Lancs, BL0 9JD.* (Ramsbottom 3162)

CARNABY, Ernest William. Moore Th Coll Syd 61. **d** 65 **p** 66 Adel. C of St Matt Kensington 65-66; P-in-c of Leigh Creek 66-69; Woomera 69-72; C of St Matt Kens 72-76; Gen Sec CMS S Austr 72-76; R of St Paul Chatswood Dio Syd from 76. *5 View Street, Chatswood, NSW, Australia 2067.* (419-2563)

CARNABY, Russell Henry. b 41. Univ of Syd. ACT ThL 68. Moore Th Coll 64. **d** 70 **p** 71 Tas. C of St Mark, Launceston 71-72; R of Ringarooma w Derby 72-74; Claremont and Chigwell Dio Tas from 74. *Rectory, Amber Street, Claremont, Tasmania 7011.* (002-49 2507)

CARNE, Brian George. b 29. Univ of Liv BCom 50. Qu Coll Birm 53. **d** 55 **p** 56 Bris. C of St Aug Swindon 55-58; St Andr w St Bart Bris 58-60; R of Lydiard Millicent w Lydiard Tregoz 60-68; V of Hartcliffe 68-74; Almondsbury Dio Bris from 74; RD of Westbury and Severnside from 80. *Almondsbury Vicarage, Bristol, BS12 4DS.* (Almondsbury 613223)

CARNE, Edward Clifton McClymont. b 17. Qu Univ Kingston Ont BTh 77. Qu Th Coll Kingston 69. **d** 70 **p** 71 Ont. R of Adolphustown 70-76; Dom Chap to Bp of Ont from 76; I of Loughboro 76-80. *1091 Lincoln Drive, Kingston, Ont, Canada.*

CARNE, Norman David John. b 27. Roch Th Coll 59. **d** 62 **p** 63 Roch. C of St Justus Roch 62-66; St Mary Strood 66-68; R of Westcote Barton w Steeple Barton 68-74; P-in-c of Enstone w Heythrop Dio Ox 74-82; V from 82. *Vicarage, Little Tew Road, Church Enstone, Oxford, OX7 4NL.* (Enstone 319)

CARNE-ROSS, Stewart Pattison. b 23. Wycl Hall Ox 58. **d** 59 **p** 60 S'wark. C of Brockley Hill 59-62; St Barn Dulwich 62-64; V of St Sav Denmark Pk 64-70; R of Culmington w Onibury 70-77; V of Bromfield 70-77; C-in-c of Stanton-Lacy 70-72; V 72-77; Hambledon 77-79; Chap HM Pris Kingston Hants from 79. *7 Hanover Court, Highbury Street, Portsmouth, Hants, PO1 2BN.* (Portsm 752698)

CARNEGIE, Kenneth Donald. Univ of Lon BA 25, 2nd cl Cl BA 27, MA 36. Gen Th Sem NY STB 56. Berkeley Div Sch USA STM 61. **d** 42 **p** 43 Ja. Hd Master of Beckford and Smith's Sch Spanish Town 42-43; C of St Luke Cross Roads 43-48; R of Vere 49-52; Annotto Bay and Port Maria Ja 52-53; in Amer Ch 54-61; Asst Master Ja Coll 61-66; Qu Sch Ja 67-69; C of Halfway Tree 65-76; Admin Asst to Bp of Ja from 76. *1 New Haven Avenue, Widcombe Heights, Kingston 6, Jamaica, W Indies.* (092-78712)

CARNELL, Canon Geoffrey Gordon. b 18. Late Scho of St Jo Coll Cam 1st cl Hist Trip pt i 39, BA (2nd cl Th Trip pt ii) 40, Lightfoot Scho, Naden Div Stud and Hughes Exhib 40, MA 44. Cudd Coll 40. **d** 42 **p** 43 Pet. C of Abington 42-49; Chap and Lect St Gabr Coll Camberwell 49-53; R of Isham 53-71; V of Gt w L Harrowden 53-71; Exam Chap to Bp of Pet and Dir of Ordin Tr from 62; Can (Non-res) of Pet from 65; R of Boughton Dio Pet from 71; Chap to HM the Queen from 81. *Boughton Rectory, Northampton, NN2 8SG.* (Northampton 842382)

CARNELLEY, Desmond. b 29. Open Univ BA 77. Ripon Hall Ox 59. **d** 60 **p** 61 Sheff. C of Aston 60-63; C-in-c of St Paul's Conv Distr Ecclesfield 63-67; V of Balby 67-73; C-in-c of Mosborough Dio Derby (Dio Sheff from 74) 73-74; V from 74; RD of Attercliffe from 79. *Mosborough Vicarage, Sheffield.* (Sheff 486518)

CARNES, Gerald Lambton. b 12. **d** and **p** 61 Bp of Haiti. (In Episc Ch in Haiti 61-68) C-in-c of Hampton Wick Dio Lon 68-74; V from 74. *Vicarage, Seymour Road, Hampton Wick, Kingston-on-Thames, KT1 4HN.* (01-977 2068)

CARNEY, David Anthony. Salford Univ BSc 77. Linc Th Coll 77. **d** 79 **p** 80 Man. C of Wythenshawe 79-81; CF from 81. *c/o Ministry of Defence, Bagshot Park, Bagshot, Surrey.*

✠ **CARNLEY, Most Rev Peter Frederick.** Univ of Melb BA 66. Em Coll Cam PhD 69. St Jo Coll Morpeth ACT ThL 62. **d** 62 **p** 64 Bath. L to Offic Dio Bath 62-64; Dio Melb 64-65; C of Parkes 66; L to Offic Dio Ely 67-69; Chap Mitchell Coll Bath 70-72; Exam Chap to Bp of Bath 70-72; Warden St Jo Coll St Lucia 72-81; Can Res of Brisb 75-81; Exam Chap to Abp of Brisb 75-81; Cons Ld Abp of Perth in St Geo Cathl Perth 26 May 81 by Abps of Melb and Brisb; Bps of NW Austr, Bunb, Willoch and Wang; and Bps Challen, Cornish, Grant and Parker; and others. *Bishop's House, 90 Mounts Bay Road, Perth, W Australia 6000.* (322 1777)

CARNLEY, Ronald Birch. b 18. Pemb Coll Ox BA and MA 47. Cudd Coll 47. **d** 49 **p** 50 Worc. C of Kidderminster 49-52; Halesowen 52-56; R of Lydiard Millicent w Lydiard Tregoz 56-60; V of Matfield 60-78; Surr 64-78. *5 Cleeve Avenue, Hawkenbury, Tunbridge Wells, Kent, TN2 4TY.*

CARPENTARIA, Lord Bishop of. *See* Jamieson, Right Rev Hamish Thomas Umphelby.

CARPENTARIA, Dean of. *See* Passi, Very Rev Dave.

CARPENTER, Canon Bruce Leonard Henry. b 32. BA (2nd cl French) Lon 54. St Chad's Coll Dur Dipl Th 59. **d** 59 **p** 60 Portsm. C of St Mark Portsea 59-63; Fareham 63-67; V of Locks Heath 67-74; RD of Alverstoke 71-77; R of H Trin Fareham Dio Portsm from 74; Warden of Readers from 77; Hon Can of Portsm Cathl from 81. *20 Osborn Road, Fareham, Hants.* (Fareham 280180)

CARPENTER, David James. b 52. St Steph Ho Ox 74. **d** 76 **p** 77 Mon. C of SS Julius & Aaron Newport 76-77; St Jas Pontypool 77-79; R Benef of Ebbw Vale Dio Mon 79-81; V from 81. *Vicarage, Badminton Grove, Beaufort, Gwent, NP3 5UN.* (0495 304516)

CARPENTER, Derek George Edwin. b 40. K Coll Lon and Warm BD and AKC 62. **d** 63 Lon **p** 64 Kens for Lon. C of Friern Barnet 63-66; Chingford 66-70; V of St Alb Dartford 70-79; R of Crayford Dio Roch from 79. *Rectory, Crayford, Kent, DA1 4RJ.* (Crayford 522078)

CARPENTER, Donald Arthur. b 35. Roch Th Coll 65. **d** 67 **p** 68 Cant. C of St Jude Thornton Heath 67-73; V of Earby 73-78; Ch Ch Skipton-in-Craven Dio Bradf from 78. *Christ Church Vicarage, Skipton, Yorks.* (Skipton 3612)

CARPENTER, Very Rev Edward Frederick. b 10. King's Exhib Lon Hist Bursary, Gladstone Pri and Barry Pri 32, Fell 54. Univ of Lon BA (1st cl Hist) 32; MA (w distinc) 34, BD 35, AKC (1st cl) 35, PhD 43. DD (Lambeth) 79. **d** 35 **p** 36 Lon. C of H Trin St Marylebone 35-41; St Mary Harrow 41-45; R of Gt Stanmore 45-51; Can of Westmr Abbey 51-74; Treas 59-74; Archd of Westmr 63-74; Dean from 74. *Deanery, Westminster, SW1.* (01-222 2953)

CARPENTER, Ven Frederick Charles. b 20. Late Exhib of SS Coll Cam, 2nd cl Hist Trip pt i 40, BA 47 (2nd cl Hist Trip pt ii), MA 49. St Cath S Ox Dipl Th 48. Wycl Hall Ox 47. **d** 49 **p** 50 Chelmsf. C of Woodford 49-51; Asst Chap Sherborne Sch 51-58; Chap 58-62; V of St Mary Moseley 62-68; Can Res of Portsm 68-77; Dioc Dir of Relig Educn Portsm 68-75; Archd of IW from 77; P-in-c of Binstead Dio Portsm from 77. *Binstead Rectory, Pitts Lane, Ryde, IW, PO33 3SU.* (Ryde 62890)

CARPENTER, Gilbert Lant. b 10. Down Coll Cam 3rd cl Hist Trip pt i 33, BA (3rd cl Hist Trip pt ii) 34, MA 38. Ely Th Coll 34. **d** 35 **p** 36 Southw. C of St Mark Mansfield 35-39; All SS E Finchley 39-41; St Andr Willesden Green 41-51; V of St Phil Tottenham 51-57; St Andr Willesden 57-76. *2 Rushbury Court, Station Road, Hampton, Middx.* (01-941 1449)

✠ **CARPENTER, Right Rev Harry James.** b 01. Univ of Lon BA (1st cl) 21. Late Southn Exhib of Qu Coll Ox 21, 1st cl Cl Mods and Hon Scho 23, BA (1st cl Lit Hum) and Liddon Stud 25, 1st cl Th 26, MA 28. Univ of Ox Hon DD 55. Cudd Coll 26. **d** 27 Win for Guildf **p** 28 Ox. C of Leatherhead 27; Tutor Keble Coll Ox 27-39; Fell 30-39; Warden 39-55; L to Offic Dio Ox 27-55; Exam Chap to Bp of Ox 39-55; Can Th of Leic 41-55; Hon Fell of Qu Coll and Keble Coll Ox from 55; Cons Ld Bp of Ox in S'wark Cathl 25 Jan 55 by Abp of Cant; Bps of S'wark; Roch; Ex; and Leic; Bps Suffr of Buckingham; Kingston T; and Dorch; res 70; Co-Chairman Anglican-Methodist Conversations 57-63; Anglican-

Orthodox Comm for Jt Doctrinal Discussions 67-73. *1 Meadow View, Baunton, Cirencester, Glos.* (Cirencester 4647)

CARPENTER, James Richard. St Bonif Coll Warm. **d** 49 **p** 50 Qu'App. V of St Jas Regina 49-52; Miss at Lytton 52-54; on leave 54-60; R of Ocean Falls 60-62; Hon C of St Cath N Vanc Dio New Westmr from 63. *2409 Philip Avenue, North Vancouver, BC, Canada.*

CARPENTER, John. b 05. Em Coll Cam BA (3rd cl Hist Trip pt ii) 27, MA 31. Ridley Hall Cam 27. **d** 29 **p** 30 S'wark. C of St John Deptford 29-31; CIM Miss Dio W China 31-36; Dio E Szech 36-39; C of Braintree 39-40; R of St Ebbe Ox 40-45; Uphill 45-54; V of Ch Ch Surbiton Hill 54-71; R of Peldon 71-74; P-in-c of Gt and L Wigborough 72-74; Hon C of Slaugham w Handcross 74-81. *8 Luxford Road, Lindfield, W Sussex, RH16 2LZ.* (Lindfield 3386)

CARPENTER, Justin David William. b 43. Univ of Dur BA (Th) 65. Westcott Ho 65. **d** 67 B & W **p** 68 Truro. C of Newlyn 67-69; Gt Marlow 69-73; Forrabury w Minster and Trevalga 73-74; Davidstow w Otterham 73-74; St Juliot w Lesnewth 73-74; Team V of Davidstow w Boscastle 74-75; P-in-c of St Mawgan-in-Pydar 75-77; R (w St Ervan and St Eval) 77-78; Chap St Wilfrid's Sch Ex from 79. *15 Union Street, St Thomas, Exeter, Devon.*

CARPENTER, Theodore George. St Jo Coll Auckld LTh 56. **d** and **p** 57 Auckld. C of Mt Roskill 57-59; V of Islands 59-61; Tuakau 61-66; Chap RNZAF 66-81; Offg Min Dio Nel 66-70; Hon C of Bulls 70-73; V of Kapiti Dio Wel from 81. *38 Hinemoa Street, Paraparaumu, NZ.*

CARPENTER, Victor Alexander. b 1897 BSc (Lon) 20. Univ of Sheff BSc (2nd cl Chem) 22, MSc 23. ARIC 22, FRIC 43. **d** 60 **p** 61 Southw. LPr Dio Southw 60-61; R of Treswell w Cottam 61-67; C of Gt Marlow 67-69; L to Offic Dio Ox from 69. *5 Meadow Close, Riverpark Drive, Marlow, Bucks.* (Marlow 3807)

CARPENTER, William Brodie. b 35. GOE 76. **d** 79 St Alb **p** 80 Hertf for St Alb. Hon C of St Mary Hemel Hempstead Dio St Alb from 79. *10 Midland Road, Hemel hempstead, herts.*

CARR, Canon Arthur Wesley. b 41. Late Exhib of Jes Coll Ox BA 64, MA 67. Jes Coll Cam BA 66, MA 70. Univ of Sheff PhD 75. Ridley Hall Cam 65. **d** 67 **p** 68 St Alb. C of Luton 67-71; Tutor Ridley Hall Cam 70-71; Chap 71-72; Univ of Sheff Research Fellow 72-74; Hon C of Ranmoor 72-74; Chap Chelmsf Cathl 74-78; Deputy Dir Cathl Centre for Research and Training Chelmsf from 74; Exam Chap to Bp of Chelmsf and Bp's Dir of Tr from 75; Can Res of Chelmsf Cathl from 78; M Gen Syn from 80. *2 Harlings Grove, Waterloo Lane, Chelmsford, CM1 1YQ.* (0245 355041)

CARR, Bernard John Bedford. b 23. Oak Hill Th Coll. **d** 61 **p** 62 St Alb. C of St Jo Bapt Bedford 61-65; R of Greenhithe 65-74; Georgeham Dio Ex from 74. *Georgeham Rectory, Braunton, Devon.* (Croyde 890326)

CARR, Christopher Patten. Univ of BC BASc 60. McGill Univ Montr BD 64. Univ of Montr MA 76. Montr Dioc Th Coll LTh 65. **d** 64 **p** 65 Montr. C of St Thos Montr 64-67; I of St Bruno 67-71; R of Cartierville Montr 71-77; I of Miss of Nativ City and Dio Montr from 77. *4041 Beaconsfield Avenue, Montreal, PQ, Canada.* (514-484 7619)

CARR, Douglas Nicholson. b 20. Jes Coll Cam BA 47, MA 50. Cranmer Hall Dur. **d** 65 **p** 66 S'wark. C of Reigate 65-69; LPr Dio S'wark from 69; Home Dir Overseas Mis Fellowship 69-77; Min from 77. *44 Croydon Road, Reigate, Surrey.* (Reigate 47771)

CARR, Frank. Dorch Miss Coll 33. **d** 35 **p** 36 Worc. C of St Andr Netherton 35-38; C-in-c of St Andr Conv Distr Wollescote 39-45; V of Amblecote 46-51; Bengeworth 51-60; P-in-c of Melville w Willagee 60-72. *11 Joseph Road, Safety Bay, W Australia 6169.* (095 27 3142)

CARR, Geoffrey. b 09. Ch Coll Cam 3rd cl Engl Trip pt i 32, BA (3rd cl Geog Trip) 33. Ridley Hall Cam 34. **d** 35 **p** 36 Lon. C of St Luke Hampstead 35-37; Chap of Corfu 37-38; Ch Ch Southport 38-41; V of St Thos Stafford 41-44; Wellington w Eyton 44-49; R of Bradfield w Buckhold 49-63; C-in-c of Stanford Dingley 54-56; RD of Bradfield 60-63; R of Arborfield 63-76; Perm to Offic Dio Guildf from 77. *15 Pewley Way, Guildford, Surrey.*

CARR, Graham Mills. St Jo Coll Morpeth ACT ThL 66. **d** 65 **p** 66 C & Goulb. C of N Goulb 65-66; Junee 67; Young 67-68. *c/o P.O. Box 58, Young, NSW, Australia.*

CARR, Harold Ernest. b 07. **d** 54 **p** 55 Ely. C of St Geo Chesterton 54-58; R of Sawtry w Upton and Copmanford 58-61; C of Farnham (in c of St Jas) 61-67; V of St Jas Croydon 67-71; R of Smarden 71-74; Perm to Offic Dio Chich from 74. *3 Pilgrims Close, Worthing, Sussex, BN14 7LP.* (0903 38987)

CARR, Henry Warren. Moore Th Coll Syd 15. **d** 17 **p** 24 Bath. C of Sofala w Hill End 17-21; Forbes 21-24; R of Geurie 24-37; Uki 37-38; Dunoon 38-48; R of Kyogle 48-59. *85 Spencer Road, Cremorne, Sydney, Australia.*

CARR, James Anthony. Em Coll Cam BA 47. St Cath S Ox Dipl Th 49. Wycl Hall Ox 48. **d** 50 **p** 51 Man. C of Gorton 50-54; R of St Geo Birm 54-62; St Mark W Gorton (w All SS from 68) Dio Man 62-76; Em Gorton from 76; C-in-c of All SS W Gorton 65-68. *Rectory, Blackwin Street, West Gorton, Manchester, M12 5LS.* (061-223 3510)

CARR, James Arthur. b 28. St Aid Coll 62. **d** 64 **p** 65 Lich. C of Cannock 64-68; V of Edensor 68-72; Caverswall Dio Lich from 72. *8 Vicarage Crescent, Caverswall, Stoke-on-Trent, Staffs, ST11 9EW.* (07818 3309)

CARR, John Dale. b 16. St Edm Hall Ox BA (3rd cl Mod Hist) 37, MA 41. Cudd Coll 38. **d** 39 **p** 40 Cant. C of Folkestone 39-40; Cranford 40-42; LDHM of H Angels Cranford 43-53; V of St Andr Uxbridge 53-80; C-in-c of St Marg, Uxbridge 65-72. *42 Cobden Close, Uxbridge, Middx.* (89 33887)

CARR, John Mabey. b 05. Late Scho of Univ Coll Dur BA (2nd cl Math) 27, MA 30. Westcott Ho Cam 27. **d** 28 **p** 29 Dur. C of Stranton 28-31; CMS Miss Tr Coll Awka 31-35; Supervisor of Schs Isoko and Sobo Distr 35-44; C-in-c of Cosham 45; V of Matlock Bank 45-54; Surr 50-54; Chap to Smedley Mem Hosp 49-54; Chap to Cameroons Development Corpn 54-56; V of St Anne Leic 56-67; Hon Can of Leic 65-67; V of Shiplake 67-74. *150 Kidmore Road, Caversham, Reading, RG4 7ND.*

CARR, John Robert. b 40. ACII 62. Oak Hill Th Coll 63. **d** 66 **p** 67 Roch. C of St Steph Tonbridge 66-70; C of St Andrew Cheadle Hulme 70-79; R of Widford Dio Chelmsf from 79. *Widford Rectory, Canuden Road, Chelmsford, Essex, CM1 2SU.* (Chelmsf 355989)

CARR, Very Rev Paul Ashley. Univ of Windsor Ont BA 66. Hur Coll BTh 69. **d** 69 **p** 70 Hur. C of St Chris Burlington 69-71; R of Chippawa 71-74; H Trin Niag Falls 74-81; Dean and R of Kenora Cathl Dio Keew from 81. *312 Main Street South, Kenora, Ont, Canada.* (807-468 7293)

CARR, Richard George. K Coll Lon and Warm AKC 65. **d** 66 **p** 67 Newc T. C of St Jas and St Basil Newc T 66-69; Alnwick 69-73; Industr Chap Dio Llan from 73. *9 Bredenbury Gardens, Nottage, Porthcawl, Mid-Glam, CF36 6NY.* (Porthcawl 5367)

CARR-HARRIS, Philip Michael. b 50. Trent Univ BA 74. Episc Div Sch Cam Mass MDiv 77. **d** 77 **p** 78 Montr. C of St Jas Ap Montr from 77-80; on leave. *c/o 1444 Union Avenue, Montreal, Quebec, Canada, H3A 2B8.*

CARRE, Canon John Trenchard. b 23. Lich Th Coll 42. Linc Th Coll 45. **d** 46 **p** 47 Guildf. C of Gt Bookham 46-48; Hodnet w Weston-under-Redcastle 48-50; Cannock (in c of Bridgtown) 50-53; V of Bodicote 53-60; Steeple Morden 60-74; Guilden Morden 60-74; RD of Shingay 67-74; R of Shingay Group (C-in-c of Croydon w Clopton; Hatley St Geo; Litlington w Abington Pigotts; Tadlow w E Hatley; Wendy w Shingay) 69-74; V of Chesterton Cam Dio Ely from 74; Hon Can of Ely Cathl from 79. *Chesterton Vicarage, Church Street, Cambridge, CB4 1DT.* (Cam 354098)

CARRELL, Brian Ruane. Univ of NZ BA 54, MA 56. Univ of Otago BD 68. Coll Ho Ch Ch. **d** 56 **p** 57 Ch Ch. C of Timaru 56-58; St Albans 58-60; V of Hororata 60-65; St Matt Dun 65-71; Gen Sec NZCMS from 71; L to Offic Dio Ch Ch 71-74; Hon C of Bryndwr Dio Ch Ch from 74. *167 Wairakei Road, Christchurch 5, NZ.* (516-415)

CARRETTE, Canon David Alan. b 38. Univ of Lon BA 3rd cl (Phil) 60. Univ of Man MA 67. Univ of Leic MA (Ed) 74. Bp's Coll Cheshunt 60. **d** 62 **p** 63 Blackb. C of Ribbleton 62-64; All SS Cheadle Hulme 64-67; V of St Luke Chadderton 67-71; R of Higham-on-the-Hill 71-75; C-in-c of Fenny Drayton 75; Youth Officer Dio Ox 76-78; Can Res of Newc T from 78; Dir of Educn and Tr Dio Newc T from 78. *Church House, Grainger Park Road, Newcastle-upon-Tyne, NE4 8SX.* (Newc T 30238)

CARRICK, Canon Ian Ross. Clare Coll Cam 3rd cl Hist Trip pt i 34, BA (3rd cl Th Trip pt i) 35, MA 39. Chich Th Coll 35. **d** 37 **p** 38 York. C of St Paul Sculcoates 37-39; Staveley 39-43; Swynnerton (in c from 44) 43-45; Min of St Barn Conv Distr Northolt 45-54; V 54-58; R of Irene 58-62; Exam Chap to Bp of Pret from 61; P-in-c of Sekhukhuniland Miss and Prin of St Francis Coll 62-66; Archd of Barberton 64-66; Pret 67-76; R of St Wilfrid Hillcrest Pret 68-76; H Trin Lynnwood Pret 76-80; Can of Pret from 76; Dir of Tr for Min Dio Pret from 80. *1 Serder Avenue, Doringkloof, Verwoordburg, Pretoria, S Africa.*

CARRINGTON, William. b 14. **d** 80 Trinid. C of St Andr Scarborough Tobago Dio Trinid from 80. *Bacolet Street, Scarborough, Tobago, WI.*

CARRIVICK, Derek Roy. b 45. Univ of Birm BSc 66. Ripon Hall Ox 71. **d** 74 Lon **p** 75 Edmon for Lon. C of St Jas Enfield Highway 74-78; Bartley Green (in c of Woodgate Valley) Dio Birm from 78. *34 Simcox Gardens, Woodgate Valley, Birmingham. B32 9RX.* (021-427 3514)

CARROLL, Ven Charles William Desmond. b 19. Trin Coll

Dub BA 43, MA 46. **d** 48 **p** 49 Carl. C of Stanwix 48-50; V 50-59; Dir Relig Educn Dio Blackb 59-73; Hon Can of Blackb 59-64; Can Res 64-75; Hon Chap to Bp of Blackb 61-64; V of Balderstone Dio Blackb from 73; Archd of Blackb from 73. *Balderstone Vicarage, Blackburn, Lancs, BB2 7LL.* (Mellor 2232)

CARROLL, Desmond Frederick. b 38. Trin Coll Dub B Soc Sc and BA 67. **d** 69 **p** 70 Cash. C of Blessed Trin Cathl Waterf 69-71; Asst Youth Officer C of I 71-76; I of Castlegar Dio Koot from 76. *117 Pinewood Drive, Castlegar, BC, Canada.*

CARROLL, Edward Ion. b 07. Keble Coll Ox BA (2nd cl Th) 28, MA 42. Cudd Coll 30. **d** 30 **p** 31 Pet. C of St Matt Northn 30-34; Asst P Pyeng-Yang 35-37; P-in-c of W Songchun 37-39; Haiju 40; C of Langley Marish 41-42; V of Airedale w Fryston 43-48; C of St Geo Claines Worc 49-51; Asst Master Pershore County Sec Mod Sch 52-55; St Geo Sch Hockley, Birm 55-56; V of The Lye 56-73. *6a Lion Street, Stourbridge, W Midl, DY8 1UE.* (Stourbridge 76387)

CARROLL, Frederick Albert. b 16. Worc Coll Ox BA (3rd cl Th) 51, MA 55. Ripon Hall Ox 46. **d** 51 **p** 52 Birm. C of Oldbury Birm 51-56; V of The Cotteridge 56-65; C-in-c of St Cuthb Conv Distr Castle Vale 65-68; V 68-74; R of Spernall and Oldberrow w Morton Bagot Dio Cov from 74; V of Coughton w Sambourne Dio Cov from 74. *Spernall Rectory, Studley, Warws, B80 7EX.* (Studley 2040)

CARROLL, John Hugh. b 31. Univ of Bris BA 57. Tyndale Hall Bris 54. **d** 58 **p** 59 Ox. C of Slough 58-61; V of St Steph S Lambeth 61-72; St Luke W Norwood 72-81; Purley Dio S'wark from 81. *38 Woodcote Valley Road, Purley, Surrey, CR2 3AJ.* (01-660 1790)

CARRUTHERS, Alan. b 15. **d** 60 **p** 61 Warrington for Liv. C of St Luke Evang Walton-on-the-Hill 60-62; St Jas Wigan 62-65; V from 65; C-in-c of St Thos Wigan 65-70; V from 70. *St James's Vicarage, Wigan, Lancs.* (Wigan 43896)

CARRUTHERS, Arthur Christopher. b 35. St Jo Coll Nottm LTh 60. **d** 60 Croydon for Cant **p** 61 Cant. C of Addiscombe 60-62; Prec of Bradf Cathl 62-64; CF from 64. *c/o Ministry of Defence, Bagshot Park, Bagshot, Surrey.*

CARRY, Edward Austin. b 18. Trin Coll Dub BA 41, MA 47. **d** 42 **p** 43 Dub. C of Drumcondra w N Strand 42-45; Sandford 45-50; R of Arklow 50-56; I of H Trin Killiney Dio Dub from 56; RD of Killiney from 80. *Holy Trinity Rectory, Killiney Road, Dublin, Irish Republic.* (Dublin 803470)

CARRY, Robert William. Univ of W Ont STh 63. Hur Coll 63. **d** 65 **p** 66 Sktn. I of Colonsay 65-67; Wynyard 67-73; Armstrong 73-77. *345 Holbrook Road West, BC, Canada.*

CARSON, Ernest. b 17. SOC 68. **d** 71 **p** 72 St Alb. C of Baldock w Bygrave and Clothall 71-75; R of Hertingfordbury Dio St Alb from 75. *Hertingfordbury Rectory, Hertford.* (Hertford 52739)

CARSON, Frederick Howard. b 39. Hur Coll Lon Ont BMin 73. **d** 73 **p** 74 Hur. I of Blyth Auburn Belgrave & Brussels 73-77; Parkland Miss Calg 77-80; St Luke Souris Dio Bran from 80. *c/o Box 728, Souris, Manit, Canada.*

CARSON, Canon Gerald James Alexander. b 24. Trin Coll Dub BA 49, MA 52. **d** 49 **p** 50 Connor. C of St Phil Belf 49-51; St Columb's Cathl Derry 51-54; I of Kilteevogue 54-57; R of Dunfanaghy 57-68; RD of Kilmacrenan W from 60; Can of Raph 67-81; Derry from 81; R of Urney w Sion Mills Dio Derry from 68; Dioc Press Officer Dio Derry from 79. *Rectory, Sion Mills, Co Tyrone, N Ireland.*

CARSON, Harold. b 05. AKC 30. **d** 30 **p** 31 S'wark. C of St Sav Battersea PK 30-36; St Jude E Brixton 36-41; Actg C-in-c of St Jas Hatcham 41-42; V of St Anne Bermondsey 42-53; PC of St Simon Plymouth 53-61; V of St Mary Priory Road Hampstead 61-71. *10 St Nicholas Road, Uphill, Weston-super-Mare, Avon.*

CARSON, Reginald Arthur. Bp's Univ Lennox BA 30, MA 31. **d** and **p** 52 Queb. I of Fitch Bay 52-55; Peninsula 55-61; Port Daniel 61-67; R of Chaleur Bay 67-71; R of Stanstead 71-72. *17581 Clermont Avenue, Pierrefonds, PQ, Canada.*

CARSON, Ven Richard Alcorn. Univ of NZ BA 34, MA 36. LTh 37. **d** 36 **p** 37 Ch Ch. C of Addington 36-38; Timaru 38-39; CMS Miss Karachi 39-47; Hon CF 41-46; Sukkur 47-53; Ch Ch Karachi 53-56; Hyderabad 57-58; V of Belfast-Styx 50-63; Hon Can of Ch Ch 62-76; V of Bryndwr 63-78; Archd of Sumner from 76; Offg Min Dio Ch Ch from 78. *6 Gregan Crescent, Christchurch 5, NZ.* (598-179)

CARSON, Richard Collingwood. b 45. Univ of Cant NZ BSc 66. BD (Lon) 71. **d** 71 **p** 72 Roch. C of St Phil and St Jas Chatham 71-74; Cashmere Hills Ch Ch 74-75; V of Hororata Dio Ch Ch from 75. *Vicarage, Hororata, Christchurch, NZ.* (Hor 858)

CARSON, Robert Andrew. Univ of W Ont BA 54. Hur Coll LTh 55. **d** 55 **p** 56 Hur. C of St Geo Sarnia 55-56; R of Paisley 56-58; I of Norway Ho 58-60; R of Forest 60-69; Lucan 69-73; Blenheim Dio Hur from 73. *Box 137, Blenheim, Ont., Canada.* (519-676 5196)

CARTER, Alfred Walton. Hatf Hall Dur BA 13, MA 19. **d** 13 **p** 14 York. C of Newington Hull 13-19; Grangetown 19-21; Asst P of Hlamankulu E Afr 21-23; Prin of St Chris Coll Lebom 22-23; C of K William's Tn 23-25; V of Bezuidenhout Valley 25-28; Prec of St Geo Cathl Capetown 28-30; R of Somerset W 30-36; Bellville 37-41; Observatory 41-52; Worcester 52-55; St Barn Capetn 55-58; Strand Dio Capetn 58-60; L to Offic Dio Capetn from 61. *PO Box 1932, Cape Town, CP, S Africa.*

CARTER, Anthony James. b 24. Sarum Th Coll 54. **d** 56 **p** 57 Guildf. C of Farncombe 56-60; Burgh Heath 60-62; V of Chessington 62-69; Walton-on-Thames 69-79; P-in-c of Lytchett Minster Dio Sarum 79-81; V from 81. *Lytchett Minster Vicarage, Poole, Dorset, BH16 6JQ.* (Lytchett Minster 622253)

CARTER, Barry Graham. b 54. AKC and BD 76. St Steph Ho Ox 76. **d** 77 **p** 78 Worc. C of Evesham 77-81; Amblecote Dio Worc from 81. *28 Sandringham Way, Withymoor Village, Brierley Hill, W Midl.* (Brierley Hill 261950)

CARTER, Brian Allan. Moore Th Coll Syd ACT ThL (2nd cl) 65. Melb Coll of Div Dipl Relig Educn 66. **d** 65 **p** 66 Syd. C of St Mark S Hurstville 65-66; P-in-c of Tarcoola Miss 66-69; Leigh Creek 69-74; P-in-c of Belconnen *D* Canberra 74-80; St Paul's Ginninderra Dio C & Goulb from 80. *124 Tillyard Drive, Flynn, ACT, Australia 2615.*

CARTER, Ven Charles Herbert. Univ of Capetn BA 48, MA (2nd cl) 49. LTh (S Afr) 51. St Paul's Th Coll Grahmstn 50. **d** 51 **p** 52 Capetn. C of Bellville 51-56; R of Clanwilliam 56-59; Goodwood 59-62; Bredasdorp 62-65; Durbanville 65-71; Archd of Paarl from 69; R of Wellington 71-76; Muizenberg Dio Capetn from 76. *Rectory, Main Road, Muizenberg, CP, S Africa.* (81-007)

CARTER, Canon Charles Trevelyan Aubrey. b 14. TCD BA 36, MA 46. **d** 37 **p** 38 Dub. C of Sandford 37-43; Chap Female Orph Ho Dub 43-52; I of St Steph Dub 52-59; St Mary Crumlin 59-67; Sandford Dio Dub from 67; RD of Garristown 64-76; St Ann from 76; Can of Ch Ch Cathl Dub from 71; Hon Sec Gen Syn 80. *Rectory, Sandford Road, Dublin 6, Irish Republic.* (Dublin 972983)

CARTER, Christopher Franklin. b 37. Wadh Coll Ox BA 59, MA 63. Wycl Hall Ox 60. **d** 64 **p** 65 Sheff. C of Clifton 64-67; Handsworth 67-70; Clun w Chapel Lawn 70-74; Perm to Offic Dio Heref 74-76; Pastoral Care of Ironbridge 76-78; V of Llansilin w Llangadwaladr and Llangedwyn Dio St A from 80. *Y Ficerdy, Llansilin, Oswestry, Salop.* (Llansilin 209)

CARTER, Clifford Stanley. b 24. Oak Hill Coll 72. **d** 74 Barking for Chelmsf **p** 75 Chelmsf. C of St Mary Becontree (in c of Hartley Brook) 74-77; V of St Paul Harold Hill Romford Dio Chelmsf from 77. *St Paul's Vicarage, Redcar Road, Harold Hill, Essex.* (Ingrebourne 41225)

CARTER, Preb Cyril Edward. b 1899. St Chad's Coll Dur BA 28. **d** 28 **p** 29 Lon. C of H Innoc Hammersmith 28-34; Poplar 34-38; V of St Paul Bow Common Lon 38-50; Chap of Bromley Ho Inst Bromley-by-Bow 38-42; V of H Trin Hounslow 50-71; RD of Heston and Isleworth 58-67; Preb of St Paul's Cathl Lon from 67. *Thatchers, West Putford, Holsworthy, Devon, EX22 7UF.*

CARTER, David John. Univ of Manit BA 58. St Jo Coll Winnipeg LTh 60 Hon DD 76. Angl Th Coll BC STB 68. **d** 60 **p** 61 Rupld. C of St Matt Winnipeg 60-61; V of St Sav Winnipeg w St Cath Bird's Hill 61-65; Chap Univ of Calg 65-69; Dean and R of Cathl Ch of Redeemer City and Dio Calg 69-79; C from 80; Exam Chap to Bp of Calg 70-79. *Carter Towers, 602-1st Street SE, Calgary, Alta, Canada.*

CARTER, David John. b 37. Chich Th Coll 64. **d** 67 Barking for Chelmsf **p** 68 Chelmsf. C of St Andr, Plaistow 67-70; Wickford 70-73; Asst Chap Runwell Hosp 71-73; Chap Basingstoke Hosp 73-80; R of E Woodhay and Woolton Hill Dio Win from 80. *Woolton Hill Rectory, Newbury, Berks.* (Highclere 253323)

CARTER, David Warren. St Jo Coll Morpeth 59. **d** and **p** 62 St Arn. C of St Paul Bend 62-64; Mildura 64-66; Perm to Offic Dio Melb 66-68 and from 70; C of St Osw Glen Iris 68-69. *Box 110, Balwayn, Vic, Australia 3103.* (836 8831)

CARTER, Dean Jonathan. b 47. Univ of Melb BTh 77. Ridley Coll Melb 74. **d** 77 Armid. C of Inverell 77-79; St Pet Campbelltown Dio Syd from 79. *Parish House, Cordeaux Street, Campbelltown, NSW, Australia 2560.* (046-25 1041)

CARTER, Canon Donald George. b 32. Keble Coll Ox BA (Th) 54, MA 57. Ely Th Coll 54. **d** 56 **p** 57 Chich. C of Ch Ch St Leonards-on-Sea 56-66; V of Mayfield Sussex 66-77; RD of Dallington 71-77; M Gen Syn Chich from 70; R of Ch Ch (and St Mary Magd from 80) Dio Chich from 77; P-in-c of St Mary Magd St Leonards-on-Sea 78-80; RD of Hastings from 78; Can and Preb of Chich Cathl from 81. *Christ Church Rectory, 17 Alfred Street, St Leonards-on-Sea, E Sussex.*

CARTER, Douglas. Kelham Th Coll 34. **d** 39 **p** 40 Bradf. C of Rawdon 39-41; St Mary Magd Bradf 41-44; St Paul Leic

44-46; Chap of Chaworth St Jas Ottershaw 46-51; C of H Sav Hitchin (in c of St Faith Walsworth) 51-53; V of Whitworth Lancs 53-58; St Alb Hull 58-68; Gen Sec Ch U 68-74; M Gen Syn Lon 70-75; V of Goldthorpe (w Hickleton from 77) 74-81; Perm to Offic Dio York from 81. *10 Golf Links Road, Hull, HU6 8RA.*

CARTER, Dudley Herbert. Peterho Cam BA 49, MA 51. Ridley Hall Cam 49. **d** 51 Sherborne for Sarum **p** 52 Sarum. C of Longfleet 51-53; Rainham Essex 54-56; Chap CCCS 56; Field Sec CCCS N Area 57-60; R of Tollard Royal w Farnham 60-64; Chap Colston's Sch Bris 65-67; Asst Master Dr Morgan's Gr Sch Bridgwater 67-73; Haygrove Comprehensive Sch Bridgwater from 73. *87 Stodden's Road, Burnham-on-Sea, Somt.* (Burnham-on-Sea 2635)

CARTER, Edgar William Pringle. b 02. Angl Th Coll BC Dipl Th 28. **d** 28 **p** 29 BC. C of Ch Ch Cathl 28-32; Port Coquitlam w Pitt Meadows 32-41; R of St Steph W Vanc 41-62; V of Boundary Bay 62-69; Hon C of St Mich Blundellsands Dio Liv from 73. *33 Cambridge Road, Liverpool, L23 7TU.*

CARTER, Eric. b 17. **d** 58 Blackb **p** 59 Lanc for Blackb. C of H Trin S Shore Blackpool (in c of St Nich Marton Moss from 59) 58-62; V of Preesall 62-69; Adlington 69-75; RD of Garstang 68-69; V of St Thos Garstang Dio Blackb from 75. *St Thomas's Vicarage, Garstang, Preston, PR3 1PA.* (Garstang 2162)

CARTER, Frank Edgar. b 19. SOC 61. **d** 64 **p** 65 S'wark. C of Carshalton 64-65; Cheam 65-68; V of H Trin Rotherhithe Dio S'wark from 68. *Holy Trinity Vicarage, Bryan Road, SE16 1HE.* (01-237 3963)

CARTER, Frank Howard James. b 23. Chich Th Coll 58. **d** 59 **p** 60 Lon. C of St Matt Bethnal Green 59-64; V of Ipstones 64-65; All SS Haggerston 65-75; St Andr Alexandra Pk Muswell Hill Dio Lon from 75. *34 Alexandra Park Road, N10 2AB.* (01-444 6898)

CARTER, Gordon Albert. b 07. Univ of Lon BA (Hons Hist) 33. Univ of Ex BA 61. St Mich Coll Llan 33. **d** 35 **p** 36 Mon. C of Mynddislwyn 35-37; Tiverton 37-41; Highweek w St Mary Newton Abbot 41-47; V of Mortehoe 47-52; R of Stoke-in-Teignhead w Combe-in-Teignhead 52-61; Stowford 61-71; V of Broadwoodwidger 61-71; V of Shaugh Prior 71-74; Publ Pr Dio Ex from 75. *The Vicarage Flat, Brampford Speke, Exeter, EX5 5DR.* (Stoke Canon 274)

CARTER, Hector Thomas. St Paul's Th Coll Grahmstn LTh 51. **d** 52 **p** 54 Natal. C of St Paul Durban 52-53; Pinetown 53-56; St Pet Pietermaritzburg 56-57; Benoni 57-59; Pinner 60; Heston 60-62; St Mary Bridgnorth 62-63; C-in-c of Ditton Priors 63-67; C of Ludford 67-70; R of Jagersfontein 71-79; St Mary w St Edw Parys Dio Bloemf from 79. *Box 48, Parys, OFS, S Africa.*

CARTER, Henry Roderick. b 13. Qu Coll Cam 3rd cl Nat Sc 34, BA 35, MA 39. Wycl Hall Ox 37. **d** 39 **p** 40 Cant. C of Em S Croydon 39-42; St Pet Woking 42-47; R of Elmdon (w Bickenhill from 52) 46-54; V of Mile Cross Nor 54-69; Min of Ch Ch Conv Distr Westbourne Bournemouth 69-74. *139a Merley Ways, Wimborne, Dorset.* (Wimborne 885988)

CARTER, Ian Sutherland. b 51. Trin Coll Ox BA 73, MA, DPhil 77. Univ of Leeds BA (Th) 80. Coll of the Resurr Mirfield 78. **d** 81 Dur. C of Shildon Dio Dur from 81. *12 Teesdale Walk, Shildon, Co Durham, DL4 2NB.*

CARTER, Ivan John. Moore Th Coll Syd 56. **d** 59 **p** 60 Tas. C of King I 59-60; R 60-62; Beaconsfield w Exeter 62-68; C in Dept of Chaps Dio Melb 68-75. *c/o Diocesan Registry, Flinders Lane, Melbourne, Australia 3000.*

CARTER, John Henry. b 24. Oak Hill Th Coll 66. **d** 68 **p** 69 Man. C of Halliwell 68-71; V of St Phil Bolton 71-76; Chap to Deaf Dios Man and Blackb from 76. *93 Highways Avenue, Euxton, Chorley, Lancs.* (Chorley 78552)

✠ **CARTER, Right Rev John Stanley.** Univ of Lon BA 47. Oak Hill Th Coll and Wycl Hall Ox. **d** 49 **p** 50 Chelmsf. C of Walthamstow 49-52; Im Streatham 52-53; R of Mowbray CP 53-56; Chap Univ of Capetn 57-63; P-in-c of Westonaria 63-68; Cons Ld Bp Suffr of Johann in St Paul's Ch Durban 17 Nov 68 by Abp of Capetn; Bps of Geo, Johann, Bloemf and Kimb K; and Bp Fosseus (Lutheran Ch); res 77; R of Fish Hoek Dio Capetn from 77; Asst Bp of Capetn from 78. *Box 100, Fish Hoek, CP, S Africa.* (82-1304)

CARTER, Ven John Wilfred. Em Coll Sktn Dipl Th 29. St Chad's Coll Regina LTh 35, DD 59. **d** and **p** 29 Qu'app. I of Dunblane 29-31; P-in-c of Mothers' U Miss Van Rockglen 31-34; R and RD of Shaunavon 34-37; I of Gull Lake 37-40; R of St Mary Regina 40-49; Lect St Chad's Coll Regina 41-50; Chap RCN 41-46; RCNR 46-68; I of St Barn Medicine Hat Dio Qu'App 49-69; Dio Calg 69-72; Synod Sec Dio Qu'App 43-67; Hon Can of Qu'App from 47; Archd of Moose Jaw 56-61; Medicine Hat 61-67; Macleod 69-72; Archd (Emer) from 72; Regr Dio Calg from 72; Dom Chap to Bp of Calg from 80. *2412 Charter Towers, 614 5th Avenue SW, Alta., Canada, T2P 0M7.* (263-5445)

CARTER, Lancelot Howard Norman. b 23. K Coll Lon and Warm. **d** 55 Guildf **p** 56 Bp Hawkes for Cant. C of Banstead 55-58; Welwyn 58-61; R of Waltham 61-67; V of St Phil w St Mark Camberwell 67-77; Whaplode Dio Linc from 77; Holbeach Fen Dio Linc from 77. *Whaplode Vicarage, Spalding, Lincs, PE12 6TD.* (Holbeach 370318)

CARTER, Leslie Alfred Arthur. K Coll Lon and Warm. **d** 54 **p** 55 Lon. C of St Barn Northolt 54-56; Chap and Asst Master St Geo Cathl Gr Sch Capetn 57-60; Hon Chap to Abp of Capetn 58-60; Dom Chap 60-62; C of Wimbledon (in c of St Jo Bapt) 63-68; Chap and Asst Master Quainton Hall Sch Harrow 68-77; Team V of The Resurr Brighton 77-81; Southend-on-Sea Dio Chelmsf from 81. *1 Sutton Road, Southend, Essex.*

CARTER, Nicholas Adrian. b 47. Ripon Hall Ox 71. **d** 74 **p** 75 Wakef. C of Sowerby 74-79; V of Hanging Heaton Dio Wakef from 79. *Hanging Heaton Vicarage, Batley, Yorks.* (Dewsbury 461917)

CARTER, Norman. b 23 Univ of Leeds BSc 48. Coll of Resurr Mirfield 48. **d** 50 **p** 51 Liv. C of Our Lady and St Nich Liv 50-54; St Marg and All H Orford 54-56; V 56-71; V of H Spirit Knotty Ash (Dovecot from 74) Dio Liv from 71; RD of W Derby from 78. *Holy Spirit Vicarage, Dovecot Avenue, Liverpool, L14 7QJ.* (051-220 6611)

CARTER, Oswald Dickin. b 09. Pemb Coll Cam BA 31, MA 38. Ely Th Coll 35. **d** 36 **p** 37 Lon. C of St Francis Isleworth 36-38; St Mary's Cathl (in c of St Pet from 40) Glas 38-44; R of H Trin Kilmarnock 44-51; Skelton w Hutton-in-the-Forest 51-58; Lazonby 58-75; Surr 59-75; L to Offic Dio Carl from 75. *Briar Cottage, Castle Carrock, Carlisle.*

CARTER, Paul Brian. b 22. AKC 49. St Bonif Coll Warm. **d** 50 **p** 51 York. C of St Columba Scarborough 50-53; Pocklington 53-55; V of Newington 55-60; Ainderby Steeple W (Yafforth from 79) and Scruton Dio Ripon from 60; M Gen Syn Ripon from 70; P-in-c of Yafforth 76-79. *Ainderby Steeple Vicarage, Northallerton, N Yorks, DL7 9PY.* (0609 3346)

CARTER, Paul Mark. b 56. Council of Nat Acad Awards BA 78. Ridley Hall Cam 79. **d** 81 Lich. C of Kidsgrove Dio Lich from 81. *42 Lamb Street, Kidsgrove, Staffs, ST7 4AL.*

CARTER, Philip George. b 45. Univ of Adel BA 67, MA 71. St Barn Coll Adel 70. **d** 72 **p** 73 Adel. C of Prospect 72-74; Tea Tree Gully 74-77; P-in-c of Ingle Farm w Pooraka 77-78; R of Renmark Dio Murray from 78. *Rectory, James Avenue, Renmark, S Australia 5341.* (085-866228)

CARTER, Raymond Timothy. b 27. Qu Coll Birm 57. **d** 59 **p** 60 Lon. C of Wembley 59-62; St Anselm Hatch End 62-67; V of St Mich AA Harrow Weald 67-79; Teddington Dio Lon from 79. *Vicarage, Twickenham Road, Teddington, Middx.* (01-977 2767)

CARTER, Richard Neville. b 35. Chich Th Coll 63. **d** 65 **p** 66 St Alb. C of St Sav St Alb 65-69; C of H Cross Empangeni 70-71; Perm to Offic Dio St Alb from 72. *4 Riverside Close, Whitbread Avenue, Bedford.* (Bedford 50401)

CARTER, Robert Desmond. b 35. Cranmer Hall Dur 62. **d** 65 **p** 66 Bradf. C of All SS Otley 65-69; C of Keighley 69-73; V of Cowling Dio Bradf from 73. *Vicarage, Gill Lane, Cowling, Keighley, W Yorks BD22 0DD.* (Cross Hills 32050)

CARTER, Robert Edward. b 44. Univ of Wales (Bangor) BSc 66. St Jo Coll Nottm 79. **d** 81 Lich. C of Caverswall Dio Lich from 81. *30 Firbank Place, Parkhall, Weston Coyney, Stoke-on-Trent, ST3 5RU.*

CARTER, Robert Thomas. b 49. Univ of Melb ThL 74. Ridley Coll Melb 73. **d** 75 Melb. C of Traralgon 75-77; P-in-c of Doveton Dio Melb from 77. *102 Power Road, Doveton, Vic, Australia 3177.* (791-5291)

CARTER, Robin. b 46. Chich Th Coll 71. **d** 74 **p** 75 Ripon. C of Wortley-de-Leeds 74-76; Hutton 76-79; Wickford (in c of St Andr) Dio Chelmsf 79-80; Team V from 80. *8 Friern Walk, Wickford, Essex, SS12 0HZ.*

CARTER, Ronald George. b 31. Univ of Leeds BA 58. Coll of Resurr Mirfield 58. **d** 60 Liv **p** 61 Warrington for Liv. C of St Anne Wigan 60-63; Prec of Wakef Cathl 63-66; V of Woodhall 66-76; M Gen Syn 75-77; Chap Qu Marg Sch York from 77. *Wheldrake Lodge, Escrick Park, Escrick, York, YO4 4JS.* (090487-282)

CARTER, Ronald William. b 01. ATCL 25. ALCD 31. **d** 31 **p** 32 Lon. C of St Mary Isl 31-32; CMS Miss Yungchowfu 33-34; Kweilin 34-38; CMS Deputn Staff 38-39; C of St Pet Staines 39-41; V 41-78; RD of Staines 68-73. *24 Vespasian Way, Chandlers Ford, Eastleigh, Hants, SO5 2DF.* (Chandlers Ford 69520)

CARTER, Samuel. b 49. St Jo Coll Dur BA 71, Dipl Th 72. Cranmer Hall Dur 73. **d** 74 **p** 75 Lich. C of St Mary Kingswinford (in c of Ascen Wall Heath) 74-77; H Cross Shrewsbury (in c of St Pet Monkmoor) Dio Lich from 77. *11 Monkmoor Avenue, Shrewsbury, SY2 5DZ.* (Shrewsbury 52493)

CARTER, Stanley Reginald. b 24. St Jo Coll Dur BA 49, Dipl Th 50. **d** 50 **p** 51 Guildf. C of Em Stoughton Guildf 50-53; Bucknall w Bagnall (in c of St Chad) 53-56; R of St Matthias w St Simon Salford 56-62; V of St Aug Highbury 62-68; St Chris Sneinton Dio Southw from 68. *Vicarage, Sneinton Boulevard, Nottingham NG2 4GL* (Nottingham 55303)

CARTER, Stephen. b 56. St D Coll Lamp BA 77. Univ of Southn BTh 81. Sarum Wells Th Coll 78. **d** 81 Colchester for Chelmsf. C of Halstead w Greenstead Green Dio Chelmsf from 81. *36 Ramsey Road, Halstead, Essex.*

CARTER, Terence John. b 31. K Coll Lon and Warm AKC and BD 57, BA (Phil) Lon 68. **d** 58 **p** 59 Lon. C of H Trin Winchmore Hill 58-60; PV of S'wark Cathl 60-63; Sacr 60-61; Succr 61-63; R of Ockham w Hatchford 63-69; Dioc Sec for Schs Dio Guildf 63-66; Schs Insp 63-69; Asst Master Bp Simpson Sch Reigate 69-76; St Bede's Sch Reigate 76-78; Publ Pr Dio S'wark from 69; Dep Hd Master Portsm Girls' Sch and L to Offic Dio Portsm from 78. *c/o 8 Tottenham Road, Portsmouth, PO1 1QL.*

CARTER, William Frederick. ACT ThL 47. **d** 47 Bp Pilcher for Syd **p** 48 Syd. C of Cook's River 47; Wallerawang 48; R 49-51; Merrylands 51-54; Windsor NSW 54-60; R of St Andr S Brisb 60-74; Can Res of Brisb 72-74; R of Canterbury 74-78; P-in-c of Hurlstone Pk 74-78; R of St Aug Hamilton Brisb 78-80; St John Dee Why Dio Syd from 80. *87 Oaks Avenue, Dee Why, NSW, Australia 2099.* (98-8694)

CARTER, William John. Ridley Coll Melb ACT ThL 51. **d** 52 **p** 53 Melb. C of H Trin Coburg 52-53; S Yarra 53-54; Min of Lara 54-56; Newport 56-60; Eltham 60-64; C of Dept of Chaps Dio Melb 64-75; Perm to Offic Dio Melb 75-80; R of NE Goldfield Dio NW Austr from 80. *1 Austin Place, Leinster, W Australia.*

CARTLEDGE, Richard James. b 40. St Jo Coll Morpeth ThDip 80. **d** 81 Tas. C of Burnie Dio Tas from 81. *PO Box 44, Burnie, Tasmania 7320.*

CARTLIDGE, Canon Harry Gee. St Jo Coll Manit 18. **d** 17 **p** 18 Moos. C of Waswanipi 17-28; I of Poplar Point 28-62; Hon Can of Rupld from 76. *440 Edmonton Street, Winnipeg 2, Manit., Canada.*

CARTMAN, James. b 10. OBE 55. Univ of Man BA 37, MA 50. Univ of Lon BD (1st cl) 44, MTh 48. Westcott Ho Cam 51. **d** and **p** 51 Roch. C of Hayes, Kent 51-53; St Luke Bromley Common 54-57; Educn Officer Ceylon Studs in UK 50-57; Hon Chap to Ceylon Forces in UK 55-57; Chap Br Ch of St Jas Oporto Portugal 57-59; V of Winchcombe w Gretton and Sudeley Manor 59-62; RD of Winchcombe 62; Sen Div Master Pate's Gr Sch Cheltm 62-66; L to Offic Dio Glouc 62-65; C-in-c of Farmington 65-69; Sen Lect Relig Stud Heref Coll of Educn 66-69; Prin Lect and Head of Dept 69-78; L to Offic Dio Heref from 69; Dios Guildf and Win from 79. *9 Handcroft Close, Crondall, Farnham, Surrey.*

CARTMELL, Richard. b 43. Cranmer Hall Dur 77. **d** 79 Lanc for Blackb **p** 80 Blackb. C of Whittle-le-Woods Dio Blackb from 79. *65 Daisy Meadow, Clayton Brook Estate, Nr Bamber Bridge, Lancs.*

CARTMILL, Ralph Arthur. b 40. St Jo Coll Dur 62. Em Coll Cam 64. Ridley Hall Cam 63. **d** 65 **p** 66 Ches. C of St Jo Evang Dukinfield 65-68; Wilmslow 68-69; Warden Walton Youth Centre Liv 69-70; Asst Master Aylesbury Gr Sch 70-74; Perm to Offic Dio Ox 72-74; V of Terriers Dio Ox from 74. *St Francis's Vicarage, Terriers, High Wycombe, Bucks.* (High Wycombe 20676)

CARTWRIGHT, Charles Henry. b 17. SOC 61. **d** 64 **p** 65 S'wark. C of St Aug Grove Pk Lee Dio S'wark 64-73; V 73-82. *c/o 336 Baring Road, SE12*

CARTWRIGHT, Cyril Hicks. b 13. Selw Coll Cam BA 35, MA 44. Linc Th Coll 36. **d** 38 Lewes for Chich **p** Chich. C of Wadhurst 38-41; Rye 41-43; Barcombe 43-45; Hayward's Heath (in c of Ch of the Presentation) 45-49; Nuthurst 49-50; Gillingham 51-52; St John Chatham 52-53; Pembury 53-54; Belvedere 54-56; Southwick 56-62; Forest Row (in c of Ashurst Wood) 62-70; V of Whitehawk 70-75; St Andr Waterloo Street Hove 75-80; Perm to Offic Dio Chich from 80. *6 Somerhill Road, Hove, BN3 1RN.* (Brighton 737814)

CARTWRIGHT, Ven Edward David. b 20. Selw Coll Cam 2nd cl Hist Trip pt i 40, BA 41, Steel Stud 41, Th Trip 2nd cl pt i 42, MA 45. Westcott Ho Cam 41. **d** 43 Grimsby for Linc **p** 44 Linc. C of Boston 43-48; V of St Leon Redfield Bris 48-52; Sec Bris Coun of Chr Chs 50-61; V of Olveston (w Aust from 54) 52-60; Proc Conv Bris 56-73; V of Bishopston 60-73; Sec Bris Dio Conf and Synod 66-73; Hon Can of Bris 70-73; Archd and Hon Can of Win from 73; V of Sparsholt w Lainston Dio Win from 73; Ch Comm from 73; M Gen Syn Dio Win from 75; Surr from 78. *Sparsholt Vicarage, Winchester, Hants, SO21 2NS.* (Sparsholt 265)

CARTWRIGHT, Frank. b 15. Chich Th Coll 47. **d** 49 **p** 50 Liv. C of Warrington 49-53; Asst Master Boteler Gr Sch 49-52; C of St Anne Wigan 53-55; V of St Mary Edge Hill 55-62; St Anne Wigan 62-73; St John Evang Walton 73-80. *38 Gaskell Street, STockton Heath, Warrington, WA4 2UN.* (Warrington 67469)

CARTWRIGHT, Hugh Benjamin Simons. b 27. Ch Coll Cam. Sarum Th Coll 56. **d** 58 **p** 59 Newc T. C of Rothbury 58-61; Walker 61-62; V of Gazeley w Dalham 62-71; R of Ringshall w Battisford and Finborough Parva 71-74; Chap at Dhahran 75-78; V of Ingrow w Hainworth Dio Bradf from 78. *St John's Vicarage, Ingrow, Keighley, Yorks, BD21 1BT.* (Keighley 604069)

CARTWRIGHT, Preb Hugh Bent. b 07. Univ of Dur 29. St Stephen Ho Ox 30. **d** 32 **p** 33 Lon. C of All SS Friern Barnet 32-36; All SS Childs Hill 37-40; LDHM of St Matthias Colindale 40-46; V of St Andr Alexandra Pk Muswell Hill Dio Lon 46-73; Preb of St Paul's Cathl Lon 69-73; Preb (Emer) from 73. *21 Queens Court, Ledbury, Herefs, HR8 2AL.* (Ledbury 3123)

CARTWRIGHT, Hugh Frederick. b 1900. St Bonif Coll Warm 35. **d** 37 **p** 39 Truro. C of E w W Looe 37-39; Linthwaite 39-41; Mirfield 41-50; Barnsley 50-53; C-in-c of Penistone 53; C of Kirkburton 53-54; Cumberworth w Denby Dale 54-55; Felkirk w Brierley 55-74. *Dulverton Hall, St Martin's Square, Scarborough.*

CARTWRIGHT, John Mountfort. b 05. Qu Coll Cam 2nd cl Hist Trip pt i 26, BA (3rd cl Anthrop Trip) 27, MA 31. Ridley Hall Cam 27. **d** 29 **p** 30 S'wark. C of Ch Ch Gipsy Hill 29-34; Battersea (in c of St Mary-le-Park) 34-35; V of St Mary-le-Park Battersea 35-43; H Trin Weston-super-Mare 43-57; Offg Chap Battersea Gen Hosp 36-43; V of Martock 57-70; RD of Martock 67-70. *Hunters End, New Road, Norton-sub-Hamdon, Somt.* (Chiselborough 271)

CARTWRIGHT, Joseph Amos Allen. St Paul's Th Coll Grahmstn. **d** 60 **p** 61 Capetn. C of Simonstown 60-79; Perm to Offic Dio Capetn from 79. *Lyndall, Glencairn, PO Simonstown, S Africa.* (82-3298)

CARTWRIGHT, Keith Nathaniel. b 58. Univ of WI BA (Th) 80. Codr Coll Barb 79. **d** 81 Nass. C of Ch the K Freeport Dio Nass from 81. *23 Eidelweiss Chalets, PO Box F87, Freeport, Grand Bahama, Bahamas.*

CARTWRIGHT, Michael John. b 42. Qu Coll Birm 67. **d** 70 **p** 71 Worc. C of Astwood Bank w Crabbs Cross 70-75; V of Dines Green 75-77; St Paul Stockton-on-Tees Dio Dur from 77. *65 Bishopton Road, Stockton-on-Tees, Cleve, TS18 4PL.* (Stockton-on-Tees 617869)

CARTWRIGHT, Canon Peter Graham. b 23. Univ of Bris BA 51. BC Coll Bris 46. **d** 51 Burnley for Blackb **p** 52 Blackb. C of Ch of Sav Blackb 51-53; BCMS Miss at Lotome 53-61; I of Moroto 61-64; C of Willowfield 64-65; I of Moville U 65-80; Dom Chap to Bp of Derry from 79; R of Conwall w Gartan Dio Raph from 80; Can of Raph from 80. *Letterkenny, Co Donegal, Irish Republic.* (Letterkenny 22573)

✠ **CARTWRIGHT, Right Rev Richard Fox.** b 13. Pemb Coll Cam BA 35, MA 39. Univ of the South, Tennessee Hon DD 69. Cudd Coll 35. **d** 36 **p** 37 S'wark. C of St Anselm Kennington Cross 36-40; Kingswood (in c of Lower Kingswood) 40-45; V of St Andr Surbiton 45-52; Proc Conv S'wark 50-52; V of St Mary Redcliffe Bristol (w Temple from 56 and St Jo Bapt from 65) 52-72; Hon Can of Bris 60-72; Cons Ld Bp Suff of Plymouth in Westmr Abbey 29 Sept 72 by Abp of Cant; Bps of Linc; Ex; B & W; Ely; St Alb; Ox; and Nor; Bps Suffr of Southn; Crediton; Croydon; Malmesbury; Edmonton; Dover; Bedford; and Huntingdon; and others; res 81. *Long Hay, Treligga, Delabole, N Cornw, PL33 9EE.* (Camelford 2506)

CARTWRIGHT, Roy Arthur. b 29. CCC Cam BA 52, MA 56. Wycl Hall Ox. **d** 54 **p** 55 Chelmsf. C of Hornchurch 54-56; Gt Clacton w L Holland 56-60; Min of St Steph Eccles Distr Prittlewell 60-69; V 69-72; Perm to Offic Dio Chelmsf from 72; Hon C of Shoebury S Dio Chelmsf from 77. *72 Raphael Drive, Shoeburyness, Southend-on-Sea, Essex, SS3 9UX.*

CARTWRIGHT, Samuel. b 27. Cudd Coll 71. **d** and **p** 72 Man. C of Rochdale 72-76; V of Roundthorn Oldham Dio Man from 76. *Roundthorn Vicarage, Clarksfield Street, Oldham, OL4 3AN.* (061-624 1007)

CARTWRIGHT, Sidney Herbert. b 1894. Ch Coll Cam BA 20, MA 23. Ridley Hall Cam. **d** 28 **p** 29 Leic. C of Loughborough 28-30; R of Stanford-on-Soar 31-32; Toft w Caldecote 32-41; Kegworth 41-56; RD of Akeley E 53-56; R of Moulton 56-64; R of Kennett 56-64; V of Gt Wilbraham 64-70; C-in-c of Horseheath 71-73. *3 The Arch, High Street, Bottisham, Cambridge.*

CARTWRIGHT, Sidney Victor. b 22. **d** 74 **p** 75 Leic. C of St Pet Braunstone Leic 74-78; P-in-c of Arnesby w Shearsby Dio Leic from 78. *Arnesby Vicarage, Leicester, LE8 3WJ.* (Peatling Magna 371)

CARTY, Very Rev Hilton Manasseh. b 21. Univ of Dur. Codr Coll Barb BA, LTh 45. **d** and **p** 45 Gui. C of All SS New Amsterdam 45-47; St Phil Georgetown 47-49; R of Anna Regina 49-52; Meten-meer-Zorg 52-59; Plaisance 59-62; C of St Agnes w St Simon Bris 62-65; Cowley (in c of St Francis) 65-73; V of Earley St Bart Reading 73-77; Dean and R of St John's Cathl Antig from 77; Exam Chap to Bp of Antig from 79. *Deanery, Box 71, St John's, Antigua, W Indies.*

CARVER, Alfred Basil. b 11. Em Coll Cam BA 33, MA 37. TD 52. Ridley Hall Cam 33. **d** 36 **p** 37 Lon. C of St Steph Paddington 36-45; CF (TA) 38-62; Men in Disp 45; Actg Chap H Trin and St Mark Florence 44-45; R of H Trin Chelsea 45-80. *The Larches, School Hill, London Road, Maresfield, E Sussex TN22 2ED.* (0825 2428)

CARVER, Arthur Tregarthen. b 15. Univ of Lon 37. Tyndale Hall Bris 37. **d** 41 **p** 42 Liv. C of Ch Ch Southport (in c from 43) 41-44; C-in-c St Matt Conv Distr Thatto Heath 44-48; V of St Mark St Helens 48-53; Marple 53-69; Proc Conv Ches 64-69; R of Uphill 69-80. *20 Hayton Street, Knutsford, Chesh, WA16 0DR.* (0565 51622)

CARVER, Bernard Nash. b 1889. Selw Coll Cam BA (3rd cl Th Trip) 11, MA 15. Wells Th Coll 11. **d** 12 **p** 13 Roch. C of Bromley 12-16; TCRN 16-19; Chap RN 19-45; Hon Chap to HM the King 43-45; V of Bradpole 46-52; Whiteparish 52-62; Perm to Offic Dio B & W 62-79. *6 Burges Close, Marnhull, Sturminster Newton, Dorset DT10 1QQ.* (Marnhull 820 025)

CARVER, Canon Clifford Henry George. b 17. Wycl Hall Ox 47. **d** 49 **p** 50 Worc. C of St Jo Bapt-in-Bedwardine Worc 49-52; V of St Pet Hindley Dio Liv 52-57; Commiss N Nig 53-67; CF (TA) 54-68; CF (TAVR) from 68; V of St Jo Bapt Claines 57-63; Putney 63-69; Treales 69-74; Industr Chap Dio Blackb 69-74; V of St Mary de Castro Leic 74-81; Chap Leic Poly 74-81; Commiss N Nig from 78; Can (Emer) in Cathl of St Mich, Kaduna, Nig from 81. *15 Castle Street, Leicester, LE1 5WN.*

CARVER, Neil Anthony Stephen. Bp's Univ Lennox BA 66, LST 69. **d** and **p** 69 Tor. P Dio Tor 69-70; C of Grace Ch, Brantford 70-71; I of Walkerton 71-74; All SS Waterloo 74-80; St John Windsor Dio Hur from 80. *3305 Sandwich Street, Windsor, Ont., Canada.*

CARVER, Walter Eric. b 23. **d** 72 St Arn. Hon C of Red Cliffs Dio St Arn (Dio Bend from 77) from 72. *6 Westcliffs Avenue, Red Cliffs, Vic, Australia 3496.* (050-24 1760)

CARVOSSO, John Charles. b 45. ACA 71. Oak Hill Th Coll 75. **d** 78 Lon **p** 79 Kens for Lon. C of St John w St Andr Chelsea Dio Lon from 78. *The Curate's Flat, St John's Church, Worldsend, King's Road, SW10.*

CASE, Peter Elliott. b 54. Qu Univ Kingston Ont BA 76. Wycl Coll Tor MDiv 79. **d** 79 **p** 80 Ont. C of Ch Ch Belleville 79-81; on leave. *Queen's University, Kingston, Ont, Canada.*

CASE, Philip Thomas Charles. b 17. Univ Coll Southn BSc (Econ) 51. Sarum Th Coll 51. **d** 53 Lon **p** 54 Kens for Lon. C of St Steph w St John Westmr 53-56; St Matt w St Hilda Ashford 56-58; C-in-c of St Hilda Conv Distr Ashford 58-61; V of St Helier Surrey 61-66; Witley Dio Guildf from 66; RD of Godalming from 79. *Witley Vicarage, Godalming, Surrey.* (Wormley 2886)

CASE, Wilfrid Michael. b 16. Worc Ordin Coll. **d** 56 **p** 57 Ripon. C of Laithkirk 56-58; V of Grinton w Marrick 59-75; Grinton w Arkengarthdale (and Downholme and Marske from 76) Dio Ripon from 75. *Reeth Vicarage, Richmond, N Yorks.* (Reeth 328)

CASEBOW, Ronald Philip. b 31. Roch Th Coll 59. **d** 61 **p** 62 Lon. C of Ch Ch Southgate 61-64; St Luke Oseney Crescent w St Paul Camden Square St Pancras 64-70; V of St Steph Colchester 70-74; Burnham-on-Crouch Dio Chelmsf from 74. *Vicarage, Burnham-on-Crouch, Essex, CM0 8DZ.* (Maldon 782071)

CASEY, Ernest George. b 14. St Chad's Coll Dur BA 36. **d** 37 **p** 38 Dur. C of Benfieldside 37-40; Winlaton (in c of High Spen) 40-44; Actg C-in-c of Cassop w Quarrington 44-45; PC of Chilton Moor 45-59; V of St Giles Dur 59-79. *7 Hampshire Road, Durham.*

CASHEL, WATERFORD, LISMORE, OSSORY, FERNS AND LEIGHLIN, Lord Bishop of. *See* Willoughby, Right Rev Noel Vincent.

CASHEL, Archdeacon of. *See* Hogg, Ven George Smith.

CASHEL, Dean of. *See* Clarke, Very Rev David George Alexander.

CASHMAN, John Harold. BD Lon 68, BA 79. Moore Th Coll Syd ACT ThL 67. **d** 67 **p** 68 Syd. C of Blacktown 67-71; Actg R of Centennial Pk 72-73; R 73-77; St Mary Balmain Dio Syd from 78. *85 Darling Street, Balmain, NSW, Australia 2041.* (82-2794)

CASHMORE, Cyril. b 01. St Aug Coll Cant 20. **d** 25 **p** 32 Truro. C of St Jo Bapt Penzance 25-26; Padstow 32-35; H Trin Weymouth 35-37; H Trin Win 37-38; R of Chillesford w Butley Capel (V) and Wantisden (V) 38-42; V of Battyeford 42-49; PC of St John Portland 49-53; Chap to HM Pris Ex 53-57; Dartmoor 57-60; Linc 60-61; V of Bardney w Southey 61-68; V of Stainfield w Apley 61-68; Bilsby w Farlesthorpe 68-71; R of Hannah w Hagnaby and Markby 68-71; Perm to Offic Dio Chelmsf from 73. *207 Front Lane, Cranham Park, Upminster, Essex, RM14 1LD.* (Upminster 29508)

✠ **CASHMORE, Right Rev Thomas Herbert.** b 1892. Codr Coll Barb. Univ of Dur BA 18. Kaisar-i-Hind Med (2nd cl) 30. **d** 17 Antig **p** 18 Chota N. Miss at Ranchi 17-23; Chap of St Jas Calc and Prin of St Jas Coll Calc 24-33; V of Holmfirth 33-42; Hon Can of Wakef Cathl 42-46; V of Brighouse 42-46; Can Missr of Wakef 46-55; Ed Wakef Dioc News 51-55; Cons Ld Bp Suffr of Dunwich in S'wark Cathl 25 Jan 55 by Abp of Cant; Bps of S'wark; Roch; B & W; Chelmsf; and Wakef; Bps Suffr of Woolwich; Pontefract; and Bp Hubback; res 67; Exam Chap to Bp of St E 55-67; Commiss Carp from 61. *Lynton, Graham Avenue, Brighton 6, Sussex.* (Brighton 553005)

CASIOT, David John. b 39. St Pet Coll Ox BA (3rd cl Th) 63, MA 67. Clifton Th Coll 63. **d** 65 **p** 66 York. C of Drypool 65-67; Barking 67-71; R of St Edm, Whalley Range Dio Man from 71. *1 Range Road, Whalley Range, Manchester, M16 8FS.* (061-226 1291)

CASON, Preb Ronald Arthur. b 28. Kelham Th Coll 48. **d** 53 Stafford for Cant **p** 54 Lich. C of Fenton Staffs 53-56; V of Brereton 56-63; Hugglescote w Donnington 63-67; Blakenall Heath 67-74; R of Stoke-on-Trent Dio Lich 74-80; Team R from 80; Preb of Lich Cathl from 75; Surr from 76; RD of Stoke-on-Trent from 78. *Rectory, Stoke-on-Trent, Staffs, ST4 1LW.* (Stoke-on-Trent 45287)

CASSAM, Victor Reginald. b 33. Chich Th Coll 59. **d** 62 **p** 63 Portsm. C of St Jo Bapt Rudmore Portsea 62-64; St Alb W Leigh Havant 64-66; St Martin Barton 66-69; Stanmer w Falmer and Moulsecoomb (in c of H Nativ Lower Bevendean) 69-73; C-in-c of Catsfield Dio Chich 73-76; R (w Crowhurst) 76-81; R and V of Selsey Dio Chich from 81. *Rectory, St Peter's Crescent, Selsey, Chichester, PO20 0NA.* (Selsey 2363)

CASSELTON, John Charles. b 43. Dipl Th (Lon) 67. Oak Hill Th Coll 64. **d** 68 **p** 69 Ex. C of St Mary Magd, Upton, Torquay 68-73; Braintree (in c of St Paul's) 73-80; V of St Jo Bapt Ipswich Dio St E from 80. *St John's Vicarage, Ipswich, Suff.* (Ipswich 78034)

CASSIDY, Cecil Ralph. b 1897. AKC 23. **d** 24 **p** 25 Roch. C of St Mary Shortlands 24-26; Witbank 26-27; Perm to Offic at Chelsfield 28-29; C of Bapchild w Tonge 29-30; Seasalter 30-35; V of Edlington w Wispington 35-38; Brothertoft w Kirton Holme 38-39; Rodmersham 39-52; Chap RNVR 41-43; V of Upwood w Gt Raveley (and L Raveley from 55) 52-56; V of L Raveley 52-55; R of Wood Walton 52-56; Nash w Thornton and Beachampton 56-60; V of Gt Waxham w Palling 60-66; C-in-c of Horsey 61-66; Perm to Offic Dio Nor from 66. *32 Brewster Court, Blofield, NR13 4JT.*

CASSIDY, Eric Lefroy. ACT ThL 27, Th Scho 36. **d** 27 **p** 28 Brisb. C of St Paul Ipswich Queensld 27-30; Perm to Offic at St Clem Barnsbury 30; St Andr Hillingdon 30-32; M of Commun of Ascen Dio Goulb 32-40; C of All SS Brisb 41-44; St Alb Auchenflower Brisb 44-47; Vice-Prin St Francis Th Coll Brisb 47-50; C of Dogura Cathl New Guinea 50-52; Warden of Newton Coll Dio New Guinea 52-70; Exam Chap to Bp of New Guinea 60-70. *Anglican Mission, Samarai, Papua, New Guinea.*

CASSIDY, George Henry. b 42. QUB BSc (Econ) 65. Univ of Lon MPhil 67. Oak Hill Th Coll 70. **d** 72 **p** 73 Bris. C of Ch Ch (w Em to 74) Clifton 72-75; V of Sea Mills 75-82; St Paul Portman Square Marylebone Dio Lon from 82. *2 St Paul's Court, 56 Manchester Street, W1M 5AH.* (01-935 3355)

CASSIDY, Herbert. b 35. Trin Coll Dub BA and Carson, Moncrieff Cox, Kyle and Downes Liturgy Pri 57, Div Test (1st cl) 58, MA 65. **d** 58 **p** 59 Connor. C of H Trin Belf 58-60; Ch Ch Derry 60-62; R of Aghavilly w Derrynoose 62-65; Hon v Cho of Arm Cathl from 63; C of Portadown 65-67; I of St Columba Portadown Dio Arm from 67. *81 Loughgall Road, Portadown, Craigavon, Co Armagh, BT62 4EG, N Ireland.*

CASSIDY, Patrick Nigel. b 40. Trin Coll Dub BA (2nd cl Div 1 Mod Lang Mod) 63, MA 66. Sarum Th Coll 64. **d** 66 **p** 67 Bradf. C of St Barn Heaton 66-68; Asst Chap Brussels 68-70; Chap SW France for CCCS and USPG 70-72; V of St Luke Oseney Crescent w St Paul Camden Square St Pancras Dio Lon from 72. *Vicarage, Camden Square, NW 1.* (01-485 3147)

CASSIDY, Ronald. b 43. BD (2nd cl) Lon 66. Tyndale Hall, Bris 63. **d** 68 Warrington for Liv **p** 69 Liv. C of St Lawr Kirkdale 68-70; Em Bolton 70-74; V of Roughtown Dio Man from 74. *Vicarage, Carrhill Road, Mossley, Ashton-under-Lyne, OL5 0SA.* (Mossley 2250)

CASSIM, Jaime. St Bart Th Coll Msumba. **d** 60 **p** 61

Lebom. P Dio Lebom 60-79; Dio Niassa from 79. *Metangula, Lago, Niassa, Mazambique.*

CASSON, Cuthbert. b 04. Late Exhib of St Cath Coll Cam 2nd cl Hist Trip Div ii, 25, BA 27, MA 31. Bps' Coll Cheshunt 28. **d** 28 **p** 29 Leic. C of Hinckley 28-31; Rugby (in c of H Trin) 31-38; V of Meriden 38-46; Chap Meriden Inst 39-46; R of Sudbourne w Orford 46-55; V of Stanford w Swinford 55-66; R of Alexton 66-76; Wardley w Belton 66-76; Perm to Offic Dio Leic from 76; L to Offic Dio Pet from 76. *8 Stamford Road, Oakham, Leics, LE15 6JA.* (Oakham 55507)

CASSON, David Christopher. b 41. Qu Coll Cam 2nd cl Hist Trip pt i 63, BA (2nd cl Th Trip pt ia) 64, MA 68. Ridley Hall Cam 65. **d** 67 Birm **p** 68 Aston for Birm. C of St Martin Birm 67-72; Luton (in c of St Francis) 72-77; V of St Francis Luton Dio St Alb from 77. *145 Hollybush Road, Luton, LU2 9HQ.* (Luton 28030)

CASSON, Donald Trench. b 12. Qu Coll Cam 3rd cl Hist Trip pt i 33, BA (3rd cl Hist Trip pt ii) 34, MA 38. Wycl Coll Ox 34. **d** 36 Bradf **p** 37 Bp Mounsey for Bradf. C of St Lawr Pudsey 36-38; CMS Miss Lui 38-40; Akot 40-41; Malek White Nile 41-45; R of Hampton Lucy 45-49; Chap and Asst Master at Arusha Sch Tang 49-52; Chap at Thika Kenya 52-60; Chap at Dusseldorf 60-63; V of Hurstbourne Tarrant (w Faccombe from 67) 63-69; P-in-c of Faccombe w Combe 64-67; V of Framfield 69-77; Perm to Offic Dio Ban from 79. *Penrhiw, Uwchygarreg, Nr Machynlleth, Powys.*

CASSON, Frank Alfred. b 06. Qu Coll Cam BA 28, MA 32. Ridley Hall Cam 28. **d** 30 Warrington for Liv **p** 31 Liv. C of St Helens 30-33; Chap Watts Naval Tr Sch Elmham 33-35; V of St Sav Liv 35-39; St Jas Alperton 39-44; Gt Baddow 44-50; R of Darfield 50-55; V of All SS Eastbourne 55-69; Perm to Offic Dio Chich from 69. *1 Roffrey Avenue, Hampden Park, Eastbourne, E Sussex, BN22 0AE.* (Eastbourne 53212)

CASSON, James Stuart. b 32. Univ of Liv BA (1st cl German) 54. Univ of Nottm MPhil 70. Ridley Hall Cam. **d** 61 Warrington for Liv **p** 62 Liv. C of Eccleston 61-64; Littleover 64-67; V of Dearham 67-76; Holme Eden Dio Carl from 76. *Holme Eden Vicarage, Warwick Bridge, Carlisle, Cumb, CA4 8RF.* (Wetheral 60332)

CASSON, Stanley Christopher. St Aid Coll 31. **d** 33 **p** 34 Ches. C Em New Brighton 33-36; H Trin Birkenhead 36-40; V of H Trin Northwich 40-53; R of Lymm 53-70. *42 Glebelands Road, Knutsford, Cheshire.*

CASSWELL, Peter Joyce. b 22. Trin Coll Cam BA 48, MA 50. Ridley Hall Cam 48. **d** 50 Dover for Cant **p** 51 Cant. C of St Mildred Addiscombe 50-53; Min of Conv Distr of St Edw K and Confessor New Addington 53-55; V 55-64; Proc Conv Cant 59-64; Chelmsf 64-70; Commiss Iran 61-70; R of Buckhurst Hill 64-78; Surr 64-78; Chap Forest Hosp 64-78; Hon Can of Chelmsf Cathl 75-78; R of Lutterworth w Cotesbach Dio Leic from 78. *Lutterworth Rectory, Leics, LE17 4SH.* (Lutterworth 2669)

CASTAING, Denis Reginald. b 40. Univ of Auckld MSc 65. St Jo Coll Auckld 70. **d** 69 **p** 70 Ch Ch. on leave from 70. *12 Rowses Road, Christchurch 7, NZ.*

CASTERTON, Michael John. b 39. St D Coll Lamp BA 62. St Mich Coll Llan 63. **d** 65 **p** 66 Roch. C of Sidcup 65-67; Brighouse 67-73; Chap Cho of Ches Cathl 73-75; V of Roberttown Dio Wakef from 75. *Roberttown Vicarage, Liversedge, W Yorks, WF15 7PF.* (Heckmondwike 402064)

CASTLE, Brian Colin. b 49. Univ of Lon BA 72. Univ of Ox BA (Th) 77. Cudd Coll Ox 74. **d** 77 **p** 78 S'wark. C of St Mich Sutton 77-80; St Pet Limpsfield Dio S'wark from 80. *15 Chichele Road, Oxted, Surrey, RH8 0AE.* (Oxted 4156)

CASTLE, Brian Stanley. b 47. Oak Hill Coll 70. **d** 73 Stepney for Lon **p** 74 Lon. C of St Andr w St Matthias Isl 73-76; St Paul Homerton 76-80; V of St Jas L Bethnal Green Dio Lon from 80. *St James the Less Vicarage, St James Avenue, E2 9JD.* (01-980 1612)

CASTLE, Charles. b 01. AKC 35. Bps' Coll Cheshunt 35. **d** 35 **p** 36 Cant. C of St Martin Croydon 35-38; H Trin Maidstone 38-42; V of H Trin Sittingbourne 42-50; R of Smarden 50-56; Chap to Ipswich and E Suff Hosp Group 56-66; V of Thurnham w Detling 66-71. *16 Pannal Ash Crescent, Harrogate, Yorks, HG2 0HT.*

CASTLE, Mervyn Edwin. b 42. St Pet Th Coll Alice Dipl Th 70. **d** 69 **p** 70 Capetn. C of St Mark, Athlone 69-72; St Geo Cathl Capetn 72-76; Prec of St Mary Virg Cathl Johann 76-77; R of Westlea Dio Johann from 77. *Box 58047, Newville, Johannesburg, S Africa.* (011-27 1797)

CASTLE, Michael David. b 38. Wells Th Coll 69. **d** 71 Aston for Birm **p** 72 Birm. C of St Mary Virg Acocks Green 71-75; Weoley Castle Dio Birm 75-78; V from 78. *Vicarage, Marston Road, Birmingham, B29 5LS.* (021-475 1194)

CASTLE, Roger James. St Jo Coll Cam 3rd cl Architecture and Fine Arts Trip pt i 61, BA (3rd cl Architecture and Fine Arts Trip pt ii) 62, MA 66. Clifton Th Coll 63. **d** 65 **p** 66 Pet. C of St Mary Rushden 65-68; Stapenhill 68-72; V of Hayfield Dio Derby from 72. *Hayfield Vicarage, Stockport, Chesh.* (New Mills 43350)

CASTLE, Vincent Clifton. b 15. St Jo Coll Dur LTh 38, BA 39. ALCD 37. **d** 39 **p** 40 Chelmsf. C of St John Moulsham 39-42; CF (EC) 42-47 (twice Men in Disp 44); Min of St Geo Conv Distr Oakdale 47-50; PC of Coalpit Heath 50-54; CF 54-58; V of Avonmouth 58-63; Chap Miss to Seamen 63-66; Sen Chap 66-71; V of Creeksea w Althorne (and Latchingdon w N Fambridge from 80) Dio Chelmsf from 71. *Althorne Vicarage, Chelmsford, Essex, CM3 6BZ.* (Maldon 740250)

CASTLE, Wilfrid Thomas Froggatt. b 11. Qu Coll Cam BA 33, MA 37. Wycl Hall Ox 33. **d** 35 **p** 36 Chelmsf. C of Ch Ch Leyton 35-38; Dover 38-39; Skipton-in-Craven 39-42; V of Cowling 42-45; 2nd Chap Cyprus 45-50; Chap at Limassol w Paphos 50-54; H Trin Cannes 54-63; Crimean Mem Ch Istanbul All SS Moda and Chap HBM Embassy Ankara 63-65; V of St Pet Bocking 65-72; R of St Barn Paisley Dio Glas 72-77; P-in-c 77-79. *2 Schaw Court, 174a Drymen Road, Bearsden, Glasgow, G61 3SG.* (041-942 6140)

CASTLE, Wilmot Rodd. St Jo Coll Auckld LTh 36. **d** 33 **p** 34 Auckld. C of Otahuhu 33-36; Bethnal Green 36; Miss Dio Melan 36-39; P-in-c of Coromandel 39-41; Chap AMF 42-45; V of Hauraki Plains 46-48; Chap RNZN 48-65; L to Offic Dio Auckld 65-66; C of Birkenhead 66-73; Hon C 73-79; Perm to Offic Dio Auckld from 79. *20a Brett Avenue, Takapuna, NZ.* (494-964)

CASTLEDINE, Canon John. b 17. AKC (1st cl) and Barry Pri 40. **d** 40 **p** 41 Ripon. C of Whitkirk 40-41; Richmond 41-43; Henfield 43-44 and 47; Chap RNVR 44-47; V of St Mich AA Lancing 48-53; Kirkby Moorside w Gillamoor 53-63; C-in-c of Bransdale w Farndale 55-60; V 60-63; Northallerton w Kirby Sigston Dio York from 63; RD of Northallerton from 63; Can and Preb of York Minster from 76. *Vicarage, Northallerton, N Yorks, DL7 8DJ.* (Northallerton 3338)

CASTLETON, David Miles. b 39. Oak Hill Th Coll 69. **d** 72 **p** 73 Stepney for Lon. C of St Steph Canonbury Islington 72-76; St Sav w Stoke-next-Guildf City and Dio Guildf from 76. *2 Joseph's Road, Guildford, Surrey, GU1 1DW.*

CASWELL, Ven Michael John. Bp's Univ Lennox BA 59, LST 61. **d** 61 Ont. C of Ch Ch Belleville 61-63; on leave 63-64; I of Sharbot Lake 64-67; Stirling 67-70; R of Trenton Dio Ont from 70; Archd of Ont from 78. *90 King Street, Trenton, Ont, Canada.* (613-392 5234)

CASWELL, Roger John. b 47. St Chad's Coll Dur BA 70. St Steph Ho Ox 75. **d** 77 **p** 78 Chich. C of The Resurr Brighton Dio Chich from 77. *6 Edinburgh Road, Brighton, Sussex.* (Brighton 602006)

CATCHPOLE, Desmond Stanley. Trin Coll Tor BA 25, BD 31, Hon DD 52. **d** and **p** 27 Koot. C of Bonnington w S Slocan 27-29; R of Rossland 29-42; Cler Sec Koot Synod and Archd of Okanagan 41-67; Can of Koot 41-67; R of Kelowna 42-67; Cler Sec to Prov Synod of BC 47-65; Exam Chap to Bp of Koot 48-67; Koot Dioc Treas 55-67; L to Offic Dio BC from 67. *Ste 406, 505 Trutch Street, Victoria, BC, Canada.*

CATCHPOLE, Geoffrey Alan. b 53. Westcott Ho Cam 76. **d** 77 **p** 78 S'wark. C of St Luke Camberwell 77-80; St Barn Dulwich Dio S'wark from 80. *The Chaplain's House, The Old College, Gallery Road, Dulwich SE21 7AD.* (01-693 9019)

CATCHPOLE, Harry Ebenezer. b 21. Roch Th Coll 64. **d** 66 **p** 67 St E. C of St Mary Stoke, Ipswich 66-69; Thorpe Episcopi 69-72; V of Gt Cornard Dio St E from 72. *Cornard Vicarage, 95 Bures Road, Sudbury, Suff, CO10 0JE.* (Sudbury 73579)

CATCHPOLE, Keith William. K Coll Lon and Warm AKC 56. **d** 57 **p** 58 Ches. C of Woodchurch 57-61; W Kirby 61-64; C-in-c of Ch of Resurr Conv Distr Upton Priory Macclesfield 64-72; R of E w Mid Lavant Dio Chich from 72; RD of Chich from 80. *Lavant Rectory, Chichester, Sussex.* (Chichester 527313)

CATCHPOLE, Roy. b 46. St Jo Coll Nottm LTh 74. **d** 74 Barking for Chelmsf **p** 75 Chelmsf. C of Rainham 74-76; Hyson Green 76-79; V of Broxtowe Dio Southw from 79. *St Martha's Vicarage, Frinton Road, Broxtowe, Nottingham, NG8 6GR.* (Nottm 278837)

CATEQUETA, Manuel. St Bart Th Coll Msumba. **d** 60 **p** 61 Lebom. P Dio Lebom. *Caixa Postal 83, Vila Cabral, Mozambique.*

CATER, Henry Derek. Chich Th Coll 49. **d** 51 **p** 52 Ripon. C of St Luke Beeston Hill Leeds 51-55; Knottingley 55-62; V of St Edw Barnsley 62-65; L to Offic Dio Gibr 65-66; Can Par Dio Wakef 66-69; L to Offic Dio Gibr (Gibr in Eur from 80) from 69. *68 Siren Street, Senglea, Malta, GC.*

CATERER, James Albert Leslie Blower. b 44. New Coll Ox BA 67, MA 81. Sarum Wells Th Coll 79. **d** 81 Tewkesbury for Glouc. C of SS Luke & John Cheltenham Dio Glouc from 81. *4 Carlton Street, Cheltenham, Glos, GL52 6AQ.*

CATES, Canon Geoffrey Charles. b 18. Univ of Leeds BA 42. Coll of Resurr Mirfield 42. **d** 44 **p** 45 Dur. C of Whitworth w Spennymoor 44-46; Brandon 46-47; Ushaw Moor 48-49; C of St Jas Clacton 49-51; Chap to Butlin's Holiday Camp Clacton-on-Sea 49-52; Bp of Accra's Chap to Chamber of Mines 52-53; V of Kumasi 54-61; Dean and R of St Geo Cathl Georgetn 61-71; R of Sacred Trin Salford Dio Man from 71; RD of Salford from 71; Hon Can of Man Cathl from 80. *52 Manchester Road, Swinton, Manchester, M27 1ET.* (061-794 8235)

CATHAN, Very Rev Paul Ambrose. b 18. St Paul's Th Coll Maur. **d** 41 **p** 42 Maur. C of St Paul Vacoas 41-45; R of St Barn Rodrigues 45-46; C of St Paul Vacoas 46-47; R of Anse Royale Sey 47-51; on leave 51-53; C of Vacoas 53-55; Sub-Dean of St Jas Cathl Port Louis 55-60; Dean from 63; R of St Barn Rodriques 60-63. *Deanery, St James's Cathedral, Port Louis, Mauritius.* (2-2354)

CATHCART, Alden Bernard. Univ of Tor BA 37. Wycl Coll Tor LTh 40. **d** 40 Tor **p** 40 Arctic for Tor. C of Apsley 40-42; R of Allandale and Innisfil 44-45; Midland 45-54; Woodbridge 54-73. *418 Hugel Avenue, Midland, Ont., Canada.*

CATHIE, Sean Bewley. b 43. Univ of Dur BA 67. Cudd Coll 67. **d** 69 Willesden for Lon **p** 70 Lon. C of Kensal Rise 69-73; H Trin w St Paul Paddington 73-75; P-in-c of Bridstow w Peterstow 75-80; L to Offic Dio Heref 80-81; Dio Lon from 81. *St Martin's Vicarage, Vicars Road, NW5 4NN.*

CATLEY, Alfred Mollett. b 10. Univ of Southn BA 61, Kelham Th Coll 28. **d** 34 **p** 35 Wakef. C of Royston 34-35; Mirfield 35-38; Hucknall Torkard 38-41; Chap RAFVR 41-46; V of Farnsfield 46-51; Chap RAF 51-57; R of Upham w Durley 57-77. *14 Ashton Close, Bishop's Waltham, Hants, SO3 1FP.* (Bp's Waltham 2087)

CATLEY, Allan Bruce. Univ of Syd BSc (Agr) 25, Walter and Eliza Hall Agr Research Fell 25-27; Univ of Wis MSc 27. Jes Coll Cam BA 37, MA 42. St Francis Coll Nundah 32. ACT ThL 34, ThD 62. **d** 32 **p** 33 Armid. C of Quirindi 32-33; Chap Boys' Sch Armid 34-35 and 38; on leave 35-37; Vice-Warden St Jo Coll Morpeth 39-46; Actg Chap C of E Gr Sch Morpeth 42-44; Hd Master All SS Coll Bath 47; Chap of St John's Coll Auckld 48-49; Sub-Warden 50-63; C of St Barn Mt Eden Auckld 65-69; Exam Chap to Bp of Auckld 67-69; Chap St Francis Coll Brisb 69-70; Perm to Offic Dio Auckld from 70. *Selwyn Village, Point Chevalier, Auckland 2, NZ.* (80-119)

CATLEY, Eric Denis. b 15. St Chad's Coll Dur BA 48, Dipl Th 50. **d** 50 **p** 51 Lon. C of Fulham 50-55; Dom Chap to Bp of Lon 55; V of St Mellitus Hanwell 56-61; Cosham 61-69; Ch of Ascen Portsea 69-79; Hon C of Parkstone Dio Sarum from 79. *19 Vicarage Court, 51 Danecourt Road, Parkstone, Dorset BH14 0PH.*

CATLEY, Frederick William. d 43 **p** 45 Calc. Chap at Asanol Dio Calc OMC Barisal 38-45; SPG Miss 46-48 (Chap Cuttack 47-48) Khargpur and Cuttack 48-51; and at Dhanbad 51-54; Chap St Paul's Cathl Calc 54-61; Can of Calc 57-62; R of St Paul's Miss Calc 61-62; V of Djakarta w Surabaja Java 62-70; P-in-c of S Distr Miss Br Hond 70-71; R of Northampton-Mullewa 71-75; Perm to Offic Dio Perth from 75. *Unit 20, Moline House, Deanmore Road, Karrinyup, W Australia 6018.* (41 3206)

CATLEY, John Howard. b 37. K Coll Lon and Warm AKC 60. **d** 61 **p** 62 Wakef. C of Sowerby Bridge w Norland 61-64; Almondbury 64-67; V of Earlsheaton 67-75; Brownhill Dio Wakef from 75. *Brownhill Vicarage, Batley, W Yorks, WF17 0NQ.* (Batley 474408)

CATLIN, John Howard. b 39. St Chad's Coll Dur BA 62. **d** 64 **p** 65 Portsm. C of St Mark N End Portsea 64-67; Fareham 67-70; P-in-c of Fresh Creek Andros Bahamas 70-71; R of Grand Turk 71-72; C of St Jo Evang Forton 72-73; V of St Mich AA Paulsgrove 73-80; St Alb Copnor Dio Portsm from 80. *St Alban's Vicarage, Copnor Road, Portsmouth, Hants, PO3 5AL.* (Portsm 662626)

CATLING, Charles Skene. Univ of Bris BA (Eng) 38. Lich Th Coll 38. **d** 40 **p** 41 Southw. C of Netherfield 40-43; Asst Chap Felsted Sch 43-45; Chap Ellesmere Coll 45-63; Perm to Offic Dio Truro 63-64; Asst Chap Univ of Keele 64-65; Ho Master Bethany Sch Goudhurst from 65; Perm to Offic Dio Cant from 71; Dio Truro from 72. *Vicarage, Devoran, Truro, Cornw, TR3 6PA.* (Devoran 863116)

CATLING, Canon Robert Mason. Late Scho and Prizeman of St Jo Coll Ox 1st cl Cl Mods 39, BA (1st cl Lit Hum) 41. 1st cl Th 42, MA 44. St Steph Ho Ox 41. **d** 43 **p** 44 Truro. C of All SS Falmouth 43-57 and 61-64; Libr of Pusey Ho Ox and L to Offic Dios Ox and Truro 57-61; Asst Chap Univ Coll Ox 57-61; V of St Barn, Beckenham 64-72; Devoran Dio Truro from 72; Hon Can of Truro from 77. *Devoran Vicarage, Truro, Cornw.* (Devoran 863116)

CATO, Percy William Frederick. b 06. AKC 35. OBE (Mil) 51. **d** 35 **p** 36 Lon. C of St Paul, Hammersmith 35-39; CF 39-64; DACG 49-60; ACG 60-64; Chap to HM the Queen 63-64; R of Cottesmore w Barrow 64-75. *4 Bailbrook Lane, Swainswick, Bath, Avon, BA1 7AH.* (Bath 26193)

CATON, David Arthur. b 25. Trin Coll Ox BA and MA 50. St Steph Ho Ox 49. **d** 51 **p** 52 Newc T. C of Seaton Hirst 51-55; St John's Cathl Umtata 55-56; Vice-Prin St Bede's Coll Umtata 57-61; V of Stapleford 61-69; Hurst 69-75; St Thos Ap Hanwell Dio Lon from 75; Commiss to Bp of St John's S Afr from 66. *182 Boston Road, W7 2AD.* (01-567 5280)

CATON, Canon Ina. b 14. Wycl Coll Tor STh 58. **d** 71 **p** 76 Sktn. Hosp Chap Dio Sktn 71-79; Can of Sktn 71-79; Can (Emer) from 79. *909-10 Hogarth Avenue, Toronto, M4K 1J9, Canada.*

CATON, Martin Oswald Hawkins. b 11. AKC 32. St Steph Ho Ox 33. **d** 34 **p** 35 Lon. C of St Francis Gladstone Park 34-39; Actg C of St Thos Shepherd's Bush 40-42; Offic C-in-c of Braybrooke and Oxendon 42-45; V of Huncote 45-48; St Mich AA Swanmore (w Havenstreet from 61) Dio Portsm from 48; C-in-c of Havenstreet IW 56-61; Chap Longford Hosp Havenstreet from 61. *St Michael's Vicarage, Wray Street, Ryde, PO33 3ED.* (Ryde 62113)

CATON, Philip Cooper. b 47. Oak Hill Coll 79. **d** Warrington for Liv. C of Much Woolton Dio Liv from 81. *39 Woolton Street, Woolton, Liverpool 25.*

CATOR, David John. b 32. St Paul's Coll Grahmstn 76. **d** 78 Bp Stanage for Johann **p** 79 Johann. C of Vereeniging Dio Johann from 78. *PO Box 3167, Three Rivers, S Africa 1935.*

CATT, Albert Henry. b 08. St Steph Ho Ox 34. **d** 37 **p** 38 Lon. C of St Mary Somers Town 37-40; CF (EC) 40-46; C of St Pet Harrow 46-48; V of St Geo Hornsey 49-74; Perm to Offic Dio Ely from 75. *48 Green Park, Chatteris, Cambs.*

CATT, Douglas Gordon. b 23. Roch Th Coll 61. **d** 63 **p** 64 Cant. C of St Martin w St Paul Cant 63-66; R of Croughton 66-75; R of Hinton-in-the-Hedges w Steane 66-75; C-in-c of Evenley 72-75; Chap S Andr Hosp Northn Dio Pet from 75. *St Andrew's Hospital, Northampton, NN1 5DG.* (Northn 21311)

CATT, Robert Stephen. b 41. St Jo Th Coll Morpeth. **d** 69 **p** 70 Newc. C of Merewether 69-70; E Maitland 70-72; Cessnock 72-75; P-in-c of Beresfield Dio Newc from 75. *Rectory, Beresfield Avenue, Beresfield, NSW, Australia 2322.* (66 1114)

CATTANACH, Alexander Hamilton Avery. Univ of Wales BA (2nd cl Latin) 37, St Mich Coll Llan 38. **d** 39 **p** 40 St D. C of St Bride's w Marloes 39-43; Pembroke Dock 43-46; St Jas Accrington 46-51; C-in-c of Lostock Hall Conv Distr 51-54; St John Conv Distr L Thornton Dio Blackb 54-61; V 61-81. *c/o Vicarage, Hawthorne Road, Thornton Cleveleys, Lancs.* (Thornton 3107)

CATTELL, Jack. Late Scho of Univ Coll Dur BA (2nd cl Cl) 37, Dipl Th 38, MA 40. BD (2nd cl) Lon 53. Sarum Th Coll 38. **d** 39 **p** 40 Wakef. C of Royston 39-41; Asst Master Dauntsey's Sch Devizes and Perm to Offic Dio Sarum 41-42; CF (EC) 42-46; Hon CF from 46; Asst Master Richmond Sch and L to Offic Dio Ripon 46-49; Chap R Wanstead Sch Dio Chelmsf 49-53; Hd Master Whitney Inst Sch Smith's Parish and LPr Dio Berm 53-60; R of H Trin Hamilton Dio Berm from 60; Archd of Berm 61-82; Exam Chap to Bp of Berm from 61; Commiss Berm 62-63 and 69. *Rectory, Bailey's Bay, Bermuda.*

CATTELL, John Eugene Brownlow. b 11. Selw Coll Cam 2nd cl Hist Trip pt i 33, BA 34, 3rd cl Th Trip pt i 35, MA 44. TD 62 Wells Th Coll 35. **d** 36 **p** 37 Chich. C of S Bersted 36-38; Soham 38-40; CF (EC) 40-45; CF (TA) 50-67; R of St Just-in-Roseland w St Mawes 45-49; Snailwell 49-65; V of Chippenham Cambs 49-65; RD of Fordham 53-65; V of Piddletrenthide w Plush, Alton Pancras (and Piddlehinton from 73) 65-74; P-in-c of Buckhorn Weston and Kington Magna 74-77. *Tredinnock, Bishops Hill Road, New Polzeath, Wadebridge, Cornwall PL27 6UF.*

CATTERALL, David Arnold. b 53. Univ of Lon BSc 74. Cranmer Hall Dur Dipl Th 78. **d** 78 **p** 79 Man. C of Swinton 78-81; St Martin Wythenshawe Dio Man from 81. *64 Blackcarr Road, Wythenshawe, Manchester, M23 8PX.*

CATTERICK, Canon John James. b 10. Univ of Lon 30. Egerton Hall Man 34. MRST 34. **d** 36 **p** 37 Man. C of St Pet Swinton 36-38; Battle (in c of Telham) 38-41; Eastbourne (in c of St Geo) 41-43; Offg C-in-c of St Pet-in-the-Forest Walthamstow 43-45; V of H Trin Waltham Cross 45-53; R of Ashwell 53-77; Hon Can of St Alb from 69. *20 Hodwell, Ashwell, Herts, SG7 5QQ.* (Ashwell 2635)

CATTLEY, Richard Melville. b 49. Trin Coll Bris Dipl Th 73. **d** 73 Penrith for Cartl **p** 74 Carl. C of St Thos Kendal 73-77; Publ Pr Dio St Alb from 77; Nat Sec of Pathfinders, Ch Pastoral Aid Soc 77-82; Ex Sec from 82. *44 Woodstock Road North, St Albans, Herts, AL1 4QF.* (St Albans 67694)

CATTON, Cedric Trevor. b 36. Wells Th Coll 70. **d** 72 **p** 73 Birm. C of Solihull 72-74; R of Hawstead w Nowton and Stanningfield w Bradfield Combust 74-79; Whepstead w Brockley 74-75; Adv for Chr Stewardship Dio St E from 77;

R of Cockfield Dio St E from 79. *Cockfield Rectory, Bury St Edmunds, Suff, IP30 0HA.* (Cockfield Green 385)

CATTON, Donald Arthur. Angl Th Coll BC LTh 66. **d** 66 New Westmr for Caled **p** 67 Caled. I of Ocean Falls 66-69; Saltcoats 69-70; Stoney Lake 70-72; St Barn Pet 72-78; St Laur City and Dio Tor from 78. *22 Wenderley Drive, Toronto, Ont, Canada.*

CAUDWELL, Charles Leopold. b 17. Sarum Wells Th Coll 75. **d** 77 **p** 78 Ex (APM). C of Offwell Group Dio Ex 77-80; Team V from 80. *Little Snodwell, Cotleigh, Honiton, Devon.*

CAUDWELL, Cyril. b 12. **d** 75 Chich **p** 76 Lewes for Chich. Hon C of St Barn Bexhill 75-78; All SS Sidley Bexhill Dio Chich from 78. *3 Bargate Close, Bexhill-on-Sea, E Sussex.* (Bexhill 210064)

CAUDWELL, Ven Rex. St Jo Coll Auckld 59. NZ Bd of Th Stud LTh 61. **d** 61 **p** 62. Waik. C of Waitara 61-62; St Pet Cathl Hamilton 62-65; Chap KS Auckld and L to Offic Dio Auckld 66-67; V of Taumarunui 68-72; W New Plymouth 72-76; Te Awamutu Dio Waik from 76; Archd of Waitomo from 76. *Box 38, Te Awamutu, NZ.* (4627)

CAULDWELL, Wallace Harrison. b 01. Paton Coll 23. Chich Th Coll 42. **d** 42 **p** 43 Pet. [f Congregational Min] C of St Jas Northampton 42-47; V of Easton Maudit 47-53; V of Grendon (w Castle Ashby from 53) 47-75. *11 The Square, Yardley Hastings, Northampton.* (Yardley Hastings 883)

CAULFEILD, Ven Arthur Edward Lampay. Bp's Univ Lennox BA 27, LST 29. **d** 29 **p** 30 Ott. C of St Geo Ott 29-30; Miss St Pet Miss Merivale Ott 30-35; R of Eastview 35-38; C of Ch Ch Cathl Ott 38-41; Chap RCAF 41-50; R of Ch of the Ascen Ott 44-50; Perth 50-57; Trin Ch St John 57-73; Can of Fred 59-64; Exam Chap to Abp of Fred 60-76; Archd of St John 64-79; Archd (Emer) from 79. *139 Sydney Street, Saint John, NB, Canada.*

CAULFIELD, David Eric. Univ of W Ont BA 54. St Chad's Coll Regina LTh 54. **d** 54 Tor for Rupld. C of St Jas Winnipeg 54-56; Attercliffe w Carbrook Sheff 56-51; P-in-c of Murdockville 58-61; R Saguenay 61-67; P-in-c of Windsor 67-69. *115 Charlotte Street, Saint John, NB, Canada.*

CAUWOOD, Phillip. b 24. K Coll Lon 47. St Bonif Coll Warm 51. **d** 51 **p** 52 Sheff. C of Balby 51-54; Doncaster 54-56; V of Lower Shiregreen Sheff 56-65; St Mary Pet 65-79; R of Ampleforth w Oswaldkirk Dio York from 79. *Ampleforth Vicarage, York, YO6 4DU.* (Ampleforth 264)

CAVAGAN, Raymond. b 36. Dipl Th (Lon) 62. Oak Hill Th Coll 60. **d** 63 **p** 64 Lon. C of St Pet U Holloway 63-66; Hurworth 66-68; V of New Shildon 68-76; St Mich-in-the-Hamlet (w St Andr from 78) Toxteth Pk Dio Liv from 76; P-in-c of St Andr Toxteth Pk 76-78. *Vicarage, St Michael's Road, Liverpool, L17 7AR.* (051-727 2601)

CAVAGHAN, Dennis Edgar. b 45. Univ of Nottm BTh 74. St Jo Coll Nottm 71. **d** 74 **p** 75 Ches. C of Hartford 74-77; St Andr Plymouth 77-80; V of Cofton w Starcross Dio Ex from 80. *Cofton Vicarage, Starcross, Exeter, Devon, EX6 8RP.* (Starcross 331)

CAVALIER, Leslie Walter. b 12. **d** 72 Ott. C of Ch Ch Cathl City and Dio Ott from 72. *1494 Kilborn Avenue, Ottawa, Ont., Canada.* (613-733 0512)

CAVALIERO, Glen Tilburn. b 27. Magd Coll Ox 2nd cl Mod Hist 48, BA 49, MA 54. Ely Th Coll 50. **d** 52 Croydon for Cant **p** 53 Cant. C of All SS Margate 52-55; St Gregory Gt Cant 55-56; Tutor Linc Th Coll 56-59; Chap 59-60; Sub-Warden 60; Chap Univ of Edin 61-64. *c/o St Catharine's College, Cambridge.*

CAVAN, Lawrence Noel. b 38. Trin Coll Bris 72. **d** 75 **p** 76 Down. C of Shankill Lurgan 75-78; Chorley Wood Dio St Alb from 78. *28 Nightingale Road, Rickmansworth, Herts.* (Rickmansworth 75850)

CAVANAGH, Charles Terrence. b 49. Univ of Oklahoma BLitt 70. Trin Hall Cam BA 74, MA 77. Ripon Coll Cudd 75. **d** 77 **p** 80 S'wark. C of St Geo Camberwell 77-78; Perm to Offic Dio S'wark 79; Hon C of Clapham Old Town Dio S'wark from 80. *34 Tasman Road, SW9.* (01-737 2269)

CAVANAGH, Kenneth Joseph. d and **p** 77 Parag. P Dio Parag. *Casilla 1124, Asuncion, Paraguay, S America.*

CAVANAGH, Peter Bernard. b 49. Sarum Wells Th Coll 71. **d** 73 Warrington for Liv **p** 74 Liv. C of St Faith Gt Crosby 73-76; St Anne Stanley Liv 76-79; V of St Columba Anfield Dio Liv from 79. *Vicarage, Pinehurst Avenue, Anfield, Liverpool, L4 2TZ.* (051-263 3031)

CAVE, Canon Alan John. b 17. Dipl Th (Lon) 65. Cudd Coll 64. **d** 65 Burnley for Blackb **p** 66 Blackb. C of St Thos St Annes-on-the-Sea 65-68; Ribbleton 68-72; V of St Cath Burnley 72-78; M Gen Syn Blackb from 75; C-in-c of St Alb w St Paul Burnley 77-78; R of Ribchester w Stydd Dio Blackb from 78; Hon Can of Blackb Cathl from 81. *Ribchester Rectory, Preston, Lancs, PR3 3XS.* (Ribchester 352)

CAVE, Brian Malcolm. St Cath Coll Ox BA 60, MA 64. Oak Hill Th Coll. **d** 63 **p** 64 S'wark. C of St Alb Streatham Pk 63-66; St Sav Herne Hill Road w St Matt Ruskin Pk 66-68; St Jas Tunbridge Wells 68-71; V of St Leon Bootle 71-75; Min of St Mary w St John Bootle 73-75; Area Sec for Leprosy Miss 75-81; V of Hurst Green Dio Bradf from 81; P-in-c of Mytton Dio Bradf from 81. *Hurst Green Vicarage, Blackburn, Lancs, BB6 9QR.* (Stonyhurst 686)

CAVE, Cyril Hayward. K Coll Lon and Warm AKC 49. Univ of Nottm MA 60, BD 63. **d** 50 **p** 51 Liv. C of Upholland 50-53; C-in-c of S Darley 53-56; V of Ticknall and Chap of Calke 56-65; Lect in Th Univ of Ex 65-80; Sen Lect from 80. *University of Exeter, Devon.*

CAVE, Douglas Lionel. b 26 Lon Coll of Div 64. **d** 66 Lon **p** 67 Stepney for Lon. C of St John U Holloway 66-69; Barking 69-73; V of St Barn Blackb 73-81; Industr Chap to E Lon Dio Lon from 81. *c/o London Diocesan House, 30 Causton Street, SW1P 4AU.*

CAVE, Eric William. b 48. St Mich Ho Crafers 73. **d** 74 **p** 75 Tas. C of Burnie 74-76; P-in-c of King I 76-78; R of fingal-Avoca w Cullenswood 78-81; Penguin & Castra Dio Tas from 81. *Rectory, Penguin, Tasmania 7316.* (004 37 2180)

CAVE, Ven Guy Newell. b 19. TCD BA and Div Test 41, MA 58. **d** 42 Bp Hind for Down **p** 43 Down. C of Knockbreda 42-45; C-in-c of Kildrumferton w Ballymachugh (w Ballyjamesduff and Castlerahan from 73) Dio Kilm from 45; RD of Ballymachugh 56-63; Dioc Sec Kilm 60-71; Can and Preb of St Patr Cathl Dub 65-72; Archd of Kilm from 72; Exam Chap to Bp of Kilm from 72. *Kildrumferton, Crosserlough PO., Co Cavan, Irish Republic.* (049-36211)

CAVE, John Edwin Dawson. b 43. Cranmer Hall Dur 71. **d** 74 **p** 75 York. C of Gt Ayton 74-77; Redcar 77-80; P-in-c of Aislaby w Ruswarp Dio York from 80. *Aislaby Vicarage, Whitby, N Yorks.*

CAVE, Robert Philip. b 23. Roch Th Coll 64. **d** 67 **p** 68 Guildf. C of St Mich Yorktown Camberley 67-71; Yaxley 71-75; R of Cottenham Dio Ely from 75. *Cottenham Rectory, Cambridge.* (Cottenham 50454)

CAVE-BROWNE-CAVE, Bernard James William. b 54. Trin Hall Cam BA 76, MA 80. Westcott Ho Cam 77. **d** 79 Huntingdon for Ely **p** 80 Ely. C of Good Shepherd Chesterton Dio Ely from 79. *19 Walker Court, Cambridge, CB4 2RU.*

✠ **CAVELL, Right Rev John Kingsmill.** b 16. Qu Coll Cam 2nd cl Hist Trip pt i 38, BA (3rd cl Th Trip pt i) and Ryle Reading Pri 39, MA 44. Wycl Hall Ox 39. **d** 40 **p** 41 Cant. C of Ch Ch Folkestone 40; Addington Croydon 40-44; Area Sec for CMS Dios Ox and Pet 44-49; Dio Ox and Tr Officer 49-52; L to Offic Dio Ox 45-52; V of Ch Ch Cheltm 52-62; St Andr Plymouth w St Mich W Hoe (w Ch Ch from 64 and East Stonehouse from 68) 62-72; RD of Plymouth 67-72; Preb of Ex Cathl 67-72; Chap Freedom Fields and Green Bank Hosps 62-72; M Gen Syn 70-72; Cons Ld Bp Suffr of Southn in Westmr Abbey 2 Feb 72 by Abp of Cant; Bps of Win; Ex; Portsm; Derby; Nor; Bps Suffr of Plymouth; Bps Howe and Cornwall; Bp to HM Pris and Borstals from 75. *Shepherds, Shepherds Lane, Compton, Winchester, Hants.* (Twyford 713285)

CAWLEY, David Lewis. b 44. AKC 71. **d** 72 **p** 73 Nor. C of Sprowston w Beeston 72-75; Chap HM Pris Nor 74-75; C of Wymondham 75-77; Buckland-in-Dover (in c of Buckland Valley) Dio Cant from 77. *St Nicholas Vicarage, Dryden Road, Dover, Kent.* (Dover 822004)

CAWLEY, Richard William Vaughan. Univ of Manit BA 59. St Jo Coll Winnipeg LTh 60. **d** 60 **p** 61 Rupld. C of H Trin Winnipeg 60-62; R of St Andrew Manitoba 62-68; Hon C of St Luke, Winnipeg 71-74; on leave 74-75. *373 Waverley Street, Winnipeg, Manit., Canada.*

CAWOOD, William. St Bonif Coll Warm 25. Univ of Dur LTh 30. **d** 30 B & W **p** 31 Bp De Salis for B & W. C of Ch Ch Frome 30-33; P-in-c of Ch of Good Shepherd and Waterberg Pret 33-38; C of Doulting w Downhead and E and W Cranmore 39-46; R of Badgworth w Biddisham 46-69; Perm to Offic Dio B & W from 79. *19 Thornbury Road, Uphill, Weston-super-Mare, Somt, BS23 4YB.* (Weston-super-Mare 21026)

CAWSTON, Arthur Cleverly. b 06. Keble Coll Ox BA 29, MA 35. Wells Th Coll 29. **d** 29 **p** 30 Linc. C of Grantham 29-33; Folkestone 33-38; Min of St Martin's Conv Distr Maidstone 38-43; V of All S Cheriton Street Folkestone 43-58; All SS Westbrook Margate 58-66; R of Lower Hardres w Nackington 66-72. *17 Heatherfield, The Pathfinder Village, Tedburn St Mary, Exeter, EX6 4)*

CAWTE, David John. b 30. St Mich Coll Llan. **d** 65 Burnley for Blackb **p** 66 Blackb. C of Chorley 65-67; All SS Boyne Hill Maidenhead (in c of Good Shepherd Cox Green) 67-74; P Missr of Conv Distr of Cox Green Maidenhead 75-78; V of Cox Green Maidenhead Dio Ox from 78. *9 Warwick Close, Cox Green, Maidenhead, Berks, SL6 3AL.* (0628 22139)

CAWTHORN, Samuel Arnold. b 1896. Univ of Dur LTh and BA 22, MA 30. Lich Th Coll 20. **d** 22 **p** 24 Lich. C of H Cross Shrewsbury 22-24; Bushbury w Essington 24-29; St Aug Hull 29-31; V of St Thos Hull 31-41; Ormesby 41-52; Watton w Beswick and Kilnwick 52-57; Newton-on-Ouse 57-61; St Thos York 61-65. *22 St Aidan Road, Bridlington, Yorks.*

CAWTHORNE, Henry Howarth. b 03. Univ of Lon BSc and AKC 24. Lich Th Coll 63. **d** 64 **p** 65 Lich. (f USPG Miss in S India). C of Wednesbury 64-67; R of Hinstock 67-75. *25 Preston Trust Homes, Preston-upon-Wealdmoors, Wellington, Telford, 3)*

CAWTHORNE, Jack. b 22. Dipl Th (Lon) 71. Cudd Coll 69. **d** 71 **p** 72 Hulme for Man. Hon C of Newchurch-in-Rossendale Dio Man from 71. *Holly House, Church Street, Newchurch, Rossendale, BB4 9EH.* (Rossendale 3305)

CAYLESS, Ven Frank Anthony. St D Coll Lamp BA and Van Mildert Exhib 53, LTh 55. **d** 55 St D for Barb **p** 56 Barb. C of St Matthias w St Laur Barb 55-59; V of St Ambrose and Chap HM Pris 60-64; R of St Geo Barb 64-73; Sec Dioc Synod 57-69; Chap Barb Ho of Assembly from 65; Dioc Sec 68-76; Can of Bridgetown Cathl 74-76; Archd of Barb from 76. *Prior Park, St James, Barbados, W Indies.*

CAYTON, John. b 32. Bps' Coll Cheshunt 54. **d** 57 **p** 58 Liv. C of All SS Hindley 57-59; Littleham w Exmouth 59-63; V of St Cath Burnley 63-72, Marton Dio Blackb from 72. *55 Vicarage Lane, Blackpool, Lancs, FY4 4EF.* (Blackpool 62679)

CAYUL, Jose. d & **p** 72 Bp Bazley. C of H Trin Temuco Dio Chile from 72. *Casilla 26D, Temuco, Chile.*

CAYUL, Canon Segundo. d 38 **p** 40 Argent for Falkd Is. Asst Chap Araucanian Miss Dio Falkd Is 38-63; Dio Chile from 63; Hon Can of Chile from 65. *Casilla 4, Cholchol, Chile, S America.*

CAYUL, Segundo. d 66 **p** 67 Chile. P Dio Chile. *Casilla 4, Cholchol, Chile, S America.*

CAYUMAN, Francisco. d 66 **p** 67 Chile. P Dio Chile. *Casilla 4, Cholchol, Chile, S America.*

CEBEKHULU, Cleopas Geoffrey. St Pet Coll Rosettenville 56. **d** 57 **p** 58 Zulu. P Dio Zulu. *Vumanhlamvu, PB 107, Nkandla, Zululand.*

CEFAS, Eugenio. d 75 N Argent. d Dio N Argent. *Casilla 187, Salta, Argentina.*

CELESTIN, Very Rev Louis Dickens. b 30. **d** and **p** 58 Haiti (Amer Ch). In Amer Ch 58-79; Dean of Sey from 80. *Box 44, Victoria, Seychelles.*

CELIZ, Edward James. b 41. St Paul's Coll Grahmstn 74. **d** 76 Bp Carter for Johann **p** 77 Johann. C of Springs 76-80; L to Offic Dio Grahmstn from 81. *PO Box 77, Grahamstown, CP, S Africa.*

CELTEL, Olaf James Edgar. b 28. St Steph Ho Ox 74. **d** 75 Stepney for Lon for Sey **p** 75 Sey (APM). P Dio Sey. *Rectory, Grand Anse, Praslin, Seychelles.*

CENTENO, Mariano. d 68 **p** 69 Argent. P Dio Argent 68-73; N Argent from 73. *Misión Chaque£na, N Argentina.*

CESPEDES, Alfredo Silverio. d 69 **p** 73 Chile. P Dio Chile 69-76. *Casilla 566, Valparaiso, Chile, S America.*

CHA, Ven Matthias. d 68 **p** 69 Seoul. P Dio Seoul; Arch P of Seoul from 77. *3 Nae Dong, Inchon Street, Kyung GI DO, 160 Korea.* (Inchon 3-3796)

CHABALA, Isaiah. d 72 **p** 73 Lusaka. P Dio Lusaka 72-79; Dio Centr Zam from 79. *Box 90475, Luanshya, Zambia.*

CHABALA, Isaiah Wilfred Noah. b 30. St Jo Sem Lusaka 68. **d** 70 Bp Mataka for Zam **p** 71 Lusaka. P Dio Lusaka. *St Joseph's Church, PO Box 134, Chipata, Zambia.*

CHABOT, Canon Arthur Lionel. Wycl Coll Tor. **d** 48 **p** 49 Alg. I of Coniston 48-54; New Liskeard 54-66; Marathon 66-75; Hon Can of Alg from 73; R of Englehart Dio Alg from 75. *Box 912, Englehart, Ont., Canada.*

CHABU, Alfred. Ho of Epiph Kuching 52. **d** 55 **p** 56 Borneo. P Dio Borneo 55-62; Dio Kuch 62-78; Can 72-78; Archd of Brunei and N Sarawak 72-78; V of St Thos Cathl Kuch 75-78. *Box 347, Kuching, Sarawak, Malaysia.* (22625)

CHACHINE, Moisés. St Chris Coll Maciene. **d** 50 **p** 52 Lebom. P Dio Lebom from 50. *Caixa Postal 63, Vila de Jo£ao Belo, Mozambique.*

CHADAMBUKA, Phineas. St Pet Coll Rosettenville 54. **d** 56 Centr Afr **p** 57 Mashon. P Dio Mashon 56-81; Dio Mutare from 81. *c/o Rectory, Jindwe, Zimbabwe.*

CHADD, Jeremy Denis. b 55. Jes Coll Cam BA 77, MA 81. Coll of the Resurr Mirfield 78. **d** 81 Bp Gill for Newc T. C of Seaton Hirst Dio Newc T from 81. *152 Newbiggin Road, Ashington, Northumberland, NE63 0TL.*

CHADD, Canon Leslie Frank. b 19. Univ of Leeds BSc (2nd cl) 41. Coll of Resurr Mirfield 41. **d** 43 **p** 44 Portsm. C of St Jo Bapt Rudmore Portsea 43-46; Chap RNVR 46-48; C of H Cross Greenford 48-54; Littlehampton 54-58; PC of All SS, Hanworth, Lon 58-65; V of SS Pet & Paul Fareham Dio Portsm from 65; Relig Adviser S Television 72-81; Hon Can of Portsm Cathl from 81. *30 Osborn Road, Fareham, Hants.* (Fareham 280256)

CHADWICK, David St Just. b 36. Bps' Coll Cheshunt 61. **d** 68 Willesden for Lon **p** 69 Lon. C of Edmonton 68-71; St Mary w St Jo Evang Edmonton 71-72; St Jo Bapt Greenhill Harrow 72-74; Dom Chap to Bp of Truro 74-79; Chap Commun of The Epiph Truro 77-79; P-in-c of St Crantock Dio Truro from 79. *Crantock Vicarage, Newquay, Cornw, TR8 5RE.* (Crantock 830294)

CHADWICK, Francis Arnold Edwin. b 30. K Coll Lon and Warm AKC 54. **d** 55 **p** 56 Ripon. C of Chapel Allerton 55-58; Hayes Kent 58-61; V of Arreton 61-67; V of Newchurch 61-67; Kingshurst 67-73; Camberley w Yorktown Dio Guildf from 73. *286 London Road, Camberley, Surrey.* (Camberley 23602)

CHADWICK, Frank. b 19. Univ of Dur LTh 35, BA 37, MA 47. Qu Coll Birm 32. **d** 36 **p** 37 Worc. C of All SS Bromsgrove 36-39; CF (TA - R of O) 39-45; Hon CF 45; C of Pershore 46-48; R of Draycott-le-Moors 50-64; V of Stoke Ferry w Wretton Dio Ely from 64; V of Whitington Dio Ely from 64. *Stoke Ferry Vicarage, King's Lynn, Norf, PE33 9SW.* (Stoke Ferry 500204)

CHADWICK, Canon George Bancroft. b 12. Linc Th Coll 40. **d** 42 **p** 43 Blackb. C of H Trin S Shore Blackpool 42-45; Hexham Abbey 45-48; All SS Gosforth 48-50; C-in-c of St Bede Newsham Blyth 50-55; V of St Geo Cullercoats 55-70; RD of Tynemouth 67-70; V of Corbridge-on-Tyne w Halton Dio Newc T from 70; Hon Can of Newc T from 74. *Vicarage, Corbridge-on-Tyne, Northumb, NE45 5DW.* (Corbridge-on-T 2128)

✠ **CHADWICK, Right Rev Graham Charles.** Keble Coll Ox (2nd Cl Th) BA 49, MA 53. St Mich Coll Llan 49. **d** 50 **p** 51 Swan B. C of Oystermouth 50-53; St Barn Masite 53-54; R of Qacha's Nek 54-59; Mohales Hoek 59-63; Chap Univ Coll Swansea 63-68; Sen Bursar Qu Coll Birm 68-69; L to Offic St Thos Hosp S'wark 69-70; Commiss Basuto 63-66; Les 63-70; Warden of Dioc Tr Centre Maseru 70-76; Cons Ld Bp of Kimb K in Cathl Ch of St Mich and St Geo Grahmstn 21 Nov 76 by Abp of Capetn; Bps of St John's, Geo, Natal, Bloemf, Johann, Grahmstn, Port Eliz, Swaz, Zulu, Pret, Les and Lebom; and others. *Bishopsgarth, Box 921, Kimberley, CP, S Africa.* (Kimberley 28702)

CHADWICK, Canon Henry. b 20. Magd Coll Cam BA, MusB 41, MA 45, DD 57. FBA 60. Univ of Glas Hon DD 57. Univ of Uppsala Hon DD 67. Yale Univ Hon DD 70. Univ of Man Hon DD 75. Univ of Leeds Hon DD 80. Ridley Hall Cam 42. **d** 43 **p** 44 Cant. C of Em S Croydon 43-45; Asst Chap Wel Coll 45-46; Chap of Qu Coll Cam 46-50; Fell 46-58; Hon Fell from 58; Select Pr Univ of Cam 47 57 and 61; Univ of Ox 53-55; Jun Proc Cam Univ 48-49; Dean of Qu Coll Cam 50-55; Hulsean Lect 55-56; Can of Ch Ch Ox and Regius Prof of Div Univ of Ox 59-69; Gifford Lect Univ of St Andr 62-64; Hon Fell Magd Coll Cam 62-79; Birkbeck Lect Univ of Cam 65; Vice-Pres Br Acad 68-69; Dean of Ch Ch Ox 69-79; Regius Prof of Div Univ of Cam from 79; Hon Can of Ely Cathl from 79. *Magdalene College, Cambridge, CB3 0AG.* (0223-61543)

CHADWICK, Martin James. b 27. Trin Hall Cam BA 51, MA 54. Cudd Coll 52. **d** 54 Kens for Lon **p** 55 Lon. C of St Cuthb Kens 54-58; Chap of Trin Hall Cam 58-63; Ch Ch Ox 63-67; V of Market Lavington w Easterton 67-79; Charlbury Dio Ox from 79; RD of Chipping Norton from 79. *Charlbury Vicarage, Oxford, OX7 3PX.* (Charlbury 810286)

CHADWICK, Martin John. b 55. Univ Coll of N Wales (Bangor) BMus 77. Coll of the Resurr Mirfield 78. **d** 81 Lich. C of Stoke-upon-Trent Dio Lich from 81. *21 Kemball Avenue, Mount Pleasant, Fenton, Stoke-on-Trent, Staffs, ST4 4LD.*

CHADWICK, Norman Alfred. b 08. St D Coll Lamp BA 36. **d** 36 **p** 37 Southw. C of St Aug New Basford 36-46; CF (R of O) from 39; CF (EC) 39-46; Men in Disp 45; Hon CF 46; V of St Lawr Mansfield 46-54; All S w Ch Ch Radford 54-68; R of Plumtree 68-79; C-in-c of Broughton Sulney 68-78; Perm to Offic Dio Southw from 79. *5 Peterscourt, 398 Woodborough Road, Nottingham.*

CHADWICK, Peter MacKenzie. b 21. Lich Th Coll 63. **d** 65 Barking for Chelmsf **p** 66 Chelmsf. C of Buckhurst Hill 65-66; Chap and Jt Hd Master Forres Sch Swanage from 66. *Forres, Swanage, Dorset.* (Swanage 2715)

CHADWICK, Roger Vernon. b 39. Univ of Dur BA 60, Dipl Th 62. Cranmer Hall Dur 60. **d** 62 **p** 63 Man. C of Swinton 62-65; St Mary Heworth 65-68; Hon C 68-74; Dioc Ordin Recruitment Officer from 68; V of St Aid w St Columba Hartlepool Dio Dur from 74. *St Aidan's Vicarage, Hartlepool, Co Durham.* (Hartlepool 73539)

CHADWICK, Rupert Pemberton. b 1887. Chich Th Coll 13. **d** 14 Nor **p** 24 Man. C of Oulton 14-16; St Mark Gorton 24-25; St Matt Preston 25-27; Haslingden 27-29; St Osw

Knuzden 29-30; Padiham w Higham 30-33; St Jo Bapt Penzance 33-37; LPr Dio Truro 37-39; C-in-c of Tresco w Bryher Conv Distr Scilly Is 39-47; V of St Issey 47-58. *Perran Bay Hotel, Perranporth, Cornw.* (Perranporth 2275)

✠ **CHADWICK, Right Rev William Frank Percival.** b 05. Wadh Coll Ox 2nd cl Cl Mods 25, BA (3rd cl Lit Hum) 27, Dipl Th 29, MA 30. Davison Scho of Harvard Univ 27. Wycl Hall Ox 28. **d** 29 **p** 30 Liv. C of St Helens 29-34; V of St Mary Widnes 34-38; Ch Ch Crouch End 38-47; Barking 47-59; Surr 47-59; Proc Conv Lon 47-50; Chelmsf 51-65; Exam Chap to Bp of Chelmsf 51-59; RD of Barking 53-59; Hon Can of Chelmsf 54-59; Pro-Prolocutor Lower Ho Conv of Cant 56-67; Cons Ld Bp Suffr of Barking in S'wark Cathl 1 May 59 by Abp of Cant; Bps of Lon; Win; Ely; Sarum; Roch; Truro; Guildf; Cov; Ex; Chich; Portsm; St E; Chelmsf; Linc; Leic; Pet; Bris; Carl; Man; and Ches; Bps Suffr of Colchester; Woolwich; Kingston T; Tewkesbury; Maidstone; Warrington; Stepney and Tonbridge; res 75; Perm to Offic Dio St E from 76. *Harvard House, Acton, Sudbury, Suffolk.*

CHADWICK, William Owen. b 16. KBE 82. St Jo Coll Cam BA 39, MA 42, BD 51, DD 55. Hon DD St Andr 60. Univ of Ox Hon DD 73. FBA 62, Pres from 81. Cudd Coll 39. **d** 40 **p** 41 Wakef. C of St John Huddersfield 40-42; Chap Wel Coll 42-46; Fell of Trin Hall Cam 47-56; Dean 49-56; Exam Chap to Bp of Lich 47-53; Win 47-56; to Abp of York 48-56; Master of Selw Coll Cam from 56; Dixie Prof of Eccles Hist 58-68; Regius Prof of Mod Hist from 68; Chairman Cam Miss to Delhi 59-66. *Master's Lodge, Selwyn College, Cambridge, CB3 9DQ.*

CHADWIN, James William. b 01. Univ of Glas MA 23. Univ of Lon BA 39. **d** 76 **p** 77 Edin (APM). Hon C of H Cross Davidson's Mains Dio Edin from 76. *25 Hillpark Road, Edinburgh, EH4 7AN.* (031-336 2247)

CHAFFEE, Alan Wilson. Wycl Coll Tor LTh 81. **d** 81 Tor. C of Ch Ch Brampton Dio Tor from 81. *4 Elizabeth Street N, Brampton, Ont, Canada, L6X 1S2.*

CHAFFEY, Kenneth Arthur. Kelham Th Coll 25. **d** 31 **p** 32 Southw. C of St Geo Nottm 31-33; St Sav Claremont S Afr 33-36; St Jas Birch-in-Rusholme 36-39; Org Sec C of E Children's S Dios Man Blackb and Carl and L to Offic Dio Man 39-41; V of Penwortham 41-44; R of De Aar 44-45; Mowbray 45-53; S Jas Sea Point 53-69; Muizenberg 69-76; Sec Capetn Dioc Bd of Miss 54-56; Can of Capetn 59-76; Exam Chap to Abp of Capetn 61-76; Perm to Offic Dio Capetn from 76. *1 Wren Way, Meadowridge, CP, S Africa.* (72-8843)

CHAFFEY, Michael Prosser. b 30. Univ of Lon BA 51. St Steph Ho Ox 53. **d** 55 **p** 56 Chelmsf. C of Ascen Vic Dks 55-59; H Trin Harrow Green and of St Aug Leytonstone 59-62; V of St Mich AA Walthamstow 62-69; P-in-c of St Thos Cov 69-75; St Jo Bapt City and Dio Cov 69-74; R from 74. *9 Davenport Road, Coventry, CV5 6QA.* (Coventry 73203)

CHAGARA, Stanley. b 28. Bp Tucker Coll Mukono 65. **d** 67 **p** 68 N Ugan. P Dio N Ugan 67-76; Dio Lango from 76. *Diocese of Lango, PO Box 6, Lira, Uganda.*

CHAIMA, Ven Enoka Suwayo. b 12. Div Sch Mori. **d** 49 **p** 51 Bp Allison for Sudan. P Dio Sudan 50-76; Dio Yambio from 76; Hon Can of Sudan 70-76; Archd of Yambio from 77; Can from 77. *ECS, Maridi, Sudan.*

CHAKA, Edwin. St Bede's Coll Umtata. **d** 57 **p** 59 Basuto. P Dio Basuto 57-66; Dio Les from 66. *St Matthew's Mission, Malealea, c/o Malealea Store, Mafeteng, Lesotho.*

CHAKWAWA, Alfred. d 72 **p** 80 Ruv. P Dio SW Tan 72-79; Dio Ruv from 79. *Ngumbo, PO Liuli, Tanzania.*

CHALCRAFT, Christopher Warine Terrell. b 37. Oak Hill Th Coll. **d** 67 **p** 68 Guildf. C of Egham 67-70; C-in-c of Slough 70-73; V in Bramerton Group Dio Nor from 73. *Rectory, Ashby St Mary, Norwich, NOR 14W.*

CHALK, Francis Harold. b 25. Lich Th Coll 61. **d** 62 Linc **p** 63 Bp Dunlop for Linc. [f Free Ch Min] C of St Nich Newport Linc 62-64; R of Kirkby Laythorpe w Asgarby 64-69; V of Ewerby w Evedon 65-69; R of Gt Gonerby Dio Linc from 69. *Great Gonerby Rectory, Grantham, Lincs.* (Grantham 5737)

CHALK, John Edward. b 33. St D Coll Lamp BA 57. **d** 58 **p** 59 St A. C of Connah's Quay 58-61; Abergele 61-65; V of Cyfarthfa 65-72; Pyle w Kenfig 72-77; Dir Notts Marriage Guidance Coun from 77. *48 Botany Avenue, The Wells Road, Nottingham.*

CHALK, Norman Albert. b 25. SOC 69. **d** 71 **p** 72 Willesden for Lon. C of St Edm Northwood Hills Pinner 71-76; R of St Laur Cowley Dio Lon from 76. *Rectory, Church Road, Cowley, Middx, UB8 3NB.* (Uxbridge 32728)

CHALK, Richard Seymour. b 05. Jun Hulme Scho of BNC Ox 24, 2nd cl Cl Mods 26, BA (2nd cl Lit Hum) 28, 2nd cl Th 29, MA 33. Wycl Hall Ox 28. **d** 32 **p** 33 Ex. C of Charles Plymouth 32-36; CMS Miss at Bhagalpur 36-51; Chap of Bhagalpur, Katihar and Purnea 37-51; Prin CMS High Sch Bhagalpur 47-50; Chap Blundell's Sch Tiverton 51-52; C-in-c of St Phil Weston Mill Devonport 52-55; V 55-59; R of Stoke Fleming 59-75; L to Offic Dio Ex from 75. *40 Mile End Road, Highweek, Newton Abbot, Devon, TQ12 1RW.* (N Abbot 67069)

CHALKLEN, John Bernard. b 43. Univ of Dur BA (2nd cl Pol and Econ) 64. Hertf Coll Ox BA 66, MA 71. Westcott Ho Cam 66. **d** 68 **p** 69 Guildf. C of Worplesdon 68-72; Chalfont St Pet (in c of All SS) 73-79; R of Hawstead w Nowton and Stanningfield w Bradfield Combust Dio St E from 79. *Rectory, Hawstead, Bury St Edmunds, Suff.* (Sicklesmere 529)

CHALKLEY, Henry Roy. b 23. St Aid Coll 58. **d** 59 **p** 60 Ches. C of Bromborough 59-63; Chap Miss to Seamen Hong Kong 63-64; Port of Spain, Trinid 65-69; Suva 69-74; Lon 74-75; Fremantle 75-79; St Austell from 79. *c/o Missions to Seamen, St Austell, Cornw.*

CHALLACOMBE, Allan James. Trin Coll Tor BA 51, LTh 54, STB 55. **d** 53 Sktn **p** 54 Tor for Sktn. Miss at Watson 54-58; Chap Trin Coll Tor 58-63; Hon C of St Martin Tor 58-63; R of All SS Sktn 63-70; Dom Chap to Bp of Sktn 64-70; Hon Can of Sktn 69-70; C of Ch Ch Calg 70-77; Exam Chap to Bp of Calg 73-77; to Bp of Edmon from 78; I of St Geo City and Dio Edmon from 78. *11737-87th Avenue, Edmonton, Alta, Canada.* (439-9798)

✠ **CHALLEN, Right Rev Michael Boyd.** Univ of Melb BSc 55. Ridley Coll Melb ACT ThL (2nd cl) 56. **d** 57 **p** 58 Melb. C of Ch Ch Essendon 57-59; Melb Dioc Centre 59-63; Dir 63-69; P-in-c of St Luke Fitzroy 59-61; St Alb N Melb 61-65; Flemington 65-69; Dir Angl Inner-City Ministry 70; Home Miss Perth 71-75; P-in-c of Lockridge w Eden Hill 73-75; Archd of the Country 76-77; Home Miss Perth 75-77; Executive Dir from 77; Cons Asst Bp of Perth in St Geo Cathl Perth 24 June 78 by Abp of Perth; Bps of Bunb and Willoch; Asst Bps of Perth, Melb and Bunb; and Bps Bryant, Muschamp and Hawkins. *Cnr Wollaston and Huddleston Roads, Mount Claremont, W Australia 6010.* (383 2774)

CHALLEN, Canon Peter Bernard. b 31. Clare Coll Cam BA 56, MA 60. Westcott Ho Cam 56. **d** 58 **p** 59 Sheff. C of Goole 58-61; V of Dalton 61-67; Proc Conv Sheff from 64-67; R of Ch Ch S'wark Dio S'wark from 67; Sen Industr Chap Dio S'wark from 67; Hon Can of S'wark Cathl from 74. *Christ Church Rectory, Colombo Street, SE1 8DP.* (01-928 4707)

CHALLEN, Victor Stanley. b 14. Bede Coll Dur BSc 39. **d** 41 Kingston T for S'wark **p** 43 S'wark. C of St Pet Vauxhall 41-44; Cheshunt (in c of St Clem Turnford) 44-50; N of Engl Area Sec UMCA 51; V of St Martin Bedford Dio St Alb from 52. *76 Clapham Road, Bedford, MK41 7PN.* (Bedford 57862)

CHALLENDER, Clifford. b 32. **d** 67 **p** 68 Connor. C of St Luke Belf 67-70; C of Kilkenny Aghour and Odagh 70-71; I of Fenagh w Myshall and Kiltennel 71-76; C-in-c of Aghade w Ardoyne 75-76; I of Fenagh w Myshall and Aghade W Ardoyne 76-79; Crosspatrick w Kilcomon Kilpipe & Preban Dio Ferns from 79. *Rectory, Tinahely, Arklow, Co Wicklow, Irish Republic.* (0402-8178)

CHALLENGER, Cyril George. b 02. Late Exhib and Scho of Peterho Cam 1st cl Cl Trip pt i 23, BA (2nd cl Cl Trip pt ii) 24. Lady Kay Scho of Jes Coll Cam 24, 2nd cl Th Trip pt ii 26, Hulsean Pri 27, MA 28. Ripon Hall Ox 26. **d** 27 **p** 28 S'wark. C of St Bart Sydenham 27-30; Caversham (in c of St Barn Emmer Green) 30-32; V of Hill St Jas 32-45; Exam Chap (for Lay Readers) to Bp of Birm 41-52; Hon Chap 44-52; V of St Cypr Hay Mill 45-52; Neen Savage w Kinlet 52-61; Dioc Insp of Ch Schs from 58; RD of Burford 60-67; Weobley 67-70; R of Burford (3rd Portion) w L Heref 61-67; V of Almeley 67-70. *52 Walliscote Road, Weston-super-Mare, Avon, BS23 1XF.* (W-s-M 26341)

CHALLENGER, Peter Nelson. b 33. St Jo Coll Cam BA (2nd cl Cl Trip pt ii) 57, MA 61. Ripon Hall Ox 57. **d** 59 Stafford for Lich **p** 60 Lich. C of Bushbury 59-62; PC of Horsley Woodhouse 62-67; V of St Barn Derby 67-75; Chap of St Paul Sao Paulo 75-80; C of New Windsor Dio Ox 80-81; Team V from 81. *73 Alma Road, Windsor, Berks, SL4 3HD.* (Windsor 53585)

CHALLICE, Cyril Eugene. b 26. Univ of Lon BSc, PhD, DSc. **d** 80 **p** 81 Calg. Hon C of Cathl Ch of the Redeemer City and Dio Calg from 80. *2916 - 14th Avenue NW, Calgary, Alta, Canada, T2N 1N1.*

CHALLICE, John Richard. b 34. ACP 65. Sarum Wells Th Coll 73. **d** 75 **p** 76 Sarum. C of Warminster 75-78; R of Longfield Dio Roch from 78. *67 Main Road, Longfield, Dartford, Kent.* (Longfield 2201)

CHALLIS, Douglas James. Selw Coll Cam BA 48, MA 55. Cudd Coll 49. **d** 51 Lon **p** 59 Ox. Perm to Offic Dio Ox 58-63; Chap St Bees Sch 63-72; Reeds Sch Cobham 73-81. *c/o Reeds School, Sandy Lane, Cobham, Surrey.* (Cobham 4573)

CHALLIS, Preb James Dobb. b 16. St Jo Coll Cam BA 38, MA 42. Ridley Hall Cam 39. **d** 40 **p** 41 Southw. C of Lenton 40-47; PC of St Chadd Derby 47-55; R of H Trin Chesterfield 55-67; V of Penn Fields 67-81; Surr 69-81; Preb of Lich Cathl 80-81; Preb (Emer) from 81. *21 Seymour Avenue, Louth, Lincs, LN11 9EW.* (Louth 602637)

CHALLIS, John Frederick. b 1887. St Cath Coll Cam BA 11, MA 15. **d** 11 **p** 12 Pet. C of St Andr Northn 11-15; St Nath Windsor W Derby 15-18; Distr Sec for N of Engl for RTS 18-21; V of St Jude Hexthorpe Doncaster 21-28; St Sav Nottm 28-39; All SS Burton-on-Trent 39-47; Trentham 47-58; L to Offic Dio Linc from 60. *Trentholme, Grove Road, Sutton-on-Sea, Mablethorpe, Lincs LN12 2NH.*

CHALLIS, Terence Peter. b 40. St Aid Coll 65. **d** 68 Bradwell for Chelmsf **p** 69 Chelmsf. C of Billericay 68-71; Bp's Chap Dio Maseno S 72-74; Admin Sec Dio Maseno S 72-75; P-in-c of Ch Ch Sparkbrook 75-80; V of St Jas Enfield Highway Dio Lon from 80. *144 Hertford Road, Enfield, Middx, EN3 5AY.* (01-804 1966)

CHALLIS, William George. b 52. Keble Coll Ox BA 73. K Coll Lon MTh 75. Oak Hill Coll 73. **d** 75 Lon **p** 76 Stepney for Lon. C of Isl 75-79; Stoke Bp 79-81; Lect Trin Coll Bris 79-81; Oak Hill Coll Lon from 82. *c/o Oak Hill College, Southgate, N14 4PS.* (01-449 0467)

CHALMERS, Arnold Lyall Roy. NZ Bd of Th Stud LTh 67. **d** 63 **p** 64 Wai. C of Dannevirke 63-65, Rotorua 65-67, V of Edgecumbe 67-69; Chap Palmerston N Hosp Dio Wel 69-74; V of Waiwhetu 75-76; St Pet Riverslea, Hastings 76-79; Waipawa Dio Wai from 79. *52 Kenilworth Street, Waipawa, NZ.*

CHALMERS, Brian. b 42. Or Coll Ox BA (Chem) 64, (Th) 71, MA 68, DPhil 70. Wycl Hall Ox 71. **d** 72 **p** 73 St Alb. C of Luton 72-76; Chap Cranfield Inst of Tech 76-81; Univ of Kent, Cant from 81. *Landon, Giles Lane, Canterbury, Kent.* (Cant 63097)

CHALMERS, Canon Reginald Paul. b 16. St Cath Coll Cam BA 38, MA 44. Westcott Ho Cam 46. **d** 48 **p** 49 Man. C of Middleton 48-51; R of St Paul Blackley 51-56; Burnage 56-59; Ed of Man Dioc Leaflet 55-65; Dioc Directory 62-68; V of Walkden 59-68; Hon Can of Man 62-74; R of Fallowfield 68-74; P-in-c of Epping Upland 74-81; Dio Communications Officer Dio Chelmsf 74-81; Hon Can of Chelmsf 78-81; Can (Emer) from 81. *13 Berwynfa, High Street, Glyn Ceiriog, Llangollen, Clwyd LL20 7HP.*

CHALONER, Stephen Mason. b 34. Univ of Dur BA (2nd cl Social Stud) 57. Ridley Coll Cam 57. **d** 59 Bp Gelsthorpe for Southw **p** 60 Southw. C of St Marg Aspley 59-62; RNR from 61; R of Bilsthorpe 62-69; C-in-c of Eakring 62-65; R 65-69; V of Radcliffe-on-Trent 69-73; Shelford 69-73; C-in-c of Holme-Pierrepont w Adbolton 69-73; Chap Saxondale Hosp Radcliffe-on-Trent 69-73; Surr 72-73; C of Rowner Portsm 73-74; Hon C 74-81; Asst Master Portsm Gr Sch 74-81; Cowes High Sch from 81; Hon Chap Miss to Seamen from 81. *12 Brookfield Gardens, Binstead, Ryde, PO33 3NP.* (Ryde 611476)

CHAMBACHAMBA, Petro. b 38. St Mark's Coll Dar-S 78. **d** 72 **p** 79 SW Tang. P Dio SW Tang. *PO Box 69, Mbozi, Tanzania.*

CHAMBE, John. **d** 74 **p** 75 Mashon. P Dio Mashon. *c/o Ngezi Council, PO Mamina, Gatooma, Zimbabwe.*

CHAMBERLAIN, Alan Thomas. b 06. Univ of Lon BSc (2nd cl Chem) 27. Dorch Miss Coll 29. **d** 30 **p** 31 York. C of S Bank 30-34; Whitby (in c of St Mich AA) 34-39; V of St Cuthb Middlesbrough 39-49; V of St Alb Stoke Heath 49-59; V of Ascen Derringham Bank Hull 59-72. *The Ilott, Illston-on-the-Hill, Leicester, LE7 9EG.* (Billesdon 346)

CHAMBERLAIN, (Bernard) David. b 28. Fitzw Ho Cam BA 51. Linc Th Coll 52. **d** 54 **p** 55 Wakef. C of Brighouse 54-57; Parson Cross Sheff 57-61; M CR from 63; Chap to Angl Students Univ of Stellenbosch CP 68-70; Commun Relns Adv to Bp of Wakef from 71. *House of the Resurrection, Mirfield, W Yorks, WF14 0BN.* (Mirfield 494318)

CHAMBERLAIN, David Murray. b 22. Cudd Coll 55. **d** 57 **p** 58 Chelmsf. C of Barkingside 57-59; in Ch in Japan 59-71; V of St Germain Edgbaston 71-76; Chap Miss to Seamen Port of Lon 76-77; Cardiff and Barry 77-79; Kobe, Japan from 79. *Kobe Mariners' Centre, 111/112 Ito-Machi, Ikuta-Ku, Kobe 651-01, Japan.*

CHAMBERLAIN, Eric Edward. b 34. Tyndale Hall Bris 62. Dipl Th (Lon) 64. **d** 65 **p** 66 Lich. C of Chell 65-73; P-in-c of St Mary Preston Dio Blackb 73-76; V from 76. *Vicarage, Brockholes View, Preston, Lancs.* (Preston 794222)

CHAMBERLAIN, Frederick George. b 19. St D Coll Lamp BA 50. Chich Th Coll 50. **d** 52 **p** 53 Guildf. C of Weybridge 52-54; St Thomas-on-the-Bourne 54-57; V of Blindley Heath 57-63; Tilshead (w Ocheston from 66 and Chitterne from 69) 63-80; P-in-c of Handley w Pentridge Dio Sarum 80-82; V from 82. *Sixpenny Handley Vicarage, Salisbury, Wilts.* (Handley 254)

CHAMBERLAIN, Neville. b 39. Univ of Nottm BA (2nd cl Th) 61, MA 73. Ripon Hall Ox 61. **d** 63 **p** 64 Birm. C of Balsall Heath 63-64; Hall Green 64-66; C-in-c of St Mich Conv Distr Gospel Lane Birm 66-69; V 69-72; M Gen Syn Birm 70-73; L to Offic Dio Linc 73-82; Sec for Social Responsibility Dio Linc 74-82; Can and Preb of Linc Cathl 79-82; R of St Jo Evang City and Dio Edin from 82. *1 Ainslie Place, Edinburgh, EH3 6AR.* (031-225 5004)

CHAMBERLAIN, Canon Roy. b 10. Selw Coll Cam 2nd cl Hist Trip 30, BA (3rd cl Th Trip) 31, MA 35. Wycl Hall Ox 32. **d** 33 **p** 34 Chelmsf. C of St Sav Westcliff 33-36; Ch Ch W Croydon 36-37; St Mary Southn 37-40; V of Greenham 40-45; St Matt Surbiton 45-58; RD of Kingston 55-58; R of Southn 58-69; Hon Can of Win 64-79; Can (Emer) from 79; V of St Matt Southn 66-69; V of Brockenhurst 69-78; RD of Lyndhurst 74-77; Adv to Bp of Win for Hosps and Hosp Chaps Dio Win from 78. *2 Cherry Close, S Wonston, Winchester, Hants.* (Winchester 880250)

CHAMBERLAIN, Russell Charles. b 51. **d** 78 Chelmsf **p** 79 Barking for Chelmsf. C of St Geo Harold Hill 78-80; Uckfield Dio Chich from 80. *Parsonage, Isfield, Uckfield, E Sussex, TN22 5TX.* (Isfield 439)

CHAMBERLAYNE, Gordon Bruce Purdon. b 55. Univ of BC BSc 77. Vanc Sch of Th MDiv 81. **d** and **p** 81 Carib. C of N Thompson Miss Dio Carib from 81. *Box 358, Barriere, BC, Canada, V0E 1E0.*

CHAMBERLAYNE, John Arthur. b 13. **d** 69 **p** 70 Glouc. C of Berkeley w Wick Breadstone and Newport 69-80. *c/o 15 Marybrook Street, Berkeley, Glos.* (Berkeley 481)

CHAMBERLEN, Lawrence Godfrey. b 1890. MC 18. BNC Ox BA 12, MA 16. Ridley Hall Cam 13. Hon CF 21. **d** 14 **p** 15 Ex. C of St Pet Tiverton 14-20; TCF 17-19; V of Buckland Monarchorum 20-24; Hildenborough 24-34; R of E Bickleigh 34-46; Butterleigh 37-46; Headley 46-50; V of Toddington Glouc 50-60; RD of Winchcombe 53-57 and 59-60. *Greenfold, Sway, Lymington, Hants.*

CHAMBERLEN, Leonard Saunders. b 1896. MC 17. BNC Ox BA 21, MA 24. Wells Th Coll 25. **d** 26 Pet for Leic **p** 27 Leic. C of St Pet Leic 26-28; Speldhurst (in c of Groombridge) 29-31; Oxted (in c of Hurst Green) 31-40; V of Wolverley 40-45; CF (EC) 42-45; V of Westwell 45-47; R of Hothfield 45-47; CF 47-53; R of Saxby 53-56; V of Horkstow 53-56; C-in-c of Toddington w Stanley Pontlarge 56-57; V of H Trin Maidstone 57-66; Perm to Offic Dio Chich from 79. *11 High Street, Heathfield, Sussex.* (Heathfield 2905)

CHAMBERS, Anthony Frederick John. b 40. Sarum Th Coll 69. **d** 71 Aston for Birm **p** 72 Birm. C of St Pet Hall Green Birm 71-74; Holdenhurst and of St Barn Queen's Pk 74-77; P-in-c of Ropley w W Tisted 77-79; V of Bp's Sutton and Ropley w W Tisted Dio Win from 79. *Vicarage, Ropley, Alresford, Hants, SO24 0DW.* (Ropley 2205)

CHAMBERS, Cyril Bertram Gerald. Ridley Coll Melb ACT ThL 21. **d** 21 **p** 22 Gippsld. C of Outtrim Vic 21-24; CMS Miss Peshawar 24-25; Multan 25-32; Furlough 35-36; Meerut 32-35 and 36-39; Perm to Offic Dio Melb 39-42; C of St Steph Richmond 42-43; Gen Sec CMS Vic 42-50; C to Dean of St Paul's Cathl Melbourne 43-50; Min of Belmont w Marshall 50-53; I of Oakleigh 53-59; Chap Dio Amrit 59-61; Perm to Offic Dio Leic 61-62; C of St John Bentleigh 62-63; St Jas w St John Miss Distr Melb 64-68; Perm to Offic Dio Syd from 71. *224 Phillip Lodge, Kilvington Village, Castlehill, NSW, Australia 2154.* (634-4780)

CHAMBERS, Ven David Houlden. Ridley Coll Melb ACT ThL 47. **d** 51 **p** 52 Melb. C of Balwyn 51-52; Min of Belgrave 52-56; St John Bentleigh 56-66; St Paul Ringwood 66-72; I of Sandringham 72-79; Archd of Brighton from 72; Dioc Consultant in Welfare and Commun Dio Melb from 79. *23 Fernhill Road, Sandringham, Vic, Australia 3191.* (03-598 5837)

CHAMBERS, Very Rev George William. b 24. Trin Coll Dub BA (3rd cl Mod) 46, Div Test (1st cl) 47, MA 57. **d** 47 **p** 48 Derry. C of Conwall 47-50; Chap Portora Royal Sch 50-51; I of Tully-Aughnish w Milford 51-61; Adare 61-81; Exam Chap to Bp of Lim from 62; Dioc Regr 62-81; Dioc Sec 65-76; Archd of Lim 69-81; Preb of Lim Cathl 69-81; Dean and R from 81; I of St Mich City and Dio Lim from 81. *7 Kilbane, Castleroy, Limerick, Irish Republic.*

CHAMBERS, Gregory. b 53. Th Sem Manila 76. **d** 80 **p** 81 Kuch. P Dio Kuch. *St Thomas Cathedral, PO Box 347, Kuching, Sarawak, E Malaysia.*

CHAMBERS, Peter Lewis. b 43. Univ of Lon BSc (Eng) 64. St Steph Ho Ox 64. **d** 66 **p** 67 Llan. C of St Pet and St Paul Cathl Llan 66-70; Chap Ch in Wales Youth Coun 70-73; Youth Chap Dio Bris 73-78; V of St Mich AA Bedminster Dio Bris from 78; RD of Bedminster from 81. *153 St John's Lane, Bedminster, Bristol, BS3 5AE.* (Bristol 776132)

CHAMBERS, Roland Arthur Blake. b 07. AKC (2nd cl) 32. **d** 32 **p** 33 S'wark. C of St Mark Plumstead 32-35; St John Angell Town Brixton 35-37; Bideford 37-44; Bp's Hatfield

44-45; St Mary's Cathl (in c of St Pet) Glas 45-46; Hitchin (in c of St Mark) 46-50; C-in-c of St Francis Conv Distr Broadfield Oxhey 50-54; V of St Leon Bedford 54-73; Perm to Offic Dio St Alb from 74. *6 Queens Road, Ampthill, Beds.* (Bedford 404629)

CHAMBERS, Sydney Percival. b 1890. Edin Th Coll. **d** 16 **p** 19 Glas. C of St Jo Evang Coatbridge 16-20; All SS Middlesbrough 20-23; Perm to Offic at St Andr Wolverhampton 24-25; C of Brandon (in c of St Agatha) 26-29; PC of Melton Ross w New Barnetby 29-43; V of St Edw Holbeck 43-47; St Matt Littleport 47-62; C-in-c of L Ouse 55-62; Perm to Offic Dio Ely from 63. *College of St Barnabas, Dormans, Lingfield, Surrey.*

CHAMBOMBE, Yonathan. St Andr Th Coll Mpondas 64. **d** 66 Malawi. d Dio Malawi 66-71; S Malawi from 71. *Box 44, Mangochi, Malawi.*

CHAMFYA, Pascal. b 25. **d** 77 Bukavu. d Dio Bukavu. *St Andrew's Church, BP 1042, Lubumbashi, Zaire.*

CHAMHENE, Richard. **d** and **p** 78 Centr Tang. P Dio Centr Tang. *Mvumi Hospital, PO Mvumi, Tanzania.*

CHAMIER, Peter Lewis Deschamps. b 13 Late Exhib of Ch Ch Ox BA (2nd cl Mod Hist) 35, 2nd cl Jurispr 37, BCL 38, MA 40. Ely Th Coll 39. **d** 39 **p** 40 Birm. C of Em Wylde Green 39-41; Holy Cross St Pancras 41-42; C-in-c of Perry Beeches 42-45; Cler Dir E Mid Area ICF 45; V of St Andr Gt Cam 45-49; Lect in Law Birm Coll of Comm 49-58; Hd of Dept of Gen Studies 55-58; Publ Pr Dio Birm 53-58; Hd Master Ld Weymouth Sch Warminster 58-60; Tutor W Region Teachers' Coll Ibad and L to Offic Dio Ibad 60-62; Actg C-in-c of Grindleton 62; Perm to Offic Dio Ches 63-65; Tutor Bp Willis Coll Ugan 66; Chap Teso Coll Aloet 67-70; Chan of Soroti 68-70; Chap Dover Coll 71; V of Sutton-on-Trent 71-80; Carlton-on-Trent 71-80; P-in-c of Normanton-on-Trent 77-80; Marnham 77-80; Actg RD of Tuxford and Norwell 80; Perm to Offic Dio Ely from 80. *9 Sherlock Road, Cambridge, CB3 0HR.* (Cambridge 354563)

CHAMP, Very Rev Cyril Bruce. b 21. TCD BA (1st cl Mod Ment and Mor Phil) 42. Abp King's Prize 42, BD 66. **d** 44 **p** 45 Dub. C of St Geo Dub 44-47; R of Baltinglass and Ballynure 47-53; Aughrim 53-75; Dean of Clonf and Kilmac from 65; I of Kilmacduagh 65-75; RD of Aughrim and Loughrea 70-81; I of Shinrone w Ettagh Dio Killaloe from 75; Aghancon w Kilcolman Dio Killaloe from 75. *St Mary's Rectory, Shinrone, Birr, Offaly, Irish Republic.* (0505 47164)

CHAMPION, Canon John Oswald Cecil. b 27. St Chad's Coll Dur BA 49, Dipl in Th 51. **d** 51 **p** 52 Worc. C of St Martin w Whittington Worc 51-53; Chap RN 53-57; C of St Martin w St Paul Cant 57-60; C-in-c of St Mich AA Eccles Distr Norton 60-64; V of Astwood Bank w Crabbs Cross 64-68; Redditch 68-75; R of Fladbury w Wyre Piddle and Moor Dio Worc from 75; RD of Pershore from 79; Hon Can of Worc from 81. *Fladbury Rectory, Pershore, Worcs, WR10 2QW.* (Evesham 860356)

CHAMPION, Sir Reginald Stuart. b 1895. KCMG 46. OBE 34. Linc Th Coll 51. **d** and **p** 52 Cant. C of All SS Maidstone 52-53; V of Chilham 53-61. *46 Chancellor House, Tunbridge Wells, Kent.* (Tunbridge Wells 20719)

CHAMPION, Russell William. Ridley Coll Melb 54. ACT ThL 56. **d** 57 **p** 58 Melb. C of Box Hill 57-59; Coburg 59; I of Leopold 59-63; Spotswood 63-67; Perm to Offic Dio Melb from 67. *3 Susan Court, Lower Templestowe, Vic, Australia 3107.* (850-3584)

CHAMPION, Thomas Eric. Moore Th Coll Syd 34. ACT ThL 46. **d** 37 **p** 38 Nel. C of Wairau Valley 37-38; V 38-40; V of Picton 40-47; CF (NZEF) 40-43; V of Stoke w Richmond 47-49; All SS Nel and Archd of Waimea 49-52; C of St John Parramatta 52-53; R of St Mary's 53-56; Petersham 56-71; Katoomba 71-72; L to Offic Dio Syd from 73. *28 Shaw Street, Petersham, NSW, Australia 2049.* (560-8275)

CHAMPNESS, George William Horace. b 11. Croix de Guerre 44. Men in Disp 45. OBE 63. Chich Th Coll 70. **d** 70 **p** 71 Portsm. C of Liss 70-75; P-in-c of Hawkley 75-77; Wroxall 77-80. *Clyde Cottage, West Street, Seaview, IW.* (Seaview 2349)

CHAMPNESS, William Arthur. **d** 43 **p** 44 Bran. C of Rivers 43-46; R of Shoal Lake 46-49; Rapid City 49-53; P-in-c of Swan River 53-59; R of Vermilion 59-61; L to Offic Dio Edmon 62-64; P-in-c of St Chad Edmon 64-66; Can Missr Dio Edmon 71-73; Perm to Offic Dio BC from 74. *303-1345 Pandora Avenue, Victoria, BC, Canada.*

CHAMPNEYS, Michael Harold. b 46. GRSM 67. Linc Th Coll 69. **d** 72 **p** 73 Stepney for Lon. C of Poplar 72-73; C of Bow 73-75; C-in-c of St Barn Bethnal Green Lon 75-76; C of Tewkesbury 76-78; V of St Mich AA Bedford Pk Dio Lon from 78. *Vicarage, Priory Gardens, W4 1TT.* (01-994 1380)

CHAMUNGU, Andrea Nhogota. St Phil Coll Kongwa. **d** 64 **p** 65 Centr Tang. P Dio Centr Tang. *PO Box 2, Mpwapwa, Tanzania.*

CHAN, Alan Chor-Choi. Union Th Coll Hong Kong. **d** 61 **p** 62 Hong. V of Kei Oi Kowloon 62-75; Lect Chung Chi Coll Hong from 75. *c/o Chung Chi College, Hong Kong.* (12-621730)

CHAN, Hin Cheung. b 44. U Th Coll Hong Kong 68. **d** 70 **p** 71 Hong. C of St Mary Hong 70-74; Relig Educn Officer Dio Hong from 75. *1 Lower Albert Road, Hong Kong.* (5-265355)

CHAN, Kai Ming. **d** and **p** 75 W Mal. P Dio W Mal. *24 Jalan Cheras, Kuala Lumpur, Malaysia.*

CHAN, Norman Ka Kwong. Trin Th Coll Sing LTh 58. **d** 58 **p** 59 Sing. P Dio Sing. *2 Dundee Road, Queenstown, Singapore 3.*

CHAN, Pak Chung. **d** 49 Hong. d Dio Hong 50-78. *9b Nassam Street, 20th Floor, Mei Foo Sun Chuen, Kowloon, Hong Kong.* (3-729 708)

CHAN, Stephen. Union Th Coll Hong Kong LTh 63. **d** 64 Hong. d Dio Hong. *St Peter's Vicarage, North Point, Hong Kong.* (5-708272)

CHAN, Tak Kin. Union Th Coll Canton 47. **d** 49 **p** 50 Sing. P-in-c of St Mary Selangor 49-50; V of All SS Selangor 59-63; P-in-c of Salak S Miss Kuala Lumpur 63-69. *Salak South Mission, Kuala Lumpur, Malaya.*

CHANCE, David Newton. b 44. St D Coll Lamp BA 68. St Steph Ho Ox 68. **d** 70 **p** 71 Cant. C of Selsdon 70-73; Plymstock 73-77; P-in-c of Northam w Westward Ho Dio Ex 77-79; Team R (w Appledore) from 79. *Northam Rectory, Bideford, Devon.* (Bideford 4379)

CHANCE, Richard James. b 47. St Jo Coll Morpeth ACT ThDip 72. **d** 73 **p** 74 N Queensld. C of St Jas Cathl Townsville 73-74; Atherton 74-76; Novice SSM 77-78; Perm to Offic Dio Adel 77-79; L to Offic from 79; Field Officer Angl Bd of Chr Educn Dio Adel from 79. *210 Archer Street, N Adelaide, S Australia 5006.* (267-1411)

CHANCELLOR, Robert John Purvis. b 25. Bps' Coll Cheshunt 61. **d** 62 Man **p** 63 Hulme for Man. C of St Benedict Ardwick 62-63; All SS and Marts Langley Lancs 63-64; St Thos W Hyde 64-69; Miss Rhod Rly Miss Matab 69-71; R of Lyttleton Pret 71-72; P-in-c of Colebrook 73-75; Down w Clannaborough 73-75; C of St Mary BV Plympton 75-76; P-in-c of Dodbrooke 76-77; E Allington 77; R of Dodbrooke 77-79; E Allington 77-79; Perm to Offic Dio Ox 79-81; Dio Ex from 72. *77 Easterdown Close, Plymstock, Plymouth, Devon.* (Plymouth 450)

CHANCELLOR, Victor David. Univ of BC BA 58. Angl Th Coll Vancouver LTh 58. **d** 58 New Westmr for Carib **p** 59 Carib. C of Lytton 58-60; P-in-c of Hazelton 60-64; R of Manzini Dio Zulu 64-68; Dio Swaz 68-70; L to Offic Dio Carib from 77. *2025 Cleasby Street, Merritt, BC, Canada.*

CHANDA, Daniel Khazan. b 28. Panjab Univ BA 57, MA 62. **d** & **p** 70 Birm. C of St Jas Handsworth Dio Birm from 70. *44 Albion Road, Handsworth, Birmingham, B21 8BG.*

CHANDI, Elias Njiru. Weithaga Bible Sch 60. **d** 61 **p** 62 Ft Hall. P Dio Ft Hall 61-65; Dio Mt Kenya 65-75; Dio Mt Kenya S 75; Dio Mt Kenya E from 76; Exam Chap to Bp of Mt Kenya E from 81. *Box 64, Sagana, Kenya.*

CHANDLER, Preb Arthur Stanley. b 06. St Edm Hall Ox 3rd cl Math Mods 27, BA (3rd cl Th) 29, MA 38. Westcott Ho Cam 29. **d** 30 **p** 31 Ox. C of Windsor 30-33; P-in-c of Broken Hill N Rhod 33-37; C of Henley-on-Thames 37-40; Hambleden (in c of Frieth and Skirmett) 40-45; R of Clovelly 45-52; V of Woolfardisworthy W 49-52; Ilfracombe Dio Ex 52-72; R (w Lee and West Down) (w Woolacombe and Bittadon from 78) from 72; Surr from 53; C-in-c of West Down Dio Ex 53-58; V 58-72; V of Lee 58-72; R of Bittadon 58-64; RD of Barnstaple 67-77; Preb of Ex from 67; R of Woolacombe 76-78. *Vicarage, Ilfracombe, Devon.* (Ilfracombe 3467)

CHANDLER, Edward John. b 05. St Aid Coll 30. **d** 35 **p** 36 Roch. C of St Mark New Brompton 35-38; St Luke Bromley Common 38-44; St Jo Evang Farncombe 44-47; V of Kirtling 47-59; R of Staple Fitzpaine w Bickenhall (and Curland from 61) 59-70. *Broadenham View, Winsham, Chard, Somt.*

CHANDLER, John Edmond Owen. b 18. St Cath S Ox 3rd cl Mod Hist BA and MA 48. Cudd Coll 68. **d** 68 Bp Parfitt for Derby **p** 69 Repton for Cant. Hon C of Quarndon 68-72; Publ Pr Dio Southw 73-78; R of Epperstone Dio Southw from 79; Gonalston Dio Southw from 79; P-in-c of Oxton Dio Southw from 79. *Rectory, Epperstone, Notts.* (Lowdham 4220)

CHANDLER, Michael John. b 45. Univ of Lon Dipl Th (Extra-Mural Stud) 75. STh (Lambeth) 80. Linc Th Coll 70. **d** 72 **p** 73 Cant. C of St Dunstan w H Cross Cant 72-75; Margate 75-78; V of Newington w Bobbing and Iwade Dio Cant from 78; Hartlip w Stockbury Dio Cant from 80. *Newington Vicarage, Sittingbourne, Kent, ME9 7JU.* (Sittingbourne 842305)

CHANDLER, Peter John. b 20. Univ of Lon BA (2nd cl Hons Hist) 41. Linc Th Coll 46. **d** 48 **p** 49 Leic. C of Aylestone 48-52; St Pet w St Swith Bournemouth 52-55; V of N Baddesley 55-64; Archd in Cyprus 64-67; Chap at Nicosia 64-67;

V of Andover w Foxcotte Dio Win from 67; Surr from 67; M Gen Syn from 80. *St Mary's Vicarage, Church Close, Andover, Hants, SP10 1DP.* (Andover 52729)

CHANDY, Sugu John Mathai. b 40. Univ of Kerala BSc 61. Univ of Serampore BD 66. Wycl Coll Tor 67. **d** 66 **p** 68 Kerala. In Ch of S India 66-74; C of St Cuthb Ormesby 74-77; Sutton-in-Holderness 77-80. *Address temp unknown.*

CHANG, Abraham Hui-won. St Mich Sem Oryudong. **d** 67 **p** 68 Taejon. P Dio Taejon 67-74; Dio Pusan from 74. *St Francis Church, Dong-Nundong, Daegu, Korea.* (Daegu 5-4112)

CHANG, Mark. St Mich Sem Oryudong 61. Soong Sil Coll BA 62. **d** 65 Korea **p** 65 Seoul. Tutor St Mich Sem Oryudong 65-71; L to Offic Dio Tor from 73. *1202-55 Emmett Avenue, Toronto, Ont, Canada.*

✠ **CHANG-HIM, Right Rev French Kitchener.** Lich Th Coll. **d** 62 Bp Gerard for York **p** 63 Maur. C of Goole 62-63; R of Praslin w St Mark's Bay Seychelles 63-67; C of St Leon Norwood 67-68; C of St Paul's Cathl Mahé Maur 68-70; Miss at Praslin 70-73; R of St Sav Anse Royale S Sey 73-79; Archd of Sey 73-79; Cons Ld Bp of Seychelles in St Paul's Cathl Vic, Mahé 25 July 79 by Abp of the Indian Ocean; Bp of Antan; and Bp G Briggs. *Box 44, Victoria, Seychelles.* (Seychelles 22432)

CHANGACH, Joseph Kimulwa. b 45. **d** 69 Maseno **p** 71 Nak. P Dio Nak from 71. *Box 79, Nandi Hills, Kenya.*

CHANING-PEARCE, David. b 32. Roch Th Coll 63. **d** 65 **p** 66 Roch. C of St Mary Plaistow Kent 65-69; Rustington 69-73; R of Slinfold Dio Chich from 73. *Slinfold Rectory, Horsham, Sussex, RH13 7QU.* (Slinfold 790377)

CHANNEL, Bertie William. b 20. Moore Coll Syd 62. **d** 79 Bp Parker for Newc. Hon C of Tor Dio Newc from 79. *77 Excelsior Parade, Cary Bay 2283, NSW, Australia.*

CHANNER, Christopher Kendall. b 42. K Coll Lon and Warm BD and AKC 64. **d** 65 **p** 66 Cant. C of St Steph Norbury 65-68; S Elmsall Wakef 68-70; V of St Edm Dartford 70-75; St Andr Bromley 75-81; Langton Green Dio Roch from 81. *Langton Green Vicarage, Tunbridge Wells, Kent.* (Langton 2072)

CHANNER, John Hugh. b 48. St Jo Coll Dur BA 72. Wycl Hall Ox 72. **d** 78 **p** 79 Wakef. C of Sandal Magna 78-81; N Stoneham w Bassett Dio Win from 81. *All Saints Lodge, Pointout Road, Bassett, Southampton.* (0703 766569)

CHANT, Edwin John. b 14. King's Coll Lon 39, Collins Pri 42, BA (Lon) 62. Clifton Th Coll 46. **d** 47 **p** 48 Roch. C of St Paul Northumb Heath, Erith 47-49; Darfield (in c of Gt Houghton) 49-51; Conisborough 51-53; St Paul Cliftonville 53-56; V of Gentleshaw 56-80; Farewell 56-80; Perm to Offic Dio Lich from 80. *19 Pineside Avenue, Cannock Wood, Gentleshaw, Rugeley, Staffs, WS15 4RG.*

CHANT, Harry. b 40. Oak Hill Coll Dipl Higher Educn 78. **d** 78 Sarum **p** 79 Bp L A brown for Sarum. C of St Jo Heatherlands Parkstone 78-81; P-in-c of Bramshaw Dio Sarum from 81; Landford w Plaitford Dio Sarum from 81. *Bramshaw Vicarage, Lyndhurst, Hants, SO4 7JF.* (Earldoms 256)

CHANT, Kenneth William. b 37. St Deiniols Libr Hawarden 67. **d** 70 **p** 71 Llan. C of Ynyshir 70-74; Bargoed and Deri w Brithdir 74; P-in-c of Aberpergwm Dio Llan 74-77; V 77-81; Cwmavon Dio Llan from 81. *Cwmavon Vicarage, Port Talbot, W Glam.* (Cwmavon 254)

CHANT, Maurice Ronald. b 26 Chich Th Coll 51. **d** 54 **p** 55 S'wark. C of St Mark Mitcham 54-57; St Matt Surbiton 57-60; C-in-c of H Trin Conv Distr Cookridge Adel 60-64; V 64-67; Chap Miss to Seamen Tilbury 67-71; Gt Yarmouth 71-77; Brisb from 77; L to Offic Dio Chelmsf 67-71; Dio Nor 71-77. *Harbour Road, Hamilton, Brisbane, Australia 4007.* (268 3495)

CHANTER, Anthony Roy. b 37. ACP 60. Open Univ BA 72. Univ of Lon MA 75. Sarum Th Coll 64. **d** 66 **p** 67 Chich. C of W Tarring 66-69; Chap St Andr Sch Worthing 69-70; Hdmaster Bp King Sch Linc 70-73; Hon PV of Linc Cathl 70-73; Hdmaster Grey Court Comprehensive Sch Richmond-upon-Thames 73-76; Hon C of Kingston T 73-76; Hdmaster Bp Reindorp Sch Guildf from 77; Perm to Offic Dio Guildf from 77. *Grasshoppers, Woodland Avenue, Cranleigh, Surrey.* (Cranleigh 3833)

CHANTLER, William Oliver. b 1900. Qu Coll Cam BA (3rd cl Th Trip pt i) 22, MA 26. Whittlesford Th Coll 37. **d** 38 Leic **p** 39 Bp Willis for Leic. C of Jas Gt Leic 38-41; Cathl Ch Leic 41-43; Actg Succr 41-44; V of St Aug Leic 44-48; Evington 48-53; R of Ibstock 53-63; Stockerston 64-75; Hallaton 64-75; RD of Gartree III 68-75; Hon Can of Leic Cathl 73-76; Can (Emer) from 76; L to Offic Dio Leic from 74. *22 Blenheim Way, Market Harborough, Leics.* (Market Harborough 67049)

CHANTRY, Richard Michael. b 31. Hertf Coll Ox BA 55, MA 57. Ridley Hall Cam 55. **d** and **p** 57 Derby. C of Boulton 57-59; Chap Ox Past and C of St Aldate Ox 59-68; Chap Hertf Coll Ox from 61; Asst Master Wycombe Girls' High Sch from 70; P-in-c of St Aldates Ox 74-75. *11 Talbot Road, Oxford, OX2 8LL.* (Oxford 58286)

CHANZI, Mpandi. **d** and **p** 77 Centr Tang. P Dio Centr Tang. *Box 82, Manyoni, Tanzania.*

CHAPA, Geoffrey. b 26. **d** 73 **p** 74 Zam (APM). P Dio N Zam. *Mutwe-na-Nkoko, Mansa, Zambia.*

CHAPEYAMA, Fanwell. **d** 74 **p** 75 Mashon. P Dio Mashon. *Rhodesia Railways, Box 552, Umtali, Zimbabwe.*

CHAPLIN, Colin. **d** 76 **p** 77 Edin (APM). C of St Jas Inverleith Row City and Dio Edin from 76. *26 Broomhill Road, Penicuik, Midlothian.*

CHAPLIN, Frederick David. b 20. CCC Ox BA (1st cl Th) 49, MA 54. Cudd Coll 49. **d** 51 **p** 52 B & W. C of Glastonbury 51-55; Chap of Wells Th Coll 55-57; Vice-Prin 57-61; LPr Dio B & W 55-61; Dean and R of H Trin Cathl Port of Spain Trinid 61-68; Exam Chap to Bp of Trinid 61-68; WCC Sec Inter-Ch Relations, Caribbean 69-72; Asst to Sec Gen of Angl Consultative Coun 72-78; Commiss Trinid from 72; Executive Sec Partnership for World Miss from 79. *24 Tufton Street, SW1P 3RB.*

CHAPLIN, George McPherson. b 13. Univ of Glas MA 34. Edin Th Coll 34. **d** 36 **p** 37 Glas. C of Baillieston 36-38; St John (in c of St Steph) Greenock 38-41; R of St Bart Gourock 41-45; St Andr Banff 45-51; St Andr Alford 51-57; H Trin Kilmarnock 57-79; Synod Clk and Can of Glas 75-79; Perm to Offic Dio Newc from 79. *19 Valencia Street, Gorokan, NSW, Australia 2263.*

CHAPMAN, Canon Albert Aidan. b 09. TD 50. Em Coll Cam BA 35, MA 39. Lon Coll of Div 35. **d** 37 **p** 38 Roch. C of St Jo Bapt Beckenham 37-39; CF (TA) 39-55; V of St Paul Northumberland Heath erith 46-50; R and V of Farnborough 50-64; Chap of Orpington Hosp 52-59; Farnborough Hosp 59-64; RD of Orpington 55-64; Sevenoaks 64-74; Hon Can of Roch 64-76; Can (Emer) from 76; V of Westerham 64-76; Perm to Offic Dio St E from 76. *41 Honeymeade Close, Stanton, Suff.*

CHAPMAN, Beverly Ann Helen. McGill Univ Montr BEducn. Univ of BC BTh. Coll of Em & St Chad Sktn. **d** 79 **p** 80 Bran. C of Grandview & Gilbert Plains 79; Dir of the Henry Budd Leadership Tr Centre Dio Bran from 80. *Box 2518, The Pas, Manit, Canada, R9A 1M3.*

CHAPMAN, Christopher Robin. b 37. Univ of Nottm Dipl Adult Educn 71. Ripon Hall Ox 72. **d** 73 **p** 74 S'wark. C of Kidbrooke 73-77; V of Hopton (w Corton from 80) Dio Nor from 77; Corton 77-80; RD of Lothingland from 80. *Vicarage, Corton, Lowestoft, Suff.* (Lowestoft 730977)

CHAPMAN, Very Rev CLifford Thomas. b 13. Univ of Lon BA (2nd cl Hist) 34, BD 35, AKC 36, MTh 40, PhD 46. Fell K Coll Lon 48. Ely Th Coll 35. **d** 36 Lon **p** 37 Willesden for Lon. C of All SS Child's Hill 36; St Paul Winchmore Hill 38-39; Pinner 36-38 and 39-42; Min of Ch of Ascen Conv Distr Preston 42-45; V of Ch Ch Chelsea 45-50; RD of Chelsea 46-50; R of Abinger 50-61; Org Adult Relig Educn Dio Guildf 52-61; Dir of Post-Ordin Tr 58-68; Dir of Relig Educn 61-63; Exam Chap to Bp of Guildf 53-73; Can Res and Sub-Dean of Guildf 61-73; Proc Conv Guildf 65-73; Dean of Ex 73-80; Dean (Emer) from 80. *Spring Cottage, Ockley Road, Cold Harbour, Dorking, Surrey.* (Dorking 6356)

CHAPMAN, Colin. Univ of St Andr MA (2nd cl Gr and Hebr) 60. BD (2nd cl) Lon 62. Ridley Hall Cam. **d** 64 **p** 65 Edin. C of St Jas L Leith 64-67; Asst Chap All SS Cathl Cairo 68-74; Perm to Offic Dio Birm 74-77. *PO Box 9481, Beirut, Lebanon.*

CHAPMAN, Colin Clifford. Em Coll Sktn. **d** 61 **p** 62 Bran. R of Elgin 61-64; Souris 64-70; Reston 64-70; St Mary's Charleswood Winnipeg 70-76; I of Portage la Priarie Dio Rupld from 76. *Box 422, Portage La Prairie, Manit, Canada.*

CHAPMAN, David. b 06. Bps' Coll Cheshunt 67. **d** 68 **p** 69 Dur. C of Bp Wearmouth 68-71; V of Merrington 71-79. *Jonifers, Farnham Road, Sheet, Nr Petersfield, Hants.*

CHAPMAN, David John. b 28. Jes Coll Ox BA 52, MA 56. Wells Th Coll 52. **d** 54 **p** 55 Lich. C of Sedgley 54-57; Cannock (in c of St Chad Chadsmoor) 57-60; V of St Matt Tipton 60-69; R of Sawley 69-79; Wells-next-the-Sea Dio Nor from 79; P-in-c of Holkham Dio Nor from 79; Warham w Wighton Dio Nor from 79. *Rectory, Wells-next-the-Sea, Norf.*

CHAPMAN, Derek. b 22. Westcott Ho Cam. **d** 53 **p** 54 Cov. C of St Barbara Cov 53-56; C of Rugby 56-58; V of E Malling 58-79; CF (TA) 60-67; R of Hever w Markbeech Dio Roch from 79; P-in-c of Four Elms Dio Roch from 81. *Hever Rectory, Edenbridge, Kent.* (Edenbridge 862249)

CHAPMAN, Edward Alexander. Bp's Univ Lennox BA 63, LST 64. **d** 64 **p** 66 Ott. C of St Matt Ott 64-70; R of Londonderry w Bass River 70-74; Hyde Park Dio Hur from 74. *Rectory, Hyde Park, Ont., Canada.* (519-471 1317)

CHAPMAN, Edwin Thomas. b 32. Univ of Man BA 60. St

Mich Coll Llan. **d** 63 **p** 64 Blackb. C of St Andr Cleveleys 63-65; St Mary Virg Ox 65-67; Chap Lady Marg Hall Ox 67-68; Asst Dir of Educn Dio York 68-75; R of E Gilling 68-76; P-in-c of Hockley 76-77; V 77-82; Quadring w Gosberton Clough Dio Linc from 82. *Vicarage, Gosberton Clough, Spalding, Lincs, PE11 4JH.* (Risegate 252)

CHAPMAN, Eric Arthur. b 02. Univ of Lon BD 49. St Aid Coll 35. **d** 37 Wakef **p** 37 Pontefract for Wakef. C of Mold Green 37-40; Golcar 40-41; C-in-c of St Paul Huddersfield 41-43; V 43-48; H Trin Runcorn 48-56; Poynton 56-63; Thurston 63-66; SPCK N Group Org 66-72; L to Offic Dio Ripon from 72. *10 Ripley Way, Harrogate, Yorks.* (Harrogate 66330)

CHAPMAN, Canon Eric Ronald. b 19. Univ of Man BA (2nd cl hons Hist) 41, BD 59. Bps' Coll Cheshunt 41. **d** 43 **p** 44 Blackb. C of St Pet Chorley 43-46; Skerton 46-51; V of St Mark Bolton 51-58; St Pet Kells Whitehaven 58-66; R of Egremont Dio Carl 66-81; Team R (w Haile) from 81; RD of Whitehaven 66-70; Hon Can of Carl Cathl from 79. *Rectory, Egremont, Cumb, CA22 2LU.* (Egremont 820268)

CHAPMAN, Preb Frederick Alexander Routley. Keble Coll Ox BA (3rd cl Th) 29, MA 33. Wells Th Coll 29. **d** 30 **p** 31 Southampton for Win. C of Eastleigh 30-32; St Mary Redcliffe (in c of St Mary L to 35) 32-37; Dom and Dioc Chap to Bp of Lich 37-40; CF (EC) 39-42; V of Bloxwich 42-46; Cannock w Chadsmoor 46-52; St Chad Shrewsbury 52-56; RD of Shrewsbury 55-56; Proc Conv Lich 55-65; R of Stoke-on-Trent 56-65; Stockton Salop 65-70; Preb of Lich Cathl from 56; RD of Stoke-on-Trent 59-65; Shifnal 69-71; V of Broughton 70-71; R of Myddle 70-71. *5 Vicars' Close, Lichfield, Staffs.*

CHAPMAN, Gorran. b 55. Univ of Dur BA. Westcott Ho Cam 78. **d** 80 **p** 81 Truro. C of Par Dio Truro from 80. *18 Trevarweneth Road, Par, Cornwall, PL24 2EA.* (Par 3721)

CHAPMAN, Canon Guy Godfrey. b 33. Univ of Southn BSc (2nd cl Eng) 57. Clifton Th Coll 60. **d** 62 **p** 63 Man. C of Ch Ch Chadderton 62-67; V of Edgeside 67-70; Shipton Bellinger Dio Win from 70; RD of Andover from 75; Hon Can of Win Cathl from 79. *St Peter's Vicarage, Shipton Bellinger, Tidworth, Hants.* (Tidworth 2244)

CHAPMAN, Harrison. Univ of Melb BSc 33. **d** 59 **p** 60 Melb. Asst Chap C of E Gr Sch Melb 59-65; C of S Yarra 59-64; Hawthorn 64; I of Flinders 65-79; Perm to Offic Dio Melb from 79. *3/15 Shakespeare Grove, Hawthorne, Vic, Australia 3122.*

CHAPMAN, Henry Davison. b 31. Univ of Bris BA (2nd cl Th) 55. Tyndale Hall Bris 52. **d** 56 Liv **p** 57 Warrington for Liv. C of St Mark St Helens 56-60; R of St Jas Clitheroe 60-67; PC of Tipton 67-68; SW Area Sec CPAS 68-72; V of St Luke Eccleston 72-78; P-in-c of Ringshall w Battisford Barking w Darmsden and Gt Bricett Dio St E 78-80; R from 80. *Rectory, Barking, Ipswich, IP6 8HJ.* (Needham Market 720394)

CHAPMAN, Hugh William. b 54. Univ of WI (Barbados) BA (Th) 79. Codr Coll Barb 75. **d** 78 **p** 79 Guy. C of St Geo Cathl Georgetown Dio Guy from 79. *80 Carmichael Street, Georgetown 2, Guyana.*

CHAPMAN, John. St Cuthb Soc Dur BA 51. St Chad's Coll Dur Dipl Th 53. **d** 53 **p** 54 Dur. C of Billingham 53-55; Harton 55-57; PC of Hedgefield 57-63; Annfield Plain 63-78; V of All S w St Jas Bolton-le-Moors Dio Man from 78. *Vicarage, Astley Street, Bolton, Lancs, BL1 8EH.* (Bolton 27269)

CHAPMAN, Canon John Charles. Moore Th Coll Syd 57. **d** 57 **p** 58 Armid. C of Moree 57-60; Youth Dir Dio Armid 60-66; Dir Armid Bd of Christian Educn 66-68; Dioc Missr Dio Syd from 68; Dir Dept of Evang Syd from 69; Can of Syd from 75. *St Andrew's House, Sydney Square, Sydney, NSW, Australia 2000.* (2-0642)

CHAPMAN, John Holland. b 54. Carleton Univ Ott BA 75. Huron Coll Lon MDiv 78. **d** and **p** 78 Ott. C of St Matthias Ott 78-79; on leave. *Huron College, London, Ont, Canada.*

CHAPMAN, John Owen. **d** 64 **p** 80 New Westmr. C of St Cath Capilano N Vanc 64-70; L to Offic Dio New Westmr from 70. *16822-14th Avenue, White Rock, BC, Canada.*

CHAPMAN, Kenneth George. St Chad's Coll Dur BA 48, Dipl Th (w distinc) 49. **d** 49 **p** 50 Chich. C of Lancing 49-55; Moulsecomb 55-66; V of St Phil Eastbourne 66-75; R of St Jo Bapt-sub-Castro Lewes 76-78. *c/o 1 The Avenue, Lewes, E Sussex.* (Lewes 3080)

CHAPMAN, Michael Robin. b 39. Univ of Leeds BA (2nd cl Gen) 61. Coll of Resurr Mirfield 61. **d** 63 **p** 64 Dur. C of St Columba Southwick 63-68; Chap RN from 68. *c/o Ministry of Defence, Lacon House, Theobalds Road, WC1X 8RY.*

CHAPMAN, Percy Frank. b 06. Univ of Bris BSc (1st cl Hons) 27, MA 31. **d** 36 **p** 37 Glouc. C of Barnwood 36-41; Asst Master Crypt Sch Glouc 31-41; Asst Chap Marlb Coll 41-65; Ho Master 50-65; V of Aldbourne 65-72; Baydon 65-72; Coombe Bissett w Homington Dio Sarum 72-81; R from 81; P-in-c of Bishopstone w Stratford Tony Dio Sarum 80-81; R from 81. *Bishopstone Rectory, Salisbury, Wilts.* (Coombe Bissett 330)

CHAPMAN, Peter Harold White. b 40. K Coll Lon and Warm AKC 64. **d** 65 **p** 66 Portsm. C of St Alb, W Leigh, Havant 65-69; Stanmer w Falmer and Moulsecoomb 69-73; Chap RN from 74. *c/o Ministry of Defence, Lacon House, Theobalds Road, WC1X 8RY.*

CHAPMAN, Peter John. b 33. Univ of Dur BA (2nd cl Th) 56, Dipl Th 59. Cranmer Hall Dur 58. **d** 59 **p** 60 Derby. C of Boulton 59-62; Tutor Buwalasi Th Coll Mbale 63-65; Warden St Andr Commun Centre Mbale 66-69; Prov Training Team Kampala 69-70; P-in-c of St Matt, Southn 71-73; Team V of Southn (City Centre) 73-78; V of Bilston Dio Lich 78-80; Team R from 80; P-in-c of St Mary Bilston 78-79. *Vicarage, Dover Street, Bilston, W Midl.* (Bilston 41560)

CHAPMAN, Raymond. b 41. Linc Th Coll 68. **d** 71 **p** 72 Derby. C of St Jo Bapt, Dronfield 71-74; Delaval 75-76; Team V of Whorlton 76-79; V of St Hilda Jesmond City and Dio Newc T from 79. *46 Sanderson Road, Jesmond, Newcastle-upon-Tyne.* (Newc T 813130)

CHAPMAN, Raymond. b 24. Jes Coll Ox BA 45, MA 59. Univ of Lon MA 47. BD (Lon) 75. PhD (Lon) 78. SOC 72. **d** 74 **p** 75 Lon. C of St Mary-le-Strand Westmr Dio Lon from 74; Perm to Offic Dio S'wark from 77. *6 Kitson Road, Barnes, SW13 9HJ.* (01-748 9901)

CHAPMAN, Canon Rex Anthony. b 38. Univ of Lon BA (2nd cl Cl) 62. St Edm Hall Ox BA (2nd cl Th) 64, MA 68. Wells Th Coll 64. **d** 65 **p** 66 Worc. C of St Thos Stourbridge 65-68; Chap Univ of Aber 68-78; Can of Aber Cathl 76-78; Select Pr TCD 77; Can Res of Carl Cathl and Bp's Adv for Educn from 78. *1 The Abbey, Carlisle, CA3 8TZ.*

CHAPMAN, Rodney Andrew. B 53. AKC 75. St Aug Coll Cant 75. **d** 76 **p** 77 Dur. C of St Aid Hartlepool Dio Dur from 76. *28 Spring Garden Road, Hartlepool, Cleve, TS25 5AD.* (Hartlepool 71105)

CHAPMAN, Roger John. b 34. K Coll Lon and Warm AKC 58. **d** 59 **p** 60 Guildf. C of Ch Ch Guildf 59-61; CMS 61-68; L to Offic Dio Maseno 63-64; Chap to Abp of E Afr 64-65; V of St Mark Nai 65-67; R of S Milford 68-77; RD of Selby 72-77; V of St Mary Beverley Dio York from 77. *15 Molescroft Road, Beverley, Yorks.* (Beverley 881437)

CHAPMAN, Sydney William. b 12. Sarum Th Coll 55. **d** 56 Chich for Win **p** 57 Win. C of Ringwood 56-60; V of Walberton w Binsted 60-81. *Grenfell, Drove Road, Chilbolton, Stockbridge, Hants.* (Chilbolton 406)

CHAPMAN, Thomas Graham. b 33. Trin Coll Bris 73. **d** 75 **p** 76 Sarum. C of St Clem Branksome 75-81; V of Quarry Bank Dio Lich from 81. *Quarry Bank Vicarage, Brierley Hill, W Midl DY5 2DN.* (Cradley Heath 65480)

CHAPMAN, Walter Godfrey. **d** 50 **p** 51 Bran. R of Rivers 50-55; Chap RCAF 55-66; CF (Canad) from 66; Perm to Offic Dio Ott from 70. *96 Bowhill Avenue, Ottawa, Ont., Canada.*

CHAPMAN, William Charles. b 11. St Chad's Coll Dur BA 33. **d** 34 **p** 35 Dur. C of Blackhill 34-37; Usworth 37-39; Crawley 39-41; Clayton w Keymer 41-44; Asst Master Bembridge Sch IoW 45-77. *69 Downland Avenue, Southwick, Brighton, BN4 4RX.*

CHAPMAN, Ven William Donald. Bp's Univ Lennox LST 58. **d** 57 **p** 58 Ott. C of St Thos, Ott 57-61; I of Mattawa 61-63; R of Vanleek Hill 65-71; St Martin City and Dio Ott from 71; Hon Can of Ott from 79; Archd of Ottawa W from 80. *2131 Neepawa Avenue, Ottawa, Ont., Canada.* (1-613-722-6077)

CHAPMAN, William Henry Stanley. b 08. OBE 58. St Chad's Coll Dur BA 31. **d** 32 **p** 33 Dur. C of St Pet Monkwearmouth 32-35; Chap RN 35-63; V of W Dean w Binderton 63-73. *Moons, Green Lane, Crowborough, Sussex, TN6 2DE.* (Crowborough 61568)

CHAPMAN, William Howard Dale. b 11. Edin Th Coll 33. **d** 38 **p** 39 Glas. C of H Trin Ayr 38-41; R of St Andr Brech 41-47; C-in-c of St John Girvan w Stranraer and Portpatrick 47; C of H Trin Ayr 47-49; R of Coverham w Horsehouse 49-53; V of Askrigg w Stalling Busk 53-60; Kemble w Poole Keynes 60-71; Brookthorpe w Whaddon and Harescombe 71-76; Perm to Offic Dio Glouc from 76. *51 Holmwood Drive, Tuffley, Gloucester, GL4 0PN.* (Glouc 417336)

CHAPMAN, William Thomas. b 44. **d** 80 Wai. Hon C of Taradale Dio Wai from 80. *31 Bristol Crescent, Tamatea, Napier, NZ.*

CHAPOTE, Hezekia. **d** and **p** 77 Centr Tang. P Dio Centr Tang. *DCT, Nghambako, Tanzania.*

CHAPPELL, Allan. b 27 Selw Coll Cam BA 51, MA 56. Coll of Resurr Mirfield 51. **d** 53 **p** 54 Bris. C of Knowle 53-57; St Alb Dar-es-Salaam 57-62; Asst P at Korogwe 62-63; C of Long Eaton 64-67; Min of St Martha Eccles Distr Broxtowe 67-73; V of Car Colston w Screveton Dio Southw from 73;

P-in-c of Flintham Dio Southw from 73. *Vicarage, Flintham, Newark, Notts.* (E Stoke 344)

CHAPPELL, Amyas George. b 04. Qu Coll Cam BA 31, MA 35. Ridley Hall Cam 31. **d** 32 **p** 33 Ex. C of Em Plymouth 32-35; St Pet Tiverton 35-37; R of E Downe 37-39; Feniton 39-53; R of Buckerell 40-53; Chap RAFVR 45-47; V of Lamerton w Sydenham Damerel 53-58; R of Hallaton 58-63; R of Stockerston 59-63; RD of Gartree iii 63-67; Warden Launde Abbey Dioc Retreat Ho 63-67; C-in-c of Loddington 63-67; R of Higham-on-the-Hill 67-71. *Straiton, Buckleigh Road, Westward Ho, N Devon.* (Bideford 4662)

CHAPPELL, Eric Richardson. b 08. Keble Coll Ox BA 30, MA 34. Cudd Coll 30. **d** 31 **p** 32 Lon. C of St Mark Teddington 31-35; St Andr Hillingdon 35-43; Chap RAFVR 43-47; RAF 47-63; V of Goodnestone-next-Wingham w Chillenden and Knowlton 64-78; P-in-c of Adisham 75-78; Perm to Offic Dio Cant from 78. *33 Sandgate Hill, Folkestone, Kent.*

CHAPPELL, Frank Arnold. b 37. Univ of Dur BA 58. Bps' Coll Cheshunt. **d** 60 **p** 61 Ripon. C of Headingley 60-65; V of Beeston Hill 65-73; R of Garforth Dio Ripon from 73. *Garforth Rectory, Leeds, LS25 1NR.* (Leeds 863737)

CHAPPELL, George. b 15. Univ of Leeds BA (2nd cl Hist) 37. Sarum Th Coll 37. **d** 39 **p** 40 Wakef. C of Hemsworth 39-44; Illingworth 44-48; R of Whitwood Mere 48-53; V of Birkenshaw w Hunsworth 53-77. *4 Mazebrook Avenue, Gomersal, Cleckheaton, W Yorks.* (Cleckheaton 878822)

CHAPPELL, Preb George Thomas. b 04. St Jo Coll Dur Th Exhib 27, LTh 28, BA 29, MA 32. Lon Coll of Div 24. **d** 28 **p** 29 Ches. C of St Mary Birkenhead 28-31; St Paul Margate 31-34; Org Sec CMS Dios Ox and Cov 34-41; Dio Pet 35-41; Offg C-in-c of St Jas Paddington 41-43; V 43-71; Surr from 44; Chap St Mary's Hosp Paddington 44-54; RD of Paddington 56-67; Westmr (Paddington) 67-69; Preb of St Paul's Cathl Lon 63-71; Preb (Emer) from 71; C of H Trin Prince Consort Rd Kens 71-74; C-in-c 74-75; L to Offic Dio Lon from 72; Perm to Offic Dios Win and Sarum from 78. *Flat 3, 19 Burton Road, Branksome Park, Poole, Dorset.* (0202-764665)

CHAPPELL, Henry Pegg. b 09. Men in Disp 41. DSC 42. St Cath Coll Cam BA 31, MA 35. Wells Th Coll 33. **d** 34 **p** 35 Lon. C of All H Barking Lon 34-39; Chap RNVR 37-58; RNR from 58; V of Tynemouth 48-63; Surr 50-76; R and RD of Ludlow 63-71; C-in-c of How Caple w Sollers Hope 71-76. *Walcote House, Pembridge, Leominster, Herefs.*

CHAPPELL, Leslie George. **d** 34 **p** 35 Yukon. Miss at Moosehide 34-35; Prin St Paul's Hostel Dawson 35-38; Miss at Moosehide 38-39; I of Ch Ch Whitehorse 40-50; Hon Can of St Paul's Cathl Dawson 43-50; I of Comox 50-55; R of All SS Vancouver 55-64; I of Hope w Yale 64-71. *1285 Kent Street, White Rock, BC, Canada.*

CHAPPELL, Michael Paul. b 35. Selw Coll Cam BA 57, MA 61. Cudd Coll. **d** 62 Bp Stuart for Worc **p** 63 Worc. C of Pershore 62-65; St Thos Cathl Kuch and Dioc Educn Sec 65-67; Chap and V Cho of Heref Cathl 67-71; Min Can of Dur Cathl 71-76; Prec 72-76; Actg Sacr 75-76; Chap H Trin and Sch Stockton Dio Dur from 76. *4 Greymouth Close, Hartburn, Stockton-on-Tees, Cleveland.* (Stockton 585749)

CHAPPLE, Reginald John. b 01. St Bonif Coll Warm 61. **d** 62 **p** 63 Ex. C of St Mark Ex 62-70; Perm to Offic Dio Ex 70-73; Publ Pr Dio Ex from 73. *21 Tarbet Avenue, Exeter, Devon, EX1 2UE.* (Ex 71637)

CHARD, Canon Albert Jesse Gauntlett. b 03. St Mich Coll Llan 26. **d** 26 **p** 27 Llan. C of St Cath Cardiff 26-28; Chap Middx Hosp 28-30; Perm to Offic as C of Stroud 30-31; C of Littleham-cum-Exmouth (in c of Littleham from 34) 31-35; Chap HM Pris Wormwood Scrubbs 35-36; Win 36-40; V of Collingbourne Kingston 40-43; Figheldean w Milston 43-48; Winterbourne Whitchurch w Winterbourne Clenstone 48-50; R of H Trin Dorchester w Frome Whitfield 50-64; Surr 57-69; Can and Preb of Sarum Cathl 62-75; Can (Emer) from 75; PC of St Thos Sarum 64-69; C of Bourne Valley 74-80. *1b St Francis Road, Salisbury, Wilts.*

CHARD, Douglas Ian. b 47. Dalhousie Univ NS BA 69. Trin Coll Tor MDiv 78. **d** 78 Bp Hatfield for NS. C of New Glas w Trenton Dio NS from 78. *228 King Street, Truro, NS, Canada, B2N 3L6.*

CHARD, Francis Eric. b 24. Univ of Dur BA (1st cl Gen) 53, Dipl Th (w Distinc) 55, MLitt 81. **d** 55 **p** 56 Blackb. C of Cleveleys 55-57; Preston 57-59; V of St Bart Ewood Blackb 59-71; Downham Dio Blackb from 71. *Downham Vicarage, Clitheroe, Lancs.* (Clitheroe 41379)

CHARD, Reginald Jeffrey. b 40. St D Coll Lamp BA 62. Coll of Resurr Mirfield 62. **d** 64 **p** 65 Llan. C of Ystrad-Mynach 64-67; St Fagan Aberdare 67-71; V of Hirwaun 71-74; Hon C of Stechford 74-78; Team V of Banbury Dio Ox from 78. *St Hugh's House, Ruskin Road, Banbury, OX16 9HU.* (Banbury 3271)

CHARE, Frederic Keith. b 16. Hatf Coll Dur LTh 38, BA 39. Edin Th Coll 35. **d** 39 **p** 40 Glas. C of St John Greenock 39-43; St John Dumfries 43-46; St John Forton 46-52; V of St Phil Camberwell 52-57; Min of St Andr Eccles Distr Barming Heath Maidstone 57-69; V 69-73; Upchurch (w Lower Halstow from 75) Dio Cant from 74; C-in-c of Lower Halstow 74-75. *Vicarage, Oak Lane, Upchurch, Sittingbourne, Kent ME9 7AT.* (Medway 367227)

CHARLES, Ven Adrian Owen. ACT ThL 50. Dipl Div (Queensld) 60. St Francis Coll Brisb 48. **d** 51 **p** 52 Brisb. Miss Chap Dio Brisb 51-52; M of Bush Bro of St Paul 52-54; Chap Southport Sch Brisb 54-56; V of Wondai 56-59; Ch Ch St Lucia Brisb 59-66; R of St Paul Ipswich Brisb 66-72; Archd of Moreton 68-71; the Downs 71-72; Chap Ch Ch Gr Sch Perth 72-73; Dean and R of St Jas Cathl Townsville 73-76; R of St D Chelmer and Graceville City and Dio Brisb from 77; Chap to ABP and Archd Dio Brisb from 81. *62 Chelmer Street East, Chelmer, Queensland, Australia 4068.* (379 2167)

CHARLES, Canon Arthur Geoffrey. b 17. Univ of Leeds BA (2nd cl Hist) 39. Coll of Resurr Mirfield 39. **d** 41 **p** 42 Liv. C of St Dunstan Edge Hill 41-44; C of St Mary Blyth 44-49; V of Ch Ch Shieldfield Newc T 49-59; R of Lambley w Knaresdale 59-66; Bellingham 66-80; C-in-c of Thorneyburn w Greystead 69-80; RD of Bellingham from 76; Hon Can of Newc T Cathl from 79; R of Bellingham-Otterburn Group Dio Newc T from 80. *Bellingham Rectory, Hexham, Northumb, NE48 2JS.* (Bellingham 20225)

CHARLES, Edward Philip Grigg. b 38. St Jo Coll Auckld LTh 73. **d** 73 **p** 74 Dun. C of Anderson's Bay 73-76; Invercargill 76-77; V of Tapanui Dio Dun from 77. *15 Forrest Street, Tapanui, NZ.* (110)

CHARLES, George Edward. St Jo Coll Morpeth ACT ThL (2nd cl) 65. **d** 66 **p** 67 Melb. C of St John Bentleigh 66-67; St Mich Broadmeadows 67-70; Min of Montmorency 70-74; I of Mooroolbark 74-81; H Trin Bacchus Marsh Dio Melb from 81. *19 Gisborne Street, Bacchus Marsh, Vic, Australia 3340.*

✠ **CHARLES, Right Rev Harold John.** b 14. Univ of Wales BA (2nd cl Welsh) 35. Keble Coll Ox BA (2nd cl Th) 38, MA 43. St Mich Coll Llan 37. **d** 38 **p** 39 St D. C of Abergwili 38-40; Bp's Messenger L to Offic Dio Swan B and Exam Chap to Bp of Swan B 40-48; Sec Swan B Dioc Conf 45-48; Warden of Ch Hostel Bangor 48-52; Exam Chap to Bp of Ban 48-54; Lect Univ Coll N Wales 48-53; V of St Jas Ban and Sec Ban Dioc Conf 52-54; Can Res of Ban 53-54; Warden of St Mich Coll Llan 54-57; Can of Llan 56-57; Dean of St A 57-71; Exam Chap to Bp of St A 57-71; Cons Ld Bp of St A in Cathl Ch of SS Pet and Paul Llan 25 March 71 by Abp of Wales; Bps of Ban; Swan B; Mon; Ches; Abp Morris; and Bps Bartlett; Richards; and Hughes; res 82. *53 The Avenue, Woodland Park, Prestatyn, Clwyd.* (Prestatyn 89528)

CHARLES, Henry Richard. Univ of Wales BA 09, MA 28. **d** 14 **p** 15 St D. C of Llansamlet 14-16; St Ishmael (in c of Ferryside) 16-28; R of Pendine w Marros 28-36; V of Abernant w Conwil-in-Elfet 36-58; RD of Carmarthen 50-58. *3 St Mary Street, Carmarthen, Dyfed.* (Carmarthen 6987)

CHARLES, Canon Hubert Edward Richard. b 09. Late Scho and Exhib of Trin Coll Cam BA 31, MA 35. Westcott Ho Cam 33. **d** 35 **p** 36 S'wark. C of St Mark Camberwell 35-37; St Phil Lambeth 37-40; St Steph Smethwick 40-42; V of St Luke Kingstanding 42-51; Arlesey w Astwick 51-59; RD of Shefford 55-59; V of Boreham Wood 59-61; All SS Oxhey 61-66; R of Dunstable 66-73; Hon Can of St Alb from 68; P-in-c of Lidlington 73-77; RD of Elstow 76-77. *46 St Albans Road, Codicote, Hitchin, Herts.* (Stevenage 820024)

CHARLES, Jack William. b 16. Bps' Coll Cheshunt 50. **d** 53 Lanc for Blackb **p** 54 Blackb. C of St Luke Skerton 53-59; St Jas Norlands Kens 59-77; Chiswick Dio Lon from 77. *37 Brackley Road, W4 2HW.* (01-995 9580)

CHARLES, John Bolton. b 10. FCA 60. Coll of Resurr Mirfield 65. **d** 66 **p** 67 S'wark. C of Richmond 66-71; R of Walkern 71-78; RD of Stevenage 75-78. *59 Woodfield Drive, Winchester, Hants, SO22 5PY.*

CHARLES, John Hugo Audley. b 04. Worc Coll Ox BA (3rd cl Jurispr) 25, MA 46. Cudd Coll 27. **d** 29 **p** 30 Sarum. C of Gillingham Dorset 29-37; Min Can and Prec of Cant Cathl and Hd Master Cathl Choir Sch 37-38; R of Stisted 38-43; V of All H Twickenham 43-62; Lyme Regis 62-74. *Haydens, Wrington, near Bristol.* (Wrington 862284)

CHARLES, Jonathan. b 42. Ripon Coll Cudd 78. **d** 79 **p** 80 St Alb. C of St Luke Leagrave 79-82; Chap Denstone Coll Uttoxeter from 82. *Denstone College, Denstone, Uttoxeter, Staffs.* (0889 590484)

CHARLES, Meedperdas Edward. b 28. United Th Coll Bangalore BD (2nd cl) 54. Fitzw Ho Cam BA (3rd cl Th Trip pt ii) 60, MA 64. **d** 54 **p** 55 Sing. C of Malacca 54-55; P-in-c of St Paul and of St Pet Sing 55-58; Perm to Offic Dio Ely 59-60; V of St Bart Sheff 60-64; Actg Gen Sec for Coun for Ch of Mal and Sing and Chap Univ of Sing 64-66; V of All SS

Gravelly Hill Erdington 66-78; St Aug Endcliffe City and Dio Sheff from 79. *Endcliffe Vicarage, Brocco Bank, Sheffield, S11 8RQ.* (Sheff 661932)

CHARLES, Philip John. **d** 68 **p** 69 Sask. I of Stanley Dio Sask from 68. *Stanley Mission, Sask., Canada.*

CHARLES, Robert Frederick George. Hur Coll Ont STh 59. **d** 58 **p** 59 Alg. P-in-c of Rosseau Dio Alg from 59. *Box 86, Rosseau, Ont., Canada.* (705-732 4255)

CHARLES, Robert Sidney James. b 40. Univ of Wales Dipl Th 65. Open Univ BA 79. St Mich Coll Llan 62. **d** 65 **p** 66 Llan. C of Merthyr Tydfil 65-68; Shotton 68-70; R of Stock Gaylard w Lydlinch 70-74; Hubberston 74-76; Asst Master Sweyne Sch Rayleigh from 81; Perm to Offic Dio Chelmsf from 81. *15 Marsh Road, Burnham on Crouch, Essex.* (0621-783016)

CHARLES, Canon Sebastian. b 32. Univ of Madras BCom 53. Serampore Coll BD (2nd cl) 64. Linc Th Coll 53. **d** 56 **p** 57 Portsm. C of St Mary Portsea 56-59; P-in-c of St John Rangoon 59-66; C of St Thos Heaton Norris 66-67; Man Industr Miss 66-67; V of St Barn Pendleton 67-74; Chap Univ of Salford 67-74; Asst Gen Sec BCC 74-78; Publ Pr Dio Man 73-74; Can of Westmr Abbey from 78. *5 Little Cloister, Westminster Abbey, SW1 3PL.* (01-222 6939)

CHARLES, Theodore Arthur Barker. b 24. Late Scho of K Coll Cam BA 45, MA 48. SOC 68. **d** 71 Lewes for Chich **p** 72 Chich. C of Cuckfield 71-77; V of Rudgwick Dio Chich from 77. *Rudgwick Vicarage, Horsham, Sussex, RH12 3DD.* (Rudgwick 2127)

✠ **CHARLES-EDWARDS, Right Rev Lewis Mervyn.** b 02. Keble Coll Ox MA 55. DD (Lambeth) 57. Lich Th Coll 22. **d** 25 **p** 26 Lich. C of Ch Ch Tunstall 25-28; St Paul Burton-on-Trent 28-31; Pontesbury (1st and 2nd portions) 31-33; V of Marchington w Marchington Woodlands 33-37; Mkt Drayton 37-44; Newark w Coddington 44-47; St Martin-in-the-Fields Trafalgar Square 47-55; RD of Hodnet 38-44; Newark 45-47; Commiss Br Hond 45-55; Select Pr Univ of Cam 49; Univ of Ox 64; Chap to HM the King 50-52; to HM the Queen 52-56; Cons Ld Bp of Worc in St Paul's Cathl 6 Jan 56 by Abp of Cant; Bps of Southw; Roch; S'wark; Heref; Guildf; Wakef; and Pittsburgh; Bps Suffr of Shrewsbury; Tewkesbury; and Pontefract; and Bps Stuart and Hamilton; res 70; Sub-Prelate O of St John of Jer from 65. *Brackenwood Cottage, East Tuddenham, Dereham, Norf, NR20 3NF.* (Nor 880590)

CHARLESWORTH, Eric Charlesworth. b 29. Kelham Th Coll 49. **d** 54 **p** 56 St E. C of Woodbridge 54-57; Asst Chap St Edm Oslo 57-59; V of Barrhead Alta 60-63; L to Offic Dio Edmon 63; R of Grand Centre Alta 64-66; Huntingfield w Cookley 66-70; Slimbridge Dio Glouc from 70. *Slimbridge Rectory, Gloucester.* (045389-233)

CHARLESWORTH, Gerald Edward. King's Coll Lon 37. **d** 41 **p** 42 Leic. C of St Aug Leic 41-44. CF (EC) 44-46; Hon CF 46; Perm to Offic at St Dunstan Stepney 47; Miss (Prin of St Thos Sch Kuching) Dio Lab 48-49; R of Croft 49-58; CF (TA) from 52; V of Liverton York 58-62; Can of Kimb Cathl 62-66; R of St Aug Kimb 62-66; Dioc Dir of Relig Educn 62-66; R of De Aar 66-72; Archd of De Aar 66-74; Exam Chap to Bp of Kimb K 69-76; R of Douglas 72-74; St Pet Mossel Bay Dio Geo from 74. *36 Marsh Street, Mossel Bay, CP, S Africa.* (2384)

CHARLEWOOD, Edward Reginald. b 02. Trin Coll Cam 3rd cl Hist Trip pt i 24, BA (3rd cl Th Trip pt i) 25, MA 29. Bps' Coll Cheshunt 25. **d** 26 Willesden for Lon **p** 27 Lon. C of All SS Edmonton 26-31; St Mary Finchley 31-33; Chap Toc H and C of All H Barking Lon 33-35; Res Chap to Bp of Lon 35-39; V of St Andr Stoke Newington 39-45; R of Cheddington 45-52; V of Mentmore 47-52; RD of Ivinghoe 51-52; Cudd 60-66; V of Horspath 52-58; R of Marsh Baldon w Toot Baldon 58-66; Brightwell Baldwin 66-71; R of Cuxham w Easington 66-71. *Flat 20, Manormead, Tilford Road, Hindhead, Surrey, GU26 6RA.* (Hindhead 5107)

CHARLEY, Julian Whittard. b 30. New Coll Ox 2nd cl Cl Mods 53, BA (1st cl Th) 55, MA 58. Ridley Hall Cam 55. **d** 57 **p** 58 Lon. C of All S w St Pet and St John St Marylebone 57-64; Lect Lon Coll of Div 64-70; Vice-Prin St Jo Coll Nottm 70-74; Warden Shrewsbury Ho Liv from 74; V of St Pet Everton Dio Liv 74-76; R from 76. *Shrewsbury House, Langrove Street, Liverpool 5.* (051-207 1948)

CHARLTON, Arthur. St Paul's Coll Grahmstn. **d** 36 **p** 37 Zulu. C of Eshowe 36-38; P-in-c of Mtunzini 38-39; R of H Cross Empangeni 39-43; P-in-c of Mtunzini Zulu 43-44; R of St Marg Witbank 44-48; P-in-c of W Suburbs Pret 48-52; C of Umhlatuzana 52-55; V of Queensburgh 55-64; R of St Mary Greyville 64-70; L to Offic Dio Natal 70-74. *2 Queensburgh Haven, Ridley Park Road, Malvern, Durban, S Africa.*

CHARLTON, Arthur David. b 23. Open Univ BA 73. Chich Th Coll. **d** 66 **p** 67 Chich. C of Rotherfield 66-70; C of Uckfield Isfield w Horsted Parva 70-72; R of Cocking w Bepton (and W Lavington from 78) Dio Chich from 72; *Cocking Rectory, Midhurst, Sussex.* (Midhurst 3281)

CHARLTON, Cecil Eskholme. b 09. Late Scho of St Chad's Coll Dur BA 30, MA 37. **d** 32 **p** 33 Dur. C of Shadforth 32-36; St Aug Wembley Park 36-47; V of St Benet and All SS Kentish Town 47-56; Potter's Bar 56-80. *64 Highview Gardens, Potters Bar, Herts, EN6 5PJ.*

CHARLTON, Colin. b 32. Em Coll Cam 3rd cl Th Trip pt i 54, BA 56, MA 60. Oak Hill Th Coll 56. **d** 58 **p** 59 Dur. C of St Geo Gateshead 58-59; Houghton-le-Spring 59-62; PC of Newbottle 62-66; Area Sec CMS Dios Chelmsf and St Alb 66-72; P-in-c of St Elis Becontree 72-78; Bentley Common Dio Chelmsf from 78; Adv for Evang Dioc Dept of Miss from 78. *Bentley Common Vicarage, Brentwood, Essex, CM14 5RZ.* (Coxtie Green 72200)

CHARLTON, James Arthur. b 47. Univ of Tas BA 75. Flinders Univ of S Austr BSocAdmin 77, Univ of Cam BA 80. St Jo Coll Nottm 80. **d** 81 Bp Jerrim for Tas. C of Devonport Dio Tas from 81. *c/o St John's Rectory, Devonport, Tasmania 7310.*

CHARLTON, John Denis Berry. Lon Coll of Div 23. **d** 26 Cashel for Killaloe **p** 27 Killaloe. C of Roscrea 26-28; Ch Ch Derry 28-30; C-in-c of Aghadowey 30-37; Chap S Afr Ch Rwy Miss Beira Dio S Rhod 37-42; CF (S Afr) 42-45; I of Newtownfertullagh w Kilbeggan 45-50; Gen Sec SPG for Ireland 50-58; Chap of St Steph Coll Balla Balla 58-62; R of Francistown 62-63; Gwanda 63-71; Perm to Offic Dio Natal from 77. *St James's Church, Morningside, Durban, S Africa.*

CHARLTON, Ralph Hedley. b 06. BA (Lon) 71. St Aid Coll 29. **d** 31 **p** 32 Ripon. C of St Mary Hunslet (in c of St Osw) 31-38; PC of Chipping Sodbury 38-46; Chap of Chipping Sodbury Inst 38-46; CF (EC) 39-46; Hon CF 46; R of Brighstone 46-72. *Huntley House, Austwick, Lancaster, LA2 8BB.*

CHARLTON, William. b 48. Chich Th Coll 76. **d** 79 **p** 80 Sheff. C of St Cecilia Parson Cross Sheff 79-80; Ch Ch Doncaster Dio Sheff from 80. *26 Thoresby Avenue, Doncaster, DN4 5BQ.* (0302 22973)

CHARMAN, Arthur Ernest. b 09. BC Coll Bris. **d** 37 **p** 38 Vic. [f Lay Miss] BCMS Miss Dio Hong 34-50; Warden Taipo Guest Ho Hongkong 50; C of Dagenham 51-53; V of St Paul Brixton 53-57; St John and St Jas Litherland 57-73. *29 Hawksworth Close Grove, Wantage, Oxon.*

CHARMAN, Canon Frederick Ernest. ALCM 37. AKC 38. **d** 38 **p** 39 Portsm. C of Ascen Portsea 38-41; Offg Chap St Cath Home Ventnor 41-43; C of Redruth 43-46; PC of St Day 46-51; V of Woodlands 51-59; C-in-c of Wimborne St Giles 53-56; R 56-59; St Jas Shaftesbury 59-67; St Thos w H Trin and St Anne St Kitts 67-73; Proc Conv Sarum 59-67; Exam Chap to Bp of Antig 71-78; Hon Can of Antig 72-78; Can (Emer) from 78; R of St Mary Antig 73-75; St Paul Antig 75-78. *Basseterre, St Kitts, WI.*

CHARNELL, John Beavan. Trin Coll Tor BA 50, LTh 53. **d** 52 BC for Qu'App **p** 53 Qu'App. C of Assiniboia 52-56; I of Pense 56-62; Indian Head 62-65; V of St Jas Regina 65-70; Exam Chap to Bp of Qu'App 66-70; Perm to Offic Dio Ott 70-80; I of Ch K Burnaby Dio New Westmr from 80. *4550 Kitchener Street, Burnaby, BC, Canada.*

CHARNLEY, John Trevor. b 12. Late Exhib of Ex Coll Ox BA 36, MA 39. Wells Th Coll 36. **d** 37 **p** 38 Liv. C of St Paul Stanley 37-39; W Derby 39-42; Banbury 42-45; V of Stanley Liv 45-53; Payhembury 53-63; RD of Ottery St Mary 60-63; V of Ashburton w Buckland-in-the-Moor Dio Ex from 63; Bickington Dio Ex from 63. *Vicarage, Ashburton, Devon.* (Ashburton 52239)

CHARNOCK, Deryck Ian. b 47. Oak Hill Coll 78. **d** 80 **p** 81 Portsm. C of Rowner Dio Portsm from 80. *49 The Curve, Peel Common, Gosport, Hants, PO13 0RA.*

CHARNOCK, Ernest Burrell. b 14. ACIS 42. AACCA 50. Dipl Th (Lon) 60. **d** 61 **p** 62 Ches. C of Bowdon 61-64; V of Buglawton 64-70; R of Tattenhall (and Handley from 77) 70-80; C-in-c of Handley 72-77. *c/o Tattenhall Rectory, Chester.* (0829 70328)

CHARNOCK, John Phethean. b 15. Worc Ordin Coll. **d** 62 **p** 63 St E. C of Gt w L Bradley 62-65; Hadleigh Suff 65-68; R of Wilby w Brundish 68-81. *c/o Wilby Rectory, Diss, Norf.* (Stradbroke 333)

CHARRETT, Geoffrey Barton. b 36. Univ of Nottm BSc 57. Ridley Hall Cam. **d** 67 **p** 68 York. C of St Phil and St Jas Clifton York 67-68; L to Offic Dio Blackb 69-80; Asst Master Forest Sch Snaresbrook and Perm to Offic Dio Chelmsf 80-81; C of St Mary Walthamstow (in c of St Steph) Dio Chelmsf from 81. *St Stephen's Vicarage, Fraser Road, Walthamstow, E17 9DD.* (01-520 1960)

CHARRINGTON, John Edmund. b 01. Dorch Miss Coll 25. **d** 28 **p** 29 B & W. C of H Trin Hendford Yeovil 28-32; St Paul Goodmayes 32-36; Brentwood 36-38; Gt Ilford (in c of St Alb) 38-41; V of St Barn Walthamstow 41-46; Bosbury

46-54; C of Amersham (in c of Coleshill) 54-62; V of N Marston w Granborough 62-69; Perm to Offic Dio Ox from 69. *Bosbury, St James' Close, Pangbourne, Berks.* (Pangbourne 3781)

CHARRINGTON, Nicholas John. b 36 Cudd Coll 60. **d** 62 **p** 63 Lich. C of St Chad Shrewsbury 62-65; Gt Grimsby (in c of St Mark) 65-72; P-in-c of Ch Ch Wellington 72-78; R of Edgmond Dio Lich from 78. *Edgmond Rectory, Newport, Salop.* (Newport 811217)

CHARTERS, Alan Charles. b 35. Trin Hall Cam 2nd cl Hist Trip pt i 59, BA (3rd cl Th Trip pt ia) 60, MA 63. Linc Th Coll 60. **d** 62 **p** 63 Linc. C of Gt Grimsby 62-65; Chap and Asst Master Eliz Coll Guernsey 65-70; L to Offic Dio Win 65-70; Dep Hd Park Sch Swindon 70-74; Perm to Offic Dio Sarum from 70; Dio Bris from 72; Chap of St Jo Sch Leatherhead 74-77; Dep Hd from 77. *Paddock House, Linden Pit Path, Leatherhead, Surrey.* (Leatherhead 72839)

CHARTERS, John Nicholson. b 27. Trin Hall Cam BA 51, MA 55. Westcott Ho Cam 51. **d** 53 **p** 54 York. C of Selby 53-55; Hornsea w Goxhill 55-57; Milton 57-60; Chap RN 60-64; R of Thorndon w Rishangles 64-68; C of Beeford Dio York from 68. *2 Alton Park, Beeford, Driffield, Yorks.* (Beeford 485)

CHARTRES, Richard John Carew. b 47. Trin Coll Cam 2nd cl Hist Trip pt i 67, BA (2nd cl Hist Trip pt ii) 68, MA 73. Linc Th Coll 72. **d** 73 St Alb **p** 74 Bedford for St Alb. C of St Andr Bedford 73-75; Dom Chap to Bp of St Alb 75-80; to Abp of Cant 80; Abp's Chap from 80. *Lambeth Palace, SE1 7JU.* (01-928 8282)

CHASE, Canon Frank Selby Mason. b 15. Univ Coll Dur BSc 37, Dipl in Th 39. St Aug Coll Cant 39. **d** 39 **p** 40 Dur. C of Shotton 39-42; Washington 42-46; PC of Greenside 46-60; RD of Chester-le-Street 57-60; PC (V from 68) of S Westoe, S Shields 60-77; Hon Can of Dur Cathl from 70; RD of Jarrow 75-77; V of Lanchester Dio Dur from 77; Chairman Ho of Clergy Dioc Syn Dur from 76. *Lanchester Vicarage, Durham.* (Lanchester 520393)

CHASE, Frederick Jack. b 14. Westcott Ho Cam 61. **d** 62 Bp Lash for Truro **p** 63 Truro. C of Newquay 62-64; R of St Denys 64-69; Melfort Mashon 69-71; P-in-c of Cranborne Mashon 69-71; V of St Columb Minor (w Colan from 73) 71-76; P-in-c of Arreton Dio Portsm from 76. *Vicarage, Arreton, Newport, IW; PO30 3AB.* (Newport 527856)

CHASE, Geoffrey Hugh. b 25. Tyndale Hall Bris 48. **d** 51 **p** 52 Lich. C of Penn Fields 51-54; Heath Town 54-57; V of W Seaton 57-62; Chap Deva Hosp Chester 62-70; W Chesh Hosp Ches from 71. *West Cheshire Hospital, Chester.* (Ches 379333)

CHASE, Stephen Henry. b 11. MC 44. Qu Coll Cam BA 33, MA 37. Linc Th Coll 33. **d** 35 **p** 36 Man. C of Prestwich 35-39; Richmond 39-40; CF (EC) 40-46; C of St Pet Limpsfield (in c of Limpsfield Chart) 46-50; R of Gamlingay 50-52; Sandon 52-62; Alfrick w Lulsley (and Suckley from 73) 62-76; C-in-c of Suckley 71-73; Leigh w Bransford 75-76. *Chapel Cottage, Orleton, Stanford Bridge, Worcester, WR6 6SU.* (Eardiston 319)

CHASSELS, Canon Donald Robert. Ch Ch Coll Ox BA (2nd cl Th) 59, MA 63. Angl Th Coll BC LTh 57, BD 66. **d** 57 New Westmr for Caled **p** 58 Ox for Caled. On leave 57-59; I of St Pet Prince Rupert 59-62; St Paul, Powell River 62-74; All SS Burnaby 74-77; St Barn Vic Dio BC from 77; Exam Chap to Bp of BC from 79; Can of BC from 79. *1522 Coldharbour Road, Victoria, BC, Canada.*

CHATER, John Leathley. b 29. Qu Coll Cam 3rd cl Engl Trip pt i 53, BA (2nd cl Th Trip pt ii) 54, MA 58. Ridley Hall Cam 54. **d** 56 **p** 57 B & W. C of Bath Abbey 56-60; V of St Anne Bermondsey 60-64; Heslington 64-69; Chap Univ of York 64-69; V of Lawrence Weston 69-73; Perm to Offic Dio Bris 74-80; P-in-c of Wraxall and Failand Dio B & W from 80. *Rectory, Wraxall, Bristol, BS19 1NA.* (Nailsea 7086)

CHATFIELD, Adrian Francis. b 49. Univ of Leeds BA 71, MA 72. Coll of Resurr Mirfield 71. **d** 72 **p** 73 Trinid. C of H Trin Cathl Port of Spain 72-77; R of St Sav Curepe Dio Trinid from 77. *St Saviour's Rectory, Curepe, Trinidad, WI.*

CHATFIELD, Canon Francis Norman. b 05. Kelham Th Coll 23. **d** 29 Bp Southwell for Chich **p** 30 Chich. C of St Bart Brighton 29-33; St Geo Nottm 33-41; V of Newstead Abbey and Colliery 41-46; Chaguanas and San Juan 46-52; R of St Joseph w San Juan 52-57; Exam Chap to Bp of Trinid 52-57 and 67-71; Chap Miss to Seamen Santos and P-in-c of All SS Santos 57-64; R of St Crispin Port of Spain 64-71; Hon Can of Trinid 67-71; Can (Emer) from 71; Commiss Trinid 71-79; C of Haywards Heath (in c of Good Shepherd) 71-79; H Sav Curepe Dio Trinid from 79. *Holy Saviour Rectory, Sellier Street, Curepe, Trinidad, WI.*

CHATFIELD, Preb Frederick Roy. b 06. **d** 32 **p** 33 Ex. C of St Thos (in c of St Andr) Ex 32-36; Budleigh Salterton 36-40; V of Thorverton 40-47; Cockington w Chelston 47-72; RD of Ipplepen 66-69; Preb of Ex from 71; Publ Pr from 73. *Warberry Cottage, Lower Warberry Road, Torquay, TQ1 1QP.* (Torquay 26033)

CHATFIELD, Norman. Fitzw Ho Cam BA 59, MA 68. Ripon Hall Ox 60. **d** 62 **p** 63 Chich. C of Burgess Hill 62-65; Uckfield 65-69; V of St Jo Evang Sandown 69-76; Locks Heath Dio Portsm from 76; Bp's Chap Post-Ordin Tr Dio Portsm from 78. *7 Church Road, Locks Heath, Southampton, SO3 6LW.* (Locks Heath 2497)

CHATFIELD, Roderick Money. b 18. Bps' Coll Cheshunt 40. **d** 44 **p** 45 Wakef. C of St Pet Barnsley 44-46; Chap Control Commiss for Germany and Austria 46-48; C of All SS Croxley Green 48-49; Ch Ch Watford 49-51; R of Hanley William w Hanley Child 51-52; CF 52-53; Perm to Offic Dios S'wark and Lon 54-55; C of St Jas Taunton 55-57; V of N Newton and St Michaelchurch 57-63; C-in-c of Thurloxton 62-63; V of Burrington 63-72; R of Ashreigney 63-72; Ilchester w Northover 72-76; Limington 72-76; C of Yarlington (in Camelot Group) 76-79; R of Stonton Wyville w Glooston, Slawston and Cranoe Dio Leic from 79. *Glooston Rectory, Market Harborough, Leics, LE16 7ST.* (E Langton 406)

CHATFIELD, Thomas William. b 19. Chich Th Coll 44. **d** 46 Lon **p** 47 Kens for Lon. C of All SS Hanworth 46-49; St Mich AA Woolwich 49-51; St Andr Eastbourne 51-55; V of St Clem Halton Hastings 55-68; P-in-c of St Mary Magd St Leon-on-Sea 68-71; R 71-78; P-in-c of Bishopstone Dio Chich from 78. *Bishopstone Vicarage, Seaford, Sussex.* (Seaford 890895)

CHATFIELD-JUDE, Canon Henry. b 09. OBE 76. AKC 32. **d** 32 **p** 33 Lon. C of St Gabr Acton 32-34; Perm to Offic at Uckfield 34-35; C of Torquay 35-37; Chap Barrackpur 37-38 and 38-40; Lebong 38; Darjeeling 40-42 and 45-47; Patna 42-45; Hon CF 46; R of Avoca and Fingal Tasmania 48-50; Chap RAF 50-57; R of Michelmersh w Eldon and Timsbury 57-62; Chap at Madeira 62-66; Br Embassy and St Geo Lisbon 66-76; Hon Can of H Trin Cathl Gibr from 71. *7 Robson Court, Robson Road, Worthing.* (Worthing 45892)

CHATHAM, Cyril Lonsdale. St D Coll Lamp BA 37. Lich Th Coll 37. **d** 39 **p** 40 Lich. C of Hednesford 39-42; St Chad Burton-on-Trent 42-43; Chap RAFVR 43-44; C-in-c of Newchapel 44-45; C of Tamworth 45-48; V of Sheen 48-50; Longnor 50-53; R of Harlaston 53-55; V of Pelsall 55-65; R of Eaglehawk 65-70; R of Castlemaine 70-77; Can of Bend 73-77; Perm to Offic Dio Melb 77 and from 80; P-in-c of Newcomb w Whittington 77-80. *28 Mouchmore Avenue, St Leonards, Vic, Australia 3223.* (052-57 1943)

CHATHAM, Richard Henry. b 28. Launde Abbey Leics 71. **d** 71 **p** 72 Leic. C of St Andr, Aylestone 71-76; C-in-c of Hoby cum Rotherby 76-77; Brooksby and Ragdale 76-77; R of Hoby cum Rotherby w Brooksby and Ragdale Dio Leic from 77. *Rectory, Church Lane, Hoby, Melton Mowbray, Leics, LE14 3DR.* (Rotherby 220)

CHATTERJI DE MASSEY, Robert Arthur Sovan Lal. Chich Th Coll 54. **d** 56 **p** 57 Chelmsf. C of Romford 56-60; R of Abberton (w Langenhoe from 61) Dio Chelmsf from 60; C-in-c of Langenhoe 60-61. *Abberton Rectory, Colchester, Essex.* (Peldon 207)

CHATUKUTA, Weston George. St Pet Coll Rosettenville 56. **d** 58 **p** 59 Mashon. P Dio Mashon. *Box 268, Sinoia, Zimbabwe.*

CHATWIN, Ronald Ernest. b 34. St Aid Coll 58. **d** 60 Dover for Cant **p** 61 Cant. C of Selsdon 60-64; Crawley (in c of St Eliz Northgate) 64-68; V of Cold Waltham 68-74; P-in-c of Woodingdean 74-75; Team V of Ovingdean w Rottingdean and Woodingdean Dio Chich from 75. *Woodingdean Vicarage, Downsway, Brighton, Sussex, BN2 6BD.* (Brighton 681582)

CHAUSA, Andrea. b 45. St Cypr Coll Ngala 75. **d** 77 Zanz T **p** 79 Bp Russell for Zanz T. P Dio Zanz T. *C.P.T. Bwembwera, PO Box 80, Muheza, Tanzania.*

CHAVANDUKA, Solomon. b 1895. **d** and **p** 70 Mashon. P Dio Mashon 70-81; Dio Mutare from 81. *Dowa 14, PO Gwangwadza, via Rusape, Zimbabwe.*

CHAVASSE, Claud Geoffrey Rowden. b 20. **d** 77 Wai. C of Rotorua Dio Wai from 77. *57 McDowell Street, Rotorua, NZ.*

CHAVASSE, Claude Lionel. b 1897. Ex Coll Ox BA (3rd cl Hist) 22, MA 25. Trin Coll Dub BLitt 40, MLitt 60. St Steph Ho Ox 27. **d** 28 **p** 29 Down. C of St Mark Dundela 28-32; C of St Luke and Chap of Home for Protestant Incurables Cork 32-34; I of Teampol-na-mbocht (the Altar) 34-40; I of Mallow 40-44; V of Kidlington 44-57; R of Hampton Poyle 45-57; C-in-c of Baltinglass w Ballynure 57-60; I 60-67; Preb of Blackrath in Oss Cathl 62-67; Preb of Tullomagimma in Leigh Cathl 62-67; Exam Chap to Bp of Oss 62-77; Perm to Offic Dio Cash from 67. *Old Sexton's House, Briska, Lemybrien, Co Waterford, Irish Republic.* (Waterford 9-1137)

CHAVASSE, Evelyn Henry. b 06. DSO 43. OBE 75. DSC 43. Cudd Coll 53. **d** 54 **p** 55 Win. C of Lymington 54-56;

Kidlington 56-58; R of Knight's Enham w Smannell 58-64; St Pet Jersey 64-73; L to Offic Dio Cyprus from 76. *PO Box 181, Kyrenia, Cyprus.*

CHEADLE, Preb Robert. b 24. MBE 71. TD 66. Univ of Leeds BA 49. Coll of Resurr Mirfield 49. **d** 51 **p** 52 Ox. C of St Jo Evang Newbury 51-55; Tunstall 55-57; V of St Luke Hanley 57-60; Bloxwich 60-72; Penkridge w Stretton Dio Lich from 72; Preb of Lich Cathl from 79; P-in-c of Dunston w Coppenhall Dio Lich from 79; Acton Trussell w Bednall Dio Lich from 80. *Penkridge Vicarage, Stafford.* (Penkridge 2378)

CHEAL, Kenneth Herbert. b 12. Sarum Th Coll 46. **d** 48 **p** 49 Bris. C of St Paul Swindon 48-53; Wotton-under-Edge 53-55; Stow-on-the-Wold w Broadwell 55-56; R of Shipton Oliffe w Shipton Sollars 57-61; Rodborough 61-77; Perm to Offic Dio Glouc from 78; Bris from 80. *6 The Ferns, Tetbury, Glos, GL8 8JE.* (Tetbury 53100)

CHEALES, Canon Henry Samuel. b 11. Univ of Dur LTh 35. Qu Coll Birm 31. **d** 34 Bp Palmer for Glouc **p** 35 Glouc. C of Lydney w Aylburton 34-37; Brockworth 37-38; Stow-on-the-Wold w Broadwell 38-47; CF (EC) 40-45; R of Wyck Rissington 47-81; L Rissington 47-81; Hon Can of Glouc from 74. *Puffits Cottage, Lansdown, Bourton-on-the Water, Glos.* (Bourton/Water 20269)

CHEALL, Henry Frederick Knowles. b 34. Ex Coll Ox BA 56, MA 60. Ripon Hall Ox 58. **d** 60 Liv **p** 61 Warrington for Liv. C of Sutton 60-63; St Mich Blundellsands 63-66; V of St Geo Kano 66-68; R of St Matt (w St Mary from 76), Crumpsall Dio Man from 68. *St Matthew's Rectory, Crumpsall, Manchester, M8 6QU.* (061-740 3106)

CHEDEGO, Yona. b 39. St Phil Coll Kongwa 75. **d** and **p** 77 Centr Tang. P Dio Centr Tang. *PO Nondwa, Tanzania.*

CHEE, Wilfred. Univ of W Austr BSc 65. Trin Th Coll Sing 67. **d** 68 **p** 69 Sing. P Dio Sing 69-70; Dio W Mal 70-74. *St Paul's Church, Jalan Utara, Petaling Jaya, Selangor, Singapore.*

CHEEK, Raymond Sidney. Wollaston Th Coll 59. **d** 60 **p** 63 Bunb. C of St Paul's Cathl, Bunb 60-61; Albany 62-64; R of Lake Grace 64-67; L to Offic Dio Bunb 67-69; P-in-c of Pingelly 69-70; Dom Chap to Bp of Bunb 70-71; L to Offic Dio Perth 72; Perm to Offic Dio Adel 73-74; P-in-c of Ravensthorpe 75-79; R of Williams Dio Bunb from 79. *Rectory, Williams, W Australia 6391.*

CHEEK, Richard Alexander. b 35. Univ of Lon RCS(Eng) LDS 60. St Steph Ho Ox 72. **d** 75 Ox **p** 76 Buckingham for Ox (APM). C of St Luke Maidenhead Dio Ox from 75. *Windrush, Sheephouse Road, Maidenhead, Berks.*

CHEESEMAN, Edgar Bertram. Qu Coll St John's 47. **d** 51 **p** 52 Newfld. C of St Mary St John's 51-54; R of Change Is 54-55; Fogo 55-59; I of New Harbour 59-67; R of Salvage 67-77; Petty Harbour Dio E Newfld from 77. *Box 9, The Goulds, Newfoundland, Canada.* (709-368 1860)

CHEESEMAN, John Anthony. b 50. Oriel Coll Ox BA 73, MA 75. Univ of Bris Dipl Th 76. Trin Coll Bris 73. **d** 76 **p** 77 Roch. C of St Nich Sevenoaks 76-79; Egham Dio Guildf from 79. *33 Grange Road, Egham, Surrey, TW20 9QP.*

CHEESEMAN, Kenneth Raymond. b 29. Roch Th Coll 63. **d** 66 **p** 67 Roch. C of Crayford 66-69; St Jas Elmers End and of St Aug Beckenham 69-75; V of St Aug Belvedere Dio Roch from 75. *St Augustine's Vicarage, Belvedere, Kent, DA17 5HH.* (01-311 6307)

CHEESEMAN, Trevor Percival. b 38. Univ of NZ BSc 60, MSc 62. Univ of Auckld PhD 64. K Coll and Warm BD (2nd cl) and AKC 67. **d** 68 **p** 69 Sheff. C of St Pet, Warmsworth, Doncaster w Edlington 68-71; Manurewa 71-73; P-in-c of Birkdale-Beachhaven Miss Dist 73-77; V of Meadowbank Dio Auckld from 77. *38 St John's Road, Meadowbank, Auckland, NZ.*

CHEESMAN, Andrew Walford. Univ of Adel BA (2nd cl Hist) 58. Cudd Coll 59. **d** 61 **p** 62 Man. C of St Aid Man 61-64; P-in-c of Keith 64-68; Prec of St Pet Cathl Adel and Chap Flinders Univ 68-69; Asst Chap St Pet Colleg Sch Adel 70-73; P-in-c of Tea Tree Gully 73-76; R of Mitcham w Torrens Pk Dio Adel from 76. *579 Fullarton Road, Mitcham, S Australia 5062.* (08-71 6858)

CHEESMAN, Peter. b 43. ACA 65, FCA 76. Ridley Hall Cam 66. **d** 69 **p** 70 Cant. C of Herne Bay 69-74; Team V of Lowestoft Group 75-81; Industr Chap Dio Glouc from 81. *Vicarage, Frampton-on-Severn, GL2 7ED.* (Glouc 740966)

CHEETHAM, Eric. b 34. Trin Hall Cam 2nd cl Law Trip pt i 56, BA (2nd cl Th Trip pt ia) 57, MA 61. Coll of Resurr Mirfield 57. **d** 59 **p** 60 Wakef. C of S Kirkby 59-62; P-in-c of H Nativ Conv Distr Mixenden Halifax 62-65; R of Fresh Creek Andros 65-67; Long I Nass 67-69; V of Grimethorpe 69-81; Featherstone Dio Wakef from 81. *Featherstone Vicarage, Pontefract, Yorks, WF7 6AH.* (Pontefract 792280)

CHEETHAM, Gilbert Stanley. b 14. Bps' Coll Cheshunt 49. **d** 52 **p** 53 Guildf. C of Thames Ditton 52-54; Cathl Par of H Trin Guildf 54-57; Farnham 57-59; R of Killamarsh 59-64; V of Basford 64-76; Clipstone Dio Southw from 76; Chap HM Pris Nottm 64-76. *Clipstone Vicarage, Mansfield, Notts.* (Mansfield 23916)

CHEEVERS, George Alexander. b 42. TCD 70. **d** 73 **p** 74 Connor. C of Carrickfergus (Bp's C of Kilroot from 78) 73-81; L to Offic Dio Connor from 81. *9 Fairview Drive, Whitehead, Antrim, N Ireland.* (Whitehead 78062)

CHELMSFORD, Lord Bishop of. *See* Trillo, Right Rev Albert John.

CHELMSFORD, Assistant Bishop of. (Vacant)

CHELMSFORD, Provost of. *see* Moses, Very Rev John Henry.

CHELTENHAM, Archdeacon of. *See* Evans, Ven Thomas Eric.

CHELTON, James Howard. b 35. Oak Hill Th Coll. **d** 67 Barking for Chelmsf **p** 68 Chelmsf. C of Pitsea 67-71; C-in-c of Nevendon 71-74; Bp's Industr Chap Basildon Dio Chelmsf 71-74; P-in-c of Harwich and Industr Chap Dio Chelmsf 74-80; Chap Miss to Seamen Dar-es-Salaam 80-81; Lagos from 81. *Chaplain's Office, Missions to Seamen, Lagos, Nigeria.*

CHEMOA, Josek. St Paul's Div Sch Limuru. **d** 54 **p** 55 Momb. P Dio Momb 55-56. *PO Box 80, Bungoma, Kenya.*

CHEMOBO, Henry. **d** 78 Nak. d Dio Nak. *c/o Box 244, Nakuru, Kenya.*

CHEMURU, Martin. b 30. **d** 75 **p** 76 Matab. P Dio Matab 75-81; Dio Lundi from 81. *Box 53, Selukwe, Zimbabwe.*

CHEMWAMIA, Isaya. b 30. **d** and **p** 74 Mbale. P Dio Mbale. *Suam, PO Bukwa, Mbale, Uganda.*

CHENG, David Ho-Ming. Union Th Coll Hong 65. **d** 67 **p** 68 Hong. C of St Barn Kowloon 67-71; P-in-c of H Nativ City & Dio Hong from 71. *Church of the Holy Nativity, Hong Kong.* (5-607469)

CHENNELL, Arthur John. b 28. St Deiniol's Libr Hawarden 77. **d** 77 **p** 78 Ches. [f CA]. C of Prenton 77-79; V of St Thos Liscard, Wallasey Dio Ches from 79. *24 Newlands Drive, Wallasey, Mer, L44 2AK.* (051-639 5278)

CHEONG, Clifford Arthur. Ridley Coll Melb ACT ThL 75. **d** 76 **p** 77 Melb. C of St Geo Malvern 76-78; Ararat 78-79; R of Nhill Dio Bal from 79. *Rectory, Nhill, Vic, Australia 3418.*

CHEONG, Geoffrey William. St Jo Coll Morpeth ThL 72. **d** 73 **p** 74 Melb. C of Ch Ch Templestow 73-75; Ormond 75-77; on leave 77-80; I of Rideau Dio Ont from 80. *Rectory, Portland, Ont, Canada.* (613-272 2360)

CHEONG, Solomon Sung Voon. b 53. Ho of the Epiph Kuch 71. **d** 76 **p** 77 Kuch. P Dio Kuch. *c/o Box 347, Kuching, Sarawak, Malaysia.*

CHEPKWESHEK, Erusaniya. b 30. Bp Tucker Coll Mukono 57. **d** 59 U Nile **p** 69 Mbale P Dio Mbale. *PO Kaproron, Sebei, Uganda.*

CHEPTAI, Yafesi. b 28. **d** and **p** 74 Mbale. P Dio Mbale. *PO Sipi, Mbale, Uganda.*

CHERERE, Stanley Njoroge. Ch Tr Centre Kapsabet 66. **d** 67 **p** 68 Nak. P Dio Nak. *Box 67, Eldama Ravine, Kenya.*

CHERRILL, John Oliver. b 33. Univ of Bath MArchit 75. Sarum Wells Th Coll 76. **d** 79 **p** 80 Portsm. C of Blackmoor Dio Portsm from 79. *7 Oaktree Road, Whitehill, Bordon, Hants, GU35 9DF.*

CHERRIMAN, Colin Wilfred. b 37. Univ of Leeds BA (3rd cl Gen) 63. Coll of Resurr Mirfield 63. **d** 65 **p** 66 Win. C of St Francis Bournemouth 65-69; M SSF from 69; LPr Dio Sarum 70-73; L to Offic Dio Chelmsf 73-75; Dio Cant 75-77; Dio Edin from 77. *Hilfield Friary, Dorchester, Dorset, DT2 7BE.* (030 03 345)

CHERRINGTON, Frank. b 01. Clifton Th Coll 38. **d** and **p** 40 Glouc. C of Wotton St Mary Without (in c of St John's Conv Distr Churchdown from 42) 40-56; Chap Glouc City and Co Mental Hosps 41-56; C of St John Cheltm 56-67; R of Tedstone Delamere w Edvin Loach and Tedstone Wafer 67-80; R of U Sapey w Wolferlow 67-80. *Tedstone Delamere, Wellington Square, Cheltenham, Glos.* (Cheltenham 515433)

CHERRINGTON, Johnson Wahi. b 18. St Jo Coll Auckld 74. **d** 74 **p** 75 Auckld. C of Whangarei 74-77; P-in-c of Waimate N Maori Past 77-81. *Box 390, Kaikohe, NZ.* (5320)

CHERRINGTON, Philip Henry. b 28. St Jo Coll Auckld 54. NZ Bd of Th Stud LTh 65. **d** 58 **p** 60 Auckld. C of Otahuhu 58-60; N Wairoa 60-62; V of Coromandel 62-67; N Wairoa 67-71; Chap Te Aute Coll Dio Wai from 71; Actg Prin 74-76. *Te Aute College, Pukekohe, Hawkes Bay, NZ.* (Otane 133)

CHERRY, Alexander William. b 08. Worc Ordin Coll 58. **d** 59 **p** 60 Worc. C of St Thos Ap Dudley 59-61; V of Wichenford 61-64; St Paul Bury 64-68; Quinton 68-71; Moreton Valence w Whitminster 71-73. *2 School Cottages, Llandwrog, Gwyn.* (Llanwnda 831157)

CHERRY, Malcolm Stephen. b 28. Sarum Th Coll 51. **d** 54

Kens for Lon **p** 55 Lon. C of John Keble Ch Mill Hill 54-57; All SS Childs Hill 57-59; Min of St Anne's Eccles Distr Colchester 59-68; V of Horndon-on-the-Hill 68-79; R of Lochgilphead Dio Arg Is from 79. *Bishopton, Lochgilphead, Argyll.* (Lochgilphead 2315)

CHERRY, Richard Stephen. Univ of Melb BSc 55, BA (1st cl Phil) 59, MA 61. Ridley Coll Melb ACT ThL 60. **d** 60 **p** 61 Melb. C of St Thos Essendon 60-61; Vermont 61-62; Min of St Mark Reservoir 62-67; I of Berwick 67-77; All SS E Malvern Dio Melb from 77. *6 Stonehaven Avenue, East Malvern, Vic., Australia 3145.* (211-1922)

CHERWARU, Ven Yovani. Buwalasi Th Coll 57. **d** 59 **p** 60 U Nile. P Dio U Nile 59-61; Dio Mbale from 61; Hon Can of Mbale from 69; Archd of Sebei from 73. *PO Box 23, Kapchorwa, Uganda.*

CHESHAM, William Gerald. b 23. MIMechE 55. Wells Th Coll 61. **d** 63 **p** 64 Cant. C of Ashford Kent 63-66; Edgbaston 66-68; V of H Trin Smethwick 68-72; L to Offic Dio Heref 73-78; Team V of Wooler Group (in c of Kirknewton) Dio Newc T from 78. *Kirknewton Vicarage, Wooler, Northumb, NE71 6XG.* (Milfield 219)

CHESTER, Lord Bishop of. *See* Baughen, Right Rev Michael Alfred.

CHESTER, Dean of. *See* Cleasby, Very Rev Thomas Wood Ingram.

CHESTER, Archdeacon of. *See* Williams, Ven Henry Leslie.

CHESTER, Philip Anthony Edwin. b 55. Univ of Birm LLB 76. St Jo Coll Dur 77. **d** 80 **p** 81 Lich. C of St Chad Shrewsbury Dio Lich from 80. *1 St Chad's Terrace, Shrewsbury, Salop.* (Shrewsbury 51130)

CHESTERFIELD, Archdeacon of. *See* Phizackerley, Ven Gerald Robert.

CHESTERFIELD, Reginald. b 15. Roch Th Coll. **d** 62 **p** 63 Bradf. C of St Clem Bradf 62-65; C-in-c of St Paul Pudsey 65-68; V 68-79; P-in-c of Manningham Dio Bradf from 79. *St Luke's Vicarage, Selborne Grove, Bradford, BD9 4NL.* (Bradf 41110)

CHESTERMAN, George Anthony. b 38. Univ of Man BSc 62. Coll of Resurr Mirfield 62. **d** 64 **p** C of Newbold w Dunston 64-68; St Thos Ap Derby 68-70; R of Mugginton Dio Derby from 70; Kedleston Dio Derby from 70; Adult Educn Officer Dio Derby 70-79; Vice-Prin E Midl Jt Tr Scheme from 79. *Mugginton Rectory, Weston Underwood, Derby, DE6 4PN.* (Brailsford 454)

CHESTERMAN, Lawrence James. b 16. K Coll Lon and Warm 48. **d** 49 **p** 50 Leic. C of Braunstone 49-52; Hayling Is w Hayling South 52-55; V of St Andr Whitwick w Thringstone 55-60; R of Thornford w Beer Hackett 60-69; C-in-c of Bradford Abbas w Clifton Maybank 61-63; V of Idmiston w Porton 69-73; R of Bourne Valley 73-81; Perm to Offic Dio Sarum from 81. *38 Pains Way, Amesbury, Salisbury, SP4 7RG.* (0980-22205)

CHESTERMAN, Peter Henry. Univ of Melb BA 60, ACT ThL 67. **d** 66 **p** 67 Melb. C of St Silas N Balwyn 66-69; Toorak 69-70; V of Carrum w Seaford 70-74; I of Armadale w Hawksburn 74; Exam Chap to Abp of Melb 74; Perm to Offic Dio Melb 76-78; Chap Firbank C of E Girls Gr Sch Dio Melb from 78. *5 Canyon Street, Balwyn, Vic, Australia 3195.* (80 3121)

CHESTERS, Canon Alan David. b 37. St Chad's Coll Dur (2nd cl Mod Hist) 59. St Cath S Ox BA (2nd cl Th) 61, MA 65. St Steph Ho Ox 59. **d** 62 **p** 63 S'wark. C of St Anne Wandsworth 62-66; Hon C 66-68; Chap Tiffin Sch Kingston-upon-Thames 66-72; LPr Dio S'wark 68-72; Hon C St Richard Ham 68-72; R of Brancepeth Dio Dur from 72; Dir of Educn Dio Dur from 72; Hon Can of Dur Cathl from 75; M Gen Syn from 75. *Rectory, Brancepeth, Durham.* (Durham 780503)

CHESTERS, Peter Durrant. b 17. ACII 52. K Coll Lon and Warm 54. **d** 56 **p** 57 S'wark. C of Crofton Pk 56-58; St Geo Camberwell 58-60; V of Stourpaine 60-66; R of Durweston 60-66; Ludgershall & Faberstown Dio Sarum from 66. *Ludgershall Rectory, Andover, Hants.* (Andover 790393)

CHESTERTON, Robert Eric. b 31. St Aid Coll 63. **d** 54 **p** 66 Leic. C of Kirby Muxloe 65-67; Miss at Cam Bay NWT 67-68; C of St Thos St Annes-on-the-Sea 68-69; V of Southminster 69-75; R of Ashcroft and Savona 75-78; V of Woodhouse Pk 78-82; Team V of Marfleet Dio York from 82. *c/o St Giles' Vicarage, Church Lane, Marfleet, Hull, HU9 5RL.*

CHETWOOD, Noah. b 14. St Jo Coll Dur BA 38, Dipl in Th 39, MA 41. Univ of Nottm MEd 58. **d** 39 **p** 40 Heref. Reader of Ludlow 39-45; Asst Master Herbert Strutt Sch Belper and L to Offic Dio Derby 45-54; Hd of Educn Dept Newland Pk Coll Chalfont St Giles 54-75; Prin Lect Bucks Coll of Higher Educn 76-78; Publ Pr Dio Ox 54-82. *10 Longfield Drive, Amersham, Bucks, HP6 5HD.* (Amersham 5259)

CHETWYND, Christopher Waller. b 13. Late Exhib of St Jo Coll Dur BA 36. Westcott Ho Cam 38. **d** 39 **p** 40 Lon. Asst Chap R Assoc in Aid of Deaf and Dumb 39-41; C of Tynemouth 41-44; Chap RNVR 44-46 and from 51; C-in-c of Benfieldside 46-47; V of Brampton 47-51; R of Simonburn 51-58; Org Sec Miss to Seamen Dio Newc T 54-58; Perm to Offic Dio Dur 54-58; Chap Miss to Seaman Fremantle 58-69; Home Sec 69-71; L to Offic Dio Lon 69-71; Chap Miss to Seamen Hamburg and I of St Thos-à-Becket Hamburg 71-73; Chap Miss to Seamen Hull 73-77; Port Said 77-78; Perm to Offic Dio York from 78. *291 Beverley Road, Anlaby, Hull, HU10 7AH.* (0482-652570)

CHETWYND, Edward Ivor. b 45. Univ of Leeds Dipl Th 68. Coll of Resurr Mirfield 68. **d** 70 **p** 71 Wakef. C of St Mich Wakef 70-74; Penistone 74-75; V of St Mich Castleford Dio Wakef from 75. *156 Smawthorne Lane, Castleford, W Yorks.* (Castleford 57079)

CHETWYND, Sydney Arthur. St Jo Coll Dur BA 41, Dipl in Th 42, MA 44. **d** 43 **p** 44 Dur. C of St Gabr Bishopwearmouth 43-48; St Marg (in c of St John Neville's Cross) Dur 48-50; C-in-c of St Osw Walker Gate Conv Distr City and Dio Newc T 50-66; Min from 66. *Vicarage, Woodhead Road, Walkergate, Newcastle upon Tyne 6.* (Wallsend 63662)

CHETWYND-TALBOT, Arthur Charles Ashton. b 07. Ch Ch Ox BA 29, MA 44. Cudd Coll 32. **d** 33 **p** 34 S'wark. C of St Jo Div Kennington 33-37; UMCA Miss at Liuli 37-40; C of Edgmond 40-43; All SS Margaret Street 43-45; R of Wrington w Redhill 45-53; V of Wantage 53-60; Surr 53-60; R of Catsfield 60-73. *Flat 2, Park Lodge, Eastbourne, Sussex, BN21 4JE.* (Eastbourne 26941)

CHEUNG, Ven John Shiu Kwai. Harvard Univ MEducn 50. Wycl Hall Ox 37. **d** 40 **p** 43 Hong. P Dio Hong from 43; Exam Chap to Bp of Hong from 51; Can of Hong 66-71; Archd of Hong from 71. *c/o Bishop's House, 1 Lower Albert Road, Hong Kong.* (5-228469)

CHEUNG, Canon Luk-Hueng. Union Th Coll Canton 38. **d** 43 **p** 44 Vic. P Dio Vic 44-50. Chap All SS Sch Kowloon 50-54; on leave 55-62; V of St Matt City and Dio Hong from 63; Can of Hong and Exam Chap to Bp of Hong from 71. *St Matthew's Vicarage, Hong Kong.* (5-484777)

CHEUNG, Peter Siu Pui. St Pet Hall and Trin Th Coll Sing LTh 58. **d** 58 **p** 59 Sing. P Dio Sing 58-70; Dio Hong from 71. *c/o Bishop Mok Sau Tseng School, Tai Po, Hong Kong.* (12-667804)

CHEUQUELAF, Maximo. b 38. **d** & **p** 72 Bp Bazley. C of Ascen Cholcol Dio Chile from 72. *Casilla 4, Cholcol, Chile.*

CHEVALIER, Harry Ensor Estienne. b 23. Mert Coll Ox BA (3rd cl Mod Hist) 49, MA 56. Ely Th Coll 49. **d** 51 **p** 52 Sarum. C of St Paul Weymouth 51-53; Broadstairs 53-55; Paignton (in c of St Andr) 55-63; V of Taddington w Chelmorton 63; C of St Mary Virg Reading (in c of St Mark) 63-66; PC of Bradninch 66-71; Perm to Offic Dio Ex from 71; C of Christchurch (in c of All SS Mudeford) 74-75; Perm to Offic Dio Win from 75. *6 Bolton Road, Southbourne, Bournemouth, Dorset, BH6 3DZ.* (Bournemouth 49623)

CHEVANNES, Gladstone Emanuel. **d** 54 **p** 55 Ja. P-in-c of Gilnock 54-55; Falmouth 55-56; C of Montego Bay 56-62; P-in-c of Kew Pk Ja 62-65; on leave 65-67; P-in-c of Mile Gully 67-76; Hosp Chap Mandeville from 76. *Rectory, Mile Gully, Jamaica, W Indies.*

CHEVERTON, David. b 22. ARIBA 55. Lon Coll of Div 65. **d** 67 **p** 68 Lon. C of Wealdstone 67-71; V of Budleigh Salterton Dio Ex from 71. *26 West Hill, Budleigh Salterton, Devon, EX9 6BU.* (Budleigh Salterton 3195)

CHEW, Creighton Desmond. Em Coll Sktn. **d** 64 **p** 65 Edmon. C of Ch Ch Edmon 64-68; V of H Nativ Calg 68-79; on leave 79-80; P-in-c of Oyen Dio Calg from 80. *Box 265, Oyen, Alta, Canada, T0J 2J0.* (664-3818)

CHEW, John Hiang Chea. Nayang Univ Sing MA 77. Univ of Lon BD 77. Trin Coll Bris. **d** 77 **p** 78 Sing. C of All SS Sing 77-79; on study leave. *51 St Albans Road, Fulwood, Sheffield, S10 4DN.*

CHEYNE, Canon John Franklin. b 06. BEM 42. MPS 30. Univ of Dur LTh 35. Qu Coll Birm 32. **d** 35 **p** 36 Cov. C of St Mark Cov 35-38; St Mary Extra (Jesus Chap) Southampton 38-44; V of St Pet Cov 44-51; R of Milton Keynes and V of Broughton 51-60; V of St Jas Camberwell 60-75; Hon Can of S'wark from 75. *5 Shelley Drive, Bletchley, Milton Keynes, Bucks, MK3 5BN.* (M Keynes 75044)

CHEYNE, Robert Douglas. b 17. Wycl Hall Ox 65. **d** 67 **p** 68 Lon. C of Oakwood 67-70; Brackley 70-72; R of Cottesbrooke w Gt Creaton (and Thornby from 74) Dio Pet from 72; C-in-c of Thornby 72-74. *Creaton Rectory, Northampton.* (Creaton 728)

CHHANGUR, Shallson Marcellene. Codr Coll Barb 46. **d** 51 **p** 53 Barb. C of St Mich Cathl Barb 51-55; R of Belfield and of Highgate 55-57. *c/o Church House, Cross Roads, Jamaica, W Indies.*

✠ **CHHOA HENG SZE, Right Rev Luke.** **d** 55 **p** 56 Sing.

P Dio Sing 56-70; Archd of N Malaya (Dio W Malaysia) 71; Cons Ld Bp of Sabah in Lambeth Palace Chap on 30 Nov 71 by Abp of Cant; Bp of Worc; Bp Suffr of Edmonton; Bps Allenby; Daly; Mabula; Saqid; and Shearburn. *Bishop's Lodge, Box 811, Kota Kinabalu, Sabah, Malaysia.* (52084)

CHIBAGO, Hosea. **d** and **p** 77 Centr Tang. P Dio Centr Tang. *PO Mvumi, Tanzania.*

CHIBALUWA, Kefa. b 35. St Phil Coll Kongwa. **d** 75 **p** 76 Centr Tang. P Dio Centr Tang. *Box 5 PO, Mpwapwa, Tanzania.*

CHIBWALE, George. b 52. **d** 81 Centr Tang. d Dio Centr Tang. *Box 264, Dodoma, Tanzania.*

CHICHESTER, Lord Bishop of. *See* Kemp, Right Rev Eric Waldram.

CHICHESTER, Assistant Bishops of. *See* Morrell, Right Rev James Herbert Lloyd; and Hunt, Right Rev William Warren.

CHICHESTER, Archdeacon of. *See* Hobbs, Ven Keith.

CHICHESTER, Dean of. *See* Holtby, Very Rev Robert Tinsley.

CHICK, Arthur Bernard. b 10. Univ Coll Dur BA (2nd cl Cl) 32, MA 35. Wells Th Coll 32. **d** 33 **p** 34 Bradf. C of Skipton 33-36; H Trin Bingley 36-40; V of Kirkby-in-Malhamdale 40-51; R of Broughton Pogis w Filkins V 51-69; C-in-c of Kencot 54-60. *1 Sundial Cottages, Downend, Horsley, Stroud, Glos GL6 0PF.*

CHICKEN, Canon John Hamilton. b 28. Wells Th Coll 55. **d** 57 **p** 58 Newc T. C of St Geo Jesmond Newc T 57-59; Hexham 59-63; V of St Paul Cullercoats 63-72; V of Bywell St Pet 72-81; Alnwick w Edlingham and Bolton Dio Newc T from 81; Hon Can of Newc T from 80; RD of Alnwick from 81. *Vicarage, Alnwick, Northumb.* (Alnwick 602184)

CHICKEN, Peter Lindsay. b 46. Univ of St Andr BSc 71. Chich Th Coll 77. **d** 79 Reading for Ox **p** 80 Ox. C of All SS High Wycombe Dio Ox from 79. *15 Brunel Road, High Wycombe, Bucks, HP13 5SR.*

CHICOGO, Matias. **d** 47 **p** 48 Lebom. P Dio Lebom. *Caixa Postal 63, Vila de Jo£ao Belo, Moçambique.*

CHIDAU, Suleman. b 44. St Phil Coll Kongwa 68. **d & p** 70 Centr Tang. P Dio Centr Tang from 70. *TTC Mpwapwa, Tanzania.*

CHIDEBELU, Joel Ikwumelu. St Paul's Coll Awka 62. **d** 62 Niger. d Dio Niger 62-71. *c/o St Peter's Church, Abagana, Nigeria.*

CHIDGEY, Geoffrey Peter. b 23. Sarum Th Coll 49. **d** 51 **p** 52 Cant. C of St Martin Maidstone 51-53; Deal 54-58; V of Chislet (with Hoath from 60) 58-64; C-in-c of Hoath 58-60; R of Gt Mongeham 64-78; Ripple 64-78; Lydd Dio Cant from 78. *Rectory, Skinner Road, Lydd, Kent, TN29 9DD.* (0679-20345)

CHIDLAW, Richard Paul. b 49. St Cath Coll Cam BA 71. Ripon Hall Ox 72. **d** 74 Worc **p** 81 Glouc. C of Ribbesford w Bewdley and Dowles 74-76; Frampton-on-Severn Dio Glouc from 81. *c/o Vicarage, Coaley, Glos.*

CHIDOGE, Leslie. St Phil Th Coll Kongwa 64. **d** 66 **p** 67 Moro. P Dio Moro. *PO Tindiga, Kilosa, Tanzania.*

CHIDOSA, Canon Filemon Nathanael. **d** and **p** 48 Centr Tang. P Dio Centr Tang 48-57; Archd of Dodoma 57-65; Mpwapwa-Kongwa 65-71; Can of Centr Tang from 71. *PO Kilimatinde, Tanzania.*

CHIDUO, Wilson Yotham. b 37. **d** 70 **p** 71 Moro. L to Offic Dio Moro 70-80; Prin Moro Bible Sch from 81. *Box 113, Morogoro, Tanzania.*

CHIDWICK, Canon Paul Field. b 30. Univ of BC BA 55. Jes Coll Cam BA 62, MA 67. Angl Th Coll STB and BD 68. **d** 58 **p** 59 New Westmr. C of St Phil Vanc 58-60; on leave 60-62; Warden Trin Coll Nairobi 62-69; Exam Chap to Bp of Nai 68-69; C of St Paul's Cathl Lon Hur 70-72; R of St Mary Gate Windsor Dio Hur from 72; Can of Hur from 75. *1983 St Mary's Gate, Windsor, Ont., Canada.* (519-252 4763)

CHIDZEY, Canon Leonard Whitehead. b 09. Ridley Hall Cam 47. **d** 48 Lon **p** 49 Stepney for Lon. Evang Sec at Ch Army HQ 42-53; C of St Mary Harrow 48-53; V of Dodderhill 53-59; St Geo Kidderminster 59-68; Chief Dioc Missr Dio Worc 60-68; Hon Can of Worc 66-68; Can (Emer) from 68; V of Gt w L Driffield 68-78. *Vicarage, Reighton, Filey, N Yorks, YO14 9RX.*

CHIGNELL, Preb Wilfred Rowland. b 08. Sarum Th Coll 31. **d** 33 **p** 34 Wakef. C of Lightcliffe 33-36; Huddersfield 36-39; PC of Cressage w Sheinton R 39-48; CF (EC) 43-46 (Men in Disp 45 and 46); V of Fownhope w Fawley and V of Brockhampton 48-56; Kington w Huntington 56-64; Surr 57-64; RD of Kington 61-64; Preb of Heref Cathl from 63; R of Whitbourne 64-73; Chap St Jas Sch W Malvern 66-77; Ed 'Heref Dioc News' from 74. *Little Stocking, Whitbourne, Worcs.*

CHIGOME, Jerome Yohana-Viane. Namasakata Th Coll 57. **d** 59 **p** 62 SW Tang. P Dio SW Tang. *Box 198, Mbeya, Tanzania.*

CHIJIOKE, Canon Joseph Igwenekwuezie Bertram. **d** 53 **p** 55 Niger. P Dio Niger 55-59; and 62-69; Dio Ow 59-61; Dio Nig Delta 61-62. Dio Enugu from 69; Hon Can of Enugu from 71. *St Luke's Parsonage, Ogui, Enugu, Nigeria.* (Enugu 3548)

CHIKABU, Obed. **d** 73 **p** 74 Centr Zam. P Dio Centr Zam. *Box 77, Kapiri, Mposhi, Zambia.*

CHIKANDIWA, Oneas. **d** 58 **p** 61 Mashon. P Dio Mashon 58-81; Dio Mutare from 81. *Rectory, Rusape, Zimbabwe.*

CHIKOKO, Haines Willett Lloyd. St Jo Th Sem Lusaka 62. **d** 64 Malawi **p** 65 Bp Mtekateka for Malawi. P Dio Malawi 64-71; Dio Lake Malawi 71-80; Can of Lake Malawi 74-80. *Mtosa Court, Benga, via Nkhotakota, Malawi, Centr Africa.*

CHIKOKOTA, Canon Alfred Joseph. St Jo Th Sem Lusaka. **d** 57 **p** 58 Nyasa. P Dio Nyasa 57-64; Dio Malawi 64-71; Dio S Malawi 71-78; Can of S Malawi 72-74; Hon Can from 78; Archd 74-78. *PO Malinde, Mangochi, Malawi.*

CHIKONJE, Gildart. b 18. **d** 74 Lake Malawi **p** 75 Bp Taylor for Lake Malawi. P Dio Lake Malawi 75-80. *Box 27, Chisemphele, Kasungu, Malawi.*

CHIKUNI, Victor Misael. St Cypr Ngala. **d** 62 **p** 64 SW Tang. P Dio SW Tang 62-70; Dio Ruv from 71. *Box 1054, Mbinga, Tanzania.*

CHIKUNIE, Abraham Okeleke Chukujindu. b 26. Trin Coll Umuahia 72. **d** and **p** 73 Benin. P Dio Benin. *St John's Parsonage, Abbi, via Abraka, Nigeria.*

CHILAMBO, Canon Nathaniel. St Andr Th Coll Likoma 50. **d** 52 **p** 55 SW Tang. P Dio SW Tang 52-71; Dio Ruv from 71; Can of Ruv from 73. *PO Mbaha, Tanzania.*

CHILD, Canon Francis Geoffrey. Ch Coll Cam BA 36, MA 54. St Aug Coll Cant 31. **d** 37 Wakef **p** 38 Pontefract for Wakef. C of Birkenshaw w Hunsworth 37-40; Graaff Reinet 40-41; St Mark's Cathl George 41-42; R of Beaufort w 42-46; Mossel Bay 46-50; Riversdale (and Ladismith 50-53) 50-61; Can of Geo 50-54 and 77-80; Hon Can from 80; Archd of Riversdale 54-62; Karoo 62-72; Geo 72-77; R of St Jas, Graaff Reinet 62-72; St Geo Knysna 72-80; Exam Chap to Bp of Geo 78-80. *PO Box 67, Knysna, CP, S Africa.*

CHILD, Garrick Lancelot. Moore Th Coll Syd 62. ACT ThL 63. **d** 63 **p** 64 Syd. C of Cabramatta 63; Engadine w Heathcote 64-66; Mosman 67; Dir of C of E Boys' S Syd 68-72 and 74-78; R of Blackheath 72-74; L to Offic Dio Syd 74-79; C of St Alb French's Forest Dio Syd from 79. *16 Lockwood Avenue, Belrose, NSW, Australia 2085.* (451-3457)

CHILD, Gerald Leonard. K Coll Lon 43. **d** 45 Barking for Chelmsf **p** 46 Chelmsf. C of L Ilford 45-47; St Edm Forest Gate 47-55; R of St Mary Maldon 55-74. *46 Gratwicke Road, Worthing, Sussex, BN11 4BH.* (Worthing 30316)

CHILD, Ven Kenneth. b 16. Univ of Leeds BA (3rd cl Cl) 39. Coll of Resurr Mirfield 39. **d** 41 **p** 42 Man. C of St Aug Tonge Moor 41-47; V 47-55; CF (EC) 44-47; Hon CF 47; Chap of Guy's Hosp Lon 55-59; Cler Sec Ch Assembly Hosp Chap Coun 59-62; R of Newmarket (w St Agnes Exning from 66) 59-69; Gt w L Thurlow and L Bradley 69-80; RD of Newmarket 63-70; Surr from 64; Proc Conv Cant from 64; Hon Can of St E from 68; Archd of Sudbury from 70. *6/7 College Street, Bury St Edmunds, Suff.*

CHILD, Kenneth Leslie. Moore Th Coll Syd ACT ThL 51. **d** and **p** 52 Syd. C of Newtown w Erskineville 52-53; R of Erskineville w Darlington 53-57; St Paul Syd 57-64; L to Offic Dio Syd 64-67; R of Marrickville 67-72; Erskineville 72-79; St Pet Rockley Dio Bath from 79. *Box 875, Bathurst, NSW, Australia 2795.*

CHILD, Rupert Henry. b 29. St John's Coll Dur. **d** 58 **p** 59 Ex. C of Tavistock 58-61; Dunstable 61-65; V of Round Green 65-74; Sawbridgeworth Dio St Alb from 74. *Vicarage, Sheering Mill Lane, Sawbridgeworth, Herts.* (Bp's Stortford 723305)

CHILD, Theodore Hilary. b 09. CCC Cam 2nd cl Hist Trip pt i 30, BA (3rd cl Th Trip) 32, MA 36. Ridley Hall Cam 32. **d** 33 Win **p** 34 Southampton for Win. C of St Mary Southampton 33-36; Sheringham 36-38; C-in-c of St Chad's Conv Distr Leic 38-40; R of W Lynn 40-47; CF (EC) 43-46; R of E w W Harling 47-59; R of Bridgham w Roudham 50-59; V of Southwold 59-74; Perm to Offic Dio St E from 74; C-in-c of Starston Dio Nor from 75. *40 Mount Street, Diss, Norf.* (Diss 3801)

CHILDERSTONE, Cyril Richard. Univ of Dur LTh 37. Oak Hill Th Coll Southgate 34. **d** 37 **p** 38 Southw. C of St John Worksop 37-42; St Pet and St Paul Mansfield 42-45; Ambleside 45-46; Tutor St Andr Coll Oyo 47-50 and 53-57; St Jo Coll Owo 51-52; Chap Oyemekun Gr Sch Akure 58-71; Chap Finasaiye Gr Sch Akure 70-80. *Address temp unknown*

✠ **CHILDS, Right Rev Derrick Greenslade.** b 18. Late Pri of Univ of Wales BA (1st cl Hist) 39. Sarum Th Coll 39. **d** 41 **p** 42 St D. C of Milford Haven 41-46; Laugharne w Llansadwrnen and Llandawke 46-51; Ed *Cymry'r Groes* 47-49; *Province* 49-67; Warden Llandaff House Penarth 51-61; Publ Pr Dio Llan 51-72; Gen Sec Ch in Wales Prov Coun Educn 55-65; Chairman from 72; Ed Sec Ch in Wales Publications 61-65; Chairman Publications Bd from 75; Chan of Llan Cathl 65-69; Prin Trin Coll Carmarthen 65-72; Can of St D 69-72; Cons Ld Bp of Mon 23 May 72 in Ban Cathl by Abp of Wales; Bps of Llan; St A; St D; Swan B; Lich; and others; Sub-Prelate O of St John of Jer from 72; Vice-Chairman NS from 73; Hon F Univ Coll Cardiff from 81. *Bishopstow, Newport, Gwent. NPT 4EA.* (Newport 63510)

CHILDS, Ernest Edmund. b 23. Lich Th Coll 63. **d** 65 **p** 66 Birm. C of Billesley Common 65-68; Elland (in c of All SS) 68-69; C of E Children's S Cler Org Sec Dios Pet, Ely, Leic 69-72; V of Staverton w Helidon and Catesby 72-76. *35 Cleaves Drive, Walsingham, Norf, NR22 6EQ.*

CHILDS, Very Rev Henry Arthur. Univ of NZ BA 30, MA 32. **d** 32 **p** 33 Ch Ch. C of Sydenham 32-35; V of Tinwald 35; P-in-c of Hokitika 40-45; V of Geraldine 45-51; Karori w Makara Wel 51-64; Hon Can of Wel 58-61; Archd of Wel 61-64; Dean and V of St Jo Evang Cathl, Napier 64-73; Dean (Emer) from 73; L to Offic Dio Wai from 73. *51 Chaucer Road, Napier, NZ.* (57-970)

CHILDS, Leonard Neil. b 43. Univ of Leeds BA (2nd cl Th) 65. Wells Th Coll 66. **d** 68 Repton for Derby **p** 69 Repton for Cant. C of Matlock w Tansley 68-72; Chesterfield 72-74; P-in-c of Stonebroom Dio Derby 74-81; V from 81; P-in-c of Morton Dio Derby 78-81; R from 81. *14 High Street, Stonebroom, Derby, DE5 6JY.* (Ripley 872353)

CHILDS, Stanley Herbert. b 1900. Late Scho of Ch Coll Cam 3rd cl Cl Trip 21, BA (1st cl Th Trip) 23, MA 26. Ridley Hall Cam 23. **d** 24 **p** 25 Win. C of St Simon Southsea 24-26; CMS Miss Tr Coll Awka 26-46; Exam Chap to Bp on the Niger 33-46; V of Welland 47-50; Grimley w Holt 50-63; RD of Martley 51-63; R of The Combertons 63-70. *14 Gretton Road, Winchcombe, Cheltenham, Glos.* (Winchcombe 602424)

CHILDS, Theodore John. b 12. Late Exhib of St Edm Hall Ox BA 34, MA 47, BLitt 47. Ripon Hall Ox. **d** 40 **p** 41 B & W. C of Yeovil w Preston Plucknett 40-48; V of Winsham w Cricket St Thos 48-61; R of Chelvey w Brockley 61-70; R of Ballaugh 70-77. *9 Ballagorry Drive, Glen Mona, Maughold, IM.*

CHILDS, William Arthur. Ch Ch Coll. **d** 67 Ch Ch **p** 68 Bp Warren for Ch Ch. C of St Alb 67-68; V of Banks Peninsula 69-72; Woodend 72-77; P-in-c of Parklands Miss Distr Dio Ch Ch from 77. *129 Queen's Park Drive, Christchurch 2, NZ.* (881-159)

CHILE and BOLIVIA, Lord Bishop in. *See* Bazley, Right Rev Colin Frederick.

CHILE and BOLIVIA, Assistant Bishops in. *See* Morrison, Right Rev Ian Archibald; and Skinner, Right Rev Brian Antony.

CHILE, BOLIVIA AND PERU, Lord Bishop in. *See* Howell, Right Rev Kenneth Walter.

CHILE, BOLIVIA AND PERU, Assistant Bishop in. *See* Bazley, Right Rev Colin Frederick.

CHILEWA, Anthony. St Phil Coll Kongwa 67. **d** 69 Moro **p** 70 Centr Tang. P Dio Centr Tang. *PO Chipogoro, Tanzania.*

CHILEWA, Meshak. **d** 62 **p** 63 Centr Tang. P Dio Centr Tang. *Nzuguni, c/o Box 233, Dodoma, Tanzania.*

CHILIMOGA, Ashery Mika. St Phil Coll Kongwa 66. **d** 68 Bp Madina for Centr Tang. **p** 68 Centr Tang. P Dio Centr Tang. *Makasuku, Kilimatinde, PO Manyoni, Tanzania.*

CHILLINGWORTH, David Robert. b 51. TCD BA 73. Oriel Coll Ox BA (Th) 75, MA 81. Ripon Coll Cudd 75. **d** 76 **p** 77 Connor. C of H Trin Belf 76-79; Ch of Ireland Youth Officer from 79. *3 Finchley Gardens, Old Holywood Road, Belfast, BT4 2JB.* (Belfast 768366)

CHILOMBE, Vincent Goodwin. St Jo Th Sem Lusaka 56. **d** 57 N Rhod. d Dio N Rhod 57-64; Dio Zam 64-70; Dio Centr Zam 71-75; Dio Lusaka 75-79; Dio Lake Malawi from 79. *P/A Benga, Nkhotakota, Malawi.*

CHILOMBO, Alfred Mushili. **d** 68 Zam **p** 68 Bp Mataka for Zam. P Dio Zam 68-70; Dio Centr Zam from 71. *Box 189, Luanshya, Zambia.*

CHILOMBO, Nicholasi Gilbert. b 24. **d** 71 S Malawi **p** 72 Lake Malawi. P Dio Lake Malawi 71-77; Dio S Malawi from 77. *PO Namwera, Malawi.*

CHILONGANI, Charles. St Phil Coll Kongwa 69. **d** and **p** 71 Centr Tang. P Dio Centr Tang. *Box 233, Dodoma, Tanzania.*

CHILONGANI, Elieza. St Phil Coll Kongwa. **d** 66 Bp Madinda for Centr Tang **p** 67 Centr Tang. P Dio Centr Tang. *Box 79, Kongwa, Tanzania.*

CHILONGOLA, Canon Ayub Chimweli. **d** 56 Bp Omari for Centr Tang **p** 57 Centr Tang. P Dio Centr Tang 56-65; Dio Moro from 65; Hon Can of Moro from 77. *PO Berega, Morogoro, Tanzania.*

CHILONGOLA, Stephen. b 44. **d** and **p** 76 Moro. P Dio Moro. *D.M. Msowero Anglican Church, PO Kilosa, Tanzania.*

CHILONJI, David. b 21. St Cypr Coll Tunduru 66. **d** 68 **p** 69 Masasi. P Dio Masasi. *KJT Mchauru, SLP 15 Newala, Mtwara Region, Tanzania.*

CHILOWAKA, Fraser. St Cypr Coll Lindi 76. **d** 77 **p** 78 Ruv. P Dio Ruv. *Box 7, Songea, Tanzania.*

CHILTON, Kenneth Chapman. St Cuthb S Dur BA 49, Dipl in Th 51. **d** 51 **p** 52 Jarrow for Dur. C of Billingham 51-53; Eaton Nor 53-57; V of Thorpe Hamlet Dio Nor from 57. *St Matthew's Vicarage, Rosary Road, Norwich, NR1 1TA.* (Nor 20820)

CHIMBELU, Emmiluis. **d** and **p** 63 N Rhod. P Dio N Rhod 63-64; Dio Zam 64-70; Dio Lusaka from 71. *St Thomas, Petauke, EP, Zambia.*

CHIMBWA, Crispin. **d** 75 Centr Zam (APM). d Dio Centr Zam. *PO Box 90506, Luanshya, Zambia.*

CHIMPANGO, Ernest. b 27. **d** 77 S Malawi. d Dio S Malawi. *PO Box 84, Blantyre, Malawi.*

CHIN, Michael Khennyap. St Mich Th Coll Crafers. **d** 55 **p** 56 Borneo. Chap and Asst Master St Thos Sch Kuching 55-57. *St Thomas's School, Kuching, Sarawak.*

CHIN, Michael Shoon Chion. Moore Th Coll Syd 60. Trin Th Coll Sing BTh 64. **d** 64 **p** 65 Sing. P Dio Sing 64-68; Perm to Offic Dio Melb 68-69; C of Rosanna 69-72; Chap Chinese Miss of Epiph Melb 73-76; Perm to Offic Dio Melb 76; Asst Chap Miss to Seamen Melb from 77. *Mission to Seamen, Flinders Street, Melbourne, Vic, Australia 3000.* (62 7083)

CHIN, Simon Chung Vun. b 43. St Jo Coll Morpeth. ACT ThL 69. **d** 70 Sabah. **p** 71 Hong. P Dio Sabah from 71. *St Paul's Church, Beaufort, Sabah, Malaysia.* (401)

CHINDANDALI, Shadrack. b 33. **d** 71 **p** 72 S Malawi. P Dio S Malawi 71-78; Dio Niassa from 78. *Coboe, Lago, Niassa, Mozambique.*

CHINYAMI, Stefano. **d** 39 **p** 41 Centr Tang. P Dio Centr Tang. *Ngara, Bugufi, Bukoba, Tanzania.*

CHINYELE, Canon Yohana. Kongwa Th Coll 53. **d** 54 **p** 55 Centr Tang. P Dio Centr Tang; Can of Centr Tang from 73. *PO Hombolo, Tanzania, E Africa.*

CHIPALA, Justin. b 20. **d** 71 **p** 72 S Malawi. P Dio S Malawi. *Box 326, Blantyre, Malawi.*

CHIPAMAUNGA, Williard. **d** 74 **p** 75 Mashon. P Dio Mashon 74-81; Dio Mutare from 81. *PB 731, Enkeldoorn, Zimbabwe.*

CHIPANDA, Canon Barnaba Cecil Leslie. St Andr Th Coll Likoma 57. **d** 59 **p** 60 Nyasa. P Dio Nyasa 59-64; Dio Malawi 64-71; Dio S Malawi from 71; Archd of Fort Johnston 70-71; Mangochi 71-78; Can of S Malawi from 78. *P Bag 514, Limbe, Blantyre, Malawi.*

CHIPANDA, Stefano. St Cypr Th Coll Tunduru. **d** 57 **p** 60 Masasi. P Dio Masasi 57-79; Dio Dar-S from 79. *PO Box 45072, Dar-es-Salaam, Tanzania.*

CHIPEMBELE, Canon Habil Matthew. St Andr Th Coll Likoma. **d** 35 N Rhod for Nyasa **p** 38 Nyasa. P Dio Nyasa 35-56; CF (E Afr) 44-46; Can of Likoma Cathl 56-61; SW Tang from 66; Archd of S Nyasa 61-66; Perm to Offic Dio Dar-S from 71. *Box 23103, Dar-es-Salaam, Tanzania.*

CHIPFUPA, Lucas. St Pet Coll Rosettenville LTh 58. **d** 57 **p** 58 Bloemf. P Dio Bloemf 57-63; Dio Kimb K 63-76; Dio Johann from 77. *3708 Martinus Smuts Drive, Diepkloof 1861, S Africa.*

CHIPLIN, Christopher Gerald. b 53. Univ of Lon BSC 75. St Steph Hq Ox BA (Th) 77, MA 81. **d** 78 Repton for Derby **p** 79 Derby. C of Chesterfield 78-80; Thorpe-Episcopi Dio Nor from 80. *14 Acacia Road, Thorpe St Andrew, Norwich, NR7 0PP.* (Norwich 35228)

CHIPLIN, Gareth Huw. b 50. Worc Coll Ox BA (Th) 71. Edin Th Coll 71. **d** 73 Edmon for Lon **p** 74 Lon. C of Friern Barnet 73-75; St Lawr Eastcote 75-79; St Mich AA Ladbroke Grove Kens Dio Lon from 79. *St Francis House, Dalgarno Way, W10 5EL.* (01-969 3813)

CHIPLIN, Michael Alfred. b 50. St Jo Coll Morpeth ACT ThDip 76. **d** 76 Newc **p** 77 Bp Parker for Newc. C of Tor 76-79; Mayfield Dio Newc from 79; Dom Chap to Bp of Newc from 81. *250 Darby Street, Newcastle, NSW, Australia 2300.*

CHIPMAN, Alfred Charles. Ridley Coll Melb ACT ThL 65. **d** 66 **p** 67 Tas. C of St John Launceston 66-68; L to Offic and Youth Org Dio Mt Kenya 69-75; Dio Mt Kenya S from 75. *PO Box 121, Murang'a, Kenya.* (Murang'a 53)

CHIPPENDALE, Peter David. b 34. Univ of Dur BA (2nd cl Geog) 55. Linc Th Coll 57. **d** 59 **p** 60 Worc. C of St Jo Bapt Claines 59-63; V of Defford w Besford 63-73; C-in-c of Eckington 66-69; V 69-73; St Geo Kidderminster 73-76; The Lickey w Blackwell Dio Birm from 76. *30 Lickey Square, Birmingham, B45 8HB.* (021-445 1425)

CHIPPENDALE, Robert William. b 42. St Francis Coll Brisb 64. **d** 67 **p** 68 Brisb. C of Maryborough 67-69; Hollinwood 70-72; V of Shaw 72-78; R of Beaudesert Dio Brisb from 79. *7 Albert Street, Beaudesert, Qld, Australia 4285.* (Beaudesert 411015)

CHIPPINGTON, George Ernest. Ch Coll Cam BA 38, MA 42. **d** 61 **p** 62 Leic. C of Glenfield 61-63; Lutterworth w Cotesbach 63-65; V of Orton-on-the-Hill w Twycross and Norton-by-Twycross 65-70; R of Milton Damerel w Newton St Petrock Abbots Bickington and Bulkworthy Dio Ex from 70. *Milton Damerel Rectory, Holsworthy, Devon.* (Milton Damerel 362)

CHIPPS, Graham Lawrence. b 47. Moore Th Coll Syd 69. ACT ThL 71. **d** 73 Perth. d Dio Perth 71-74. *Wollaston College, Mt Claremont, W Australia 6010.*

CHIPUDHLA, Joseph. St Jo Sem Lusaka. **d** 70 **p** 71 Mashon. C of St Mich Hararf 70-75; St Mary and All SS Cathl Salisbury Dio Mashon from 76. *Box 981, Salisbury, Zimbabwe.*

CHIRIMUUTA, Elijah. St Jo Th Sem Lusaka 56. **d** 58 **p** 60 Mashon. P Dio Mashon. *160 Muririangenze Street, Mufakose, Salisbury, Zimbabwe.*

CHISALUNI, Habel. b 20. **d** 74 **p** 75 Centr Tang. P Dio Centr Tang. *c/o Box 15, Dodoma, Tanzania.*

CHISHOLM, David Whitridge. b 23. Keble Coll Ox (2nd cl Th) BA 48, MA 48. Linc Th Coll 48. **d** 50 **p** 51 Lon. C of Sudbury Middx 50-53; Jes Ch Forty Hill Enfield 53-57; V of St Aldhelm Edmon 57-66; St Alb N Harrow 66-72; St Jas Paddington Lon 72-78; Area Dean of Westmr (Paddington) 74-79; V of Hurley Dio Ox from 79. *Hurley Vicarage, Maidenhead, Berks, SL6 5LT.* (Littlewick Green 4892)

CHISHOLM, Harold Venn. b 17. St Chad's Coll Dur BA 38, Dipl in Th 39, MA 49. **d** 40 **p** 41 Dur. C of St Mary Tyne Dk 40-45; St Mary Heworth 45-48; V of South Moor 48-53; Deaf Hill w Langdale 53-58; St Alb Heworth 58-73; St Osw Hebburn-on-Tyne 73-82. *28 King Street, Pelaw, Tyne & Wear.*

CHISHOLM, Ian Keith. b 36. K Coll Lon and Warm AKC 62. **d** 63 **p** 64 Lich. C of St Chad Lich 63-66; Sedgley 66-69; V of St Martin Rough Hills Wolverhampton 69-77; Harrow Weald Dio Lon from 77. *175 Uxbridge Road, Harrow Weald, Middx, HA3 6TP.* (01-954 0247)

CHISHOLM, Ian Stuart. b 37. ALCD 63. **d** 63 Bp Gelsthorpe for Southw **p** 64 Southw. C of St John Worksop 63-66; Succr Sheff Cathl 66-68; Chap Social Responsibility 68-72; Tutor Wycl Hall Ox 72-76; C of St Andr Ox 72-76; V of Conisborough Dio Sheff from 76. *Conisborough Vicarage, Doncaster, S Yorks.* (Rotherham 864695)

CHISHOLM, Canon Reginald Joseph. Trin Coll Dub BA 40, MA 51, Jun and Sen Comp Pri and Past Th Pri 41, Downes Prem 42, Abp King's Pri 42; Div Test 42. **d** 42 Arm for Down **p** 43 Down. C of St Donard 42-45; Bangor 45-48; I of Ardglass w Dunsford 48-51; Newtownards Dio Down from 51; Surr from 52; Min Can of Belf Cathl 52-65; RD of Ards 71-73; Can and Treas Down Cathl from 80. *Rectory, Newtownards, Co Down, N Ireland.* (Newtownards 812527)

CHISHOLM, Timothy Martyn. b 45. St Jo Coll Auckld. **d** 76 Bp McKenzie for Wel **p** 77 Wel. C of Ch Ch Wanganui 76-80; V of Eketahuna Dio Wel from 80. *9 Church Street, Eketahuna, NZ.*

CHISINA, Canon Isaka. St Phil Th Coll Kongwa. **d** 57 Centr Tang **p** 58 Bp Omari for Centr Tang. P Dio Centr Tang 58-65; Dio Moro from 65; Hon Can of Moro from 77. *Box 31, Rubeho, Kilosa, Tanzania.*

CHISINA, Yeremiya. **d** and **p** 63 Centr Tang. P Dio Centr Tang 63-65; Dio Moro from 65. *Box 36, Mikumi, Tanzania.*

CHISLETT, David Edward. b 52. Univ of Syd BA 73. **d** 79 **p** 80 Bal. C of Ch Ch Cathl Bal 79-80; Warrnambool Dio Bal from 80. *71 Fairy Street, Warrnambool, Australia 3280.*

CHISNELL, Harry Reginald. b 10. Selw Coll Cam 2nd cl Th Trip pt i 33, BA (2nd cl Th Trip pt i) 34, MA 39. Ely Th Coll 34. **d** 35 **p** 36 Ripon. C of All S, Leeds 35-39; Bedale 39-44; St Barn Heigham 44-46; R of Acle 46-56; C-in-c of Beighton w Moulton 53-56; V of Happisburgh w Walcot 56-65; C-in-c of Ridlington 56-61; R of E Bergholt 65-75. *46 Kent Road, Harrogate, N Yorks.*

CHISOKOLE, Andrea Alderson. St Cyprian Coll Ngala 67. **d** 69 Bp Mlele for S W Tang **p** 70 S W Tang. P Dio S W Tang 70-71; Dio Ruv from 71. *Nkili, PO Liuli, Tanzania.*

CHISOKOLE, Andrew. St Paul's Coll Liuli. **d** 55 **p** 66 SW Tang. P Dio SW Tang 66-70; Dio Ruv from 71. *Kwambe, PO Mbamba Bay, Tanzania.*

✠ **CHISONGA, Right Rev Gayo Hilary.** St Cypr Th Coll Namasakata 46. **d** 47 **p** 50 Masasi. P Dio Masasi 47-59; Can of Masasi 59-68; Archd of Luatala 65-68; Cons Ld Bp of Masasi in St Mary Virg and St Bart Cathl Ch Masasi 21 Dec 68 by Abp of E Afr; Bp of Dar S; Asst Bps of Masasi; and SW Tang; and Bp Thorne; Dean of Masasi Cathl from 68. *Private Bag, PO Masasi, Tanzania.*

CHISOTI, Patrick Benaiah. St Cypr Th Coll Namasakata 58. **d** 60 **p** 62 SW Tang. P Dio SW Tang 60-66; Dio Dar-S 66-69; Dio SW Tang 69-70; Dio Ruv from 71. *PO Liuli, Tanzania.*

✠ **CHISWELL, Right Rev Peter.** Univ of NSW BEng 55. Moore Th Coll Syd ACT ThL (2nd cl) 58. **d** 58 **p** 59 Armid. C of Quirindi 58-59; Narrabri 59-61; V of Bingara 61-68; Gunnedah 68-76; Hon Can of Armid 70-72; Archd of NW Armid 72-76; Exam Chap to Bp of Armid 72-76; Cons Ld Bp of Armid in St Andr Cathl Syd 1 Nov 76 by Abp of Syd; Bps of Newc, Graft and C & Goulb; and Bps Kerle, Dain, Reid, Short, Cameron and Chynoweth. *Bishopscourt, Box 198, Armidale, NSW, Australia 2350.* (72-4555)

CHISWELL, Russell James. b 52. St D Coll Lamp BA 73. Wycl Hall Ox 74. **d** 76 **p** 77 Llan. C of Gabalfa 76-80; V of Hirwaun Dio Llan from 80. *Vicarage, High Street, Hirwaun, Aberdare, CF44 9SL.* (Hirwaun 811316)

CHIT HLA, Augustine. **d** 40 **p** 62 Rang. P Dio Rang. *St John's Church, Rangoon, Burma.*

CHIT SHWE, **d** 40 **p** 41 Rang. P Dio Rang from 40. *St Paul's Church, Danoung Chaung, Delta, Burma.*

CHIT HLA, Augustine. H Cross, Rang 37. **d** 40 **p** 62 Rang. P Dio Rang. *St Augustine's Church, Moulmein, Burma.*

CHIT SHWE, James. **d** 40 **p** 41 Rang. P Dio Rang from 40. *Danonchaung, Myaungmya District, Delta, Burma.*

CHITALYA, Elieza. **d** and **p** 76 Centr Tang. P Dio Centr Tang. *Box 462 PO, Dodoma, Tanzania.*

CHITAMBO, Canon Walter. St Pet Rosettenville 55. **d** 57 **p** 58 Mashon. P Dio Mashon; Can of Mashon from 71. *P.O. Box UA7, Salisbury, Zimbabwe.*

CHITELELA, Nathan. **d** 41 **p** 42 N Rhod. P Dio N Rhod 41-64; Dio Zam 64-70; Dio Centr Zam 71-75. *PO Box 172, Ndola, Zambia.*

CHITEMASI, Nelson. b 47. St Phil Coll Kongwa. **d** 75 **p** 76 Centr Tang. P Dio Centr Tang. *427, Chilonwa, Tanzania.*

CHITEMASI, Samson. **d** and **p** 78 Centr Tang. P Dio Centr Tang. *PO Mlowa Barabarani, Dodoma, Tanzania.*

✠ **CHITEMO, Right Rev Gresford.** St Paul's Coll Limuru 57. Moore Th Coll Syd 58. **d** 57 Centr Tang **p** 58 Bp Hilliard for Syd for Centr Tang. P Dio Centr Tang 57-65; Cons Ld Bp of Moro in H Trin Cathl Moro 30 Nov 65 by Abp of E Afr; Bps of Centr Tang; Vic Nyan; W Tang; and Dar-S; Asst Bps of Centr Tang; and Zanz T. *PO Box 320, Morogoro, Tanzania.*

CHITTENDEN, Charles Edward de Cummins. b 21. Ex Coll Ox MA 47. St Deiniol's Libr Hawarden 78. **d** 78 Birm **p** 79 Aston for Birm (APM). Hon C of St Agnes Moseley Dio Birm from 78; Chap for the Deaf Dio Birm from 78. *258 Yardley Wood Road, Moseley, Birmingham, B13 9JN.*

CHITTENDEN, John Bertram d'Encer. b 24. AIAC 57. Lon Coll Div 56. **d** 58 **p** 59 S'wark. C of St Mary at Lambeth 58-64; R of Hawkinge Dio Cant from 64; R of Acrise Dio Cant from 64. *Hawkinge Rectory, Folkestone, Kent.* (Hawkinge 2369)

CHITTENDEN, Reginald Henry. b 18. Bps' Coll Cheshunt 46. **d** 49 **p** 50 Cov. C of Westwood 49-54; V of Eastern Green 54-58; R of Upton w Skilgate 58-61; V of Countisbury w Lynmouth 61-69; R of Meavy w Sheepstor Dio Ex from 69. *Meavy Rectory, Yelverton, Devon, PL20 6PJ.* (Yelverton 3147)

CHITTENDEN, Roy Norman. b 29. St Chad's Coll Dur BA 53. **d** 54 B & W for Ex **p** 55 Ex. C of St Thos N Keyham 54-57; Miss Dio Nyasa 57-59; C of Ashburton 59-61; Asst Master Gillingham G Sch 61-70; Perm to Offic Dio Roch 61-65; Hon C of St Aug Gillingham 65-70; Hon C of St Chad Saddleworth 70-73; Asst Master Blue Coat Sch Oldham 70-73; R of St Mary Aber 73-75. *13 Normandy Way, St Budeaux, Plymouth, Devon.*

CHITTICK, Robert William. St Jo Coll Morpeth ThL 68. **d** 69 **p** 70 Graft. C of Coff's Harbour 69-70; C of Wyan w Rappville and of Casino 70-72; V of Copmanhurst 72-75; Hosp Chap Dio Bend from 75. *79 Nolan Street, Bendigo, Vic, Australia.* (054-43 7888)

CHITTLEBOROUGH, Colin Carew. St Barn Coll Adel 23. ACT ThL 25. **d** 25 **p** 26 Adel. C of St Aug Renmark 25-28; P-in-c of Mukawa 28-33; R of Balaclava 34-36; St Jude Brighton 36-49; Port Adelaide 49-56; Crafers 56-66; Can of Adel 57-66; C of St Steph Willunga 66-70; L to Offic Dio The Murray from 70. *William Street, Port Willunga, S Australia 5173.* (56 5078)

CHITTLEBOROUGH, Canon Gordon Arthur. **d** and **p** 63 Centr Tang. P Dio Centr Tang 63-64; Can of Centr Tang 63-66; W Tang and Dioc Regr 66-72; V of Ch Ch Arusha 72-77; Hon Can of Nai from 78; Lect Kenya Lang Sch Nai from 78. *Box 49898, Nairobi, Kenya.*

CHITTLEBOROUGH, Keith Stanley. Univ of Dur BA 60. Crafers Th Coll 47. ACT ThL 51. **d** and **p** 51 Adel. Gen L to Offic Dio Adel 51-56; and 60-63; Tutor and Chap SSM Th Coll Crafers 52-56; Ho of Sacred Miss Kelham 56-60; Publ Pr Dio Southw 56-60; Tutor SSM Th Coll Crafers 60-63; P-in-c of Woomera 63-67; R of Millicent 67-69; Sub-Warden St Barn Th Coll Belair 70-76; P-in-c of Parkside Dio Adel from 77; Dir of Post Ordin Tr Dio Adel from 77; Exam Chap to Abp of Adel from 79. *7 St Ann's Place, Parkside, S Australia 5063.* (71-3254)

CHITTLEBOROUGH, Martin Carew. St Jo Coll Morpeth 57. ACT ThL 59. Univ of Queensld BA 72. **d** 60 **p** 61 Adel. C of Mt Gambier 60-62; P-in-c of Tailem Bend Miss 62-65; Agenehambo 66-72; Archd of N Papua 70-74; Dir Chr Tr Centre Haruro Dio Papua 73-76; R of Waikerie 76-77; Austrn Executive Sec World Chr Action from 77; Perm to Offic Dio Syd from 78. *199 Clarence Street, Sydney, NSW, Australia 2000.* (29-2215)

CHITTLEBOROUGH, Ven Wilfrid James. St Barn Coll Adel ACT ThL 44. **d** and **p** 45 Adel. C of Ch Ch Mt Gambier 45-48; P-in-c of Koolunga 48-51; Robe 51-55; R of Renmark 55-59; R of Glen Osmond 59-78; Magill Dio Adel from 78; Hon Can of Adel 73-79; Can from 79; Archd of Eliz from 79. *8 Church Street, Magill, S Australia 5072.* (08-31 2494)

CHITTY, Preb Ernest Hedley. b 11. K Coll Lon and Warm AKC 48. **d** 48 Lon **p** 49 Stepney for Lon. C of Isleworth 48-50; Heston 50-53; PC of St Jo Bapt Tottenham 53-62; V of All S Hampstead 62-77; Bp of Edmonton's Chap for Post-Ordin Tr from 71; RD of N Camden 73-77; Preb of St Paul's Cathl Lon from 77; R of St Geo Bloomsbury Dio Lon from 77. *Flat 2, 8 Adamson Road, NW3 3HR.* (01-722 1992)

CHITTY, Philip Crofts. b 27. Roch Th Coll 61. **d** 63 Bp McKie for Cov **p** 64 Cov. C of St Luke Holbrooks 63-68; V of Long Itchington w Bascote 68-77; C-in-c of Ufton 68-69; R 69-77; P-in-c of St Marg City and Dio Cov from 77. *St Margaret's Vicarage, Stoke Park, Coventry, Warws.* (Coventry 457344)

CHITTY, William Paul Thomas. b 43. Linc Th Coll 68. **d** 71 Glouc **p** 72 Hulme for Man. C of St Mary Yate 71-72; St Francis Newall Green Wythenshawe 72-74; Harrow Weald 74-81. *Address temp unknown.*

✠ **CHIU, Right Rev Ban It.** Univ of Lon LLB 41. Westcott Ho Cam 43. **d** 45 **p** 46 Birm. [f Barrister-at-Law] C of St Francis Bournville 45-47; C of St Andr Cathl Sing 50-52; P-in-c of St Hilda Katong 52-55; Regr Dio Sing 52-56; Hon Can of Sing 56-59; V of Selangor 55-59; Home Sec ABM and L to Offic Dio Syd 59-62; Sec for Laymen World Coun of Chs 62-65; Fell St Aug Coll Cant 65-66; Cons Ld Bp of Sing in Sing Cathl 1 Nov 66 by Bp of Kuch; Bps of Jess; Kalg; Taiwan (USA); and Madras (Ch of S India); Bp Coadj of Philippines (USA); and Bps Envall (Swedish Lutheran); and Ga (Philippine Ind Ch). *Bishopsbourne, 4 Bishopsgate, Singapore 10.* (64-1661)

CHIU, Peter Lin Chun. Ming Hwa Th Coll Hong Kong 55. **d** 57 **p** 61 Hong. P Dio Hong. *71 Bonham Road, Hong Kong.* (5-461212)

CHIVERS, Eric Frank. b 21. Qu Coll Birm 69. **d** 69 Bp Cornwall for Win **p** 70 Win. C of Maybush 69-76; V of St Alb Southn Dio Win from 76. *357 Burgess Road, Southampton.* (Southn 554231)

CHIVERS, Ronald. b 27. Univ of Dur BA 52. Oak Hill Th Coll 52. **d** 53 Lancaster for Blackb **p** 54 Blackb. C of All SS Blackpool 53-57; V of St Nath Windsor W Derby 57-60; PC of Samlesbury 60-61; N Sec CCCS Prov of York from 61; L to Offic Dio Ripon 61-65; Dio Blackb 66-71; V of Woodside Dio Ripon from 71. *Vicarage, 1 Scotland Close, Horsforth, Leeds, LS18 5SG.* (0532-582433)

CHIVERS, Thomas Harry. b 19. Clifton Th Coll 60. **d** 60 **p** 61 S'wark. C of St Matt Surbiton 60-64; Keighley 64-65; C-in-c of St Barn Conv Distr Thwaites Brow Keighley 65-70; V of Oxenhope Dio Bradf from 70. *Oxenhope Vicarage, Keighley, W Yorks, BD22 9SA.* (Haworth 42529)

CHIVERS, William Herbert. b 20. Univ of Wales BA (2nd cl Hist) 42. Coll of Resurr Mirfield 42. **d** 44 **p** 45 Llan. C of St Sav Cardiff 44-48; Pontlottyn 50-51; Peterston-super-Ely 51-53; Bushey 53-58; V of St Jo Bapt Bollington 58-60; R of Bushey 60-81; Surr 61-81; Carnarvon Dio NW Austr from 81. *3 Glass Street, Carnarvon, W Australia 6701.* (099-83 1351)

CHIVERTON, Dennis Lionel Dunbar. b 26. Late Scho of St D Coll Lamp BA 51. **d** 53 **p** 54 Llan. C of St Mary Cardiff 53-54; Dowlais 54-57; Bargoed 57-61; C-in-c of Cymmer w Abercregan 61-67; R of Llanfabon Dio Llan from 67. *Nelson Rectory, Treharris, Mid Glam.* (Nelson 335)

CHIWANGA, Simon Peter. St Paul's Th Coll Limuru 62. **d** 64 **p** 65 Centr Tang. P Dio Centr Tang 65-70; MP Govt of Tanzania from 70; L to Offic Dio Centr Tang from 70. *Box 9121, Dar-es-Salaam, Tanzania.*

CHIWANGO, Marriot Stefano. St Paul's Coll Liuli. **d** 55 SW Tang. d Dio SW Tang 55-71; Dio Ruv from 71. *PO Liuli, Tanzania.*

CHIWEYO, Peter. b 45. **d** 72 **p** 73 Lake Malawi. P Dio Lake Malawi. *Box 294, Lilongwe, Malawi.*

CHIYUMBE, Richard. St Phil Th Coll Kongwa. **d** 64 **p** 65 Centr Tang. P Dio Centr Tang. *Box 15, Dodoma, Tanzania.*

CHIZA, William Neera. **d** 57 Bp Omari for Centr Tang. d Dio Centr Tang 57-66; Dio W Tang from 66. *Box 102, Kakonko, Kibondo, Tanzania.*

CHIZITO, Dunstan Marriott. St Andr Th Coll Likoma 57. **d** 59 **p** 60 Nyasa. P Dio Nyasa 59-64; Dio Malawi 64-71; Dio Lake Malawi 71-79; Can of Lake Malawi 74-79. *Box 2, Mkhotakota, Malawi.*

CHO, Augustine Kumhwan. b 42. St Mich Sem Seoul 70. **d** 73 **p** 75 Seoul. P Dio Seoul. *c/o 3 Chong dong, Chung Ku, Seoul 100, Korea.*

CHO, Francis. b 39. St Mich Sem Oryudung 69. **d** and **p** 70 Seoul. P Dio Seoul 70-74. *3533 North Albany, Chicago, Il, USA.*

CH'OE, Leo Chaung. b 50. Chungang Univ BA 72. St Mich Sem Seoul 75. **d** and **p** 79 Seoul. C of St Bede Seoul 79-81; St Paul Dio Seoul from 81. *234-55 Youngdu dong, Tongdaemun Ku, Seoul 131, Korea.*

CH'OE, Stephen Yongsei. b 45. St Mich Sem Seoul 70. **d** 73 Seoul. d Dio Seoul 73-77. *234-55 Yongdu Dong, Seoul 131, Korea.*

CHOGE, Job. Maseno Bible Sch 58. **d** 61 **p** 64 Nak. P Dio Nak. *PO Emgwen, Kenya.*

CHOGOLO, Yohana Chimya. **d** 64 **p** 65 Centr Tang. P Dio Centr Tang. *TTC Mpwapwa, Tanzania.*

CHOI, Stephen Yongsei. b 44. St Mich Sem Seoul 70. **d** 73 Seoul. d Dio Seoul. *Anglican Church, 3 Chong dong, Seoul 120, Korea.*

✠ **CHOI, Right Rev William Chul-Hi.** Rikkyo Univ Tokyo MA 72. St Mich Sem Seoul 52. **d** 54 **p** 56 Korea. P Dio Korea 54-57; V of Ch'ungju 57-62; Pusan 62-63; Chap of St Bede Ho 63-65; Archd of Seoul 65-66; Chap H Cross Conv 66-68; Prin St Mich Sem Korea 68-72; on leave 72-74; Cons Ld Bp of Pusan (or Busan) in St Nich Cathl Seoul 1 June 74 by Bp of Seoul; Bps of Kuch, Sabah, Vic Hong Kong and W Mal; and others. *PO Box 441, Pusan 600, Korea.* (Pusan 42-5846)

CHOMBE, Boaz. b 45. Bp Tucker Coll Mukono 74. **d** 78 M & W Nile. d Dio M & W Nile. *PO Box 370, Arua, Uganda.*

CHOMOLA, Richard. St Phil Coll Kongwa 60. **d** 60 Bp Wiggins for Centr Tang **p** 61 Centr Tang. P Dio Centr Tang. *PO Box 30, Itigi, Tanzania.*

CH'ON, Gregory Kwangil. b 44. St Mich Sem Seoul. **d** 72 **p** 74 Taejon. P Dio Taejon. *309 Byoungchon, Chonwonkun 330, Chungnam, Korea.*

CHON, Sebastian Samgwang. b 46. St Mich Sem Seoul 70. **d** 74 **p** 75 Seoul. P Dio Seoul. *58-76, 3Ka Munrae Dong, Yongdungp'o, Seoul 150, Korea.*

CHONG, En Shin. Div Coll Kwang Tang. **d** 47 Lab **p** 50 Borneo. P Dio Borneo 47-62; Dio Kuch 62-68. *c/o Bishop's House, PO Box 347, Kuching, Sarawak.*

CHONG, Jude Man-duk. St Mich Sem Oryudong. **d** 68 **p** 69 Taejon. P Dio Taejon. *Anglican Church, 35 Somun-Dong, Sangju 642, Korea.*

CHOO, Canon Dunstan. St Pet Coll Rosettenville. **d** 46 **p** 47 Pret. P Dio Pret 47-63; Dio Nyasa 63-64; Archd of Likoma 64-70; Hon Can of Lake Malawi from 73. *Anglican Church, PO Chintheche, Nkhata Bay, Malawi.*

CHOPPING, Reginald Eric. b 26. Coll of Min Canberra 79. **d** 81 Tas. On study leave. *c/o Church House, 125 Macquarie Street, Hobart, Tasmania 7000.*

CHOTE, Canon Arthur Abel. Wycl Coll Tor LTh 48, BA 49, Hon DD 79. **d** 48 **p** 49 Tor. C of Port Whitby 48-50; R of Cavan 50-53; Richmond Hill 53-57; Ch of the Messiah Tor 57-69; Can of Tor from 66; Chap N York Hosp Tor 69-72; R of St Phil Etobicoke Tor 72-80. *40 High Park Avenue, Toronto, M6P 2S1, Ont., Canada.*

CHOU, Ven John Mung Chow. Union Th Coll Canton. **d** 43 **p** 44 Hong. P Dio Hong; Can of Hong 71-73; Exam Chap to Bp of Hong from 71; Archd of Hong from 73. *All Saints' Ho-mun-tin, Kowloon, Hong Kong.* (3-319944)

CHOULES, Edward Frank. b 16. St Steph Ho Ox. **d** 78 **p** 79 Reading for Ox (NSM). C of All SS Boyne Hill Maidenhead 78-80. *6 Gables Close, Ray Lea Road, Maidenhead, Berks, SL6 8QD.*

CHOVAZ, Ven Albert Earl. Hur Coll LTh 68. **d** 67 **p** 68 Hur. P-in-c of Ch Ch Lon 67-73; Admin Asst Dio Hur 73-74; Sec-Treas from 74; Archd without Territorial Jurisd from 74. *33 Nottinghill Crescent, London, Ont., Canada.* (519-434 6893)

CHOW, James Leslie Ewing. Ch Coll Cam BA 16, MA 49. **d** 50 Hong **p** 53 Gui. L to Offic Dio Hong 50-53; C of St Geo

Cathl. Georgetown 53-56. *8 Belle Smythe Street, Woodbrook P.O., Trinidad, W Indies.*

CHOW, Thomas. b 38. Union Th Coll Hong Kong 67. **d** 70 **p** 71 Hong. Miss to Seamen Dio Hong 70-74 and from 75. *11 Middle Road, Kowloon, Hong Kong.*

CHOW, Thomas Wing-Fu. b 51. Chinese Univ of Hong Kong BA 76. Chung Chi Coll Hong 75. **d** 77 Hong. d Dio Hong. *397 Block 4, Lady Grantham Villa, Sycamore Street, Kowloon, Hong Kong.*

CHOW, Ting Suie Roy. b 46. Sarum Wells Th Coll 70. **d** 72 Man **p** 73 Middleton for Man. C of St Luke w All SS Weaste Salford 72-75; Swinton 75-78; R of St Paul Blackley Dio Man from 78; Sec SPCK Man from 80. *Rectory, Erskine Road, Blackley, Manchester, M9 2RB.* (061-740 1518)

CHOWN, Alfred. b 1896. St Aug Coll Cant 54. **d** 55 **p** 56 B & W. C of Wellington w W Buckland 55-58; R of Fordwich 58-66. *207 Cromwell Road, Whitstable, Kent, CT5 1NE.*

CHOWN, Ernest John Richard. b 17. St Steph Ho Ox 48. **d** 51 **p** 52 Ox. C of St Paul Ox 51-53; St Paul Brighton 53-65; V of St Mary, Swanley 65-72; St Andr Worthing Dio Chich from 72. *St Andrew's Vicarage, Victoria Road, Worthing, Sussex, BN11 1XB.* (Worthing 33442)

CHOWN, William Richard Bartlett. b 27. K Coll Lon and Warm AKC 54. **d** 55 **p** 56 Carl. C of Egremont 55-58; Upminster 58-61; R of St Andr, Romford 61-78; Newton Longville w Stoke Hammond, Whaddon and Tattenhoe Dio Ox from 78. *Newton Longville Rectory, Milton Keynes, Bucks, MK17 0BH.* (Milton Keynes 77847)

CHRISTCHURCH, Lord Bishop of. *See* Pyatt, Right Rev William Allan.

CHRISTCHURCH, Dean of. *See* Underhill, Very Rev Michael Leeke.

CHRISTCHURCH, N.Z., Dean of. *See* Underhill, Very Rev Michael Leeke.

CHRISTENSEN, Norman Peter. b 37. St D Coll Lamp BA 63. Ridley Hall Cam 63. **d** 65 **p** 66 Ches. C of Barnston 65-70; V of St Jo Evang Over 70-77; R of Bromborough Dio Ches from 77. *Rectory, Mark Rake, Bromborough, Wirral, L62 2DH.* (051-334 1466)

CHRISTENSEN, William Niels. Trin Coll Tor BA 63, STB 66. Univ of Windsor MA 68. **d** 66 **p** 67 Tor. Chap Cant Coll Windsor Ont 66-68; P-in-c of St Mark Edmon 68-74; Perm to Offic Dio Koot from 78. *2938 Coleman Street, Penticton, BC, Canada.*

CHRISTIAN, Anthony Clive. b 46. Univ of Kent Cant BA (Phil) 74. St Aug Coll Cant 74. **d** 76 **p** 77 Cant. C of faversdham 76-79; St Laurence-in-Thanet (in c of St Chris Newington) Dic Cant from 79; *St Christopher's House, Kimberley Road, Newington, Ramsgate, Kent.* (0843 54160)

CHRISTIAN, Gerald. b 29. Qu Coll Birm 74. **d** and **p** 77 Birm (APM) 77-82. C of Stirchley 77-82; Asst to Archd of E Transv from 82. *St Margaret's Church House, 33 Montgomery Avenue, Witbank, Tvl, S Africa.*

CHRISTIAN, Richard. b 37. Univ of Nottm Dipl Educn 74. MA (Oxon) 81. K Coll Lon and Warm AKC 62. **d** 63 **p** 65 S'wark. C of St Mich AA w All S Camberwell 63-66; Woolwich 66-70; Chap and Lect Bp Lonsdale Coll of Educn Derby 70-74; Keble Coll Ox 74-76; P-in-c of Hurley 76-79; Chap Lancing Coll W Sussex from 79. *c/o Lancing College, Lancing, W Sussex, BN15 0RW.*

CHRISTIAN, (Lawrence) Robert Christopher Graham. b 10. Magd Coll and Fitzw Ho Cam BA 38, MA 41. Chich Th Coll 39. M SSF 66. **d** 40 **p** 41 S'wark. C of St Paul Newington 40-42; Warden of Well Coll Miss Walworth 42-48; C of St Alphage Burnt Oak 49-50; Co-Warden of St Anne's Ho Soho 50-54; C-in-c of St Paul Camden Sq St Pancras 54-55; C of St Luke Oseney Crescent St Pancras (in c of St Paul Camden Sq) 55-56; C-in-c of St Pet Limehouse 56-57; V 57-66; L to Offic Dio Sarum from 66. *St Mary At the Cross, Glasshampton, Shrawley, Worcester, WR6 6TQ.*

CHRISTIAN, Canon Ronald George. b 20. AKC 48. St Bonif Coll Warm. **d** 49 **p** 50 Southw. C of Mansfield Woodhouse 49-52; Margate 52-56; V of Bramford (w Burstall 56-63) Dio St E from 56; Dioc Ecumen Officer from 66; Hon Can of St E Cathl from 75. *Bramford Vicarage, Ipswich, Suff.* (Ipswich 41105)

CHRISTIAN-EDWARDS, Michael Thomas. b 36. Down Coll Cam BA 60, MA 64. Clifton Th Coll 60. **d** 62 **p** 63 Ex. C of St Leon Ex 62-67; V of St Thos Trowbridge 67-75; R of Wingfield 67-75; P-in-c of St Paul Fisherton Anger City and Dio Sarum from 75. *St Paul's Rectory, Salisbury, Wilts.* (Salisbury 4005)

CHRISTIANSON, Carl Eric. Univ of Queensld BA 63. ACT ThL 57. St Francis Th Coll Brisb. **d** and **p** 57 Brisb. C of Coorparoo Brisb 57; St Luke Toowoomba 57-59; P-in-c of Biggenden 59-61; Chap R Pk Psychiatric Hosp Melb 61-65; Melb C of E Gr Sch 65-66; Min of Buleen 66-71; on leave 71-74; I of Kilsyth 74-79; C in Dept of Evang and Ex Dio Melb from 79. *238 Maroondah Highway, Ringwood, Vic, Australia 3134.* (870 3940)

CHRISTIANSON, Rodney John. b 47. St Paul's Coll Grahmstn Dipl Th 72. **d** 72 **p** 73 Natal. C of St Sav Cathl Pmbg Natal 72-76; Asst Chap Flying Angel Club Denton 76-80; Chap from 80; Sen Chap Port of Lon from 81. *Flying Angel Club, Missions to Seamen, Denton, Gravesend, Kent.* (Gravesend 63383)

CHRISTIE, Canon Graham. Univ of Leeds BA (2nd cl Hist) 31. Coll of Resurr Mirfield 31. **d** 33 **p** 34 Man. C of Swinton 33-36; St Jas Ex 36-37; St Marg Hollinwood 37-38; V of St Mary Magd Winton 38-45; R of Roos w Tunstall-in-Holderness 46-60; C-in-c of Garton-in-Holderness w Grimston and Hilston 48-58; V 58-60; Proc Conv York 55-70; RD of S Holderness 58-60; Pocklington 60-74; V of Pocklington w Yapham-cum-Meltonby and Owsthorpe w Kilnwick Percy 60-81; Millington w Gt Givendale 60-81; Can and Preb of York Minster from 62. *66 Wold Road, Pocklington, York.* (Pocklington 4200)

CHRISTIE, Leonard Douglas. b 16. AKC 39. Bps' Coll Cheshunt 39. **d** 39 **p** 40 S'wark. C of St Mark Camberwell 39-42; St Martin Epsom (in c of St Stephen Epsom Downs) 42-45; I of St Ambrose Oldham 45-50; V of Arncliffe w Halton Gill 50-53; Chap NE Lancs Welfare Assoc for Deaf Bp of Blackb's Chap for Deaf and Sacrist of Blackb Cathl 53-56; Supt of Adult Deaf in Derby and Derbys 56-63; LPr Dio Derby 56-63; Supt and Chap St Alb Dioc Assoc for Deaf 63-69; L to Offic Dio Guildf 70-76; V of Easington w Skeffling and Kilnsea Dio York from 76. *Easington Vicarage, Hull, Humb, HU12 0TE.* (Spurn Point 203)

CHRISTIE, Canon Thomas Richard. b 31. CCC Cam BA 53, MA 57. Linc Th Coll 55. **d** 57 **p** 58 Portsm. C of St Mark Portsea 57-60; St Andr Cherry Hinton (in c of St Jas) 60-62; Min of St Jas Conv Distr Cherry Hinton 62-66; V of St Aug Wisbech 66-73; Whitstable (w St Pet from 75) 73-80; M Gen Syn Ely 70-73; Cant 75-80; Pet from 80; Can Res, Chan and Libr of Pet Cathl from 80; Exam Chap to Bp of Pet from 80. *Prebendal House, Minster Precincts, Peterborough, PE1 1XX.* (Pet 69441)

CHRISTIE, Ven William Douglas McLaren. Bp's Univ Lennox BA 38. **d** 35 Queb for Ott **p** 36 Ont for Ott. C of Bury PQ 35-36; Miss of Montague w Franktown 36-39; I of Vankleek Hill 39-43; R of Renfrew 43-46; All SS Westboro Ott 46-58; Cornw Ont 58-67; St Bart City and Dio Ott from 72; Archd of Cornw 58-67; Dioc Archd 67-78; Archd (Emer) from 79; Dir of Program Dio Ott 67-72; Chap to Bp of Ott 67-77. *2-23 Mackay Street, Ottawa, Ont., Canada.*

CHRISTMAS, Alan Frederick. b 29. K Coll Lon and Warm AKC and BD 57. **d** 58 **p** 59 S'wark. C of St Sav w All H S'wark 58-61; PV of S'wark Cathl 58-61; V of All SS S Wimbledon 61-66; Industr Chap to Bp of Ox from 66. *26 Lansdowne Avenue, Slough, Berks, SL1 3SJ.* (Slough 30230)

CHRISTMAS, Ernest Hugh. St Chad's Coll Regina. **d** 40 **p** 42 Qu'App. C of Empress 40-43; I of Alsask 43-44; Milden 44-47; Wolseley 47-51; Estevan 51-54; Chap RCAF 54-73; L to Offic Dio Calg 60-67 and from 75; I of Ch of Good Shepherd Calg 73-75. *3302 50th Street, NW, Calgary, Alta, Canada.* (286-8495)

CHRISTOPHER, George Whitmore. ACT ThL 43. Moore Coll Syd. **d** and **p** 44 Syd. C of E Balmain 44-45; Chap AIF 45-46; C of St Paul Chatswood 46; Gen Sec CMS SA Branch 47-48; C-in-c of Par Distr Abbotsford w Russell Lea 48-50; R of St Leon 50-52; CMS Gen Sec Dio Tas 50-52; L to Offic Dio Syd 50-52; C of H Trin Hobart 52-55; C-in-c of St Barn Punchbowl 62-66; R 66-68; All SS Oatley W 68-72; Strathalbyn Dio Murray from 73. *Rectory, East Terrace, Strathalbyn, S Australia 5255.* (085-36 2030)

CHRISTOPHER, Henry Mansfield. b 22. **d** 80 Trinid. C of All SS Port of Spain Dio Trinid from 80. *48 Alyce Glen, Petit Valley, Diego Martin, Trinidad, WI.*

CHU, Bernard Kwong Chung. Trin Th Coll Sing. **d** 64 **p** 65 Kuch. P Dio Kuch 64-76; Dio Hong from 76. *St Peter's, Castle Peak, New Territories, Hong Kong.* (12-819182)

CHU, James. Union Th Coll Hong LTh 63. **d** 66 **p** 67 Hong. C of St Paul Hong 67-69; V of St Jas Hong 70-77; Perm to Offic Dio BC 77-80; I of St Pet Chinese Par City and Dio Ott from 80. *Box 2843, Ottawa, Ont, K1P 5W8, Canada.* (613-238 3429)

CHUBB, John Nicholas. b 33. St Cath S Ox BA 55, MA 58. Qu Coll Birm 57. **d** 59 **p** 60 York. C of Kirby Moorside 59-62; Scarborough 62-64; V of Potterspury w Furtho and Yardley Gobion 64-69; Brixworth (w Holcot from 74) 69-81; Hampton Hill Dio Lon from 81; C-in-c of Holcot 73-74. *St James's Vicarage, Hampton Hill, Middx. TW12 1DG.* (01-979 2069)

CHUBB, Richard Henry. b 45. Univ of Wales (Cardiff) Mus Bac 67. Linc Th Coll 67. **d** 70 **p** 71 Malmesbury for Bris. C of Chippenham Bris 71-72; Stockwood Conv Distr Brislington 72-73; Stockwood 73-76; Perm to Offic Dio Bris 76-79;

Min Can & Succr Bris Cathl and Publ Pr from 79. *45 Claremont Road, Bishopston, Bristol, BS7 8DN.*

CHUCHUNI, Alfred. **d** 78 **p** 79 Centr Melan. P Dio Centr Melan. *Tasiboko District, Guadalcanal, Solomon Islands.*

CHUDLEY, Cyril Raymond. b 29. BA (Engl Lit) (Lon) 53. Wells Th Coll 70. **d** 72 **p** 73 Southw. C of Newark-on-Trent 72-75; Egg Buckland 75-77; P-in-c of St Aug Plymouth Dio Ex 77-80; V from 80. *St Augustine's Vicarage, Lipson Vale, Plymouth, Devon.* (Plymouth 660618)

CHUKUEZI, Ven Felix Efiefula. Trin Coll Umuahia 54. **d** 56 **p** 57 Niger. P Dio Niger 56-59; P Dio Nig Delta 59-69; Dio Ow from 69; Archd of Ow 69-71; Okigwe-Orlu from 71. *Archdeacon's House, Nkwerre, Orlu, Nigeria.*

CHUKUIGWE, Ven Samuel Yemen. St Paul's Coll Awka 55. **d** 55 **p** 57 Nig Delta. P Dio Nig Delta; Archd of Port Harcourt from 72. *PO Box 53, Port Harcourt, Nigeria.* (Port Harcourt 21561)

CHUKUKA, Christopher Ifediora Nwoye. Trin Coll Umuahia. **d** 61 **p** 62 Niger. P Dio Niger. *Parsonage, Nawfija, Awka, Nigeria.*

CHUKUKA, James Ndubisi. Trin Coll Umuahia 49. **d** 51 Niger **p** 53 N Nig. P Dio N Nig 51-59; Dio Ow 59-66; Dio Niger from 67. *St Philip's Parsonage, Ogidi, Via Onitsha, Nigeria.*

CHUKWUKEZIE, Michael Uchenna. b 47. Trin Coll Umuahia 74. **d** 76 Niger. d Dio Niger. *St Matthew's Parsonage, Ozubulu, Nnewi, Nigeria.*

CHULU, Maurice. **d** 77 **p** 78 Matab. P Dio Matab. *Box 49, Madumabisa, Wankie, Zimbabwe.*

CHUMA, Ernest Edward. St Phil Th Coll 46. **d** 65 **p** 66 Bp Kahurananga for W Tang. P Dio W Tang. *PO Box 15, Kibondo, Tanzania.*

CHUN, Stephen. St Mich Th Coll Korea. **d** 38 **p** 39 Korea. P Dio Korea 39-62; Archd of Centr Korea 56-62. *c/o Young Shik Kim, 8-34 Yongmoon-Dong, Wonhyo-Ro, Yongsan-Koo, Seoul, Korea.*

CHUNG, Abel. Trin Th Coll Sing 60. **d** 63 **p** 64 Sing. P Dio Sing 63-70; Dio W Mal 70-75; Dio Syd 76-80. *c/o Mission to Seamen, 11 Macquarie Place, Sydney, Australia 2000.* (241-3555)

CHUNG, Anthony Yon Woo. b 35. St Mich Sem Oryudong 68. **d** and **p** 69 Seoul. P Dio Seoul. *23-37; 3 Ka Chungang Ro, Chunch'on 200, Korea.*

CHUNG, Ka-lok. b 44. Bible Coll of Vic Dipl Th 76. **d** 78 Hong. d Dio Hong. *All Saints Church, Pak Po Street, Kowloon, Hong Kong.*

CHUNG, Ven Matthew. b 40. Univ of Yonsei ThB 68. St Mich Sem 70. **d** 70 **p** 71 Seoul. P Dio Seoul; Sec to Bp of Seoul 70-71; Dioc Sec 77-80; P-in-c of Kumho Dong 78-79; St Bede City and Dio Seoul from 79; Archd P Dio Seoul from 79. *32 Yongon Dong, Chong No Ku, Seoul 110, Korea.*

CHUNG, Ven Yan Laap. U Th Coll Canton. **d** 27 **p** 28 Hong. V of Canton 27-34; St Steph Hong Kong 34-42; St Paul and Chap of St Jo Cathl Hong Kong 42-45; Sec Dioc Standing C'ttee 45-51; P Chinese Miss Wadestown Wel 51-56; V of Macao 56-63; All SS Yaumati Kowloon 63-68; Can of Hong from 58; Archd 65-68; Archd (Emer) from 68; P-in-c of Chinese Miss Wel 68-69; L to Offic Dio Wel from 69. *14 Danube Street, Wellington, NZ.* (836-379)

CHURCH, Albert George. Ridley Coll Melb ACT ThL 40. **d** 40 **p** 41 St Arn. C of Murrayville 40-41; V 41-44; R of Birchip 44-46; Merbein 46-48; Kallista 48-50; Frankston Dio Melb from 50. *22 High Street, Frankston, Vic, Australia 3199.* (78-3 3085)

CHURCH, Geoffrey Arthur. b 09. Clare Coll Cam BA 31, MA 35. Wells Th Coll 31. **d** 32 **p** 33 S'wark. C of Lambeth 32-36; H Trin Waltham Cross 36-38; St Mary L Cam 39; R of Witton w Brundall (and Bradeston from 51) 40-52; V of Patrixbourne w Bridge 52-57; R of Harbledown 57-67; V of Boughton Monchelsea 67-70; C of Ch Ch Watford 70-76; L Berkhamsted w Bayford, Essendon and Ponsbourne 76-81. *Address temp unknown.*

CHURCH, Canon George Harold Christian. CBE 75. ALCD 37. **d** 37 **p** 38 St Alb. C of Ware 37-39; Chap RAF 39-65; (Men in disp 45); Asst Chap-in-Chief 58-65; Hon Chap to HM the Queen 62-65; Chap St Mark Florence 65-75; Can of Malta 71; Archd of Malta 71-75; Hon Can of Malta from 75. *Diesbach Strasse 5, 3012 Bern, Switzerland.* (Bern 245004)

CHURCH, Graeme Leslie. b 45. Univ of Vic Wel BA. St Jo Coll Auckld 77. **d** 78 **p** 79 Wai. C of St Aug Distr Dio Wai from 78. *194 Vigor Brown Street, Napier, NZ.*

CHURCH, Howard Joseph. b 05. Em Coll Cam BA 28, MA 33. Ridley Hall Cam 29. **d** 30 **p** 31 S'wark. C of St Jo Evang Blackheath 30-33; CMS Miss Kabare 33-35; Kabete 35-37; Weithaga 38-39; Embu 39-46; Actg RD of N Highlands 45-46; St Mark Parklands Nai 48-53; Special Emergency Duty Dio Momb 53-57; V of Sparkbrook 57-59; Wisley w Pyrford 59-69; Nakuru 69-72. *Courts Close, Holne, Newton Abbot, Devon.*

CHURCH, Canon Ivor Frederick. Ridley Coll Melb BA 46, ACT ThL 38. St Edm Hall Ox BA (2nd cl Th) 50, MA 53. **d** 39 **p** 40 Melb. C of All SS St Kilda 39-42; Chap RAAF 42-46; C of St Pet Melb 46-47; Tutor at Cudd Coll 50-51; L to Offic at Ch Ch Brunswick Dio Melb 51; Prin of St Francis Th Coll Brisb from 51; Can Res of Brisb Cathl from 56; Commiss Polyn 62-69; Kuch 63-69. *St Francis College, Milton, Brisbane, Queensland, Australia 4064* (36 4286)

CHURCH, Canon William Harold Morrison. Bp's Univ Lennox BA 29, LST 32. **d** 32 **p** 33 Ott. C of All SS Ott 32-33; I of Port Elmsley 33-37; Dom Chap to Bp of Queb 37-60; Miss Dio Queb 37; R of Levis and S Shore Miss 37-38; I of Valcartier Miss 39-41; Shawinigan Falls 41-44; Coaticook 44-49; R of Drummondville Dio Queb 49-55 and 61-68; Wakeham 55-61; Can of Queb 54-75; Hon Can from 76; I of Scotstown 69-72; R of Stanstead 72-75. *RR3, Ayer's Cliff, PQ, Canada.*

CHURCHILL, Arthur Wallace. Mem Univ Newfld BA 63. Qu Coll Newfld LTh 63. **d** 62 **p** 63 Newfld. C of Flower's Cove Dio Newfld 62-65; I 65-70; R of Bay of Is Dio Newfld (W Newfld from 76) from 70. *453 Curling Street, Corner Brook, Newfoundland, Canada.* (709-785 5055)

CHURCHILL, Canon Aubrey Gilbert Roy. b 12. Sarum Th Coll 37. **d** 39 Portsm **p** 40 Bp Kitching for Portsm. C of St Pet and St Paul Fareham 39-42; Horfield (in c of St Francis) 42-45; St Mary Banbury (in c of St Paul Neithrop) 45-47; St Jo Bapt Cov 47-51; V of Wilmcote (w Billesley from 55) 51-76; RD of Alcester 59-69; Hon Can of Cov 72-76; Can (Emer) from 76. *Wilmcote Lodge, Harbury, Leamington Spa, CV33 9LX.* (Leamingtn Spa 613309)

CHURCHILL, Gerald Thomas. Bp's Univ Lennox BA 61, LST 63. **d** 63 **p** 64 Ott. C of St Thos Ap Ott 63-66; I of Winchester 66-70; R of N Gower 70-73; Resurr Ott 73-76; Ch of H Sav Waterloo Dio Hur from 76. *190 Mary Street, Waterloo, Ont., Canada.* (519-743 8772)

CHURCHILL, Very Rev John Howard. b 20. Late Exhib of Trin Coll Cam 1st cl Math Trip pt i 41, BA (2nd cl Th Trip pt i) 42, MA 46. Linc Th Coll 42. **d** 43 Kingston T for S'wark **p** 44 S'wark. C of St Geo Camberwell 43-48; All H Tottenham 48-53; Chap and Lect K Coll Lon and L to Offic Dio Lon 53-60; V of St Geo (w St Steph 60-64) Sheff 60-67; Lect Univ of Sheff 60-67; Exam Chap to Bp of Sheff 60-67; to Bp of St E and Dioc Dir of Ordins and Clergy Training 67-73; Can Res of St E 67-73; Lady Margaret Pr Univ of Cam 69; M Gen Syn from 70; Dean of Carl from 73. *Deanery, Carlisle, Cumb.* (Carlisle 23335)

CHURCHILL, Walter Bowen. **d** 40 **p** 41 Perth. C of Toodyay 40-41; R of W Northam and P-in-c of Goomalling 41-44; R of Beverley 44-52; Kelmscott-Armadale 52-54; P-in-c of Gingin and of Swan 54-59; Chap at Stoneville Farm Sch 59-63; R of Rosalie 63-71; Perm to Offic Dio Perth from 71. *30 Jameson Street, Mosman Park, W Australia 6012.* (31 2192)

CHURCHMAN, David Ernest Donald. b 21. BC Coll Bris 45. **d** 48 **p** 49 Blackb. C of All SS Preston 48-49; Braintree 50-52; V of St Pet Harold Wood 52-59; St Jude Southsea Portsea 59-74; M Gen Syn Portsm 70-74; V of Cockfosters Dio Lon from 74; Area Dean of Enfield 75-81; M Gen Syn Lon 75-80. *Christchurch Vicarage, Chalk Lane, Cockfosters, Herts, EN4 9JQ.* (01-441 1230)

CHURCHUS, Eric Richard Ivor. b 28. Univ of Lon BSc, MSc 56. **d** 78 **p** 79 Heref. C of Sutton St Nich w St Mich Dio Heref from 78; Withington w Westhide & Weston Beggard Dio Heref from 78. *Colnebrook, Millway, Sutton St Nicholas, Hereford, HR1 3BQ.*

CHURCHWARD, Kenneth Percy. Moore Th Coll Syd ACT ThL 54. **d** and **p** 55 Syd. C of Wollongong 55-57; C-in-c of Baulkham Hills 57-61; R of Mittagong 61-66; C-in-c of Sylvania Heights Provis Distr 66-68; R of Kingsgrove 68-73; Perm to Offic Dio Melb 74-78; R of St Andr Summer Hill Dio Syd from 79. *2 Henson Street, Summer Hill, NSW, Australia 2130.* (798-6149)

✠ **CHYNOWETH, Right Rev Neville James.** Moore Th Coll ACT ThL 49. Univ of Syd BA 54, MA 57. Melb Coll of Div BD 70. **d** and **p** 50 Syd. C of St Mich Syd 50-51; R of Kangaroo Valley 51-52; C of St D Surry Hills and Hosp Chap Syd 52-54; R of Dee Why 54-63; St Anne Strathfield 63-66; R of All SS Canberra 66-71; St Paul Canberra 71-74; Archd of Canberra 73-74; Cons Asst Bp of C & Goulb in St Andr Cathl Syd 18 Oct 74 by Abp of Syd; Bps of C & Goulb and Graft; and Bps R Arthur, G Delbridge, F Hulme-Moir, G Muston, F Parker, J Reid and D Robinson Apptd Bp of Gippsld 80. *Bishop's Court, Box 383, Sale, Vic, Australia 3850.* (051-44 2046)

CIANCHI, Dalbert Peter. b 28. Univ of Lon BSc 57. Westcott Ho Cam 69. **d** 70 **p** 71 St Alb. C of Harpenden 70-74;

P-in-c of Wavendon w Walton 74-80; Lavendon w Cold Brayfield Dio Ox from 80; Team V of Woughton 74-80; Clifton Reynes 81. *Lavendon Rectory, Olney, Milton Keynes, MK46 4EX.* (Bedford 712647)

CIDAHE, Reuben. **d** 32 **p** 33 Centr Tang. P at Buigiri 32-40; Burunge 40-48. *CMS, Buigiri, Kikombo, Tanzania.*

CIRCUS, Robert William. b 19. Wycl Hall Ox 52. **d** 54 **p** 55 Chelmsf. C of Rayleigh 54-56; V of St Andr Northn 56-60; Werrington 60-70; R of The Quinton 70-76; P-in-c of Wolverley Dio Worc from 76; Cookley Dio Worc from 81. *Wolverley Vicarage, Kidderminster, DY11 5XD.* (Kidderminster 851133)

CIRIMUUTA, Elijah. St Jo Sem Lusaka 56. **d** 58 **p** 60 Mashon. P Dio Mashon. *St Paul's Church, P.O. Box 268, Sinoia, Rhodesia.*

CITASHE, Justice. St Bede's Coll Umtata 72. **d** 73 Port Eliz. C of Ch of Ascen City and Dio Port Eliz from 73. *Box 681, Cradock, S Africa.* (Cradock 479)

CITELELA, Nathan. **d** 41 **p** 42 N Rhod. P Dio N Rhod 41-64; Dio Zam from 64. *USPG, Fiwila, Zambia.*

CIZA, Antoine. **d** 75 **p** 76 Buye. P Dio Buye. *Buhiga D/S 127, Bujumbura, Burundi.*

CLAASENS, Charles. b 54. St Pet Coll Natal. **d** 78 **p** 79 Geo. P Dio Geo 78-80; C of Bonteheuwel Dio Capetn from 81. *Priest's House, David Profit Street, Bonteheuwel 7764, CP, S Africa.*

CLACEY, Derek Phillip. b 48. St Jo Coll Nottm 76. **d** 79 Barking for Chelmsf **p** 80 Chelmsf. C of Gt Parndon Dio Chelmsf from 79. *23 Little Cattins, Sumners, Harlow, Essex.*

CLACK, Joseph John. b 14. Univ of Dur LTh 38. Clifton Th Coll 34. **d** 37 Bp Mounsey for Bradf **p** 38 Bradf. C of Slaidburn 37-40; Ingrow w Hainworth 40-42; St John Thornham w Gravelhole (in c of St Jas) 42-43; V of Austwick 43-52; Farsley 52-61; V of Kelbrook 61-76; P-in-c of Weston w Denton 76-81. *Flat 2, 23 St Mark's Avenue, Harrogate, N Yorks.*

CLACK, Canon Maurice Hammond. Univ of Lon BSc 24. Bps' Coll Cheshunt 25. **d** 27 **p** 28 Lon. C of St Matt Bethnal Green 27-31; Chap S Afr Ch Rly Miss Dio Pret 31-34; V of St Mary Lowgate Hull 34-39; C of St Mary's Cathl Johann 39-41; P-in-c of St Alb Miss Johann 41-45; R of St Wilfrid Hillcrest Pret 45-56; St Mark E Lon CP 56-64; St Francis Port Eliz 64-71; Archd of Port Eliz 68-72; R of Somerset E 71-74; Can of Port Eliz from 72; L to Offic Dio Bloemf 74-81; Perm to Offic Dio Pret from 81. *Irene Homes, Irene, 1675, S Africa.*

CLAGUE, Ven Arthur Ashford. b 15. St Jo Coll Dur BA 38, MA 41. Bp Wilson Th Coll IM 33. **d** 38 **p** 39 Man. C of St Mary Crumpsall 38-40; Lect of Bolton 40-44; R of Ch Ch Harpurhey 45-49; Golborne 49-69; Surr 52-69; V of Lezayre Dio S & M from 69; RD of Ramsey 72-78; Can of St German Cathl Peel from 77; Archd of Man from 78; Exam Chap to Bp of S & M from 78. *Lezayre Vicarage, Ramsey, IM.* (Ramsey 812500)

CLANCY, Michael. b 24. **d** 79 **p** 80 Glas. Hon C of St Silas City and Dio Glas from 79. *17 Williamwood Park, Netherlee, Glasgow, G44 3TD.*

CLAPHAM, John. **p** 81 Ex. b 47. Open Univ BA 76. Sarum Wells Th Coll 77. **d** 80 **p** 81 Ex. Dep PV Ex Cathl from 80. *7 Guildford Close, Exwick, Exeter, Devon.*

CLAPHAM, Kenneth. b 47. Trin Coll Bris 76. **d** 78 **p** 79 Liv. C of St Mark Newtown Pemberton Dio Liv from 78. *125 Victoria Street, Newtown, Wigan, Lancs.*

CLAPP, Nicholas Michel Edward. b 48. Univ of Wales (Cardiff) Dipl Th 74. St Mich AA Llan 71. **d** 74 **p** 75 Lich. C of St Gabr Fullbrook Walsall 74-77; St Cath Burnley 77-80; C-in-c of St Alb w St Paul Burnley 77-80; R of H Trin Blackley Dio Man from 80. *Holy Trinity Rectory, Blackley, Manchester, M9 1FE.* (061-205 2879)

CLAPSON, Clive Henry. b 55. Univ of Leeds BA 76. Trin Coll Tor 79. **d** 79 **p** 80 Ont. C of St Thos Belleville 79-80; I of Loughboro Dio Ont from 80. *Box 144, Sydenham, Ont, Canada.*

CLARE, Arthur Hargreaves. b 14. St Aid Coll 46. **d** 48 **p** 49 Glas. C of Ch Ch Glas 48-50; R 50-54; St Bart Gourock 54-60; Miss P Glenrothes and P-in-c of Ascen Leslie 60-64; V of Sutton Chesh 64-77; Aston-by-Sutton Dio Ches from 77. *Aston Vicarage, Sutton Weaver, Runcorn, Chesh.* (Aston 225)

CLARE, Lionel Philip. b 19. St Aid Coll 46. **d** 49 **p** 50 Ripon. C of St Chad Far Headingley Leeds 49-52; Low Harrogate 52-54; R of Addingham 54-66; V of Sunnyside w Bourne End 66-74; Kirkbymoorside w Gillamoor Farndale and Bransdale Dio York from 74. *Vicarage, Kirkbymoorside, York, YO6 6AZ.* (Kirkbymoorside 31452)

CLARE, Thomas Charles Hunter. b 10. Selw Coll Cam BA 33, MA 37. Bede Coll Dur 37. **d** 38 **p** 39 Dur. C of Ch Ch Gateshead 38-42; Ch Ch Morningside Edin 42-46; Birstall and Wanlip 46-48; St Aug New Basford 48-50; R of Saxelbye w Grimston and Shoby Dio Leic from 51. *Saxelbye Rectory, Melton Mowbray, Leics.* (Asfordby 213)

CLAREY, Harry. b 09. Worc Ordin Coll 65. **d** 66 **p** 67 Linc. C of Thornton w Martin 66-70; P-in-c of Nettleton Dio Linc from 70; Swallow w Cabourn Dio Linc from 70. *School House, Caistor, Lincoln.* (Caistor 851494)

CLARINGBULL, Denis Leslie. b 33. K Coll Lon and Warm BD and AKC 57. Knowling Sermon Pri & Clothworkers Co Exhib Univ of Lon. **d** 58 Croydon for Cant **p** 59 Cant. C of St Aug Croydon 58-62; Industr Chap to Bp of Croydon 62-71; Industr Chap Dio Cov and Chap of Cov Cathl 71-75; Succr of Cov Cathl 72-75; V of St Phil Norbury 75-79; Sen Industr Chap Dio Birm from 79. *197 Russel Road, Moseley, Birmingham, B13 8RR.* (021-449 1435)

CLARK, Canon Albert Ethelbert. **d** 24 **p** 26 Gippsld. C of Gormandale 24-26; V of Alberton 26-29; Bruthen 29-32; R of Trafalgar 32-37; RD of Warragul 36-37 and from 43; R of Toora 37-43; RD of Toora 39-43; P-in-c at Warragul 43-46; R 46-50; Hon Can of St Paul's Cathl Sale 49-56; Can (Emer) from 56; R of Lakes Entrance 50-55; Perm to Offic Dio Gippsld from 55. *Williams Road, Lakes Entrance, Vic., Australia 3909.* (051-55 1943)

CLARK, Albert Percival. b 17. Late Exhib of Hatf Coll Dur LTh and BA 39. St Bonif Coll Warm 36. **d** 40 **p** 41 Linc. C of Wildmore 40-42; St Aid New Cleethorpes 42-44; St Boltoph Linc 44-46; V of Strubby w Woodthorpe and Maltby R 46-50; R and Dir of Miss Wepener 50-52; V of Newc 52-57; Pinetown 57-61; R of The Quinton 61-70; V of Werrington 70-77; R of St Jas Dundee, Natal 77-80; Chipping Warden w Edgcote and Aston-le-Walls Dio Pet from 80. *Chipping Warden Rectory, Banbury, Oxon.* (Chipping Warden 256)

CLARK, Alexander Rees. St D Coll Lamp BA 48. **d** 51 Bp R W Jones for Llan **p** 52 St D. C of Yspytty-Ystwth w Ystradmeurig 51-53; Eglwys Newydd 53-55; V of Gwynfe w Llanddeusant 55-61; Pontyates 61-74; Surr from 61; V of Yspytty-Cynfyn w Llantrisant Dio St D from 74. *Yspytty-Cynfyn Vicarage, Ponterwyd, Aberystwyth, Dyfed.*

CLARK, Alfred Reeves. b 06. MC 44. Mil Knight of Windsor 71. Lon Coll of Div 53. **d** 55 Sarum for Lah **p** 57 Lah. CMS Miss Dio Lah 56-63; Chap HM Pris Liv 64; HM Pris Parkhurst 65-69; L to Offic Dio Sarum 70-71; Dio Ox from 71. *16 Lower Ward, Windsor Castle, Berks.*

CLARK, Arthur David. Bps' Coll Cheshunt 65. **d** 65 **p** 66 Ox. C of St Mich Tilehurst 66-72; Perm to Offic Dio Sarum 71-77; P-in-c of E Grafton, Tidcombe & Fosbury 77-79; C of Edington 79-81; Sidbury Dio Ex from 81. *Cotford Rise, Sidbury, Sidmouth, Devon.*

CLARK, Arthur Towers. OBE 45. AKC 36. **d** 36 Bradf **p** 37 Bp Mounsey for Bradf. C of Guiseley 36-40; V of Esholt w Hawksworth 40-48; Chap RAF 48-50; Chap Lon Hosp 50-51; C of Leeds and Chap Leeds Gen Infirm 51-56; V of Robert Town 56-58. *17 Pledwick Lane, Sandal, Wakefield, Yorks.*

CLARK, Bernard Charles. b 34. Open Univ BA 81. SOC 65. **d** 68 Warrington for Liv **p** 69 Liv. C of Pemberton 68-71; Winwick 71-73; P-in-c of St Barn Warrington 73-76; V 76-78; Hindley Dio Liv from 78. *Hindley Vicarage, Wigan, Lancs, WN2 3XA.* (Wigan 55175)

CLARK, Bruce Lee. St Jo Coll Morpeth 44. ACT ThL 48. **d** 47 Bath **p** 64 Melb. C of Coonambie 47-48; Hon C of St Jas Turramurra 49-51; St Jas E Malvern 52; Asst Master Geelong Gr Sch 53-54; Sen Master Knox Gr Sch 55-60; Hon C of St Paul Frankston 64-66; Chap Peninsula Sch Mt Eliza from 64. *39 Foote Street, Frankston, Vic, Australia 3199.* (03-783 2537)

CLARK, Bruce Quinton. St Francis Coll Brisb ACT ThL 63. **d** 63 Bp Hudson for Brisb **p** 63 Brisb. C of All SS Chermside Brisb 63-65; St Matt Groveley Brisb 65-67; V of Miles 67-70; R of Gayndah 70-76; Gympie Dio Brisb from 76. *St Peter's Rectory, Gympie, Queensland, Australia 4570.* (82 2629)

CLARK, Charles Gordon Froggatt. b 07. Em Coll Cam BA 29, MA 33. Wycl Hall Ox 29. **d** 31 **p** 32 Lon. C of St John Ealing Dean 31-33; St Matt Bayswater 33-35; R of Ilmington 35-40; PC of Somercotes 40-43; R of Barton Seagrave 43-48; V of Crowborough 48-67; Chap Crowborough Hosp 59-67; Kent and Sussex Hosp and Homoeopathic Hosp Tunbridge Wells Dio Roch 67-80; C of Penshurst & Fordcombe Dio Roch from 80; Chap Tunbridge Wells and Distr Maternity Home 74-77; Commis Ekiti from 66; L to Offic Dio Roch from 67; Perm to Offic Dios Cant and Chich from 67. *Froggatt Edge, Orchard Rise, Groombridge, Tunbridge Wells, TN3 9RZ.* (Groombridge 777)

CLARK, Colin Ashley. BD (Lon) 61. Moore Th Coll Syd 61. ACT ThL (2nd cl) 62. **d** 61 Bp Kerle for Syd **p** 62 Syd. C of Manly 61-64; V of Te Ngawai 64-67; C of St John Darlinghurst Syd 67-68; Asst Master Gr Sch for Girls Darlinghurst 68-72; Prin Moss Vale Gr Sch 72-75; Perm to Offic Dio

C & Goulb from 75. *9 Lyster Place, Melba, ACT, Australia 2615.*

CLARK, David George Neville. Linc Coll Ox BA 49, MA 59. Wells Th Coll 49. **d** 51 **p** 52 S'wark. C of Sanderstead 51-54; St Jo Bapt Southend Lewisham 54-59; V of St Barn, Sutton New Town 59-72; R of Charlwood Dio S'wark from 72; Sidlow Bridge Dio S'wark from 77. *Charlwood Rectory, Horley, Surrey, RH6 0EE.* (0293-862 343)

CLARK, David Gordon. b 29. Clare Coll Cam BA 52, MA 57. Ridley Hall Cam 52. **d** 54 **p** 55 Chelmsf. C of St Jo Evang Walthamstow 54-57; St Andr Gt Ilford 57-60; V of St Jo Evang Walthamstow 60-69; R of Stansted Dio Roch from 69. *Rectory, Fairseat, Sevenoaks, Kent.* (Fairseat 822494)

CLARK, David Humphrey. b 39. G and C Coll Cam BA 60. Wells Th Coll 62. **d** 64 **p** 65 Man. C of Leigh 64-68; Prec and Min Can of Man Cathl 68-70; C-in-c of St Clem w St Edm and St Geo Colegate Nor 70-76; St Sav w St Paul Nor 70-76; Industr Chap Dio Nor from 70; Hon Min Can of Nor Cathl 74-79; R of Norwich Over-the-Water 76-79; Hon C of St Pet Mancroft City and Dio Nor from 79. *42 Heigham Road, Norwich, NR2 3AU.* (Norwich 25734)

CLARK, Dennis Henry Graham. b 26. St Steph Ho Ox. **d** 55 **p** 56 Lon. C of St Geo Southall 55-58; St Steph Worc 58-61; Chap RAF 61-78; Asst Chap in Chief from 78; Chap St Clem Danes Lon from 79. *c/o Ministry of Defence, Adastral House, WC 1.*

CLARK, Donald Burbidge. K Coll NS BA 50. Dalhousie Univ MA 51. Trin Coll Tor LTh 58; **d** 57 **p** 58 Ott. I of Lanark Miss 58-60; R of Hawkesbury 60-64; V of St Bart Cathl B'pore 64-67; Dom Chap to Bp of B'pore 64-67; Sec for Asia and Pacific Angl Ch of Canada 67-78; I of Fitzroy Harbour Dio Ott from 78. *Fitzroy Harbour, Ont, Canada.* (613-623 3882)

CLARK, Donald Waltfred. N Texas State Coll BA 48. Trin Coll Tor LTh 52, STB 54. **d** and **p** Dallas 52. [f in Amer Ch] C of St Thos Tor 65-67; R of St Cuthb Oakville Niag 67-70; R of All SS, Windsor 70-75; P-in-c of St Jude Tor 76-77; All H Tor 77-81; on leave. *c/o Box 279, Peace River, Alta, Canada.*

CLARK, Douglas Austin. b 15 Univ of Dur LTh 41. Univ of Lon BA 51. Oak Hill Th Coll 38. **d** 41 **p** 42 Lon. C of St Luke Kilburn 41-43; Chap RAFVR 43-48; C of Ch Ch Cockfosters Trent Park (in c of St Paul Hadley Wood) 48-52; V of St Cuthb Chitts Hill Wood Green 52-58; St Jo Bapt Folkestone 58-66; St Matt Rugby 66-81; Commiss Moro 65-81. *c/o Balfour Court, Glen Waverley, Vic, Australia 3150.*

CLARK, Ven Earl Norville. McMaster Univ Ont BA 41. Trin Coll Tor LTh 43. **d** 42 **p** 43 Niag. I of Fonthill and Port Robinson 43-50; R of St Mark Hamilton 50-53; St Mary Hamilton Dio Niag from 53; Exam Chap to Bp of Niag 63-73; Dom Chap 75-78; Hon Can of Niag 64-78; Archd of Hamilton from 78. *42 Owen Place, Stoney Creek, Ont., Canada.* (416-561 8086)

CLARK, Edward Robert. b 39. Late Exhib of Ex Coll Ox BA (2nd cl Th) 61, MA 65. St Steph Ho Ox 61. **d** 63 **p** 64 Birm. C of Solihull 63-67; Perm to Offic Dio Bris 67-69; Dio Leic 69-71; Dio Ox 71-80; Dio St Alb from 80. *13 Warmark Road, Hemel Hempstead, HP1 3PZ.* (0442 46305)

CLARK, Eric Douglas Colbatch. b 08. MBE 62, OBE 66. St Jo Coll Ox BA 29. Wycl Hall Ox 39. **d** 40 Lon for Col Bp **p** 41 Niger. Prin Dennis Mem Sch Onitsha 37-50; Prin CMS Gr Sch Freetown 51-52; Prin Rural Tr Centre Asaba 52-56 and 59-66; Sec for Overseas Visitors CMS 57-59; Dom Chap to Bp of Sier L 66-70; CMS Rep Dio Sier L 66-70; Actg Dir Overseas Stud Commendation Centre Lon 70-71; Warden Stud Res Centre Wimbledon from 72. *35 Arterberry Road, SW20 8AG.*

CLARK, Ernest Stanley Edward. b 10. Worc Ordin Coll 60. **d** 62 Bp Stuart for Worc **p** 63 Worc. C of Halesowen (in c of St Pet Lapal) 62-65; R of Leadenham (w Welbourn from 67) Dio Linc 65-71; C-in-c of Welbourn 65-67; R of Shaw-cum-Donnington 71-76; Perm to Offic Dio Pet from 76; Dio Ox from 78. *21 Townsend Lane, Thorpe Mandeville, Banbury, Oxon OX17 2EU.*

CLARK, Frederick Albert George. b 15. MBE (Mil) 68. ACP 66. **d** 67 **p** 68 Glouc. C of Stroud Dio Glouc from 67. *2 Terrace Cottages, Thrupp, Stroud, Glos.* (Brimscombe 882060)

CLARK, Gerald Hurley. Univ of NZ BSc 54, Univ of Cant BA 65. NZ Bd of Th Stud LTh 67. Univ of Kent MA 70. **d** 58 **p** 59 Centr Tang. Asst Master Alliance Sch Dodoma 58-61; C of Dodoma Cathl 59-61; Hd Master Livingstone Coll Kigoma 62-67; Perm to Offic Dio Cant 68-69; L to Offic Dio Auckld 70-71; Hon C of Ch Ch Ellerslie 71-73; Prin Samuel Marsden Colleg Sch Wel from 74; Offg Min Dio Wel 74-78; Hon C of Karori Dio Wel from 78. *Samuel Marsden School, Karori, Wellington, NZ.* (769-454)

CLARK, Harold Clive. St Paul's Th Coll Grahmstn. **d** 54 **p** 55 Johann. C of Orange Grove 54-56; Springs 56-68; R of Mayfair Johann 58-60; C of Morden Surrey 60-62; R of Verulam 62-68; Chap Michaelho Sch Natal 68-77; V of Green I Dio Dun from 77. *15 Muir Street, Green Island, Dunedin, NZ.* (883-220)

CLARK, Henry. b 23. K Coll Lon and Warm AKC 52. **d** 53 Glouc **p** 54 Bp Barkway for Cant. C of St Barn Tuffley Glouc 53-56; C of High Wycombe (in c of St John) 56-63; V of St Chad Middlesbrough Dio York from 63. *9 Emerson Avenue, Middlesbrough, Cleve.* (Middlesbrough 819854)

✠ **CLARK, Most Rev Howard Hewlett.** Univ of Tor BA 32. Trin Coll Tor DD (*jure dig*) 45. Em Coll Sktn Hon DD 55. Bp's Univ Lennox Hon DCL 60. Univ of Manit Hon LLD 66. **d** 30 **p** 32 Ott. C of St John Norway Tor 30-32; Ch Ch Cathl Ott 32-38; P-in-c 38; R 39-54; Can of Ott 41-45; Dean of Ott 49-54; Cons Ld Bp of Edmon in All SS Cathl Edmon 25 Jan 54 by Abp of Rupld (Primate); Bps of Sask; Bran; Athab; Sktn; Calg; and Keew; Elected Primate of All Canada 59; Trld to Rupld 61; Res 70; Episc Can of Colleg Ch Jer 60-70; Chan Univ Trin Coll Tor from 71. *252 Glenrose Avenue, Toronto 290, Ont., Canada.*

CLARK, Hugh Lockhart. b 44. Oak Hill Th Coll 69. **d** 72 **p** 73 Stepney for Lon. C of St Jude Mildmay Pk Islington 72-75; N Walsham 75-78; Team V of S Molton 78-81; CF from 81. *c/o Ministry of Defence, Bagshot Park, Bagshot, Surrey, GU19 5PL.*

CLARK, Ian. b 31. Lich Th Coll 63. **d** 65 **p** 66 Man. C of Droylsden 65-68; St Thos Bedford-Leigh 68-70; V of Broughton Moor 70-80; R of Kirton Dio Southw from 80; V of Walesby Dio Southw from 80; P-in-ic of Egmanton Dio Southw 80-81; V from 81. *Walesby Vicarage, Newark, Notts, NG22 9PA.* (Mansfield 860522)

CLARK, Ian Duncan Lindsay. b 35. K Coll Cam BA 59, MA 63, PhD 64. Linacre Ho Ox BA 62, Dipl Th (w distinc) 63. Ripon Hall Ox 62. **d** 64 **p** 65 Newc T. C of Willington-on-Tyne 64-66; Lect Bp's Coll Calc 66-76; Vice-Prin 69-76; Chap St Cath Coll Cam 76-78; Tutor from 78; Dean of Chap from 80. *St Catharine's College, Cambridge, CB2 1RL.*

CLARK, Ian Mortimer. b 46. St Jo Coll Morpeth 78. **d** and **p** 80 Newc. C of Cessnock Dio Newc from 80. *Rectory, Mulbring Street, Averdare 2325, NSW, Australia.*

CLARK, Ivor Herbert. Univ of Wales BA 38. St Mich Coll Llan 37. **d** 38 **p** 39 Mon. C of H Trin Newport 38-40; CF (EC) 40-46; R of Shabani 46; Asst Master and Chap at Guinea Fowl Sch S Rhod 46-61; Chingola High Sch Zambia 61-63; Ch Gr Sch Launceston Tas 64-67; Bal Coll from 68. *Ballarat College, Ballarat, Vic. 3350, Australia.*

CLARK, Jack. b 14. St Andr Coll Pampisford 47. **d** 49 **p** 50 S'wark. C of St Jo Evang E Dulwich 49-52; Merstham 52-59; V of St Barn Southfields 59-75; C of Kingswood 75-80; Perm to Offic Dio S'wark from 80. *7 White Knobs Way, Caterham, Surrey, CR3 6RH.* (Caterham 47653)

CLARK, James David. St Jo Coll Morpeth 66. **d** 68 **p** 69 C & Goulb. C of Wagga Wagga S 68-73; R of Marulan 7376; P-in-c of Belconnen C Canberra Dio C & Goulb from 76. *136 Drake Brockman Drive, Holt, ACT, Australia 2615.*

CLARK, John David. b 40. Univ of Manit BA 65, BTh 68. **d** 67 **p** 68 Bran. Sec of Synod Bran 69-72; Hon C of St Chad Winnipeg 73-80; Reg Coordinator of Pastoral Services Dio Tor from 80. *Box 12000, Barrie, Ont, Canada.*

CLARK, John David Stanley. b 36. Univ of Dur BA (Social Stud) 64. Ridley Hall Cam 64. **d** 66 Hulme for Man **p** 67 Man. C of Benchill 66-69; Beverley Minster 69-74; Perm to Offic Dio Southw 74-76; L to Offic 76-77; Chap Miss to Seamen Port of Lon 77-80; L to Offic Dio Chelmsf 77-80; Perm to Offic Dio York from 80. *33 Bagdale, Whitby, N Yorks, YO21 1QL.* (Whitby 603254)

CLARK, John Edward Goodband. b 49. Chich Th Coll 70. **d** 73 **p** 74 Nor. C of Thorpe-Episcopi 73-76; St Anne Earlham 76-78; Chap RN from 78. *c/o Ministry of Defence, Lacon House, Theobalds Road, WC1X 8RY.*

CLARK, John Leslie. Em Coll Sask BA and LTh 44. **d** 44 **p** 45 Sask. I of Paddockwood 44-47; Ashcroft and Clinton 47-51; Hon Can of Carib 50-51; R of All SS Miss New Westmr 51-54; W Field Sec GBRE 54-59; R of Sapperton Dio New Westmr 59-69; Exam Chap to Bp of New Westmr 66-71; R of White Rock 70-76; St Helen Surrey Dio New Westmr from 76. *10787 128th Street, Surrey, BC, Canada.*

CLARK, John Mansell. b 19. Sarum Wells Th Coll 78. **d** 80 Chich **p** 81 Horsham for Chich (NSM). C of Warnham Dio Chich from 80. *Goosegreen Farm, Broadbridge Heath Road, Warnham, Horsham, Sussex, RH12 3RS.*

CLARK, John Nicholson. Bps' Coll Cheshunt. **d** 64 **p** 65 Ox. C of St Pet Maidenhead 64-67; V of Cranbourne 67-74. *3 Prince Albert Drive, King's Ride, Ascot, Berks.* (Ascot 21828)

CLARK, John Patrick Hedley. b 37. St Cath Coll Cam 2nd cl Mod Lang Trip pt ii BA 61, MA 65. Worc Coll Ox BA (Th)

63, MA 72, BD 74. St Steph Ho Ox 61. **d** 64 **p** 65 Birm. C of Highter's Heath 64-67; Eglingham 67-72; P-in-c of St Ann Newc T 72-77; V of Long Framlington w Brinkburn Dio Newc T from 77. *Long Framlington Vicarage, Morpeth, Northumb, NE65 8AQ.* (Long Framlington 200)

CLARK, John Ronald Lyons. b 47. Trin Coll Dub BA 69, MA 72. Div Hostel Dub 67. **d** 70 **p** 71 Down. C of St Mark Dundela Belf 70-72; CF 72-75; C of St Aid Belf 75-76; R of Stranorlar w Kilteevogue and Meenglass 76-81; Chap Wythenshawe Hosp Man from 81. *8 Heath Road, Timperley, Cheshire, WA15 6BH.*

✠ **CLARK, Right Rev John Thomas.** CBE 76. Univ of Dur BA 39. St Pet Coll Ja 33. **d** 33 **p** 35 Ja. C of Golden Grove w Bath 33-34; Halfway Tree 34-37; C-in-c of Balaclava w Keynsham 37-38; C of St Luke Cross Roads 39; St Geo Kingston 40-46; Hambleden w Frieth 46-47; R of Halfway Tree 47-68; Exam Chap to Bp of Ja 50-68; P-in-c of Swallowfield Miss 50-54; Hon Can of Ja 51-68; Cons Ld Bp Suffr of Kingston in Cathl Ch of St Jago de la Vega Spanish Town Ja 30 Nov 68 by Abp of W Indies; Bps of Hond; Antig; Ja; and Puerto Rico (USA); res 76. *Dunscomb, Friary Hill PO, Jamaica, W Indies.* (099-33432)

CLARK, Keith Noel. Univ of Queensld BA (2nd cl Hist) 61. St Jo Coll Morpeth ACT ThL 56. **d** 60 **p** 61 Newc. C of Taree 60-63; E Maitland 63-68; R of The Entrance Dio Newc from 68. *287 The Entrance Road, The Entrance, NSW, Australia 2261.* (043-32 2374)

CLARK, Canon Kenneth James. b 22. DSC 44. St Cath S Ox BA 48, MA 52. Cudd Coll 52. **d** 52 Malmesbury for Bris **p** 53 Bris. C of Brinkworth 52-53; Cricklade w Latton 53-56; C-in-c of H Cross Conv Distr Filwood Park Bris 56-59; V of H Cross, Inns Court, Bris 59-61; Westbury-on-Trym 61-72; St Mary Redcliffe w Temple and St Jo Bapt Bedminster Dio Bris from 72; RD of Bedminster 73-79; P-in-c of St Mich AA Bedminster 73-78; Hon Can of Bris from 74; M Gen Syn from 80. *10 Redcliffe Parade West, Bristol, BS1 6SP.* (Bris 291962)

CLARK, Lance Edgar Dennis. b 52. Linc Th Coll 74. **d** 77 **p** 78 Southw. C of Arnold Dio Southw from 77. *27 Churchmoor Lane, Arnold, Nottingham, NG5 8HL.*

CLARK, Malcolm Aiken. b 05. Lich Th Coll 32. **d** 34 **p** 35 Glas. C of St John Greenock (in C of St Steph Carsdyke) 38; R of All SS Lockerbie 38-49; All SS Langholm 39-42; Chap RAFVR 42-46; P-in-c of St Mary Dalkeith 49-56; R of Good Shepherd Edin 56-77; Chap St Vincent Chap Edin from 77. *1 Darnaway Street, Edinburgh, EH3 6DW.*

CLARK, Martin Hudson. b 46. K Coll Lon BD 68, AKC 68. St Aug Coll Cant 70. **d** 71 **p** 72 S'wark. C of H Trin, S'wark 71-74; St Pet Parkstone 74-77; V of E Wickham Dio S'wark from 77. *St Michael's Vicarage, Upper Wickham Lane, Welling, Kent DA16 3AP.* (01-304 1214)

CLARK, Neville Shirley. b 51. Univ of Birm BA 72. Cudd Coll Ox 72. **d** 75 **p** 76 Cant. C of St Mich AA Croydon Dio Cant from 75. *St Michael's Vicarage, Poplar Walk, Croydon, Surrey, CRO 1UA.* (01-688 0694)

CLARK, Percy. Coll of Resurr Mirfield 32. **d** 34 **p** 35 Glas. C of H Trin Paisley 34-36; Ch Ch Newc T 36-37; P-in-c of Cambusland 37-39; V of St Matt Hutts Gate 38-44; R of St Paul Capetn 44-54; Groot Drakenstein 54-61; Ch K Claremont 61-66; Wellington 66-71; Perm to Offic Dio Capetn from 73. *17 Riverside Mews, Somerset West 7130, CP, S Africa.*

CLARK, Peter. b 39. Ch Coll Cam BA 61, MA 65. Chich Th Coll 61. **d** 63 **p** 64 Wakef. C of Huddersfield 63-67; St Jo Evang (in c of All SS w St Columb) Notting Hill Kens 67-74; R of St Patr Grenada Windw Is 75-79; P-in-c of St Patr Hove Dio Chich from 79; Ch Ch Brighton Dio Chich from 80. *30 Cambridge Road, Hove, E Sussex, BN3 1DF.* (Brighton 733151)

CLARK, Peter Norman. b 53. Qu Coll Cam BA 79. Westcott Ho Cam 78. **d** 80 **p** 81 Bris. C of St Mary Redcliffe Bedminster Dio Bris from 80. *2 Colston Parade, Bristol, BS1 6RA.*

CLARK, Peter William. b 49. Moore Th Coll Syd ThL 78. **d** 78 **p** 79 Armid. V of Mungindi Dio Armid from 78. *Vicarage, Bucknell Street, Mungindi, NSW, Australia 2406.*

CLARK, Peter William Footner. b 1895. Kelham Th Coll. M SSM 22. **d** 24 **p** 25 Linc. C of St Swithin Linc 24-26; Publ Pr Dio Southw from 26. *St Paul's Priory, Quernmore, Lancaster.*

CLARK, Reginald. Moore Th Coll Syd 62. **d** 63 **p** 64 Syd. C of St Mark S Hurstville 63-64; St Andr Wahroonga 64-66; Liverpool 66-67; P-in-c of St Mark Green Valley 67-71; S Pilbara 71-75; R of Denistone E w Marsfield 76-80; Pris Chap Dio Syd from 81. *5 Prince Edward Street, Malabar, NSW, Australia 2036.* (661-4519)

CLARK, Ven Reginald Harlan. AKC 38. St Aug Coll Cant 39. **d** 39 Tewkesbury for Glouc **p** 40 Glouc. C of Dursley 39-42; P-in-c of St Columba Miss Bulawayo 42-49; Darambe 49-56; R of Umtali 56-76; Hon Can of Mashon 64-65; Can of St Mary and All SS Cathl Salisbury from 65; Archd of Umtali 65-66; Mashon from 75; R of Ruwa Dio Mashon from 77. *Box 122, Ruwa, Zimbabwe.*

CLARK, Reginald Isaac. b 16. AKC 47. **d** 47 Bp Walsh for Ely **p** 48 Ely. C of Somersham w Pidley and Colne 47-49; Luton 49-53; Min of St Chris Eccles Distr Round Green 53-59; V 59-65; Chap Shenley Hosp from 65. *Shenley Hospital, Radlett, Herts, WD7 9HB.* (Radlett 5631)

CLARK, Richard Eugene. W Washington State Coll BA 52. Berkeley Bapt Div Sch BD 55. **d** and **p** 60 Calg. C of St Steph Calg 60-61; I of H Nativ Calg 61-67. *c/o Anglican Church House, 881a 17th Avenue South West, Calgary, Alta., Canada.*

CLARK, Ven Richard Rex. Univ of NZ BA 37, MA 40. NZ Bd of Th Stud LTh 38. **d** 39 **p** 40 Auckld. C of St Mary's Cathl Auckld 39-42; Chap NZMF 42-47; C of St Pet Ealing 48-49; Chap and Hd Master St Mich Sch Kobe Japan 49-52; V of Waitara 53-57; Claudelands 57-76; Katikati 76-79; Can of Waik 60-62; Archd of Waitomo 62-76; Archd (Emer) from 76; Perm to Offic Dio Wai from 80. *Ruamoana Place, Omokoroa, RD2, Tauranga, NZ.*

CLARK, Canon Robert James Vodden. b 07. Edin Th Coll 40. **d** 41 **p** 42 Edin. C of St Paul and St Geo (in c of St Barn Miss) Edin 41-44; R of St Andr Fort William 44-48; Warden of the Scottish Centre of Outdoor Tr and L to Offic Dio Moray (in c of St Jo Bapt Miss Rothiemurchus) 48-49; C-in-c of St D of Scotld Pilton Edin 49-54; CF (TA) 50-60; R of Ch Ch Falkirk 54-69; Can of Edin 62-76; Hon Can from 76; Dean of Edin 67-76; R of Lasswade 69-79. *15 North Street, St Andrews, Fife.*

CLARK, Robin. b 27. Univ of Lon BA (2nd cl French) 49. BD (Lon) 69, M Phil (Lon) 77. St Jo Coll Dur Dipl Th 54. **d** 54 **p** 55 Man. C of Newton Heath 54-58; Asst Master Woodhouse Gr Sch Sheff 58-61; R of Brant Broughton w Stragglethorpe Dio Linc from 61; C-in-c of Welbourn 65-66; RD of Loveden from 72. *Rectory, Brant Broughton, Lincoln, LN5 0SL.* (Loveden 72449)

CLARK, Preb Roland Mark Allison. b 21. St Cath Coll Cam BA 48, MA 53. Wells Th Coll 48. **d** 50 **p** 51 S'wark. C of St Paul Battersea 50-52; St Alfege w St Pet Greenwich 52-56; Chap RNVR 53-56; PC of Wilton 56-68; V 68-79; RD of Taunton S 60-65; Preb of Wells Cathl from 63; Proc Conv B & W from 64; R of Backwell Dio B & W from 79; RD of Portishead from 82. *Backwell Rectory, Bristol, BS19 3JJ.* (Flax Bourton 2391)

CLARK, Ronald Percy. b 14. **d** 79 **p** 80 Wai. Hon C of St Jo Cathl Napier from 79. *Morse Street, Napier, NZ.*

CLARK, Roy. b 21. MBE (Mil) 64. Roch Th Coll 65. **d** 67 Grantham for Linc **p** 68 Linc. C of New Sleaford 67-70; V of Eastville and New Leake w Midville 70-72. *Address temp unknown.*

CLARK, Ven Sidney Harvie. b 05. Jes Coll Cam BA 27, MA 31. Westcott Ho Cam 29. **d** 30 **p** 31 Dur. C of St Mary Gateshead 30-34; St Mary Portsea 34-36; R of Jarrow 36-40; St Jo Evang Edin 40-47; Wishaw 47-48; V of Harborne 48-67; Archd of Birm and Hon Can of Birm 47-67; Proc Conv Birm 47-67; Archd of Stow 67-75; V of Hackthorn w Cold Hanworth 67-75; Can and Preb of Linc Cathl 67-77; Archd and Can (Emer) from 77. *Stow House, Skillington, Grantham, Lincs.* (Grantham 860447)

CLARK, Stephen. b 52. Adel Coll of Advanced Educn Dipl Th 75, BTh 79. St Barn Th Coll Adel 77. **d** 80 **p** 81 Adel. C of St Mary South Road Dio Adel from 80. *50 English Avenue, Clovelly Park, S Australia 5041.*

CLARK, Stephen Barry. Univ of Syd BA 59, MA 68, MEducn 68. **d** 72 Newc. Hon C of The Entrance Dio Newc from 72. *21 Trade Street, Newtown, NSW, Australia 2042.*

CLARK, Canon Thomas Russell Hope. Univ of Melb BA 36, ACT ThL 37. **d** 38 **p** 39 Melb. C of Ch Ch Brunswick 38-40; St Andr Brighton 40-41; Chap RAAF 41-46; V of St John Croydon 46-47; I of Ch Ch Brunswick Melb 48-52; Hampton 52-55; St John E Malvern 56-62; St John Camberwell 62-77; Can of Melb from 63; C in Dept of Evang and Ex Dio Melb from 77. *6-429 Glenferrie Road, Hawthorn, Vic., Australia 3122.* (818-8572)

CLARK, Trevor Bartholomew. b 44. Qu Coll Birm 68. **d** 71 **p** 72 Sheff. C of Maltby 71-75; V of New Rossington 75-80; Campsall Dio Sheff from 80. *Campsall Vicarage, Doncaster, S Yorks.* (Doncaster 700286)

CLARK, Vivian George. b 08. Chich Th Coll 31. TD 56. **d** 34 **p** 36 Truro. C of St Mary Truro and PV of Truro Cathl 34-37; C of St Sav w St Pet S'wark and PV of S'wark Cathl 37-41; Succr of S'wark Cathl, Dom Chap to Bp of S'wark and Offg Chap Guy's Hosp 39-41; CF (EC) 41-48; CF (TA) 48-62; Hon Sen CF from 62; V of Cardiston w Alberbury 48-52; R of Ightfield w Calverhall 52-59; V of Shifnal 59-74; V of Boningale 59-74; C-in-c of Stirchley 59-72; Surr from 60;

RD of Shifnal 70-74; C of Acton Burnell w Pitchford Dio Heref from 74. *The Glebe House, Cound, Shrewsbury, Shropshire* (Cross Houses 360)

CLARK, Wilfred. b 19. St Geo Windsor. **d** 56 **p** 57 Sheff. C of Aston w Aughton 56-60; V of St Pet Hoyland Dio Sheff from 60. *104 Hawshaw Lane, Hoyland, Barnsley, S Yorks, S74 0HH.* (Barnsley 742279)

CLARK, William. Qu Coll Birm 64. **d** 64 **p** 65 Matab. C of St Jo Bapt Cathl Bulawayo 64-67; L to Offic Dios Matab and Mashon 67-75; R of Saxby w Stapleford Garthorpe and Wyfordby 75-81. *Dulverton Hall, St Martin's Square, Scarborough, Yorks.*

CLARKE, Alan Clive. ACT ThL (2nd cl) 60. St Francis Coll Brisb 58. **d** 60 **p** 61 N Queensld. C of St Matt Townsville 60-63; Ayr 63-65; Cairns 65-66; R of Ganmain 66-69; C-in-c of St Phil Collingwood 69-72; St Matthias N Richmond 69-72; I of Black Rock 72-77; Perm to Offic Dio Melb 77-81; I of St Steph Gardenvale Dio Melb from 81. *111 North Road, Gardenvale, Vic, Australia 3185.*

CLARKE, Alan John. b 55. St Jo Coll Dur BA 77. Westcott Ho Cam 78. **d** 80 **p** 81 Dur. C of St Mary Heworth Dio Dur from 80. *Northfield, High Lanes, Heworth, Gateshead, T & W.*

CLARKE, Alfred Charles Reginald. b 19. ACII. Qu Coll Birm 71. **d** and **p** 74 Birm. C of Hay Mill 74-80; Packwood w Nuthurst and Hockley Dio Birm from 81. *15 Newton Road, Knowle, Solihull, W Midl.* (Knowle 3861)

CLARKE, Alfred Eugene. FTCL 44. **d** 60 Nass. C of Ch Ch Cathl Nass 60-67. *P.O. Box 653, Nassau, Bahamas, W Indies.*

CLARKE, Canon Anthony Ivan. Univ of Otago LLB 62. Selw Coll Dun. **d** 64 Bp McKenzie for Wel **p** 65 Wel. C of Levin 64-68; Chap HM Pris Te Awamutu 68-74; Can of Waik from 74; P-in-c of Hamilton Maori Past Dio Waik from 74. *2 Lyons Street, Hamilton, NZ.* (77-338)

CLARKE, Arthur. b 34. BD (Lon) 66. Univ of Nottm MPhil 75. Sarum Wells Th Coll 75. **d** 76 **p** 77 Southw. C of Wollaton 76-79; R of Sutton Bonington Dio Southw from 79; P-in-c of Normanton-on-Soar Dio Southw from 79. *Rectory, Sutton Bonington, Loughborough, Leics, LE12 5PF.* (Kegworth 2236)

CLARKE, Arthur. b 07. Wycl Coll Tor. **d** 33 **p** 34 Tor. C of Haliburton 33-35; I of Beeton w Tottenham and Polgrave 35-37; Chap (Eccles Est) Chakrata 37; Naini Tal 37-38; Jhansi 38; Fyzabad 39; Meerut 40-42; CF 42-46; Hon CF 46; Agra 46-48; V of Claybrooke W Wibtoft 49-51; Cl Org Sec C of E Children's S for Dios Derby Linc Sheff and Southw 51-59; V of Bleasby w Halloughton 59-69; C of Witheridge 69-73. *The Long House, Upper Westwood, Bradford-on-Avon, Wilts, BA15 2DF.*

CLARKE, Barry Bryan. b 52. McGill Univ Montr BTh 77. Montr Dioc Th Coll 76. **d** 78 **p** 79 Montr. C of St Matthias Westmount Montr 78-80; R of St Bruno Dio Montr from 80. *2075 Bedford Street, St Bruno, Quebec, Canada, J3V 4A9.* (514-653 9582)

CLARKE, Benjamin Albert. St Francis Coll Brisb 72. **d** 73 **p** 74 Brisb. C of Wynnym Brisb 73-74; St Luke Toowoomba 74-76; P-in-c of Allora Dio Brisb from 76. *St David's Rectory, Allora, Queensland, Australia 4362.* (076-69 3343)

CLARKE, Benjamin Blanchard. b 08. Univ of Birm Ascough Sch 28 and 30, BSc (1st cl Geol and Geog) and Panton Geol Pri 31, MSc 34. St Cath S Ox BA (2nd cl Th) 33, MA 37. Ripon Hall Ox 31. **d** 33 **p** 34 Birm. C of St Germain Edgbaston 33-37; St Barn (in c of St Marg) Erdington 37-40; V of St Matthias Birm 40-46; R of Byford w Mansell Gamage 46-55; Seq of Preston-on-Wye 46-55; V of Padstow 55-73; RD of Pydar 58-61; Perm to Offic Dio Truro from 73. *4 Athelstan Park, Bodmin, Cornwall, PL31 1DS.* (Bodmin 3989)

CLARKE, Bernard Ronald. b 53. Ridley Hall Cam 74. **d** 77 **p** 78 Portsm. C of Leigh Park 77; St Pet Petersfield w Sheet 78-81; Chap RN from 81. *Ministry of Defence, Lacon House, Theobalds Road, WC1X 8RY.*

CLARKE, Bert Richard. b 32. **d** 78 Bp Spence for Auckld **p** 79 Auckld. Hon C of Managere Miss Distr Dio Auckld from 78. *30 Jordan Road, Mangere, Auckland, NZ.* (57 476)

CLARKE, Christopher George. b 43. Sarum Th Coll 67. **d** 68 Thetford for Nor **p** 69 Nor. C of Sprowston 68-72; V of Hemsby 72-77; Sutton Courtenay w Appleford Dio Ox from 77. *Sutton Courtenay Vicarage, Abingdon, Oxon, OX14 4BD.*

CLARKE, Colin David Emrys. b 42. Wells Th Coll 67. **d** 68 S'wark **p** 69 Woolwich for S'wark. C of St Nich Plumstead 68-71; K Lynn 71-75; Asst Chap HM Pris Wakef 75-77; V of Birkenshaw w Hunsworth Dio Wakef from 77. *876 Bradford Road, Birkenshaw, Bradford, Yorks.* (Bradford 683776)

CLARKE, Cyril. Univ of Lon BA 24. Linc Th Coll 26. **d** 27 **p** 28 Linc. C of All SS Gainsborough 27-30; Crosby 30-34; V of Ancaster 34-39; R of Barnoldby-le-Beck 39-42; V of Ewerby w Evedon R 43-55; RD of Lafford N 53-73; R of Bloxholme w Digby 54-81; V of Ashby de la Launde 55-81; Rowston 59-81; Dioc Insp of Schs 57-81. *Address temp unknown.*

CLARKE, Daniel. b 17. Trin Coll Dub BA 39, MA 44, BD 66. **d** 41 **p** 42 Dub. C of St Bart Dublin 41-44; Dioc C of Killaloe 44-46; C-in-c of Corbally 46-49; Chap Roscrea Insts 46-49; I of Borrisokane w Ardcroney and Aglishclohane 49-59; RD of Lower Ormond (B) 51-58; Ely O'Carroll 58-59; Asst Master Robert Bloomfield CSM Sch Shefford 59-62; Reigate Gr Sch from 62; Chap from 73. *4 Orchard Way, Reigate, Surrey.* (Reigate 46169)

CLARKE, Very Rev David George Alexander. b 23. Trin Coll Dub BA 47, MA 51, BD 55, PhD 57. **d** 48 **p** 49 Clogh. C of Dromore 48-49; C-in-c of Drum 49-50; I of Clonbroney w Killoe 50-51; Clogher 52-54; C of Skibbereen 55-57; R of Usworth 57-61; Kilrossanty 61-73; RD of Dungarvan, Waterf and Lism 65-67; Can and Preb of St Patr Cathl Dub from 65; Prec of Waterf and Lism 67-73; Dean of Cash and R of St Jo Bapt City and Dio Cash from 73. *Deanery, Cashel, Co Tipperary, Irish Republic.* (062-61232)

CLARKE, David Leslie. b 10. Univ of S Wales & Mon BSc 32, MSc 34. **d** 73 **p** 74 Mon (APM). Asst Master Howardian High Sch Cardiff 53-75. *46 Llyswen Road, Cyncoed, Cardiff, CF2 6PP.* (Cardiff 753455)

CLARKE, Canon David Robert Lancelot. Univ of Tor BA 34. Trin Coll Tor LTh 36. **d** 36 Hur for Tor **p** 37 Tor. C of St Alb Tor 36-37; St Thos Tor 37-43; Chap RCAF 43-46; R of St Phil, City and Dio Tor from 46; Can of Tor from 72. *197 Caribou Road, Toronto 12, Ont., Canada.* (416-783 5606)

CLARKE, Douglas Charles. b 33. Bps' Coll Cheshunt 65. **d** 66 **p** 67 Chelmsf. C of Chingford 66-72; V of Ascen Collier Row 72-79; Bembridge Dio Portsm from 79. *Vicarage, Bembridge, IW, PO35 5NA.* (Bembridge 2175)

CLARKE, Dudley Barrington. Em Coll Cam BA 46, MA 48. Ridley Hall Cam 46. **d** 48 **p** 49 Guildf. C of H Trin Aldershot 48-50; Chap Monkton Combe Sch 50-58; Asst Master Hutchin's Sch Hobart 59-61; Hd Master Peninsula Sch Mt Eliza 61-71; Hutchins Sch Sandy Bay Dio Tas from 71. *99 Nelson Road, Sandy Bay, Tasmania 7005.* (002-25 2274)

CLARKE, Duncan James Edward. b 54. Wycl Hall Ox 75. **d** 78 **p** 79 Mon. C of St Andr Lliswerry Newport Mon 78-81. *Address temp unknown*

CLARKE, Edmund Wilson. Em Coll Sktn LTh 62. **d** 62 **p** 63 Calg. I of Coutts 62-66; Vulcan 66-72; on leave 73-74; R of St Andr Calg 74-80; Ch of Good Shepherd City and Dio Edmon from 80. *13428-127 Street, Edmonton, Alta, T5L 1B1, Canada.*

CLARKE, Edward. b 02. Univ of Dur LTh 28. St Jo Coll Dur BA 30, MA 32. St Aid Coll 25. **d** 29 **p** 30 Wakef. C of St Pet Huddersfield 29-34; V of Newsome 34-46; Golcar 46-51; Lupset 51-64; Kirkburton 64-70. RD of Kirkburton 68-70. *11 Rowley Drive, Lepton, Huddersfield, Yorks.*

CLARKE, Edward Pattison William. Univ of Perth BA 19, MA 23. ACT ThL 27, Th Scho 33. **d** and **p** 33 Adel. C of St Pet Glenelg and Asst Tutor St Barn Coll Adel 33; Asst Chap Trin Gr Sch Kew 33-35; L to Offic Dio Syd 36-37; and from 67; R of St Mary Waverley 37-67. *Mowll Memorial Village, Castle Hill Road, Castle Hill, NSW, Australia 2154.*

CLARKE, Edwin Joseph Alfred. b 18. Ripon Hall Ox 64. **d** 66 **p** 67 Birm. C of Yardley 66-70; R of Nether Whitacre w Lea Marston Dio Birm from 70. *Nether Whitacre Rectory, Coleshill, Birmingham, B46 2DU.* (Furnace End 81252)

✠ **CLARKE, Right Rev Edwin Kent.** Bp's Univ Lennox BA 54, LST 56. Hur Coll Ont DD. **d** 56 **p** 57 Ott. C of All SS Westboro 56-59; Dir of Christian Educn Dio Ott 60-66; R of St Lambert Montr 66-73; Dioc Sec Dio Niag 73-76; Archd of Niag 73-76; Cons Bp Suffr of Niag in Ch Ch Cathl Hamilton 30 May 76 by Abps of Ont and Rupld and Abp E W Scott (Primate); Bps of Niag, Ott, Hur, Caled, Alg and Bran; and others; Trld to Edmon 79. *10033-84th Avenue, Edmonton, Alta, T6E 2G6, Canada.* (403-439 7344)

CLARKE, Elwyn Keith. St Jo Coll Morpeth ACT ThL 41. **d** 37 Newc **p** 41 New Guinea. C of Scone 37-39; Mukawa 39-45; H Trin Fortitude Valley 45-46; Wingham 46-48; R of Jerry's Plains 48-52; Nabiac 51-58; V of Springsure 58-65; R of Killarney 65-73; C of Beaudesert 73-75. *29 Tina Street, Beaudesert, Queensland, Australia 4285.*

CLARKE, Eric Samuel. Univ of Nottm BSc 51. St Cath Coll Ox BA and MA 69. Wycl Hall Ox 51. **d** 54 **p** 55 Southw. C of Gedling 54-57; St Pet w St Jas Nottm 57-69; Asst Master of Nottm Bluecoat Sch 57-62; John Port Sch Derbys from 62; Perm to Offic Dio Derby from 63. *16 Menin Road, Kedleston Road, Derby.*

CLARKE, Frederick. King's Coll Lon AKC. Ely Th Coll 46. **d** 46 **p** 47 Sheff. C of H Trin Darnall 46-48; Cambrois 48-50; C-in-c of Moor Ends Conv Distr 50-56; V 56-58; Chap HM Borstal Inst Hatfield Yorks 56-58; V of Malin Bridge

58-62; R of Margaret River 62-66; Carlisle 66-78; Perm to Offic Dio Perth from 78. *5 Kennedya Road, Walliston, W Australia 6076.* (291 8006)

CLARKE, Geoffrey Spencer. Univ of Syd BA 49, LLB 52. Moore Th Coll Syd ACT ThL (1st cl) 57. **d** 58 Syd **p** 58 Bp Hilliard for Syd. C of Pymble 58-60; C-in-c of Keiraville 60-63; Regents Pk and Birrong Provisional Par 63-71; Putney Provisional Distr 71-77; Chap Concord Repatriation Hosp Dio Syd from 77. *26 Morrice Street, Lane Cove, NSW, Australia 2066.* (427-2474)

CLARKE, Gervais Angelo Morales. Univ of W Indies LTh 68, BA 74. Princeton Th Sem ThM 81. St Pet Coll Ja. **d** 66 **p** 67 Ja. C of Cross Roads 66-70; Chap Miss to Seamen Kingston from 68; R of St Geo Kingston Dio Ja from 70; Chap Bellevue Hosp from 70; Chap to Bp of Ja from 74. *34 Orane Avenue, Meadowbrook Mews, Kingston 19, Jamaica, WI.* (809 92 54343)

CLARKE, Gregory Neville. b 48. St Jo Coll Morpeth ThDip 75. **d** 75 **p** 76 Newc. C of Cessnock 75-77; E Maitland 77-78; New Lambton 78-80; R of Clarence Town Dio Newc from 80. *127 Queen Street, Clarence Town, NSW, Australia 2321.*

CLARKE, Harold. Sarum Th Coll 30. **d** 32 **p** 33 Dur. C of Beamish 32-35; Herrington (in c of St Chad) 35-38; PC of St Geo E Boldon 38-40; St Edm Bearpark 40-48; St Osw Hebburn-on-Tyne 48-57; V of Firtree (or Howden-le-Wear) 57-73; Perm to Offic Dio Dur from 73. *6 Swinburn Avenue, Darlington, Co Durham.*

CLARKE, Harold George. b 29. St D Coll Lamp 58. **d** 61 **p** 62 Mon. C of Ch Ch Ebbw Vale 61-64; St German, Roath 64-73; V of Glyntaff Dio Llan from 73; Chap Glamorgan Poly 73-74. *Glyntaff Vicarage, Pontypridd, Mid-Glam, CF37 4AS.* (Pontypridd 402535)

CLARKE, Harold Godfrey Coddrington. b 26. SOC 71. **d** 74 **p** 75 S'wark. C of Redhill 74-79; V of Blindley Heath Dio S'wark from 79. *Blindley Heath Vicarage, Nr Lingfield, Surrey, RH7 6HJ.* (Lingfield 832337)

CLARKE, Herbert Alan. b 23. Ely Th Coll 53. **d** 55 **p** 56 Ches. C of H Trin Ches 55-58; Ch Ch Ellesmere Port 58-59; R of Garveston w Thuxton 59-62; V of Plemstall w Guilden Sutton 62-67; St Thos Hyde 67-77; Wrenbury w Baddiley Dio Ches from 77. *Wrenbury Vicarage, Nantwich, Chesh.* (Crewe 780398)

CLARKE, Ven Herbert Lewis. b 20. Late Exhib of Jes Coll Ox BA (2nd cl Lit Hum) 43, 2nd cl Hons Th 45, MA 46. Union Th Sem NY STM *(magna cum laude)* 50. Linc Th Coll 44. **d** 45 **p** 46 St D. C of Llanelli 45-48; PV of Wells Cathl 48-49; Lect Wells Th Coll 48-49; Lect St D Coll Lamp 50-52; Lect Bp's Univ Lennox 52-54; Asst Prof 54-57; C-in-c of Barry I 57-59; Sub-Warden St Mich Coll Llan 59-67; L Exam Chap to Bp of Mon 61-73; to Bp of Llan from 65; R of Caerphilly 67-77; Surr from 68; Can of Llan Cathl 75-77; Archd of Llan from 77; R of St Fagan's w Michaelston-super-Ely Dio Llan from 77. *St Fagan's Rectory, Cardiff, CF5 6EL.* (Cardiff 565869)

CLARKE, Hilary James. b 41. St D Coll Lamp BA (2nd cl Th) 64. St Steph Ho Ox 64. **d** 66 **p** 67 Leic. C of Kibworth-Beauchamp w Kibworth Harcourt 66-68; Chap Miss for Deaf and L to Offic Dio Leic 68-71; Missr Miss for Deaf Walsall 71-73; L to Offic Dio Lich 71-73; Dio Leic from 73; Prin Officer Leic and Co Miss for Deaf from 73. *Leic & County Miss for the Deaf, 135 Welford Road, Leicester, LE2 6BE* (Leic 556776)

✠ **CLARKE, Right Rev James Charles MacLeod.** Trin Coll Tor BA 44, LTh 44. **d** 49 Tor for Calg **p** 50 Calg. C of St Steph Calg 49-51; Miss Fort Chimo 51-74; Hon Can of Arctic 62-65; Archd of Ungava 65-74; Dioc Archd Dio Arctic 74-79; Cons Bp Suffr of the Arctic at Frobisher Bay 30 Nov 79 by Abps of Rupld and Ont; Bps of the Arctic and Sktn; and Bp G Snell. *1055 Avenue Road, Toronto, Ont, M5N 2C8, Canada.*

CLARKE, John. St Aid Coll 62. **d** 65 Warrington for Liv for Nass **p** 66 Nass. C of Ch Ch Cathl Nass 65-66; P-in-c of Inagua 66-69; C of Ch Ch Cathl Nass 69-70; P-in-c of St Steph Eight Mile Rock Grand Bahama 70-74; R of St Marg Nass 75-77; C of St Ann I and Dio Nass from 77. *Box N-1569, Nassau, Bahamas.* (35100)

CLARKE, John Cecil. b 32. St Jo Coll Dur BA 70, Dipl Th 71. **d** 75 **p** 76 Ches. Hon C of St Mary Ches 75-78; Chairman Ches Co of Chs 75-79; Ecumen Officer Dio Ches from 75; Sec Chesh Ch Leaders Consultation from 76; R of Barrow Dio Ches from 78. *Rectory, Mill Lane, Great Barrow, Chester, CH3 7JF.* (Tarvin 40263)

CLARKE, John Graham. Ridley Coll Melb 60. **d** 62 **p** 63 Armid. C of St John Tamworth 62-68; V of Emmaville 68-71; Min of Gunnedah 71-74; I of Avondale Heights 74-78; St John Heidelberg Dio Melb from 78. *St John's Court, Burgundy Street, Heidelberg, Vic, Australia 3084.* (45 1144)

CLARKE, John Lester. b 17. Univ of Manit BScEE 50. St Jo Coll Winnipeg. **d** 81 Rupld. Hon C of St Matt Winnipeg Dio Rupld from 81. *211-30 Strauss Drive, Winnipeg, Manit, Canada, R3J 3S6.*

CLARKE, John Martin. b 52. Hertf Coll Ox Ba 73. Univ of Edin BD 76. Edin Th Coll 73. **d** 76 **p** 77 Newc T. C of Kenton 76-79; Prec St Ninian's Cathl Perth 79-81. *Address temp unknown*

CLARKE, John Percival. b 44. TCD BA (2nd cl Mod Ment and Mor Sc) 67. **d** 69 **p** 70 Connor. C of St Simon, Belf 69-72; Dom Chap to Bp of Connor 69-72; C of Monkstown 72-76; Asst Chap TCD 76-78; R of Durrus w Rooska Dio Cork from 79. *Rectory, Durrus, Co Cork, Irish Republic.* (Durrus 11)

CLARKE, John Philip. b 31. Trin Hall Cam 3rd cl Hist Trip pt i 53, BA (3rd cl Th Trip pt I) 54, MA 62. Linc Th Coll **d** 57 **p** 58 S'wark. C of Lady Marg w St Mary Magd Walworth 57-59; Warlingham w Chelsham and Farleigh 59-62; Mottingham (in c of St Alb Coldharbour) 62-67; St Luke Eltham 67-72; Chap Leeds Gen Infirm from 72. *75 Weetwood Lane, Leeds, LS16 5NF.* (Leeds 759526)

CLARKE, John Philip. b 36. Univ of Hull BA 60. Univ of Bris MLitt 75. Tyndale Hall Bris. **d** 62 **p** 63 Bradf. C of St Steph Bowling 62-65; Hampreston 65-68; CF from 68. *c/o Gronwen, 4 Pen-y-Gaer, Deganwy, Gwyn, LL31 9RF.*

CLARKE, John Robert. Univ of W Ont BA 61. Hur Coll LTh 64. **d** 63 Hur for Moos **p** 64 Bp Clarke for Moos. d Dio Moos 63-64; C of St Mich AA Tor 64-66; I of Moosonee Dio Moos from 67. *Church of the Apostles, Moosonee, Ont., Canada.* (705-336 2321)

CLARKE, John Stephenson. b 09. VRD 44. G and C Coll Cam BA 32, MA 52. Lich Th Coll 32. **d** 35 **p** 36 Ex. C of Em Plymouth 35-39; Chap RNVR 38-60; RNR 60-64; PC of St Barn Devonport 46-53; H Trin Rotherfield Greys 53-76. *The Cottage, Turkdean, Cheltenham, Glos, GL54 3NU.*

CLARKE, Joseph Holmes. b 57. Univ of Dalhousie BA 78. Univ of Tor MDiv 81. Trin Coll Tor 78. **d** 81 NS. C of Westphal Dio NS from 81. *72 Symonds Street, Cartmouth, NS, Canada, B3A 3L9.*

CLARKE, Joseph Willoughby Lloyd George. Codr Coll Barb. **d** 55 **p** 56 Barb. C of St Mich Cathl Barb 55-59; V of St Anne I and Dio Barb from 59. *St Anne, St Michael, Barbados, W Indies.*

CLARKE, Kenneth Herbert. b 49. TCD BA (Phil) 71. Div Hostel Dub 70. **d** 72 **p** 73 Down & Drom. C of Magheralin 72-75; Dundonald 75-78; SAMS Miss in Chile from 78. *Casilla 451, Valdivia, Chile.* (Valdivia 2455)

CLARKE, Canon Knolly Ulric Alexander. Codr Coll Barb. **d** 60 Barb for Trinid **p** 61 Trinid. C of Prince's Tn 60-67; R 67-74; Hon Can of H Trin Cathl Port of Spain from 74. *St Agnes's Rectory, Port of Spain, Trinidad.*

CLARKE, Canon Leslie Reginald Minchin. b 10. TCD BA 40, MA 46. **d** 40 **p** 41 Oss. C of Kilnamanagh 4044; I of Aughrim w Clontushert and Kiltormer 44-46; CMS Miss Dio Ugan 46-60; Dio Nam 61-63; Asst Educn Sec Gen Dio Ugan 56-60; Dio Nam 61-63; I of Timoleague 63-66; Abbeystrewry 66-71; Dioc C and Sec Cork from 71; Can of St Mich and of Inniskenny in Cork Cathl 76-80; Can of Brigown in St Colman's Cathl Cloyne 76-80. *Adamstown, Fivemilebridge, Ballinhassig, Co Cork.* (021-888165)

CLARKE, Canon Malcolm Methuen. b 08. Late Cho Scho of K Coll Cam BA 36, MA 40. Cudd Coll 37. **d** 38 **p** 39 Pet. C of St Matt Northn 38-49; V of Wellingborough 49-78; Surr from 50; RD of Wellingborough 52-69; and 73-76; Can (Non-res) of Pet 57-78; Can (Emer) from 78. *11a Kingsley Road, Northampton, NN2 7BN.*

CLARKE, Martin Geoffrey. b 45. Univ of Dur BA 66. Wells Th Coll 67. **d** 69 Bp McKie for Cov **p** 70 Cov. C of Atherstone 69-72; Keresley w Coundon 72-75; R of Scorborough w Leconfield 75-79; P-in-c of Lockington w Lund 78-79; R of Lockington and Lund and Scorborough w Leconfield 79-81; Romsley Dio Worc from 81. *Rectory, St Kenelm's Road, Romsley, Halesowen, Worcs B62 0PH.* (Romsley 710216)

CLARKE, Martin Howard. b 47. AKC 70. St Aug Coll Cant 70. **d** 71 Bradwell for Cant **p** 72 Chelmsf. C of Saffron Walden 71-74; H Trin w St Mary Ely 74-78; V of Messing w Inworth Dio Chelmsf from 78. *Messing Vicarage, Colchester, Essex, CO5 9TN.* (Tiptree 815434)

CLARKE, Maurice Fulford Lovell. b 12. Late Exhib of Clare Coll Cam 2nd cl Cl Trip pt i 33, BA (2nd cl Cl Trip pt ii) 34, 1st cl Th Trip pt i 35, MA 38. Wells Th Coll 35. **d** 36 **p** 37 Newc T. C of Benwell 36-46; CF (EC) 40-46; CF (TA) 48-54; Vice-Prin Sarum Th Coll and LPr Dio Sarum 46-53; V of St Swith Hither Green 54-65; Chap Hither Green Hosp 54-65; R of Ashley 65-77; C-in-c of Hales 65-73. *8 St Mary's Mews, Ludlow Shropshire, SY8 1DZ.*

CLARKE, Maurice Gordon. b 29. Univ of Lon BSc 52, MSc 79. Westcott Ho Cam 52. **d** 54 **p** 55 St Alb. C of Hitchin

54-58; St Jo Bapt Chipping Barnet 58-62; Dir Pastoral Counselling and Publ Pr Dio S'wark 64-69. *Rivendell, Hillside Road, Chorleywood, Rickmansworth, Herts WD3 5AP.*

CLARKE, Maurice Harold. b 30. Univ of Sussex MA 79. LCP 69. Cudd Coll 65. **d** 67 **p** 68 Portsm. C of Waterlooville 67-70; Fareham 70-72; Hd Master Lower Sch Co Secondary Sch Cowplain 67-72; Dep Hd Master Thamesview High Sch Gravesend 72-80; Hd Master Eltham Green Comprehensive Sch from 80; Hon C of Higham w Merston Dio Roch from 72. *1 Holbrook Lane, Chislehurst, Kent.* (01-467 8551)

CLARKE, Michael. Ely Th Coll 60. **d** 62 **p** 63 Win. C of St Mary S Stoneham 62-64; All H, Greenford 64-67; Hereford 67-69; Milton Portsm 69-74; Chap St Jas Hosp Portsm from 69. *Locksway Road, Miltron, Portsmouth, PO4 8LD.*

CLARKE, Michael Charles. b 12. Ch Ch Ox BA 36, MA 38. TD 59. Cudd Coll 36. **d** 37 **p** 38 Lich. C of Stoke-on-Trent 37-46; CF (EC) 40-46; V of Uttoxeter w Bramshall 46-53; CF (TA) 47-62; (TA - R of O) from 62; V of Churston Ferrers w Goodrington 54-57; R of Easthampstead 57-64; V of Eastbury w Garston E Dio Ox from 64; V of Woodlands Dio Ox from 64; C-in-c of Gt Shefford 69-72. *Eastbury Vicarage, Newbury, Berks, RG16 7JN.* (0488 71655)

CLARKE, Norman. b 28. Keble Coll Ox BA (2nd cl Th) 52, MA 58. St Steph Ho Ox 52. **d** 54 Stockport for Ches **p** 55 Ches. C of Ellesmere Port 54-57; St Mary Virg Kettering 57-60; Chap and Tutor St Monica Mampong 60-62; C of All SS Friern Barnet 62-63; L to Offic Dio Leic 63-74; C of St Mary Magd Knighton Leic 74-81; P-in-c of Sproughton w Burstall Dio St E from 81; Dioc Communications Officer from 81. *Sproughton Rectory, Ipswich, Suff.* (Ipswich 47681)

CLARKE, Oliver Fielding. b 1898. Late Scho of Hertf Coll Ox BA (2nd cl Hist) 21, 1st cl Th 23, MA 25, BD 50. Ripon Hall Ox 22. **d** 24 **p** 25 Ox. C of St Aldate Ox 24-26; Chap Worc Coll Ox 26-27; Sec SCM Ox 24-27; Miss P (CSS) at Poona 27-29; Chap All SS Malabar Hill and St Geo Hosp Bom 29-30; C of St Paul Knightsbridge 30-33; C of St Geo Hanover Sq and Chap of Liddon Ho 33-36; Perm to Offic at St Clem Barnsbury 36-37; St Jude on the Hill Hampstead Garden Suburb 37-38; Chap St Andr Hosp Clewer 38-41; V of H Trin Crockham Hill 41-51; Chap St Jas Hosp Balham 51-57; Stephenson Fell at Sheff Univ and L to Offic at St Geo Sheff 58-60; V of Hazelwood 60-67; Exam Chap to Bp of Derby 60-67; L to Offic Dio Derby from 68. *42 St John Street, Wirksworth, Derby.* (Wirksworth 2678)

CLARKE, Oswald Reeman. b 12. Univ of Liv BA 35. St Cath S Ox BA (3rd cl Th) 37, MA 40. Ripon Hall Ox 34. **d** 36 **p** 37 Carl. C of H Trin w Ch Ch Whitehaven 36-37; Addingham 37-38; Perm to Offic at H Trin Carl 38-39; C of St Mary Wavertree 39-43; C-in-c of St Mary Widnes 43-44; V of St Sav Liv 44-53; Tulse Hill 53-58; St Simon Zelotes Chelsea Dio Lon from 58. *34 Milner Street, SW3.* (01-589 5747)

CLARKE, Canon Peter. b 25. Univ of Lon BSc (Econ 2nd cl) 49. St Chad's Coll Dur Dipl in Th (w distinc) 51. **d** 51 **p** 52 Linc. C of St Giles Linc 51-53; Gt Grimsby 53-60; PC of All SS Linc 60-68; V of Bardney w Southrey 68-75; PC of Stainfield w Apley 68-69; V 69-75; St Nich w St John Newport City and Dio Linc from 75; RD of Christianity from 78; Can and Preb of Linc Cathl from 79. *St Nicholas's Vicarage, 103 Newport, Lincoln, LN1 3EE.* (Lincoln 25653)

CLARKE, Peter Gerald. b 38. Cudd Coll 75. **d** 76 B & W **p** 77 Taunton for B & W. C of Marston Magna w Rimpton (w Qu & W Camel & Corton Denham from 79) Dio B & W from 76. *Kyle, Church Lane, Marston Magna, Nr Yeovil, Somt BA22 8DG.* (Marston Magna 850547)

CLARKE, Peter John. Late Exhib of Qu Coll Ox BA 60, MA 64. Clifton Th Coll 60. **d** 62 **p** 63 S'wark. C of St Matthias U Tulse Hill 62-64; CMJ Miss Buenos Aires Dio Argent from 64. *Pedro Morán 4414, Buenos Aires, Argentina.*

CLARKE, Canon Reginald Gilbert. b 06. Qu Coll Cam BA 29, MA 34. Wycl Hall Ox 30. **d** 31 **p** 32 Wakef. C of St Pet Huddersfield 31-36; V of Ch ch Mt Pellon 36-45; St Pet Sowerby 45-48; V of St Jo Div Thorpe 46-48; H Trin Huddersfield 48-56; Asst RD of Huddersfield 53-65 and 60-68; V of Pontefract 56-60; Hon Can of Wakef 58-68; Can (Emer) from 68; V of Almondbury 60-68; Leck 68-71; L to Offic Dio Blackb from 79; Dio Carl from 79. *Brook Cottage, Holme, Carnforth, Lancs, LA6 1QN.* (0524 781601)

CLARKE, Richard Francis. **d** 60 **p** 63 C & Goulb. C of Cooma 60-62; Cootamundra 62-65; R of Pambula 65-74; Adelong Dio C & Goulb from 74. *Box 28, Adelong, NSW, Australia 2729.* (0648-46 2013)

CLARKE, Richard Leon. b 37. Sarum Th Coll 62. **d** 65 **p** 66 Sarum. C of Fordington 65-68; St Richard Haywards Heath 68-72; Goring (in c of St Richard) 72-76; P-in-c of St Andr Portslade 76-77; St Pet Southwick 76-77; V of St Pet and St Andr Portslade 77-80; R of Clayton w Keymer Dio Chich from 80. *Keymer Rectory, Hassocks, W Sussex.* (Hassocks 3570)

CLARKE, Richard Lionel. b 49. TCD BA 71, MA 79. K Coll Lon AKC and BD 75. **d** 75 **p** 76 Down. C of Holywood 75-77; St Bart w Ch Ch Leeson Pk Dub 77-79; Min Can St Patr Cathl Dub from 77; Chap TCD from 79. *Trinity College, Dublin, Irish Republic.*

CLARKE, Robert George. Univ of Dur BA 65, Dipl Th 67. Cranmer Hall Dur 62. **d** 67 Bp Cornwall for Win **p** 68 Win. C of Basingstoke 67-70; R of Ixopo 71-74; C of H Nativ Cathl Pmbg Dio Natal from 76. *274 Alexandra Road, Pietermaritzburg, Natal, S Africa.*

CLARKE, Robert George. b 49. **d** 79 **p** 80 Pret. C of St Steph Lyttelton Dio Pret from 79. *153 Station Road, Verwoerdburg 0140, S Africa.*

CLARKE, Robert James. b 22. ACP 58. GOE. **d** 69 **p** 70 Connor, C of St Mary, Belf 69-70; C & Min Can St Mary's Cathl Lim 70-72; Asst Chap & Master Wilsons Hosp Sch Multyfarnham Westmeath from 72. *Wilson's Hospital, Multyfarnham, Co Westmeath, Irish Republic.*

CLARKE, Robert Michael. b 45. BD (Lon) 71. Sarum Wells Th Coll 77. **d** 78 Taunton for B & W **p** 79 B & W. C of Glastonbury 78-81; Chap Felsted Sch Dunmow from 81. *Felsted School, Dunmow, Essex.*

CLARKE, Robert Sydney. b 35. K Coll Lon and Warm AKC 64. **d** 65 **p** 66 Lon. C of Hendon 65-69; Langley Marish 69-70; Chap of New Cross Hosp Wolverhampton 70-74; Herrison Hosp Dorchester 74-80; Westmr Hosp & Med Sch from 80. *Chaplain's Office, Westminster Hospital, SW1 2AP.* (01-828 9811)

CLARKE, Robert Thorneycroft. b 10. Late Exhib of St Jo Coll Dur BA (3rd cl Th) 36. **d** 36 **p** 37 Liv. C of St Mary Wavertree 36-38; St Cath Wigan 38-40. *43 College Road, Great Crosby, Liverpool, L23 0RL.*

CLARKE, Roger Grenville. b 21. Fitzw Ho Cam BA (Agric) 49, MA 61. ARICS 70. **d** 71 **p** 72 St E. C of St Jo Evang St E 71-75; St Geo Bury St E Dio St E from 75. *76 Hardwick Lane, Bury St Edmunds, Suffolk.* (Bury St Ed 3766)

CLARKE, Roland. b 22. St Aid Coll 49. **d** 52 **p** 53 Man. C of St Agnes Birch-in-Rusholme 52-54; Flixton 54-56; V of Langold 56-59; Ch Ch Pendlebury 59-78. *c/o Christ Church Vicarage, Pendlebury, Manchester, M27 1AZ.* (061-794 2962)

CLARKE, Ronald George. b 31. Oak Hill Th Coll. **d** 64 **p** 65 Southw. C of Carlton-in-the-Willows 64-68; V of St Matt Bestwood 68-75; St Andr (w St Matthias to 77 and H Trin from 79 and All SS from 81) Isl Dio Lon from 75; P-in-c of H Trin Isl 75-79; All SS Battle Bridge Caledonian Road w St Jas Pentonville Isl 79-81. *45 Thornhill Road, N1 1JS.* (01-607 4552)

CLARKE, Roy Langridge. b 21. St Chad's Coll Dur BA 48, Dipl Th 50. **d** 51 **p** 52 Jarrow for Dur. C of St Osw Dur and Chap Bow Sch Dur 51-68; Chap Caldicott Sch Farnham Royal 68-69; Hon C of All SS Boyne Hill Maidenhead (in c of St Geo Larchfield) 69-81; Perm to Offic Dio Ox from 69. *26 Furrow Way, Maidenhead, Berks.*

CLARKE, Royston James. b 33. ALCD (2nd cl) 58. **d** 58 **p** 59 Guildf. C of St Sav Guildf 58-61; Otley 61-65; R of Stockton 65-72; C-in-c of St Mary Leamington Dio Cov 72-75; V from 75. *St Mary's Vicarage, Leamington, Warws, CV31 1JP.* (Leamington 25927)

CLARKE, Stewart Horatio. Bp's Univ Lennox BA 56, LST 59. **d** 58 **p** 59 Ott. C of St John Smith's Falls 58-62; CF (Canad) from 62. *c/o Dept of National Defence, Canadian Forces HQ, Ottawa 4, Ont., Canada.*

CLARKE, Thomas Percival. b 15. Univ of Wales BA 39. Lich Th Coll 39. **d** 41 **p** 42 Llan. C of St Mary the Virgin Cardiff 41-45; Ch Ch Walcot 45-48; St Mary the Virgin. Bathwick 48-49; V of H Trin Hendford Yeovil 49-52; UMCA Area Sec for E Counties 52-56; Metrop Area Sec and Perm to Offic Dios Lon S'wark and Ox 56-59; C of St Steph Glouc Rd lon 56-59; V of Blackheath 59-72; Chap Leighton Hosp Ches 72-73; Charing Cross Hosp Fulham 73-81; L to Offic Dio Glouc 81. *15 Crescent Way, Brockley, SE4.*

CLARKE, Vernon Douglas. b 18. Jes Coll Cam BA 48, MA 50. Bps' Coll Cheshunt 47. **d** 49 **p** 50 Southw. C of Bulwell 49-51; Ambleside 51-54; V of Aspatria 54-63; Surr 56-74; V of H Trin Millom 63-71; Cockermouth 71-74; Commiss Fulham and Gibr 75; P-in-c of Kirkland Dio Carl from 75; Gt Salkeld Dio Carl 79-80; C-in-c from 80. *Birchfield, Great Salkeld, Penrith, Cumbria, CA11 9LW.* (Lazonby 380)

CLARKE, Wallace Frederick Carlile. b 01. Late Exhib of Keble Coll Ox 3rd cl Cl Mods 22, BA (3rd cl Lit Hum) 24, MA 30. Coll of Resurr Mirfield 24. **d** 26 Willesden for Lon **p** 27 Lon. C of St Clem Barnsbury 26-30; St Mary Magd Newark-on-Trent 30-33; PC of St Cath Nottm 33-37; Prec of Cathl Ch Blackb and Exam Chap to Bp of Blackb 37-45; V of St Paul Blackb 39-45; Tottenham 45-62; Chap St Kath Coll 45-59; Chap Prince of Wales Hosp Tottenham 48-62; Min of St Mich Conv Distr Beaconsfield 62-69. *2 Hillwood Close, Warminster, Wilts.* (Warminster 212527)

CLARKE, William Gascoyne. St Paul's Coll Grahmstn 55.

d 57 Grahmstn. C of H Trin K William's 57-60. *108 Alexandra Road, King William's Town, CP, S Africa.*

CLARKE, William Martin. d 30 **p** 31 Keew. C of Dryden 30-32; Miss at Churchill 32-34; C of Gt w L Driffield 35-47; V of Lowthorpe w Rushton Parva 37-44; R of Preston-in-Holderness 44-61; R of Sproatley 53-61; V of Owthorne w Rimswell 61-67; Hutton Cranswick w Skerne 67-76; R of Winstead 61-67; Perm to Offic Dio York from 76. *Top Flat, 1 Railway Crescent, Withernsea, Hull.*

CLARKSON, Alan Geoffrey. b 34. Ch Coll Cam BA (2nd cl Mech Sc Trip pt i) 57, MA 61. Wycl Hall Ox 57. **d** 59 Shrewsbury for Lich **p** 60 Stafford for Lich. C of Penn 59-60; Oswestry 60-63; Wrington 63-65; V of Chewton Mendip w Emborrow 65-74; Glastonbury w Godney Dio B & W from 74; C-in-c of W Pennard Dio B & W from 80; Meare Dio B & W from 81; M Gen Syn B & W 70-75. *St John's Vicarage, Glastonbury, Somt, BA6 8BY.* (Glastonbury 32362)

CLARKSON, Eric George. b 22. St Jo Coll Dur BA 48, Dipl in Th 50. **d** 50 **p** 51 Liv. C of St John Birkdale 50-52; St Mary Grassendale 52-54; PC of St Luke W Derby 54-66; V of St Mich AA (w St Jo Evang from 75) Blackb 66-75; Chapeltown Dio Sheff from 75. *Vicarage, Housley Park, Chapeltown, Sheffield, S30 4UE.* (Sheff 467295)

CLARKSON, Geoffrey. b 35. K Coll Lon and Warm AKC 61. **d** 62 **p** 63 Dur. C of Shildon 62-65; Asst Chap HM Pris Liv 65-66; Chap HM Borstal Inst Feltham 66-71; Development Officer Br Assoc of Settlements Lon 71-74; L to Offic Dio Lon from 71; Dir Commun Projects Found from 74. *16 Ormond Crescent, Hampton, Middx.* (01-979 2377)

CLARKSON, Ivon George Townley. b 1900. Jes Coll Cam 3rd cl Hist Trip pt i 24, 3rd cl Hist Trip pt ii 26, BA 27, MA 33. King's Coll Lon 35. **d** 39 Ox **p** 40 Dorch for Ox. C of Aylesbury 39-41; Perm to Offic Dio Pet 41; Dio S'wark 42-43; Dio Lon 42-43 and 45; Dio Ox 44-45 and 66-67; Dio Ex 64-66; Dio Chich from 67; C of St Mich Camden Town 45-48; Beckenham 51; All SS Benhilton 51-52; Stroud Green 52-61; Wolborough 63-64; St Agnes Hove 67-70; Actg C-in-c 70-71; Perm to Offic Dio Chich from 71. *47 Denmark Villas, Hove, E Sussex, BN3 3TD.* (0273 732349)

CLARKSON, John Gorman. d 52 **p** 53 S Calif. In Amer Ch 49-69; Tutor United Th Coll of WI 69-72; P-in-c of Mona Heights Ja 69-70; Tower Hill St Andr Dio Ja from 72. *26 Daisy Avenue, Kingston 6, Jamaica, W Indies.* (093-79302)

CLARKSON, John Thomas. b 30. K Coll Lon and Warm. **d** 54 **p** 55 St Alb. C of St Sav (in c of St Mich and St Geo from 56) Luton 54-59; M Bush Bro of St Barn Dio N Queensld 59-64; V of Mundingburra 64-72; St Mary Dallington Northn 73-77; R of W Wyalong Dio Bath from 77. *Rectory, West Wyalong, NSW, Australia 2671.* (069-7212 163)

CLARKSON, Richard Michael. b 38. Univ of Dur BA 60, Dipl Th 62. Cranmer Hall Dur 60. **d** and **p** 63 Blackb. C of St Annes-on-the-Sea 62-66 and from 70; Lanc 66-68; Asst Master Kirkham Gr Sch from 68. *35 Westby Street, Lytham, Lancs, FY8 5JF.* (Lytham 733719)

CLARRIDGE, Donald Michael. b 41. Oak Hill Th Coll. **d** 67 **p** 68 Newc T. C of St Barn w St Jude, Newc T 67-70; St Pancras w St Martin Pennycross 70-77; V of Bampton Dio Ex from 77; R of Huntsham Dio Ex from 77; Clayhanger Dio Ex from 77; Petton Dio Ex from 77. *Vicarage, Bampton, Tiverton, Devon.* (Bampton 31385)

CLASPER, John. b 42. K Coll Lon and Warm AKC 67. **d** 68 **p** 69 Ripon. C of All H w St Simon Leeds 68-71; Hawksworth Wood (in c of Moor Grange) 71-74; Team V & Idustr Chap of Jarrow Dio Dur from 74. *St Andrew's House, Borough Road, Jarrow, T & W, NE32 5XW.* (Jarrow 893279)

CLASPER, Paul. b 23. Taylor Univ Indiana BA 44. S Bapt Sem Kentucky BD 47. U Th Sem NY STM 50, ThD 52. **d** 75 Bp Myers (Calif) **p** 75 Hong. P Dio Hong. *Chung Chi College, Shatin, Hong Kong.*

CLATTENBURG, Maxwell Davis. d 57 **p** 58 NS. C of Truro 57-59; I of Rawdon 59-61; Lockeport 61-67; Aylesford w Berwick 67-74; New Glasgow Dio NS from 74; Trenton 74-79; Waverley Dio NS from 79. *Box 183, Waverley, NS, Canada.*

CLATWORTHY, Jonathan Richard. b 48. Univ of Wales BA 70. Sarum Wells Th Coll 71. **d** 76 Man **p** 77 Middleton for Man. C of The Resurr Man 76-78; Bolton-le-Moors 78-81; V of St Pet Ashton Dio Man from 81. *St Peter's Vicarage, Chester Square, Ashton-under-Lyne, OL7 OLB.* (061-330 4285)

CLATWORTHY, Thomas Donald Vaughan. b 08. Univ of Wales BA (3rd cl Fr) 30. St Mich Coll Llan 31. **d** 33 **p** 34 Mon. C of Fleur de Lys 33-35; U Grangetown 35-38; Minehead 38-40; All SS Clevedon 40-42; CF (EC) 42-46; PC of Catcott 47-51; Burtle 47-51; V of Pensford w Publow 51-71; RD of Chew Magna 62-71; V of All SS Weston-super-Mare 71-77; Perm to Offic Dio Ex from 77. *51 Greenway Lane, Budleigh Salterton, Devon.*

CLAUGHTON, Dennis Peter. St Francis Coll Brisb ThL 79. **d** 79 **p** 80 Brisb. C of St Barn Ithaca Dio Brisb from 79. *23 Rothesay Street, Kenmore, Queensland, Australia 4069.* (378 8309)

CLAUSEN, John Frederick. b 37. Sarum Th Coll 65. **d** 68 Willesden for Lon. **p** 69 Lon. C of Kentish Town 68-71; Rainham 71-77; R of Stone Dio Roch from 77. *Rectory, Stone, Greenhithe, Kent, DA9 9BE.* (Greenhithe 842076)

CLAWSON, Derek George. b 35. Qu Coll Birm 63. **d** 66 Warrington for Liv **p** 67 Liv. C of Ditton 66-70; Speke (in c of All SS) 70-72; V of Hindley Green Dio Liv from 72. *St John's Vicarage, Atherton Road, Hindley Green, via Wigan, WN2 4SA.*

✠ **CLAXTON, Right Rev Charles Robert.** b 03. Qu Coll Cam BA 26, MA 33. DD (Lambeth) 60. Ridley Hall Cam 26. **d** 27 **p** 28 Chelmsf. C of St John Stratford 27-29; St John Redhill 29-33; V of H Trin Bris 33-38; Hon Chap to Bp of Bris 38-46; Hon Can of Bris 42-46; Hon Chap to Bp of Roch; Publ Pr Dio Roch and Home Sec of Miss Coun of Ch Assem 43-46; C of St Martin-in-the-Fields 44-46; R of W Derby 46-48; Cons Ld Bp Suffr of Warrington in Liv Cathl 7 April 46 by Abp of York; Bps of Man; Liv; Ches; Portsm; Blackb; Sheff; Wakef; S & M; Lah; Centr Tang; Bps Suffr of Penrith; Lanc; Pontefract; Burnley; Barking; Bps Maxwell; Sara; Sherwood Jones; Stanton Jones; Tubbs; and Mosley; Dioc Can of Liv 46-60; Proc Conv Liv 47-60; R of Halsall 48-59; Trld to Blackb 60; res 71; Asst Bp of Ex from 72. *6 The Lawn, Budleigh Salterton, Devon.* (Budleigh 2193)

CLAXTON, Leslie Edward Mitchell. b 11. MC 46. Peterho Cam Math Trip pt i 31, BA (Th Trip pt ii) 33, MA 48. LRSM 59. ARCM 61. Cudd Coll 34. **d** 35 **p** 36 Lon. C of H Trin Hounslow 35-38; Dartford 38-39; CF 39-68; DACG 58-64; ACG 64-68; Hon Chap to HM the Queen 67-68; R of St Olave Hart Street and All H Staining w St Cath Coleman City and Dio Lon from 68. *8 Hart Street, Mark Lane, EC3R 7NB.* (01-488 4318)

CLAXTON, Louis Allen. b 15. Worc Ordin Coll 62. **d** 63 **p** 64 B & W. C of Ascen S Twerton 63-66; Padstow 66-68; PC of Pencoys 68-71; C-in-c of Carmenellis 68-71; Chap Miss to Seamen Rotterdam 71-74; Chap of Ch of the Ascen Cadenabbia 74-77; Costa Blanca 77-78; P-in-c of St Andr Bexhill Dio Chich from 78. *18 Woodville Road, Bexhill, TN39 3EU.* (Bexhill 215460)

CLAY, Christopher Henry Leigh. b 42. Trin Coll Cam BA 64, MA 69. Clifton Th Coll 67. **d** 69 Chich **p** 70 Lewes for Chich. C of Broadwater 69-73; P-in-c of St Pet Macclesfield Dio Ches 73-77; V from 77. *175 Windmill Street, Macclesfield, SK11 7LB.* (Macclesfield 22591)

CLAY, Colin Peter. b 32. Ch Coll Cam 2nd cl Hist Trip pt i 54, BA (2nd cl Hist Trip pt ii) 55, MA 59. Wells Th Coll 55. **d** 57 **p** 58 S'wark. C of St Jas Malden 57-59; Epiph Sudbury Ont 59-60; R of St Jas w St Geo Sudbury Ont 60-64; St Jas Sudbury w St Thos French R 64-69; Capreol 70-77; Exam Chap to Bp of Alg 74-77; Chap Univ of Sask from 77. *St Andrew's College, College Drive, Saskatoon, Sask, S7N 0W3, Canada.* (343-5963)

CLAY, John Herbert Julian. b 09. Keble Coll Ox BA 34, MA 65. Cudd Coll 52. **d** 53 **p** 54 Newc T. C of Monkseaton 53-55; V of St Aid Newc T 55-59; Felton 59-68; St Luke Wallsend 68-71; Alwinton w Holystone Kidland and Alnham 71-76; Perm to Offic Dio Guildf from 76. *22 Littleton, Guildford, Surrey.*

CLAY, Peter Herbert. b 31. Lich Th Coll 62. **d** 64 **p** 65 Heref. C of Ross-on-Wye 64-67; Leamington Priors 67-70; C-in-c of Temple Grafton w Binton 70-73; R 73-75; C-in-c of Exhall w Wixford 70-73; R 73-75; Team V of Centr Telford Dio Lich from 75. *9 Chiltern Gardens, Dawley, Telford, Salop.* (Telford 504999)

CLAYDEN, David Baldwin. ACT ThDip 72. Ridley Coll Melb 60. **d** 61 **p** 62 St Arn. C of Bealiba 61-65; V 65-66; R of Sea Lake 66-71; Avoca 71-74; Red Cliffs Dio St Arn (Dio Bend from 77) from 74. *Rectory, Heath Street, Red Cliffs, Vic, Australia 3496.* (050-24 1062)

CLAYDEN, David Edward. b 42. Oakhill Coll 74. **d** 76 **p** 77 Southw. C of St Jo Evang Worksop 76-79; V of Clarborough w Hayton Dio Southw from 79. *Clarborough Vicarage, Retford, Notts, DN22 9NA.* (Retford 704781)

CLAYDEN, William James Baldwin. Ridley Coll Melb ACT ThL 29. **d** 29 Bp Stephen for Melb **p** 30 Melb. C of Ch Ch S Yarra 29-31; R of Heyfield 31-35; Warragul 35-42; C-in-c of Bairnsdale 42-43; Chap RAAF 43-46; R of Yarram 46-52; H Trin Kensington 52-54; Coburg 54-62; I of St Mark Fitzroy 62-65; Chap Ellerslie Home Hawthorn Dio Melb from 65. *14 Harcourt Street, Hawthorn, Vic 3122, Australia.*

CLAYDEN, William John. Univ of Melb BA 55. ACT ThL (2nd cl) 55. **d** 56 **p** 57 Melb. C of Ashburton 56-58; Min of Lorne 58-61; R of Alexandra 61-66; V of Aberfeldie 66-72; Strathmore 73-81; Perm to Offic Dio Melb from 81. *353 Glenferrie Road, Malvern, Vic, Australia 3144.*

CLAYDON, David. Univ of Syd BEcon 58. Melb Coll of Div BD 71. **d** and **p** 79 Syd. Hon C of St Swith Pymble 79-80; C of St Alb Lindfield Dio Syd from 80. *12 Gould Avenue, St Ives, NSW, Australia 2075.*

CLAYDON, Graham Leonard. b 43. K Coll Lon BA (1st cl Hist) 65. Clifton Th Coll 66. **d** 68 Bradwell for Chelmsf **p** 69 Chelmsf. C of Walthamstow 68-73; All S Langham Place, Marylebone 73-81; V of Isl Dio Lon from 81. *St Mary's Vicarage, Upper Street, N1.* (01-226 3400)

CLAYDON, John Richard. b 38. St Jo Coll Cam 3rd cl Nat Sc Trip pt i BA 61, MA 65. Univ of Bris Dipl Th 72. Trin Coll Bris 71. **d** 73 Edmon for Lon **p** 74 Lon. C of Ch Ch Finchley 73-76; Asst Chap K Edw Sch Witley 76-77; C of Macclesfield 77-81; V of All SS Marple Dio Ches from 81. *Vicarage, Church Lane, Marple, Stockport, SK6 7LD.* (061-427 2378)

CLAYPOLE WHITE, Douglas Eric. b 29. FCA. St Alb Ministerial Tr Scheme 77. **d** 80 St Alb **p** 81 Hertf for St Alb. C of Sharnbrook Dio St Alb from 80. *Homelands, Turvey, Bedford, MK43 8DB.*

CLAYTON, Anthony Edwin Hay. Sarum Th Coll 61. **d** 63 **p** 64 S'wark. C of All SS Tooting Graveney 63-68; Perm to Offic Dio Leic 69-74; Dio Southw 73-78; Hon C of Lockington w Hemington 74-75; Hon C-in-c 75-80; P-in-c of Eaton Dio Leic from 80; Eastwell Dio Leic from 80. *Vicarage, Eaton, Grantham, NG32 1SP.* (Knipton 329)

CLAYTON, Chan Charles Henry Ernest. b 15. Trin Coll Dub BA 44, MA 47. **d** 44 **p** 45 Down. C of St Clem Belfast 44-46; Min Can Down Cathl 46-52; C-in-c of Annahilt 52-56; R 56-59; R of Cathl Ch of Ch the Redeemer Drom Dio Drom from 59; RD of Drom 60-71; Preb of Dromara in Drom Cathl 63-64; Treas 64-66; Prec 66-71; Chan from 71. *Rectory, Dromore, Co Down, N Ireland.* (Dromore 692275)

CLAYTON, Frederick John. b 18. LCP 54. Nor Ordin Course 73. **d** 76 **p** 77 Nor (APM). Hon C of H Trin Caister 76-77; Ormesby St Mich Dio Nor from 77. *The Pines, Ormesby St Michael, Gt Yarmouth, NR29 3LW.*

CLAYTON, Geoffrey Buckroyd. b 26. Univ of Newc T BA (2nd cl Swedish Stud) 67. Roch Th Coll 62. **d** 64 **p** 65 Newc T. C of St Geo Jesmond Newc T 64-67; St Anthony Byker Newc T 67-68; Cheddleton 69-72; V of Arbory IM Dio S & M from 72. *Arbory Vicarage, Ballabeg, Isle of Man.* (0624-823595)

CLAYTON, Canon Giles. b 21. Keble Coll Ox BA 42, MA 47. St Steph Ho Ox 42. **d** 44 **p** 45 S'wark. C of St Jas Riddlesdown 44-46; Plymstock 46-49; Littleham w Exmouth (in c of St Andr) 49-52; PC of Durrington 52; RD of Avon 67-70; R of St Martin City and Dio Sarum from 69; RD of Salisbury 72-77; Can and Preb of Sarum Cathl from 73. *St Martin's Rectory, Salisbury, Wilts, SP1 2JJ.* (Salisbury 5895)

CLAYTON, Canon John. b 11. Univ of Leeds BA (2nd cl Hist) 33, MA 43. Wells Th Coll 34. **d** 35 **p** 36 Wakef. C of Dewsbury Moor 35-38; Halifax 38-41; Lect 40-41; V of St Geo Lupset 41-51; Chap Snapethorpe Hosp 49-51; V of St Jas Bolton 51-65; RD of Calverley 56-65; Otley 68-73; Proc Conv Bradf 58-75; Hon Can of Bradf 63-76; Can (Emer) from 76; V of Otley 65-76; Perm to Offic Dios Bradf and Ripon from 76. *10 Sandy Walk, Bramhope, Leeds, LS16 9DW.*. (Leeds 611388)

CLAYTON, John. St Mich Coll Crafers 60. **d** 65 **p** 66 Adel. Asst Chap Qu Eliz Hosp Adel 65-66; C of St Patr Perth 67; P-in-c of N Beach 68-69; Perm to Offic Dio Perth 69-70. *24 Panton Crescent, Karrinyup, W Australia 6018.*

CLAYTON, Michael John. b 32. **d** 79 **p** 80 Buckingham for Ox. C of St Paul Wokingham Dio Ox from 79. *33 St Paul's Gate, Wokingham, Berks, RG11 2YP.*

CLAYTON, Norman James. b 24. K Coll Lon and Warm AKC 52. **d** 53 **p** 54 Newc T. C of Long Benton 53-55; R of Lomagundi Rhod 55-60; Chap St Geo Home Johann 60-78; L to Offic Dio Johann 65-78; P-in-c of Risley Dio Derby from 78; Dioc Communications Officer from 78. *Diocesan Communications Office, Derby Church House, Full Street, Derby, DE1 3DR.* (Derby 382232)

CLAYTON, Robert Oswald. Ridley Coll Melb ACT ThL 65. **d** 64 **p** 65 St Arn. C of Ch Ch Cathl St Arn 64-66; Swan Hill 66-67; Bairnsdale 67-69; Hon C of Morwell Dio Gippsld 69-75. *7 Switchback Road, Churchill, Vic. 3842, Australia.*

CLAYTON, Sydney Leigh. b 38. Late Exhib Pemb Coll Ox BA 62, MA 65. BD (Lon) 65. Linc Th Coll. **d** 65 **p** 66 Man. C of St Jas Birch-in-Rusholme 65-68; Hulme Lect of Bolton-le-Moors 68-76; V of Denshaw Dio Man from 77. *Denshaw Vicarage, Saddleworth, Oldham, OL3 5SB.* (Saddleworth 4575)

CLAYTON, Wilfred. b 10. Worc Ordin Coll 57. **d** 59 Bp Sinker for Derby **p** 60 Derby. C of St Phil Chaddesden 59-61; Chesterfield 61-63; PC of Marlpool 63-68; R of Whitwell 68-73; P-in-c of Calow 74-77. *The Haven, Hodthorpe, Worksop, Notts.* (Worksop 720006)

CLAYTON, William Alan. Univ of Liv BSc (2nd cl Biochem) 54. BD (2nd cl) Lon 60. **d** 63 **p** 64 Ches. C of Wallasey 63-67; R of Burton Agnes w Harpham 67-69; V of St Thos Batley 69-72; Asst Mast Richmond Comprehensive School from 73; L to Offic Dio Ripon from 73. *Swaledale House, The Green, Reeth, Richmond, N Yorks.*

CLAYTON, William Terence. b 42. K Coll Lon and Warm AKC 66. Univ of Lon BSc 71, MSc 73, MSc (Psychol Educn) 76. **d** 67 **p** 68 S'wark. C of Rotherhithe 67-71; Hon C of St Mich AA Grosv Pk Camberwell 71-76; St Paul Newington 71-76; Winterslow Dio Sarum 76. *Dungarth, Middleton Road, Middle Winterslow, Salisbury, SP5 1QL.*

CLAYTON-JONES, Roger Francis. b 39. K Coll Lon and Warm AKC 64. **d** 66 **p** 67 Ches. C of Oxton 66-70; Asst Chap R Hosp Sch Ipswich 70-71; Chap Decarteret Coll Mandeville Ja 71-73; CF from 73. *c/o Royal Army Chaplains Dept, Bagshot Park, Bagshot, Surrey.*

CLEALL, Ven Aubrey Victor George. b 1898. Selw Coll Cam BA 22, MA 26. Trin Coll Dub MA *(ad eund)* 47. Wells Th Coll 23. **d** 24 **p** 25 B & W. C of Crewkerne 24-28; Waltham Abbey (or Holy Cross) w St Thos Upshire 28-29; V 29-59; Dioc Insp of Schs 32-46; Surr 34-69; St Antholin Lect (City of Lon) 37-57; RD of Chigwell 46-59; Hon Can of Samuel Harsnett Abp in Chelmsf Cathl 49-59; R of Wickham St Paul w Twinstead 59-63; Archd of Colchester 59-69; Archd (Emer) from 69. *189 Seaside, Eastbourne, BN22 7NP.*

CLEAR, Peter Basil. b 13. Late Exhib of New Coll Ox BA 35, MA 40. Chich Th Coll 35. **d** 36 **p** 37 Lon. C of St Mary Graham Terrace Pimlico 36-39 and 46-48; Chap RNVR 39-46; Chap Conv of Reparation Woking 49-50; C-in-c of N Perrott 50-52; R of Pen Selwood 52-68. *21 Portland Court, Lyme Regis, Dorset.* (Lyme Regis 2273)

CLEASBY, Very Rev Thomas Wood Ingram. b 20. Late Exhib of Magd Coll Ox BA and MA 47 (3rd cl Mod Hist). Cudd Coll 47. **d** 49 **p** 50 Wakef. C of Huddersfield 49-52; Dom Chap to Abp of York 52-56; Chap of Nottm Univ and Southw Lect 56-63; C of St Mary Nottm 56-63; Commiss Melb 61-68; V of Chesterfield 63-70; Hon Can of Derby from 63; Surr 63-78; Archd of Chesterfield 63-78; Exam Chap to Bp of Derby 64-78; R of Morton 70-78; Dean of Ches from 78. *Deanery, 7 Abbey Street, Chester, CH1 2JF.* (Chester 25920)

CLEATOR, Canon Kenneth Irving. McMaster Univ Ont BA 40, BD 43. U Th Sem NY STM 47. Ch Div Sch USA. **d** 59 **p** 60 Calif. [f in Amer Ch] I of Cooksville S 61-65; R of St Barn Danforth Avenue Tor 65-67; St Geo, City and Dio Montr from 67; Hon Can of Montr from 74. *575 Roslyn Avenue, Westmount, Montreal, PQ, Canada.* (514-489 1977)

CLEAVER, Gordon Philip. **d** 78 Truro (APM). C of St Ruan w St Grade Dio Truro from 78. *Bryn-Mor, Cadgwith, Ruan Minor, Helston, Cornwall, TR12 7JZ.* (The Lizard 328)

CLEAVER, John Martin. b 42. K Coll Lon and Warm BD and AKC 64. **d** 65 **p** 66 Roch. C of Bexley 65-69; W Ealing 69-71; Belvedere (in c of St Andr Bostall Heath) 71-76; V of Green Street Green Dio Roch from 76. *46 World's Lane, Green Street Green, Orpington, Kent.* (Farnborough 52905)

CLEEVE, Martin. b 43. ACP 67. Open Univ BA 80. Oak Hill Th Coll 69. **d** 72 **p** 73 Cant. C of H Trin Margate 72-76; V of Southminster Dio Chelmsf from 76. *Vicarage, Southminster, Essex.* (Maldon 772300)

CLEGG, David. b 46. N Ordin Course 77. **d** 80 **p** 81 Blackb. C of Briercliffe Dio Blackb from 80. *3 Finsley View, Burnley Road, Harle Syke, Burnley, Lancs BB10 2JG.*

CLEGG, Canon David Nigel Astley. b 26. Ch Coll Cam BA 48, MA 53. Trin Coll Dub Abp King Pri and Div Test (1st cl) 51, Th Exhib 52, BD 68. **d** 52 **p** 53 Man. C of St Matt Stretford 52-56; C-in-c of Conv Distr of St Jas Thornham 56-60; V of St Marg, Prestwich Dio Man from 60; Proc in Conv 69-80; Exam Chap to Bp of Man from 71; Hon Can of Man from 78. *St Margaret's Vicarage, Prestwich, Manchester, M25 5QB.* (061-773 2698)

CLEGG, Frank Cooper. b 01. **d** 64 Stafford for Lich **p** 64 Lich. C of Stoke-upon-Trent 64-73; L to Offic Dio Lich from 73. *16 Kirkup Walk, Longton, Stoke-on-Trent, Staffs.*

CLEGG, Herbert. b 24. Fitzw Ho Cam BA 59, MA 63. Univ of Bris MA 65. Sarum Th Coll 52. **d** 54 Taunton for B & W **p** 55 B & W. C of Street 54-56; Perm to Offic Dio Ely 56-59; Tutor St Pet Th Coll Kingston Jamaica 59-61; R of Newington Bagpath w Kingscote and Ozleworth 61-65; Prin Bp Willis Coll Iganga 65-69; C-in-c of Aldsworth 70-75; Sherborne w Windrush 70-75; V of Marcham w Garford Dio Ox from 75. *Marcham Vicarage, Abingdon, OX13 6NP.*

CLEGG, John Anthony Holroyd. b 44. Kelham Th Coll 65. **d** 70 **p** 71 Lanc for Blackb. C of St Anne's-on-Sea 70-74; Lancaster Priory 74-76; V of Lower Darwen 76-79; Team V of Shaston Dio Sarum from 79. *St James' Vicarage, Tanyard Lane, Shaftesbury, Dorset, SP7 8HW.* (0747 2193)

CLEGG, John Lovell. b 48. Qu Coll Ox BA 70, MA 74. Dipl Th (Bris) 75. Trin Coll Bris 72. **d** 75 Penrith for Carl **p** 76 Carl. C of St Mark Barrow-F 75-79; R of St Andr Levenshulme Dio Man from 79. *27 Errwood Road, Levenshulme, Manchester, M19 2PN.* (061-224 5877)

CLEGG, Roger Alan. b 46. St Jo Coll Dur BA 68. Univ of Nottm Dipl Th 76. St Jo Coll Nottm 75. **d** 78 **p** 79 Man. C of Harwood 78-81; Team V of Sutton & Wawne Dio York from 81. *Wawne Vicarage, 50 Main Street, Wawne, Hull, HU7 5XH.* (Hull 836635)

CLEGHORN, Matthew. d 59 **p** 59 NS. R of Falkland 59-64; Dominion and of New Waterford 65-67. *330 Stanhope Road, South Shields.*

CLELAND, James Johnston. b 09. Edin Th Coll 31. **d** 35 **p** 36 Brech. C of St Salvador Dundee 35-39; P-in-c of H Trin Riddrie Glas 39-42; P-in-c of St Ninian's Miss Dundee 42-43; R of St Salvador Dundee 43-48; Perm to Offic at Ch Ch Glas 49-50; C of the Ascen Lavender Hill 50-54; Old St Paul Edin 54-56; P-in-c of St Ninian Edin 56-64; R of St Bride, Glas 64-73; Perm to Offic Dio Edin from 73. *34 Dean Park, Peebles, EH45 8DD.*

CLELAND, Richard. b 26. MPS 47. St Aid Coll 58. **d** 60 **p** 61 Connor. C of Ch Ch Lisburn 60-63; St Jude Belf 63-66; St Paul Portman Square St Marylebone 66-67; V of Ilkley Dio Bradf from 67. *Vicarage, Ilkley, Yorks.* (Ilkley 607615)

CLEMENT, David Elwyn. b 17. St D Coll Lamp BA 39. St Mich Coll Llan 46. **d** 46 **p** 48 Swan B. C of Ystalyfera 46-52; Llangyfelach w Morriston 52-55; V of Ystradfellte w Pontneathvaughan 55-59; Llansamlet 59-60; R of Gladestry 60-81. *Address temp unknown.*

CLEMENT, Very Rev James Orlando. Codr Coll Barb. **d** 49 Gui for Antig **p** 51 Antig. C of Dominica 49-50; St Anthony Montserrat 50-52; P-in-c of St Geo Montserrat 52-59; Anguilla 59-64; St Bart's Antig 62-64; St Paul w St John and St Mary St Kitts 64-67; V of Lodge 67-77; Dean and R of St Geo Cathl Georgetn Dio Guy from 77. *Deanery, Carmichael Street, Georgetown 2, Guyana, S America.* (02-65067)

CLEMENT, Morgan Lewis. b 17. St D Coll Lamp BA 46. **d** 46 **p** 47 Llan. C of St Fagan Aberdare 46-51; St Paul Newport 51-54; V of St Andr Lliswerry Newport 54-62; Blackwood 62-78; RD of Bedwellty 72-78; V of St Mary Abergavenny w Llanwenarth Citra Dio Mon from 78. *St Mary's Vicarage, Abergavenny, Gwent,* (Abergavenny 3168)

CLEMENTS, Alan Austin. b 39. AIB 66. Linc Th Coll 74. **d** 76 Dorchester for Ox **p** 77 Ox. C of Woodley 76-79; Wokingham Dio Ox from 80. *2a Norreys Avenue, Wokingham, RG11 1TU.* (Wokingham 780820)

CLEMENTS, Andrew. b 48. BD and AKC 72. St Aug Coll Cant 72. **d** 73 **p** 74 Man. C of All SS & Marts Langley 73-76; St Bart Westhoughton 76-81; R of Thornton Dale w Ellerburne and Wilton Dio York from 81. *Rectory, Thornton Dale, Pickering, N Yorks.* (Pickering 74244)

CLEMENTS, Anthony John. b 37. K Coll Lon and Warm AKC 60. **d** 61 **p** 62 Birm. C of Highters Heath 61-63; St Nich Guildf 63-66; King's Lynn (in c of St Edm N Lynn) 66-70; P-in-c of Tilney All SS 78-79. *2 Pingles Road, North Wootton, Kings Lynn, Norfolk.* (K Lynn 674164)

CLEMENTS, Edwin George. b 41. Chich Th Coll 77. **d** 79 Reading for Ox **p** 80 Ox. C of St Pet Didcot Dio Ox from 79. *52 Edwin Road, Didcot, Oxon, OX11 8LE.*

CLEMENTS, Harold Denis. b 08. Lich Th Coll 36. **d** 38 **p** 39 Lich. C of Tamworth 38-45 (in c of Hopwas 41-45); Abington (in c of St Alban) 45-47; R of All SS Jordanhill Glas 47-49; Writhlington 49-54; V of Ascen S Twerton 54-71; Ch Ch Bath 71-76; C-in-c of H Trin Bath 74-76. *14 St Michael's Road, Melksham, Wilts.* (Bath 704711)

✠ **CLEMENTS, Right Rev Kenneth John.** Univ of Syd BA (2nd cl Hist) 33. St Jo Coll Morpeth 27. ACT ThD 49. **d** 33 **p** 34 River. Regr Dio River 33-37; C of St Paul's Pro-Cathl Hay 35-37; P-in-c of Narrandera 37-39; R of Tumbarumba 39-43; Gunning 43-44; Dir of Studies Canberra Gr Sch 45-46; Regr and Archd of Goulb 46-56; Exam Chap to Bp of Goulb 47-56; Cons Bp Coadj of Goulb in St Andr Cathl Syd 29 June 49 by Abp of Syd; Abp of Brisb; Bps of Bath; Armid; Goulb; River; Bps Hilliard and Pilcher; VG Dio C & Goulb 49-56; Apptd Bp of Graft 56; Trld to C & Goulb 61; res 71; Perm to Offic Dio C & Goulb 72-74; Dio Brisb from 74. *Mowbray, Mons School Road, Buderim, Queensland, Australia 4556.*

CLEMENTS, Philip Christian. b 38. Late Pri of K Coll Lon and Warm BD (2nd cl) and AKC (2nd cl) 64. **d** 65 **p** 66 Cant. C of St Mark S Norwood 65-68; Chap and Asst Master (Ho Master from 72) R Russell Sch Croydon 68-75; Asst Chap Denstone Coll Uttoxeter 75-76; Chap 76-81; Lancing Coll from 81. *Lancing College, Sussex, BN15 0RW.*

CLEMENTS, Roy Adrian. b 44. Univ of Dur BA 68, Dipl Th 69. St Chad's Coll Dur 65. **d** 69 Pontefract for Wakef **p** 70 Wakef. C of Royston 69-73; V of Clifton 73-77; St Matt Rastrick Dio Wakef from 77. *St Matthew's Vicarage, Ogden Lane, Brighouse, W Yorks, HD6 3HF.* (Brighouse 713386)

CLEMENTS, Roy Clifford. Univ of NZ BA 55, MA 56. St Jo Coll Auckld 60. **d** 61 **p** 62 Waik. C of St Aid Claudelands 61-63; Te Awamutu 63-64; Gen Sec NZ Studs Christian Movement from 65; L to Offic Dios Auckl and Wai 65-70; Dio Wel from 65. *P.O. Box 742, Wellington, NZ.*

CLEMENTS, Very Rev Thomas. b 16. Trin Coll Dub BA 38, Div Test 39, BD 54. **d** 39 Tuam for Down **p** 40 Down. C of St Donard Belf 39-41; St Anne's Cathl (in c of Miss Distr) Belf 41-43; C-in-c of Kildrumfertin w Ballymachugh 43-45; Mullaghdun 45-48; I of Finner 48-50; Enniskillen (and Trory to 56) Dio Clogh from 50; Preb of Donacavey in Clogh Cathl 57-60; RD of Enniskillen from 57; Chan of Clogh Cathl 58-60; Prec 60-66; Dean from 66. *Rectory, Enniskillen, Co Fermanagh, N Ireland.*

CLEMENTSON, John William. b 08. **d** and **p** 40 gui. C of St Jo Georgetown 40; St Geo Cathl Georgetown 40-42; R of Anna Regina 42-45; V of Priors Marston 45-47; Priors Hardwick 45-47; R of Brampton Ash w Dingley 47-49; P-in-c of St Geo Montserrat 49-52; Chap to Leper Hosp and V of St Jo Bapt Barb 52-57; St Faith Wandsworth 57-62; R of Weeley 62-70; C-in-c of Beaumont w Moze 62-68. *Manormead Nursing Home, Tilford Road, Hindhead, Surrey.*

CLEMETSON, Thomas Henry. b 22. **d** 62 **p** 63 Ches. C of Timperley 62-66; V of Hurdsfield 66-76; St Sav Stockport Dio Ches from 76. *St Saviour's Vicarage, Great Moor, Stockport, Ches.* (061-483 2633)

CLEMETT, Peter Thomas. b 33. St D Coll Lamp BA 60. Sarum Th Coll 59. **d** 61 **p** 62 Mon. C of Tredegar 61-63; Chap of St Woolos Cathl Newport 63-66; CF from 66. *c/o Ministry of Defence, Lansdowne House, Berkeley Square, W 1.*

CLENDON, David Arthur. b 33. Em Coll Cam 2nd cl Hist Trip pt i 55, BA (2nd cl Th Trip pt i) 56, MA 61. Wells Th Coll 56. **d** 58 **p** 59 St Alb. C of All SS Hockerill 58-62; Digswell 62-63; Ch Ch Luton 63-65; V of Caddington 65-71; C-in-c of Ch Ch w St Pet Luton 71-76; Pirton Dio St Alb from 75. *Pirton Vicarage, Hitchin, Herts.* (Pirton 230)

CLENNETT, Raymond Theodore. St Jo Coll Winnipeg. **d** 51 **p** 52 Edmon. V of Mannville 52-53; Marwayne 53-54; Clandonald 54-55; Miss at Frog Lake 55-60; I of Haines Junction and of Champagne 60-69; Alaska Highway 62-69; Can of Yukon 65-76; Exam Chap to Bp of Yukon 65-76; C of Whitehorse Yukon 69-70: R 70-76; Hudson Bay Dio Sask from 76. *Box 274, Hudson Bay, Sask, Canada.*

CLERKE, Christopher John. Moore Th Coll Syd ACT ThL 69. **d** 69 Syd. C of St Aug Neutral Bay 69-71; Hunter's Hill 71-72; P-in-c of Menindee 72-77; Missr at Leigh Creek and N Area Dio Willoch from 77. *Box 52, Leigh Creek, S Australia 5731.* (Leigh Creek 46)

CLEVELAND, Archdeacon of. *See* Southgate, Ven John Eliot.

CLEVERDON, Ven Harold Dawe. d 34 **p** 35 Tor. C of Ch of Messiah Tor 34-35; I of Mulmur 35-37; R of Beeton w Tottenham and Palgrave 37-40; I of Lakeview 40-42; Chap CASF 42-46; R of Ch Ch Oshawa 46-68; Archd of Scarborough 56-68; Archd (Emer) from 69. *3 Larry Avenue, RR 2, Oshawa, Ont., Canada.*

CLEVERLEY, Michael Frank. b 36. Univ of Man BSc (Tech) 57. Wells Th Cll 61. **d** 63 **p** 64 Wakef. C of St Aug Halifax 63; St Jo Evang Huddersfield 63-66; Brighouse 66-69; V of Gomersal Dio Wakef from 69. *St Mary's Vicarage, Gomersal, Cleckheaton, W Yorks, BD19 4LS.* (Cleckheaton 872131)

CLEWES, Henry. Lich Th Coll 54. **d** 55 **p** 56 Lich. C of Hednesford 55-58; V of U Gornal 58-64; Milton 64-70; R of Tatenhill 70-77; P-in-c of Dresden Dio Lich from 77. *Dresden Vicarage, Longton, Staffs.*

CLIBBENS, Mervyn Arthur Roy. d 61 Bunb **p** 69 Bris. C of St Bonif Cathl Bunb 61-66; Perm to Offic Dio Bris from 66. *14 Maple Close, Stockwood, BS14 8HX.* (Whitchurch 838912)

CLIFF, Bruce Stanley. b 42. Ridley Coll Melb 70. **d** 72 **p** 73 Gippsld. C of Bruthen 72-75; R of Stratford Dio Gippsld from 75. *Rectory, Stratford, Vic, Australia 3862.*

CLIFF, Frank Graham. b 38. Clifton Th Coll Dipl Th 66. **d** 66 Bp Horstead for Leic **p** 67 Leic. C of St Chris Conv Distr Pk Estate Leic 66-69; Whitton w Thurleston and Akenham 69-71; in Amer Ch from 71. *4902 Jason, Houston, Texas 77035, USA.*

CLIFF, Julian Arnold. b 41. Cranmer Hall Dur 63. **d** 66 **p** 67 Ches. C of Bowdon 66-69; Poynton 69-73; C-in-c of St Barn Crewe Dio Ches 73-74; V 75-80. *c/o Vicarage, West Street, Crewe, Chesh.* (Crewe 2418)

CLIFF, Philip Basil. b 15. Univ of Lon BSc 61. **d** and **p** 77 Birm. Hon C of St Laur Northfield Dio Birm from 77. *4 Fox Hill Close, Birmingham, B29 4AH.*

CLIFFORD, Edward Aemilius Homfray. Trin Coll Tor BA 40, LTh 47. **d** and **p** 47 Tor. C of St Cuthb Tor 47-50; P-in-c of St Laur Miss Tor 50-56; I of St Jas Tor 53-54; Chap of Sunnybrook Hosp Tor 56-57; C of St Aug of Cant City and Dio Tor from 57. *5 Stibbard Avenue, Toronto, Ont., Canada.*

CLIFFORD, Garth. d 75 Tor for Keew **p** 80 Keew. On

leave 75-80; I of Atikokan Dio Keew from 80. *Box 554, Atikokan, Ont, Canada.*

CLIFFORD, Henry Albert. b 02. Dorch Miss Coll 25. **d** 29 **p** 30 Derby. C of St John Long Eaton 29-32; Gt Clacton 32-36; V of Steeple Bumpstead 36-46; R of Rayne 46-73. *19 Connaught Road, Fleet, Aldershot, Hants, GU13 9RA.* (Fleet 3381)

CLIFFORD, Peter Gilbert. Moore Th Coll Syd ACT ThL 62. **d** 61 **p** 62 Adel. C of St Luke Adel 61-62; SAMS Miss Dio Argent 63-69; Dio Parag 70-73; SAMS M 73-77; Min of St Jas Minto Dio Syd from 78. *Kent Street, Minto, NSW, Australia.* (605-4425)

CLIFT, Canon David. b 34. Trin Coll Ox BA (3rd cl Lit Hum) 58, MA 62. Cudd Coll 58. **d** 60 **p** 61 Birm. C of St Paul w St Mark Birm 60-63; Caversham 63-67; V of U Arley and Industr Chap in Kidderminster 67-72; Industr Chap in Maidstone and E Kent from 73; Hon Can of Cant Cathl from 79. *41 Buckland Hill, Maidstone, Kent, ME16 0SA.* (Maidstone 52062)

CLIFT, Canon John Wilfred. b 04. MBE 65. St Paul's Coll Burgh 29. **d** 30 Southw for Col Bp **p** 31 Perth. C of St Geo Cathl Perth 30; St John Fremantle 30-44; Chap Miss to Seamen and SPCK Port Chap Fremantle Dio Perth 30-44; Sen Chap Port of Lon and Dio Chelmsf 44-49; Miss to Seamen Southn and L to Offic 49-72; C of St Jas Southn Docks 50-52; Commiss Bunb, Perth, Kalg and NW Austr 45-72; Hon Can of Perth from 51. *34 Priory Close, Beeston Regis, Sheringham, Norf.*

CLIFT, Norman Charles. b 21. Kelham Th Coll 40. **d** 45 **p** 46 Chelmsf. C of St. Marg Leytonstone 45-54; Min of St Alb Conv Distr Gt Ilford 54-58; V 58-61; V of St Marg w St Columba Leytonstone 61-74; V of Gt w L Bardfield Dio Chelmsf from 75. *Great Bardfield Vicarage, Braintree, Essex.* (Dunmow 810267)

CLIFTON, Gregory Keith. b 45. Moore Coll Syd ThL 71. **d** 73 Syd **p** 73 Bp Delbridge for Syd. C of Gymea 73-75; Epping 75-77; R of Harris Pk 77-80; St Barn Fairfield Dio Syd from 80. *10 Frederick Street, Fairfield, NSW, Australia 2165.* (72-1628)

CLIFTON, Roger Gerald. b 45. ACA 70. Sarum Wells Th Coll 70. **d** 73 Bp Malmesbury for Bris **p** 74 Bris. C of Winterbourne 73-76; P-in-c of St Cuthb Brislington Dio Bris from 76. *35 Wick Crescent, Brislington, Bristol, BS4 4HG.* (Bris 776351)

CLINCH, Canon Arthur Harold Gordon. b 1885. Westcott Ho Cam 24. **d** 26 **p** 27 Worc. C of Pershore 26-30; V of Claines 30-56; Proc Conv Worc 44-51; RD of Worc 44-56; Hon Can of Worc 47-56; Can (Emer) from 56; C of Bournemouth (in c of St Swith) 57-63; Dir Bournemouth and Distr Samaritans 62-70. *1 Richmond Park Crescent, Bournemouth, Dorset.* (Bournemouth 36847)

CLINCH, Kenneth Wilfred. b 22. Bps' Coll Cheshunt 62. **d** 64 **p** 65 Chich. C of Old w New Shoreham 64-67; St Mich AA Lancing (in c of Ch of Good Shepherd) 67-73; R of St Jo Evang U St Leonards Dio Chich from 73. *St John's Rectory, Brittany Road, St Leonards-on-Sea, Sussex.* (0424 423367)

CLINGO, John Francis. b 20. Lich Th Coll 52. **d** 54 **p** 55 Birm. C of Olton 54-59; V of Llangarron w Llangrove 59-65; Ivington w Monkland Dio Heref from 65; C-in-c of Dilwyn w Stretford 72-73. *Monkland Vicarage, Leominster, Herefs.* (Ivington 274)

CLITHEROW, Andrew. b 50. St Chad's Coll Dur BA 72. Sarum Wells Th Coll 78. **d** 79 St Alb **p** 80 Hertford for St Alb. Hon C of Ch Ch Bedford Dio St Alb from 79; Asst Chap Bedford Sch from 79. *c/o The Common Room, Bedford School, Burnaby Road, Bedford.*

✠ **CLITHEROW, Right Rev Richard George.** b 09. CCC Cam 2nd cl Th Trip pt i A 34, BA (2nd cl Th Trip pt i B) 35, MA 39. Wells Th Coll 35. **d** 36 **p** 37 S'wark. C of St Aug S Bermondsey 36-40; CF (EC) 40-46; Can of Guildf 46-58; Dioc Missr and Exam Chap to Bp of Guildf 46-58; Proc Conv Guildf 51-58; Cons Ld Bp Suffr of Stafford in Cant Cathl 11 June 58 by Abp of Cant; Bps of Birm; Guildf; and Lich; Bps Suffr of Shrewsbury; Maidstone; Dover; Bps Hawkes and Dale; res 74; Preb of Tachbrook in Lich Cathl 58-67; Proc Conv Lich from 67; Hon Can of Lich from 68. *37 Fairbanks Walk, Swynnerton, Stone, Staffs, ST15 0PF.*

CLODE, Arthur Raymond Thomas. b 35. Roch Th Coll 67. **d** 69 **p** 70 Birm. C of Blackheath 69-72; V of Londonderry 73-75; R of Bride 75-78. *c/o Rectory, Bride, Ramsey, IM.* (Kirk Andreas 351)

CLOETE, Richard James. b 47. AKC 71. St Aug Coll Cant 72. **d** 72 **p** 73 S'wark. C of St Matt Redhill 72-75; V of St Paul Furzedown Streatham Dio S'wark from 75. *Vicarage, Chillerton Road, SW17 9BE.* (01-672 5536)

CLOGHER, Lord Bishop of. *See* McMullan, Right Rev Gordon.

CLOGHER, Archdeacon of. *See* Skuce, Ven Francis John Leonard.

CLOGHER, Dean of. *See* Clements, Very Rev Thomas.

CLONFERT, Bishop of. *See* Limerick.

CLONFERT and KILMACDUAGH, Archdeacon of. *See* Bredin, Ven Thomas Andrew Noble.

CLONFERT and KILMACDUAGH, Dean of. *See* Champ, Very Rev Cyril Bruce.

CLONMACNOISE, Dean of (Dio Meath). *See* Bredin, Very Rev Thomas Andrew Noble.

CLOSE, Brian Eric. b 49. St Chad's Coll Dur BA 74, MA 76. Ridley Hall Cam 74. **d** 76 **p** 77 Ripon. C of Far Headingley 76-79; St Wilfrid Harrogate 79-82; P-in-c of Alconbury w Weston and of Buckworth and of Upton Dio Ely from 82. *Vicarage, Alconbury, Cambs.* (Alconbury 890284)

CLOSE, David Barrie. d and **p** 59 Bath. C of Mudgee 59-61; P-in-c of Coolah 61-62; R 62-66; C of Gosford 66-69; P-in-c of Beresfield 69-73. *c/o Diocesan Registry, Tyrrell House, Newcastle, NSW, Australia.*

CLOSE, Edric George. b 10. Chich Th Coll 38. **d** 41 Linc **p** 42 Grimsby for Linc. C of St Jo Evang in Spittlegate Grantham 41-46; V of St Matt Sutton Bridge 46-53; Morton w Hacconby 53-67; R of Thorpe-on-the-Hill 67-78; N Scarle 68-78; V of Eagle 68-78. *4 Mill Moor Way, North Hykeham, Lincoln, LN6 9PQ.*

CLOSS-PARRY, Canon Selwyn. b 25. St D Coll Lamp BA 50. St Mich Coll Llan 50. **d** 52 **p** 53 Ban. C of Dwygyfylchi w Penmaenmawr 52-58; V of Treuddyn 58-66; R of Llangystennin 66-71; V of Holywell 71-77; Cursal Can of St A Cathl from 76; V of Colwyn Dio St A from 77. *Vicarage, Old Colwyn, Colwyn Bay, Clwyd.* (Colwyn Bay 55079)

CLOTHIER, Gerald Harry. b 34. Oak Hill Th Coll 75. **d** 78 Chelmsf **p** 79 Bradwell for Chelmsf. C of Highwood 78-79; Writtle w Highwood Dio Chelmsf from 79. *Agape, Loves Green, Highwood, Chelmsford, CM1 3QG.*

CLOTHIER, Canon Harry Legg. b 05. G and C Coll Cam BA 27, MA 36. Ely Th Coll 28. **d** 29 **p** 30 Dur. C of St Mary Tyne Dk 29-32; St Ives Hunts 32-33; Earsdon (in c of St Mary Holywell) 33-36; V of Cuthb Newc T 36-38; R of Aspley Guise 38-49; RD of Fleete 43-47; V of Braughing 49-54; C-in-c of Westmill 49-54; V of Sharnbrook 54-69; R of Knotting w Souldrop 54-69; Hon Can of St Alb 62-69; Can (Emer) from 69; L to Offic Dio St D from 69. *Glenview, Aberporth, Cardigan, Dyfed, SA43 2ER.*

CLOUDSDALE, Arthur Cygnet. Christ's Coll Tas ACT ThL 47. **d** 47 **p** 48 Tas. C of H Trin Hobart 47-50; Miss at Dodoma 50-53; Mpwapwa Tang 53-55; I of Geeveston w Port Esperance Tas 55-58; R of Sheff Tas 58-60; P-in-c Hopetoun w Beulah and Rainbow 60-66; R 66-68; St Paul Launceston 68-72; Brighton 72-77; Howrah Dio Tas from 77. *1 Lorne Crescent, Howrah, Tasmania 7018.* (002-479700)

CLOUGH, Alfred Frederick. b 03. St Jo Coll Manit 25. **d** 29 Rupld **p** 30 Warrington for Liv for Rupld. C of St Chrys Winnipeg 29-31; Houghton-le-Spring 31-35; Newburn (in c of Throckley) 35-39; R of Whitfield 39-48; V of St Mary Berwick-on-Tweed 48-67; Warter w Huggate 67-71. *12 Bardney Road, Hunmanby, Filey, York.*

CLOUGH, Harry. b 11. AKC (1st cl) 39. **d** 39 **p** 40 Man. C of St Mary Hulme 39-42; St Gabr Hulme 42-44; St Mich Wakef 44-48; Rashcliffe 48-49; V of Battyeford w Knowl 49-67; U Hopton 68-77; Perm to Offic Dio Wakef from 77. *2 Kirkgate Lane, South Hiendley, Barnsley, S Yorks, S72 9DS.*

CLOUGH, Ven John Cyril. Trin Coll Tor BA 30. **d** 32 Niag for Tor **p** 33 Tor. C of Ch Ch Deer Pk Tor 32-37; R of Port Perry 37-40; I of N Tor Miss Area 40; Chap CASF 40-45; R of the Good Shepherd Mt Dennis 40-52; St Luke Winnipeg 52-63; Can of Rupld 58-62; R of St John Pet Tor 62-74; Can of Tor 64-72; Archd of Pet Tor 72-74; Archd (Emer) from 75. *17 Abbott Boulevard, Cobourg, Ont., Canada.*

CLOUGH, Richard. b 1898. Keble Coll Ox BA (3rd cl Mod Hist) 21, MA 25. Wells Th Coll 28. **d** 29 **p** 30 Chich. C of Cuckfield 29-33; St Sav Leic 33-35; R of Seagrave 35-37; CF (EC) 40-42; Hon CF from 42; Perm to Offic Dio Ox 43; Dio York 38 and 43-44; Offg C-in-c of Bedford Chap Ex 44-45; V of Yarcombe 45-51; Perm to Offic Dio S'wark 51-52; R of Lowick (w Sudborough from 55) 52-59; RD of Thrapston 56-59; PC of Underbarrow w Helsington 59-69; L to Offic Dio Carl from 69. *Pye Howe, Great Langdale, Ambleside, Cumb, LA22 9JS.* (Langdale 202)

CLOUT, Ronald Charles. Moore Th Coll Syd 61. ACT ThL 62. **d** 62 **p** 63 Syd. C of Nowra 62-64; R 64-77; H Trin Miller's Point Syd 77-81; on leave. *c/o 50 Lower Fort Street, Miller's Point, Sydney. Australia 2000.* (27-2664)

CLOWES, John. b 45. K Coll Lon and Warm AKC 67. **d** 68 **p** 69 Pet. C of St Columba, Corby 68-71; R of Itchen Stoke w Ovington and Abbotstone 71-74; V of Acton and L w Gt Waldingfield 74-80; Team V of Southend-on-Sea Dio

Chelmsf from 80. *93 Cambridge Road, Southend-on-Sea, SS1 1EP.*

CLOYNE, Archdeacon of. *See* Gordon, Ven Arthur.

CLOYNE, Bishop of. *See* Cork.

CLOYNE, Dean of. (Vacant)

CLUBLEY, Clifford. b 06. Univ of Leeds BA 39, MA 46. Univ of Hull PhD 65. Lich Th Coll 30. **d** 32 **p** 33 Bradf. C of Keighley 32-35; St Aug Hull 35-36; Baildon 36-40 and 45-46; CF (EC) 40-45; V of Ault Hucknall 46-51; Perm to Offic Dio Linc 53-55; C-in-c of St John's Conv Distr Bracebridge Heath 55-65; PC of Chapel St Leon 65-68; V 68-72; L to Offic Dio Linc from 72. *203 Rookery Lane, Lincoln.*

CLUCAS, Robert Stephen. Rhodes Univ Grahmstn BA 48. St Paul's Th Coll Grahmstn LTh (w Distinc) 50. **d** 50 **p** 51 Kimb K. C of St Cypr Cathl, Kimb 50-52; P-in-c of Prieska 52-55; LPr Dio Grahmstn 55-58; C of Pietersburg W Miss 58-59; L to Offic Dio Johann 59-60 and 63-76; C of Ferreiras Tn 60-63; Perm to Offic Dio Capetn from 76. *93 Station Road, Observatory, CP, S Africa.*

CLUER, Donald Gordon. b 21. SOC 61. **d** 64 **p** 65 S'wark. C of St Jas New Malden 64-68; Bexhill 68-73; V of Shoreham Beach 73-77; St Richard Heathfield Dio Chich from 77. *St Richard's Vicarage, Heathfield, E Sussex.* (Heathfield 2744)

CLUES, Raymond William. b 12. MBE (Mil) 61. Roch Th Coll. **d** 61 **p** 62 Win. C of Basingstoke 61-63; CF (TA) 62-67; CF (TAVR) 67-75; Hon CF from 75; R of Swarraton w Northington Brown Candover and Chilton Candover 63-72; V of St Denys Southn 72-78; Perm to Offic Dio Ely from 79. *92 Grounds Avenue, March, Cambs, PE15 9BA.* (55826)

CLUETT, Frank. Mem Univ Newfld BA 69. McMaster Univ Hamilton MA 71. Qu Coll Newfld LTh 61. **d** 59 **p** 60 Newfld. I of Topsail 59-60; R of Greenspond 60-65; I of Buchans 65-68; on leave 69-71; C of Corner Brook 71-79; Exam Chap to Bp of W Newfld from 76; L to Offic Dio E Newfld from 79. *Queen's College, Prince Philip Drive, St John's, Newfoundland, Canada.*

CLUETT, Vernon. Qu Coll Newfld LTh 53. **d** 51 **p** 53 Newfld. Miss at White Bay, Newfld 51-57; R of Trinity 57-62; Port Dufferin 62-65; St Martin's 65-70; St Pet, Halifax Dio NS from 70. *6 Dakin Drive, Rockingham, NS, Canada.* (443-1296)

CLUTTERBUCK, Herbert Ivan. b 16. Ch Coll Cam 3rd cl Cl Trip pt i 37, BA (3rd cl Th Trip pt i) 38, MA 42. Chich Th Coll 38. **d** 39 Bp Linton Smith for Roch **p** 40 Roch. C of H Trin Lamorbey 39-41; CF (EC) 41-44; LPr Dio Ely 44-47; Chap to Wellingborough Sch 44-47; Chap RN 47-62; V of Lanteglos-by-Fowey 62-66; Org Sec Ch U 66-74; Chap Qu Marg Sch York 74-76; Chap and Dir of Relig Stud Roedean Sch Brighton 76-81; Master St John's Hosp City and Dio Lich from 82. *Master's House, St John's Hospital, Lichfield, Staffs, WS13 6PB.* (Lichfield 24169)

CLUTTERBUCK, John Michael. b 28. Qu Coll Ox BA (2nd cl Engl) 53, 2nd cl Th 55. St Steph Ho Ox 53. **d** 56 **p** 57 Glouc. C of Tewkesbury 56-59; H Redeemer Clerkenwell 59-64; R of Filton 65-72; Frampton Cotterell Dio Bris from 72. *Frampton Cotterell Rectory, Bristol, BS17 2BP.* (Winterbourne 772112)

CLYDE, John. b 39. Div Hostel Dub 70. **d** 71 **p** 72 Connor. C of St Aid Belf 71-74; R of St Barn Belf 74-80; H Trin Belf Dio Connor from 80. *313 Ballysillan Road, Belfast, BT14 6RD.* (Belfast 743958)

CLYNES, William. b 33. Sarum Wells Th Coll 78. **d** 79 **p** 80 Bris. C of St Mich Winterbourne Dio Bris from 79. *31 High Street, Winterbourne, Bristol, BS17 1JG.*

CLYNICK, Peter Charles. b 17. **d** 40 **p** 41 Ex. C of Alphington 40-42; Woodbury 42-43; St Luke Torquay 43-46; C-in-c of St Mich AA Pimlico (Conv Distr from 50) Torquay 46-53; PC of St Mary Virg Laira Plymouth 53-58; C-in-c of St Mary Cable St Stepney Dio Lon 58-68; V from 68. *385 Cable Street, E1 0AH.* (01-790 3141)

COAD, Gordon John. ACT ThL 50. **d** 47 Bend for Bal **p** 48 Bal. Prin St Cuthb Home for Boys Colac 47-50; V of Warracknabeal 50-53; Surrey Hills 53-57; Warden CA Tr Coll Newc 58-60; R of Wallsend 60-67; P-in-c of Charlestown 67-72; R 72-75; Mayfield 75-79; Perm to Offic Dio Newc from 79; Dio Armid from 80. *5 Souter Street, Bundarra, NSW, Australia 2359.*

COALDRAKE, Keith James. ACT ThL 45. **d** 46 **p** 47 Melb. C of St Paul Frankston 46-48; Chap of Forrest River Miss 48-56; Supt 48-54; C-in-c of Paterson 56-57; R of Kendall 57-63; V of Aramac 63-70; Hon Can of Rockptn 69-74; V of Dawson Valley 70-74; Merriwa 74-80. *Ditchley's, Deep Creek Road, Hannam Vale, NSW, Australia.*

COANGAE, Jeremiah. St Pet Coll Rosettenville. **d** 51 **p** 52 Bloemf. C of St Francis Miss Kroonstad 51-54; Thaba'Nchu 54-58; Dir Springfontein Miss 58-68; Senekal Miss 68-76. *Box 9, Thaba 'Nchu, OFS, S Africa.*

COATES, Calvin John. b 31. **d** 79 **p** 80 Centr Newfld. C of Lewisporte Dio Centr Newfld from 79. *1 First Avenue, Lewisporte, Newfoundland, Canada, A0G 3A0.*

COATES, Canon Francis Gustav. b 10. G and C Coll Cam BA 32, MA 36. OBE 63. Ridley Hall Cam 32. **d** 52 Ugan **p** 54 Worc for Col Bp. [f CMS Lay Miss] CMS Miss at Mwiri 52-65; C of St Paul Worthing 65-68; C-in-c of Wickmere w Wolterton and L Barningham 68-71; R of Heydon w Irmingland Dio Nor from 68; C-in-c of Booton w Braniston Dio Nor from 71; Hon Can of Busoga from 81. *Heydon Rectory, Norwich, Norf, NR11 6AD.* (Saxthorpe 218)

COATES, Glenn Curwood. b 50. Bp's Univ Lennoxville BA 76. Wycl Coll Tor LTh 79. **d** 79 **p** 80 Queb. C of Magdalen Is Dio Queb from 79. *Leslie Post Office, Grosse Ile, Magdalen Islands, Que, Canada, G0B 1M0.*

COATES, John David Spencer. b 41. Univ of Dur BA 64, Dipl Th 66. Cranmer Hall Dur 64. **d** 66 **p** 67 Glouc. C of Chipping Campden 66-69; CF from 69. *c/o Royal Army Chaplain's Dept Centre, Bagshot Park, Bagshot, Surrey, GU19 5PL.*

COATES, Canon Kenneth Will. b 17. St Jo Coll Dur LTh 45, BA 46. Tyndale Hall Bris 39. **d** 42 **p** 43 Man. C of St Geo Mart Daubhill 42-44; Perm to Offic Dio Bris 44-45; C of Cheadle (in c of St Andr) 47-49; V of All SS Preston 49-60; St Helens Dio Liv from 60; Surr from 62; Proc Conv Liv 64-70; Hon Can of Liv from 71. *Vicarage, St Helens, Mer, WA10 6LA.* (St Helens 22067)

COATES, Maxwell Gordon. b 49, Trin Coll Bris 75. **d** 77 **p** 78 S'wark. C of Blackheath Park Dio S'wark from 77. *1a Pond Road, Blackheath Park, SE3 9JL.*

COATES, Peter Frederick. b 50. AKC and BD 79. St Steph Ho Ox 79. **d** 80 Chelmsf **p** 81 Barking for Chelmsf. C of St Barn Woodford Dio Chelmsf from 80. *36a Greenstead Gardens, Woodford Green, Essex.* (01-504 9009)

COATES, Raymond Frederick William. b 14. AKC (1st cl) and Whichelow Pri 39. Bps' Coll Cheshunt 39. **d** 39 Bedford for St Alb **p** 40 St Alb. C of All SS w St John Hertford 39-41; C of St Steph St Alb 41-44; CF 44-64; Cf (R of O) 64-69; Hon CF from 69; V of Shepshed 64-69; King's Somborne w Ashley 69-81. *Kingston House, Stowmarket Road, Needham Market, Suff.* (Needham Market 720791)

COATES, Robert James. b 16. Lon Coll of Div 57. **d** 59 **p** 60 Chich. [f CMS Miss] C of St Leon St Leonards-on-Sea 59-62; V of Brimscombe 62-67; Chap St Geo Hosp Stafford 67-81. *17 Haywood Grange, Little Haywood, Stafford, ST18 0UB.* (L Haywood 881508)

COATES, Stuart Murray. b 49. Univ of Lon BA 70. Wycl Hall Ox 72. **d** 75 Warrington for Liv **p** 76 Liv. C of Rainford 75-78; Orrell Dio Liv 78-79; V from 79. *St Luke's Vicarage, Lodge Road, Orrell, Wigan, Lancs.* (Up Holland 623410)

COATH, Richard Kenneth Routh. b 14. AKC 42. **d** 42 **p** 43 Ches. C of St Mary Stockport 42-46; Dawlish 46-50; R of Cotleigh w Monkton 50-53; Sennen 53-58; Talaton 58-67; V of Escot 58-67; Bampton 67-76; R of Huntsham 68-76; Clayhanger 68-76; V of Petton 68-76; RD of Tiverton 75-76; R of Feniton Dio Ex from 76; P-in-c of Buckerell Dio Ex 76-78; R from 78. *Feniton Rectory, Honiton, Devon, EX14 0ED.* (Honiton 850253)

COATHAM, Canon Sydney. b 16. Univ of Leeds BA 40. Coll of Resurr Mirfield 40. **d** 42 **p** 43 Blackb. C of St Pet Fleetwood 42-44; St John Southend (in c of St Barn Downham) 44-49; V of Robert Town 49-55; St Jo Evang Cleckheaton 55-63; Lindley Dio Wakef from 63; Hon Can of Wakef Cathl from 80. *Lindley Vicarage, Huddersfield, Yorks.*

COATS, Leonard George. b 1896. Univ of Bris BA (1st cl Econ) 22. Sarum Th Coll 22. **d** 24 **p** 25 Ex. C of St Mark Ford 24-27; Totnes 27-30; Paignton 30-31; V of E Coker 31-40; C of St Mary Warw 40-45; V of Upton w Skilgate R 45-46; Henstridge 46-53; R of Shipham w Rowberrow 53-61. *Ladymead Cottage, Pound Lane, Bishops Lydeard, Taunton, Somt.*

COATSWORTH, Nigel George. b 39. Trin Hall Cam BA 61. Cudd Coll 61. **d** 63 **p** 64 Nor. C of Hellesdon 63-66. *Ewell Monastery, West Malling, Kent.*

COBB, Anthony Bernard Joseph. b 15. Univ of Leeds BA (2nd cl Gen) 37. Coll of Resurr Mirfield 37. **d** 39 Willesden for Lon **p** 40 Lon. C of St Paul Bow Common 39-46; V of St Mich AA Bromley-by-Bow 46-51; C-in-c of St Mich AA Conv Distr Bedford Dio St Alb 51-56; Min 56-66; V from 66. *St Michael's Vicarage, Faldo Road, Bedford, MK42 0EH.* (Bedford 66920)

COBB, Bruce Ian. b 02. St Aid Coll 46. **d** 48 **p** 49 Chelmsf. C of Hermon Hill South Woodford 48-53; V of St Erkenwald Barking 53-64; V of Shrub End 64-72. *7 Chaucer Way, Lexden, Colchester, Essex, CO3 4HA.*

COBB, Douglas Arthur. b 25. Kelham Th Coll. **d** 54 **p** 55 Lon. C of St Mich AA w Ch Ch N Kens 54-57; S Ruislip 57-63; V of St Silas Mart, St Pancras Dio Lon from 63; P-in-c of St Martin w St Andr Kentish Town Dio Lon from 81. *11 St Silas Place, NW5 3QP.* (01-485 3727)

COBB, George Reginald. b 50. Oak Hill Th Coll BA 81. **d** 81 St Alb. C of Ch Ch Ware Dio St Alb from 81. *42 Barley Ponds Road, Ware, Herts, SG12 7EZ.*

COBB, John Newbert. b 21. E Midl Min Tr Course 79. **d** 81 Sheff (NSM). C of Intake Dio Sheff from 81. *40 Sandall Rise, Wheatley Hills, Doncaster, S Yorks, DN2 5NL.*

COBB, John Philip Andrew. b 43. Univ of Man BSc (2nd cl Math) 65. New Coll Ox BA (2nd cl Th) 67, MA 71. Wycl Hall Ox 66. **d** 68 **p** 69 Ox. C of St Jo Evang w St Steph Reading 68-71; Ch of Good Shepherd Romford 71-73; SAMS Miss Dio Chile from 73; Exam Chap to Bp of Chile from 75; Dioc Admin and Treas from 80. *Iglesia Anglicana, Casilla 675, Santiago, Chile.*

COBB, Michael Hewett. K Coll Lon and Warm 53. **d** 54 St Alb **p** 56 Chich. C of Leavesden 54-55; St Mich AA Brighton 55-60; S Ruislip 60-61; Warden of Albion Ho Boys' Club 61-67; Uppingham Corby Boys' Club 67-69; Warden Quest Commun from 70; Perm to Offic Dio Birm from 71. *398 Alum Rock Road, Birmingham, B8 3DA.*

COBB, Peter George. b 37. Ch Ch Ox BA (2nd cl Hist) 59, 2nd cl Th 61, MA 63. St Steph Ho Ox 64. **d** 65 **p** 66 Birm. C of Solihull 65-69; Libr Pusey Ho Ox 69-71; L to Offic Dio Ox from 69; Sen Tutor St Steph Ho Ox 71-76; Custodian of Libr Pusey Ho Ox 76-78; V of Midsomer Norton Dio B & W from 78; Clandown Dio B & W from 78. *83 North Road, Midsomer Norton, Bath, BA3 2QH.* (Midsomer Norton 412118)

COBB, Peter Graham. b 27. St Jo Coll Cam BA 48, MA 52. Ridley Hall Cam 66. **d** 68 Bp T M Hughes for Llan **p** 69 Llan. C of Porthkerry w Barry 68-71; C-in-c of Penmark Dio Llan 71-72; V (w Porthkerry) 72-81; Magor w Redwick and Undy Dio Mon from 82. *Vicarage, Magor, Gwent, NP6 3PZ.* (Magor 880266)

COBB, Canon Robert John. b 08. Fitzw Ho Cam 2nd cl Econ Trip pt i 31, BA (2nd cl Th Trip pt i) 33, MA 37. Lon Coll of Div 33. **d** 34 **p** 35 Lon. Tutor Lon Coll of Div 33-39; Lect and L to Offic Dio Chich 40-43; V of St Matt Rugby 43-45; Surr 43-45; Exam Chap to Bp of Cov 44-45 and 47-54; Prin Clifton Th Coll 46-49; Chap to Rio Tinto Mines Huelva Spain 49-50; V of St Andr Burgess Hill 50-56; PC of H Trin Brighton 56-61; Can and Preb of Chich Cathl from 56; Dioc Officer for Adult Relig Educn 56-66; Proc Conv Chich 59-64; V of Rustington 61-78; Surr 65-78; RD of Arundel 68-75. *Flat 4, Fern Lodge, 33a Lyndhurst Road, Hove, BN3 6FB.* (0273-779901)

COBBETT, David George. St Jo Coll Morpeth 48. ACT ThL 50. **d** 51 **p** 53 Newc. C of New Lambton 51-54; Taree 54-56; R of Kendall 56-57; P-in-c of Pusan 57-65; Archd of Pusan 61-65; R of St Barn Orange 65-68; Warrnambool 68-73; I of Burwood 73-79; R of Glenelg Dio Adel from 79. *10 Augusta Street, Glenelg, S Australia 5045.* (295 2382)

COBERN, Canon Charles John Julian. b 14. Keble Coll Ox BA 36, MA 62. Cudd Coll 36. **d** 37 **p** 38 St Alb. C of St Mary Apsley End 37-41; St Mark Noel Pk 41-49; V of H Sav Hitchin 49-68; Woburn Sands 68-79; RD of Hitchin 62-68; Hon Can of St Alb 64-79; Can (Emer) from 79. *Flat 2a, 2 Walton Street, St Albans, Herts, AL1 4DQ.* (St Albans 33645)

COBHAM, George Albert Anthony Douglas. St Jo Coll Auckld LTh 55. **d** 56 **p** 57 Auckld. C of St Matt Auckld 56-57; Warrington Dio Liv 58-59; Mt Roskill 59-60; Chap Auckld Hosp 60-62; V of Kaitaia 62-67; Auckl City Missr 67-71; V of Forest Lake 67-71; Chap New Plymouth Hosp Dio Waik 71-78; Wel Hosps from 78. *22 Rua Street, Lyall Bay, Wellington, NZ.*

COBHAM, John Hargreaves Ashworth. b 06. CCC Cam BA 30, MA 34. Wells Th Coll 30. **d** 31 **p** 32 Southw. C of St Jo Evang Mansfield 31-34; Chap of Aysgarth Sch 34-38; R of Stockton-on-the-Forest w Holtby and Warthill 39-47; Chap RNVR 42-46; Chap to Nautical Coll Pangbourne 47-57; R of Barningham 58-80; C-in-c of Wycliffe w Hutton Magna 77-80. *c/o Barningham Rectory, Richmond, N Yorks, DL11 7DW.* (Barningham 217)

COBHAM, Ven John Oldcastle. b 1899. CCC Cam BA 21, 2nd cl Th Trip pt i 23, MA 25. Westcott Ho Cam 24. **d** 26 **p** 27 Win. C of St Thos Win 26-30; Vice-Prin Westcott Ho Cam and L to Offic Dio Ely 30-34; Select Pr Univ of Cam 33 and 40; Exam Chap to Bp of Southw 32-41; to Bp of Ex 45-48; to Bp of Dur 53-66; to Bp of Wakef 59-68; Prin Warden and Chap Qu Coll Birm 34-53; Hon Chap to Bp of Birm 36-53; V of St Benedict Cam 40-45; CF (EC) 43-45; Hon CF 45; Hon Can of Derby 50-53; Select Pr Univ of Ox 52-54; Can Res and Archd of Dur 53-69; Archd (Emer) from 69; Perm to Offic Dio St E from 69. *5 Church Close, Aldeburgh, Suff, IP15 5DY.* (Aldeburgh 2803)

COCHLIN, Maurice Reginald. b 19. GTC BTh 80. ACP (Lon) 60. STh (Lambeth) 74. Chich Th Coll 70. **d** 70 **p** 71 Portsm. C of St Jo Bapt Rowlands Castle 70-72; Asst Master and Chap at Paulsgrove Sch Cosham 71; C of Warblington w Emsworth 72-75; S w N Bersted (in c of N Bersted) 75-78; Hdmaster U Sch Littlemead, Chich 78-79; C of Saltdean Dio Chich from 79. *129 Rodmell Avenue, Saltdean, Brighton, BN2 8PH.* (Brighton 31639)

COCHRAN, Edward Brenton Nicol. K Coll NS BA 36, LTh 50, DD 58. **d** 37 **p** 38 NS. C of La Have 37-41; R of cornwallis 41-45; St Geo Sydney 45-53; St Mark Halifax 53-58; Dean and R of All SS Cathl Halifax NS 58-79; Exam Chap to Bp of NS from 70. *c/o Deanery, 1350 Tower Road, Halifax, NS, Canada.*

COCHRANE, Kenneth Wilbur. Trin Coll Dub BA 58, MA 61. **d** 58 **p** 59 Connor. C of St Aid Belf 58-61; St Nich Belf 61-62; Ch Ch Lisburn 62-63; C-in-c of St Paul Lisburn Dio Connor 63-65; R from 66. *St Paul's Rectory, Ballinderry Road, Lisburn, Co Antrim, BT28 1UD, N Ireland.* (Lisburn 3520)

COCHRANE, Norman John Michael Antony Ferguson. b 24. Late Scho of QUB BA (3rd cl French) 46. Linc Th Coll 49. **d** 51 **p** 52 Lon. C of St Geo Headstone Hatch End 51-56; C of Horsham (in c of H Trin) 56-76; V of Aldwick Dio Chich from 76. *Vicarage, Gossamer Lane, Aldwick, Bognor Regis, W Sussex.* (Pagham 2049)

COCHRANE, Canon Roy Alan. b 25. K Coll Lon and Warm AKC 53. **d** 54 **p** 55 Linc. C of St Faith Linc 54-56; Skegness (in c of St Clem) 56-59; R of Thurlby w Norton Disney 59-65; V of Swinderby 59-65; Chap HM Borstal Inst Morton Hall Swinderby 59-65; R of N Coates 65-69; V of Marsh Chapel 65-69; PC of Grainthorpe w Conisholme 65-69; V of Glanford Bridge (or Brigg) Dio Linc from 69; RD of Yarborough 76-81; Can and Preb of Linc Cathl from 77. *Vicarage, Glanford Road, Brigg, S Humb, DN20 8DJ.* (Brigg 53989)

COCHRANE, William Griffith. St Jo Coll Morpeth 26. **d** 27 **p** 28 Newc. C of Adamstown 27-28; Hamilton 28-31; L to Offic (Col Cl Act) at St Luke Bermondsey 31-32; St Aug Bermondsey 32-33; C of St John Farnworth 33-34; R of Nabiac 34-38; P-in-c of Belmont 38-42; R of Wingham 42-51; Wickham 51-60; The Entrance 60-68; Perm to Offic Dio Newc from 68. *98 Main Road, Toukley, NSW, Australia 2263.*

COCKAYNE, Michael. d 69 C & Goulb. C of St Jo Bapt Canberra 69-73; R of Koorawatha 73-76; P-in-c of Moruya 76-77; R of Queanbeyan Dio C & Goulb from 78. *Box 103, Queanbeyan, NSW, Australia 2620.*

COCKBURN, Bruce Alister. b 30. St Jo Coll Auckld LTh 74. **d** 74 Wel **p** 75 Bp McKenzie for Wel. C of Feilding 74-77; V of Patea 77-80; Epiph Masterton S Dio Wel from 80. *15 Intermediate Street, Masterton, NZ.* (85-333)

COCKBURN, Norman John. b 06. Univ of Edin MA 28, BD (distinc in Eccles Hist) 31, PhD 51. Edin Th Coll 28. **d** 30 **p** 31 Edin. C of H Trin Stirling 30-33; Chap of St Mary's Cathl (in c of H Trin Dean Bridge) Edin 33-36; Vice-Prin Edin Th Coll 36-41; Can and Vice-Prov of Edin Cathl 41-53; Gen Sec BFBS 53-67; L to Offic Dio S'wark from 68. *College of St Barnabas, Blackberry Lane, Lingfield, Surrey, RH7 6NJ.*

COCKBURN, Sidney. b 14. Univ of Leeds BA 36. Coll of Resurr Mirfield 36. **d** 38 **p** 40 Dur. C of St Jas W Hartlepool 38-39; Perm to Offic at St German Roath 39-40; C of St Paul Gateshead 40-42; St Mary the Virgin Newc T 42-43; Serving w RAFVR 43-47; C of Heanor (in c of All SS Marlpool) 47-51; PC (V from 68) of St John, Long Eaton Dio Derby from 51. *59 Trowell Grove, Long Eaton, Nottingham, NG10 4AY.* (Long Eaton 4819)

COCKCROFT, Basil Stanley. Univ of Leeds BSc 49. Wells Th Coll 64. **d** 66 **p** 67 Wakef. C of Featherstone 66-69; Norton Dur 69-71; C-in-c of Eldon Dur 71-75; L to Offic Dio Wakef from 75. *9 Dene Close, South Parade, Elland, W Yorks.*

COCKE, James Edmund. b 26. Wadh Coll Ox 3rd cl Mod Hist 49, BA 50, MA 55. Wells Th Coll 50. **d** 52 **p** 53 Win. C of Christchurch 52-57; V of Highfield City and Dio Ox from 57; Chap Wingfield-Morris Hosp Ox (Nuffield Orthopaedic Centre) from 57. *85 Old Road, Headington, Oxford, OX3 7LB.* (Oxford 62536)

COCKERELL, David John. b 47. Univ Coll Cardiff BA 71. Univ Coll Swansea MA 74. Qu Coll Cam BA 75. Westcott Ho Cam 73. **d** 76 **p** 77 Ripon. C of Chapel Allerton 76-79; Farnley 79-81; Team V of Hitchin (in c of St Faith) Dio St Alb from 81. *St Faith's Vicarage, Franklin Gardens, Hitchin, Herts.*

COCKERTON, John Clifford Penn. b 27. Univ of Liv BA (2nd cl Geog) 48. St Cath S Ox BA (2nd cl Th) 54, MA 58. Wycl Hall Ox 51. **d** 54 **p** 55 Liv. C of St Helens 54-58; Tutor Cranmer Hall Dur 58-60; Chap 60-63; Warden from 68; L to Offic Dio Dur from 58; Vice-Prin St Jo Coll Dur 63-70; Prin 70-78; Exam Chap to Bp of Dur 71-72; R of Wheldrake Dio York from 78; M Gen Syn from 80. *Wheldrake Rectory, York, YO4 6AW.* (Wheldrake 230)

COCKIN, Canon Charles Munby. b 12. MBE (Mil) 46.

Late Scho of Em Coll Cam BA 34, 1st cl Th Trip pt i 35, MA 38. MBE (Mil) 46. Westcott Ho Cam 46. **d** and **p** 48 Southw. C of Radcliffe-on-Trent 48-50; V of Stanground 50-56; R of Empingham 56-63; V of Oundle w Ashton 63-77; Surr from 63; RD of Oundle from 67-72; Hon Can of Pet 70-77; Can (Emer) from 77; M Gen Syn Pet 70-75; Hon C of Much Hadham Dio St Alb from 77. *Horseshoe Cottage, Much Hadham, Herts.* (027984-3217)

✠ **COCKIN, Right Rev George Eyles Irwin.** b 08. Univ of Leeds BA 31. Linc Th Coll 52. **d** 53 **p** 54 Sheff. [F Lay Miss CMS Nigeria 33-52] C of Kimberworth 53-55; Sen Supervisor of Schs to Dios Niger and Nig Delta 55-59; Cons Ld Bp of Ow in All SS Cathl Onitsha 25 Jan 59 by Abp of W Afr; Bps of Niger; Nig Delta; Lagos; Ibad; Ondo-B; and N Nig; Bps Nkemena, Awosika and Afonya; res 69; Asst Bp in Dio York from 69; R of Bainton 69-78; RD of Harthill 73-78. *42 Carr Lane, Willerby, Hull.* (Hull 653086)

COCKING, Albert. b 1893. MBE 17. AKC 23. Leeds Cl Scho 23. **d** 23 **p** 24 Lon. C of St John Ealing Dean 23-25; H Trin St Austell 25-26; V of Treverbyn 26-33; Tuckingmill 33-36; Org Sec CPAS for Metrop Distr and LPr Dio Lon 36-41; Chap RAf 41-50; R of Uffington 50-64; C-in-c of Tallington 52-54; V 54-61; RD of Ness 55-59; Chap Allnut's Hosp Goring Heath 64-70. *12 St John's Hospital, Heytesbury, Warminster, Wilts.* (Sutton Veny 404)

COCKING, Kermode Neil. b 48. Sarum Wells Th Coll 71. **d** 74 **p** 75 Birm. C of Shirley 74-76; Ch the Sav Ealing 76-78; CF (TAVR)from 75; Offg CF from 81; Hon C of Ch Ch Streatham 78-81; St Paul Deptford Dio S'wark from 81. *21 St Albans House, Leigham Court Road, Streatham, London, SW16 2RF.* (01-677 9056)

COCKINGS, Noel Kingsley. Ridley Coll Melb ACT ThL 59. **d** 60 **p** 61 Melb. C of St John Bentleigh 60-64; P-in-c of St Andr Glen Waverley 64-66; V 66-70; N Dandenong 70-74; I of H Trin Lara Dio Melb from 74. *Vicarage, Lara, Vic, Australia 3212.* (052-821 273)

COCKRAM, David McEwan. b 51. St Jo Coll Morpeth ACT ThDip 76. **d** and **p** 77 Perth. on leave 77; C of Belmont 78-79; R of Kambalda-Norseman Dio Perth from 79. *3 Sandalwood Lane, Kambalda, W Australia 6442.* (090-27 1030)

✠ **COCKS, Right Rev Francis William.** b 13. St Cath Coll Cam 2nd cl Hist Trip pt i 34, BA (2nd cl Hist Trip pt ii) 35, MA 43. CB (Mil) 59. Westcott Ho Cam 35. **d** and **p** 37 Win. C of Ch Ch Portswood 37-39; Chap RAFVR 39-45; Chap RAF 45-65; Asst Chap-in-Chief 50-59; Chap-in-Chief and Archd 59-65; Hon Chap to HM the Queen 59-65; Preb and Can of St Botolph in Linc Cathl 59-65; Can (Emer) from 65; Select Pr Univ of Cam 60; R of Wolverhampton 65-70; RD of Wolverhampton 65-70; Surr 65-70; C-in-c of All SS Wolverhampton 66-70; C-in-c of St Geo Wolverhampton 67-70; Preb of Curborough in Lich Cathl 68-70; Hon Can of Lich from 70; Cons Ld Bp Suffr of Shrewsbury on 24 Feb 70 in Westmr Abbey by Abp of Cant; Bps of Lon; Win; Birm; Ches; Ely; Guildf; Leic; Lich; Linc; Portsm; Roch; St E; S'wark; Bps Suffr of Sherborne and Stafford; Bps Allenby; Armstrong; Holderness; res 80. *41 Beatrice Avenue, Felixstowe, Suff.* (Felixstowe 3574)

COCKS, Howard Alan Stewart. b 46. St Barn Coll Adel. **d** 80 Bal. C of Portland Dio Bal from 80. *2 View Street, Portland, Australia 3305.*

COCKS, Canon John Cramer. b 14. Univ of Lon BD 50. ALCD 50. **d** 50 **p** 51 Ox. C of St Pet Iver 50-53; Org Sec CMJ Lon Distr 53-56; V of Woodford Halse 56-62; RD of Culworth 58-62; V of Rothwell w Orton Dio Pet from 62; RD of Rothwell 62-70; Can of Pet from 77; Sub Warden Kettering Dioc Readers' Assoc from 76. *Vicarage, Rothwell, Kettering, Northants, NN14 2BQ.* (Kettering 710268)

COCKS, Michael Dearden Somers. Univ of NZ BA 49, MA (2nd cl Phil) 50. St Cath S Ox BA 53, MA 57. Ripon Hall Ox. **d** 53 **p** 54 Ch Ch. C of Merivale 53-56; Geraldine 56-58; V of Ross and S Westland 58-60; V of Hinds 60-63; C of Opawa 63; V of St Martin's 63-70; Barrington Street Dio Ch Ch from 70. *10 Deloraine Street, Christchurch 2, NZ.* (35-049)

COCKS, Norman Henry Fulcher. b 05. **d** 70 **p** 71 Tas. [f Congregational Min] C of St Jas New Town and Sec Tas Coun of Ch Dio Tas 70-77. *33 Forest Road, West Hobart, Tasmania 7000.* (002-34 1923)

CODD, Ernest Appleby. St Barn Coll Adel 27. **d** 31 **p** 32 Adel. C of St Aug Unley 31-34; Miss at Vureas 34-35; Warden of Siota Coll 35-38; R of Harvey 38-40; Chap AIF 40-44; Perm to Offic Dio Perth 42-44; R of St Andr Subiaco 44-49; R of Mt Gambier 49-55; Hon Can of Adel 50-66; Archd of Mt Gambier 49-66; Adel 66-70; Org Chap Bp's Home MS 55-59; R of Toorak Gardens 59-70; Exam Chap to Bp of Adel 66-70; L to Offic Dio Adel from 70. *18 James Street, Prospect, S Australia 5082.* (44-8652)

CODRINGTON, Canon George Herbert. b 13. St Jo Coll Dur BA and LTh 36, MA 39. ALCD 34. **d** 36 **p** 37 Lon. C of H Trin E Finchley 36-40; St Anselm Belmont 40; Chap RNVR 40-46; RN 46-48; C of St Martin, Birm 48-52; V of St Andr Brighton Melb 52-65; Archd of Kew 60-62; Brighton 62-65; V of Melton Mowbray w Burton Lazars, Freeby, Sysonby, Welby, Thorpe Arnold and Brentingby 65-71; R 71-80; RD of Framland ii 65-79; Surr 65-80; Commiss Perth 69; Hon Can of Leic 70-80; Can (Emer) from 80; C of St Weonards w Orcop Dio Heref from 80; Tretire w Michaelchurch and Pencoyd Dio Heref from 80. *Rectory, Welsh Newton, Nr Monmouth, Gwent.* (Llangarron 395)

COE, David. b 45. **d** 69 **p** 70 Connor. C of St Matt Shankill Belf 69-72; St Donard Belf 72-75; R of Tullylish 75-81; St Jo Evang Lurgan Dio Drom from 81. *St John's Rectory; Sloan Street, Lurgan, Craigavon, BT66 8NT, N Ireland.* (Lurgan 2770)

COE, John Norris. b 31. Oak Hill Th Coll 57. **d** 59 **p** 60 Guildf. C of Em Stoughton 59-61; St Michel du Valle Guernsey 61-63; Norbiton 63-67; V of Widcombe Bath Dio B & W from 67. *65 Prior Park Road, Bath, BA2 4NL.* (Bath 310580)

COEY, David Stuart. b 19. Trin Coll Dub BA (2nd cl Mod Lang) 41, Div Test 42, MA 53, BD 54. **d** 42 **p** 43 Lon. C of Ch Ch Hampstead 42-44; CF 44-69; DACG 64-69; Asst Master Lanc R Gr Sch from 69. *54 Quernmore Road, Caton, Lancs.* (Caton 770210)

COFFEE, Joseph Owen Edward. b 16. Oak Hill Th Coll 55. **d** 57 **p** 58 Cant. C of St Jo Bapt Folkestone 57-60; V of Havering-atte-Bower 60-68; R of Stapleford Abbots 60-68; Spaxton w Charlynch 68-74. *Cobwebs, Drayton, Nr Langport, Somt.* (Curry Rivel 459)

COFFEY, Hubert William. MBE 46. Trin Coll Dub BA 37, MA 40. **d** 38 **p** 39 Arm. C of Errigle Keerogue 38-41; Chap RNVR 41-47; R of Milltown 47-52; Asst Chap Miss to Seamen Belfast 52-53; Chap at Fremantle 53-59; Asst Chap Melb 59-61; V of St Luke S Melb 64-80; Perm to Offic Dio Melb from 80. *23 Hawthorn Avenue, Caulfield North, Vic, Australia 3161.*

COFFIN, James Allan. Mem Univ of Newfld LTh 59. **d** 57 **p** 58 Newfld. R of Lamaline 57-60; R of Belleoram 60-62; Bay L'Argent 62-66; I of New Harbour 66-75; Carbonear Dio Newfld (E Newfld from 76) from 75. *PO Box 915, Carbonear, Newfoundland, Canada.* (709-596-6187)

COFFIN, Owen Walter. Mem Univ of Newfld BA and LTh 59. Qu Coll Newfld BD 62. **d** 58 **p** 59 Newfld. I of Bonne Bay 58-64; Burin 64-70; R of Channel 70-78; Foxtrap Dio E Newfld from 78. *Foxtrap, Kelligrews, Newfld, Canada.* (709-834 2269)

COFFIN, Ven Peter Robert. b 46. King Coll Halifax BA 68. Trin Coll Tor STB 71. **d** and **p** 71 Ott. C of St Matt, Ott 71-73; Lect Ho of Epiph Dio Kuch 73-76; R of Hull Dio Ott from 76; Archd of W Queb from 79. *44 Hadley Crescent, Hull, PQ, Canada.* (819-776 1759)

COFFIN, Stephen. b 52. Univ of Ox MA. Trin Coll Bris. **d** 77 **p** 78 Truro. C of Illogan 77-80; Liskeard Dio Truro from 80. *Barnfield House, Station Road, Liskeard, PL14 4DT.* (Liskeard 42136)

✠ **COGGAN of CANTERBURY and of SISSINGHURST, Most Rev and Right Hon Frederick Donald.** b 09. PC 61. Late Scho of St Jo Coll Cam 1st cl Or Lang Trip pt i 30, BA (1st cl Or Lang Trip pt ii), Jeremie Sept Pri and Naden Div Stud 31. Tyrwhitt Hebr Scho and Mason Pri 32, MA 35, Hon Fell 61, Hon DD 62. Wycl Coll Tor BD 41, DD (*hon causa*) 44. DD (Lambeth) 57. Univ of Leeds Hon DD 58. Univ of Aber Hon DD 63. Univ of Tokyo Hon DD 63. Univ of Sask Hon DD 63. Hur Coll Hon DD 63. Univ of Hull Hon DD 63. Westmr Choir Coll Princeton Hon DHum 66. Univ of Lanc Hon DLitt 67. Gen Th Sem NY STD (*hon causa*) 67. Univ of Man Hon DD 72. Univ of Liv Hon LLD 72. Univ of Cant Hon DCL 75. Univ of York Hon D 75. FKC 75. Moravian Th Sem Hon DD 76. Wycl Hall Ox 34. **d** 34 **p** 35 Lon. C of St Mary Isl 34-37; Prof of NT Wycl Coll Tor 37-44; Prin Lon Coll of Div 44-56; Macneil Prof of Bibl Exegesis LCD 52-56; Exam Chap to Bp of Linc 46-56; Man 51-56; S'wark 54-56; Ches 55-56; Proc Conv Lon 50-56; Cons Ld Bp of Bradf in York Minster 25 Jan 56 by Bp of Sheff; Bps of Dur; Newc T; Liv; Carl; Ripon; Man; Wakef; Blackb; and Ches; Bps Suffr of Selby; Knaresborough; Stockport; Middleton; Hulme; Whitby; Burnley; and Lanc; and Bps Gerrard; Weller; Hardy; Gelsthorpe; and T S Jones; Trld to York (Abp, Primate of England, and Metrop) 61; Chap and Sub-Prelate O of St John of Jer 60-67; Prelate from 67; Select Pr Univ of Ox 60-61; Chairman Liturgical Comm 60-64; Chairman Coll of Prs 60-80; Trld to Cant (Abp, Primate of All England, and Metrop) 74; res Jan 80; Created Life Baron 80.

Kingshead House, Sissinghurst, Cranbrook, Kent, TN17 2JE. (0580-714443)

COGGINS, Edwin Stanley Claude. b 14. Univ of Bris BSc 36. **d** 64 **p** 65 Leic. Hon C of Knighton 64-72; Hd Master Gartree High Sch Oadby 51-72; V of Barlestone 72-77; Hon P-in-c of W Beckham Dio Nor from 78. *The Old Chapel, West Beckham, Holt, Norf, NR25 6PE.*

COGGINS, Richard James. b 29. Ex Coll Ox BA (Mod Hist) 50, MA 54, Dipl Th 53, BD 75. St Steph Ho Ox 52. **d** 54 **p** 55 Ex. C of Withycombe Raleigh 54-57; Tutor at St Steph Ho Ox 57-60; Chap 60-62; Asst Chap Ex Coll Ox 57-62; L to Offic Dios Ox and Bris 57-62; Chap Magd Coll Ox 60-62; Sub-Warden Th Hostel K Coll Lon 62-67; Lect 62-81; Sen Lect from 81; L to Offic Dio Lon from 64. *8 Gateley Road, SW9.*

COGGINS, Stephen Ernest. b 41. Univ of NSW BA 69. Moore Coll Syd ThL 73. **d** 74 **p** 75 Melb. C of St Jude Carlton 74-76; St Columb Hawthorn 76-78; P-in-c of Mt Dandenong Dio Melb from 78. *Vicarage, Olinda, Vic, Australia 3788.* (751 1053)

COGHLAN, Patrick John. b 47. Down Coll Cam BA 69, Univ of Nottm MA 73. ALCD 72. St Jo Coll Nottm. **d** 73 Doncaster for Sheff **p** 74 Sheff. C of St Thos Crookes Sheff 73-79; SAMS Miss from 79. *Caixa Postal 69, Salvador BA 40.000, Brazil.*

COGMAN, Canon Frederick Walter. b 13. AKC (2nd cl) 38. Univ of Lon BD 38. **d** 38 Ox **p** 39 Dorch for Ox. C of Upton w Chalvey 38-42; Chap of St Geo Sch Harpenden 42-48; R of St Martin Guernsey 48-76; Dean of Guernsey 67-78; Hon Can of Win 67-79; Can (Emer) from 79; R of St Pet Port Guernsey 76-78. *Oriana Lodge, Forest, Guernsey, CI.*

COHEN, Clinel Ewen Vivian. St Pet Coll Ja 65. **d** 65 Kingston for Ja **p** 66 Ja. C of Montego Bay 65-69; on leave 69-72; C of St Jas Montego Bay 72-76; R 76-78; CF (Ja) from 78. *Defence Force, Kingston 5, Jamaica, WI.*

COHEN, Clive Ronald Franklin. b 46. AIB 71. Sarum Wells Th Coll 79. **d** 81 Guildf. C of Esher Dio Guildf from 81. *Hazel Cottage, Hillbrow Road, Esher, Surrey, KT10 9UD.*

COHEN, David Mervyn Stuart. b 42. Univ of Syd BA 63, MA 79. **d** 67 **p** 68 Maur. Dep Gen Sec Bible S in NZ 70-72; Gen Sec 72; Reg Sec for Afr 72-75; Perm to Offic Dios Auckl, Ch Ch, Dun, Nel, Wai and Waik 70-72; C-in-c of St Mark Sylvania 75-77; R of Manly Dio Syd from 78. *30 Addison Road, Manly, NSW, Australia 2095.* (977-6249)

COHEN, Henry Cecil. b 1889. AKC 12. M CR 51. **d** 13 **p** 14 Lon. C of St Mary Whitechapel 13-16; TCF 16-18; C of St Mich Cricklewood 18-20; M of Bush Bro Charleville Queensld 21-25; on leave 25-26; Asst Chap Southport Sch 26-29; M of Commun of Ascen Goulb from 29; Supr 36-40; Perm to Offic Dio Goulb 30-42; R of Cumnock 42-44; Perm to Offic Dio Bath 44-49; Prof Commun of the Resurr Mirfield from 51. *House of the Resurrection, Mirfield, W Yorks, WF14 0BN.*

COHEN, Herbert John. Montr Dioc Th Coll LTh 63. **d** 62 **p** 63 Montr. I of Grenville 62-66; High Level 66-71; Hinton 71-72; Mayerthorpe Dio Edmon from 72. *Box 487, Mayerthorpe, Alta., Canada.* (403-786 3589)

COHEN, Ian Geoffrey Holland. b 51. Univ of Nottm BA 74. Ripon Coll Cudd 77. **d** 79 **p** 80 Nor. C of Sprowston Dio Nor from 79. *48 Rosemary Road, Sprowston, Norwich, NR7 8ER.* (Nor 47655)

COHEN, Leon David. St Jo Coll Morpeth ACT ThL 61. **d** 58 **p** 59 River. C of St Pet Broken Hill 58-61; Corowa 61-63; P-in-c of Moama 63-66; R of St Jo Bapt Cathl Kalgoorlie 66-68; Prec of St Bonif Cathl Bunb 68-69; L to Offic Dio Perth 69-74; Chap St Mary's Gr Sch Mt Yokine 72-74. *32 Bourke Street, Mt Yokine 6060, W Australia.*

COHEN, Malcolm Arthur. b 38. Canberra Coll of Min ThDip 79. **d** and **p** 79 C & Goulb. C of Moruya 79-80; Cootamundra Dio C & Goulb from 81. *204 Thompson Street, Cootamundra, NSW, Australia 2590.*

COHEN, Timothy Giles. b 54. Ridley Coll Melb ThDip 77. **d** 77 **p** 78 Gippsld. Prec St Paul's Cathl Sale Dio Gippsld from 77. *155 Cunninghame Street, Sale, Vic, Australia 3850.*

COHEN, Vernon Leslie. St Jo Coll Morpeth ACT ThL 52. **d** 52 Geelong for Melb **p** 53 Melb. C of Ch Ch Essendon 52-54; V of Inverleigh 54-56; I of Cheltm 56-64; Mitcham 64-66; Warden Avalon Commun Lara from 66. *Avalon Community, Lara, Vic, Australia 3212.* (052-82 1206)

COHN, Colin Jessop. Moore Th Coll Syd ACT ThL 41. **d** 42 **p** 43 Syd. C of St Steph Kembla 42-44; Min of Melton 44-48; I of Yarraville 48-53; Elsternwick 53-65; Vermont 65-74; C of St Jas w St John Miss Distr Melb 74-75; on leave 76-80; Perm to Offic Dio Melb from 80. *3-68 Riversdale Road, Hawthorn, Vic, Australia 3132.* (03-81 8625)

COHN, Lionel James. Ridley Coll Melb ACT ThL 44. **d** 43 **p** 44 Melb. C of St Steph Richmond 43-44; Chap AIF 44-46; Min of Broadmeadows 47-50; I of St Matt Geelong 50-57; Thornbury 57-69; Dingley 69-76; Perm to Offic Dio Melb from 77. *107 Dare Street, Ocean Grove, Vic, Australia 3226.* (052-55 2406)

COISH, Colin Joseph. Univ of Melb BA (Hons) 48. St Columb's Hall Wang ACT ThL 43. BD (Lon) 57. **d** 47 **p** 48 Wang. C of Milawa 47-49; R of Bethanga 49-50; Yarrawonga 50-58; Nagambie 58-60; Priv Chap to Bp of Wang 58-60; Min of Pascoe Vale 60-64; Perm to Offic Dio Melb 64-71; Assoc Dir Gen Bd of Relig Educn 71-73; P-in-c of Balaclava 73-77; I 77-80; Ch Ch Ormond Dio Melb from 80. 73-77; I from 77. *436 North Road, Ormond, Vic, Australia 3204.*

COKE, William Robert Francis. b 46. St Edm Hall Ox BA 68, MA 79. BD (Lon) 78. Trin Coll Bris 75. **d** 79 Burnley for Blackb **p** 80 Blackb. C of Ch of the Sav City and Dio Blackb from 79. *72 Lytham Road, Blackburn, Lancs, BB2 3JT.*

COKER, Barry Charles Ellis. b 46. K Coll Lon BD and AKC (2nd cl) 69. St Aug Coll Cant 69. **d** 70 Jarrow for Dur **p** 71 Dur. C of Newton Aycliffe 70-74; R of H Cross Marabella Trinid 74-78; Matson Dio Glouc from 78. *Matson Rectory, Gloucester, GL4 9DX.* (Glouc 22598)

COKER, Richmondson Bankole Ethelbert. Univ of Dayton Ohio BA 64. Kenyon Coll Ohio BD 67. **d** 67 S Ohio for Sier L **p** 68 Sier L. P Dio Sier L. *4 Ross Road, Freetown, Sierra Leone.* (Freetown 24666)

COKER, Stephen Paul. b 53. St Steph Ho Ox 78. **d** 81 Sheff. C of St Leon & St Jude Doncaster Dio Sheff from 81. *21 Rochester Row, Scawsby, Doncaster, DN5 8PE.*

COLACINO, Robert Charles. Moore Th Coll Syd 76. **d** 78 Syd **p** 79 Bp Robinson for Syd. C of Carlingford 78-80; St Matt W Pennant Hills Dio Syd from 80. *5 New Line Road, West Pennant Hills, NSW, Australia 2120.* (84-2753)

COLBERT, Keith Stanley William. St Francis Th Coll Brisb 62. **d** 63 Bp Hudson for Brisb **p** 64 Brisb. C of H Trin, Fortitude Valley, Brisb 63-64; Wynnum, Brisb 64-67; Bush Bro of St Paul Quilpie 67-69; R of Childers w Howard 69-73; Mundubbera 73-80; St Matt Grovely City and Dio Brisb from 80. *PO Box 99, Everton Park, Queensland, Australia 4053.* (355 1314)

COLBORNE, Walter John. b 1897. K Coll Lon. **d** and **p** 44 Glouc. C of Thornbury 44-46; R of Oldbury-on-Severn 46-50; Bittadon w W Downe V 50-53; C-in-c of St Phil Conv Distr Kelsall 53-57; V 57-60; Firbank w Howgill and Killington 60-68; L to Offic Dio Bradf from 68. *38 Greenacres, Skipton, Yorks.* (Skipton 4401)

COLBOURN, John Martin Claris. b 30. Selw Coll Cam BA (2nd cl Hist Trip pts i and ii) 52, MA 56. Ridley Hall Cam 52. **d** 54 Stockport for Ches **p** 55 Ches. C of Cheadle 54-58; V of St Thos Trowbridge 59-65; St Jo Evang Fareham Dio Portsm from 65. *3a St Michael's Grove, Fareham, Hants, PO14 1DN.* (Fareham 280762)

COLBOURN, William George Martin Claris. b 01. St Jo Coll Dur LTh 26. Lon Coll of Div 23. **d** 27 **p** 28 S'wark. C of H Trin Redhill 27-31; Crowborough 31-34; Asst Master Monkton Combe Sch Bath 34-39; V of St Jas Bath 39-42; R of Walcot Bath 42-51; V of H Trin, Redhill 51-58; St Luke Parkstone 58-70. *20 Montague Road, Boscombe, Bournemouth, BH5 2EP.*

COLBOURNE, Walter Gerald. Qu Coll Newfld LTh 65. **d** 64 **p** 65 Newfld. C of St Jo Bapt Cathl St John's 64-65; R of Battle Harbour 65-67; Grand Falls Hermitage 70-74; Bay d'Espoir Dio Newfld (Centr Newfld from 76) from 74. *PO Box 9, Bay D'Espoir, Milltown, Newfoundland, Canada.* (709-4271)

COLBY, David Allan. b 33. St Steph Ho Ox 78. **d** 81 Buckingham for Ox (NSM). Perm to Offic Dio Ox from 81. *43 Beech Close, Faringdon, Oxon, SN7 7EN.*

COLBY, Robert James. b 31. Roch Th Coll 62. **d** 64 **p** 65 St Alb. C of Ch Ch w St Pet Luton 64-68; Chirbury 68-70; P-in-c 70-78; V 78-79; P-in-c of Marton-in-Chirbury 70-78; V 78-79; P-in-c of Trelystan w Leighton 70-78; V 78-79; P-in-c of Whitbourne Dio Heref from 79; Tedstone Delamere w Edvin Loach and Tedstone Wafer Dio Heref from 80; U Sapey w Wolferlow Dio Heref from 80. *Whitbourne Rectory, Worcester.* (Knightwick 285)

COLCHESTER, Lord Bishop Suffragan of. *See* Coote, Right Rev Roderick Norman.

COLCHESTER, Archdeacon of. *See* Roxburgh, Ven James William.

COLCHESTER, Halsey Sparrowe. b 18. CMG 68. OBE 60. Magd Coll Ox BA 39, MA 45. Cudd Coll 72. **d** 73 **p** 74 Glouc. C of Minchinhampton 73-76; V of Bollington 76-81; P-in-c of Gt w L Tew Dio Ox from 81. *Great Tew Vicarage, Oxford, OX7 4OB.* (Gt Tew 293)

COLCHESTER, John Charles Markham. b 26. Bps' Coll Cheshunt 65. **d** 67 **p** 68 S'wark. C of St Matt, Brixton 67-71; Team V of Thamesmead 71-78; V of All SS and St Barn S Lambeth 78-80; St Anne (and All SS from 80) S Lambeth Dio S'wark from 78. *179 Fentiman Road, SW8 1JY.*

COLCLOUGH, Michael John. b 44. Univ of Leeds BA

(2nd cl Engl and Relig Stud) 69. Cudd Coll 69. **d** 71 **p** 72 Lich. C of St Werburgh Burslem 71-75; St Mary S Ruislip 75-79; P-in-c of St Anselm Hayes Dio Lon from 79. *St Anselm's Vicarage, Nield Road, Hayes, Middx. UB3 1SQ.* (01-573 0958)

COLDERWOOD, Alfred Victor. b 26. Bps' Coll Cheshunt 58. **d** 60 **p** 61 Lon. C of Oakwood 60-63; St Jas Enfield Highway 63-66; V of St Aldhelm Edmon Dio Lon from 66. *St Aldhelm's Vicarage, Windmill Road, N18 1PA.* (01-807 5336)

COLDWELLS, Alan Alfred. b 30. Univ Coll Ox BA 55, MA 57. Wells Th Coll 53. **d** 55 **p** 56 Cov. C of Rugby 55-62; V of Sprowston 62-73; R of Beeston 62-73; Rugby Dio Cov from 73; RD of Nor 70-72; Rugby 73-78. *Rectory, Clifton Road, Rugby, Warws.* (Rugby 2936)

COLE, Alan Ernest. Univ of Syd BVSc 50. **d** 55 **p** 70 C & Goulb. C of Young 55-72. *c/o Diocesan Church House, George Street, Sydney, Australia.*

COLE, Alan John. b 35. Bps' Coll Cheshunt. **d** 66 St Alb **p** 67 Bedford for St Alb. C of Boreham Wood 66-69; St Mich St Alb 69-72; V of Redbourn 72-80; R of Thorley w H Trin Bp's Stortford Dio St Alb from 80. *Thorley Rectory, Bishop's Stortford, Herts.* (0279-54955)

COLE, Alan Michael. b 40. Univ of Melb BA 74. Act ThDip 67. St Francis Coll Brisb. **d** 66 **p** 67 Bal. L to Offic Dio Brisb 66-67; C of Horsham 67-69; Colac 69-70; Perm to Offic Dio Melb 71-75; L to Offic Dio Cant from 76; Chap Bp Otter Coll Chich 76-77; St Sav Coll Ardingly 77-82; at Bonn & Cologne Dio Gibr in Eur from 82. *c/o British Embassy, Bonn, BFPO 19.*

COLE, Brian Robert Arthur. b 35. Univ of Nottm BA (3rd cl Econ and Social Hist) 57. Ridley Hall Cam 59. **d** 61 **p** 62 Chelmsf. C of Tye Green w Netteswell 61-64; Keighley 64-67; V of Copley 67-72; Chap Halifax Gen Hosp 67-73; R of Gt w L Dunham Dio Nor from 73; Gt w L Fransham Dio Nor from 74; P-in-c of Sporle w Gt & L Palgrave Dio Nor from 81. *Rectory, Great Dunham, King's Lynn, Norf, PE32 2LQ.* (Litcham 466)

COLE, Charles Vincent. b 26. Kelham Th Coll 47. **d** 51 **p** 52 Dur. C of St Pet Harton 51-54; St Jas Gateshead 54-56; V of Blackhall Dio Dur from 56. *Blackhall Vicarage, Hartlepool, Cleveland.* (Peterlee 864202)

COLE, David. b 40. Qu Coll Birm 66. **d** 66 Kens for Lon **p** 67 Lon. C of St Helen w H Trin Kens 66-69; Altham w Clayton-le-Moors 69-72; C-in-c of St Luke Preston 72-75; V of Inskip 75-80; C of St Clem (in c of St Aug) Castle Bromwich Dio Birm from 80. *St Augustine's Vicarage, Anglesey Avenue, Chelmsley Wood, B36 0NS.*

COLE, David Henry. ALCD 56. **d** 56 **p** 57 Guildf. C of Ashtead 56-59; Farnham 59-60; R of Simonds, NB 60-67; Hon C of St Luke, St John 67-73; on leave. *10922-79a Avenue, Delta, BC, Canada.*

COLE, Donald. b 24. Edin Th Coll. **d** 59 **p** 60 Edin. C of Ch Ch Morningside Edin 59-62; R of Lasswade 62-69; St Cuthb City and Dio Edin from 69. *6 Westgarth Avenue, Edinburgh 13.* (031-441 3557)

COLE, Edmund Keith. Univ of Syd BA 46, MA 49, BD 50. Moore Th Coll Syd ACT ThL 43, Th Scho 48, ThD 65. **d** and **p** 44 Syd. C of St Steph Newtown 44-45; St Phil Syd 44-50; CMS Miss Dio Momb 50-60; Dio Ft Hall 61-63; Exam Chap to Bp of Momb 52-60; to Bp of Ft Hall 61-63; Prin St Paul's Th Coll Limuru 55-60; Archd of Centr Kenya 61-63; Vice-Prin Ridley Coll Melb 64-72; Commiss Mt Kenya 66-75; Mt Kenya S from 75; C of E Kew 64-72; Hon C of Ch Ch Cathl Darwin 73-77; Dir of Th Educn Dio Bend from 78. *28 Woodbury Street, Bendigo, Vic., Australia 3550.*

COLE, Eric Saxon Wall. Em Coll Sktn. **d** 34 Sktn for Sask **p** 35 Sask. C of Onion Lake 34-35; I of Arborfield 35-38; Wakef 38-40; Chap CASF 40-46; Prin of St Cypr Sch and Miss Peigan Res 46-47; Miss on Blackfoot Reserve and Prin of Old Sun Sch 47-55; on leave 55-56; Prin of Chooutla Ind Sch Carcross 56-59; in Amer Ch 59-63; I of Grand Rapids 63-71; H Trin Cumb 72-76. *Box 289, Victoria Island, BC, Canada.*

COLE, Graham Arthur. b 49. Univ of Syd BA 71. BD (Lon) 76. Moore Th Coll Syd ACT ThL 75. **d** 77 Bp Dain for Syd **p** 77 Syd. C of St Paul Chatswood 77-78; St Jas Turramurra 79-80; Lect Moore Th Coll Syd from 80. *Moore Theological College, Carillon Avenue, Newtown, NSW, Australia 2042.*

COLE, Harry Edmead. **d** 65 **p** 66 Bend. C-in-c of Loddon 65-68; R of Elmore Dio Bend from 68. *44 Michie Street, Elmore, Vic, Australia 3558.* (325211-58)

COLE, Henry Frederick Charles. b 23. ALCD 52. **d** 52 **p** 53 Roch. C of Ch Ch Bexley-Heath 52-55; P-in-c of Wigmore w Hempstead Conv Distr 55-56; Min 56-59; V of Lawkholme 59-67; Chap Sheff Industr Miss 67-72; V of Wadsley Dio Sheff from 72. *Wadsley Vicarage, Sheffield, S6 4BB.* (Sheffield 344002)

COLE, Canon Howard Stacey. b 12. Univ of Bris BSc 38. Ridley Hall Cam 38. **d** 40 **p** 41 B & W. C of St Mark Lyncombe 40-41; CF (EC) 41-44; CF 44-70; DACG 60-64; ACG 64-70; Hon Chap to HM the Queen 67-70; R of Barcombe 70-73; Can and Chan of St Paul's Cathl Valetta 73-77; Hon Can from 81. *St Paul's Anglican Cathedral, Valetta, Malta.*

COLE, John Gordon. b 43. Magd Coll Cam BA 65, MA 69. Cudd Coll 66. **d** 68 **p** 69 Ripon. C of Leeds 68-71; Moor Allerton (in c of Alwoodley) 71-75; Communications Officer Dio Blackb from 75; P-in-c of Pendleton-in-Whalley Dio Blackb from 75. *Pendleton Vicarage, Clitheroe, Lancs, BB7 1PT.* (0200-22449)

COLE, John Leopold. b 23. **d** 73 **p** 76 Antig (APM). C of St Jas Nevis 73-75; St John's Cathl Antig 75-78; R of St Paul Falmouth Dio Antig from 78. *St Paul's Rectory, Falmouth, Antigua, WI.*

COLE, John Spensley. b 39. Clare Coll Cam BA 62, MA 66. FCA 65. Univ of Nottm Dipl Th 79. Linc Th Coll 78. **d** 80 **p** 81 Portsm. C of St Mary Cowes Dio Portsm from 80; All SS Gurnard Dio Portsm from 80. *22 The Avenue, Gurnard, Cowes, Isle of Wight, PO31 8HA.*

COLE, John Wilfrid. b 06. Keble Coll Ox BA 30, Dipl in Th 31, MA 34, Dipl in Psychol 48, BSc 51. Wycl Hall Ox 30. **d** 32 **p** 33 S'wark. C of Ch Ch Purley 32-34; St Barbara Earlsdon 34-36; R of Hinton Waldrist 36-44; Pusey 36-54; V of Lyford (w Charney from 47) 44-71. *35 Norham Road, Oxford.* (Oxford 57927)

COLE, Lawrence Howard. b 09. ALCD 39. Univ of Dur BA 47. **d** 39 **p** 40 S'wark. C of Bermondsey 39-42; Lect and C of Watford 42-43; CF (EC) 43-46; C of St Nich Durham 46-47; R of Hawkwell 47-51; V of St Jas-the-Less Bethnal Green and Chap Lon Chest Hosp Bethnal Green 51-60; PC of Cogges 60-68; V 68-77; Perm to Offic Dio Ox from 77. *Turret Thatch, Hempton, Oxford, OX5 4QY.* (Deddington 38969)

COLE, Melvin George Merriman. b 05. Fourah Bay Coll Freetown. **d** 48 Ely for Lon **p** 53 Sier L. C of St Mildred Addiscombe 48-50; St Thos Norbury Ches 50-51; St Steph Norbury Dio Cant 51-53; V of Bp Crowther Mem Ch Freetown Sier L 53-56; C of St Jude Thornton Heath 56-61; St Matt Croydon 61-63; Minister-in-Sheppey 64-67; St Pet Paddington 67-69; V of Kissey Sier L 69-76; Perm to Offic Dio S'wark from 76. *101 Pendle Road, SW16.*

COLE, Michael Berkeley. b 44. Cudd Coll 70. **d** 72 **p** 73 Leic. C of Shepshed 72-76; V of St Chad Leic 76-80. *c/o 145 Coleman Road, Leicester, LE5 4LH.* (Leic 766062)

COLE, Michael George. Lich Th Coll 58. **d** 60 **p** 61 Sheff. C of Ch Ch Doncaster 60-63; Chap RAF 63-68; in RC Ch 68-70; C of St Wilfrid Tor 70-72; CF (Canad) 72-78; R of Belleville Dio Ont from 78. *79 Bridge Street East, Belleville, Ont., Canada.* (613-962 3000)

COLE, Michael John. b 34. St Pet Hall Ox BA (3rd cl Hist) 56, MA 60. Ridley Hall Cam 56. **d** 58 Lon **p** 59 Knaresborough for York. C of Ch Ch Finchley 58; St Geo Leeds 58-61; Trav Sec for Inter-Varsity Fellowship 61-64; V of St Thos Crookes Sheff 64-71; R of Rusholme 71-75; V of Woodford Wells Dio Chelmsf from 75. *All Saints' Vicarage, Woodford Wells, Essex.* (01-504 0266)

COLE, Norman George. b 05. Late Scho of St Jo Coll Dur BA 27, MA 30, Dipl Th 28. **d** 28 **p** 29 S'wark. C of St Matthias U Tulse Hill 28-31; St Sav Nottm (in c of St Marg) 31-35; PC of Hulland 35-52; R of Atlow 42-52; Croscombe 52-60; V of Stainland 60-63; Asst Master Devonport High Sch for Boys 63-70; Perm to Offic Dio Ex 63-75. *20 Mostyn Avenue, Lipson, Plymouth, Devon.*

COLE, Canon Peter George Lamont. b 27. Pemb Coll Cam BA 49, MA 52. Cudd Coll 50. **d** 52 **p** 53 Guildf. C of St Mich Aldershot 52-55; St Jo Cathl Bulawayo 55-59; P-in-c of All SS Riverside Bulawayo 55-59; R 59-62; Chap St Steph Coll Balla Balla S Rhod 63-65; V of St Andr Bromley 65-72; Folkestone Dio Cant from 72; Hon Can of Cant Cathl from 80. *Vicarage, Priory Gardens, Folkestone, Kent.* (Folkestone 52947)

COLE, Reginald Joshua. b 08. Univ of Liv BA (2nd cl Hist Hons) 30. Wycl Hall Ox 33. **d** 34 **p** 35 Liv. C of St Luke Gt Crosby 34-36; Ch Ch Ince-in-Makerfield 36-38; All SS Southport 38-40; CF (EC) 40-45; V of H Trin Runcorn 45-48; St Steph Bowling 48-52; Surr 48-52; CF 52-60; V of Fordham 60-73; Perm to Offic Dio St E 78-80; Dio Blackb from 80. *17 Skipton Avenue, Crossens, Nr Southport, Lancs.*

COLE, Richard Leslie. b 08. Late Scho of Ball Coll Ox BA 31, Ellerton Th Essay Pri 32, MA 35. St Steph Ho Ox 32. **d** 32 **p** 33 Portsm. C of St Mark Portsea 32-34; Gillingham Kent 35-44; Chap RNVR 44-46; Vice-Prin Chich Th Coll and L to Offic Dio Chich 46-48; Perm to Offic Dio Llan 48-50; Lect St Mich Coll Llan 49-56; C of Llanblethian 50-56; St Sav and St Mark Wilmington Hull 56-61; C of Bartica Dio Guy 61-63; V 68-71; C-in-c of Leguan w Wakenaam and Essequibo I

63-68; Teigngrace 72-75; R of E Bank Demerara Dio Guy from 75. *Rectory, Eccles, East Bank, Demerara, Guyana.* (02-61832)

COLE, Canon Robert Alan. TCD BA 44, PhD 48. Univ of Lon BD (1st cl) 49, MTh 51. Oak Hill Th Coll 46. **d** 50 **p** 51 S'wark. C of St Luke Deptford 50-51; CIM Miss 52-62; C of Kuala Lumpur Sing 52-53; Dio Honolulu 53-56; Miss at Mambang Di-Awan S Perak 56-61; Sen Lect Moore Th Coll Syd 61-62 and 69-72; CMS Miss 62-68; Lect St Pet Hall Mt Sophia Sing 62-68; C of St Matt Sing 64-68; Exam Chap to Bp of Sing 65-68; Chap Robert Menzies Coll Macquarie Univ 73-79; Hon Can of Syd from 79; Federal Sec CMS from 79. *93 Bathurst Street, Sydney, NSW, Australia 2000.* (267-3711)

COLE, Ronald Berkeley. b 13. Bps' Coll Cheshunt 40. **d** 42 **p** 43 Leic. C of Braunstone 42-48; Succr of Leic Cathl 48-50; V St Phil, Leic 50-73; Hon Chap to Bp of Leic 49-53; Archd of Loughborough 53-63; Leic 63-80; Surr 53-80; Exam Chap to Bp of Leic 56-80; Can Res of Leic Cathl 77-80. *70 Cromer Road, Sheringham, Norf, NR26 8RT.* (Sheringham 824955)

COLE, Thomas. St Aid Th Coll Bal ACT ThL (2nd cl) 09. Th Scho 32. **d** 09 **p** 10 Bal. C of Wycheproof 09; Hamilton 10-12; P-in-c of Natimuk 12-16; V of Mortlake Vic 16-20; C of St Jas Melb 20-23; Min of Ch of Epiph Northcote 23-35; Commiss to Bp of St Arn 29-49; I of Ivanhoe 35-49; Perm to Offic Dio Melb from 49. *16 Harcourt Street, Hawthorn East, Vic, Australia 3123.* (82-3253)

COLE, Canon Victor Roland. Moore Th Coll Syd ACT ThL 61. **d** 61 Bp Kerle for Syd **p** 62 Syd. C of Pymble 61-64; C-in-c of Mona Vale 64-69; R of St Mary Magd St Mary's 69-77; Can of St John's Prov Cathl Parramatta 70-77; R of Forestville Dio Syd from 77. *697 Warringah Road, Forestville, NSW, Australia 2037.* (451-5242)

COLE, Ven Vincent. Montr Dioc Coll 41. **d** 41 **p** 42 Edmon. C of St Luke Mayerthorpe 41-42; I of St John Sedgewick 42-44; Itin P Dio Edmon 45-46; V of Mannville 46-50; Tofield 50-57; Leduc 58-64; R of Wainwright 64-71; Hon Can of Edmon 59-63; Archd of Strathcona 63-76; R of Ft Sask 71-76; Executive Archd and Dioc Sec and Treas Dio Edmon 76-80; Archd (Emer) from 80. *905-10135 Saskatchewan Drive, Edmonton, Alta, Canada T6E 4Y9.*

COLE, Walter John Henden. b 04. Bps' Coll Cheshunt 25. **d** 27 **p** 28 Roch. C of All SS Frindsbury 27-31; St Benet Fink Tottenham 31-33; St Mark Regent's Pk 33-41; V of St Mark Marylebone Rd Lon 41-52; Stone-in-Oxney w Ebony 52-55; St Jas W Hampstead 55-76. *87 College Road, Isleworth, Middx.* (01-568 2708)

COLE, William Gbenka. d 68 **p** 70 Sier L. P Dio Sier L. *Kabala, Sierra Leone.*

COLE, William Pritchard. b 09. St D Coll Lamp BA 32. MBE (Mil) 45. OBE (Mil) 51. **d** 33 **p** 35 Swan B. C of St Matt Greenhill Swansea 33-35; St Thos Swansea 35-36; H Trin Windsor 36-39; TCF 39; CF 43-59; DACG 50-59; Chap U Chine Sch Shanklin 65-76. *27 Burton Road, Bridport, Dorset, DT6 4JD.* (Bridport 56289)

COLE-LEWIS, Peter Athanasius. d 35 **p** 41 Sier L. P Dio Sier L 35-69. *4 Mammy Yoko Street, Freetown, Sierra Leone.*

COLEBROOK, Bryan Andrew. b 54. Codr Coll Barb 73. **d** 78 Nass. C of St Geo Nass 78-81; R of St Phil Inagua Dio Nass from 81. *Rectory, Matthew Town, Inagua, Bahamas.*

COLEBROOK, Canon John Ridley. b 26. Ball Coll Ox BA 47, MA 51. Coll of Resurr Mirfield 51. **d** 53 Lon **p** 54 Kens for Lon. C of St Alb Mart Holborn w St Pet Saffron Hill Lon 53-58; St Francis Bournemouth 58-60; V of St Mary (w St Clem from 64) Bournemouth 60-68; St Mich AA Andover Dio Win from 68; Hon Can of Win Cathl from 81. *Vicarage, The Avenue, Andover, Hants.* (Andover 2553)

COLEFAX, Stanford Ronald. St Jo Coll Morpeth Dipl Th 64. **d** and **p** 65 C & Goulb. C of Cootamundra 65-67; R of Koorawatha 67-68; Chap Miss to Seamen Newc 69-73; C of St Alb Epping 73-74; R of Concord and Burwood 74-80; St John Ashfield Dio Syd from 80. *74 Bland Street, Ashfield, NSW, Australia 2131.* (798-6313)

COLEMAN, Alan. b 22. DFC 44 and Bar 45. Wells Th Coll 65. **d** 66 Hulme for Man **p** 67 Man. C of St John, Bury 66-68; V of Wilton-in-Cleveland 69-73; Sen Chap Miss to Seamen Middlesbrough 69-73; V of Flamborough 73-75; R of Coleford w Holcombe Dio B & W from 75. *Coleford Vicarage, Bath, Somt.* (Mells 812300)

COLEMAN, Very Rev Arthur Edmund. K Coll NS BA 25, LTh and Div Test 31, Hon DCnL 52. **d** 27 **p** 28 Fred. Miss of Wilmot Wicklow and Peel 27-31; Bp's Missr Ch Extension Work 31-35; R of St Jo Div Verdun 35-40; Ascen Montr 40-48; R of Trin Ch St John 48-57; Dean and R of H Trin Cathl Queb 57-69; Dean (Emer) from 72. *Apt 1001, 133 Erskine Avenue, Toronto, Ont, M4P IY3, Canada.*

COLEMAN, Beverley Warren. b 20. Univ of Leeds, BA 43. Coll of Resurr Mirfield. **d** 43 **p** 44 Lon. C of H Cross Greenford 43-46; St Dunstan and All SS Stepney 46-47; CF 47-52; Hon CF 52; CF (TA) from 52; PC of Barrow Gurney 52-54 V of Malacca 54-56; Miss in Java 56-58; V of Java w Sumatra 58-63; C-in-c of Albrighton 63-64; V 64-71; R of St Sav Jersey Dio Win from 71. *St Saviour's Rectory, Jersey, C.I.* (Central 36679)

COLEMAN, Brian James. b 36. K Coll Cam BA 58, MA 61. Ripon Hall Ox 58. **d** 60 **p** 61 Derby. C of Allestree (in c of St Nich) 60-65; PC of St Nich Allestree 65-69; Chap and Lect Coll of Sarum St Mich 69-77; P-in-c of Matlock Bank Dio Derby from 77. *All Saints Vicarage, Matlock, Derbys, DE4 3JG.* (Matlock 2235)

COLEMAN, Charles Romaine Boldero. b 10. Clifton Th Coll 36. **d** 39 **p** 40 Bris. C of Downend 39-41; Keynsham 41-43; R of Felthorpe w Haveringland 43-49; Waxham w Palling 49-55; R of Horsey 52-55; Buckenham w Hassingham and Strumpshaw 55-61; Sampford Brett 61-77. *Address temp unknown.*

COLEMAN, David. b 49. AKC and BD 72. St Aug Coll Cant 72. **d** 73 Stepney for Lon **p** 74 Lon. C of Ch Ch and St John w St Luke Poplar 73-76; H Cross Greenford 76-79; V of Cricklewood Dio Lon from 79. *25 Basing Hill, NW11.* (01-455 5173)

COLEMAN, Edward William. b 20. Lon Coll of Div 62. **d** 64 **p** 65 Lon. C of Ch Ch Fulham 64-67; Barking 67-70; Dagenham 70-78; P-in-c of High Laver w Magdalen Laver and L Laver Dio Chelmsf from 78. *Lavers Rectory, Magdalen Laver, Ongar, Essex, CM5 0ES.* (Harlow 33311)

COLEMAN, Frederick Philip. b 11. Univ of Lon BSc (Econ) 33. St Steph Ho Ox 38. **d** 40 S'wark **p** 41 Kingston T for S'wark. C of St Alphege S'wark 40-42 and 55-64; St Steph Lewisham 42-48; V of Nunhead 48-52; Ellesmere Port 52-55; Surr 54-55; Gen Sec Ch U 55-68; Proc Conv S'wark 59-64; Lon 64-70; Commiss Nass from 62; Hon C of St Andr-by-the-Wardrobe Lon 64-68; Warden Commun of St Jo Bapt Clewer 68-79; R of St Andrew-by-the-Wardrobe City and Dio Lon from 71; Area Dean of the City of Lon 79-82. *St Andrew's House, St Andrew's Hill, EC4V 5DE.* (01-248 7546)

COLEMAN, John Edward Noel. b 15. St Chad's Coll Dur BA 37, MA 49, Dipl Th 39. **d** 39 **p** 40 Ches. C of St Jas Latchford 39-48; V of Allithwaite 48-55; Silverdale Dio Blackb from 55. *Silverdale Vicarage, Carnforth, Lancs.* (Silverdale 701268)

COLEMAN, Kenneth Armstrong. d 50 **p** 51 Ont. C of N Augusta 50-54; Chap at Ajnala 54-68; R of Cataraqui Dio Ont from 68. *998 Sydenham Road, Kingston, Ont, Canada.* (613-542 8229)

COLEMAN, Kenneth George. Moore Th Coll Syd ACT ThL 69. **d** 69 Syd. C of Avalon 69-72; Miss at Sarawak 72-74; Perm to Offic Dio Syd 75; Dio Brisb 76-79. *c/o 19 Bolger Street, Upper Mount Gravatt, Queensland, Australia 4122.*

COLEMAN, Lyman Russell. Angl Th Coll BC 51. **d** and **p** 54 Ont. I of N Frontenac 54; R of Bath 56-58; CF (Canad) from 58. *c/o Chaplain General's Office, Canadian Forces HQ, Ottawa 4, Ont., Canada.*

COLEMAN, Norman John Henry George. b 09. Tyndale Hall Bris 51. **d** 52 **p** 53 Ches. C of Cheadle 52-56; V of Balderstone Rochdale 56-64; C of St Columba Drypool 70-78; Perm to Offic Dio Bradf from 78. *17 Rayner Avenue, Bradford, BD8 9PP.*

COLEMAN, Ven Peter Everard. b 28. Univ of Lon LLB and AKC 53. (Called to Bar Middle Temple 66). Univ of Bris MLitt 76. Westcott Ho Cam 53. **d** 55 **p** 56 Bris. C of St Francis Bedminster 55-58; Sec SCM and C of St Helen Bishopsgate Lon 58-60; Chap and Lect K Coll Lon 60-66; Chap Univ of Bris 66-71; V of St Paul Ap Clifton 66-71; Can Res of Bris Cathl 71-81; Worc Cathl from 81; Dir of Ordin Tr and Exam Chap to Bp of Bris 71-81; M Gen Syn Dio Bris 74-81; Dir Bris & Glouc Sch for Min 77-81; Archd of Worc from 81. *7 College Yard, Worcester, WR1 2LA.* (0905 25046)

COLEMAN, Philip John. AKC. **d** 12 **p** 13 S'wark. C of All SS Blackheath 12-14; St Paul Kingston Hill 14-16; Newquay 16-19; St Just-in-Roseland (in c of St Mawes) 19-25; Asst Chap at St John Mentone 25-26; PC of Mount Hawke 27-33; V of Marazion 33-36; Chap of Estoril 36-45; Madeira 45-50; Palma 51-59. *Hotel Paris, Estoril, Portugal.*

COLEMAN, Robert William Alfred. b 16. Ch Coll Cam BA 39, MA 42. BC Coll Bris 39. **d** 40 **p** 41 Chich. C of Broadwater 40-42; CF (EC) 42-46; V of St Geo Tiverton 46-50; St John Ealing Dean 50-59; Chap K Edw Hosp Ealing 50-59; Springfield Hosp Tooting 59-60; Seaford Coll 60-81. *Villa Forence, West Drive, Middleton-on-Sea, Bognor Regis, Sussex.* (Middleton-on-Sea 3410)

COLEMAN, Ronald Leslie. Moore Th Coll Syd ACT ThL 59. **d** and **p** 60 Syd. C of Pagewood 60-62; Kiama w Jamberoo 62-63; C-in-c of Canley Vale 63-70; R of Belmore 70-77; Mona Vale Dio Syd from 77. *105 Darley Street, Mona Vale, NSW, Australia 2103.* (99-2062)

✠ **COLEMAN, Right Rev William Robert.** Univ of Tor BA 40, MA 43, BD 46, STM 48, DD 52. **d** 42 **p** 43 Alg. C of Ch of Epiph Sudbury 43-44; P-in-c 44-45; L to Offic Dio Ely 47; Lect Wycl Coll Tor 47-49; Perm to Offic Dio Ely 49-50; Dean of Div B'ps Univ Lennox 50-52; Prin of Hur Coll 52-60; Can of Hur 60; Cons Ld Bp of Koot in Ch Ch Cathl Victoria BC 6 Jan 61 by Abp of BC (Metrop); Bps of New Westmr; Carib; Caled; Yukon; Olympia and Spokane; and Bps Sovereign, Rhea, Martin and Mandeville; Res 65; Dean of Pro-Cathl of St Sav Nelson BC 61-63. *2129 Perron Drive, Mississauga, Ont., Canada.*

COLERIDGE, Francis Arthur Wilson. b 10. Clifton Th Coll 58. **d** 59 **p** 60 Win. C of St Paul Bournemouth 59-61; R of Berrington w Betton Strange 61-68; Perm to Offic Dio Chich from 69. *68 Kings Avenue, Eastbourne, E Sussex, BN21 2PD.*

COLES, Very Rev David John. b 43. Univ of Auckld BA 65, MA 67. Univ of Otago BD 69, MTh 71. Univ of Man PhD 74. St Jo Coll Auckld 66. **d** 68 **p** 69 Auckld. C of St Mark Remuera Auckld 68-70; Asst Chap Selw Coll Dun 70-71; C of Fallowfield 72-73; Chap Hulme Hall Univ Man 73-74; V of Glenfield 74-76; Takapuna 76-80; Exam Chap to Bp of Auckld from 74; Dean and V of St John's Cathl Napier Dio Wai from 80. *Deanery, Church Lane, Napier, NZ.* (57-862)

COLES, Edward Charles. b 19. **d** 79 Bp Stanage for Johann. M CR from 79. *PO Box 49027, Rosettenville, S Africa 2130.*

COLES, Francis Herbert. b 35. Selw Coll Cam BA 59, MA 63. Coll of Resurr Mirfield. **d** 61 **p** 62 Ox. C of Wolvercote 61-65; Farnham-R 65-69; V of Lynton w Brendon (R Martinhoe and Parracombe from 73) 69-73; R 73-76; R of Countisbury w Lynmouth 70-76; C-in-c of Iffley City and Dio Ox from 76. *30 Abberbury Road, Oxford, OX4 4ES.* (Oxford 773516)

COLES, Geoffrey Herbert. b 38. N Ordin Course 77. **d** 80 **p** 81 Bradf. Hon C of Shelf Dio Bradf from 80. *12 Cooper Grove, Shelf, Halifax, W Yorks, HX3 7RF.*

COLES, John Spencer Halstaff. b 50. Hertf Coll Ox BA 72, MA 76. Wycl Hall Ox 72. **d** 75 **p** 76 Reading for Ox. C of Greyfriars Reading 75-79; Ch Ch Clifton 79-82; V of St Barn Woodside Park Finchley Dio Lon from 82. *St Barnabas's Vicarage, Westbury Road, N12 7PD.* (01-445 3598)

COLES, Robert Charles. b 41. Bps' Coll Cheshunt 66. **d** 68 Pet **p** 69 Bp Graham-Campbell for Pet. C of St Alb Mart, Northn 68-72; Durrington 72-74; Portslade 74-78; Horsham Dio Chich from 78. *St John's House, Church Road, Broadbridge Heath, W Sussex, RH12 3LD.* (Horsham 65238)

COLES, Stephen Richard. b 49. Univ Coll Ox BA 70, MA 74. Univ of Leeds BA 80. Coll of the Resurr Mirfield 78. **d** 81 Stepney for Lon. C of St Mary Stoke Newington Dio Lon from 81. *Rectory Flat, Stoke Newington Church Street, N16 9ES.*

COLES, Thomas William. b 01. Late Scho and Pemberton Exhib of Univ Coll Dur BSc 28. Wycl Hall Ox 28. **d** 30 **p** 31 Carl. C of St Nich Whitehaven 30-32; C-in-c of Currock Conv Distr Carl 32-37; Min 37; R of Moresby 37-49; V of Luddendenfoot 49-52; St Geo Ovenden Halifax 52-65; Grosmont (w Egton from 66) 65-71; C-in-c of Egton 65-66. *61 St James's Drive, Burton, nr Carnforth, Lancs, LA6 1HY.* (0524 781703)

COLES, William Dennis. b 17. St Cath S Ox 3rd cl Math Mods 36, 2nd cl Math 38, BA 40. QUB PhD 71. Edin Th Coll 38. **d** 40 **p** 41 Glas. C of H Trin Paisley 40-42; H Spirit Beeston Hill 42-43; Asst Master Clayesmore Sch 43-51; Hd Master St Jo Coll Nass 51-53; Asst Master Northn Gr Sch 53-55; Lect Nig Coll of Arts Sc and Technology Ibad 55-61; Perm to Offic Dio Arg Is from 56; Lect Ealing Technical Coll 61-64; Magee Univ Coll Londonderry 64-81. *Caraminish, An-t-Ob, Na Hearadh, W Isles, Scotland PA83 3UD.*

COLEY, Frederick Albert. b 13. Lich Th Coll 65. **d** 66 **p** 67 Worc. C of Headless Cross 66-68; Tardebigge w Webheath 68-72; C-in-c of Stoke Bliss w Kyre Wyard (and Hanley William w Hanley Child from 73) 72-79; Hanley William w Hanley Child Dio Worc 72-73. *Greenfields, Kyre Wood, Tenbury Wells, H & W.* (T Wells 810961)

COLEY, Samuel Bernard. b 13. Jes Coll Cam BA 34, MA 38. Ridley Hall Cam 35. **d** 37 **p** 38 Sheff. C of Conisborough 37-39; St Mary Bearwood Smethwick 40-41; Chap RAFVR 41-46; C of St Paul Birm 47-48; V of Foy 48-50; Chap HM Borstal Inst Borstal 50-54; HM Pris Wandsworth 54-59; V of Rowley Regis 59-70; R of Long Whatton 70-73. *8 Elvaston Drive, Long Eaton, Notts, NG10 3BQ.*

COLIN, Desmond Eric. b 16. TCD BA (2nd cl Ment and Mor Sc Mod) 38, MA 51. **d** 39 Cash **p** 40 Dub for Cash. C of St Mary Clonmel w Innislonagh 39-40; Leigh U 41-43; I of St Edm Dunmanway 43-45; R of Clonenagh w Roskelton 45-51; C of St aug Ipswich 51-53; Dewsbury 53-55; V of Colbury 55-81; Surr 75-81. *29 Brook Hall Road, Boxford, Suff.*

COLIN, Emmanuel Paul. Warner Th Coll Buye 67. **d** 69 Bur D Dio Bur. *c/o PO Box 58 Ngozi, Burundi, Centr Africa.*

✠ **COLIN, Right Rev Gerald Fitzmaurice.** b 13. Trin Coll Dub Found Scho and Bernard Pri 33, BA (1st cl Mod), Wray Pri, Downes Oratory Pri, Downes Comp Pri and Ryan Pri 34, Bp Forster Pri 35, Div Test (1st cl) 36, Elrington Th Pri 38, MA 46. **d** 36 **p** 37 Down. C of Ballywillan 36-38; St Geo Dub and Chan V St Patr Cathl Dub 38-47; Chap RAFVR 39-47; V of Frodingham 47-66; Proc Conv Linc 59-64 and 66-78; Can and Preb of Milton Ecclesia in Linc Cathl from 60; RD of Manlake 60-66; Cons Ld Bp Suffr of Grimsby in S'wark Cathl 6 Jan 66 by Abp of Cant; Bps of Linc; Ely; S'wark; and Portsm; Bps Suffr of Maidstone; Buckingham; Grantham; and Warrington; Bps Walsh; Dunlop; Martin; Chase; Healey; and Bp of Calif; res 78; Asst Bp of Linc from 79; Abp's Dir of Butlin's Camp Chap Service 70-79. *Orchard Close, St Mary's Lane, Louth, Lincs, LN11 0DT.* (0507-602600)

COLLARD, Fred. b 25. Wycl Hall Ox. **d** 61 York for Sing **p** 63 Ipoh for Sing. Miss 0MF 61-81; C of St Paul Slim River 63; Cameron Highlands 63-68; P-in-c of Perak 69-75; Home Staff OMF 75-81; Perm to Offic Dio Ox 71-81; Team V of Cheltm Dio Glouc from 81. *4 Albert Road, Cheltenham, Glos, GL52 2QX.* (0242-24572)

COLLARD, Harold. b 27. Wycl Hall Ox 51. **d** 53 **p** 54 Chelmsf. C of Rainham Essex 53-56; Hull 56-59; V of Ch Ch U Armley 59-67; R of H Trin Chesterfield 68-77; P-in-c of Matlock Bath Dio Derby from 77. *Vicarage, Matlock Bath, Derbys, DE4 3PU.* (Matlock 2947)

COLLARD, John Cedric. b 30. Pemb Coll Cam BA 53, MA 76. St Alb Ministerial Tr Scheme 77. **d** 80 St Alb **p** 81 Hertf for St Alb. C of Roxton w Gt Barford Dio St Alb from 80. *68 Barford Road, Blunham, Bedford, MK44 3ND.*

COLLARD, Norton Harvey. b 22. Open Univ BA 80. Roch Th Coll 63. **d** 65 **p** 66 Roch. C of St Mary Virg Swanley 65-67; Dartford 67-70; V of St Anne Grantham Dio Linc from 70. *St Anne's Vicarage, Harrowby Road, New Somerby, Grantham, Lincs, NG31 9ED.* (Grantham 2822)

COLLAS, John Paul. St Jo Coll Morpeth 60. ACT ThL (2nd cl) 62. **d** 62 **p** 63 Adel. C of Mt Gambier 62-64; P-in-c of Norton Summit 64-66; Kangaroo I 66-71; R of Glenunga 71-77; Tea Tree Gully 77-78; Glen Osmond Dio Adel from 78. *2 Pridmore Road, Glen Osmond, S Australia 5064.* (79 1494)

COLLAS, Canon Victor John. b 23. Late Scho of Pemb Coll Ox BA 44, MA 48. Wycl Hall Ox. **d** 51 **p** 52 Win. C of St Mary Magd Milton 51-58; R of St Andr Guernsey 58-81; Hon Can of Win Cathl 78-81- Can (Emer) from 81. *c/o Paradis, Vale, Guernsey, CI.* (0481-44450)

COLLETT, Alan Wilfred. b 37. St Barn Coll Adel 79. **d** 81 The Murray. C of O'Halloran Hill Dio The Murray from 81. *45 Paterson Drive, Hackham, S Australia 5163.* (08-382 5604)

COLLETT, Albert Ernest Jack. b 15. SOC 62. **d** 65 **p** 66 S'wark. C of St Jo Bapt Southend Lewisham 65-73; Min of St Phil Conv Distr Reigate Dio S'wark from 73. *102a Nutley Lane, Reigate, Surrey, RH2 9HA.*

COLLETT, Ian Haldane Ewart. Univ of Capetn BA 65. St Paul's Coll Grahamstn 66. **d** 68 **p** 69 Grahmstn. C of St Mich and St Geo Cathl Ch Grahmstn 68-70; St Mich AA Queenstown 70-73; R of Cathcart 73-77; St Jo Bapt Ft Beaufort Dio Grahmstn from 77; P-in-c of H Trin Ft Beaufort Dio Grahmstn from 78. *66 Campbell Street, Fort Beaufort, CP, S Africa.*

COLLETT, Lloyd Parsons. Qu Coll Newfld 59. **d** 61 **p** 62 Newfld. C of Fogo 61-64; I of Cow Head 64-65; Twillingate 65-70; R of Bay St George Dio Newfld (W Newfld from 76) from 70. *Rectory, Robinson's Bay, St George, Newfoundland, Canada.* (709-645-2024)

COLLETT, Maurice John. b 28. SOC 76. **d** 79 Kens for Lon **p** 80 Lon. C of Feltham Dio Lon from 79. *58 Shakespeare Avenue, Feltham, Middx, TW14 9HX.*

COLLETT, Wilfrid Arthur. b 06. K Coll Lon and Warm 56. **d** 57 **p** 58 S'wark. C of St Andr w All SS Peckham 57-59; Freshwater 59-65; V of Seaview 65-72. *7 St Mary's Close, Upton Road, Ryde, IW, PO33 3HJ.*

COLLETT-WHITE, Derek Arthur. Bp's Univ Lennox BA 62. McGill Univ Montr BD 64. **d** 64 Ja for Carib **p** 64 Carib. C of Lytton Ind Miss 64-66; I of Lillooet 66-67; P-in-c of Southfield 67-68; R of Bluefields 69-76. *c/o Rectory, Southfield, Jamaica, W Indies.*

COLLETT-WHITE, Thomas Charles. b 36. Trin Coll Cam BA 61. Ridley Hall Cam 60. **d** 62 **p** 63 Roch. C of St Mark Gillingham 62-66; Normanton 66-69; V of St Aug Highbury Lon 69-76; R of Huntingdon w Ormstown Queb 76-79; V of St Mark Gillingham Dio Roch from 79. *St Mark's Vicarage, Canterbury Street, Gillingham, Kent.* (Medway 51818)

COLLEY, Graham Albert. b 46. St Jo Coll Auckld 67. **d** 70

Monteith for Auckld **p** 71 Auckld. C of Ch Ch Papakura 70-73; P-in-c 73; V of Waimate N 73-81; Thames Dio Auckld from 81. *603 Mackay Street, Thames, NZ.*

COLLEY, Sidney James. Em Coll Sktn 52. **d** 53 **p** 55 Sktn. R of Delisle 53-56; Sec Treas and Trav Miss Dio Sktn 56-57; Chap RCAF from 57. *c/o Air Force HQ, Ottawa, Ont., Canada.*

COLLIE, Bertie Harold Guy. b 28. Univ of Glas MB ChB 56. **d** 76 **p** 77 Glas. Hon C of H Trin Ayr Dio Glas from 76. *Hillside, Cargill Road, Maybole, Ayrshire.* (Maybole 82255)

COLLIE, John Norman. b 25. Em Coll Cam BA 51, MA 56. Ridley Hall Cam 52. **d** 54 **p** 55 Leic. C of H Ap Leic 54-57; C of Melton Mowbray 57-59; Chap of Lee Abbey 59-62 V of Im w St Anselm Streatham 62-68; Ecclesall Dio Sheff from 68. *Ecclesall Vicarage, Sheffield 11.* (Sheffield 360084)

COLLIE, Robert William Strickland. b 45. Ridley Coll Melb ThL 60. **d** 60 **p** 61 Melb. C of Toorak 60-62; St Mary Caulfield 62-63; Min of Ferntree Gully 63-67; I of St Mark Forest Hill 67-78; Greythorn Dio Melb from 78. *32 Ardgour Street, Balwyn North, Vic, Australia 3104.* (857 6719)

COLLIER, Albert Horace. Em Coll Sktn 63. **d** and **p** 64 Calg. C of Carbon 64-67; St Luke Red Deer 64-70; R of Rocky Mountain Ho 70-80. *4045-39th Street, Red Deer, Alta, Canada, T4N 0Y8.*

COLLIER, Alfred Stanley. b 1899. BA (Lon) 22. **d** 59 Ex **p** 60 Crediton for Ex. C of St Matthias Plymouth 59-61; R of Sutcombe 61-62; C of Ashtead 62-63; Perm to Offic Dio Ex 63-64; Dio Ely 64-68; C of Freshwater 68-70; Perm to Offic Dio St Alb from 70; Ely from 75; Chelmsf from 77. *11 Spencer Road, Great Chesterford, Essex, CB10 1PZ.*

COLLIER, Anthony Charles. b 45. Peterhouse Cam BA (Hist) 68, MA 72. Or Coll Ox Dipl Th 70. Cudd Coll 68. **d** 71 Dorking for Guildf **p** 72 Guildf. C of St Jo Evang North Holmwood 71-75; Perm to Offic Dio S'wark 75-79; Hon C of St Jo Evang Shirley Dio Cant from 80. *38 Firsby Avenue, Shirley, Croydon.*

COLLIER, David Charles. b 24. Gregorian Univ Rome (Engl Coll) PhL 50, STL 54. **d** and **p** 53 RC Cardinal Traglia. Rec into Angl Ch in Perth Cathl 68. R of St Andr Claremont 68-70; Perm to Offic Dio Perth 70-71; Chap Aiglon Coll Villars, Switzerland from 73. *Aiglon College, 1885 Chesières-Villars, Switzerland.*

COLLIER, Leonard Cyril. b 20. **d** 78 Southn for Win **p** 79 Basingstoke for Win. C of Lockerley & E Dean w E & W Tytherley Dio Win from 78. *School House, Butts Green, Lockerley, Romsey, Hants.*

COLLIER, Michael Francis. b 29. Wycl Hall Ox 71. **d** 73 **p** 74 Birm. C of Hamstead 73-75; P-in-c of Castleton 75-80; Hope Dio Derby 78-80; V (w Castleton) from 80. *Vicarage, Hope, Sheffield, S30 2RN.* (Hope Valley 20534)

COLLIER, Richard John Millard. b 45. E Anglian Min Tr Course 78. **d** 81 Nor. Hon C of St Pet Mancroft City and Dio Nor from 81. *11 The Close, Norwich, Norfolk, NR1 4DH.*

COLLIER, Robert Howard. b 25. St Cath S Ox BA (2nd cl Mod Hist) 46, MA 50. **d** 54 Lon **p** 55 Kens for Lon. C of K Chas Mart S Mymms 54-57; St Geo Hanover Square Lon 57-59; V of Shabbington Dio Ox from 78; V of Worminghall Dio Ox from 78; C-in-c of Ickford Dio Ox from 78; RD of Waddesdon 66-73. *c/o Shabbington Vicarage, Aylesbury, Bucks.* (Long Crendon 201154)

COLLIER, Stanley Milne. Em Coll Cam 3rd cl Hist Trip pt i 23, BA (2nd cl Hist Trip pt ii) 24, MA 28. Westcott Ho Cam 24. **d** 25 **p** 26 Cov. C of St Mark Cov 25-28; Hd Master St Mich Sch Sandakan 27-28; Asst P at Sandakan 28-30; Actg Hd Master St Thos Sch Kuching 30-31; R of All SS Jesselton 31-46; V of St Geo Penang and Archd of Penang 46-50; SPG Sec SW Area 50-52; Perm to Offic Dio Truro 50-52; C of Chalfont St Peter 52-56; V of Hawley and of Minley 56-60; R of N Cadbury 60-65; V of Brent-Knoll 65-70. *The Bank Flat, St James Street, South Petherton, TA13 5BN.* (0460 41413)

COLLIN, Anthony Garth. b 27. Roch Th Coll 64. **d** 66 **p** 67 Chich. C of Haywards Heath 66-69; C of Hove 69-72; R of Rumboldswyke 72-75; Chap to Chich Hosps from 75. *Chaplain's Office, St Richard's Hospital, Chichester, Sussex.* (Chichester 788122)

COLLIN, Terry. b 39. St Aid Coll 65. **d** 67 **p** 68 Bradf. C of St Jas Bolton 67-71; Keighley 71-73; V of Greengates Dio Bradf from 74. *Greengates Vicarage, 138 New Line, Bradford, W Yorks, BD10 0BK.* (Bradf 613111)

COLLING, Canon James Oliver. b 30. Late Scho Univ of Man BA (2nd cl Hist) 50. Cudd Coll 52. **d** 54 **p** 55 Liv. C of Wigan 54-59; V of Padgate 59-71; R 71-73; R of Warrington Dio Liv from 73; RD of Warrington from 70; Can of Liv Cathl from 76. *Rectory, Warrington, Chesh, WA1 2TL.* (Warrington 35020)

COLLINGS, John Reuben. Ch Coll Tas ACT ThL 52. **d** 52 **p** 53 Tas. C of St Mary Moonah 52-54; R of Geo Town 54-57; Kingston 57-63; Dir of Christian Educn Dio Newc 63-66; Perm to Offic Dio Melb 67-70; P-in-c of Prov Distr Belconnen *B* Canberra 70-72; Chap Coll of Advanced Educn Canberra 72-74. *237 Antill Street, Watson, ACT, Australia 2602.*

COLLINGS, Preb Neil. b 46. K Coll Lon BD and AKC 69. St Aug Coll Cant 69. **d** 70 **p** 71 Ex. C of Littleham w Exmouth 70-72; Team V 72-74; Chap of Westmr Abbey 74-79; R of St Nich City and Dio Heref from 79; Dioc Dir of Ordinands and Dir of Post-Ordin Tr Dio Heref from 79; Preb of Heref Cathl from 79. *St Nicholas's Rectory, Breinton Road, Hereford.* (Hereford 273810)

COLLINGS, Robert Frank. Univ of Lon BD 53. ALCD 52. **d** 52 **p** 53 Lon. C of St Matt Bayswater 52-55; Portsdown 55-59; R of St Lawr IW 59-66; CF (TA) 63-66; R of Williams 66-69; Mandurah 69-71; Boyup Brook 71-74; Harvey 74-79; Bridgetown Dio Bunb from 79. *Rectory, Bridgetown, W Australia 6255.* (097-61 1031)

COLLINGS, Robert Sidney John. St Jo Coll Morpeth. **d** 71 **p** 72 Gippsld. C of Traralgon 71-75; P-in-c of Heyfield 75-76; R of Loch 76-79; Orbost Dio Gippsld from 79. *Box 77, Orbost, Vic, Australia 3888.*

COLLINGS, Thomas William Ralph. b 38. St Pet Coll Ox BA (Maths) 61, BA (Th) 63, MA 65. U Th Sem NY STM 65. Univ of Essex MSc 70. **d** 79 Glas for Rupld **p** 80 Rupld. C of St John's Cathl Winnipeg Dio Rupld from 80. *64 St Cross Street, Winnipeg, Manit, Canada, R2W 3X8.*

COLLINGWOOD, John Jeremy Raynham. b 37. CCC BA 60, MA 68. Univ of Lon BD 78. (Called to Bar Gray's Inn 64) Trin Coll Bris 75. **d** 78 **p** 79 Bris. C of Henleaze 78-80; P-in-c of H Trin Hotwells w St Andr L and St Pet Clifton Dio Bris 80-81; V from 81. *Holy Trinity Vicarage, Clifton, Bristol, BS8 4RA.* (Bristol 34751)

COLLINS, Adelbert Andrew. Lich Th Coll **d** 61 Shrewsbury for Lich **p** 62 Lich. C of Sedgley 61-77; P-in-c of Enville Dio Lich from 77. *Enville Rectory, Stourbridge, W Midl.* (Kinver 3733)

COLLINS, Arthur Lionel. b 04. Bps' Coll Cheshunt 65. **d** 66 Win **p** 67 Bp Cornwall for Win. C of St Luke, Southn 66-72; Perm to Offic Dio Win 72-76; Hon C of Woolston 76-81; Perm to Offic Dio Win from 81. *5 Chine Avenue, Bitterne, Southampton, SO2 7JF.* (Southampton 449592)

COLLINS, Barry Douglas. b 47. Kelham Th Coll 66. **d** 70 **p** 71 Man. C of Peel Green 70-73; St Phil w St Steph Salford 73-75; R of H Trin Blackley 75-79. *Address temp unknown.*

COLLINS, Christopher. b 46. K Coll Lon BSc and AKC 67. Pemb Coll Ox BA 70. St Steph Ho Ox 68. **d** 71 Dur **p** 72 Jarrow for Dur. C of St Thos Conv Distr Pennywell Bp Wearmouth 71-74; St Luke Bp Wearmouth, St Mary Magd Millfield 74-76; W Harton 76-78; Team V Winlaton w Rowland's Glen High Spen Dio Dur from 78. *Vicarage, High Spen, Rowlands Gill, Tyne & Wear, NE39 2AA.* (Rowlands Gill 2815)

COLLINS, Christopher David. b 43. Univ of Sheff BA (2nd cl Econ) 64. Tyndale Hall Bris 65. **d** 68 **p** 69 Man. C of Rusholme 68-71; Bushbury 71-74; V of St Jo Div Fairfield Liv 74-81; St John Tunbridge Wells Dio Roch from 81. *1 Amherst Road, Tunbridge Wells, Kent.* (Tunbridge Wells 21183)

COLLINS, Christopher Robin. St Jo Coll Morpeth. ACT ThL 62. **d** 62 **p** 63 Bath. C of E Orange 63-68; R of Cobar 68-70; Chap of Bloomfield Hosp Dio Bath from 70. *Bloomfield Hospital, Orange, NSW, Australia 2800.* (62-4309)

COLLINS, Canon Donald Martin. b 20. K Coll Lon. **d** 43 Lewes for Chich **p** 44 Chich. C of St Nich Arundel w St Stoke and Tortington 43-46; St Geo Cathl Perth W Austr 46-47; Forest Row (in c of Ashurst Wood) 48-50; CF 50-58; R of Middleham 58-77; V of Thornton Steward 58-76; Hon Can of Ripon 75-77; Can (Emer) from 77; P-in-c of Doddington Dio Ches 77-78; V from 78. *Doddington Vicarage, Nantwich, Chesh.* (Bridgmere 236)

COLLINS, Frederick Spencer. b 36. Univ of Birm Dipl Th 67. FACCA. Ripon Hall Ox. **d** 67 **p** 68 Bp T G S Smith for Leic. C of Evington 67-71; Hall Green 71-73; V of Ch Ch Ward End 73-79; Birm Dioc Stewardship Adv from 79. *340 Yardley Wood Road, Moseley, Birmingham, B13 9JX.*

COLLINS, George Martyn. b 36. Univ of Bris BA (2nd cl Hist) 58. Coll of Resurr Mirfield. **d** 62 **p** 63 Portsm. C of Wymering w Widley 62-64; St Mark's Conv Distr Kingstanding 64-69; V of Weoley Castle 69-78; R of Curdworth Dio Birm from 78. *Rectory, Glebe Fields, Curdworth, Sutton Coldfield, B76 9ES.* (0675-70384)

COLLINS, Harold Victor Norman. b 20. Div Hostel Dub 70. **d** 71 **p** 72 Connor. C of Jordanstown Dio Connor from 71. *683 Shore Road, Jordanstown, Newtownabbey, Co Antrim, N Ireland.*

COLLINS, Ian Geoffrey. b 37. Univ of Hull BA 60. Sarum Th Coll 60. **d** 62 **p** 63 Linc. C of Gainsborough 62-65; Min Can of St Geo Chap Windsor 65-81; Succr 67-81; Asst Master St Geo Sch Windsor 68-81; R of Kirkby-on-Ashfield Dio

Southw from 81. *12 Church Street, Kirkby-in-Ashfield, Nottingham, NG17 8LE.* (Mansfield 753790)

COLLINS, James Edward. b 49. Gordon Coll Mass USA BA 71. **d** 74 Mass for Moos **p** 75 Moos. C of St Thos Moose Factory 74-76; I of Mistassini Dio Moos from 76. *Mistassini, Baie du Poste, PQ, Canada.*

COLLINS, James Frederick. b 10. St Jo Coll Cam 2nd cl Hist Trip pt i 33, BA (3rd cl Th Trip pt i) 34, MA 38. Westcott Ho Cam 34. **d** 35 **p** 36 Newc T. C of Benwell 35-38; Chap Miss to Seamen Port Sudan 38-41; Chap RNVR 36-46; C of All SS Milford 46-47; V of Rothwell w Orton 47-51; R of Bromham 51-62; Surr 48-51; V of Chiseldon w Draycot Foliat 62-68; Dir of Ordinands Dio Sarum 68-73; Publ Pr Dio Sarum from 68; C of Devizes 68-75. *19 King's Court, Beach Green, Shoreham-by-Sea, Sussex, BN4 5YD.*

COLLINS, John. Moore Th Coll Syd ACT ThL 68. **d** 69 **p** 70 Syd. C of Kiama 69-72; R of Mulgoa Dio Syd from 72. *Rectory, Mulgoa, NSW, Australia 2750.* (Mulgoa 73-8270)

COLLINS, John Brenton. b 06. Trin Coll Cam BA 28, MA 32. Ridley Hall Cam 30. **d** 33 **p** 34 Sarum. C of St Jas Poole 33-35; Chap of Canford Sch 35-47; V of Canford Magna 36-47; CF (EC) 40-45; Hon CF from 45; R of Marnhull 47-53; V of Market Lavington 53-57; PC of Easterton 53-57; Chap Dauntsey's Sch 54-57; Proc Conv Sarum 55-59; R of Hever (w Markbeech from 69) 57-73; C-in-c of Markbeech 66-69. *Handley Gate Cottage, Garway Hill, Hereford, HR2 8HD.*

COLLINS, John Gilbert. b 32. SOC 67. **d** 71 **p** 72 S'wark. C of St Jo Evang, Coulsdon 71-75; Chap St Francis and Hurstwood Pk Hosps Haywards Heath from 75; Roftez Pk Hosp Horsham from 80. *Oakhurst, Hurstwood Lane, Haywards Heath, W Sussex, RH17 7SH.* (H Heath 51881)

COLLINS, John Theodore Cameron Bucke. b 25. Clare Coll Cam BA 49, MA 52. Ridley Hall Cam 49. **d** 51 **p** 52 Lon. C of All S Langham Place 51-57; V of St Mark Gillingham 57-71; Chap Medway Hosp 70-71; Commiss Centr Tang 61-77; V of Canford Magna 71-80; RD of Wimborne 79-80; H Trin Brompton Road w St Paul Onslow Sq Kens Dio Lon from 80. *73 Princes Gate Mews, SW7 2PP.* (01-589 4153)

COLLINS, Kenneth Marritt. b 13. FRCO 44. Sarum Th Coll. **d** 63 **p** 64 Win. C of Ringwood 63-66; V of Hatherden w Tangley 66-77. *Geffery's House, London Road, Hook, Hants.*

COLLINS, Canon Lewis John. b 05. Late Scho of SS Coll Cam 3rd cl Math Trip 25, BA (2nd cl Th Trip pt i) 27, 1st cl Th Trip pt ii and Carus Gk Test Pri 28, MA 31. Or Coll Ox MA (by incorp) 38. Westcott Ho Cam 27. **d** 28 Dover for Cant **p** 29 Cant. C of Whitstable 28-29; Chap SS Coll Cam 29-31; Min Can of St Paul's Cathl Lon and Dep P-in-Ord to HM the King 31-34; P-in-Ord 34-35; Lect in Th K Coll Lon 32-34; Hulsean Pr Cam 36-37; Vice-Prin Westcott Ho Cam 34-37; Lect and Chap Or Coll Ox 37-38; Fell 37-48; Dean 38-48; Exam Chap to Bp of Newc T 38-57; Chap RAFVR 40-45; Can Res of St Paul's Cathl Lon 48-81; Can (Emer) from 81; Chan 48-54; Libr 51-52; Prec 54-70; Treas from 70; Select Pr Univ of Ox 66-67. *Mill House, Chappel Rad, Mount Bures, Suffolk.* (0787 227 388)

COLLINS, Maurice Arthur Reily. Clare Coll Cam BA 41, MA 45. Westcott Ho Cam 45. **d** 47 **p** 48 St Alb. C of Bishop's Stortford 47-50; Rugby (in c of St John) 50-51; Perm to Offic Dio Guildf 52-53; R of Ockley Dio Guildf from 53; P-in-c of Okewood w Forest Green Dio Guildf from 82. *Ockley Rectory, Dorking, Surrey.* (Dorking 711550)

COLLINS, Maurice Frank. b 44. St Francis Coll Brisb. **d** 69 **p** 71 Brisb. C of All SS, Chermside 69-70; St Pet Southport 71-73; V of Mitchell 73-77; Par Distr of Carina-Belmont City and Dio Brisb from 77. *12 Sankey Street, Carina, Queensland, Australia 4152.* (398 8069)

COLLINS, Neville Eustace. Moore Th Coll Syd. **d** 61 **p** 62 Armid. C of Moree 61-63; P-in-c of Baradine 63-69; V of Manilla 69-77; W Tamworth Dio Armid from 77. *Box W73, West Tamworth, NSW, Australia.*

COLLINS, Norman Hilary. b 33. Former Postmaster of Merton Coll Ox 1st cl Cl 53, BA (2nd cl Lit Hum) 55, 3rd cl Th 56, MA 58. Wells Th Coll 58. **d** 60 **p** 61 Llan. C of Ystrad Mynach 60-62; Gelligaer 62-67; V of Maerdy 67-77; R of Penarth w Lavernock Dio Llan from 77. *Rectory, Hickman Road, Penarth, S Glam, CF6 2AJ.* (Penarth 709463)

COLLINS, Paul David Arthur. b 50. AKC and BD 72. St Aug Coll Cant 72. **d** 73 **p** 74 S'wark. C of Rotherhithe 73-76; St Luke Stocking Farm City and Dio Leic 76-78; V from 78. *St Luke's Vicarage, Halifax Drive, Stocking Farm, Leicester.* (Leic 353206)

COLLINS, Paul Myring. b 53. St Jo Coll Dur BA 75. St Steph Ho Ox BA (Th) 78. **d** 79 **p** 80 Lich. C of H Trin Meir Dio Lich from 79. *142 Broadway Meir, Stoke-on-Trent, Staffs.* (0782-311390)

COLLINS, Canon Peter Churton. b 13. Univ of Lon BD 35. Ely Th Coll 35. **d** 36 **p** 37 Roch. C of Crayford 36-42; V of St Alb Dartford 42-60; R of Crayford 60-79; RD of Dartford 61-64; Erith from 64; Hon Can of Roch from 63; Surr from 64; Proc Conv Roch 64-70; Chap of Huggens Coll Northfleet Kent from 79. *Huggens College, Northfleet, Kent, DA11 9DL.* (0474 52428)

COLLINS, Peter John. b 33. Open Univ BA. Oak Hill Th Coll 64. **d** 66 Colchester for Chelmsf **p** 67 Chelmsf. C of St Mary, Leyton 66-69; Portsdown 69-72; V of St Paul Gatten Shanklin 72-79; P-in-c of Ingrave 79-81. *c/o Rectory, St Stephen's Crescent, Brentwood, Essex, CM13 2AT.*

COLLINS, Philip Howard Norton. b 50. AKC 73. St Aug Coll Cant 73. **d** 74 Lon **p** 75 Stepney for Lon. C of St Thos Clapton Common 74-78; Ramsey 78-81; Upwood w Gt and L Raveley 78-81; R of Leverington Dio Ely from 81. *Leverington Rectory, Wisbech, Cambs.* (Wisbech 581486)

COLLINS, Rodney Harry. b 20. Open Univ BA 74. SOC 75. **d** 78 **p** 79 Roch. C of St Mary Swanley Dio Roch from 78. *16 Stanhope Road, Sidcup, Kent, DA15 7HA.* (01-302 0867)

COLLINS, Roger Richardson. b 48. W Midl Min Tr Course 78. **d** 81 Birm (NSM). C of The Cotteridge Dio Birm from 81. *6 Chesterfield Court, Middleton Hall Road, Birmingham, B30 1AF.*

COLLINS, Ronald Dowse. St Francis Coll Brisb. ACT ThL 42. **d** 41 **p** 42 N Queensld. C of H Trin Mackay 41-45; Atherton N Queensld 45-46; L to Offic at St Phil Newc T 47; St Paul Ruislip Manor (Col Cl Act) 48-49; R of Prosperine N Queensld 49-51; Home Hill 52-53; Mareeba 53-56; W Mackay 57-62; L to Offic Dio N Queensld from 63. *48 Jack Street, Atherton, N. Queensland, Australia.*

COLLINS, Canon Ronald William. St Chad's Coll Dur Long Reading Pri 31, Long Declamation Pri 32, BA 32. St Steph Ho Ox 32. **d** 32 **p** 33 Lon. C of St Mary Magd Chiswick 32-34; Chap RN 34-39; C of Sawbridgeworth 39-40; Newport Pagnell 40-43; V of Olney Dio Ox from 43; RD of Newport 54-67; C-in-c of Chicheley 56-61; Hon Chap Showman's Guild of Gt Britain from 58; Hon Can of Ch Ch Cathl Ox from 66. *Vicarage, Olney, Bucks.* (Bedford 711317)

COLLINS, Canon Trevor. b 30. K Coll Lon and Warm BD (2nd cl) and AKC (1st cl) 56. **d** 57 **p** 59 Linc. C of New Sleaford 57-59; Grantham 59-60; Gt Grimsby (in c of St Mark) 60-65; V of Witham-on-the-Hill 65-68; Dir of Educn Linc 68-75; Preb and Can of Linc Cathl from 73; V of Boston Dio Linc from 75; RD of Holland E 75-80. *Vicarage, Boston, Lincs.* (Boston 62864)

COLLINS, Vernon James Edward. **d** 79 Wang. Perm to Offic Dio Wang from 79. *c/o Bishop's Registry, Wangaratta, Victoria, Australia.*

COLLINS, William Arthur. Univ of W Ont BA 58. Hur Coll LTh 59. **d** 58 **p** 59 Hur. C of St D Lon 58-59; St Geo Walkerville 59-60; R of Merlin 60-62; Caracas Venezuela 62-71. *Apartardo 61, 116 del Est, Caracas, Venezuela, S America.*

COLLINS, William Arthur Donovan. b 21. K Coll Lon and Warm AKC (2nd cl) 49. **d** 50 **p** 51 Wakef. C of St Jo Evang Huddersfield 50-52; R of Rustenburg 52-57; Nelspruit and White River w Plaston 57-61; C of All SS Friern Barnet 61-62; V of Kellington w Whitley 62-66; R of Ch the King Claremont 66-75; St Barn Capetn 75-77; Observatory Capetn 77-80; Archd of Capetn 75-80; V of Birchington w Acol Dio Cant from 80; Commiss St Hel from 79. *Vicarage, Minnis Road, Birchington, Kent, CT7 9SE.* (Thanet 41117)

COLLINS, William Cecil. b 03. Tyndale Hall Bris. **d** 46 **p** 47 Bris. C of St Luke Bris 46-50; V of Summerstown 50-54; St Luke Wolverhampton 54-81. *c/o 122 Goldthorn Hill, Wolverhampton, Staffs.*

COLLINS, William Francis Martin. b 43. St Cath Coll Cam BA 66, MA 70. Cudd Coll 68. **d** 70 **p** 71 Man. C of Vic Pk 70-73; P-in-c of All SS Ancoats Man 73-78; L to Offic Dio Man and Commun Chap Abraham Moss Centre Hr Crumpsall Man from 78; Hon C of St Luke Cheetham City and Dio Man from 81. *23 Mariman Drive, Hr Crumpsall, Manchester, M8 6PS.* (061-740 2031)

COLLINS, William John. St Francis Coll Brisb. **d** 60 **p** 62 Brisb. C of Ipswich Brisb 60-66; V of Surat 66-70; R of Crow's Nest 70-76; CF (Austr) from 76. *Jungle Training Centre, Canungra, Queensland, Australia 4275.*

COLLINS, Winfield. b 41. **d** 76 Pontefract for Wakef for Barb. Asst Chap HM Pris Wakef 76. *St John's Church, St John, Barbados, W Indies.*

COLLINSON, Alfred Edward. b 06. Lich Th Coll 27. **d** 30 **p** 31 Newc T. C of Howdon Panns 30-35; Cambois 35-37; Eldon 37-38; Harton 38-39; Hensingham 39-42; C of Wormhill 42-48 (in c of Wormhill 43-47; in c of Peak Dale 47); V of Kirk-Hallam 48-53; Greenhead 53-59; Shilbotel 59-66; Lucker 66-70. *14 West Acres, Alnwick, Northumb.* (Alnwick 2417)

COLLINSON, Brian William. b 55. Univ of Calgary BA 77. Huron Coll Ont MDiv 81. **d** 81 Bp CM Mitchell for Niag.

C of St Paul Fort Erie Dio Niag from 81. *c/o St Paul's Church, 303 Niagara Boulevard, Fort Erie, Ont,*

COLLINSON, Ernest John. ALCD 36. **d** 36 **p** 37 Lon. C of St John Southall 36-38; CMS Miss at Akot 38-40; Lui 40-46; R of Graveley w Chivesfield 46-48; V of Laleham 48-52; AIM Miss Gel River 52-54; V of St Jo Evang Penge 54-63; Deputn Sec Ruanda Miss 63-64; Gen Sec 64-66; V of St Geo Tiverton 66-73; Publ Pr Dio Ex from 74. *13 St John's Road, Exmouth, Devon.* (03952-3050)

COLLIS, Falkiner Stephen. b 30. **d** 77 **p** 79 Grahmstn (APM). C of Cathl Ch of St Mich & St Geo Grahmstn 77-80; Asst Chap Rhodes Univ from 80. *3 Harrismith Street, Grahamstown 6140, S Africa.*

COLLIS, Henry Frederick Edward. b 08. **d** 72 **p** 73 S'wark. Hon C of Kidbrooke Dio S'wark from 72. *174 Wricklemarsh Road, Blackheath, SE3.*

COLLIS, Michael Alan. b 35. K Coll Lon and Warm BD and AKC 60. **d** 61 **p** 62 Worc. C of St Martin Worc 61-63; St Thos Dudley (in c of St Luke) 63-66; St Pet-in-I of Thanet (in c of St Andr Reading Street) 66-70; V of H Trin Selhurst Croydon 70-77; P-in-c of Norbury Dio Cant 77-81; V from 81. *Vicarage, Warwick Road, Thornton Heath, Surrey, CR4 7NH.* (01-684 3820)

COLLIS, Ronald George. b 14. ALCD 56. **d** 56 **p** 57 S'wark. C of Norbiton 56-60; V of St Aid Southcoates Drypool 60-71; Thornton w Bagworth 71-79; Asst Chap HM Borstal Glen Parva Leic from 81. *37 Stanley Drive, Scraptoft Lane, Leicester, LE5 1EB.* (Leicester 766415)

COLLISHAW, Arthur Beecroft. Qu Coll Cam BA 35, MA 48. Chich Th Coll 38. **d** 40 **p** 41 Southw. C of St Jo Evang Carrington 40-43; CF (EC) 43-46; C of Ashington 47-49; St Bart Brighton 49-54; Chap Adisadel Coll 54-57; Achimota Coll 57-60; Bernard Mizeki Coll 61-66; St Anne's Sch Goto 66-68; Achimota Sch from 69. *Achimota School, P.O. Box 11, Achimota, Ghana, W Africa.*

COLLISON, Christopher John. b 48. Oak Hill Th Coll 68. **d** 72 **p** 73 Nor. C of Cromer & Gresham 72-75; Costessey 75-78; Heckmondwike 78-79; P-in-c of Shepley Dio Wakef from 79; Dioc Communications Officer Dio Wakef from 79. *Shepley Vicarage, Huddersfield, HD8 8AE.* (Huddersfield 602640)

COLLISON, Frank Joshua. b 35. **d** 77 Caled. C of St John Masset Dio Caled from 77. *Box 233, Masset, B.C, Canada.*

COLLISON, Geoffrey Norman. Univ of Syd BSc. Univ of Lon BD. Moore Th Coll Syd LTh. **d** 81 Syd. C of St Paul Chatswood Dio Syd from 81. *1/7 View Street, Chatswood, NSW, Australia 2067.*

COLLISON, Kenneth Maxwell. Vanc Th Coll. **d** 48 **p** 49 Caled. Miss at Vanderhoof 48-52; CF (Canad) 53-56; V of Strathmore 56-59; R of Lacombe 59-65; Dawson Creek 65-73; Hon Can of Caled 71-73; I of W Coast Miss BC 73-76; R of St Martin-in-the-Fields Vic Dio BC from 77. *745 Cowper Street, Victoria, BC, Canada.* (604-385 3748)

COLLIS SMITH, Charles Philip. b 39. St Cath Coll Cam BA 61. Lich Th Coll 61. **d** 63 **p** 64 Lich. C of Wednesfield 63-66; Hednesford 66-71; V of High Offley (w Knightley from 74) 71-80; Broughton Dio Lich from 80; R of Myddle Dio Lich from 80. *Myddle Rectory, Shrewsbury, Salop.* (0939-290811)

COLLYER, David John. b 38. Westcott Ho Cam. **d** 63 Bp Warner for Birm **p** 64 Birm. C of Perry Beeches 63-65; Bp's Chap (for Special Youth Work) Dio Birm 65-70; C-in-c of Deritend 66-70; Bps Youth Chap and Dioc Youth Officer 70-73; R of Northfield 73-78; Hon Chap Birm Cathl from 78; Hon C of St Geo City and Dio Birm from 81. *23 Teazel Avenue, Bournville, Birmingham, W Midl.*

COLLYER, John Gordon Llewellyn. b 15. Univ of Lon BA. Sarum Th Coll 69. **d** 70 **p** 71 Porstm. C of Porchester 70-74; All SS Portsea (in c of St Jo Bapt Rudmore) 74-75; Team V of Davidstow w Boscastle 75-77; C of Pitsea 78-79; Perm to Offic Dio St E 79-80; P-in-c of Copdock w Washbrook Dio St E from 80. *4 Charlottes, Washbrook, Ipswich, Suff.*

COLMAN, Cyril Vickers. b 14. ALCD 40. **d** 40 Carl **p** 41 Penrith for Carl. C of St Mark Barrow-F 40-45; St Leon Deal 45-48; R of Bromsberrow 48-53; V of Boughton under Blean 53-55; R of Blaisdon w Flaxley 55-58; Orlestone w Ruckinge 58-70; V of Lower Halstow 70-72; St Matt Cobo Guernsey Dio Win from 72. *St Matthew's Vicarage, Cobo, Guernsey, CI.* (Guernsey 56447)

COLMAN, Geoffrey Hugh. b 29. Univ of Ox BA (2nd cl Phil Pol and Econ) 53, MA 68. Wells Th Coll 67. **d** 68 **p** 69 Chelmsf. C of Wanstead 68-72; V of St Erkenwald Barking 72-77; Ed 'Essex Churchman' from 76; Youth Officer Colchester Archd 78-80; Dioc Youth Officer and Publ Pr Dio Chelmsf from 80. *Old Deanery, Deanery Hill, Bocking, Braintree, Essex.*

COLMAN, John Keane. b 06. ALCD 33 (LTh from 74). **d** 33 **p** 34 York. C of St Paul York 33-35; Stapleford 35-42; Drypool Hull 42-43; PC of Chell 43-48; V of St Bede Toxteth Pk 48-52; Gentleshaw 52-5; V of Fairwell 52-55; Firbank w Howgill 55-60; Austwick 60-62; Barmby Moor w Fangfoss 62-70; Ellerton Priory w Aughton and E Cottingwith 70-74. *Gate Helmsley House, Gate Helmsley, York.* (Stamford Bridge 71753)

COLMAN, Thomas Rushton. b 05. Linc Coll Ox BA 29, MA 31. Wells Th Coll 30. **d** 30 **p** 31 S'wark. C of St Geo Camberwell 30-34; Chap S Afr Ch Rly Miss Naauwpoort 34-37; Beira 37-38; C of Mortlake (in c of E Sheen) 38-39; R of Asby w Ormside 39-44; Chap RNVR 44-46; V of Bridekirk 46-50; Henlow 50-56; RD of Shefford 54-55; R of St Mary Bedford 56-59; Hardwicke 59-63; C of Sandringham 63-67; PC of St Lawr Mansfield 67-68; V 68-71; Hon Min Can of Nor Cathl from 76. *1 Queen Elizabeth Close, Palace Plain, Norwich.* (Norwich 618159)

COLMER, Malcolm John. b 45. Univ of Sussex MSc 67. Univ of Nottm BA 73. St Jo Coll Nottm 71. **d** 73 Dorking for Guildf **p** 74 Guildf. C of Egham 73-76; St Mary Chadwell 76-79; V of S Malling Dio Chich from 79. *Vicarage, S Malling, Lewes, Sussex.* (Lewes 4387)

COLQUHOUN, Canon Frank. b 09. Univ Coll Dur LTh 32, BA 33, MA 37. BC Coll Bris 29. **d** 33 **p** 34 Cant. C of St Faith Maidstone 33-35; Ch Ch New Malden 35-39; V of St Mich AA Blackheath Pk 39-46; Ed Sec Nat Ch League and LPr Dio S'wark 46-52; Ed of 'The Churchman' 46-52; C-in-c of Ch Ch Woburn Square Bloomsbury 52-54; Ed Sec World Evang Alliance 52-54; V of Wallington 54-61; Hon Can of S'wark 59-61; Can Res of S'wark 61-73; Prec 61-66; Chan 66-73; Exam Chap to Bp of S'wark 61-73; Prin SOC 66-71; Can Res of Nor 73-78; Can (Emer) from 78; Vice Dean 74-78. *21 Buckholt Avenue, Bexhill-on-Sea, E Sussex, TN40 2RS.* (Bexhill 221138)

COLSON, Alexander Francis Lionel. b 21. Men in Disp 45. St Jo Coll Cam BA 43, MA 61. MBE (Mil) 45. Tyndale hall Bris 60. **d** 62 **p** 63 Ox. C of St Paul, Slough 62-65; R of Elmswell 65-73; V of St Luke w St Simon and St Jude W Kilburn Dio Lon from 73. *19 Macroom Road, London W9 3HY.* (01-969 0876)

COLSTON, John Edward. b 43. Lich Th Coll 65. **d** 68 **p** 69 Worc. C of All SS Bromsgrove 68-71; Tettenhall Wood 71-74; V of Alrewas w Fradley Dio Lich from 74; Wychnor Dio Lich from 74. *Alrewas Vicarage, Burton-on-Trent, Staffs, DE13 7BT.* (B-on-T 790486)

COLTHURST, Canon Alan St George. b 1897. Late Exhib of CCC Cam BA 21, MA 27. Westcott Ho Cam 24. **d** 24 **p** 25 Wakef. C of Kirkburton 24-26; Huddersfield (in c of St Mark) 26-29; Chap Toc H for W and S Yorks and L to Offic Dio Wakef 29-34; Dio Ripon 32-34; R of St Swith London Stone w St Mary Bothaw Lon 34-36; V of St Paul Bedford 36-46; Aldenham 46-67; Surr 47-67; Commiss Gambia 37-75; Chap Delrow Ho Approved Sch Aldenham 49-62; Hon Can of St Alb 63-67; Can (Emer) from 67; C-in-c of E Quantoxhead 67-75. *Cormeilles, Back Lane, Bredon, Tewkesbury, Glos, GL20 7LJ.* (Bredon 72385)

COLTHURST, Patrick Beadon. b 1898. Selw Coll Cam BA 24, MA 33. Ely Th Coll 24. **d** 25 **p** 26 Lon. C of St Aug Stepney 25-33; Missr of Clare Coll Miss Rotherhithe 33-40; serving w Army 40-45; Perm to Offic Dios Lich and St A 40-45; CF 45-48; C of St Matt and St John Limehouse 48-51; V of St Mich AA Bromley-by-Bow 51-56; C-in-c of All SS Andros 56-57; P-in-c of Long I 57-63; Inagua 65-66; Chap Princess Marg Hosp 63-64; Commun St Mary Virg Spelthorne 66-70; Perm to Offic Dio Roch from 70. *22 Fromandez Drive, Horsmonden, Kent, TN12 8LN.* (Brenchley 2920)

COLTHURST, Reginald William Richard. b 22. TCD BA 44, Div Test (1st Cl) 45, Carson Bibl Pri 44, Lambert Greek Pri 45. **d** 45 **p** 46 Arm. C of St Mark Portadown 45-48; All SS Belf 48-55; R of Ardtrea w Desertcreat 55-66; Richhill Dio Arm from 66; RD of Kilmore from 79. *Rectory, Richhill, Armagh, N Ireland.* (Richhill 871232)

COLVEN, Christopher George. b 45. Univ of Leeds BA (2nd cl Engl and Hist) 66. Coll of Resurr Mirfield 66. **d** 68 Willesden for Lon **p** 69 Lon. C of St Paul Tottenham 68-74; St Mich AA Ladbroke Grove w Ch Ch Notting Hill Kens 74-76; V of St Jas W Hampstead 76-81; P-in-c of All S Loudoun Rd Hampstead 78-81; N and W and E Barsham Dio Nor from 81; Admin of Shrine of Our Lady of Walsingham from 81. *The College, Walsingham, Norfolk, NR22 6EF.* (032-872 266)

COLVER, Canon John Lawrence. b 14. Keble Coll Ox BA (2nd cl Th) 36, MA 40. Cudd Coll 36. **d** 37 Linc **p** 38 Grimsby for Linc. C of St Nich w St John Newport Linc 37-40; St Jo Evang E Dulwich 40-42; St Nich Plumstead 42-45; V of L Coates 45-52; Caistor w Holton-le-Moor and Clixby 52-63; RD of Caistor 54-63; PC of Easington Colliery 63-65; V of Bembridge 65-79; Proc Conv Portsm 68-69; RD of E Wight

70-75; Hon Can of Portsm 76-79; Can (Emer) from 79. *35 Henley Road, Southsea, Hants, PO4 0HS.* (Portsm 736941)

COLWELL, Ven Donald Wetmore. K Coll NS BA 33, LTh 35. **d** 33 NS for Fred **p** 34 Fred. Miss of Hillsboro w Hopewell and Harvey 34-40; R of Newcastle 40-43; Shediac 43-55; Lancaster 55-74; Exam Chap to Bp of Fred 60-74; Can of Ch Ch Cathl Fred 64-68; Archd of St Andr 68-74; Archd (Emer) from 74. *55 Magazine Street, Saint John, NB, Canada.*

COLWILL, Raymond William. b 06. Ripon Hall Ox 71. **d** 71 B & W **p** 71 Bp Wilson for B & W. C of Wilton Dio B & W from 71. *Hamara, Comeytrowe Lane, Taunton, Somerset.* (Taunton 81833)

COLYER, Alan Stewart. b 46. Ridley Coll Melb 74. **d** 75 **p** 76 Tas. C of St Mark Launceston 75-76; P-in-c of Fingal w Avoca and Cullenswood 76-78; R of Franklin Tas 78-80; CF (Austr) from 80; Perm to Offic Dio Wang from 80. *Army Chaplaincy, Puckapunyal, Vic, Australia.*

COLYER, Raymond Henry Day. Ridley Coll Melb 55. ACT ThL 59. **d** 59 **p** 60 Melb. C of Kingsville 59-61; C of Traralgon 61-62; Moe w Newborough 62-64; P-in-c of Moondarra 64-68; V of Bass 68-72; R of Carnarvon 72-78; Carlisle Dio Perth from 78. *239 Orrong Road, Carlisle, W Australia 6101.* (361 1305)

COMBE, John Charles. b 33. TCD BA 53, MA 56, BD 57, MLitt 65, PhD 70. **d** 56 **p** 57 Cork. C of St Luke w St Ann Cork 56-58; Ballynafeigh 58-61; I of St Jas Bray 61-66; Hon Cler V of Ch Ch Cathl Dub 63-66; C of St Bart Belf 66-70; R of St Barn Belf 70-74; I of Portadown Dio Arm from 74. *Rectory, Portadown, Co Armagh, N Ireland.* (Portadown 32368)

COMBER, Ven Anthony James. b 27. Univ of Leeds BSc 49, MSc 52. St Chad's Coll Dur 53. **d** 56 **p** 57 Ripon. C of Manston 56-60; V of Oulton 60-69; Hunslet and Stourton (Hunslet from 73) 69-77; RD of Armley 72-75 and 79-81; R of Farnley N Yorks 77-82; Hon Can of Ripon Cathl from 80; Archd of Leeds from 82. *c/o Ripon Diocesan Office, St Mary Street, Leeds, LS9 7DP.* (Leeds 487487)

COMBER, Keith Charles. b 15. Wycl Hall Ox 71. **d** 73 **p** 74 Birm. C of Walmley 73-76; V of Barston 76-79. *29 School Road, Runcton Holme, King's Lynn, PE33 0AN.*

COMBER, Michael. b 35. **d** 71 (Evang Ch) Carl **p** 72 Carl. [f CA]. C of H Trin, St Barn and St Luke's Carl 71-72; St Jo Bapt Upperby Carl 73-76; V of Dearham 76-81; St Elisabeth Harraby City and Dio Carl from 81. *St Elizabeth's Vicarage, Harraby, Carlisle, CA1 3QA.* (Carl 26440)

COMBER, Thomas Graham. b 09. Pemb Coll Cam BA 31. Cudd Coll 32. **d** 33 **p** 34 Chelmsf. C of St Matt Vic Dks 33-37; St Bonif Germiston 37-41; R of St Mary Jeppestown Johann 41-50; Ermelo 50-56; P-in-c of Ferreira's Town Miss Johann 56-59; Chap Univ of Witwatersrand and St Mary's Sch Johann 59-63; R of St Andr Kens Johann 63-64; Chap Sch of St Helen and St Kath, Abingdon 64-72; C of N Hinksey 72-74; C-in-c of St Frideswide Ox 76-79; Binsey Ox 76-79. *c/o 32 Alexandra Road, Oxford, OX2 0DB.* (Oxford 44632)

COMBES, Roger Matthew. b 47. K Coll Lon LLB 69. Ridley Hall Cam 72. **d** 74 Lon **p** 75 Kens for Lon. C of St Paul Onslow Sq Kens 74-77; H Trin Brompton 76-77; H Sepulchre w All SS Cam Dio Eli from 77. *9 Victoria Street, Cambridge, CB1 1JP.* (0223-59314)

COMEAU, Maurice Aldham Paston. Univ of Birm BA 39. Ripon Hall Ox 39. **d** 40 **p** 41 Birm. C of St Hilda Warley Woods 40-46; Actg C-in-c of St Geo w St Paul Stonehouse 46-47; R of Bow (Nymet Tracy w Broad Nymet) 47-52; Bradford Devon 52-57; Thornbury Devon 51-57; V of Yealmpton Dio Ex from 57. *Yealmpton Vicarage, Plymouth, Devon.* (Yealmpton 229)

COMER, Michael John. b 30. St Mich AA Llan 79. **d** 81 Ban for St A. C of Bistre Dio St A from 81. *52 Briar Drive, Buckley, Clwyd, CH7 2AW.*

COMERFORD, Henry Montgomery. Univ of Tor BA, MD. Wycl Coll Tor. **d** 70 **p** 80 Bran. C of St Matt's Cathl Bran 79-81; Moose Lake Dio Bran from 81. *Moose Lake, Manit, Canada, R0B 0Y0.*

COMERFORD, Peter Morris. b 35. K Coll Lon and Warm. **d** 62 **p** 63 S'wark. C of Catford 62-65; St Mary Virg w St Clem Bournemouth 65-66; Berry Pomeroy w Bridgetown 66-68; Asst Chap HM Pris Wormwood Scrubs 68-69; Chap HM Pris Grendon 69-74; HM Borstal Feltham 74-78; HM Pris Brixton from 78. *c/o HM Prison, Jebb Avenue, SW2.* (01-674 9811)

COMERFORD, Philip Henry. Em Coll Sktn. **d** 63 **p** 64 Sask. C of Fort a la Corner Reserve 63-64; La Ronge 64-65; I of Hines Creek 65-68; R of Radisson 68-79. *1a 28th Street, Long Branch, Toronto, Ont, Canada.*

COMERY, Arthur Clayton. b 48. St Jo Coll Auckld 74. **d** 74 **p** 75 Auckld. C of Manurewa 74-78; P-in-c of New Lynn Dio Auckld from 78. *8 Islington Avenue, Auckland, NZ.* (874 416)

COMFORT, Canon John. Bp's Univ Lennox LST 32. **d** 31 **p** 32 Queb. C of St Pet Sherbrooke 31-32; Kirkdale w S Dur 32-33; Malbay 33-36; I of Sandy Beach w York Miss 36-41; R of Maple Grove w Lower Ireland 41-43; Chap RCAF 43-45; I of W Sherbrooke 45-50; R of Magog 50-57; Cler Sec Queb Dioc Synod 50-61; Can of Queb 54-57; Hon Can from 75; R and Archd of Gaspé 57-72. *3-217 Westminster Avenue, Montreal West, PQ, Canada.*

COMLEY, Thomas Hedges. b 36. Univ of Leeds BA (2nd cl Gen) 62. Coll of Resurr Mirfield. **d** 64 **p** 65 Dur. C of Leadgate 64-67; Shirley 67-71; V of St Alb Smethwick 71-76; Perm to Offic Dio Birm 76-82; V of St Cuthb N Wembley Dio Lon from 82. *St Cuthbert's Vicarage, Carlton Avenue West, N Wembley, Middx.* (01-904 7657)

COMMANDER, Reginald Arthur. b 20. Qu Coll Birm 75. **d** 78 **p** 79 Lich (APM). Hon C of St Chad Wolverhampton Dio Lich from 78. *6 Claremont Road, Penn Fields, Wolverhampton, W Midl.* (Wolverhampton 332895)

COMMIN, Robert William. b 47. St Paul's Coll Grahmstn Dipl Th 71. **d** 70 **p** 71 Capetn. C of Claremont 70-74; Bellville Capetn 74-76; Asst Chap Dioc Coll Rondebosch 76-78; Chap from 78; L to Offic Dio Capetn from 76. *The Lodge House, Diocesan College, Rondebosch, CP, S Africa.*

COMMISKEY, Canon Norman Victor. Trin Coll Dub BA 40, MA 43. **d** 40 **p** 41 Lim. C of St Mary's Cathl Lim 40-44; Harold's Cross Dub 44-50; I of St Cath Dub 50-62; Min Can of St Patr Cathl Dub 50-62; R of Holmpatrick w Kenure 61-77; Chan V of St Patr Cathl Dub from 61; RD of Finglas 69-77; V of Ch Ch Cathl Group City and Dio Dub from 77; Can from 78. *30 Philsborough Road, Dublin 7, Irish Republic.*

COMPTON, Barry Charles Chittenden. b 33. Linc Th Coll 60. **d** 62 **p** 63 S'wark. C of Beddington 62-65; Limpsfield w Titsey 66-68; R of Ash w Ridley 69-70; Hon C Limpsfield Dio S'wark from 71. *Highlands, Limpsfield Chart, Oxted, Surrey.* (Limpsfield Chart 2121)

COMPTON, Christopher Moore. Brisb Th Coll ACT ThL 37. **d** 38 **p** 39 Brisb. C of St Andr S Brisb 38-39; M of Bro of St Paul Brisb 40-42; Chap AIF 42-45; Chap Southport Sch Dio Brisb 45-51; R of Gayndah 51-54; Stanthorpe 54-63; St D Chelmer and Graceville Brisb 63-77; Perm to Offic Dio Brisb from 77. *114 Brighton Terrace, Sandgate, Brisbane, Queensland, Australia 4017.*

COMPTON, Frank Edward. b 12. St Jo Coll Dur BSc (2nd cl Physics) 34. St Cath S Ox BA (2nd cl Th) 36, MA 40. Ripon Hall Ox 34. **d** 36 **p** 37 Birm. C of Acock's Green 36-39; Harborne 39-44; Dioc Chap Birm (in c of St Anne Duddeston and St Cath Nechells) 44-48; RD of E Birm 46-48; R of The Quinton 48-60; Hon Chap to Bp of Birm 49-60; V of Caynham 60-77. *School House, Leysters, Leominster, Herefs, HR6 0HS.*

COMYNS, Clifford John. b 28. TCD BA 50, Higher Dipl Educn and MA 53, BD 67. **d** 51 **p** 52 Dub. C of St Jude Dub 51-55; CF 55-75; Asst Master Estbourne Coll from 75. *Eastbourne College, Eastbourne, E Sussex, BN21 4JY.*

CONDELL, Joseph Alfred Ambrose. b 48. Div Hostel Dub 70. **d** 73 **p** 74 Dromore. C of Donaghcloney 73-76; I of Tubbercurry w Kilmactigue and Achonry 76-79; Roscrea Dio Killaloe from 79; Bourney Dio Killaloe from 79. *St Cronan's Rectory, Roscrea, Co Tipperary, Irish Republic.* (Roscrea 86)

CONDER, Paul Collingwood Nelson. b 33. Late Exhib of St Jo Coll Cam 2nd cl Cl Trip pt i 55, BA 56, 2nd cl Th Trip pt ii 57, MA 60. Ridley Hall Cam 56. **d** 58 Warrington for Liv **p** 59 Liv. C of Grassendale 58-61; Tutor St Jo Coll Dur 61-67; L to Offic Dio Dur 62-67; V of Sutton St Helens 67-74; R 74-75; Thames Ditton Dio Guildf from 75. *Vicarage, Summer Road, Thames Ditton, Surrey, KT7 0QQ.* (01-398 3446)

CONDO, Richard Stafford. Univ of Manit BComm 67. Vanc Sch of Th STB 71. **d** 71 Rupld. C of St Aid Winnipeg 71-73; Portage Plains 73-75; I 76-78; Virden w Elkhorn Dio Bran from 78. *Box 15, Virden, Manit, Canada.*

CONEY, Christopher Thomas. b 32. Magd Coll Cam BA 56, MA 60. Cudd Coll 68. **d** 69 Dorking for Guildf. **p** 70 guildf. C of Farnham 69-72; Chap of Pangbourne Coll from 72. *Pangbourne College, Pangbourne, Berks.*

CONEY, Gerald Frederick. St Paul's Th Coll Grahmstn. **d** 63 **p** 64 Waik. Chap St Pet Sch Cam Dio Waik 63-75; C of All SS Somerset W 75-79; Offg Min Dio Waik from 79. *6 Mokena Flats, Boundary Street, Te Aroha, NZ.* (48-118)

CONEY, Canon Harold Robert Harvey. b 1889. Keble Coll Ox BA (sc Th w distinc) 20, MA 24. Cudd Coll 20. Men in Disp 16. **d** 20 **p** 21 S'wark. C of Bermondsey 20-23; Warden of Caius Coll Cam Miss Battersea 23-28; V of Felkirk w Brierley 28-37; Can Missr and Can of St Richard of Hampole in Wakef Cathl 37-40; Hon Can 40-61; Can (Emer) from 61; R of Thornhill 40-61; Ed Wakef Dioc News 41-48; RD of Dewsbury 47-61; C of Coonamble Dio Bath 61-63; Perm to Offic Dio B & W 63-69; Dio Brisb 69-75. *Ellesborough Manor, Butlers Cross, Aylesbury, Bucks, HP17 0XF.*

CONEY, Peter Norman Harvey. b 28. Keble Coll Ox BA 51, MA 55. Cudd Coll 51. **d** 53 **p** 54 York. C of Northallerton 53-56; C and Sacr of All SS Cathl Wakef 56-59; V of Milverton 59-65; Chap K Coll Taunton 65-70; V of Martock w Ash Dio B & W from 70; RD of Martock from 80. *Vicarage, Martock, Somt, TA12 6JN.* (Martock 822579)

CONEYBEARE, John Thomas. Univ of Tor BA 43. Wycl Coll Tor LTh 46. **d** 45 **p** 46 Tor. C of St Paul Tor 46-49; I of Port Perry and Brooklin 49-50; R of All SS Niagara Falls 50-56; R of Dunnville 56-64; Etobicoke 64-73; C of St Mary Richmond Hill and Richvale 73-74; P-in-c of Richvale 74-75; on leave. *129 Braemar Avenue, Toronto, Ont., Canada.*

CONGDON, John Jameson. b 30. St Edm Hall Ox BA (3rd cl Th) 53, MA 57. Wycl Hall Ox 53. **d** 55 **p** 56 Southw. C of Aspley 55-58; C-in-c of St Mark's Conv Distr Woodthorpe Nottm 59-63; V 63-69; St Mary Spring Grove Osterley Isleworth Dio Lon from 69. *Osterley Vicarage, Isleworth, Middx.* (01-560 3555)

CONLIFFE, Clement Christopher. Univ of Dur (Codr Coll Barb) BA 25, MA 29. **d** 24 **p** 25 Barb. C of St Mich Cathl Barb 24-28; V of St Aug Barb 28-33; St Mary Bridgetown Barb 33-48; St Pet Barb 48-52; Can of Barb 51-56; R of St Geo Barb 52-56; Pakenham 56-69. *136 First Avenue, Ottawa, Ont., Canada.*

CONLIFFE, David Augustine. Bp's Univ Lennox BA 53. McGill Univ Montr BD 56. **d** and **p** 56 Montr. C of Beaconsfield and Pointe Claire 56-58; R of St Mary Beaconsfield Montr 58-67; Greenfield Pk 68-77; Vaudreuil Dio Montr from 77; Sec of Synod Dio Montr 72-75. *Box 666, Hudson Heights, PQ, Canada.* (514-458 5372)

CONLIFFE, Mark Shankland. Montr Dioc Th Coll LTh 60. **d** 60 Ott for Alg **p** 61 Alg. C of St John Port Arthur 60-62; I of W Thunder Bay 62-68; R of St Mich AA Thunder Bay Dio Alg from 68. *675 Red River Road, Thunder Bay, Ont., Canada.* (807-344-9471)

✠ **CONLIN, Right Rev John Fletcher Stout.** Univ of Sask BA 57. Em Coll Sktn LTh 57. **d** 57 **p** 58 Bran. C of Gilbert Plains 57-61; R of H Trin Killarney 61-63; St Jas Sktn 63-69; Dean and R of St Matt Cathl Bran 69-75; Cons Ld Bp of Bran in St Matt Cathl Bran 1 May 75 by Abp of Qu'App; Bps of Rupld and Sktn. *341 13th Street, Brandon, Manit., Canada, R7A 4P8.*

CONN, Alistair Aberdein. b 37. Down Coll Cam BA 60, MA 64. Linc Th Coll 60. **d** 62 **p** 63 Dur. C of St Paul W Hartlepool 62-65; Chap Busoga Coll Jinja 65-66; Shrewsbury Sch 66-73; L to Offic Dio Lich 66-73; R of Coupar Angus 73-78; V of Ravenshead Dio Southw from 78. *55 Sheepwalk Lane, Ravenshead, Nottingham.* (Blidworth 2716)

CONN, Robert Edwin. b 14. Trin Coll Dub BA 38, MA 44. **d** 39 Bp Kennedy for Down **p** 40 Down. C of Trin Coll Dub Miss Belf 39-42; Maralin 42-45; C-in-c of Kilwarlin 45-53; I 53-63; C-in-c of Killyleagh Dio Down 63-65; I from 65. *Killyleagh Rectory, Co Down, N Ireland.* (Killyleagh 231)

CONNELL, Canon Ernest Oldham. b 03. St Jo Coll Cam BA 25, MA 29. **d** 53 **p** 54 Edin. Hon Super Dio Edin 53-78; Hon Can of Edin from 73. *5 Dreghorn Loan, Edinburgh, EH13 0DF.* (031-441 2565)

CONNELL, Neville Allan. St Mich Coll Crafers ACT ThL (2nd cl) 64. **d** 65 **p** 66 Adel. C of Port Lincoln 65-67; Betong Dio Kuch 67-69; P-in-c 69-70; Org Sec ABM Adel 70-72; P-in-c of St Chris Saigon 72-74; R of Alberton 74-77; P-in-c of Modbury 77-80; V of Creswick w Clunes Dio Bal from 81. *St John's Vicarage, Creswick, Vic, Australia 3363.*

CONNELL, Canon Philip Minton. Ridley Coll Melb ACT ThL 37, Th Schol 53. **d** 39 **p** 40 Melv. C of St Mary Caulfield 39-42; V of Wyan w Rappville 42-45; Penong 45-47; P-in-c of Ceduna 47-50; Streaky Bay 50-57; R of Strathalbyn 57-68; Balaklava 69-79; Can of Willoch 76-79; Can (Emer) from 79. *Box 34, Hanley Bridge, S australia 5401.*

CONNELL, Robert Mitchinson St John. d 71 Windw Is. C of Georgetown St Vincent Dio Windw Is from 71. *Box 569, Kingstown, St Vincent, W Indies.*

CONNER, Charles Borthwick. b 20. Keble Coll Ox BA 43 (1st cl Mod Hist 47, 1st cl Th 49), MA 49. St Steph Ho Ox 48. **d** 50 **p** 51 York. C of Saltburn-by-the-Sea 50-52; Chap Ely Th Coll 52-53; CF 53-70; Perm to Offic Dio Sarum from 80. *c/o Williams & Glyn's Bank Ltd., Whitehall, SW 1.*

CONNER, David John. b 47. Univ of Ox BA 69, MA 77. St Steph Ho Ox 69. **d** 71 Buckingham for Ox **p** 72 Ox. C of St Mich AA Summertown Dio Ox 71-76; Team V (w Wolvercote) 76-80; Asst Chap St Edw Sch Ox 71-73; Chap 73-80; Sen Chap Win Coll from 80. *12 Kingsgate Street, Winchester, SO23 9PD.* (Win 62237)

CONNER, John Charles Maunsell. Keble Coll Ox BA 37, MA 40. AKC 40. **d** 40 **p** 41 Lon. C of St Andr Stoke Newington 40-43; Chap RAFVR 43-47; PC of All H N Greenford Lon 48-50; R of Ballymartle 50-52; Kilmocomogue (Bantry) Dio Cork from 52; Surr from 53. *Bantry Rectory, Co Cork, Irish Republic.* (Bantry 94)

CONNOCK, Gilbert Ronald. b 14. St Cath S Ox BA (2nd cl Th) 49, MA 53. St Steph Ho Ox. **d** 49 **p** 50 Wakef. C of S Kirkby 49-52; Chap Miss to Seamen Hamburg 52-54; Swansea 54-56; Sen Chap Glas 57-63; Sec for Scotld 60-63; Cands' Sec Lon 63-68; R of Hayes 68-77; V of Gt and R of L Samford Dio Chelmsf from 77. *Little Sampford Rectory, Saffron Walden, Essex.* (Gt Sampford 427)

CONNOLLY, Sydney Herbert. b 40. Univ of Leeds BA (2nd cl Engl and Th) 66. Coll of Resurr Mirfield 66. **d** 68 Warrington for Liv **p** 69 Liv. C of W Derby 68-71; C of Prescot (in c of St Paul Bryer Estate) 71-74; V of Burtonwood 74-80; Walker Dio Newc T from 80. *Walker Vicarage, Newcastle-upon-Tyne, NE6 3DS.* (Wallsend 623666)

CONNOR, Lord Bishop of. *see* McCappin, Right Rev William John.

CONNOR, Archdeacon of. *See* Stevenson, Ven Richard Clayton.

CONNOR, Dean of. *See* Barr, Very Rev William Norman Cochran.

CONNOR, Dennis George Austin. b 16. Univ of Lon BD and AKC 40. **d** 40 **p** 41 Lon. C of St Leon Shoreditch 40-42; John Keble Ch Mill Hill 42-47; Enfield 47-52; V of Harefield Dio Lon from 52; Chap Harefield Hosp from 52; RD of Hillingdon 70-75. *Harefield Vicarage, Middx.* (Harefield 3221)

CONNOR, Ellis Jones. b 16. Univ of Wales BA 38. St Mich Coll Llan 38. **d** 39 **p** 41 St A. C of Broughton 39-43; Llandegfan w Beaumaris 43-48; V of St Chris Norris Green 48-55; R of Desford 55-73; North Hill 73-75; V of Lewannick 73-75; R of Llanddewi Skirrid and Llanvetherine and Llangattock Lingoed w Llanfair Chap 75-78; C of St Jo Bapt Spalding Dio Linc from 79. *44 West Parade, Spalding, PE11 1HD.* (Spalding 61486)

CONNOR, Geoffrey. b 46. AKC and BD 73. St Aug Coll Cant 73. **d** 74 **p** 75 Dur. C of Cockerton 74-79; Dioc Recruitment Officer for Ordinands from 79. *107 Jedburgh Drive, Branksome, Darlington, Co Durham, DL3 9UP.* (Darlington 69382)

CONNOR, George Howard Douglas. St Jo Coll Auckld NZ Bd of Th Stud LTh (1st cl) 65. **d** 65 **p** 66 Waik. C of Tokoroa 65-66; Te Awamuta 66-67; Tutor St Pet Coll Siota 67-71; Tutor Patteson Th Centre Kohimarama 70-73; C of Tauranga 73-75; V of Te Ngae Maori Past 75-81; Turangi-Whangara Past Dio Wai from 81; Commiss Centr Melan from 76. *Box 3033, Gisborne, NZ.*

CONNOR, Patrick Francis Latham. b 25. Ex Coll Ox BA 47, MA 52. Gen Th Sem NY STB 53. **d** and **p** 53 Quincy. [f in Amer Ch] R of N Tamerton 55-59; in Amer Ch 59-62; R of St Ive 62-64; Sparkford w Weston Bampfylde Dio B & W from 64; C-in-c of Sutton Montis Dio B & W from 70. *Weston Bampfylde Rectory, Sparkford, Yeovil, Somt, BA22 7HT.* (North Cadbury 40273)

CONNORS, Oliver Charles. b 31. **d** 72 **p** 73 St Arn. Hon C of Merbein 72-74; V of Ouyen Dio St Arn (Dio Bend from 77) from 74. *Rectory, Martin Street, Ouyen, Vic, Australia 3490.* (050-92 1107)

CONOLLY, David John. St Jo Coll Morpeth ACT ThL (2nd cl) 64. **d** and **p** 64 Melb. C of Glenroy 64-65; Cheltm 65-67; Perm to Offic Dio Lon 69-70; I of E Thornbury 70-77; St John E Malvern Dio Melb from 77. *7 Finch Street, East Malvern, Vic, Australia 3145.* (211-6616)

CONRAD, Paul Derick. b 54. Worc Coll Ox BA (Th) 76, MA 82. St Steph Ho Ox 78. **d** 80 Chelmsf **p** 81 Barking for Chelmsf. C of St Mary Virg w Ch Ch Wanstead Dio Chelmsf from 80. *The Master's House, High Street, Wanstead, E11.* (01-530 3182)

CONRAD, Richard Leo. b 34. **d** 72 Ott **p** 75 Edmon. L to Offic Dio Edmon 73-75; I of Sedgewick Dio Edmon from 75. *PO Box 111, Sedgewick, Alta., Canada.*

CONRAN, Wallace James. St Jo Coll Armid ACT ThL 18. **d** 17 **p** 19 Bath. M of Bro of the Good Shepherd Bourke 17-22; R of Bourke 19-22; Kandos 22-23; Coolan 23-26; W Wyalong 26-34; Parkes 34-43; Can, Sub-Dean and R of Ch Ch Cathl Graft and Chap to Bp of Graft 43-47; Archd of Graft and Dioc Regr Dio Graft 46-47; R of Adaminaby 47-48; Berridale 49-50; Tumut 50-54. *Flat A, Harriman Court, Nuffield Village, Castle Hill, NSW 2154, Australia.*

CONSTABLE, Douglas Brian. b 40. Univ of Lon BA 62. Linc Th Coll 63. **d** 65 **p** 66 Bris. C of Stockwood Conv Distr 65-70; Hon C of St Paul, Clifton 70-72; Asst Chap Univ of Bris 70-72; Chap Lee Abbey, Lynton 72-77; V of St Thos Derby Dio Derby from 77. *159 Pear Tree Road, Derby.* (Derby 43470)

CONSTANCE, Andrew Laurence. b 48. Canberra Coll of Min ACT ThDip 75. **d** and **p** 76 C & Goulb. C of N Albury 76-78; Young 78-81; St Paul Manuka Dio C & Goulb from

81. *28 Warramoo Crescent, Narrabundah, NSW, Australia 2604.*

CONSTANT, Arden. K Coll Cam BA 32, MA 36. Cudd Coll. **d** 34 **p** 35 Wakef. C of King Cross 34-39; Lowestoft (in c of St Andr) 39-43; Chap RNVR 41-46; I of H Trin Nuwara Eliya w Ch Ch Ragalla Ceylon 47-59; V of Heaton 59-66; Kirkby-in-Malhamdale 66-73. *c/o Kirkby Malham Vicarage, Skipton, Yorks.* (Airton 215)

CONSTANT, Ernest. b 43. **d** 77 Bran. C of The Pas Dio Bran from 77. *Box 3006, The Pas, Manitoba, R9A 1M2, Canada.*

CONSTANT, Robert William. **d** 54 Lon for Col Bp **p** 57 Graft. C of Kempsey 56-59; V of Woodenbong 59-62; R of Bowraville 62-70; Bellingen 70-79. *Rectory, Bellingen, NSW, Australia.* (55 1475)

CONSTANTINE, Leonard. b 30. K Coll Lon and Warm AKC 57. **d** 58 **p** 59 Dur. C of St Aid W Hartlepool 58-61; St Geo w St Steph Sheff 61-62; R of Lilongwe 62-65; Zomba 66-69; V of W Pelton 69-73; Shotton 73-78; Stillington 78-81; Grindon and Stillington Dio Dur from 81. *Stillington Vicarage, Stockton-on-Tees, Co Durham.*

CONWAY, Alfred Sydney. b 22. Kelham Th Coll 40. **d** 45 **p** 46 Lon. C of St Aug Fulham 45-49; PC of Allenton 49-55; St Phil Chaddesden 55-63; V of Croxley Green 63-81; St Jo Evang Walton-on-the-Hill Dio Liv from 81. *St John's Vicarage, Rice Lane, Liverpool, L9 2BW.* (051-525 3458)

CONWAY, Glyn Haydn. b 38. St Mich Coll Llan Dipl Th 65. **d** 65 **p** 66 St A. C of Wrexham 65-71; Team V 71-77; V of Holywell Dio St A from 77. *Vicarage, Fron Park Road, Holywell, Clwyd.* (Holywell 710010)

CONWAY, Irvine Claude. b 31. Em Coll Cam BA 56, MA 60. ACP 62. Univ of Sheff MA 73. Qu Coll Birm 72. **d** 75 **p** 76 Lich (APM). Hon C of Ch Ch City and Dio Lich from 75. *1 Preedy's Close, Abbots Bromley, Rugeley, Staffs.* (Burton 840513)

CONWAY, Owen Arnott. b 35. Univ of Dur BA (3rd cl Music) 58. St Steph Ho Ox 58. **d** 60 **p** 61 Ripon. C of Manston 60-64; V of St Phil Osmondthorpe Leeds 64-70; Warden of Dioc Ho Barrowby 70-73; V of Armley w New Wortley 73-81; Headingley Dio Ripon from 81. *Headingley Vicarage, Shire Oak Road, Leeds, LS6 2DD.* (Leeds 751526)

CONWAY, Reginald Henry. b 02. St Aid Coll 29. **d** 33 **p** 34 Southw. C of St Steph Hyson Green 33-36; H Trin Nottm 36-37; St Mary Rushden 37-39; CF (R of O) 39-46; V of Woodford Halse 46-56; Ch Ch Northn 56-63; Holme 64-69; R of Conington 64-69. *Address temp unknown.*

CONWAY, Robert Arthur. b 48. Univ of Tor BA 78. Trin Coll Tor MDiv 81. **d** 81 Tor. C of St Marg W Hill Dio Tor from 81. *4130 Lawrence Avenue East, West Hill, Ont, Canada, M1E 4R4.*

CONWAY-LEE, Stanley. b 17. Linc Th Coll 68. **d** 70 **p** 71 Bradwell for Chelmsf. C of Dedham 70-72; L Ilford 72-74; V of Tollesbury (w Salcot Virley from 75) 74-79; St Pet Bocking Dio Chelmsf from 79; Surr from 81. *St Peter's Vicarage, Bocking, Braintree, Essex, CM7 6AR.* (Braintree 22698)

CONYARD, Canon Kenneth Johnson. Univ of W Ont BA 54, MA 57. Hur Th Coll BTh 57. **d** 57 **p** 58 Hur. I of St Geo Kitchener 57-61; R of St Geo Lon 61-67; Galt Dio Hur from 67; Exam Chap to Bp of Hur from 71; Can of Hur from 72. *14 Blair Road, Galt, Ont., Canada.* (519-621 8860)

COOGAN, Robert Arthur William. b 29. Univ of Tas BA 51. St Jo Coll Dur Dipl Th 53. **d** 53 **p** 54 Chelmsf. C of St Andr Plaistow 53-56; R of Bothwell Tas 56-62; V of N Woolwich 62-73; C-in-c of St Barn, Silvertown, Vic Dks 62-73; Commiss Tas from 68; V of St Steph Hampstead (w All H from 77) Dio Lon from 73; P-in-c of All H Gospel Oak St Pancras 74-77; Old St Pancras w St Matt Oakley Square 76-80; St Martin w St Andr Kentish Town Dio Lon 78-81; RD of Camden S 75-81; Camden N from 78. *27 Thurlow Road, NW3 5PP.* (01-435 5890)

COOK, Alan. b 27. St Deiniol's Libr Hawarden 79. **d** 80 Ches **p** 81 Stockport for Ches. C of Gatley Dio Ches from 80. *26 Burnside Road, Gatley, Cheadle, Cheshire, SK8 4NA.*

COOK, Alan John Newton. b 12. Ch Coll Cam BA 37, MA 41. Ridley Hall Cam 37. **d** 39 **p** 40 S'wark. C of new Malden w Coombe 39-42; R of Toft w Caldecote and Chap Cam Past 42-45; V of H Trin Aldershot 45-51; Warden C of E Soldiers' Inst 45-51; V of Bp Hannington Mem Ch w H Cross Hove 51-65; Proc Conv Guildf 50-51; R of St Pet-upon-Cornhill City and Dio Lon from 65; Chap City of Lon Poly from 66; RD of City 73-76; C-in-c of St Andr Undershaft w St Mary Axe Lon 76-78. *Vestry, St Peter-upon-Cornhill, EC 3.* (01-626 9483)

COOK, Allen Francis. Sir Geo Williams Univ Montr BA 59. Bp's Univ Lennox LST 57. **d** 57 **p** 59 Montr. C of St Lambert 57-61; R of Erin 61-65; Beamsville 65-73; P-in-c of Smithville 65-73; R of Glanford Dio Niag from 73. *Box 134, Mount Hope, Ont, Canada.* (416-679 4135)

COOK, Arthur James. St Jo Coll Morpeth ACT ThL 44. Moore Th Coll Syd. **d** 44 **p** 45 Newc. C of W and E Maitland 44-45; Adamstown 46-49; P-in-c of Charlestown 49-53; R of Wollombi 53-61; Stroud 61-75; Rockley Dio Bath from 75. *Rectory, Rockley, NSW, Australia 2795.* (3791 12)

COOK, Brian Edwin. b 36. Sarum Wells Th Coll 78. **d** 80 **p** 81 S'wark. C of St Mich E Wickham Dio S'wark from 80. *19 Saltash Road, Welling, Kent, DA16 1HD.*

COOK, Charles Emerson. **d** 65 Hur. Hon C of Trin Ch St Thos 65-67. *73 Metcalfe Street, St Thomas, Ont., Canada.*

COOK, Charles Peter. b 32. St Jo Coll Dur BA 54, Dipl Th 58. **d** 58 **p** 59 York. C of H Trin Hull 58-64; Prec 61-64; V of St Paul Elswick Newc T 64-74; St Andr Cheadle Hulme Dio Ches from 74. *St Andrew's Priory, Cheadle Road, Cheadle Hulme, Chesh, SK8 5EU.* (061-485 1112)

COOK, Charles Thomas. b 16. Roch Th Coll. **d** 62 **p** 63 Birm. C of St Mary w St Ambrose Edgbaston 62-64; Oldbury (in c of St John Langley) 64-67; V of St Paul, Lozells 67-69; R of St Dennis from 69. *Rectory, Carne Hill, St Dennis, St Austell, Cornw, PL26 8AZ.* (St Austell 822317)

COOK, Christopher. b 44. Qu Coll Birm 68. **d** 69 Colchester for Chelmsf **p** 70 Chelmsf. C of St Mary Virg Gt Ilford 69-72; Corringham 72-77; R of E Donyland Dio Chelmsf from 77. *Rectory, Rowhedge, Colchester, Essex.* (Colchester 867517)

COOK, Ven Christopher Arthur. Edin Th Coll 53. **d** 56 **p** 58 Glas. C of Motherwell 56-59; C of Clydesdale 59-60; Matatiele 60-61; R of Idutywa S Afr 61-64; Area Sec USPG Dios Wakef and Sheff 65-70; R of St Matt Miss w Ch Ch Keiskammahoek Dio Grahmstn from 70; Archd Dio Grahmstn from 80. *St Matthew's Mission, PO St Matthew's, CP, S Africa.* (St Matt 12)

COOK, David. b 46. Hertf Coll Ox BA, MA 72. Wycl Hall Ox 69. **d** 73 **p** 74 Dur. C of Stranton 74-75; Lect Queen's Coll Birm from 75. *c/o Queen's College, Somerset Road, Birmingham, B15 2QH.* (021-454 1527)

COOK, David Blake. b 52. Ripon Coll Cudd 75. **d** 78 **p** 79 Ex. C of Crediton 78-81; Barnstaple w Goodleigh & Landkey Dio Ex from 81. *15 Britten Drive, Barnstaple, EX32 8AQ.* (Barnstaple 76811)

COOK, David Charles Murray. Univ Coll Ox BA (2nd cl Mod Hist) 64, MA 67. Wycl Hall Ox. **d** 67 **p** 68 Roch. C of St Phil and St James Chatham 67-71; Script U in S Afr 71-78; L to Offic Dio Natal 73-78; C of St John Wynberg 78-80; Ch Ch Kenilworth Dio Capetn from 80. *3 Mathew Mews, 3rd Avenue, Kenilworth 7700, CP, S Africa.* (64-1688)

COOK, David Reginald Edmund. b 25. Wells Th Coll 65. **d** 67 Barking for Chelmsf **p** 68 Chelmsf. C of Gt Ilford 67-71; C-in-c of Langdon Hills 71-75; R 75-79; RD of Basildon 76-79; R of W Bergholt Dio Chelmsf from 79. *Rectory, West Bergholt, Colchester, Essex, CO6 3JF.* (Colchester 240273)

COOK, David Smith. b 47. Lich Th Coll 68. **d** 71 Dur **p** 72 Jarrow for Dur. C of St Andr Spennymoor 71-75; St Mary Virg w St Pet Conv Distr Bp Wearmouth 75-77; V of Copley 77-80; Birstall Dio Wakef from 80. *Birstall Vicarage, Batley, W Yorks.* (Batley 473715)

COOK, Derek Edward. b 23. K Coll Lon and Warm AKC 51. **d** 52 **p** 53 St Alb. C of Radlett 52-56; Hatfield Hyde 56-64; V of St Paul Luton 64-78; P-in-c of Stanbridge w Tilsworth 78-80; V of Totternhoe w Stanbridge and Tilsworth Dio St Alb from 80. *Stanbridge Vicarage, Mill Road, Leighton Buzzard, Beds, LU7 9HX.* (Leighton Buzzard 210253)

COOK, Donald Reginald. Waterloo Lutheran Univ BA 69. Wycl Coll Tor. **d** 59 BC **p** 60 Tor. C of Cedar Hill 59-60; All SS Pet Ont 60-66; I of Washago 66-76; St Eliz Queensway City and Dio Tor from 76. *964 The Queensway, Toronto, Ont., Canada.*

COOK, Douglas. b 18. **d** 77 S Malawi. d Dio S Malawi. *Box 1, Thyolo, Malawi.*

COOK, Canon Edward Rouse. b 28. Linc Coll Ox BA (2nd cl Mod Hist) 51, MA 55. Linc Th Coll 51. **d** 53 **p** 54 Linc. C of Louth 53-56; Crosby 56-57; Lect of Boston 58-60; V of L Coates 60-67; Saxilby w Ingleby Dio Linc from 67; R of Broxholme Dio Linc from 70; P-in-c of Burton-by-Linc Dio Linc from 78; Can and Preb of Linc Cathl from 79. *Saxilby Vicarage, Lincoln, LN1 2PT.* (Lincoln 702427)

COOK, Francis Arthur. Em Coll Sktn LTh 36. **d** 36 **p** 37 Qu'App. C of Hodgeville 36; Cabri 37-38; Wadena 38-41; I of Balcarres 41-43; Gull Lake 43-44; R of Navan 44-47; Manotick 47-54; Kincardine 54-59; St Jas Brantford 59-74. *100 Wilkes Street, Brantford, Ont., Canada.*

COOK, Frederick Walter. Ridley Coll Melb 59. **d** 63 **p** 64 Gippsld. C of Korumburra 63-64; Morwell 64-65; St Barn Balwyn 65-66; V of Moonee Ponds Dio Melb from 66. *58 Derby Street, Moonee Ponds, Vic, Australia 3039.* (03-37 5935)

COOK, Frederick Walter Batchelor. St Jo Coll Auckld LTh 54. **d** 55 **p** 56 Auckld. C of Mount Roskill 55-57; Bay of Islands 57-61; V of Fitzroy 61-66; Cambridge 66-79; Can of

Waik 74-79; Exam Chap to Bp of Waik 77-79; V of Kelburn Dio Wel from 79. *103 Upland Road, Wellington, NZ.* (759-338)

COOK, George Basil Frederick. b 21. K Coll Lon BA (2nd cl French) 42. St Cath S Ox BA (1st cl Th) 48, MA 52. Ripon Hall Ox 46. **d** 49 **p** 50 Ox. C of St Luke Maidenhead 49-52; St Paul w St Mary Camberley 52-53; Upton w Chalvey (in c of St Laur) 53-55; V of St Barn Mitcham Dio S'wark from 55. *Vicarage, Thirsk Road, Mitcham, Surrey, CR4 2BD.* (01-648 2571)

COOK, George Pilkington. b 1893. **d** 39 Aotearoa for Wel **p** 40 Wel. C of Karori Wel 39-41; St Paul's Cathl Wel 41-42; V of Mangatainoka w Pongaroa 42-43; Patea 43-50; Bulls w Rongotea 50-51; Greytown 51-60; P-in-c of Wairarapa Maori Distr 60-63; L to Offic Dio Wel from 63. *10 Rexwood Street, Carterton, NZ.*

COOK, Henry. d 67 **p** 68 Sask. I of Pelican Narrows 67-76. *La Ronge, Sask, Canada.*

✠ **COOK, Right Rev Henry George.** Univ of W Ont BA 35, Hon DD 48. Hur Coll Ont. **d** 35 Hur for Athab **p** 36 Arctic for Athab. Miss at Fort Simpson 35-42; Can of Athab 42-43; C of St Paul Tor 43-44; I of S Porcupine 44-45; Archd of James Bay 45-51; Prin Bp Horden Mem Sch Moose Factory 45-51; Supt Indian C of E Schs 52-63; Cons Bp Suffr of The Arctic in All SS Cathl Edmon 6 Jan 63 by Abp of Rupld (Metrop); Bps of Bran; Arctic; Keew; Sask; Edmon, Qu'App, Ott, Yukon; and Bp Suffr of Rupld; Apptd Bp Suffr of Athab 66; Trld to Episc Distr of The Mackenzie 71; res 75. *15 Plainfield Court, Stittsville, Ont, K0A 3G0, Canada.*

COOK, Ian Bell. b 38. NW Ordin Course 70. **d** 73 Man **p** 74 Hulme for Man. C of St Paul Oldham 73-75; C-in-c of St Wilfred and St Anne Newton Heath and Industr Chap Dio Man 76-79; V of Middleton Junction Dio Man from 79. *Vicarage, Greenhill Road, Middleton Junction, Manchester, M24 2BD.* (061-643 5064)

COOK, Ian Brian. b 38. Univ of Aston in Birm MSc 72. Univ of Birm MA 76. Kelham Th Coll 58. **d** 63 **p** 64 Ox. C of Langley Marish 63-66; Stokenchurch w Cadmore End 66-68; V of Lane End 68-72; C-in-c of Ibstone w Fingest 68-72; Tutor W Brom Coll of Com & Techn 72-74; Sen Lect 74-79; Perm to Offic Dio Lich 75-77; P-in-c of St Pet W Bromwich 77-80; St Jo Evang Wednesbury Dio 80; St Jas Wednesbury 80; R of SS Jas & John Wednesbury Dio Lich from 80. *Rectory, Hollies Drive, Wednesbury, W Midl, WS10 9EQ.* (021-556 0645)

COOK, James Christopher Donald. b 49. Ch Ch Ox BA 70, MA 74. St Steph Ho Ox 79. **d** 80 Dorchester for Ox **p** 81 Ox. C of Witney w Curbridge and Wood Green Dio Ox from 80. *17 Chestnut Close, Witney, Oxon.* (Witney 5061)

COOK, John. b 09. Univ of Glas MA 29, BD 50. Edin Th Coll 29. **d** 32 **p** 33 Edin. C of St Jas w St Phil Edin 32-35; Soham w Barway 35-38; St Pet (in c of St John) St Alb 38-43; N Stoneham (in c of Chilworth) 43-46; V of Impington 46-54; R of Wimpole 54-69; V of Arrington 54-69; R of Orwell 54-69; V of Crawley Down 69-74. *68a Tudor Close, Seaford, Sussex, BN25 2LY.*

COOK, John Edward. b 35. K Coll Lon and Warm AKC 61. **d** 62 **p** 63 Guildf. C of Yorktown Camberley 62-67; L to Offic Dio Sing 67-68; C of St Andr Cathl Sing and Chap St Marg Secondary Sch 68-71; V of St Pet Sing 72-77; P-in-c of Beoley Dio Worc from 77. *Beoley Vicarage, Redditch, Worcs.* (Redditch 63976)

COOK, John Henry. b 11. Mert Coll Ox BA 34, BSc 35, MA 39, MSc 81. Clifton Th Coll 36. **d** 38 Ox **p** 39 Dorch for Ox. C of Faringdon 38-42; Newbury 42-45; V of Winkfield 45-52; St Pet Maidenhead 52-68; R of Witney 68-78; Hon C from 79. *9 Church View Road, Witney, Oxon.* (Witney 4609)

COOK, John Michael. b 48. Coll of The Resurr Mirfield 72. **d** 74 Sarum **p** 75 Sherborne for Sarum. C of H Trin Weymouth 74-76; St Jo Bapt Felixstowe 76-79; P-in-c of Gt w L Whelnetham Dio St E from 79. *Whelnetham Rectory, Bury St Edmunds, Suff.* (Sicklesmere 332)

COOK, Canon Kenneth Hugh. b 30. K Coll Lon & Warm AKC 55. **d** 56 **p** 57 Southw. C of Netherfield 56-59; Newark w Coddington 59-61; V of St Aid Basford 61-67; Gargrave 67-77; Dir of Ordinands Dio Bradf from 77; Can Res of Bradf Cathl from 77; Exam Chap to Bp of Bradf from 77. *3 Cathedral Close, Stott Hill, Bradford, BD1 4EG.* (Bradf 27720)

COOK, Kenneth Robert. b 42. Chich Th Coll 66. **d** 68 **p** 69 Ox. C of St Mary Upton w Chalvey Slough 68-72; Duston 72-76; V of St Hilda Halifax 76-79; Chap Huddersfield Poly from 79. *c/o Huddersfield Polytechnic, Huddersfield, W Yorks.*

COOK, Marcus John Wyeth. b 41. Chich Th Coll 67. **d** 70 **p** 71 Willesden for Lon. C of St Jas Friern Barnet 70-73; Hon C of St Geo-in-the-E Whitechapel Dio Lon from 73. *St George-in-the-East Church, Cannon Street Road, E1 0BH.*

COOK, Paul Raymond. Wollaston Coll W Austr 63. **d** 66 Perth **p** 67 NW Austr. C of H Cross Cathl Geraldton 66-68; Carnarvon 69-70; P-in-c 70-72; V of St Mark Seremban 72-75; Exam Chap to Bp of W Mal 75; R of Kens Perth 76-79; Narrogin Dio Bunb from 79. *Rectory, Narrogin, W Australia 6312.*

COOK, Peter John Arthur. b 42. Univ of Reading BA (2nd cl Mod Hist & Pol) 64. Brandeis Univ USA MA 65. Qu Univ Belf PhD 81. Tynd Hall Bris 68. **d** 71 Warrington for Liv **p** 72 Liv. C of St John w St Chrys and Em Everton 71-74; Chap and Lect (Sen Lect from 78) Stranmillis Coll of Educn Belf from 74; Hon C of All SS Belf Dio Connor from 81. *Stranmillis House, Stranmillis College, Belfast, BT9 5DY.*

COOK, Richard John Noel. b 49. Univ Coll Ox BA 70, MA 74, BA (Th) 77. Wycl Hall Ox 75. **d** 78 Doncaster for Sheff **p** 79 Sheff. C of Ch Ch Fulwood Sheff 78-80; St Paul w Em Bolton Dio Man from 81. *208 Derby Street, Bolton, BL3 6JN.* (Bolton 393282)

COOK, Robert Bond. Univ of Dur BSc (2nd cl Agr) 54. Ripon Hall Ox 54. **d** 56 **p** 57 Newc T. C of St Jas Benwell Newc T 56-60; Sugley (in c of H Spirit Denton) 60-64; V of Denton Newc T 64-74; Haltwhistle Dio Newc T from 74. *Vicarage, Haltwhistle, Northumb.* (Haltwhistle 215)

COOK, Canon Robert John. AKC 42. **d** 42 **p** 43 Ches. C of Frankby 42-44; Ellesmere Port 44-47; Earley (in c of St Nich) 47-52; R of Gnowangerup w Borden and Ongerup 52-55; Collie 55-59, Can of Bunb 58-67, R of Harvey 59-64, Busselton 64-67; Dalkeith 67-75; Vic Pk Dio Perth from 75; Can of St Geo Cathl Perth from 76. *15 Leonard Street, Victoria Park, W Australia 6100.* (361-1233)

COOK, Ronald Thomas. b 50. Univ of Ox BA 79. St Steph Ho Ox 77. **d** 80 **p** 81 Willesden for Lon. C of St Andr Willesden Green and of St Francis Gladstone Pk Dio Lon from 80. *110 Ellesmere Road, NW10 1JS.*

COOK, Russell Victor. St Jo Coll Auckld 59. **d** 60 **p** 61 Waik. C of New Plymouth 60-63; V of Ohura 63-65; Inglewood 65-66; Asst Dir Christian Educn Dio Auckld 66-70; V of Sandringham 70-74; St Andr Epsom City and Dio Auckld from 74. *Vicarage, St Andrew's Road, Epsom, Auckland 3, NZ.* (688-264)

COOK, Trevor Vivian. b 43. Sarum Th Coll 67. **d** 69 **p** 70 S'wark. C of St Phil Lambeth 69-73; St Buryan w St Levan and St Sennen 73-75; V of The Ilketshalls 75-77; R 77-79; P-in-c of Rumburgh w S Elmham 75-79; Ilketshall St John 75-79; V of Rumburgh w S Elmham w The Ilketshalls Dio St E from 79. *Rectory, Rumburgh, Halesworth, Suff, IP19 0JX.* (Ilketshall 472)

COOK, William. d 60 **p** 61 Moos. I of King Kirkland 61-62; R of Virginiatown 62-67; Kirkland Lake 67-75; Forest 75-80; Southn and Port Elgin Dio Hur from 80. *Box 584, Southampton, Ont., Canada.*

COOK, Canon William George. b 14. St Jo Coll Dur LTh 36, BA 37. St Aid Coll 33. **d** 37 **p** 38 Derby. C of Elmton w Creswell 37-40; CF (EC) 40-46; R of Bonsall 46-51; PC of Stanley Derbys 51-56; R of Aston-on-Trent w Weston-on-Trent 56-68; RD of Melb 67-68; V of Allestree 68-79; Hon Can of Derby 78-79; Can (Emer) from 79; Perm to Offic Dio St E from 79. *79 Bucklesham Road, Ipswich, Suff, IP3 8TR.* (Ipswich 76893)

COOKE, Alan. b 50. Univ of Nottm BTh 74. Kelham Th Coll 69. **d** 75 **p** 76 Man. C of Tyldesley 75-78; St Clem Ordsall Salford 78; All SS & Marts Langley Dio Man from 80. *Church Flat, Wood Street, Langley, Middleton, Manchester, M24 3GL.* (061-653 9797)

COOKE, Canon Alfred Gordon. b 05. St Edm Hall Ox 24. AKC (1st cl) and Barry Pri 28. Ripon Hall Ox 29. **d** 29 **p** 30 Birm. C of St John Ladywood 29-32; Aston (in c of St Martin Perry Common) 32-35; C-in-c of Billesley Conv Distr 35-37; V 37-41; V of H Trin N Harborne Smethwick 41-49; Cler Sec Dioc Conf Dio Birm 43-49; R of St Columb Major (w St Wenn from 72) Dio Truro from 49; RD of Pydar 55-58; Hon Can of Truro from 57. *Rectory, St Columb Major, Cornw.* (St Columb 252)

COOKE, Alfred Hunt. b 08. Univ of Lon MRCS and LRCP 35. **d** 68 Willesden for Lon. **p** 69 Lon. C of Hendon Dio Lon from 68. *74 Brent Street, NW4 2EF.* (01-202 8414)

COOKE, Almerick Constantine. St Pet Th Coll Ja 50. **d** 52 **p** 53 Ja. R of Trinityville 52-57; St Margaret's Bay 57-58; P-in-c of Montpelier 58-67; R of Manchioneal Dio Jamaica from 67. *Long Bay, P.O., Jamaica, W Indies.*

COOKE, Arthur Lewis. b 16. Keble Coll Ox BA (3rd cl Th) 38, MA 43. Univ of Wales BD 48. St Mich Coll Llan 39. **d** 39 Ban **p** 41 Swan B for Ban. C of Llandysilio 39-41; Festiniog w Maentwrog 41-43; St Jas Ban 43-50; V of Llanidan w Llanedwen and Llanddaniel-fab 50-59; R of Hope 59-81. *144 Gresford Road, Singret Heights, Llay, Wrexham, Clwyd.*

COOKE, Charles James. Trin Coll Dub BA (2nd cl Math Mod) 54, Downes Pri in Written Comp 55 and 56, MA 61, Higher Dipl Educn (2nd cl) 59. **d** 56 Down for Connor **p** 57

Connor. C of Ballymena 56-58; Cler V of Ch Ch Cathl Dub 58-63; Perm to Offic Dio Derby from 65. *Matlock College of Education, Matlock, Derbys.*

COOKE, Christopher Kingston Hamel. b 21. CCC Ox BA 49, MA 52. Cudd Coll 49. **d** 50 **p** 51 S'wark. C of Roehampton 50-53; Temple Balsall (in c of St Pet Balsall Common) 53-57; Dean's V of Lich Cathl 57-59; Hon PV 59-69; V of St Mark w St Barn Cov 59-69; RD of Cov E 63-69; V of St Andr Bedford 69-79; C-in-c of St Mary Bedford 70-75; R of St Marylebone w H Trin Dio Lon from 79. *21 Beaumont Street, W1N 1FF.* (01-935 8965)

COOKE, David John. b 31. Linc Th Coll 60. **d** 62 **p** 63 Chich. C of Good Shepherd Preston Sussex 62-65; Clayton w Keymer 65-70; R of Stone (w Bishopstone to 77 and Dinton from 77) w Hartwell Dio Ox from 70; P-in-c of Dinton 72-77. *Stone Rectory, Aylesbury, Bucks.* (Aylesbury 748215)

COOKE, Edward Alan. b 18. St D Coll Lamp BA 41. **d** 46 **p** 47 Mon. C of Blaenavon 46-48; Trevethin 48-50; CF 50-73; R of Ightfield w Calverhall Dio Lich from 73; P-in-c of Ash Dio Lich from 78. *Calverhall Rectory, Whitchurch, Salop.* (Calverhall 638)

COOKE, Frederic Ronald. b 35. Selw Coll Cam 3rd cl Nat Sc Trip pt i 58, BA (Th Trip pt ii) 60, MA 62. Ridley Hall Cam. **d** 61 **p** 62 Man. C of Flixton 61-64; C-in-c of St John's Conv Distr Flixton 64-67; V 68-74; R of Ashton-under-Lyne 74-77; Chap of Ch Ch Jer 77-81; V of Ch Ch Walmsley Dio Man from 80; RD of Walmsley from 81. *Walmsley Vicarage, Egerton, Bolton, Lancs, BL7 9RZ.* (Bolton 54283)

COOKE, Geoffrey. b 38. Sarum Th Coll 61. **d** 64 **p** 65 B & W. C of St Jo Bapt Bridgwater 64-67 and 71-76; Chap RAF 67-71; R of N Newton w St Michaelchurch and Thurloxton (and Durston from 78) Dio B & W from 76. *Rectory, Thurloxton, Taunton, Somt, TA2 8RH.* (West Monkton 412479)

COOKE, George Frederic. b 13. Univ of Wales BA 38. St Mich Coll Llan 47. **d** 49 **p** 50 St A. C of Hawarden 49-54; Staveley 54; PC of Stoney Middleton (and Curbar from 57) 54-68; V 68-79. *5 Park Lane, Retford, Notts, DN22 6TX.* (0777 702223)

COOKE, Gordon Ewart. b 28. Univ of Lon BSc (Econ) 57, MSc 64. Lich Th Coll 59. **d** 60 **p** 61 Worc. C of Kidderminster 60-62; Hagley 62-66; R of Brinklow 66-75; Areley-Kings Dio Worc from 75. *Rectory, Areley-Kings, Stourport-on-Severn, Worcs.* (Stourport 2868)

COOKE, Canon Greville Vaughan Turner. b 1894. Late Exhib of Ch Coll Cam Stewart of Rannoch Scho for Sacr Mus 13, BA and BMus 16, MA 20. ARAM 13, FRAM 27. Ridley Hall Cam 16. **d** 18 **p** 19 Ex. C of Tavistock 18-20; Dep Min Can of St Paul's Cathl 20-21; C of St Mary Ealing 21; V of Cransley 21-56; Can (Non-res) of Pet 55-56; Can (Emer) from 56; R of Buxted 56-71. *Waveney, West Close, Middleton-on-Sea, Bognor Regis, Sussex.*

COOKE, Harry Burford. b 18. **d** 64 **p** 65 Glouc. C of Slad w Uplands 64-68; Chap Marling Sch Stroud 68-78. *181 Bisley Road, Stroud, Glos.* (Stroud 3953)

COOKE, Henry John Shellabear. **d** 24 Bris for Kimb K **p** 25 Kimb K. Dom Chap to Bp of Kimb K 24-26; C of St Cypr Cathl Kimb K 26-27; St Jo Bapt (in c of All SS) Eastover, Bridgwater 27-30; Perm to Offic at St Pet (in c of St Hilda) Leic 30-31; R of Treborough and PC of Withiel Florey 31-32; C of Margate (in c of St Aug) 32-35; V of St Oswin S Shields 35-46; C of Twickenham 46-49; R of Fritton w Morningthorpe 49-55; V of Shapwick w Ashcott 55-57; Leigh Woods 57-60. *St Anthony, Highdale Avenue, Clevedon, Somt.* (Clevedon 2036)

COOKE, Hereward Roger Gresham. b 39. ACA 64. K Coll Lon BD 69, AKC 70. **d** 70 **p** 71 Cov. C of St Andr Rugby 70-76; Dir ICF from 76; P-in-c of St Kath Cree Lon 76-82; St Edm K Lombard Street City and Dio Lon from 82. *St Edmund the King, Lombard Street, EC3.* (01-623 6970)

COOKE, Ian Kirk Hamel. b 17. Univ of Birm BA (2nd cl Engl) 39. Chich Th Coll 39. **d** 41 **p** 42 Bris. C of St Francis Ashton Gate 41-43; All SS Alton 43-48; V of N Baddesley 48-55; R of Hartest w Boxted 55-63; V of Addlestone 63-75; RD of Chertsey 68-73; R of Tittleshall w Godwick, Wellingham (and Weasenham from 76) Dio Nor from 75; C-in-c of Weasenham 75-76; Rougham Dio Nor from 75. *Tittleshall Rectory, King's Lynn, Norf, PE32 2PN.* (Tittleshall 268)

COOKE, James Percy. St D Coll Lamp BA 51. **d** 52 **p** 54 St A. C of Prestatyn 52-57; R of Derwen w Llanelidan Dio St A from 57. *Llanelidan Rectory, Ruthin, Clwyd.* (Clawdd-newydd 633)

COOKE, James Whitehead. Keble Coll Ox BA 26, MA 30. Wycl Hall Ox 26. **d** 27 **p** 28 Ripon. C of St Aug Wrangthorn 27-30; Burley 30-31; V of Sutton-on-the-Hill 31-34; Whitfield 34-41; St Geo Sutton 41-50; Moor Allerton 50-69; C-in-c of Weeton 69-81. *c/o Whitegate, East Keswick, Leeds.* (Collingham Bridge 2341)

COOKE, John. b 21. BD (Lon) 60. Univ of Man MA 65. **d** 44 **p** 45 RC Abp of Liv. Rec into C of E by Bp of Ches 53. Hon C of St Thos Eccleston 68-71; C of Rainhill 71-76; V of St Thos Eccleston 76-81; R of Caston w Griston, Merton and Thompson Dio Nor from 81; P-in-c of Stow-Bedon w Breckles Dio Nor from 82. *Rectory, Caston, Attleborough, Norf.* (Caston 222)

COOKE, John Frederick. b 51. Sarum Wells Th Coll 72. **d** 75 **p** 76 Sheff. C of St Cecilia Parson Cross Sheff 75-78; Goldthorpe w Hickleton Dio Sheff from 78. *St Michael's House, Barnsley Road, Goldthorpe, Rotherham, S Yorks S63 9AP.* (Rotherham 892003)

COOKE, John Stephen. b 35. K Coll Lon and Warm BD and AKC 58. **d** 59 Stafford for Lich **p** 60 Lich. C of St Francis Friar Pk W Bromwich 59-62; Chalfont St Pet (in c of All SS) 62-66; V of Cross Heath 66-72; R of Haughton from 72; C-in-c of Ranton Dio Lich from 72. *Haughton Rectory, Stafford.* (Stafford 780236)

COOKE, Kenneth John. Linc Coll Ox BA (3rd cl Th) 53, MA 57. Ely Th Coll 53. **d** 55 **p** 56 Cov. C of St Mary Virg Nuneaton 55-58; St Thos Cov 58-61; V of Willenhall w Whitley 61-66; Meriden 66-76; St Geo City and Dio Cov from 76. *St George's Vicarage, Moseley Avenue, Coventry, CV6 1HR.* (Cov 591994)

COOKE, Michael David. b 46. New Coll Ox BA 68, MA 71, DPhil 71. **d** 78 Reading for Cant for Ox **p** 79 Buckingham for Ox (APM). C of Newport Pagnell Dio Ox from 78. *10 Westbury Lane, Newport Pagnell, Bucks, MK16 8JA.* (Newport Pagnell 612961)

COOKE, Michael John. **d** 80 **p** 81 Aber (NSM). Perm to Offic Dio Aber 80-81; Chap Miss to Seamen Immingham from 81. *Seafarers' Centre, Immingham Dock, Grimsby, DN40 8DH.*

COOKE, Phillip Revett. Ridley Coll Melb 45. ACT ThL 49. **d** 50 **p** 51 Melb. C of Heidelberg 50-53; P-in-c of Timboon 53-57; Min of Rosanna 57-60; C of Melb Dioc Centre 61-65; Chap Ivanhoe Gr Sch Dio Melb from 65. *2 St James's Road, Rosanna, Vic, Australia 3084.* (03-45 6222)

COOKE, Raymond. b 34. Univ of Liv BSc 56. Wells Th Coll 58. **d** 60 **p** 61 Man. C of All SS Newton Heath 60-64; P-in-c of H Family Lord Lane Conv Distr Failsworth Dio Man 64-75; R from 75. *Holy Family Rectory, Lord Lane, Failsworth, Manchester, M35 0PG.* (061-681 3644)

COOKE, Walter Louis. b 1886. **d** 09 **p** 10 RC Bp of Nottm. Rec into Angl Communion July 17. CF 15-17; C of St Pet Leic 17-23; V of St Sav Leic 23-29; Somerford Keynes w Sharncote 29-31; Miss Br Honduras 31-32; CF (R of O) 26-41; Hon CF 41. *Address temp unknown.*

COOKE, William Henry. b 32. St Aid Coll 62. **d** 64 **p** 65 Bradf. C of Otley 64-67; V of Burley Dio Ripon from 67. *271 Burley Road, Leeds LS4 2EL.* (Leeds 785872)

COOKMAN, Alan George. b 26. Keble Coll Ox BA (3rd cl Th) 50, MA 56. St Steph Ho Ox 50. **d** 52 **p** 53 Ex. C of St Pet Plymouth 52-60; St Jo Div Richmond 60-61; R of Ascen Lower Broughton Salford 61-65; V of The Ascen Lavender Hill 65-72; R of Lympstone 72-81; V of Laira Plymouth Dio Ex from 81. *Vicarage, Federation Road, Laira, Plymouth, Devon.* (Plymouth 663210)

COOKSON, Graham Leslie. b 37. Sarum Th Coll 64. **d** 67 **p** 68 Ches. C of H Ascen Upton Chesh 67-69; Timperley 69-75; V of Godley w Newton Green Dio Ches from 75. *Godley Vicarage, Sheffield Road, Hyde, Chesh.* (Hyde 2159)

COOLING, Derrick William. b. 35. Univ of Wales MEd 81. K Coll Lon and Warm AKC 58. BD (Lon) 69. **d** 59 **p** 60 Liv. C of St Jas Gt Haydock 59-61; St Barn Hove 61-63; V of Llangattock-Vibon-Avel w Llanvaenor and St Maughan 63-68; R of Aberystruth (Blaina) 68-70; Asst Master Fynamore Sch Calne 70-74; Perm to Offic Dio Sarum 70-74; Dio Mon 79-81; Chap Windsor Girls' Sch Hamm 74-75; Asst Master Croesyceiliog Sch Cwmbran 75-81; Chap & Asst Master Epsom Coll Guildf from 81. *Epsom College, Guildford, Surrey.*

COOLING, Graham Harry. St Jo Coll Morpeth 57. ACT ThL 60. **d** 60 **p** 61 Adel. C of Eliz Miss 60; Prospect 61-62; P-in-c of Pinnaroo 63-68; R of Port Adel 68-72; Chap RAN from 73. *HMAS Leeuwin, Preston Point Road, Fremantle, W Australia 6160.* (059-83 9403)

COOMBE, Donald James. Seager Hall Ont Dipl Th 63. **d** and **p** 63 Niag. C of Ch Ch Niagara Falls 63-67; I of Woodburn 67-74; St Alb Hamilton Dio Niag from 74. *21 Edith Avenue, Hamilton, Ont., Canada.* (416-389 7880)

COOMBE, James Anthony. b 31. Em Coll Cam 2nd cl Math Trip pt i 51, BA (1st cl Math Trip pt ii) 53, MA 57. BD (2nd cl) Lon 60. Tyndale Hall Bris 57. **d** 60 **p** 61 Man. C of Ch Ch Chadderton 60-63; St Geo Worthing 63-65; V of St Mich AA Southfields 65-74; C-in-c of Warboys Dio Ely 74-76; R from 76. *15 Church Road, Warboys, Cambs, PE17 2RJ.* (Ramsey 822237)

COOMBE, (Martin) John Morrell. b 25. Chich Th Coll 56. **d** 57 **p** 58 Sarum. M SSF from 49; LPr Dio Sarum 57-59;

C-in-c of Hilfield w Hermitage 59-66; Asst Chap Ellesmere Coll and L to Offic Dio Lich 66-69; Chap Ranby Ho Sch Retford 69-71; V of St Benedict Cam Dio Ely from 71. *15 Botolph Lane, Cambridge, CB2 3RD.* (Cam 353903)

COOMBE, Kenneth Harry Southcott. b 24. Clifton Th Coll 61. **d** 63 **p** 64 Ex. C of Cullompton 63-66; C-in-c of Elburton Conv Distr Plymstock Dio Ex 66-73; V from 73. *St Matthew's Vicarage, Elburton, Plymouth, Devon, PL9 8DQ.* (Plymouth 42771)

COOMBE, Michael Thomas. b 31. BA (Lon) 64. St Steph Coll Ox 73. **d** 75 Ox **p** 76 Buckingham for Ox (APM). Chap St Piran's Sch Maidenhead 75-81; Hon C of St Pet Maidenhead 76-81; Asst Chap St Edm Oslo Dio Gibr in Eur from 81. *c/o British Embassy, Heftyes Gt 8, Oslo 2, Norway.*

COOMBER, Ian Gladstone. b 47. Univ of Southn BTh 79. Sarum Wells Th Coll 73. **d** 76 **p** 77 Southn for Win. C of Weeke 76-79; Team V of Saffron Walden w Wendens Ambo and Littlebury Dio Chelmsf from 79. *Vicarage, Church Walk, Littlebury, Saffron Walden, CB11 4TT.*

COOMBER, Maurice Bunduka Zadok. Fourah Bay Th Coll 49. **d** 52 Sier L. d Dio Sier L. *Makeni, Sierra Leone.*

COOMBES, Derek Fennessey. b 42. Edin Th Coll 61. **d** 65 **p** 66 Moray. Prec of St Andr Cathl Inverness 65-68; Perm to Offic Dio Nor 76-79; V of Happisburgh w Walcot Dio Nor from 79; P-in-c of Hempstead w Lessingham and Eccles Dio Nor from 79. *Happisburgh Vicarage, Norwich, NR12 0AB.* (Walcott 650313)

COOMBES, Edward David. b 39. Univ of Dur BA 61. Univ of Birm Dipl Th 63. Qu Coll Birm 61. **d** 63 **p** 64 Worc. C of St Jo Bapt Claines Worc 63-65; Halesowen w Hasbury 65-69; V of Beoley 72-76; Edgbaston Dio Birm from 78; Chap Univ of Birm from 78. *Vicarage, Arthur Road, Edgbaston, Birmingham, B15 2UW.* (021-454 0070)

COOMBES, Frederick Ernest. **d** 58 **p** 60 Tas. C of Clarence 58-61; R of The Channel 61-64; Sorell 64-68; Cooee 68-77. *15 Umina Park, Mooreville Road, Burnie, Tasmania 7320.*

COOMBS, Canon John Ames. Trin Coll Tor BA 46, LTh 49, BD 51. **d** 49 Queb for Tor **p** 50 Tor. C of H Trin Cathl Queb 49-51; St Jas Cathl Tor 51-61; R of St Thos Kingston Ont 61-71; Can of Ont from 71; C of St Geo Cathl Kingston 72-76; V 76-77; on leave; Exam Chap to Bp of Ont from 75. *68 Earl Street, Kingston, Ont, Canada.* (613-546 7541)

COOMBS, John Kendall. b 47. Culham Coll Ox BEducn 73. Sarum Wells Th Coll 75. **d** 77 **p** 78 Portsm. C of H Trin w St Columba Fareham 77-80; Petersfield w Sheet Dio Portsm from 80. *Parsonage, Inmans Lane, Petersfield, Hants, GU32 2AN.* (Petersfield 3673)

COOMBS, Maurice Alfred. ACT ThL 66. **d** 66 **p** 67 NW Austr. Chap to Bp of Perth 67-69; Dom Chap to Abp in Jer and Dioc Regr 69-73; in Amer Ch from 73. *c/o Grace Church, Brooklyn Heights, New York, USA.*

COOMBS, Ven Peter Bertram. b 28. Univ of Bris BA (2nd cl Th) 58, MA 61. Clifton Th Coll 55. **d** 60 Tonbridge for Cant **p** 61 Roch. C of Ch Ch Beckenham 60-63; R of St Nich Nottm 63-68; V of New Malden w Coombe 68-75; RD of Kingston 71-75; Archd of Wandsworth from 75. *68 Wandsworth Common North Side, SW18 2QX.* (01-874 5766)

COOMBS, Richard John. b 29. K Coll Lon and Warm BD and AKC 53. **d** 54 **p** 55 Ripon. C of Methley 54-57; St Thos-on-the-Bourne 57-60; in Amer Ch 60-61; V of Burghill 61-70; Chap St Mary's Hosp Heref 61-70; CF (TA) 62-70; CF from 70. *c/o Ministry of Defence, Bagshot Park, Bagshot, Surrey.*

COOMBS, Stephen Harry. Trin Coll Tor LTh 58. **d** 57 Yukon for Niag **p** 58 Niag. R of Erin 57-60; C of St Geo St Catherines 60-63; R of St Bart Hamilton 63-70; on leave 71-75; Hon C of St Matt Burlington Dio Niag from 76. *700 Cherrywood Drive, Burlington, Ont., Canada.* (416-639 3534)

COOMBS, Walter James Martin. b 33. Keble Coll Ox BA (3rd cl Eng) 57, 3rd cl Th 59, MA 61. Cudd Coll 59. **d** 61 **p** 62 S'wark. C of Kennington 61-64; Chap Em Coll Cam 64-68; Dom Chap to Bp of S'wark 68-70; V of St Jo Evang E Dulwich 70-77; Pershore w Pinvin, Wick and Birlingham Dio Worc from 77. *Vicarage, Pershore, Worcs.* (Pershore 552071)

COOMER, Martin Lee. b 45. St Jo Coll Nottm 78. **d** 80 **p** 81 Bp Swartz for Capetn. C of St Marg Fish Hoek Dio Capetn from 80. *5 Fifth Avenue, Fish Hoek, Cape 7975, S Africa.*

COON, Clayton Hollis. b 37. Univ of Calif Berkeley BA 60. Episc Th Sch Cam Mass BD (MDiv) 66. **d** 66 **p** 67 Bp of Calif. In Amer Ch 66-71; C of St Jo Bapt Hove 71-74; St Paul Brighton 74-79; V of Linthwaite Dio Wakef from 79. *Linthwaite Vicarage, Huddersfield, Yorks, HD7 5TA.* (Huddersfield 842591)

COONEY, Michael Patrick. b 55. City of Lon Poly BA 77. Ripon Coll Cudd 77. **d** 80 Bp McKie for Cov **p** 81 Cov. C of Cov E Team Min Dio Cov from 80. *58 George Eliot Road, Coventry, CV1 4HU.*

COONEY, William Barry. b 47. St Aug Coll Cant 69. **d** 70 **p** 71 Lich. C of W Bromwich 70-73; Wolverhampton 73-75; Rugeley 75-78; V of Sneyd Green Dio Lich from 78. *St Andrew's Vicarage, Granville Avenue, Sneyd Green, Stoke-on-Trent, ST1 6BH.* (0782-25139)

COOPER, Albert Frederick George. b 05. Linc Th Coll 45. **d** 45 **p** 46 Bradf. C of Ch Ch Windhill Shipley 45-48; H Trin Bingley 48-50; V of All SS L Horton Bradf 50-71; Chap St Luke's Hosp Bradf 50-71; RD of Horton 58-71; Hon Can of Bradf 63-71; Perm to Offic Dio Linc from 77. *58 Eton Drive, Bottesford, Scunthorpe, S Humb, DN17 2PH.*

COOPER, Alfred Philip. b 50. Univ of Bris BA 71. **d** 77 Chile. d Dio Chile. *Casilla 675, Santiago, Chile.*

COOPER, Andrew John Gearing. b 48. Univ of Lon BSc 70. Ripon Coll Cudd 73. **d** 76 Knaresborough for Ripon **p** 77 Ripon. C of Potternewton 76-80; St John's Cathl Antig 80-81; R of St Mary Anguilla Dio Antig from 81. *St Mary's Rectory, The Valley, Anguilla, W Indies.*

COOPER, Arthur Robert. St Jo Coll Auckld 60. **d** 62 **p** 63 Auckld. C of Otahuhu Auckld 62-65; Whangarei Auckld 65-67; NCC Pris Chap Dio Auckld 68-75; Hon C of St Matt Auckld 71-75; P-in-c of Kawakawa and S Bay Is 75-81; V of St Martin Mt Roskill Dio Auckld from 81. *1352 Dominion Road, Mount Roskill, Auckland, NZ.*

COOPER, Barry Jack. Sarum Th Coll 59. **d** 61 **p** 62 Cant. C of St Osw Norbury 61-64; Crook 64-68; R of Cheriton (w Newington to 78) Dio Cant from 68. *St Martin's Rectory, Horn Street, Folkestone, Kent.* (Folkestone 38509)

COOPER, Bede Robert. b 42. Univ of Ex BA (2nd cl Th) 69. Coll of Resurr Mirfield 69. **d** 71 **p** 72 Sarum. C of H Trin Weymouth 71-74; V of Wootton Bassett Dio Sarum from 74; Broad Town 74-80. *Wootton Bassett Vicarage, Swindon, Wilts, SN4 7DU.* (Swindon 853272)

COOPER, Brian Hamilton. b 35. Late Scho of Keble Coll Ox 1st cl Cl Mods 56, BA (1st cl Lit Hum) 58, 1st cl Th 60, MA 67. Ripon Hall Ox 58. **d** 60 **p** 61 S'wark. C of Woolwich 60-64; Prof Systematic Th Angl Th Coll BC 64-66; Vice Prin Westcott Ho Cam from 66-71; R of Downham Market w Bexwell Dio Ely from 71. *Rectory, Downham Market, Norf, PE38 9LE.* (Downham Mkt 2187)

COOPER, Cecil Clive. b 26. TD 75. K Coll Lon and Warm AKC 52. **d** 53 Glouc **p** 54 Bp Barkway for Cant. C of Chipping Campden 53-55; Cheltm 55-60; PC of Stroud 60-65; CF (TAVR) 63-75; R of Woodmansterne Dio S'wark from 65; RD of Sutton from 80. *Woodmansterne Rectory, Banstead, Surrey.* (Burgh Heath 52849)

COOPER, Cecil William Marcus. b 32. Trin Coll Dub BA 58, MA 66. **d** 59 **p** 60 Cork. C of St Fin Barre and St Nich Cork 59-62; Bp's V and Libr of St Canice's Cathl and Regr Dios Oss, Ferns and Leigh 62-64; C of Knockbreda 65-67; Asst Ed Ch of Ireland Gazette from 66; R of Magheradroll Dio Drom from 67; Regr Dios Down and Drom from 81. *Magheradroll Rectory, Ballynahinch, Co Down, N Ireland.* (Ballynahinch 562289)

COOPER, Christopher. b 09. Worc Coll Ox 3rd cl Cl Mods 30, BA 31, MA 35. Lon Coll of Div 33. **d** 34 **p** 35 Lon. C of St Andr Whitehall Pk 34-36; Chap Clifton Th Coll 36-38; Chap Moshi and Arusha 39-41; Hon CF 40-43; Miss at Dodoma 41; Berega 41-43; Uha 43-44; Kongwa 44-46; V of Birling 46-50; P-in-c of Kongwa and Prin St Phil Th Coll 50-54; Exam Chap to Bp of Centr Tang 52-54; P-in-c of Wallaroo 54-57; R of Kadina 54-61; P-in-c of Norton Summit [f Morialta] 61-64 and 69-73; R of Magill 64-69; C of Ch Ch Hampstead 73-79; Perm to Offic Edmon Area Dio Lon from 79. *1 Windmill Hill, NW3 6RU.* (01-435 4450)

COOPER, Christopher Neville. Univ of Cant BEng 65. Ch Ch Coll. **d** 68 **p** 69 Wel. C of Hawera 68-71; L to Offic Dio Auckld from 71. *c/o Diocesan Office, 40 Shortland Street, Auckland, NZ.*

COOPER, Clive Anthony Charles. b 38. Univ of Lon BEducn 74. ALCD 62 (LTh from 74). **d** 62 **p** 63 S'wark. C of Morden 62-65; Miss SAMS Dio Argent 65-71; Asst Master Cranleigh C of E Middle Sch from 74; Hon C of Cranleigh 78-79; SS Pet & Paul Ewhurst Dio Guildf from 80. *20 Longpoles Road, Cranleigh, Surrey, GU6 7JZ.* (Cranleigh 4056)

COOPER, Colin Charles. b 40. Oak Hill Th Coll 62. **d** 66 Lon **p** 67 Stepney for Lon. C of St Andr Islington 66-69; Sandys Berm 69-71; P-in-c 71-72; R 72-76; V of Gorleston Dio Nor from 77. *Vicarage, Duke Road, Gorleston, Great Yarmouth, NR31 6LL.* (Gt Yarmouth 63477)

COOPER, David. b 44. K Coll Lon AKC 69. **d** 69 **p** 70 Ripon. C of Wortley-de-Leeds 69-73; CF from 73. *c/o Ministry of Defence, Bagshot Park, Bagshot, Surrey.*

COOPER, David Jonathan. b 44. Sarum Wells Th Coll 70. **d** 74 **p** 75 Cant. C of St Pet & St Paul Charlton Dover 74-79; Team V of Wednesfield Dio Lich from 79. *St Alban's Vicarage, Griffiths Drive, Ashmore Park, Wednesfield, WV11 2LJ.* (Wolverhampton 732317)

COOPER, David Robin. St Jo Coll Morpeth ACT ThL (2nd cl) 63. **d** 63 **p** 64 Bath. C of All SS Cathl, Bath 63-65; Dubbo 65-68; Asst Chap All SS Coll Bath 69-71; R of Gilgandra 72-76; Cowra Dio Bath from 76. *Kendal Street, Cowra, NSW, Australia 2794.* (42 1409)

COOPER, Dennis Bradley. b 29. New Coll Ox BA 52, MA 57. Cudd Coll 52. **d** 54 **p** 55 St Alb. C of St Mary Bedford 54-56; St Mary of Eton Hackney Wick 56-59; V of St Chad York 59-67; St Martin Middlesbrough 67-74; Norton-juxta-Malton Dio York from 74. *Norton Vicarage, Malton, Yorks, YO17 9AE.* (Malton 2741)

COOPER, Dennis Howard. b 11. Bps' Coll Cheshunt 57. **d** 58 St Alb **p** 59 Bedford for St Alb. C of Hemel Hempstead 58-61; V of Rye Pk 61-66; Woodside (w E Hyde from 76) 66-79. *New Mill End Farm, East Hyde, Luton, Beds.* (Harpenden 61703)

COOPER, Derek Edward. b 30. Bps' Coll Cheshunt 61. **d** 62 **p** 63 St Alb. C of Bp's Stortford 62-66; V of St Cedd and the Saints of Essex Westcliff-on-Sea Dio Chelmsf from 66. *122 Mendip Crescent, Westcliff-on-Sea, Essex, SS0 0HN.* (Southend-on-Sea 525126)

COOPER, Donald Martin. K Coll Lon Jun Wordsworth Pri 33, Trench Gk Test Pri, AKC and BD 35, MTh 40, PhD 44. **d** 35 Ex **p** 36 Crediton for Ex. C of Barnstaple 35-38; Brampford Speke (in c of Cowley Chap) 38-41; Landkey 41-44; PC of Stanford Bp 44-51; Chap Tooting Bec Hosp 51-77. *82 Nork Way, Banstead, Surrey, SM7 1HW.* (Burgh Heath 53163)

COOPER, Ven Edwin Angus. Ridley Coll Melb ACT ThL 49. **d** 51 **p** 52 Melb. C of St Andr Brighton 51-52; John Keble Ch Mill Hill Lon 53-55; R of Alexandra Vic 56-61; R of Euroa 61-72; Dom Chap to Bp of Wang 64-77; R of Kilmore 72-79; Rutherglen Dio Wang from 79; Archd Dio Wang from 77. *St Stephen's Rectory, High Street, Rutherglen, Vic, Australia 3685.*

COOPER, Eric John. b 22. Em Coll Cam BA 48. Chich Th Coll 51. **d** 53 **p** 54 Lon. C of St Paul Tottenham 53-55; Hillingdon 55-62; St Martin Knowle 62-65; V of St Osw Bedminster Down 66-72. *6 Deveron Grove, Bristol, BS18 1UJ.*

COOPER, Frank. b 14. **d** 45 Gui for Trinid **p** 45 WI for Trinid. Chap HM Prison and Hosp Trinid 45-48; C of H Trin Cathl Port of Spain 46-48; R of St Chris Siparia 48-56; V of Butleigh 56-59; Area Sec SPG 59-62; Promotion and Tr Sec SPG Lon 62-64; USPG 65; R of St Sav Guernsey Dio Win from 65. *St Saviour's Rectory, Guernsey, CI.* (0481 63045)

COOPER, Frank Howard Score. wycl Coll Tor LTh 61. **d** 61 **p** 64 Tor. C of All S Tor 61-65; St Marg 65-70; I of St Jas Humber Bay Tor 70-74; St Wilfrid Islington City and Dio Tor rom 74. *1315 Kipling Avenue, Islington, Toronto, Ont., Canada.* (416-231 4232)

COOPER, Frederick. b 30. Cranmer Hall Dur 68. **d** 70 **p** 71 Blackb. C of All SS Preston 70-72; Preston (in c of St Steph) 72-76; Team V 76-78; V of Higher Walton Dio Blackb from 78. *Vicarage, Higher Walton, Preston, Lancs.* (Preston 35406)

COOPER, Frederick James. b 05. K Coll Lon and Warm. **d** 51 **p** 52 Dover for Cant. C of St Martin w St Paul Cant 51-55; V of Eastry 55-80. *3 Aumbry Cotts, Eastry, Kent.* (Eastry 323)

COOPER, George Conway. b 25. Carleton Univ Ott BA 74. Montr Dioc Coll LTh 76. **d** and **p** 76 Ott. I of Eganville Dio Ott from 76. *Box 212, Eganville, Ont., Canada.*

COOPER, George Daniel. b 50. Carleton Univ Ott BA 76. Huron Coll Lon Ont MDiv 79. **d** and **p** 79 Ott. C of St Thos City and Dio Ott from 79. *c/o 2345 Alta Vista Drive, Ottawa, Ont, Canada, K1H 7M6.*

COOPER, George Frank. b 19. St Aid Coll 41. **d** 45 Stepney for Lon **p** 46 Lon. C of W Drayton 45-47; St Steph Avenue Road w St Andr St John's Wood 47-48; Perm to Offic at St John's Wood Chap 47-48; Succr of S'wark Cathl and in c of All H S'wark 48-50; Min of St Barn Old Heath Distr Colchester 50-57; Chap Hostel of Good Shepherd Colchester 51-57; V of Barkestone W Plungar 57-61; Dioc Sec NS Leic from 59; Dioc Insp of Schs Leic 60-78; V of Countesthorpe w Foston 61-74; RD of Framland I 60-61; R of Thurlaston (w Peckleton and Kirkby Mallory from 76) Dio Leic from 74; P-in-c of Stoney Stanton and of Croft Dio Leic from 82. *Rectory, Stney Stantn, Leics, LE9 6LR.* (Sapcote 2360)

COOPER, Gilbert Macduff. d 37 Blackb for Col Bp **p** 38 Brisb. C of Toowoomba 38; St Paul Stanthorpe 38-39; St Paul Ipswich 39-42; V of Holland Pk 42-45; Elvaston w Thurlaston and Ambaston 46-49; Hartington 49-70; PC of Biggin 49-70; Perm to Offic Dio Derby from 74. *Fern Rock Cottage, Chelmorton, Buxton, Derbys.*

COOPER, Gordon Robert. b 16. Oak Hill Th Coll 36. Univ of Dur LTh 39. **d** 39 **p** 40 York. C of Selby Abbey 39-42; Chap RAFVR 42-47; V of Stainton-in-Cleveland 47-58; V of Brompton w Deighton 58-81; Chap HM Borstal Inst Northallerton 58-63; HM Pris 63-81; Perm to Offic Dio Dur from 81. *Carlbury Grove, High Coniscliffe, Darlington, DL2 2LP.* (Piercebridge 653)

COOPER, Graham Denbigh. b 48. Univ of Nottm BTh 75. St Jo Coll Nottm LTh 75. **d** 75 **p** 76 Man. C of The Sav Man 75-78; Stambermill Dio Worc 79-80; V of The Lye and Stambermill from 80. *Vicarage, High Street, Lye, Stourbridge, W Midl.* (Lye 3142)

COOPER, Very Rev Harry Rhodes. K Coll Halifax NS BA 46, BSLitt 48. **d** 47 **p** 49 NS. C of All SS Cathl Halifax 47-50; R of New Waterford and Dominion 50-54; St Phil Halifax 54-63; St Thos St John's Newfld 63-72; Dean of Fred from 72; Commiss Fred 72-75; Exam Chap to Bp of Fred from 74. *808 Brunswick Street, Fredericton, NB, Canada.*

COOPER, Preb Henry. b 08. Kelham Th Coll 29. **d** 34 **p** 35 St Alb. C of Knebworth 34-37; St Sav St Alb 37-40; St Paul Bedford 40-41; C-in-c of St Christopher's Conv Distr Round Green Luton 41-43; R of St Serf Burntisland w Aberdour and Kinghorn (in c of St Pet Inverkeithing 45-46) 43-48; V of St Mich Shoreditch 48-53; CF (TA) 51-64; Proc Conv Lon 51-77; V of St Pet Ealing 53-63; Surr 54-64; Ed *Chrism* from 54; M BCC from 56; Delegate WCC 61 and 68; RD of Ealing 60-63; Tower Hamlets 66-68; Master of R Found of St Kath 63-68; Vice-Chairman Ch Assembly Ho of Cl 65-71; R of St Geo Bloomsbury 68-77; Preb of St Paul's Cathl Lon 69-77; Preb (Emer) from 77; Sec Abp's Comm on RC Relns 69-71; Abp's Adv from 71; RD of Camden S 71-75; Vice-Pres Dioc Syn Lon 71; Chairman Gen Syn 72-75; Exam Chap to Bp of Edmon from 72; Perm to Offic Dio Ox from 77. *106 Woodstock Road, Witney, Oxon, OX8 6DY.* (Witney 4582)

COOPER, Herbert William. b 29. Chich Th Coll 77. **d** 79 **p** 80 Portsm. C of St Francis Leigh Park 79-82; C-in-c of St Pet Conv Distr Hayling N Dio Portsm from 82. *117 Havant Road, North Hayling, Hants, PO11 0LE.* (Hayling Is 3377)

COOPER, Ian Clive. b 48. FCA. Univ of Ex BA 76. Linc Th Coll 76. **d** 78 Lon **p** 79 Kens for Lon. C of St Mary Sunbury 78-81; P-in-c of Astwood Bank Dio Worc from 81. *Vicarage, Church Road, Astwood Bank, Redditch, Worcs, B96 4EH.* (Astwood Bank 2489)

COOPER, Ian Douglas Lewis. Coll Ho Ch Ch NZ 49. NZ Board of Th Stud LTh 66. **d** 51 **p** 52 Ch Ch. C of St Pet Riccarton 51-53; Sydenham 53-55; V of Malvern 55-59; Otaio w Blue Cliffs 59-63; Morchwiel 63-67; Te Awamutu 67-76; Claudelands 76-80; St Matt Masterton Dio Wel from 80; Can of Waik 78-80. *43 Church Street, Masterton, NZ.* (86-566)

COOPER, Jack. b 44. St Jo Coll Nottm 76. **d** 78 **p** 79 Ripon. C of St Edm Roundhay 78-81; All SS w St John Ripley Dio Ripon from 81. *15 Lime Avenue, Ripley, Derbys, DE5 3HO.* (Ripley 43799)

COOPER, Jack. b 11. Univ of Dur LTh 37. Clifton Th Coll 34. **d** 37 **p** 38 Linc. C of Bottesford w Ashby 37-43; New Sleaford 43-48; PC (V from 68) of Martin 48-80. *10 Hawthorn Close, Ruskington, Sleaford, Lincs, NG34 9BX.*

COOPER, Jeremy John. b 45. Kelham Th Coll 65. **d** 71 Repton for Derby **p** 72 Derby. C of St Luke Derby 71-76; Team V of Malvern Link w Cowleigh 76-79; P-in-c of Claypole 79-80; Westborough w Dry Doddington & Stubton 79-80; C of Eye w Braiseworth & Yaxley Dio St E from 80. *Occold Rectory, Eye, Suffolk, IP23 7PW.*

COOPER, Jesse Philip. b 10. Em Coll Sktn Testamur 37. **d** 37 **p** 38 Bran. C of Elgin 37-38; R 38-41; Chap RCAF 41-47; Chap RAF 47; L to Offic Dio York 67; Ripon 69. *High Fold, Dacre Top, Harrogate, N Yorks.* (0423-780270)

COOPER, John. b 47. Sarum Wells Th Coll 71. **d** 74 Lon **p** 75 Kens for Lon. C of St Mary Spring Grove Osterley Isleworth 74-77; St Steph w St Thos Shepherd's Bush Dio Lon from 77. *Curate's Maisonette, St Stephen's Vicarage, Coverdale Road, W12 8JJ.* (01-743 4515)

COOPER, John Edward. b 40. K Coll Lon and Warm BD and AKC 63. **d** 64 **p** 65 Chelmsf. C of Prittlewell 64-67; Up Hatherley 67-69; St Phil Eccles Distr Dorridge 69-71; C-in-c of Alkmonton w Yeaveley 71-76; R of Longford 71-76; Team V of Canvey I Dio Chelmsf from 76. *St Anne's House, St Anne's Road, Canvey Island, Essex.*

COOPER, John Leslie. b 33. BD (Lon) 65, M Phil (Lon) 78. Chich Th Coll 59. **d** 62 **p** 63 Birm. C of King's Heath 62-65; Asst Chap HM Pris Wandsworth 65-66; Chap HM Borstal Portland 66-68; HM Pris Bris 68-72; Research Fell Qu Coll Birm 72-73; P-in-c of St Paul Balsall Heath Dio Birm 73-81; V from 81; Exam Chap to Bp of Birm from 81. *26-28 Lincoln Street, Balsall Heath, Birmingham, B12 9EX.* (021-440 2219)

COOPER, John Richard. b 34. Dipl Th (Lon) 60. Bps' Coll Cheshunt 60. **d** 62 **p** 63 Lon. C of St Anne Brookfield 62-66; Old St Pancras w St Matt Oakley Square 66-70; Chap Nat Hosp Qu Sq Lon 70-71; C of Old St Pancras w St Matt Oakley Sq 71-74. *54 Longlands Road, Welwyn Garden City, Herts.*

COOPER, Joseph Newman. b 17. **d** 72 **p** 74 Newfld (APM).

C of Flower's Cove Dio Newfld (W Newfld from 76) from 72. *1805 Larch Street, Main Brook, White Bay North, Newfoundland, Canada.*

COOPER, Joseph Trevor. b 32. Linc Th Coll 65. **d** 67 Bp McKie for Cov **p** 68 Cov. C of St Jas Fletchamstead 67-69; Industr Chap Dio Cov from 69. *16 Trevor Close, Tile Hill Village, Coventry CV4 9HP.* (Cov 462341)

COOPER, Kenneth Cantlay. b 17. Qu Coll Cam BA 39, MA 43. Ridley Hall Cam 39. **d** 41 **p** 42 Sarum. C of St Mary Melcombe Regis 41-46; Broadwater 46-50; V of Cumnor 50-65; Surr 59-65; R of St Paul Fisherton Anger 65-74; P-in-c of Fovant and Sutton Mandeville Dio Sarum 74-79; R (w Teffont Evias and Teffont Magna) from 80; P-in-c of Teffont Evias w Magna 75-79. *Fovant Rectory, Salisbury, Wilts.* (Fovant 246)

COOPER, Leslie Martin. b 17. Jes Coll Cam BA 39, MA 43. Lon Coll of Div 39. **d** 40 **p** 41 Man. C of St Mary Droylsden 40-43; St Cath Neasden w Kingsbury 43-44; CF (EC) 44-47; Dioc Chap in c of St Geo and of St Edw w St Nich (from 47) and St Matthias Birm 48-49; R of St Geo Birm 49-53; King's Stanley 53-64; Chap St Jo Sch Leatherhead 64-71; Chap Wrekin Coll Wellington Salop 71-79. *87 Corinium Gate, Cirencester, Glos.* (Cirencester 4094)

COOPER, Malcolm Tydeman. b 37. Pemb Coll Ox BA (2nd cl Botany) 61, MA 64. Linc Th Coll 63. **d** 63 **p** 64 Ripon. C of Spennithorne 63-66; Caversham 66-71; Perm to Offic Dio Ox 71-74, Dio Sarum 74-76; Dio B & W from 76. *Spring Cottage, Middle Road, Cossington, Bridgwater, TA7 8LH.* (Chilton Polden 722763)

COOPER, Maxwell Edgar. Jes Coll Cam BA 37, MA 41. CD 63. Wycl Hall Ox 37. **d** 39 **p** 40 Lich. C of Meole Brace 39-41; CF (EC) 41-46; CF 46-54; Hon CF 54; R of St Mary Virg S Hill S Vanc 55-62; Hon Synod Cler Sec Dio New Westmr 61-64; R of Chilliwack 62-71; St Mark Vanc 71-76. *RR1, Mill Bay Road, Mill Bay, BC, VOR 2PO, Canada.*

COOPER, Canon Michael Leonard. b 30. St Jo Coll Cam 2nd cl Mod Lang Trip pt i 51, BA (2nd cl Mod Lang Trip pt ii) 53, MA 58. Cudd Coll 53. **d** 55 Croydon for Cant **p** 56 Cant. C of Croydon 55-61; V of All SS Spring Pk Croydon 61-71; Boxley Dio Cant from 71; RD of Sutton 74-80; Hon Can of Cant Cathl from 76; P-in-c of Detling Dio Cant from 77. *Boxley Vicarage, Maidstone, Kent, ME14 3DX.* (Maidstone 58606)

COOPER, Michael Sydney. b 41. St D Coll Lamp BA 63. Westcott Ho Cam 63. **d** 65 **p** 66 Portsm. C of Farlington 65-69; Cathl Ch Lahore 70-71; Personal Asst to Bp of Maur and P-in-c of Curepipe Maur 72-73; P-in-c of St Pet Conv Distr Hayling N 74-81; V of Carisbrooke Dio Portsm from 81; St Nich-in-Castro Carisbrooke Dio Portsm from 81. *Carisbrooke Vicarage, Newport, PO30 1PA, IW.* (Newport 522095)

COOPER, Milton Norbert. b 48. Nashotah Ho Wisc USA MDiv 76. **d** 75 **p** 76 Nass. P-in-c of Ch of Good Shepherd Grand Bahama 77-80; in Amer Ch. *4241 West Washington Boulevard, Chicago, Illinois 60624, USA.*

COOPER, Norman Mortimer. b 32. St Mich Coll Llan 63. **d** 65 **p** 66 Llan. C of Llangynwyd w Maesteg 65-70; C-in-c of Matthewstown w Ynysboeth 70-72; V of Oakwood 72-79; Cadoxton-Juxta-Neath Dio Llan from 79. *Cadoxton Vicarage, Neath, W Glam.* (Neath 4625)

COOPER, Peter David. b 48. Sarum Wells Th Coll 70. **d** 73 **p** 74 Win. C of Yateley 73-78; Christchurch 78-81; P-in-c of St Mark Southn Dio Win from 81. *St Mark's Vicarage, 10 Ranelagh Gardens, Southampton, SO1 2TH.* (Southn 36425)

COOPER, Richard Thomas. b 46. Univ of Leeds BA 69. Coll of Resurr Mirfield 69. **d** 71 **p** 72 Ripon. C of H Trin, Rothwell 71-75; Adel 75-78; Knaresborough (in c of H Trin) Dio Ripon from 78. *9 Castle Yard, Knaresborough, N Yorks.* (Harrogate 864678)

COOPER, Robert Edward. b 28. St Cath Coll Ox BA 51, MA 56. **d** 75 Repton for Derby **p** 76 Derby (APM). [f Bapt Min] Hon C of Buxton Dio Derby from 75. *1 Broad Walk, Buxton, Derbys, SK17 6JE.*

COOPER, Robert James. b 52. Univ of Bris BA 75. Ridley Hall Cam 76. **d** 78 Taunton for B & W **p** 79 B & W. C of Street w Walton Dio B & W from 78; Greinton Dio B & W from 79. *6 Bowling Green, Street, Somerset, BA16 0AH.* (Street 45393)

COOPER, Robert Tamlyn. St Francis Coll Bris ACT ThL 65. **d** 65 **p** 66 Brisb. C of St Jas Toowoomba 65-68; St Mary Virg Kuala Lumpur 68-70; V of Malacca 70-72; Chap C of E Gr Sch Canberra 72-81; L to Offic Dio C & Goulb 75-81; R of Kambah Dio C & Goulb from 81. *63 Bissenberger Crescent, Kambah, ACT, Australia 2902.*

COOPER, Roderick Alfred David. Angl Th Coll BC LTh 64. **d** 64 New Westmr. Miss E Coast Miss Dio BC 64-70; Hon C Chilliwack Dio New Westmr from 70. *46149 Hope River Road, Chilliwack, BC, Canada.*

COOPER, Roger Charles. b 48. GRSM 69. Coll of the Resurr Mirfield 79. **d** 81 Bp Gill for Newc T. C of St Mary Virg Monkseaton Dio Newc T from 81. *12 Richmond Terrace, Whitley Bay, Tyne & Wear, NE26 1SG.*

COOPER, Stephen. b 54. Chich Th Coll 74. **d** 77 **p** 78 Wakef. C of Horbury (w Horbury Bridge from 78) 77-81; St Mary Barnsley Dio Wakef from 81. *33 Queen's Drive, Barnsley, S75 2QG.* (Barnsley 84775)

COOPER, Sydney Bernard Nikon. K Coll Lon BD (2nd cl) and AKC (1st cl) 49, **d** 51 **p** 52 Lon. C of Ch Ch St Marylebone 51-54; Palmer's Green 54-58; Min of Ch Ch Staines 58-66; V of Woodberry Down 66-76; R of Chigwell Row Dio Chelmsf from 76. *Chigwell Row Rectory, Chigwell, Essex, IG7 4QD.* (01-500 2805)

COOPER, Te Waru Hakiapi. b 36. **d** 79 **p** 80 Wai. Hon C of Waipatu-Moteo Dio Wai from 79. *1013 Bledisloe Street, Hastings, NZ.*

COOPER, Thomas. b 20. Univ of Man BA 42. Edin Th Coll 42. **d** 44 **p** 45 Blackb. C of St John Sandylands 44-46; Burnley 46-49; St Geo Chorley 49-51; V of St Jas Chorley 51-57; PC of St Jas Blackb 57-63; CF (TA) 59-67; V of Bolton-le-Sands Dio Blackb from 63. *Bolton-le-Sands Vicarage, Carnforth, Lancs.* (Hest Bank 822335)

COOPER, Trevor John. b 51. Wycl Hall Ox 75. **d** 79 Portsm. C of St Pet Southsea Dio Portsm from 79. *c/o The Vicarage, Playfair Road, Southsea, Hants.*

COOPER, Vincent Norman. b 07. ALCD 30. **d** 30 **p** 31 Ox. C of Chesham 30-34, I of St Silas Glas 34-39, V of St Mary Becontree 39-45; St Jo Evang Carl and Chap Carl City Gen Hosp 45-56; V of Rodbourne-Cheney 56-58; Cler Asst Sec CPAS 58-72; Perm to Offic Roch 58-72; Dio Chich from 72. *10 Amberley Drive, Hove, Sussex, BN3 8JS.* (Brighton 70129)

COOPER, Wallace Peter. b 24. Kelham Th Coll 45. **d** 51 **p** 52 St Alb. C of St Mich AA Watford 51-52; St Barn Ealing 52-54; St Luke New Brompton 54-56. *10 Mortoncourt, Christchurch Road, Reading, Berks.* (Reading 860528)

COOPER, William Brunyee. b 42. Univ of Tor BA 64, STB 68. **d** 68 **p** 69 Tor. C of H Trin Tor 68-70; I of Mono 70-76; on leave. *RR1, Pickerng, Ont., Canada.*

COOPER, Canon William Gough Porter. Trin Coll Dub BA 37, MA 40, Div Test 37. MC 43. **d** 38 **p** 39 Dub. C of Monkstown 38-40; CF (EC) 40-46; Hon CF 46; I of Inch 46-49; Malahide w Portmarnock and St Doulagh's Dio Dub from 49; Can of Ch Ch Cathl Dub from 72. *Rectory, Malahide, Co Dublin, Irish Republic.* (Dublin 350239)

COOPER, William Henry Vere. b 24. Trin Coll Dub BA 46, Div Test 47. **d** 47 **p** 48 Down. C of Ballymacarrett 47-50; Coleraine 50-53; I of Arboe 53-55; R of Lissan 55-65. *23 Drumnacross Road, Cookstown, Co Tyrone, BT80 9DT, N Ireland.*

COOPER, Very Rev William Hugh Alan. b 09. Ch Coll Cam BA (2nd cl Hist Trip pts i and ii) 31, MA 35. Lon Coll of Div 31. **d** 32 **p** 33 S'wark. C of Lee 32-36; H Trin Cam 36-38; CMS Miss and Dioc Missr Dio Lagos 38-41; C of Farnham 41-42; R of Ashtead 42-51; V of St Andr Plymouth 51-62; C-in-c of Ch Ch Plymouth 61-62; Surr from 52; Preb of Ex Cathl 58-62; Proc Conv Ex 59-62; Bradf from 62; Provost and V of Cathl Ch Bradf 62-76; in Ch of Pakistan 76-81; P-in-c of Chrishall Dio Chelmsf from 81. *Chrishall Vicarage, Royston, Herts.* (Chrishall 312)

COOPER-SMITH, Alfred Riddington. b 13. TD 63. St Deiniols Hawarden 74. **d** 74 **p** 75 Bp Horstead for Leic **p** 75 Leic. Hon C of Smeeton Westerby w Saddington 74-80; Perm to Offic Dios Leic & Pet from 80. *63 Stockerston Crescent, Uppingham, Oakham, Leics, LE15 9UA.* (Uppingham 2412)

COOTE, Bernard Albert Ernest. b 28. Univ of Lon BD 53. Chich Th Coll 54. **d** 55 Croydon for Cant **p** 56 Cant. C of Addiscombe 55-57; Hawkhurst 57-59; Sanderstead 59-63; V of Sutton Valence w E Sutton 63-76; Chap HM Borstal E Sutton Pk 63-74; C-in-c of Chart Sutton 71-76; Prin and Chap R Sch for Blind Leatherhead from 76. *Royal School for the Blind, Leatherhead, Surrey.* (Leatherhead 73086)

COOTE, Denis Ivor. b 08. CBE (Mil) 51. Sarum Th Coll 62. **d** 63 **p** 64 Sarum. C of Sherborne w Castleton and Lillington 63-65; R of E Stoke w E Holme 65-67; St Jas Shaftesbury 67-73. *12 Belle Vue Road, Parkstone, Dorset, BH14 8TW.*

COOTE, Herbert Edward Lloyd. b 41. **d** 72 Bp Greenwood for Alg **p** 76 Alg. M SSJE 72-74; I of Wawa 75-79; Port Sydney Dio Alg from 79. *Christ Church Rectory, Port Sydney, Ont, Canada.*

COOTE, Robert Horton. K Coll NS. **d** 61 **p** 62 Bp W W Davis for NS. R of Rawdon 61-65; Mahone Bay 65-72; Timberlea w Lakeside 72-74; Dartmouth N Dio NS from 74. *68 Micmac Drive, Dartmouth, NS, Canada.* (469-8009)

✠ **COOTE, Right Rev Roderic Norman.** b 15. Trin Coll Dub BA (2nd cl Mod Ment and Mor Sc) 37, Div Test (1st cl) 38, MA 41, DD 54. **d** 38 **p** 39 Dub. C of St Bart Dub 38-41;

Hon Cler V of Ch Ch Cathl Dub 41; SPG Miss Dio Gambia 41-51; Cons Ld Bp of Gambia and the Rio Pongas in St Geo Cathl Freetown Sierra Leone 15 April 51 by Abp of Cant; Bps of Accra; Lagos; Sier L; and Niger; Bps Akinyele; Phillips; Hall; Dimeari; Jones; Wilson and Lasbrey; Prov Sec to Abp of W Africa 55-57; Trld to Fulham (in c of the jurisd of N and Cent Europe) 57; to Colchester 66; Archd of Colchester 69-72. *Bishop's House, 32 Inglis Road, Colchester, Essex, CO3 3HU.* (Colchester 72856)

COOZE, Cyril Wakelin. St Jo Coll Auckld. **d** 60 Bp Rich for Wel **p** 61 Wel. C of Gonville 60-64; Ruapehu 64-67; V 67-69; Lyall Bay Wel 69-78; Marton Dio Wel from 78. *Vicarage, Maunder Street, Wellington, NZ.* (8494)

COPE, Anthony William Groves. b 08. Ex Coll Ox BA (3rd cl Mod Hist) 32, MA 36. Wycl Hall Ox 32. **d** 34 **p** 35 S'wark. C of H Trin Tulse Hill 34-36; Putney (in c of St John) 36-39; CF (TA) 38-39; R of Feltwell 39-53; Offg Chap RAF 39-40; Chap RAFVR 40-46; RD of Feltwell 44-53; R of Upwell St Pet 53-65; V of Hovingham 65-73; R of Slingsby 66-73; L to Offic Dio Ban from 73. *Pen-y-Bryn, Dinas, Pwllheli, Gwynedd, LL53 8SY.* (Tudweiliog 616)

COPE, Gilbert Frederick. b 10. Univ of Birm BSc (2nd cl Biochem) 31, MSc 32, PhD (Th) 60. St Cath S Ox Dipl Th 34. Ripon Hall Ox 32. **d** 34 **p** 35 Birm. C of Sutton Coldfield 34-38; C-in-c of Highter's Heath Conv Distr 38-40; PC 40-45; V of St Thos, Cov 45-47; Lect Univ of Birm 47-76; Dep Dir Inst for Study of Worship and Relig Archit 62-76; Hon Fell from 76; LPr Dio Birm 49-76. *Dragonyard, Church Lane, Barford, CV35 8ES.* (0926-624620)

COPE, Canon Henry William. Ja Ch Th Coll 08. **d** 09 **p** 11 Ja. C of St Geo Kingston Ja 09-11; P-in-c of Woburn Lawn w Trinityville 11-13; R of Santa Cruz 13-15; Savanna la Mar 15-55; Hon Can of Ja 33-50; Can (Emer) from 50. *109 Old Hope Road, Kingston 6, Jamaica, W Indies.*

COPE, Peter John. b 42. Mert Coll Ox BA (2nd cl Th) 64, MA 68. Univ of Lon MSc 74. Cudd Coll 64. **d** 66 **p** 67. C of St Matt Chapel-Allerton 66-69; Industr Chap NW Lon 69-76; Worc 76-79; Sen Chap Worcs Industr Miss from 79; Min Can of Worc from 76. *19 Athelstan Road, Worcester, WR5 2BW.* (Worc 352328)

COPE, Ralph Bruce. Sir Geo Williams Univ Montr BA 60. McGill Univ Montr BD 62. **d** 60 **p** 61 Ont. I of N Augusta 60-62; Sharbot Lake w Parham 62-64; Chap RCAF from 64. *RR7, Perth, Ont, Canada.*

COPE, Tasman Duncan. ACT ThL 62. **d** 61 **p** 62 Perth. C of Subiaco 61-63; Rabaul 64; Miss Dio New Guinea 64-71; Dio Papua 71-73; R of St Hilda City and Dio Perth from 74. *Box 86, N Perth, W Australia 6006.* (2715239)

COPELAND, Christopher Paul. b 38. K Coll Lon and Warm AKC 64. **d** 65 **p** 66 St Alb. C of St Andr Luton 65-67; St Nich w St Pet Droitwich 67-71; King's Norton 71-72; Team V 72-78; V of St Edm Tyseley City and Dio Birm from 78. *Vicarage, Reddings Lane, Tyseley, Birmingham, B11 3DD.* (021-777 2433)

COPELAND, Derek Norman. b 38. Worc Coll Ox BA (2nd cl Th) 62, MA 68. Westcott Ho Cam 63. **d** 64 **p** 65 Portsm. C of St Mary Portsea 64-71; P-in-c of Avonmouth 71-77; M of Bris Dioc Soc & Industr Dept from 71; P-in-c of St Paul Chippenham w Langley Burrell 77-79; R of St Paul Chippenham w Hardenhuish and Langley Burrell Dio Bris from 79; Kington St Mich Dio Bris from 79. *9 Greenway Park, Chippenham, Wilts, SN15 1QG.* (Chippenham 653839)

COPELAND, Norman. b 1900. OBE (Mil) 54, Men in Disp 45. Univ Coll Dur BA 25, MA 30. **d** 25 **p** 26 Dur. C of Beamish 25-28; CF 29-54; DACG 48-54; R of Gotham 54-71; Chap St Jo St Mary Magd and Ch Hosps Win 71-79. *16 Normans, Normans Road, Winchester, SO23 9PP.* (Win 62186)

COPELAND, Peter John. Wollaston Coll W Austr 57. **d** 59 **p** 60 Perth. C of St Mary S Perth 59-63; R of Cunderdin 63-68; P-in-c of Spearwood w Hilton Pk 68-73; Perm to Offic Dio Perth from 74. *27 Dericote Way, Greenwood, W Australia 6024.* (35 1898)

COPESTAKE, Leslie. ALCD 39. **d** 39 **p** 40 Ches. C of Ch Ch Macclesfield 39-42; Mottram-in-Longdendale w Broadbottom 42-45; St Geo Stockport 45-47; V of Hurdsfield 47-51; Area Sec CMS Dios Worc Lich and Heref 51-55; V of Norris Green 55-61; St John Beckermet 61-71; Egton w Newland 71-78. *Haverthwaite House, Haverthwaite, Ulverston, Cumb, LA12 8AE.* (Newby Bridge 31819)

COPESTAKE, Victor Henry. b 1897. Qu Coll Cam 2nd cl Hist Trip pt i 22, BA (3rd cl Th Trip pt i) 23. Westcott Ho Cam 24. **d** 25 **p** 26 St E. C of St Mary Mildenhall 25-27; Ch Ch Rotherhithe 27-29; Dunster (in c of Alcombe) 30-35; R of Foxcote w Shoscombe 35-47; V of Huish Episcopi 47-57. *Address temp unknown*

COPINGER, Stephen Hubert Augustine. b 18. BA (3rd cl Hist) Lon 48. Ely Th Coll 60. **d** 62 **p** 63 Ely. C of St Benedict, Cam 62-64; M SSF from 65; LPr Dio Sarum from 68; C-in-c of Hilfield w Hermitage 68-76; Gen L Dio Connor from 76; L to Offic Dio Meath and Kild from 78. *75 Deerpark Road, Belfast, BT14 7PW, N Ireland.* (0232-743480)

COPLAND, Canon Charles McAlester. b 10. CCC Cam 3rd cl Hist Trip pt 1 31, BA (3rd cl Th Trip pt i) 33, MA 36. Cudd Coll 33. **d** 34 **p** 35 Pet. C of St Jo Bapt Pet 34-38; Miss in Chanda Dio Nagp 38-42; Hd 42-53; Can of Nagp 52-53; R of St Mary Arbroath 53-59; Can of St Paul's Cathl Dundee 53-59; R and Provost of St Jo Div Cathl Oban 59-79; Hon Can from 79; Dean of Arg Is 77-79. *Fir Cottage, South Crieff Road, Crieff, Scotland.*

COPLAND, Frank Frederick. Moore Th Coll Syd 61. ACT ThL 62. **d** 62 **p** 63 Syd. C of St Sav Punchbowl 62-63; St Steph Coorparoo Brisb 63-65; C-in-c of Old Guildf Dio Syd from 65. *64 Broughton Street, Old Guildford, NSW, Australia 2161.* (632-9301)

COPLAND, Ian William. b 46. St Jo Coll Morpeth ThL 80. **d** and **p** 80 Newc. C of Charlestown Dio Newc from 80. *52 Waratah Street, Kahibah, NSW, Australia 2290.*

COPLAND, William Samuel. Univ of Leeds BSc 32. Coll of Resurr Mirfield 32. **d** 34 **p** 35 York. C of St Mary Sculcoates 34-36; Uitenhage 36-39; R of Barkly E 39-43; St John E Lon 43-48; Fort Beaufort 48-50; C of Hayes Middx 50-52; R of Norseman w Esperance 52-53; Williams 53-55; S Bunb 55-58; Brunswick 58-65; Wagin 65-71; Can of Bunb 67-72; R of Carey Pk 71-72; Perm to Offic Dio Bunb from 72. *9 Buckby Road, Harvey, W Australia 6220.* (097-290 582)

COPLEY, Anthony Walter. ACT ThL 68. Ridley Coll Melb 65. **d** 75 **p** 76 Melb. C of Rosanna 75-77; St John Blackburn 77-79; P-in-c of Clayton Dio Melb from 79. *Vicarage, Dixon Street, Clayton, Vic., Australia 3168.* (544 1525)

COPLEY, Colin. b 30. Kelham Th Coll 51. **d** 55 **p** 56 Linc. C of St Swith Linc 55-58; Bottesford w Ashby 58-60; Chap Hollesley Borstal Inst 60-66; HM Pris Walton Liv 66-70; HM Pris Styal Ches 70-73; Reg Chap HM Prisons and Borstals N Region 70-73; Midl Region from 73; L to Offic Dio Ches 70-73; Dio Lich from 73; Chap HM Pris Drake Hall, Eccleshall 73-75; Asst Chap Gen from 81. *Home Office, Prison Dept, Midland Regional HQ, Calthorpe House, r.* (021-455 9855)

COPLEY, David Judd. b 15. Linc Coll Ox BA (3rd cl Mod Hist) 48, MA 53. Wycl Hall Ox 48. **d** 50 **p** 51 Worc. C of Old Swinford 50-53; Priv Chap to Bp of Worc 52-55; Min of AA Eccles Distr Norton Worc 53-56; R of Romsley 56-67; V of Tardebigge 67-81. *220 Bromsgrove Road, Hunnington, Halesowen, W Midl.* (Romsley 710247)

COPLEY, Edmund Miles. b 27. BSc (Eng) Lon 50. Univ of Birm Dipl Th 57. Qu Coll Birm 55. **d** 57 **p** 58 Derby. C of Allestree 57-61; R of Banff 61-65; Portsoy 61-65; Uggeshall w Sotherton Wangford and Henham Dio St E from 65. *Wangford Vicarage, Beccles, Suff.* (Wangford 235)

COPLEY, Canon Richard Bevis. b 07. K Coll Lon AKC 34. **d** 34 **p** 35 Portsm. C of St Marg Eastney 34-41; V of St Sav-on-the-Cliff Shanklin 41-61; RD of E Wight 57-61; Hon Can of Portsm 58-67; Can (Emer) from 67; V of H Spirit Southsea Portsea 61-67. *141 Broomfield Avenue, Worthing, Sussex.*

COPNER, Thomas Herbert Woodward. b 08. Bp Wilson Th Coll IM 36. **d** 38 **p** 39 S & M. C of St Geo Douglas 38-45; Offg C-in-c of Kirk Onchan 41-45; V of Kirk Patrick 45-59; Kirk Lonan 59-75. *Crossag Villa, Ballasalla, IM.*

COPPEN, Peter Euan. b 39. Ripon Coll Cudd 79. **d** 81 Grantham for Linc. C of New Sleaford Dio Linc from 81. *29 St Denys Avenue, Sleaford, Lincs.*

COPPEN, Robert George. b 39. Univ of Capetn BA 66. St Jo Coll Dur 79. **d** 81 **p** 82 S & M. C of St Geo & St Barn w All SS Douglas Dio S & M from 81. *46 Albany Road, Douglas, Isle of Man.*

COPPIN, Canon Ronald Leonard. b 30. Univ of Birm BA (Hist) 52. Ridley Hall Cam 54. **d** 56 **p** 57 Lon. C of All SS Harrow Weald 56-59; Dom Chap to Bp of Man and LPr Dio Man 59-63; Chap St Aid Coll 63-65; Vice-Prin 65-68; Exam Chap to Bp of Man 64-74; to Bp of Derby from 75; Selection and Min Sec ACCM 68-71; Selection Sec and Sec of C'tte of Th Educn of ACCM 71-74; Can Res of Dur from 74; Dir of Clergy Tr Dio Dur from 74; Warden NE Ordin Course from 76. *3 The College, Durham.* (Durham 2415)

COPPING, John Frank Walter Victor. b 34. K Coll Lon and Warm BD and AKC 58. **d** 59 **p** 60 Lon. C of Hampstead 59-62; Bray 62-65; PC of Langley Mill 65-71; V of Cookham Dean Dio Ox from 71. *Cookham Dean Vicarage, Maidenhead, Berks.*

COPPING, Raymond. b 36. Wycl Hall Ox 72. **d** 74 Dorchester for Ox **p** 75 Ox. C of St Andr Hatters Lane High Wycombe 74-77; Team V of High Wycombe Dio Ox from 77. *199 Cressex Road, High Wycombe, HP12 4PZ.* (High Wycombe 30134)

COPSEY, Preb Harry Charles Frederick. b 05. Linc Th

Coll 31. **d** 34 **p** 35 Leic. C of Em Loughborough 34-36; St Jo Bapt Bognor Regis 36-38; Chap at Arosa 37-39; V of Lower Beeding 39-43; Willingdon 43-54; E Grinstead 54-75; Chap Qu Vic Hosp E Grinstead 55-75; Sackville Coll E Grinstead 56-75; Preb of Chich Cathl from 70. *Town House, South Pallant, Chichester, Sussex, PO19 1SY.* (Chich 784509)

COPSEY, Nigel John. b 52. AKC and BD 75. St Aug Coll Cant 72. **d** 76 Chelmsf **p** 77 Barking for Chelmsf. C of St Francis Barkingside 76-78; Vic Dks Dio Chelmsf from 78. *Clergy House, Baxter Road, E16.* (01-476 3784)

COPSON, Michael Roland. Chich Th Coll 72. **d** 73 **p** 74 Worc. C of Malvern Linc w Cowleigh 73-77; St John's Cathl Buenos Aires 78-80; Team V of St Pet and St Andr Corby w Gt and L Oakley Dio Pet from 80. *Kingswood Vicarage, 26 Kingsbrook, Corby, Northants, NN18 9HY.* (Gt Oakley 743234)

COPUS, Brian George. K Coll Lon and Warm AKC 59. **d** 60 Maidstone for Cant **p** 61 Cant. C of St Mich AA Croydon 60-63; St Mark Swindon 63-69; V of Colebrooke 69-73; C-in-c of Hittisleigh 69-73; R of Perivale 73-82; V of St Mary S Ruislip Dio Lon from 82. *9 The Fairway, South Ruislip, Middx.* (01-845 3485)

COPUS, James Lambert. b 19. Edin Th Coll 47. **d** 50 **p** 51 Derby. C of Fairfield 50-52; C-in-c of St Ninian Dundee 52-55; C of Ch Ch Sutton Surrey 55-57; W Norwood 57-58; V of All SS and St Barn S Lambeth 58-78; Team V of Totton 78-80. *3 Park Avenue, Wakefield, W Yorks, WF2 8DS.*

COPUS, Jonathan Hugh Lambert. b 44. BNC Ox BA (Th) 66, MA 71. SOC 68. **d** 71 Dorking for Guildf **p** 72 Guildf. C of Horsell 71-73; Publ Pr Dio Win from 74; Producer Relig Programmes BBC Radio Solent from 73. *55 Lower Ashley Road, Ashley, New Milton, Hants, BH25 5QF.*

CORBAN, Donald Arthur. b 39. **d** 77 **p** 78 Waik. C of Te Awamutu 77-78; V of Ngaruawahia Dio Waik from 78. *13 Galileo Street, Ngaruawahia, NZ.* (8852)

CORBEIL, Robert Calixte. d 59 Caled. I of Miller Bay 59-61; Hon C of St Geo Ott 63-65; St John Ott 65-70; Perm to Offic Dio Ott from 70. *20 Chesterton Drive, Ottawa, Ont., Canada.*

CORBET-MILWARD, Canon Richard George Corbet. b 12. K Coll Cam 2nd cl Hist Trip pt i 34, BA 36, MA 40. Cudd Coll 37. **d** 38 **p** 39 S'wark. C of St Sav w St Pet S'wark 38-41; PV of S'wark Cathl and Sacr 39-41; C of All SS Heref 41-43; Romsey 43-48; V of St Alb Copnor Portsea 48-74; H Trin Ryde 74-79; Surr 60-79; RD of Portsm 65-69; Hon Can of Portsm from 68; RD of E Wight 75-78; Perm to Offic Dio Portsm from 79. *2 Pembroke Close, Old Portsmouth, Hants, PO1 2NX.*

CORBETT, Albert Ernest. b 20. FCA 62. Qu Coll Birm 71. **d** and **p** 74 Birm. Hon C of Sheldon 74-77; Coleshill Dio Birm from 77. *39 Dorchester Road, Solihull, Warwicks, B91 1LW.* (021-705 6538)

CORBETT, Canon Charles Eric. b 17. Jes Coll Ox BA (2nd cl Th) 39, MA 43. Wycl Hall Ox 39. **d** 40 **p** 41 St A. C of Gresford 40-44; CF (EC) 44-47; C of Eglwys-Rhos 47-49; R of Harpurhey 49-54; V of St Cath Wigan 54-61; Surr from 50; V of St Luke Farnworth 61-71; RD of Farnworth 64-71; Archd of Liv 71-79; Can Res of Liv from 71; Treas from 79. *The Cathedral, Liverpool, L1 7AZ.*

CORBETT, George. b 18. BC Coll Bris 47. **d** 50 **p** 51 Lich. C of Heath Town 50-52; R of St Matthias w St Simon Salford 52-55; N Area Sec BCMS and Perm to Offic Dios Ches, Man and York 55-58; V of St Steph Lambeth 58-61; Assoc Home Sec BCMS 61-63; V of Hatherleigh 63-78; P-in-c of Ringmore w Kingston Dio Ex from 78. *Rectory, Ringmore, Kingsbridge, Devon, TQ7 4HR.* (Bigbury-on-Sea 565)

CORBETT, Henry St John Spens. b 53. CCC Cam BA 75. Wycl Hall Ox Dipl Th 78. **d** 78 **p** 79 Liv. C of St Pet Everton Dio Liv from 78. *54 Milburn Heights, Conway Street, Liverpool L5 3NJ.* (051-207 1465)

CORBETT, Ian Deighton. b 42. St Cath Coll Cam 2nd cl Hist Trip pt i 63, BA (2nd cl Hist Trip pt ii) 64, MA 68. Westcott Ho Cam 67. **d** 69 Hulme for Man **p** 70 Man. C of St Jas New Bury Farnworth 69-72; St Pet Bolton-le-Moors (in c of H Trin) 72-75; Chap Bolton Inst of Tech 72-75; Dioc Further Educn Officer from 74; R of Vic Pk Lancs 75-80; Chap Univ of Salford from 80. *c/o University House, University of Salford, M5 4WT.* (061-736 5843)

CORBETT, John David. b 32. Or Coll Ox BA 55, MA 59. St Steph Ho Ox 55. **d** 57 **p** 58 Ex. C of St Pet (in c of All SS from 60) Plymouth 57-64; PC (V from 68) of Marldon 64-74; Team V of St Steph Bournemouth Dio Win from 74. *St Stephen's Vicarage, St Stephen's Way, Bournemouth, Dorset, BH2 6JZ.* (Bournemouth 24355)

CORBETT, Maxwell Thomas. Univ of Syd BA 74, MA 78. Moore Th Coll Syd ACT ThL 51. **d** and **p** 52 Syd. C-in-c of St Barn Punchbowl 52-54; Miss at Kilimetinde 54-60; Chap at Dodoma 60-64; Arusha 64-67; Can of Centr Tang 66-70; CMS Rep Dio Centr Tang 68-70; R of Summer Hill 70-74; L to Offic Dio Syd 74-76; Asst Master Barker Coll 76; R of St Andr Wahroonga Dio Syd from 77. *2 Water Street, Wahroonga, NSW, Australia 2076.* (48-3278)

CORBETT, Sidney Charles. b 13. Univ of Wales BA 38. St Mich Coll Llan 39. **d** 41 **p** 42 Llan. C of Llanddewi Rhondda 41-44; Tonyrefail 44-45; St Cath Canton Cardiff 45-47; Chap and Dep Hd Master of Wm Baker Tech Sch Goldings 47-56; Chap of Trent Coll Long Eaton from 56; Sen Master Bp Wand Sch Sunbury-on-Thames 70-76; Hon C of St Mary Sunbury 70-76; C of Ludlow 76-80. *70 Bringewood Rise, Ludlow, SY8 2NE.*

CORBETT-JONES, Michael Anthony. Moore Th Coll Syd ACT ThL (2nd cl) 64. **d** 64 **p** 65 Syd. C of Turramurra 64-67; P-in-c of Tawau 67-71; C of St Andr Kowloon 72-77; St John's Cathl Hong Kong 77-80; Dir Angl Marriage and Family Counselling Centre Syd from 80. *491 Kent Street, Sydney, Australia 2000.* (267-3946)

CORBIN, Harry Sinclair Parker. K Coll Halifax NS BA 48, MA 49, LTh 49. **d** 49 **p** 50 NS. R of Indian Harbour 49-59; Mahone Bay 59-65; Bedford Dio NS from 65. *PO Box 160, Bedford, NS, Canada.* (835-3117)

CORBIN, Robert Charles Henry. b 17. K Coll Lon & Warm AKC 49. **d** 49 Win **p** 50 Southn for Win. C of St Alb Southn 49-52; St Aldhelm Branksome 52-55; R of Hilperton w Whaddon 55-69; C of St Andr Boscombe Bournemouth 69-72; St Pet (in c of St Swith) Bournemouth 72-74; P-in-c of Newton Valence w Selborne 74-79, Old Alresford 79-80; Chap Commun of The Sacred Passion and Homes and Hosp of St Giles E Hanningfield from 80. *St Giles Lodge, East Hanningfield, Chelmsford, CM3 5AS.* (Danbury 2077)

CORBY, John Booth. St Jo Coll Morpeth ACT ThL (2nd cl) 67. **d** 68 **p** 69 Melb. C of Broadmeadows 68-69; St John Bentleigh 69; R of Yackandandah 69-73; C of Home Miss Dept of Chaps Dio Melb 73-80; I of St Matt Glenroy Dio Melb from 80. *30 Widford Street, Glenroy, Vic, Australia 3046.*

CORDELL, Derek Harold. b 34. Chich Th Coll 57. **d** 60 Croydon for Cant **p** 61 Cant. C of Whitstable 60-63; Moulsecoomb (in c of St Mary Magd) 63-69; Chap in Bucharest 69-71; V of St Wilfrid Brighton 71-74; Chap HM Borstal Roch 74-80; Asst Chap HM Pris Strangeways 80-81; Chap HM Pris The Verne Portland from 81. *42 Elwell Street, Upwey, Weymouth, Dorset.* (0305 812721)

CORDELL, Oliver Tristram. Univ of Syd BA 25. ACT ThL 25, Th Scho 46. **d** 24 **p** 25 Bath. C of St Steph Newtown Syd 24-26; R of Hill End 26; Maldon Vic 27-28; Hd Master CMS Centr Sch Dodoma 28-35; Dioc Insp of Schs and Miss at Kongwa 35-41; Prin Teachers' Tr Sch Dodoma 41-43; C of St Martin Kens 44-45; Chap Arusha 46-50; Can of Centr Tang 48-59; Exam Chap to Bp of Centr Tang 48-56; Archd of Dodoma 50-57; Mpwapwa 57-58; Centr Tang Dioc Sec 52-56; Perm to Offic Dio Momb 59-61; Dio Nak 61-62; L to Offic Dio Syd from 63. *22 Alexander Parade, Roseville, NSW, Australia 2069.* (41-3989)

CORDEN, Canon Thomas Hugh. b 11. Univ Coll Dur BA 35, MA 38. **d** 37 **p** 38 Dur. C of S Westoe 37-40; CF (EC) 40-46; Hon CF 46; PC of Beamish 46-56; R of Gateshead 56-66; C-in-c of St Aid Gateshead 56-57; PC 57-66; C-in-c of H Trin Gateshead 56-57; V 57-66; Hon Can of Dur 56-79; Can (Emer) from 79; RD of Gateshead 60-66; V of Shildon 66-79; C-in-c of Eldon 66-71; Commiss Venez 73-76. *29 Watling Road, Bishop Auckland, Co Durham.*

CORDES, Albrecht Johannes Martin Friedrich. b 08. St Geo, Windsor. **d** 56 **p** 57 Derby. C of Melb Derbys 56-58; Matlock w Tansley 58-59; V of Corringham w Springthorpe 59-66; R of Heapham 61-66; V of Scunthorpe 66-71; V of Appleby 71-77. *Address temp unknown.*

CORDINGLEY, Brian Lambert. b 30. St Aid Coll 55. **d** 57 **p** 58 Sheff. C of Clifton 57-61; Industr Miss Dio Sheff 57-63; Rotherham 61-63; R of St Cuthb Trafford Pk Dio Man from 63; Industr Missr Dio Man from 63; Dioc Officer for Urban and Industr Miss from 77; V of All SS Hamer, Rochdale Dio Man from 81. *All Saints' Vicarage, Rochdale, Lancs, OL12 0ES.* (Rochdale 355591)

CORDINGLEY, Francis André Annandale. b 26. **d** 67 **p** 68 Newc T. C of Wooler 67-70; V of Broadhembury 70-73; Rillington (w Scampston, Wintringham and Thorpe Bassett from 77) Dio York from 73; Scampston 74-77; C-in-c of Wintringham 74-77. *Rillington Vicarage, Malton, Yorks.* (Rillington 317)

CORDINGLEY, Fred. b 11. Late Exhib of St Jo Coll Dur BA (2nd cl Th) 40, MA 43. **d** 40 **p** 41 Man. C of St Jas Higher Broughton 40-42; All SS Maldon 42-48; V of Bilsdale Midcable 48-59; C-in-c of Hawnby 49-53; V of St Hilda Bilsdale 54-59; R of Birdbrook (w Sturmer from 63) 59-71; C-in-c of Sturmer 59-63. *8 Ashwood Close, Helmsley, Yorks, YO6 5HW.*

CORDY, Gordon Donald. b 30. Roch Th Coll 61. **d** 63 **p** 64 Nor. C of Kirkley 63-65; Stroud 66-68; V of Badgeworth w

Shurdington 68-71; Coleford w Staunton 71-73; C of Digswell 73-75; V in Shingay Group 75-78; R of St John March Dio Ely from 78. *St John's Rectory, March, Cambs.* (March 3525)

COREA, Michael Hippolit. BD (Rome) 52. BSc (Lon) 68. **d** 51 **p** 52 RC Abp of Colom. Rec into Angl Commun 57. C of St Paul Sing 59-62; V of All SS Taiping 62-66; Kelantan w Tregganu 66-71; L to Offic Dio Sing from 71. *82 Braemar Drive, Singapore 19.*

COREY, William Wallace. Wycl Coll Tor 72. **d** 71 Fred. C of Petersville and Greenwich 71-73; on leave 74-75; R of Cam and Waterborough 75-80; St Jas St John Dio Fred from 80. *32 Wildwood Court, St John, NB, Canada.*

CORFE, David Robert. b 35. Pemb Coll Cam BA 58, MA 62. Lambeth Dipl Th 70. Cudd Coll 58. **d** 60 **p** 61 Liv. C of All SS Wigan 60-63; SPG Miss Dio Chota N 63-68; on leave 68-69; in Ch of N India 70-75; C of Em Northwood 75; R of Eastwell w Boughton Aluph 75-80; V of Westwell 75-80; Hildenborough Dio Roch from 80. *194 Tonbridge Road, Hildenborough, Kent.* (Hildenborough 833596)

CORFIELD, John Bernard. b 24. Jes Coll Cam BA 49, MA 51. Ridley Hall Cam 64. **d** 66 **p** 67 Ely. C of St Jo Evang Cam 66-69; P-in-c of Bledlow Ridge 69-75; Bradenham 71-75; R of Sherington w Chicheley and N Crawley w Astwood and Hardmead Dio Ox from 75. *Rectory, Sherington, Newport Pagnell, Bucks.* (Newport Pagnell 610521)

CORFMAT, Percy Thomas Walter. b 14. K Coll Lon AKC 47. **d** 47 **p** 48 Guildf. Chap to Deaf and Dumb Dio Guildf 47-50; L to Offic at St Francis Ch for Deaf and Dumb Redhill 48-50; Chap E Lon Distr Deaf and Dumb 50-53; L to Offic at All SS Ch for Deaf and Dumb W Ham 50-53; Chap to Deaf and Dumb Dio St Alb 53-63; Dio Cant 63-72; Chap Miss for Deaf and L to Offic Dio Leic 72-73; Chap Coun for Deaf Dio Ox from 73. *36 Aplin Road, Aylesbury, Bucks, HP21 7BT.*

CORIN, Alan Paul. b 08. Late Gainer Scho of Pemb Coll Ox 3rd cl Cl Mods 29, BA (3rd cl Lit Hum 31), MA 35. MBE 45. Westcott Ho Cam 31. **d** 32 **p** 33 Wakef. C of King Cross Halifax 32-36; V of St Thos Huddersfield 36-46; CF (R of O) 39-45; V of St Mary of Eton Hackney Wick (w St Aug from 53) 46-58; Ch the Sav Ealing 58-81. *27 Arcadia Road, Burnham-on-Crouch, Essex.* (Maldon 784301)

CORK, Archdeacon of. *See* Hutchinson, Ven John Desmond.

CORK, Dean of. *See* Carey, Very Rev James Maurice George.

CORK, CLOYNE and ROSS, Lord Bishop of. *See* Poyntz, Right Rev Samuel Greenfield.

CORKE, Francis Boniface. b 33. Sarum Th coll 62. **d** 64 **p** 65 Newc T. C of St Paul Alnwick 64-68; V of Horton w Piddington 68-79; C-in-c of Preston Deanery 68-72; Team V of Scilly Is Dio Truro from 79. *The Parsonage, Tresco, TR24 0QG.* (Scillonia 22880)

CORKE, John Harry. b 29. K Coll Lon & Warm AKC 55. **d** 56 **p** 57 Cov. C of Stockingford 56-58; Nuneaton 58-60; V of Hartshill 60-80; R of Hampton Lucy w Charlecote and Loxley Dio Cov from 80. *Charlecote Vicarage, Warwick, CV35 9EW.*

CORKER, John Anthony. b 37. K Coll Lon and Warm AKC 63. **d** 64 **p** 65 Wakef. C of Lindley 64-68; V of Brotherton 68-72; Perm to Offic Dio York from 76. *16 St Nicholas Crescent, Copmanthorpe, York, N Yorks.* (York 706691)

CORKER, Ronald. b 30. Ely Th Coll 51. **d** 54 **p** 55 Dur. C of Whitworth w Spennymoor 54-58; Min of St Nich Eccles Distr Dunston 58-65; V 65-68; Chap Dunston Hill Hosp 58-68; R of Willington (w Sunnybrow from 75) 68-80; C-in-c of Sunnybrow 73-75; V of Billingham Dio Dur from 80. *St Cuthbert's Vicarage, Billingham, Cleve, TS23 1BW.* (Stockton 553236)

CORKETT, Canon Cecil Harry. b 10. Univ of Dur LTh 41. Sarum Th Coll 32. **d** 35 **p** 36 Wakef. C of St Pet Morley w Churwell All SS 35-38; Felkirk (in c of Brierley) 38-43; V of Cleckheaton-Whitechapel 43-80; Hon Can of Wakef 71-80; Can (Emer) from 80. *c/o Whitechapel Vicarage, Cleckheaton, Yorks.* (Cleckheaton 872869)

CORKHILL, James Hampton. St Chad's Coll Regina 29. **d** 32 **p** 33 Qu'App. C of Bethune 32; I of Milden 32-33; R 33-36; I of Wadena 36-38; Arcola 39-44; Manor 43-44; Raymore 44-45; R of Fort Qu'App 45-64; Hon Can of Qu'App 56-58; Can 57-64. *1425 College Avenue, Regina, Sask., Canada.*

CORLESS, Keith Ronald. b 37. GIMarE 66. Edin Th Coll 58. **d** 61 Glouc **p** 62 Tewkesbury for Cant. C of All SS Cheltm 61-64; St Phil and St Jas Leckhampton 66-69; R of Ashchurch Dio Glouc from 69. *Ashchurch Rectory, Tewkesbury, Glos.* (Tewkesbury 293729)

CORLISS, Roland Charles. b 06. Chich Th Coll 38. **d** 40 **p** 41 Lich. C of Ch Ch Tunstall 40-43; Ch Ch E Greenwich 43-48; Wimbledon (in c of St Jo Bapt) 48-50; V of St Bart Camberwell 50-54; Rushton Spencer 54-60; Hanford 60-64; R of Ch Eaton 64-70. *10 Newquay Avenue, Weeping Cross, Stafford.* (Stafford 662870)

CORMACK, Wilfrid Howard. b 1887. Univ of Man BA 09, MA 10. Wycl Hall Ox 10. **d** 12 **p** 13 Ripon. C of H Trin Ripon 12-15; Thornthwaite w Braithwaite 16-19; w CA Egypt and Palestine 17-18; Ch Ch Cockermouth 19-21; PC of Mallerstang 21-24; Mungrisdale 24-31; V of Bampton (w Mardale from 35) 31-49; Leck 49-61; L to Offic Dio Carl 62-68. *16 Westwood Road, SW 13.*

CORNECK, Warrington Graham. b 35. Clifton Th Coll. **d** 65 **p** 66 Lon. C of St Jude Mildmay Pk Islington 65-67; St Mary Southgate Crawley (in c of St Andr Furnace Green) Chich 67-73; P-in-c of St Luke Deptford 73-76; V of St Nich (w Ch Ch to 76 and St Luke from 76) Deptford Dio S'wark from 73. *41 Creek Road, SE8 3BU.* (01-692 2749)

CORNELIO, Antonio. b 40. **d** 68 Argent **p** 71 Parag for Argent. P Dio Argent 68-73; N Argent from 73. *Parsonage, Yuto, N Argentina.*

CORNELIUS, Canon Cecil Ryan. Univ of Rang BA 40. **d** 42 **p** 44 Lah. Asst Chap Bp Cotton Sch Simla 42-43; Moghalpura 43-47; St Andr w St Osw Lah 47-49; R of Dunoon 49-52; Mullumbimby 53-76; Hon Can of Graft 70-76; Can (Emer) from 76; Perm to Offic Dio Graft from 76. *Newrybar, Bangalow, NSW, Australia 2479.*

CORNELIUS, Donald Bruce. St Jo Coll Morpeth ACT ThL (2nd cl) 57. **d** 57 **p** 58 Adel. C of St Paul Naracoorte 57-59; P-in-c of Pinnaroo 59-62; R of Bordertown 62-65; C of Ch Ch St Laur Syd 65-69; R of Narrandira 69-72; Henley Beach Dio Adel from 72. *188 Military Road, Henley Beach, S Australia 5022.* (08-356 8301)

CORNELL, Frederick William. b 12. St Coll Coll Ox BA (Engl) 34, MA 38. Wells Th Coll 38. **d** 40 **p** 41 Wakef. C of Birkenshaw w Hunsworth 40-42; St Thomas on the Bourne Farnham 43-44; Chap RNVR 44-48; C of St Kath Southbourne-on-Sea 48-50; R of Easthampstead 50-53; Chieveley w Winterbourne Oare and Curridge 53-56; Bathealton w Stawley and Kittisford 56-60; R of Puckington w Stocklynch (w Bradon from 64) 61-77; V of Barrington 61-77; Perm to Offic Dio Ex from 79. *Pinneys Cottage, Chardstock, Axminster, Devon.* (S Chard 20883)

CORNELL, John Lister. b 12. St Pet Hall Ox BA 34, MA 39. Wycl Hall Ox 35. **d** 35 **p** 36 S'wark. C of St Anne Bermondsey 35-40; Putney 40-44; R of Spexhall w Wissett 44-53; Mickleham 53-78. *Staddles, Windmill Hill, Ashill, Ilminster, TA19 9NT.* (0823 480012)

CORNELL, Neil. b 45. Ripon Coll Cudd 79. **d** 81 Guildf. C of Gt Bookham Dio Guildf from 81. *19 The Lorne, Bookham, Leatherhead, Surrey, KT23 4JY.* (Bookham 53729)

CORNES, Andrew Charles Julian. b 49. CCC Ox BA 70, BA (Th) 72. St Jo Coll Dur Dipl Th 73. Cranmer Hall Dur 72. **d** 73 **p** 74 York. C of St Mich-le-Belfrey w H Trin York 73-76; Dir of Training & C of All S Langham Place St Marylebone Dio Lon from 76. *12 De Walden Street, W1M 7PH.*

CORNES, Canon James. b 1898. Qu Coll Ox BA (3rd cl Cl Mods) 21, Dipl Th (w Distinc) 22, MA 25. MC w bar 18. **d** 23 **p** 24 Ripon. C of St Bart (in c of St Dunstan) Armley 23-26; St Andr (in c of St Phil) Rugby 26-28; V of St Marg Cov 28-44; R of Harborough Magna 44-58; R of Churchover 44-58; RD of Rugby 49-56; Hon Can of Cov 51-65; Can (Emer) from 65; V of Leek Wootton 58-65. *Flat 1, Heathlands, Alma Lane, Sidmouth, Devon.*

CORNESS, Dennis William. Univ of Alta BSc 53. St Jo Coll Winnipeg LTh 60. **d** 60 **p** 61 Athab. C of Wembley 60-62; I of Boyle 62-65; All SS Vancouver 65-69; on leave. *2648 Oxford Street, Vancouver, BC, Canada.*

CORNESS, Leslie Albert. Em Coll Sktn LTh 54, BA 61. **d** 54 **p** 55 Edmon. C of All SS Cathl Edmon 54-56; V of Drayton Valley 56-57; Frobisher Bay 57-61; C of H Trin Edmon 61-62; St John Woking 62-63; Chap Miss to Seamen Rotterdam 63-64; Lagos 64-65; Area Sec Berks 65-66; C of Stoneycroft 66-67; Perm to Offic Dio Edmon from 76. *9908-108th Street, Fort Saskatchewan, Alta, Canada.*

CORNEY, Peter James. Ridley Coll Melb ACT ThL 62. **d** 63 Bp Sambell for Melb **p** 64 Melb. C of Doncaster 63-65; St Hilary Kew 65-67; Dioc Youth Chap Dio Melb 67-73; C of H Trin Doncaster 73-75; I of St Hilary Kew Dio Melb from 75. *John Street, Kew, Vic, Australia 3101.* (03-80 1546)

CORNISH, Anthony. b 30. Roch Th Coll 64. **d** 67 Barking for Chelmsf **p** 68 Chelmsf. C of Goodmayes 67-71; Buckhurst Hill 71-73; V of St Andr Westcliff-on-Sea Dio Chelmsf from 73. *65 Electric Avenue, Westcliff-on-Sea, Essex, SS0 9NN.* (Southend-on-Sea 42868)

CORNISH, Canon Basil Desmond. b 22. Clare Coll Cam BA 48, MA 50. Ridley Hall Cam 48. **d** 50 **p** 51 Derby. C of Norton 50-52; CF (TA) 51-62; C of Chelmsf Cathl 52-57; Prec 53-57; V of St Jo Evang Seven Kings 57-62; Selection Sec CACTM 62-66; R of Danbury 66-81; Exam Chap to Bp of Chelmsf from 67; Dioc Dir of Ordinands 67-72; RD of

Chelmsf 78-81; Hon Can of Chelmsf from 78; V of S Weald Dio Chelmsf from 81. *South Weald Vicarage, Brentwood, Essex, CM14 5QP.* (Brentwood 212054)

CORNISH, Canon Edward Maurice John. b 14. TD 51. Qu Coll Birm 46. **d** 48 **p** 49 St Alb. C of Hatfield 48-50; R of Gt Bircham w Bircham Newton and Bircham Tofts 50-56; V of St Geo Chorley 56-70; Hon Chap to Bp of Blackb 66-70; Commiss Bloemf 68-79; R of Ribchester w Stydd 70-78; Dom Chap to Bp of Blackb 70-78; Hon Can of Blackb 74-81; Can (Emer) from 81. *16 Ripon Road, Ansdell, Lytham St Anne's, Lancs, FY8 4DS.*

CORNISH, Francis John. b 14. Hertf Coll Ox BA 36, MA 42. Wycl Hall Ox 37. **d** 38 **p** 39 Cant. C of Shirley 38-40; Phillack w Gwithian Hayle 40-42; St Andr Plymouth 42-46; V of Buckland Monachorum 46-57; R of Edburton 57-79; R of Poynings 57-79. *Four Winds, Clapham, Worthing, Sussex, BN13 3UU.* (Patching 359)

CORNISH, John Douglas. b 42. Lich Th Coll 67. **d** 70 **p** 71 Willesden for Lon. C of L Stanmore 70-73; Harefield Dio Lon from 73. *23 High Street, Harefield, Middx, UB9 6BX.* (Harefield 2510)

CORNISH, Philip Gordon Pym. b 01. K Coll Lon AKC and Whichelow Reading Pri 25, BD 28. **d** 26 **p** 27 S'wark. C of H Trin Roehampton 26-29; C of St Steph Edmon Alta 29-31; R of Edson 31-33; C of St Jo Evang U St Leon 33-37; R of St Clem Hastings 37-44; V of Danehill 44-59; Surr 39-67; RD of Uckfield 56-59; R of L Waltham 59-67; Perm to Offic Dio Sarum from 67. *75a Penn Hill Avenue, Parkstone, Poole,* (Parkstone 747085)

CORNISH, Stanley James. b 13. AKC 39. Ely Th Coll 39. **d** 39 **p** 40 Portsm. C of H Trin Ryde 39-45; Chap RAFVR 45-48; V of St Mark Notting Hill Kens 48-54; Chap Princess Louise Hosp Lon 48-54; V of W Wycombe 54-69; Thatcham 69-79; Chap St Mary's Sch Gerrard's Cross 59-67; Perm to Offic Dio Truro & Ex from 80. *1 Quarry Cottages, Gunnislake, Cornwall, PL18 9ND.*

CORNWALL, Archdeacon of. *See* Wood, Ven Arnold.

CORNWALL, Canon John Whitmore. b 1900. Cudd Coll 29. **d** 31 **p** 32 S'wark. C of Streatham 31-33; UMCA Miss Dio Masasi 33-54; V of Gorsley w Cliffords Mesne 55-59; Minchinhampton 59-72; Hon Can of Glouc 69-74; Can (Emer) from 74. *The Orchard House, Park Road, Stroud, Glos.*

✠ **CORNWALL, Right Rev Nigel Edmund.** b 03. CBE 55. Or Coll Ox BA (3rd cl Mod Hist) 26, MA 30. Cudd Coll 26. **d** 27 **p** 28 Dur. C of St Columba Southwick 27-30; Dom Chap to Bp of Colom 31-38; Perm to Offic at St Wilfrid Brighton 38-39; UMCA Miss Dio Masasi 39-49; Hd Master of Chidya 44-49; Cons Ld Bp of Borneo in Westmr Abbey 1 Nov 49 by Abp of Cant; Bps of Lon; Win; S'wark; Glouc; Truro; Derby; Sarum; Ely; Cov; Newc T; and Brech; Bps Suffr of Willesden; and Knaresborough; and Bps Carey; Carpenter-Garnier; Roberts; Risdale; and Hollis; res 62; Asst Bp in Win and Can Res of Win 63-73; Commiss Kuch from 63. *The Hermitage, Cheriton Road, Winchester, SO22 5HW.* (Win 64518)

CORNWALL-JONES, Canon Guy Rupert. b 30. Jes Coll Cam BA 54, MA 59. Westcott Ho Cam 55. **d** 57 **p** 58 Lich. C of Longton 57-60; St Chad Cov 60-64; R of Weddington w Caldecote Dio Cov from 64; RD of Nuneaton from 79; Hon Can of Cov Cathl from 80. *Weddington Rectory, Church Lane, CV10 0EX.* (Nuneaton 386028)

CORNWELL, Christopher Richard. b 43. Univ of Dur BA 67. Cudd Coll 67. **d** 69 **p** 70 Lich. C of Cannock 69-75; C-in-c of Hadley 75-80; V 80-81; Dom Chap to Bp of Lich from 81. *14a The Close, Lichfield, Staffs, WS13 7LD.* (Lich 51231)

CORNWELL, Peter Raphael. b 34. Late Scho of Worc Coll Ox BA (2nd cl Th) 57. Cudd Coll 57. **d** 59 **p** 60 York. C of St Mich AA Hull 59-62; Cuddesdon 62-66; Chap Cudd Coll 62-65; Vice-Prin 65-66; PC of Silksworth 66-68; V 68-72; Barnard Castle 72-75; St Mary Virg w St Cross and St Pet-in-the-E City and Dio Ox from 75; Exam Chap to Bp of Ox from 79. *12 Mansfield Road, Oxford, OX1 3TA.* (Oxford 59676)

CORNWELL, Canon Reginald George. b 09. St Edm Hall Ox BA (3rd cl Mod Hist) 31, Dipl Th 32, MA 35. Cudd Coll 32. **d** 33 **p** 34 Portsm. C of Ch of Ascen Portsea 33-36; Stoke-On-Trent (in c of St Paul) 36-40; V of Pleshey 40-46; Surr 46-59; R of Warsop w Sookholm 46-55; V of Bawtry w Austerfield 55-59; V of Misson 55-59; RD of Bawtry 55-59; V of St Andr (w St Luke from 62) Grimsby 59-68; V of St Luke Grimsby 59-62; Proc Conv Linc 64-70; Can Res Newc T and Industr and Commun Adv to Bp of Newc T 68-76; Hon Can from 76; M Gen Syn Newc T 70-75; Perm to Offic Dios Newc T and Dur from 76. *Sherburn House, Durham, DH1 2SE.* (Durham 720205)

CORRADINE, John. St Aid Coll. **d** 58 **p** 59 Ches. C of Tarporley 58-61; Wilmslow 61-64; V of Moulton Dio Ches from 64. *Moulton Vicarage, Northwich, Chesh.* (Winsford 3355)

CORRELL, Canon Roger Sinclair. St Barn Coll Adel 35. ACT ThL 37. **d** 38 **p** 39 Adel. C of Ch Ch Mt Gambier 38-40; P-in-c of Penola and Chap AMF 40-51; Chap RAAF 41-46; R of Kadina and of Wallaroo 46-54; Ch Ch Cathl and Can of Bal 54-58; R of Hawthorn 58-75; Hon Can of Adel from 70; L to Offic Dio Adel from 75. *68 Monmouth Street, Westbourne Park, Adelaide, Australia 5041.* (71 9037)

CORREY, William Henry. b 14. Univ of Liv BA (2nd cl Hist) 37. ALCD 49. **d** 49 **p** 50 Liv. C of St Helens 49-52; Claughton w Grange 52-54; V of Lawkholme 54-58; Westgate-on-Sea 58-66; PC (V from 68) of St Gabr, Bp Wearmouth 66-73; R of Gt Parndon 73-80; V of Hatfield Broad Oak and Bush End Dio Chelmsf from 80. *Hatfield Broad Oak Vicarage, Bishop's Stortford, Herts.* (Hatfield Broad Oak 274)

CORRICK, Peter David. b 33. Univ of Bris BA 54. ACP 75. **d** 67 **p** 68 B & W. C of Wedmore 67-69; Westbury-sub-Mendip 69-77; Perm to Offic Dio B & W 77-78; L to Offic 78-80; C of Rodney-Stoke w Draycott Dio B & W from 80. *Sedany, The Street, Draycott, Cheddar, BS27 3TH.* (Cheddar 742742)

CORRIE, John. b 48. Univ of Lon BSc 69, MSc 70, PhD 73, Dipl Th (Extra-Mural Stud) 77. Trin Coll Bris 74. **d** 77 Penrith for Carl. C of St Thos Kendal 77-80; Attenborough w Toton Dio Southw from 80. *120 Seaburn Road, Toton, Beeston, NG9 6HJ.* (Long Eaton 5655)

CORRIE, Paul Allen. b 43. St Jo Coll Nottm 77. **d** 79 **p** 80 York. C of Beverley Minster Dio York from 79. *38 Highgate, Beverley, N Humb, HU17 0DN.*

CORRIGAN, Ven Thomas George. b 28. Trin Coll Dub 56. **d** 58 **p** 59 Kilm. C of Cavan and Drung 58-60; I of Drung 60-67; St Mich Belf 67-70; Enniskeen (Kingscourt) Dio Meath from 70; Archd of Meath from 81. *St Ernan's Rectory, Kingscourt, Co Cavan, Irish Republic.* (Dundalk 67255)

CORSER, Peter Robert Mosse. b 18. Bps' Coll Cheshunt 47. **d** 49 **p** 50 Wakef. C of Lindley 49-51; Morley 51-54; Miss at Seoul 54-56; Sang Chu 56; on leave 57-58; C of Seacroft 58-60; V of St Alb Rochdale 60-66; R of Wainfleet 66-74; V of St Mary Wainfleet 66-74; Holland Fen w Amber Hill and Chap Hill 74-80; R of Westborough w Dry Doddington and Stubton w Claypole Dio Linc from 81. *Rectory, Rectory Lane, Claypole, Newark, Notts. Claypole 224)*

CORSON, John Henry. b 38. Canberra Coll of Min 77. **d** 79 **p** 80 C & Goulb. C of St John Canberra Dio C & Goulb from 79. *1 Amaroo Street, Reid, ACT, Australia 2601.*

CORSTON, Thomas Alexander. b 49. Lakehead Univ Ont Ba 72. Wycl Coll Tor MDiv 75. **d** 74 **p** 75 Moos. C of St John Foleyet 74-75; I 76-78; Long Lac Dio Moos from 78. *Box 635, Long Lac, Ont, Canada.*

CORTEEN, Robert. b 18. Coll of the Resurr Mirfield 77. **d** 79 **p** 80 Man (APM). Hon C of St Clem Chorlton-cum-Hardy Dio Man from 79. *23 Meadow Bank, Manchester, M21 2EF.* (061-881 1118)

COSENS, William Edward Hyde. Lich Th Coll 61. **d** 64 **p** 65 Lon. C of W Drayton 64-68; Roehampton 68-70; Chap Miss to Seamen Vic Dk Lon 70; Rotterdam 70-72; Tilbury 72-76; Dampier Seafarers Centre NW Austr 76-81; Auckland Flying Angel Club from 81. *Box 465, Auckland, NZ.* (734-352)

COSH, Roderick John. b 56. Univ of Lon BSc 78. St Steph Ho Ox 78. **d** 81 Bris. C of Swindon New Town Dio Bris from 81. *St Saviour's House, Ashford Road, Swindon, Wilts, SN1 3NR.*

COSSAR, David Vyvyan. b 1934. Univ of Lon BA 63. Chich Th Coll 63. **d** 65 **p** 66 Lon. C of St Matt U Clapton 65-68; Withycombe Raleigh w Exmouth 68-72; Team V of All SS Exmouth 72; V of St Francis Honicknowle Plymouth 72-78; Brixham w Churston Ferrers Dio Ex from 78. *Vicarage, Durleigh Road, Brixham, Devon, TQ5 9JJ.* (Brixham 4924)

COSSAR, John Robert Mackenzie. b 26. Oak Hill Th Coll. **d** 56 **p** 57 Chelmsf. C of Rainham 56-59; St Mary-in-Castle and of Em Hastings 59-61; C-in-c of Madehurst Dio Chich 61-62; V from 62; Bp's Youth Chap Dio Chich 61-78; P-in-c of Slindon w Eartham Dio Chich from 81. *Slindon Rectory, Arundel, Sussex.* (Slindon 275)

COSSERAT, Algernon Willford Peloquin. b 15. Hatf Coll Dur LTh 37, BA 38, St Aug Coll Cant 34. **d** 38 **p** 39 Dur. C of St Cuthb Hebburn 38-42; Boldon 42-45; V of St Aid Gateshead 45-50; PC of Hebburn-on-Tyne 50-68; R of Boldon 68-79; Hon C of Swanage 79-81. *34 Taunton Avenue, Northampton.*

COSSINS, John Charles. b 43. Univ of Hull BSc 65. Oak Hill Th Coll 65. **d** 67 Bp McKie for Cov **p** 68 Cov. C of St Jo Evang Kenilworth 67-70; C of St Geo Huyton 70-73; Team V of Maghull 73-79; Chap Oakwood Hosp Maidstone from 79. *28 Silverdale, Barming, Maidstone, ME16 9JG.* (Maidstone 29829)

COSSINS, Roger Stanton. b 40. K Coll Lon and Warm BD and AKC 67. **d** 68 **p** 69 Ripon. C of Bramley Yorks 68-71; West End 71-76; V of Bramley Dio Win from 76. *Bramley Vicarage, Basingstoke, Hants, RG26 5DQ.* (Basingstoke 881373)

COSSLETT, Desmond Neil. b 44. Ripon Hall Ox 68. **d** 71 Warrington for Liv **p** 72 Liv. C of West Derby 71-76; Team V of Gateacre Dio Liv from 76. *St Mark's Vicarage, Cranwell Road, Liverpool, L25 1NX.* (051-487 9634)

COSSLETT, Ronald James. b 38. St D Coll Lamp Dipl Th 70. **d** 70 **p** 71 Mon. C of St Teilo Newport 70-74; St Barn Epsom 74-78; Shrewsbury 78-80; V of Smallthorne Dio Lich from 80. *Smallthorne Vicarage, Stoke-on-Trent, Staffs.* (S-on-T 85941)

COSTELLOE, Ven Alfred George. Ch Coll Tas ACT ThL 45. **d** 45 Tas **p** 46 River. C of St D Cathl Hobart 45-46; Cerby 46-50; R of Wynyard 50-67; Ulverstone 67-69; Archd of Darwin from 67; Launceston from 70; R of Carrick Dio Tas from 69. *Rectory, Carrick, Tasmania 7257.* (003-93 6120)

COSTELOE, Frederick John. b 14. Trin Coll Dub BA 41, MA 45. **d** 40 Carl **p** 41 Penrith for Carl. C of H Trin w Ch Ch Whitehaven 40-42; Chap RAFVR 42-46; C of St Nich Blundellsands 46-47; V of N Grimston w Wharram Percy and Wharram-le-Street 48-51; Lawkholme 51-54; St John Bowling 54-60; Kewstoke (w Milton 60-65) 60-75; Brent Knoll 75-80. *3 Regency Close, Burnham-on-sea, Somt.*

COSTER, Ven Arthur Selwyn. K Coll Halifax NS BA 23, MA 24, DD 61. **d** 26 **p** 27 Fred. C of Moncton 26-29; Sen Master Rothesay Colleg Sch 29-39; R of Ch Ch St Anne's Fred 39-69; Exam Chap to Bp of Fred 39-72; Can of Fred 51-60; Archd of Fred 60-70; Archd (Emer) from 70. *165 Parkside Drive, Fredericton, NB, Canada.*

COSTERTON, Alan Stewart. b 40. Univ of Bris BA (2nd cl Th) 67. Clifton Th Coll 67. **d** 69 **p** 70 S'wark. C of Peckham 69-73; St Sav Forest Gate w St Matt W Ham 73-76; Team V (in c of St Matt) 76-79; V of Thornton w Bagworth Dio Leic from 79. *Thornton Vicarage, Leicester, LE6 1AF.* (Bagworth 268)

COSTERTON, John Henry Fisher. Univ of BC BA 60. Angl Th Coll BC LTh 63. **d** 63 Koot **p** 64 Edmon for Koot. C of Ch Ch Edmon 63-65; V of Windermere 65-70; P-in-c of Grand Forks 71-78; Quesnel Dio Carib from 78. *481 Nadeau Street, Quesnell, BC, Canada.*

COSTIN, Arthur John. b 10. Selw Coll Cam BA 35, MA 39. Ely Th Coll 35. **d** 36 **p** 37 S'wark. C of Newington 36-38; St Paul (in c of St Mary Virg) Camberley 38-50; V of St Jo Bapt W Byfleet Guildf 50-72; Chap Commun of St Jo the Evang St Davids 72-78; Perm to Offic Dio St D from 72. *3 St Non's Close, St Davids, Dyfed.*

COTGROVE, Alan Edward. b 26. K Coll Lon and Warm AKC 51. M SSJE 58. **d** 52 **p** 53 Lon. C of St Cuthb Earl's Court 52-55; Perm to Offic Dio Ox 56-58; L to Offic Dio Ox 58-62; and 65-76; Dio Bom 62-65; Dio Lon from 76. *22 Great College Street, SW1P 3QA.* (01-222 9234)

COTGROVE, Edwin John. b 23. Kelham Th Coll **d** 47 **p** 48 Bris. C of St Jude w St Matt Bris 47-50; St Geo Southall 50-52; R and Dir of Odendaalsrus 52-56; Chap St Mark's Sch Mbabane 56-57; V of St Mich AA Bromley by Bow 57-64; All SS Hampton 64-82; RD of Hamptn 72-82; V of Linton Dio Cam from 82; R of Bartlow Dio Cam from 82. *Vicarage, Linton, Cambs, CB1 6JX.* (Cam 891291)

COTGROVE, Norman James. CCC Cam BA 53, MA 57. Kelham Th Coll. **d** 50 Bp Walsh for Ely **p** 51 Ely. L to Offic Dio Ely 50-53; Chap of Peterho Cam 53; C of Cherry Hinton 53-60; R of Ashingdon w S Fambridge 60-80; P-in-c of Wakes Colne w Chappel Dio Chelmsf from 80; Gt Tey Dio Chelmsf from 80. *Rectory, Colchester Road, Wakes Colne, Colchester, CO6 2BY.* (Earls Colne 2385)

COTMAN, John Sell Granville. b 44. St Jo Coll Dur BA 69. Sarum Wells Th Coll 70. **d** 73 Man **p** 74 Hulme for Man. C of Leigh 73-76; C-in-c of H Trin Coldhurst, Oldham 76-78; Team V of Oldham Dio Man from 78. *The Flat, St Andrew's Parish Hall, Winterbottom Street, Oldham, Gtr Man.* (061-620 8901)

COTTEE, Christopher Paul. b 54. Univ of Newc T BSc 75. Wycl Hall Ox 77. **d** 80 Liv **p** 81 Warrington for Liv. C of Woolton Dio Liv from 80. *School Cottage, Church Road South, Woolton, Liverpool L25.*

COTTER, Bernard. b 17. Lon Coll of Div 66. **d** 68 **p** 69 Guildf. C of Farnborough Hants 68-71; V of Okewood and Forest Green 71-77; Ottershaw Dio Guildf from 77. *Ottershaw Vicarage, Chertsey, Surrey, KT16 0PA.* (Ottershaw 3160)

COTTER, Charles Graham. Trin Coll Tor BA 46, MA 47, PhD 52, LTh 58. **d** 57 **p** 58 Tor. Hon C of St Simon Tor 57-65; Executive Sec Tor Dioc Coun for Soc Serv 58-65; R of St Mark Parkdale City and Dio Tor from 65; Dir of Dioc Marriage Serv from 65. *27 Tyndall Avenue, Toronto 3, Ont., Canada.* (416-535 8240)

COTTER, Graham Michael. b 50. Coll of N Wales (Bangor) BA 72. Ridley Hall Cam 75. **d** 78 **p** 79 Guildf. C of Headley 78-81; St Andr Plymouth Dio Ex from 81. *117 Lipson Road, Lipson, Plymouth, Devon.* (Plymouth 661334)

COTTER, James England. b 42. G and C Coll Cam BA 64, MA 67. Linc Th Coll 65. **d** 67 **p** 68 Man. C of St Matt Stretford 67-70; Lect Linc Th Coll 70-73; L to Offic Dio Lon 73-74; Chap Gonville and Caius Coll Cam 74-77; C of Leavesden Dio St Alb from 77. *1 Kingswood Road, Watford, Herts, WD2 6EE.* (Garston 73129)

COTTER, James Myrtle. b 12. Wycl Hall Ox 66. **d** 67 **p** 68 Ex. C of Lydford w Bridestowe and Sourton 67-69; V of Stockland w Dalwood 69-73; Santan 73-77; Sec Dioc Syn S & M 73-77; C of Malborough w S Huish Dio Ex from 78. *26 Weymouth Park, Hope Cove, Kingsbridge, Devon.*

COTTER, John Beresford Dolmage. b 20. Trin Coll Dub BA and Div Test (1st cl) 47, BD 55. **d** 47 **p** 48 Down. C of Glencraig 47-49; Chap in N Chile and Bolivia 49-53; Lobitos Oilfields Peru 53; R of Tempo N Ireland 54-55; Garrison 55-60: I of Donagh 60-67; Dromore 67-69; Can of Clogh 62-69; Donaghmore in St Patr Cathl Dub 69; Exam Chap to Bp of Clogh 62-69; Dir of Ordins Dio Clogh 62-69; V of Bahrain 69-75; V of Zennor Dio Truro from 76; Towednack Dio Truro from 76. *Vicarage, Zennor, St Ives, Cornw, TR26 3BY.* (Penzance 796955)

COTTIER, John Ballantyne Cameron. Univ of Queensld BA 75. Ridley Coll Melb ACT ThL 59. **d** 60 **p** 61 Melb. C of Coburg 60-61; Footscray 61-62; Miss P at Kumbun 62-65; Simbai 65-68; Dir of Relig Educn New Guinea 68-73; I of E Bentleigh 73-78; Dir Dept of Chr Educn Dio Melb from 78. *53 Drummond Street, Carlton, Vic, Australia 3053.* (347 7788)

COTTINGHAM, Peter John Garnet. b 24. Wadh Coll Ox BA 48, MA 50. Ridley Hall Cam 48. **d** 50 **p** 51 Ches. C of St Mary Cheadle 50-55; R of St Clem Ox 55-68; V of Ch Ch Mymms Barnett 68-81; St Pet w Ch Ch & H Trin City and Dio Derby from 81. *16 Farley Road, Derby, DE3 6BX.* (Derby 47821)

COTTINGHAM, Ronald Frederick. Bps' Coll Cheshunt 55. **d** 58 **p** 59 St Alb. C of Biscot 58-60; Bushey Heath 60-64; C-in-c of St Giles Conv Distr Enfield 64-68; C of K Chas Mart S Mymms 68-69; R of Hardwycke Dio Pet from 70; V of Mears Ashby Dio Pet from 70. *Vicarage, Mears Ashby, Northampton, NN6 0EE.* (Northn 810298)

COTTON, Canon John Alan. b 24. Qu Coll Ox BA (2nd Cl Phil Pol and Econ) 48, 2nd cl Th 49. MA 52. Chich Th Coll 50. **d** 51 **p** 52 Sheff. C of Doncaster 51-54; Ifield 54-56; C-in-c and Seq of Jevington 56-57; R 57-60; Chief Org Sec SPCK 60-63; Chap Univ of Sussex 63-69; V of Fairwarp Dio Chich from 69; Dir of Educn Dio Chich 72-78; Can and Preb of Chich Cathl from 72; Exam Chap to Bp of Chich from 75; Bp's Adv on Min and Dir of Ordinands from 79. *Fairwarp Vicarage, Uckfield, Sussex, TN22 3BL.* (Nutley 2277)

COTTON, John Horace Brazel. b 28. St Jo Coll Cam BA 50, MA 76. MIMechE. St Alb Min Tr Scheme 78. **d** 81 St Alb. C of L Berkhamsted w Bayford, Essendon and Ponsbourne Dio St Alb from 81. *49 Sherrardspark Road, Welwyn Garden City, Herts.*

COTTON, John Kenneth. b 25. Westcott Ho Cam 57. **d** 58 **p** 59 Linc. C of S Ormsby 58-61; R of Wrentham w Benacre Covehithe and Henstead 61-68; Sotterley w Willingham 63-68; R of Shadingfield 63-68; P-in-c of Port Alice and Port McNeil BC 68-69; L to Offic Dio BC 69-71; V in Sandringham Group 71-76; P-in-c of Assington Dio St E from 80; Newton Dio St E from 80; L Cornard Dio St E from 80. *Assington Vicarage, Colchester.* (Boxford 210485)

COTTON, John Wallis. b 31. Wells Th Coll 57. **d** 59 **p** 60 Lon. C of Stepney 59-64; All SS Hanworth 63-67; V of St Sav Hammersmith 67-74; Lancing w coombes Dio Chich from 74. *63 Manor Road, Lancing, West Sussex.* (Lancing 3212)

COTTON, Norman Joseph. b 39. Kelham Th Coll 59. **d** 64 **p** 65 Dur. C of St Helen Bp Auckland 64-67; St Chris Withington 67-68; Hucknall Torkard 69-71; Team V (in c of St Pet and St Paul) 71-73; Fenny Stratford 73-81; P-in-c of Broughton w Milton Keynes Dio Ox from 81; Wavendon w Walton Dio Ox from 81. *Broughton Rectory, Milton Keynes, MK10 9AA.* (Pineham 5298)

COTTON, Patrick Arthur William. b 46. Univ of Essex BA (1st cl) 67. Linc Th Coll 68. **d** 71 Thetford for Nor **p** 72 Nor. C of St Anne, Earlham Nor 71-73; Chap Downing Coll Cam 73-78; V of Eaton Socon Dio St Alb from 78. *19 Bushmead Road, Eaton Socon, Huntingdon, Cambs, PE19 3BP.* (Huntingdon 212219)

COTTON, Peter John. b 45. BNC Ox BA 66. Cudd Coll 67. **d** 69 Hulme for Man **p** 70 Man. C of St Phil w St Steph, Salford 69-73; Asst Educn Officer St Alb 73-75; C of St Geo E Bris 75-76; P-in-c of St Geo Conv Distr Portsea 76-80; Dioc

Social Responsibility Adv Dio Portsm from 78. *Rectory, Bones Lane, Buriton, Petersfield, GU31 5SE.* (Petersfield 2012)

COTTON, Richard William. b 35. Hertf Coll Ox BA 58, MA 62. Clifton Th Coll 58. **d** 60 **p** 61 Chelmsf. C of St Pet Harold Wood 60-64; Higher Openshaw 64-67; N Trav Sec Ch Youth Fellowships Assoc and Pathfinders 67-71; L to Offic Dio Man 67-71; Sec CPAS Pathfinders 71-76; L to Offic Dio St Alb 73-76; V of Ch Ch Chislehurst Dio Roch from 76. *Vicarage, Lubbock Road, Chislehurst, Kent.* (01-467 3185)

COTTON, Roy William. b 29. Jes Coll Ox BA 53, MA 61. Chich Th Coll 66. **d** 66 **p** 67 Portsm. C of Eastney 66-71; R of Harting 71-74; P-in-c & Seq of St Andr Eastbourne Dio Chich 74-76; V from 76. *St Andrew's Vicarage, 425 Seaside, Eastbourne, Sussex, BN22 7RT.* (Eastbourne 23739)

COTTRELL, Bertram Lionel. b 23. Lich Th Coll 51. **d** 54 **p** 56 Glouc. C of Lynworth 54-56; St Aldate Glouc 56-57; Gt Yarmouth (in c of St Luke) 57-58; Mill Hill 58-61; Christchurch (in c of Mudeford) 61-63; V of St Jo Bapt Isleworth Dio Lon from 63. *Vicarage, St John's Road, Isleworth, Middx.* (01-560 4916)

COTTRELL, Francis St John. b 02. St Chad's Coll Dur BA 27, Dipl Th 28, MA 30. **d** 28 **p** 29 Mon. C of St Jo Bapt Newport 28-38; PC of St Mark Lakenham 38-69; V of St John de Sepulchre Nor 54-61; Perm to Offic Dio Ches 69-70; Dio Nor from 70. *24 Neville Street, Norwich, NR2 2PR.*

COTTRELL-DORMER, Harry Clement Upton. **d** 42 **p** 43 Syd. C of Kangaroo Valley 42-43; R 43-44; CMS Miss 44-46; Perm to Offic Dio Syd 46-50 and 56-73; C-in-c of Wilberforce Par Distr 50-53; C of Ryde 55-56; Ch Ch Blacktown 73-76; L to Offic Dio Syd from 76. *24 Statham Avenue, Faulconbridge, NSW, Australia 2776.* (047-513178)

COUCH, Andrew Nigel. b 48. K Coll Lon BD and AKC 70. St Aug Coll Cant 70. **d** 71 **p** 72 Truro. C of St Ives 71-74; St Martin-in-the-Fields Trafalgar Sq 74-78; USPG Miss Argent from 78. *Duart House, Montevideo, Uruguay.*

COUCHMAN, Anthony Denis. b 37. Sarum Th Coll 66. **d** 69 Colchester for Chelmsf **p** 70 Chelmsf. C of St Francis of Assisi Barkingside 69-71; C of Chingford (in c of St Francis) 71-76; P-in-c of St Barn w St Jas Gtr Walthamstow Dio Chelmsf 76-80; V from 80. *Vicarage, St Barnabas Road, E17 8JZ.* (01-520 5323)

COUCHMAN, Maurice Lionel. b 1891. Qu Coll Cam BA 13, MA 16. Bp's Hostel, Farnham 14. **d** 15 **p** 16 Ox. C of Binfield 15-21; TCF 17-19; R of Heidelberg Transv 21-24; V of Bezuidenhout Valley Johann 24-25; C of St Mary Eastbourne 26-29; Hon CF 19-28; CF (R of O) 28-50; Hon CF 50; Chap Qu Alex Hosp Roehampton 30-33; V of Raynes Pk 29-36; Kingsthorpe 36-45; Broadwater Down 45-59; RD of Etchingham 51-57; Surr 53-58. *22 Allington Road, Newick, Lewes, Sussex.* (Newick 2204)

COULBECK, Albert Edward. b 06. AKC 34. Linc Th Coll 34. **d** 35 **p** 36 Pet. C of Ch Ch Northn 35-37; St Paul Jarrow 37-41; V of St Hilda Millfield 41-43; R of Creed 47-50; St Just-in-Roseland 50-69; C-in-c of Philleigh 56-69; C of Sidmouth 69-71; Publ Pr Dio Ex from 71. *16 Connaught Road, Sidmouth, Devon, EX10 8TT.*

COULING, Albert James. b 10. Linc Th Coll 43. **d** 44 **p** 45 Linc. C of Boston (in c of St Jas 45-47) 44-47; V of Long Bennington w Foston 47-59; R of Bleadon 59-78; Perm to Offic Dio B & W from 79. *36 Brockley Crescent, Bleadon Hill, Weston-s-Mare, Avon, BS24 9LL.* (Bleadon 812056)

COULING, David Charles. b 36. Qu Coll Birm 61. **d** 63 **p** 64 Birm. C of St Faith and St Laur Harborne 63-66; St Mary Virg E Grinstead 66-70; V of Copthorne 70-75; St Mich AA Eastbourne Dio Chich from 75. *35 Carew Road, Eastbourne, BN21 2JN.* (Eastbourne 24060)

COULSHAW, Leonard. b 1896. MC 17. CB 49. AKC and Whichelow Reading Pri 23. Ely Th Coll. **d** 23 **p** 24 Chelmsf. C of St Andr, Romford 23-27; Chap RN 27-52; Chap of the Fleet and Archd of the Royal Navy 47-52; Hon Chap to HM the King 48-52; HM the Queen 52; Fell of K Coll Lon from 49; V of Westend 52-54; Frensham w Dockenfield 54-65; Perm to Offic Dio Portsm 74-80. *4 Ashurst Court, Alverstoke, Gosport, Hants, PO12 2TZ.* (Gosport 82467)

COULSON, Isaiah Andrew. b 38. St Pet Coll Alice 66. **d** 69 **p** 70 Capetn. C of Matroosfontein Dio Capetn from 70. *PO Box 5, Ravensmead, CP, S Africa.*

COULSON, John Keyworth. St Jo Coll Auckld 62. **d** 63 **p** 64 Auckld. C of Manurewa 63-66; St Aid Remuera Auckld 66-67; Timaru 67-68; V of Akaroa 68-71; L to Offic Dio Wel 71-73; Hon C of Wanganui E 73-78; Offg Min Dio Wel from 78; Chap Wanganui Colleg Sch from 79. *c/o Collegiate School, Private Bag, Wanganui, NZ.* (55-932)

COULSON, Louis Morton. b 36. K Coll Lon BA (2nd cl Engl) 59. Wells Th Coll 59. **d** 61 **p** 62 S'wark. C of Ch Ch w St Andr and St Mich E Greenwich 61-64; St Paul Furzedown Streatham 64-67; PV of Truro Cathl 67-70; R of Gidleigh (w Throwleigh from 72) 70-77; P-in-c of Throwleigh 70-72; Hartland w Welcombe Dio Ex 77-80; V from 80. *Hartland Vicarage, Bideford, Devon.* (Hartland 240)

COULSON, Robert Gustavus. b 1899. Wycl Th Coll Ox 45. **d** 45 **p** 45 Roch. C of Hildenborough 45; V of St Marg Underriver 45-50; R of Stansted 50-61; Perm to Offic Dio Guildf from 61; Dio Ox from 63; Dio Glouc from 66. *The Old Vicarage, Moulsford, Wallingford, Oxon.* (Cholsey 651368)

COULSON, Thomas Stanley. b 32. Trin Coll Dub BA 54, Div Test 55, MA 68. **d** 55 **p** 56 Derry. C of Maghera 55-62; R of Aghalurcher and Tattykeeran 62-63; Woodschapel Dio Arm from 63. *Woodschapel Rectory, Magherafelt, Co Londonderry, N Ireland.* (Ballyronan 230)

COULSON, Tony Erik Frank. b 32. St Edm Hall Ox BA (3rd cl French) 55, Dipl Th 56, MA 59. Wycl Hall Ox 55. **d** 57 **p** 58 Chelmsf. C of Walthamstow 57-60; St John Reading 60-63; PC of Iver Dio Ox 63-68; V from 68. *Vicarage, Iver, Bucks, SL0 9JY.* (Iver 653131)

COULTAS, George Newham. b 10. Worc Ordin Coll 65. **d** 67 **p** 68 York. C of St Luke Thornaby-on-Tees 67-68; St Barn Linthorpe Middlesbrough 68-71; C-in-c of Carlton Miniott w Sand Hutton 71-73; Team V (w Thirsk and S Kilvington) 73-75; V of Hemingbrough 75-81. *97 Albert Avenue, Anlaby Road, Hull.* (Hull 53786)

COULTER, John James. TCD BA and Div Test (2nd cl) 32. **d** 32 **p** 33 Clogh. C of Monaghan w Tyholland 32-34; Ellesmere 34-40; CF (EC) 40-47, CF 47-57; V of Cauldon 57-78; V of Waterfall 57-78. *31 Lapworth Way, Newport, Salop.* (Newport 810230)

COULTER, Richard Samuel Scott. b 09. Univ of Dur LTh 39. Clifton Th Coll 35. **d** 38 **p** 39 Liv. C of H Trin Parr Mount 38-40; CF (EC) 40-46; C of Huyton (in c of St Gabr) 46-50; Chap to County Hosp Whiston 47-50; V of St Bridget Wavertree 50-61; Upton Snodsbury w Broughton Hackett (w Naunton Beauchamp from 72) 61-77; P-in-c of Naunton Beauchamp 70-72. *29 Greenheart Way, Southmoor, Abingdon, Oxon.*

COULTHARD, John Richard. b 11. Qu Coll Ox BA (2nd cl Mod Hist) and Holwell Stud 34, MA 39, Dipl Th 35. Bps' Coll Cheshunt 35. **d** 36 **p** 37 Truro. C of Falmouth 36-38; Porlock and Stoke Pero 38-41; Dawlish 41-42; CF (EC) 42-46; Hon CF 46; C of St Brelade (in c of St Aubin) Jersey 46-48; Leeds 48-51; Chap Leeds Gen Infirm 48-51; PC of Mungrisdale 51-56; R of Charlton-on-Otmoor 56-59; Perm to Offic Dio Ox from 62. *Box Villa, Charlton-on-Otmoor, Oxford, OX5 2UF.*

COULTHARD, Roy Edward. Univ of NZ BA 46. Moore Th Coll Syd ACT ThL 48. **d** 48 **p** 49 Ch Ch. C of Sumner 48-51; V of Malvern 51-55; Otaio w Blue Cliffs 55-59; Linc 59-67; Shirley 67-78; Woolston Dio Ch Ch from 78. *10 St John Street, Christchurch 6, NZ.* (841-737)

COULTON, David Stephen. b 41. Sarum Th Coll. **d** 67 **p** 68 Guildf. C of H Trin Guildf 67-71; Asst Chap Radley Coll Ox from 71. *Radley College, Abingdon, Oxon.*

COULTON, Nicholas Guy. b 40. Univ of Lon BD 72. Cudd Coll 65. **d** 67 **p** 68 Worc. C of Pershore 67-70; Chap to Bp of St Alb 71-75; C of St Paul Bedford Dio St Alb 75-79; V from 79. *12 The Embankment, Bedford.* (Bedford 52314)

COULTON, Philip Ernest. b 31. St Cath Coll Cam BA 54, MA 58. Trin Coll Dub BD 68. Ely Th Coll 55. **d** 57 **p** 58 Southw. C of Newark-on-Trent 57-61; Min Can and Sacr of Cant Cathl 61-63; Min Can and C of Ripon Cathl 63-68; Asst Master Ashton-u-L Gr Sch 69-80; Ashton Sixth Form Coll from 80. *63 Green Lane, Hollingworth, Hyde, Chesh, SK14 8JQ.* (Mottram 62507)

COUND, David Bryan. b 32. St D Coll Lamp BA 52. St Mich Coll Llan. **d** 55 **p** 56 Llan. C of St Fagan Aberdare 55-60; St Sav Roath 60-61; Llandaff 61-63; V of Porth 63-68; C-in-c of Englefield 68-73; R 73-75; Asst Dioc Youth Officer Ox 68-75; Tr Officer Berks Youth & Commun Service from 75; L to Offic Dio Ox from 75. *St Mark's House, Englefield, Reading, Berks.* (Reading 302227)

COUNSELL, Garth Quinton. b 53. St Paul's Grahmstn 77. **d** 79 **p** 80 Capetn. C of St John Wynberg Dio Capetn from 79. *60 Ottery Road, Wynberg 7800, CP, S Africa.*

COUNSELL, Michael John Radford. b 35. Pemb Coll Cam BA 59, MA 63. Ripon Hall Ox 59. **d** 61 **p** 62 Birm. C of Handsworth 61-63; St Andr Cathl (in c of St Pet) Sing 64-66; V of St Pet Sing 66-68; Chap Mekong (Vietnam and Cambodia) 68-72; P-in-c St Paul's Cathl Mahé Seychelles 72-73; Dean 73-76; V of Harborne Dio Birm from 76. *Harborne Vicarage, Old Church Road, Birmingham, B17 0BB.* (021-427 1949)

COUPAR, Thomas. b 50. **d** 80 Edin **p** 81 (NSM). Hon C of Haddington Dio Edin from 80; Hdmaster Pencaitland Primary Sch E Lothian 80-81; King's Meadow Sch from 81. *5 Vetch Park, Haddington, E Lothian, EH41 3LH.*

COUPE, George William Frederick. b 13. Trin Coll Cam BA 36, MA 42. Bps' Coll Cheshunt 36. **d** 38 Lon **p** 39

Willesden for Lon. C of All SS Poplar 38-42; Chap of SS Coll Cam and L to Offic Dio Ely 42-46; Chap to Papworth Village Settlement and Hosp 46-55; R of Papworth Everard 49-55; RD of Bourn 53-55; R of Somersham w Pidley-cum-Fenton and Colne 55-59; Chap HM Pris Holloway 59-63; HM Pris Win 63-68; HM Pris Reading 68-74; V of St Laur, Reading 68-74; RD of Reading 70-74; Bradfield 75-78; C-in-c of Yattendon w Frilsham 74-78. *Farley Cottage, Tas Combe Way, Willingdon, Eastbourne, E Sussex, BN20 9JA.* (Eastbourne 55526)

COUPER, Donald George. b 21. Tyndale Hall Bris 39. St Jo Coll Dur BA and LTh 44. **d** 45 **p** 46 Blackb. C of Ch Ch Blackpool 45-48; R of St Cath Collyhurst 48-52; Org Sec CPAS in NW Engl 52-55; V of Hunmanby (w Muston from 69) 55-74; C-in-c of Muston 59-69; V of Ledsham w Fairburn Dio York from 74. *11 Main Street, Ledston, Castleford, W Yorks.* (Castleford 556946)

COUPER, Jonathan George. b 51. St Jo Coll Dur Ba 73. Wycl Hall Ox 73. **d** 75 **p** 76 York. C of SS Phil & Jas Clifton York 75-78; Darfield 78-81; V of Ch Ch Bridlington Dio York from 81. *2 Quay Road, Bridlington, N Humb, YO15 2AP.* (Bridlington 73538)

COUPER, Roger Benson. Univ of NZ BA 61. NZ Bd of Th Stud LTh 62. **d** 62 Bp McKenzie for Wel **p** 63 Wel. C of Lower Hutt 62-67; W Wickham 67-68; P-in-c of Waiwhetu 68-69; V of Hunterville 69-72; Chap K Sch Auckld from 72; Hon C of St Aid Remuera Dio Auckld from 77. *c/o Kings School, Remuera Road, Auckland 5, NZ.* (501-517)

COUPLAND, Robert William Brydon. Univ of Tor BA 34. Wycl Coll Tor. **d** 37 Tor for NS **p** 38 NS. C of Country Harbour 37-42; U La Have 42-51; R of New London 51-53; Morning's Hills 53-55; Port Rowan 55-59; Meaford 59-68; Kingsville 68-74. *RR3, Bridgewater, NS, Canada.*

COURAGE, Anthony John. b 38. Angl Th Coll BC Dipl Th 71. **d** 71 **p** 72 Carib. C of U Fraser Miss 71-73; All SS Cathl Edmon 73-75; Geraldine 75-76; Ashburton 76-77; V of Oxford-Cust Dio Ch Ch from 78. *Vicarage, Church Street, Oxford, Canterbury, NZ.* (24-538)

COURAGE, John James. Mem Univ Newfld BA 77. Atlantic Sch of Th Halifax 80. **d** 81 E Newfld. C of Happy Valley Dio E Newfld. *Happy Valley, Labrador, Canada, A0P 1E0.*

COURAGE, Roy Kenneth. b 25. ACCS 63. ACIS 70. St D Coll Lamp 67. **d** 69 **p** 70 Mon. C of Blaenavon w Capel Newydd 69-71; R of Aberystruth (Blaina) 71-78; V of Blackwood Dio Mon from 78. *Vicarage, South View Road, Blackwood, Gwent, NP2 1HR.* (Blackwood 224214)

COURATIN, Canon Arthur Hubert. b 02. Late Found Scho of CCC Ox 1st cl Cl Mods 23, BA (2nd cl Lit Hum) and Haigh scho 25, 2nd cl Th 26, MA 27. St Steph Ho Ox 25. **d** 26 **p** 27 Llan. C of St Sav Roath 26-30; St Steph Lewisham 30-35; Jun Chap Mert Coll Ox 36-39; Chap of St Steph Ho Ox 35-36; Vice-Prin 36; Prin 36-62; Hon Chap to Bp of Ox 46-62; Commiss Nass 46-62; Kalg 51-67; St John's 56-77; Select Pr Univ of Cam 55; Exam Chap to Bp of S'wark 59-80; to Bp of Dur 62-67; Hon Can of Ox 61-62; Can and Libr of Dur 62-74; Can (Emer) from 74. *7 Pimlico, Durham, DH1 4QW.* (Durham 64676)

COURSE, John Earl. b 54. Brock Univ Ont BA 77. Huron Coll Lon Ont MDiv 80. **d** 80 Niag **p** 81 Bp CM Mitchell for Niag. C of St Mark Orangeville Dio Niag from 80. *c/o St Mark's Church, 5 First Avenue, Orangeville, Ont, Canada L9W 1H7.* (519-941 0640)

COURSE, John Edward. Seagar Hall Ont. **d** and **p** 61 Niag. C of Dundas 61-63; C-in-c of W Flamboro 61-65; St Brandan Port Colborne 65-71; R of Jordan 71-80; St John Weston City and Dio Tor from 80. *51 Gratton Street, Weston, M9N 3J6, Ont, Canada.*

COURT, Arthur Albert. b 12. Univ of Sask BA 37. Em Coll Sktn LTh 37. **d** 37 **p** 38 Sktn. Miss of Perdue 37-39; V of St Mary Edgerton 39-44; CF (Canad) 44-46; C of Waltham Abbey (in c of St Thos Upshire) 46-49; V of St Lawr Brentford (w St Paul from 52 w St Geo from 61) Dio Lon from 49. *3 The Butts, Brentford, Middx., TW8 8BJ.* (01-560 7411)

COURT, Denis. b 09. Wells Th Coll 47. **d** 49 **p** 50 Carl. C of Penrith 49-52; V of Holme Cultram 52-56; Milburn w Newbiggin 56-61; R of Dufton 56-61; V of Beetham 61-80. *118 Birchwood Drive, Ulverston, Cumb, LA12 9NY.*

COURT, Jack Arthur. b 14. AKC 40. **d** 40 **p** 41 S'wark. C of St Andr Stockwell Green 40-44; St Luke Kingston T 44-47; St Pet St Helier Morden (in c of Bp Andrewes's Ch) 47-51; Minehead 51-56; PC of St Mich AA Yeovil 56-66; C-in-c of Chilton Cantel w Ashington 57-66; R of Walton-in-Gordano 66-80. *14 Channel Road, Clevedon, Avon, BS21 7DR.* (Clevedon 874846)

COURT, Kenneth Reginald. b 36. K Coll Lon and Warm AKC 60. **d** 61 **p** 62 Ripon. C of Garforth 61-63; St Wilfrid Harrogate 63-65; V of Thornbury, Yorks 65-73; Prec of St Martin's Cathl Leic 73-76; L to Offic Dio Leic 73-76; V of St Matt Douglas Dio S & M from 76. *Vicarage, Alexander Drive, Douglas, IM.* (Douglas 6310)

COURTAULD, Augustine Christopher Caradoc. b 34. Trin Coll Cam Econ Trip pt i 54, BA (Th Trip pt ii) 58. Westcott Ho Cam 58. **d** 60 **p** 61 Man. C of Oldham 60-63; Chap Trin Coll Cam 63-68; Lon Hosp 68-78; V of St Paul Knightsbridge Dio Lon from 78. *32 Wilton Place, SW1X 8SH.* (01-235 1810)

COURTENAY, John Manifold. b 08. Keble Coll Ox BA 39, MA 45. Ripon Hall Ox 39 and 45. **d** 45 **p** 46 Liv. C of Warrington 45-49; V of Offley 49-55; CF (TA) from 52; C-in-c of Lilley 54-55; Chap St Edm's Sch Cant 56-60; R of Adwell w S Weston 60-64; V of Lewknor 60-64; C of S Ormsby 64-66; V of Long Buckby (w Brington 66-69; w Watford from 72) 66-75; C of St Mary Oxted Dio S'wark from 75. *41 Johnsdale, Oxted, Surrey.* (Oxted 5681)

COURTIE, John Malcolm. b 42. BNC Ox BA 65, DPhil 73. St Jo Coll Dur 74. **d** 77 **p** 78 Liv. C of St Matt & St Jas Mossley Hill 77-80; V of St Paul Hatton Hill, Litherland Dio Liv from 80. *St Paul's Vicrage, Watling Avenue, Liverpool, L21 9NU. (051-928 2705)*

COURTLEY, Alec Parker. b 27. Keble Coll Ox BA 52, MA 55. Wells Th Coll 52. **d** 54 **p** 55 Wakef. C of Brighouse 54-59; C-in-c of Lundwood Eccles Distr 59-60; V of Lundwood 60-71; R of Ackworth Dio Wakef from 71. *Rectory, Ackworth, Pontefract, Yorks.*

COURTNEY, Brian Joseph. b 44. Div Hostel Dub 70. **d** 73 **p** 74 Down. C of Willowfield Dio Down from 73. *1 Delaware Street, Belfast, N Ireland, BT6 8ET.*

COURTNEY, Michael Monlas. b 19. Coll of Resurr Mirfield 58. **d** 60 **p** 61 Lich. C of St Chad, Shrewsbury 60-63; PC (V from 68) of St Thos N Keyham, Devonport 63-73; Team V of Sidmouth, Woolbrook and Salcombe Regis (and Branscombe from 79) Dio Ex from 74. *Branscombe Vicarage, Seaton, EX12 3DW.* (Branscombe 328)

COUSINS, Herbert Ralph. b 13. Bps' Coll Cheshunt 52. **d** 54 **p** 55 St Alb. C of St Luke Leagrave Luton 54-58; R of Maulden 58-63; RD of Ampthill 62-63; C-in-c of Lewsey Conv Distr Luton 63-65; Min 65-67; V 67-70; V of Southill 70-71; R of Clophill 71-78. *Evensong, Sand Road, Sand Bay, Weston-s-Mare, Avon BS22 9UF.*

COUSINS, Philip John. b 35. K Coll Cam BA (2nd cl Mod and Med Lang Trip pt ii) 58, MA 62. Cudd Coll Ox 59. **d** 61 **p** 62 Blackb. C of Marton 61-63; PV of Truro Cathl 63-67; Chap Truro Cathl Sch 63-66; Addis Ababa 67-75; V of Henleaze Dio Bris from 75; RD of Clifton from 79. *Vicarage, The Drive, Henleaze, Bristol, BS9 4LD.* (Bristol 623196)

COUSINS, Stanley Frank. b 07. Cudd Coll 66. **d** 67 **p** 68 Chich. C of Billingshurst 67-72. *Five Ashes, The Haven, Billingshurst, Sussex.*

COUSLAND, Andrew Oliver. b 41. Edin Th Coll 62. **d** 65 **p** 66 Brech. C of Broughty Ferry 65-68; H Trin Ayr 68-70; R of Renfrew 70-75; Hon C of St Mary Stoke Ipswich 75-81. *Address temp unknown.*

COUSSENS, Mervyn Haigh Wingfield. b 47. Univ of Nottm BTh 74. St Jo Coll Nottm 70. **d** 74 **p** 75 Bris. C of Ch Ch Clifton 74-77; St Lawr Morden Dio S'wark from 77. *151 Camborne Road, Morden, Surrey.* (01-542 2966)

COUSSMAKER, Canon Colin Richard Chad. b 34. Worc Coll Ox BA 57, BSc 58, MA 63. Chich Th Coll 59. **d** 60 Win **p** 61 Southn for Win. C of St Luke, Southn 60-64; Ch Ch (in c of St Agnes), Reading 64-67; Chap at Istanbul 67-72; Sliema Malta 72-77; Antwerp Dio Gibr (Gibr in Eur from 80) from 77; Can of H Trin Cathl Brussels from 81. *39 Gretrystraat, Antwerp, Belgium.* (031-393339)

COUTTS, James Walter Cargill. b 35. St D Coll Lamp BA (2nd cl Lit, Hist and Phil) 57. CCC Cam BA (2nd cl Th Trip pt ii) 59. St Mich Coll Llan 59. **d** 60 **p** 61 Llan. C of St Mary Virg Cardiff 60-63; Gt Greenford 63-67; St Gabr Swansea 67-71; V of Llanwrtyd w Llandulas in Tir Abad and Eglwys-Oen-Duw w Llanfihangel-Abergwessin and Llanddewi 71-78; Exam Chap to Bp of Swan B from 69; V of St D Brecon (or Llanfaes) Dio Swan B from 78. *St David's Vicarage, Brecon, LD3 8DR.* (Brecon 4734)

COUTTS, John. b 13. Late Exhib of Ex Coll Ox 2nd cl Cl Mods 34, BA (2nd cl Lit Hum) 36, MA 39, BLitt 41. Ripon Hall Ox 40. **d** 40 **p** 41 Liv. C of Haigh w Aspull 40-43; Banbury 43-46; St Pet w St Swithin Bournemouth 46-52; V of Holybourne w Neatham 52-78; Exam Chap to Bp of Win 69-77; Perm to Offic Dio Ox from 79. *37 St James Close, Pangbourne, Berks, RG8 7AP.*

COUTTS, Robert Thomas. b 24. **d** 71 **p** 72 Graft. C of Kempsey w U Macleay 71-74; R of Byron Bay Dio Graft from 74. *Rectory, Byron Bay, NSW, Australia 2481.* (85 6431)

COVE, Kenneth John. b 34. Lich Th Coll 58. **d** 60 **p** 61 Wakef. C of Crosland Moor 60-63; Halifax 63-65; V of St Jo Bapt Wakef 65-73; Appleby 73-78; RD of Appleby 74-78; V of Ambleside w Brathay Dio Carl from 78. *Vicarage, Ambleside, Cumb, LA22 9DH.* (Ambleside 3205)

COVE, Tom Griffiths William. b 10. M OSB 59. **d** 64 **p** 65 Ox. L to Offic Dio Ox from 65. *Nashdom Abbey, Burnham, Bucks, SL1 8NL.*

COVENEY, John Andrews. St Jo Coll Auckld 57. NZ Bd of Th Stud LTh 60. **d** 60 **p** 61 Waik. C of Taumarunui 60-62; Matamata 62-63; V of Mokau 63-64; C of Frankton and Asst Chap Waik Publ Hosp 64-66; Asst Chap Miss to Seamen Suva 66-68; Chap Miss to Seamen in Queensld 68-72; V of Taumarunui 72-78; Otahuhu Dio Auckld from 78. *20 Mason Avenue, Otahuhu, NZ.* (64-808)

COVENTRY, Lord Bishop of. *See* Gibbs, Right Rev John.

COVENTRY, Assistant Bishop of. *See* McKie, Right Rev John David.

COVENTRY, Provost of. (Vacant).

COVENTRY, Archdeacon of. *See* Bridges, Ven Peter Sydney Godfrey.

COVENTRY, Preb Frank. b 13. K Coll Lon BA (1st cl Engl) and Geo Smith and Inglis Studs 35. Em Coll Cam PhD 42. Linc Th Coll 45. **d** 46 **p** 47 S'wark. C of All SS West Dulwich 46-48; Chap of K Coll Lon 48-53; V of St Mary Magd Enfield 53-58; RD of Enfield 56-58; St Marylebone 59-67 and 74-78; R of St Marylebone w H Trin 58-78; Exam Chap to Bp of Lon 60-73; Preb of St Paul's Cathl Lon 73-78; Preb (Emer) from 79. *2b Upper Park Road, NW3 2UP* (01-722 7298)

COVINGTON, Michael William Rock. b 38. Open Univ BA 78. Sarum Th Coll 60. **d** 63 **p** 64 Pet. C of Daventry 63-66; Woolwich 66-68; Northn 68-71; V of Longthorpe Dio Pet from 71; Hon Min Can of Pet from 75. *Longthorpe Vicarage, Thorpe Road, Peterborough, PE3 6LU.* (Pet 263016)

COWAN, Brian Alexander James. Univ of BC Angl Th Coll of BC. **d** and **p** 60 BC. I of Galiano and Mayne Is 60-63; R of St Martin-in-the-Fields Vic 63-70; R of Qualicum Beach Dio BC from 71. *Box 137, Qualicum Beach, BC, Canada.* (604-752 9571)

COWAN, Bruce Edgar. b 52. Univ of Tor BA 74. Univ of Trin Coll Tor MDiv 78. **d** and **p** 78 Queb. C of Schefferville w Matemikosh Dio Queb from 78. *CP 843, Schefferville, PQ Canada, G0G 2T0.*

COWAN, Hugh Donald. b 36. ACT ThL 68. St Mich Ho Crafers 67. **d** 68 Newc **p** 69 Armid. Chap the Armid Sch 69-72; Miss in Saigon 73-74; Novice SSF Brisb and Auckld 74-75; P-in-c of Mangere E 75-76; L to Offic Dio Waik 76; Assoc P of Hamilton Past 77-79; Chap St Paul's Colleg Sch Hamilton 79-80; City Missr Dio Auckld from 80. *Box 6779, Auckland 1, NZ.*

COWAN, James Arnold Jackson. b 51. Nashotah Ho Wisc MDiv 77. **d** 76 **p** 77 Qu'App. C of Kamsack 76; St Mich Regina Dio Qu'App from 76. *215 Smith Street North, Regina, Sask, Canada.*

COWAN, Canon Kenneth Reginald. Univ of Tor BA 40. Trin Coll Tor. **d** 41 **p** 42 Ott. C of Trin Ott 41-42; I of Combermere 42-44; R of Eganville 44-50; I of St Martin Ott 50-62; R of St Matt Winnipeg 62-71; Can of Rupld 66-71; R of Bell's Corners Dio Ott from 71; Can of Ott from 77. *3865 Richmond Road, Bell's Corners, Ottawa, Ont., Canada.* (1-613-828-0007)

COWAN, Michael Alexander. b 42. St Jo Coll Auckld 76. **d** 79 Bp Wiggins for Wel **p** 80 Wel. C of All SS Palmerston N 79-81; V of Foxton Dio Wel from 81. *PO Box 42, Foxton, NZ.*

COWAN, Canon Robert Wesley. Univ of Tor BA 35. Trin Coll Tor LTh 37. **d** 38 **p** 39 Tor. C of Stanhope 38-39; St Thos Hamilton 39-40; Ch Ch Niag Falls 40-42; Actg Warden St Chad's Coll Regina 42-43; C of Pro-Cathl Calg 43-44; V of St Mary Lethbridge (w Lethbridge N Miss 44-61) 44-81; Hon Can of Calg from 56. *1912-21st Avenue North, Lethbridge, Alta, Canada.*

COWARD, Colin Charles Malcolm. b 45. Westcott Ho Cam 75. **d** 78 **p** 79 S'wark. C of St Geo Camberwell 78-82; V of St Faith Wandsworth Dio S'wark from 82. *16 Alma Road, Wandsworth, SW18 1AA.* (01-874 8567)

COWARD, Frederic Edward. b 06. Univ of Man BA 31. Ripon Hall Ox 30. **d** 31 **p** 32 Liv. C of Mossley Hill 31-33; Perm to Offic at St Phil Liv 33-35; St Edm Sedgefield (in c of St Cath Fishburn) 35-37; V of St Clem 37-46; Probus w Cornelly 46-60; R of Moreton Dorset 60-66; V of Clyffe Pypard (w Tockenham from 73) 66-80; R of Tockenham 66-73. *Old Vicarage, Clyffe Pypard, Swindon, Wilts, SN4 7PY.* (Broad Hinton 309)

COWDREY, Herbert Edward John. b 26. Trin Coll Ox BA (1st cl Mod Hist) 49, 2nd cl Th 51, MA 51. St Steph Ho Ox 50. **d** 52 **p** 53 Ox. Tutor St Steph Ho Ox 52-54; Chap 54-56; Asst Chap Ex Coll Ox 52-56; Fell, and Tutor in Mod Hist St Edm Hall Ox from 56; Chap 56-78; Lect in Medieval Hist St Pet Coll Ox 57-68; L to Offic Dio Ox from 52. *St Edmund Hall, Oxford.* (Ox 45511)*; and 30 Oxford Road, Old Marston, Oxford.* (Ox 43360)

COWDRY, Gilbert. b 26. Wells Th Coll 70. **d** 72 **p** 73 B & W. C of Twerton-on-Avon 72-76; V of Long Sutton w Long Load Dio B & W from 76. *Long Sutton Vicarage, Langport, Somt.* (Long Sutton 260)

✠ **COWDRY, Right Rev Roy Walter Frederick.** AKC 41. **d** 41 **p** 42 Lon. C of St Nich Perivale 41-44; Ch Ch Ealing 44-50; Dom Chap to Abp of Capetn 50-57; Chap of Capetn City Pris 52-58; Cons Asst Bp of Capetn in Capetn Cathl 2 Mar 58 by Abp of Capetn; Bps of Grahmstn; Pret; George; and Bps Lavis, Peacey, and Browne; Bp Suffr from 61; res 64; Archd of the Cape 58-64; Asst Bp of Grahmstn 65-70; Asst Bp of Port Eliz from 70; R of St Cuthb Port Eliz Dio Grahmstn 64-70; Dio Port Eliz from 70; R of St Phil Port Eliz 66-68. *24 Westbourne Road, Port Elizabeth, CP, S Africa.* (041-332526)

COWELL, Arthur John. b 10. Wycl Hall Ox 40. **d** 41 **p** 42 S'wark. C of Horley 41-43; W Cheam (in c of St Alb from 44) 43-48; V of St Jas Camberwell 48-51; V of St Jo Evang Kingston Surrey 51-54; CF (TA) 53-65; Org Sec Miss to Seamen SW Engl and Publ Pr Dio Sarum 54-60; Min of St Pet Eccles Distr Prittlewell 60-63; V 63-80; Chap Southend Gen Hosp 68-80. *183 Shaftesbury Avenue, Thorpe Bay, Essex.*

COWELL, Brian. b 47. N-W Ordin Course 72. **d** 75 **p** 76 Ches. C of Timperley 75-77; Chap RAF 77-81; P-in-c of Newnham & Nately Scures and mapledurwell w Up Nateley Dio Win from 81. *Rectory, Up Nately, nr Basingstoke, Hants, RG27 9PR.* (Hook 2021)

COWELL, Dennis Aubrey. NZ Bd of Th Stud LTh 49. **d** 54 **p** 55 Waik. C of Cambridge 54-56; Chap of St Pet Sch Cambridge 54-60; Hd Master 60-61; V of Putaruru 61-63; L to Offic Dio Waik 63; Dio Wai 63-69; Dio Auckld from 69. *64 Raleigh Road, Northcote, Auckland 9, NZ.*

COWELL, Harold George Dench. b 07. AKC 34. **d** 34 **p** 35 Cant. C of Teynham 34-37; H Trin Sheerness 37-45; V of Leysdown w Harty 45-53; Brenzett w Snargate and Snave 53-62; Sholden 62-74. *2 Grassmere, St Mary's Bay, Romney Marsh, Kent.*

COWELL, Lyall John. b 49. St Francis Coll Brisb 69. **d** 72 **p** 73 N Queensld. C of Ayr 72-75; St Mark Warwick 75; V of Ch Ch St Geo 75-77; R 77-79; P-in-c of Algester Dio Brisb from 79. *Vicarage, Ormskirk Street, Calamvale, Queensland, Australia 4116.*

COWELL, Trevor Grant. Ridley Coll Melb ACT ThL (2nd cl) 62. **d** 62 Bp Barrett for Tas **p** 64 Tas. C of St John Launceston 62-66; R of Stanley Dio Tas from 66. *Rectory, Stanley, Tasmania.*

COWEN, Brian. b 45. Univ of Nottm BTh 77. Linc Th Coll 73. **d** 77 **p** 78 Newc T. C of Hexham Abbey 77-80; Ledbury 80-81; Team V of Wooler Dio Newc from 81. *2 Queen's Road, Wooler, Northumberland, NE71 6DR.*

COWEN, Peter Stewart. b 42. K Coll Lon and Warm AKC 65. **d** 67 **p** 68 S'wark. C of St Paul, Wimbledon 67-71; Warden of Ayia Napa Monastery and Refugee Projects Officer for Middle E Coun Chs 71-75; Hon C of St Paul Haringay 75; Chap of St Paul Nicosia w Larnaca 75-78; V of Harringay 78-80. *c/o Vicarage, Wightman Road, N4 1RW.* (01-340 6592)

COWEN, Selwyn. Or Coll Ox 4th cl Th 29, BA 31, MA 48. Sarum Th Coll 29. **d** 31 **p** 32 Ripon. C of St Bart Armley 31-34; St Francis Bournville 34-35; M of Bush Bro of St Paul Charleville Queensld 35-40; Chap AIF 40-46; P-in-c of Blackhall 46-53; R of Barcaldine 53-59; Callide Valley 59-63; Exam Chap to Bp of Rockptn 59-63; Hon Can of Rockptn 62-65; R of Stanthorpe 63-65. *4 Evenden Street, Warwick, Queensland, Australia 4370.*

COWGILL, John Wilfrid Alban. b 06. Late Squire Scho and Exhib of Ex Coll Ox 3rd cl Cl Mods 26, BA (2nd cl Th) 28, MA 34. Ely Th Coll 28. **d** 29 **p** 30 Southw. C of St Mary and St Cuthb Worksop 29-41; V of Misterton 41-49; E Drayton and Stokeham (w Askham to 56) 49-74; R of Headon w Upton 51-74; RD of Tuxford 65-70; Perm to Offic Dio Southw from 74. *90 Camborne Crescent, Hallcroft, Retford, Notts, DN22 7RF.* (Retford 705853)

COWHAM, Hugh Nicholas Gerard. b 26. Selw Coll Cam BA 51, MA 77. **d** 78 **p** 79 Moray. Hon C of H Trin Elgin Dio Moray from 78; Chap Gordonstoun Sch 78-80; St Hilda Sch Southport from 80. *3 Ellen Street, Southport, Queensld, Australia 4215.*

COWIE, Derek Edward. b 33. SOC 70. **d** 73 **p** 74 Chelmsf. C of Maldon 73-76; R of Bowers Gifford w N Benfleet 76-79; V of Ch of Ascen City and Dio Chelmsf from 79. *The Ascension Vicarage, Maltese Road, Chelmsford, Essex, CM1 2PB.* (0245-51803)

COWIE, Leonard Wallace. b 19. Exhib Pemb Coll Ox BA (2nd cl Mod Hist) 41, Dipl in Th 43, MA 46. Univ of Lon MA

48, PhD 54. Ripon Hall Ox 42. **d** 43 **p** 44 Ox. C of High Wycombe and Asst Master R Gr Sch High Wycombe 43-45; Chap and Tutor Coll of St Mark and St John Chelsea 45-47; Tutor 47-68; Whitelands Coll Putney from 68. *38 Stratton Road, Merton Park, SW19*. (01-542 5036)

COWLAN, William Thomas. b 12. OBE 79. **d** and **p** 79 Ex. Hon C of Kenton Dio Ex from 79. *4 Court Hall, Kenton, Devon*.

COWLAND, Peter Claude. Sarum Th Coll 66. **d** 69 Sherborne for Sarum **p** 70 Sarum. C of St Fred **p** 63 Fred. C of Waterford 62-63; R 63-65; Burton 65-73; Oromocto 73-76. *424 Covert Street, Oromocto, NB, Canada*.

COWLE, Maxwell Pressland. St Barn Coll Adel ACT ThL 36. **d** 37 **p** 38 Adel. C of St Cuthb Prospect 37-39; Chap Tatiara Miss 39-41; R of St John Maitland and Chap AMF 41-42; R of St Mary The Burra 42-48; Perm to Offic Dio Melb 48-50; Chap Miss to Seamen Wel 50-54; V of Eaglehawk 54-57; Cobden 57-66; I of Brunswick 66-75; Perm to Offic Dio River from 76; Dio Wang from 79. *1/23 Newby Street, Numurkah, Vic, Australia 3636*.

COWLEY, Bruce Tucker. b 29. Newman Coll Edmon BTh 77. **d** 73 **p** 74 Rupld. P Dio Rupld 73-74; C of All SS Cathl Edmon 75-78; Hon C from 78; Chap Edmon City Police from 78. *14505-95 Avenue, Edmonton, Alta, Canada T5N 0B1*. (454-0815)

COWLEY, Charles Frederick. b 27. Trin Coll Cam BA 53, MA 56. Wells Th Coll 53. **d** 55 **p** 56 St E. C of All SS Newmarket 55-58; Chap Aycliffe Approved Sch 58-61; V of Aldringham w Thorpe Dio St E from 61. *Aldringham Vicarage, Leiston, Suff*. (Leiston 830632)

COWLEY, Canon Colin Patrick. b 02. Late Exhib of Hertf coll Ox 3rd cl Mod Hist 24, BA 25, MA 28. Wells Th Coll. **d** 26 **p** 27 Sarum. C of Bridport 26-28; St Mary Abbots Kens 28-35; R of Shenfield 35-50; CF (EC) 40-46; Can Res and Treas of Win 50-54; Hon Can 55-71; Can (Emer) from 71; R of Wonston 55-71. *42 Cheriton Road, Winchester*.

COWLEY, Geoffrey Willis. b 17. St Alb Min Tr Scheme. **d** 80 St Alb **p** 81 Hertf for St Alb. Hon C of Stevington Dio St Alb from 80. *The Cottage, High Street, Carlton, Bedford, MK3 7LA*.

COWLEY, Herbert Kenneth. b 20. **d** 79 **p** 80 Glouc. C of Lydney w Aylburton Dio Glouc from 79. *17 Kimberley Drive, Lydney, Glos*. (Dean 42880)

COWLEY, Ian Michael. b 51. Univ of Natal BComm 72, BA 75. Wycl Hall Ox 76. **d** 78 Bp Hallowes for Natal **p** 79 Natal. C of Scottsville Dio Natal from 78. *PO Box 10282, Scottsville, Pietermaritzburg 3209, S Africa*.

COWLEY, Leslie. b 22. St Jo Coll Bramcote 70. **d** 71 **p** 72 Southw. C of St Jo Evang Worksop 70-73; P-in-c of Awsworth w Cossall 74-77; V of Basford Dio Southw from 77. *152 Perry Road, Basford, Nottingham*. (Nottm 605602)

COWLEY, Roger Wenman. b 40. St Jo Coll Cam BA 61. MA 64, BD 80. **d** 76 **p** 77 Egypt. P Dic Egypt 76-78; Dio Jer 78-79; Tutor Oak Hill Coll from 79. *23 Orchard Close, Watford, Herts, WD1 3DU*. (Watford 43421)

COWLING, Canon Douglas Anderson. b 19. Univ of Leeds BA (2nd cl Engl) 40. Coll of Resurr Mirfield. **d** 42 Grimsby for Linc **p** 43 Linc. C of St Andr Linc 42-45; Habrough w Immingham 45-47; R of Candlesby w Scremby 47-53; Carlton-Scroop w Normanton 53-61; V of St Paul Spalding Dio Linc from 61; Hon Can of Linc Cathl from 77. *St Paul's Vicarage, Spalding, Lincs*. (Spalding 2532)

COWLING, John Francis. b 32. K Coll Cam 2nd cl Cl Trip pt i 55, BA (2nd cl Cl Trip pt ii) 56. Linc Th Coll 56. **d** 58 **p** 59 Man. C of Leigh Lancs 58-61; Sec SCM in Schs Liv and Ches 61-65; V of St Matt (w St Barn from 71) Bolton-le-Moors 65-75; H Trin Southport Dio Liv from 75. *37 Queens Road, Southport, Mer, PR9 9EX*. (Southport 38560)

COWLING, Ronald Austin. b 12. Jes Coll Cam 2nd cl Hist Trip pt i 33, BA (2nd cl Hist Trip pt ii) and Lady Kay Scho 34, 3rd cl Th Trip pt ii 35, MA 38. Wells Th Coll 35. **d** 36 **p** 37 Bris. C of St Barn Knowle 36-38; Stoke Bp 38-40: Henlease 40-41; Downend 41-44; Chap RAFVR 44-47; C of St John Greenhill Harrow 47-48; V of Rounds Green 48-52; C-in-c of St Mark's Conv Distr Kingstanding 52-59; R of Kimcote w Walton (and Bruntingthorpe from 75) 59-79; Perm to Offic Dio Leic from 81. *60 Main Street, Cosby, Leicester*.

COWLING, Wilfred Edmund. b 14. KC Univ of Dur BA 38, MA 42. St Aid Coll 38. **d** 40 **p** 41 Newc T. C of St Aid Newc T 40-43; Asst Chap Miss to Seamen Glasgow 43-45; C of St Geo Leeds 45-47; P-in-c of St Thos Scarborough 47-57; V of Garton-on-the Wolds Dio York from 57; Kirkburn Dio York from 57; RD of Harthill 63-73; Actg RD of Harthill 79-81. *Garton-on-the-Wolds Vicarage, Driffield, E Yorks, YO25 0EW*. (Driffield 43349)

COWMEADOW, Derek Lowe. b 28. Wells Th Coll 68. **d** 70 **p** 71 Heref. C of Ledbury 70-72; Llanrhos 72-74; V of Bringhurst w Gt Easton and Drayton 74-77; P-in-c of Quenington w Coln St Aldwyns Hatherop 77-81; V of Coln St Aldwyns Hatherop, Quenington, Eastleach and Southrop Dio Glouc from 82. *Coln St Aldwyns Vicarage, Cirencester, Glos, GL7 5AG*. (Coln St Aldwyns 207)

COWPER, Christopher Herbert. b 44. Open Univ BA 76. K Coll Lon and Warm AKC 67. **d** 68 **p** 69 Sheff. C of Ch Ch Pitsmoor Sheff 68-71; Ulverston 71-74; R of Kirklinton w Hethersgill 74-79; C-in-c of Scaleby 75-79; R of Kirklinton w Hethersgill and Scaleby Dio Carl from 79. *Kirklinton Rectory, Carlisle, Cumb*. (Kirklinton 363)

COWPERTHWAITE, John. b 20. St Jo Coll Dur **d** 53 **p** 54 Dur. C of Castletown 53-56; Em Loughborough 56-59; V of Breedon-on-the-Hill w Isley Walton 59-65; PC of Ryhill 65-68; V 68-74; Royston Wakef 74-80; Felkirk w Brierley Dio Wakef from 80. *26 Poplar Avenue, Shafton, Barnsley, W Yorks*. (Barnsley 711974)

COX, Alan. b 44. St Chad's Coll Dur BSc 65, Dipl Th 68. **d** 68 **p** 69 Man. C of N Reddish 68; St Agnes Birch-in-Rusholme 69-71; St Crispin Withington 71-74; R of St Thos Ardwick Man 74-78. *c/o Rectory, Ardwick Green North, Manchester, M12 6FZ*. (061-273 5585)

COX, Alan John. b 34. ALCD 65 (LTh from 74). **d** 65 **p** 66 Wakef. C of Kirkheaton 65-67; Keynsham w Qu Charlton 67-71; R of Chipstable w Raddington and Huish Champflower w Clatworthy 71-76; Team V of St Francis Strood Dio Roch 76-79; V from 79. *St Francis Vicarage, Galahad Avenue, Strood, ME2 2YS*. (Medway 77162)

COX, Alexander James. b 12. Pemb Coll Ox BA 34, MA 43. Westcott Ho Cam 34. MCR 63. **d** 36 **p** 37 Wakef. C of Liversedge 36-39; St Andr Handsworth 39-41; St Mary Virg Acocks Green 41-45; C of Weoley Castle (in c of Bartley Green) 45-50; Min of St Mich Cov Distr Bartley Green 50-52; Chap United Birm Hosps and L to Offic Dio Birm 52-56; R of Fort Wellington Guy 56-60; Tutor Codr Coll Barb 64-69; L to Offic Dio Barb 64-69; P-in-c of St Bart Barb 70-75. *c/o House of the Resurrection, Mirfield, W Yorks*.

COX, Anthony Chilton. St Jo Coll Morpeth ACT ThL 65. **d** 65 **p** 66 Adel. C of Plympton 65-67; Burnside 67-68; Kogarah 68-73. *38 Gladstone Street, Kogarah, NSW, 2217, Australia*.

COX, Anthony David. b 46. Chich Th Coll 76. **d** 79 Stafford for Lich **p** 80 Lich. C of Fenton Dio Lich from 79. *14 Maud Street, Fenton, Stoke-on-Trent, Staffs, ST4 2JU*.

COX, Anthony James Stuart. b 46. BNC Ox BA (Th) 68. Univ of Birm Dipl Th 70. Qu Coll Birm 69. **d** 71 Aston for Birm **p** 72 Birm. C of St Matt w St Chad Smethwick 71-75; Chap Malosa Sch Kasupe Dio S Mal from 75. *Malosa Secondary School, PO Kasupe, Malawi*.

COX, Arthur Charles. b 09. Wycl Hall Ox 59. **d** 60 **p** 61 Ox. C of Glympton 60-61; R 61-70; V of Wormingford Dio Chelmsf from 70; P-in-c of Mt Bures Dio Chelmsf from 70. *Wormingford Vicarage, Colchester, Essex*. (Bures 227398)

COX, Athol Henry Arthur. b 14. **d** 76 **p** 77 Gippsld. C of Bairnsdale Dio Gippsld from 76; P-in-c of Nowa Nowa Dio Gippsld from 76. *62 Newlands Drive, Paynesville, Vic, Australia*.

COX, Benjamin Leopold. b 44. Sarum Wells Th Coll 72. **d** and **p** 75 Nass. C of H Cross Nass 75-76; R of St Steph Fresh Creek, Andros 76-79; St Steph Grand Bahama Dio Nass from 79. *Box F2063, Freeport, Grand Bahama, Bahamas*. (3482135)

COX, Bernard Sheffield. Moore Th Coll Syd ACT ThL 56. **d** 56 **p** 58 Nel. C of Ch Ch Cath Nel 56-58; All SS Nel 58; Greymouth 58-60; V of Reefton 60-66; Collingwood 66-68; Perm to Offic Dio Auckld 68-70; Hon C of Manurewa 71-75; CF (NZ) from 75. *Burnham Military Camp, Burnham, NZ*. (256-766)

COX, Bryan Leslie. b 41. Qu Coll Birm 77. **d** 79 Reading for Ox **p** 80 Ox. C of Stantonbury Dio Ox from 79. *56 Glazier Drive, Neath Hill, Milton Keynes, MK14 6HQ*.

COX, Canon Christopher George Stuart. b 17. St Jo Coll Dur BA 38, Dipl in Th 39, MA 41. **d** 40 **p** 41 S'wark. C of St Luke Deptford 40-42; CMS Miss 43-46; CMS Area Sec Dios Dur and Newc T 48-51; Dios Birm Cov and Leic 51-54; LPr Dio Birm 51-54; V of Kirby Muxloe 55-69; St Jo Bapt Knighton Leic 69-77; RD of Sparkenhoe iii 64-69; Hon Can of Leic from 65; Surr from 69; R of Appleby Magna Dio Leic from 77; Swepstone w Snarestone Dio Leic from 81. *Appleby Magna Rectory, Burton-on-Trent, Staffs, DE12 7BQ*. (Measham 70482)

COX, Cyril Edwin. b 16. Univ of Lon BD (1st cl Hons) 39. AKC (1st cl) 39, MTh 45. **d** 39 Willesden for Lon **p** 40 Lon. C of St Dionis Fulham 39-41; St Alb N Harrow 41-46; Lect in Th at St D Coll Lamp 46-49; Lect in Div and Chap St Mary's Coll and St Paul's Coll Cheltm 49-53; Chap and Asst Master of Highgate Sch Lon 53-62; Lect in Educn Univ of Birm 62-68; Sen Lect (Educn) Univ of Lon Inst of Educn 68-70 and 71-76; Reader in Educn from 76; Prof of Educn Mem Univ of Newfld 70-71. *Stone House, Welton, Daventry, Northants*. (Daventry 2269)

COX, David. b 20. SS Coll Cam BA 46, MA 48, Burney Pri 48, BD 57. Qu Coll Birm 47. **d** 48 **p** 49 Southw. C of Warsop w Sookholm 48-51; Loughton 51-53; Chislehurst 53-55; V of All SS Chatham 55-75; St Thos Southborough Dio Roch from 75. *St Thomas's Vicarage, Southborough, Tunbridge Wells, Kent.* (Tun Wells 29624)

COX, David John. b 51. Qu Coll Birm 76. **d** 79 **p** 80 Sheff. C of Brampton Bierlow Dio Sheff from 79. *3 Brampton Road, Wath-upon-Dearne, Rotherham, S63 6AN.*

COX, Desmond Maitland. b 47. St Jo Coll Morpeth 70. **d** and **p** 74 Perth. C of Carl-Rivervale 74-77; P-in-c of Esperance 77; R of E Avon 78-80; Balga Dio Perth from 80. *24 Climping Street, Balga, W Australia 6061.* (349-2573)

COX, Eric George Ernest. Univ of Manit BA 60, LTh 58. **d** and **p** 58 Rupld. R of St Andrew's 58-61; V of St Chrys Winnipeg 61-63; L to Offic Dio Rupld 63-75. *66 St Cross Street, Winnipeg 4, Manit., Canada.*

COX, Canon Eric Hector. b 16. LCD 46. MBE 46. **d** 48 **p** 49 Ex. C of Stoke Damarel (in c of St Bart) 48-52; Min of St Aid Eccles Distr Wheatley Hills Doncaster 52-57; V 57-61; Norton Lees Sheff 61-69; Surr 60-69; R of Corscombe 69-71; R of Tankersley 71-78; Hon Can of Sheff Cathl from 77; V of St Osw Millhouses City and Dio Sheff from 78; Dioc Adv for Chr Stewardship from 81. *St Oswald's Vicarage, Bannerdale Road, Sheffield, S7 2DL.* (Sheff 550793

COX, Eric William. b 30. Univ of Dur BA 54. Wells Th Coll 54. **d** 56 **p** 57 Southw. C of Sutton-in-Ashfield 56-59; Asst Chap of United Angl Ch Brussels 59-62; V of Winnington 62-71; Middlewich (w Byley from 77) Dio Ches from 71; P-in-c of Byley w Lees 73-76; R of Byley Dio Ches from 76. RD of Middlewich from 80. *Vicarage, Middlewich, Chesh, CW10 9AR.* (Middlewich 3124)

COX, Frank Allen. b 09. Lon Coll of Div 29. Univ of Dur LTh 51. **d** 32 **p** 33 Lon. C of St Jas U Edmonton 32-35; St Jas W Teignmouth 35-37; St Jas Alperton 37-39; St John March 39-43; St Pet Bedford 43-46; V of Upwood w Gt Raveley 46-51; Raveley 49-51; R of Gaulby w King's Norton and Stretton Parva 51-55; Markfield w Stainton-under-Bardon 55-57; PC of St Geo Gt Yarmouth 57-59; V of Linstead w Chediston 59-70; Min of St Jo Bapt, Ashbourne 70-74. *11 Oakley Drive, Spalding, Lincs, PE11 2BN.*

COX, Geoffrey Sidney Randel. b 33. Merton Coll Ox BA (2nd cl Mod Lang) 56, MA 60. Tyndale Hall Bris. **d** 58 **p** 59 Roch. C of St Barn Conv Distr Cray 58-61; Ch Ch Bromley 61-64; V of Gorsley w Clifford's Mesne 64-79; Hucclecote Dio Glouc from 79. *Hucclecote Vicarage, Gloucester, GL3 3SB.* (Gloucester 66339)

COX, George Ernest Pritchard. b 03. Late Scho of Jes Coll Cam 22, 1st cl Cl Trip pt i and Stewart of Rannoch Scho 24, BA (1st cl Cl Trip pt ii) and Lady Kay Scho 25, 1st cl Th Trip pt ii 27, MA 29. St Steph Ho Ox 27. **d** 28 **p** 29 Man. C of St Mary Virg Bury 28-31; Tue Brook 31-36; V of Haigh w Aspull 36-46; Exam Chap to Bp of Liv 46-63; Chap and Lect at St Kath Tr Coll Liv 46-63; Hon Can of Liv 56-63; V of Babraham 63-66; V of Pampisford 63-66; Select Pr Univ of Ox 65; R of Beckley 66-76. *24 Ghyll Side Road, Northiam, Rye, TN31 6QG.* (079-74 2171)

COX, Gerald Arthur. b 42. Chich Th Coll 73. **d** 76 Repton for Derby **p** 77 Derby. C of St Phil Chaddesden 76-81; Team V of Cowley (in c of St Jas) Dio Ox from 81. *St James's House, Beauchamp Lane, Cowley, Oxford, OX4 3LF.* (Ox 779262)

COX, Hugh Teversham. b 42. Moore Coll Syd ACT ThL 68, Th Scho 71. **d** 69 **p** 70 C & Goulb. C of St Paul Canberra 70-71; P-in-c of Kameruka 71-74; on leave 75-76; P-in-c of Ch Ch Canberra Dio C & Goulb from 76. *31 Ross Smith Crescent, Scullin, ACT, Australia 2614.*

COX, Ian William. b 43. Ridley Coll Melb ACT ThL 70. **d** 71 **p** 72 Melb. C of St Mary Caulfield 71-73; H Trin Adel 73-76; R of St Clem Lalor Pk Dio Syd from 77. *13 Freeman Street, Lalor Park, NSW, Australia 2147.* (624 3684)

COX, James Edward Thomas. b 20. Univ of Sheff BA 47. Cudd Coll 47. **d** 49 **p** 50 Cant. C of Boxley 49-52; Min of St Nich Buckland Valley Conv Distr Dover 52-59; R of Hawkinge 59-64; R of Acrise 59-64; Chap RAF Hawkinge 59-62; Abbey Sch Malvern 64-79; V of L Malvern Dio Worc from 65. *18 Kings Road, Malvern Wells, Worcs, WR14 4HL.* (Malvern 64392)

COX, Canon James Gordon. b 12. Univ of Poitiers Diplôme d'Etudes Françaises, 31. Hertf Coll Ox BA (2nd cl Mod Hist) 34, MA 38. Cudd Coll 37. **d** 38 Grimsby for Linc **p** 39 Linc. C of St Mary and St Jas Grimsby (in c of St Martin Nunsthorpe from 40) 38-42; Cheam (in c of St Osw) 42-45; Chap of Horton Hosp and the Manor Epsom 45-51; R of Walpole St Pet 51-59; C-in-c of Kirkby Laythorpe w Asgarby 59-60; R 60-63; V of Ewerby and Evedon 59-63; Dioc Insp of Schs Dio Linc 60-63; Dioc Dir of Educn Dio Pet 63-76; R of Thorpe Malsor 63-76; Can of Pet Cathl 75-80; Can (Emer) from 80; V of Warmington 76-80; L to Offic Dio Pet from 80; Perm to Offic Dio Ely from 80. *9 De Vere Road Thrapston, Kettering, Northants, NN14 4JN.* (Thrapston 3553)

COX, John Anthony. b 45. Univ of Hull BA (Th) 67. Univ of Birm Dipl Th 72. Qu Coll Birm 71. **d** 73 Buckingham for Ox **p** 74 Ox. C of Buckingham 73-76; Ch Ch Whitley Reading 76-81; V of St Agnes w St Paul Reading Dio Ox from 81. *St Agnes Parsonage, Northumberland Avenue, Reading, RG2 8DE.* (Reading 81847)

COX, John Christopher. b 52. Univ of Capetn BA 77. Wycl Hall Ox 78. **d** 81 Bp Matolengwe for Capetn. C of St Sav Claremont Dio Capetn from 81. *3 Corona Court, Church Street, Claremont 7700, Cape Town, S Africa.*

COX, John Edgar. b 26. Univ of Lon BSc (Eng) 50, MSc 69. MIEE 56. Bps' Coll Cheshunt 67. **d** 68 Bradwell for Chelmsf **p** 69 Chelmsf (APM). C of St Mary Magd Harlow 68-76; Perm to Offic Dio Chelmsf from 76; C of S Petherwyn w Trewen Dio Truro 77-79; P-in-c from 79; Lezant Dio Truro from 81; Lawhitton Dio Truro from 81. *South Petherwin Vicarage, Launceston, Cornw, PL15 7JA.* (Launceston 3782)

COX, John Hamilton. b 23. Univ Coll of S Wales, BA (2nd cl Hist) 48. St Mich Coll Llan 49. **d** 51 **p** 52 Llan. C of Merthyr Tydfil 51-56; Skewen 56-61; V of Tylorstown Dio Llan from 61; Surr from 77. *Vicarage, Tylorstown, Ferndale, Rhondda, Mid Glam.* (Ferndale 730518)

COX, John Stuart. b 40. Fitzw Ho Cam BA 62, MA 66. Linacre Coll Ox BA 67. Wycl Hall Ox 64. **d** 68 Warrington for Liv **p** 69 Liv. C of Prescot 68-71; St Geo Birm 71-73; R 73-78; Selection Sec ACCM from 78; Hon C of All SS Orpington Dio Roch from 78. *Church House, Dean's Yard, SW1P 3NZ.*

COX, Leonard James William. b 27. Sarum Wells Th Coll 79. **d** 81 Cant. C of Hythe Dio Cant from 81. *34 martello Drive, Hythe, Kent.*

COX, Paul Graham. b 40. Univ of Keele Dipl Educn 62. Westcott Ho Cam 77. **d** 78 **p** 79 Roch (APM). C of Kemsing w Woodlands 78-80; Hd Master St Mich Sch Otford from 81. *St Michael's School, Otford, Kent.*

COX, Percy Campbell. b 22. Bps' Coll Cheshunt 50. **d** 53 **p** 54 St Alb. C of St Andr Luton 53-55; St Paul St Alb 55-56; V of H Trin, N Harborne, Smethwick 60-61; CF 56-60 and 61-74; DACG Cyprus 74; N-W Distr 75-76; V of Castletown 76-77; P-in-c of Hickling 78-80; Kinoulton 78-80; Broughton Sulney 78-80; V of St Paul S Ramsey Dio S & M from 80. *St Paul's Vicarage, South Ramsey, IM.* (Ramsey 812275)

COX, Peter Allard. b 55. St D Coll Lamp BA 76. Wycl Hall Ox 77. **d** 79 **p** 80 Llan. C of All SS Penarth Dio Llan from 79. *84 Coleridge Avenue, Penarth, S Glam, CF6 1SR.*

COX, Robert Roland. b 24. TCD BA 48, MA 55. **d** 49 **p** 50 Down. C of Dundonald 49-51; St Nich Belf 51-55; I of Kilbride 55-63; R of Ch Ch Belf 63-74; I of Kilbride Dio Connor from 74. *Kilbride Rectory, Doagh, Ballyclare, Co Antrim, N Ireland.* (Ballyclare 40225)

COX, Ronald Thomas. b 12. Dorch Miss Coll 38. **d** 41 **p** 42 Man. C of Our Lady of Mercy and St Thos of Cant Gorton 41-44; Miss Dio Masasi 44-52; P-in-c of Nachingwea 52-56; Mtwara 56-62; Procurator Cathl Ch of St Mary Virg and St Bart Masasi 63-72; V of Ermington Dio Ex from 73; Commiss Masasi from 78. *Ermington Vicarage, Ivybridge, Devon, PL21 9NT.* (Modbury 830409)

COX, Selwyn. St Edm Hall Ox BA and MA 28. Wells Th Coll 29. **d** 29 **p** 31 Lon. C of All SS Fulham 29-32; CF 32-54; Chap R Hosp Chelsea 51-54; V of Hampton Wick 54-60; St Phil Earls Court Road Kens 60-71; Perm to Offic Dio St E from 71; Dio Lon & Guildf from 80. *9 Lindley Court, 9 Glamorgan Road, Hampton Wick, Kingston-upon-Thames,*

COX, Stephen. b 38. Open Univ BA 80. Bp's Coll Cheshunt 65. **d** 68 Lynn for Nor **p** 69 Nor. C of Gaywood w Bawsey and Mintlyn 68-72; Kings Lynn Dio Nor from 73; Youth Chap Lynn Dio Nor from 72. *Great Bircham Rectory, King's Lynn, Norfolk.* (Syderstone 306)

COX, Stephen John Wormleighton. b 54. New Coll Ox MA 79. Fitzw Coll Cam Ba 79. Ridley Hall Cam 77. **d** 80 **p** 81 Stepney for Lon. C of All S Clapton Pk Dio Lon from 80. *All Souls Vicarage, Overbury Street, E5 0AJ.*

COX, Vernon James Frederick. b 37. Sarum Th Coll 66. **d** 69 Sherborne for Sarum **p** 70 Sarum. C of St Francis, Sarum 69-72; C-in-c of Winterbourne Earls w Winterbourne Dauntsey and Winterbourne Gunner 72-73; Team V of Bourne Valley 73-81; Chap Rubery Hill, John Conolly and Sheldon Hosps Birm 81. *Address temp unknown.*

COX, Victor Nelson. b 23. **d** 68 **p** 69 Edmon. Chap Camsell Hosp Edmon from 69. *15232 94th Street, Edmonton, Alta., Canada.*

COX, Wallace Francis. b 13. Univ of Bris BA 34. Sarum Th Coll 33. **d** 36 **p** 37 Worc. C of St Pet Cradley 36-39; CF (TA) 39-46; C of Claines 46; V of St John Dudley 46-48; R of St Leon Bridgnorth w Tasley 48-56; V of H Trin Southport 56-63; Chap and Lect St Kath Coll Scarisbrick 59-63; V of Kidderminster 63-71; RD of Kidderminster 68-70; V of Burrington 71-78; Perm to Offic Dio B & W from 79. *Knapps, Knapps Drive, Winscombe, Bristol.* (Winscombe 3109)

COX, Treas William Arthur Moncrieff. b 13. TCD BA 35, MA 50. **d** 37 **p** 38 Down. C of Cathl Ch Drom 37-39; Santry w Glasnevin Cloghran and Coolock 39-44; Hon Cler V of Ch Ch Cathl Dub 43-44; I of Castledermot w Kinneagh 44-56; Brinny w Templemartin 56-60; RD of Omurthy 50-56; St Canice 68; I of Mothel 60-68; Bunclody Dio Ferns from 68; Preb of Ferns Cathl 80-81; Treas from 81. *Rectory, Bunclody, Enniscorthy, Co Wexford, Irish Republic.* (Enniscorthy 77139)

COX, William John Francis. b 24. **d** 77 **p** 78 Truro (APM). C of Liskeard w St Keyne Dio Truro from 77. *43 Highwood Park, Dobwalls, Liskeard, Cornwall.*

COX, William Robert. b 14. TCD BA 38, MA 48. **d** 48 Dub for Blackb **p** 49 Blackb. C of Preston 48-50; CF 50-61; V of Ch Ch Reading 61-71; Chap HM Pris Bris from 72. *56 College Court, College Road, Fishponds, Bristol, BS16*

COXHEAD, Ross Herbert. ACT ThL 72. Moore Coll Syd. **d** 74 Syd **p** 74 Bp Robinson for Syd. C of Carlingford Dio Syd from 74. *218 Pennant Hills Road, Carlingford, NSW, Australia 2118.* (630-3562)

COXON, Gerald Stanley. St Barn Coll Adel ACT ThL (2nd cl) 39. **d** 39 **p** 40 Perth. C of Carl 39-41; R 41-43; Three Springs 43-45; Chap AIF 45-46; R of Kalgoorlie 46-55; Archd of Goldfields 51-55; CF (Austr) 55-60; I of Glen Iris 60-66; P-in-c of Midland 66-67; R of Kalamunda 67-71; Perm to Offic Dio Perth from 72. *30a Canning Road, Kalamunda, W Australia 6076.* (293 3416)

COYLE, Ven Frank Robert. Trin Coll Tor BA 43. Gen Th Sem STB 50. **d** 49 Tor for Bran. C of Swan River 49-50; R 50-54; Birtle 54-56; Thistletown 56-59; Englehart 59-65; St Jo Evang Sault Ste Marie Dio Alg from 65; Hon Can of Alg 73-76; Archd of Alg from 76. *134 John Street, Sault Ste Marie, Ont., Canada.* (705-256-3060)

COYLE, Matthew Ernest. b 11. Lon Coll of Div 31. **d** 34 **p** 35 Lon. C of St D W Holloway 34-36; St Martin Worc 36-39; V of St Aug Vic Pk 39-42; R of Motherwell 42-44; Sampford Peverell 44-62; C-in-c of Uplowman 50-53; R 53-62; Weare Gifford w Landcross 62-69. *3 Fulford Road, Exeter, Devon, EX1 2UA.*

COYNE, John Edward. b 55. Coun for Nat Acad Awards BA (Th) 79. Oakhill Coll Lon 76. **d** 79 **p** 80 Ches. C of St Andr Cheadle Hulme 79-81; St Mich AA Macclesfield Dio Ches from 81. *10 Regent Avenue, Macclesfield, Cheshire.* (Macclesfield 26131)

COYNE, Terence Roland Harry. Chich Th Coll 64. **d** 66 **p** 67 Lich. C of Meir 66-69; Horninglow 69-72; V of St Gabr Fullbrook Walsall Dio Lich from 72. *St Gabriel's Vicarage, Walstead Road, Walsall, Staffs.* (Walsall 22583)

COZENS, Daniel Harry. b 44. Dipl Th (Lon) 70. Oak Hill Th Coll 68. **d** 71 **p** 72 Roch. C of St Barn Cray 71-74; St Nich (w Ch Ch to 76 and St Luke from 76) Deptford 74-78; Rees Missr Dio Ely frpm 78. *Rectory, High Street, Coton, Cambridge, CB3 7PL.* (Madingley 210239)

COZENS, Ronald James. **d** 80 **p** 81 Melb. C of St Paul Ringwood Dio Melb from 80. *24 Walter Street, Glen Waverley, Vic, Australia 3150.*

✠ **CRABB, Most Rev Frederick Hugh Wright.** b 15. Univ of Lon BD (1st cl) 39. Wycl Coll Tor DD (*hon causa*) 60. St Andr Coll Sktn DD (*hon causa*) 67. Coll of Em & St Chad DD (*hon causa*). ALCD 39. **d** 39 B & W for Ex **p** 40 Ex. C of W Teignmouth 39-41; St Andr Plymouth 41-42; CMS Miss at Akot, Sudan 42-45; Prin of Bp Gwynne Coll Mundri Sudan 45-51; Exam Chap to Bp in Sudan 49-51; to Bp of Calg 68-75; Vice-Prin LCD and LPr Dio Lon 51-57; Commiss Sudan 56-76; Prin of Em Coll Sktn 57-67; Hon Can of Sktn 65-67; C of Ch Ch Calg 67-71; R of St Steph, Calg 71-75; Cons Ld Bp of Athab in St Jas Cathl Peace River 4 March 75 by Bp of Edmon (Actg Abp); Bps of Calg, Rupld, Sask and Sktn; Elected Abp and Metrop of Prov of Rupld 77. *Bishop's Lodge, PO Box 279, Peace River, Alta, TOH 2XO, Canada.* (403-624 2419)

CRABB, John Anthony. b 29. Ely Th Coll 57. **d** 59 **p** 60 Wakef. C of Hebden Bridge 59-62; Barnsley 62-64; V of Grimethorpe 64-69; Stanley 69-78; St Jo Evang Huddersfield Dio Wakef from 78. *75 St Johns Road, Huddersfield, HD1 5EA.* (Huddersfield 27071)

CRABTREE, Stephen. b 56. Univ of Nottm BTh 80. Linc Th Coll 76. **d** 80 Burnley for Blackb **p** 81 Blackb. C of St Pet Chorley Dio Blackb from 80. *50 Corporation Street, Chorley, Lancs, PR6 0DP.* (Chorley 63627)

CRABTREE, Victor. b 18. Kelham Th Coll 36. **d** 43 Bp O'Ferrall for Derby **p** 44 Derby. C of H Trin Shirebrook 43-46; St Paul Burton-on-Trent 46-50; PC of Shirebrook 50-56; Bradwell Derbys 56-66; R of Shirland Dio Derby from 66; P-in-c of Brackenfield 77-80. *Shirland Rectory, Derby, DE5 6BB.* (Alfreton 3231)

CRACE, John Allan. b 21. DSC 43. Wells Th Coll 62. **d** 64 **p** 65 Sarum. C of Westbury 64-67; V of Milton Lilbourne w E Royal Dio Sarum from 67; R of Wootton Rivers Dio Sarum from 71; RD of Pewsey from 79. *Milton Lilbourne Vicarage, Pewsey, Wilts.* (Pewsey 3457)

CRACKNALL, Canon Garth Younghusband. Ridley Coll Melb ACT ThL 50. **d** 49 **p** 50 St Arn. P-in-c of Bealiba 49-50; V of Dunolly 50-51; R of Red Cliffs 51-65; Can of St Arn Cathl 60-65; V of St Pet City and Dio Bal 65-67; R from 67; Hon Can of Bal 68-74; Can 74-80; Can (Emer) from 80; P-in-c of Skipton Dio Bal from 80. *Rectory, Skipton, Vic, Australia 3361.* (053-32 3929)

CRACKNELL, Albert Samuel. St Jo Coll Perth. ACT ThL 09. **d** 09 **p** 10 Perth. C of Kalg 09-14; R of Mt Magnet w Yalgoo 14-16; Dom Chap to Bp of Kalg 14-19; R of Meekatharra 16-20; Coolgardie 20-24; Esperance 24-28; Wagin 28-31; Karridale 31-32; Margaret River 32-33; Wickepin 33-35; Collie 35-50; Perm to Offic Dio Perth 50-70. *11 Elvire Street, North Beach, W Australia 6020.* (47 1133)

CRACKNELL, Lloyd George. **d** 57 **p** 58 Hur. I of St Jude Lon Dio Hur from 57; Dom Chap to Bp of Hur 71-74. *4 Daleview Crescent, London, Ont., Canada.* (519-434 9414)

CRADDOCK, Brian Arthur. b 40. Chich Th Coll 67. **d** 70 **p** 71 Lich. C of Stoke-upon-Trent 70-74; Pembroke Dio Berm from 75. *2 St John's Place, Langton Hill, Pembroke, Bermuda.*

CRADDOCK, Sydney Thomas. b 09. BC Coll Bris. 29. **d** 32 **p** 33 Rang. BCMS Miss at Minbya 32-35; C of Ch Ch Norris Green 35-41; V of All H Leeds 41-42; Ch Ch Kens Liv 42-47; N Petherwyn 47-61; RD of Trigg Major from 53; PC of Mithian w Mt Hawke 61-77; Perm to Offic Dio Truro from 77. *Blake House, Penberthy Road, Portreath, Redruth, TR16 4LP.*

CRADDUCK, Martin Charles. b 50. Univ of Hull BSc 71. St Jo Coll Nottm Dipl Th 77. **d** 79 **p** 80 Lon. C of W Kilburn Dio Lon from 79. *Flat 2, St Luke's Church Centre, Fernhead Road, W9.* (01-969 1752)

CRAFT, Ernest Charles. b 10. MBE 45. Keble Coll Ox BA 32, MA 58. Wells Th Coll 32. **d** 33 **p** 34 Blackb. C of St Pet Burnley 33-38; TCF 38-40; CF 40-49; Min of Conv Distr of Hersden 49-52; R of Westbere w Hersden 52-63; E Horsley 63-76; RD of Leatherhead 67-72; Perm to Offic Dio Cant from 76. *Upton Lodge, Worth, Nr Deal, Kent.* (Sandwich 613061)

CRAFT, Nickless Hugh. Moore Th Coll Syd ACT ThL 63. **d** 63 **p** 64 Syd. C of Kingsgrove 63-66; Chatswood 67-68; on leave. *c/o Diocesan Church House, George Street, Sydney, NSW 2000, Australia.*

✠ **CRAGG, Right Rev Albert Kenneth.** b 13. Jes Coll Ox BA (2nd cl Mod Hist) 34, Ellerton Th Pri 37, MA 38, Green Mor Phil Pri 47, DPhil 50. Hur Coll Hon DD 63. Tyndale Hall Bris 34. **d** 36 Man for Ches **p** 37 Ches. C of St Cath Tranmere 36-39; Chap at Beirut 39-47; Asst Prof of Phil Amer Univ of Beirut 42-47; Warden of St Justin's Ho Beirut 42-47; R of Longworth 47-51; Ed *The Muslim World* 52-60; Prof of Arabic and Islamics Hartford Sem USA 51-56; Can Res of St Geo Colleg Ch Jer 56-59; Hon Can 65-73; Cant 61-80; Exam Chap to Bp in Jordan 58-75; to Abp of Cant 61-67; Fell of St Aug Coll Cant 59-60; Sub-Warden 60-61; Warden 61-67; Select Pri Univ of Cam 61; TCD 62; Ox 74; Commiss Jer 62-68; Proc Conv Cant 64-68; Bye-Fell G and C Coll Cam 69-74; Cons Asst Bp in Jer Abpric in St Geo Colleg Ch Jer on 15th Feb 70 by Abp in Jer; and Bps in Jordan and Iran; res 73; Asst Bp of Chich 73-78; Wakef 78-81; 78; Reader in Relig Stud Univ of Sussex 73-78; V of Helme 78-81. *Appletree Cottage, Ascott-under-Wychwood, Oxon, OX7 6AG.* (0993-830911)

CRAGG, Ian Charles. St Francis Coll Brisb ThDip 79. **d** 79 **p** 80 Brisb. C of St Barn Sunnybank 79-80; Gympie Dio Brisb from 80. *17 Church Street, Gympie, Queensld, Australia 4570.*

CRAGG, John George Hawley. b 1899. St Paul's Coll Burgh 31. **d** 34 **p** 35 Linc. C of New Sleaford 34-38; V of Swineshead 38-75; V of Brothertoft w Kirton Holme 66-72; CF (R of O) 38-54; Hon CF from 54. *3 King John Road, Swineshead, Boston, Lincs, PE20 3EH.* (Boston 820564)

CRAGG, Leonard Albert. b 28. TCD BA 53, MA 56. Cudd Coll 54. **d** 55 Blackb **p** 56 Lanc for Blackb. C of St Barn Morecambe 55-57; St Luke Skerton 57-60; V of Brierfield 60-63; Chap Whittingham Hosp 63-69; V of Padiham w Higham 69-81; *c/o 1 Arbory Drive, Padiham, Burnley, Lancs. BB12 8JS.*

CRAGGS, Michael Alfred. b 43. Open Univ BA 79. St Mich AA Coll Llan 66. **d** 69 Grimsby for Linc **p** 70 Linc. C of Clee 69-72; Old Brumby 72-76; Team V of Kingsthorpe w Northn Dio Pet from 76. *Vicarage, Evenley Road, Northampton, NN2 8JR.* (0604-846215)

CRAGO, Geoffrey Norman. b 44. Linc Th Coll 67. **d** 70 **p**

71 Glouc. C of Matson Glouc 70-75; V of Drybrook 75-80; P-in-c of Huntley w May Hill Dio Glouc from 80. *Huntley Rectory, Gloucester, GL19 3DZ.* (Glouc 830363)

CRAIG, Alan Stuart. b 38. Univ of Leeds BA (3rd cl Gen) 59. Univ of Dur Dipl Th 61. Cranmer Hall Dur. **d** 61 **p** 62 Lich. C of Newc L w Butterton 61-65; Scarborough 65-67; V of Werrington, Staffs 67-72; Asst Chap HM Pris Man 72-73; Chap Hindley Borstal Inst 73-77; HM Pris Acklington from 78. *HM Prison, Acklington, Morpeth, Northumberland.* (Red Row 411)

CRAIG, Ven Alexander Barlow. Bp's Univ Lennox BA 41. **d** 41 Niag for Koot **p** 42 Niag. C-in-c of W Flamboro w Rockton 41-43; I of Salmon Arm 43-50; V of Creston 50-51; Centr W Field Sec Gen Bd of Relig Educn 51-59; R of Newc w Nelson 59-63; St Paul St John 63-69; Newcastle w Nelson Dio Fred from 69; Can of Ch Ch Cathl Fred 71-75; Res Can from 75; Dioc Regr Dio Fred from 76; Archd of Fred from 80. *23 Main Street, Fredericton, NB, Canada E3A 1B7.*

CRAIG, Eric. b 39. Univ of Birm BA (3rd cl Th) 62, Dipl Th 63. Qu Coll Birm 62. **d** 64 **p** 65 Wakef. C of Todmorden 64-68; Hurstpierpoint 68-70; Cobham Surrey 70-73; V of St Jerome Dawley, Hillingdon 73-76; Stainland Dio Wakef from 76. *Vicarage, Stainland, Halifax, W Yorks, HX4 9EX.* (Elland 74767)

CRAIG, Gillean Weston. b 49. Univ of York BA 72. Qu Coll Cam BA 76, MA 80. Westcott Ho Cam 76. **d** 77 Lon **p** 78 Bp Woollcombe for Lon. C of St Mark (w Ch Ch and St Paul from 78) St Marylebone Dio Lon from 77. *St Paul's House, 9a Rossmore Road, NW1 6NJ.* (01-402 1000)

CRAIG, Graham Fetherstonhaugh. b 06. Late Exhib of TCD BA 29, MA 35. **d** 29 **p** 30 Down. C of St Anne's Cathl Belf 29-38; Dean's V Cho 31-35; Min Can 31-39 and 51-58; I of St Jo Bapt Upper Falls Belf 38-51; CF (EC) 41-46; I of St Jas Belf 51-66; Can of St Anne's Cathl Belf 58-66; R of Drumbo 66-70. C of St Anne's Cathl Belfast Dio Connor from 71. *8 Prince Edward Drive, Belfast, BT9 5GB* (Belfast 667171)

CRAIG, James Alexander. b 09. Univ of Aber MA 32, Pri 36, BD 39. Edin Th Coll 34. **d** 36 **p** 37 Aber. Chap of St Andr Cathl Aber 36-39; R of St Andr Banff 39-44; V of Ainstable 44-47; PC of Armathwaite 44-47; Chap at Bordeaux 47-51; St Andr Santiago 51-55; V of Lavington (or Lenton) w Osgodby, Keisby, Hanby, and Ingoldsby 55-59; R of Willoughby w Sloothby 59-61; Prin Bp's Sch Amman 61-64; R of Burghclere w Newtown 66-77. *32 Bromley College, Bromley, Kent.*

CRAIG, Canon James Hannington. Univ of BC BA 25. Univ of Tor MA 30. Trin Coll Tor LTh 30, BD 32, DD (*jure dig*) 45. **d** 30 **p** 31 Hur. I of St Luke Broughdale Lon Ont 30-35; St Mary Kerrisdale New Westmr 35-44; Exam Chap to Bp of New Westmr 40-44; Dean of Algoma 44-51; R of St Luke's Pro-Cathl Sault Ste Marie 44-51; Exam Chap to Bp of Alg 47-51; Dean of Calg 51-53; R of Grace Ch-on-the-Hill 53-72; Can of Tor from 56. *56 Deloraine Avenue, Toronto, Ont, Canada.*

CRAIG, John Maxwell. b 25. **d** 69 Tor **p** 72 Alg. C of St Marg New Tor 69-71; St John Chapleau 71-73; I of Kinmount 73-75; St Mark Oshawa 75-80; Orillia S Dio Tor from 80. *28 Charles Road, Orillia, Ont, Canada.*

CRAIG, John Newcome. b 39. Selw Coll Cam BA 63, MA 67. Linc Th Coll 63. **d** 65 **p** 66 Lich. C of Cannock 65-71; V of Gt Wyrley 71-79; Team R of Wednesfield Dio Lich from 79. *9 Vicarage Road, Wednesfield, Wolverhampton, WV11 1SB.*

CRAIG, Patrick Thomas. St D Coll Lamp BA 59. Bps's Coll Cheshunt. **d** 61 **p** 62 Connor. C of St Mary Belf 61-65; St Pet Belf 65-69; CF from 69. *c/o Ministry of Defence, Lansdowne House, Berkeley Square, W 1.*

CRAIG, Richard Harvey. b 31. Em Coll Cam BA 58. Linc Th Coll. **d** 60 **p** 61 Linc. C of Bottesford w Ashby (in c of St Cath from 62) 60-65; Industr Chap to Bp and L to Offic Dio Linc 65-69; Dioc Adv Laity Tr Dio Bris 69-74; V of Whitchurch Dio Bris from 74. *780 Whitchurch Lane, Whitchurch, Bristol, BS14 0EU.* (Whitchurch 832380)

CRAIG, Robert Henry. b 13. St Jo Coll Dur BA 47, Dipl Th 49. **d** 49 **p** 50 Cant. C of Herne Bay 49-51; Ch Ch Folkestone 51-55; H Trin Folkestone 51-55; V of Exning w Landwade 55-58; Walsham-le-Willows 58-62; R of Waldershare w Coldred 62-68; Mersham 68-78; V of Tilmanstone 62-68; P-in-c of Bilsington 74-78. *2 Aston Court, Trinity Cardens, Folkestone, Kent, CT20 2RP.*

CRAIG, Robert Joseph. B 43. TCD BA 65, Div Test 66. **d** 66 **p** 67 Connor. C of Carrickfergus 66-69; Asst Master R Acad Belfast 70-72; Qu Mary's Coll Basingstoke 72-74; Chap Lord Wandsworth Coll Dio Win from 75. *Kimbers, Lord Wandsworth College, Long Sutton, Basingstoke, Hants.* (L Sutton 206)

CRAIGHEAD, John Miller. Ch Ch Coll 64. NZ Bd of Th Stud LTh 67. **d** 66 Nel. C of Ch Ch Cathl Nel 66-69; Chap Wanganui Colleg Sch 69; L to Offic Dio Nel 69-70; V of Hanmer Dio Nel from 70. *Vicarage, Hanmer Springs, NZ.* (Hanmer Springs 86)

CRAIGIE, Douglas John. Trin Coll Dub BA 43. **d** 43 **p** 44 Down. C of St Clem Belfast 43-44; CF from 44. *41 Dorchester Waye, Hayes, Middx.*

CRAIGIE, James Reid. St Francis Th Coll Brisb. **d** 58 **p** 59 Brisb. C of St Steph Coorparoo 58-60; H Trin Fortitude Valley 60-61; P-in-c of Killarney 61-64; C of St Jas Toowoomba 64-67; R of St John's Mundubbera 67-69; Chap to R Brisb Hosp 69-72; C of Toowoomba 72-73. *34 Russell Street, Moffat Beach, Caloundra, Queensland, Australia 4551.*

CRAIN, David Lindsay. Univ of Syd BA 61. BD (Lon) 65. St Jo Coll Morpeth ACT ThL (1st cl) 64. **d** 64 Newc **p** 66 Bp Stibbard for Newc. C of Maitland 64-67; Cessnock 68-71; P-in-c of Birm Gardens 71-75; R 75-79. *Holy Trinity Rectory, Keck Street, Bendigo, Vic, Australia 3550)*

CRAMP, Brian George Willard. b 28. Pemb Coll Cam BA 50, MA 55. Westcott Ho Cam 50. **d** 52 **p** 53 Man. C of St Phil, Salford 52-55; Chap St Jo Coll Cam and L to Offic Dio Ely 55-57; R of St Wilfrid Newton Heath 57-62; Dioc Youth Officer Man 62-68; LPr Dio Man 62-77; Prin Lect Man Poly 70-77; Brighton Poly from 77. *Balcombe House, Varley Hall of Residence, Coldean Lane, Brighton BN1 9GR.* (Brighton 696385)

CRAMPTON, John Leslie. b 41. Div Hostel Dub. **d** 67 **p** 68 Down. C of Shankill Lurgan 67-71; Dundela 71-73; Umtali 73-76; R of Fort Vic Dio Mashon (Dio Lundi from 81) from 76. *Box 331, Fort Victoria, Zimbabwe.*

CRAMPTON, Richard Laurence. b 08. Univ of Dur LTh 36. **d** 34 **p** 35 Roch. C of Crayford 34-37; V of Levuka 37-38; Supt Indian Miss Labasa 38-45; V of Vanua Levu 38-45; C of Weybridge (in c of St Mich AA) 45-47; Min of Conv Distr of St Aug Aldershot 47-50; V of Reepham 50-55; Sec Polyn Dioc Assoc 47-56; Commiss Polyn 48-59; R of Gt Gonerby 55-59; Spridlington w Saxby and Firsby 59-62; V of Hackthorn w Cold Hanworth 59-62; R of Beaufort W 62-66; R of Vic W 62-66; V of Nocton 67-73; V of Dunston 66-73. *3 Tor-o-Moor Gardens, Woodhall Spa, Lincs, LN10 6RX.* (Woodhall Spa 52679)

CRAN, Preb Alexander Strachan. b 09. St Jo Coll Dur BA (3rd cl Th) 31, MA 43. St Aid Coll 31. **d** 32 **p** 33 Blackb. C of St Andr Ashton-on-Ribble 32-36; St Silas Blackb 36-38; V of Ch Ch Preston 38-48; Surr 46-48; V of Congresbury (w Wick St Lawr 48-54) 48-73; RD of Locking 59-72; Preb of Wells Cathl from 61; C-in-c of Puxton w Hewish and Wick 71-73. *Rowan Wick, Wolvershill Road, Banwell, Weston-super-Mare, Somt.* (Banwell 823209)

CRANCH, Peter Kenneth. b 47. St Chad's Coll Dur BA 70, Dipl Th 71. **d** 73 Crediton for Ex **p** 74 Ex. C of Tavistock w Gulworthy 73-78; Team V of Centr Torquay 78-80; C of Heavitree w St Paul City and Dio Ex from 80. *The School House, South Lawn Terrace, Exeter, Devon, EX1 2SN.* (Ex 54284)

CRANCH, Ven William Maxwell. St Jo Coll Auckld LTh 66. **d** 64 **p** 65 Auckld. C of Whangarei 64-67; N Wairoa 67-70; V of Helensville 70-73; Hosp Chap Dio Auckld from 73; Archd of Waimate from 80. *124 Puriri Park Road, Whangarei, Auckland, NZ.* (81-910)

CRANE, Bryant Frederick Francis. b 13. Qu Coll Cam 3rd cl Hist Trip Pt i 34, BA 35, MA 39. Ridley Hall Cam 35. **d** 37 **p** 38 Nor. C of E Dereham w Hoe and Dillington 37-39; King's Lynn (in c of St Nich) 39-44; V of St Mark Kempt Town Brighton 44-52; Chap St Mary's Hall Brighton 47-53; Chap of St Dunstan's Tr Centre Ovingdean 46-52; V of Em Southport 52-63; R of Astbury w Smallwood 63-78; Perm to Offic Dio Ches from 78; Dio Lich from 81. *6 Ridgefields, Biddulph Moor, Stoke-on-Trent, ST8 7JE.* (S-on-T 513752)

CRANE, Canon David Henry Melrose. Wycl Coll Tor BA 43, LTh 46, BD 48. **d** 45 **p** 46 Tor for Niag. C of All SS Tor 45-46; Ch of Ascen Hamilton 46-48; R of Hagersville 48-51; C of Grace Ch Tor 51-53; R of Penetanguishene 53-55; I of St Chris Tor 55-60; R of Ch of Transfig Tor 61-72; St Simon City and Dio Tor from 72; Can of Tor from 72. *40 Howard Street, Toronto 5, Ont., Canada.* (416-923 8714)

CRANE, Harold William. St Paul's Coll Grahmstn 61. **d** 63 **p** 64 Matab. C of Raylton Bulawayo 63-69; Pris Chap and L to Offic Dio Matab 69-74; R of St Marg Bulawayo 74-77; C of Gwelo 77; R of Selukwe Dio Matab (Dio Lundi from 81) from 77. *Rectory, Selukwe, Zimbabwe.* (Selukwe 316)

CRANE, Hubert. b 02. Kelham Th Coll 19. **d** 25 Lon **p** 26 Willesden for Lon. C of St Mary Magd Munster Sq 25-31; St Mich AA Barnes 31-34; St Mich AA S Beddington 34-45; CF (R of O) 39-45; Perm to Offic at St Mich Camberwell 45; at St Giles Camberwell 45-46; C-in-c of St Anselm Streatham 46-49; P-in-c of Livingstone N Rhod 49-53; Fiwila 53-56; P-in-c of The Ascen Mosspark Glas 56-64; R of St Aid Clarkston 64-71; Perm to Offic Dio Sarum from 71. *7 York Close, Charminster, Dorchester, Dorset, DT2 9QJ.*

CRANE, John. b 32. Chich Th Coll. **d** 58 Southw **p** 59 Bp

Gelsthorpe for Southw. C of Forest Town 58-60; St Mary Virg Primrose Hill 60-64; PC of All H N Greenford 64-67; Min Can and Chap of St Geo Chap Windsor from 67; Chap St Geo Sch Ascot 67-79; Perm to Offic Dio Worc from 80. *Holland House, Cropthorne, Nr Pershore, Worcs.*

CRANE, Robert Bartlett. b 14. Clare Coll Cam 2nd cl Hist Trip pt i 35, BA (2nd cl Hist Trip pt ii) 36, MA 40. Qu Coll Birm 37. **d** 39 York **p** 40 Selby for York. C of Acomb 39-44; Chap RNVR 44-46; V of Laxton 47-51; V of Blacktoft 47-51; Kingstanding 51-57; Balsall Heath 57-66; R of Port Antonio 66-69; Area Sec USPG Dio S'wark from 70; Hon C of St Dunstan Bellingham Dio S'wark from 79. *Flat 1, 22 Oaklands Road, Bromley, Kent, BR1 3SL.* (01-460 4578)

CRANE, Vincent James. b 10. St Aid Coll 62. **d** 64 **p** 65 Lich. C of Penn 64-70; V of Swindon 70-78; R of Himley 70-78. *26 Sandringham Road, Wombourne, Wolverhampton, Staffs.*

CRANK, James William. b 1896. Bps' Coll Cheshunt 34. **d** 36 **p** 37 Lon. C of Feltham 36-38; St Paul Foleshill 38-40; V of St Alb Stoke Heath 40-49; St Jo Bapt Leamington 49-61; Radway w Ratley 61-64. *8 Clifton Drive, Lytham, Lytham-St-Annes, Lancs, FY8 5RE.* (7253 73410)

CRANKSHAW, Ronald. b 41. Coll of Resurr Mirfield 74. **d** 76 **p** 77 Liv. C of St Andr Orford 76; N Meols 76-79; V of St Jo Evang Abram Dio Liv from 79. *Vicarage, Lee Lane, Abram, Wigan, Gtr Man.*

CRANSTON, Robert William. b 23. Univ of Bris BSc 47. Oakhill Th Coll 76. **d** 79 **p** 80 Ex. C of Heanton-Punchardon w Marwood Dio Ex from 79. *Broom Cottage, Middle Marwood, Barnstaple, N Devon.* (0271 72426)

CRANSTON, Wendy Beryl. b 46. Univ of Auckld BA 67, MA 69. St Jo Coll Auckld LTh 71. **d** 71 **p** 77 Auckld. C of Howick 71-78; Chap Univ of Auckld from 78; L to Offic Dio Auckld 78-79; Hon C of St Paul City and Dio Auckld from 79. *54c Stamford Park Road, Auckland, NZ.*

CRANSWICK, James Harvard. Univ of Melb BA (1st cl Hist) 47. St Cath S Ox BA (3rd cl Th) 50, MA 54. Wycl Hall Ox 49. **d** 50 **p** 51 Man. C of St Thos Werneth 50-52; St Pancras 52-54; St Alb Dartford 54-56; V of Birregurra 56-59; Ararat 59-66; C of Raynes Pk 69-72; Missr Dio Lon 72-75; I of All SS Preston 75-78; C in Dept of Evang and Ex Dio Melb from 78. *The Pines, Locarno Avenue, Kallista, Vic, Australia 3791.* (750 1136)

CRANSWICK, Rupert Loraine. Ch Ch Ox BA (3rd cl Mod Hist) 21, MA 26. Cudd Coll 22. **d** 23 **p** 24 Worc. C of Kidderminster 23-26; St Jo Bapt Bulawayo 26-30; V of Plumtree 30-37; R of Groot Drakenstein 37-43; Nigel 43-48; Chap Fairbridge Mem Sch and L to Offic Dio S Rhod 48-50; Asst P at Umtali 50-51; R of Avondale 51-63; Hon Can of Mashon 61-67; R of Famona 63-67; L to Offic Dio Matab from 67. *P.O. Box 65, Selukwe, Rhodesia.*

CRARY, Denham. d 49 **p** 51 Hong. Supt Taipo Orph 49-55; V of St Jas Wanchai 55-63; L to Offic Dio Hong 63-65; P-in-c of Ch Ascen Kowloon Dio Hong from 65; P-in-c of Kam Tin Dio Hong from 69. *Flat A, 7th Floor, 34/36 Nullah, Kowloon, Hong Kong.* (12-982813)

CRASKE, Leslie Gordon. b 29. K Coll Lon and Warm AKC 54. STh (Lambeth) 80. **d** 55 **p** 56 S'wark. C of Malden 55-58; Streatham 58-60; R of Gwanda 60-63; P-in-c of St Patr Miss Gwelo 63-66; Prin SPCK Tr Coll Gwelo 64-66; V of St Jo Evang U Norwood Dio Cant from 67. *2 Sylvan Road, SE19.* (01-653 0378)

CRASTON, Canon Richard Colin. b 22. Univ of Bris BA (2nd cl Gen) 49. Univ of Lon BD (2nd cl) 51. Tyndale Hall Bris 46. **d** 51 Dur **p** 52 Jarrow for Dur. C of St Nich Dur 51-54; V of St Paul (w Em from 77) Bolton Dio Man from 54; C-in-c of Em Bolton Dio Man 64-66; V 66-77; Hon Can of Man from 68; M Gen Syn Man from 70; RD of Bolton from 72. *174 Chorley New Road, Bolton, BL1 4PF.* (Bolton 42303)

CRATCHLEY, Canon William Joseph. b 08. Univ of Bris BSc (Chem) 29, MA 33, PhD 36. Or Coll Ox BLitt 38, BA (2nd cl Th) 39, MA 42. Trin Coll Dub BD 53, DD 57. Sarum Th Coll 29. **d** 31 Bris **p** 32 Malmesbury for Bris. C of St Geo Brandon Hill Bris 31-33; St Adhelm Bedminster 33-36; Perm to Offic at W Hendred 36-37; Chap and Tutor of Ripon Hall Ox 36-38; Sen Tutor 38-39; L to Offic Dio Ox 37-39; V of St Jo Evang w St Anselm Clifton 39-49; New Swindon (W St Paul Swindon from 65) 49-74; Chap to Bris Homoeopathic Hosp 47-49; Hon Chap to Bp of Bris 50-64; Hon Can of Bris 50-74; Can (Emer) from 74; Exam Chap to Bp of Bris 53-74; Surr 53-73; Proc Conv Bris 55-60; Select Pr Trin Coll Dub 58; RD of Cricklade 61-70. *Amberley House, Northleach, Cheltenham, Glos, GL54 3ET.* (Northleach 223)

CRATE, Canon George Frederick Jackson. b 28. Univ of Lon BD 56. ALCD 55. **d** 56 **p** 57 Roch. C of St Jo Evang Penge 56-58; St Steph Tonbridge 58-60; R of Knossington w Cold Overton 60-64; V of Owston w Withcote 60-64; Ch Ch Mountsorrel Dio Leic from 64; RD of Akeley E from 75; Hon Can of Leic from 80. *Christ Church Vicarage, Mountsorrel, Loughborough, LE12 7JU.* (Leicester 302235)

CRAVEN, Archdeacon of. *See* Rogers, Ven David Palmer.

CRAVEN, Allan. b 35. BD (Lon) 72. St D Coll Lamp BA 57. Chich Th Coll 57. **d** 59 St A for Ban **p** 60 Ban. C of Blaenau Festiniog 59-61; Milford Haven 61-65; V of Llwynhendy 65-68; R of Nolton w Roch Dio St D from 68. *Nolton Rectory, Broad Haven, Haverfordwest, Dyfed.* (Camrose 213)

CRAVEN, Gordon Forster. b 26. Qu Coll Cam BA 50, MA 55. Wells Th Coll 51. **d** 53 **p** 54 Wakef. C of Castleford 53-57; V of Fairfield 57-72; PC of King Sterndale Derby 57-68; V 68-72. *41 Southover, Wells, Somt.* (Wells 72282)

CRAVEN, Joseph. St Paul's Coll Burgh. **d** 20 Bp Goldsmith for Bunb **p** 21 Bunb. Bro of St Bonif Miss Bunb 20-26; R of Manjimup 26-29; Pingelly 29-36; Donnybrook 36-38; Wiluna 38-39; Kelmscott-Armadale 39-42; Chap AMF 42-46; R of St Alb Highgate Perth 46-55; Hosp Chap Dio perth 55-66; L to Offic Dio Perth 66-67. *Riley House, Shenton Park, W Australia 6008.* (81-5791)

CRAVEN, William Robert. Em Coll Sktn LTh 36. **d** 36 Sask **p** 37 Sktn for Sask. C of Turtleford 36-38; I of Big River 38-41; Serving w RCAF 41-45; Miss at Lashburn 45-48; I of St Andr Hamilton Beach 49-52; Medonte 52-55; R of Cavan 55-56. *169 West Street, Goderich, Ont., Canada.*

CRAVEN, William Robert Dillon. Univ of Tor BA 59. Hur Coll BTh 62. **d** 62 Bp Appleyard for Hur **p** 63 Hur. C of St Paul's Cathl Lon 62-4; R of Pot Lambton 64-70; Thamesville 70-76; St John St Thomas Dio Hur from 76. *24 Flora Street, St Thomas, Ont., Canada.* (519-631 7368)

CRAVEN-SANDS, Colin de Clouet. b 17. MBE 75. ACT ThL 40. Moore Th Coll 38. **d** 41 **p** 42 Syd. C of St Steph Port Kembla 41-42; Chap RAN 42-46; C of Ch Ch Chadderton 46-47; V of Ch Ch Lannarth 47-51; R of Castle Hill 51-53; Chap Miss to Seamen Syd 53-65; Sen Chap 65-80; State Sec Miss to Seamen 66-73 and 77-80; Chap Correspondent Miss to Seamen from 80. *25 Southtown Road, Great Yarmouth, NR31 0DT.* (Gt Yarmouth 2019)

CRAWFORD, Albert Edward. Trin Coll Dub BA 37, MA 43. Div Test 39. **d** 37 **p** 38 Liv. C of St Andr Southport 37-42; Perm to Offic at St Andr Maghull 42-44; Chap RAFVR 44-47; C-in-c of Inismacsaint 47-52; I of Milltown 52-65; R of Camlough 65-78. *54 Edenvale Avenue, Newry Road, Banbridge, Co Down, N Ireland.* (Banbridge 22924)

CRAWFORD, Arthur Edward. Trin Coll Dub BA 39, MA 51. **d** 40 **p** 41 Clogh. C of Aghabog w Killeevan and Newbliss 40-43; C-in-c of Errigal Trough w Errigal Shanco 43-47; I of Donagh (w Tyholland from 51) 47-55; Killabban U (w Luggacurren from 61) 55-66; Clara w Kilcleagh (Moate) Dio Meath from 66. *Clara House, Clara, Offaly, Irish Republic.* (Clara 31199)

CRAWFORD, Canon Benjamin. b 1898. MBE 71. QUB BA 23. Trin Coll Dub Div Test (2nd cl) 25. **d** 25 Man **p** 26 Man for Blackb. C of H Trin Darwen 25-28; Harewood (in c of E Keswick) 28-34; V of Crakehall w Langthorne 34-75; Hornby 46-75; RD of Bedale from 56; Hon Can of Ripon 62-75; Can (Emer) from 75; V of Patr Brompton w Hunton 71-75. *Rosscatt, Crakehall, Bedale, N Yorks.* (Bedale 2872)

CRAWFORD, David Hugh. Moore Th Coll Syd ACT ThL 52. **d** and **p** 53 Syd. C of St Matt Manly 53-54; C-in-c of Miranda 54-58; R of St Matt Bondi 58-65; Malabar Dio Syd from 65. *2a Victoria Street, Malabar, NSW, Australia 2036.* (661-2055)

CRAWFORD, Ernest Douglas Oldaker. Univ of Syd BA 45. Moore Th Coll Syd ACT ThL 46. **d** and **p** 47 Syd. C of All SS Woollahra 47-48; C-in-c of Homebush w Flemington 49-51; R of Concord N 50-56; All SS N Parramatta Dio Syd from 56. *All Saints' Rectory, Elizabeth Street, Parramatta, NSW, Australia 2150.* (630-1567)

CRAWFORD, Janet Estridge. b 43. Univ of Auckld BA 64, BD 78. St Jo Coll Auckld. **d** 78 **p** 79 Waik. C of Te Awamutu 78-80; WCC Consultant from 80. *Box 66, CH1211 Geneva 20, Switzerland.*

CRAWFORD, John. b 22. Trin Coll Dub BA 50. **d** 51 **p** 53 Connor. C of St Colman Dunmurry 51-58; Monaghan 58-60; St Luke Kens 60-63; St Mary Stoke Newington 63-65; Wickford 65-67; L Marlow Dio Ox from 67. *7 Churchill Close, Flackwell Heath, High Wycombe, Bucks.* (Bourne End 20679)

CRAWFORD, John William Rowland. b 53. AKC 75. Div Hostel Dub 75. **d** 76 **p** 77 Down. C of Dundela Dio Down from 76. *217 Holywood Road, Belfast, BT4 2DH.* (Belfast 654090)

CRAWFORD, Lionel Anderson St Clair. Codr Coll Barb 61. **d** 62 **p** 63 Barb. C of St John Barb 62-66; V of St Clem w St Swith Barb 66-69; R of St Matt Barb 69-70; St Jos Barb 70-75; St Paul I and Dio Barb from 76. *Rectory, Bay Street, St Michael, Barbados, W Indies.*

CRAWFORD, Norman. St Aid Th Coll Bal ACT ThL (2nd

cl) 14. **d** 14 Bal **p** 15 Melb for Bal. C of Beeac 14-15; Ouyen 15-16; P-in-c of Dimboola 16-17; Sea Lake 17-19; Bursar of St Aid Coll Bal 22-23; Asst Chap BHMS and Org Sec CE Immig C'tte of S Austr 23-24; C of St Pet Glenelg 24-28; P-in-c of Plympton Miss (w Glandore from 28) 24-32; Perm to Offic (Col Cl Act) at Wargrave 32-34; L to Offic Dio Cant 35-36; Succr of St Pet Cathl Adel 39-43; P-in-c of St Cypr N Adel 43-60; Northfield 60-64; L to Offic Dio Adel from 65. *56 High Street, Grange, S Australia 5022.* (356 4477)

CRAWFORD, Peter. b 22. Trin Coll Cam 2nd cl Engl Trip pt i 48, BA (2nd cl Th Trip pt i) 49, MA 54. Wycl Hall Ox 49. **d** 51 **p** 52 Man. C of Ashton-u-Lyne 51-54; V of St Jo Evang Pendlebury 54-60; Chap R Man Children's Hosp Pendlebury 54-60; V of Masham (w Healey from 75) 60-79; RD of Ripon 70-75; R of E Bergholt Dio St E from 79. *Rectory, White Horse Road, East Bergholt, Suff, CO7 6TR.* (Colchester 298076)

CRAWFORD, Peter Campbell. b 50. Monash Univ Vic BEcon 71, LLB 73. BD (Lon) 76. ACT ThL 76. Ridley Coll Melb 74. **d** 77 **p** 78 Melb. C of St John Toorak 77-79; St Columb Hawthorn 79-81; I of St Mark Emerald Dio Melb from 81. *Vicarage, Church Street, Emerald, Vic, Australian 3782.*

CRAWFORD, Philip Hugh Southern. Univ of Lon BA 40. Chich Th Coll 41. **d** 42 **p** 43 Ox. C of w Wycombe 42-46; Bro of Good Shepherd Nyngan NSW 46-52; PC of Lane End Bucks 52-60; V of Healaugh w Wighill and Bilbrough 60-78; P-in-c of Hovingham Dio York from 78; Slingsby Dio York from 78; RD of Bulmer and Malton from 80. *Hovingham Vicarage, York, YO6 4JZ.* (Hovingham 245)

CRAWFORD, Robin. b 33. Pemb Coll Cam BA 57, MA 61. **d** 67 Accra **p** 80 Win. Hd Master of Navrongo Sch Accra 67-69; Dep Sec Chrs Abroad 69-73; Dep Hd Priory Sch Lewes 73-76; Prin Govt Teachers Coll Nigeria 77-78; Perm to Offic Dio Win 78-80; Hon C of H Trin City and Dio Win from 80. *Magnolia House, Park Road, Winchester, SO22 6AA.*

CRAWFORD, Ven Thomas Henry. Trin Coll Dub BA (2nd cl Hist and Pol Sc Mod) 56. **d** 57 Derry **p** 58 Abp Barton for Dub. C of St Aug Derry 57-59; Ch Ch Cathl Hamilton 59-63; R of St Columba St Cath 63-69; Port Colborne 69-74; Hon Can of Niag 72-79; R of St Chris Burlington Dio Niag from 74; Dom Chap to Bp of Niag 77-79; Archd of Trafalgar from 79. *662 Guelph Line, Burlington, Ont, Canada.* (416-634 6780)

CRAWFORD, William Ihinga. b 42. **d** 78 **p** 79 Wai. Hon C of Tolaga Bay Dio Wai from 78. *PO Tolaga Bay, NZ.*

CRAWFORD-NUTT, Desmond Haig. Univ of S Africa BA 73, MA 75. St Paul's Coll Grahmstn LTh 47. **d** 49 **p** 50 Johann. C of Krugersdorp 49-51; Benoni 51-52; R of Standerton 53-57; Brixton w Newlands Johann 58-77. *57 Fulham Road, Rossmore, Johannesburg, S Africa.*

CRAWLEY, David. b 47. St Steph Ho Ox 75. **d** 78 **p** 79 Birm. C of Solihull 78-81; Team V of Newbury Dio Ox from 81; P-in-c of Speen Dio Ox from 81. *St Mary's Vicarage, London Road, Newbury, Berks, RG13 1LA.*

CRAWLEY, Ven David Perry. Univ of Manit BA 58. Univ of Kent MA 68. St Jo Coll Winnipeg LTh 61. **d** 61 **p** 62 Edmon. C of Sherwood Pk 61-62; I 62-66; on leave 66-68; C of All SS Cathl Edmon 68-70; Can Missr of Edmon 69-70; R of St Matt Winnipeg 71-77; Archd of Winnipeg 74-77; Dioc Archd Dio Rupld from 77. *66 St Cross Street, Winnipeg, Manit, R2W 3XB, Canada.*

CRAWLEY, David Stuart. b 49. Carleton Univ Ott BA 70. St Jo Coll Nottm. **d** and **p** Ott. C of Pembroke 77-79; I of Mattawa Dio Ott from 79. *Box 205, Mattawa, Ont, Canada.* (705-744 5477)

CRAWLEY, John Lloyd Rochfort. b 22. Selw Coll Cam BA (2nd cl Th Trip pt 1) 47, MA 52. Cudd Coll 47. **d** 49 **p** 50 Newc T. C of H Cross Fenham Newc T 49-52; V of St Anthony Byker Newc T 52-59; Longhoughton w Howick 59-69; Master St Thos Mart Newc T 69-74; Chap Univ of Newc T 69-74; P-in-c of Cockermouth Dio Carl 74-77; R (w Embleton and Wythop) from 77. *Rectory, Cockermouth, Cumb, CA13 9DU.* (090-082 3269)

CRAWLEY, Leonard Frank. b 38. N-W Ordin Course 74. **d** 77 **p** 78 Bradf (APM). C of Lidget Green Dio Bradf from 77. *185 Highgate, Bradford, W Yorks, BD9 5PU.* (Bradford 47249)

CRAWLEY, Malcolm Leonard. **d** 63 **p** 64 Wang. C of Benalla 63-66; Corryong 66-68; R 68-72; Euroa 72-77; Beechworth Dio Wang from 77. *Rectory, Ford Street, Beechworth, Vic, Australia 3747.* (061-28 1472)

CRAWLEY, Robert Cecil. Angl Th Coll BC. **d** 65 New Westmr for Caled **p** 66 Caled. C of Burn's Lake Miss 65-67; I of Ladysmith 67-72; C of Ch Ch Cathl Vic Dio BC from 72. *912 Vancouver Street, Victoria, Bc, Canada.* (604-598 6809)

CRAWLEY, Simon Ewen. b 31. Em Coll Cam BA 57, MA 60. Ridley Hall Cam 56. **d** 58 **p** 59 Carl. C of St Jas Carl 58-61; PC of St Steph Cinderford 61-67; V of H Trin Margate 67-74; H Trin w Ch Ch Folkestone 74-81; R of Patterdale Dio Carl from 81. *Patterdale Rectory, Penrith, Cumb.* (Glenridding 209)

CRAWLEY-BOEVEY, Robert Arthur. b 12. Hertf Coll Ox BA 34, MA 38. Cudd Coll 35. **d** 37 Buckingham for Ox **p** 38 Ox. C of Farnham R 37-43; Chap RNVR 43-46; R of Waltham-on-the-Wolds 47-51; V of Stonesby 47-51; Cuddington w Dinton 51-59; V of Seer Green 59-78. *Deer's Leap, 3 St Michael's Close, Urchfont, Devizes, Wilts, SN10 4QJ.*

CRAWSHAW, Charles Barritt. b 14. Univ of Leeds BA 36. Coll of Resurr, Mirfield 36. **d** 38 **p** 39 Man. C of St Clem Ordsall 38-41; Atherton 41-46; C-in-c 46-47; V of St Pet Westleigh 47-53; Hon Chap to Bp of Birm 53-60; V of H Trin Smethwick 54-60; Lect Coll of Further Educn Ashton L 60-63; Bris Tech Coll 63-69; Bris Polytech 69-71; Brunel Tech Coll (Bris) 71-80; L to Offic Dio Bris from 80. *30 Hillcrest Road, Portishead, Bristol.* (Bristol 842659)

CRAWSHAW, Geoffrey Colin. St Jo Coll Auckld 62. NZ Bd of Th Stud LTh 64. **d** 64 **p** 65 Waik. C of Tokoroa 64-65; Claudelands 65-68; V of Katikati 68-71; Chartwell Dio Waik 75-78; Taumarunui Dio Waik from 78. *Box 256, Taumarunui, NZ.* (8116)

CRAWSHAW, Henry Michael Aitken. b 15. Late Scho of Em Coll Cam BA 37, MA 43, Westcott Ho Cam 39. **d** 40 **p** 41 Nor. Publ Pr Dio Nor 40-43, Chap of Uppingham Sch 43-48; V of Stourport 48-51; R of Knebworth 51-57; Chedgrave w Hardley and Langley 57-64; RD of Loddon 61-64; R of Barnham Broom w Bixton Kimberley and Carleton Forehoe 64-70; L Brandon 64-70; PC of Wramplingham w Barford 64-70; PC of Coston w Runhall 64-70; PC of Hardingham 64-70; PC of Garveston w Thuxton 64-70; R of Burnham Deepdale 70-80; Brancaster (w Burnham Deepdale and Titchwell from 80) Dio Nor from 70; C-in-c of Titchwell 74-80. *Brancaster Rectory, King's Lynn, Norf.* (Brancaster 268)

CRAWSHAW, John Stuart. b 48. Grey Coll Dur BSc 70. Wycl Hall Ox 75. **d** 78 Repton for Derby **p** 79 Derby. C of St Barn City and Dio Derby from 78. *38 Cobden Street, Derby, DE3 3GX.* (Derby 371050)

CRAWTE, William Richard. b 30. Trin Coll Dub BA 54. **d** 55 Connor **p** 56 Down for Connor. C of St Aid Belf 55-57; Newc Dio Drom 57-59; CF 59-79. *Address temp unknown.*

CRAY, Graham Alan. b 47. Univ of Leeds BA 68. St Jo Coll Nottm 69. **d** 71 **p** 72 Roch. C of St Mark Gillingham Roch 71-75; CPAS N Area Co-Ordinator Youth Dept 75-78; C of St Mich-le-Belfrey City and Dio York from 78. *13 Hempland Drive, Heworth, York, YO3 0AY.* (York 28539)

CRAYMER, Samuel Maitland. Montr Dioc Th Coll STh 44. **d** 43 **p** 44 Alb. C of Bala 43-48; R of Bracebridge 49-52; St John Port Arthur 52-57; Ch of Epiph Sudbury Alg 57-74; Hon Can of Alg 60-71; Archd of Nipissing 71-74. *1250 Ramsey View Court, Apt 811, Sudbury, Ont., Canada.* (705-522-9247)

CRAZE, Canon Oswald Romilly. Hertf Coll Ox BA 34, MA 37. Wells Th Coll 34. **d** 37 **p** 38 Worc. C of Wollaston 37-39; C-in-c 39-45; Chap RAFVR 45-48; V of Mortomley 48-51; St Pet the Gt 51-56; Priv Chap to Bp of Worc 52-55; R of Upton-on-Severn 56-64; Surr 56-64; V of St Barn Rainbow Hill Worc 64-75; R (w Ch Ch Tolladine) 76-77; V of Ch Ch Tolladine Worc 64-75; RD of Worc 65-77; Hon Can of Worc from 67. *59 Woolhope Road, Worcester.* (Worc 356381)

CREAGH, George Terence. St Jo Coll Auckld LTh 61. **d** 61 **p** 62 Auckld. C of All SS Auckld 61-65; New Lynn 65-66; V of Hokianga 66-69; Glenfield 70-75; P-in-c of Avondale 75-77; Exam Chap to Bp of Auckld 75-76; Lect St Jo Coll Auckld from 77; Hon C of Meadowbank Dio Auckld from 77. *129 St John's Road, Auckland 5, NZ.*

CREAL, Kenneth Howard Michael. Univ of BC BA (1st cl Hist) 48, MA 49. Trin Coll Tor STB 53. **d** 52 **p** 53 Niag. R of Winona 52-55; Dioc Missr and LPr Dio Niag 55-61; Exam Chap to Bp of Niag 56-61; Can of Niag 59-70; L to Offic Niag 61-70; (on leave from Niag). *214 Lawrence Avenue East, Toronto, Ont., Canada.*

CREAL, Canon Murray Alexander Mark Macdonald. Univ of Manit BA 38. St Jo Coll Manit LTh 39. **d** 40 **p** 41 Rupld. C of St Mary Portage la Prairie 40-43; R of Carman 43-48; St Mark St Vital Winnipeg 48-60; St Paul Hamilton Dio Niag from 60; Hon Can of Niag 70-72 and from 77; Archd of Hamilton 72-77; Exam Chap to Bp of Niag 73-74. *42 Dromore Crescent, Hamilton, Ont., Canada.* (416-529 6933)

CREARY, George Lemuel. **d** 59 Ja **p** 60 Kingston for Ja. C of St Phil Whitfield Town 59-66. *5 Kingswood Avenue, Kingston 10, Jamaica, W Indies.*

CREASER, Canon David Edward. b 35. St Cath Coll Cam 3rd cl Law Trip pt i 57, BA (2nd cl Th Trip pt ia) 58, MA 62. Clifton Th Coll 59. **d** 61 **p** 62 Ches. C of Cheadle 61-67; V of Weston (w Denton from 69) 67-74; and from 82; C-in-c of

Denton 67-69; V of Frizinghall 74-81; Dioc Dir of Educn Dio Bradf from 73; Hon Can of Bradf from 80. *Vicarage, Askwith, Otley, W Yorks, LS21 2HX.* (Otley 461139)

CRECY, Hugh. b 05. Worc Ordin Coll 56. **d** 57 **p** 58 Worc. C of Malvern 57-59; R of Kimpton w Thruxton and Fyfield 59-62; Bentworth w Shalden 62-77; Perm to Offic Dio Ex from 77. *2 Weirfield Road, St Leonards, Exeter, EX2 4DN.* (0392-36777)

CREDITON, Lord Bishop Suffragan of. *See* Pasterfield, Right Rev Philip John.

✠ **CREEGGAN, Right Rev Jack Burnett.** Qu Univ Kingston, BA 25. Bp's Univ Lennox LST 27, DCL (*hon causa*) 71. **d** 27 **p** 28 Ont. C of Bancroft 27-29; St Aid Tor 29-31; I of Sharbot Lake Miss 31-33; R of N Augusta 33-39; Picton 39-43; St John Precott 43-50; Ch Ch Belleville 50-62; Can of Ont 51-53; Archd of Ont 53-62; Frontenac 62-68; R of Gananoque and of S Lake 62-70; Bp's Commiss Ont 67-70; Archd of Kingston 69-70; Cons Ld Bp of Ont in St Geo Cathl Kingston Ont 18 May 70 by Abp of Alg; Abp of Rupld; Bps of Moos; Tor; Bps Suffr of Hur; Moos; and Tor; Bp of Centr NY; Bp Suffr of Albany; Bp Nieminski (Polish Catholic Ch); res 74. *67 Sydenham Street, Kingston, Ont, Canada.* (613-542 5319)

CREERY-HILL, Anthony Thomas. b 23. BNC Ox BA (2nd cl Jurisp) 49, MA 54. Ridley Hall Cam 49. **d** 51 **p** 52 Lon. C of Ch Ch Highbury 51-53; Travelling Sec CSSM 53-58; Asst Master Red Ho Sch Moor Monkton 58-59; Chap Dean Close Jun Sch Cheltm 59-74; Sen Master Larchfield Sch Helensburgh 75-78. *St Andrew's School, Turi, Kenya.*

CREES, Geoffrey William. b 35. Cranmer Hall Dur 65. **d** 67 **p** 68 St Alb. C of Hoddesdon 67-70; Harwell and of Chilton 70-73; V of Greenham Dio Ox from 73. *Greenham Vicarage, Newbury, Berks.* (Newbury 41075)

CRELLIN, Howard Joseph. b 30. Late Exhib of Magd Coll Cam BA 52, MA 56. Magd Coll Ox BA (by incorp) 54, Dipl Th 55, MA 56. Wycl Hall Ox 53. **d** 55 **p** 56 Chelmsf. C of Dovercourt 55-58; R of Theydon Garnon 58-70; Select Pr Univ of Ox 68; Chap St Marg Hosp Epping 59-70; Perm to Offic Dio Ox 70-74; Asst Master K Chas I Sch Kidderminster 74-80. *Address temp unknown.*

CRESSEY, Roger Wilson. b 35. Chich Th Coll 72. **d** 74 Pontefract for Wakef **p** 75 Wakef. C of Pontefract 74-80; Dewsbury Dio Wakef from 77; Chap of Wakef Hosps from 80. *Pinderfields General Hospital, Aberford Road, Wakefield.*

CRESSWELL, Howard Rex. b 31. Ely Th Coll 56. **d** 59 **p** 60 Chelmsf. C of Dovercourt 59-61; Ascen Vic Dks Dio Chelmsf 61-64; V 64-71; Felsted Sch Missr 64-71; Surr 65-71; V in Harling Group 71-72; Quidenham Group 72-75; V of Trowse Dio Nor from 75; Arminghall Dio Nor from 75; R of Caistor w Markshall Dio Nor from 75. *Trowse Vicarage, Norwich, NR14 8TN.* (Nor 21732)

CRESSWELL, Canon Jack Joseph. b 11. Qu Coll Cam BA 39, MA 43. Wycl Hall Ox 39. **d** 40 **p** 41 Liv. C of St Helens 40-46; V of Iver 46-56; R of Windlesham 56-62; Sec Guildf Dioc Conf 61-70; V of Horsell 62-70; Hon Can of Guildf 69-78; Can (Emer) from 78; R of Busbridge 70-78; Sec Guildf Dioc Syn 70-75. *12 Eastleach, Cirencester, Glos, GL7 3NQ.* (Southrop 261)

CRESSWELL, Jeremy Peter. b 49. St Jo Coll Ox BA (Th) 72, MA 78. Ridley Hall Cam 73. **d** 76 **p** 76 Guildf. C of Wisley w Pyrford 75-78; Weybridge Dio Guildf from 75. *2 Cricket View, Princes Road, Weybridge, Surrey.* (Weybridge 51957)

CRESSWELL, Preb Kenneth Benjamin. b 17. St D Coll Lamp BA 50. **d** 51 **p** 52 Lich. C of Porthill 51-55; R of St Jo Bapt Longton 55-67; V of Horninglow 67-81; Preb of Lich Cathl from 80; Team V of Stoke-upon-Trent Dio Lich from 81. *All Saints' Vicarage, Leek Road, Hanley, Stoke-upon-Trent, ST1 3HH.* (Stoke-upon-Trent 264886)

CREW, Richard John. b 42. Trin Coll Bris 79. **d** 81 Penrith for Carl. C of St Jo Evang City and Dio Carl from 81. *68 Greystone Road, Carlisle, CA1 2DG.* (Carlisle 20893)

CRIBB, Canon Fred. St Jo Coll Dur BA and LTh 23, MA 27. Lon Coll of Div 22. **d** and **p** 24 Roch. C of St Pet and St Paul Tonbridge 24-26; Prin CMS Sch Momb 27-28; Chap Momb Cathl 29-30; Prin CMS Normal Sch Butere 29-30; Chap Miss to Seamen Momb 32-46; Hon Chap to Bp of Momb 42-46; Chap Miss to Seamen Lourenco Marques 47-48; E Africa Area 48-53; Chap Trans-Nzoia 53-64; Can of Nak 61-64; Hon Can from 64; Exam Chap to Bp of Nak 61-64. *Kaptien, PO Box 92, Nandi Hills, Kenya.*

CRIBB, Nicholas Llanwarne. b 12. Univ of Dur LTh 38. BA (Lon) 59; BD 2nd cl (Lon) 71. Lich Th Coll 32. **d** 35 **p** 36 Lon. C of All H Bromley-by-Bow 35-37; St Sav Brockley Rise 37-39; Asst Chap (Miss to Seamen) Port of Lon and Publ Pr Dio Chelmsf 39-40; Asst Chap Port of Man and Ship Canal 40-41; V of Kenton w Ashfield and Thorpe 41-52; Chap RNVR 43-46; R of Worlingworth w Tannington 52-55; Chap RAF 55-58; Lect & Chap Nottm Regional Coll of Tech 59-70; Warden of Dryden Hostel 59-63; Chap and Lect Trent Poly 70-77; Sen Lect 75-77; Publ Pr Dio Southw 59-77. *High Barn, Drinkstone, Bury St Edmunds, Suffolk.* (Rattlesden 396)

CRICHLOW, Very Rev Harold Edmund. St Chad's Coll Dur BA (2nd cl Th) 60. Codr Coll Barb 56. **d** 60 **p** 61 Barb. C of Ch Ch Barb 60-66; Hd Master Ch Ch High Sch Barb 60-66; L to Offic Barb 66;70; Asst Master Combermere Sch Barb 66-69; Sen Chap Univ of WI Ja 69-72; Dean of St Mich Cathl Barb from 72; Hon Chap of St Pet Leeds Dio Ripon from 80. *Flat 2, St Peters House, Kirkgate, Leeds LS2 7DJ.* (Leeds 454012)

CRICHLOW, Neville Joseph. b 40. Univ of Sask BA 73. Em & St Chad's Coll Sktn LTh 72. **d** 74 **p** 75 Sktn. I of Rosthern 74-75; St Matt City and Dio Sktn from 76. *811 Egbert Avenue, Saskatoon, Sask, Canada.*

CRICHTON, Harry. Edin Th Coll 43. **d** 45 **p** 46 Wakef. C of Featherstone 45-47; St Pancras 47-48; Aintree (in c of St Giles) 48-49; V of Cressing 49-56; Chap Black Notley Sanat 49-54; R of Highgate St Mary Ja 56-57; V of Nether Hoyland 57-59; Linton 59-71; Chap Linton Hosp 59-71; V of St Jo Bapt Sevenoaks 71-76; R of Lavenham Dio St E from 76. *Lavenham Rectory, Sudbury, Suff.* (Lavenham 247244)

CRICHTON, James Kenneth. b 35. Glouc Sch of Min 78. **d** and **p** 80 Glouc (APM). Hon C of Minchinhampton Dio Glouc from 80. *7 Market Square, Minchinhampton, Stroud, Glos, GL6 9BW.*

CRICK, Peter. b 39. BD (Lon) 68. Wells Th Coll 66. **d** 67 **p** 68 Chich. C of Horsham 67-71; Asst Dioc Youth Officer Ox 71-75; R of Denham Dio Ox from 75. *Rectory, Denham Village, Uxbridge, UB9 5BB* (Denham 832771)

CRICK, Philip Benjamin Denton. b 33. Univ of Bris BA (3rd cl Th) 63. Clifton Th Coll 60. **d** 64 **p** 65 Lon. C of Clerkenwell 64-67; CF from 67-72; C of St John Southall 72-75; C-in-c of H Trin Southall Dio Lon from 75. *Holy Trinity Vicarage, Uxbridge Road, Southall, Middx, UB1 3HH.* (01-574 3762)

CRIGAN, Alexander Charles Hamilton. Moore Th Coll Syd ACT ThL 46. **d** and **p** 47 Syd. C of Enfield 47; Asst Chap Miss to Seamen Syd 48-50; Perm to Offic Dios Glas and Cant 50-51; Asst Chap Miss to Seamen Melb 52-55; Min of St Mark W Preston 55-59; W Reservoir 59-61; I of H Trin E Melbourne 61-70; I of Mt Eliza 70-81; St Jas Point Lonsdale Dio Melb from 81. *Vicarage, Point Lonsdale, Vic, Australia 3225.*

CRIGAN, Conway Duncan. ACT ThL 17. **d** 18 **p** 19 Bal. C of Talbot Vic 18-19; P-in-c 19-20; Chalton 20-22; V 22-24; R of Balranald 24-26; P-in-c Of Creswick 26-30; V of Warracknabeal 30-51; Chap to Bp of Bal 42-51; RD of Stawell 46-51. *Iona, Crigan Road, Point Lonsdale, Vic. 3225, Australia.*

CRIGHTON, Andrew Charles. b 41. Univ of Glas MA 64. Edin Th Coll 77. **d** 79 **p** 80 Glas. C of Ayr 79-81; R of Laurencekirk, Drumtochty & Fasque Dio Brech from 81. *Beattie Lodge, Laurencekirk, Kincardineshire.* (Laurencekirk 380)

CRIGHTON, Roswell Carman. Univ of Tor BA 49. Vic Univ Tor BD 52. **d** 60 **p** 61 Alg. I of Burk's Falls 60-62; St Jas Orillia 62-68; R of St Mary Virg City and Dio Tor from 68. *42 Westmoreland Avenue, Toronto 173, Ont., Canada.* (416-536 9151)

CRINGLE, William Edward James. Univ of Lon BD 40. **d** and **p** 41 S & M. C of St Geo Douglas 41-49; V of Foxdale 49-55; R of Kirk Bride 55-61; V of St Olave Ramsey 61-80; Surr 64-80; Exam Chap to Bp of S & M 67-80. *3 Queens Drive West, Ramsey, IM.*

CRIPPS, Harold Ernest. b 04. AKC 47. **d** 47 **p** 48 Liv. C of St Elphin Warrington 47-52; C-in-c of New Springs 52-53; V 53-59; Burtonwood 59-74. *15 Bignor Close, Rustington, Littlehampton, Sussex.* (Rustington 2603)

CRIPPS, Keith Richard John. b 21. Trin Coll Cam 1st cl Cl Trip pt i, 42, BA (2nd cl Th Trip pt i) 43, MA 47. Univ of Newc T PhD 80. Ridley Hall Th Coll 43. **d** 45 Man **p** 47 Birm. C of St Chrys Man 45-47; Man Inter-Coll Sec SCM 45-47; C of Aston Juxta Birm 47-50; R of St Ambrose Chorlton-on-Medlock 50-60; Chap Angl Fellowship Univ of Man 51-60; Lect Univ of Man 52-60; Chap and Lect Ripon Tr Coll 60-65; L to Offic Dio Ripon 60-65; Dio Newc T from 65; Lect Kenton Lodge Coll Newc T from 65; Newc T Coll of Educn from 71; Newc T Poly 74-79. *9 Pentlands Court, Pentlands Close, Cambridge.* (Cambridge 354216)

CRIPPS, Michael Frank Douglas. b 28. Ch Ch Ox BA (2nd cl Mod Hist) 50, MA 53. Ridley Hall Cam 58. **d** 59 **p** 60 Ely. C of St Mary Gt Cam 59-62; Chap Trin Coll Kandy 62-66; P-in-c of St Paul's Conv Distr Covingham Swindon 66-72; V of St Paul's Covingham Swindon 72-73; P-in-c of Aldbourne 73; Baydon 73; Team V of Whitton 74-81; C of Marlborough

Dio Sarum from 81. *9 Silverless Street, Marlborough, Wilts, SN8 1JQ.*

CRIPPS, Thomas Royle. **d** 68 Zam **p** 68 Bp Mataka for Zam. C of St Geo Kabwe 68-70; R of Roodebloem 70-75; Devil's Peak 73-75; Worcester 75-78; Ixopo Dio Natal from 78. *Box 45, Ixopo, Natal, S Africa.*

CRISFIELD, Ven Roy Lacy. St Jo Coll Winnipeg BA 48, BD 50. **d** 50 **p** 51 Calg. C of St Mich AA Calg 50-52; I of Colinton 52-55; High Prairie 56-59; Dean and R of St Jas Cathl Peace River 59-64; R of Duncan 64-66; Lethbridge 66-73; All SS Regina 73-81; Exam Chap to Bp of Qu'App from 74; Archd of Assiniboia from 77; Dioc Executive Sec Dio Qu'App from 81. *1501 College Street, Regina, Sask, Canada.* (306-527 8606)

CRISP, Canon John Edward. b 19. Univ of Dur LTh 47. St Pet Hall Ox BA 52, MA 55. St Aug Coll Cant. **d** 44 Lon **p** 45 Stepney for Lon. C of St Matt Willesden 44-48; St Marg Ox 48-52; V of St Mark w St Luke St Marylebone 52-63; Newport Pagnell 63-70; R of Lathbury 63-70; RD of Newport 67-70; V of High Wycombe 70-75; R 75-77; RD of Wycombe 74-77; V of N Hinksey Dio Ox from 77; Hon Can of Ch Ch Ox from 79. *81 West Way, Botley, Oxford, OX2 9JY.* (Oxford 42345)

CRISP, Ronald Leslie. Worc Ordin Coll. **d** 56 **p** 57 Worc. C of Redditch 56-59; St Luke Dudley 59-63; V of St Jo Evang Dudley Wood Dio Worc from 63. *Vicarage, Lantern Road, Dudley Wood, Dudley, Worcs DY2 0DL.* (Cradley Heath 69018)

CRISPE, Denis Geoffrey Wingate. St Jo Coll Morpeth 59. **d** 63 **p** 64 Adel. C of Prospect 63-65; Miss Chap Northfield 65-68; P-in-c of Elliston 68-72; R of Pet w Terowie 72-74; L to Offic Dio Adel from 75; Asst Chap St Pet Coll Adel 78-80; Chap from 80. *639 Grange Road, Grange, S Australia 5022.* (08-356 8430)

CRISTOBAL, Canon Ariel Dario. Buenos Aires Sem Dipl Th 54. **d** 55 **p** 59 Argent. C of St Paul Buenos Aires 55-59; Chap 59-67; Asst Chap St Sav Belgrano Buenos Aires 67-68; Hon Can of St Jo Bapt Cathl Buenos Aires from 68. *25 De Mayo 282, 1002, Buenos Aires, Argentina.*

CRITCHLEY, Colin. b 41. Univ of Dur BA 63. Univ of Liv MA 69. N-W Ordin Course 75. **d** 78 **p** 79 Liv. Hon C of Halewood Dio Liv from 78. *53 Elwyn Drive, Halewood, Merseyside, L26 0UX.*

CRITCHLEY, Ronald John. b 15. Kelham Th Coll 31. **d** 38 **p** 39 Bradf. C of Ch Ch Skipton 38-40; Actg C of Ilkley 40-41; C 41-42; Chap RAFVR 42-47; PC of St Sav Fairweather Green 47-52; R of Barton-le-Street 52-63; V of Salton 52-63; Fylingdales 63-80; V of Hawsker 63-80. *4a North Promenade, Whitby, N Yorks, YO21 3JX.*

CRITCHLOW, John Webster. b 1895. Egerton Hall Man 32. **d** 33 **p** 34 Man. C of St John Old Trafford 33-35; All SS Newton Heath 35-38; R of St Paul (w St Luke from 62) Chorlton-on-Medlock 38-67. *The Lodge, London Road, Newark-on-Trent, Notts.*

CRITTALL, Richard Simon. b 47. Univ of Sussex BA (Russian) 69. Linacre Coll Ox BA (Th) 71. St Steph Ho 69. **d** 72 **p** 73 Lich. C of H Trin Oswestry 72-75; St Mary E Grinstead 75-78; Team V of The Resurr Brighton Dio Chich from 78. *St Alban's Vicarage, Natal Road, Brighton, BN2 4BN.*

CRITTLE, Wilfrid. b 04. Univ of Birm BCom 24. **d** 30 Rang **p** 31 Birm for Rang. BCMS Miss at Kamaing 30-36; and 37-42; Exam Chap to Bp of Rang 39-43; Chap at Saugor 43-44; CF (Ind) 44-46; Miss at Mohnyin 47-49; V of Worthing 49-74; Perm to Offic Dio Chich from 74. *Address temp unknown.*

CROAD, Arthur Robert. b 35. Down Coll Cam BA 58, MA 61. Clifton Th Coll. **d** 61 **p** 62 Southw. C of St Chris Sneinton 61-64; Kinson 64-72; R of Sherfield English (w Awbridge from 74) Dio Win from 72. *Sherfield English Rectory, Romsey, Hants.* (West Wellow 22352)

CROAD, David Richard. b 31. Univ of Reading BSc 55. Clifton Th Coll. **d** 57 **p** 58 Ox. C of Iver 57-60; Rushden 60-63; V of Loudwater 63-72; Sec CPAS in SW Area 72-78; Publ Pr Dio Bris 72-78; V of Bovingdon Dio St Alb from 78. *Vicarage, Bovingdon, Hemel Hempstead, Herts, HP3 0LP.* (0442-833298)

CROCKER, Eric George Martin. b 1896. Selw Coll Cam BA 21, MA 25. Westcott Ho Cam 21. **d** 22 **p** 23 Leic for Pet. C of All SS Northn 22-25; Chap RN 25-54; Hon Chap to HM the King 46-52; HM the Queen 52-54; V of Ermington 54-61. *Flat 2, Stoneleigh House, South Street, Totnes, Devon.*

CROCKER, Keith Gwillam. b 49. Lanchester Poly Cov BSc 70. Dipl Th (Extra-Mural Stud) 78. Oak Hill Coll 74. **d** 77 Bp McKie for Cov **p** 78 Cov. C of Whitnash 77-80; St Jo Evang Gt Horton City and Dio Bradf from 80. *4 Lesmere Grove, Bradford, BD7 4DY.* (Bradf 573261)

CROCKER, Robert John. Trin Coll Tor BA 47, LTh 50. **d** 49 Tor for Calg **p** 50 Calg. C of Lethbridge 50-52; V of Taber 52-55; Miss to Blackfoot Reserve 55-56; I of Wiarton 56-58; Trin Sarnia 58-64; R of St Steph Brantford 64-72; St Jas St Mary's 72-76; Goderich Dio Hur from 76. *87 North Street, Goderich, Ont., Canada.* (519-524 9961)

CROCKETT, Canon Benjamin Stephen Walcott. b 13. Bp Wilson Th Coll IM 34. **d** 37 **p** 38 Ex. C of Ottery St Mary 37-40; C of Gt Torrington 40-41; R of W Camel 41-44; V of North Kelsey 44-45; Mickleover Dio Derby from 45; Hon Can of Derby from 78. *All Saints Vicarage, Etwall Road, Mickleover, Derby, DE3 5DL.* (Derby 513793)

CROCKETT, Bruce Thomas Allison. Sir Geo Williams Univ Montr BSc 60. Hur Coll LTh 63. **d** 63 Montr for Niag. C of St Mary Hamilton 63-66; R of St Matt Hamilton 66-70; H Trin, Hamilton 70-73; Aylmer 73-79; Archd of W Queb 77-79; I of St Richard City and Dio Ott from 79. *Abingdon Drive, Nepean, Ont, K2H 7M5, Canada.*

CROCKETT, Peter James Sinclair. b 44. Sarum Wells Th Coll 74. **d** 77 **p** 78 Ex. C of Heavitree Ex 77-80; Team V of Em in Team Min of St Thos & Em City and Dio Ex from 80. *49 Okehampton Road, Exeter, Devon.* (Exeter 72908)

CROCKETT, Philip Anthony. b 45. K Coll Lon BA (Cl) 67, BD and AKC 70. St Mich Coll Llan 70. **d** 71 **p** 72 Llan. C of Aberdare 71-74; Whitchurch 74-78; V of Llanfihangel-y-Creuddyn w Llanafan-y-Trawscoed Dio St D from 78. *Llanafan-y-Trawscoed Vicarage, Aberystwyth, Dyfed.* (Crosswood 253)

CROCKETT, William Robert Kirkpatrick. Univ of Tor BA 56. Trin Coll Tor STB 60. Univ of Chicago MA 63, PhD 71. **d** 60 **p** 61 Tor. C of St John Weston 60-63; Lect Angl Th Coll of BC (Vanc Sch of Th from 71) from 64. *6000 Iona Drive, Vancouver 8, BC, Canada.*

CROFT, Bernard Theodore. b 10. Kelham Th Coll 30. **d** 35 **p** 36 Sheff. C of Conisborough 35-37; St Mary's Cathl Glas 37-39; St Jas (in c of St Francis) Cowley Ox 39-42; RAFVR 42-46; Chap Radley Coll Berks 47-48; L to Offic Dio Ox 48-49; R of Saxby 49-51; V of Horkstow 49-51; Chap RAF 51-54; Chap and Asst Master Woolpit Sch Ewhurst 54-60; L to Offic Dio Guildf 56-60; V of St Jude Birm 60-68; Reighton w Speeton 68-75; Perm to Offic Dio York from 75. *4 Freeman's Court, Water Lane, York, YO3 6PR.* (0904 56611)

CROFT, Harold John. b 17. St Aid Coll. **d** 47 **p** 48 Bradf. C of Ch Ch Skipton 47-50; V of Ingleton w Chapel-le-Dale 51-57; Cler Deputn Sec Dr Barnardo's Homes N Area 50-51; R of Heydon w L Chishill 57-81; V of Gt Chishill 57-81. *1 Green Street, Royston, Herts, SG8 7BB.* (Royston 42751)

CROFT, John Alexander. b 26. Wells Th Coll 67. **d** 69 Sherborne for Sarum **p** 70 Sarum. C of H Trin Trowbridge 69-73; V of St Pet Devizes Dio Sarum from 74. *St Peter's Vicarage, Devizes, Wilts.* (Devizes 2621)

CROFT, John Armentières. b 15. MC 44. Sarum Th coll 56. **d** 57 **p** 58 Truro. C of Madron w Morvah 57-60; V of Gwinear 60-70; Perm to Offic Dio Truro from 70; Dio Ex from 77. *Oakhurst, Beaston, Broadhempston, Totnes, Devon.*

CROFT, John Frederick. b 25. BSc (Lon) 52, PhD (Lon) 59. **d** 74 **p** 78 Nor. C of Cringleford Dio Nor from 74. *34 Brettingham Avenue, Cringleford, Norwich, NR4 6XQ.*

CROFT, Peter Gardom. b 25. St Jo Coll Cam BA 48, MA 50. Wells Th Coll 50. **d** 52 **p** 53 Cov. C of St Andr Rugby 52-58; V of Stockingford 58-65; R of Washington 65-78; Dioc Information Officer Dio Sheff from 78. *32 Clarendon Road, Sheffield, S10 3TR* (Sheff 306759)

CROFT, Reid Lionel. b 44. Montr Dioc Th Coll 74. **d** 75 Montr. C of Greenfield Park 75-76; on leave. *261 D'Avignon Street, Dollard des Ormeaux, Quebec, Canada.* (514-683 9819)

CROFT, Ronald. b 30. St Aid Coll 61. **d** 63 Middleton for Man **p** 64 Man. C of St Mich AA Lawton Moor 63-65; St Crispin Withington 65-66; St Marg Prestwich 66-67; V of St Ambrose Oldham 67-71; C-in-c of St Jas Oldham 67-68; V 68-71; V of St Hilda Prestwich 71-74; R of St Crispin Withington Dio Man from 74. *2 Hart Road, Manchester, M14 7LE.* (061-224 3452)

CROFT, Simon Edward Owen. b 51. St Steph Ho Ox 75. **d** 78 **p** 79 Ex. C of St Mich AA Heavitree (in c of St Paul from 81) City and Dio Ex from 78. *St Paul's Vicarage, Milton Road, Exeter, Devon.* (Ex 54783)

CROFT, Thomas Denman. Univ of Syd BA 54. Moore Th Coll Syd ACT ThL 52. **d** and **p** 53 Syd. C of Hurstville 53-54; Roseville 54; St Mich Wollongong 54-55; C-in-c of Toongabbie 55-58; R of Harris Pk 58-65; Bellevue Hill Dio Syd from 65. *Rectory, Bellevue Park Road, Bellevue Hill, NSW, Austrlia 2023.* (389-9615)

CROFT, Thomas Geoffrey. Moore Th Coll Syd ACT ThL 58. **d** 58 Bp Loane for Centr Tang **p** 59 Centr Tang. CMS Miss Dio Centr Tang 58-63; Dio Vic Nyan 64-67; C-in-c of Baulkham Hills Dio Syd 67-71; R from 71. *295 Windsor Road, Baulkham Hills, NSW, Australia 2153.* (639-4089)

CROFT, Warren David. St Francis Coll Brisb 59. ACT ThL 62. **d** 61 Syd for N Queensld **p** 62 N Queensld. C of Ayr 62-63; Sec for Youth and Miss Dio N Queensld 63-64; C of

Innisfail 64-66; P-in-c of Proserpine 66-68; R of Madang 68-72; Dir Angl Centre Madang 72-77; C of Mottingham (in c of St Alb) 77-78; Field Officer ABM in NSW from 79; Perm to Offic Dio Syd from 79; Dio C & Goulb from 80. *91 Bathurst Street, Sydney, NSW, Australia 2000.*

CROFT, William Alan. b 15. Lich Th Coll 55. **d** 57 **p** 58 Ex. C of St Thos Ex 57-59; R of Ashprington 59-73; V of Cornworthy 59-73; R of E Woolfardisworthy, Cheriton-Fitzpaine, Kennerleigh, Washford Pyne, Puddington, Poughill, Stockleigh English, Stockleigh Pomeroy (w Morchard Bp from 74 and Down St Mary and Clannaborough from 77) 73-80. *Ty'r Cae, Brechfa, Carmarthen, Dyfed.*

CROFT, William Hammond. b 08. Late Scho of Jes Coll Ox BA (2nd cl Mod Hist) 30, 3rd cl Th 31, MA 35. Wells Th Coll 31. **d** 31 **p** 32 Llan. C of St Fagan Aberdare 31-33; Coity w Nolton 34-37; Wolborough 37-39; V of Whipton 39-47; Dawlish 47-54; R of Alphington 54-73; RD of Kenn 59-63. *Frogs, Longmeadow Road, Lympstone, Exmouth, Devon.* (Exmouth 3551)

CROFT, William Stuart. b 53. Trin Hall Cam BA 76, MA 79. Ripon Coll Cudd BA (Th) 80. **d** 80 **p** 81 Edmonton for Lon. C of St Jas Gt Friern Barnet Dio Lon from 80. *2 Church House, Friern Barnet Road, N11 3BS.* (01-361 1292)

CROFTON, Edwin Alan. b 46. Univ Coll Ox BA 68, MA 72. Cranmer Hall Dur Dipl Th 72. **d** 73 **p** 74 York. C of Newland (St John Hull from 77) 73-77; St Jo Evang Worksop 77-81; V of Scarborough Dio York from 81. *Vicarage, The Crescent, Scarborough, N Yorks, YO11 2PP.*

CROFTS, Charles Arthur. b 14. Late Williams Exhib of Ball Coll Ox BA (2nd cl Phil Pol and Econ) 38, MA 48. Lich Th Coll 38. **d** 39 **p** 40 Lich. C of St Chad Shrewsbury 39-41; Tettenhall 42-48; Min Can of Worc and Asst Master of K Sch Worc 48-50; V of St Cross Holywell (w St Pet in the East from 57) 51-62; CF (TA) 54-64; V of Crowhurst 62-68; Hexton 69-76; Dioc Insp Sch Dio S'wark 62-68; Dir of Relig Educn St Alb 69-71; Hon Can of St Alb 69-76; C of Merstham w Gatton Dio S'wark from 77. *Epiphany House, Mansfield Drive, Merstham, Surrey, RH1 3JP.* (Merstham 2815)

CROMBIE, William Ian. b 52. Ex Coll Ox BA 76, MA 79. Ripon Coll Cudd 76. **d** 78 **p** 79 Sarum. C of Warminster 78-81; Fleetwood Dio Blackb from 81. *98b Poulton Road, Fleetwood, Lancs.* (Fleetwood 5396)

CROMPTON, Joseph. Paton Th Coll 33. **d** 43 Chelmsf **p** 43 Colchester for Chelmsf. C of St Pet Colchester 43-45; All SS, Goodmayes 45-47; V 47-52; R of St Mary Magd, Colchester 52-56; V of High Beach w Upshire 56-80. *12 Mornington Road, Chingford, E4 7DS.* (01-529 4379)

CROOK, David Creighton. b 37. Trin Coll Cam 2nd cl Cl Trip pt i 60, BA (2nd cl Th Trip pt ia) 61, MA 68. Cudd Coll 61. **d** 63 **p** 64 Carl. C of Workington 63-66; Penrith 66-70; V of St Jas Barrow-F 70-78; Maryport 78-81; Team V of Greystoke Dio Carl from 81. *Vicarage, Matterdale, Penrith, Cumbria.* (Glenridding 301)

CROOK, Dennis Eric. b 40. K Coll Lon and Warm AKC (2nd cl) 65. **d** 66 **p** 67 Blackb. C of Penwortham 66-69; Kirkham 69-71; V of St Jo Evang Accrington Dio Blackb from 72. *11 Queens Road, Accrington, Lancs, BB5 6AR.* (Accrington 34587)

CROOK, Frederick Herbert. b 17. Oak Hill Th Coll. **d** 52 **p** 53 Win. [f Lay Miss Niger] C of St Jo Evang Boscombe Bournemouth 52-55; V of H Trin Margate 55-66; Sec CCCS 66-79; L to Offic Dio Lon 70-71; I of St Paul Halifax 71-79; Trin E City and Dio Tor from 79. *425 King Street East, Toronto, Ont, Canada.* (416-367 0272)

CROOK, Graham Leslie. b 49. Chich Th Coll 74. **d** 76 Bp Hanson for Man **p** 77 Man. C of St Crispin Withington 76-80; St Marg Prestwich Dio Man from 80. *c/o St Margaret's Vicarage, Prestwich, Manchester, M25 5QB.*

CROOK, James Gordon. b 11. Selw Coll Cam 2nd cl Th Trip pt i 32, BA (3rd cl Th Trip pt i) 33, MA 38. Wells Th Coll 33. **d** 34 **p** 35 Lich. C of St Bart Wednesbury 34-36; R of Bluff Point 37-44; Chap Miss to Seamen Geraldton 37-44; Townsville N Queensland 44-47; Asst Chap Tyne 47-48; Port Chap Hull 48-50; Glas and Clyde 50-56; R of Patrington (w Winestead 67-75) 56-75. *50 Southcliff Road, Withernsea, Hull, HU19 2HX.* (Withernsea 3303)

CROOK, John Michael. b 40. St D Coll Lamp BA 62. Coll of Resurr Mirfield 62. **d** 64 Stafford for Lich **p** 65 Lich. C of Horninglow 64-66; Bloxwich 66-70; R of St Mich AA Inverness 70-74; Ed Moray Dioc Magazine and Dioc Press Officer 72-78; St Jo Evang (w St Mich AA from 74) Inverness 74-78; Aberfoyle Dio St Andr from 78; Callander Dio Dunk from 78; Doune Dio St Andr from 78. *St Mary's Rectory, Aberfoyle, Stirling, FK8 3UJ.* (Aberfoyle 252)

CROOK, Rowland William. b 39. Dipl Th (Lon) 63. Tyndale Hall Bris 61. **d** 64 **p** 65 Lich. C of St Phil Penn Fields 64-68; St Clem w St Matthias Salford 68-70; Bucknall w Bagnall 70-76; V of New Shildon Dio Dur from 76. *All Saints Vicarage, New Shildon, Co Durham, DL4 2JT.* (Shildon 2785)

CROOKES, Canon Richard John. b 17. Pemb Coll Cam BA 38, MA 42. Linc Th Coll 39. **d** 41 **p** 42 Pet. C of Abington 41-44; CF (EC) 44-47; Hon CF 47; C of Grimsby (in c of St Martin) 47-52; CF (TA) 48-76; Min of Good Shepherd Conv Distr Little Coates 52-60; V of Cleethorpes 60-75; Surr 63-75; RD of Grimsby and Cleethorpes 64-73; Can and Preb of Linc Cathl from 72; R of Binbrook Dio Linc from 75; Swinhope w Thorganby Dio Linc from 75; P-in-c of Kelstern w Calcethorpe and E Wykeham Dio Linc from 81. *Rectory, Binbrook, Lincs, LN3 6BJ.* (Binbrook 227)

CROOKS, David William Talbot. b 52. TCD BA 75, MA 78. **d** 77 **p** 78 Derry. C of Glendermott Dio 77-81; Old St Paul City and Dio Edin from 81. *59 Jeffrey Street, Edinburgh, EH1 1DH.* (031-556 9597)

CROOKS, Eric. b 34. Oak Hill Th Coll 68. **d** 70 **p** 71 Man. [f in Ch Army] C of Ch Ch, Chadderton 70-73; St Paul Deansgate Bolton 73-75; Shankill Lurgan 75-77; R of Aghaderg w Donaghmore 77-80; Dundonald Dio Down from 80. *Rectory, Dundonald, Co Down, N Ireland.* (Dundonald 3153)

CROOKS, Frederick Walter. b 18. TCD BA 41, MA 45. **d** 41 **p** 42 Oss. Dean's V of St Canice's Cathl and C of Kilkenny 41-43; Chap RNVR 43-46; C of High Wycombe (in c of St Andr) 46-48; V of St Paul Dock Street w St Mark Whitechapel 48-52; Cobham 52-62; R of Haslemere 62-69; RD of Godalming 67-69; V of Epsom 69-74; Shalfleet 74-80; Thorley 75-80; Hon Can of Guildf 69-74; RD of Epsom 70. *Millstream Cottage, Station Road, Yarmouth, IW, PO41 0QT.* (Yarmouth 760240)

CROOKS, Henry Cecil. b 15. Edin Th Coll 71. **d** and **p** 72 St Andr. P-in-c of Kinross 72-75; R 75-81; P-in-c of Dollar 76-81; C of E Bris Dio Bris from 81. *St Leonard's Vicarage, Parkfield Avenue, Bristol, BS5 8DP.*

CROOKS, Ian Barry. St Jo Coll Morpeth ACT ThL 69. **d** 69 River. C of St Alb Griffith 69-71; Perm to Offic Dio Brisb 72-74; Dio Bath from 75. *77 Esrom Street, Bathurst, NSW, Australia 2795.*

CROOKS, Very Rev John Robert Megaw. b 14. TCD BA and Div Test 38, MA 48. **d** 38 **p** 39 Dub. C of St Pet Dub 38-43; Min Can of St Patr Cathl and Catechist Dub High Sch 39-43; C of Leighlin Group 43-44; R of Killylea 44-56; V Cho of Arm Cathl 56-73; Dioc Sec 63-79; Hon Sec Gen Syn from 70; Preb of Ballymore 71-72; Mullabrack 72-73; Archd of Arm 73-79; Dean & Keeper of Publ Libr Arm from 79; Dean of St Patr Cathl Arm from 79. *44 Abbey Street, Armagh, BT61 7DZ, N Ireland.* (Armagh 522540)

CROOKS, Louis Warden. Trin Coll Dub BA 33, Div Test 35, MA 57. **d** 36 **p** 37 Derry. C of Templemore 36-42; CF (EC) 39-46; CF (TA) 46-51; SCF (TA) 51-63; TD 55; R of Conwall U (w Gartan from 58) 46-80; Archd of Raph 57-80; Exam Chap to Bp of Derry and Raph 57-80. *c/o Letterkenny, Co Donegal, Irish Republic,* (Letterkenny 72)

CROOKS, Peter James. b 50. St Jo Coll Cam BA 72. Cranmer Hall Dur 74. **d** 76 Lon **p** 77 Kens for Lon. C of St Paul Onslow Sq Kens 76-79; H Trin Brompton Road Kens 78-79; St Jo Evang Wembley 79-82. *20 Swinderby Road, Wembley, HA0 4SF.* (01-902 5803)

CROOKS, Very Rev Samuel Bennett. b 20. OBE 81. Trin Coll Dub BA 43, MA 47. TD 64. **d** 43 Connor **p** 44 Bp Hind for Connor. C of St Anne's Cathl Belf 43-49; Dean's V 43-47; v Cho 47-49; Min Can 52-63; R of St John Laganbank and Orangefield Belf 49-63; RD of Hillsborough 53-63; I of Shankhill (Lurgan) 63-70; SCF (TA) from 63; Archd of Drom 64-70; Can of St Anne's Cathl Belf 64-70; Dean of St Anne's Cathl Belf and V of Belf from 70. *St Anne's Vicarage, Donegall Street, Belfast, BT1 2HB.* (Belf 28332)

CROOKSHANK, Richard Graham. b 06. **d** 32 **p** 34 Truro. C of Creed 32-34; St Paul Herne Hill 34-36; C-in-c of Tresco w Bryher Is of Scilly 36-38; V of Tresmere w Treneglos and Tremaine 38-44; CF (R of O) 39-44; R of Calstock 44-47; Bere Ferrers w Bere Alston 47-56. *Voss, Trematon, Saltash, Cornw.* (Saltash 4458)

CROOKSHANK, Stephen Graham. b 08. Univ of Lon BA 37. Westcott Ho Cam 39. **d** 40 **p** 41 S'wark. C of St Barn Dulwich 40-43; Kingswood (in c of Tadworth) 43-47; Min of Conv Distr of Tadworth 47-50; R of Mottingham 50-58; Min of H Trin Eccles Distr Twydall Gillingham Kent 58-64; V 64-66; Seal 66-73; L to Offic Dios of Cant Roch and S'wark 73-76; Perm to Offic Dio Roch from 76. *23 Vinson Close, Orpington, Kent, BR6 0EQ.* (Orpington 38729)

CROSBIE, Kenneth Antonio. d and **p** 77 Qu'App. C of New Sumner Dio Qu'App from 77. *Box 89, Saltcoats, Sask, Canada.*

CROSFIELD, Very Rev George Philip Chorley. b 24. Selw Coll Cam BA (1st cl Th Trip pt i) 50. 2nd cl Hist Trip pt ii 51, MA 55. Edin Th Coll 46. **d** 51 **p** 52 Edin. C of St D Pilton

51-53; St Andrews 53-55; R of Hawick 55-60; Chap Gordonstoun Sch 60-67; Vice-Provost and Can of St Mary's Cathl Edin 68-70; Provost from 70. *8 Lansdowne Crescent, Edinburgh, EH12 5EQ.* (031-225 2978)

CROSLAND, George Lindley. b 16. Univ of Leeds BA 38. ARCM 51. LRAM 54. Ely Th Coll 39. **d** 40 **p** 41 Wakef. C of St Mich Castleford 40-43; Saltney 43-47; V of St Luke Dukinfield 47-56; Werneth (or Compstall) Dio Ches from 56; Surr from 54. *Compstall Vicarage, Stockport, Chesh.* (061-427 1259)

CROSS, Very Rev Aidan Harrison. Univ of Leeds BA (2nd cl Engl) 39. Coll of Resurr Mirfield 39. **d** 41 Tewkesbury for Glouc **p** 41 Glouc. C of St John, Cinderford 41-43; St Sav, Maritzburg 43-51; V of Karkloof 51-56; St Phil Lambeth 56-58; R and Dean of Bloemf Cathl from 58; Archd of Bloemf City and Can of Bloemf from 58. *Deanery, Salzmann Street, Bloemfontein, OFS, S Africa.* (051-73649)

CROSS, Alan. b 43. Chich Th Coll 68. **d** 70 **p** 71 Birm. C of St Osw Bordesley 70; St Mich AA S Yardley Birm 70-73; St Jas w All SS St Nich & St Runwald Colchester 73-77; V of St Jas Leigh Dio Chelmsf from 77. *St James' Vicarage, Blenheim Chase, Leigh-on-Sea, Essex.* (Southend-on-Sea 73603)

CROSS, Christopher Francis. b 02. New Coll Ox BA 24, MA 27. Cudd Coll 26. **d** 27 **p** 28 Glouc. C of Cirencester w H Trin Watermoor 27-31; Sydenham 31; V of Waihao NZ 31-35; R of Bucknell Oxon 36-40; Mixbury w Finmere 40-48; Aston Tirrold w Aston Upthorpe 48-61. *Field Barn, Rectory Road, Streatley, Berks.* (Goring 872419)

✠ **CROSS, Right Rev David Stewart.** b 28. Trin Coll Dub BA (Resp) 52, MA 56. Westcott Ho Cam 52. **d** 54 **p** 55 Newc T. C of Hexham 54-57; St Alb Abbey St Alb 57-63; Prec 60-63; C of St Ambrose Chorlton-on-Medlock and Asst Chap Man Univ 63-67; Producer Relig Broadcasting BBC N and L to Offic Dio Man 68-76; Cons Ld Bp Suffr of Doncaster in York Minster 2 July 76 by Abp of York; Bps of Wakef, Man, Sheff, Bradf and Ripon; Bps Suffr of Jarrow, Stockport, Burnley, Penrith, Pontefract, Selby, Knaresborough, Sherwood, Hulme, Whitby, Warrington and Hertf; and others; Trld to Blackb 82; Chairman BBC Sheff Local Radio Advisory Coun 80-82; Chs Advisory Comm on Local Broadcasting 80-82. *Bishop's House, Claytn-le-Dale, Blackburn, Lancs, BB1 9EF.* (Blackburn 48234)

CROSS, Edward Charles. **d** 69 **p** 71 Bath. C of H Trin Orange Dio Bath from 71. *9 Windred Street, Orange, NSW, Australia 2800.* (62-2146)

CROSS, Frederick Albert. Univ of Tor BA 55. Trin Coll Tor LTh 59. **d** 59 **p** 60 Tor. C of St Clem N Tor 59-63; R of Bramalea 63-65; St Chris-on-the-Heights Downsview City and Dio Tor from 65; Exam Chap to Bp of Tor from 74. *171 Delhi Avenue, Downsview, Ont., Canada.* (416-635 8307)

CROSS, Canon Frederick Harford. b 02. Univ of Birm BA (Hist) 24. Univ of Lon BD 43. Kelham Th Coll 26. **d** 30 Barking for Chelmsf **p** 31 Colchester for Chelmsf. C of St Matt Custom Ho Victoria Dks 30-33; St Paul Brighton 33-34; C-in-c of H Cross Conv Distr Aldrington 34-38; Chap of St Kath Tr Coll Tottenham 38-42; V of St Jas Gt Bethnal Green 42-46; Dir of Relig Educn Dio Linc 46-50; Proc Conv Linc 47-55; Can and Preb of St Mary Crackpool in Linc Cathl 48-54; Dioc Missr 50-53; R of Flixborough w Burton-on-Stather 53-54; Warden of Whalley Abbey and Can of Blackb 54-59; Dir of Relig Educn Dio Blackb 54-59; Dio Glouc 59-64; Hon Can of Glouc 59-71; Can (Emer) from 71; L to Offic Dio Glouc 59-64; Exam Chap to Bp of Glouc from 60; V of St Steph Cheltenham 64-71; Perm to Offic Dio Chich from 72. *38 Links Road, Bexhill-on-Sea, Sussex.*

CROSS, Greville Shelly. b 49. Sarum Wells Th Coll 73. **d** 76 Dudley for Worc **p** 77 Worc. C of St Mary & All SS Kidderminster 76-80; P-in-c of St Mark-in-the-Cherry-Orchard Worc 80-81; Team V of Worc SE City and Dio Worc from 81. *St Mark's Vicarage, Bath Road, Worcester, WR5 3EP.*

CROSS, James Stuart. b 36. Magd Coll Ox BA (2nd cl Th) 65, MA 72 Ripon Hall Ox 62. **d** 65 **p** 66 Glouc. C of St Phil and St Jas Leckhampton 65-67; CF from 67. *c/o National Westminster Bank Ltd, Priory Road, Monmouth.*

CROSS, Jeremy Burkitt. b 45. St Pet Coll Ox BA (3rd cl Th) 68, MA 71. Wycl Hall Ox 67. **d** 69 Dunwich for St E **p** 70 St E. C of Mildenhall 69-72; Lindfield 72-77; V of Framfield Dio Chich from 77. *Framfield Vicarage, Uckfield, Sussex.* (Framfield 365)

CROSS, John Henry Laidlaw. b 30. Peterho Cam BA 53, MA 57. Ridley Hall Cam 53. **d** 55 Kens for Lon **p** 56 Lon. C of St John Ealing Dean 55-58; Gt Baddow 58-60; PC of Maidenhead 60-68; News Ed C of E Newspaper 68-71; C of St Pet-on-Cornhill City and Dio Lon from 68; Assoc Ed Chr Weekly Newspapers Ltd 71-72; Ed 72-75; Dir 71-79; C of All SS Chelsea (Old Ch) Dio Lon from 76. *23 Calonne Road, SW19.*

CROSS, Leslie Howard. b 10. ACP 65. Cranmer Hall Dur 63. **d** 64 **p** 65 Newc T. C of St Jo Evang Percy Tynemouth 64-70; Benwell (in c of Old Benwell) 70-72; V of Matfen 72-78; P-in-c of Stamfordham 76-78; V of Stamfordham w Matfen 78-80; Hon C of Bywell Dio Newc from 81. *14 Birkdene, Painshawfield Road, Stocksfield, Northumberland, NE43 7EN.* (Stocksfield 3245)

CROSS, Michael Anthony. b 45. Univ Leeds BA (Phil and Engl) 67, BA (Th) 69. Coll of Resurr Mirfield 68. **d** 70 **p** 71 Bloemf. C of Bloemf Cathl 70-73; Adel 74-76; Chap Birm Univ 76-81; V of Chapel Allerton Dio Ripon from 81. *Chapel Allerton Vicarage, Wood Lane, Leeds, LS7 3QF.* (Leeds 683072)

CROSS, Michael Harry. b 28. Univ of Liv BVSc 50. Cudd Coll 74. **d** 76 **p** 77 Heref. C of Ledbury 76-79; P-in-c of Bosbury Dio Heref from 79; Coddington Dio Heref from 79; Wellington Heath Dio Heref from 79. *Bosbury Vicarage, Ledbury, Herefs.* (Bosbury 225)

CROSS, Ronald Charles. St Jo Coll Morpeth. **d** 65 **p** 66 Melb. C of St Mark Camberwell 65-67; Murrumbeena 67-70; Min of Dallas 70-73; in Dept of Chaps Dio Melb from 73. *20 Surfers Avenue, Ocean Grove, Vic, Australia 3226.* (052-55 1285)

CROSS, Walter Alan. b 07. ALCD 32. **d** 32 **p** 33 Guildf. C of H Trin Aldershot 32-35; Chap N Prov Tang Terr 35-39; C of Ch Ch Ramsgate 39-40; CF (EC) 40-46 (twice Men in Disp 44); Org Sec CMS for Dios Birm Cov and Leic 46-50; V of The Martyrs Leic 50-72; Perm to Offic Dio Cant from 72. *149 Sandown Road, Deal, Kent, CT14 6NX.*

CROSSE, Canon Michael Selby. b 09. Linc Th Coll 29. **d** 33 **p** 34 Derby. C of St John Derby 33-36; Grantham 36-38; Chap of All SS Cathl Ch Derby 38-41; C-in-c of Riddings 39-41; Sec Dioc Coun of Youth 40-41; Chap RAFVR 41-46; Dom Chap to Bp of Linc 46-47; V of Lenton w Ingoldsby 47-51; St Faith Linc 51-57; Dom Chap to Bp of Dur 57-64; V of Taddington w Chelmorton 64-68; Hazelwood 68-74; RD of Duffield 70-74; Hon Can of Derby Cathl 74; Can (Emer) from 74; Perm to Offic Dio Glouc from 75. *8 Lansdown Terrace, Cheltenham, Glos, GL50 2JT.*

CROSSLAND, Felix Parnell. b 20. Univ of Wales (Swansea) BSc 49. MIMechE 57, CEng St Deiniol's Libr Hawarden 73. **d** 75 Bp Poole-Hughes for Llan **p** 76 Llan. C of Skewen 75-78; Neath w Llantwit Dio Llan from 78. *21 Cimla Road, Neath, W Glam, SA11 3PR.* (Neath 3560)

CROSSLEY, Dennis Thomas. K Coll Lon and Warm AKC 52. **d** 53 **p** 54 S'wark. C of Crofton Park 53-56; Beddington 56-59; St Mark Talbot Village (in c of St Thos Ensbury Pk) 59-62; R of Finchampstead Dio Ox from 62. *Finchampstead Rectory, Wokingham, Berks, RG11 3SE.* (Eversley 732102)

CROSSLEY, George Alan. b 34. Univ of Dur BA 56, Dipl Th 60. Cranmer Hall Dur. **d** 60 Burnley for York **p** 61 Blackb. C of St Steph Blackb 60-63; Ashton-on-Ribble 63-65; V of St Paul Oswaldtwistle 65-72; C-in-c Milburn w Newbiggin 72-73; R of Long Marton w Dufton & Milburn 72-76; C-in-c of St John Beckermet Dio Carl 76-78; V (w St Bridget and Ponsonby) from 78. *St John's Vicarage, Beckermet, Cumb, CA21 2YB.* (Beckermet 327)

CROSSLEY, Hugh Vaughan. b 20. AKC 42. Bps' Coll Cheshunt. **d** 47 **p** 48 Chelmsf. C of Loughton 47-49; R of Mohales Hoek 49-52; Chap Miss to Seamen and R of St Steph and St Lawr, Lourenço Marques 52-57; Org Sec Miss to Seamen E Distr 57-58; v of Shalford 58-60; R of Witbank 60-66; R of H Trin Middelburg 61-66; P-in-c of St Francis Miss Middelburg 61-66; Archd of Mafeking and R of Mafeking 66-70; C-in-c St Mark's Lobatse 66-70; R of Welkom 70-73; Odendaalsrus 70-73; P-in-c of Orsett Dio Chelmsf 73; R from 73; P-in-c of Bulphan Dio Chelmsf from 77. *Orsett Rectory, Grays, Essex, RM16 3JT.* (Grays Thurrock 891254)

CROSSLEY, James Salter Baron. b 39. Linc Th Coll 70. **d** 72 Repton for Derby **p** 73 Derby. C of Chesterfield 72-75; Chap to R Infirm St Cath's Hosp and Tickhill Road Hosp Doncaster from 75; Hon C Intake Dio Sheff from 78. *2 Avoca Avenue, Intake, Doncaster.* (Doncaster 66666)

CROSSLEY, Kenneth Symonds. Univ of Melb BA 39. St Jo Coll Morpeth. ACT ThL 43. **d** and **p** 38 Goulb. Asst Chap Canberra Gr Sch 38; C of Cathl Ch Goulb 38-39; R of Barmedman 39-42; Chap AIF 42-46; R of Kameruka 46-49; furlough 49; Asst Master Canberra Gr Sch 50-55; All SS Coll Bath 55-65; Chap 56-59; Asst Chap 60-65; R of Braidwood 65-67; Queanbeyan 67-78; Perm to Offic Dio C & Goulb from 78; Dio Syd from 80. *26 Ringwood Road, Exeter, NSW, Australia 2580.*

CROSSLEY, Robert Scott. b 36. BSc (Lon) 61. BD (Lon) 68. PhD (Lon) 75. ALCD 64. **d** 64 **p** 65 Roch. C of St Jo Bapt Beckenham 64-68; Morden 68-72; Chap Ridley Hall Cam 72-75; V of St Paul w St Mary Camberley Dio Guildf from 75;

RD of Surrey Heath from 81. *St Paul's Vicarage, Crawley Ridge, Camberley, Surrey.* (Camberley 22773)

CROSSLEY, William Laurance Raymond. b 49. Oak Hill Coll 71. **d** 74 Ox **p** 75 Reading for Ox. C of Gerrard's Cross 74-77; Langley Marish 77-79; CF from 79. *c/o Ministry of Defence, Bagshot Park, Bagshot, Surrey, GU19 5PL.*

CROSSMAN, Leslie Ronald. St Jo Coll Morpeth 35. **d** 37 **p** 38 Bath. M of Bro of Good Shepherd 37-41; Chap AIF 41-46; V of Coraki 46-50; R of Bellingen 50-55; Bulimba 55-77; Perm to Offic Dio Brisb from 77. *14 Epsom Street, Macgregor, Queensland, Australia 4109.*

CROSTHWAIT, Ven Terence Patrick. Trin Coll Tor BA 30, MA 32. **d** 32 Niag for Tor **p** 33 Tor. C of St John Norway Tor 32-33; Grace Ch Tor 33-41; R of St Mark Port Hope 41-45; St Alb Tor 45-56; Dom Chap to Bp of Tor 48-56; Can of Tor 52-57; R of St Clem Eglington Tor 56-70; Archd of York 57-71; Tor 71-72; Archd (Emer) from 72. *182 Brooke Avenue, Toronto 12, Ont, Canada.*

CROSTHWAITE, George Roger. b 38. Univ of Dur BSc 62. Ridley Hall Cam 62. **d** 65 **p** 66 Bradf. C of St Pet Cathl Bradf 65-67; St Aldate 67-70; Youth Adv CMS 70-73; P-in-c of St Werburgh Derby 73-78; V 78-81; P-in-c of Cherbury 81-82. *c/o Longworth Rectory, Abingdon, Oxon, OX13 5DX.*

CROSTHWAITE, Howard Wellesley. b 37. Univ of Dur BA 59. St Steph Ho Ox 59. **d** 61 Penrith for Carl **p** 62 Carl. C of Workington 61-63; R of St John w St Mark Grenada 63-64; C of Barnsley 64-67; V of Milnsbridge 68-70; Thurgoland 70-79; Chap of Stainborough 70-76. *185 Woolley Road, Stocksbridge, Sheffield, S30 5GF.*

CROUCH, Jack Sydney. Wycl Coll Tor. **d** 54 Bp Wilkinson for Tor **p** 57 Tor. C-in-c of Pickering 54-56; I of Bolton 56-60; R of St Barn Tor 60-62; C of All SS Kingsway Tor 62-65; R of St Bede Tor 65-69; St Jo Div Scarborough Tor 70-74; Copper Cliff Dio Alg from 74. *PO Box 661, Copper Cliff, Ont., Canada.* (705-682-2623)

CROUCH, Keith Matheson. b 45. AKC 70. St Aug Coll Cant 71. **d** 72 **p** 73 Birm. C of St Jas Hill Birm 72-75; Bartley Green (in c of Woodgate Valley) 76-78. *13 Charlton Rise, Sheet Road, Ludlow, Salop.*

CROUCH, Raymond. b 21. Cudd Coll 66. **d** 68 **p** 69 Ox. C of Bracknell 68-71: P-in-c of Littlemore 71-78; C of Boxgrove 78-81; Oving w Merston 78-81; Tangmere 78-81; V of Winkfield w Chavey Down Dio Ox from 81; P-in-c of Cranbourne Dio Ox from 81. *Winkfield Vicarage, Windsor, Berks.* (Winkfield Row 2322)

CROUCHMAN, Eric Richard. b 30. Bps' Coll Cheshunt. **d** 66 **p** 67 St E. C of H Trin Ipswich 66-69; All Hallows Ipswich 69-72; V of Crowfield w Stonham Aspal (and Mickfield from 73) 72-81; R of Combs Dio St E from 81. *135 Poplar Hill, Combs, Stowmarket, Suff, IP14 2AY.* (Stowmarket 2076)

CROUSE, Robert Darwin. King's Coll NS BA 51. Harvard Univ STB 54. Trin Coll Tor MTh 57. **d** 54 **p** 55 NS. P Dio NS 54-60; Asst Prof of Ch Hist Bp's Univ Lennox 60-64; Exam Chap to Bp of NS from 70. *Dalhousie University, Halifax, NS, Canada.*

CROW, Arthur. b 26. St Chad's Coll Dur BA 51, Dipl Th 52. **d** 52 **p** 53 Wakef. C of Thornhill 52-54; Holmfirth 54-57; V of Shelley 57-63; Flockton w Denby Grange Dio Wakef from 63. *Flockton Vicarage, Wakefield, W Yorks, WF4 4DH.* (Wakef 848349)

CROW, Michael John. b 35. K Coll Lon and Warm AKC (2nd cl) 63. **d** 64 **p** 65 St Alb. C of Welwyn Garden City 64-67; Sawbridgeworth 67-69; Biscot Luton 69-71; V of St Aug Limbury 71-79; Team R of Borehamwood Dio St alb from 79. *94 Shenley Road, Borehamwood, Herts.* (01-953 2554)

CROWDER, Canon Norman Harry. b 26. St Jo Coll Cam BA 48, MA 52. Westcott Ho Cam 50. **d** 52 Bp Weller for Southw **p** 53 Southw. C of St Mary Radcliffe-on-Trent 52-55; Res Chap to Bp of Portsm 55-59; Asst Chap Canford Sch 59-64; Chap 64-72; V of St John Oakfield Ryde 72-75; Can Res of Portsm and Dioc Dir of Relig Educn Dio Portsm from 75. *1 Pembroke Close, Portsmouth, Hants, PO1 2NX.* (Portsm 818107)

CROWDER, Ven Robert Burn. Em Coll Sktn LTh 51. **d** 42 Arctic for Sktn **p** 43 Sktn. C of Maymont 42-44; Lintlaw 44-47; Colonsay 47-50; R of Battleford 50-51; Wilkie 51-56; C of Ch Ch Calg 56-57; I of St Phil Elboya Calg 57-65; Archd of Calg from 65; Bp's Commiss Calg from 66; Regr Dio Calg 68-69; Commiss Moro from 68; Exam Chap to Bp of Calg from 70; R of St Barn City and Dio Calg from 72. *22 Malibou Road SW, Calgary, Alta., Canada.* (255-4398)

CROWE, Anthony Murray. b 34. St Edm Hall Ox BA (2nd cl Th) 58, MA 61. Westcott Ho Cam 57. **d** 59 **p** 60 Cov. C of Stockingford 59-62; All SS New Eltham 62-66; V of St Jo Evang, Clapham S'wark 66-73; R of St Luke Charlton Dio S'wark from 73. *Rectory, Charlton Church Lane, SE7 7AA.* (01-858 0791)

CROWE, Eric Anthony. b 29. St Jo Coll Dur BA 53. Cudd Coll 53. **d** 55 **p** 56 Wakef. C of St Jo Evang Huddersfield 55-58; St Pet Barnsley 58-60; R of High Hoyland 60-68; V of Battyeford w Knowle 68-75; C-in-c of Pitminster w Corfe Dio B & W 75; V from 76. *Pitminster Vicarage, Taunton, Somt.* (Blagdon Hill 232)

CROWE, John Yeomans. b 39. Keble Coll Ox BA (Th) 62, MA 66. Linc Th Coll 62. **d** 64 **p** 65 Lich. C of Tettenhall Regis 64-67; Caversham 67-71; V of Gt and L Hampton 72-76; C-in-c of Leek Dio Lich 76-79; Team R from 79. *6 Church Street, Leek, Staffs, ST13 6AB.* (Leek 382515)

CROWE, Laurence. b 32. Linc Th Coll 60. **d** 61 **p** 62 Cov. C of St Jo Bapt Cov 61-66; V of New Bilton 66-75; Washwood Heath Dio Birm from 75. *266 Washwood Heath Road, Birmingham, B8 2XS.* (021-327 1461)

CROWE, Lionel Cyril Gordon. St Francis Coll Brisb 39. ACT ThL 41. **d** 40 **p** 41 N Queensld. C of Charters Towers 40-43; M Bush Bro of St Barn 43-46; R of St Pet West End townsville 47-50; C (Col Cl Act) of St Matt Bethnal Green and of St Sav Pimlico 51; St John Hampstead 52; Beckenham 53-54; R of St John Forbes 54-72; Cumnock 72-75. *84 Bungay Road, Wingham, NSW, Australia 2429.*

CROWE, Canon Norman Charles. b 23. **d** 63 **p** 64 Leic. C of Marts Leic 63-66; Min of St Chad's Eccles Distr Leic 66-68; V 68-73; Market Harborough Dio Leic from 73; RD of Gartree I 76-81; Hon Can of Leic from 80. *Vicarage, Market Harborough, Leics.* (Market Harborough 63441)

CROWE, Philip Anthony. b 36. Selw Coll Cam BA 60, MA 64. Ridley Hall Cam 60. **d** 62 **p** 63 Lon. C of Cockfosters 62-65; Tutor Oak Hill Th Coll 62-67; Ed C of E Newspaper 67-71; Lect at St Martin Birm 71-76; R of Breadsall Dio Derby from 77; Dioc Miss Dio Derby from 77. *Breadsall Rectory, Derby, DE7 6AL.* (Derby 831352)

CROWE, Sydney Ralph. b 32. Edin Th Coll 61. **d** 63 **p** 64 Bradf. C of H Trin Bingley 63-66; Bierley 66-69; V of St Chad Manningham Dio Bradf from 69. *54 Toller Lane, Bradford, W Yorks, BD8 8QH.* (Bradford 43957)

CROWHURST, David Brian. b 40. Qu Coll Birm 77. **d** 80 **p** 81 Worc (NSM). C of Ribbesford w Bewdley & Dowles Dio Worc from 80; Hon Chap Birm Cathl from 81. *Innage Lea, Bewdley, Worcs.*

CROWIE, Hermon John. b 41. Kelham Th Coll 61. **d** 69 **p** 73 Southw. C of St Cypr Sneinton 69; Balderton 72-75; V of St Aid Basford 75-78; R of Everton w Mattersey and Clayworth Dio Southw from 78. *Rectory, Mattersey, Doncaster, Yorks, DN10 5DX.* (Wiseton 364)

CROWLEY, Brian Golland. b 01. Keble Coll Ox BA (2nd cl Hist) 23, MA 28. Westcott Ho Cam 26. **d** 27 **p** 28 Liv. C of St Phil Liv 27-29; Lect U Christian Coll Alwaye Travancore 29-45; V of Shedfield 45-54; Clifton Hampden (w Burcote from 63) 54-69. *2 Woodlands Paddock, Penn Road, Wolverhampton.*

CROWSON, Richard Charles Marriott. b 39. Down Coll Cam BA 62, MA 66. Lich Th Coll. **d** 64 **p** 65 Birm. C of Londonderry Smethwick 64-67; V of St Andr Nottingham 67-74; Commun Relns Officer Pet from 74. *112 Eyrescroft, Bretton, Peterborough, PE3 8EU.* (Pet 41061)

CROWTHER, Alfred Eric Keston. St Chad's Th Coll Regina 24. **d** 26 **p** 27 Qu'App. C of Heward 26-28; R of Wolseley 28-36; Kamsak 36-40; Melville 40-43; St Pet Regina 43-56; Exam Chap to Bp of Qu'App 45-52; Hon Can of Qu'App 47-56; Sktn 57-63; R of St Jas Sktn 56-63; All SS Medicine Hat 63-67. *83 Sioux Square, Hiawatha Park, Kelowna, BC, Canada.*

CROWTHER, Frank. b 28. Qu Coll Birm 68. **d** 69 **p** 70 Southw. C of Bulwell 69-72; Team V of St Francis Clifton 72-77; V of St Thos Kirkby-in-Ashfield Dio Southw from 77. *St Thomas Vicarage, Kirkby-in-Ashfield, Notts, NG17 7DX.* (Mansfield 752259)

CROWTHER, Ronald. b 22. Sarum Th Coll. **d** 53 **p** 54 Guildf. C of Hawley Green w Blackwater 53-55; Chap RAF 55-58; I of Valcartier PQ 58-60; R of Baie Comeau 60-63; Fugglestone w Bemerton 63-67; V of All SS Tooting Graveney 67-73; R of Burrough Green w Brinkley and Carlton 73-80; P-in-c of Westley Waterless 78-80; R of Brandon w Wangford Santon Downham and Santon Dio St E from 80. *Rectory, London Road, Brandon, Suff, IP27 0EL.* (Thetford 811221)

CROWTHER, Thomas William Facey. Univ of NB BSc 47. K Coll Halifax LTh 56. **d** 56 NS **p** 57 Fred. R of Canterbury w Benton 57-62; Westfield 62-66; St Geo Moncton Dio Fred from 66. *101 Alma Street, Moncton, NB, Canada.*

CROWTHER-ALWYN, Benedict Mark. b 53. Univ of Kent at Cant BA 74. Qu Coll Birm 74. **d** 77 Buckingham for Ox **p** 78 Reading for Ox. C of Fenny Stratford 77-80; Moulsecoomb Dio Chich 80-81; Team V from 81. *Coldean Vicarage, Selham Drive, Brighton, BN1 9EL.* (Brighton 61854)

CROWTHER-GREEN, John Patrick Victor. b 18. Late Exhib of Hatf Coll Dur LTh 41, BA 42. St Bonif Coll Warm

39. **d** 42 **p** 44 Cant. C of H Trin Selhurst 42-44; H Trin Windsor 44-49; R of Congerstone 49-53; V of Willoughby Waterleys w Peatling Magna and Ashby Magna 53-58; St Sav Leic 58-73; R of Blaby Dio Leic from 73; RD of Guthlaxton I from 81. *Blaby Rectory, Wigston Road, Blaby, Leicester, LE8 3FA.* (Leicester 771679)

CROWTHER-GREEN, Michael Leonard. b 36. K Coll Lon and Warm 56. **d** 60 **p** 61 S'wark. C of Caterham 60-64; St John Southend Lewisham (in c of St Mark Downham) 64-69; Chr Aid Area Sec Berks Oxon and Bucks 69-78; L to Offic Dio Ox from 78. *8 Egerton Road, Reading, Berks, RG2 8HQ.* (Reading 82502)

CROYDON, Lord Bishop Suffragan of. *See* Snell, Right Rev Geoffrey Stuart.

CROYDON, Archdeacon of. *See* Hazell, Ven Frederick Roy.

CROYLE, John Alan. St Jo Coll Morpeth 60. **d** 62 **p** 63 Armid. C of St Paul W Tamworth 62-64; St Pet Cathl Armid 64-66; Asst Chap Miss to Seamen Brisb 66-67; C of All SS Cathl Bath 67-68; R of Nyngan 68-71; Chap Miss to Seamen Kobe 71-75; R of Bourke w Brewarrina 75-81; Perm to Offic Dio Armid from 81. *12 Glen Innes Road, Armidale, NSW, Australia 2350.*

CRUICKSHANK, Canon James David. Univ of Minnesota BA 59. Em Coll Sktn 59. **d** 62 **p** 63 Carib. V of U Fraser 62-65; Dir Angl Lay Tr Centre, Sorrento 65-72; Exam Chap to Bp of Carib from 75; Hon Can of Carib from 81. *6000 Iona Drive, Vancouver 8, BC, Canada.*

CRUICKSHANK, Jonathan Graham. b 52. AKC and BD 74. St Aug Coll Cant 75. **d** 76 Dorchester for Ox **p** 77 Ox. C of Stantonbury 76-79; Burnham Dio Ox from 79; Chap RNR from 80. *85 Sandringham Court, Cippenham, Slough, SL1 6JU.* (Burnham 65373)

CRUMP, Douglas Gerald. Em Coll Sktn. **d** 65 Sask. Miss at Stanley 65-67; Montr Lake 67-68; I of Cumberland House 68-71; Hudson Bay 71-76; Williams Lake Dio Carib from 75. *549a Carson Drive, Williams Lake, BC, Canada.* (392-7622)

CRUMP, John. b 27. K Coll Lon and Warm AKC (2nd cl) 54. **d** 55 **p** 56 Chelmsf. C of H Trin Wanstead 55-58; Min of St Geo Eccles Distr Harold Hill, Romford 58-65; V of All SS, Highams Pk 65-78; RD of Waltham Forest 75-78; R of Lambourne w Abridge and Stapleford Abbotts Dio Chelmsf from 78. *Lambourne Rectory, Romford, Essex.* (Theydon Bois 4254)

CRUMP, Peter David Longton. Univ of NZ BCom 52, BA 55. Coll Ho Ch Ch. **d** 56 Wel. C of St Pet Palmerston N 56. *5 Hughes Avenue, Palmerston North, NZ.*

CRUMP, Stephen Thomas. Trin Coll Cam BA 52, MA 56. Westcott Ho Cam. **d** 68 **p** 69 Lon. C of Chelsea Old Ch (All SS) 68-69; Limehouse 69-70; L to Offic Dio Lon 70-71; Chap to Bp of Stepney 70-71; Lect Univ of Amsterdam from 72. *c/o Universiteit van Amsterdam, Keizergracht 397, Amsterdam C, Holland.*

✠ **CRUMP, Right Rev William Henry Howes.** Univ of W Ont BA 24. Trin Coll Tor BD 27, Hon DD 60. Em Coll Sktn Hon DD 60. Hur Coll Hon DD 60. **d** 26 **p** 27 Bran. C of Wawanesa 26-27; R of Glenboro 27-31; Holland 31-33; Boissevain 33-35; St Aid Winnipeg 35-44; Ch Ch Calg 44-60; Can of Calg 49-60; Exam Chap to Bp of Calg 52-60; Cons Ld Bp of Sask in St Alb Cathl Prince Albert 24 Feb 60 by Abp of Rupld (Metrop); Apb of Edmon (Primate); Bps of Bran; Athab; Calg; Keew; and Sktn; res 70. *RR2 Whitby, Ont., Canada.*

CRUMPTON, Colin. b 38. K Coll Lon and Warm AKC 61. **d** 64 **p** 65 Dur. C of Billingham 64-66; Shirley Birm 66-69; V of Mossley 69-75; Chap-Supt Miss to Seamen Mersey 75-77; V of St Paul Burslem Dio Lich from 77. *St Paul's Vicarage, Burslem, Stoke-on-Trent, Staffs, ST6 4DL.* (S-on-T 88932)

CRUMPTON, Michael Reginald. b 33. Chich Th Coll 66. **d** 69 **p** 70 Lich. C of St Mary and St Chad Longton Lich 69-72; Rugeley 72-76; Min of St Mary Kingswinford Dio Lich from 76. *28 Foundry Road, Wall Heath, Brierley Hill, W Midl, DY6 9BD.* (Kingswinford 3961)

CRUSE, Jack. b 35. Sarum Wells Th Coll 76. **d** 79 **p** 80 Ex (NSM). C of W Teignmouth Dio Ex from 79. *30 Ferndale Road, Teignmouth, Devon.*

CRUSHA, Edwin Herbert William. b 12. St Cath Coll Ox BA (2nd cl Mod Hist) 35, MA 38. Univ of Bris BA 36. St Steph Ho Ox 39. **d** 40 Dorch for Ox **p** 41 Ox. Chap of Magd Coll Sch Ox 40-44; Asst Master Ardingly Coll 44-45; C of Worksop 46-52; V of Saltley 52-63; R of Charlton-on-Otmoor (w Oddington from 65) 63-78; C-in-c of Oddington 64-65; Perm to Offic Dio Nor from 78. *31 Pyghtle Close, Trunch, North Walsham, Norfolk, NR28 0QF.* (Mundesley 721219)

CRUST, John Allen. Linc Th Coll. **d** 68 Grantham for Linc **p** 69 Linc. C of Spalding 68-73; St Geo Cullercoats 73-75; V of St Marg Scotswood Newc T 75-81. *Leake Vicarage, Boston, Lincs, PE22 9NS.* (Old Leake 662)

CRUTTWELL, Canon Norman Edward Garry. St Edm Hall Ox BA (1st cl Nat Sc) 38, MA 44. Cudd Coll 38. **d** 40 **p** 41 Win. C of St Mich Basingstoke (in c of All SS from 43) 40-46; Miss P Dio New Guinea 46-47; P-in-c Menapi 47-65; Agaun 65-74; Can of Dogura Cathl New Guinea from 63; R of Goroka Dio Aipo from 77. *Box 576, Goroka, Papua New Guinea.* (72-1695)

CRYER, Gordon David. b 34. St D Coll Lamp BA 63, Dipl Th 64. **d** 64 **p** 65 S'wark. C of Mortlake w E Sheen 64-67; Godstone (in c of St Steph S Godstone) 67-70; R of Stoke Damerel Devonport Dio Ex from 71. *Rectory, Penlee Way, Stoke Damerel, Plymouth, Devon PL3 4AW.* (Plymouth 52348)

CRYER, Neville Barker. b 24. Hertf Coll Ox BA 48, MA 49. Ridley Hall Cam 48. **d** 50 **p** 51 Derby. C of St Werburgh Derby 50-52; Ilkeston 52-54; R of St Pet Blackley 54-59; V of Addiscombe 59-67; Sec Conf Br Miss Societies from 67; Gen Sec BFBS 70-73; Gen Dir from 73; L to Offic Dio Lon from 71. *5 Meadway, Epsom, Surrey.* (Epsom 28118)

CRYER, Percival. b 11. AKC 39. **d** 39 **p** 40 Bradf. C of St Aug Bradf 39-42; St Jo Bapt Knighton 42-44; Pris Chap Leic 43-44; V of St Barn New Humberstone Leic 44-52; Chap to Towers Hosp 44-52; R of Barwell w Stapleton and Potters Marston 52-62; Surr from 56; Chap Leybourne Grange Hosp W Malling and Princess Christian's Hosp Hildenborough 62-81. *4 The Orpines, Wateringbury, Maidstone, ME18 5BP.* (Maidstone 812812)

CTERCTEKO, Harold Ernest. Moore Th Coll Syd ACT ThL 47. **d** 47 **p** 48 Syd. Chap Herne Bay Housing Settlement 47-48; R of Canley Vale w Cabramatta 48-52; Port Kembla 52-57; Botany 57-60; Sans Souci Dio Syd from 60. *325 Rocky Point Road, Sans Souci, NSW, Australia 2219.* (529-6141)

✠ **CUBA'IN, Right Rev Najib Atallah.** **d** 28 **p** 32 Jer. P Dio Jer 31-51; Hon Can of St Geo Colleg Ch Jer 51-58; Exam Chap to Bp in Jer 52-58; Cons Ld Bp in Jordan, Lebanon and Syria in St Geo Colleg Ch Jer 6 Jan 58 by Abp in Jer; Bps in Iran; Sudan; and Bp Deng; res 75. *PO Box 19122, Jerusalem, Israel.*

CUFFE, John Norman. St Francis Coll Brisb ACT ThDip. **d** 80 Bal. C of St Steph Portland & Asst Chap Miss to Seamen Dio Bal 80; C of St Andr Lutwyche Dio Brisb from 80. *54 Khartoum Street, Gordon Park, Qld, Australia 4031.*

CUIR, Henry Riak. St Paul's Th Coll Limuru 66. **d** 67 **p** 69 N Ugan. P Dio N Ugan from 69. *PO Box 232, Gulu, Uganda.*

CULBERTSON, Eric Malcolm. b 54. Ch Ch Ox BA 76, MA 80. Edin Th Coll 78. **d** 80 **p** 81 Edin. C of St Thos Corstophine City and Dio Edin from 80. *54 Kaimes Road, Edinburgh, EH12 6LN.*

CULL, Ernest Geoffrey. b 20. Coll of Resurr Mirfield 57. **d** 57 **p** 58 Heref. C of H Trin Heref 57-61; PC of Barrow Hill Chesterfield 61-70; V of St Paul Derby 71-80; St Francis Mackworth Dio Derby from 80. *Vicarage, Collingham Gardens, Mackworth, Derby, DE3 4FQ.* (Derby 47690)

CULL, Francis Cyril Duncan. b 15. Univ of Natal BA 63. Univ of York MPhil 73. Univ of S Afr DLitt 79. Clifton Th Coll 35. **d** 38 **p** 39 Chelmsf. C of Waltham Abbey (or H Cross) 38-40; St Paul Furzedown Streatham 40-42; Newington 42-45; E Wickham (in c of St Mary Virg Welling) 46-47; Min of Legal Distr of St Mary Virg Welling 47-52; V of St Steph, Battersea 52-57; Chap Battersea Gen Hosp 52-57; P-in-c of Maseru 58-61; Dioc Sec Basuto 58-61; P-in-c of St Aid Durban 61-62; Chap St John's Conv Pietermaritzburg 62-65; Asst Master Durban High Sch 65-66; L to Offic Dio Natal 65-66; Dio Grahmstn 66-74; Dio Johann 74-75; Lect and Warden Coll Ho Rhodes Univ 66-74; L to Offic Dio York 71-73; Sen Lect Univ of Witwatersrand 74-80; C of St Mary's Cathl Johann 75-78; R of Germiston Dio Johann from 78. *65 Fourth Avenue, Lambton, Germiston 1401, S Africa.* (34-1299)

CULL, John. b 31. Oak Hill Th Coll. **d** 59 Sherborne for Sarum **p** 60 Sarum. C of Radipole 59-66; Chap Mariners' Ch Glouc 66-70; R of Woodchester 70-81. *c/o Woodchester Rectory, Stroud, Glos.* (Amberley 2266)

CULL, Stafford Guy. Coll Ho Ch Ch NZ Bd of Th Stud LTh 64. **d** 59 Wel **p** 60 Bp Rich for Wel. C of Ch Ch Wanganui 59-63; V of Hunterville 63-67; Makara w Karori W 67-73; Chap Nel and Ngawhatu Hosps 73-78; Hutt Hosps Dio Wel from 79. *32 Hinau Street, Lower Hutt, NZ.* (661-646)

CULLEN, Clifford Lloyd. St Jo Coll Auckld LTh 51. **d** 51 **p** 52 Auckld. C of St Luke Mt Albert 52-53; V of Hokianga South 53-56; C of St Aid Auckld 56-60; V of Avondale 60-66; Papatoetoe Dio Auckld from 66. *Vicarage, Miles Avenue, Papatoetoe, NZ.* (27-83 412)

CULLEN, Henry D'Aubri. b 17. Univ of Leeds, BA 39.

Coll of Resurr Mirfield 39. **d** 41 **p** 42 Derby. C of St Lawr Long Eaton 41-43; Brimington 43-45; Bamford-in-the-Peak 45-46; Bakewell (in c of Over Haddon) 46-47; Whitfield (in c of St Luke) 47-50; PC of Barrow Hill 50-55; V of Wragby 55-57; St Geo Over Darwen 57-66; R of Shottisham w Sutton Dio St E from 66. *Shottisham Rectory, Woodbridge, Suff, IP12 3HG.* (Shottisham 411679)

CULLEN, Henry William Robert. b 08. Univ of Liv BA (2nd cl Med and Mod Hist) 31. Fitzw Ho Cam BA (2nd cl Th Trip pt i) 34, MA 38. Ely Th Coll 34. **d** 34 Warrington for Liv **p** 35 Liv. C of Warrington 34-39; Chap RAFVR 39-48; RAF 48-62; V of N w S Rauceby 62-78; R of Cranwell 62-78. *9 Victoria Avenue, Sleaford, Lincs.* (Sleaford 304964)

CULLEN, John Austin. b 43. Univ of Auckld BA 67. Univ of Otago BD 76. St Jo Coll Auckld 66. **d** 69 **p** 70 Auckld. C of Papatoetoe 69-73; Assoc P of St Luke Mt Albert 73-75; P-in-c 74; Hon C of St Aid Remuera Auckld 75-78; L to Offic Dio Ox from 78; Actg Chap Keble Coll Ox 79; Asst Chap from 80. *Keble College, Oxford, OX1 3PG.* (Ox 59201)

CULLIFORD, Michael. b 26. Qu Coll Birm 56. **d** 58 **p** 59 Ches. C of St Jas Birkenhead 58-60; Bollington 60-62; V of Heald Green 62-80; Asst Dioc Insp of Schs 64-76. *c/o 11 Neal Avenue, Heald Green, Cheadle, Cheshire.* (061-436 4309)

CULLINGFORD, Cecil Howard Dunstan. b 04. Late Scho of CCC Cam 1st cl Cl Trip pt i 25, BA (1st cl Cl Trip pt ii) 26, 1st cl Hist Trip pt ii 27, MA 30. Clifton Th Coll. **d** 33 **p** 34 Bris. Vice-Prin Clifton Th Coll 32-34; Asst Chap 33-34; Chap Oundle Sch 35-46; CF (R of O) 39-45; Hon CF 45; Hd Master Mon Sch 46-56; Lect RNC Dartmouth 57-60; Chap St Jo Sch Leatherhead 60-64; St Mich Sch Limpsfield 64-67; V of Stiffkey w Morston 67-72; L to Offic Dio St E 72-76; RD of Beccles 72-76. *The Staithe, Beccles, Suffolk, NR34 9AV.* (Beccles 712182)

CULLIS, Andrew Stanley Weldon. b 48. Hertf Coll Ox BA 69. St Jo Coll Nottm 70. **d** 73 **p** 74 S'wark. C of Reigate 73-79; Yateley Dio Win from 79. *51 Woodbridge Road, Darby Green, Camberley, Surrey, GU17 0BS.* (Yateley 87717)

CULLWICK, Christopher John. b 53. Univ of Hull BA 75. Univ of Ox BA (Th) 80. Wycl Hall Ox 78. **d** 81 Southw. C of St Jude Mapperley Nottm Dio Southw from 81. *3 Gordon Rise, Mapperley, Nottingham, NG3 5GB.* (Nottm 605328)

CULLY, Joseph. Edin Th Coll. **d** 63 Down **p** 64 Tuam for Down. C of St Donard Belf 63-66; Newtownards 66-68; C-in-c of Knocknagoney 68-74; I of St Jo Evang Lurgan 74-81. *16 Chippendale Park, Bangor, Co Down, BT20 4PU.* (Bangor 52455)

CULLY, Wilfred. b 1897. Bps' Coll Cheshunt 29. **d** 32 **p** 33 Newc T. C of Sleekburn 32-36; Long Benton 36-40; St Jas and St Basil (in c of H Trin Cowgate) Newc T 40-43; V of Willington 43-61; Dinnington 61-68. *8 Ilfracombe Avenue, Newcastle upon Tyne, NE4 8RU.*

CULPIN, Albert. b 16. Open Univ BA 75. St Deiniol's Libr Hawarden 76. **d** 77 **p** 78 Ches (APM). C of Bidston Dio Ches from 77. *27 Derwent Road, Meols, Hoylake, Wirral, Mer, L47 8XY.*

CULROSS, James Fred. b 17. Univ of Lon BD 51. Bps' Coll Cheshunt 47. **d** 50 **p** 51 Ripon. C of Pateley Bridge 50-54; Romaldkirk 54-55; V of St Cross Middleton 55-62; R of St Jas Springburn Glas 62-65; C of Bramley 65-67; Chap R Wanstead Sch 67-71; Chap Sir R Manwood Sch Sandwich 71-79; R of Barrowden and Wakerley w S Luffenham Dio Pet from 79. *Barrowden Rectory, Oakham, Leics.* (Morcott 248)

CULVER, Frederick Lloyd. b 12. K Coll Lon BA 34. BD (Lon) 58. **d** 75 Bp Ambo for Papua. d Dio Papua. *PO Box 35, Popondota, Papua New Guinea.*

CULVERWELL, Keith Francis. b 57. Univ of Leeds BA 78. St Steph Ho Ox 79. **d** 81 Leic. C of St Mary Magd Knighton City and Dio Leic from 81. *43 Knighton Church Road, Leicester, LE2 3JN.*

CULVERWELL, Martin Phillip. b 48. Sarum Wells Th Coll 72. **d** 75 Kens for Lon **p** 76 Lon. C of St Hilda Ashford 75-78; Chelsea 78-80; Chap RN from 80. *c/o Chaplain of the Fleet, Lacon House, Theobalds Road, WC1X 8RY.*

CUMBERBATCH, Lionel Alfred. b 28. Codr Coll Barb 72. **d** 72 **p** 73 Barb. C of St Lawr Barb 72-75; R of Falmouth Dio Ja from 75. *PO Box 24, Falmouth, Jamaica, WI.*

CUMBERBATCH, Stephen Kenneth. Codr Coll Barb 39. **d** 41 **p** 42 Antig. C of St John's Cathl Antig 41-44; P-in-c of St Mary Antig 44-45; R of Ch Ch Stann Creek 45-48; V of St Patr Tobago 48-54; R of Sangre Grande 54-58; Tacarigua 58-68; San Fernando 68-71; St Crispin Port of Spain 71-79; Hon Can of Trinid 65-69; Archd and VG 69-79. *27b Cascade Road, St Ann's, Trinidad, W Indies.*

CUMBERLAND, Leslie Hodgson. b 15. Univ of Leds BA (2nd cl Hist) 37. Coll of Resurr Mirfield 37. **d** 39 **p** 40 Dur. C of Birtley 39-44; Medomsley 44-49; Min of Kimblesworth Distr 49-55; V of St Columba Horton Bradf 55-64; L to Offic Dio Bradf from 64. *29 Union Road, Low Moor, Bradford, BD12 0DW.* (Bradford 676138)

CUMBERLAND, WEST, Archdeacon of. *See* Hodgson, Ven Thomas Richard Burnham.

CUMBERLEGE, Francis Richard. b 41. K Coll Lon and Warm AKC 65. **d** 66 **p** 67 Portsm. C of Leigh Pk Conv Distr 66-71; P-in-c of Gona 71-75; Archd of N Papua 74-81; R of Popondetta 79-81; R of Hastings Dio Chich from 81. *106 High Street, Hastings, E Sussex.* (0424-422023)

CUMBRAE, Provost of. *See* Douglas, Very Rev George James Cosmo.

CUMING, Canon Geoffrey John. b 17. Or Coll Ox Bible Clerk Scho 36, 2nd cl Cl Mods 38, 3rd cl Lit Hum 40, BA 40, MA 43, DD 62. Westcott Ho Cam 45. **d** 47 Burnley for Blackb **p** 48 Blackb. C of St Steph Burnley 47-50; Tutor St Jo Coll Dur 50-52; Vice-Prin 52-55; V of Billesdon w Goadby and Rolleston 55-62; RD of Gartree iii 57-62; V of St Mary Humberstone Leic 63-74; Exam Chap to Bp of Leic 63-80; Hon Can of Leic 65-71; M of Liturgical Comm from 65; Commiss Ch Ch from 67; Lect K Coll Lon 69-80; Can Th of Leic 71-80; Can (Emer) from 80; Lect Ripon Coll Cudd 74-81; Proc Lon Univ 75-80; C of Cudd 75-80. *Water Lane Cottage, Steeple Aston, Oxford.*

CUMING, Kenneth Gordon. b 12. MRCS (Lon) and LRCP (Engl) 43. Wells Th Coll. **d** 59 Guildf **p** 60 Bp Dale for Cant. C of Bramley 59-62; R of Woodborough w Manningford Bohune and Beechingstoke 62-69; Chap Kerin Trust Burrswood 74-75; Warden 75-77. *3 Bethany Place, St Just, Penzance, Cornwall, TR19 7HB.*

CUMING, Mark Alexander. b 53. AKC 75. Westcott Ho Cam 76. **d** 77 **p** 78 Newc T. C of Fenham Dio Newc T from 77. *2a Lanercost Drive, Newcastle-upon-Tyne, NE5 2QP.*

CUMINGS, Llewellyn Frank Beadnell. b 29. Univ of Natal BA 50. St Cath Coll Cam Certif Educn 53. Ridley Hall Cam 65. **d** 67 Bp McKie for Cov **p** 68 Cov. C of St Mary Leamington 67-70; PC of All SS Lobley Hill Gateshead 70-74; R of Denver Dio Ely from 74; Ryston w Roxham Dio Ely from 74. *Denver Rectory, Downham Market, Norf.* (Downham Market 2127)

CUMMING, Nigel Patrick. b 42. St Jo Coll Nottm 73. **d** 75 **p** 76 Ches. C of H Trin Castle Hall Stalybridge 75-78; Tadley 78-82; R of Overton & Laverstoke w Freefolk Dio Win from 82. *54 Lordsfield Gardens, Overton, Basingstoke, Hants, RG25 3EW.* (Basingstoke 770207)

CUMMINGS, Alfred Henry. Em Coll Sktn LTh 43. Univ of Sask BA 45, BD 50. **d** 41 **p** 42 Bran. C of St Mary Virden 41-42; I 42-49; C of Ch Ch Cathl Vic BC 49-50; R of St Geo Bran 50-51; St Phil Dunbar Heights Vanc 51-67; St Aug Vanc 67-76; Can of New Westmr 64-76. *c/o 1161 West 67th Avenue, Vancouver, BC, V6P 2S9, Canada.*

CUMMINGS, George Osmond. b 21. St Chad's Coll Dur BA 43, MA 48, Dipl in Th 45. **d** 45 **p** 46 York. C of St Jo Evang Middlesbrough 45-49; St Sav Wilmington 49-51; V of St Paul Sculcoates 51-55; St Lawr w St Nich and New Fulford York 55-62; Bentley 62-67; C-in-c of New Cantley Conv Distr Doncaster 67-72; V of Campsall 72-80; Arksey Dio Sheff from 80. *Arksey Vicarage, Doncaster, Yorks, DN5 0SD.* (Doncaster 874445)

CUMMINGS, Richard Vivian Payn. b 21. Univ of Lon BSc (2nd cl Eng.) 41. Chich Th Coll 51. **d** 53 **p** 54 Pet. C of All SS Pet 53-55; Wellingborough 55-60; V of Wollaston w Strixton 60-69; St Barn, Wellingborough 69-73; RD of Wellingborough 70-73; R of Collingtree w Courteenhall (and Milton Malsor from 80) Dio Pet from 73; C-in-c of Milton Malsor 73-80. *Collingtree Rectory, Northampton.* (Northampton 61895)

CUMMINGS, Walter Raymond. b 18. BD (Lon) 52. Cudd Coll 71. **d** 71 **p** 72 Win. C of H Sav Bitterne 71-79; P-in-c of Felbrigg w Metton and Sustead 79-80; Roughton Dio Nor 79-80; R (w Felbrigg, Metton and Sustead) from 80. *Rectory, Roughton, Norwich, Norfolk.*

CUMMINGS, William Alexander Vickery. b 38. Late Scho of Ch Ch Ox 2nd cl Cl Mods 59, BA (3rd cl Lit Hum) 62, 2nd cl Th 63, MA 64. Wycl Hall Ox 61. **d** 64 **p** 65 Chelmsf. C of Leytonstone 64-67; Writtle 67-71; R of Stratton St Mary w St Mich (and Wacton from 73) Dio Nor from 71; Wacton Magna w Parva 71-73; RD of Depwade from 81. *Stratton St Mary Rectory, Norwich, NR15 2TS.* (Long Stratton 30238)

CUMMINS, James Ernest. b 32. Westcott Ho Cam 57. **d** 60 **p** 61 Lich. C of Berkswich w Walton 60-64; V of Hales w Heckingham 64-70; R of Raveningham Group 70-76. *Skyborry, Knighton, Powys, LD1 1TW.*

CUMMINS, Nicholas Marshall. b 36. **d** 67 **p** 68 Connor. C of Ballymena 67-70; C of St Nich Belf 70-73; Dom Chap to Bp of Connor 71-73; R of Buttevant Dio Cloyne from 73; Mallow Dio Cloyne from 78. *Rectory, Mallow, Co Cork, Irish Republic.* (Mallow 21473)

CUMMINS, William Frederick. b 17. St Pet Hall Ox BA (2nd cl Mod Lang) 39, Dipl in Th 40, MA 44. Wycl Hall Ox 39. **d** 41 **p** 42 Man. C of St Matt Stretford 41-43; St Paul Kersal 43-46; V of St Barn Pendleton 46-49; St Jude Blackb

49-52; St Paul Preston 52-60; Chap Preston R Infirm 52-60; V of Pendleton-in-Whalley 60-67; Dioc Youth Chap Blackb 60-67; Chap R Gr Sch Worc from 67; C-in-c of Peopleton 70-75; White Ladies Aston w Churchill & Spetchley 75-78; R of Peopleton and White Ladies Aston w Churchill & Spetchley Dio Worc from 78. *Peopleton Rectory, Pershore, Worcs, WR10 2EE.* (Worcester 840243)

CUMPSTY, John Sutherland. Univ of Dur BSc (1st cl Mining) 53. PhD 56, Dipl Th 60. Carnegie Inst of Technology, Pittsburgh, USA MSc 58. Cranmer Hall Dur 58. **d** 60 **p** 61 Wakef. [f Barrister-at-Law] C of Normanton 60-62; Asst Tutor and Research Fell Cranmer Hall Dur and L to Offic Dio Dur 63-66; Lect Univ of Glas and Perm to Offic Dio 66-70; Prof of Relig Stud at Univ of Capetn and L to Offic Dio Capetn from 70. *Warden's Lodge, University of Cape Town, Rondebosch, S Africa.* (65-6412)

CUNDY, Ian Patrick Martyn. b 45. Trin Coll Cam 3rd cl Math Trip pt ia 65, BA (2nd cl Th Trip pt ii) 67, MA 71. Tyndale Hall Bris 67. **d** 69 Stepney for S'wark **p** 70 S'wark. C of New Malden w Coombe 69-73; Lect Oak Hill Th Coll Southgate 73-77; R of Mortlake w E Sheen Dio S'wark from 77; Exam Chap to Bp of S'wark from 78. *170 Sheen Lane, SW14 8RL.* (01-876 4816)

CUNDY, Reginald Charles Stuart.. b 1893. St Aid Coll 19. **d** 22 **p** 23 Man. C of St Phil Hulme 22-24; St Thos Ardwick 24-25; Chap Miss to Seamen Rosario 25-26; Org Sec Miss to Seamen NW Area 25-32; LPr Dios Man Blackb Carl and Ches 26-32; Perm to Offic Dio Liv 35-36; C-in-c of St D W Derby 36-40; Chap RAFVR 40-45; L to offic Dio Ches 46-50; V of Winnington 50-62; L Budworth 62-68. *10 Zig Zag Road, West Derby, Liverpool.*

CUNINGHAM, John Copeland. b 1900. Trin Coll Dub 21. Wells Th Coll 28. **d** 29 **p** 30 B & W. C of Chard 29-32; Combe Down 32-34; V of Stoke St Mich (or Stoke Lane) 34-38; Condover 38-45; PC of Burrington 45-51; V of Shirburn w Pyrton 51-60; Perm to Offic Dio B & W 60-71; Dio Ox 71-79. *2 St Aubyn's Villas, Canal Hill, Tiverton, Devon.*

CUNLIFFE, Gerald Thomas. b 35. Linc Th Coll 74. **d** 76 **p** 77 Roch. C of St Jo Evang Sidcup Dio 76-80; Pembury Dio Roch from 80. *9 Knight's Close, Pembury, Tunbridge Wells, TN2 4EL.* (Pembury 2654)

CUNLIFFE, Harold. St Aid Coll 57. **d** 60 Liv **p** 61 Warrington for Liv. C of Hindley 60-64; V of St Chad w Ch Ch Everton 64-69; R of Golborne Dio Liv from 70. *Rectory, Golborne, Nr Warrington, Lancs, WA3 3TH.* (Ashton-in-Makerfield 728305)

CUNLIFFE, William Richard. Univ of NZ BA 42, LTh 43. St Jo Coll Auckld. **d** 41 **p** 42 Waik. C of St Pet Cathl Hamilton 41-42; Putaruru 42-43; C-in-c of Par Distr of H Trin Ngaruawahia 43-44; V of Ohura 44-46; CF (NZ) 46-47; C of All SS Palmerston North 48-50; V of Taita 50-54; Taihape 54-56; Frankton 56-61; Te Aroha 61-67; Te Kuiti 67-74; Exam Chap to Bp of Waik 56-74; Can of Waik 58-74; V of Te Ngawai Dio Ch Ch from 74. *St Albans Vicarage, Pleasant Point, S Canterbury, NZ.* (P.P. 748)

CUNNINGHAM, Douglas Frederick. Univ Coll Ox BA 49, MA 56. Edin Th Coll 49. **d** 51 **p** 52 Glas. C of St Jo Evang Greenock 51-53; R of St Mich Govan Glas 53-55; C of St Marg Newlands 55-57; Asst Master of Craigflower Sch Torryburn Fife from 57; L to Offic Dio St Andr from 57. *Address temp unknown.*

CUNNINGHAM, James Simpson. Wycl Coll Tor BA 46, LTh 50, MA 59. St Cath S Ox BA (2nd cl Th) 54. **d** 49 **p** 50 Tor. C of Ch of Transfig Tor 49-52; on Leave 52-54; C of St Paul Bloor St Tor 54-55; Chap at Hart Ho Univ of Tor 55-60 and from 64; P-in-c of St Andr-by-the-Lake Tor 62-63; P-in-c of St Edw Tor 69-72. *30 Glencairn Avenue, Toronto 310, Ont., Canada.*

CUNNINGHAM, John. b 23. McGill Univ Montr BA 46. Qu Coll Birm 46. **d** 48 **p** 49 Ex. C of Paignton 48-51; Chap Kelly Coll Tavistock 51-55; R of Shobrooke 55-62; R of Stockleigh Pomeroy 57-62; Newdigate 62-69; V of Pirbright Dio Guildf from 70; RD of Woking from 77. *Pirbright Vicarage, Woking, Surrey.* (Brookwood 3332)

CUNNINGHAM, John Colpoys. b 10. Or Coll Ox BA 34, MA 37. Cudd Coll 34. **d** 35 **p** 36 S'wark. C of Eltham 35-39; St Geo Hanover Sq 39; Serving w the RAF 39-46; Asst Chap Tonbridge Sch 46-50; Chap and Asst Master Oundle Sch 50-54; Chap Bromsgrove Sch 54-63; R of Hanbury 63-68; Churchill-in-Halfshire w Blakedown 68-77. *7a Devonshire Crescent, Leeds, LS8 1AX.* (Leeds 666148)

CUNNINGHAM, Robert Stewart. b 16. **d** 59 **p** 60 Connor. C of St Mary Belf 59-62; All SS Belf 62-63; R of Portglenone 63-74; R of Whiterock Dio Connor from 74. *194 Ballygomartin Road, Belfast, N Ireland.* (Belfast 747458)

CUNNINGHAM, Walter Borden. Hur Coll Ont. **d** 27 **p** 28 Hur. C of St Luke Yarmouth Heights 27-29; R of Millbank w Milverton 29-36; I of Glencoe Wardsville and Newbury 36-41; Ascen Windsor 41-69. *460 Lafferty Avenue, Windsor 40, Ont., Canada.*

CUNNINGHAM-BURLEY, Theodore. b 18. Lon Coll of Div 68. **d** 70 **p** 71 Lon. C of St Andr Enfield 70-72; St Mary Magd Enfield 72-74; V of St Mich-at-Bowes Bowes Pk 74-76; All SS E Finchley Dio Lon from 76. *1 Twyford Avenue, N2 9NH.* (01-883 9315)

CUNNINGTON, Edgar Alan. b 37. Oak Hill Th Coll 68. **d** 70 **p** 71 Stepney for Lon. C of Highbury 70-73; C-in-c of St D W Holloway 73-76; V of Martham Dio Nor from 76; W Somerton Dio Nor from 76. *Martham Vicarage, Great Yarmouth, Norf.* (Great Yarmouth 740240)

CUPIDO, David Arthur. b 20. **d** 77 Capetn. C of Good Shepherd Maitland Dio Capetn from 77. *125 9th Street, Kensington Estate, Maitland 7405, Cape, S Africa.*

CUPITT, Don. b 34. Trin Hall Cam 2nd cl Nat Sc Trip pt i 54, BA (2nd cl Th Trip pt ia) 55, 1st cl Th Trip pt iii 58, MA 59. Westcott Ho Cam 57. **d** 59 **p** 60 Man. C of St Phil Salford 59-62; Vice-Prin Westcott Ho Cam 62-66; Fell and Dean of Em Coll Cam from 66; L to Offic Dio Ely from 63; Stanton Lect Univ Cam 68-71; Asst Lect in Div Univ Cam 68-73; Lect from 73. *Emmanuel College, Cambridge, CB2 3AP.* (Cambridge 65411)

CURGENVEN, Peter. b 10. CCC Cam 2nd cl Hist Trip pt i 31, 2nd cl Mod Lang Trip pt i BA 33, MA 36. Cudd Coll 48. **d** 49 **p** 50 Chich. C of Goring-by-Sea 49-51; Chap Cudd Coll 51-53; Recruitment Sec CACTM 53-54, Gen Sec 54-59; V of Goring 59-70; R of Rotherfield 70-79; RD of E Grinstead 75-77. *Tretawn, Church Hill, Marnhull, Sturminster newton, Dorset DT10 1PU.*

CURIHUAL, Segundo. d 74 **p** 75 Bp Bazley for Chile. P Dio Chile. *Casilla 4, Chol-Chol, Chile.*

CURLING, Arthur Sylvester. b 23. **d** 71 Br Hond **p** 81 Bel. C of St Mary Bel Dio Br Hond (Bel from 73) from 71. *22 Sixth Street, King's Park, Belize City, British Honduras.*

CURNEW, Brian Leslie. b 48. Qu Coll Ox BA 69, DPhil 77, Dipl Th 78. Ripon Coll Cudd 77. **d** 79 Reading for Ox **p** 80 Ox. C of Sandhurst Dio Ox from 79. *65 Mickle Hill, Sandhurst, Camberley, Surrey, GU17 8QU.* (Crowthorne 6237)

CURNOW, Andrew William. b 50. Univ of Melb BComm 70, BD 74. **d** 73 **p** 74 Bend. R of Milloo 73-75; Lockington Dio Bend from 75. *St Mary's Rectory, Willis Street, Lockington, Vic, Australia 3563.* (054-86 2466)

CURNOW, Canon Kevin. Univ of Melb BA 55. Ridley Th Coll Melb ACT ThL 54. **d** 55 **p** 56 Melb. C of Hawthorn 55-57; P-in-c of St Mary Melb 57-59; CMS Home Sec and Hon C of Melb Cathl 59-64; V of Blackb 64-70; Commiss Centr Tang from 64; I of Greythorn 70-77; St John Camberwell Dio Melb from 77; Can of Melb from 81. *552 Burke Road, Camberwell, Vic, Australia 3124.* (82 4851)

CURNOW, Terence Peter. b 37. St D Coll Lamp BA 62, Dipl Th 63. **d** 63 **p** 64 Llan. C of Llanishen w Lisvane 63-71; Dioc Youth Chap Llandaff 67-71; Asst Chap K Coll Taunton 71-74; Chap Taunton Sch from 74. *Taunton School, Taunton, Somt, TA2 6AD.* (Taunton 84359)

CURRAH, Michael Ewart. b 31. Down Coll Cam BA 54, MA 58. Sarum Th Coll 54. **d** 56 **p** 57 Sarum. C of Calne 56-60; PC of Southbroom 60-69; Perm to Offic Dio Sarum from 70; Asst Master Woodroffe Sch Lyme Regis from 71. *55 Victoria Grove, Bridport, Dorset.* (Bridport 22488)

CURRAN, Luis Oliver. Univ of Sask. BA 66. Em Coll Sktn LTh 66. **d** and **p** 66 Bp Greenwood for Carib. C of St Paul's Cathl Kamloops 66-69; I of Savona 67-69; R of St Thos Vanc 69-72; St Anselm Vanc 72-80; on leave. *203-5450 University Boulevard, Vancouver, BC, Canada.*

CURRAN, Thomas Heinrich. b 49. Univ of Tor BA 72. Dalhousie Univ NS MA 75. Atlantic Sch of Th NS 75. **d** 78 NS. Dean of Residence Univ of K Coll NS from 78. *University of King's College, Halifax, NS B3H 2A1, Canada.*

CURRAN, William Arthur. St Barn Coll Adel Act ThL (2nd cl) 34. **d** 34 **p** 35 Adel. C of Ch Ch Adel 34-36; Miss Chap Millicent 37-39; R of St Paul Naracoorte 39-43; St Marg Woodville 43-57; Glenelg 57-79; L to Offic Dio Adel from 79. *3 Allen Terrace, Glenelg East, S Australia 5045.* (294 5933)

CURRIE, John Thomas. d 63 **p** 64 Melb. C of St Luke Frankston E 63-65; Melb Dioc 65-66; Perm to Offic Dio Syd from 79. *2/2 Victoria Parade, Manly, NSW, Australia 2095.* (977-4371)

CURRIE, Piers William Edward. b 13. BNC Ox BA (2nd cl Lit Hum 35, 2nd cl Jurispr 36), MA 62. E Anglian Min Tr Course 79. **d** 80 **p** 81 Nor (APM). Hon C of Holt Dio Nor from 80; Edgefield Dio Nor from 80. *Westward House, Woodlands Close, Holt, Norfolk.*

CURRIE, Royston Alexander Fairlie. Em Coll Sask. **d** 47 **p** 48 Athab. C-in-c of Sexsmith 47-49; R of High Prairie 49-51; Chap RCAF 51-71; R of Ox Ont 71-77. *2006 Naskapi Drive, Ottawa, Ont, Canada.*

CURRIE, Thomas Eric. St Barn Coll N Adel ACT ThL 37.

d 37 Perth **p** 38 Bunb for Perth. C of Vic Pk 37-39; R of Narembeen w Corrigan 39-43; St Mark Bassendean 43-47; Prin St Gabriel's Sch Pudu Sing 47-56; C-in-c of Smarden Kent 56; Knebworth Herts 56; R of Harvey W Austr 56-59; Dir Relig Educn in Secondary Schs Dio Perth 59-65; R of Gingin 65-67; Actg Prin St Columba Sch Miri 68-69; St Aid Sch Miri 69; Perm to Offic Dio Perth from 70. *87 Shenton Road, Swanbourne, W Australia 6010.* (31 5589)

CURRIE, Canon Wilfred Bennetto. b 08. Univ of Edin MA (1st cl Cl) 31. Edin Th Coll 31. **d** 33 Edin for Aber **p** 34 Aber. C of St John Aber 33-36; P-in-c of St Mark Aber 36-45; CF (EC) 40-45; R of St Jo Evang Longside 45-47; H Trin Stirling 47-55; Provost of St Ninian's Cathl Perth 55-69; Hon Can from 69; R of St Pet Peebles 69-76; Perm to Offic Dio St Andr from 76. *1 Kinness Place, St Andrews, Fife.* (St Andrews 75980)

CURRIE, William George. b 08. Clifton Th Coll 38. **d** 41 **p** 42 Chelmsf. C of Chadwell Heath 41-44; C-in-c of St Alb Becontree 44-45; R of Holton w Bratton St Maurice 45-51; Templecombe 51-60; V of Shapwick 60-63; V of Kingston Lacy (w Shapwick from 63) 60-65; Gt Bedwyn 65-81; L Bedwyn 65-81; Savernake Forest 65-81. *c/o Great Bedwyn Vicarage, Marlborough, Wilts.* (Bedwyn 267)

CURRY, Anthony Bruce. b 31. Late Scho of St Edm Hall Ox BA (1st cl Mus) 53, MA 57. ARCO 49. Wells Th Coll 53. **d** 55 Taunton for B & W for Roch **p** 56 Roch. C of All SS Perry Street Northfleet 55-56; Chap of K Sch Cant 56-61; R of Penshurst 61-75; L to Offic Dio Ex from 76; Dio Truro from 77; Dir of Mus Kelly Coll Tavistock from 76. *Kelly College, Tavistock, Devon.*

CURRY, Bruce. b 39. Univ of Dur BA 61. Wells Th Coll 61. **d** 63 **p** 64 B & W. C of Shepton Mallet 63-67; Cheam (in c of St Alb) 67-71; R of W Walton 71-77; V of St Neots Dio Ely from 77. *St Neots Vicarage, Church Street, Huntingdon, Cambs, PE19 2BU.* (Huntingdon 72297)

CURRY, Carl Wesley. Codr Coll Barb LTh 37. **d** 36 **p** 37 Barb. C of Ch Ch Barb 36-38; V of St Clem and St Swith 38-42; C of St Mich Cathl 42; St Matthias and St Lawrence Barb 42-44; V of St Patr Barb 44-56; R of St Thos I and Dio Barb from 56. *St Thomas's Rectory, Barbados, W Indies.*

CURRY, David John. b 24. St Cath Coll Cam BA 48, MA 58. Oak Hill Coll 73. **d** 74 **p** 75 St Alb. C of Watford 74-77; V of St Andr Whitehall Pk U Holloway Dio Lon from 77. *86 Hornsey Lane, N6 5LT.* (01-272 4746)

CURRY, David Leslie. St Francis Coll Brisb 77. **d** 79 **p** 80 Brisb. C of St John Gympie 79-80; Bundaberg Dio Brisb from 80. *58 Crofton Street, Bundaberg, Queensld, Australia 4670.*

CURRY, Canon George Christopher. TCD BA (2nd cl Mod Ment and Mor Sc) 42, MA 55. **d** 44 Kilm **p** 45 Elph. C of Roscommon 44-47; Camus-Juxta-Mourne 47-57; C-in-c of Edenderry Dio Derry 57-64; I from 64; RD of Omagh from 60; I of Clanabogan Dio Derry from 64; Can of St Columb Cathl Derry from 79. *Edenderry Rectory, Omagh, Co Tyrone, N Ireland.* (Omagh 2248)

CURRY, George Robert. b 51. Bede Coll Dur BA 72. Cranmer Hall Dur Dipl Th 74. Oak Hill Coll 75. **d** 76 Penrith for Carl **p** 77 Carl. C of St Jas Denton-Holme 76-81; V of St Steph Low Elswick City and Dio Newc T from 81. *St Stephen's vicarage, Clumber Street, Low Elswick, Newcastle-on-Tyne, NE4 7RD.* (0632-734680)

CURRY, Norman George. Univ of Melb BA (Engl) 51, B Educn 58, M Educn 65. Univ of Lon PhD 68. Ridley Coll Melb 59. **d** 61 **p** 62 Melb. C of St Paul's Cathl City and Dio Melb 61-65 and from 67; Perm to Offic Dio Lon 65-66. *20 Hodgson Street, Kew, Vic, Australia 3101.* (03-86 8989)

CURRY, Thomas Christopher. b 47. Sarum Wells Th Coll 71. **d** 74 **p** 75 Sarum. C of Bradford-on Avon 74-77; Asst Chap Hurstpierpoint Coll from 78. *Hurstpierpoint College, Hassocks, BN6 9JS.*

CURSON, James Desmond. b 30. Keble Coll Ox BA 54, MA 60. **d** 56 **p** 57 Lon. C of Teddington 56-58; Ruislip 58-62; V of St Paul Tottenham 62-67; Hockley 67-75; Chap HM Borstal Bullwood Hall 68-75; V of Treverbyn 75-79; P-in-c of Marazion Dio Truro from 79; St Hilary w Perranuthnoe Dio Truro from 81. *Rectory, St Hilary, Churchtown, Penzance, Cornwall, TR20 9DQ.* (Penzance 710294)

CURTIS, Albert William. b 05. Hatf Coll Dur BA and LTh 27. St Bonif Coll Warm 23. **d** 28 Malmesbury for Bris **p** 29 Bris. C of St Matt Moorfields Bris 28-30; Coorow (W Austr) 30-34; R of York 34-39; E Claremont 39-42; Chap AMF 40-43; R of Fremantle 43-46; C of All SS Friern Barnet 46-49; PC of Ch of Ascen Hanger Hill 49-74; RD of Ealing 63-67. *41 Edward Road, West Bridgford, Notts, NG2 5GE.*

CURTIS, Clement Ernest. b 09 Late Exhib of Ch Coll Cam 3rd cl Engl Trip 31, BA (3rd cl Geog Trip) 32, MA 36. Ely Th Coll 32. **d** 33 **p** 35 S'wark. C of Ascen Plumstead 33-37; All SS Poplar 37-38; St Aug Stepney 38-46; V of Wrawby 46-61; PC of St Chad Bensham Gateshead 61-68; V 68-74. *Greystones, Duddleswell, Uckfield, Sussex.*

CURTIS, Canon Douglas Henry. St Cath Coll Cam 3rd cl Hist Trip pt i 31, BA (3rd cl Th Trip pt i) 32, MA 36. Westcott Ho Cam 32. **d** 33 **p** 34 Blackb. C of H Trin S Shore Blackpool 33-38; V of St Jo Bapt Gannow 38-50; Surr 38-50; CF (EC) 40-45; Gen Sec of Inter Ch Aid and Refugee Dept Br Coun of Chs 50-53; V of Towcester w Easton Neston 53-81; RD of Towcester 53-81; 54-69; Surr from 55; Can of Pet from 61. *c/o Vicarage, Towcester, Northants.* (Towcester 459)

✠ **CURTIS, Right Rev Ernest Edwin.** b 06. CBE 76. Univ of Lon BSc 27. ARCSC 27. Wells Th Coll 32. **d** 33 **p** 34 St Alb. C of H Trin Waltham Cross 33-36; Civil Chap Rose Hill and Prin of St Paul's Coll Maur 37-44; C of St Mary Portsea 44-47; V of All SS Portsea 47-55; C-in-c of St Agatha Portsea 54-55; Chap R Portsm Hosp 47-55; Commiss Maur 48-66; V of Locks Heath 55-66; RD of Alverstoke 64-66; Cons Ld Bp of Maur in S'wark Cathl 1 Nov 66 by Abp of Cant; Bps of Lon; Nor; Ely; and Porstm; Bps Suffr of Fulham; and Buckingham; and Bps O'Ferrall; Otter-Barry; Anderson; Trapp; Clarke; and Chamberlain; Elected Abp and Metrop of Indian Ocean 73; res 76; Hon Asst Bp of Portsm from 76; P-in-c of Whitwell Dio Portsm from 76. *Whitwell Vicarage, Ventnor, IW, PO38 2PP.* (Niton 730922)

CURTIS, Frederick John. b 36. SS Coll Cam MA 64. Ridley Hall Cam 77. **d** 79 McKie for Cov **p** 80 Cov. C of Chilvers-Coton w Astley Dio Cov from 79. *126 Coventry Road, Nuneaton, CV10 7AD.*

CURTIS, Geoffrey John. b 35. Univ of Dur BA (2nd cl Engl) 57, Ripon Hall Ox 59. **d** 61 **p** 62 Portsm. C of Ch Ch, Gosport 61-65; Bedhampton 65-68; Producer Schs Broadcasting Dept BBC Lon from 68; C-in-c of Grayswood Dio Guildf from 75; Dioc Communications Adv Dio Guildf from 75. *Grayswood Vicarage, Haslemere, Surrey.* (Haslemere 4208)

CURTIS, Graham. b 30. Chich Th Coll 71. **d** 73 **p** 74 Bris. C of Penhill 73-76; Winterbourne Down Dio Bris from 76. *21 Church Road, Winterbourne Down, Bristol, BS17 1BX.* (Winterbourne 772115)

CURTIS, Harry Austin. b 22. **d** 77 **p** 78 Edin (APM). C of H Cross Davidson's Mains Dio Edin from 77. *27 Barnton Park Avenue, Edinburgh, EH4 6ES.* (031-336 4002)

CURTIS, John Barry. Trin Coll Tor. **d** 58 **p** 59 Ott. C of H Trin Pembroke 58-61; R of S March 61-65; Buckingham 65-68; All SS Westboro Ott 69-79; Can of Ott 79-80; Dir of Program 78-80; R of Ch Ch City and Dio Calg from 80. *3032 Glencoe Road SW, Calgary, Alta, Canada.*

CURTIS, John Durston. b 43. Lich Th Coll 65. **d** 68 **p** 69 Lich. C of Coseley 68-71; Sedgley 71-74; CF 74-79; P-in-c of Newton Valence w Selborne Dio Win 79-80; V (w E Tisted and Colmer) from 81. *St Mary's Vicarage, The Plestor, Selborne, Alton, Hants, GU34 3JB.* (Selborne 242)

CURTIS, Neville Leighton. Ridley Coll Melb 58. ACT ThL 61. **d** 61 **p** 62 Melb. C of Ivanhoe 61-62; Toorak 62-63; Williamstown 63-64; R of St Jude Carlton 64-67; V of St Edw S Blackb 67-74; I of N Dandenong Dio Melb from 74. *1472 Heatherton Road, Dandenong, Vic, Australia 3175.* (03-792 4925)

CURTIS, Peter Bernard. b 35. St Pet Hall Ox BA (2nd cl Th) 60, MA 64. Westcott Ho Cam 60. **d** 62 **p** 63 Southw. C of Warsop w Sookholme 62-65; Chap Grey Van Mildert and St Aid Colls Univ of Dur 65-69; V of Worle 69-78; R of Crewkerne w Wayford Dio B & W from 78. *Rectory, Crewkerne, Somt.* (Crewkerne 72047)

CURTIS, Philip. b 17. Late Scho of Ball Coll Ox 2nd cl Cl Mod 37, BA (2nd cl Lit Hum) 39, 2nd cl Th 40, MA 42. **d** 40 **p** 41 Liv. C of Warrington 40-43; Asst Master Giggleswick Sch 43-52; Chap from 55; Libr of Pusey Ho 52-55; Asst Chap Pemb Coll Ox 53-55. *Giggleswick School, Settle, N Yorks.*

CURTIS, Terrence Peter. Wollaston Coll W Austr 65. ACT ThL 67. **d** 68 Bp Macdonald for Perth **p** 69 Perth. C of City Beach 68-69; Scarborough 69-71; C of St Patr Perth 71-72; Willagee 72-74; Chap Perth Coll 75-79; Newc Gr Sch and Prec of Ch Ch Cathl Newc from 80. *43 Wolfe Street, Newcastle, NSW, Australia 2300.* (22575)

CURTIS, Thomas John. b 32. Pemb Coll Ox BA 55, MA 59. BD (Lon) 58. Clifton Th Coll 55. **d** 58 **p** 59 S'wark. C of Wandsworth 58-61; SAMS Chile Dio Argent 61-63; Dio Chile 63-71; Exam Chap to Bp of Chile 64-71; Hon Can of St Andr Cathl Santiago 70-71; R of Saxmundham 71-77; V of St Mark Cheltm Dio Glouc from 77. *St Mark's Vicarage, Fairmount Road, Cheltenham, Glos.* (Cheltm 580036)

CURTIS, Very Rev Wilfred Frank. b 23. K Coll Lon and Warm AKC 51. **d** 52 **p** 53 Ox. C of High Wycombe 52-55; CMS Area Sec Dios Ex and Truro 55-65; SW Regional Sec 62-65; L to Offic Dio Ex 55-74; Perm to Offic Dio Truro 55-65; Dio Lon 65-74; Home Sec CMS 65-74; V and Provost of Cathl Ch (w St Paul and St Jude Moorfields) City and Dio Sheff from 74. *Provost's Lodge, 22 Hallam Gate Road, Sheffield, S10 5BS.* (0742-662373)

CURTIS, Wilfrid Fitz-Harold. b 23. St Aug Coll Cant 47. Linc Th Coll 49. **d** 51 **p** 52 Linc. C of New Sleaford 51-53; Skegness 53-57; Chap Butlin's Holiday Camp Skegness 53 and 60-62; Filey 54 and 55; Chap Actors' Ch U from 53; V of St Paul Westcliff-on-Sea 57-60; CF (TA) from 58; R of Ingoldmells W Addlethorpe 60-67; V of Filey Dio York from 67. *Vicarage, Filey, Yorks, YO14 9AD.* (Filey 512745)

CURWEN, Cecil Eldred. b 1897. Kelham Th Coll 20. **d** 25 **p** 26 Heref. C of St Leon Bridgnorth 25-27; H Trin Reading 27-30; St Anne (in c of St Mary) Wandsworth 30-36; V of All SS Surrey Sq 36-42; PC of Ch Ch Hendon 42-45; V of Finsbury 45-52; (w St Matt City Road and St Barn King's Sq Lon 52) C-in-c of St Matt City Road and St Barn King's Sq Lon 45-52; R of Perivale 52-59; V of All S Brighton 59-64; C-in-c of St Patr and Seq Hove 64-69. *3 Nevill Close, Hove, Sussex, BN3 7QT.* (Brighton 501425)

CURWEN, David. b 38. St Cath Coll Cam 2nd cl Engl Trip pt i 61, BA (2nd cl Engl Trip pt ii) 62. Cudd Coll 62. **d** 64 Warrington for Liv **p** 65 Liv. C of St Andr Orford 64-67; Industr Chap to Bp of Croydon 67-77; C of Ch Ch S'wark Dio S'wark from 77; Admin S Lon Industr Miss from 77. *Vicarage, Clayhill Road, Leigh, Nr Reigate, Surrey RH2 8NN.* (Dawes Green 224)

CUSH, Charles Alexander. **d** 67 **p** 71 Guy. C of Mackenzie 67-73; V of Skeldon Dio Guy from 73. *Vicarage, Skeldon, Corentyne, Guyana.*

CUSSEN, Ven Colin Francis. ACT ThL 56. **d** 55 **p** 57 N Queensld. C of St Matt Townsville 56-60; Dioc Missr and Min of W Townsville 60-61; C of Herberton 61-65; Bursar and Chap St Mary's Sch Herberton 61-74; R of Sarina 65-70; Ingham 70-74; Can of N Queensld 72-74; R of Cairns 74-78; Archd of Cairns 74-78; Townsville from 78; Exam Chap to Bp of N Queensld from 76; Commiss N Queensld from 79. *Box 1244, Townsville, Queensland, Australia.*

CUTCHER, Canon George Charles. b 20. VRD 65. Qu Coll Cam BA 48, MA 53. Ridley Hall Cam 48. **d** 51 **p** 52 Liv. C of St John Birkdale 51-53; St Paul Warrington 53-59; Chap RNR 54-75; V of Hatcham S'wark 59-74; RD of Deptford from 73; V of St Paul Kingston Hill 74-81; RD of Kingston 75-81; Hon Can of S'wark Cathl from 76; V of St Bart Leigh Dio S'wark from 81. *Leigh Vicarage, Reigate, Surrey, RH2 8NN.* (Dawes Green 224)

CUTCLIFFE, Edgar Merland. St Jo Coll Armid ACT ThL 23. **d** 23 **p** 24 Armid. C of Gunnedah Armid 23-26; P-in-c of Nundle 26-28; Berridale 29-34; Binda 34-36; R of Bombala 36-42; Chap AIF 40-47; C of Wagga Wagga 47-50; R of Braidwood 50-55; Boorowa 55-61; L to Offic Dio Syd from 61. *3 St Augustine's Lodge, Mowll Memorial Village, Castle Hill, NSW, Australia 2154.*

CUTCLIFFE, John Edward. b 44. St Francis Coll Brisb 67. **d** 70 **p** 71 Brisb. C of St Mary Redcliffe 70-72; Bundaberg 72-74; V of Taroom 74-78; R of Killarney Dio Brisb from 78. *Rectory, Acacia Street, Killarney, Queensland, Australia 4373.*

CUTHAND, Adam. Em Coll Sktn. **d** 53 **p** 55 Sask. Miss at Montr Lake 54-60; John Smith's Reserve 60-63; Hon Can of Sask 61-65; Miss Loon Lake 63-64; V of Dynevor 64-67; L to Offic Dio Rupld from 67; Archd of St Peter 70-73; Hon C of H Trin Winnipeg 73-78; Consultant Native Affairs Ch Ho Tor from 77. *600 Jarvis Street, Toronto, Ont., Canada.*

CUTHAND, Stanley. Univ of Winnipeg Hon DD 70. Em Coll Sktn LTh 44. **d** 44 **p** 45 Sask. C of Lac La Ronge w Stanley and Pelican Narrows 44-50; Miss at Mont Nebo 50-55; Lac la Ronge 55-59; I of Cardston 59-67; Touchwood Hills 67-69; L to Offic Dio Sktn 71-73; on leave 74-75 and from 79; Hon C of Good Shepherd Winnipeg 76-79. *50 Newcastle Road, Winnipeg, Sask., Canada.*

CUTHBERT, Frederick Norton. b 07. Worc Ordin Coll 67. **d** 68 Cov **p** 69 Bp Daly for Cov. C of St Marg Cov 68-73; St Mich Stoke (Caludon Team Min from 76) (in c of St Cath) Cov 73-79; Hon C from 79. *2 Harefield Road, Coventry, CV2 4DF.* (Cov 452248)

CUTHBERT, John Hamilton. b 34. St D Coll Lamp BA 59. Coll of Resurr Mirfield 59. **d** 61 **p** 62 Cov. C of St Pet Cov 61-64; M Bush Bro of St Barn N Queensld 64-69; St Andr Willesden 69-72; St Cecilia Parson Cross Sheff 72-74; V of Lavender Hill Dio S'wark from 74. *The Ascension Clergy House, Pountney Road, SW11 5TU.* (01-228 5340)

CUTHBERTSON, Christopher Martin. b 48. AKC and BD Univ of Lon MTh 80. St Aug Coll Cant 75. **d** 76 **p** 77 Cant. C of Whitstable 76-79; Asst Master Princess Marg R Free Sch Windsor from 79. *Princess Margaret School, Bourne Avenue, Windsor, Berks, SL4 3JP.* (Windsor 62017)

CUTHBERTSON, John Dickon. b 19. Univ of Lon BSc 49. Oak Hill Th Coll 51. **d** 53 Stafford for Cant **p** 54 Lich. C of Penn Fields 53-56; R of High Halstow w St Mary Hoo 56-62; V of St Cuthb W Hampstead 62-69; St Jo Evang U Holloway 69-77; R of Stanstead w Shimplingthorne and Alpheton Dio St E from 77; P-in-c of Lawshall Dio St E from 80. *St James' Rectory, Stanstead, Sudbury, Suff.* (Glemsford 280738)

CUTHBERTSON, Raymond. b 52. AKC 75. Coll of Resurr Mirfield 76. **d** 77 **p** 78 Dur. C of St Mark w St Paul Darlington 77-81; H trin Usworth Dio Dur from 81. *61 Marlborough Road, Sulgrave, Washington, T & W.* (Wash 475627)

CUTHBERTSON, Canon Ross Gray. Univ of Natal BA 54. St Paul's Coll Grahmstn LTh 56. **d** 56 **p** 57 Natal. C of St Sav Cathl Pietermaritzburg 56-60; V of Drakensberg 60-61; York w Ravensworth 61-62; P-in-c of Mobeni 63-64; R of Wentworth Dio Natal 64-80; Can of Natal from 80. *28 Essex Street, Jacobs, Natal, S Africa.*

CUTHBERTSON, Trevor Albert. Univ of Syd BA 63. Moore Th Coll Syd ACT ThL 62. **d** 62 **p** 63 Syd. C of St Geo Hurstville 62-64; Port Kembla 64-66; C-in-c of Merrylands W 66-69; The Oaks 69-72; Peakhurst w Lugarno 73; L to Offic Dio Syd from 74. *43 Pacific Avenue, Werri Beach, NSW, Australia 2534.*

CUTHBERTSON, Warwick James. b 49. St Jo Coll Morpeth ACT ThDip 76. **d** 77 **p** 78 Tas. C of Burnie 77-78; P-in-c of King I 78-80; R of Sorell & Tasman Peninsula Dio Tas from 80. *Rectory, Sorell, Tasmania 7172.* (002 65 2445)

CUTLER, Francis Bert. b 15. Kelham Th Coll 32. **d** 38 **p** 39 Ches. C of Coppenhall 38-41; Ch Ch Timperley (in c of St Andr) 41-46; V of W Pinchbeck 46-64; R of Croyland or Crowland 64-80. *35 St Andrew's Road, Spalding, Lincs.*

CUTLER, Herbert. b 06. Kelham Th Coll 26. **d** 31 **p** 32 Dur. C of St Pet Stockton-on-Tees 31-34; Hd Master St Mich Sch Sandakan N Borneo 34-38; C of St Paul Ruislip Manor 38-42; Stoke-on-Trent 42-43; R of St Mich AA Prince Geo BC 43-47; Maple Ridge BC 47-53; PC of Northmoor 54-58; V of Stanton Harcourt 54-58; V of Stewkley 58-64; Dunsden 64-70; Chap Jesus Hosp Bray from 70; L to Offic Dio Ox from 70. *The Chaplain's House, Jesus Hospital, Bray, Maidenhead, Berks.* (M'head 20026)

CUTLER, Robert Francis. b 37. BSc (Lon) 57. Clifton Th Coll 62. **d** 64 **p** 65 S'wark. C of Peckham 64-68; H Trin Redhill 68-70; Trav Sec Inter-Coll Christian Fellshp of IVF 70-81. *Address temp unknown.*

CUTLIFFE, Neil Robert. b 50. New Univ of Ulster BA 72. TCD 72. **d** 75 **p** 76 Connor. C of St Mary Belf Dio Connor from 75. *5 Silvio Street, Crumlin Road, Belfast 13.*

CUTT, Chan Samuel Robert. b 25. Late Scho of Selw Coll Cam 1st cl Th Trip pt i 49, BA (1st cl Th Trip pt ii) 50, Wordsworth Stud 50, 2nd cl Th Trip pt iii 51, MA 54. Cudd Coll 51. **d** 53 **p** 54 Dur. C of St Aid W Hartlepool 53-56; Tutor St Bonif Coll Warm 56-59; Sub-Warden 59-65; Publ Pr Dio Sarum 57-65; Lect and Tutor Chich Th Coll 65-71; PV of Chich Cathl and L to Offic Dio Chich 66-71; Min Can of St Paul's Cathl Lon 71-79; Succr 74-79; Warden Coll of Min Cans 74-79; LPr Dio Lon 71-79; Lect K Coll Lon 73-79; P-in-Ord to HM the Queen 75-79; Chan and Can Res of Wells Cathl from 79; Dir of Ordinands Dio B & W from 79; Exam Chap to Bp of B & W from 80. *8 The Liberty, Wells, Somt, BA5 2SU.* (Wells 78763)

CUTTELL, Colin. OBE 77. Bp's Univ Lennox BA 37, STM 68. **d** 37 **p** 38 Edmon. Miss of Wabamun 37-42; Quebec 42-43; CF 43-44; Dom Chap to Bp of Queb 42-43; PV of S'wark Cathl 45-49; C of St Sav w St Pet S'wark 49-50; Commiss Qu'App 51-76; Industr Missr Dio S'wark 48-63; Can Res and Libr of S'wark Cathl 54-63; V of All H Barking-by-the-Tower w St Dunstan-in-E Lon 63-76; Field Comm Toc H 62-63; Dep Admin Padre 63-76. *Penn Mead, Penn, Bucks.* (049481-5682)

CUTTELL, Maurice John. b 05. Qu Coll Birm 46. **d** 48 **p** 49 Sheff. C of Conisborough 48-50; Goole (in c of St Paul) 50-53; V of Wincobank 53-61; R of Bradwell 61-77; Perm to Offic Dio Nor from 78. *3 Hannant Road, North Walsham, Norf, NR28 9ES.*

CUTTER, Harry Gordon. b 1900. St Chad's Coll Dur BA 23. **d** 24 Bp Wood for Newc T **p** 25 Newc T. C of Rothbury 24-27; St Andr Newc T 27-33; Rothbury (in c of Hepple and Thropton) 33-36; V of Shilbotel 36-45; Kirk Hammerton 45-69; C-in-c of Nun Monkton 49-52; V 52-69; RD of Boroughbridge 59-66. *26 Great Hales Street, Market Drayton, Salop.* (Market Drayton 3127)

CUTTER, John Douglas. b 31. BD (Lon) 61. Chich Th Coll 56. **d** 59 **p** 60 Newc T. C of St Mary Blyth 59-62; Rugeley 62-65; V of Rocester 65-73; V of St Giles Shrewsbury Dio Lich from 73. *St Giles Vicarage, Abbey Foregate, Shrewsbury, Salop, SY2 6LY.* (Shrewsbury 56426)

CUTTING, Peter Ralph. b 25. Ridley Hall Cam 70. **d** 72 Ely **p** 73 Huntingdon for Ely. C of St Martin Cam 72-74; P-in-c of Bury Dio Ely 74-75; R from 75; Wistow Dio Ely 74-75; R from 75. *Rectory, Bury, Huntingdon, Cambs.* (Ramsey 812514)

CUTTRISS, Ven Frank Leslie. OBE 74. ACT ThL 41. **d** 42 Geelong for Melb **p** 43 Melb. C of Ch Ch S Yarra 42-44;

Chap RAAF 44-46; Can Res and R of St Paul's Pro-Cathl Hay 46-48; Hon Can 48-51; R of Leeton 48-50; Mentone and Parkdale 51-56; Hampton 56-60; Dir Dioc Task Force Dio Melb 60-62; Can of Melb 61-62 and from 79; R of St Jas Syd 62-75; Hon Can of Syd 74-75; I of St Jas Dandenong 75-81; St Phil Avondale Dio Melb from 81; Archd of Essendon from 81. *11 Somerset Street, Avondale Heights, Vic, Australia 3034.*

CUTTS, David. b 52. Van Mildert Coll Dur BSc 73. Univ of Nottm BA (Th) 79. St Jo Coll Nottm 77. **d** 80 **p** 81 St E. C of St Matt Ipswich Dio St E from 80. *9 Wellington Street, Ipswich, Suffolk, IP1 2NT.*

CUTTS, Montague Fox Gapper. Hur Th Coll LTh 53. **d** 53 Hur for Ont **p** 54 Ont. R of Lansdowne Front 53-58; Wolfe I 58-60; I of Dunham 60-63; St D Dio Fred from 63. *Oak Bay, NB, Canada.*

✠ **CUTTS, Right Rev Richard Stanley.** K Coll Lon and Warm 47. **d** 51 **p** 52 Guildf. C of Godalming 51-56; Etalaneni Miss 56-57; Dir 57-63; Kambula Miss 63-65; Dir of Miss and R of St Mar Kuruman 65-71; Archd of Kuruman 70-71; Dean of St Mary and All SS Cathl Salisbury Mashon 71-75; Archd of Salisbury City 75; Cons Ld Bp in Argent and E S Amer w Falkld Is in St John's Cathl Buenos Aires 12 Oct 75 by Bps of N Argent and Colombia; Bps Flagg and Leake; Abp of Cant Commiss in Falkld Is from 78. *25 de Mayo 282, 1002 Buenos Aires, Argentina.*

CUYLER, Canon Arthur Robert. Angl Th Coll BC 51. **d** 53 **p** 54 New Westmr. I of Deep Cove 53-56; C of St Paul Vancouver 56-59; R of Sundridge 62-66; New Liskeard 66-69; Sec Coun for social Service Tor 69-73; Dir of Co-ordin Bp of Commun Services Tor 73-74; Dir of Dioc Services Dio Tor from 74; Can of Tor from 77. *135 Adelaide Street East, Toronto, Ont., Canada.* (416-363 6021)

CUZNER, Arthur Edward. K Coll NS BA 52. St Chad's Coll Regina 54. **d** 54 **p** 55 Qu'App. C of St Matt Regina 54-55; I of Eston 55-56; Moose Jaw 56-60; Lethbridge 60-65; I of Castor 65; on leave 65-68; L to Offic Dio Qu'App 68-74. *12 Foxglove Crescent, Regina, Sask., Canada.* (306-586 6529)

CYPRUS and the GULF, Lord Bishop in. *See* Ashton, Right Rev Leonard James.

CYPRUS and the GULF, Provost of. *See* Henry, Very Rev Bryan George.

CYSTER, Canon Raymond Frederick. b 13. CCC Ox 1st cl Math Mods 33. BA (2nd cl Physics) 35, MA 40. Wycl Hall Ox 40. **d** 42 **p** 43 St E. C of St Jo Bapt Ipswich 42-45; Chap and Lect at Norwich Tr Coll 45-64; L to Offic Dio Nor 58-64; R of Fenny Compton w Wormleighton 64-76; Hon Can of Cov Cathl 74-80; Can (Emer) from 80; C-in-c of Hampton Lucy w Charlecote 76-79; R (w Loxley) 79-80. *47 Cherry Orchard, Stratford-on-Avon, Warws, CV37 9AP.*

D

DAAGI, Clement. St Pet Coll Siota. **d** 53 Melan. d Dio Melan 53-75. *Utupua, British Solomon Islands.*

DABA, Layton Mziwabantu. St Francis Coll Sekhukhuniland 62. **d** 64 **p** 65 Pret. C of Waterberg 65-68; R of Matlala 68-73; St Pet Witbank 73-78; P-in-c of Alexandra 78-80. *Box 225, Begvliet, Johannesburg, S Africa.*

DABBS, Roger Stevens. b 09. Bp Wilson Th Coll IM 29. **d** 32 **p** 33 Birm. C of St Thos Birm 32-35; Chap Toc H for E Midld Area 35-38; V of Cosby 38-47; H Trin Ashby-de-la-Zouch 47-53; RD of Akeley W 48-53; R of Grouville Jersey 53-74; Perm to Offic Dio Ex from 74. *9 Highfield, Walden Meadows, Honiton, Devon.*

DABINYABA, Hannington Puimba. Newton Th Coll Dogura 59. **d** 61 **p** 63 New Guinea. P Dio New Guinea 61-71; Dio Papua from 71. *PO Box 36, Popondetta, Papua New Guinea.*

DABIRI, Zaccheus Adekunle. b 37. **d** 74 Lagos **p** 76 Ijebu. d Dio Lagos 74-76; P Dio Ijebu from 76. *St Michael's Church, Owo-Ijebu, Owu/Ikija PA, via Ijebu-Ode, Nigeria.*

DABORN, Robert Francis. b 53. Keble Coll Ox BA 74, MA 78. Fitzwm Coll Cam BA 77. Ridley Hall Cam 75. **d** 78 **p** 79 S'wark. C of Mortlake 78-81; Chap Grey and Collingwood Colls Univ of Dur from 82. *Collingwood College, South Road, Durham, DH1 3LT.*

DACK, Paul Marven. K Coll Lon and Warm BD and AKC 51. **d** 52 **p** 53 Glouc. C of Leckhampton 52-55; R of Bourton-on-the-Hill 55-61; Quedgeley 61-82; Hasfield w Tirley and Ashleworth Dio Glouc from 82. *Hasfield Rectory, Gloucester, GL19 4LQ.* (Tirley 360)

da COSTA, Very Rev John Robert. Kelham Th Coll. **d** 57 S'wark for Cant for Col Bp **p** 59 S'wark. d Dio Accra 57-58; C of St Marg Qu Streatham Hill 58-61; St Cypr Cathl Kimb 61-62; R and Dir of Douglas 62-65; R of St Mark Capetn 65-72; Dir of Miss Prov of S Africa 72-75; Hon Can of Kimb K 73-75; Commiss St Hel 73-79; L to Offic Dio Johann 73-75; Dean of St Mary and All SS Cathl Salisbury Dio Mashon from 75. *Box 981, Salisbury, Zimbabwe.* (70 2251)

DACRE, Roy Aubrey. b 17. AKC (2nd cl) 41. Univ of Lon BD (2nd cl) 41. Linc Th Coll 41. **d** 41 **p** 42 Win. C of Basingstoke 41-47; CF 47-51; Hon CF 51; R of Newnham w Hook, Rotherwick, Nately Scures, Mapledurwell and Greywell w Up Nately 51-55; Rotherwick, Hook and Greywell 55-59; V of Alton 59-66; Chap at Alton Gen Hosp 59-66; Surr 59-66; RD of Alton 63-66; Asst Master Wombwell High Sch 66-82; L to Offic Dio Sheff from 66. *Parsonage, Hemingfield, Barnsley, Yorkshire.*

DADD, Alan Edward. St Jo Coll Nottm 77. **d** 78 **p** 79 Bris. C of Bishopsworth Dio Bris from 78. *St Dunstan's Vicarage, Bedminster Down Road, Bristol BS13 7AA.*

DADD, Peter Wallace. b 38. Univ of Sheff BA (2nd cl Hist) 59. Qu Coll Birm 59. **d** 61 **p** 62 Chelmsf. C of Grays 61-65; Grantham (in c of Ascen Harrowby) 65-72; Team V 72-73; V of Haxey Dio Linc from 73. *Haxey Vicarage, Doncaster, Yorks, DN9 2HY.* (Haxey 752351)

✠ **DADSON, Right Rev Joseph Kobina.** b 27. Univ of Ghana BA 71. Wells Th Coll 55. **d** and **p** 58 Accra. P Dio Accra; CF (Ghana) 75-81; Chap Gen 78-81; Archd of Accra 78-81; VG Dio Accra 80-81; Cons Ld Bp of Sunyanikamala 18 Oct 81. *c/o Box 23, Sunyani, Ghana.*

D'AETH, Narbrough Hughes. b 01. CB 51. CBE 43. Linc Th Coll. **d** 57 **p** 58 Ox. C of Crowthorne 57-59; R of E Langdon w Guston 59-60; Furneaux Is 60-65; L to Offic Dio Syd 65-67; Dio Perth 71-72; P-in-c of Midl Junction w Swan 67-71; Perm to Offic Dio Ex from 73. *11 Exmoor Way, Minehead, Somt.*

DAFFA, Vohana. St Cypr Th Coll Ngala 60. **d** 62 Zanz. d Dio Zanz 62-65; Dio Zanz T from 65. *PO Muheza, Tanzania.*

DAFFURN, Lionel William. b 19. DFC 43. AKC 49. **d** 50 **p** 51 Cov. C of Rugby 50-53; V of St Thos Cov 53-57; R of St Thos Brampton Derby 57-74; C-in-c of Hindon w Chicklade and Pertwood 74-76; E Knoyle (and Hindon w Chicklade and Pertwood from 76) Dio Sarum from 74. *Hindon Vicarage, Salisbury, Wilts.* (Hindon 362)

✠ **DAFIEWHARE, Right Rev John Onyaene.** Trin Th Coll Umuahia 55. **d** 57 **p** 58 Niger. P Dio Niger 57-63; C of Glen Parva w S Wigston Leic 63-65; P Dio Benin 65-79; Dom Chap to Bp of Benin 66-77; Can of Benin 69-79; Cons Bp of Warri 79. *PO Box 396, Warri, Bendel State, Nigeria.*

DAGAA, Zephaniah. **d** 60 Centr Tang **p** 60 Bp Wiggins for Centr Tang. P Dio Centr Tang. *PO Kintinku, Tanzania.*

DAGGER, John Henry Kynaston. b 07. Selw Coll Cam 3rd cl Hist Trip pt i 30, BA (3rd cl Th Trip pt i) 31, MA 35. Cudd Coll. **d** 32 **p** 34 Lich. C of St Pet Wolverhampton 32-37; W Bromwich 37-40; Chap RAFVR 40-46; RAF 46-61; R of Sutton w Bignor 61-77; Barlavington 62-77. *Greenways, Copthorne Lane, Fawley, Southampton, So4 1DP.* (Fawley 891582)

DAGGER, Kenneth. b 46. Cranmer Hall Dur 73. **d** 76 Burnley for Blackb **p** 77 Blackb. C of St Jas Blackb 76-79; St Bart Colne 79-81; R of Hesketh w Becconsall Dio Blackb from 81. *Hesketh Rectory, Hesketh Bank, Preston, Lancs PR4 6SQ.* (Hesketh Bank 2345)

DAGLEISH, John. b 38. AIB 74. SOC 75. **d** 78 **p** 79 S'wark. Hon C of Riddlesdown Dio S'wark from 78; Perm to Offic Dio Lon from 81. *29 Lower Barn Road, Purley, Surrey, CR2 1HY.* (01-660 6060)

DAGLISH, John David. b 44. R Mil Coll of Sc BSc 70. Cranmer Hall Dur 76. **d** 77 **p** 78 York. C of Ormesby Dio York from 77. *22 Coronation Green, Ormesby, Cleveland, T53 0LT.*

DAGNALL, Bernard. b 44. AKC 65, BSc 65, CChem MRIC 75. Univ of Ox BA 75, MA 78. St Steph Ho Ox 72. **d** 75 Ripon **p** 76 Man. C of Stanningley 75-76; Lightbowne 76-78; St Alphage Hendon Dio Lon from 78. *St Augustine's House, Great Field, NW9 5SY.* (01-205 1979)

DAGNALL, Radford Henry. b 14. Univ of Lon Plumptre Pri (K Coll Lon) 38, BD 39, AKC 39. Univ of Leeds, MA 41. **d** 39 **p** 40 Wakef. C of St Pet Horbury 39-43; Battyeford 43-44. *10 Abbots Road, Leicester.*

d'AGUIAR, Carlos. b 20. St Chad's Coll Dur BA 43, Dipl Th 44. **d** 44 **p** 45 Ripon. C of St Pet w St Mary Leeds 44-47; St Aug Woodston 47-51; Min Can of Ripon Cathl 51-55; V of Thornthwaite w Darley and Thruscross 55-64; Bowes (w Startforth from 80) Dio Ripon from 64. *Startforth Vicarage, Barnard Castle, Co Durham.* (Teesdale 37371)

DAH BYA, d 32 **p** 35 Rang. P Dio Rang. *St Luke's School, Toungoo, Burma.*

DAHL, Grant Stanley. Em Coll Sktn LTh 64. **d** 63 **p** 64 Qu'App. C of Mortlach 63-64; St John Moose Jaw 64-65; I of Maple Creek 65-68. *231 9th Avenue, Calgary, Alta., Canada.*

DAHL, Canon Murdoch Edgcumbe. b 14. Late Scho of St Jo Coll Dur BA (2nd cl Th) 36, MA 56. **d** 37 **p** 38 Man. C of St Paul Astley Bridge 37-39; Fallowfield 39-43; Happenden 43-49; V of Arlesey and R of Astwick 49-51; Min of St Osw Conv Distr Croxley Green 51-56; V of Gt w L Hormead 56-60; R of Wyddial 56-60; Exam Chap to Bp of St Alb 59-79; Dir of Cler Stud Dio St Alb 60-71; Hon Can of St Alb 63-65; Can Res 65-79; Can Th 69-79; Can (Emer) from 79. *52 Fleet Street, Beaminster, Dorset.*

DAI, Canon Kiwami. St Paul's Th Coll Thurs Is 48. **d** 49 **p** 51 Carp. C of St Paul's Miss Moa 49-51; Torres Straits Miss 51-52; Miss at Cowal Creek 52-54; Thursday I 54-56; Badu I 56-61; L to Offic Dio Carp 61-75; Hon Can of Carp from 71; P-in-c of Yam I 75-78; Saibai I Dio Carp from 78. *c/o Box 79, Thursday Island, Queensland, Australia 4875.*

DAILEY, Arthur John Hugh. b 25. Univ of Lon BSc 45. Clifton Th Coll 63. **d** 65 **p** 66 S'wark. C of All SS Wandsworth 65-70; V of H Trin Frogmore St Alb 70-81; RD of Aldenham 75-78; C of St Paul City and Dio St Alb from 82. *46 Brampton Road, St Albans, Herts, AL1 4PT.* (St Alb 50639)

DAIMOND, John Ellerbeck. b 39. Univ of Dur BA (3rd cl Phil) 61. Ripon Hall Ox 61. **d** 63 **p** 64 Lich. C of Caverswall 63-66; Chap RAF from 66. *c/o Ministry of Defence, Adastral House, WC1 8RU.*

✠ **DAIN, Right Rev Arthur John.** OBE 79. Ridley Hall Cam **d** 59 Chelmsf for Cant for Syd **p** 59 Syd. Federal Sec CMS of Austr and Tas 59-65; L to Offic Dio Syd 59-65; Exam Chap to Abp of Syd 65-76; Commiss Maseno from 63; Cons Asst Bp of Syd in St Andr Cathl Syd 20 April 65 by Abp of Syd; Abp of Melb; Bps of Newc; C & Goulb; Graft; Armid; and Bath; Bps Coadj of Syd (Loane and Hulme-Moir); Asst Bp of Newc; and Bp Moyes; Archd of Syd w E Syd 75-79. *St Andrew's House, Sydney Square, Sydney, NSW, Australia 2000.* (269-0642)

DAIN, Frederick Ronald. OBE 80. Jes Coll Ox BA (1st cl Math) 31, MA 43. St Aug Coll Cant. **d** 62 **p** 64 Momb. Hon C of All SS Cathl Nai 62-65; Chap Kenyatta Coll Nai 65-67 and 68-77; Executive Officer CORAT Afr from 77. *PO Box 42493, Nairobi, Kenya.*

DAINES, John Muir. Univ of Witwatersrand BA 60. St Paul's Th Coll Grahmstn LTh 63. **d** 62 **p** 63 Johann. C of Linden 62-68; R of Belgravia Dio Johann from 68; R of Jeppe 68-72; CF (S Afr) 72-76; Perm to Offic Dio Pret 74-76; R of Voortrekkerhoogte Dio Pret from 76. *Box 77, Voortrekkerhoogte, Pretoria, S Africa.* (71-1379)

DAINES, John Wilfrid. Univ of Lon BD 36, AKC 36, MTh 45, Teachers' Dipl 46. PhD 49. **d** 36 **p** 37 S'wark. C of Ch Ch Battersea 36-39; Coulsdon (in c of St Bart from 40) 39-41; Chap HM Pris Wakef 41-42; V of H Trin Haverstock Hill 42-47; Div Lect Derby Tr Coll and LPr Dio Derby 47-58; Tutor Univ of Nottm from 58; Hon C of Ockbrook Dio Derby from 79. *161 The Ridings, Ockbrook, Derby.*

DAINES, Norman Steele. b 26. Univ of Aber MA (Educn) 76. Chich Th Coll 51. **d** 55 Ex. OSB 76. C of Whipton 55-56; Dep Hdmaster and Chap Hollingbury Court Sch Brighton 56; Asst Master Elmhurst Sch S Croydon 58-66; Hon C of St Barn Hove 60-62; C of Good Shepherd Brighton 64-68; Asst Master Old Gr Sch Lewes 68-70; Battle Abbey Sch 70-72; Lect Hastings Coll Further Educn 72-74; Hon C of St Jo Evang U St Leonards 75; St John Aber 75-76. *Weston Lodge, Glyne Ascent, Bexhill-on-Sea, Sussex, TN40 2NX.*

DAINTITH, Canon Richard. b 09. Lich Th Coll 37. **d** 39 **p** 40 Ches. C of St Paul Tranmere 39-41 and 42-46; Presteigne w Discoyd 41-42; Actg C of Stoke-on-Trent (in c of All SS) 46-47; C of St John Ches 47-49; V of St Jas Latchford 49-53; St Paul S Tranmere 53-69; C-in-c of Lower Tranmere 69-71; RD of Birkenhead 62-65 and 68-71; Hon Can of Ches 69-74; Can (Emer) from 74; Surr from 69; V of Wybunbury 71-74; C of W Kirby 74-77; Perm to Offic Dio Ches from 78. *3 Bedford Drive, Rock Ferry, Birkenhead, Chesh.* (051-645 3082)

DAINTREE, Geoffrey Thomas. b 54. Univ of Bris BSc 77. Trin Coll Bris 78. **d** 81 Worc. C of Old Hill Dio Worc from 81. *15 Highland Road, Cradley Heath, Warley, W Midl, B64 5NB.*

DAINTY, James Ernest. b 46. Dipl Th (Lon) 68. **d** 73 Pontefract for Wakef **p** 74 Wakef. C of Normanton 73-76; St Mark Gillingham 76-78; V of St Geo Barnsley Dio Wakef from 78. *St George's Vicarage, Dodworth Road, Barnsley, S Yorks, S70 6HL.* (Barnsley 203870)

DAISLEY, John Charles. Em Coll Sktn LTh 38. **d** 38 Sktn for Sask **p** 39 Sask. C of Nipawin w White Fox 38-41; Leask 42; Chap CASF 42-46; I of Birch Hills 46-51; V of Strathmore 51-52; CF (Canad) 52-64; I of Taber 64-75. *Box 77, Taber, Alta., Canada.* (223-3942)

DAKADA, Solomon Xela. St Bede's Coll Umtata 40. **d** 41 **p** 44 Grahmstn. Asst Miss O of Ethiopia Dio Grahmstn 41-60; Prov 60-79. *P.O. Box 2, Lady Frere, CP, S Africa.*

DAKAMELA, Solomon Magonya. d 78 **p** 79 Matab. P Dio Matab. *193 Barbourfields, Bulawayo, Zimbabwe.* (65608)

DAKIN, Canon John Edward Clifford. b 10. AKC and Whichelow Pri 40. **d** 40 **p** 41 Southw. C of E Retford 40-42; CF (EC) 42-46; V of Bircotes 46-50; Colston Bassett 50-57; R of Langar w Barnstone 50-57; Thrapston 57-78; Surr 58-78; RD of Thrapston 59-70; Can (Non-res) of Pet 71-78; Can (Emer) from 78; L to Offic Dio Pet from 78. *8 Derling Drive, Raunds, Nr Wellingborough, Northants, NN9 6LF.*

DAKIN, Reginald James Blanchard. b 25. SOC 66. **d** 70 **p** 71 Willesden for Lon. C of Ascen Wembley 70-74; St Jo Bapt Greenhill Harrow 74-76; C-in-c of Littleton Dio Lon from 76. *Littleton Rectory, Squires Bridge Road, Shepperton, Middx.* (59328 62249)

DAKIN, Stanley Frederick. b 30. Roch Th Coll 63. [f CA . **d** 65 **p** 66 Lich. C of Meole-Brace 65-68; V (and R of Sutton) 68-72; Hosp Chap Nai 72-75; P-in-c of Nettlebed (w Highmore from 78) Dio Ox 75-81; R (w Bix) 81; Bix w Pishill 77-81; V of St John W Ealing Dio Lon from 81; P-in-c of St Jas W Ealing Dio Lon from 81; Commiss Momb from 81. *23 Culmington Road, W13 9NJ.* (01-567 4164)

DALBY, Francis Bruce. b 01. Late Scho of Keble Coll Ox 2nd cl Cl Mods 21, BA (2nd cl Lit Hum) 23. Qu Coll Birm 23. M SSJE 42. **d** 24 **p** 25 Ex. C of St Pet Plymouth 24-30; Heavitree 30-39; L to Offic Dio Ox 40-64; Supr-Gen SSJE Cowley St John Ox 49-64 and 73-75; St Cuthb Miss Dio St John's 65-74; Proc Conv Ox 57-64. *Box 660, Bracebridge, Ont., Canada.*

DALBY, John. Cudd Coll 72. **d** 74 **p** 75 Bradf. C of Baildon 74-78; P-in-c of Austwick Dio Bradf from 78. *Vicarage, Austwick, Via Lancaster.* (Clapham 313)

DALBY, John Mark Meredith. b 38. Late Exhib of Ex Coll Ox BA (2nd cl Th) 61. MA 65. Univ of Nottm PhD 77. Ripon Hall Ox 61. **d** 63 **p** 64 Ox. C of Hambleden 63-68; Fawley Fingest Medmenham and Turville 66-68; V of St Pet Birm 68-75; RD of Birm City 73-75; Selection Sec and Sec of Committee of Th Educn of ACCM 75-80; Hon C of Tottenham 75-80; V of Worsley w Ellenbrook Dio Man from 80; Exam Chap to Bp of Man from 80. *Worsley Vicarage, Manchester, M28 4WH.* (061-790 2362)

DALBY, Canon Victor Ivor. b 15. Univ of Lon BA (2nd cl Engl) 36. Dorch Miss Coll 36. **d** 38 **p** 39 Derby. C of Shirebrook 38-42; St Mary and St Jas Grimsby (in c of St Hugh) 42-48; V of St Giles Linc 48-64; R of Boultham Dio Linc from 64; Chap HM Pris Linc 48-49; RD of Christianity 57-78; Can and Preb of Biggleswade in Linc Cathl from 61. *Rectory, St Helen's Avenue, Boultham, Lincoln.* (Lincoln 682026)

DALE, David William. b 35. Open Univ BA 74. Wells Th Coll 61. **d** 63 **p** 64 Guildf. C of Weybridge 63-66; Lect Bolton-le-Moors 66-67; C of Farnham 67-69; V of Leintwardine w Adforton 69-76; C-in-c of Downton-on-the-Rock w Burrington Aston and Elton 69-76; Brampton Bryan 69-76; Wigmore w Leinthall Starkes 72-76; V of H Trin Heref 76-81; Chap Shiplake Coll Henley-on-Thames from 81. *Shiplake College, Henley-on-Thames, Oxon.*

DALE, Eric Stephen. b 24. Roch Th Coll 63. **d** 65 **p** 66 Ripon. C of Kippax w Gt Preston 65-67; Fulford York 67-69; V of Askham Bryan (w Askham Richard from 71) 69-78; V of Askham Richard 69-71; Chap HM Pris Askham Grange 69-78; Wakef 78-79; Gartree from 79. *HM Prison, Gartree, Market Harborough, Leics.*

DALE, Gerald Arnold Montague. b 05. **d** 57 **p** 58 Newc T. C of Hexham 57-59; R of Allendale 59-61; C of St Pet Lutton Place Edin 61-63; L to Offic Dio Edin 63-66; R of W Linton 66-69; C of St Pet, Lutton Place Edin 69-71; L to Offic Dio Edin 71-78; Hon C of St Martin Scarborough Dio York from 80. *Dulverton Hall, Scarborough, N Yorks, YO11 2DQ.*

DALE, Grant Edward. Univ of BC BA 46. Angl Th Coll Vancouver LTh 44, BD 55. **d** and **p** 46 Athab. R of Fort Chipewyan 46-49; C of All SS Vernon 49-50; I of Princeton 50-55; R of Dawson Creek 55-65; Hon Can of Caled 63-65; R of St Marg Vanc 65-74; St Alb Richmond Dio New Westmr from 74; Cler Sec of Syn Dio New Westmr from 76. *7251 St Alban Road, Richmond, BC, Canada.*

DALE, John Anthony. b 42. Qu Coll Birm 72. **d** 75 **p** 76 Worc. Dioc Regr and Hon C of Elmley Castle 75-81; P-in-c of Elmley Castle w Netherton, Bricklehampton and the Combertons Dio Worc from 81. *Little Comberton Rectory, Pershore, Worcs, WR10 3EP.* (Elmley Castle 240)

DALE, John Clifford. b 18. St D Coll Lamp BA 40. St Mich Coll Llan 40. **d** 42 **p** 43 Llan. C of Cymmer w Porth 42-48; Ledbury 48-52; V of Dixton w Wyesham 52-57; V of Holmer w Huntington Dio Heref from 57. *Holmer Vicarage, Hereford.* (Hereford 3200)

DALE, Peter Ernest. b 41. St Pet Coll Ox BA 62, MA 68. Univ of Sussex DPhil 65. BD (2nd cl) Lon 68. Tyndale Hall Bris 65. **d** 68 Ely **p** 69 Huntingdon for Ely. C of St Paul Cam 68-71; Bletchley w Water Eaton 71-78. *Address temp unknown.*

DALES, Douglas John. b 52. Ch Ch Ox BA (Mod Hist) 74, BA (Th) 76, MA 78. Cudd Coll 74. **d** 77 Kens for Lon **p** 78 Lon. C of Shepperton 77-81; H Trin w St Mary City and Dio Ely from 81. *44 Northwold, Ely, Cambs.* (Ely 5084)

DALEY, George Chatterton. b 27. Em & St Chad's Coll Sktn 53. **d** 55 **p** 56 Keew. P Dio Keew 55-69; on leave 70-74; R of Kashechewan 75-78; I of Foleyet 78-80; Creemore Dio Tor from 80. *St Luke's Rectory, Creemore, Ont, Canada.*

DALEY, Leslie Eugene. Em Coll Sktn STh 64. **d** 60 **p** 61 Bran. C of Grand View 60-64; R of Elgin 64-68; Glenboro 68-70; Shoal Lake 70-75; Kelwood 75-78; P-in-c of Vulcan w Carmangay 79-80. *10 Glen Everest Road, Scarborough, Ont, Canada.*

DALEY, Peter Andrew. b 44. Linc Univ Penn BA 70. Yale Univ MDiv 72. Codr Coll Barb 62. **d** and **p** 72 Antig. P Dio Antig 72-73; on leave 73-74; Dir of Chr Educn Dio Antig from 75; Exam Chap to Bp of Antig from 76. *PO Box 1245, St John's, Antigua, WI.* (20261)

DALEY, Victor Leonard. b 38. Chich Th Coll 76. **d** 78 Horsham for Chich **p** 79 Chich. C of Durrington 78-81; Charlton Adam w Charlton Mackrell and Kingsdon Dio B & W from 81; Somerton w Compton Dundon Dio B & W from 81. *Rectory, Charlton Adam, Somerton, Somt, TA11 7NQ.* (Charlton Mackrell 3282)

DALLAS, Robert Washington. Univ of Sheff BA (2nd cl Hist) 27, MA and Dipl Educn 28. Ely Th Coll 59. **d** 60 **p** 61 York. C of Howden 60-62; Woodston 62-64; R of Coveney 64-72. *10 Chariot Way, Thorpe Audlin, Pontefract, W Yorks, WF8 3EZ.*

DALLAWAY, Joan Anne. b 36. St Jo Coll Auckld. **d** 77 **p** 79 Auckld. Educn Officer Dio Auckld 77-78; Hon Asst to Dir of Chr Educn Dio Auckld 78-80; C of St Paul City and Dio Auckld from 80. *38 Edenvale Road, Mount Eden, Auckland 3, NZ.*

DALLAWAY, Philip Alan. b 48. Chich Th Coll 80. **d** 81 Reading for Ox. C of St Nicolas Newbury Dio Ox from 81. *51 Gloucester Road, Newbury, Berks.*

DALLIMORE, Hugh de Clifford. Lon Coll of Div. **d** 13 River **p** 18 Sheff. C of Wilcannia 13-15; Orange 15-16 (both in NSW); Conisborough 16-20; Perm to Offic at Exning (in c of St Phil) 20-21; C of St Paul Dorking 22-25; Wiggenhall St German (in c of St Pet) 25-28; Thorney Abbey 28-30; R of Barnwell 30-43; L Massingham 43-51. *27 Megalong Road, Nedlands, W Australia.*

DALLING, Alfred Thomas Everitt. Moore Th Coll Syd ACT ThL 52. **d** 54 **p** 56 Gippsld. C-in-c of Newborough 54-56; V of Omeo 56-60; Asst Chap Miss to Seamen Syd and L to Offic Dio Syd 60-62; Chap Miss to Seamen Dio Newc 62-68; RANR from 64; Asst Chap Miss to Seamen Melb 68-72; I of Diamond Creek 72-78; Hamlyn Heights Dio Melb from 78. *Vicarage, Beulah Street, Hamlyn Heights, Vic, Australia 3218.* (78 3822)

DALLING, Antony Fraser. b 26. Magd Coll Cam MA 50. Westcott Ho Cam 64. **d** 65 Dunwich for St E **p** 66 St E. C of St Mary-le-Tower Ipswich 65-67; Hemel Hempstead 67-70; Industr Chap Dio St Alb 70-76; Dio Roch from 76. *30 Maiden Erlegh Avenue, Bexley, Kent, DA5 3PD.*

DALRIADA, Archdeacon of. *See* McKinney, Ven Wilson.

DALTON, Canon Arthur Benjamin. b 07. Univ Coll Lon BA (2nd cl Hist) 27. Univ of Ox BA (2nd cl Th) 30, MA 35. Ripon Hall Ox 27. **d** 30 **p** 31 Ox. C of Caversham 30-34; Wandsworth 34-42; V of All SS S Lambeth 42-49; St Aug Honor Oak Pk 49-75; Surr from 66; Hon Can of S'wark 71-75; Can (Emer) from 75. *43 Empress Drive, Chislehurst, Kent, BR7 5BQ.* (01-467 8727)

DALTON, (Patrick) Edmund George Arthur Henry. b 11. M OSB 32. **d** 38 **p** 41 Ox. L to Offic Dio Ox 41-47 and from 65; in Amer Ch 47-65. *Nashdom Abbey, Burnham, Slough, SL1 8NL.*

DALTON, James Lawrence. Angl Th Coll BC LTh 43. **d** 43 **p** 44 Koot. C of Vernon 43-46; P-in-c of St Faith Vanc 46-50; V of Lumsden 51-53; R of St Luke Regina 53-60; Archd of Regina 58-60; R of Maple Ridge 60-63; Haney 63-67; St Geo Vanc 67-73; Drumheller 73-81. *Carbon, Alta., Canada.* (823-2594)

DALTON, John Leonel. Angl Th Coll LTh 43. **d** 43 Koot for Carib **p** 44 Carib. C of Lytton 43-45; Trail 45-46; Miss Ind Sch Gleichen 46; Vice-Prin Ind Sch Moose Factory 46-47; C of St Paul Vancouver 47-48; R of N Surrey 48-54; Prin St Mich Ind Sch Alert Bay 54-63; R of Revelstoke 63-66; Kimberley 66-69; on leave 69-72; R of Strathmore 72-81. *114-13th Avenue NW, Calgary, Alta, Canada.*

DALTON, Kevin. b 32. TCD BA 65, Div Test 66. Ch Div Sch USA BD 67. **d** 66 **p** 67 Dub. C of Stillorgan 66-72; R of Drumcondra w N Strand and St Barn Dub 72-79; Monkstown Dio Dub from 79. *62 Monkstown Road, Monkstown, Co Dublin, Irish Republic.* (Dub 806596)

DALTON, Lawrence Richard. b 18. Qu Coll Birm. **d** 58 Pontefract for Wakef **p** 59 Wakef. C of Lupset 58-60; V of Paddock 60-64; Chap Miss to Seamen Port Harcourt 64-68; Antwerp 68-71; V of Birstall 71-79; Darrington w Wentbridge Dio Wakef from 79. *Darrington Vicarage, Pontefract, W Yorks, WF8 3AB.* (Pontefract 704744)

DALTON, Ronald. b 20. **d** 61 **p** 62 York. C of N Ferriby 61-64; V of Rillington 64-73; Scampston 64-73. *15 Ambrey Close, Hunmanby, Filey, N Yorks, YO14 0LZ.* (Hunmanby 890037)

DALY, Canon Dorothy Isabel. b 40. Vanc Sch of Th BTh 74. **d** 64 Bp Hunt for Tor **p** 77 Caled. Perm to Offic Dio Tor 64-65; C of St Aug w St Phil Stepney 65-66; All SS Hanworth 66-71; Perm to Offic Dio Caled 71-72; Hon C H Trin Vanc 73-75; All SS Whitby 75-76; I of Ch of Transfig Chetwynd Dio Caled from 77; Hon Can of Caled from 81. *Box 326, Chetwynd, BC, Canada, V0C 1J0.*

✠ **DALY, Right Rev John Charles Sydney.** b 03. K Coll Cam BA 24, MA 28. Cudd Coll 25. **d** 26 Jarrow for Dur **p** 27 Dur. C of St Mary Tyne Dk 26-29; C-in-c of Airedale Conv Distr Castleford 29-30; I of Airedale w Fryston 30-35. Cons Ld Bp of Gambia and the Rio Pongas in All H Barking-by-the-Tower 1 May 35 by Abp of Cant; Bps of Wakef; Sarum; S Rhod; and Masasi; Bp Suffr of Pontefract; and Bps G L King, Boutflower and Radford, Trld to Accra 51; to Korea 55; to Taejon 65; res 68; Asst Bp of Cov 68-75; C-in-c of Honington w Idlicote and Whatcote 68-70; V of Bp's Tachbrook 70-75. *Rye Croft, Honington, Shipston-on-Stour, Warws, CV36 5AA.* (0608-62140)

DALZELL, Donald Paul. **d** 80 **p** 81 Melb. C of All SS Geelong Dio Melb from 80. *113 Noble Street, Newtown, Geelong, Vic, Australia 3220.*

DAMANT, Derek George. Univ of S Afr BA 61, MA 73, DLitt & DPhil 77. Kelham Th Coll 52. **d** 56 **p** 58 Basuto. Asst Chap St Andr Sch Bloemf 56-58; Chap 59-64; Peka High Sch Basuto 58-59; Hd Master Dioc High Sch Mohales Hoek 64-70; Chap St Alb Coll Pret and L to Offic Dio Pret 71-75; Exam Chap to Bp of Pret 75-79; to Bp of Geo from 80; Dean and R of St Alb Cathl Pret 75-79; R of St Geo Knysna Dio Geo from 80. *Box 67, Knysna, CP, S Africa.* (Knysna 53)

DAMARALAND, Diocese of. *See* Namibia.

DAMASANE, Matthias Elijah. St John's Sem Lusaka 51. **d** 53 **p** 54 Matab. P Dio Matab from 53. *St Francis Mission, Tjololyo, Rhodesia.*

DAMES, Louis Roscoe. Sarum Wells Th Coll 70. **d** and **p** 73 Nass. C of St Geo Nass 73-74; P-in-c of Governor's Harbour Eleuthera 75-77; Dioc Treas Dio Nass from 77. *Box N-656, Nassau, Bahamas.* (23015)

DAMMERS, Very Rev Alfred Hounsell. b 21. Late Scho of Pemb Coll Cam Kilby Pri 41, BA 45, 1st cl Th Trip pt i 46, MA 47. Westcott Ho Cam 46. **d** 48 **p** 49 Blackb. C of Adlington 48-50; Edgbaston 50-53; Lect at Qu Coll Birm 50-53; Ch of S India 53-57; V of H Trin Millhouses Sheff 57-65; Exam Chap to Bp of Sheff 58-65; Select Pr Univ of Cam 63; Can Res of Cov 65-73; Dean of Bris from 73; Select Pr Univ of Ox 75. *Deanery, Charlotte Street, Bristol, BS1 5PZ.* (Bristol 22443)

DAMPIER, Robert Cecil Walter. b 19. Pemb Coll Cam BA 40, MA 47. Ely Th Coll 46. **d** 48 **p** 49 S'wark. C of St Giles Camberwell 48-52; Min of Legal Distr of St Mary Virg Welling Kent 52-55; V 55-60; St Steph Lewisham 60-67; Tettenhall Wood Dio Lich from 67; Hon Chap to Bp of S'wark 61-67. *Tettenhall Wood Vicarage, Compton, Wolverhampton, W Midl, WV6 8LZ.* (Wolverhampton 751116)

DAMS, Edward Lamprey. Ch Ch Ox BA 33. Wells Th Coll 34. **d** 35 **p** 36 Lon. C of St Matt Yiewsley 35-38; Chalfont St Pet Bucks 38-50; Bush Bro of St Barn Dio N Queensld 50-55; Miss P Dio New Guinea 56-67; Dio Papua 71-77; Dio Aipo from 77. *Anglican Church, PO Box 101, Bulolo, New Guinea.*

DAMS, John Lockton. b 17. Late Scho of King's Coll Lon AKC 45. FRCO 40. **d** 46 **p** 47 OX. C of St Nich Newbury 46-49; PV of Ex Cathl 49-73; Succr 62-73; DPV from 73; C-in-c of Doddiscombsleigh 56-65; St Mary Maj w St Geo, St John and St Petrock Ex 66-69; St Petrock w St Mary Maj Ex 69-74; Team V of Ex Centr 74-78. *4 Wonford Road, Exeter, Devon. EX2 4EQ.* (Exeter 71448)

DANA, Dalindyebo Kehle Qakata. St Bede's Coll Umtata 56. **d** 57 **p** 58 St Jo Kaffr. P Dio St John's. *PB 232, Tsomo, Transkei, S Africa.*

DANA, Canon Edmund Francis Kinnaird. b 15. ALCD 40. **d** 40 **p** 41 Glouc. C of St Paul Cheltm 40-45; C-in-c of Sheet Petersfield 45-49; R of Shanklin 49-62; V of Crofton 62-63; R of Northwood IW 63-80; RD of W Wight 73-77; P-in-c of H Trin Cowes 77-78; V 78-80; Hon Can of Portsm 77-80; Can

(Emer) from 81. *15 Littlestairs Road, Shanklin, IW.*

DANCE, Peter Patrick. b 31. Em Coll Sktn. **d** and **p** 69 Edmon. R of Mannville 69-71; C of Hednesford 71-75; P-in-c of Westcote Barton w Steeple Barton (R w Duns Tew and Sandford St Martin from 77) Dio Ox from 75; Sandford St Martin 76-77. *Westcote Barton Rectory, Middle Barton, Oxford, OX5 4AA.* (Steeple Aston 40510)

DANCE, Terrance Arthur. b 52. Univ of W Ont BA 73. Hur Coll Lon MDiv 76. **d** and **p** 77 Bp Robinson for Hur. C of St Jo Evang Lon 77-78; P-in-c of Westmount Exper Min Lon Ont 78-80; I of Chesley Dio Hur from 80. *Box 359, Chesley, Ont, Canada.*

DAND, Robert William Scrymgour. b 17. Pemb Coll Ox BA MA 45. Cudd Coll. **d** 47 **p** 48 Portsm. C of St Mary Portsea 47-50; V of Finchingfield 50-59; R of Woodbridge Dio St e 59-60; Chap at Br Embassy and St Geo Lisbon 60-66; PC of Bracknell 66-68; V 68-72; C of Upton cum Chalvey Slough Dio Ox from 73. *43 Lascelles Road, Slough, Bucks, SL3 7PW.* (Slough 21004)

DANDASE, Graham. Newton Coll Dogura 70. **d** 72 Bp Kendall for Papua. d Dio Papua. *Newton College, PO Dogura, via Boroko, Papua, New Guinea.*

DANE, Henry Arthur. b 12. Univ of Lon BSc and DIC 35. ARCS 34. Clifton Th Coll 37. **d** 39 **p** 40 S'wark. C of St Steph Clapham Pk 39-43; R of Langar w Barnstone 43-49; V of Worthington w Newbold and Griffy Dam Dio Leic 49-72; RD of Akeley W 63-69; Asst Master Newbridge High Sch Coalville 72-78; L to Offic Dio Leic 72-78; P-in-c of Kirk Langley Dio Derby from 79; Mackworth Dio Derby from 79. *131 Lower Road, Mackworth, Derby, DE3 4NG.* (0332-48262)

DANE, William Edward Pye. Linc Coll Ox BA 40, MA 47. Wycl Hall Ox 42. **d** 42 Glouc **p** 43 Tewkesbury for Glouc. C of Westbury-on-Severn 42-45; Wotton-under-Edge 45-53; Henbury 53-57; V of Forest Hill w Shotover 57-80; R of Stanton St John 58-80. *c/o Forest Hill Vicarage, Oxford.* (Stanton St John 340)

DANES, Charles William. b 28. Chich Th Coll 54. **d** 56 **p** 57 Lon. C of All H Greenford 56-59; Caversham 59-63; V of Walsgrave-on-Sowe 63-65; PC of All SS Hanworth 65-67; V 68-76; St Jas Littlehampton 76-78; P-in-c of St Mary Littlehampton 76-78; All SS Wick 76-78; V of St Jo Div W Worthing Dio Chich from 78. *15 Reigate Road, West Worthing, Sussex.* (Worthing 47340)

DANG, Canon David Sing Hiong. Trin Coll Sing LTh 56. **d** 56 **p** 57 Sing. P Dio Sing 56-61 and 63-77; Perm to Offic Dio Melb 61-63; Hon Can of Sing 70-77; Can (Emer) from 77; Commiss Sabah from 71; Perm to Offic Dio Auckld from 78. *44 Harania Avenue, Favona Mangere, Auckland, NZ.* (57-791)

DANGERFIELD, John Bubb. St Aug Coll Cant 57. **d** 58 **p** 59 Pet. C of St Mary Virg Far Cotton Northn 58-62; V of Rathwell 62-64; C of St Geo Winnipeg 64-67; L to Offic Dio BC 67-69; R of Saturna I Dio BC from 69. *Saturna Island, BC, Canada.*

DANI, Daniel. St Pet Coll Siota 54. **d** 56 **p** 59 Melan. P Dio Melan 56-75; Dio Ysabel from 75. *Poro, Gao, Santa Ysabel, Solomon Islands.*

DANIA, Canon Josiah Lewis Olayinka. **d** 69 Ibad **p** 70 Benin. P Dio Benin from 70; Can of Benin from 74. *Teacher Training College, PO Box 345, Benin City, Mid Western State, Nigeria.*

DANIEL, Abraham Paul. **d** 47 **p** 48 Tinn. Ch of S India 47-52; P Dio Sing 52-70; Dio W Mal 70-75. *14 Lorong Abdullah, Jalan Bungsar, Kuala Lumpur, Malaysia.*

DANIEL, Alan Noel. b 09. AKC (1st cl) 35. Ripon Hall Ox 35. **d** 36 **p** 37 S'wark. C of St Jo Evang Kingston T 36-39; H Trin U Tooting 39-47; V of St Sav Brockley Rise 47-58; Dormansland 58-76. *31 Large Acres, Selsey, Sussex, PO20 9BA.* (Selsey 4566)

DANIEL, Arthur Guy St John. b 12. King's Coll Cam BA 33, MA 37. Cudd Coll 34. **d** 35 **p** 36 Sarum. C of Blandford Forum 35-38; St Giles-in-Reading 38-40; Marlow 40-46; PC of Colnbrook 46-67; V 68-78; Team V of Riverside 78-80. *2 Gervis Court, Penwerris Avenue, Osterley, Middx.* (01-572 1848)

DANIEL, Carol Watcyn. b 09. St D Coll Lamp BA 36. **d** 37 **p** 38 B & W. C of St Luke S Lyncombe 37-42; CF (EC) 42-46; St Mk Lyncombe 46-49; R of Clutton 49-56; V of Fivehead w Swell 56-75; Hon CF from 64. *26 St Mary's Park, Huish Episcopi, Langport, Somt.*

DANIEL, George Francis. St Paul's Coll Grahmstn LTh 56. **d** 56 **p** 57 Pret. C of St Wilfrid Hillcrest Pret 56-60. *1099 South Street, Hatfield, Pretoria, S Africa.*

DANIEL, Henry Felix Jeyaraj. Univ of Madr BA (2nd cl Econ) 46, MA 47. Qu Coll Birm. **d** 49 **p** 50 Newc T. C of St Thos Mart Newc T 49-51; Sec SCM for NE Engl 49-51; Sec World Student Christian Federation 51-53; Gen Sec SCM India 54-61; Miss in India 61-68; Sec Urban Industr Miss E Asia Chr Conf Sing 68-70; WCC Geneva 70-73; Assoc Gen Sec Chr Conf of Asia Sing from 74. *480 Lorong 2, Toa Payoh, Singapore 12.*

DANIEL, Herrick Haynes. b 38. Open Univ BA 81. Trin Coll Bris 73. **d** 75 Lon **p** 76 Willesden for Lon. C of St Mark Harlesden 75-78; St Andr Livesey 78-81; P-in-c of St Barn City and Dio Blackb from 81. *24 Adelaide Terrace, Blackburn, Lancs, BB2 6ET.* (Blackb 56587)

DANIEL, Isaac Thomas. Univ of Wales BA 34. St D Coll Lamp 35. **d** 36 **p** 37 Sheff. C of St Swith Sheff 36-37; St Andr Sheff 37-40; Chap RAFVR 40-46; R of Castle Frome w Frome's Hill 46-55; V of St Chad Wolverhampton 55-76. *113 Bryniau Road, West Shore, Llandudno, Gwynedd.*

DANIEL, James. **d** 78 Windw I. C of H Trin Georgetown St Vinc Dio Windw I from 78. *Sandy Bay, St Vincent, W Indies.*

DANIEL, Leslie Mills. Univ of Wales, BA 39. St Mich Coll Llan 40. **d** 41 **p** 42 St A. C of Holywell 41-48; Llangollen 48-54; R of Bangor Monachorum Dio St A from 54. *Rectory, Bangor-on-Dee, Wrexham, Clwyd.* (Bangor-on-Dee 273)

DANIEL, Michael George. b 23. Magd Coll Cam BA 49, MA 52. BSc (Lon) 64. Univ of Lon MPhil 67. Linc Th Coll 49. **d** 51 **p** 52 St Alb. C of Welwyn Gdn City 51-56; Asst Master Collyer's Sch Horsham 56-57; V of Warnham 57-61; C of St Mich w St Phil Ches Square Westmr 61-64; Adviser to R Found of St Kath 64-66; Hd of Soc Dept Southlands Coll Wimbledon from 66. *8 Westmoreland Terrace, SW 1.* (01-828 0468)

DANIEL, Rajinder Kumar. b 34. St Steph Coll Delhi 55. Westcott Ho Cam 61. **d** 63 Delhi for S'wark **p** 64 S'wark. C of St Barn Purley 63-66; St Pet Battersea 66-67; St Alb N Harrow (in c of St Martin) 67-72; Team V of Beaconsfield (in c of St Thos Holtspur) 72-75; V of St Matt w St Chad Smethwick Dio Birm from 75. *St Matthew's Vicarage, Smethwick, Warley, B66 3TN.* (021-558 1653)

DANIEL, Walter Campbell. Angl Th Coll BC LTh 27. **d** and **p** 27 New Westmr. V of Langley 27-32; White Rock 32-34; St Agnes N Vancouver 34-42; Chap RCAF 42-45; L to Offic Dio New Westmr 45-63. *515 East 8th Street, N Vancouver, BC, Canada.*

DANIEL, Wilfrid Artnell. b 45. Codr Coll Barb 71. **d** and **p** 74 Antig. C of St John's Cathl Antig 74-76; R of St Pet Montserrat 76-79; St Anne and St Paul w St Thos Sandypoint Dio Antig from 79. *St Anne's Rectory, Sandypoint, St Kitts, W Indies.*

DANIELS, Abraham Chelliah. **d** 49 **p** 50 Sing. P Dio Sing. *Our Saviour's Mission, M 15, Havelock Road, Singapore 3.*

DANIELS, Alan Henry. b 14. Keble Coll Ox BA 35, BSc and MA 39. Wycl Hall Ox 63. **d** 64 **p** 65 Portsm. C of Rowner 64-67; R of Yarmouth Dio Portsm from 67. *Rectory, Yarmouth, Isle of Wight, PO41 0NU.* (Yarmouth, IW 760247)

DANIELS, David Martin. b 52. St Pet Coll Alice Dipl Th 74. **d** 75 **p** 76 Capetn. C of Bonteheuwel 75-76; P-in-c of St Helena Bay 76-80; R of Hanover Pk Dio Capetn from 80. *St Dominic's House, Lonedown Road, Hanover Park 7764, CP, S Africa.* (67-3163)

DANIELS, Geoffrey Gregory. b 23. St Pet Coll Ox BA 48, MA 53. Lambeth Dipl Th 60. Linc Th Coll 73. **d** 73 Nor **p** 75 Lewes for Chich. Hon C of Diss 73-74; Bexhill Dio Chich from 74. *20 Richmond Grove, Bexhill-on-Sea, Sussex.* (Bexhill 211719)

DANIELS, Henry Charles. b 10. **d** 79 **p** 80 Bal. Hon C of Colac Dio Bal from 79. *Churchill Square, Colac, Australia 3250.*

DANIELS, Hubert Frederick. Qu Coll Birm 51. **d** 52 **p** 53 Lon. TD 50. C of Enfield 52-55; Chap at Cologne and Bonn 55-60; R of Croughton 60-66; R of Hinton-in-the-Hedges w Steane 60-66; C-in-c of Newbottle w Charlton 60-65; V of Alfriston w Lullington Dio Chich from 66. *The New Vicarage, Sloe Lane, Polegate, Sussex, BN26 5UY.* (Alfriston 376)

DANIELS, Kenneth Percival Thomas. b 17. AKC 50. St Bonif Coll Warm 50. **d** 51 **p** 52 S'wark. C of St Luke Eltham Pk 51-54; St Helier Surrey 54-58; V of H Redeemer Lamorbey 58-75; Kemsing w Woodlands Dio Roch from 75. *Kemsing Vicarage, Sevenoaks, Kent.* (Sevenoaks 61351)

DANIELS, Leonard. Univ of Lon BA 13. Sarum Th Coll 19. **d** 20 **p** 21 Win. C of Ch Ch Woking 20-22; R of Wilcannia 22-32; Lithgow 32-40; St Steph Kurrajong 40-59; L to Offic Dio Syd from 59. *102 Farrer Brown Court, Nuffield Village, Castle Hill, NSW, Australia 2154.* (634-6237)

DANIELS, Louis Victor. b 47. Univ of Tas BA 73. St Mich Ho Crafers 75. **d** 74 **p** 75 Tas. Hon C of Moonah 74-75; in Dept of Miss Dio Tas 76-81; C of Cathl Ch of Tas from 81. *11 Windsor Street, Glenorchy, Tasmania 7010.*

DANIELS, Norman. b 38. Univ of Leeds BA (Hist) 60. St Mich AA Coll Llan 71. **d** 73 **p** 74 Mon. C of Pontynewynydd 73-76; Chap of Qu Sch Rheindahlen Germany from 76. *Queen's School, BFPO 40.*

DANIELS, Philip William. b 11. Late Exhib of Keble Coll Ox 3rd cl Mod Hist 34, BA 35, MA 44. St Andr Coll Whittlesford 35. **d** 35 **p** 36 Carl. C of Lowther w Askham 35-37; H Trin Southport 37-40; CF (EC) 40-45; C of All SS Netherton Maryport 46; CF (EC) 46-48; CF 48-66; R of Moreton 66-77; R of Woodsford w Tincleton 66-77. *15 Broodside, Milborne Port, Sherborne, Dorset, DT9 5RB.*

DANIELS, Richard Hubert FitzLawrence. b 15. Codr Coll Barb 70. **d** and **p** 73 Guy. C of Skeldon 73-76; R of Leguan w Wakenaam Dio Guy from 76. *Rectory, Leguan, Essequibo Islands, Guyana.*

DANIELS, Ronald Edward. b 37. **d** 79 Bp Ndwandwe for Johann **p** 80 Johann (NSM). C of Westlea Dio Johann from 79. *32 Heathfield Crescent, Eldorado Park Extension 4, S Africa 1812.*

DANKS, Alan Adam. b 41. Edin Th Coll 61. **d** 64 **p** 65 Glas. C of St Jo Evang Dumfries 64-67; Tutor St Cath Cumberland Lodge Windsor 67-68; C of St Cuthb Kens 68-71; St Steph Walbrook and Warden of St Steph Ho Lon 71-74; C of St Mary Brookfield Lon 74-76; St Mary Hendon Dio Lon from 76. *The Parsonage, Holders Hill Road, NW4.* (01-346 5882)

DANN, Charles Edward. b 13. Univ of Lon BA 38. Ripon Hall Ox 38. **d** 39 **p** 40 York. C of St Aug Newland Hull 39-45; Chap Hull Trinity Ho from 41; Cottingham 45-47; V of Hedon (w Paull from 55) 47-79; C-in-c of Paull 47-54. *414 Main Road, Wyton, Bilton, Hull, Yorks, HU11 4DH.*

DANN, Ven Robert Philip. Univ of NB BA 37. **d** 40 **p** 41 Fred. I of Wilmot Wicklow and Peel 40-41; C of Trin Ch St John 42-44; I of N Essa 44-47; R of Islington 47-60; Archd of Etobicoke 53-60; Dir of Ch Extension Dio Tor 53-56; R of St Paul Bloor Street City and Dio Tor from 60; Hon Can of Tor 60-71; Archd of Tor E from 70. *Rectory, 227 Bloor Street East, Toronto, Ont., Canada.* (416-961 8116)

✠ **DANN, Most Rev Robert William.** Univ of Melb ACT ThL 42. BA 45. **d** 45 **p** 46 Melb. C of St Paul's Cathl Melb 45-46; Dir of Youth and Educn Dio Melb 46-51; I of Cheltenham 51-56; I of Malvern 56-61; St John Footscray 61-63; Exam Chap to Abp of Melb 60-61; Archd of Essendon 61-69; Can of St Paul's Cathl Melb 62-69; Dir of Evang Ex Dio Melb 63-77; Cons Bp Coadj of Melb in St Paul's Cathl Melb 1 Nov 69 by Abp of Melb; Bps of St Arn; Bend; Bal; and Wang; and Bp Coadj of Melb; apptd Abp of Melb (Metrop of Prov of Vic) 77. *Bishop's Court, Clarendon Street, E Melbourne, Vic, Australia 3002.* (03-41 3621)

DANNER, David Lawrence. b 51. Lawrence Univ Wisc USA BA 73. Trin Coll Tor MDiv 76. **d** 76 Bp Read for Tor **p** 77 Tor. C of Ch Ch Oshawa 76-81; Chap York Centr Hosp Richmond Hill from 81. *York Central Hospital, Trench Street, Richmond Hill, Ont, Canada.*

DANO, Elgie. St Bede's Coll Umtata 63. **d** 64 **p** 65 Natal. P Dio Natal; Archd Dio Natal 79-81. *Box 583, Port Shepstone, Natal, S Africa.*

DA NOH, H Cross Coll Rang. **d** 67 Rang. d Dio Rang 67-70; Dio Pa-an from 70. *St Mark's Church, New Thandaung, Burma.*

DANSKIN, William Campbell. b 35. Edin Th Coll 78. **d** 80 **p** 81 Glas. C-in-c of St Bart Gourock Dio Glas from 80. *86 Albert Road, Gourock, Renfrewshire, PA19 1NN.*

DAODU, Jacob Monday. Im Coll Ibad. **d** 68 **p** 69 Ekiti. P Dio Ekiti. *St Stephen's Vicarage, Aiyetoro-Ekiti, Nigeria.*

DAR-ES-SALAAM, Lord Bishop of. *See* Sepeku, Right Rev John.

DARAMOLA, Ven Joseph Orisadare. Melville Hall Ibad. **d** 48 **p** 49 Lagos. P Dio Lagos 48-52; Dio Ibad 52-58; Hon Can of Ibad 58-63; Can 63-69; Archd of Ekiti S from 69. *St Peter's Vicarage, Ikere-Ekiti, Nigeria.*

DARAMOLA, Samson Folorunso. b 40. Im Coll Ibad. **d** 74 **p** 75 Lagos. P Dio Lagos 74-76; Dio Egba from 76. *Box 1438, Abeokuta, Nigeria.*

DARBY, Anthony Ernest. b 26. Linc Th Coll 74. **d** 76 Bp Daly for Cov **p** 77 Cov. C of Chilvers-Coton 76-79; P-in-c of Longford Dio Cov 79-81; V from 81. *Vicarage, Hurst Road, Longford, Coventry, CV6 6EL.* (Cov 361042)

DARBY, Cyril Owen. b 01. OBE 52. Em Coll Sktn 22, Div Test 27. **d** 27 **p** 28 New Westmr for Caled. Miss of Massett 27-33; Chap RN 33-56 and 56-61; R of Greenhithe 56-65; Chap Stone House Hosp from 61; Chap and Warden Huggens Coll Northfleet from 65; Hon C of St Jo Evang Sidcup Dio Roch from 74. *St John's Lodge, The Green, Sidcup, Kent.* (01-300 2510)

✠ **DARBY, Right Rev Harold Richard.** b 19. St Jo Coll Dur BA 49. **d** 50 **p** 51 Chelmsf. C of Leyton 50-51; Harlow 51-52; C-in-c of Berechurch 53-54; V 54-59; All SS Stanway 53-59; Chap St Mary's Sch Colchester 57-59; Chap to Bp of Colchester 59; V of Waltham Abbey 59-70; Chap Honey Lane Hosp 60-70; Dean and V of Battle 70-75; Cons Ld Bp Suffr of Sherwood in York Minster 24 June 75 by Abp of York; Bps of Leic, Southw, Ripon, Man, Carl and Wakef; Bps Suffr of Jarrow, Stockport, Penrith, Pontefract, Selby, Knaresborough and Lanc. *Applegarth, Halam, Southwell, Notts.* (Southwell 814041)

DARBY, Ian Douglas. b 41. Univ of Natal MA 77, PhD 81. CA (SA) 65. K Coll Lon and Warm BD (2nd cl) and AKC (2nd cl) 68. **d** 69 **p** 70 S'wark. C of Lewisham 69-73; St Jas Durban 73-74; R of York w Ravensworth 74-78; Lect Federal Th Sem Plessislaer and L to Offic Dio Natal from 78. *Private Bag, Imbali 4503, S Africa.*

DARBY, Michael Barwick. b 34. St D Coll Lamp BA 61. Tyndale Hall Bris 61. **d** 63 **p** 64 Lon. C of St Andr Islington 63-66; St John Ealing Dean 66-68; V of Broomfleet w Faxfleet 68-73; Em Paddington Lon 73-77; Area Sec CCCS Dios York and Sheff 68-72; L to Offic Dio Sheff 69-73; Chap of Khuzistan 77-78; Ahwaz Dio Iran 78-80; Perm to Offic Dio Cant from 80. *Address temp unknown.*

DARBY, Nicholas Peter. b 50. Sarum Wells Th Coll 71. **d** 74 **p** 75 Guildf. C of Walton-on-Thames 74-78; Horsell 78-80; Perm to Offic Dio Cant from 81. *12 The Precincts, Canterbury, Kent, CT1 2EH.* (Canterbury 63060)

DARBY, Philip William. b 44. Univ of Birm Dipl Th 70. Qu Coll Birm 67. **d** 70 **p** 71 Worc. C of St Geo Kidderminster 70-74; V of St John Dudley 74-80; Catshill Dio Worc from 80. *Catshill Vicarage, Bromsgrove, Worcs.* (Bromsgrove 72547)

DARBY, Walter Frederick. Univ of Lon BD (2nd cl) and AKC 40. Ely Th Coll 40. **d** 40 **p** 41 S'wark. C of St Mark East Street Walworth 40-44; Ascen Lavender Hill 44-50; CF 50-56; L to Offic Dio Momb 51-56; Archd of Magila 57-60; Can of Zanz 57-63; Chap St Andr Coll Minaki 60-63; Treas Dio SW Tang 63-72; P-in-c of Njombe 64-76; Mufindi 70-76; Can and Chan of SW Tang 73-76; Sub-Dean 76; P-in-c of Praslin 76-78. *PO Masasi, Mtwara Region, Tanzania.*

DARCUS, Roy Lionel Heath. b 43. Univ of BC BA 65, MA 67. Concordia Univ Queb PhD 81. **d** and **p** 72 Montr. C of St Geo Montr 72-74; R of Sutton 74-76; on leave 77-80; Chap Montr Gen Hosp from 81. *Box 236, Cote St Luc, Montreal, PQ, Canada.*

DARDIS, Frank Fletcher. b 1885. Sarum Th Coll. **d** 26 **p** 27 Sarum. C of Westbury Wilts 26-29; Director ICFN Area and LPr Dio Blackb 29-31; C of Bowdon 31-33; V of St Jude Preston Lancs 33-36; R of Stedham 36-46; V of Newnham Cant 46-56; L to Offic Dio Cant 56-65. *5 Dardis Close, Bethany Homestead, Kingsley Road, Northampton.*

DARE, Charles Gilbert Francis. b 22. Univ of Dur BA 48. St Jo Coll Dur 46. **d** 48 **p** 49 Bris. C of St Barn Swindon 48-50; H Trin Winchmore Hill 50-54; V of St Paul Haggerston 54-60; St Paul S Harrow 60-74; St Pet Ealing 74-81; Wisborough Green Dio Chich from 81. *Vicarage, Wisborough Green, Billingshurst, Sussex.* (Wisborough Green 339)

DARE, Canon Michael Dada. Im Coll Ibad 64. **d** 66 **p** 67 Ondo. P Dio Ondo; Hon Can of Ondo from 76. *PO Box 4, Ondo, Nigeria.* (Ondo 2034)

DARGAVILLE, Anderson Douglas. Univ of Tas BSc (2nd cl Chemistry) 50. Trin Coll Melb ACT ThL (2nd cl) 57. **d** 58 **p** 59 Melb. C of St Geo Malvern 58-62; Leader Tr Officer Dept of Youth and Relig Educn Dio Melb 58-62; I of Werribee 62-66; Perm to Offic Dio Melb 66-67; C of Chadstone E 67-78; L to Offic Dio Melb from 78. *40 Grandview Road, Chadstone, Vic, Australia 3148.* (03-277 3711)

DARLEY, Derrick Charles. b 30. St Chad's Coll Dur BA (2nd cl Th) 55. Wells Th Coll. **d** 56 **p** 57 York. C of St Columba Scarborough 56-59; All SS Sculcoates 59-61; C-in-c of St Silas, Sculcoates 61-63; V of Craghead 63-75; Chap Holmside and S Moor Hosp 63-75; V of St Leon and St Jude Doncaster Dio Sheff from 75. *Vicarage, Barnsley Road, Doncaster, DN5 8QE.* (Doncaster 784858)

DARLEY, Shaun Arthur Neilson. b 36. Univ of Dur BA (2nd cl Pol and Econ) 61, Dipl Th 63. Univ of Reading MSc 75. Cranmer Hall Dur 61. **d** 63 **p** 64 St Alb. C of Luton 63-67; L to Offic at St Thos Mart Bedminster 67-71; Lect and Chap Bris Tech Coll 67-69; Bris Polytech 69-75; Chap and Sen Lect from 75; Cathl Chap from 69. *24 Downs Park East, Westbury Park, Bristol, BS6 7QD.* (Bristol 629219)

DARLING, Edward Flewett. b 33. TCD BA (Resp) 55, MA 58. **d** 56 Down for Connor **p** 57 Connor. C of St Luke Belf 56-59; Orangefield 59-62; C-in-c of St Gall Carnalea 62-72; Chap Ban Hosp 63-72; R of St John Malone Belf Dio Connor from 72. *86 Maryville Park, Belfast, BT9 6LQ.*

DARLING, Grant Delbert. Univ of W Ont BA 51. Hur Th Coll LTh 53. **d** 53 **p** 54 Hur. I of St Mark Brantford 53-56; St Matt Windsor 56-60; R of All SS Lon 60-69; St Jude Brantford 69-80; Delhi and Otterville Dio Hur from 80. *209 James Street, Delhi, Ont, Canada N4B 2A1.*

DARLING, John. b 47. Sarum Wells Th Coll 76. **d** 79 Sarum **p** 80 Ramsbury for Sarum (NSM). C of St Thos Trowbridge Dio Sarum from 79; Wingfield Dio Sarum from 79. *24 Eastbourne Road, Trowbridge, Wilts, BA14 7HN.*

DARLINGTON, Preb David John. b 14. Oak Hill Th Coll

33. **d** 37 **p** 38 Lon. C of H Trin Isl 37-39; BCMS Miss Burma 39-42 and 56-63; C of H Trin Rusholme 48-49; Miss Kachin State Burma 49-56; V of St Mark (w St Anne from 65) Holloway 63-81; V of St Anne Holloway 63-65; Preb (Emer) of St Paul's Cathl Lon from 79. *39 Grasmere Road, Luton, Beds, LU3 2DT.* (0582-591547)

DARLINGTON, Canon John. b 1899. Magd Coll Ox BA (3rd cl Th) 22, MA 27. Leeds Cl Scho 23. **d** 24 **p** 25 Lon. C of St John Hoxton 24-31; LDHM All H N Greenford 31-32; Min 32-48; V of Newton Valence 48-74; Selborne 48-74; Chap to Treloar Hosp Alton 55-74; RD of Alton 66-74; Hon Can of Win 71-74; Can (Emer) from 74. *Fannyfield, Evanton, Ross-shire.*

DARLINGTON, John Henry. Moore Th Coll Syd ACT ThL (2nd cl) 55. **d** 56 **p** 57 Syd. C of Lindfield 56-58; CF (Austr) 58-65; R of Penshurst Dio Syd from 65. *43 Laycock Road, Penshurst, NSW, Australia 2222.* (57-1217)

DARLINGTON, Wallace Garnett. Ch Ch Coll Ch Ch 67. **d** 68 Bp Warren for Ch Ch. C of Sydenham w Beckenham 68-71; C of Timaru 71-72; V of Ross w S Westland 72-77; C of Blenheim Dio Nel from 77. *90 Weld Street, Blenheim, NZ.*

DARNLEY, Warren Robert. b 47. St Jo Coll Morpeth 76. **d** 77 Rockptn. C of Gladstone Dio Rockptn from 77. *c/o St Saviour's Rectory, PO Box 72, Gladstone, Qld, Australia 4680.*

DARRAH, Reginald Geoffrey. b 30. Jes Coll Ox BA (3rd cl Th) 54. Coll of Resurr Mirfield 54. **d** 56 **p** 57 Dur. C of Ryhope 56-58; St Hilda Leeds 58-62; V of Shelf 62-68; R of Winfarthing Group (R of Winfarthing w Shelfanger) 68-79; V of St Anne w St Eliz Earlham Dio Nor from 79. *St Anne's Vicarage, Bluebell Road, Earlham, Norwich, NR4 7LP.* (Norwich 52922)

DARRALL, Charles Geoffrey. b 32. Univ of Nottm BA (2nd cl Th) 55, MA 57. Qu Coll Birm 56. **d** 57 **p** 58 Carl. C of Cockermouth 57-63; V of St John-in-the-Vale w Wythburn Dio Carl from 63; Chap Carl Dioc Youth Centre from 63. *St John-in-the-Vale's Vicarage, Naddle, Keswick, Cumb, CA12 4TF.* (Keswick 72542)

DARRALL, John Norman. b 34. Univ of Nottm BA (2nd cl Hist) 57. Ripon Hall Ox 57. **d** 60 **p** 61 Southw. C of Nottm 60-65; Chap Nottm Children's Hosp 64-65; V of Bole w Saundby 65-66; V of Sturton-le-Steeple w Littleborough 65-66. *Southland, Cartmel, Grange-over-Sands, Lancs.*

DARROCH, Ronald Humphrey. b 45. Trin Coll Cam BA 67, MA 71. Ch Ch Ox BA (by incorp) 67, MA 71. Ripon Hall Ox 67. **d** 70 **p** 71 York. C of St Nich Hull Dio York 70-73; Hon C 73-74; St Jo Perth Dio Dunk from 74. *17 Viewlands Terrace, Perth, Scotland.* (Perth 28880)

DART, John Peter. b 40. St Jo Coll Ox BA 63. Cudd Coll 62. **d** 64 **p** 65 Dur. C of St Aid W Hartlepool 64-67; C of Alverthorpe 67-70; Youth & Commun Worker (Educn Dept) Wakef 70-74; Youth Org from 74; L to Offic Dio Wakef from 70. *11 Pinders Grove, Wakefield, Yorks.* (Wakef 71156)

DART, Thomas Henry. b 08. Trin Hall Cam BA 30, MA 34. Cudd Coll 31. **d** 31 **p** 32 Birm. C of St Paul Balsall Heath 31-34; Lect Bp's Coll Calc 34-42; Chap Eccles Est St Paul's Cathl Calc 42-45; V of St Pet Handsworth 45-51; SPG Org Sec Dio Ox 51-55; V of Aldershot 55-68; Hon Sec Guildf Dioc Overseas Coun 57-66; RD of Aldershot 60-65; Commiss B'pore 60-70; Sub-Warden Commun of St Pet Woking 68-71; Warden 71-81; Chap St Columba's House Woking 68-81; Smiles and Bernard Sunley Homes from 74. *6 Creston Avenue, Goldsworth Park, Near Woking, Surrey.* (Brookwood 80237)

DARVILL, Geoffrey. b 43. Oak Hill Th Coll Dipl Higher Educn 81. **d** 81 Barking for Chelmsf. C of St Marg Barking Dio Chelmsf from 81. *48 Sunningdale Avenue, Barking, Essex, IG11 7QF.*

DARVILL, George Collins. b 36. Kelham Th Coll 56. **d** 61 **p** 62 York. C of St Chad Middlesbrough 61-64; Manston 64-66; V of Kippax w Gt Preston 66-79; Catterick w Tunstall Dio Ripon from 79; RD of Richmond from 80. *Catterick Vicarage, Richmond, N Yorks, DL10 7LN.* (Richmond 811462)

✠ **DARWENT, Right Rev Frederick Charles.** b 27. Wells Th Coll 61. **d** 63 Warrington for Liv **p** 64 Liv. C of Pemberton 63-65; R of Strichen 65-71; R of New Pitsligo 65-78 Fraserburgh 71-78; Can of St Andr Cathl Aber 71-78; Dean of Aber and Ork 73-78; Cons Ld Bp of Aber and Ork in St Andr Cathl Aber 13 Jan 78 by Bp of Edin (Primus); Bps of St Andr, Moray, Glas Brech and Arg Is; and Bps R N Russell, Begg and Easson. *Bishop's Lodge, 15 Morningfield Road, Aberdeen, AB2 4AP.* (Aberdeen 34765)

DARWIN, Oliver Maurice. Bps' Coll Cheshunt. **d** 57 **p** 58 St E. C of St Mary Bury St Edms 57-59; R of Tostock 59-62; R of Drinkstone 59-62; V of All SS Ipswich 62-68; R of Jollimore NS 68-72; C of Spondon 72-74; V of Manea Dio Ely from 74; R of Wimblington Dio Ely from 74. *Manea Vicarage, March, Cambs.* (Manea 415)

DASH, Walter Eric. Univ of Dur (Codr Coll) LTh 11. **d** 12 **p** 13 Barb. C of St Lucy Barb 12-14; R of Rivière Dorée St Lucia 14-18; St Andr Grenada 18-22; C of Cathl St Vincent 22-23; V of St Mark and St Kath Barb 23-25; R of St Andr Barb 25-31; St Jas Barb 31-47; C of Ch Ch Barb 50-53; L to Offic Dio Barb from 53. *Cherhill, 11 Mount Clapham, St Michael, Barbados, W Indies.*

DASHFIELD, Edward Maurice. Coll Ho Ch Ch 51. NZ Bd of Th Stud LTh 65. **d** 51 **p** 52 Wel. C of Masterton Dio Wel 52-55; Cannock (Col Clergy Act) Dio Lich 55-57; V of Tinui 57-64; Carterton 64-69; Prin St Matt Colleg Sch Masterton 69-80. *16 Upper Plain Road, Masterton, NZ.*

DATE, Robert Samuel. St Jo Coll Morpeth ACT ThL 56. **d** and **p** 57 Graft. C of Graft Cathl 57-59; Casino 59-61; V of Dunoon 61-64; R of Byron Bay 64-71; Macksville Dio Graft from 71. *Rectory, Macksvill, NSW, Australia 2447.* (68 1035)

DAU, Frederick John. St Columb's Coll Wang. 31. ACT ThL 34. **d** 34 **p** 35 Wang. C of Milawa 34-35; Junee NSW 35-36; Shepparton 36-37; Chiltern 37-39; Junee 39-41; R of Cobargo 41-46; C of St Sav Cathl Goulb 46-48; R of Tumbarumba 48-55; Tumut 55-62; C of St Paul Canberra 62-66; R of Adaminaby 66-69; L to Offic Dio C & Goulb 69-74; Can of St Sav Cathl Goulb 72-76; C of St Paul Canberra 74-76; Perm to Offic Dio C & Goulb from 76. *Box 165 Tumut, NSW, Australia 2720.*

DAUBNEY, Kenneth Crocker. b 18. Cudd Coll 69. **d** 70 **p** 71 Bris. C of New Swindon 70-73; Highcliffe w Hinton Admiral 73-75; C-in-c of Froyle Dio Win from 75. *40 Rookswood, Alton, Hants, GU34 2LD.* (Alton 86993)

DAUBUZ, Michael Claude. b 19. Trin Coll Cam BA 40, MA 53. Wells Th Coll 40. **d** 42 **p** 43 Portsm. C of St Pet and St Paul Fareham 42-47; Perm to Offic at Blandford Forum 47-50; C of Gillingham w E and W Stower 50-53; V of Brading w Yaverland 53-59; Perm to Offic Dio Win 62-64; C of Twyford 64-70; V of Colden Common Dio Win from 70. *Colden Common Vicarage, Winchester, Hants.* (Twyford 713277)

DAUGAARD, Peter William. b 41. Moore Th Coll Syd 67. **d** 70 **p** 71 Syd. C of St Anne Ryde 70-72; Nowra 72-74; CF (Austr) from 74. *1 Recruit Training Centre, Kapooka, Wagga Wagga, Australia 2661.* (069-251111)

DAUGHTRY, Norman. b 26. St Chad's Coll Regina 51. **d** 53 **p** 54 Qu'App. C of Ogema 53-54; V of Cabri 54-56; R and RD of Grenfell 56-59; St Mark Edmon 59-61; Ponoka Alta 61-63; V of St Mich Castleford 63-65; R of Hinton w Edson 65-67; C of Claxby w Normanby-le-Wold 67-69; V of Taddington w Chelmorton 69-73; P-in-c of Dalbury w Long Lane and Trusley 73-77; Radbourne 74-77; Chap Pastures Hosp Mickleover 77-81; R of Clifton Dio Derby from 81; Norbury w Snelston Dio Derby from 81. *Clifton Vicarage, Ashbourne, Derbys, DE6 2GJ.* (Ashbourne 2199)

DAULMAN, John Henry. b 33. Lich Th Coll 60. **d** 62 **p** 63 Newc T. C of St Mary Virg Monkseaton 62-65; Prec and C of St Nich Cathl Newc T 65-67; Chap Crumpsall and Springfield Hosps Man 67-73; V of Tyldesley 73-81; Turton Dio Man from 81. *Vicarage, High Street, Turton, Bolton, BL7 0EH.* (Turton 852222)

DAUNT, William Henry. Late Scho of Trin Coll Dub BA (1st cl Ment and Mor Sc Mod) 40, MA 62. **d** 42 Tuam for Down **p** 43 Oss. C of St Anne's Cathl Belf 42-43; Carlow 43-44; Chap RNVR 44-47; Asst Dioc C Cork Cloyne and Ross 47-48; Chap RAF 48-52; V of Brough w Stainmore 52-60; I of Warw 60-63; Point Edw 63-70; Mitchell w Sebringville 70-74; Colchester Dio Hur from 75. *RR1, Harrow, Ont., Canada.* (519-738 2950)

DAUNTON-FEAR, Andrew. b 45. Univ of Tas BSc (Chem) 64. Qu Coll Cam BA (2nd cl Th Trip pt ii) 67, MA 72. ACT ThL 68. Univ of St Andr BPhil 76. Ridley Hall Cam 67. **d** 68 **p** 70 Melb. C of Thomastown 68-71; Lect Ridley Coll Melb 68-70; Hon C of Islington 71-75; C-in-c of H Trin Islington 71-75; Asst Libr Univ Coll Lon 73-75; Perm to Offic Dio St Andr 75-76; C of Stoke Bp 76-79; R of Thrapston Dio Pet from 79. *Rectory, Thrapston, Northants, NN14 4PD.* (Thrapston 2393)

DAUNTON-FEAR, Ven Richard Daunton. ALCD 31 (LTh from 74). Qu Coll Cam 35. St Chad's Coll Regina LTh 38, Hon DD 46. Univ of Bris Research Stud 40, MA 44. **d** and **p** 32 S'wark. C of St John Deptford 32-33; R of Aspenden 35-36; Denton w S Heighton and Tarring Neville 36-38; V of Lindfield 38-40; R of Street 40-44; Commiss Geo 40-52; Lect Univ of Bris 40-43; V of H Trin Malvern and Chap Malvern Girls' Coll 44-48; R of Gravesend 48-53; Surr 48-53; RD of Gravesend 49-53; Preb of St Mary-in-the-Castle Ex from 53; V of St Phil Hove 53-59; Sen Chap to Abp of Capetn 59-60; Commiss Capetn 60-65; Armid from 65; V of Tamworth NSW 60-65; Archd of Tamworth 60-65; (Emer) of Armid from 65; Gawler 66-70; Perm to Offic Dio Chich 65-66; Org Chap Bp's Home Miss S Dio Adel 66-70; Perm to Offic Dio Adel 70-72; Dio Win from 72; Hon C of St Matt Millbrook Jersey 72-79. *105 Rouge Bouillon, St Helier, Jersey, CI.* (Jersey Central 32833)

DAVENPORT, James Clifford. Angl Th Coll of BC LTh 56. **d** 56 New Westmr for Koot **p** 56 Koot. V of Fruitvale 56-60; I of Agassiz 60-63; I of French Creek 68-81; Port Alice Dio BC from 81. *Box 159, Port Alice, BC, Canada.*

DAVENPORT, Michael Arthur. b 38. Lich Th Coll 60. **d** 62 **p** 63 Southw. C of Bilborough w Strelley 62-66; St Mary Virg (in c of St Jo Evang) Kettering 66-69; V of St Benet Fink Tottenham Dio Lon from 69. *Vicarage, Walpole Road, N17 6BH.* (01-888 4541)

DAVENPORT, Canon Richard. Univ of BC BA 51. Angl Th Coll BC LTh 54. **d** 54 **p** 55 BC. C of Comox 54-55; P-in-c Denman I 55-56; V of Cumb 55-59; C of Ch Ch Calg 59-61; V of Castor 61-63; R of Innisfail 64-67; L to Offic Dio Calg from 66; Hosp Chap Dio Calg from 67; Hon Can of Calg from 80. *435 Willingdon Boulevard SE, Calgary, Alta., Canada.* (271-0492)

DAVENPORT, Terence Hope. b 1900. Egerton Hall Man 28. **d** 30 **p** 31 Man. C of St Edm Whalley Range 30-33; Perm to Offic at Yardley (in c of St Mich) 33-34; R of Bubbenhall 34-36; Harborough Magna 36-38; V of L Leigh 38-44; St Barn Warrington 44-49; Surr 44-49; Nether Whitley 49-53; Perm to Offic Dio Ches from 75. *6 Abbey Green, Chester.*

DAVEY, Andrew John. b 53. Univ Coll Cardiff Dipl Th 76. St Mich AA Llan 75. **d** 77 Willesden for Lon. **p** 78 Lon. C of St John Gt Stanmore Dio Lon from 77. *11 Elm Park, Stanmore, Middx.* (01-954 4616)

DAVEY, Canon Clive Herbert George. b 09. St Jo Coll Dur BA (3rd cl Th) 31, MA 34. Wycl Hall Ox 31. **d** 32 **p** 33 Dur. C of St Mary-le-Bow Dur and Chap of St Jo Coll Dur 32-36; C of Middleton Lancs 36-41; R of St John Moston 41-46; V of St Faith Maidstone 46-54; Asst Chap HM Pris Maidstone 47-54; V of Faringdon w L Coxwell 54-63; RD of Vale of White Horse 61-63; V of Ch Ch Guildf 63-78; RD of Guildf 73-78; Hon Can of Guildf 75-78; Can (Emer) from 78; Perm to Offic Dio Ex from 78. *10 Somerset Court, Mount Pleasant Road, Brixham, Devon, TQ5 9RX.* (Brixham 7251)

DAVEY, Colin Hugh Lancaster. b 34. Late Scho of Em Coll Cam 1st cl Cl Trip pt i 55, BA (2nd cl Cl Trip pt ii) 56, 2nd cl Th Trip pt ia 57, MA 60. Cudd Coll 59. **d** 61 Aston for Birm **p** 62 Birm. C of St Agnes Moseley 61-64; L to Offic Dio Gibr 64-65; Sub-Warden St Bonif Coll Warm and L to Offic Dio Sarum 66-69; C of St Jo Evang Weston B & W 69-70; Asst Gen-Sec C of E Coun on Foreign Relations 70-71; Sec Angl-RC Comm 71-74; C of St Dunstan-in-the-West, Lon 71-73; St Jo Div Kennington 73-74; Asst Chap Abp of Cant's Counsellors on Foreign Relns 72-74; V of St Paul S Harrow 74-80; St Jas Paddington Dio Lon from 80. *6 Gloucester Terrace, W2 3DD.* (01-723 8119)

DAVEY, Canon Deryck Harry Percival. b 23. St Jo Coll Dur BA 48, Dipl Th 50. **d** 50 Truro **p** 51 Ugan for Cant. C of Madron w Morvah 50-53; V of Paul 53-59; Liskeard w St Keyne (and St Pinnock from 76) Dio Truro from 59; C-in-c of St Pinnock 62-76; RD of W Wivelshire 65-68 and 71-73; Hon Can of Truro Cathl from 75; P-in-c of Morval Dio Truro from 80. *Vicarage, Liskeard, Cornw, PL14 3AQ.* (Liskeard 42178)

DAVEY, Eric Victor. b 28. Wycl Hall Ox 53. Ridley Hall Cam. **d** 56 **p** 57 Dur. C of Stockton-on-Tees 56-59; Stretford 59-61; V of Slaithwaite w E Scammonden 61-67; Pontefract Dio Wakef from 68; Surr from 68. *Vicarage, The Mount, Pontefract, Yorks.* (Pontefract 70 2218)

DAVEY, Frederick Hutley David. b 14. Cranmer Hall Dur 58. **d** 60 **p** 62 Dur. C of St Nich Bp Wearmouth 60-62; St Giles Dur 62-64; Chap at Dibrugarh and Jorhat 64-68; Hon Can of Assam 66-68; P-in-c of Chittagong 68-72; Chap Miss to Seamen Pusan 73-77; De Beer from 77. *International Seamen's Centre, De Beer, West Rozenburg, Netherlands.*

DAVEY, Garry Richard. b 45. Univ of Melb BA 67, MA 70. Trin Coll Melb ACT Th Scho 69. **d** 70 **p** 71 Melb. C of St Luke E Frankston 70-71; Ch Ch Berwick 71-72; Perm to Offic Dio Melb 72-73; P-in-c of St Jas St Kilda E 73-75. *435 Inkerman Street, East St Kilda, Vic, Australia 3183.*

DAVEY, John. b 35. Chich Th Coll 67. **d** 69 **p** 70 Chich. C of St Eliz Eastbourne 69-72; St Mary Eastbourne 72-73; V of W Wittering 74-77; Chap and Min Can of St Geo Chap Windsor 77-81; R of the Rissingtons Dio Glouc from 81. *Great Rissington Rectory, Cheltenham, Glos.*

DAVEY, John Michael. b 31. St Chad's Coll Dur BA 54, Dipl Th 56. **d** 56 **p** 61 Dur. C of Southwick 56-57; Harton 60-64; Bawtry w Austerfield and Misson 64-67; PC of Stillington Dur 67-68; V 68-70; L to Offic Dio Dur 70-78; Perm to Offic Dio Sheff from 78. *254 Albert Road, Sheffield, S8 9RB.* (0742-588734)

DAVEY, Julian Metherall. b 40. Late Exhib of Jes Coll Ox (2nd cl Cl Mods 60), BA (2nd cl Th) 62, MA 65. Wells Th Coll 62. **d** 64 **p** 65 B & W. C of Weston-s-Mare 64-66; Asst Master St Alb Sch 66-68; Chap 68-73; Merchant Taylors' Sch Crosby from 73. *28 Windsor Road, Formby, Liverpool, L37 6DY.* (Formby 73614)

DAVEY, Julian Warwick. b 45. Qu Coll Birm 78. **d** 81 Worc (NSM). C of Ipsley Dio Worc from 81. *2 Meeting Lane, Alcester, Warwicks.*

DAVEY, Preb Norman John. b 23. Bps' Coll Cheshunt 51. **d** 53 **p** 54 Ex. C of Highweek w Abbotsbury 53-57; R of Ashreigney 57-62; V of Burrington 57-62; RD of Chulmleigh 60-62; R of Shobrooke 62-66; R of Stockleigh Pomeroy 62-66; Dioc Youth Chap Dio Ex 62-70; C of St Martin w St Steph (in c of St Steph) 67-70; Chap Ex Sch 67-75; R of St Mary Arches w St Pancras Ex 70-73; Ex Centr 73-77; C-in-c of Ide 75-77; Preb of Ex Cathl from 77; V of Holcombe Burnell Dio Ex from 77; Dir of Educn Dio Ex from 77. *Holcombe Burnell Vicarage, Exeter, Devon, EX6 7SW.* (Longdown 261)

DAVEY, Peter Francis. b 40. Trin Coll Cam BA 63, MA 68. Cudd Coll 63. **d** 65 Hulme for Man **p** 66 Man. C of Atherton 65-69; Leesfield 69-71; V of High Crompton 71-79; Blackrod Dio Man from 79; Sec SPCK Rochdale from 80. *St Katherine's Vicarage, Blackhorse Street, Blackrod, BL6 5EN.* (Horwich 68150)

DAVEY, William Edwin. b 15. TCD BA 39, MA 42. **d** 41 **p** 42 Down. C of Ch Ch Lisburn 41-44; C-in-c of Tamlaght O'Crilly Lower 44-48; I of Muff 48-53; Urney 53-67; Commiss Ja 56-67; RD of Strabane 60-67; V of St John Gt Harwood 67-72; R of Mamble w Bayton 72-80. *Flat 2, The Holt, Staddon Road, Appledore, Bideford, Devon EX39 1RG.* (Bideford 77334)

DAVID, Colin Mackie. b 20. St Mich Coll Llan 46. **d** 48 **p** 49 Llan. C of St Martin Roath 48-52; Newcastle w Laleston 52-60; R of Llanfabon 61-67; Merthyr Dyfan Dio Llan from 67; Surr from 61; Commiss Kimb K from 77. *10 Buttrills Road, Barry, S Glam, CF6 6AB.* (Barry 735943)

DAVID, Conrad Frederick Adam. NZ Bd of Th Stud LTh 40. **d** 40 **p** 41 Ch Ch. C of Fendalton 40-42; Sydenham 42-45; Perm to Offic Dio Auckld 45-50; Perm to Offic (Col Cl Act) at St Eliz Eastbourne Dio Chich 50; at St Mary Magd S Molton 51; St Geo Mart Qu Sq Lon 51-54; C of St Mary Port Elizabeth 54-57; P-in-c of Bedford 57-58; R 59-68; Hon C of St Jude's Rondwick Syd 68-69; on leave 70-73; L to Offic Dio Auckld from 73. *322 Lichfield Building, Selwyn Village, Target Street, Point Chevalier, Auckland, NZ.* (860-119)

DAVID, Edmund Watcyn Rees. b 15. St D Coll Lamp BA 37. **d** 38 **p** 39 Blackb. C of Fleetwood 38-41; St Marg Burnley 41-43; C of Skerton 43-44; CF (EC) 44-47; Chap Accra 47-48; P-in-c of Wiawso 48-53; Chap at Cape Coast 53-55; Accra 55-56; Can & Treas of H Trin Cathl Accra 53-57; V of Much Dewchurch w Llanwarne and Llandinabo 56-59; Much Wenlock w Bourton 59-65; Sub-Warden Commun of St Pet Woking 65-68; V of Shoreham 68-80; RD of Shoreham from 77. *Chapmans, North Street, St Leonards-on-Sea, E Sussex, TN38 0EY.* (Hastings 715385)

DAVID, Evan David Owen Jenkin. b 10. St D Coll Lamp BA 34. **d** 34 **p** 35 Ban. C of Machynlleth 34-41; V of Llwydiarth 41-53; R of Llandyrnog (w Llangwyfan from 67) 53-77. *26 South Drive, Rhyl, Clwyd.*

DAVID, Frederick. b 47. Trin Th Coll Sing BTh 80. **d** 81 Sabah. d Dio Sabah. *PO Box 17, Sandakan, Sabah, Malaysia.*

DAVID, John Sidney Lewis. Qu Coll Cam BA 25, MA 29. Ridley Hall Cam 25. **d** 26 **p** 27 Chelmsf. C of St Mary Magd Colchester 26-29; Res Tutor BCMT Coll Clifton Bris 29-30; Chap 30-32; Chap and Bursar Clifton Th Coll 32-33; Lect 33-35; V of H Trin Tewkesbury 33-37; CCCS Chap Ch Ch Madr 38-42; Org Sec CCCS for Midld Distr and LPr Dio Derby 43-48; Perm to Offic Dios Sheff Southw Birm Lich Cov Ely Leic Heref and Worc 43-48; R of Galby w King's Norton and Stretton Parva 48-50; Bluntisham w Earith 51-52. *Langarth, Mill Lane, Yateley, Camberley, Surrey.* (Yateley 873288)

DAVID, Kenith Andrew. b 39. Univ of Natal BA 64. Coll of Resurr Mirfield 64. **d** 66 St Alb **p** 67 St Alb for Natal. C of Harpenden 66-69; R of Ch of Epiph Chatsworth Durban 69-71; Th Educn Sec Chr Aid 72-81; L t Offic Dio S'wark 72-81; Project Officer for India and Bangladesh Chr Aid 76-81; Prov Sec Ch of Prov of Centr Africa from 81; L to Offic Dio Botswana from 81. *PO Box 769, Gaborone, Botswana.*

DAVID, Michael Anthony Louis. b 29. K Coll Lon and Warm AKC 58. **d** 59 **p** 60 Lon. C of St Jo Bapt Greenhill Harrow 59-63; V of St Mary Gravesend 63-78; Repton 78-81; Foremark 78-81; Team V of Buxton Dio Derby from 81. *12 Ecclesbourne Drive, Buxton, Derbys.* (Buxton 4179)

DAVID, Philip Evan Nicholl. b 31. Jes Coll Ox BA (2nd Cl Mod Hist) 53, MA 57. Univ of Wales BA (2nd cl Hebr) 61. St

Mich Coll Llan 56. **d** 57 **p** 58 Llan. C of Llanblethian w Cowbridge 57-60; St Jo Bapt Cardiff 60-64; Chap Ch Coll Brecon 64-74; C-in-c of Aberyskir w Llanfihangel-Nantbran 70-74; Chap Loretto Sch Musselburgh from 75. *Chaplain, Loretto School, Musselburgh, Midlothian.*

DAVID, Polycarp Matong. **d** 63 **p** 64 Bloemf. P Dio Bloemf 63-76. *2536 Melk Street, Bochabela, Bloemfontein, S Africa.*

DAVIDGE, Peter Henry. b 24. Roch Th Coll 61. FCII 51. **d** 63 **p** 64 Roch. C of Orpington 63-68; V of Green Street Green 68-76; R of Harrington Dio Carl from 76. *Rectory, Primrose Crescent, Harrington, Workington, Cumb CA14 5PP.* (Harrington 830215)

DAVIDS, Christoffel. b 41. St Pet Coll Alice Dipl Th 71. **d** 71 **p** 72 Capetn. C of Bonteheuwel 71-74; P-in-c Hanover Park 74-80; R of Mitchell's Plain Dio Capetn from 80. *Rectory, Park Avenue, Westridge, Mitchell's Plain 7785, CP, S Africa.* (31-0119)

DAVIDSON, Alexander Hampton. b 25. **d** 78 **p** 79 Wai. Hon C of Otumoetai Dio Wai from 78. *103 Beach Road, Otumoetai, Tauranga, NZ.*

DAVIDSON, Alfred William. b 12. **d** 77 **p** 78 Caled. C of St John Masset Dio Caled 77-78; I from 78. *Box 51, Masset, BC, Canada.*

DAVIDSON, Charles Alexander. b 54. Codr Coll Barb 73. **d** 77 Barb for Guy **p** 78 Stabroek for Guy. C of All SS New Amsterdam 77-81; H Trin Cathl Port of Spain Dio Trinid from 81. *30a Abercromby Street, Port of Spain, Trinidad, W Indies.*

DAVIDSON, Canon Charles Hilary. b 29. St Edm Hall Ox BA 52, MA 56. Lich Th Coll 52. **d** 54 **p** 55 Pet. C of Abington 54-59; St Jo Bapt Pet 59-60; R of Sywell w Overstone 60-66; Maidwell w Draughton (and Scaldwell and Lamport w Faxton from 77) 66-79; R of Scaldwell 66-77; C-in-c of Lamport w Faxton 66-77; Hon Min Can of Pet Cathl from 70: RD of Brixworth 77-79; Can of Pet Cathl from 79; V of Roade Dio Pet from 79. *Roade Vicarage, Northampton, NN7 2NT.* (Northampton 862284)

DAVIDSON, George Morley. b 10. AKC (1st cl) 33. **d** 33 **p** 34 Lon. C of St John w Hendon 33-35; Wybunbury 35-46; CF (EC) 40-46; V of Bredbury 46-48; R of Guysborough NS 48-49; Ch Ch Winnipeg 49-50; St Jas Winnipeg 50-53; V of Plemstall w Guilden Sutton 53-55; Runcorn 55-60; RD of Frodsham 60; V of Marcham w Garford 60-68; Clavering w Langley 68-75. *7 Lordsmill Road, Shavington, Crewe, Chesh, CW2 5ET.*

DAVIDSON, Canon George Philip. b 25. BA (2nd cl Engl) Lon 50, BSc (2nd cl Econ) Lon 57, BD (Lon) 60. **d** 63 Bp Gelsthorpe for Southw **p** 64 Southw. C of Holme Pierrepont w Adbolton (in c of Tythby w Cropwell Butler) 63-65; C-in-c of Langar w Barnstone 65-67; R 67-72; C-in-c of Tythry w Cropwell Butler 65-72; Colston Bassett 67-72; Cropwell Bishop 71-72; Granby w Sutton and Elton-on-the-Hill 71-72; Med Admin Angl Coun Malawi 72-74; Sec Zambia Angl Coun 74-81; Hon Can of Lusaka 78-81; Can (Emer) from 81; Commiss Centr Zam from 81; R of Houghton-on-the-Hill and Keyham Dio Leic from 81. *Houghton-on-the-Hill Rectory, Leicester, LE7 9GD.*(Leic 415828)

DAVIDSON, Graeme John. b 42. Vic Univ Wel BA 64, MA 65. Linacre Coll Ox BA (3rd cl Th) 69. St Steph Ho Ox 67. **d** 67 **p** 71 Ox for Wel. C of St Luke Maidenhead 70-73; Hon C of I Bay 74-78; on leave. *9 Oku Street, Wellington, NZ.* (836-092)

DAVIDSON, Ian George. b 32. Univ of Lon BSc (Econ) 53. Linc Th Coll 55. **d** 58 **p** 59 St Alb. C of Waltham Cross 58-60; C of St Alb Cathl 61-63; Dioc Youth Chap Dio S'wark and Hon PV of S'wark Cathl 63-67; V of Gt Cornard 67-72; V of L Cornard 67-70; L to Offic Dio St E 72-79; P-in-c of Witnesham w Swilland and Ashbocking Dio St E from 79. *Witnesham Rectory, Ipswich, Suff.* (Witnesham 318)

DAVIDSON, Isaac Emmanuel. b 1888. Trin Coll Dub Hebr Prem 16, BA 18, MA 24. **d** 18 **p** 19 Clogh. C of Clones 18-20; N Sec of CI Aux to LJS 20-24; Miss LJS Dio Lon 24-26; Dir Barbican Miss to Jews 26-68; C-in-c of St Pet Chap Seven Trees Chislehurst 41-67. *35 Woodride, Petts Wood, Orpington, Kent.*

DAVIDSON, John. b 1895. Edin Th Coll 24. Univ of Dur LTh 26. **d** 26 Carl **p** 27 Barrow-F for Carl. C of St John Barrow-F 26-27; All SS Cockermouth 27-31; St Geo Millom 31-35; R of Bolton 35-48; V of St Steph Carl 48-61; R of Kirkbride w Newton Arlosh 61-66; L to Offic Dio Carl 66-71; Perm to Offic from 74; C of Southend-on-Sea 71-74. *5 St George's Crescent, Carlisle.*

DAVIDSON, John Lindsay. b 27. Trin Coll Dub LRCP 51. St Cath S Ox Dipl Th 57. St Steph Ho Ox. **d** 58 Croydon for Cant **p** 59 Cant. C of St Mich AA Croydon 58-61; P-in-c of H Cross Miss 62-66; V of St Steph Lewisham 67-70; V of St Mich AA Croydon 70-81; R of E Woolfardisworthy, Cheriton-Fitzpaine, Kennerleigh, Washford Pyne, Puddington, Poughill, Stockleigh English, Stockleigh Pomeroy, Morchard Bishop, Down St Mary and Clanna-Borough Dio Ex from 81. *Rectory, Cheriton Fitzpaine, Crediton, Devon, EX17 4JB.* (Cheriton Fitzpaine 352)

DAVIDSON, Canon John Noble. b 15. Edin Th Coll 52. **d** 54 **p** 55 Carl. C of H Trin Carl 54-57; V of Netherton w Grasslot 57-63; Walney I 63-69; RD of Dalton 68-69; Surr 68-69; V of H Trin Southport 69-75; Rockliffe w Cargo 75-78; P-in-c of Blackford 75-78; Hon Can of Pro-Cathl of St Paul Valletta Dio Gibr in Eur from 81. *6 Etterby Terrace, Carlisle, Cumb.* (Carlisle 37106)

DAVIDSON, John Stuart. b 27. Linc Th Coll 62. **d** 64 **p** 65 Newc T. C of Hexham 64-66; CF 66-77; P-in-c of Rockcliffe w Cargo 78-79; Blackford 78-79; V of Rockcliffe and Blackford Dio Carl from 79. *Rockcliffe Vicarage, Carlisle, Cumb, CA6 4AA.* (Rockcliffe 209)

DAVIDSON, John Wilmur. McGill Univ BA 54, BD 57. **d** and **p** Montr 57. P-in-c of Iron Hill 57-59; Brome w Iron Hill 59-64; R 64-79; Waterloo Dio Montr from 79. *Box 508, Waterloo, PQ, Canada J0E 2N0.* (514-539 2078)

DAVIDSON, Jonathan Eric. b 18. Trin Coll Dub BA 41, MA 65. **d** 42 Tuam for Down **p** 43 Down. C of Antrim 43-45; Drumragh and Mountfield 45-47; C-in-c of Ballynascreen 47-51; I of Kildress Dio Arm from 51. *Kildress Rectory, Cookstown, Co Tyrone, N Ireland.* (Tulnacross 215)

DAVIDSON, Paul James. b 33. St Jo Coll Auckld 74. **d** 75 **p** 76 Wai. C of Havelock North 75-78; V of Otane 78-80; C of Ch Ch Wanganui Dio Wel from 80. *4 Gibson Crescent, Wanganui, NZ.*

DAVIDSON, Canon Ronald Ralph. b 31. Wycl Coll Tor LTh 63. **d** 61 **p** 62 Tor. R of Ch K Tor 70-74; Ch Ch Deer Pk City and Dio Tor from 74; Can of Tor from 77. *1570 Yonge Street, Toronto, Ont., Canada.* (416-920 5211)

DAVIDSON, Sinclair Melville. b 22. CBE 68. CEng 50. Chich Th Coll 79. **d** 81 Chich. C of High Hurstwood Dio Chich from 81. *Moy Cottage, Fielden Lane, Crowborough, E Sussex.*

DAVIDSON, Stanley Guest. b 05. Clifton Th Coll 39. **d** 42 **p** 43 Bris. C of St Lawr Bris 42-45; C-in-c 45-49; R of Swerford w Showell 49-62; C-in-c of Gt Rollright 58-62; R of High Halstow w Hoo St Mary 62-74; Perm to Office Dio Ox from 79. *102 Oxford Road, Banbury, Oxon.*

DAVIDSON, Thomas James. Bp's Univ Lennox BA 61, LST 63. **d** 62 **p** 63 Alg. d Dio Alg 62-63; I of Capreol 63-68. *81 Highland Avenue, Belleville, Ont., Canada.*

DAVIDSON, Victor Adolphus. St Pet Coll Ja. **d** 65 **p** 66 Ja. C of St Geo Kingston 65-70; R of Buff Bay Dio Ja from 70. *Buff Bay PO, Jamaica.*

DAVIDSON, William Ivan Windsor. St Francis Coll Brisb ACT ThL (2nd cl) 66. **d** 66 **p** 67 Brisb. C of All SS Chermside Brisb 66-69; L to Offic Dio Brisb 69-70; C of St Matt, Sherwood Brisb 70-72; V of Wondai 72-78; C of Mossman Dio Carp from 78. *c/o The Rectory, Mossman, Queensland, Australia 4873.*

DAVIDSON, William Watkins. b 20. Wadh Coll Ox BA 48, MA 53. Westcott Ho Cam 49. **d** 50 **p** 51 Southw. C of Radcliffe-on-Trent 50-53; Chap RN 53-57; R of Esher 57-65; V of St Steph w St Jo Westmr Dio Lon from 65. *21 Vincent Square, SW1P 2NA.* (01-834 8981)

DAVIE, Keith Maitland. Univ Coll OX BA (4th cl Mod Hist) 22, MA 26. Cudd Coll 23. M CR 42. **d** 23 **p** 24 Lon. C of St Jas Gt Bethnal Green 23-26; Asst Master C of E Gr Sch Guildf W Austr 26-27; R of Wyalkatchem 27-28; P-in-c of Coolgardie w Kurrawang 28-29; Gen L Dio Gibr 29-30; C of Petworth 30-33; St Nich Brighton 33-34; St Mary Hendon 34-36; V of St Alphage Hendon 36-42; Miss Sophiatown 46-47; P-in-c of Orlando 47-50; Chap Baragwanath Hosp Johann 49-52; L to Offic Dio Lon 57-59; Miss P at Sophiatown Johann 59-63; R of Alice 63-66; L to Offic Dio Johann 66-80. *Priory of St Peter, Rosettenville, Johannesburg, S Africa.* (011-26 1933)

DAVIE, Peter Edward Sidney. b 36. Univ of Lon BSc (2nd cl Econ) 57, M Phil 78. Univ of Birm MA (Th) 73. Coll of Resurr Mirfield 57. **d** 60 **p** 61 Kens for Lon. C of St Pet De Beauvoir Town W Hackney 60-63; C-in-c of St Alb Godshill 63-67; R of Upton St Leon 67-73; Sen Lect Ch Ch Coll Cant from 73. *27 St Stephen's Road, Canterbury, Kent, CT2 7JD.*

DAVIES, Adrian Paul. b 43. K Coll Lon and Warm. **d** 69 Southw **p** 70 Sherwood for Southw. C of Nottm 69-73; Gt w L Billing 73-74; R of Castor (w Sutton and Upton from 75) 75-82; P-in-c of Marholm 75-82; V of St Mich Byker City and Dio Newc T from 82. *St Michael's Vicarage, Headlam Street, Byker, Newcastle upon Tyne, NE6 2DX.* (Newc T 653720)

DAVIES, Alcwyn Ivor. Univ of Wales BA (2nd cl Civic Stud) 32, Dipl Educn 33. St D Coll Lamp 36. **d** 38 Llan **p** 39 Swan B for Llan. C of St D Llanddewi Rhondda 38-41; St Pet and St Paul Wisbech 41-44; R of Hamerton 44-48; V of Winwick 44-48; Friday Bridge 48-53; V of Coldham 48-53; R of Fowlmere 53-76; V of Triplow 53-76; RD of Barton 62-67.

17 Station Road, Lode, Cambridge, CB5 9HB. (Cambridge 811867)

DAVIES, Aldwyn Ivan. b 09. St D Coll Lamp BA 31. **d** 32 **p** 33 Swan B. C of Ch Ch Swansea 32-36; Milford Haven 36-39; Asst Chap Mersey Miss to Seamen 39-43; R of Gladestry w Colva 43-46; Chap Miss to Seamen Swansea 46-54; V of Lidget Green 54-56; Chap to Mersey Miss to Seamen 56-57; R of Halwill w Beaworthy 57-63; Chap Miss to Seamen Glas and Sec for Scotld 63-69; R of Rhossili (w Port Eynon and Llanddewi from 72) 69-74; Prov Sec Miss to Seamen in Wales 69-78; V of Llangennith 75-77. *43 Eastlands Park, Bishopston, Swansea.* (Bishopston 2942)

DAVIES, Alexander Richard. b 12. **d** 64 **p** 65 St A. C of Llangollen 64-69; V of Llanfihangel Crucorney Cwmyoy and Llanthony and R of Oldcastle 69-77; Perm to Office Dio St A from 77. *4 Gwyn Fryn Terrace, Llangollen, LL20 8HD.* (Llangollen 861321)

DAVIES, Canon Alfred Joseph. b 23. St D Coll Lamp BA 49. **d** 50 **p** 51 St D. C of Llanegwad 50-53; Ch Ch Llanelly 53-54; V of Llangeler 54-74; Cardigan Dio St D from 74; RD of Emlyn 70-73; Can of St D Cathl from 79. *Vicarage, Cardigan, Dyfed.* (Cardigan 2722)

DAVIES, Alick John. St Jo Coll Morpeth 55. **d** 57 **p** 58 Adel. C of St Geo Magill 57-59; P-in-c of Elliston 59-62; P-in-c of Waikerie 62-66; R of Kapunda 66-71; South Road Dio Adel from 71. *1167 South Road, St Mary's, S Australia 5042.* (08-276 2693)

DAVIES, Alun Edwards. b 18. Univ of Wales BA 40. St D Coll Lamp. **d** 46 **p** 47 Llan. C of St Matthias Treharris 46-48; St Mary Cardigan 48-50; CF 50-56; Hon CF 56; R of Byford w Mansel Gamage 56-58; C-in-c of Preston-on-Wye 56-58; V of Birch-in-Hopwood 58-62; R of St Thos Lower Crumpsall Dio Man from 62. *St Thomas' Rectory, Hazelbottom Road, Manchester, M8 7GQ.* (061-205 3342)

DAVIES, Very Rev Alun Radcliffe. b 23. Univ of Wales BA 45. Keble Coll Ox BA (2nd cl Th) 47, MA 51. St Mich Coll Llan 47. **d** 48 **p** 49 Llan. C of Roath 48-49; Lect St Mich Coll Llan 49-53; Bp's Messenger Dio Llan 50-59; Dom Chap to Abp of Wales 52-57; Chap RNVR 53-58; RNR 58-60; Exam Chap to Bp of Llan from 54; Dom Chap 57-59; V of Ystrad-Mynach 59-75; Chan of Llan Cathl 69-71; Archd of Llan 71-77; Can Res of Llan Cathl 75-77; Dean and V from 77. *Deanery, Cathedral Green, Llandaff, Cardiff, S Glam.* (Cardiff 561545)

DAVIES, Anthony John. b 41. New Coll Ox BA (3rd cl Mod Hist) 65, MA 71. St Steph Ho Ox 64. **d** 66 **p** 67 Lich. C of St Mary and St Chad Longton 66-68; Trent Vale 68-72; V of Cross Heath Dio Lich from 72. *19 King Street, Cross Heath, Newcastle, Staffs, ST5 9HQ.* (Newc 617241)

DAVIES, Arthur Cadwaladr. b 19. Univ of Wales BA 41. Wells Th Coll 41. **d** 43 **p** 44 St A. C of Broughton 43-48; Llanrhos 48-52; V of St Paul Spalding 52-57; Ch Ch Ches 57-64; Stockton Heath Dio Ches from 64; RD of Gt Budworth from 81. *Stockton Heath Vicarage, Warrington, Lancs.* (Warrington 61396)

DAVIES, Arthur Cecil Francis. b 11. Keble Coll Ox BA 34, MA 42. Bps' Coll Cheshunt 35. **d** 37 Bradf **p** 38 Ripon for Bradf. C of Keighley Bradf 37-42; Min Can of Worc 42-45; L to Offic Dio Worc 42-45; Prec of Blackb Cathl 45-48; C and Prec of St Jo Bapt Croydon 48-52; PC of Eastville w Midville 52-59; V of Horncastle w Low Toynton 59-79; Surr from 59; Warden Brown's Hosp Stamford from 80; Perm to Offic Dio Pet from 80. *Warden's House, Brown's Hospital, Stamford, Lincs, PE9 1PF.* (Stamford 2406)

DAVIES, Arthur Gerald Miles. b 29. Univ Coll of N Wales BA 51. St Mich Coll Llan. **d** 53 **p** 54 St A. C of Shotton 53-60; R of Nannerch 60-63; V of Llansilin w Llangadwaladr 63-71; Llanfair Caereinion w Llanllugan 71-75; Team V of Wrexham Dio St A from 75. *Vicarage, Princess Street, Wrexham, Clwyd.* (Wrexham 566145)

DAVIES, Arthur Leslie. Em Coll Sktn. **d** 34 **p** 35 Sktn. C of Perdue 34-35; I of Paynton 35-37; C of St Matt Winnipeg 37-39; I of St Mary Magd St Vital 39-40; St John Manitou Manit 40-42; Prin of St John Ind Sch Wabasca 42-50; I of Alert Bay 50-53; Maple Ridge 53-56; R of St Thos Vanc 56-63; I of Ocean Pk w Crescent 63-68; St Andr Burnaby 68-71; R of St Matt Vanc 69-71. *3560 Cambie Street, Vancouver, BC, Canada.*

DAVIES, Arthur Lloyd. b 31. Univ of Wales BA 55. Cudd Coll 55. **d** 57 Swan B for Wales **p** 58 Llan. C of Llwynypia 57-59; Merthyr Dyfan 59-62; Amersham (in c of St Geo) 62-65; PC (V from 68) of St Geo Tilehurst 65-73; R of St Paul Wokingham Dio Ox from 73. *St Paul's Rectory, Wokingham, Berks.* (Wokingham 780629)

DAVIES, Arthur Philip. b 1899. Lon Coll of Div 24. **d** 27 **p** 28 S'wark. C of H Trin Richmond 27-29; St Mary Battersea 29-30; Baldock w Bygrave (in c of Clothall) 30-32; Chap of Bilbao 32-36; V of Buildwas 36-40; Ketley 40-69; RD of Wrockwardine 61-66; Perm to Offic Dio Heref from 70. *The Gafflat, Foy, Ross-on-Wye, Herefs.*

DAVIES, Basil Tudor. b 18. Keble Coll Ox BA 40, MA 48. Westcott Ho Cam 40. **d** 42 **p** 43 S'wark. C of St Luke w St Paul Old Charlton 42-44; St Andr Stockwell Green 44-49; Ox Miss to Calc 49-53; C of Wantage 53-57; V of Wigston Magna 57-73; R of Upwell St Pet 73-77; C-in-c of Nordelph 75-77; Perm to Offic Dio Ox from 77. *10 Denchworth Road, Wantage, Oxon, OX12 9AU.* (Wantage 2289)

DAVIES, Bernard. b 34. BD (Lon) 63. Oak Hill Th Coll 59. **d** 63 Hulme for Man **p** 64 Man. C of Rawtenstall 63-69; Trav Sec Ruanda Miss 69-71; R of Widford 71-78; V of Braintree Dio Chelmsf from 78. *St Michael's Vicarage, Marshalls Road, Braintree, Essex.* (Braintree 22840)

DAVIES, Bruce Edmund. b 22. Univ of Wales BA 44. S Mich Coll Llan 44. **d** 46 **p** 47 Llan. C of St Luke Canton Cardiff 46-48; St Agnes Roath 48-56; C-in-c of St Dyfrig Cardiff 56-66; Chap Univ Coll Cardiff 56-78; R of Peterston-super-Ely w St Brides-super-Ely Dio Llan from 78. *Peterston-super-Ely Rectory, Cardiff.* (P-s-E 760297)

DAVIES, Cadoc Trevor. b 28. Keble Coll Ox BA 52, MA 57. Cudd Coll 57. **d** 57 **p** 58 Glouc. C of St Steph Cheltm 57-60; Shalford 60-64; V of Water Orton Dio Birm from 64. *Water Orton Vicarage, Birmingham.* (021-747 2751)

DAVIES, Clifford Morgan. Univ of Wales BA 41. St Mich Coll Llan 41. **d** 43 **p** 44 Llan. C of Gabalfa 43-46; St Cath Pontypridd 46-51; All SS Bournemouth 51-56; R of S Tidworth w Shipton Bellinger 56-61; Chap Duke of York's R Mil Sch Dover 61-77. *110 Send Road, Send, Woking, Surrey.*

DAVIES, Clifford O'Connor. Univ of Lon BCom (2nd cl) 37. St Aug Coll Cant 42. **d** 44 **p** 45 Roch. C of H Trin Lamorbey 44-46; Cathl Ch Grahmstn 46-49; P-in-c of Zoutpansberg 49-52; R of W Suburbs Pret 52-57; R of Florida Transv 57-71; Yeoville City and Dio Johann from 71. *50 Dunbar Street, Yeoville, Johannesburg, S Africa.* (011-43 2047)

DAVIES, Conway. b 1889. Selw Coll Cam BA 11, MA 38. Ridley Hall Cam 12. St Mich Coll Llan 24. **d** 25 **p** 26 Llan. C of Pentrebach (Treodyrhiw) 25-26; Perm to Offic at Richmond Surrey 26-27; V of Bradwell 27-60; L to Offic Dio Dun 65-66. *Kingswood Hall, Kington, Herefs.*

DAVIES, Canon David. b 1887. Late Phillips Scho of St D Coll Lamp BA 16. **d** 16 Ban for St D **p** 17 St D. C of St John Clydach 16-20; Llanbadarn-Fawr 20-23; V of Capel Bangor 23-31; Llanegwad 31-43; Henfynyw 43-58; RD of Glyn Aeron 51-58; Surr from 43; Can of St D from 57. *Bryntirion, Penglais Road, Aberystwyth, Dyfed.* (Aberystwyth 3737)

DAVIES, David Arthur Guy Hampton. St Jo Coll Ox BA 50, Dipl Th 51, MA 55. Ely Th Coll 51. **d** 53 **p** 54 Lon. C of Somers Town 53-55; Cranford 55-60; C of H Cross Shrewsbury 60-62; R of St Mary Stamford Dio Linc from 62. *St Mary's Rectory, Stamford, Lincs.* (Stamford 3142)

DAVIES, David Barry Grenville. b 38. Univ of Dur BA 60. MA 78. Sarum Th Coll 61. **d** 63 **p** 64 St D. C of Abth 63-66; Min Can of St D Cathl 66-72; R of Stackpole Elidor w St Petrox Dio St D from 72. *Stackpole Rectory, Pembroke, Dyfed, SA71 5BZ.* (Lamphey 672215)

DAVIES, David Christopher. b 52. BSc (Lon) 73. Dipl Th (Leeds) 75. Coll of Resurr Mirfield 73. **d** 76 Lon **p** 77 Stepney for Lon. C of St Jo w St Bart Bethnal Green 76-80; P-in-c of St Geo Conv Distr Portsea Dio Portsm 80-81; V from 81. *3 Victory Road, Portsmouth.* (Portsm 812215)

DAVIES, Canon David Eldred. b 18. St Edm Hall Ox St Mich Coll Llan 46. **d** 49 **p** 50 St A. C of Newtown w Llanllwchaiarn 49-51; Louth w Welton-le-Wold 51-53; R of Barrowby 53-56; V of Spilsby w Hundleby 56-61; C-in-c of Hagworthingham w Asgarby and Lusby 61; RD of Hill (South) 58-61; Surr 58-61; R of Mkt Deeping Dio Linc from 62; C-in-c of W Deeping 62-65; V of Langtoft 65-71; Hon Can of Linc Cathl from 77; RD of Aveland and Ness w Stamford 77-80. *Market Deeping Rectory, Peterborough.* (Market Deeping 342237)

DAVIES, David Francis Jeffrey. b 01. Keble Coll Ox BA 22, MA 40. Sarum Th Coll 24. **d** 26 **p** 27 Sarum. C of Warminster w St John Boreham 26-30; Temple (or H Cross) Bedminster 30-31; Ch Ch Cheltenham 31-35; V of Nailsworth w Inchbrook and Shortwood 35-55; Upton St Leon 55-67. *Romanway, Church Lane, North Woodchester, Stroud, Glos. GL5 5NE.*

DAVIES, David Garfield. Univ of Wales BA 08. St Mich Coll Llan 10. **d** 11 **p** 12 Llan. C of Rhymney 11-16; Longridge 16-17; Gannow 17-23; St Andr Burnley 23-28; V of Haslingden Grane 28-31; Perm to Offic at Skerton 31-33; Pendleton 33-34; Methley 34-36; R of Kirkhaugh 36-38; V of St Pet Allendale 38-53. *46 Colinmander Gardens, Aughton Park, Ormskirk, Lancs.*

DAVIES, David Geoffrey George. b 24. Univ of Wales (Bangor) BA 49. BD (Lon) 55. St Mich Coll Llan 49. **d** 51 **p** 52 Swan B. C of Brecon w Battle 51-55; Min Can 53-55; C of

Oystermouth 55-59; V of Cwm Flints 59-63; Ruabon w Penylan 63-70; Warden of Ordinands 62-70; Hon Can of St A Cathl 66-69; Cursal Can of Ricardi Harrison in St A Cathl 69-70; Asst Master Netherley Compr Sch Liv 70-72; Deanery High Sch Wigan 73-81; Perm to Offic Dio Liv 71-81; Team V of Bourne Valley Dio Sarum from 81. *Vicarage, Allingtn, Salisbury, SP4 0BZ.* (Idmiston 610663)

DAVIES, Canon David Hywel. b 13. Univ of Wales BA 40. St Mich Coll Llan 41. **d** 42 **p** 43 Llan. C of St Andr Llwynpia (w Tonypandy) 42-47; St Andr Major w Dinas Powis 47-53; V of Monkton Pembroke 53-67; Carmarthen Dio St D from 67; USPG Area Sec Dio St D from 56; Can of St D from 72. *Vicarage, Carmarthen, Dyfed.* (Carmarthen 7117)

DAVIES, Canon David Ioan Gwyn. Univ of Wales BA 41, MA 54. Lich Th Coll 41. **d** 43 **p** 44 Swan B. C of Llandilo Talybont (Pontardulais) 43-47; Llansamlet 47-49; Blackpool 49-53; V of St Mich AA Blackb 53-56; St Jude Preston 56-59; St Paul Blackpool Dio Blackb from 59; RD of Blackpool from 73; Hon Can of Blackb from 77. *St Paul's Vicarage, Egerton Road, Blackpool, FY1 2NP.* (Blackpool 25308)

DAVIES, David Jeremy Christopher. b 46. Late Cho Exhib of CCC Cam Engl Trip pt i 66, BA (2nd cl Engl Trip pt ii) 68, 2nd cl Th Trip pt ii 70, MA 72. Westcott Ho Cam 68. **d** 71 **p** 72 Stepney for Lon. C of Stepney 71-74; Dep Min Can of St Paul's Cathl Lon from 74; Chap Qu Mary Coll Lon 74-78; Sen Chap Univ Coll Cardiff and Poly of Wales from 78. *Anglican Chaplaincy, 61 Park Place, Cardiff, CF1 3AT.* (Cardiff 32550)

DAVIES, David John. b 1900. Univ of Wales (Cardiff) BA 28. St D Coll Lamp. **d** 28 **p** 29 St D. C of St Mary Cardigan 28-30; Gorslas (in c of St Anne Cross Hands) 30-33; Llandefeilog (in c of St Anne Cwmffrwd) 33-36; V of Llanfynydd 36-50; C-in-c of Merthyr 50-58; V of Llandyfriog w Llanfair-Trelygen (and Troedyraur from 62 and R of Langynllo from 70) 58-71. *Glyn-Telori, Bronwydd, Carmarthen, Dyfed.*

DAVIES, David John. b 36. St Cath S Ox BA (2nd cl Engl) 58, MA 62. St D Coll Lamp 58. **d** 60 **p** 61 St A. C of Rhosddu 60-68; Chr Aid Area Sec for Glos, Herefs, and Worcs from 68; Reg Co-ordinator for Midl from 78. *16 Rosefield Crescent, Newtown, Tewkesbury, Glos, GL20 8EH.* (Tewkesbury 292491)

DAVIES, David Jones. b 06. Univ of Wales BA 33. St Mich Coll Llan 35. **d** 35 **p** 36 Llan. C of Llangynwyd w Maesteg 35-38; Wrexham 38-44; Perm to Offic Dio Birm from 44; Chap to the Welsh War-workers in Midlands 44-47; C of Trealaw 47-48; Cowbridge w Llanbeddian 48-49; R of Llangranog 49-57; V of Kenfig Hill 57-76; Perm to Offic Dio Llan from 79. *Bryn Eglwys, Pyle Road, Pyle, Bridgend, Mid Glam.* (Kenfig Hill 740484)

DAVIES, David Leslie Augustus. b 25. St D Coll Lamp BA 50. **d** 51 Bp R W Jones for Wales **p** 52 St D. C of St Mich Abth 51-55; St Paul Llanelly 55-56; V of Castlemartin w Warren 56-61; R of Eglwysilan 61-65; Chap Mayday and Qu Hosps Croydon 65-71; V of Penrhyncoch w Elerch 71-74; Chap R Berks and Reading Distr Hosps from 74. *79 The Mount, Christchurch Road, Reading, Berks, RG1 5HL.* (Reading 84365)

DAVIES, David Michael Cole. St D Coll Lamp. **d** 68 **p** 69 St D. C of Carmarthen 68-72; R of Dinas w Llanllawer 72-77; V of Tycroes w Saron Dio St D from 77. *Tycroes Vicarage, Ammanford, Dyfed, SA18 3LF.* (Ammanford 2384)

DAVIES, David Philip. b 09. St Aid Coll 34. **d** 36 **p** 37 Blackb. C of Ch Ch Accrington 36-38; Sunninghill 38-40; St Andr Cobham 40-45; Min All SS Conv Distr Lightwater (Windlesham) 45-51; V of West End Chobham 51-74; C-in-c of Bisley 56-57; Perm to Offic Dio St Alb from 74. *25 Hilton Avenue, Dunstable, Beds, LU6 3QF.* (Dunstable 67655)

DAVIES, David Protheroe. b 39. Late Exhib of CCC Cam 2nd cl Cl Trip pt i 61, BA (2nd cl Th Trip pt ia) 62, MA 66. Powis Exhib 62, 63. CCC Ox BA (by incorp) 62, MA and BD 69, Hall-Houghton Jun Gr Test Pri 63, Sen 64. Ripon Hall Ox 62. **d** 64 **p** 65 Swan B. C of Swansea 64-67; Lect in Th St D Coll Lamp 67-75; Dean of Faculty of Th 75-77; of Arts from 77; Perm to Offic Dio St D from 67. *St David's Univ College, Lampeter, Dyfed, SA48 7ED.* (Lamp 422351)

DAVIES, David Rees. b 1900. St D Coll Lamp BA 28. **d** 28 **p** 29 Swan B. C of Llandilo-Talybont 28-30; Llansamlet 30-36; V of Nantmel 36-50; Llanwrtyd w Llanddulas in Tir Abad 50-71; RD of Builth 61-71. *2 Bryn Morfa, Temple Drive, Llandrindod Wells, Powys.* (Llandrindod 2016)

DAVIES, David Saunders. b 08. St D Coll Lamp BA 31. **d** 32 **p** 33 St A. C of Flint 32-38; Hope 38-46; V of Caerfallwch (or Rhosesmor) 46-54; Brymbo 54-64; Surr from 54; R of Marchwiel 64-75. *The School House, Bowling Bank, Wrexham, Clwyd.* (Wrexham 61565)

DAVIES, David Thomas. b 09. St D Coll Lamp BA 31. Jes Coll Ox BA 33, MA 36. St Steph Ho Ox. **d** 33 **p** 34 St D. C of St Paul Llanelly 33-36; St D Carmarthen 37-40; C-in-c of Walton W w Talbenny 40; CF (EC) 40-46; V of Llanllwni 46-49; R of Llangybi w Llanarmon 49-52; V of Glanogwen 52-60; RD of Arllechwedd 57-60; Llifon and Talybolion 66-75; V (R from 71) of Holyhead 60-77; Can Res of Ban Cathl 62-65; Preb of Llanfair 65-77. *17 Alban Road, Llanelli, Dyfed, SA15 1EP.*

DAVIES, David Vernon. b 14. Univ of Wales BA 35, BD 38. St Cath S Ox BA 40, MA 44. PhD (Lon) 56. St D Coll Lamp 41. **d** 41 **p** 42 St D. C of Ch Ch Llanelly 41-46; Asst Master St Jo Coll Nassau 47-50; Chap Cane Hill Hosp Coulsdon 50-61; Lect St Luke's Coll Ex 62-68; Llan Coll of Educn 68-77; L to Offic Dio Ex 62-68; Dio Llan from 68; Sen Lect Univ Coll Cardiff 77-79. *41 Cefn Coed Avenue, Cyncoed, Cardiff, CF2 6HF.* (Cardiff 757635)

DAVIES, Dennis William. b 24. Univ of Leeds BA (2nd cl Hist) 46. K Coll Lon and Warm AKC 54, BD 65. **d** 54 Reading for Cant **p** 55 Ox. C of Aylesbury 54-58; Asst Master Quarrendon Sch Aylesbury from 59; Perm to Offic Dio Ox 60-61 and 69-70; L to Offic Dio Ox 61-68 and from 70. *48 Brook Street, Aston Clinton, Aylesbury, Bucks.*

DAVIES, Dewi Caradog. b 14. St D Coll Lamp BA 35. **d** 38 **p** 39 Llan. C of Abercynon 38-44; Cilybebyll 44-49; C-in-c of Crynant Conv Distr 49-54; V of Llwynypia w Tonypandy 54-66; Surr from 56; R of Canton 66-79. *10 Insole Gardens, Llandaff, Cardiff.*

DAVIES, Dillwyn. b 30. St Mich Coll Llan 52. **d** 54 **p** 55 St D. C of Laugharne 54-57; Chap Miss to Seamen and L to Offic Dio Dur 57-58; Chap Miss to Seamen Colom 58-62; R of Winthorpe 62-71; V of Langford w Holme-by-Newark 62-71; V of Mansfield Woodhouse Dio Southw from 71. *Vicarage, Butt Lane, Mansfield Woodhouse, Notts, NG19 9JS.* (Mansfield 21875)

DAVIES, Canon Dilwyn Morgan. b 10. Univ of Wales BA (3rd cl Hist) 32, Dipl Educn 33. St Mich Coll Llan 32. **d** 34 **p** 35 Llan. C of Dinas and Penygraig 34-36; Bassaleg 36-40; CF (EC) 40-46; V of Finham 46-54; R of Stoke Cov 54-61; Rugby 61-72; Hon Can of Cov from 65; P-in-c of Ilmington w Stretton-on-Fosse and Ditchford 72-80. *6 Manor Farm Barns, Ilmington, Shipston-on-Stour, Warws, CV36 4LS.*

DAVIES, Donald Alfred. b 11. Linc Th Coll 62. **d** 63 **p** 64 Ex. C of Honiton 63-65; R of Bow w Broad Nymet 65-77; C-in-c of Colebrooke 75-77; Perm to Offic Dio Ex from 79. *5 Homefield Close, Ottery S Mary, Devon.* (Ott S Mary 2562)

DAVIES, Don Burnett. Moore Th Coll Syd ACT ThL 63. **d** 63 **p** 64 Syd. C of St Andr Wahroonga 63-64; Pymble 64-67; C-in-c of Matraville w Phillip Bay Provisional Distr 67-68; Perm to Offic Dio Syd from 79. *31 Cowen Road, St Ives, NSW, Australia.* (44-5479)

DAVIES, Douglas James. b 47. St Pet Coll Ox BLitt 72. St Jo Coll Dur Ba 69, BA (Th) 73. Univ of Nottm PhD 80. Cranmer Hall Dur 71. **d** 75 **p** 76 Southw. C of St Leon Wollaton Dio Southw from 75; Lect Nottm Univ from 74. *University of Nottingham, Dept of Theology, University Park, Nottingham, NG7 2RD.*

DAVIES, Douglas Puckle. ACT ThL 51. St Mich Th Coll Crafers. **d** 51 Adel for Perth **p** 51 Kalg for Perth. C of Kalg Cathl 51-53; R of Southern Cross 53-56; P-in-c of Leonora-Gwalia 56-57; C of Chiswick Dio Lon 57-59; R of Gnowangerup 59-64; Chap Guildf Gr Sch 64-70; Ment Health Services of W Austr from 70; Sen Chap Dio Perth 81. *45 Waverley Street, South Perth, W Australia 6151.* (3674378)

DAVIES, Douglas Tudor. b 20. Univ of Wales BA 44. Coll of Resurr Mirfield. **d** 46 **p** 47 Swan B. C of Ch Ch Swansea 46-52; Oystermouth 52-57; V of Llangynllo 57-63; R of Bleddfa 57-63; C-in-c of St Alb Conv Distr Treboeth Dio Swan B 63-66; V from 66; RD of Penderi from 78. *St Alban's Vicarage, Treboeth, Swansea, W Glam.* (Swansea 71332)

DAVIES, Ebenezer Thomas. b 03. Univ of Wales BA (1st cl Hist) 27, MA 40. St Mich Coll Llan 35. **d** 36 **p** 37 Mon. C of Basaleg 36-40; Chepstow 40-43; V of Mathern 43-48; R of Llangibby 48-73; Dir of Relig Educn Mon 49-73; Can of Mon 53-73; Exam Chap to Bp of Mon from 52; Swan B from 54; RD of Usk 63-72; P-in-c of Llanover w Llanfair Kilgeddin Dio Mon from 77. *Llanover Vicarage, Abergavenny, Gwent, NP7 9BY.* (Gobion 238)

DAVIES, Edmund Alfred. d 69 **p** 70 Sktn. I of St Luke City and Dio Sktn from 69. *607 28th Street West, Saskatoon, Sask., Canada.*

DAVIES, Edward William Llewellyn. b 51. Univ of Nottm BTh 77. St Jo Coll Nottm 73. **d** 78 **p** 79 Portsm. C of St Jude Southsea Portsea 78-81; St Mary Alverstoke Dio Portsm from 81. *30 Burney Road, Alverstoke, Gosport, Hants.* (Gosport 82523)

DAVIES, Canon Edwin Isaac. b 21. Univ of Wales BA 42 (2nd cl Hist) 43. St Mich Coll Llan 43. **d** 45 **p** 46 Llan. C of Merthyr Tydfil 45-48; Cathl Ch Llan 48-57; Surr from 57; V of Llantrisant 57-78; St Jo Bapt Cardiff Dio Llan from 78; Res Can of Llan Cathl from 78; Offg Chap for Wales O of St

Jo of Jer from 78; Chap Actors' Ch U from 78. *Vicarage, Cathedral Road, Cardiff, S Glam.* (Cardiff 30692)

DAVIES, Ernest Frank Vaughan. d 55 Tor. C of St Thos City and Dio Tor from 55. *315 Oriole Parkway, Toronto 197, Ont., Canada.*

DAVIES, Evan James. b 1898. St D Coll Lamp BA 24. **d** 25 **p** 26 St D. C of Gorslas 25-27; St Paul Llanelly 27-33; V of Ystradffin 33-37; R of Llangoedmore 37-53; Llanllwchaiarn (New Quay) 53-71; Surr from 54; RD of Glynaeron 62-71. *Erw Lon, Llanarth, Dyfed.*

DAVIES, Evan Wallis. b 08. Bps' Coll Cheshunt. **d** 42 **p** 43 St Alb. C of Biggleswade 42-45; Loughor 45-46; Cuffley 46-48; V of Pirton 48-52; Publ Pr Dio St Alb 52-65. *7 Treetops, Swiss Valley Park, Llanelli, Dyfed.*

DAVIES, Francis James Saunders. b 37. Univ of Wales BA (2nd cl Welsh) 60. Selw Coll Cam BA (2nd cl Th Trip pt ii) 62, MA 66. Univ of Bonn 63. St Mich Coll Llan 62. **d** 63 Llan for Ban **p** 64 Ban. C of Holyhead w Rhoscolyn 63-67; Cathl Chap Ban 67-69; R of Llanllyfni w Talysarn and Penygroes 69-75; Can Missr Dio Ban 75-78; V of Gorseinon Dio Swan B from 78. *Vicarage, Princess Street, Gorseinon, W Glam.* (Gorseinon 892849)

DAVIES, Frank. b 25. K Coll Lon 52. **d** 55 **p** 56 Lich. C of Porthill 55-59; V of Smallthorne 59-67; R of St Jo Bapt Longton 67-75; V of St Werburgh Burslem Dio Lich from 75. *St Werburgh's Presbytery, Haywood Road, Burslem, Stoke-on-Trent, ST6 7AH.* (S-on-T 87582)

DAVIES, Frank Ernest. b 13. Univ of Dur LTh 43. Clifton Th Coll 39. **d** 43 Liv **p** 44 Warrington for Liv. C of St Luke Evang Walton-on-the-Hill 43-45; St Jo Evang Ravenhead St Helens 45-48; Ch Ch W Didsbury 48-50; R of St Thos Ardwick Man 50-56; V of St Aug Plymouth 56-60; R of Bigbury Dio Ex from 60. *Bigbury Rectory, Kingsbridge, Devon, TQ7 4AP.* (Bigbury-on-Sea 386)

DAVIES, Frederick Edward. b 1900. Clifton Th Coll. **d** 60 **p** 61 Lon. C of St Mary Hornsey Rise 60-63; R of W Woodhay Ox 63-70. *50 Mousehole Lane, Bitterne Park, Southampton.*

DAVIES, Gary. b 37. K Coll Lon and Warm AKC (1st cl) 62. **d** 63 **p** 64 Chelmsf. C of Dovercourt 63-65; St Phil Lambeth 65-68; C-in-c 68-70; V of St Mary The Boltons Kens Dio Lon from 70; Area Dean of Chelsea 76-80; Dir of Post-Ordin Tr Kens Episc Area from 79. *43 Gilston Road, SW 10.* (01-352 9620)

DAVIES, Geoffrey Colin. St Aug Coll Cant. **d** 35 **p** 36 Capetn. C of Plumstead 35-37; R of Calvinia 37-40; CF (S Afr) 40-43; Chap RAFVR 43-45; R of Ingoldmells w Addlethorpe 45-47; Sen Chap for Butlin's Holiday Camps 47-48; C of Bloemf Cathl 48-49; in Amer Ch 50-53; R of H Trin U Paarl 53-54; Simonstown 54-59; St Barn Capetn 59-63; Somerset W 63-66; Lon Area Sec USPG 66-68; Chap at Baghdad 68-75; Tripoli 75-77. *c/o British Embassy, Tripoli, Libya.*

DAVIES, Geoffrey Francis. b 41. Univ of Capetn BA 62. Em Coll Cam BA (3rd cl Th Trip pt ii) 67, MA 71. Cudd Coll 67. **d** 69 Lon **p** 70 Kens for Lon. C of St Mary The Boltons Kens 69-72; P-in-c of Serowe Botswana 72-76; R of Kalk Bay 76-81; L to Offic Dio Johann from 81. *Box 4849, Johannesburg 2000, S Africa.*

DAVIES, Geoffrey Lovat. b 30. St Aid Coll. **d** 62 **p** 63 Ches. C of Davenham 62-65; Higher Bebington 65-67; V of Witton 67-80; R of Lymm Dio Ches from 80. *Rectory, Lymm, Chesh, WA13 0AL.* (Lymm 2164)

DAVIES, Geoffrey Michael. b 43. St D Coll Lamp Dipl Th 70. **d** 70 **p** 71 Swan B. C of Brynmawr 70-73; St Sav Claremont 73-76; R of The Strand Dio Capetn from 76. *Rectory, The Strand, CP, S Africa.* (3-1208)

DAVIES, Canon George Colliss Boardman. b 12. St Cath Coll Cam 2nd cl Hist Trip pt i 33, BA (3rd cl Hist Trip pt ii) 34, MA 38, BD 47, DD 51. Trin Coll Dub MA and DD *(ad eund)* 59. Univ of Ox DD 81. Lon Coll of Div 34. **d** 37 **p** 38 Guildf. C of Woking 37-39; Perm to Offic Dio Ely 39-40; R of St Clem w St Edm and St Geo Colegate Nor 40-42; N Tamerton 43-51; Kingham 51-56; Beresford Prof of Eccles Hist Trin Coll Dub 56-63; Prof of Pastoral Th 60-63; C-in-c of St Andr Dub 57-60; Treas of St Patr Cathl Dub 62-63; Res Can of Worc 63-77; Can (Emer) from 77; Libr 64-70; Proc Conv Worc 64-70; M Gen Syn 70-75; Vice-Dean 70-74; Treas 70-77; Commiss Kimb K 68-76; Exam Chap to Bp of Worc 71-77; Dir of Post Ordin Stud Dio Worc 71-75; Perm to Offic Dio Ox from 77; Lect Wycl Hall Ox from 78. *53 Blenheim Drive, Oxford, OX2 8DL.* (Oxford 56297)

DAVIES, George Luther Rogers. b 1897. Down Coll Cam BA 20, MA 28. **d** 21 **p** 22 St D. C of Yspytty Ystwyth w Ystradmeurig 21-24; Llandilofawr 24-27; C-in-c of Glais Llansamlet 27-31; R of Llangynllo 31-37; V of Mortletwy w Lawrenny Minwear Newton N and Coedceulas 37-55; Amroth 55-69. *Mör-Awelon, Amroth, Narberth, Dyfed.*

DAVIES, George Vivian. b 21. CCC Cam BA 47, MA 49. Ely Th Coll. **d** 49 **p** 50 Cant. C of St Martin Maidstone 49-51; Folkestone 51-56; V of Leysdown w Harty 56-59; R of Warehorne w Kenardington 59-74; W & E Rounton and Welbury Dio York from 74. *West Rounton Rectory, Northallerton, N Yorks.* (E Harisey 238)

DAVIES, Canon Gideon. Bp Wilson Th Coll IM 33. **d** 36 **p** 37 S & M. C of Malew and Chap of St Mark 36-38; C of Andreas and Chap of St Jude Andreas 38-40; V of Kirk Lonan IM 40-44; C-in-c of St Marg Hasbury 44-45; R of St Andr w St Mary de Witton Droitwich 45-69; R of St Nich w St Pet Droitwich 64-69; C-in-c of Hadzor w Oddingley 64-69; V of Elmley Castle w Netherton and Bricklehampton (and the Combertons from 73) 69-81; RD of Droitwich 52-69; Surr 54-81; Hon Can of Worc from 63; C-in-c of The Combertons 70-73. *c/o Little Comberton Rectory, Pershore, Worcs WR10 3EP.* (Elmley Castle 240)

DAVIES, Glanmor Adrian. b 51. St D Coll Lamp Dipl Th 73. Bp Burgess Hall Lamp 69. **d** 73 **p** 75 St D. C of Llanstadwell 73-78; R of Dinas w Llanllawer Dio St D from 78. *Rectory, Dinas Cross, Dyfed.* (Dinas Cross 348)

DAVIES, Glyn Richards. b 28. **d** 79 **p** 80 Mon (NSM). [Solicitor]; L to Offic Dio Mon from 79. *Yew Tree Cottage, Penylan, Nr Bassaleg, Gwent, NP1 9RW.*

DAVIES, Glenn Naunton. b 50. Univ of Syd BSc 72, BD 79. Moore Th Coll Syd ThM. **d** 81 Syd. C of St Steph Willoughby Dio Syd from 81. *86 Laurel Street, Willoughby, NSW, Australia 2068.*

DAVIES, Graham James. b 35. St D Coll Lamp BA 56. St Mich Coll Llan 56. Episc Th Sch Massachusetts 58. **d** 59 **p** 60 St D. C of Steynton w Johnston 59-61; Llangathen 62-64; Min Can of St D Cathl 64-66; R of Burton 66-71; R of Hubberton 71-74; C of Lenham w Boughton Malherbe 74-80; V of Cwmdeuddwr w Nantgwyllt, St Harmon and Llanwrthwl Dio Swan B from 80. *Cwmdeuddwr Vicarage, Rhayader, Powys, LD6 5AP.* (Rhayader 810574)

DAVIES, Harry Bertram. b 11. Chich Th Coll 70. **d** 70 **p** 71 Portsm. C of Fareham 70-74; R of Lowick w Sudborough and Slipton 74-81; P-in-c of Islip 78-81. *2 Collindale Court, Kingswinford, W Midl.*

DAVIES, Hedleigh Llewelyn. b 17. Worc Coll Ox BA (3rd cl Th) 40, MA 44. Westcott Ho Cam 40. **d** 41 **p** 42 Mon. C of Beaufort 41-48; CF (EC) 43-48; Hon CF 48; C of St Luke W Norwood 48-49; V of St Barn Mitcham 49-54; PC of Motcombe w Enmore Green 54-59; V of Old Catton 59-66; St Andr Nor 66-72; C-in-c of St Mich-at-Pleas w St Pet Hungate Nor 66-72; V of St Mary-in-the-Marsh Nor 67-72; Hon Min Can of Nor 60-66; and from 78; Sacr 66-71; V of Kirstead w Langhale and Brooke Dio Nor from 72. *Brooke Vicarage, Norwich, NR15 1JU.* (Brooke 378)

DAVIES, Canon Henry George Bankole. Univ of Dur (Fourah Bay Coll) BA 41. **d** 42 **p** 43 Sier L. C of St Geo Cathl Freetown 42-47; Miss at Lunsar 47-50; V of St Mich Waterloo 50-52; Tutor at Ora Gr Sch 52-56; Tutor and Chap at CMS Gr Sch Freetown Dio sier L from 56; Can of Sier L from 75. Sier L from 75. *8 Earl Street, Freetown, Sierra Leone.*

DAVIES, Henry Joseph. b 38. Univ of Wales BSc 61. St Mich AA Coll Llan 75. **d** 76 **p** 77 Mon. C of Griffithstown 76-79; V in R Benef of Cwmbran Dio Mon from 80. *Vicarage, Llantarnam, Cwmbran, Gwent, NP44 3BW.*

DAVIES, Canon Henry Lewis. St Jo Coll Dur BA 42, Dipl in Th 43, MA 45. **d** 43 **p** 44 Worc. C of Upton-on-Severn 43-47; St John Dudley 47-49; Halesowen 49-52; V of Cradley 52-65; R of Old Swinford Dio Worc from 65; Hon Can of Worc Cathl from 76. *Old Swinford Rectory, Stourbridge, Worcs.* (Stourbridge 5410)

DAVIES, Herbert Lewis Owen. b 08. Keble Coll Ox BA 31, MA 36. St Steph Ho Ox 31. CBE (Mil) 61. **d** 32 **p** 33 Mon. C of St Paul, Newport 32-35; CF 35-61; Hon Chap to HM the Queen 59-61; R of Newent 61-68; Bourton-on-the-Hill 68-75. *16 Tree Lane, Iffley, Oxford.*

DAVIES, Horace. b 15. Univ of Wales BA 36. St D Coll Lamp 37. **d** 38 Llan **p** 39 Swan B for Llan. C of Treherbert 38-41; Eglwysilan 41-44; Chap of Mon Cathl Ch 44-50; V of Abersychan 50-55; St John Ebbw Vale 55-58; Griffithstown 58-70; RD of Pontypool 62-74; Chepstow from 78; R of Itton and V of St Arvan's and Penterry Dio Mon from 70; R of Kilgwrrwg w Devauden Dio Mon from 81. *St Arvan's Vicarage, Chepstow, Gwent.* (Chepstow 2064)

✠ **DAVIES, Right Rev Howell Haydn.** b 27. ARIBA 55. Tyndale Hall Bris 56. **d** 59 **p** 60 Heref. C of St Pet Heref 59-61; Miss at Kitale 62-63; Warden Ch Tr Centre Kapsabet 64-70; C of Emgwen 69-70; BCMS Field Rep from 69; V of Kericho 70-71; Archd of N Maseno 71-74; Exam Chap to Bp of N Maseno 71-74; to Abp of Nai 74-79; Provost of All SS Cathl Nairobi 74-79; Commiss Maseno N from 79; V of Woking 79-81; Cons Ld Bp of Karamoja in St Phil Pro-Cathl Moroto 27 Sept 81 by Abp of Uganda; Bps of Nam, Ruw, Lango,

Mbale and Soroti. *Karamoja Diocese, Private Bag, PO Kapenguria, Via Kitale, Kenya.*

DAVIES, Hugh Middlecott. b 19. Worc Ordin Coll 58. **d** 59 Stafford for Lich **p** 60 Lich. C of Whitchurch 59-61; R of Scarning w Wendling 61-66; R of Ightfield w Calverhall 66-72; Chap HM Borstal Stoke Heath 70-72; R of Catfield 72-74; Chap Norf and Nor Hosp 74-75; Asst Chap HM Pris Nor 74-77; R of Bunwell w Carleton Rode 75-77; Master of the Charterho Hull 77-80; Lect St Mary's Lowgate 77-80; Chap Addenbrookes Hosp Cam 80-81. *90 Church Lane, Beeston Regis, Sheringham, Norfolk, NR26 8BY.* (0263-824574)

DAVIES, Hugh Richard Howells. b 34. St D Coll Lamp BA 59. **d** 60 **p** 61 Mon. C of St Jo Evang Maindee 60-61; Abergavenny w Llanwenarth Citra 61-64. *46 Beaufort Avenue, Mumbles, Swansea.*

DAVIES, Ian Charles. b 51. Sarum Wells Th Coll 78. **d** 81 Kens for Lon. C of St Mary Virg Bedfont Dio Lon from 81. *77 West Road, Bedfont, Middx. TW14 8JG.*

DAVIES, Ieuan. Univ of Lon BSc (Sociology) 60. K Coll Cam 60. New Coll Ox 63. St Steph Ho Ox 63. **d** 65 **p** 66 Lon. C of St Gabr w All SS Pimlico 65-68; in Amer Ch from 68. *903a Waterside Towers, 901 6th Street, Washington DC, USA.*

DAVIES, Iorwerth Vernon. b 34. Univ of Wales BA (2nd cl Welsh) 55. Fitz Ho Cam BA (2nd cl Th) 57, MA 62. St Mich Coll Llan. **d** 58 **p** 59 Ban. C Glanadda 58-61; Llangefni 61-63; R of Llanllyfni w Talysarn and Penygroes 63-65; Lect Trin Coll Carmarthen 65-72; Dean of Men 72-74; Dep Prin from 74. *Trinity College, Carmarthen, Dyfed.*

DAVIES, Ven Ivor Gordon. b 17. Univ of Wales BA (2nd cl Gr) 39. Univ of Lon BD 51. St Steph Ho Ox 39. **d** 41 **p** 42 Llan. C of St Paul Grangetown 41-44; Cf (EC) 44-47; C of St Jo Bapt Felixstowe 47-49; PC of St Thos Ipswich 49-57; Can Res of S'wark Cathl and Dioc Missr 57-72; Proc Conv S'wark from 64; Archd of Lewisham from 72. *2 St Austell Road, SE13 7EQ.* (01-852 3649)

DAVIES, Canon Ivor Llewelyn. b 23. Univ of Wales BA (2nd cl Phil) 49. St Cath S Ox Dipl Th 52, Fitzw Ho Cam BA (2nd cl Th Trip pt iii) 56, MA 60. Wycl Hall Ox 49. **d** 51 **p** 52 Swan B. C of Knighton w Heyope 51-54; St Andr Gt Cam 54-56; C-in-c of Llanwrthwl w Elan Valley 56-59; R of Llanveigan w Llanthetty and Glyn-Collwng 59-70; C-in-c of Llansantffraed-juxta-Usk 67-70; V of Hay (and Llanigon w Capel-y-Ffin from 72) Dio Swan from 70; RD of Hay from 73; Hon Can of Brecon Cathl 76-79; Can from 79. *Vicarage, Hay-on-Wye, Hereford, HR3 5DQ.* (Hay-on-Wye 820612)

DAVIES, Ivor Llewellyn. b 35. Univ of Wales BA (2nd cl Lat) 56. St Cath S Ox BA (3rd cl Th) 58, MA 63. Wycl Hall Ox 56. **d** 62 **p** 63 St A. C of Wrexham 62-64; Miss in India 65-71; V of Connah's Quay 71-79; P-in-c of Gorsley w Clifford's Mesne and Dioc Dir of Ordinands Dio Glouc from 79. *Gorsley Vicarage, Ross-on-Wye, Herefs, HR9 7SP.* (Gorsley 261)

DAVIES, James Charles. b 16. Worc Ordin Coll. **d** 65 **p** 66 Pet. C of Duston 65-68; R of Yardley Hastings Dio Pet from 68; V of Denton Dio Pet from 68. *Yardley Hastings Rectory, Northampton.* (Yardley Hastings 263)

DAVIES, James Owen. b 26. St Aid Coll 60. **d** 61 Shrewsbury for Lich **p** 62 Stafford for Lich. C of Mkt Drayton 61-65; V of St Jo Evang Tipton 65-70; C-in-c of L Drayton Dio Lich 70-73; V from 73. *Little Drayton Vicarage, Market Drayton, Shropshire, TF9 1DY.* (Mkt Drayton 2801)

DAVIES, James Trevor Eiddig. b 17. St D Coll Lamp BA 39. AKC 41. **d** 41 **p** 42 Mon. C of Rhymney 41-44; St Andr Newport 44-47; C-in-c 47-51; C-in-c of Nash 50-51; R of Bettws Newydd w Trostrey and Kemeys Commander 51-58; V of Blaenavon w Capel Newydd 58-68; Llanfihangel-Llantarnam 68-71; R of Cwmbran Dio Mon from 71; Surr from 76. *Rectory, Clomendy Road, Cwmbran, Gwent, NP4 3LS.*

DAVIES, James William. b 51. Trin Hall Cam BA 72, MA 76. St Jo Coll Dur BA 79. **d** 80 **p** 81 Cant. C of Ch Ch Broad Green Croydon Dio Cant from 80. *15 Chatfield Road, Croydon, Surrey, CR0 3LA.* (01-688 8635)

DAVIES, John. Moore Th Coll 49. **d** 50 **p** 51 C and Goulb. C-in-c of Taralga 50-52; R of Moruya 52-54; Battow w Wondalga 54-57; R of Thuddungra 57-59; on leave 59-60; V of Dromana, Rosebud and McRae 60-74. *6 Currawong Street, Mornington, Vic., Australia 3931.*

DAVIES, John Arthur. St Aid Coll 11. Wycl Coll Tor LTh 18. ED 47. **d** 13 **p** 14 Qu'App. Miss Dio Qu'App 13-14; R of St Paul Dawson 14-19; Roslin 22; Clarksburg w Collingwood Township 22-26; St John St Thos 26-32; RD of Elgin 30-32; R of Kingsville w Grainger 32-48; Dom Chap to Bp of Hur 42-45; Exam Chap 45-54; R of Old St Paul Woodstock 48-55. *774 Grosvenor Street, Woodstock, Ont., Canada.*

DAVIES, Canon John Arthur. b 06. Late Scho of St D Coll Lamp BA (2nd cl Th) 37. Qu Coll Birm 37. **d** 38 **p** 39 Ches. C of All SS Hoole 38-41; CF (EC) 41-46; C-in-c of St Pet Aston-by-Sutton 46-47; V 47-54; Lindow 54-61; PC of Fernilee 61-66; R of Taxal (w Kettleshulme 61-66; w Fernilee from 66) 61-73; Hon Can of Ches 71-73; Can (Emer) from 74; C of Chapel-en-le-Frith 73-75. *53 Milldale Avenue, Buxton, Derbys, SK17 9BG.* (Buxton 2050)

DAVIES, John Atcherley. b 27. St Jo Coll Dur BA 55. Wycl Hall Ox. **d** 57 **p** 58 Chich. C of St Jo Evang Eastbourne 57-61; Chap RN 61-82. *c/o Ministry of Defence, Lacon House, Theobald's Road, WC1X 8RY.*

DAVIES, John Aubrey. b 15. St D Coll Lamp BA 37. **d** 41 Blackb **p** 42 Burnley for Blackb. C of St Paul Preston 41-43; Tring 43-47; V of Nettleden w Potten End 47-64; R (P-in-c from 75) of Essendon w Woodhill 64-76; R of L Berkhamsted (w Bayford, Essendon and Ponsbourne from 76) 75-80. *7 St Nicholas Way, Coggeshall, Essex, CO6 1PX.* (Coggeshall 62462)

DAVIES, John Barden. b 47. Univ of Wales (Ban) Dipl Th 70. Burgess Hall Lamp 70. **d** 71 **p** 72 St A. C of Rhosllanerchrugog 71-75; R of Llanbedr-y-Cennin w Dolgarrog, Trefriw and Llanrhychwyn Dio Ban from 75. *Llanbedr Rectory, Conway, Gwyn.* (Tyngroes 231)

DAVIES, John Byron. b 38. St D Coll Lamp BA 60. Dipl Th 62. **d** 62 **p** 63. St D. C of Ch Ch Llanelly 62-67; V of Llanpumsaint 67-74; Dafen Dio St D from 74. *Dafen Vicarage, Llanelly, Dyfed.* (Llanelly 4730)

DAVIES, Preb John Conway de la Tour. b 16. Late Scho of Jes Coll Cam 2nd cl Nat Sc Trip pt i 37, BA 38, 3rd cl Th Trip pt i and Lady Kay Scho 39, MA 42. Ripon Hall Ox 39. **d** 40 **p** 41 Ox. C of Chipping Norton and Heythrop 40-44; CF 44-52; Hon CF 52; V of Highter's Heath 52-57; Peterchurch Dio Heref from 57; V of Vowchurch w Turnastone Dio Heref from 57; P-in-c of Bredwardine w Brobury, of Moccas and of Dorstone Dio Heref from 77; RD of Abbeydore from 78; Preb of Heref Cathl from 79. *Vicarage, Peterchurch, Herefs, HR2 0SJ.* (Peterchurch 374)

DAVIES, Canon John Dudley. b 27. Trin Coll Cam 2nd cl Engl Trip pt i 50, BA (2nd cl Th Trip pt 1a) 51, MA 63. Linc Th Coll 52. **d** 53 **p** 54 Ripon. C of Halton 53-56; Yeoville Transv 57; R of Evander Transv 57-61; R and Dir of Empangeni 61-63; Chap Univ of Witwatersrand Johann 63-71; Sec for Chaplaincies in Higher Educn C of E Bd of Educn 71-74; Perm to Offic Dio S'wark 72-74; Chap Univ of Keele 74-76; C-in-c of Keele 74-76; Prin Coll of Ascen Selly Oak Birm 76-81; Preb of Lich Cathl from 76; Res Can of St A Cathl and Dioc Missr Dio St A from 82. *1 Llys Trewithan, Mount Road, St Asaph, Clwyd, LL17 0DF.* (0745-582882)

DAVIES, Ven John Edward. b 08. Univ of Wales BA (2nd cl Welsh) 31. Jes Coll Ox 32. St Mich Coll Llan 34. **d** 35 **p** 36 St A. C of Wrexham 35-39; Abergele 39-42; V Cho of St A Cathl 42-44; V of Llanasa 44-54; Mold 54-73; Cursal Can of Johannes Griffith in St A Cathl 65-69; Preb of Meliden in St A Cathl from 69; Archd of Wrexham 69-78; Exam Chap to Bp of St A from 71; V of Llanrhaeadr-yng-Nghinmerch and Prion 73-78; Archd (Emer) from 78. *Rectory, Llandyrnog, Denbigh, Clwyd.* (Landyrnog 578)

DAVIES, John Edward. Univ of NSW BSc 60. BD (2nd cl) Lon 65. Moore Th Coll Syd ACT ThL 65. **d** 65 **p** 66 Syd. C of St Paul Wahroonga 66; Asst Master Abbotsleigh Sch 66; Caringbah 67-71; C-in-c of Jannali w Como Provisional Par 71-74; R 74-78; Northbridge Dio Syd from 78. *17 Tunks Street, Northbridge, NSW, Australia 2063.* (95-5794)

DAVIES, John Edwards Gurnos. b 18. Ch Coll Cam 3rd cl Cl Trip pt i 39. BA (3rd cl Th Trip pt i) 41, MA 45. Westcott Ho Cam 40. **d** 42 **p** 43 Ches. C of St Paul Portwood 42-44; CF (EC) 44-46; CF 46-73; ACG 70; Hon Chap to HM the Queen 72; V of Monk Sherborne w Pamber 73-76; R of The Sherbornes w Pamber Dio Win from 76. *Sherborne St John Rectory, Basingstoke, Hants, RG24 9HX.* (Basingstoke 850434)

DAVIES, Canon John Evan. b 05. Univ of Wales BA 34. St Mich Coll Llan 34. **d** 36 **p** 37 St D. C of Hubberston 36-38; Min of St Padarn Welsh Ch Isl 38-40; C of Brynamman 40-42; V of Mynachlogddu w Llangolman 42-47; Llanrhystid (w Llanddeiniol from 56) 47-62; RD of Glynaeron 58-62; V of Llandybie 62-70; Penbryn w Blaen-Porth 70-74; Hon Can of St D Cathl from 72. *Leeside, Cwmcoy, Newcastle Emlyn, Dyfed.*

DAVIES, Canon John Gordon. b 19. Ch Ch Ox BA 2nd cl Th 42, MA 45, BD 46, DD 56. Univ of St Andr Hon DD 68. Westcott Ho Cam 42. **d** 43 Kingston-T for S'wark **p** 44 S'wark. C of Rotherhithe 43-48; L Pr Dio Birm from 48; Asst Lect in Th Univ of Birm 48-50; Lect 50-56; Sen Lect 56-59; Reader 59-60; Prof and Hd Dept of Th from 60; Dir Inst Study of Worship and Relig Archit from 62; Select Pr Univ of Cam 61; Univ of Ox 79; Hon Can of Birm from 65. *28 George Road, Birmingham, B15 1PJ.* (021-454 6254)

DAVIES, John Gwylim. b 27. Ripon Hall Ox. **d** 70 **p** 71 Ox. C of St Mich Ox 70-72; Team V of New Windsor 73-77; R of

Hagley Dio Worc from 77. *Church Centre, St Saviour's, Hagley, Stourbridge, W Midl, DY9 0NS.* (Hagley 886363)

DAVIES, John Gwyn. b 12. St Cath Coll Cam 3rd cl Hist Trip pt i 35, BA (3rd cl Th Trip pt i) 36, MA 40. Ely Th Coll 36. **d** 37 **p** 38 Blackb. C of St Pet Fleetwood 37-39; Wyken 39-44; C-in-c 44-45; V 45-54; Rowington 54-77; Chap to K Edw VII Chest Hosp Warw from 68; L to Offic Dio Cov from 78. *Lapwater, Pinley, Claverdon, Warwick, CV35 8NA.* (Claverdon 2597)

DAVIES, Canon John Howard. b 29. Late Scho of St Jo Coll Cam 1st cl Mus Trip pt i 49, BA 50, 1st cl Th Trip pt ii 51, 2nd cl Th Trip pt iii 52, MA 54. BD (Nottm) 62. Westcott Ho Cam 54. **d** 55 **p** 56 Derby. Succr Derby Cathl 55-58; Chap Westcott Ho Cam 58-63; Perm to Offic Dio Ely 61-63; Lect (Sen from 74) in Th Univ of Southn 63-81; Dir of Stud from 81; L to Offic Dio Win from 63; Can Th Win Cathl from 81. *13 Glen Eyre Road, Southampton.* (Southn 769359)

DAVIES, Canon John Howard. b 35. Ely Th Coll 62. **d** 64 **p** 65 Worc. C of All SS Bromsgrove 64-67; Astwood Bank w Crabbs Cross 67-70; R of St Martin (w St Pet from 74) Worc 70-79; C-in-c of St Pet Worc 72-74; M Gen Syn from 75; RD of Worc E 77-79; R of Malvern Link w Cowleigh Dio Worc from 79; Hon Can Worc Cathl from 81. *12 Lambourne Avenue, Malvern Link, Worcs, WR14 1NL.* (Malvern 3834)

DAVIES, John Hywel Morgan. b 45. St D Coll Lamp BA 71, LTh 73. Bp Burgess Hall Lamp 71. **d** 73 **p** 74 St D. C of Milford Haven 73-77; R of Castlemartin w Warren, Angle and Rhoscrowdder w Pwllcrochan Dio St D from 77. *Rectory, Angle, Pembroke, Dyfed.* (Angle 443)

DAVIES, John Ifor. b 20. **d** 80 Liv **p** 81 Warrington for Liv. C of Allerton Dio Liv from 80. *20 Calderstones Road, Liverpool, L18.*

DAVIES, John James. b 12. St D Coll Lamp BA 33. **d** 40 **p** 42 Llan. C of Michaelston-super-Avon 40-44; Eglwysilan (in c of St Jas Taffs Well) 44-48; Llangynwyd w Baiden and Maesteg 48-53; V of Tylorstown 53-61; V of All SS Darlaston 61-67; Hednesford 67-77; P-in-c of Kynnersley, of Tibberton and of Preston Wealdmoors 77-78; R of Tibberton w Kynnersley and Preston Wealdmoors Dio Lich from 78. *Tibberton Rectory, Newport, Salop.* (Sambrook 409)

DAVIES, John Lewis. St D Coll Lamp BA 20. **d** 21 Llan **p** 22 Mon. C of St Dingat New Tredegar 21-26; Ormesby St Marg w Scratby and Ormesby St Mich 26-28; V of Binham (w Cockthorpe from 29) 28-34; R of L Cressingham w Threxton 34-54; RD of Breckles 50-54; Heacham 56-64; V of Sedgeford w Southmere R 54-64. *2 Victoria Avenue, Hunstanton, Norf.*

DAVIES, John Melvyn George. b 37. Wycl Hall Ox 68. **d** 71 **p** 72 Ches. C of Norbury 71-75; Heswall 75-78; V of Claughton w Grange Dio Ches from 78. *7 Palm Grove, Birkenhead, Mer, L43 1TE.* (051-652 5647)

DAVIES, John Neville Milwyn. b 27. MBE (Mil) 45. Univ of Wales BA (2nd cl Hist) 37. St Steph Ho Ox 37. **d** 38 Mon **p** 39 Llan for Mon. C of St Mary Virg Mon 38-40; Roath 40-41; Perm to Offic Dio St D 41-42; CF 42-72; DACG 1 Corps BAOR 62-66; Asst Chap Gen N Commd 66-71; L to Offic Dio York 66-71; V of H Spirit Clapham 72-80; SCF from 80. *Whatmer House, 81 Island Road, Sturry, Canterbury, Kent, CT2 0EF.*

DAVIES, John Oswell. b 27. St D Coll Lamp 74. **d** 75 **p** 76 St D. C of Henfynyw w Aberaeron & Aberarth 75-76; P-in-c of Eglwysnewydd w Yspytty-Ystwyth Dio St D 76-77; V from 77. *Eglwysnewydd Vicarage, Cwm Ystwyth, Aberystwyth, Dyfed.* (Pontrhydygroes 233)

DAVIES, John Rees. b 07. St D Coll Lamp BA 38. **d** 41 **p** 42 Llan. C of Nantymoel 41-44; Dowlais 44-48; Skewen 48-54; V of Maerdy 54-67; Resolven 67-77. *24 Broniestyn Terrace, Trecynon, Aberdare, Mid-Glam, CF44 8EG.*

DAVIES, Ven John Roberts. Univ of Dalhousie NS MA 36. Trin Coll Tor LTh 31. **d** 30 **p** 31 NS. C of All SS Cathl Halifax 30-34; St Thos Tor 34-38; R of Yarmouth 38-42; I of Kentville 42-51; Liv 51-58; Can of St Pet Cathl Charlottetown 58-67; R 58-67; Archd of PEI 62-67; Archd (Emer) from 67; C of All SS Cathl Halifax Dio NS from 67. *1165 Rockliffe Street, Halifax, NS, Canada.* (429-3151)

DAVIES, John Stewart. b 43. Univ of Wales (Bangor) BA 72. Qu Coll Cam MLitt 75. Westcott Ho Cam 72. **d** 74 **p** 75 St A. C of Hawarden 74-78; V of Rhosymedre Dio St A from 78. *Rhosymedre Vicarage, Wrexham, Clwyd.* (Ruabon 822125)

DAVIES, John Treharne. b 14. St D Coll Lamp BA 36. **d** 38 **p** 39 Swan B. C of St Matt w Greenhill Swansea 38-42; Calne 42-52; V of Bradpole 52-59; Potterne 59-73; V of Worton 67-73; RD of Devizes 65-73; C-in-c of Ramsbury w Axford 73-74; R of Whitton 74-81; Can and Preb of Sarum Cathl 72-81. *16 Lambourne Close, Ledbury, Herefs.*

DAVIES, John Vernon. b 16. Late Exhib of Or Coll Ox BA (3rd cl Th) 40, MA 43. Cudd Coll 40. **d** 41 **p** 42 Llan. C of Llantwit Fardre 41-44; St Martin Roath 44-45; Peterston-super-Ely 47-51; C-in-c of Flemingston and Gileston Dio Llan 51-54; R 54-56; Org Sec for SPCK Dio Llan 55-64; V of St Andr w St Teilo Cardiff 56-69; R of Radyr Dio Llan from 69. *Rectory, Radyr, Cardiff.* (Cardiff 842 417)

DAVIES, John Vernon. b 20. Clifton Th Coll 66. **d** 68 **p** 69 S'wark. C of Ch Ch, Surbiton Hill 68-70; St Jo Evang Heatherlands Parkstone 70-75; V of St Mich AA Southfields Dio S'wark from 75. *73 Wimbledon Park Road, SW18 5TT.* (01-874 7682)

DAVIES, John William. b 38. Ridley Coll Melb 77. **d** and **p** 81 Gippsld. P-in-c of Nowa Nowa w Lake Tyers Dio Gippsld from 81. *Clergy House, Nowa Nowa, Vic, Australia 3887.*

DAVIES, Johnston ap Llynfi. b 28. St D Coll Lamp BA 51. St Mich Coll Llan. **d** 53 **p** 54 Swan B. C of Ch Ch Swansea 53-55; Sketty 55-57; Bp's Chap to Mining Commun N Nig 57-61; Exam Chap to Bp of N Nig 57-61; R of Whittington Derbys 61-64; Chap Broadmoor Hosp 64-66; Perm to Offic Dio Ox 67-72; Dio York from 72. *6 Greenlands, Hutton Rudgy, Yarm, Cleve, TS15 0JQ.* (Stokesley 700240)

DAVIES, Joseph Henry. b 17. St D Coll Lamp BA 40. St Mich Coll Llan 40. **d** 41 **p** 42 St A. C of Rhosllanerchrugog 41-46; Llanrhos (in c of Deganwy) Llandudno 46-49; V of Fauls 49-52; St Alkmund Shrewsbury and Chap R Salop Infirm 52-57; R of Mucklestone 57-66; V of Barlaston 66-78; R of Mucklestone Dio Lich from 78. *Mucklestone Rectory, Market Drayton, Salop.* (Ashley 2132)

DAVIES, Canon Josiah Jones. b 15. MBE 74. St D Coll Lamp BA 36. Univ of Wales Hon MA 72. **d** 38 **p** 39 Swan B. C of Llanguicke 38-43; Chap RNVR 43-46; V of Llywel (w Traenglas) from 53) Dio Swan B from 47; RD of Brecon ii 58-76; Hon Can of Brecon Cathl from 72. *Llywel Vicarage, Trecastle, Powys, LD3 8UW.* (Sennybridge 481)

DAVIES, Canon Kenneth. b 14. Univ of Wales BA 37. Dorch Miss Coll 37. **d** 39 Tewkesbury for Glouc **p** 40 Glouc. C of St Barn Tuffley 39-41; Actg C of St Mary Stafford 41-42; St Anselm Belmont 42-45; Knighton 45-50; V of St Alb Leic 50-78; Hon Can of Leic 65-81; Can (Emer) from 81; Master of Wyggeston's Hosp and L to Offic Dio Leic from 78. *Wyggeston's Hospital, Hinckley Road, Leicester, LE3 0UX.* (Leic 548682)

DAVIES, Kenneth John. b 42. Ripon Coll Cudd 79. **d** 80 Dorch for Ox **p** 81 Ox. C of Buckingham Dio Ox from 80. *5 Chandos Close, Buckingham, MK18 1AW.*

DAVIES, Laurence Gordon. b 28. Down Coll Cam BA 52, MA 56. Linc Th Coll 52. **d** 54 **p** 55 S'wark. C of St Jo Evang E Dulwich 54-57; All SS Maidenhead 57-61; V of Brigstock w Stanion 61-69; R of Gt w L Billing Dio Pet from 69. *Great Billing Rectory, Northampton, NN3 4ED.* (Northn 407163)

DAVIES, Lawford Idwal. b 32. St D Coll Lamp Dipl Th 63. **d** 63 **p** 64 St D. C of Llanelly 63-70; Team V of Tenby (V of Penally) 70-78; R of St Florence w Redberth Dio St D from 78; V of Penally Dio St D from 78. *Vicarage, Penally, Tenby, Dyfed, SA70 7PN.*

DAVIES, Lawrence. b 14. Late Scho and Exhib of St D Coll Lamp BA (2nd cl Hist) 36. Chich Th Coll 36. **d** 38 **p** 39 St A. C of Ruabon 38-45; Chap RNVR 45-48; RN 48-53; V of Longdon (w Bushley and Queenhill w Holdfast from 78) Dio Worc from 54; Queenhill 54-78; RD of Upton from 81. *Longdon Vicarage, Tewkesbury, Glos, GL20 6AT.* (Birtsmorton 256)

DAVIES, Lawrence. b 20. BEM 45. Tyndale Hall Bris 46. **d** 49 Dunwich for Ely **p** 50 Bp Walsh for Ely. C of St Paul Cam (in c of St Martin from 50) 49-54; V of St Ann Nottm and Chap Coppice Hosp Nottm 54-61; V of All SS Preston 61-73; St Mich-on-Wyre Dio Blackb from 73. *Vicarage, St Michael's-on-Wyre, Preston, Lancs, PR3 0TQ.* (Michael-on-Wyre 242)

DAVIES, Lawrence John David Llewellin. b 16. Jes Coll Ox BA 39, MA 43, Schoolmaster Stud 67. Univ of Bonn ThD 58. Ripon Hall Ox 39. **d** 39 **p** 40 St D. C of Narberth w Robeston Wathen and Mounton 39-48; Chap RM Signalling Sch 44-46; RN Arms Depot Trecwn 46-48; TA (R of O) 47-48; RAF 48-57 Perm to Offic Dio Ox 57-62, 66-67 and from 81; L to Offic 62-66 and 67-81; Dean of Chap and Hd Div Dept Slough Technical High Sch (The Herschel High Sch from 71) 59-80. *Deans Lodge, Hollybush Hill, Stoke Poges, Slough, SL2 4PZ.* (Fulmer 2495)

DAVIES, Lawrence Stanley Richard Gilbert. **d** 56 **p** 57 Win. C of St Jo Evang Boscombe Bournemouth 56-58; V of Cosby Leics 58-61; R of Emu Plains w Castlereagh 61-62; Pris Chap Emu Plains 61-62; R of Rockingham w Safety Bay 62-65; V of Metfield w Withersdale 65-70. *10 Chatsworth Road, Highgate, W Australia 6000.*

DAVIES, Lawrence Vercoe. b 40. Lich Th Coll 67. **d** 70 Bp T M Hughes for Llan **p** 71 Llan. C of Glan Ely 70-77; Insp for Schs Dio Lan 75-77; V of St Paul Grangetown Cardiff Dio Llan from 77. *St Paul's Vicarage, Grangetown, Cardiff.* (Cardiff 28707)

DAVIES, Canon Leslie Lobbett John. Keble Coll Ox BA (3rd cl Mod Hist) 30, MA 38. MC 43. Wells Th Coll 33. **d** 34

p 35 Swan B. C of Kilvey 34-36; St Mary Brecon and Min Can of Brecon Cathl 36-39; CF TA (R of O) 36-38; CF (TA) from 38; CF (EC) 39-45; V of St D Brecon (w Llanilltyd from 51) 45-54; Surr from 46; C-in-c of Llanilltyd 51-54; V of Milford Haven 54-68; St Mary Haverfordwest 68-77; Hon Chap Miss to Seamen from 54; Can of St D Cathl from 65. *Boyne House, Cardigan Road, Haverfordwest, Dyfed.*

DAVIES, Canon Lorys Martin. b 36. Late Scho and Exhib. St D Coll Lamp BA (2nd cl Hist) 57. ALCM 52. Wells Th Coll 57. **d** 59 **p** 60 St D. C of Tenby 59-62; Asst Chap Brentwood Sch 62-66; Chap Solihull Sch and Perm to Offic Dio Birm 66-68; V of Moseley 68-81; Surr from 74; Hon Can of Birm Cathl 81; Can Res from 81; Dioc Dir of Ordinands from 82. *119 Selly Park Road, Birmingham, B29 7HY.*

DAVIES, Malcolm Thomas. b 36. St Mich Coll Llan 71. **d** 73 **p** 74 St D. C of Bettws w Ammanford 73-76; V of Cilycwm w Ystradffin, Rhandirmwyn and Llanfair-ar-y-Bryn 76-80; Llangyfelach Dio Swan B from 80. *Vicarage, Swansea Road, Llangyfelach, W Glam.* (Swansea 74120)

DAVIES, Mervyn Morgan. b 25. Univ Coll of S Wales BA 49. Coll of Resurr Mirfield 49. **d** 51 **p** 52 Llan. C of Penarth w Lavernock 51-58; L to Offic Dio Wakef 58-60; C of Port Talbot 60-63; V of Pontycymmer w Blaengarw 63-69; Fairwater Dio Llan from 69; RD of Llandaff from 81. *St Peter's Vicarage, St Fagan's Road, Fairwater, Cardiff.* (Cardiff 562551)

DAVIES, Meurig Ceredig. Univ of Wales BA 43. St Mich Coll Llan. **d** 45 **p** 46 St D. C of Llangeler 45-47; Llanfihangel-Geneu'r-Glyn 47-49; Llandyry Pembrey 49-51; V of Gwynfe w Llanddeusant 51-55; CF 56-59; V of Clydach Vale 59-61; Perm to Offic Dio Pet 64-74; V of St Dogmael's w Llantood (w Moylgrove and Monington from 77) Dio St D from 74. *St Dogmael's Vicarage, Cardigan, Dyfed.* (Cardigan 2030)

DAVIES, Morgan Llewellyn. b 05. Univ of Wales BA 35. St Mich Coll Llan 35. **d** 37 **p** 38 St D. C of St Paul Llanelly 37-40; Ch Ch Llanelly 40-41; C-in-c of Bosherton w St Twynnell 41-44; R of Ludchurch 44-49; PC of Templeton 44-49; V of Cwmamman 49-72; Surr 54-72; RD of Llandilo 58-65; Duffryn Aman 65-72; Can of St D Cathl 67-72. *11 Stepney Road, Garnant, Dyfed.*

DAVIES, Mostyn David. b 37. K Coll Lon and Warm AKC 64. **d** 65 **p** 66 Pet. C of St Columba, Corby 65-69; Industr Chap Dio Pet from 69; P-in-c of St Barn City and Dio Pet from 81. *16 Swanspool, Ravensthorpe, Peterborough PE3 7LS.*

DAVIES, Myles Cooper. b 50. Sarum Wells Th Coll 71. **d** 74 Warrington for Liv **p** 75 Liv. C of W Derby 74-77; Seaforth Dio Liv 77-80; V from 80. *St Thomas's Vicarage, Elm Road, Seaforth, Liverpool, L21 1BH.* (051-928 1889)

DAVIES, Neil Anthony Bowen. b 52. Univ of Ex BSc 74. Westcott Ho Cam 75. **d** 78 Bp Reece for Llan **p** 79 Llan. C of Llanblethian w Cowbridge 78-80; Aberdare Dio Llan From 80. *9 College Street, Aberdare, Mid Glam, CF44 0RN.* (Aberdare 872765)

DAVIES, Nigel Eric. b 20. Codr Coll Barb 39. **d** 43 **p** 44 Barb. C of St Leon Barb 43-46; Ch Ch Barb 46; Gt w L Driffield 47-50; Skelton-in-Cleveland and Upleatham 50-56; Ash w Ash Vale 56-57; V of Leeming Dio Ripon from 57. *Leeming Vicarage, Northallerton, Yorks. DL7 9SS.*

DAVIES, Norman Edward. b 37. Worc Coll Ox 2nd cl Cl Mods 60, BA (2nd cl Th) 62, Denyer and Johnson Pri 63. Cudd Coll 62. **d** 64 **p** 65 S'wark. C of Mottingham Dio S'wark 64-75; Asst Master Crown Woods Sch 71-75; Hd Master W Hatch Sch Chigwell from 76; Exam Chap to Bp of S'wark from 77; Hon C of Trin Eltham Dio S'wark from 77. *23 Beechhill Road, SE9 1HJ.* (01-850 8595)

DAVIES, Oliver. b 04. St Jo Coll Dur 50. **d** 52 **p** 53 Worc. C of St Andr (in c of St Pet) Dudley 52-56; R of Knightwick w Doddenham and Broadwas 56-72; Chap Knightwick Sanat 56-63. *Cartref, The Strand, Charlton, Pershore, Worcs, WR10 3JZ.* (Evesham 860157)

DAVIES, Paul Martin. b 35. Univ of Lon BD 75. Sarum Wells Th Coll 75. **d** 75 **p** 76 Chelmsf. C of St Mary w St Steph Walthamstow 75-79; CMS Miss Dio Nak from 79. *c/o Box 56, Nakuru, Kenya.*

DAVIES, Percy Sharples. b 10. Univ of Wales BA 32. St Steph Ho Ox 32. **d** 34 **p** 35 St A. C of Hanmer (in c of St Mary Magd Tallarn Green) 34-40; St Geo Perry Hill 40-44; C-in-c of St Paul Forest Hill 44-51; V of St Mark (w St Marg from 67) Plumstead 51-77. *149a Middle Street, Deal, Kent.*

DAVIES, Peter Hassall. **d** 57 **p** 59 C & Goulb. C of Young 57-59; R of Koorawatha 59-63; Tarcutta 63-66; Binda 66-69; Longreach 69-73; Hon Can of Rockptn 71-77; R of St Matt Pk Avenue Rockptn 73-77; Yass Dio C & Goulb from 77. *Box 25, Yass, NSW, Australia 2582.* (062-26 1089)

DAVIES, Peter Richard. b 32. St Jo Coll Ox 3rd cl Cl Mods 53, BA (2nd cl Th) 55, MA 58. Westcott Ho Cam. **d** 58 Lich **p** 59 Stafford for Lich. C of Cannock 58-62; Asst Chap Prince of Wales Sch Nai 63-66; Chap Nai Sch 66-76; Bedford Sch from 76. *Bedford School, Bedford.*

DAVIES, Peter Timothy William. b 50. Univ of Leeds BSc 74. Oak Hill Coll 75. **d** 78 **p** 79 S'wark. C of Kingston Hill 78-81; Bp Hannington Mem Ch w H Cross Hove Dio Chich from 81. *19 Rutland Gardens, Hove, E Sussex.* (Brighton 734165)

DAVIES, Philip Bertram. b 33. Cudd Coll 61. **d** 63 Hulme for Man **p** 64 Man. C of Atherton 63-66; V of Winton 66-71; R of St Phil w St Steph Salford 71-75; V of Radlett Dio St Alb from 76; RD of Aldenham from 79. *13 Christ Church Crescent, Radlett, Herts, WD7 8AG.* (Radlett 6606)

DAVIES, Ramond Emlyn Peter. b 25. St Mich Coll Llan 51. **d** 53 **p** 54 llan. C of Llangeinor 53-58; Llanishen w Lisvane Dio Llan 58-62 and 65-68; V of Avan Vale 62-65; Penrhiwceiber 68-72; C of Whitchurch 72-73; V of Childs Ercall 73-81; R of Stoke-on-Tern 73-81; R of Mavesyn Ridware Dio Lich from 81; Hamstall Ridware Dio Lich from 81; V of Pipe Ridware Dio Lich from 81. *Rectory, Uttoxeter Road, Hill Ridware, Rugeley, Staffs.* (Armitage 490984)

DAVIES, Raymond Thomas Edward. b 15. Late Scho and Exhib of St D Coll Lamp BA (1st cl Hist) 38. St Mich Coll Llan 38. **d** 39 Ban for Llan **p** 41 Llan. C of St Jo Bapt Cardiff 39-41; Treherbert 41-46; Aberaman 46-48; Bedlinog 48-53; V of Colwinston 53-58; Chap at Morgannwg Hosp Bridgend from 58. *Morgannwg Hospital, Bridgend, Mid Glam.* (Bridgend 3391)

DAVIES, Rees Jeffrey. b 1883. Hatf Coll Dur LTh 08, BA 13, MA 17. **d** 08 **p** 09 Dur. C of Cassop w Quarrington 08-10; Coxhoe 10-15; Whitburn 15-22; R of Norris Bank 22-36; Weston-Colville 36-75; Westley Waterless 36-38. *c/o Westley Rectory, Newmarket, Suff.* (Stetchworth 263)

DAVIES, Reginald Charles. b 33. Tyndale Hall Bris 58. **d** 64 **p** 65 Man. C of St Jas Heywood 64-66; Drypool 66-69; V of Denaby Main Dio Sheff from 69. *Denaby Main Vicarage, Doncaster, Yorks.* (Rotherham 862297)

DAVIES, Rendle Leslie. b 29. St Chad's Coll Dur BA 52, Dipl Th 54. **d** 54 **p** 55 Mon. C of Monmouth 54-58; V of Llangwm Uchaf 58-63; Usk w Monkswood Glascoed and Gwehelog Dio Mon from 63; Chap HM Borstal Inst Usk from 63. *Vicarage, Usk, Gwent, NP5 1AA.* (Usk 2653)

DAVIES, Richard Henry. b 44. Mansfield Coll Ox BA (Th) 72, MA 78. St Steph Ho Ox 68. **d** 72 Bp Graham-Campbell for Cant for Pet **p** 73 Pet. C of Higham Ferrers w Chelveston 72-80; Cantley Dio Sheff from 80. *200 Cantley Lane, Doncaster, S Yorks.* (Doncaster 55133)

DAVIES, Richard Henry Heard Lloyd. Em Coll Sktn 60. **d** 60 **p** 61 Sktn. I of Wilkie and of Kerrobert 60-63; Miss at Kytton 63-67; R of Ashcroft 67-69; V of Abberly 69-70; L to Offic Dio Koot 70-75; P-in-c of St Mary Virg City and Dio Bran from 75. *415 1st Street, Brandon, Manit., Canada.*

DAVIES, Richard James. b 42. Peterho Cam BA 64, MA 68. St Steph Ho Ox 67. **d** 69 Chich for Matab **p** 70 Matab. C of Nyamandhlovu 69-72; St Mich Southwick 72-74; P-in-c of Westport 75; C of Stoke 75-76; V of Atawhai-Hira 77-78; Exam Chap to Bp of Nel 76-78; Perm to Offic Dio Nel from 78. *4 Tory Street, Nelson, NZ.*

DAVIES, Richard Paul. b 48. Wycl Hall Ox 72. **d** 75 Warrington for Liv **p** 76 Liv. C of St Sav w St Cuthb Everton 75-78; Asst Chap Basingstoke Distr Hosp 78-80; Team V of Basinstoke Dio Win from 80. *62 Cumberland Avenue, Basingstoke, RG22 4BQ.* (Basinstoke 65666)

DAVIES, Robert. **d** 60 **p** 61 Ban. C of Llanllyfni 60-63; C-in-c of Llangurig 63-65; R of Trefriw w Llanrhychwyn 65-71; V of Llangwyllog w Coedana 71-75; Llannerchymedd w Rhodgeidio w Gwredog 71-75; R of Maentwrog w Trawsfynydd 75-77; Perm to Offic Dio Ban from 77. *31 Bro Infryn, Glasinfryn, Bangor.*

✠ **DAVIES, Right Rev Robert Edward.** CBE 81. Univ of Queensld MA 52. St Jo Coll Morpeth ACT ThL 36, ThD 60. **d** 37 **p** 38 Newc. C of Cathl Ch Newc 37-41; Chap Toc H 41-42; Chap RAAF 42-45; Miss Chap Brisb 46-48; Vice-Warden St Jo Coll Brisb 46-48; R of Canberra 49-53; Archd of Canberra 49-53; R and Archd of Wagga Wagga 53-60; Warden St Jo Coll Morpeth 60-63; Hon Can of Newc 60-63; Cons Asst Bp of Newc in St Andr Cathl Syd 7 June 60 by Abp of Syd; Bps of C & Goulb; Armid; Newc; Graft; Bath; Wang; and Rockptn; Bps Kerle; Loane; Hudson; and Arthur; Apptd Ld Bp of Tas 63; res 81. *12 Elboden Street, Hobart, Tasmania 7000.*

DAVIES, Robert Mark. b 53. Univ of Nottm BTh 79. St Jo Coll Nottm 76. **d** 79 **p** 80 Roch. C of SS Pet & Paul Tonbridge Dio Roch from 79. *6 London Road, Tonbridge, Kent, TN10 3AH.*

DAVIES, Canon Robert Thomas Cecil. b 05. Univ of Wales BA 31. **d** 30 **p** 31 St A. C of Rhosddu 30-40; CF (EC) 40-45; Hon CF 45; C of Wrexham 45-48; V of Holt (w Isycoed from 55) 48-59; Gwersyllt 59-75; RD of Wrexham 66-75; Cursal

Can of St Asaph Cathl from 70. *15 Acton Road, Wrexham.* (Wrexham 56489)

DAVIES, Roger Charles. b 46. Univ of S Wales & Mon BD 73. St Mich AA Coll Llan 69. **d** 73 **p** 74 Llan. C of Llanfabon 73-76; CF (TAVR) from 75; C of Llanblethian 76-78; CF from 78. *c/o Ministry of Defence, Bagshot Park, Bagshot, Surrey, GU19 5PL.*

DAVIES, Canon Ronald. Univ of Wales BA 36. St Steph Ho Ox 36. **d** 39 Llan for Mon **p** 40 Mon. C of St Mary Mon 39-42; Ch Ch Newport 42-44; St Jas Tredegar 44-48; V of St Matt Maindee Newport 48-60; V of H Trin Abergavenny Dio Mon from 60; RD of Abergavenny from 67; Surr from 76; Can of Mon from 77. *Holy Trinity Vicarage, Baker Street, Abergavenny, Mon.* (Abergavenny 203)

DAVIES, Ronald Owen. St Mich Th Coll Crafers 50. ACT ThL 55. **d** 53 **p** 54 Perth. C of St Hilda Perth 53-56; R of Dalwallinu 56-62; Belmont 62-68; Beaconsfield 68-74; Macarthur 74-80; Beaufort Dio Bal from 80. *Rectory, Beaufort, Vic, Australia 3373.*

DAVIES, Roswell Morgan. b 22. St D Coll Lamp BA 46. **d** 48 **p** 49 Swan B. C of St Thos Swansea 48-50; St Pet Cockett Swansea 50-56; R of Bryngwyn w Newchurch Llanbedr-Painscastle and Llanddewi Fach 56-63; V of Rhayader (w Nantmel from 76) Dio Swan B from 63. *Vicarage, Rhayader, Powys.* (Rhayader 810223)

DAVIES, Roy Basil. b 34. Univ of Bris BA (2nd cl Hist) 55. Westcott Ho Cam 57. **d** 59 St E **p** 60 Dunwich for St E. C of St Mary-le-Tower Ipswich 59-63; C of Clun w Chapel Lawn 63-70; V of Bp's Castle w Mainstone Dio Heref from 70; P-in-c of More w Lydham Dio Heref from 70; Snead Dio Heref from 70; RD of Clun Forest from 72. *Vicarage, Bishop's Castle, Salop, SY9 5AF.* (Bp's Castle 445)

DAVIES, Roy Gabe. Dipl Th (Wales) 64. St Mich Coll Llan 61. **d** 64 **p** 65 St D. C of St Issells 64-65; Milford Haven 65-67; Codsall 67-70; V of St Steph Wolverhampton 70-79; St Julian Newport Dio Mon from 79. *41 St Julian's Avenue, Newport, Gwent, NPT 7JT.* (Newport 58046)

DAVIES, Roy Thomas. b 34. Late Scho of St D Coll Lamp BA (1st cl Welsh) 55. Late Meyricke Grad Scho of Jes Coll Ox Dipl Th 58, BLitt 59. St Steph Ho Ox 57. **d** 59 **p** 60 St D. C of St Paul Llanelly 59-64; V of Llanafan-y-Trawscoed w Gwnnws 64-67; C of Abth 67-69; Team V 69-73; Angl Chap Univ Coll of Wales Abth 67-73; Exam Chap to Bp of St D 71-73; Sec Prov Coun for Miss and Unity and L to Offic Dio Llan 73-79; V of St D Carmarthen Dio St D from 79. *St David's Vicarage, Carmarthen, Dyfed.* (Carmarthen 7662)

DAVIES, Samuel Maelor. b 08. Univ of Wales 34. Ripon Hall Ox 37. **d** 39 **p** 40 Wakef. C of Southowram 39-40; Todmorden (in c of St Mary) 40-41; C-in-c of Wrangbrook 41-45; St Thos St Annes-on-the-Sea 45-48; V of St Laur Morecambe 48-56; Bampton w Mardale 56-62; Grange-over-Sands 62-73; L to Offic Dio Carl from 73. *Greystones, Levens, Kendal, Cumb, LA8 8ND.*

DAVIES, Sidney. St D Coll Lamp BA 40. **d** 41 **p** 42 St D. C of Llandyssul 41-44; Llanfihangel-ar-Arth 44-53; V of Llanerch-aeron w Ciliau-aeron (w Dihewyd from 69) Dio St D from 53. *Ciliau-aeron Rectory, Lampeter, Dyfed.* (Aeron 268)

DAVIES, Ven Sidney John Philip. Bp's Univ Lennox BA 38. **d** 38 **p** 39 Ott. C of Navan 38-39; R of Alberton 39-43; Milton 43-48; New London 48-50; Newfld Distr Sec BFBS 50-54; C of St Thos St John's 54-57; R 57-62; Dioc Comm Dio NS 62-65; Hon Can of All SS Cathl Halifax NS 62-74 and from 79; R of Amherst 65-69; Joggins 68-69; N Sydney 69-74; Waverley 74-79; Archd of Northumb 65-69; Cape Breton 69-74; Archd (Emer) from 75. *Port Williams, Waverley, NS, Canada.*

DAVIES, Stanley James. b 18. MBE (Mil) 54. Late Scho and Pri of St Chad's Coll Dur BA 40, MA 44, Dipl in Th 41. **d** 41 **p** 42 Liv. C of St Marg Belmont Road Anfield 41-42; Wigan 42-45; CF 45-73; DACG Rhine Area 66-68; ACG Lon 68-70; ACG BAOR 70-73; Hon Chap to HM the Queen from 72; R of Uley w Owlpen and Nympsfield Dio Glouc from 73; Commiss to Bp of Seoul from 73. *Rectory, Uley, Glos, GL11 5SN.* (Dursley 860249)

DAVIES, Stephen Walter. b 26. K Coll Lon and Warm AKC 54. **d** 55 **p** 56 Ex. C of Plympton 55-58; St Mark Ex 58-61; Chap RAF 61-77; R of Feltwell Dio Ely from 79. *Feltwell Rectory, Thetford, Norf, IP26 4DB.* (Feltwell 828631)

DAVIES, Stuart Simeon. b 13. St Chad's Coll Dur BA 41. Dipl in Th 42, MA 44. Knutsford Test Sch Hawarden 37. **d** 42 **p** 43 Liv. C of St Columba Anfield 42-44; St Barn Epsom 44-47; Chieveley (in c of Curridge) 47-52; V of St Swith Kennington 52-65; R of Fifield w Idbury 65-74. *86 St John's Priory, Lechlade, Glos, GL7 3HN.*

DAVIES, Sydney Herbert. Dorch Miss Coll. **d** 23 Southw **p** 26 Willesden for Lon. C of Bulwell 23-24; St Ann Stamford Hill 26-27; St Luke Camberwell 27-30; P-in-c of Elliston 30-44; Laura and Dioc Sec Dio Willoch 44-61; R of Inglewood 61-63. *9 Paddington Road, Oakleigh, Vic., Australia.*

DAVIES, Terence. St D Coll Lamp BA (2nd cl Engl) 56. Wycl Hall Ox. **d** 58 **p** 59 Mon. C of Panteg 58-60; Caerphilly 60-62; Halesowen w Hasbury and Lapal 62-64; Chap Rothesay Colleg Sch Dio Fred 64-75; Hon C of St Barn Dulwich 75-77; Chap St Mich Univ Sch Vic from 79. *3400 Richmond Road, Victoria, Vancouver Island, BC, Canada.*

DAVIES, Canon Thomas. b 15. Univ of Man BA 38. Ridley Hall Cam 38. **d** 40 **p** 41 Man. C of St Bart Westhoughton 40-43; Worsley (in c of Ellenbrook w Boothstown) 43-45; R of Ch Ch Bradf 45-49; V of Tyldesley 49-53; Westhoughton 53-80; Hon Can of Man Cathl 70-80; Can (Emer) from 80; RD of Deane 74-80. *9a College Avenue, Rhos-on-Sea, Colwyn Bay, Clwyd, LL28 4NT.* (Colwyn Bay 49339)

DAVIES, Thomas Brynmor. Univ of Wales BA 39. St Steph Ho Ox 33. **d** 34 **p** 35 Llan. C of Cymmer w Porth 34-36; Rhyl 36-41; R of Llansannan (w Bylchan 47-50) 41-50; V of Minera w Coedpoeth 50-59; Chap HM Pris Lewes 59-63; R of Presteigne w Discoyd 63-76; Surr 63-76; Perm to Offic Dio Heref from 78. *Church Close, Broad Street, Presteigne, Powys.*

DAVIES, Preb Thomas Derwent. b 16. St D Coll Lamp Traherne Scho 37, BA (2nd cl Engl) 38. St Mich Coll Llan 39. **d** 39 Ban for Llan **p** 41 Llan. C of St Cath Pontypridd 39-45; Bideford 45-48; Asst Sec Ex Dioc Bd of Finance 48-51; L to Offic Dio Ex 48-51; V of St Mark Ford Devonport 51-58; Surr 51-81; R of Bideford 58-74; Preb of Ex Cathl from 69; V of Thorverton 74-81; Cadbury 74-81; Ex Dioc Clergy Widows' Officer from 79. *12 Blagdon Rise, Crediton, Devon.*

DAVIES, Thomas John Egbert. Late Scho and Pri of St D Coll Lamp BA 30. **d** 30 **p** 31 Swan B for St D. C of Llandilo-Fawr 30-34; Eglwysrhos (in c of St Paul's Mem Ch) 34-48; R of St Geo Abergele 48-70. *49 The Beeches, Llandysul, Dyfed.*

DAVIES, Thomas John Ward. Univ of Lon BSc (Eng) 35. St Cath S Ox BA 42. Cudd Coll 40. **d** 41 **p** 42 Mon. C of Trevethin 41-42; Machen 42-44; Trevethin 44-47; Stoke-on-Trent 47-50; PC of St Werburgh Burslem 50-56; V of Stonnall 56-79; V of Wall 56-79. *7 Brook End, Longdon, WS14 3PS.*

DAVIES, Thomas Neville James. b 27. St Mich Coll Llan 54. **d** 56 **p** 57 St A. C of Wrexham 56-62; V of Bettisfield w Bronington 62-65; CF from 65. *c/o Ministry of Defence, Bagshot Park, Bagshot, Surrey.*

DAVIES, Canon Thomas Philip. St Mich Coll Llan 55. **d** 56 **p** 57 St A. C of Ruabon 56-60; Prestatyn 60-62; V of Penley 62-69; Holt w Isycoed 69-77; RD of Wrexham 76-77; Dioc Dir of Educn Dio St A from 76; R of Hawarden Dio St A from 77; Can of St A Cathl from 79. *Hawarden Rectory, Deeside, Clwyd.* (Hawarden 531103)

DAVIES, Thomas Richard. St Paul's Coll Grahmstn 58. **d** 58 **p** 59 Mashon. C of St Mary's Cathl Salisbury Rhod 58-62; Sub-Warden St Pet Home Grahmstn 62-64; L to Offic Dio Mashon 64-77; Dio Grahmstn from 77. *27 Melville Heights, St James Road, East London, CP, S Africa.*

DAVIES, Thomas Samuel. b 02. Late Scho of Univ of Wales BA (2nd cl Welsh) 33. St Mich Coll Llan 33. **d** 35 **p** 36 St D. C of Llanfihangel-Geneu'r-Glyn 35-38; Llandefeilog 38-41; R of Bangor Teifi w Henllan 41-53; RD of Emlyn 49-53; V of Llanychaiarn 53-72; Can of St D Cathl 64-72. *Felindre Fach, Abermeurig, Lampeter, Dyfed.* (Aeron 470545)

DAVIES, Thomas Stanley. b 10. **d** 37 **p** 38 Lon. C of St Cath Coleman N Hammersmith 37-40; St Mich Shoreditch 40-41; St Francis Isleworth 41-45; C of St Paul (in c of St Margaret) Burton-on-Trent 45-47; R of Gt Sutton 47-55; V of Shopland 47-55; V of St Jas Leigh 55-71; Stansted Mountfitchet 71-78; Surr 72-78; Perm to Offic Dio Chelmsf from 78. *54 Newbiggen Street, Thaxted, Essex, CM6 2QT.* (Thaxted 830110)

DAVIES, Tommy. b 16. St D Coll Lamp. **d** 39 **p** 40 Ban. C of Harlech w Llanfair-juxta-Harlech 39-54; V of Llanfihangel-y-Pennant w Talyllyn 54-63. *Gwynfro, Ciliau Aeron, Lampeter, Dyfed.*

DAVIES, Canon Trevor Gwesyn. b 28. Univ of Wales (Cardiff) BEducn 73. St Mich Coll Llan 55. **d** 56 **p** 57 St A. C of Holywell Flints 56-63; V of Cwm, Flints 63-74; Colwyn Bay Dio St A from 74; Dioc Sec for Social Work Dio St A from 75; Can of St A Cathl from 79. *Vicarage, Colwyn Bay, Clwyd.* (Colwyn Bay 2403)

DAVIES, Tudor Elvey. b 1899. Univ of Wales BA 22. St Mich Coll Llan. **d** 33 **p** 34 St D. C of Abernant w Conwil Elvet 33-38; Chap Trin Coll Carmarthen 38-39; Bp's Messenger Dio St D 39-41; V of Abergwili w Llanfihangel-Uwch-Gwili 41-70; RD of Carmarthen 60-67. *Lynwood, College Road, Carmarthen, Dyfed.*

DAVIES, Victor George. b 08. St Jo Coll Dur BA (2nd cl Th Hons) 33, MA 36, Gabbett Pri 37. **d** 34 **p** 35 Liv. C of St Paul Widnes 34-36; St Mary-le-Bow Dur and Asst Chap St Jo Coll Dur 36-38; C of Em Southport 38-40; V of St Chris Norris Green 40-48; Gateacre 48-59; Proc Conv York 55-60;

V of Walton 59-73. *15 Wennington Road, Southport, Lancs.*

DAVIES, Vincent Anthony. b 46. St Mich AA Coll Llan 71. **d** 73 **p** 74 Dur. C of St Jas Owton Manor 73-76; St Faith Wandsworth 76-78; V 78-81; St Jo Evang Walworth Dio S'wark from 81. *Vicarage, Larcom Street, SE17.* (01-703 4375)

DAVIES, Vincent James. St D Coll Lamp BA 48. **d** 50 **p** 51 Swan B. C of Loughor 50-58; V of Llangorse (w Cathedine from 72) Dio Swan B from 58; RD of Brecon I from 77. *Vicarage, Llangorse, Brecons.* (Llangorse 298)

DAVIES, Canon Walter Emlyn. St D Coll Lamp BA (Hons) 30. St Mich Th Coll Llan. **d** 31 **p** 32 St D. C of St Pet Carmarthen 31-38; V of Myddfai (or Mothvey) 38-57; Bettws w Ammanford 57-64; Cler Sec St D Dioc Conf and Sec Dioc Bd of Patr from 63; V of Llanbadarn-Fawr 64-72; RD of Llanbadarn-Fawr 67-71; Can of Mathry in St D Cathl 68-72. *Bourne House, Trinity Road, Aberystwyth, Dyfed.*

DAVIES, Walter Hugh. b 28. **d** 66 **p** 67 Ban. C of St Mary Ban 66-69; C-in-c of Rhosybol w Llandyfrydog 70; Team V of Amlwch and Rhosybol w Llandyfrydog 71-74; R of Llanfaethlu w Llanfwrog Llanrhuddlad Llanfair-yng-Nghornwy and Llanrhwydros Dio Ban from 74; Surr from 81. *Llanfaethlu Rectory, Holyhead, Anglesey, Gwyn, LL65 4PB.* (Llanfaethlu 251)

DAVIES, Canon Walter Merlin. St D Coll Lamp BA (2nd cl Th) 36. Westcott Ho Cam 37. **d** 38 **p** 39 Bris. C of St Mich AA Windmill Hill Bris 38-40; SCM Chap Cant Univ Dio Ch Ch 41-44; Prec of Ch Ch Cathl and Vice-Prin Ch Ch Coll 41-44; Exam Chap to Abp of NZ 42-44; Sec SCM for Wales 45-46; Dir of Relig Educn Dio Bris 46-49; V of Berkswich w Walton 49-59; Avonside 59-75; Archd of Akaroa and Ashburton 59-69; Dir of Post Ordin Tr Dio Ch Ch 59-75; Exam Chap to Bp of Ch Ch 60-75; Archd of Sumner 69-75; Warden St Jo Coll Auckld 75-76; Hon Can of Auckld 75-76; Can (Emer) from 77; Perm to Offic Dio Auckld from 77. *20 Queen Street, Northcote, Auckland 9, NZ.* (487-225)

DAVIES, William Bertram. b 1899. AKC 35. **d** 35 **p** 36 Lon. C of St Andr Sudbury (in c of St Cuthb Wembley from 39) 35-44; V of St Martin Lower Edmonton 44-50; Jesus Ch Forty Hill Enfield 50-68. *Ty Gwyn, Doyle Road, St Peter Port, Guernsey, CI.*

DAVIES, William Daniel. Lon Coll of Div. **d** 15 **p** 18 Llan. C of Dowlais 15-18; St Andr Llwynypia 18-23; Llandefeilog w Cwmffrwd 23-27; R of Capel Cynon w Talgarreg 27-31; V of Llanddewi-Brefi (w Llanbadarn Odyn 31-52) 31-57. *Belair, Queen's Road, Aberystwyth, Dyfed.*

DAVIES, William David. b 19. Univ of Bris BA (2nd cl Hist) 41. St Mich Coll Llan. **d** 43 **p** 44 Mon. C of Ch Ch Ebbw Vale 43-46; St Matthew Buckley 46-48; C of Cathl Ch 48-50; C-in-c of St Pet Conv Distr Fairwater 50-67; V 67-68; R of Porthkerry w Barry Llan 68-72; R of Barry Dio Llan from 72; RD of Penarth and Barry from 75. *Rectory, Barry, S Glam.* (Barry 734629)

DAVIES, Canon William Hopkin Septimus. b 06. Univ Coll Dur LTh 29. Lon Coll Div 28. **d** 29 **p** 30 Mon. C of All SS Newport 29-32; St Pet Worc 32-35; Hartlebury 35-37; R of Shelsley Beauchamp w Shelsley Walsh 37-47; CF (EC) 40-46; Hon CF 46; RD of Bredon 47-56; R of Severn Stoke 47-56; Hartlebury w Bp's Wood 56-74; Hon Can of Worc Cathl 73-74; Can (Emer) from 74. *Thorngrove Cottage, Grimley, Near Worcester, WR2 6NP.* (Worc 640091)

DAVIES, William John. St D Coll Lamp Butler Scho 30, BA (Hist Hons) and Traharne Scho 31. **d** 31 **p** 32 Llan. C of Gellygaer (in c of St Marg Gilfach) 31-33; Old Swinford 33-35; Edgmond 35-40; CF (EC) 40-46; R of Sampford Spiney w horrabridge (V) 46-55; V of Twickenham 55-78; Surr 55-78. *6 Tavistock, Devonshire Place, Eastbourne, E Sussex, BN21 4AG.*

DAVIES, William John. b 07. Late Scho of St D Coll Lamp BA 31. St Mich Coll Llan 31. **d** 32 **p** 33 St D. C of Hubberston 32-34; Cardigan 34-36; Llannon 36-38; V of St Mary Bronllys 38-54; R of Cefnllys w Llandrindod 54-75; RD of Melineth (and Elwell 65-70) 58-74; Can of Brecon Cathl 60-72; Prec 72-75. *Paxton House, Llandeilo Road, Cross Hands, Llanelli, Dyfed.*

DAVIES, Canon William John Morgan. b 10. St D Coll Lamp BA 32. **d** 36 **p** 37 Swan B. C of Loughor 36-41; Ystradgynlais 41-47; V of Crickadarn w Gwenddwr 47-54; Devynock w Rhydybriw and Llandilo'r Fan Dio Swan B from 54; RD of Builth 54-55; RD of Brecon ii 76-80; Can of Brecon Cathl from 78. *Vicarage, Defynnog, Brecon, Powys, LD3 8SB.* (Sennybridge 226)

DAVIES, (Edgar) William Kenneth. b 24. St Pet Hall Ox BA 47, MA 50. Wycl Hall Ox. **d** 50 **p** 51 Worc. C of St Andr Netherton 50-53; CF 53-57; C-in-c of Birchen Coppice Conv Distr Kidderminster 57-61; R of Stoke Bliss w Kyre Wyard 61-69; M SSF from 69; Perm to Offic Dio Ely 72-73; L to 73-75; Perm to Offic Dio Worc from 75; L to Offic Dio Liv 77-80; Perm to Offic Dio Ely 80-81; L from 81. *St Francis House, 15 Botolph Lane, Cambridge, CB2 3RD.* (0223-353903)

DAVIES, William Llewelyn. b 17. **d** 43 **p** 45 Worc. C of St Jas Gt Dudley 43-45; C-in-c of Llangian 45-57; C of Llangeod 47-49; Llandegfan 49-54; R of Mallwyd (w Llanymawdduy from 63 and Cemmaes from 70) 54-75; Llanfwrog w Efenechtyd Dio St A from 75. *Rectory, Mwrog Street, Ruthin, Clwyd, LL15 1LE.*

DAVIES, William Martin. b 56. Univ of Wales (Cardiff) BSc 78. Wycl Hall Ox 78. **d** 81 Llan. C of St Mark Gabalfa Dio Llan from 81. *27 Pen-y-Bryn Road, Gabalfa, Cardiff, CF4 3LG.*

DAVIES, William Morris. b 19. Late Scho of St D Coll Lamp BA (2nd cl Hist) 41, Welsh Ch Scho and Powis Exhib 41. Jes Coll Ox BA (3rd cl Th) 43, MA 47. LCP 56. Univ of Liv MEd 68. St Mich Coll Llan 43. **d** 44 Wales **p** 45 St D. C of Yspytty Ystwyth w Ystrad Meurig 44-49; V 49-57; Asst Master Ystrad Meurig Gr Sch 44-49; Hd Master 49-57; Chap and Asst Master Sandbach Sch 57-65; L to Offic Dio Ches from 57; Lect in Div Crewe Coll Educn 65-68; Sen Lect 68-71; Hd of Dept 71-75; Tutor Crewe & Alsager Coll of Higher Educn 75-79; Open Univ from 78; V of Norley Dio Ches from 79. *Vicarage, Norley, Warrington, WA6 8NE.* (Kingsley 88363)

DAVIES, William Morris. b 23. St Mich Coll Llan 66. **d** and **p** 68 Swan B. C of Llanguicke (Pontardawe) 68-72; R of Bryngwyn w Newchurch and Llanbedr Painscastle w Llanddewi Fach 72-77; Bedwas Dio Mon from 77. *Rectory, Bryn Goleu, Bedwas, Newport, Gwent, NP1 8AU.* (Caerphilly 885220)

DAVIES, William Paul Seymour. b 27. Ex Coll Ox 2nd cl Cl Mods 50, BA 51, 3rd cl Lit Hum 52, MA 55. St Mich Coll Llan 53. **d** 54 **p** 56 St A. C of Chirk 54-55; Minera 55-57; V of Bwlchgwyn 57-61; R of Llandrinio w Criggion 61-66; Chap Tristan da Cunha 66-68; R of Pont Robert w Pont Dolanog 68-71; V of Llansilin w Llangadwaladr and Llangedwyn 71-80; Meifod w Llangynyw Dio St A from 80. *Vicarage, Meifod, Clwyd.* (Meifod 231)

DAVIES, William Thomas Henry Basil. Fitzw Ho Cam BA 47, MA 52. Ripon Hall Ox. **d** 49 St D **p** 53 Win. C of Laughharne w Llansadwrnen 49; Perm to Offic at Cwmamman 50-52; C of Andover w Foxcot 52-55; R of Melton Constable w Swanton Novers 55-57; V of Briningham 55-57; R of Beckington w Standerwick (w Berkley, Rodden, Lullington and Orchardleigh from 78) Dio B & W from 57; P-in-c of Berkley, Rodden, Lullington and Orchardleigh 77-78. *The Priory, Beckington, Bath, Somt.* (Beckington 314)

DAVIES, Winton James Detheridge. Coll Ho Ch Ch LTh 64. **d** 57 **p** 59 Wel. C of St Pet Palmerston N 57-61; Karori w Makara Wel 61-62; V of Waverley-Waitotara 62-67; Chap Wel Hosp 67-71; V of Ngaio Wel 71-79; Wanganui Dio Wel from 79. *Box 4050, Wanganui, NZ.* (53-096)

DAVIES, Zacchaeus Hennessy Kurrah-Harry. Fourah Bay Coll 49. **d** 52 **p** 55 Sier L. C of St Geo Cathl Freetown 52-57; Dom Chap to Abp of Sierra L 55-59; V of Bp Crowther Mem Ch Freetown 57-59; H Trin Freetown 59-61; Wilberforce 61-63; St Mark Lumley 63-65. *17 Montague Street, Freetown, Sierra Leone.*

DAVIES-FREME, Evan Thomas. b 03. Univ of Wales BA 30. Lich Th Coll 28. **d** 28 Maenan for St A **p** 30 St A. C of Cerrig-y-Drudion 28-30; St Andr Newport 30-33; Bassaleg (in c of St John Rogerstone) 33-36; V of Padbury 36-42; Lelant 42-59; CF (EC) 44-46; R of Pelynt w Llansallos 59-61; C of Paignton 61-63; V of Shaugh Prior 63-67; Perm to Offic Dio Ex from 67. *53 Preston Down Road, Paignton, Devon, TQ3 2RL.* (Paignton 523116)

DAVIS, Alan. b 34. Univ of Birm BSc 56. **d** 75 Ox **p** 76 Buckingham for Ox (APM). C of Chesham 75-80; Gt Chesham Dio Ox from 80. *18 Cheyne Walk, Chesham, Bucks, HP5 1AY.*

DAVIS, Alan John. b 33. St Alb Ministerial Tr Scheme 77. **d** 80 St Alb **p** 81 Hertf for St Alb. C of Goldington Dio St Alb from 80. *15 Bamburgh Drive, Bedford, MK41 8JD.*

DAVIS, Alan Norman. b 38. Open Univ BA 75. Lich Th Coll. **d** 65 **p** 66 Birm. C of St Luke Kingstanding 65-68; C-in-c of St Paul's Conv Distr (St Paul's Wordsworth Ave from 72) Ecclesfield 68-72; V 72-73; St Paul's Wordsworth Ave Sheff 73-75; Lower Shiregreen 75-80; Maltby Dio Sheff 80-81; Team R from 81. *69 Blyth Road, Maltby, Rotherham, Yorks, S66 7LF.* (0709-812684)

DAVIS, Canon Alfred Henry. Univ of Tor BA 30. Wycl Coll Tor Hon DD 55. **d** 30 Rupld **p** 31 Bp Matheson for Rupld. C of Westbourne 30; I of St Mary Magd St Vital 30-32; C of St Jas Poole 32-33; Assoc Sec Dr Barnardo's Homes and Perm to Offic Dios Win Sarum Ex and Portsm 33-35; C of Ascen Hamilton Ont 35-36; R of Hagersville w Cheapside 36-40; P-in-c of H Trin Welland 40-41; R 41-43; RD of Lincoln and Welland 47-50; Hon Can of Niag 48-50 and 53-69; Can (Emer) from 70; Archd of Lincoln and Welland 50-53; Field Sec Miss S of Angl Ch of Canada 53-59; Gen Sec 59-69. *55 Belmont Street, Toronto, Ont., Canada.*

DAVIS, Allan. b 15. ALCD 54. **d** 54 **p** 55 Chelmsf. C of Good Shepherd Romford 54-58; Min of St Paul's Conv Distr Parkeston 59-67; V of St John Colchester 67-80; Perm to Offic Dio St Alb from 80. *5 Pipit Close, Flitwick, Beds.*

DAVIS, Andrew Fisher. b 46. St Chad's Coll Dur BA 67. St Steph Ho Ox 68. **d** 70 **p** 71 Roch. C of St Jas Elmers End Beckenham 70-74; St Mary Abbots Kens 74-79; V of St Andr Sudbury Dio Lon from 80. *956 Harrow Road, Sudbury, Middx,* (01-904 4016)

DAVIS, Anthony David Hugh. b 52. Univ of Southn BTh 80. Chich Th Coll 75. **d** 78 **p** 79 Llan. C of St German Roath Dio Llan from 78. *St German's Clergy House, Metal Street, Roath, Cardiff, CF2 1LA.*

DAVIS, Canon Anthony William. LTh (S Afr) 61. St Paul's Th Coll Grahmstn 61. **d** 61 Pret for Johann **p** 61 Johann. C of Yeoville 61; R of Nigel 63-67; Stilfontein 67-69; Beaufort W 69-72; R of Vic W 69-72; Formosa 72-74; Plettenberg Bay Dio Geo from 74; Can of Geo from 80. *PO Box 18, Plettenberg Bay, CP, S Africa.* (Plettenberg Bay 8)

DAVIS, Arthur Vivian. b 24. Clifton Th Coll 60. **d** 62 **p** 63 Derby. C of St Chad Derby 62-65; St Andr L Cam (in c of St Steph) 65-68; V 68-75; Wood Ditton w Saxon Street Dio Ely from 75; Kirtling Dio Ely from 75. *Wood Ditton Vicarage, Newmarket, Suff, CB8 9SG.* (Stetchworth 282)

DAVIS, Barry Henry. b 40. St Barn Th Coll Adel 75. **d** 80 **p** 81 Adel. C of St Aug Unley Dio Adel from 80. *75 Clifton Street, Malvern, S Australia 5061.*

DAVIS, Canon Bernard Rex. b 33. Univ of Syd BA 55. Univ of Newc MA 67. Coll of Resurr Mirfield. Gen Th Sem NY MDiv 60. **d** 57 **p** 58 Guildf. C of St Nich Guildf 57-59; in Amer Ch 59-61; R of Wickham 62-66; Sec Div Stud Austrn Coun of Chs 66-68; Dio Syd 66-68; Sec World Coun of Chs Geneva 68-77; Can Res, Subdean and Preb of Linc Cathl from 77. *Subdeanery, Lincoln, LN2 1PX.*

DAVIS, Bertie John. b 1893. St Paul's Coll Burgh 23. **d** 24 **p** 25 Fred. C of Queensbury w Southampton NB 24-26; Harrow Green (in c of St Alb) 26-28; St Paul Addlestone 28-30; Hagley 30-31; PC of Tilty w Duton Hill 31-34; V of Wilburton 34-35; Birling 35-46; R of Shalstone w Biddlesden 46-49; Seaforth 49-50; Sackville 50-57. *9 Anglesea Terrace, St Leonards-on-Sea, Sussex.* (0424-437804)

DAVIS, Brian. b 40. AKC and BD 69. St Aug Coll Cant 69. **d** 70 **p** 71 Leic. C of St Mary Humberstone 70-73; Kirby Muxloe 73-74; V of Countesthorpe w Foston Dio Leic from 74. *Countesthorpe Vicarage, Leicester, LE8 3TB.* (Leicester 774441)

✠ **DAVIS, Right Rev Brian Newton.** Univ of NZ BA 57, MA (1st cl Geog) 60. NZ Bd of Th Stud LTh 65. Ch Ch Coll. **d** 60 Bp Rich for Wel **p** 61 Wel. C of St Mark Wel 60-62; Karori w Makara 62-64; V 64-67; Dannevirke 67-73; Dean and V of St Jo Evang Cathl Napier 73-80; Cons Ld Bp of Waik in St Pet Cathl Hamilton 30 Sept 80 by Abp of NZ; Bps of Nel, Ch Ch, Wel, Polyn, Dun, Wai and Aotearoa; and others. *Bishop's House, 3 Domain Drive, Hamilton, NZ.*

DAVIS, Christopher Eliot. b 28. Pemb Coll Cam BA (3rd cl Th Trip pt i) 50, MA 55. Wells Th Coll 53. **d** 54 **p** 55 Bp Stuart for Worc. C of St Aug Holly Hall Dudley 54-56; Bromyard 56-57; Min Can and Sacr of Carl Cathl 57-59; Min Can Prec and Sacr of Worc Cathl 59-62; L to Offic Dio Worc from 59; PV of Lich Cathl 65-67; C-in-c of St Mary Lich 65-66; Perm to Offic Dio Lich 65-63 and from 77; Chap Magd Coll Ox 71-74. *28 Newbridge Crescent, Wolverhampton, WV6 0LH.* (Wolverhampton 758588)

DAVIS, Claude. Ely Th Coll 54. **d** 56 **p** 57 St Alb. C of St Andr Bedford 56-58; R of Sutton Beds 58-63; V of Eyeworth 58-63; Publ Pr Dio Syd from 64. *39 Pennant Hills Road, North Parramatta, Sydney, NSW, Australia.*

DAVIS, Clinton Ernest Newman. b 46. Wycl Hall Ox 78. **d** 80 **p** 81 Cant. C of H Trin Margate Dio Cant from 80. *84 Millmead Road, Margate, Kent, CT9 3QL.*

DAVIS, Cyril Jonathan. b 51. St Pet Coll Alice. **d** 76 **p** 77 Capetn. C of All SS Somerset W 76-80; Groot Drakenstein Dio Capetn from 80. *Box 12, Groot Drakenstein, CP, S Africa.*

DAVIS, David Graham. Univ of Syd LLB 51. Univ of New Engl BA 78. Moore Th Coll ACT ThL 53. **d** 53 Nel **p** 54 Wel for Nel. C of All SS Nel 53-55; Org Sec Bd of Educn Syd 55-58; Asst Dir of Educn Syd 58-59; C-in-c of Ch Ch Provisional Distr St Ives w Terrey Hills 60-66; R 66-71; R of Lindfield 71-80; St Phil York Street City and Dio Syd from 80. *Rectory, York Street, Sydney, NSW, Australia 2000.* (27-1071)

DAVIS, David John. b 35. St Steph Ho Ox 79. **d** 81 Reading for Ox. C of St Mark Reading Dio Ox from 81. *29 Prince of Wales Avenue, Reading, RG3 2UH.*

DAVIS, Donald Henry Kortright. b 41. BD (Lon) 65. Codr Coll Barb 61. **d** 65 **p** 66 Antig. C of St Geo St Kitts 65-67; R of St Pet w St John Montserrat 67-69; Lect Codr Coll 70-71; Vice-Prin from 72; Exam Chap to Bp of Antig 71-75; Commiss Antig from 80. *St Bartholomew's Rectory, Christ Church, Barbados.*

DAVIS, Edmund. Univ of WI BA (Th) 74. United Th Coll of WI 69. **d** 69 **p** 70 Ja. C of St Luke Cross Roads 69-72; Ch Ch Vineyard Town 73-74; on leave 74-75; P-in-c of Bridgeport Miss Dio Ja from 75. *Lot 346, Basie Avenue, Bridgeport, Jamaica, WI.* (098-81499)

DAVIS, Edwin John Charles. b 36. Univ of Dur. BA 60. St Cath S Ox BA (2nd cl Th) 62, MA 66. Ripon Hall Ox 60. **d** 62 **p** 63 Heref. C of Kington w Huntington 62-65; Lect Lich Th Coll 65-66; Chap Edin Th Coll 66-70; Hon Chap St Mary's Cathl Edin 66-70; P-in-c of Middleton 70-78; V 78-81; P-in-c of Hope w Shelve 70-78; R 78-81; P-in-c of Worthen 75-78; R 78-81; V of S w New Hinksey Dio Ox from 81. *New Hinksey Vicarage, Oxford, OX1 4RD.* (Ox 45879)

DAVIS, Canon Eldon Stanley. Bp's Univ Lennox BA 37, MA 39. **d** and **p** 38 Ott. C of Pemb and Petawawa 38-41; Chap CASF 41-45; C of St John Ott 45-47; Miss MSCC Dio Lah 47-53; Dio Amrit 53-62; R of St Steph Ott 62-71; Can of Ott Cathl from 71; Dioc Counselling Min Ott 75-81. *988 Watson Street, Ottawa 4, Ont., Canada.* (1-613-828-6624)

DAVIS, Eric Ronald. b 25. **d** 78 Ndwandwe for Johann **p** 79 Johann (NSM). C of Bryanston Dio Johann from 78. *PO Box 69855, Bryanston, S Africa 2021.*

DAVIS, Eustace Bowater. b 07. Univ of Bris BA 31. Tyndale Hall Bris 31. **d** 32 **p** 33 Liv. C of St Nath Windsor W Derby 32-34; Perm to Offic at St Jas W Streatham 34-35; BCMS Miss Dio W China 35-37; Dio E Szech 37-52; R of Wingfield 52-57; Overseas Sec BCMS 57-65; Hon C of Ch Ch Bromley 60-65; V of Ch Ch Camberwell Dio S'wark from 65. *79 Asylum Road, SE15 2RJ.* (01-639 5662)

DAVIS, Frederick James Charles. b 03. K Coll Lon and Warm 52. **d** 53 **p** 54 St Alb. C of All SS Luton 53-55; V of Riseley 55-73. *18 Marsh Lane, Milton Ernest, Bedford.* (Oakley 3072)

DAVIS, Frederick William Frank. b 1896. Trin Coll Dub. **d** 65 **p** 66 Kilm. C of Mohill and of Outeragh 65-66; St Matthias Canning Town 66-68; Perm to Offic Dio Chelmsf 68-75; Dio Win 75-80; Dio Ox from 80. *Manyara, Packhorse Road, Gerrard's Cross, Bucks.*

DAVIS, Geoffrey. b 47. St Jo Coll Nottm 79. **d** 81 Cant. C of St Luke Maidstone Dio Cant from 81. *75 Snowden Avenue, Maidstone, Kent.*

DAVIS, Canon Gordon Henry Donne. b 10. St Cath Coll Cam 3rd cl Engl Trip pt i 35, BA (2nd cl Archaeol and Anthrop Trip) 36, MA 40. Wycl Hall Ox 36. **d** 37 **p** 38 S'wark. C of Morden 37-40; Chap RAFVR 40-46; R of St Helen Ipswich 45-50; V of St Pet Norbiton 50-72; RD of Kingston 58-63; Hon Can of S'wark 62-72; Can (Emer) from 73. *15 Sutton Avenue, Rustington, W Sussex, BN16 2ES.* (Rustington 71680)

DAVIS, Harold Horace. b 19. Worc Ordin Coll 66. **d** 67 Barking for Chelmsf **p** 68 Chelmsf. C of Gt Clacton w L Holland 67-73; V of Heybridge w Langford 73-76; C-in-c of W Hanningfield Dio Chelmsf 76-78; R from 78. *Rectory, West Hanningfield, Chelmsford, Essex.* (Chelmsford 400148)

DAVIS, Hector Percival Harold. **d** 66 **p** 67 Wel. Hon C of Stokes Valley Dio Wel from 66. *40 Kamahi Street, Stokes Valley, NZ.* (Stokes Valley 8716)

DAVIS, Herbert Roger. b 36. Kelham Th Coll 60. **d** 65 Barking for Chelmsf **p** 66 Chelmsf. C of St Francis of Assisi Barkingside 65-69; Harpenden 69-73; C-in-c of Eaton Bray 73-75; V (w Edlesborough) 75-81; RD of Dunstable 77-81; R of Gt Berkhamstead Dio St Alb from 81. *Rectory, Berkhamsted, Herts, HP4 2DH.* (Berkhamsted 4194)

DAVIS, Ivor Leslie. b 23. Trin Coll Dub BA 48, MA 53. Div Test 48. **d** 48 Drom **p** 49 Connor for Down. C of Aghalee 48-50; Willowfield 50-53; Chap RAF 53-59; C of Halsall 59; C-in-c of St Jas Conv Distr Eccleston Pk Dio Liv 59-60; Min 60-61; V 61-70; Maghull Dio Liv 70-72; Team R from 72. *20 Damfield Lane, Maghull, Liverpool, L31 6DD.* (051-526 5017)

DAVIS, James Raymond. b 17. Late Squire Scho of Mert Coll Ox (3rd cl Cl Mods) 38, BA (2nd cl Th) 40, MA 44. Wells Th Coll 40. **d** 41 **p** 42 Llan. C of Roath 41-48; St Alb Miss Johann 48-54; R of Nigel Dio Johann 54-59; Chap St Marg Conv E Grinstead 59-65; Perm to Offic Dio Chich 65-66; V of Borden Dio Cant from 66. *Borden Vicarage, Sittingbourne, Kent, ME9 8JS.* (Sittingbourne 72986)

DAVIS, Canon John. St Paul's Coll Grahmstn 60. **d** 62 Grahmstn. C of St Mich AA Port Eliz 62-64; K William's Town 64-66; St Mary Port Eliz 66-69; Chap Miss to Seamen Port Eliz 67-69; C of St Mich and St Geo Cathl, Grahmstn 69-72; P-in-c of Sidbury 69-72; R of Barkly E 72-75; St Nich Beacon Bay E Lon 75-79; St Mark E Lon Dio Grahmstn from 79; Can of Grahmstn from 79. *7 Elizabeth Road, Cambridge, East London, CP, S Africa.*

DAVIS, John Brian. b 33. Linc Th Coll 72. **d** 75 **p** 76 St E. C of Bungay Dio St E from 75. *The Cherry Tree House, Bungay, Suffolk, NR35 1DY.* (Bungay 3854)

DAVIS, John Harold. b 54. St Jo Coll Dur BSc 76, Dipl Th 78. Cranmer Hall Dur 76. **d** 79 **p** 80 York. C of St Mark Marske-in-Cleveland Dio York from 79. *78 High Street, Marske-by-the-Sea, Redcar, Cleveland, TS11 7BE.* (Redcar 478039)

DAVIS, John Cameron. b 47. Univ of Adel BA 69. McMaster Univ Ont MA 71. Trin Coll Melb BD 78. **d** 79 **p** 80 Melb. C of St John Toorak 79-81; St Pet City and Dio Melb from 81. *c/o Vicarage, Albert Street, Eastern Hill, Vic, Australia 3002.*

DAVIS, John Stephen. b 51. N Staffs Poly BSc 75. Wycl Hall Ox 75. **d** 78 **p** 79 Lich. C of Meole Brace 78-81; Bloxwich Dio Lich from 81. *9 Sanstone Road, Bloxwich, Walsall, W Midl.* (0922-79160)

DAVIS, Kenneth Gordon. b 18. Selw Coll Cam BA 40, 3rd cl Th Trip pt i 41, MA 43. Qu Coll Birm 40. **d** 42 **p** 43 Portsm. C of St Steph Portsea 42-46; Milton 46-51; C-in-c of St Mich AA Conv Distr Andover 51-56; V of St Mich AA Norton 56-63; R of Exbury (w Beaulieu from 77) Dio Win from 63. *Beaulieu Vicarage, Brockenhurst, Hants.* (Beaulieu 612242)

DAVIS, Kenneth William. b 25. Ripon Hall Ox 60. **d** 62 **p** 63 B & W. C of St Pet Lyngford Taunton 62-65; R of Axbridge 65-72; V of St Cuthb Wells w Ch Ch Coxley (and Wookey Hole from 73) Dio B & W from 72; RD of Shepton Mallet from 80. *Vicarage, St Cuthbert Street, Wells, Somerset.* (Wells 73136)

DAVIS, Leslie Augustin. Ch Coll Cam 3rd cl Cl Trip pt i 36, BA (2nd cl Th Trip pt i) 38, MA 41. Qu Coll Birm 38. **d** 39 **p** 40 Portsm. C of St Mark North End Portsea 39-47; Chap RNVR 44-46; C of Northn 47-48; St Sav Claremont CP 48-50; R of St Steph Pinelands CP 50-58; in Amer Ch 58-59; Chap Dio Mashon 59-63; R of St Luke Salisbury E 63-66; Asst Chap O of St John of Jer from 62; Chap Guild of St Raphael 66-68; Chap R Found of St Kath 66-68; Bernard Mizeki Coll Dio Mashon 68-78; Hd Master 75-78; R of Klerksdorp Dio Johann from 78. *Box 548, Klerksdorp 2570, Transvaal, S Africa.*

DAVIS, Manuhiri Louis. b 06. **d** and **p** 74 Wai. Hon C of Te Kaha Dio Wai from 74. *c/o Post Office, Torere, Bay of Plenty, NZ.*

DAVIS, Maxwell Pelham. b 45. St Jo Coll Morpeth 72. **d** 75 **p** 76 Newc. C of Gosford 75-77; Singleton 77-79; Gosford Dio Newc from 80; on leave 79-80. *14 Tangerine Street, Springfield, NSW, Australia 2250.*

DAVIS, Michael James Burrows. b 36. St Deiniol's Libr Hawarden 72. **d** and **p** 72 Berm (APM). C of H Trin Cathl Hamilton Dio Berm from 72. *Box 74, Southampton, Bermuda.*

DAVIS, Norman. b 38. FCII 66. Oak Hill Coll 77. **d** 79 **p** 80 St E. C of Walton Dio St E from 79. *27 Treetops, Felixstowe, Suffolk, IP11 9ER.* (Felixstowe 3307)

DAVIS, Norman John. b 41. Oak Hill Th Coll 63. **d** 66 **p** 67 Lich. C of All SS Wel 66-70; C of St Clem Higher Openshaw 70; R of St Andr Levenshulme 72-79; P-in-c of Berrow w Pendock and Eldersfield Dio Worc 79-81; V from 81. *Vicarage, Berrow, Nr Malvern, Worcs.* (Birtsmorton 237)

DAVIS, Paul Montague. b 29. St Jo Coll Dur BA 52. Ely Th Coll 52. **d** 54 **p** 55 S'wark. C of St Jas Malden 54-56; Boreham Wood 56-57; St Jas Colchester 57-61; CF 61-63; Asst Master Hockley Co Sch Essex 63-70; C of Leigh Essex 63-67; Hockley 67-70; Hon C of St Jas Colchester 72-81; V of L Horkesley Dio Chelmsf from 81. *Little Horkesley Vicarage, Fishponds, Great Horkesley, Colchester, Essex.*

DAVIS, Peter William. b 44. TCD BA 65, MA 68. St Jo Coll Auckld 71. **d** 72 **p** 73 Ch Ch. C of Sydenham-Beckenham 72-74; Chap Univ of Auckld 75-78; Perm to Offic Dio Auckld from 75; Dio Wai from 78; Dir of Communications Angl Ch of NZ from 78. *Box 2668, Auckland, NZ.* (30-138)

DAVIS, Richard Glyn. Univ of Wales BA (2nd cl Engl) 61. Clifton Th Coll 61. **d** 63 **p** 64 Sarum. C of Kinson 63-66; Perm to Offic Dio Lich from 67. *30 Richmond Road, Sedgley, Dudley, Worcs.*

DAVIS, Robert Malcolm. St Mich Th Coll Crafers 51. ACT ThL 55. **d** 54 **p** 55 St Arn. C of Mildura 55-58; V of Nyah 58-64; Ouyen 64-65; R 65-68; Mildura 68-77; Castlemaine 77-80; Can of St Arn 71-76; Ch Ch Old Cathl St Arn 77-80; I of St Geo Reservoir Dio Melb from 80. *Vicarage, Ralph Street, Reservoir, Vic, Australia 3073.*

DAVIS, Ronald Frank. b 26. Oak Hill Th Coll 62. **d** 64 **p** 65 Ripon. C of Bilton 64-68; R of N w S Otterington 68-77; C-in-c of S Hornchurch Dio Chelmsf from 77. *St John's Parsonage, South End Road, Rainham, Essex.*

DAVIS, Ronald Huthwaite. b 03. Univ of Lon BSc 23. **d** 43 **p** 44 Pet. Chap Win Ho Sch Brackley Dio Pet from 43. *Winchester House School, Brackley, Northants.*

DAVIS, Russell Earls. Univ of Syd LLB 50. Moore Th Coll ACT ThL 52. **d** 52 **p** 53 Tas. C of H Trin Launceston 52-54; Prec and Min Can of St Geo Cathl Perth 54-60; Chap Hale Sch Perth from 60; L to Offic Dio Perth from 60. *51 Cromarty Road, Floreat Park, W Australia 6014.* (387 2334)

DAVIS, Stephen Charles. b 19. St Cath S Ox BA (*sc* 2nd cl Th) 50, MA 54. AKC 48. Wycl Hall Ox. **d** 50 **p** 51 Ox. C of Slough 50-52; R of Brixton w Newlands Johann and Chap Univ of Witwatersrand 52-57; w SPG Lon 57-58; V of H Trin Leic and Chap HM Pris Leic 58-64; Dioc Sec CEMS Dio Leic 58-64; R of St Marg City and Dio Dur from 64; Commiss Papua from 71. *St Margaret's Rectory, South Street, Durham, DH1 4QP.* (Durham 43623)

DAVIS, Vincent Paul. b 06. Linc Coll Ox BA (3rd cl Hist) 28, MA 32. Cudd Coll 30. **d** 31 **p** 32 S'wark. C of St Olave Mitcham 31-34; Queenstown 34-38; L to Offic Dio Guildf 38-44; V of St Mary Virg Ewell 44-68; Skillington 68-73; R of Stainby w Gunby 68-73. *6 Lawn Road, Guildford, Surrey, GU2 5DE.* (Guildf 31787)

DAVIS, Walton Wheremu. b 29. St Jo Coll Auckld 80. **d** 80 Wel. C of Porirua Dio Wel from 80. *136 Driver Crescent, Canon's Creek, Porirua, NZ.*

DAVIS, William Charles. Montr Dioc Th Coll LTh 67. **d** and **p** 67 Tor. C of St Geo Willowdale 67-69; R of Beeton 69-74; St Pet Scarborough City and Dio Tor from 74. *776 Brimley Road, Scarborough, Toronto, Ont., Canada.* (416-267 2741)

DAVIS, William Gerald. b 25. Trin Coll Dub BA 49, MA 53. **d** 49 **p** 51 Connor. C of Ch Ch Lisburn 49-52; St Phil Booterstown 52-55; Chap RAF 55-59; I of Muckross w Templecarne 59-63; R of Norris Bank Dio Man from 63. *Rectory, Norris Bank, Stockport, SK4 2JE.* (061-432 3537)

DAVIS, William Henry. b 17. Bps' Coll Cheshunt. **d** 67 **p** 68 Lon. C of Sudbury 67-70; V of Wickhambrook (w Stradishall and Denston) Dio St E from 70; C-in-c of Stansfield 76-78. *Wickhambrook Vicarage, Newmarket, Suffolk.* (Wickhambrook 288)

DAVIS, William Maxwell. b 28. FCA 53. Moore Coll Syd 68. **d** 78 **p** 80 Graft. Hon C of Coffs Harbour Dio Graft from 78. *Westwood, Dairyville Road, Upper Orara, NSW, Australia 2450.*

✠ **DAVIS, Most Rev William Wallace.** Bp's Univ Lennox BA (1st cl Th) 31, BD 34, DCL 58. Univ K Coll Halifax NS Hon DD 54. **d** and **p** 32 Ott. C of St Matt Ott 32-39; R of Coaticook 36-38; St Matt Queb 38-52; Exam Chap to Bp of Queb 43-52; Archd of Queb 48-52; Dean and R of All SS Cathl Halifax 52-58; Exam Chap to Bp of NS 53-58; Cons Bp Coadj of NS in All SS CAthl Halifax NS 25 Feb 58 by Abps of Queb and Alg; Bps of NS; Montr; Ott; Fred; and Newfld; Bps Suffr of Moos; and Massachusetts (USA); Apptd Ld Bp of NS 63; Elected Abp and Metrop of Prov of Canada 72; res 75; Asst to Bp of Ott from 75. *Apt 712, 1465 Baseline Road, Ottawa, Canada.*

DAVIS-JONES, Noel Jenkin. b 10. Late Scho of St D Coll Lamp BA (2nd cl Engl) 32. **d** 33 **p** 34 Swan B. C of Llansantffraed-juxta-Usk w Llanddetty and Glyncollwng 33-40; Chap RAFVR 40-46; V of Ludford Magna w Ludford Parva R 46-51; Kelstern w Clacethorpe and E Wykeham 46-51; Chap RAF 51-54; R of Caracas Venezuela and Chap to Br Embassy Venezuela 54-60; R of Southn Berm 60-65; V of Luddington w Garthorpe 65-76; R of Amcotts 65-76; RD of I of Axholme 69-76; C-in-c of Althorpe w Keadby 70-76; P-in-c of Llandewi and Abbey Cwmhir Dio Swan B from 76. *Llandewi Vicarage, Llandrindod Wells, Powys.* (Penybont 424)

DAVISON, Colin Keith Hay. b 35. St Edm Hall Ox BA 59, MA 63. Cudd Coll 58. **d** 60 **p** 61 S'wark. C of St Faith N Dulwich 60-63; St Alb Cathl Pret 63-64; R of Rustenburg 65-69; Dir Chr Inst of SA and L to Offic Dio Johann 70-71; Chap K Coll Cam 71-72; Group Work Officer C of E Bd of Educn 72-77; Consultant and Research Fell in Ch Stud, Grubb Inst 78-80; V of Stapleford Dio Ely from 80; Bp's Adv for Research and Tr Dio Ely from 80. *Vicarage, Stapleford, Cambridge, CB2 5BG.* (Shelford 2150)

DAVISON, Canon David Edward. b 09. TD 76. St Jo Coll Dur BA 31, MA 35. **d** 32 **p** 33 Dur. C of All SS Stranton 32-35; Birtley Co Dur 35-39; Min of Eccles Distr of St Mark Darlington 39-49; CF 39-46; Hon CF from 46; V of W Harton 49-61; Chap S Shields Gen Hosp 49-61; V of Shotton 61-72; RD of Easington 63-72; Hon Can of Dur Cathl 71-80; Can (Emer) from 80; Master of Sherburn Hosp 72-77; C-in-c of Pittington 72-77. *312 Coniscliffe Road, Darlington, Co Durham.*

DAVISON, Canon Paul. Ex Coll Ox BA 37, MA 41. Ripon Hall Ox 37. **d** 39 **p** 40 Roch. C of St Alb Dartford 39-42; Crayford 42-45; Chap R Merchant Navy Sch Bear Wood 45-53; C of Crayford 53-55; R of Hawkedon and Stansfield

55-64; V of Needham Mkt w Badley Dio St E from 64; RD of Bosmere 70-78; Hon Can of St E Cathl from 75; C-in-c of Creeting (St Mary) Dio St E from 75. *Vicarage, Needham Market, Suff.* (0449-720316)

DAVISON, Peter Wood Asterley. Ball Coll Ox BA (3rd cl Th) 59, MA 62. Cudd Coll 59. **d** 61 Lon for Montr **p** 61 Montr. C of Trin Mem Ch Montr 61-64; R of St Johns Montr 64-67; P-in-c of Iberville 64-67; R of Aylmer 67-73; St Faith Vanc 73-79; Bp Cronyn Mem Lon Dio Hur from 79. *442 William Street, London, Ont, Canada N6B 3E2.*

DAVISON, Ralph Guild. b 13. Ely Th Coll 33. **d** 36 Taunton for B & W **p** 37 B & W. C of St Jo Evang Taunton 36-40; CF (EC) 40-45; V of H Trin Taunton 45-47; Chap Taunton and Somerset Hosp 46-47; V of H Trin Bury 47-53; R of Mamhead 53-62; Ashcombe 53-62; P-in-c of W Bagborough 62; R 63-78. *Posbury St Francis, Crediton, Devon, EX17 3QF.* (Crediton 3280)

DAVISON, Richard Ireland. b 42. St Chad's Coll Dur BSc 63. Linc Th Coll 64. **d** 66 Jarrow **p** 67 Dur. C of Cockerton 66-70; Houghton-le-Spring 70-73; V of St Alb Heworth 73-80; St Mary Ascen I Dio St Hel from 80. *St Mary's Vicarage, Ascension Island, S Atlantic Ocean.*

DAVISON, Richard John. b 32. St Andr Univ MA 56. Linc Th Coll. **d** 58 **p** 59 Dur. C of S Shields 58-61; St Cuthb Dur 61-63; R of Wyberton Dio Linc from 63. *Wyberton Rectory, Boston, Lincs.* (Boston 62296)

DAVISON, Canon Roger William. b 20. Kelham Th Coll 46. **d** 51 **p** 52 Man. C of Tonge Moor 51-55; V 55-65; Hon Can of Man 63-65; Can (Emer) from 65; V of Higham Ferrers (w Chelveston from 68) Dio Pet from 65; C-in-c of Chelveston 65-68; Commiss Taejon 68-74; Pusan (or Busan) from 74; Surr from 69. *Clergy House, Wood Street, Higham Ferrers, Wellingborough, NN9 8DL.* (Rushden 2433)

DAVISON, Thomas Alfred. b 28. St Chad's Coll Dur 52. **d** 60 **p** 61 Glouc. C of Tetbury 60-62; Malvern Link 62-65; R of Coates Cirencester (w Rodmarton & Sapperton w Frampton Mansell from 75) 65-78; Chap to R Agric Coll Cirencester 67-78; C-in-c of Bleadon 78-81; Asst Chap HM Pris Leeds from 81. *Chaplain's Office, HM Prison, Armley, Leeds.* (Leeds 636411)

DAVISON, William. b 18. St D Coll Lamp 58. **d** 60 **p** 61 Linc. C of Horsington w Stixwould 60-62; R of Welby 62-65; V of Heydour w Culverthorpe 62-65; R of Offord D'Arcy w Offord Cluny 65-66; Mareham-le-Fen (and Revesby from 76) 66-77; L to Offic Dio Linc 77-78; P-in-c of Barkestone w Plungar and Redmile 78; R 78-81. *65 New Beacon Road, Grantham, Lincs, NG31 9JS.* (Grantham 61696)

DAVY, Kenneth Thomas. NZ Bd of Th Stud LTh 65. Ch Ch Coll. **d** 54 **p** 65 Ch Ch. C of Avonside 64-66; St Pet U Riccarton 66-69; V of Fairlie 69-73; Amberley 73-74; P-in-c of Marchwiel Dio Ch Ch 75; V from 75. *213 Selwyn Street, Timaru, NZ.* (Tim 7205)

DAW, Ven Allan Graham. St Barn Coll Adel 40. ACT ThL 42. **d** and **p** 43 Adel. C of St Aug Unley 43-44; St Barn Clare 44-45; P-in-c of Koolunga w St Phil Pt Broughton 45-48; R of Minlaton 48-53; Dioc Sec Dio New Guinea and R of Samarai 53-58; Can of Dogura Cathl 56-58; R of Prospect (w Prospect N from 66-69) 58-69; Commiss Polyn 65-70; R of Grange 69-77; Campbelltown Dio Adel from 77; Can of Adel 73-79; Archd of Eliz 76-79; Adel from 79; Org Chap Bp's Home Miss S Dio Adel from 79. *44 Rostrevor Avenue, Rostrevor, S Australia 5073.* (267 1411)

DAWANI, Salem. d 66 Jordan. d Dio Jordan 66-75; Dio Jer from 76. *PO Box 15, Salt, Jordan.* (Salt 23)

DAWANI, Suheil Salman. b 51. **d** 76 **p** 77 Jer. P-in-c of Bir Zeit w Ramallah Dio Jer from 76. *St Andrew's Episcopal Church, PO Box 112, Ramallah, Israel.*

DAWE, Clement George. b 02. Ex Coll Ox BA 26, MA 30. Wells Th Coll 26. **d** 27 **p** 28 Ex. C of St Marychurch (in c of St Martin from 30) 27-31; V of King's Kerswell 31-41; Cockington w Chelston 41-47; RD of Ipplepen 38-42; PC of Budleigh Salterton 47-58; Surr from 48; V of Bampton Proper w Bampton Lew 58-67; V of Bampton Aston w Shifford 64-67; R of Emberton w Tyringham and Filgrave 67-71; Perm to Offic Dio Ex 71-78; L to Offic Dio Ex from 79. *45 Barn Hayes, Woolbrook, Sidmouth, EX10 9EE.* (Sidmouth 5303)

DAWE, David Fife Purchas. b 20. Keble Coll Ox BA (Hist) 41, MA 45. Wells Th Coll 41. **d** 43 **p** 44 Lich. C of Wolstanton 43-46; Meole-Brace Shrewsbury 46-47; All SS Leek 47-50; Tardebigge w Webheath 50-52; R of Stoke Bliss w Kyre Wyard 52-54; Jackfield 54-61; PC of Buildwas 54-61; V of Criftins-by-Ellesmere 61-77; Dudleston 63-77; P-in-c of Alkmonton w Yeaveley Dio Derby 77-82; V from 82; Cubley w Marston Montgomery Dio Derby 77-82; V from 82. *Alkmonton Vicarage, Longford, Derby, DE6 3DL.* (Gt Cubley 382)

DAWE, Harold Brien. Linc Th Coll. **d** 67 **p** 68 Pet. C of St Pet and St Andr Corby 67-69; Sherborne w Castleton and Lillington 69-73; V of West Moors 73-79. *c/o West Moors Vicarage, Wimborne, Dorset, BH22 0JF.* (Ferndown 2310)

DAWES, Alexander Barton. b 09. Bps' Coll Cheshunt 44. **d** 46 **p** 47 Roch. C of St Alb Dartford 46-48; Evesham 48-50; V of Norton w Lenchwick 50-54; All SS St John's Wood 54-69; R of Quendon w Rickling 69-70; V of Pill 70-74. *3 Woodhill Court, Portishead, Avon, BS20 9EU.* (0272-842948)

DAWES, Cyprian Osborne. b 13. United Th Coll of WI 69. **d** 70 **p** 71 Ja. P-in-c of Frankfield 70-73; Chap Kingston Hosp Dio Ja from 74. *67 Garden Boulevard, Mona Heights, Kingston 6, Jamaica, W Indies.* (093-77607)

DAWES, Hugh William. b 48. Late Exhib and Scho Univ Coll Ox BA (Mod Hist) 71, MA 76. Cudd Coll 71. **d** 74 **p** 75 S'wark. C of St Mark Woodcote Purley 74-77; Chap G and C Coll Cam from 77; L to Offic Dio Ely from 78. *Gonville and Caius College, Cambridge, CB2 1TA.* (Cam 312211)

DAWES, Julian Edward. b 27. Bps' Coll Cheshunt 58. **d** 59 **p** 60 Lon. C of St Aug of Cant Whitton 59-62; Chap RAF 62-65; V of Overbury w Teddington Alston and Washbourne 65-70; Cropthorne w Charlton 70-75; Chap Exe Vale Hosp Group from 76. *c/o Chaplain's House, Exe Vale Hospitals, Exminster, Exeter, EX6 8AB.* (0392-71337)

DAWES, Peter Martin. b 24. **d** 81 Doncaster for Sheff **p** 81 Sheff. C of Ch Ch Dunscroft Dio Sheff from 81. *162 Station Road, Dunscroft, nr Doncaster, S Yorks.* (0302 841328)

DAWES, Ven Peter Spencer. b 28. Hatf Coll Dur BA 52. Tyndale Hall Bris 48 and 53. **d** 54 Kens for Lon **p** 55 Lon. C of St Andr Whitehall Pk 54-57; St Ebbe Ox 57-60; Tutor Clifton Th Coll and L to Offic Dio Bris 60-65; V of Ch of Good Shepherd Romford 65-80; Exam Chap to Bp of Chelmsf from 70; M Gen Syn Chelmsf from 70; Commiss Chile 72-77; Hon Can of Chelmsf 78-80; Archd of W Ham from 80. *15 Wallenger Avenue, Gidea Park, Romford, Essex, RM2 6EP.* (Romford 21866)

DAWES, Victor. b 18. Wycl Hall Ox 63. **d** 64 **p** 65 Bradf. C of Guiseley 64-67; V of Jurby 67-73; Chap of St Jude Andreas 67-73; Min of Div Healing Dio S & M from 73. *Stanleyville, Laxey, IM.*

DAWES, William Henry. b 41. K Coll Lon 65, AKC 68. **d** 69 Capetn **p** 73 Edmon for Lon. C of St Mark Noel Park 72-76; All H N Greenford 76; St Andr Uxbridge 76-78; Perm to Offic Dio Birm from 78. *533 Stratford Road, Shirley, Solihull, W Midl.* (021-745 4153)

DAWIDI, Manasse Binyi. St Paul's Th Coll Limuru 66. **d** 67 **p** 69 N Ugan. d Dio Sudan. *c/o Clergy House, Box 153, Khartoum, Sudan.*

DAWKES, Peter. b 31. Roch Th Coll 64. **d** 66 Repton for Derby **p** 67 Derby. C of Newbold w Dunston 66-69; Buxton Derby 69-72; V of Somercotes Dio Derby from 72. *Somercotes Vicarage, Derby.* (Leabrooks 602840)

DAWKINS, Canon Alan Arthur Windsor. b 26. Univ of Lon Dipl Th 54. St Aid Coll 53. **d** 55 **p** 56 Blackb. C of Em Ch Preston 55-57; H Trin S Shore Blackpool 57-59; V of Slade Green 59-61; St Mary w St Paul Cray 61-63; R of Pebmarsh 63-66; R of White Colne 63-66; C-in-c of Mt Bures 65-66; V of Westgate-on-Sea 66-74; Herne Bay Dio Cant from 74; Hon Can of Cant from 79; Dioc Adv for Miss and Unity from 76. *38 Beltinge Road, Herne Bay, Kent, CT6 6BU.* (Herne Bay 4906)

DAWKINS, Anthony Norman. b 32. N-W Ordin Course 70. **d** 73 Man **p** 74 Hulme for Man. C of Clayton 73-74; St Werburgh Chorlton-cum-Hardy 74-76; St Martin Scarborough 76-78; P-in-c of Kexby w Wilberfoss Dio York from 78. *Vicarage, Ings Road, Wilberfoss, York, YO4 5NG.* (07595-426)

DAWKINS, Cecil Brian. Em Th Coll Sktn 57. **d** 57 **p** 58 Sktn. I of St Matt Sktn 57-62; C of Ch Ch Edmon 62-63; I of St Albert 63-68; Leduc 68-79; Drayton Valley Dio Edmon from 79. *Box 299, Drayton Valley, Alta., Canada.* (403-542 5033)

DAWKINS, Cuthbert Howard. Peterho Cam BA 32, MA 47. St Andr Coll Pampisford. **d** 47 **p** 48 Glouc. C of St Mark Cheltenham 47-50; Miss (BCMS) at Addis Ababa 51-52; Dio Sudan 52-56; Perm to Offic Dio Momb 56-61; Perm to Offic Dio Maseno 61-70; Dio S Maseno from 70. *Trinity Fellowship, P.O. Box 376, Kisumu, Kenya.*

DAWKINS, David Michael. Ridley Coll Melb ACT ThL 63, Dipl Relig Educn 65. **d** 65 **p** 66 Melb. C of Rosanna 65-67; St John Blackburn 67-69; Asst Chap Monash Univ from 69; Perm to Offic Dio Melb from 69. *Flat 3, 74 Wellington Road, Clayton, Vic. 3168, Australia.*

DAWKINS, Michael Howard. Tyndale Hall Bris 67. **d** 69 and **p** 69 York. C of Drypool 69-71; St Jas Bermondsey 71-72; Chap Desford Sch Leic 72-74; CF 74-80; P-in-c of Figheldean w Milston Dio Sarum from 80; Bulford Dio Sarum from 80. *Vicarage, Figheldean, Salisbury, Wilts, SP4 9BE.*

DAWSON, Alan. b 28. St Jo Coll Dur BA 54. Univ of Liv MA 67. Clifton Th Coll 54. **d** 56 **p** 57 Bradf. C of St Steph Bowling 56-59; Attenborough w Bramcote and Chilwell (in c of St Barn Inham Nook) 59-62; V of St Jo Evang Everton 62-69; Birkdale Dio Liv from 69. *2 St Peter's Road, Birkdale, Southport, PR8 4BY.* (Southport 68448)

DAWSON, Arthur Roger. b 38. Sarum Th Coll 64. **d** 66 Croydon for Cant **p** 66 Cant. C of St Mildred, Addiscombe 66-67; Cove w Hawley 67-69; P-in-c of Newton-in-Makerfield Dio Liv 75-76; R from 76. *Rectory, Wargrave Road, Newton-le-Willows, Mer, WA12 8RR.* (N-l-W 4920)

DAWSON, Barry. b 38. Univ of Lon Dipl Th 65. Oak Hill Th Coll 63. **d** 66 Kens for Lon **p** 67 Lon. C of St Mary Hammersmith Road Fulham 66-69; All S Langham Place St Marylebone 69-73; Dom Chap to Bp of Nor 73-76; Gen Sec C of E Men's Society 76-81; V of Rye Pk Dio St Alb from 81. *Rye Park Vicarage, Ogard Road, Hoddesdon, Herts.* (Hoddesdon 63168)

DAWSON, Brian. b 33. Univ of Leeds BA (2nd cl Engl) 54. Dipl Th (Lon) 57. Coll of Resurr Mirfield 56. **d** 58 **p** 59 Man. C of Hollinwood 58-62; Rawmarsh 62-63; V of St Anne Longsight Royton 63-75; Urswick Dio Carl from 75; Bardsea Dio Carl from 75. *Urswick Vicarage, Ulverston, Cumb.* (0229-56254)

DAWSON, Clifford Mildmay Asquith. b 22. Wycl Hall Ox. **d** 58 **p** 59 Liv. C of Sutton 58-60; R of Laceby 60-68; Irby-upon-Humber 64-68; Bradfield 68-77; V of Brodsworth w Hooton Pagnell, Frickley, Clayton and Marr 77-80; Wentworth Dio Sheff from 80. *Wentworth Vicarage, Rotherham, Yorks, S62 7TW.* (Barnsley 742274)

DAWSON, Cyril. b 34. St Chad's Coll Dur BA (3rd cl Th) 58, Dipl Th 59. **d** 59 Ex **p** 60 Crediton for Ex. C of St Francis Honicknowle Devonport 59-63; Paignton (in c of St Andr) 63-66; V of Heptonstall 66-71; Surr from 70; V of Todmorden Dio Wakef from 71; RD of Calder Valley from 75; P-in-c of Walsden Dio Wakef from 81. *Vicarage, Todmorden, Lancs, OL14 7BS.* (Todmorden 3180)

DAWSON, Edmund Smuts. b 16. ACommA 52. **d** 71 **p** 72 Damar. C of Walvis Bay 71-74; Fort Beaufort and Adel 75-76; Perm to Offic Dio Grahmstn from 81. *Central Garage, Campbell Street, Fort Beaufort, CP, S Africa.*

DAWSON, Francis Andrew Oliver Duff. b 48. Keble Coll Ox BA 70, MA 74. St Jo Coll Nottm 74. **d** 76 **p** 77 Chelmsf. C of Billericay 76-80; Chap St Kath Coll Liv from 80; C of Childwall Dio Liv from 80. *55 Woolacombe Road, Liverpool, L16 9JG.* (051-722 0153)

DAWSON, Frederick William. b 44. Univ of Dur BA (2nd cl Hist) 66. Univ of Nottm MTh 74. Linc Th Coll 67. **d** 69 **p** 70 Ox. C of Caversham 69-72; Ranmoor Sheff 72-79; R of Kibworth-Beauchamp Dio Leic from 79; P-in-c of Smeeton-Westerby w Saddington Dio Leic from 80. *Rectory, Church Road, Kibworth Beauchamp, Leics.* (Kibworth 2294)

DAWSON, George Alfred. b 1898. K Coll Lon 21 and 31. **d** 22 **p** 23 Dun. C of Winton w Otautau 22-24; V of Otautau 24-25; CTA 25; V of Wyndham w Fortrose 25-28; Tapanui 28-31; C of St Pet w St Mary Marlborough 32-34; St Agnes Sefton Park 34-35; Elmton w Creswell 35-37; St Pet Belper (in c of St Mark Openwoodgate) 37-39; Odd Rode w Mow Cop 39-42; V of Tolleshunt D'Arcy 42-72. *17 Barnhall Road, Tolleshunt Knights, Maldon, Essex.*

DAWSON, George Cuming. b 17. Ch ch Ox BA 38. TCD BA *(ad eund)* 56. **d** 58 **p** 59 Dub. C of S Thos w St Barn Dub 58-62; Drumcondra w N Strand 62-67; Hon Cler V of Ch Ch Cathl Dub from 68; C-in-c of St Werburgh's Dub 74-79. *Kilronan, Cloghran, Co Dublin, Irish Republic.* (Dub 401224)

DAWSON, Very Rev Harry James. Bp's Univ Lennox BA 63. Hur Coll BTh 65. **d** 65 Niag. C of St Geo, St Catharine's 65-68; R of Acton 68-74; St Jas Guelph 74-81; Hon Can of Niag from 79; Dean and R of All SS Cathl Edmon from 81. *10023-103rd Street, Edmonton, Alta, Canada T5J 0X5.* (403-422 4234)

DAWSON, John. b 1879. **d** 46 **p** 47 Man. C of St Thos Bedford-Leigh 46-50; C-in-c 50-51; C-in-c of Lostock Conv Distr 51-54; L to Offic Dio St A 54-60 and from 64; C of Eglwys-Rhos 60-64. *17 Trafford Park, Penrhyn Bay, Llandudno, Gwynedd.* (Llandudno 49234)

DAWSON, Neil. b 49. Ripon Hall Ox 71. **d** 74 **p** 75 S'wark. C of Putney 74-78; Camberwell 78-80; Team V of N Lambeth Dio S'wark from 80. *1 Havilland House, Sancroft Street, SE11.*

DAWSON, Norman William. b 41. K Coll Lon and Warm BD and AKC 63. **d** 65 Hulme for Man **p** 66 Man. C of St Phil w St Steph Salford 65-68; Ch Ch Heaton 68-70; R of Longsight (w Kirkmanshulme from 75) Dio Man from 70. *Rectory, St John's Road, Longsight, Manchester, M13 0WU.* (061-224 2744)

DAWSON, Ven Peter. b 29. Keble Coll Ox BA 52, MA 56. Ridley Hall Cam 52. **d** 54 **p** 55 S'wark. C of Morden 54-59; V of Barston 59-63; R of St Clem Higher Openshaw 63-68; Morden 68-77; RD of Merton 75-77; Archd of Norf from 77. *Intwood Rectory, Norwich, NR4 6TG.* (Norwich 51946)

DAWSON, Peter. b 34. E Midl Jt Ordin Tr Scheme 73. **d** 76 **p** 77 Linc. C of Blyton and Pilham 76-80; Laughton w Wildsworth 76-80; E Stockwith 77-80; St Mary Blyth Dio Newc T from 80. *74 Marine Terrace, Blyth, Northumb, NE24 2LR.* (Blyth 69482)

DAWSON, Peter Donald. Moore Th Coll Syd ACT ThL 56. **d** and **p** 57 Syd. C of Penrith 57-59; Chap at Mwanza 59-65; Msalato Bible Sch 65-74; Can of Centr Tang 70-74; Overseas Sec CMS and L to Offic Dio Syd from 74. *2 Skinner Parade, Roseville, NSW, Australia 2069.* (467-1751)

DAWSON, Richard Frailick. St Jo Coll Manit BA (1st cl) 26. St Aug Coll Cant 26. **d** 28 **p** 29 Chelmsf. C of St Jo Evang Seven Kings 28-31; R of Flin Flon w Sheridon Manit 31-33; V of St Jo Evang Ford End 33-42; R of St Andr Levenshulme 42-48; Lockport 48-50; Gen Miss Rupld 50-56; R of Charleswood 56-61; St Patr Winnipeg 61-65; Hon Can of St Jo Cathl Winnipeg 62-66. *4325 Cedar Hill Road, Victoria, BC, Canada.*

DAWSON, Ronald Eric John. b 27. BD (Lon) 64. Bp's Coll Cheshunt. **d** 62 **p** 63 Roch. C of Dartford 62-66; St Etheldreda Fulham 66-74; V of St Faith Brentford 74-80. *13 Birkbeck Road, Ealing, W5 4ES.* (01-560 3564)

DAWSON, William John. b 26. ACP 68. Div Hostel Dub 77. **d** 80 **p** 81 Conner (APM). C of St Paul Lisburn Dio Conner from 80. *55 Thornleigh Drive, Lisburn, Co Antrim, BT28 2DA.* (Lisburn 70252)

DAWSON, William Norman. b 27. Univ of Leeds BA (3rd cl Hist) 50. Coll of Resurr Mirfield 50. **d** 52 **p** 53 Blackb. C of St Steph Blackpool 52-57; V of St Bede Nelson-in-Marsden 57-63; Min of H Cross Eccles Distr Blackpool Dio Blackb 63-65; V from 65. *Holy Cross Vicarage, Central Drive, Blackpool, Lancs.* (South Shore 41263)

DAWSON-WALKER, Eric Dawson. b 07. St Jo Coll Dur BA (2nd cl Mod Hist) 29, MA 32. Ripon Hall Ox 31. **d** 32 **p** 33 Ox. C of H Trin Windsor 32-35; CF Aldershot 35-36; Tidworth 36-45; R of H Trin Windsor 45-72; Surr 46-72; Perm to Offic Dio Dur from 73. *Address temp unknown.*

DAXTER, Gregory. b 42. Dipl Th (Lon) 66. Oak Hill Th Coll 64. **d** 68 **p** 69 Ex. C of St Paul Preston Paignton Ex 68-72; Woodford Wells 72-75; Hon C of Harold Hill 75-78; Perm to Office Dio Roch from 79. *17 Gothic Close, Wilmington, Dartford, DA1 1TR.*

DAY, Algernon James. b 1895. Univ of Dur 21. Lich 70354) Coll 22; Bps' Coll Cheshunt 44. **d** 44 **p** 45 Leic. Hon C of Little Bowden 44-47; R of Knossington w Cold Overton 47-55; V of Measham w Willesley 55-82. *6 Wells Road, Ashby-de-la-Zouch, Leics.*

DAY, Cecil Ronald. **d** 59 **p** 60 Keew. C of Emo 59-62; I of Castlegar 62-65; R of Merritt 65-69; Cobble Hill Dio BC from 69. *RR 1, Cobble Hill, BC, Canada.*

DAY, Charles Ian. b 48. Univ of Wales (Bangor) BA 72. St Mich AA Llan 73. **d** 75 **p** 76 St A. C of Llanrhos 75-79; V of Mochdre Dio St A from 79. *Mochdre Vicarage, Nr Newtown, Powys.* (Newtown 27483)

DAY, Clark Edward. b 42. Lakehead Univ Thunder Bay Ont BA 74. Univ of Sask BEducn 77. Coll of Em and St Chad LTh & MDiv 77. **d** and **p** 77 Keew. I of Em Ch Ignace 77-80; Churchill Dio Keew from 80. *Box 57, Churchill, Manit, Canada.*

DAY, Colin Michael. b 40. Univ of Lon BSc (1st cl) and AKC 62. Em Coll Cam BA (3rd cl Th Trip pt ii) 66, MA 71. Ridley Hall Cam 65. **d** 67 **p** 68 York. C of H Trin, Heworth w St Cuthb, Peaseholme York 67-70; St Clem Ox 70-76; V of Kidsgrove Dio Lich from 76. *Kidsgrove Vicarage, Stoke-on-Trent, Staffs, ST7 1AG.* (Kidsgrove 2821)

DAY, David William. b 37. Univ of St Andr MA 58, BD 61. **d** 76 St Andr **p** 77 Brech. C of All SS St Andr 76-77; P-in-c of St Ninian Dundee Dio Brech from 77. *St Ninian's Church House, Kingsway East, Dundee.*

DAY, Fergus William. Trin Coll Dub BA 40, MA 45. **d** and **p** 41 Clogh. Dioc C Dio Clogh 41; C of Enniskillen 41-43; St Michan Dub 43-45; I of Drumcondra w N Strand 45-54; Ch Ch Kingstown (w Mariner's Ch from 59) 54-67; Dean and Libr of Waterf and Sec to Bp of Cash 67-79. *Elgar, Glenageary Terrace, Dun Laoghaire, Co Dublin.* (Dub 800101)

DAY, Frank Henry. b 18. St Jo Coll Dur 37. Clifton Th Coll 40. **d** 43 **p** 44 Bris. C of St Ambrose Bris 43-46; St Paul Chippenham 46-50; Brinkworth 50-52; R of Stanton St Quintin 52-59; C-in-c of Seagry 53-54; V 54-59; R of Grittleton w Leigh Delamere (w Stanton St Quintin from 68 and Hullavington and Norton from 77) 59-81; C-in-c of Kington St Mich 64-65; Stanton St Quintin 65-68; Hullavington 73-77; Norton 73-77; L to Offic Dio Bris from 81. *17 Avon Mead, Monkton Park, Chippenham, Wilts, SN15 3PP.* (0249-57929)

DAY, Frederick James. NZ Bd of Th Stud LTh 64. **d** 50 **p** 51 Waik. C of Te Awamutu 50-52; V of Taumarunui 52-55; Mangakino 55-58; Otorohanga 59-63; on leave 63-65; C of Fitzroy 65-66; P-in-c of Kawhia Miss Distr 66-68; Mokau Miss Distr 68-76; Perm to Offic Dio Waik 76-78; Hon C of Te

Kuiti Dio Waik from 78. *Box 309, Te Kuiti, NZ.* (1554)

DAY, George Chester. b 45. Univ of Ex BA 66. BD (Lon) 70. Clifton Th Coll 67. **d** 71 Reading for Ox **p** 72 Ox. C of St Jo Evang w St Steph Reading 71-75; St Lawr Morden 75-81; Jt Sec for Min CPAS from 81. *c/o Falcon Court, 32 Fleet Street, EC4Y 1DB.*

DAY, Hilary Paul Wilfrid. b 13. Qu Coll Birm. **d** 48 **p** 49 Lich. C of Broadway and Pye Green Cannock (in c of Chadsmoor) 50-52; V of Stubbins Lancs 52-55; R of St Chad Moston 55-62; V of Slade Green 62-71; R of Milton-next-Gravesend Dio Roch from 71. *Milton Rectory, Church Walk, Gravesend, Kent.* (Gravesend 533434)

DAY, Canon James Alfred. b 23. DFC 44. AKC 49. St Bonif Coll Warm. **d** 50 **p** 51 Lon. C of St Aug Wembley Pk 50-52; Chap at H Trin Rose Hill and to St Andr Sch Dio Maur 52-57; R of E w W Ravendale and Hatcliffe and R of Beelsby 57-60; PC of St Paul W Marsh Grimsby 60-66; R of Coningsby 66-80; PC (V from 68) of Tattersal w Thorpe 66-80; Offg Chap RAF Coningsby from 66; RD of Horncastle 73-80; Hon Can of Linc Cathl from 77; V of Heckington w Howell and Burton Pedwardine Dio Linc from 80. *Vicarage, Heckington, Sleaford, NG34 9RW.* (Sleaford 60302)

DAY, Canon James Laughton. b 07. Univ of Dur LTh 40. Qu Coll Birm 27. **d** 30 **p** 31 Linc. C of New Sleaford 30-33; R of Brauncewell w Dunsby and Anwick (V) 33-52; CF (EC) 40-45; R of Asterby w Goulceby 52-77; Donington-on-Bain 52-77; Stenigot 52-77; V of Scamblesby w Calkwell 52-77; RD of Horncastle 57-77; R of Gayton-le-Wold w Biscathorpe 60-77; Can and Preb of All SS Thorngate in Linc Cathl from 61; C-in-c of Benniworth w Market Stainton and Ranby 70-73; R 73-77. *Thorngate, Goulceby, Louth, Lincs, LN11 9UR.* (Stenigot 270)

DAY, Canon John Alfred. b 25. TCD BA 51, Div Test 51. **d** 51 **p** 52 Clogh. C of Enniskillen and Trory 51-54; R of Clontibret w Tullycorbet 54-58; Drumkeeran 58-67; Maguiresbridge w Derrybrusk Dio Clogh from 67; Can of Clogh from 78; Exam Chap to Bp of Clogh from 78. *Rectory, Maguiresbridge, Co Fermanagh, N Ireland.* (Lisnaskea 21250)

DAY, John Ashley Garnet. Univ of NZ BA 37. **d** 39 Waik for Polyn **p** 42 Dun. Perm to Offic Dio Waik 39-40; Hd Master All SS Sch Labasa 40-42; C of All SS Dun 42-44; V of Bluff w Stewart Is 44-47; Balclutha 47-48; Perm to Offic Dio Wel 48-49; P-in-c of Otorohanga 49-51; V of Forest Lake 51-61; Mornington 61-67; Fitzroy 67-71; Waihi 71-74; Perm to Offic Dio Waik from 74. *11 Forest Lake Road, Hamilton, NZ.* (395-875)

DAY, John Cuthbert. b 36. Sarum Th Coll 66. **d** 68 **p** 69 Portsm. C of Bedhampton 68-72; V of Froxfield (w Privett from 73) 72-77; Ch Ch Warm 77-81; R of Pewsey Dio Sarum from 81. *Rectory, Church Street, Pewsey, Wilts, SN9 5DL.* (067-26 3203)

DAY, John Nathaniel. b 36. Kelham Th Coll 59. **d** 64 **p** 65 Southw. C of St Mark Mansfield 64-69; C of W Wycombe (in c of Downley) 69-75; Team V of High Wycombe 75-77; P Missr of St Geo Conv Distr Britwell Farnham Royal 77-78; Team V of W Slough Dio Ox from 78. *St George's House, Long Furlong Drive, Britwell, Slough, SL2 2LX.* (Slough 25935)

DAY, Michael. b 37. RCA MA 81. K Coll Lon and Warm AKC 61. **d** 62 Hulme for Man **p** 63 Man. C of St Phil Hulme Man 62-65; Asst Chap Univ of Newc T 65-70; Chap Univs in Lon from 70. *80a Old Brompton Road, SW7.* (01-589 9919)

DAY, Patrick Austin. St Mich Coll Crafers 47. ACT ThL 51. **d** and **p** 51 Adel. Gen L Dio Adel 51-52; C of Hawthorn 51-54; Miss at Kilburn 54-57; R of Naracoorte 57-63; Bp's V St Pet Cathl Adel 63-64; Chap R Adel Hosp 63-64; R of Ch Ch St Laurence City and Dio Syd from 64; Commiss Kuch from 64. *507 Pitt Street South, Sydney, NSW, Australia 2000.* (211-0560)

DAY, Paul Geoffrey. b 51. Univ of Dur BEducn 75. Trin Coll Bris 76. **d** 78 Willesden for Lon **p** 79 Lon. C of Ch Ch Roxeth Harrow 78-82. *c/o 69 Southdown Crescent, Roxeth, S Harrow, Middx HA2 0QT.*

DAY, Philip Maurice. b 45. TCD BA 69, MA 78. Div Sch TCD 69. **d** 70 **p** 71 Dub. C of Crumlin 70-73; Asst Chap K Hosp Sch Dub 73-76; I of Mountmellick Dio Kild from 76. *Rectory, Mountmellick, Portlaoise, Leix, Irish Republic.*

DAY, Robert Clifford. b 08. **d** 70 **p** 71 Willesden for Lon. C of L Stanmore 70-75. *10 Forge Lane, Blakedown, Kidderminster, Worcs, DY10 3JF.* (Kiddermin 700205)

DAY, Ronald Stribling. **d** 61 **p** 62 Johann. C of Springs 61-65; R of Vanderbijl Pk 65-71; Florida Dio Johann from 71. *Box 65, Florida, Transvaal, S Africa.* (011-672 2203)

DAY, Roy Frederick. b 24. SOC 63. **d** 67 **p** 68 S'wark. C of St Paul Newington 67-70; Radlett 70-72; C-in-c of Ponsbourne 72-74; R of Campton Dio St Alb from 76; V of Shefford Dio St Alb from 76. *Vicarage, Shefford, Beds, SG17 5BD.* (Hitchin 813228)

DAY, Canon Samuel Richard. b 15. Univ of Reading BSc 36. Ch Ch Ox BA (2nd cl Th) 48, MA 52, DPhil 56. St D Coll Lamp 37. **d** 38 **p** 39 Liv. C of St John, Birkdale 38-40; CF (EC) 40-46; C of St Mich-at-the-N Gate Ox 46-49; R of Chinnor 49-66; R of Emmington 50-66; C-in-c of St Mary Sydenham 51-66; Lect in Ch Hist Ripon Hall Ox 57-62; Proc Conv Ox 59-75; V of Gt Marlow Dio Ox from 66; RD of Wycombe 68-74; Hon Can of Ch Ch Ox from 70. *Vicarage, Marlow, Bucks.* (Marlow 2660)

DAY, Terence Patrick. ALCD 59. Univ of Lon BD 60, MTh 62, PhD 66; **d** 60 **p** 61 Chich. C of Polegate 60-63; Chap St Jo Coll Agra 66-75; Hon C of Good Shepherd Winnipeg Dio Rupld from 75. *31 Temple Bay, Winnipeg, Manit., R3T 2V1, Canada.*

DAYBELL, Canon Cecil John Richmond. b 16. Univ Coll Ox BA (3rd cl Mod Hist) 38, MA 47. Westcott Ho Cam 39. **d** 40 **p** 42 Leic. C of Hinckley 40-42; St Mary Magd Knighton 42-48; V of St Aug Leic 48-54; Chap and Sub-Warden of Aberlour Orph 54-58; V of Dalby-on- the-Wolds or Old Dalby 58-61; C-in-c of Nether Broughton 60-61; V of Old Dalby w Nether Broughton Dio Leic from 61; Surr from 65; Hon Can of Leic Cathl from 70; RD of Framland II from 79. *Old Dalby Vicarage, Melton Mowbray, Leics.* (Melton Mowbray 822272)

DAYKIN, Timothy Elwin. b 54. Univ of Lon BSc 75. Univ of Dur Dipl Th 77, MA 81. Cranmer Hall Dur 75. **d** 78 **p** 79 Guildf. C of St Thos-on-the-Bourne 78-81; Chap K Alfred's Coll Win from 82. *King Alfred's College, Winchester, Hants, SO22 4NR.* (Win 64724)

DAYNES, Andrew John. b 47. Jes Coll Cam BA 69, MA 73. Westcott Ho Cam 69. **d** 72 **p** 73 St Alb. C of Radlett 72-76; Chap of Cathl and Abbey Ch St Alb 76-80; St Alb Sch 76-80; Bryanston Sch Dorset from 80. *Bryanston School, Blandford, Dorset.*

DAYNES, Anthony Geoffrey Norman. b 24. Oak Hill Th Coll 57. **d** 59 Thetford for Nor for Rang **p** 60 Momb. C of St Mich Oulton 59; Miss at Maralal Kenya 59-62; C-in-c of Swanton Abbott w Skeyton 62-64; R 64-74; C-in-c of Scottow 62-65; V 65-74; R of Mileham 74-81; C-in-c of Beeston-next-Mileham 74-75; R 75-81; C-in-c of Stanfield 74-75; R 75-81; P-in-c of Cranworth w Letton and Southbergh Dio Nor from 81; Reymerston Dio Nor from 81; Whinburgh w Westfield Dio Nor from 81. *Rectory, Reymerston, Norwich, NR9 4AG.*

DDUMBA, Leubeni Male. Bp Tucker Coll Mukono 61. **d** 66 **p** 67 W Bugan. P Dio W Bugan 66-72; Dio Kamp from 72. *PO Box 335, Kampala, Uganda.*

DE BOWEN, Alfred William. b 24. St Paul's Coll Grahmstn 78. **d** 78 Grahmstn (APM). d Dio Grahmstn from 78. *PO Hogsback 5705, CP, S Africa.*

DE GROOT, John. b 48. Moore Coll Syd BTh 79. **d** 80 **p** 81 Tas. C of Devonport 80; P-in-c of King I Dio Tas from 80. *The Rectory, Currie, King Island, Tasmania 7256.*

DE STADLER, Dennis John. b 50. Univ of S Africa BTh 80. St Bede's Coll Umtata 78. **d** 80 **p** 81 Grahmstn. C of St Mark E Lon Dio Grahmstn from 80. *9 Church Lane, Cambridge, E London 5247, CP, S Africa.*

DEACON, (Angelo) Donald. Chich Th Coll 66. **d** 68 **p** 69 Sarum. M SSF from 68. L to Offic Dio Man 69-70; in Amer Ch 70-72; C of St Jo Div Kennington 72-74; St Paul Knightsbridge 74-75; Angl-Franciscan Rep Ecumen Centre Assisi Dio Gibr 75-79; M SSF from 79. *The Friary, Hilfield, Dorchester, Dorset.*

DEACON, Edwin William Frederick. Oak Hill Th Coll 46. **d** 48 **p** 49 Ex. C of Highweek w St Mary Newton Abbot 48-51; Tiverton St Pet and Chevithorne 51-52; St D Ex 52-54; R of E Woolfardisworthy w Kennerleigh 54-60; R of Washford Pyne w Puddington 55-60; V of St Matt Ex 60-69; Chap R Devon and Ex Hosp 66-69; Dep PV of Ex Cathl 66-69; R of Lustleigh Dio Ex from 69. *Lustleigh Rectory, Newton Abbot, Devon, TQ13 9TE.* (Lustleigh 304)

DEACON, Frederick George Raymond. b 15. Tyndale Hall Bris 63. **d** 65 **p** 66 Bris. C of H Trin Kingswood 65-69; St Phil and St Jas Leckhampton 69-71; V of Longcot w Fernham (and Bourton from 72) 71-77; C-in-c of Bourton Wilts 71-72; Hd of Railway Miss Dio Matab 77-80; P-in-c of Cressage w Sheinton 80-81; Harley 80-81; Team V of Wenlock Dio Heref from 81. *Cressage Vicarage, Shrewsbury, Salop.* (Cressage 355)

DEACON, Jonathan. b 49. St Jo Coll Auckld. **d** 78 Bp Spence for Auckld **p** 79 Auckld. C of Epsom Dio Auckld from 78. *85 Onslow Avenue, Epsom, Auckland 3, NZ.* (688-932)

DEACON, Peter Olford. K Coll Lon and Warm 48. **d** 52 **p** 53 S'wark. C of Lewisham 52-58; E Cowes w Whippingham 58-61; Chap Saunders-Roe Osborne 58-61; Chap City of Lon Freemen's Sch Ashstead Pk 61-62; Min of Gurnard Conv

Distr 62-68; Chap RN from 68. *c/o Ministry of Defence, Lacon House, Theobalds Road, WC1X 8RY.*

DEACON, Timothy Randall. b 55. Univ of Ex BA 78. Chich Th Coll 79. **d** 80 **p** 81 Ex. C of Whitleigh Dio Ex from 80. *99 Shrewsbury Road, Whitleigh, Plymouth, PL5 4EY.* (Plymouth 785608)

DEAKIN, John Hartley. b 27. K Coll Cam BA 50, MA 63. Univ of Dur Dipl Th 65. Cranmer Hall Dur. **d** 65 **p** 66 Lich. C of St Geo Newc L 65-70; V of Cotes Heath Dio Lich from 70; P-in-c of Standon Dio Lich from 79. *Cotes Heath Vicarage, Stafford.* (Standon Rock 268)

✠ **DEAKIN, Right Rev Thomas Carlyle Joseph Robert Hamish.** b 17. Wadh Coll Ox BA 38, MA 42. Wells Th Coll 38. **d** 40 **p** 41 Glouc. C of St Lawr Stroud 40-44; V of H Trin Forest of Dean 44-49; Charlton Kings 49-73; RD of Cheltm 63-73; Hon Can of Glouc from 66; Cons Ld Bp Suffr of Tewkesbury in St Paul's Cathl 1 Nov 73 by Abp of Cant; Bps of Lon, Birm, Chich, Derby, Glouc, Linc, Nor, Ox and Portsm; Bps Suffr of Dorking, Dorch, Doncaster, Huntingdon, Taunton and Croydon; and others. *Green Acre, Hempsted, Gloucester.* (Gloucester 21824)

DEALY, Thomas William. b 05. Linc Th Coll 65. **d** 66 **p** 67 Linc. C of Deeping St Jas 66-69; St Faith Linc 69-72; V of Brothertoft (w Kirton Holme 72-75) 72-76; Langrick w Wildmore 75-76; Perm to Offic Dio Linc from 77. *46 Fern Grove, Cherry Willingham, Lincoln, LN3 4BG.* (Lincoln 51042)

DEAN, Alan. b 38. Univ of Hull BA (2nd cl Psychology and Sociology) 61. Univ of Birm Dipl Th 63. Qu Coll Birm 61. **d** 63 **p** 64 Blackb. C of Clitheroe 63-67; Burnley 67-68; CF from 68. *3 Longfield, Penwortham, Preston, Lancs.*

DEAN, Alan Shacklock. b 24. Univ of Lon BSc 54. St Jo Coll Dur 79. **d** 81 Burnley for Blackb. C of All SS Habergham Burnley Dio Blackb from 81. *1 Southern Avenue, Ightenhill, Burnley, Lancs, BB12 8AH.* (0282-28691)

DEAN, Andrew Duncan. b 40. Sarum Th Coll 62. **d** 64 **p** 65 Ches. C of Stockton Heath 64-68; Mottram-in-Longendale w Woodhead (in c of Broadbottom) 68-71; P-in-c of Over Tabley w High Legh 71-73; V 73-78; R of Astbury w Smallwood Dio Ches from 79. *Astbury Rectory, Nr Congleton, Chesh.* (02602-2625)

DEAN, Archibald Charles. b 13. Wycl Hall Ox 52. **d** 54 B & W **p** 55 Taunton for B & W. C of Yeovil 54-61; R of Odcombe Dio B & W from 61; Lufton Dio B & W from 61; Brympton D'Evercy Dio B & W from 61; P-in-c of Montacute Dio B & W from 78. *Rectory, Odcombe, Yeovil, Somt.* (West Coker 2224)

DEAN, Dana Grant Lawrence. b 48. Univ of Windsor Ont BA 70. Trin Coll Tor 73. **d** 74 NS. On study leave 74-75; I of Liscombe Dio NS from 75. *Rectory, Sherbrooke, NS, Canada.*

DEAN, Canon Desmond Keable. b 06. S Jo Coll Dur LTh 30, BA 31, MA 37, BD 41. ALCD 30. **d** 30 **p** 31 Lon. C of H Trin Isl 30-32; Tutor Tyndale Hall Bris 32-35; C of St Bart Bris 33-35; V of St Pet U Holloway 35-41; Chap RAFVR 41-45; R of St Clem Higher Openshaw 45-51; Surr from 46; Exam Chap to Bp in N Africa 50-54; R of Tooting Graveney 51-76; Chap Fountain Hosp 51-61; Grove Hosp 54-58; Surr 53-76; Exam Chap to Bp of S'wark 62-76; Hon Can of S'wark 63-76; Can (Emer) from 76; Proc Conv S'wark 64-70; RD of Tooting 65-75. *68 Milland Road, Harmers Hay, Hailsham, E Sussex, BN27 1TY.* (0323-843910)

DEAN, Eric William Alfred. ALCD 41. Univ of Lon BD (2nd cl) 41. **d** 41 **p** 42 Southw. C of St Ann Nottm 41-44; H Trin Wallington 44-45; Bedworth 45-49; V of St Andr Lambeth (in C of St Thos Lambeth) 49-51; Chap to Fairbridge Mem Coll Bulawayo 51-59; Glenmuir High Sch Dio Ja from 64. *Glenmuir High School, May Pen, Jamaica, W Indies.*

DEAN, Francis John Michael. b 15. Univ Coll Ox BA (2nd cl Mod Hist) 38, MA 42. Cudd Coll 38. **d** 39 **p** 40 Bris. C of All SS Clifton 39-46; Hd Master of All SS Sch Clifton 43-46; Exam Chap to Bp of Glouc 46-52; Chap of Ch Ch Cathl Ox 46-52; Libr of Pusey Ho Ox 46-52; V of St Steph Bournemouth 52-57; R of Cranford 57-64; St Antholin Lect at St Mary Aldermary Lon 58-62 and 74-75; V of St Mark Prince Albert Road St Pancras 64-81. *Flat 4, 9 Hendon Avenue, Finchley N3 1UL.* (01-346 5111)

DEAN, Frank Arthur. b 22. Univ of Lon BD 49. ALCD (2nd cl) 49. **d** 49 **p** 50 Liv. C of Em Everton 49-52; St Mark St Helens 52-55; V of St Matt Thatto Heath 55-64: Earlestown 64-70; St Paul Newbarns w Hawcoat Barrow-F Dio Carl from 70. *353 Abbey Road, Barrow-in-Furness, Lancs.* (Barrow-F 21546)

DEAN, John Milner. b 27. SOC 69. **d** 72 **p** 73 S'wark. C of Lewisham 72-75; Merton 75-77; V of S Beddington Dio S'wark from 77. *St Michael's Vicarage, Milton Road, Wallington, SM6 9RP.* (01-647 1201)

DEAN, Malcolm. b 34. Tyndale Hall Bris 67. **d** 69 **p** 70 Middleton for Man. C of St Geo Mart Daubhill Bolton 69-73; C-in-c of Constable Lee 73-74; V 74-79; St Sav w St Cuthb Everton Dio Liv from 79; P-in-c of Anfield Dio Liv from 81. *69 Anfield Road, Liverpool, L4 0TQ.* (051-263 2518)

DEAN, Canon Maurice. b 12. Univ of Birm BA 37. Ripon Hall Ox 37. **d** 38 **p** 39 Birm. c of St Paul Balsall Heath 38-40; Chap RNVR 40-46; V of Shaw Hill 46-47; Relig Broadcasting Organizer Midland Region 47-53; V of Hanley Castle w Hanley Swan 53-59; R of St Olave Hart Street and All H Staining w St Cath Coleman Lon 59-68; V of Bromsgrove 68-77; RD of Bromsgrove 73-77; Hon Can of Worc Cathl 76-77; Can (Emer) from 77. *45 Somers Park Avenue, Malvern, WR14 1SE.* (Malvern 2687)

DEAN, Michael Horace. Wollaston Th Coll W Austr 57. **d** and **p** 64 Perth. P-in-c of Wyalkatchem 64-66; R 66-67; Bruce Rock 67-70; Asst Chap Miss to Seamen Fremantle 70-74; Perm to Offic Dio Perth from 75. *13 Beach Street, Mosman Park, W Australia 6012.* (384 6685)

✠ **DEAN, Most Rev Ralph Stanley.** Univ of Lon BD 38, MTh 44. ALCD 38. Wycl Coll Tor Hon DD 53. Em Coll Sktn Hon DD 57. Angl Th Coll Bc Hon DD 65. Hur Coll Hon DD 66. Trin Coll Hartford Conn Hon STD 66. **d** 38 Lon **p** 39 Willesden for Lon. C of St Mary Isl 38-41; Watford (in c of St Luke) 41-45; Chap and Tutor Lon Coll Div 45-47; Vice-Prin 47-51; Prin of Em Coll Sktn 51-56; I of Sutherland and Hon Can of Sktn 55-56; Cons Ld Bp of Carib in Ch Ch Cathl Vic BC 6 Jan 57 by Abp of BC; Bps of Athab; Caled; Calg; Koot; New Westmr; Sktn; and Spokane; and Bp Ragg; res 73; Executive Officer Angl Communion 64-69; Elected Abp and Metrop of Prov of BC 71; res 73; in Amer Ch from 74. *Christ Church, Greenville, South Carolina, USA.*

DEAN, Preb Raymond Charles. b 27. Univ of Bris BA 51. Wycl Hall Ox 51. **d** 53 **p** 54 B & W. C of Weston-s-Mare 53-59; V of St Pet Lyngford Taunton 59-70; Burnham Dio B & W from 70; Preb of Wells Cathl from 73. *Vicarage, Burnham-on-Sea, Somt.* (Burnham-on-Sea 782991)

DEAN-JONES, Keith Michael. b 52. Macquarie Univ NSW BA 74. St Jo Coll Morpeth ACT ThL 76. **d** 76 Newc **p** 77 Bp Parker for Newc. Prec of Ch Ch Cathl Newc 77-79; C of E Maitland 80-81; St Chad City and Dio Leic from 82. *c/o 145 Coleman Road, Leicester, LE5 4LH.*

DEANE, Arthur Davidson. Moore Th Coll Syd. **d** and **p** 49 Syd. C of Summer Hill 49-50; Chap of Cranbrook Sch 50-52; Youth Chap Dio Syd 52-56; R of Castle Hill 56-59; Vice-Prin Syd Miss and Bible Coll 59-65; Prin from 65; L to Offic Dio Syd 59-69; Perm to Offic from 69. *43-45 Badminton Road, Croydon, NSW, Australia.*

DEANE, Gilbert Ernest. b 06. Univ of Lon BD (2nd cl hons) 38. Lon Coll of Div 34. **d** 38 **p** 39 Ex. C of Dawlish 38-40; Budleigh Salterton 40-47; Chap RAFVR 42-47; V of Countess Weir and Chap Ex Ment Hosp 47-55; Chap RAF 55-61; Asst Master Graham Road Boys' Secondary Sch Bexleyheath 61-63; Forest Girls' Sch Horsham 64-75. *Address temp unknown.*

DEANE, Nicholas Talbot Bryan. b 46. Bris Univ BA (2nd cl Th) 69. Trin Coll Bris 70. **d** 72 **p** 73 Blackb. C of Ch Ch Accrington 72-77; Miss Dio Seoul from 77. *Box 347, Kwang Hwa Moon, Seoul 110, Korea.*

DEANE-HALL (formerly HALL), Henry Michael. b 21. Univ of Leeds BA 46. Coll of Resurr Mirfield 47. **d** 49 Kens for Lon **p** 50 Lon. C of St Sav Poplar 49-51; Kirkley 51-53; St Mary (in c of St Mark) Reading 53-56; Chap of St Gabr Sch Sandleford Priory Newbury 56-62; V of Hermitage 58-65; Kirk Patrick 65-67; R of Boughton 67-71; Duloe w Herodsfoot 71-79; V of Morval 71-79; P-in-c of Donhead and of Donhead St Mary w Charlton 79-80; R of The Donheads Dio Sarum from 80. *Rectory, Donhead St Andrew, Shaftesbury, Dorset.* (9788 370)

DEANS, John Guy. b 37. St Aid Coll 59. **d** 62 Bp McKie for Cov **p** 63 Cov. C of St Mary Warw 62-65; Styvechale 65-67; Uttoxeter 67-70; Chap HM Borstal Stoke Heath 70-74; HM Borstal Glen Parva and L to Offic Dio Leic from 74. *5 Eden Close, Oadby, Leics.*

DEAR, Graham Frederick. b 44. Wycl Hall Ox 67. **d** 70 **p** 71 Bradwell for Chelmsf. C of Chigwell 70-73; Chingford 73-75; V of Ch Ch Southchurch Dio Chelmsf from 75. *Christ Church Vicarage, Warwick Road, Thorpe Bay, Essex, SS1 3BN.* (Southend-on-Sea 582585)

DEARDEN, James Varley. b 22. Wycl Hall Ox 61. **d** 62 **p** 63 York. C of Drypool 62-66; V of Transfig N Newington 66-75; H Trin Huddersfield Dio Wakef from 75. *132 Trinity Street, Huddersfield, HD1 4DT.* (Huddersfield 22998)

DEARDEN, Philip Harold. b 43. K Coll Lon and Warm AKC and Barry Pri 65. **d** 66 Lanc for Blackb **p** 67 Blackb. C of Haslingden 66-69; Burnley 69-71; V of Langho w Old St Leon Whalley 71-78; Team R of St Pet Darwen w Hoddlesden Dio Blackb from 78; Surr from 78. *Rectory, St Peter's Close, Darwen, Lancs, BB3 2EA.* (Darwen 72411)

DEARING, Trevor. b 33. BD (Lon) 58. Qu Coll Birm MA 63. **d** 61 **p** 62 Wakef. C of Todmorden 61-63; V of Silkstone 63-66; Northowram 66-68; C of Harlow New Town w L Parndon 68-70; V of Hainault 70-75; Dir of Healing Miss Dio Chelmsf 75-79; Hon C of St Andr Great Ilford 75-79; Perm to Offic Dio Linc 80-81; in Amer Ch. *c/o St Luke's Rectory, Seattle, Washington, USA.*

DEARNALEY, Fred Arthur John. d 62 Bp Redding for Melb **p** 63 Melb. C of Mentone 62-63; St Andr Brighton 63-66; V of Lara 66-74; I of Sunshine Dio Melb from 74. *49 Sun Crescent, Sunshine, Vic, Australia 3020.* (03-311 1659)

DEARNALEY, William Darryl. Ridley Th Coll Melb ACT ThL 62. **d** 64 **p** 65 Bend. C of St Paul Bend 64-67; P-in-c of Raywood 67-68; R of Kangaroo Flat Dio Bend from 68. *Rectory, Melbourne Road, Kangaroo Flat, Vic, Australia.*

DEARNE, Peter. b 1893. **d** 49 **p** 50 Dur. C of Usworth 49-53; R of Penshaw 53-57; PC of Evenwood 57-61; V of S Moor 61-69. *50 Harmer Green Lane, Digwell, Welwyn, Herts.*

DEARNLEY, Patrick Walter. b 34. Univ of Nottm BA (Engl) 55. ALCD 64 (LTh from 74). **d** 64 **p** 65 S'wark. C of New Malden 64-68; Ch Ch Portswood (or Highfield) Southn 68-71; St Geo Leeds 71-74; Hon C of St Nich Nottm 74-77; P-in-c of Em w St Barn Holloway Dio Lon from 77; RD of Isl from 80. *9 Jackson Road, N7 6ES.* (01-607 6255)

DEAS, Graeme Donald Martin. St Paul's Th Coll Grahmstn 60. **d** 63 **p** 64 Grahmstn. C of St John E Lon 63-67; P-in-c of All SS Port Eliz 66-68; R of Humansdorp 68-70; Good Shep E Lon Dio Grahmstn from 71. *10 Elton Street, Southernwood, East London, S Africa.* (2-1137)

DEASEY, Randal Hugh. Univ of Melb BA (2nd cl Cl) 38. Univ of Harvard M Publ Admin 55. Wells Th Coll 59. **d** 60 **p** 61 Melb. C of St Andr Brighton 60-61; I of Glenroy 61-71; Archd of Essendon 70-78; Can of Melb 71-78; I of Essendon 71-81; Kingsville w Yarraville Dio Melb from 81. *295 Somerville Road, Kingsville, Vic, Australia 3012.*

DEASEY, Canon William Keith. Moore Th Coll Syd ACT ThL 34. **d** 35 **p** 36 Syd. C of St Mich Wollongong 35-36; St Paul Syd 36-38; Chap Norf I 38-39; P-in-c of Cabramatta 39-41; R of Belmore 41-45; Cook's River 45-50; West Manly 50-68; Hon Can of Syd from 65; Dir of Chaps Dio Syd 68-75; R of St Mich Syd 70-72; L to Offic Dio Syd from 75. *7/30 Bellevue Parade, Hurstville, NSW, Australia 2220.*

DEASY, Roy Denis. b 21. Trin Hall Cam BA 48, MA 52. Westcott Ho Cam 47. **d** 49 **p** 50 Lon. C of St Jo Bapt Greenhill 49-53; Chap Portsm Cathl 53-55; CF (TA) from 54; V of Harrow Weald 55-62; St Andr Holborn 62-64; Dir Youth Service Dio Lon 62-64; Commiss Capetn 63-64; Perm to Offic Dio Ex 79-81; Hon C of Kenton w Mamhead Dio Ex from 81. *3 Pennsylvania Park, Exeter, EX4 6HD.* (Ex 72986)

De BEER, John Michael. b 45. Univ of the Witwatersrand BSc 67. Linacre Coll Ox BA (Th) 69, St Paul's Coll Grahmstn 72. **d** 72 Bp Carter for Johann **p** 73 Johann. C of Springs 72-75; L to Offic Dio Johann 75-77. *PO Box 49027, Rosettenville, Johannesburg, S Africa.*

DEBENHAM, Christopher Temple. St Jo Coll Armid ACT ThL (1st cl) 20. **d** 20 **p** 21 Goulb. C of Tumut NSW 20-22; P-in-c of Hume Reservoir Miss 22-24; C of Wagga Wagga 24-28; Asst Chap C of E Gr Sch N Syd 28-33; C of St Andr S Brisb 33-34; Asst Chap C of E Gr Sch Brisb 34-38; R of Ch Ch Boonah 38-52; Chap RAAF 42-46; R of N Ipswich 53-67. *16 Bentinck Street, Sherwood, Queensland, Australia 4075.* (379-6875)

de BERRY, Andrew Piers. b 44. St Jo Coll Dur BA 66. Ripon Hall Ox 70. **d** 74 Buckingham for Ox **p** 75 Ox. C of H Trin Aylesbury 74-77; In Amer Ch 78; Team V of Clyst Valley 78-80; Asst Chap HM Pris Wormwood Scrubs 80-82; Chap HM Pris Sudbury from 82. *c/o HM Prison, Sudbury, Derby.* (Sudbury 511)

de BERRY, Canon Oscar Keith de la Tour. b 07. St Jo Coll Cam 2nd cl Hist Trip pt i 28, BA (3rd cl Engl Trip pt ii) 29, MA 33. Ball Coll Ox MA 52. Ridley Hall Cam 29. **d** 30 **p** 31 Lon. C of St Mary Islington 30-35; V of St Geo Battersea w St Jas Nine Elms 35-39; Immanuel (in c of St Anselm) Streatham 39-52; Chap Belmont Hosp 40-52; Sen Chap Ox Past 52-74; R of St Aldate (w H Trin from 56) Ox 52-74; Surr from 52; V of H Trin Ox 55-56; Commiss Argent from 63; Proc Conv Ox from 64; Hon Can of Ch Ch Cathl Ox from 70; Hon C of St Mich w St Phil Ches Sq Dio Lon from 74. *9 Wilton Place, Hyde Park Corner, SW1 X8RL.* (01-235 5583)

de BERRY, Robert Delatour. b 42. Qu Coll Cam 2nd cl Econ Trip pt i 62, BA (2nd cl Th Trip pt ii) 64, MA 68. Ridley Hall Cam 65. **d** 67 **p** 68 Bradf. C of St Pet Cathl Bradf 67-70; Youth Worker CMS Uganda 71-75; V of Attercliffe w Carbrook Dio Sheff from 75. *St Albans Church House, Chapelwood Road, Sheffield 9.* (Sheffield 41873)

de BLANK, John. b 44. ACT ThDip 77. Ridley Coll Melb 74. **d** 78 **p** 79 Melb. C of St D Moorabbin 78-80; St Jude Carlton Dio Melb from 80. *630 Canning Street, Carlton, Vic, Australia 3053.*

DEBNEY, Wilfred Murray. b 26. ACA 48, FCA 60, Wycl Hall Ox 58. **d** 60 **p** 61 Leic. C of H Ap Leic 60-65; V of St John Thorpe Edge 65-69; V of Shingay Group 69-75; R of Brampton Dio ely from 75. *Brampton Rectory, Huntingdon, PE18 8PF.* (Huntingdon 53341)

DEBOO, Alan John. b 45. City Univ Lon MSc 69. Qu Coll Cam BA 73, MA 77. Westcott Ho Cam 72. **d** 74 **p** 75 Pet. C of Brackley 74-77; Perm to Offic Dio Sarum from 81. *Mayzell's Cottage, Collingbourne Kingston, Marlborough, Wilts, SN8 3SD.* (Collingbourne Ducis 683)

de BRETT, Rodney John Harry. b 13. Wells Th Coll 63. **d** 64 **p** 65 B & W. C of Wells 64-66; PC of Stoke St Gregory 66-68; V (w Burrowbridge from 75 and Lyng from 78) 68-81; RD of Taunton N 73-78. *106 Whipton Lane, Exeter, EX1 3DJ.*

de BRISAY, Robert Michael Delacour. b 31. K Coll Lon and Warm Relton and Plumtre Pris and AKC 55. **d** 56 **p** 57 Lon. C of St Steph Ealing 56-59; Heston 59-61; M of Bro of St Barn and Chap All S Sch Charters Towers Queensld 62-66; Asst Chap Worksop Coll 67-68; Chap 68-77; L to Offic Dio Southw 67-76; Chap St Edm Sch Cant 77-81; L to Offic Dio Cant 77-81; V of H Trin Northwood Dio Lon from 81. *6 Wildwood Dene Road, Northwood, Middx, HA6 2DB.* (65 25732)

de BURGH-THOMAS, George Albert. b 30. Univ Coll of N Wales (Ban) BA 50. St Mich Coll Llan 51. **d** 53 **p** 54 St A. C of Hawarden 53-56; St Martin Roath 56-58; Llangeinor 58-60; Hawarden 60-63; V of Bampton w Mardale 63-70; Fritwell (w Souldern and Ardley w Fewcot from 82) Dio Ox from 70; R of Souldern 70-82; C-in-c of Ardley w Fewcot (and Stoke Lyne to 76) 72-82. *Fritwell Vicarage, Bicester, Oxon.* (Fritwell 220)

de CAEN, St John Robert. b 24. Univ of Lon BA 52. Monash Univ Vic BEducn 77. Melb Coll of Div ThL 72. Wycl Hall Ox 50. **d** 52 **p** 53 Chelmsf. Chap Dockland Settlement E Lon 52-54; CF 66-63; Asst Master Tonbridge Sch 63-64; Trin Grammar Sch Kew 64-69; Ringwood High Sch 70-72; Boronia High Sch 73-77; Bacchus Marsh High Sch 78-79; C of Ch Ch Cathl Bal from 79. *1 Darling Street, Ballarat, Vic, Australia 3350.*

de CANDOLE, Charles Patrick. b 07. Chich Th Coll 34. **d** 34 **p** 36 S'wark. C of St Mark Walworth 34-37; Chap RN 37-62; R of Witchampton w Long Crichel and Moor Crichel (and Hinton Parva from 80) Dio Sarum from 62; Hinton Parva 79-80. *Witchampton Rectory, Wimborne, Dorset, BH2 15AP.* (Witchampton 354)

de CANDOLE, Canon Donald Vully. Linc Th Coll 37. **d** 38 Linc for Wel **p** 39 Bp Sprott for Wel. C of All SS Palmerston N 38-42; CF (NZ) 42-46; V of Waverley w Waitotara 46-50; Carterton 50-60; Harston w Hauxton Cambs 60-66; C of Wainuiomate (in C of St John) 66-67; V of St John Wainuiomata 67-77 Hon Can of Wel 71-77; Can (Emer) from 77; Perm to Offic Dio Wel from 77. *4 Kereru Street, Waitana, NZ.*

de CASABIANCA, Louis Edward Philip. b 09. Codr Coll Barb LTh (Dur) 38. **d** 38 **p** 39 Derby. C of Burbage (in c of St Jas Harpur Hill) 38-41; Chesterfield 41-44; C-in-c of Bamford 44-45; C of St Mark N Audley Str 45-47; R of Bulwick w Laxton 47-55; C-in-c of Bulwick 55-57; Woodford (w Twywell from 67) 55-57; R 57-80; C-in-c of Twywell 66-67. *2 Birch Drive, Attleborough, Norf.*

DECEMBER, Frederick Eustace. d 64 **p** 71 Gui. C of Port Mourant 64-70; Kitty 70-72; V of Enmore Dio Guy from 72. *St Mark's Vicarage, Enmore, ECD, Guyana.* (029-276)

de CHAZAL, John Robert. b 16. Wycl Hall Ox 53. **d** 55 **p** 56 Bris. C of St Sav Redland 55-57; St Anne Brislington 57; Boxwell w Leighterton 58-60; Newington Bagpath w Kingscote and Ozleworth 58-60; C-in-c 60; Chap at Baghdad and at Kirkuk 61-64; Hon Chap Br Embassy Baghdad 61-64; V of Caldecote 64-71; R of Bradford Peverell w Stratton (and Frampton and Sydling St Nicholas from 77) 72-80. *Lavender Cottage, Sydling St Nicholas, Dorchester, Dorset.*

DECK, Michael C. b 50. Ch Div Sch of the Pacific Calif 75. **d** 76 Bp Meyers (USA) for New Westmr **p** 76 New Westmr. C of Fraser Cheam 76-80; I of St Mich Surrey Dio New Westmr from 80. *7347 Whitby Place, Delta, BC, Canada.*

DECKER, James Burton. b 43. Univ of Tor BA 65. Trin Coll Tor MDiv 79. **d** 79 Bp Read for Tor **p** 80 Tor. C of St Marg W Hill 79-80; I of St Pet Oshawa Dio Tor from 81. *258 Thomas Street, Oshawa, Ont, Canada, L1J 1M1.*

de CORNEILLE, Roland. Amherst Coll Mass BA 46. Gen Th Sem New York 47-49. Trin Coll Tor LTh 53, STB 54, MTh 61. **d** 52 **p** 53 Tor. C of St John W Tor 52-53; St Jo Evang Montr 53-55; R of St Andr Tor 55-56; St Laur Tor 56-63. *9 Berwick Road, Willowdale, Ont, Canada.*

de DEAR, David Leon. Moore Th Coll Syd ACT ThL 57.

d 56 **p** 57 Gippsld. C of Traralgon 57-58; Bairnsdale 58-60; V of Foster 60-64; R of Gulgong 64-68; C of All SS Cathl Bath 68-72; I of Ocean Grove 72-74; St Geo E Ivanhoe 74-75. *Box 226, Toorak, Vic, Australia 3142.*

DEDMAN, Roger James. b 45. Oak Hill Th Coll 68. **d** 71 Repton for Derby **p** 72 Derby. C of Ch Gresley w Linton 71-74; St Francis Ipswich 74-78; P-in-c of Bildeston w Wattisham Dio St E from 79; Lindsey Dio St E from 79. *Bildeston Rectory, Ipswich, Suff.* (Bildeston 740530)

DEDMAN, Stanley Charles. b 13. SOC 62. **d** 65 **p** 66 Guildf. C of Farncombe 65-73; P-in-c of Wishford Magna 73-80; Libr of Sarum Cathl 73-80. *East Barn, Hobgoblins, Iwerne Minster, Dorset, DT11 8LP.*

DEEBLE, William Ernest. Univ of S Afr BA 51. St Paul's Th Coll Grahmstn LTh 53. **d** 53 **p** 54 Johann. C of Benoni 53-55; Rosettenville 55-57; Durban N 57-69; R of St Marg Northlands Durban 69-81; L to Offic Dio Natal from 81. *34 Ambleside Avenue, La Lucia 4051, Natal, S Africa.*

DEEDES, Canon Arthur Colin Bouverie. b 27. Bede Coll Dur BA 51. Wells Th Coll 51. **d** 53 Bp Kitching for Portsm **p** 54 Portsm. C of St Jas Milton 53-58; Worplesdon (in c of St Alb) 58-60; V of All SS Weston 60-66; Fleet 66-73; RD of Aldershot 69-73; R of Bournemouth 73-80; RD of Bournemouth 74-80; Hon Can of Win Cathl from 78; Master of St Cross Hosp and Min of St Faith City and Dio Win from 80. *Master's Lodge, St Cross, Winchester, Hants.*(Winchester 2888)

DEEKS, Norman Spencer. b 06. Peterho Cam BA 27, MA 35. Univ of Lon BSc 27. Ridley Hall Cam 45. **d** 48 **p** 49 B & W. [f Teacher and CMS Miss] C of S Lyncombe 48-52; V of St Jo Evang Kilburn 52-60; St Geo Enfield 60-71; C of Ch Ch Malvern 71-74. *64 Church Road, Mavern, Worcs, WR14 1NH.*

DEETH, William Stanley. b 38. St Pet Coll Ox BA 59, MA 67. St Steph Ho Ox 66. **d** 68 **p** 69 Chich. C of Eastbourne 68-71; St Jas Benwell (in c of Ven Bede) Newc T 71-75; C-in-c of St Martin Conv Distr Byker Newc T 75-76; St Martin Byker Newc T 76-82. *c/o St Martin's Parsonage, Roman Avenue, Newcastle upon Tyne.*

DE FORTIS, Paul Maurice Georges Pierre Guichot. b 53. AKC and BD 80. Ridley Hall Cam 80. **d** 81 Stepney for Lon. C of W Hackney Dio Lon from 81. *306b Amhurst Road, N16.*

DEFTY, Grahame John. Moore Th Coll Syd ACT ThL (2nd cl) 60. **d** 60 Syd **p** 61 Bp Kerle for Syd. C of Lindfield 60-63; Vaucluse 63-64; W Wollongong 65-66; CMS Miss Dio W Tang 66-75; Dio Centr Tang 75; Min of Housing Distr Glenquarie 76-79; R of Berrima w Moss Vale Dio Syd from 79. *5 Brownley Street, Moss Vale, NSW, Australia 2577.* (048-91 1052)

DEFTY, Henry Gordon. b 14. St Chad's Coll Dur BA 38, MA and Dipl in Th 41. **d** 39 **p** 40 Dur. C of St Mary Cockerton 39-43; Ferryhill 43-48; V of Hedgefield 48-51; PC of St Aid W Hartlepool 51-68; V 68-73; Can Res of Ches Cathl 73-74; V of Gainford 74-80; C-in-c of Winston 74-76; R 76-80; Perm to Offic Dio Dur from 80. *39 Crossgate, Durham, DH1 4PS.* (Durham 44334)

DEGG, Ralph William. b 26. BSc (Lon) 57. Wells Th Coll 61. **d** 63 **p** 64 Birm. C of Sutton Coldfield 63-66; The Lickey (in c of St Cath Blackwell) 66-71; R of Grendon 71-78; V of Salter Street Dio Birm from 78. *Salter Street Vicarage, Earlswood, Solihull, Warws, B94 6DH.* (Earlswood 2579)

De GROOSE, Leslie John. b 28. Oak Hill Th Coll 62. **d** 64 **p** 65 Nor. C of Gunton 64-67; Chap RN from 67. *c/o Ministry of Defence, Lacon House, Theobalds Road, WC1X 8RY.*

De GRUYTHER, Albert Alfred. b 14. Magd Coll Ox BA (2nd cl Phil Pol Econ) 48, MA 60. Ridley Hall, Cam. **d** 50 **p** 51 Liv. C of St Helens 50-53; C-in-c of St Jas Conv Distr Eccleston Pk 53-59; V of H Trin Ulverston 59-67; R of Ulverston 67-73; Gt Salkeld 73-79. *The Mill House, Lindale, Grange-over-Sands, Cumbria.*

DEHLE, Robert John. b 54. SSM Th Coll Adel 76. **d** 81 Adel. C of St Andr Walkerville Dio Adel from 81. *1 Reece Avenue, Klemzig, S Australia 5086.*

De HOOP, (Tom) Thomas. b 38. Bp's Univ Lennox BA and LTh 63. **d** 68 **p** 69 Moos. C of Paint Hills 68-70; I of Mistassini Moos 70-72; R of La Tuque 73-75; C of Roxboro-Pierrefonds 75-79; M SSF from 79. *Society of St Francis, St Mary-at-the-Cross, Glasshampton, Shrawley, Worcs.*

✠ **DEHQANI-TAFTI, Right Rev Hassan Barnaba.** b 20. Virginia Th Sem DD 81. Ridley Hall Cam 47. **d** 49 **p** 50 V of St Luke Isfahan 49-61; Cons Ld Bp in Iran in Colleg Ch of St Geo Mart Jer 25 Apr 61 by Abp in Jer; Bps in Sudan; and Jordan; and Bp Thompson; Episc Can of St Geo Jer from 76; Elected Pres of Centr Syn of the Episc Ch in Jer and the Middle E 76; Re-elected 80; Asst Bp in Dio Win from 82. *Bishop's House, PO Box 12, Isfahan, Iran; and c/o 14 Great Peter Street, SW1P 3NQ.*

DEIGHTON, Ian Armstrong. b 19. Univ of Glas MA 40. Edin Th Coll 40. **d** 43 **p** 44 Glas. C of H Trin Paisley 43-45; P-in-c of St Bride Nether Lochaber Argyll w St Paul Kinlochleven 45-47; Chap to Bp Arg Is 45-47; P-in-c of St Mark Kinning Park Glas 47-52; R of Clydebank 52-57; St Pet Musselburgh Dio Edin from 57; P-in-c of Prestonpans Dio Edin from 76. *12 Windsor Gardens, Musselburgh, Midlothian.* (031-665 2925)

DEIGHTON, William John. b 44. K Coll Lon and Warm AKC 68. **d** 69 **p** 70 Truro. C of St Kenwyn w Tregavetham 69-72. *c/o 20 Western Terrace, Falmouth, Cornw.*

DEIN, Terence Kemball. Univ of NSW BComm 64. Moore Th Coll Syd ACT ThL 69. **d** 69 **p** 70 Syd. C of Willoughby 69-73; Youth Dir Dio Syd 74-79; R of St Mark Yagoona Dio Syd from 79. *211 Auburn Road, Yagoona, NSW, Australia 2199.* (705-6281)

de JAGER, Frank. b 33. St Pet Coll Alice 72. **d** 74 Kimb K for Geo **p** 75 Geo. C of All SS Mossel Bay 74-77; P-in-c of St Matt Beaufort W 77-78; R of St Steph Paarl Dio Capetn from 78. *Rectory, Yellowwood Avenue, New Orleans, Paarl 7646, CP, S Africa.* (0251 22857)

De JONGE, Frank Hermann. b 03. Or Coll Ox BA (Engl Lit) 24, MA 45. DTh (*hon causa*) Univ of Kiel 49. Ely Th Coll 25. **d** 26 Willesden for Lon **p** 27 Lon. C of St Sav Poplar 26-29; L to Offic Dio Lon 29-31; C of St Alb Holborn 32-37; Chap of Commun of St Mary's Abbey W Malling 37-39; C of H Cross St Pancras 39-50; Chap RAFVR 40-47; Field Officer in Germany for Christian Reconstr in Eur 46-50; V of Somers Town 50-56; L to Offic Dio Lon 56-62; Travelling Sec for Inter-Ch Aid and Refugee Service of Br Coun of Chs 56-57; Bro of R Found of St Kath Stepney 58-62; R of Hitcham 62-73. *Oriel House, Thames Road, Goring-on-Thames, Oxon, RG8 9AH.* (Goring 2134)

DEJONGE, Jacob. b 38. St Paul's Coll Grahmstn Dipl Th 73. **d** 73 **p** 74 Pret. C of Hillcrest 73-76; R 76-78; Nelspruit w Waterval Boven Dio Pret from 78. *PO Box 298, Nelspruit, Transvaal 1200, S Africa.*

DE KEYSER, Nicholas David Llewellyn. b 49. Univ of Nottm BTh 75. St Jo Coll Nottm 71. **d** 75 **p** 76 Southn for Win. C of Highfield Southn 75-77; Yateley 77-81; Team V of Grantham Dio Linc from 81. *Vicarage, The Grove, Grantham, Lincs, NG31 7PU.* (Grantham 71270)

DELACOUR, Arthur Winter. b 14. Univ of Lon BSc (Econ) 52. Sarum Wells Th Coll 79. **d** 80 Malmesbury for Bris **p** 81 Bris (APM). C of Colerne 80-81; Hon C of Gtr Corsham Dio Bris from 81. *Neston Vicarage, Corsham, Wilts, SN13 9TA.* (Hawthorn 810572)

de la HOYDE, Denys Ralph Hart. b 33. G and C Coll Cam BA 57, MA 61. Westcott Ho Cam 57. **d** 59 **p** 60 Man. C of Ch Ch Moss Side 59-60; Chap of G and C Coll Cam 60-64; P-in-c of Naini Tal; Bhowali; Almora; and Raniket 64-68; C of H Trin Eltham 68-69; Chap Bromsgrove Sch 69-71; Asst Master Harrogate High Sch and L to Offic Dio Ripon 71-78. *119 Wetherby Road, Harrogate, N Yorks.*

de la MARE, Benedick James Hobart. b 38. Trin Coll Ox BA 63, MA 67. Trin Coll Cam MA (by incorp) 68. Cudd Coll 63. **d** 65 **p** 66 Newc T. C of All SS Gosforth 65-68; Chap Trin Coll Cam 68-73; V of St Gabr Heaton 73-81; St Osw w St Mary-Le-Bow and St Mary L City and Dio Dur from 81. *St Oswald's Vicarage, Church Street, Durham, DH1 3DE.* (Dur 64313)

de la MOUETTE, Norman Harry. b 39. Univ of Southn BEducn 73. Sarum Wells Th Coll 76. **d** 79 Basingstoke for Win **p** 80 Southn for Win (APM). C of St Lawr w St Swith City and Dio Win from 79. *146 Greenhill Road, Winchester, Hants, SO22 5DR.*

DELANEY, Lloyd Jackson. Trin Coll Tor BA 39, LTh 46, BD 47. **d** 41 **p** 42 Tor. C of St Mich Tor 41-42; R of Perrytown w Gores Landing and Harwood 43-48; Lakefield 48-57; Chap Grove Sch Lakefield 48-50; R of Midland 57-68. *290 King Street, Midland, Ont, Canada.*

DELANEY, Peter anthony. b 37. K Coll Lon and Warm AKC 65. **d** 66 Lon **p** 67 Willesden for Lon. C of St Marylebone 66-70; Chap Univs in Lon 70-73; L to Offic Dio Lon 70-73; Can Res and Prec of S'wark Cathl 73-76; V of All H Barking-by-the Tower w St Dunstan-in-E Dio Lon from 76; M Gen Syn from 81. *The Parish Office, All Hallows Church, Byward Street, EC3R 5BJ.* (01-481 2928)

DELANEY, Timothy John. b 49. York Univ Ont BA 74. Trin Coll Tor MDiv 78. **d** and **p** 78 Alg. C of Nipigon, Red Rock, Dorion & Schreiber 78-81; I of Schreiber Dio Alg from 81. *Box 520, Schreiber, Ont, Canada.*

DELBRIDGE, Noel. Moore Th Coll Syd ACT ThL 50. **d** and **p** 51 Syd. C of Coogee 51-53; R of S Hurstville 53-60; Dir of Christian Educn Dio Newc and L to Offic Dio Newc 60-63; R of St Luke Mosman 63-73; Dir Dept of Chr Educn Melb 73-78; Archd of Essendon 78-81; Pastoral Consultant to Abp of Melb from 78. *27 McKean Street, North Fitzroy, Vic, Australia 3068.*

DELEVINGNE, Gordon Gresswell. b 21. Oak Hill Th Coll 59. **d** 61 **p** 62 Southw. C of Carlton-in-the-Willows 61-63; Normanton-by-Derby (in c of St Steph) 63-65; V of St Matt W Ham 65-72; R of Langley 72-79. *33 Culverden Avenue, Tunbridge Wells, Kent.*

DELIGHT, Preb John David. b 25. Open Univ BA 75. Oak Hill Th Coll 49. **d** 52 **p** 53 S'wark. C of Tooting Graveney 52-55; Wallington 55-58; Trav Sec for Inter-Varsity Fellowship 58-61; LPr Dio Man 58-61; Min of St Chris Conv Distr Leic 61-68; Chap HM Pris Leic 62-67; V 68-69; R of Aldridge Dio Lich from 69; Preb of Lich Cathl from 80; RD of Walsall from 81. *14 The Green, Aldridge, Walsall, Staffs, WS9 8NH.* (Aldridge 52414)

DELIGHT, Paul Charles. b 31. Oak Hill Th Coll 59. **d** 62 **p** 63 Ches. C of Ch Ch Macclesfield 62-65; Ho Master Mobberley Approved Sch Knutsford and Perm to Offic Dio Ches 65-68; Asst Master Mile Oak Sch Portslade and Perm to Offic Dio Chich 68-71; Dep-Prin Thorntoun Sch Kilmarnock and Perm to Offic Dio Glas 71-75; R of Snodland w Lower Birling 75-81; V of H Trin Guernsey Dio Win from 81. *Holy Trinity Vicarage, Brock Road, St Peter Port, Guernsey, CI.* (Guernsey 24382)

DE LISLE, Michael Hirzel. b 21. Univ of Capetn MA 46. Univ of Ox MA 53. **d** 80 **p** 81 Pret. C of St Alb Cathl Pret 80-81; All SS Silverton Dio Pret from 81. *454 Joseph Bosman Street, Silverton, 0184, S Africa.*

DELL, Murray John. Univ of Capetn BA 51, BSc 54. Univ of Edin MB and ChB 59. Westcott Ho Cam 63. **d** and **p** 65 Natal. C of Kloof 65-70; Dean and R of St Geo Cathl Windhoek 71-80; V of Lyme Regis Dio Sarum from 80. *Vicarage, Lyme Regis, Dorset,* (Lyme Regis 3134)

DELL, Ven Robert Sydney. b 22. Em Coll Cam 2nd cl Hist Trip pt i 45, BA 46, 2nd cl Th Trip pt i 47, MA 50. Ridley Hall Cam 46. **d** 48 Lon **p** 49 Stepney for Lon. C of St Mary Islington 48-50; H Trin Cam 50-53; Asst Chap Wrekin Coll and L to Offic Dio Lich 53-55; V of Mildenhall w Beck Row 55-57; Vice Prin Ridley Hall Cam 57-65; L to Offic Dio Ely 57-65; V of Chesterton Cam 66-73; Proc in Conv and M Gen Syn 70-73; Archd of Derby from 73; Hon Can of Derby 73-81; Can Res from 81; Exam Chap to Bp of Derby from 73; M Gen Syn from 78; Visiting Fell St George's Ho Windsor Castle from 81. *72 Pastures Hill, Littleover, Derby, DE3 7BB.* (0332-512700)

de LONG, Frederick Paul. K Coll Halifax NS LTh. **d** 49 **p** 51 Fred. Miss at Cambridge w Waterborough 51-54; Chap RCAF from 54; Hon C of St Mary Winnipeg Dio Rupld from 76. *CFB Winnipeg, Manit, Canada.*

DELUMO, Samuel Adeola. Fourah Bay Coll BA (Dur) 13. OBE 57. **d** 13 **p** 15 W Eq Afr. CMS P Dio Lagos. Can of Lagos Cathl 39-57; Archd of Abeokuta 53-57. *Ibadan Road, Abeokuta, Nigeria.*

DELVE, Albert William John. b 15. Univ of Leeds BA (2nd cl Hist) 38. Coll of Resurr Mirfield 38. **d** 40 **p** 41 Ex. C of All SS Brixham 40-43; Tavistock 43-47; C-in-c of Burnt House Lane Conv Distr 47-55; Chap St Loye's Tr Coll and Orth Hosp Ex 47-55; V of Dawlish 55-69; RD of Kenn 68-69; R of Thurlestone Dio Ex from 69; P-in-c of S Milton Dio Ex from 81. *Thurlestone Rectory, Kingsbridge, Devon.* (Thurlestone 232)

DELVES-BROUGHTON, Simon Brian Hugo. b 33. Ex Coll Ox BA (3rd cl Th) 56, MA 64. Kelham Th Coll 56. **d** 59 Linc for Calc **p** 60 Calc. Miss OMC Calc 59-64; C of Skirbeck 64-67; Chap of Chittagong 67-69; P-in-c of St Thos Pro-Cathl Dacca 69-74; V of Ch Ch Northn Dio Pet from 74. *3 Christchurch Road, Northampton, NN1 5LL.* (Northn 33254)

de MAAR, Canon Robert. Bp Gray Coll Capetn LTh 59. **d** 59 **p** 60 Grahmstn. C of St Mich Port Eliz 59-66; R 66-73; P-in-c of Hanover Pk 73; Manenberg tn 73-79; Can of Capetn from 77; R of Good Shepherd Maitland Dio Capetn from 80. *Rectory, Ariel Street, Maitland 7405, CP, S Africa.* (51-5375)

DEMADEMA, Ven Aidan. St Jo Th Sem Lusaka 60. **d** 62 **p** 64 Matab. P Dio Matab; Archd of Matab from 78. *Rectory, Npopoma, Bulawayo, Zimbabwe.* (68188)

DEMANT, Vigo Auguste. b 1893. Armstrong Coll Dur BSc 13. Ex Coll Ox BLitt 24, DLitt 40. Univ of Dur Hon DD 74. Ely Th Coll 19. **d** 19 **p** 20 Ox. C of St Thos Ox 19-23; St Mich AA Summertown Ox 23-24; St Nich Plumstead 24-26; All SS Highgate 26-29; St Silas Kentish Town 29-33; V of St Jo Div Richmond 33-42; Can of St Paul's Cathl Lon 42-49; Chan 42-48; Treas 48-49; Can of Ch Ch Ox 49-71; Regius Prof of Moral and Past Th in Univ of Ox 49-71; Gifford Lect Univ of St Andr 57-58; Select Pr Univ of Ox 61. *31 St Andrew's Road, Old Headington, Oxford.*

De MEL, Basil. Keble Coll Ox BA (3rd cl Geog) 41, MA 47, BLitt 47. Westcott Ho Cam 41. **d** 43 **p** 44 Lon. C of All H Tottenham 43-46; Cowley 47-48; H Trin Headington Quarry 48-50; Iffley 50-53; Chap Manor Hosp Epsom from 53. *Manor Hospital, Epsom, Surrey.*

de MELLO, Gualter Rose. b 34. Ridley Hall Cam 63. **d** 64 **p** 65 Lon. C of St John w Ch Ch S Hackney 64-66; Chap Toc H Hackney 66-72; Perm to Offic Dio Lon from 73. *Director, Friends Anonymous Service, Friendship House, 27 Hackney Grove, E8 3NR.* (01-986 2233)

De METZ, Jacques. St Paul's Coll Grahmstn 66. **d** 68 **p** 69 Grahmstn. C of K William's Town 68-71; St John E Lon 71-72; R of Barberton 72-75; Middleburg w Belfast and Machadodorp Dio Pret from 75. *PO Box 699, Middleburg, East Transvaal, S Africa. Middleburg 5131)*

DEMPSEY, Gordon John. Vic Univ of Wel BA 60. NZ Bd of Th Stud LTh 66. **d** 65 Bp McKenzie for Wel **p** 66 Wel. C of Ch Ch Wanganui 65-71; V of Otaki Dio Wel from 71. *Vicarage, Te Rauparaha Street, Otaki, NZ.* (Otaki 7099)

DEMPSEY, Winston Henry. St Jo Coll Morpeth, 60. **d** 60 Armid. C of Inverell 60-61; Quirindi 61-65; W Tamworth 65-68; P-in-c of Boggabilla 69-73; V of Warialda 73-74. *c/o Box 198, Armidale, NSW, Australia.*

DEN BLAAUWEN, Pieter. St Paul's Coll Grahmstn. **d** 63 **p** 64 Johann. C of Springs 63-66; R of St Pet Brakpan Dio Johann from 66. *97 Hastings Avenue, Brakpan, Transvaal, S Africa.* (011-55 2808)

DENBY, Paul. b 47. N-W Ordin Course 73. **d** 76 **p** 77 Man. C of All SS Stretford 76-80; V of Stalybridge Dio Man from 80. *St George's Vicarage, 2 Tintagel Court, Astley Road, Stalybridge, SK15 1RA.* (061-338 2368)

DENCH, Hugh Brian Douglas. b 49. Univ of W Ont BA 71. Trin Coll Tor MDiv 74. **d** 74 **p** 75 Tor. C of St Geo-on-the-Hill Tor 74-76; on leave. *993 O'Connor Drive, Toronto, Ont., Canada.*

DENDE, Nicholas Titus. b 28. **d** 76 Centr Zam. d Dio Centr Zam. *PO Box 42, Kabwe, Zambia.*

DENDY, David Reginald. b 19. Late Scho of Qu Coll Ox 2nd cl Cl Mods 39, BA (2nd cl Lit Hum) 41, 2nd cl Th 42, MA 45, BD 55. St Steph Ho Ox 41. **d** and **p** 43 Glouc. C of Cirencester 43-45; Clewer St Steph 45-48; Sunninghill 48-51; Chap and Prec of Ch Ch Ox and Hd Master of Cathl Choir Sch 51-59; V of Bledington 59-79. *Address Temp unknown.*

DENERLEY, John Keith Christopher. b 34. Late Scho of Qu Coll Ox 2nd cl Cl Mods 56, BA (3rd cl Lit Hum) 58, 2nd cl Th 60, MA 61. St Steph Ho Ox 58. **d** 61 **p** 62 Wakef. C of Airedale w Fryston 61-64; Chap Sarum Th Coll 64-68; C of St Mich Cathl Cov 68-76; Chap Lanchester Poly Cov 70-76; Chap Dorothy Kerin Trust from 76. *Burrswood, Groombridge, Tunbridge Wells, Kent, TN3 9PY.* (Groombridge 353)

DENFORD, Keith Wilkie. b 35. K Coll Lon and Warm AKC 62. **d** 63 **p** 64 Lon. C of Gunnersbury 63-66; Brighton 66-71; Sacr and Min Can of Cant Cathl 71-75; R of W Tarring Dio Chich from 75. *West Tarring Rectory, Glebe Road, Worthing, W Sussex, BN14 7PF.* (Worthing 35043)

✠ **DENG, Right Rev Daniel.** **d** 41 **p** 43 Bp Gelsthorpe for Egypt. P Dio Egypt 41-45; Dio Sudan 45-55; Can of All SS Cathl Khartoum 53-55; Cons Asst Bp to Bp in the Sudan 15 May 55 in St Paul's Cathl Kampala by Abp of Cant; Bps of Sudan; Momb; Centr Tang; Ugan; U Nile; Nig Delta; Zanz; Bps Balya Brazier Lutaya Tomusange and Bp C E Stuart; res 61. *ECS, Malek, Bor District, Upper Nile Province, Sudan.*

DENG, Nakanora Acienkuc. Bp Tucker Mem Coll. **d** 50 Bp Allison for Sudan **p** 52 Sudan. P Dio Sudan from 50. *P.O. Box 110, Juba, Equatoria Province, Sudan.*

DENHAM, Albert Philip. b 08. Clifton Th Coll 33. **d** 37 **p** 38 Sheff. C of Owlerton 37-39; Framlingham w Saxtead 39-42; V of Bentley 42-49; Offg C-in-c of Gt Wenham 43-44; R of Sloley w Westwick 49-62; C-in-c of Worstead 49-56; V 56-62; Tinsley 62-69. *1 Smelter Wood Court, Sheffield, S13 8RY.*

DENHAM, Austin Douglas. St Paul's Coll Grahmstn 64. **d** 66 **p** 67 Johann. C of Rosettenville 67-69; C of Springs 69-70; C of Vereeniging 70-72; L to Offic Dio Johann 72; C of Regent Hill 73-81; St Mary Virg Cathl City and Dio Johann from 81. *57 George Street, Rosettenville, Johannesburg, S Africa.*

DENHAM, Thomas William. b 17. Wycl Hall Ox 58. **d** 59 Bp Stannard for Roch **p** 60 Roch. C of St Jo Evang Bexley 59-62; CMS Area Sec Dios Liv and Man 62-82; Perm to Offic Dio Liv 62-73; C-in-c of St Gabr Bp Wearmouth 73-82. *c/o St Gabriel's Vicarage, Sunderland, T & W, SR4 7TF.*

DENHOLM (formerly DENHOLM-YOUNG), Edward Godfrey Denholm. b 08. AKC 34. **d** 35 **p** 36 Lon. C of St Clem Barnsbury 35-36; Perm to Offic at St Simon Zelotes Bethnal Green 36-37; C of Ch Ch St Geo-in-the-East 37-40; St Mich AA w All SS Paddington 40-43; Min of Conv Distr of St Nich Perivale 43-51; Perm to Offic Dio Lon 52-54; C-in-c of Old St Pancras Lon 54-55; V of St Mich AA w All SS Paddington 55-63; V of Paddington Green 60-63; Chap Commun of St

Kath Parmoor 68-73. *Round Lodge, Godstone, Surrey, RH9 8DB.*

DENHOLM, Robert Jack. b 31. Edin Th Coll 53. **d** 56 **p** 57 Brech. C of St Mary Magd Dundee 56-59; St Pet Edin 59-61; R of St Sav Bridge of Allan 61-69; St Baldred N Berwick 69-80; Gullane 76-80; St Mark Portobello Dio Edin from 80. *27 Argyle Crescent, Portobello, Edinburgh, EH15 2QF.* (031-669 3452)

DENING, John Cranmer. b 21. Clare Coll Cam BA 48, MA 52. Qu Coll Birm 50. **d** 52 Warrington for Liv **p** 53 Liv. C of Allerton 52-55; St Andr Bournemouth 55-58; Leamington 59-60; Yeovil (in c of St Jas) 61-67; St John Moulsham Chelmsf 69-70; St Jas W Teignmouth 70-73; N Stoneham w Bassett 73-79; Sholing Dio Win from 79. *93 Spring Road, Sholing, Southampton, SO2 7QH.* (Southn 444301)

DENISON, Keith Malcolm. b 45. Down Coll Cam BA 67, MA 71, PhD 71. Westcott Ho Cam 70. **d** 71 **p** 72 Mon. C of St Mary, Chepstow 71-72; Bassaleg 72-75; V of Mathern and Mounton (w St Pierre from 80) Dio Mon from 75; Dioc Dir of Post-Ordination and In-Service Training from 75. *Mathern Vicarage, Chepstow, Gwent, NP6 6JA.* (Chepstow 2317)

DENLEY, David. b 32. St Jo Coll Morpeth. ACT ThL 68. **d** 67 **p** 68 River; C of Leeton 68-70; P-in-c of Wentworth 71-72; R 72-76; P-in-c of St Geo Canberra Dio C & Goulb from 77. *8 Dalrymple Street, Red Hill, ACT, Australia 2603.*

DENMAN, Frederick George. b 46. Chich Th Coll 67. **d** 70 **p** 71 Lich. C of Stafford 70-72; Ascot Heath 72-75; P-in-c of Sutton Courtenay w Appleford 75-77; Culham 75-78; Clifton Hampden 77-78; Team V of Dorchester 78-81; P-in-c of West Hill Dio Ex from 82. *West Hill Vicarage, Ottery St Mary, Devon.* (Ottery St Mary 2094)

DENMAN, Preb Ronald. b 19. St Chad's Coll Dur LTh 44, BA 46. St Aug Coll Cant. **d** 44 **p** 45 Roch. C of St Aug Gillingham 44-47; Clevedon 47-51; TCF from 50; R of N w S Barrow 51-57; PC of Lovington 51-57; V of Cheddar Dio B & W from 57; Preb of Wells Cathl from 76. *Vicarage, Cheddar, Somt, BS27 3RF.* (Cheddar 742535)

DENNE, Arthur Roy. b 08. Univ of Leeds BA (2nd cl Hist) 29. Coll of Resurr Mirfield 29. **d** 31 **p** 32 Sheff. C of St Steph Eastwood 31-33; H Trin Hulme 33-35; St Jas Oldham 35-38; R of St Andr Ancoats Man 38-45; V of St Marg Hollinwood 45-51; C of Skerton 51-53; V of Dolphinholme 53-70. *3 Grammah Avenue, Cronk Sumark, Port Erin, IM.*

DENNEN, Lyle. b 42. Harvard Univ LLB 67 (Juris D from 69) Trin Coll Cam BA (2nd cl Th Trip pt ii) 70, MA 75. Cudd Coll 72. **d** 72 **p** 73 S'wark. C of St Anne S Lambeth 72-75; St Mary Richmond 75-78; V of St Jo Div Kennington (w St Jas Ap from 79) Dio S'wark from 78. *92 Vassall Road, SW9.* (01-735 9340)

DENNETT, John Edward. b 36. Tyndale Hall Bris 66. **d** 68 **p** 69 Lich. C of Chell 68-71; Bispham 71-73; Ch Ch Cheltm 73-75; V of Coppull 75-79; R of Parkham, Alwington and Buckland Brewer Dio Ex from 79. *Rectory, Parkham, Bideford, Devon, EX39 5PL.* (Horns Cross 204)

DENNETT, Stephen Frederic James. b 1895. Linc Th Coll 29. **d** 34 **p** 35 Newc T. C of Seaton Hirst 34-40; V of Horton w Cowpen and New Delaval 40-41; R of Attleborough Major and Min 41-47; V of Bamburgh 48-73. *The Red Barns, Bamburgh, Northumb.* (Bamburgh 298)

DENNIS, Alan Godfrey. b 55. St Pet Coll Natal 76. **d** 78 **p** 79 Capetn. C of St John Belville S Dio Capetn from 78. *1 Denneboom Road, Belhar, CP 7500, S Africa.*

✠ **DENNIS, Right Rev John.** b 31. St Cath Coll Cam BA 54, MA 59. Cudd Coll 54. **d** 56 **p** 57 Ripon. C of Armley 56-60; Kettering 60-62; V of Ch of Ch and St John w St Luke I of Dogs Poplar 62-71; V of John Keble Ch Mill Hill 71-79; RD of W Barnet 73-79; Preb of St Paul's Cathl Lon 77-79; Cons Ld Bp Suffr of Knaresborough in York Minster 10 Oct 79 by Abps of York and the Indian Ocean; Bps of Dur, Ripon, Bradf, Brech, Chich, Carl and S & M; Bps Suffr of Taunton, Kingston T, Tonbridge, Plymouth, Doncaster, Whitby, Lanc, Stockport, Warrington, Hull, Sherwood, Jarrow, Reading and Edmon; and others; Dioc Dir of Ordinands from 80; Episc Guardian of Angl Focolari from 81. *16 Shaftesbury Avenue, Roundhay, Leeds 8.* (Leeds 664800)

DENNIS, John Daniel. b 20. St D Coll Lamp BA 41, LTh 43. **d** 43 St D **p** 44 Wales. C of St Mary and St Thos Haverfordwest 43-48; St Mark Newport 48-54; V of New Tredegar 54-62; R of Worthenbury w Tallarn Green 62-71; V of Chirk Dio St A from 71; RD of Llangollen from 74. *Chirk Vicarage, Wrexham, Clwyd, LL14 5HD.* (Chirk 2421)

DENNIS, John William. b 13. St Pet Hall Ox BA (3rd cl Th) 38, MA 45. Linc Th Coll 38. **d** 39 **p** 40 Dur. C of St Cuthb Hebburn 39-45; St Nich w St John Newport (in c of St Matthias) Linc 45-49; PC of St Paul W Marsh Grimsby 49-60; V of St Andr Linc 60-68; PC (V from 68) of St Swith City and Dio Linc from 60. *St Swithin's Vicarage, Croft Street, Lincoln, LN2 5AZ.* (Linc 27540)

DENNIS, Patrick John. b 44. Linc Th Coll 67. **d** 70 **p** 71 Bradf. C of Eccleshill 70-72; Ponteland 73-75; Chr Aid Org Leic and Linc 75-78; Team V of Cullercoats Dio Newc T from 78; Dioc Ecumen Adv from 79. *29 Billy Mill Lane, North Shields, Tyne & Wear, NE29 8BZ.*

DENNIS, Canon Peter Gwyn Morgan. b 1899. Univ of Bris BA 26. **d** 31 **p** 32 Dur. C of S Westoe 31-33; CF (TA) 32-40; V of Firtree 33-44; Craghead 44-46; Heworth 46-55; R of Ingram 55-58; Ilderton 55-58; V of Long Benton 58-72; RD of Newc E 64-72; Hon Can of Newc T 66-72; Can (Emer) from 72. *The Langley Flat, Sherburn House, Durham.*

DENNIS, Robert Ernest. b 08. TCD BA (Resp) and 2nd Eccles Hist Pri 34. Downes Liturgy Pri 34. MA 38. **d** 35 **p** 36 Down. C of St Patr Ballymacarrett 35-38; St Mary Newry 38-39; C-in-c of Termonmaguirke 39-42; R of Killylea 42-44; I of St Pet Cork 44-48; Drumcree 48-61; V of Ch Ch Bootle 61-75; C of Ormskirk Dio Liv from 75. *288 Liverpool Road South, Burscough, Ormskirk, Lancs, L40 7TD.* (Burscough 895275)

DENNIS, Trevor John. b 45. St Jo Coll Cam 1st cl Cl Trip pt i 66, BA (1st cl Th Trip pt ii) 68, MA 71, PhD 74. **d** 72 Buckingham for Ox **p** 73 Reading for Ox. C of Newport Pagnell 72-75; Chap Eton Coll from 75. *Eton College, Windsor, Berks.*

DENNIS, Wilfrid Edwin. St Francis Coll Brisb. **d** 60 **p** 61 Brisb. C of Sandgate 60-62; Roma 62; Miss Chap Surat 62-65; R of Loxton 65-69; Perm to Offic Dio Adel 70-73; C of Campbelltown 73-74; St John Salisbury 74-80; P-in-c of Parafield Gdns Dio Adel from 80. *7-9 Lamorna Parade, Parafield Gardens, S Australia 5107.*

DENNISON, Philip Ian. b 52. Univ of Nottm BTh 81. St Jo Coll Nottm 77. **d** 81 Stockport for Ches. C of H Trin & Ch Ch Stalybridge Dio Ches from 81. *2 Sunbury Close, Fur Tree Crescent, Dukinfield, Cheshire, SK16 5HP.*

DENNISON, Thomas. b 10. St Andr Dioc Ordin Course 71. **d** 73 **p** 74 St Andr. Hon C of dunfermline (W Fife Group) Dio St Andr from 73. *Old Schoolhouse, North Queensferry, Fife, KY11 1JJ.*

DENNISS, Ronald John. b 25. St Mich AA Llan 77. **d** 78 **p** 79 Mon. C of Bassaleg 78-80; V of St Andr Lliswerry Newport Dio Mon from 80. *Vicarage, Brookfield Close, Lliswerry, Newport, Gwent.* (Newport 271904)

DENNISTON, Robin Alastair. b 26. Ch Ch Ox MA 48. **d** 78 **p** 79 Worc (APM). C of Clifton-on-Teme Dio Worc from 78. *The Hope Farm, Clifton-on-Teme, Worcester.*

DENNO, Basil. b 52. Univ of Dundee BSc 74, BA 81. Oak Hill Coll. **d** 81 Repton for Derby. C of St Mary Chaddesden Dio Derby from 81. *24 Ordish Avenue, Chaddesden, Derby, DE2 6QF.*

DENNY, Laurence Eric. b 29. Oak Hill Th Coll 54. **d** 57 **p** 58 S'wark. C of Wallington 57-61; V of St Edw Leyton 61-64; C-in-c 65-69; V of St Mary (w St Edw from 69) Leyton Dio Chelmsf 64-72; St Pancras Pennycross, Plymouth Dio Ex from 72. *Vicarage, Glentor Road, Hartley, Plymouth, Devon.* (Plymouth 774332)

DENNY, Laurence John. Univ of Cant NZ BA 59. Ch Ch Coll 56. NZ Bd of Th Stud LTh 66. **d** 59 **p** 60 Dun for Ch Ch. C of Avonside 59-62; Papanui 62-63; Merivale 63; on leave 63-64; V of Fairlie 65-69; Belfast-Styx 69-75; C of St Pet Cathl Hamilton Dio Waik 75-79; Hon C from 79. *110 Knighton Road, Hamilton, NZ.* (63-321)

DENNY, Michael Thomas. b 47. St Jo Coll Nottm 71. **d** 73 **p** 74 Birm. C of St Mich Gospel Lane 73-77; C-in-c of Frankley Dio Birm 77-81; R from 81. *Rectory, Church Hill, Frankley, Birmingham, B32 4BG.* (021-475 3724)

DENNY, Peter Bond. b 17. Univ of Lon BA (2nd cl Hist) 41. Bps' Coll Cheshunt 41. **d** 43 St Alb **p** 44 Bp Heywood for St Alb. C of St Pet Bushey Heath 43-45; Calstock 52-56; V of St Newlyn East Dio Truro from 56; RD of Pydar 61-64 and 74-81. *St Newlyn East Vicarage, Newquay, Cornw.* (Mitchell 383)

DENNY, Trevor Clifton. b 44. York Univ Ont BA 71, MDiv 72. Wycl Coll Tor 72. **d** 72 **p** 73 tor. C of St Geo Oshawa 72-75; R of Haliburton Dio Tor from 75. *Box 92, Haliburton, Ont., Canada.* (705-457 2074)

DENT, Christopher Mattinson. b 46. K Coll Lon BA (1st cl Hist) 68, AKC 68, MTh 69. Late Scho Jes Coll Cam BA 1st cl Th Trip pt ii 72, MA 76. New Coll Ox MA (by incorp) 76, DPhil 80. Westcott Ho Cam 70. **d** 72 **p** 73 Kens for Lon. C of Chelsea 72-76; Asst Chap New Coll Ox 76-79; Fell, Dean of Div and Chap from 79; L to Offic Dio Ox from 77. *New College, Oxford, OX1 3BN.* (Oxford 48451)

DENT, Gordon Lloyd. St Jo Coll Morpeth ACT ThL 50. **d** 48 **p** 49 Armid. C of Glen Innes 48-50; V of Emmaville 50-55; R of Wentworth 55-63; C of Henley Beach 62-63; R of St Geo Alberton 63-74; Woodend 74-76; P-in-c of Eliz Downs 76-79;

R of Norton Summit Dio Adel from 79. *Rectory, Norton Summit, S Australia 5136.* (30 1799)

DENT, Michael Christopher Avis. b 45. K Coll Lon and Warm AKC 67. **d** 68 **p** 69 Portsm. C of All SS Ryde 68-71; St Jo Evang Hollington 71-73; C-in-c of All SS Conv Distr Gurnard 73-76. *c/o 2 Solent View Road, Gurnard, Cowes, IW.* (Cowes 3900)

DENT, Raymond William. b 47. Ridley Hall Cam 70. **d** 73 **p** 74 Ches. C of Hyde 73-76; Eastham 76-79; Team V of E Runcorn w Halton 79-80; V of St Mark Hallwood Dio Ches from 80. *Vicarage, off Old Northwich Road, Sutton Park, Brookvale, Runcorn, Cheshire WA7 6PE.* (0928-713101)

DENT, Richard William. b 32. Down Coll Cam BA 56, MA, LLB 59. **d** 77 **p** 78 Bris (APM). C of Southmead 77-81; Henleaze Dio Bris from 81. *9 Henleaze Gardens, Bristol, BS9 4HA.*

DENTITH, Eric Leonard. b 14. Univ of Birm BA (3rd cl French) 35. St Steph Ho Ox 36. **d** 38 **p** 39 Pet. C of St Mich AA Northn 38-42; St John Wolverhampton 42-46; Walsall Wood 46-49; C-in-c of Birches Head Conv Distr 49-54; PC 54-56; R of Kingsley 56-61; V of St Aug Dudley 61-69; Ipstones 69-80; C-in-c of Onecote w Bradnop 76-80. *34 East Bank Ride, Forsbrook, Stoke-on-Trent, ST11 9DS.* (Blythe Bridge 6322)

DENTON, Kenneth Percival. b 14. Clifton Th Coll 54. **d** 55 **p** 56 Bradf. C of Buttershaw 55-57; Otley Yorks 57-59; Morpeth 59-62; R of Winteringham 62-69; V of St Thos Middlesbrough 69-73; C of Rufforth w Moor Monkton 73-76; C-in-c of Escrick 76-80. *46 Pedlars Grove, Packsaddle Way, Frome, Somt, BA11 2SX.*

DENTON, Peter Brian. b 37. Kelham Th coll 57. **d** 62 **p** 63 Ches. C of Ellesmere Port 62-66; Chap Hollesley Bay Borstal Inst 66-69; CF from 69. *c/o Allways, Glatton, Huntingdon, Cambs.*

DENTON, Peter Charles. Late Scho and Exhib of St Jo Coll Dur BA (2nd cl Th) 52. Oak Hill Th Coll 49. **d** 52 Jarrow for Dur **p** 53 Dur. C of Ushaw Moor 52-54; C-in-c of St Mary's Conv Distr Throckley 54-58; V of Longhorsley 58-67; Lect City of Newc T Coll of Educn from 67; Perm to Offic Dio Dur from 67; Sen Lect Newc T Poly from 75. *10 Whitesmocks Avenue, Durham.* (Durham 43247)

DENYER, Allen Stewart. b 16. Univ of Leeds BA 39, BD 42, MA 50. **d** 74 **p** 75 Ex. C of Centr Torquay 74-78; P-in-c of Combe-in-Teignhead w Stoke-in-Teignhead Dio Ex from 78. *Rectory, Combe-in-Teignhead, Newton Abbot, Devon, TQ12 4RF.* (Shaldon 3493)

DENYER, Edwin Alfred. b 22. ThDip 78. **d** and **p** 80 Newc. C of Gosford and Chap to Centr Coast Dio Newc from 80. *62 Yowie Avenue, Caringbah, NSW, Australia 2229.*

DENYER, Paul Hugh. b 46. Univ of Lon BA 68. Ripon Coll Cudd 74. **d** 77 **p** 78 Bris. C of H Trin Horfield Dio Bris from 77. *31 Rosling Road, Horfield, Bristol, BS7 8SX.* (Bristol 514299)

✠ de PINA CABRAL, Right Rev Daniel Pereira dos Santos. Univ of Lisbon Licenciado (Law) 47. Lon Coll of Div. **d** 47 **p** 49 Arm. [f in Lusitanian Ch of Portugal] Cons Ld Bp Suffr of Lebom in St Paul's Lusitanian Cathl Lisbon 25 May 67 by Abp of Capetn; Bps of Lebom; Glas; Southw; Gibr; Rhode I (USA) and Puerto Rico (USA); and Bps Pereira (Lusitanian Ch); Urs Küry (Old Catholic Ch); Bayne; and Boys; Apptd Ld Bp of Lebom 68; res 76; Asst Bp of Gibr (Gibr in Eur from 80) from 76; Hon Can of Gibr from 79. *Rua de Damiao Peres, 41-Hab 161, 4100 Porto, Portugal.* (667 929)

DEPPEN, Jay Ralph. b 18. Gen Th Sem NY MDiv 44, STD 67. **d** 43 **p** 44 Harrisburg (USA). In Amer Ch 43-75; P-in-c of Woburn and of Battlesden w Pottesgrove 76-78. *Address temp unknown.*

De PURY, Andrew Robert. b 28. K Coll Lon and Warm BD and AKC 57. **d** 58 **p** 59 Chelmsf. C of Epping 58-60; Loughton 60-65; V of St Geo Harold Hill Romford 65-72; Missr to Swan Par Group 72-76; R of Swan Dio Ox from 76. *Grendon Underwood Rectory, Aylesbury, Bucks, HP18 0SY.* (Grendon Underwood 240)

DER, Edmund Bowen. Nat Taiwan Univ BA 58. Ch Div Sch of the Pacific Calif BD 61. **d** 61 W Virg **p** 62 Hong. C of St Mary Hong 61-64; V of Un Long Hong 64-67; In Amer ch 67-76; V of H Trin Kowloon Dio Hong from 76. *135 Ma Tau Chung Road, Kowloon, Hong Kong.*

DERBRIDGE, Roger. b 39. Clifton Th Coll. **d** 66 S'wark **p** 69 Kingston T for S'wark. C of Ch Ch Surbiton Hill 66-67; Ch Ch Richmond Surrey 67-70; Team V Desig of St Philemon w St Gabr Toxteth Pk Dio Liv 70-75; Team V from 75. *2 Steble Street, Liverpool, L8 6QH.* (051-708 7751)

DERBY, Lord Bishop of. *See* Bowles, Right Rev Cyril William Johnston.

DERBY, Assistant Bishops of. *See* Parfitt, Right Rev Thomas Richards; and Hudson, Right Rev Arthur William Goodwin.

DERBY, Archdeacon of. *See* Dell, Ven Robert Sydney.

DERBY, Provost of. *See* Lewers, Very Rev Benjamin Hugh.

DERBY, William Vinton. b 46. Rutgers Univ NJ BA 68. Episc Th Sch Cam Mass MDiv 72. **d** 72 NY **p** 73 Bp Wetmore for NY. C of St Lambert Montr 72-76; R of All SS Verdun City and Dio Montr from 76. *7365 Ouimet Avenue, Verdun, Queb H4H 2J6, Canada.*

DERBYSHIRE, Alan George. b 16. Univ of Lon BA 41. Linc Th Coll 41. **d** 43 **p** 44 St Alb. C of Dunstable 43-47; CF 47-67; R of Merrow 67-81. *Feldemore, Old Orchard Lane, Colwall, Malvern, Worcs, WR13 6HU.*

DERBYSHIRE, Arnold Sydney. b 06. **d** 50 E Szech **p** 52 Sarum. Miss (CIM) at Yingshan Dio E Szech 50-51; C of Heatherlands Parkstone 51-54; R of Cotton w Wickham Skeith 54-61; Horsington 61-75; Perm to Offic Dio B & W from 76. *Sutledge House, Langford, Bristol, BS18 7HP.* (Wrington 862271)

DERBYSHIRE, Douglas James. b 26. **d** 81 Stockport for Ches. C of Heald Green Dio Ches from 81. *91 East Avenue, Heald Green, Cheadle, Cheshire, SK8 3BR.*

DERBYSHIRE, Noel William. Univ of Otago BCom 65. NZ Bd of Th Stud LTh 68. St Jo Coll Auckld. **d** 68 **p** 69 Dun. C of Invercargill 68-70; V of Riverton 70-73; Resources Officer Dio Dun 73-74; V of Taieri 74-76; Prov Sec Papua and Hon C of Lae 77-79; V of Gore Dio Dun from 80. *15 Trafford Street, Gore, NZ.* (Gore 7366)

DERISLEY, Canon Albert Donald. b 20. Ely Th Coll. **d** 62 **p** 63 Nor. C of Gt Yarmouth 62-66; V of Gt w L Plumstead 66-72; N Elmham w Billingford Dio Nor from 72; RD of Brisley and Elmham from 77; Hon Can of Nor from 78. *North Elmham Vicarage, Dereham, Norf.* (Elmham 244)

DERMOTT, David John. b 34. Univ of Hull BA (1st cl Th) 60. Cudd Coll 67. **d** 68 **p** 69 York. C of Howden 68-71; W Acklam 71-74; Team V of Thornaby-on-Tees 74-79; R of Hinderwell w Roxby Dio York from 79. *Rectory, Hinderwell, Saltburn, Cleve, TS13 5JH.* (0947-840249)

DERRETT, Jack. Moore Th Coll Syd ACT ThL 54. **d** and **p** 55 Syd. C of Marrickville 55-56; R of Wallerawang 56-59; C-in-c of St Phil Caringbah w St Steph Taren Pt 59-64; R 64-66; St Mark W Wollongong 66-74; Gymea Dio Syd from 75. *129 Gymea Bay Road, Gymea, NSW, Australia 2227.* (524-6225)

DERRETT, Canon Leslie John. b 14. Late Gisborne Scho St Jo Coll Dur BA (3rd cl Th) 41, MA 45. **d** 41 **p** 42 Chelmsf. C of Grays Thurrock 41-43; Walthamstow 43-44; Chap of Ellesmere Coll 44-45; Chap of Dur Sch 45-48; L to Offic Dio Dur 45-48; V of St Nich Whitehaven 48-54; PC of Hedworth 54-58; V of E Ham 58-68; Witham 68-76; Surr 58-79; V of Thorpe-le-Soken 76-80; Hon Can of Chelmsf 76-80; Can (Emer) from 80; Perm to Offic Dio Chelmsf from 80. *15 Larkfield Road, Great Bentley, Essex, CO7 8PX.* (995-251315)

DERRIMAN, Graham Scott. b 39. Bps' Coll Cheshunt 63. **d** 66 **p** 67 S'wark. C of St Mich Wandsworth Common 66-70; Merton 70-74; V of Earlsfield 74-81; St Luke Camberwell Dio S'wark from 81. *123 Farnborough Way, SE15 6HL.* (01-703 5587)

DERRY, Archdeacon of. *See* Willoughby, Ven George Charles.

DERRY, Dean of. *See* Good, Very Rev George Fitzgerald.

DERRY, Eric Leonard Stobart. b 15. Worc Ordin Coll 62. **d** 64 **p** 65 Wakef. C of Mirfield 64-67; Almondbury 67-68; V of Luddenden 68-73; Dodworth Dio Wakef from 73. *Dodworth Vicarage, Barnsley, Yorks.* (Barnsley 203838)

DERRY, Hugh Graham. b 10. Or Coll Ox BA 35, MA 50. Ely Th Coll 46. **d** 48 **p** 49 Ex. C of St Pet Plymouth 48-50; St Mich AA Summertown Ox 50-51; Chap Radcliffe Inf Ox 51-56; L to Offic Dio Ox 52-58; C of H Cross Pondoland 58-65; P-in-c of Maclear 65-72; C of Mt Fletcher 65-72; Perm to Offic Dio Ex from 74. *Beech Tree Cottage, Cheriton Fitzpaine, Crediton, Devon.*

DERRY, Wilfred Reginald. b 11. Mert Coll Ox BA (2nd cl Mod Hist) 32, 2nd cl Th 34, MA 60. St Steph Ho Ox 34. **d** 34 Taunton for B & W **p** 35 Bp De Salis for B & W. Chap of Wells Th Coll 34-38; Asst Master and Asst Offg Chap Lancing Coll 38-45; Offg Chap 45-54; C of St Geo Hanover Sq (in c of Grosvenor Chap) and Warden of Liddon Ho 54-67; Commiss Masasi 61-68; Vice-Provost S Div Woodard Corp 62-67; Provost Midl Div 68-80. *Edgmond Priory, Newport, Shropshire.* (Newport 810731)

DERRY and RAPHOE, Lord Bishop of. *See* Mehaffey, Right Rev James.

DE SARAM, Brian John Hector. b 13. OBE 78. Univ of Lon BSc (2nd cl Chem) 33. Ridley Hall Cam 58. **d** 59 Sudan **p** 60 Willesden for Lon. CMS Miss at Juba Sudan 59; Ch Ch Crouch End Hornsey 60; CMS Men Cands' Sec 59-63; Afr Sec 63-70; CMS Miss Cairo 70-77; Provost of All SS Cathl

Cairo 72-77; C of Crowborough 77-81. *Norfolk Lodge, Crowborough Hill, Crowborough, E Sussex, TN6 2SE.* (Crowborough 61420)

de SATGE, John Cosmo. b 28. Ch Ch Ox BA (2nd cl Mod Hist) 51, Dipl Th 52, MA 55. ALCD 54. **d** 54 Kens for Lon **p** 55 Lon. C of H Trin Brompton 54-57; Chap Wycl Hall Ox 57-63; Exam Chap to Bp of Sheff 62-72; Can Res of Sheff and Dir of Ordinands Dio Sheff 63-72; Exam Chap to Bp of Truro from 77. *Hele Linhay, Ashburton, Nr Newton Abbot, Devon TQ13 7NW.* (0364 52319)

De SAUSMAREZ, Canon John Havilland Russell. b 26. MA (Lambeth) 81. Wells Th Coll 54. **d** 56 **p** 57 Nor. C of King's Lynn 56-58; Hythe 58-61; V of St Martin Maidstone 61-68; St Pet in I-of-Thanet 68-81; RD of Thanet 74-81; Hon Can of Cant 78-81; Can Res from 81. *22 The Precincts, Canterbury, Kent.*

DESCH, Roland Cecil. b 12. MBE (Mil) 46. AKC 34. Westcott Ho Cam 34. **d** 35 **p** 36 Cant. C of St Pet Croydon 35-38; Bognor Regis 38-40; CF (EC) 40-46; V of Portslade w Hangleton (R) 46-48; Thurston 48-52; CF (TA) 49-55; R of Earl Soham and V of Cretingham 52-55; CF 55-60; R of St Steph Hackington Cant 60-67; Sutton Veny 67-71; V of Norton Bavant 67-71; Thurston 71-73; C-in-c of Chute w Chute Forest 73-77. *Linden Cottage, Eddington, Hungerford, Berks.* (Hungerford 2160)

DESERT, Thomas Denis. b 31. Bps' Coll Cheshunt 54. **d** 56 **p** 57 St Alb. C of Goldington 56-60; C-in-c of Lewsey Conv Distr Luton 60-63; C of St Sav St Alb 63-65; Cheshunt 65-68; V of All SS Bedford Dio St Alb from 68. *87 Beverley Crescent, Bedford.* (Bedford 66945)

DESGRAND, Christopher John. **d** 78 **p** 79 N Queensld. C of St Luke Sarina Dio N Queensld from 78. *St Luke's Rectory, PO Box 74, Sarina, Qld, Australia 4737.*

De SILVA, Gamage Samuel. **d** 54 **p** 55 Kurun. P Dio Kurun 54-74; C of H Trin Cookridge Adel Ripon 74-78. *Address temp unknown.*

✠ De SOUZA, Right Rev Neville Wordsworth. St Pet Coll Ja 56. **d** 58 Kingston for Ja **p** 60 Ja. C of Porus 58-62; R of Grange Hill 62-66; May Pen 67-73; Cons Ld Bp Suffr of Montego Bay in Ch of St Jas Gt Montego Bay 24 Feb 73 by Abp of WI; Bps of Barb; Ja, Br Hond, Nass, Windw Is, Antig, Trinid and Venez; and Bps Suffr of Kingston, Mandeville, Stabroek and others; Elected Bp of Ja 79. *Church House, 2 Caledonia Avenue, Kingston 5, Jamaica, W Indies.*

DESPARD, Canon Eric Herbert. b 17. TCD BA (2nd cl Mods) 40, 2nd cl Div Test 41, BD 48. **d** 41 **p** 42 Kilm. C of Roscommon 41-43; St Pet Dublin 43-51; I of Blessington w Kilbride 51-65; Leixlip w Lucan Dio Glendal from 65; RD of Rathdrum 63-77; Ballymore from 77; Can of Ch Ch Cathl Dub from 73. *Rectory, Lucan, Co Dublin, Irish Republic.* (Lucan 280339)

DETE, Gideon Takaruza. **d** 78 **p** 79 Matab. P Dio Matab. *Methuen Barracks, PO Llewellin, Zimbabwe.*

DEUCHAR, John. b 24. Or Coll Ox BA (2nd cl Mod Hist) 49, MA 50. Westcott Ho Cam 49. **d** 51 **p** 52 Cov. C of St Andr Rugby 51-55; V of St Andr Bournemouth 55-61; Eastleigh 61-68; Surr 61-68; R of Woolwich 68-72; V of Ch Ch Reading Dio Ox from 72. *Christchurch Vicarage, 4 Vicarage Road, Reading, Berks, RG2 7AJ.* (0734-871250)

DEVAMANIKKAM, Trevor. b 47. Ripon Hall Ox 74. **d** 76 Knaresborough for Ripon **p** 77 Ripon. C of St Jas Manston 76-79; Moor Allerton 79-81; St Wilfrid and St Luke Harrogate Dio Ripon from 81. *59 Coppice Way, Harrogate, N Yorks.* (Harrogate 522194)

DEVAPIRAGASAM, J. Villie. b 29. Trin Th Coll Sing 68. **d** 72 **p** 73 Sing. V of St Paul Sing 72-79; Ch Ch City and Dio Sing from 79. *Christ Church, Dorset Road, Singapore 0802.*

DEVENNEY, Raymond Robert Wilmont. b 47. TCD BA 69, MA 73. Div Test 70. **d** 70 **p** 71 Connor. C of Ballymena 70-75; Ballyholme 75-81; R of Killinchy U Dio Down from 81. *Rectory, Whiterock Road, Killinchy, Co Down, N Ireland.* (Killinchy 541249)

✠ DEVENPORT, Right Rev Eric Nash. b 26. Open Univ BA 74. Kelham Th Coll 46. **d** 51 **p** 52 Leic. C of St Mark Leic 51-54; St Matt Barrow-F 54-56; Succr of Leic Cathl 56-59; V of Shepshed 59-64; Oadby 64-73; Proc Conv Leic 64-80; Surr 67-80; Hon Can of Leic Cathl from 73; Dioc Missr Dio Leic 73-80; Cons Ld Bp Suffr of Dunwich in St Paul's Cathl Lon 30 Sept 80 by Abp of Cant; Bps of Lon, Leic, St E, Birm, Chelmsf, Derby, Ex, Ox, Cov and Worc; Bps Suffr of Edmon, Stafford and Thetford; and Bps Allenby, Bulley, Franklin, Porter, Daly and Riches. *Old Newton House, 52 Church Road, Old Newton, Stowmarket, IP14 4ED.* (044-970332)

DEVER, John Curzon. b 34. St Aid Coll. **d** 63 Middleton for Man **p** 64 Man. C of Lightbowne 63-65; R of St Thos Grand Turk I 65-69; C of Brixham 69-71; Team V of Melton Mowbray w Thorpe Arnold 71-76; P-in-c of Scalford (V w Goadby Marwood from 77) Dio Leic from 76; Goadby Marwood 76-77; Sec Nass Assoc from 76. *Scalford Vicarage, Melton Mowbray, Leics.* (Scalford 205)

de VERE, Anthony George Augustine. b 31. Ch Ox BA 54, MA 58. St Steph Ho Ox 54. **d** 56 **p** 57 Lon. C of Poplar 56-59; Capetn Cathl 59-60; Chap Bp Gray Th Coll Capetn 61-63; P-in-c of Faure 64-71; V of Elsfield Dio Ox from 71; C-in-c of Horton w Studley Dio Ox from 71; Beckley Dio Ox 71-73; V from 73. *Vicarage, Elsfield, Oxford, OX3 9UH.* (Stanton St John 260)

DEVEREUX, Canon John Ernest Donald. b 1897. Or Coll Ox 15, BA 20, MA 22. Ridley Hall Cam 20. **d** 21 **p** 22 Birm. C of St John Sparkhill 21-23; Lect and C of Watford Herts 24-25; V of St Steph Hull 25-29; St Pet Paddington 29-35; Offg Chap Lon Lock Hosp 30-35; Paddington Hosp 30-34; Chap 34-35; Chap of Ch Ch Brussels 35-40; to Br Embassy Brussels 38-40; V of Macclesfield 40-47; RD of Macclesfield 42-47; V of Hoylake 47-67; Hon Can of Ches 47-67; Can (Emer) from 67; RD of Wirral North 53-67. *Field Cottage, Church Lane, Corton, Suff.* (Lowestoft 730385)

DEVEREUX, John Swinnerton. BSc (2nd cl Physics) Lon 53. Wells Th Coll. **d** 58 **p** 59 Liv. C of St Mich AA Wigan 58-60; Goring 60-69; Industr Chap Dio Chich from 69. *4 The Driveway, Shoreham-by-Sea, Sussex, BN4 5GG.*

de VIAL, Raymond Michael. b 35. Oak Hill Coll 77. **d** 80 **p** 81 Roch (APM). C of St Jo Bapt Beckenham Dio Roch from 80. *20 Whitmore Road, Beckenham, Kent, BR3 3NT.*

DEVITT, Walter William. **d** 66 **p** 67 NW Austr. C of Geraldton 66-68; Derby w Broome Cockatoo I and Koolan I 68-72; Perm to Offic Dio Perth 72-74. *15 Willis Street, East Victoria Park, W Australia 6101.*

DEVLIN, Edward John. b 1893. Trin Coll Dub BA 16, MA 24. **d** 18 **p** 19 Dub. C of Dunganstown w Redcross 18-20; Mariners' Ch Kingstown 21-27; Hd Master Kingstown Sch 27-64. *1 Glenageary Terrace, Dunlaoghaire, Co Dublin, Irish Republic.* (Dublin 802791)

DEVLIN, Geoffrey John. Wollaston Th Coll W Austr 62. **d** 64 **p** 65 Perth. C of Carl 64-65; Mosman Pk 66; St Luke Cottesloe 66-67; P-in-c of Gingin 67-70; R 70-71; R of Cunderdin 71-73; R of Quairading 71-73; Asst Chap Miss to Seamen Fremantle 74-76. *PO Box 79, Fremantle, W Australia 6160.* (35 5000)

4 Knighton Drive, Leicester, LE2 3HB.

DEVONSHIRE, Albert Edward. b 05. ALCD 30. **d** 30 **p** 31 Cant. C of St Geo Mart Deal 30-34; H Trin Tulse Hill (in c of St John Guernsey Grove) 34-38; V of St Paul Greenwich 38-45; Offg Chap Miller Hosp and John Penn Almshos 40-45; C-in-c of St Pet Greenwich 44-45; V of Ferneux Pelham w Stocking Pelham 45-49; Royston 49-75; Surr 48-75; RD of Baldock 65-75. *57 Cromer Road, Holt, Norf.*

DEVONSHIRE, Very Rev William Wynn. St Jo Coll Morpeth ThL 48. **d** 49 **p** 50 Newc. C of Cessnock 49-51; Mayfield 51-52; Waratah 52-53; R of Kendall 53-56; St Paul Maitland 56-57; Payneham and P-in-c of Hillcrest 57-64; Bp's V of St Pet Cathl Adel 64-66; R of Unley 66-72; Dean of Bal 72-79; Dean (Emer) from 79; Chap Bal and Qu Gr Sch Bal from 79. *Ballarat Grammar School, Ballarat, Vic, Australia 3350.* (053-31 2601)

de VRIES, Bren. Hur Coll. **d** 55 **p** 57 Hur. C-in-c of Blyth 55-58; R of Ex 58-63; Hespeler 64-71; on leave 72-76; I of New Hamburg 76-81; Chap Port of Queb from 81. *1053 Ch Guiana, Cap Rouge, PQ, Canada G0A 1K0.*

DEW, Robert David John. b 42. St Pet Coll Ox BA (2nd cl Th) 63. St Steph Ho Ox 63. **d** 65 **p** 66 Pet. C of Abington 65-69; Chap St Jo Sch Tiffield 69-71; Bp's Chap for Industry Dio Pet 71-79; Industr Chap Dio Liv from 79. *Church House, 1 Hanover Street, Liverpool, L1 3DW.*

DEW, Canon William Harold. b 02. Late Scho of St Jo Coll Cam 1st cl Nat Sc Trip pt i 23, BA (1st cl Nat Sci Trip pt ii) 24, MA 28. Univ of Lon BSc (1st cl) 24. Westcott Ho Cam 25. **d** 26 **p** 27 Southw. C of St Mary Nottm 26-29; H Trin Formby 29-30; C of Ch Ch Hoxton and Warden St Jo Coll Miss Maurice Hostel 30-34; Asst Chap Bede Coll Dur and Chap of St Hilda's Coll Dur 34-36; L to Offic Dio Dur and Lect Bede Coll Dur 34-37; V of St Hilda Millfield 36-41; Barrow-on-Soar 41-64; RD of Akeley E 56-64; Hon Can of Leic 60-70; Can (Emer) from 70; R of Medbourne w Holt 64-70; Ed Leic Dioc Cal 65-69; L to Offic Dio Leic from 70. *56 Northleigh Grove, Market Harborough, Leics, LE16 9QX.* (Market Harbro' 64717)

de WAAL, Hugo Ferdinand. b 35. Pemb Coll Cam BA 58, MA 63. Ridley Hall Cam 59. **d** 60 **p** 61 Birm. C of St Martin Birm 60-64; C-in-c of Dry Drayton 64-68; R (includng Bar Hill Ecumen Team) 68-73; Chap Pemb Coll Cam 64-68; V of Blackpool 74-78; Prin Ridley Hall Cam from 78. *Principal's Lodge, Ridley Hall, Cambridge, CB3 9HG.*

de WAAL, Very Rev Victor Alexander. b 29. Late Exhib Pemb Coll Cam 1st cl Mod Lang Trip pt i 47, BA (2nd cl Mod Lang Trip pt ii) 49, MA 53. Ely Th Coll 50. **d** 52 **p** 53 Lon. C of St Mary Virg Isleworth 52-56; Chap Ely Th Coll and L to Offic Dio Ely 56-59; Chap and Succr K Coll Cam 59-63; Chap Univ of Nottm 63-69; Hon C of Nottm 63-69; Select Pr Univ of Cam 64 and 74; Univ of Ox 77; Chan and Can and Preb of Linc Cathl 69-76; Exam Chap to Bp of Linc 69-76; to Bp of Derby 70-76; Dean of Cant from 76. *Deanery, Canterbury, Kent.* (Canterbury 60083)

DEWAR, Francis John Lindsay. b 33. Late Exhib of Keble Coll Ox 2nd cl Cl 55, BA (3rd cl Lit Hum) 58. Cudd Coll 58. **d** 60 **p** 61 York. C of Hessle 60-63; St Chad Stockton-on-Tees 63-66; PC of St Chad Sunderland 66-81; Hon C of All SS Newton Hall Dio Dur from 82. *2 Lumley Road, Newton Hall, Durham, DH1 5NP.* (Durham 41509)

DEWAR, John. b 32. Chich Th Coll 58. **d** 61 **p** 62 Ripon. C of St Hilda Leeds 61-65; St Geo Cullercoats (in c of St Hilda Marden) 65-69; V of St Bede Newsham Blyth 69-75; Kenton Dio Newc T from 76. *Vicarage, Creighton Avenue, Kenton, Newcastle-upon-Tyne, NE3 4UN.* (Newc T 857803)

DEWAR, Michael Willoughby. b 21. Late Exhib and Pri of Em Coll Cam BA (2nd cl Archaeol and Anthrop Trip B) 47, MA 49. Dipl Th (Lon) 57. QUB PhD 60. St Aid Coll 47. **d** 49 **p** 50 Drom. C of Shankill 49-51; L to Offic at St Mary Castle Street Reading 51-52; C of Ballymacarrett 52-55; R of Scarva 55-60; Chap and Jt Hd Master Harcourt Sch Weyhill Andover 60-64; L to Offic Dio Win 60-64; Perm to Offic Dio Cant from 61; C-in-c of Magherally w Annaclone 64-73; R of Helen's Bay Dio Down from 73; Exam Chap to Bp of Down 71-73 and from 80. *Rectory, Helen's Bay, Bangor, Co Down, N Ireland.* (Helen's Bay 852245)

De WEEVER, Bertie Christopher Horatio. b 07. Codr Coll Barb 72. **d** 63 Guy **p** 73 Stabroek for Guy. C of Beterverwagting 63-72; Providence w Agricola 72-75; R of Suddie w Queenstown 75-76; V of Kitty Dio Guy from 76. *St James-the-Less Vicarage, David Street, Kitty, Guyana.* (02-63696)

DEWEY, David Malcolm. b 43. Univ of Lon BA 72. Westcott Ho Cam 76. **d** 78 Lon **p** 79 Edmon for Lon. Hon C of St Mich AA Enfield Dio Lon from 78; Sen Lect Middlesex Poly from 72; Hon C of St Steph Bush Hill Park Dio Lon from 79. *29 Orchard Crescent, Enfield, Middx, EN1 3NS.* (01-366 8479)

DEWEY, Haydn Greenwood. b 06. ALCD 35. **d** 35 **p** 36 Blackb. C of H Trin Darwen 35-39; Morecambe 39-43; V of St Thos Barrowford 43-60; R of Rufford 60-71; Perm to Offic Dio Bradf from 71. *1 Falcon Gardens, Settle, N Yorks.*

DEWEY, Meredith Ballard. b 07. Late Scho of Pemb Coll Cam 1st cl Nat Sc Trip pt i 27, BA 28, 1st cl Nat Sc Trip pt ii 29, MA 32. Ely Th Coll 29. **d** 31 **p** 32 Liv. C of Wigan 31-35; Fell and Dean of Pemb Coll Cam 36-73; Life Fell from 73; Chap RNVR 39-45; Select Pr Univ of Cam 47 and 51; Univ of Ox 49-50; Exam Chap to Bp of S'wark 49-58. *19 Millington Road, Cambridge, CB3 9HW.*

DEWEY, Peter Lewis. b 38. Wycl Hall Ox. **d** 71 **p** 72 Kens for Lon. C of St Sav, Shepherds Bush 71-73; Dom Chap to Bp of Kens 73-75; C (in c of All SS) of Isleworth 75-81; Team V of Dorchester Dio Ox from 81; P-in-c of Long Wittenham w Little Wittenham Dio Ox from 82. *Vicarage, Clifton Hampden, Abingdon, Oxon, OX14 3EF.* (Clifton Hampden 7784)

DEWEY, William Robert. b 07. Hatf Coll Dur Capel Cure Pri 31, BA 32, Dipl in Th (w distinc) 33, MA 35. **d** 33 **p** 34 Linc. C of Skegness 33-37; V of Humberston 37-49; RD of Grimsby S 44-49; R of Branston 49-61; Chap Branston Sanat 49-61; R of Mablethorpe w Stane 61-64; C of Ashburton NZ 64; V of Akaroa NZ 65-68; C of Parkstone 69-71; St Kath Southbourne Bournemouth 72-73. *38 Seafield Road, Southbourne, Bournemouth, Hants.* (B'mth 426479)

DEWHURST, George. b 34. TD 76. K Coll Lon and Warm AKC 58. **d** 59 Blackb **p** 60 Lanc for York. C of St Pet Chorley 59-61; P-in-c of All SS Conv Distr Oswaldtwistle 61-65; CF (TA) 63-67; CF (TAVR) from 67; V of Shevington Dio Blackb from 65. *St Anne's Vicarage, Shevington, Wigan, Lancs.* (Appley Bridge 2136)

DEWHURST, George Gabriel. b 30. **d** 59 **p** 60 RC Bp of Hexham & Newc. Rec into Angl Ch by Bp of Dur 69. C of St Jo Evang Darlington 70; St Nich Bp Wearmouth 71-73; C-in-c of St Mark's Conv Distr Stockton-on-Tees 73-81; V of Harton Dio Dur from 81. *182 Sunderland Road, South Shields, T & W, NE34 6AH.* (S Shields 561855)

DEWHURST, John Bertram. Ridley Coll Melb. **d** 58 Bal **p** 60 St Arn for Bal. C of Ch Ch Cathl Bal 58-59; Horsham 59-60; H Trin Coburg 61-62; P-in-c of Merino 62-64; V 64-66; R of Macarthur 66-73; Casterton 73-80; Chap Qu Gr Sch Bal from 80. *4 Hampden Street, Ballarat, Vic, Australia 3350.*

DEWING, Richard William David. b 13. Selw Coll Cam BA 34, MA 38. Cudd Coll 34. **d** 36 **p** 37 York. C of Hessle 36-38; Scarborough 38-43; C-in-c of St Luke's Conv Distr Scarborough 43-44; V of Yaxley 44-47; R of Rustenburg 47-52; P-in-c of Rustenburg E Nat Miss 48-52; R of Boksburg 52-63; St Pet Warmsworth Doncaster (w Edlington to 67) 63-73; V of Binsted 73-79. *6 Quinnettes, Churt, Farnham, Surrey, GU10 2NU.* (0428-713071)

DEWIS, Harry Kenneth. b 19. N-W Ordin Course 75. **d** 78 **p** 79 Ripon. C of Bedale Dio Ripon from 78. *11 Masham Road, Bedale, N Yorks, DL8 2AF.* (Bedale 23588)

De WIT, John. b 47. Oriel Coll Ox BA 69, MA 73. Clare Coll Cam BA 78. Westcott Ho Cam 75. **d** 78 **p** 79 Birm. C of Quinton 78-81; Team V of Solihull Dio Birm from 81. *St Michael's House, 2 Cheltondale Road, Solihull, W Midl.* (021-704 4730)

De WOLF, James Edward. K Coll NS BA 37. **d** 39 **p** 40 NS. C of Ch Ch Dartmouth 39-44; R of Musquodoboit Harbour 44-47; Weymouth 47-52; I of Cardston 52-55; Miss at Blood Reserve 52-63; Prin of La Tuque Ind Res Sch 65-68; on leave. *69 Pine Street, Brockville, Ont., Canada.*

DEWSBURY, Michael Owen. St Aid Coll. **d** 57 **p** 58 Nor. C of Hellesdon 57-60; Speke 60-62; R of L w Gt Glemham 62-67; St Pet W Lynn King's Lynn 67-68; L to Offic Dio Perth 68; P Sacr Perth Cathl 69; R of Dongara w Greenough-Walkaway 69-71; Nollamara 71-76; Assoc Chap R Perth Hosp 76-79; Chap Fremantle Hosp from 79. *250 Walcott Street, Mount Lawley, W Australia 6050.* (271 0892)

DEXTER, Eric Henry Vincent. b 22. Univ of Manit BSc 42. **d** 74 **p** 75 Rupld. Hon C of River N Pars 74-76; I of Woodsdale 77-78; R of Kelowna Dio Koot from 78. *608 Sutherland Avenue, Kelowna, BC, Canada.*

DEXTER, Frank Laurence. b 45. Em Coll Sktn 70. **d** 71 Rupld. C of Pond Inlet 72-82; Miss at All SS Arctic Bay Dio Arctic from 82. *All Saint's Mission, Arctic Bay, NWT, Canada.*

DEXTER, Frank Robert. b 40. Cudd Coll 66. **d** 68 Bp Ramsbotham for Newc T **p** 69 Newc T. C of H Cross Fenham 68-71; Whorlton 71-73; V of Ch the Carpenter City and Dio Pet 73-80; St Phil City and Dio Newc T from 80; RD of Newc W from 81. *St Phillip's Vicarage, Newcastle upon Tyne, NE4 5JE.* (Newc T 737407)

DEY, Charles Gordon Norman. b 46. Dipl Th (Lon) 70. Lon Coll Div. **d** 71 **p** 72 Wakef. C of Almondbury 71-76; V of Mixenden Halifax Dio Wakef from 76. *Vicarage, Mixenden, Halifax, HX2 8RX.* (Halifax 244761)

DEY, John Alfred. b 33. ALCD 57. **d** 57 **p** 58 Man. C of Albert Mem Ch Man 57-60; Pennington Lancs 60-62; V of Mosley Common 62-69; Em Chadderton 69-79; St John Flixton Dio Man from 79. *St John's Vicarage, Irlam Road, Flixton, Manchester, M31 3WA.* (061-748 6754)

DHIKANGE, Nasanaeri. Bp Tucker Coll Mukono. **d** 63 **p** 64 Nam. P Dio Nam from 63. *Anglican Church, Waibuga, Uganda.*

DHLADHLA, Ven Lyman William Mntukaterjwa. Rosettenville Th Coll 45. **d** 48 **p** 49 Zulu. C of Kambula Miss 48-50; Paulpietersburg 50-57; Etalaneni 57-62; Can of Zulu 62-73; R of Chwezi 62-70; St Aug Miss Dio Zulu from 70; Archd of W Zulu from 73. *St Augustine's Rectory, PO St Augustine's, Via Dundee, Natal, S Africa.* (St Augustine's 2)

DHLAMINI, Isaac Mtembeni. St Bede's Coll Umtata 64. **d** 66 **p** 67 Zulu. C of St Matt Ntshiza 69-73; R of Hlazakazi 73-78; Chwezi 78-81; St Faith Durban Dio Natal from 81. *80 Carlisle Street, Durban 4001, S Africa.*

DHLODHLO, Daniel Mpehlo Zembe. **d** 66 **p** 68 Matab. P Dio Matab. *St Peter's Rectory, Madinare, Rhodesia.*

DHLULA, Canon Elliott. b 22. Univ of S Afr BA 65. **d** 70 **p** 71 Matab. P Dio Matab from 70; Can of Matab from 77; Archd of the Midlands 78-79; Prin St Columba Sch Bulawayo from 79. *Box 521, Bulawayo, Zimbabwe.* (64208)

DIAB, Victor. **d** 73 **p** 74 Jordan. C of Ch of Redeemer Amman Dio Jordan 73-75; Dio Jer from 76. *PO Box 598, Amman, Jordan.* (25383)

DIACON, Francis John. Ch Coll Hobart. **d** 66 **p** 67 Tas. P-in-c of Furneaux Is 66-68; Chap St Paul's Sch Bald Hills, Brisb 69-73; R of Sandgate Dio Brisb from 74. *58 Rainbow Street, Sandgate, Queensland, Australia 4017.* (269 1148)

DIALA, Arthur. **d** and **p** 72 Papua. P Dio Papua. *Anglican Church, Korisata, Papua New Guinea.*

DIALE, David Soloman. Coll of the Resurr Rosettenville 45. **d** 47 **p** 48 Johann. C of Orlando Miss Distr 47-52; P-in-c of Ventersdorp Miss Distr 52-58; Springs Miss Distr 58-62; R of Kagiso 62-63; L to Offic Dio Johann 63-66; C of Atteridgeville 67-71; Saulsville 71-75; L to Offic Dio Pret from 78. *c/o PO Box 96, Ga Rankuwa 0208, Transvaal, S Africa.*

DIAMOND, Canon David John. b 35. Univ of Leeds BA 60. St Steph Ho Ox 60. **d** 62 Warrington for Liv **p** 63 Liv. C of Tue Brook 62-68; R of St Paul w St Mark Deptford Dio S'wark from 68; Hon Can of S'wark Cathl from 73. *St Paul's Rectory, Deptford High Street, SE8 3PQ.* (01-692 1419)

DIAMOND, Gordon Ernest. b 08. ALCD 37. **d** 36 **p** 37 Glouc. C of Nailsworth 36-38; All S (in c of St Luke) Harlesden 38-40; V of Ch Ch New Catton Nor 40-45; H Trin

Sydenham 45-50; St Geo Worthing 50-56; Chap Worthing Hosp 54-56; R of Newick 56-73; RD of Uckfield 64-73; Hon C of Battle Dio Chich from 74. *Whispers, North Trade Road, Battle, Sussex, TN33 0HW.* (Battle 3466)

DIAMOND, Michael Lawrence. b 37. St Jo Coll Dur BA 60, MA 74. ALCD 62 (LTh from 74). **d** 62 **p** 63 S'wark. C of St Mich AA Southfields 62-64; All SS Patcham 64-69; R of Hamsey 70-75; C-in-c of St Andr L Cam Dio Ely from 75. *Vicarage, Parsonage Street, Cambridge, CB5 8DN.* (Cam 353794)

DIANI, Very Rev Jean Baguma. b 41. **d** 79 **p** 80 Boga-Z. P Dio Boga-Z 79-80; Dean from 80. *EAZ Boga, BP 154, Bunia, Zaire.*

DIAZ, Carlos. b 1900. **d** and **p** 66 Argent. P Dio Argent 66-73; N Argent from 73. *Parsonage, San Luis, N Argentina.*

DIBBENS, Hugh Richard. b 39. BA (Lon) 63. St Pet Coll Ox BA 65, MA 74. Univ of Lon MTh 67. Oak Hill Th Coll. **d** 67 Lon **p** 68 Willesden for Lon. C of St Geo Mart Qu Square Holborn 67-72; CMS Miss Birm 73-74; Hokkaido Japan 74-77; R of Chigwell Dio Chelmsf from 78. *Rectory, High Road, Chigwell, Essex, IG7 6QB.* (01-500 3510)

DIBBS, Canon Geoffrey. Univ Coll Man BA (Th) 51, ThD 69. Wycl Hall Ox 51. **d** 53 **p** 54 Man. C of Droylsden 53-56; V of St Luke Chadderton 56-59; R of Burton Agnes w Harpham 59-66; C of St Jas Stratford 66-68; R of St Alb Lon 68-76; Can of Hur from 75; Hon C of St Paul's Cathl Lon Ont 76-78; R of St Aid Lon Dio Hur from 78. *4-220 Dundas Street, London, Ont., Canada.*

DIBDEN, Alan Cyril. b 49. Univ of Hull LLB 70. Fitzw Coll Cam 2nd cl Th Trip pt ii BA 72, MA 76. Westcott Ho Cam 70. **d** 73 **p** 74 S'wark. C of St Luke Camberwell 73-77; Team V of Walworth 77-79; Langley Marish Dio Ox from 79. *2 Woodstock Avenue, Slough, Berks.* (Slough 79654)

DICK, Alexander Walter Henry. b 20. BSc (Lon) 49. BSc Econ (Lon) 56. Sarum Wells Th Coll 73. **d** 74 **p** 75 Ex. C of Totnes 74-77; Publ Pr Dio Ex 77-80; V of Estover 80-81; P-in-c of Lifton Dio Ex from 81; Kelly w Bradstone Dio Ex from 81; Broadwoodwidger Dio Ex from 81. *Rectory, Lifton, Devon, PL16 0BJ.* (Lifton 291)

DICK, Cecil Bates. b 42. Selw Coll Cam BA 68, MA 72. E Midl Jt Ordin Tr Scheme 73. **d** 76 **p** 78 Southw (APM). Hon C of Cinderhill 76-79; Asst Master Nottm High Sch 72-79; Chap The Dame Allan's Schs Newc T from 79. *25a Low Gosforth Court, Newcastle upon Tyne, NE3 5QA.* (Wideopen 367660)

DICK, Raymond Owen. b 53. Univ of Edin BD 77. Edin Th Coll 73. **d** 77 **p** 78 Glas. C of St Mary's Cathl City and Dio Glas from 77. *45 Oakfield Avenue, Glasgow, G12 8LL.*

DICKEN, Eric William Trueman. b 19. Ex Coll Ox BA (Mod Lang) 39, MA 46, Junior Hall Gr Test Pri 48, 1st cl Th 48, DD 64. Cudd Coll 49. **d** 49 **p** 50 Southw. C of Hucknall Torkard 49-54; V of Caunton 54-65; V of Maplebeck 54-65; Warden Lenton Hall 65-80; Lect Dept of Th Univ of Nottm 65-70; Sen Lect 70-80; R of Maidwell w Draughton and Scaldwell and Lamport w Faxton Dio Pet from 80. *Maidwell Rectory, Northampton, NN6 9JF.* (Maidwell 223)

DICKENS, Philip Henry Charles. b 28. SOC 76. **d** 79 **p** 80 Guildf. Hon C of All SS Headley Dio Guildf 79-81; C from 81. *Stephen's Orchard, Grayshott, Hindhead, Surrey.*

DICKENS, Timothy Richard John. b 45. Univ of Leeds BSc 68. Westcott Ho Cam 68. **d** 71 Lich. C of Meole Brace 71-74; P-in-c of Ch Ch Conv Distr Stamford 74-80; V of Anlaby Dio York from 80. *St Peter's Vicarage, Church Street, Anlaby, N Humb, HU10 7DG.* (Hull 653024)

DICKENSON, Arthur John. **d** 76 **p** 77 Brisb. Hon C of St Andr Indooroopilly Dio Brisb from 76. *35 Francis Street, Taringa, Queensland, Australia 4068.* (370 9601)

DICKENSON, Charles Gordon. b 29. Bps' Coll Cheshunt 53. **d** 56 **p** 57 Ches. C of Ellesmere Port 56-61; V of St Columba Egremont Wallasey 61-68; Latchford 68-74; P-in-c of Hargrave 74-79; Chap to Bp of Ches 75-79; V of St Jas w St Bede Birkenhead Dio Ches from 79. *56 Tollemache Road, Birkenhead, Merseyside.* (051-652 1016)

DICKENSON, Geoffrey. b 20. Kelham Th Coll 38. **d** 44 **p** 45 Southw. C of Averham w Kelham 44-47; All SS Sedgley 47-49; Fenton 49-53; Welkom S Afr 53-57; C of Gt Greenford 57-59; R of Sandiacre 59-67; PC of Frecheville 67-70; RD of Staveley 69-70; V of Scarcliffe 70-75; R of Walton-on-Trent and Croxall w Oakley Dio Derby from 75. *Walton Rectory, Burton-on-Trent, Staffs, DE12 8NA.* (Barton-under-Needwood 2442)

DICKENSON, Canon George Harris. Codr Coll Barb. **d** 42 **p** 43 Barb. C of St Mich Cathl Barb 42-46; P-in-c of St Mary Antig 46-50; V of Boscobel Barb 50-51; All SS Barb 51-62; R of St Jos Barb 62-69; St Jas I and Dio Barb from 69; Can of Barb from 76. *St James's Rectory, Barbados, W. Indies.*

DICKENSON, Oswald Clare. b 08. Qu Coll Newfld 32. **d** 37 **p** 38 Newfld. C of St Thomas Newfld 37; I of Random 37-39; C of St Anthony Byker 40-43; C-in-c of St Mary Holywell 43-47; R of Grand Bahama 47-49; V of Lambley 50-56; R of Knaresdale 50-56; PC of W Pelton 56-63; V of Ch Ch Clapham 63-77; Perm to Offic Dio Dur from 77; Newc T from 78. *9 Burn Terrace, Rosehill, Wallsend-on-Tyne, NE28 7BJ.* (Wallsend 627068)

DICKER, David. b 31. St Pet Hall Ox BA 57, MA 59. Linc Th Coll 55. **d** 57 Sherborne for Sarum **p** 58 Sarum. C of Wootton Bassett and of Broad Town 57-60; H Trin Weymouth 60-63; All SS Antig 63-64; V of Tisbury 64-71; Hon Sec Sarum Dio Conf 64-67; R of St Mark's Hurlingham w Villa Devoto Buenos Aires Argent 71-78; Chap Miss to Seamen Newport Gwent 78-81; Dunkirk from 81. *The Missions to Seamen, Princess Alice House, 130 Rue de L'Ecole*.

DICKER, John Hamilton. Bp's Univ Lennox LST 32. **d** 32 **p** 34 Queb. C of St Jo Bapt Cathl Belize 32-33; H. Trin. Cathl Queb 33-34; St Clem Miss Labrador 34-39; V of Kitscoty Alta 39-40; Hardisty 41-42; Wabamun 42-43; Chap CASF 43-46; V of Mayerthorpe 46-53; Ashmont 53-55; Miss Sandy Lake 55-60; Frog Lake 60-65; Onion Lake 60-65; Chap Prince Albert Ind Sch 66-68. *Lakeside Road, Hampton Village, NB, Canada.*

DICKER, Ven Percival Hensby. OBE 72. Trin Coll Melb BA (2nd cl Phil) Bromby Gr Prize and Dipl Educn (1st cl) 20, Bromby Hebr Prize 21, MA (Hons) 22. ACT ThL (1st cl) 21. Univ of Lon BD 34. **d** 21 **p** 22 Gippsld. C of Yallourn 21-25; on leave 24; St Andr Brighton Vic 26; Min of N Geelong 27-29; Prin Geelong Boys' Prep Sch Melb 27-32; Ho Master and Chap Geelong Gr Sch 33; on leave 34-35; Can of Wang Cathl and R of Wang 35-65; Archd of Wang and Exam Chap to Bp of Wang 57-67; Archd (Emer) from 67. *Wangaratta, Vic., Australia.*

DICKERSON, Cedric Winston. b 41. St Paul's Coll Grahmstn 78. **d** 80 **p** 81 Grahmstn. C of St Sav E Lon Dio Grahmstn from 80. *14 Belgravia Crescent, E London 5201, CP, S Africa.*

DICKERSON, Richard Keith. b 31. McGill Univ Montr BD 61. Montr Dioc Th Coll. **d** and **p** 60 Montr. C of St Matt Montr 60-63; R of Waterloo 63-69; on leave; C of Canvey Island 73-76; Perm to Offic Dio Queb from 78. *Box 58, Georgeville, PQ, Canada.*

DICKIE, James Graham Wallace. b 50. Worc Coll Ox BA 72, MA, Blitt 77. Westcott Ho Cam 78. **d** 81 Reading for Ox. C of Bracknell Dio Ox from 81. *15 Oakwood Road, Bullbrook, Bracknell, Berks.*

DICKIE, William Acworth. Univ of Glas BSc 26. Down Coll Cam BA 29, MA 33, Bps' Coll Cheshunt 31. **d** 32 **p** 33 Wakef. C of Outwood 32-34; Miss at Pamua 34; Pawa Sch Ugi 34-40; C of Lythe 40-42; V of Westerdale 42-48; Acaster-Selby w Appleton Roebuck 48-53; Hon C of Canning Town 69-73; Perm To Offic Dio Chich from 80. *210 Bannings Vale, Saltdean, Brighton, BN2 8DJ.*

DICKIN, Canon Gordon Clark. CD 67. Univ of W Ont BA 45. Hur Coll LTh 45. **d** 44 **p** 45 Hur. I of Muncey Chippewa and Oneida 45-49; R of Sandwich S w Oldcastle 49-54; Fort Macleod 54-58; St Cypr Calg 58-81; Hon Can of Calg from 73. *c/o 2812 19th Street NW, Calgary, Alta, Canada, T2M 3V8.* (289-3226)

DICKIN, Canon William Charles. b 10. Jes Coll Ox BA 31, MA 45. St Steph Ho Ox 31. **d** 33 **p** 34 Maenan for St A. C of Denbigh 33-35; Berriew 35-40; CF (EC) 40-46; R of Castle Caereinion 46-53; V of Chirk 53-70; RD of Llangollen 65-70; Cursal Can of St A Cathl 66-77; R of Hawarden 70-77; Prec of St A Cathl 74-77. *Sherwood, Northop Hall, Mold, Clwyd.*

DICKINSON, Arthur Edward. b 02. Pemb Coll Cam BA 27, MA 30. Bp's Coll Cheshunt 28. **d** 30 **p** 31 Lon. C of St Phil Kens 30-32; Gt Malvern 32-34; V of Elmley Castle w Netherton and Bricklehampton 34-37; Longhirst w Hebron 37-47; R of Salle 47-63; R of Heydon w Irmingland 47-63; Brockdish w Thorpe Abbotts 63-66. *48 Cliff Parade, Hunstanton, Norfolk.*

DICKINSON, Donald Herbert. b 36. Lon Coll of Div 61. **d** 64 **p** 65 Ely. C of Wisbech 64-67; St John, March 67-71; V of Guyhirn w Rings End 71-79; St Bede Morris Green, Bolton Dio Man from 79. *St Bede's Vicarage, Normanby Street, Morris Green, Bolton, BL3 3QR.* (Bolton 61496)

DICKINSON, Douglas Johnson. ACT ThL 59. **d** and **p** 59 C & Goulb. C of Temora 59-60; R of Pambula 60-65; Gunning 65-66; V of Ch Ch Heathmont 66-72; I of Templestowe 72-77; St Paul Kew 77-78; Ferntree Gully Dio Melb from 79; Warden Miss to Streets and Lanes Melb from 80. *6 Burke Road, Ferntree Gully, Vic, Australia 3156.* (758 1068)

DICKINSON, Gerard Brian. Sarum Th Coll 52. **d** 54 Lanc for Blackb **p** 55 Blackb. C of St Matt Burnley 54-56; Miss P Dio New Guinea 56-60; C of St Mary Wellingborough 60-61; Chap Emscote Lawn Sch Warw 61-64; Prin Forrest Lodge Hostel Geraldton 64-66; Prec of H Cross Cathl Geraldton 64-66; Dean and R 66-69; Asst Master Guildf Gr Sch Dio

Perth from 69. *45 Terrace Road, East Guildford, W Australia 6055.* (279-1135)

DICKINSON, Gilbert. b 08. ARIBA 32. Westcott Ho Cam 65. **d** 66 **p** 67 York. Hon C of H Trin w St Jo Evang St Martin and St Greg Micklegate York 66-68; C of W Acklam 68-71; V of Kexby w Wilberfoss 71-74; Perm to Offic Dio York from 75. *1 Deangate, York, YO1 2JB.* (York 52675)

DICKINSON, Hon Hugh Geoffrey. b 29. Trin Coll Ox BA 53, Dipl Th 54, MA 56. Cam MA (*by incorp*) Cudd Coll 54. **d** 56 **p** 57 Sarum. C of Melksham 56-58; Chap Trin Coll Cam 58-63; Win Coll 63-69; Select Pr Univ of Cam 61; P-in-c of Old Milverton 69-77; V of St Mich City and Dio St Alb from 77. *Vicarage, St Michael's Street, St Albans, Herts.* (St Alb 53810)

DICKINSON, James Bernard. b 46. St Chad's Coll Dur BA 64, Dipl Th 69. **d** 70 Repton for Derby **p** 71 Derby. C of Newbold w Dunstan 70-73; Team V of Staveley w Barrow Hill 73-76; C of Ilkeston 76-77; V of Allenton and Shelton Lock Dio Derby from 77. *Vicarage, Sinfin Avenue, Derby, DE2 9JA.* (Derby 701194)

DICKINSON, John Compton. b 12. Late Exhib of Keble Coll Ox Goldsmith Stud and BA 34, MA 38, BLitt 38. FRHistS 42. Linc Th Coll 48. **d** 48 **p** 49 Ely. Fell Em Coll Cam 47-50; L to Offic Dio Ely from 49; Select Pr Univ of Cam 50-58; Exam Chap to Bp of Pet from 50; Fell and Chap of Pemb Coll Cam 50-60; Select Pr Univ of Ox 57-58; Lect in Th Univ of Birm 60-62; Sen Lect 62-73; Perm to Offic Dio Worc 60-75; L to Offic Dio Birm 62-75; Hon Can of Pet 70-73; Perm to Offic Dio Carl from 80. *Yewtree Cottage, Bangarth, Cartmel, Grange-over-sands, S Cumb.* (Cartmel 302)

✠ **DICKINSON, Right Rev John Hubert.** b 01. Late Exhib of Jes Coll Ox 2nd cl Cl Mods 21, 3rd cl Lit Hum 23, BA 24, MA 28. Cudd Coll 24. **d** 25 **p** 26 York. C of St John Middlesborough 25-29; SPG Miss Dio S Tokyo 29-31; Cons Asst Bp of Melan in St Paul's Pro-Cathl Wel 30 Aug 31 by Abp of NZ; Bps of Wel; Ch Ch; Dun; Nel; Waik; Wai; and Melan; res 37. V of Felkirk w Brierley 37-42; Warkworth Northumb 42-59; Hon Can of Newc T Cathl 47-71; V of Chollerton w Thockrington 59-71. *52 Station Close, Riding Mill, Northumb.* (Riding Mill 589)

DICKINSON, Matthew Lewis. b 22. Launde Abbey Leic 77. **d** 79 Bp Garrett for Leic **p** 80 Leic. C of St Anne Leic 79-81; St Mary Humberstone City and Dio Leic from 81. *c/o Humberstone Vicarage, Leicester, LE5 1EE.*

DICKINSON, Robert Edward. b 47. Univ of Nottm BTh 74. St Jo Coll Nottm 70. **d** 74 **p** 75 Birm. C of St Martin Birm 74-78; P-in-c of St Bride w St Sav City and Dio Liv 78-81; Team V from 81. *8 Bedford Walk, Liverpool.* (051-708 8969)

DICKINSON, Victor Tester. b 48. Univ of Wales (Cardiff) BSc 70. St Steph Ho Ox 70. **d** 73 **p** 74 Llan. C of Neath w Llantwit 73-76; Asst Chap Univ Coll Cardiff 76-79; Team V of Willington Team Parish Dio Newc T from 79. *47 Norman Terrace, Willington Quay, Wallsend, NE28 6SP.* (Wallsend 623574)

DICKINSON, Wilfrid Edgar. b 21. AKC 42. Univ of Lon BD 42. Linc Th Coll. **d** 44 Chelmsf **p** 45 Barking for Chelmsf. C of Prittlewell 44-47; Chingford 47-49; Saffron Walden 49-51; V of Gt Wakering 51-54; Chigwell 54-74; R 74-78: Surr from 55; V of Hatfield Heath Dio Chelmsf from 78. *Hatfield Heath Vicarage, Bishops Stortford, Herts, CM22 7EA.* (Hatfield Heath 288)

DICKS, Terence Henry. Moore Th Coll Syd ACT ThL 57. **d** 57 Syd for Tas **p** 58 Tas. C of St John Launceston 57-60; C-in-c of Abbotsford NSW 60-62; R of Fairfield 62-67; Waverley Dio Syd from 67. *240 Birrell Street, Waverley, NSW, Australia 2024.* (389-3077)

DICKSON, Brian John. b 19. Univ of Reading BSc 41. Univ of Birm Dipl in Th 51. **d** 51 **p** 52 S'wark. C of H Trin S Wimbledon 51-53; Sec SCM Th Colls Dept 53-55; Chap Hulme Gr Sch Oldham 55-60; L to Offic Dio Worc and Chap K Sch Worc 60-67; Min Can of Worc Cathl 60-67; Chap Colston Sch Bris 67-73; L to Offic Dio Bris 67-74; V of Bishopston Dio Bris from 74; RD of Horfield from 80. *Bishopston Vicarage, Bristol 7.* (Bris 44359)

DICKSON, Canon Colin Frazer. Angl Th Coll Vancouver 54. **d** and **p** 57 Carib. I of Shulus Ind Miss 57-67; Lytton Ind Miss Dio Carib from 67; Hon Can of Carib from 64; Chap St Geo Ind Sch Lytton 70-78. *PO Box 67, Lytton, BC, Canada.* (455-2404)

DICKSON, George Norton. b 21. Trin Coll Dub BA (2nd cl Mods) 43. **d** 45 **p** 47 Kilm. C of Drumgoon and Ashfield 45-48; Woodhouse 48-50; R of Rathcormac 50-55; Clascarrig 55-71; I of Leskinfere Dio Ferns from 71. *Ballycanew Rectory, Gorey, Co Wexford, Irish Republic.* (Ballycanew 4)

DICKSON, Richard. b 48. Ch Coll Cam BA 70, BChir 73, MB 74. Coll of Resurr Mirfield 74. **d** 77 **p** 78 Portsm. C of Paulsgrove 77-80; Forton Dio Portsm from 80. *39 Heaton Road, Gosport, Hants.*

DICKSON, Samuel Mervyn James. b 41. Div Hostel Dub. **d** 66 **p** 67 Down. C of Ballyholme 66-70; Knockbreda 70-75; R of Clonallon w Warrenpoint Dio Drom from 75. *Warrenpoint Rectory, Newry, Co Down, N Ireland.* (Warrenpoint 2267)

DIEGO SUAREZ, Diocese of. *See* Antsiranana.

DIENYE, Franklin Inomo. b 26. Trin Coll Umuahia. **d** 63 **p** 64 Nig Delta. P Dio Nig Delta. *Isiokpo, via Port Harcourt, Nigeria.*

DIGGLE, Michael John. b 31. K Coll Lon and Warm AKC 58. **d** 59 Bp Gelsthorpe for Southw **p** 60 Linc. C of Bawtry 59; St Andr and St Luke Grimsby 59-63; V of Roxby w Risby 63-68; Lawkholme 68-72; V of Kellington w Whitley 75-77; Industr Chap Dio Wakef 72-77; Dio Liv from 77. *16 Bewsey Road, Warrington, Chesh, WA2 7LW.*

DIGHT, Harri Jandrell. b 13. Fitzw Ho Cam BA 39; Bps' Coll Cheshunt 38. **d** 43 **p** 44 Southw. C of St Mary Magd Newark 43-45; C-in-c of All SS Coddington 45-48; V of Billinghay w Walcot and Dogdyke 48-53; R of N w S Claypole 53-55; PC of St Jo Evang Grantham 55-59; V of Saxilby w Ingleby 59-66; R of Broxholme 60-66; V of Kilby 66-78; Wistow w Newton Harcourt 66-78. *The Birches, Wirksworth Road, Whatstandwell, Matlock, Derbys.* (Wirksworth 3096)

DIGNAN, Leslie Arnold. **d** 48 **p** 49 NS. C of Port Hill Dio NS 48-49; R 49-52; CF (Canada) 52-63; I of Lakeside w Timberlea 63-68; Blandford 68-71. *PO Box 107, Waverley, NS, Canada.*

DIJKMAN, Jan Hendrik Leonard. Rhodes Univ Grahmstn BA 59, BD 61. Fitzw Ho Cam BA (3rd cl Th Trip pt iii) 62. Westcott Ho Cam. **d** and **p** 63 Johann. C of Rosebank Johann 63-67; Springs 67-68; R of Westonaria 68-72; Roodepoort 72-77; C of Parktown Dio Johann and Chap Univ of Witwatersrand from 77. *13 Seymour Avenue, Parktown, Johannesburg, S Africa.*

DIKE, Levi Arazu. **d** 43 **p** 44 Bp Patterson for Niger. P Dio Niger 43-65; Hon Can 65-72. *c/o St Mary's Church, Uruagu-Nnewi, Nigeria.*

DIKO, Thompson. **d** 79 **p** 80 Centr Melan. P Dio Centr Melan. *Lunga Village Honiara, Solomon Islands.*

DIL, Pierre Joseph. Bp Gray Th Coll Capetn LTh 62. **d** 63 Capetn **p** 64 Bp Cowdry for Capetn. C of Somerset W 63-65; St Alb Cathl Pret 65-67; H Cross Cathl Lusaka 67-69; P-in-c of the Team Min of Lusaka W Dio Lusaka from 71. *P.O. Box RW 258, Lusaka, Zambia.*

DILL, Peter Winston. b 41. ACP 66. AKC and BD 72. St aug Coll Cant 72. **d** 73 **p** 74 Southw. C of Warsop w Sookholme 73-75; Rhyl 75-77; Oxton 77-78; V of Newton-in-Mottram Dio Ches from 78. *Vicarage, Bradley Green Road, Newton-in-Mottram, Hyde, SK14 4NA.* (061-368 1489)

DILLAM, Canon Walter. b 12. St Chad's Coll Dur LTh 42. **d** 42 **p** 43 Wakef. C of St John Huddersfield 42-45; Prec of Leeds 45-50; V of Manston 50-63; St Wilfrid Harrogate 63-72; RD of Harrogate 70-72; Ripon 75-79; Can Res of Ripon Cathl 72-80; Can (Emer) from 80; P-in-c of Nidd Dio Ripon from 81. *1 The Almshouses, Ripley Road, Nidd, Harrogate, HG3 3BP.* (Harrogate 771269)

DILLISTONE, Canon Frederick William. b 03. Late Scho of BNC Ox 1st cl Math Mods 22, BA (2nd cl Math) 24, Dipl Th 25, MA 28, BD 33, DD 51. Wycl Coll Tor Hon DD 57. Episc Th Sch Cam Mass Hon DD 67. Wycl Hall Ox 25. **d** 27 Win for Portsm **p** 28 Portsm. C of St Jude Southsea 27-29; Tutor Wycl Hall Ox 29-31; CMS Miss N India Th Coll Saharanpur 31-32; PC of St Jas Alperton 32-34; V of St Andr Ox 34-38; Prof of Systematic Th Wycl Coll Tor 38-45; Vice-Prin Lon Coll Div 45-47; Prof of Th Episc Th Sch Cam Mass 47-52; Can Res and Chan of Liv Cath 52-56; Can (Emer) from 63; Hulsean Pr Univ of Cam 53; Select Pr Univ of Ox 53-55; Dean of Liv 56-63; Chap O of St John of Jer from 59; Select Pr Univ of Cam 60; Commiss Wai from 61-70; Fell and Chap Or Coll Ox 64-70; Fell (Emer) from 70; Bampton Lect Univ of Ox 68. *15 Cumnor Rise Road, Oxford, OX2 9HD.* (Cumnor 2071)

DILLON, Cecil William. Moore Th Coll Syd 27. **d** 27 **p** 28 Syd. C of Castle Hill w Baulkham Hills and Dural 27-28; furlough 29; Hornsby 30-31; Strathfield w Homebush 31-34; R of St Andr, Stratfield 34-71; L to Offic Dio Syd from 71. *39 Fitzroy Street, Leura, NSW, Australia 2781.* (047-84 1678)

DILLON, Howard Frederick. Moore Th Coll Syd ACT ThL 63. BD (Lon) 66. **d** 63 **p** 65 Syd. C of St Steph Willoughby 63-66; CF (Austr) 66-73; L to Offic Dio Wang 67-73; R of Bowrall 73-78; I of Ivanhoe Dio Melb from 78. *18 Noel Street, Ivanhoe, Vic, Australia 3079.* (49 1158)

DILLON, Peter Rudolph. Moore Th Coll Syd 63. **d** 66 **p** 67 Graft. C of Ch Ch Cathl Graft 66-67; P-in-c of Dunoon 67-69; L to Offic Dio Graft 70-80; Perm to Offic Dio Brisb from 80. *70 Belclare Street, The Gap, Queensld, Australia 4061.*

DILLON, Canon Rudolph Frederick. Moore Th Coll Syd

ACT ThL 30. **d** 31 **p** 32 Syd. C of St Alb Ultimo 32; H Trin Erskinville 32-35; St Steph Willoughby 35-36; C-in-c of St Thos Auburn 36-38; I of St Luke Clovelly 38-40; R of H Trin Erskineville 40-45; St Hilda Katoomba 49-50; Campsie 50-57; Hurstville 59-64; Hon Can of Syd from 63; L to Offic Dio Syd from 64. *62 Pacific Avenue, Werri Beach, NSW, Australia 2534.* (042-341292)

DILNOT, John William. b 36. Selw Coll Cam BA 60, MA 64. Cudd Coll 60. **d** 62 **p** 63 Lich. C of Stafford 62-66; Stoke-on-Trent 66-67; V of All SS Leek 67-74; Leeds w Broomfield 74-79; P-in-c of Aldington Dio Cant 79-81; R (w Bonnington and Bilsington) from 81; Bonnington w Bilsington 79-81. *Aldington Rectory, Ashford, Kent, TN25 7EF.* (Aldington 480)

DILWORTH, Arthur. b 1899. Late Scho of Worc Coll Ox 2nd cl Cl Mods 21, BA 22, 2nd cl Lit Hum 23, MA 33. Wycl Hall Ox 23. **d** 24 **p** 25 Wakef. C of Birstall 24-27; SPG Miss Burma 27-39; Chap of Bassein and Exam Chap to Bp of Rang 34-39; V of Thurstonland 39-43; C of St Mary Magd Knighton 43-45; St Barn Hove 45-47; V of Cross Stone 47-51; Airedale w Fryston 51-53; R of Hoggeston w Dunton 53-56; V of Whaddon w Tattenhoe 56-62; R of Gt Horwood 62-64; RD of Mursley 60-64; Perm to Offic Dio Sarum 64-67; Dio Ox 67-74; Dio Wakef 74-79; Dio York from 79. *Dulverton Hall, St Martin's Square, Scarborough, YO11 2DQ.*

DIMAS, Jonathan Mambwe. b 30. St Jo Sem Lusaka 68. **d** 70 Bp Mataka for Zam **p** 71 Centr Zam. P Dio Lusaka 70-71; Dio Centr Zam from 71. *PO Box 172, Ndola, Zambia.*

✠ **DIMIEARI, Right Rev Ebenezer Tamunoteghe.** CBE 54. St Andr Coll Oyo 10. St Jo Coll Dur 34. **d** 22 **p** 24 Bp Howells for Niger. P Dio Niger 22-49; Archd of the Niger Delta 39-46; Bonny 46-48; Delta 48-49; Aba 49; Cons Asst Bp on the Niger in St Paul's Cathl 29 June 49 by Abp of Cant; Bps of Win; Truro; Cov; and Bris; Bp Suffr of Stepney; and Bps N Sherwood Jones; Hall; Lasbrey; T Sherwood Jones; Wilson; Smith; and Roberts; Apptd Ld Bp on the Niger Delta 52; res 61. *c/o Bishop's House, Aba, Nigeria.*

DIMMER, Harry James. b 12. Chich Th Coll 73. **d** and **p** 73 Portsm (APM). C of H Trin Fareham Dio Portsm from 73. *9 Bradley Road, Fareham, Hants, PO15 5BW.*

DIMOLINE, Keith Frederick. b 22. Clifton Th Coll 48. **d** 51 **p** 52 St Alb. C of Ch Ch Watford 51-54; Corsham 54-59; C-in-c of St Jo Bapt Conv Distr Park Swindon 59-62; V 62-65; Coalpit Heath 65-74; Hanham w Hanham Abbots Dio Bris from 74. *Vicarage, Church Road, Hanham, Bristol, BS15 3AF.* (Bristol 673580)

DIMOND, Edward William. b 27. Trin Coll Dub BA 50, Div Test 51. **d** 51 **p** 52 Connor. C of St Mary Belf 51-54; Chap Miss to Seamen Immingham and LPr Dio Linc 54-55; C of Portadown 55-59; R of St Jas Higher Broughton Salford Dio Man from 59. *St James's Rectory, Higher Broughton, Salford 7, Lancs.* (061-792 1208)

DIN, Esuva. St Pet Th Coll BSI. **d** 41 **p** 46 Melan. P Dio Melan 41-74. *Vanua Lava, Banks Islands, New Hebrides.*

DINA, Jonathan Bolaji. b 18. **d** 81 Ijebu. d Dio Ijebu. *St Matthew's Church, Ijebu-Igbo, Nigeria.*

DINEEN, Harvey Arthur Joseph. St Jo Coll Morpeth ACT ThL (2nd cl) 62. **d** 62 Melb **p** 63 Bp Sambell for Melb. C of St Geo Reservoir 62-64; Murrumbeena 64-65; Melb Dioc Centre 65-67; V of Inglewood 67-71; R of Kilcoy 71-75; Stanthorpe Dio Brisb from 75. *Rectory, Corundum Street, Stanthorpe, Queensland, Australia 4380.* (Stanthorpe 81 1083)

DINES, Anthony Bernard. b 25. Clifton Th Coll 57. **d** 60 Lon **p** 61 Kens for Lon. C of Highbury 60-63; St Jo Evang Weymouth 63-67; R of St Silas Glas 67-78; St Pet Gunton Dio Nor from 78. *36 Gunton Church Lane, Lowestoft, Suff.* (Lowestoft 2600)

DING, Frank. **d** and **p** 77 New Hebr. P Dio New Hebr 77-80; Dio Vanuatu from 80. *Mosina, Vanua Lava, Banks Islands, Vanuatu.*

DINGIR, Butros Kuku. **d** 71 **p** 72 Sudan. P Dio Sudan 71-76; Dio Omdurman from 76. *Box 65, Omdurman, Sudan.*

DINGLE, Adrian Kenneth. b 44. St Barn Coll Adel 77. **d** 78 **p** 79 Willoch. C of Port Linc 78-80. *17 Eden Street, Port Lincoln, S Australia 5606.*

DINGLE, Edwin Richard Doidge. **d** 64 **p** 66 New Westmr. Asst Chap Miss to Seamen Vanc 64-69; P-in-c of St Jas L New Westmr 70-75. *514 First Street, New Westminster, BC, Canada.*

DINGLE, Geoffrey Philip Warren. b 27. Trin Hall Cam BA 51, MA 55. Westcott Ho Cam 51. **d** 53 **p** 54 Cov. C of H Trin Leamington 53-57; Rottingdean 57-60; V of St Paul Warw 60-66; R of Berkswell Dio Cov from 66. *Berkswell Rectory, Near Coventry, W Midl.* (Berkswell 32321)

DINGLE, John Rodger. b 14. Keble Coll Ox BA 37, MA 41. Westcott Ho Cam 38. **d** 39 **p** 40 Dur. C of Billingham 39-42; L to Offic Dio Worc 42-43; C of H Trin Hartlepool 43-44; Shadforth 44-46; St Swith (St Martin in The Cornmarket from 78) City and Dio Worc from 76. *34 Beech Avenue, Worcester, WR3 8PY.* (Worc 53053)

DINGWALL, Canon Ian MacLeod. Univ of BC BA 60. Angl Th Coll Vanc LTh 61. **d** 61 **p** 62 New Westmr. C of St Paul Vanc 61-63; I of Agassiz 63-66; R of St Faith Vanc 66-72; St Jude Oakville Dio Niag from 72; Exam Chap to Bp of Niag from 73; Hon Can of Niag from 77. *Box 446, Oakville, Ont., Canada.* (416-845 2223)

DINNEN, John Frederick. b 42. TCD BA 65, BD 72. **d** 66 **p** 67 Connor. C of All SS Belf 66-68; ICM Dub 69-71; C of Carnmoney 71-73; Asst Chap QUB from 73; Dean of Residences QUB from 74. *22 Elmwood Avenue, Belfast, BT9 6AY.* (Belf 667754)

DINNIS, Richard Geoffrey. b 40. K Coll Lon and Warm AKC Barry & Whichelow Pri 63. **d** 64 **p** 65 Ex. C of St Pet Plymouth 64-68; St Mich Tividale 68-70; V of Goldenhill 70-79; R of Letchworth Dio St Alb from 79. *93 Pixmore Way, Letchworth, Herts, SG6 3TP.* (Letchworth 4822)

DINSDALE, Norman Vincent. b 09. AKC (2nd cl) 34. **d** 34 **p** 35 Bradf. C of Guiseley 34-38; C-in-c of Horton Bank Top Conv Distr 38-40; V of Tosside 40-44; Ingleton w Chapel-le-Dale 44-50; Sec Dioc Conf 47-50; PC of Macclesfield Forest w Wildboarclough 50-51; V of Stoke St Milburgh w Heath 51-54; PC of Hopton Cangeford 51-54; Seq of Cold Weston 51-54; NE Engl Area Sec CECS 54-62; R of Skelton Yorks 62-67; Org Sec C of E Children's S 66-71; V of Leake w Over and Nether Silton and Kepwick 71-79; C-in-c of Cowesby 71-79. *10 South Parade, York, YO2 2BA.* (York 53949)

DIROKPA, Balufuga. b 39. **d** 80 Boga-Z. d Dio Boga-Z. *C.A.Z. Bukavu, BP 2876, Bakuvu, Zaire.*

DISEKO, Daniel Molefe. St Francis Th Coll Sekhukhuniland 62. **d** 64 **p** 65 Pret. C of St Francis Mamelodi 64-69; Ga-Rankuwa 69-71; R of Mabopane Dio Pret from 71. *1728 Mabopane, Pretoria District, Transvaal, S Africa.*

DISNEY, Peter James. Univ of BC BA 36, Angl Th Coll BC LTh 37. **d** 37 **p** 38 Edmon. C of Hardisty 37-42; I of All SS w St Marg Vanc 42-46; C of St Mary Magd Wandworth 46-47; Dufton 47-48; V of Godmanchester 48-57; All SS Ipswich 57-63; Distr Sec BFBS Essex and Herts 63-69; Surrey 65-69; V of H Trin Halstead 69-78; Perm to Offic Dio St E from 78. *16 Lower Byfield, Monks Eleigh, Ipswich, Suff, IP7 7JJ.*

DISS, Ronald George. Sarum Th Coll 58. **d** 61 **p** 62 S'wark. C of Greenwich 61-65; Perm to Offic Dio Lon 65-68; L to Offic 68-77; Dio S'wark 65-80; Chap Univ of Lon 68-71; Asst Candidates' Sec CMS 71-77; Bps' Chap Dio Win 77-80; V of Maybush Dio Win from 80. *Vicarage, Sedbergh Road, Millbrook, Southampton, SO1 9HJ.* (Southn 771996)

DITTMER, Michael William. b 17. St Edm Hall Ox BA (3rd cl Th) 39, MA 43. Sarum Th Coll 40. **d** 41 Bp Mann for Roch **p** 42 Roch. C of St Andr Bromley 41-43; Horfield (in c of St Francis) 43-49; P-in-c of Conv Distr of St Francis Lockleaze 49-52; R of Yatton Keynell Dio Bris from 52; R of Castle Combe Dio Bris from 52; R of Biddestone w Slaughterford Dio Bris from 52; RD of Chippenham 66-76; R of W Kington Dio Bris from 75. *Yatton Keynell Rectory, Chippenham, Wilts.* (Castle Combe 782286)

DITTRICH, Douglas. Univ of Tor BA 60. Wycl Coll Tor. **d** and **p** 62 Tor. P-in-c of Frobisher Bay 62-67; Inuvik 67-76; I of St Geo Kamloops Dio Carib from 76. *1099 La Roque Street, Kamloop, BC, V2B 5L6, Canada.* (376-7707)

DIVALL, David Robert. b 40. New Coll Ox BA (Maths) 62, BA (Th) 64. Univ of Sussex DPhil 74. Sarum Wells Th Coll 75. **d** 77 **p** 78 Portsm. C of Catherington w Clanfield Dio Portsm from 77. *17 Pipers Mead, Clanfield, Portsmouth, PO8 0ST.*

DIWI, John. **d** 77 Zanz T **p** 81 Bp Russell for Zanz T. P Dio Zanz T. *Box 123, Tanga, Tanzania.*

DIX, Canon Thomas Hooton Michael. b 08. AKC 40. ARCO 34. Bps' Coll Cheshunt 40. **d** 40 **p** 41 St Alb. C of St Sav St Alb 40-43; UMCA Miss Dio Zanz 43-44; P-in-c of Msalabani 44-51; Miss at Tanga 51-54; Archd of Zanz and P-in-c of Ch Ch Cathl Zanz 54-59; V of Harrold 59-63; C-in-c of Carlton w Chellington 60-63; RD of Felmersham 62-63; V of Flamstead 63-74; Hon Can of St Alb 70-74; Can (Emer) from 74. *28 Sheridan Mansions, Sheridan Terrace, Hove, W Sussex.*

DIXIE, Philip Oswald Strathmore. Univ of Capetn BA 61, B Soc Sc 68. St Paul's Coll Grahmstn LTh 64. **d** 64 **p** 65 Capetn. C of St Thos Rondebosch 64-66; Clanwilliam 66-67; L to Offic Dio Capetn 68-74; Dio Johann from 74. *University of Witwatersrand, Braamfontein, Johannesburg, S Africa.* (011-724 1311)

DIXON, Aidan Geoffrey Wilson. b 15. Bp Wilson Coll IM. **d** 44 **p** 45 Ches. C of St Geo Stockport 44-47; V of Thwaites 47-54; Dacre 54-60; Surr from 60; Appleby w Murton and Hilton 60-72; R of Kynnersley 72-76; Tibberton 72-76; Preston 74-76; Perm to Offic Dio Lich from 76. *Sidney House, Kynnersley, Wellington, Salop.* (Telford 603224)

DIXON, Alan Ernest. b 31. Wadh Coll Ox BA (2nd cl Eng) 52, MA 56. MICE 64. Tyndale Hall Bris 64. **d** 66 Hulme for Man **p** 67 Man. C of Ch Ch Chadderton 66-71; V of Edgeside 71-78; Hon C of Bradley Dio Wakef from 78. *12a Grasmere Road, Marsh, Huddersfield.* (Huddersfield 47895)

DIXON, Canon Anthony. Univ of Man BSc 23. Leeds Cl Scho 23. **d** 24 **p** 25 Liv. C of St Mary Bootle 24-26; Hd Master Boys' High Sch and Chap at Panchgani 26-34; C-in-c of Cleeve-in-Yatton 35; C of St Osw Winwick 35-37; V of St John Ainsdale 37-66; Hon Can of Liv 64-66; Can (Emer) from 66; Chap at Madeira 66-72. *Rua Do Quebra Costas 20, Funchal, Madeira.*

DIXON, Ben Oswald Good. d and **p** 42 Yukon. C of Moosehide 42-44; Prin Ind Sch Elkhorn 44-47; Alert Bay 47-48; LPr Dio BC 48-55; C of Nanaimo 55-56; I of Harewood 56-72. *Cassidy, BC, Canada.*

DIXON, Blair Allison. Dalhousie Univ BA 64. K Coll NS LTh 66. **d** 66 **p** 67 Ott. C of All SS Westboro 66-70; R of Vanleek Hill 70-72; on leave 72-74; In Amer Ch 74-77; C of St Jas Lon Ont 77-70; I of Ch Ch Lon Dio Hur from 80. *22 Marla Crescent, London, Ont., Canada.*

DIXON, Bruce Richard. b 42. Univ of Lon BSc (Eng) 63. Sarum Th Coll 66. **d** 68 Warrington for Liv **p** 69 Liv. C of Walton-on-the-Hill 68-70; Harnham 70-73; Streatham 73-76; R of Thurcaston Dio Leic from 76. *Thurcaston Rectory, Leicester, LE7 7JA.* (Leic 362525)

DIXON, Canon Charles Harwood. Univ of St Andr BSc (2nd cl Nat Phil) 47 BD 53. Edin Th Coll. **d** 49 **p** 50 Brech. C of St Paul's Cathl Dundee 49-51; Prec 51-53; C of Umtata 53-55 and 57-58; Sub-Warden St Jo Coll Umtata 56 and 59-67; Dean of St John's Cathl 67-72; Can (Emer) from 73; C of St Jas Graaf Reinet 73-78. *Parsonage Street, Graaf Reinet, CP, S Africa.* (Graaf Reinet 868)

DIXON, Charles William. b 41. NOC 78. **d** 81 Pontefract for Wakef. C of Almondbury Dio Wakef from 81. *14 Wormald Street, Almondbury, Huddersfield, HU5 8NQ.*

DIXON, David. b 19. Lich Th Coll 57. **d** 58 Penrith for Carl **p** 59 Carl. C of St Luke w St Perran Barrow-F 58-61; V of St Mary Westfield Workington 61-68; Warden Rydal Hall Dio Carl from 68; P-in-c of Rydal Dio Carl from 78. *Rydal Hall, Ambleside, Cumb, LA22 9LX.* (Ambleside 2050)

DIXON, Canon Donald Harry. d 40 **p** 41 Alg. Miss at Espanola 40; St Joseph's I 40-54; R of L Current 54-78; Hon Can of Alg from 60. *RR1, Richards Landing, Ont., Canada.*

DIXON, Douglas Arthur. b 17. Edin Th Coll 43. **d** 46 **p** 47 Chelmsf. C of Collier Row 46-48; St Marg Ilford 48-49; St Mich Gidea Park 49-53; V of St Jas L Westmr 53-56; Cressing 56-61; St Jo Div Mawneys Romford 61-77; Perm to Offic Dio Portsm from 77. *30 St John's Crescent, Sandown, IW.*

DIXON, Edward Ashby. b 15. AKC (2nd cl), Relton Pri and Trench Gt Pri 40, BD (2nd cl) 45. **d** 40 **p** 41 Birm. C of St Benedict Bordesley 40-46; Clewer 46-49; St Matthias-at-the-Link Malvern 49-53; R of St Matt Coates 53-59; Chap of R Agr Coll Cirencester 53-59; PC of All SS Glouc 59-66; V of Frampton-on-Severn (w Whitminster from 74) 66-80; C-in-c of Arlingham 66-80; RD of S Glouc 68-79. *2 Grange Close, Minchinhampton, Stroud, Glos, GL6 9DF.* (Brimscombe 882560)

DIXON, Edward Michael. b 42. St Chad's Coll Dur BA 64, Dipl Th 66. **d** 66 Jarrow for Dur **p** 67 Dur. C of H Trin Hartlepool 66-70; Howden 70-73; Chap HM Pris Liv 73; Onley 74-82; Dur from 82. *c/o HM Prison, Frankland, Durham.*

DIXON, Eric. b 31. MPS. E Midl Min Tr Course 78. **d** 81 Repton for Derby (NSM). C of Mackworth Dio Derby from 81; Kirk Langley Dio Derby from 81. *92 Radbourne Street, Derby, DE3 3BU.*

DIXON, Francis Charles. St Aid Th Coll Bal, ACT ThL 27, Th Scho 34. **d** 27 **p** 28 Bal. C of Ararat 27-29; P-in-c of The Otway Forest 29-30; V of Edenhope 30-32; R of Mullewa 32-35; Supt of Forrest River Miss 35-36; R of Wiluna 36-37; Carnarvon 38-41; Northampton 41-44; Bluff Point and Chap Miss to Seamen Geraldton 44; Asst Chap Miss to Seamen Fremantle 44-45; Perm to Offic Dio Melb 45-46; Org Sec Victoria Miss to Seamen Dio Melb 47-50; P-in-c of Hillston and P-in-c of Lake Cargelligo 50-51; Actg Dio Sec 50; Dioc Commiss Dio River from 51; L Offic Dio Bal from 57; Dio St Arn 64-66. *72 Geelong Road, Ballarat, Vic., Australia.* (053-31 3379)

DIXON, Geoffrey Howard George. b 43. Oak Hill Th Coll 68. **d** 71 **p** 72 Ches. C of Ch Ch Macclesfield 71-75; Miss at Holman 75-78; at All SS Aklavik Dio Arctic from 81. *Box 28, Aklavik, NWT, Canada.*

DIXON, Gilbert Melville. d 70 **p** 71 Ja. C of Montego Bay 70; St Mary Maverley 71-72; R of Old Harbour 72-74; P-in-c of Harewood 74-77. *5 Fairfax Drive, Kingston 8, Jamaica, WI.* (092-44378)

DIXON, Gordon Arthur. b 45. Univ of Sask BA 73. Em & St Chad's Coll LTh 72. **d** 73 **p** 74 Calg. C of St Mich AA Calg 73-75; I of Ch of Good Shepherd Calg 75-80; C of St Pet City and Dio Calg from 80. *75 Deer Lane Place SE, Calgary, Alta, Canada.* (252-0393)

DIXON, Canon Guy Kenneth. b 08. Hertf Coll Ox BA 30, MA 34. Cudd Coll 30. **d** 31 **p** 32 Man. C of St Jas Birch-in-Rusholme 31-34; Ranmoor 34-36; C-in-c of St Jas Clifton 36-37; V 37-45; R of Thrybergh 45-73; Asst RD of Rotherham 47-73; Hon Can of Sheff 64-73; Can (Emer) from 73; L to Offic Dio Chich from 73. *20 Alderton Court, West Parade, Bexhill-on-Sea, E Sussex, TN39 3HF.* (Bexhill 218834)

DIXON, Hubert Clift. Univ of Syd BEducn 37. Moore Th Coll ThL 42. **d** 41 **p** 42 Syd. C of Ultimo 41; Mosman 41-42; Chap RAAF 42-46; Chap of Barker Coll Hornsby Dio Syd 47-80; L to Offic Dio Syd 64-80. *3 Dunlop Street, Hackett, ACT, Australia 2602.*

DIXON, John Henry Milward. b 03. Edin Th Coll 41. **d** 43 **p** 44 Dur. C of Coundon (in c of Leeholme Miss Ch) 43-49; Brandon (in c of St Agatha Brandon Colliery) 49-53; R of Lyons 53-57; Perm to Offic Dio Lon 58-59; C of All SS Notting Hill Kens 59-68; L to Offic Dio St E 68-76; C-in-c of St Mary-at-Elms Ipswich Dio St E from 76. *68 Black Horse Lane, Ipswich, IP1 2EF.* (Ipswich 211097)

DIXON, John Kenneth. b 40. Linc Th Coll 79. **d** 81 Alb. C of Goldington Dio St Alb from 81. *2 Ballinghall Close, Goldington, Bedford, Beds.* (0234-213468)

DIXON, John Martin. b 43. Lich Th Coll 69. **d** 72 **p** 73 Ches. C of Ellesmere Port 72-74; Bredbury 74-75; C (in c of St Anne Greenlands) of St Steph Blackpool Dio Blackb from 75. *St Anne's Church, Salmesbury Avenue, Bispham, Lancs, FY2 0PR.* (0253-53900)

DIXON, John Ridgewell. St Jo Coll Morpeth 66. **d** 66 **p** 67 Newc. C of New Lambton 66-67; Taree 68-70; Wyong 70-72; Prec St Paul's Cathl Rockptn 72-73; V of Springsure 73-77; C of Waratah Dio Newc from 80. *11 Myall Road, Waratah, NSW, Australia 2298.* (68 3378)

DIXON, John Stanfield. b 14. St Jo Coll Dur LTh 39, BA 40. St Aid Coll 36. **d** 40 **p** 41 Dur. C of Blackhall 40-42; Willington 42-47; Staindrop w Cockfield 47-49; V of Lynesack 49-55; PC of Chilton 55-60; L to Offic Dio Dur from 60; Asst Master Bp Auckland Gr Sch 60-77. *85 Lambton Drive, Bishop Auckland, Co Durham.*

DIXON, Canon John Wickham. b 18. St Aid Coll 38, LTh 41. St Jo Coll Dur BA (1st cl Th) 43, MA 46. **d** 43 **p** 44 Blackb. C of St Andr Ashton-on-Ribble 43-46; Tutor St Aid Coll 46-50; Chap Wycl Hall Ox 51-54; V of St Steph Blackb Dio Blackb from 54; Exam Chap to Bp of Blackb from 55; Can Res of Blackb 65-73; Hon Can from 73. *285 Whalley Old Road, Blackburn, Lancs, BB1 5RS.* (Blackburn 51258)

DIXON, Kenneth William. b 22. ACT ThDip 70. St Barn Coll Adel. **d** 71 **p** 72 Adel. C of St Aug, Unley 71-73; P-in-c of Eliz Downs 73-75; R of Yankalilla 75-78; Balhannah Dio Murray from 78. *Rectory, Balhannah, S Australia 5242.* (08-3884222)

DIXON, Lewis Sandison. Seager Hall Ont. **d** 64 **p** 65 Hur. C of New St Paul Woodstock 64-66; R of Ridgetown 66-70; St Jas Windsor Dio Hur from 70. *4276 Roseland Drive East, Windsor 22, Ont., Canada.* (519-969 4472)

DIXON, Nicholas Scarth. b 30. G and C Coll Cam 2nd cl Hist Trip pt i 53, BA (3rd cl Th Trip pt ia) 54, MA 63. Westcott Ho Cam 54. **d** 56 **p** 57 Carl. C of I of Walney 56-59; CF 59-62; V of H Trin w Ch Ch Whitehaven 62-69; R of Blofield w Hemblington 70-77; P-in-c of Bowness-on-Solway 77-79; R 79-81; V of Frizington and Arlecdon Dio Carl from 81. *Arlecdon Vicarage, Frizington, Cumb, CA26 3UB.* (Lamplugh 353)

DIXON, Peter. b 36. Qu Coll Ox BA 58, MA 62. Univ of Birm Dipl Th 60, BD 65, PhD 75. Qu Coll Birm 58. **d** 60 **p** 61 Llan. C of Mountain Ash 60-63; Penrhiwceiber w Tyntetown and Ynysboeth 63-68; C-in-c of Matthewstown w Ynysboeth 68-70; V of Bronllys w Llanfilo and Llandefaelog Tre'rgraig Dio Swan B from 70. *Vicarage, Bronllys, Brecon, LD3 0HS.* (Talgarth 711200)

DIXON, Peter David. b 48. Univ of Edin BSc 71. **d** 79 **p** 80 Edin. C of Musselburgh and of Prestonpans Dio Edin from 79. *18 New Street, Musselburgh, Midlothian.*

DIXON, Phillip. b 48. Univ of Leeds BSc 69. St Jo Coll Nottm 77. **d** 80 **p** 81 Bris. C of Soundwell Dio Bris from 80. *59 Middle Road, Kingswood, Bristol, BS15 4XJ.*

DIXON, Philip Roger. b 54. CCC Ox BA 77, MA 80. Oak Hill Coll Ba 80. **d** 80 **p** 81 Man. C of St Mary Droylsden Dio Man from 80. *4 Willow Walk, Droylsden, Manchester, M35 7DP.* (061-301 4704)

DIXON, Richard Russell. b 32. Univ of Dur BA 60. Chich Th Coll 60. **d** 62 **p** 70 York. C of St Martin Scarborough 62-63; Thirsk 69-73; C-in-c of Swine 73-81; Dioc Youth Officer York 73-78; V of St Nich Beverley Dio York from 81.

St Nicholas Vicarage, Beverley, N Humb, HU17 0ER. (0482 881458)

DIXON, Robert. b 50. St D Coll Lamp BA (Th) 80. Chich Th Coll 80. **d** 81 **p** 82 Cant. C of St Martin Maidstone Dio Cant from 81. *78 Plains Avenue, Maidstone, Kent.* (0622 64019)

DIXON, Roger John. b 33. Univ of Cam MA. **d** 79 **p** 80 Nor (APM). Hon C of Fakenham Dio Nor from 79. *14 Westmead Road, Fakenham, Norfolk.* (Fakenham 2714)

DIXON, Roy Dennison. Ch Coll Hobart ACT ThL 61. **d** 61 **p** 62 Tas. C of St Steph Hobart 61-62; P-in-c of Risdon Vale Miss Distr 62-64; R of Sheffield 64-68; Geeveston 68-69; L to Offic Dio Tas 70-77; P-in-c of Zeehan-Rosebery 77-81; Carrick Dio Tas from 81. *Rectory, Carrick, Tasmania 7257.* (003 93 6120)

DIXON, Royston Clarence. Univ of Leeds BA (2nd cl Gen Hons) 36. Coll of Resurr Mirfield 36. **d** 38 Ox **p** 39 Dorch for Ox. C of Thatcham 38-44; St Mary Slough 44-49; Wolborough 49-53; V of Appledore 53-72; C-in-c of Lundy I 53-72; RD of Hartland 62-67; V of Exwick City and Dio Ex from 72. *Exwick Vicarage, Exeter, Devon.* (Exeter 73597)

DIXON, Thomas Stanley. b 1897. FRCO 18. **d** 53 Glouc **p** 54 Tewkesbury for Cant. Hon C of Stonehouse 53-58; R of Medbourne w Holt 58-64. *Aldreth, Pearcroft Road, Stonehouse, Glos.*

DIXON, Victor. b 08. BC Coll Bris 37. **d** 38 **p** 40 Egypt. Vic Miss Dio Hong Kong 38-44; Perm to Offic (Col Cl Act) as C of Conv Distr of Southmead Bris 45; St Paul Hyson Green 45-47; V of Hawksworth Scarrington 47-51; Willoughby-on-the-Wolds w Wysall 51-60; St Matt Cam 60-70; Cler Sec Ely Dioc Conf 64-70; R of Winteringham 70-75. *12 Bradley Road, Grimsby, S Humberside.* (Grimsby 79800)

DIXON, William George St Clair. b 39. Univ of the WI BA (Th) 76. Codr Coll Barb 71. **d** and **p** 75 Barb. P-in-c of St Chris I and Dio Barb from 75. *St Christopher's Lodge, Enterprise, Christ Church, Barbados, WI.*

DIXON, William Gordon Murray. b 41. St Jo Coll Auckld 69. **d** 71 **p** 72 Auckld. C of Grey Lynn 71-74; V of Helensville 74-76; Chap RNZAF from 77. *4 Kupe Avenue, Whenuapai, NZ.*

DIXON, Canon William Thomas. St D Coll Lamp BA 34. **d** 36 **p** 37 Blackb. C of St Geo Chorley 36-40; Offg C-in-c of St Jo Bapt Burnley 40-42; V of St Jo Evang Darwen 42-47; CF (EC) 43-47; R of Haworth 47-59; Hon Can of Bradf 54-59; V of St Jo Bapt German 59-77; Hon Dioc Chap to Bp of S & M from 60; Can of S & M 63-77; Can (Emer) from 77; RD of Peel 66-76. *The Garth, Main Road, Colby, IM.*

DJAMU, Thomasi. Bp Tucker Coll Mukono 55. **d** 56 Ugan. d Dio Ugan 56-60; Dio Ruw from 60. *Anglican Church, Mulobya, Uganda.*

DLAMINI, Alfred Starkey Smakuhle. b 40. St Pet Coll Alice 73. **d** 75 **p** 76 Grahmstn. C of St Mich Miss Herschel 75-78; St Mich Queenstown and St Pet Lanti 78-80; R of St Pet Peddie Dio Grahmstn from 80. *Box 30, Peddie 5640, CP, S Africa.*

DLAMINI, Canon David Philemon. St Bede's Coll Umtata. **d** 57 **p** 59 Zulu. P Dio Zulu 59-68; Dio Swaz from 68; Can of Swaz 70-79; Hon Can from 79; Archd of W Swaz 73-76; Swaz 76-79. *Box 1311, Mbabane, Swaziland.*

DLAMINI, Gideon. b 14. **d** 75 **p** 77 Swaz (APM). P Dio Swaz 75-81. *Box 9, Ezulwini, Swaziland.*

✠ **DLAMINI, Right Rev Jacob Zambuhle Bhekuyise.** St Bede's Coll Umtata. **d** 61 **p** 63 Zulu. P Dio Zulu 61-78; Prov Co-Dir Dept of Miss S Africa 78-80; L to Offic Dio Johann 78-80; Cons Ld Bp Suffr of St John's in Kwa Magwaza Par Ch Zulu 3 July 80 by Abp of Capetn; Bps of Swaz, St John's, Zulu and Natal; Bps Suffr of Natal, Capetn, Johann and Pret. *Box 174, Umtata, Transkei, S Africa.*

DLAMINI, Kenrick Moses Vezi. St Bede's Coll Umtata. **d** 64 **p** 66 Natal. P Dio Natal. *Box 36224, Ntokozweni 4066, Natal, S Africa.*

DLAMINI, Petros Josiah. **d** 74 **p** 75 Swaz (APM). P Dio Swaz. *Ngwempisana School, PO Mankayana, Swaziland.*

DLAMINI, Phendu Joseph Jeremiah. **d** 72 **p** 74 Swaz. C of Usuthu Miss 72-75; P-in-c of Shiselweni Dio Swaz 75-79; Sobantu 79-81; R of Greytown Dio Natal from 81. *Box 98, Greytown 3500, Natal, S Africa.*

DLAMINI, Simon Douglas. **d** 70 Swaz. d Dio Swaz from 70. *Box 149, Mbabane, Swaziland, S Africa.*

DLAMINI, William Nkosi. **d** 71 **p** 72 Swaz (APM). C of Epiphany 71-80. *Box 9, Ezulwini, Swaziland, S Africa.*

D'MORIAS, Sydney James. b 07. Univ of Madr BA 29. Serampore Coll BD 32. Bp's Coll Calc 30. **d** 32 Bp Pakenham-Walsh for Madr **p** 33 Madr. Asst Chap of All SS Bangalore 32-35; Chap 35-36; Chap of Nellore w Bitragunta 36-45; St Matthias Vepercy 45-55; C of St Barn Southfields Surrey 55; V of All SS Kharagpur 56-57; St Jas Calc 58-61; C of Hornsey 61-67; V of St Thos Finsbury Park 67-78. *c/o 106 Queen's Drive, N4.* (01-802 1749)

DOAK, Wilbur Angus. Moore Th Coll Syd ACT ThL 50. **d** 50 **p** 51 Graft. C of Casino 50-53; Lismore 53; V of Mallanganee 53-55; Bowraville 55-56; R of Nimbin 56-61; Tweed Heads 61-66; Ballina Dio Graft from 66; Hon Can of Graft from 76. *Rectory, Ballina, NSW, Australia 2478.* (86 2094)

DOBB, Canon Arthur Joseph. b 31. ARIBA 54. Oak Hill Th Coll. **d** 58 **p** 59 Man. C of St Paul Bolton 58-60; Rawtenstall 60-62; V of Birtle (or Bircle) 62-72; Harwood Dio Man from 72; Hon Can of Man Cathl from 81. *Harwood Vicarage, Bolton, Lancs.* (Bolton 25196)

DOBB, Christopher. b 46. Univ of Dur BA 68. Cudd Coll Ox 68. **d** 70 **p** 71 Portsm. C of Portsea 70-73; L to Offic Dio S'wark 73-77; Perm to Offic Dio Bris 77-79; Publ Pr 79-81; V of St Aug Swindon Dio Bris from 81. *Vicarage, Morris Street, Swindon, Wilts, SN2 2HT.* (Swindon 22741)

DOBB, William Leslie. b 12. St Chad's Coll Dur BA 34, MA 47, Dipl Th 35. **d** 35 **p** 36 Win. C of St Alb Southampton 35-39; Bridport w West Bay 39-42; Cler Deputn Sec Dr Barnardo's for SW Distr 42-47; HQ Cler Org Sec Dr Barnardo's Homes 47-49 and 53-56; V of Wick Bris 49-53; C-in-c of Doynton 51-53; Chap of Dr Barnardo's Village 53-54; HQ Chap 53-56; R of Gussage St Mich 56-59; V of All SS Gussage 56-59; PC of Colehill 59-62; R of Insch 62-65; Forgue 62-65; Folla-Rule 62-65; St Jas Aber 65-66; St Drostan, Old Deer 66-74; St John Longside 66-74; Strichen 71-74; Perm to Offic Dio Sarum from 74. *12 Walnut Close, Urchfont, Devizes, Wilts.*

DOBBIN, Charles Philip. b 51. Jes Coll Cam BA 73, MA 77. Oriel Coll Ox BA 75. St Steph Ho Ox 74. **d** 76 **p** 77 Cant. C of New Addington 76-79; Melton Mowbray Dio Leic from 79. *17 Ankle Hill, Melton Mowbray, Leics, LE13 0QJ.* (Melton Mowbray 69973)

DOBBIN, Harold John. b 47. Univ of Liv BSc 69. St Steph Ho Ox 70. **d** 73 **p** 74 Derby. C of Newbold w Dunston 73-77; St Phil and St Jas Leckhampton 77-80; V of Hebburn Dio Dur from 80. *St Cuthbert's Vicarage, Hebburn, T & W, NE31 2SG.* (Hebburn 832038)

DOBBS, Clifford Leslie. Univ of NZ BA 28. **d** 28 **p** 29 Wel. C of Hawera 28-30; Wanganui 30-34; V of Ohakune w Raetihi 34-38; Tinui 38-41; St Matt Brooklyn Wel 41-48; St Albans NZ 48-62; Southbridge 62-66; Prec of Ch Ch Cathl 66-67; L to Offic Dio Ch Ch from 67. *Diamond Harbour, NZ.* (D Harbour 653)

DOBBS, George Christopher. b 43. Linc Th Coll 66. **d** 68 **p** 69 Linc. C of N and S Hykeham 68-71; Asst Master Heneage Sch Grimsby 71-78; Perm to Offic Dio Southw 78-80; Team V of Chelmsley Wood Dio Birm from 80. *17 Aspen Drive, Chelmsley Wood, Birmingham, B37 7QX.* (021-770 5918)

DOBBS, John Hedley. b 03. Late Scho of Magd Coll Cam 1st cl Cl Trip pt i 24, BA (1st cl Cl Trip pt ii) 26, MA 32. Ridley Hall Cam 26. **d** 27 **p** 28 Sarum. Asst Chap and Asst Master Marlborough Coll 27-32; Dom Chap to Bp of Sarum 32-36; LPr Dio Sarum 35-37; C of Andover 36-38; V of St Paul, Southn 38-41; King's Somborne w Ashley 41-46; PC of Iffley 46-59; V of Durnford 59-74; RD of Avon 70-74. *Drovers Way, London Road, Stockbridge, Hants.* (Stockbridge 671)

DOBBS, Kildare Dixon Borrowes. b 1899. TCD 17. Sarum Th Coll 20. St Chad's Coll Dur LTh 23. **d** 24 **p** 25 Sarum. C of Mere 24-28; St Geo w St Aid St Aug and Free Ch Dub and Asst Chap Mountjoy Pris Dub 28-44; C-in-c of Kill Dio Dub 44-50; R 50-72. *30 Northumberland Avenue, Dun Laoghaire, Co Dublin, Irish Republic.*

DOBBS, Michael John. Linc Th Coll 74. **d** 77 **p** 78 Southw. C of Warsop w Sookholme Dio Southw from 77. *11 Alexandra Street, Warsop, Mansfield, Notts, NG20 0BA.*

DOBINSON, William Garry. b 49. FTCL 72. York Univ of Tor BA 74, BEducn 76. Wycl Coll Tor 79. **d** 81 Alg. C of St Thos Thunder Bay Dio Alg from 81. *322 N Edward Street, Thunder Bay, Ont, Canada, P7C 4P2.*

DOBNEY, Frederick John. St Chad's Coll Regina 60. **d** 63 **p** 64 Alg. C of St Paul Fort William 63-68; I of Norway Ho Dio Keew from 68. *Box 34, Norway House, Manit, Canada.*

DOBSON, Geoffrey Norman. b 46. ACP 70. Open Univ BA 73. Wells Th Coll 71. **d** 74 Barking for Chelmsf **p** 75 Chelmsf. C of S Woodford 74-76; Halstead 76-78; Colchester Archd Youth Officer 76-78; P-in-c of Kirkandrews-on-Eden w Beaumont and Grinsdale Dio Carl from 78; Dioc Youth Officer Dio Carl from 78. *Rectory, Kirkandrews-on-Eden, Carlisle.* (Burgh-by-Sands 302)

DOBSON, Canon Howard. b 1891. Univ of Man BA 12. Cudd Coll 13. **d** 14 **p** 15 Southw. C of Ordsall 14-19; Pleasley 19-22; Proc Conv Southw 22; PC of Clay Cross 22-29; R of Huntingfield w Cookley 29-66; Proc Conv St E from 38; Hon Can of St Edm K and Mart in St E Cathl 46-70; Can (Emer) from 70; RD of S Dunwich 60-65; Surr 60-65; Pro-Prolocutor of Lower Ho of Conv of Cant 63-72. *Manormead Nursing Home, Tilford Road, Hindhead, Surrey, GU26 6RA.*

DOBSON, John Douglas Alexander. Univ of Tor BA 49, M Educn 62. Vic Univ Tor BD 52. **d** and **p** 64 Niag. C of St Thos St Catherine's 64-67; R of Arthur 67-72; Combermere 72-77; Centr Dundas Dio Ott from 77. *Box 516, Winchester, Ont, Canada.* (613-774 2236)

DOBSON, John Francis Alban. d 38 Cardiff (RC) **p** 45 Chich. Asst Master York Blue Coat Sch 41-42; Asst Chap and Master Brighton Coll 43-48; R of Trayning 48; Bencubbin Nungarin 48-49; Hd Master of Ch Ch Gr Sch Claremont W Australia 49-50; Chap St Andr Sch Bloemf 50-55; Hd Master of St Mark's Sch Mbabane and LPr Dio Zulu 55-56; V of Groombridge Sussex 57-58; R of Harbour I Nass 58-59; Chap Lakefield Prep Sch Ont and L to Offic Dio Ont 59-63; R of Ch of Good Shepherd Mt Dennis Tor 63-78; Mulmer 78-81; Alliston and W Essa Dio Tor from 81. *Box 429, Alliston, Ont, Canada.*

DOBSON, John Haselden. b 29. Mert Coll Ox BA 52, MA 55. BD (Lon) 58. Oak Hill Th Coll 54. **d** 56 **p** 57 Cov. C of St Matt Rugby 56-59; St Luke Hampstead 59-60; Prin Archd Tr Centre Ochoko 61-65; Tutor Bp Tucker Coll Mukono 66-72; Assoc Min of Gorleston 73-77; R of Saxlingham-Nethergate Dio Nor from 77; V of Shotesham Dio Nor from 77. *Saxlingham Nethergate Rectory, Norwich. NR15 1AJ.* (Hempnall 454)

DOBSON, John Mackenzie. Univ of W Ont BA 25. **d** 26 **p** 27 Hur. C of Princeton Ayr and Drumbo 26-27; I 27-29; L to Offic Dio Hur 29-49; I of Walter's Falls 49-51; R of Shelburne w Primrose 51-67. *22 Vincent Street, Niagara-on-the-Lake, Ont., Canada.*

DOBSON, John Watson. b 29. **d** 78 **p** 79 Swaz. P Dio Swaz. *All Saints Rectory, PO Box 34, Mbabane, Swaziland.*

DOBSON, Kenneth Shuard. b 26. Oak Hill Th Coll 53. **d** 56 **p** 57 S'wark. C of Hatcham 56-59; St Mary Wimbledon 59-62; R of St Pet w Lynn King's Lynn 62-66; L to Offic Dio Nor 66-68; P-in-c of Deopham 68-74; Chap Eccles Hall Sch Quidenham 74-78; R of Elveden Dio St E from 78; Icklingham Dio St E from 78; Eriswell Dio St E from 78; RD of Mildenhall 80-81. *Elveden Rectory, Thetford, Norf.* (Elveden 204)

DOBSON, Reginald Maurice. Univ of W Ont BA 54. Hur Th coll LTh 55. **d** 55 **p** 56 Hur. I of St John Chatham 55-61; St Clair Beach 61-68; R of Essex 68-75. *1453 Prince Road, Windsor, Ont., Canada.*

DOBSON, Robert Christopher. b 28. Univ of Reading BSc (Agr) 49. Clifton Th Coll 65. **d** 67 **p** 68 Lich. C of Bilston 67-70; Cromer 70-74; R of S Walsham 74-81; V of Upton (w Fishley to 77) 74-81; Chap R Albert Hosp Lanc from 81. *1 Hibbert Terrace, Lancaster, LA1 5AB.* (Lanc 2855)

DOBSON, Robert William. Univ of Wales BA (2nd cl Hons Welsh) 41. Coll of the Resurr Mirfield 41. **d** 43 **p** 44 St A for Ban. C of Llandudno 43-46; P-in-c of Abaco 47-51; Asst Master St Jo Coll Nassau 51-52; Hd Master 52-54; Chap Sch of St Helen and St Katherine Abingdon 55-62; Chap and Lect St Mary's Coll Ban 62-77; Commiss Nass 58-63; V of Holt and Isycoed Dio St A from 77. *Holt Vicarage, Wrexham, Clwyd.* (Farndon 318)

DOBSON, Theodore Edward. b 16. K Coll Cam BA 38, MA 42. Ridley Hall Cam. **d** 40 Roch **p** 41 Bp Mann for Roch. C of St Jo Evang Penge 40-42; CMS Miss Uganda 42-53; RD of Toro Distr 46-50; C-in-c of Rainworth Conv Distr Blidworth 53-56; R of St Paul Fisherton Anger 56-65; V of Wembley 65-74; P-in-c of Stradbroke w Horham and Athelington 74-78; R 78-81; RD of Hoxne 78-81. *34 Empire Road, Salisbury, Wilts, SP2 9DF.* (Salisbury 332663)

DOBSON, William. b 14. Univ of Edin MA 39. Vanc Sch of Th STB 71. **d** 71 **p** 72 BC. I of Harewood Miss BC 71-72; Brentwood Mem Chap BC 73-81. *1036 Nagle Street, Duncan, BC, Canada.*

✠ DOCKER, Right Rev Ivor Colin. b 25. Univ of Birm BA 46. St Cath S Ox BA 49, MA 52. Wycl Hall Ox 46. **d** 49 **p** 50 Wakef. C of Normanton 49-52; Lect of Halifax 52-54; CMS Area Sec Dios Derby Linc and Southw 54-58; Metrop Sec (S) 58-59; V of Midhurst 59-64; R of Woolbeding 61-64; Surr from 60; RD of Midhurst 61-64; Seaford from 64; V of Seaford w Sutton 64-71; Eastbourne 71-75; Can and Preb of Colworth in Chich Cathl 66-81; RD of Eastbourne 71-75; M Gen Syn 70-75; Cons Ld Bp Suffr of Horsham in Westmr Abbey 31 Jan 75 by Abp of Cant; Bps of Ox, Nor, Sarum, Chich, Wakef, Derby, Chelmsf, Heref, Bris, Linc, St E and Nam; Bps Suffr of Edmon, Kens, Basingstoke, Southn, Woolwich and Lewes; and others. *Bishop's Lodge, Worth, Crawley, W Sussex, RH10 4RT.* (Crawley 883051)

DOCKRELL, George Thomas. b 29. Trin Coll Dub BA 51, MA 66. **d** 51 **p** 53 Connor. C of St Luke Belf 51-54; Portadown 54-59; R of Newtownhamilton w Ballymoyer 59-63; CMS Area Sec Dios Ox and Win from 63; V of St Andr Jersey 68-80; Asst Chap HM Pris Pentonville 80-81; Chap HM Pris Coldingley Bisley from 81. *3 South Road, Bisley, Woking, Surrey.*

DODD, Charles Nathanael. Westcott Ho Cam. **d** 57 **p** 58 Portsm. C of Milton 57-62; Maryborough Vic 62-63; R of Manangatang 63-68; Dir Coun of Chr Educn Dio St Arn 65-68; R of Trafalgar 68-76; Dom Chap to Bp of Gippsld 72-81; Perm to Offic Dio Gippsld from 76. *66 Davidson Street, Traralgon, Vic, Australia 3844.*

DODD, Cyril. b 20. Coll of the Ven Bede MA 48. Coll of the Resurr Mirfield 80. **d** 81 Bradf. Hon C of Guiseley Dio Bradf from 81. *37 Croft Park, Menston, Ilkley, W Yorks, LS29 6LY.*

DODD, Edward Vivian. Univ of Wales BA 29. St Mich Coll Llan 29. **d** 30 **p** 32 Mon. C of Llanhilleth 30-33; St Mary Seven Sisters 33-35; Neath w Llantwit 35-40; CF (EC) 40-45; C-in-c of Crynant 46-49; V of Llantwit Fardre 49-66; R of Llansannor w Llanfrynach and Penllyn 66-73. *24 Crymlyn Road, Skewen, Neath, W Glam.*

DODD, Ian Neville. b 16. Montr Dioc Th Coll. **d** 67 **p** 68 Montr. C-in-c of Lakefield Dio Montr 67-68; P-in-c 68-70; R of Knowlton Montr 70-74; C of St Mark Kingstanding 74-75; P-in-c of Smallburgh w Dilham and Honing w Crostwight 75-80; R 80-81. *Address temp unknown.*

DODD, John. Univ of Edin MA 50. Wycl Hall Ox 50. **d** 52 **p** 53 Win. C of St Jas Shirley Dio Win 52-54; H Trin Cathl Suva 55-56; V of Levuka 56-58; C of Roslyn 58-59; V of Waitaki 59-64; Green I w Brighton 64-67; H Trin Wainuiomata 67-72; Hunterville 72-79; Gonville Dio Wel from 79. *75 Koromiko Road, Wanganui, NZ.* (57-101)

DODD, John Dudley. b 15. Univ of Liv BA (1st cl Hons) 36. Univ of Lon BD 51, Dipl Educn (Lon) 54. Westcott Ho Cam 54. **d** 54 **p** 55 Win. C of St Helier Jersey 54-59; Asst Master Vic Coll Jersey 54-61; Jersey Coll for Girls 61-69; Lect of St Helier 69-78; Hon P-in-c St Martin Gouray Jersey Dio Win from 78. *Gouray Vicarage, St Martin, Jersey, CI.* (Jersey 53255)

DODD, John Granger. b 25. St D Coll Lamp BA 50. Chich Th Coll 50. **d** 52 Lich **p** 53 Stafford for Cant. C of Cannock (in c of St John Heath Hayes from 54) 52-58; V of U Tean Dio Lich from 58. *Tean Vicarage, Stoke-on-Trent, ST10 4LE.* (Tean 2227)

DODD, John Stanley. b 24. Hur Th Coll. **d** 50 **p** 51 Hur. C of Elmira Galt and Kitchener 50-51; I of St Columb Kitchener Elmira Dio Hur 51-52; Perm to Offic (Col Cl Act) at Leeds (in c of St Jo Evang) 52-54; C of Harrogate 54-58; V of Stainburn w N Rigton 58-65; Weeton 58-64; Meanwood Dio Ripon from 65. *9 Parkside Green, Leeds, LS6 4NY.* (Leeds 757885)

DODD, Lawrence Walter. b 04. St Edm Hall Ox 24. Wells Th Coll 45. **d** & **p** 47 Glouc. C of Prestbury 47-49; PC of Capesthorne w Siddington 49-55; RD of Macclesfield 52-55; Stratton 63-66; V of Stratton 55-69. *Sliggon Field, Trebetherick, Wadebridge, Cornwall.*

DODD, Malcolm Ogilvie. b 46. Univ of Dur BSc 67. Edin Th Coll 67. **d** 70 **p** 71 Chich. C of Hove 70-73; Crawley 73-79; Dioc Youth Adv Dio Chich from 78; P-in-c of Rusper Dio Chich from 79. *Rectory, Rusper, Horsham, W Sussex, RH12 4DX.*

DODD, Michael Christopher. b 33. Ch Coll Cam BA 55, MA 59. Ridley Hall Cam 57. **d** 59 **p** 60 Birm. C of Stechford 59-62; V of St Bonif Birm 62-72; Team V of Paston 72-77; R of Hodge Hill Dio Birm from 77. *Rectory, Hodge Hill Common, Birmingham, B36 8AG.* (021-747 2094)

DODD, Percy Charles. St Chad's Coll Regina 50. **d** 53 **p** 54 Qu'App. I of Major 53-55; Ogema 55-56; Milden 56-58; C of St Barn Medicine Hat 58-59; I of Crow's Nest 59-60; R of Dutton 60-67; Thamesford 67-69; on leave 69-72; R of Gorrie 72-74; Chatsworth 74-78; St Geo Windsor Dio Hur from 78. *1267 Kildare Road, Windsor, Ont, Canada.* (519-254 1834)

DODD, Peter Curwen. b 33. St Jo Coll Cam 3rd cl Th Trip pt i 55, BA (2nd cl Th Trip pt ii) 57. Linc Th Coll 58. **d** 60 **p** 61 Sheff. C of Eastwood Yorks 60-63; Chap Sheff Industr Miss 63-67; Industr Chap to Bp of Newc T from 67; RD of Newc E from 78. *26 The Oval, Benton, Newcastle upon Tyne.*

DODD, Peter Lawrence. b 38. Univ of Leeds BA (2nd cl Th) 61. Univ of Birm Dipl Th 62. Qu Coll Birm 61. **d** 63 **p** 64 York. C of Marske-in-Cleveland 63-67; Prec of All SS Cathl Jess 67-69; R of Likas Sabah 69; CF from 70. *RAChD, Bagshot Park, Bagshot, Surrey, GU19 5PL.*

DODD, Roy. b 30. SOC 67. **d** 70 Dorking for Guildf **p** 71 Guildf. C of St Mark's, Farnborough 70-75; Walton-on-Thames 75-76; Perm to Offic Dio Guildf 76-81; C of Woodham Dio Guildf from 81. *32 Madeira Road, West Byfleet, Weybridge, Surrey.* (Byfleet 51122)

DODD, Walter Herbert. b 1896. Qu Coll Birm 33. **d** 35 **p** 36 Lich. C of H Cross Shrewsbury 35-37; Walsall Wood 37-40; V of Weston-on-Trent 40-63. *32 Glynderwen Close, Sketty, Swansea, W Glam.* (Swansea 206819)

DODD, William Harold Alfred. b 1899. Univ of Liv ChM 27. FRCS 27. Lon Coll of Div 69. **d** 70 **p** 71 Willesden for Lon. Hon C of All S Langham Place 70-80. *Flat 22, Campden Hill Gate, Duchess of Bedford's Walk, W8.* (01-937 9297)

DODD, William Samuel. b 31. Oak Hill Th Coll 64. **d** 66 Colchester for Chelmsf **p** 67 Chelmsf. C of Dagenham 66-67; Stratford 67-70; Woodford Wells 70-72; V of St Paul E Ham 72-77; Perm to Offic Dio Chelmsf 77-82; V of Harwich Dio Chelmsf from 82. *Vicarage, King's Quay Street, Harwich, Essex, CO12 3EE.* (Harwich 2817)

DODD, William Thomas. b 08. St D Coll Lamp BA 34. **d** 34 **p** 35 Llan. C of St Cynfelyn Caerau 34-36; St John Canton 36-43; V of Cwmbach 43-46; Chap Netherne Hosp Coulsdon 46-66; Min of St Luke Conv Distr Netherne Coulsdon 51-66; C-in-c of Kilpeck 66-73; C-in-c of St Devereux w Wormbridge 66-73; C-in-c of Tretire w Michaelchurch and Pencoyd 67-73; Perm to Offic Dio Llan 74-79. *3 Marsh Court, Station Road, Abergavenny, Gwent.* (Abergavenny 6091)

DODDS, Canon Arthur Whitfield. b 20. Qu Coll Ox BA 48, MA 53. Wells Th Coll 49. **d** 50 **p** 51 S'wark. C of St Bart Horley 50-53; R of Honiley w Wroxall 53-58; V of Atherstone 58-64; Chedworth w Stowell and Yanworth (w Coln St Denys & Coln Rogers from 75) Dio Glouc from 64; RD of Northleach from 73; Hon Can of Glouc from 78. *Chedworth Vicarage, Cheltenham, Glos, GL54 4AA.* (Fosse Bridge 392)

DODDS, Brian Martin. b 37. K Coll Lon and Warm AKC (2nd cl) 62. **d** 63 **p** 64 Newc T. C of Morpeth 63-67; Georgetn Cathl 67-69; V of Morawhanna 69-71; Willington-on-Tyne 71-74; Team V of Brayton w Barlow 75-79; All SS Gravelly Hill Erdington Dio Birm from 79. *Gravelly Hill Vicarage, George Road, Birmingham 23.* (021-373 0730)

DODDS, Edmund Hanbury Lee. b 14. Kelham Th Coll 30. **d** 38 **p** 39 S'wark. C of H Trin S Wimbledon 38-41; St Steph Redditch 41-43 (in c of St Pet Crabbs Cross Headless Cross 42-43); R of Brockdish w Thorpe Abbotts 43-55; CF 51-54; V of Veryan 55-81; C-in-c of Ruan Lanihorne 55-81; Dioc Insp of Schs Dio Truro 60-70; RD of Powder 69-74; Perm to Offic Dio Truro from 81. *Montroc, Station Road, Drakewalls, Gunnislake, Cornw, PL18 9DY.* (Tavistock 833495)

DODDS, Neil Sutherland. b 35. Keble Coll Ox BA 59, Dipl Th 61, MA 63. ARCO 59. Linc Th Coll 60. **d** 62 **p** 63 Birm. C of St Jas Handsworth 62-65; V of Highter's Heath 65-75; Olton Dio Birm from 75; RD of Solihull from 79. *Olton Vicarage, Solihull, W Midl, B92 7JU.* (021-706 2318)

DODDS, Norman Barry. b 43. Div Hostel Dub 73. **d** 76 **p** 77 Down. C of Ballynafeigh 76-80; R of St Mich Belf Dio Connor from 80. *37 Indiana Avenue, Belfast, BT15 5BZ. N. Ireland.*

DODGSON, Ronald. b 27. Sarum Wells Th Coll 72. **d** 74 Sarum **p** 75 Sherborne for Sarum. Sub-Warden of The Barnabas Fellowship Dio Sarum from 74; Hon C of Canford Magna Dio Sarum from 78. *36 Knights Road, Bearwood, Bournemouth, Dorset, BH11 9SY.* (Bournemouth 578754)

DODI, Simeon. **d** 78 Aipo. d Dio Aipo. *Koinambe PMB, via Mount Hagen, Papua New Guinea.*

DODMAN, Donald Andrew. b 37. Angl Th Coll BC LTh 68. **d** 68 Caled. Miss at Burns Lake 68-71; V of All SS Cathl Edmon 71-73; Hon C of H Trin Edmon 73-74; I of Schefferville 75-77; St Albert Dio Edmon from 78. *212-47 Sturgeon Road, St Albert, Alta, Canada.* (458-5488)

DODOWANE, Silas. **d** 79 **p** 80 Centr Melan. P Dio Centr Melan. *Makira, Solomon Islands.*

DODSON, Gordon. b 31. Em Coll Cam BA 54, LLB 55, MA 58. Barrister-at-Law (Gray's Inn) 56. Ridley Hall Cam 57. **d** 59 **p** 60 Chelmsf. C of All SS Belhus Pk 59-60; Barking 60-63; CMS Miss 63-67; C of New Malden 67-69; V of Snettisham 69-81; M Gen Syn Dio Nor from 75; RD of Heacham and Rising 76-81; P-in-c of Reepham w Hackford, Whitwell and Kerdiston Dio Nor from 81; Thurning w Wood Dalling Dio Nor from 81; Salle Dio Nor from 81. *Reepham Rectory, Norwich, NR10 4RA.* (Reepham 220)

DODSON, James Peter. b 32. Lich Th Coll 58. **d** 61 **p** 62 Lich. C of Chasetown 61-63; Hednesford 63-67; V of St Hilda Halifax 67-75; Upperthong Dio Wakef from 76. *St John's Vicarage, Holmfirth, Huddersfield, HD7 1BQ.* (Holmfirth 3131)

DODSON, Canon Robert George Everard. b 04. Em Coll Cam 2nd cl Hist Trip pt i 30, BA (2nd cl Hist Trip pt ii) 31, 2nd cl Th Trip pt i 32, MA 38. Ridley Hall Cam 31. **d** 33 **p** 34 Chelmsf. C of St Luke Walthamstow 33-35; Org Sec CPAS for SE Distr 35-38; Youth Sec CPAS Chap Ox Pastorate and Chap Wadh Coll Ox 38-39; Chap RAFVR 39-46; Cler Asst Sec CPAS 46-53; L to Offic Dio Guildf 36-53; R of Gressenhall (w Longham and Bittering Parva from 61) 53-69; C-in-c of Longham and of Bittering Parva 56-61; Chap Beech Ho Gressenhall from 54; RD of Elmham 63-69; Brisley 68-69; Hon Can of Nor 68-69; Hon Can (Emer) from 69; Perm to Offic Dio Arg I from 69; Hon Can of St John's Cathl Oban from 80. *8 Grosvenor Crescent, Connel, Argyll, PA37 1PQ.* (Connel 318)

DODSON, Victor Sidney. Ridley Coll Melb 30. ACT ThL 31. **d** 31 **p** 33 Bend. C of St Paul Bend 32-34; St Nich Deptford 34-37; Chap RAF 38-46; V of Tugby w Skeffington Leic 46-50; Asst Master Malvern Mem Gr Sch 50; Essendon Gr Sch 51; Wadhurst Melb C of E Gr Sch 52-65; on leave 66-73; Perm to Offic Dio Melb from 73. *5 Bethela Street, Burwood, Vic, Australia 3125.* (29 2744)

DODSWORTH, George Brian Knowles. b 34. Dipl Th (Wales) 62. St Mich Coll Llan 59. **d** 62 **p** 63 Worc. C of Kidderminster 62-67; Asst Chap HM Pris Man 67-68; Chap HM Pris Eastchurch 68-70; Love Lane Wakefield 70-74; Wormwood Scrubs Lon from 74. *158 Du Cane Road, W12 0TX.* (01-743 4749)

DODWELL, Percy Malby. b 04. OBE (Mil) 58. Univ of Lon BD 29. Late Exhib of Or Coll Ox BA (Th) 31, MA 35. Lon Coll of Div 24. **d** 28 **p** 29 Ox. C of St Ebbe Ox 28-32; Chap RN 32-60; R of Easton w Martyr Worthy 60-73; Perm to Offic Dio Auckld 73-74; L to Offic Dio Win from 73. *23 Saxon Road, Winchester, Hants, SO23 7DJ.* (Win 69577)

DOE, Francis Harold. b 22. SOC 68. **d** 71 **p** 72 Chich. C of Sompting 71-74; Stopham 74-78; Asst to Archd of Horsham from 74; Hardham 74-78; P-in-c Sutton w Bignor 78-81; Barlavington 78-81; V of Warnham Dio Chich from 81. *Vicarage, Warnham, Sussex, RH12 3QW.* (Horsham 65041)

DOE, Gilbert Kent. Carleton Univ Ott BA 64. Trin Coll Tor STB 67. **d** 67 **p** 68 Ott. C of Cornwall 67-71; P-in-c of Long Sault 71-75; R of Blackburn 75-78; St Marg Vanier Ott 78-79; St Paul's City and Dio Ott from 79. *35 Acacia Avenue, Ottawa, Ont, Canada.* (613-744 1151)

DOE, Michael David. b 47. St Jo Coll Dur BA (2nd cl Gen Stud) 69. Ripon Hall Ox 69. **d** 72 **p** 73 S'wark. C of St Helier Dio S'wark 72-76; Hon C 76-81; Youth Sec in Ecumen Affairs Div BCC 76-81; P Missr of Conv Distr of Blackbird Leys City and Dio Ox from 81. *1 Cuddesdon Way, Blackbird Leys, Oxford.* (Oxford 778728)

DOE, William Frank. b 11. K Coll Lon AKC 46 Knowling Pri 46. **d** 46 **p** 47 Ox. C of St Luke Maidenhead 46-48; Farnham 48-50; C-in-c of New Cathl Conv Distr Guildf 50-55; V of Teynham (w Buckland from 57) 55-60; St Osw Norbury 60-68; St Martin Maidstone 68-72; Preston-next-Faversham (and Goodnestone w Graveney from 73) 72-78; C-in-c of Goodnestone w Graveney 72-73; RD of Ospringe 76-78; Perm to Offic Dio Cant from 79; Dio Guildf from 81. *11 Woodfield Close, Ashtead, Surrey.* (Ashtead 75824)

DOERING, Roderick Edmund. **d** 55 **p** 56 NS. R of Falkland 56-59; I of Lockeport 59-60; R of Parrsboro 60-64; Canning 65-70; St Martin's w Black River 70-73. *Anglican Church Homes, Sussex, NB, Canada.*

DOGGETT, Stanley William. Qu Coll Cam Hist Trip pt i 32, BA (Hist Trip pt ii) 33, MA 37. TD 50. MBE 62. Ridley Hall Cam 33. **d** 35 Bedford for St Alb **p** 36 St Alb. C of Ch Ch Ware 35-38; Chap of Wrekin Coll Wellington 38-71; (in army 40-46); R of N w S Kilworth Dio Leic from 71. *North Kilworth Rectory, Lutterworth, Leics, LE17 6HA.* (Market Harborough 880436)

DOGURA, Lord Bishop of. *See* Sanana, Right Rev Rhynold Ewaruba.

DOHERTY, Ven Raymond William Patrick. b 39. TCD BA 63, MA 71. **d** 65 **p** 66 Derry. C of All SS Clooney 65-67; Conwall 67-70; I of Drumholm 70-75; R of Tralee Dio Ardf from 75; Ballymacelligott Dio Ardf from 75; RD of Tralee 78-79; Archd of Ardf and Aghadoe from 79. *Rectory, Ashe Street, Tralee, Kerry, Irish Republic.* (Tralee 22245)

DOHERTY, Robert Brendan. TCD Carson Bibl Pri 26, BA and Div Test 27, MA and BD 49. **d** 35 **p** 36 Cork. C of St Luke Cork 35-36; I of Drimoleague 36-37; Kilgariffe w Templeomalus 37-39; Chap (Eccles Est) Ghorpuri 39-45 and 46-47; Chap at Kirkee 47; Deolali 47-48; R of Castletownroche 48-49; I of Ballydehob 49-51; Innishannon 51-60; Fermoy 60-64; Moviddy w Kilmurry 64-75; Can of St Mich in Cork Cathl and of Brigown in Cloyne Cathl 65-67; Cahirlag in Cork Cathl 67-68; Treas of Cloyne 67-68; Cork 68-75. *Wroxham, Forge Hill, Crosshaven, Co Cork, Irish Republic.*

DOHERTY, Samuel William Olantunbosun. Im Coll Ibad 64. **d** 67 **p** 68 Lagos. P Dio Lagos 67-76; L to Offic Dio N Nig 76-80; Dio Kaduna from 80; CF (Nigeria) from 76. *Ministry of Defence, Sokoto, Nigeria.*

DOHERTY, Terence William. b 30. St Jo Coll Dur BA 56. Ripon Hall Ox. **d** 58 **p** 59 Heref. C of Ch Stretton 58-60; Halesowen 60-62; L to Offic Dio Worc 62-64; R of Hagley 64-69; Perm to Offic Dio Worc from 69; Warden Ches Dioc Con Centre and L to Offic Dio Ches 69; Asst Master Churchill Sch Somt 70-78; Perm to Offic Dio B & W from 73; R of Sutton-in-Holderness w Wawne Dio York from 78. *Sutton Rectory, Hull, N Humb, HU7 4TL.* (Hull 782154)

DOHERTY, Thomas Alexander. b 48. Chich Th Coll 73. **d** 76 **p** 77 Derry. V Cho S Columb's Cathl Derry 76-79; C of

Llan Cathl from 79. *9b The Cathedral Green, Llandaff, CF5 2EB.*

DOHM-SMIDT, Martin. b 35. Vanc Sch of Th 70. **d** 73 **p** 74 Caled. C of Terrace Caled 73-75; Departure Bay & Lantzville 75-79; I of St Phil Lantzville Dio BC from 79. *Box 298, Lantzville, BC, Canada.*

DOIDGE, Ven John Nicholls. Univ of W Ont BA 38. Montr Dioc Th Coll Hon DD 80. Hur Coll Ont LTh 39. **d** 38 **p** 39 Hur. C of St Jas Lon 38-39; I of Nor w Ox 39-41; C of St Geo St Catharines 41-43; Chap CASF 43-45; C of St Paul's Cathl Lon 45-47; R of Tillsonburg and Culloden 47-50; St Geo Lon 50-53; Ch Ch Chatham 53-55; Exam Chap to Bp of Hur 51-54; R of St Matt Winnipeg 55-62; Hon Can of Rupld 58-62; R of St Matthias City and Dio Montr from 62; Hon Can of Montr 66-70; Archd of Montr from 70. *370 Kensington Avenue, Westmount, Montreal 215, PQ, Canada.* (514-933 9611)

DOIG, Cecil Victor. Univ of the Witwatersrand Johann BA 25. Bend Th Coll 26. ACT ThL 36. **d** 27 **p** 29 Lich. C of Cobridge 27-31; St Andr Wakef 31-34; H Trin Sheerness 35-37; V of Rye Harbour w Camber and Broomhill 37-45; Offg C-in-c of St Matt, Brighton 40-45; R of Beaconsfield and Exeter, Tas 46-47; V of Ch Ch Gt Warley Essex 47-53; Min of Belmont Vic 53-59; Healesville 59-68; I of Mt Dandenong w Olinda 68-72; Perm to Offic Dio Melb from 72. *65 Flinders Street, Queenscliff, Vic, Australia 3225.* (052-52 1863)

DOIG, Ernest Theodore. b 1888. Univ Coll Dur 08. **d** 14 **p** 15 S & M. Chap St Luke Braddon IM 14-16; served in RAMC 16-19; C of St Luke Skerton 19-24; St Geo Millom (in c of St Luke Haverigg) 25-27; V of Flimby 27-34; Wigton 34-41; Chap RAFVR 41-49; R of Ashley w Silverley 49-54; V of St John Bradshaw Halifax 54-56; Perm to Offic Dio Ely from 56. *329 Histon Road, Cambridge.*

DOLAIASI, Nathanael. St Pet Coll Melan. **d** 46 **p** 50 Melan. P Dio Melan 46-75. *Dala, N Malaita, Solomon Islands.*

DOLD, John Dennis Gilbert. St Paul's Coll Grahmstn Dipl Th 66. **d** 66 **p** 67 Mashon. C of St Mary and All SS Cathl Salisbury 66-68. *P.O. Box 1056, Johannesburg, S Africa.*

DOLLI, Ven Bullen A. b 45. St Paul's Coll Limuru 65. **d** 67 **p** 69 N Ugan. P Dio N Ugan 67-75; Dio Rumbek from 76; Archd of Rumbek from 77. *Episcopal Church of the Sudan, Rumbek, S Sudan.*

DOLMAN, Albert Hans Werner. b 07. St Jo Coll Dur BA (3rd cl Cl) 30, Or Coll Ox BA (2nd cl Th) 34, MA 54. St Aid Coll 30. **d** 31 **p** 32 Ox. C of St Clem Ox 31-34; Chap Bps' Coll Cheshunt 34-37; C of Tring 37-41; Asst Master St Pet Sch Weston-s-Mare 41-54; C of St Jo Bapt Weston-s-Mare 44-54; PC of Barrow Gurney 54-59; Perm to Offic Dio Birm 59-72; Asst Master Moseley Gr Sch Birm 59-72; C of West Heath Dio Birm from 72. *19 Saffron House, Redditch Road, Birmingham 38.* (021-458 6103)

DOLPHIN, Geoffrey Horace. Codr Coll Barb 72. **d** and **p** 74 Stabroek for Guy. C of New Amsterdam 74-77; R of Suddie w Queenstown Dio Guy from 77. *Rectory, Suddie, Essequibo, Guyana.* (074-215)

DOMINEY, Canon John Herbert. b 11. Bps' Coll Cheshunt 38. **d** 40 **p** 41 Lon. C of St Mary Ealing 40-46; Bushey 47-50; PC of Goff's Oak 50-52; V of Apsley End 52-62; Biggleswade 62-78; Surr 62-78; RD of Biggleswade 67-75; Hon Can of St Alb 70-78; Can (Emer) from 78. *91 London Road, Biggleswade, Beds.* (Biggleswade 312939)

DOMINY, Peter John. Qu Coll Ox BA (2n cl Phil Pol and Econ) 60, MA 64. Oak Hill Th Coll 60. **d** 62 Bp McKie for Cov **p** 63 Cov. C of Bedworth 62-66; Miss SUM Dio N Nig 67-72; V of St Piran Jos Dio N Nig from 72. *c/o Sudan United Mission, P.O. Box 643, Jos, N Nigeria.*

DOMKEL, Charles Noah. Patteson Th Coll Kohimarama. **d** 72 Melan. d Dio Melan 72-75; Dio New Hebr from 75. *Merig, Banks Islands, New Hebrides.*

DOMMETT, Canon Richard Radmore. b 19. St Jo Coll Ox BA 41, MA 45. Wells Th Coll 41. **d** 43 **p** 44 S'wark. C of St Jo Evang E Dulwich 43-48; St Chrys Peckham 48-51; V of St Pet Clapham 52-60; R of Caister-on-Sea 60-81; RD of Flegg 64-78; Hon Can of Nor from 77; P-in-c of Saxthorpe w Corpusty Dio Nor from 81; Oulton Dio Nor from 81; Blickling Dio Nor from 81. *Saxthorpe Vicarage, Norwich, NR11 7BJ.* (Saxthorpe 228)

DON, Bruce William. Coll Ho Ch Ch 49. **d** 52 **p** 53 Ch Ch. C of Fendalton 52-54; Sumner 54-59; P-in-c of Lyttleton 59; V of Methven 59-63; C of Sydenham w Beckenham 63-68; V of Hinds Dio Ch Ch from 68. *P.O. Box 5, Hinds, NZ.*

DONALD, Andrew William. St Jo Coll Morpeth ACT ThL 50. **d** 49 **p** 50 Perth. C of Ch Ch Claremont 49-50; St Geo Cathl Perth 50-52; R of Wyalkatcham 52-56; Perm to Offic (Col Cl Act) at St Pet Kens Pk Road Lon 57-58; Chap at Gothenburg 58-65; Lausanne 65-68; C of St Patr Mt Lawley Perth 68-70; R of Bellevue w Darlington 70-79; Toodyay/Goomalling Dio Perth from 79. *Rectory, Fiennes Street, Toodyay, W Australia 6566.* (096-26 2203)

DONALD, Dennis Curzon. b 38. Oak Hill Th Coll 68. **d** 70 **p** 71 Carl. C of St Jo Evang Carl 70-73; Warden Blaithwaite Ho Chr Conf Centre Wigton from 73; L to Offic Dio Carl from 73. *Blaithwaite House, Wigton, Cumb, CA7 0AZ.*

DONALD, Malcolm Collighan. b 15. Keble Coll Ox 34. Chich Th Coll 37. **d** 40 Roch **p** 41 Bp Mann for Roch. C of St Aug Belvedere 40-42; Chap RAFVR 42-46; C of Cobham (in c of St Matt Hatchford) 47-52; C-in-c of Ockham 49-52; V of Lower Cam 52-64; Stow Bardolph w Wimbotsham 64-77; RD of Fincham 65-73; C-in-c of Crimplesham w Stadsett 68-73; Surr from 70; R of Fowlmere Dio Ely from 77; V of Triplow Dio Ely from 77. *Fowlmere Rectory, Royston, Herts.* (Fowlmere 221)

DONALD, Robert Francis. b 49. Univ of Nottm BTh 75. St Jo Coll Nottm 72. **d** 75 **p** 76 St Alb. C of St Jas New Barnet 75-79; St Paul (In C of St Luke) City and Dio St Alb from 79. *St Luke's Parsonage, Cell Barnes Lane, St Albans, Herts, AL1 5QJ.* (St Albans 65399)

DONALD, Very Rev Walter James. Angl Th Coll BC LTh 67. **d** 67 **p** 68 BC. C of Ch Ch Cathl, Vic Dio BC 67-68; Hon C 69-73; P-in-c of St Sav W Vic 73-80; Chap Univ of Vic 78-80; Dean and R of St Sav Cathl Nelson Dio Koot from 80. *723 Ward Street, Nelson, BC, Canada.* (352-6844)

DONALD, William. b 30. Dipl Th (Lon) 61. Tyndale Hall Bris 58. **d** 61 **p** 62 Derby. C of Stapenhill 61-63; Perm to Offic Dio Ox 63-66; L to Offic Dio Bris 66-70; C of St Mark Cheltm 70-77; St Jas City and Dio Glouc from 77. *27 Midland Road, Gloucester, GL1 4UH.*

DONALDSON, Christopher William. b 17. Univ of Lon BD 49. Kelham Th Coll. **d** 42 Croydon for Cant **p** 43 Cant. C of St Steph Norbury 42-46; St Andr Buckland-at-Dover 47-51; R of St Mary-in-the-Marsh 51-55; R and V of Newchurch 51-55; V of Birchington w Acol 55-63; R of St Martin w St Paul Cant 63-76; Six Pr in Cant Cathl 72-78. *Ashleigh, Horn Ash, Clapton, Somt.*

DONALDSON, Harry. Wycl Coll Tor 43. **d** 44 **p** 45 Abp of Tor for Episc Supervisor of Dio Falkd Is. Supt SAMS Miss Chile 45-50; Chap of Ascen Cholchol 49-50; I of Cookstown 51-53; St Columba Kitchener 53-59; R of Seaforth 59-67; Delhi and Scotland Ont 69-75. *277 Main Street, Delhi, Ont., Canada.*

DONALDSON, James Melvin. **d** 45 **p** 46 Moos. Miss at Fort Albany 45-49; V of Rupert's Ho 49-51; I of Matheson 51-56; Cainsville 56-62; R of Woodhouse 62-69; Paris Ont 69-76; Wiarton 76-79; Ch Ch Port Stanley Dio Hur from 79. *Box 708, Port Stanley, Ont., Canada.*

DONALDSON, John Colvin. b 22. TCD BA 49, MA 57. **d** 50 **p** 51 Dub. C of St Pet w St Audoen Dub 50-52; St Faith Linc 52-54; R of St Clem Longsight 54-57; L to Offic Dio Ex from 57; Area Sec UMCA in SW Engl 57-59; V of Ilsington 59-72; RD of Moreton 69-72; V of Cockington w Chelston Dio Ex from 72; RD of Ipplepen from 78. *Cockington Vicarage, Torquay, Devon.* (Torquay 605177)

DONALDSON, Maurice Coburne. Univ of Wales BA 40. St Mich Coll Llan 41. Univ of Lon BD (2nd cl) 47. **d** 42 **p** 43 Ban. C of Blaenau Festiniog 42-44; Conway w Gyffin 44-47; Llandysilio 47-49; C-in-c of Llanfachraeth w Llanynghenedl and Llanfugael 49-53; V of Ynyscynhaiarn w Penmorfa 53-57; Yspytty Ystwyth w Ystrad Meurig 57-70; Ruabon w Penylan 70-77; Abergele Dio St A from 77; Hd Master St Jo Coll Ystrad Meurig 57-70. *Vicarage, Abergele, Clwyd, LL22 7SU.* (Abergele 823132)

DONALDSON, Roger Francis. b 50. Jes Coll Ox BA 71, MA 75. Westcott Ho Cam 72. **d** 74 **p** 75 St A. C of Mold 74-78; V of Denio Dio Ban from 78; Abererch Dio Ban from 78. *Vicarage, Pwllheli, Gwyn.* (Pwllheli 2305)

DONALDSON, Walter Sloan. Trin Coll Dub BA 47. **d** 48 **p** 49 Arm. C of Derryloran 48-56; I of Arboe 56-75; Kilsaran Dio Arm from 75. *Kilsaran Rectory, Castlebellingham, Co Louth, Irish Republic.* (042-72245)

DONAT, Luc Rex Victor. Univ of Delhi BA 59. St Paul's Coll Maur LTh 64. **d** 64 Maur. USPG Miss Dio Maur from 64. *Duperré Avenue, Quatre Bornes, Mauritius.* (4-4808)

DONCASTER, Bishop Suffragan of. (Vacant)

DONCASTER, Archdeacon of. *See* Harland, Ven Ian.

DONCASTER, Ven Edward William. b 31. St Jo Coll Morpeth 54. **d** 56 Kalg for Perth **p** 57 Perth. C of Vic Pk 56-59; R of Bluff Point 59-64; Carnarvon 64-68; Archd of the NW 66-68; R of Gascoyne-Ashburton 68-70; R of S Cross 70-72; Mundaring 72-75; Floreat Pk Dio Perth from 75; Can of Perth 79-80; Archd of Swan from 80. *49 Berkeley Crescent, Floreat Park, W Australia 6014.* (387-1304)

DONCASTER, Kenneth Terrance. b 48. St Thos Univ Fred BA 74. Atlantic Sch of Th Halifax 72. **d** 75 **p** 76 Fred. I of St Clem, St John 76-79; Ketepec, St John Dio Fred from 79. *Box 59, Morva Heights, St John West, NB, Canada E2L 3W7.*

DONCASTER, Reginald Arthur. b 23. Univ of Leeds BA 48. Coll of Resurr Mirfield. **d** 50 Derby **p** 51 Bp O'Ferrall for Derby. C of Chesterfield 50-54; R of Pleasley w New Houghton 54-73; V of Ardleigh Dio Chelmsf from 73. *Ardleigh Vicarage, Colchester, Essex, CO7 7LD.* (Colchester 230231)

DONE, Robert Howard. b 43. Univ of New Engl BRurSc 66. St Barn Coll Adel 71. **d** and **p** 73 River. C of Broken Hill 74-76; P-in-c of Lake Cargelligo 76-80; R of Corowa Dio River from 80. *St John's Rectory, Corowa, NSW, Australia 2646.* (33 1124)

DONKIN, Robert. b 50. Univ of Wales (Cardiff) Dipl Th 74. St Mich AA Llan 71. **d** 74 **p** 75 Llan. C of Mountain Ash 74-77; Coity w Nolton 77-79; V of Oakwood Dio Llan from 79. *Vicarage, Oakwood, Pontrhydyfen, Port Talbot, SA12 9SD.* (Port Talbot 896249)

DONNAN, William Henry. b 18. St Pet Hall Ox BA 39, MA 42. Wycl Hall Ox 39. **d** 41 **p** 42 Blackb. C of St Paul Blackpool 41-43; CF (EC) 43-45; C of Kenilworth 45-47; St Paul N Shore Blackpool 47-49; Shalford 49-50; R of H Trin Keith 50-52; C of Mildenhall 52-54; C-in-c of Eriswell 54-57; R 57-61; R of Worlingworth w Tannington (w Southolt from 78 and Bedfield w Monk Soham from 79) Dio St E from 61; P-in-c of Bedfield w Monk Soham 77-79. *Worlingworth Rectory, Woodbridge, Suff.* (Worlingworth 244)

DONNELLY, Alfred Charles. Ridley Coll Melb ACT ThL 35. **d** 36 **p** 37 Melb. C of St Cath Caulfield 36-37; Min of Emerald 37-39; Belmont 39-40; Chap RAAF 40; Min of Lilydale 40-43; Vic Sec Bush Ch Aid Soc 43-45; I of Romsey 45-48; Preston West 48-53; Yarraville 53-57; V of Cant 57-71; on leave 71-75. *1/69 Wattle Valley Road, Canterbury, Vic, Australia 3126.* (03-83 4126)

DONNELLY, Canon Arthur Ferguson. b 14. St Jo Coll Dur BA and Jenkyns Scho 36, MA 39. **d** 37 **p** 38 Newc T. C of St Luke Wallsend 37-41; C-in-c of St Silas Newc T 41-44; Chap (Eccles Est) St Paul's Cathl Calc 44-47; Fort William 46-47; Chap Presidency Gen Hosp Calc 44-47; C-in-c of St John's Conv Distr Wallsend 48-56; R of Whitfield 56-65; Hartburn w Meldon Dio Newc T from 65; V of Netherwitton Dio Newc T from 65; RD of Morpeth from 76; Hon Can of Newc T from 77. *Hartburn Vicarage, Morpeth, Northumb.* (Hartburn 276)

DONNELLY, James Alexander. b 20. TCD BA (Mod Hist and Pol Sc 2nd cl) 42. **d** 43 **p** 44 Down. C of Ballymacarrett 43-45; St Donard Belf 45-49; CMS Sudan 49-53; I of Saintfield 53-64; Saul w Inch Dio Down from 64. *Saul and Inch Rectory, Downpatrick, Co Down, N Ireland, BT30 6SE.* (Downpatrick 3101)

DONNELLY, Robert James. **d** 57 **p** 58 Wang. C of Wadonga (in c of Bethanga) 57-60; R of Yackandandah and of Kiewa 60-65; Chap Miss to Seamen Melb 65-68; Sen Chap 68-72; I of Bellarine 73-80; Perm to Offic Dios Melb and Wang from 80. *4 Bartlett Street, Corryong, Vic, Australia 3707.*

DONOHOO, Alan Frederick. Moore Th Coll Syd ACT ThL 58. **d** 59 Bp Hilliard for Syd **p** 59 Syd. C of St Clem Mosman 59-60; Rozelle 60-63; R of Cook's River 63-69; Leichhardt 69-80; Assoc R of St Pet Cooks River 76-80; St Mich Flinders Street Syd 77-78; R of H Trin Peakhurst Dio Syd from 81. *671 Forest Road, Peakhurst, NSW, Australia 2210.* (53-8683)

DONOVAN, Maurice Stanton. Trin Coll Tor BA 48, MA 51. Knox Th Coll Tor 50. **d** 52 **p** 53 Tor. C of St Leon Tor 52-55. *Adelphi College, Garden City, Long Island, New York, USA.*

DONOVAN, Philip. b 18. BA Lon 49. Lich Th Coll. **d** 62 Heref **p** 73 St A. (APM). C of Rushbury 62-63; Sen Master Kingshott Sch Hitchin 63-65; Asst Chap and Master Lowther Coll Bodelwyddan 65-75; C of St Asaph Cathl 73-75; Llangollen 75-77; Chap Miss to Seamen E Lon Grahmstn 78-79; Dunkirk from 79; R of St Pet E Lon Grahmstn 78-79. *Missions to Seamen, Rue de l'Ecole Maternelle, Dunkirk, France.* (650420)

DOOLAN, Brian James. b 43. ACP 65. St Steph Ho Ox 66. **d** 68 Southn for Win **p** 69 Win. C of Milton 68-71; St Pet Bournemouth 71-73; St Aug Kilburn 73-76; V of St Osw Bordesley Dio 76-82; Surr 81; P Dio Guy from 82. *c/o St Mark's Clergy House, Bandywood Crescent, Kingstanding, Birmingham, B44 9JX.*

DOOLAN, Ven John George Meara. Univ of Tor BA 45. Wycl Coll Tor. **d** 48 **p** 49 Alg. I of Minnow Lake w Lockerby 48-59; R of Chapleau 59-66; Onaping 66-74; Resurr Sudbury Dio Alg from 74; Hon Can of Alg 74-76; Archd of Sudbury from 76. *353 Eyre Street South, Sudbury, Ont., Canada.* (705-674-4674)

DOOLEY, Brian James. Univ of Syd BA 28. ACT ThL 53. Moore Th Coll Syd 50. **d** 51 Armid **p** 52 Syd. C of Tamworth 51; Randwick 52-54; C-in-c of Mortdale 54-61; R of Glenbrook 61-70; L to Offic Dio Syd from 70. *60 Cambridge Street, Penshurst, NSW, Australia 2222.* (57-3065)

DOOLEY, Roy Wilfred. b 30. Westcott Ho Cam. **d** 57 **p** 58 Lon. C of St Barn Woodside Pk Finchley 57-60; Belmont 60-64; Min of St Jude's Conv Distr Pet 64-69; V 69-71; Badby w Newnham Dio Pet from 71. *Badby Vicarage, Daventry, Northants, NN11 6AP.* (Daventry 2622)

DOONAN, Robert John. b 13. Trin Coll Dub BA 36. **d** 37 **p** 38 Clogh. C of Carrickmacross and Killaney 37; Magheraculmoney and Drumkeeran 37-39; Urney 39-41; I of Newtowngore w Drumreilly and Carrawallen 41-44; Swanlinbar 44-50; R of Garvary 50-53; Magheraculmoney (w Muckross and Templecarne from 70 and Drumkeeran from 72) 53-78; RD of Kesh 57-78; Can of Clogh and Exam Chap to Bp of Clogh 68-78. *Crevenish Road, Kesh, Co Fermanagh, N Ireland.*

DORAN, Anthony Alan. b 42. Univ of New Engl BSc 64, PhD 70. BD (Lon) 72. Moore Coll Syd 70. **d** 73 Syd **p** 73 Armid. Chap Univ of New Engl Armid 73-74. *17 Garibaldi Street, Armidale, NSW 2350, Australia.*

DORAN, Patrick George. b 46. McMaster Univ Hamilton Ont BA 71. Trin Coll Tor MDiv 79. **d** 79 **p** 80 Niag. C of Grace Ch St Catharines Dio Niag from 79. *65 Lowell Avenue, St Catharines, Ont, Canada L2R 2C9.*

DORAN, Sidney William. b 12. AKC and Knowling Pri 40. **d** 40 **p** 41 Lon. C of St Pet Edmon 40-43; Caversham (in c of St Andr Caversham Heights) 43-51; V of Uffington w Woolstone (w Baulking from 52) 51-58; Bray (w Braywood from 61) 58-77; Surr 59-77; RD of Maidenhead 74-77; Perm to Offic Dio Truro from 77; Dio Ex from 80. *St Michael's, Combe Lane, Widemouth Bay, Bude, Cornw EX23 0AA.* (Widemouth Bay 386)

DORBER, Adrian John. b 52. St Jo Coll Dur BA 74. Westcott Ho Cam 76. **d** 79 Reading for Ox **p** 80 Ox. C of Easthampstead Dio Ox from 79. *St Michael's House, Crowthorne Road, Bracknell, Berks, RG12 4ER.*

DORCHESTER, Lord Bishop Suffragan of. *See* Meyer, Right Rev Conrad John Eustace.

DORE, Preb Robert Edward Frederick. b 28. Univ of Birm BCom 51. Wycl Hall Ox. **d** 58 **p** 59 Glouc. C of Ch Ch Cheltm 58-62; St Mary Magd Bridgnorth 62-67; R of Chetton w Deuxhill and Glazeley Dio Heref from 67; R of Billingsley w Sidbury Dio Heref from 67; R of Middleton Scriven Dio Heref from 67; RD of Bridgnorth 71-78; Preb of Heref Cathl from 75; P-in-c of Chelmarsh Dio Heref from 81. *Sidbury Rectory, Bridgnorth, Salop.* (Stottesdon 625)

DORION, James Kenrick. Wycl Coll Tor LTh 66. **d** 67 Keew. C of Rainy River 67-72; L to Offic Dio Moos from 73. *Box 335, Noranda, PQ, Canada.*

DORITTY, Donald Owen. Univ of Tor BA 53. Trin Coll Tor STB 56. **d** 56 **p** 57 WNY. [f in Amer Ch] Hon C of St Andr Scarborough Tor 63-69; St Clem Eglinton City and Dio Tor from 69. *93 Craighurst Avenue, Toronto 12, Ont., Canada.*

DORKING, Lord Bishop Suffragan of. *See* Evans, Right Rev Kenneth Dawson.

DORKING, Archdeacon of. (Vacant)

DORMAN, Canon Denis John Brennian. Univ of NZ BA 36, MA 39, LTh 40. Selw Coll Dun. **d** 38 **p** 39 Dun. C of St Martin NE Valley 38-41; V of Waitaki 41-45; Wyndham 45-51; V of Winton 52-57; Mornington 57-61; Exam Chap to Bp of Dun 58-71; Hosp Chap Dio Dun 61-70; Hon Can of Dun 66-76; Can (Emer) from 76; V of Tuapeka 70-73; Maniototo 73-77; Hon C of All SS w Port Chalmers Dio Dun from 77. *188e Queen Street, Dunedin, NZ.* (773-132)

DORMAN, Canon John Richard. Keble Coll Ox 2nd cl Mod Hist 37, BA 38, MA 55. Ely Th Coll 38. **d** 39 **p** 40 Carl. C of Dalston 39-42; Maryport 42-44; C-in-c of Threlkeld 44-46; R 46-57; V of Bartica 57-68; Kamarang Dio Guy from 68; Can of St Geo Cathl Georgetown from 65. *Vicarage, Kamarang, Upper Mazaruni River, Guyana.*

DORMAN, Milton Forrest. Sir Geo Williams Univ Montr BA 61. Trin Coll Tor STB 63. **d** 64 **p** 65 Queb. I of Magdalen Is 64-69; Grand Manan 69-74; Lancaster Dio Fred from 74; Exam Chap to Bp of Fred from 77. *1004 Manawagonish Road, Saint John West, NB, Canada.*

DORMAN, Paul Wilfrid. b 14. Keble Coll Ox BA (4th cl Th) 36, MA 46, Ely Th Coll 36. **d** 38 **p** 39 Ely. C of Woodston 38-41; Downham w Bexwell 41-47; Chap RAFVR 43-46; V of Whittlesey 47-54; R of St John March 54-68; V of St Helen Nor 68-69; L to Offic Dio Nor 69-75; Dioc Stewardship Adv from 69; R of Caston (w Griston and Merton from 78) 75-81; V of Griston 75-78; C-in-c of Tompson 75-81; Merton 75-78. *c/o Rectory, Caston, Attleborough, Norf.* (Caston 222)

DORMER, Christopher Robert. b 39. Univ of Bris BA (2nd cl Engl) 61. Lich Th Coll 61. **d** 63 **p** 64 Sheff. C of St Cecilia Parson Cross Sheff 63-67; Greenford 67-69; M of St Barn, Bush Bro Queensld 69-74; Actg Sec USPG Ireland 74-75; R of Catton w Stamford Bridge 75-81; C-in-c of Skirpenbeck 76-78; R 78-81; Scrayinham w Leppington 78-81; Actg RD of

Pocklington 80-81; RD 81; Itin P Dio Moray from 81. *25 Market Street, Ullapool, Ross-shire, IV26 2XE.* (Ullapool 2143)

DORMOR, Duncan Stephen. b 36. St Edm Hall Ox BA 60. Cudd Coll Ox 60. **d** 62 **p** 63 Ox. C of Headington 62-66; in Amer Ch 66-72; R of St Andr Hertford Dio St Alb from 72; RD of Hertford from 77. *43 North Road, Hertford.* (Hertford 52726)

DORMOR, William Henry. b 06. King's Coll Lon 28. Lich Th Coll 32. **d** 33 **p** 34 Lich. C of Cheddleton 33-36; Withycombe-Raleigh 36-39; Chap Ex City Mental Hosp 37-39; PC of Beer 39-62; Chap RNVR 42-46; RD of Honiton 54-59; PC of St John Torquay 62-67; C 67-69; V of Ide 69-74; L to Offic Dio Ex from 74. *13 Beech Park, West Hill, Ottery St Mary, Devon, EX11 1TY.*

DORRINGTON, Brian Goodwin. b 32. **d** 66 **p** 67 Ches. C of Poynton 66-71; Hd Master Veryan VP Sch Dio Truro from 71; Perm to Offic Dio Truro 71-78; Hon C of Veryan Dio Truro from 78. *Tomdoun, Roseland Gardens, Veryan, Truro, TR2 5QR.* (Veryan 484)

DORRINGTON, Richard Bryan. b 48. Linc Th Coll 79. **d** 81 Lich. C of Streetly Dio Lich from 81. *6 Ferndale Road, Streetly, Sutton Coldfield, W Midl, B74 3PU.* (021-353 9508)

DORSET, Archdeacon of. (Vacant)

DOS SANTOS, Edwin. Sir Geo Williams Univ Montr BA 51. Wycl Coll Tor LTh 54. **d** 54 Tor for Fred **p** 55 Fred. C of St Luke Portland St John 54-56; R of Cambridge NB 56-61; P-in-c of Old Harbour Ja 61-63; V of Mandeville 63; R of Kingston NB 63-70; Trin St Steph 70-73; St Martin's w Black River 73-81; Petersville and Greenwich Dio Fred from 81. *RR1, Westfield, NB, Canada.*

DOSSETOR, Roberts Francis. b 14. St Pet Hall Ox BA (3rd cl Engl) 37, MA 62. BA (2nd cl Phil) Lon 63, MA 67. Ripon Hall Ox 37. **d** 37 **p** 38 S'wark. C of St Matt Surbiton 37-39; Putney 39-41; R of Black Torrington 41-48; Hartwell w Stone 48-53 and 54-59; Chap Co Mental Hosp Stone 48-54; CF (EC) 43-46; Chap Windsor Sch Hamm 53-54; Chap City of Lon Freemen's Sch Ashtead Pk 59-61; V of St Andr Lower Streatham 61-80; Pastoral Care of Tilshead, Orcheston and Chittern Dio Sarum from 80. *Vicarage, Tilshead, Salisbury, Wilts.*

DOSSETT, Edward James. McGill Univ STh 48. CEM 51. CD 57. **d** 47 **p** 48 Montr. Dean of Residents Montr Dioc Th Coll 47-49; I of Aylmer and P-in-c of Gatineau 49-51; CF (Canad) 51-63; R of St Matthias Vancouver 63-69; Chap Shaughnessy Hosp Vanc 69-77. *7642 Hudson Street, Vancouver 14, BC, Canada.*

DOSUMU, Ven Ebenezer O. Im Coll Ibad 64. **d** 66 **p** 67 Ondo. P Dio Ondo 66-79; Dio Ijebu from 79; Archd Dio Ijebu from 80. *Emmanuel Church, Isonyin, via Ijebu-Ode, Nigeria.*

✠ **DOTIRO, Right Rev Yeremaya Kufuta.** Div Sch Mori. **d** 47 Sudan **p** 50 Bp Allison for Sudan. P Dio Sudan 47-62; Cons Asst Bp in the Sudan in Juba Par Ch 25 Jan 63 by Abp in Jer; Bp in Sudan; and Bp of W Bugan; Apptd Bp of Yambio 76; Archd of Bari Zande 63-70. *Episcopal Church of the Sudan, Western Equatoria Province, Yambio, Sudan.*

DOUBLE, (Samuel) Richard Sydney. b 47. K Coll Lon BD and AKC 69. St Aug Coll Cant 69. **d** 70 **p** 71 Warrington for Liv. C of Walton-on-the-Hill 70-75; M SSF from 75; L to Offic Dio Sarum from 75; Publ Pr Dio Man from 77. *Heathfield, Manchester Road, Ashton-under-Lyme.* (061-370 2181)

DOUBTFIRE, Samuel. b 33. Edin Th Coll. **d** 66 Pontefract for Wakef **p** 66 Wakef. C of Knottingley 66-68; V of Ripponden w Rishworth 68-76: Crosthwaite Keswick 76-81; St Matt Barrow-in-Furness Dio Carl from 81. *St Matthew's Vicarage, Highfield Road, Barrow-in-Furness, Cumb, LA14)*

DOUGLAS, Alexander Joseph. Trin Coll Dub BA and Div Test 45, MA 61. **d** 45 **p** 46 Connor. C of St Mary Belf 45-49; R of St Sav Connor 49-51; I of Magheralin (or Maralin) 51-63; R of St Jo Div Orangefield Dio Down from 63. *397 Castlereagh Road, Belfast, N Ireland, BT5 6AB.*

DOUGLAS, Anthony Victor. b 51. St Jo Coll Nottm 74. **d** 76 **p** 77 Liv. C of St Luke Gt Crosby 76-79; Team V of Fazakerley (in c of St Geo) Dio Liv from 79. *St George's Vicarage, Stopgate Lane, Fazakerley, Lancs.*

DOUGLAS, Canon Archibald Sholto. b 14. Selw Coll Cam BA 37, MA 46. TD 50. Wells Th Coll 38. **d** 47 **p** 48 Ches. C of Macclesfield (in c of St Andr from 49) 47-51; CF (TA) 49-61; SCF (TA) 61-64; C of St Mary Magd Ashton-on-Mersey 51-52; V of Wharton 52-55; Capesthorne w Siddington (w Marton from 69) Dio Ches from 55; C-in-c of Marton 65-69; Hon Can of Ches Cathl from 78. *Fanshawe Vicarage Siddington, Macclesfield, Chesh.* (Marton Heath 243)

DOUGLAS, Charles David. b 29. Univ of Leeds BSc 50. Linc Th Coll 68. **d** 70 Hulme for Man **p** 71 Man. C of St Anne Longsight Royton 70-73; V of Edenfield Dio Man from 73. *Edenfield Vicarage, Church Lane, Ramsbottom, Bury, Lancs BL0 0QL.* (Ramsbottom 3125)

DOUGLAS, Colin Kenneth. AKC 35. **d** 35 **p** 36 Chelmsf. C of St Andr Westcliff 35-36; Grays Thurrock 36-39; Sprowston 39-42; St Botolph (in c of St Steph) Colchester 42-45; R of W Bergholt 45-78; Chap St Mary's Hosp Colchester 46-73. *49 Madeira Road, Holland-on-Sea, Clacton-on-Sea, Essex, CO15 5NE.* (Clacton 814933)

DOUGLAS, George Gawain. b 35. Keble Coll Ox 56. Qu Coll Birm 59. **d** 61 Bp Graham for Carl **p** 62 Carl. C of St John Workington 61-64; Upperby Carl 64-67; C-in-c of St Luke's Conv Distr Morton Carl 67-68; V 68-72; Aspatria w Hayton Dio Carl from 72. *Vicarage, King Street, Aspatria, Carlisle, CA5 3AL.* (Aspatria 20398)

DOUGLAS, Ian Alexander. b 11. St Aug Coll Cant 71. **d** 71 **p** 72 Edmon for Lon. C of St Jo Evang Palmers Green 71-81. *62 Compton Road, Winchmore Hill, N21 3NS.* (01-360 3472)

DOUGLAS, James Shanks. b 32. Edin Th Coll 53. **d** 56 **p** 57 Brech. C of Arbroath 56-58; St Geo Cathl Kingstown St Vinc 58-61; R of Barrouallie 61-70; St Patr Grenada 70-72; Georgetn St Vinc 73-74; Chap HM Pris Pentonville 74-75; HM Pris Camp Hill 75-80. *c/o 86 Quarry View, Camp Hill, Newport, IW.* (Newport 527661)

DOUGLAS, John Beresford. b 36. Southern Dioc Min Tr Scheme 78. **d** 81 B & W (NSM). C of St Mary w St Jo Bapt Bathwick Bath Dio B & W from 81. *242 Bailbrook Lane, Bath, Avon, BA1 7AA.*

DOUGLAS, John Howard Barclay. b 23. St Jo Coll Dur BA 48. Bps' Coll Cheshunt. **d** 50 **p** 51 Dur. C of St Hilda Hartlepool 50-53; Ch Ch Woodhouse 53-55; PC of St Edm Gateshead 55-60; V of Thirkleby w Kilburn and Bagby Dio York from 60. *Kilburn Vicarage, York, YO6 4AH.* (Coxwold 234)

DOUGLAS, Peter John McKechnie. b 13. Sarum Wells Th Coll 72. **d** 73 Crediton for Ex **p** 74 Ex. C of Okehampton Dio Ex from 73. *125 Station Road, Okehampton, Devon.*

DOUGLAS, Robert Vernon. b 24. Pemb Coll Cam BA 48. Wells Th Coll 48. **d** 50 **p** 51 Man. C of Worsley (in c of Ellenbrook) 50-53; Pendleton and of Brindle Heath 53-55; Min of St Phil and St Jas Eccles Distr Chatham 55-62; PC 62-65; R of N Cray 65-80; V of St Mary Virg Platt Dio Roch from 80. *Platt Vicarage, Comp Lane, Sevenoaks, Kent, TN14 8NR.* (Borough Green 885482)

DOUGLAS, William Gurwood McDonald. b 26. Lich Th Coll 57. **d** 59 **p** 60 Cov. C of St Jo Bapt Cov 59-61; St Paul The Hythe Egham 61-64; Chap Cotswold Commun Ashton Keynes 65-80. *c/o Cotswold Community, Ashton Keynes, Swindon, Wilts.* (Ashton Keynes 239)

DOUGLAS-JONES, Ian Elliot. b 14. Trin Hall Cam BA 35, MA 39. Wycl Hall Ox 35. **d** 37 **p** 38 Lon. C of Ch Ch Highbury 37-40; H Trin Tunbridge Wells 40-41; Chap RAFVR 41-46; Men in Disp 45; V of St Jo Evang Penge (w Ch Ch from 52) 46-54; Surr 46-63; R of St Mary Rushden 54-63; C-in-c of Newton Bromswold 60-63; V of Fulwood Sheff 63-68; Mayfield 68-79. *32 Hanley Road, Malvern Wells, Worcs.*

DOUGLASS, Ven Cedric William. ACT ThL 54. St Jo Coll Morpeth. **d** 54 **p** 56 Newc. C of Cessnock 54-56; Merewether 56; Waratah 56-58; R of Nabiac 58-61; Toronto 61-70; Cessnock 70-81; Woy Woy Dio Newc from 81; Can of Newc from 79; Archd of the Centr Coast from 81. *Rectory, Burge Street, Woy Woy, NSW, Australia 2256.*

DOUGLASS, Donald Marsh. Moore Th Coll ACT ThL 53. **d** and **p** 54 Syd. C-in-c of Berowra 54-56; R of Hedland 56-61; Booval 61-65; St Pet, N Neutral Bay 65-70; Chap N Ryde Hosp from 70. *23 Holland Street, Chatswood, NSW, Australia 2067.* (412-1374)

DOUGLASS, John Edward. b 20. St D Coll Lamp 60. **d** 62 **p** 63 Mon. C of Maindee 62-66; R of Llanddewi Skirrid w Llanvetherine Llangattock Lingoed and Llanfair Chap 66-70; R of H Trin Pillgwenlly Newport 70-75; V of St Steph Newport 70-75; R of St Steph w H Trin Newport 75-76; V of Trellech and R of Cwmcarvan Dio Mon from 76. *Vicarage, Trellech, Gwent.*

DOUGLIN, Hugh Arthur. Codr Coll Barb 43. **d** 47 **p** 49 Trinid. [f in Amer Ch] R of Anna Regina 66-71; V of Ch Ch Georgetn 71-74; Kitty 74-76; R of St Jude Arima Dio Trinid from 77. *St Jude's Rectory, Arima, Trinidad, WI.*

DOUGLIN, Very Rev Rawle Ernest. Kelham Th Coll 55. **d** 59 **p** 60 Trinid. C of All SS Port-of-Spain 59-63; R of Princes Town 63-67; Tunapuna w St Juan 67-71; All SS Port of Spain 71-73; Hon Can of Trinid 71-73; Exam Chap to Bp of Trinid from 73; Dean and R of H Trin Cathl Port of Spain Dio Trinid from 73. *Deanery, Abercromby Street, Port of Spain, Trinidad, W Indies.*

DOULIN, Patrick Brian Harry. b 36. Linc Th Coll 67. **d** 70 **p** 71 Chich. C of Hurstpierpoint 70-73; Albourne 71-73; Southport Queensld 73; R of Madang 73-75; Chap Balob Coll Dio Papua 75-76; Perm to Offic Dio Brisb 76-77; Chap

St Hilda Sch Southport 77; P-in-c of Slacks Creek Dio Brisb from 77. *Boronia Street, Slacks Creek, Queensland, Australia 4127.* (208 9867)

DOULTON, Dick. b 32. St Cath Coll Cam BA 60, MA 64. Ridley Hall Cam 61. **d** 63 Bp Gelsthorpe for Southw **p** 64 Southw. C of Gedling 63-65; Danbury 65. *Thornton Hall, Thornton, Milton Keynes, Bucks.* (Buckingham 5272)

DOUPE, Henry Festus. b 13. Oak Hill Th Coll 54. **d** 56 **p** 57 Liv. C of Fazakerley 56-58; V of St Thos Wigan 58-61; Higher Walton 61-78; Hon C of Fulwood 78-79. *38 Stratford Drive, Fulwood, Preston, Lancs, PR2 3HU.*

DOUST, James Athol John. Moore Th Coll Syd ACT ThL 62. **d** 61 **p** 62 Brisb. C of St Steph Coorparoo Brisb 61-64; Chap AMF 64-68; C of St Aug Neutral Bay 68-69; Youth Dir Dio Syd 69-73; L to Offic Dio Syd 69-73; Perm to Offic Dio Gippsld 73-77; Dio Newc from 79; Chap RAAF from 73. *RAAF Base, Williamtown, NSW, Australia 2301.* (049-28 6423)

DOUTHWAITE, William Ernest. b 15. Univ of Edin MA 35. Edin Th coll 36. **d** 38 **p** 39 Moray. Prec of St Andr Cathl Inverness 38-40; Dioc Super 39-40; C of St Marg Lochee 40-42; Perm to Offic Dio S'wark 42-43; Asst Miss CCC Cam Miss Camberwell 43-47; C of Mortlake (in c of All SS) 47-50; V of St Bart Battersea 50-58; PC of Twyford w Poundon and Charndon 58-65; R of Lavendon w Cold Brayfield 65-80. *12 Langlands Lavendon, Olney, Milton Keynes, MK46 4EL.* (Bedford 712716)

DOVE, Canon John. McGill Univ BA 36. Dioc Th Coll Montr. **d** 41 **p** 42 Montr. C of Ch Ch Cathl Montr 41-44; I of Greenfield Pk 44-56; R of St Luke Montr 56-78; Hon Can of Montr 68-78; Can (Emer) from 78. *718 Oxford Street East, London, Ont, Canada.*

DOVE, Canon Reginald George James Thomas. Univ of Leeds BA 38. Coll of Resurr Mirfield 38. **d** 40 **p** 41 Newc T. C of St Mary Blyth 40-43; Orlando and Pimville Miss Distr 43-47; P-in-c of Pimville Miss Distr Johann 47-52; R of Leribe and Dir of Hlotse Miss 52-71; Can of Basuto 59-66; Lesotho 66-71; Can (Emer) from 71; R of Edenvale Dio Johann from 74. *59 7th Avenue, Edenvale, Transvaal, S Africa.* (011-53 3346)

DOVER, Lord Bishop Suffragan of. *See* Third, Right Rev Richard Henry McPhial.

DOVER, Canon Oswald Leslie Simpson. b 18. Edin Th Coll 46. **d** 47 **p** 48 Edin. C of H Trin Stirling 47-49; P-in-c of St Cath Bo'ness w St Mildred Linlithgow and Blackness 49-51; C of St Wilfrid Harrogate 51-53; R of Galashiels 53-59; H Trin Melrose Dio Edin from 59; Hon Can of Edin from 77. *Rectory, Melrose, Roxburghs.* (Melrose 2626)

DOW, Andrew John Morrison. b 46. Univ Coll Ox BA 67, MA 71. Oak Hill Th Coll 69. **d** 71 **p** 72 St Alb. C of St Luke Watford 71-74; Chadderton 74-77; V of St Paul Leamington Dio Cov from 78. *St Paul's Vicarage, 15 Lillington Road, Leamington Spa, CV32 7RW.* (Leamington Spa 35331)

DOW, Geoffrey Graham. b 42. Qu Coll Ox BA 63, BSc 65, 2nd cl Th 66, MA 68. Univ of Birm Dipl Th 74. Clifton Th Coll 66. **d** 67 **p** 68 Roch. C of Tonbridge 67-72; Chap Stud of St Jo Coll Ox 72-75; Lect St Jo Coll Nottm 75-80; V of H Trin City and Dio Cov from 80. *Vicarage, Davenport Road, Coventry, Warws, CV5 6PS.* (Coventry 74996)

DOW, George Francis. b 11. Univ of Lon 29. ALCD 32. **d** 34 **p** 35 Win. C of St Matt Southampton 34-36; St Helier Jersey 37-38; Pulborough 38-40; CF (EC) 40-46; V of Ifield 46-53; Fernhurst 53-66; Manaccan w St Anthony-in-Meneage 66-76; Perm to Offic Dio Ox from 76. *24 Meadow Close, Lower Way, Thatcham, Newbury, Berks.*

DOW, Ronald Edgar Forbes. b 19. St Chad's Coll Regina 52. **d** 53 **p** 54 Qu'App. I of Stoughton 53-55; St Mich Regina Dio Qu'App 55-56; C of H Trin Bingley 56-57; V of St Sav Harden Bingley 57-60; C-in-c of Wilsden 57-60; Area Sec UMCA S Midls 60-62; R of Kingsley 62-71; V of Horton Leek 71-73; C-in-c Rushton Spencer 71-73; V of Rocester 73-77; P-in-c of Dilhorne Dio Lich from 77. *Dilhorne Vicarage, Stoke-on-Trent, Staffs, ST10 2PQ.* (Blythe Bridge 2199)

DOWDELL, Alfred Falconer. Bp's Univ Lennox BA 27, LST 29. **d** 29 **p** 30 Ont. C of Bancroft 29-30; St Geo Tor 30-31; I of Cardiff w Monmouth Ont 31-32; P-in-c of N Frontenac 32-35; R of Lansdowne Front 35-49; Ox Mills 49-58; Chap Tyendinaga 58-65; R of Deseronto 65-69. *135 Chapel Street, Coburg, Ont, Canada.* (416-372 6367)

DOWDEN, Gordon Frederick. b 25. Selw Coll Cam BA 51, MA 55. Chich Th Coll 51. **d** 53 **p** 54 Sarum. C of St Mich Sarum 53-56; St Neots 56-58; Gt w L Paxton and Toseland 56-58; R of St Phil (Ascen from 70) Hulme Man 58-78; RD of Hulme 73-78; M Gen Syn 74-75; P-in-c of Holybourne w Neatham Dio Win from 78; RD of Alton from 80. *Holybourne Vicarage, Alton, Hants, GU34 4HD.* (Alton 83240)

DOWDEN, Victor Boyd. Trin Coll Tor STB 61. **d** 61 Edmon. C of St Faith's Miss Edson 61-62; R of Winfield 62-64; Edson 64-66. *10808 15th Street, Dawson Creek, BC, Canada.*

DOWDING, Edward Brinley. b 47. St D Coll Lamp BA 71. St Mich Coll Llan 70. **d** 72 **p** 73 Llan. C of St Cath Canton 72-75; Aberdare 75-78; V of H Trin Aberavon Dio Llan from 78. *Holy Trinity Vicarage, Fairway, Sandfields, Port Talbot, W Glam, SA12 7HG.* (Port Talbot 884409)

DOWDING, Stanley Frederick. b 10. St Jo Coll Dur BA and LTh 33. ALCD 32. **d** 34 **p** 35 Bris. C of St Silas Bris 34-37; Downend 37-39; Portland (in c of St Pet) 39-42; C-in-c of St Phil Weston Mill 42-46; V of St Luke Preston 46-55; Chap HM Pris Preston 51-52; V of Nelson-in-Marsden 55-75; Surr 65-75; RD of Burnley 68-70; Pendle 70-75. *Hillside Avenue, Reedley, Burnley, Lancs, BB10 2NF.* (Nelson 693030)

DOWE, Francis Samuel. b 20. **d** 72 Ott. C of Ch of Resurr City and Dio Ott from 72. *211 Wurtemburg Street, Apt 411, Ottawa K1N 8L9, Ont., Canada.*

DOWE, Philip John. Univ of Syd BA 52, BD 67. St Jo Coll Morpeth. **d** 56 Newc **p** 57 Syd. C of Muswellbrook 56-59; Marrickville 58-59; V of Walgett 60-69; Uralla 69-79; Narrabri Dio Armid from 79. *13 Dewhurst Street, Narrabri, NSW, Australia 2390.*

DOWEL, William Richard. Ridley Coll Melb ACT ThL 50. **d** 51 **p** 52 Melb. Chap Victoria Miss to Seamen 51-52; C of St Paul's Cathl Melb 52-54; Chap Miss to Seamen Port of Lon 54-56; Walvis Bay 56-60; V of Inverleigh 60-64; Sen Chap Miss to Seamen Vic Austr 64-68; I of Ch Ch Brunswick 68-75; St Phil W Heidelberg 75-79; Balwyn Dio Melb from 79. *86 Balwyn Road, Balwyn, Vic, Australia 3103.* (836 4107)

DOWELL, Graham Moffat. b 26. Magd Coll Cam BA 48, MA 53. Ely Th Coll 51. **d** 53 **p** 54 Derby. C of All SS Cathl Derby 53-56; Chap at Nicosia 56-59; Chap Univ of Sheff 59-63; C of St Geo Sheff 59-63; USPG Chap Addis Ababa 64-67; Chap Univ of Zambia 68-70; Univs in Lon 70-74; L to Offic Dio Lon 70-74; V of St John Hampstead Dio Lon from 74. *14 Church Row, NW3.* (01-435 0553)

DOWKER, Ven George Hasted. Univ of Manit BA 22, MA 23. Angl Th Coll of BC LTh 27. St Jo Coll Winnipeg DD (*hon causa*) 54. Wycl Coll Tor DD (*hon causa*) 69. **d** and **p** 27 New Westmr. C of St Paul Vancouver 27-30; R of St Phil Dunbar Heights Vancouver 30-33; H Trin Cathl New Westmr 33-39; St Geo Winnipeg 39-44; Exam Chap to Bp of Rupld 41-44; R of Grace Church-on-the-Hill Tor 44-53; Can of Tor 51-53; Dean and R of Ch Ch Cathl Montr 53-60; Archd of Bow Valley and R of Ch Ch Calg 60-66; Archd (Emer) from 79; Exam Chap to Bp of Calg 61-66; Hon C of St Paul Tor 66-69; Perm to Offic Dio BC 71-79. *687 Falkland Road, Victoria, BC, Canada.*

DOWKER, John Hasted. Montr Dioc Coll LTh 57. **d** 57 Montr **p** 58 Rupld. C of St Luke Winnipeg 57-60; V of Whytewold 60-62; Miss Blackfoot Reserve Miss and R of Strathmore 62-64; Hon C of St Paul Tor 66-69; L to Offic Dio BC 71-72; on leave 73-75; C of Shanty Bay 75-77. *Rectory, Shanty Bay, Ont., Canada.*

DOWLAND, Martin John. b 48. BD (Lon) 70. Wycl Hall Ox 75. **d** 77 **p** 78 Newc T. C of Clayton Mem Ch Jesmond 77-80; Chadderton Dio Man from 80. *1 Fountain's Walk, Denton Lane, Chadderton, Oldham, OL9 8PX.* (061-624 0278)

DOWLEN, Edward Mark. b 25. Cranfield Inst Tech MSc 49. St Jo Coll Dur 78. **d** 79 **p** 80 St A. Hon C of Rhyl 79-81; M SSM from 81; L to Offic Dio St A from 81. *26 Laburnum Drive, Rhyl, Clwyd.*

DOWLING, Donald Edward. b 43. Univ of St Andr MA 66. St Jo Coll Dur Dipl Th 74. **d** 74 Dorchester for Ox **p** 75 Ox. C of Thame and Towersey 74-78; Norton 78-80; V of Wilbury Dio St Alb from 81. *103 Bedford Road, Letchworth, Herts.* (Letchworth 79236)

DOWLING, James William. b 15. Lich Th Coll. **d** 57 **p** 58 Newc T. C of St Aid Newc T 57-60; Long Benton (in c of St Mary Magd) 60-63; V of Lynemouth 63-81; Cresswell 71-81. *2 Moor End Villas, Newbiggin, Northumb.* (Ashington 817563)

✠ **DOWLING, Right Rev Owen Douglas.** Univ of Melb BA 55. ACT ThL (2nd cl) 61. **d** 60 **p** 61 Melb. C of Sunshine Melb 60-62; Min of St Phil w Heidelberg 62-65; Prec of St Sav Cathl Goulb 65-68; R of S Wagga Wagga 68-73; St Jo Bapt Canberra 73-81; Archd of Canberra 74-81; Exam Chap to Bp of C & Goulb from 74; Cons Asst Bp of C & Goulb in St Andr Cathl Syd 25 March 81 by Abps of Syd and Melb; Bps of C & Goulb, Graft, Newc, River and Armid; and others. *Jamieson House, Constitution Avenue, Reid, ACT, Australia 2601.* (062-48 0811)

DOWLING, Ronald Lindsay. b 47. St Jo Coll Morpeth ThL 72. **d** 73 **p** 74 Melb. C of St Geo Malvern 73-76; P-in-c of Merlynston 76-80; St Marg Eltham Dio Melb from 80. *Vicarage, John Street, Eltham, Vic, Australia 3095.*

DOWMAN, John Frederick. b 26. K Coll Lon and Warm AKC 52. **d** 53 **p** 54 Linc. of Frodingham 53-55; Clee w

Cleethorpes 55-57; Horncastle w Low Toynton 57-59; PC of S w N Kyme 59-64; V of Legbourne w L Cawthorpe (and Muckton w Burwell and Walmsgate from 81) Dio Linc from 64; R of Muckton w Burwell and Walmsgate 64-81; P-in-c of Raithby and Hallington 79-81; Tathwell w Haugham 79-81; Withcall 79-81; R of Raithby Dio Linc from 81. *Legbourne Vicarage, Louth, Lincs.* (Louth 2535)

DOWN, Archdeacon of. *See* Macourt, Ven William Albert.

DOWN, Dean of. *See* Good, Very Rev James Herbert Rosmond.

DOWN, Martin John. b 40. Jes Coll Cam BA 62, MA 68. Westcott Ho Cam 63. **d** 65 Hulme for Man **p** 66 Man. C of Bury 65-68; Leigh 68-70; R of Fiskerton 70-75; V of Corby Glen w Irnham (and Swayfield w Swinstead from 79) Dio Linc from 75. *Corby Glen Vicarage, Grantham, Lincs, NG33 4NJ.* (Corby Glen 263)

DOWN, Peter Michael. b 54. AKC and BD 78. Coll of the Resurr Mirfield 78. **d** 79 **p** 80 Bris. C of Ch Ch Swindon Dio Bris from 79. *71a Bath Road, Swindon, Wilts, SN1 4AU.* (Swindon 36005)

DOWN, Wilfred Samuel. b 26. Keble Coll Ox BA 50, MA 54. Linc Th Coll. **d** 51 **p** 52 Bris. C of St Jo Div Fishponds 51-56; Horfield 56-59; V of St Osw Bedminster Down 59-65; St Steph Southmead 65-69; R of Monkton Farleigh w S Wraxall 69-76; Marlborough Dio Sarum from 76. *Rectory, Rawlingswell Lane, Marlborough, Wilts, SN8 1AU.* (0672 52357)

DOWN, William John Denbigh. b 34. St Jo Coll Cam BA (2nd cl Mod Lang) 57, MA 61. Ridley Hall Cam 57. **d** 59 **p** 60 Sarum. C of Fisherton Anger 59-63; Chap Miss to Seamen S Shields 63-65; Hull 65-71; Chap Flying Angel Club Fremantle 71-74; Dep Gen Sec Miss to Seamen 75; Gen Sec from 76; Chap St Mich Paternoster R City and Dio Lon from 76; Perm to Offic Dio St Alb from 78. *Missions to Seamen, St Michael Paternoster Royal, College Hill, EC4R 2RL.* (01-248 5202)

DOWN AND DROMORE, Lord Bishop of. *See* Eames, Right Rev Robert Henry Alexander.

DOWNER, Canon Alfred Wallace. Wycl Coll Tor. **d** 29 Niag **p** 31 Tor. C of Erin 29-31; Miss Scarboro Junction 31-35; I of Batteau w Duntroon 35-75; Chap CASF 42-45; Can of Tor from 75. *263 Beech Street, Collingwood, Ont., Canada.*

DOWNER, Cuthbert John. b 18. SOC 60. **d** 74 Chich **p** 75 Horsham for Chich. C of Kirdford 74-77; Linstead w Chediston and Halesworth 77-79; P-in-c of Knodishall w Buxlow 79-80; Friston 79-80; R of Bacton w Wyverstone Dio St E from 80; P-in-c of Cotton Dio St E from 80. *Bacton Rectory, Stowmarket, Suff.* (bacton 245)

DOWNER, Donald. b 47. Univ of Guelph BA 69. Trin Coll Tor MDiv 73. **d** and **p** 74 Niag. C of St Jude Oakville 74-76; R of St Marg Hamilton Dio Niag from 76. *67 Harold Court, Hamilton, Ont, Canada.* (416-522 1888)

DOWNER, Philip William. Univ of Lon 27. Late Scho of Univ of Tor. BA 32, MA 33. Wycl Coll Tor LTh 34. **d** 33 **p** 34 Tor. C of St Anne Tor 33-35; Dean of Res and Prof Em Coll Sktn 35-37; I of Meota w Langmeade 37-40; Humboldt and Mancroft 40-42; R of Colonsay Elstow and Viscount 42-47; Exam Chap to Bp of Sktn 45-50; R of Florence 49; Tilbury 49-56; Collingwood 56-73. *1 Royal Orchard Boulevard, Thornhill, Ont., Canada.*

DOWNEY, John Stewart. b 38. Open Univ BA 76. Oak Hill Th Coll 63. **d** 66 **p** 67 Derry. C of St Aug Londonderry 66-71; I of Dungiven w Bovevagh Dio Derry from 71; Dom Chap to Bp of Derry from 75. *Dungiven, Londonderry, N Ireland.*

DOWNEY, Philip Gladstone. Univ of NZ MB ChB 48. Moore Th Coll Syd 60. **d** 62 **p** 63 Ch Ch. C of Fendalton 62-63; Sumner-Heathcote 64-65; on leave. *139 Fendalton Road, Christchurch 4, NZ.*

DOWNEY, Richard Kenneth. b 41. Univ of Tor BSc 63, MA 65, Trin Coll Tor MDiv 73. **d** 73 **p** 74 Tor. C of Ch Ch Brampton 73-75; I of Fenlon Falls and Ch Ch Coboconk 75-79; St Barn Pet Dio Tor from 79. *171 Marina Boulevard, Peterborough, Ont., Canada.*

DOWNEY, Very Rev Thomas Edward. Trin Coll Tor BA 43, LTh 46, DD 74. **d** 45 **p** 46 Ott. I of Aultsville 46-47; C of St Matt Ott 47-50; R of Navan 50-55; Manotick 55-58; All SS Westboro Ott 58-63; St Geo St Catharines Dio Niag from 63; Hon Can of Niag 66-70; Dom Chap to Bp of Niag 67-70; Dean and R of Ott Cathl from 70. *439 Queen Street, Ottawa, Ont., Canada.* (1-613-722-6625)

DOWNHAM, Peter Norwell. b 31. Univ of Man BA (2nd cl Econ) 52. Ridley Hall Cam 54. **d** 56 **p** 57 Ches. C of Cheadle 56-62; V of Rawtenstall 62-68; St Jas Denton Holme Carl 68-79; Chap Rossendale Gen Hosp 62-68; V of Greyfriars Reading Dio Ox from 79. *Greyfriars Vicarage, Friar Street, Reading, RG1 1EH.* (Reading 53822)

DOWNIE, Canon Malcolm Alan Frank. Ch Coll Hobart Tas ACT ThL 35. **d** 36 **p** 37 Tas. C of St Jas New Town 36-37; Burnie 37-40; P-in-c of Furneaux Is 40-42; R of Beaconsfield and Exeter 42-46; Cressy 46-51; Queenstown 51-54; Chap to Bp of Tas 50-54; R of Franklin 54-59; Can Missr Tas 59-81; Can (Emer) from 81; Dir of Overseas Dept Tas 59-66; R of Lindisfarne 66-74; Campbell Town and Ross 74-81. *42 Pottery Road, Lenah Valley, Tasmania 7008.*

DOWNING, Edward Nalder. b 10. Late Exhib of Worc Coll Ox 2nd cl Cl Mods 31, BA (2nd cl Lit Hum) 33, 3rd cl Th 34, MA 36. Westcott Ho Cam 34. **d** 35 **p** 36 Bris. C of St Jo Evang w St Anselm Clifton 35-37; Chap Toc H Man and L to Offic Dio Man 37-39; Birm and L to Offic Dio Birm 39; TCF 39-45; Chap St Ninian's Cathl Perth 45-47; CF 47-55; V of Shelton and Oxon 55-58; R of High Ham 58-64; C-in-c of Low Ham 58-64; R of St Mary w St Paul Hulme Man 64-68; V of Shaw 68-72; C-in-c of Heaton Norris 72-75; Hon C of Ch Ch Davyhulme 75-77; Hon C-in-c of Rosslyn Chap Dio Edin from 77. *51 Moat View, Roslin, Midlothian, EH25 9NZ.* (031-440 1678)

DOWNING, Francis Gerald. b 35. Qu Coll Ox BA (1st cl Th) 56, MA 60. Linc Th Coll. **d** 58 **p** 59 Bris. C of H Cross Filwood Pk 58-60; Tutor Linc Th Coll 60-64; L to Offic Dio Linc 60-64; V of Unsworth 64-80; Henson Lect Ox 73-74; on staff of N Ordin Course from 80; L to Offic Dio Man from 80. *44 Cleveland Road, Crumpsall, Manchester, M8 6QU.* (061-740 1200)

DOWNING, Nicholas Probert. b 11. MBE 55. Ripon Hall Ox 58. **d** 59 **p** 60 Cov. C of Bilton 59-63; V of Ettington 63-78; Loxley 63-78; Perm to Offic Dio Cov from 80. *Oldborough Farm Cottage, Loxley, Warwick, CV35 9JW.*

DOWNS, Albert Victor. b 05. Lon Coll of Div 50. **d** and **p** 51 Chich. [f Free Ch Min] C of St Matt St Leonards-on-Sea 51-53; Cranleigh 53-56; Wimbledon (in c of Ch Ch) 56-59; R of Denton w S Heighton and Tarring Neville 59-66; V of Heathfield 66-73; C of Bodiam 73-74; Salehurst 73-74; Ewhurst 74-78; Perm to Offic Dios Cant and Chich from 78. *93 High Street, Tenterden, Kent, TN30 6LB.* (Tenterden 2076)

DOWNS, Ivan Frederick. b 26. Chich Th Coll 65. **d** 66 **p** 67 Newc T. C of Corbridge-on-Tyne 66-70; Tynemouth 70-74; V of Walker 74-79; Dudley Dio Newc T from 79. *Vicarage, Dudley, Cramlington, Northumb, NE23 7HR.* (Newc T 500251)

DOWNS, Thomas Greaves. b 19. Qu Coll Birm 74. **d** 76 Heref **p** 79 Penrith for Carl. C of Tenbury Wells 76-78; Crosthwaite Keswick 79-81; Perm to Offic Dio Carl from 81. *Woodlands, Edenhall, Penrith, Cumbria, CA11 8SR.* (Penrith 63131)

DOWSE, Edgar. b 10. Univ of Dur LTh 35. Univ of Lon BD 37, 1st cl Hons 39. Fitzw Ho Cam (1st cl Th Trip 41) BA 72, MA 74. Clifton Th Coll 32. **d** 35 **p** 36 Bris. Asst Chap and Tutor Clifton Th Coll 35-36; C of St Andr Chippenham 36-40; Tutor St Andr Th Coll Whittlesford and L to Offic Dio Ely 40-42; C of St Mich AA Bournemouth 42-45; C-in-c of Ch of Epiph Moordown Bournemouth 45-51; R of Freemantle 51-57; V of St Bart Bethnal Green 57-70; Lect Lon Bible Coll 60-61; St Antholin Lect at St Mich, Cornhill Lon 60-63; at St Steph Walbrook Lon 65-68; at St Dunstan-in-the-W Lon 70-71; C-in-c of St Alb Acton Green 71-72; V 72-75; Hon C of St John Isleworth Dio Lon from 75. *87 College Road, Isleworth, Middx.* (01-568 2548)

DOWSE, Ivor Roy. b 35. St Deiniol's Libr Hawarden. **d** 68 **p** 70 Willesden for Lon. C of St Pet, Harrow 68-69; Sudbury Middx 69-71; Weeke 71-73; Chap Ban Cathl 73-78; V of Hollym w Welwick and Holmpton 78-81; R of Bearwood Dio Ox from 81. *Rectory, St Catherine's Close, Sindlesham, Wokingham, Berks, RG11 5BZ.* (Wokingham 791763)

DOWSE, Canon Leonard. b 17. Univ of Wales, BA 39. St Mich Coll Llan 39. **d** 40 **p** 41 Llan. C of Cadoxton-juxta-Barry 40-44; Llanishen w Lisvane 44-50; P-in-c of St Dyfrig Cardiff 50-56; V of Llanishen w Lisvane Dio Llan from 56; Surr from 56; RD of Caerphilly from 63; Can of St Nich in Llan Cathl from 69. *Llanishen Vicarage, Cardiff.* (Cardiff 752545)

DOWSE, Richard Henry. b 1900. TCD Hebr Pri and Wall Bible Scho 21, Syriac and Aramaic Pri 22, BA (Sen Mod) 23, Bibl Gr Pri 24, Div Test 26, MA 34. **d** 26 **p** 27 Down. C of Bangor 26-29; St Ann Dub 29-34; I of St Pet w St Audoen Dub 34-75; RD of St Pet 45-75; Commiss Delhi 61-66; Can and Preb of St Patr Cathl Dub 62-73; Prec 73-75. *16 Earlsfoot Terrace, Dublin, Irish Republic.* (Dublin 65314)

DOWSETT, Alan Charles. b 27. Selw Coll Cam BA 51, MA 55. Cudd Coll 51. **d** 53 **p** 54 Portsm. C of Portsea 53-57; Wokingham 57-60; V of Water Orton 60-64; Chap Colston's Sch Stapleton Bris from 64; C of Stoke Bp 64-67; LPr Dio Bris from 69. *23 Upper Cranbrook Road, Redland, Bristol, BS6 7UW.* (Bristol 43227)

DOWSON, Roger Christopher. b 32. Clifton Th Coll 60. **d** 63 **p** 64 Guildf. C of Virginia Water 63-66; Darfield 66-68; V of Thorpe Edge 68-80; Wyke Dio Bradf from 80. *Vicarage, Vicarage Close, Wyke, Bradford, W Yorks.*

DOWTHWAITE, Robert Hedley. b 09. Late Exhib of St Jo Coll Dur LTh 31. BA 32. St Aid Coll 28. **d** 32 **p** 33 Liv. C of Rainford 32-39; St Geo Wigan 39-44; V of Abram 44-78. *23 Eccleston Street, Wigan, Lancs.*

DOWTHWAITE, Robert William. BD (Lon) 58. Moore Th Coll Syd ACT ThL (2nd cl) 57. **d** 58 **p** 60 Bp Morris. In C of E in S Afr 58-65 and 68-69; C of Mittagong 69-71; R of Sutton Forest 71-75; Perm to Offic Dio C & Goulb 75-76; Dio Syd from 76; Gen Sec Afr Evang Fellowship from 76. *Box 292, Castle Hill, NSW, Australia 2154.* (634-4682)

DOXSEY, Roy Desmond. St D Coll Lamp 64. **d** 67 **p** 68 St D. C of Pembroke 67-70; Milford Haven 70-73; Loughton 73-75; Chap Llandovery Coll 75-81; Miss at Luanshya Dio Centr Zam from 81. *Box 90189, Luanshya, Zambia.*

DOYLE, Canon Alan Holland. b 22. Univ of Lon BD 55. Wycl Hall Ox 52. **d** 52 **p** 53 S & M. C of Braddan 52-54; St Geo Douglas IM 54-55; V of St Andr Oldham 55-59; Chap Dioc Prep Sch for Boys Ruzawi 59-62; V of Chaddesley Corbett 62-66; St Jo Bapt Kidderminster 66-67; R of Salwarpe 67-74; CF (TA) 63-67; RD of Droitwich 69-78; P-in-c of Himbleton w Huddington 74-78; Hon Can of Worc from 74; R of Ombersley w Doverdale Dio Worc from 78. *Ombersley Rectory, Droitwich, Worcs, WR9 0DR.* (Worc 620950)

DOYLE, Canon Alfred Thomas Laurence. b 10. St Jo Coll Dur BA 32, Dipl in Th 33, MA 35. **d** 33 **p** 34 Chelmsf. C of All SS Leyton 33-36; St Jo Bapt (in c of St Mark) Southend 36-40; V of St Barn Birm 40-50; St Mary and St Ambrose Edgbaston 50-75; Hon Can of Birm 69-75; Can (Emer) from 75; Perm to Offic Dios Truro and Ex from 75. *Norr Rock, The Cleave, Kingsand, Cornw, PL10 1NF.* (Plymouth 822944)

DOYLE, Graham Thomas. ACT ThL 73. St Barn Coll Adel 72. **d** 73 **p** 74 Riv. C of Leeton 73-76; Broken Hill 76-77; St D Cathl Hobart 77-79; P-in-c of Latrobe Dio Tas 79-80; R from 80. *Rectory, Latrobe, Tasmania 7307.* (004-26 1104)

DOYLE, John Ernest. b 1889. St Jo Coll Winnipeg. **d** 17 **p** 18 Rupld. C of Gladstone 17-18; I 18-22; C of Camus-juxta-Mourne 22-26; C-in-c of Convoy 26-31; I of Donagheady 31-37; Killygarvan w Glenalla 36-62; Sec Bd of Relig Educn Dio Derry and Raph 37-62; RD of Kilmacrenan E 46-60; Can of Raph 49-60; Dean 60-62. *10 Ennismore Avenue, Guildford, Surrey.* (Guildford 5586)

DOYLE, Robert Colin. b 47. Univ of Syd BSc 70. Moore Coll Syd ACT ThL 74. BD (Lon) 75. **d** and **p** 76 Syd. C of St Steph Willoughby NSW 76-78; P-in-c of St Clem Aber 79-81; Lect Moore Th Coll Syd from 82. *Moore Theological College, Carillon Avenue, Newtown, NSW, Australia.*

DOYLE, Robin Alfred. b 43. Univ of Dur BA 65. Westcott Ho Cam 66. **d** 68 Bp Sinker for Birm **p** 69 Birm. C of St Geo Edgbaston 68-70; Erdington 70-73; P-in-c of Oldbury 73-81; V of Maker w Rame Dio Truro from 81. *Maker Vicarage, Fore Street, Kingsand, Cornw, PL10 1NB.* (Plymouth 822302)

DRACKLEY, John Oldham. b 36. Em Coll Cam BA 57, MA 61. Wells Th Coll 57. **d** 59 Bp Sinker for Derby **p** 60 Derby. C of Eckington 59-62; Good Shepherd Lee 62-63; Thos Ap Derby 63-67; Matlock w Tansley 67-77; P-in-c of Dalbury and Long Lane Dio Derby from 77; Radbourne Dio Derby from 77; Longford Dio Derby from 77. *Long Lane Vicarage, Dalbury Lees, Derby.* (Kirk Langley 560)

DRAGE, Michael Campbell. b 36. Fitzw Coll Cam BA 67, MA 70. Ridley Hall Cam 64. **d** 67 Nor **p** 68 Lynn for Nor. C of Eaton 67-71; Relig Educn Adv Dio Cant 71-74; Asst Master John Bentley Comprehensive Sch Calne from 74. *John Bentley School, Calne, Wilts.* (Calne 814449)

DRAIN, Walter. b 39. ACP 66. Open Univ BA 76. N-W Ordin Course 76. **d** 79 **p** 80 Ches (APM). C of Cheadle (in c of St Cuthb) Dio Ches from 79. *St Cuthbert's Curatage, Cuthbert Road, Cheadle, Chesh, SK8 2DT.* (061-428 3983)

DRAKE, Bryan Douglas. St Jo Coll Auckld NZ BD of Th Stud LTh (2nd cl) 65. **d** 65 **p** 66 Auckld. C of St Andr Epsom Auckld 65-68; Papakura 68-70; V of Bombay Auckld 71-73; Blockhouse Bay 73-75; Ascen Sing 75-81; Ellerslie Dio Auckld from 81. *167 Ladies Mile, Ellerslie, Auckland 5, NZ.*

DRAKE, Francis Mackworth. b 01. Late Exhib of Ex Coll Ox BA 24, MA 32. Wycl Hall Ox 40. **d** 40 **p** 41 Lich. Chap of Wrekin Coll Wellington 40-45; Hd Master Bp Cotton Sch Simla 45-49; Prin Monnaie Sch Guernsey and Perm to Offic Dio Win 50-60; Chap Burrswood Nursing Home and Healing Centre Groombridge 60-62; Perm to Offic Dio Win from 64; Warden Monnaie Home of Rest and Healing 64-68; C of St Andr Guernsey (in c of Ch the Healer) Dio Win from 68. *Le Gron Cottage, St Saviour's, Guernsey, CI.*

DRAKE, Graham Rae. b 45. Fitzw Coll Cam 3rd cl Geo Trip pt i 67, pt ii 68, BA 68, MA 72. Qu Coll Birm 70. **d** 73 Buckingham for Ox **p** 74 Ox. C of New Windsor 73-77; Team V of New Windsor 77-78; C-in-c of Ascen Bath 78-81; Team V of Marlbrook, Bath Dio B & W from 81. *Ascension Vicarage, Bath, Avon.* (Bath 21971)

DRAKE, John Paul. b 19. Late Scho of Qu Coll Ox BA 41, MA 44. Cudd Coll 46. **d** 47 Lon **p** 48 Stepney for Lon. C of St Dunstan w All SS Stepney 47-54; Chap to Lon Hosp 51-54; V of All S Brighton 54-59; Chap to St Edw Sch Ox 59-69; V of Stewkley (w Soulbury & Drayton Parslow from 75) Dio Ox from 69; C-in-c of Drayton-Parslow 69-75; Soulbury 72-75; RD of Mursley from 77. *Stewkley Vicarage, Leighton Buzzard, Beds, LU7 0OH.* (Stewkley 287)

DRAKE, Leslie Sargent. b 47. Univ of Boston Mass BA 69, ThM 72. Univ of Hull BPhil 74. Coll of the Resurr Mirfield 78. **d** 78 **p** 79 Man. C of Oldham 78-81; Team V of Rochdale Dio Man from 81. *498 Manchester Road, Sudden, Rochdale, Gtr Man, OL11 3HE.* (Rochdale 31812)

DRAKE, William Brereton. b 1885. Trin Coll Ox BA 07, MA 10. Cudd Coll 07. **d** 08 S'wark **p** 09 Woolwich for S'wark. C of St Jo Div Kennington 08-11; Miss at Quesnel BC 11; C of St Jo Div Kennington 12-19; L Houghton w Brafield-on-the-Green 19-22; V of Dorchester w Burcott Oxon 22-25; Soulbury 25-51; RD of Ivinghoe 47-51; C of St Mary Arches Ex 51-61; Hon C of St Matt City and Dio Ex and Perm to Offic Dio Ex from 61-69. *27 Southernhay East, Exeter, Devon.* (Exeter 71137)

DRAKE, William Nevill. Ch Coll NZ. **d** 40 Ch Ch for Wai **p** 42 Auckld for Wai. C of H Trin Gisborne 40-44; CF (NZ) 44-46; Actg V of Whakatane 46-47; V of Pukekohe 47-56; St Alb Auckld 56-65; St Pet Onehunga 65-73; S Hokianga 73-74; Min 74-76; Offg Min Dio Wai from 76. *75 Rifle Range Road, Taupo, NZ.*

DRAKE-BROCKMAN, Archibald David. b 12. Late Scho of Magd Coll Cam 1st cl Cl Trip pt i w Distinc 32, BA (1st cl Cl Trip pt ii w distinc) and Lady Kay Scho Jes Coll Cam 34, 1st cl Th Trip pt ii and Sen Scholefield Pri 35, MA 37. Ely Th Coll 35. **d** 36 **p** 37 Ox. C of St Mary Virg Ox 36; Asst Master Eton Coll 36-38; L to Offic Dio Ox 36-39; Chap Bradfield Coll 38-41; Asst Master 41-48; V of Framfield 48-49; Asst Master Bedford Sch from 49; Chap 49-65; L to Offic Dio St E from 70. *Rosemary Cottage, Grundisburgh, Woodbridge, Suff, IP13 6RA.*

DRAKE-BROCKMAN, David Richard. b 33. Wells Th Coll 65. **d** 67 **p** 68 Bris. C of H Nativ Knowle 67-69; P-in-c of St Barn Georgetn 69; V of NE La Penitence 69-70; C of Lymington 70-73; Chap Miss to Seamen Suva, Fiji 73-76; V of Longwood Dio Wakef from 76. *313 Vicarage Road, Longwood, Huddersfield, HD3 4HJ.* (Huddersfield 653576)

DRAKELEY, Stephen Richard Francis. b 51. Univ of Aston in Birm BSc 73. Chich Th Coll 76. **d** 76 **p** 77 Birm. C of Yardley Wood 76-79; V of Rednal Dio Birm from 79. *Vicarage, Edgewood Road, Rednal, Birmingham, B45 8SG.* (021-453 3347)

DRAKES, Christopher St Clair. b 35. Em & St Chad's Coll Sktn 67. **d** and **p** 71 Trinid. C of St Paul Sanfernando 71-72; R of St Patr Mt Pleasant 73-80; Sangre Grande Dio Trinid from 80. *Rectory, Sangre Grande, Trinidad, W Indies.*

DRAKU, Girisimu. b 47. Bp Tucker Coll Mukono 75. **d** 76 **p** 77 M & W Nile. P Dio M & W Nile. *PO Box 370, Arua, Uganda.*

DRAKU, Semi. b 42. Bp Tucker Coll Mukono 76. **d** 77 **p** 78 M & W Nile. P Dio M & W Nile. *PO Box 370, Arua, Uganda.*

DRALEA, Sitefano. **d** 66 **p** 67 N Ugan. P Dio N Ugan 66-69; Dio M & W Nile from 69. *Box 37, Arua, Uganda.*

DRAMANI, Manaseh. b 36. Bp Tucker Coll Mukono 63. **d** 73 M & W Nile. d Dio M & W Nile. *Box 169, Arua, Uganda.*

DRAPER, Ven Alfred James. b 23. Univ of Natal BA 50. St Paul's Coll Grahmstn LTh 54. St Aug Coll Cant Dipl Th 59. **d** and **p** 54 Natal. C of St Paul Durban 54-58; V of Umkomaas 60-63; PC of St Pet Tile Cross Yardley 63-68; V 68-72; Olton 72-75; R of St Paul Durban Dio Natal from 75; Archd Dio Natal from 79. *St Paul's Church, Church Street, Durban, Natal, S Africa.* (Durban 23770)

DRAPER, Charles John. Wycl Coll Tor. **d** 30 **p** 31 Hur. I of Ripley and Pine River 30-31; St John Walpole I 31-34; Wiarton w Hepworth 34-40; C-in-c of St John Sarnia 40-41; I of Milverton w Millbank and Elma 41-46; St Pet Ohsweken w St Paul and St Barn Kanyengeh 46-47; I of Thamesville Dresden and Moraviantown 47-51; St Mark Windsor 51-56; C of St Mary Walkerville 56-59; St Mary Windsor 69-70. *2 Cecil Street, Ridgetown, Ont., Canada.*

DRAPER, Derek Vincent. b 38. Linc Th Coll 65. **d** 68 **p** 69 Roch. C of Orpington 68-72; Bramley 72-74; Min of Transfig Conv Distr Kempston 74-76; P-in-c of Transfig Kempston Dio St Alb 76-79: V from 79; RD of Bedford from 79. *132 Bedford Road, Kempton, Beds.* (Bedford 854788)

DRAPER, Jack William. b 18. Oak Hill Th Coll 51. **d** 53 **p** 54 Nor. C of New Catton 53-54; R of Colney w Earlham 54-57; V of W Ashton 57-62; C-in-c of Heywood 60-62; R of

Bramerton w Surlingham 62-70; Bramerton Group 70-75; RD of Loddon 71-75; P-in-c of Hoxne w Denham St John Dio St E 75-79; V (w Syleham) from 79; P-in-c of Syleham 76-79; Surr from 81. *Hoxne Vicarage, Eye, Suff.* (Hoxne 246)

DRAPER, James William. b 46. Unit of Tor BA 68. Trin Coll Tor STB 71, MTh 73. **d** 71 **p** 73 Tor. On leave 71-72; Tutor & Lect Bp Patteson Th Centre Melan 73-75; Lect St Jo Coll Winnipeg 75-78; Actg Dean of Div 78-80; Dean from 80; C of Good Shepherd Winnipeg Dio Rupld from 81. *St John's College, 400 Dysart Road, Winnipeg, Manit, Canada, R3T 2M5.*

DRAPER, Jonathan Alfred. b 49. Univ of Dur BA 71. Rhodes Univ Grahmstn BD 78. St Paul's Coll Grahmstn 74. **d** 77 **p** 78 Zulu. C of Empangeni Dio Zulu from 77. *PO Box 55, Empangeni 3880, S Africa.*

DRAPER, Canon Jonathan Ernest. b 1895. St Paul's Miss Coll Burgh 15. Univ of Dur LTh 21. **d** 21 Lon for Col **p** 22 Wai. C of Dannevirke 21-23; Hastings 23-25; V of Opotiki 25-30; Ch of H Sepul Auckld 30-36; R of Halton Holgate 37-43; Toynton St Pet w All SS 43-52; RD of Bolingbroke 43-52; Commiss Auckld 49-60; V of Willoughton 52-60; R of Blyborough 52-60; RD of Aslackhoe 53-60; Can and Preb of Heydour w Walton in Linc Cathl 54-66; Can (Emer) from 66; R of Caythorpe 60-66; RD of Loveden 60-64; Chap and Warden St Anne's Bedehouses Linc 66-72. *17 Chellaston Lane, Aston on Trent, Derby, DE7 2AX.*

DRAPER, Martin Paul. b 50. Univ of birm BA 72. Univ of Southn BTh 79. Chich Th Coll 72. **d** 75 Lon **p** 76 Edmon for Lon. C of St Mary Virg Primrose Hill Hampstead 75-79; St Matt Gt Pet Street Westmr Dio Lon from 79. *20 Great Peter Street, SW1.* (01-222 7466)

DRAPER, Raymond James. b 48. Ex Coll Ox BA 70, MA 75. Em Coll Cam BA 73, MA 78. ridley Hall Cam 71. **d** 74 Doncaster for Sheff **p** 75 Sheff. C of Sheff Manor 74-78; Chap Sheff Industr Miss from 78. *28 Aldred Street, Rotherham, S Yorks, S65 2AL.*

DRAPER, Canon William. **d** 51 Knaresborough for Alg **p** 51 Alg. C-in-c of All SS White River 51-52; I of Red Rock w Nipigon 52-54; C of St Jo Bapt St John 54-55; Moncton 55-56; Miss Gordon 56-58; I of Coverdale w Hillsboro 58-67; Simmonds 67-71; Marysville w Maugerville Dio Fred from 71; Dom Chap to Bp of Fred from 76; Can of Fred from 81. *169 Canada Street, Marysville, NB, Canada E3A 3Z7.*

DRATI LEE, Enoka. b 40. Bp Tucker Coll Mukono 70. **d** 73 M & W Nile. d Dio M & W Nile. *Box 52, Moyo, Uganda.*

DRAVU, Aron. Buwalasi Th Coll 56. **d** 59 U Nile **p** 61 N Ugan. P Dio N Ugan 59-69; Dio M and W Nile from 69. *PO Koboko, Uganda.*

DRAY, Robert William. b 30. Wells Th Coll 62. **d** 64 **p** 65 St Alb. C of Bushey Heath 64-68; C-in-c of H Cross Conv Distr Marsh Farm Luton 68-71; V of Hatfield Hyde Dio St Alb from 71. *Vicarage, Ludwick Way, Welwyn Garden City, Herts.* (Welwyn Garden City 22313)

DRAYCOTT, Christopher John Philip. Cudd Coll 77. **d** 79 **p** 80 Lich. C of Horninglow Dio Lich from 79. *Vicarage Flat, Rolleston Road, Horninglow, Burton-on-Trent DE13 0JZ.*

DRAYCOTT, Derrick. b 16. St Aid Coll 54. **d** 56 **p** 57 Sheff. C of Wadsley 56-59; C-in-c of All SS Sheff 59-61; C of Darfield 61-63; V of Barnby dun 63-68; Cowick 68-72; Kilnhurst 72-80. *Address temp unknown.*

DRAYSON, Nicholas James Quested. b 53. Keble Coll Ox BA. **d** 79 Bp Marino for N Argent **p** 79 N Argent. Chap Chorote Ch Dio N Argent from 79. *Casilla 30, 4560 Tartagal, Salta, Argentina.*

DRAYTON, John Leslie. Moore Th Coll Syd ACT ThL 54. **d** and **p** 55 Syd. C of Port Kembla 55-57; Manly 57-58; C-in-c of Forestville w Narraweena 58-61; Flemington w Homebush 61-70; Newport Dio Syd 70-74; R from 74. *4 Foamcrest Avenue, Newport Beach, NSW, Australia 2106.* (99-1495)

DRAYTON, Kenneth John. Ridley Coll Melb 60. **d** 62 **p** 63 Armid. C of Moree 62-66; P-in-c of Tambar Springs 66-69; R of Trayning 69-73; Maylands Dio Perth from 73. *2 Rowlands Street, Maylands, W Australia 6051.* (71 1263)

DREDGE, David John. b 32. Cranmer Hall Dur 69. **d** 71 **p** 72 Sheff. C of Goole 71-74; V of Whitgift w Adlingfleet (and Eastoft from 77) 74-78; C-in-c of Eastoft 74-77; V of Walkley 78-81; Team V of Bicester w Bucknell, Caversfield and Launton Dio Ox from 81. *St Peter's Vicarage, Severn Close, Bicester, OX6 8NN.* (Bicester 43941)

DREDGE, William Thomas. b 1890. Univ of Wales BA 13. St Mich Coll Llan 15. **d** 15 **p** 16 Llan. C of St Jas Tredegar 15-17; Aberavon 18-24; C-in-c of St Agnes Conv Distr Port Talbot 24-30; Chap Rampton State Inst 30-54; R of Flintham w Kneeton 54-57; Perm to Offic Dio Linc 57-59; C of St Mary le Wigford w St Martin Linc 59-65. *114 Doddington Road, Lincoln.* (Lincoln 63377)

DREW, Arthur O'Neill. b 1896. CCC Ox BA 20, MA 22. Westcott Ho Cam 37. **d** 37 **p** 38 Liv. C of St Luke Eccleston 37-39; R of Clayhanger 39-43; PC of Petton Chap 39-43; V of Letcombe Regis w Bassett R 43-61; Dioc Insp of Schs Dio Ox 44-58; C of Albury w St Martha 63-73. *Ramsay Hall, Byron Road, Worthing, Sussex.*

DREW, Emlyn Floyd. b 06. Lich Th Coll. **d** and **p** 57 Ex. C of Paignton 57-59; V of Christow 59-68; Branscombe 68-71; Perm to Offic Dio Ex from 73. *3 James Close, Elburton, Plymouth.* (Plymouth 41411)

DREW, Gerald Arthur. b 36. Bps' Coll Cheshunt 59. 61 Bedford for St Alb **p** 62 St Alb. C of H Trin, Lyonsdown, New Barnet 61-67; Tring 67-71; R of Bramfield w Stapleford and Waterford 71-78; Langleybury Dio St Alb from 78. *Vicarage, Watford Road, Langleybury, Kings Langley, Herts WD4 8QR.* (Kings Langley 63169)

DREW, Gordon William. b 04. Kelham Th Coll 26. **d** 29 **p** 30 Worc. C of Bromsgrove 29-31; Tideswell 31-34; R of Intwood w Keswick 34-55; CF 40-45; Chap Highcroft Hall Hosp Birm 55-62. *Meadow Cottage, Bleasby Moor, Market Rasen, Lincs.*

DREW, John Whatley. b 24. CCC Cam BA 54, MA 58. Kelham Th Coll 46. **d** 51 **p** 52 Ely. C of St Andr Gt Cam 51-54; St Barn Northolt 54-57; St Jas Gt w St Jude Bethnal Green 57-60; V of Thorington w Wenhaston 60-76; Leiston w Sizewell Dio St E from 76. *Vicarage, Leiston, Suff.* (Leiston 830640)

DREW, Joseph Harold. b 09. Late Scho of St D Coll Lamp BA (3rd cl Engl) 30. St Mich Coll Llan. **d** 32 **p** 33 Mon. C of Blaenavon 32-35; St Sav. Roath 35-38; St Jo Bapt Newport Mon 38-39; V 39-50; Chap HM Borstal Inst Feltham 50-55; HM Pris Man 55-58; Pentonville 58-63; Chap-Sec Ch Assembly Pris Chap Coun and ACG HM Pris Dept 64-74. *58 Cambridge Drive, Lee, SE12 8AJ.* (01-852 8031)

DREW, Michael Edgar Cecil. b 31. Or Coll Ox BA (2nd cl Mod lang) 55, MA 59. St Steph Ho Ox. **d** 57 **p** 58 Ex. C of St Pet Plymouth 57-63; Missr at Pemb Coll Cam Miss (St Chris Conv Distr) Walworth 63-67; Asst Chap Allhallows Sch Rousdon 67-75; L to Offic Dio Ex 67-76; Perm to Offic from 76; Asst Master Honiton Coll 75-80; Chap All H Sch Rousdon 80-81; Ex Sch from 81. *3 Friars Walk, Exeter.*

DREWER, Sydney Walter. St Jo Hall Dur BA 13. Lon Coll of Div 11. **d** 14 **p** 15 Sarum. C of St John Weymouth 14-17; Wimbledon 17-18; served in Artists Rifles 18-19; C of Ch Ch Clifton 19-21; V of St Pet Clifton Wood 21-26; Poughill 26-34; St Luke Bedminster 34-51; Poughill 51-59. *Tindage, Poughill, Bude, Cornw.* (Bude 2824)

DREWETT, Francis Edward. b 12. Univ of Bris BSc 36. St Mich Coll Llan 36. **d** 37 **p** 38 Swan B for Llan. C of St Anne Ynyshir 37-39; St Thos w Immanuel Birm 39-42; St Mary Handsworth 42-43; V of Langley 43-50; CMS Area Sec Dios Chich Guildf and Portsm 50-54; V of St Matt Croydon 54-79. *10 Larkfield Avenue, Chepstow, Gwent.*

DREWETT, Canon Mervyn Henry. b 27. Wadh Coll Ox BA 50, MA 53. Linc Th Coll 52. **d** 54 Malmesbury for Bris **p** 55 Bris. C of Filwood Pk 54-58; Bishopston 58-61; V of St Chris Brislington 61-67; Henbury w Hallen 67-80; RD of Westbury and Severnside 79-80; Hon Can of Bris Cathl from 80; Team R of Gtr Corsham Dio Bris from 80. *Rectory, Lacock Road, Corsham, Wilts, SN13 9HS.*

DREWETT, Robert John. b 40. Ripon Hall Ox 64. **d** 66 Bris **p** 67 Malmesbury for Bris. C of St Jo Div Fishponds 66-70; Oldland 70-74; C-in-c of Coalpit Heath 74-76. *c/o Vicarage, Coalpit Heath, Bristol.* (Winterbourne 772270)

DREWLO, Elizabeth Jean. **d** 74 **p** 78 Bran. C of Easterville w Grand Rapids Miss 78-81; on leave. *c/o Church House, 600 Jarvis Street, Toronto, Ont, Canada, M4Y 2J6.*

DRILLEN, Canon Thomas Hubert. K Coll NS BA 42, BLitt 44. **d** 43 **p** 44 Fred. C of New Bandon Dio Fred 43-44; R from 44; Can of Fred from 74. *Box 1000, Bathurst, NB, Canada.*

DRINKWATER, Arthur Leopold. Pemb Coll Ox BA 17. Ridley Hall Cam 17. **d** 17 **p** 19 Glouc. C of Woodside Cinderford 17-22; Perm to Offic Dio St Alb and Asst Master Lon Orphan Sch Watford 22-24; Org Sec CCCS for NE Distr 24-27; for S Distr 27-29; R of L Bookham 29-58; Perm to Offic Dio Guildf from 58. *90 Links Road, Ashtead, Surrey.*

DRINKWATER, Frank. b 10. K Coll Lon BSc 32, AKC 34. **d** 34 Knaresborough for Ripon **p** 35 Ripon. C of St Pet Hunslet Moor 34-36; CMS Miss Dio Niger 37-55; Prin Awka Coll Dio Niger 46-52; Exam Chap to Bp on the Niger 46-54; to Bp on Nig Delta 52-54; Hon Can of Niger and Educn Sec Dio Niger 52-54; Lect St Mary's Tr Coll and Asst Chap Cheltm Tr Colls 55-61; Commiss Niger 55-69; Benin 64-76; V of St Lawr Mansfield 61-67; Chap Bp King Secondary Sch Linc 67-69; C of Earley 69-72; V of Coley 72-77; RD of Brighouse and Elland 74-77. *59 York Road, Tewkesbury, Glos.*

DRISCOLL, David. b 42. Univ of Lon BSc 64. Univ of

Nottm Dipl Th 69. Linc Th Coll 68. **d** 71 **p** 72 Barking for Chelmsf. C of St Jo Evang Walthamstow 71-76; Chap NE Lon Poly 71-79; C-in-c of Plaistow 76-79; P-in-c of Stratford Dio Chelmsf from 79. *20 Deanery Road, E15 4LP.* (01-534 8388)

DRISCOLL, Edward Llewellyn. b 09. Kelham Th Coll 33. **d** 38 **p** 39 Sarum. C of Warminster 38-42; V of Longbridge Deverill w Crockerton and Hill Deverill Warminster 42-45; Chap RNVR 45-46; V of St Jas Burnley 46-56; Ribbleton 56-67; Fairhaven 67-74; RD of Preston 64-67. *32 Ashley Road, Lytham St Anne's, Lancs, FY8 3As.*

DRIVER, Anthony. b 28. Chich Th Coll 76. **d** 76 Bp Isherwood for Gibr **p** 77 Fulham for Gibr. Prec & Port Missr Cathl Ch of H Trin Gibr 76-78; C of Harton Dio Dur from 78. *84 Canterbury Avenue, South Shields, T & W, NE34 6SF.* (S Shields 561747)

DRIVER, Arthur John Roberts. b 44. SS Coll Cam MA 70. Univ of Nottm Dipl Th 75. Linc Th Coll 74. **d** 76 **p** 77 S'wark. C of H Trin w St Matt S'wark 76-80; Team V of N Lambeth Dio S'wark from 80. *47 Walcot Square, SE11 4UB.* (01-735 4902)

DRIVER, Bruce Leslie. b 42. LLB (Lon) 73. Dipl Th (Nottm) 77. Linc Th Coll 76. **d** 78 **p** 79 St Alb. C of Dunstable 78-81; Team V from 81. *c/o 20 Friars Walk, Dunstable, LU6 3JA.*

DRIVER, Jeffrey William. b 51. Ridley Coll Melb 76. **d** 77 Bath. C of Reservoir 77. *c/o 30 Ralph Street, Reservoir, Vic., Australia 3073.*

DRIVER, Canon Stuart Clare. b 15. Ch Coll Cam BA 37, MA 41. Ridley Hall Cam 37. **d** 38 **p** 39 Man. C of St Luke Weaste 38-45; V of St Thos Werneth 45-80; Hon Can of Man 76-80; Can (Emer) from 80; RD of Oldham 76-80. *9 Brookside Lane, High Lane, Stockport, SK6 8HL.* (Disley 2263)

DROMORE, Archdeacon of. *See* Crooks, Ven Samuel Bennett.

DROMORE, Bishop of. *See* Down.

DROMORE, Dean of. *See* Lockhart, Very Rev Robert Joseph Norman.

DRONYI, Ven John. **d** 43 **p** 44 U Nile. P Dio U Nile 43-61; Hon Can 58-61; N Ugan 61-69; M & W Nile 69-70; Archd of Moyo 70-76; Koboko from 76. *PO Koboko, Uganda.*

DROUGHT, John Smerger. Trin Coll Melb BA 15, Dipl in Educn 23. ACT ThL 20. **d** 20 Melb **p** 21 Gippsld for Melb. Asst Chap Geelong Grammar Sch 20-21; C of All SS St Kilda 21-22; furlough 22-23 and 27-28; Min of Somerville 23-26; C of St Gabr Pimlico 27-28; I of Queenscliffe 28-34; Min of St Dunstan Middle Camberwell 34-44; I of St Paul Malvern 44-50; Chap-Gen Commun of H Name Melb 46-60; Actg Prin St Aid Coll Dogura 60-61; C of Moorabbin 61; I of Burwood 61-65; Perm to Offic Dio Melb from 65; Dio Murray from 72. *197 Archer Street, N Adelaide, S Australia 5006.*

DROUGHT, Thomas Godfrey. Univ of Melb BA 52. St Jo Coll Morpeth ACT ThL 52. **d** and **p** 53 Adel. C of Gawler 53-55; Miss Chap at Woodville Gdns 55-58; P-in-c of Morgan w Waikerie 58-59; R of Burra 59-64; P-in-c of Lockleys (w Kidman Pk 64-72) 64-75. *9 Douglas Street, Lockleys, S Australia 5032.* (08-43 8286)

DROWLEY, Arthur. b 28. Oak Hill Th Coll 54. **d** 56 Sherborne for Sarum **p** 57 Sarum. C of Longfleet 56-59; Wallington 59-62; V of St Jas Taunton 62-73; RD of Taunton North 72-73; V of Rodbourne Cheney Dio Bris from 73. *298 Cheney Manor Road, Swindon, SN2 2PF.* (Swindon 22379)

DROWN, Richard. b 19. BNC Ox BA (3rd cl Th) 41, MA 45. Wycl Hall Ox 41. **d** 42 **p** 43 Liv. C of St Helens 42-45; CMS Miss Budo Ugan 45-52; Chap and Tutor K Coll Budo 57-64; Hd Master St Andr Sch Turi 65-73; Edin Ho Sch New Milton from 73; L to Offic Dio Nak 67-73; Dio Win from 73. *Edinburgh House School, New Milton, Hants.*

DRUCE, Brian Lemuel. b 31. Bps' Coll Cheshunt 58. **d** 60 **p** 61 Lon. C of St Aug Whitton 60-63; Minehead 63-66; R of St Agnes, Birch-in-Rusholme 66-70; V of Overbury w Teddington, Alstone and Little Washbourne 70-81; Agr Chap Worcs Industr Miss from 81. *Madge Hill, Severn Stoke, Worcester, WR8 9JN.* (Severn Stoke 260)

DRUCE, James Milton. b 10. Em Coll Cam BA 33, MA 76. Wycl Hall Ox 75. **d** 76 Taunton for B & W **p** 77 B & W. C of Ch Ch Clevedon Dio B & W 76-80; Hon C from 80. *26 Edward Road South, Clevedon, Avon, BS21 7JA.*

DRUCE, John Perry. b 34. Em Coll Cam BA 57, MA 61. Wycl Hall Ox 57. **d** 59 Stafford for Lich **p** 60 Lich. C of St Bart Wednesbury 59-62; Bushbury 62-64; V of Walsall Wood 64-74; R of Farnborough Kent Dio Roch from 74. *Rectory, Farnborough, Kent, BR6 7EQ.* (Farnborough 53471)

DRUDE, Bismarck Frederick. St Pet Coll Alice. **d** 65 **p** 66 Kimb K. C of St Barn Kimb 65-68; R of St Thos De Aar 68-77; St Andr Riversdale Dio Geo from 77. *PO Box 28, Riversdale, CP, S Africa.* (Riversdale 45)

DRUETT, Albert Edward. b 05. BSc (Lon) 30. Cudd Coll. **d** 64 **p** 65 Ox. C of Wendover 64-67; Bramley Surrey 67-68; C-in-c of Loughton w Bradwell 68-71; C-in-c of Shenley 68-71; C of St Jas Riddlesdown 71-75; Perm to Offic Dio S'wark 75-77. *Address temp unknown.*

DRUITT, Geoffrey Poulter. b 05. Lon Coll of Div 28. Men in Disp 43 and 45. CBE 46. **d** 30 **p** 31 Chelmsf. C of Walthamstow 30-34; CF 34-53; DCG 44-46 and 50-53; ACG 46-50; Hon Chap to HM the King 51-52; to HM the Queen 52-53; V of Woodhouse Eaves 53-58; Chap HM Pris Linc 58-60; Dartmoor 60-64; Chap H Trin Cannes 64-69. *Border Cottage, 54 College Road, College Town, Camberley, Surrey.*

DRUITT, Canon Kenneth Harwood. b 1900. St Jo Coll Dur BA 26, MA 29. Dipl in Th 27. **d** 27 **p** 28 Chelmsf. C of West Ham 27-30; V of St Luke Deptford 30-51; RD of Greenwich and Deptford 44-51; Surr from 50; Hon Can of S'wark Cathl 50-51; V of Walthamstow Dio Chelmsf from 51; RD of Walthamstow and Chingford 52-75; Proc Conv Chelmsf 55-64; Hon Can of Chelmsf from 61. *Vicarage, Church Hill, Walthamstow, E17 3BD.*

DRUMMOND, Christopher John Vaughan. b 26. Magd Coll Ox BA (2nd cl Th) 51, MA 51. Magd Coll Cam MA (*by incorp*) 56. Ridley Hall Cam 51. **d** 53 **p** 54 Chelmsf. C of Barking 53-56; Tutor at Ridley Hall Cam 56-59; L to Offic Dio Ely 57-62; Chap Clare Coll Cam and Chas Simeon Chap to Univ 59-62; Lect Im Th Coll Ibad 63-67; Vice-Prin 67-69; L to Offic Dio Ibad 63-69; V of St Jo Evang Walthamstow 69-74; Commiss Ibad from 71; C-in-c of Stantonbury Dio Ox 74-75; Team R from 75. *Rectory, Great Linford, Milton Keynes, MK14 5BD.*

DRUMMOND, Canon Harold John. b 1881. Trin Coll Cam BA 03, MA 07. Ridley Hall Cam 03. **d** 05 **p** 06 York. C of St Mich and St Leon Malton 05-10; H Trin Bridlington 10-12; St Mary Wheatley Doncaster 12-13; V of Ch Ch Leic 14-56; C-in-c of St Luke Leic 36-43; Hon Can of Leic 37-58; Can (Emer) from 58. *51 Evington Drive, Leicester.* (Leicester 737137)

DRUMMOND, John Eric Mark. b 09. Univ of Allahabad BA 31. Bp's Coll Calc 33. **d** 36 **p** 37 Luckn. Dioc Chap Mussoorie 36; Allahabad 36-37; Saharanpur 37-38; Moradabad 38-39; Gorakhpur 39; Saharanpur and Roorkee 40-46; Chakrata 46-47; Mussoorie 47; Chap at Lucknow 48-52; C of St Gabr Plymouth 52; U Sunbury 52-53; Horfield 53-56; PC of St Anne Brislington 56-69; V of St Sav Woolcott Pk Clifton 69-74; L to Offic Dio Bris from 74. *9 Colston Parade, Redcliffe Hill, Bristol, BS1 6RA.*

DRUMMOND, John Malcolm. b 44. Edin Th Coll 68. **d** 71 Man **p** 72 Hulme for Man. C of St Thomas Kirkholt 71-74; St Pet Westleigh 74-76; Asst Master Leigh High Sch and L to Offic Dio Man from 76. *2 Eden Grove, Leigh, Lancs.* (Leigh 606879)

DRUMMOND, Josceline Maurice Vaughan. b 29. Dipl Th (Lon) 58. BD (Lon) 70. Wycl Hall Ox. **d** 58 **p** 59 Roch. C of St John Tunbridge Wells 58-60; Walthamstow 60-62; V of Oulton 62-68; St Cath Leyton Dio Chelmsf from 71; M Gen Syn from 80. *St Catherine's Vicarage, Fairlop Road, Leytonstone, E11 1BL.* (01-539 6361)

DRUMMOND, William Balfour. Trin Coll Dub BA 35, MA 62. **d** 36 **p** 37 Down. C of St Paul Belf 36-41; C-in-c of St Brendan Sydenham Belf Dio Down 42-62; R 62-70; C-in-c of Loughinisland Dio Down from 71. *Naghan Lodge, Seaforde, Downpatrick, Co Down.* (Seaforde 230)

DRURY, Esmond Peter. b 24. Univ of Sheff BSc 43. Univ of Newc T Dipl Educn 64. Coll of Resurr Mirfield. **d** 49 **p** 50 Derby. C of Alfreton 49-54; Long Eaton 54-55; Beighton 55-57; Min of Ch Ch Eccles Distr Hackenthorpe Beighton 57-60; Asst Master King's Sch Tynemouth 60-63; Lect Coll of Further Educn Newc T from 64. *74 Beach Road, Tynemouth, North Shields, T & W, NE20 2QW.* (North Shields 74350)

DRURY, John Henry. b 36. Trin Hall Cam 1st cl Hist Trip pt i 59, BA (2nd cl Th Trip pt ii) 61. Westcott Ho Cam 61. **d** 63 **p** 64 Lon. C of St John's Wood Ch 63-66; Chap Down Coll Cam 66-69; Chap, Fell and Lect Ex Coll Ox 69-73; Selet Pr Univ of Ox 73; and Univ of Cam 81; Can Res of Nor Cathl 73-79; Exam Chap to Bp of Nor 73-79; M Doctrine Comm C of E 77-81; Vice Dean of Nor 78-79; Lect Univ of Sussex 79-81; Exam Chap to Bp of Chich 80-81; Dean of K Coll Cam from 81. *King's College, Cambridge.*

DRURY, Michael Dru. b 31. Trin Coll Ox BA (2nd cl Geog) 55, MA 59, Dipl Th 57. Wycl Hall Ox 56. **d** 58 **p** 59 Lon. C of St Mary Fulham 58-62; St Jo Evang Blackheath 62-64; Asst Chap Canford Sch Wimborne 64-72; Chap 72-80; Chap Fernhill Manor Sch New Milton 80-81; C-in-c of Stowe Dio Ox from 82; Asst Chap and Asst Master Stowe Sch from 82. *Stowe icarage, Dadford, Buckingham, MK18 5JX.* (Buckingham 2285)

DRURY, Peter Alexander. b 44. St Jo Th Coll Auckld Jt Bd of Th Stud LTh 70. **d** 70 Bp Monteith for Auckld **p** 71 Auckld. C of St Phil, St Heliers Bay 70-72; Hon C of All SS Ponsonby Auckld 73-77; C of Milford 77-79; Chap Univ of Cant Ch Ch from 79. *20 Puriri Street, Christchurch 4, NZ.* (486-483)

DRURY, Thomas Frank. Westcott Ho Cam **d** 45 **p** 46 Heref. C of Ledbury 45-48; R of St Luke Miles Platting 48-52; V of Tonge w Breightmet 52-56; R of Kessingland 56-64; V of St Giles w St Benedict Nor 64-76; Chap W Nor Hosp 64-76; Bethel Hosp Nor 65-76; C-in-c of St Laur w St Greg Nor 66-75; Chap St Nich Hosp Gt Yarmouth from 76; Gen Hosp Gt Yarmouth from 78; Hon C of Caister Dio Nor from 78. *17 Brooke Avenue, Caister-on-Sea, Norf, NR30 5RN.*

DRURY, William. b 30. Qu Coll Cam BA 53, MA 56. Trin Coll Tor STB 61. **d** and **p** 61 Carib. P-in-c of Ashcroft w Clinton 61-62; V of Ashcroft 62-66; Clinton 62-63 and 65-66; C of Ashford 66-70; V of Milton Regis-next-Sittingbourne Dio Cant from 70. *Milton Regis Vicarage, Sittingbourne, Kent.* (Sittingbourne 72016)

DRY, John Malcolm. Ely Th Coll 53. **d** 55 Guildf **p** 56 Bp Hawkes for Cant. C of Farnham 55-59; Banstead 59-62; Weybridge 62-64; PC of Calow 64-67; St Thos-on-the-Bourne 67-71; Andover 71-74; P-in-c of Knight's Enham 74-75; R 76-78; P-in-c of Hatherden w Tangley Dio Win 78-81; V (w Weyhill and Penton Mewsey) from 81; P-in-c of Weyhill and Penton Mewsey 78-81. *Vicarage, Penton Mewsey, Andover, Hants.*

DRYBURGH, Canon Alexander Huntly. Coll Ho Ch Ch LTh 64. **d** 52 **p** 54 Wel. C of Hawera 53-55; V of Shannon 55-59; Youth Dir Wel 59-62; Dir Christian Educn Coun Dio Wel 62-71; V of Feilding 71-76; Taradale Dio Waik from 76; Can of Wai from 78. *23 Puketapu Road, Taradale, NZ.* (442-998)

DRYDEN, Albert Frederick. St Jo Coll Morpeth 35. ACT ThL 37. **d** 37 **p** 38 Bath. M of Bro of Good Shepherd Dubbo 37-41; Chap AIF 41-46; C of St Paul Burwood 46-47; L to Offic Dio Syd 50-52; Asst Master Pulteney Gr Sch and LPr Dio Adel 52-54; R of Coonamble 54-57; E Orange 57-60; Chap All SS Coll Bath 60-68; Perm to Offic Dio Syd from 69. *304 Camellia Court, Hopetoun Village, Castle Hill 2154.*

DRYDEN, Canon Leonard. b 29. MI MechE 59. MIEE 59. Univ of Lon BD 64. Univ of Bath MSc 73. Ridley Hall Cam. **d** 61 **p** 62 St Alb. C of Luton 61-65; C-in-c of St Thos Mart Bedminster 65-74; Social and Industr Adv to Bp of Bris 65-74; Bp's Cathl Chap 66-70; Hon Can of Bris 70-74; Can (Emer) from 74; Dir of Admin Stud, Chr Org Research and Advisory Trust 74-76; Team Leader and Convener of Lon Industr Chap from 76. *St Katharine Cree, Leadenhall Street, EC3A 3DH.* (01-283 5733)

DRYE, Douglas John. b 37. Univ of Man BSc 61. Clifton Th Coll. **d** 63 Middleton for Man **p** 64 Man. C of St Edm Whalley Range 63-66; Drypool 66-68; V of Worsbrough Common Dio Sheff from 68. *6 Mount Vernon Road, Barnsley, S Yorks, S70 4DJ.* (Barnsley 82619)

DRYLAND, James Paul. Moore Th Coll Syd 19. ACT ThL (1st cl) 19, Th Scho 26. **d** 19 **p** 20 Syd. C of Enmore NSW 19-21; All SS Leichhardt 21-24; R of Mortdale and Penshurst w Oatley and Peakhurst 24-28; St John Bishopthorpe Syd 28-53; LPr Dio Syd from 53. *24 Colane Street, Concord West, NSW 2138, Australia.*

DRYSDALE, Munro. Univ of Otago NZ BA 60, MA 61, BD 65. St Jo Coll Auckld 61. **d** 64 **p** 65 Auckld. C of Otara 64-67; Perm to Offic Dios Lon and S'wark 67-68; C of Papatoetoe 68-70; V of Wellsford 70-73; Team V of Mangere Miss Distr Auckld 73-76; R of Wentworth 77-81; Salisbury Dio Adel from 81. *Box 97, Salisbury, S Australia 5108.*

DUA-AWERE, George. **d** 76 **p** 77 Kum. P Dio Kum. *Box 17, Mampong, Ashanti, Ghana.*

DUAYBIS, Canon Khalil Ibrahim. Amer Univ of Beirut BA 53. Near East Sch of Th Beirut LTh 53. **d** 53 **p** 54 Jer. P Dio Jer; Hon Can of Nain in St Geo Colleg Ch Jer from 70. *Box 47, Nablus, Israel.*

DUBA, Ambrose Mbutana. St Bede's Coll Umtata. M CR 50. **d** 48 **p** 49 St Jo Kaffr. P Dio St Jo Kaffr; L to Offic Dio Johann 48 and 52-54; Miss P at Sophiatown City and Dio Johann from 54. *St Mary's Priory, Orlando, Johannesburg, S Africa.*

DUBE, Alson. St Jo Coll Umtata 46. **d** 48 **p** 49 Zulu. C of Mbabane Miss 48-53; Vryheid Miss 53-57; Bremersdorp and C-in-c of Ingwavuma 58-59; C of Rosettenville 59-61; Mafitleng 61-66; R 66-74; Etalaneni Dio Zulu from 74. *Etalaneni, PO Nkandla, Zululand.* (Thandanani 2)

DUBE, Richard. b 22. **d** 75 **p** 76 Matab. P Dio Matab 75-81; C of Coity w Nolton Dio Llan from 81. *13 Cae Odin, Brackla, Bridgend, Mid Glam.*

DUBE, Seth Lotyi. **d** 62 **p** 63 Zulu. P Dio Zulu 62-68; Dio Swaz from 68. *PO Box 6, Bunya, Swaziland.*

DUBLIN, Lord Archbishop of, Lord Bishop of Glendalough, Primate of Ireland, and Metropolitan. *See* McAdoo, Most Rev Henry Robert.

DUBLIN, Archdeacon of. *See* Warke, Ven Robert Alexander.

DUBLIN, Dean of (Christ Church). *See* Salmon, Very Rev Thomas Noel Desmond Cornwall.

DUBLIN, Dean of (St Patrick's). *See* Griffin, Very Rev Victor Gilbert Benjamin.

DUBY, Laurence Gene. Waterloo Lutheran Univ Ont BA 64. Trin Coll Tor STB 67. **d** 67 Niag. C of H Trin Welland 67-70; R of Good Shepherd St Catharines 70-75; Waterdown Dio Niag from 75. *182 Main Street North, Waterdown, Ont., Canada.* (416-689 4756)

DUCE, Alan Richard. St Pet Coll Ox BA 65, MA 68. Cudd Coll 65. **d** 67 **p** 68 Linc. C of Boston 67-71; Chap to St Geo Hosp Lon 71-75; HM Pris Pentonville 75-76; HM Pris The Verne Portland 76-81; HM Pris Linc from 81. *Chaplain's Office, HM Prison, Greetwell Road, Lincoln.* (0522 33633)

DUCHESNE, David George. Univ of New Engl Armidale BA 70. Moore Th Coll Syd ACT ThL 57. **d** and **p** 57 Syd. C of Nowra 57-59; C-in-c of Old Guildf and E Fairfield 59-62; R of St Jas S Cant 62-64; Dapto 68-74; Chap Trin Gr Sch Summer Hill 64-68; Asst Master Syd C of E Gr Sch from 74. *Sydney Grammar School, Blue Street, North Sydney, Australia 2060.* (92-5646)

DUCKER, Vere Townshend. b 04. Wadh Coll Ox BA 26, 3rd cl Th 27, MA 30. Wycl Hall Ox 27. **d** 28 **p** 29 Ripon. C of All H Leeds 28-31; Prittlewell 31-33; C-in-c of St Pet Conv Distr Prittlewell 33-36; V of All SS w St John Hertford 36-42; Chap Ch Hosp Sch Hertford 38-42; Tideswell 42-61; R of Hanborough 61-66; Perm to Offic Dio Guildf from 66; Dio Chich from 69; on Staff of BCC 67-68. *Paddock Corner, Farnham Lane, Haslemere, Surrey, GU27 1HB.* (Haslemere 2827)

DUCKETT, Canon Alfred George. b 10. Univ Coll Dur BA 31, Dipl in Th 32, MA 35. Wells Th Coll 32. **d** 33 **p** 34 B & W. C of Ilminster w Whitelackington 33-37; S Norwood (in c of H Innoc) 37-41; St Sav w St Pet S'wark PV of S'wark Cathl and Chap of Guy's Hosp 41-43; V of St Faith Wandsworth 43-50; St Olave Mitcham 50-57; St Marg Qu Streatham Hill 57-66; St Andr Coulsdon 66-74; Commiss Berm 64-70; Hon Can of S'wark 68-74; Can (Emer) from 74; Hon C of Belmont Dio S'wark from 74. *65 Downs Road, Sutton, Surrey.* (01-642 9775)

DUCKETT, Brian John. b 45. ALCD 70. **d** 70 **p** 71 S'wark. C of St Steph S Lambeth 70-73; St Luke W Norwood 73-75; Bushbury 75-77; Team V 77-79; V of St Martin Dover Dio Cant from 79. *339 Folkestone Road, Dover, CT17 9JG.* (Dover 205391)

DUCKETT, Edward. b 36. Keble Coll Ox BA 59, MA 61. Cudd Coll 59. **d** 61 **p** 62 Portsm. C of St Cuthb Copnor 61-65; Rotherham 65-68; L to Offic Dio Portsm 68-75; Hon Chap of Portsm Cathl 69-75; Perm to Offic Dio Ely from 75. *29 Margetts, Hemingford Grey, Cambs.*

DUCKETT, John Dollings. b 41. Univ of Nottm BA 62. Linc Th Coll 79. **d** 81 Grantham for Linc. C of Boston Dio Linc from 81. *23 Church Street, Boston, Lincs.*

DUCKETT, John Michael. b 35. Chich Th Coll 62. **d** 64 **p** 65 Newc T. C of St Geo Cullercoats 64-67; St Aid Benwell Newc T 67-71; V of St Lawr Newc T 71-79; St Aug City and Dio Newc T from 79. *119 Brighton Grove, Newcastle upon Tyne, NE4 5NT.* (Newc T 735859)

DUCKWORTH, Derek. b 29. Fitzw Ho Cam BA (2nd cl Nat Sc Trip pt i) 52, MA 58. Univ of Lanc PhD 72. Oak Hill Th Coll 52. **d** 54 Lanc for Blackb **p** 55 Blackb. C of All SS Preston 54-57; Sutton Lancs 57-58; Asst Master Qu Eliz Gr Sch and C of St Jo Bapt Wakef 58-60; Asst Master R Gr Sch for Boys Clitheroe 60-63; Publ Pr Dio Blackb 61-64; Asst Master High Sch for Girls Accrington 63-73; C of Whalley 64-73; Sen Research Officer Nat Found for Educl Research 73-77; Research Fell Univ of Kent from 77; C of Newbury 73-80; Perm to Offic Dio Ox from 80; Dio Cant from 81. *Glebe Cottage, Church Walk, Headcorn, Kent.* (Headcorn 890143)

DUCKWORTH, Canon Edward Broughton Parr. b 08. Late Rustat Scho of Jes Coll Cam 2nd cl Hist Trip pt i 28, BA (1st cl Th Trip pt i) and Lady Kay Scho 29, 2nd cl Th Trip pt ii and Steel Stud 30, MA 33. Ridley Hall Cam 30. **d** 31 **p** 32 York. C of Northallerton 31-35; PC of The Ascen Derringham Bank 35-46; Chap Hull City Mental Hosp 38-46; CF (TA-R of O) 39-45; R of Sutton-on-Derwent 46-51; Exam Chap to Abp of York 46-51 and 53-56; Dir of Relig Educn Dio York 46-51; Dean Chap and Sen Lect Coll of Technology Kumasi Gold Coast 51-53; R of St Mary Bishophill Sen w St Clem York 53-56; Capenhurst 56-71; Hon Can and Dir of Relig Educn Dio Ches 56-74; Can (Emer) from 74; Exam Chap to Bp of Ches 58-74; Proc Conv Ches 58-70; L to Offic

Dio Ches 71-74; Perm to Offic Dio York from 75. *Rosedene, Moor Lane, Knayton, Thirsk, N Yorks, YO7 4AZ.* (Thirsk 537393)

DUCKWORTH, Frank Gordon. **d** 66 **p** 71 Hur. Hon C of St John St Thomas 66-70; P-in-c of Oneida Reserve 71-76. *37 Yarwood Street, St Thomas, Ont., Canada.*

DUCKWORTH, Canon William George Sumner. b 05. Selw Coll Cam 2nd cl Hist Trip pt i 25, BA (3rd cl Hist Trip pt ii) 26, MA 30. Wells Th Coll 28 **d** 28 Hull for York **p** 29 York. C of Northallerton 28-31; CMS Miss at Masindi Ugan 31-36; R of S Otterington 36-38; Org Sec CMS Dios Liv and Man from 38; Dios Sheff S & M and Wakef from 40; Publ Pr Dio Man 39-41; R of Kirk Bride 41-48; V of St Thos Douglas 48-54; Kirk Maughold 54-72; RD of Ramsey 59-71; Can of S & M 73-78; Can (Emer) from 78. *Dalkeith, Cronkbourne Avenue, Douglas, IM.* (Douglas 23298)

DUDDING, Barry John. Moore Coll Syd ThL 69. **d** and **p** 72 Syd. C of St Paul Redfern 72-73; R 73-76; Cleve w Cowell and Kimba Dio Willoch from 77. *Box 142, Cleve, S Australia 5640.* (Cleve 142)

DUDDING, (Gregory) Edward Leslie. b 30. Univ of Auckld MSc 52. St Jo Th Coll Auckld LTh 56. **d** and **p** 57 Auckld. C of Takapuna 57-58; Asst Missr Dio Auckld 58-60; L to Offic Dio Chich from 62; M CSWG from 62; Father Supr from 73. *CSWG, Monastery, Crawley Down, Sussex.*

DUDLEY, Lord Bishop Suffragan of. *See* Dumper, Right Rev Anthony Charles.

DUDLEY, Archdeacon of. *See* Campling, Ven Christopher Russell.

DUDLEY, Harold George. b 14. St Mich Coll Llan 68. **d** and **p** 70 Mon. C of Fleur-de-Lys 70-73; V of Goldcliff w Whitson and Nash Dio Mon from 73. *Whitson Vicarage, Newport, Gwent, NP6 2PG.* (Newport 278106)

DUDLEY, Herbert George. Wycl Coll Tor 13. **d** 19 **p** 20 Moos. Miss at Hearst 19-21; I of Onedega Middleport and Ohsweken 21-23; P-in-c of Queensport 23-27; Perm to Offic at Langley Birm 27-29; St Jas Southbroom 31-33; Chap Roundway Hosp Devizes 29-57; Toc H Devizes 36-57; Perm to Offic Dio Sarum from 57. *1 St George's Close, West Harnham, Salisbury, Wilts.*

DUDLEY, John Rea. b 31. Pemb Coll Cam 2nd cl Engl Trip pt i 53, BA 54, 3rd cl Th Trip pt ii 55, MA 58. St Steph Ho Ox. **d** 57 **p** 58 S'wark. C of St Jo Div Kennington 57-61; Merstham w Gatton 61-68; V of N Gosforth 68-79; St Jo Bapt City and Dio Newc T from 79; RD of Newc Centr from 77; M Gen Syn from 80. *5 Summerhill Grove, Newcastle-upon-Tyne, NE4 6EF.* (Newc T 327194)

DUDLEY, Martin Raymond. b 53. AKC and BD 77, MTh 78. St Mich AA Llan 78. **d** 79 **p** 80 Llan. C of Whitchurch Dio Llan from 79. *16 Saint John's Crescent, Whitchurch, Cardiff, CF4 7AF.*

DUDLEY, Canon Ralph Edward Hughes. b 13. Pemb Coll Cam Chich Th Coll. **d** 39 **p** 40 Colom. C of Ch Ch Cathl Colom 39-49; V of W Wratting 49-54; V of W Wickham 49-54; PC of Edington w Imber 54-68; V 68-81; C-in-c of E Coulston 66-67; R 67-81; Can and Preb of Highworth in Sarum Cathl 70-81; Can (Emer) from 82. *4 Goose Street, Southwick, Trowbridge, Wilts, BA14 9RQ.*

✠ **DUDLEY-SMITH, Right Rev Timothy.** b 26. Pemb Coll Cam BA 47, MA 51. Ridley Hall Cam 48. **d** 50 **p** 51 Roch. C of St Paul Northumb Heath 50-53; Hd of Cam Univ Miss Bermondsey 53-55; Hon Chap to Bp of Roch 53-60; Publ Pr Dio Roch 53-73; Dio S'wark 53-62; Ed Sec Evang Alliance 55-59; Asst Sec CPAS 59-65; Sec 65-73; Commiss Syd 71-81; Exam Chap to Bp of Nor from 71; Archd of Nor 73-81; Cons Ld Bp Suffr of Thetford in St Paul's Cathl Lon 7 Jan 81 by Abp of Cant; Bps of Lon, Nor, Derby, Birm, Edin, Guildf, Iran, Lich, Liv, Man, Ox, Portsm, St Alb, St E, Sarum, S'wark and Truro; Bps Suffr of Aston, Bedford, Buckingham, Edmon, Hertf, Knaresborough, Huntingdon, Lynn, Maidstone, Malmesbury, St Germans, Stepney, Kingston T, Taunton, Tonbridge, Warwick and Willesden; and others. *Rectory Meadow, Bramerton, Norwich, NR14 7DW.* (Surlingham 251)

DUDMAN, Ven Robert William. b 25. Univ of Hull BA (2nd cl Sociology and Th) 68. Linc Th Coll 50. **d** 52 **p** 53 Sheff. C of St Jas Shiregreen Sheff 52-53; Wombwell 53-55; Frodingham 55-57; Industr Chap to Bp of Linc from 57; L to Offic Dio Linc 57-60; R of Scotton w Northorpe 60-71; Can and Preb of Linc Cathl from 68; Archd of Lindsey and Can Res of Linc Cathl from 71; Treas of Linc Cathl from 75. *The Archdeaconry, Cantilupe Chantry, Lincoln, LN2 1PX.* (0522 25784)

DUFF, Adam Alexander Howard. b 16. Linc Coll Ox BA 38, Dipl in Th 43, MA 46. Wycl Hall Ox 42. **d** 43 **p** 44 Birm. C of Langley 43-45; St Andr Enfield 45-47; Asst Master Ch Ch Cathl Sch Ox 47-49; L to Offic Dio Ox 48-54; Dio Ripon 51-54; Org Dir West Midls Area ICF 49-51; Asst Dir Lon and SE Engl 54-59; Toc H Area Padre W Riding Yorks 51-52; E Lon Area 52-54; C of St Mary Abbots Kens 59-62; V of H Trin w St Paul Paddington 62-79; C of St Aug w St John Kilburn Paddington 79-81. *Cedar Cottage, Water Eaton Road, Summertown, Oxford, OX2 7QQ.* (0865 58621)

DUFF, Canon Harold Patterson. b 23. Edin Th Coll 48. **d** 51 **p** 52 Glas. C of H Trin Motherwell 51-54; P-in-c of St Columba Bathgate 54-56; R of St Jas Springburn Glas 56-62; P-in-c of St Martin Dundee 62-75; R of St Salvador, Dundee Dio Brech from 69; Can of St Paul's Cathl Dundee from 76. *14 William Street, Dundee, DD1 2NL.* (Dundee 26444)

DUFF, William Edgar. Univ of Tor BA 55. Em Coll Tor BD 62. **d** 64 Bp Hunt for Tor **p** 65 Tor. C of St Paul Bloor Street Tor 64-67; I of St Paul Winnipeg 70-80; St Aug Lethbridge Dio Calg from 80. *409 11th Street South, Lethbridge, Alta, Canada, T1J 2N9.* (327 2406)

DUFFETT, Paul Staton. b 33. Keble Coll Ox BA 55, Dipl Th 58, MA 59. Ripon Hall Ox 57. **d** 59 **p** 60 Portsm. C of St Cuthb Copnor 59-63; Inhlwathi 63-65; R of Isandhlwana 65-68; Hosp Chap Nqutu 68-70; R of Vryheid 71-79; Can of Zulu 77-79; P-in-c of Greatham w Empshott Dio Portsm from 79. *Greatham Rectory, Liss, Hants, GU33 6HA.* (Blackmoor 474)

DUFFIELD, Ian Keith. b 47. AKC and BD 71, MTh 73. St Aug Coll Cant 71. **d** 73 **p** 74 St Alb. C of Broxbourne 73-77; Harpenden 77-81; Team V of Sheff Manor Dio Sheff from 81. *St Swithun's Vicarage, Cary Road, Sheffield, S2 1JP.*

DUFFIELD, Robert Winston. Univ of Adel BEcon 61. Moore Th Coll Syd ACT ThL 66. **d** 67 **p** 68 Adel. C of Lockleys w Kidman Pk 67-68; Kens 69-71; Perm to Offic Dio Melb 71-74; L to Offic 74-75; Dir C of E Boys S Dio Melb from 71; I of Spotswood Dio Melb from 75. *622 Melbourne Road, Spotswood, Vic, Australia 3015.* (03-391 3183)

DUFFY, Ven Alex Edward. St Jo Coll Auckld 52. **d** and **p** 55 Dun. C of Oamaru 55-57; V of Tapanui 57-62; Balclutha 62-64; Winton w Otautau 64-70; Wairarapa Maori Past 71-76; Aotea-Kurahaupo Maori Past 76-81; Eltham Dio Wel from 81; Archd of Waitotara from 78. *Box 178, Eltham, NZ.* (8119)

DUFFY, James Walter. b 17. Univ of Leeds BA 48. Coll of Resurr Mirfield 48. **d** 50 **p** 51 Birm. C of St Chad Rubery 50-56; PC of St Steph Eccles Distr Rednal 56-57; V 57-60; V of St Osw Bordesley 60-64; R of Curdworth 64-70; Ballachulish 70-74; Glencoe 70-74; Auchterarder Dio St Andr from 74. *Rectory, Auchterarder, Perthshire, Scotland.* (Auchterarder 2525)

DUFFY, Thomas Patrick. Clifton Th Coll 55. **d** 57 **p** 58 Bp Morris. In C of E in S Afr 57-60; C of Ch Ch Addington Durban 60-62; St Pet Pietermaritzburg 62; V of York w Ravensworth S Afr 63-64; C of Mildenhall 64-66; R of Mooi River 66-69; V of St Mary, Ascen I 69-73; R of St Barn Port Eliz 73-78; Chap of St Andr Gothenburg 78-80; Chap Miss to Seamen Gothenburg 78-80; R of Acton and L w Gt Waldingfield Dio St E from 80. *Rectory, Acton, Sudbury, Suff.*

DUFTON, Francis Trevor. b 29. Trin Coll Cam BA 51, MA 55. Ridley Hall Cam 51. **d** 53 **p** 54 St A. C of Ch Ch Ware 53-56; V of Ch Ch Bengeo 56-67; R of Wenden Lofts w Elmdon 67-80; Strethall 67-80; P-in-c of Bottisham Dio Ely from 80; Swaffham Bulbeck Dio Ely from 80. *Bottisham Vicarage, Cambridge, CB5 9BA.* (Cam 811245)

DUGDALE, Dennis. b 19. OBE 78. Worc Ordin Coll. **d** 68 **p** 69 Guildf. C of Shalford 68-70; V of Sandon w Wallington and Rushden 71-74; Chap at Ghent and Ypres Dio (Gibr in Eur from 80) Lon (N and C Eur) from 74. *Apartment Majestic, 57 Frere Orbanlaan, Ghent, Belgium.* (091-233706)

✠ **DUGGAN, Right Rev John Coote.** b 18. Late Scho of Trin Coll Dub BA (1st cl Mod) 40, Div Test (2nd cl) 41, BD 47. **d** 41 **p** 42 Cork. C of St Luke Cork 41-43; Taney 43-48; R of Portarlington 48-55; Glenageary 55-69; Exam Chap to Abp of Dub 61-69; R of Aughaval (Westport) 69-70; Archd of Tuam 69-70; Cons Ld Bp of Tuam Killala and Achonry in St Patr Cathl Dub 2 Feb 70 by Abps of Arm and dub; Bps of Down; Cashel; Ossory; Limerick; Kilmore; Connor; Cork; and Meath. *Bishop's House, Knockglass, Crossmolina, Co Mayo, Irish Republic.* (096-31317)

DUGMORE, Clifford William. b 09. Ex Coll Ox BA (3rd cl Or Langs) 32, MA and James Mew Rabbinical Hebr Scho 35, BD 40, DD 57. Qu Coll Cam BA (*by incorp*) 33, MA 36, Norrisian Pri 40. Wycl Hall Ox 32. **d** 35 **p** 36 Liv. C of H Trin Formby 35-37; Sub Warden St Deiniol's Libr Hawarden 37-38; R of Ingestre w Tixall 38-43; Chap to Earl of Shrewsbury 38-43; Chap of Alleyn's Coll Dulwich 43-45; R of Bredfield w Boulge 45-47; Dir of Relig Educn Dio St E 45-46; Sen Lect (Eccles Hist) Univ of Man 46-58; Select Pr Univ of Cam 56; Prof of Eccles Hist Univ of Lon 58-76; Prof (Emer) from 76; Hulsean Lect Univ of Cam 58-60; M Univ of Lon Senate 64-71; Dean of Faculty of Th 74-76; M Gen Syn 70-75.

Thame Cottage, The Street, Puttenham, Guildford, Surrey, GU3 1AT. (Guildford 810460)

du HEAUME, Cecil Cabot. b 04. Keble Coll Ox BA 29, MA 40. Wycl Hall Ox 27. **d** 31 **p** 32 Glouc. C of St Cath Glouc 31-34; CMS Miss Dio Jer 34-49; Chap Blundell's Sch Tiverton 49-51; V of Portbury 51-56; Sec Leprosy Miss (Ireland) 56-74; C-in-c of Glympton 74-80. *Hillgrove, Rockfield, Monmouth, Gwent, NP5 4EZ.* (Monmouth 3806)

DUIKER, Ven William Marutsaneng. St Pet Coll Rosettenville. **d** 41 **p** 42 Johann. C of Sophiatown Miss Johann 41-45; St Mary's Miss Orlando 45-47; P-in-c of Koster Miss Distr Johann 47-52; Pimville Johann 52-56; Asst P St Columba Miss Bulawayo 56-64; P-in-c 67-70; P-in-c of H Cross Miss Bulawayo 64-69; R of Francistown Dio Matab (Dio Botswana from 72) from 70; Archd of Botswana from 73. *Box 102, Francistown, Botswana.*

DUKE, Alan Arthur. b 38. Tyndale Hall Bris 59. **d** 64 Hulme for Man **p** 65 Man. C of St Marg Whalley Range 64-67; H Trin Folkestone 67-71; V of Queenborough 71-76; Bearsted Dio Cant from 76; P-in-c of Thurnham Dio Cant from 77. *Vicarage, Church Lane, Bearsted, Maidstone, Kent.* (Maidstone 37135)

DUKE, Brian Peter. b 33. Pemb Coll Cam BA 55, MA 59. Ely Th Coll. **d** 57 **p** 58 Newc T. C of St Mary Blyth 57-61; St Andr Newc T 61-63; Perm to Offic at Fleet Dio Guildf from 64; St Alb from 69. *24 Regent Close, Fleet, Aldershot, Hants, GU13 9NS; and Merchant Taylors' School, Sandy Lodge, Northwood, Middx. HA6 2HT.*

DUKE, Frederick. b 02. Bps' Coll Cheshunt 39. **d** 41 **p** 42 Guildf. C of All Ss Weston 41-48; CF (EC) BAOR 48-49; V of St Paul Egham Hythe 49-70; RD of Chertsey 63-68; C-in-c of Claydon w Mollington Dio Ox from 70. *Wayside Mollington, Banbury, Oxon.* (Cropredy 557)

DUKE-BAKER, Canon Philip Howard. b 03. Late Organ Scho of Qu Coll Cam BA 28, MA 32. Westcott Ho Cam 28. **d** 29 **p** 30 Portsm. C of E Cowes 29-34; V of St Marg Eastney 34-43; R of Havant 43-62; Surr 44-81; RD of Havant 49-62; Hon Can of Portsm 52-76; Can (Emer) from 76; Chap Havant War Mem Hosp 50-62; R of Botley 62-70; RD of Bp's Waltham 62-67; Perm to Offic Dio Portsm from 70. *15 St George's Road, Hayling Island, PO11 0BS.* (Hayling 2702)

DULFER, John Guidi. b 37. Lich Th Coll 62. **d** 64 **p** 65 Ox. C of Fenny Stratford 64-67; Cheshunt 67-68; St Anselm Kennington Cross 68-74; North Lambeth 74-76; P-in-c of St Phil Earls Court Road Kens Dio Lon 76-78; V from 78. *48 Pembroke Square, W8.* (01-937 0248)

DULLEY, Arthur John Franklyn. b 32. Mert Coll Ox BA 54, MA 57. St Jo Coll Nottm 69. **d** 71 **p** 72 Southw. Lect St Jo Coll Nottm from 71; Hon C of Chilwell 71-73; C of Penn Fields 73-74; Chap Aldenham Sch Elstree 74-79; V of Langham Dio Pet from 79. *Langham Vicarage, Oakham, Leics.* (Oakham 2969)

DUMA, Andrew Thabo. St Bede's Coll Umtata 63. **d** 64 **p** 65 Basuto. P Dio Basuto 64-66; Dio Les from 66. *All Saints' Mission, Mikia, PO Lejones, Lesotho, S Africa.*

DUMBRELL, Allen Strong. St Jo Coll Morpeth ACT ThL 47. **d** 48 Bath for Newc **p** 48 Newc. C of Mayfield 48-50; Singleton 50-51; P-in-c of The Entrance 51-55; R of Aberdeen 55-56; Sarina 56-64; C of Kogarah 64-66; Asst Chap Miss to Seamen and L to Offic Dio Syd from 67. *11 Macquarie Place, Sydney, NSW, Australia 2000.* (241-3555)

DUMBRELL, William John. Univ of Syd BA 55, MA 58. BD (Lon) 61, MTh (Lon) 66. Harvard Univ Mass ThD 70. Moore Th Coll Syd 62. **d** 56 **p** 57 Syd. C of Parramatta 56-58; Penrith 58-60; C-in-c of Ermington w Rydalmere 60-63; Lect Moore Th Coll Syd 63-66; Sen Lect 71-74; Vice-Prin from 75; on leave 66-71. *44 Carillon Avenue, Newtown, NSW, Australia.* (519-5506)

DUMEKO, Mhlabeni. b 48. St Bede's Coll Umtata 73. **d** 74 **p** 75 St John's. P Dio St John's 74-80; Dio Johann from 81. *Box 237, Ermelo 2350, Transvaal, S Africa.*

DUMEZWENI, Canon John Geoffrey. St Bede's Coll Umtata 60. **d** 61 **p** 62 St John's. P Dio St John's 61-70; Dio Port Eliz from 71; Can of Port Eliz from 75. *Box 681, Cradock, CP, S Africa.* (0482 479)

DUMGAN SINWA, Timothy. **d** 60 Rang. d Dio Rang 60-70; Dio Mand from 70. *Emmanuel Divinity School, Mohnyin, Myitkyina District, Burma.*

✠ **DUMPER, Right Rev Anthony Charles.** b 23. Ch Coll Cam BA 45, MA 48. Westcott Ho Cam. **d** 47 **p** 48 S'wark. C of Ch Ch E Greenwich 47-49; V of South Perak 49-57; Archd of N Malaya 55-64; V of St Geo Penang 57-64; Hon Can of Sing 63-64; Can (Emer) from 70; Dean and V of St Andr Cathl Sing 64-70; Exam Chap to Bp of Sing 64-70; V of St Pet Stockton 70-77; RD of Stockton 70-77; Commiss Sing from 73; C-in-c H Trin Stockton 76-77; Cons Ld Bp Suffr of Dudley in Westmr Abbey 31 March 77 By Abp of Cant; Bps of Lon, Dur, Worc, Glouc, Guildf, Lich, Ely, Portsm, Roch and Bradf; Bps Suffr of Buckingham, Dorch, Edmon, Grimsby, Hertf, Horsham, Huntingdon, Jarrow, Kingston, Knaresborough, Malmesbury, Selby, Sherborne, shrewsbury, Stafford, Tonbridge and Willesden; and others. *Bishop's House, Halesowen Road, Cradley Heath, W Midl.* (021-550 3407)

DUNANT, Charles Edward. St Jo Coll Cam BA 34. King's Coll Lon 38. **d** 40 **p** 41 Lon. C of St Sav Poplar 40-47; Chap RN 47-59; Chap at Ch Ch Vienna 60-62; V of H Trin N Shields 62-66. *Ashover, Gilham Grove, Deal, Kent.*

DUNBAR, David Cartwright. Univ of W Ont BA 56. Wycl Coll Tor. **d** 59 **p** 60 Carib. C of St Paul's Cathl Kamloops 59-61; I of Princeton 61-66; on leave. *Box 139, Marysville, BC, Canada.*

DUNBAR, George Alban Charles. b 08. AKC 40. **d** 40 **p** 41 Lon. C of St Mark Teddington 40-44; Chap RAFVR 44-47; V of Ch Ch Isle of Dogs (w St Cuthbert Millwall w St Luke Millwall and St Jo Evang Isle of Dogs from 52) Lon 47-53; C-in-c of St Luke Millwall 47-52; V of St Barn Kentish Town and of H Trin St Pancras 53-56; St Jo Ap Whetstone 56-81. *11 Avenue Road, Grantham, Lincs.*

DUNBAR, Peter Lamb. b 46. Bede Coll Dur Dipl Educn 68. STh (Lambeth) 77. N Ordin Course 78. **d** 81 Knaresborough for Ripon. C of Knaresborough Dio Ripon from 81. *St John's Cottage, Knaresborough, N Yorks.*

DUNBAR, William Don Clavell. Brisb Th Coll ACT ThL 32. **d** 32 **p** 33 Brisb. C of St Paul Ipswich 32-35; R of Kojonup 35-39; C of St Aug Hamilton 39-40; V of Wondai 40-42; Chap RAAF 42-46; V of St Paul Taringa Brisb 46-47; R 47-52; St Aug Hamilton Brisb 52-73; Hon Can of Brisb 63-73; Commiss Rockptn 60-69; Perm to Offic Dio Brisb from 73. *46 Drane Street, Clayfield, Queensland, Australia 4011.* (262-1667)

DUNBLANE, *See* St Andrews.

DUNCAN, Andrew Anderson. b 40. St Barn Coll Belair 76. **d** and **p** 79 River. C of Griffith 79-81; Deniliquin Dio River from 81. *Flat 2, 425 Harfleur Street, Deniliquin, NSW, Australia 2710.* (058 812599)

DUNCAN, Anthony Douglas. b 30. Chich Th Coll 60. **d** 62 Tewkesbury for Cant **p** 63 Glouc. C of Tewkesbury w Walton Cardiff 62-65; V of Parkend 65-69; R of Highnam w Lassington and Rudford 69-73; Hon Chap to Bp of Ox from 72; V of St Jo Bapt Newc T 73-79; Warkworth Dio Newc T from 79; Acklington Dio Newc T from 79. *Warkworth Vicarage, Morpeth, Northumb, NE65 0UR.* (0665-711217)

DUNCAN, Bruce. b 38. Univ of Leeds BA 60. Cudd Coll 65. **d** 67 Knaresborough for Ripon **p** 68 Ripon. C of Armley 67-69; Dir Children's Relief Internat 69-70; L to Offic Dio Ely 69-70; Asst Chap St Hilda's Sch Whitby 70-71; Chap Br Embassies Vienna; Budapest; Prague; and Chap Ch Ch Vienna 71-75; V of Crediton Dio Ex from 75; Posbury Chap Dio Ex from 75; RD of Cadbury 76-81; P-in-c of Shobrooke Dio Ex from 81. *Vicarage, Crediton, Devon, EX17 2AF.* (Crediton 2669)

DUNCAN, Christopher Robin. b 41. AKC 71. St Aug Coll Cant 71. **d** 72 **p** 73 Cant. C of Allington Maidstone (in c of St Pet from 75) 72-76; P-in-c of Wittersham Dio Cant from 76. *Wittersham Rectory, Tenterden, Kent.* (Wittersham 227)

DUNCAN, Colin Henry. b 1897. Univ of Melb BA 39, MA 40. Ridley Coll Melb ACT ThL 41, Fell 61. BD (Lon) 52. Fitzw Ho Cam PhD 59. **d** 42 Geelong for Melb **p** 43 Melb. C of St Mary Caulfield 42-43; Chap AIF 43-46; Min of St Thos Winchelsea 46-49; V of St Aug Moreland 49-52; Hawthorn 52-56; Vice-Prin Ridley Coll Melb 50-51; Lect 52-56; Sen Lect 60-62; C of Ch Ch Cam 56-58; C-in-c of Impington 59; V of N Carlton 60-62; Regr Austr Coll of Theology 61-73; C of Toorak 63-81; Can of St Paul's Cathl Melb 63-81; Perm to Offic Dio Melb from 81. *21 Stanley Street, Box Hill, Vic, Australia 3128.* (03-88 5650)

DUNCAN, Canon Douglas Alexander. b 1897. MC 19. OBE 61. Keble Coll Ox BA 21, MA 26. Commdr R O of K Geo I of Greece 60. Cudd Coll 22. **d** 23 **p** 24 Worc. C of St Mary and All SS Kidderminster 23-27; CF 27-47; Chap Br Embassy Athens 47-60; Can of St Paul's Angl Cathl Malta 55-60; Can (Emer) from 60; R of Mersham 60-64; Chap HM Detention Centre Aldington 61-64; Chap at Milan 64-67. *Address temp unknown.*

DUNCAN, George Ballie. b 12. Univ of Edin MA 32. BC Coll Bris and Th Coll Clifton 35. **d** 37 **p** 38 Chich. C of Broadwater 37-40; V of St Jas Denton Holme 40-44; R of St Thos Edin 44-51; V of Cockfosters 51-58. *Little Shepherds, Coleman's Hatch, Hartfield, E Sussex, TN7 4HF.* (Forest Row 4295)

DUNCAN, Harold Norton. b 03. Univ of Lon 24. BC Coll Bris 28. **d** 29 Montr for Moos **p** 37 S'wark. BCMS Miss at Pond Inlet 29-35; Gen Supt Mr Fegan's Homes 35-37; C of Bermondsey and Hd of CUM Bermondsey 37-40; Actg Hd CUM Bermondsey 40-45; Asst Master Monkton Combe Sch 41-47; Hd Master Cloverley Hall Sch (formerly Maesfen Hall

Sch) 48-66; Perm to Offic Dio Lich 49-59; Dio Ches 49-66; Dio Heref 64-66; L to Offic Dio Lich 60-66; R of Easton w Letheringham 66-72; Chap ICM Dio Dub 72-75; C-in-c of St Thos Dub 72-75; Cler Sec S Engl from 75; L to Offic Dio Cant from 75. *238 Selsdon Road, S Croydon, CR2 7AA.* (01-688 6679)

DUNCAN, Harold Osmond. b 08. Late Scho of Trin Coll Dub BA (2nd cl Mod) 30, Div Test 32, MA 40. **d** 32 **p** 33 Dur. C of St Paul Hendon Dur 32; St Hilda Hartlepool 32-35; Perm to Offic at Ven Bede Monk Wearmouth 35-36; C of Kempston (in c of St John 36; Transfig 40) 36-42; R of Stella 42-53; CF 45-47; R of St Marg Dur 53-63; Surr Chap Dryburn and Crossgate Hosps 53-63; V of Chiselhampton w Stadhampton 63-68; R of Drayton St Leon 63-68; Bp Middleham 68-74; Chap Co Hosp Dur from 73. *39 South Street, Durham.* (Durham 61027)

DUNCAN, James Montgomerie. b 29. Edin Th Coll 53. **d** 56 **p** 57 Edin. C of St Pet Edin 56-59; Old St Paul Edin 59-60; Clydesdale CP 60-61; P-in-c of Indawana 61-65; Prov Youth Org Episc Ch Scotld 65-69; R of St Salvador and Chap HM Pris City and Dio Edin and Chap HM Pris City and Dio Edin from 69. *Rectory, Stenhouse Street West, Edinburgh, EH11 3QU.* (031-443 2228)

DUNCAN, John. b 22. Roch Th Coll 64. **d** 66 **p** 67 Linc. C of Gainsborough 66-68; Boultham 68-71; V of W Pinchbeck 72-76; Miss at Ft Smith 76-81; R of Ridgewell w Ashen, Birdbrook and Sturmer Dio Chelmsf from 81. *Ridgewell Vicarage, Halstead, Essex, CO9 4SA.* (Ridgewell 355)

DUNCAN, John Finch. b 33. Univ Coll Ox BA 57, MA 63. Cudd Coll 57. **d** 59 **p** 60 York. C of S Bank 59-61; SSF 61-62; C of St Pet Birm 62-65; Chap Univ of Birm 65-76; V of Kings Heath Dio Birm from 76; Exam Chap to Bp of Birm from 81. *Vicarage, Kings Heath, Birmingham, B14 7RB.* (021-444 1207)

DUNCAN, Leslie James. St Francis Coll Brisb ACT ThL 68. **d** 67 **p** 68 Brisb. C of St Bart Mt Gravatt Brisb 67-72; V of St John U Mt Gravatt Brisb 72-74; R 74-77; Perm to Offic Dio Brisb from 77. *Main Western Road, North Tambourne, Queensland, Australia 4270.*

DUNCAN, Malcolm Nugent Samuel. b 13. TD 53. LRCP (Lon) 38. MRCS (Engl) 38. FRCGP 75. **d** and **p** 72 Portsm. Hon C of Eastney 72-77; Milton Dio Portsm from 77. *5 Selsey Avenue, Southsea, Hants.*

DUNCAN, Peter Harold Furlong. b 25. BA (Lon) 68. Goldsmith's Coll Lon BA (Soc) 71. M Phil (Soc) 79. K Coll Lon and Warm AKC 52. **d** 53 **p** 54 Sheff. C of St Geo w St Steph Sheff 53-56; Wealdstone 56-57; V of St Pet Battersea 57-64; Industr Chap Port Harcourt 64-66; L to Offic Dio Lon from 67; Perm to Offic Dio Chelmsf from 67; Bp of Lon Industr Chap for Dks 67-73; Sen Lect (Soc) City of Lon Poly from 73; P-in-c of Gt Canfield Dio Chelmsf from 80. *Rectory, Great Canfield, Dunmow, Essex, CM6 1JX.*

DUNCAN, Ronald Edward. b 46. Sir Geo Wm's Univ Montr BA 67. Mem Univ Newfld MEducn 73. Sarum Wells Th Coll 75. **d** 76 **p** 77 W Newfld. C-in-c of Seal Cove Dio W Newfld from 76. *Rectory, Baie Verte, White Bay, Newfoundland, Canada.*

DUNCAN, William Albert. b 30. TCD BA (2nd cl Hist and Pol Sc Mod) 53, Div Test (1st cl) 54, MA 61, BD 66. **d** 54 **p** 55 Down. C of Bangor Abbey 54-57; Larne 57-61; Hd of Trin Coll Miss Belf 61-66; R of Rasharkin w Finvoy 66-78; Ramoan Dio Connor from 78. *Rectory, Novally Road, Ballycastle, Co Antrim, N Ireland.* (Ballycastle 62461)

DUNCAN-JONES, Andrew Roby. b 14. St Edm Hall Ox BA 38, MA 41. Linc Th Coll 39. **d** 40 **p** 41 Derby. C of Bolsover 40-42; Chap and Succr of Edin Cathl 42-45; Hd Master Prebendal Sch Chich and PV and Succr of Chich Cathl 45-51; Chap of St Thos Cathl and of All SS Bom and Chap of Gujarat 51-53; V of Amport St Mary w Monxton 53-56; Hd Master St Chad's Cathl Sch Lich 57-70; Exam Chap to Bp of Lich 57-64; Preb of Curborough in Lich Cathl 67-68; R of Lochgilphead w Kilmartin 70-79. *Barrachourin, Kilmartin, Lochgilphead, Argyll.*

DUNCANSON, Derek James. b 47. Open Univ BA 80. K Coll Lon AKC 69. St Aug Coll Cant 69. **d** 70 **p** 71 Cant. C of St Osw Norbury 70-72; CF (TAVR) from 71; C of Woodham 72-76; CF 76-79; V of Burneside Dio Carl from 79. *Vicarage, Burneside, Kendal, Cumb, LA9 6QX.* (Kendal 22015)

DUNDAS, Edward Thompson. b 36. Trin Coll Dub BA 63. **d** 64 **p** 65 Derry. C of Conwall U 64-67; R of Kilbarron 67-78; Donagheady Dio Derry from 78. *Earlsgift, Donemana, Strabane, Co Tyrone, N Ireland.*

DUNDEE, Provost of. *See* Rogan, Very Rev John.

DUNDON, Colin George. BD (2nd cl) Lon 65. Moore Th Coll Syd ACT ThL 65. **d** and **p** 66 Syd. C of Dapto 66-67; Parramatta 67-68; CMS Miss 69-80; Exam Chap to Bp of Mt Kenya 72-75; Mt Kenya S 75-76; Tutor St Paul's United Th Coll Limuru 76-78; Vice-Prin 78-80; R of St Paul Lithgow Dio Syd from 81. *2 Roy Street, Lithgow, NSW, Australia 2790.* (063-51 3070)

DUNEDIN, Lord Bishop of. *See* Mann, Right Rev Peter Woodley.

DUNEDIN, Dean of. *See* Mills, Very Rev Robert Scott.

DUNFORD, Ernest Charles. b 09. St Cath S Ox BA 33, MA 37. Cudd Coll 34. **d** 35 **p** 36 Ox. C of Gt Marlow 35-37; St Paul Knightsbridge 37-39; V of Gt Missenden 39-76; RD of Wendover 59-67; Perm to Offic Dio Ox from 77. *26 Bacombe Lane, Wendover, Aylesbury, Bucks, HP22 6EQ.*

DUNFORD, Evelyn Cecil Braley. b 11. Jes Coll Cam 2nd cl Hist Trip pt i 32, Lady Kaye Scho 33, BA (2nd cl Th Trip pt ii) 34, MA 39. Hatf Coll Dur Dipl Th 35. Wells Th Coll 36. **d** 37 **p** 38 Leic. C of St Mich Belgrave 37-40; All S Leic 40-45; Chap RAFVR 41-46; Perm to Offic Dio Leic 46; Chap Sarum Th Coll 46-53; Asst V Cho of Sarum Cathl 48-53; Publ Pr Dio Sarum 46-53; R of Teffont Ewyas w Teffont Magna 53-55; V of Dinton 53-55; Lect Sarum Th Coll 52-55; V of All S Leic 55-62; Chap Leic R Infirm 56-62; R of Marhamchurch 62-76; Perm to Offic Dio Truro from 76. *Vine Cottage, Port Isaac, Cornw.* (Port Isaac 422)

DUNFORD, Malcolm. b 34. FCA 74. E Midl Jt Ordin Tr Scheme 73. **d** 76 **p** 77 Linc. C of Frodingham Dio Linc from 76. *57 Rowland Road, Scunthorpe, S Humb, DN16 1SP.*

DUNFORD, Paul Arnold. b 38. St D Coll Lamp. **d** 67 **p** 68 Carl. C of St John Workington 67-71; V of Crosscrake 71-74; CF 75-79; Perm to Offic Dio Bradf 80-81; Team V in R Benef of Hawarden Dio St A from 81. *Carlton, Aston Hill, Deeside, Clwyd, CH5 3AL.*

DUNFORD, Reginald John. b 15. Worc Ordin Coll. **d** 60 **p** 61 Southw. [f in CA] C of Selston 60-61; V of St Matt Bestwood 61-68; Lenton 68-80. *33 Cowlane, Bramcote, Nottingham.* (Bramcote 256841)

DUNGAN, Eric Noel. Trin Coll Dub BA 47, MA 53, Div Test 48. **d** 48 **p** 49 Dub. C of St Werburgh and Crumlin 48-55; St Pet Pietermaritzburg 55-61; Enniscorthy 61-62; R of Westmorland NB 62-63; St Jas Moncton 63-70; Advent City & Dio Montr from 70. *422 Wood Avenue, Westmount, Montreal 217, PQ, Canada.* (514-935 2160)

DUNGAN, Victor Samuel. b 17. Trin Coll Dub BA 39, 1st cl Hebr 40, BD 42, Pastoral Th Pri 40, Abp King's Div Pri (1st) 40, 1st cl Div Test 41. **d** 42 Tuam for Down **p** 43 Down. C of Derriaghy 42-45; I of Killanne w Templeludigan 45-48; Kilnamanagh U 48-49; C of Zion Ch Rathgar Dub 49-53; I of Dunganstown U 53-59; R of Ch Ch Leeson Pk Dub 59-71; Killiney Dio Dub from 71; Dean of Residence Univ Coll Dub 65-72; Chap Molyneux Home for the Blind 59-79. *Killiney Rectory, Ballybrack, Co Dublin, Republic of Ireland.* (Dub 852228)

DUNGE, Gabriele Omba. Bp Gwynne Coll Mundri. **d** 53 **p** 54 Sudan. P Dio Sudan. *c/o ECS, Parish Church, Rokon, Juba, Equatoria, Sudan.*

DUNGEY, Roy Andrew. Univ of W Ont BA 65. Hur Coll BTh 68. **d** 67 **p** 68 Hur. Chap St Leon Ho Lon Ont 67-77; on leave. *452 East 7th Street, Vancouver, BC, Canada.*

DUNGGAT, Ambrose. Ho of Epiph Kuching 52. **d** 55 **p** 56 Borneo. P Dio Borneo 56-62; Dio Kuch from 62. *St Stephen's Church, Simunjan, Sarawak, Malaysia.*

DUNGLISON, Edmond Francis. St Francis Coll Brisb ACT ThL (2nd cl) 58. **d** 57 **p** 58 Brisb. C of St Paul Ipswich 57-60; M of Bush Bro of St Paul Charleville 60-63; C of St Mary of Eton Hackney Wick 63-64; Youth Chap Dio Brisb 64-66; C of H Trin Fortitude Valley Brisb 64-66; R of Chinchilla 66-71; Boonah 71-73; Chap St Paul's Sch Bald Hills 74-78; Ecumen Chap Dio Brisb 78-80; Perm to Offic Dio Brisb from 80. *39 Froude Street, Banyo, Queensland, Australia 4014.* (267 7184)

DUNHAM, John Charles. b 1889. Trin Coll Dub BA 12, MA 15. **d** 12 **p** 13 Meath. C of Athboy 12-14; Drumcondra 14-15; Org Sec S Amer MS for Ireland and Gen L Dio Dub 15-22; Org Sec S Amer MS for SE Distr 22-24; V of L Horwood 24-28; Chap of N Prov Dio Centr Tang 28-33; N Nigeria Dio Lagos 33-35; V of Ansley 36-47; CF (EC) 41-45; Hon CF 45; V of St Paul Leamington 47-62. *178 Cubbington Road, Leamington Spa, Warws.* (Leamington Spa 23420)

DUNHILL, Robin Arnold. b 15. BNC Ox BA 38, MA 46. Cudd Coll 41 and 46. **d** 46 **p** 47 Pet. C of All SS Pet (in c of Ch of Christ the Carpenter Dogsthorpe) 46-53; V of All SS Wellingborough 53-63; St Jude-on-the-Hill Hampstead Garden Suburb 63-73; RD of W Barnet 70-73; L to Offic Dio Pet from 74. *Market Cross, Bridge Street, Kingscliffe, Peterborough, PE8 6XH.*

DUNK, Peter Norman. b 43. Sarum Th Coll 67. **d** 69 Sheff **p** 70 Bp Gerard for Sheff. C of St Mary Sheff 69-71; Margate 71-74; Youth Officer Dio Birm 74-78; R of The Ascen and St Mary Hulme City and Dio Man from 78. *Church of The Ascension, Royce Road, Manchester, M15 5FQ.* (061-226 5568)

DUNKELD, *See* St Andrews.

DUNKERLEY, James Hobson. Kelham Th Coll 58. **d** 64 **p** 65 Birm. C of Stirchley 64-66; Perry Barr 66-70; In Amer Ch from 72. *621 Belmont Avenue, Chicago, Ill, USA.*

DUNKERLEY, John Spencer. Late Scho of K Coll Cam 1st cl Hist Trip pt i 36, BA (1st cl Hist Trip pt ii) 37, MA 45. Gladstone Prize 39. Coll of Resurr Mirfield 48. **d** 51 **p** 52 Cov. C of St Mary Magd Cov 51-53; All SS Notting Hill 53-55; Hd of Bush Bro of St Paul Charleville 55-60; Chap St Mark's Coll Adel 61-64; Asst Chap 64-80; L to Offic Dio Adel from 64; P-in-c of St Mary Magd Adel 74-75; Commiss Jer from 77. *156 Flinders Street, Adelaide, S Australia 5000.*

DUNKINSON, Henry. b 04. Wycl Hall Ox 66. **d** 67 **p** 68 Blackb. C of Colne 67-69; St John Gt Harwood Dio Blackb from 69. *Lyndon House, Harwood Lane, Great Harwood, Blackburn, Lancs.* (Great Harwood 884365)

DUNKLEY, Charles Nathaniel. d 75 Ja (APM). P Dio Ja. *Box 668, Kingston 8, Jamaica, WI.*

DUNKLEY, Christopher. b 52. Univ of Edin MA 74. Univ of Ox BA 77. St Steph Ho Ox 75. **d** 78 Repton for Derby **p** 79 Derby. C of Newbold Dio Derby from 78. *80 Highfield Lane, Chesterfield, Derbys.*

DUNKLEY, Reginald Alfred Lorenz. b 13. Clifton Th Coll 56. **d** 58 **p** 59 Roch. C of Meopham 59-60; Belvedere 60-63; R of Longfield 64-78. *33 Sheriff Drive, Walderslade, Chatham, Kent.*

DUNLOP, Canon Arthur John. b 27. K Coll Lon and Warm AKC 52. **d** 53 **p** 54 Chelmsf. C of St Jo Bapt Loughton 53-57; C-in-c of All SS Conv Distr Chelmsf 57-62; Min 62-65; R of Laindon w Basildon 65-72; RD of Basildon 65-72; V of Maldon Dio Chelmsf from 72; RD of Maldon from 73; Hon Can of Chelmsf from 80; M Gen Syn from 80. *Vicarage, Maldon, Essex.* (Maldon 54179)

DUNLOP, Canon Ian Geoffrey David. b 25. New Coll Ox BA (3rd cl Mod Hist) 48, MA 56. Linc Th Coll 54. **d** 56 **p** 57 St Alb. C of Bp's Hatfield 56-60; Chap Westmr Sch 60-62; V of Bures 62-72; Can Res and Chan of Sarum Cathl from 72; Dir of Post Ordin Tr from 72; Dioc Dir of Ordin Dio Sarum from 73; Tutor Sarum & Wells Th Coll 76-78. *24 The Close, Salisbury, Wilts, SP1 2EH.* (Salisbury 6809)

DUNLOP, James Arnold. d 51 **p** 52 Ont. I of Parham 51-56; Newboro 56-62; R of St Marg Belleville 62-74; P-in-c of Pelee I 75-76; Tyendinaga 76-77. *Apt 805, Belleville, Ont, Canada.*

DUNLOP, Peter John. b 44. Trin Coll Dub BA 68, MA 72. Univ of Dur Dipl Th 70. **d** 71 **p** 72 Chelmsf. C of Barking 71-75; Ch Ch Malvern 76-78; Chap K Sch Tynemouth from 78. *The King's School, Tynemouth, North Shields, T & W, NE30 4RF.* (N Shields 74066)

DUNLOP, Rodney Owen. b 42. St Jo Coll Auckld LTh 69. **d** 68 **p** 70 Waik. C of Claudelands 68-69; Cambridge 69-71; V of Katikati 71-76; Perm to Offic Dio Sarum from 78. *Post Green, Lytchet Minster, Poole, Dorset.*

DUNN, Alastair Matthew Crusoe. b 40. Univ of Lon LLB 64, AKC 64. Wycl Hall Ox 78. **d** 80 **p** 81 Birm. C of Yardley Dio Birm from 80. *422 Church Road, Yardley, Birmingham, B33 8PB.*

DUNN, Albert Reginald. d 26 **p** 27 Bloemf. Asst Master St Andr Sch Bloemf 21-52; Chap 26-37; Asst Chap 37-52; P-in-c of Winburg 52-54; Dom Chap to Bp of Damar and Chap to St Geo Sch Windhoek 54-59; L to Offic Dio Damar 60-70; Hon Can of St Geo Cathl Windhoek 65-75. *c/o Grand Hotel, Harrismith, S Africa.* (Harrismith 33)

DUNN, Brian. b 40. St Aid Coll 66. **d** 69 Blackb **p** 70 Lanc for Blackb. C of H Trin Darwen 69-71; Burnley 71-74; V of St Barn Over Darwen Dio Blackb from 74. *St Barnabas Vicarage, Darwen, Lancs.* (Darwen 72732)

DUNN, Christopher George Hunter. b 28. Pemb Coll Cam BA 49, MA 53. Oak Hill Th Coll 51. **d** 53 **p** 54 Roch. C of H Trin Tunbridge Wells 53-54; Broadwater 54-58; R of Garsdon w Lea and Cleverton 59-74; V of St Geo Tiverton Dio Ex from 74; Surr from 76. *St George's Vicarage, Tiverton, Devon.* (Tiverton 252184)

DUNN, David. b 42. Univ of Wales Dipl Th 65. St Mich Coll Llan 62. **d** 66 **p** 67 Chich. C of St Wilfrid Brighton 66-69; St Barn Tunbridge Wells 69-74; Team V of The Resurr Brighton 74-77; V of H Spirit Southsea, Portsea Dio Portsm from 77. *26 Victoria Grove, Southsea, Hants, PO5 1NE.* (Portsm 736063)

DUNN, David Michael. b 47. K Coll Lon AKC 70. St Aug Coll Cant 70. **d** 71 Warrington for Liv **p** 72 Liv. C of Ch Ch Padgate 71-74; St Marg Halliwell Bolton 74-76; V of Lever Bridge Dio Man from 76. *Lever Bridge Vicarage, Bolton, BL2 1NZ.* (Bolton 28300)

DUNN, Canon Donald Kinglake. St Francis Th Coll Brisb ACT ThL 38. **d** 38 **p** 40 Rockptn. C of St Sav Gladstone 38-40; M of Bush Bro and P-in-c of Wowan 40-43; Dawson and Callide Valley 43-45; C of St Jas Ivanhoe 45-46; St Andr Brighton 46-47; P-in-c of Rainbow w Jeparit 47-50; V of Rupanyup 50-56; R of Gladstone 56-73; Mt Morgan 73-78; Hon Can of Rockptn from 76. *43 Darcy Street, Mount Morgan, Queensland, Australia 4714.*

DUNN, Frederick. d 74 **p** 75 Rang. Chap Miss to Blind Dio Rang from 74. *c/o Anglican Religious Training Centre, 196 Kyundaw Road, Rangoon.*

DUNN, George Mervyn. b 41. Div Hostel Dub 71. **d** 73 **p** 74 Down. C of St Jo Evang Orangefield 73-76; Knockbreda 76-79; Bp's C of Ardglass w Dunsford Dio Down from 79. *Rectory, High Street, Ardglass, Downpatrick, Co Down, BT30 7TU, N Ireland.* (Ardglass 841311)

DUNN, Hubert Woodham. b 09. King's Coll Cam 3rd cl Cl Trip pt i, 30, BA (2nd cl Th Trip pt i) 32, MA 35. Cudd Coll 32. **d** 33 **p** 34 Roch. C of H Trin Penge 33-35; Gravesend 35-36; Min Can of St Geo Chap Windsor 37-48; V of Ogbourne St Geo 48-74; Ogbourne St Andr 51-74. *18 Orchard Avenue, Cambridge, CB4 2AH.*

DUNN, John. St Pet Coll Rosettenville LTh 49. **d** 49 **p** 50 Natal. C of Good Shepherd Miss Howick 49-64; R of Inhlosane 64-65; C of St Faith Durban 65-66; R of St Phil Stanger 66-74; Perm to Offic Dio Natal from 74. *55a Ogle Road Flats, Austerville, Natal, S Africa.*

DUNN, John Frederick. b 44. Trin Coll Bris 71. **d** 74 Penrith for Carl **p** 75 Carl. C of St Jo Evang Carl 74-77; St Nich Tooting Dio S'wark from 77. *6 St Nicholas Glebe, Rectory Lane, SW17 9QH.*

DUNN, John Martin. St Paul's Th Coll Grahmstn LTh 61. **d** 61 **p** 62 Grahmstn. C of St Mich AA Queenstown 61-64; St Hugh Port Eliz 65; Dom Chap to Abp of Capetn 66-67; P-in-c of St Marg Port Eliz Dio Grahmstn 68-70; Dio Port Eliz from 70. *505 Cape Marina, Summerstrand, Port Elizabeth, S Africa.* (041-8193)

DUNN, Julian. St Aug Coll Cant 70. **d** 71 **p** 72 Kens for Lon. C of All SS Hanworth 71-74; Kidlington 74-76; Cleethorpes (in c of St Francis) Dio Linc 76-77; Team V from 77. *St Francis' House, Sandringham Road, Cleethorpes, Lincs.* (Cleethorpes 691215)

DUNN, Michael Henry James. b 34. Em Coll Cam BA 56, MA 62. Cudd Coll. **d** 62 **p** 63 Roch. C of St Steph Chatham 62-66; Bromley 66-70; V of St Justus City & Dio Roch from 70. *Vicarage, 1 Binnacle Road, Rochester, Kent, ME1 2XR.* (Medway 41183)

DUNN, Nicholas John Eaton. b 12. Keble Coll Ox BA 36, MA 46. **d** 68 **p** 69 Heref. C of Leebotwood w Longnor 68-80; Dorrington 72-80; Stapleton 72-80; L to Offic Dio Heref from 80. *Bungey Hall, Longnor, Shrewsbury, Shropshire, SY5 7PP.* (Dorrington 219)

DUNN, Paul Everley. Ridley Coll Melb ACT ThL 51. **d** 52 **p** 53 Melb. C of H Trin Kew 52-54; R of Pemberton 54-56; C of St Matt Moorfields Bris 57-58; V of Bunyip 58-61; R of Heyfield 61-66; Korumburra 66-68; Field Officer Adult Educn Dio Bath 68-71; Dio Newc 71-74; Perm to Offic Dio Newc 74-81; Dio Adel from 81; Reg Dir Inter Ch Trade Miss NSW 74-81. *14 Korana Street, South Plympton, S Australia 5038.*

DUNN, Reginald Wallace. b 1899. AKC 25. **d** 23 Heref **p** 28 Chich. C of H Trin Minsterley 23-24; Asst Master Bp's Stortford Sch 25-27; Chap 26-27; Perm to Offic Dio Chich 28-31; LPr 31-32; Asst Master Hurstpierpoint Coll 28-32; Perm to Offic Dio Lon 32-33; V of Witham Friary 33-46; R of Seaborough 46-53; Wayford 46-53; R and Arch P of Haccombe w Coffinswell 53-65; Perm to Offic Dio Ex from 65. *6a Hawkins Drive, Teignmouth, Devon, TQ14 8LT.* (Teignmouth 3753)

DUNN, Sidney Albert. b 06. K Coll Lon. **d** 42 **p** 43 Glouc. C of Dursley w Woodmancote 42-46; V of Hawkesbury 46-48; PC of Wotton St Mary-Without 48-60; St Pet Cheltm 60-63; V of St Osw Coney Hill Glouc 63-67; R of Huntley w May Hill 67-74. *37a St Mary's Square, Gloucester.* (Glouc 412808)

DUNN, Struan Huthwaite. b 43. Moore Coll Syd ACT ThL 68. **d** 70 **p** 71 Roch. C of Ch Ch Orpington 71-74; Cheltenham 74-76; C of Welling (in c of Bp Ridley Ch) 76-79; Chap at Barcelona Dio Gibr (Gibr in Eur from 80) from 79. *Calle San Juan de la Salle 41, Moracio, Barcelona, Spain.*

DUNN, Stuart Francis. Montr Dioc Th Coll LTh 66. **d** 66 Montr for Fred **p** 67 Fred. C of Petersville w Greenwich Dio Fred 66-67; I 67-70; Canterbury w Benton 70-74; Madawaska Dio Fred from 74. *34 Dube Street, Edmundston, NB, Canada.*

DUNN, Ven Terence James. b 33. Univ of Alta BA 55, LLB 56. Angl Th Coll BC STB 69. **d** 69 **p** 70 Calg. C of St Pet Calg 69-70; R of Oyen 70-72; All SS w H Trin Medicine Hat 72-76; St Leon-on-the-Hill Red Deer Dio Calg from 76; Archd of Rocky Mountain from 77. *4241-44th Street, Red Deer, Alta, Canada.* (346-6769)

DUNNETT, Robert Curtis. b 31. SS Coll Cam 2nd cl Hist Trip pt i 53, BA (2nd cl Econ Trip pt ii) 54, MA 58. Oak Hill Th Coll 56. **d** 58 **p** 59 Leic. C of Markfield w Stanton-under-Bardon 58-60; Bucknall w Bagnall 60-73; Perm to

Offic Dio Birm from 74. *16 Carpenter Road, Edgbaston, Birmingham, B15 2JW.*

DUNNILL, Michael Holmes. d 59 **p** 60 Alg. I of White River 59-63; Cobalt 63-66; Gore Bay Alg 66-71; on leave from 74. *46 Oakdale Drive, Oshawa, Ont., Canada.*

DUNNING, Douglas Frederick. d 62 **p** 63 Ont. C of Trenton 62-64; R of Adolphustown 64-71; Amherst I 69-71; St Paul Kingston 71-77. *RR2, Napanee, Ont, Canada.* (613-373 2622)

DUNNING, George Henry John. b 27. Sarum Th Coll 57. **d** 59 **p** 60 Newc T. C of Seaton Hirst 59-61; Hedworth 61-64; V of St Pet Bp Auckland 64-75; Clay Cross Dio Derby from 75. *Clay Cross Vicarage, Chesterfield, Derbys, S45 9AQ.* (Chesterfield 862136)

DUNNING, Harold Frederick. b 1893. Clifton Th Coll. **d** 51 **p** 52 Lon. C of St Jas Gt Clapton 51-53; C-in-c of Uxbridge 53-54; V 54-62; C-in-c of St John Uxbridge Moor 54-58; Chap St Jo Hosp Hillingdon 55-62. *35 Newport Road, Barnstaple, N Devon.*

DUNNING, John Stanley. b 19. Univ of Lon BSc 41. E Midl Tr Course 78. **d** 81 Sherwood for Southw. C of St Pet w St Jas Nottm Dio Southw from 81. *12 Brookhill Drive, Wollaton, Nottingham, NG8 2PS.*

DUNNINGHAM, Very Rev Selwyn David Eden. Univ of NZ BA 44, MA 47. St Jo Coll Auckld LTh 48. **d** 48 **p** 49 Ch Ch. C of St Mich Christchurch 48-51; Chap RNZN 51-52; V of Warkworth 52-57; Exam Chap to Bp of Auckld 57-72; and from 78; V of Otahuhu 57-70; St Helier's Bay 70-79; Archd of Tamaki 65-76; Archd (Emer) from 77; Dean and V of St Pet Cathl Hamilton Dio Waik from 79; Exam Chap to Bp of Waik from 79. *Deanery, Tisdall Street, Hamilton, NZ.* (393-551)

DUNNINGS, Reuben Edward. b 36. Clifton Th Coll 62. **d** 66 **p** 67 Sarum. C of Longfleet 66-70; Melksham 70-73; Team V 73-78; V of Holt Dio Sarum from 78; R of Broughton Gifford w Gt Chalfield Dio Sarum from 78. *Holt Vicarage, Trowbridge, Wilts, BA14 6PZ.* (N Trowbridge 782289)

DUNS, Charles Maxwell James. Ridley Coll Melb ACT ThL 64. **d** 61 **p** 62 Melb. C of Surrey Hills 61-62; Min of Par Distr Bellarine 62-65; I of St Jas E Thornbury 65-70; Surrey Hills 70-77; Aberfeldie 77-79; Perm to Offic Dio Melb 79-81. *11/375 Abbotsford Street, N Melbourne, Vic, Australia 3051.*

DUNSBY, Cyril Frederick. b 12. Univ of Leeds BA 33. Coll of Resurr Mirfield 33. **d** 35 **p** 36 Liv. C of St Geo Wigan 35-39; St Pet Swinton 39-43; Chap RNVR 43-46; C of Wigan 47-48; V of St D Childwall 48-66; St Mich Wigan 66-78; Chap Broadgreen Hosp 57-66; Wigan R Infirm 66-78. *21 Hinds Head Avenue, Wrightington, Wigan, Lancs.*

DUNSTAN, Canon Alan Leonard. b 28. Wadh Coll Ox BA 49, MA 52. Ripon Hall Ox 50. **d** 52 **p** 53 Cov. C of Barford and Asst Chap Warwick and Hertford Hill Hosps 52-55; C of H Trin Brompton Kens 55-57; V of St Mary Gravesend 57-63; Chap Wycl Hall Ox 63-66; Vice-Prin 66-70; Chap of Keble Coll Ox 70-71; Assoc P of St Cross w St Pet-in-the-East Dio Ox 70-78; Vice-Prin of Ripon Hall Ox 71-74; Actg Prin 74-75; Vice-Prin Ripon Coll Cudd 75-78; L to Offic Dio Ox 63-78; Can Res of Glouc from 78. *8 College Green, Gloucester, GL1 2LX.* (Glouc 23987)

DUNSTAN, Canon Gordon Reginald. b 17. Univ of Leeds BA (1st cl Hist) and Rutson Scho 38, MA (w distinc) 39. Univ of Ex Hon DD 73. Coll of Resurr Mirfield 39. **d** 41 **p** 42 Wakef. C of King Cross Halifax 41-45; Huddersfield 45-46; Sub Warden St Deiniol's Libr Hawarden 46-49; L to Offic Dio St A 46-52; Lect William Temple Coll 46-49; Ripon Hall Ox 53-55; V of Sutton Courtenay w Appleford 49-55; Cler Sec C of E Coun for Social Work 55-63; Sec Ch Assembly Jt Bd of Stud 63-66; Min Can of St Geo Chap Windsor 55-59; Westmr Abbey 59-67; Dep P-in-Ord to HM the Queen 59-64; P-in-Ord 64-76; Commiss Melb 59-68; Select Pr Univ of Cam 60 and 77; Ed 'Theology' 65-75; Can Th of Leic from 66; Prof of Moral and Social Th K Coll Lon 67-82; Exam Chap to Bp of Derby from 70; Chap to HM the Queen from 76; Perm to Offic Dio Ex from 81. *9 Maryfield Avenue, Pennsylvania, Exeter, EX4 6JN.* (0392-214691)

DUNSTAN, Harold Clive. Moore Th Coll Syd ACT ThL 33. **d** 33 Bp Kirkby for Syd **p** 35 Syd. C of St Paul Lithgow 33-35; St Luke Mosman 36-37; St Mich Wollongong 37-38; R of St John Wallerawang 38-40; V of St John Wilberforce 40-41; R of St Barn Mill Hill Waverley 41-79; L to Offic Dio Syd from 79. *39 Fraser Avenue, Hillsdale, NSW, Australia 2036.* (344-0426)

DUNSTAN, Norman Edward. b 33. St Jo Coll Winnipeg 78. **d** and **p** 80 Keew. I of Fort Alexander w L Black River & Wanipigow Dio Keew from 80. *Box 659, Pine Falls, Man, R0E 1M0, Canada.*

DUNSTAN, Sydney James. b 33. St Deiniol's Libr Hawarden 71. **d** 72 **p** 73 Llan. C of Llangynwyd w Maesteg 72-75; V in R Benef of Ystradyfodwg 75-79; Llanbradach Dio Llan from 79. *Vicarage, Church Street, Llanbradach, Mid Glam, CF8 3LS.* (Caerphilly 862202)

DUNSTER, Horace Romulus. d 51 **p** 52 Athab. I of Fort McMurray 51-62; L to Offic Dio BC from 62. *10031 Brock Avenue, Victoria, BC, Canada.*

DUNWICH, Lord Bishop Suffragan of. *See* Devenport, Right Rev Eric Nash.

DUNWOODY, Derek Cecil. b 34. Trin Coll Dub. **d** 63 **p** 64 Kilm. C of Swanlinbar w Templeport 63-65; Bp's V and Regr Dios Oss Ferns and Leigh 65-67; C of St Lambert 67-70; I of Thorndale Pierrefonds 70-71; C of Gt Grimsby (in c of St Mark) 72; I of Hodgson-Peguis 72-74; St Mary Magd Winnipeg Dio Rupld from 74. *3 St Vital Road, Winnipeg, Manit, R2M 1Z2, Canada.*

DUNWOODY, Thomas Herbert Williamson. b 35. Trin Coll Dub BA 58, MA 64, Downes Comp Pri (1st) and Div Test (1st cl) 59. **d** 59 **p** 60 Down. C of St John Newc Co Down 59-61; St Martin Miss Distr Ballymacarrett 61-63; C of Lurgan 63-66; I of Ardglass w Dunsford 66-74; V of Urmston Dio Man from 74. *Vicarage, Urmston, Manchester, M31 1HH.* (061-748 3972)

du PLESSIS, Michael. St Pet Coll Alice 65. **d** 68 **p** 69 Geo. C of All SS Mossel Bay 68-70; St Mich Port Eliz 70-72; R of St Mark and St John City and Dio Port Eliz from 73. *Rectory, Parkside, Port Elizabeth, S Africa.* (041-422780)

DUPLOCK, Canon Peter Montgomery. OBE 76. Qu Coll Cam BA 38, MA 42. Ridley Hall Cam 38. **d** 40 **p** 41 S'wark. C of Morden 40-43; CF (EC) 43-47; R of St Nich Nottm 47-52; Loddington (w Harrington from 54) 52-55; R of Harrington 52-54; V of St Andr Kettering 55-64; Chap at Geneva 65-71; H Trin Brussels 71-81; RD of Belgium and Luxembourg 71-77; Archd of Belgium, Luxembourg and the Netherlands 77-80; NW Eur 80-81; Chan of H Trin Cathl Brussels 81; Hon Can from 81; V of Breamore Dio Win from 81. *Breamore Rectory, Fordingbridge, Hants.* (Breamore 219)

du PRE, Wilfrid de Vaumorel. b 04. St Paul's Coll Maur LTh 30. **d** 28 Maur **p** 30 Madag for Maur. C of Curepipe 28-31; P-in-c of St Paul Mahé Seychelles 31-32; C of St Mich AA Walthamstow 32-34; V of Woodford Bridge 34-35; St Simon Jersey 35-49; R of Northampton NW Austr 52-53; C of St Mary & All SS Walsall 55-56; R of Dumbleton w Wormington 58-60; Hon C of Northwood Hills Pinner 71-72; Publ Pr Dio Chelmsf from 73. *10 Blenheim Court, Horn Lane, Woodford Green, Essex, IG8 9AQ.*

DURAND, Sir Henry Mortimer Dickon Marion St George. b 34. Sarum Th Coll 66. **d** 69 **p** 70 Kens for Lon. C of All SS Fulham 69-72; Heston 72-75; Upper Sunbury (in c of St Benedict) 75-79; I of Kilbixy U 79-82; Youghal Dio Cloyne from 82. *Rectory, Youghal, Co Cork, Irish Republic.* (024-2350)

DURAND, Noel Douglas. b 33. Jes Coll Cam BA 57, MA 61. BD (Lon) 76. Westcott Ho Cam 72. **d** 74 Lynn for Nor **p** 75 Thetford for Nor. C of Eaton 74-78; V of Cumnor Dio Ox from 78. *Cumnor Vicarage, Oxford.* (Cumnor 2198)

DURANT, Robert Ashton. St D Coll Lamp BA 47. **d** 48 Swan B **p** 49 Mon. C of Brynmawr 48-49; Fleur-de-Lis 49-51; Bassaleg 51-56; CF (TA) 53-55; V of Trellech 56-69; Strete Dio Ex from 69; Slapton Dio Ex from 69. *Strete Vicarage, Dartmouth, Devon.* (Stoke Fleming 378)

DURANT, Stanton Vincent. b 42. SOC 69. **d** 72 **p** 73 Willesden for Lon. C of Ickenham 72-76; Em Paddington Dio Lon 76-78; V from 78. *28 Windermere Avenue, NW6 6LN.* (01-969 0438)

DURANT, William John Nicholls. b 55. **d** 80 **p** 81 S'wark. C of W Norwood Dio S'wark from 80. *12 Chestnut Road, W Norwood, Se27 9LF.* (01-670 2400)

DURDEN, Bernard Arthur John. b 15. Clifton Th Coll 37. **d** 42 **p** 43 Chelmsf. C of St Geo Becontree 42-46; Plympton 46-51; V of Holbeton 51-57; Cler Org Sec C of E Children's S for Dios S'wark, Guildf, Lon and Chelmsf 57-74; Chief Cler Org Sec 74-78. *11 Poplar Drive, Filby, Nr Great Yarmouth, Norf.*

DURHAM, Lord Bishop of. *See* Habgood, Right Rev John Stapylton.

DURHAM, Assistant Bishop of. (Vacant)

DURHAM, Archdeacon of. *See* Perry, Ven Michael Charles.

DURHAM, Dean of. *See* Baelz, Very Rev Peter Richard.

DURHAM, John Francis Langton. b 03. Keble Coll Ox 22. TD 50. Ely Th Coll 27. **d** 28 **p** 29 Lon. C of St Mary Stoke Newington 28-33; Sec CETS and Police Court Miss Dio S'wark 33-37; Sec for Publicity S Lon Ch Fund and S'wark Dioc Bd of Finance 35-37; Warden and Chap The Boys' Shelter Home Camberwell 34-39; Gen Sec Nat Police Court Miss 37-39; CF (TA) 39-45; Toc H Staff 45-55; Dep V of All H Barking-by-the-Tower 55-60; V of St Andr Sudbury 60-68. *E India Sports & Public Schs Club, 16 St James's Square, SW1.*

DURIE, David Frew. Univ of Syd BA 50. Austrn Nat Univ MA 77. Univ of Melb BD 53, BEducn 63. **d** 59 **p** 61 New Guinea. Actg Prin St Aid Coll Dogura 59-60; Prin 61-64; V of Charleville 64-65; Vice Prin St Francis Coll Brisb 66-68; Asst Master Canberra Gr Sch 68-71; CI Tr Dir Dio C & Goulb from 71; Exam Chap to Bp of C & Goulb from 72. *5 Amaroo Street, Reid, Canberra, ACT, Australia 2601.*

DURN, Edward Nelson. b 06. St Francis Coll Brisb 62. **d** 63 Carp **p** 63 Brisb. C of Katherine 63-64; Bundaberg 64-66; C-in-c of Gin Gin 66-67; Perm to Offic Dio Ox 67-69; Dio Blackb 69-72; C of Preston 70-72; H Trin Cov 73-75; Cainscross w Selsley 75-78. *Lyttleholme, Selsley West, Stroud, Glos, GL5 5LG.* (Stonehouse 4105)

DURNELL, John. b 32. St Aid Coll. **d** 66 **p** 67 Lich. C of Newport 66-69; P-in-c of Church Aston 69-72; R 72-77; V of The Lodge (Weston Rhyn) Dio Lich from 77. *Weston Rhyn Vicarage, Oswestry, Shropshire, SY10 7RE.* (Chirk 773328)

DURNFORD, John Edward. b 30. CCC Cam 3rd cl Cl Trip pt i 52. BA (3rd cl Th Trip pt ia) 53, MA 61. Linc Th Coll 53. **d** 55 Selby for York **p** 56 York. C of Selby 55-58; Newland Yorks 58-62; Umtali Mashon 62-64; R of Mazoe Valley 64-76; V of Hebden Bridge Dio Wakef from 76. *Vicarage, Hebden Bridge, W Yorks, HX7 6DL.* (Hebden Bridge 842138)

DURNFORD, Peter Jeffrey. b 20. Bps' Coll Cheshunt 63. **d** 65 **p** 66 Lon. C of St Alphege Edmon 65-67; Chap St Bonif Bad Godesberg and All SS Cologne 67-69; R of St Just-in-Roseland w St Mawes Dio Truro from 70; P-in-c of Philleigh Dio Truro from 70. *Rectory, St Just-in-Roseland, Truro, Cornw, TR2 5JD.* (St Mawes 270248)

DUROSE, Harry Vernon. b 01. **d** 54 **p** 55 Natal. C of St Cypr Durban 54-56; Chap St John's Conv Pietermaritzburg 56-58; C of Ch K Claremont 58-60; Chap Groote Schuur and Conradie Hosps Capetn 60-62; V of Boxted 62-69. *Dolf Cottage, Plains Farm, Boxted, Colchester, Essex.*

DURRANS, Anthony. b 37. Univ of Leeds BA (3rd cl French) 59. Linc Th Coll 60. **d** 62 **p** 63 Ripon. C of Stanningley 62-64; St Ambrose Chorlton-on-Medlock 64-69; SCM Field Sec Man 64-66; NW Sec 66-68; Asst Gen Sec 68-69; R of St Jo Evang Old Trafford 69-80; M Gen Syn from 75; V of All SS and Marts Langley Dio Man from 80. *All Saints Vicarage, Wood Street, Langley, Middleton, Manchester.* (061-643 5013)

DURRANT, Reginald Francis Warburton. b 10. Pemb Coll Cam BA 32, MA 36. Westcott Ho Cam 34. **d** 36 Bp Golding-Bird for Guildf **p** 37 Guildf. C of St Paul Nork 36-39; St Nich Guildf 39-49; Chap RAFVR 40-46; V of Hindhead 49-56; Waresley 56-59; V of Abbotsley 56-59; Shrivenham w Watchfield 59-68; Surr 59-66; RD of Vale of White Horse 63-68; V of S Ascot 68-73. *17 Glebeland Close, West Stafford, Dorchester, Dorset.* (Dorchester 65122)

DURRANT, Reginald Patrick Bickersteth. AKC 64. **d** 65 **p** 66 Ox. C of St Mich AA Summertown Ox 65-68; Ascot Heath 68-71; Heene Worthing 71-76; V of Burwash Dio Chich from 76. *Burwash Rectory, Etchingham, TN19 7BH.* (Burwash 882301)

DURRETT, Lionel Payne. Bp's Coll Lennox BA 63, LST 61. **d** 62 **p** 63 Ott. P Dio Ott 62-63; I of Antrim 63-68; on leave; R of Long Sault 75-80; Sec and Treas Dio Ont from 80. *90 Johnston Street, Kingston, Ont, K4L 1X7.* (613-544 4774)

DURSTON, Aubrey George. b 10. Univ of Dur LTh 43. Clifton Th Coll 34. **d** 36 **p** 37 Bris. C of St Werburgh Bris 36-39; Highworth w Sevenhampton 39-44; St Mich Bris 44-46; V of Stanton Lacy 46-54; R of Westbury 54-58; Hemington w Hardington 58-76; R of Laverton 62-76; Perm to Offic Dio Heref from 76. *Hotspur, Bromfield Road, Ludlow, Salop.* (Ludlow 2243)

DURSTON, David Michael Karl. b 36. Em Coll Cam BA 60, MA 64. Clifton Th Coll 61. **d** 63 **p** 64 Lich. C of Heath Town 63-66; Project Officer Grubb Inst Lon 68-78; P-in-c of St Paul W Bromwich Dio Lich from 78. *St Paul's Vicarage, Bagnall Street, Harvills Hawthorn, W Bromwich, W Midl B70 0TS.* (021-557 2025)

DURUIBE, Emmanuel Enyioma. b 34. **d** 76 **p** 77 Aba. P Dio Aba. *St Michael's Cathedral, PO Box 818, Aba, Nigeria.*

DUSTAN, Thomas Mitchell. Trin Coll Tor BA 40, LTh 42, BD 45, DD 56. **d** 42 Tor **p** 43 Suffr Bp of Tor for Tor. C of St Matt Tor 42-43; Ch Ch Cathl Hamilton 43-46; w MSCC in India 47-63; Prin St Paul's High Sch Palampur 47-56; Exam Chap to Bp of Amrit 54-63; Hd Master Bp Cotton Sch Simla 58-63; R of Milton 63-68; St Steph Calg 68-70; Exam Chap to Bp of Calg 68-70; Perm to Offic Dio Newfld 70-76; Dio W Newfld 76-80; Dio New Westmr from 80. *87-1133 Pipeline Road, Coquitlam, BC, Canada.*

DUTFIELD, Canon Alan. b 20. Linc Th Coll 54. **d** 55 **p** 56 Sheff. C of Kimberworth 55-60; V of New Rossington 60-71; St Hugh Old Brumby Dio Linc 71-77; R from 77; Can and Preb of Linc Cathl from 81. *114 Ashby Road, Scunthorpe, Lincs.* (Scunthorpe 3064)

DUTHIE, Elliot Malcolm. b 31. Clifton Th Coll 63. **d** 66 Warrington for Liv **p** 67 Liv. C of St Luke Eccleston 66-69; Overseas Miss Fellowship Dio W Mal 70-75; P-in-c of St Leon Bootle 76-78; V 78-81; H Ap Charlton Kings Dio Glouc from 81. *Holy Apostles Vicarage, Langton Grove Road, Charlton Kings, Cheltenham, ham 512254)*

DUTHIE, Stanley. b 08. Tyndale Hall Bris 34. **d** 37 Blackb **p** 38 Man. C of St Mark Preston 37-38; St Clem Higher Openshaw 38-41; Bucknall w Bagnall 41-43; R of St Bart Salford 43-46; Burlingham St Edm w Lingwood V Nor 46-50; Chap Lingwood Inst 46-50; V of St Philemon Toxt Pk 50-58; C-in-c of St Silas Toxt Pk 52-58; V of St Thos Lanc 58-73; L to Offic Dio Blackb from 74. *36 Station Road, Thornton, Blackpool, FY5 5HZ.* (Cleveleys 867550)

DUTHIE, Struan James. b 47. Univ of Cant NZ BA 70. St Jo Coll Auckld LTh 70. **d** 70 **p** 71 Ch Ch. C of Sydenham-Beckenham Ch Ch 70-72; Avonside 72-74; P-in-c of Otaio-Blue Cliffs Dio Ch Ch 74-75; V from 75. *St Andrews Vicarage, S Canterbury, NZ.* (St A 730)

DUTSON, Bruce Martin. b 45. Univ of Man BA 67. Univ of Nottm Dipl Th 69. Chich Th Coll 67. **d** 70 **p** 71 Ex. C of St Pet Plymouth 70-73; St Alb Mart w St Patr Bordesley Dio Birm from 73. *30 Alexandra Rad, Edgbaston, Birmingham, B57 NJ.*

DUTTON, Canon Alan Gordon. Kelham Th Coll St Mich Th Coll Crafers. **d** 56 Blackb for Melan **p** 57 Adel for Melan. Asst Master St Mary's Boys' Sch Marovovo 57-58; Hd Master St Barn Sch Alangaula 58-59; Asst Warden St Pet Th Coll Siota 59-62; Warden 62-67; Can of Melan 64-68; Org Sec ABM Dio Adel 68-70; R of Broadview 70-73; Chap Ch Ch Gr Sch Perth 74-78; R of Mosman Pk Dio Perth from 78; Can of Perth from 80. *22 Monument Street, Mosman Park, W Australia 6012.* (384 0108)

DUTTON, Arthur Mander. b 10. Univ of Dur 36. St Aid Coll 37. **d** 39 **p** 40 Sheff. C of Anston and Woodsetts 39-41; Blakenall Heath 41-42; Cannock 42-44; V of Buckminster w Sewstern 44-48; V of St Jo Div Leic 48-49; Aslackby w Kirkby Underwood R 49-52; R of Baxterley 52-55; V of Merevale 52-55; R of Newington Bagpath w Kingscote 55-58; R of Nympsfield 55-58; Perm to Offic Dio Lich 58-62; V of Ipstones 62-64; L to Offic Dio Lich from 64. *Greaves Bungalow, Draycott-in-the-Clay, Derby, DE6 5BY.* (Burton on Trent 820298)

DUTTON, Frederick John. St Mich Coll Llan. **d** 64 Malmesbury for Bris **p** 65 Bris. C of Oldland w Longwell Green 64-71; Perm to Offic Dio BC 72-75; and from 78; Dio B & W 75-77. *1801 San Pedro Avenue, Victoria, BC, Canada.*

DUTTON, Horace Allison. Wooster Coll Ohio BA 42. Oberlin Coll Ohio BD 45. **d** 65 Mexico **p** 67 Hong. L to Offic Dio Hong 67-70. *10b Stanley Beach Road, Stanley, Hong Kong.*

DUTTON, Leonard Arthur. b 35. Bps' Coll Cheshunt, 63. **d** 66 Bp Horstead for Leic **p** 67 Leic. C of St Jo Bapt Knighton 66-70; Chilvers Coton w Astley 70-73; R of Hathern 73-79; V of H Trin Ashby-de-la-Zouch Dio Leic from 79. *Holy Trinity Vicarage, Station Road, Ashby-de-la-Zouch, Leics, LE6 5GL.* (Ashby 412180)

• **DUTTON, Richard Alfred Rowley.** b 42. ACT ThDip 79. St Barn Coll Belair 76. **d** and **p** 79 River. C of Broken Hill 79-80; P-in-c of Lake Cargelligo Dio River from 80. *Rectory, PO Box 63, Lake Cargelligo, NSW, Australia 2672.* (068-9821 82)

DUVAL, Canon David. b 14. Ch Ch Ox BA (2nd cl Mod Hist) 36, MA 41. Wells Th Coll 36. **d** 38 **p** 39 Chelmsf. C of Wanstead 38-41; Hurstpierpoint 41-42; Cuckfield 42-45; Heathfield 45-47; V of Lyminster 47-49; Barton Gt 49-59; RD of Thingoe 54-62; Hadleigh 67-71; R of Fornham All SS 59-62; Hadleigh Suff (w Layham w Shelley from 66) 62-73; Dean of Bocking 62-73; Hon Can of St E from 62; Surr 63-79; C-in-c of Layham w Shelley 65-66; R of Withersfield Dio St E 73-79; C-in-c from 79; P-in-c of Gt Wratting Dio St E from 77. *c/o Withersfield Rectory, Haverhill, Suff.* (Haverhill 702307)

DUVAL, Canon Philip Ernest. b 18. Mert Coll Ox BA and MA 45. MBE (Mil) 45. Westcott Ho Cam 47. **d** 47 **p** 48 S'wark. C of All SS Tooting 47-51; Raynes Pk 51-55; V of St Mary Balham and Chap Weir Hosp 55-66; R of Merstham w Gatton Dio S'wark from 66; Hon Can of S'wark Cathl from 78. *Rectory, Merstham, Surrey.* (Merstham 3236)

DUVALL, Michael James. B 31. **d** 79 St Alb **p** 80 Hertf for St Alb. C of King's Langley Dio St Alb from 79. *6 Avenue Approach, Kings Langley, Herts, WD4 8DW.*

DUWANI, Suheil. b 51. **d** 76 **p** 77 Jer. P-in-c of Ramallah & Bir Zeit Dio Jer from 76. *PO Box 112, Ramallah, West Bank, Jerusalem.*

DUXBURY, James Campbell. b 33. Tyndale Hall, Bris 58. **d** 61 **p** 62 Warrington for Liv. C of St Simon and St Jude Southport 61-65; V of Tittensor 65-70; Good Shepherd w St Jo Evang W Bromwich 70-75; M Gen Syn Dio Lich from 70; V of Wellington w Eyton Dio Lich from 75; Surr from 76; Ch

Comm from 78. *Vicarage, Crescent Road, Wellington, Telford, TF1 3DW.*

DWANE, Ndabankulu. AKC & BD 70. Univ of Lon MTh 71. St Bede's Coll Umtata 38. **d** 40 St Jo Kaffr **p** 43 Grahmstn. M O of Ethiopa. C of St Barn E Lon 41-43; Miss Bengu 43-52; St Matt Grahmstn 52-61; Dio Kimb K 61-64; Dio Grahmstn 64-70 and 76-77; Dio Port Eliz 70-76; Prin St Pet Coll Pmbg from 76. *P/B X505, Plessislaer 4500, Natal, S Africa.*

DWANE, Sigqibo. St Pet Coll Alice 63. **d** 66 Grahmstn **p** 68 Lon for Grahmstn. C of Keiskama Hoek 66-67; H Trin Kingsway Lon 67-69; St Mary Virg Primrose Hill 69-70; St Paul and St Martin Cant 71; St Mich Miss Herschel 71-73; Chap St Pet Coll and Tutor Federal Th Sem 73-76; Prin St Pet Coll Alice 76-77; L to Offic Dio Natal from 77. *Private Bag X 505, Plessislaer 4500, S Africa.*

DWE, Daniel. H Cross Coll Rang 71. **d** 75 **p** 76 Rang. P Dio Rang. *St Michael's Church, Nysung-ngu, Wakema District, Burma.*

DWE, Yakobo. **d** 61 **p** 62 N Ugan. P Dio N Ugan. *Church of Uganda, Palabek, Uganda.*

DYANTYI, Canon Nathaniel Mongezi. **d** 63 **p** 65 Grahmstn. C of St Matt Miss 65-69; R of St Anne Uitenhage 70-74; C of Fort Beaufort 75-76; R of St Phil Grahmstn 76-81; Can of Grahmstn from 76; R of St Cypr Macubeni Dio Grahmstn from 81. *Box 34, Indwe 5445, CP, S Africa.*

DYAS, Stuart Edwin. b 46. Univ of Lon BSc 67. Ridley Hall Cam 78. **d** 80 B & W **p** 81 Taunton for B & W. C of St Jo Evang Weston w Kelston Bath Dio B & W from 80. *20 Foxcombe Road, Bath, BA1 3ED.* (0225 311513)

DYE, Ralph Sawford. b 1900. Ch Coll Cam BA 23, MA 51. Bps' Coll Cheshunt 27. **d** 27 **p** 28 St Alb. C of Dunstable 27-30; Hitchin 30-36; Chap Toc H W Yorks Area 36-39; Chap at Ypres 39-40; C of Rhayader 40-45; Chap CCG 48-51; Chap at H Trin Sliema Malta 51-62; H Cross Palermo Sicily 62-66; R of Everdon w Farthingstone 67-74; Perm to Offic Dio Nor from 74. *3 Queen Elizabeth Close, Palace Plain, Norwich, Norf, NR3 1RY.*

DYE, William Earle. K Coll Halifax NS. **d** 60 **p** 61 NS. C-in-c of Arichat 60-65; R of Port Medway 65-72; Mahone Bay Dio NS from 72. *Rectory, Mohone Bay, NS, Canada.* (624-9021)

DYER, Harold Herbert. b 08. Hatf Coll Dur BA and LTh 33. St Bonif Coll Warm 29. **d** 34 **p** 35 Leic. C of St Pet Leic 34-36; Miss at Shwebo Burma 37-38; Irrawaddy Delta 38-42; Chap at Indore 42-45; on leave 45-47; Chap Kalaw and Oilfields Burma 47-48; Chap Rangoon Cathl 48-49; R of W Tarring 49-58; V of Lynchmere 58-68. *43 Kingsdon, Somerton, Somt.* (Ilchester 840538)

DYER, Ivan Richard. b 55. Trent Univ Ont BA 78. Univ of Nottm Dipl Th 79. Wycl Coll Tor MDiv 80. **d** 81 Bp Read for Tor. C of St Geo-on-the-Hill City and Dio Tor from 81. *4600 Dundas Street West, Islington, Ont, Canada, M9A 1A5.*

DYER, James Henry. ALCD 39. **d** 39 Willesden for Lon **p** 40 Lon. C of S Hackney 39-43; Ch Ch New Malden and Coombe 43-50; V of Murchison NZ 50-56; Collingwood 56-59; Spring Creek 60-67; Amuri 67-70; Motupiko 70-78; Perm to Offic Dio Nel from 78. *41 Oxford Street, Richmond, NZ.*

DYER, John Alan. Linc Coll Ox BA 53, MA 57. BD (Lon) 58. Tyndale Hall Bris 53. **d** 56 **p** 57 B & W. C of Ch Ch Weston-s-Mare 56-60; V of St Geo w St Andr Battersea 60-69; P-in-c of Narraweena Dio Syd 69-74; R from 74. *9 Janice Place, Narraweena, NSW, Australia 2099.* (981-3758)

DYER, John Henry. b 12. **d** and **p** 71 Rupld. Hon C of St Paul, Winnipeg and St Cypr Teulon 71-78. *1701 Cedar Hill Cross Road, Victoria, BC, Canada.*

DYER, Paul. Univ of Cant BA 68. NZ Bd of Th Stud LTh 68. **d** 68 **p** 69 Nel. C of Ch Ch Cathl 68-71; Blenheim 71-73; V of Granity 73-75; C of Motueka 76-78; Dir of Chr Educn and Stewardship Dio Wel from 78. *Box 12002, Wellington, NZ.* (696-659)

DYER, Philip. b 48. Univ of Cant NZ BA 73. St Jo Coll Auckld LTh 75. **d** 75 **p** 76 Ch Ch. C of Fendalton 75-77; Timaru 77; V of Mayfield-Mt Somers Dio Ch Ch from 78. *Vicarage, Mayfield, NZ.* (Mayfield 114)

DYER, Sydney Charles George. St Jo Coll Dur LTh 33, BA 34, MA 38. ALCD 33. **d** 34 **p** 35 S'wark. C of St Jas Malden 34-36; St Sav Raynes Pk (in c of Holy Cross) 36-40; V of St Jo Evang Clapham Rise 40-45; S Paul Herne Hill 45-55; St Jo Evang Redhill 55-69; Chap at Tenerife Dio Gibr from 72. *Apartado 28, Puerto de la Cruz, Tenerife, Canary Islands.* (371638)

DYER, Canon Walter John. Wycl Coll Tor. **d** 54 Coadj Bp for Tor **p** 55 Tor. I of Creemore 54-58; St Geo Barrie 58-64; R of St Marg West Hill Tor 64-78; P-in-c of St Edw Tor 76-78; I of Cavan and Manvers Dio Tor from 78; Can of Tor from 78. *PO Box 187, Millbrook, Ont, Canada.* (705-932 2897)

DYKE, Kenneth Aubrey. Sarum Th Coll 61. **d** 63 **p** 64 Birm. C of Bournville 63-66; Chap RAF from 66. *c/o Ministry of Defence, Adastral House, WC1.*

DYKES, Frederick Alfred. Univ of BC BA 51, BD 56. Univ Coll Ox 58. Angl Th Coll Vancouver LTh 53. **d** 53 **p** 54 Calg. C of St Barn Calg 53-55; R of Crow's Nest w Coleman 55-58; I of Carbon 59-63; R of St Gabr Calg 63-70; St Aug w St Luke Calg 71-80; Exam Chap to Bp of Calg 64-68; Hon Can of Calg 74-81; L to Offic Dio Calg 80-81; on leave. *133 Madeira Way SE, Galgary, Alta, Canada.*

DYKES, Lawrence Gregson Fell. Wycl Hall Ox. **d** 34 **p** 35 Ripon. C of Meanwood 34-36; St Pet Hunslet Moor 36-40; V of Cartmel 40-51; CF 42-46; (Men in Disp 45 and Hon CF 54); R of Hartfield 51-76; Perm to Offic Dio Carl from 77. *The Garden Cottage, Holker Hall, Cark in Cartmel, Grange-over-Sands, Cumb.*

DYKES, Michael David Allan. b 42. Chich Th Coll 68. **d** 71 York **p** 72 Hull for York. C of Pocklington 72-75; Howden 75-77; V of Eskdaleside (or Sleights) w Ugglebarnby (and Sneaton from 81) Dio York from 77; P-in-c of Sneaton 79-81. *22 Eskdaleside, Sleights, Whitby, N Yorks, YO22 5EP.* (Whitby 810349)

DYKES, Richard Owen. Moore Th Coll Syd ACT ThL 53. **d** and **p** 54 Syd. C-in-c of Pagewood 54-57; R of Port Kembla 57-60; Penrith 60-66; Turramurra 66-77; Dean of All SS Cathl Bath 77-80; Dir and Sen Chap Miss to Seamen NSW from 80. *11 Macquarie Place, Sydney, NSW, Australia 2000.* (241-3555)

DYMOCK, Michael James Paul. b 45. K Coll Lon AKC 69. St Aug Coll Cant 70. **d** 70 **p** 71 S'wark. C of Benhilton 70-73; V of St Jo Evang Clapham (w Ch Ch from 77) 73-80; All SS N Beddington Dio S'wark from 80. *Vicarage, New Road, Mitcham Junction, Surrey, CR4 4JL.* (01-648 3650)

DYMOKE-MARR, Cyprian. b 06. Qu Coll Cam BA 28, MA 32. Westcott Ho Cam 29. **d** 29 **p** 30 Dur. C of St Mary Magd Millfield 29-32; St Nich W Boldon 32-35; Min of St Francis Eccles Distr S Shields 35-43; R of Clewer w All SS Dedworth Green and St Agnes Spital 43-71; Proc Conv Ox 64-71; Perm to Offic Dios Ox and Sarum from 71; Hon C of Swanage Dio Sarum from 71. *Clewer Cottage, Sunnydale Road, Swanage, BH19 2JA.* (Swanage 3941)

DYSART, Harry. K Coll NS BA 32. **d** 33 NS for Fred **p** 34 Fred. R of Norton 34-36; St Mary York Co 36-45; Dean of K Coll NS 45-55. *Box 1321, Halifax, NS, Canada.*

DYSON, Anthony Oakley. b 35. Em Coll Cam BA 59, MA 63. Ex Coll Ox BA (by incorp) 59, MA 64, BD 64, DPhil 68. Ripon Hall Ox 59. **d** 61 **p** 62 S'wark. C of Putney 61-63; Chap Ripon Hall Ox 63-68; Prin 69-74; L to Offic Dio Ox from 65; Select Pr Univ of Ox 71; Henson Lect Ox 72-73; Exam Chap to Bp of Carl from 73; to Bp of Sheff from 77; Can of Windsor 74-77; Lect Univ of Kent 77-80; L to Offic Dio Cant 78-80; Dios Man and Ches from 80; Prof of Social and Pastoral Th Univ of Man from 80. *43 Hill Top Avenue, Cheadle Hulme, Cheshire, SK8 7HZ.*

DYSON, Frank. Oak Hill Th Coll 60. **d** 62 Warrington for Liv **p** 63 Liv. C of Parr 62-65; V of Newchapel 65-77; R of Bunwell w Carleton Rode (and Tibenham from 80) 77-81; P-in-c of Tibenham 78-81; R of Pakefield Dio Nor from 81. *Pakefield Rectory, Lowestoft, Suff, NR33 0JZ.* (Lowestoft 4040)

DYSON, Norman Colbeck. b 12. Westcott Ho Cam. **d** 57 Man **p** 58 Middleton for Man. C of St Mark Glodwick 57-64; Missr to Deaf and Dumb Oldham 49-64; Dioc Missr for Deaf Dio Leic 64-67; Dio Truro 67-71; R of St Phil Gorton 71-77; Chap Oldham R Infirmary from 78. *12 Malvern Close, Royton, Oldham, Lancs.*

DYSON, Peter Whitely. b 51. Univ of Man BA 73, LLB 75. Qu Coll Birm Dipl Th 80. **d** 81 Bris. C of Ch Ch Swindon Dio Bris from 81. *58 Upham Road, Swindon, Wilts, SN3 1DN.*

DYSON, Philip. b 45. K Coll Lon and Warm AKC 67. **d** 68 **p** 69 S'wark. C of St Jo Div Kennington 68-71; Petersham and of St Richard Ham 71-74; V of Ponders End 74-80; St Mary Virg Somers Town, St Pancras Dio Lon from 80; P-in-c of Old St Pancras Dio Lon from 80. *St Mary's Church House, Eversholt Street, NW1.* (01-387 7301)

DYSON, Canon Ronald Arthur. St Jo Coll Morpeth ACT ThL 60. **d** 52 **p** 53 Armid. C of Moree 52-54; St Pet Cathl Armid 54-56; R of Dorrigo 56-61; R of Macksville 61-66; Tweed Heads 66-81; Kempsey Dio Graft from 81; Hon Can of Graft from 76. *Rectory, West Kempsey, NSW, Australia 2440.*

DYSON, Stanley Senior. b 20. N-E Ordin Course 76. **d** 79 **p** 80 Newc T (APM). Hon C of St Pet Cowgate City and Dio Newc T from 79. *45 Burnfoot Way, Kenton, Newcastle-upon-Tyne, NE3 4TL.*

DYSON, Ven Thomas. Univ of Man BA 38. Univ of Lon BD 44. St Edm Hall Ox BA 50, MA 53, Dipl in Educn 47. Ely Th Coll 38. **d** 40 **p** 41 S'wark. C of St Anselm Kennington

Cross 40-43; Chap RNVR 43-47; V of St Pet-in-the-East w St Jo Bapt Ox 47-55; Asst Chap St Edm Hall Ox 47-55; Chap and Asst Master at Hamm BAOR 55; R of Colne Lancs 55-57; Warwick Dio Berm from 57; Chap to Bp of Berm 60-68; Exam Chap from 64; Syn Sec Dio Berm from 70; Can of Berm from 73; Archd from 82. *Rectory, Warwick East, Bermuda.*

DZIMGWE, Alfred Uukani. b 26. **d** 79 **p** 80 St John's (APM). P Dio St John's. *Private Bag 9001, Mount Frere, Transkei.*

E

EADE, Henry George. b 11. **d** 63 **p** 64 St E. C of St Marg Ipswich 63-66; R of Bucklesham w Brightwell and Foxhall 66-75; Combs 75-81. *2 Hillyfields, Woodbridge, Suffolk.*

EADE, John Christopher. b 45. Ch Coll Cam, BA 68, MA 72. Linc Th Coll 68. **d** 70 Bp Woolmer for Portsm **p** 71 Portsm. C of St Mark, N End Portsea 70-73; Henleaze 73-77; V of Uplands w Slad Dio Glouc from 77. *Vicarage, 167 Slad Road, Stroud, Glos, GL5 1RD.* (Stroud 4833)

EADE, Stephen David. b 29. Wells Th Coll 67. **d** 69 Bris **p** 70 Malmesbury for Bris. C of Soundwell 69-72; St Paul Chippenham w Langley Burrell 72-75; P-in-c of Pilning w Severn Beach and Northwick 75-80; C of Twerton-on-Avon Bath 80-81; Team V of Marlbrook, Bath Dio B & W from 81. *St Peter's Vicarage, High Street, Twerton-on-Avon, Bath, BA2 1DB.* (Bath 27966)

EADES, Jonathan Peter. b 51. Univ of Dundee MA 74. Univ of Edin BD 77. Edin Th Coll 74. **d** 77 **p** 78 Brech. Chap St Paul's Cathl Dundee Dio Brech from 77; Univ of Dundee from 79. *18 Whitehall Crescent, Dundee.* (Dundee 2774)

EADIE, Robert Henry. b 41. Univ of Tor BA 64. Trin Coll Tor MDiv 78. **d** and **p** 78 E Newfld. C of U I Cove 78-79; Mt Pearl Dio E Newfld from 79. *24 Harnum Crescent, Mount Pearl, Nfld, Canada.*

EAGLE, John Frederick Laurence. St Chad's Coll Dur BA 39, Dipl in Th 40, MA 42. **d** 41 **p** 41 Southw. C of Greasley 41-43; Bestwood Park 43-47; Malden 47-53; Mortlake (in c of All SS E Sheen) 53-58; R of Stanwick (w Hargrave from 72) Dio Pet from 58; C-in-c of Hargrave 59-72. *Stanwick Rectory, Wellingborough, Northants.* (Raunds 2317)

EAGLE, Julian Charles. b 32. Qu Coll Cam BA 56, MA 60. Westcott Ho Cam. **d** 58 **p** 59 Dur. C of St Aid Billingham 58-61; Eastleigh 61-65; Bp's Industr Chap S Hants Dio Win from 65. *The Old Vicarage, Chilworth, Southampton.* (Soton 768072)

EAGLES, Canon Albert Robert. Bp's Univ Lennox LST 34. **d** 34 Niag for Koot **p** 34 Lon for Col. C of Fulham 34-37; V of Golden 37-41; Chap CASF 41-46; V of Fernie and Michel 46-49; R of Kimberley 49-52; Penticton 52-64; Can of Koot 54-64; Can (Emer) from 64; L to Offic Dio BC from 65. *1270 Dallas Road, Victoria, BC, Canada.*

EALES, Howard Bernard. b 46. Sarum Wells Th Coll 73. **d** 76 **p** 77 Ches. C of Timperley 76-78; St Thos Stockport Dio Ches from 78. *90 Richardson Street, Hillgate, Stockport, SK1 3JL.* (061-429 7643)

EALES, William Bernard. b 07. Kelham Th Coll 25. **d** 30 **p** 31 Man. C of Ch of Ascen Lower Broughton 30-34; H Trin Hartlepool 34-37; R of Darwin 37-40; Asst Chap St Andr Cath Sing 40-41; Chap of Malacca 41-45; V of St Chris Johore Bahru 47-49; Succr St Andr Cathl Sing 49-52; V of Blackrod 52-58; PC of Gt Harwood 58-72. *39 Hurst Avenue, Worthing, W Sussex, BN11 5NZ.*

EALES-WHITE, Donald James. b 16. St Jo Coll Ox BA and MA 44. MC 45. **d** 61 **p** 62 Aber. C of Fraserburgh (in c of All SS Strichen) 61-62; R of All SS Strichen 62-64; New Pitsligo 62-64; Ballachulish 64-66; R of Glencoe 65-66; Dioc Insp Schs Aber 62-64; Dio Arg Is 65-66; R of Bardwell 68-69; L to Offic Dio Arg is 69-71 and 74-77 and 79-81; V of Mendham 71-72; C-in-c Metfield w Withersdale 71-72; Perm to Offic Dio St E 73-74; R of Dalbeattie 77-79; P-in-c of Brora and Dornoch Dio Moray from 81. *Fernlea, High Street, Dornoch, Sutherland.* (Dornoch 636)

EAMES, Arthur Robert. b 1889. Chich Th Coll 19. Univ of Dur LTh 22. **d** 22 **p** 23 Southampton for Win. C of St Sampson Guernsey 22-27; New Milton 27-35; V of Salter Street 35-53; R of Clapham w Patching 53-59. *Middleton, Combe Martin, Ilfracombe, Devon.*

EAMES, Hubert Hardisty. Univ of NZ BA 53. St Jo Coll Auckld 54. **d** 56 **p** 57 Wai. C of Rotorua 56-58; Tauranga 58-61; V of Waikohu 61-65; Wai Dioc Dir of Chr Educn 65-68; L to Offic Dio Wai 69; Dio Wel from 73; C of Lower Hutt 69-73. *305 Dowse Avenue, Maungarakei, Lower Hutt, NZ.* (661-989)

✠ **EAMES, Right Rev Robert Henry Alexander.** b 37. QUB LLB (2nd cl) 60, PhD (Law) 63. TCD Div Test. **d** 63 Down **p** 64 Tuam for Down. C of Bangor 63-66; I of Gilnahirk 66-74; Dom Chap to Bp of Down 70-72; Exam Chap 73-75; R of St Mark Dundela Belf 74-75; Cons Ld Bp of Derry and Raphoe in St Patr Cathl Armagh 9 June 75 by Abp of Arm; Bps of Connor, Down, Kilm, Lim, Clogh, Killaloe and Tuam; Trld to Down and Drom 80. *The See House, 32 Knockdene Park South, Belfast, BT5 7AB, N Ireland.*

EARDLEY, John. b 38. Ch Coll Cam BA 61, Ridley Hall Cam 60. **d** 62 **p** 63 Ches. C of Barnston 62-65; Wilmslow 65-67; V of Hollingworth 67-75; Leasowe Wallasey Dio Ches from 75. *123 Reeds Lane, Leasowe, Moreton, Wirral, Mer L46 1QT.* (051-677 6550)

EARDLEY, John Barry. b 35. K Coll Lon and Warm AKC 62. **d** 63 **p** 64 S'wark. C of St Jas Merton 63-66; St Pet St Helier (in c of Bp Andrewes Ch) 66-69; Bilton Warws 69-70; Min of St Steph Conv Distr Canley 70-74; P-in-c of Ch Lawford w K Newnham 74-79; Dioc Educn Officer Dio Cov from 80. *244 b Dunchurch Road, Rugby, Warws.* (Rugby 816419)

EARDLEY, Paul Wycliffe. b 19. ALCD (1st cl Hons) 42. **d** 42 Burnley for Blackb **p** 43 Blackb. C of St Luke Brierfield 42-44; St Mary Virg Somers Town 46-48; Chap at Guy's Hosp 48-49; Warden of Stanford Priory Stanford-le-Hope 49-50; Warden of Edw Wilson Ho 50-55; C of St Ethelburga Bpsgate Lon 55-57; L to Offic Dio Chich and Warden of Danehurst 57-62; R of Ripe w Chalvington 62-71; V of St Mark w St Matt Kemp Town Brighton Dio Chich from 71. *27 Church Place, Brighton, BN2 5JN.* (Brighton 681652)

EARDLEY, Stephen Roy. Kelham Th Coll 58. **d** 63 Dunwich for Antig **p** 64 Antig. C of St John's Cathl Antig 63-68 and 69-70; R of St Geo Montserrat 68-69; St Phil Antig 71-75; St Paul Cote de Neiges Montr 75-78; St Phil Montr W Dio Montr from 78. *3400 Connaught Avenue, Montreal West, PQ, Canada.* (481-4871)

EARIS, Stanley Derek. b 50. Univ Coll Dur BA 71, BCL 80. Ripon Hall Ox BA 73, MA 80. **d** 74 **p** 75 York. C of Sutton-in-Holderness 74-77; St Steph Acomb York 77-81; V of Skelmanthorpe Dio Wakef from 81. *Skelmanthorpe Vicarage, Huddersfield, W Yorks, HD8 9AQ.* (Huddersfield 863232)

EARL, Very Rev David Kaye Lee. b 28. TCD BA 54. **d** 55 **p** 56 Dub. C of St Jude Dub 55-58; R of Rathkeale 58-65; Killarney 65-79; RD of Tralee 71-77; Prec and Preb of Lim Cathl 77-79; Dio Sec 77-79; Dean of Ferns from 79. *Deanery, Ferns, Co Wexford, Irish Republic.* (Ferns 6124)

EARL, Kenneth Stuart. St Chad's Coll Regina. **d** 63 **p** 64 Qu'App. C of Nokomis 63-64; I of Punnichy 65-67; Lumsden 67-78; St Matt Regina Dio Qu'App from 78. *2161 Winnipeg Street, Sask, Canada.* (523-8810)

EARL, Victor Charles. Coll of Ven Bede Dur BA (1st cl Cl and Gen Lit) 49. ALCD 51. **d** 51 **p** 52 Birm. C of Stechford 51-54; St Paul Newbarns Barrow-F 54-57; R of Plumbland w Gilcrux 57-61; St Phil w St Mark Man 61-67; L to Offic Dio Man from 67. *59 Norfolk Avenue, Denton, Manchester, M34 2WL.* (061-336 2387)

EARLE, Charles Walter. b 08. Keble Coll Ox BA (3rd cl Mod Hist) 31, MA 35. Linc Th Coll 31. **d** 32 **p** 33 Southw. C of St Mich AA Sutton-in-Ashfield 32-35; St Pet w St Jas Nottm 35-37; C-in-c of Bircotes Conv Distr 37-42; Chap RNVR 42-46; V of St Anne Worksop 46-56; C-in-c of Scofton w Osberton 51-56; R of Chipping Barnet 56-69; RD of

Barnet 59-66; Hon Can of St Alb 68-69; R of Newent 69-76. *10 Orchard Road, St Michaels, Tenterden, Kent, TN30 6ED.* (Tenterden 2836)

EARLE, Cyril Wall. Montr Dioc Th Coll LTh 34. **d** 34 **p** 35 Montr. C-in-c of River Desert 35-37; I of Papineauville 37-40; P-in-c of St Alb Montr 40-41; Chap CASF 41-44; I of Aylmer 44-49; RD of Clarendon 46-49; R of St Jas Hull and P-in-c of Chelsea 49-58; Hon Can of Montr 53-58; I of St Timothy-by-the-Humber Tor 59-61; R of Morrisburg 61-73. *Apt 1, 45 Mille Roches Road, Long Sault, Ont., Canada.*

EARLE, Ven Edward Ernest Maples. b 1900. Univ of Dur Th Exhib and LTh 24, BA 27, MA 30. Lon Coll of Div. **d** 24 **p** 25 Roch. C of Crayford 24-27; Keston 27-32; C-in-c of St Jo Evang Conv Distr Bexley 32-37; V 37-39; Rainham 39-44; Min Can Roch Cathl Dom Chap to Bp of Roch 44-48; Sec Roch Dioc Appeal C'tte 44-49; Sec Roch Dioc Reorganization C'tte 44-53; Hon Can Roch from 49; R of Chatham 50-52; Proc Conv Roch 50-53; R of Wrotham 52-59; Archd of Tonbridge 53-77; Archd (Emer) from 78; V of Shipbourne Dio Roch from 59. *Shipbourne Vicarage, Tonbridge, Kent.* (Plaxtol 810478)

EARLE, Canon George Halden. St Chad's Coll Dur LTh 39, BA 40, MA 44. Qu Coll Newfld 35. **d** 38 **p** 39 Newfld. L to Offic Dio Newfld 38-40; C of St Pet Monkseaton 40-45; R of Falstone 45-52; V of Choppington 52-57; Prin of Qu Coll St John's Newfld 57-79; Can of St Jo Bapt Cathl Newfld from 72. *Box 275, Topsail, Conception Bay, Newfoundland, Canada.* (709-753 0116)

EARLE, Harry Oake. **d** 78 **p** 79 Matab. C of Que Que 78-81. *c/o Diocesan Office, Box 4019, Durban, S Africa.*

EARLE, John Chipman. KCNS. **d** 60 NS **p** 61 Bp Davis for NS. C of Westville 60-64; R of Musquodoboit Harbour 64-68; French Village Dio NS from 69. *RR1, Armidale, NS, Canada.* (826-2154)

EARLE, John Nicholas Francis. b 26. Trin Coll Cam BA 46, 1st cl Th Trip pt i 50, MA 54. Westcott Ho Cam 50. **d** 52 **p** 53 Bris. C of St Matt Moorfields Bris 52-59; St Botolph Aldgate w H Trin Minories Lon 59-61; Asst Master Dulwich Coll 61-71; Publ Pr Dio S'wark 61-71; Hd Master of Bromsgrove Sch from 71. *Bromsgrove School, Bromsgrove, Worcs.* (Bromsgrove 32774)

EARLE, Jonathan Patrick. b 42. R Mil Coll of Canada BA 66. Wycl Coll Tor MDiv 73. **d** 73 **p** 74 Alg. C of Lake of Bays 73-74; on leave. *Greenlanes, Henley-in-Arden, Solihull, Warws.*

EARLE, Joseph Edward. b 12. St Jo Coll Dur LTh 40, BA 42, MA 46. St Aid Coll 36. **d** 39 Bp Linton Smith for Roch **p** 40 Roch. C of Ch Ch Luton Chatham 39-42; Beamish 42-45; V of Ch Ch Healey 45-52; St Paul Oldham 52-58; St Cath Horwich 58-66; Norton St Phil (R w Hemington, Hardington and Laverton from 76) 66-78; Hinton Charterhouse 66-76; RD of Frome 72-78; Perm to Offic Dio B & W from 78. *69 Lane End, Corsley, Warminster, Wilts, BA12 7PG.* (Chapmanslade 515)

EARLE, Kenneth Noel Morris. b 07. St D Coll Lamp BA 30. St Mich Th Coll Llan 30. **d** 31 **p** 32 Swan B. C of Llandilo-Talybont 31-32; Sketty 32-34; St Mich AA Plumstead 34-35; St Andr Stockwell Green 35-39; Chap R Assoc in Aid of Deaf and Dumb from 39; L to Offic in St Mellitus Prittlewell and St Cedd Moulsham 40-42; Chap R Assoc in Aid of Deaf and Dumb in N Lon 42-50; St Alb Dioc Miss 50-53; Northants and Rutland Miss to Deaf and Dumb and L to Offic Dio Pet 53-72. *27 Mayfield Road, Northampton, NN3 2RE.* (Northampton 44481)

EARLE, Virgil Francis. **d** 65 **p** 66 Ont. I of Roslin 65-69; I of Tweed 67-74; Belleville Dio Ont from 74. *25 Oriole Park Avenue, Belleville, Ont, Canada.* (613-962 2064)

EARNEY, Graham Howard. b 45. K Coll Lon and Warm AKC 67. **d** 68 **p** 69 Dur. C of St Helen Bp Auckland 68-72; Corsenside 72-76; P-in-c 76-79; Team V of Willington Dio Newc T from 79. *Battle Hill Vicarage, Berwick Drive, Battle Hill Estate, Wallsend, Tyne & Wear.*

EARNSHAW, Alan Mark. b 36. ALCD 60 (LTh from 74). **d** 60 Liv **p** 61 Warrington for Liv. C of Em Fazakerley 60-65; V of St Geo Ovenden Halifax 65-79; L to Offic Dio Wakef from 80. *89 Savile Park Road, Halifax, W Yorks.*

EARNSHAW, Robert Richard. b 42. NOC 78. **d** 81 Liv. C of All S Springwood City and Dio Liv from 81. *17 Archerfield Road, Liverpool, Mer, L18 7HS.* (051-724 4443)

EARNSHAW, Thomas Gibson. b 16. **d** 74 Johann. C of Springs Dio Johann from 74. *10 Ariston Court, Ariston Avenue, Selcourt Tvl 1560, S Africa.* (011-56 1602)

EARP, John William. b 19. Jes Coll Cam Rustat Scho 2nd cl Cl Trip 40, BA 42, 2nd cl Th Trip 42, MA 45. Ridley Hall, Cam 42. **d** 43 **p** 44 Lon. C of St Paul Portman Square Lon 43-46; Tutor Ridley Hall Cam 46-48; Chap 48-51; Vice Prin 51-56; Select Pr Cam 49 and 53; Jun Proc Univ of Cam 54-55; Exam Chap to Bp of Lich 50-57; to Bp of Win 62-76; Asst Master and Chap of Eton Coll 56-62; V of Hartley Wintney w Elvetham (and Winchfield and Dogmersfield from 76) Dio Win from 62; Surr from 66; RD of Odiham from 76. *Hartley Wintney Vicarage, Basingstoke, Hants.* (Hartley Wintney 2670)

EARWAKER, Canon Clifford George. b 02. St D Coll Lamp BA 31. **d** 31 **p** 32 S'wark. C of Em Camberwell 31-37; Eastbourne (in c of St Geo) 37-41; V of Littlehampton 41-53; Dioc Insp of Schs 43-53; RD of Arundel 47-53; Battle and Bexhill 56-59; Horsham 59-68; Surr from 47; R of Bexhill 53-59; Crawley 59-68; Can and Preb of Chich Cathl 60-78; Can (Emer) from 78; V of Lynchmere 68-74. *3 Kewhurst House, Little Common, Bexhill-on-Sea, Sussex.* (Cooden 2415)

EARWAKER, John Clifford. b 36. Keble Coll Ox BA (3rd cl Th) 59, MA 63. Univ of Man MEd 71. Linc Th Coll 59. **d** 61 Sheff **p** 62 Bp Gerard for Sheff. C of Ecclesall Sheff 61-64; Succr of St Mary's Cathl Edin 64-65; Div Master at Ashton L Gr Sch and L to Offic Dio Man 65-69; Lect (Sen Lect from 73) Sheff City Coll of Educn from 69; Sen Lect Sheff City Poly from 76; L to Offic Dio Sheff from 69. *41 Hallam Grange Crescent, Fulwood, Sheffield, S10 4BB.* (Sheffield 303421)

EARWAKER, Victor Hyde. b 34. K Coll Lon 56. Sarum Th Coll 69. **d** 70 **p** 71 Edmonton for Lon. C of All SS, Friern Barnet 70-75; New Alresford w Ovington and Itchen Stoke 75-77; V of E w W Worldham and Hartley Mauditt w Kingsley and Oakhanger Dio Win from 77. *East Worldham Vicarage, Alton, Hants.* (Alton 82392)

EASON, Cyril Edward. Univ of Leeds BA 43, MA 67. Coll of Resurr Mirfield 43. **d** 45 **p** 46 Man. C of St Aug Tonge Moor 45-51; H Cross S Shore Blackpool 51-53; V of Lever Bridge 53-65; Area Sec USPG Dio B & W from 65; Dios Ex and Truro from 75; Perm to Offic Dio Ex from 75; Dio Truro from 75. *2 The Liberty, Wells, Somt, BA5 2SU.* (0749-74702)

EASON, Glenn Owen. b 53. Concordia Univ Montr BSc 77. McGill Univ Bth 79. Montr Dioc Th Coll 77. **d** 80 **p** 81 Montr. C of St Phil Montr W Dio Montr from 80. *52 Ronald Drive, Montreal West, Quebec, Canada, H4X 1M8.* (514-486 4064)

✠ **EASSON, Right Rev Edward Frederick.** b 05. Univ of St Andr BSc 27, MA (2nd cl Math and Chem Hons) 28, Hon DD 62. Edin Th Coll 31. **d** 33 **p** 34 Edin. C of St Pet (in c of St Aid Niddrie Mains from 36) Edin 33-39; R of St Pet Peterhead and Chap Peterhead Pris 39-48; St Devenick Bieldside 48-56; Insp of Schs Dio Aber 45-56; Can of Aber 46-56; Dean of Aber and Ork 53-56; Cons Ld Bp of Aberdeen and Orkney in St Andr Cathl Aber 25 Apr 56 by Bp of Arg Is (Primus); Bps of Brech; Edin; Glas; Moray; and St Andr; and Bp of Connecticut; res 72. *25 Corbiehill Avenue, Edinburgh, EH4 5DX.* (031-336 2580)

EAST, Alfred Laurence Roy. b 17. Lich Th Coll 37. **d** 40 **p** 41 Dur. C of St Paul Jarrow 40-44; Norton 44-47; St Nich w St John Linc 47-49; R of Escrick 49-61; Chap Qu Marg Sch Escrick Pk 49-61; V of Thornton-le-Street (w N Otterington to 64) Thornton-le-Moor and Thornton-le-Beans 61-67; R of Kirby Misperton w Barugh Habton and Ryton 67-80. *14 Springfield Garth, Norton on Derwent, Malton, N Yorks, YO17 9EL.*

EAST, John Michael. b 39. Univ of Bris BA 67. Qu Coll Birm 75. **d** 77 Bp McKie for Cov. C of H Trin City and Dio Cov from 77. *22 William Bristow Road, Cheylesmore, Coventry, CV3 5LQ.*

EAST, Reginald Walter. b 16. St Jo Coll Dur BA 49, Dipl Th 50. **d** 50 **p** 51 Chelmsf. C of St Mary Virg Loughton 50-52; Bp's Youth Chap Chelmsf 52-57; V of W Mersea 57-71; R of E Mersea 57-71; C of Winterbourne Whitechurch 71-75; Warden Barn Fellowship 71-75; Publ Pr Dio Sarum from 80. *Shepherds Cottage, Whatcombe, Blandford Forum, Dorset, DT11 0NZ.* (Milton Abbas 880190)

EAST, William Gordon. b 48. Keble Coll Ox BA 69, MA 77 Dipl Th 77. Yale Univ MPhil 71, PhD 74. St Steph Ho Ox 77. **d** 78 **p** 79 S'wark. C of St Mary Newington 78-81; St Jo Div w St Jas Ap Kennington Dio S'wark from 81. *6 Calais Street, SE5.* (01-274 0777)

✠ **EASTAUGH, Right Rev Cyril.** b 1897. MC 17. Ch Ch Ox BA 28, MA 32. Cudd Coll 28. **d** 29 **p** 30 S'wark. C of St Jo Div Kennington 29-31; Chap Cudd Coll 31-34; Vice-Prin 34-35; V of St Jo Div Kennington 35-49; R of St Andr Undershaft w St Mary Axe Lon 50-53; Commiss Bloemf 35-52; Proc Conv S'wark 43-49; Hon Can of S'wark Cathl 45-49; Cons Ld Bp Suffr of Kensington in Westmr Abbey 1 Nov 49 by Abp of Cant; Bps of Lon; Win; S'wark; Glouc; Truro; Derby; Heref; Linc; Cov; B & W; and Brech; Bp Montgomery Campbell; Bps Suffr of Kingston T; Stepney; and Woolwich; and Bps Palmer, Warman, and Ridsdale; Trld to Pet 61; res 72; Prin S of Faith from 72; Hon Asst Bp of Portsm from 76. *Blackmoor House, Liss, Hants, GU33 6DA.* (Bordon 3777)

✠ **EASTAUGH, Right Rev John Richard Gordon.** b 20. Univ of Leeds BA 42. Coll of Resurr Mirfield. **d** 44 Lon **p** 45 Stepney for Lon. C of All SS Poplar 44-51; R of W Hackney 51-56; C-in-c of St Barn Shacklewell 54-55; R of Poplar 56-63; V of Heston 63-67; St Pet Eaton Square 67-74; Commiss Polyn 63-70; Archd of Middx 66-74; Cons Ld Bp of Heref in Westmr Abbey 24 Jan 74 by Abp of Cant; Bps of Ox, Worc, Ely, Glouc, Birm, Pet, Bradf, Guildf and Derby; Bps Suffr of Edmon, Kens, Tonbridge, Dorking, Basingstoke and Sherborne; and others; Sub Prelate of the O of St John of Jer from 78. *Bishop's House, The Palace, Hereford, HR4 9BN.* (Hereford 2823)

EASTELL, John Kevin. b 42. Univ of Liv Dipl Adult Educn 80. Wells Th Coll 65. **d** 66 Wakef **p** 67 Pontefract for Wakef. C of Horbury 66-69; Armley 70-72; V of St Marg Toxt Pk Liv 72-76; Formby Dio Liv from 76. *Church House, Green Lane, Formby, Liverpool, L37 DJ.* (Formby 73369)

EASTEN, Edmund John Attlee. b 07. CCC Cam BA 29, MA 33. Bps' Coll Cheshunt 29. **d** 30 Win **p** 31 Southampton for Win. C of Bitterne Park 30-34; I of Badulla 34-39; Perm to Offic at King's Lynn 39-44; C of St Marg w St Nich King's Lynn 44-46; V of Burley 46-61; R of Thurning w Wood Dalling 61-79; Perm to Offic Dio Nor from 79. *Church Hill Cottage, Reepham, Norwich, NR10 4JL.*

EASTER, Brian James Bert. b 33. Dipl Th (Lon) 55. St Aug Coll Cant 56. **d** 57 **p** 58 Lich. C of Tipton 57-59; Area Sec BCMS 59-64; Perm to Offic Dios Worc; Derby; Leic; Birm; Heref; Cov; Lich; Pet; Linc and Southw 59-64; Dio Glouc 62-64; V of Barston 64-72; Chap Monyhull and Middlefield Hosps Birm from 72. *995 Yardley Wood Road, Birmingham, B14 4BS.* (021-474 2622)

EASTER, Stephen Talbot. b 22. St Cath Coll Cam BA 47, MA 53. Ely Th Coll. **d** 50 Croydon for Cant **p** 51 Cant. C of Whitstable 50-53; Chap SA Ch Rly Miss Bulawayo 53-56; V of Wymynswold 56-61; Min of Aylesham Conv Distr 56-61; V of St Marg-at-Cliffe w W Cliffe (and E Langdon w W Langdon from 75) Dio Cant from 61. *St Margaret's-at-Cliffe Vicarage, Dover, Kent, CT15 6AB.* (Dover 852179)

EASTGATE, John. b 30. Kelham Th Coll 47. **d** 54 **p** 55 Lon. C of St Pet Ealing 54-58; Min of St Gabr Eccles Distr Belgrave 58-64; V 64-69; Glen Parva w S Wigston 69-74; Asst RD of Christianity 64-69; V of Woodley Dio Ox from 74. *Vicarage, Church Road, Woodley, Reading, Berks.* (Reading 692316)

EASTHAM, John. b 1894. Can Scho Linc 21. **d** 23 **p** 24 Southw. C of St Andr Derby 23-28; Brighton 28-35; V of St Jo Evang Brighton 35-47; R of Horsted Keynes 47-64; Hon C of Tarvin 64-80; Perm to Offic Dio Blackb from 80. *The Haven, Neville Street, Longridge, Preston, PR3 3DF.*

EASTMAN, Canon Derek Ian Tennent. b 19. Ch Ch Ox BA 41, MA 46. MC 45. Cudd Coll 46. **d** 48 **p** 49 Wakef. C of Brighouse 48-51; Caversham 51-56; V of St Andr Headington Ox 56-64; Banbury w Neithrop 64-70; Surr from 57; Proc Conv Ox 64-70; V of Chilton w Dorton 70-77; Archd of Buckingham 70-77; M Gen Syn 75-77; Can of Windsor from 77. *4 The Cloisters, Windsor Castle, Berks, SL4 1NJ.* (Windsor 64142)

EASTMAN, Patrick William Henry. b 37. St Steph Ho Ox 65. **d** 68 **p** 69 Dur. C of St Mary Magd Millfield 68-71; C-in-c of Hedworth Dio Dur 71-72; V from 72; M Gen Syn 75-80. *St Nicholas House, Hedworth Lane, Bolden Colliery, T & W, NE35 9JA.* (Bolden 367552)

EASTOE, Robin Howard Spenser. b 53. AKC and BD 75. Coll of the Resurr Mirfield 77. **d** 78 Chelmsf **p** 79 Barking for Chelmsf. C of St Mary Ilford 78-81; St Sav Walthamstow Dio Chelmsf from 81. *212 Markhouse Road, Walthamstow, E17 8EP.* (01-556 2968)

EASTON, Edward George. b 01. St Paul's Miss Coll Burgh. **d** 27 Grantham for Linc for Masasi **p** 29 Masasi. UMCA Asst Miss Dio Masasi 27-35; P-in-c of Lumesule and Mbaya 35-37; Mindu w Lumesule 37; Chap Sneaton Castle Sch 37-38; Org Sec UMCA for NE Area 38-41; V of Tattershall 39-45; Chap RAFVR (E Afr) 42-46; V of Bp's Teignton 46-50; R of Lusaka 50-58; V of Strete and of Slapton 59-61; R of Port Alfred S Afr 61-64; Marwood 64-68; R of Bittadon 64-68; L to Offic Dio Ex 69-72; C of Shirwell w Loxhore 72-77; Newport 77-79; RD of Shirwell 73-77; L to Offic Dio Ex from 79. *Rose Ash, Sentry Lane, Bishop's Tawton, Barnstaple, Devon, EX32 0BW.*

EASTON, John. b 34. St Cath S Ox BA (2nd cl Engl) 59, MA 63. Chich Th Coll 59. **d** 61 **p** 62 Lich. C of Rugeley 61-64; All SS Shrewsbury 64-66; Chap Industr Miss Dio Sheff 66-72; V of Rugeley Dio Lich from 72. *Vicarage, Rugeley, Staffs.* (Rugeley 2149)

EASTON, Richard Huntingford. Or Coll Ox BA and MA 51. Westcott Ho Cam 53. **d** 54 **p** 55 Bris. C of St Ambrose Bris 54-57; V of Northland w Wilton 57-78; Exam Chap to Bp of Wel 67-73; Offg Min Dio Auckld from 79. *Muriwai Road, RD1, Waimauku, NZ.*

EASTWAY, David Edwin. Moore Coll Syd ThL 71. **d** 71 **p** 72 Syd. C of Blacktown 71-73; Castle Hill 73-76; P-in-c of Wilcannia 76-77; Menindee 77-78; Sec Bush Ch Aid S and Nat Home Miss Fund S Austr from 79; Hon C of Norwood Dio Adel from 79. *10 Pitt Street, Paradise, S Australia 5075.*

EASTWOOD, Arthur Christopher John. b 17. St Edm Hall Ox 3rd cl Math Mods 38, BA 45, MA 45. Westcott Ho Cam 45. **d** 47 **p** 48 Chelmsf. C of Gt Ilford 47-50; St Mary Portsea 50-54; C-in-c of St Wilfrid's Conv Distr Cowplain Dio Portsm 54-62; V from 62; Dioc Insp of Schs Dio Portsm 61-68. *Vicarage, Padnell Road, Cowplain, Portsmouth, Hants PO8 8DZ.* (Waterlooville 2295)

EASTWOOD, Colin Foster. b 34. Univ of Leeds BA (2nd cl Th) 56, MA 66. Linc Th Coll 65. **d** 67 **p** 68 York. C of Cottingham 67-70; Darlington (in c of All SS Blackwell) 70-75; V of Eighton Banks 75-81; St Jas Sutton Dio Ches from 81. *St James Vicarage, Sutton, Nr Macclesfield, Chesh.* (Sutton 2228)

EASTWOOD, Canon Dennis Townend. b 05. Univ of Man BA 29. Wells Th Coll 29. **d** 30 **p** 31 Man. C of St Paul Bury 30-34; St Jas Accrington 34-36; PC of St Geo Darwen 36-44; V of St Paul Bury 44-63; Hon Can of Man 63; Can (Emer) from 63; V of Hart w Elwick Hall 63-73. *Bishop Stichill Cottage, Greatham, Hartlepool, Cleve, TS25 2HR.* (0429 870888)

EASTWOOD, Harry. b 14. St Aid Coll 39. **d** 41 **p** 42 Wakef. C of St Mich Wakef 41-44; Liversedge (in c of Hightown) 44-48; PC of St John Cleckheaton 48-55; R of Elland 55-63; Middleton-on-the-Wolds 63-67; C-in-c of N Dalton 63-67; Hollym w Withernsea 67-68; C-in-c of Owthorne w Rimswell Dio York 67-68; V (w Withernsea) 68-73; RD of S Holderness 67-74; C-in-c of Halsham 70-73; V of Goathland 73-79; Perm to Offic Dio York from 79. *9 Brooklands, Filey, N Yorks, YO14 9BA.*

EATHER, Gregory Bruce. b 53. Univ of NSW BA 77, BTh 80. Canberra Coll of Min 77. **d** 79 **p** 80 C & Goulb. C of St Paul Turvey Park Dio C & Goulb from 79. *2a Blakemore Street, Ashmont, Wagga Wagga, NSW, Australia 2650.*

EATOCK, John. b 45. Lich Th Coll 67. **d** 70 **p** 71 Hulme for York. C of Crumpsall 70-73; Atherton 73-74; Ribbleton 74-77; V of Ingol Dio Blackb from 77. *St Margaret's Vicarage, Tag Lane, Ingol, Preston, PR2 3XA.* (Preston 727208)

EATON, Canon Albert William. b 05. St Paul's Coll Grahmstn LTh 30. **d** 30 **p** 31 Johann. [f in CA] C of St Dunstan Benoni 30-35; R of Malvern 35-41; Ch Ch Mayfair Johann 41-46; V of St Pet w St Hilda Leic 46-60; Ed Leic Dioc Leaflet 49-60; Commiss Johann 49-50; Hon Sec Leic Coun of Chs 50-60; Hon Can of Leic 53-60; Surr 50-60; Proc Conv Leic 57-60; R of Kitwe Zam 60-67; RD of Copperbelt and Katanga 60-66; Hon Can Lusaka 63; Can (Emer) from 63; V of St Laur Morecambe 67-74; Can Miss Dio Blackb 67-74; Perm to Offic Dio Sarum from 75. *Manormead Nursing Home, Tilford Road, Hindhead, Surrey, GU26 6RA.*

EATON, David John. b 45. Univ of Nottm BTh 74. St Jo Coll Nottm 70. **d** 74 **p** 75 Guildf. C of All SS Headley 74-77; Industr Chap in Halesowen 77-82; V of Rowledge Dio Guildf from 82. *Vicarage, Rowledge, Farnham, Surrey.*

EATON, Very Rev Derek Lionel. b 41. Trin Coll Bris 70. **d** and **p** 71 Jer. C of St Luke Bris 71-72; Chap St Geo Tunis 72-78; Provost of All SS Cathl Cairo from 78. *c/o Box 87, Distribution Zamalek, Cairo, Egypt.*

EATON, Edwin Francis. K Coll NS STh 63. **d** 61 **p** 63 Fred. C of Restigouche 61-63; R of Gladstone 63-67; Kingsclear 67-70; New Maryland 67-70. *550 Dufferin Street, Fredericton, NB, Canada.*

EATON, Eric. b 13. St D Coll Lamp 47. **d** 50 **p** 51 Llan. C of Gellygaer 50-54; Flint (in c of Oakenholt) 54-57; V of St Jas Wigan 57-65; C-in-c of St Thos Wigan 61-65; R of Ashton-in-Makerfield 65-80; Surr 67-80; Perm to Offic Dio Liv from 80. *1 Hale Road, Hale, Liverpool, L24 5RB.* (051-425 4235)

EATON, Henry Jackson. Ch Ch Coll 66. **d** 66 **p** 67 Ch Ch. C of Sumner-Heathcote 66-69; St Pet U Riccarton 69-70; V of Waiho Downs 70-73; Rakaia 73-76; Perm to Offic Dio Ch Ch from 76. *72 Wiggins Street, Christchurch 8, NZ.* (Sum 6066)

EATON, Howard. Univ of W Austr BA 69, BEducn 75. ACT BTh 78. **d** and **p** 79 Perth. C of Claremont Dio Perth from 79. *2a Queenslea Drive, Claremont, W Australia 6010.* (384 8445)

EATON, Oscar Benjamin. b 37. Episc Th Coll of the Carribbean Puerto Rico STB 66. **d** 66 **p** 67 Bp Reed (Ecuador). In Amer Ch 66-69; C of St Anne Wandsworth 69-71; St Leon Aldrington 71-73; Secr for Higher Educn of Ch Aid 73-74; Team V of Littleham w Exmouth 74-79; R of Alphington Dio Ex from 79. *Rectory, Alphington, Exeter, Devon.* (Exeter 72115)

EATON, Ross Seymour. Univ of NZ BA 45, MA 49. Coll Ho Ch Ch. **d** 55 **p** 56 Ch Ch. C of Merivale 55-59; St Paul Haggerston 59-60; St Paul Covent Garden 60-62; Linwood-Aranui 63; V of Warrington 63-69; Assoc Chap Ch Ch Pris 69-73; Chap from 73. *75 Glandovy Road, Christchurch 5, NZ.* (518-766)

EATON, Sara Lucretia. b 28. Univ of Tor BA 49. Montr Dioc Coll LTh 80. **d** and **p** 80 Ott. C of All SS Westboro City and Dio Ott from 80. *35 Foothills Drive, Nepean, Ont, Canada, K2H 6K6.*

EAVES, Alan Charles. b 37. Tyndale Hall Bris 62. Dipl Th (Lon) 64. **d** 65 Warrington for Liv **p** 66 Liv. C of St Simon and St Jude Southport 65-66; Eccleston 66-70; V of Earlestown 70-79; Ch Ch Orpington Dio Roch from 79. *Vicarage, Charter House Road, Orpington, Kent.* (Orpington 70923)

EAVES, Brian Maxwell. b 40. Tyndale Hall Bris 66. **d** 69 **p** 70 Lich. C of St Jude Wolverhampton 69-72; Fazeley 72-75; Team V of Ipsley 75-79; Chap at Amsterdam Dio (Gibr in Eur from 80) Lon (N and C Eur) from 79. *Christ Church, Groenburgwal 42, Amsterdam, Netherlands.* (24 88 77)

EAVES, Lindon John. Univ of Birm BSc (1st cl Genetics) 66. Cudd Coll 66. **d** 68 Bp Sinker for Birm **p** 69 Birm. C of St Faith w St Laur Harborne 68-72; L to Offic Dio Birm from 73. *101 Wood Lane, Harborne, Birmingham, B17 9AY.*

EBBITT, Francis Simon. b 20. Trin Coll Dub BA 42, MA 49, BD 56. **d** 43 **p** 44 Down. C of St Mary Magd Belf 43-46; Shankill Lurgan 46-48; Bangor 48-50; R of Ballee w Bright 50-53; Aghalee 53-59; V of Stanwix 59-65; Rainhill 65-74; Stanford-in-the-Vale w Goosey and Hatford 74-80; St Pet Maidenhead Dio Ox from 80; RD of Vale of White Horse 75-80. *259 Courthouse Road, Maidenhead, Berks.* (Maidenhead 21961)

EBIAU, Yoasi. Bp Tucker Coll Mukono 67. **d** 69 Soroti. d Dio Soroti. *PO Otuboi, Teso, Uganda.*

EBO, Joel Iheanyichuku Daberechuku. b 46. Trin Coll Umuahia 71. **d** 74 **p** 75 Ow. P Dio Ow. *Box 194, Mbieri, Owerri, Nigeria.*

✠ **EBO, Right Rev Samuel Chukuma Nwokorie.** Univ of Nig Nsuka BA 65. Trin Coll Umuahia 56. **d** 58 Niger for N Nig **p** 59 N Nig. P Dio N Nig 59-69; Dio Ow 70-79; Archd of Ow 71-75; Exam Chap to Bp of Ow 71-79; Prov of All SS Cathl Egbu 75-79; Cons Ld Bp of Jos in St Mich Cathl Kaduna 6 Jan 80 by Abp of Nigeria; Bps of Aba, Ow, Asaba, Benin, Egba-Egbado, Enugu, Ijebu, Ilesha, Kwara, Lagos, Niger, Nig Delta and Ondo. *Bishopscourt, Box 12, Jos, Plateau State, Nigeria.*

EBOH, Edwin Eriemiatoi. b 26. **d** 73 **p** 74 Benin. P Dio Benin. *St Michael's Parsonage, Owa-Alero, Agbor, Nigeria.*

EBONG, Paul. **d** 77 Lango. d Dio Lango. *PO Aloi, Apala, Lira, Uganda.*

EBSARY, Edwin Reginald Kenneth. b 55. St Francis Xavier Univ NS BSc 77. Atlantic sch of Th Halifax NS MDiv 80. **d** 80 NS. C of Sherbrooke Dio NS from 80. *St James Anglican Rectory, Sherbrooke, NS, BOJ 3C0, Canada.*

EBSARY, George Roy Frederick. St Jo Coll Winnipeg. **d** 48 **p** 49 Bran. C-in-c of Rivers 48-50; R of Belmont 50-52; Crapaud 52-58; Tangier 58-63; I of Chester 63-67; St Geo Sydney Dio NS from 67. *52 Nepean Street, Sydney, NS, Canada.* (564-4335)

EBSWORTH, Michael Paul. b 46. Univ of Calg BA 67, MA 73. Trin Coll Tor MDiv 76. **d** 76 **p** 77 Calg. I of Hanna 77-81; St Mary Lethbridge Dio Calg from 81. *537-12th C Street North, Lethbridge, Alta., Canada.*

EBUGU, Sira. **d** 76 **p** 77 Soroti. P Dio Soroti. *Kaberamaido County, Central Teso, Soroti, Uganda.*

ECCLES, Ernest Pattison. b 23. Kelham Th Coll. **d** 50 **p** 51 Sheff. C of St Leon Norwood Sheff 50-54; C-in-c of Elsecar 54; L to Offic Dio Sheff 54-56; R of Braithwell Dio Sheff from 56; C-in-c of Ravenfield 62-75. *Braithwell Rectory, Rotherham, S Yorks, S66 7AS.* (Rotherham 812665)

ECCLESTON, Bryan Arthur. Th Coll Crafers, 53. **d** 56 Geelong for Adel **p** 57 Perth. L to Offic Dio Adel 56-57; C of Walkerville 57-59; Asst Chap St Pet Coll Adel 60-64; Dir Dioc Bd Relig Educn Perth 65-68; Perm to Offic Dio Perth from 65; Asst Master Guildf Gr Sch Dio Perth from 69. *Guildford Grammar School, Guildford, W Australia 6055.* (279 1135)

ECCLESTON, Frederick Ernest. **d** 41 **p** 42 Lah. Bp Cotton Sch Simla E 41-44; Lah Cathl 44-45; Karachi 45-46; Hon CF 46; Master Guildford Gr Sch Perth 47-48; R of Bassendean 47-50; St Mary West Perth 50-55; Chap Ch Ch Sch Claremont 55-69. *35b Raleigh Road, Marmion, W Australia 6020.*

ECCLESTONE, Alan. b 04. Late Scho of St Cath Coll Cam 1st cl Hist Trip pt i, 24, BA (1st cl Engl Trip) 25, MA 29. Wells Th Coll 30. **d** 31 **p** 32 Carl. [f Lect Univ of Dur] C of St Aid w Ch Ch Carl 31-34; St Jo Evang Barrow-F 34-36; V of Frizington 36-42; H Trin Darnall Sheff 42-69; Proc Conv Sheff 45-48; L to Offic Dio Carl from 69. *Raceside Cottage, Wellington, Gosforth, Seascale, Cumb.*

ECHE, Thankgod Ndunburuoke Ihendinihu. b 51. Trin Coll Umuahia 75. **d** 78 Aba. d Dio Aba. *St Silas Parsonage, Old Umuahia, Nigeria.*

ECHEFU, Godson Chinyere. Trin Th Coll Umuahia, 62. **d** 64 **p** 65 Ow. P Dio Ow; Synod Sec Dio Ow from 73. *PO Box 37, Owerri, Nigeria.* (Owerri 177)

ECHENDU, Canon Michael Chiagozie. Trin Coll Umuahia 62. **d** 64 **p** 65 Niger. P Dio Niger; Hon Can of Niger from 81. *Parsonage, Fegge, Onitsha, Nigeria.*

ECHENDU, Timothy Anyiam. St Paul's Coll Awka, 55. **d** 55 **p** 57 Niger. P Dio Niger 55-65; Dio Ow 65-80. *Christ Church, Ezihe, via Okigwe, Nigeria.*

ECHENIM, Charles Alika. **d** 47 **p** 49 Niger. P Dio Niger 50-62; Dio Benin 62-77; Dio Asaba from 77; Archd of Asaba 62-73 and 78-79. *St John's Parsonag, Agbor, Nigeria.*

ECKERSLEY, Canon Charles Alfred Wright Ryley. b 16. Keble Coll Ox BA (2nd cl Hist) 38, MA 44. Linc Th Coll 38. **d** 40 **p** 41 Carl. C of St Geo Barrow-F 40-42; C of St Mich Workington 42-44; R of St Andr Holyrood Road Edin 44-46; Haddington 46-51; V of St Pet Kells Whitehaven 51-58; Maryport 58-66; St John Workington 66-69; St Geo w St Luke and St Perran Roose Barrow-F 69-73; Hayton w Talkin 73-78; Hon Can of Carl from 72; Dir of Ordinands Dio Carl 73-78. *13 Etterby Lea Road, Stanwix, Carlisle, CA3 9JW.* (Carlisle 38033)

ECKERSLEY, Canon James Holland. b 11. Keble Coll Ox BA 34. Linc Th Coll 33. **d** 35 Barrow-F for Carl **p** 36 Carl. C of Workington 35-41; Chap RAFVR 41-43; C of St John Keswick 43-44; V of H Trin Millom 45-49; St Mary Walney I 49-55; Chap Selly Oak Hosp Birm 55-57; V of King's Heath 57-61; St Jo Bapt Upperby Carl 61-63; Wreay 63-70; Hon Can of Carl from 69; L to Offic Dio Carl from 70. *5 Moorhouse Road, Belle Vue, Carlisle, Cumb.* (Carl 21641)

ECKERSLEY, Richard Hugh. Trin Coll Cam BA 48, MA 50. Chich Th Coll 49. **d** 51 **p** 52 Portsm. C of St Jo Bapt Rudmore Portsea 51-57; St Mark Portsea 57-62; PC (V from 69) of St Mich AA Paulsgrove Wymering 62-73; V of St Nich Brighton Dio Chich from 73. *6 Montpelier Villas, Brighton, Sussex, BN1 3DH.* (Brighton 23412)

EDAH, Lawson. b 27. **d** 76 Nig Delta. d Dio Nig Delta. *Holy Trinity Church, Rumuapara, PO Box 213, Port Harcourt,Rivers State, Nigeria.*

EDDERSHAW, Lionel Francis Trevor. Down Coll Cam BA 58, MA 62. Linc Th Coll 58. **d** 60 **p** 61 Newc T. C of St Luke Wallsend 60-63; St Pet Conv Distr Balkwell Tynemouth 63-68; R of Falstone 68-75; St John Lee Dio Newc T from 75. *St John Lee Rectory, Hexham, Northumb.* (Hexham 2220)

EDDISON, Frederick Donald Buchanan. b 19. Trin Coll Cam BA 41, MA 46. Ridley Hall, Cam 47. **d** 48 Lon **p** 49 Stepney for Lon. C of St Matt Fulham 48-51; All S Langham Place w St Andr Wells Street 51-53; Asst Chap and Asst Master Forres Sch Swanage 53-56; Chap CSSM and Perm to Offic Dio Chich 56-65; V of St John Tunbridge Wells 65-80. *43 East Cliff Road, Tunbridge Wells, Kent, TN4 9AG.* (Tunbridge Wells 20991)

EDDISON, Robert John Buchanan. b 16. Trin Coll Cam 3rd cl Hist Trip pt i, 37, BA (2nd cl Hist Trip pt ii) 38, MA 42. Ridley Hall Cam 38. **d** 39 Bp Linton Smith for Roch **p** 40 Roch. C of St John Tunbridge Wells 39-43; Travelling Sec to the Scripture Union 42-80; Chap to Bp of Roch 47-60; LPr Dio Roch 47-81; Dio Chich from 81. *Durham Lodge, Crowborough, E Sussex.* (Crowborough 2606)

EDDLESTON, William. St Jo Coll Dur BA (2nd cl Th) 31, MA 34. Wycl Hall Ox 31. **d** 32 **p** 33 Blackb. C of Colne 32-36; Poulton-le-Fylde 36-38; V of Walton-le-Dale 38-44; St Pet Salesbury 44-65; Dioc Insp of Schs 44-65; R of Shillingstone 65-72; C-in-c of Okeford Fitzpaine 67-72; Perm to Offic Dio Ex from 72. *25 Springfields, Colyford, Colyton, Devon, EX13 6RE.*

EDE, Albert Alfred. Univ of Dur LTh 44, BA 45. Clifton Th Coll 36. **d** 39 **p** 40 Newc T. C of Walker 39-41; Embleton 41-43; Rolleston (in c of Anslow) 43-46; R of Greetham w Ashby Puerorum and Fulletby Dio Linc from 46; C-in-c of High Toynton Dio Linc 49-52; PC 52-68; V from 68; PC of Mareham-on-the-Hill Dio Linc 57-68; V from 68; R of Hameringham w Scrafield and Winceby Dio Linc from 63. *Greetham Rectory, Horncastle, Lincs.* (Winceby 202)

EDE, Dennis. b 31. Univ of Nottm BA (2nd cl Th) 55. Univ of Birm MSocSc 73. Ripon Hall Ox 55. **d** 57 **p** 58 Birm. C of Sheldon 57-60; Castle Bromwich (in c of St Phil and St Jas Hodge Hill) 60-64; Min of St Phil and St Jas Eccles Distr Hodge Hill 64-70; R of Hodge Hill Team Min 70-76; M Gen Syn 75-76; V of W Bromwich Dio Lich from 76; C-in-c of Ch Ch W Bromwich 76-79; RD of W Bromwich from 76; M Gen Syn from 80. *90 Hall Green Road, W Bromwich, B71 3LB.* (021-588 3698)

EDE, Preb Oswald George. b 16. Lich Th Coll 37. **d** 39 **p** 40 Lich. C of Cheadle 39-46; V of Marchington w Marchington Woodlands Dio Lich from 46; RD of Uttoxeter 66-76; Preb of Lich Cathl from 73. *Vicarage, Marchington, Uttoxeter, Staffs.* (Burton-on-Trent 820304)

EDEBOHLS, William Ernest. b 54. Univ of Melb BTh. Trin Coll Melb. **d** 78 **p** 79 Bal. C of S Bal 78-80; V of Timboon Dio Bal from 81. *St Jude's Church, Timboon, Vic, Australia 3268.*

EDEKI, Imevbore. Univ of Dur (Fourah Bay Coll) BA 53, MA 57. **d** 58 **p** 59 Ondo-B. P Dio Ondo-B 58-62; Dio Benin from 62. *PO Box 28, Benin City, Nigeria.*

EDELSTON, James Greenwood. Wells Th Coll 67. **d** 69 Tewkesbury for Glouc **p** 70 Glouc. C of Stonehouse 69-71; Standish w Hardwicke and Haresfield 71-74; R of Alderton w Gt Washbourne Dio Glouc from 74. *Alderton Rectory, Tewkesbury, Glos.* (Alderton 238)

EDEN, Dennis. b 34. **d** 73 **p** 76 Kimb K. P Dio Kimb K. *14 Clifford Street, West End, Kimberley, CP, S Africa.* (Kimberley 91581)

EDEN, Leslie Thomas Ernest. b 19. SOC. **d** 69 **p** 70 S'wark. C of Kidbrooke Dio S'wark from 69. *47 Begbie Road, SE3.*

EDGAR, David. Univ of NZ BA 56, MA (2nd cl Engl) 57. NZ Bd of Th Stud L Th (1st cl) 59. St Jo Coll Auckld. **d** 60 Bp Rich for Wel **p** 61 Wel. C of Lower Hutt 60-62; Petone 62-64; Gonville 64-65; Chap RNZN 65-66; L to Offic Dio Auckld 65-67; C of Paraparaumu 66-68; V of Foxton 68-72; Pauatanahui 72-81; Makara-Karori W Dio Wel from 81. *1 Woodhouse Road, Karori, Wellington 5, NZ.* (767-121).

EDGAR, Donald Haslam. Univ of Melb BA 63. Trin Coll Melb ACT ThL 64. **d** 63 **p** 64 Wang. C of H Trin Cathl Wang 63-66; Perm to Offic Dio Gibr 67; Dio River 68-69; Dio Melb 69; L to Offic Dio N Terr 69-72; Hon C of Ch Ch Cathl Darwin 72-73; Perm to Offic Dio Brisb 74; V of Inala 74-77; L to Offic Dio Rockptn from 78. *State School, Woorabinda, Queensland, Australia 4702.*

EDGAR, Canon Granville George. b 25. St Pet Hall Ox BA (4th cl Th) 46, MA 50. St Mich Coll Llan 46. **d** 48 **p** 49 Mon. C of St Mary Monmouth 48-50; Chap of St Woolos Cathl Ch Newport 50-59; V of St John Ebbw Vale 59-65; St Paul Newport 65-69; Llantilio Crossenny w Llanfihangel-Ystern-Llewern 69-73; Dir of Relig Educn Dio Mon from 73; R of Llangybi Dio Mon from 73; Can of Newport Cathl from 75. *Llangybi Rectory, Usk, Gwent, NPT5 1NL.* (Tredunnock 214)

EDGAR, Timothy Roy. b 56. AKC and BD 78. Coll of the Resurr Mirfield 79. **d** 80 **p** 81 Edmon for Lon. C of St Jude Hampstead Garden Suburb 80-82; St Wilfred Cantley Doncaster Dio Sheff from 82. *40 Cantley Manor Avenue, Doncaster, S Yorks, DN4 6TN.* (0302-51520)

EDGAR, Wyndham. b 06. Dorch Miss Coll 36. **d** 39 **p** 40 Chelmsf. C of St Pet Becontree 39-40; Leighton Buzzard 40-43; V of Edlesborough 43-51; Linslade 51-61; Surr from 51; RD of Ivinghoe 52-61; V of St Mary Virg w All SS St Sav St Mark and St Matt Reading 61-71; L to Offic Dio St Alb from 71; Perm to Offic Dio Ox from 71. *The Plantations, Plantation Road, Leighton Buzzard, Beds.* (Leighton Buzzard 377157)

EDGE, John Francis. b 32. Late Hasker Scho of Ex Coll Ox BA (2nd cl Lit Hum) 54, 2nd cl Th 56, Liddon Stud 57, MA 58. St Steph Ho Ox 54. **d** 58 Lich **p** 59 Stafford for Lich. C of H Trin Oswestry 58-62; Tutor Lich Th Coll 62-64; L to Offic Dio Lich 62-64; V of H Trin Oswestry 64-79; Warden Ho of Epiph Th Coll Kuch from 79. *c/o Box 347, Kuching, Sarawak, Malaysia.*

EDGE, John Henry. b 06. **d** 63 Bp Gelsthorpe for Southw **p** 64 Southw. Publ Pr Dio Southw 63-66; R of Gamston w Eaton and W Drayton 66-73; Perm to Offic Dio Linc from 74. *10 The Meadows, Trusthorpe, Mablethorpe, Lincs, LN12 2QP.*

EDGE, Michael MacLeod. b 45. Univ of St Andr BSc 68. Qu Coll Cam Ba 70. MA 74. Westcott Ho Cam 68. **d** 72 Warrington for Liv **p** 73 Liv. C of Allerton 72-76; R of Bretherton 76-82; Team R of Ewyas Harold Dio Heref from 82; P-in-c of Kilpeck Dio Heref from 82; St Devereux w Wormbridge Dio Heref from 82. *Rectory, Ewyas Harold, Hereford, HR2 0EY.* (Golden Valley 240484)

EDGE, Philip John. b 54. Ripon Coll Cudd 77. **d** 80 **p** 81 Willesden for Lon. C of St Alb N Harrow Dio Lon from 80. *29 The Ridgeway, N Harrow, Middx, HA2 7QL.* (01-429 0763)

EDGELL, Edward Brian. b 02. Worc Coll Ox BA 24, MA 28. Wells Th Coll 36. **d** 38 **p** 39 Portsm. C of St Jas Milton 38-46; V of Bushley 46-49; St Jas Dudley 49-54; H Trin Worc 54-58; R of St Clem Worc 58-60; V of Arlesey w Astwick 60-65; R of Holywell w Needingworth 65-68. *5 Tollgates, Battle, Sussex.* (Battle 2511)

EDGELL, Hugh Anthony Richard. b 31. K Coll Lon and Warm AKC 57. **d** 58. **p** 59 Nor. C of King's Lynn 58-64; R of S Walsham 64-74; V of Upton w Fishley 64-74; R of Hingham Dio Nor from 74; Asst Chap O of St John of Jer from 79; P-in-c of Scoulton and Woodrising Dio Nor from 80. *Hingham Rectory, Norwich, Norf, NR9 4HP.* (Hingham 211)

EDGELL, William John Raymond. b 15. St Aid Coll 63. **d** 65 Warrington for Liv **p** 66 Liv. C of Sutton (in c of All SS from 66) Lancs 65-68; V of St Paul Bury 68-77. *c/o Vicarage, Parsonage Street, Bury, Lancs, BL9 6BG.* (061-764 8839)

EDGINGTON, Charles Spenser. K Coll Lon 30. Wycl Hall, Ox 34. **d** 36 **p** 37 Lon. C of St Mich AA Stoke Newington 36-39; N Walsham 39-40; CF (EC) 40-46; V of Waltham St Lawr 46-51; R of Gt w L Whelnetham 51-54. *c/o Canadian Imperial Bank of Commerce, 4473 West 10th Avenue, Vancouver 8, BC Canada.*

EDGINGTON, Harold James Figg. b 05. LCP 49. Cudd Coll 60. **d** 60 **p** 61 Ox. Hd Master Wendover Sch 48-64; C of Whaddon 60-61; C-in-c of Preston Bissett 61-64; C-in-c of Barton-Hartshorn w Chetwode 61-64; Chap at Bahrain 64-67; R of Boyton w Sherrington 67-76; Hon C of Bladon w Woodstock 76-80; C-in-c of Cottisford and of Hardwick Dio Ox from 80. *St Fergus, Cottisford, Brackley, Northants, NN13 5SW.* (Finmere 418)

EDINBURGH, Lord Bishop of. *See* Haggart, Most Rev Alastair Iain Macdonald.

EDINBURGH, Dean of. *See* Brady, Very Rev Ernest William.

EDINBURGH, Provost of. *See* Crosfield, Very Rev Philip Chorley.

EDMISTON, Canon Douglas Seymour. Coll Ho Ch Ch 5, LTh 64. **d** 51 **p** 52 Wel. C of Lower Hutt 51-53; V of Mangaweka 53-58; Tawa-Linden 58-67; C of St Mark Dalston 67-68; V of Naenae-Epuni 68-81; Can (Emer) of Wel from 81; C of Palmerston N Dio Wel from 81. *34 Birmingham Street, Palmerston North, NZ.* (72-394)

EDMONDS, Bernard Bruce. b 10. Ch Coll Cam BA 32, MA 36. St Steph Ho Ox 36. **d** 37 **p** 38 Lon. C of St Mary Virg Kenton (in c of Miss of H Spirit from 41) 37-48; V of St Matt Oxhey 48-61; C-in-c of St Jas Watford 54-60; V of Caxton 61-72; Perm to Offic Dio Pet from 73; Dios Ox and St Alb from 74. *The Schoolhouse, Marston St Lawrence, Banbury, Oxon, OX17 2DA.* (Banbury 710331)

EDMONDS, Clive. b 42. ACII. SOC 78. **d** 81 Guildf. C of Horsell Dio Guildf from 81. *6 Waldens Park Road, Horsell, Nr Woking, Surrey.*

EDMONDS, Douglas Graham. b 44. Univ of Monash Melb BA 65. ACT BTh 78. St Barn Coll Adel 76. **d** 79 **p** 80 Melb. C of St Steph Mt Waverley 79-81; H Trin Surrey Hills Dio Melb from 81. *368 Mont Albert Road, Mont Albert, Vic, Australia 3127.*

EDMONDS, Canon John Herbert. b 16. Late Colquitt Exhib of BNC Ox 3rd cl Mods 36, BA (3rd cl Lit Hum) 38, 2nd cl Th 39, MA 41. Cudd Coll 39. **d** 40 **p** 41 Lon. C of St Mary Northolt 40-44; Chap and Asst Master Woodbridge Sch Suff 44-47; K Sch Cant 47-56 and from 78; L to Offic Dio Cant from 47; Min Can of Cant Cathl 49-56; Hd Master Jun K Sch Cant 56-78; Hon Can of Cant from 74. *15 Burgate, Canterbury, Kent.* (Canterbury 55840)

EDMONDS, Joseph William. b 12. Bps' Coll Cheshunt, 46. **d** 49 **p** 50 Lon. C of St Paul Tottenham 49-54; V of St Alphege Edmonton 54-66; R of Dickleburgh w Langmere (and Thelveton and Frenze from 69 w Shimpling from 80) 66-81; P-in-c of Thelveton w Frenze 66-69; RD of Redenhall 73-81; P-in-c of Shimpling 80. *Linlee, Snow Street, Roydon, Diss, Norf.*

EDMONDS, Richard Henry. b 11. Em Coll Cam BA 34, MA 39. Chich Th Coll 35. **d** 36 **p** 37 Lon. C of St Aug Kilburn 36-38; St Paul Chich 38-39; Wimborne Minster 39-41; CF 41-43; V of Handley w Pentridge R 43-49; R of E Horsley 49-54; C-in-c of St Mich AA Conv Distr Torquay 54-67; PC (V from 69) of St Jo Evang Torquay 67-74; Surr 68-77; R of Centr Torquay 74-77; Publ Pr Dio Ex from 77. *446 Babbacombe Road, Torquay, Devon, TQ1 1HW.*

EDMONDS, Sidney. b 20. Oak Hill Th Coll. **d** 58 **p** 59 Lon. C of St Geo Mart w H Trin Holborn (w St Bart Gray's Inn Road from 60) 58-61; Chap HM Pris Walton Liv 61-63; Dur 63-69; Parkhurst 69-74; Reading from 74; V of Aldworth w Ashampstead Dio Ox from 74. *Vicarage, Ashampstead, Reading, Berks, RG8 8SH.* (Compton 355)

EDMONDSON, Christopher Paul. b 50. Univ of Dur BA 71, MA 81. St Jo Coll Dipl Th 72. **d** 73 **p** 74 Wakef. C of Kirkheaton 73-79; V of St Geo Ovenden Dio Wakef from 79. *St George's Vicarage, Lee Mount, Halifax, Yorks.* (Halifax 54153)

EDMONDSON, Christopher Talbot. b 32. Wycl Hall Ox 64. **d** 66 Barking for Chelmsf **p** 67 Chelmsf. C of Buckhurst Hill 66-70; V of Leytonstone Dio Chelmsf from 70; Surr from 72. *44 Hartley Road, Leytonstone, E11 3BL.* (01-989 5447)

EDMONDSON, Gerald Paul. Montr Dioc Th Coll LTh

67. **d** 67 **p** 68 Montr. C of St Phil W Montr 67-69; R of Sorel 69-71; I of Thorndale-Pierrefonds 71-74; Granby 74-78; St Paul Chatham Dio Hur from 78. *26 Dolsen Road, Chatham, Ont., Canada.* (519-354 1317)

✠ **EDMONDSON, Right Rev Herbert Da Costa.** St Pet Coll Ja 47. BA (Lon) 50, BD 54. **d** 49 **p** 50 Ja. R of Snowdon w Providence (and Pratville from 52) 50-57; Dir of Angl Schs Dio Ja 57-61; in Amer Ch 62-71; Cons Ld Bp Suffr of Mandeville in Cathl Ch of St Jago de la Vega Spanish Town Ja on 25 April 72 by Abp of W Indies; Bps of Ja; Windw Is; Antig; Trinid; Bps Suffr of Stabroek; and New Providence; and others; Elected Bp of Ja 75; res 79; in Amer Ch. *St Timothy's Rectory, Datona Beach, Florida, USA.*

EDMONDSON, The Right Hon John Cyril. *See* Sandford, Baron.

EDMONDSON, Canon Norman Ross. b 16. St Jo Coll Dur BA (3rd cl Th) 39. **d** 39 **p** 40 Dur. C of Annfield Plain 39-43; Chap RAFVR 43-47; V of Chilton 48-55; R of Crook 55-72; RD of Stanhope 61-72; Surr from 60; C-in-c of Stanley Dur 64-72; Hon Can of Dur from 66; R of Sedgefield Dio Dur from 72; RD of Sedgefield from 78. *Sedgefield Rectory, Stockton-on-Tees, Cleve.* (Sedgefield 20274)

EDMONDSON, Ronald Jack. b 14. Univ of Dur LTh 46. St Aid Coll 43. **d** 46 **p** 47 Blackb. C of Chorley 46-49; Min Can and Sacr of Carl Cathl 49-52, V of Bassenthwaite 52-56; R of W w E Allington and Sedgebrook 56-58; PC of Mithian w Mt Hawke 58-60; R of Mapperton 60-65; V of Melplash 60-65; R of Spetisbury w Charlton Marshall 65-67; V of Martin 67-70; R of Melbury Osmond w Melbury Sampford and Stockwood 70-74. *1 Hastings House, Holyrood Lane, Ledsham, S Milford, Leeds LS25 5LL.* (S Milford 684591)

EDMONSON, David Arthur. b 30. **d** 80 Tas. Hon C of All SS Hobart Dio Tas from 80. *4 Carlton Street, Lenah Valley, Tasmania 7008.*

EDMONTON, Lord Bishop of (Province of Rupert's Land). *See* Clarke, Right Rev Edwin Kent.

EDMONTON, Dean of (Province of Rupert's Land). *See* Dawson, Very Rev Harry James.

EDMONTON, Lord Bishop Suffragan of (Diocese of London). *See* Westwood, Right Rev William John.

EDMUNDS, Gerald. b 12. AIB 34. Glouc Th Course 70. **d** 72 **p** 73 Glouc. C of Tewkesbury w Walton Cardiff Dio Glouc from 72. *29 Manor Park, Tewkesbury, Glos.*

EDMUNDS, Canon Kenneth Crayden. b 05. Late Exhib of G and C Coll Cam 2nd cl Hist Trip pt i 26, BA (3rd cl Th Trip pt ii) 27, MA 31. Ridley Hall Cam 27. **d** 28 **p** 29 S'wark. C of St Pet Brockley 28-30; Chap HMS *Conway* 30-35; Bradfield Coll 35-38; K Coll Budo Ugan (CMS) 38-46; St John Entebbe 39-46; R of Bishop's Cleeve w Southam 47-82; Hon Can of Glouc Cathl from 71. *c/o Rectory, Bishop's Cleeve, Cheltenham, Glos.* (Bishop's Cleeve 2070)

EDMUNDS, Ven William Milton. Univ of Wales BA (1st cl Engl) 34, Dipl in Educn 35 Clifton Th Coll 37. **d** 38 **p** 39 S'wark. C of St Mary Summerstown 38-42; All SS w H Trin Wandsworth 42-44; V of Weston (Herts) 44-49; Opotiki Dio Wai 49-54; Wairoa 54-76; Archd of Wai 66-76; Archd (Emer) from 76; Exam Chap to Bp of Wai 69-76; L to Offic Dio Wai from 76. *Box 382, Napier, NZ.* (434-495)

EDMUNDSON, Canon Edmund James. b 14. Univ of Glas. [f Min in Reformed Episc Ch] **d** 55 **p** 56 Chelmsf. C of Harlow 55-58; V of Exning Dio St E from 58; RD of Newmarket 70-73; Hon Can of St E from 77. *Exning Vicarage, Newmarket, Suff, CB8 7HF.* (Exning 324)

EDMUNDSON, Thomas. b 09. Oak Hill Th Coll 58. **d** 59 Bp Gelsthorpe for Southw **p** 60 Southw. C of St Paul Hyson Green 59-61; V of Halliwell 61-75; L to Offic Dio Blackb from 79. *2 Higher Hill Cottages, Tockholes, Blackburn, Lancs.* (Darwen 71309)

EDNEY, William Franklyn. Wycl Coll Tor STh 61. **d** 60 Bp Hunt for Tor **p** 63 Tor. C of St Columba Tor 60-64; R of Stayner 64-74; Unionville Dio Tor from 74. *Box 1, Unionville, Ont., Canada.* (416-297 1991)

EDNEY, William Henry. b 13. Univ of Birm BA 34. Qu Coll Birm 77. **d** 78 **p** 79 Cov. C of St Geo City and Dio Cov from 78. *20 Loudon Avenue, Coundon, Coventry, CV6 1JH.*

EDOKPOLO, Emmanuel Ayemwenre. Im Coll Ibad 74. **d** 76 **p** 77 Ondo. P Dio Ondo. *Vicarage, Ijagba, Ondo, Nigeria.*

EDOKPOLO, Kempshall Charles. **d** 49 **p** 50 Lagos. P Dio Lagos 49-52 and 56-67; Dio Ondo-B 52-56; Can of Benin 67-68; Archd 68-73; Provost 73-76. *PO Box 40, Benin City, Nigeria.*

EDRIDGE, Peter Jack. b 38. St Jo Coll Auckld LTh 70. **d** 70 **p** 71 Nelson. C of Stoke 70-74; V of Murchison 74-77; Wairau Valley 77-81; Newlands-Paparangi, Dio Wel from 81. *100 Kenmore Street, Newlands, Wellington 4, NZ.* (788-471)

EDSFORTH, Gilbert Fielding. K Coll NS BA 22, MA 23. **d** 25 **p** 26 Fred. Miss Canning w Shipman 25-28; C of Cathl Ch Fred 28-30; R of Norton 30-33; Grand Manan 33-42; St Marg Fred 44-49; Hammond River 49-67. *Grand Bay, NB, Canada.*

EDWARDS, Canon Alan Henry. b 07. Qu Coll Ox BA 30, MA 33. Westcott Ho Cam 33. **d** 34 **p** 35 Portsm. C of Havant 34-37; Chap Cho and Prec of Ches Cathl 38-42; C-in-c of All SS Weston 42-45; C of Cathl Ch of H Trin w St Mary Guildf 45-49; V of Bickerton 49-62; PC of Bosley w N Rode 62-69; Hon Can of Ches 65-74; Can (Emer) from 74; V of Marbury 69-74; Perm to Offic Dio Lich from 75. *5 Kenilworth Close, The Longlands, Market Drayton, Salop.*

EDWARDS, Albert. b 03. Westcott Ho Cam 44. **d** 44 Dover for Cant **p** 45 Cant. C of H Trin Margate 44-46; CF (EC) 46-49; L to Offic Dio Ripon 49; R of St Clem Ordsall Salford 50-54; V of Crawshawbooth 54-60; Mabe 60-67; R of St Gerrans w St Anthony-in-Roseland 67-72. *12 Poltair Road, Penryn, Cornwall.* (Penryn 73409)

EDWARDS, Preb Albert. b 20. St D Coll Lamp BA 48. St Mich Coll Llan 48. **d** 50 St D for Wales **p** 51 St A. C of Welshpool 50-54; V of Stanton-on-Hine Heath 54-58; R of Hanley w Hope 58-64; RD of Stoke N 63-64; Tamworth 69-81; V of Tamworth w Glascote and Hopwas Dio Lich from 64; Surr from 65; Preb of Lich Cathl from 73. *Vicarage, Tamworth, Staffs.* (Tamworth 62446)

EDWARDS, Albert Charles. St Jo Coll Melb. **d** 12 **p** 14 Bend. C of White Hills 12-13; Perm to Offic Dio Melb 13-15; P-in-c of Coramba 15-18; Natimuk 18-20; R of Cobram 21-24; Numurkah 25-28; Boort 55-57; Perm to Offic Dio Bend 57-66. *44 Mackenzie Street, Bendigo, Vic, Australia.*

EDWARDS, Aled. b 55. St D Coll Lamp BA 77. Trin Coll Bris 77. **d** 79 **p** 80 Ban. C of Glanogwen Dio Ban from 79. *4 Erw Las, Bethesda, Bangor, Gwyn, LL57 3HN.*

EDWARDS, Andrew David. b 42. Tyndale Hall Bris 67. **d** 70 **p** 71 Blackb. C of Ch Ch Blackpool 70-73; St Jas (in c of Ch Ch) W Teignmouth 73-76; P-in-c of St Phil and St Jas Ilfracombe Dio Ex from 76; Lundy I Dio Ex from 79. *St Philip and St James Vicarage, Hillsborough Road, Ilfracombe, N Devon.* (Ilfracombe 63519)

EDWARDS, Andrew James. b 54. Univ of York BA 76. Wycl Hall Ox 77. **d** 80 **p** 81 Roch. C of St Jo Bapt Beckenham Dio Roch from 80. *21 Glanfield Road, Beckenham, Kent, BR3 3JS.* (01-650 4061)

EDWARDS, Anthony Stuart. b 40. Univ of Queensld BA 60. Linacre Coll Ox BA 65, MA 70. Univ of Lon MA (Educn) 77; St Steph Ho Ox 63. **d** 66 Lon **p** 68 S'wark. C of St Gabr Pimlico 66-67; Balham 68-69; St Andr Bedford 69-73; St Paul Bedford 73-75; Chap Bancroft's Sch Woodford Green 75-81; Publ Pr Dio Chelmsf from 75; Asst Master Davenant Found Sch Loughton from 81. *25 Newlands Road, Woodford Green, Essex.* (01-504 6571)

EDWARDS, Anthony Terence. b 40. Univ of Manit BA 65. St Chads Coll Dur Dipl Th 67. **d** 67 Bp Cornwall for Win for Bran **p** 68 Bran. C of St Matt Cathl Bran 67-69; I of Fairford 69-70; on leave; Hon C of St Julian Newport Dio Mon from 73. *c/o Newport High School, Bettws, Newport, Gwent.*

EDWARDS, Arthur John. b 42. Univ of Lon BA (2nd cl Hist) 64, M Phil 68. St Mich Coll Llan 66. **d** 68 **p** 69 Mon. C of St Woolos Cathl Ch Newport 68-71; V of Llantarnam 71-74; Chap and Asst Master Bp of Llan High Sch Cardiff 74-78; V of Griffithstown Dio Mon from 78. *Vicarage, Griffithstown, Gwent.* (Pontypool 3641)

EDWARDS, Charles Grayson. b 37. Macalester Coll USA BSc 59. Ripon Hall Ox 64. **d** 66 **p** 67 Ox. C of Bletchley 66-68; Ware 68-73; Team V of Basingtoke 73-79; P-in-c of Sandford w Upton Hellions Dio Ex from 79. *Sandford Rectory, Crediton, Devon.* (Crediton 2530)

EDWARDS, Charles Phillip. b 29. Univ of Tor LTh 71. Wycl Coll Tor 68. **d** 71 **p** 72 Tor. C of Georgina 71-73; R 73-79; St D Lawrence City and Dio Tor from 79. *1796 Lawrence Avenue, Toronto, Ont, M6L 3B7, Canada.*

EDWARDS, Charles Wilberforce. **d** 76 Ja (APM). C of Port Maria Dio Ja from 76. *PO Box 54, Port Maria, Jamaica, W Indies.*

EDWARDS, Cyril Arthur. b 28. Ripon Hall Ox 54. **d** 56 **p** 57 Sheff. C of Rotherham 56-61; Publ Pr Dio Bris from 61; Asst Master Cotham Gr Sch 61-64; St Mary Redcliffe and Temple Sch from 65. *1a Colston Parade, Bristol, BS1 6RA.* (Bristol 22770)

EDWARDS, Cyril Herbert Charles. b 03. AKC (2nd cl) 31. **d** 31 **p** 32 Ox. C of Ch Ch Reading (in c of St Paul Lower Whitley) 31-34; Banbury (in c of Easington) Hawridge w Cholesbury 61-73; Hon C of Reading Dio Ox from 73. *7 Warwick Road, Reading, Berks.*

EDWARDS, David Arthur. b 26. Wadh Coll Ox BA 50, MA 51. Wycl Hall Ox 50. **d** 52 **p** 53 Man. C of Em Didsbury 52-55; Chap to Univ of Liv and Dioc Sec SCM 55-58; R of St Nich Burnage 58-65; V of Yardley 65-73; Org Sec for CECS in Dios Man Carl and Blackb 73-78; R of The Resurr Man 78-81; V of Lorton and Loweswater w Buttermere Dio Carl from 81. *Loweswater Vicarage, Cockermouth, Cumb, CA13 0RU.* (Lorton 237)

EDWARDS, David Forsyth. Late Stud of Selw Coll Cam BA 37, MA 41. Ridley Hall Cam 37. **d** and **p** 41 Southw. C of St Marg Aspley 41-44; Prin BCMS Bible Sch Dio Momb 48-52; PC of St Aug Derby 53-58; Asst Master Alliance Secondary Sch Dodoma 58-62; L to Offic Dio Mashon 63-66; Dio Matab from 66. *Box 553, Bulawayo, Zimbabwe.* (19-81975)

EDWARDS, David Henry Oswald. b 16. St D Coll Lamp BA 38. **d** 41 **p** 42 St D. C of Letterston 41-44; Chap RN 44-71; C of Fishguard w Llanychaer 71-81. *Walmer House, West Street, Fishguard, Dyfed.*

EDWARDS, David Idwal. St D Coll Lamp BA 29. **d** 29 **p** 30 St A. C of Mold 29-34; Offg C-in-c of Henllan-Amgoed w Llangan 34-36; C of Brynamman 36-40; C-in-c of Walwyn's Castle w Robeston W 40-45; R of Llanfyrnach 45-57; St Lawr w Ford 57-76. *Garreg-Wen, Llanfyrnach, Dyfed, SA35 0BA.* (Crymych 460)

EDWARDS, Very Rev David Lawrence. b 29. Late Demy of Magd Coll Ox BA (1st cl Mod Hist) 52, MA 56. Westcott Ho Cam 53. **d** 54 **p** 55 Ely. Fell of All S Coll Ox 52-59; Tutor Westcott Ho Cam 54-55; C of St John Hampstead 55-58; St Martin-in-the-Fields Westmr 58-66; Sec SCM 55-58; Ed SCM Press 59-66; Gen Sec SCM 65-66; Select Pr Univ of Cam 60; Ox 72 and 74; Exam Chap to Bp of Man 65-72; to Bp of Dur 68-72; to Bp of Bradf 72-78; to Bp of Lon 74-78; to Abp of Cant 75-78; Fell and Dean of K Coll Cam 66-70; Hulsean Lect Univ of Cam 66-68; Asst Div Lect 67-70; Six Pr Cant Cathl 69-76; Can of Westmr 70-78; Sub-Dean 74-78; R of St Marg Westmr 70-78; Chairman of Chr Aid 71-78; Chap to Speaker of Ho of Commons 72-78; Dean of Nor from 78. *Deanery, Norwich, Norf, NR1 4EG.* (Norwich 23846)

EDWARDS, Donald Ross. Univ of Queensld BD 71. **d** and **p** 73 Brisb. C of St Francis Nundah Brisb 73-76; P-in-c of St Paul's Taringa Brisb 76-79; Chap St Francis Coll Milton from 79. *St Francis College, Milton, Brisbane, Queensland, Australia 4064.*

EDWARDS, Douglas. b 33. St Mich Coll Llan 60. **d** 62 Hulme for Man **p** 63 Man. C of St Luke w All SS Weaste 62-66; St Paul Kersal Salford 66-71; V of Gedney 71-80. *c/o Gedney Vicarage, Spalding, Lincs.* (0406 362230)

EDWARDS, Dudley James Milne. b 15. AKC 38. **d** 38 **p** 39 Southw. C of Beeston 38-42; N Hinksey 42-44; St Luke Maidenhead 44-46; I of St Phil Port Eliz 46-49; V of St Andr Wigan Lancs 49-51; Asst P of St Aid Miss Bembesi Dio S Rhod 51-52; P-in-c of St Aid Miss Matab 52-61; St Mary Famona Bulawayo 61-63; R of Barlborough 63-68; V of St Francis Mackworth 68-75; R of Ashwick and Oakhill w Binegar 75-80. *Trefechan, The Street, Draycott, Cheddar, Somt BS27 3TH.*

EDWARDS, Emrys Llewelyn. b 14. St D Coll Lamp BA 37. **d** 39 **p** 41 St A. C of Wrexham 39-44; Lampeter-pont-Stephen 44-47; V of Gartheli w Bettws Leiki 47-60; RD of Ultra Aeron 58-60; Kidwelly from 65; V of Ch Ch Llanelly 60-72; Can of St D Cathl 72-79; R of Llanbadarn Fawr 72-79. *Llys-y-Coed, New Quay, Dyfed.* (New Quay 560143)

EDWARDS, Frank Benjamin. b 22. **d** 77 Antig. C of St Geo Dominica Dio Antig from 77. *6 Shillingford Crescent, Goodwill, Dominica, W Indies.*

EDWARDS, Frank Raymond. **d** 79 Rupld. Hon C of St Geo Transcona Dio Rupld from 79. *3 Lethbridge Bay, Winnipeg, Manit, Canada, R2C 2A5.*

EDWARDS, Geoffrey Frank. b 11. BSc (Lon) 31. Glouc Th Course 70. **d** 71 **p** 72 Heref. C of St Mary, Ross-on-Wye 71-80. *The Shrubbery, Camp Road, Ross-on-Wye, Herefs.* (Ross-on-Wye 2641)

EDWARDS, Canon Geoffrey Lewis. b 14. Univ of Lon BD 39. AKC 39. **d** 39 Willesden for Lon **p** 40 Lon. C of All H Twickenham 39-44; Bushey 44-47; V of Mill End w Heronsgate 47-72; V of West Hyde 47-72; Asst RD of Watford 63-68; RD 68-70; Rickmansworth 70-72; V of Hockerill Dio St Alb from 72; RD of Bp's Stortford from 74; M Gen Syn 75-80; Hon Can of St Alb from 76. *Hockerill Vicarage, Bishops Stortford, Herts.* (0279 54930)

EDWARDS, George Walter. Ridley Th Coll Melb ThL 42. **d** 42 **p** 43 Gippsld. C of Noojee Tangil Bren 42; P-in-c 43-44; V of Blackwood Forest and Bass 44-48; C of Bairnsdale 48-50; C of H Trin Cathl Wang 50-70; P-in-c of Marysville Dio Wang from 70. *Rectory, Marysville, Vic 3799, Australia.* (059-63 3281)

EDWARDS, Geraint Wyn. b 47. St D Coll Lamp Dipl Th 70. **d** 71 **p** 72 Ban. C of Llandudno 71-73; St Mary Ban 73-74; V of Penisa'rwaun w Llanddeiniolen (w Llandinorwig from 77) 74-78; R of Llanfechell w Bodewryd Rhosbeirio and Llanfflewin w Llanbadrig Dio Ban from 78. *Rectory, Llanfechell, Amlwch, Gwyn.* (Cemaes Bay 356)

EDWARDS, Gerald Claude Francis. b 04. Keble Coll Ox BA (3rd cl Th) 27, MA 31. Cudd Coll 27. **d** 28 **p** 29 Wakef. C of Staincliffe 28-30; St Edm Northn 30-33; Uttoxeter 33-35; Perm to Offic at Sedgley 35-37; Dio Lich 37-38; C of Ch Ch w St John St Marylebone 38-40; R of Beyton 40-44; Wear Giffard w Landcross 44-51; Hinxworth w Edworth 51-54; Blunham 54-70; Perm to Offic Dio Ex from 70. *The Priory, Halberton, Tiverton, Devon.* (Sampford Peverell 820665)

EDWARDS, Gerald Lalande. b 30. Univ of Bris MEducn 72. Glouc Ordin Course 75. **d** and **p** 76 Glouc. C of All SS Cheltenham 76-79; St Mich Cheltenham Dio Glouc from 79. *26 Monica Drive, Cheltenham, GL50 4NQ.* (Cheltenham 516863)

EDWARDS, Graham Arthur. b 32. St D Coll Lamp. **d** 61 **p** 62 St D. C of Betws w Ammanford 61-65; V of Castlemartin w Warren 65-69; R (w Angle Rhoscrowther and Pullcrochan) 69-77; V of St Clears w Llanginning and Llanddowror Dio St D from 77; Chap (TAVR) from 78. *Vicarage, St Clears, Dyfed.* (St Clears 230266)

EDWARDS, Harold James. b 50. W Midl Min Tr Scheme 78. **d** 81 Birm (NSM). C of The Quinton Dio Birm from 81. *48 Vicarage Road, Harborne, Birmingham, B17 0SP.* (021-426 4760)

EDWARDS, Harry. b 06. **d** 33 **p** 34 Lon. C of Ch Ch Turnham Green 33-35; Ch Ch Southgate 35-38; V of St Andr Muswell Hill 38-46; St Mich Highgate 46-73; Offg Chap Highgate Cem from 47; RD of Hornsey 61-73; Preb of St Paul's Cathl Lon 67-73. *46 Manor Road, Bexhill-on-Sea, Sussex.*

EDWARDS, Harry Joseph Augustus. Moore Th Coll Syd ACT ThL 50. **d** 49 **p** 50 Syd. C of Dulwich Hill 49-51; C-in-c of Flemington w Homebush 51-54; R of Lithgow 54-58; C-in-c of Pagewood Syd 58-65; R 65-70; St Thos N Syd Dio Syd from 70. *PO Box 132, North Sydney, NSW, Australia 2060.* (929-2432)

EDWARDS, Harry Steadman. St Aid Coll 64. **d** 66 **p** 67 Birm. C of St Jas Handsworth Dio Birm from 66. *32 Grafton Road, Handsworth, Birmingham 21.*

EDWARDS, Henry St John. Ripon Hall Ox. **d** 59 **p** 60 Chelmsf. C of Wickford 59-62; R of Woodburn 62-65; Educn Officer Dio Graft 65-69; Dean and R of Ch Ch Cathl Graft 69-79; I of St Steph Mt Waverley Dio Melb from 79. *Vicarage, High Street Road, Mount Waverley, Vic, Australia 3149.* (277 3168)

EDWARDS, Henry Victor. b 48. AKC 71. St Aug Coll Cant 72. **d** 73 **p** 74 Portsm. C of St Alb w Leigh Conv Distr Havant 73-77; V of Cosham Dio Portsm from 77. *St Philip's Vicarage, Hawthorn Crescent, Cosham, Hants.* (Cosham 376579)

EDWARDS, Herbert Joseph. b 29. Univ of Nottm BA 51. Wells Th Coll 54. **d** 56 **p** 57 Leic. C of St Pet w St Hilda Leic 56-61; Min of St D Conv Distr Broom Leys Whitwick 61-65; V 65-68; Lect Lich Th Coll 68-71; L to Offic Dio Lich 69-71; USPG Miss Dio Mashon 71-80; Dio Botswana 74; V of Bloxwich Dio Lich from 80. *Vicarage, Elmore Row, Bloxwich, W Midl, WS3 2HR.* (Bloxwich 76598)

EDWARDS, Ian Carncross. St Jo Coll Auckld NZ Bd of Th Stud LTh 38. **d** 38 Wel **p** 39 Bp Sprott for Wel. C of St Mark Wel 38-42; Masterton 42-43; C-in-c of Pahiatua 43-46; V of Manaia 46-52; Pauatahanui 52-54; Henderson 54-61; C of Howick 61-71; Chap Private Hosps Auckld from 71; Perm to Offic Dio Auckld from 80. *72 Litten Road, Howick, NZ.* (53-49458)

EDWARDS, James Frederick. b 36. ALCD 62. **d** 62 **p** 63 Truro. C of St Kenwyn w Tregavethan 62-68; V of Tuckingmill 68-76; St Columb Minor w Colan Dio Truro from 76. *Vicarage, St Columb Minor, Newquay, Cornw.* (Newquay 3496)

EDWARDS, James Nathaniel. b 28. Codr Coll Barb. **d** 77 **p** 78 Antig. C of St John's Cathl Antig 78-80; R of St Jas Nevis Dio Antig from 80. *St James's Rectory, Nevis, W Indies.*

EDWARDS, John Gregory. b 29. Univ of Wales BA (2nd cl Engl) 49, MA 53. St Steph Ho Ox 64. **d** 66 **p** 67 Lon. C of Ch Sav Ealing 66-70; Great Greenford (in c of St Edw Perivale Park) 70-75; P-in-c of Poundstock Dio Truro from 75; Week St Mary and of Whitstone Dio Truro from 82. *Rectory, The Glebe, Week St Mary, Holsworthy, Devon.* (028884 265)

EDWARDS, John Malcolm. ACT ThL 68. St Barn Coll Adel 65. **d** 67 **p** 68 Adel. C of Prospect 67-69; P-in-c of Warradale w Darlington 69-71; R of Kapunda 71-74; C of St Pet Southport 74; Chap St Hilda's Sch Southport Brisb 74-76; P-in-c of Eliz S (Eliz from 80) Dio Adel from 76. *16 Swan Crescent, Elizabeth South, S Australia 5112.* (255 3173)

EDWARDS, John Russell. St Chad's Coll Dur BA 33, MA 37. **d** 35 Sarum for Ches **p** 36 Ches. C of Neston 35-43; V of St Steph Congleton 43-48; St Mark Dunham Massey Dio Ches from 48; C-in-c of H Trin Bollington 65-73. *St Mark's Vicarage, Dunham Massey, Altrincham, Chesh.* (Altrincham 2311)

EDWARDS, Canon Jonathan Gilbert. b 19. Keble Coll Ox BA 41, MA 50. Linc Th Coll 41. **d** 43 **p** 44 Roch. C of St Jas Elmers End 43-46; Our Lady and St Nich Liv 46-50; Leatherhead (in c of All SS) 50-56; V of Hale 56-67; R of Gt Bookham 67-80; RD of Leatherhead 77-80; Hon Can of Guildf from 78; V of Bramley (w Grafham from 81) Dio Guildf from 80; RD of Cranleigh from 81. *Bramley Vicarage, Guildford, Surrey.* (Bramley 2109)

EDWARDS, Joseph Henry. b 05. St Aid Coll 25. **d** 28 **p** 29 St A. C of Wrexham 28-30; Brotton Parva (in c of Carlin How) 30-31; C-in-c of St Hilda Thurnscoe 31-35; V 35-37; R of St Aid Man 37-50; Chap Ancoats Hosp Man 37-50; Chap to S Man Group of Hosps 50-66. *21 Hurst Avenue, Cheadle Hulme, Chesh, SK8 7PQ.* (061-439 3686)

EDWARDS, Kenneth Barnsley. b 19. Univ of Birm BSc (Anatomy & Physiol) 48. Wells Th Coll 70. **d** 72 **p** 73 Ox. C of St Pet Furze Platt Maidenhead 72-74; Henley-on-Thames 74-77; C-in-c of Hatch- Beauchamp w Beercrocombe and of W Hatch 77-81; Curry Mallet 79-81. *11 Richmond Terrace, Clifton, Bristol.*

EDWARDS, Leigh Cameron. b 17. St Cath S Ox BA (3rd cl Mod Hist) 38, MA 42. St Steph Ho Ox 38. **d** 40 **p** 41 Llan. C of Roath 40-43; C-in-c of Gwernesney and Llangeview 43-46; St Mary Bournemouth 46-49; V of St Jas Southn 49-54; V of St Jo Bapt w Winnall Win 54-58; R of Carshalton Dio S'wark from 58. *Rectory, Carshalton, Surrey.* (01 647 2366)

EDWARDS, Leslie. b 27. Univ of Wales Dipl Th 54. St D Coll Lamp 54. **d** 55 **p** 56 St A. C of Rhyl 55-59; V of Llawr-y-Bettws w Bettws Gwerfil Goch and Dinmael 59-62; Caerfallwch Dio St A from 62; R of Halkyn Dio St A from 66; P-in-c of Rhesycae Dio St A from 74. *New Rectory, Halkyn, Holywell, Clwyd, CH8 8BU.*

EDWARDS, Malcolm Ralph. b 27. Univ of Man 49. Cranmer Hall Dur 57. **d** 59 **p** 60 Man. C of Withington 59-62; Chadderton 62-64; R of Longsight 64-70; V of St Thos Halliwell 70-81; Milnrow Dio Man from 81. *Milnrow Vicarage, Eafield Avenue, Milnrow, Rochdale, Lancs.* (Rochdale 42988)

EDWARDS, Michael Norman William. St Paul's Th Coll Grahmstn 62. **d** 63 **p** 65 Capetn. C of Woodstock 63-66; Plumstead 66-69; C-in-c of All SS Lansdowne 69-72; R of Hoetjes Bay 73-78; St Marg Parow 78-80; P-in-c of Tristan Dio Cunha Dio Capetn from 80. *Island of Tristan Da Cunha, South Atlantic.*

EDWARDS, Mostyn George. BD (2nd cl) Lon 68. Moore Th Coll Syd 65. **d** 69 Bp Macdonald for Perth **p** 69 Perth. C of Riverton 69-71; Mt Hawthorn 71-72; R of Balcatta 72-76. *c/o 30 Eversley Street, Balcatta, W Australia 6021.* (49 1070)

EDWARDS, Neil Russell. Univ of Syd BA 42, MEducn 62. **d** 42 **p** 43 Goulb. C of St Sav Cathl Goulb 42-46; R of Cobargo 46-49; Adelong 49-50; LPr Dio Syd 50-61; Educn Liaison Officer Austr Ho Lon 64-72; Perm to Offic Dio C & Goulb from 72. *301 Bandjalong Crescent, Aranda, ACT, Australia 2614.*

EDWARDS, Nicholas John. b 53. Univ of E Anglia BA 75. Fitzwm Coll Cam BA (Th) 77, MA (Th) 80. Westcott Ho Cam 75. **d** 78 **p** 79 Liv. C of Kirkby 78-81; V of St Jude Cantril Farm City and Dio Liv from 81. *168 Round Hey, Cantril Farm, Liverpool, L28 1RQ.* (051-220 4524)

EDWARDS, Norman. Wycl Coll Tor 69. **d** 72 Moos **p** 73 Abp Scott for Moos. C of Long Lac 72-74; I of Chibougamau 74-78; Noranda Dio Moos from 78. *Box 326, Noranda, PQ, Canada.*

EDWARDS, Peter Aubrey. Qu Coll Birm. **d** 58 **p** 59 Derby. C of Ilkeston 58-61; Aylesbury (in c of St John) 61-65; V of St Pet Didcot 65-73; P-in-c of Letcombe Regis w Letcombe Bassett 73-77; Childrey 75-77; Sparsholt w Kingston Lisle 75-77; R of Ridgeway Dio Ox from 77; RD of Wantage from 77. *Letcombe Regis Rectory Wantage, Oxon, OX12 9LD.* (Wantage 3805)

EDWARDS, Peter Graham. b 50. St Steph Ho Ox 72. **d** 75 Kens for Lon **p** 76 Lon. C of SS Pet & Paul Teddington 75-81; USPG Miss at H Cross Cathl Lusaka from 81; Sec Ordin Selection Conf Dios Lusaka, Centr and N Zam from 81. *Deanery, Box 30477, Lusaka, Zambia.* (Lusaka 250484)

EDWARDS, Canon Peter John Smallman. b 48. Univ of Wales (Bangor) BD 72, MTh 75. Linc Th Coll 72. **d** 73 **p** 74 St D. C of Llanelli 73-76; Prec of St Andr Cathl Inverness 76-77; R of Walton W w Talbenny and Haroldston W 77-81; Exam Chap to Bp of St D 78-81; to Bp of Moray from 81; Prin Moray Ordin Course and Can Th of Inverness Cathl from 81; P-in-c of St Ninian Invergordon Dio Moray from 81. *132 High Street, Invergordon, Ross, IV18 0AE.* (Invergordon 852392)

EDWARDS, Philip John. b 28. Univ of Lon MRCS and LRCP 51. Chich Th Coll 58. 1 60 Tonbridge for Cant **p** 61 Roch. C of St Andr Orpington 60-67; Mayfield 67-71; V of St Richard Haywards Heath Dio Chich from 71. *Vicarage, Queens Road, Hayward's Heath, W Sussex, RH16 1EB.* (Hayward's Heath 413621)

EDWARDS, Philip Osbert Clifford. b 11. St Jo Coll Ox BA 33, MA 47. Wycl Hall Ox 35. **d** 35 **p** 36 Lon. C of St Matt Bayswater 35-38; St Luke Chelsea 38-39; C of Ch Ch Woburn Sq 39-41; Chap RAFVR 41-47; Chap of Ch Coll Ch Ch NZ 47-54; Oundle Sch Pet 54-69; St Chris Hospice Sydenham 69-74; C-in-c of Stoke Doyle 60-63; Chap at Algarve Portugal 74-77; Perm to Offic Dio Pet from 77; Dio Ex from 78. *Abbots, Combe Raleigh, Honiton, Devon.*

EDWARDS, Phillip Gregory. b 52. Univ of Lon BSc. Univ of Birm Dipl Th 80. Qu Coll Birm 78. **d** 81 Cov. C of Lillington Dio Cov from 81. *1 Severn Close, Lillington, Leamington Spa, Warws, CV32 7BZ.* (Leam Spa 313580)

EDWARDS, Raymond Augustus. b 11. Ch Coll Cam BA 31, MA 35. Ridley Hall Cam 31. **d** 34 **p** 35 Lich. C of St Leon Bilston 34-37; C and Prec of Cathl Ch Cov 37-41; CF (EC) 41-46; V of Frosterley 46-49; Ch Ch Bp Wearmouth 49-52; Surr 50-52; Select Pr Univ of St Andr 50; Asst Master Pownall Hall Wilmslow 52-57; C of Wilmslow 53-57; V of Kirklington w Hockerton 57-66; Asst Master Rodney Sch Kirklington 58-66; C-in-c of Winkburn 62-66; R of Instow 66-77; Perm to Offic Dio Ex from 78. *1 Fosketh Terrace, Westward Ho!, Bideford, N Devon.* (Bideford 5580)

EDWARDS, Raymond Lewis. Late Univ Squire Scho Keble Coll Ox BA 46, MA 47. St Deiniol's Libr Hawarden 69. **d** 70 **p** 71 Bangor. Hon C of Dwygyfylchi 70-81; P-in-c of Llandwrog w Groeslon Dio Ban from 81. *Vicarage, Groeslon, Gwyn.*

EDWARDS, Reginald Keith. Univ of Melb BEE 55. St Francis Coll Brisb ACT ThL 63. **d** and **p** 64 Brisb. C of All SS Chermside Brisb 64-66; Bundaberg 66-68; M Bush Bro of St Paul Brisb 68-73; R of Longreach 73-74; Yea 74-77; Euroa Dio Wang from 77. *Rectory, Euroa, Vic, Australia 3666.*

EDWARDS, Rhys Meurig. b 16. St D Coll Lamp BA 37. **d** 39 Ban for Llan **p** 41 Llan. C of Garw Valley 39-41; St Mich AA Harrow Weald 41-44; St Luke W Norwood 44-48; R of Wongan Hills 48-51; Kensington 51-52; Mundaring 52-55; V of Kenley 55-74; Kingston Vale Dio S'wark from 74. *Vicarage, Robin Hood Lane, Kingston Vale, SW15 3PY.* (01-546 4079)

EDWARDS, Richard Sinclair. b 46. Univ of Leeds BA 68, Dipl Th 70. Coll of Resurr Mirfield 68. **d** 71 **p** 72 St Alb. C of St Jas Bushey 71-75; H Sav (in c of St Faith's) Hitchin 75-76; Team V 77-81. *Address temp unknown.*

EDWARDS, Robert James. b 24. St Deiniol's Libr Hawarden 68. **d** 70 **p** 71 St A. C of Eglwys-Rhos 70-74; R of Llanfynydd 74-80; R of Caerwys Dio St A from 80; Bodfari Dio St A from 80. *Rectory, Caerwys, Mold, Clywd, CH7 5AQ.* (Caerwys 223)

EDWARDS, Ronald. b 14. DSO 44. St D Coll Lamp BA 37. **d** 38 **p** 39 Man. C of St Geo Tyldesley 38-41; St John Old Trafford 41-42; CF (EC) 42-46; R of St Paul Blackley 46-50; V of Ashton-on-Ribble 50-52; CF 52-65; Chap Licensed Victualler's Sch Slough 65-76; L to Offic Dio St D 76-80; Perm to Office Dio Ox from 80. *33 Saltdean Drive, Saltdean, Brighton, Sussex.*

EDWARDS, Canon Ronald William. Kelham Th Coll 37. **d** 43 **p** 44 Roch. C of All SS Perry Street Kent 43-46; Chap of St Matt Coll Grahmstn 46-52; R of Seymour w Winterburg 53-57; V of Godmanchester 57-62; R of Cunderdin 62-63; Bassendean 63-67; Claremont 67-74; Exam Chap to Abp of Perth 66-74; Archd of the Coast 71-74; Dean of All SS Cathl Bath 74-77; L to Offic Dio Perth from 77; Hon Can of Perth 79; Can from 79. *2/31 Park Street, Como, W Australia 6152.* (450 1668)

EDWARDS, Rufus Isaac Nathaniel. b 09. St Jo Coll Dur BA (3rd cl Th) 33, MA 43. **d** 33 **p** 34 Man. C of St Mary Rawtenstall 33-36; All SS Elton Lancs 36-38; R of St Mary Beswick 38-45; St Andr Blackley 45-48; Surr 45-48; V of Broughton w Croxton 48-52; Montford w Shrawardine 52-60; R of Whitestone 60-63; PC of Oldridge 60-63; Asst Master Ex Cathl Sch from 60; R of Plymtree 63-81. *c/o Plymtree Rectory, Cullompton, Devon.* (Plymtree 227)

EDWARDS, Stephen Zachary. b 04. Down Coll Cam BA 30, MA 33. Ridley Hall Cam 29. **d** 31 **p** 32 Liv. C of St Helens 31-34; V of Stokesay 34-39; Bullinghope w Grafton 39-42; R of Dewsall w Callow 39-42; V of Cockfield w Staindrop 42-56; Ch Coniston 56-65; C-in-c of Torver 63-65; R of Siddington w Preston 65-69. *Llys Tanwg, Harlech, Gwyn.* (Harlech 780567)

EDWARDS, Stuart. b 36. Ch Ch Coll LTh 61, Dipl Th 70. **d** 60 Bp Rich for Wel **p** 61 Wel. C of Masterton 60-64; V of Mangaweka 64-68; Te Ngawai 68-73; P-in-c of Aranui-Wainoni 73-75; V 75-79; Opawa Dio Ch Ch from 79. *100 Opawa Road, Christchurch 2, NZ.* (327-384)

EDWARDS, Stuart. b 46. Dipl Th (Lon) 70. Univ of Lanc BA 73. Kelham Th Coll 66. **d** 71 **p** 72 Lanc for Blackb. C of

St Luke Skerton 71-75; Ribbleton Dio Blackb 75-80; Team V from 80. *450 Watling Street Road, Brookfield, Preston, Lancs.*

EDWARDS, Thomas Erwyd Pryse. St D Coll Lamp BA 56. St Mich Coll Llan. **d** 58 **p** 59 Ban. C of Llanbelig w Caernarvon 58-63; Asst Chap St Geo Hosp Group Lon 63-66; Chap K Coll Hosp Lon 66-72; V of Penmon w Llangoed and Llanfihangel-Din-Silwy 72-75; Llandysilio (Menai Bridge) 75-81; Glanadda Dio Ban from 81. *St David's Vicarage, Glanadda, Bangor, Gwyn, LL57 2LL.* (Bangor 53405)

EDWARDS, Thomas Harold David. Late Exhib of Jes Coll Ox Gladstone Mem Pri 37, BA (2nd cl Mod Hist) 38, MA 46. St Aug Coll Cant 58. **d** 58 Bris for Sarum **p** 59 Sarum. C of Southbroom 58-61; V of H Trin U Tooting 61-64; Bledlow (w Saunderton and Horsenden from 73) Dio Ox 64-73; R from 73; RD of Aylesbury 72-77. *Bledlow Rectory, Aylesbury, Bucks.* (Princes Risborough 4762)

EDWARDS, Thomas Victor. b 27. St D Coll Lamp BA (2nd cl Phil) 52, LTh 54. Univ of Birm MA 57. **d** 54 **p** 55 Mon. C of Griffithstown 54-56; SSC Dio Lich 56-57; C of St Mary Kingswinford 57-59; V of St Jo Evang Tipton 59-65; V of Oxley 65-71; R of Kingsley Dio Lich from 71. *Kingsley Rectory, Stoke-on-Trent, Staffs, ST10 2BA.*

EDWARDS, Thomas Wallace. b 1891. Univ Coll Dur LTh 21, BA 22, MA 32. Lich Th Coll 19. **d** 21 **p** 22 York. C of St Columba Middlesbrough 21-25; V of Kamo NZ 25-30; Miss at Raga Melan 30-32; V of Lastingham 32-40; R of Terrington 40-57; R of Dalby w Whenby 52-57; RD of Malton 51-57; V of E Harsley 57-64; V of Ingleby Arncliffe 57-64; Perm to Offic Dio York from 64. *Springfield, Throxenby, Scarborough, Yorks.* (Scarborough 60548)

EDWARDS, Trevor William. Univ of Syd BA 72. Univ of Lon BD 77. Moore Th Coll Syd ThL 76. **d** 78 Syd **p** 78 Bp Short for Syd. C of Caringbah 78-80; St Barn Broadway City and Dio Syd from 80. *37 Arundel Street, Forest Lane, NSW, Australia 2037.* (692-0030)

EDWARDS, William Christopher. b 04. Univ of Leeds BSc 27. Coll of Resurr Mirfield 23. **d** 29 **p** 30 Lon. C of St Paul Bow Common 29-31; Southbourne-on-Sea 31-35; St Jas Southampton 36-38; V of Bransgore 38-46; R of Medstead (w Wield from 49) 46-52; PC of Testwood 52-68; V of Binsted 68-73. *30 Courtlands Drive, Biggleswade, Beds.* (313536)

EDWARDS, William Emrys. b 13. Univ of Wales BA (Latin) 35. St Mich Coll Llan 35. **d** 36 **p** 37 Ban. C of Portmadoc 36-42; Llanengan w Llangian 42-45; V of Aberdaron w Bodferin 45-52; Asst Master Caernarvon Gr Sch 52-72; L to Offic Dio Ban 52-72 and from 78; R of Llandwrog w Groeslon 72-78. *Menai, Campbell Road, Caernarfon, Gwyn.*

EDWARDSON, Joseph Philip. Univ of Dur BA 52. Wells Th Coll 61. **d** 63 **p** 64 Ches. C of Macclesfield 63-66; V of St John Egremont Wallasey 66-72; Eastham Ches 72-81; St Luke Poulton Wallasey Dio Ches from 81. *St Luke's Vicarage, Mill Lane, Wallasey, Mer, L44 3BP.* (051-638 4663)

EDYE, Ian Murray. b 21. SOC 66. **d** 69 **p** 70 Chich. C of E Grinstead Dio Chich from 69. *Thrush Field, Coombe Hill Road, E Grinstead, W Sussex, RH19 4LY.*

EFEMEY, Raymond Frederick. b 28. Late Exhib of Ball Coll Ox BA (2nd cl Mod Lang) 51, MA 64. Cudd Coll 51. **d** 53 Croydon for Cant **p** 54 Cant. C of St Mich AA W Croydon 53-57; H Trin Yeovil (in c of St Mary) 57-60; V of U Arley and Industr Chap Kidderminster 60-66; Dudley 66-75; C-in-c of St Jas Gt Dudley 66-69; Perm to Offic Dio Man 75-76; C of All SS Stretford Dio Man from 76. *15 Marlborough Road, Stretford, Manchester, M32 0AW.* (061-865 7522)

EFEREKAYA, David Aminobire Ubiomo. d 69 **p** 70 Benin. P Dio Benin 69-77; Dio Warri from 77. *Box 396, Warri, Nigeria.*

EFFI, Gabriel. b 17. **d** 73 **p** 74 Benin. P Dio Benin 73-77; Dio Warri 77-80; Dio Lagos from 80. *c/o Box 13, Lagos, Nigeria.*

EFUNBOADE, Timothy Oderemi. Im Coll Ibad 58. **d** 61 **p** 63 Ibad. P Dio Ibad. *PO Box 182, Ibadan, Nigeria.*

EGAIRO, Samuel Wapon. Newton Coll Dogura 70. **d** 74 Bp Kendall for Papua **p** 74 Papua. P Dio Papua 74-77; Dio Aipo 77-78; Dio Dogura from 78. *Anglican Church, PO Dogura, Papua New Guinea.*

EGAN, Desmond Russell. St Francis Coll Brisb. **d** 60 **p** 61 Bath. C of St Jo Bapt Wel 60-63; Dubbo 63-65; R of Cumnock 65-69; Trundle w Tottenham 69-79; R of Cant w Hurlstone Pk Dio Syd from 79. *72 Hardy Street, Canterbury, NSW, Australia 2193.* (798-3165)

EGAN, Henry Alfred Ernest. b 09. TCD Hebr Pri 29 and 30, BA 31, Hebr Pri 32, Downes Pri (Oratory) and 2nd cl Div Test 33, MA 36. **d** 33 **p** 34 Derry. C of Ch Ch Londonderry 33-37; I of Castledawson 37-75; RD of Maghera 43-75; Exam Chap to Bp of Derry 61-75; Can of Derry 65-75. *St Ninian's, Whithorn, Wigtownshire, DG8 8PD.* (Whithorn 232)

EGBA-EGBADO, Lord Bishop of. *See* Akintayo, Right Rev Titus Ilori.

EGBA-EGBADO, Provost of. *See* Olomodosi, Very Rev Adeneye Olufemi.

EGBUEDO, Caleb Ahuchama. b 25. St Paul's Coll Awka 78. **d** and **p** 79 Aba. P Dio Aba. *St Simon's Parsonage, c/o PO Box 694, Aba, Nigeria.*

EGBUJO, Edwin Anyaelesim. Trin Coll Umuahia, 56. **d** 58 Niger **p** 67 Ow. P Dio Ow from 58. *Parsonage, Onicha, via Owerri, Nigeria.*

EGERTON, Canon Charles Hubert Sorel. St Jo Coll Morpeth ACT ThL 30. **d** 30 **p** 31 Graft. C of Murwillumbah 30-32; Casino 32; U Clarence 32-33; P-in-c of Coffs Harbour 35-38; R of Murwillumbah 38-47; RD of Murwillumbah 46-47; R of All SS Kempsey 47-70; Hon Can of Graft 55-70; Can (Emer) 70. *RMB 71, Woolgoolga Road-Side, Coffs Harbour 2450, NSW, Australia.*

EGERTON, Canon Ernest Prior. b 08. AKC 35. St Steph Ho Ox 35. **d** 35 **p** 36 Ches. C of St Jas Latchford 35-37; Audlem 37-38; V of Frankby 38-46; St Jo Egremont 46-53; Weaverham 53-74; Chap Grange Hosp from 59; Hon Can Ches Cathl 70-74; Can (Emer) from 74; Perm to Offic Dio Ches from 74; Dio Lich from 75. *4 Copthorne Drive, Audlem, Crewe, Chesh, CW3 0EQ.* (Audlem 811569)

EGERTON, George. b 28. SOC 70. **d** 73 Dorking for Cant for Guildf **p** 74 Guildf. C of Shere w Peaslake Dio Guildf from 73. *Barncroft, Shere, Guildford, Surrey.* (Shere 2549)

EGERTON, Ronald. b 14. Late Scho of St D Coll Lamp BA (Hist) 37. St Mich Coll Llan 37. **d** 38 Bp Wentworth-Shields for St A **p** 39 St A. C of Newtown 38-42; Hanmer (in c of Tallarn Green) 42-47; V of Welshampton 47-54; Lyneal w Colmere 52-54; Silverdale 54-63; R of Selattyn 63-77; Rhydycroesau 63-77; RD of Oswestry 76-77; V of Chewton Mendip w Emborough, Ston Easton and Litton 77-80. *10 Rosehill Close, Whittington, Oswestry, Salop, SY11 4DY.*

EGGERT, Max Alexander. MIPM 81. K Coll Lon and Warm AKC 67. Univ of Lon BSc 74. **d** 67 **p** 68 Lon. C of St Aug Whitton 67-69; Hon C of Hackney 72-74; Llantwit Major 74-75; St Richard Haywards Heath Dio Chich from 76. *94 High Street, Lindfield, Haywards Heath, RH16 2HP.* (Lindfield 3057)

EGGINGTON, William Charles. b 10. Univ of Lon BSc 31. Coll of Resurr Mirfield 32. **d** 34 **p** 35 Leic. C of St Matt Leic 34-39; St Jo Bapt Aldenham 39-40; CF (EC) 40-46; V of Abbots Langley 46-50; C of St Mary Hitchin (in c of St Mark) 50-60; PC (V from 69) of St Mark Barnet Vale 60-80. *Holwell Rectory, Hitchin, Herts, SG5 3SS.* (Pirton 307)

EGGLESTON, Egan Moulton. Univ of Melb LLB 30. ACT LTh 41. Ridley Coll Melb. **d** 41 Melb **p** 42 Geelong for Melb. C of St Jas Ivanhoe 41-42; Min of Belgrave 42-47; St Paul E Kew 47-51; V of Box Hill 51-61; I of Dandenong 61-72; All SS Malvern E 72-77; Perm to Offic Dio Melb from 77. *Avenel, Main Road, Warburton East, Vic, Australia 3799.* (059-66 2268)

EGLIN, Ian. b 55. St Jo Coll Dur BA 76. Coll of the Resurr Mirfield 77. **d** 79 Bp McKie for Cov **p** 80 Cov. C of St Mary Magd City and Dio Cov from 79. *118 Sir Thomas White's Road, Coventry, CV6 8DR.* (Cov 711335)

EGLIN, Reginald Martin. b 1897. Bps' Coll Cheshunt 29. **d** 31 **p** 32 Cant. C of All SS Birchington 31-33; Twerton-on-Avon 33-38; V of Stoke St Mich 38-42; R of Donyatt 42-48; Kingsdon w Podymore-Milton 48-61; C-in-c of Yeovilton 60-61; V of Offton w Willisham and Nettlestead 61-74. *70 Springfield Road, Somersham, Ipswich, IP8 4PQ.*

EGLINGTON, Sidney Ralph. b 20. **d** 71 Graft. Hon C of Kingscliff Dio Graft from 71. *15 McPhail Avenue, Kingscliff, NSW, Australia 2413.*

EGLINGTON, Terence Percy. Univ of Capetn BA (distinc in Ethics) 46. BC Coll Bris. **d** and **p** 49 Syd. C of St John Sutherland 49-50; St Clem Mosman 50-51; R of Wingecarribee w Robertson 51-55; Redfern 55-74; L to Offic Dio Syd from 74. *126 Falls Road, Wentworth Falls, NSW, Australia 2782.*

EGOLUM, Patrick Obidigbo. Trin Coll Umuahia 49. **d** 51 **p** 52 Niger. P Dio Niger 51-59 and 63-79; Dio Ow 59-63; Archd of Awka 71-79. *c/o St Mary's Church, NR1, Awka, East Central State, Nigeria.*

EGONDI, Abedunago. d 54 **p** 56 U Nile. P Dio U Nile 54-61; Dio Mbale 61-72; Dio Bukedi from 72. *Church of Uganda, Busikho, Uganda.*

EGWEDE, Patient Whisky Daniel. Trin Coll Umuahia. **d** 61 Niger **p** 62 Benin. P Dio Benin. *Ozoro, Nigeria.*

EGWUATU, Christopher Nwosa Chukwunyelu. b 34. Univ of Nigeria BA 67. Im Coll Ibad 71. **d** 71 **p** 72 Niger. P Dio Niger. *St Augustine's Church, Umunze, Nigeria.*

EGYPT WITH LIBYA, NORTH AFRICA and ETHIOPIA, Lord Bishop of. *See* Musaad, Right Rev Ishak.

EISEMAN, Stewart Alexander. b 25. St Francis Coll Brisb 77. **d** 78 **p** 79 Brisb. C of St Pet Wynnum 78-80; P-in-c of Surat

Dio Brisb from 80. *27 Cordelia Street, Surat, Queensld, Australia 4417.*

EJAA, Nasanairi. Buwalasi Th Coll 65. **d** 66 Soroti. d Dio Soroti. *Church of Uganda, Kotido, Karamoja, Uganda.*

EJIOGU, Nathanial Egbufo. b 36. Trin Coll Umuahia 77. **d** 80 Aba. d Dio Aba. *Christchurch Parsonage, Akwete, Ndoki, Nigeria.*

EJIVA, Teofilo Caraa. d 63 **p** 66 Ruw. P Dio Ruw 63-72; Dio Bunyoro from 73. *Box 20, Hoima, Uganda.*

EJODAME, Philip Obo. Melville Hall Ibad. **d** 50 **p** 51 Lagos. P Dio Lagos 50-52; Dio Ondo-B 52-62; Dio Benin from 62; Archd 67-73. *St Andrew's Vicarage, Ekpoma, via Benin, Nigeria.*

EJOTU, Joshua. b 32. Bp Tucker Coll Mukono 70. **d** 71 **p** 73 Soroti. P Dio Soroti; Prin Kaberamaido Bible Sch from 77. *Box 10, Kaberamaido, Uganda.*

EKADU, Isiraeri. CMS Tr Coll Buwalasi. **d** 43 **p** 44 U Nile. P Dio U Nile 43-60; Dio Soroti 60-80; Hon Can of Soroti 72-80. *c/o PO Box 107, Soroti, Uganda.*

EKE, Robert Foord Stansfield. b 17. AKC (1st cl) 39. Univ of Lon BD (2nd cl) 39. Ely Th Coll 40. **d** 40 **p** 41 Carl. C of St Aid w Ch Ch Carl 40-43; St Clem Bournemouth 43-46; Wimbledon (in c of St Matt) 46-54; V of Ch Ch Clapham S'Wark 54-62; R of St Paul Nevis 62-71; Exam Chap to Bp of Antig 71-72; V of Alton Dio Win from 72; Commiss Antig from 72; M Gen Syn from 80; Ecumen Officer Dio Win from 80. *Vicarage, Church Street, Alton, Hants.* (Alton 83234)

EKEH, Emmanuel Okechukwu. b 34. Trin Coll Legon 69. **d** 73 **p** 74 Enugu. P Dio Enugu. *All Saints Parsonage, Box 112, Abakaliki, ECS, Nigeria.*

EKELEME, James Odoemela. b 37. Trin Coll Umuahia 76. **d** and **p** 79 Aba. P Dio Aba. *St Mary's Parsonage, Ogwe, via Aba, Nigeria.*

EKEYI, Innocent Nwokike. b 48. Trin Coll Umuahia 78. **d** 81 The Niger. d Dio The Niger. *St Stephen's Anglican Church Onitsha, Anambra State, Nigeria.*

EKIN, Tom Croker. b 29. Linc Th Coll 59. **d** 60 **p** 61 Cov. C of Leamington 60-63; R of Ilmington w Stretton-on-Fosse and Ditchford 63-72; St Jas Durban 72-77; R of Batsford w Moreton-in-Marsh Dio Glouc from 77. *Rectory, Moreton-in-Marsh, Glos.* (Moreton 50389)

EKIRIAT, Ezekieri. Mukono Coll Ugan 56. **d** 56 **p** 58 U Nile. P Dio U Nile 56-60; Dio Soroti from 70. *Kamod, Uganda.*

EKITI, Lord Bishop of. *See* Adetiloye, Right Rev Joseph Abiodun.

EKOH, Elijah Omodele. Im Th Coll Ibad 52. **d** 59 **p** 60 Ondo-B. P Dio Ondo-B 59-62; Dio Ondo from 62. *Vicarage, Oba-Akoko, Nigeria.*

EKOH, Jacob Idowu. d 51 Lagos **p** 52 Ondo-B. P Dio Lagos 51; Dio Ondo-B 52-62; Dio Ondo 62-66; Dio Ekiti from 66. *St Paul's Vicarage, Emure, Ekiti, Nigeria.*

EKOL, Icaka. d 64 **p** 66 N Ugan. P Dio N Ugan 64-76; Dio Lango from 76. *Orum, PO Aloi, Lira, Uganda.*

EKPRIKPO, Wilfred George. Trin Coll Umuahia. **d** 67 **p** 68 Nig Delta. P Dio Nig Delta. *St Augustine's Parsonage, Box 29, Abonnema, Nigeria.*

EKSTEEN, Ven George Johannes. Bp Gray Th Coll Capetn 59. **d** 61 **p** 63 Geo. C of St Paul Geo 61-64; All SS Mossel Bay 64-71; R 71-77; Can of Geo from 74; R of Heidelberg Dio Geo from 77; Archd of Geo from 80. *Rectory, Heidelberg, CP, S Africa.*

EKUNDAYO, Joseph Francis. d 30 **p** 31 Lagos. P Dio Lagos 30-55; Dio Ibad 55-65. *c/o Vicarage, Olanla, via Ikereku, Ibadan, Nigeria.*

EKUWI, Dishon. d 65 **p** 66 Maseno. P Dio Maseno 65-69; Dio N Maseno from 70. *Anglican Church, Namulungu, PO Box 26, Mumias, Kenya.*

EKWENCHI, Canon Edward Enyeana. Univ of Nigeria, BA (2nd cl Th) 64. Trin Coll Umuahia, 55. **d** 57 **p** 58 Niger. P Dio Ow 57-67; Dio Niger from 67; Hon Can of Niger from 72; Synod Sec 72-76. *Boys' High School, Adazi, Nigeria.*

EKWUE, John. b 34. Trin Coll Umuahia 72. **d** 74 Niger. d Dio Niger. *St Faith's Church Awka, E.C.S., Nigeria.*

EKWUFOLU, Chukwudozie Stephen Ndukaku. b 55. Trin Coll Umuahia 78. **d** The Niger. d Dio The Niger. *St John's Church, Ekwulobia, Aguata LGA, Anambra State, Nigeria.*

EKWULUGO, Alfred Me-ka-ogbo. d 23 **p** 26 Niger. P Dio Niger 23-32 and from 36; Dio Lagos 32-36; Supt Ife Distr 43-48; Udi Distr from 48. *Emmanuel Church, Umuabi, Nigeria.*

ELBORNE, William. b 1892. G and C Coll Cam. **d** 44 **p** 45 Pet. C of Uppingham w Ayston 44-47; R of Tinwell 47-55; L to Offic Dio Ripon from 55; Dio Pet from 66; Perm to Offic Dio York 59-80. *Address temp unknown.*

ELBOURNE, Keith Marshall. b 46. Univ of Nottm BTh 74. BD (Lon) 76. St Jo Coll Nottm 70. **d** 74 Barking for Chelmsf **p** 75 Chelmsf. C of Good Shepherd Collier Row Romford 74-78; St Luke Vic Docks Dio Chelmsf 78-81; P-in-c from 81. *St Luke's Vicarage, Tarling Road, Canning Town, E16 1HN.* (01-476 2076)

ELBOURNE, Raymond Nigel Wilson. b 43. Univ of Dur BA 66. Linc Th Coll 67. **d** 69 **p** 70 Ches. C of St Mary Liscard Wallasey 69-72; V of Hattersley 72-77; R of Odd Rode Dio Ches from 77. *Odd Rode Rectory, Scholar Green, Stoke-on-Trent, Chesh, ST7 3QN.* (Alsager 2195)

ELCOAT, Canon George Alastair. b 22. Qu Coll Birm. **d** 51 **p** 52 Newc T. C of St Andr Corbridge 51-55; V of Spittal 55-62; Chatton w Chillingham 62-70; Sugley 70-81; RD of Newc W 77-81; Hon Can of Newc T Cathl from 79; P-in-c of Tweedmouth Dio Newc T from 81. *Vicarage, Tweedmouth, Berwick-on-Tweed.* (Berwick 6150)

ELCOCK, George William. b 01. AKC (1st cl) 26. **d** 26 Willesden for Lon **p** 27 Lon. C of All H E India Docks 26-31; St Matthias Stoke Newington 31-35; Feltham 35-40; V of St Sav U Sunbury 40-48; St Aug Wembley Park 48-54; R of Gt Casterton w Pickworth and Tickencote (and L Casterton from 61) 54-62; RD of Ketton 55-62; V of All H Gospel Oak St Pancras 62-70; Perm to Offic Dio Cant from 70. *174 Faversham Road, Kennington, Ashford, Kent.* (Ashford 26641)

ELDER, David. b 28. **d** 79 **p** 80 Brech (APM). Hon C of St Salvador Dundee Dio Brech from 79. *21 Law Road, Dundee, Angus.*

ELDER, Eric Raymond. Univ of Syd BA (1st cl) Phil and Prof Wood Hist Prizes 22. ACT ThL (1st cl) 23. **d** 23 Syd **p** Bp Langley for Syd 24. C of Ultimo 23-26; R of Erskineville 26-28; SPG Miss at Nukualofa 28-29; P-in-c of Ind Miss Labasa 29-38; V of Levuka 38-41; VG Dio Polyn 41-45; L to Offic Dio Newc 45-46; R of Mt Vincent 46-50; Merriwa 50-53; St John Newc 53-62; Hon Can of Newc 55-62; Prin Austr Bd of Miss Tr Coll Dio Syd 62-64. *23 Mimosa Avenue, Saratoga, NSW, Australia 2251.*

ELDER, Nicholas John. b 51. Hatfield Poly BA 73. Cudd Coll 73. **d** 76 **p** 77 St Alb. C of St Pet Mill End w St John Heronsgate (and St Thos of Cant W Hyde from 77) Rickmansworth 76-79; Team V of Borehamwood Dio St Alb from 79. *Holy Cross Vicarage, Warren Grove, Borehamwood, Herts.* (01-953 2183)

✠ **ELDER, Right Rev Philip Edward Randolph.** Codr Coll Barb 48. **d** 51 Barb for Gui **p** 52 WI. C of St Geo Cathl Georgetn 51-56; R of Suddie 56-62; Plaisance 62-66; Can of Gui 63-76; Cons Ld Bp Suffr of Stabroek in St Geo Cathl Georgetn 20 Feb 66 by Abp of W Indies; Bps of Trinid; Barb; Berm; Georgia; and Puerto Rico; Bp Coadj of Alabama; and Bps Suffr of Kingston and Mandeville; res 76. *1002 4th Avenue, Ashbury Park, NJ 07712, USA.*

ELDERKIN, Denys Frank. b 23. **d** 76 **p** 77 Mon (APM). C of Goytre Dio Mon from 76. *Mon Abri, Plough Road, Goytre, Pontypool, Gwent, NP4 0AL.*

✠ **ELDON, Right Rev Michael Hartley.** St Cath Coll Cam BA 52. St Steph Ho Ox 52. **d** 54 **p** 55 Nass. C of St Matt and Asst Master St Jo Coll Nass 54-63; P-in-c of St Mary Magd W End Grand Bahama 63-64; R of St Steph w St Mary Magd Grand Bahama 64-71; Archd of Grand Bahama 67-71; Cons Ld Bp Suffr of New Providence in Ch Ch Cathl Nass 24 June 71 by Abp of WI; Bps of Ja; Br Hond; Nass; Antig; Trinid and others; Apptd Ld Bp of Nass 72. *Box N-7107, Nassau, Bahamas.* (52647)

ELDRED, Michael Coriell. b 47. Univ of the South Tenn USA BA 69. Trin Coll Tor 72. **d** 75 **p** 76 Alg. C of Ch of Epiph Sudbury 75-77; I of St Jos I Dio Alg from 77. *Box 105, Richards Landing, Ont., Canada.*

ELDRED-EVANS, Peter. b 18. St Jo Coll Dur 48. **d** 51 Dur **p** 52 Jarrow for Dur. C of Chester-le-Street 51-53; Gt Barr (in c of St Chad's Pheasey) 53-56; V of Ipstones 56-61; R of Bolas Magna Dio Lich from 61; R of Waters Upton Dio Lich from 61. *Bolas Magna Rectory, Telford, Shropshire, TF6 6PQ.* (Great Bolas 270)

ELDRID, John Gisborne Charteris. b 25. K Coll Lon and Warm AKC 52. **d** 53 **p** 54 Lon. C of St Geo-in-the-East Lon 53-56; St Mary Virg E Grinstead 56-58; St Steph Walbrook 58-64; V of All SS Portsea 64-72; C-in-c of St Jo Bapt Rudmore Portsea 69-72; C of St Steph Walbrook City and Dio Lon and Gen Consultant (Director from 74) to Lon Samaritans from 72; L to Offic Dio Lon from 82. *The Samaritans, 39 Walbrook, EC4N 8BP.* (01-283 3400)

ELDRIDGE, Ernest Douglas. Univ of Tor Wycl Coll Tor 55. **d** 57 Tor for Alg **p** 58 Alg. I of Sundridge 57-60; C of St Mary Kerrisdale Vanc 60-63; R of St Thos Vanc 63-69; St Matthias Vanc Dio New Westmr from 69. *5628 Ash Street, Vancouver 13, BC, Canada.*

ELDRIDGE, Ernest James Morritt. b 1896. OBE (Mil) 19. St Aid Coll 29. **d** 30 Warrington for Liv **p** 31 Liv. C of St Thos Wavertree 30-34; V of St Cleopas Toxteth Pk 34-39; St Luke

Walton 39-41; St Jas Cheltm 41-65; Surr 58-65. *The Mill, Mill Lane, Prestbury, Cheltenham, Glos.*

ELDRIDGE, Francis Henry Bixby. b 16. AKC (2nd cl) 47. **d** 48 Dover for Cant **p** 49 Cant. C of St Sav Folkestone 48-50; Rickmansworth 50-54; V of H Trin Northn 54-68; St Mary Kettering 68-78; R of Walgrave w Hannington and Wold Dio Pet from 78. *Walgrave Rectory, Northampton, NN6 9QF.* (Walgrave St Pet 377)

ELDRIDGE, Richard Henry. b 21. Univ of Lon BSc (2nd cl Physics) 48, MSc 50. BD (Lon) 61. Ridley Hall Cam 56. **d** 58 **p** 59 Liv. C of Knotty Ash 58-61; V of St Matt Luton 61-67; L Heath 67-76; P-in-c of Belper Dio Derby from 76; RD of Duffield from 81. *St Peter's Vicarage, Belper, Derbys, DE5 1FD.* (Belper 2148)

ELELE, Stephen Uwaeyionu. b 30. **d** 76 **p** 77 Aba. P Dio Aba. *St Matthew's Parsonage, Mgbedeala, Owerrinta, Nigeria.*

ELEM, Isaya. b 19. **d** 78 Lango. d Dio Lango. *PO Abako, Lira, Uganda.*

ELENWA, Canon Samuel Obu Onyuku. b 33. Univ of Nigeria BA 73. Im Coll Ibad Dipl Th 68. **d** 56 **p** 57 Lagos. P Dio Lagos 56-76; Dio Nig Delta from 77; Exam Chap to Bp of Nig Delta from 77. *PMB 5208, Port Harcourt, Nigeria.*

ELERS, Peter Charles Edward. b 30. St Cath S Ox BA 52, MA 56. Coll of Resurr Mirfield, 52. **d** 54 **p** 55 Chelmsf. C of St Jas w All SS Colchester 54-57; Wanstead 57-60; V of Kelvedon 60-73; Thaxted Dio Chelmsf from 73; M Gen Syn from 75. *50 Newbiggen Street, Thaxted, Essex, CM6 2QT.* (Thaxted 830221)

ELESU, Yakobo. Bp Tucker Coll Mukono 67. **d** 69 Soroti. d Dio Soroti. *PO Otuboi, Teso, Uganda.*

ELEY, John Edward. b 49. Sarum Wells Th Coll 74. **d** 77 **p** 78 Sarum. C of Sherborne 77-80; Min Can of Carl Cathl from 80. *7 The Abbey, Carlisle, Cumb, CA3 8TZ.* (Carlisle 46325)

ELEY, Ven Neville James. St Jo Coll Morpeth, 47. ACT ThL 49. **d** 50 **p** 51 Armid. C of Quirindi 51-52; Chap of Lockhart River Miss 52-55; P-in-c of Baradine 55-58; State Sec ABM for NSW and L to Offic Dio Syd 58-64; Org Sec Angl Miss Coun of W Austr and L to Offic Dio Bunb 64-67; R of Dubbo 67-75; Archd of Long 71-75; Newc from 75; Can of Newc from 75. *48 Church Street, Newcastle, NSW, Australia 2300.* (2 1311)

ELEZIE, Nathaniel Onyebuchi. b 35. **d** 72 **p** 73 Aba. P Dio Aba. *St Thomas's Parsonage, Umuosu, Nigeria.*

ELFORD, Robert John. b 39. Univ of Man MA (Th) 71. Univ of Ex PhD 74. Ridley Hall Cam 66. **d** 68 **p** 69 Man. C of St Lawr Denton 68-71; C-in-c Gwinear 71-74; R of Phillack w Gwithian and Gwinear 74-78; Lect Univ of Man from 78; Publ Pr Dio Man 78-79; Exam Chap to Bp of Leic from 78; Hon C of Withington Dio Man from 79; Warden St Anselm Hall Univ of Man from 82. *St Anselm Hall, Victoria Park, Manchester, M14 5BX.*

ELFRED, Michael William. b 48. Coun for Nat Acad Awards BA (Th) 76. Linc Th Coll 77. **d** 79 **p** 80 Linc. C of Boultham Dio Linc from 79. *35 Park Avenue, Swanpool, Lincoln, LN6 0BY.*

ELGAR, Frederick Stanton. b 20. K Coll Lon and Warm AKC 56. **d** 56 **p** 57 Southw. C of Mansfield 56-60; C-in-c of St Barn Conv Distr Pound Hill 60-81. *c/o St Barnabas House, Crawley Lane, Pound Hill, Crawley, W Sussex RH10 4EB.*

ELIAS, David James. St D Coll Lamp BA 50. **d** 52 **p** 53 Llan. C of Ynyshir 52-56; Aberavon 56-59; Llanfrechfa 59-61; V of Magor w Redwick 61-64; Cwm 64-72; Fleur-de-Lys Dio Mon from 72. *Fleur-de-Lys Vicarage, Pengam, NP2 1TX.*

ELIAS, Louis Elias. Bp's Univ Lennox 52. **d** and **p** 55 Queb. P-in-c of Labrador Miss 55-58; Miss at Magd Is 58-60; P-in-c of Scotstown 60-62; R of St Paul Charlottetown 62-69; Bear Brook 70-76; St Luke City and Dio Ott from 76. *760 Somerset Street West, Ottawa, Ont., Canada.* (613-234 5757)

ELIDA, Emanuel. **d** 77 Lango. d Dio Lango. *PO Adukie, Chawente, Lira, Uganda.*

ELING, John Warren. Assumpn Univ Ont BA 61. Trin Coll Tor STB 64. **d** and **p** 64 Bp Snell for Tor. C of St Jas Cathl Tor 64-73; R of St Jude Wexford Tor 73-81; St Anne City and Dio Tor from 81. *661 Dufferin Street, Toronto, Ont., Canada.*

ELIOT, Harlovin Harwood ffolliott. St Cath S Ox BA 36, MA 37, Ripon Hall Ox 34. **d** 37 **p** 39 St E. C of Leiston w Sizewell 37-39; Cockington 39-40; R of Benacre w Easton Bavents and Covehithe 40-52; C-in-c of Henstead w Hulver 42-52; Chap St Felix Sch Southwold 45-49; R of Therfield 52-70; Kelshall 52-70; V of Witham Friary 70-71; C-in-c of Marston Bigot 70-71. *Address temp unknown.*

ELIOT, Ven Peter Charles. b 10. Magd Coll Cam BA 31, MA 35. Westcott Ho Cam 53. **d** 54 **p** 55 Lon. C of St Martin-in-the-Fields Lon 54-57; V of Cockermouth 57-61; RD of Cockermouth and Workington 60-61; Archd of Worc 61-75; Archd (Emer) from 75; V of Cropthorne w Charlton 61-65; Hon Can of Worc 61-65; Can Res 65-75; Can (Emer) from 75; Exam Chap to Bp of Worc 62-75. *The Old House, Kingsland, Leominster, Herefs, HR6 9QS.* (Kingsland 285)

ELIOT, Whately Ian. b 12. **d** 39 **p** 40 Ex. C of Wolborough 39-48; V of Thorverton 48-55; C-in-c of St Paul's Conv Distr Burnthouse Lane Ex 55-64; Min 64-69; V 69-77; RD of Christianity 68-70; Publ Pr Dio Ex from 77. *21 Rydon Lane, Countess Wear, Exeter, Devon.*

ELIOTT, Canon George Vivian Heyman. b 10. Late Scho of Trin Coll Ox BA (2nd cl Lit Hum) 33, 2nd cl Th 34, MA 36. Wycl Hall Ox 33. **d** 34 **p** 35 Wakef. C of Normanton 34-37; CMS Miss Dio W Szech 38-44; R of St Nich Burnage 45-51; V of St Luke Heywood 51-62; RD of Bury 56-62; V of Horwich 62-72; Hon Can of Man 68-75; Can (Emer) from 75; V of Crawshawbooth 72-75; Chap of Bolton Gen Hosp from 75. *13 Ferns Grove, Bolton, Lancs.* (Bolton 491345)

✠ **ELISEE, Right Rev Jean Rigal.** b 27. Philadelphia Div Sch MDiv 70. Episc Th Sem Haiti 52. **d** & **p** 52 Bp Voegli. In Amer Ch 52-71; Cons Bp of Gambia and the Rio Pongas (Gambia and Guinea from 80) 23 Jan 72 in St Geo Cathl Freetown by Abp of W Afr; Bps of Ibad; Lagos; Niger; Bp Arthur; and Bp of Liberia (USA). *PO Box 51, Banjul, Gambia.*

ELKIN, Adolphus Peter. CMG 66. Univ of Syd BA 15, MA 22. Univ of Lon PhD (Anthrop) 27. **d** 15 **p** 16 Newc. C of Newc Cathl NSW 15-16; Gundy 16-18; R of Wallsend 18-19; Asst Warden St Jo Coll Armid 19-21; R of Wollombi 22-25; R of Morpeth 29-37; L to Offic Dio Newc 21-22 and 37-61; Exam Chap to Bp of Newc 31-73; Lect Univ of Syd 33; Prof of Anthrop 34-56; Prof (Emer) from 56; Fell of Senate from 59. *15 Norwood Avenue, Lindfield, NSW 2070, Australia.*

ELKINGTON, David John. b 51. Univ of Nottm BTh 76. St Jo Coll Nottm 73. **d** 76 **p** 77 Leic. C of the Martyrs Leic 76-78; Kirby Muxloe 78-80; Asst Chap Univ of Leic from 80; C of H Spirit City and Dio Leic from 82. *Flat 1, 40 Knighton Drive, Leicester.* (Leic 707689)

ELKINGTON, John Robert Samuel Wilmot. b 04. Ripon Hall Ox 57. **d** and **p** 58 Roch. C of Darenth 58-60; R of Chiddingstone 60-73. *Address temp unknown.*

ELKINS, Alan Bernard. b 47. Sarum Wells Th Coll 70. **d** 73 **p** 74 Sarum. C of Wareham 73-77; P-in-c of Codford w Upton Lovell and Stockton 77-79; Boyton w Sherrington 77-79; R of Bishopstrow and Boreham Dio Sarum from 79. *8 Rock Lane, Warminster, Wilts.* (Warminster 213000)

ELKINS, Patrick Charles. b 34. St Chad's Coll Dur BA 57, Dipl Th 60. **d** 60 **p** 61 Win. C of St Jo Bapt Moordown Bournemouth 60-63; Basingstoke 64-66; V of Bransgore Dio Win from 67. *St Mary's Vicarage, Ringwood Road, Bransgore, Christchurch, Dorset BH23 8JH.* (Bransgore 72327)

ELLABY, Geoffrey Russell. b 09. AKC (2nd cl) and Relton Pri 31. Wells Th Coll 31. **d** 32 Taunton for B & W **p** 33 B & W. C of Weston-s-Mare 32-34; Bromyard 34-36; Emsworth (in c of Warblington) 36-37; R of L Barford 37-40; Buckworth 40-44; Upton w Compmanford 40-44; St Mich w All SS Long Stanton 44-50; Barton Bendish 50-54; R of Beachamwell w Shingham 50-54; V of Manea 54-60; Terrington St Clem 60-64; Lode 64-76. *14 Berrylands, Milton Road, Cambridge, CB4 1XW.* (Cambridge 356700)

ELLAM, William John. Univ of W Ont BA 59. Hur Coll LTh 61. **d** 61 **p** 62 Alg. I of Garson Dio Alg from 61; I of Ascen Sudbury Alg 66-74; St Luke Thunder Bay 74-78; Ch Ch N Bay Dio Alg from 78. *999 Clarence Street, North Bay, Ont, Canada.*

ELLARD-HANDLEY, Philip Ellard. b 11. St Cath Coll Cam BA 32, MA 36. Lich Th Coll 33. **d** 34 **p** 35 Bradf. C of H Trin Queensbury 34-37; Chap of Orleton Sch and C of St Martin Scarborough 37-38; Chap (Eccles Est) Dinapore 38-42; Chap RAFVR 42-44; Perm to Offic at Stanstead 44-45; Hd Master Prebendal Sch and PV and Succr Chich Cathl 45-46; Perm to Offic at Lyminster 45-46; R of N Scarle 46-49; Stow w Sturton and V of Coates 49-56; R of Willingham-by-Stow 51-56; V of Sark 56-77. *64 Laurel Avenue, Onchan, IM.*

ELLEL, Thomas Fielding. b 20. Cranmer Hall, Dur. **d** 63 **p** 64 Blackb. C of Colne 63-66; C-in-c of St Marg Conv Distr Hapton 66-67; V of Huncoat 67-74; Worsthorne Dio Blackb from 74. *Worsthorne Vicarage, Burnley, Lancs.* (Burnley 28478)

ELLEM, Kevin George. St Jo Coll Morpeth. **d** 69 **p** 70 Graft. C of Ch Ch Cathl Graft 69-70; Lismore 70-73; R of Mallanganee 73-76; Perm to Offic Dio Brisb 76-78; R of Booval Dio Brisb from 78. *144 Brisbane Road, Booval, Queensland, Australia 4304.* (282-1471)

ELLEN, Albert Edward. b 01. St George's Windsor. **d** 53 Hull for York **p** 53 Selby for York. C of Newington Yorks 53-56; V of Caxton 56-60; Master of Charterho Hull from 60;

L to Offic Dio York 60-72. *26 The Charterhouse, Hull, Yorks.* (Hull 218943)

ELLERMAN, Brian Walter. **d** 54 **p** 70 C and Goulb. C of Young Dio C and Goulb from 54. *Box 172, Young, NSW, Australia.*

ELLERY, Arthur James Gabriel. b 28. St Jo Coll Dur BSc (Hons Physics) 49. Linc Th Coll 51. **d** 53 Croydon for Cant **p** 54 Cant. C of Milton Regis 53-56; St Laur-in-I-of-Thanet w Manston 56-58; Darlington 58-62; V of Tanfield 62-70; Chap St Olave's Sch York 70-78; V of Gt Ayton w Easby and Newton-in-Cleveland Dio York from 78. *Great Ayton Vicarage, Middlesbrough, Yorks.* (Gt Ayton 2333)

ELLERY, Robert Martin. b 53. Jesus Coll Ox BA 76. St Mich AA Coll Llan 74. **d** 77 **p** 80 S'wark. C of St Jo Div Earlsfield 77-80; Clapham Old Town Dio S'wark from 80. *c/o 20 North Side, Clapham Common, SW4 0RQ.*

ELLINGFORD, Harold David. b 04. Univ of Leeds BA 29. Coll of Resurr Mirfield 24. **d** 31 **p** 32 Lon. C of St Sav Poplar 31-43; R of Thruxton w Kingstone 43-51; V of Winksley w Grantley 51-67; PC of Aldfield w Studley 51-67; V of Healey Ripon 67-74. *Healey House, 4 Park Street, Masham, Ripon, Yorks HG4 4HN.* (Masham 406)

ELLINGSEN, Martin Julius. b 08. Linc Th Coll 33. **d** 35 **p** 36 Dur. C of Seaham w Seaham Harbour 35-36; Dom Chap to Bp of Dur 36-39; L to Offic Dio Dur 37-39; C of St Cuthb Darlington (in c of Blackwell) 39-43; Hon Chap to Bp of Dur 40-51; V of St Hilda Millfield Sunderland 43-51; Perm to Offic Dio Edin 51-52; P-in-c of St Columba Bathgate 52-53; Angl Chap Bangour Hosp Broxburn 52-53; C of St Werburgh Derby 54-55; V of Stanwick w Aldborough 55-60; R of Melsonby 55-60; Exam Chap to Bp of Ripon 58-61; V of Aldeburgh w Hazlewood 60-64; Perm to Offic Dio Dur 64-67; C of Darlington (in c of St Columba) 67-68; V of Coniscliffe Dur 68-73. *5 Elton Road, Darlington, Co Durham.*

ELLINGTON, David John. b 39. Or Coll Ox BA (3rd cl Th) 63. Cudd Coll 63. **d** 65 **p** 66 Shef. C of St Mark Broomhall Sheff 65-68; Timperley 68-72; C-in-c of St Jo Evang Altrincham 72-74; V 74-80. *80 The Downs, Altrincham, Chesh.*

ELLIOT, Hugh Riversdale. b 25. Bps' Coll Cheshunt. **d** 62 **p** 65 Nor. C of Swaffham 62-64; Kessingland 64-67; Mutford w Rushmere 65-67; C-in-c 67-68; C-in-c of Gisleham 67-68; Welborne 68-72; V (in Dereham Group) of Yaxham 68-80; N Tuddenham and Hockering 72-80; R of E Harling w W Harling Dio Nor from 80; Bridgham w Roudham Dio Nor from 80. *East Harling Rectory, Norwich, NR16 2NB.* (E Harling 717235)

ELLIOT, Canon Raymond Elver. Ridley Coll Melb ACT ThL (2nd cl) 52. **d** 53 **p** 54 Gippsld. C of Yallourn 53-54; V of Neerim S 54-58; R of Yarram 58-63; Warragul 63-71; V of Foster 71-74; Dom Chap to Bp of Gippsld 61-73; Hon Can of St Paul's Cathl Sale 69-71; Archd of S Gippsld 71-74; Dean of St Paul's Cathl Sale Dio Gippsld 74-78; Exam Chap to Bp of Gippsld 75-78; Can of All SS Cathl Bendigo from 78. *116 Mundy Street, Bendigo, Vic., Australia 3550.*

ELLIOT-NEWMAN, Christopher Guy. b 43. Westcott Ho Cam 67. **d** 70 **p** 71 Warrington for Liv. C of Ditton 70-73; Hazlemere (in c of Good Shepherd) 73-77; R of Stockton-on-the-Forest w Holtby and Warthill Dio York from 77. *Stockton-on-the-Forest Rectory, York, YO3 9UW.* (York 400337)

ELLIOTT, Brian. b 49. Univ of Dur BA 73. Coll of Resurr Mirfield 73. **d** 75 **p** 76 York. C of Nunthorpe-in-Cleveland 75-77; CF from 77. *c/o Ministry of Defence, Bagshot Park, Bagshot, Surrey.*

ELLIOTT, Charles. b 15. BA (Lon) 55. St Steph Ho Ox 51. **d** 53 Stafford for Cant **p** 54 Lich. C of St Chad Shrewsbury 53-56; Min of Birches Head Eccles Distr 56-61; V of Lower Gornal 61-80; L to Offic Dio Lich from 80; Dio Worc from 81. *1 The Village, Kingswinford, Dudley, W Midl, DY6 8AY.* (Kingswinford 279360)

ELLIOTT, Christopher John. b 44. Sarum Th Coll. **d** 69 Barking for Chelmsf **p** 70 Chelmsf. C of St Pet Walthamstow 69-71; Witham 71-74; P-in-c of Gt w L Bentley 74-79; R of Ch Ch w St Mary Virg Colchester Dio Chelmsf from 80. *Christ Church Rectory, Cambridge Road, Colchester, Essex, CO3 3NS.* (Colchester 74642)

ELLIOTT, Christopher John. b 46. St Mich Ho Crafers 72. **d** 74 **p** 75 Graft. C of Port Macquarie 74-77; P-in-c of Lockhart River 77-79; C of St Pet Coolangatta Dio Brisb from 79. *32 Lanham Street, Coolangatta, Queensland, Australia 4225.* (36 3004)

ELLIOTT, Ven Clark Russell. K Coll NS BA 37. **d** 40 **p** 41 NS. C of H Trin Liverpool NS 40-43; Pugwash 43-46; R of Bridgetown 46-56; Lantz 56-63; St John Halifax 63-68; Liverpool 69-76; St John Halifax Dio NS from 76; Archd of S Shore 69-76; Archd (Emer) from 77; Hon Can of NS from 80. *3433 Dutch Village Road, Halifax, NS, Canada.* (454-4061)

ELLIOTT, Ven Clement Henry. **d** and **p** 24 Accra. P-in-c of Tarkwa 24-29; Koforidua 29-37; Ch Ch Cape Coast 37-49; Tutor Prince of Wales Coll Achimota 49-60; Archd of Sekondi 51-60; Archd (Emer) from 73; Hon Can of Accra 60-72; L to Offic Dio Accra 60-72. *PO Box 373, Cape Coast, Ghana.* (Cape Coast 373)

ELLIOTT, Canon Colin. b 23. St Pet Coll, Ox 2nd cl Phil Pol Econ BA 48, Dipl Th 49, MA 52. Wycl Hall, Ox 48. **d** 49 Liv **p** 50 Warrington for Liv. C of St Cath Wigan 49-52; St Nich Blundellsands (in c of St Steph Hightown) 52-55; V of St Paul Southport 55-59; R of Windermere Dio Carl from 59; Surr from 61; RD of Windermere from 79; Hon Can of Carl Cathl from 81. *Rectory, Glebe Road, Windermere, Cumb, LA23 3HB.* (Windermere 3063)

ELLIOTT, Colin David. b 32. K Coll Lon and Warm AKC 55. **d** 56 Dover for Cant **p** 57 Cant. C of W Wickham 56-59; Dover 59-64; V of Linton 64-66; H Trin Gillingham 66-81; Belvedere Dio Roch from 81. *Vicarage, Nuxley Road, Belvedere, Kent.* (Erith 32169)

ELLIOTT, Very Rev David. b 31. Bps' Coll Cheshunt, 60. **d** 63 **p** 64 Chelmsf. C of St Anne Chingford 63-64; Woodford 64-66; Chap of Qatar, Trucial States, Muskat and Oman 67-69; Prec St Alb Cathl 69-71; Dean of Ndola Cathl 72-75; Vicar Gen of Centr Zam 72-75; Hon Can of H Nativ Cathl Ndola from 75; V of Borehamwood 75-79; Team R 79; Dean of St Geo Cathl Ch Jer from 79. *Box 19018, Jerusalem, Israel.* (Jer 282167)

ELLIOTT, Derek John. b 26. Pemb Coll Cam 2nd cl Hist Trip pt i, 49, BA (2nd cl Hist Trip pt ii), 50, MA 55. Oak Hill Th Coll 48. **d** 51 Lon **p** 53 Cov. C of St John W Ealing 51-53; New Milverton 53-55; St John Boscombe 55-57; V of Biddulph 57-63; Surr 60-68; R of Rushden 63-68; RD of Higham 66-68; Chap Bedford Modern Sch from 68. *268 Kimbolton Road, Bedford.* (Bedford 68831)

ELLIOTT, Derrick. **d** 79 St Alb **p** 80 Bedford for St Alb (APM). C of St Nich Harpenden (in c of St Mary Kinsbourne Green from 80) Dio St Alb from 79. *86 Tuffnells Way, Harpenden, Herts, AL5 4QH.* (Harpenden 62485)

ELLIOTT, Preb Eric Patrick Moore. b 16. St Edm Hall Ox BA (2nd cl Mod Hist) 38, MA 44. Westcott Ho Cam 38. **d** 44 **p** 45 Clogh. C-in-c of H Trin Garvary 44-50; Dio Sec Dio Clogh 47-50; Educn Officer for Ch of Ireland in N Ireland 50-57; R of Ch Ch Belf 57-63; Chief Insp of Schs Dios Down and Drom and Connor 58-61; RD of Mid-Belf 60-63; Chap Stranmillis Coll Belf 61-67; R of St Thos Belf Dio Connor from 63; Preb of Rathmichael in St Patr Cathl Dub from 64. *St Thomas's Parsonage, Eglatine Avenue, Belfast 9, N Ireland.*

ELLIOTT, Frank Robert. St Jo Coll Morpeth. **d** 56 **p** 57 Newc. C of Merewether 56-58; V of Nundle 58-69; Moree Dio Armid from 69. *Vicarage, Moree, NSW, Australia 2400.* (52-1103)

ELLIOTT, George Evan. b 17. Sarum Th Coll. **d** 58 **p** 59 Blackb. C of Padiham 58-61; Cleveleys 61-63; Min of Kimblesworth Eccles Distr Dio Dur 63-64; V 64-71; St Jas Sutton 71-78; St Edm Sutton 71-78; R of Wadingham w Snitterby 78-80; V of Bp Norton w Atterby (w Wadingham and Snitterby from 80) Dio Linc from 78. *Vicarage, Bishop Norton, Lincoln.* (Bp Norton 663)

ELLIOTT, George Henry. b 20. Lich Th Coll 51. **d** 54 **p** 55 Newc T. C of Haltwhistle 54-56; St Gabr Heaton Newc T 56-61; V of Amble 61-63; Long Framlington w Brinkburn 63-68; Hon C of St Pet Monkseaton Dio Newc T 68-70; L to Offic Dio Newc T from 70. *83 Beverley Road, Monkseaton, Whitley Bay, Northumb, NE25 8JQ.* (Whitley Bay 29457)

ELLIOTT, Gordon. Qu Coll Newfld. **d** 11 **p** 13 Newfld. C of Random 11-12; Bonavista 12-13; I of Rose Blanche 13-17; R of Badger's Quay 17-18; I of Tack's Beach 18-24; whitbourne 24-28; R of Port de Grace 28-31; Change Is 31-37; C of Ramsgate 37-39; V of Shoulden 39-47; R of Foxtrap 47-59. *Twillingate, Notre Dame Bay, Newfoundland, Canada.*

ELLIOTT, Gordon. b 25. St Aid Coll 63. **d** 65 **p** 66 Ches. C of St Jas Latchford 65-68; St Jo Bapt Bollington 68-70; V of St Mark Dukinfield 70-73; Team V of Tenbury Wells 74-78; Burford I II III 74-78; R of Culmington w Onibury Dio Heref from 78; V of Bromfield Dio Heref from 78; Stanton Lacy Dio Heref from 78. *Bromfield Vicarage, Ludlow, Salop.* (Bromfield 234)

ELLIOTT, Harry. b 04. LTh (Dur) 30. St Aug Coll Cant 26. **d** 30 **p** 32 Ripon. C of St Mary Hunslet 30-35; R of Kondinin w Wickepin 35-39; C of All SS Leeds 39-41; Chap RAFVR 41-48; C of St Jo Bapt Adel Leeds 48-50; Laister Dyke 50-51; V of Horton-in-Ribblesdale 51-58; Embsay w Eastby 58-70; Rathmell-in-Craven w Wigglesworth 70-73. *22 Grassington Road, Skipton, Yorks.*

ELLIOTT, Ian David. b 40. Qu Coll Cam BA 61, MA 65. Tyndale Hall Bris 64. **d** 66 Warrington for Liv **p** 67 Liv. C of Halewood 66-71; Gt Crosby 71-74; C-in-c of St Mark's Conv

Distr Dallam, Warrington Dio Liv 74-80; V from 80. *141a Longshaw Street, Dallam Estate, Warrington, Chesh, WA5 5JE.* (Warrington 31193)

ELLIOTT, James Andrew Theodore. Em Coll Sktn. **d** 34 **p** 35 Sktn. C of Senlac 34-35; I of Radisson 35-37; Kinistino 37-39; Wynyard 39-45; Beachburg 45-49; R of Ashton 49-56; Chesley 56-60; Colchester 60-72; Wheatley 72-74; C of St Jo Evang Niag Falls Dio Niag from 75. *Apt 308, 39 Leaside Drive, St Catharines, Ont., Canada.*

ELLIOTT, John George. b 15. Qu Coll Ox BA 37, MA 46. Westcott Ho Cam 46. **d** 47 **p** 48 Ches. C of St Sav Oxton Chesh 47-51; Chap St Thos Coll Gurutalawa 51-52; Trin Coll Kandy Ceylon 52-61; Loughborough Gr Sch 61-80. *14 Victoria Street, Loughborough, Leics, LE11 2EN.* (Loughborough 63365)

ELLIOTT, John Philip. b 37. Univ of Salford CEng. MIChemE 61. Glouc Sch for Min 79. **d** and **p** 80 Glouc (APM). C of Brimscombe 80-82. *69 Bownham Park, Rodborough Common, Stroud, Glos.*

ELLIOTT, Ven John Stoddart. **d** and **p** 50 Syd. Asst Chap Miss to Seamen Syd 51-52; Chap to RAAF from 52; Prin Chap from 75; Archd in RAAF from 75. *485 Bourke Street, Melbourne, Vic, Australia 3000.* (03-60 0261)

ELLIOTT, Joseph William. Chich Th Coll. **d** 66 Jarrow for Dur **p** 67 Dur. C of Whickham 66-72; V of Lamsley 72-78; R of Usworth Dio Dur from 78. *4 Highbury Close, Springwell, Gateshead, T & W, NE37 1NW.*

ELLIOTT, Keith. VC 42. Coll Ho Ch Ch. **d** 47 **p** 48 Wel. C of All SS Palmerston N 47-50; Asst Missr Wel City Miss 50-52 and 66-73; V of Pongaroa 52-56; Pohangina 56-59; of Wainuia-arua Maori Past 59-63; Aotea-Kurahaupo Maori Past 63-66; Asst Missr Wel City Miss 66-73; V of Makara w Karori W 73-81; Perm to Offic Dio Wel from 81. *36 Tiromoana Road, Raumati, NZ.*

ELLIOTT, Leslie Aidan. b 13. Qu Coll Cam BA 35, MA 39. Trin Coll Dub Downe's Comp Pri 36 and 37, Newport White Pri 37. **d** 37 **p** 38 Down. C of Cathl Ch Lisburn 37-40; Zion Ch Rathgar 40-43; I of Celbridge w Straffan 44-50; Finglas 50-59; Greystones 59-73; Durrus 73-78; Kilmoe U Dio Cork from 78; Can of Ch Ch Cathl Dub 66-73. *Altar Rectory, Toormore, Schull, Co Cork, Irish Republic.*

ELLIOTT, Matthew George Holden. b 49. Univ of Tor BA 72. Wycl Coll Tor MDiv 79. **d** 79 Bp Read for Tor **p** 80 Tor. C of St Thos Mississauga 79-80; I of St Paul Minden Dio Tor from 81. *Box 83, Minden, Ont, Canada, K0M 2K0.*

ELLIOTT, Michael Cowan. b 38. Univ of Auckld BA 63. NZ Bd of Th Stud LTh 61. Episc Th Sch Mass BD 66. St Jo Coll Auckld 59. **d** 61 **p** 62 Auckld. C of New Lynn 61-64; Thames 65; Warden Pemb Coll Cam Miss Walworth 66-70; Dir St Luke's Centre Haifa 70-74; C (in c of Coleshill) of Amersham 74-75; Dir Ecumen Development NZ and Hon C of St Matt City and Dio Auck from 76. *Box 5038, Wellesley Street, Auckland, NZ.* (74-433)

ELLIOTT, Peter. b 41. Hertf Coll Ox BA (3rd cl Mod Hist) 63, MA 68. Linc Th Coll. **d** 65 **p** 66 Newc T. C of All SS Gosforth 65-68; St Pet Balkwell Tynemouth 68-72; V of St Phil Newc T 72-80; N Gosforth Dio Newc T from 80. *North Gosforth Vicarage, Wideopen, Newcastle upon Tyne, NE13 6NH.* (Wideopen 362280)

ELLIOTT, Peter Gordon. b 54. Trent Univ Peterborough Ont BA 76. Episc Div Sch Cam Mass MDiv 80. **d** 80 Niag **p** 81 Bp CM Mitchell for Niag. C of Ch Ch Cathl Hamilton Dio Niag from 80. *c/o Christ's Church Cathedral, 252 James Street North, Hamilton, Ont, 3239)*

ELLIOTT, Peter Wolstenholme. b 31. N-E Ordin Course 78. **d** 81 York (NSM). C of Yarm Dio York from 81. *48 Butterfield Drive, Eaglescliffe, Stockton-on-Tees, Cleve, TS16 0EZ.* (Eaglescliffe 782788)

ELLIOTT, Raymond Harold. b 43. Univ of Monash BSc 66. Trin Coll Melb ThL 69. Melb Coll of Div BDiv 72. **d** 70 **p** 71 Melb. C of St David's Moorabbin 70-71; M in Dept of Chr Educn Dio Melb 71-73; Field Officer 74-77; L to Offic Dio Melb 74-77; Chap Trin Gr Sch Kew from 77. *14 Heather Court, East Hawthorn, Vic, Australia 3123.* (86-6204)

ELLIOTT, Raymond Paul. b 56. Univ of Ex BA (Th) 78. St Steph Ho Ox 79. **d** 81 Ches. C of St Mich Coppenhall Crewe Dio Ches from 81. *38 Evans Street, Crewe, Cheshire.* (Crewe 212430)

ELLIOTT, Richard Timothy. b 47. Univ of W Ont BA 68. Gen Th Sem NY MDiv 71. **d** 77 Bp Read for Tor **p** 78 Tor. C of St Geo-on-the-Hill Tor 77-80; I of All SS King Dio Tor from 80. *Box 33, King City, Ont, L0G 1K0, Canada.*

ELLIOTT, Robert George. **d** 48 **p** 49 Montr. C of St Clem Verdun Montr 48-50; I of Aylwin and of River Desert 50-52; R of Shawville and of N Clarendon 52-60; St Paul Côte des Neiges Montr 60-66; I of Two Mountains Montr 66-77; P-in-c of St Eustache-sur-le-Lac 66-77. *Box 386, Maxville, Ont, Canada.*

ELLIOTT, Roland Jack. b 12. Clifton Th Coll 52. **d** 53 Glouc **p** 54 Bp Barkway for Cant. C of St Jas Glouc 53-55; H Trin Stroud 55-57; R of Littledean 57-78; RD of S Forest 70-75. *7 Bells Place, Ruspidge, Cinderford, Glos, GL14 3BA.* (Cinderford 23550)

ELLIOTT, Stanley Griffin. b 19. Univ of Lon BA 50. Ridley Hall Cam 50. **d** 52 **p** 53 Man. C of St Paul Astley Bridge 52-54; St Thos Bedford-Leigh 54-56; R of St Cypr Ordsall Salford 56-59; Ashton-on-Mersey 59-80; V of Tile Hill Dio Cov from 80. *Vicarage, Jardine Crescent, Coventry, CV4 9PL.* (Cov 465072)

ELLIOTT, Thomas. b 08. Late Scho of Selw Coll Cam 2nd cl Hist Trip pt i, 29, BA (2nd cl Hist Trip pt ii) 30, 2nd cl Th Trip pt ii, 32, MA 38. Ridley Hall, Cam 31. **d** 33 **p** 34 Dur. C of S Westoe 33-36; Vice-Prin Bp Wilson Coll IM 36-38; Tutor 38-42; R of Ballaugh 38-48; Prin of Bp Wilson Coll IM 42-43; Dom Chap to Bp of S & M 42-48; R of N Creake 48-77; P-in-c 77-78; RD of Burnham 56-68; C-in-c of Waterden 57-69. *Dunelm House, South Creake, Fakenham, Norf, NR21 9PG.*

ELLIOTT, Trevor Michael. St Jo Coll Winnipeg. **d** 63 **p** 64 Edmon. d Dio Edmon 63-64; I of Edgerton 64-71; St Faith City and Dio Edmon from 71. *53 Ridgewood Terrace, St Albert, Edmonton, Alta., Canada.* (403-459 5889)

ELLIOTT, William. b 20. BA (2nd cl Hist) Lon 56. Ripon Hall, Ox. **d** 61 **p** 62 Worc. C of Kidderminster 61-70; V of Far Forest 70-78; Rock w Heightington and Far Forest Dio Worc from 78. *Far Forest Vicarage, Kidderminster, Worcs.* (Rock 266580)

ELLIOTT, William Charles. b 10. **d** 67 **p** 68 Ches. C of Saltney (or Lache) 67-69; Harlington 69-72; C-in-c of Ch Ch Conv Distr Harlington 72-76. *35 Station Road, Harpenden, Herts.*

ELLIOTT, William Edmund Hartley. St Paul's Th Coll Grahmstn 59. **d** 60 **p** 61 St John's. C of St John's Cathl Umtata 60-61; Matatiele 61-65; P-in-c of Swartberg 65-76. *Box 33, Matatiele 4730, S Africa.* (Matatiele 89)

ELLIOTT, William Henry Venn. b 34. K Coll Cam BA 55, MA 59. Wells Th Coll. **d** 61 **p** 62 Wakef. C of Almondbury 61-66; V of Bramshaw 66-81; Mere w W Knoyle and Maiden Bradley Dio Sarum from 81; P-in-c of Landford w Plaitford 77-81. *Vicarage, Angel Lane, Mere, Warminster, Wilts, BA12 6DH.* (Mere 860292)

ELLIOTT, William James. b 38. Jes Coll Cam 3rd cl Cl Trip pt i, 61, BA (3rd cl Th Trip pt ia) 62, MA 66. Univ of Birm MA (Th) 69, PhD 74. Qu Coll Birm 62. **d** 64 **p** 65 Lon. C of Mill Hill 64-67; St Pancras 67-69; C-in-c of St Paul Preston 69-73; R of Elstree Dio St Alb from 73. *Rectory, Elstree, Herts.* (01-953 1411)

ELLIOTT, William Norman. b 20. Kelham Th Coll 37. **d** 43 **p** 44 Lich. C of St Mich Tividale Tipton 43-50; St Mary Barnsley (in c of St Paul) 50-55; V of St Mich Castleford 55-63; S Crosland Dio Wakef from 64. *South Crosland Vicarage, Huddersfield, W Yorks.* (Huddersfield 661080)

ELLIS, Arthur Norman. Qu Coll Cam 2nd cl Cl Trip pt i, 32, BA (2nd cl Engl Trip pt ii) 33, 2nd cl Th Trip pt i, 34, MA 45. Univ of W Ont BD 55. Ridley Hall, Cam 33. **d** 35 **p** 36 Liv. C of St Ann Warrington 35-37; Bootle 37-39; V of Ch Ch Waterloo Lancs 39-52; R of Brussels Ont 52-56; Courtright 56-60; Harrow 60-64; All SS City and Dio Tor from 64. *101 Roehampton Avenue, Toronto 12, Ont., Canada.* (416-368 7977)

ELLIS, Bruce William. b 45. Coll of Em and St Chad Sktn 78. **d** 80 **p** 81 Calg. C of St Jas City and Dio Calg from 80. *c/o St James' Church, 6351 Ranchview Drive NW, Calgary, Alta, Canada, T3G 1B5.*

ELLIS, Bryan Stuart. b 31. Qu Coll Cam BA 54, MA 58. **d** 57 **p** 58 Cant. C of St Luke Ramsgate 57-59; Herne Bay 59-62; V of Burmantofts 62-81; St Andr w St Mary City and Dio Wakef from 81; RD of Wakef from 81. *31 Peterson Road, Wakefield, W Yorks, WF1 4DU.* (Wakef 375600)

ELLIS, Charles Harold. b 50. NOC 78. **d** 81 Man. C of St Mary Davyhulme Dio Man from 81. *95 Davyhulme Road, Urmston, Manchester, M31 2BU.*

ELLIS, Christopher Charles. b 55. Univ of Edin BD 78. Univ of Hull MA 80. Edin Th Coll 76. **d** 79 **p** 80 York. C of Abbey Ch of Our Lord St Mary and St Germain Selby Dio York from 79; Ecumen Adv Dio York from 81. *24 Londesborough Street, Selby, N Yorks, YO8 0AW.*

ELLIS, Clarence Douglas. McGill Univ BA (1st cl Cl and Medal) 44, PhD 54. Univ of Tor MA 46. Trin Coll Tor LST 48. Yale Univ MA 49. Selw Coll Cam BA 51. **d** 47 **p** 48 Montr. Perm to Offic Dio Ely 50-51; C of St Matthias Montr 51-54; w MSCC 54-55; I of Albany 55-58; Prof of Linguistics McGill Univ from 69. *5205 Hingston Avenue, Montreal 253, PQ, Canada.* (514-488 0298)

ELLIS, Craig Tullo. b 51. St Jo Coll Morpeth 76. **d** 80 Tas. Hon C of Howrah 80; C of Cressy Dio Tas from 80. *The Rectory, Cressy, Tasmania 7302.*

ELLIS, David Arthur. Univ of Tor BA 52, MA 55. Trin Coll Tor STB 55. **d** 55 **p** 56 Ott. Miss at Sugluk 55-60; I of

Athab 60-64; Dean and R of St Jas Cathl Peace River 64-69; R of St Columba St Cath 70-71; Okotoks 73-78; Banff Dio Calg from 78. *Box 309, Banff, Alta, Canada.* (762-3694)

ELLIS, David Craven. b 34. Univ of Man BA (2nd cl Engl) 56, MA 57. St Aid Coll 59. **d** 61 **p** 62 Liv. C of Gt Crosby Liv 61-65; Chap Dioc Boys' Sch Kowloon and C of Ch Ch Kowloon Dio Hong 65-69; C-in-c of Sawrey 69-74; Dioc Youth Officer Carl 69-74; V of St Aug Halifax Dio Wakef from 74. *Vicarage, Hanson Lane, Halifax, Yorks.* (Halifax 65552)

ELLIS, David Edward. b 06. St Mich Coll Llan 46. **d** 48 **p** 49 Ban. C of Llanllechid 48-50; Penmaenmawr 50-52; Llanberis 52-55; V of Clynog Fawr 55-76. *3 Lon Ddwr, Talybont, Bangor, Gwyn.*

ELLIS, Edmund Mackay. b 04. Sarum Th Coll 27. **d** 29 **p** 30 Wakef. C of St Jas Heckmondwike 29-35; St Mark Portsea 35-39; Newport 39-40; V of Langrish (w Privett from 52) Dio Portsm 40-73. *12 Barnfield Road, Petersfield, Hants.* (Petersfield 4342)

ELLIS, Edward Charles. K Coll Halifax NS BA 61, BST 64. BD 66. **d** 64 **p** 65 NS. R of Port Morien 64-68; E Passage Dio NS from 68. *Rectory, Eastern Passage, Dartmouth, NS, Canada.* (469-6607)

ELLIS, Frank Stephen. b 57. St Mich Ho Crafers 76. **d** 80 **p** 81 The Murray. C of Murray Bridge Dio The Murray from 80. *4 Clara Street, Murray Bridge, S Australia 5253.* (085 32 3680)

ELLIS, Howard William. St Jo Coll Morpeth. **d** 30 **p** 31 Bath. M of Bro of Good Shepherd Dubbo 30-36; C of St Mary w Ch Ch Scarborough 36-37; R of Narromine 37-42; Chap RAAF 42-44; R of Gulgong 44-50; Kelso 50-75; Archd of Barker 52-54; Broughton 54-74. *110 Brilliant Street, Bathurst, NSW, Australia 2795.*

ELLIS, Ian Gordon. Ridley Coll Melb 59. ACT ThL 61. **d** 62 Bp Redding for Melb **p** 63 Melb. CMS Youth Sec and Hon C of St Paul's Cathl Melb 62-65; C of St Silas N Geelong 65-66; Dept of Chaps Melb 66-72; Dep Dir and Supt of Child Care St John's Homes Cant Dio Melb 73-76; Dir from 76. *18 Balwyn Road, Canterbury, Vic, Australia 3126.* (83-9461)

ELLIS, Ian Morton. b 52. Qu Univ Belf BD 75. Trin Coll Dub **d** 77 **p** 78 Arm. C of St Columba Portadown 77-79; Armagh and Chap Armagh R Sch Dio Arm from 79. *6 Ashley Avenue, Armagh, BT60 1HD, N Ireland.*

ELLIS, Ieuan Pryce. Fitzw Ho Cam Th Trip pt i 56, BA (Th Trip pt ii) 58, Th Trip pt iii 60, MA 62. Trin Coll Ox BA 60, BLitt 63. BD (Lon) 63. Cudd Coll 64. **d** 65 **p** 66 York. C of St Alb Hull 65-69; Lect in Th Univ of Hull from 65. *c/o Dept of Theology, University, Hull, Yorks.*

ELLIS, John. TCD BA 64. **d** 66 **p** 67 Connor. C of Ch Ch Cathl Lisburn 66-69; Norbiton 69-72; New Clee Dio Linc from 72. *83 Harrington Street, Cleethorpes, Humb.* (Cleethorpes 66521)

ELLIS, John Anthony. b 47. Open Univ BA 80. St D Coll Lamp Dipl Th 70. Coll of Resurr Mirfield 70. **d** 72 Mon for Swan B **p** 73 Swan B. C of Sketty 72-75; Duston 75-80; R of Lichborough w Maidford and Farthingstone Dio Pet from 80. *Maidford Rectory, Towcester, Northants, NN12 8HG.*

ELLIS, John Beaumont. b 45. St D Coll Lamp BA 67, LTh 69. **d** 69 **p** 70 Mon. C of Abergavenny w Llanwenarth Citra 69-72; St Gabr Swansea 72-75; V of Llanbister w Llanbadarn-Fynydd and Llananno 75-77; St Andr Lliswerry Newport 77-80; Risca Dio Mon from 80. *Vicarage, Gelli Crescent, Pontymister, Gwent, NP1 6QG.* (Risca 612307)

ELLIS, John Francis. Ch Army Tr Coll 31. **d** and **p** 48 Ex. C of St Pet (in c of St Paul from 49) Sticklepath Conv Distr Barnstaple 48-53; V of New Brighton NZ 53-59; Sydenham and Beckenham 59-71; L to Offic Dio Ch Ch 71; Dio Nel 72; P-in-c of Otaio 71; Bishopdale w Harewood 72. *12 Herbert Street, Richmond, NZ.* (27-8942)

ELLIS, John Franklyn. b 34. Univ of Leeds, BA (3rd cl Gen) 58. Linc Th Coll 58. **d** 60 **p** 61 Man. C of St Chad Ladybarn 60-63; St Geo Stockport 63-66; V of High Lane 66-81; Chelford Dio Ches from 81. *Chelford Vicarage, Macclesfield, Chesh, SK11 9AH.* (Chelford 231)

ELLIS, John Frederick Alexander. b 23. Sarum Th Coll 50. **d** 52 **p** 53 Bris. C of Fishponds 52-55; SSF 55-57; St Mary Redcliffe w Temple Bedminster 57-62; V of St Jo Bapt Leamington 62-65; Harnham 65-80; RD of Salisbury 77-80; Hon Can of Sarum Cathl 77-80; of S Tawton w S Zeal 80-81; Belstone w Sticklepath Chap 80-81; V of S Tawton w Belstone Dio Ex from 81. *Vicarage, South Tawton, Okehampton, EX20 2LQ.* (Sticklepath 337)

ELLIS, John George. b 31. Worc Coll Ox BA 54, MA 56. Wells Th Coll. **d** 58 **p** 59 Lon. C of Poplar 58-65; V of Diddlebury w Bouldon and Westhope 65-72; R of Munslow w Broadstone 67-72; V of St Kath N Hammersmith Dio Lon from 72. *St Katharine's Vicarage, Westway, W12 0SD.* (01-743 3951)

ELLIS, John Roland. b 32. Wells Th Coll 67. **d** 69 **p** 70 Pet. C of Kettering 69-71; Kingsthorpe 71-73; Team V 73-74; V in R Benef of Ebbw Vale 74-76; V of Llanddewi-Rhydderch w Llavapley, Llanfihangel Gobion and Llangattock-Juxta-Usk Dio Mon from 76. *Llanddewi-Rhydderch Vicarage, Abergavenny, Gwent.* (Gobion 373)

ELLIS, John Wadsworth. b 42. TCD BA 64. **d** 66 **p** 67 Connor. C of Lisburn Cathl 66-69; St Pet Norbiton 69-72; St Jo and St Steph New Clee Dio Linc 72-77; jt C-in-c from 77. *161 Carr Lane, Grimsby, DN32 8JF.*

ELLIS, Joseph. Univ of Lon BA (3rd cl Hist Hons) 30. Sarum Th Coll 32. **d** 33 **p** 34 S'wark. C of St Andr Earlsfield 33-36; H Trin S Wimbledon 36-38; St John Woking (in c of H Trin Knaphill) 38-44; R of Shackleford 44-65; R of Peper Harow 44-65; Fonthill Bp w Berwick St Leon Dio Sarum from 65; R of Fonthill Gifford Dio Sarum from 65. *Fonthill Gifford Rectory, Tisbury, Wilts, SP3 6PX.* (Tisbury 870382)

ELLIS, Joseph Walter. b 08. St D Coll Lamp BA 32. **d** 32 **p** 33 Man. C of St Mary Droylsden 32-36; Oldham 36-40; V of St Steph and All Mart Oldham 40-50; Royton 50-64; Gt w L Chesterford 64-77. *5 Southfield, Back Lane, Ickleton, Cambs.*

ELLIS, Joseph Walter. CD 64. Angl Th Coll of BC. **d** and **p** 41 Yukon. C of Old Crow 41-45; I of All SS Hanna 45-47; Prin of Ind Res Sch Carcross 47-50; R of St Marg Cedar Cottage Vanc 50-60; St Paul Vanc 60-74; Team V of Langley New Westmr 74-77. *4598 Saddlehorn Crescent, Aldergrove, BC, Canada.*

ELLIS, MacAllister Scott. McGill Univ Montr LTh 52. Montr Dioc Th Coll 50. **d** 52 **p** 53 Montr. C of St Columba Montr 52-55; In Amer Ch 55-66; R of Pugwash 66-75; R of River John 66-75; Yarmouth Dio NS from 75. *65 William Street, Yarmouth, NS, Canada.* (742-2145)

ELLIS, Malcolm. b 51. St Paul's Coll Grahmstn 72. **d** 74 **p** 76 Natal. C of Westville 74-79; Chap Univ of Natal from 79. *5 Princess Anne Place, Glenwood, Durban 4001, S Africa.*

ELLIS, Malcolm Railton. b 35. St D Coll Lamp BA 56. LTCL 71. Sarum Th Coll 56. **d** 58 **p** 59 Llan. C of Llangynwyd w Maesteg and Troedrhiw Garth 58-61; Llantrisant 61-67; V of Troedrhiw Garth 67-70; PV of Truro Cathl 70-73; V of Egloshayle 73-81; Margam Dio Llan from 81. *Margam Vicarage, Port Talbot, W Glam.* (Port Talbot 891067)

ELLIS, Mark Durant. b 39. Univ of Ex BA (2nd cl Th) 62. Cudd Coll 62. **d** 64 **p** 65 B & W. C of St Pet Lyngford Taunton 64-67; PC of Bournville Weston-s-Mare 67-76; Team V of Yeovil Dio B & W from 76. *St Michael's Vicarage, Yeovil, Somt.* (Yeovil 5752)

ELLIS, Patrick Richard. Univ of BC BA 36. Angl Th Coll BC LTh 38. **d** 37 **p** 38 New Westmr. C of Ch Ch Cathl Vanc 37-38; I of St Cuthb Princeton w Hedley and Copper Mountain 38-40; C of St Geo Vanc 40-42; Chap RCAF 42-46; I of Lulu Is 46-51; R of St Paul Vanc 51-60; Supt Columb Coast Miss Dios New Westmr and BC 60-65; Archd of Quatsino 60-65; R of S Westmr 65-76; Perm to Offic Dio BC from 76. *RR1, Duncan, BC, Canada.*

ELLIS, Peter Andrew. b 46. St D Coll Lamp 65. **d** 69 **p** 70 St D. C of Milford 69-71; V of Walwyn's Castle w Robeston W 71-74; Asst Port Chap Hong Kong 74-75; Port Chap Sing from 75. *Missions to Seamen, 4 Prince Edward Lane, Singapore 2.*

ELLIS, Reginald John Grant. Univ of S Afr BA 34. St Paul's Coll Grahmstn LTh (S Afr) 37. **d** 37 **p** 39 Zulu. C of Empangeni 37-38; R of Fort Vic 38-43; I of Que Que 43-46; P-in-c of St Sav Port Eliz 46-54; R of Cambridge 54-56; CF (S Afr) 56-58; V of Greytown 58-61; R of St Jas Durban 61-71; L to Offic Dio Natal 71-77; Perm to Offic 77; R of Richmond Dio Natal from 77. *Box 171, Richmond, Natal, S Africa.*

ELLIS, Robert Albert. b 48. K Coll Lon AKC and BD 70. St Aug Coll Cant 70. **d** 72 Liv **p** 73 Warrington for Liv. C of Our Lady and St Nich Liv 72-76; P-in-c of Meerbrook and Relig Programmes Producer BBC Radio Stoke-on-Trent 76-80; V of All SS Highgate 80-81; P-in-c of Longdon Dio Lich from 81; Dioc Communications Officer from 81. *Longdon Vicarage, Rugeley, Staffs.* (Armitage 490307)

ELLIS, Robert Charles Ross-Lewin. b 06. TCD Erasmus Smith Suppl Exhib 24, BA and Abp King's Pri 28, Div Test 29. **d** 29 **p** 30 Down. C of St John Whitehouse 29-32; C-in-c of St Colman Dunmurry (w St Hilda Kilmakee 58-64) 32-45; R 45-79; RD of Lisburn 60-67; Derriaghy 67-71; Preb of Connor in Connor Cathl 61-65; Treas 65-73; Prec 73-79. *27 Glenshesk Park, Dunmurry, Belfast, N Ireland.* (Belfast 621266)

ELLIS, Ven Robin Gaeth. b 35. Late Scho of Pemb Coll Ox, Winter Williams Law Scho 56, BA (2nd cl Jurispr) 57, BCL 58, MA 62. Chich Th Coll 58. **d** 60 **p** 61 Man. C of Swinton 60-63; Asst Chap Worksop Coll 63-66; V of Swaffham Prior w Reach 66-74; Asst Dir Relig Educn Dio Ely 66-72; V of St Aug Wisbech 74-82; Yelverton Dio Ex from 82;

M Gen Syn from 80; Archd of Plymouth from 82. *Vicarage, Yelverton, Plymouth, Devon, PL20 6AE.* (Yelverton 852362)

ELLIS, Rodney Norman. b 49. Univ of Natal BA 74. Univ of Nottm Dipl Th 75. St Jo Coll Nottm 76. **d** 77 **p** 78 Natal. C of Ch Ch Addington 77-79; R of Queensburgh Dio Natal from 79. *26 Kingston Road, Escombe, Queensburgh, Natal, S Africa.*

ELLIS, Roger Henry. b 40. Univ of Natal BA 61. Selw Coll Cam BA 64, MA 68. Linacre Coll Ox BLitt 69. **d** 66 Ox **p** 67 Ox for Natal. C of St Mich Ox 66-68; Hon C of St Sav Cathl Pmbg 68-76; Sen Lect in Div Univ of Natal 68-76; Exam Chap to Bp of Natal 71-76; C-in-c of Wortham 77; V of St Aid Doncaster Dio Sheff from 77. *St Aidan's Vicarage, Central Boulevard, Wheatley Hills, Doncaster, DN2 5PE.* (Doncaster 62047)

ELLIS, Stanley. Univ of Tor BA 59. Trin Coll Tor STB 62. **d** 61 **p** 62 Calg. C of Ch of Redeemer Calg 62-64; R of Fort Qu'App 64-68; I of Craik Dio Qu'App from 68. *St Agnes's Vicarage, Craik, Sask, Canada.*

ELLIS, Timothy William. b 53. AKC 75. St Aug Coll Cant 75. **d** 76 **p** 77 Man C of St Jo Evang Old Trafford 76-80; V of Pendleton and Chap Salford Coll of Tech Dio Man from 80. *14 Eccles Old Road, Salford, M6 7AF.* (061-737 2107)

ELLIS, Canon Vorley Michael Spencer. b 15. Late Squire Scho of St Edm Hall, Ox 3rd cl Cl Mods 36, BA (3rd cl Th) 38, MA 41. St Steph Ho Ox 37. **d** 39 **p** 40 St A. C of Llanrhos 39-42; CF (EC) 42-47; L to Offic Dio St A 47-48; C of Hawarden (in c of St John Pentrobin and St Mary Broughton) 48-49; V of St Jo Evang Keswick Dio Carl from 49; Surr from 56; Hon Can of Carl from 78; P-in-c of Threlkeld Dio Carl from 78. *St John's Vicarage, Keswick, Cumb, CA12 4DN.* (Keswick 72130)

ELLISON, Christian Waldemar. b 04. Univ of Lon BSc 25, BD 29. Lon Coll of Div 26. **d** 29 **p** 30 Lon. C of St Jude Mildmay Pk 29-31; Miss (CIM) Dio E Szech 32-51; Dio Sing 52-72; Hon C of St Jude Mildmay Pk Isl 73-76. *62 Hook Road, Epsom, Surrey, KT19 8TR.* (Epsom 242323)

ELLISON, Cyril Crowden. b 13. Late Sizar of Trin Coll Dub BA 35, Div Test (1st cl) 36, MA 40. **d** 36 **p** 37 Birm. C of St Thos Birm 36-38; St Giles Newc L 38-40; I of Tashinny w Shrule 40-45; R of Kilcleagh U 45-54; C-in-c of Ferbane 52-54; I of Navan U 54-69; Meath Dioc Regr 58-77; Can of Meath 66-69. *40 Haddon Way, Carlyon Bay, St Austell, Cornwall, PL25 3QG.*

✠ **ELLISON, Right Rev and Right Hon Gerald Alexander.** b 10. PC 73. KCVO 81. New Coll Ox BA 32, Dipl in Th 34, MA 36. DD (Lambeth) 55. Westcott Ho Cam 34. **d** 35 **p** 36 Sarum. C of Sherborne 35-37; Dom Chap to Bp of Win and Sec Dioc Youth Movement Dio Win 37-42; Chap RNVR 39-43 (Men in Disp 42); Dom Chap to Abp of York 43-46; Hon Chap 46-50; V of St Mark Portsea 46-50; Surr 47-50; Exam Chap to Bp of Portsm 49-50; Can of Portsm 50; C-in-c of St Botolph Bishopsgate Lon 50-53; Cons Ld Bp Suffr of Willesden in St Paul's Cathl 21 Sept 50 by Abps of Cant and York; Bps of Lon; Win; Portsm; Roch; Guildf; Blackb; Gibr; Bps Suffr of Stepney; Croydon; Kens; and Fulham; and Bps Kitching and Lovett; Sub-Prelate of O of St Jo of Jer from 52; Trld to Ches 55; to Lon 73; res 81; Select Pr Univ of Ox 40, 61, 72; of Cam 57; Dean of Chapels Royal and Prelate of OBE 73-81; Prelate of Soc of KB from 73; Episc Can of St Geo Jer 76-81. *Billeys House, 16 Long Street, Cerne Abbas, Dorset.* (Cerne Abbas 247)

ELLISON, John Alexander. ALCD 67. **d** 67 **p** 68 Guildf. C of St Paul Woking 67-74; St Sav Belgrano Dio Argent from 80. *Rio Del Garcia 2655, 1429 Nunez, Buenos Aires, Argentina.*

ELLISON, John Rowland. Univ of Dur LTh 35. Bp Wilson Th Coll IM 32. **d** 35 **p** 36 Liv. C of H Trin Walton Breck 35-38; St Paul Widnes 38-41; C-in-c of St Jas Conv Distr Eccleston Park 41-47; V of All SS Newton-le-Willows 47-50; St Paul Widnes 50-54; PC of H Trin Ripon 54-59; V of St Nich Wallasey 59-78. *Address temp unknown.*

ELLISTON, John Ernest Nicholas. b 37. ALCD 61. **d** 61 **p** 62 S'wark. C of Gipsy Hill 61-64; Whitton 64-68; C-in-c of New Clee 68-71; V of St Steph Grimsby 71-75; New Clee 75-76; Mildenhall 76-77; Team R of Barton-Mills, Beck Row w Kenny Hill, Freckenham, Mildenhall w Red Lodge, W Row and Worlington Dio St E from 77; RD of Mildenhall from 81. *Rectory, Mildenhall, Suff.* (Mildenhall 712128)

ELLMORE, Robert. b 37. St Jo Coll Morpeth 76. **d** 77 Bath. C of Parkes Dio Bath from 77. *PO Box 86, Parkes, NSW, Australia 2870.*

ELLSLEY, Howard. b 23. Roch Th Coll 65. **d** 67 **p** 68 Glas. C of St Marg Newlands Glas 67-71; R of Dalbeattie 71-77; Team V of Melton Mowbray 77-78; R of Balcombe Dio Chich from 78. *Balcombe Rectory, Haywards Heath, Sussex.* (Balcombe 249)

ELLSON, Harry. Ridley Coll Melb 46. ACT ThL 47. **d** 47 **p** 48 Bend. C of Castlemaine 48; V of White Hills 48-52; Rochester 52-55; P-in-c of Lautoka 55-57; R of Murchison 57-60; C of Vermont (in c of Bayswater) 60-61; V of Bayswater 61-66; Chap Dept of Industr Chaps Melb 66-72; I of Lancefield 73-80; Perm to Offic Dio Melb from 80. *Hopetoun Street, Rochester, Vic, Australia 3561.*

ELLWOOD, Keith Brian. b 36. ACP 65. Bp's Coll Cheshunt 64. **d** 64 **p** 65 Chelmsf. C of Wanstead 64-66; Chap R Wanstead Sch 64-66; CF 66-70; Chap St Paul's C0-Ed Coll Hong 70-71; C-in-c of Bicknoller 71-73; Chap and Asst Master Roedean Sch Brighton 73-76; Windsor Boys' Sch Hamm, W Germany 76-79; Perm to Offic Dio B & W 74-79; Chap Trin Coll Glenalmond 79-81; Hd Master St Chris Sch Burnham-on-Sea and Perm to Offic Dio B & W from 82. *St Christopher's School, Burnham-on-Sea, Somt.*

ELMORE, Graeme Martin. b 47. Sarum Wells Th Coll 71. **d** 74 **p** 75 Cant. C of St Osw Norbury 74-77; P-in-c of St Allen 77-79; St Erme 77-79; V of Newlyn Dio Truro from 79. *Newlyn Vicarage, Penzance, Cornwall, TR18 5HT.* (Penzance 2678)

ELMSLIE, Stewart Kayser Bayntin. b 08. K Coll Lon AKC 40. **d** 40 **p** 41 Lon. C of All SS Queensbury 40-42; St Nich Chiswick 42-46; V of St John Whetstone 46-49; in Amer Ch 49-56; V of All H Gospel Oak St Pancras 56-61; All SS Friern Barnet 61-74. *38 Trent Drive, Northmoor Park, Wareham, Dorset, BH40 4DF.* (Wareham 3754)

ELPHICK, Robin Howard. b 37. ALCD 63. **d** 64 **p** 65 S'wark. C of St Barn Clapham Common 64-67; Woking 67-71; R of Rollesby w Burgh and Billockby (W Ashby, Oby, Thurne and Clippesby from 81) Dio Nor from 71; P-in-c of Ashby, Oby and Thurne w Clippesby 79-81. *Rollesby Rectory, Great Yarmouth, Norf, NR29 5HJ.* (Gt Yarmouth 740323)

ELPHIN, Bishop of. *See* Kilmore.

ELPHIN and ARDAGH, Archdeacon of. *See* Bond, Ven Thomas James.

ELPHIN and ARDAGH, Dean of. *See* Bolton, Very Rev George Holmes Gibson.

ELSAM, Thomas Charles. b 13. Kelham Th Coll 30. **d** 36 **p** 37 Ripon. M SSM 36-62; C of St Aid Leeds 36-39; Perm to Offic Dio Liv 39 and 40-41; Southw 40; L to Offic Dio Liv 42; C of St Cecilia Parson Cross 42-45; St Andr Rowbarton 45-46; Tutor at St Mich Ho Crafers S Australia and Perm to Offic Dio Adel 46-47; Perm to Offic at St Andr Rowbarton 47-48; St Jo Evang Clevedon 48-49; C of St Geo Nottingham 49-53; Parson Cross 53-54; Ch Ch Poplar 54-55; P-in-c St Marg Bloemf 55-56; Asst Sec Korean Miss 56-60; Sec 60-71; Perm to Offic Dio Lon 56-71; C of Bow w Bromley St Leonard 71; Team V of H Trin Mile End 71-72; P-in-c of St Alb (w St Mary from 77) Teddington 72-79. *8 Clifford Haigh House, 280 Fulham Palace Road, SW6 6HP.* (01-385 2539)

ELSDON, Bernard Robert. b 29. Roch Th Coll. **d** 67 **p** 68 Ches. C of Wallasey 67-71; Our Lady and St Nich Liv 71-72; V of St Marg Anfield Dio Liv from 73; Dioc Executive Dir for Chr Responsibility 78-81. *Vicarage, Rocky Lane, Liverpool, L6 4BA.* (051-263 3118)

ELSEY, Cyril. b 08. Ridley Hall, Cam 65. **d** 66 **p** 67 Lich. C of Rolleston and of Anslow 66-69; R of Petton w Cockshutt 69-75; Perm to Offic Dio Win 75-79; Dio Chelmsf 79-81; Dio Ex from 82. *3 Cricket Field Lane, Budleigh Salterton, Devon, EX9 6PB.* (Salterton 5504)

ELSON, Christopher John. b 52. AKC and BD 75. St Aug Coll Cant 75. **d** 76 **p** 77 Guildf. C of New Haw 76-79; H Trin w St Mary City and Dio Guildf from 79. *27 Pewley Way, Guildford, Surrey, GU1 3PX.*

ELSON, George William. b 24. Wycl Coll Tor 72. **d** 73 **p** 74 Ont. I of N Hastings 73-78; Tyendinaga Dio Ont from 78. *Mohawk Rectory, Deseronto, Ont, Canada.* (613-396 3119)

ELSON, John Frederick. Roch Th Coll 62. **d** 64 **p** 65 Cant. C of Tenterden w Small Hythe 64-68; C-in-c of Chart Sutton 68-71; V of Fletching Dio Chich from 71. *Fletching Vicarage, Uckfield, Sussex, TN22 3SR.* (Newick 2498)

ELSON, Peter Stanley. St Francis Coll Brisb. **d** 79 Brisb. Perm to Offic Dio Brisb from 79. *16 Hetherington Street, Herston, Queensland, Australia 4006.* (52 1414)

ELSTON, Philip Herbert. b 35. RD 80. Univ of Leeds MA 76. K Coll Lon and Warm AKC 63. **d** 64 **p** 65 Leic. C of Ch Ch Thurnby Lodge 64-66; Hon C 66-67; Chap RNR from 67; Chap Malosa Secondary Sch Likwenu Malawi 68-75; APM of Far Headingley 75-79; Chap Leeds RN Assoc 76-79; V of Knowl Hill w Littlewick Dio Ox from 79. *St John's Vicarage, Littlewick Green, Maidenhead, Berks, SL6 3QR.* (Littlewick Green 2732)

ELSTONE, John Kenrick. b 15. AKC 49. St Bonif Coll Warm 49. **d** 50 **p** 51 Ripon. C of All SS Leeds 50-56; St Jo Evang Middlesbrough Dio York 56-79; V from 79. *114 Marton Road, Middlesbrough, Cleve, TS1 2DY.* (Middlesbrough 245073)

ELTON, Clarence Edward. b 09. ALCD 36. **d** 36 **p** 37 Sheff. C of Fulwood 36-38; Actg C of Ch Ch Ramsgate 38-39; Org Sec CCCS for Midl Area 39-43; L to Offic Dio Worc 42; V of Boulton 43-47; Chap Amsterdam 47-49; RD of Holland 48-49; Org Sec CPAS for Metrop Distr 49-51; L to Offic Dio S'wark 49-51; Perm to Offic Dio Ox from 50; PC of Belper 51-53; Asst Sec of CCCS 53-57; R of Hambledon 57-74; Perm to Offic Dio Guildf from 74. *76 Church Road, Milford, Godalming, Surrey, GU8 5JD.* (Godalming 7959)

ELTON, Derek Hurley. b 31. Univ of Lon BSc 52. Wycl Hall Ox 53. **d** 55 **p** 56 Blackb. C of Ashton-on-Ribble 55-58; in Ch of S India 58-71; R of Wickmere w L Barningham and Itteringham 71-79; Gt w L Ellingham Dio Nor from 79; P-in-c of Rockland St Pet w All SS Dio Nor from 81. *Rectory, Great Ellingham, Norf, NR17 1LD.* (Attleborough 453200)

ELUK, Very Rev Washington. b 38. Bp Tucker Coll Mukono 70. **d** 72 **p** 73 N Ugan. P Dio N Ugan 72-76; Dio Lango from 76; Dean of Lango from 72. *Box 6, Lira, Uganda.*

ELVES, William Edward. b 07. St Aug Coll Cant 27. **d** 32 **p** 33 Roch. C of Stone 32-35; St Anne Maitland 35-37; R of Namaqualand 37-42; R of All SS Roodebloem 42-48; C of St Etheldreda Bp's Hatfield (in c of St Mich Birchwood) 49-52; R of St Paul Bradf Man 52-57; V of Ch Ch Dukinfield 57-73; C of Hertingfordbury Dio St Alb from 73. *St John's Parsonage, Woolmers Lane, Letty Green, Hertford.* (07072-61463)

ELVIN, Keith Vernon. b 24. Univ of Bris BSc (2nd cl Geog) 52. **d** and **p** 65 Truro. C of St Clem Dio Truro 65-66; Hon C 68-80; Chap Truro Cathl Sch 66-67; Asst Master Truro Co Gr Sch 68-78; Asst Master Richard Lander Sch from 78; Hon C of St Paul Truro 79-80; Vice Prin and Tutor of the Chan Sch and Publ Pr Dio Truro from 80. *37 Edward Street, Truro, Cornw.* (Truro 74632)

ELVY, Canon Peter David. b 38. Univ of Lon BA (2nd cl Hist) 62. Fitzw Ho Cam BA (2nd cl Th Trip pt ii) 64, MA 68. Ridley Hall Cam. **d** 65 **p** 66 Cant. C of Herne 65-66; New Addington 66-68; St Mildred Addiscombe 69-71; Youth Chap Dio Chelmsf and Asst Dir Relig Educn 71-80; Publ Pr 72-75; V of Gt Burstead Dio Chelmsf from 75; Can of Chelmsf Cathl from 80. *111 Church Street, Billericay, Essex, CM11 2TR.* (Billericay 53138)

ELWIN, Ernest John. b 31. Selw Coll Cam BA 54, MA 58. Ridley Hall, Cam 54. **d** 56 **p** 57 S'wark. C of Wandsworth 56-59; St Paul Harlow 59-61; Asst Master Tidworth Down Sch 61-63; V of Soundwell 63-66; Asst Master Seldown Sch Poole 66-68; Wareham Modern Sch 68-69; Perm to Offic Dio Sarum from 66; Lect S Dorset Tech Coll from 70. *Penn, Bradford Peverell, Dorchester, Dorset.* (Martinstown 223)

ELWIS, Malcolm John. b 42. St Jo Coll Morpeth 69. **d** 70 Melb **p** 72 Gippsld. [f Bapt Min] C of St Jo Bentleigh 70-72; St Paul's Cathl Sale 72-73; Perm to Offic Dio Melb from 73. *7 Leslie Street, E St Kilda, Vic, Australia 3183.* (527 7780)

ELY, Lord Bishop of. *See* Walker, Right Rev Peter Knight.

ELY, Assistant Bishop of. (Vacant).

ELY, Archdeacon of. *See* Walser, Ven David.

ELY, dean o. (vacant)

EMAN, Willem Albert. Univ of Leiden Cand Th. **d** 56 **p** 58 Sing. C of Malacca 56-58; P-in-c 58-63; C of Ch Ch Epsom 63-68; Chap at Den Helder Dio Lon (N and C Eur) from 70. *c/o Groenburgwal 42, Amsterdam, Holland.*

EMASU, Patrick. b 52. **d** 78 **p** 79 Soroti. P Dio Soroti. *PO Box 107, Soroti, Uganda.*

EMBLETON, Harold. b 21. Ch Coll Cam BA 47, MA 52. Qu Coll Birm. **d** 49 **p** 50 Worc. C of Kidderminster 49-52; Wimbledon (in c of St Jo Bapt) 52-53; CF (TA) 50-52; Chap RN 53-76; Hon Chap to HM the Queen from 74; V of Bognor Dio Chich from 76; RD of Arundel and Bognor from 77; Chairman Angl and E Chs Assoc from 77. *17 Victoria Drive, Bognor, W Sussex, PO21 2RH.* (Bognor 821423)

EMBLEY, Roy Frederic. Univ of Manit BA 60, B Educn 65. St Jo Coll Winnipeg, LTh 59. **d** 59 **p** 60 Rupld. C-in-c of Emerson 59-64; H Trin Winnipeg 64-66; St Marg St Hubert 66-68; R of Dalhousie 68-72; I of Simonds 72-76; Fred Junction Dio Fred from 76. *Hoyt, NB, Canada.*

EMBLING, Christopher John. b 33. St Paul's Coll Grahmstn 69. **d** 71 **p** 72 Grahmstn. C of St Mich and St Geo Cathl Ch Grahmstn 71-75; R of Barkly E 75-78; H Trin Belvidere Dio Geo from 78. *Rectory, Belvidere, CP, S Africa.*

EMELUGO, Charles Nwanko. Awka Th Coll 47. **d** 48 Bp Onyeabo for Niger **p** 49 Niger. P Dio Niger. Archd of Onitsha 71-76. *St Andrew's Parsonage, Onitsha, Nigeria.*

EMERSON, Arthur Edward Richard. b 24. Lich Th Coll 69. **d** 72 **p** 73 Linc. C of Barton-on-Humber 72-74; V of Chapel St Leonard Dio Linc from 75; P-in-c of Hogsthorpe Dio Linc from 76. *Vicarage, Chapel St Leonard, Skegness, Lincs.* (Skegness 72666)

EMERSON, John Hall. **d** 78 **p** 80 N Queensld. C of St Jas Cathl Townsville Dio N Queensld from 78. *30 Hooper Street, Belgian Gardens, Qld, Australia 4810.*

EMERSON, Kenneth Winter. b 11. St Andr Coll Pampisford. **d** 43 **p** 44 Sheff. C of St Swith Sheff 43-47; Eastwood (in c of St Sav) 47-49; Bolsterstone Stocksbridge (in c of Deepcar) 49-52; V of St Hilda Thurnscoe E 52-72; Hooton Pagnell 72-76; C-in-c of Hickleton 72-76; Perm to Offic Dio Sheff from 76. *Address temp unknown.*

EMERSON, Norman Neil. Moore Th Coll Syd ThL 77. **d** 78 Syd **p** 78 Bp Short for Syd. C of St Mich Cathl Wollongong 78-79; St Steph Normanhurst Dio Syd from 80. *92 Duffy Avenue, Westleigh, NSW, Australia 2120.* (848-9427)

EMERTON, John Adney. b 28. CCC Ox BA (1st cl Th) 50, Liddon Stud and Hall Jun Gr Test Pri 50, Hall-Houghton Jun Septuagint Pri 51, Kennicott Hebr Fellowship and 1st cl Or Stud 52, Houghton Syriac Pri 53, Hall-Houghton Sen Septuagint Pri and MA 54. CCC Cam MA (by incorp) 55, BD 60, DD 73, Univ of Edin Hon DD 77. FBA 79. Wycl Hall Ox 50. **d** 52 Birm **p** 53 Bp Linton for Cant. C of St Phil Cathl Birm and Asst Lect in Th Univ of Birm 52-53; Lect in Hebrew Univ of Dur 53-55; Visiting Prof Trin Coll Tor 60; Lect in Div Univ of Cam and L to Offic Dio Ely 55-62; Reader in Semitic Philology Univ of Ox 62-68; Select Pr Univ of Cam 62 and 71; Fell St Pet Coll Ox 62-68; L to Offic Dio Ox 62-68; Dio Ely from 68; Regius Prof of Hebr Univ of Cam from 68; Fell St Jo Coll Cam from 70. *34 Gough Way, Cambridge, CB3 9LN.*

EMERY, Ernest John. Moore Th Coll Syd ACT ThL 57, ThScho 68. **d** 58 Syd **p** 58 Bp Hilliard for Syd. C of Wollongong 58-59; St Clem Mosman 60-61; C-in-c of Dundas w Telopea 62-69; CF (Austr) 70; L to Offic Dio Syd 70; Actg R of Ashbury 71-72; R 72-77; St Steph Mittagong 77-79; Perm to Offic Dio Syd from 79. *c/o Box 464, Penrith, NSW, Australia 2750.*

EMERY, Frank. b 07. **d** 67 **p** 68 Ban. C of Holyhead 67-80. *16 Seabourne Road, Holyhead, Anglesey, Gwynedd, LL65 1AL.* (Holyhead 2491)

EMERY, Graham. St Jo Coll Ox 2nd cl Mod Hist 58, Dipl Th 59, MA 62. Linc Th Coll 61. **d** 63 **p** 64 Worc. Asst Master and Chap R Gr Sch Worc 63-67; Linc City Sch 67-71; Asst Master Dame Allan's Sch Newc T from 71; Hon C of St Martin Worc 63-65; L to Offic Dio Newc T from 71. *97 Nuns Moor Road, Newcastle-on-Tyne, NE4 9BA.*

EMES, Leonard Bingham. b 10. Wycl Hall Ox 69. **d** & **p** 70 Ox. C of Thame 70-73; P-in-c of Tetsworth 73-77; Adwell w S Weston 73-77; Perm to Offic Dio St E from 77. *27 Green Willows, Lavenham, Sudbury, Suff.*

EMESI, Josiah Oluchukwu Akpuafor. b 28. Trin Coll Umuahia Dipl Th 74. **d** 73 **p** 74 Niger. P Dio Niger. *St Luke's Parsonage, Ibolo Oraifite via Nnewi, ECS, Nigeria.*

EMILE, Joseph. b 43. St Aug Past Coll Mahanoro 63. **d** 70 Tam. d Dio Tam from 70. *Sahorama, Nosy-Varika, Mananjary, Madagascar.*

EMLY, Archdeacon of. *See* Limerick.

EMLY, Bishop of. *See* Limerick.

EMLY, Dean of. *See* Limerick.

EMM, Robert Kenneth. b 46. K Coll Lon and Warm BD and AKC 68. **d** 69 Lon. **p** 70 Kens for Lon. C of St Mich and St Geo Conv Distr White City Hammersmith 69-72; Keynsham 72-75; Yeovil 75-80; Team V of Gt Grimsby Dio Linc from 80. *St Mark's Vicarage, Winchester Avenue, Grimsby, S Humb.* (Grimsby 77900)

EMMANUEL, Rees. b 07. St D Coll Lamp BA 33. **d** 33 **p** 34 Llan. C of Troedyrhiw 33-35; St Cadoc Bedlinog 35-42; V 42-46; R of Cilybebyll 46-60; V of Bargoed 60-67; Surr 47-67; C of Christchurch w Mudeford 67-70; V of Tonyrefail 70-73; RD of Rhondda 72-73; L to Offic Dio Llan and Swan B from 73. *17 Gwyn Street, Alltwen, Pontardawe, W Glam.* (Pontardawe 863655)

EMMEL, Malcolm David. b 32. Qu Coll Birm Dipl Th 58. **d** 58 **p** 59 York. C of Hessle 58-62; Miss at Cam Bay 62-66; V of Catterick w Tunstall 66-73; Pateley Bridge w Greenhow Hill 73-77; C-in-c of Middlesmoor w Ramsgill 76-77; V of Upper Nidderdale Dio Ripon from 77; RD of Ripon from 79. *Pateley Bridge Vicarage, Harrogate, HG3 5LQ.* (Harrogate 711414)

EMMERSON, Peter Barrett. b 29. Fitzw Ho Cam BA 54, MA 58. Tyndale Hall, Bris 50. **d** 54 Warrington for Liv for York for Arctic **p** 57 Arctic. Miss at Coppermine 54-55; Cambridge Bay 55-58; V of St Nath Fazakerley Walton-on-the-Hill 59-64: Distr Sec BFBS for Northumb and Co Dur 64-70; Staffs, Warws and Birm 70-72; Perm to Offic Dios Newc T, Dur and Liv 64-70; Dios Cov and Lich from 70; Publ Pr Dio Birm 71-74; Hon C of Boldmere 71-74; Reg Sec BFBS Midl Region 72-74; P-in-c of Crown E Conv Distr 74-77; Crown E and Rushwick 77-81; V of Stoke Prior w Wychbold and Upton Warren Dio Worc from 81. *Stoke Prior Vicarage, Bromsgrove, Worcs.* (Bromsgrove 32501)

✠ **EMMERSON, Right Rev Ralph.** b 13. AKC (2nd cl) 38.

Univ of Lon BD (2nd cl Hons) 38. Westcott Ho Cam 38. **d** 38 Ripon **p** 39 Knaresborough for Ripon. C of St Geo Leeds 38-41; C-in-c of New Seacroft Conv Distr Leeds 41-48; C of St Osw Methley (in c of St Marg Mickletown) 48-49; C-in-c of Methley 49-52; R 52-56; C-in-c of Mickletown 49-52; V 52-56; PC of Headingley 56-66; Hon Can of Ripon 64-66; Can Res and Can Missr 66-72; Cons Ld Bp Suffr of Knaresborough in York Minster 1 May 72 by Abp of York; Bps of Ches; Ripon; Wakef; Man; Southw; Sheff; Blackb; Lich; and others; res 79. *24 Laburnum Road, Wakefield, WF1 3QS.* (Wakef 369455)

EMMET, Herbert Gerald. b 18. Trin Coll Cam BA 40. Linc Th Coll 40. **d** 42 **p** 43 Leic. C of St Pet Leic 42-44; St Andr Melksham 44-48; St Sav St Alb 48-51; V of St Nich Leic 51-56; Industr Chap Dio Leic 51-53; PC of Hatfield Hyde 56-64; V of St Jo Bapt Harpenden 64-73; King's Langley 73-80; RD of Wheathampstead 70-72. *39 Linwood Grove, Leighton Buzzard, Beds.*

EMMETT, Kerry Charles. b 46. St Jo Coll Dur BA 68. St Jo Coll Nottm 71. **d** 73 **p** 74 Southw. C of Attenborough w Chilwell 73-74; Chilwell w Inham Nook 74-76; Wembley 76-79; V of St Richard of Chich Hanworth Dio Lon from 79. *35 Forge Lane, Hanworth, Middx, TW13 6UN.* (01-898 0241)

EMMETT, Thomas. b 40. Chich Th Coll 67. **d** 70 Bp Ramsbotham for Newc T **p** 71 Newc T. C of Shiremoor, Tynemouth 70-73; Haltwhistle 73-75; V of Ch Ch Shieldfield (w St Ann from 80) City and Dio Newc T from 75; P-in-c of St Ann Newc T 77-80 *St Ann's Vicarage, Gibson Street, Newcastle-upon-Tyne, NE1 6PY.* (Newc T 320516)

EMMOTT, David Eugene. b 41. St Chad's Coll Dur BA 63, Dipl Th 66. **d** 66 **p** 67 Bradf. C of H Trin Bingley 66-69; St Marg Anfield 69-70; Kirkby 70-75; Asst Master Ruffwood Sch 70-75; Chap Newc T Poly 75-78; Hon C of St Marg Toxteth Pk 78-80; Team V of Up Holland (in c of Ch the Servant Digmoor) Dio Liv from 80. *208 Birkrig, Skelmersdale, WN8 9HW.* (Skelmersdale 28176)

EMMOTT, Douglas Brenton. b 45. AKC and BD 78. Linc Th Coll 79. **d** 80 **p** 81 York. C of St Alb Hull Dio York from 80. *43 Fairfield Road, Hull, HU5 4QX.*

EMMOTT, Frederick William. b 10. St Aid Coll 57. **d** 58 **p** 59 Dur. C of St Gabr Bp Wearmouth 58-61; PC of Chilton 61-68; V 68-80. *72 Loraine Crescent, Darlington, Co Durham.*

EMOJONG'O, Livingstone. b 49. St Paul's Coll Limuru. **d** 74 **p** 75 Maseno N. P Dio Maseno N. *PO Box 143, Kimilili, Kenya.*

EMORDI, Daniel Ngozichukwu. b 45. Trin Coll Umuahia 77. **d** 80 **p** 81 Asaba. P Dio Asaba. *All Saints Cathedral, PO Box 69, Asaba, Bendel State, Nigeria.*

EMPEY, Canon Clement Adrian. b 42. TCD BA 64, MA 68, PhD 71. Div Hostel Dub 72. **d** 74 **p** 75 Dub. C of St Ann Dub 75-76; R of Kells-Inistioge Group Dio Oss from 76; Can of Oss from 80. *The Priory, Kells, Co Kilkenny, Irish Republic.* (Kilkenny 28115)

✠ **EMPEY, Right Rev Walton Newcombe Francis.** b 34. TCD BA 57. K Coll Halifax BD 69. **d** 58 **p** 59 Dub. C of St Paul Glenageary 58-60; I of Grand Falls 60-63; R of Madawaska 63-66; I of Stradbally 66-71; Dean & R of Lim Cathl 71-81; I of St Mich Lim 71-81; Can and Preb of St Patr Cathl Dub 73-81; Cons Ld Bp of Lim and Killaloe in St Mary's Cathl Lim 25 March 81 by Abp of Dub; Bps of Meath, Cork and Cash. *Bishop's House, North Circular Road, Limerick, Irish Republic.* (Limerick 51532)

EMSLEY, John Stobart. Qu Coll Birm 39. **d** 41 S'wark **p** 41 Kingston T for S'wark. C of St Luke W Norwood 41-44; St Luke w St Paul Old Charlton 44-46; St Marg Ilkley 46-51; V of St Osw Bradford 51-71; St Andr Yeadon 71-79. *Oak Cottage, Dacre Banks, Harrogate, N Yorks.*

EMUDUKO, Gideon. **d** 76 **p** 77 Soroti. P Dio Soroti. *Ngariam, Usuk County, North Teso, Soroti, Uganda.*

EMUKAH, Daniel Okerafo. **d** 61 **p** 62 Ow. P Dio Ow. *Parsonage, Akabo, Owerri, Nigeria.*

EMURIA, Stephen. **d** 65 **p** 66 Maseno. P Dio Maseno 65-70; Dio Maseno N from 70. *PO Box 5056, Funyula, Kenya.*

ENDEAN, James Edwin Murray. Moore Coll Syd ACT ThL 73. **d** 75 Bp Robinson for Syd **p** 76 Syd. C of St Luke Liverpool 75-77; R of Dulwich Hill 78-81; Asst Res Min of Tregear Dio Syd from 81. *19 Fleetwood Street, Shalvey, NSW, Australia.*

ENDICOTT, Oliver Brian. Sarum Th Coll. **d** 57 **p** 58 Chelmsf. C of St Barn L Ilford 57-60; Barking 60-66; V of Gt w L Saling 66-70. *1005a Boyd Ave, Newton, Kansas, USA.*

ENDICOTT, Orville Richard. Univ of BC BA 54. Dalhousie Univ MA 67. Angl Th Coll BC LTh 57, BD 61. **d** 56 **p** 57 Koot. C of Creston 56-57; I of Golden 57-61; R of Fernie-Michel 61-63; Fernie 64-65; Can of Koot 64-68; I of Jollimore 66-68. *10 Elm Street, Yarmouth, NS, Canada.*

ENEASATO, Adolphus Ifeanyichuku. b 38. Trin Coll Umuahia 71. **d** 73 **p** 74 Enugu. P Dio Enugu. *St Andrew's Church, Ibagwa PA, Naukka, ECS, Nigeria.*

ENEMO, Lawrence Nwekemezie. b 34. Trin Coll legon ThL 72. **d** 72 Niger. d Dio Niger. *St Faith's Church, Box 96, Awka, Nigeria.*

ENGEL, Kevin Francis. Moore Th Coll Syd ACT ThL 51. **d** and **p** 52 Syd. C of Enfield 52-53; Corrimal 53-54; Dodoma Cathl 54-60; Can 65-70; P-in-c of Morogoro 60-62; Chan Dio Centr Tang 63-70; Asst Gen Sec CMS NSW 71-72; L to Offic Dio Syd from 71; Consultant Austr Chr Lit S and CMS from 73. *8 Duraba Place, Caringbah, NSW, Australia 2229.* (525-6263)

ENGLAND, Robert Gordon. b 39. TCD BA 62. **d** 66 **p** 67 Dub. C of Raheny w Coolock 66-72; Ch Ch Lisburn 72-73; Asst Master Belf Royal Acad 73-74. *Address temp unknown.*

ENGLISH, Peter Gordon. Univ of Edin MA (2nd cl Math) 55. Ripon Hall, Ox 59. **d** 61 **p** 62 Bradf. C of Bingley 61-64; V of Cottingley 64-66; Chap Nabumali High Sch 66-70; Lect Makerere Univ Coll Dio Nam from 70. *PO Box 7062, Kampala, Uganda.*

ENGLISH, Peter Redford. b 26. Ridley Hall Cam 70. **d** 72 Man **p** 73 Middleton for Man. C of Tyldesley 72-74; Worsley 74-76; R of St Mark Levenshulme 76-81; Heytesbury and Sutton Veny w Tytherington, Knock and Norton Bavant Dio Sarum from 81. *Sutton Veny Rectory, Bests Lane, Sutton Veny, Warminster, Wilts BA12 7AU.* (Sutton Veny 713)

ENGLISH, Robert William. Univ of Manit BA 56. St Jo Coll Winnipeg, LTh 60. **d** 59 **p** 60 Bran. R of Holland 59-63; C of St Aid Winnipeg 63-64; R of St Thos Winnipeg 64-75; Good Shepherd Winnipeg Dio Rupld from 75; Exam Chap to Bp of Rupld from 80. *673 Silverstone Avenue, Winnipeg, Manit, Canada.*

ENGORU, Yokana. **d** 52 Bp Tomusange for U Nile **p** 54 U Nile. P Dio U Nile 54-71; Dio Soroti 71-80. *Kamudu, Soroti, Uganda.*

ENGWAU, Enosi. **d** 76 **p** 77 Soroti. P Dio Soroti. *Attira, Serere County, Central Teso, Soroti, Uganda.*

ENIMA, Timoteo. **d** 62 **p** 63 N Ugan. P Dio N Ugan 63-69; Dio M & W Nile from 69. *Oluko, PO 37, Arua, Uganda.*

ENITILO, Zacheus Awoyemi. Im Coll Ibad 59. **d** 61 Ibad **p** 62 Lagos. P Dio Lagos. *Igbein, Abeokuta, Nigeria.*

ENNIS, Alfred Reginald. b 07. Late Sizar and Exhib of Trin Coll Dub Townsend Mem Pri 26, 1st cl Maths and Logic Mod 26 and 27, Math Scho 28, BA (3rd cl Phil Mod) 29, Downes Div Pri (Oratory) 30, MA 34, BD 35. **d** 34 **p** 35 Southw. C of St John Mansfield 34-35; H Ap Charlton Kings 35-36; Selby Abbey 36-38; V of Monk Fryston 38-45; CF (TA) 39-45; Hon CF 45; Asst Master Bedford Sch 45-49; Chap 46-49; V of Milton Ernest 49-54; RD of Felmersham 50-54; C-in-c of Bletsoe; of Pavenham; of Stevington and of Thirleigh 52-54; V of Earl Shilton w Elmsthorpe 54-56; Dalby-on-the-Wolds 56-58; All H W Bridgford 58-60; R of Stanton-by-Bridge w Swarkestone 60-80; Exam Chap to Bp of Derby 60-67. *14 Beechbank, Unthank Road, Norwich, NR2 2AR.* (0603 55930)

ENOCH, William Frederick Palmer. for Derby **p** 80 Derby b 30. E Midl Jt Ordin Tr Scheme Nottm 76. **d** 79 Repton for Derby **p** 80 Derby (APM). C of Ilkeston Dio Derby from 79. *33 Oakwell Drive, Ilkeston, Derbys, DE7 5GL.*

ENRIGHT, James Leslie. b 06. **d** and **p** 66 Lim. C of Dromod 66-67; I 67-76; Prec and Preb of Lim Cathl 72-76. *8 Seafield Drive, Newtown Hill, Tramore, Co Waterford, Irish Republic.* (051-81855)

ENSOR, Arthur George. b 13. Univ of Dur L Th 38. St Bonif Coll Warm 35. **d** and **p** 39 Glouc. C of Winchcombe w Gretton and Sudeley Manor 39-42; Wotton-under-Edge 42-43; Westcote 43-45; St Aug Kimberley (in c of St Mary Barkly W) 45-47; C of Queenstown 47-52; Perm to Offic Dio St E 53-56; R of Newton 56-66; Homersfield w St Cross S Elmham 66-76; Perm to Offic Dio St E from 77. *27 Morley Avenue, Woodbridge, Suff, IP12 4AZ.* (Woodbridge 4190)

ENSOR, David Alec. b 25. Univ of Capetn BA 67. Cudd Coll 48. **d** 50 **p** 51 Capetn. C of Woodstock 50-56; P-in-c of Hout Bay CP 56-60; V of Enmore w Cane Grove Br Gui 60-61; St Barn Georgetn Br Gui 61-64; St Barn Warrington 64-68; Quadring 68-73; St Aug Grimsby Dio Linc from 73; St Andr w St Luke Grimsby 73-74. *145 Legsby Avenue, Grimsby, S Humb, DN32 0LA.* (Grimsby 77109)

ENSOR, Keith Victor. Univ of Dur LTh 32. Lon Coll of Div 27. **d** 31 **p** 32 Lon. C of St Jas Holloway 31-34; Org Sec BCMS for N Prov 34-38; L to Offic Dio Liv 37-38; BCMS Miss at Algiers 38-39; Chap RAFVR 39-47; Men in Disp 44 and 45; V of Wolvey w Burton Hastings 47-50; Chap RAF 50-63; R of Horton w L Sodbury Dio Glouc from 64. *Horton Rectory, Chipping Sodbury, Bristol.* (Chipping Sodbury 3256)

ENSOR, Stephen Herbert Paulett. St Jo Coll Dur LTh 31,

BA 32. ALCD 31. **d** 32 **p** 33 Blackb. C of Leyland 32-35; C of St Bart Bris 35-36; Tutor BCMS and Th Coll Bris 35-40; Org Sec BCMS for SW and Midlds 36-40; V of Patcham 40-48; R of Bispham 48-69; Bedworth 70-81; RD of Bedworth 71-76. *Druid's Hall, South Cray, Castle Cray, Somt, BA7 7ES.*

ENSOR, Terence Bryan. b 45. AKC and BD 78. Westcott Ho Cam 78. **d** 79 **p** 80 S'wark. C of St Hugh's Conv Distr Borough & Dio S'wark from 79. *35 Eastwell House, Tabard Gardens Estate, Weston Street, SE1 4DH.* (01-403 3483)

ENTWISLE, George Barry. b 43. St Jo Coll Ox BA 66, MA 73. Linc Th Coll 73. **d** 75 **p** 76 Sheff. C of Rawmarsh w Parkgate 75-78; Ashburton 78-80; V of U Clutha Dio Dun from 80. *24 Blyth Street, Cromwell, NZ.* (50-292)

ENTWISTLE, Alan. b 41. ACP 69. Open Univ BA 80. N-W Ordin Course 72. **d** 75 Man **p** 76 Hulme for Man. C of H Trin Bury 75-78; Publ Pr Dio Man from 78; Hdmaster Hazlehurst Sch Bury from 78. *1 Alderwood Grove, Edenfield, Bury, Lancs, BLq 0HQ.* (Ram 4221)

ENTWISTLE, Frank Roland. b 37. Univ of Dur BA (2nd cl Th) 59, Dipl Th (w distinc) 60. Cranmer Hall, Dur 59. **d** 61 Aston for Birm **p** 62 Birm. C of St Jo Bapt Harborne 61-65; S Area Sec BCMS 65-66; Educn Sec 66-73; Hon C of Wallington S'wark 68-73; Ch Ch Ware 73-76; H Trin City and Dio Leic from 76. *157 Shanlin Drive, Leicester, Le2 3QG.* (Leic 700759)

ENTWISTLE, Harry. b 40. St Chad's Coll Dur BSc 61, Dipl Th 63. **d** 63 **p** 64 Blackb. C of Fleetwood 63-69; C-in-c of Hardwicke 69-74; Aston-Abbots w Cublington 69-74; Chap HM Pris Aylesbury 69-74; HM Pris Lewes 74-76; Remand Centre Risley 76-81; HM Pris Wandsworth from 81. *c/o 7 Frewin Road, Wandsworth, SW18 3LR.*

ENTWISTLE, Howard Rodney. b 36. Late Exhib of Ball Coll Ox BA 61. Linc Th Coll 61. **d** 63 Hulme for Man **p** 64 Man. C of St Aid Conv Distr Langley 63-64; All SS and Marts Langley 64-66; V of St Martin Wythenshawe 66-73; R of St Matt Stretford Dio Man from 73. *39 Sandy Lane, Stretford, Manchester, M32 9DB.* (061-865 2535)

ENTWISTLE, Keith. Dipl Th (Lon) 58. Qu Coll Birm 49. **d** 50 **p** 51 Sheff. C of Clifton 50-53; V of Wankie S Rhod 53-57; C of Goole (in c of Airmyn and Hook) 57-58; V of Hook and C-in-c of Airmyn 58; V of Legbourne w L Cawthorpe 58-62; R of Muckton w Burwell 60-62; V of Stainton by Langworth w Newball Colstead and Reasby 62-65; PC of Barlings w Langworth 62-65; R of S Cross 65-68; Archd of the Goldfields 68-72; Dean and R of Kalg Cathl 68-72; Perm to Offic Dio Perth from 74. *34 Robinson Street, Inglewood, W Australia 6052.* (71 0807)

ENTWISTLE, Ronald William Hurst. b 06. St Aid Coll 27. **d** 30 **p** 31 Blackb. C of St Chad Poulton-le-Fylde 30-35; Lanc 35-38; V of All SS Blackpool 38-46; Surr from 38; Chap RAFVR 43-46; V of Caton w Littledale 46-66; Tunstall 66-71. *3 Monteagle Square, Hornby, Lancaster, LA2 8LZ.*

ENUGU, Lord Bishop of. *See* Otubelu, Right Rev Gideon Nweke.

ENUKU, Nathaniel Akporouabe. b 33. Im Coll Ibad 64. **d** 67 **p** 68 Benin. P Dio Benin. *Holy Trinity Parsonage, Box 108, Asaba, Nigeria.*

ENYAGU, George Noel. b 37. Univ of Bris BA 71. Bp Tucker Coll Mukono Dipl Th 68. **d** 64 **p** 66 Soroti. P Dio Soroti; Lect at Bp Tucker Coll Mukono from 72; Exam Chap to Bp of Nam from 76. *c/o Bishop Tucker Theological College, PO Box 4, Mukono, Uganda.* (Mukono 231)

ENYIA, Emmanuel Oriaku. b 34. **d** 77 Aba. d Dio Aba. *Teacher Training College, Ihie, via Nbawsi, Nigeria.*

ENYINDAH, Alexander Ogbu. Trin Coll Umuahia 58. **d** 60 **p** 61 Nig Delta. P Dio Nig Delta 60-65; and from 72; Dio N Nig 65-72. *HQ Garrison, Nigerian Army, Jos, Nigeria.*

EPELLE, Amos Tuonimi Joseph. b 18. **d** 75 **p** 76 Aba. P Dio Aba. *St Andrew's Parsonage, Ohuru, Asa, Nigeria.*

EPERSON, Canon Donald Birkby. b 04. Late Scho of Ch Ch Ox 1st cl Math Mods 25, BA (1st cl Maths) 27, MA 30. Ripon Hall, Ox 30. **d** 30 **p** 31 Sarum. Asst Chap Sherborne Sch 30-38; V of Charminster and Chap Dorset Co Mental Hosp 38-53; Can and Preb of Netherbury in Ecclesia in Sarum Cathl 51-53; Can (Emer) from 53; Chap and Lect at Bp Otter Tr Coll Chich 53-64; Hon PV Chich Cathl 54-64; Sen Lect Ch Ch Coll Cant 64-69; L to Offic Dio Cant from 64; Hon Min Can of Cant 67-72. *12 Puckle Lane, Canterbury, Kent.* (Canterbury 66477)

EPOLOTO, Frederick. Maseno Bible Sch 58. **d** 59 Momb **p** 62 Maseno. P Dio Momb 59-61; Dio Maseno 62-69; Dio N Maseno from 70. *Katakwa, PO Myanga, Kenya.*

EPPINGSTONE, Rudolph Oscar Herbert. b 19. Kelham Th Coll 47. **d** 51 **p** 52 S'wark. C of St Paul w St Mark Deptford 51-55; Worth 55-59; R of Clovelly 59-78; RD of Hartland 67-74; V of W Woolfardisworthy w Buck Mills 77-78; V of Beer Dio Ex from 78. *Beer Vicarage, Barline, Seaton, Devon.* (Seaton 20996)

EPPS, Gerald Ralph. b 31. Open Univ BA 79. K Coll Lon 54. **d** 57 **p** 58 Roch. C of Slade Green 57-60; V of Freethorpe w Wickhampton 60-70; C-in-c of Halvergate w Tunstall 62-67; V 67-70; R of St Mary Magd Pulham (w St Mary Virg from 80) Dio Nor from 70; P-in-c of Alburgh 76-77; Denton 76-77; St Mary Virg Pulham 76-80. *Rectory, Pulham Market, Diss, Norf, IP21 4TE.* (Pulham Mkt 256)

EPPS, Stanley Moorcroft. b 1900. St Jo Coll Cam BA 22, MA 26. Univ of Lon BD K Coll Lon 22. 53. **d** 23 **p** 24 Roch. C of St Mark New Brompton 23-26; Gravesend (in c of St Mary) 26-30; V of St Mary Virg Strood 30-36; Chap RN 36-49; Chap Portsm Cathl 49-51; V of St Osw Coney Hill Glouc 51-57; Wimborne Minster 57-66; Surr 57-66; L to Offic Dio B & W from 67. *5 Powlett Court, Bath, BA2 6QJ.* (Bath 66778)

EPUS, Zachaeus. **d** 74 **p** 76 Maseno N. P Dio Maseno N. *Box 83, Malakiji, Kenya.*

EQUEALL, David Edward Royston. b 41. St Mich Coll Llan 68. **d** 71 **p** 72 Llan. C of St Marg Mountain Ash 71-74; Gabalfa 74-77; Asst Chap Univ Hosp of Wales Cardiff 77-79; Chap N Gen Hosp Sheff from 79. *Northern General Hospital, Herries Road, Sheffield, S5 7AU.*

ERAI, Edgar. **d** 74 Bp Ambo for Papua **p** 74 Bp Kendall for Papua. P Dio Papua 74-76. *Anglican Church, Aione, via Madang, Papua New Guinea.*

ERASTO, Samuel. b 23. **d** and **p** 66 Argent. P Dio Argent 66-73; N Argent from 73. *Parsonage, San Luis, N Argentina.*

ERB, John Edwin. b 32. Waterloo Univ Coll BA 62. Trin Coll Tor STB 65. **d** and **p** 65 Bp Snell for Tor. C of St Aid Tor 65-67; Dir Dioc Youth Centre and L to Offic Dio Guy 67-70; Dio S'wark 70-73; Youth Sec USPG 70-73; C of Grace Ch-on-the-Hill Tor 73-77; I of St Luke Tor 77-81; St Mich AA W Tor Dio Tor from 81. *611 St Clair Avenue West, Toronto, Ont, Canada.*

EREAUT, Arthur. Wells Th Coll 31. **d** 31 **p** 32 B & W. C of W Monkton 31-35; V of Lyng 35-60. *Maison Alexandre, High Street, St Aubin, Jersey, CI.*

EREH, Peter Ofobukueta. Im Coll Ibad. **d** 63 **p** 64 Benin. P Dio Benin. *St Matthew's Vicarage, Box 4, Eko-Abetu, Benin City, Nigeria.*

ERETAN, Eleazer Olawumi. b 37. **d** 74 **p** 76 Ondo. P Dio Ondo. *St Paul's Church, Idi-Ogba, Nigeria.*

ERETT, Leslie Alexander. b 1900. Trin Coll Dub 28. ALCD 31. **d** 31 Bp De Salis for B & W **p** 33 B & W. C of St Mark Lyncombe 31-34; St Paul Clifton 34-36; V of St Aug Swindon 36-43; Warden of St John's Centre and C-in-c of St Aubyn St Jo Bapt St Paul and St Steph Devonport 43-48; CF (EC) 40-42; Chap Devonport Hosp 44-47; R of Stoke-Fleming 47-54; Kidbrooke 54-63; Sherborne St John 63-71; RD of Basingstoke 69-71. *Clarehaven, Mount Pleasant, Hartley Wintney, Hants.* (Hartley Wintney 2583)

ERHAHON, Mosis Enina Ojo. Im Coll Ibad 78. **d** 81 Benin. d Dio Benin. *c/o Registrar, PO Box 82, Benin City, Nigeria.*

ERINLE, Samuel Obatola. **d** 41 **p** 43 Lagos. P Dio Lagos 41-52; Dio Ondo-B 52-61; Dio Ibad 61-66. *Vicarage, Old Ikeji, Ilesha, Nigeria.*

ERINOSO, Oyekanmi Albert. Univ of Ibad BA 72. Im Coll Ibad 73. **d** 73 **p** 74 Lagos. P Dio Lagos. *c/o Igbobi College, Yaba, Nigeria.*

ERIOBUNAH, Felix Anedum Agwuncha. b 38. Trin Coll Umuahia. **d** 68 **p** 70 Niger. P Dio Niger from 70. *St Silas' Church, Ihiala, Nigeria.*

ERLE-DRAX, George Wanley Sawbridge. b 1900. Ch Ch Ox BA 22, MA 61. Cudd Coll 23. **d** 24 **p** 25 Lon. C of St Mary of Eton Hackney Wick 24-27; Miss (UMCA) Ch Ch Cathl Zanz 27-31; P-in-c of Dar-S 31-32; Miss Chipili 34-35; Perm to Offic Dio Lon 36-38; P-in-c of St Mary's Pro-Cathl Bathurst 38-39; Offg C-in-c of Eastry and Tilmanstone 40-42; Perm to Offic at H Trin Lamorby 42-46; C 46-49; Perm to Offic at St Anne Wandsworth 49-51; St Pet w All SS Berkhamsted 51-54; Chap SSC Tymawr 54-60; C of All SS Falmouth 60-61; St Jo Bapt Cov 61-68; Tenterden 68-69; Perm to Offic Dio Cant from 69. *Orchard Cottage, Godmersham, Canterbury, Kent, CT4 7DY.* (Chilham 234)

ERNEST, Ven Gerald Edward. Coll of the Resurr Mirfield 46-47. **d** 50 **p** 52 Maur. C of St Paul Plaine Verte 50-52; St Paul Vacoas 52-53; R of St Barn Rodrigues 54-59; P-in-c of St Paul Vacoas 60-61; C of H Trin Rosehill 61-64; R of Mahebourg 64-73; Beau Bassin Dio Maur from 73; Archd and VG of Maur from 77. *St Thomas's Rectory, Beau Bassin, Mauritius.* (4-4286)

ERREY, Albert George. b 18. Univ of Lon BA (2nd cl Phil) 44, MA 48, BD (1st cl) 50. Cudd Coll. **d** 65 Bp McKie for Cov **p** 66 Cov. Hon C of H Trin Leamington Priors 65-72; C 72-74; C-in-c of Wolverton w Norton Lindsey and Langley Dio Cov from 74; R from 78. *Wolverton Rectory, Stratford-on-Avon, Warws, CV37 0HF.* (Snitterfield 278)

ERRIDGE, David John. b 45. Dipl Th (Lon) 68. Tyndale Hall Bris 66. **d** 69 Warrington for Liv **p** 70 Liv. C of St Matt

Bootle 69-72; Horwich 72-77; R of Blackley Dio Man from 77. *Rectory, Churchdale Road, Higher Blackley, Manchester, M9 3ND.* (061-740 2961)

ERSKINE, Canon Samuel Thomas. b 19. Trin Coll Dub BA Resp 42, MA 46, Div Test (2nd cl) 42. **d** 43 **p** 44 Chelmsf. C of Ch Good Shepherd Romford 43-44; Barking 45-47; Bishop's Chap for Youth 47-52; V of St Andr Ilford 52-60; Chap to Bp of Barking 59-60; Proc Conv 59-64; V of Mortlake w E Sheen 60-68; Prittlewell Dio Chelmsf from 68; RD of Canewdon and Southend from 68; Hon Can of Chelmsf from 70; C-in-c of Sutton w Shopland 72-75. *489 Victoria Avenue, Southend-on-Sea, Essex, SS2 6NL.* (Southend-on-Sea 43470)

ERSON, William Kingston. St Jo Coll Auckld 49. **d** 53 **p** 54 Auckld. C of St Heliers Bay 53-56; on leave 56-61; C of Sophiatown 61-62; Chap Baragwaneth Hosp 62-65; Perm to Offic Dio Auckld 65-67; C of St Aug Miss Penhalonga 67-71; L to Offic Dio Johann 71-74; R of St Pet Rosettenville Dio Johann from 75. *PO Box 49027, Rosettenville, Johannesburg, S Africa.* (011-26 1933)

ERUBA, Abulamu. Bp Tucker Coll Mukono. **d** 64 **p** 65 Mbale. P Dio Mbale 64-72; Dio Bukedi from 72. *Budumba, PO Tororo, Uganda.*

ERWAU, George William. **d** 76 **p** 77 Soroti. P Dio Soroti. *Soroti Cathedral, PO Box 107, Soroti, Uganda.*

ERWIN, John Desmond. Selw Coll Dun. **d** 57 **p** 58 Dun. C of Caversham 57-60; V of Milton 60-64; Waitaki 64-70; Waitaki N Oamaru 70-74; Hampden-Maheno 74-77; St Kilda Dio Dun from 77. *17 Ajax Street, St Kilda, Dunedin, NZ.* (54-015)

ESCRITT, Michael William. b 35. Univ of Birm Dipl Th 67. Qu Coll Birm 64. **d** 67 **p** 68 York. C of All SS Huntington York 67-69; Dom Chap to Abp of York 69-72; V of Bishopthorpe Dio York from 72; V of Acaster Malbis Dio York from 72. *Bishopthorpe Vicarage, York, YO2 1QG.* (York 706476)

ESDAILE, Adrian George Kennedy. b 35. Mert Coll Ox BA 57, MA 61. Wells Th Coll 59. **d** 61 **p** 62 S'wark. C of St Pet St Helier 61-64; Wimbledon 64-68; Proc Conv S'wark 64-75; V of All SS N Beddington 68-80; RD of Sutton 76-80; R of Chipping Barnet w Arkley Dio St Alb from 80. *118 Wood Street, Barnet, Herts, EN5 4DA.* (01-449 3894)

ESELEH, Ven Jonathan Oni. Melville Hall, Ibad 54. **d** 55 **p** 56 Ondo-B. P Dio Ondo-B 55-62; Dio Benin from 62; Archd of Benin from 75. *PO Box 1, Ekpoma, Nigeria.*

ESLING, Edwin. b 07. Qu Coll Birm 33. **d** 36 **p** 37 Southw. C of Old Basford 36-40; C-in-c of Bestwood 40-43; 36-40; L Pr Dio Southw (in c of Arnold) 43-46; V of Walkeringham 46-51; PC of N Wilford 51-58; V of Castle Bytham and R of L Bytham Lincs 58-60; R of St Leonards 60-65; Deloraine 65-69; V of Alvingham w N & S Cockerington 70-73; R of Yarburgh 71-73. *The Wing, Thurlby Hall, Lincoln.*

ESSERY, Eric Albert. b 28. TD. ED (TAVR) 78. St D Coll Lamp BA 53. St Mich Coll Llan 53. **d** 55 **p** 56 Llan. C of Skewen 55-57; Oakwood w Bryn 57-59; St Mary Sunbury-on-Thames 59-63; Industr Chap of Crawley 63-64; C-in-c of Lowfield Heath Crawley 63-64; V of Hammersmith 64-73; Surr from 65; CF (TAVR) from 65; V of Shinfield Dio Ox from 73. *Shinfield Vicarage, Reading, Berks, RG2 9BY.* (Reading 883363)

ESSEX, William Anthony. b 49. Univ of Sask BA 73. **d** 75 Newfld. P-in-c of Upper I Cove 75-78; Fort St John Dio Caled from 78. *1403-101 Street, Fort St John, BC, Canada.*

ESSIEN, Bassey Effiong. b 46. **d** 76 Nig Delta. d Dio Nig Delta. *3 Infantry Division Headquarters, Nigerian Army, Jos, Nigeria.*

ESTDALE, Francis Albert. b 26. ALCD 53. **d** 53 Stafford for Cant **p** 54 Lich. C of Penn 53-56; Ch Ch Watford 56-61; V of Stopsley Dio St Alb from 61. *702 Hitchin Road, Stopsley, Luton, Beds.* (Luton 29194)

ESTES, James Gray. b 34. New Engl Coll NH BA 58. Yale Univ BD 61. **d** & **p** 61 New Hampshire. In Amer Ch 61-66; Chap and Asst Master St Steph Coll Hong from 67; L to Offic Dio Hong from 67. *St Stephen's College, Stanley, Hong Kong.* (5-93360)

ESTRADA, Ezequiel. b 30. **d** 68 **p** 69 Argent. P Dio Argent 68-73; N Argent from 73. *Parsonage, Embarcación, N Argentina.*

ETCHELLS, Peter. b 26. Kelham Th Coll 48. **d** 52 **p** 53 Ely. C of St Geo Chesterton 52-55; St Marg Leic 55-58; R of Willoughby Waterleys w Peatling Magna and Ashby Magna Dio Leic from 58; Ed Leic Dioc Cal from 69. *Ashby Magna Vicarage, Lutterworth, Leics, LE17 5NF.* (Leire 209406)

ETCHES, Haigh David. b 45. St Jo Coll Dur BA 71, Dipl Th 72. **d** 73 **p** 74 Cov. C of Whitnash 73-77; Wallingford Dio Ox from 77. *33 Wantage Road, Wallingford, OX10 0LR.* (Wallingford 36353)

ETCHES, Richard Geoffrey Adderley. b 05. St Pet Coll Ja. **d** 36 **p** 37 Ja. C of St Andr Halfway Tree Ja 36-39; Fladbury 39-42; C-in-c of Wribbenhall 42-43; V of Leek Wootton 43-47; R of Snowdon 47-49; Felton w Preston Wynne 49-51; Stourmouth 51-58; L to Offic Dio Cant from 58. *13 Marten Road, Folkestone, Kent.* (Folkestone 52104)

ETEMESI, Very Rev Fanuel. St Paul's Dioc Div Sch. **d** 49 **p** 51 Momb. P Dio Momb 49-61; Dio Maseno 61-70; Dio Maseno N from 70, Hon Can of Maseno 68-70; Maseno N from 70; Dean of Maseno N from 76. *Box 100, Butere, Kenya.*

ETERHERE, John Aleluya. Trin Coll Umuahia. **d** and **p** 66 Benin. P Dio Benin. *St Barnabas's Parsonage, PA Owhrode, Warri, Nigeria.*

ETHERDEN, Frederick William. Bp's Univ Lennox BA 57. Hur Coll LTh 59. **d** and **p** 59 Niag. C of St Geo St Catharines and C-in-c of Weller Pk 59-60; R of St Eliz Burlington 61-67; Hon C of St Jude Wexford Tor 67-70; on leave. *95 Dreyer Road, Ajax, Ont., Canada.*

ETHERIDGE, Richard Thomas. b 32. BD (Lon) 62. ALCD (2nd cl) 61. **d** 62 **p** 63 Roch. C of Wilmington 62-65; Rainham 65-69; V of St John Langley Dio Birm from 69. *Vicarage, St John's Road, Oldbury, Warley, W Midl, B68 9RP.* (021-552 5005)

ETHERIDGE, Terry. b 44. Wells Th Coll 68. **d** 70 **p** 71 Carl. C of St Jo Evang, Barrow-F 70-73; Wilmslow 73-75; V of St Cross Knutsford Dio Ches from 76. *St Cross Vicarage, Knutsford, Chesh.* (Knutsford 2389)

ETHERINGTON, Ernest Hugh. b 12. CCC Cam BA 34, MA 39. Linc Th Coll 34. **d** 35 **p** 36 Win. C of Iford 35-39; Bromborough 39-41; CF (EC) 41-48; Christian Reconstruction in Eur 48-50; C of Haywards Heath 50-53; R of Southwick Sussex 53-58; Asst Master Wakef Tutorial Sch 58-61; Horbury Secondary Sch 61-77. *4 Southfield Close, Horbury, Wakefield, WF4 5AZ.* (Wakef 274612)

ETHERINGTON, Robert Barry. b 37. Univ of Man BA (Th) 62. Linc Th Coll 62. **d** 64 **p** 65 Linc. C of St Jo Bapt Ermine Linc 64-67; Frodingham 67-69; V of Reepham 69-78; Ind Chap to Bp of Linc 70-78; Industr Chap in Herts and Beds Industr Miss Team from 78; L to Offic Dio St Alb from 78. *10 Turnberry Walk, Bedford.* (0234-58173)

ETHRIDGE, Gordon William. Qu Coll Newfld. **d** 51 **p** 52 Newfld. I of Battle Harbour 51; C of St Mich St John's 52; I of St Anthony 52-58; Random 58-67; R of Trinity 67-71; I of Gambo Dio Newfld (Centr Newfld from 76) 71-78. *c/o Box 239, Dark Cove, Gambo, Newfoundland, Canada.* (709-674-4488)

ETIANG, Canon Stanley. Buwalasi Th Coll. **d** 52 **p** 54 U Nile. P Dio U Nile 52-61; Dio Soroti 61-66; Hon Can from 66. *Church of Uganda, Bukedea, Uganda.*

ETTERLEY, Peter Anthony Gordon. Wells Th Coll 66. **d** 68 **p** 69 Roch. C of St Aug Gillingham 68-71; Miss Dio Papua 71-77; Dio New Guinea Is 77-80; V of Cleeve w Chelvey & Brockley Dio B & W from 80. *106 Main Road, Cleeve, Bristol, BS19 4PN.* (Yatton 833161)

ETTLINGER, Max Brian. b 28. Sarum Wells Th Coll 70. **d** 72 **p** 73 Edmon for Lon. C of John Keble Ch Mill Hill 72-74; Min of L St Pet Conv Distr Cricklewood 74-78; R of Monken Hadley Dio Lon from 78. *Rectory, Hadley Common, Barnet, Herts, EN5 5QD.* (01-449 2414)

ETTRICK, Peter Alured. TD 56. OBE (Mil) 67. Ch Coll Cam 2nd cl Econ Trip pt i 34, BA (2nd cl Th Trip pt i) 36, MA 41. Qu Coll Birm 36. **d** 37 **p** 38 Man. C of St Thos Werneth 37-39; Offg C-in-c of St Pet Blackley 39-40; Ch Ch Ashton-L 40-42; CF (EC) 42-47; R of Heaton Norris 47-52; SCF (TA) 48-62; DACG (TA) 62-66; R of Flixton 52-61; V of Gaydon w Chadshunt 61-65; Asst Dir of Relig Educn Dio Cov 61-65; V of St Nich Cov 65-70; Bisley 70-79. *Meiktila, The Ridge, Bussage, Stroud, Glos.* (Brimscombe 883272)

ETWAP, Eliakim. **d** 76 Lango. d Dio Lango. *PO Cegere, Apach, Uganda.*

ETWELL, Eric John. b 37. Massey Univ NZ BSA 63. **d** 78 Ch Ch. Hon C of Highfield Dio Ch Ch from 78. *Hadlow, 4rd, Timaru, NZ.*

EURICH, Hugh Frederick Albrecht. b 10. St Pet Hall, Ox BA (2nd cl Mod Lang) 34, MA 38. Ripon Hall, Ox 34. **d** 36 **p** 37 Newc T. C of Bedlington 36-39; Allerton 39-41; C-in-c of St Mary Widnes 41-43; V of St Phil Liv 43-51; Chap at Utrecht 51-55; Amsterdam 55-56; V of Kilby 56-62; Wistow w Newton Harcourt 56-62; Tockwith 62-72; Bilton-in-Ainsty 62-72; Bubwith 72-74; C of All SS Pavement York 74-76; Team V 76-79; C of St Denys York 74-76. *5 Lilac Avenue, Hull Road, York, YO1 3AS.* (York 411364)

EUROPE, Diocese in. *See* Gibraltar in Europe.

EUROPE NORTH WEST, Archdeacon of. *See* Duplock, Ven Peter Montgomery.

EUROPE, NORTH and CENTRAL, Anglican Bishop for. Part of Diocese of Gibraltar in Europe from 80.

EUSTACE, Donald John. Bp's Univ Lennox LST 64. **d** 64 **p** 65 Queb. R of E Angus 64-67; E Sherbrooke 67-70; Hagersville w Cheapside 70-77; Deep River Dio Ott from 77.

Box 426, Deep River, Ont, Canada. (613-584 3710)

EUSTICE, Peter Lafevre. b 32. K Coll Lon and Warm AKC 56. **d** 57 **p** 58 Lon. C of Finsbury Pk 57-60; Redruth 60-63; PC of Treslothan 63-71; V of All SS Falmouth 71-76; R of St Steph-in-Brannel Dio Truro from 76. *Rectory, St Stephen, St Austell, Cornw, PL26 7RL.* (St Austell 822236)

EVA, Nigel James. b 29. Pemb Coll Cam 2nd cl Mod Lang Trip pt i 52, BA (2nd cl Mod Lang Trip pt ii) 53, MA 57. Ely Th Coll 53. **d** 55 **p** 56 S'wark. Asst Missr Pemb Coll Miss Walworth 55-57; C of Greenwich 57-60; Mottingham 60-62; V of H Trin Eltham 62-80; R of Portishead Dio B & W from 80. *Rectory, Portishead, Bristol, BS20 9PU.* (Portishead 842284)

EVA, Canon Owen Vyvyan. b 17. Selw Coll Cam BA 39, MA 43. Ridley Hall, Cam. **d** 47 **p** 48 Liv. C of St Mich Garston 47-51; V of Edge Hill 51-57; St Andr Kowloon Hong Kong 57-61; C-in-c of H Trin Warrington 61-62; R of Halewood Dio Liv from 62; RD of Farnworth 71-81; Hon Can of Liv from 74. *Halewood Rectory, Liverpool, L26 6LA.* (051-487 5610)

EVANS, Alan David Carter. b 35. Clifton Th Coll 62. **d** 65 Barking for Chelmsf **p** 66 Chelmsf. C of Gt Baddow 65-68; Walthamstow 68-71; V of St Mark Forest Gate 71-76; Chadwell Heath Dio Chelmsf from 76. *10 St Chad's Road, Chadwell Heath, Romford, Essex, RM6 6JB.* (01-590 2054)

EVANS, Alan Morewood. b 54. Qu Univ Kingston Ont BA 76. Atlantic Sch of Th Halifax MDiv 80. **d** 80 **p** 81 Ont. C of St Geo Trenton Dio Ont from 80. *130 Lorne Avenue, Trenton, Ont, Canada, K8V 5C2.* (613-394 4511)

EVANS, Alfred Leslie. b 09. Univ of Wales, BA (2nd cl Phil) 37. St Mich Coll Llan 37. **d** 38 **p** 39 St D. C of Llandilo Fawr 38-41; Pembrey 41-49; V of Elerch 49-50; St Ann Llandegai 50-55; R of Machynlleth w Llanwrin 55-74; Surr 60-74; RD of Cyfeiliog and Mawddwy 62-67; Hon Can of Ban Cathl 71-74. *26 Felindre, Pennal, Gwyn, SY20 9DP.* (Pennal 676)

EVANS, Alun Wyn. b 47. Downing Coll Cam 2nd cl Geog Trip pt i 68, BA (2nd cl Th Trip pt ii) 70. MA 73. Cudd Coll 70. **d** 72 **p** 73 Llan. C of Bargoed w Brithdir (and Deri from 74) 72-75; Coity w Nolton 75-77; V of Michaelstone-super-Avon 77-81; Llangynwyd w Maesteg Dio Llan from 81; Warden of Ordinands Dio Llan 80-81. *33 Brynmawr Place, Maesteg, Bridgend, Mid Glam.* (Maesteg 733194)

EVANS, Anthony Nigel. b 53. Univ of Nottm BA 74. Fitzwm Coll Cam Ba 76. Westcott Ho Cam 74. **d** 77 **p** 78 Southw. C of St Cypr Carlton Hill Sneinton 77-80; Worksop Priory Dio Southw from 80. *8 Coleridge Road, Kilton, Worksop, Notts.* (Worksop 472112)

EVANS, Benjamin John. b 13. St Mich AA Llan 75. **d** 76 **p** 77 Llan. C of Barry Dio Llan from 76. *167 Pontypridd Road, Barry, S Glam, CF6 8LW.*

EVANS, Brian. b 34. Univ of Wales (Cardiff) Dipl Th 58. St Deiniol's Libr Hawarden 70. **d** 71 Swan B for Llan **p** 72 Llan. C of Porthkerry w Barry 71-72; All SS Barry 72-75; V of Abercynon Dio Llan from 75. *Vicarage, Abercynon, Mid-Glam.* (Abercynon 740207)

EVANS, Brian Allen. Montr Dioc Th Coll LTh 67. **d** 67 Montr. C of Trin Mem Ch Montr 67-69; I of Ile-Perrot Dorian 69-72; Mascouche 70-75; R of St Clem Verdun Dio Montr from 75. *4322 Wellington Street, Verdun, PQ, Canada.* (514-769 5373)

✠ **EVANS, Right Rev Bruce Read.** Oak Hill Th Coll 54. **d** 57 **p** 58 S'wark. C of H Trin Redhill 57-59; St Paul Portman Square Lon 59-62; St John Wynberg 62-69; R 69-75; Can of Capetn 73-75; Cons Ld Bp of Port Eliz in St Geo Cathl Capetn 1 June 75 by Abp of Capetn; Bps of Geo, Natal, Bloemf and Grahmstn; Bps Suffr of Capetn; and others. *14 Buckingham Road, Port Elizabeth, CP 6001, S Africa.* (041-33 1949)

EVANS, Cadwaladr Gwilym Jones. b 03. St D Coll Lamp BA 27. **d** 28 **p** 29 Swan B. C of St Matt Swansea w Greenhill 28-30; St Mary Whitchurch 30-36; Chap RN 36-58; R of W Tanfield 58-74. *Carlingwark, Mickley, Ripon, Yorks.*

EVANS, Charles Wyndham. b 28. Late Exhib of Univ Coll of N Wales BA (1st cl hons Phil) 49. St Cath S Ox BA (3rd cl Th) 51, MA 55. St Steph Ho Ox 49. **d** 52 **p** 53 St A. C of Denbigh 52-56; Chap and Tutor at Llandovery Coll 56-58; Ho Master 58-67; Chap and Lect Trin Coll Carmarthen 67-79; LPr Dio St D 56-79; V of Llanrhaeadr-yng-Nghinmerch and Prion Dio St A from 79. *Llanrhaeadr Vicarage, Denbigh, Clwyd.* (Llanynys 250)

EVANS, Christopher Francis. b 09. CCC Cam (2nd cl Cl Trip pt i 30), BA (1st cl Th Trip pt i), and Jeremie Hellenistic Pri 32, MA 38. Linc Th Coll 33. Univ of Ox MA 48 (by incorp). Univ of Southn Hon DLitt 77. St Deiniol's Libr Hawarden 33-34. **d** 34 Southn for Win **p** 35 Win. C of St Barn Southn 34-38; Tutor Linc Th Coll 38-44; Chap and Lect Dioc Training Coll 44-48; L to Offic Dio Linc 39-48; Chap Fell and Lect in Div at Corpus Christi Coll Ox 48-58; Chap to Bp of Derby at Univ of Ox 49-58; Exam Chap to Bp of Bris 48-58; Select Pr Univ of Ox 55-57; Univ of Cam 59-60; Proc Conv Ox 55-58; Lightfoot Prof of Div Univ of Dur 58-62; Can Res of Dur 58-62; Exam Chap to Bp of Dur 59-62; to Abp of Cant 62-75; to Bp of Lich 68-75; Prof of NT Stud K Coll Lon 62-77; Prof (Emer) from 77; F K Coll Lon from 70. *4 Church Close, Cuddesdon, Oxford, OX9 9EX.* (Wheatley 4406)

EVANS, Christopher Idris. b 51. Chich Th Coll 74. **d** 77 **p** 78 Llan. C of Gelligaer 77-80; St Andr Major w Michaelston-le-Pit 80-81; V of Llangeinor Dio Llan from 81. *Vicarage, Ogmore Vale, Bridgend, Mid Glam.* (Ogmore Valley 298)

EVANS, Christopher Jonathan. b 43. K Coll Lon and Warm AKC 67. **d** 68 **p** 69 Lich. C of Wednesfield 68-71; St Phil Eccles Distr Dorridge 71-73; V of Marston Green 73-80; Acocks Green Dio Birm from 80. *34 Dudley Park Road, Birmingham, B27 6QR.*(021-706 9764)

EVANS, Clifford John George. Episc Th Sem Kentucky LTh 77. **d** 77 **p** 78 Fred. R of Gagetown 77-80; Tamworth Dio Ont from 80. *Rectory, Tamworth, Ont, Canada K0K 3G0.* (613-379 2204)

EVANS, Canon Colin Rex. b 24. Univ of Reading, BA 49. Linc Th Coll. **d** 57 **p** 58 Linc. C of Boultham 57-59; St Nich w St John Linc 59-62; V of St Mary le Wigford w St Martin Linc 62-66; C in c of St Faith Linc 63-66; R of Bassingham 66-73, V of Aubourn w Haddington 66-73; Carlton-le-Moorland w Stapleford 66-73; R of Skinnand 66-73; Thurlby w Norton Disney 66-73; RD of Graffoe 69-73; Elloe E from 74; V of Holbeach Dio Linc from 74; Can and Preb of Linc Cathl from 74. *Holbeach Vicarage, Spalding, Lincs, PE12 7DT.* (Holbeach 22185)

EVANS, Cuthbert Ralph. St Jo Coll Morpeth ACT ThL 36. **d** 37 **p** 38 Armid. C of Tamworth 37-38; Narrabri 38-40; P-in-c of Tingha 40-42; Chap AIF 42-45; P-in-c of Wee Waa 45-53; V of Barbara 53-59; Inverell 59-76; Perm to Offic Dio Brisb from 78. *Tosti Street, Sorrento, Queensland, Australia 4220.* (075-31 6280)

EVANS, Daniel Jones. St D Coll Lamp BA 33. **d** 33 **p** 35 Swan B. C of Cockett (St Pet Swansea) 33-39; Actg C of Cefncoed (in c of Nantddu) 39-41; V of Llangennith 41-50; St Jude Swansea 50-77. *c/o St Jude's Vicarage, Swansea, W Glam.*

EVANS, Daniel Trevor. b 11. Late Scho of St D Coll Lamp BA (3rd cl Cl) 34. St Mich Coll Llan 34. **d** 35 **p** 36 St A. C of Colwyn Bay 35-39; St Mich AA Watford 39-44; Ch Ch Luton 44-45; Biggleswade 45-48; R of Wrestlingworth 48-53; V of Dunton Beds 48-53; Bromham w Oakley 53-77. *26 Burrow Down, Eastbourne, E Sussex, BN20 8ST.* (Eastbourne 35707)

EVANS, David. b 37. Late Exhib of Keble Coll Ox BA (2nd cl Hist) 60, 3rd cl Th 62, MA 65. BD (2nd cl) Lon 64. Wells Th Coll 62. **d** 64 **p** 65 Swan B. C of Brecon w Battle 64-68; Min Can of Brecon Cathl 64-68; Chap Univ Coll Swansea 68-71; C of St Mary Swansea 68-71; Bp's Chap for Samaritan and Social Work Birm 71-75; Joint Gen Sec Samaritans from 75; L to Offic Dio Ox from 75. *20 Haywards Close, Henley-on-Thames, RG9 1UY.* (Henley 4146)

EVANS, David. b 37. St Mich Coll Llan 65. Open Univ BA 73. **d** 67 **p** 68 Swan B. C of St Pet Cockett Swansea 67-70; St Austell 70-74; R of Purley Dio Ox from 75. *Purley Rectory, Reading, Berks, RG8 8DE.* (Reading 21003)

EVANS, David Alexander Noble. b 13. Pemb Coll Ox 2nd cl Cl Mods 34, BA (2nd cl Mod Hist) 36, MA 41. Wells Th Coll 38. **d** 40 **p** 41 Ripon. C of Leeds 40-44; CF (EC) 44-47; on Staff of Univ Coll Sch Frognal 47-50; V of Eton w Eton Wick and Boveney 50-66; PC of Sunningdale 66-68; V 68-80; Perm to Offic Dio Ex from 80. *High Bank, Manaton, Newton Abbot, Devon, TQ13 9UA.*

EVANS, David Aylmer. b 28. St D Coll Lamp BA 49, LTh 51. **d** 51 **p** 52 Swan B. C of St D Brecon 51-53; Colwyn Bay 53-54; Macclesfield 54-56; V of Lostock Gralam 56-59; Chap Endsleigh Sch 59-65; Publ Pr Dio Chelmsf 59-65; Perm to Offic Dio Ox 65-73; Asst Master Wokingham Gr Sch 65-73; Counsellor S Molton Sch & Commun Coll Devon from 73. *4 Burlington Close, Barnstaple, Devon, EX32 9BP.*

EVANS, David Burton. b 35. Edin Th Coll 60. **d** 62 Ripon **p** 63 Knaresborough for Ripon. C of St Hilda (w St Sav from 64) Leeds 62-67; Min Can of Dur 67-71; L to Offic Dio Dur 67-71; PV of Chich Cathl and Chap of Prebendal Sch 71-74; R of Lynch w Iping Marsh 74-79; Chap K Edw VII Hosp Midhurst from 77; V of Easebourne Dio Chich from 79. *Easebourne Priory, Midhurst, W Sussex, GU29 0AJ.* (Midhurst 3341)

EVANS, Canon David Conrad. b 16. St D Coll Lamp BA 40. **d** 42 **p** 43 Swan B. C of Llandilo Talybont 42-45; CF (EC) 45-48; Hon CF 48; C of Gorseinon 48-50; St Mich Aberystwyth 50-53; V of Beddgelert 53-56; R of Llangelynin 56-59; Llanllyfni 59-63; V of Llanfihangel-Abercowin Dio St

D from 63; RD of St Clears from 77; Surr from 78; Hon Can of St D Cathl from 79. *Llanfihangel Vicarage, St Clears, Dyfed.* (St Clears 378)

EVANS, David Douglas Lloyd. b 08. CBE 56. Wells Th Coll. **d** 65 B & W **p** 65 Taunton for B & W. C of Bath Abbey w St Jas Bath 65-66; R of Steeple w Tyneham and Church Knowle w Kimmeridge 66-75. *3 Bramar Court, 41 Westcliff Road, Bournemouth, Dorset.*

EVANS, David Eifion. b 11. Univ of Wales BA 32, MA 51. St Mich Coll Llan. **d** 34 **p** 35 St D. C of Llanfihangel-ar-Arth 34-36; Llanbadarn Fawr 36-40; CF (EC) 40-45; V of Llandeloy w Llanrheithan 45-48; Penrhyncoch (w Elerch from 52) 48-57; Aberystwyth 57-67; Llanafan-y-Trawscoed w Gwnnws 67-69; RD of Llanbadarn-Fawr 57-67; Surr 57-79; Can of Caerfai in St D Cathl 63-67; Preb of Llandyfriog 67-79; Archd of Cardigan 67-79; V of Newcastle Emlyn 69-79. *31 Bryncastell, Bowstreet, Dyfed.*

EVANS, David Elwyn. b 43. St Mich Coll Llan 71. **d** 73 **p** 74 St D. C of Llandebie 73-75; Llanelli 75-78; V of Trelech-a'r-Bettws Dio St D from 78. *Trelech Vicarage, Penybont, Carmarthen, Dyfed.* (Maddox 335)

EVANS, David Frederick. b 15. Univ of Wales BA 36. St D Coll Lamp 36. **d** 38 Lon **p** 39 Willesden for Lon. C of St Geo Enfield 38-41; Ch Ch Chester 41-44; Tarporley (in c of St Cross Cotebrook) 44-46; V of Alvanley 46-52; St Mary Tottenham Dio Lon from 52. *St Mary's Vicarage, Lansdowne Road, N17.* (01-808 6644)

EVANS, David Frederick Francis. b 35. Univ of Wales BSc 59. Wells Th Coll 59. **d** 61 **p** 62 S'wark. C of Eltham 61-64; Banbury 64-69; V of Brize Norton w Carterton 69-73; St Geo Tilehurst Dio Ox from 73. *98 Grovelands Road, Reading, Berks.* (Reading 54901)

EVANS, David Geraint. Univ of Wales BA 47. St D Coll Lamp 49. **d** 49 **p** 50 St D. C of St Ishmael w Ferryside and Llansaint 49-54; Llandilo Vawr w Llandyfeisant 54-58; V of Strata-Florida 58-68; R of Ystradgynlais Dio Swan B from 68. *Ystradgynlais Rectory, Swansea, W Glam.* (Glantawe 843200)

EVANS, David James. b 51. Univ of the Witwatersrand BA 73. St Paul's Th Coll Grahmstn 76. **d** Bp Stanage for Johann **p** 79 Johann. C of Springs Dio Johann from 78. *PO Box 949, Springs, S Africa 1560.*

EVANS, David John. b 49. Univ of Wales (Bangor) BSc 72. Dipl Th (Leeds) 77. Coll of the Resurr Mirfield 75. **d** 78 **p** 79 S'wark. C of St Anne Wandsworth 78-81; Angell Town Brixton Dio Lon from 81. *73 Baytree Road, Brixton, SW2 5RR.* (01-274 6907)

EVANS, David Leslie Bowen. b 28. St D Coll Lamp BA 52, LTh 54. **d** 54 **p** 55 St D. C of Cardigan 54-57; Llangathen w Llanfihangel Cilfargen 57-58; Betws w Ammanford 58-60; V of Bettws Evan w Bryngwyn 60-64; Burry Port w Pwll 64-76; Eglwys Dewi Sant Cardiff Dio Llan from 76; Dep Chap HM Pris Cardiff from 76. *51 Heath Park Avenue, Cardiff, CF4 3RF.* (Cardiff 751418)

EVANS, David Morgan. Lich Th Coll 26. **d** 29 **p** 30 St A. C of Llanrwst 29-38; R of Moulsoe Dio Ox from 38; C-in-c of Milton Keynes 60-64; C-in-c of Broughton 60-64. *Moulsoe Rectory, Newport Pagnell, MK16 0HL.* (Pincham 5249)

EVANS, David Rhys. b 42. **d** 73 **p** 74 Bunb. C of St Bonif Cathl Bunb 73-74; P-in-c of Lake Grace 74-79; V of Miri Dio Kuch from 79. *Box 233, Miri, Sarawak, Malaysia.*

EVANS, David Richard. b 31. K Coll Lon and Warm AKC 55. **d** 56 Dover for Cant **p** 57 Cant. C of St Sav Folkestone 56-59; St Matt Bethnal Green 59-62; St Jo Evang Kensal Green 62-64; V of Hibaldstow 64-71; Burgh-le-Marsh 71-78; Orby 71-78; Welton-le-Marsh w Gunby 71-78; R of Bratoft w Irby-in-the-Marsh 71-78; Chap RADD from 78. *412a Clapham Road, SW9 9DA.* (01-622 3566)

EVANS, David Richard. b 47. St Steph Ho Ox 68. **d** 72 **p** 73 Llan. C of St Jo Bapt Cardiff 72-76; PV of Llan Cathl 76-81; V of Cleeve Prior w The Littletons Dio Worc from 81. *South Littleton Vicarage, Evesham, Worcs, WR11 5JJ.* (Evesham 830397)

✠ **EVANS, Right Rev David Richard John.** b 38. G and C Coll Cam BA 63, MA 66. Clifton Th Coll 63. **d** 65 **p** 66 Lon. C of Cockfosters 65-68; C of H Trin Lomad de Zamora 69-73; Asst Min 74-77; Chap Ch of Good Shepherd Lima 77-78; Cons Ld Bp of Peru in Ch of Good Shepherd Lima 14 May 78 by Bps of Chile and Parag; and Bp D Leake. *Avenida Santa Cruz 491, Miraflores, Lima 18, Peru.*

EVANS, David Russell. Univ of Liv BA (2nd cl Engl) 57. Ripon Hall Ox 59. **d** 61 **p** 62 Liv. C of St Osw Conv Distr Netherton 61-65; Asst Chap Can Slade Gr Sch Bolton from 65; L Pr Dio Man from 65; Perm to Offic Dio Liv from 76. *2 Rushford Grove, Bolton, Lancs.*

EVANS, David Thomas Pugh. St Aid Coll 41. **d** 44 Bp Tubbs for Ches **p** 45 Ches. C-in-c of St Winifred's Welsh Ch Birkenhead Dio Ches from 44; V of H Trin Birkenhead 54-74. *33 Harcourt Street, Birkenhead, Merseyside.* (051-652 4617)

EVANS, David Vincent. b 22. Keble Coll Ox BA 43, MA 47. Wells Th Coll 45. **d** 47 **p** 48 Portsm. C of H Trin Fareham 47-51; Chap RN 51-81; Hon Chap to HM the Queen 75-77. *22 The Ridgeway, Fareham, Hants, PO16 8RE.* (Fareham 233791)

EVANS, Denys Roberts. b 22. K Coll Lon AKC and BD 47. **d** 47 **p** 48 Bris. C of St Luke Brislington 47-50; St Mich AA w Ch of Good Shepherd Bishopston 50-54; V of Stoke Gifford and Chap Stoke Pk Hosp Stapleton 54-61; Chap Magd Coll Sch Ox from 61. *4 Staunton Road, Headington, Oxford.* (Oxford 62784)

EVANS, Derek. St D Coll Lamp 65. **d** 68 **p** 69 St D. C of Pemb Dk 68-74; V of Ambleston w St Dogwell and E Walton w Llysyfran 74-78; Wiston (and Ambleston w St Dogwells and Walton East and Spittal w Tregarn from 81) Dio St D from 78. *Wiston Vicarage, Clarbeston Road, Haverfordwest, Dyfed.* (Clarbeston 266)

EVANS, Preb Derek Courtenay. b 29. Late Exhib of Down Coll Cam 2nd cl Cl Trip pt i 51, BA (2nd cl Cl Trip pt ii) 52, MA 56. St Aid Coll 55. **d** 57 Taunton for B & W **p** 58 B & W. C of Taunton 57-61; V of Trull 61-77; RD of Taunton S 72-77; R of Street (w Walton from 78) Dio B & W from 77; C-in-c of Walton 77-78; Preb of Wells Cathl from 77; RD of Glastonbury from 79; P-in-c of Greinton Dio B & W from 80. *Rectory, Vestry Road, Street, Somt, BA16 0HX.* (Street 42671)

EVANS, Desmond. b 26. St D Coll Lamp BA 48. St Cath S Ox BA (2nd cl Th) 50, MA 54. St Steph Ho Ox 48. **d** 51 **p** 52 Swan B. C of Clydach 51-54; Chap and Asst Master Cranleigh Sch and L to Offic Dio Guildf 54-59; Div Lect St Mary's Coll Ban 59-78; Perm to Offic Dios Ban and Llan 59-78; Dioc Inspector of Schs 78; V of Llanwrtyd w Llandulas in Tir Abad and Eglwys Oen Duw w Llanfihangel Abergwessin and Llanddewi 78-82; RD of Builth-Elwell 79-82; V of Clydach Dio Swan B from 82. *Vicarage, Clydach, Swansea, W Glam.* (Clydach 843203)

EVANS, Dilwyn Morgan. St D Coll Lamp BA 41, LTh 43. **d** 43 **p** 44 St D. C of Laugharne w Llansadurnen and Llandawke 43-47; Griffithstown 47-49; Bedwas 49-51; V of Llanfihangel-y-Creuddyn 56-58; Asst Master Portsm Tech Sch 58-67. *Eryl, Llanrhystyd, Dyfed.*

EVANS, Donald Henry. b 13. St D Coll Lamp BA 35. **d** 36 **p** 37 St A. C of Wrexham 36-48; R of Worthenbury w Tallarn Green 48-61; V of Towyn Denbighs 61-64; Seighford w Derrington and Creswell 64-78. *3 Highfields Avenue, Audlem, Crewe, Chesh.*

EVANS, Douglas Haig. b 18. Late Scho of St D Coll Lamp BA (2nd cl Hist) 39, LTh 60. **d** 46 **p** 47 St D. C of Pembroke Dk 46-48; C-in-c of Capel Tygwydd 48-49; V of Gt and L Badminton w Acton Turville and Priv Chap to Duke of Beaufort 49-58; CF (TA) 54-58; V of St Paul Ches 58-69; Henbury Dio Ches from 69. *Henbury Vicarage, Macclesfield, Chesh, SK11 9NN.* (0625 24113)

EVANS, Edward John. b 47. Univ of Wales (Cardiff) Dipl Th 71. St Mich Coll Llan 67. **d** 71 **p** 72 Llan. C of Llantwit Fardre 71-77; R of Eglwysilan Dio Llan from 77. *Rectory, Brynhafod Road, Abertridwr, Caerphilly, Mid Glam CF8 2BH.* (Senghenydd 830220)

✠ **EVANS, Right Rev Edward Lewis.** b 04. Univ of Lon BD 34, MTh 39. Bps' Coll Cheshunt 35. **d** 37 **p** 38 Chelmsf. C of Prittlewell 37-40; Warden of St Pet Coll Ja 40-49; Exam Chap to Bp of Ja 40-60; Can of Ja 43-50; P-in-c of Ch Ch Vineyard Pen 44-49; R of Kingston 49-52; Archd of Surrey and Commiss in Ja 50-57; R of Woodford w Craigton 52-57; Cons Ld Bp Suffr of Kingston (Ja) in Spanish Town Cathl on 25 March 57 by Abp of W Indies; Bps of Nassau, Ja; Br Hond; and Haiti; Trld to Barb 60; res 71; P-in-c of Marley Ja 71-72; Commiss Antig from 72; Ja from 77. *Bungalow 1, Terry's Cross, Woodmancote, Henfield, BN5 9SX.* (Henfield 3334)

EVANS, Edward Percy. b 07. Worc Ordin Coll 64. **d** 66 **p** 67 Win. C of Overton w Laverstoke and Freefolk 66-74. *Pear Tree Cottage, Sheep Street, Chipping Campden, Glos, GL55 6DS.* (Evesham 840809)

EVANS, Elwyn David. b 36. Keble Coll Ox 3rd cl Cl Mods 56, BA (3rd cl Lit Hum) 58, MA 62. St Mich Coll Llan 60. **d** 61 **p** 62 St D. C of H Trin Aberystwyth 61-63; St Paul Llanelly 63-66; St German Roath 66-69; V of Crynant 69-78; R of Llanilid w Pencoed Dio Llan from 79. *Rectory, Coychurch Road, Pencoed, Bridgend, Mid Glam, CF35 5NA.* (0656 860337)

EVANS, Elwyn Thomas. Univ of Wales, BA 36. St D Coll Lamp 37. **d** 38 Llan **p** 39 Swan B for Llan. C of Ystrad Mynach 38-40; Caeru w Ely 40-52; V of St Clem Nechells 52-64; PC of St Edm Tyseley Birm 64-68; V 68-78. *c/o Vicarage, Reddings Lane, Birmingham, 11.*

EVANS, Emrys. b 17. St D Coll Lamp BA 41. **d** 42 Glouc **p** 43 Tewkesbury for Glouc. C of Tidenham w Beachley and

Lancaut 42-46; St Mary Charlton Kings 46-50; V of Viney Hill 50-55; All SS Glouc 55-59; All SS Twickenham 60-81. *c/o Vicarage, Campbell Road, Twickenham, Middx, TW2 5BY.*

EVANS, Ernest. b 1889. Univ of Glas MA (1st cl Cl) 10, John Clark Fell 09-11, Ferguson Scho 12, Hon DD 45. Late Exhib of Ch Ch Ox 2nd cl Cl Mods 11, BA (2nd cl Lit Hum) 13, Jun Gr Test Pri and 1st cl Th 14, MA 16, BD 25, DD 52. **d** 14 **p** 15 Glouc. C of Chipping Campden 14-17; Cirencester 17-21; St Aid Leeds 21-23; Sub-Warden St Aug Coll Cant 23-32; V of Hellifield 32-64; Lect and Exam in Th Univ of Dur 34-47; Hon Can of St John of Beverley in Bradf Cathl 39-64; RD of Settle 41-52; Exam Chap to Bp of Bradf 56-65; Lect and Exam in Th Univ of Leeds 47-59. *Crimbles Court, Scalby, Scarborough, Yorks.* (Scarborough 65537)

EVANS, Ernest Lloyd Parry. St D Coll Lamp BA (2nd cl Hist) 37. Keble Coll Ox BA (3rd cl Th) 39, MA 45. St Mich Coll Llan 39. **d** 40 **p** 41 St D. C of St Paul Llanelly 40-43; Chap RAF 43-69; V of Frensham 69-80. *2 Kimbers Lane, Farnham, Surrey.* (0252 714914)

EVANS, Ernest Percival. b 16. Keble Coll Ox BA (3rd cl Th) 38, MA 43. TD 60. Ely Th Coll 38. **d** 39 Llan for Mon **p** 40 Mon. C of H Trin Abergavenny 39-41; St Jo Bapt Newport 41-46; CF (TA) 47-61; SCF (TA) 61-66; DACG (TA) 66-67; Bp's Messenger 46-52; Hon Chap to Bp of Mon 47-63; V of Chepstow (w St Arvans and Penterry to 59) 52-64; Can of Mon 57-63; RD of Chepstow 62-63; V of Llantilio Crosseny w Llanfihangel-Ystern-Llewern 64-69; Archd of Mon 63-73; Newport 73-76. *27 Woodville Road, Newport, Gwent.*

EVANS, Evan. b 04. **d** 39 **p** 40 Glouc. C of Westbury-on-Severn 39-42; Berkeley (in c of Sharpness) 42-47; V of Parkend 47-56; Awre w Blakeney 56-61; Churcham w Bulley 61-69; C of St Jas Glouc 70-74. *4 Oxstalls Way, Gloucester.* (Glouc 24620)

EVANS, Canon Evan Austin. b 02. Keble Coll Ox BA 24, MA 31. St D Coll Lamp. **d** 25 **p** 26 St D. C of Bettws w Ammanford 25-27; St Sav Roath 27-30; St Aug Penarth 30-32; PV of Llan Cathl 32-37; V of Glyntaff 37-64; Surr 37-64; RD of Rhondda 56-64; Can of Llan Cathl 61-72; V of Llancarfan 64-72. *30 Bron Awelon, Barry, S Glam.* (Barry 734837)

EVANS, Evan Walter. b 16. Men in Disp 46 and 55. MBE (Mil) 65. Late Scho and Exhib of St D Coll Lamp BA (2nd cl Hist) 36. **d** 39 **p** 40 St D. C of Cellan w Llanfair Clydogau 39; Narberth w Robeston Wathen 39-40; St Mary Cardigan 40-42; CF (EC) 42-47; C of Llandyssul 47; R of Didmarton w Oldbury on the Hill and Sopworth 47-52; CF (TA) 50-52; CF 52-72; Chap Royal Hosp Chelsea 72-81. *36 Mumbles Road, Blackpill, Swansea, SA3 5AU.* (0792-202139)

EVANS, Frank Bertram. b 04. Linc Th Coll 43. **d** 45 Lon for Cant **p** 46 Cant. C of St Mary Addington 45-48; C-in-c of Bacton 48-51; R 51-57; Wyverstone 51-57; RD of S Hartismere 56-57; V of Aylsham 57-70; RD of Ingworth 63-65; C-in-c of Alby w Thwaite 64-70; Perm to Offic Dio Nor from 70. *Lime Tree Walk, Blickling Hall, Norwich, NR11 6NH.* (Aylsham 2173)

EVANS, Frank Dennis. b 09. Lich Th Coll 29. **d** 32 **p** 33 Lich. C of St John Longton 32-36; Caverswall 36-42; R of Putley 42-50; V of Knowbury 50-52; R of St Geo Folla-Rule w Tillymorgan 52-61; PC of Eastville w Midville 61-69; Perm to Offic Dio Linc 69-76; Dio Lich from 76. *2 Queensway Court, Broadway, Meir, Stoke-on-Trent, Staffs ST3 5PE.*

EVANS, Frank Owen. b 23. Univ of Wales, BA 44. St D Coll Lamp 44. **d** 46 **p** 63 St D. C of Hubberston 46; Llanelly Dio St D from 63; Asst Master Coleshill Secondary Sch 49-74; Hd Master from 74; Dep Hd Master Bryngwyn Comprehensive Sch Llanelli from 77. *27 Maes-y-Parc, Kidwelly, Dyfed, SA17 4UE.*

EVANS, Frederic John Everard. b 11. Keble Coll Ox BA 32, MA 36. Wells Th Coll 34. **d** 35 **p** 36 S'wark. C of St Alb Streatham Pk 35-39; St Jas Kidbrooke 39; Bermondsey 40-42; PC of H Trin Louth 42-50; V of Keddington 45-50; St Jo Evang Bexley 50-74; Chilham Dio Cant from 74. *Chilham Vicarage, Canterbury, Kent, CT4 8BY.* (Chilham 235)

EVANS, Frederick James Stephens. b 21. Qu Coll Cam BA (3rd cl Hist) 42, MA 46. St D Coll Lamp LTh 44. **d** 44 **p** 45 Birm. C of St Jas Shirley 44-47; R of Scotter (w E Ferry from 54) 47-64; CF (TA) 48-51; V of Chalfont St Pet 64-79; Rustington Dio Chich from 79. *Vicarage, Chaigmar Road, Rustington, Sussex, BN16 2NL.* (Rustington 4749)

EVANS, Frederick John Margam. b 31. Magd Coll Ox BA 53, MA 57. St Mich Coll Llan 53. **d** 54 **p** 55 Mon. C of New Tredegar 54-58; Chepstow 58-60; Asst Chap United Sheff Hosps 60-62; Chap Brookwood Hosp Woking 62-70; V of Crookham Dio Guildf from 70; RD of Aldershot from 78. *14 Gally Hill Road, Church Crookham, Aldershot, Hants, GU13 0LH.* (02514 7130)

EVANS, Gareth Milton. b 39. Univ of Bris LLB 60. St Cath Coll Ox BA 62, Nubar Pasha Pri 63, MA 66. Ripon Hall, Ox 60. **d** 63 **p** 64 Bris. C of Ch Ch Hengrove 63-65; Prec and Min Can of Bris Cathl 65-68; Exec Sec Bris Coun of Chr Chs 65-68; C of Bishopston (in c of Good Shepherd) 68-71; Sec Fellowship of St Alban & St Sergius from 71; C of St Jo Evang Notting Hill Dio Lon from 71. *52 Ladbroke Grove, W11 2PB.* (01-727 7713)

EVANS, Ven Geoffrey Bainbridge. St Mich Coll Llan 56. **d** 58 **p** 59 Llan. C of All SS Conv Distr Llan 58-60; All SS Llan N 60-67; V of Skeldon w Leeds 67-71; Chap at Paramaribo 67-71; Morawhanna 71-73; Izmir and Bornova Turkey Dio Gibr (Dio Gibr in Eur from 80) from 73; Archd of the Aegean from 78; Can of Malta Cathl from 78. *1402 Sokak 6 No 7, Izmir, Turkey.* (Izmir 149969)

EVANS, Geoffrey David. b 44. K Coll Lon BD and AKC 69. St Aug Coll Cant 69. **d** 70 **p** 71 Malmesbury for Bris. C of Lawrence Weston 71-73; Chap Grenville Coll Bideford 74-79; Eastbourne Coll from 79. *41 Blackwater Road, Eastbourne, BN21 4JX.* (Eastbourne 34329)

EVANS, Geoffrey Raymond. Ridley Coll Melb ThL 68. **d** 68 Bp Sambell for Melb **p** 69 Melb. C of Dandenong 68-70; Greensborough 70-73; P-in-c of Warburton 73-74; I of Blackburn S Dio Melb from 74. *15 Cluney Court, Blackburn South, Vic, Australia 3130.* (03-877 3665)

EVANS, Canon George William. b 1892. AKC 18, MBE 45. Bps' Coll Cheshunt 18. **d** 19 **p** 20 Lon. C of All SS Friern Barnet 19-24; Chap Miss to Seamen S Shields 24-26; Dunkerque 26-32, Chap Toc H S Area 32-35; Chap-Supt Mersey Miss to Seamen 35-58; Can Dioc of Liv Cathl 50-57; Can (Emer) from 57; C-in-c of St Mich U Pitt Street Liv 52-57; Chap Dreadnought Seamen's Hosp Greenwich 58-59; Whiteley Village Walton-on-Thames 60-62; Kent and Sussex Hosp Tunbridge Wells 62-67. *The Flat, Camoys Court, Barcombe, Lewes, Sussex.* (Barcombe 400544)

EVANS, Gerald Arthur. b 35. Univ of Wales (Swansea) BA 57. SOC 74. **d** 77 Chich **p** 78 Horsham for Chich (APM). C of Balcombe 77-79; Cuckfield Dio Chich from 79. *16 Bramble Mead, Balcombe, Sussex, RH17 6HU.* (Balcombe 491)

EVANS, Canon Glyn. b 10. Univ of Wales BA (3rd cl Lat) 33. St Steph Ho Ox 33. **d** 34 **p** 35 Ban. C of Dolgelley 34-39; Llanfairfechan 39-43; R of Llanallgo w Llaneugrad 43-55; V of St Issell 55-80; RD of Narberth 65-80; Can of St D Cathl from 69; Treas 77-80. *c/o St Issell's Vicarage, Saundersfoot, Dyfed.* (Saundersfoot 812375)

EVANS, Glyn Peter. b 54. Univ of Leeds BA (Th) 75. Ripon Coll Cudd 76. **d** 77 Bp McKie for Cov **p** 78 Cov. C of Binley w Coombe Fields 77-80; Clifton-on-Dunsmore w Brownsover and Newton Dio Cov from 80. *43 Grasmere Close, Brownsover, Rugby, Warws.* (Pavilion 6439)

EVANS, Canon Gwilym Gerallt. St D Coll Lamp BA 34, Ely Th Coll 35. **d** 36 Lon for Col **p** 37 Willoch. M of St Steph Bush Bro Quorn 36-41; R of Waikerie 41-43; Ch Ch Kadina w Parkeville and P-in-c of Wallaroo and Moonta 43-45; C of St Matt Bethnal Green 46-49; Chap Man R Infirm 49-54; United Man Hosps from 54; Hon Can of Man from 69. *c/o Royal Infirmary, Oxford Road, Manchester, 13.* (061-273 3300)

EVANS, Gwilym Owen. b 06. St D Coll Lamp BA 29, BD 55. **d** 29 **p** 30 Ban. C of Conway w Gyffin 29-31; Llandudno 31-34; Kingsbury (in c of Dosthill) 34-36; St Annes-on-the-Sea 36-38; V of Fence-in-Pendle 38-44; St Steph Preston 44-56; Bilsborrow 56-58; C of Rhyl 58-61; V of Whitford 61-66; Chap to Gr Sch and Hosps St Johns Antigua WI 66-67; L to Offic Dio St A from 67. *2 Vicarage Close, Bodelwyddan, Rhyl, Clwyd.* (St Asaph 583010)

EVANS, Gwydol Morgan. Late Exhib of St D Coll Lamp BA (2nd cl Hist) 36. Jes Coll Ox 2nd cl Th 38. St Mich Coll Llan 38. **d** 39 Swan B for Llan **p** 40 Llan. C of Troedyrhiw 39-41; Cefn Coed w Nanttdu 41-43; St Pet Cockett 43-48; L to Offic Dio Swan B 48-50; C of St Paul St Alb 50-55; Perm to Offic Dio St Alb from 55. *23 Abbots Park, London Road, St Albans, Herts.* (St Albans 57578)

EVANS, Harold Vincent. b 1899. St D Coll Lamp Bates Pri 22, Butler Scho 23, BA (Th) 25. **d** 25 St D **p** 26 Mon. C of Laugharne w Llansadwrnen 25-26; Ch Ch Ebbw Vale 26-30; Trevethin (in c of St John Wainfelin) 30-36; V of Crumlin 36-37; Llanddewi Rhydderch 37-45; Beaufort 45-46; R of Henllys w Bettws 46-50; V of Llantilio Crossenny and R of Llanfihangel-Ystern-Llewern 50-58; RD of Raglan 55-58. *Grosvenor House, Gloucester Road, Ross-on-Wye, Herefs.* (Ross 2469)

EVANS, Hector Wynne. b 17. Univ of Wales, BA 39. Coll of Resurr Mirfield 39. **d** 41 **p** 42 Ban. C of Conway w Gyffin 41-43; Llandudno 43-48; Chap RNVR 46; C of Llandegfan w Beaumaris 48-51; V of Aberaman 51-65; RD of Aberdare 58-65; R of Newton-Nottage w Porthcawl Dio Llan from 65. *64 Victoria Avenue, Porthcawl, Mid Glam.* (Porthcawl 2042)

EVANS, Canon Henry Thomas Platt. b 28. Selw Coll Cam BA 51, MA 55. Linc Th Coll 51. **d** 53 **p** 54 Chelmsf. C of St Barn L Ilford 53-56; C-in-c of St Luke's Conv Distr Stocking

Farm Leic 56-58; Min 58-66; V 66-67; R of St Matt Stretford 67-72; V of St Mary Knighton City and Dio Leic from 73; Hon Can of Leic from 76; RD of Christanity S from 81. *Knighton Vicarage, Leicester, LE2 3WG.* (Leicester 706332)

EVANS, Ven Hugh Arfon. b 13. St D Coll Lamp BA 35. St Mich Coll Llan 35. **d** 36 Mon for Ban **p** 37 Ban. C of Holyhead 36-43; V of Capel Curig 43-52; Llanfairisgaer 52-73; Surr from 53; RD of Arfon 58-73; Hon Can of Ban 65-66; Can Treas 66-73; Archd of Ban from 73. *31 Trefonwys, Bangor, Gwyn, LL57 2HU.* (Bangor 355515)

EVANS, Hywel Victor. b 14. Univ of Wales BA 36. St Steph Ho Ox 36. **d** 38 Llan **p** 39 Swan B for Llan. C of Merthyr Dyfan 38-42; Chap RNVR 42-46; C-in-c of Conv Distr of St Agnes Port Talbot 46-56; V of E Markham w Askham 56-61; C-in-c of H Trin Conv Distr New Clifton Notts 61-66; V of Bunny w Bradmore 66-74; Surr 69-79; V of Walesby 74-79; R of Kirton 74-79; P-in-c of Egmanton 77-79; Perm to Offic Dio Southw 79-81; Hon C of Caerphilly 81-82. *c/o St Andrew's Church House, Troeda'r Bryn, Penyrheol, Caerphilly, Mid-Glamorgan.*

EVANS, Ifor Wynne. b 06. Univ Coll Ox BA 28, MA 31. St Mich Coll Llan 32. **d** 33 Llan for Mon **p** 34 Mon. C of St Andr Newport 33-36; Trevethin 36-44; V of Newbridge 44-52; White Ladies Aston w Spetchley and Churchill 54-57; Ampfield 57-74. *Ridgemount Haccups Lane, Michelmersh, Romsey, Hants.*

EVANS, Ivor. b 1890. St Edm Hall Ox BA 15, MA 17. Ely Th Coll 14. **d** 15 **p** 16 St D. C of Ch Ch Swansea 15-17; Pembroke Dock 17-20; New Sleaford 20-25; Lamphey 25; Aysgarth 25-27; Monkton 27-29; R of Nolton w Roch V 29-63. *c/o 13 Elm Road, Kirriemuir, Angus, DD8 4DG.*

EVANS, James. b 08. St D Coll Lamp BA 31. **d** 31 Bris **p** 32 Malmesbury for Bris. C of H Trin w St Philip Bris 31-34; Ch Ch Ellacombe Torquay 34-36; All SS Fishponds 36-43; V of St Aug Swindon 43-47; St Barn Ashley Road Bris 47-54; Pilning w Northwick 54-63; C of Portchester 63-65; R of Gatcombe w Chillerton 65-73. *Orchard Cottage, Ashlake Copse Lane, Fishbourne, Ryde, IW, PO33 4EY.* (Wooton Bdge 882194)

EVANS, John. b 10. St D Coll Lamp BA 34. **d** 34 **p** 35 Ban. C of Llangian 34-37; Aberdovey 38-42; R of Penmachno 42-51; Penegoes (w Darowen from 55 and Llanbryn-Mair w Dylife from 72) 51-78; RD of Cyfeiliog and Mawddwy 68-78. *Brynhyfryd, Llwyngwril, Meirion Gwynedd, LL37 2QB.* (Fairbourne 473)

EVANS, Ven John Barrie. b 23. St D Coll Lamp BA (1st cl Cl) St Edm Hall, Ox (2nd cl Th) BA 49, MA 54. St Mich Coll Llan 50. **d** 51 **p** 52 Mon. C of Trevethin 51-57; V of Caerwent w Dinham 57-64; R of Llanfair Discoed 57-64; V of Chepstow 64-79; Can of Mon 71-77; Archd of Mon from 77; R of Llanmartin w Wilcrick and Langstone Dio Mon from 79. *Llanmartin Rectory, Newport, Gwent, NP6 2EB.* (Llanwern 412661)

EVANS, John Ceri Owen. b 48. St D Coll Lamp Dipl Th 70. Wycl Hall Ox 70. **d** 71 **p** 72 St A. C of Denbigh 71-75; V of Llanfair Caereinion and Llanllugan Dio St A from 75. *Vicarage, Llanfair Caereinion, Welshpool, Powys.* (Llanf-C 810282)

EVANS, John Daryll. b 39. Univ of Wales (Abth) BSc 61. Univ of Wales (Cardiff) MA 68, PhD 72. **d** 73 **p** 74 Mon (APM). Sen Lect S Glam Inst of Higher Educn from 73. *6 Sluvad Road, Panteg, Pontypool, Gwent, NP4 5PX.*

EVANS, John Emrys Clayton. b 07. St D Coll Lamp BA 31. **d** 32 **p** 33 St D. C of Llanwnda w Manorowen 32-34; Llanegwad 34-35; Llandilo-Talybont 35-39; V of Capel Coelbren 39-47; Magor w Redwick 47-61; RD of Netherwent 54-61; PC of Theale 61-68; V 68-74; PC of Henton Dio B & W 61-68; V 68-74. *39 Cissbury Road, Broadwater, Worthing, Sussex.* (Worthing 207412)

EVANS, John Eric. b 14. St D Coll Lamp BA 38. **d** 38 **p** 39 Lich. C of St Andr Wolverhampton 38-41; Ogley Hay w Brownhills 41-42; Hednesford 42-46; V of Bayston Hill 46-53; St Martin 53-64; Churchstoke w Hyssington (and Sarn from 77) 64-79; P-in-c of Sarn 66-77. *71 Oaklands Road, Chirk Bank, Wrexham, Clwyd.*

EVANS, John Griffiths. b 37. GOC 76. **d** and **p** 77 Glouc. C of Hartpury w Corse and Staunton Dio Glouc from 77. *Gadfield Elm House, Staunton, Gloucester.*

EVANS, John Heber. b 07. St Cath S. Ox BA (2nd cl Phil Pol & Econ) 36, MA 40. **d** and **p** 70 Nel. C of Suburban N 70-72; Dom Chap to Bp of Nel from 70-78; V of Atawhai-Hira 72-77; Perm to Offic Dio Nel from 77. *Whakamarina Valley, Canvastown, Marlborough, NZ.* (Havelock 116)

EVANS, Canon John Hopkin. b 17. St D Coll Lamp BA 41. **d** 42 **p** 44 St A. C of Llanycil w Bala 42-51; V of Llanwddyn 51-60; R of Llanfechain (w Bwlch-y-Cibau 67 to 80) Dio St A from 60; RD of Llanfyllin from 73; Hon Can of St A Cathl from 76. *Rectory, Llanfechain, Powys, SY22 6UT.* (Llansantffraid 446)

EVANS, Canon John Mascal. b 15. BNC Ox BA 37, MA 43. Wells Th Coll 37. **d** 38 **p** 39 Bp Golding-Bird for Guildf. C of Epsom 38-43; Min of Conv Distr of St Jo Bapt Stoneleigh 43-48; PC of Stoneleigh 48-52; V of Fleet 52-60; Walton-on-Thames 60-68; Hon Can of Guildf 63-80; Can (Emer) from 80; Commiss Barb 65-72; RD of Emly 66-68; Archd of Surrey 68-80; M Gen Syn 75-80; M C of E Pensions Bd from 76; Team V of Ridgeway Dio Sarum from 80. *Ogbourne St George Vicarage, Marlborough, Wilts, SN8 1SU.*

EVANS, John Morgan. b 14. St D Coll Lamp BA 35. **d** 37 **p** 38 Swan B. C of St Mary Brynmawr 37-46; CF (EC) 46-48; V of Glascombe w Rhulen 48-54; Llangenny 54-79; CF from 55. *1 St John's Road, Brecon.* (Brecon 4054)

EVANS, John Norfolk. Univ of Manit BA 38. St Jo Coll Manit 35. **d** 39 **p** 40 Rupld for Moos. C of Hearst 39; Miss at Fort Hope 40-42; serving w Army 42-46; Miss at Mistassini 47-48; Cedar Lake 48-50; Rupert's House 54-58; I of Fairford 58-64; on leave 64-67; Miss at Kincolith 67-70. *Pelican Rapids, Manit, R0L 1L0, Canada.*

EVANS, John Oliver. b 20. St D Coll Lamp BA 40. K Coll Lon AKC 42. **d** 43 **p** 44 St D. C of Llanelly 43-51; V of Rosemarket 51-58; Llanfihangel-ar-Arth Dio St D from 58; RD of Carmarthen from 74. *Vicarage, Llanfihangel-ar-Arth, Pencader, Dyfed.* (Pencader 230)

EVANS, John Price. b 13. Jes Coll Ox 2nd cl Cl Mods 33, BA (2nd cl Lit Hum) 35, MA 50. St Mich Coll Llan 35. **d** 36 **p** 37 Mon. C of Ch Ch Ebbw Vale 36-39; Bedwas 39-41; serving w RAF 41-46; Chap of Reed's Sch Cobham 46-50; L to Offic Dio Guildf 48-50; V of Bishopton w Gt Stainton 50-58; Chap Stockton Gr Sch 58-62; L to Offic Dio Dur 59-62; V of Casterton 62-75; Chap Casterton Sch 62-75; P-in-c of Crosscrake 75-78. *Beech Cottage, Burton, Via Carnforth, Lancs, LA6 1HX.* (Burton 781394)

EVANS, John Rhys. b 45. Univ of Hull BSc 66. Sarum Wells Th Coll 77. **d** 79 **p** 80 Win. C of St Lawr Alton Dio Win from 79. *146 Greenfield Avenue, Alton, Hants, GU34 2HX.*

EVANS, John Ronald. b 16. Univ of Wales BA 40. St Mich Coll Llan 41. **d** 42 **p** 44 St A. C of Rhosllanerchrugog 42-45; Holywell 45-54; V of Glyndyfrdwy 54-81; RD of Ederyrnion 63-81; surr 64-81; Dioc Sec SPCK 66-81. *21 Bryn Hyfryd, Nant Parc, Johnstown, Wrexham, Clwyd LL14 1PR.*

EVANS, John Thomas. b 43. Univ of Wales Dipl Th 66. St Mich Coll Llan 66. **d** 67 **p** 68 St A. C of Connah's Quay 67-71; Llanrhos 71-74; Chap of Rainhill Hosp 74-78; Team V of Wrexham Dio St A from 78. *37 Acton Gate, Garden Village, Wrexham.* (Wrexham 51143)

EVANS, John Trevor. b 10. St D Coll Lamp BA 38. **d** 39 **p** 40 Swan B. C of Llandilo Talybont 39-43; Gowerton w Waunarlwydd 43-51; V of Trallwng w Bettws Penpont 51-58; Manselton Swansea 58-63; Gorseinon 63-77. *7 Druid's Close, Castle Acre, Mumbles, Swansea, SA3 5TY.* (Swansea 61384)

EVANS, Ven John Walter. b 19. Univ of Dur BA (2nd cl Th) 41, MA 44. Cudd Coll 41. **d** 42 **p** 43 Llan. C of St Marg Roath 42-47; Chap Barnard Castle School 47; C of St Nich near Cardiff 47-49; C-in-c of Abercwmboi 49-51; C of Aberavon 51-53; Chap Bisley Sch Woking 53-58; Latymer U Sch Hammersmith 58-65; V of St Pet Hammersmith 65-75; RD of Hammersmith 72-75; Archd of Malta 75-78; Italy from 78; Chap of St Mark Florence 75-81; Can of Malta from 76; Chan of St Paul's Cathl Valletta Dio Gibr in Eur from 81. *St Paul's Cathedral, Valletta, Malta.*

EVANS, John Wyn. b 46. Univ of Wales (Cardiff) BA 68 (Archaeol), BD 71. Powis Exhib 68. St Mich Coll Llan 68. **d** 71 **p** 72 St D. C of St D Cathl from 71; Min Can 72-75; R of Llanfallteg w Castell Dwyran, Clynderwen, Henllan-Amgoed and Llangan Dio St D from 77; Exam Chap to Bp of St D from 77; Dioc Warden of Ordinands from 78. *Llanfallteg Rectory, Whitland, Dyfed.* (Clynderwen 584)

EVANS, Joseph Henry Godfrey. b 31. St D Coll Lamp BA 51. Qu Coll Birm 53. **d** 55 **p** 56 Lon. C of St John Hackney 55-58; Stonehouse 58-60; V of Selsley 60-65; St Pet Cheltenham 65-73; R of Willersey w Saintbury 73-77; Chap Tiffin Sch Kingston T from 77. *300 Raeburn Avenue, Surbiton, Surrey, KT5 9EF.* (01-390 0936)

EVANS, Kenneth. b 50. Bp Burgess Hall Lamp Dipl Th 74. **d** 74 **p** 75 Ban. C of Llanaber and Caerdeon (w Bontddu from 77) 74-79; St Thos Clapton Common Dio Lon from 79. *20 Moresby Road, E5 9LF.* (01-806 2430)

✠ **EVANS, Right Rev Kenneth Dawson.** b 15. Clare Coll Cam BA 37, MA 41. Ripon Hall Ox 37. **d** 38 **p** 39 Pet. C of St Mary Far Cotton Northn 38-41; All SS w St Kath Northn 41-45; R of Ockley 45-49; V of St Martin Dorking 49-63; R of Ranmore 49-63; Ed Guildf Dioc Gazette 48-61; Hon Can of Guildf 55-63; and from 79; RD of Dorking 57-63; Can Res 63-68; Archd of Dorking 63-68; Cons Ld Bp Suffr of Dorking in H Spirit Cathl Guildf 28 Oct 68 by Abp of Cant; Bps of Lon; Chich; Roch: and Guildf; Bps Suffr of Dorch; Stafford;

Buckingham; and Horsham; and Bps Usher-Wilson; Stannard; Pike; and White. *13 Pilgrims Way, Guildford, Surrey.* (Guildford 67978)

EVANS, Kenneth Percy. b 16. Keble Coll Ox BA 37, MA 41. OBE 68. Wells Th Coll 38. **d** 39 **p** 40 S'wark. C of St Aug S Bermondsey 39-41; Chap RN 41-72; Hon Chap to HM the Queen from 69; V of Bradninch Dio Ex from 72; RD of Cullompton 77-81. *Bradninch Vicarage, Exeter, Devon, EX5 4QS.* (Hele 264)

EVANS, Kenneth Roy. b 47. BSc (Lon). Ridley Hall Cam 79. **d** and **p** 81 Cov. C of H Trin Stratford-upon-Avon Dio Cov from 81. *33 College Street, Old Town, Stratford-upon-Avon. Warws.*

EVANS, Kenwyn Harries Price. b 29. St D Coll Lamp BA 52. St Mich Th Coll Llan 56. **d** 57 **p** 58 Swan B. C of St Nich-on-the-Hill Swansea 57-58; C-in-c of Rhayader 58-61; Chap Miss to Seamen Cardiff 61-62; C of Llangynwyd w Maesteg 62-65; V of Nantymoel w Wyndham 65-71; Pwllgwaun (w Llandewi Rhondda from 75) Dio Llan from 71. *Vicarage, Llanelay Crescent, Pontypridd, CF37 1JB.* (Pontypridd 402417)

EVANS, Laman Evan Cox. b 1896. Keble Coll Ox BA 20, BCL 23. Wycl Hall Ox 52. **d** and **p** 54 Roch. C of Cobham w Luddesdowne 54-56; Perm to Offic Dio Cant from 56. *Great Maytham Hall, Rolvenden, Kent.* (Rolvenden 437)

EVANS, Leslie John. Univ of Wales, BA 39. St Mich Coll Llan 40. **d** 41 **p** 42 St D. C of Pembroke Dock 41-43; C-in-c of St Mich Pembroke 43-46; V of Llanhowell (w Carnhedrin 46-52; w Llandeloy and Llanrheithan from 52) 46-56; R of Mount Barker 56-61; Millen Dio Perth from 61. *20 Whittlesford Street, East Victoria Park, W Australia 6101.* (61-3931)

EVANS, Lewys Thomas Gareth. St Mich Coll Llan. **d** 58 **p** 59 Swan B. C of Clydach 58-65; R of Vaynor w Capel Taffechan 65-80. *c/o Vaynor Rectory, Cefn Coed, Merthyr Tydfil, Mid Glam.*

EVANS, Malcolm Charles. Westcott Ho Cam 59. **d** 61 Ont for Niag **p** 61 Niag. C of Thorold 61-63; R of St Hilda Oakville 63-67; Stamford 67-69; Dir Planning and Program Dio Niag 69-72; C of Chap of H Spirit Hamilton 69-72; R of Grace Ch-on-the-Hill Tor 72-81; Can of Tor 75-81; Chap Bp's Coll Sch Lennoxville from 81. *Bishop's College School, Lennoxville, PQ, Canada J1M 1Z8.*

EVANS, Mark Desmond. b 48. Univ of NSW BSc 68. Austr Nat Univ ThL 70. **d** and **p** 79 Gippsld. C of Traralgon Dio Gippsld from 79. *149 Grey Street, Traralgon, Vic, Australia 3844.*

EVANS, Michael Courtenay. b 31. Oak Hill Th Coll 60. **d** 64 **p** 65 Ox. C of Maidenhead 64-69; All SS Patcham 69-76; R of St Silas City and Dio Glas from 78. *4 Banavie Road, Glasgow, G11 5AN.* (041-357 0486)

EVANS, Nathaniel. Univ of Wales, BA 35. **d** 38 **p** 40 Dur. C of Cornforth 38-46; Newhaven 46-49; V of Durrington 49-75. *31 Mulberry Lane, Goring-by-Sea, Worthing, W Sussex.*

EVANS, Patrick Alexander Sidney. b 43. Linc Th Coll 70. **d** 73 **p** 74 St Alb. C of H Trin Lyonsdown, Barnet 73-76; Royston 76-78; V of Gt Gaddesden Dio St Alb from 78; Dioc Stewardship Adv Dio St Alb from 78. *Great Gaddesden Vicarage, Hemel Hempstead, Herts.* (H Hempstead 52672)

EVANS, Percy. b 12. St D Coll Lamp BA 33. St Mich Coll Llan. **d** 35 **p** 36 St D. C of Llanegwad 35-38; St Pet Carmarthen 38-43; R of Manordeifi (and Llangoedmor w Llechryd from 78) Dio St D from 43. *Manordeifi Rectory, Llechryd, Cardigan, Dyfed.* (Llechryd 239)

EVANS, Peter. b 40. SOC 75. **d** 75 **p** 76 S'wark. C of Welling 75-78; Sutton New Town 78-81; Kingston-upon-Thames Dio S'wark from 81. *St John's House, Springfield Road, Kingston, Surrey, KT1 2SA.* (01-546 3096)

EVANS, Peter. b 35. St Aid Coll 57. **d** 60 **p** 61 Ches. C of Higher Bebington 60-63; W Kirby 63-66; C-in-c of Lower Tranmere 66-68; V of Flimby 68-74; Kirkby Ireleth 74-79; P-in-c of Kirkbride w Newton Arlosh Dio Carl 79-80; R from 80. *Kirkbride Rectory, Carlisle, Cumb, CA5 5HY.* (Kirkbride 256)

EVANS, Peter Anthony. b 36. Univ of Lon BSc (Eng) 57. St Cath S Ox Dipl Th 59. St Steph Ho Ox 58. **d** 60 **p** 61 S'wark. C of St Mark Surbiton 60-63; Asst Chap Univ of Lon 63-64; C of St Luke Kens 64-68; Surbiton 68-69; Loughton 69-74; C-in-c of St Geo Becontree Dio Chelmsf from 74. *St George's Vicarage, Rogers Road, Dagenham, Essex, RM10 8JX.* (01-592 1339)

EVANS, Canon Peter Ceredig. Univ of Wales, BA (2nd cl Phil) 35. St Cath S Ox BA (2nd cl Th) 37, MA 41. Ripon Hall, Ox 35. **d** 38 Llan **p** 39 Swan B for Llan. C of St Andr Cardiff 38-40; Rumney 40-42; CF (EC) 42-46; CF (TA) 48-55; CF (TA - R of O) 55-68; Hon CF from 68; C of St Mark Newport 46-48; V of Mathern 48-55; Dioc Insp of Schs Dio Mon 49-55; Lect in Th Univ of Wales 49-55; R of Paget 55-81; Can of Berm 72-81; Can (Emer) from 81. *c/o Rectory, Paget, Bermuda.*

EVANS, Peter Gerald. b 41. K Coll Lon and Warm AKC 64. Univ of Man BA (Psychol) 72. **d** 65 **p** 66 S'wark. C of St Jas Kidbrooke 65-69; H Innoc Fallowfield 69-72; Brockley Hill 72-75; R of St Botolph w H Trin and St Giles Colchester Dio Chelmsf from 75. *50 Priory Street, Colchester, Essex.* (Colchester 868043)

EVANS, Peter Kenneth Dunlop. b 38. Bp Burgess Hall Lamp 72. **d** 74 **p** 75 Llan. C of Roath 74-77; V of Buttington and Pool Quay Dio St A from 77. *Buttington Vicarage, Welshpool, Powys.* (Welshpool 3351)

EVANS, Raymond Ellis. b 08. St D Coll Lamp BA 29. Casberd Exhib of St Jo Coll Ox 31, BA 33, MA 35. **d** 34 **p** 35 Mon. C of Penmaen 34-36; St Jo Evang Newport 36-44; V of St Andr Newport (Liswerry) 44-47; Exam Chap to Bp of Mon from 46; V of Blackwood 47-52; Sec Mon Dioc Conf 51-54; V of St Mark Newport 52-53; Dean of Mon and V of St Woolos Cathl Ch Newport 53-75. *23 Stelvio Park Drive, Newport, Gwent.* (Newport 51153)

EVANS, Redvers Christopher. Univ of Dur BA 22. **d** 24 **p** 25 Llan. C of Fochriw and Deri 24-26; Merthyr Tydfil 26-32; Caerau w Ely Dio Llan 32-33; V 33-71; Surr 36-71. *46 Parsonage Barn Lane, Ringwood, Hants.*

EVANS, Canon Rees Caerionydd. St D Coll Lamp BA 42. St Mich Coll Llan 42. **d** 43 **p** 44 St A. C of Prestatyn 43-52; V of Llangernyw (w Llanddewi and Gwytherin from 55) 52-66; Rhosllanerchrugog 66-76; Can of St A Cathl from 74; V of Tremeirchion Dio St A from 76; R of Bodfari 76-80. *Tremeirchion Vicarage, St Asaph, Clwyd.* (Bodfari 234)

EVANS, Reginald Arthur. b 07. Univ of Bris BA 38. Sarum Th Coll 38. **d** 40 **p** 41 Bris. C of St Aldhelm Bedminster 40-43; H Trin Cathl Guildf 43-45; V of St Andr Stoke Newington 45-49; Batheaston 49-77; RD of Keynsham 59-71; Preb of Ilton in Wells Cathl 63-77. *15 Downham Mead, Monkton Park, Chippenham, Wilts, SN15 3LN.* (Chippenham 3663)

EVANS, Reginald Henry. St Francis Coll Brisb. **d** 64 Bath **p** 75 Graft. C of Bourke 64-65; Hon C of Kempsey and Lismore 75; C of Casino 76; P-in-c of Culcairn-Henty 76-79. *Box 68, Lockhart, NSW, Australia 2656.*

EVANS, Richard Alan. b 15. Univ of Wales BA 37. **d** 38 **p** 39 Swan B. C of Ch Ch Swansea and Asst Chap Swansea Pris 38-41; All SS Oystermouth (in c of Clyne Castle Chap Blackpill from 42) 41-52; V of Newbridge-on-Wye w Llanfihangel-Brynpabuan 52-58; St Thos Swansea (w Kilvey from 65) 58-80. *135 Penfilia Road, Brynhyfryd, Swansea, SA5 9HX.*

EVANS, Richard Edward Hughes. b 14. Univ of Wales, BA 44. St Mich Coll Llan. **d** 45 **p** 46 Llan. C of St Pet Nantymoel 45-48; Pontyberem 48-50; Llandilo Fawr (in c of Maesteilo) 50-53; V of Yspytty Cynfyn 53-64; Llanwenog w Llanwnen 64-72; Llanychaiarn 72-79. *Tan-yr-Allt, Pontrhydygroes, Ystrad, Meurig, Dyfed.*

EVANS, Richard Edward Victor. b 21. Linc Th Coll 66. **d** 68 **p** 69 Sheff. C of Aston w Aughton 68-71; Prestwich 71-74; R of St John Moston Dio Man from 74. *Rectory, Railton Terrace, Moston, Manchester, M9 1WW.* (061-205 4967)

EVANS, Richard Gregory. b 50. Univ of Wales (Cardiff) Dipl Th 72. St Mich AA Coll Llan 69. **d** 73 **p** 74 Swan B. C of Oystermouth 73-76; Clydach 76-79; V of Llanddew w Talachddu Dio Swan B from 79; Bp's Chap for Dio Swan B from 79. *Vicarage, Llanddew, Brecon.* (Brecon 3011)

EVANS, Richard Lee. b 47. Univ of Wales (Cardiff) BA 71. St D Coll Lamp 71. **d** 73 **p** 74 Llan. C of Llantwit Major 73-74; St Sav Roath 74-77; Penarth w Lavernock 77-78; P-in-c of Clydach Vale 78; Rhydyfelin Dio Llan from 78. *6 Fairfield Lane, Hawthorn, Pontypridd, CE37 5LN.* (Treforest 2298)

EVANS, Richard Neville. b 15. Qu Coll Cam 2nd cl Mod Lang Trip pt i 35, BA (3rd cl Th Trip pt i) 36, MA 44. Ripon Hall, Ox 36. **d** 38 **p** 39 S'wark. C of St Mich E Wickham 38-43; Chap RNVR 43-46; C of St Andr Surbiton 46-47; R of Southacre w Westacre 47-55; V of Castleacre w Newton by Castleacre 49-55; Chap R Free Hosp Gray's Inn Road Lon 55-60; V of Gt St Andr Cam 60-72; Waterbeach 72-74; Perm to Offic Dio Ely from 75; Asst Chap Addenbrooke's Hosp from 81. *12 Acrefield Drive, Cambridge, CB4 1JP.* (Cam 62796)

EVANS, Richard Trevor. b 33. Jes Coll Ox MA 58. **d** and **p** 76 St Andr (APM). C of St Marg Leven Dio St Andr from 76. *Marsfield, Shore Road, Anstruther, Fife.* (Anstruther 310498)

EVANS, Robert Arthur. b 24. Univ of Wales, BA (3rd cl Lat) 48. St Mich Coll Llan. **d** 50 Bp Jones for Llan **p** 51 Llan. C of St Fagan Aberdare 50-53; Roath 53-57; Llan 58-61; Chap Mersey Miss to Seamen 61-62; Supt 62-74; Chap-Supt from 79; Chap RNR from 67; V of Rainhill 74-79. *Mersey Missions to Seamen, Kingston House, James Street, Liverpool, L2 7PG.* (051-236 2432)

EVANS, Robert Ernest. Moore Th Coll Syd. ACT ThL 51. **d** and **p** 52 Syd. C of W Manly 52-53; Castle Hill 53-54; C-in-c of Baulkham Hills 54-57; R of Cant 57-62; Ch Ch N Syd 62-65; Asst Gen Sec Home Miss S 65-67; L to Offic Dio Syd from 65; Asst Master Shore Sch N Syd from 67. *9 Long Avenue, North Ryde, NSW, Australia 2113.* (88-2436)

EVANS, Robert George Roger. Trin Coll Bris 74. **d** 77 **p** 78 Blackb. C of All H Bispham 77-80; St Mary Chadwell Dio Chelmsf from 80. *7 Cedar Road, Chadwell St Mary, Grays, Essex, RM16 4ST.* (Tilbury 70877)

EVANS, Robert Rowland. b 1900. St D Coll Lamp BA 25. **d** 25 **p** 26 Swan B. C of Llandilo Talybont 25-27; St Mark Ford Devonport 28; Chap RN 28-50; R of Gt Warley 50-64; Freston w Woolverstone 64-70. *15 Winston Drive, Port Stewart, Co Londonderry, N Ireland, BT55 7NW.*

EVANS, Ronald Wilfred Andrew. b 32. Lich Th Coll 55. **d** 58 **p** 60 B & W. C of Ch Ch Frome 58-59; St Sav Weston-s-Mare 59-63; PC of W Pennard (w Bradley and Lottisham from 65) 63-69; PC of W Bradley w Lottisham 63-65; V of Alveley 69-74; C-in-c of Milton Abbas w Winterbourne Whitchurch and Winterbourne Clenston 74-75; Team V in Upper Kennet 75-77; R 77-80. *c/o Broad Hinton Vicarage, Swindon, SN4 9PA.* (Broad Hinton 310)

EVANS, Ron Wilson. b 47. Trin Coll Tor BA 69. **d** 72 NS. R of Springhill 74-76; Chap Univ of PEI Charlottetown from 76. *University of PEI, Charlottetown, PEI, Canada.*

EVANS, Roy Baker. d 67 **p** 71 Fred. C of Richmond 67-71; R 71-75; Upham 75-81; Gagetown Dio Fred from 81. *Rectory, Gagetown, NB, Canada.*

EVANS, Very Rev Seiriol John Arthur. b 1894. CBE 69. Late Choral Scho of K Coll Cam 3rd cl Hist Trip pt i 15, BA (3rd cl Med and Mod Lang Trip pt i) 16, MA 23. Sarum Th Coll. **d** 20 **p** 21 Worc. C of St Mary and All SS Kidderminster 20-22; Min Can and Sacr of Glouc and Asst Master K Sch Glouc 22-23; Prec and Sacr of Ely and Hd Master of Choir Sch 23-29; R of Ch Ch Upwell 29-47; Chap RNVR 40-45; Proc Conv Ely 40-47; Ch Comm 48-68; Archd of Wisbech 45-53; R of Upwell St Pet 47-53; Select Pr Univ of Cam 49, 61 and 73; Dean of Glouc 53-72; Dean (Emer) from 72; Fell St Mich Coll Tenbury 61; Chairman Coun for Care of Chs 54-71; Commiss Berm 56-63. *The Old Manor, Fulbourn, Cambridge.*

EVANS, Simon. d 80 **p** 81 b 55. Univ of Newc T BA 77. St Steph Ho Ox 78. **d** 80 **p** 81 Pet. C of St Jude City and Dio Pet from 80. *57 Brookfurlong, Peterborough, Cambs.*

EVANS, Canon Stanley. b 20. K Coll Lon 55. **d** 55 **p** 56 S'wark. C of Ch Ch S'wark 55-58; St Luke Reigate (in c of St Pet Dovers Green) 58-60; V of St Mark Battersea 60-67; Perry Hill 67-76; RD of W Lewisham 73-76; Hon Can of S'wark from 75; V of Kingswood Dio S'wark from 76. *Vicarage, Woodland Way, Kingswood, Tadworth, Surrey.* (Mogador 832164)

EVANS, Stanley Munro. b 30. K Coll Lon and Warm AKC 53. **d** 54 Croydon for Cant **p** 55 Cant. C of St Osw Norbury 54-57; St Lawr in I of Thanet 57-63; V of Bredgar (w Bicknor and Huckinge from 71) 63-72; St Sav Westgate-on-Sea Dio Cant from 72; P-in-c of Bicknor 67-71; Huckinge 69-71. *Vicarage, Thanet Road, Westgate-on-Sea, Kent, CT8 8PB.* (Thanet 31869)

EVANS, Very Rev Sydney Hall. b 15. CBE 76. Late Scho and Pri of St Chad's Coll Dur BA (1st cl Cl) and Lightfoot Scho 37, Bp Robertson Div Pri 38, 1st cl Th 39, MA 40, BD 45. DD (Lon) 78. DD (Lambeth) 78. **d** 39 **p** 40 Dur. C of St Andr Bp Auckland 39-41; Ferryhill 41-43; Chap RAFVR 43-45; Chap and Lect of K Coll Lon 45-48; L to Offic Dio Lon 47-48 and 56-77; Warden of K Coll Lon Post-Graduate Coll Warminster 48-56; L to Offic Dio Sarum 48-56; Select Pr Univ of Cam 52 and 65; Univ of Ox 73; Fell of K Coll Lon from 55; Dean 56-77; Exam Chap to Bp of S'wark 56-78; to Bp of Chelmsf from 58; to Bp of Truro 61-73; to Bp of Dur 68-73; To Bp of Lon 74-78; Commiss Kimb K 61-65 and 73-78; Capetn 61-64; Ekiti from 71; Hon Can of S'wark 59-78; Pr of Gray's Inn 60-77; Dean of Sarum from 77. *Deanery, 7 The Close, Salisbury, Wilts.* (Salisbury 22457)

EVANS, Terence. b 35. St Mich Coll Llan 67. **d** 69 **p** 70 Swan B. C of Loughor 69-73; Gowerton w Waunarlwydd 73-77; V of Llanbister w Llanbadarn-Fynfydd and Llananno Dio Swan B from 77. *Llanbister Vicarage, Llandrindod Wells, Powys, LD1 6TN.* (Llandrindod Wells 83682)

EVANS, Thomas Emrys. b 1900. Univ of Wales, BSc 28. St Mich Coll Llan 28. **d** 29 **p** 30 Llan. C of Llantrisant 29-33; St Paul Grangetown Cardiff 33-38; Llangathen w Llanfihangel Cilfargen (in c of St Mary Court Henry) 38-40; V of Trefeglwys 40-55; Talley w Taliaris 55-68. *1 Trehelyg, Llansawel, Llandeilo, Dyfed, SA19 7JW.*

EVANS, Ven Thomas Eric. b 28. St D Coll Lamp BA 50. St Cath Coll Ox BA (3rd cl Th) 53, MA 57. St Steph Ho Ox. **d** 54 Croydon for Cant **p** 55 Cant. C of Margate 54-58; St Pet Bournemouth 58-62; Youth Chap Dio Glouc 62-69; Hon Min Can of Glouc 62-69; Hon Chap to Bp of Glouc 64-70; Can Missr and Can Res of Glouc Cathl from 69; M Gen Syn Glouc from 70; Archd of Cheltm from 75; M Bd of Governors of Ch Comm from 78. *9 College Green, Gloucester, GL1 2LX.* (Glouc 20620)

EVANS, Thomas Ewart. Univ of Wales, BA 39. St D Coll Lamp 39. **d** 42 Bradf **p** 43 Bp Mownsey for Bradf. C of St Aug Undercliffe Bradf 42-45; R of Peterstow 45-51; Moreton-on-Lugg w Pipe and Lyde 51-66; RD of Weston 64-72; V of Lugwardine w Bartestree 66-79. *Alderley, Roman Road, Bobblestock, Hereford, HR4 9QW.*

EVANS, Thomas Howell. b 13. St Cath S Ox BA 37, MA 40. Ripon Hall, Ox 36. **d** 37 **p** 38 Leic. C of Loughborough 37-40; V of Prestwold w Hoton 40-49; R of Hoby w Rotherby 49-58; Anstey 58-74; V of Brent Pelham w Meesden 58-74; P-in-c of Albury 74-79. *Home Farm Lodge, Clavering, Saffron Walden, Essex.* (Clavering 600)

EVANS, Ven Thomas John. b 14. St D Coll Lamp BA 42. **d** 43 **p** 44 St D. C of Dafen w Llwynhendy 43-48; Llanelly 48-59; V of Llangynnwr Dio St D from 59; Ed of St D Dioc Year Book from 63; RD of Carmarthen 72-74; Archd of Carmarthen and Preb of St D Cathl from 74. *Llangynnwr Vicarage, Carmarthen, Dyfed.* (Carmarthen 6435)

EVANS, Canon Thomas Norman. b 30. K Coll Lon and Warm BA (2nd cl French) 51, BD 53, AKC 54. **d** 56 **p** 57 Sheff. C of Handsworth Yorks 56-59; Mexborough 59-61; V of Denaby Main 61-65; V of Woodhouse Pk 65-78; RD of Withington 72-78; Radcliffe and Prestwich from 78; R of Prestwich Dio Man from 78; Hon Can of Man from 79. *Rectory, Church Lane, Prestwich, Manchester, M25 5AN.* (061-773 2912)

EVANS, Thomas Rowland. b 09. Univ of Wales, BA 41. Coll of Resurr Mirfield 41. **d** 43 **p** 44 Llan. C of Newton Nottage w Porthcawl 43-57; C-in-c of St Agnes Conv Distr Port Talbot Dio Llan 57-60; V 60-78. *128 Victoria Avenue, Porthcawl, Mid Glam, CF36 3HA.*

EVANS, Canon Trefor Rhys. b 06. Univ of Wales BA (2nd cl Hebr) 32. St Mich Th Coll Llan 33. **d** 33 **p** 34 Llan. C of Llantrisant 33-35; Chap of St D Cathl 35-38; R of Llangeitho 38-43; Llandyssul 43-56; Surr from 47; V of Lampeter-Pont-Stephen U Dio 56-74; Can of St D from 70. *56 Penbryn, Lampeter, Dyfed.*

EVANS, Preb Trevor Owen. b 37. Univ. of Wales BSc (2nd cl Geology) 59. Coll of Resurr Mirfield 59. **d** 61 **p** 62 Ban. C of Llanaber w Barmouth and Caerdeon 61-64; Llandudno (Team V from 70) 64-75; V of Llanidloes w Llangurig Dio Ban from 75; RD of Arwystli from 75; Preb of Ban Cathl from 82. *Vicarage, Llanidloes, Powys, SY18 6HZ.* (Llanidloes 2370)

EVANS, Urien. b 18. Oak Hill Th Coll 38. **d** 41 **p** 42 Man. C of St Sav Chorlton-on-Medlock Man 41-43; St Martin Castleton Moor 43-46; R of Steph Hulme 46-48; C-in-c of St Mark Hulme 46-48; R of St Andr Blackley 48-53; V of Deeping St Jas 53-60; Breage w Germoe 60-70; R of Ludgvan 70-75; V of St Merryn 75-78; L to Offic Dio Truro from 78. *Gulls Way, Seameads, Praa Sands, Penzance, Cornwall, TR20 9TA.* (Germoe 2498)

EVANS, Vernie Leslie Tudor. b 20. Late Scho of St D Coll Lamp BA (2nd cl Hist) 40, LTh 42. **d** 43 **p** 44 St D. C of Hubberston w Hakin 43-46; Gorslas (in c of St Anne Cross Hands) 46-50; Llandilo 50-53; R of St Lawr w Ford 53-56; V of Llangathen 56-59; Asst Master Blackdown High Sch Leamington Spa and Perm to Offic Dio Cov 59-61; Wirral Gr Sch and Perm to Offic Dio Ches 61-64; Horsham Girls' High Sch and Perm to Offic Dio Chich 64-70; Glouc Girls High Sch and Perm to Offic Dio Glouc 70-76; Perm to Offic Dio Swan B from 76. *46 Mayals Avenue, Blackpill, Swansea, W Glam.*

EVANS, Victor Arthur. Univ of Syd BA 38. Moore Th Coll Syd ACT ThL 39. **d** 40 **p** 41 Syd. C of St John Ashfield 40-42; All SS Parramatta 42-43; Mortdale and Penshurst w Oatley and Peakhurst 43-47; R of Dapto 48-58; Kogarah Dio Syd from 58. *Box 63, Kogarah, NSW, Australia 2217.* (587-5951)

EVANS, Walter James. b 29. Hur Coll LTh 58. **d** 58 **p** 59 Tor. C of Ch of Redeemer Tor 58-60; I of Manvers 60-61; C of Cobourg 61-63; Wolborough w Newton Abbot 63-65; R of Chilthorne Domer and Thorne Coffin (w Yeovil Marsh from 67) 65-70; V of Chalford Dio Glouc from 70. *Chalford Vicarage, Stroud, Glos, GL6 8QB.* (Brimscombe 883375)

EVANS, Walter William. b 05. **d** 55 **p** 56 Leic. C of Melton Mowbray 55-58; R of Sharnford w Wigston Parva Dio Leic from 58. *Sharnford Rectory, Hinckley, Leics.* (Sapcote 2230)

EVANS, William Arthur. b 14. St D Coll Lamp BA (2nd cl Engl) 35. St Mich Coll Llan 37. **d** 37 **p** 38 Llan. C of Whitchurch 37-40; St Paul Newport 40-48; V of Penmaen 48-57; R of Portskewett w St Pierre and Sudbrook 57-79; Chap at

Tangier Dio Gibr (Gibr in Eur from 80) from 79. *St Andrew Church, Rue d'Angleterre 50, Socco, Tangier, Morocco.* (21211)

EVANS, William Artro. b 05. Univ of Wales BA (2nd cl Fr) 25. St Mich Coll Llan 33. **d** 33 **p** 34 Ban. C of St Ann Llandegai 33-39; V of St Mark Brithdir (w Bryncoedifor from 51) 39-52; Aberdaron w Bodferin 52-59; Surr from 52; V of Abererch 59-74. *Ael y Don, South Beach, Pwllheli, Gwyn, LL53 5AL.*

EVANS, Canon William Brewster. b 15. Trin Coll Dub BA and Div Test 37, MA 43. **d** 38 **p** 39 Derry. C of Ch Ch Londonderry 38-44; I of Cumber Upper w Learmount 44-60; R of Castlerock U Dio Derry from 60; Can of Derry from 72. *Castlerock Rectory, Coleraine, BT51 4RA. N Ireland.* (Castlerock 242)

EVANS, William Hill. b 01. Clifton Th Coll 35. **d** 37 **p** 38 Truro. C of Illogan 37-41; C-in-c of Stythians w Perran-ar-Worthal 41-43; V of St Giles-in-the-Heath w Virginstow 43-48; R of Buscot 48-73; Eaton Hastings 49-73. *Cotswold, Burford Road, Lechlade, Glos, GL7 3ER.* (Faringdon 52696)

EVANS, William James Lynn. b 30. Bp Burgess Hall 828427) **d** 75 **p** 76 St D. P-in-c of Penbryn w Blaenporth 75-77; V 77-79; Betws Evan w Brongwyn 77-79; Penrhyncoch w Elerch Dio St D from 79. *Penrhyncoch Vicarage, Aberystwyth, Dyfed.* (Abth 828427)

EVANS, William Maynard. St Mich Coll Llan 55. **d** 56 **p** 57 Swan B. C of Ystradgyn-lais 56-60; Abercrave w Callwen 60-63; R of Aberyskir w Llanfihangel-Nantbran 63-70. *Oxford House, Ystradgynlais, Swansea, W Glam.* (Glantawe 3217)

EVANS, William Noel. b 03. St D Coll Lamp BA 26. Qu Coll Ox 3rd cl Lit Hum 29, BA and MA 37. **d** 29 **p** 30 St A. C of Llangollen 29-32; Llangattock-vibon-Avel w St Maughan 32-35; R of Llanglydwen w Kilymaenllwyd 35-42; V of St Paul Llanelly 42-49; L to Offic Dio St D 49-69; Hd Master Abermad Sch Aberystwyth 49-69. *Dolgelynen Trawscoed Aberystwyth, Dyfed.* (Crosswood 212)

EVANS, William Penrhys. b 35. K Coll Lon and Warm AKC 63. **d** 64 **p** 65 Man. C of Hurst 64-67; Leigh Lancs 67-68; C-in-c of St Anne Newton Heath Dio Man from 68; R of H Trin Failsworth Dio Man from 71. *103 Oldham Road, Failsworth, Manchester, M35 0BR.* (061-682 7901)

EVANS, Preb Trevor Owen. Univ of Leeds BA 31. Coll of Resurr Mirfield 31. **d** 33 **p** 34 Chelmsf. C of Romford 33-35; St Paul Rondebosch 35-38; P-in-c of Dioc Miss to Moslems Capetn 39-41; Sec Dioc 75; of Miss 40-41; CF (S Afr) 41-46; Chap Toc Preb of Ban Cathl from 82. H and L to Offic Dio Natal 46-54; C of Pietermaritzburg Cathl 54-56; V of Karkloof 56-61; R of Springs 61-75; Archd of SE Transv 71-75; Hon Can of Johann from 75; R of Brixton Dio Johann from 78. *57 Fulham Road, Brixton, Johannesburg, S Africa.* (011-35 3509)

EVANS, William Thomas. b 10. Univ of Wales BA 37. St D Coll Lamp 37. **d** 40 **p** 41 St D. C of Monkton 40-42; Llandygwydd (in c of Capel Tygwydd) 42-48; R of Freystrop w Haroldstone 48-64; V of St Clears w Llanginning (and Llanddowror from 69) 64-76. *27 Danlan Road, Pembrey, Dyfed.*

EVANS-PUGHE, Thomas Goronwy. b 29. Wycl Hall Ox 59. **d** 61 Warrington for Liv **p** 62 Liv. C of Grassendale 61-63; C-in-c of Mossley Hill 63-64; C 64-65; Prec of Chelmsf Cathl 66-69; R of Birchanger Dio Chelmsf from 69. *Birchanger Rectory, Bishop's Stortford, Herts.* (Bp's Stortford 812310)

EVASON, Andrew Brian. b 32. St D Coll Lamp BA 57. St Mich Coll Llan. **d** 59 **p** 60 Swan B. C of Llangyfelach w Morriston 59-66; R of Llangammarch w Garth Llanfechan and Llanlleonfel 66-73; Bishopston Dio Swan B from 73. *Bishopston Rectory, Swansea, W Glam.* (Bishopston 2140)

EVASON, Stuart Anthony. b 44. Univ of Salford BSc. Chich Th Coll 79. **d** 81 Heref. C of St Martin City and Dio Heref from 81. *3 Beaufort Avenue, Hereford, HR2 7PZ.*

EVE, Cedric Robert Sutcliff. b 18. Lon Coll of Div 63. **d** 65 **p** 66 S'wark. C of St Jo Bapt w St Jas (w St Paul from 68) Plumstead 65-69; Ipsley 69-73; Team V 73-78; R of Harvington and Norton and Lenchwick Dio Worc from 78. *Harvington Rectory, Evesham, Worcs.* (Evesham 870241)

EVE, David Charles Leonard. b 45. AKC 74. St Aug Coll Cant 74. **d** 75 **p** 76 Birm. C of Ascen Hall Green 75-79; Team V of King's Norton Dio Birm from 79. *53 Wychall Park Grove, King's Norton, Birmingham, B38 8AG.* (021-458 1836)

EVE, Ian Halliday. St Paul's Coll Grahmstn LTh 59. **d** 59 **p** 60 Capetn. C of St Sav Claremont 59-63; R of Malmesbury 63-67; C of Dumfries 67-68; R of Parow 68-72; St Sav Claremont 72-80; P-in-c of Salcombe 80-81; R of Constantia Dio Capetn from 81. *Box 162, Constantia 7848, CP, S Africa.*

EVE, Noel Robert Samuel. b 41. St Jo Coll Morpeth 73. **d** 75 **p** 77 Newc. On study leave 75-76; C of Cardiff 76-79; Gosford 79-80; P-in-c of Gateshead Dio Newc from 80. *Rectory, Talinga Close, Windale, NSW, Australia 2306.*

EVELEIGH, Raymond. b 36. Univ of Wales (Cardiff) BSc 58. N-W Ordin Course 73. **d** 76 **p** 77 York. C of S Cave and Ellerker w Broomfleet 76-79; P-in-c of St Mary Virg Lowgate Hull and Chap Coll of Further Educn Hull Dio York from 79. *c/o 223 Cottingham Road, Hull, HU5 4AU.* (0482-43182)

EVELYN, Ven Randolph. Dipl Th (Lambeth) 62. Codr Coll Barb. **d** 61 Barb for Windw Is **p** 62 Windw Is. C of St Geo Grenada 61-65; P-in-c of St John w St Mark Grenada Is 65-69; R 69-75; Can of St Geo Cathl St Vincent from 73; R of H Trin St Lucia Dio Windw Is from 75; Archd of St Lucia from 79. *PO Box 40, Castries, St Lucia, W Indies* (4485)

EVENDEN, Canon Clyde James. St Jo Coll Morpeth. **d** 53 **p** 54 Armid. C of Gunnedah 54-55; C-in-c of Ashford 55-61; C of Mudgee 61-64; R of Millthorpe 64-69; Grenfell 69-76; Blayney Dio Bath from 76; Can of Bath from 75. *Rectory, Blayney, NSW, Australia 2799.*

EVENDEN, Edwin James. b 48. St Jo Coll Morpeth 70. **d** 73 **p** 74 Bath. C of H Trin Orange Dio Bath from 73. *Box 174, Orange, NSW, Australia 2800.* (62-1367)

EVENING, Donovan Victor. Wells Th Coll 56. **d** 56 **p** 57 Sarum. C of Gillingham w Stour and Milton 56-58; R of Sutton Veny 58-63; V of Norton Bavant 59-63; Downton 63-72; R of Odstock w Nunton and Bodenham 72-77; L to Offic Dio Sarum from 77. *28 St Gregory's Avenue, Salisbury, Wilts, SP2 7JP.* (Salisbury 5799)

EVENS, Robert John Scott. b 47. AIB 74. Trin Coll Bris 74. **d** 77 **p** 78 Portsm. C of St Simon Southsea 77-79; Portchester Dio Portsm from 79. *190 Dore Avenue, Portchester, PO16 8EP.* (Fareham 288716)

EVERALL, Mervyn Stanley. Univ of Tor BA 60. Wycl Coll Tor BTh 63. **d** 62 **p** 63 Tor. C of St John W Tor 62-64; R of Fort Nelson 64-65. *27 Howard Avenue, Lindsay, Ont, Canada.*

EVERALL, Canon Thomas Roy. St Jo Col Auckld LTh (1st cl) 51. ACT Th Sch 58. **d** 51 **p** 52 Auckld. C of Whangarei 51-55; V of Papakura 55-63; Dir of Christian Educn Dio Auckld 63-69; P-in-c of Otara Miss Distr 64-65; V of St Aid Remuera City and Dio Auckld from 69; Archd of Manukau 74-81; P-in-c of Manurewa Dio Auckld from 78; Can of Auckld from 81. *6 Ascot Avenue, Remuera, Auckland 5, NZ.* (502-574)

EVEREST, Harold William. b 26. Univ of Lon BD 54. Tyndale Hall Bris 51. **d** 54 **p** 55 Sheff. C of St Thos Crookes Sheff 54-57; St Andr Leyland 57-59; V of St Barn Over Darwen 59-67; St Jo Evang Park Sheff 67-78; Tinsley Dio Sheff from 78. *24 Highgate Tinsley, Sheffield, S9 1WL.* (Sheffield 441740)

EVEREST, John Cleland. b 45. Sarum Th Coll 66. **d** 68 **p** 69 Chich. C of Moulsecomb w Stanmer and Falmer 68-71; Easthampstead 71-74; Southwick (in c of All S) 74-77; Adv in Commun Service Dio Worc from 77. *10 Highclere Drive, Bewdley, Worcs, DY12 2EY.* (Bewdley 404169)

EVERETT, Bryan John. b 25. ALCD 54. **d** 54 **p** 55 Roch. C of H Trin Beckenham 54-56; Gorleston 56-59; V of E w W Beckham 59-62; R of Bodham 59-62; CMS Area Sec Dios Derby and Lich 62-69; R of Nether Seale w Over Seale 69-80; V of Lullington 69-80; P-in-c of Longstone Dio Derby from 80. *Great Longstone Vicarage, Bakewell, Derbys.* (Gt Longstone 257)

EVERETT, Colin Gerald Grant. b 44. Open Univ BA 77. Ripon Coll Cudd 79. **d** 81 Sheff. C of Aston w Aughton Dio Sheff from 81. *1 Rosegarth Avenue, Aston-cum-Aughton, Sheffield.*

EVERETT, David Gordon. b 45. Pemb Coll Ox BA 67. Lon Coll of Div 68. **d** 70 **p** 71 S'wark. C of Hatcham 70-73; St Jo Evang w St Steph Reading 73-77; Team V of Fenny Stratford w Water Eaton Dio Ox from 77. *20 Ribble Crescent, Bletchley, Milton Keynes, Bucks.* (Milton Keynes 72723)

EVERETT, John Wilfred. b 37. Qu Coll Cam BA Nat Sc Trip pts i & ii 61, MA 65. Cudd Coll 64. **d** 66 **p** 67 S'wark. C of St Helier 66-69; Yeovil 69-73; R of Wincanton Dio B & W from 73; Pen Selwood Dio B & W from 79. *Rectory, Wincanton, Somt, BA9 9LQ.* (Wincanton 33367)

EVERETT, Robin Nigel. b 34. Univ of Dur BA 55, Dipl Th 59. Cranmer Hall Dur 57. **d** 59 Leic **p** 60 Bp Maxwell for Leic. C of St Barn New Humberstone 59-62; Humberstone 62-66; V of Quorn 66-74; Castle Donington Dio Leic from 74; P-in-c of Lockington w Hemington Dio Leic from 81. *Vicarage, Delven Lane, Castle Donington, Derby, DE7 2LJ.* (Derby 810364)

EVERETT-ALLEN, Clive. b 47. AKC 70. St Aug Coll Cant 69. **d** 70 **p** 71 St A. C of Minera 70-72; St Cath Hatcham 72-75; Team V (in c of St Thos Holtspur) of Beaconsfield Dio Ox from 75. *St Thomas' House, Holtspur, Beaconsfield, Bucks, HP9 1UF.* (Beaconsfield 2750)

EVERITT, Alan Kenneth. St Jo Coll Auckld LTh 69. **d** 68 Wel. C of St Pet Palmerston N 68-71; V of Patea 71-75; Martinborough Dio Wel from 75. *59 Jellicoe Street, Martinborough, NZ.* (Martinborough 51)

EVERITT, Frank George. b 04. BSc (Lon) 25. MIEE 46. **d** 67 **p** 68 Bp Smith for Leic. C of Castle Donington 67-72; Perm to Offic Dio Leic 72-80. *Sylvelin, Muriau Estate, Criccieth, Gwyn.*

EVERITT, Mark. b 34. Late Scho of Linc Coll Ox BA (1st cl Mod Lang) 58, MA 62. Wells Th Coll. **d** 60 **p** 61 Chich. C of Hangleton 60-63; Fell, Chap and Tutor in Mod Lang Mert Coll Ox from 63. *Merton College, Oxford.*

EVERITT, William Frank James. b Dioc Univ of Dur BA 68, Dipl Th 69. FCA 63. Cranmer Hall Dur 65. **d** 69 **p** 70 Leic. C of St Phil Leic 69-73; C-in-c of Prestwold w Hoton 73-77; N Grimston w Wharram Percy and Wharram-le-Street 77; R of Settrington w N Grimston and Wharram Dio York from 77; M Dioc Syn York from 77; RD of Buckrose from 80. *Settrington Rectory, Malton, N Yorks, YO17 8NP.* (North Grimston 275)

EVERS, Harold Edward. Univ of Queensld BA 42. St Francis Coll Brisb ACT ThL (2nd cl) 43. **d** 44 **p** 45 Brisb. C of All SS Brisb 44-46; R of Alice Springs 46-50; V of Ascen Morningside Brisb 50-62; P-in-c of Crow's Nest 62-63; V of Taroom 63-68; Pialba 68-70; Perm to Offic Dio Brisb from 70. *32 Orana Street, Carina, Queensland, Australia 4152.* (398 6298)

EVERSON, Owen Neville. b 32. St Jo Coll Cam BA 56, 1st cl Th Trip pt iii 57, MA 61. Wycl Hall Ox. **d** 58 **p** 59 Birm. C of S Aug Edgbaston 59-63; Tutor Wycl Hall Ox 63-66; Chap 66-67; Exam Chap to Bp of Birm 63-69; to Bp of S'wark from 68; V of Good Shepherd w St Pet Lee Dio S'wark from 67. *47 Handen Road, SE12 8NR.* (01-852 5270)

EVERY, Canon Edward. b 09. Late Postmaster of Mert Coll Ox BA (2nd cl Mod Hist) 30, 2nd cl Th 32, MA 46. Linc Th Coll 36. **d** 36 **p** 37 Linc. C of Caistor w Holton-le-Moor and Clixby 36-38; St Pet Burnley 38-40; St Paul Glouc 40-41; Chap RAFVR 41-46; Field Officer Chr Recon in Eur Greece 46-47; C of St Pet St Helier Morden 48-49; Chap St Geo Colleg Ch Jer 50-52; Exam Chap to Bp in Jer 52-57 and 75-79; to Abp in Jer 57-75; to Bp in Jordan 58-75; Can Res of St Geo Colleg Ch Jer 52-79; Can (emer) from 79; Chan 70-79; Actg Dean 78-79; M Angl-Orthodox Jt Doctrinal Comm 73-82. *Stanhope Court Hotel, Stanhope Gardens, SW7 5RT.*

EVISON, George Edward. St Chad's Coll Dur BA 56. **d** 58 **p** 59 Ripon. C of Manston 58-61; St George (in c of St David's I) Berm 61-64; R of Methley w Mickletown 64-69; P-in-c of N Lomagundi 69-70; C of St Jo Bapt Cathl Bulawayo 70-74; I of St Alb Winnipeg Dio Rupld from 75. *486 Rathgar Avenue, Winnipeg, Manit., Canada.*

EWAGATA, Jonathan. St Paul's Div Sch Limuru, 46. **d** 49 **p** 51 Momb. P Dio Momb 51-61; Dio Maseno 61-69; Dio N Maseno from 70. *PO Alupe, Busia, Kenya.*

EWALD, Dennis Ernest Samuel. Univ of W Ont BA 58. Hur Coll BTh 61. **d** 61 Hur **p** 62 Bp Townshend for Hur. C of Preston 61-63; R of Ridgetown 63-66; St Luke Preston Ont 66-69. *66 Roberts Crescent, Kitchener, Ont, Canada.*

EWBANK, Very Rev Robert Arthur Benson. Late Scho of Qu Coll Ox 1st cl Cl Mods 43, BA (2nd cl Lit Hum) 45, 1st cl Th 47, Liddon Stud 46-48; Jun Denyer and Johnson Scho 48, MA 50. Cudd Coll 46. **d** 48 **p** 49 Linc. C and Lect of Boston 48-52; Chap and Asst Master Uppingham Sch 52-57; Prin of Cyrene Secondary Sch Bulawayo from 57; P-in-c of Figtree Conv Distr 60-82; Can of St John's Cathl Bulawayo 64-80; Can Theologian from 80; Dean of St Jo Bapt Cathl Bulawayo from 82. *45a Leander Avenue, Hillside, Bulawayo, Zimbabwe.*

EWBANK, Robin Alan. b 42. Ex Coll Ox BA (2nd cl Phys) 64. BD (Lon) 68. Clifton Th Coll 66. **d** 69 Barking for Chelmsf **p** 70 Chelmsf. C of Woodford Wells 69-72; Warden Cam Univ Miss Bermondsey 72-76; Team V of Sutton-in-Holderness w Wawne 76-82; R of Bramshott w Liphook Dio Portsm from 82. *Bramshott Rectory, Liphook, Hants, GU30 7AA.* (Liphook 723119)

EWBANK, Ven Walter Frederick. b 18. Late Scho of Ball Coll Ox 1st cl Cl Mods 38, BA (2nd cl Th) 45, MA 45, BD 52. Bps' Coll Cheshunt. **d** 46 **p** 47 Carl. C of St Martin Windermere 46-48; V of Hugill (or Ings) 49-52; Youth Chap Dio Carl 49-52; V of Casterton and Chap Casterton Sch 52-62; Proc Conv Carl 57-70; Hon Chap to Bp of Carl 61-71; V of Raughton Head w Gatesgill 62-66; St Cuthb Carl 66-71; Dom Chap to Bp of Carl 62-66; Dioc Dir of Ords & Post-Ord Tr 62-66; Hon Can of Carl 66-77; Res Can from 77; RD of Carl 70-71; Archd of Westmorland and Furness 71-77; V of Winster 71-77; Archd of Carl from 77. *3 The Abbey, Carlisle, CA3 8TZ.* (Carlisle 21834)

EWEN, Keith John McGregor. b 43. Sarum Wells Th Coll 77. **d** 79 Heref **p** 80 Bp Wood for Heref. C of Kington w Huntington Dio Heref from 79; Old Radnor w Kinnerton Dio Heref from 79. *14 Church Street, Kington, Herefs, HR5 3AZ.*

EWER, (Jonathan) Edward Sydney John. ACT ThL (2nd cl) 63. Univ of New Engl BA 69. St Mich Ho Crafers M SSM 68. **d** 62 **p** 63 Newc. C of New Lambton 62-65; Waratah 65; Chap and Tutor St Mich Ho Crafers 66-71 and from 76; Chap Univ of W Austr 71-76; Perm to Offic Dio Adel 76-81; L to Offic from 81. *St Michael's House, Summit Road, Crafers, S Australia 5152.*

EWETADE, Simeon Olanrewaju. b 54. Im Coll Ibad 78. **d** 81 Ijebu. d Dio Ijebu. *St John's Church, Itele, via Ijebu-Ode, Nigeria.*

EWING, Edward Leonard Frank. b 14. **d** 69 Bp Wilkinson **p** 71 Niag. C of St John Cayuga 71-73; R of Acton 74-79. *Milton Towers, Apt 202, 81 Millside Drive, Milton, Ont, Canada.*

EWINGTON, John. b 43. ARICS 68. Chich Th Coll 74. **d** 78 Chelmsf **p** 79 Barking for Chelmsf. C of St Jo Evang Walthamstow 78-81; I of Bougainville Dio New Guinea Is from 81. *Box 621, Arawa, North Solomans Province, Papua New Guinea.*

EXALL, John Aubrey. b 20. Univ Coll Lon BSc 41. Cudd Coll 46. **d** 48 **p** 49 Win. C of Bitterne Park 48-53; Romsey 53-56; C-in-c of St Barn Southn Dio Win 56-57; V from 57. *42 The Avenue, Southampton.* (Southampton 23107)

EXCELL, Robin Stanley. b 41. K Coll Lon and Warm AKC 64. **d** 65 **p** 66 St E. C of St Mary Stoke Ipswich 65-68; Melton Mowbray 68-71; R of Gt and L Blakenham w Baylham (and Nettlestead from 76) Dio St E from 71. *Great Blakenham Rectory, Ipswich, Suffolk.* (Ipswich 830325)

EXELL, Ernest William Carter. b 28. Qu Coll Cam BA 52. Tyndale Hall, Bris 49. **d** 52 **p** 53 S'wark. C of H Trin Sydenham 52-54; St Paul E Ham 54-57; AIM Ch of Uganda 57-65; Chap St Marg Moshi Centr Tang 66-70; R of Abbess Roding w Beauchamp Roding Dio Chelmsf from 70; C-in-c of White Roding Dio Chelmsf 70-71; R from 71; RD of Roding 75-79. *Abbess Roding Rectory, Ongar, Essex.* (White Roding 313)

EXETER, Lord Bishop of. *See* Mercer, Right Rev Eric Arthur John.

EXETER, Assistant Bishops of. *See* Armstrong, Right Rev John; Claxton, Right Rev Charles Robert; Key, Right Rev John Maurice; Westall, Right Rev Wilfrid Arthur Edmund.

EXETER, Archdeacon of. *See* Richards, Ven John.

EXETER, Dean of. *See* Eyre, Very Rev Richard Montague Stephens.

EXHAM, Kenar Edgar Arthur. Univ of Alta BEducn 57. Trin Coll Tor LTh 58. **d** 58 **p** 59 Edmon. C-in-c of St Faith's Miss Edson 58-61; I of Evansburg 61-65; Old Crow 65-70; R of Vermilion 70-78; Ponoka Dio Edmon from 78. *Box 1118, Ponoka, Alta, Canada.* (403-783 3612)

EXLEY, Malcolm. b 33. Cranmer Hall Dur. **d** 67 **p** 68 York. C of Sutton-in-Holderness 67-73; V of Mappleton w Goxhill 73-77; Market Weighton Dio York from 77; C-in-c of Goodmanham Dio York 77; R from 78. *Vicarage, Market Weighton, York, YO4 3JH.* (Mkt Weighton 3230)

EYDEN, Canon Eric Westley. b 09. Univ of Lon BA (2nd cl Hist) 31, BD 34. AKC (1st cl) and Knowling (sermon) Pri 33. **d** 33 **p** 34 S'wark. C of St Matt Newington Surrey 33-36; All SS Kingston-on-Thames 37-39; V of St Steph Battersea 39-44; St Sav Raynes Pk 44-54; Org Sec S'wark Youth Coun 37-39; Hon Sec 39-53; Proc Conv S'wark 50-55; RD of Wimbledon 53-54; Shepton Mallet 57-64; R of Shepton Mallet 54-64; Prec, Can Res and Preb of Heref Cathl 64-75; Can (Emer) from 75. *Peppercorn Cottage, Chilton Polden Hill, Bridgwater, Somt.* (Chilton Polden 722622)

EYDEN, Montague John. b 03. Univ Coll Lon BA 22. St Steph Ho Ox 31. **d** 32 **p** 33 Lon. C of St Mary Virg Somers Town 32-41; Chap and Hdmaster Quainton Hall Sch 34-69; C of Cranford 41-65; St Jo Bapt Greenhill Harrow 65-69; St Jo Bapt Sevenoaks 70-74; Perm to Offic Dio Roch from 74. *Stable Flat, Otford Court, Sevenoaks, Kent, TN14 5SA.* (Otford 2364)

EYERS, (Laurence) Frederick Thomas. b 12. Ridley Coll Melb ACT ThL 38. M SSM 50. **d** 39 **p** 40 Melb. C of Ch Ch S Yarra 39-42; Chap AMF 42-46; C of St John E Malvern 46; SSM Kelham 46-48 and 50; C of St Cecilia Parson Cross Sheff 48-50; SSM at Crafers and L to Offic Dio Adel 50-60; Prior SSM Priory Perth and L to Offic Dio Perth 60-73; Hon Can of Perth 64-73; Prior SSM Priory Lanc 74-82; SSM Priory Canberra from 82. *Box 421, Woden, ACT, Australia 2606.* (Canb 814505)

EYIANROMI, Amos Adebodun. b 26. **d** 71 **p** 74 Lagos. P Dio Lagos. *St Peter's Church, Ajido-Badagry, Box 7, Badagry, Nigeria.*

EYLES, Anthony John. b 34. Univ of Bris BSc (1st cl) 57. Sarum Th Coll 61. **d** 63 **p** 64 B & W. C of Wel w W Buckland and Nynehead 63-67; Wilton 67-74; Industr Chap Dio Dur from 74. *1 Holly Terrace, South Moor, Stanley, Co Durham, DH9 7AA.*

EYLES, David William. b 45. Sarum Wells Th Coll 75. **d** 77 Knaresborough for Ripon **p** 78 Ripon. C of Knaresborough 77-80; Chapel Allerton 80-82; P-in-c of W Tanfield and Well w Snape and of N Stainley Dio Ripon from 82. *Rectory, West Tanfield, Ripon, Yorks.* (Well 321)

EYNON, Canon Ettrick Harold. b 15. St D Coll Lamp BA 36. TD 64. **d** 38 **p** 39 Bris. C of St Aldhelm Bedminster 38-41; Keynsham 41; CF (EC) 41-46; Men in Disp 45; Hon CF 46-52 and from 64; CF (TA) 52-60; DACG (CF) 60-64; C of St Paul Cheltenham 46-47; V of H Trin Stroud 47-58; V of St Phil and St Jas Leckhampton (w St Jas Cheltm from 72) 58-81; C-in-c of St Jas Cheltm 65-72; Hon Can of Glouc Cathl from 73; RD of Cheltm 75-76. *1 Mead Close, Mead Road, Cheltenham, Glos.*

EYOU, Canon Danieri. **d** 50 **p** 53 Bp Tomusange for U Nile. P Dio U Nile 50-60; Dio Soroti 60-76; Hon Can 66-76; Can (Emer) from 77. *Kaberamaido, Teso, Uganda.*

EYRE, Very Rev Richard Montague Stephens. b 29. Or Coll Ox 2nd cl Cl Mods 51, BA (3rd cl Lit Hum) 53, 2nd cl Th 55, MA 56, Can Hall Sen Gr Test Pri 57. St Steph Ho Ox 53. **d** 56 **p** 57 Portsm. C of St Mark Portsea 56-59; Tutor Chich Th Coll 59-61; Chap 61-62; Eastbourne Coll 62-65; V of Arundel w S Stoke and Tortington 65-73; Good Shepherd Preston 73-75; Dioc Dir of Ordinands Dio Chich 75-79; Archd of Chich 75-81; Treas of Chich Cathl 78-81; Dean of Ex from 81. *Deanery, Exeter, Devon, EX1 1HT.* (Exeter 72697)

EYRE, Richard Stuart. b 48. Univ of Bris BEd 81. Linc Th Coll 74. **d** 77 **p** 78 Bris. C of Henbury 77-81; Bedminster Dio Bris from 81. *St Dunstan's Vicarage, Bedminster Down Road, Bristol, BS13 7AA.* (Bris 666351)

EYRE-WALKER, John Benson. b 15. St Pet Hall, Ox BA 40, Dipl in Th 41, MA 44. Wycl Hall Ox. **d** 42 **p** 43 Roch. C of Ch Ch Beckenham 42-44; Bp Hannington Mem Ch Distr Hove 44-48; V of Leigh Kent 48-57; Burton Chesh 57-80. *Address temp unknown.*

EYRES, Canon Leslie. AKC 41. **d** 41 **p** 42 Liv. C of St Phil Litherland 41-45; C-in-c of Huyton w Roby 45-51; PC of St Luke W Derby 51-54; V of Rainhill 54-65; R of St Mich Aughton 65-78; Hon Can of Liv 74-78; Can (Emer) from 78. *25 Montrose Drive, Southport, Merseyside, PR9 7JA.* (Southport 27776)

EYTON-JONES, Hugh Arthur. Jes Coll Cam BA 13, MA 17. Ridley Hall, Cam 13. **d** 14 **p** 15 Lon. C of St John Paddington 14-17; St Mary Le-Park Battersea 17-18; Org Sec CPAS for NW Distr 18-21; Metrop Distr 21-25; V of St John Walthamstow 25-30; St Antholin Lect at St Mary Aldermary Lon 28-30; PC of St Geo Brighton and Offg Chap St Dunstan Brighton 30-39; V of St Alb Streatham Pk 39-42; St Simon Southsea 42-52; RNVR 43-46; V of Crofton 52-61; H Trin Cowes 61-76; Hon Chap Miss to Seamen Dio Portsm 62-76. *11 Shandon Close, Tunbridge Wells, Kent, TN2 3RE.* (0892-22913)

EZE, Jonathan Nwaka. b 38. St Paul's Coll Awka 75. **d** 76 **p** 77 Enugu. P Dio Enugu. *St Luke's Parsonage, Amufie, Enugu Ezike, via Nsukka, Nigeria.*

EZE, Reuben John Umeonyirioha. St Paul's Th Coll Awka 63. **d** 63 **p** 64 Ow. P Dio Ow. *Parsonage, Umueshi, Uruala, Nigeria.*

EZE, Ven Samuel Ata. Trin Coll Umuahia 57. **d** 59 **p** 60 Niger. P Dio Niger 59-69; Dio Enugu from 70; Hon Can of Enugu 75-78; Archd of Enugu from 78. *Christ Church Parsonage, Uwani, Enugu, Nigeria.*

EZE, Canon Stephen Ibekwe. Melville Hall Ibad. **d** 57 **p** 58 N Nig. P Dio N Nig 57-70; Dio Enugu from 71; Hon Can of Enugu from 75. *Christ Church Parsonage, PO Achi, Nigeria.*

EZEANATA, Raphael. b 43. Trin Coll Umuahia 72. **d** 74 Niger. d Dio Niger. *St Peter's Church, Okija, Nigeria.*

EZEANI, Levi Onwugamba. Trin Coll Umuahia 53. **d** 55 **p** 57 Niger. P Dio Niger. *Parsonage, Nibo, Nigeria.*

EZEKWO, Joshua. **d** 75 **p** 76 Niger. P Dio Niger. *c/o Box 361, Onitsha, Nigeria.*

EZENWA, Canon David Igwedinma. b 20. Trin Coll Umuahia 68. **d** 68 **p** 70 Niger. P Dio Niger; Hon Can of Niger from 81. *St Paul's Church, Oba, Nr Onitsha, Nigeria.*

EZEONYEODU, Christopher Okafor. Im Coll Ibad 62. **d** 64 **p** 65 Nig. P Dio N Nig 64-69; Dio Enugu from 69. *St Luke's Parsonage, Amufie, Enugu-Ezike, Nigeria.*

EZIKE, Daniel Anuche. Trin Coll Umuahia 62. **d** 63 **p** 64 Niger. P Dio Niger. *St John's Parsonage, Oko, Box 12, Aguata, Nigeria.*

EZIRIM, Ven Daniel Nmezi. Trin Coll Umuahia 54. **d** 56 **p** 57 Niger. P Dio Niger 56-69; Dio Ow from 70; Hon Can of Ow from 73; Archd from 77. *Box 6, Nkwerre, Imo State, Nigeria.*

EZUOKE, Ugochukwu Uwaoma. b 48. Trin Coll Umuahia 73. **d** 75 **p** 76 Aba. P Dio Aba. *St Michael's Cathedral, Box 818, Aba, Nigeria.*

EZURUIKE, John Nnadiegbulem. **d** 62 **p** 63 Ow. P Dio Ow. *Parsonage, Umuariam, Obowo, Nigeria.*

EZZY, Gregory Sibson. Ridley Coll Melb. ACT ThL 66. **d** 66 **p** 67 Brisb. C of St Andr S Brisb 66-69; St Luke Ekibin 69-70; R of Blackwater 70-74; Dalby Dio Brisb from 74; Sec Bush Ch Aid S Queensld from 74. *Rectory, Cunningham Street, Dalby, Queensland, Australia 4405.* (Dalby 62 2071)

F

FABIAN, Reginald Thomas. ACT ThL 40. **d** 38 **p** 39 Bend. C of Murrabit 38-39; V of Koondrook 39-40; St Paul Bendigo 40-41; Chap AIF 41-45; CMF 49-61; R of Elmore 46-56; Woodend 56-64; Dom Chap to Bp of Bend 56-64; Can of Bend 57-64; R of Port Fairy 64-72; Perm to Offic Dio Bal from 72. *Unit 2, Fairway Terrace, Ballarat, Vic., Australia 3350.*

FABIYI, Joseph Abidoye Asola. Im Coll Ibad. **d** 70 **p** 71 Lagos. P Dio Lagos. *St Paul's Vicarage, Box 43, Ago Iwoye, Nigeria.*

FABIYI, Timothy Falodun. Fourah Bay Coll Sierra Leone BA 61. **d** 68 **p** 69 Ekiti. P Dio Ekiti 68-72; L to Offic Dio Ibad from 72. *Modakeke High School, Ile-Ife, Nigeria.*

FABULUJE, Daniel Folayemi. Melville Hall Ibad 52. **d** 53 **p** 54 Ibad. P Dio Ibad 53-62; Dio Ondo from 62. *c/o PO Box 25, Ondo, Nigeria.*

FABULUJE, Canon Jeremiah Olagbamigbe Aivewumi. Univ of Ibad BA 67. Im Coll Ibad. **d** 62 Ondo-B **p** 63 Ondo. P Dio Ondo; Hon Can of Ondo from 75; Prin Vining Tr Centre Akure from 77. *Box 3, Akure, via Ondo, Nigeria.* (Akure 2021)

FACEY, Canon Edward Lincoln. b 13. St Aug Coll Cant 33. **d** 38 **p** 39 Chelmsf. C of Upminster 38-41; CF (EC) 41-46; V of Paddock 46-53; St Bart Marsden 53-66; Crosland Moor 66-77; Asst RD of Huddersfield 60-68; RD of Blackmoorfoot 68-77; Surr from 62; Hon Can of Wakef from 71; Master Abp Holgate's Hosp Hemsworth Dio Wakef from 77. *Master's Lodge, Archbishop Holgate's Hospital, Hemsworth, Pontefract, W Yorks.*

FACEY, Samuel Dyke. b 04. Ball Coll Ox BA (3rd cl Lit Hum) 27. Linc Th Coll 55. **d** 55 **p** 56 Sarum. C of Westbury 55-58; R of Compton Bassett 58-67. *Court Place, Misterton, Crewkerne, Somt.* (Crewkerne 2898)

FADALMULA, Stephen. **d** 72 **p** 73 Sudan. P Dio Sudan 72-76; Dio Yambio from 76. *ECS, Maridi, Sudan.*

FADEYI, Joshua Oyewole. b 28. Im Coll Ibad 68. **d** 71 **p** 72. P Dio Ibad. *St Barnabas Vicarage, Apomu, Box 47, Ikire, Nigeria.*

FADEYIBI, John Omotosho. b 10. **d** 77 Ilesha. d Dio Ilesha. *St Mary's Church, Oke Owa, Ipetu Ilesha, Nigeria.*

FADIL, Harun. **d** 72 Sudan. d Dio Sudan 72-76; Dio Omdurman from 76. *Box 8, Kadugli, Sudan.*

FADIPE, James. b 36. Im Coll Ibad. **d** 68 **p** 69 Lagos. P Dio Lagos. *St Andrew's Church, Box 125, Ibara-Abeokuta, Nigeria.*

FAGAN, Brian Lorentz. Ridley Coll Melb ACT ThL 57. **d** 57 **p** 58 Adel. C of St Luke Adel 57-59; Mvumi 60; Katoke 61; Kibondo 62-64; Kilimatinde 65; Lect St Phil Th Coll Kongwa and L to Offic Dio Centr Tang 66-73; Perm to Offic Dio Adel 74-75; R of Norwood Dio Adel from 75. *77 Beulah Road, Norwood, S Australia 5067.* (08-42 2227)

FAGAN, John Raymond. b 32. BD (Lon) 69. Ripon Hall Ox 71. **d** 72 Man **p** 73 Middleton for Man. C of Stalybridge 72-74; Madeley 74-79; V of Shuttington w Amington Dio Birm from 79. *Amington Vicarage, Tamworth, Staffs.* (Tamworth 62573)

FAGAN, Thomas. b 27. NOC 78. **d** 81 Liv. Hon C of Rainhill Dio Liv from 81. *Wensleydale Avenue, Rainhill, nr Prescott, Mer, L35 4NR.*

FAGBEMI, Festus Olaleye. Fourah Bay Coll BA 44, Dipl in Th 44. **d** and **p** 46 Lagos. P Dio Lagos. *c/o PO Box 13, Lagos, Nigeria.*

FAGBEMI, Johnson Babatunde. b 42. Im Coll Ibad 77. **d** 80 **p** 81 Egba. P Dio Egba. *St John's Church, Igbein, Abeokuta, Nigeria.*

FAGBEMI, Very Rev Seth Oni. Dipl Th (Lon) 58. Univ of Ibad BA 68. Melville Hall Ibad. **d** and **p** 57 Ondo-B. P Dio Ondo-B 57-62; Dio Ondo from 62; Hon Can of Ondo 69-72; Exam Chap to Bp of Ondo from 70; Archd of Ondo 72-76; Dioc Sec from 77; Provost of St Steph Cathl Ondo from 77. *Box 4, Ondo, Nigeria.* (Ondo 2034)

FAGBOLAGUN, Gabriel Akinlulu. Im Coll Ibad 58. **d** 60 **p** 61 Ondo-B. P Dio Ondo-B 60-62; Dio Ondo 62-66; Dio Ekiti from 66. *St Mary's Vicarage, Ode-Ekiti, Nigeria.*

FAGERSON, Joseph Leonard Ladd. b 35. Harvard Univ BA (Hist *cum laude*) 57. Dipl Th (Lon) 62. Ridley Hall Cam 61. **d** 63 **p** 64 Roch. C of Tonbridge 63-67; V of Kabul Afghan

67-74; C-in-c of Marbury 74-75; Chap Rannoch Sch Dio St Andr from 75. *Rannoch School, Rannoch, Perthshire, PH17 2QQ.* (088-22235)

FAGG, Alan Gordon. b 06. K Coll Lon and Warm 54. **d** 55 **p** 56 S'wark. C of St Geo Camberwell 55-58; Chap HM Pris Maidstone 58-63; V of Forest Row 63-70; Tutor and Chap of Whittington Coll Felbridge 70-78; Perm to Offic Dio Chich 70-78; Hon C of St Barn Bexhill Dio Chich from 78. *37 Egerton Road, Bexhill-on-Sea, E Sussex, TN39 3HJ.* (Bexhill 218730)

FAGG, Norman Leslie. Moore Th Coll Syd BTh 79. **d** and **p** 80 Syd. C of St Andr Sans Souci Dio Syd from 80. *1 Newcombe Street, Sans Souci, NSW, Australia 2219.* (529-6141)

FAGG, Ven Thomas Francis. Coll Ho Ch Ch 34. NZ Bd of Th Stud LTh 36. **d** 36 **p** 37 Wel. C of St Jas Lower Hutt 36-39; St Pet Wel 39-42; V of Berhampore 42-50; Eketahuna 50-54; St Andr Napier 54-65; Rotorua 65-72; Archd of Tauranga 66-72; Archd (Emer) from 72; V of Riverslea 72-76; L to Offic Dio Wai from 76. *Flat 3, 9 Meeanee Quay, Westshore, Napier, NZ.*

FAGOROYE, Samuel Akin. Im Coll Ibad 62. **d** 64 **p** 65 Ondo. P Dio Ondo. *Box 44, Okitipupa, Nigeria.*

FAHEY, Canon Michael Wainright. Univ of NZ BA 60. St Jo Coll Auckld NZ Bd of Th Stud LTh 62. **d** 61 **p** 62 Wel. C of Feilding 61-65; V of Whakatane 65-72; Te Hapara 72-76; Taupo 76-80; Te Puke Dio Wai from 80; Can of Wai from 80. *47 Jocelyn Street, Te Puke, NZ.* (37-970)

FAHIE, Richard Whittington. b 25. **d** 77 **p** 80 Antig. C of St Mary Anguilla 77-81; I of St Luke I and Dio Antig from 81. *St Boniface House, Martin's Village, W Indies.*

FAIFU, Manasseh. St Pet Coll Siota. **d** 69 **p** 72. P Dio Melan 69-75; Dio Malaita from 75. *Fiu, N Malaita, Solomon Islands.*

FAIR, James Alexander. Trin Coll Dub BA (2nd cl Mod Mental and Mor Sc) 48, MA 59. **d** 49 **p** 50 Clogh. C of Monaghan w Tyholland 49-52; Portadown 52-56; R of Woodschapel 56-60; Dean's V of St Anne's Cathl Belf 60-62; C-in-c of Rathcoole 62-68; R of Larne w Inver Dio Connor from 68. *Rectory, Larne, Co Antrim, N Ireland.* (Larne 2788)

FAIR, William Patrick John. b 11. Chich Th Coll 53. **d** 53 **p** 54 Linc. C of New Sleaford 53-56; R of Thelveton w Frenze 56-60; Tivetshall 60-63; Flordon w Hapton 63-79; Hon Chap Nor Cathl 65; SSC 68. *22 Arundel Road, Wymondham, NR18 0JE.*

FAIRBAIRN, Ven Alan. Bp's Univ Lennox LST 67. **d** and **p** 67 Queb. C of Windsor 67; I of Cookshire 67-77; Archd of St Francis from 77; R of Sherbrooke Dio Queb from 77. *200 Montreal Street, Sherbrooke, PQ, Canada.*

FAIRBANK, Brian Douglas Seeley. b 53. AKC 75. St Steph Ho Ox 77. **d** 78 **p** 79 Dur. C of Newton Aycliffe 78-81; St Luke Stocking Farm City and Dio leic from 81. *347 Thurcaston Road, Mowmacre Hill, Leicester, LE4 2RF.* (0533 356681)

FAIRBROTHER, Robin Harry. Wells Th Coll. **d** 69 **p** 70 St A. C of Wrexham 69-74; Welshpool 74-77; V of Bettws Cedewain and Tregynon (w Llanwyddelan from 81) Dio St A from 77. *Bettws Vicarage, Newtown, Powys.* (Tregynon 345)

FAIRBROTHER, Ronald Peter. St Steph Ho Ox 59. **d** 61 **p** 62 Ex. C of Dawlish 61-69; R of Newton Ferrers w Revelstoke Dio Ex from 69. *Newton Ferrers Rectory, Plymouth, Devon.* (Newton Ferrers 530)

FAIRBURN, Peter. b 16. St Chad's Coll Dur 38. Linc Th Coll 42. **d** 42 **p** 43 Linc. C of St Faith Linc 42-46; St Wilfrid Harrogate 46-51; V of Downholme 51-54; C-in-c of Hudswell 51-53; PC 53-54; R of Goldsborough Dio Ripon from 54; V of Arkendale Dio Ripon from 54; V of Allerton Mauleverer Dio Ripon 54-70; C-in-c 70-71; RD of Boroughbridge 66-71. *Goldsborough Rectory, Knaresborough, N Yorks, HG5 8NR.* (Harrogate 863009)

FAIRCHILD, Thomas Samuel. b 09. Linc Th Coll 44. **d** 46 **p** 47 B & W. C of Ilminster w Whitelackington 46-49; Crewkerne w Easthams and Hewish 49-52; R of Bleadon 52-59; V of St Sav Weston-s-Mare 59-80. *Flat 2, 2 Ashcombe Gardens, Weston-super-Mare, Avon, BS23 2XA.* (Weston-s-Mare 25715)

FAIRCLOUGH, Canon Francis Stanley. b 08. St Jo Coll Dur BA 30 Dipl Th 31 MA 34. · 31 **p** 32 Sheff. C of Pitsmoor 31-34; Perm to Offic at Sharrow Sheff 34-37; C of Chesterfield 37-38; R of Newbold w Dunston 38-47; V of Hathersage 47-67; Bretby w Newton Solney 67-70; RD of Eyam 56-67; Surr 56-70; Hon Can of Derby 63-70; Can (Emer) from 70. *30 Penn Lane, Melbourne, Derby, DE7 1EQ.*

FAIRHEAD, Arthur Gerald. Univ of Tor BA (Sc) 48. Wycl Coll Tor LTh 57. **d** 56 **p** 57 Tor. C of St John W Tor 56-58; R of Elmvale 58-61; Trin Queb 61-65; I of St Timothy Lon 65-72; Wallaceburg Dio Hur from 72. *707 James Street, Wallaceburg, Ont., Canada.* (519-627 1302)

FAIRHEAD, Robert Alexander. Wycl Coll Tor. **d** 68 **p** 69 Edmon. I of Ch of Good Shepherd Edmon 68-74; I of St Albert Edmon 68-74; R of Humboldt Dio Sktn from 74. *Box 758, Humboldt, Sask, Canada.*

FAIRHURST, Canon Alan Marshall. b 30. Clare Coll Cam 3rd cl Cl Trip pt i, 51, BA (2nd cl Cl Trip pt ii) 52, MA 56. BD (Lon) 56. Wycl Hall Ox 55. **d** 56 **p** 57 Dur. Tutor St Jo Coll Dur 56-60; C of St Geo Stockport 60-62; V of Ch Ch Galle Face Colom 62-66; Exam Chap to Bp of Colom 65-66; R of Ashley w Silverley 67-71; St Mary Stockport Dio Ches from 71; Hon Can of Ches from 81. *224 Dialstone Lane, Stockport, Chesh.* (061-483 7544)

FAIRHURST, John. b 1893. **d** 56 Lanc for Blackb **p** 57 Blackb. C of Croston 56-60; Tarporley (in c of Cotebrook) 60-67. *23 Beechfield, Hilldale, Parbold, Wigan, Lancs.*

FAIRHURST, Ronald Hardman. b 31. Qu Coll Birm 77. **d** 80 **p** 81 Lich (APM). C of Cheadle Dio Lich from 80. *49 Ness Grove, Cheadle, Stoke-on-Trent, Staffs, ST10 1TA.*

FAIRLEY, Ian Stratford. b 05. TCD BA 45. Univ of Glas BL 48. Wycl Hall, Ox. **d** 50 **p** 51 Roch. C of Gravesend 50-52; Strood (in c of St Francis Conv Distr) 52-53; V of Sporle w Gt and L Palgrave 53-65; R of Barningham w Matlaske 65-75; C-in-c of Bessingham 68-75; Perm to Offic Dio Nor from 75. *14 Beechwood Avenue, Aylmerton, Norwich, NR11 8QQ.*

FAIRLIE, Donald Cameron. Ridley Coll Melb 74. **d** 76 **p** 77 Melb. C of H Trin Doncaster 76-78; Box Hill 78-80; I of St Paul Inverleigh Dio Melb from 81. *St Paul's Vicarage, High Street, Inverleigh, Vic, Australia.*

FAIRLIE, William James. McMaster Univ BA 64. Union Th Sem BD 68. **d** 68 Hur **p** 69 Bp D J Campbell (USA) for Hur. *74 South Common Street, Lynn, Mass 01902, USA.*

FAIRWEATHER, David James. b 35. Univ of Keele BEd 79. Wycl Hall Ox 70. **d** 72 **p** Lich. C of Trentham 72-76; Cheddleton 76; Hnaley 77-79; Rugeley Dio Lich from 79. *1 Gorseburn Way, Etching Hill, Rugeley, Staffs, SW15 2XA.* (Rugeley 5728)

FAIRWEATHER, Canon Eugene Rathbone. McGill Univ BA 41. Univ of Tor MA 43. Trin Coll Tor BD 45. Union Th Sem. New York STM 48, ThD 49. **d** 43 **p** 44 Tor. C of St Matt Tor 43-47; Assoc Prof of Dogmatic Th Trin Coll Tor 49-64; Keble Prof of Div from 64; Exam Chap to Bp of Tor from 65; Can of Tor from 69. *Trinity College, Toronto, Canada.*

FAIRWEATHER, John. b 39. K Coll Lon and Warm AKC 66, BD 72. **d** 67 **p** 68 Ex. C of St Jas L Ham Plymouth 67-69; Dartmouth 69-73; V of Corringham w Springthorpe 73-78; C-in-c of Blyborough 73-78; Heapham 73-78; Willoughton 73-78; V of Pinchbeck Dio Linc from 78. *Pinchbeck Vicarage, Spalding, Lincs, PE11 3UD.* (Spalding 2084)

FAIRWEATHER, Canon Karl. Univ of Tor BA 37. Wycl Coll Tor LTh 37. **d** 37 **p** 38 Fred. C of Ch Ch Fred 37-39; R of Denmark 39-78; Grand Falls 39-60; Can of Ch Ch Cathl Fred from 64; Dom Chap to Bp of Fred from 64. *New Denmark, NB, Canada.*

FAIRWEATHER, Norman Perley. K Coll NS 21. **d** 21 **p** 23 Fred. C of Musquash NB 21-23; Min 23-25; R of St Mary York Co 25-28; Douglas 28; St Jude St John 28-42; CF (Canad) 42-46; R of Campobello 46-64. *Box 972, Sussex, NB, Canada.*

FAIRWEATHER, Walter Henry. Codr Coll Barb 47. **d** 50 Trinid **p** 50 Br Hond. Miss Dio Br Hond 50-54; V of St Clem w St Swith Barb 54-57; St Luke Barb 57-69; St Lucy I and Dio Barb from 69. *St Lucy's Rectory, Barbados, W Indies.*

FAJEBE, James Ayinde Olumuyiwa. b 34. **d** 79 **p** 81 Egba. P Dio Egba. *St Paul's Church, Owode, Egbado, Nigeria.*

FAJEMIROKUN, Emmanuel Ijigbola. St Andr Coll Oyo. **d** 52 **p** 53 Ibad. P Dio Ibad 52-72. *c/o St Luke's Church, Okeigbo, Ondo, Nigeria.*

FAJEMISIN, Canon Rowland Adetomi. Melville Hall, Oyo 38. **d** 39 **p** 41 Lagos. P Dio Lagos 39-52; Dio Ibad 52-77; Hon Can of Ibad 58-63; Can from 63. *Z114, Ijofi Street, Ilesha, Nigeria.*

FAJI, Very Rev josiah Oladele. **d** 56 **p** 57 Lagos. P Dio Lagos 56-80; Admin and Sec Assoc of Angl Dios in Nigeria from 74; Can of Lagos 76-80; Provost of H Trin Cathl Kano and Exam Chap to Bp of Kano from 80; Dioc Sec from 81. *Box 180, Kano, Nigeria.*

FAKA, Luke. b 49. Bp Patteson Th Centre Kohimarama 71. **d** 74 Melan. d Dio Melan 74-75; Centr Melan from 75. *Tikopia Island, Temotu Region, Solomon Islands.*

FAKAFU, Robert. **d** 57 **p** 59 Melan. P Dio Melan 57-75; Dio Ysabel 75-76; Dio Centr Melan from 76. *Lavasa Vaturanga, Guadalcanal, Solomon Islands.*

FAKAIA, William. St Pet Coll Siota 66. **d** 68 **p** 70 Melan. P Dio Melan 68-75; Dio Malaita from 75. *Pelau, Malaita, Solomon Islands.*

FALAIYE, Michael Taiwo. Im Coll Ibad 56. **d** 58 **p** 60 Ibad. P Dio Ibad. *Ikeji-Ile, Nigeria.*

FALASE, Ven Emanuel Akinrolabu. Melville Hall Ibad. **d** 48 **p** 49 Lagos. P Dio Lagos 48-70; Dio Ibad 71-74; Dio Kwara from 75; Can of Lagos 65-70; Ibad 71-74; Archd Dio

Ilorin from 75. *Box 2, Ilorin, Kwara, Nigeria.*

FALCONER, Colin Ross. St Jo Coll Auckld. **d** 77 **p** 78 Wel. C of Palmerston N 77-79; V of Opunake Dio Wel from 79. *Vicarage, Tasman Street, Opunake, NZ.*

FALCONER, Ian Geoffrey. b 40. Late Exhib of BNC Ox BA (2nd cl Hist) 62. Cudd Coll 62. **d** 64 **p** 65 Lon. C of Chiswick 64-68; C-in-c of Good Shepherd Conv Distr Hounslow 68-76; V of St Matt Sinclair Road W Kens Dio Lon from 76. *113 Sinclair Road, W14 0NP.* (01-603 9769)

FALCONER, John Geikie. b 13. Selw Coll Cam 2nd cl Hist Trip pt i, 32, BA (2nd cl Geog Trip pt i) 33, MA 37. Lon Coll of Div 33. **d** 36 **p** 37 Carl. C of St Paul Silloth 36-37; Lowther w Askham 37-39; Chap RN 39-60; Perm to Offic Dio Dub 61-62; Deputn Sec Leprosy Miss 62-70; Perm to Offic Jurisd of Kens from 72. *10 Hounslow Avenue, Hounslow, Middx.* (01-898 1122)

FALCONER, Noel Barzillai. St Pet Coll Ja, 57. **d** 58 Kingston for Ja **p** 59 Ja. C of St Geo Kingston 58-59. *7 Gibson Drive, Hope Pastures, Kingston 6, Jamaica, W Indies.* (093-76100)

FALKINGHAM, Ven John Norman. Trin Coll Melb BA (Hons) 39. ACT ThL (1st cl) 40, Hey Sharp Pri 40, Stuart Pri and Bromby Pri 42. **d** 41 Melb **p** 42 Geelong for Melb. C of H Trin Surrey Hills 41-44; Chap Trin Coll Melb 44-50; V of Malvern 50-61; Exam Chap to Abp of Melb 47-61; Lect Trin Coll Melb 50-61, Commiss River 52-61; Can of Melb 59-61; Dean of Newc 61-75; Lect St Jo Coll Morpeth 61-75; R of St Paul Canberra Dio C & Goulb from 75; Can of St Sav Cathl Goulb 76-81; Archd Dio C & Goulb from 81. *Box 417, Manuka, ACT, Australia 2603.* (062-95 9009)

FALKLAND ISLANDS, *See* Argentina and Eastern South America with the Falkland Islands.

FALKNER, Jonathan Michael Shepherd. b 47. Open Univ BA 74. St Jo Coll Dur 76. **d** 79 Penrith for Carl **p** 80 Carl. C of Penrith Dio Carl from 79. *4 Barco Terrace, Penrith, Cumbria, CA11 8NB.*

FALKNER, Richard Eric. b 26. Ex Coll Ox BA 47, MA 51. Wells Th Coll 47. **d** 49 **p** 50 Ex. C of Ilfracombe 49-52; Woodham 52-57; Chap of Reed's Sch and L to Offic Dio Guildf 57-60; V of Ch Ch Epsom 60-66; Englefield Green Dio Guildf from 66. *Englefield Green Vicarage, Egham, Surrey.* (078-43 32553)

FALL, Harry. b 17. Univ of Leeds BA 40, BD 51. Univ of Dur BA 42, MA 48. **d** 42 **p** 43 Man. C of St Mary Eccles 42-44; Ch Ch Heaton Norris 44-45; St Barn Linthorpe (in c of St Jas Middlesbrough) 45-49; V of Danby-in-Cleveland 49-54; Harden Bingley 54-57; R of Scrayingham w Leppington and Howsham 57-71; R of Full Sutton w Skirpenbeck 57-67; V of Bossall w Buttercrambe 67-71; R of H Trin w St Jo Evang Micklegate and St Martin-cum-Gregory City and Dio York from 71. *Holy Trinity Rectory, Micklegate, York, YO1 1LE.* (York 23798)

FALL, John David McPherson. St Paul's Coll Grahmstn LTh 64. **d** 64 **p** 65 Mashon. C of Lomagundi 64-66; Umtali 66-69; L to Offic Dio Mashon from 69. *c/o Diocesan Office, PO Box 7, Salisbury, Rhodesia.*

FALLE, Francis Aylmer. Montr Dioc Th Coll LTh 67. **d** 67 **p** 68 Sask. I of Spiritwood 67-73; Glaslyn w Medstead 73-75; L to Offic Dio Sktn 75-76; R of H Trin City and Dio Sktn from 76. *23-208 Lindsay Place, Saskatoon, Sask, Canada.*

FALLOWES, Richard Prince. b 01. Pemb Coll Cam 3rd cl Th Trip pt ii, 22, BA (3rd cl Th Trip pt i) 23, MA 27. Dorch Miss Coll. **d** 24 **p** 25 S'wark. C of St Jo Evang E Dulwich 24-29; Miss at Maravovo 29-30; Bugotu 30-36; C of St Martin Scarborough 39-41; C-in-c of St Alb Hull 41-45; CF (EC) 45-50; V of Whatton-in-the-Vale w Aslockton 50-59; R of Gingindhlovu 59-61; St Pet Vryheid 61-68; Can of Zulu 63-68; L to Offic Dio Swaz from 71. *PO Box 137, Nhlangano, Swaziland.* (Nhlangano 24)

FALLOWS, Stuart Adrian. b 50. **d** 78 **p** 79 Moray. Hon C of St John Forres 78-81; Elgin w Lossiemouth Dio Moray from 81. *2 Grangehall Farm Cottages, Forres, Moray, IV36 0TR.*

FALODE, Canon Benjamin Ayotunde. **d** 26 Bp Oluwole for Lagos **p** 28 Lagos. P Dio Lagos 26-52; Dio N Nig 52-55; Dio Ibad 55-79; Hon Can of Lagos 44-55; Ibad 55-63; Can from 63. *13 Iporo-Ake Street, Abeokuta, Nigeria.*

✠ **FALOPE, Right Rev John Adegbehin Ibitayo.** **d** 55 Bp Oyebode for Ondo-B **p** 55 Ondo-B. P Dio Ondo-B 55-64; Dio Ondo 68; Hon Can of Ondo 61-71; L to Offic Dio Lagos 69-71; Can of Ibad 71-72; Archd of Ilesha 72-74; Cons Ld Bp of Ilesha in St Jas Cathl Ibad 27 Oct 74 by Abp of W Afr; Bps of Accra, Niger, Aba, Benin, Lagos, Ibad, Kum, Ow, Enugu, N Nig, Ekiti, Ondo, Nig Delta and Gambia; and others; res 81. *Box 28, Ilesha, Nigeria.*

FALTENI, Lucas Danson Livingstone. b 34. St Bede's Coll Umtata 70. **d** 70 **p** 72 St John's. C of H Cross Miss 70-76; Clydesdale 77-79; P-in-c of Cibini Dio St John's from 79. *Box 408, Matatiele 4730, S Africa.*

FALUSI, Canon Gabriel Kolawole. Univ of Lon Dipl Th (Extra-Mural) 61. Univ of Ibad BA 68. Melville Hall Ibad 58. **d** 60 **p** 61 Ibad. P Dio Ibad 60-63; Dio Sier L 63-66; Dio Ekiti 66-74; Ibad from 74; Exam Chap to Bp of Ekiti 67-74; Hon Can of Ibad from 80. *University of Ibadan, Ibadan, Nigeria.* (62550)

FALUSI, John Bodunde. Melville Hall Ibad. **d** 48 **p** 49 Lagos. P Dio Lagos 48-62; Hon Can of Lagos 62-76. *Oke Ilefi Compound, Odo Quarters, Ise-Ekiti, Nigeria.*

FAMEWO, Canon Ezekiel Oloruntola. Melville Hall Ibad 51. **d** 52 **p** 53 Ondo-B. P Dio Ondo-B 52-62; Dio Ondo 62-66; Dio Ekiti from 66; Can of Ekiti from 68. *St Mark's Vicarage, Ise-Ekiti, Nigeria.*

FAMEWO, James Oladimeji. b 52. Im Coll Ibad 66. **d** 69 **p** 70 Ibad. P Dio Ibad. *St James's Cathedral, Oke-Bola, Ibadan, Nigeria.*

FAMEWO, Ven John Kayode. St Andr Coll Oyo. **d** 46 **p** 47 Lagos. P Dio Lagos 46-52; Dio Ondo-B 52-62; Hon Can of Ondo 59-66; Provost of Ekiti from 66; Archd of Ekiti Centr from 66; Exam Chap to Bp of Ekiti from 67. *Emmanuel Cathedral, PO Box 12, Ado-Ekiti, Nigeria.*

FAMUDI, Edward Kofoe. Newton Coll Dogura 71. **d** 74 **p** 75 Papua. P Dio Papua 74-77; Dio Aipo from 77. *Anglican Church, Kenainj, Papua New Guinea.*

FANE, Clifford Charles. b 39. Kelham Th Coll 62. **d** 67 Lon **p** 68 Kens for Lon. C of Heston 67-73; St Mich AA Bedminster 73-77; Gaywood 77-81; V of St John Top o' th' Moss Bolton-le-Moors Dio Man from 81. *St John's Vicarage, Alford Close, Breightmet, Bolton, Lancs.* (Bolton 31191)

FANIYI, George Aderemi. b 45. Im Coll Ibad 73. **d** 76 **p** 77 Ibad. P Dio Ibad. *St Peter's Anglican Church, Gbongan, Nigeria.*

FAPOHUNDA, Festus Ojo. **d** 52 **p** 53 Ondo-B. P Dio Ondo-B 52-62; Dio Ondo from 62. *Vicarage, Okeagbe-Akoko, Ondo, Nigeria.*

FAPOHUNDA, Samuel Adedodoye. b 38. Im Coll Ibad Dipl Th 70. **d** 70 **p** 71 Ondo. P Dio Ondo. *Vicarage, Ikare-Akoko, Nigeria.*

FARAH, Ven Rafiq Amin. Amer Univ of Beirut BA 45. **d** 46 **p** 48 Jer. C of St Paul Jer 46-47; Nablus 47-48; V of St John Haifa 48-64; Exam Chap to Abp in Jer 64-74; to Bp in Jordan 66-75; C of Jer 66-68; V of Beirzeit Dio Jordan 68-77; Can Res of St Geo Colleg Ch Jer 71-74; Hon Can from 76; Archd Dio Jordan 74-75; Dio Jer 76-77; in Beirut from 78; Chap at Beirut Dio Jer from 78. *PO Box 2211, Beirut, Lebanon.*

FARAH, Shafiq Amin. Amer Univ of Beirut BA 53. Near E Sch of Th LTh 53. **d** 53 **p** 54 Jer. P-in-c of Nablus 53-56; Ramallah and Beir Zeit 56-59; Beirut and Damascus 59-65; Amman 65-78; Exam Chap to Bp in Jordan 59-72; Hon C of St Geo Willowdale Tor 78-79; R of The Annunc City and Dio Tor from 79. *157 Florence Avenue, Willowdale, Toronto, Ont, M2N 4G3, Canada.*

FARAHANE, Gabriel. **d** and **p** 75 Lebom. P Dio Lebom 75-79; Dio Niassa from 79. *Lago, Niassa, Mozambique.*

FARAHANE, Jaime. **d** and **p** 75 Lebom. P Dio Lebom 75-79; Dio Niassa from 79. *Lago, Niassa, Mozambique.*

FARBRIDGE, Nicholas Brisco. b 33. Sarum Wells Th Coll 75. **d** 77 Dorking for Guildf **p** 78 Guildf. C of Gt Bookham 77-81; St Mary Virg Ewell Dio Guildf from 81. *Danehurst, Epsom Road, Ewell, KT17 1JL.* (01-393 6367)

FARDON, Raymond George Warren. b 30. St Pet Hall Ox BA 52, MA 56. Ridley Hall Cam 54. **d** 59 **p** 60 Ox. C of High Wycombe 59-63; Chap Bedford Modern Sch 63-68; Dep Hd Brewer's Hill Secondary Sch Dunstable 68-72; Hd Master K Sch Grantham 72-82. *26 Kingland Road, Poole, Dorset.* (Poole 5609)

FARGUS, Gavin James Frederick. b 30. K Coll Lon and Warm AKC 54. **d** 55 **p** 57 Sarum. C of St Mark Salisbury 55-57; Wareham 57-60; Marlborough (in c of Ch Ch Savernake) 60-63; C-in-c of Davidstow w Otterham 63-65; C-in-c of Lesnewth 63-65; R of St Bride Nether Lochaber w St Paul Kinlochleven 65-81; Dioc Youth Chap Arg Is 66-72. *c/o St Bride's, Onich, Fort William, Invernesshire, PH33 6RZ.* (Onich 204)

FARGUS, Maxwell Stuart. b 34. Linc Coll Ox BA 57, MA 61. Cudd Coll 57. **d** 59 **p** 60 Newc T. C of St Francis High Heaton Newc T 59-62; Rothbury 62-64; R of Kirkby Wiske w Maunby 64-76; Dioc Youth Adv Dio Ripon 64-76; Perm to Offic Dios Wakef and Sheff from 77. *Community Education Centre, Station Road, Bolton-upon-Dearne, Rotherham, S Yorks S63 8AB.*

FARIYIKE, Joseph Olabode. b 22. Im Coll Ibad 70. **d** and **p** 73 Ekiti. P Dio Ekiti 73-76; Dio Ibad from 76. *Vicarage, Olorunda Baba-Sale, Ibadan, Nigeria.*

FARLEIGH, Gerald Gibson. Moore Th Coll Syd. **d** 65 **p** 66 C & Goulb. C of St Paul Canberra 65-70; Cooma 70-73; R of Murrumburrah 73-81; Temora-Barmedman Dio C & Goulb from 81. *Box 125, Temora, NSW, Australia 2666.*

FARLEY, Edward Albert. b 36. Univ of Lon BSc (1st cl Geology) 59, ARCS 59. Em Coll Cam BA 61. Ridley Hall Cam 60. **d** 62 **p** 63 Win. C of Bitterne 62-65; Ch Ch Swindon 65-68; V of Dunston w Coppenhall 68-71; Blurton Dio Lich from 71. *Blurton Vicarage, Longton, Stoke-on-Trent, Staffs.*

FARLEY, Graham Clifford James. Moore Th Coll Syd. **d** and **p** 73 Armid. C of Gunnedah 73-74; St Pet Cathl Armid 75-77; V of Manilla 77-80; Wee Waa Dio Armid from 80. *Vicarage, Wee Waa NSW, Australia 2388.*

FARLEY, Lawrence Russell. b 54. Trin Coll Tor BA 76. Wycl Coll Tor MDiv 79. **d** 79 Bp Stiff for Sask **p** 79 Sask. C of Turtle River Dio Sask from 79. *PO Box 352, Turtleford, Saskatchewan, Canada, S0M 2Y0.*

FARLEY, Lionel George Herbert. b 10. Univ of Dur 31. Chich Th Coll 32. **d** 35 Sarum **p** 36 Sherborne for Sarum. C of St Osmund Parkstone 35-39; St Francis of Assisi Bournemouth 39-46; St Austell 46-48; V of Lewannick 48-51; V of Marazion 51-78; RD of Penwith 65-67. *32 Chestnut Way, Gillingham, Dorset.*

FARLEY, Ronald Alexander. b 30. Oak Hill Coll 76. **d** 79 Stepney for Lon **p** 80 Lon. C of St Matthias Stoke Newington Dio Lon from 79. *20 Chaucer Court, Howard Road, N16 8TS.*

FARLIE, David Gordon. St Jo Coll Morpeth 60. **d** 61 **p** 63 Gippsld. C of Leongatha 62-64; P-in-c of Cann River 54-56; V of Poowong w Loch 66-69; C of Sans Souci 70; St Mich Surrey Hills 70-71; I of Fawkner 71-75; Perm to Offic Dio Melb from 75. *1/14 Stradbrok Avenue, Heidelberg, Vic, Australia 3084.*

FARLIE, Hugh. b 29. Univ of Lon BSc 53. Linc Th Coll 53. **d** 55 **p** 56 Lich. C of Bilston 55-58; Woodberry Down 58-63; Asst Chap Univ of Bris and L to Offic Dio Bris 63-68; Chap Bris Coll Sc and Technology 63-65; Univ of Bath 65-73; L to Offic Dio B & W 68-73; C-in-c of St Barn Knowle Dio Bris from 73. *Vicarage, Daventry Road, Bristol, BS4 1DQ.* (Bristol 664139)

FARMBOROUGH, James Laird McLelland. b 22. Magd Coll Cam BA 49, MA 54. Tyndale Hall, Bris. **d** 52 **p** 53 Lich. C of St Luke Wolverhampton 52-55; St Mary Magd Holloway Lon 55-56; St Mary Broadwater 56-58; Chap All SS Niteroi Brazil 58-64; Org Sec SAMS 65-70; V of Marple 70-80; Chap of St Pet Vina del Mar Dio Chile from 81. *Casilla 561, Pje Jaxsop, 347 Chorrillos, Vina del Mar, Chile.*

✠ **FARMBROUGH, Right Rev David John.** b 29. Linc Coll Ox BA (2nd cl Mod Hist) 51, MA 53. Westcott Ho Cam 51. **d** 53 **p** 54 St Alb. C of Bp's Hatfield (in c of St John Hatfield New Town from 57) 53-63; V of Bp's Stortford 63-74; Surr 63-81; Chap Bp's Stortford Hosp 63-74; Hon Chap to Bp of Roch 63-74; M Gen Syn 72-81; RD of Bp's Stortford 73-74; Archd of St Alb 74-81; Cons Ld Bp Suffr of Bedford in Cathl and Abbey Ch of St Alb 27 Oct 81 by Abp of Cant; Bps of Lon, St Alb, Roch, Lich, Newc T and Lusaka; Bps Suffr of Hertf, Stafford, Warwick, Buckingham, Tonbridge and Bradwell; and Bp Pytches. *168 Kimbolton Road, Bedford, MK41 8DN.* (Bedford 57551)

FARMER, George Wilson. b 37. Lich Th Coll 62. **d** 65 **p** 66 S'wark. C of Kingston-T 65-70; Heston 70-74; Southmead 74-75; Bedminster 75-80; Team V of Langley Marish Dio Ox from 80. *180 Langley Road, Langley, Slough, Berks.*

FARMER, John. K Coll NS. **d** 54 **p** 55 Fred. C of St Marg Fred 54-59; Stanley 59-60; CF (Canad) from 60. *c/o Chaplain General's Office, Canadian Forces HQ, Ottawa, Ont, Canada.*

FARMER, Kenneth William. b 29. Ripon Coll Cudd 75. Launde Abbey Leic 76. **d** 77 Bp Garrett for Leic **p** 78 Leic. C of St Denys Evington 77-80; V of Wymeswold and Prestwood w Hoton Dio Leic from 80. *Wymeswold Vicarage, Clay Street, Loughborough, Leics, LE12 6TY.* (Wymeswold 880275)

FARMER, Canon William John Cotton. b 19. St Jo Coll Dur BA 43. LTh 42. St Aid Coll. **d** 43 Roch for St E **p** 44 St E. C of St Aug Ipswich 43-45; St Mary Warwick 45-49; Solihull 49-54; V of Blackheath Staffs 54-64; Packwood w Hockleyheath 64-81; Hon Can of Birm Cathl 80-81; Can (Emer) from 81. *28 Winchcombe Road, Alcester, Warwicks, B49 6QL.* (Alcester 762918)

FARNCOMBE, Edgar Basil Turberville. b 01. St Jo Coll Ox BA and MA 25. Ripon Hall Ox 26. **d** 27 **p** 28 Birm. C of St Pet Harborne 27-34; V of St Geo Edgbaston Birm 34-50; R of Nafford w Birlingham 52-59; V of Hanley Castle w Hanley Swan 59-64; Perm to Offic Dio Worc from 64; Dio Heref from 68. *Vernon Lodge, Harcourt Road, West Malvern, Malvern, Worcs.* (Malvern 4875)

FARNELL, Reginald James. b 52. St Mich Ho Crafers 72. **d** 76 **p** 77 Graft. C of All SS Murwillumbah 76-79; Wendouree 79-81; R of Balmoral Dio Bal from 81. *Rectory, Balmoral, Vic, Australia 3407.*

FARNSWORTH, Charles Redden. b 31. **d** and **p** 77 Ont. Chap Grenville Chr Coll Brockville Ont from 77. *Grenville Christian College, Box 610, Brockville, Ont, Canada, K6V 5V8.*

FARNWORTH, Godfrey Frankland. b 18. Selw Coll Cam BA 40, MA 46. Westcott Ho Cam 40. **d** 42 Chich **p** 43 Lewes for Chich. C of Horsham 42-47; Storrington 47-50; CF 50-72; Team V of Blakeney Group (in c of Hindringham and Binham w Cockthorpe) 72-77; R of Hindringham and Binham Dir Nor from 77. *Hindringham Vicarage, Fakenham, Norf, NR21 0QA.* (Thursford 338)

FAROUNBI, Daniel Olaoye. b 13. **d** 72 **p** 73 Ekiti. P Dio Ekiti. *Emmanuel Anglican Church, Agbado, Ekiti, Nigeria.*

FARQUHARSON-ROBERTS, Donald Arthur. b 21. Bps' Coll Cheshunt 64. **d** 65 **p** 66 Sarum. C of Preston w Sutton Poyntz 65-68; R of Pimperne Dio Sarum from 68; P-in-c of Stourpaine Dio Sarum from 77. *Pimperne Rectory, Blandford Forum, Dorset, DT11 8UB.* (Blandford 53425)

FARR, Arthur Ronald. b 24. St Mich AA Coll Llan 77. **d** 80 **p** 81 Llan (NSM). C of All SS Penarth Dio Llan from 80. *3 Cymric Close, Ely, Cardiff, CF5 4GR.*

FARR, Canon Beverley Huron. Univ of W Ont BA 34. Hur Coll Ont LTh 35. **d** 33 **p** 35 Hur. C of St John London Township 33-35; I of Hensall w Staffa 35-36; R of Dorchester Glanworth and Belmont 36-39; I of St D Lon 39-42; Chap CASF 42-45; I of St Geo Goderich 45-52; RD of Hur from 47; R of St John Sarnia 52-71; Can of Hur 54-71; Can (Emer) from 71. *12 Ranson Drive, London, Ont., Canada.*

FARR, Michael David Huron. b 43. Univ of Sask BA 70. Em Coll Sktn LTh 70. **d** 70 **p** 71 Hur. C of Port Lambton 70-71; I 71-73; R of St Hilda w St Luke, St Thos 73-77; Good Shepherd Woodstock Dio Hur from 77; Dom Chap to Bp of Hur 78-80. *857 Warwick Avenue, Woodstock, Ont., Canada.* (519-537 3360)

FARRAN, Brian George. b 44. Austr Nat Univ BA 69. St Jo Coll Morpeth ACT ThL 64. **d** 67 **p** 68 River; C of St Phil Canberra 67-68; Griffith 68-72; P-in-c of Lake Cargelligo 72-75; R of St Barn N Rockptn Dio Rockptn from 75; Exam Chap to Bp of Rockptn from 78. *Rectory, Musgrave Street, Rockhampton, Queensland, Australia 4701.*

FARRAN, George Orman. b 35. Late Exhib of Worc Coll Ox BA (2nd cl Th) 58, MA 62. Wycl Hall Ox 58. **d** 60 Hulme for Man **p** 61 Man. C of Tyldesley 60-62; Tutor Wycl Hall Ox 62-64; V of St Osw Netherton 64-73; R of Sephton 69-73; Surr 70-73; R of Credenhill, Mansel Lacey, Yazor and Brinsop w Wormesley Dio Heref from 73; Rd of Heref Rural from 81. *St Mary's Rectory, Credenhill, Hereford.* (Heref 760687)

FARRANCE, William Kenneth. b 22. Univ Coll of N Wales 46. Bps' Coll Cheshunt 49. **d** 52 **p** 53 Newc T. C of St Gabr Heaton Newc T 52-58; V of St Bede Newsham Blyth 58-63; Heddon-on-the-Wall 63-78; Chap Tynemouth Hosps from 79. *15 Walton Avenue, North Shields, T & W.* (N Shields 574925)

FARRANT, Very Rev John Frederick Ames. b 30. Univ of Aber MA 51, BD 58. Edin Th Coll 51. **d** 53 **p** 54 Brech. C of St Mary Magd Dundee 53-58; R of Clydebank 58-65; Motherwell 65-70; Lae Papua 70-73; St Bride Glas 73-81; Can of Glas Cathl 77-81; Exam Chap to Bp of Glas 78-81; Dean and R of Rabaul Cathl Dio New Guinea Is from 81; Exam Chap to Bp of New Guinea Is from 81. *Box 159, Rabaul, New Britain, Papua New Guinea.*

FARRANT, (Basil) Jonathan. St Mark's Coll Dar-S 72. M SSF from 74. **d** 73 **p** 74 Dar-S. P Dio Dar-S 73-78; L to Offic Dio Heref from 78. *31 Madresfield Vicarage, Great Malvern, Worc.*

FARRANT, Martyn John. b 38. K Coll Lon and Warm AKC 61. **d** 62 **p** 63 Lon. C of Hampton 62-65; Shere 65-67; V of Stoneleigh 67-75; Addlestone Dio Guildf from 75. *Vicarage, Addlestone, Surrey, KT15 1SJ.* (Weybridge 42879)

FARRAR, James Albert. TCD BA 55, Div Test 56, MA 67. **d** 56 **p** 57 Dub. C of Drumcondra w N Strand 56-59; Rathmines 59-61; I of Ballinaclash 61-72; Dunganstown w Redcross (and Conary from 73) 72-79; Warden Ch Min of Healing Ireland from 79. *Divine Healing Chapel, St Andrew's Church, Suffolk Street, Dublin 2,*

FARRE, Andrew. St Paul's Coll Grahmstn 35. LTh (S Afr) 37. **d** 37 Kimb K **p** 41 Geo. C of St Cypr Cathl Kimberley 37-40; St Andr Riversdale 40-43; Knysna 43-46; R of Jagersfontein 46-53; Kuruman and Dir of Kuruman Miss Distr 53-60; Upington Dio Kimb K 60-61. *Healing Home, Kearsney, Natal, S Africa.*

FARREL, Graham Robert. Univ of Queensld BA 77. ACT ThL 68. **d** 63 **p** 64 Bal. C of Creswick w Clunes 63-64; V 64-66; P-in-c of Dimboola Dio Bal 66-68; R 68-70; L to Offic Dio Papua 70-73; Perm to Offic Dio Brisb from 74. *10 Diamantina Street, Chapel Hill, Queensland, Australia 4069.* (378 8260)

FARRELL, Anthony Wesley. b 50. St Paul's Coll Grahmstn 71. **d** 75 Bp Nye for Pret **p** 76 Pret. C of Pietersburg 75-76; Lyttelton 77-78; R of Pret N w Brits 78-81; N Suburbs

City and Dio Pret from 81. *424, 24th Avenue, Villieria, Pretoria, S Africa.*

FARRELL, Peter Godfrey Paul. b 39. Sarum Wells Th Coll 72. **d** 74 **p** 75 Truro. C of St Just-in-Roseland 74-77; Kenwyn w Tregavethan 77-80; V of St Jo Bapt Knighton City and Dio Leic from 80. *9 Springfield Road, Leicester, LE2 3BB.* (Leic 706097)

FARRELL, Canon Ray Kelvin. Univ of W Ont BA 58. Hur Coll BTh 61. **d** 61 Hur **p** 62 Bp Townshend for Hur. R of Thedford 61-64; H Trin Lon Ont 64-68; I of St Matt Windsor 68-71; Trin Ch St Thos 72-78; St Jo Evang Lon Dio Huron from 78; Exam Chap to Bp of Hur from 75; Can of Hur from 77. *280 St James Street, London, Ont, Canada.*

FARRELL, Robert Andrew. Moore Coll Syd ThL 70. **d** 71 Syd **p** 72 Bp Delbridge for Syd. C of St Anne Ryde 71-73; L to Offic Dio Armid 73-74; and 75-78; C of Barradine 74-75; Perm to Offic Dio Syd from 78. *Lot 26, York Street, Tahmoor, NSW, Australia.*

FARRELL, Thomas Stanley. b 32. BD (Lon) 71. Ridley Hall Cam. **d** 71 Warrington for Liv **p** 72 Liv. C of St Pet Woolton 71-73; Gt Sankey 73-74; Asst Chap Dulwich Coll 74-76; Chap 76-81; P-in-c of Wonersh Dio Guildf from 81. *Wonersh Vicarage, Guildford, Surrey.* (Bramley 3131)

FARRER, Michael Robert Wedlake. St Pet Hall Ox BA 52, MA 57. Tyndale Hall Bris 47. **d** 52 **p** 53 Roch for Ox. C of St Ebbe Ox 53-56; Tutor Clifton Th Coll Bris 56-65; R of Barton Seagrave (w Warkton from 73) 65-78; V of St Paul Cam Dio Ely from 78. *St Paul's Vicarage, Cambridge, CB1 2EZ.* (Cam 354186)

FARRER, Ralph David. St Barn Th Coll Adel 65. ACT ThL (2nd cl) 69. **d** 68 **p** 69 Adel. C of Plympton 68-71; P-in-c of Hillcrest 71-73; C of St Pet Melb 73-75; I of Brunswick Dio Melb from 75. *8 Glenlyon Road, Brunswick, Vic, Australia 3056.* (38-1064)

FARRER, Simon James Anthony. b 52. St Cath Coll Cam MA 77. AKC and BD 78. Coll of the Resurr Mirfield 78. **d** 79 Bp Woollcombe for Lon **p** 80 Lon. C of St John's Wood Dio Lon from 79. *3 Cochrane Street, NW8.*

FARRINGTON, Arthur Stanley. Ripon Hall Ox 65. **d** and **p** 66 Birm. C of St Mary w St Ambrose Edgbaston 66-68; St Pet Harborne 68-80. *19 Green Meadow Road, Weoley Hill, Birmingham, B29 4DD.* (021-475 1413)

FARRINGTON, David Clifford Frank. b 43. Univ of Bris BA (3rd cl Lat) 64. **d** 67 Warrington for Liv **p** 68 Liv. C of St Mich Liv 67; St Philemon Toxt Pk Liv 70-74; St Mark Newtown Pemberton (in c of St Barn Marsh Green) 74-77; C-in-c of Hardington Mandeville w Pendomer Dio B & W 77-81; R (w E Chinnock) from 81; P-in-c of E Chinnock 77-81. *Hardington Mandeville Rectory, Yeovil, Somt.* (W Coker 2267)

FARRINGTON, Harold Ernest. b 08. Ex Coll Ox BA (2nd cl Mod Hist) 30. Ely Th Coll 38. **d** 39 **p** 40 Lon. C of All SS Poplar (in c of St Steph 42-43) 39-43 V of St Gabr Warw Square w All SS Pimlico 43-50; St Francis of Assisi Gladstone Pk and Chap of Haberdashers' Aske's Sch 50-55; R of St Geo-in-the-E 55-57; C-in-c of H Angels Cranford 61-66; C of Malvern Link (in c of Ascen) 66-75; Team V (w Cowleigh) 75-76; Perm to Offic Dio Heref from 78. *35 Lower Road, Ledbury, Herefs, HR8 2DH.* (Ledbury 3591)

FARRINGTON, Peter Colson. Moore Th Coll Syd. **d** 63 **p** 64 Gippsld. C of Warragul 63-64; Leongatha 64-66; V of Neerim S 66-69; Stratford 69-75; R of Eugowra Dio Bath from 75. *Box 50, Eugowra, NSW, Australia 2806.* (068-5911 63)

FARROW, Edward. b 38. Sarum Th Coll 69. **d** 71 **p** 72 Sarum. C of St Pet Parkstone w Brownsea I 71-74; R of Tidworth 74-79; P-in-c of W Lulworth and E Lulworth 79-80; Winfrith Newburgh w Chaldon Herring 79-80; R of The Lulworths, Winfrith Newburgh and Chaldon Dio Sarum from 80. *Rectory, West Road, West Lulworth, Wareham, Dorset, BH20 5RY.* (092941 550)

FARROW, Ian Edmund Dennett. b 38. SOC 70. **d** 72 **p** 73 Roch. C of St John Tunbridge Wells 72-78; P-in-c of Walsoken Dio Ely 78-80; R from 80. *Walsoken Rectory, Wisbech, Cambs, PE13 3RA.* (Wisbech 3740)

FARROW, Peter Maurice. b 44. St Chad's Coll Dur BSc 65, Dipl Th 68. **d** 68 Lynn for Nor **p** 69 Nor. C of Gt Yarmouth 68-71; King's Lynn 71-75; P-in-c of Sculthorpe w Dunton and Doughton 75-78; Perm to Offic Dio Nor from 81. *3 Mousehold Avenue, Norwich, Norf.*

FARROW, Philip Montague. b 50. St Aug Coll Cant 74. **d** 75 Bp Poole-Hughes for Llan **p** 76 Llan. C of Bargoed 75-79; St Gabr Swan 79-82; V of Gilfach Goch w Llandyfodwg Dio Llan from 82. *Vicarage, Gilfach Goch, Porth, Mid Glam.*

FARTHING, Michael Thomas. b 28. St Steph Ho Ox STh 81. **d** 58 **p** 59 Lon. C of St Mark w St Luke St Marylebone 58-63; Newport Pagnell (in c of St Luke) 63-68; R of Standlake 69-76; R of Yelford 69-76; C-in-c of Stanton Harcourt w Northmoor 75-76; R of Lower Windrush Dio Ox from 76. *Standlake Rectory, Witney, Oxon, OX8 7SG.* (Standlake 252)

FARTHING, Ronald Edward. b 27. Oak Hill Th Coll. **d** 58 **p** 59 Lon. C of St Mark and of St Anne Holloway 58-61; V of Clodock and Longtown w Crasswall and Llanveynoe 61-67; R of Langley 67-71; V of Bapchild w Tonge and Rodmersham 72-80; Team V of Widecombe-in-the-Moor, Leusden and Princetown w Postbridge and Huccaby Chaps Dio Ex from 80. *New Vicarage, Leusden, Poundsgate, Newton Abbot, Devon.* (Poundsgate 453)

FARWELL, Roland. Qu Coll Newfld. **d** 33 **p** 37 Newfld. sick leave 33-37; C of Corner Brook 37; P-in-c of Port de Grave 37-38; R 38-43; C of Grand Falls Newfld 43-52; R of Carbonear 52-54; Bridgewater 54-67; Stellarton 67-74; R of Westville 67-74. *174 Lincoln Road, Grand Falls, Newfoundland, Canada.*

FASAWE, Samson Omilegan. **d** 77 Egba. d Dio Egba from 77. *Box 26, Okenla-Ifo, Nigeria.*

FASHOLE-LUKE, Edward William. Univ of Dur BA (2nd cl Th) 63. Cranmer Hall Dur 61. **d** 62 **p** 63 Dur. C of St Cuthb Dur 62-64; Asst Lect in Th Fourah Bay Coll Sier L from 65. *Fourah Bay College, Sierra Leone, W Africa.* (Freetown 27372)

FASIPE, Jacob Olasunkanmi. b 44. Im Coll Ibad 74. **d** 77 Ibad. d Dio Ibad. *c/o Box 3075, Ibadan, Nigeria.*

FASOGBON, Nathaniel Olusola. b 40. Im Coll Ibad Dipl Th 70. **d** 70 **p** 71 Ondo. P Dio Ondo. *University of Ife, Ile-Ife, Nigeria.*

FASUGBE, Isaac Taiye. b 48. Im Coll Ibad 72. **d** 75 Ilesha. d Dio Ilesha. *St Peter's Vicarage, Erinmo, via Ilesha, Nigeria.*

FASUNON, Joseph Adeleye. BA (Lon) 64. St Andr Coll Oyo. **d** 69 Ibad. d Dio Ibad. *Ijesha High School, PO Box 16, Ilesha, Nigeria.*

FASUSI, Daniel Owolabi. b 35. **d** 74 **p** 76 Ondo. P Dio Ondo. *St David's Vicarage, Afo, via Owo, Nigeria.*

FASUYI, Michael A Rinbinu. St Andr Coll Oyo. **d** 23 **p** 24 Bp Oluwole for Lagos. P Dio Lagos. *5 Gbogi Street, Ondo, Nigeria.*

FATAI, Nelson. St Pet Coll Siota 54. **d** 56 **p** 59 Melan. P Dio Melan 56-75. *Ngongosila, Malaita, Solomon Islands.*

FATHERS, Derek Esmond. b 27. Magd Coll Ox BA (2nd cl Mod Lang) 50, MA 52. St Aid Coll 55. **d** 56 **p** 57 Ches. Tutor St Aid Coll 56-59; C of W Kirby (in c of St Mich Newton) 59-63; V of Thornton Hough Dio Ches from 63; Exam Chap to Bp of Ches from 65; RD of Wirral S from 78. *Vicarage, Thornton Hough, Wirral, Mer, L65 1JP.* (051-336 3429)

FATILE, Elias Orimolade. b 46. Im Coll Ibad Dipl Th 72. **d** 72 **p** 73 Ondo. P Dio Ondo. *Vicarage, Ipogun, Ondo, Nigeria.*

FATOKI, Canon Jacob Babalola Oladele. Im Coll Ibad 64. **d** 66 Bp Jadesimi for Ibad **p** 67 Ibad. P Dio Ibad 66-80; Dio Kaduna from 80; Can from 81. *PO Box 46, Minila, Nigeria.*

FATUASE, Adebayo Solomon. b 43. Im Coll Ibad Dipl Th 72. **d** 72 **p** 73 Ekiti. P Dio Ekiti. *Emmanuel Anglican Church, Igogo, Ekiti, Nigeria.*

FATUKASI, Moses Akinlose Akingbule. Im Coll Ibad 61. **d** 63 **p** 64 Ondo. P Dio Ondo. *Vicarage, Supare-Akoko, Ondo, Nigeria.*

FAUCHON, Ian Edward. b 37. Moore Th Coll Syd Thl 76. **d** 77 Bp Dain for Syd **p** 77 Bp Robinson for Syd. C of St Paul Riverstone 77-80; C-in-c of St Steph Kellyville Dio Syd from 80. *17 President Road, Kellyville, NSW, Australia 2153.* (629-1453)

FAULDS, John Parker. b 33. Edin Th Coll 55. **d** 57 **p** 58 Edin. C of St D Edin 57-58; St Jo Evang Edin 58-60; Dioc Super Dio Brech and Hosp Chap in Dundee 60-63; Chap Qu Coll Dundee 60-63; Lect Dundee Coll of Educn 62-63; Publ Pr Dio Birm 65-66; C-in-c of Aston Brook 66-69; V of St Pet Handsworth Dio Birm from 69. *45 Holly Road, Birmingham, 20.* (021-554 6723)

FAULKNER, Cecil Joseph William. b 1899. Moore Th Coll Syd 29. **d** 31 **p** 32 Syd. C of St Nic Coogee 31-32; St Steph Newtown 32-33; St Anne Strathfield 34; Canberra 35-37; Asst Chap Miss to Seamen Sydney 34-35; Org Sec for EC Area 37-40 and 47-53; Port Chap Grimsby 40-45; Hong Kong 46-47; R of Harlestone 53-79; C-in-c of Brington 53-56. *Hotel Palace, Lucerne, Switzerland.*

FAULKNER, David Ernest. b 43. St D Coll Lamp Dipl Th 65. St Mich Coll Llan. **d** 66 Llan for St D **p** 67 St D. C of Aberystwyth 66-68; Tenby w Gumfreston 68-69; Burry Port w Pwll 69-73; R of Jeffreyston w Reynalton and E Williamston Dio St D from 73; Loveston Dio St D from 78. *Jeffreyston Rectory, Kilgetty, Dyfed.* (Carew 269)

FAULKNER, Donald Ernest. OBE 49. Wells Th Coll 58. **d** 58 Bp Dale for Guildf **p** 59 Guildf. C of Godalming 58-62; V of Wyke 62-67; R of Donnybrook 67-70; Mt Barker 70-71; Denmark 72-76. *17 Enid Road, Kalamunda, W Australia 6076.*

FAULKNER, Henry Odin. b 35. G and C Coll Cam BA 56, MA 60. St Jo Coll Nottm Dipl Th 73. **d** 74 **p** 75 Nor. Hon C of H Trin Heigham 74-76; C of Heeley Sheff 76-80; Team V of Netherthorpe City and Dio Sheff from 80. *Netherthorpe Vicarage, Burgoyne Road, Sheffield, S6 3QB.* (Sheff 336977)

FAULKNER, John William Harper. Selw Coll Cam BA 28, MA 32. Bps' Coll Cheshunt 28. **d** 29 **p** 30 Cov. C of St Nich Nuneaton 29-32; Buckingham 32-34; V of Seer Green 34-45; R of Lillingstone Dayrell w Lillingstone Lovell 45-51; V of Aston Abbotts w Cublington 51-56; C of St Pet Bedford 56-64; H Trin Bedford 65-68. *196 Foster Hill Road, Bedford.* (Bedford 66657)

FAULKNER, Peter Charles. b 37. Chich Th Coll 72. **d** 74 **p** 75 Ripon. C of Armley 74-76; St Mich (in c of St Birinus, Calcot) Tilehurst 76-80; V of Calcot Dio Ox from 80. *St Birinus House, Langley Hill, Calcot, Reading, RG3 5QX.* (Reading 22828)

FAULKNER, Robert Henry. b 20. St Edm Hall Ox BA 48, MA 53. Wycl Hall Ox 48. **d** 50 **p** 51 Ches. C of Macclesfield 50-53; Hoylake 53-55; V of St Barn Crewe 55-60; Thame (w Towersey from 73) Dio Ox from 60; V of Towersey w Aston Sandford 60-73; R of Aston Sandford Dio Ox from 73; RD of Aston 74-81. *Vicarage, Thame, Oxon.* (Thame 2225)

FAULKNER, Roger Kearton. b 36. K Coll Lon and Warm AKC 62. **d** 63 **p** 64 Ches. C of Oxton 63-67; Ellesmere Port 67-69; V of H Trin Runcorn 69-73; Team V of E Runcorn w Halton 73-76; V of Altrincham Dio Ches from 76. *St George's Vicarage, Altrincham, Ches.* (061-928 1279)

FAULKS, Ronald Stuart. Angl Th Coll BC LTh 34. **d** 34 **p** 35 Edmon. C-in-c of St Mary Barhead 34-37; I of Clandonald 37-40; St Pet w Good Shepherd Edmon 40-51; Can of Edmon 50; R of St Jo Div Centr Pk S Burnaby 51-63; St D Powell River 63-74; Archd of Sechelt 64-74. *3484 La Fleur Street, Port Coquitlam, BC, Canada.*

FAULL, Bernard Maxwell. b 49. St John's Coll Auckld 74. **d** 76 **p** 77 Waik. C of St Mary New Plymouth 76-79; V of Taranaki E Dio Waik from 79. *RD 22 Toko, Stratford, NZ.*

FAULL, Cecil Albert. b 30. Trin Coll Dub BA (2nd cl Mod Hist and Pol Sc) 52. **d** 54 **p** 55 Dub. C of Zion Ch Dub 54-57; St Geo Dub 57-59; Hon Cler V of Ch Ch Cathl Dub 58-63; C of Dun Laoghaire 59-63; R of Portarlington U 63-71; St Geo & St Thos Dub 71-81; I of Clondalkin w Rathcoole Dio Dub from 81. *5 Monastery Road, Clondalkin, Co Dublin, Irish Republic.* (Dublin 592160)

FAULL, William Baines. b 29. Univ of Lon BSc 51. N-W Ordin Course 77. **d** 79 Ches **p** 80 (APM). C of Willaston 79-80; Neston Dio Ches from 80. *Tioman, Briardale Road, Willaston, S Wirral, Cheshire, L64 1TD.*

FAUNCH, Paul. St Jo Coll Dur 51. **d** 53 **p** 54 Man. Lect of Bolton 53-55; V of Bradshaw 55-58; Chap St Geo Sch Ascot 58-59; Prec Guildf Cathl 59-60; C of St Jo Bapt Southend-on-Sea (in c of St Mark) 60; V of Gt Wakering 60-65; R of E Donyland 65-75; Chap and Lect Buckingham Coll Harrow 75-76; Perm to Offic Dios Lon and Chelmsf from 75; Hon C of Kentish Tn 76-77; St Gabr w All SS Pimlico Dio Lon from 78. *66 Claverton Street, Pimlico, SW1.* (01-821 1997)

FAURE, Michael Newbury Abercrombie. Univ of Leeds BA 61. Coll of Resurr Mirfield 62. **d** 63 **p** 64 St John's. C of H Cross Miss 65-68; St Mary Colleg Ch Port Eliz 68-75; Chap Univ of Port Eliz 71-75; R of All SS Mbabane 75-78; C of Linden Dio Johann from 78. *Box 44108, Linden 2104, Johannesburg, S Africa.*

FAVELL, Brian Jeffrey. b 23. Cudd Coll 64. **d** 66 **p** 67 Birm. C of Rubery 66-69; L to Offic Dio Birm 70-76; V of Cwmtillery Dio Mon from 76; P-in-c of Six Bells Dio Mon from 77. *St Paul's Vicarage, Cwmtillery, Gwent, NP3 1LS.* (Abertillery 212365)

FAVELL, John Walter Allen. b 25. **d** 72 **p** 73 Pet. C of St Pet Northn Dio Pet from 72; Dioc Chap to Deaf Dio Pet from 73. *66 Main Road, Duston, Northampton, NN5 6JN.* (Northampton 54694)

FAWCETT, Frederick William. Trin Coll Dub BA 49, Div Test (2nd cl) 50, MA 52. **d** 50 **p** 51 Connor. C of St Aid Belf 50-52; C-in-c of Ballynascreen 52-59; R 59-60; Upper Cumber w Learmount Dio Derry from 60; Exam Chap to Bp of Derry from 79. *87 Cumber Road, Claudy, Derry, N Ireland.* (Claudy 214)

FAWCETT, James Ralph Llewelyn Rees. b 12. AKC 38. **d** 38 Lon **p** 39 Willesden for Lon. C of H Innoc Kingsbury 38-44; St Martin Ruislip 44-52; V of Brandeston w Kettleburgh 52-65; R of Tittleshall w Godwick and Wellingham 65-74; C-in-c of Weasenham 67-74; Rougham 70-74; R of Stiffkey (and Cockthorpe from 76) w Morston and Bp's Langham Dio Nor from 74. *Langham Vicarage, Holt, Norf.* (Binham 246)

FAWCETT, John. b 10. St Aid Coll 31. TD 54. **d** 35 **p** 36 Blackb. C of St Geo Chorley 35-37; Skerton 37-39; CF (TA-R of O) 39-46; V of St Cath Burnley 46-48; Dormanstown 48-55; CF (TA) 49-53; SCF (TA) from 53; V of Marton 55-72. *9 Calder Road, Blackpool, FY2 9TX.* (Blackpool 54734)

FAWCETT, Kenneth. b 17. **d** 40 **p** 41 Graft. C of S Graft 40-42; P-in-c of Liston 42-43; Chap AIF 43-46; C of Tong w Tong Street 46-48; Chap to HM Pris Wandsworth 48-50; HM Pris Leeds and L to Offic Dio Ripon 50-52; V of St Mary of Bethany New Wortley w H Trin Armley Hall 53-58; Shadwell 58-61; Chap Miss to Seamen Durban 61-64; V of Fewston w Blubberhouses Dio Bradf from 64. *Fewston Vicarage, Harrogate, Yorks, HG3 1SU.* (Blubberhouses 282)

FAWCETT, Timothy John. b 44. K Coll Lon and Warm BD (2nd cl) 66, AKC 67, PhD 71. **d** 67 Lanc for Blackb **p** 68 Blackb. C of St Steph Blackpool 67-70; Hon C of All SS Marg Street St Marylebone 68-70; Bowes Pk 70-72; Sacr of Dur Cathl 72-75; V of Wheatley Hill 75-79; Torrisholme Dio Blackb from 79. *Torrisholme Vicarage, Michaelson Avenue, Morecambe, Lancs.* (Morecambe 413144)

FAWCETT, William Henry Carr. b 21. Univ of Lanc MA 72. Kelham Th Coll 38. **d** 45 Southw for Sheff **p** 46 Sheff. C of St Cecilia Parson Cross 45-48; SPG Korean Miss 49-52; Warden of St Mich Th Coll Chong Chu 52-55; C of St Mary Wellingborough 55-56; Lanc Priory Ch 56-58; V of St Barn Morecambe 58-66; Melling w Tatham Dio Blackb from 66. *Town End House, Melling, Nr Carnforth, Lancs, LA6 2RB.*

FAWEHINMI, Daniel Adeyemi. **d** 16 **p** 20 Bp Johnson for W Equat Afr. CMS P Dio Lagos 16-52; Dio Ondo-b 52-59; Hon Can of Ondo-B 55-58. *Oke Ado, Ibadan, Nigeria.*

FAWELL, Herbert Edmund. ACT ThL 31. St Aid Th Coll Bal 29. **d** 31 **p** 32 Bal. C of Swan Marsh 31-32; P-in-c 32-37; P-in-c of Rainbow 37-39; Apollo Bay 39-42; Chap RAN 42-62; Perm to Offic Dio Melb 54-64; Archd of RAN 60-62; I of Ch Ch Geelong 64-77; Perm to Offic Dio Melb from 77. *50 Dare Street, Ocean Grove, Vic., Australia 3226.* (052-55 2792)

FAWKES, Edward George Dalton. b 03. OBE 53. Keble Coll Ox BA (1st cl Engl Lang and Lit) 25, MA 29. St Steph Ho Ox. **d** 27 Southampton for Win **p** 28 Win. C of St Luke Southampton 27-34; Chap RN 34-58; Hon Chap to HM the Queen 56-58; R of Compton w Shawford 58-73. *Hunter's Hill, Twyford, Winchester, Hants, SO21 1QU.*

FAYE, Very Rev John Colley. MBE 47. **d** 47 **p** 73 Gambia. C of St Mary's Pro-Cathl Bath and of Ch Ch Serreh-Kunda Kombo 47-52; L to Offic Dio Gambia 52-67; C of St Mary's Pro-Cathl Banjul 67-74; Dioc Sec Dio Gambia from 74; Provost of St Mary's Pro-Cathl Banjul from 77. *Box 136, Banjul, Gambia.*

FAYEMI, Emmanuel Bamidele Oladejo. b 36. Im Coll Ibad 76. **d** 77 **p** 79 Ilesha. P Dio Ilesha. *Emmanuel Church, Idofin, Esa-Oke, Ilesha, Nigeria.*

FAYERS, Henry Douglas Freeman. b 03. Lich Th Coll 55. **d** 56 **p** 57 Wakef. C of Halifax 56-58; Normanton 58-59; V of Kenton w Ashfield and Thorpe 59-62; R of Westerfield (w St Martin Tuddenham from 71) 62-73; Perm to Offic Dio St E from 78. *52 Pier Avenue, Southwold, Suff.*

FAYOMI, Joseph Ayinde. b 40. Im Coll Ibad 73. **d** 75 **p** 76 Ibad. P Dio Ibad. *All Saints Church Vicarage, PO Box 26, Osogbo, Nigeria.*

FEARN, Anthony John. b 34. Lich Th Coll 58. **d** 61 **p** 62 Worc. C of Redditch 61-64; Bladon w Woodstock 64-66; PC of Ruscombe w Twyford Dio Ox 66-67; V from 68. *Ruscombe Vicarage, Reading, Berks RG10 9UD.* (0734 341685)

FEARN, Preb Hugh. b 18. Selw Coll Cam 2nd cl Hist Trip pt i, 47, BA (2nd cl Hist Trip pt ii) 48, MA 52. Univ of Sheff MA 52. St Ant Coll Ox MA (by incorp) 56. Univ of Lon PhD 57. FRHistS 60. **d** and **p** 58 Accra. Academic Regr and chap Univ Coll of Ghana and L to Offic Dio Accra 58-62; Lect in Hist 60-62; V of St Olave Woodberry Down 62-65; H Trin Northwood 65-81; Surr from 66; Commiss Accra 69-74; Warden of Readers Dio Lon from 70; Preb of St Paul's Cathl Lon from 77; R of St Clem Eastcheap w St Martin Orgar City and Dio Lon from 81. *7 Bishop Street, N1 8PH.* (01-226 6992)

FEARN, Robert Benjamin. Bps' Coll Cheshunt 62. **d** 64 **p** 65 Southw. C of Newark-on-Trent 64-68; V of St Aid Basford 68-74; Beckingham w Walkeringham Dio Southw from 74. *Beckingham Vicarage, Doncaster, Yorks.* (Saundby 266)

FEARON, Ebenezer Zaccheus. Melville Hall Oyo 37. **d** 39 **p** 41 Lagos. P Dio Lagos 39-60; Dio Ibad 60-65; Dio Niger from 65. *St Paul's Parsonage, Box 11, Onitsha, Nigeria.*

FEAST, Robert Butler. b 08. Trin Hall Cam BA 30, MA 36. Cudd Coll 30. **d** 31 **p** 32 York. C of Guisborough 31-35; Earlham w Bowthorpe 35-36; V of St Mary Thetford 36-42; Chap of Thetford Inst 38-39; Chap RNVR 39-46; R of Somerleyton w Ashby 46-53; Litcham w Kempston and of E w W Lexham 53-56; Newton Flotman w Swainsthorpe 56-69; Chap Vale Hosp Swainsthorpe 59-69; R of N Lew w Ashbury 69-73. *Rose Cottage, Boddington Lane, Witney, Oxon.*

FEAST, Willis Mansfield. b 02. CCC Cam BA 24, MA 36. Cudd Coll 24. **d** 26 **p** 27 Nor. C of Swaffham 26-29; Babbacombe 29-30; R of Heilbron w Parys 30-31; Jagersfontein

31-32; Wepener 32-35; R of Booton w Brandiston 35-71. *1 Bracondale Court, Norwich, NOR 58B.* (Norwich 21698)

FEATHAM, Lawrence William Carson. b 53. AKC 74. SSM Lanc 77. **d** 78 **p** 79 Liv. C of St Columba Anfield Dio Liv from 78. *17 Victoria Road, Liverpool 13.*

FEATHERSTON, William Roger. St Mich Th Coll Crafers 63. ACT ThL 67. **d** 68 **p** 69 Melb. C of All SS Geelong 68-71; C-in-c of Warrandyte 71-72; I 72-74; C of Liti Levu W 74-76; I of Pascoe Vale Dio Melb from 76. *26 Pleasant Street, Pascoe Vale, Vic, Australia 3044.* (35-6575)

FEATHERSTONE, Andrew. b 53. St Chad's Coll Dur BA 74. Sarum Wells Th Coll 78. **d** 80 Newc T **p** 81 Bp Gill for Newc T. C of H Cross Fenham Dio Newc T from 80. *2a Lanercost Drive, Newcastle-upon-Tyne, NE5 2DE.* (0632 749574)

FEATHERSTONE, Gray. b 42. Univ of Stellenbosch BA 62, LLB 64. Cudd Coll 65. **d** 67 **p** 68 Capetn. C of Woodstock 67-70; Asst Master Waterford Sch Mbabane and L to Offic Dio Swaz 70-72; Chap Miss to Seamen and P-in-c of St Steph and St Lawr Maputo 73-76; Chap Miss to Seamen Gravesend 77-80; V of St Matt U Clapton Dio Lon from 80; St Thos Clapton Common Dio Lon from 80. *37 Clapton Common, E5 9AA.* (01-806 1463)

FEATHERSTONE, John. b 23. Kelham Th Coll 40. **d** 46 Man **p** 47 Hulme for Man. C of St Pet Swinton 46-51; V of Glodwick 51-55; Dormanstown 55-61; R of Roos w Tunstall-in-Holderness 61-66; V of Garton-in-Holderness w Grimston and Hilston 61-66; Alkmonton w Yeaveley 66-70; R of Longford 66-70; V of St Phil Chaddesden 70-72; Denby 72-77; R of Whitwell Dio Derby from 77; RD of Bolsover and Staveley 78-81. *Whitwell Rectory, Worksop, Notts.* (Worksop 720220)

FEATHERSTONE, John. Univ of Man BA (2nd cl French) 53. St Cath S Ox BA (2nd cl Th) 60. Wycl Hall Ox 57. **d** 60 **p** 61 York. C of St Aug Newland Hull 60-62; H Innoc Kidderminster 62-65. *14 Stabler's Walk, Old Earswick, York.*

✠ **FEAVER, Right Rev Douglas Russell.** b 14. Late Scho of Keble Coll Ox BA (1st cl Mod Hist and Liddon Stud) 35, 1st cl Th 37, MA 39. Wells Th Coll 37. **d** 38 **p** 39 St Alb. C of Abbey Ch St Alb 38-42; Chap RAFVR 42-46; Can and Sub-Dean of St Alb Cathl 46-58; Surr from 48; Exam Chap to Bp of St Alb 48-58; to Bp of Portsm 60-72; Proc Conv St Alb 51-58; V of Nottm 58-72; RD of Nottm 58-72; Hon Can of Southw 58-72; Treas Southw Chapter 60-67; Surr 69-72; Proc in Conv Southw 70-72; Cons Ld Bp of Pet in S'wark Cathl 1 Nov 72 by Abp of Cant; Bps of Lon, Portsm, Leic, Derby, and Nor; Bps Suffr of Willesden, Edmon, Buckingham, Bradwell, and others. *The Palace, Peterborough, PE1 1YA.* (Peterborough 62492)

FEDDEN, Canon Patrick Vincent. b 17. Ex Coll Ox BA 40, MA 43. Westcott Ho Cam 40. **d** 41 **p** 42 Bris. C of St Matt Moorfields Bris 41-46; Dom Chap to Bp in Egypt 46-49; V of St Barbara Earlsdon Cov 50-59; Totteridge 59-72; RD of Barnet 66-72; V of Stourport Dio Worc from 72; RD of Stourport 75-80; Hon Can of Worc from 79. *Vicarage, Stourport-on-Severn, Worcs, DY13 9DD.* (Stourport 2041)

FEDIGHA, Crispin Nathaniel. b 14. St Paul's Coll Awka. **d** 74 **p** 75 Nig Delta. P Dio Nig Delta. *St Paul's Parsonage, Ogboloma Taylor Creek, c/o P.A. Okolobiri, via Ahoada, Nigeria.*

FEE, George Bertram. Trin Coll Tor LTh 41. **d** 39 **p** 40 Tor. C of St Geo Tor 39-40; St Mary Virg Bran 40; Chap RCAF 52-78; Shaughnessy Hosp Vanc from 78. *4414 West 4th Avenue, Vancouver, BC, Canada V6R 1R1.*

FEHELEY, Allan Paul. Univ of Tor MusBac 75. Trin Coll Tor MDiv 78. **d** 78 **p** 79 Tor. C of St Clem Eglinton Tor 78-80; Caledon E Dio Tor from 80. *Box 93, Caledon East, Ont, Canada.*

FEHRE, Charles Derwent. ACT ThL 60. Ridley Coll Melb. **d** and **p** 61 Tas. C of Claremont 61-62; R of Swansea 62-66; Sandford 66-76; Glenorchy Dio Tas from 76. *476 Main Road, Glenorchy, Tasmania 7010.* (002-727638)

FEHRENBACH, Donald Joseph. Selw Coll Cam BA 49, MA 53. Qu Coll Birm 49. **d** 51 **p** 52 York. C of Beverley Minster 51-54; V Cho Sarum Cathl 54-59; Min Can of St Geo Chap Windsor 59-65; PC of Sandford-on-Thames Dio Ox 65-67; V from 68; Chap Ch Ch Cathl Ox 70-73. *Field Cottage, 26 Henley Road, Sandford-on-Thames, Oxford.*

FEIST, Nicholas James. b 45. [f Solicitor] St Jo Coll Nottm LTh 76. **d** 76 Man **p** 77 Middleton for Man. C of St Jas & Em Didsbury 76-80; V of Friar Mere Dio Man from 80. *37 Huddersfield Road, Delph, Oldham, Lancs, OL3 5EG.* (Saddleworth 4209)

FEIT, Michael John. b 24. FICE 73. FIStructE 73. SOC. **d** 69 **p** 71 Kens for Lon. C of Feltham 69-74; Ashford 74-77; N Hykeham 78-81; R of Leasingham and Brauncewell Dio Linc from 81; V of Cranwell Dio Linc from 81. *Leasingham Rectory, Sleaford, Lincs.* (Sleaford 2406)

FELCE, Brian George. b 30. Jes Coll Ox BA 54, MA 57. Oak Hill Th Coll. **d** 58 **p** 59 Lon. C of St Steph E Twickenham 58-60; St Luke Ramsgate 60-64; R of Bedingfield w Southolt 64-73; V of All SS Preston Dio Blackb from 73. *94 Watling Street Road, Fulwood, Preston, PR2 4BP.* (Preston 700672)

FELDMAN, Ralph Carlisle. ACA 57. Moore Th Coll Syd ACT ThL (2nd cl) 59. **d** and **p** 60 Syd. C of St Anne Strathfield 60-62; C-in-c of St Aid Hurtsville Grove 63-66; R of St Luke Concord w Burwood 66-74; Leura Dio Syd from 74. *137a Megalong Street, Leura, NSW, Australia 2781.* (047-84 1195)

FELIX, H Cross Coll Rang 68. **d** 70 **p** 71 Rang. P Dio Rang. *196 Kyundaw Road, Sanchaung PO., Rangoon, Burma.*

FELIX, Donald Cameron. b 24. St Aid Coll 64. **d** 65 **p** 66 Lich. C of Walsall 65-68; V of St Mary Pype Hayes Erdington 68-73; St Paul Burslem 73-76; Bloxwich 76-79; P-in-c of Seighford w Derrington and Cresswell Dio Lich 79-81; V from 81. *Seighford Vicarage, Stafford, ST18 9PQ.* (Seighford 324)

FELL, Alan William. b 46. Ball Coll Ox BA 69. Univ of Leeds Dipl Th 70. Coll of Resurr Mirfield 68. **d** 71 **p** 72 Ches. C of H Cross Woodchurch 71-74; St Cross w St Paul Clayton 74-75; St Marg Prestwich 75-77; V of St Thos Hyde 77-80; R of Tattenhall and Handley Dio Ches from 80. *Tattenhall Rectory, Chester.* (0829-70328)

FELL, Stephen. St Jo Coll Dur BA 42, LTh 41. Oak Hill Th Coll. **d** 42 Burnley for Blackb **p** 43 Blackb. C of Em Preston 42-46; All H Tottenham 46-49; St Mary Luton 49-52; R of Toddington 52-58; Castleford Dio Wakef from 58. *Rectory, Castleford, Yorks.* (Castleford 2401)

FELL, Willis Marshall. b 29. N-W Ordin Course 73. **d** 75 Repton for Derby **p** 76 Derby. C of Bolsover 75-78; Clay Cross 78-80; V of St Mark Brampton Dio Derby from 80. *27 Shaftesbury Avenue, Chesterfield, Derbys.* (Chesterfield 34015)

FELLINGHAM, John. b 25. Lon Coll Div 52 **d** 55 **p** 56 Nor. C of Pakefield 55-59; R of Coltishall w Gt Hautbois 59-70; C-in-c of Horstead 62-65; RD of Ingworth 65-70; Chap HM Pris Nor 69-73; C-in-c of St Helens, Nor 70-73. *22 Market Place, Hingham, Norwich, NR9 4AF.* (Hingham 549)

FELLOWES, Norman Bennett. **d** 57 **p** 59 C & Goulb. C of Cootamundra 57-58; Wagga Wagga 58-59; Batlow 59-60; Cooma 60-62; P-in-c of Barmedman 62-66; Tarcutta 66-67; L to Offic Dio Syd 70; P-in-c of St Anne Strathfield 70-72; P-in-c of Culcairn 72-74; R 74-76; Lockhart 76-77; The Rock Dio River from 78. *St Peter's Rectory, The Rock, NSW, Australia 2655.* (069-2015 35)

FELLOWES-BROWN, Eldred Joscelyn Fellowes. b 03. Ch Ch Ox BA 25, MA 32. Cudd Coll 26. **d** 27 **p** 28 Lon. C of St Mary of Eton Hackney Wick 27-34; St Nich Chiswick 34-37; V of St Jo Evang Hammersmith 37-43; Ch Ch Isle of Dogs Lon 43-47; LDHM of K Chas Mart S Mymms 47-49; PC 47-53; V of St Mich AA Mill Hill 53-60; Isleworth 60-64; Worstead w Westwick and Sloley 64-69; C of St Mich Wood Green 69-70; St Mich (in c of Calcot) Tilehurst 70-71; Perm to Offic Dio Lon 73-75; C of Burnham Thorpe w Burnham Overy 75-77; Hon C of St Andr Southgate 77-80; Perm to Offic Dio Nor 80-81. *18 New Barns Road, Ely, Cambs, CB7 4PN.* (Ely 61528)

FELLOWS, Canon Arthur Gregory. St Francis Coll Brisb ACT ThL (2nd cl) and John Forster Pri 50. **d** 50 **p** 51 Rockptn. C of N Rockptn 50-53; V of Springsure 53-57; Callide Valley 57-59; R of Oakey 59-62; Roma 62-68; St Alb Auchenflower 68-73; Org Sec ABM Brisb from 73; Hon Can of Brisb from 75. *83 Payne Road, The Gap, Queensland, Australia 4061.* (30 3428)

FELLOWS, Grant. b 56. AKC and BD 77. Coll of Resurr Mirfield 79. **d** 80 **p** 81 Cant. C of Addington Dio Cant from 80. *St Mary's Church Hall Flat, Addington Village Road, Croydon, CR0 5AS.*

FELLOWS, John Michael. b 46. Oriel Coll Ox MA 77. Coll of Resurr Mirfield 74. **d** 77 **p** 78 Birm. [f Barrister]. C of King's Heath 77-80; Team V of E Ham Dio Chelmsf from 80. *1 Norman Road, East Ham, E6.* (01-471 8751)

FELLOWS, Ronald Samuel. Univ of W Ont BA 54. Hur Coll LTh 55. **d** 55 **p** 56 Hur. C of All SS Windsor 55-57; R of Merlin 57-60; St D and St John Sarnia 60-65; in Amer Ch 65-69; on Nat Staff Angl Ch of Canada from 69. *600 Jarvis Street, Toronto, Ont., M4Y 2J6, Canada.*

FELLOWS, Roy. b 30. Keble Coll Ox BA (2nd cl Mod Hist) 53, 3rd cl Th 55, MA 57. St Steph Ho Ox 53. **d** 56 **p** 57 Man. C of Tonge Moor 56-61; St Phil Hulme Man 61-63; R of St Crispin Withington 63-73; V of St Luke Southport 74-78; St Thos Bedford-Leigh 78-81; Warden of Company of

Miss Priests from 81. *St Helen's Rectory, Hemsworth, Nr Pontefract, W Yorks.* (0977-610507)

FELSTEAD, Canon Kenneth Walter Harry. b 14. Univ of Sheff BSc (2nd cl Hons) 35, MSc 36. Lich Th Coll 35. **d** 37 **p** 38 Derby. C of St John Long Eaton 37-39; Chap and Lect King Alfred's Coll Win and L to Offic Dio Win 39-40; Perm to Offic at Weston 40-45; Dioc Insp of Schs 42-45 and 49-58; C-in-c of St Mich w H Rood St Lawr and St John Southn 45-46; V (w St Jas from 68) 46-70; Surr from 52; RD of Southn 58-70; Proc Conv Win 59-75; Hon Can of Win 62-79; Can (Emer) from 79; Master of St Cross Hosp and Min of St Faith Win 70-79; RD of Win 73-78; Heytesbury from 80; Ch Comm 73-78. *29 Damask Way, Warminster, Wilts.*

FELTHAM, Geoffrey Hayes. Univ of Syd BA 47. Moore Th Coll Syd ACT ThL 43. **d** 45 Syd **p** 46 Bp Pilcher for Syd. C of St Cuthb Langlea 45-46; St Steph Newtown 47-49; C-in-c of Belmore 49-50; Burwood E 50; Hosp Chap Camperdown 50-52; R of Milton 52-54; Austinmer 54-58; Lithgow 58-60; Chap Ment Hosps Syd 59-65; Univ of NSW 65-69; L to Offic Dio Syd 63-69; R of Epping Dio Syd from 69. *3 Pembroke Street, Epping, NSW, Australia 2121.* (86-3362)

FELTHAM, Keith. b 40. Dipl Th (Lon) 66. **d** 75 Ex **p** 76 Plymouth for Ex. [f Bapt Min] C of Plympton 75-79; Team V of Northam w Westward Ho and Appledore Dio Ex from 79. *Vicarage, Appledore, Bideford, N Devon, EX39 1RJ.* (Bideford 4610)

FELTON, Philip Leonard. b 31. St D Coll Lamp BA 53. **d** 55 **p** 56 St D. C of St Ishmael w Llansaint and Ferryside 55-64; V of Gwaun-Cae-Gurwen 64-79. *Address temp unknown.*

FENN, Norman Alexander. b 20. Kelham Th Coll 37. **d** 43 **p** 44 Lich. C of Ch Ch Tunstall 43-47; Leek 47-51; V of Tilstock 51-55; Milton 55-61; Ellesmere Dio Lich from 61; V of Welsh Frankton Dio Lich from 62; RD of Ellesmere from 70; Surr from 72. *Vicarage, Ellesmere, Salop, SY12 0HB.* (Ellesmere 2571)

FENN, Roy William Dearnley. b 15. Jes Coll Ox BA (2nd cl Th) 54, MA 59, BD 68. St Mich Coll Llan 54. **d** 56 **p** 57 Swan B. C of Swansea 57-59; St Jo Bapt Cardiff 59-60; Bridgend 60-63; V of Glascwm w Rhulon (w Cregrina to 68) 63-74; P-in-c of Letton w Staunton-on-Wye, Byford, Mansel Gamage and Monnington-on-Wye 75-81. *c/o Letton Rectory, Hereford.* (Eardisley 343)

FENN, Canon Walter James. St Jo Coll Morpeth ACT ThL 56. **d** 56 **p** 57 River. C of Leeton 56-58; R of Lake Cargelligo 58-65; Wentworth 65-69; V of Fawkner 69-71; Chap Geelong Hosp and Pris 71-72; R of Narrandera Dio River from 72; Hon Can of River from 78. *PO Box 50, Narrandera, NSW, Australia 2700.* (060-59 2089)

FENNELL, Canon Alfred Dennis Charles. b 15. Bp's Coll Calc 35. **d** 38 **p** 39 Luckn. Chap St Pet Charbagh Luckn 38-46; St Nich Naini Tal 47-48; C of St Helen N Kens 48-50; Min of All SS Queensbury 50-54; V 54-62; Prec of Birm Cathl 62-64; V of Hay Mill 68-80; Hon Can of Birm Cathl from 78. *12 Cedarhurst, Tennal Road, Harborne, Birmingham, B32.*

FENNELL, Francis Vincent. St D Coll Lamp BA 48. **d** 49 **p** 50 Mon. C of Tredegar 49-54; V of Crumlin 54-59; Chap Auckld Psychiatric Hosp 59-63; L to Offic Dio Auckld 59-63 and from 68; Dio Dub 63-67; Dir Family Guidance Centre Auckld 68-71; Chap Kingseat and Raventhorpe Hosps Dio Auckld 71-80. *102 Beach Road, Papakura, NZ.* (84-739)

FENNEMORE, Nicholas Paul. B 53. Wycl Hall Ox 76. **d** 79 **p** 80 St Alb. C of N Mymms Dio St Alb from 79. *21 Bulls Lane, Welham Green, Hatfield, Herts.* (Hatfield 65751)

FENNING, George Charles. Hur Coll LTh 46. **d** and **p** 41 Hur. I of Florence w Aughrim and Bothwell 41-42; St D Lon Ont 42-50; R of St Paul Kamloops 50-52; St D Tor 52-60; Ch Ch Scarborough Tor 60-75. *Apt 803, 10 Roanoke Road, Don Mills, Ont., Canada.*

FENTON, Canon Albert George. Linc Th Coll 42. **d** 43 Linc for Sarum **p** 44 Sarum. C of St Paul Weymouth 43-46; C of Bloemf Cathl 46-48; Miss to Free State Gold Fields 48-52; V of Stanger 52-59; Can of Bloemf 59-61; R of Harrismith 59-61; Archd of Harrismith 59-61; R of Coates Ely 61-62; St Steph Durban 62-71; All SS Ladysmith 71-75; Archd of Ladysmith 71-75; R of St Cypr Durban 75-76; Hon Can of Natal from 75; C of St Martin Durban N 76-78; Perm to Offic Dio Natal from 78. *400a Currie Road, Durban 4001, Natal, S Africa.*

FENTON, Christopher Miles Tempest. b 28. Qu Coll Cam BA 50, LLB 51, MA 56. Ridley Hall Cam 52. **d** 54 **p** 55 Roch. C of St John Welling 54-57; Chap Malsis Prep Sch Keighley and L to Offic Dio Bradf 57-63; C of Bp Hannington Mem Ch Hove 64-65; V of Ch Ch Ramsgate 65-71; C of Mottingham (in c of St Alb) 71-73; Perm to Offic Dio Ely from 73; Hd of Dept of Groupwork Westmr Pastoral Found from 73. *3 Talls Lane, Fenstanton, Huntingdon, Cambs, PE18 9JJ.* (St Ives 62489)

FENTON, Francis. b 1897. Linc Th Coll. **d** 62 **p** 63 Linc. C of St Pet-at-Gowts w St Andr Linc 62-75. *St Paul's Nursing Home, Waddington, via Lincoln.*

FENTON, Gordon Douglas. b 56. Univ of Man BA, MDiv. St Jo Coll Winnipeg 78. **d** 80 **p** 81 Keew. C of Ear Falls Dio Keew from 80. *Box 305, Ear Falls, Ont, P0V 1T0, Canada.*

FENTON, Graham Richard Cooper. St Jo Coll Nottm. **d** 74 **p** 75 Natal. C of Ch Ch Addington 74-77; St John Wynberg Dio Capetn from 77. *35 Wetton Road, Wynberg 7800, CP, S Africa.* (777856)

FENTON, Ian Christopher Stuart. b 40. K Coll Lon and Warm AKC 62. **d** 63 **p** 64 Guildf. C of Banstead 63-67; V of N Holmwood Dio Guildf from 67. *North Holmwood Vicarage, Dorking, Surrey.* (0306 882135)

FENTON, Canon John Charles. b 21. Qu Coll Ox BA (2nd cl Th) 43, MA 47, BD 53. Linc Th Coll 43. **d** 44 Warrington for Liv **p** 45 Liv. C of All SS Hindley 44-47; Chap Linc Th Coll 47-51; Sub-Warden Linc Th Coll 51-54; V of Wentworth 54-58; Exam Chap to Bp of Sheff 56-58; to Bp of Lich 59-68; to Bp of Dur 65-66 and 68-72; Prin Lich Th Coll 58-65; St Chad's Coll Dur 65-78; Select Pr Univ of Cam 62; Univ of Ox 62 and 79; Can of Ch Ch Ox from 78. *Christ Church, Oxford, OX1 1DP.*

FENTON, Michael John. b 42. Linc Th Coll 67. **d** 69 **p** 70 Bradf. C of Guiseley 69-72; Heswall 72-75; Team V of Birkenhead Priory 75-81; V of Alvanley Dio Ches from 81. *Alvanley Vicarage, Warrington, Chesh, WA6 9HD.* (Helsby 2012)

FENTON, Richard James. St Jo Coll Auckld LTh 40. **d** 40 **p** 42 Auckld. C of Ellerslie 40-43; Pukekohe 43-47; P-in-c 47; V of Clevedon 47-54; Bay of Islands 54-57; Northcote 57-63; St Columba Grey Lynn 63-73; Royal Oak Dio Auckld from 73. *17 Crown Street, Auckland 3, NZ.* (657-482)

FENTON, Wallace. b 32. Trin Coll Dub. **d** 64 **p** 65 Connor. C of Glenavy 64-67; R of Tullaniskin Dio Arm from 67. *275 Coalisland Road, Dungannon, Co Tyrone, BT71 6ET.* (Coalisland 40370)

FENTY, Peter Decourcy. b 51. Univ of the WI LTh 75. Codr Coll Barb 72. **d** and **p** 75 Barb. C of St Matthias I and Dio Barb from 75. *11 Graeme Hall, Christ Church, Barbados, WI.*

FENWICK, Edward Hartwig. b 05. Fitzw Coll Cam 3rd cl Hist Trip pt 1 31, BA (3rd cl Th Trip pt i) 33, MA 43. Westcott Ho Cam 32. **d** 33 **p** 34 Newc T. C of St Aid Newc T 33-35; St Andr Roker 35-38; PC of Benfieldside 38-60; I of St Jas Delhi 46-47; Chap Shotley Bridge Hosp 40-60; R of Lapworth 60-76; Baddesley Clinton 60-76; Perm to Offic Dio Birm from 78. *1 St Alphege Close, Solihull, West Midl.*

FENWICK, Canon Jeffery Robert. b 30. Pemb Coll Cam BA 53, MA 57. Linc Th Coll 53. **d** 55 **p** 56 Liv. C of St Thos Upholland 55-58; P-in-c of Daramombe S Rhod 58-64; Area Sec USPG Dio Ox 64-65; R of All SS Gatooma 65-67; Salisbury E 67-75; Exam Chap to Bp of Mashon 66-75; P-in-c of Mabvuku 68-70; Archd of Charter 73-75; Bulawayo 75-78; Dean and R of St Jo Bapt Cathl Bulawayo 75-78; VG of Matab 75-78; Can Res of Worc Cathl from 78. *10 College Yard, Worcester, WR1 2LA.* (Worc 24874)

FENWICK, John Robert Kipling. b 51. Van Mildert Coll Dur BSc 72. Univ of Nottm BA (Th) 74, MTh 78. St Jo Coll Nottm 72. **d** 77 Penrith for Carl **p** 78 Carl. C of Dalton-in-Furness 77-80; Lect Trin Coll Bris from 80. *Trinity College, Stoke Hill, Bristol, BS9 1JP.* (Bristol 682803)

FENWICK, Malcolm Frank. b 38. Cranmer Hall, Dur 62. **d** 65 **p** 66 Newc T. C of St Paul Cullercoats 65-68; St Pet Bywell 68-73; V of Alnmouth (w Lesbury from 75) 73-80; Delaval Dio Newc T from 80; CF (TAVR) from 75. *Delaval Vicarage, Seaton Sluice, Whitley Bay, Northumb.* (Seaton Delaval 481982)

FENWICK, Richard David. b 43. St D Coll Lamp BA 66. TCD BMus 79. FLCM 68. FTCL 76. Ridley Hall Cam 66. **d** 68 **p** 69 Bp T M Hughes for Llan. C of Skewen 68-72; Penarth w Lavernock 72-74; PV Succr and Sacr of Roch Cathl 74-78; Min Can and Jun Cardinal of St Paul's Cathl Lon from 78; Succr from 79. *6 Amen Court, EC4.* (01-248 6115)

FERGUSON, Alan John Halliday. Univ of Tor BA 59. Trin Coll Tor STB 62. **d** and **p** 62 Sktn. I of Watson 62-67; I of Pathlow 62-67; C of St Clem Eglinton 67-70; I of Thompson 70-76; Archd of York 74-76; R of St Bede Scarborough Tor 76-80; St Marg New Tor Dio Tor from 80. *156-6th Street, Toronto, M8V 3A5.*

FERGUSON, Anthony David Norman. b 51. Wycl Hall Ox 75. **d** 78 **p** 79 Lich. C of St Matt Tipton Dio Lich from 78. *97a Dudley Road, Tipton, W Midlands, DY4 8EB.* (021-557 4096)

FERGUSON, David Ernest. Seager Hall Ont STh 61. **d** 61 Hur for Sktn **p** 62 Sktn. R of St Steph Sktn 61-67; Maitland 68-69; I of Shelburne 69-76; C of Ch Ch Dartmouth Dio NS from 76. *12 Rose Street, Dartmouth, NS, Canada.*

FERGUSON, Donald Thomas. St Jo Coll Auckld LTh 56.

d 56 **p** 57 Wai. C of St Aug Napier 56-59; Rotorua 59-62; V of Opotiki 62-65; R and Sub-Dean of All SS Cathl Honiara 65-70; Hon Can of All SS Cathl Honiara 69-72; V of Gate Pa Dio Wai 70-76; Archd of Tauranga 72-77; Hon C of Whakatane Dio Wai from 77. *Titoki Road, RD2, Whakatane, NZ.* (6503)

FERGUSON, Ian John. b 51. Univ of Aber BD 77. Trin Coll Bris 77. **d** 78 **p** 79 Cant. C of St Jo Bapt Folkestone Dio Cant from 78. *126 Lucy Avenue, Folkestone, Kent.*

FERGUSON, James Paterson. b 07. Univ of Glas MA 29. Qu Coll Ox BA 33. Wycl Hall Ox 33. **d** 33 **p** 34 B & W. C of St Swith Walcot Bath 33-36; CMS Miss Khatauli 36-38; St Jo Coll Agra 38-45; Sikandra 45-51; V of Stretton-on-Dunsmore 52-55; Lect Fourah Bay Coll 55-61; Sen Lect in Phil Univ Coll Sier L 60-69; Warden of Studs 60-64; Exam Chap to Bp of Sier L 57-69; Can of St Geo Cathl Freetown 65-69; Admin Adult Chr Educn Manzini Dio Swaz 70-71. *Cregneish, Albany Road, Douglas, IM.* (Douglas 3130)

FERGUSON, John. b 36. Univ of Lon BSc 67, PhD 70. Oak Hill Coll 73. **d** 76 **p** 77 St Alb. C of Ch Ch Watford Dio St Alb from 76. *84 Tudor Drive, Watford, Herts.*

FERGUSON, John Aitken. b 40. Univ of Glas BSc 64. Univ of Strathclyde PhD 74. MICE, CEng, Linc Th Coll 79. **d** 81 Bp Gill for Newc T. C of Morpeth Dio Newc T from 81. *18 Northbourne Avenue, Morpeth Northumberland, NE61 1JG.*

FERGUSON, John Duncan. b 31. Clare Coll Cam BA 54, MA 58. Kelham Th Coll 54. **d** 59 **p** 60 S'wark. C of Old Charlton 59; L to Offic Dio Accra 63-72; Asst Master and Chap Navrongo Sch Ghana 63-72; St Monica Sch Mampong Ghana 73-75; L to offic Dio Kum 73-75; Perm to Offic Dio Pet 75-76; Dio Ox 75-77; V of Hessenford Dio Truro from 77. *Hessenford Vicarage, Torpoint, Cornw, PL11 3HR.* (Widegates 317)

FERGUSON, John Meredith. b 14. **d** 69 **p** 70 Bloemf. C of Bloemf Cathl and Bp's Chap 69-70; St Marg Bloemf 70-73; P-in-c of Springfontein 70-72; R of St Jo Bapt Harrismith 73-76; Umhlanga Dio Natal from 76. *45 Marine Drive, Umhlanga Rocks, Natal, S Africa.*

FERGUSON, John Richard Preston. b 34. TCD 63. **d** 65 **p** 66 Down. C of Dundela 65-70; I of Annahilt 70-76; St Brendan Belf Dio Down from 76. *36 Circular Road, Belfast, BT4 2GA, N Ireland.*

FERGUSON, Canon Mark. K Coll Dur BA 38, MA 41. Cudd Coll 41. **d** 43 Hull for York **p** 44 York. C of St Jo Evang Middlesbrough 43-45; All SS Sydenham 45-46; Esh w Langley Pk 46-50; C-in-c of St Cuthb Conv Distr Cleadon Pk 50-52; Min 50-54; Chap of Cleadon Pk Sanat 50-54; R of Westville NS 54-57; All SS Cathl Halifax 57-59; Summerside 59-64; Hon Can of NS from 63; Hosp Chap Halifax 64-67; Exam Chap to Bp of NS 66-70; on leave 70-74; R of Musquodoboit 74-76; Falmouth Dio NS from 76. *RR2, Falmouth, Hants Co, NS, Canada.* (798-4865)

FERGUSON, Peter Carr. b 22. Cranmer Hall, Dur 62. **d** 63 **p** 64 York. C of Newington Dio York 63-66; V (w Dairycoates from 69) 66-73; St Thos w St Maurice York 73-79; Lythe Dio York from 79. *Lythe Vicarage, Whitby, Yorks.* (Sandsend 252)

FERGUSON, Peter Thomas Devlin. Moore Th Coll Syd ACT ThL 60. **d** 60 **p** 61 C & Goulb. C of Wagga Wagga 60-63; P-in-c of Lake Bathurst 63-65; R of Clanwilliam 65-72; St Mark Capetn 72-73; Melville 73-80; E Vic Pk w Bentley Dio Perth from 80. *20 Whittlesford Street, East Victoria Park, W Australia 6101.* (361-3931)

FERGUSON, Richard Archie. b 39. Univ of Dur BA 62. Linc Th Coll 62. **d** 64 Middleton for Man **p** 65 Man. C of St Matt Stretford 64-68; Dom Chap to Bp of Dur 68-69; C of St Geo Jesmond 69-71; V of St Mark w Ch Ch Glodwick Oldham 71-77; Tynemouth Dio Newc T from 77. *26 Cleveland Road, N Shields, T & W, NE29 0NG.* (N Shields 571721)

FERGUSON, Robert Garnett Allen. b 48. Univ of Leeds LLB 70. Cudd Coll 71. **d** 73 Pontefract for Wakef **p** 74 Wakef. C of All SS Cathl Wakef 73-76; V of Lupset Dio Wakef from 76. *Lupset Vicarage, Broadway, Wakefield, W Yorks, WF2 8AA.* (Wakefield 373088)

FERGUSON, Robin Sinclair. b 31. Worc Coll Ox BA (3rd cl Mod Hist) 53, MA 57. Certif Educn (Lon) 63. ALCD 55. Wycl Coll Tor 56. **d** 57 **p** 58 Lon. C of H Trin Brompton 57-60; St Matt Brixton 60-63; Asst Master St Mich AA Sch Framlingham 63-65; Place Farm Primary Sch Haverhill 65-67; Hon C of Framlingham 63-65; Haverhill 65-67; Chap St Mary Magd Secondary Sch Richmond 67-75; C of Richmond 67-76; Chap Croft Ho Sch Shillingstone from 76; R of Shillingstone Dio Sarum from 76. *Rectory, Shillingstone, Blandford, Dorset.* (0258-860261)

FERGUSON, Ronald Allan. Em Coll Sktn. **d** 58 Edmon **p** 61 Caled. On leave 58-61; C of Burns Lake 61-62; I of Chetwynd 62-65. *Box R, Innisfail, Alta, Canada.*

FERGUSON, Ronald Leslie. b 36. Chich Th Coll 65. **d** 68 Warrington for Liv **p** 69 Liv. C of St Marg Toxt Pk 68-72; C of Oakham 72-74; Asst Chap Dorothy Kerin Trust Burrswood 74-76; Castleside Dio Dur from 76. *Castleside Vicarage, Consett, Co Durham.* (Castleside 242)

FERGUSON, Wallace Raymond. b 47. Div Hostel Dub 76. **d** 78 **p** 79 Down. C of Shankill Lurgan 78-80; V of Movilla Abbey Ch Newtownards Dio Down from 80. *27 Old Movilla Road, Newtownards, Co Down, N Ireland.*

FERGUSON, William Alexander. RMC (Canada) BA 53. Univ of W Ont BA 55, MA 64. **d** 67 **p** 70 Tor. Hon C of All SS Tor 67-70; St Chad Tor 70-74; Perm to Offic Dio Carib 74; I of Jasper 74-79; Hinton 76-79; P-in-c of Ch of Nativ Malvern City and Dio Tor from 79. *127 Purvis Crescent, Scarborough, Ont, Canada.*

FERGUSON-DAVIE, Sir Arthur Patrick, Bt. b 09. Linc Coll Ox BA 39, MA 45. TD 54. Ely Th Coll 33. **d** 34 **p** 35 Ex. C of Littleham w Exmouth 34-37; CF (TA) 37; LPr Dio Ox 37-38; C of St Aug Kilburn 38-39; RA ChD Gibr 40-43; BNAF 43-44; CMF 44-45; Hon CF 46; PC of St John Torquay 45-48; L to Offic Dio Ex 49-74; Hon Chap to Bp of Ex 49-73; RD of Cadbury 66-67; L to Offic Dio Cyprus from 76. *Skalatos, Klepini, Kyrenia, Cyprus.*

FERGUSSON, James Bartram. Univ of Manit BA 59. Angl Th Coll BC LTh 63. **d** 63 **p** 64 New Westmr. C of Pender Harbour 63-64; Sechelt w Pender Harbour 64-66; R of Mission w Steelhead 66-68; Dir Relig Educn Dio Ja 68-76; Lect Ch Coll Mandeville from 76. *Box 41, Mandeville, Jamaica, W Indies.* (096-22601)

FERLEY, Canon John Harold. b 07. Lon Coll of Div 25. **d** 30 **p** 31 Lon. C of St Jo Bapt Hoxton 30-32; St Mark Leic 32-36; Kingston T 36-37; V of St Edm Dudley 37-50; Surr 41-50; V of St Jas w Pockthorpe Nor 50-52; C-in-c of St Martin-at-Palace Nor 50-52; V of St Edm Hunstanton 52-72; Surr from 53; RD of Heacham 66-72; Hon Can of Nor from 70; C-in-c of St Geo Tombland City and Dio Nor from 72. *10 Kingsley Road, Norwich, Norf, NR1 3RB.* (Nor 610268)

FERMER, Michael Thorpe. b 30. Univ of Lon BSc (2nd cl Maths) 52. ARCS 52. St Cath S Ox BA (2nd cl Th) 54. Wycl Hall Ox 52. **d** 54 Kens for Lon **p** 55 Lon. C of All SS Tufnell Pk Holloway 54-57; St Andr Plymouth 57-59; V of Tamerton Foliot 59-63; Asst Chap United Sheff Hosps 63-64; Sen Chap 64-66; Asst Master Thornbridge Secondary Sch Sheff 66-73; L to Offic Dio Sheff 66-73; V of Holmesfield 73-79; R of Old Brampton and Loundsley Green Dio Derby from 79. *Old Brampton Rectory, Chesterfield, Derbys, S42 7JG.* (Chesterfield 6422)

FERMOR, Alan Lewis. b 16. Worc Ordin Coll. **d** 65 Bp McKie for Cov **p** 66 Cov. C of Lillington 65-68; R of Barton-on-the-Heath 68-74; V of Wolford w Burmington 68-74; Burton Dassett w North End Dio Cov from 74; Gaydon w Chadshunt Dio Cov from 74. *Vicarage, North End, Leamington Spa, Warwicks, CV33 0TH.* (Fenny Compton 400)

FERN, John. b 36. Univ of Nottm BA (2nd cl Social Administration) 57. Coll of Resurr Mirfield. **d** 59 **p** 61 Southw. C of St Jo Bapt Carlton 59-61; Hucknall Torkard (in c of St Paul) 61-68; V of Rainworth Dio Southw from 68. *Vicarage, Southwell Road East, Rainworth, Nr Mansfield, Notts, NG21 0BW.*

FERNANCE, Don Robert. Moore Th Coll Syd. **d** 65 **p** 66 Bath. Bro of Good Shepherd Bourke 65-71; R of Condobolin 71-77; Gulgong Dio Bath from 77. *Box 17, Gulgong, NSW, Australia 2852.* (7422 44)

FERNENCE, Leslie Thornton. b 42. **d** and **p** 80 Armid. V of Lightning Ridge Dio Armid from 80. *PO Box 440, Lightning Ridge, NSW, Australia 2392.*

FERNLEY, Barry James. b 45. Melb Coll of Div LTh 76. **d** and **p** 75 C & Goulb. C of Albury 75-77; R of Holbrook 77-81; Brunswick Junction Dio Bunb from 81. *Rectory, Shines Crescent, Brunswick Junction, W Australia 6224.* (097-261051)

FERNS, Archdeacon of. *See* Ruddell, Ven Joseph Frith William.

FERNS, Bishop of. *See* Cashel.

FERNS, Dean of. *See* Earl, Very Rev David Kaye Lee.

FERNSBY, Jack. b 08. St Chad's Coll Dur. Long Pri 37, BA 39. Dipl Th 40. MA 42. **d** 40 **p** 41 Dur. C of St Cuthb Billingham 40-42; St Jo Div Kennington 42-46; Res Chap K Coll Hosp Denmark Hill 42-46; Perm to Offic at All SS Marg Street 46-47; St Jo Evang U Norwood 47-48; V of Weoley Castle w Bartley Green 48-51; Chap Shenley Fields Homes 50; V of Nether Stowey 51-55; Perm to Offic Dio Lich from 72. *15 Twmpath, Gobowen, Oswestry, Salop, SY10 7AQ.* (Oswestry 50473)

FERNYHOUGH, Ven Bernard. b 32. Late Scho of St D Coll Lamp BA (2nd cl Th) 53. **d** 55 **p** 56 Ja for Barb. C of Trinid Cathl 55-61; R of Stoke Bruerne w Grafton Regis and Alderton 61-67; RD of Preston 65-67; Haddon from 68; V of

E Haddon 67-68; V of Ravensthorpe (w E Haddon and Holdenby from 68) 67-77; R of Holdenby 67-68; RD of Brixworth 71-77; Can of Pet 74-77; Can Res from 77; Archd of Oakham from 77; Exam Chap to Bp of Pet from 77. *18 Minster Precincts, Peterborough.* (Peterborough 62762)

FERRABY, Canon Heneage. b 09. Clare Coll Cam BA (2nd cl Th Trip) 31, MA 35. Westcott Ho Cam 32. **d** 33 **p** 34 Ripon. C of St Geo w St Phil Leeds 33-37; V of Woodlands 37-44; R of Handsworth 44-81; Cler Sec Sheff Dioc Conf 44-70; RD of Attercliffe 46-78; Hon Can of Sheff 59-81; Can (Emer) from 81; Vice Pres Sheff Dioc Syn 70-78. *19 Spencer Gardens, East Sheen, SW14 7HA.* (01-878 6010)

FERREY, Quentin David. Rhodes Univ BA 63. St Paul's Coll Grahmstn 64. **d** 65 **p** 66 Johann. C of Rosebank 65-70; R of Auckland Pk 70-73; L to Offic Dio Johann 73-78; C of Krugersdorp Dio Johann from 78. *95 York Street, Krugersdorp, Johannesburg, S Africa.*

FERRIDAY, Donald Martin. b 30. St D Coll Lamp BA 55. Qu Coll Birm 55. **d** 57 **p** 58 Ches. C of St Sav Stockport 57-59; Heswall 59-64; V of All SS Cheadle Hulme 64-72; R of Ches (Team Parish from 72) 72-77; W Kirby Dio Ches from 77. *St Bridget's Rectory, West Kirby, Mer, L48 7HL.* (051-625 5229)

FERRIE, Russell Arnold. Em Coll Sktn. **d** 61 **p** 62 Sask. C of Loon Lake 61-63; R of Shellbrook 63-68; Yellowknife 69-73; Williams Lake 73-75; Team V of Langley Dio New Westmr from 76. *20853 Newlands Drive, Langley, BC, Canada.*

FERRIER, Malcolm. b 38. St Mich Coll Llan 67. **d** 69 **p** 70 Birm. C of Solihull 69-73; E Grinstead 73-75; V of Saltley Dio Birm from 75. *Saltley Vicarage, St Saviour's Road, Birmingham, B8 1HN.* (021-327 0570)

FERRIS, George William. b 47. McMaster Univ BA 69. Huron Coll Ont BTh 71. **d** 71 **p** 72 Hur. C of Six Nations Reserve W 71-72; I 72-76; Walkerton Dio Huron from 76. *Box 112, Walkerton, Ont., Canada.*

FERRIS, Ven John Homer. McMaster Univ Ont BA 40. Trin Coll Tor LTh 44, Hon DD 78. **d** and **p** 42 Niag. C of St Geo Guelph 42-44; R of Arthur 44-49; Milton 49-52; Port Colborne 52-59; Grace Ch Hamilton 59-64; Grimsby 64-77; Can of Niag 60-64; Dom Chap to Bp of Niag 61-63; Exam Chap to Bp of Niag 63-73; Archd of Niag and from 77; Linc 74-77; Dioc Regr Dio Niag from 77. *67 Victoria Avenue, South Hamilton, Ont, Canada.* (416-632 7809)

✠ **FERRIS, Right Rev Ronald Curry.** b 45. Univ of W Ont BA 70. Huron Coll Hon DD 82. **d** 70 **p** 71 Yukon. C of Old Crow 70-73; I of St Steph Lon, Ont 73-81; Cons Ld Bp Yukon in Ch Ch Cathl Whitehorse 1 March 81 by Actg Abp of BC; Bps of BC, Koot, Carib, Caled and Hur; and Bps March and Frame. *Box 4247, Whitehorse, Yukon Territory, Y1A 3T3, Canada.* (403-667 2247)

FERRIS, Royden Kenneth. K Coll NS LTh 64. **d** and **p** 65 Fred. C of Cambridge w Waterborough 65-66; I of Bright 66-70; R of Gagetown 70-76; Canning and Chipman Dio Fred from 76. *Newcastle Bridge, NB, Canada.*

FERRIS, William. **d** 73 Queb. C of St Clem Miss Labrador 73-74; R of New Carl 75-77; St Richard Vanc Dio New Westmr from 77. *1351 West 15th Street, N Vancouver, BC, Canada.*

FERRY, Francis James. **d** 15 **p** 17 Nel. C of Murchison NZ 15-16; V 16-18; P-in-c of Suburban N 18-20; V of Sounds 20-22; Takaka 22-24; LPr Dio Nel 24-26; Offg Min Dio Auckld 26-31; V of Mosgiel 31-35; Maniototo 35-42; Balclutha 42-45; Havelock w Pelorus 49-50; L to Offic Dio Nel 50-79; Perm to Offic Dio Wel from 79. *12 Kohutuhutu Road, Raumati Beach, NZ.*

FERRY, Raymond James. b 52. Univ Tor BSc 75. Wycl Coll Tor MDiv 80. **d** 80 Bp Read for Tor **p** 81 Tor. C of St Mich AA City and Dio Tor from 80. *611 St Clair Avenue West, Toronto, Ont, Canada.*

FESOBI, Robert Ekundayo. Im Coll Ibad 59. **d** 61 Ondo-B **p** 62 Ondo. P Dio Ondo-B 61-62; Dio Ondo from 62. *c/o Bishopscourt, PO Box 25, Ondo, Nigeria.*

FETENI, Hamilton Bozozo. b 39. **d** 80 Port Eliz. C of B Mizeki Miss New Brighton Dio Port Eliz from 80. *c/o PO Box 50, Kwazakele, Port Elizabeth 6205, S Africa.*

FETHNEY, John Garside. b 27. Linc Coll Ox BA 53. Linc Th Coll 51. **d** 53 Lon **p** 54 Kens for Lon. C of W Hackney 53-55; C-in-c 56; C of Cathl Ch of Resurr Lah 57 and 67-68; C-in-c of Pattoki Dio Lah 57-67; RD of Pattoki 63-67; Area Sec USPG and L to Offic Dio York 68-70; Dio Lon from 70; Deputn Sec USPG from 73; C of St Nich Cole Abbey Lon 73-80; Perm to Offic Dio Chich from 80. *21 Plover Close, East Wittering, Chichester, PO20 8PW.* (Bracklesham Bay 670145)

FEWKES, Jeffrey Preston. b 47. Wycl Hall Ox 72. **d** 75 **p** 76 Dur. C of Chester-le-Street 75-78; St Mark Kennington 78-81; V of St Jo Div Bulwell Dio Southw from 81. *St John's Vicarage, Squires Avenue, Bulwell, Nottingham, NG6 8GH.*

FFOLLIOTT, John Patrick. Em Coll Sktn 61. **d** 61 **p** 62 Rupld. R of Manitou 61-65; St Aug Grande Prairie 65-68; Commiss Ind Miss Dio Sktn 68-74; I of Deer Creek w Ft Pitt and Onion Lake 74-78. *c/o Church House, Cross Roads, Kingston, Jamaica.*

FFRENCH-BEYTAGH, Canon Gonville Aubie. b 12. St Paul's Coll Grahmstn LTh 38. **d** 38 **p** 39 Johann. C of Springs 38-41; Germiston 41-44; R 44-51; Dioc Sec of Johann Evang Coun 51-52; Can of Johann 52-54; P-in-c of St Alb Johann 52-54; Dean and R of Salisbury Rhod 54-64; Dean of Johann 65-71; Archd of Johann Centr 65-71; Hon Can of Johann from 72; Cant from 73; Chairman Transv, Rhod and Botswana Assoc 72-74; C of St Matt Westmr 73; R of St Vedast *alias* Foster City and Dio Lon from 74. *Rectory, Foster Lane, EC2V 6HH.* (01-606 3998)

FIANDER, Edward Joseph. K Coll NS BA 61, LTh 63. **d** 62 **p** 63 NS. I of New Lon 62-68; R of Springhill 68-74; Exam Chap to Bp of NS 75-79; Hosp Chap Halifax from 75. *1348 Tower Road, Halifax, NS, Canada.* (429-2334)

FIANDER, Lochleigh. b 30. **d** 75 Newfld (APM). C of Grand Bank Fortune Lamaline Dio Newfld (E Newfld from 76) from 75. *Fortune, FB, Newfoundland, Canada.*

FIDDAMAN, Ernest Robert. b 13. Chich Th Coll 77. **d** 78 Chich **p** 78 Horsham for Chich. C of St Jo w St Pet Preston Dio Chich from 78. *27 Chester Terrace, Brighton, Sussex, BN1 6GB.*

FIDDLER, Charles. b 40. **d** 77 Sask. C of Cumberland Ho Dio Sask from 77. *Cumberland House, Sask, Canada.*

FIDGIN, Canon Douglas Michael. b 15. Men in Disp 45. Linc Th Coll 46. **d** 49 **p** 50 Leic. C of St Pet Leic 49-52; S Afr Rly Miss Grahmstn 52 and Dio Pret 52-55; C of St Jo Bapt Greenhill Harrow 55-57; V of All SS Swindon 57-62; St Steph Hounslow 62-69; R of Owermoigne w Warmwell 70-76; Portland w Southw 76-81; Can of Sarum Cathl from 81; P-in-c of Urchfont w Stert Dio Sarum from 81. *Vicarage, Urchfont, Devizes, Wilts.* (Chirton 672)

FIDOE, Sidney. b 1892. Univ of Dur LTh 16. dorch Miss Coll 12. **d** 16 **p** 17 Ripon. C of H Spirit Beeston Hill Leeds 16-19; TCF 18-19; C of St Aid Leeds 19-20; V of St Barn Moose Jaw 20-26; C of Epping 26-27; CF (Canad) 24-26; C of Gt Ilford (in c of St Alb) 27-32; V of St Columba Wanstead Slip 32-44; R of Ch Ch Smeeton Westerby 44-65; L to Offic Dio Leic from 65. *13 The Oval, Market Harborough, Leics.*

FIELD, David Hibberd. b 36. K Coll Cam 1st cl Cl Trip pt i 56, BA (2nd cl Th Trip pt ii) 58. Oak Hill Th Coll 58. **d** 60 **p** 61 Guildf. C of H Trin Aldershot 60-63; H Trin Margate 63-66; Sec Th Studs Fellowship 66-68; Tutor Oak Hill Th Coll from 68; Vice-Prin from 79. *Oak Hill College, Chase Side, N14.* (01-440 3225)

FIELD, Donald Charles. b 21. Univ of Lon BSc 50. **d** 66 **p** 67 Glouc. C of Stonehouse 66-69; Tewkesbury 69-72; V of Standish (w Hardwicke to 74) and Haresfield (and Moreton Valance from 74) 72-79; P-in-c of Forthampton w Chaceley 79-80; Deerhurst w Apperley Dio Glouc 79-80; V (w Forthampton and Chaceley) from 80. *21 Apperley Park, Apperley, Gloucester, GL19 4EB.* (Tirley 506)

FIELD, Ernest John. b 1894. Em Coll Cam 2nd cl Hist Trip pt i, 22, BA (2nd cl Hist Trip pt ii) 23, MA 27. Westcott Ho Cam 23. **d** 25 **p** 26 Cant. C of St Sav Croydon 25-27; Asst Chap of Pro-Cathl Cairo 27-28; Chap of Suez 28-30; Heliopolis (and OCRAF) 30-31; C of Margate 32-34; Lyminge 34-35; V of Leysdown w Harty (and OCRAF Eastchurch) 35-43; V of St Sav Croydon 43-56; Chap Mayday Hosp 43-49; R of Chartham 56-66; Perm to Offic Dio Cant from 66. *22 St Stephen's Hill, Canterbury, Kent, CT2 7AX.* (Canterbury 61776)

FIELD, Geoffrey Alder. Ely Th Coll. **d** 47 Wakef **p** 48 Pontefract for York. C of St Paul King Cross Halifax 47-50; H Trin w St Mary (in c of St Pet) Ely 50-54; V of Whittlesey 54-75; Foxton 75-81. *14 Poplar Close, Great Sheldon, Cambridge, CB2 5LY.* (0223 842099)

FIELD, Gerald Gordon. b 54. AKC and BD 75. Coll of Resurr Mirfield 76. **d** 77 Lanc for Blackb **p** 78 Blackb. C of Broughton 77-79; St Steph Blackpool Dio Blackb from 79. *17 St Stephen's Avenue, Blackpool FY2 9RB.* (Blackpool 54273)

FIELD, Michael Alan. b 35. Oak Hill Th Coll 68. **d** 70 **p** 71 Lon. C of Ch Ch, Finchley 70-73; St Paul (in c of St Luke) St Alb 73-79; Min of St Paul Jersey Dio Win from 79. *Resthaven, Highlands Lane, St Saviour, Jersey, CI.* (Jersey 76129)

FIELD, Richard Colin. b 33. St Cath S Ox BA (2nd cl Mod Lang) 54, MA 63. Clifton Th Coll 63. **d** 65 **p** 66 Lon. C of Highbury 65-70; V of St Ann Stamford Hill Dio Lon from 70. *Vicarage, South Grove, N15 5QG.* (01-800 3506)

FIELD, Thomas Sidney. b 07. SOC 61. **d** 64 **p** 65 S'wark. C of S'wark Cathl 64-72; Hon C of Pewsey Dio Sarum from 72.

Little Ann Cottage, Milton Road, Pewsey, Wilts, SN9 5JW. (Pewsey 2344)

FIELD, William Jenkin. b 25. **d** 66 **p** 67 Llan. C of St Jo Bapt Cardiff 66-72; V of Llancarfan w Llantrithyd Dio Llan from 72. *Llancarfan Vicarage, Barry, S Glam.* (St Athan 241)

FIELDEN, Robert. b 32. Linc Th Coll 65. **d** 67 **p** 68 Linc. C of Bassingham 67-71; R of Anderby w Cumberworth Dio Linc from 72; P-in-c of Huttoft Dio Linc from 72; Mumby Dio Linc from 77. *Anderby Rectory, Skegness, Lincs, PE24 5YF.* (Huttoft 248)

FIELDER, Canon Arthur John. b 14. Univ of Lon (Richmond Coll) Dipl in Th 48. Bps' Coll Cheshunt. **d** 46 **p** 47 St Alb. C of All SS Luton 46-48; St Mary Magd Taunton 48-50; Bexhill 50-56; V of All SS Luton 56-61; Dioc Youth Chap Dio Leic 61-67; Dir Dioc Bd of Educn 67-77; L to Offic Dio Leic 61-78; Hon Can of Leic 67-77; Can (Emer) from 77; Master of Wyggeston's Hosp Leic 68-78. *185 Oliver Street, Ampthill, Beds, MK45 2SF.* (0525-402489)

FIELDER, Lloyd Bannerman. b 08. **d** 65 **p** 66 Portsm. Hon C of Botley 65-68; C of Warblington w Emsworth Dio Portsm 68-72; Hon C from 72. *Copsford, Park Crescent, Emsworth, Hants.*

FIELDGATE, John William Sheridan. b 44. **d** 79 Ox **p** 80 Buckingham for Ox (NSM). C of Haddenham w Cuddington & Kingsey Dio Ox from 79. *Candlemas Cottage, Flint Street, Haddenham, Aylesbury, HP17 8Al.*

FIELDING, Harold Ormandy. b 12. Magd Coll Cam 2nd cl Geog Trip pt i 34, BA (2nd cl Geog Trip pt ii) 35, MA 39. Ripon Hall Ox 35. **d** 36 **p** 37 Man. C of St Mary Virg Leigh 36-40; St Paul Walkden 40-44; V of St Jas New Bury 44-65; Chap Bolton Distr and Townleys Hosps 44-65; Bolton R Infirm from 65; V of Bolton-le-Moors Dio Man from 65; Can of Man 65-72; RD of Bolton 65-72; Surr from 65; Archd of Rochdale 72-82; M Gen Syn from 80. *Vicarage, Churchgate, Bolton, BL1 1PS.* (Bolton 33847)

FIELDING, John Joseph. b 29. TCD BA 53, Div Test 54, MA 65. **d** 54 **p** 55 Connor. C of St Luke Belf 54-57; St Mary Magd Belf 57-60; Chap Windsor Boys' Sch Hamm 61-69; St Edw Sch Ox 69-73; V of St Mich Highgate Dio Lon from 73. *10 The Grove, Highgate, N6 6LB.* (01-340 7279)

FIELDING, Canon Kenneth Edgar. b 14. Late Exhib of Ch Ch Ox BA (2nd cl Phil Pol and Econ) 36, MA 40. Ely Th Coll 39. **d** 40 **p** 41 Derby. C of Chesterfield 40-44; All SS King's Heath 44-45; Actg C-in-c of Perry Beeches 45-47; V of Shaw Hill 47-51; St Steph Smethwick 51-62; St Andr Handsworth 62-81; Hon Can of Birm Cathl from 71; RD of Handsworth 73-77. *12 High Beeches, Newton Road, Great Barr, Birmingham, B34 8AQ.*

FIELDING, Ven Ronald Jeffrey. Univ of Lon BSc 38. Qu Coll Birm 40. **d** 42 **p** 43 Birm. C of St Mary Selly Oak 42-46; H Cross E Pondoland 46-47; St Barn Ntlaza W Pondoland 47-49; P-in-c of Clydesdale 49-54; St Barn W Pondoland 54-57; Pret Miss Distr 57-61; P-in-c of All SS Silverton 61-63; Miss at Kwazakele Port Eliz 63-64; P-in-c of St Simon and St Jude Peddie 64-70; Dir of Relig Educn Dio Grahmstn 65-74; Archd of K Williams Tn 68-70; Albany 70-74; E Lon from 74; R of St Sav E Lon Dio Grahmstn from 75. *13 Belgravia Crescent, East London, CP, S Africa.* (2-3842)

FIELDING, William. b 35. St Jo Coll Dur BA 60. Ridley Hall, Cam. **d** 62 **p** 63 Blackb. C of St Mich AA Ashton-on-Ribble 62-64; Broughton 64-67; V of Knuzden 67-75; St Cuthb Darwen Dio Blackb from 75; RD of Darwen from 77. *St Cuthbert's Vicarage, Darwen, Lancs.* (Darwen 72793)

FIELDING-FOX, John Alfred. b 21. Univ of Wales BA 42. **d** 48 **p** 49 Llan. C of St Jo Evang Canton Cardiff 48-50; St Andr Cardiff 50-59; C-in-c of Barry Is Conv Distr 59-66; V of Hammerwich Dio Lich from 66. *Hammerwich Vicarage, Walsall, Staffs.* (Burntwood 6088)

FIELDSEND, John Henry. b 31. Univ of Nottm BSc (2nd cl Eng) 54. Univ of Lon BD 61. ALCD 59. **d** 61 **p** 62 Man. C of Pennington 61-64; Ch Ch W Didsbury 64-66; C-in-c of Bayston Hill Dio Lich 66-67; V from 67. *Bayston Hill Vicarage, Shrewsbury, Salop.* (Bayston Hill 2164)

FIENNES, *See* Twisleton-Wykeham-Fiennes.

FIFE, Canon John Ross. Univ of Sask BA 38. Em Coll Sktn LTh 38, Hon DD 72. Ball Coll Ox BA 47, MA 51. Chevalier de l'O de Léopold II avec palme (Belgian) and Croix de Guerre avec palme (Belgian) 40. **d** 38 **p** 39 Sktn. Miss at Carrangana 38-39; C of Ch Ch Cathl Vic 39-42; Chap CASF 42-45; on staff of Em Coll Sktn 47-74; Exam Chap to Bp of Sktn 53-74; I of H Trin Sktn 68-70; Hon Can of Sktn 73-79; Can (Emer) from 79; Lect Pacific Th Coll Suva 74-79; Offg Min Dio Polyn 74-79; R of Huntingdon-Ormstown Dio Montr from 79. *62 Wellington Street, Huntingdon, PQ, Canada.* (514-264 3475)

FIFIELD, Cecil. Qu Coll Newfld LTh 61. **d** 61 **p** 62 Newfld. C of Corner Brook 62-69; R of Lewisporte 69-77; Hon C of St Jo Bapt Cathl St John's Dio E Newfld 78-81; C from 81. *52 Forbes Street, St John's, Newfoundland, Canada.*

FIFIELD, William Herbert. b 04. Univ of Wales BA 26. Ripon Hall Ox 27. **d** 28 **p** 29 Swan B. C of St Mark Swansea 28-30; St Andr Cardiff 30-34; Ch Ch Brondesbury 34-35; Aston-juxta- Birm (in c of St Martin Perry Common) 35-39; V of Attleborough 39-79. *102 Lutterworth Road, Nuneaton, Warws.* (Nuneaton 342308)

FILBY, John Michael. b 34. Oak Hill Th Coll 56. **d** 60 **p** 61 Roch. C of St Jo Evang Penge 60-64; St Jo Bapt Folkestone 64-66; Perm to Offic Dio Roch 66-68; Dio Guildf 68-71; Dio Chelmsf 71-75; R of Broxted w Chickney, Tilty and L Easton Dio Chelmsf from 75. *Rectory, Little Easton, Dunmow, Essex.* (Great Dunmow 2509)

FILBY, Canon William Charles Leonard. b 33. Univ of Lon BA 58. Oak Hill Th Coll 53. **d** 59 **p** 60 Chich. C of All S Eastbourne 59-62; St Jo Bapt Woking (in c of H Trin Knaphill) 62-65; V of H Trin Richmond 65-71; Bp Hannington Mem Ch w H Cross Hove 71-79; M Gen Syn from 75; R of Broadwater Dio Chich from 79; RD of Worthing from 80; Can and Preb of Chich Cathl from 81. *Broadwater Rectory, Worthing, Sussex.* (Worthing 33182)

FILE, Ronald Sidney Omer. b 20. Bps' Coll Cheshunt 58. **d** 60 Croydon for Cant **p** 61 Cant. C of St Steph Norbury 60-62; St Jo Bapt Croydon 62-66; C of Clee Grimsby 68-72; R of Trusthorpe 72-75; V of Bardney w Southrey Dio Linc 76-78; Stainfield w Apley 76-78; R of Gautby and Waddingworth 76-78; R of Bardney 78-80; Dir of Chr Counselling Centre Hong Kong from 80. *St John's Cathedral, Hong Kong.*

FILE, Roy Stephen. Univ of Leeds BA 50. Coll of Resurr Mirfield 50. **d** 53 **p** 54 Liv. C of Par Ch Liv 53-55; St John Pemberton 55-57; V of St Olave Mitcham 57-66; R of Plumstead Capetn 66-76; Somerset W, Capetn 76-80; V of St Marg Ilkley Dio Bradf from 80. *Vicarage, St Margaret's Terrace, Ilkley, LS29 9NA.* (Ilkley 607015)

FILER, Victor John. b 43. Sarum Th Coll 66. **d** 69 **p** 70 S'wark. C of Mortlake Dio S'wark from 69. *3 Christchurch Road, SW 14.*

FILER, Ven William Alfred. Wycl Coll Tor. **d** 24 **p** 25 Niag. Miss at Omagh and Palermo 24-25; C of St Anne Tor 26-27; Epiph Ch Tor 29-30; I of St Paul w St Luke Brantford Ont 30-31; C of St Luke St John 31-33; R 33-41; All SS Peterborough 41-47; RD of Peterborough 43-47; R of St Pet Hamilton Dio Niag 47-64; Hon C from 76; Archd of Hamilton 62-67; Archd (Emer) from 68. *38 Sunning Hill Avenue, Hamilton 56, Ont, Canada.* (416-389 7260)

FILLERY, Robert James. b 11. Tyndale Hall Bris 47. **d** 48 **p** 49 S'wark. C of Hatcham 48-51; Watford 51-56; Min of St Luke's Legal Distr Watford 56-59; V of Walmley 59-67; R of Kirby Cane 67-71; R of Ellingham (w Kirby Cane from 69) 67-78. *31 St James's Crescent, Belton, Great Yarmouth, Norf, NR31 9JN.* (Gt Yarmouth 781713)

FILLERY, William Robert. b 42. Univ of Wales BA (Engl) 65. St D Coll Lamp BD 69. **d** 68 **p** 69 Swan B. C of Llangyfelach w Morriston 68-71; Morriston 71-72; Hon C 72-73; Asst Master Cefn Hengoed Sch Swansea 72-73; Cox Green Sch Maidenhead 73-76; L to Offic Dio Ox 73-76; Chap and Asst Master Windsor Girls' Sch Hamm, W Germany 76-81; OCF Hamm 79-81; Chap Reeds Sch Cobham from 81. *Reeds School, Sandy Lane, Cobham, Surrey, KT11 2ES.* (Cobham 4057)

FILLINGHAM, Ven Robert Gordon. MBE 80. Moore Th Coll Syd ACT ThL 44. **d** and **p** 45 Syd. C of Kangaroo Valley 45; St Jo Bapt Milson's Point 45-46; C-in-c of Ashbury 46-47; S Canterbury Par 47-48; Gen Sec Home Miss S Dio Syd 49-64 and from 75; Hon Can of Syd 60-64; Archd of Parramatta (w N Syd from 67) 64-75; N Sydney from 75. *St Andrew's House, Sydney Square, Sydney, NSW, Australia 2000.* (2-0642)

FINCH, Alfred John. b 10. Trin Coll Dub BA and Div Test (2nd cl) 33, MA 36. **d** 33 **p** 34 Down. C of Kilmegan w Maghera 33-37; Ch Ch Belf 37-43; R of Tyrella w Rathmullen 43-55; Knocknamuckley 55-75. *4 Shimnavale, Newcastle, Co Down, N Ireland.* (Newcastle 22202)

FINCH, Barry Marshall Palmer. b 23. Hertf Coll Ox BA 47, MA 48. Westcott Ho Cam 47. **d** 49 **p** 50 Lich. C of Alrewas w Fradley 49-51; Birchington 51-56; R of Harrietsham 56-66; Chap Westmr Hosp Lon 66-73; V of Chipping Sodbury w Old Sodbury Dio Glouc from 73; Surr from 75. *Chipping Sodbury Vicarage, Bristol, BS17 6ET.* (Chipping Sodbury 313159)

FINCH, Christopher. b 41. Univ of Lon BA (2nd cl Engl) and AKC 63. BD (Lon) 69. Sarum Th Coll 63. **d** 65 **p** 66 Ox. C of High Wycombe 65-69; Prec of St Martin's Cathl Leic 69-73; C-in-c of L Bowden 73; R 73-81; V of Evington Dio Leic from 81. *Evington Vicarage, Leicester.* (Leic 712032)

FINCH, Canon Edward Alfred. b 23. BSc (Lon) 50. Sarum Th Coll 50. **d** 52 **p** 53 Lon. C of Wealdstone 52-55; E Grinstead 55-59; V of St Pet Walthamstow 59-70; Can Res of

Chelmsf and Bp's Adv for Social Work from 70; Dir Dept of Miss from 77. *St Clare, Links Drive, Chelmsford, Essex.* (Chelmsf 353914)

FINCH, Frank. b 33. Qu Coll Birm 72. **d** 74 **p** 75 Lich. C of St Leon Bilston 74-78; R of Sudbury w Somersal Herbert Dio Derby from 78; Chap HM Pris Sudbury Pk from 78; HM Detention Centre Foston Hall from 80. *Sudbury Rectory, Derby, DE6 5HS.* (Sudbury 302)

FINCH, Frederick. b 22. Lon Coll of Div 59. **d** 60 **p** 61 Man. C of St Pet Halliwell 60-63; V of Tonge Fold 63-68; W Midl Area Sec CPAS 68-71; V of Ch Ch Blackpool 71-77; C of Greenfield Pk, Queb 78-79; P-in-c of St Jos of Nazareth Brossard Dio Montr from 80. *5590 Varin Street, Brossard, Montreal, J4W 1E3, Canada.*

FINCH, Ven Geoffrey Grenville. b 23. St Pet Hall Ox Nat Sc Hons 43, BA 47, 2nd cl Th 49, MA 49. Wycl Hall Ox 48. Wells Th Coll 50. **d** 50 Warrington for Liv **p** 51 Liv. C of Wigan 50-54; V of St Pet Westleigh 54-60; R of Milton 60-71; Proc Conv Win from 64; RD of Christchurch 66-71; Archd of Basingstoke from 71; V of Preston Candover w Nutley and Bradley 71-76; M Gen Syn Win 73-80. *3 Crossborough Hill, Basingstoke, Hants, RG21 2Ag.* (Basingstoke 28572)

FINCH, John. b 20. Bps' Coll Cheshunt, 59. **d** 61 **p** 62 York. C of St Paul Middlesbrough 61-64; V of Easington w Skeffling and Kilnsea 64-68; St Matt Habergham Eaves Burnley 68-75; Garstang Dio Blackb from 75. *St Helen's Vicarage, Garstang, Preston, PR3 0HS.* (Garstang 2294)

FINCH, Paul William. b 50. Dipl Th (Lon) 73. Oak Hill Coll 73. **d** 75 **p** 76 Ches. C of Hoole 75-78; Charlesworth Dio Derby from 78. *St John's Vicarage, Charlesworth, Hyde, Chesh, SK14 6DA.* (Glossop 2440)

FINCH, Richard Michael. b 22. Selw Coll Cam BA (2nd cl Th Trip pt ia) 47, MA 49. Cudd Coll. **d** 49 **p** 50 Chelmsf. C of Maldon 49-52; Finchley 52-56; Min of H Cross Distr Woodingdean 56-62; V of Westfield 62-79; P-in-c of Laughton w Ripe and Chalvington Dio Chich from 79. *Rectory, Shortgate Lane, Laughton, Lewes, E Sussex, BN8 6DQ.* (Ripe 491)

FINCH, Ronald. b 15. Qu Coll Birm 79. **d** and **p** 80 Glouc. C of Welford w Weston and Clifford Chambers Dio Glouc from 80. *Harmony, Luddington, Straford-on-Avon, Warwicks, CV37 9SJ.*

FINCH, Stanley James. b 31. Mert Coll Ox 2nd cl Cl Mods 53, BA (2nd cl Lit Hum) 55, MA 58. Wells Th Coll 55. **d** 57 **p** 58 Blackb. C of Lanc 57-61; C and Prec of Leeds 61-65; V of Habergham 65-73; H Trin S Shore Blackpool Dio Blackb from 73. *Holy Trinity Vicarage, South Shore, Blackpool, Lancs.* (Blackpool 42362)

FINCH, Thomas. Univ of Lon BD (2nd cl) 57. Edin Th Coll 48. **d** and **p** 51 Aber. Chap St Andr Cathl Aber 51-55; St Cypr Clarence Gate 55-58; V of Warmington 58-67; St Mary Wellingborough Dio Pet from 67; RD of Oundle 62-67. *St Mary's Vicarage, Wellingborough, Northants.* (Wellingborough 222461)

FINCHAM, Frank Goldworth. b 1896. **d** 24 **p** 25 Truro. C of St Paul Truro 24-26; St Mark Leic 26-29; Somersham (in c of Pidley and Fenton) 29-32; Brighton 32-36; V of E Preston w Kingston 36-69; Perm to Offic Dio Chich from 69. *53 Norfolk Gardens, Littlehampton, Sussex.* (Rustington 4588)

FINCHER, John Farram. St Jo Coll Armid. **d** 48 **p** 49 Armid. C of Gunnedah 48-52; V of Walgett 52-55; Bingara 55-60; Quirindi Dio Armid from 60. *Vicarage, Quirindi, NSW, Australia 2343.* (Quirindi 59)

FINDLAY, Brian James. b 42. Univ of Wellington BA 62, MA 63, BMus 66. Univ of Birm Dipl Th 71. Magd Coll Ox MA 75. Qu Coll Birm 69. **d** 72 **p** 73 S'wark. C of St Paul w St Mark Deptford 72-75; Fell and Dean of Div Magd Coll Ox from 75. *Magdalen College, Oxford.*

FINDLAY, Melvin John. K Coll Halifax NS BA 53, BS Litt 54. **d** and **p** 54 NS. R of Port Hill 54-59; Martin's Point 59-65; Wilmot Dio NS from 65. *244 Main Street, Middleton, NS, Canada.* (825-3128)

FINDLAY, Robert Campbell. ACT ThL 37. **d** 28 **p** 36 Melb. C of St Aug Moreland 28-29; St Columb Hawthorn 29-31; St Bart Burnley 32-33; Perm to Offic Dio Melb 33-35; C of St Thos Essendon 35-36; Min of Inverleigh w Meredith 36-41; All SS Preston 42-46; I of St Alb Armadale 46-65. *92 Roslyn Street, Burwood, Vic, Australia 3125.* (03-288 6558)

FINDLAYSON, Bryan. Moore Coll Syd ThL 70. **d** 71 **p** 72 Syd. C of Narrabeen 71; Cronulla 72-75; St Geo Engadine 75-78; C-in-c of Helensburgh Dio Syd from 78. *72 Walker Street, Helensburgh, NSW, Australia.* (042-94 1024)

FINDLEY, Canon Frederick. AKC 34. Sarum Th Coll 34. **d** 35 Lich for Cov **p** 36 Cov. C of St Jo Bapt Cov 35-37; R of Ficksburg 37-45; Dir of Ficksburg Miss 41-45; R of St Marg Bloemf 45-49; R and Sub-Dean of Bloemf Cathl 49-50; R and Dean 51-58; Archd of Bloemf City 51-58; Can of Bloemf 49-58; Can (Emer) from 58; R of Stellenbosch and Chap to Univ 58-67; Can of Capetn 61-63; Archd of Paarl 63-70; R of St Alb Green Point 67-75; Ed of *Seek* 69-78; R of Ch K Claremont 75-78; Perm to Offic Dio Capetn from 78. *5 Carbrook Avenue, Claremont, CP, S Africa.* (61-3214)

FINDLOW, Oliver Lofgren Calrow. b 1897. Worc Ordin Coll 55. **d** 56 **p** 57 Lich. C of H Trin Burton-on-Trent 56-58; Chap Industr Chr Fellowship 58-60; C of K Lynn 60-62; V of St Mark Walsall 62-70. *The Poplars, Norwich Road, Cromer, Norf, NR27 0HZ.*

FINDON, John Charles. b 50. Keble Coll Ox BA 71, MA 75, Dipl Th 76, DPhil 79. Ripon Coll Cudd 75. **d** 77 Man **p** 78 Bp Hulme for Man. C of Middleton 77-80; Lect of Bolton-le-Moors Dio Man from 80. *63 Bradford Street, Bolton, BL2 1HT.* (Bolton 393615)

FINEANGANOFO, Sosaia Ala. St John's Coll Suva, 63. **d** 65 **p** 67 Polyn. P Dio Polyn. *PO Box 31, Nuku'alofa, Tonga.*

FINKENSTAEDT, Harry Seymour. b 23. Yale Univ Conn BA 49. Univ of Mass MA 68, Episc Th Sch Mass BD 50. **d** 53 Bp Donegan NY **p** 54 Bp Kennedy Honolulu. In Amer Ch 53-71; C of Hazlemere 71-73; Huntingdon 73-75; V of Shudy Camps Dio Ely from 75; R of Castle Camps Dio Ely from 75; P-in-c of Horseheath 79-81; W Wickham Dio Ely from 79. *Shudy Camps Rectory, Cambridge, CB1 6RB.* (Ashdon 260)

FINLAY, Donald. St Mich Th Coll Crafers, 49. **d** 53 Adel **p** 53 Perth. C of Willagee 54-56; P-in-c of Merredin 56; R 57-58; Boyup Brook 58-60; St Paul's Cathl Bunb 60-64; Hon Chap to Bp of Bunb 60-78; R of Corrigin-Kondinin 64-68; Kojonup 68-73; Gnowangerup 73-75; Marg River 75-78; L to Offic Dio Bunb from 78. *220 Bussell Highway, W Busselton, W Australia 6280.*

FINLAY, Michael Stanley. b 45. NOC 78. **d** 81 Liv. C of Padgate Dio Liv from 81. *15 Woodpecker Close, Oakwood, Birchwood, Warrington, WA3 6RQ.*

FINLAY, Ven Terence Edward. Univ of W Ont BA 59. Jes Coll Cam BA 64, MA 68. Hur Coll BTh 62. **d** 61 Hur **p** 62 Bp Townshend for Hur. On leave 62-64; I of All SS Waterloo 64-66; St Aid Lon 66-68; R of St Jo Evang Lon 68-78; Exam Chap to Bp of Hur 70-78; Can of Hur 75-78; Archd of Brant from 78; R of Grace Ch Brantford Dio Hur from 78. *15 Albion Street, Brantford, Ont., Canada.* (519-752 6814)

FINLAYSON, Duncan. b 24. **d** and **p** 76 St Andr (APM). C of Bridge of Allan Dio Dunb from 76. *29 Cawder Road, Bridge of Allan, Stirling, FK9 4JJ.* (Bridge of Allan 3074)

FINN, Gordon Frederick. b 33. Univ of Dur BA (2nd cl German) 60. Ely Th Coll 60. **d** 62 **p** 63 Lich. C of St Mary Kingswinford 62-65; St Mary Virg Northn 65-67; Chap Barnsley Hall and Lea Hosps Bromsgrove 67-71; C of Swanage 71-73; P-in-c Ford End 73-79; V of St Oswin's S Shields Dio Dur from 79. *Vicarage, St Oswin's Street, South Shields, T & W, NE33 4SE.* (S Shields 553072)

FINNAMORE, Albert John. b 26. Trin Coll Dub BA 49, Div Test (2nd cl) 51, Higher Dipl in Educn 53, MA 57. **d** 51 **p** 52 Ferns. C of Wexford 51-53; Asst Master Dundalk Gr Sch 53-54; Hd Master from 54; L to Offic Dio Arm from 54. *Dundalk Grammar School, Co Louth, Irish Republic.*

FINNEMORE, Ernest Harold. b 28. Keble Coll Ox BA (2nd cl Math) 49, MA 53, Dipl Th 52. St Steph Ho Ox 51. **d** 53 **p** 54 Wakef. C of Almondbury 53-55; Talke 55-57; V of Longnor w Reapsmoor Newtown and Hollinsclough 57-64; Hanford Dio Lich from 64. *Hanford Vicarage, Stoke-on-Trent, Staffs.* (Stoke-on-Trent 57848)

FINNEY, Ven Charles William. b 27. **d** 59 **p** 60 Oss. C of Dunleckney 59-62; I of Abbeyleix 62-72; R of Edenderry Dio Kild from 72; Clonsast w Clonbulloge Rathangan and Thomastown Dio Kild from 72; RD of Kild 75-76; Can and Treas of St Brigid's Cathl Kild 76-79; Archd of Kild from 79. *Rectory, Edenderry, Offaly, Irish Republic.*

FINNEY, David. b 41. St Mich Coll Llan 68. **d** 70 Hulme for York **p** 71 Man. C of Wm Temple Ch Woodhouse Pk 70-73; St Thos Bedford-Leigh 73-75; V of St Anne Longsight Royton 75-81; Dearnley Dio Man from 81. *Dearnley Vicarage, Littleborough, Gtr Man, OL15 8NJ.* (Littleborough 78466)

FINNEY, Fred. b 17. Univ of Bris BA (2nd cl Engl) 38, Dipl Educn 39. Wycl Hall Ox 61. **d** 62 Warrington for Liv **p** 63 Liv. C of Gt Crosby 62-66; V of St Thos Ashton-in-Makerfield Dio Liv from 66. *St Thomas's Vicarage, Ashton-in-Makerfield, Wigan, Lancs.* (Ashton 77275)

FINNEY, Gordon Hurd. b 49. Univ of Tor BA 72, MA 75. Wycl Coll Tor MDiv 78. **d** 78 **p** 79 Tor. C of St Paul Bloor Street Tor 78-80; I of Elmvale Dio Tor from 80. *Box 162, Elmvale, Ont, Canada.*

FINNEY, John Thomas. b 27. Univ of Sheff BA 51. Ripon Hall Ox 60. **d** 62 Hulme for Man **p** 63 Man. C of Leigh 62-65; V of Peel 65-69; Chap Hockerill Coll Bp's Stortford 69-74; V of Astley Dio Man from 74. *Vicarage, Astley, Manchester.* (Atherton 883313)

FINNEY, John Thornley. b 32. Hertf Coll Ox BA (2nd cl Jurispr) 55, Dipl Th 57. Wycl Hall Ox. **d** 58 **p** 59 Ox. C of All SS Highfield Ox 58-61; Weston Turville 61-65; Tollerton 65-71; V of Aspley 71-80; Surr from 72; Sec of Dioc Syn

Southw 73-77; Asst Sec from 77; Bp's Adv on Evang Dio Southw from 80. *14 Devonshire Road, Sherwood, Nottingham, NG5 2EW.* (Nottm 620272)

FINNEY, Melva Kathleen. d 56 **p** 78 Ch Ch. dss Dio Lon 56-59; Novice of the Sisters of the Love of God Fairacres Ox 59-61; C of Fendalton 61-63; Chap Princess Marg & Sunnyside Hosps Ch Ch from 63. *22 Gunns Crescent, Christchurch 2, NZ.* (327-100)

FINNIMORE, Keith Anthony. b 36. K Coll Lon and Warm AKC 59. **d** 60 **p** 61 Chelmsf. C of H Trin Hermon Hill 60-63; Kingswood 63-65; V of Bolney 65-67; Elmstead 67-75; R of Foxearth w Pentlow Liston and Borley 73-77. *c/o Foxearth Rectory, Sudbury, Suff.* (Sudbury 75697)

FIRBY, Herbert. Clifton Th Coll. **d** 33 **p** 34 York. C of St Matt Hull 33-36; V of Eastrington 36-42; Hedon 42-47; Kirk Levington 47-55; V of High w Low Worsall 47-55; Kilham 55-57; Mapleton 57-59. *Address temp unknown.*

FIRMAGE, David Edward. Moore Th Coll Syd ACT ThL 65. **d** 66 Bp Loane for Syd **p** 67 Syd. C of Punchbowl 66-70; St Mark Darling Point Syd 70-71; Chap Norfolk I 71-74; C-in-c of Berowra Dio Syd from 75. *Berowra Waters Road, Berowra, NSW, Australia 2081.* (451-1285)

FIRMAN, Lewis Edward. Ridley Coll Melb ACT ThL 53. **d** and **p** 54 Melb. C of Ivanhoe 54-56; Min of Gisbourne 56-58; R of E Preston 58-60; Perm to Offic Dio Melb 60-63; Dio Perth 63-65; CF (Austr) 66-70 and 75-78; V of Golden Square 70-74; L to Offic Dio Perth 74-78; Chap St Mary's Girls' Sch Perth from 79. *38 Elmwood Avenue, Woodlands, W Australia 6018.* (341-1022)

FIRTH, Barry. b 37. FCA 71. N-W Ordin Course 74. **d** 77 **p** 78 Wakef. C of Brighouse 77-81; V of St Thos Batley Dio Wakef from 81. *St Thomas' Vicarage, Rutland Road, Batley, W Yorks.*

FIRTH, Christopher John Kingsley. b 37. Univ of Wales Dipl Th 66. St Mich Coll Llan 63. **d** 66 **p** 67 Southw. C of Sutton-in-Ashfield 66-70; V of Langold 70-74; C of Falmouth 74-77; P-in-c of Mabe Dio Truro 77-81; V from 81. *Vicarage, Rajel, Church Road, Mabe, Penryn, TR10 9HN.* (Penryn 73201)

FIRTH, Cyril Bruce. b 05. Fitzw Ho Cam BA 28, MA 32. Cheshunt Coll Cam 25. **d** 65 **p** 66 Win. Hon C of Wellow Dio Win from 65; Asia Sec Conf of Miss S of Gt Britain and Ireland 65-74. *Steplake Cottage, Sherfield English, Romsey, Hants, SO5 0EP.*

FIRTH, George Cuthbert. b 19. Keble Coll Ox BA 41, MA 45. Lich Th Coll 41. **d** 43 **p** 44 Lich. C of Shelton 43-46; Miss to the Deaf and Dumb and L to Offic Dio Ox 46-49; L Pr Dio Man and Supt of Rochdale and Distr Adult Deaf and Dumb S 49-52; Chap Wilts and Dorset Assoc for Deaf and Dumb 52-58; R of Steeple Langford 58-64; Welfare Officer Cornw 64-66; Perm to Offic Dio Truro 64-66; Chap and Sen Welfare Officer S Staffs and Salop 66-74; L to Offic Dio Lich 66-71; C-in-c of Patshull 71-73; Dioc Chap to the Deaf Staffs 72-74; Ex from 74; L to Offic Dio Ex from 74. *15 Thornton Hill, Exeter, EX4 4NN.* (Ex 75568)

FIRTH, Graham Alfred. b 38. Univ of Man BA 60. Ripon Hall Ox. **d** 62 Bp Gerard for York **p** 63 Sheff. C of St Paul Norton Lees 62-65; C-in-c of St John's Conv Distr Kimberworth Pk Dio Sheff 65-69; V 69-71; Laxton 71-77; C-in-c of Egmanton 71-77; Dioc Adv in Chr Stewardship Dio Southw 71-81; R of Elston Dio Southw from 77; V of E Stoke w Syerston Dio Southw from 77; Sibthorpe Dio Southw from 77. *Elston Rectory, Newark, Notts.* (E Stoke 383)

FIRTH, Canon Harold. b 13. St Aug Coll Cant 35. **d** 39 **p** 40 Wakef. C of Liversedge 39-41; Ripponden (in c of Rishworth) 41-43; Chap RNVR 43-46; RN 46-55; R of H Trin Elgin 55-71; Educn Adv Dio Moray 60-71; Can of Inverness Cathl 61-71; Hon Can from 71; Ed Dioc Quarterly 62-71; V of Charlbury w Shorthampton 71-79; RD of Chipping Norton 74-79. *65 Fosseway Avenue, Moreton-in-Marsh, Glos, GL56 0EB.* (M-in-M 50218)

FIRTH, Leonard Peter. b 51. Ridley Coll Melb ThL 74. **d** and **p** 75 Perth. C of Claremont 75-77; R of Trayning Dio Perth from 77. *Box 29, Trayning, W Australia 6488.*

FIRTH, Canon Peter James. b 29. Late Exhib of Em Coll Cam (2nd cl Mod and Med Lang Trip pt i) 52, 3rd cl Hist Trip pt i, 51, BA 52, MA 63. St Steph Ho Ox 53. **d** 55 **p** 56 Worc. C of St Steph Barbourne Worc 55-58; Malvern Link 58-62; R of St Geo Abbey Hey 62-66; Relig Broadcasting Asst N Region BBC 66-67; Sen Producer Relig Programmes Bris and L to Offic Dio Bris from 74; Can of Bris from 74. *Broadcasting House, Whiteladies Road, Bristol 8.*

FIRTH, Ronald Mahlon. Linc Th Coll 60. **d** 61 **p** 62 York. C of Marske-in-Cleveland 61-64; Thornaby-on-Tees 64-66; V of St Thos York 66-73; Marton-in-Cleveland Dio York from 73. *Marton-in-Cleveland Vicarage, Middlesbrough, TS7 8JU.* (Middlesbrough 36201)

FISH, Winthrop. b 40. Dalhousie Univ NS BA 63. Univ of Birm BPhil 76, MEd 78. **d** 64 **p** 65 NS. I of Arichat 64-66; Neil's Harbour 66-67; I of Baddeck 66-67; Cut Knife 68-70; Perm to Offic Dio NS 70-74; Dio Birm from 74; Dio Cov from 79; Asst Chap Solihull Sch Birm from 77; Chap Wroxall Abbey Sch from 79. *17 Westbourne Road, Olton, Solihull, W Midl, B92 8AT.* (021 706 9736)

FISHER, Adrian Charles Procter. b 24. Trin Coll Dub BA 48, Div Test 48, MA 62. **d** 49 **p** 50 Leigh. C of Carlow 49-52; CF 52-57 and 62-69; I of Fethard U Wexf 57-62; C-in-c of N Stoke w Ipsden and Mongewell Dio Ox from 70. *Vicarage, North Stoke, Oxford, OX9 6BG.* (Wallingford 35077)

FISHER, Arthur Stanley Theodore. b 06. Univ of Ox Abbott Scho 24. Ch Ch Ox BA 27, MA 31. Cudd Coll 28. **d** 31 **p** 32 Sarum. Chap Bryanston Sch Blandford 31; C of Bassaleg (in c of St John Rogerstone) 32-33; V of Wells Cathl 34; Asst Master Leeds Gr Sch 37-43; Perm to Offic Dio Ripon 37-38; L to Offic 38-43; Asst Master De Aston Sch Market Rasen and LPr Dio Linc 43-46; Chap and Asst Master Magd Coll Sch Ox 46-60; L to Offic Dio Ox 46; Fellows' Chap Magd Coll Ox 50-58; R of Westwell w Holwell 61-73; Hon Sec Ox Dioc Adv C'tee from 79. *72 Rosamund Road, Wolvercote, Oxford, OX2 8NX.* (Ox 56978)

FISHER, David Benjamin. b 52. Chich Th Coll 75. **d** 78 **p** 79 Liv. C of Dovecot 78-81; St Paul Weymouth Dio Sarum from 81. *49e Abbotsbury Road, Weymouth, Dorset, DT4 0AQ.*

FISHER, Eric William. b 30. Univ of Birm BA (Hist) 53. Coll of Resurr Mirfield 70. **d** 72 **p** 73 Cov. C of Styvechale 72-75; Chesterfield 75-78; Team V of Buxton Dio Derby from 78. *2a New Market Street, Buxton, Derbys, SK17 9AN.*

FISHER, Ernest George Reginald. b 15. St Aid Coll 66. **d** 68 **p** 69 Derby. C of St Thos Brampton 68-71; C-in-c of Langley Mill 71-79. *3 Love Lane, Berwick-upon-Tweed, Northumb, TD15 1AR.* (Berwick 4011)

FISHER, Ernest William. St Jo Coll Dur BA 56, Dipl Th 58. Cranmer Hall Dur 58. **d** 58 Worc for Hong **p** 59 Hong. Asst Chap St Jo Cathl Hong 58-60; Chap and Asst Master Dioc Boys' Sch Hong Kong 60-65; St Paul's Coll Hong Kong 65-70; C of Whiston 70-71; Chap St Paul's Coll Hong Kong from 71; L to Offic Dio Hong from 72. *c/o St Paul's College, Bonham Road, Hong Kong.* (5-462241)

FISHER, Francis Vivian. Selw Th Coll **d** 18 **p** 19 Dun. C of All SS Dun 18-21; V of Wyndham 21-24; Winton 24-25; Roxburgh 25-29; Mornington 29-37; Addington 37-48; Hinds 48-52; RD of Centr Ch Ch 41-48; L to Offic Dio Ch Ch 52-59; Hon Can Ch Ch 56-59; C of Opawa 59-66. *23 Chancellor Street, Shirley, Christchurch, NZ.*

FISHER, George Arthur. St Jo Coll Morpeth, LTh 34. **d** 33 **p** 34 Newc. C of Morpeth 33-35; Hamilton 36; Gosford 36-37; Woy Woy 37-40; P-in-c of Coopernook 41-43; Terrigal 44-53; Merriwa 53-60; Birm Gardens 60-71; R of Clarence Town 72-78; Perm to Offic Dio Newc from 78. *68 Grey Street, Clarence Town, NSW, Australia 2321.*

FISHER, Gordon. b 44. N-W Ordin Course 74. **d** 77 **p** 78 Wakef. Hon C of Airedale w Fryston 77-81; C of Ripponden w Rishworth and of Barkisland w W Scammonden Dio Wakef from 81. *Vicarage, Barkisland, Halifax, W Yorks, HX4 0DE.*

FISHER, Harry. b 26. Roch Th Coll 60. **d** 61 Bp McKie for Cov **p** 62 Cov. C of Finham 61-63; Attenborough w Bramcote and Chilwell 63-64; CF 64-68; V of Bickerstaffe Dio Liv from 68. *Bickerstaffe Vicarage, Ormskirk, Lancs, L39 0HW.* (Skelmersdale 22304)

FISHER, Henry John. Lich Th Coll 64. **d** 66 **p** 67 Birm. C of King's Norton 66-70; Weston-super-Mare (in c of H Trin from 72) 70-75; C-in-c of Leigh-on-Mendip (w Stoke St Mich from 78) 75-80; Stoke St Mich 75-80; P-in-c of Downhead 78-80; C of Wilton (in c of Galmington) Dio B & W from 80. *1 Comeytrowe Lane, Galmington, Taunton, TA1 5PA.* (0823 87458)

FISHER, Jack. b 10. Bp Wilson Th Coll IM. **d** 36 **p** 37 York. C of St Barn Hull 36-41; RAFVR 41-46; V of Norton 46-62; Sherburn-in-Elmet w Barkston 62-71; R of Burton Agnes w Harpham 71-76. *19 Northway, Middleton Road, Pickering, N Yorks.*

FISHER, James Atherton. b 09. Late Exhib of SS Coll Cam 3rd cl Cl Trip 30, BA (1st cl Th Trip pt i) 31, Scho 1st cl Th Trip pt ii and Sen Scholfield Pri 32, MA 45. Cudd Coll 32. **d** 33 **p** 34 St Alb. C of St Matt Oxhey 33-36; Dunstable 36-39; Chap Bedford Sch 39-43; V of St Paul Pet 43-53; Asst Relig Broadcasting Dept BBC 53-58; Can and Treas of St Geo Chap Windsor 58-78. *Hillgate, Gedney Hill, Spalding, PE12 0NW.*

FISHER, James Victor. b 35. Sarum Wells Th Coll 75. **d** 77 **p** 78 Bris. C of Corsham 77-80; Stockwood Dio Bris from 81. *20 Durweston Walk, Stockwood, Bristol.* (Whitchurch 834715)

FISHER, John Bertie. b 15. Trin Coll Dub BA 36. Carson Bibl Pri 2nd Abp King Pri and 1st cl Eccles Hist 38. 2nd Bibl Gr Pri and 1st cl Div Test 39, BD 44. **d** 39 Tuam for Down **p**

40 Down. C of Glenavy 39-41; C-in-c of Bannow w Duncormick 41-44; I of Kiltegan w Stratford 44-51; R of Kilternan Dio Dub from 51; RD of Killiney 77-80. *Kilternan Rectory, Co Dublin, Irish Republic.* (Dublin 894559)

FISHER, Preb John Douglas Close. b 09. Late Scho of SS Coll Cam 2nd cl Cl Trip pt i 30, BA (2nd cl Cl Trip pt ii) 31, MA 47, BD 66. Lich Th Coll 36. **d** 38 **p** 39 Chich. C of Horsham 38-44; Brighton 44-47; PC of Burwash Weald 47-51; V of St Matthias Preston Sussex 51-58; Proc Conv Chich 51-80; of Aldrington 58-67; Can and Preb of Chich Cathl from 66; V of Cuckfield 67-77; P-in-c of St John Bapt Hove 77-81. *Flat 2, 10 Brunswick Square, Hove, Sussex, BN3 1EG.* (Brighton 738080)

FISHER, Canon John Howard Warren. Univ Coll Dur LTh 30. St Aug Coll Cant. **d** 30 **p** 31 Glouc. C of Wotton-under-Edge 30-33; Slad 33-34; V of Stone w Woodford 34-45; Hill 39-45; Chap RAFVR 41-46; V of Berkeley w Sharpness 45-67; Rangeworthy 67-75; Surr 47-75; Hon Can of Glouc from 53. *Greenacres, Church Lane, Rockhampton, Berkeley, Glos, GL13 9DX.* (Falfield 260470)

FISHER, John Samuel. Univ of NZ BA 59. NZ Bd of Th Stud LTh 65. Ch Ch Coll 64. **d** 64 **p** 65 Ch Ch. C of St Alb 64-67; Belfast-Styx 67-68; V of Chatham I 68-70; Woodend 70-71; L to Offic Dio Ch Ch 71-77; C of Andersons Bay 77; Asst Chap Ch Ch Hosp 77-78; on leave 78-81; C of St Jo Div Invercargill Dio Dun from 81. *9 Jenkin Street, Invercargill, NZ.* (84-945)

FISHER, John Victor. b 33. Coll of Resurr Mirfield 66. **d** 68 **p** 69 Lon. C of Stepney 68-71; E Ham w Upton Pk 71-73; C-in-c of St Pet Becontree Dio Chelmsf from 73. *Vicarage, Warrington Road, Dagenham, Essex.* (01-590 2740)

FISHER, Joseph Reuben. b 10. TCD BA 31, Hebr Pri, Bp Forster Pri (2nd) and Abp King Pri (2nd) 32, Div Test (1st cl) 33. **d** 33 **p** 34 Dub. C of Santry w Glasnevin and Coolock 33-39; C-in-c of Ballyboy w Kinnity 39-46; I of Dunboyne w Moyglare, Maynooth and Kilcock (w Dunshaughlin and Ballymaglasson from 71) 46-79; RD of Skryne and Ratoath from 64; Can of Meath 64-79; Archd of Meath 69-79; Bp's Commiss from 74. *c/o Rectory, Maynooth, Co Kildare, Irish Republic.*

FISHER, Kenneth Francis McConnell. b 36. K Coll Lon and Warm 57. **d** 61 Sheff **p** 62 Bp Gerard for York. C of St Geo w St Steph Sheff 61-63; Chap Univ of Sheff 64-69; Univ Chap SE Lon 69-75; P-in-c of Dean 75-80; Dioc Officer for Social Responsibility 75-80; Team R of Melksham Dio Sarum from 80. *Rectory, Melksham, Wilts, SN12 6LX.* (Melksham 703262)

FISHER, Ven Leslie Gravatt. b 06. ALCD 33. **d** 33 **p** 34 Lon. C of Em Northwood 33-36; V of St Mich AA Blackheath Pk 36-39; R of Bermondsey 39-47; C-in-c of Ch Ch Bermondsey 42-47; Chap Bermondsey Med Miss Hosp 46-47; Home Sec CMS and L Pr Dio S'wark 47-65; L to Offic at Bromley 48-65; Archd of and Can Res of Ches Cathl 65-75; Archd (Emer) from 75; Vice Dean 73-75; Publ Pr Dio Ex from 79; RD of Okehampton from 79. *14 Lamb Park, Chagford, Newton Abbot, Devon.* (Chagford 3308)

FISHER, Mark. b 52. AKC and BD 76. M SSF 71-80. **d** and **p** 78 Chelmsf. Hon C of Ch of Ascen Vic Dock 78-79; Publ Pr Dio Chelmsf from 78; Perm to Offic Dio Ox from 79; Chap Lady Marg Hall Ox from 80. *Lady Margaret Hall, Oxford, OX2 6QA.* (Ox 54353)

FISHER, Michael Emory. b 42. Univ of Missouri BA 64. Episc Th Sem of SW Texas MDiv 68. **d** 68 **p** 68 Missouri. In Amer Ch 68-72; C of Foxtrap Newfld 73-74; I of Port Saunders 74-75; C of Bonne Bay Dio Newfld (W Newfld from 76) from 75. *Box 59, Woody Point, Newfoundland, Canada.*

FISHER, Michael Harry. b 39. Univ of Ex BA (3rd cl Th) 61. St Steph Ho Ox 61. **d** 63 **p** 64 Lich. C of Wolverhampton 63-67; Newquay 67-70; V of Newlyn 70-75; C-in-c of St Steph and St Thos by Launceston Dio Truro from 75. *St Stephen's Vicarage, Launceston, Cornw.* (Launceston 2679)

FISHER, Michael John. b 43. Univ of Leic BA 64. Univ of Keele MA 67. Qu Coll Birm 75. **d** 78 **p** 79 Lich (APM). C of Stafford Dio Lich from 78. *35 Newland Avenue, Stafford, ST16 1NL.* (Stafford 45069)

FISHER, Nigel Anthony. b 42. Univ of Edin MA (2nd cl Engl) 64. Late Squire Scho at Linacre Coll Ox BA (2nd cl Th) 68, MA 72. St Steph Ho Ox 66. **d** 69 Knaresborough for Ripon **p** 70 Ripon. C of St Aid Leeds 69-71; Asst Chap Middx Hosp Lon 71-73; C of St Clem w St Mary (in c of St Mary) Bournemouth 73-77; V of St Bede Nelson-in-Marsden 77-82; Chap Commun of St Pet Woking Dio Guildf from 82. *West Hill Lodge, Maybury Hill, Woking, Surrey, GU22 8AD.* (Woking 60896)

FISHER, Paul Vincent. b 43. Worc Coll Ox BA 66, MA 70. Univ of Birm Dipl Th 68. Qu Coll Birm 67. **d** 70 **p** 71 Worc. C of Redditch 70-73; St Ambrose Chorlton-on-Medlock 73-79; Executive Sec Div of Commun Affairs BCC 79-81; Dioc Dir of Lay Tr and P-in-c of Raughton Head Dio Carl from 81. *Raughton Head Vicarage, Carlisle, Cumb.* (Raughton Head 249)

FISHER, Peter Timothy. b 44. Univ of Dur BA 68, MA 75. Cudd Coll 68. **d** 70 **p** 71 St Alb. C of St Andr Bedford 70-74; Chap Univ of Surrey 74-78; Sub-Warden Linc Th Coll from 78. *23 Drury Lane, Lincoln, LN1 3BN.* (Linc 23227)

✠ **FISHER, Right Rev (Michael) Reginald Lindsay.** b 18. MA (Lambeth) 78. Westcott Ho Cam 51. **d** 53 **p** 54 Ely. M SSF 42. L to Offic Dio Ely 54-62; Dio Newc T 62-67; Dio Sarum 67-79; European Prov Min SSF from 67; Cons Bp Suffr of St Germans in St Paul's Cathl Lon 25 April 79 by Abp of Cant; Bps of Truro, Heref, Ox, Chich, Derby, Leic, Newc T, Nor and St E; Bps Suffr of Barking, Dorch, Dudley, Fulham and Gibr, Grantham, Grimsby, Hertf, Jarrow, Lewes, Stafford and Taunton; and others. *32 Falmouth Road, Truro, Cornw.*

FISHER, Robert St John. b 05. St Edm Hall Ox BA (2nd cl Th) 27, MA 35. Cudd Coll 27. **d** 28 **p** 29 Blackb. C of Fleetwood 28-30; Preston 30-33; All SS Clayton-le-Moore 33-35; St Mich-in-the-Hamlet Toxteth Pk 35-37; Ch Ch Bootle 37-38; R of Newton Reigny 38-53; V of Dearham 53-62; R of Sebergham w Welton 62-70. *6 Trafalgar Street, Carlisle, Cumb.*

FISHER, Roy Percy. b 22. Linc Th Coll 51. **d** 53 **p** 54 S'wark. C of St Jo Bapt Southend Lewisham 53-56; Min of Clare Coll Miss Rotherhithe 56-59; V of Boughton-under-Blean 59-66; St Sav Westgate-on-Sea 66-71; R of Staplegrove 71-79; Eckington w Renishaw, Handley and Ridgeway Dio Derby from 79. *Eckington Rectory, Sheffield, S Yorks.* (Eckington 2196)

FISHER, Terence Arthur. b 48, St Paul's Coll Grahmstn 77. **d** 79 **p** 80 Grahmstn. C of H Trin K Wm's Tn Dio Grahmstn from 79. *PO Box 356, King William's Town 5600, CP, S Africa.*

FISHER, Thomas Ruggles. b 20. Cranmer Hall Dur 58. **d** 60 Bp Maxwell for Leic **p** 61 Leic. C of Melton Mowbray 60-63; R of Husbands Bosworth (w Mowsley and Knaptoft from 74) (and Theddingworth from 79) Dio Leic from 63; C-in-c of Mowsley and Knaptoft 72-74. *Husbands Bosworth Rectory, Lutterworth, Leics, LE17 6LY.* (Market Harborough 880351)

FISHER, Trevor Lester. St Jo Coll Auckld. **d** 75 **p** 76 Nel. C of Blenheim 75-77. *91 Parker Street, Blenheim, NZ.*

FISHER-JOHNSON, Edwin Warwick. Moore Th Coll Syd ACT ThL 47. **d** and **p** 47 Syd. C of St Anne Ryde 47-48; R of Wilcannia 48-50; C-in-c of Par Distr of Abbotsford w Russell Lea 50-52; R of Berry 52-54; Blacktown 54-60; Lidcombe 60-62; Richmond 63-76; L to Offic Dio Syd from 76. *Box 512, Orange, NSW, Australia 2800.* (063-62 5778)

FISHLEY, Canon George Reuben. b 04. Univ of Lon BA 23. Wells Th Coll 28. **d** 29 **p** 30 Lich. Chap R Orph Wolverhampton 29-38; Hd Master Jun Sch 37-38; Chap Mental Hosp Winwick 38-46; Chap of Highcroft Hall and Erdington Cottage Homes 46-50; V of Hunningham and V of Wappenbury w Weston-under-Weatherley 50-60; Chap Weston Hosp 50-56; Dir of Relig Educn Dio Cov 57-72; R of Ladbroke w Radbourne 60-76; Hon Can of Cov 65-67; Can Th 67-72; Can Th (Emer) from 72; RD of Southam 67-76. *4 Margetts Close, Kenilworth, Warws.*

FISK, Charles James. Bp's Univ Lennox BA 53, LST 54. **d** 53 **p** 54 Queb. C of Sherbrooke 53-55; I of Port Neuf 54-55; Waterville 56-59; H Trin Tor 63-77; on leave. *469 St Clements Avenue, Toronto, Ont., Canada.*

FISK, Paul. b 35. St Jo Coll Cam BA 60, MA 64. Wells Th Coll 60. **d** 62 **p** 63 St E. C of H Trin Ipswich 62-65; Wrentham w Benacre Covehithe and Henstead and of Sotterley w Willingham and Shadingfield 65-67; R of Copdock w Washbrook and Belstead 67-73; Brantham 73-75; RD of Samford 73-75. *c/o 11 Woodstone Avenue, Ipswich, Suff.*

FISK, Canon William Ernest Gyde. b 09. TD 51. Linc Th Coll. **d** 47 **p** 48 Dur. C of Washington 47-49; Herrington (in c of Thorney Close) 49-51; CF (TA) 49-59; C-in-c of St Pet Thorney Close Conv Distr 51-53; R of Norbury w Snelston 53-59; Sudbury w Somersal Herbert 59-77; RD of Longford 59-71; Chap HM Pris Sudbury Pk 59-77; Hon Can of Derby 68-77; Can (Emer) from 77. *17 Chestnut Grove, Etwall, Derbys.* (Etwall 3272)

FISKE, Eben Horsford. b 10. Harvard Univ AB 35. Late Scho of Trin Coll Cam BA (3rd cl Hist Trip) 37, MA 42. Cudd Coll 38. **d** 40 **p** 41 Dur for Lon. C of St Jas W Hartlepool 40-44; Prec of Wakef Cathl 44-57; Wakef Dio Youth Chap 57-58; C of Castleford 57-58; C-in-c of Kinsley Dio Wakef from 58. *Kinsley Vicarage, Fitzwilliam, Pontefract, Yorks, WF9 5BX.* (0977-610497)

FISKE, Paul Francis Brading. b 45. St Jo Coll Dur BA 68, PhD 72. Wycl Hall Ox Dipl Th 72. **d** 73 Warrington for Liv **p** 74 Liv. C of Sutton St Helens 73-76; Cheltenham 76; Team

V of Cheltm 76-80; C of Cowplain (in c of Hartplain) Dio Portsm from 80. *61 Hartplain Avenue, Cowplain, Portsmouth, PO8 8DZ.*

FISON, Geoffrey Robert Martius. b 34. Univ of Dur BA 59. Ely Th Coll 59. **d** 61 **p** 62 Ex. C of Heavitree 61-64; Bro of St Barn N Queensld 64-69; C of Maybush 70-73; Team V of All SS and St Mary Strood 73-79; Dorcan Swindon Dio Bris from 79. *27 Kershaw Road, Swindon, Wilts, SN3 6BS.*

FITCH, Canon John Ambrose. b 22. Late Scho of CCC Cam BA (1st cl Hist Trip pt i; 2nd cl Th Trip pt i) 44, MA 48. Wells Th Coll 45. **d** 47 Chelmsf for St E **p** 48 St E. C of All SS Newmarket 47-50; V of Reydon 51-70; Chap St Felix Sch Southwold 51-69; R of Brandon w Santon Downham 70-80; Hon Can of St E Cathl from 75; RD of Mildenhall 78-80; R of Monks Eleigh w Chelsworth and Brent Eleigh w Milden Dio St E from 80. *Rectory, The Street, Monks Eleigh, Ipswich, Suff IP7 7AU.*

FITITEI, Ellison. b 31. bp Patteson Th Centre Kohimarama 71. **d** 73 **p** 74 Melan. P Dio Melan 73-75; Centr Melan from 75. *Luesaleba, Santa Cruz, Solomon Islands.*

FITZGERALD, Gerald. Otago Univ NZ BA 50. Trin Coll Ox BA 52, MA 56. Westcott Ho Cam 52. **d** 54 Man **p** 55 Middleton for Man. C of St Phil and of St Steph Salford 54-57; St Pet Riccarton U 57-59; V of Malvern 59-62; Hokitika 62-66; V of Linwood 66-67; L to Offic Dio Ch Ch from 71. *12 Idris Road, Christchurch 12, NZ.* (516-766)

FITZ-GERALD, Gerald O'Connell. b 07. K Coll Cam BA 29, MA 33. Ely Th Coll 29. **d** & **p** 31 S'wark. C of St Jo Evang Walworth 30-32; Leatherhead 32-34; St Aug Queen's Gate Kens 34-38; PV of Ex Cathl 38-40; Chap RNVR 40-46; C of Paignton (in c of St Andr) 46-49; Chap of Sliema Malta 49-51; Perm to Offic at St Mary Bourne Street Lon 51-52; V of St Aug Highgate 52-70. *3/41 Ventnor Villas, Hove, E Sussex, BN3 3DA.* (0273 772249)

FITZGERALD, John Edward. b 44. Oak Hill Coll 74. **d** 76 Chelmsf **p** 77 Barking for Chelmsf. C of Rainham 76-78; St Andr L Cam Dio Ely from 79. *St Stephen's Parsonage, Coldham's Lane, Cambridge.* (Cam 248148)

FITZGERALD, Knightley Purefoy. St Bonif Coll Warm 34. **d** 34 Sherborne for Sarum for Col Bp **p** 35 Melan. Miss at Arawe 34-35; Siota 35-36; Maravovo 36-37; Rabaul 37-40; Perm to Offic (Col Cl Act) at St Anne Wandsworth 40-44; C of St Luke West Norwood 44-46; Christchurch (in c of All SS Mudeford) 46-49; P-in-c of St Steph Grand Bahamas 49-54; R of Grand Turk Nass 54-57; V of Kilmeston w Beauworth 57-66; Commiss Nass 58-63. *Downfield West, Alresford Road, Winchester, Hants.* (Winchester 63853)

FITZGERALD, Thomas Martin William. b 30. Trin Coll Bris 72. **d** 72 **p** 73 Bris. C of Stapleton 72-75; Gt Yarmouth (in c of St Paul) 75-77; P-in-c of Tasburgh 79-82; Tharston 79-82; Forncett St Mary w Forncett St Pet 79-82; Flordon 79-82. *c/o Joshua Trust, Plot 52, Underwood Road, E1.*

FITZGIBBON, Kevin Peter. b 49. Univ of Nottm BTh 81. St Jo Coll Nottm 77. **d** 81 Pet. C of St Columba Corby Dio Pet from 81. *214 Rowlett Road, Corby, Northants, NN17 2BX.*

FITZHARRIS, Barry. b 47. Univ of Lon BA 69. AKC and BD 72. Univ of W Ont MA 73. St Aug Coll Cant 72. **d** 73 **p** 74 Cant. C of Whitstable 73-76; Perm to Offic Dio Cant 76-77; Hon C of Clapham Old Town 77-79; Asst Chap Abp Tenison's Gr Sch from 78; Hon C of Ch Ch Streatham Dio S'wark from 80. *c/o 20 North Side, Clapham Common, SW4 0RQ.*

FITZHERBERT, David Henry. b 18. Lich Th Coll 62. **d** 63 **p** 64 Derby. C of Ashbourne w Mapleton 63-66; R of Dennington 66-77; P-in-c of Bedfield w Monk Soham 71-77. *Address temp unknown.*

FITZHUGH, Francis Coulbourn. b 28. Bp's Univ Lennox BA 49. Cudd Coll 50. **d** and **p** 56 Queb. C of St Matt Queb 56-58; St Mich Cathl Bridgetown 58-59; V of St Simon Barb 59-60; R of Bimini Nass 60-63; C of Leigh-on-Sea Essex 63-65; C of St Mary's Cathl Johann 65-67; Chap to St Jo Coll Dio Johann 67-74; C of St D Ex 74-79; in Amer Ch. *Address temp unknown.*

FITZPATRICK, John Hunter. St Jo Coll Auckld 57. **d** 57 **p** 58 Dun. C of Gladstone 57-60; V of Riverton 60-63; CF (NZ) 63-66; Offg Min Dio Wel 65-66; C of St Marg Hillsborough 66-71; Chap Green Lane and Nat Women Hosps Dio Auckld from 71. *7 Boakes Road, Auckland 6, NZ.*

FITZPATRICK, Richard William. b 1896. TCD BA 20, MA 21, Abp King Pri 21, Div Test (2nd cl) and Downes Pri 22. **d** 22 **p** 23 Dub. C of St Paul Glengeary 22-26; CF 26-55; ACG Lon Distr and Chap to Household Bde 47-55; Hon Chap to HM the Queen 53-55; R of Ashwell w Burley 56-75. *50 Sandymount Avenue, Ballsbridge, Dublin 4, Irish Republic.* (Dublin 691735)

FITZWILLIAMS, Mark Morshead. b 36. Trin Coll Cam BA 59, MA 64. Westcott Ho Cam 59. **d** 61 Kens for Lon **p** 62 Lon. C of St John's Wood Ch 61-64; Hempnall 64-70; V of Newport Pagnell 70-78; R of Lathbury 70-78; Team R of Beaconsfield Dio Ox from 78; RD of Newport 73-78. *Rectory, Wycombe End, Beaconsfield, Bucks, HP9 1NP.* (Beaconsfield 3949)

FLACK, John Robert. b 42. Univ of Leeds BA 64. Coll of Resurr Mirfield. **d** 66 **p** 67 Ripon. C of Armley 66-69; St Mary Virg Northn 69-72; V of St Jas Chapelthorpe 72-81; Ripponden w Rishworth Dio Wakef from 81; Barkisland w W Scammonden Dio Wakef from 81. *Vicarage, Ripponden, Sowerby Bridge, W Yorks, HX6 4DF.* (Ripponden 2239)

FLAGG, David Michael. b 50. CCC BA 71, MA 75. Univ of Nottm BA (Th) 76. St Jo Coll Nottm 74. **d** 77 Chich **p** 78 Lewes for Chich. C of St Leon Hollington 77-80; Woodley Dio Ox from 80. *35 Highgate Road, Woodley, Reading, Berks.* (Reading 696157)

FLAGG, Ven Ernest Geoffrey. CD 67. Univ of Sask BA (w distinc) 40. Em Coll Sktn LTh (w distinc) 41, BD 58, DD (*hon causa*) 67. **d** 41 **p** 42 Sktn Miss at Radisson 41-44; CF (Canad) 44-46; I of Macklin 46-47; R of Fort Macleod w Claresholm 47-53; C of Grace Ch Tor 53-54; R of Red Deer 54-63; Hon Can of Calg 58-63; Dean and R of St Andr Cathl Prince Rupert 63-70; R of Naniamo 70-81; Archd of Naniamo 71-81; Archd (Emer) from 81. *Site E, RR3, Naniamo, BC, Canada.* (754-5889)

✠ **FLAGG, Right Rev John William Hawkins.** b 29. **d** 59 **p** 61 Argent. C of Asuncion Paraguay 59-64; Field Supt SAMS Dio Argent 64-69; Archd of N Argent 65-69; Cons Ld Bp in Paraguay and N Argent in St Jo Bapt Cathl Buenos Aires 21 Dec 69 by Bps of Argent; and Chile; and Bp Bazley; Res 73; Presiding Bp Angl Coun of S Amer 73-77; Asst Bp in Chile 73-77; Bp of Peru 77; Asst Bp in Liv from 78; V of St Cypr w Ch Ch Toxteth Dio Liv from 78; Commiss Peru from 78. *52 Deane Road, Liverpool, L7 OET.* (051-263 4170)

FLAGLER, Canon John Russel. Wycl Coll Tor BA 42. **d** 42 Bran **p** 43 Tor for Bran. C of Hamiota 42-43; St Mary w St Geo Bran 43-45; R of St Geo Bran 45-50; RD of Brandon 47-50; R of St Mary Hamilton 50-52; I of Wainwright 55-59; R of St Faith Edmon 59-69; Dom Chap to Bp of Edmon 60-69; Can of Edmon 63-69; R of St Phil Elboya City and Dio Calg from 69; Hon Can of Calg from 78; Dom Chap to Bp of Calg from 79. *4903-4th Street SW, Calgary, Alta., Canada.* (243-3084)

FLANAGAN, Fraser Kelvin. b 42. Univ of Cant BA 71. Melb Coll of Div LTh 68. **d** 70 **p** 71 Ch Ch. C of Shirley 70-72; St Pet Riccarton 72-74; Mansfield 75-76; P-in-c of Riccarton 76; Highfield 77; V of Methven Dio Ch Ch from 77. *Vicarage, Methven, Canterbury, NZ* (Ash 28254)

FLATAU, Cyrus Raymond. Moore Th Coll Syd 42, ACT ThL 42. **d** and **p** 43 Syd. C of St John Parramatta 43; I of St Paul Lithgow 43-46; C of St Clem Marrickville 46-47; CIM Miss China 47-53; Miss in Malaya 53-71; C-in-c of Blakehurst 71-74; Rooty Hill 74-77; R 77-78; S Cant Dio Syd from 78. *14 Mons Street, Canterbury, NSW, Australia 2193.* (78-1176)

FLATHER, Peter George. b 29. Sarum Th Coll. **d** 59 **p** 60 Win. C of Fordingbridge 59-63; Lyndhurst 63-65; R of E w W Bradenham 65-72; P-in-c of All SS Speke 72-73; Sharrington Dio Nor from 73; R of Gunthorpe w Bale Dio Nor from 73; P-in-c of Gt w L Snoring Dio Nor from 77. *Bale Rectory, Fakenham, Norf.* (Thursford 292)

FLATMAN, Martin Edward. b 46. Univ of Hull BA 68. Cudd Coll 69. **d** 71 Buckingham for Ox **p** 72 Reading for Ox. C of St Giles Reading 71-75; Team V of Newbury 75-81; V of Cowley St John City and Dio Ox from 82. *276 Cowley Road, Oxford, OX4 1UR.* (Ox 42396)

FLATT, Donald Clifford. b 15. Worc Ordin Coll 63. **d** 65 **p** 66 St Alb. C of Tring 65-67; V of Wigginton 67-75; Biddenham Dio St Alb from 75; Chap HM Pris Bedford from 75. *Vicarage, Biddenham, Bedford.* (Bedford 54433)

FLATT, Roy. b 47. Episc Th Coll Edin 78. **d** 80 **p** 81 St Andr. C of St Andr St Andrews Dio St Andr from 80; Elie Dio St Andr from 80; Pittenweem Dio St Andr from 80. *30 James Street, Pittenweem, Anstruther, Fife.*

FLAVELL, Benjamin. b 42. **d** 79 **p** 80 Wai. Hon C of Ruatoki-Whakatane Dio Wai from 79. *7 Pohutukawa Drive, Murupara, NZ.*

FLAVELL, Benjamin. St Mich Th Coll Llan 25. **d** 27 **p** 28 Llan. C of Cadoxton-juxta-Barry 27-30; All SS Clevedon 30-35; CF (TA) from 30; Hd Master and Asst Chap R Sch of the Blind Leatherhead 35-36; C of H Trin Taunton 36-39; CF (EC) 39-45; Hon CF 45; V of All SS Rockwell Green Wellington w Thorne-St-Margaret 45-52; V of Haselbury Plucknett w N Perrott 52-68. *7 St Barnabas Houses, Newland, Malvern, Worcs.* (Malvern 4639)

FLAVELL, Paul William Deran. b 44. Univ of Wales Dipl Th 66. St Mich Coll Llan 67. **d** 68 **p** 69 N Queensld. C of W Cairns 68-71; Blaenavon w Capel Newydd 71-74; V of Ynysddu 74-78; P-in-c of Waimate N Par Distr Dio Auckld from 78. *c/o Vicarage, Kaikohe, NZ.*

FLAVELL, Timoti Hami Paihana. St Jo Coll Auckld 56. **d** 61 **p** 62 Waik. C of Morrinsville 61-62; Taumarunui 62-64; P-in-c of Taranaki Maori Past 64-67; Waik Maori Past 67-79; Waitomo Maori Past Dio Waik from 79. *10 St Luke's Crescent, Te Kuiti, NZ.*

FLEETWOOD, John Arnold. b 10. K Coll Lon Robertson Pri 38, AKC and BD (2nd cl) 39. **d** 39 **p** 40 Chelmsf. C of All SS Leyton 39-42; Barking (in c of St Patr from 43) 42-45; V of St Andr Leytonstone 45-57; Canvey I 57-73; Navestock 73-78; R of Kelvedon Hatch 73-78. *15 Orchard Piece, Blackmore, Ingatestone, Essex, CM4 0RX.* (Blackmore 822683)

FLEISCHER, Kenneth Noel. d 53 **p** 54 Capetn. Warden of St John's Hostel Capetn 54-67; C of Hermanus 67-77; Perm to Offic Dio Capetn from 77. *c/o PO Box 110, Hermanus, CP, S Africa.* (Hermanus 364)

FLEMING, David. b 37. Kelham Th Coll. **d** 63 Warrington for Liv **p** 64 Liv. C of Walton-on-the-Hill 63-67; V of Gt Staughton 68-75; Chap Gaynes Hall Borstal Inst from 68; RD of St Neots 72-76; V of Whittlesey Dio Ely from 76; RD of March from 77. *Whittlesey Vicarage, Church Street, Whittlesey, Peterborough, PE7 1DB.* (Peterborough 202200)

FLEMING, Desmond. TCD **d** 55 Connor **p** 56 Down for Arm. C of St Mary Magd Belf 55-57; St Jude Ballynafeigh 57-61; I of Ardglass w Dunsford 61-66; C of St Chris Burlington 66-68; Min Can Down Cathl 68-69; R of All SS Niagara Falls 69-74; St Monica Niagara Falls 70-73; St Steph Hamilton Dio Niag from 74. *39 Grandfield Avenue, Hamilton, Ont., Canada.* (416-388 8620)

FLEMING, Canon Edward Daniel. Montr Th Coll LTh 57. **d** 56 **p** 57 Ont. C of Westport 57-58; R 58-61; Merrickville 61-65; Carleton Place 65-70; St Thos City and Dio Montr from 70; Exam Chap to Bp of Montr from 76; Hon Can of Montr from 79. *6897 Somerled Avenue, Montreal 265, PQ, Canada.* (514-488 5517)

FLEMING, George. b 39. **d** 78 **p** 79 Down. C of Donaghcloney w Waringstown 78-80; St Pet St Owen & St Jas City and Dio Heref from 80. *23 St James Road, Hereford, HR1 2QS.*

FLEMING, John Irving. St Barn Th Coll Adel 67, ACT ThL (2nd cl) 68. **d** 69 **p** 70 Adel. C of Brighton Adel 69-71; Chap Univs of Adel and Flinders 71-76; P-in-c of St Paul Adel 71-76; Asst Chap St Mark's Coll Adel 76; C of Chiswick 77-78; R of Plympton Dio Adel from 78. *15 Clayton Avenue, Plympton, S Australia 5038.* (293 5050)

FLEMING, Very Rev John Robert William. b 07. TCD BA (3rd cl Cl Mod) 30, MA 33. Div Test 40, BD (Lon) 63. **d** 40 Meath **p** 41 Kilmore for Meath. Vice-Warden of Wilson's Hosp Multyfarnham and L to Offic Dio Meath 40-43; C of Leighlin Group 43-44; Hd Master Bp Foy Sch Waterford 44-52; I of Agnold U 52-56; C of Chilvers Coton 56-59; R of Midleton 59-78; Castlemartyr 59-78; Can and Preb of St Patr Cathl Dub from 72; Treas of Cork from 76; Dean and I of Ross Cathl from 78; Chan of Cork Cathl from 78; Exam Chap to Bp of Cork from 78. *Deanery, Rosscarbery, Co Cork, Irish Republic.* (Bandon 48166)

FLEMING, Mary Charlotte. b 53. Univ of Tor MusBac 75. Wycl Coll Tor MDiv 79. **d** 79 **p** 80 Niag. C of St Jas Dundas Dio Niag from 79. *c/o St James' Church, 137 Melville Street, Dundas, Ont, Canada L9H 2A6.* (416-627 1424)

FLEMING, Matthew James. Wycl Coll Tor Dipl Th 65. **d** 65 **p** 66 Bran. Vice Prin Mackay Ind Resid Sch 65-66; R of MacGregor and of Carberry 66-69. *c/o Box 234, MacGregor, Manit, Canada.*

FLEMING, Richard Gordon. McGill Univ Montr BSc 51, BD 54. Selw Coll Cam BA 56, MA 61. Montr Th Coll LTh 54. **d** 53 Ont **p** 55 Ely for Col Bp. LPr Dio Ont 53-56; R of Marmora 56-62; Ch Ch Bellevlle 62-64; Dean and R of St Geo Cathl Kingston Ont 64-76; on leave. *11 Robert Wallace Drive, Kingston, Ont, Canada.* (613-542 1666)

FLEMING, Robert Michael. b 47. Carleton Univ Ott BA 73. Trin Coll Tor MDiv 76. **d** and **p** 76 Ott. I of Bearbrook 76-80; C of St Jo Evang City and Dio Ott from 80. *1539 Nothdale Avenue, Ottawa, Ont, Canada.*

FLEMING, Ronald Thorpe. b 29. Codr Coll Barb. **d** 56 **p** 57 Barb. C of St Mary Barb 57-58; V of St Marg Barb 58-60; St Jo Bapt Barb 60-61; C of Delaval 61-64; V of Cambois 64-69; Ancroft w Scremerston 69-81; Longhirst w Hebron Dio Newc T from 81. *Longhirst Vicarage, Morpeth, Northumb, NE61 3LU.* (Morpeth 790253)

FLEMING, William Edward Charlton. b 29. Trin Coll Dub BA 51, Div Test (1st cl) 52, MA 65. **d** 52 **p** 53 Dub. C of Santry 52-56; St Mark Arm 56-61; I of Tartaraghan (w Diamond from 80) Dio Arm from 61; Prov Regr Arm from 79. *Tartaraghan Rectory, Portadown, N Ireland.* (Annaghmore 851289)

✠ **FLEMING, Right Rev William Launcelot Scott.** b 06. KCVO 76. Trin Hall Cam BA (1st cl Nat Sc Trip pt ii) 28, MA 32. Univ of Yale MS 31. DD (Lambeth) 50. FRSE 71. Univ of E Anglia Hon DCL 76. Westcott Ho Cam 31. **d** 33 **p** 34 Bp Price for Ely. Chap of Trin Hall Cam 33-34; Chap and Geol Br Graham Land Exped 34-37; Fell of Trin Hall Cam 33-49; Dean and Chap 37-49; Hon Fell from 56; Exam Chap to Bp of S'wark 37-49; St Alb 39-45; Heref 42-49; Chap RNVR 40-44; Hon Chap from 50; Dir of Service Ordination Candidates 44-46; Select Pr Univ of Cam 46 and 53; Dir of Scott Polar Research Inst Cam 46-49; Chairman C of E Youth Coun 50-61; Cons Ld Bp of Portsm in S'wark Cathl 18 Oct 49 by Abp of Cant; Bps of Nor; S'wark; Sarum; Ely; Linc; and Ripon; Bps Suffr of Kingston T; Dunwich; and Croydon; and Bps Lovett; Karney; Kitching; Barkway; and Holland; Trld to Nor 59; res 71; Dean of Windsor and Dom Chap to HM the Queen 71-76; Register O of the Garter 71-76. *Tithe Barn, Poyntington, Sherborne, Dorset, DT9 4LF.* (Corton Denham 479)

FLENLEY, Kenneth Bernard. b 17. TD 62, 1st clasp 69. St Pet Hall Ox 3rd cl Cl Mods 38, BA 41, MA 43. Wycl Hall Ox 44. **d** 45 **p** 46 Liv. C of St Paul Widnes 45-46; Keynsham 46-50; CF (TA) 49-67; CF (TAVR) 67-80; V of Bathford 50-79. *85 Dovers Park, Bath, BA1 7UE.* (Bath 858763)

FLETCHER, Albert Reginald. b 20. Univ of Leeds BA 50. **d** 51 **p** 52 Bradf. C of Skipton 51-54; Charlwood (in c of Lowfield Heath) 54-57; P-in-c of Rosyth and of Inverkeithing 57; C of Limpsfield (in c of St Andr) 57-63; V of St Luke Whyteleafe Dio S'wark from 63. *8 Whyteleafe Hill, Whyteleafe, Surrey, CR3 0AA.* (01-660 4015)

FLETCHER, Anthony Joseph. Sarum Th Coll 32. **d** 35 **p** 36 Wakef. C of Kirkburton 35-38; Chap RN 38-47; P-in-c of Pouce Coupe Dio Caled 55-59. *Box 323, Pouce Coupe, BC, Canada.*

FLETCHER, Anthony Peter Reeves. b 46. Ridley Hall Cam 71. **d** 74 **p** 75 St Alb. C of Luton 74-78; Chap RAF from 78. *c/o Ministry of Defence, Adastral House, WC1.*

FLETCHER, Arthur William George. b 24. Univ of Leeds BA 50. Coll of Resurr Mirfield 50. **d** 52 **p** 53 Lon. C of Bush Hill Pk 52-55; Chap RAF 55-58 and 61-72; V of Topcliffe w Dalton 58-61; R of Challoch w Newton Stewart 72-75; Kilmacolm w Bridge of Weir Dio Glas from 75. *Rectory, Kilmacolm, Renfrew.* (Kilmacolm 2044)

FLETCHER, Charles. St Aid Coll 28. **d** 31 **p** 32 Heref. C of St Mich Madeley 31-35; V of Cardington Salop 35-39; St Cuthb Darwen 39-50; Longridge 50-64. *83 Woodplumpton Lane, Woodplumpton, Preston, Lancs, PR4 0AQ.* (Broughton 864275)

FLETCHER, Christopher Raymond Drayson. b 41. Vanc Sch of Th 75. **d** 79 **p** 80 Yukon. C of Atlin Carcross Dio Yukon from 79. *Box 73, Atlin, BC., Canada, V0W 1A0.*

FLETCHER, Colin William. b 50. Trin Coll Ox BA 72. BA (Th) 74, MA 76. Wycl Hall Ox 72. **d** 75 **p** 76 Bradf. C of St Pet Shipley 75-79; Tutor Wycl Hall Ox from 79; Hon C of St Andr City and Dio Ox from 79. *Wycliffe Hall, Oxford, OX2 6PW.*

FLETCHER, David Clare Molyneux. b 32. Worc Coll Ox BA 55, MA 59. Wycl Hall Ox. **d** 58 **p** 59 Lon. Hon C of Islington Dio Lon from 58. *4 Burfield Road, Chorleywood, Herts, WD3 5NS.*

FLETCHER, Douglas. b 40. Coll of Resurr Mirfield 67. **d** 68 Lon **p** 69 Kens for Lon. C of St Jo Evang Notting Hill Kens 68-74; St Mary L Cam 73-74; St John Fulham Dio Lon from 74. *40 Racton Road, SW6.* (01-385 3644)

FLETCHER, Francis Cecil. b 12. Clifton Th Coll 33. **d** 36 **p** 38 Lich. C of Ch Ch Burton-on-Trent 36-39; Chasetown 39-44; Gresley 44-46; V of St Julian Shrewsbury 46-49; All SS Darlaston 49-54; Hammerwich 54-66; Weston-on-Trent 66-75. *38 Brocton Road, Milford, Stafford.*

FLETCHER, Geoffrey Mitchell. Moore Th Coll Syd ACT ThL 47. **d** 47 **p** 48 Syd. C of St Andr Summer Hill 47-50; C-in-c of Kingsgrove w Bexley N 50-51; R 51-55; Gen Sec NSW Branch of CMS 53-63; L Pr Dio Syd 56-63; R of Northbridge 63-66; Dioc Missr Dio Syd 66-68; L to Offic Dio Syd from 68. *133 Bathurst Street, Sydney, NSW, Australia 2000.* (26-2007)

FLETCHER, George Henry Yorke. b 11. Wycl Hall Ox 58. **d** 59 **p** 60 Birm. C of Yardley Wood 59-62; V of Hursley w Pitt 62-67; St Pet Hall Green Birm 67-75; Clive w Grinshill 75-80; Perm to Offic Dio Lich from 80. *4 Croft Close, Bomere Heath, Shrewsbury, Salop.* (Bomere Heath 290337)

FLETCHER, Gordon Wolfe. Edin Th Coll. **d** 62 **p** 63 York. C of Eston w Normanby 62-65; W Harton 65-68; V of Pelton 68-81; Ryhope Dio Dur from 81. *St Paul's Vicarage, Ryhope, Sunderland, SR2 0HH.* (Sunderland 210238)

FLETCHER, Harry Maurice. b 43. St Steph Ho Ox 71. **d** 74 Roch **p** 75 Tonbridge for Roch. C of the Annunc Chislehurst 74-77; Chap Quainton Hall Sch Harrow from 77. *95 Hindes Road, Harrow, Middx.*

FLETCHER, James Anthony. b 36. St Edm Hall Ox BA 60, Dipl Th 61, MA 66. St Steph Ho Ox 60. **d** 62 **p** 63 S'wark. C of St Pet Streatham 62-65; St Mary's Conv Distr Hob's

Moat Solihull 65-68; Cowley St John (in c of St Alb Mart) Ox 68-76; V of All SS Hanworth Dio Lon from 76. *All Saints' Vicarage, Uxbridge Road, Feltham, Middx, TW13 5EE.* (01-894 9330)

FLETCHER, John Alan Alfred. b 33. Oak Hill Th Coll 58. **d** 61 **p** 62 Roch. C of St Paul Erith 61-64; Rushden 64-67; R of Hollington Dio Chich from 67. *Hollington Rectory, 6 Swallow Bank, St Leonards-on-Sea, Sussex.* (Hastings 52257)

FLETCHER, John Sidney. b 21. **d** 72 **p** 73 Ont. C of Marysburg 72-73; I 73-75; I of Quinte Dio Ont from 75. *Box 428, Deseronto, Ont, Canada.* (613-396 2829)

FLETCHER, Jonathan James Molyneux. b 42. Hertf Coll Ox BA (2nd cl Lit Hum) 66, MA 68. Wycl Hall Ox. **d** 68 Willesden for Lon **p** 69 Lon. C of Cockfosters 68-72; H Sepulchre (w All SS from 73) Cam 72-76; St Helen Bishopsgate Lon 76-81. *33 Ellington Street, N7.* (01-607 7678)

FLETCHER, Keith. b 47. Univ of Man Dipl Th 72. Chich Th Coll 79. **d** 80 **p** 81 Dur. C of St Paul Hartlepool Dio Dur from 80. *96 Grange Road, Hartlepool, Cleve.*

FLETCHER, Robin Geoffrey. b 32. Univ of Nottm BA (3rd cl Th) 57. Ridley Hall Cam 57. **d** 59 **p** 60 Lon. C of Ch Ch Barnet 59-64; V of Wollaton Pk 64-71; St Phil and St Jas Clifton City and Dio York from 71. *Clifton Vicarage, York, YO3 6BH.* (York 55071)

FLETCHER, Stanley Philip. b 27. St Jo Coll Dur BA 52, MA 73. **d** 54 **p** 55 Leic. C of St Jo Bapt Knighton 54-58; V of Fleckney w Saddington 58-61; Tutor Ibad Gr Sch 61-64; Vice-Prin and Chap 64-66; V of Bishopton w Gt Stainton 66-76; Cornforth Dio Dur from 76. *Vicarage, West Cornforth, Co Durham, DL17 9HU.* (Ferryhill 54242)

FLETCHER, Timothy. b 27. Univ of Reading BSc (Agr) 48. Linc Th Coll 50. **d** 52 **p** 53 Guildf. C of Oatlands 52-57; Miss Dio Korea 57-61; V of Kirkby Ravensworth w Dalton 61-67; R of Binfield 67-81; Barcombe Dio Chich from 81. *Rectory, Church Lane, Barcombe, Lewes, E Sussex, BN8 5TW.* (Barcombe 400260)

FLETCHER, Valentine. b 14. Or Coll Ox BA 38, MA 64. Cudd Coll 38. **d** and **p** 39 Bradf. C of Sedbergh 39-43; St Mary Virg All SS and St Mich Elland (in c of All SS from 45) 43-47; Chap and Prec of St Paul's Cathl Dundee 47-49; R of St Mich Govan Glas 49-52; Montrose w Inverbervie 52-56; CF (TA) 50-63; (TA-R of O) 63-69; V of Lidget Green 56-58; R of Duxford 58-64; V of Littlemore 64-71; R of Stratton Audley w Godington (in c of Stoke Lyne) 71-74; Perm to Offic Dio Sarum from 75; Hon C of Blandford-Forum Dio Sarum from 76. *Chase Cottage, Tollard Royal, Salisbury, SP5 5PW.* (Tollard Royal 266)

FLETCHER, Walter Raémond. b 47. Trent Univ BA 70. Trin Coll Tor MDiv 72. **d** 72 Tor **p** 75 Queb. C of St Paul Thunder Bay 72; Malbay 73-75; R 75-76; I of La Tuque 76-79; Aylmer Dio Ott from 79. *101 Charles Street, Aylmer, PQ, Canada.* (613-684 3073)

FLETCHER, William Harry Gregory. b 16. St Cath S Ox BA 38, MA 43. BD (Lon) 70. Wycl Hall Ox 71. **d** 71 **p** 72 Leic. C of Loughborough 71-74; V of Newtown Linford Dio Leic from 74. *Newtown Linford Vicarage, Leicester, LE6 0HB.* (Markfield 2955)

FLETCHER-JONES, Canon Basil Mills. b 13. Pemb Coll Ox BA (2nd cl Phil Pol and Econ) 36, MA 39. Sarum Th Coll 38. **d** 40 **p** 41 Win. C of Lymington 40-46; Youth Org Dio Perth 46-50; C of St Geo Cathl Perth 47-48; Chap Perth Coll 48-50; Chap and Sub-Warden St Geo Coll Perth 50-54; Asst Sec CACTM 54-60; Sec Ordin Cands C'tte CACTM 60-62; R of Walton-on-the-Hill 62-80; RD of Walton 66-75; Hon Can of Liv 70-81; Can (Emer) from 81; Hon C of Good Shepherd Preston Dio Chich from 81. *56 Reigate Road, Brighton, BN1 5AH.* (Brighton 509721)

FLEURY, Franquefort Eccles. **d** 20 **p** 21 Wel. C of All SS Kilbirnie NZ 20-21; V of Mangatainoka and Pongaroa 22-26; Martinborough 26-36; Kiwitea 36-48; Perm to Offic Dio Wel from 48. *c/o D E Fleury, Box 26, Kimbolton, NZ.*

FLEWELLEN, James Joseph. **d** 45 **p** 46 Ch Ch. C of New Brighton 45-47; Linwood 47-52; Avonside 52-58; L to Offic Dio Ch Ch from 58. *68 Woodham Road, Christchurch, NZ.*

FLEWKER, David William. b 53. Univ of Birm BA 75. Wycl Hall Ox 76. **d** 78 **p** 79 Liv. C of Netherton Dio Liv from 78. *34 Park Lane West, Netherton, Bootle, Merseyside.*

FLIGHT, Michael John. b 41. Sarum Th Coll 68. **d** 71 Sherborne for Sarum **p** 72 Sarum. C of Wimborne Minster 71-75; R of Tarrant Gunville 75-78; Tarrant Hinton 75-78; V of Tarrant Monkton w Tarrant Launceston 75-78; P-in-c of Tarrant Rushton w Tarrant Rawston 77-78; Tarrant Keynston w Tarrant Crawford 77-78; R of Tarrant Valley 78-80; V of Westbury w Westbury Leigh and Dilton Dio Sarum from 80. *Vicarage, Bitham Lane, Westbury, Wilts, BA13 3BU.* (Westbury 822209)

FLINDALL, John Franklin. Univ of W Ont BA 59. Hur Coll LTh 62, BD 66. **d** 62 **p** 63 Caled. I of Kitkatla 62-65; Cataraqui 65-68; R of Bath w Collins Bay 68-73; Chap Kingston Penit Dio Ont from 73. *203 East Street, Napanee, Ont, Canada.*

FLINN, John Robert Patrick. b 30. **d** 65 **p** 66 Dub. C of Rathfarnham 65-67; I of Baltinglass w Ballynure and Stratford-on-Slaney 67-77; Castlepollard and Oldcastle Dio Meath from 77. *Rectory, Castlepollard, Co Meath, Irish Republic.*

FLINN, Reuben Bishop. b 1887. St Jo Coll Dur 20. **d** 20 **p** 22 Lon for Col Bp. CMS Miss at Yambio Sudan 21-22; C of H Trin Heigham 22-23; CMS Miss at Mpwapwa 23-28; Kilimatinde 29-31; Buigiri 31-33; Perm to Offic at St Helen (in c of St Mary) 34-35; V of St Thos Barnsbury 35-41; C of St John Wynberg 41-42; Actg C of St Paul Canonbury 42-43; V of Ch Ch Ore 43-62; Perm to Offic Dio Chich from 62. *35 Park View, Hastings, Sussex.* (3058-7864)

FLINT, David Moore. Univ of Tor BA 59, MA 68. Trin Coll Tor STB 62. **d** 62 **p** 63 Bran. R of Birtle 62-66; on leave 67-78; C of St John York Mills City and Dio Tor from 78. *15 Danean Drive, Willowdale, Ont, Canada.*

FLINT, Elwyn Henry. Univ of Brisb BA (1st cl Mod Lang and Lit) 36. Brisb Th Coll ACT ThL 36. **d** 37 **p** 38 Brisb. C of St Andr Lutwyche Brisb 37-40; V of Monto 40-43; Chap AIF 43-46; L to Offic Dio Brisb and Lect Univ of Queensld from 46. *Box 48, University Post Office, St Lucia, Queensland, Australia 4067.* (266 6856)

FLINT, Howard Harrison. Trin Coll Tor STh 55. **d** 55 **p** 56 Ont. I of Marysburgh 56-58; R of Augusta 58-78. *Box 125, Maitland, Ont, Canada.* (613-348 3269)

FLINT, John Edgar Keith. b 03. Univ of Lon. 28. **d** 39 Dorch for Ox **p** 40 Ox. [f Congregational Min]. C of Waddesdon w Over Winchendon and Fleet Marston 39-43; Leighton Buzzard 43-49; V of Heath w Reach 49-54; Jamestown St Hel 54-63; Chap Tristan da Cunha 63-66; St Kath Conv Parmoor 67-68; C of Tenbury 68-80; Chap Commun of St Jo Evang St D from 80. D from 80. *Community of St John Evangelist, The Priory, St David's, Dyfed.*

FLINT, John Hedley. b 32. Edin Th Coll 55. **d** 57 **p** 58 Glas. C of Ch Ch Glas 57-60; Motherwell 60-62; P-in-c of St Gabr Govan Glas 62-65; C-in-c of St Ninian's Conv Distr Harlow Green 65-73; V of Gannow Burnley 74-76; Chap R Assoc in Aid of Deaf and Dumb Dio S'wark 76-79; C-in-c of Idridgehay Dio Derby from 79; Kirk Ireton Dio Derby from 79. *Kirk Ireton Rectory, Derby, DE4 4LE.*

FLINT, Louis Thomas. b 47. **d** 80 Bp Ndwandwe for Johann (NSM). C of Florida Dio Johann from 80. *6 Sandikiaat Street, Weltevreden Park, Florida, S Africa 1710.*

FLINT, Maurice Sidney. Tyndale Hall Bris. Univ Coll Tor BA 50. Wycl Coll Tor LTh 50. Boston Univ STM 51 PhD 64. **d** 36 Lon for Col Bp **p** 40 Tor for Arctic. Miss at Pond Inlet 36-40; Chap RAF 40-45; Rep of Script U and CSSM Canada 45-47; C of Ch of Messiah Tor 47-50; C-in-c Trin E Tor 51-53; R 53-63; Tutor Wycl Coll Tor 63-69. *Maplewood, RR 2 Oakville, Ont, Canada.*

FLITCROFT, John. b 14. Late Scho and Pri of Univ of Man BA (1st cl Hist) and Jones Scho 36, MA 37. Bps' Coll Cheshunt 37. **d** 38 **p** 39 Man. C of H Rood Swinton 38-40; St Luke Benchill 40-42; St Chrys Vic Pk 42-44; V of St Thos Bury 44-48; Ashton-on-Ribble 48-50; LPr Dio Man 50-66; Warden Hulme Hall Univ of Man 50-64; Lect Eccles Hist Univ of Man 51-72; Hon C of St Ann Man 64-66; V of Lytham 66-79. *5 Greenhey, Lytham St Annes, Lancs, FY8 4HL.* (Lytham 733849)

FLOAT, Wilfrid Laurence Palk. b 1885. Clare Coll Cam Jun Opt 06, BA LLB (2nd cl Law Trip pt ii) 07, 2nd Cl Th Trip pt i 09, MA 11. Ridley Hall Cam. **d** 09 Woolwich for S'wark **p** 10 S'wark. C of Ch Ch Gipsy Hill 09-12; V of N Stainley w Sleningford 12-20; Dom Chap to Bp of Ripon 12-20; Lect Ridley Hall Cam 21; Ex Dioc Tr Coll 22; R of H Trin Chesterfield 22-25; Chap to Chesterfield and N Derbys U 23-25; V of High Wycombe 25-50; Surr 25-50; Perm to Offic Dio Chich From 50. *39 Dean Court Road, Rottingdean, Sussex.* (Brighton 32724)

FLOATE, Herbert Frederick Giraud. b 25. Keble Coll Ox BA (2nd cl Geog) 50, MA 54. Qu Coll Birm 50. **d** 61 Maur **p** 63 Linc. C-in-c of Anse Royale Seychelles 61; Asst Master Carre's Gr Sch Sleaford 63-65; Hon C of Quarrington w Old Sleaford 63-65; P-in-c of Mareham-le-Fen 65-66; Asst Chap Ch Ch Gr Sch Claremont 66-67; Lect Univ of W Austr 67-72; R of Harlaxton w Wyville and Hungerton 72-74; Stroxton 72-74; Lect Shenstone New Coll Worc 74-78; P-in-c of St Geo Redditch 78-79. *c/o USPG, 15 Tufton Street, SW1P 3QQ.*

FLOOD, Claude Edward. b 08. Roch Th Coll **d** 62 **p** 63 St E. C of St Mary Bury St Edms 62-66; V of Wood Ditton w Saxon Street 66-74; V of Stetchworth 66-74. *69 Orchard Way, Burwell, Cambs.*

FLOOD, Eric Malcolm Edward. b 36. St D Coll Lamp BA (2nd cl Hist) 60. St Cath Coll Ox BA (3rd cl Th) 62, MA 66. St Steph Ho Ox 60. **d** 63 **p** 64 Blackb. C of St Pet Accrington 63-66; St Steph Blackpool 66-71; V of Haslingden w Haslingden Grane 71-76; Thornton-le-Fylde Dio Blackb from 76. *Vicarage, Meadows Avenue, Thornton-le-Fylde, Blackpool, Lancs.* (Cleveleys 855099)

FLOOD, Frederick Horace. Clifton Th Coll 52. **d** 54 **p** 55 S'wark. C of Tooting 54-57; R of St Sav Chorlton-on-Medlock 57-65; S Normanton 65-79. *121 Coronation Drive, South Normanton, Derby.*

FLOOK, James Richard. St Jo Coll Morpeth. **d** 47 Bath **p** 50 Newc. Regr Dio Bath 47-48; C of St Pet E Maitland 49-50; R of St John Wollombi 50-54; Charlestown 54-55; Waratah 55-56; P-in-c of Boolaroo 56-61; R of Gresford 61-67; L to Offic Dio Syd 69-80. *Unit 130, Blues Point Tower, McMahon's Point, North Sydney, NSW, Australia 2060.* (92-3959)

FLORANCE, Lyall Peace. b 18. **d** 64 **p** 65 Wai. C of Havelock N 64-67; Gisborne 67-70; P-in-c of Turangi Miss Distr 70-74; Team V of Gisborne 75-80; Offg Min Dio Wai from 80. *The Birches, Koura Street, Turrangi, NZ.* (8842)

FLORENT, Zakariasy. **d** 49 **p** 52 Madag. P Dio Madag. *Ampasimanjeva, Sahasinaka, Madagascar.*

FLORY, John Richard. b 35. Clare Coll Cam BA (Nat Sci Trip) 59, MA 63. Westcott Ho Cam 69. **d** 71 **p** 72 Bris. C of St Mary Shirehampton 71-74; V of Patchway Dio Bris from 74. *Vicarage, Southsea Road, Patchway, Bristol, BS12 5DP.* (Bristol 692935)

FLOWER, Brian Harold. b 32. St Jo Coll Auckld 77. **d** 79 **p** 80 Auckld. C of St Heliers Bay Dio Auckld from 79. *92 Riddell Road, Glendowie, Auckland 5, NZ.*

FLOWER, Neil Ashbrook. Moore Th Coll Syd ThL 66. **d** 66 **p** 67 Syd. C of St Andr Wahroonga 66-69; Youth Sec CMS for NSW 70-74; R of Cabramatta Dio Syd from 74. *42 Cumberland Street, Cabramatta, NSW, Australia 2166.* (72-1630)

FLOWER, Roger Edward. b 45. K Coll Lon and Warm AKC 68. **d** 69 Willesden for Lon **p** 70 Lon. C of Gt Stanmore 69-72; Wells w Coxley & Wookey Hole 72-77; V of Tatworth 77-82; P-in-c of St Andr Taunton Dio B & W from 82. *St Andrew's Vicarage, Rowbarton, Taunton, Somt.* (Taunton 2081)

FLOWERDAY, Edward Arthur. b 04. Richmond Th Coll 28. **d** and **p** 43 Nor. C of S Lynn 43-45; V of Hopton 45-50; Scalby 50-58; St Steph Acomb 58-74; RD of York 62-66. *14 Barton View, Penrith, Cumbria, CA11 8AV.*

FLOWERDEW, George Douglas Hugh. b 10. MBE (Mil) 44. Wycl Hall Ox 66. **d** 67 Win **p** 68 Southn for Win. C of Chandler's Ford 67-70; R of Baughurst w Ramsdale 70-80; Bp's Ecumen Officer Dio Win 74-80. *3 Lovelace Road, Summertown, Oxford.*

FLOWERS, John Henry. b 33. Qu Coll Birm 63. **d** 65 **p** 66 Llan. C of St Fagan Aberdare 65-68; Llantrisant 68-72; V of Nantymoel w Wyndham 72-76; Chap HM Pris Wormwood Scrubs 76-78; Winson Green Birm 78-81; HM Pris Albany IW from 81. *c/o HM Prison, Albany, Isle of Wight.* (Newport 524055)

FLOWERS, Leroy Norman. b 49. Codr Coll Barb 76. **d** 75 **p** 77 Bel. On study leave 75-77; P-in-c of Toledo Dio Bel from 77. *Anglican Mission House, Mango Creek, Independence, Belize.*

FLOWERS, Robert Thomas. Univ of Tor BA 60. Wycl Coll Tor LTh and BTh 63. **d** 63 Bp Snell for Tor **p** 63 Tor for Keew. C of Ch of the Messiah Tor 63-65; Ignace 65-68; R of Brighton 69-75; Lively Dio Alg from 75. *Box 284, Lively, Ont., Canada.*

FLOYD, Stephen Walter. b 10. Late Scho of Pemb Coll Cam BA (Wrangler) 31, MA 35. Ely Th Coll 32. **d** 33 **p** 34 Liv. C of St Mich AA Wigan 33-36; UMCA Miss Dio Zanz 36-39; C of Gt Grimsby 39-42; Chap RNVR 40-42; Asst Master St Jas Choir Sch Grimsby 42-44 and 56-67; R of Hameringham w Scrafield and Winceby 44-47; Asst Master Fettes Coll Edin 47-50; Min of S Queensferry 50-56;V of Thornton Curtis 56-67; R of Wilsford w Kelby 67-78; V of N Rauceby Dio Linc from 78. *4 Penarwyn Woods, Par, Cornwall.* (Par 5168)

FLOYD, Thomas Henry. Trin Coll Tor. **d** 25 **p** 26 Tor. C of St Jo Evang Tor 25-26; I of Caledon E w Sandhill and Cambell's Cross 27-31; R of Ch Ch Campbellford 31-38; I of Pet S w Graystock 38-42; Chap RCAF 42-46; C of St John Peterborough Tor 46-47; Hosp Chap Kingston Ont 47-49; I of Creemore Banda and Lisle 49-50; Chap of Hosp Whitby 49-69; Hon C of St Geo Oshawa 60-69; St Mark Pet Dio Tor from 70. *823 Armour Road, Peterborough, Ont, Canada.*

FLUCK, Paul John Martin. b 46. Hertf Coll Ox BA 69, MA 78. Cranmer Hall Dur Dipl Th 72. **d** 73 **p** 74 Ripon. C of Burmantofts 73-76; Kingswood 76-79; Team V of Ipsley Dio Worc from 79. *Winyates Vicarage, Winforton Close, Redditch, Worcs, B98 0JX.* (0527-27296)

FLUCK, Peter Ernest. b 29. Linc Th Coll. **d** 61 **p** 62 Cant. C of Maidstone 61-64; R of Uffington 64-70; V of Tallington 64-70; C-in-c of Barholme w Stowe 65-66; V 66-70; St Nich w St John Newport Linc 70-75; R of S Ormsby w Ketsby Calceby and Driby Dio Linc from 75; C-in-c of Harrington w Brinkhill Dio Linc from 75; Oxcombe Dio Linc from 75; Ruckland w Farforth and Maidenwell Dio Linc from 75; Somersby w Bag Enderby Dio Linc from 75; Tetford w Salmonby Dio Linc from 75; Haugh Dio Linc from 75. *South Ormsby Rectory, Louth, Lincs, LN11 8QT.* (Swaby 236)

FLUDE, Maurice Haddon. b 41. St Aid Coll 66. **d** 69 Woolwich for S'wark **p** 70 S'wark (APM). C of Mottingham 69-74; Perm to Offic Dio S'wark 76-81. *19 Simmonds Way, Danbury, Essex.* (Danbury 3074)

FLUKE, John Ronald. b 12. St Mich Coll Llan 46. **d** 48 **p** 49 Llan. C of Tylorstown 48-51; Llantrissant 51-57; V of Penmaen 57-63; Pawlett 63-73; Newbridge 73-79. *c/o St Mary's Vicarage, Crumlin, Gwent, NP1 4FW.* (Newbridge 245368)

FLUMERFELT, Donald Bruce. b 47. Mt Allison Univ NB BA 69. McGill Univ Montr BTh 74. Montr Dioc Th Coll 74. **d** 75 **p** 76 Montr. C of Beaconsfield Kirkland 75-77; R of Stanbridge E Dio Montr from 77. *Box 1, Stanbridge East, Quebec, Canada.*

FLUX, Brian George. b 39. Oak Hill Th Coll 68. **d** 71 Man **p** 72 Hulme for Man. C of Ch Ch Chadderton 71-74; All SS Preston 74-76; Min of St Luke Preston 76-81; CF (TAVR) from 78; R of St Clem Higher Openshaw Dio Man from 81. *Rectory, Ashton Old Road, Manchester, M11 1HJ.* (061-370 1538)

FLYNN, Peter Alfred. Univ of Manit BA 60. St Jo Coll Winnipeg BTh 65. **d** 64 Bp Anderson for Rupld **p** 65 Rupld. Chap Univ of Manit 64-72; St Jo Coll Winnipeg 67-72; on Leave 73-75; Hon C of St Mark Winnipeg 75; Assoc P of River N Angl Pars Dio Rupld 76-79; P Supervisor from 79. *292 Scotia Street, Winnipeg, Manit, Canada.*

FLYNN, Peter Murray. b 35. Oak Hill Coll 76. **d** 79 Edmon for Lon **p** 80 Lon. C of St Mary Finchley Dio Lon from 79. *34 Bunns Lane, Mill Hill, NW7 2DU.*

FLYNN, William Russell. Trin Coll Tor. **d** 58 Bp Snell for Tor **p** 60 Tor. C of St Columba Tor 59-61; R of Shanty Bay 61-70; Brooklin 70-76; St Ninian Tor 76-81; on leave. *49 Simpson Avenue, Bowmanville, Ont, Canada.*

FOIZEY, Michael John. b 24. Trin Coll Cam BA 45, MA 65. Westcott Ho Cam 45. **d** 47 **p** 48 Lon. C of St Mary Magd Munster Square 47-53; V of St Matt Willesden 53-60; R of St Pet Lon Dks w St John Wapping Dio Lon from 60; Commiss Bal from 75. *St Peter's Clergy House, Wapping Lane, E1 9RW.* (01-481 2985)

FOLEY, Geoffrey Evan. Univ of New Engl Armid BA 71. St Jo Coll Morpeth ACT ThL 53. Univ of Queensld Dipl Div 65. **d** 53 **p** 54 Graft. C of Murwillumbah 54-59; R of Mallanganee 59-65; Woodburn 65-72; Hon C of Ch Ch Cathl City and Dio Graft from 72; Exam Chap to Bp of Graft from 73. *68 Bacon Street, Grafton, NSW, Australia 2460.* (42 4078)

✠ **FOLEY, Right Rev Ronald Graham Gregory.** b 23. St Jo Coll Dur BA 49, Dipl Th 50. **d** 50 **p** 51 Blackb. C of H Trin S Shore Blackpool 50-54; V of St Luke Blackb 54-60; R of Brancepeth Dio Dur from 60; Dir of Relig Educn Dio Dur 60-70; Hon Can of Dur 65-70; V of Leeds 71-82; Hon Can of Ripon from 71; Chap to HM the Queen from 77; Cons Ld Bp Suffr of Reading in Ch Ch Cathl Ox 22 July 82 by Abp of Cant. *Diocesan Church House, North Hinksey, Oxford, OX2 0NB.* (Ox 44566)

FOLEY, Timothy David. b 41. Trin Coll Tor BA 67. **d** 70 **p** 71 Tor. C of St John York Mills 71-72; R of Erin Mills S 72-80; Dom Chap to Bp of Tor from 77; I of Redeemer City and Dio Tor from 80. *162 Bloor Street West, Toronto, M5S 1M4, Ont, Canada.*

FOLKARD, John Lancelot. b 07. Univ of Dur 32. St Aid Coll 32. **d** 35 **p** 36. C of St Steph Hull 35-39; Bromley 39-42; R of N Tamerton 42-43; V of Sewerby w Marton Grindall and Ergham 43-54; C-in-c of H Trin Bridlington 47-54; V 54; R of Ulcombe 54-80. *1 Merrals Wood Road, Strood. Rochester, ME2 2PP.* (Medway 74332)

FOLKARD, Laurence Goring. b 08. Univ of Bris BA (Phil and Econ Hons Aegr) 34, MA 47. Qu Coll Birm 36. **d** 37 **p** 38 Birm. C of Hall Green 37-39; Farlington 39-41; Rusthall 41-42; C-in-c of Goldhanger w L Totham 42-44; R of Woodham Mortimer w Hazeleigh 44-54; Dioc INSp of Schs Dio Chelmsf 46-62; Chap to St Pet Hosp Maldon 48-54; R of Foxearth w Pentlow 54-65; Surr from 55; V of Longnor w Reapsmoor Newtown and Hollinsclough 65-73; RD of Alstonfield 70-73; C-in-c of Quarnford 73. *68 Portland Crescent, Shrewsbury.* (Shrewsbury 61683)

FOLKARD, Oliver Goring. b 41. Univ of Nottm BA (Phil) 63. Lich Th Coll 64. **d** 66 **p** 67 Southw. C of Carlton 66-67; Worksop 67-68; Brewood 68-71; Folkingham 72-75; V of Whaplode Drove Dio Linc from 75; P-in-c of Gedney Hill Dio Linc 75-77; V from 77. *Vicarage, Whaplode Drove, Spalding, Lincs.* (W Drove 392)

FOLKS, Andrew John. b 42. St Jo Coll Dur BA 65, Dipl Th

69. **d** 69 **p** 70 Dur. C of Stranton 69-72; Chap Sandback Sch from 73; Perm to Offic Dio Ches from 74. *2 Dane Close, Sandbach, Chesh.*

FOLKS, Peter William John. b 30. FRCO 56. Launde Abbey Leic 72. **d** 72 Leic **p** 73 Bp Mort for Leic. C of St Aid Leic 72-76; V of St Aug City and Dio Leic from 76. *1a Tetuan Road, Leicester, LE3 9RT.* (Leic 59679)

FOLLAND, Ronald George. b 14. AKC (2nd cl Hons) 48. St Bonif Coll Warm 48. **d** 49 **p** 50 Ex. C of Tavistock 49-52; King's Heath 52; St Steph St Alb 52-56; R of Ashwater 56-65; RD of Holsworthy 62-65; V of E Teignmouth 66-79; Surr 66-79; Publ Pr Dio Ex from 80. *67 The Marles, Exmouth, Devon, Ex8 4NE.*

FOLLENT, John William. b 13. Univ of Syd MB BS 40. **d** 70 Graft. C of Tweed Heads Dio Graft from 70. *Box 18, Tweed Heads, NSW 2485, Australia.*

FOLLIS, George Raymond Carlile. b 23. DFC 45. Lich Th Coll 63. **d** 65 **p** 66 Lich. C of Walsall Wood 65-69; R of New Fishbourne Dio Chich from 69. *12 Fishbourne Road, Chichester, Sussex.* (Chichester 83364)

FOLLIS, Henry Horatio. b 16. St D Coll Lamp BA (1st cl Hist) 37. BD (Lon) (2nd Cl) 57. Ripon Hall, Ox. **d** 39 **p** 40 Lich. C of St Jas Wolverhampton 39-42; Caverswall 42-45; Madeley 45-47; C-in-c of Canwell Conv Distr Lich 47-51; Treas V of Lich Cathl 51-54; Dean's V 54-57; V of Little Aston 52-69; St Mary Shrewsbury 69-71; V of St Alkmund Shrewsbury 69-71; Broadway 71-73; R of Blymhill w Weston-under-Lizard 73-80; P-in-c of Tong 74-76. *67 Maes-y-Castell, Llanrhos, Llandudno, Gwyn, LL30 1NG.* (0492 83144)

FOLORUNSO, Elkanah Olurinde. Im Coll Ibad. **d** 60 **p** 61 Lagos. P Dio Lagos. *c/o Bible Society of West Africa, PO Box 68 Apapa, Lagos, Nigeria.*

FONSECA, Eugene Guillaume. b 13. **d** 50 Gui **p** 74 Starbroek for Guy. d Dio Guy 50-74; C of Ch Ch Georgetown 74-75; P-in-c of H Spirit Miss Prashad Nagar 75-80; Perm to Offic Dio Guy from 80. *62 Fourth Avenue, Subryanville, Guyana.*

FOOD, Frank Herbert. Wycl Hall Ox 37. **d** 38 Lon **p** 39 Willesden for Lon. C of St Mary Islington 38-41; V of St Matt Cam 41-45; H Trin-Heworth York 45-52; Leyton and Surr 52-58; Perm to Offic Dio Leic 61; R of Markfield w Stanton-under-Bardon 61-71; Chap Torbay Hosp 71-77; Perm to Offic Dio Ex from 77. *15 St Michael's Road, Torquay, Devon.* (Torquay 35530)

FOOKES, Roger Mortimer. b 24. VRD 63. Ch Ch Ox BA (3rd cl Th) 49, MA 53. Wells Th Coll. **d** 50 **p** 51 Bris. C of Westbury-on-Trym 50-53; Frome Selwood 53-55; Chap RNVR 51-58; RNR 58-74; R of Barwick 55-62; R of Closworth 55-62; V of Midsomer Norton 62-78; RD of Midsomer Norton 72-78; M Gen Syn B & W 70-78; C-in-c of Stratton-on-the-Fosse 74-78; Clandown 75-78; V of Wotton-under-Edge w Ozleworth and N Nibley Dio Glouc from 78. *Vicarage, Wotton-under-Edge, Glos.* (Wotton-under-Edge 2175)

FOORD, Claude Victor. b 07. Worc Ordin Coll. **d** 56 **p** 57 Worc. C of St Clem Worc 56-58; Old Swinford 58-60; R of St Clem Worc 60-64; V of Cleeve Prior 64-72. *11 Greenhill Gardens, Greenhill, Evesham, Worcs.* (Evesham 2147)

FOORD, Dudley Tucker. Univ of Syd BSc 50, MSc 53. BD (Lon) 59. ACT ThL 57, Th Scho 68, Moore Th Coll Syd. **d** 58 Syd **p** 58 Bp Hilliard for Syd. C of Manly 58-59; Ashbury and Gladesville 59-60; R of Kingsgrove 60-65; Chap to Univ of NSW 60-64; Univ of Syd 65-67; Dean and Lect of Moore Th Coll Syd and L to Offic Dio Syd 65-72; R of St Ives Dio Syd from 72. *7 Walker Avenue, St Ives, NSW, Australia 2075.* (44-5545)

FOOT, Daniel Henry Paris. b 46. Peterho Cam BA 67, MA 74. Ridley Hall Cam 77. **d** 79 **p** 80 Pet. C of Werrington Dio Pet from 79. *63 Hall Lane, Werrington, Peterborough, PE4 6RA.* (0733-74268)

FOOT, Edward Percival. b 09. Trin Coll Dub BA and Div Test 32, MA 44. **d** 32 **p** 33 Clogh. C of Enniskillen 32-35; Dioc C Dio Clogh 35-36; C-in-c of Garvary 36-39; Donaghmore w Monellan 39-44; I of Tamiaghtard w Aghanloo 44-47; CF 47-49; C of Yeovil w Preston Plucknett 52-60; Stoke-on-Trent 60-62; I of Fertagh U 62-79; RD of St Canice and Kells 77-79. *The Residence, Church Street, Templemore, Co Tipperary, Irish Republic.*

FOOT, Leslie Frank. b 07. Univ of Dur 30. St Bonif Coll Warm 27. **d** 32 **p** 33 Brech. C of St Jo Bapt Dundee 32-35; M of St Steph Bush Bro Quorn 35-38; St Mich Colom 38-40; CF (EC) 40-46; Hon CF 46; R of E Stoke 46-47; PC of E Holme 46-47; CF 47-50; Chap RAF 50-63; R of Eastergate 63-75; Perm to Offic Dio Chich from 75. *120 Little Breach, Chichester, Sussex, PO19 4TZ.* (Chichester 789640)

FOOT, Leslie Robert James. b 33. Univ of Bris BSc 54. Wells Th Coll 67. **d** 69 B & W **p** 70 Bp Wilson for B & W. C of Yeovil 69-76. *21 Holm Oaks, Butleigh, Glastonbury, Somt.* (Baltonsborough 50870)

FOOT, Luxmore Knethel. **d** 79 N Queensld (NSM). C of St Thos Hughenden Dio N Queensld from 79. *Hann Highway, Hughenden, Qld, Australia 4821.*

FOOT, Paul. b 41. Univ of Lon BA (2nd cl Hist) 64. Chich Th Coll 65. **d** 67 **p** 68 Portsm. C of St Mark N End Portsea 67-71; Grimsbury 71-74; V of St Cury w St Gunwalloe 74-80; P-in-c of Port Isaac Dio Truro from 80; St Kew Dio Truro from 80. *Vicarage, Trewetha Lane, Port Isaac, Cornw, PL29 3RN.*

FOOT, William Henry. b 1896. **d** 71 **p** 72 Sask. C of Kinistino Dio Sask from 71. *RR1 Weldon, Sask, Canada.*

FOOT, William Verner. b 11. Trin Coll Dub BA 33, Div Test 34, MA 65. **d** 34 **p** 35 Derry. C of Maghera 34-37; C-in-c of Kilteevogue 37-42; Chap RNVR 42-46; RN 46-66; R of Bradford Peverell w Stratton 66-70. *Courshay Cottage, Hawkchurch, Axminster, Devon, EX13 5XE.* (Hawkchurch 450)

FOOTE, John Bruce. b 18. G and C Coll Cam BA 39, MA 43, MD 51. St Jo Coll Nottm 78. **d** 79 **p** 80 Sheff (APM). C of St Thos Crookes City and Dio Sheff from 79. *67 St Thomas Road, Crookes, Sheffield 10.*

FOOTE, Keith Athelstane. St Francis Coll Brisb. **d** 66 **p** 67 Brisb. C of St Pet Wynnum 66-70; St Mark Warwick Dio Brisb 70; Perm to Offic Dio Brisb from 70. *5 Osric Street, Yeronga, Queensland, Australia 4104.* (48 3551)

FOOTE, Reuben Athelstane. Brisb Th Coll ACT ThL 33. **d** 33 **p** 34 Brisb. C of St John Dalby 33-35; St Mark Eidsvold 35-36; St Paul Maryborough 36-38; V of St Pet Milmerran 38-42; R of Laidley 42-45; Brisbane Valley 45-52; St Mich AA Kingaroy 52-57; St Mary Kangaroo Point Brisb 57-78; Perm to Offic Dio Brisb from 78. *36 Jolly Street, Clayfield, Queensland, Australia 4011.*

FOOTE, William Walter. b 53. Univ of Waterloo BA 74. Hur Coll Lon MDiv 77. **d** 77 Bp Parke-Taylor for Hur **p** 78 Hur. C of St Paul's Cathl Lon Ont 77-79; I of St Luke and St John Brantford Dio Hur from 79. *24 Hill Crest Avenue, Brantford, Ont, Canada N3T 2C7.*

FOOTITT, John Michael. b 35. Dipl Th (Lon) 62. St Aid Coll 60. **d** 62 **p** 63 Worc. C of Dudley 62-69; V of St Barn Dudley 69-75. *16 Romsley Court, Westley Street, Dudley, W Midlands.*

FOOTTIT, Anthony Charles. b 35. K Coll Cam 2nd cl Cl Trip pt i 56, BA (2nd cl Cl Trip pt ii) 57, MA 70. Cudd Coll 59. **d** 61 **p** 62 Nor. C of Wymondham 61-64; Blakeney w L Langham 64-67; V in Blakeney Group (C-in-c of Hindringham w Binham and Cockthorpe) 67-71; R of N Cadbury 71-76; C-in-c of Yarlington 71-76; S Cadbury 75-76; R of Camelot 76-81; St Hugh's Missr for Lincs from 81. *Claythorpe Old Rectory, Grantham, Lincs, NG32 3DU.*

FOOTTIT, John Guy. b 11. Jes Coll Cam 3rd cl Hist Trip pt i 33, BA 34. Wycl Hall Ox 34. **d** 35 **p** 36 Pet. C of St Giles Northn 35-39; Kingsthorpe 40-45; Sec Pet Dioc Youth Coun 43-45; V of Comberton 45-51; R of Whatfield w Semer 51-77; RD of Hadleigh 62-66; P-in-c of Nedging w Naughton 74-77. *6 Robert Street, Harrogate, HG1 1HP.*

FORAE, Mark Boloje. Im Coll Ibad. **d** and **p** 66 Benin. P Dio Benin. *St Matthew's Parsonage, Okpara, via Sapele, Nigeria.*

FORAN, John William. ACT ThL 72. Moore Coll Syd 72. **d** 74 Syd **p** 74 Bp Robinson for Syd. C of Dural 74-76; St Steph Penrith 76-77; R of Westmead Dio Syd from 77. *75 Hawkesbury Road, Westmead, NSW, Australia 2145.* (635-5669)

FORBES, Douglas Stewart. b 12. Edin Th Coll 59. **d** 61 Arg Is for Edin **p** 62 Edin. C of St Mark Portobello 61-63; R of Cruden 63-68; Fraserburgh 68-71; Forres 71-79. *14 Whinnieknowe Gardens, Nairn, IV12 5EL.* (Nairn 54849)

FORBES, Francis James. Edin Th Coll 55. **d** 58 **p** 59 Brech. C of St Ninian Dundee 58-60; Hatfield (in c of St Francis Waterfalls) 61-64; R of Waterfalls 64-69; Arcadia Dio Mashon from 69. *129 Montgomery Drive, Prospect, Salisbury, Rhodesia.*

FORBES, Frank Agar. b 05. Lon Coll of Div 50. **d** 52 **p** 53 S'wark. C of Streatham Vale 52-55; V of H Trin w St Paul Greenwich and Chap Miller Gen Hosp 55-61; V of Tudeley w Capel 61-74; Hon C of Hordle 75-81; L to Offic Dios Win & Sarum from 81. *2 Ashley Court, Kenilworth Close, New Milton, Hants.*

FORBES, Graham John Thomson. b 51. Univ of Aber MA 73. Univ of Edin BD 76. Edin Th Coll 73. **d** 76 **p** 77 Edin. C of Old St Paul City and Dio Edin from 76. *41 Jeffrey Street, Edinburgh, EH1 1DH.*

FORBES, Very Rev John Franey. K Coll Lon and Warm AKC 57. **d** 58 **p** 59 Dur. C of H Trin Darlington 58-62; St Geo Cathl Capetn 62-65; R of Hoetjes Bay 65-69; Warden Zonnebloem Coll Capetn 69-75; Exam Chap to Abp of Capetn 69-75; Commiss Damar 71-76; Dean and R of H Nativ Cathl

Pmbg Dio Natal from 76. *Deanery, PO Box 1639, Pietermaritzburg, Natal, S Africa.* (2-5848)

FORBES, Patrick. b 38. Linc Th Coll 64. **d** 66 **p** 67 B & W. C of Yeovil 66-69; Wm Temple Ch Conv Distr Abbey Wood 69-70; M Thamesmead Ecumen Group Min 71-74; Team V of Thamesmead 74-78; P-in-c of Offley w Lilley Dio St Alb from 78; Dioc Communications Officer from 78. *Offley Vicarage, Hitchin, Herts.*

FORBES, Raymond John. b 34. ALCD (2nd Cl) 58. **d** 58 **p** 59 S'wark. C of St Steph Wandsworth 58-61; Kewstoke (in c of St Jude Milton) 61-63; V of Fordcombe 63-73; R of Ashurst 64-73; P-in-c of Morden w Almer and Charborough 73-76; Bloxworth 73-76; V of Red Post Dio Sarum from 76. *Morden Vicarage, Wareham, Dorset, BH20 7DR.* (092-945 244)

FORBES, Stuart. b 33. BD (Lon) 59. Oak Hill Th Coll 56. **d** 61 **p** 62 Man. C of St Pet Halliwell 61-64; C-in-c of H Trin Wicker w Neepsend Sheff 64-69; V of Stainforth 69-77; All SS Salterhebble Dio Wakef from 77. *All Saints' Vicarage, Salterhebble, Halifax, HX3 0LS.* (Halifax 65805)

FORBES ADAM, Stephen Timothy Beilby. b 23. Ball Coll Ox. Chich Th Coll 59. **d** 61 **p** 62 York. C of Guisborough 61-64; R of Barton-in-Fabis 64-70; V of Thrumpton 64-70; Hon C of S Stoke Dio B & W from 74. *Brewery House, South Stoke, Bath, Avon.*

FORCE-JONES, Graham Roland John. b 41. Sarum Th Coll 65. **d** 68 **p** 69 Sarum. C of Calne w Blackland Dio Sarum 68-74; Team V of Oldbury 73-76; P-in-c 76-78; R 78-80; Team R of Upper Kennet Dio Sarum from 80. *West Overton Vicarage, Marlborough, Wilts, SN8 4ER.*

FORD, Adam. b 40. Univ of Lanc MA 72. K Coll Lon and Warm. BD (2nd Cl) and AKC 63. **d** 65 Tewkesbury for Glouc **p** 65 Glouc. C of Cirencester w Watermoor 65-70; V of Hebden Bridge 70-76; Chap St Paul's Girls Sch Hammersmith from 77. *55 Bolingbroke Road, W14.*

FORD, Canon Alfred Carr. b 17. Kelham Th Coll 34. Trin Coll Mus ATCL 46. **d** 40 **p** 41 Roch. C of All SS Perry Street Northfleet 40-43; Gillingham w Upberry 43-46; Min Can Roch Cathl 44-49; CF 47-50; Youth Chap to Bp of Roch 46-52; R of Fawkham Dio Roch from 49; Chap Old Downs Hartley from 58; Hon Can of Roch 79-82; Can (Emer) from 82. *Fawkham Rectory, Longfield, Kent, DA3 8LX.* (Longfield 2152)

FORD, Arthur Edward. b 05. Ch Ch Ox Heath Harrison Trav Scho 25, BA (2nd Cl Mod Lit) 26, MA 31. Cudd Coll 28. **d** 30 **p** 31 S'wark. C of St Andr Catford 30-31; Streatham 31-34; Chap to Bp of Gibr 34-36; C of St Mary Portsea (in c of St Wilfred) 36-40; Chap RNVR 40-48; C of Bradford-on-Avon 48-49; Chipping Campden 49-50; R of Merrow 50-66; V of Kilmeston w Beauworth 66-72. *Mayford, Beeches Hill, Bishop's Waltham, Southampton, SO3 1FE.* (Bp's Waltham 3476)

FORD, Brian Brakefield. b 49. Coll of Em & St Chad Sask 71. **d** 75 Bp Stiff for Arctic. C of Port Harrison 75-78; Miss at Baker Lake Dio Arctic from 78. *St Aidan's Mission, Baker Lake, NWT, Canada.*

FORD, Christopher Simon. b 51. AKC 74. St Aug Coll Cant. **d** 75 **p** 76 Man. C of Wm Temple Woodhouse Park 75-77; St Jas New Bury Farnworth 77-80; R of St Jo Evang Old Trafford Dio Man from 80. *Rectory, Lindum Avenue, Old Trafford, Manchester, M16 9NQ.* (061-872 0500)

FORD, Colin David. b 28. MIMechE 59. Oak Hill Th Coll 60. **d** 62 **p** 63 Cant. C of St Martin Dover 62-67; V of Goodnestone w Graveney 67-71; Ch Ch Broad Green Croydon Dio Cant from 71. *21 Elmwood Road, Croydon, Surrey.* (01-684 2880)

FORD, Colvin Leslie. b 47. St Jo Coll Morpeth 71. **d** 71 **p** 72 Newc. C of Singleton 71-75; R of Kendall 75-77; Dungog Dio Newc from 77. *Rectory, Myles Street, Dungog, NSW, Australia 2420.*

FORD, Canon David George. b 37. ALCD 61 (LTh from 74). **d** 61 **p** 62 Chelmsf. C of St Barn Walthamstow 61-64; Wisbech 64-66; C-in-c of St Jas Conv Distr Cherry Hinton 66-73; V of St Jas Cam 73-80; Can Res of Ripon Cathl from 80. *St Peter's House, High St Agnesgate, Ripon, HG4 1QR.* (Ripon 4108)

FORD, David John. b 38. BD (Lon) 68. Lon Coll of Div 67. **d** 69 Woolwich for S'wark **p** 70 S'wark. C of St Jo Evang Blackheath 69-71; Westlands 71-75; V of St Steph w St Phil and St Anne Sheff 75-77; Team R of St Steph and St Bart (and St Nath from 80) Netherthorpe City and Dio Sheff from 77. *115 Upperthorpe Road, Sheffield, S6 3EA.* (Sheffield 77130)

FORD, Derek Ernest. b 32. St Mich Coll Llan 56. **d** 58 **p** 59 Llan. C of St Martin Roath 58-61; Newton Nottage 61-67; V of Abercanaid 67-70; Perm to Offic Dio Win 70-80; M SSF 72-80; Publ Pr Dio Sarum 73-80; L to Offic Dio Newc T 75-80; In Amer. Ch. *Society of St Francis, Little Portion Friary, PO Box 399, Mt Sinai, NY 11766, USA.*

FORD, Donald Robert. b 50. Mem Univ Newfld BA 70. Trin Coll Tor MDiv 74. **d** & **p** 74 Newfld. C of Burin 74-76; I of Twillingate 77-80; St Jude Brantford Dio Hur from 80. *79 Peel Street, Brantford, Ont, Canada.*

✠ **FORD, Right Rev Douglas Albert.** Univ of BC BA 39, BD 48. Angl Th Coll BC LTh 41. Coll of Em and St Chad Sask Hon DD 70. **d** 41 **p** 42 New Westmr. C of St Mary Kerrisdale 41-42; St Geo Vancouver 42-44; V of Strathmore 44-49; R of Okotoks 49-52; Vermilion 52-55; St Mich AA Calg 55-62; Hon Can of Calg 59-66; R of Lethbridge 62-66; Dean and R of St Jo Evang Cathl 66-70; Cons Ld Bp of Saskatoon in St Jo Evang Cathl 30 Nov 70 by Abp of Rupld; Bps of Keew; Sask; Arctic; Athab; Bran; Calg; and Koot; and Bp Cook; res 81; I of Cochrane Dio Calg from 81. *Box 1043, Cochrane, Alta, Canada.*

FORD, Preb Douglas William Cleverley. b 14. Univ of Lon BD 36. ALCD 36, MTh 41. **d** 37 **p** 38 Lon. Tutor Lon Coll of Div 37-39; C of Bridlington 39-42; V of H Trin Hampstead 42-55; Lect Lon Coll of Div 42-43 and 52-58; CMS Women's College 47-48; CA Tr Coll 53-60; V of H Trin Kensington Gore w All SS Ennismore Gardens 55-74; Commiss Ugan 53-60; Hon Dir Coll of Prs 60-73; RD of Westmr 65-67; Westmr (St Marg) 67-75; Preb of St Paul's Cathl Lon 68-80; Preb (Emer) from 80; Prov Can of York from 69; Chap to HM the Queen from 73; Sen Chap to Abp of Cant 75-80; Lect Wey Inst of Relig Studies Guildf from 80. *Rostrevor, Lingfield, Surrey, RH7 6BZ.* (0342-832461)

FORD, Eric Charles. b 31. Ely Th Coll 56. **d** 59 **p** 60 Pet. C of St Mary Virg (in c of St John from 61) Kettering 59-65; R of Bowers Gifford 65-69; V of St Barn w St Jas Gtr Walthamstow 69-76; St Edm Chingford Dio Chelmsf from 76; Commiss Gambia from 78. *Vicarage, Larkswood Road, E4 9DS.* (01-529 5226)

FORD, Eric Copeland. b 20. Linc Th Coll 68. **d** 70 Pontefract for Wakef **p** 71 Wakef. C of Lupset 70-73; V of Cornholme 73-78; Wragby w Sharlston Dio Wakef from 78. *Vicarage, Sharlston, Wakefield, W Yorks.* (Wakefield 862414)

FORD, Frank Albert. Univ of Tor BASc 51. Trin Coll Tor STB 66. **d** 66 **p** 67 Tor. C of St Clem Eglinton Tor 66-68; R of Haliburton 68-73; Woodbridge 73-75; on leave. *99 Humbervale Boulevard, Ont., Canada.*

FORD, Ven Frederick John. NZ Bd of Th Stud LTh (2nd cl) 51. **d** 49 **p** 50 Nel. C of Blenheim 50-53; V of Collingwood 53-56; Murchison 56-65; Can of Nel 62-71; V of Awatere 65-76; Spring Creek Dio Nel from 76; Archd of Marlborough from 71; VG Nel from 75. *Vicarage, Spring Creek, NZ.* (728)

FORD, Gordon Rex. b 28. Coll Ho Ch Ch 53, LTh 64. **d** 54 **p** 55 Nel. C of Motupiko 54-55; Blenheim 55-57; V of Havelock and of The Sounds 57-64; Kaikoura 64-69; Picton 69-77; Wadestown City and Dio Wel from 77. *55 Pitt Street, Wellington 1, NZ.* (736-472)

FORD, Guy Arthington. b 02. Sarum Th Coll 25. **d** 27 **p** 28 Guildf. C of Frimley 27-32; St Mich Yorktown Camberley 32-36; All SS Portland (in c of St Pet) 36-39; V of Shoreham 39-44; R of Balsham 44-67. *Enfield Heath Road, Norton, Bury St Edmunds, Suff.* (Pakenham 30633)

FORD, Henry Malcolm. b 33. Em Coll Cam BA 54, MA 58. Ely Th Coll 58. **d** 59 **p** 69 Dunwich for St E. C of St Matt Ipswich 59-61; St John Bury St Edms 66-76; Hawstead Dio St E from 76; M Gen Syn 75-80. *Cross Green, Cockfield, Bury St Edmunds, Suff.* (Cockfield Green 828479)

FORD, Hubert. b 14. Kelham Th Coll 30. **d** 38 **p** 39 Lon. C of St Dunstan Stepney 38-42; St Pet St Helier (in c of St Francis) 42-46; Chap Miss to Seamen Sunderland Seaham and Hartlepool 46-50; Port of Lon 50-52; V of Ch Ch Bp Wearmouth 52-63; Surr 52-63; Chap Sunderland Eye Infirm 52-63; Min of St Jo Evang Conv Distr Hurst Green Oxted 63-64; V 64-79. *88 Barrington Road, Worthing, W Sussex.* (Worthing 44428)

FORD, John. b 15. Linc Th Coll 38. **d** 40 **p** 41 Bris. C of Stoke Bp 40-42; Cirencester w H Trin Watermoor 42-43; Tewkesbury w Walton Cardiff 43-44; R of Wolverton Stratford-on- Avon 44-45; V of Seathwaite 45-46; Eskdale 46-50; Wigton 50-56; Wootton Courtenay 56-61; R of Luccombe 57-61; V of Brampton 61-67; R of Aikton 67-72; C-in-c of St Jo Evang Waterloo Rd Lambeth 72-76. *c/o St John's Vicarage, Waterloo Road, SE1.* (01-928 4470)

FORD, John. b 31. Sarum Th Coll. **d** 61 **p** 62 Chelmsf. C of Saffron Walden 61-64; Chingford 64-67; V Chor of Southw Minster 67-72; R of N and S Wheatley w W Burton 72-78; P-in-c of Sturton le Steeple w Littleborough 72-78; Bole w Saundby 72-78; V of Edwinstowe Dio Southw from 78. *Vicarage, West Lane, Edwinstowe, Mansfield, Notts, NG21 9QT.* (Mansfield 822430)

FORD, Preb John Albert. b 13. Trin Coll Dub BA 35, Div Test 36, MA 38. **d** 36 **p** 37 Arm. C of Derryloran 36-39; Arm

39-44; I of St Sav Portadown 44-61; Drumcree Dio Arm from 61; Preb of Arm Cathl from 75. *78 Drumcree Road, Portadown, Craigavon, Co Armagh, N Ireland, BT62 1PE.* (Portadown 33711)

FORD, John David. Qu Coll Newfld BA and LTh 55. **d** 54 **p** 55 Newfld. C of St Mich AA St John's 54-59; Bay St Geo 59-64; Chap K Coll Sch Windsor Dio NS from 64. *King's College School, Windsor, NS, Canada.* (798-2270)

FORD, John Francis Stewart. Bp's Univ Lennox BA 33. **d** 35 Queb for Edmon **p** 36 Edmon. C of St Phil Westlock Alta 35-37; I of Kenogami 37-42; W Sherbrooke 42-45; R of St Paul S Porcupine 45-46; Cochrane 46-51; CF (Canad) 51-62; R of Deep River 62-66; St Luke Ott 66-71; on leave 71-75; I of St Clem Miss St Aug Duplessis 76-77; Sept Is 77-80. *1007-1485 Baseline Road, Ottawa, Ont, Canada.*

FORD, John Frank. b 52. Chich Th Coll 76. **d** 79 **p** 80 S'wark. C of Ch Ch Forest Hill Dio S'wark from 79. *9 Grassmount, Taymount Rise, SE23.*

FORD, Laurance Duncombe. b 1895. Wycl Hall Ox 57. **d** 57 **p** 58 Roch. C of Meopham 57-59; Tutor Roch Th Coll 59-66; Min Can of Roch Cathl 59-66; C of Winchelsea (in c of St Richard) 66-78. *9 Harold Grove, Frinton-on-Sea, Essex.*

FORD, Leonard John. ACT ThL 69. Moore Th Coll Syd. **d** 70 **p** 71 Syd. C of Campbelltown 70-72; C-in-c of Lurnea 73-78; C-in-c of Liv S Dio Syd from 78. *152 Graham Avenue, Lurnea, NSW, Australia 2170.* (601-5526)

FORD, Leslie Charles. b 08. SOC 65. **d** 68 **p** 69 S'wark. C of St Luke w Norwood 68-76. *St Mark's College, Audley End, Essex, CB11 4JB.*

FORD, Lionel Peter. b 32. St Mich Coll Llan 57. **d** 60 **p** 61 Worc. C of Ribbesford w Bewdley 60-63; St Mary-in-the-Marsh 63-67; V of Elmsted w Hastingleigh 67-71; New Romney w Hope and St Mary's Bay (and St Mary in the Marsh from 78) Dio Cant from 71; RD of S Lympne 75-81; P-in-c of St Mary-in-the-Marsh 76-78; Old Romney Dio Cant from 81. *Vicarage, New Romney, Kent.* (New Romney 2308)

FORD, Lionel Summer Kynge. b 07. St Jo Coll Ox BA (1st cl Th) 31, MA 46. Cudd Coll 32. **d** 33 **p** 34 S'wark. C of Rotherhithe 33-35; SPG Miss at Peking 35-38; Ch'ung Te Sch Peking 38-39; Actg Chap British Embassy 39-40; C-in-c of Yung Ch'ing 40-41; Asst Master Tientsin Gr Sch 41-42; Chap Felsted Sch 43-57; Prin Teachers' Tr Coll Nyakasura 57-64; V of Bp's Frome 64-72; C-in-c of Castle Frome 64-72. *Dan y Bryn, Rhulan, Builth Wells, Powys.*

FORD, Lionel Widdicombe. b 18. Univ of Leeds, BA (2nd Cl Hist) 40. Coll of Resurr Mirfield, 37. **d** 42 **p** 43 S'wark. C of St Jo Evang E Dulwich 42-45; Crediton 45-48; Townstal w St Sav Dartmouth 48-50; V of Exminster 50-57; R of Diptford 57-68; R of N Huish (w Avonwick from 60) 58-68; V of Stonehouse Dio Glouc from 68. *Vicarage, Stonehouse, Glos., GL10 2NP.* (Stonehouse 2332)

FORD, Peter. ACP 75. Linc Th Coll 76. **d** 78 **p** 79 Dur. M OGS from 72; C of H Trin Hartlepool 78-81. *Address temp unknown.*

FORD, Peter Collins. b 23. Roch Th Coll 60. **d** 62 **p** 63 Bradf. C of Keighley 62-64; Gravesend 64-65; Hon C 67-68; V of St Aid Buttershaw 65-67; Ch Ch Milton-next-Gravesend 69-72; V of Gosfield Dio Chelmsf from 72; RD of Halstead & Coggeshall from 79. *Gosfield Vicarage, Halstead, Essex.* (Halstead 473857)

FORD, Canon Peter Hugh. St Cath Coll Cam BA 65, MA 69. Cudd Coll 65. **d** 67 **p** 68 Lon. C of Ch of Ch and St John w St Luke I of Dogs Poplar 67-70; Tillsonburg 70-71; St Thos St Cath 71-73; P-in-c Resurr Thorold S 71-73; R of St Brendan Port Colborne 73-78; Grace Ch Milton 78-80; Can of Ch Ch Cathl Hamilton Dio Niag from 80. *252 James Street North, Hamilton, Ont, Canada L8R 2L3.* (416-527 3239)

FORD, Richard Graham. b 39. K Coll Lon and Warm AKC 65. **d** 66 **p** 67 Newc T. C of Morpeth 66-71; Fordingbridge 71-73; Team V of Whorlton 73-80; V of Choppington Dio Newc T from 80. *Vicarage, Choppington, Northumb.* (Bedlington 822216)

FORD, Robert Holden. St Francis Th Coll Nundah, 28. **d** 31 Rockptn **p** 33 Newc. C of St Paul's Cathl Rockptn 31-32; Adamstown 32-34; Perm to Offic Dio Melb 34-35; M of Bro of St Andr 35-40; P-in-c of Dawson and Callide Miss Distr 35-36; Longreach 36-37; Mt Morgan 37-38; C of Clermont 39-40; P-in-c 40-42; R 42-48; V of Cobram 48-50; R of Bright 50-52; Beechworth 52-56; C of Melb Dioc Centre 56-62; Min of Kilsyth Montrose and Mooroolbark 62-68; I of Lancefield w Romsey 68-72; Perm to Offic Dio Melb from 72. *St John's Court, Mooroolbark, Vic, Australia 3138.* (03-723 3628)

FORD, Stanley Bruce. St Jo Coll Morpeth ACT ThL 52. **d** and **p** 53 C & Goulb. C of Temora 53-54; St Paul Canberra 54-56; Chap RAAF from 56; Perm to Offic Dio Brisb 59-63 and from 68. *25 Dandenong Street, Jamboree Heights, Queensland, Australia 4074.* (376 3231)

FORDE, Basil Augustus. b 14. St Chad's Coll Dur BA 36, MA and Dipl in Th 39. **d** 37 **p** 38 Carl. C of St Jas Barrow-F 37-38; Aspatria 38-39; St John Keswick 39-42; Newburn (in c St Mary Throckley) 42-45; V of Sutton St Edm 45-49; Wellingore w Temple Bruer 49-54; PC of Alvingham w N and S Cockerington 54-56; R of Snelland w Snarford 56-61; V of Winthorpe 61-76; C-in-c of Bratoft 64-70; Perm to Offic Dio Linc from 77. *10 Horace Street, Boston, Lincs.*

FORDER, Ven Charles Robert. b 07. Late Exhib of Ch Coll Cam 1st cl Math Trip pt i 26, BA (Sen Opt pt ii) 28, MA 32. Ridley Hall Cam 28. **d** 30 **p** 31 Ripon. C of St Pet Hunslet Moor 30-33; St Matthias Burley 33-34; V of H Trin Wibsey 34-40; St Clem Bradf 40-47; Drypool Hull 47-55; C-in-c of St Pet Drypool 48-51; Chap to HM Pris Hull 49-51; HM Borstal Inst Hull 51-52; Proc Conv York 54-57; R of Routh 55-57; V of Waghen 55-57; Sec York Dioc Ch Bldg Appeal 54-76; Archd of York 57-72; Archd (Emer) from 74; Can and Preb of York Minster 57-76; Can (Emer) from 76; R of Sutton-on-Derwent 57-63; Ch Comm 58-73; R of H Trin w St Jo Evang St Martin and St Greg Micklegate York 63-66; Perm to Offic Dio Nor 76-79; Dio York from 79. *Dulverton Hall, St Martin's Square, Scarborough, YO11 2DQ.* (Scarborough 73082)

FORDER, Harry Walter. b 16. AKC 39. **d** 39 **p** 40 S'wark. C of St Mark Battersea Rise 39-42; St Luke Battersea 42-44; St Dunstan Cheam 44-48; Cobham Surrey 48-53; R of W Horsley Dio Guildf from 53. *West Horsley Rectory, Leatherhead, Surrey.* (East Horsley 2173)

FORDHAM, Frank Henry Vernon. Kelham Th Coll 37. **d** 37 **p** 38 Cant. C of All SS Maidstone 37-43; St Laur-in-I of Thanet 43-45; V of Milton Regis w St Paul 45-49; C-in-c of Elmley w Iwade 48-49; V of St Mich AA Maidstone 49-63; Birchington w Acol 63-79. *6 Green Dell, Hales Place, Canterbury, Kent.*

FORDHAM, Canon James Charles Horace Adcock. b 11. MBE (Mil) 47. TD 61. St Aid Coll 39. **d** 41 **p** 42 Blackb. C of H Trin South Shore Blackpool 41-44; CF (EC) 44-47; Hon CF 47-82; V of Em Ch Preston Blackb 47-82; Hon Can of Blackb from 72. *23 The Row, Silverdale, Nr Carnforth, Lancs.*

FORDHAM, Philip Arthur Sidney. b 51. St Steph Ho Ox 80. **d** 81 Barking for Chelmsf. C of Wanstead Dio Chelmsf from 81. *2 Church Path, Wanstead, E11.*

FOREMAN, Frederick George. b 12. ALCD 34. **d** 35 **p** 36 Lon. C of St Barn Holloway 35-38; Morden 39-40; V of All SS w St John Islington 40-45; St John U Holloway 45-58; Runham 58-64; Abberton and Bishampton (w Throckmorton from 74) 73-77; R of Stokesby w Herringby 58-64; Ipsley 64-73. *32 Bleachfield Street, Alcester, Warws, B49 5BA.*

FOREMAN, Patrick Brian. b 41. St Jo Coll Nottm 77. **d** 79 Grimsby for Linc **p** 80 Linc. C of All SS Gainsborough Dio Linc from 79. *6 Connaught Road, Gainsborough, Lincs, DN21 2QU.*

FOREMAN, Roy Geoffrey Victor. b 31. Oak Hill Th Coll 62. **d** 64 **p** 65 Lon. C of St Cuthb Chitts Hill Wood Green 64-67; Rodbourne Cheney 67-70; Walthamstow Dio Chelmsf from 71. *13 Orford Road, Walthamstow, E17.* (01-520 6168)

FOREMAN, Sydney Robert. **d** 44 **p** 45 Queb. I of Kingsey 44-47; Inverness 47-50; R of Bury 50-53; Chap RCAF 53-55; R of St Mary Magd Winnipeg 55-74; P Assoc of St Jas Winnipeg Dio Rupld from 74. *1004-77 University Crescent, Winnipeg, Manit, Canada.*

FORESTER, Leslie Troone. b 57. Univ of Newc BA 77, ThL 81. St Jo Coll Morpeth 77. **d** and **p** 81 Newc. C of New Lambton Dio Newc from 81. *3 March Street, Kotara 2288, NSW, Australia.*

FORGIE, Neil Angus. b 44. St Barn Coll Adel ACT Dipl Th 71. **d** 69 Willoch **p** 70 Bp Rosier. Missr Point Pearce Reserve 69-73; on leave 73-75; R of Pet Orroroo 75-76; L to Offic Dio Willoch from 76. *Box 13, Melrose, S Australia 5483.* (086-66 2183)

FORGRAVE, William James. b 23. **d** 81 Fred (APM). Perm to Offic Dio Fred from 81. *114 Marlewood Drive, Moncton, NB, Canada E1A 2N4.*

FORMAN, Alastair Gordon. b 48. St Jo Coll Nottm 78. **d** 80 **p** 81 Ex. C of St Pancras Fennycross Plymouth Dio Ex from 80. *23 Pennycross Park Road, Peverell, Plymouth, PL2 3NP.*

FORRER, Michael Dennett Cuthbert. St Pet Hall, Ox BA (Th) 59, MA 63. Wycl Hall Ox 59. **d** 60 **p** 61 Cov. C of Westwood 60-63; Asst Industr Chap Cov 63-69; Sen Chap 69-71; C of St Mich Cathl Cov 63-71. *2 Old Burlington, Church Street, W4.*

FORREST, Edward William. b 09. Univ of Man BA (Com) 34. Bps' Coll Cheshunt. **d** 62 Hulme for Man **p** 63 Man. C of Bury 62-65; V of St Paul Ramsbottom 65-76; Perm to Offic Dio Man from 77; Chap Ramsbottom Cottage Hosp from 70. *14 Wellington Road, Bury, Lancs, BL9 9BG.* (061-764 9578)

FORREST, John Sagar. b 15. Ridley Hall, Cam 65. **d** 66

Hulme for Man **p** 67 Man. C of St Jas New Bury Farnworth 66-69; R of St Pet w St Jas L Man 69-75; St Paul New Cross Man 72-75; Chap Wythenshawe and Christie Hosps Man 75-80; L to Offic Dio Man 75-81. *Address temp unknown.*

FORREST, Kenneth Malcolm. b 38. Linc Coll Ox BA (2nd Cl Mod Hist) 61, MA 65. Wells Th Coll 60. **d** 62 Warrington for Liv **p** 63 Liv. C of Walton-on-the-Hill 62-65; Asst Chap Univ of Liv 65-67; R of Wavertree and Chap Blue Coat Sch Liv 67-75; R of Wigan Dio Liv from 75. *The Hall, Wigan, Lancs.* (Wigan 44459)

FORREST, Leslie David Arthur. b 46. TCD BA (2nd cl Mod Hebr and Semitic Lang) 68, Div Test 70. **d** 70 Derry. C of Conwall 70-73; I of Tullyaughnish 73-80; Dom Chap to Bp of Derry 75-80; R of Galway and Kilcummin Dio Tuam from 80; Athenry w Monivea Dio Tuam from 80. *Rectory, Taylor's Hill, Galway, Irish Republic.* (091-21914)

FORREST, Leslie Grundell. b 05. Peterho Cam BA 26, MA 35. Westcott Ho Cam 26. **d** 28 **p** 29 Sheff. C of St Mary Sheff 28-30; St Luke Battersea 30-34; Soham 34-35; Chap Miss to Seamen Hamburg 35-39; Ghent 39-40; Asst Chap Tyne and L to Offic Dio Dur 40-42; V of St Matt Gosport 42-48; Cherry Hinton 48-72. *40 Greenacres Park, Meysey Hampton, Cirencester, Glos.*

FORREST, Michael Barry Eric. Chich Th Coll NZ Bd of Th Stud LTh 62. **d** 66 **p** 67 Roch. C of St Jas Elmers End Beckenham 66-70; P-in-c of Cape Vogel 70-73; Alotau 74; R of Lae 74-76; C of Altarnon w Bolventor 77-78; Lewannick 77-78; Team V of North Hill 78-79; R of St Martin-by-Looe Dio Truro from 79. *Rectory, St Martin-by-Looe, Cornwall, PL13 1NX.* (Looe 3070)

FORREST, Robin Whyte. b 33. Edin Th Coll 58. **d** 61 **p** 62 Glas. C of St Mary's Cathl Glas 61-66; R of Renfrew 66-70; Motherwell 70-79; St Andr Wishaw 75-79; Forres Dio Moray from 79; Nairn Dio Moray from 79. *Rectory, Victoria Road, Forres, Moray.* (Forres 2856)

FORRESTER, Herbert Howarth. b 19. Univ of Liv LLB 46. Wycl Hall Ox 65. **d** 67 Warrington for Liv **p** 68 Liv. C of Blundellsands 67-70; V of St Phil (w St D from 76) City and Dio Liv from 70. *55 Sheil Road, Liverpool, L6 3AD.* (051-263 6202)

FORRESTER, James Oliphant. b 50. SS Coll Cam BA 72, MA 76. Wycl Hall Ox 73. **d** 76 **p** 77 York. C of St John Newland Hull 76-80; Fulwood City and Dio Sheff from 80. *18 Blackbrook Road, Lodge Moor, Sheffield, S10 4LP* (Sheff 305271)

FORRESTER, Kenneth Merville. Codr Coll Barb 57. **d** 61 Barb for Trinid **p** 62 Trinid. C of St Andr Scarborough Tobago 61-65; R of St D Plymouth Tobago Dio Trinid from 65. *St David's Rectory, Plymouth, Tobago, W Indies.*

FORRESTER, Kenneth Norman. Ely Th Coll 46. **d** 49 **p** 50 Ely. C of H Trin w St Mary Ely 49-51; Wymondham 51-53; V of Shotesham 53-56; R of St Jo Evang Inverness and Chap to Inverness Hosps and Pris 56-60; Itin P Dio Moray 60-61; P-in-c of St Pet and H Rood Thurso 61; V of Tilney 61-68; C of St Bart Brighton 68-71; Chap at St Jo Evang Montreux 71-79; St Geo Malaga 79-81; St Andr Pau w Biarritz Dio Gibr in Eur from 81. *Le Manor, ave Honore Baradat, Pau, France.* (59-023858)

FORRESTER, Matthew Agnew. Univ of Wales (Cardiff) BA (2nd cl Econ) 64. Univ of Lon Dipl Th 72. Trin Coll Bris 70. **d** 72 **p** 73 Roch. C of Tonbridge 72-77; Chap Elstree Sch Woolhampton 77-78; Chap Duke of York's R Mil Sch Dover from 78. *Gloucester House, Duke of York's Royal Military School, Dover, Kent, CT15 5EQ.* (Dover 210019)

FORRESTER, Robert Lowe Birkley. St Aug Coll Cant 35. **d** 37 **p** 38 Lon. C of H Trin Northwood 37-40; Chap RAFVR 40-46; Chap and Asst Master at St Geo Gr Sch Capetn 46-47; Hd Master of St Mark's Sch Mbabane Zulu 47-54; L to Offic Dio Zulu 54-68; Dio Swaz 68-70; R of Mhlume-Tshaneni 70-74; C of All SS Mbabane 74-76. *Box 1210, Mbabane, Swaziland.*

FORRYAN, John Edward. b 31. Wells Th Coll 58. **d** 60 **p** 61 Glouc C of St Phil and St Jas Leckhampton 60-63; Cirencester w Watermoor 63-68; V of St Paul Glouc 68-78; R of Rodborough Dio Glouc from 78. *Rectory, Walkley Hill, Rodborough, Stroud, Glos, GL5 3TX.*

FORSE, Canon Edward John. b 07. CCC Cam 3rd cl Hist Trip 28, BA (3rd cl Th Trip) 30, MA 33. Wells Th Coll 30. **d** 31 **p** 32 Portsm. C of St Jas Milton 31-34; Ryde 34-39; C-in-c of St Wilfrid's Conv Distr Cowplain 39-45; Offg Chap Qu Alexandra Hosp Cosham 39-41; CF (EC) 41-46; R of Rowlands Castle (f Redhill) 46-74; RD of Havant 62-72; Hon Can of Portsm 70-76; Can (Emer) from 76. *12 Newnham Road, Binstead, Ryde, IW, PO33 3TD.* (Ryde 66402)

FORSE, Reginald Austin. b 43. Oak Hill Th Coll 77. **d** 79 **p** 80 Portsm. C of H Rood Crofton Dio Portsm from 79. *46 Carisbrooke Avenue, Stubbington, Fareham, Hants, PO14 3PR.* (Stubbington 3672)

FORSGATE, Canon Noel John. b 1892. **d** 35 **p** 36 Centr Tang. Miss at Buigiri 35-38; Dodoma 38-46; Hon Can and P-in-c of Cathl of H Spirit Dodoma 46-47; Provost 47-49; Can (Emer) from 52; V of Gt w L Tey 49-68; RD of Coggeshall and Tey 56-68; Surr 64-68. *112 Layer Road, Colchester, Essex, CO2 7JN.* (Colchester 73504)

FORSHAW, David Oliver. b 27. Trin Coll Cam BA 50, MA 52. Qu Coll Birm. **d** 53 Bp Hollis for Cant **p** 54 Leic. C of S Wigston 53-55; Chap St Andr Sch Sing 55-59; V of Heptonstall 59-66; St Nich Whitehaven 66-76; Surr 66-76; C-in-c of H Trin w Ch Ch Whitehaven 73-76; V of Benchill Dio Man from 76. *Vicarage, Brownley Road, Benchill, Manchester, M22 4PT.* (061-998 2071)

FORSHAW, Eric Paul. Ridley Hall Cam 69. **d** 70 **p** 71 Birm. Univ of Birm MA (Th) 78. C of Yardley 70-72; Industr Chap Dio Birm 72-78; C of St Geo Edgbaston 72-78; Bp's Adv on Industr S Dio Southw from 78; Chap C of E Men's S Dio Southw from 78. *11 Clumber Crescent North, The Park, Nottingham, NG7 1EY.* (Nottm 47156)

FORSTER, Bennet Fermor. b 21. BNC Ox BA 48, MA 53. Cudd Coll. **d** 51 **p** 52 Lon. C of St Dunstan Stepney 51-53; Petersfield (in c of St Mary Sheet) 53-57; V of St Cuthb Copnor 57-65; Chap Bedford Sch 65-72; L to Offic Dio St Alb 65-72 and 73-78; P-in-c of Froxfield w Privett and of Hawkley w Priors Dean Dio Portsm from 78. *Vicarage, Hawkley, Liss, Hants, GU33 6NF.* (Hawkley 459)

FORSTER, Brian John. b 39. Chich Th Coll 64. **d** 68 Warrington for Liv **p** 69 Liv. C of St Andr Orford 68-71; H Spirit Knotty Ash 71-74; V of St Mark Kirkby Northwood 74-79; St Paul Stoneycroft City and Dio Liv from 79. *St Paul's Vicarage, Carlton Lane, Liverpool, L13 6QS.* (051-228 1041)

FORSTER, Canon Charles Alfred. b 04. OBE 58. Late Scho of Univ Coll Dur BA 26, MA 29. Ridley Hall, Cam 26. **d** 27 **p** 28 Bris. C of Downend 27-30; Prin Dennis Mem Gr Sch Onitsha 31-37; Gen Manager of Schs Onitsha Archdy 37-46; Sec CMS Niger Miss and Synod Sec Dio Niger 41-53; Archd of Onitsha 49-53; Can of Niger 53-57; Sec Christian Coun of Nigeria and Educnl Adviser to Prot Miss 53-57; Commiss Niger 54-60; Ow 60-69; R of Wylye w Stockton and Fisherton Delamere 57-69; Hon Can of Niger from 64; RD of Wylye 65-69. *Green Gate, Knights Lane, All Saints, Axminster, Devon.*

FORSTER, Charles Clifford. b 34. K Coll Lon and Warm AKC 59. **d** 60 **p** 61 York. C of Marske-by-the-Sea 60-63; St Andr w St Anne Bp Auckld 63-65; V of Brafferton w Pilmoor and Myton-on-Swale 65-72; Ascen Derringham Bank Hull 72-81; Brompton w Snainton Dio York from 81. *Brompton Vicarage, Scarborough, Yorks, YO13 9DP.* (Scarborough 85400)

FORSTER, Eric Lindsay. b 11. Worc Coll Ox BA 33, MA 38. Wycl Hall, Ox 34. **d** 39 **p** 40 Man. C of The Sav Bolton 39-41; Actg C of Mottram-in-Longdendale (in c of Broadbottom) 41-42; C of Ch Ch Skipton 42-44; St Geo Redditch 44-47; V of St Jo Evang Bacup 47-52; St Bede Nelson-in-Marsden 52-57; C-in-c of Woolley 57-65; V of Spaldwick w Barham (and Woolley from 65) 57-75; C-in-c of Easton 57-58; V 58-75; Surr 58-75. *17 Needham Crescent, Ely, CB7 4QW.*

FORSTER, George. b 04. Armstrong Coll Dur BSc 25. Wycl Hall Ox 29. **d** 30 **p** 31 Newc T. C of St Mich Byker 30-32; St Geo Jesmond 32-35; CF (TA) 32-36; I of H Cross Fenham 35-48; V of Long Benton 48-57; CF (EC) 40-42; Surr 49-57; Insp of Sch Dio Newc T 55-57; R of Nympsfield 57-66; R of Uley w Owlpen (w Nympsfield from 66) 57-73; RD of Dursley 66-73. *3 Durbin Park Road, Clevedon, Avon, BS21 7EU.* (Clevedon 875860)

FORSTER, Gregory Stuart. b 47. Worc Coll Ox BA (2nd cl Th) 69, MA 73. Wycl Hall Ox 69. **d** 72 **p** 73 B & W. C of Walcot 72-74; Em Bolton 74-77; St Paul w Em Bolton 77-79; R of Northenden Dio Man from 79. *Northenden Rectory, Manchester, M22 4QN.* (061-998 2615)

FORSTER, Ian Robson. b 33. K Coll Lon and Warm AKC 59. **d** 60 **p** 61 Man. C of St Mary Virg Leigh 60-62; St Werburgh Chorlton-cum-Hardy 62-64; St Geo Grenada 64-66; P-in-c of Riviére Dorée Windw Is 66-69; V of Ford Herefs 69-76; P-in-c of Alberbury w Cardeston 69-76; Commiss Windw Is from 70; C of St Chad Wolverhampton Dio Lich 76-78; Team V from 78. *St Chad's Vicarage, Manlove Street, Wolverhampton, WV3 0HG, W Midl.* (Wolverhampton 26580)

FORSTER, Joseph. St Francis Coll Brisb ACT ThL 48. **d** 41 **p** 42 Rockptn. C of St Paul Rockptn 41-47; P-in-c of Weston w Abermain 47-50; Asst Chap Miss to Seamen Melb 50-54; Min of Mitcham 54-64; V of St Osw Glen Iris 64-79; Perm to Offic Dio Melb from 79. *Vicarage, Lorne, Vic, Australia 3232.* (052-89 1222)

FORSTER, Leslie. b 08. St Chad's Coll Dur BA 31, Dipl in Th 32, MA 34. **d** 32 **p** 33 Dur. C of St Hilda S Shields 32-35; St Luke W Hartlepool 35-38; PC of Dipton 38-43; V of Ch Ch

Dunston 43-74. *Flat 8, Blythswood, Osborne Road, Jesmond, Newcastle-upon-Tyne, NE2 2AZ.*

FORSTER, Canon Leslie John. b 17. MBE 80. ALCD 40. **d** 40 **p** 41 Liv. C of St John and St Jas Litherland 40-42; Warrington (in c of St Geo Mission Ch) 42-47; V of Hollinfare 47-52; R of Warburton 52-56; V of H Trin w St Luke Warrington 56-61; Gt Budworth 61-75; Antrobus 67-75; RD of Gt Budworth 71-81; R of Grappenhall Dio Ches from 75; Hon Can of Ches Cathl from 75. *Grappenhall Rectory, Warrington, Chesh, WA4 3EP.* (Warrington 61546)

FORSTER, Peter Robert. b 50. Merton Col Ox MA (Chem) 73. Edin Univ BD 77. Edin Th Coll 77. **d** 80 Liv **p** 81 Warrington for Liv. C of Mossley Hill Dio Liv from 80. *Mosslake Lodge, Rose Lane, Mossley Hill, Liverpool, L18 8DB.*

FORSTER, Roger John. b 43. Trin Coll Tor LTh 79. **d** 79 **p** 80 Niag. R of St Philip-by-the-Lake Grimsby Dio Niag from 79. *7 Grand Avenue, Grimsby, Ont, Canada L3M 2R6.* (416-945 5022)

FORSTER, Thomas William Norman. b 1897. Ripon Hall Ox 55. **d** 56 **p** 57 Lon. C of St Phil Kens 56-59; R of Gissing 59-77; C-in-c of Burston w Shimpling 59-77; V in Winfarthing Group 68-77. *12 The Street, Tivetshall St Mary, Norf, NR15 2BU.* (037 977 297)

FORSTER, Canon Victor Henry. b 17. Trin Coll Dub BA 45, MA 49. **d** 45 **p** 46 Down. C of Maralin 45-47; C-in-c of Garrison w Slavin 47 51; Bp's C of Ballybay 51 52; I of Killeevan 52-59; Rathgraffe 59-67; Aghalurcher w Tattykeeran and Cooneen w Mullaghfad Dio Clogh from 67; RD of Clogher from 73; Preb of Tullycorbet and Can of Clogh from 80. *Colebrooke Rectory, Fivemiletown, Co Tyrone, N Ireland.*

FORSYTH, Alan George. b 41. Univ of Perth BA 64. St Mich Ho Crafers. **d** 68 Bunb. C of Pinjarra 68-70; St Bonif Cathl Bunb 70-72; P-in-c of Ravensthorpe 72-75; Perm to Offic Dio Perth 75-76; R of Woomera 76-80; P-in-c of Whyalla 80; Port Augusta Dio Willoch from 81. *Box 152, Port Augusta, S Australia 5700.*

FORSYTH, John Warren. b 38. Univ of W Austr BA 62. St Mich Ho Crafers ThL 65. **d** 65 **p** 66 Bunb. C of Busselton 65-68; R of Kondinin 68-72; C of St Mary Warw 72-74; St Pet Lutton Place Edin 74-76; R of E Fremantle w Palmyra 76-79; Chap to Abp of Perth and Warden Wollaston Th Coll from 79; Dioc Regr Dio Perth from 80. *Wollaston College, Mount Claremont, W Australia 6010.* (384 4731)

FORSYTH, Robert Charles. Univ of Syd BA 72. Moore Coll Syd ACT ThL 74. BD (Lon) 75. **d** 76 Syd **p** 76 Bp Robinson for Syd. C of St Pet Glenbrook 76-77; H Trin City and Dio Adel from 77. *87 North Terrace, Adelaide, S Australia 5000.* (51-3862)

FORSYTH, William. b 10. Lich Th Coll 55. **d** 56 **p** 57 Newc T. C of St Jas and St Basil Newc T 56-59; V of Cleator 59-65; Netherton w Grasslot 65-70; Levens 70-78. *2 Vicarage Road, Levens, Kendal, Cumb.* (Sedgwick 60926)

FORSYTHE, John Leslie. b 27. Trin Coll Dub. **d** 65 **p** 66 Connor. C of Ch of Ascen Cloughfern 65-67; Carnmoney 67-71; R of Mossley 71-80; V of Antrim Dio Connor from 80. *Vicarage, Antrim, N Ireland.* (Antrim 2186)

FORT, Sidney John. **d** 44 **p** 46 Capetn. Actg C of St Luke Salt River 44-47; Dioc Chap Dio Capetn 47-53. *Southernwood, Glebe Road, Rondebosch, CP, S Africa.*

FORTCHIMO, Sidney Amos. b 45. **d** 75 **p** 76 Moos. C of St Jo Bapt Paint Hills Dio Moos from 75. *Anglican Church, Paint Hills, PQ, via Moosonee, Ont, JOM 1LO, Canada.*

FORTH, David Selwyn. McGill Univ Montr BA 53, BD 56. Selw Coll Cam PhD 59. **d** 56 Montr **p** 67 Ely for Montr. C of St Giles Cam 57-59; Ch Ch Sorel PQ 59-60; Asst Prof of Systematic Th Bp's Univ Lennox 60-64; Asst Prof of Phil Laurentian Univ Sudbury Ont 64-69; on leave. *1714 Wallace Street, Stroudsburg, Pa 18360, USA.*

FORTUNE, Eric Montague. b 13. St Aid Coll 43. **d** 44 **p** 45 Chelmsf. C of Great Ilford 44-47; CF 47-68; R of Berrow w Pendock 68-78. *66 Badsey Lane, Evesham, Worcester.* (Evesham 47508)

FORWARD, Eric Toby. b 50. Univ of Nottm BEducn 72. Cudd Coll 74. **d** 77 **p** 78 S'wark. C of Ch Ch Forest Hill 77-80; Chap Goldsmith's Coll Lon from 80. *20 Shardeloes Road, SE14 6NZ.* (01-691 3064)

FORWARD, Canon Ronald George. b 25. Selw Coll Cam BA 50, MA 54. Ridley Hall Cam 50. **d** 52 **p** 53 Carl. C of St Jas Carl 52-55; C-in-c of St Andr Conv Distr Mirehouse Whitehaven 55-61; V 61-66; St Thos Kendal Dio Carl from 66; Crook Dio Carl from 78; Hon Can of Carl Cathl from 79. *St Thomas's Vicarage, Kendal, Cumb, LA9 4PL.* (Kendal 21509)

FOSBUARY, David Frank. b 32. Univ of Leeds, BA (3rd cl Phil and Hist) 63. Coll of Resurr Mirfield, 63. **d** 65 Blackb **p** 66 Lanc for Blackb. C of Fleetwood 65-68; St Jas Maseru 69-71; Masite 71; R of St Sav Leribe 72-76; C of Dovercourt 76-79; Team V of Basildon Dio Chelmsf from 79. *23 Claremont Road, Laindon, Basildon, Essex, SS15-5QB.*

FOSDIKE, Lewis Bertram. b 23. Keble Coll Ox BA (2nd cl Phil Pol and Econ) 52, MA 56. Wells Th Coll 52. **d** 54 **p** 55 Bris. C of Westbury-on-Trym 54-58; V of St Francis Ashton Gate Bedminster 58-64; Summertown Ox 64-76; R of Wolvercote w Summertown City and Dio Ox from 76. *Vicarage, Lonsdale Road, Oxford.* (Oxford 56079)

FOSKETT, Eric William. b 29. Qu Coll Birm 75. **d** 78 **p** 79 Birm. C of Billesley Common Dio Birm from 78. *1204 Yardley Wood Road, Solihull Lodge, Shirley, Solihull, W Midl B90 9JY.*

FOSKETT, John Herbert. b 39. St Cath Coll Cam BA 62. Chich Th Coll 62. **d** 64 **p** 65 S'wark. C of Malden 64-70; V of St Jo Evang Kingston T 70-76; Chap to Bethlem R Hosp Beckenham & Maudsley Hosp Denmark Hill from 76. *Bethlem Royal Hospital, Monk's Orchard Road, Beckenham, Kent, BR3 3BX.* (01-777 6611)

FOSS, David Blair. b 44. Univ of Bris BA (2nd cl Hist) 65. Univ of Dur MA 66. Fitzw Coll Cam BA (1st cl Th Trip pt ii) 68, MA 72. St Chad's Coll Dur 68. **d** 69 **p** 70 Dur. C of Barnard Castle 69-72; Lect Fourah Bay Coll and L to Offic Dio Sier L 72-74; Chap and Lect St Jo Coll York 74-75; Ch Ch Coll Cant 75-80; Chap & Asst Master Elmslie Girls' Sch Blackpool from 80; Hon C of St Steph Blackpool Dio Blackb from 81. *6 Erith Grove, Bispham, Blackpool, Lancs, FY2 9AR.* (0253 53407)

FOSS, William Cecil Winn. b 40. Univ of Man BA 68. Dipl Th (Lon) 66. BD (Lon) 76. Wells Th Coll 64. **d** 68 **p** 69 S'wark. C of St Geo Mart S'wark 68-73; Asst Master Crewe Co Boys' Gr Sch from 73; Perm to Offic Dio Ches 73-79; V of Ch Ch Crewe Dio Ches from 79. *3 Heathfield Avenue, Crewe, Chesh, CW1 3BA.* (Crewe 213148)

FOSTER, Alan John. b 53. ACT BTh 78. St Jo Coll Morpeth 76. **d** 78 **p** 79 Melb. C of H Trin Surrey Hills 78-80; on leave. *368 Mont Albert Road, Mont Albert, Vic, Australia 3127.*

FOSTER, Albert Edward John. b 29. Lich Th Coll 52. **d** 55 **p** 56 Lon. C of Ch Ch Isle of Dogs 55-58; St Mich AA Ladbroke Grove Kens 58-60; St Matt Bethnal Green (in c of St Jas Gt w St Jude) 60-62; C-in-c of St Jas Gt w St Jude Bethnal Green 62-69; V of St Mary Paddington Green Dio Lon from 69. *6 Park Place Villas, W2.* (01-723 1968)

FOSTER, Antony John. b 39. Down Coll Cam 2nd cl Nat Sc Trip pt i 60, BA (2nd cl Chem Trip pt ii) 61, 2nd cl Th Trip pt ii 63, MA 65. Ridley Hall Cam 65. **d** 66 **p** 67 Wakef. C of Sandal Magna w Newmillerdam 66-69; Chap Teso Coll Aloet Soroti 69-74; V of Ch Ch Mt Pellon Dio Wakef from 74. *Christ Church Vicarage, Mount Pellon, Halifax, W Yorks, HX2 0EF.* (Halifax 65027)

FOSTER, Charles George Peebles. b 10. St Jo Coll Dur BA 33. **d** 34 **p** 35 Down. C of St Mary Newry 34-38; Thurles 39-41; I of Killorglin U 41-56; Tallow U 56-63; Preb of Kilrosanty and Treas of Lism Cathl 61-63; Preb of St Patr and Treas of Waterf Cathl 61-63; I of Knockmourne 63-72; Innishannon U 72-79. *Glebe Cottage, Blind Gate, Kinsale, Co Cork, Irish Republic.* (021-72757)

FOSTER, Christopher Richard James. b 53. Univ Coll Dur BA 75. Univ of Man MA (Econ) 77. Trin Hall Cam BA 79. Westcott Ho Cam 78. **d** 80 **p** 81 Lich. C of Tettenhall Regis Dio Lich from 80. *45 Lower Street, Tettenhall, Wolverhampton, WV6 9LR.* (Wolv 755292)

FOSTER, David Brereton. b 55. Selw Coll Cam BA (Mod Langs) 77, MA 81. Univ of Ox BA (Th) 80. Wycl Hall Ox 78. **d** 81 St Alb. C of St Mary Luton Dio St Alb from 81. *72 Crawley Green Road, Luton, Beds, LU2 0QU.* (Luton 35548)

FOSTER, David Johnstone. b 04. **d** 64 Penrith for Carl **p** 65 Carl. C of Greystoke 64-74; Hon C of St Kentigern Crosthwaite Dio Carl from 74. *The Close, Vicarage Hill, Crosthwaite, Keswick, Cumb.*

FOSTER, Donald Wolfe. b 24. Late Exhib of St Cath Coll Cam 1st cl Eng Trip pt i 47, BA (1st cl Eng Trip pt ii) 48, MA 50. Trin Coll Dub BD 56. **d** 50 Leigh **p** 51 Oss. C of Dunleckney U 50-52; Coseley 52-54; St Aug Newland 54-58; V of St Mary Virg Lowgate Hull 58-62; Chap HM Borstal Inst Hull 58-62; V of Osbaldwick w Murton 62-67; Sec York Dio Conf 65-67; Asst Chap Loughborough Gr Sch 67-80; Chap from 80. *267 Nanpantan Road, Loughborough, Leics.* (Loughborough 39219)

FOSTER, Edward James Graham. b 12. St Jo Coll Cam BA 34, MusBac 35, MA 38. Wells Th Coll 35. **d** 37 **p** 38 Worc. C of Kidderminster 37-43; Feckenham w Astwood Bank 43-45; Chap and Lect Dioc Tr Coll Ches 45-51; V of Balby 51-67; Surr 61-67: PC (V from 68) of Ashford w Sheldon 67-78. *Montrose, Ashford Road, Bakewell, Derby DE4 1GL.*

FOSTER, Edward Philip John. b 49. Trin Hall Cam BA 70, MA 74. Ridley Hall Cam 77. **d** 79 **p** 80 Lon. C of Ch Ch Finchley Dio Lon from 79. *618a High Road, Finchley, N12 0NU.* (01-445 6988)

FOSTER, Eric George. **d** 60 **p** 61 Caled. I of Fort Nelson 60-64; Cassiar 64-70; R of Fort Nelson 70-71; Perm to Offic Dio BC from 74. *3800 Cedar Hill Road, Victoria, BC, Canada.*

FOSTER, Francis Desmond. b 11. ALCD 33. **d** 34 **p** 35 Cant. C of St Phil Norbury 34-39; Faversham 39-48; V of Throwley (and Stalisfield w Otterden from 75) 48-78; C-in-c of Stalisfield w Otterden 73-75. *43 Milton Road, Eastbourne, E Sussex, BN21 1SH.*

FOSTER, Gareth Glynne. b 44. Chich Th Coll 66. **d** 69 **p** 70 Llan. C of Fairwater 69-71; in R Benef of Merthyr Tydfil (and Cyfartha from 72) Dio Llan 71-76; V from 76. *19 The Walk, Merthyr Tydfil, Mid Glam.* (Merthyr 2375)

FOSTER, Georgina Doris. b 53. Carlton Coll Ott BA 75. Hur Coll Lon Ont MDiv 78. **d** 79 Bp Parke-Taylor for Hur **p** 80 Bp Robinson for Hur. C of Trin Ch St Thomas Dio Hur from 79. *59 Gladstone Avenue, St Thomas, Ont, Canada, N5R 2L7.*

FOSTER, Graham. Moore Th Coll Syd ACT ThL (2nd cl) 65. Melb Coll of Div Dipl Relig Educn 68. **d** 67 **p** 68 Melb. C of Rosanna Dio Melb from 67. *130 Sommers Avenue, MacLeod, Vic. 3085, Australia.*

FOSTER, Harold Bede. b 07. **d** 70 Graft. Hon C of Tweed Heads 70-75; Perm to Offic Dio C & Goulb from 75. *4 Burara Crescent, Waramanga, ACT, Australia 2611.*

FOSTER, John Anthony. b 18. Ridley Hall Cam 62. **d** 64 **p** 65 Heref. C of Bromyard 64-67; V of Nassington w Yarwell 67-73; R of Taxal w Fernilee Dio Ches from 73. *Taxal Rectory, Whaley Bridge, Stockport, Chesh.* (Whaley Bridge 2696)

FOSTER, John Augustus Cory. Ridley Coll Melb ACT ThL 30. **d** 30 **p** 31 Melb. C of St Steph Richmond 30-34; Epping 34-35; Min of Broadmeadows 35; C of St John Ryde 38-41; CF (EC) 42-54; Hon CF 54; Perm to Offic Dio Melb 59-61; C of Epiph Northcote 61-64; St Steph Richmond 64-65; P-in-c of N Carlton 65-72; Perm to Offic Dio Melb from 73. *171 Howard Street, North Melbourne, Vic, Australia 3051.*

FOSTER, John Cameron. b 04. Univ of Edin MA (2nd cl Engl) 26. Edin Th Coll 65. **d** 66 **p** 67 Edin. C of Ch Ch Morningside Edin 66-68; St Jas Aber 68-69; P-in-c of All SS Hilton 69-71; Hon C of St Jas Aber 71-75; Perm to Offic Dio Aber from 75. *45 Seafield Road, Aberdeen.* (Aberdeen 35370)

FOSTER, John Edward. b 01. St Cath Coll Cam BA 25, MA 29. Bps' Coll Cheshunt 25. **d** 26 **p** 28 Sheff. C of St Pet Abbeydale 26-31; V of St Mich AA Neepsend 31-47; CF (EC) 41-45; Hon CF 45; V of St Mary Bishophill Jun (w All SS North Street from 58) York 47-60; C-in-c of All SS North Street York 51-58; V of Reighton w Speeton 60-67. *Dulverton Hall, St Martin's Square, Scarborough, Yorks.* (0723-73082)

FOSTER, John Francis. b 13. Chich Th Coll 47. **d** 49 **p** 50 Man. C of Atherton 49-52; St Marg Halliwell 52-53; V of Briercliffe 53-59; Kirk Michael 59-64; St Paul S Ramsey 64-79; P-in-c of Leck Dio Blackb from 79. *Leck Vicarage, Cowan Bridge, Carnforth, Lancs.* (Kirkby Lonsdale 71496)

FOSTER, Very Rev John William. b 21. St Aid Coll 51. **d** 54 **p** 55 Leic. C of Loughborough 54-57; Chap St Jo Cathl Hong Kong 57-60; Prec 60-64; Dean of Hong Kong 64-73; Hon Can from 73; V of Lythe 73-78; Dean of Guernsey and R of St Pet Port Guernsey Dio Win from 78; Hon Can of Win from 79. *Deanery, St Peter Port, Guernsey, CI.* (Guernsey 20036)

FOSTER, Kenneth John. b 12. Univ of Dur 32. St Pauls Coll Burgh. **d** 36 **p** 37 Lon. C of St Paul Brentford 36-40; Eccleshall 40-60; V of Rushton Spencer 60-68; Milwich Dio Lich from 68 *Milwich Vicarage, Stafford.* (Hilderstone 308)

FOSTER, Kenneth Richard. Moore Coll Syd ThL 70. **d** 71 Syd for Armid **p** 72 Armid. C of Moree 71-74; V of Warialda 74-81; Armid Dio Armid from 81. *54 Gordon Street, Armidale, NSW, Australia 2350.*

FOSTER, Leon Joseph Alexander. b 45. St Pet Coll Alice Dipl Th 69. **d** 69 Grahmstn **p** 70 Port Eliz. C of St Mich Port Eliz 70-73; Hosp Chap Dio Port Eliz 74-80; P-in-c of Ch K Gelvandale City and Dio Port Eliz from 80. *Box 16083, Gelvandale, S Africa.*

FOSTER, Michael John. b 52. St Steph Ho Ox 76. **d** 79 Edmon for Lon **p** 80 Lon. C of St Mich Wood Green Dio Lon from 79. *20 Belsize Avenue, N13 4JS.* (01-889 1750)

FOSTER, Neville Colin. b 34. Univ of Aston Birm BSc 67. Qu Coll Birm 78. **d** 81 Birm (NSM). C of St Clem Castle Bromwich Dio Birm from 81. *20 Marlborough Road, Castle Bromwich, Birmingham, B36 0EH.*

FOSTER, Oswald Leslie. St Chad's Coll Regina. **d** 43 Qu'App **p** 53 Calg. C-in-c of Maryfield 43-44; Milestone 44; I of Canmore 53-55; Okotoks 55-58; S Saanich 58-71; Gulf Is 71-74. *402-1065 Burdett Avenue, Victoria, BC, Canada.*

FOSTER, Phillip Deighton. b 38. BD (Lon) 70. St Aid Coll 62. **d** 66 Hulme for Man **p** 67 Man. C of Castleton Moor 66-70; V of Facit 70-76; R of St Phil w St Steph Salford Dio Man from 76. *6 Encombe Place, Salford, M3 6FJ.* (061-834 2041)

FOSTER, Ven Raymond Samuel. b 20. Late Exhib Univ of Lon BD (2nd cl) 41. ALCD (1st cl) 41. K Coll Lon 43. Univ of Nottm PhD 52. ACT ThD 67. **d** 43 **p** 44 Southw. C of Old Basford 43-45; Newark 45-47; Lect Linc Th Coll 46-52; Lect Nottm Univ 47-52; R of Elston w Elston Chap 47-52; V of Sibthorpe 47-52; Chap Alleyn's Coll of God's Gift Dulwich 52-56; Chap and Lect Fourah Bay Coll Sier L 56-60; L to Offic Dio Sier L 56-60; Dio St A from 72-73; Exam Chap to Abp of W Afr 57-61; to Bp of Pet 60-62; to Bp of St A from 74; to Abp of Wales 75-78; V of Whittlebury w Silverstone 60-62; Dir of Ordin Tr Dio Pet 60-62; Warden St Jo Coll Auckld 62-72; Commiss Polyn from 62; Hon Can of Auckld 62-72; Ed Austr and NZ Th Review 64-71; Sec for Home Miss and Research SPCK 72-73; Warden and Libr of St Deiniol's Libr Hawarden 73-77; Hon Can of St A 76-77; R of Wrexham Dio St A from 77; Preb of St A Cathl from 77; Prec 77-81; Treas from 78; Archd of Wrexham from 78; Warden of Ordinands Dio St A from 81. *7 Westminster Drive, Wrexham, Clwyd, LL12 7AT.* (Wrexham 263905)

FOSTER, Robert Banks. Univ of Vic BC 64. Univ of Syracuse USA MA 70. Episc Div Sch Mass MDiv 75. **d** 75 Centr NY **p** 76 Rupld. C of St John's Cathl Winnipeg 75-76; C of St Matt Winnipeg 76-80; Tutor St Jo Coll Winnipeg 77-80; on leave. *General Delivery, Woodlands, Manit, Canada.*

FOSTER, Robert Wood. Hur Coll. **d** and **p** 59 Niag. C-in-c of Winona 59-62; R of Jordan 62-68; Milton 68-73; Grace Ch Hamilton 74-78; Ch of Redeemer Lon Dio Hur from 78. *889 Adelaide Street, London, Ont, Canada.* (519-439 1581)

FOSTER, Robin. b 46. ACP 70. Univ of Nottm BTh 75. Linc Th Coll 71. **d** 75 Burnley for Blackb **p** 76 Blackb. C of Briercliffe 75-77; Asst Dir of Relig Educn and P-in-c of Tockholes 77-80; L to Offic Dio Blackb from 80; Asst Master Sudell Sch Darwen from 80. *55 Park Road, Darwen, Lancs, BB3 2LB.* (Darwin 774684)

FOSTER, Ronald George. b 25. Univ of Bris BSc 51. K Coll Lon and Warm 49, AKC 51. **d** 52 **p** 53 Glouc. C of Lydney w Aylburton 52-54; Leighton Buzzard 54-60; Chap And Asst Master Bear Wood Coll Wokingham from 60. *48 Lakeside, Earley, Reading, Berks.* (Reading 65171)

FOSTER, Stephen Arthur. b 54. GLCM 75. Coll of the Resurr Mirfield 75. **d** 78 **p** 79 Ches. C of H Trin City and Dio Ches from 78. *51 The Parade, Blacon, Chester.* (Ches 376307)

FOSTER, Steven. b 52. Wadham Coll Ox BA 75, MA 80. Ridley Hall Cam 76. **d** 79 **p** 80 Worc. C of Ipsley Dio Worc from 79. *12 Winforton Close, Winyates, Redditch, Worcs, B98 0JX.* (Redditch 21552)

FOSTER, Steven Francis. b 55. AKC and BD 76. Coll of the Resurr Mirfield 77. **d** 78 Chelmsf **p** 79 Barking for Chelmsf. C of St Edw Romford 78-80; St Clem Leigh Dio Chelmsf from 80. *109 Oakleigh Park Drive, Leigh-on-Sea SS9 1RR.* (Southend 74352)

FOSTER, Stuart Jack. b 47. Coun for Nat Acad Awards BA 80. Oak Hill Coll 77. **d** 80 **p** 81 Win. C of Worting Dio Win from 80. *7 Swallow Close, Kempshott, Basingstoke, Hants, TG22 5QA.*

FOSTER, Thomas Andrew Hayden. b 43. Div Hostel Dub 70. **d** 73 **p** 74 Dub. C of Clontarf 73-78; P-in-c of Polstead 78; R of Drumcliffe 78-80; Kilscoran Dio Ferns from 80. *Rectory, Killinick, Co Wexford, Irish Republic.* (Wexford 28959)

FOSTER, Thomas Arthur. b 23. Late Scho of St D Coll Lamp BA (2nd cl Th) 47. Cudd Coll Ox 47. **d** 49 **p** 50 Mon. C of Risca 49-52; H Trin Win 52-55; Rumney 55-56; V of Cwmtillery 56-59; R of Llanfoist and Llanelen Dio Mon from 59. *Llanfoist Rectory, Abergavenny, Gwent.* (Abergavenny 78168)

FOSTER, William Basil. b 23. Worc Ordin Coll 65. **d** 67 **p** 68 Linc. C of Folkingham 67-71; V of Whaplode Drove 71-75; C-in-c of Gedney Hill 71-75; R of Ropsley w L Humby Dio Linc from 75; Sapperton w Braceby Dio Linc from 75; Somerby w Gt Humby Dio Linc from 75; Welby 75-77; V of Heydour w Culverthorpe 75-77; Londonthorpe 75-76. *Ropsley Rectory, Grantham, Lincs.* (Ingoldsby 255)

FOSTER, William Charles. b 05. LGSM 36. Wycl Hall Ox 43. **d** 43 Glouc **p** 44 Dur. C of Caincross 43; Chap Barnard Castle Sch 43-44; L to Offic Dio Dur 44-45; C of St Giles Newc L (in c of St Andr Westlands) 45-47; All H Twickenham 47-49; St Jas Kidbrooke (in c of St Nich) 49-51; V of St Mary-le-Pk Battersea 51-54; St Paul Furzedown Streatham 54-63; Worle 63-69; Perm to Offic Dio Cant from 69, *47 Tanners Hill Gardens, Hythe, Kent, CT21 5HX.* (Hythe 66275)

FOSTER, William Ernest. b 19. Keble Coll Ox BA (3rd cl

Mod Lang) 41, MA 45. Cudd Coll 41. **d** 43 **p** 44 Lon. C of Poplar 43-47; St Luke Enfield 47-49; PV of Lich Cathl and C of St Mich Lich 49-52; V of Weoley Castle and Chap Shenley Fields Homes 52-60; Witton 60-80; P-in-c of Croxton w Broughton Dio Lich from 80; Adbaston Dio Lich from 80. *Broughton Vicarage, Stafford, ST21 6NR.* (Wetwood 231)

FOTHERGILL, Anthony Page. b 36. Univ of Dur BA 60, Dipl Th 62. Cranmer Hall Dur 60. **d** 62 **p** 63 Lich. C of St Mark Wolverhampton 62-66; Chasetown 66-69; V of St Luke Wel Hanley 69-77; Team V of H Evang Hanley 77-78; V of Rocester Dio Lich from 78. *Rocester Vicarage, Uttoxeter, Staffs, ST14 5JZ.* (Rocester 590424)

FOTHERGILL, Guy Sherbrooke. Lon Coll of Div. **d** 47 **p** 48 Roch. C of Sevenoaks 47-50; Edgware (in c of St Andr Broadfields) 50-52; V of St Laur Kirkdale 52-57; PC of St Paul Slough 57-65; V of Drax 65-72; Eldersfield 72-77; Perm to Offic Dio Glouc from 77. *96 Colesbourne Road, Benhall, Cheltenham, Glos, GL51 6DN.* (Cheltm 27884)

FOTHERGILL, Leslie Gurth. b 09. Tyndale Hall, Bris 46. **d** 49 **p** 50 S & M. C of St Ninian Douglas 49-50; St Mark Cheltenham 50-54; R of Barton Seagrave 54-65; V of Poughill Truro 65-74. *Magnolia Cottage, Kingscott, Torrington, Devon, EX38 7JJ.* (Torrington 3554)

FOULDS, Canon Dennis. b 07. Univ of Leeds BA (2nd cl Hist) 33. Coll of Resurr Mirfield 33. **d** 35 **p** 36 S'wark. C of St Paul Clapham 35-37; C of St Luke Reigate and Chap of Surrey Co Hosp Redhill 37-40, C of St Paul Bluckb 40-41; Chertsey 42-47; V of Caxton 47-55; R of Stretham w L Thetford 55-66; V of Littleport 66-73; RD of Ely 71-82; Hon Can of Ely from 74. *34 Northwold, Ely, CB6 1BG.* (Ely 4753)

FOULKES, Francis. Univ of NZ MSc (1st cl Math) 47, BA 48. Ball Coll Ox BA (1st cl Th) 51, MA and BD 56. Wycl Hall Ox 50. **d** 53 Chelmsf for Cant for Col **p** 53 Ibad. Tutor Melville Hall Ibad 53-59; Prin Vining Centre Akure 60-63; Warden Federal Tr Coll CMS Austr 63-67; Perm to Offic Dio Melb 64-67; Chap St Andr Hall Parkville 67-74; Hon C of Te Atatu 74-77; P-in-c of Massey E 78; Lect Univ of Auckld from 74; Offg Min Dio Auckld from 79. *179b St Johns Road, Meadowbank, Auckland 5, NZ.* (584-078)

FOULKES, John David. b 50. AKC 72. St Aug Coll Cant 72. **d** 73 Cant. C of Sheerness 73-81. *Address temp unknown.*

FOULKES, Canon Meurig. b 21. Late Organ Scho of St D Coll Lamp BA 46. St Mich Coll Llan 46. **d** 47 Ban **p** 48 St A for Ban. C of Llanbeblig w Caernarvon 47-55; Private Chap to Bp of Ban 55-58; V of Harlech w Llanfair-Juxta-Harlech 58-66; RD of Ardudwy 64-76; R of Llanaber w Barmouth and Caerdeon 66-76; Llandegfan w Beaumaris and Llanfaes w Penmon and Llangoed w Llanfihangel Dinsylwy Dio Ban from 76; Can of Ban Cathl from 71; Treas from 74. *Rectory, Beaumaris, Anglesey, Gwyn.* (810146)

FOUNTAIN, Alfred Raymond. b 13. St Pet Hall Ox BA 35, Dipl in Th 36, MA 39. Wycl Hall Ox 35. **d** 37 **p** 38 S'wark. C of Ch Ch Gipsy Hill 37-41; Chap RAFVR 41-46; Chap Bradf Cathl 46-49; Succr 49-51; V of Hildenborough 51-59; St Paul Newbarns w Hawcoat Barrow-F 59-70; Faringdon w L Coxwell 70-76; P-in-c of Lamplugh w Ennerdale 76-80. *3 Tudor Close, East Blatchington, Seaford, E Sussex, BN25 2LU.* (0323 892186)

FOURNIER, Henri. Univ of Liège 28. **d** and **p** 32 Liège (RC). Rec into Angl Communion by Bp of Sask 49. Miss at Lac la Ronge 49-56; I of Hudson's Bay 55-57; Kamsack 57-64; Outlook 64-74; L to Offic Dio Calg from 74. *Box 975, Lacombe, Alta., Canada.* (782-2916)

FOUTS, Arthur Guy. b 44. Univ of Washington BA 72. Ridley Hall Cam 78. **d** 81 Willesden for Lon. C of St Jas Alperton Dio Lon from 81. *1 Norwood Avenue, Alperton, Wembley, Middx.*

FOWELL, Canon Milton David. St Jo Coll Morpeth ACT ThL 59. **d** 59 **p** 60 Newc. C of Gosford 59-61; Waratah 62-63; P-in-c of Charlestown 64; N Lake Macquarie 64-69; Home Miss Chap and L to Offic Dio Newc 69-75; R of Charlestown Dio Newc from 75; Can of Newc from 79. *Rectory, Canberra Street, Charlestown, NSW, Australia 2290.* (43-4500)

FOWKE, Thomas Randall. Chich Th Coll 52. **d** 54 **p** 55 Chich. C of Haywards Heath 54-57; V of Fletching 57-63; St Aug Preston Brighton 63-76. *6 Lower Road, Pontesbury, Salop, SY5 0YH.*

FOWKE, Canon Walter Henry. b 06. Keble Coll Ox BA (2nd cl Th) 28, MA 32. Cudd Coll 30. **d** 30 **p** 31 Pet. C of Oakham 30-33; M of Bush Bro of St Barn Dio N Queensld 33-39; Chap RAFVR 39-46; R of Halwill w Beaworthy 46-51; Chap at Bangkok 51-55; V of Newton St Cyres 55-66; C-in-c of Cowley Chap 58-66; V of Chaddesley Corbett 66-76; RD of Cadbury 65-66; RD of Kidderminster 72-76; Hon Can of Worc 75-76; Can (Emer) from 76. *Fordgate Cottage, Ford, Wiveliscombe, Taunton, TA4 2RH.*

FOWKES, Eric. Lich Th Coll 54. **d** 55 **p** 56 Wakef. C of Sowerby Bridge 55-58; V of All SS Pontefract Dio Wakef from 58. *All Saints' Vicarage, Pontefract, Yorks.* (Pontefract 2286)

FOWLE, Ian. b 36. Sarum Wells Th Coll 74. **d** 76 **p** 77 S'wark. C of H Trin w St Pet S Wimbledon 76-80; St Luke w H Trin Charlton Dio S'wark from 80. *73 Elliscombe Road, Charlton, SW7 7PF.* (01-858 0296)

FOWLER, Arthur Daniel Adair. St Jo Coll Morpeth ACT ThL 52. Austr Nat Univ BA 68. **d** 52 **p** 53 Newc. C of Scone 52-53; Aberdeen 53-54; Mayfield 54-56; R of Aberdeen 56-60; Miss P Dio New Guinea 60-65; L to Offic Dio C & Goulb 65-68; C of Manuka 68-69; V of Brunei 69-71; Chap St Thos Sch Kuch 71-72; Chap Geelong Gr Sch Melb 73-77; C of Albury 77-78; P-in-c 78-80; Tumut Dio C & Goulb from 80. *55 Reign Street, Bradfordville, NSW, Australia 2580.*

FOWLER, David Mallory. b 51. Trin Coll Bris 75. **d** 78 **p** 79 Liv. C of Rainhill 78-81; St John Houghton Dio Carl from 81. *224 Kingstown Road, Carlisle, CA3 0DE.* (0228 34711)

FOWLER, Hugh Charles Stephen. b 41. Trin Hall, Cam 2nd cl Hist Trip pt i 62, BA (3rd cl Hist Trip pt ii) 63. Westcott Ho Cam 64. **d** 66 **p** 67 S'wark. C of Sanderstead 66-68; St Ambrose 68-70; Stockwood 70-72; Bishopston 75-77; R of St Gerrans w St Anthony-in-Roseland Dio Truro from 77. *St Gerrans Rectory, Portscatho, Truro, Cornw.* (Portscatho 277)

FOWLER, John Douglass. b 22. Worc Ordin Coll 61. **d** 63 **p** 64 B & W. C of Portishead 63-67; C-in-c of Huish Champflower w Clatworthy 67-71; C-in-c of Chipstable w Raddington 67-71; R of Chelvey w Brockley 71-73; Asst Chap Is of Scilly 73; Team V 74-78; C-in-c of Ashbrittle w Bathealton, Stawley and Kittisford Dio B & W from 78; Team V of Wellington and Distr from 81. *Ashbrittle Vicarage, Wellington, Somt, TA21 0LF.* (Greenham 672495)

FOWLER, Very Rev John Richard Hart. Trin Coll Tor BA 58, STB 62, Hon DD 79. St Cath S Ox BA 60, MA 65. St Steph Ho Ox. **d** 61 **p** 62 Ott. C of St Thos Ott 61-63; Fell and Tutor in Div Trin Coll Tor 63-68; C of Oakville 68-69; Chap and Lect Qu Coll St John's 69-70; L to Offic Dio Niag 70-71; I of Dryden 72-74; Archd of Keew S 74; Dean and R of St Matt Cathl Timmins Dio Moos from 75. *65 Hemlock Street, Timmins, Ont., Canada.* (705-264 0915)

FOWLER, John Ronald. b 30. Ely Th Coll 55. **d** 58 **p** 59 S'wark. C of St Andr Surbiton 58-62; V of Morawhanna 62-65; R of Plaisance 65-70; V of Beterverwagting 69-70; All SS Sydenham 70-81; Commiss to Abp of W Indies 77-79; to Bp of Guy from 80; V of St Chad City and Dio Cov from 81. *Vicarage, Hillmorton Road, Coventry, CV2 1FY.* (Cov 612909)

FOWLER, Canon John Sims. b 25. Late Scho and Pri of Trin Coll Cam 1st cl Mech Sc Trip 45, BA 46, MA 50. Clifton Th Coll 48. Univ of Lon BD (1st cl) 52. **d** 52 **p** 53 Bris. C of Rodbourne-Cheney 52-55; CMS Miss from 55; Chap to Bp of Lagos 56-60; Actg Tutor CMS Tr Coll Chislehurst 60-61; CMS Yoruba Miss 61-62; Dir Inst of Ch and Soc Ibad 63-72; Hon Can of Ibad Cathl from 71; Lagos from 72; R of St Columba Crieff 73-78; Muthill 74-78; Comrie 77-78; Warden Leasow Ho Selly Oak from 78. *Leasow House, Crowther Hall, Weoley Park Road, Selly Oak, Birmingham, B29 6QT.* (021-472 4228)

FOWLER, John Stephen. b 1891. Men in Disp 18. Bp Wilson Th Coll IM 36. **d** 38 **p** 39 Glouc. C of Coleford w Staunton 38-43; St Cuthb Wells 43-45; R of Axbridge 45-49; Chap at Mem Chs Ypres Lille and Arras 49-58; Huggens' Coll Northfleet 58-64; Stone Ho Hosp Dartford 58-61; L to Offic Dio Roch from 64. *20 Hillside Avenue, Fridsbury, Rochester, Kent.* (Medway 79015)

FOWLER, Russell Charles. Moore Th Coll Syd ACT ThL (2nd cl) 59. **d** and **p** 60 Syd. C of Wollongong 60-62; R of Miranda 62-68; Chap NSW Dept of Child Welfare 68-72; Chap Royal N Shore Hosp from 72. *32 Millwood Avenue, Chatswood, NSW, Australia 2067.* (419-4028)

FOWLER, Stuart John. Univ of Lon BSc (Econ) 64. Wells Th Coll. **d** 68 Bp Sinker for Birm **p** 69 Birm. C of Old Ch Smethwick 68-71; Bracebridge Heath 71-74; L to Offic Dio Linc 74-76; Perm to Offic Dio Edin from 76. *Address temp unknown.*

FOWLER, Thomas Edward. b 03. Clifton Th Coll 33. **d** 30 **p** 31 Rang. BCMS Miss at Mohnyin Burma 30-32; V of Rainham 33-39; Tibshelf 39-45; St Aug Derby 45-53; V of St Paul Jersey 53-65; R of Knight's Enham w Smannell 65-69. *19 West Street, Scarborough, N Yorks.*

FOWLES, Christopher John. b 31. Lich Th Coll 54. **d** 58 Kingston T for Guildf **p** 59 Guildf. C of Englefield Green 58-63; Worplesdon 63-69; V of Chessington 69-77; Horsell Dio Guildf from 77. *Horsell Vicarage, Woking, Surrey, GU21 4QQ.* (Woking 72134)

FOWLES, Peter. b 30. St Deiniols Libr Hawarden 71. **d** 72 **p** 73 St A. C of Connah's Quay 72-76; V of Towyn Dio St A from 76. *Towyn Vicarage, Abergele, Clwyd.* (Rhyl 1211)

FOWLOW, Guy. Qu Coll Newfld. **d** 39 **p** 40 Newfld. C of Bonavista 39-40; R of Burgeo 40-46; Bay Roberts 46-55;

Hearts Content 55-58; Corner Brook 58-71; Spaniard's Bay 71-76. *106 Topsail Road, St John's, Newfoundland, Canada.*

FOX, Albert. b 06. **d** 73 **p** 74 Bris. C of St Ambrose Bris 73-75; E Bristol Dio Bris 75-79; Perm to Offic Dio Bris from 79. *20 New Brunswick Avenue, St George, Bristol 5.* (Bristol 672632)

FOX, Alex. b 39. **d** 77 **p** 78 Keew. C of St Pet Bearskin Lake Dio Keew from 77. *St Peter's Church, Bearskin Lane, Ont, POV 1EO, Canada.*

FOX, Alex Maurice. St Francis Coll Brisb. **d** 60 **p** 61 Brisb. C of St Andr Indooroopilly 60-63; Dalby 63-64; V of Jandowae 64-65; R of Stanthorpe 65-71; Perm to Offic Dio Brisb 71; Archd of Carp 71-73; Exam Chap to Bp of Carp 71-73; P-in-c of Weipa 71-73; St Andr Longreach 74; R of St Paul E Brisb 74-77; Perm to Offic Dio Brisb from 77. *3 Rosecliffe Street, Highgate Hill, Queensland, Australia 4101.* (44 8403)

FOX, Alfred Henry Purcell. b 1895. AKC 21. **d** 22 **p** 23 S'wark. C of St Barn Dulwich 22-25; St Phil Stepney 25-29; Hawarden (in c of St Mary Broughton) 29-34; Chap Brompton Hosp 34-42; Chap RAFVR 42-45; Salisbury Gen Infirm 45-47; V of Downton 47-55; R of Ashmore 55-59; V of Cragg Vale 59-65; PC of Cothelstone 65-72. *151a High Street, Spaxton, Bridgwater, Somt.*

FOX, Bernard John Gurney. b 07. Hertf Coll Ox BA (3rd cl Hist) 28, MA 35. Cudd Coll 31. **d** 32 **p** 33 Dur. C of St Mary Magd Millfield 32-35; CPSS Poona 35-41; Math Acharya 38-41; S Bank 41-44; PC of Grangetown 44-49; V of Selangor and Pahang Dio Sing 49-54; C-in-c of St Pet Thorney Close Conv Distr 54-58; Commiss Bom 57-62; R of Winlaton 58-67; V of Acklington (w Warkworth from 68) 67-73; Commiss Ja 69-70. *13 Thornhill Terrace, Sunderland.* (Sunderland 57713)

FOX, Cecil George. b 15. Trin Coll Dub BA 47, MA 64. **d** 48 **p** 49 Cash. C of Thurles 48-50; R of Newport w Killoscully and Abington 50-54; Killarney 54-64; Can of Lim 63-64; Chap HM Pris Man 64-66; Lewes 66-70; V of Charsfield (w Debach and Monewden w Hoo from 77) Dio St E from 70; R of Monewden w Hoo 70-77. *Charsfield Vicarage, Woodbridge, Suff.* (Charsfield 253)

FOX, Canon Charles Alfred. St Aid Coll 31. **d** 33 **p** 34 Bradf. C of St Pet Bradf 33; St Jo Evang Gt Horton Bradf 33-35; St John Stratford Essex 35-37; V of Em Leyton 37-58; CF (TA) from 37; CF (R of O) 39-45; Men in Disp 46; Commiss to Abp of W Africa 53-56; to Bp of Lagos 56-60; V of Stratford (w Ch Ch Stratford from 62 and St Jas Forest Gate from 66) 58-78; C-in-c of Ch Ch Stratford 58-62; Surr 58-78; Hon Can of Chelmsf 63-78; Can (Emer) from 78; Hon Sec Chelmsf Dioc Conf from 66; Perm to Offic Dio Lich from 78. *5 Limewood Close, Blythe Bridge, Staffs, ST11 9NZ.* (Blythe Bridge 5164)

FOX, Charles Edward. b 36. Lich Th Coll 62. **d** 66 **p** 67 York. C of S Bank 66-69; Stokesley 69-72; V of Egton w Grosmont Dio York from 72; C-in-c of Ugthorpe Dio York from 72. *Egton Vicarage, Whitby, Yorks.* (Whitby 85264)

FOX, Colin George. b 46. Univ of Southn Dipl Th 75. Sarum Wells Th Coll 73. **d** 75 Lon **p** 76 Kens for Lon. C of St Kath Westway Hammersmith 75-79; Heston 79-81; Team V of Marlborough Dio Sarum from 81. *22 West Manton, Marlborough, Wilts.* (06725-3408)

FOX, Douglas James. b 30. Univ of Tor BA 53, MA 68, PhD 75. Knox Coll Tor BD 62. **d** and **p** 80 Hur. C of Chap of St Jo Evang Hur Coll Lon Ont from 80. *Huron College, 1349 Western Road, London, Ont, Canada, N6G 1H3.*

FOX, Douglas John. b 55. Univ of Regina BA 75. Univ of Sask MDiv 81. Em & St Chad's Coll Sktn 79. **d** 81 Qu'App. C of Prairie Cross Dio Qu'App from 81. *c/o Synod Office, 1501 College Avenue, Regina, Sask, Canada, S4P 1B8.*

FOX, George Shipman. b 1898. Univ of Dur 23. Chich Th Coll 23. TD 50. **d** 25 **p** 26 Sheff. C of St Mich AA Neepsend 25-27; Frome 27-30; Aylesbury 30-33; Perm to Offic at St Aid Gateshead 33-34; C of St Cuthb Newc T 34-38; Seghill (in c of Seaton Delval) 38-39; CF (TA - R of O) 39-46; Chap St Mich Home Axbridge 46-49; V of W Harptree 49-57; C-in-c of Compton Martin 50-53; Hon CF from 53; R of Stepleton 57-60; V of Dorrington 57-60; Eaton 60-64; Perm to Offic Dio B & W 64-78. *South Ferriz Hall, Barton on Humber, S Humb.*

FOX, Harvey Harold. b 27. Lich Th Coll 58. **d** 60 Birm **p** 61 Aston for Birm. C of Birchfield 60-62; Boldmere 62-65; V of Em Sparkbrook 65-71; Dordon w Freazley 71-77; Four Oaks 77-82; Packwood w Nuthurst & Hockley Heath Dio Birm from 82. *Nuthurst Vicarage, Hockley Heath, Solihull, W Midl B94 5RP.* (Lapworth 3121)

FOX, Herbert Frederick. b 26. Univ of Leeds BA 50. Coll of Resurr Mirfield 50. **d** 52 **p** 53 Man. C of St Thos Bury 52-55; V of Unsworth 55-61; Turton 61-72; Farnworth 72-78; R of E Farnworth and Kearsley Dio Man from 78; RD of Farnworth from 77. *Farnworth Rectory, Bolton, Lancs, BL4 8AQ.* (Farnworth 72819)

FOX, Ian James. b 44. Selw Coll Cam 2nd cl Th Trip pt i 64, BA (3rd cl Th Trip pt ii) 66. Linc Th Coll 66. **d** 68 **p** 69 Man. C of St Phil w St Steph Salford 68-71; Kirk Leatham 71-73; Team V of Redcar 73-77; V of St Pet Bury Dio Man from 77. *St Peter's Vicarage, Bury, BL9 9QZ.* (061-764 1187)

FOX, Jonathan Alexander. b 56. St Jo Coll Nottm LTh, BTh 81. **d** 81 Lich. C of Chasetown Dio Lich from 81. *7 Hill Lane, Chase Terrace, Walsall, WS7 8LS.* (Burntwood 4124)

FOX, Canon Joseph Denis. St Edm Hall, Ox BA (2nd cl Th) 28, MA 33. Cudd Coll 28. **d** 29 Lon for Guildf **p** 30 S'wark. C of St Nich Guildf 29-30; St Jo Evang E Dulwich 30-35; St Aldhelm Branksome 35-36; PC of Wardington w Williamscote and Coton 36-51 V. of Happisburgh w Walcot 51-54; C-in-c of Ridlington 51-54; Vice-Prin of Cudd Coll 53-54; Chap Eastbourne Coll 54-62; R of Neatishead w Irstead 62-76; RD of Tunstead 68-76; P-in-c of Barton Turf 74-76; Hon Can of Nor 75-77; Can (Emer) from 77. *Seaward, Verriotts Lane, Morcombelake, Bridport, Dorset, DT6 6DX.* (Chideock 397)

FOX, Joseph William. b 08. Sarum Th Coll 52. **d** 52 **p** 53 Ex. C of Widecombe-in-the-Moor 52-56; Leusden 59-61; Perm to Offic Dio Ex from 74. *Pease Close, Throwleigh, Okehampton, Devon.*

FOX, Leonard. b 41. K Coll Lon and Warm AKC 66. **d** 67 **p** 68 Man. C of Stowell Mem Ch Salford 67-68; St Phil Hulme (Ascen Hulme from 70) 68-72; All SS and St John Portsea 72-75; V of St John Ryde Dio Portsm from 75. *1 High Park Road, Ryde, IW, PO33 1BP.* (Ryde 62863)

FOX, Maurice Henry George. b 24. BD (Lon) 58. St Aid Coll. **d** 49 **p** 50 Bradf. C of St Luke Eccleshill 49-52; Bingley 52-56; V of Cross Roads w Lees 56-62; Sutton-in-Craven 62-79; Grange-over-Sands Dio Carl from 79. *Vicarage, Grange-over-Sands, Cumb.* (G-0-S 2757)

FOX, Michael John. b 42. Univ of Hull BSc (Chem) 63. Coll of Resurr Mirfield 64. **d** 66 Barking for Chelmsf **p** 67 Chelmsf. C of St Eliz Becontree 66-70; H Trin S Woodford 70-72; V of Ascen Vic Dks 72-76; All SS Borough and Dio Chelmsf from 76. *Vicarage, King's Road, Chelmsford, Essex, CM1 4HP.* (Chelmsf 352005)

FOX, Michael John Holland. b 41. BD (Lon) 68. Oak Hill Th Coll 64. **d** 69 Bp Boys for S'wark **p** 70 S'wark. C of Reigate 69-73; St Sav Guildf 73-76; Reigate Dio S'wark from 76; Asst Chap Reigate Gr Sch from 81. *71 Blackborough Road, Reigate, Surrey, RH2 7BU.* (0732 49017)

FOX, Michael John Howard. Linc Coll Ox. Coll of Resurr Mirfield, 56. **d** 58 **p** 59 Dur. C of St Thos Conv Distr Pennywell Bp Wearmouth 58-60; Birtley 60-62; Asst Master Fairchilds Secondary Modern Boys' Sch New Addington Croydon 63-66; L to Offic Dio Centr Tang 66-68; Dio Dar-S 68-70; Dio Lusaka 70-74; Dio Cyprus 75-79. *Address temp unknown*

FOX, Canon Michael Storrs. b 05. Em Coll Cam BA (2nd cl Hist Trip pt ii) 28, MA 32. Bps' Coll Cheshunt 31. **d** 33 **p** 34 York. C of Bolton Percy 33-35; SPG Miss at Cawnpore 35-49; Chap St Nich Naini Tal; St D Bhowali; St Mark Almora; and Ranikhet 49-57; V of Egton 57-64; V of Grosmont 57-64; Can and Preb of York Minster from 62; R of Barton-le-Street 64-77; V of Salton 64-77. *Hawthorn Cottage, Coneysthorpe, York, YO6 7DD.*

FOX, Nigel Stephen. b 35. Sarum Th Coll 59. **d** 62 Bp Stuart for Worc. **p** 63 Worc. C of St Barn Rainbow Hill Worc 62-65; St Geo Kidderminster 65-67; Min of St Wulstan Eccles Distr Warndon Worc 67-69; V 69-74; R of Callington w S Hill Dio Truro from 74; RD of E Wivelshire 78-81. *Rectory, Callington, Cornw, PL17 7PD.* (Callington 3341)

FOX, Norman. BEM 79. Moore Th Coll Syd ACT ThL 51. **d** 26 **p** 27 Syd. C of St Phil Auburn 27-28; St Andr Summer Hill 28-32; R of St John Shoalhaven 32-37; St Mich Syd 37-47; R of Lismore 47-48; Five Dock 48-54; Killara 54-74; C of St Phil York Street Syd 74-80. *6/1 Marian Street, Killara, NSW, Australia 2071.* (498-2203)

FOX, Norman Stanley. b 39. Univ of Wales Dipl Th 64. St Mich Coll Llan 61. **d** 64 **p** 65 Lich. C of Brierley Hill 64-67; Tettenhall Regis 67-70; V of Cradley 70-73; Asst Chap HM Pris Wakefield 73-74; Chap HM Pris Verne 74-76; R of Clayton W w High Hoyland 76-81; R of Cumberworth w Denby Dale Dio Wakef from 81. *Rectory, Hollybank Avenue, Upper Cumberworth, Huddersfield, Yorks HD8 8NY.* (Huddersfield 606225)

FOX, Peter John. b 52. AKC 74. St Aug Coll Cant 74. **d** 75 Nor **p** 76 Lynn for Nor. C of Wymondham 75-80; P-in-c of Gerehu Dio Port Moresby from 80. *Box 806, Port Moresby, Papua New Guinea.*

FOX, Raymond. b 46. Qu Univ Belf BSc 69. Trin Coll Dub Div Test 71. **d** 71 **p** 72 Down. C of Holywood 71-75; Min Can of Down Cathl 75-78; I of Killinchy w Kilmood 78-81; St Mary Belf Dio Connor from 81. *St Mary's Rectory, Crumlin Road, Belfast, BT14 7GL.*

FOX, Sidney. b 47. Univ of Nottm BTh 79. Linc Th Coll 75. **d** 79 **p** 80 York. C of St Osw Middlesbrough Dio York 79-81; P-in-c from 81. *St Oswalds Vicarage, Lambton Road, Middlesbrough, Cleve.* (Middlesbrough 816156)

FOX, Timothy William Bertram. b 37. CCC Cam 3rd cl Hist Trip pt i 60, BA (3rd cl Th Trip pt ia) 61. Qu Coll Birm 66. **d** 68 **p** 69 Lich. C of Cannock 68-72; Bilston 72-75; V of Essington 75-81; Buildwas and Leighton w Eaton Constantine and Wroxeter Dio Lich from 81. *Eaton Constantine Rectory, Shrewsbury, SY5 6RF.* (Cressage 333)

FOX-DAVIES, Mortimer Edmond. b 11. Worc Ordin Coll 61. **d** 62 **p** 63 Roch. C of Crofton 62-66; R of Horsmonden 66-72; Perm to Offic Dio Cant from 73. *44 Reculver Avenue, Birchington-on-Sea, Kent, CT7 9NU.* (Thanet 42338)

FOX-WILSON, Francis James. b 46. Univ of Nottm BTh 73. Linc Th Coll 69. **d** 73 Chich **p** 74 Lewes for Chich. C of St Eliz Eastbourne 73-76; Seaford 76-78; P-in-c of Hellingly and U Dicker Dio Chich from 78. *Hellingly Vicarage, Hellingly, Hailsham, E Sussex.* (Hellingly 844236)

FOXCROFT, James. b 05. St Andr Coll Pampisford 47. **d** and **p** 49 Bhag. [f in CA]. Miss Dio Bhag 49-55; Actg Rep CMS and CEZMS for Bhag 53-54; R of Folke w Long Burton N Wootton and Haydon 56-59; CMS Area Sec Dio Linc 59-64; Dios Derby and Southw 59-62; Dio Ely 62-64; V of Woodborough 64-65; PC of H Trin w St Marg Keddington Louth 65-70; R of Cattistock w Chilfrome 70-73; Perm to Offic Dio Southw from 74. *47 The Holme, Westhorpe, Southwell, Notts. NG25 0NF.* (Southwell 813910)

FOXCROFT, Robert Gill Bentley. b 40. Chich Th Coll 66. **d** 68 Kens for Lon **p** 69 Lon. C of Chiswick 68-72; CF 72-75; V of St Pet Hammersmith Dio Lon from 75. *6 St Peter's Square, W6 9AB.* (01-748 1781)

FOXWELL, John Graham. b 17. Sarum Th Coll 46. **d** 49 **p** 50 S'wark. C of Wandsworth Common 49-50; Battersea 50-52; Burgess Hill 52-54. *6 Church Close, Lower Kingswood, Tadworth, Surrey.*

FRALICK, Allan John Albert. K Coll Halifax NS Syd 49, LTh 51. **d** 51 **p** 52 NS. R of Seaforth 51-57; I of Jollimore and Purcell's Cove and P-in-c of Terrance Bay 57-58; CF (Canad) from 58. *CFB Uplands, Ottawa, Ont, Canada.*

FRALICK, Canon John Ronald. Univ of Tor BA 51. Wycl Coll Tor. **d** 54 Tor **p** 54 Coadj Bp for Tor. C of St John W Tor 54-55; I of Elmvale 55-58; St Jo Div Tor 58-69; Orillia Dio Tor from 69; Can of Tor from 72. *57 Neywash Street, Orillia, Ont., Canada.* (705-325 2742)

✠ **FRAME, Right Rev John Timothy.** Univ of Tor BA 53. Trin Coll Tor LTh 57, STB 62, DD 68. **d** 57 Tor for Caled **p** 58 Caled. Miss at Burns Lake 57-68; Hon Can of Caled 65-68; Cons Ld Bp of Yukon in Ch Ch Cathl Vic 6 Jan 68 by Abp of BC; Bps of New Westmr; Caled; and Koot; Asst Bp of Carib; and Bps Coleman and I I Curtis (USA); res 80; Dean and R of Ch Ch Cathl Vic Dio BC from 80. *912 Vancouver Street, Victoria, BC, Canada, V8V 3V7.* (604-383 3616)

FRAMPTON, Gerald Reginald. b 43. **d** 73 **p** 74 Newfld (APM). C of New Harbour Dio Newfld (E Newfld from 76) from 73. *Chapel Arm, Trinity Bay, Newfoundland, Canada.* (709-592 2193)

FRAMPTON, Kenneth John. Peterho Cam BA 49, MA 54. Wycl Coll Tor BTh 57. **d** 56 **p** 57 Tor. C of Ch of Redeem Tor 56-58; I of Orillia S 58-63; R of Bowmanville 63-68; St Clem Riverdale Tor 69-71; I of Our Sav Don Mills Tor 71-81; Assoc P of St Clem Eglinton City and Dio Tor from 81. *59 Briar Hill Avenue, Toronto, M4R 1H8, Ont, Canada.*

FRANCE, Evan Norman Lougher. b 52. Jes Coll Cam BA 74, MA 78. Wycl Hall Ox 76. **d** 79 **p** 80 Birm. C of Ascen Hall Green Dio Birm from 79. *91 School Road, Hall Green, Birmingham, B28 8JQ.*

FRANCE, Geoffrey Charles. b 23. Ripon Hall, Ox 57. **d** 59 Bp Gelsthorpe for Southw **p** 60 Southw. C of St Mark Mansfield 59-61; V of Rainworth 61-68; St Cypr Sneinton Dio Southw from 68. *Vicarage, Marston Road, Nottingham.* (Nottingham 248502)

FRANCE, George Edward. Atlantic Sch of Th Halifax NS 80. **d** 81 NS. Perm to Offic Dio NS from 80. *37 Dipper Crescent, Halifax, NS, Canada, B3M 1W5.*

FRANCE, Malcolm Norris. b 28. Ch Ch Ox BA 54, MA 57. Univ of Essex PhD 75. Westcott Ho Cam. **d** 55 **p** 56 St E. C of St Mary-le-Tower Ipswich 55-58; V of Esholt w Hawksworth 58-64; Chap Univ of Essex 64-73; Perm to Offic Dio Chich from 77. *New House Farm, Bodiam, Robertsbridge, E Sussex, TN32 5UP.* (Staplecross 637)

FRANCE, Richard Thomas. b 38. Ball Coll Ox 1st cl Cl Mods 58, BA (2nd cl Lit Hum) 60, MA 63. BD (1st cl) Lon 62. Univ of Bris PhD 67. Tyndale Hall Bris 60. **d** 66 Huntingdon for Ely **p** 67 Ely. C of St Matt Cam 66-69; Lect Relig Stud Ife Univ Nigeria 69-73; Ahmadu Bello Univ Nigeria from 76; Libr Tyndale Ho Cam 73-76. *Ahmadu Bello University, Zaria, Nigeria.*

FRANCE, William Michael. b 43. Univ of Syd BA 68. BD (Lon) 72. Moore Coll Syd ThL 70. **d** and **p** 73 Syd. C of Turramurra 73-77; Barton Seagrave Pet from 77-78; R of St Andr Dundas Dio Syd from 79. *7 St Andrew's Place, Dundas, NSW, Australia 2117.* (638-3968)

FRANCIS, Arthur John Hugh. b 15. St Jo Coll Dur LTh 38, BA 39. ALCD 38. **d** 39 **p** 40 Pet. C of St Giles Northn 39-43; Ch Ch Reading 43-45; Farnham 45-48; St Jo Bapt Pet 48-50; R of Clifton Reynes w Newton Blossomville 50-55; CF 55-69; R of Easton-on-the-Hill Dio Pet from 69. *Rectory, Easton-on-the-Hill, Stamford, PE9 3LS.* (Stamford 2616)

FRANCIS, Claude Vernon Eastwood. b 15. Univ of Wales BA 38. Ripon Hall Ox 38. **d** 40 **p** 41 Llan. C of Cilybebyll 40-44; Treorchy 44-46; Whitchurch 46-49; Winscombe w Sandford 49-55; R of E Pennard w Pylle (w Ditcheat from 75) 55-80. *Millbank, Mill Lane, Alhampton, Ditcheat, Somt.*

FRANCIS, Clement Emmanuel. b 45. Trin Coll Tor 73. **d** 75 Bp Read for Tor **p** 76 Tor. C of St Mich AA Tor 75-78; P-in-c of All SS Westboro 78-79; C 79-80; I of Bearbrook-vars-Russell Dio Ott from 80. *Box 609, RR3, Navan, Ont, Canada.* (613-835 2288)

FRANCIS, Cyril. ACT ThL (2nd cl) 33. **d** and **p** 34 Newc. C of Adamstown 34-35; Gosford 35-36; Hamilton 36-37; R of Wollombi and P-in-c of Ellalong 37-40; Chap AIF 40-44; R of Gosford 44-57; Muswellbrook 57-69; Can of Newc 69; Perm to Offic Dio Newc from 70. *PO Box 54, Muswellbrook, NSW, Australia 2333.*

FRANCIS, David Everton. St Deiniol's Libr Hawarden 76. **d** 77 **p** 78 Swan B. C of Llangyfelach 77-78; Llansamlet 78-80; V of Llanrhaeadr-ym-Mochnant Llanarmon Mynydd Mawr Dio St A from 80. *Berwynfa, Llanrhaeadr-ym-Mochnant, Oswestry, Salop.* (Llanrhaeadr 247)

FRANCIS, David Lloyd. b 01. St Jo Coll Auckld. St Jo Coll Morpeth 34. **d** 35 Melan **p** 37 Waik for Melan. Miss at Aoba 35-37; C of Cam NZ 37-38; Miss At Raga 38-40; CF (NZ) 41-44; P-in-c of Kamo-Hikurangi 44-45; Deputn Staff NZABM 45-46; Deputn Staff Melan Miss Lon 47-49; Sec New Guinea Miss 49-54; C of H Trin Chelsea 55-59; Chap Westmr Hosp 61-66. *54 Wordsworth Street, Hove, Sussex.*

FRANCIS, Donald. b 31. Univ of Bris BA 52. St Mich Coll Llan 52. **d** 54 **p** 55 Mon. C of St Julian Newport 54-59; St Jas Pokesdown Bournemouth 59-61; R of Wolvesnewton w Kilgwrrwg and Devauden 61-74; V of Llantilio-Pertholey w Bettws Dio Mon from 74. *St Teilo's Vicarage, Llantilio Pertholey, Abergavenny, Gwent, NP7 6NY.* (Abergavenny 4323)

FRANCIS, Donald Elliott. Ridley Coll Melb 60. ACT ThL (2nd cl) 62. **d** 63 **p** 64 Willoch. C of Pt Pirie 63-67; P-in-c of Quorn 67-70; C of Ivychurch 70-72; R of H Cross Canberra 72-77; Cooma Dio C & Goulb from 77. *Box 43, Cooma, NSW, Australia 2630.* (0648-2 1544)

FRANCIS, Ven Edward Reginald. b 29. Roch Th Coll 59. **d** 61 **p** 62 Roch. C of Frindsbury 61-64; C-in-c of St William Conv Distr Chatham 64-67; Min 67-71; V 71-73; Rochester 73-79; RD of Roch 73-78; Archd of Bromley and M of Kent Industr Chap from 79; M Gen Syn from 81. *6 Horton Way, Farningham, Kent.* (Farningham 864522)

FRANCIS, Ernest Walter. b 08. MBE 45. BC Coll Bris 29. **d** 36 **p** 37 Rang. BCMS Miss Burma and India 36-45; Paletwa 47-65; CF (India) 42-46; S Area Sec BCMS 67-74; Perm to Offic Dios Chelmsf; Chich; Guildf; Portsm; St Alb; S'wark; and Win from 67; Dio Cov from 76. *7 Margetts Close, Barrowfield Lane, Kenilworth, CV8 1EN.* (Kenilworth 52560)

FRANCIS, Garfield. b 12. Univ of Wales (Swansea) 34. St D Coll Lamp. **d** 42 **p** 43 Ripon. C of St Mary Hunslet 42-49; Chap St Jas Hosp Leeds and LPr Dio Ripon 49-59; R of Grafton Flyford w N Piddle (and Flyford Flavell from 62) 59-77; C-in-c of Flyford Flavell 59-62. *Llangennith Vicarage, Swansea, W Glam.*

FRANCIS, Gerald Edward. St Paul's Coll Grahmstn 66. **d** 68 **p** 69 Capetn. C of Parow 68-70; L to Offic Dio Port Eliz 70-75; C of Milnerton 76-78; Matroosfontein 78-80; Perm to Offic Dio Capetn from 80. *22 Charles Court, Ficus Road, Thornton 7460, CP, S Africa.* (21-5057)

FRANCIS, Graham John. b 45. Univ of Wales (Cardiff) Dipl Th 70. St Mich Th Coll Llan 66. **d** 70 Bp Hughes for Llan **p** 71 Llan. C of Llanblethian w Cowbridge and Llandough w St Mary Ch 70-76; V of Penrhiwceiber w Matthewstown and Ynysboeth Dio Llan from 76. *Vicarage, Penrhiwceiber, Mountain Ash, Mid Glam, CF45 3YF.* (Mountain Ash 473716)

FRANCIS, Graham Louis. Lich Th Coll 55. **d** 56 **p** 57 Ches. C of St John Wallasey 56-60; V of St Mark Dukinfield 60-65; R of St Pet Ches 65-72; C-in-c of St Mich w St Olave Ches 65-72; L to Offic Dio St A 72-80; V of Berse w Southsea Dio St A from 80. *Vicarage, Southsea, Wrexham, LL11 6PN.*

FRANCIS, Hilton Barrington. b 23. Selw Coll Cam BA 46, MA 48. Ridley Hall, Cam 61. **d** 62 **p** 63 Nor. C of Eaton 62-67; V of Trowse 67-69; PC of Arminghall 67-69; Lect Nor

City Coll 69-75; Tutor Adult Educn 75-81; P-in-c of Gt w L Plumstead Dio Nor from 81. *Vicarage, Lawn Crescent, Thorpe End, Norwich, NR13 5BP.* (Nor 34778)

FRANCIS, James. St Pet Coll Rosettenville LTh 46. **d** 45 **p** 46 Natal. C of St Paul Ind Miss Maritz 45-48; St Faith's Miss Durban 48-52; C-in-c of Ch Ch Sydenham Durban 52-61; P-in-c of St Aid Durban 62-64; R 64-78; C of St Pancras w St Jas & Ch Ch Dio Lon from 78. *3 St Pancras Church House, 1 Lancing Street, NW1 1NA.* (01-387 8250)

FRANCIS, Jeffrey Merrick. b 46. Univ of Bris BSc 69. Qu Coll Birm 72. **d** 76 **p** 77 Bris. C of Stockwood 76-79; Bishopston Dio Bris from 79. *26 King's Drive, Bristol, BS7 8JP.* (Bris 43424)

FRANCIS, John Harris. St Aid Coll 39. Univ of Dur LTh 42. **d** 42 **p** 43 Wakef. C of Darton 42-45; Sandal Magna 45-47; PC of Ironville 47-76; RD of Heanor 59-76; Surr from 59. *62 Southgate Road, Southgate, Penard, Swansea.*

FRANCIS, John Sims. St D Coll Lamp BA 47, LTh 49. Fitzw Ho Cam BA (3rd cl Th Trip pt ii) 54, MA 58. **d** 49 **p** 50 Swan B. C of St Barn Swansea 49-52; Chesterton Cambs 52-54; St Mary Swansea 54-58; V of Newbridge-on-Wye 58-65; R of Willingham Dio Ely from 65; RD of N Stowe from 78. *Willingham Rectory, Cambridge.* (Willingham 60379)

FRANCIS, Jon. b 49. Univ of Birm BEducn 75. Ripon Hall Ox Dipl Th 74. **d** 74 **p** 75 Worc. C of St Jo Bromsgrove 74-75; Evesham 75-77; St Pet Eaton Square 78-80. *c/0 33 Buckmaster Road, SW11.*

FRANCIS, Kenneth. b 30. Em Coll Cam 2nd cl Th Trip pt i 54, BA (2nd cl Th Trip pt ii) 56, MA 60. Coll of Resurr Mirfield. **d** 58 **p** 59 Lon. C of St Pet De Beauvoir Town W Hackney 58-61; Sub-Warden St Jo Th Sem Lusaka 62-65; Chap 65-70; P-in-c of St Phil Lusaka 62-70; V of St Mary Magd Harlow 70-76; St Jo Bapt Felixstowe Dio St E from 76. *St John's Vicarage, Felixstowe, Suff.* (Felixstowe 4226)

FRANCIS, Kenneth Charles. b 22. Oak Hill Th Coll. **d** 50 **p** 51 S'wark. C of Wandsworth 50-53; V of St Nich w Ch Ch Deptford 53-61; St Mary Summerstown 61-77; R of Cratfield w Heveningham and Ubbeston w Huntingfield and Cookley Dio St E from 77. *Cratfield Vicarage, Halesworth, Suff, IP19 0BU.* (Ubbeston 275)

FRANCIS, Canon Kenneth Edgar. b 15. St D Coll Lamp BA 38. **d** 39 **p** 40 Ban. C of Criccieth w Treflys 39-47; Towyn 47-48; R of Llanymawddy 48-55; V of Aberdovey 55-80; Beddgelert Dio Ban from 80; Hon Can of Ban Cathl from 81. *Vicarage, Beddgelert, Gwyn.*

FRANCIS, Leslie John. b 47. Pembroke Coll Ox BA 70, MA 74. Qu Coll Cam PhD 76. Univ of Nottm MTh 76. Univ of Lon MSc 77. Westcott Ho Cam 70. **d** 73 **p** 74 St E. C of Haverhill 73-78; P-in-c of Gt Bradley Dio St E from 78; L Wratting Dio St E from 79. *Rectory, Great Wratting, Haverhill, Suff.* (Thurlow 272)

FRANCIS, Martin Rufus. b 37. Pemb Coll Ox BA 60, MA 64. Linc Th Coll 60. **d** 63 **p** 64 Dur. C of St Paul W Hartlepool 63-67; Yeovil 67-69; Sen Chap Tonbridge Sch from 69; L to Offic Dio Roch from 69. *27 Dry Hill Park Road, Tonbridge, Kent.* (Tonbridge 352802)

FRANCIS, Noel Charles. b 14. St D Coll Lamp BA 36. **d** 38 **p** 39 St D. C of Llanegwad 38-40; St D Carmarthen 40-42; Penistone 42-51; St Andr Riversdale 51-52; R of Victoria W 52-55; Beaufort W 55-58; St Pet Mossel Bay 58-65; I of Muckross w Templecarne 65-68; Perm to Offic Dio St Andr 68-69; V of St Paul w St Jude Manningham 69-81. *Address temp unknown.*

FRANCIS, Paul Edward. b 52. Sarum Wells Th Coll 78. **d** 81 Roch. C of Biggin Hill Dio Roch from 81. *22 Foxearth Close, Biggin Hill, Westerham, Kent, TN16 3HQ.*

FRANCIS, Peter Brereton. b 53. Univ of St Andr MTh 77. Qu Coll Birm 77. **d** 78 Dudley for Worc **p** 79 Worc. C of Hagley 78-81; Chap Qu Mary Coll Lon from 81. *Queen Mary College, Mile End Road, E1.*

FRANCIS, Peter Phillip. b 48. St Jo Coll Dur BA 73. Wycl Hall Ox 73. **d** 75 **p** 76 Cant. C of St Jo Bapt Folkestone 75-78; St Lawr Morden (in c of St Geo) Dio S'wark from 78. *Church Farm Cottage, London Road, Morden, Surrey.* (01-648 3105)

FRANCIS, Canon Roger. b 07. Univ of Man BSc (Tech) 29. Ely Th Coll 29. **d** 30 **p** 31 S'wark. C of St Mark East Street Walworth 30-33; St Andr Croydon 33-38; Aldershot (in c of St Aug) 38-44; Min of St Aug Conv Distr Aldershot 44-47; R of Areley-King's 47-74; RD of Mitton 53-71; Proc Conv Worc 55-64; C of St Martin London Rd City and Dio Worc from 74; Hon Can of Worc 69-75; Can (Emer) from 75. *131 Victoria Avenue, Worcester, WR5 1EE.* (Worcester 356275)

FRANCIS, Canon William Albert Paynter. b 13. St D Coll Lamp BA 40. St Aid Coll 41. **d** 41 Blackb **p** 42 Burnley for Blackb. C of Thornton-le-Fylde 41-43; Chap RAFVR 43-48; V of Musbury 48-56; Kirkham 56-80; Chap Kirkham Pris 62-74; RD of Fylde 74-80; Hon Can of Blackb Cathl 74-80; Can (Emer) from 80. *11 Beech Drive, Poulton-le-Fylde, Blackpool, Lancs.* (883449)

FRANCIS, William Mervyn Bowen. b 10. ALCD 31. **d** 33 Stepney for Lon for St Alb **p** 34 St Alb. C of Ch Ch Watford 33-35; St Mich St Alb 35-37; Ch Ch Reading 37-39; V of Holt 39-46; R of E Horsley 46-49; V of Pentridge w Handley 49-51; Ravenstone w Weston Underwood 51-56; R of Langton Herring w Buckland Ripers 56-59; C of Haslemere 59-62; R of Bisley 62-75; Perm to Offic Dio Sarum from 75. *3 Pier Terrace, West Bay, Bridport, Dorset.*

FRANCOM, Edward James. Univ of W Ont BA 56. Hur Coll BTh 63. **d** 62 **p** 63 Alg. I of Lake of Bays 63-66; Chap Univ of W Ont 67-71. *386 St Vincent Street, Stratford, Ont., Canada.*

FRANK, Richard Egon. b 15. Univ of Lon BSc (Econ) 37. Qu Coll Birm. **d** 48 **p** 49 Lon. C of St Mary Bryanston Square Lon 48-51; Friern Barnet 51-53; H Trin Twickenham 53-54; Heston 54-56; R of Ingham w Sutton 56-59; V of Westbury (w Turweston from 60) 59-65; R of Kingsnorth 65-70; R of Shadoxhurst 65-71; V of St Geo Shirley 71-78. *3 Wyatt Court, Hinton St George, TA17. 8SS.* (0460 73702)

FRANK, Richard Patrick Harry. b 40. St Chad's Coll Dur BA 66, Dipl Th 68. **d** 68 **p** 69 Dur. C of H Trin Darlington 68-72; St Andr Roker, Monkwearmouth 72-74; P-in-c of St Ninian's Conv Distr Harlow Green 74-79; R of Skelton and Hutton-in-the-Forest w Ivegill Dio Carl from 79. *Skelton Rectory, Penrith, CA11 9SE.* (Skelton 295)

FRANKHAM, Very Rev Harold Edward. b 11. Lon Coll of Div 39. **d** 41 **p** 42 St Alb. C of Luton 41-44; H Trin Brompton 44-46; V of Addiscombe 46-52; R of Middleton Lancs 52-61; Commiss Gippsld from 51; RD of Middleton 58-61; Luton 67-70; V of Luton L w E Hyde 61-70; Surr 61-70; Hon Can of St Alb from 67; R of St Sav w All H Borough and Dio S'wark from 70; Provost of S'wark Cathl from 70. *Provost's Lodging, 51 Bankside, SE1.* (01-928 6414)

FRANKLAND, John Ashlin. b 12. Hatf Coll Dur LTh 36, BA 37, MA 47. Edin Th Coll 35. **d** 37 **p** 38 Carl. C of St Matt Barrow-F 37-40; St Mary Ulverston 40-42; St Pet Parr 42-44; St Ann Warrington 44-48; CMS Miss at Yambio Sudan 48-51; Tutor Union Coll Bunumbu 53-59. *27 Warwick Road, Hale, Chesh.* (061-928 5178)

FRANKLAND, William. b 1894. Egerton Hall, Man 38. **d** 40 **p** 41 Blackb. C of St John Sandylands 40-43; Ch Ch Adlington 43-44; St Pet Heysham 44-46; V of Overton 46-52; Newchurch-in-Pendle 52-60. *15 Grindleton Road, West Bradford, Clitheroe, Lancs.*

FRANKLIN, Archibald William. b 01. Univ of Lon BD 32. AKC (1st cl) Jelf Pri and Trench Pri 32. **d** 32 **p** 33 Portsm. C of St Mary Portsea 32-40; V of St Mary Virg Hawksworth Wood Leeds 40-61; Camberley w Yorktown 61-66; Pool (w Arthington from 74) Yorks 66-77. *56 New Adel Lane, Leeds, LS16 6AN.* (Leeds 610796)

FRANKLIN, Arthur Harrington. b 03. Late Scho of Linc Coll Ox 2nd cl Cl Mods 24, BA (3rd cl Lit Hum) 26, MA 29. MBE 45. TD 51. Bps' Coll Cheshunt 34. **d** 34 **p** 35 Lon. [f Barrister] C of St Gabr Pimlico 34-38; St Steph Roch Row, Westmr 38-39; Asst Master Westmr Sch 26-39; CF (TA) 39-45 (Men in Disp 45); R of Gt Leighs 45-70; Hon CF (2nd cl) from 58; RD of Roding 62-70; Surr 63-70. *Hea Corner, Mill Road, Felsted, Essex, CM6 3HQ.* (0371-820519)

FRANKLIN, Eric Edward Joseph. b 29 St Pet Hall, Ox BA (2nd cl Th) 53, MA 58. Qu Coll Birm Dipl Th 55. **d** 55 **p** 56 Leic. C of Knighton 55-60; Chap and tutor Brasted Place Westerham 60-66; Tutor St Chad's Coll Dur 66-72; L to Offic Dio Roch 61-66; Dio Dur 66-72; Tutor Chich Th Coll 72-74; C of Margate Dio Cant from 74. *40 Addiscombe Road, Margate, Kent, CT9 2SU.* (Thanet 22074)

FRANKLIN, Geoffrey Eric. b 18. AKC 49. **d** 49 **p** 50 York. C of St Matt Grangetown 49-52; Boosbeck w Moorsholm 52-53; C of High Wycombe (in c of St John) 53-56; V of St Pet Accrington 56-65; Carnforth 65-81. *175 Yealand Road, Warton, Carnforth, Lancs.*

FRANKLIN, Preb Henry Laurence. b 12. Ex Coll Ox BA (2nd cl Th) and Amelia Jackson Sen Stud 34, BLitt 35, MA 39, MLitt 79. **d** 35 **p** 36 Ex. C of Okehampton 35-38; C-in-c of Honicknowle Conv Distr 38-42; Offg CF 38-42; CF (TA) 55-78; V of Newport Devon 42-49; Dioc Insp of Schs 45-50; Dir of Relig Educn and Sec Dioc Educn C'tte Dio B & W 49-77; V of Felton Common 50-80; Preb of Wells Cathl from 51; Proc Conv B & W 64-70; Sub-Dean of Wells Cathl from 70; RD of Chew Magna 77-80; Bp's Chap for Ret Clergy Wells from 81. *8 Vicars' Close, Wells, Somt.*

FRANKLIN, Herbert Cecil. b 04. St Aid Coll 32. **d** 35 **p** 36 Man. C of St Clem Urmston 35-38; St Phil Cam 38-40; CF (EC) 40-46; L to Offic Dio Ely 47-50; Immigrants' Chap to SPCK at Austr Ho Lon 49-50; V of Swavesey 50-60; R of Milton 60-78; Perm to Offic Dio Ely from 79. *26 Minster Precincts, Peterborough.*

FRANKLIN, Canon John Douglas Reginald. St Aug Coll

Cant 39. **d** 40 Guildf for Gui **p** 41 Gui. C of St Phil Georgetn 41-43; V of Skeldon w Leeds Br Guiana 43-48; I of Port Daniel w Shigawake Queb 48-52; Kenogami 52-60; R of St Pet Sherbrooke 61-77; Exam Chap to Bp of Queb 64-77; Can of Queb 67-77; Hon Can from 77; Hon C of St Leon City and Dio Tor from 78. *51 Kappele Avenue, Toronto, Ont, Canada.*

FRANKLIN, Kenneth Douglas. b 20. Worc Ordin Coll 61. **d** 62 **p** 63 Lon. C of St Cuthb N Wembley 62-63; Prin St Agnes Sch Kota Kinabalu 64-66; R of Sandakan 66-67; Chap St Luke's Secondary Sch Portsm 67-68; V of St Pet Sing 69-72; St Pet Southsea 72-78; St Pet w St Luke Sing 78-80; Chap Qu Alexandra Hosp Cosham from 81. *Queen Alexandra Hospital, Cosham, Hants.*

FRANKLIN, Leonard Patrick. ACT ThL 25. **d** 26 **p** 27 Graft. M of Bush Bro of Our Sav Dio Graft 25-27; P-in-c of Lower Macleay 27-28; C of Wickham 28-30; Perm to Offic at St Barn Pimlico 30-31; St Alb Holborn 31-32; C of St Pet Lon Dks (for St Geo Hosp Chap) 33-35; L to Offic Dio Syd 35-36; P-in-c of St Mary Miss Fitzroy 36-39; V of Bardon 40-47; Chap Royal Hosp Adel 47-48; Chap of Hosps 48-49; R of Portland Dio Bath 49-53; C of St Gabr Warwick Square Pimlico 53-55; Perm to Offic Dio Nor 55-56; C-in-c of St Benet and All SS St Pancras 56-59; R of Sudbrooke w Scothern 59-62; L to Offic Dio Nor 62-64; Perm to Offic Dio Syd 64-73; Dio Newc from 73. *5 Brunswick Road, Terrigal, NSW, Australia 2260.*

FRANKLIN, Lewis Owen. b 46. Univ of Natal BSc 67. St Paul's Coll Grahmstn 72. **d** 73 **p** 74 Natal. C of St Paul Durban 73-76; R of H Trin Newcastle 76-80; C of St Geo Cathl and Dir of St Geo Cathl Centre Capetn from 80. *39 Glynn Street Gardens, Cape Town 8001, S Africa.* (021-45 2685)

FRANKLIN, Richard Charles Henry. b 48. Sarum Wells Th Coll 75. **d** 78 **p** 79 Worc. C of Pershore w Pinvin, Wick and Birlingham 78-80; Educn Chap Dudley from 80. *332 Himley Road, Gornal Wood, Dudley, DY3 2PY.*

FRANKLIN, Richard Heighway. b 54. Univ of Southn BA (Th) 75. Sarum Wells Th Coll 75. **d** 78 Buckingham for Ox **p** 79 Ox. C of Thame 78-81; Asst Angl Chap Univ of Southn from 81. *Chaplaincy Centre, The University, Southampton.* (0703 559122 ext 511)

FRANKLIN, Simon George. b 54. Univ of Bris BA 75. Ridley Hall Cam 77. **d** 79 **p** 80 S'wark. C of Woodmansterne Dio S'wark from 79. *92 Chipstead Way, Woodmansterne, Nr Banstead, Surrey.* (Burgh Heath 51192)

FRANKLIN, Canon Theodore Robert. b 11. AKC 34. Wells Th Coll 34. **d** 35 **p** 36 Chich. C of S Bersted 35-38; Chap S Afr Ch Rly Miss Dio Pret from 38; at Naauportt 41-42; CF (S Afr) 42-46; C of Moulescomb 46-47; V of St Jo Evang Brighton 47-54; R of Hurstpierpoint 54-64; RD of Hurst 56-64; Surr from 61; R of Uckfield 64-69; R of Isfield 64-69; R of Horstead Parva 64-69; Can and Preb of Chich Cathl 64-82 Can (Emer) from 82; V of Sidlesham 69-77; RD of Chich 70-76. *7 The Grove, Felpham, Bognor Regis, PO22 7EY.* (Bognor 825388)

✠ **FRANKLIN, Right Rev William Alfred.** b 16. OBE 64. Kelham Th Coll 33. **d** 40 **p** 41 Lon. C of St Jo Evang Bethnal Green 40-42; St John Palmers Green 42; Asst Chap St Sav Belgrano 45-48; Chap H Trin Lomas de Zamora 48-58; Dom Chap to Bp of Argent 52-57; Chap St Andr Santiago 58-64; Hon Can, Sub Dean & R of St Andr Cathl Ch Santiago 64-65; in Amer Ch 65-78; Cons Bp of Colombia 72; Res 78; Asst Bp of Pet from 78; Can (Non-Res) of Pet Cathl from 78. *4 Penfold Drive, Great Billing, Northampton.* (Northampton 407839)

FRANKS, Dennis Leslie. b 24. BEM 55. Bps' Coll Cheshunt 65. **d** 67 **p** 68 York. C of St Mark Anlaby 67-70; V of Ascen Middlesbrough 71-75; C-in-c of Whorlton Dio York 75-77; V (w Carlton and Faceby) from 77. *18 Church Lane, Swainby, Northallerton, N Yorks, DL6 3EA.* (Stokesley 700321)

FRANKS, John Edward. b 29. **d** 61 **p** 62 Ex. C of St Matthias Plymouth 61-66; V of Upton Grey w Weston Patrick and Tunworth (and Herriard w Winslade from 76) 66-79; P-in-c of Wolverton w Ewhurst and Hannington 79-81; R of Baughurst and Ramsdell w Wolverton, Ewhurst and Hannington Dio Win from 81. *Wolverton Rectory, Basingstoke, Hants, RG26 5RU.* (Kingsclere 298008)

FRANZ, Kevin Gerhard. b 53. Univ of Edin MA 74. Episc Th Coll Edin 76. **d** 79 **p** 80 Edin. C of St Martin City and Dio Edin from 79. *13 Wardlaw Place, Edinburgh, EH11 1UD.*

FRASER, Alexander. b 07. AKC (2nd cl) 32. **d** 32 **p** 33 Blackb. C of St Pet Blackb 32-35; St Aid Leeds 35-36; C-in-c of St Gabr Conv Distr Fullbrook 36-40; PC 40-48; Stoney Middleton 48-54; V of Pilsley 54-57; R of Hasland 57-71; PC of Temple Normanton 57-71; V of Osmaston w Edlaston 71-73. *7 Belvedere Avenue, Walton, Chesterfield, Derbys, S40 3HY.*

FRASER, Alister Douglas. b 26. Qu Coll Cam BA 49, MA 55. Tyndale Hall, Bris. **d** 68 Sherborne for Sarum **p** 69 Sarum. C of St Jo Evang Weymouth 68-72; R of Kingswood 72-80; V of St Steph Cinderford Dio Glouc from 80. *St Stephens Vicarage, St Annal's Road, Cinderford, GL14 2AS.* (Cinderford 22286)

FRASER, Arthur James Alexander. MBE 78. Moore Th Coll Syd 05. **d** 05 **p** 06 Syd. C of Springwood w Glenbrook Lawson and Wentworth Falls 06-08; R of Jamberoo w Shellharbour 08-12; C-in-c of Conv Distr of Auburn 12-14; R of St Phil Auburn 14-15; Leura 15-24; Haberfield 24-39; C of St Thos N Syd 39; Sub-Dean, Can and V of St Pet Cathl Armid 40-45; Sec Austr Bd of Miss for NSW 45-49; LPr Dio Syd from 46. *39 Phillip's Lodge, Kilvington Village, Castle Hill, NSW, Australia 2154.* (634-5425)

FRASER, Bruce William. **d** 56 **p** 57 Alg. I of All SS Sault Ste Marie 57-59; St Theodore Tor 59-67; Hon C of St Mary Richmond Hill Dio Tor from 67. *178 Royal Orchard Boulevard, Thornhill, Ont, Canada.*

FRASER, David Ian. b 32. Em Coll Cam BA 54, MA 58. Oak Hill Th Coll 56. **d** 58 **p** 59 St Alb. C of St Jo Bapt Bedford 58-61; St Andr Cheadle Hulme 61-64; R of Fringford w Hethe, Newton Purcell w Shelswell 64-67; V of St Luke Preston 67-71; Ch Ch Surbiton Hill Dio S'wark from 71. *34 The Avenue, Surbiton, Surrey. KT5 8JG.* (01-399 3444)

FRASER, Ernest William Emerson. b 04. AKC (1st cl) and Barry Pri 27. Westcott Ho Cam 28. **d** 28 Roch **p** 29 Bp King for Roch. C of Ch Ch Tunbridge Wells 28-32; Gt Malvern 32-37; Perm to Offic Dio Roch 38-39; V of Hildenborough 39-51; Downe 51-57; Perm to Offic Dio Chich from 57. *The Goodalls, Ellerslie Lane, Bexhill-on-Sea, Sussex.* (Bexhill 211141)

FRASER, Geoffrey Michael. b 29. Sarum Th Coll. **d** 59 **p** 60 Guildf. C of Thames Ditton 59-63; Shere 63-65; C of Dunsford w Doddiscombsleigh 65-70; V of Uffculme Dio Ex from 70. *Uffculme Vicarage, Cullompton, Devon, EX15 3AX.* (Craddock 40215)

FRASER, Henry Paterson. b 07. KBE 61. CB 53. AFC 37. Pemb Coll Cam BA 29, MA 73. **d** 77 **p** 78 S & M (APM). Hon C of Ramsey Dio S & M from 77. *803 King's Court, Ramsey, IM.* (Ramsey 813069)

FRASER, Hugh Kenneth. St Mich Th Coll Crafers, 50. ACT ThL 55. Univ of Melb BA 62. **d** 54 **p** 55 Adel. LPr Dio Adel 54-58; Tutor SSM Th Coll Crafers 56-58; Perm to Offic Dio Melb 58-62; Tutor Kelham Th Coll 63-63; C of Old St Pancras w St Matt Oakley Square Lon 63; Milawa 64; R 65-66; Chiltern 66-69; Lect and Tutor St Columb's Hall Wang 65-69; Perm to Offic Dio Melb 69-79. *Flat 23, 34 Neill Street, Carlton, Vic. 3053, Australia.*

FRASER, James Garfield. Univ of Melb BA 61, MA 65, PhD 70. Melb Coll of Div BD 65. ACT ThL (2nd cl) 55, Th Scho 65. Ridley Coll Melb. **d** 60 **p** 62 Melb. C of St Phil Heidelberg W 60-62; Alphington 62-64; Spotswood 64; Tutor Ridley Coll Melb 62-66; Perm to Offic Dio St Andr 68-69; Dio Melb 69-72; P-in-c of Alphington Dio Melb from 72. *13 Lowther Street, Alphington, Vic, Australia 3078.* (03-49 2683)

FRASER, James Stuart. b 26. Em Coll Cam BA 50, MA 53. Westcott Ho Cam 52. **d** 54 Bp H A Wilson for St E **p** 55 St E. C of St Thos Ipswich 54-57; V of St Andr Rushmere 57-70; St Mary w All SS Putney Dio S'wark from 70. *45 St John's Avenue, SW15 6AL.* (01-788 4575)

FRASER, John Keys. b 15. Trin Coll Dub BA (2nd cl Mod Hist and Pol Sc) 38, Div Test (1st cl) 39. **d** 39 Dub for Liv **p** 40 Liv. C of St Benedict Everton 39-41; CF 41-46; C of St Mary Stoke Newington 46-47; V of St Clem Bradf 47-54; RD of Bradf 53-54; V of Shipley 54-64; Scarborough 64-81; RD of Scarborough 64-72; Can and Preb of York Minster 76-81. *10 North Leas Avenue, Scarborough, N Yorks, YO12 6LN.* (Scar 77982)

FRASER, Canon John Sheean. b 23. Trin Coll Dub BA 47, MA 52. **d** 47 **p** 50 Dub. C of St Geo Dub 47-48; St Steph Dub 50-52; I of Leney and Kilbixy 52-59; Killucan U 59-65; V of St Mary's Cathl Lim 65-67; Can Res and Preb of Lim Cathl from 67; Sub-Dean from 74; RD of Askeaton from 67. *5 Ashbrook, Ennis Road, Limerick, Irish Republic.* (Limerick 45714)

FRASER, Leslie. b 34. ALCD 62. **d** 62 Warrington for Liv **p** 63 Liv. C of St Matt Thatto Heath 62-64; Em Fazakerley 64-67; R of St Osw w St Cath Collyhurst 67-72; C-in-c of St Jas Collyhurst 67-72; R of the Sav Collyhurst 72-74; Perm to Offic Dio Blackb from 79. *Address temp unknown.*

FRASER, Ralph William James. Moore Th Coll Syd ACT ThL 50. **d** and **p** 51 Syd. C of Eastwood 51-53; Miss at Morogoro 53-55; Gen Sec CMS Brisb 55; Home Sec CMS in NSW 56-57; R of Greenwich 57-59; Immigration Chap Dio Syd 59-63; R of Berrima w Moss Vale 63-68; Chap St Vincent's and Lewisham Hosps Syd 68-74; R of Woollahra Dio Syd from 75. *81 Ocean Street, Woollahra, NSW, Australia 2025.* (32-1504)

FRASER, Ross Dominic. b 24. St Jo Coll Morpeth. **d** 47 **p** 48 Bath. Chap All SS Coll 47-51; C of Cairns 51-55; Min of St Pet Townsville Queensld 55-59; C of St Helen Bp Auckland (in c of Witton Pk) 59-60; V of Witton Pk 60-61; V of Ryhope 61-74; Elton 74-75; C-in-c of Medomsley Dio Dur 75-76; V from 76. *Medomsley Vicarage, Consett, Co Durham.* (Ebchester 560289)

FRASER-SMITH, Keith Montague. b 48. St Jo Coll Dur BA 70. Trin Coll Bris Dipl Th 72. **d** 73 **p** 74 Bris. C of Bishopsworth 73-76; CMS Miss Dio Egypt 76-80; Bp's Chap 79-80; Chap Ch of Redeemer Amman Dio Jer from 80. *c/o Church of Redeemer, Box 598. Amman, Jordan.*

FRAWLEY, Canon William John. Ridley Coll Melb. **d** and **p** 54 Gippsld. P-in-c of Poowong w Loch 54-61; R of Lang Lang 61-62; Chap Pentridge Pris 62-64; C of Melb Dioc Centre 64-69; R of Korumburra 69-80; Can of St Paul Cathl Sale 71-74; Archd of S Gippsld 74-80; Hon Can of Gippsld from 80; Perm to Offic Dio Gippsld from 80. *20 Malcliff Road, Newhaven, Vic, Australia 3925.*

FRAY, John Stoffel. b 43. **d** 76 Natal. C of St Matt Escourt 76-80; Sydenham Dio Natal from 80. *80 Rippon Road, Sydenham, Natal, S Africa.*

FRAYLING, Nicholas Arthur. b 44. Univ of Ex BA (2nd cl Theol) 69. Cudd Coll 69. **d** 71 **p** 72 S'wark. C of St Jo Peckham 71-74; V of All SS Tooting Dio S'wark from 74. *Vicarage, Franciscan Road, SW17 8DQ.* (01-672 3706)

FRAYNE, David. b 34. St Edm Hall, Ox BA (2nd cl Phil Pol and Econ) 58, MA 62, Univ of Birm Dipl Th 60. Qu Coll Birm 58. **d** 60 **p** 61 S'wark. C of E Wickham 60-63; St Jo Bapt Southend Lewisham (in c of St Barn) 63-67; V of N Sheen 67-73; R of Caterham Dio S'wark from 73; RD of Caterham from 80. *Rectory, Whyteleafe Road, Caterham, Surrey, CR3 5EG.* (Caterham 42062)

FRAYNE, Dennis George. b 44. Trin Coll Tor BA, LTH 68. **d** 68 **p** 69 Sask. C of All SS Pet Ont 68-70; I of Meadow Lake 70-77; Loon Lake 70-77; Claresholm Dio Calg from 77. *Box 436, Claresholm, Alta, Canada.* (235-2732)

FRAYNE, Derek Arthur Vivian. b 30. Univ Coll Swansea BA (2nd cl Engl) 52. Wells Th Coll 52. **d** 54 **p** 55 Llan. C of Aberdare 54-58; Chap Llan Cathl 58-64; V of Llanharan w Peterston-super-Montem 64-79; R of Canton Dio Llan from 79. *Canton Rectory, Romilly Road, Cardiff, CF1 9HB.* (Cardiff 29683)

FRAZER, Ven Albert Henry Victor. b 14. Trin Coll Dub BA and Div Test 38, MA 62. **d** 38 Down **p** 39 Bp Kennedy for Down. C of St Steph Belf 38-43; I of Donoughmore w Donard 43-66; Rathdrum w Glenealy (and Derralossary from 70) Dio Glendal from 66; Can of Ch Ch Cathl Dub 59-70; RD of Omurthy from 60; Archd of Glendalough from 70. *Rectory, Rathdrum, Co Wicklow, Irish Republic.* (Wicklow 6160)

FRAZER, James Stewart. b 27. TCD 55. **d** 57 **p** 58 Connor. C of Whiterock 57-59; St Matt Belf 59-61; R of Lack 61-64; Mullaglas 64-65; Milltown 65-70; Heathcote 70-72; Kangaroo Flat 72-74; I of Dromore Dio Clogh from 74; RD of Kesh from 78; Dioc Chr Stewardship Adv Dio Clogh from 81. *Rectory, Dromore, Co Tyrone, N Ireland.* (Dromore 300)

FRAZER, Milburn Ronald. b 18. Worc Ordin Coll 63. **d** 65 **p** 66 Worc. C of St Barn Rainbow Hill Worc 65-67; Bexhill 67-71; R of Tillington 71-78; Chap U Chine Sch Shanklin I-o-W from 78. *Upper Chine School, Shanklin, I-o-W.* (Shanklin 2297)

FREAM, Benjamin. d 31 **p** 32 NS. Miss of Country Harbour 32-35; R of New London 35-42; Round Hill 42-44; Crapaud NS 44-49; Westphal 49-54; Neil's Harbour 54-58; Joggins 58-68; I of Gulf Is 68-71. *24c Rupert Street, Amherst, NS, Canada.* (667-7469)

FREAR, Philip Scott. b 45. St D Coll Lamp BA 66. **d** 80 **p** 81 Bris. C of Purton 80-81; Rodbourne Cheney Dio Bris from 81. *54 Furlong Close, Swindon, Wilts.*

FREATHY, Nigel Howard. b 46. BA (Lon) 68. Sarum Wells Th Coll 79. **d** 81 Ex. C of Crediton Dio Ex from 81. *79 Willow Walk, Crediton, Devon.*

FREDERICK, Canon Charles James Buchan. Codr Coll Barb BA and LTh 06, MA 48. **d** 08 **p** 09 Barb. C of St Lucy Barb 08-10; Miss at Demerara River Br Gui 10-12; C of Cathl Ch Barb 12-13; V of St Sav Barb 13-16; St Phil L Barb 16-18 and 23-26; St Leon Barb 18-22; All SS Barb 26-43; St Pet Barb 43-47; RD of St Pet 45-47; Chap Westbury Cem Barb 49-54; L Pr Dio Barb 54-60; C of St Matthias I and Dio Barb from 60; Hon Can of Barb from 68. *Haggatt Hall, St Michael's, Barbados, W Indies.*

FREDERICK, John Bassett Moore. b 30. Princeton Univ NJ BA 51, Gen Th Sem NY MDiv 54. Univ of Birm PhD 73. **d** 54 Conn USA **p** 55 Bp Hatch for Conn USA. In Amer Ch 54-56; and 61-71; C of All H Barking-by-the-Tower 56-58; SS Phil & Jas Ox 58-60; on study leave 71-74; R of Bletchingley Dio S'wark from 74; Surr from 78. *Bletchingley Rectory, Redhill, Surrey, RH1 4LR.* (0883-843252)

FREDERICTON, Lord Archbishop of, and Metropolitan of Ecclesiastical Province of Canada. *See* O'Neil, Most Rev Alexander Henry.

FREDERICTON, Lord Bishop of. *See* Nutter, Most Rev Harold Lee.

FREDERICTON, Dean of. *See* Cooper, Very Rev Harry Rhodes.

FREDRIKSEN, Martin. b 47. St Chad's Coll Dur BA 69, Dipl Th 70. **d** 70 **p** 71 Ex. C of Bideford 70-73; St Nicolas Guildf 73-76; V of Woolavington Dio B & W from 76; R of Cossington Dio B & W from 76. *Woolavington Vicarage, Bridgwater, Somt.* (Puriton 683408)

FREE, Canon James Michael. b 25. AKC (1st cl) 50, BD (2nd cl) 50. St Bonif Coll Warm 50. **d** 51 Bris **p** 52 Malmesbury for Bris. C of Corsham 51-54; R of St Patr Tobago 54-58; Diego Martin 58-62; V of St Barn Knowle 62-67; Pilning w Severn Beach and Northwick 67-75; C-in-c of Lydiard Millicent w Lydiard-Tregoz 75-82; Hon Can of Bris 76-82; Res Can, Prec & Sacr Bris Cathl from 82. *28 Woodfield Road, Redland, Bristol, BS6 6JQ.* (Bris 35632)

FREEBORN, John Charles Kingon. b 30. G and C Coll Cam BA 52, MA 56. Ridley Hall Cam 53. **d** 55 **p** 56 Sheff. C of Doncaster 55-57; Tutor Wycl Hall Ox 57-61; R of Flixton 61-72; C of H Ap Leic 72-73; E Crompton 73-74; Ashton-under-Lyne 74-76; Perm to Offic Dio Man 77-80; Hd Master H Trin Junior Sch Halifax from 80; L to Offic Dio Wakef from 80. *27 Crossley Hill, Halifax, W Yorks.*

FREELAND, Brian Desmond. St Patr Coll Ott BCom 47. Trin Coll Tor LTh 50, BD 51. **d** 50 **p** 51 Ott. C of All SS Ott 50-52; St Jo Evang Montr 52-54; Long Branch 54-57; Hon C of St Thos City and Dio Tor from 57. *Apt 1417, 31 Alexander Street, Toronto 5, Ont., Canada.*

FREEMAN, Canon Alan John Samuel. b 27. SS Coll Cam BA (3rd cl Mech Sc Trip) 48, MA 52. Sarum Th Coll 50. **d** 52 **p** 53 Lon. C of West Green Tottenham 52-55; Harpenden 55-60; R of Aspley Guise 60-75; RD of Fleete 67-70; Surr from 69; RD of Ampthill 70-75; Hon Can of St Alb from 74; M Gen Syn from 74. V of Boxmoor Dio St Alb from 75. *10 Charles Street, Hemel Hempstead, Herts, HP1 1JH.* (Hemel Hempstead 55382)

FREEMAN, Anthony John Curtis. b 46. Ex Coll Ox BA 68, MA 72. Cudd Coll 70. **d** 72 **p** 73 Worc. C of St Martin Worc 72-75; Dom Chap to Bp of Chich 75-78; P-in-c of St Wilfrid Conv Distr Parklands City and Dio Chich from 78. *St Wilfrid's House, Durnford Close, Chichester, W Sussex, PO19 3AG.* (Chich 783853)

FREEMAN, Arnold Grainger. b 15. Down Coll Cam BA 37, MA 41. Wycl Hall Ox 37. **d** 39 **p** 40 Ches. C of Grappenhall 39-41; Ch Ch Folkestone 42-44; St Matt Cambridge 44-45 (in c 45); St Jo Evang Cambridge 45-48; V of Standon 48-51; CMS Area Sec Dios Chelmsf and St E 51-52; Metrop Sec 52-61; C of St John Downshire Hill Hampstead 61-62; St Mark Hamilton Terrace St John's Wood 62-65; Hendon 65-68; Stepney 68-70; Tattenham Corner and Burgh Heath 70-73; W Hackney 73-75; R of Lydgate w Ousden (w Cowlinge from 76) 75-77; *72 Rembrandt Way, Bury St Edmunds, Suff, IP33 2NT.* (Bury St Edmunds 3171)

FREEMAN, Canon Douglas Charles. b 29. Univ of Lon BD 54. AKC (2nd cl) 54. **d** 55 **p** 56 Lon. C of Ch Ch I of Dogs 55-59; V of Guyhirn w Ring's End 59-63; C-in-c of Coldham 60-63; R of Duloe w Herodsfoot 63-70; V of Morval 66-70; St Ives Dio Truro from 70; M Gen Syn Truro from 70; P-in-c of Lelant 78-80; Hon Can of Truro Cathl from 80. *Vicarage, St Ives, Cornw, TR26 1AH.* (Penzance 796404)

FREEMAN, Gerald Douglas Langston. b 42. Sarum Th Coll 72. **d** 81 Wolverhampton for Lich **p** 81 Lich. C of St Thos Wednesfield Dio Lich from 81. *18 Duke Street, Wednesfield, Wolverhampton.* (0902 733501)

FREEMAN, James Henry. b 14. **d** 79 **p** 80 S'wark. Hon C of St Steph Wandsworth Dio S'wark from 79. *43 Oakhill Road, Putney, SW15 2QJ.*

FREEMAN, John Philip. b 50. St John's Coll Morpeth 75. **d** and **p** 78 Bp Parker for Newc. C of Wallsend 78-80; Hamilton Dio Newc from 80. *27 Chatham Road, Hamilton, NSW, Australia 2303.* (61 4204)

FREEMAN, Luke Edward Wheway. b 09. Late Scho of Ex Coll Ox Squire Scho 28, 3rd cl Cl Mods 30, BA (2nd cl Th) 32. Lich Th Coll 33. **d** 34 **p** 35 Lich. C of Cannock 34-37; Tutor Lich Th Coll 37-45; Chap 40-45; C of St Mary Shrewsbury 45-48; V of Moxley 48-52; Hanford 52-60; St Mary Virg Tunstall 60-75. *St Mary's Cottage, St Mary's Place, Shrewsbury, Salop.* (Shrewsbury 53557)

FREEMAN, Malcolm Douglas. b 49. Trin Coll Melb 76. **d** and **p** 79 Melb. C of Sunshine 79; Ararat 80-81. *St Mark's Church, Sunshine, Vic, Australia.*

FREEMAN, Michael Charles. b 36. Magd Coll Cam 2nd cl Cl Trip pt i 60, BA (2nd cl Th Trip pt ia) 61, MA 68. BD (Lon) 69. Clifton Th Coll 67. **d** 69 **p** 70 Cov. C of Bedworth 69-72;

Morden 72-76; V of Westcombe Pk Dio S'wark from 76. *89 Westcombe Park Road, SE3.* (01-858 3006)

FREEMAN, Michael Curtis. b 51. Univ of Lanc BA 72. Cudd Coll 72. **d** 75 Warrington for Liv **p** 76 Liv. C of Walton-on-the-Hill 75-78; Hednesford 78-81; Team V of Solihull Dio Birm from 81. *52 Redlands Close, Elmdon Heath, Solihull, W Midl.* (021-705 3234)

FREEMAN, Philip Martin. b 54. Westcott Ho Cam 76. **d** 79 **p** 80 Liv. C of St Anne Stanley City and Dio Liv from 79. *8 Derwent Square, Liverpool, L13 6QT.* (051-228 5252)

FREEMAN, Philip Michael. b 25. Jes Coll Cam 2nd cl Hist Trip pt i 49, BA (2nd cl Th Trip pt i) 50, MA 54. Qu Coll Birm. **d** 52 **p** 53 Linc. C of Gainsborough 52-58; V of Messingham w E Butterwick 58-65; Goxhill 65-66; Bottesford w Ashby 66-73; R 73-75; P-in-c of St Nich Warwick Dio Cov 75-76; Team V (w St Mary) from 76. *St Nicholas's Vicarage, Brooke Close, Bridge End, Warwick, CV34 6PE.* (Warw 492909)

FREEMAN, Richard Norman. b 33. St Jo Coll Morpeth 74. **d** 74 **p** 75 Riv. C of Griffith 75-78; P-in-c of Hillston Dio River from 78. *Box 162, Hillston, NSW, Australia 2675.*

FREEMAN, Robert John. b 52. St Jo Coll Dur BSc 74. Fitzwm Coll Cam BA 76. Ridley Hall Cam 74. **d** 77 **p** 78 Blackb. C of Blackpool 77-81; Team V of Chigwell Dio Chelmsf from 81. *Vicarage, St Winifred's Church, Manor Road, Chigwell, Essex IG7 5PS.* (01-500 4608)

FREEMAN, Ronald Mercer. b 24. Trin Coll Cam BA 45, MA 50. Wycl Hall, Ox 47. **d** 49 **p** 50 Man. C of Worsley 49-52; Prin St Paul's Sch Zaria 52-56; I of S Zaria 57-62; V of St Barn Pendleton 62-67; R of St Paul Kersal Salford 67-78; V of Walmersley Dio Man from 78. *Walmersley Vicarage, Bury, Lancs, BL9 5JE.* (061-797 9273)

FREEMAN, Terence. b 40. Wells Th Coll 67. **d** 70 **p** 71 Bris. C of Hanham 70-74; Cockington w Chelston 74-77; R of Sampford Spiney w Horrabridge Dio Ex from 77. *Rectory, Horrabridge, Yelverton, Devon, PL20 7RF.* (Yelverton 2528)

FREEMAN, William John. b 04. Lon Coll of Div 31. **d** 34 Taunton for B & W **p** 35 Bp de Salis for B & W. Chap Sec Somt Dioc Miss to Deaf and Dumb 34-43; V of Stowey w Bp Sutton 40-45; Tilshead 45-54; W Parley 54-69. *133 Heathfield Road, West Moors, Wimborne, Dorset, BH22 0DE.* (Ferndown 875029)

FREEMAN, William Thomas Manuel. St Pet Coll Alice. **d** 66 **p** 67 Capetn. C of Silvertown 66-68; Bonteheuwel 68-69; Bp Lavis Matroosfontein 69-74; P-in-c of Lotus River 74-78; Perm to Offic Dio Capetn from 78. *c/o St George's Rectory, Groot Drakenstein, CP, S Africa.*

FREER, Andrew Selwyn Bruce. b 26. Wells Th Coll 55. **d** 57 **p** 58 Birm. C of Yardley 57-62; R of Byfield 62-71; V of Brackley 71-81; Surr 79-81; R of Bincombe w Broadwey, Upwey and Buckland Ripers Dio Sarum from 81. *526 Littlemore Road, Broadwey, Weymouth, Dorset, DT3 5PA.* (Upwey 2542)

FREER, Bernard. b 22. St Aid Coll 60. **d** 62 **p** 63 Derby. C of Boulton 62-65; PC of Stanley Derby 65-68; V 68-73; V of Marston-on-Dove (w Scropton from 74) Dio Derby from 73; Scropton 73; RD of Longford from 81. *Marston Vicarage, Hilton, Derby, DE6 5GJ.* (Etwall 3433)

FREER, Charles Kindersley. b 15. Linc Coll Ox BA (3rd cl Th) 41, MA 45. Wycl Hall Ox 41. **d** 42 S'wark **p** 43 Kingston T for S'wark. C of H Trin Tulse Hill 42-44; Sanderstead 45; Perm to Offic Dio Worc 46; Dio Ox 47; C of Thame 47-52; R of Hawksworth w Scarrington 52-56; C of St Mary Bryanston Square St Marylebone 56-61; Perm to Offic Dio Lon 61-62; C of Alvechurch 62-64; St Andr w St Mary and of St Nich w St Pet Droitwich 64-67; Calne w Blackland 67-68; Canning Town 69-73; Perm to Offic Dio Ox 73-82. *21 Middle Row, Chipping Norton, OX7 5NH.* (Ch Norton 3410)

FREESTONE, Herbert Keith. b 14. Ripon Hall Ox. **d** 65 **p** 66 Roch. [f Bapt Min] C of H Trin Bromley Common 65-68; C-in-c of Erith 68-73; Sec Dioc Miss & Ecumen Coun Roch 72-78; R of Horsmonden 73-79; Perm to Offic Dio Chich from 79. *51 Ashdown Road, Worthing, W Sussex, BN11 1DE.* (Worthing 34956)

FREETH, Barry James. b 35. Univ of Birm BA (3rd cl Th) 60. Tyndale Hall Bris 60. **d** 62 **p** 64 Birm. C of Selly Hill 62-63; St John Ladywood 63-71; Chap RAF 71-75; P-in-c of Crudwell w Ashley 75-81; Lanreath and of Pelynt Dio Truro from 81. *Lanreath Rectory, Looe, Cornw, PL13 2NU.* (Lanreath 310)

FREETH, John Stanton. b 40. Selw Coll Cam BA 62, MA 66. Ridley Hall, Cam. **d** 66 **p** 67 Roch. C of St Mark Gillingham 66-72; Chap Univ of York from 72; Team V of Heslington 72-80; R of St John Wynberg Dio Capetn from 80. *St John's Rectory, Waterloo Green, Wynberg, CP 7800, S Africa.* (77-4147)

FREETH, Richard Hudson de Wear. b 13. Worc Ordin Coll. **d** 64 **p** 65 Chelmsf. C of St Jo Bapt (in c of St Mark) Southend-on-Sea 64-67; V of Mayland 67-76; R of Steeple 67-76. *Flat 11, Calpe, Alicante, Spain.*

✠ **FREETH, Right Rev Robert Evelyn.** Late Scho of Selw Coll Cam BA (2nd cl Cl Trip) 08, MA 12. ACT ThD 61. Ridley Hall, Cam 08. **d** 09 St Alb for Melan **p** 10 Melan. Miss at Banks Is 09-13; C of Ch Ch N Adel 13-14; P-in-c of Angaston 14-15; Asst Chap of KS Parramatta 15-16; Chap and Ho Master 18-20; Sen Cl Master 19-20; Prec of St Andr Cathl Syd and Prin of Cathl Choir Sch Syd 16-18; Asst Master CE Gr Sch N Syd 20-26; Hd Master Prep Sch and Ho Master Jun Ho 26-27; Auth to Offic Dio Syd 20-27; Hd Master Gr Sch Guildf Perth 28-49; Can of Perth Cathl 41-49; L to Offic Dio Perth 50-52; Archd of Perth 53-61; Cons Asst Bp of Perth in St Geo Cathl Perth 2 Feb 57 by Bp of Kalg; Bps of NW Austr and Bunb; and Bps Elsey and Riley; res 63; L to Offic Dio Perth from 67. *142 Victoria Avenue, Dalkeith, W Australia 6009.* (386 2106)

FRENCH, Ven Basil Charles Elwell. Edin Th Coll 41, LTh 44. **d** 45 **p** 46 Edin. C of Ch Ch Falkirk 45-46; St Aid Bris 46-49; H Trin Henford Yeovil 49-51; PC of Ash-in-Martock 51-58; P-in-c of Long Load 57-58; Asst P at Ndola 59-60; Chap Rhod and Nyasa Rly Miss 60-61; P-in-c of Arcadia and Cranbourne 61-69; R of Umvukwes Dio Mashon from 69; Archd of Th Gt Dyke from 80. *c/o Box UA7, Salisbury, Zimbabwe.*

FRENCH, Clive Anthony. b 43. AKC and St Aug Coll Cant 70. **d** 71 Bp Ramsbotham for Newc T **p** 72 Newc T. C of Monkseaton 71-73; Asst to Dir Relig Educn Dio Newc T 73-76; Chap RN from 76. *c/o Ministry of Defence, Lacon House, Theobalds Road, WC1X 8RY.*

FRENCH, David John. d 59 **p** 60 C & Goulb. C of Temora 59-61; All SS E St Kilda 62-63; Point Lonsdale 63-64; St Pet Box Hill 64-66; I of Kingsville 66-68; Chap RAAF from 68; Perm to Offic Dio Adel from 81. *RAAF Base Edinburgh, S Australia 5111.*

FRENCH, Dendle Charles. b 29. Univ of Lon BD 56. ALCD (1st cl) 55. **d** 56 **p** 57 Nor. C of Gt Yarmouth 56-63; Chap De Carteret Coll Mandeville Jamaica 63-66; V of Sedgeford w Southmere 66-71; C-in-c of Gt Ringstead 66-67; R 67-71; V in Thetford Group 71-74; Chap Hockerill Coll Bp's Stortford 74-78; P-in-c of St Paul's Walden Dio St Alb from 78. *Vicarage, Whitwell, Hitchin, Herts.* (Whitwell 658)

FRENCH, Donald Samuel. Wycl Coll Tor. **d** 59 **p** 60 Tor. C of St Andr-by-the-Lake 59-60; I of Stayner 60-64; St Geo Barrie 64-69. *14 Marwendy Drive, Barrie, Ont, Canada.*

FRENCH, Canon Francis Melvin. K Coll NS. **d** 39 **p** 40 NS. C of St Jas Halifax 39-43; New Germany 43-44; R of Sydney Mines 44-68; Hon Can of NS 61-65 and from 75; Can 65-75; R of St Mark Halifax 69-74; on leave. *15 Deepwood Crescent, Halifax, NS, Canada.* (443-0068)

FRENCH, John Daniel. d 63 **p** 68 C & Goulb. C of Tumut 63-69; Temora 69-71; R of Adaminaby 71-75; Perm to Offic Dio C & Goulb from 75. *84 Russell Street, Tumut, NSW, Australia 2720.*

FRENCH, Norman. St Jo Coll Auckld LTh 64. **d** 61 **p** 62 Auckld. C of Kohimarama Distr Auckld 61-64; Otara Miss Distr 64-65; P-in-c 65-68; V 68-70; Otahuhu 70-77; St Geo Epsom Dio Auckld from 77. *15 Ranfurly Road, Epsom, Auckland 3, NZ.* (544-424)

FRENCH, Owen John Jason. b 01. K Coll Lon 34. **d** 38 **p** 39 Chelmsf. C of St Mary Virg Loughton 38-40; St Andr Westcliff 40-42; V of Mayland 42-47; Wimbish w Thunderley 47-52; Gt w L Maplestead 53-59; Chap St Mary's Dioc Home Gt Maplestead 57-59; Asst Chap O of St John of Jer 56-60; Sub-Chap from 60; V of Mucking 59-61; R of High Easter w Marg Roding 61-69; V of Good Easter 61-69. *22 Kingston Square, Norwich, NR4 7PF.*

FRENCH, Richard John. b 34. Tyndale Hall Bris 62. **d** 64 **p** 65 Chich. C of Rustington 64-68; H Trin Aylesbury (in c of Good Shepherd) 68-72; V of Grove Berks Dio Ox from 72. *Vicarage, Grove, Wantage, Oxon.* (Wantage 66484)

FRENCH, Robert. b 05. St Paul's Coll Burgh 30. **d** 33 **p** 34 Lich. C of Brierley Hill 33-35; St Jude S Shields 35-38; Blyth (in c of Ranskill and Barnby Moor) 38-45; H Trin Carl 45-47; R of Asby w Ormsdie 47-57; V of St Cuthb Holme Cultram 57-68; Mosser 68-71. *Address temp unknown.*

FRENCH, William Alfred. ALCD 40. **d** 40 **p** 41 Newc T. C of St Paul Newc T 40-43; Rothbury (in c of Hepple and Thropton) 43-46; Org Sec NE Distr CPAS from 46; Perm to Offic Dio Newc T 46-47; L to Offic Dio Ripon 47; V of St Matthias Burley 47-52; P-in-c of Labasa Dio Polyn 52-57; V of Kamo 57-60; Helensville 60-64; Royal Oak 64-73; Min of Glendene 73-76; Hon C of Henderson 76-79; Offg Min Dio Auckld from 79. *Selwyn Park, Maunu, Whangarei, NZ.*

FRERE, Christopher Michael Hanbury. b 21. Roch Th Coll 65. **d** 67 Grantham for Linc **p** 68 Linc. C of Spilsby w Hundleby 67-70; V of N Kelsey 70-75; Cadney w Howsham 70-75; Ingham w Cammeringham 75-79; Fillingham 75-79; Ingham w Cammeringham and Fillingham Dio Linc from 79;

P-in-c of Aisthorpe w Scampton and W Thorpe 75-79; Brattleby 75-79; R of Aisthorpe w Scampton and Thorpe le Fallows w Brattleby Dio Linc from 79; RD of Lawres from 78. *Vicarage, Ingham, Lincoln.* (Linc 730254)

FRESTON, John Samuel Kern. b 28. Lich Th Coll 70. **d** 72 **p** 73 Lich. C of Walsall 72-75; Team V of Trunch Dio Nor from 75. *Rectory, Southrepps, Norwich, NR11 8NJ.* (Southrepps 404)

FREWER, Kenneth Gilbert. Univ of Syd BA 67. ACT ThL 72. BD (Lon) 74. Moore Coll Syd 73. **d** and **p** 74 Syd. C of Vaucluse 74-76; CMS Miss from 76; Perm to Offic Dio Syd 77. *d/a STT GKI, Kotak Pos 125, Jayapura, Irian Jaya, Indonesia.*

FREWIN, Terence Gwynne. St Jo Coll Morpeth. **d** 73 **p** 76 Newc. C of Taree 73-75; Singleton 75-77; Hamilton 77-79; P-in-c of W Wallsend Dio Newc from 79. *47 Brown Street, West Wallsend, NSW, Australia 2286.* (53 2960)

FRIARS, Robert John. b 32. Trin Coll Cam BA (2nd cl Hist Trip pt ii) 55, MA 59. Wells Th Coll 55. **d** 57 **p** 58 Lon. C of Hackney 57-62; St Andr Holborn (Guild Ch) 62-70; Youth Tr Officer Dio Lon 62-65; Sen Youth Chap 65-70; Team V of Hackney 70-79; V of Sompting Dio Chich from 79. *Sompting Vicarage, Lancing, W Sussex, BN15 0AZ.* (Worthing 34511)

FRICKER, Canon David Duncan. b 27. Univ of Lon BA 53. Ridley Hall, Cam 53. **d** 55 **p** 56 Sheff. C of Ecclesfield 55-58; Luton 58-61; PC of St Paul Luton 61-64; R of St Pet (w St Cuthb from 75) Bedford Dio St Alb from 64; RD of Bedford 69-78; Surr from 71; Hon Can of St Alb from 74; C-in-c of St Paul Bedford 75-79. *St Peter's Rectory, Bedford, MK40 2TP.* (Bedford 54543)

FRICKER, Very Rev Joachim Carl. Univ of W Ont BA 51. Hur Coll LTh 52, Hon DD 74. **d** and **p** 52 Niag. C-in-c of Hannon w St Aug Hamilton 52-59; I of St D Welland 59-65; Dundas 65-73; Hon Can of Ch Ch Cathl Hamilton 64-73; Dean and R of Ch Ch Cathl Hamilton Dio Niag from 73. *Christ Church Cathedral, James Street N, Hamilton, Ont., Canada.* (416-525 5862)

FRIEND, Graham Arthur. b 39. Chich Th Coll 60. **d** 63 **p** 64 Leic. C of Syston 63-65; St Pet w H Trin Barnstaple 65-67; Clewer 67-74; R of E & W Hendred 74-77; Wantage Downs from 77. *East Hendred Rectory, Wantage, Oxon, OX12 8LA.* (East Hendred 235)

FRIEND, James Alan. Univ of Syd MSc 47. Trin Hall Cam PhD 51. ACT ThL 60. **d** and **p** 60 Tas. Lect Univ of Tas 60-61; L to Offic Dio Ox 61-62; Hon C of St Pet Sandy Bay 64-66; L to Offic Dio Trinid 69-75; Warden Ch Coll Hobart 75-80; Asst Registr ACT NSW from 81. *Australian College of Theology, New College, Kensington, NSW, Australia 2033.* (662-6066)

FRIEND, John Arthur. Univ of Syd BEng 26. **d** 61 Bp Kerle for Syd **p** 62 Syd. Asst Court Chap Syd 61-63; L to Offic Dio Syd from 64; Chap Lidcombe State Hosp 64-67; Rydalmere Psychiatric Hosp 67-68. *Girral Park, Curragh Road, Trunkey, NSW, Australia 2741.*

FRIEND, Robert John. Univ of Syd BSc (Agr) 55. Moore Th Coll Syd 57. **d** 58 Bp Loane for Centr Tang **p** 59 Centr Tang. CMS Miss and Educn Sec Bukoba 58-61; Lect Livingstone Coll Kigoma 61-63; Lect Mitchell Coll City and Dio Bath from 69; Hon C of All SS Cathl Bath 71-77; S Bath Dio Bath from 77. *8 Pioneer Street, Bathurst, NSW, Australia 2795.* (31 3273)

FRIESLAAR, Henry Frank. St Paul's Th Coll Grahmstn 59. **d** 62 Grahmstn for Capetn **p** 63 Bp Thorne for Capetn. C of All SS Bredasdorp 62-66; R of Roodebloem 66-69; V of St Paul Geo 69-73; R of St Marg Bloemf 73-77; H Trin Paarl Dio Capetn from 77; Can of Bloemf 75-77. *Rectory, Auret Street, Paarl, CP, S Africa.* (Paarl 22522)

FRIESS, Herbert Friedrich. b 09. Leipzig Univ BD 34. **d** and **p** 42 Sheff. C of Attercliffe 42-48; V of Elsecar 48-54; St Luke Brighton 54-59; R of W Blatchington 59-64; I of Crossmolina U 64-73; Can and Preb of St Patr Cathl Killala 66-68; Dean of Killala 68-73; I of Killala U 68-73; Achill U 73-79. *Mulvanny, Co Mayo, Irish Republic.*

FRIGGENS, Maurice Anthony. Univ of Sheff BA (Bibl Hist and Lit) 65. Westcott Ho Cam 65. **d** 67 **p** 68 Sheff. C of Stocksbridge 67-70; St Buryan St Levan and Sennen Dio Truro 70-72; R from 72. *St Buryan Rectory, Penzance, Cornw.* (St Buryan 216)

FRIGGENS, Robert Walter. b 05. **d** 72 Graft. Hon C of Port Macquarie Dio Graft from 72. *9 Surf Street, Port Macquarie, NSW, Australia 2444.*

FRISBY, Peter William. b 24. St Chad's Coll Dur BA 52. Bp's Coll Cheshunt 52. **d** 54 Lon **p** 55 Kens for Lon. C of All SS Fulham 54-58; Hendon (in c of St Mary Magd Holders Hill) 58-61; V of St Alb Dartford 61-70; St Luke Gillingham 70-78; Lyddington w Stoke Dry and Seaton 78-80; Team V of Basildon w Laindon and Nevendon Dio Chelmsf from 80. *c/o 7 Botelers, Lee Chapel South, Basildon, Essex, SS16 5SE.* (Basildon 417865)

FRITH, Algernon Jasper. b 01. RM Coll Sandhurst. St Andr Coll Pampisford. **d** 48 **p** 49 B & W. C of Norton-sub-Hamdon 48-51; V of Burrington 51-57; Compton Dando 57-67; R of Chelwood 57-67; C of Ringwood 72-79. *5 New Road, Moortown, Ringwood, Hants.*

FRITH, Charles Richard. ACT ThL (2nd cl) 62. Moore Th Coll Syd 62. **d** 62 **p** 63 Syd. C of Hunters Hill 62-64; St Clem Mosman 64-67; Ch Ch Cathl Graft 67-68; L to Offic Dio Graft from 70. *c/o Diocesan Office, PO Box 4, Grafton, NSW, Australia.*

FRITH, Christopher John Cokayne. b 44. Ex Coll Ox BA (3rd cl Hist) 65, MA 69. Ridley Hall Cam 66. **d** 68 **p** 69 Sheff. C of St Thos Crookes Sheff 68-71; H Trin Rusholme 71-74; R of St Mary Virg Haughton Dio Man from 74. *Haughton Green Rectory, Meadow Lane, Denton, Manchester, M34 1GD.*

FRITH, John Griffith. Cudd Coll 46. **d** 47 **p** 48 Sarum. C of Wareham 47-49; V of Lacock (w Bowden Hill from 55) 49-57; C of Ch Ch Cathl Montr 59-60; R of Alberni 60-64; Hon C of St Steph W Vanc 65-66; St Paul Vanc Dio New Westmr from 73. *205-1555 Esquimalt, West Vancouver, BC, V7V 1R5, Canada.*

FRITH, Lawrence Edward Cokayne. Univ of Manit BA 13, BSc 21. **d** 38 **p** 40 Alg. M SSJE Bracebridge 38-47; Miss at Sorrento 47-49; SSJE Bracebridge Dio Alg from 49. *c/o Mission House, Bracebridge, Ont., Canada.* (705-645 5291)

FRITH, Richard Michael Cokayne. b 49. Fitzw Coll Cam BA 72, MA 76. St Jo Coll Nottm. **d** 74 **p** 75 S'wark. C of Mortlake w E Sheen 74-78; Team V of Thamesmead Dio S'wark from 78. *5 Finchale Road, Abbey Estate, SE2.* (01-310 5614)

FRITH, Canon Roger Cokayne. b 11. Wadh Coll Ox 30. Ely Th Coll 32. **d** 35 **p** 36 Pet. C of St Lawr Northn 35-38; Downham Cambs 38-40; Offg C-in-c of Offord d'Arcy w Offord Cluny 40-43; R of Sawtry 43-53; R of Upton w Copmanford 50-53; Feltwell 53-69; Long Stanton 69-81; RD of Feltwell 65-69; Hon Can of Ely from 68; P-in-c of Fen-Drayton 72-78. *Northfields, Norwich Road, Yaxham, Dereham, Norf NR19 1AB.*

FRITH, Roger Eatherley. b 12. St Jo Coll Dur BA 37, MA 40. **d** 38 **p** 39 York. C of Heworth and St Mary Castlegate w St Mich Spurriergate York 38-40; Cheadle 40-42; V of St Chad Handforth 42-51; Chap Styal Cottage Homes 42-51; R of Arthuret 51-60; V of Jesmond 60-72; St Jo Evang Carl 72-80; P-in-c of Westward w Rosley and Welton Dio Carl from 80. *31 Gosling Drive, Kingstown, Carlisle, Cumb.* (0228 44940)

FRIZELLE, Thomas Herbert. b 07. TCD BA 36, MA 40. **d** 38 **p** 39 Tuam for Down. C of Maralin 38-40; Cathl Ch Lisburn 40-43; C-in-c of Ardkeen 43-46; I of Annolong 46-51; Dundonald 51-80; RD of Holywood 68-72; Can of St Anne's Cathl Belf 71-73; Treas of Down 74-80. *24 Killeaton Park, Dunmurry, Belfast 17, N Ireland.*

FROGGATT, Alan. b 16. Nor Ordin Course 73. **d** 76 **p** 77 Lynn for Nor (APM). Hon C of St Andr Gorleston Dio Nor from 76. *15 Clarke's Road, Gorleston, Gt Yarmouth, Norfolk NR31 7AG.*

FROGGATT, Geoffrey Samuel. b 12. Qu Coll Ox BA 34, MA 44. Wycl Hall, Ox 35. **d** 37 **p** 38 Chich. C of St Leon Aldrington 37-42; S Bersted 42-43; Chap RAFVR 43-46; C of St Leon Aldrington 46-47; V of St Phil Eastbourne 47-53; Ifield 53-55; Old w New Shoreham 55-77. *17 Windsor Close, Minehead, Somt.*

FROGGATT, Jeffrey. b 27. Ch Coll Cam 2nd cl Hist Trip pt i 47, BA 48, MA 52. Ridley Hall Cam 49. **d** 51 **p** 52 Linc. C of Scunthorpe 51-53; St Jas Doncaster 53-56; V of New Edlington 56-62; Malin Bridge 62-73; Wortley 73-79; R of Todwick Dio Sheff from 79. *Todwick Rectory, Sheffield, Yorks, S31 0HL.* (Worksop 770283)

FROMMURZE, Ivan Anthony. St Paul's Coll Grahmstn 61. **d** 63 **p** 64 Pret. C of Pietersburg 63-66; P-in-c of Nelspruit 66-68; C of St Marg Witbank 68-69; R of Sabie w Lydenburg 69-76; Pret N w Brits 76-78; Mtubatuba Dio Zulu from 78. *Box 49, Mtubatuba, Zululand, S Africa.*

FROOM, Ian Leonard John. b 42. Sarum Th Coll 69. **d** 71 Sherborne for Sarum **p** 72 Bp MacInnes for Sarum. C of St Mary Virg, Gillingham 71-75; St Pet Parkstone 75-78; V of St Mary Hurst Hill Sedgley Dio Lich from 78. *St Mary's Vicarage, Hurst Hill, Sedgley, Dudley, W Midl.* (Sedgley 3310)

FROST, Alan Sydney. b 26. AKC 50. Univ of Lon BD 50. St Bonif Coll Warm 50. **d** 51 Dover for Cant **p** 52 Cant. C of St Sav Folkestone 51-56; St Steph w St Alb Sneinton 56-59; L of Offic (in c of St Alb Sneinton) Dio Southw 59-60; C of St Luke Woodside Croydon 60-63; Asst Chap Mersey Miss to Seamen 63-66. *8 Erskine Court, Wallwood Road, E11.*

FROST, Bruce Alan. b 31. St Barn Coll Adel 74. **d** 76 **p** 77

Willoch. C of Broughton Valley w Crystal Brook Dio Willoch 76-79; R from 79. *55 Brandis Street, Crystal Brook, S Australia 5523.* (086 362070)

FROST, Daveth Harold. b 56. Univ Coll Dur BSc 77. Ripon Coll Cudd 77. **d** 80 **p** 81 Dur. C of Cockerton Dio Dur from 80. *St Mary's Vicarage, Newton Lane, Cockerton, Darlington, Co Durham, DL3 9EX.*

FROST, Derek Charles. b 47. Lich Th Coll 69. **d** 71 Ox. C of Woodley 71-76; V of Bampton w Clanfield 76-81; Minster Lovell w Brize Norton Dio Ox from 81. *Vicarage, Burford Road, Minster Lovell, Oxon, OX8 5RA.* (Ashall Leigh 312)

FROST, Donald Ian. Univ of Tas BSc 48. Ridley Coll Melb ACT ThL (2nd cl) 54. **d** 55 **p** 56 Geelong for Melb. C of Em Oakley 55-57; R of Emu Plains w Castlereagh 57-58; C-in-c of Flemington w Homebush 58-61; Chap Caulfield Gr Sch Melb 61-69; Chap Hutchins Sch Hobart and L to Offic Dio Tas 69-72. *240 Steele Street, Devonport 7310, Tasmania.*

FROST, Eric Griffin. d 77 **p** 78 Matab. C of Gwelo Dio Matab (Dio Lundi from 81) from 77. *Box 1349, Gwelo, Zimbabwe.*

FROST, George. b 35. Univ of Dur BA 56, MA 61. Linc Th Coll 57. **d** 60 **p** 61 Chelmsf. C of Barking 60-64; Min of St Mark's Eccles Distr Marks Gate Chadwell Heath 64-70; V of St Matt Tipton 70-77; Penn Dio Lich from 77. *Penn Vicarage, Wolverhampton, WV4 5JD.* (Wolverhampton 341399)

FROST, John Peter. b 16. Sarum Th Coll 51. **d** 52 Dover for Cant **p** 53 Cant. C of St Mich AA Maidstone 52-56; Knysna Dio Geo 56-58; Chap Slade Sch Warwick Brisb 58-60; Asst P of St Mark's Cathl Geo 61-65; R of Amanzimtoti 66-71; Holcot 72; Margate, Natal 73-74; Drakensberg 74-77; Perm to Offic Dio Natal from 77. *c/o Box 132, Underberg, Natal, S Africa.*

FROST, Julian. b 36. Univ of Bris BA (2nd cl Th) 61, MA 65. Clifton Th Coll 64. **d** 65 **p** 66 Roch. *f Solicitor* C of Welling Roch 65-69; Hon C 69-73; Dep Dir of Schs Coun Project on Relig Educn Univ of Lanc 73-78; V of St Paul Beckenham Dio Roch from 78. *Vicarage, Brackley Road, Beckenham, Kent.* (01-650 3400)

FROST, Norman Baldwin. d 65 **p** 66 C & Goulb. C of H Cross Provisional Distr Hackett 65-66; Junee 66-67; R of Batlow 67-71; Gunning 71-74; Perm to Offic Dio C & Goulb from 74. *26 Paterson Street, Ainslie, ACT, Australia 2602.*

FROST, Philip Frederick Wainwright. b 20. Keble Coll Ox BA 42, MA 46. Qu Coll Birm 46. **d** 48 **p** 49 Derby. C of Ilkeston 48-51; Holmfirth 51-53; V of New Mill 53-69; Thurstonland 63-69; Ainstable w Armathwaite 69-74; Flimby 74-79; Allithwaite Dio Carl from 79. *Allithwaite Vicarage, Grange-over-Sands, Lancs.* (Grange-over-Sands 2437)

FROST, Russell Gilbert. b 51. Univ of Man BA 72. Lambeth STh 77. St Steph Ho Ox 72. **d** 75 Chich **p** 76 Lewes for Chich. C of Mayfield 75-78; Perm to Offic Dio Nor 78-80; Asst Admin Shrine of Our Lady Walsingham from 80; C of St Jo Bapt Sevenoaks Dio Roch from 81. *62 Quakers Hall Lane, Sevenoaks, Kent, TN13 3TX.* (0732 51710)

FROST, Samuel Norman Hartley. b 07. Univ Coll Dur LTh 28, BA 29, MA 35. Edin Th Coll 25. **d** 30 Edin **p** 31 Derby. C of St Pet Edin 30-31; St Thos Derby 31-33; St Paul Derby 33-35; C-in-c of St Mark Conv Distr Derby 35-37; PC 37-39; V of Stokesay 39-48; SPCK Port Chap and Org Sec Liv 48-54; V of Froxfield 54-72; C-in-c of Hawkley w Priors Dean 59-66; V 66-72. *Address temp unknown.*

FROST, Thomas Laurence. b 20. Linc Th Coll 60. **d** 62 Bp McKie for Cov **p** 63 Cov. C of Bulkington 62-64; Leeds 64-66; C-in-c of H Trin Knaresborough 66-69; V 69-78; R of Stoke Climsland 78-80; Chap of H Trin Sliema, Malta 80-81; R of Kirriemuir Dio St Andr from 81. *St Mary's Rectory, Kirriemuir, Angus.* (Kirriemuir 2730)

FROST, William Henry. b 10. Univ of Dur LTh 37. Clifton Th Coll 33. **d** 36 **p** 37 Man. C of St John Failsworth 36-41; St Mark St Helens 41-43; Drypool 43-45; V of St Mark Victoria Pk Lon 45-51; R of St Osw Collyhurst Man 51-56; V of St Phil w St Jacob and Em Bris 56-59; Sea Mills 59-75; Surr 67-75; Perm to Offic Dio B & W and Bris from 79. *44 Locking Road, Weston-super-Mare, BS23 3DN.* (W-s-M 23666)

FROST, William Joshua Theodore. St Barn Coll Adel 74. **d** 74 **p** 75 Willoch. Chap Miss to Seamen Port Pirie Dio Willoch 74-80; P-in-c of Port Pirie 76-77; C of Gateacre Liv 80-81; V of Widnes Dio Liv from 81. *St Mary's Vicarage, St Mary's Road, Widnes, Chesh.* (051-424 4233)

FROST, Preb William Selwyn. b 29. Wells Th Coll 61. **d** 62 Stafford for Lich **p** 63 Shrewsbury for Lich. C of Cheddleton 62-67; R of Rodington Dio Lich from 67; V of Longdon-on-Tern Dio Lich from 67; RD of Wrockwardine from 77; P-in-c of Wrockwardine and of Uppington Dio Lich from 80; Preb of Lich Cathl from 81. *Wrockwardine Vicarage, Wellington, Telford, Shropshire.* (Telford 42267)

FROSTICK, Alan Norman. Ripon Hall Ox 74. **d** 75 **p** 76 B & W. C of Crewkerne 75-78; C-in-c of Brompton Regis w Withiel Florey, Upton and Skilgate 78-80; V of St Aid Buttershaw Dio Bradf from 80. *St Aidan's Vicarage, Lastingham Green, Buttershaw, Bradford, BD6 3SD.* (Bradford 679488)

FROSTICK, Canon John George. b 23. Wells Th Coll 52. **d** 54 **p** 55 Leic. C of St Pet Loughborough 54-57; Knighton 57-58; V of Frisby-on-the-Wreake w Kirby Bellars 58-71; Shepshed Dio Leic from 71; Hon Can of Leic from 80. *Shepshed Vicarage, Loughborough, Leics, LE12 9RH.* (Shepshed 2255)

FROSTICK, Paul Andrew. b 52. Ripon Coll Cudd 75. **d** 77 Taunton for B & W **p** 78 B & W. C of Shepton Mallet 77-80; Team V of Barton-Mills Dio St E from 80. *Vicarage, The Street, Barton Mills, Bury St Edmunds, Suffolk, IP28 6AP.* (Mildenhall 716044)

FROUD, James George. b 23. **d** 54 **p** 55 Hong. Chap of St Jo Cathl Hong Kong 54-58; C of All H Barking-by-the-Tower 58-61; Chap at Durning Hall Christian Commun Centre from 58; C-in-c of St Jas Forest Gate 61-66; Chap Forest Gate Hosp 61-69. *Durning Hall, Earlham Grove, E7.* (01-555 0142)

FROUD, Canon John Dakers. Univ of NZ BCom 37. **d** 37 **p** 38 Ch Ch. [f Accountant] C of Fendalton 37-38; Sydenham 38-40; P-in-c of Banks Peninsula 40-45; CF (NZ) 42-45; V of Kensington w Otipua 46-49; New Brighton 49-53; Ashburton 53-60; Addington 60-69; Commiss Melan 63-74; Centr Melan from 76; Hon Can of Ch Ch 68-78; Can (Emer) from 78; C of Merivale 69-74; Hon C of St Luke Ch Ch 74-78; Merivale Dio Ch Ch from 78. *32 Pitcairn Crescent, Christchurch 5, NZ.* (517-730)

FRY, Christopher David. b 49. St D Coll Lamp Dipl Th 74. Bp Burgess Hall Lamp 71. **d** 74 **p** 75 Llan. C of Ynyshir w Wattstown 74-75; Barry 76-79; V of Llansawel w Briton Ferry 79-81; C of Llanishen w Lisvane Dio Llan from 81. *8 Cherry Tree Close, Lisvane, Cardiff.* (Cardiff 756400)

FRY, David John. b 36. BSc (2nd cl Eng) Lon 59. Wells Th Coll 61. **d** 62 **p** 63 B & W. C of Radstock 62-64; Kettering (in c of St Mich AA) 64-66; Asst Master Amery Hill Sch Alton Hants 66-69; Ho Master 69-73; Hd Master Middle Sch Swinton Comprehensive Mexborough 73-78. *c/o Britannia Inn, Elterwater, Ambleside, Cumbria, LA22 9HP.* (Langdale 210)

FRY, Frank. K Coll NS BA 22, MA 24. **d** 23 **p** 24 NS. C of Port Dufferin 23-25; R of Falmouth 25-30; Petite Riviere 30-36; Horton 36-54; I of St Steph Beverley Hills Tor 54-65; Hon Can of NS 53-54; Hon C of Grace Ch-on-the-Hill Tor 65-78. *Box 1288, Alliston, Ont, Canada.*

FRY, Hugh Selwyn. b 08. OBE 63. Trin Coll Cam BA 30, MA 34. **d** 32 **p** 33 St Alb. C of Abbey Ch St Alb 32-37; Publ Pr Dio St Alb 37-39; Dioc Chap to Bp of St Alb 37-46; V of Nettleden w Potten End 39-46; Chap RNVR 43-47; Chap RN 47-63; V of Stanford-in-the-Vale w Goosey and Hatford 63-73. *10 Cliff Road, Sherston, Malmesbury, Wilts, SN16 0LN.* (Sherston 456)

FRY, James Reinhold. b 30. St Cuthb Soc Dur BSc 53, MA 70. Oak Hill Th Coll 55. **d** 57 **p** 58 Roch. C of St Jo Evang Bromley 57-60; V of St Luke Deptford 60-66; Chalk Dio Roch from 66; RD of Gravesend from 81. *Chalk Vicarage, Gravesend, Kent.* (Gravesend 67906)

FRY, Leslie. b 02. FIB 57. St Aug Coll Cant 63. **d** 64 **p** 65 Roch. C of Belvedere 64-67; V of St Paul Chatham 67-74; Hon PV of Roch Cathl 75-81. *10 Morley Place, Tarrants Hill, Hungerford, Berks, RG17 0HS.*

FRY, Lionel David. Moore Th Coll Syd ACT ThL (2nd cl) 66. Melb Coll of Div Dipl Relig Educn 69. **d** 66 **p** 67 Newc. C of Maitland 66-69; New Lambton 69-71; Mayfield 71-72; R of Nabiac (Wallamba from 73) Dio Newc from 72. *Rectory, Bent Street, Tuncurry, NSW, Australia 2428.* (065-54 8351)

FRY, Roger Joseph Hamilton. b 29. Em Coll Cam 2nd cl Econ Trip pt i 50, BA (2nd cl Th Trip pt ii) 52, MA 56. Clifton Th Coll 52. **d** 54 **p** 55 B & W. C of Walcot 54-57; Ch Gresley (in c of Ch Ch Linton) 57-61; V of St Jo Evang Bowling Dio Bradf from 61; C-in-c of St Bart w St Luke Bowling 61-65. *96 Lister Avenue, Bradford, W Yorks, BD4 7QS.* (Bradford 20660)

FRY, Roger Owen. b 30. Sarum Th Coll 58. **d** 60 **p** 61 B & W. C of St Mich AA Yeovil 60-63; R of Portishead 64-80; Clapton-in-Gordano 64-71; C-in-c of Weston-in-Gordano 64-71; V of Weston Zoyland Dio B & W from 80. *Weston Zoyland Vicarage, Bridgwater, Somt, TA7 0EP.* (W Zoyland 251)

FRYAR, Godfrey Charles. b 50. St Francis Coll Brisb 70. **d** 73 Bp Hudson for Brisb **p** 74 Brisb. M of Bush Bro of St Paul Cunnamulla 73-75; P-in-c of Quilpie Distr 75-76; R of Dawson Valley Dio Rockptn from 76. *Box 102, Theodore, Queensland, Australia 4719.*

FRYAR, John Davies. b 53. St Steph Ho Ox 77. **d** 80 **p** 81 Ches. C of Bidston 80-81; Thame Dio Ox from 81. *8 Victoria Mead, Thame, Oxon.* (Thame 3491)

FRYE, John. b 42. Rhodes Univ MA 68. Univ of Leic MA 73. St Paul's Coll Grahmstn Dipl Th 78. **d** 79 **p** 80 Capetn. R of Clanwilliam Dio Capetn from 79. *PO Box 6, Clanwilliam 8135, CP, S Africa.*

FRYER, Alfred Nathaniel. b 1894. Lon Coll of Div. **d** 21 **p** 23 Chelmsf. C of Dagenham 21-24; St John Walthamstow 24-26; H Trin Scarborough 26-28; V of St Andr Leeds 28-38; Eastwood 38-44; Lothersdale 44-64. *8 Abbeyfield, Woodlands Drive, Gargrave Road, Skipton, N.Yorks.* (Skipton 3659)

FRYER, Anthony Charles. b 18. R Mil Acad Woolwich 37. Wycl Hall Ox. **d** and **p** 60 Ox. C of St Pet Maidenhead 60-62; V of Shinfield 62-73. *Beddings Gully, Hatch Lane, Chapel Row, Reading, RG7 6NX.* (Woolhampton 3346)

FRYER, Charles Eric John. b 14. BA (1st cl Hist) Lon 54. Linc Th Coll 62. **d** 63 Bp McKie for Cov **p** 64 Cov. C of Finham 63-66; Lect Eaton Hall Coll Retford 66-79; Perm to Offic Dio Southw 66-75; Publ Pr 75-79; P-in-c of Killin and of Lochearnhead Dio St Andr from 79. *The Shieling, Crianlarich, Perthshire.*

FRYER, George. b 33. St Jo Coll Cam BA 57, MA 61. M RTPI 65. Ox Ordin Course 73. **d** 76 **p** 77 Reading for Ox (APM). C of Wallingford 76-79; St Paul Wokingham 79-81. *Address temp unknown.*

FRYER, Kenneth Wesley. K Coll Lon and Warm AKC 59. **d** 60 **p** 61 Wakef. C of Heckmondwike 60-62; St Phil Osmondthorpe Leeds 62-65; All S Ancoats Man 65-66; V of Tinsley 73-77; P-in-c of Scarcliffe 77-80; V of Newhall Dio Derby from 80. *Newhall Vicarage, Burton-on-Trent, Staffs.* (B-on-T 213860)

FRYER, Canon Leonard Charles. Univ of Manit BA 40, LTh 47. **d** 47 **p** 48 Keew. Miss at Jack River 47-54; I of Rainy River 54-60; Lac du Bonnet 60-71; Hon Can of Keew 62-71; I of Stonewall Dio Rupld from 71; P-in-c of Woodlands 72-80; Can of Rupld 78-80; Hon Can from 80. *Box 176, Stonewall, Manit., Canada.*

FRYER, Neil William Kingston. b 44. St Francis Coll Brisb 72. **d** 75 **p** 76 Rockptn. C of Wandal 75-77; M Bush Bro of St Paul Brisb 77-79; C of Horsham 79-81; R of Dimboola Dio Bal from 81. *Rectory, Dimboola, Vic, Australia 3414.*

FRYER, Peter Hugh. b 25. Linc Th Coll 58. **d** 60 **p** 61 Ex. C of Tavistock 60-64; R of St Buryan 64-72; R of St Levan 66-72; St Sennen 70-72; H Trin Elgin w St Marg Lossiemouth 72-76; Offg Chap RAF Lossiemouth 72-76; P-in-c of North Hill 76-78; Lewannick 76-78; Altarnon w Bolventor 76-78; R of North Hill w Altarnon, Bolventor and Lewannick Dio Truro from 78; P-in-c of Laneast w St Clether & Tresmeer Dio Truro from 80. *Rectory, North Hill, Launceston, Cornw, PL15 7PQ.* (Coads Green 394)

FUBARA, Nelson Vidal. b 22. Im Coll Ibad 72. **d** 72 **p** 73 Nig Delta. P Dio Nig Delta. *St Paul's Parsonage, Opobo Town, Nigeria.*

✠ **FUBARA, Right Rev Yibo Alalibo.** Trin Coll Umuahia 48. **d** 50 **p** 51 Niger. P Dio Niger 50-52 and 60-63; Dio Nig Delta 52-60; Can of Nig Delta 63-71; Archd of Aba 71; Cons Ld Bp on the Nig Delta in All SS Cathl Onitsha 29 Sept 71 by Abp of Sier L Bps of Accra; Lagos; Niger; Ibadan; N Nig; Ow; Benin; Ekiti; Enugu; and Bp Afonya. *Bishop's Lodge, PO Box 115, Port Harcourt, Nigeria.* (Port Harcourt 773)

FUDGE, Alton William. Qu Coll Newfld. **d** 38 **p** 39 Newfld. Miss at Battle Harbour 38-46; C of Bell Island 46-47; R of Pushthrough 47-52; Badger's Quay 52-57; Botwood 57-63; Ship Harbour 63-72; Falmouth 72-76. *2770 Spring Garden Road, Halifax, NS, Canada.*

FUDGER, David John. b 53. Coll of Resurr Mirfield 76. **d** 77 **p** 78 Southw. C of St Mary Sutton-in-Ashfield 77-80; Duston 80-81; V of All S w Ch Ch and St Mich AA Old Radford Dio Southw from 81. *164 Lenton Boulevard, Nottingham.* (Nottm 785364)

FUDGER, Michael Lloyd. b 55. AKC and BD 77. Coll of the Resurr Mirfield 77. **d** 78 **p** 79 Pet. C of Weston Favell Dio Pet from 78. *5 Greenway, Weston Favell, Northampton.* (Northampton 405946)

FUGE, Douglas Neil. Univ of Otago BA 59, MA 64. St Jo Coll Auckld LTh 63. **d** 63 **p** 64 Auckld. C of E Coast Bays 63-66; St Luke Mt Albert Auckld 66-69; V of Hokiango N 69-72; Papakura Dio Auckld from 73. *38 Coles Crescent, Papakura, NZ.* (87-493)

FUGGLE, Francis Alfred. Selw Coll Cam 3rd cl Hist Trip pt i 33, BA (2nd cl Archaeol and Anthrop Trip) 34, MA 38. Wells Th Coll 35. **d** 36 **p** 37 Lon. C of St Andr Kingsbury 36-38; St Aug Zulu 38-39; R of Nongoma 39-48; Vryheid 48-59; Can of Zulu 53-59; V of Kingsway 59-61; R of All SS Ladysmith 62-71; Woodlands w Montclair, Durban Dio Natal from 71. *6 Delalle Road, Woodlands, Durban, Natal, S Africa.* (Durban 421481)

FUGUI, Leslie. b 43. St Jo Coll Suva 66. **d** 67 **p** 68 Melan. P Dio Melan 67-75; L to Offic Dio Centr Melan 75-77; Dio Malaita from 77. *Auki, Malaita, Solomon Islands.*

FUHRMEISTER, Henry George. Moore Th Coll Syd. **d** 48 **p** 49 Syd. C of St Matt Manly 48-50; P-in-c of Minnipa 50-56; V of Quorn 56-63; R of Lang Lang 63-71; V of Rosedale 71-78; R of Wilcannia Dio River from 78. *Rectory, Wilcannia, NSW, Australia 2836.*

FULHAM, Lord Bishop Suffragan of. *See* Masters, Right Rev Brian John.

FULLAGAR, Michael Nelson. b 35. SS Coll Cam 3rd cl Mod Lang Trip pt i 55, BA (3rd cl Mod Lang Trip pt ii) 57, MA 61. Chich Th Coll 57. **d** 59 **p** 60 S'wark. C of Camberwell 59-61; St Barn Northolt 61-64; Hythe 64-66; R of Chipata 66-70; P-in-c of Livingstone 70-75; Chingola 75-78; R of Freemantle Dio Win from 78. *125 Paynes Road, Freemantle, Southampton.* (Southn 21804)

FULLER, Colin Spencer. b 34. Qu Coll Birm 60. **d** 63 **p** 64 Lich. C of Walsall 63-68; C-in-c of St Chad's Conv Distr Pheasey Gt Barr 68-75; V of Pheasey 75-76; Team V of Cockermouth (w Embleton and Wythop from 77) Dio Carl from 76. *1 Fern Bank, Cockermouth, Cumb, CA13 0DF.* (Cockermouth 823068)

FULLER, David William George. b 47. Univ of Vic BC BSc 70, MDiv 74. Vanc Sch of Th 71. **d** 73 **p** 74 BC. C of St Matt Vic 73-80; I of Sidney Dio BC from 80. *Box 2253, Sidney, BC, Canada.*

FULLER, Douglas Harold Traies. Hur Th Coll LTh 51. CD 64. **d** 51 **p** 52 Hur. C-in-c of Bervie 51; Walpole I 51-53; I of Gorrie 53-54; Jamestown Ont 54-56; Chap RN (Canad) 56-74; R of St Paul and St John Chatham 74-77; Listowel 77-80; St John Simcoe and Port Ryerse Dio Hur from 80. *RR3, Simcoe, Ont, Canada.*

FULLER, Edgar William. McGill Univ Montr BA 48. Wycl Coll Tor LTh 53, BD 55. Yale Univ STM 57. **d** 53 **p** 54 Tor. C of York Mills Tor 53-56; R of Port Perry 57-63. *1382 Lillian Boulevard, Sudbury, Ont., Canada.*

FULLER, Ernest Albert. b 1895. Mert Coll Ox BA and MA 27. Wycl Hall, Ox 27. **d** 27 **p** 28 Liv. C of St Helens 27-31; V of Kenninghall 31-37; St Paul w St Sav Nor 37-57; St Sav w St Paul Nor 57-60. *Address temp unknown.*

FULLER, Canon Frank William. b 22. Chich Th Coll 53. **d** 54 **p** 55 St E. C of Risby 54-55; C-in-c of Lackford and of W Stow w Wordwell 55-58; R of Culford w W Stow and Wordwell 58-61; Cockfield 61-72; RD of Lavenham 64-72; Surr from 64; Hon Can of St E from 67; V of Bungay Dio St E from 72; RD of Beccles w S Elmham from 76. *Vicarage, Bungay, Suff.* (Bungay 2110)

FULLER, Frederick Walter Tom. b 17. St Cath Coll Cam BA 48, MA 53. U Th Sem NY Smith-Mundt Fell and Fulbright Scho STM 54. Univ of Bris MLitt 72. Univ of Ex PhD 74. Cudd Coll 49. **d** 51 **p** 52 York. C of Helmsley 51-53; Asst Chap Qu Mary Sch 52-53; in Amer Ch 53-54; Chap RAF (Supervisor Ord Cands to 58) 55-59; Lect and Chap St Luke's Coll Ex 59-78; Warden 60-78; Dep PV of Ex Cathl from 62; Perm to Offic Dio Bris from 54; L to Offic Dio Ex from 59; C of Swindon New Town (in c of St Sav) Dio Bris from 79. *29 Oxford Road, Stratton St Margaret, Swindon, Wilts, SN3 4HP.* (Swindon 824980)

FULLER, Graham Drowley. b 33. K Coll Lon and Warm AKC 58. **d** 59 **p** 60 Chich. C of E Grinstead 59-62; St Andr Coulsdon 62-64; Chap RN 64-68; V of St Luke Battersea 68-75; S Stoneham w Swaythling Dio Win from 75. *South Stoneham Vicarage, Wessex Lane, Southampton, SO2 2JS.* (Southn 555487)

FULLER, Canon Howel Pascal. b 20. St D Coll Lamp BA 47. **d** 49 **p** 50 St D. C of Pembrey 49-51; C of Newtown w Llanllwchaiarn 51-54; Chap RAF 54-60; R of Ashton w Hartwell 60-70; V of Camrose 70-73; R of Prendergast w Rudbaxton Dio St D from 73; RD of Daugleddy from 78; Can of St D Cathl from 80. *Prendergast Rectory, Haverfordwest, Dyfed, SA61 2PL.* (Haverfordwest 2625)

FULLER, John Hugh Latimer. b 17. Rhodes Univ Coll Grahmstn BA and MA 38, **d** 72 **p** 73 Matab. C of Essexvale Dio Matab 72-75; P-in-c from 75. *Box ESX 5806, Essexvale, Zimbabwe.* (Essexvale 263)

FULLER, John James. b 38. SS Coll Cam 1st cl Hist Trip pt i 61, BA (2nd cl Th Trip pt ii) 63. U Th Sem NY STM 64. Chich Th Coll 63. **d** 65 Kens for Lon **p** 66 Lon. C of St Steph Roch Row w St Jo Evang Westmr 65-71; Tutor Cudd Coll 71-75; Ripon Coll Cudd 75-77; Dir S Dios Ministerial Tr Scheme from 77. *Sarum & Wells Theological College, The Close, Salisbury, Wilts.* (Salisbury 332235)

FULLER, Reginald Harry. b 32. St John's Coll Winnipeg. **d** 80 **p** 81 Rupld. Hon C of St Jas Winnipeg Dio Rupld from 80. *503 Winona Street, Winnipeg, Manit, Canada, R2C 2N7.*

FULLER, Robert James. Univ of Lon BD (2nd cl) 53. **d** 55 **p** 56 Southw. [f Solicitor] C of St Andr Nottm 55; W Bridgford 55-58; R of Sparkford w Weston Bampfylde 58-61; V of Exmoor 61-75; R of Challacombe 61-75. *Brenchoillie Farmhouse, By Inveraray, Argyll.* (Furnace 642)

FULLER, Robert Peter. b 49. Trin Coll Bris 72. **d** 75 **p** 76 Roch. C of Tonbridge 75-79; Welling Dio Roch from 79. *Bishop Ridley House, The Green, Welling, Kent.* (01-303 9998)

FULLER, Terence James. b 30. Univ of Bris BA 55. Clifton Th Coll 55. **d** 56 **p** 57 B & W. C of Uphill (in c of St Barn Old Mixon from 58) 56-59; V of St Jude Mildmay Pk Islington 59-66; V of St Mary Southgate Crawley 66-79; R 79-80; Stoke Climsland Dio Truro from 80. *Stoke Climsland Rectory, Callington, Cornw, PL17 8NZ.* (Stoke Climsland 501)

FULLER, Vernon Maurice. *See* Harvey-Fuller, Vernon Maurice.

FULLERTON, Hamish John Neville. b 45. Ball Coll Ox BA 68, MA 73. SOC 76. **d** 79 **p** 80 S'wark. Hon C of St Paul Clapham Dio S'wark from 79; Asst Master Abp Tenison's Sch Kennington Oval from 79. *21 Offerton Road, SW4 0DJ.*

FULLJAMES, Michael William. b 36. K Coll Lon and Warm AKC 60. **d** 61 **p** 62 Ripon. C of Armley 61-64; St Thos Wells 64-67; R of Stanningley 67-73; Chap St Aug Hosp Chartham from 73. *The Limes, Chartham Downs, Canterbury, Kent.* (Chartham 382)

FULLJAMES, Owen Ralph. b 01. VRD 54. Late Stud and Exhib of St Jo Coll Cam BA (2nd cl Hist Trip pt i) 23, MA 27. Ridley Hall Cam 25. **d** 26 **p** 27 S'wark. C of St Jo Evang Redhill 26-29; Chap RN 29-36; RNVR 36-56; Asst Master Rugby Sch 36-39; Chap 46-54; R of Hornsey 54-59; P-in-c of H Trin Kingsway w St Jo Evang Drury Lane Lon 59-60; V 60-73; Hon Chap to Bp of Lon 59-73; Dep Min Can of St Paul's Cathl Lon 59-81. *9 Warren Close, Hayling Island, Hants, PO11 0HP.* (07016-4526)

FULLJAMES, Peter Godfrey. b 38. Late Scho of BNC Ox BA (2nd cl Phys) 60, MA 64. Univ of Birm Dipl Th 62. Qu Coll Birm 60. **d** 62 Bp Gerard for Sheff **p** 63 Sheff. C of Mexborough 62-65; Chap and Lect Union Christian Coll Alwaye India 65-69; L to Offic Dio Lich from 70; Asst Master Wednesfield High Sch Wolverhampton 69-71; Moorside Comprehensive Sch Werrington from 71. *76 Chatsworth Drive, Werrington, Stoke-on-Trent.*

FULLWOOD, William. b 11. St Aid Coll. **d** 48 **p** 49 Bradf. C of All SS Little Horton Bradf 48-51; St Pet Shipley 51-53; V of Earby 53-64; Blacktoft 64-68; V of Laxton (w Blacktoft from 68) 64-74; Rudston w Boynton 74-77. *11 Ambrey Close, Hunmanby, Nr Filey, N Yorks, YO14 0LZ.* (Scarborough 891027)

FULTON, Jeffrey. b 14. St Jo Coll Dur BA (3rd cl Engl) 37, MA 41. **d** 38 **p** 39 Dur. C of S Westoe 38-41; Chap Miss to Seamen W Hartlepool and L to Offic Dio Dur 42-46; Chap RNVR 46; RN 46-69; Asst Master Tech High Sch Portsm 69-79. *3 Jubilee Terrace, Southsea.* (Portsmouth 27096)

FULTON, John William. b 49. Ex Coll Ox BA 71, MPhil 72, BA (Th) 74, MA 75. Wycl Hall Ox 72. **d** 76 **p** 77 Roch. C of Ch Ch Bexleyheath 76-79; St John W Ealing Dio Lon from 79. *127 Coldershaw Road, W13.*

FULTON, Robert Roland Richard. b 29. St Jo Coll Auckld 77. **d** 79 **p** 80 Wel. C of St Mary Karori Dio Wel from 79. *9 Donald Street, Karori, Wellington 5, NZ.*

FUNDE, Joseph Gadi. St Pet Coll Alice 63. **d** 65 **p** 66 Grahmstn. O of Ethiopia. P Dio Grahmstn 65-76; Dio Port Eliz from 77. *25 Third Avenue, Xaba, CP, S Africa.*

FUNDIRA, Phineas. b 42. **d** 71 **p** 72 Matab. P Dio Matab 71-72 and from 78; Mashon 72-78. *Box 28, Gokwe, Zimbabwe-Rhodesia.* (Gokwe 21)

FUNG, Kenneth Kar-Leung. **d** 68 **p** 69 Hong. P Dio Hong 68-73; Dio Tor from 73. *14 Orley Avenue, Toronto, Ont., Canada.* (416-423 6922)

FUNNELL, Canon Allan Harold. Moore Th Coll Syd ThL 41, **d** 42 **p** 43 Syd. C of St Jo Evang Campsie 42-43; Chap RAAF 43-45; C-in-c of Prov Distr of S Canterbury 46-47; R of Kembla 47-52; Enfield 52-56; Summer Hill 56-65; Eastwood 65-72; Can of Syd from 67; R of St Swith Pymble 72-76; L to Offic Dio Syd from 76. *15 Ray Road, Epping, NSW, Australia 2121.* (869-8853)

FUNNELL, Norman Richard James. b 40. St D Coll Lamp BA (3rd cl Ancient Hist and Lit) 64. Ripon Hall Ox. **d** 66 **p** 67 Lon. C of Hackney 66-70; Hon C from 71; Asst Master Hackney Downs Sch from 71. *8 Sutton Place, E9.* (01-985 6548)

FUONGO, Keliopa. **d** 72 **p** 73 Sudan. P Dio Sudan 72-76; Dio Yambio from 76. *ECS, Madebe, Ibba, Sudan.*

FURLONG, Andrew William Ussher. b 47. TCD BA (Ment & Mor Sc) 69. Jes Coll Cam BA 71. Westcott Ho Cam 70. **d** 72 **p** 73 Down. C of Dundela 72-76; St Anne and of St Steph City and Dio Dub from 76. *33 Wellington Road, Ballsbridge, Dublin 4, Irish Republic.* (Dublin 684903)

FURLONGER, Maurice Frank. b 25. K Coll Lon and Warm AKC 50. **d** 51 **p** 52 S'wark. C of Hither Green 51-54; Chap RAF 54-57; V of Fillongley 57-62; R of St Levan 62-65; Gt Bookham 65-67; V of St Minver w St Mich and St Enodoc 67-70; St Gluvias 70-74; Team V of Seacroft 74-77; V of Hunslet 77-81; In Amer Ch. *1725 11th Avenue, Delano, Calif 93215, USA.*

FURMEDGE, John Michael. Ridley Coll Melb 54, ACT ThL 56. **d** 57 **p** 58 Melb. C of Hampton 57-59; Glenroy 59-60; Dioc Task Force 60; P-in-c of St Phil Heidelberg W 61-62; Min of Diamond Creek 62-66; Perm to Offic Dio Melb 66-68; I of St John Frankston w Carrum Downs 68-71; C of St Matt Cheltenham 70-73; I of Chelsea 73-81; St Jas Syndal Dio Melb from 81. *380 Blackburn Road, Syndal, Vic, Australia 3149.*

FURNEAUX, Thomas Harold. b 10. AKC 40. **d** 40 **p** 41 Chelmsf. C of St John Stratford 40-42; Ingatestone (in c of Ch Ch Buttsbury) 42-45; V of St Andr Walthamstow 45-54; R of Chigwell Row 54-76; Pastoral Care of Ocle Pychard and Ullingswick 76-81; Perm to Offic Dio Heref from 81. *42 Eckroyd Park, Credenhall, Hereford, HR4 7EL.* (Hereford 760702)

FURNELL, Very Rev Raymond. b 35. Linc Th Coll 63. **d** 65 **p** 66 Lich. C of Cannock 65-69; V of Clayton 69-75; R of St Mark Shelton 75-77; RD of N Stoke 75-81; C-in-c of Hanley w Hope 75-77; Etruria 75-77; R of H Evang Hanley 77-81; Provost and V of St Jas Cathl Ch Bury St Edms Dio St E from 81. *Provost's House, Bury St Edmunds, Suff.* (Bury St E 4852)

FURNESS, Archdeacon of. *See* Westmorland and Furness.

FURNESS, Colin. b 43. Lich Th Coll 65. **d** 68 **p** 69 Sheff. C of New Bentley 68; St Cecilia Parson Cross Sheff 68-74; V of New Edlington 74-78; Team V of Heavitree City and Dio Ex from 78. *St Lawrence Vicarage, Lower Hill Barton Road, Exeter, EX1 3EH.* (Ex 66302)

FURNESS, Edward Joseph. b 41. SOC 74. **d** 77 **p** 78 S'wark. Hon C of St Steph S Lambeth Dio S'wark from 77; Warden Mayflower Family Centre Canning Town from 82. *Mayflower Family Centre, Vincent Street, Canning Town, E16 1LS.* (01-476 1171)

FURNESS, Edward Peter Alexander. b 29. St Edm Hall, Ox BA (2nd cl Geog) 52, MA 56. St Aid Coll 52. **d** 54 **p** 55 Blackb. C of Ashton-on-Ribble 54-57; Storrington and of Sullington 57-59; V of Worsthorne 59-64; Longridge Dio Blackb from 64. *Longridge Vicarage, Preston, Lancs.* (Longridge 3281)

FURNESS, John Alfred. b 31. Chich Th Coll 60. **d** 62 **p** 63 Ripon. C of St Aid Leeds 62-66; Rickmansworth 66-73; R of Wymington (w Podington from 75) 73-79; C-in-c of Podington w Farndish 74-75; V of Waltham Cross Dio St Alb from 79. *Vicarage, Longlands Close, Cheshunt, Waltham Cross, Herts, EN8 8LW.* (Waltham Cross 33243)

FURNIVALL, Charles Guy. b 06. Late Scho of Trin Coll Cam 1st cl Cl Trip pt i, 27, BA (1st cl Cl Trip pt ii) 28, MA 37. Westcott Ho Cam 37. **d** 38 **p** 39 St Alb. C of Ch Ch Luton 38; St Andr Luton 38-41; Chap Shrewsbury Sch 41-66; Crete 66-68; L to Offic Dio Chich from 69. *The Barn, Angel Street, Petworth, W Sussex, GU28 0BG.* (Petworth 42454)

FURUTA, Francois. **d** 74 Bur **p** 75 Buye. P Dio Buye. *c/o BP 23 Muyinga, Burundi.*

FUSSELL, Henry Stephen. b 1890. **d** and **p** 29 Waik. C of Te Awamutu and Dom Chap to Bp of Waik 29; P-in-c Piopio w Aria 29-32; V of Waitara 32-35; C of Tisbury 35-38; R of Chilmark 38-45; PC of Dilton Marsh 45-52; V of Hindon w Chicklade and Pertwood 52-56; R of Sutcombe 56-61; Perm to Offic Dio Ex 61-63; L to Offic from 63. *Flint House, Netheravon, Salisbury, Wilts.*

FUSSELL, Preb Laurence Walkling. b 14. Keble Coll Ox BA (2nd cl Th) 35, MA 39. Wells Th Coll 36. **d** 37 **p** 38 S'wark. C of Lambeth 37-39; All SS Weston 39-44; V of Wellow and PC of Hinton Charterhouse 44-59; R of Wraxall w Failand 59-79; Preb of Wells Cathl from 69. *25 West Town Road, Backwell, BS19 3HE.*

FUTSAKA, John Wepukhulu. Buwalasi Th Coll 64. **d** 66 **p** 67 Mbale. P Dio Mbale. *PO Box 614, Mbale, Uganda.*

FUTTER, Ivan Herbert. Roch Th Coll 62. **d** 64 **p** 65 Chelmsf. C of Buckhurst Hill 64-66; Chap Columb Coast Miss 66-71; R of S Saanich Dio BC from 71. *8056 McPhail Road, RR2, Saanichton, BC, Canada.* (604-652 3860)

FUTTER, John McLean. St Paul's Th Coll Grahmstn LTh 61. **d** 61 **p** 62 Johann. C of Orange Grove 61-65; Germiston 65-67; St Aug Kilburn Lon 68-70; R of Malvern 71-72; C of St Mary Cathl Johann 72-75; R of Stilfontein 75-79; Primrose Dio Johann from 79. *Box 2044, Primrose 1416, S Afica.*

FWANICHI, Gerald. St Andr Th Coll Likoma 50. **d** 52 SW Tang **p** 55 Myasa. P Dio SW Tang 52-55; Dio Myasa 55-61; Dio Lebom from 61. *Msumba, Fort Johnston, Malawi.*

FYFE, Arthur Douglas Cummine. b 1898. St Aug Coll Cant. **d** 60 **p** 61 Lon. C of St Mary Virg Primrose Hill Hampstead 60-65; R of Bardwell 65-68; C-in-c of Thorpe-by-Ixworth 65-68; Perm to Offic Dio Chich from 69. *27 The Lawns, Sompting, Lancing, Sussex, BN15 0DT.* (Lancing 4840)

FYFFE, Robert Clark. b 56. Univ of Edin BD 78. Edin Th

Coll 74. **d** 79 **p** 80 Edin. C of St John Princes Street City and Dio Edin from 79. *76 Thirlestane Road, Edinburgh, EH9 1AR.*

FYFFE, Timothy Bruce. b 25. New Coll Ox BA and MA, 54. Westcott Ho Cam 54. **d** 56 **p** 57 S'wark. C of Lewisham 56-60; V of All SS Enugu 60-68; Team V of Lowestoft Group 69-80; Tettenhall Regis Dio Lich from 80; Chap HM Pris Blundeston 70-77; RD of Lothingland 77-80. *Church Cottage, Church Road, Tettenhall, Wolverhampton, WV6 9AJ.* (Wolverhampton 751941)

FYLES, Gordon. b 39. Trin Coll Bris 76. **d** 77 Lon **p** 78 Bp Howell for Lon. C of St Mary Isl 77-81; Ex Sec BCMS from 81. *c/o 251 Lewisham Way, SE4 1XF.*

FYNN, Sidney Alfred. b 38. **d** 79 Bp Stanage for Johann **p** 80 Johann (NSM). C of Westlea Dio Johann from 79. *4 Peperboom Street, Bosmont, S Africa 2093.*

FYOTO, Ven Stefano. Warner Th Coll Buye, 58. **d** 60 **p** 61 Rwanda B. P Dio Rwanda B 60-66; Dio Bur 66-75; Dio Buye from 75; Archd of N Bur from 77. *Anglican Church, Buhiga, Bujumbora, Burundi, Centr Africa.*

G

GABB, Roy. d 64 **p** 65 Melb. C of E Brighton 64-66; Min of Diamond Creek 66-72; P-in-c of Glenroy Dio Melb from 72. *30 Widford Street, Glenroy, Vic, Australia 3046.* (03-306 9528)

GABB-JONES, Adrian William Douglas. b 43. ARICS. Ripon Coll Cudd 80. **d** 81 Willesden for Lon. C of St Barn Northolt Pk Dio Lon from 81. *3 Vernon Rise, Greenford, Middx.*

GABBOTT, Stephen Leonard. Univ of NSW BSc 64. BD (Lon) 67. Moore Th Coll Syd ACT ThL 68. **d** 68 **p** 69 Syd. C of Ryde 68-70; C of St Mark Darling Point Syd 71; CMS Miss Tanzania 71-76; Kenya 76-79; R of Ch Ch Kiama Dio Syd from 80. *Terralong Street, Kiama, NSW, Australia 2553.* (32-2066)

GABE, Eric Sigurd. b 15. Univ of Lon BA 52. St Aid Coll 54. **d** and **p** 55 Ches. [f BJS Miss] C of St Andr W Kirby 55-56; Lect St Aid Coll 56-60; C of Hoylake 56-60; V of St Mich Cricklewood 60-72; V of St Anne w H Trin Brondesbury 72-80; Exam Chap to Bp of Willesden 72-80. *21 Cromer Road, New Barnet, Herts.* (01-449 6779)

GABORONE, Ishmael Matshidiso. b 35. St Pet Coll Alice 70. **d** 72 **p** 73 Johann. C of Natalspruit 72-75; R of Delareyville Dio Johann from 75. *Box 148, Sannieshof, Delareyville, Transvaal, S Africa.*

GABRIEL, Canon Edmund Brookes. Qu Coll Newfld STh 37. **d** 23 **p** 24 Newfld. C of Tack's Beach Miss 23-26; P-in-c of Badger's Quay 26-33; R of Louisbourg 33-38; P-in-c of Annapolis 38-48; R of St Geo Halifax 48-58; Hosp Chap Halifax 58-64; Can of NS 58-64; Hon Can from 64. *271 Lockhart Avenue, Ottawa 13, Ont, Canada.*

GABRIEL, Michael Hunt. d 57 **p** 58 Dub. C of Ch Ch Cathl Waterf 57-60; H Trin Windsor 60-62; Ch Ch St Pancras 62-63; R of Gt w L Shefford 63-67; C of Hillingdon Dio Lon from 67. *91 Harlington Road, Hillingdon, Uxbridge, Middx.*

GABULA, Morriat Nceba. St Bede's Coll Umtata 63. **d** 63 **p** 65 St John's. P Dio St John's. *St Andrew's Mission, Lusikisiki, Transkei, S Africa.*

GACANJA, Canon Elijah. Dioc Div Sch Freetown 28. **d** 29 **p** 35 Momb. CMS P Dio Momb; RD of St Highlands 50-55; Tairobi Distr 55-61; Hon Can of Momb 58-64; Can (Emer) from 64; Chap St Paul's U Th Coll Limuru 63-64; Hon Can of Nai from 64. *Anglican Church, Nyakianga, PO Kangema, Kenya.*

GACHARO, Frederick. d 78 **p** 79 Ruw. P Dio Ruw. *c/o Box 1401, Kamwenge, Uganda.*

GACHOCHA, Josiah. b 55. St Phil Coll Kongwa LTh 79. **d** and **p** 79 Vic Nyan. P Dio Vic Nyan. *PO Box 64, Geita, Tanzania.*

GACIRA, Canon Nathaniel. St Paul's Div Sch Limuru, 33. **d** 34 U Nile for Momb **p** 39 Momb. CMS P Dio Momb; RD of Embu 53-57; Ft Hall 57-61; Hon Can of Ft Hall 61-64; Mt Kenya 64-75; Mt Kenya S from 75. *PO Box 66, Fort Hall, Kenya.*

GADD, Alan John. b 44. Univ of Lon BSc 65, PhD 69. **d** 71 **p** 72 Kens for Lon. Asst Chap to Univs in Lon 71-72; Priest-Worker Dio S'wark from 72; Exam Chap to Bp of S'wark from 77. *25 The Chase, SW4 0ND.*

GADD, Frederick Arthur. St Jo Coll Dur BA 40, MA 43. **d** 40 **p** 41 Liv. C of Em Southport 40-43; All H Allerton 43-44; C-in-c of St Geo Conv Distr Knowsley 44-47; V of Burscough Bridge 47-52; St Mark (w H Trin from 55) Brompton Kent 52-57; R of Dutton Ont 57-60; St Mark St John 60-66; I of Campobello 66-72; R of Hampton 72-80. *c/o Hampton Village, NB, Canada.*

GADEBO, Isaac Ruaita. Newton Coll Dogura 66. **d** 69 **p** 70 New Guinea. C of Rabaul 70-73; P-in-c of Stettin Bay 74-80; Exam Chap to Bp of New Guinea Is 77-80. *Pacific Theological College, Suva, Fiji.*

GADEN, John Robert. Trin Coll Melb BA 64. ACT ThL 64, ThSchol 66. **d** 63 Bath **p** 64 Melb for Bath. Perm to Offic Dio Melb 64-65; C of Mudgee 65-68; on leave 68-71; Chap Melb C of E Gr Sch 72-73; Chap Monash Univ 74-76; Lect Trin Coll and Abp's Consultant Theologian Melb from 77. *Trinity College, Royal Parade, Parkville, Vic., Australia 3052.* (347 9902)

GADEN, Stanley Simeon Victor. St Andr Coll Whittlesford, 41. **d** 42 **p** 43 Sheff. C of Goole 42-44; Rawmarsh 44-48; V of H Trin Wicker Sheff 48-51; Moe 51-52; R of Molong 52-60; Maclean 60-73; L to Offic Dio Graft 74-75; Dio Syd from 75. *4/2 Merchant Street, Stanmore, NSW, Australia 2048.*

GADI, Yosiya. d 52 **p** 55 Ugan. P Dio Ugan 52-60; Dio W Bugan from 60. *Namutumba, Uganda.*

GAGE, Robert Edward. b 47. Whitman Coll Wash USA BA 69. Cudd Coll BA (Th) 75, MA 81. **d** 76 **p** 77 St Alb. C of Cheshunt 76-79; Harpenden 79-81; V of St Giles S Mymms Dio St Alb from 81; C-in-c of St Marg Ridge Dio St Alb from 81. *Vicarage, South Mymms, Herts, EN6 3PE.* (Potters Bar 43142)

GAGG, Percival Stanley. b 03. Ely Th Coll. **d** 39 **p** 40 Southw. [f Methodist Min] C of W Bridgford 39-45; PC of Shirebrook 45-50; V of Prestwold w Hoton 50-54; R of Nailstone w Carlton 54-56; Calstock w Gunnislake 56-60; V of Lelant 60-71; L to Offic Dio Ex from 71. *15 Decoy Road, Newton Abbot, Devon.* (Newton Abbot 5939)

GAHENGA, John. Warner Mem Th Coll Ibuye, 56. **d** 58 **p** 59 Bp Brazier for Ugan. P Dio Ugan 58-60; Dio Rwanda B 60-66; Dio Bur 66-75; Dio Buye from 75; Archd of S Bur 66-75. *Ibuyi, Ngozi, Burundi, E Africa.*

GAINER, Jeffrey. b 51. Jes Coll Ox BA (Hist) 73, BA (Th) 76, MA 77. Wycl Hall Ox 74. **d** 77 Llan **p** 78 Bp Reece for Llan. C of Baglan 77-81; V of Cwmbach Dio Llan from 81. *Vicarage, Bridge Road, Cwmbach, Mid Glam, CF44 0LS.* (Aberdare 878674)

GAINES, George Yorke. b 15. St Aid Coll 59. **d** 61 **p** 62 York. C of Bridlington 61-64; V of Kilham 64-77; V of Lowthorpe w Ruston Parva 64-77; C-in-c of Kirk Fenton Dio York from 77. *Church Fenton Vicarage, Tadcaster, Yorks.* (Barkston Ash 387)

GAINEY, Alfred Tom. b 08. **d** 62 Tewkesbury for Glouc **p** 63 Glouc. C of Bisley 62-65; C-in-c of Bussage 65-68; V of Saul w Fretherne and Framilode Dio Glouc from 68. *Vicarage, Saul, Gloucester.* (Glouc 740311)

GAINS, Peter Eric. b 21. St Cath S Ox BA (2nd cl Th) 48, MA 52. LRAM 51. Wycl Hall, Ox 48. **d** 50 **p** 51 Man. C of St Matt Stretford 50-52; Asst Chap to Liv Coll 52-53; C of Northenden 53-55; V of Macclesfield Forest w Wilboarclough 55-59; Ch Minshull w Leighton and Minshull Vernon Dio Ches from 59. *Vicarage, Minshull Vernon, Crewe, CW1 4RD.* (027-071 213)

GAISEY, Isaac Yaw. b 40. **d** and **p** 75 Accra. P Dio Accra. *Box 94, Sefwi-Awaso, Ghana.*

GAISFORD, Canon John Scott. b 34. Late Exhib of St Chad's Coll Dur BA (2nd cl Th) 59, Dipl Th (w Distinc) 60. Univ of Dur MA 76. **d** 60 **p** 61 Man. C of St Hilda Audenshaw 60-62; C of Bramhall 62-65; V of St Andr Crewe Dio Ches from 65; RD of Nantwich from 74; M Gen Syn from 75; Hon Can of Ches Cathl from 80. *St Andrew's Vicarage, Nantwich Road, Crewe, Chesh.* (Crewe 69000)

GAIT, David James. b 48. BNC Ox BA 71, BSc 72, MA 77. Ridley Hall Cam 71. **d** 74 Warrington for Liv **p** 75 Liv. C of St Paul Hatton Hill Litherland 74-77; Farnworth (in c of St John) 77-80; V of St John Widnes Dio Liv from 80. *St John's House, Greenway Road, Widnes, Lancs, WA8 6HA.* (051-424 3134)

GAIT, Canon James. b 08. Univ of Aber MA 29. Edin Th Coll 29. **d** 31 **p** 32 Glas. C of St Marg Newlands Glas 31-36; R of St Ninian Prestwick 36-39; CF (EC) 39-43; Actg R of H Trin Ayr 43-44; V of St Martin Potternewton 44-54; Chap to Min of Pensions Hosp Leeds 44-54; R of Laurencekirk Drumtochty and Fasque 54-81; Hon Can of St Paul's Cathl Dundee from 79; Perm to Offic Dio Brech from 81. *6 Old Mains Cottages, Fasque, Laurencekirk, Kincardineshire.* (Fettercairn 417)

GAITA, Charles Gaikia. St Paul's Th Coll Limuru 75. **d** 75 **p** 76 Nak. P Dio Nak. *Box 217, Nyahururu, Kenya.*

GAKOMBE, Francois. d 80 Kiga. d Dio Kiga. *BP 20, Nyamata, Rwanda.*

GAKUYA, Nephat. b 47. **d** 71 **p** 72 Mt Kenya. P Dio Mt Kenya 71-75; Dio Mt Kenya S from 75. *Njumbi, Box 35, Gikoe, Kenya.*

GAKWARE, Festus. Warner Mem Coll Ibuye, 53. **d** 54 Bp Brazier for Ugan **p** 55 Ugan. P Dio Ugan 54-60; Dio Rwanda B 60-66; Dio Rwa 66-75; Archd of S Rwa 64-75. *BP 225, Butare, Rwanda.*

GALANA, Gabriel. b 11. St Aug Coll Madag 63. **d** 70 Tam. d Dio Tam from 70. *Lavakianja, Ambinanindrano, Mahanoro, Madagascar.*

GALANE, Solomon. St Francis Coll Sekhukhuniland. **d** 67 **p** 68 Pret. C of Pietersburg 67-71; Mamelodi E Pret 71; R of Rethabile 71-79; C of Temba Dio Pret from 79. *PO Box 36, Temba, Pretoria, S Africa.*

GALBRAITH, John Angus Frame. b 44. Sarum Th Coll 68. **d** 71 **p** 72 S'wark. C of Richmond 71-74; Chap W Lon Colls 74-78; R of H Trin w St Matt S'wark Dio S'wark from 78. *Holy Trinity Rectory, Merrick Square, SE1 4JB.* (01-407 1707)

GALBRAITH, John Watson Joseph Denham. b 19. Univ of Glas MA 41. Bps' Coll Cheshunt 47. **d** 48 St Alb **p** 49 Bedford for St Alb. C of Biggleswade 48-49; Tring 49-51; All SS Challoch (in c of Stranraer and Portpatrick) 51-53; CF 53-72; DACG 67-72; R of Hodnet w Weston-under-Redcastle and Peplow 72-77; V of Deeping St Jas 77-81; Chap of St Jas Oporto Dio Gibr in Eur from 81. *Rua Campo Allegre 640-50-D, Oporto, Portugal.*

GALE, Allan Norman. b 05. **d** 73 **p** 77 Calg. C of St Aug Calg 73-77; L to Offic Dio Calg from 77. *1220 Memorial Drive SE, Calgary, Alta., Canada.* (262-7441)

GALE, Charles Turner. Univ of Manit BA 57, LTh 60. **d** 60 **p** 61 Rupld. C of St Jas Winnipeg 60-62; V of Woodlands 62-67; St Matt Barb 67-68; C of St Aug Lethbridge 68-70; I of Crows Nest Pass 70-73; L to Offic Dio Calg 73-74; Hon C of St Steph Edmon 75-78; St Albert Dio Edmon from 79. *Site 3, RR1, St Albert, Alta, Canada.*

GALE, Christopher. b 44. ALCD 67. **d** 68 **p** 69 Southw. C of Balderton 68-72; St Jo Bapt Bilborough 72-75; P-in-c of Colwick 75-77; V of St Pet Old Radford Dio Southw from 78. *Old Radford Vicarage, Nottingham.* (Nottingham 784450)

GALE, Colin Edward. b 49. St Jo Coll Nottm LTh, BTh 73. **d** 79 **p** 80 Ches. C of Hoole Dio Ches from 79. *8 Park Drive, Hoole, Chester, CH2 3JS.* (Ches 311104)

GALE, Daudi. **d** 70 M & W Nile. d Dio M & W Nile. *c/o PO Box 190, Nyangilia Koboko, via Arua, W Nile, Uganda.*

GALE, Denys Jearrad Pickmore. b 08. St Chads' Coll Dur BA 29. **d** 39 Chich **p** 42 Lewes for Chich. C of Felpham w Middleton 39-40; St Jo Bapt Bognor 40-44; Hd Master Northcliffe Ho Sch Bognor 44-62. *Orchard Gate, Parsons Hill, Arundel, Sussex.*

GALE, Edwin Donald. b 12. AKC 40. **d** 40 **p** 41 Lon. C of All H Barking-by-the-Tower 40-41; St Matt Westmr 41-43; Chap RNVR 43-46; C of Dursley 46-47; Chap RAF 47-51; and 53-62; V of All SS Perry Street Northfleet 51-53; R of Marsham and Burgh next Aylsham 62-68; C of Camp Hill w Galley Common 68-69; V of St Osw Hebburn-on-Tyne 69-73. *6 The Peacheries, Chichester, W Sussex.*

GALE, John. b 34. St D Coll Lamp 67. **d** 69 **p** 70 Llan. C of Aberdare 69-71; Merthyr-Dyfan 71-74; St Jo Bapt Walmer 74; R of St Sav Walmer Dio Port Eliz from 74; P-in-c of St Aug Walmer Dio Port Eliz from 74. *24 Heugh Road, Walmer, Port Elizabeth, CP, S Africa.* (041-512288)

GALE, Keith George. b 44. Sarum Th Coll 69. **d** 70 **p** 71 Bp Gerard for Sheff. C of St Cuthb, Firvale Sheff 70-77; St Martin City and Dio Birm from 77. *2/91 Sir Harry's Road, Birmingham, B5 7QH.* (021-440 4168)

GALE, Ronald Jack. b 08. AKC (2nd cl) 35. **d** 35 **p** 36 Glas. C of H Trin Paisley 35-38; St Bart Brighton 38-42; St Steph Barborne 42-44; St Martin Knowle 44-48; R of St Martin Polmadie 48-50; St Modoc Doune 50-52; Chap at Basra 52-54; Miss to Seamen Kobe Japan 54-57; R of St Mary Hamilton 57-60; St Jo Evang Inverness 60-74; Chap Inverness Hosps and Pris 60-74; Can of St Andr Cathl Inverness 73-74. *20 Comiston Terrace, Edinburgh, EH10 6AH.*

GALENA, Gabriel. Mahanoro Past Coll 70. **d** 71 **p** 72 Tamatave. P-in-c of Befotaka Dio Tam from 71. *Befotaka, Mahanoro, Malagasy Republic.*

GALES, Alan. b 29. Sarum Th Coll 56. **d** 59 **p** 60 Dur. C of Greenside 59-60; Peterlee 60-63; V of Marley Hill Dio Dur from 63; Dep Chap HM Pris Dur 74-81; *Marley Hill Vicarage, Newcastle upon Tyne, NE16 5DJ.* (Whickham 887887)

GALES, Bernard Henry. b 27. Univ of Lon BSc (Econ) 51. Wells Th Coll 62. **d** 64 Southn for Win **p** 65 Win. C of Sholing 64-67; Fordingbridge w Ibsley 67-71; C of S Molton 71-73; Thelbridge 73-80; R of Colebrooke Dio Ex from 80; Bow w Broad Nymet Dio Ex from 80; Zeal Manochorum Dio Ex from 80. *Bow Rectory, Crediton, Devon.*

GALEY, Leonard Joseph. K Coll NS BA 53, LTh 54. **d** 54 **p** 55 Fred. I of Dalhousie 54-61; R of Hardwicke 61-64; All SS E St John 64-74; Assoc P of Portland Dio Fred from 74. *536 Champlain Street, Saint John, NB, Canada.*

GALILEE, George David Surtees. b 37. Or Coll Ox BA 60, MA 64. Westcott Ho Cam 61. **d** 62 **p** 63 Leic. C of Knighton 62-67; V of St Luke Stocking Farm Leic 67-69; Tutor Westcott Ho and Homerton Coll Cam 69-71; V of Sutton 71-80; P-in-c of St Mildred Addiscombe Dio Cant 80-81; V from 81. *Vicarage, Sefton Road, Croydon, CRO 7HR.* (01-654 3569)

GALIWANGO, Besweri. **d** 39 **p** 41 Ugan. P Dio Ugan 39-61; Dio Nam 61-73. *PO Box 16047, Kampala, Uganda.*

GALLAGHER, Hubert. b 31. Linc Th Coll 78. **d** 80 **p** 81 Wakef. C of Lupset Dio Wakef from 80. *341 Horbury Road, Lupset, Wakefield, W Yorks.*

GALLAGHER, John James. b 25. St Francis Coll Brisb 77. **d** 78 **p** 79 Brisb. C of St Osw Banyo 78-80; Perm to Offic Dio Brisb from 80. *60 Mott Street, Enoggera, Queensld, Australia 4051.*

GALLAGHER, Neville Roy. b 45. AKC 70. Univ of Lon BD 76. St Aug Coll Cant 70. **d** 71 **p** 72 Cant. C of Folkestone 71-74; Sutton Valence w E Sutton 74-76; Team V of Centr Telford 76-78; P-in-c of Gt Mongeham Dio Cant 78-80; R (w Ripple and Sutton-by-Dover) from 80; P-in-c of Ripple 78-80. *Great Mongeham Rectory, Deal, Kent.* (Deal 5319)

GALLAGHER, Robert. Univ of W Ont BA 62. Trin Coll Tor STB 65. **d** 65 Niag. C of Ch of H Redeemer Stoney Creek 65-67, I of St Marg Hamilton W 67-71; R of Georgetown 71-78; Grace Ch Hamilton Dio Niag from 78. *32 Grosvenor Avenue South, Hamilton, Ont, Canada.* (416-545-9030)

GALLAGHER, Robert. St Chad's Coll Dur BSc 65, Dipl Th 67. **d** 67 Pontefract for Wakef **p** 68 Wakef. C of Crosland Moor 67-69; Huddersfield 69-71; Chap Huddersfield Poly 71-79; Min in Coulby Newham Ecumen Project Middlesbrough Dio York from 79. *c/o Church House, Grange Road, Middlesbrough, Cleve, TS1 2LR.*

GALLARDO, Bartolo. **d** 66 **p** 67 Chile. P Dio Chile. *Casilla 4 Cholchol, Chile, S America.*

GALLETLY, Thomas. b 23. St Chad's Coll Dur BA 50, Dipl Th 52. **d** 52 **p** 53 Newc T. C of Woodhorn w Newbiggin 52-55; Chap Aycliffe Approved Sch and L to Offic Dio Dur 56-57; Chap and Warden of Chailey Heritage Craft Sch and Hosp from 57; L to Offic Dio Chich from 59. *Beech House, North Chailey, Lewes, Sussex.* (Newick 2168)

GALLEY, Giles Christopher. b 32. Qu Coll Cam 3rd cl Cl Trip pt i 55, BA (3rd cl Th Trip pt ia) 56 MA 60. Linc Th Coll 56. **d** 58 Nor **p** 59 Thetford for Cant C of Gt Yarmouth 58-62; King's Lynn 62-66; Leeds 66-69; V of St Mich AA Hull 70-79; Strensall Dio York from 79. *Strensall Vicarage, York, YO3 5UB.* (York 490683)

GALLICHAN, Charles Alan. Bp's Univ Lennox BA 63. Trin Coll Tor STB 68. **d** 68 **p** 69 Ott. C of St Matt Ott 68-71; I of Eganville 71-75; Carleton Place Dio Ott from 75. *Box 43, Carleton Place, Ont, Canada.* (613-257 1477)

GALLICHAN, Henry Ernest. b 45. Sarum Wells Th Coll 70. **d** 72 **p** 73 Newc T. C of Kenton Dio Newc T 72-76; L to Offic Dio Zanz T 76-80. *Karibu, Trevelmond, Liskeard, Cornwall.* (Drobwalls 20530)

✠ **GALLIFORD, Right Rev David George.** b 25. Late Organ Scho of Clare Coll Cam BA 49, MA 51. Westcott Ho Cam. **d** 51 **p** 52 York. C of St John Newland Hull 51-54; Min Can of Windsor and C of Eton 54-56; V of St Osw Middlesbrough 56-61; R of Bolton Percy w Colton 61-71; Can and Preb of York Minster 69-75; Can Res and Treas of York Minster 70-75; Cons Ld Bp Suffr of Hulme in York Minster 18 Oct 75 by Abp of York; Bps of Wakef, Man, Southw and Blackb; Bps Suffr of Middleton, Jarrow, Aston, Hull, Pontefract, Whitby and Knaresborough; and others. *31 Bland Road, Prestwich, Manchester, M25 8NW.* (061-773 1504)

GALLON, Edward George. b 16. St Steph Ho Ox 64. **d** 66 Colchester for Chelmsf **p** 67 Chelmsf. C of All SS Southend-on-Sea 66-69; Hockley 69-74; R of Takeley w L Canfield Dio Chelmsf from 74. *Takeley Vicarage, Bishops Stortford, Herts.* (Bp's Stortford 870837)

GALLOP, Alfred Henry. Moore Th Coll Syd 10. **d** 10 **p** 11 Syd. C of St Steph Rookwood w St Phil Auburn 10-12; St Steph Newtown 13-15; Ch Ch Kiama w Gerringong 15-16 (all in NSW); TCF 16-19; R of Jamberoo w Shellharbour 20-26; C of All SS Woollahra 26-42; Chap AIF 42-46; C of St Luke Liv 46-49; Parramatta 49-58; L of Offic Dio Syd from 58. *96 Stella Street, Collaroy Plateau, NSW 2098, Australia.*

GALLOWAY, Bishop of. *See* Glasgow.

GALLOWAY, Charles Bertram. b 41. Univ of Lon Ba (3rd cl Cl) 62. Univ of Birm Dipl Th 64. Qu Coll Birm 64. **d** 64 **p** 65 Dur. C of H Trin Darlington 64-68; Industr Chap Dur 68-77; Sen Industr Chap Dio Liv from 77. *Church House, 1 Hanover Street, Liverpool, L1 3DW.*

GALLOWAY, Canon Douglas Victor. b 12. Univ of Wales, BA (2nd cl Phil) 36. Sarum Th Coll 36. **d** 38 **p** 39 Sarum. C of

H Trin Weymouth 38-41; Shepton Mallet 41-44; R of Clutton 44-49; Bincombe w Broadway 49-55; V of Westbury w Westbury Leigh and Dilton 55-62; Beaminster 62-77; Proc Conv Sarum 62-64; Surr 64-77; RD of Beaminster 66-74; Can and Preb of Sarum Cathl from 70. *10 Pike Hills Mount, Copmanthorpe, York, YO2 3UU.*

GALLOWAY, Michael Edward. Chich Th Coll 72. **d** 74 **p** 75 Chich. C of Aldwick 74-77; St Clem Boscombe (in c of St Mary Virg) Dio Win from 77. *49 Thistlebarrow Road, Bournemouth, Dorset.* (Bournemouth 38376)

GALLUP, Peter Whitfield. b 06. Sarum Th Coll 51. **d** 53 Bp Kitching for Portsm **p** 54 Portsm. C of St Mary Portsea 53-61; R of Buriton 61-74; Hon Chap of Win Cathl from 79. *16 St Swithun Street, Winchester.*

GALSWORTHY, William Donald. Fitzw Ho Cam BA 28, MA 38. Ch Ch Ox MA (by incorp) 60. Linc Th Coll 38. **d** 39 **p** 40 Sarum. C of Bradford-on-Avon 39-43; C-in-c of Conv Distr of St Geo Oakdale 43-45; Chap of Barnard Castle Sch 45-47; PC of Ch Ch Bradford-on-Avon 47-55; Hd Master of Kingwell Court Prep Sch Bradford-on-Avon 55-59; Ch Ch Cathl Choir Sch 59-64; Prec 59-64; R of Graveley w Yelling (and Papworth St Agnes from 76) 64-77; C-in-c of Papworth St Agnes Ely 64-65; R 65-76. *17 Lea Road, Hemingford Grey, Huntingdon, Cambs.* (St Ives 63340)

GALT, Ian Ross. b 34. Univ of Leeds BSc 56. **d** 76 **p** 77 Mon (APM). C of St Julian Newport Dio Mon from 76. *47 Brynglas Avenue, Newport, Gwent, NPT 5LR.*

GAMBIA, Lord Bishop of. *See* Elisee, Right Rev Jean Rigal.

GAMBLE, Brian Michelson. Univ of Tor BA 59. Wycl Coll Tor LTh 59, BD 64. **d** 58 Tor **p** 59 Carib. I of Lillooet 58-64; Hon C of St D Lawr Ave Tor 65-68. *Apt 121, 16 The Links, Willowdale, Ont, Canada.*

GAMBLE, David Lawrence. b 34. K Coll Lon and Warm AKC (2nd Cl) 61. **d** 62 **p** 63 Chelmsf. C of All SS Eccles Distr Belhus Pk 62-65; St Jas Gtr w All SS, St Nich and St Runwald Colchester 65-69; C-in-c of Hatfield Heath 69; V of St Andr Chelmsf 69-73; C of Hatfield Heath 74-77; Team V of Hemel Hempstead Dio St Alb from 77. *7 Tollpit End, Gadebridge, Hemel Hempstead, Herts.* (Hemel Hempstead 54061)

GAMBLE, Norman Edward Charles. b 50. Trin Coll Dub BA 72, PhD 78. Div Hostel Dub 76. **d** 79 **p** 80 Down. C of Bangor Dio Down from 79. *109 Old Gransha Road, Bangor, Co Down, N Ireland.*

GAMBLE, Peter John. b 20. St Cath S Ox BA 51, MA 55. Ripon Hall Ox 48. **d** 52 **p** 53 Birm. C of Erdington 52-54; Asst Chap Embassy Ch Paris 54-55; Chap and Ho Master Milton Abbey Sch 55-59; Chap and Tutor Millfield Sch 59-62; Sen Chap and Tutor 62-67; Prin Anglo-Amer Coll Alvescot 67-71; Perm to Offic Dio Lon from 60; Dio Ox 67-71; Asst Master Harrow Sch from 72. *38 Crown Street, Harrow-on-the-Hill, Middx, HA2 0HR.* (01-422 0546)

GAMBLE, Robin Philip. b 53. Oak Hill Coll 74. **d** 77 **p** 78 Bradf. C of Laisterdyke Dio Bradf from 77. *15 Keswick Street, Laisterdyke, Bradford, Yorks, BD4 8PX.*

GAMBLE, Thomas Richard. b 42. K Coll Lon and Warm BD and AKC 64. **d** 65 Barking for Chelmsf **p** 66 Chelmsf. C of St Jo Evang Seven Kings 65-68; Hon C 68-73; Asst Master Pettits Secondary Sch Romford 68-73; Hall Mead Sch Upminster 73-75; Tabor High Sch Braintree 76-77; Chap Warm Sch Wilts 77-80. *34 Thornhill Road, Warminster, Wilts, BA12 8EF.* (Warm 215331)

GAMBLING, William Wreyford. **d** and **p** 73 Qu'App. C of Stoughton 73-79; I of Assiniboia 79-81; Rainy River Dio Keew from 81. *General Delivery, Rainy River, Ont, Canada.*

GAMESTER, Sidney Peter. Late Scho of SS Coll Cam 1st cl Law Trip pt i 50, BA (1st cl Law Trip pt ii) 51, MA 55. Oak Hill Th Coll 56. **d** 58 **p** 59 S'wark. C of Ch Ch Surbiton Hill 58-61; H Trin Worthing (in c of St Matt) 61-69; R of St Matt St Leonards-on-Sea Dio Chich from 69. *St Matthew's Rectory, St Leonards-on-Sea, Sussex.* (Hastings 423790)

GAMON, John Stott. b 01. Bps' Coll Cheshunt, 35. **d** 36 **p** 37 Ches. C of Witton 36-40; Chap RNVR 40-45; V of Chelford 45-55; R of Tattenhall 55-65; Norbury w Snelston 65-73. *Tatlow's Cottage, Trusley, Sutton-on-the-Hill, Derby, DE6 5JG.* (Etwall 3396)

GAN, Boon Guan. b 05. **d** 73 **p** 74 Sing (APM). P Dio Sing. *18-A, Blk 97 Commonwealth Crescent, Singapore 3.*

GANAAFA, Ven William. **d** 74 **p** 75 Ank. P Dio Ank 74-77; Dioc Regr, Sec and Treas Dio W Ank 77-78; Dom Chap to Bp of W Ank 78-80; Archd Dio W Ank from 80. *Box 2027, Rwashamaire, Uganda.*

GANASA, Giles Magibuaga. b 32. **d** 64 New Guinea. d Dio New Guinea 64-71; Dio Papua from 71. *Anglican Church, Kumbun, via Kandrian, New Guinea.*

GANDIYA, Chad. **d** 79 **p** 80 Mashon. P Dio Mashon. *c/o Anglican Diocesan Offices, PO Box UA7, Salisbury, Rhodesia.*

GANDIYA, David. St Jo Coll Lusaka 70. **d** 72 **p** 73 Mashon. P Dio Mashon 72-81; Dio Mutare from 81. *Rectory, Chimvuri, Zimbabwe.*

GANDON, Andrew James Robson. b 54. St Jo Coll Dur BA (Th) 76. Ridley Hall Cam 76. **d** 78 **p** 79 Birm. C of Aston Dio Birm from 78. *22 Brantley Road, Witton, Birmingham, B6 7DR.*

GANDON, Percy James. b 22. ALCD 53. **d** 53 Bp Hollis for Cant **p** 54 Leic. C of St Barn Leic 53-56; H Trin Leic 56-57; Chap at Tororo 57-60; V 60-63; Hoddesdon Dio St Alb from 63; RD of Cheshunt from 81. *Vicarage, Hoddesdon, Herts.* (Hoddesdon 62127)

GANE, Christopher Paul. b 33. Qu Coll Cam BA 57, MA 61. Ridley Hall Cam 57. **d** 59 **p** 60 Chelmsf. C of Rainham 59-62; Farnborough Hants 62-64; V of St Paul Erith 64-71; St Marg Ipswich Dio St E from 71. *32 Constable Road, Ipswich, Suff, IP4 2UW.* (Ipswich 53906)

GANGARABWE, John. **d** 78 **p** 80 Matab. P Dio Matab. *PB 9030, Gwelo, Zimbabwe.*

GANJE-HNEMA, Daniel Michael. **d** 58 **p** 60 Mashon. P Dio Mashon. *St Augustine's Priory, Penhalonga, Rhodesia.*

GANLEY, Donald Andrew. Ridley Coll Melb ACT ThL 37. **d** 38 **p** 40 Bend. C of St Paul Bend 38-39; St Jas and St John Miss Distr Melb 39-40; V of Serpentine 40-42; Chap AIF 42-45; V of St Alb Mooroopna 46-47; C of St Jas and St John Miss Distr Phillip Is and Asst Master at Boys' Tr Home Newhaven 47-50; V of Broadmeadows 50-52; C of Melb Dioc Centre 52-59; V of Belmont 59-62; Chap Miss to Seamen Dio Brisb 62-67; Buenos Aires Dio Argent 68-69; Dio Chile 69-72; Dio Melb 72-78; Perm to Offic Dio Melb 72-78; Dio Bend from 78. *George Street, Serpentine, Vic., Australia 3517.*

GANN, Canon Anthony Michael. b 37. Trin Coll Dub BA (2nd cl Mod) 60, MA and BD 64. **d** 62 **p** 63 Derry. V Cho of Derry Cathl 62-66; Chap and Lect in Th Univ of Botswana Les and Swaz 66-74; Exam Chap to Bps of Bloemf, Les and Kimb K 69-74; P-in-c of Bampton w Mardale 75-80; Dioc Officer Carl Miss and Unity 75-80; Hon Can of Les from 77; Team V of Centr Telford Dio Lich from 80. *15 Carwood, Stirchley, Telford, TF3 1YA.* (Telford 595482)

GANN, John West. b 29. Ex Coll Ox BA (2nd cl Th) 55, MA 59. Wells Th Coll 55. **d** 57 **p** 58 Ox. C of Wendover 57-59; Walton-on-the-Hill Liv 59-62; R of Didcot 62-70; St Nich Newbury (w St Jo Evang Newbury, Speenhamland and Wash Common from 73) 70-78; V of Twickenham Dio Lon from 78; Dir of Ordinands Kens Episc Area Dio Lon from 81. *St Mary's Vicarage, Riverside, Twickenham. Middx, TW1 3DT.* (01-892 2318)

GANS, Arthur Elliott. b 36. Univ of Washington Seattle BA 57. Lehigh Univ Penn MA 70. Ch Div Sch of Pacific Calif BD 60. **d** 60 Bp Pike (Calif) **p** 61 Bp Shires (Calif). In Amer Ch 60-71; V of Battleford Sktn 71-74; Westlock 74-78; CF (Canad) from 78. *19 Rutledge Court, Oromocto, NB, Canada.*

GANT, Brian Leonard. b 45. St Aug Coll Cant 72. **d** 73 Bp McKie for Cov. **p** 74 Cov. C of Hillmorton 73-75; St Geo Cov 75-76; P-in-c of St Mary Maldon 76-79; R of St Columba Crieff 79-81; Comrie 79-81; Muthill 79-81; Ed 'Outlook' 79-81; V of St Paul Walsall Dio Lich from 81. *57 Mellish Road, Walsall, W Midl.* (Walsall 24963)

GANT, Peter Robert. b 38. Late Scho of BNC Ox BA 60, MA 64. G and C Coll Cam BA 62, MA 67. Ridley Hall Cam 61. **d** 63 **p** 64 Portsm. C of St Mary Portsea 63-67; V of Blackheath Birm 67-73; Perm to Offic Dio Birm 73-75; Dio Guildf from 75. *8 Sandon Close, Esher, Surrey, KT10 8JE.* (01-398 5107)

GANT, Ven Waverley Drake. St Jo Coll Manit BA 37, LTh 40. **d** and **p** 41 Rupld. C of St Matt Winnipeg 41-45; R of Wakefield and I of Winnipeg Beach 46-49; Charleswood and Headingley 49-52; Meota Pars Dio Calg from 52; Hon Can of Calg 60-66; Archd of Bow Valley 66-72; Macleod from 72; Exam Chap to Bp of Calg 66-68. *General Delivery, Black Diamond, Alta., Canada.* (933-7617)

GANTUNU, Phinehas. Buwalasi Th Coll 65. **d** 66 Ankole-K. d Dio Ank K 66-67; Dio Ank 67-76; Dio E Ank from 76. *PO Box 14, Mbarara, Uganda.*

GANYANA, Yakabo. Bp Tucker Coll Mukono. **d** 56 Ugan **p** 58 Balya for Ugan. P Dio Ugan 56-60; Dio W Bugan from 60. *Church of Uganda, Nanggoma, PO Bukola, Tanzania.*

GANZ, Timothy Jon. b 36. Univ Coll Ox BA (3rd cl French) 58, 4th cl Th 60, MA 62. ARCM 63. St Steph Ho Ox 58. **d** 61 **p** 62 Lich. C of H Cross Shrewsbury 61-65; Asst Chap Hurstpierpoint Coll 65-69; Chap 69-73; Perm to Offic Dio Swan B 73; Chap Univ Coll Swansea and C of Swansea 74-75; P-in-c of All SS Hanley 75-80; V of Tutbury Dio Lich from 80. *Tutbury Vicarage, Burton-on-Trent, Staffs.* (B-on-T 813127)

GAO, Malachi. **d** 37 **p** 44 Melan. P Dio Melan 37-74. *Lolowai, New Hebrides.*

GAO, Ven Timon. St Pet Coll Siota. **d** 70 **p** 71 Melan. P Dio Melan 70-75; Dio New Hebr 75-80; Dio Vanuatu from 80;

VG 76-78; Archd of Vanuatu from 80. *Lolowai, Aoba, Vanuatu.*

GARAE, Paul. d 76 **p** 78 New Hebr. P Dio New Hebr 76-80; Dio Vanuatu from 80. *Lolosiwoi, Longana, Vanuatu.*

GARBUTT, Arthur. b 09. St Paul's Miss Coll Burgh 32. **d** 33 **p** 34 York. C of St Mary Bishopshill Sen w St Clem York 33-35; PV of St Steph and St Lawr Pro-Cathl Lourenço Marques 35-39; C of Guisborough 39-46; CF (EC) 41-46; V of Ravenscar w Stainton Dale 46-50; Brafferton w Pilmoor (and Myton-on-Swale from 57) 50-62; C-in-c of Myton-on-Swale 53-57; R of Catton w Stamford Bridge 62-74; Perm to Offic Dio York from 74. *35 Fossway, Stamford Bridge, York, YO4 1DS.* (Stamford Bridge 71436)

GARBUTT, Gerald. b 41. St Aid Coll 65. **d** 67 **p** 68 Man. C of All SS Stretford 67-70; Youth Worker All SS Newton Heath from 70; L to Offic Dio Man 70-72; R of St Bart Oldfield Rd Salford 72-74; V of St Aid Kersal, Salford 74-79; Team R of St John w St Bart Bethnal Green Dio Lon from 79. *St John's Vicarage, Victoria Park Square, Bethnal Green, E2 0HU.* (01-980 1742)

GARBUTT, Hedley George Wilesmith. b 19. St Mich Coll Llan 54. **d** 56 **p** 57 Swan B. C of Loughor 56-65; R of Llanfihangel Talyllyn w Llanywern and Llangasty Talyllyn Dio Swan B from 65. *Rectory, Llanfihangel Talyllyn, Brecon, Powys, LD3 7TG.* (087-484 633)

GARDENER, Canon Michael George. Univ of Reading BA (2nd cl Psychology) 53. Wycl Hall, Ox 53; **d** 55 S'wark for Cant for Arctic **p** 57 Arctic. Miss at Lake Harbour 55-63; Hon Can of Arctic from 63; I of Cape Dorset 63-70; Miss at Pangnirtung 70-81; Frobisher Bay Dio Arctic from 81; Exam Chap to Bp of the Arctic from 75. *Box 57, Frobisher Bay, NWT, Canada.*

GARDIN, Edward. Univ of Dur LTh 32. Edin Th Coll 29. **d** 32 **p** 33 Glas. C of St Mary's Cathl Glas 32-34; St Aug Chesterfield 34-35; C-in-c of St Mark's Conv Distr Lower Brampton 35-48; C of Clee w Cleethorpes 48-51; R of Firsby w Gt Steeping 51-61; R of L Steeping 51-61; Carlton Scroop w Normanton 61-69. *Address temp unknown.*

GARDINER, Alan. Bp's Univ Lennox BA 23, MA 24. Trin Coll Tor LTh 26, BD 28. **d** 26 **p** 27 Ott. C of Win 26-27; St Matt Ott 27-31; V of St Sav Vic W 31-33; R of St Paul Esquimalt 33-36; P-in-c of St Matthias Miss 36-39; Chap CASF 39-43; Chap of Brentwood Coll 43-45; R of Cranbrook 45-49; Waterford 49-54; St Steph Lon 54-60; Port Dover 60-65; L to Offic Dio Hur from 65. *1059 The Parkway, London, Ont, Canada.*

GARDINER, Anthony Reade. Univ of Cant NZ BA 59. Cudd Coll 60. **d** 62 **p** 63 Newc T. C of All SS Gosforth 62-65; V of Waikohu 65-69; Edgecumbe 69-74; Eltham 74-78; Trentham Dio Wel from 78. *1 Moonshine Road, Upper Hutt, NZ.* (Upper Hutt 85588)

GARDINER, Arthur John. Ch Ch Ox BA 46, MA 50. Ely Th Coll 49. **d** 50 **p** 51 Lon. C of H Cross Greenford 50-54; Chap of Milton Abbey Sch Dorset 54-55; C of E Chap Univ of Lon 55-57; Chap Ardingly Coll 57-58; Bloxham Sch 58-64; Prin Teachers' Tr Coll Daramombe Dio Mashon from 64; P-in-c of Daramombe w Enkeldoorn and Umvuma 67-78; Hd Master Ch K Sch Daramombe 73-78; Exam Chap to Bp of Mashon 74-81; Can of Mashon 77-81; R of Rushton w Pipewell, Glendon and Thorpe Malsor Dio Pet from 81. *Rushton Rectory, Kettering, Northants.* (Kettering 710415)

GARDINER, Edmund Austin. b 1898. K Coll Lon BSc and AKC 23. OBE 52. St George's Windsor 53. **d** and **p** 53 Guildf. C of Hersham 53-55; R of Seale 55-62; C of Farnham 63-73; L to Offic Dio Guildf 62-63 and from 73. *Manormead Nursing Home, Tilford Road, Hindhead, Surrey.* (Hindhead 5226)

GARDINER, George John. St Francis Coll Milton. **d** 53 **p** 54 Bath. C of All SS Cathl Bath 53-56; R of Warren 56-61; L to Offic Dio C & Goulb 64-68; Dio Syd from 75. *6 Oatway Parade, North Manly, NSW, Australia 2100.* (939-7379)

GARDINER, James Carlisle. b 18. St Jo Coll Dur LTh 48. Tyndale Hall, Bris. **d** 49 **p** 50 Blackb. C of Ch Ch Blackpool 49-52; Rushen Man 52-56; R of Ditton Kent Dio Roch from 56. *2 The Stream, Ditton, Maidstone, Kent, ME20 6AG.* (W Malling 842027)

GARDINER, James Gordon. Univ of Tor BA 43, LTh 46. Trin Coll Tor. **d** 46 **p** 47 Tor. C of St Geo Tor 46-49; St Faith Miss Edson 49-56; R of St Bede Winnipeg 57-66; Can of St John's Cathl Winnipeg 63-66; R of St Jas Vancouver Dio New Westmr from 66. *303 East Cordova Street, Vancouver 4, BC, Canada.*

GARDINER, John. b 15. Clifton Th Coll 67. **d** 68 **p** 69 Man. C of St Pet Halliwell 68-71; V of Monton Eccles 71-80; Hoghton Dio Blackb from 80. *Hoghton Vicarage, Preston, Lancs, PR5 0RY.* (Hoghton 2529)

GARDINER, John Kingsmill. b 18. OBE (Mil) 52. Bps' Coll Cheshunt 53. **d** 55 **p** 56 Lon. C of St Helen w H Trin Kens 55-57; V of St Olave Woodberry Down 57-62; R of Harden-huish 62-68; L to Offic Dio Bris from 69; Tutor Nat Marriage Guidance Coun from 69. *Combe Head, Giddeahall, Chippenham, Wilts, SN14 7ES.* (Castle Combe 782497)

GARDINER, Kenneth Ashton. b 27. SOC 60. **d** 63 **p** 64 S'wark. C of H Trin Sydenham 63-67; Macclesfield 67-70; V of St Phil and St Jas Chatham Dio Roch from 70. *289 Walderslade Road, Chatham, Kent.* (Medway 62498)

GARDINER, Kent Hornick. b 30. Wycl Coll Tor LTh 69. **d** 69 Hur **p** 70 Ont. I of Marysburg 69-72; Chatsworth 72-74; Port Lambton Dio Hur from 74. *Box 4, Port Lambton, Ont., Canada.* (519-677 5586)

GARDINER, Thomas Alfred. b 30. St Cuthb S Dur BA 52, MA 56. Ridley Hall, Cam 54. **d** 56 **p** 57 Ches. C of St Geo Stockport 56-60; Asst Chap Brentwood Scho 60-62; Chap from 62. *Mitre House, 6 Shenfield Road, Brentwood, Essex.* (Brentwood 5484)

GARDINER, William Gerald Henry. b 46. BD (Lon) 72. Oak Hill Th Coll 68. **d** 72 **p** 73 Roch. C of St Jo Bapt Beckenham 72-75; St Mary Cheadle 75-80; P-in-c of Swynnerton Dio Lich from 81; Tittensor Dio Lich from 81. *Vicarage, Stone Road, Tittensor, Stoke-on-Trent, ST12 9HE.* (Barlaston 2312)

GARDNER, Albert Edward Charles. Univ of Syd BA 40. Moore Th Coll Syd ACT ThL 32. **d** 32 Syd **p** 33 Bath for Goulb. C of St Alb Ultimo 32-33; Asst Master Canberra Gr Sch and Perm to Offic Dio Goulb 33-38; Perm to Offic Dio Syd 38-40; Chap Canberra Gr Sch 40-50; LPr Dio Syd from 53; Dio Newc 56-58; C of St Jas Syd 59-63; Hon C of Petersham Dio Syd from 63. *4-15 Orpington Street, Ashfield, NSW Australia 2131.* (798-0867)

GARDNER, Alfred. b 04. **d** and **p** 55 Cov. C of St Mich Stoke Cov 55-58; V of Bp's Itchington 58-64; Marton w Birdingbury 64-72. *1 Margetts Close, Kenilworth, Warws.*

GARDNER, Anthony Brian. b 32. Lon Coll of Div 62. **d** 64 Bp McKie for Cov **p** 65 Cov. C of St Mich Stoke Cov 64-68; R of Whitnash Dio Cov from 68; RD of Leamington 78-79; Warw and Leamington from 79. *Whitnash Rectory, Leamington, Warws.* (Leamington 25070)

GARDNER, Charles Graham. AKC 49. St Bonif Coll Warm. **d** 50 **p** 51 S'wark. C of Clapham 50-54; Chap St Matt Coll Grahmstn 54-57; Warden 57-62; Miss St Mich Miss Herschel 62-74; Archd of Aliwal N 70-81; R of Aliwal N and Burgersdrop 74-81; St Marg City and Dio Bloemf from 81. *1 Cromwell Road, Bloemfontein 9301, S Africa.*

GARDNER, Canon Christopher John. b 23. Jes Coll Cam BA 47, MA 53. Ely Th Coll. **d** 50 **p** 51 Lon. C of St Paul Ruislip Manor 50-54; Malvern Link 54-58; Missr at St Chris Conv Distr (Pemb Coll Cam Miss) Walworth 58-63; R of Orton Waterville Dio Ely from 63; RD of Yaxley from 79; Hon Can of Ely Cathl from 81. *Orton Waterville Rectory, Peterborough, PE2 0EQ.* (Peterborough 231876)

GARDNER, Ven Clifton Gordon. b 15. Univ of Tor BA 36. Univ of Lon BD 39. AKC 39. **d** 39 Dorch for Ox **p** 40 Ox. C of St Luke Maidenhead 39-41 and 46-47; Chap RNVR 41-46; PC of St Pet Furze Platt Dio Ox 47-52; R of St Luke St Thomas Dio Hur 52-56; Chap Westmr Hosp Lon Ont 56-74; Exam Chap to Bp of Hur 60-70; Hon Cler Sec Hur 64-73; Can of St Paul's Cathl Lon Ont 64-74; R of Dorchester 74-76; Archd of Middx Ont 74-76; Archd (Emer) from 76. *1 Shepherd's Way, Saffron Walden, Essex, CB10 2AH.*

GARDNER, David Edward. b 21. Oak Hill Th Coll 44. **d** 49 **p** 50 Lon. C of St Cuthb Chitts Hill Wood Green 49-52; Ch Ch S Mymms Barnet 52-55; Chap of Dockland Settlement Canning Town 55-57; Mayflower Family Centre Canning Town 58-60; Trav Chap Boys' Covenanter U and L to Offic Dio Lon from 60. *6 Hillside Gardens, Barnet, Herts.*

GARDNER, David Lewis. b 20. Oak Hill Th Coll 49. **d** 52 **p** 53 S'wark. C of Morden 52-54; New Malden w Coombe 54-56; PC of Chaddesden 56-60; Missr of St Paul Valparaiso 60-62; V of Alne w Aldwark 62-65; C of St Mary Walthamstow 77-78; P-in-c of Ramsden Crays and Ramsden Bellhouse Dio Chelmsf from 79. *Rectory, Church Lane, Crays Hill, Billericay, CM11 2UN.*

GARDNER, Douglas George. b 22. Univ of Leeds BA 46. Coll of Resurr Mirfield 46. **d** 49 **p** 50 Cov. C of St Mark Cov 49-52; St Martin U Knowle 52-58; V of St Paul Swindon 58-65; C-in-c of Conv Distr of Covingham Swindon 65-66; V of Langley Fitzurse (or Kington Langley) Dio Bris from 66; R of Draycot Cerne Dio Bris from 66. *Kington Langley Vicarage, Chippenham, Wilts, SN15 5NJ.* (Kington Langley 231)

GARDNER, Geoffrey Maurice. b 28. K Coll Lon BA (2nd cl Hist) 51. Univ of Dur Dipl Th 59. Cranmer Hall, Dur 57. **d** 59 **p** 60 Bradf. C of St John Bowling 59-62; Asst Master Ch Sch Ado-Ekiti 62-68; Tutor Im Coll Ibad 68-70; Prin 70-72; C of St Luke Bath 72-81. *17 St Winifred's Drive, Combe Down, Bath, Avon.*

GARDNER, Glenn Stewart. Moore Th Coll Syd ACT ThL 69. **d** 69 **p** 70 Syd. C of St Barn, Roseville E 69-72; Eastwood

72-74; R of Lane Cove Dio Syd from 74. *6 Finlayson Street, Lane Cove, NSW, Australia 2066.* (42-1163)

GARDNER, Ian Douglas. b 34. St Pet Hall Ox BA (2nd cl Russian) 58, MA 62. Oak Hill Th Coll 58. **d** 60 **p** 61 Lich. C of Biddulph 60-63; St Jo Evang Weston, Bath 64; L to Offic Dio Nig Delta 65-76; P-in-c of Hurstbourne Tarrant w Faccombe Dio Win 77-79; V (w Vernham Dean and Linkenholt) from 79; P-in-c of Vernham Dean w Linkenholt 78-79. *Hurstbourne Tarrant Vicarage, Andover, Hants.* (Hurstbourne Tarrant 222)

GARDNER, John Ernest. Carleton Univ Ott BA 61. Trin Coll Tor STB 64. Coll of Resurr Mirfield, 61. **d** 64 Bp Snell for Tor **p** 64 Tor. C of St Barn Danforth Tor 64-66; St Mich Cathl Barb 66-67; I of St Jas Humber Bay 67-70; R of St Mark Port Hope 70-79; St Luke Pet Dio Tor from 79. *2708 Farmcrest Avenue, Peterborough, Ont, K9H 1R9, Canada.*

GARDNER, John Philip Backhouse. b 21. St Aid Coll 49. **d** 52 **p** 53 Guildf. C of Ashtead 52-55; Bromley 55-57; V of New Hythe 57-63; St Justus Roch 63-69; V of Wisley w Pyrford Dio Guildf from 69. *Pyrford Vicarage, Aviary Road, Woking, Surrey, GU22 8TH.* (Byfleet 52914)

GARDNER, Leslie John Thomas. b 15. Wells Th Coll 68. **d** 69 **p** 70 Ex. C of Tiverton 69-70; Thornton 70-72; C-in-c of Wilne w Draycott 72-74; C of Fordingbridge w Ibsley 74-75; Welwyn 75-78; Em Plymouth Dio Ex from 78. *22 Lisson Grove, Mutley, Plymouth, Devon.* (Plymouth 21553)

GARDNER, Paul Douglas. AKC and BA 72. Reformed Th Sem Miss USA MDiv 79. Ridley Hall Cam 79. **d** 80 **p** 81 Ely. C of St Martin Cam Dio Ely from 80. *31 Kelvin Close, Cambridge, CB1 4DN.*

GARDNER, Richard Beverley Twynam. b 11. Chich Th Coll 33. **d** 36 **p** 37 Linc. C of St Jo Div Gainsborough 36-38; St Giles Linc 38-39; Horsell 39-42; Chap RNVR 42-46; Perm to Offic at Horsell 46-47; C of Yorktown 47-48; V of St Paul East Molesey 48-54; Botleys w Lyne 54-71; Long Cross 56-71; Ewshott 71-76. *Cappacrucis, Hillside Road, Weybourne, Farnham, Surrey.*

GARDNER, Robert Christopher. b 21. Tufts Univ Mass BA 42. Episc Th Sch Mass STB 52. **d** and **p** 52 Mass. In Amer Ch 52-74; Nat Co-ordinator Inter-Ch Committee Canada for World Development Educn from 75. *c/o 600 Jarvis Street, Toronto, Ont, Canada.*

GARDNER, Robert George. St Pet Coll Ja. **d** 48 Kingston for Ja **p** 49 Ja. C of St Luke Cross Roads 49-51; R of Balaclava 51-53; C of Montego Bay 53; R of St Phil Grimsby Beach 61-73; Cayuga Dio Niag from 74; Dom Chap to Bp Suffr of Niag from 80. *Box 8, Cayuga, Ont., Canada.* (416-772 5077)

GARDNER, Ronald Frederick. b 25. Univ of Dur BA 51, Dipl Th 52. Univ of Man MA 79. **d** 52 Knaresborough for Ripon **p** 53 Ripon. C of Horsforth 52-56; Whitchurch w Dodington 56-58; V of Malins Lee 58-64; R of Talke 64-69; V of Forsbrook Dio Lich from 69. *Forsbrook Vicarage, Stoke-on-Trent, Staffs.* (Blythe Bridge 2259)

GARDNER, Ronald Leslie. b 1885. Late Scho of Qu Coll Cam BA 07. **d** 08 **p** 09 S'wark. C of St Chrys Peckham 08-10; Lavenham 10-14; Hadleigh 14-16; TCF 16-20; R of Chelsworth 20-23; V of Exning w Lanwade 23-38; R of Brandon Ferry w Wangford 38-43; RD of Mildenhall 40-43; V of Foxton w Gumley R 43-55; RD of Gartree i 49-56; R of Stonton Wyville w Glooston (w Slawston and Cranoe from 56) 55-73; C-in-c of Slawston w Cranoe 55-56; L to Offic Dio Leic from 73. *The Cottage, Stonton Wyville, Market Harborough, Leics.*

GARDNER-BROWN, Gerald Edward Miles. b 10. Pemb Coll Cam 3rd cl Hist Trip pt i 31, BA (2nd cl Hist Trip pt ii) 32, MA 38. TD 50. Westcott Ho Cam 32. **d** 34 Newc T **p** 36 Heref. C of H Sav Tynemouth 34-35; Ch Stretton 35-38; R of Pontesbury (3rd portion) 38-48; PC of Longden 38-48; V of Lydbury North 48-77; CF (TA) 39-49; CF (TA - R of O) 49-65; Hon CF from 65; Surr 57-77; P-in-c of Edgton 62-77. *Heathmynd, Mainstone, Bishop's Castle, Salop.* (Bishop's Castle 654)

GARDNER-SMITH, Percival. b 1888. Jes Coll Cam BA (1st cl Th Trip Pt i) and Crosse Scho 09, 1st cl Th Trip pt ii 11, MA 13, BD 27. Ridley Hall Cam 10. **d** 11 **p** 12 Worc. C of New Milverton 11-16; V of Comberton Cambs 16-22; BEF (w CA) 18; Pro-Proc Cam 23-24; Proc 24-25; Dean of Jes Coll Cam 22-56; Fell from 23; Pres 48-58; Lect Univ of Cam 26-53; Select Pr Univ of Cam 34, 38, 45 and 54; Ox 40-42. *Jesus College, Cambridge; and 11 Cranmer Road, Cambridge.* (Cambridge 356028)

GARDOM, Francis Douglas. b 34. Trin Coll Ox BA (3rd Cl Th) 55, MA 59. Wells Th Coll 58. **d** 60 Kingston T for S'wark **p** 61 S'wark. C of Greenwich 60-68; St Steph w St Mark Lewisham Dio S'wark 68-77; Hon C from 77; Publ Pr Dio S'wark from 77. *79 Maze Hill, SE 10.* (01-858 7052)

GAREEBA, Seduraka. **d** 50 **p** 52 Bp Stuart for Ugan. P Dio Ugan 50-60; Dio Ankole-K 60-67; Dio Kig from 67. *Kizinga, PO Box 3, Kabale, Kigezi, Uganda.*

GARGERY, Edwin John. Lich Th Coll. **d** 22 **p** 24 Lich. C of St Mark Wolverhampton 22-25; St Dunstan Cheam 25-33; V of Limpenhoe w Southwood (and Cantley from 40) 33-45; Tong 45-54; Ivinghoe w Pitstone 54-62. *Shepway Lodge, Walmer, Kent.*

GARIHA, Kingsford. **d** 71 Bp Ambo for Papua **p** 72 Papua. P Dio Papua. *Box 36, Popondota, Papua, New Guinea.*

GARLAND, Christopher John. b 47. Univ of Ex BA (Th) 69, PhD 72. Qu Coll Birm 78. **d** 80 **p** 81 Roch. C of St Jas Elmers End Beckenham Dio Roch from 80. *6 Lloyds Way, Elmers End, Beckenham, Kent.*

GARLAND, Deryck Barnard. b 16. Late Scho of Worc Coll Ox 2nd cl Cl Mods 37, BA (3rd cl Lit Hum) 39, Dipl Th 40, MA 46. Wycl Hall Ox 39. **d** 41 **p** 42 Liv. C of St Jo Evang Ravenhead 41-43; St Luke Gt Crosby 43-48; Blundellsands (in c of St Steph Hightown) 48-51; V of St Mary Bootle and Chap Bootle Gen Hosp 51-57; V of All S Southport 57-65; R of Kirkandrews-on-Eden w Beaumont and Grinsdale 65-72; V of Wreay Dio Carl from 72; Chap of Cumb Infirm from 71. *Wreay Vicarage, Carlisle, Cumb, CA4 0RL.* (Southwaite 463)

GARLAND, Harry Earle. b 01. St Bonif Coll Warm. **d** 49 **p** 50 St E. C of H Trin and St Mary Bungay 49-50; V of Parham w Hacheston 51-69. *Rose Cottage, Hacheston, Woodbridge, Suff.* (Framlingham 723561)

GARLAND, James Ralph. b 39. Gordon Coll Mass BA (Hist) 64. Wycl Coll Tor LTh and BTh 67, ThM 75. **d** 67 **p** 68 Tor. C of Coburg 67-69; R of Cavan Tor 69-73; on leave 73-75; I of St Steph Beverley Hills City and Dio Tor from 75. *2259 Jane Street, Downsview, Ont, Canada.*

GARLAND, Michael. b 50. St D Coll Lamp Dipl Th 72. Sarum Wells Th Coll 72. **d** 73 **p** 74 Swan B. C of St Thos Swansea w Kilvey 73-76; Boldmere 76-79; V of Kingshurst Dio Birm from 79. *Vicarage, Overgreen Drive, Kingshurst, Birmingham, B37 6EY.* (021-770 3972)

GARLAND, Peter. b 32. **d** 75 **p** 76 S Malawi. P Dio S Malawi. *c/o PO Kasupe, Malawi.*

GARLICK, David. b 37. Univ of Nottm BA Th) 62. St Steph Ho Ox 62. **d** 64 **p** 65 S'wark. C of St Jo Div Kennington 64-66; Hon C of St Paul Newington and Warden Crossed Swords Youth Centre Lorrimore Square 66-68; C-in-c of St Pet Vauxhall 68-79; V of Lewisham Dio S'wark from 79. *48 Lewisham Park, SE13 6QZ.* (01-690 2682)

GARLICK, Ernest Victor. b 04. Worc Ordin Coll 64. **d** 65 **p** 66 Ex. [f Congregational Min] C of Budleigh Salterton 65-68; R of Down St Mary w Clannaborough 68-73; Perm to Offic Dio Ex from 73. *17 School Close, Shobrooke, Crediton, Devon.* (Crediton 4042)

GARLICK, Peter. b 34. K Coll Lon and Warm AKC 57. **d** 58 **p** 59 Bris. C of St Mark Swindon 58-63; R of St Thos w H Trin and of St Anne St Kitts 63-66; V of Heyside 66-73; R of All SS Stretford 73-79; M Gen Syn Man 75-79; V of Dustan Dio Pet from 79; RD of Wootton from 79; Surr from 79. *Duston Vicarage, Northampton, NN5 6JB.* (Northampton 52591)

GARLICK, Canon Wilfrid. b 10. Qu Silver Jubilee Med 77. Univ of Man BSc 31, MA (*hon causa*) 68. Egerton Hall Man 31. **d** 33 **p** 34 Man. C of St Andr Ancoats 33-35; St Clem Chorlton-cum-Hardy 35-38; R of St Nich Burnage 38-44; Sec Man Dioc Youth Coun 43-44; V of St Geo Sheff 44-48; St Geo Stockport 48-75; Hon Can of Ches from 58; RD of Stockport 64-72; Chap to HM the Queen 64-80; R of Alderley Dio Ches from 75. *Rectory, Nether Alderley, Macclesfield, Chesh.* (Alderley Edge 3134)

GARMAN, Canon Bernard Wilfred. b 16. Edin Th Coll 47. **d** 49 **p** 50 Edin. C of St Mary Grangemouth 49-51; Rothbury 51-57; R of Bellingham 57-66; V of (Bywell to 73) w Riding Mill 66-77; Hon Dioc Tr Asst Newc T Dioc Educn Bd from 77; Hon Can of Newc T from 77. *Thropton Hill, Physic Lane, Thropton, Morpeth, Northumberland, NE65 7HU.* (Rothbury 20840)

GARNER, Carl. Rhodes Univ BA (1st cl Eccles Hist) 62. Keble Coll Ox BA (2nd cl Th) 65. St Paul's Coll Grahmstn 66. **d** 67 **p** 68 Pret. C of Pietersburg 67-71; R of Louis Trichardt 71-75; Chap St Paul Th Coll Grahmstn from 75. *St Paul's College, PO Box 77, Grahamstown 6140, S Africa.*

GARNER, David Henry. b 40. Trin Coll Bris 70. **d** 73 **p** 74 Man. C of Tunstead 73-75; Fazeley and of Drayton Bassett 75-78; V of Sparkhill Dio Birm from 78. *St John's Vicarage, Phipson Road, Sparkhill, Birmingham, B11 4JE.* (021-449 2760)

GARNER, Eric. St Francis Coll Sekhukhuniland. **d** 65 **p** 66 Pret. Dioc Sec Dio Pret 65-75; C of Irene 66-70; R of Pretoria N w Brits 70-75; Sundays River Valley 75-79; Alexandria w Kinkelbos and Paterson Dio Port Eliz from 79. *Box 13, Alexandria, CP, S Africa.*

GARNER, Geoffrey Walter. b 40. Ripon Hall Ox 69. **d** 71

p 72 Cov. C of St Mich Stoke 71-76; V of Tile Hill 76-80; Team V of Hackney Dio Lon from 80. *21 Blurton Road, E5 0NL.* (01-986 4348)

GARNER, Gordon George. Univ of Melb BA 60. Ridley Coll Melb ThL 49. Melb Coll of Div BD 67. **d** 49 Bal **p** 51 Melb. C of Warrnambool 49-51; V of Sale 51-53; Cann River 53-55; Lect Archaeol Soc of Melb 55-66; Univ of Melb 57-60; Perm to Offic Dio Melb 60-66; Tutor Ridley Coll Melb 66-73; C of Doncaster 66-73; on leave 73-75; Perm to Offic Dio Melb from 76. *c/o 104 Grandview Grove, Rosanna, Vic, Australia 3084.* (45-1521)

GARNER, Martin Wyatt. b 39. Sarum Th Coll 66. **d** 66 Sarum for Connor **p** 67 Connor. C of Coleraine 66-70; St Martin Cam 70-72; V of St Nath Windsor W Derby 72-73; St Nath (Windsor from 75) Edge Hill 72-80; C-in-c of Burton Dio Carl from 80. *Vicarage, Burton-in-Westmorland, Carnforth, Lancs, LA6 1NW.* (Burton 781391)

GARNER, Canon Maurice Heath. b 08. Em Coll Cam BA 30, MA 34. Ridley Hall Cam 30. **d** 32 Warrington for Liv **p** 33 Man for Liv. C of St Chrys Everton 32-34; Miss W Nile Distr Ugan 34-39; V of Whittle-le-Woods 39-47; R of St Mary Weymouth 47-70; Surr from 51; Hon Chap to Bp of Sarum 53-70; Chap Weymouth Distr Hosp 58-61; Can and Preb of Sarum 61-70; Can (Emer) from 71; Proc Conv Sarum 64-70; V of Steyning 71-78; R of Ashurst 71-78. *3 Southfield Avenue, Weymouth, Dorset.*

GARNER, Peter. b 33. BSc (Lon) 56. Wycl Hall Ox 56. **d** 58 **p** 59 Chelmsf. C of St Jo Evang Walthamstow 58-61; Min of St Paul's Eccles Distr Hainault 61-63; V 63-70; R of Theydon Garnon 70-73; P-in-c of Kirby-le-Soken Dio Chelmsf 73-74; V from 74. *Vicarage, Thorpe Road, Kirby Cross, Essex, CO13 0LT.* (Frinton-on-Sea 5997)

GARNER, Richard. b 43. K Coll Lon and Warm. **d** 69 Bp Ramsbotham for Newc T **p** 70 Newc T. C of Tynemouth Dio Newc T 69-73; St Jas and St Basil Newc T 73-76; V of St Bernard Hamstead 76-80; Greytown Dio Wel from 81. *Vicarage, West Street, Greytown, NZ.* (Greytown 44)

GARNER, Rodney George. b 48. Univ of Birm Dipl Th 77. Qu Coll Birm 75. **d** 78 Birkenhead for Ches **p** 79 Ches. C of St Paul w St Luke Higher Tranmere 78-81; V of St Thos Eccleston Dio Liv from 81. *21 St George's Road, St Helens, Mer.* (St Helens 22295)

GARNETT, David Christopher. b 45. Univ of Nottm BA 67. Fitzw Coll Cam (Th Trip pt iii) BA 69, MA 73. Westcott Ho Cam 67. **d** 69 **p** 70 York. C of Cottingham 69-72; Fell and Chap of Selw Coll Cam 72-77; R of Patterdale 77-80; Dir of Ordinands Dio Carl 78-80; V of Heald Green Dio Ches from 80. *Vicarage, Outwood Road, Heald Green, Cheadle, Chesh, SK8 3JS.* (061-437 4614)

GARNETT, James Arthur. b 42. N Ordin Course 77. **d** 80 **p** 81 Liv. C of St Mark Kirkby Dio Liv from 80. *12 Melling Way, Old Hall Estate, Kirkby, Merseyside, L32 1TP.*

GARNETT, Joseph William. b 20. AKC (1st cl) 48. Edin Th Coll 48. **d** 49 **p** 50 Glas. C of St Mary's Cathl Glas 49-51; P-in-c of St Matt Possilpark Glas 51-56; R of Montrose w Inverbervie 56-64; V of Flookburgh 64-69; St Aid w Ch Ch Carl 69-73; R of Nairn 73-78; St Jo Evang Greenock 78-80; Castle Douglas Dio Glas from 80. *St Ninian's Rectory, Whitepark Road, Castle Douglas, Kirk, DG7 1EX.* (Castle Douglas 2424)

GARNETT, Peter. b 17. Bps' Coll Cheshunt 49. **d** 51 Whitby for York **p** 52 York. C of South Bank 51-55; Miss P w SA Rly Miss Dio Pret 55-57; w Rhod and Nyasa Rly Miss Dios Matab and N Rhod 57-58; C of Blechingley 59-61; St Matt Lomagundi 61-64; Asst P at Fort Vic 64-65; C-in-c of St Marg Burnley 67-69; C of St Mary and All SS Cathl Salisbury Mashon 69-71; Malden 73-77; Headington Quarry Dio Ox from 77. *20 Binswood Avenue, Headington, Oxford.* (Oxford 68509)

GARNETT, Ralph Henry. b 28. Cudd Coll 58. **d** 60 **p** 61 Heref. C of Broseley w Benthall 60-64; V of Leintwardine w Adforton 64-69; C-in-c of Downton-on-the-Rock w Burrington Aston and Elton 66-69; R of Burford 2nd Portion, Whitton w Greete and Hope Bagot 69-74; V of Tenbury Wells 69-74; R of Burford 3rd Portion w L Heref 69-74; RD of Ludlow 72-75; C-in-c of Burford 1st Portion, Nash and Boraston 72-74; R of Tenbury Wells Team Min Dio Heref from 74. *Vicarage, Tenbury Wells, Worcs.* (Tenbury Wells 810702)

✠ **GARNSEY, Right Rev David Arthur.** Univ of Syd BA (1st cl Lat and Gr) 30. Rhodes Scho 31. New Coll Ox BA (2nd cl Lit Hum) 33, 2nd cl Th 34, MA 37. ACT ThD (*hon causa*) 55. Ripon Hall Ox 33. **d** 34 **p** 35 Ox. C of St Mary Virg (Univ Ch) Ox 34-38; St Sav Cathl Goulb 38-41; R of Young 41-45; Gen Sec Austr SCM 45-48: Exam Chap to Bp of Goulb 39-45; and 48-58: Perm to Offic Dios Melb and Goulb 45-48; Hd Master Canberra Gr Sch 48-58; Can of St Sav Cathl Goulb 49-58; Cons Ld Bp of Gippsld in St Paul's Cathl Melb 2 Feb 59 by Abp of Melb; Bps of C & Goulb; Tas; Wang; Graft; St Arn; and Bend; and Bps McKie; Omari; Booth; Stephenson; Blackwood; and Reading; res 74; Perm to Offic Dio C & Goulb from 74. *33 Dutton Street, Dickson, ACT, Australia 2602.*

GARNSEY, George Christopher. Univ of Syd BA 58. Qu Coll Ox BA 63. **d** and **p** 60 C & Goulb. C of St Phil Canberra 60; Wagga Wagga 60-61; St Phil Canberra 64-68; Chap Austrn Nat Univ 68-71; L to Offic Dio Goulb 71-75; R of St Phil Canberra 75-78; on leave 78-80; Prin St Jo Coll Morpeth from 80. *St John's College, Morpeth, NSW, Australia 2321.*

✠ **GARNSWORTHY, Most Rev Lewis Samuel.** Univ of Alta BA 43. Wycl Coll Tor DD (*hon causa*) 69. **d** 45 Tor for NS **p** 46 Tor. C of St Jo Bapt Tor 45-48; R of Birchcliffe 48-56; Transfig Tor 56-60; St John York Mills Tor 60-68; Hon Can of Tor 64-68; Cons Ld Bp Suffr of Tor in St Jas Cathl Tor 30 Nov 68 by Abp of Alg; Bps of Tor; Hur; Ont; Moos; and Ott; Bps Suffr of Moos; Tor; and Hur (Appleyard and Queen); Bps of W New York (USA); Erie (USA) and Bps Nieminski (Polish Nat Catholic Ch) and Wilkinson; Apptd Bp of Tor 72; Elected Abp and Metrop of Prov of Ont 80; R of H Trin City and Dio Tor from 77. *135 Adelaide Street East, Toronto, Ont., Canada.* (416-363 6021)

GARRARD, Horace George. M SSJE 43. **d** 41 **p** 43 Alg. SSJE Miss at Bracebridge Dio Alg from 43. *Mission House, Bracebridge, Ont., Canada.* (705 645 5291)

GARRARD, Canon Richard. b 37. K Coll Lon and Warm BD and AKC 60. **d** 61 **p** 62 S'wark. C of Woolwich 61-66; St Mary Gt Cam 66-68; Chap and Lect Keswick Hall Coll Nor 68-74; Prin CA Tr Coll Blackheath 74-79; Dir of Tr Dio S'wark from 79; Can and Chan of S'wark Cathl from 79. *29 Shooter's Hill Road, SE3.* (01-858 1514)

GARRARD, Robert Ernest. b 12. St Aid Coll 37. **d** 39 **p** 40 Bradf. C of St John Clayton 39-41; V of St Andr Bradf 41-45; PC of St John Wimborne 45-65; Asst Sec BFBS and L to Offic Dio Sarum 65-80; Perm to Offic Dio Sarum from 80. *Firswood, Colehill, Wimborne, Dorset.* (Wimborne 882590)

GARRATT, Bernard John. b 43. BA (2nd cl French) Lon 65. Linacre Coll Ox BA (2nd cl Th) 67, MA 71. St Steph Ho Ox 65. **d** 68 Kens for Lon **p** 69 Lon. C of St Jo Evang Notting Hill Kens 68-71; Fareham (in c of St Francis Funtley) 71-73; Chap City of Lon Poly 73-79; V of H Trin Trowbridge Dio Sarum from 79. *Holy Trinity Vicarage, Trowbridge, BA14 9AA.* (Trowbridge 3326)

GARRATT, David. b 44. K Coll Lon and Warm AKC (2nd cl) 68. **d** 69 Southw **p** 70 Sherwood for Southw. C of St Andr Nottm 69-71; St Matt Boughton and Ollerton 71-75; V of Esh 75-79; Hamsteels 75-79; Woodborough Dio Southw from 79. *Woodborough Vicarage, Nottingham, NG14 6DX.* (Nottm 652250)

GARRATT, George. Wycl Coll Tor. **d** 56 **p** 57 Tor. C of St D Lawrence Avenue Tor 56-57; St Columba Tor 57-59; I of Apsley 59-63; St Timothy-by-the-Humber Tor 63-72; Lucknow Dio Hur from 72. *Box 402, Lucknow, Ont., Canada.* (519-528 2339)

GARRATT, John William. b 11. **d** and **p** 78 Kens for Lon. C of H Trin Hounslow Dio Lon from 78. *183 Bath Road, Hounslow, TW3 3BU.* (01-570 6009)

GARRATT, Peter James. b 37. ALCD 64. **d** 64 **p** 65 Southw. C of Bingham 64-67; Mansfield 67-69; V of St Andr Purlwell, Batley 69-73; R of Kirk Sandall (and Edenthorpe from 79) Dio Sheff from 73. *Kirk Sandall Rectory, Doncaster, Yorks.* (Doncaster 882861)

GARRATT, Roger Charles. b 50. St Jo Coll Dur BA 72, Dipl Th 73. Cranmer Hall Dur 73. **d** 74 Cov **p** 75 Bp McKie for Cov. C of St Paul Leamington 74-77; Chap Emscote Lawn Sch Warwick from 77. *16 Hadrian Close, Lillington, Leamington Spa, CV32 7ED.*

GARRAWAY, James. d 78 Windw I. C of Canouan The Grenadines, S Vinc Dio Windw I from 78. *Canouan, S Grenadines, St Vincent, W Indies.*

GARRETT, Christopher Hugh Ahlan. b 35. Sarum Wells Th Coll 72. **d** 75 **p** 76 Cant. C of St Mildred Addiscombe 75-81; V of St Jude w St Aidan Thornton Heath Dio Cant from 81. *11 Dunheved Road North, Thornton Heath, Surrey, CR4 6AH.* (01-684 1630)

GARRETT, Edgar Ashton. b 20. SOC 62. **d** 65 **p** 66 Guildf. C of Horsell 65-70; V of Send 70-79; Asst Master Chich High Sch for Boys from 79. *14 Crosbie Close, Chichester, W Sussex.* (Chich 789770)

GARRETT, Canon Frederick Henry. b 18. Trin Coll Dub BA 43. **d** 43 **p** 44 Down. C of Dromore 43-45; Rathkeale and Nantenan 45-49; I of Murragh w Killowen 49-55; Mallow U (w Kilshannig from 57. Castlemanger from 71) 55-74; RD of Midleton 65-75; I of Glengariff w Berehaven Dio Ross from 74; Can of Dromdaleague and Kilnaglory in Cork Cathl and of Island in Ross Cathl from 76. *Rectory, Glengariff, Co Cork, Irish Republic.* (Glengariff 36)

GARRETT, Canon John Charles. Trin Coll Tor BA 43. Bp's Univ Lennox LST 47. **d** 47 **p** 48 Ott. C of Cornwall 47-49; I of Lanark 49-53; North Gower 54-56; Hawkesbury 56-60; R of St Richard Ott 60-69; St Pet Brockville 69-80; Dom Chap to Bp of Ont 76-80; Can of Ont from 77. *RR1 Oxford Station, Ont, Canada.*

GARRETT, Canon John Robert. b 12. Hertf Coll Ox BA 34, MA 43. Cudd Coll 35. **d** 36 **p** 37 Chelmsf. C of Ascen Vic Dks 36-42; Org Sec Ely Dioc Youth Coun and L to Offic Dio Ely 42-45; R of Eynesbury 45-52; Proc Conv Ely 50-55; R of Hilgay 52-60; Papworth Everard 60-81; Rd of Bourn 62-72; Hon Can of Ely from 74. *15 Shelford Park Avenue, Great Shelford, Cambridge, CB2 5LU.*

GARRETT, John Watkins. b 09. St Chad's Coll Dur BA 35. **d** 36 **p** 37 Leic. C of St Mary de Castro Leic 36-38; H Trin Win 38-42; Staveley 42-44; St Barn Derby 44-48; V of St Jas Aylestone Pk Leic 48-59; Chap Carlton Hayes Ment Hosp Narborough from 54; Enderby Ho Narborough 61-71; R of Narborough 59-75; L to Offic Dio Leic from 75. *5 Keats Close, Enderby, Leicester, LE9 5QP.* (0533-864666)

GARRETT, William Edward Richard. b 29. Trin Coll Dub. **d** 67 **p** 68 Kilm. C of Drumlease 67-71; I of Kildallon w Newtowngore and Corrawallen 72-75; Bailieborough w Mullagh Dio Kilm from 75; Knockbride w Shercock Dio Kilm from 75. *Rectory, Bailieborough, Co Cavan, Irish Republic.* (Bailieborough 36)

GARRITY, Canon Robert Pete. b 15. St Jo Coll NZ. **d** 42 **p** 43 Wai. C of Tauranga 42-44; Hd Master St Patr Scho Lolawai 44-47; C of St Mary's Cathl Parnell 47-48; V of Birkenhead NZ 48-50; Miss at Honiara 50-53; R of Cathl, Honiara 53-56; Deputn Sec Melan Miss Lon 56-57; Gen Sec 57-75; Hon Can of St Barn Cathl Honiara from 58; Perm to Offic Dio S'wark from 76; Dio Chich from 80. *Address temp unknown.*

GARSIDE, Canon Howard. b 24. Univ of Leeds BA 49. Coll of Resurr Mirfield, 49. **d** 51 **p** 52 Wakef. C of St Pet Barnsley 51-53; St Barn Linthorpe Middlesbrough 53-56; V of St Aid Middlesbrough 56-64; Manston 64-78; RD of Whitkirk 70-78; V of St Wilfrid and St Luke from 80) Harrogate Dio Ripon from 78; P-in-c of St Luke Harrogate 78-80; Hon Can of Ripon from 78. *51b Kent Road, Harrogate, N Yorks, HG1 2EU.* (Harrogate 503259)

GARSTIN, Norman Elliott. Trin Coll Dub BA and Div Test 18, MA 23. **d** 18 **p** 19 Clogh. C of Monagnan 18-20; Castlerock 20-24; C-in-c of Moville U 24-27; I of Drumholm (w Rossnowlagh from 42) 27-58; Can of Raph Cathl 57-58. *Main Street, Ballintra, Co Donegal, Irish Republic.*

GARTON, Derek John. b 33. ALCD 59. **d** 59 Roch **p** 60 Tonbridge for Cant. C of St Aug Bromley Common 59-62; St Aid Gravesend 62-66; Hon C of Gravesend 66-73; Chap Plymouth Coll and Perm to Offic Dio Ex from 77. *Mannamead Flat, Ford Park, Plymouth.* (Plymouth 28239)

GARTON, John Henry. b 41. Worc Coll Ox BA 66, Dipl Th 67, Ellerton Pri 68. Cudd Coll 67. **d** 69 Ox for Cant. CF 69-73; Lect Linc Th Coll 73-78; R of Cov E Team Min Dio Cov from 78. *St Peter's Rectory, Charles Street, Coventry, CV1 5NP.* (Coventry 25907)

GARTON, Richard John. b 07. Late Scho of Worc Coll Ox 2nd cl Cl Mods 28, 2nd cl Th 30, BA 31, MA 39. Egerton Hall, Man 30. **d** 31 **p** 32 Blackb. C of Cathl Ch Blackb 31-36; PC of Longton 36-42; R of High Ham (w Low Ham Chap from 43) 42-57; Cameley w Temple Cloud 57-75. *12 Tor Street, Wells, Somt.* (Wells 73762)

✠ **GARTRELL, Right Rev Frederick Roy.** McMaster Univ Ont BA 35. Wycl Coll Tor LTh 38, BD 44, Hon DD 62. **d** 38 **p** 39 Montr. C of St Jas Montr 38-40; I of Noranda 40-44; C of St Paul Tor 44-45; R of St Geo Winnipeg 45-62; Archd of Winnipeg 58-62; Dean and R of Ott Cathl 62-70; Cons Ld Bp of BC in Ch Ch Cathl Vic BC 7 May 70 by Abp of BC; Bps of Koot; Dur; Bps Barfoot; Sexton; Calvert; F H Wilkinson; Greenwood; and Bp of Olympia (USA); res 80; Pres Columb Coast Miss 70-80; Perm to Offic Dio BC from 80. *1794 Barrie Road, Victoria, BC, Canada.* (604-477 3293)

GARUBA, Frederick Ade. b 33. **d** 73 **p** 74 Benin. P Dio Benin. *St James's Church, Ibillo, via Auchi, Nigeria.*

GARWELL, John Arthur. b 25. K Coll Lon and Warm. **d** 52 **p** 53 Ripon. C of St Mark Woodhouse 52-55; St Aid Leeds 55-56; All SS Alton 56-60; Chap RN 60-76; C of St Nicolas Guildf 76-77. *446 Fulham Road, SW6 1DT.* (01-385 2110)

GARWOOD, Albert Wells. Ripon Hall, Ox. **d** 59 Bp Stannard for Roch **p** 60 Roch. C of Dartford 59-60; R of Iken 60-64; C-in-c of Tunstall 60-64; I of St Jo Evang Crapaud 64-66; Musquash 72-75. *20 O'Brien Street, Saint John West, NB, Canada.*

GARWOOD, (Damian) David John Shirley. Univ of Leeds BA (3rd cl Gen) 59. M CR 69. Coll of Resurr Mirfield. **d** 61 **p** 62 Lich. C of Meir 61-66; L to Offic Dio Wakef 67-71; C of Stellenbosch Dio Capetn from 71. *8 Heldenburg Street, Stellenbosch, CP, S Africa.*

GASCOIGNE, Harry. b 1894. K Coll Lon. **d** and **p** 41 Glouc. C of H Trin Cheltm 41-42; R of Stokesby w Herringby 42-53; C-in-c of Rollesby 50-53; R 53-62; C-in-c of Burgh St Marg w Billockby 53-62. *19 Barnfield Road, Harpenden, Herts. AL5 5TH.* (Harpenden 4797)

GASCOIGNE, Philip. b 27. Oak Hill Th Coll. **d** 62 **p** 63 Blackb. C of Ch Ch Blackpool 62-65; V of St Leon Bootle 65-71; Staff Evang CPAS 71-74; V of St Mark St Helens 74-77; Ch Ch (w All SS from 81) Blackpool Dio Blackb from 77. *23a North Park Drive, Blackpool, Lancs.* (Blackpool 31235)

GASH, Wilfred John. b 31. Dipl Th (Lon) 62. St Aid Coll 60. **d** 62 **p** 63 Roch. C of St Mary Cray w St Paul's Cray 62-65; St Jo Evang Bexley 65-67; R of Levenshulme 67-72; V of Clifton City and Dio Man from 72; Area Dean of Eccles from 81. *Vicarage, Clifton, Manchester, M27 2PP.* (061-794 1939)

GASHEGU, Daniel. Warner Mem Coll Ibuye 53. **d** 54 Bp Brazier for Ugan. d Dio Ugan 53-60; Dio Ankole-K 60-67; Dio Ank from 67. *PO Box 129, Mbarara, Uganda.*

GASI, Zeburona. Bp Gwynne Coll Mundri, 61. **d** 65 Sudan. d Dio Sudan. *ECS, Yambio, Equatoria Province, Sudan.*

GASKELL, Anthony. b 17. Pemb Coll Ox BA 42, MA 44. Egerton Hall, Man 40. **d** 43 **p** 44 Wakef. C of St Mich Thornhill 43-46; Castleford 46-48; V of Airedale w Fryston 48-51; R of High Hoyland 51-60; V of Clifton-in-Workington 60-68; Rampside 68-76; Dendron 68-76; P-in-c of Aldingham 74-76; R of Aldingham and Dendron and Rampside Dio Carl from 76. *Aldingham New Rectory, Ulverston, Cumb, LA12 9RT.* (Bardsea 305)

GASKELL, David. b 48. BD (Lon) 76. Trin Coll Bris 72. **d** 76 **p** 77 Liv. C of Ch Ch Eccleston 76-80; Rainhill Dio Liv from 80. *72 Bishopdale Drive, Rainhill, Prescot, Mer.* (051-426 7276)

GASKELL, Ian Michael. b 51. Univ of Nottm BTh 81. Linc Th Coll 77. **d** 81 Wakef. C of St Jo Bapt City and Dio Wakef from 81. *47 Newton Close, Newton Hill, Wakefield, WF1 2QQ.*

GASKELL, John Bernard. b 28. Jes Coll Ox BA (2nd cl Th) 52, MA 58. Chich Th Coll 59. **d** 60 Tonbridge for Cant **p** 61 Tonbridge for Roch. C of St Jas Elmers End Beckenham 60-64; All SS Margaret Street St Marylebone 64-68; St Geo Hanover Square (in c of Grosvenor Chap) and Warden Liddon Ho 68-79; V of St Alb Mart Holborn w St Pet Saffron Hill Dio Lon from 79; Area Dean of S Camden from 81. *St Alban's Clergy House, Brooke Street, EC1N 7RD.* (01-405 1831)

GASKILL, Ernest Raymond. b 17. St Chad's Coll Dur BA (2nd cl Hist) 39, Dipl Th 41, MA 42. **d** 41 **p** 42 Sheff. C of St Hilda Shiregreen Sheff 41-43; Wath-on-Dearne 43-46; Perm to Offic at H Redeemer Clerkenwell 46-47; H Cross Greenford (in c of St Edw Perivale Park) 47-53; V of Goldthorpe Sheff 53-62; Chap Mampong Conv and L to Offic Dio Accra 62-63; V of St Cuthb Birkby Huddersfield 63-66; Ch Ch Doncaster Dio Sheff from 66. *45 Thorne Road, Doncaster, Yorks.* (Doncaster 4271)

GASON, Edward John Garratt. St Jo Coll Morpeth ThL 64. **d** 66 **p** 67 Melb. C of Moorabbin 66-67; Niddrie 67-69; Belmont 69-70; P-in-c of Inverleigh 70-71; I 71-81; Em Oakleigh Dio Melb from 81. *26 Abbeygate Street, South Oakleigh, Vic, Australia 3167.*

GASON, John Vance. Ridley Coll Melb 26. ACT ThL 31. **d** 31 **p** 33 Melb. C of H Trin Coburg 31-33; St Geo Malvern 33-34; St Pet w St Mary Marlborough 34-36; Asst Chap St Andr Lah 36-38; Chap Dagshai 38-39; Asst Chap (Eccles Est) Quetta 39-43; Simla 43-44; Ferozepur 44-46; Simla 46-47; Hon CF 46; furlough 48; Perm to offic Dio Natal 48-49; Dio Melb 49-52; V of Ch Ch Hawthorn 52-59; I of All SS Geelong 59-77; Actg Archd of Geelong 70-71; Archd 71-77; Perm to Offic Dio Melb from 77. *St George's Vicarage, Queenscliff, Vic, Australia 3225.* (052-52 1532)

GATABAZI, James. **d** 65 Rwanda B **p** 66 Rwa. P Dio Rwa 65-75; Dio Kiga from 75. *Anglican Church, PO Box 43, Gikongero, Rwanda, Centr Africa.*

GATAMBO, Julius. b 39. St Paul's Coll Limuru 70. **d** 72 **p** 74 Mt Kenya. P Dio Mt Kenya 72-75; Dio Mt Kenya S from 75. *Box 31, Murang'a, Kenya.*

GATANAZI, Emmanuel. b 53. **d** 79 Kiga. d Dio Kiga. *BP 61. Kigali, Rwanda.*

GATE, Alan Bertram. Univ of Queensld BA 62. St Francis Coll Brisb. ACT ThL (2nd cl) 60. **d** 60 **p** 61 Brisb. C of All SS Chermside Brisb 60-62; St Jas Toowoomba 62-64; V of Miles 64-67; Miss N Guinea 67-69; R of Eidsvold w Mundubbera 69-73; Cleveland Dio Brisb from 73. *Rectory, Cross Street, Cleveland, Queensland, Australia 4163.* (286 1037)

GATEHOUSE, Arthur Ferdinand. b 1900. St Aid Coll. **d** 25 **p** 26 Heref. C of Ross 26-28; TCF Aldershot 28; CF 28-47; V of Piddington 47-76; V of Ambrosden 49-72; Perm to Offic

Dio Ox from 76. *The Glebe Cottage, Bucknell, Bicester, Oxon.*

GATENBY, Denis William. b 31. Ex Coll Ox BA (2nd cl Mod Lang) 54, Dipl Th (w distinc) 55, MA 58. Wycl Hall Ox 54. **d** 56 **p** 57 Man. C of Deane 56-60; Bradf Cathl 60-63; V of St Matt Bootle 63-72; Horwich Dio Man from 72. *Vicarage, Horwich, Lancs.* (Horwich 68263)

GATENBY, Paul Richard. b 32. Univ of Dur BA 55. Univ of Birm Dipl Th 64. Qu Coll Birm 62. **d** 64 **p** 65 Pet. C of St Barn Wellingborough 64-68; V of Braunston w Brooke 68-71; C of Langley Marish 71-72; Team V of Laindon w Basildon 72-77; R of Isham w Pytchley Dio Pet from 77. *Isham Rectory, Kettering, Northants, NN14 1HQ.* (Burton Latimer 2371)

GATER, William George Herbert. b 05. AKC 35. Chich Th Coll 35. M SSJE 60. **d** 35 Bp Crick for Derby **p** 36 Derby C of H Trin Ilkeston 35-38; Perm to Offic Dio Ox 38-40; Chap RNVR 40-46; Chap Heritage Craft Sch 46-49; C of Abourthorne 49; V of Codnor 49-55; PC of Chinley w Buxworth 55-60; L to Offic Dio Ox 60-67; Dio Lon from 76. *22 Great College Street, SW1P 3QA.*

GATES, Alan Clason. b 07. Late Exhib of CCC Cam 2nd cl Hist Trip pt i 28, BA (3rd cl Th Trip pt i) 30, MA 33. Ely Th Coll 30. **d** 31 Win **p** 32 Southn for Win. C of Eastleigh 31-33; Chap to Bp of Lah and Chap at Moghalpura 33-36; C of St Alb Bournemouth 36-37; Chap RAF 37-46; Men in Disp 43; R of Lambourne w Abridge and Asst Master Chigwell Sch 46-49; R of Wanstead 49-62; RD of Wanstead and Woodford 53-62; Walsingham 62-70; Hon Can of Chelmsf 61-62; R of Blakeney Group (R of Blakeney w Langham Parva from 62) 64-74; C-in-c of Stiffkey w Morston 62-74; Hindringham w Binham and Cockthorpe 64-67; Barningham w Matlaske 76-79; Chap Runton Hill Sch from 78. *Runton Hill School, West Runton, Cromer, Norf.* (W Runton 661)

GATES, Alan Michael. b 43. St Steph Ho Ox 64. **d** 67 **p** 68 S'wark. C of St Jo Evang E Dulwich 67-69; St Marg King's Lynn 69-71; Hon Min Can of Worc Cathl 73-78; Chap at Muscat Oman 78-80; C M S Miss, Sultanate of Oman Dio Cyprus from 80. *Box 4982, Ruwi, Sultanate of Oman.*

GATES, Andrew Edward. b 43. Univ of BC BA 70. Vanc Sch of Th STB 71. **d** 71 **p** 72 BC. I of Gold River 72-77; R of Cordova Bay Dio BC from 77. *5186 Cordova Bay Road, Victoria, BC, Canada.* (604-658 8078)

GATES, Charles John Newton. b 1898. Univ of Lon Dipl Th 49. LCP 41. **d** 53 St E **p** 54 Bp HA Wilson for St E. C of St Jo Evang Bury St Edms 53-55; R of Elveden 55-68; Hon C of St Jo Bapt Felixstowe Dio St E from 69. *42 Brook Lane, Felixstowe, Suff.* (Felixstowe 5016)

GATES, Edward Hugh Mitchell. b 43. St Paul's Coll Grahmstn 77. **d** 79 **p** 80 Grahmstn. C of St Sav E Lon Dio Grahmstn from 79. *66 Recreation Road, Southernwood, E London 5201, CP, S Africa.*

GATES, John Michael. b 35. Univ of Dur BA 56, Dipl Th 60. Cranmer Hall, Dur 58. **d** 60 Dunwich for St E **p** 61 St E. C of St Jo Bapt Felixstowe 60-67; R of Boyton w Capel St Andr and Hollesley Dio St E from 67. *Hollesley Rectory, Woodbridge, Suff, IP12 3RE.* (Shottisham 252)

GATES, John Richard. b 47. Oak Hill Coll Dipl Th 73. **d** 73 **p** 74 Ox. C of Iver 73-76; Broadwater (in c of St Steph) 76-79; Dioc Youth Officer Dio Nor 79-81; V of Cosby Dio Leic from 82. *Cosby Vicarage, Leicester, LE9 5UU.* (0533-862313)

GATES, Kenneth George. AKC 13. **d** 14 **p** 15 Lon. C of St Luke Milwall 14-17; TCF 17-19; C of St Mary Stafford 19-20; Warrington 20-24; V of St Matt Liv 24-28; CF (TA) from 26; V of St Chad Everton 28-34; Cathl Chap Liv Cathl 31-34; R of Ballaugh IM 34-37; Cler Org Sec CECS Dios Liv Man and Blackb and Publ Pr Dio Man 37-39; Dio Carl 39-42; N Prov 39-42; Pub Pr Dio Ripon 40-42; R of Lightbowne 42-51; V of Armitage Bridge 51-55; R of Kirk Smeaton 55-60; L to Offic Dio Perth from 67. *6 Avon Court, Avonmore Terrace, Mosman Park, W Australia 6012.* (31 4684)

GATES, Peter Harvey. b 34. St Step Ho Ox. **d** 61 **p** 62 Lon. C of St Kath Coleman N Hammersmith 61-65; St Jo Bapt Moordown Bournemouth 65-67; C-in-c of St Alb Conv Distr Godshill 67-71; V of St Phil Earls Court Road Kens 71-75; St Mark S Farnborough Dio Guildf from 75. *Vicarage, St Marks Close, Reading Road, Farnborough, Hants, GU14 6PP.* (Farnborough 44711)

GATFORD, Ian. b 40. K Coll Lon and Warm AKC 65. **d** 67 **p** 68 Southw. C of Clifton w Glapton Dio Southw 67-71; Team V 71-75; V of Sherwood Dio Southw from 75. *Vicarage, Trevose Gardens, Sherwood, Nottingham.* (Nott'm 607547)

GATHERCOLE, Canon John Robert. b 37. Fitzw Ho Cam BA 59, MA 63. Ridley Hall Cam 59. **d** 62 **p** 63 Dur. C of St Nich Dur 62-66; Croxdale 66-69; Social and Industr Adviser to Bp of Dur 66-70; L to Offic Dio Dur 66-70; Industr Chap Redditch and L to Offic Dio Worc from 70; RD of Bromsgrove from 77; Hon Can of Worc Cathl from 80. *182 Birchfield Road, Redditch, Worcs.* (Redditch 45656)

GATHERER, Edward Godson. Codr Coll Barb 47. **d** 51 **p** 52 Barb. C of St Joseph 51-53; V of St Anne Barb 53-59; R of St Andr I and Dio Barb from 59. *St Andrew's Rectory, Barbados, W Indies.*

GATLIFFE, David Spenser. b 45. Keble Coll Ox BA 67. Fitzw Coll Cam BA 69. Westcott Ho Cam 67. **d** 69 Bp Boys for S'wark **p** 70 S'wark. C of Oxted 69-72; Roehampton 72-75; Hon C of St Mich AA S Beddington 75-77; Team V of St Paul Clapham Dio S'wark from 78; P-in-c of Ch Ch & St John Clapham Dio S'wark from 81. *ST Paul's Vicarage, Rectory Grove, SW4 0DX.* (01-622 2128)

GATU, Patteson. MBE 80. St Pet Coll Siota. **d** 52 **p** 57 Melan. P Dio Melan 52-75; Dio Centr Melan from 75; Hd Master Catechists' Sch Melan 57-63. *Aola, Guadalcanal, Solomon Islands.*

GATUNGU, John Isaac. b 43. St Paul's Th Coll Limuru 72. **d** 74 Nak. d Dio Nak 74-78; on leave. *Box 1253, Nakuru, Kenya.*

GAUDIN, William John. NZ Bd of Th Stud LTh 66. Ch Ch Coll. **d** 62 Bp McKenzie for Wel **p** 63 Wel. C of Nae Nae 62-64; Masterton 64-67; P-in-c of Spreydon 67-68; Bishopdale 68-72; V of Oxford-Cust 72-74; Featherston 74-77; N Invercargill Dio Dun from 77. *80 Antrim Street, Invercargill, NZ.* (77-219)

GAUL, Reginald Clifford. Univ of Man BA 34. Lich Th Coll 36. **d** 36 **p** 37 Man. C of St Matt Stretford 36-38; St Jas Milnrow 38-40; All SS Newton Heath 40-42; R of Rand w Fulnetby 48-77; V of Goltho w Bullington 51-77; Perm to Offic Dio Linc from 77. *3 St Helen's Avenue, Lea, Gainsborough, DN21 5EJ.*

GAULT, Cecil. b 1898. CCC Ox BA 26, MA 30. St Steph Ho Ox 25. **d** 26 Willesden for Lon **p** 27 Lon. C of St Mary Somers Town and Asst Miss Magd Coll (Ox) Miss 26-32; V of St Mary Magd Paddington 32-39; St Columba Seaton Burn N Gosforth 40-48; R of Bishopstone w Stratford Tony V 48-51; V of St Mich AA Ch Ch NZ 51-63. *Posbury St Francis, Crediton, Devon, EX17 3QF.* (Crediton 2262)

GAUNT, Arthur Raymond. b 15. St Aid Coll 47. **d** 49 **p** 50 Bradf. C of St Marg Thornbury 49-51; Ch Ch Skipton-in-Craven 51-52; C-in-c of St Jas Conv Distr Pudsey 52-55; V of H Trin Bingley 55-58; Glaisdale 58-63; R of H Trin York 63-66; V of Kexby w Wilberfoss 66-71; Clergy Widows Officer Dio York from 68; St Columb Scarborough 71-78; Clergy Retirement Officer Dio York from 74. *3 Hill Top Close, Embsay, Skipton, N Yorks, BD23 6PA.* (0756-4952)

GAUNT, Eric Emmerson. Sarum Th Coll 65. **d** 67 **p** 68 Lon. C of St Anselm Hatch End 67-74; V of Neasden (w St Paul Oxgate from 80) Dio Lon from 74. *Vicarage, Tanfield Avenue, NW2 7RX.* (01-452 7322)

GAUNT, George Herbert. b 14. **d** 78 **p** 79 Huntingdon for Ely (APM). C of St Edm K Downham Market 78-80; P-in-c of Crimplesham w Stradsett Dio Ely from 80. *Lynwood, Market Lane, Crimplesham, King's Lynn, Norf.*

GAUNT, Canon Howard Charles Adie. b 02. K Coll Cam BA 25, MA 27. Cudd Coll 54. **d** 54 **p** 55 Win. Asst Master Win Coll 53-63; Chap and Sacr of Win Cathl 63-66; Prec 66-73; Hon Can 66-74; Can (Emer) from 74. *57 Canon Street, Winchester, Hants.*

GAUNT, Roger Cecil. b 30. K Coll Cam 2nd cl Cl Trip pt i 51, BA (2nd cl Th Trip pt i) 52. Westcott Ho Cam 53. **d** 55 **p** 56 Dur. C of Barnard Castle 55-58; St Jo Bapt Newc T 58-61; V of St Barn Coulsdon 61-66; St Helier 66-68; R of Limpsfield w Titsey 68-77; Dir Educn Dio St Alb 77-79; Can Res of St Alb Cathl 77-79. *16 Lincoln Road, Dorking, Surrey.*

GAUNTLETT, Gilbert Bernard. b 36. Or Coll Ox 2nd cl Cl Mods 57. BA (2nd cl Lit Hum) 59, Dipl Th (w distinc) 60, MA 62, Wycl Hall Ox 59. **d** 61 **p** 62 Ox. C of Maidenhead (in c of St Mary Magd) 61-64; St Ebbe Ox 64-68; R of St Nich Nottm 68-72; Asst Master Leys High Sch Redditch 73-79; Stourport High Sch from 79. *4 Teal Road, Studley, Warwicks, B80 7LF.*

GAUSDEN, Peter James. b 32. Qu Coll Birm 57. **d** 60 **p** 61 S'wark. C of St Pet Battersea 60-63; St Pet-in-I-of-Thanet 63-68; V of Sturry Dio Cant 68-74; R (w Fordwich and Westbere w Hersden) from 74; C-in-c of Westbere w Hersden 70-74; Fordwich 73-74. *Rectory, Sturry Hill, Sturry, Canterbury, Kent.* (Canterbury 710320)

GAW HTOO, May. b 47. **d** 74 **p** 75 Pa-an. P Dio Pa-an. *c/o Lankoktaya Quarters, Toungoo, Burma.*

GAWE, Ven James. St Pet Coll Alice, 62. **d** 64 **p** 65 Grahmstn. C of St Mich Miss Dio Grahmstn 64-70; R of Zwelitsha 70-75; Can of Grahmstn 74-75; Archd of Mdantsane from 76. *Box 90, Mdantsane, CP, S Africa.*

GAWITH, Alan Ruthven. b 24. Lich Th Coll 54. **d** 56 **p** 57 Carl. C of Appleby 56-59; Newton Aycliffe 59-61; C-in-c of St Jas Conv Distr Owton Manor W Hartlepool 61-67; V of St

Geo Kendal 67-74; LPr Dio Man from 74. *27 Blackfriars Road, Salford, M3 7AQ.* (061-832 5253)

GAWNE, Murray Eden. b 07. Bps' Coll Cheshunt, 34. **d** 35 **p** 36 Chelmsf. C of St Pet Upton Cross 35-37; Saffron Walden 37-40; Chap Toc H for E Anglia 40-43; Perm to Offic Dio Ely 40-43; Chap RAFVR 43-46; R of Heydon w L Chishill 46-56; V of Gt Chishill 47-56; C of Pembroke Berm 57-59; R of Devonshire and Chap Hamilton City Goal Berm 59-66; R of Chilbolton w Wherwell 66-77. *Touch Down, Cow Lane, Kimpton, Andover, Hants.* (Weyhill 2670)

GAWNE-CAIN, John. b 38. G and C Coll Cam BA 61, MA 66. Cudd Coll 74. **d** 76 Dorchester for Ox **p** 77 Ox. C of Cowley 76-80; C-in-c of St Giles City and Dio Ox from 80. *1 Norham Gardens, Oxford, OX2 6PS.* (Oxford 59833)

GAY, Colin James. b 37. St D Coll Lamp BA 63. Chich Th Coll 63. **d** 65 **p** 66 Lon. C of W Hackney 65-69; H Sav Hitchin (in c of St Faith) 69-74; C-in-c of Apsley End 74-80; Team V of Chambersbury, Hemel Hempstead Dio St Alb from 80. *31 Chipperfield Road, Aspley End, Hemel Hempstead, Herts.* (Hemel Hempstead 61610)

GAY, David Charles. b 46. CCC Cam BA (Nat Sc) 68, MA 72, PHD 71. CCC Ox MA, DPhil 79 (by incorp). Dipl Th (Leeds) 74. Coll of Resurr Mirfield 72. **d** 75 **p** 76 Sheff. C of St Mark Broomhall Sheff 75-78; Bp's Chap for Graduates and Libr Pusey Ho Ox 78-80; L to Offic Dio Sheff from 80. *62 Kingfield Road, Sheffield, S11 9AU.*

GAY, John Dennis. b 43. St Pet Coll Ox BA (2nd cl Geog) 64, Dipl Th 65, MA 68, DPhil 69, MSc 78. Ripon Hall Ox 64. **d** 67 **p** 68 Lon. C of St Jas Paddington 67-70; C-in-c 71-72; Chap and Lect Culham Coll of Educn 72-79; Lect Univ of Ox (Educn Stud) 78-80; Dir Culham Coll Inst for Ch Educn from 81. *8 Mattock Way, Abingdon, Oxon, OX14 2PB.* (Abingdon 25662)

GAYA, James Mbuti. b 35. St Bede's Coll Umtata 71. **d** 72 Kimb K **p** 75 St John's. P Dio St John's 72-76; Dio Damar from 76. *c/o Box 57, Windhoek, SW Africa.*

GAYE, Douglas Bruce. b 03. RMC Sandhurst 21. Ridley Hall Cam 52. **d** 53 Ox **p** 54 Chelmsf for Cant. C of H Trin Aylesbury 54-56; V of Gt w L Saling 56-61; R of Wivenhoe 61-75. *39 Horsecastles Lane, Sherborne, Dorset, DT9 6BU.* (Sherborne 2927)

GAYLARD, Horace Malcolm. St Paul's Coll Grahmstn 29, LTh (S Afr) 32. **d** 32 **p** 34 St Jo Kaffr. C of All SS Engcobo 32-35; St Barn Ntlaza 35-36; Clydesdale 36-37; L to Offic Dio Johann 37-38; R of Waterberg Distr (w Potgietersrust from 42) 38-45; Pret W Suburbs 45-48; V of Richmond Natal 49-51; C-in-c of Molepolole 51-52; C of St Jo Bapt Bulawayo 52-53; Hillside 53-54; R of Witbank 54-59; Regent Hill 59-63; L to Offic 67-69; C of Orange Grove 69-71; R of Eersterus w Silverton 71-74. *PO Twenty-Four Rivers, Vaalwater 0530, S Africa.*

GAYLER, Roger Kenneth. b 44. Lich Th Coll 68. **d** 70 **p** 71 Barking for Chelmsf. C of St Anne Chingford 70-75; P-in-c of Marks Gate Chadwell Heath Dio Chelmsf from 75. *187 Rose Lane, Marks Gate, Romford, Essex, RM6 5NR.* (01-599 0415)

GAZE, Canon Arthur Philip Atkinson. St Jo Coll Ox BA 36, MA 47. Linc Th Coll 39. **d** 41 **p** 42 Chelmsf. C of Romford (in c of St Thos and St Geo Noak Hill 44-48) 41-48; Asst Master and Chap Cumnor House Sch 48-50; R of Puttenham w Wanborough 50-57; V of Horsell 57-62; Green I w Brighton 62-64; Exam Chap to Bp of Dun 63-73; V of All SS Dun 64-80; Hon Chap Selw Coll Dun 64-78; Hon Can of Dun from 75; L to Offic Dio Dun 80-81; C of Roslyn Dio Dun from 81. *18 Drivers Road, Maori Hill, Dunedin, NZ.* (774-951)

GAZE, George Henry. St John's Coll Dur BA 50, Dipl Th 51, MA 56. **d** 51 Bp O'Ferrall for Derby **p** 52 Derby. C of Stapenhill 51-55; St Luke Ramsgate 55-56; R of Slaidburn Dio Bradf from 56. *Slaidburn Rectory, Clitheroe, Lancs, BB7 3ER.* (Slaidburn 238)

GAZZARD, Richard George Edward. b 40. Lich Th Coll. **d** 67 **p** 68 S'wark. C of Lewisham 67-71; Ch Ch Milton-next-Gravesend (in c of H Family) 71-74; V of H Family Gravesend 74-79; R (w St Marg Ifield) 79-81; V of Ch Ch S Ashford Dio Cant from 81. *Vicarage, Beaver Road, South Ashford, Kent, TN23 1SR.* (Ashford 20600)

GBAAWA, Obeole. d 72 **p** 73 Sudan. P Dio Sudan 72-76; Dio Yambio from 76. *ECS, Yambio, Sudan.*

GBONDA, Joseph Bockarie. d 66 **p** 67 Sier L. P Dio Sier L. *St Stephen's Vicarage, Gobaru, Sierra Leone.*

GBONIGI, Emmanuel Bolanie. Im Coll Ibad 56. **d** 59 **p** 60 Ibad. P Dio Ibad 59-65; Chap to Bp of Ibad 65-66; Tutor Im Coll City and Dio Ibad from 66; Exam Chap to Bps of Ijebu and Ibad from 77; Ondo from 78; Hon Can of Ibad from 78. *Immanuel College, PO Box 515, Ibadan, Nigeria.*

GEACH, Michael Bernard. b 26. Qu Coll Cam BA 51, MA 56. Westcott Ho Cam 51. **d** 53 Truro **p** 54 Bp Wellington for Truro. C of Kenwyn 53-56; Bodmin and Helland 56-59; R of St Dominic 59-65; Chap Cotehele Ho Chap 60-65; Dioc Youth Chap Bodmin 61-66; V of Linkinhorne Dio Truro from 65. *Linkinhorne Vicarage, Callington, Cornw.* (Rilla Mill 62279)

GEAKE, Christopher Laidman. b 53. St Mich & AA Llan 75. **d** 79 **p** 80 Llan. C of Coity w Nolton 79-81; Newton Nottage Dio Llan from 81. *18 Picton Avenue, Porthcawl, Mid Glam, CF36 3AJ.*

GEAKE, Peter Henry. b 17. Late Exhib of Trin Hall Cam 1st cl Math Trip pt i 37, BA (2nd cl Th Trip pt i) 39, MA 46. Cudd Coll 45. **d** 47 **p** 48 Portsm. C of St Mary Portsea 47-50; St Jas Southbroom Devizes 50-52; R of Clovelly 52-55; Chap Canford Sch 55-62; V of Tattenham Corner and Burgh Heath 62-72; R of Fulbeck 72-82; P-in-c of Carlton Scroop w Normanton 72-82. *c/o Fulbeck Rectory, Grantham, Lincs, NG32 3JS.* (Loveden 72305)

GEAR, John Arthur. b 37. St Aid Coll 62. **d** 64 Bp McKie for Cov. **p** 66 Cov. C of Attleborough 64-66; Attercliffe w Carbrook Sheff 66-68; Sheerness (in c of St Paul) 68-73; Publ Pr and Asst Youth Adv Dio S'wark 73-78; Dioc Youth Officer Dio Lich from 78. *The Old Vicarage, Burnhill Green, Wolverhampton, WV6 7HU.* (Ackleton 618)

GEAR, Michael Frederick. b 34. Univ of Dur BA 59, Dipl Th 61. Cranmer Hall Dur 59. **d** 61 **p** 62 Roch. C of Bexleyheath 61-64; St Aldate Ox 64-67; V of Clubmoor 67-71; R of Avondale 71-76; Tutor Wycliffe Hall Ox 76-80; V of Macclesfield Dio Ches from 80. *85 Beech Lane, Macclesfield, Chesh, SK10 2DZ.* (Macclesfield 26110)

GEARY, Sidney Thomas William. b 11. **d** 80 Bp Mort for Leic **p** 81 Leic (APM). C of Syston Dio Leic from 80. *Cedarwood, Sixhills Road, Ragdale, Melton Mowbray, Leics.*

GEATER, Edgar James. b 01. Late Scho of Peterho Cam BA (Sen Opt) 23, MA 27. Ridley Hall Cam 23. **d** 24 **p** 25 Ex. C of St Andr Plymouth 24-32; V of St Bonif Devonport 32-47; Clavering w Langley 47-53; Min Can of Heref Cathl 53-66; C of Ch Ch Watford 66-70; Perm to Offic Dio Chich from 70. *1 Homestead Cottages, Sea Lane, Ferring, Worthing, W Sussex BN12 5DZ.* (Worthing 501335)

GEBADI, Canon Ephraim. St Paul's Coll Moa I 50. **d** 56 **p** 57 Carp. P Dio Carp from 57; Prec of All S Cathl Thursday I Dio Carp 69-71; Can of Carp from 71; P-in-c of Edward River 74-79; Yam I Dio Carp from 79. *Yam Island, Queensland, Australia.*

GEBAUER, George Gerhart. b 25. Sarum Wells Th Coll 71. **d** 73 **p** 74 Portsm. C of Portsdown 73-78; V of Purbrook Dio Portsm from 78. *Purbrook Vicarage, Portsmouth, Hants.* (Waterlooville 2307)

GEBBIE, John Hewitt. b 05. QUB BA 27. Lon Coll of Div 27. **d** 31 **p** 32 Down. C of St Mary Belf 31-35; St Jude Ballynafeigh 35-36; C-in-c of Ardstraw 36-39; R 39-72; Surr 37-72; RD of Newtownstewart 54-72; Can of Derry 65-72. *5 Princetown Road, Bangor, Co Down, N Ireland.* (Bangor 3489)

GEBBIE, Thomas Wilson. b 06. QUB BA 31. Lon Coll of Div 37. **d** 38 Down **p** 39 Tuam for Down. C of St Phil (Drew Mem) Belf 38-40; Ballymacarrett 40-42; C-in-C of Glenties w Ardara 42-46; I 46-48; C of Ballymacarrett 48-51; I of Kircubbin 51-64. *111 Wiston Avenue, Worthing, Sussex.*

GEDDES, Gordon David. b 38. St Chad's Coll Dur BA (2nd cl Th) 59. Dipl Th 60. **d** 61 **p** 62 Dur. C of St Mary Virg w St Pet Conv Distr Bp Wearmouth 61-65; Jarrow (in c of Monkton) 65-68; Asst Master Crewe Boys Gr Sch 68-78; Ruskin Sch Crewe from 78; L to Offic Dio Ches from 68. *6 Richmond Close, Elworth, Sandbach, Chesh, CW11 9TX.* (Sandbach 7484)

GEDDES, Leonard Frederick. b 05. Late Scho of Pemb Coll Ox Squire Scho 24, 3rd cl Cl Mods 26, BA 29, MA 31. Wycl Hall Ox 28. **d** 29 Roch **p** 30 Bp King for Roch. C of Erith 29-32; CMS Lah 33-34; Dera Ismail Khan 34-36; Chap (Eccles Est) Quetta 36-38; Lah Cathl Prec and Choirmaster 38-39 42-44 and 46; Kohat 39-40 44-46; Simla 40; Hazara 40-42; Gulmarg 44; Hon CF 46; New Delhi Cathl 47; Peshawar w Kabul 47-48; V of St Geo w Steph Sheff 48-50; Wentworth 50-54; R of U Hardres w Stelling 54-60; Bishopsbourne w Kingston 60-73; Perm to Offic Dio Cant from 73; Embassy Chap Algiers 73-74; Tunis 78-79. *8 Burgate House, Canterbury, Kent, CT1 2HB.* (Canterbury 52276)

GEDGE, Peter Maurice Sydney. b 10. K Coll Cam BA 32, MA 39. Coll of Resurr Mirfield 73. **d** 73 Hull for York **p** 74 York. C of Scarborough Dio York from 73; Actg RD of Scarborough from 81. *Pasture Howe, Hutton Buscel, Scarborough, N Yorks, YO13 9LL.* (Scarborough 863151)

GEDGE, Simon John Francis. b 44. Keble Coll Ox BA (2nd cl Th) 67, MA 73. Cudd Coll 67. **d** 69 **p** 70 Birm. C of Perry Barr 69-73; St Andr Handsworth 73-75; V of St Pet Birm 75-81. *60 Lime Tree Avenue, Coventry.*

GEE, Arthur. b 13. ALCD 37. Univ of Lon BD 38. **d** 37 **p** 38 Lon. C of St Luke W Kilburn 37-41; CF 41-47; C of Bilston 47-48; V of Basford Staffs 48-62; R of Hodnet w

Weston-under-Redcastle and Peplow 62-71; V of Moxley 71-75. *5 Newport Croft, Brewood, Stafford, ST19 9DU.* (Brewood 850833)

GEE, Edward. b 28. **d** 61 **p** 62 Wakef. C of Hanging Heaton 61-65; V of Brownhill 65-75; Alverthorpe Dio Wakef from 75. *Alverthorpe Vicarage, St Paul's Drive, Alverthorpe, Wakefield, WF2 0BT.* (Wakefield 71300)

GEE, Frank Richard. Univ of Syd BA 72. ACT ThL 72. BD (Lon) 74. Moore Coll Syd 72. **d** and **p** 74 Syd. C of Beecroft 74-76; CMS Miss from 76. *Box 125, Abepura, Irian Jaya, Indonesia.*

GEE, Michael Terence. b 29. Univ of Dur BSc 54. Tyndale Hall Bris 60. **d** 62 **p** 63 Blackb. C of St Thos Blackpool 62-64; Selston 64-68; V of Brimscombe 68-80; Tidenham w Beachley and Lancaut Dio Glouc from 80. *Tidenham Vicarage, Gloucester Road, Tutshill, Chepstow, Gwent.* (Chepstow 2442)

GEE, Norman. b 11. Univ of Lon BA (2nd cl Phil Hons) 33. St Cath S Ox BA (2nd cl Th) 35, MA 42. Wycl Hall, Ox 33. **d** 35 **p** 36 Lon. C of St Mary Kilburn 35-38; Youth Sec CMJ 38-41; C-in-c of St Barn Woodside Pk 40-41; V 41-49; St Thos Oakwood 49-58; Lyncombe (St Bart Bath from 72) and Chap of St Mary Magd Holloway Bath 58-73; Curry Rivel 73-78; Perm to Offic Dio B & W from 79. *2 Highbridge, Williton, Somt, TA4 4RN.*

GEEN, James William. b 50. Chich Th Coll 76. **d** 79 Jarrow for Dur **p** 80 Dur. C of St John Brandon Dio Dur from 79. *The Clergy House, Sawmill Lane, Brandon, Durham, DH7 6NS.*

GEERING, Anthony Ernest. b 43. Dipl Th (Lon) 66. Kelham Th Coll 62. **d** 68 Bp McKie for Cov **p** 69 Bp Daly for Cov. C of St Mary Magd Cov 68-71; Howick Auckld 71-75; P-in-c of Brinklow 75-81; Harborough Magna 75-81; Monks Kirby (w Pailton and Stretton-under-Fosse from 77) 76-77; V 77-81; V of Pilton w Ashford Dio Ex from 81. *Pilton Vicarage, Northfield Lane, Barnstaple, Devon.* (Barnstaple 42734)

GEESON, Brian Alfred. b 30. Qu Coll Ox BA (2nd cl Math) 51. Qu Coll Birm 54. **d** 55 **p** 56 Derby. C of Newbold w Dunston 55-59; PC of Calow 59-64; R of Broughton-in-Airedale 64-71; Team V of Seacroft 71-77; Hon C of Hanging Heaton Dio Wakef from 77. *30 Ullswater Avenue, Dewsbury, W Yorks.*

GEGEYO, Cephas. **d** 76 Bp Ambo for Papua **p** 77 Aipo. P Dio Aipo. *Anglican Church, Simbai, via Madang, Papua New Guinea.*

GEILINGER, John Edward. BSc (Lon) 53, BD 58, BA (Lon) 76, MPhil (Lon) 79. Tyndale Hall Bris. **d** 59 **p** 60 Ex. C of St Jude Plymouth Dio Ex 59-61; Lect Trin Th Coll Umuahia 63-72; Th Coll of N Nig Jos 72-77; Perm to Offic Dio Portsm from 79. *Raymond Villa, York Road, Totland Bay, I o W.*

GEILS, Canon Percival William Alston. St Paul's Coll Grahmstn 32. LTh (S Afr) 33. **d** 34 **p** 35 Natal. C of St Jas Durban 34-37; V of Mooi River 37-42; Ladysmith 42-46; St Jas Durban 46-61; Capitular Can of St Sav Cathl Pietermaritzburg 50-61; R of Curdworth Birm 61-63; Sen Hosp Chap Durban 63-76; Hon Can of Natal from 64; Synod Sec Dio Natal 64-76; Perm to Offic Dio Natal from 77. *7 Inyoni Drive, Hillcrest, Durban, Natal, S Africa.* (78-7426)

GEIPEL, Henry Cecil. b 1899. Late Scho of Univ Coll Dur BA (2nd cl Th) 21, MA 24. **d** 22 **p** 23 Southw. LPr Dio Southw and Asst Master St Cuthb Sch Worksop 22-25; C of Streatham 25-26; Chap Worksop Coll Dio Southw 26-32; V of Sewerby w Marton Grindall and Ergham 32-39; Horkstow 39-49; R of Saxby 39-49; RD of Yarborough 47-49; R of Waltham and RD of Grimsby S 49-60; R of N Lew w Ashbury 60-69; L to Offic Dio Ex from 69. *St John's, Barton Hill Road, Torquay, TQ2 8LX.*

GELDARD, Mark Dundas. b 50. Univ of Liv BA 71. Univ of Bris MA 75. Trin Coll Bris 73. **d** 75 Warrington for Liv **p** 76 Liv. C of Ch Ch Aughton 75-78; Tutor Trin Th Coll Bris and Publ Pr Dio Bris from 78. *Flat No 9, Bartlett Court, Clifton, Bristol, BS8 3ET.* (Bris 741283)

GELDARD, Peter John Esdale. b 45. AKC 69. St Aug Coll Cant 70. **d** 71 Maidstone for Cant **p** 72 Cant. C of H Trin w St Paul Sheerness 71-78; Gen Sec Ch U from 78; L to Offic Dio Lon from 79; M Gen Syn from 80. *Faith House, 7 Tufton Street, SW1P 3QN.* (01-222 6952)

GELDART, John William. Ridley Coll Melb. **d** 68 **p** 69 Bend. C of All SS Cathl Bend 68-70; V of Maldon 70-73; Tatura Dio Bend from 73; Dom Chap to Bp of Bend from 70. *2a Francis Street, Tatura, Vic, Australia.* (058-24 1170)

GELDING, John Edward. Moore Th Coll Syd ACT ThL (2nd cl) 65. **d** 65 **p** 66 Syd. C of Castle Hill 66-68; H Trin Adel 68-71; R of Normanhurst 71-77; Ryde Dio Syd from 78. *46 Church Street, Ryde, NSW, Australia 2112.* (80-4114)

GELDING, Norman McLean. Univ of Syd BA 42. Moore Th Coll Syd 37. ACT ThL 38. **d** 40 **p** 41 Syd. C of Ch Ch Gladesville 40-42; C-in-c of Prov Distr of Langlea 42-45; R of Sutherland 45-48; CMS Miss Dio Centr Tang. Kongwa 48; Mpwapwa 48-51; Dioc Treas 51-52; Murgwanza 53-54; Berega 54-57; Prin St Phil Th Coll Kongwa 58-62; CMS Dioc Sec 58-62; C-in-c of W Lindfield 63-72; R 72-81; Rep Angl Home Miss S Syd from 81. *c/o Box Q190. Queen Victoria Building, Sydney, NSW, Australia 2000.*

GELL, Reginald Arthur Patrick. b 10. ALCD 32. **d** 33 **p** 34 Southw. C of Ch Ch Newark-on-Trent 33-35; Heworth and St Mary Castlegate w St Mich Spurriergate York 35-37; V of St Steph Newc T 37-44; All SS Hoole 44-63; Ch Ch Paignton Dio Ex from 63. *Christ Church Vicarage, Paignton, Devon.* (Paignton 556311)

GELLING, Canon John Drury. b 22. Pemb Coll Ox BA 44, Dipl Th 45, MA 48. Wycl Hall Ox 44. **d** 54 **p** 55 Man. Hd Master Eccles High Sch 50-64; C of Irlam 54-59; V of Rushen 64-77; Surr from 64; RD of Castletown 71-77; Exam Chap to Bp of S & M from 74; P-in-c of Kirk Michael Dio S & M 77-78; V from 78; R of Ballaugh Dio S & M from 77; Can of S & M from 80. *Rectory, Ballaugh, IM.* (Sulby 7873)

GELSTON, Anthony. b 35. Keble Coll Ox 2nd cl Cl Mods 55, BA (1st cl Th) 57, Pusey and Ellerton Scho 58, 2nd cl Or Stud 59, MA and Houghton Syriac Pri 60, Hall-Houghton Sen Septuagint Pri 61. Ridley Hall Cam 59. **d** 60 **p** 61 Ox. C of Chipping Norton 60-62; Lect in Th Univ of Dur 62-76; Sen Lect from 76; Dean of Faculty of Div 77-79; L to Offic Dio Dur from 62. *Lesbury, Hetton Road, Houghton-le-Spring, T & W, DH5 8JW.* (Houghton 842256)

GEMMELL, Ian William Young. b 52. St Jo Coll Nottm LTh 77. **d** 77 **p** 78 Worc. C of H Trin Worc 77-81; Selly Pk Dio Birm from 81. *927 Pershore Road, Selly Park, Birmingham, B29 7PS.*

GENDALL, Patrick John. **d** 78 **p** 79 Matab. C of Hillside 78-81; R of St Luke Que Que Dio Lundi from 81. *Box 75, Que Que, Zimbabwe.*

✠ **GENDERS, Right Rev (Anselm) Roger Alban Marson.** b 19. Late Scho of BNC Ox BA (Lit Hum) and MA 47. Coll of Resurr Mirfield 48. M CR 52. **d** and **p** 52 Wakef. LPr Dio Wakef 52-55; Exam Chap to Bp of Barb 55-65; Vice Prin of Codr Coll Barb 55-57; Prin 57-65; Treas and C of St Aug Miss Penhalonga 66-75; Archd of E Distr Mashon 70-75; Asst Bursar CR Mirfield 75-77; Cons Ld Bp of Berm in St Paul's Cathl Lon 18 Oct 77 by Abp of Cant; Bps of Lon, St Alb, Linc, Lich and Nor; Bps Suffr of Fulham & Gibr, Stepney, Buckingham, Horsham, Pontefract, Sherborne and Tonbridge; and Bps J Armstrong, M Hodson and E Trapp; and others. *Bishop's Lodge, Box 769, Hamilton, Bermuda.* (2-2967)

GENGE, David. Dalhousie Univ BSc 50. Mem Univ Newfld BA 65. Qu Coll Newfld. **d** 56 **p** 57 Newfld. R of Gander Bay 56-60; C of St Thos St John's 60-64; P-in-c of Foxtrap 64-70; R of St Geo w Pennfield 70-76; L to Offic Dio E Newfld 76-79; I of St Geo Carleton Dio Fred from 79. *183 Duke Street, Saint John West, NB, Canada.*

GENGE, Hubert Thomas. St Jo Coll Armid ACT ThL 24. **d** 24 **p** 25 Bath. C of Dubbo 24-26; R of Wyalong 26-30; Pambula 30-35; Koorawatha 35-45. *30 Barton Road, Artarmon, NSW, Australia.*

GENGE, Canon Kenneth Lyle. Univ of Sask BA 58. Em Coll Sktn LTh 57. **d** 57 **p** 58 Sask. I of Fort Pitt 57-59; R of Shellbrook 59-62; Miss At Yellowknife 62-69; R of St Mich AA Calg 69-74; St Barn, St Lambert Dio Montr from 74; Hon Can of Montr from 79. *95 Lorne Avenue, St Lambert, PQ, Canada.* (514-672 2277)

✠ **GENGE, Right Rev Mark.** St Chad's Coll Dur BA 55, MA 71. Qu Coll Newfld 47. **d** 51 **p** 52 Newfld. C-in-c of Stephenville 52-53; on leave 53-55; Vice Prin Qu Coll St John's Newfld 55-57; Exam Chap to Bp of Newfld 57-69; C of St Mary St John's 57-59; R of Foxtrap 60-64; Battle Harbour 64-65; Burgeo 65-69; Marbleton 69-71; I of Port de Grave and of Brigus w Salmon Cove 71-73; Newfld Distr Sec Canad Bible S and Perm to Offic Dio Newfld 73-76; Cons Ld Bp of Centr Newfld at Gander 20 June 76 by Abp of Prov of Canada; Bps of NS, W Newfld, NB and Queb; and Bps Meaden and Maguire. *34 Fraser Road, Gander, Newfoundland, Canada.* (709-256 2372)

GENJIM, David. Newton Coll Dogura 70. **d** 73 Bp Meredith for Papua **p** 74 Papua. P Dio Papua 73-77; Dio Aipo from 77. *Anglican Church, Simbai, via Madang, Papua New Guinea.*

GENOWER, Arthur Herbert. Univ of Leeds BA 30. Ripon Hall 33. **d** 33 **p** 34 S'wark. C of Mortlake 33-36; St Marg Putney 36-40; R of Wootton, Portsm 40-68. *26 Grange Crescent, St Michaels, Tenterden, Kent.* (Tenterden 3488)

GENT, Anthony Leonard. b 20. Sarum Th Coll. **d** 67 **p** 68 Truro. C of Forrabury w Minster and Trevalga Dio Truro from 67; Davidstow w Otterham Dio Truro from 67; St Juliot w Lesnewth 67-70; V of St Minver w St Enodoc and St Mich

Dio Truro from 70; RD of Trigg Minor from 73. *St Minver Vicarage, Wadebridge, Cornw.* (Trebetherick 3356)

GENTLE, David Paul. b 45. St Francis Coll Brisb 67. **d** 69 **p** 70 Rockptn. C of Callide Valley 70-73; Perm to Offic Dio Rockptn from 73. *238 Flanagan Street, North Rockhampton, Queensland, Australia 4701.* (079-28 1776)

GENTLES, Javan. **d** 60 **p** 61 Ja. C of Spanish Tn Cathl 60-61; P-in-c of Somerset Hall 61-68; R of Chapelton 68-71; Trinityville Dio Ja from 71. *Rectory, Trinityville, Jamaica, W Indies.*

GENTRY, Francis George. b 03. St Aid Coll 46. **d** and **p** 47 Ches. C of Ellesmere Port 47-49; Davenham 49-52; V of Ch Ch Crewe 52-60; Surr from 54; V of Gailey w Hatherton 60-73. *Address temp unknown.*

GEOGHEGAN, John George Frederick. St Jo Coll Morpeth ACT ThL 60. **d** 59 **p** 60 Graft. C of Coff's Harbour 59-60; Casino 60-62; V of Woodenbong w Liston 62-66; Macksville 66-71; R of Woodburn (Mid-Richmond from 73) 71-81; S Graft Dio Graft from 81. *Box 20, South Grafton, NSW, Australia 2461.*

GEORGANTIS, Canon Anthony George. Univ of NZ BA 49, MA 50. Coll Ho Ch Ch Lth 51. **d** 51 **p** 52 Ch Ch. C of Sydenham 51-53; Ashburton 53-54; St Alb Ch Ch 54-55; V of Ross w S Westland 55-58; C of Shirley Surrey 58-61; V of Fairlie 61-64; Opawa 64-69; Wadestown 69-77; Waiwhetu Dio Wel from 77; Hon Can of St Paul's Cathl Wel from 79. *28 Guthrie Street, Waiwhetu, Lower Hutt, NZ.* (662-002)

GEORGE, Lord Bishop of. *See* Manning, Right Rev William James.

GEORGE, Assistant Bishop of. *See* Schuster, Right Rev James Leo.

GEORGE, Dean of. *See* Witts-Hewinson, Very Rev William Edwin.

GEORGE, Alec. b 29. Lich Th Coll 56. **d** 59 **p** 60 Cov. C of St Luke Holbrooks Cov 59-65; R of Ascen Lower Broughton Salford 65-71; V of Hollinwood Dio Man from 71. *St Margaret's Vicarage, Chapel Road, Hollinwood, Oldham, Lancs.* (061-681 4541)

GEORGE, Alexander Robert. b 46. K Coll Lon BD and AKC 69. St Aug Coll Cant 69. **d** 70 **p** 71 St E. C of Newmarket w Exning 70-74; Swindon 74-76; St Mary Henbury 76-79; Publ Pr Dio Bris 79-80; Team V of Oldland Dio Bris from 80. *89 Ellacombe Road, Longwell Green, Bristol, BS15 6BP.* (Bitton 2414)

GEORGE, Barry Stewart. Moore Th Coll Syd ACT ThL 63. **d** 63 **p** 64 Syd. C of Liverpool 63-64; Narrabeen 64-66; C-in-c of W Cabramatta 66-68; CMS Miss Dio Centr Tang 69-73; R of St Thos Kingsgrove 74-80; Asst Gen Sec CMS, NSW from 80. *93 Bathurst Street, Sydney, Australia 2000.* (267-3711)

GEORGE, Cedric James Noel. b 17. Worc Coll Ox BA (3rd cl Th) 39, MA 43. Ripon Hall Ox. **d** 40 **p** 41 Guildf. C of Ch Ch Epsom Common 40-45; Leatherhead 45-47; V of Cornworthy and R of Ashprington 48-57; RD of Totnes 54-57; V of Seaton Dio Ex from 57; RD of Honiton 62-65. *Vicarage, Seaton, Devon, EX12 2DF.* (Seaton 20391)

GEORGE, Charles Dennis. b 18. Tyndale Hall Bris 46. **d** 49 **p** 50 Sheff. C of St Thos Crookes Sheff 49-51; Sec CPAS NE Area 51-55; V of St Mark Siddal Halifax 55-61; R of Treeton 61-78; V of Pollington w Balne Dio Sheff from 78. *Balne Vicarage, Pollington, Goole, Yorks, DN14 0DZ.* (Goole 85663)

GEORGE, Charles Roy. b 32. St Edm Hall Ox BA 55, MA 59. Cudd Coll 55. **d** 57 **p** 58 Blackb. C of Chorley 57-60; Norton 60-64; V of St Barn Eltham S'wark 64-74; Milton Dio Portsm from 74. *c/o Milton Vicarage, Portsmouth, Hants.* (Portsmouth 732786)

GEORGE, Colin Harry. b 46. K Coll Lon AKC 69. St Aug Coll Cant 69. **d** 70 **p** 71 Roch. C of St Barn Gillingham 70-73; Leigh Park 73-75; Petersfield w Sheet 75-79; R of Wickham Dio Portsm from 79. *Wickham Rectory, Fareham, Hants, PO17 6HR.* (Wickham 832134)

GEORGE, David Michael. b 45. Selw Coll Cam 2nd cl Engl Trip pt i 65, BA (2nd cl Engl Trip pt ii) 66, MA 70. Chich Th Coll 70. **d** 73 **p** 74 Kens for Lon. C of Chiswick 73-76; St Mary Abbots (in c of Ch Ch) Kens 76-78; St Barn Northolt Pk 78-81. *Address temp unknown.*

GEORGE, Eric Joscelyn. b 06. Ch Coll Hobart 62. **d** 63 **p** 64 Tas. C of Ross 63; R of Cygnet Tas 64-66; C of Wirksworth w Carsington 66-67; V of Horsley Woodhouse Dio Derby from 67. *Horsley Woodhouse Vicarage, Derby.* (Derby 880666)

GEORGE, Frederick. St Mich Ho Crafers 72. **d** 72 N Queensld. Asst Master All S Sch Charters Towers N Queensld 72-76; Hd Master St Jas Sch Kuala Belait and L to Offic Dio Kuch 76-80; Prin Marina Sch Banjul from 80. *Marina School, Banjul, Gambia.*

GEORGE, Hubert Edgar. b 12. Univ of Sheff BA 33. Lich Th Coll 33. **d** 35 **p** 36 Dur. C of Shotton 35-39; St Thos Bp Wearmouth 39-41; C-in-c of Hetton-le-Hole 41-45; V of Annfield Plain 45-53; Surr 48-53 and 66-77; V of Walkey Sheff 53-66; RD of Hallam 60-66; V of Polesworth w Birchmoor 66-77; Perm to Offic Dio St E 78-80; Dio Linc 80-81; Dio Lich from 81. *Parsonage, Church Drive, Hopwas, Nr Tamworth, Staffs, B78 3AL.* (0827-62983)

GEORGE, Canon Ian Gordon. Univ of Adel LLB 56. Gen Th Sem NY STB 64. **d** and **p** 64 NY for Adel. in Amer Ch 64-65; C of Burnside 66-67; P-in-c of Woomera 67-69; Sub-Warden and Chap St Geo Coll Perth 69-73; Dean of Brisb 73-81; Can of C & Goulb from 81; R of St John Canberra Dio C & Goulb from 81. *Box 219, Canberra City, ACT, Australia 2601.*

GEORGE, Ignatio. b 43. St Cypr Th Coll Rondo 71. **d** 74 **p** 75 Masasi. P Dio Masasi. *KJT Mangaka, Private Bag Masasi, Mtwara Region, Tanzania.*

GEORGE, Preb John Thomas. b 17. St D Coll Lamp BA 42. Selwyn Coll Cam BA 44, MA 47. Westcott Ho Cam 44. **d** 45 **p** 46 St D. C of Llanstadwell 45-48; C of St Thos Ap Eastville Bris 48-50; PV of Wells Cathl and C of St Cuthb Wells and Asst Master Cathl Sch Wells 50-52; V of Cheddar 52-57; C-in-c of Priddy 55-57; CF 57-60; V of Thornton w Allerthorpe, Melbourne, Waplington and Storwood 60-62; R of Backwell 62-72; RD of Portishead from 68; V of Wellington w W Buckland and Nynehead 72-75; Team R of Wellington and Distr Dio B & W from 75; Can and Preb of Wells Cathl from 78. *Rectory, Wellington, Somt, TA21 8RF.* (Wellington 2248)

GEORGE, Keith Mervyn. St Jo Coll Morpeth ACT ThL 62. **d** 62 **p** 63 Adel. C of Plympton 62-64; P-in-c of O'Halloran Hill Miss 64-66; C of Hartcliffe 66-68; P-in-c of Hillcrest 68-71; Producer Chr TV Adel 71-75; Chap Hillcrest Hosp Dio Adel 71-78. *3 Cecil Street, Rostrevor, S Australia 5074.*

GEORGE, Maclean Nyemiearigbo Ekeke. b 29. **d** 72 **p** 73 Aba. P Dio Aba. *St Michael's Parsonage, Okaiuga, Nigeria.*

GEORGE, Peter Frederick. ACT ThL 60. Moore Th Coll Syd 58. **d** 60 Syd **p** 61 Bp Kerle for Syd. C of Baulkham Hills 61-63; St Thos Essendon 63-65; P-in-c of St Mich N Dandenong 65-67; V 67-70; P-in-c of Outer Mt Isa 70-73; Prahran Dio Melb 73-77; I from 77. *48 The Avenue, Windsor, Vic, Australia 3181.* (03-51 5483)

✠ **GEORGE, Right Rev Randolph Oswald.** Codr Coll Barb 46. **d** 50 **p** 51 Barb. C of St Pet Barb 50-52; V of St Phil L Boscobel Barb 52-53; C of Leigh Lancs 53-55; St Benedict Ardwich Man 55-57; St Mich AA Kens 57-58; Lavender Hill 58-60; Dom Chap to Bp of Trinid 60-62; Chap Col Hosp Dio Trinid 60-62; R of Couva 62-67; All SS Port of Spain 67-71; Hon Can of Trinid 68-71; Dean and R of St Geo Cathl Georgetn 71-76; Cons Ld Bp Suffr of Stabroek in St Geo Cathl Georgetn 28 Oct 76 by Abp of W Indies; Bps of Windw Is, Trinid, Antig, Nass, Ja, Barb, Bel and Venez; Bps Suffr of Montego Bay and Mandeville; and others; Apptd Bp of Guy 80. *Austin House, Georgetown 1, Guyana, S America.* (02-64239)

GEORGE, Robert William. Moore Coll Syd ACT ThL 74. **d** and **p** 75 Syd. C of St Bede Beverly Hills 75-76; St Mich Wollongong 76-77; P-in-c of Winton Dio Rockptn from 78. *Box 142, Winton, Qld, Australia 4735.*

GEORGE, Thomas Igwebike. Awka Tr Coll. **d** 45 **p** 47 Niger. P Dio Niger 45-75. *St Mary's Church, Obosi, Onitsha, Nigeria.*

GEORGE, Walter. Univ Coll Dur LTh 36, BA 37, MA 39. St Aug Coll Cant 32. **d** 37 **p** 38 Sarum. C of Wareham 37-39; Tutor St Jo Coll Palamcottah 40-44; SPG Miss Dio Tinn 44-47; Ch of S India 47-52; R of King's Worthy 52-74; Headbourne Worthy 67-74; C-in-c of Bighton 78-80. *11 Dorian Grove, Alresford, Hants, SO24 9QR.* (Alresford 2977)

GEORGE, William Donald. b 24. Univ of Tulane USA BA 50. Seabury-Western Th Sem LTh 53, BD 54 (MDiv from 71). **d** 53 Bp Noland for La USA **p** 54 La USA. In Amer Ch 53-68; P-in-c of St David Barb 68-69; St Mary Barb 69-72; R of St Lucy I and Dio Barb from 72. *The Rectory, St Lucy, Barbados, WI.*

GEORGE, William Havard. b 15. St D Coll Lamp BA 37. St Mich Coll Llan 38. **d** 41 **p** 42 Blackb. C of St Cuthb Preston 41-43; Gt Yarmouth 43; Chap RNVR 43-46; CF 47-53; Hon CF 53; C of St Paul Llanelly 53-54; Chap Miss to Seamen Port of London 54-55; C of Woodhorn w Newbiggin 55-56; V of Bassenthwaite (w Isel and Setmurthy from 72) Dio Carl from 57. *Bassenthwaite Vicarage, Keswick, Cumb, CA12 4QG.* (Bassenthwaite Lake 410)

GEORGE, William Llewelyn John. b 16. St Chad's Coll Dur BA (2nd cl Hist) 37, Dipl Th 38, MA 40. **d** 39 **p** 40 Swan B. C of St Mary Swansea 39-43; Org Sec C of E Children's S for NE Area 43-47; for S Area 47-58; Publ Pr Dio Ripon 43; Perm to Offic Dios Newc T, Wakef, Bradf, Dur, Sheff, York and Southw 43-47; Dios Cant, Roch, Portsm and Win 47-58;

LPr Dio Chich 47-58; V of Lillington 58-66; Hon Dir Samaritans Dio Cov 62-66; R of Cherington w Stourton and Sutton-under-Brailes 66-73; R of Barcheston 66-73; Chap HM Pris Wormwood Scrubs 73-74; HM Pris Ford 74-79. *12 Beach Court, Irvine Road, Littlehampton, W Sussex. BN17 5JF.* (Littlehampton 22429)

GEORGE, William Ronald. b 08. TD 57. Univ of Wales BSc 30. St Mich Coll Llan 30. **d** 31 **p** 32 Llan. C of Gilfach Goch 31-32; Coity w Nolton 32-34; St Donat Abercynon 34-35; Burythorpe w Acklam and Leavening 35-37; Driffield 37-42; CF (EC) 42-47; Hon CF 47; V of Burstwick (w Thorngumbald from 55) 47-60; C-in-c of Thorngumbald 47-55; CF (TA) 48-58; TA (R of O) 58-63; V of Sand Hutton w Gate and U Helmsley 60-74; C-in-c of Bossall w Buttercrambe 72-74; Hon C of Driffield Dio York from 75. *58 Middle Street North, Driffield, N Humb.* (Driffield 42827)

GEORGE-JONES, Canon Gwilym Ifor. b 26. K Coll NS 56. **d** and **p** 57 NS. [f Methodist Min] R of St Jas Seaforth NS 57-61; V of Kirton-in-Lindsey 61-71; R of Manton 61-71; R of Grayingham 61-71; V of Alford w Rigsby and Ailby Dio Linc from 71; R of Maltby-le-Marsh Dio Linc from 71; Well Dio Linc from 71; V of Bilsby w Farlesthorpe Dio Linc from 71; Hannah and Hagnaby w Markby Dio Linc from 71; R of Saleby and Thoresthorpe w Beesby-in-the-Marsh Dio Linc from 71; RD of Calcewaithe and Candleshoe from 77; Can and Preb of Linc Cathl from 81. *Vicarage, Alford, Lincs.* (Alford 2488)

GEORGETOWN, Dean of. *See* George, Very Rev Randolph Oswald.

GEORGIAN BAY, Bishop of. *See* Appleyard, Right Rev Harold Frederick Gaviller (Bp Suffr of Hur).

GERALDTON, Dean of (Dio NW Austr). *See* Kyme, Very Rev Brian Robert.

GERARD, Clive Inglis. b 42. Univ of Syd BEcon 66, BA 76. St Jo Coll Morpeth ThL 77. **d** 78 **p** 79 Armid. C of Glen Innes Dio Armid from 78. *78 Meade Street, Glen Innes, NSW, Australia 2370.*

✠ **GERARD, Right Rev George Vincent.** b 1898. CBE 44. MC 18. BNC Ox BA 21, MA 25. Bd of Th Stud NZ LTh 26. **d** 22 **p** 23 Ch Ch. C of Timaru 22-26; Perm to Offic at St Sav Croydon 27-28; St Marg Barking 28-29; V of Pahiatua 29-32; Petone 32-36; St Matt Auckld 36-38; Cons Ld Bp of Wai in St John's Cathl Napier 28 Oct 38 by Abp of Auckld; Bps of Ch Ch; Dun; Waik; Wel; and Nel; res 44; Sen Chap NZ Forces 40-45; V of Rotherham 45-60; RD of Rotherham 45-60; Asst Bp of Sheff 47-71; Hon Can of Sheff 47-60; Chap of Rotherham Hosps 45-60; Proc Conv Sheff 50-51 and 52-70; Commiss Dun 54-75; Wai 56-70; Can Res of Sheff 60-69; Vice-Chairman Ch Assembly Ho of Cl 61-65; Chairman 65-70. *18 Barton Court Avenue, Barton-on-Sea, New Milton, Hants, BH25 7HD.* (New Milton 614964)

GERARD, John William. b 23. BNC Ox BA 47, MA 52. **d** and **p** 51 Niag. C of Ch Ch Niag Falls 51-53; I of Ridgeway Ont 53-61; Perm to Offic Dio Chelmsf from 74. *11 Wycke Lane, Tollesbury, Essex.*

GERBER, Earl Christian Newstead. Univ of Tor BA 50. Wycl Coll Tor LTh 53, BD 64. **d** 53 Tor for Arctic **p** 54 Arctic. Miss at Port Harrison 54-60; I of Washago 60-66; Oak Ridges 66-77; Streetsville Dio Tor from 77. *69 Queen Street South, Streetsville, Ont., Canada.* (416-826 1901)

GERBER, Gordon Bruce. ED 65. Moore Th Coll Syd ACT ThL 43. **d** and **p** 43 Syd. C of St Clem Marrickville 43-44; C-in-c St John Sutherland 44-45; Homebush 45-46; Chap of Norfolk I 46-48; R of St Sav Redfern 48-52; Belmore 52-69; Chap CMF 51-69; R of Drummoyne 69-79; Asst Min of Nowra Dio Syd from 79. *17 Hawke Street, Huskisson, NSW, Australia 2540.* (044-415755)

GEREA, John Richardson. St Pet Coll Siota 64. **d** 68 **p** 69 Melan. P Dio Melan 68-75; Dio Malaita from 75. *Fiu, N Malaita, Solomon Islands.*

GERLACH, Alfred John. **d** and **p** 30 Syd. C of Eastwood 50-51; Cammeray 51-52; P-in-c of Wyan w Rappville 52-58; R of Bellingen 58-62; Kilkivan 63-73; V of Palmwoods 73-74; R from 74. *Vicarage, Hill Street, Palmwoods, Queensland, Australia 4555.* (Palmwoods 45 9019)

GERMAN, Canon Ian MacDonald. b 09. Egerton Hall Man 34. **d** 34 Carl **p** 35 Barrow-F for Carl. C of Ch Ch Cockermouth 34-36; St Mary and St Paul Carl 36-38; Min of St Herbert Distr Currock Carl 38-43; CF (EC) 43-46; V of St Columba Broughton Moor 46-49; R of Egremont 49-66; Surr from 50; RD of Whitehaven 53-66; Hon Can of Carl 61-74; Can (Emer) from 74; V of Maryport 66-70; Bampton w Mardale 70-74; RD of Appleby 70-74; Dioc Officer Carl Miss 71-75. *Fairways, Egremont Road, St Bees, Cumb, CA27 0AS.* (St Bees 552)

GERMOND, Brian Charles. b 47. St Paul's Coll Grahmstn 74. **d** 76 Bp Carter for Johann **p** 77 Johann. C of Rosebank Dio Johann from 76. *PO Box 52139, Saxonwold 2132, S Africa.* (011-42 3559)

GERMOND, Charles Alfred. b 18. St Paul's Th Coll Grahmstn 80. **d** 80 Bp Stanage for Johann. C of Vereeniging Dio Johann from 80. *PO Box 3167, Three Rivers, S Africa, 1935.*

GERRARD, Brian James. b 38. Wycl Hall Ox 72. **d** 74 Warrington for Liv **p** 75 Liv. C of St Ditton 74-78; V of Lydiate Dio Liv from 78. *Lydiate Vicarage, Liverpool, L31 4HL.* (051-526 0512)

GERRARD, David Keith Robin. b 39. St Edm Hall Ox BA (1st cl Geog) 61. Linc Th Coll 61. **d** 63 **p** 64 Lon. C of Woodberry Down 63-66; St Mary Virg Primrose Hill Hampstead 66-69; V of St Paul Newington 69-79; Surbiton Dio S'wark from 79. *St Mark's Vicarage, Church Hill Road, Surbiton, Surrey, KT6 4UG.* (01-399 6053)

GERRARD, George Ernest. b 16. FCCS (FCIS from 70) 60. Ridley Hall Cam. **d** 68 Lynn for Nor **p** 69 Nor. C of Hilborough w Bodney 68-70; Ramsey 70-75. *99 Norwich Road, Watton, Thetford, Norfolk, IP25 6DH.* (0953-882732)

GERRISH, David Victor. b 38. St Jo Coll Dur BSc 61, MA 64. Oak Hill Th Coll 61. **d** 64 **p** 65 Portsm. C of St Jo Evang Fareham 64-67; Asst Chap K Sch Roch 67-71; Chap Bryanston Sch 71-77; Mon Sch from 77. *Monmouth School, Monmouth, Gwent, NP5 3DE.*

GERRY, Dylan John Rowland. b 38. Oak Hill Th Coll 69. **d** 71 Bradwell for Cant. **p** 72 Chelmsf. C of Hawkwell 71-74; St Geo w St Andr Battersea 74-77; St Sav Battersea Pk 74-77; V of Axmouth w Musbury Dio Ex from 77. *Axmouth Vicarage, Seaton, Devon.* (Seaton 20989)

GERRY, Canon Thomas Melville Pearce. ACT ThL 06. **d** 08 **p** 09 Syd. C of St Matthias Paddington NSW 08-09; St Thos Balmain 09-10; Armidale 11-13; V of Mid-Clarence 13-18; Byron Bay 18-28; R 28-44; Can of Graft 29-64; Can (Emer) from 64; RD of Murwillumbah 32-42; I of Port Macquarie 44-58; Archd of Southern Rivers 48-54; L to Offic Dio Graft 58-70. *131 Picton Parade, Wynnum, Queensland, Australia.*

GETHYN-JONES, Canon John Eric. b 09. MBE 45. TD 50. Univ of Bris MA 66, Qu Coll Birm 32. **d** 34 Bp Palmer for Glouc **p** 35 Glouc. C of St Cath Glouc 34-37; Kempley 37; Dymock w Kempley (w Preston from 41) 37-55; R of Dymock w Donnington 55-67; CF (TA) 38-61; Hon Chap to HM the Queen 59-61; RD of N Forest 60-67; V of Berkeley w Wick, Breadstone and Newport 67-76; Hon Can of Glouc from 68. *Canonbury House, Canonbury Street, Berkeley, Glos.* (Dursley 810296)

GHEST, Richard William Iliffe. b 31. Em Coll Cam BA 53, MA 57. Univ of Lon BA (2nd cl Sanskrit) 66. Wells Th Coll 53. **d** 55 **p** 56 Taunton for B & W. C of Weston-s-Mare 55-57; Chap to Bp of Bhag and I of Bhag 58-63; Dioc Sec 59-63; Dioc Treas 60-63; C of St Geo Mart Qu Square w H Trin and St Bart Gray's Inn Road Holborn 63-67; Combe Down 68-74; R of Tickenham Dio B & W from 74. *Tickenham Rectory, Clevedon, Avon.* (Nailsea 853278)

GHINN, Edward. b 45. Oak Hill Th Coll 71. **d** 74 **p** 75 S'wark. C of Purley 74-77; Chap at Santiago 77-79; Concepcion Dio Chile from 79. *Casilla 1973, Concepcion, Chile.*

GHOSH, Dipen. b 43. Univ of Burdwan W Bengal BSc 63. St Jo Coll Nottm 71. **d** 74 **p** 75 Lich. C of Bushbury 74-77. *c/o 27 Morrison Avenue, Bushbury, Wolverhampton, WV10 9TZ.*

GIBB, William. b 35. **d** 76 Queb. Perm to Offic Dio Quebec from 76. *2223 Brulart Street, Sillery, Quebec, G1T 1G2, Canada.*

GIBB, William Arthur James. b 26. Chich Th Coll 53. **d** 56 Bp Hawkes for Cant **p** 57 Guildf. C of Fleet Hants 56-59; Hangleton 59-61; V of Hadlow Down 61-67; R of Etchingham 67-71; C-in-c of Hurst Green 67-71; V of Scaynes Hill Dio Chich from 71. *Vicarage, Scaynes Hill, Haywards Heath, Sussex, RH17 7PB.*

GIBBARD, Charles Ernest Roger. b 14. Univ of Lon BSc (2nd cl Botany) 36, ARCS 36. Wycl Hall Ox 63. **d** 64 **p** 65 Roch. HdMaster Hayesbrook Sch Tonbridge 64-74; Hon C of St Paul Crofton Orpington 64-75; R of Medbourne w Holt and Stockerston w Blaston 75-78; Perm to Offic Dio B & W from 78. *3 Stanchester Way, Curry Rivel, Langport, Somt, TA10 0PS.* (Langport 250935)

GIBBARD, Roger. b 48. Univ of Southn BA 73. Cudd Coll 73. **d** 75 **p** 76 Portsm. C of St Mary Portsea 75-79; New Addington (in c of St Geo) 79-81; Team V of Ditton Dio Liv from 81. *20 Deepdale, Widnes, WA8 9WN.* (051-420 4963)

GIBBARD, Sydney Mark. Late Scho of Selw Coll Cam 1st cl Th Trip pt i 31, BA (2nd cl Th Trip pt ii) 32, MA 37. Cudd Coll 33. M SSJE 43. **d** 33 **p** 34 Pet. C of All SS Wellingborough 33-37; Chap and Lect St Bonif Coll Warm 37-41; Lect Bps' Coll Cheshunt 41-46; LPr Dio Ox from 44; Select Pr Univ of Cam 59-60; Commiss Colom from 65; Malawi from 68; Lect Berkeley Div Sch New Haven 68-69; Gen Th Sem

NY 70-71; Asst Chap Ex Coll Ox 71-75; in USA 75-76; M Gen Syn Dio Cant 75-76; Lect Bp's Coll Calc 77-78; St Jo Coll Morpeth 78-79; St Jo Coll Auckld 79-80; in Amer Ch 80-81. *St Deiniol's Library, Hawarden, Deeside, Clwyd, CH5 3DF.*

GIBBES, Robin Brooke Blower. Moore Th Coll Syd ACT ThL 44. **d** and **p** 45 Syd. Asst Chap Miss to Seamen Dio Syd 45-47; C of Port Kembla 47-48; R of Guildf 48-58; Sutton Forest 58-71; CMS Miss Umbakumba 71-75; L to Offic Dio Syd from 75. *78 Walder Road, Hammondville, NSW, Australia 2170.* (601-7517)

GIBBIN, Robert William. b 28. Jes Coll Cam BA 52, 2nd cl Th Trip pt ii 53, MA 56. Westcott Ho Cam 53. **d** 55 **p** 56 Wakef. C of Huddersfield 55-59; Mufulira 60-62; Lusaka 62-67; V of St Wilfrid Mereside Blackpool 67-72; Prec and Can Res of Guildf Cathl 73-77; V of Oatlands Dio Guildf from 77. *5 Beechwood Avenue, Oatlands, Weybridge, Surrey, KT13 9TE.* (Weybridge 47963)

GIBBON, Andrew Kerr. b 06. Ball Coll Ox BA 28, MA 41. Wycl Hall Ox 39. **d** 41 **p** 42 Sheff. C of Rotherham 41-44; Putney 45-49; All S Springwood 49-51; R of Standlake 51-68; R of Yelford 52-68. *18 Portland Road, Oxford.* (Oxford 59837)

GIBBON, Edward Herbert Morgan. b 15. St D Coll Lamp BA 37. St Mich Coll Llan 38. **d** 40 **p** 41 Llan. C of St Luke Canton 40-42; St Steph Ealing 42-44; CF (EC) 44-47; R of Pitsea 48-50; Chap RAf 50-66; V of Sunninghill 66-79. *10 Trebor Avenue, Farnham, Surrey, GU9 8JH.* (Farnham 713636)

GIBBON, Gordon Percy. b 17. Oak Hill Th Coll 63. **d** 64 **p** 65 Lon. C of St Andr Whitehall Pk U Holloway 64-68; V of St Gabr Walthamstow Dio Chelmsf from 68. *31 Upper Walthamstow Road, E17 3QG.* (01-520 3411)

GIBBON, Canon Robert Geoffrey. b 01. Late Postmaster of Merton Coll Ox BA (1st cl Mod Hist) 21, MA 25. Wells Th Coll 33. **d** 34 **p** 35 S'wark. C of St Pet St Helier 34-36; St John Bulawayo 37-38; R of Plumtree 38-41; C of St Mary and All SS Cathl Salisbury Rhod 41-47; R of Avondale 47-51; Highlands 51-58; Can of Mashon 53-65; Hon Can from 65; R of Borrowdale S Rhod 58-65; V of Somerford Keynes w Sharncote 65-71; Commiss Mashon 66-71. *Edgehill, Stockwell Lane, Cleeve Hill, Cheltenham, GL52 3PU.*

GIBBONS, Cecil Bryan. b 02. OBE (Mil) 53. Worc Ordin Coll 57. **d** 57 **p** 58 Cov. C of Farnborough w Avon Dassett 57-60; V of Wolvey w Burton Hastings and Stretton Baskerville 60-72. *21 Knox Crescent, St Nicolas Park Estate, Nuneaton, Warws.* (Nuneaton 384195)

GIBBONS, Cecil Wilson. b 02. Univ Coll Lon BSc 32. Ridley Hall Cam 34. **d** 35 **p** 36 Chelmsf. C of Walthamstow 35-37; C-in-c of Earls Colne 37-38; V of Feering 38-40; Selside 40-49; Seq of Skelsmergh 40-49; V of Barrington 49-70. *13 Croft Lodge, Barton Road, Cambridge.* (Cam 62819)

GIBBONS, Eric. b 47. Sarum Th Coll 69. **d** 72 **p** 73 Dorking for Guildf. C of New Haw 72-76; P-in-c of Blackheath and Chilworth Dio Guildf from 79. *Blackheath Vicarage, Guildford, Surrey, GU4 8QT.* (Guildf 893129)

GIBBONS, John. b 31. K Coll Lon 52. Oak Hill Th Coll 55. **d** 57 **p** 58 Lon. C of St Steph Islington 57-60; Rolleston and of Anslow 60-63; V of Bobbington Dio Lich from 63. *Bobbington Vicarage, Stourbridge, W Midl, DY7 5DD.* (038-488 247)

GIBBONS, Ven Kenneth Harry. b 31. Univ of Man BSc 52. Cudd Coll 54. **d** 56 **p** 57 Blackb. C of Fleetwood 56-60; Sec SCM in Schs NE Region 60-62; Hon C of Leeds 60-62; Perm to Offic Dio York 61-62; C of St Martin in the Fields Westmr 62-65; V of New Addington 65-70; Portsea 70-81; RD of Portsm 73-78; M Gen Syn 74-80; Hon Can of Portsm 76-81; Archd of Lanc from 81; P-in-c of Weeton Dio Blackb from 81. *St Michael's Vicarage, Weeton, Preston, Lancs, PR4 3WD.* (Weeton 249)

GIBBONS, Paul James. b 37. Chich Th Coll 63. **d** 65 **p** 66 Cant. C of St Mich AA Croydon 65-72; V of St Mich Maidstone Dio Cant from 72. *St Michael's Vicarage, Tonbridge Road, Maidstone, Kent, ME16 8JS.* (Maidstone 52710)

GIBBONS, Peter Robert. b 49. Ridley Coll Melb 73. **d** and **p** 74 Perth. C of Kalamunda 74-76. *15 Girawheen Drive, Gooseberry Hill, W Australia 6076.* (60 5861)

GIBBONS, Tony Francis Hector. Wollaston Coll W Austr ACT ThL 67. **d** 67 Perth **p** 69 Bp Rosier for Perth. C of Graylands 67; Kwinana 67-69; Northam 69-71; P-in-c of Swan 71-74; R of Cunderdin w Quairading 74-78; Esperance Dio Perth from 78. *Box 295, Esperance, W Australia 6450.* (71 2126)

GIBBONS, William Simpson. b 32. TCD BA 60, MA 64. **d** 61 **p** 62 Derry. C of Ch Ch Londonderry 61-65; I of Drumholm and Rossnowlagh 65-70; C of St Ann w St Steph Dub 70-72; I of Kill o' the Grange Dio Dub from 72; Adv on Chr Stewardship Dio Dub from 75. *Rectory, Kill o' the Grange, Co Dublin, Blackrock, Irish Republic.* (Dublin 801721)

GIBBS, Charles Harold. Bp's Univ Lennox LST 32. **d** 32 **p** 33 Berm. C of Pembroke 32-33; Paget 33-34; I of Michel 34-37; C of Kelowna 37-38; St Jo Evang Montr 39-40; L to Offic Dio Berm 40-42; C-in-c of Golden 42-44; C of Kelowna 44-46; I of Gibson's Landing 46-48; Squamish 48-63; on leave 63-64; R of St Matt Vancouver 64-68. *1296 East 17th Avenue, Vancouver 10, BC, Canada.*

GIBBS, Colin Wilfred. b 39. Univ of Man BA 62. St Jo Coll Nottm 71. **d** 73 Horsham for Chich **p** 74 Lewes for Cant for Chich. C of Crowborough 73-76; Rodbourne Cheney 76-77; Bickenhill w Elmdon Dio Birm from 77. *Church House, Church Lane, Bickenhill, Solihull, W Midlands.* (Hampton in Arden 2412)

GIBBS, Derek Norman. b 38. Kelham Th Coll. **d** 62 **p** 63 Newc T. C of Ch Ch Shieldfield Newc T 62-65; St Mark's Conv Distr Shiremoor 65-67; V of New Bentley 67-68; St Cecilia Parson Cross Sheff 68-80; Cantley Dio Sheff from 80; RD of Ecclesfield 75-80. *Cantley Vicarage, Doncaster, S Yorks.* (Doncaster 55135)

GIBBS, Edmund. b 38. BD (Lon) 62. Fuller Th Sem Calif DMin 81. Oak Hill Th Coll 58. **d** 63 **p** 64 S'wark. C of Wandsworth 63-66; Chap at Santiago 66-68; Quilpue 68-70; Sec SAMS 70-73; Educn Sec 73-77; Ch Programmes Manager BFBS from 77; Perm to Offic Dio St Alb from 78. *139 Windsor Road, Lawns, Swindon, SN3 1LJ.*

GIBBS, Ian Edmund. b 47. Univ of Lon BEducn 69. St Steph Ho Ox 72. **d** 75 Buckingham for Ox **p** 76 Ox. C of Stony Stratford 75-79: V of Forest Town Dio Southw from 79. *Vicarage, Old Mill Lane, Forest Town, Mansfield, Notts.* (Mansfield 21120)

✠ **GIBBS, Right Rev John.** b 17. Univ of Bris BA 42. Univ of Lon BD 48. Linc Th Coll 55. **d** 55 **p** 56 Bris. C of St Luke Brislington 55-57; Chap and Lect Coll of St Matthias Fishponds Bris 57-64; Vice-Prin 61-64; Prin Keswick Hall C of E Coll of Educn 64-73; L to Offic Dio Nor 64-73; Exam Chap to Bp of Nor 67-73; Hon Can of Nor from 68; Cons Ld Bp Suffr of Bradwell in Westmr Abbey 19 June 73 by Abp of Cant; Bps of Ely, Heref, Chelmsf, Nor and Mon; Bps Suffr of Kens, Colchester, Barking, Doncaster, Plymouth and Lynn; and others; trld to Cov 76. *Bishop's House, Davenport Road, Coventry, W Midl, CV5 6PW.* (Cov 72244)

GIBBS, Kenneth Graham. Wycl Coll Tor 61. **d** and **p** 61 Alg. R of Nipigon 61-66; Chapleau 66-71; Elliot Lake 71-80; Exam Chap to Bp of Alg from 77; I of St John N Bay Dio Alg from 80. *301 Main Street East, North Bay, Ont, Canada.*

GIBBS, Martin Franck. b 12. St Steph Ho Ox 32. **d** 35 **p** 36 Ox. C of Wantage 35-43; V of Wootton Berks 43-57; R of Brightwell w Sotwell 57-67; RD of Wallingford 61-67; V of St German Roath 67-77; Perm to Offic Dio B & W from 77; Dio Llan from 78. *Pennycot, George and Crown Cottages, Hinton St George, Crewkerne, Somt.* (0460-72158)

GIBBS, Canon Philip Roscoe. b 33. Codr Coll Barb 57. **d** 60 Barb **p** 61 Br Hond. C of St John's Cathl Belize 61-63; P-in-c of S Distr Missions Dio Br Hond 63-70; St Matt Pomona 70-71; Corozal 71-74; Hon Can of Br Hond (Bel from 73) from 71; V of St Mich AA Stoke Newington Common Dio Lon from 74; Commiss Bel from 77. *55 Fountayne Road, N16 7ED.* (01-806 4225)

GIBBS, Robert John. b 43. Univ of Dur BA (2nd cl Th) 64. Westcott Ho Cam 66. **d** 68 Lynn for Nor **p** 69 Nor. C of Costessey 68-71; Halesowen w Hasbury and Lapal 71-75; Team V 75-76; V of St Jas Gt Dudley Dio Worc from 77. *Vicarage, The Parade, Dudley, W Midlands.* (Dudley 53570)

GIBBS, Roderick Harold. b 25. Univ of Leeds BA (2nd cl Hist) 49. Coll of Resurr Mirfield 49. **d** 51 **p** 52 Lon. C of St Phil and St Jas Whitton 51-56; V of St Steph Hammersmith 57-65; R of Stepney 65-72; Dep Hd Master Laindon Sch 72-76; Hdmaster Wm Forster Sch Tottenham from 77; Hon C of Langdon Hills 74-78; St Gabr Bounds Green Edmonton Dio Lon from 78. *26 Brownlow Road, N11 2DE.* (01-889 5760)

GIBBS, Thomas Reginald. b 02. Cudd Coll 26. **d** 27 York **p** 28 Whitby for York. C of S Bank 27-31 and 34-38; UMCA Miss P Chipil 31-34; C of Whitby (in c of St Ninian) 38-44; V of S Bank 44-49; Cjhap St Hilda's Middle Sch Whitby 49-69; C of Ascen Derringham Bank Hull 70-72. *Adelaide House, W Malvern, Worcs.*

GIBBS, William Gilbert. b 31. Bps' Coll Cheshunt 55. **d** 58 **p** 59 B & W. C of Wellington 58-61; St Mary Abbots Kens (in c of St Geo from 63) 61-68; V of Guilsborough w Hollowell (and Cold Ashby from 75) Dio Pet from 68; C-in-c of Cold Ashby 69-74. *Guilsborough Vicarage, Northampton.* (Guilsborough 297)

GIBBY, Thomas Rees. b 12. Late Scho and Exhib of St D Coll Lamp BA 33, BD 42. St Mich Coll Llandaff 33-35. **d** 35

p 36 Llan. C of Llangeinor 35-39; Llantrisant 39-44; Bideford w St Pet Chap 44-45; R of Langtree 45-58; C-in-c of L Torrington 49-55; R 55-58; V of Bradworthy 58-62; C-in-c of W w E Putford 59-62; V of Ivybridge 62-75; R of Harford 63-75; RD of Plympton 66-71. *Penlon, Cwmann, Lampeter, Dyfed, SA48 8DU.*

GIBLING, Derek Vivian. b 31. Wadh Coll Ox BA 56, MA 63. Wycl Hall Ox 70. **d** 72 **p** 73 Sarum. C of St Paul Fisherton Anger, Sarum 72-74; Yatton Keynell 74-77; Castle Combe 74-77; Biddestone w Slaughterford 74-77; P-in-c of Youlgreave w Middleton Dio Derby from 77; Stanton-in-the-Peak w Birchover Dio Derby from 77. *Youlgreave Vicarage, Bakewell, Derby, DE4 1WL.* (Youlgreave 285)

GIBRALTAR IN EUROPE, Lord Bishop of. *See* Satterthwaite, Right Rev John Richard.

GIBRALTAR IN EUROPE, Lord Bishop Suffragan of. *See* Weekes, Right Rev Ambrose Walter Marcus.

GIBRALTAR, Dean of H Trin Cathl Ch. *See* Rowlands, Very Rev Daniel John.

GIBRALTAR, Archdeacon of. *See* Ney, Ven Reginald Basil.

GIBSON, Alan. b 35. Univ of Birm BSc 56. Univ of Man MSc 72. N-W Ordin Course 72. **d** 74 **p** 75 Ches. C of Sale 74-77; V of St Mich AA Runcorn Dio Ches from 77. *145 Greenway Road, Runcorn, Chesh, WA7 4NR.* (Runcorn 72417)

GIBSON, Canon Alan Gordon. b 18. AKC (2nd cl) 48. St Bonif Coll Warm. **d** 48 **p** 49 S'wark. C of St Mary Lewisham 48-52; Vice-Prin of Qu Coll St John's Newfld 52-55; V of Crofton Pk (w St Cypr Brockley from 60) 55-64; Commiss Newfld from 56; V of St Mich AA S Beddington 64-76; RD of Sutton 70-76; W Lewisham from 79; Hon Can of S'wark from 74; V of Perry Hill Dio S'wark from 76. *2 Woolstone Road, SE23.* (01-699 2778)

GIBSON, Alan Henry. b 11. MBE 44. Late Exhib of Univ of Lon BD 37, K Coll Lon Jun Wordsworth Lat Pri 35, AKC (1st cl) 37. Ely Th Coll 37. **d** 37 **p** 38 S'wark. C of Ascen Balham Hill 37-40; St Steph Battersea 40-42; CF 42-64; V of Sandgate 64-76. *207 Shorncliffe Road, Folkestone, Kent.* (Folkestone 57813)

GIBSON, Alexander Douglas. b 21. Wycl Hall Ox 60. **d** 62 Warrington for Liv **p** 63 Liv. C of St Helens 62-65; V of Ch Gresley w Linton 65-77; Biggin 77-78; Hartington (and Biggin from 78) Dio Derby from 77. *Hartington Vicarage, Buxton, Derbys, SK17 0AW.* (Hartington 280)

GIBSON, Arthur John. b 22. **d** 64 **p** 76 Gippsld. d Dio Graft 64-76; P-in-c of Neerim S 76-80; R of Foster Dio Gippsld from 80. *Rectory, Foster, Vic, Australia 3960.*

GIBSON, David Innes. b 31. Oak Hill Th Coll 56. **d** 59 Bp Rose for Cant **p** 60 Cant. C of Em S Croydon 59-62; Washfield 62-63; Asst Chap Blundells Sch 63-64; Sutton Valence Sch 64-68; Dean Close Sch 68-76; Ho Master from 75. *Dean Close School, Cheltenham, Glos.*

GIBSON, Donald William. Univ of Melb 55. ACT ThL 54. Ridley Coll Melb. **d** 56 Gippsld **p** 58 Melb for Gippsld. C of Yallourn 56-57; Boolarra 57-62; V of Bunyip 62-64; R of Numurkah 64-77; Shepparton Dio Wang from 77. *Rectory, Maude Street, Shepparton, 3630.*

GIBSON, Very Rev Edward George. Ridley Coll Melb. **d** 56 **p** 58 Bunb. C of Narrogin 56-57; St Paul's Cathl Bunb 57-59; R of Lake Grace 59-62; Mt Barker 62-65; V of Moe 65-70; R of Drouin 70-76; Hon Can of Gippsld 73-78; R of Leongatha 76-78; Dean of St Paul's Cathl Sale Dio Gippsld from 78; VG and Exam Chap to Bp of Gippsld from 81. *Deanery, Marley Street, Sale, Vic, Australia 3850.* (051-44 2020)

GIBSON, Garry Stuart. b 36. Univ of Lon BA (2nd cl Hebr) 62, PhD 75, BA (2nd cl Phil) 79. Oak Hill Th Coll 62. **d** 64 **p** 65 St Alb. C of Watford 64-67; Lect Cambs Coll of Arts and Tech 67-69; Middx Poly from 70. *20 Chalk Lane, Cockfosters, Barnet, Herts, EN4 9HJ.* (01-449 0474)

GIBSON, George Francis. b 1898. Trin Coll Dub BA Div Test and Downes Pri 28, MA 31. **d** 28 Down for Arm **p** 29 Arm. C of Dundalk 28-31; Wexford 31-33; I of Ballyfin 33-35; Fertagh 35-38; Lickmolassy 38-42; Arm. U 42-55; RD of Aughrin and Loughrea 40-42; Exam Chap to Bp of Cash 54-60; Can and Treas of Waterf Cathl 55-56; Chan of Waterf Cathl and Preb of Rossduff 56-60; I of Clonmel U 55-60; Newtown Fetullagh 60-67. *17 Cathedral Square, Waterford, Irish Republic.*

GIBSON, George Granville. b 36. Cudd Coll 69. **d** 71 Bp Ramsbottom for Newc T **p** 72 Newc T. C of St Paul Cullercoats (or Whitley Bay) 71-73; Team V of Cramlington 73-77; V of Newton Aycliffe Dio Dur from 77; M Gen Syn from 80. *St Clare's Vicarage, Newton Aycliffe, Co Durham.* (Aycliffe 313613)

GIBSON, Canon George Henry. b 04. Univ of Bris BA (1st cl Phil and Econ) 33, MA 36. Univ of Lon PhD 45. Westcott Ho Cam 34. **d** 35 **p** 36 S'wark. C of St Mark (in c of St Hilda) Camberwell 35-40; V of Lodsworth 40-44; Pastor and Leader of Commun of St Hilda in the Fields Nuthurst 40-58; R of Nuthurst 44-57; Prin of Gaveston Hall Sch Nuthurst 45-58; Guest Prof Rikkyo Univ Tokyo 55-56; V of Findon 57-59; Prof and Chap Momoyama Univ Osaka 59-64; Visiting Prof Rikkyo, Aoyama and Toritsu Univs Tokyo 65-68; Hon Can of Kobe 68-73; V of Stone 69-73; Perm to Offic Dio Man from 77. *13 Swann Way, Broadbridge Heath, Nr Horsham, W Sussex, RH12 3NQ.*

GIBSON, Henry Edward. b 15. Keble Coll Ox BA 41, MA 46, Dipl Th 42. St Steph Ho 41. **d** 43 **p** 44 Ox. C of St Mich AA Summertown Ox 43-49; Warden of Youth Ho and Youth Org for the Episc Ch in Scotld 49-51; C of Farlington 51-56; V of H Trin Ryde 56-63; Waterlooville 63-81. *8 Worcester Road, Chichester, Sussex.* (Chich 779194)

GIBSON, Jack Hodgetts. b 03. St Cath Coll Cam 2nd cl Hist Trip pt i 25, BA (2nd cl Th Trip pt i) 26, MA 31. Westcott Ho Cam. **d** 27 Southw **p** 28 Bp Abraham for Southw. C of St Steph Sneinton 27-31; St Marg Ilkley 31-35; St Jo Bapt (in c of St Barn) Ches 35-36; Hucknall Torkard (in c of St Pet) 36-41; PC of Kirkby Woodhouse 41-47; V of Netherfield 47-61; R of Colwick 56-61; Keyworth 61-69; Perm to Offic Dio Southw from 69. *398/6 Woodborough Road, Nottingham, NG3 4JF.* (Nottingham 608794)

GIBSON, James Douglas. b 19. **d** 74 **p** 75 Tas. C of Burnie 74-75; P-in-c of Ringarooma w Derby 75-77; R of Cooee Dio Tas from 77. *5 Poke Street, Cooee, Tasmania 7320.* (004-31 1053)

GIBSON, John Chad. b 05. AKC (2nd cl) 34. **d** 34 **p** 35 S'wark. C of St Jo Evang E Dulwich 34-36; St Anne (in c of St Mary) Wandsworth 36-39; Welwyn 39-43; V of Sundon w Streatley 43-49; Sawbridgeworth 49-62; RD of Bp's Stortford 61-62; R of Stedham w Iping 62-68; Rumboldswyke Chich 68-72; C of Leamington Priors 72-73; Chilvers Coton w Astley 73-77; Perm to Offic Dios Sarum and B & W from 77. *33 Parham Road, Ensbury Park, Bournemouth, BH10 4BB.* (0202-511952)

GIBSON, John George. b 20. Chich Th Coll 47. **d** 50 **p** 51 Lon. C of St Mich AA w Ch Ch Notting Hill 50-53; St Mary Virg Kenton 53-58; V of Gunnersbury 58-70; SS Pet and Paul Teddington Dio Lon from 70. *Vicarage, Bychurch End, Teddington, Middx, TW11 8PS.* (01-977 3330)

GIBSON, John Houston Arthur. St Jo Coll Morpeth ACT ThL 68. **d** 68 **p** 69 C & Goulb. C of St Jo Bapt Canberra 68-70; Albury 70-72; Havant Portsm 72-74; R of Gunning 74-79; Kooringal Dio C & Goulb from 79. *83 Grove Street, Kooringal, NSW, Australia 2650.*

GIBSON, John Murray Hope. b 35. Univ of Dur BA 58, Dipl Th 60. Cranmer Hall Dur 58. **d** 60 **p** 61 Dur. C of Chester-le-Street 60-63; Stockton-on-Tees 63-68; V of Denton w Ingleton 68-75; Swalwell Dio Dur from 75. *Swalwell Vicarage, Newcastle upon Tyne, NE16 3JL.* (Whickham 887538)

GIBSON, Murray John. b 36. **d** 81 Pret. C of St Steph Lyttelton Dio Pet from 81. *27 George Street, Eldoraigne, Verwoerdburg 0140, S Africa.*

GIBSON, Paul Saison. Bps' Univ of Lennox BA 56. St Chad's Coll Regina LTh 57. **d** 56 Ox for Cant for Niag **p** 57 Lon for Niag. C of Bloomsbury and Chap Univ of Lon 57-59; R of Hannon Ont 59-60; Chap McMaster Univ Ont 59-60; McGill Univ Montr 60-66; Prin U Th Coll Hong Kong and L to Offic Dio Hong 66-72; Educn Consultant Gen Syn Angl Ch of Canada from 72. *c/o 600 Jarvis Street, Toronto 285, Ont., Canada.* (416-924 9192)

GIBSON, Philip Nigel Scott. b 53. St Jo Coll Dur BA 78. Cranmer Hall Dur Dipl Th 79. **d** 79 **p** 80 Birm. C of Yardley Dio Birm from 79. *424 Church Road, Yardley, Birmingham, B33 8PB.*

GIBSON, Canon Ralph Thexton. Wycl Coll Tor. **d** 40 **p** 41 Keew. Miss at Churchill 40-44; Prin of All SS Res Sch Aklavik 44-55; Can of Arctic 52-55; R of Clarksburg 55-75; Can of Hur 72-75; Can (Emer) from 76. *PO Box 225, Clarksburg, Ont, Canada.*

GIBSON, Raymond. b 23. Ely Th Coll 60. **d** 62 **p** 63 Leic. C of St Jas Gtr Leic 62-67; Chap Leic R Infirm and Succr Leic Cathl 67-68; Chap City, Heathfield, Sherwood and St Francis Hosps Nottm from 68. *10 Breck Hill Road, Woodthorpe, Nottingham.* (Nottm 265929)

GIBSON, Raymond Frank. b 34. Tor Bible Coll BTh 61. Tyndale Hall Bris 62. **d** 64 **p** 65 Bradf. C of St Jo Evang Gt Horton Bradf 64-67; Otley 67-72; V of Fairlight Dio Chich from 72. *Fairlight Vicarage, Hastings, Sussex.* (Pett 3104)

GIBSON, Robert Swinton. b 26. Wadh Coll Ox BA 50, MA 55. Wells Th Coll 50. **d** 53 **p** 54 S'wark. C of Greenwich 53-61; Hon Chap to Bp of S'wark 56-67; Industr Missr Dio S'wark 55-62; Sen Chap S Lon Industr Miss 62-67; Dean of Port Harcourt Chr Coun Project Nigeria 67-69; R of Guisborough Dio York from 69; RD of Guisborough from 73. *Rectory, Guisborough, Cleve.* (Guisborough 2588)

GIBSON, Ronald Ross. Moore Th Coll Syd. **d** and **p** 49 Syd. C of Marrabeen 49-50; L to Offic Dio Syd 50-51; Org Sec CMS Dio Perth 51-55; R of Harris Pk 55-58; Austinmer 58-68; Bexley 68-78; L to Offic Dio Syd from 78. *20 Bellevarde Parade, Mona Vale, NSW, Australia 2207.* (99-3619)

GIBSON, Terence Allen. b 37. Jes Coll Cam 2nd cl Nat Sc Trip pt i 60, BA (2nd cl Th Trip pt ia) 61, MA 65. Cudd Coll 61. **d** 63 Warrington for Liv **p** 64 Liv. C of Kirkby 63-66; Warden of Centre 63 Kirkby 66-75; Area Youth Chap 66-72; Team V of Kirkby Dio Liv 72-75; R from 75; RD of Walton from 79. *Rectory, Sherwood, Mill Lane, Kirkby, Liverpool L32 2AX.* (051-547 2155)

GIBSON, Thomas Thomson. b 23. Sarum Th Coll 62. **d** 63 **p** 64 Sarum. C of E w W Harnham 63-66; V of Rowde 66-75; R of Poulshot 67-75; V of Gt and L Badminton w Acton Turville Dio Glouc from 75; P-in-c of Hawkesbury w Hawkesbury Upton Dio Glouc from 81. *Vicarage, Badminton, Glos.* (Badminton 427)

GIBSON, Timothy Maxwell. b 47. Univ of Syd BSc 69. Univ of NSW MESc 71. ACT BTh 78. St Barn Coll Adel 76. **d** 79 **p** 80 Melb. C of St paul Frankston 79-81; St John Toorak Dio Melb from 81. *12 Ruabon Road, Toorak, Vic, Australia 3142.*

GIBSON, Canon William Henry. St Chad's Coll Regina STh 56. **d** 53 **p** 53 Moos. Miss at Cadillac 53-56; Rouyn 56-60; R of S Porcupine Dio Moos from 60; Exam Chap to Bp of Moos from 60; Hon Can of Moos from 77. *Box 847, South Porcupine, Ont., Canada.* (705-235 3103)

GIBSON, William John. b 29. Univ of Dur BA (3rd cl Th) 58, Dipl Th 59. **d** 59 **p** 60 Wakef. C of Elland 59-62; St Jo Evang Huddersfield 62-66; V of Sowerby Dio Wakef from 66. *Sowerby Vicarage, Towngate, Sowerby Bridge, Yorks.* (Halifax 31036)

GICHURU, Daniel Ng'ang'a. **d** 63 **p** 65 Nak. P Dio Nak. *Box 217, Thomson's Falls, Kenya.*

GICK, Alan Gladney. Trin Coll Dub BA 38, MA 58. **d** 40 **p** 41 Derry. C of Conwall 40-44; C-in-c of Donaghmore w Monellan 44-60; I of Lislimnaghan 60-80. *15 Fernhill Crescent, Greenmount, Coleraine, Co Derry, BT51 3QS.*

GIDDENS, Leslie Vernon. b 29. Bps' Coll Cheshunt 54. **d** 56 **p** 57 Lon. C of St Pet Harrow 56-58; St Benet Fink Tottenham 58-63; P-in-c of St Nich Conv Distr Hayes Dio Lon from 63. *Vicarage, Raynton Drive, Hayes, UB4 8BG.* (01-573 4122)

GIDDEY, Canon William Denys. b 17. Univ of Leeds, BA (2nd cl Hist) 39. Coll of Resurr Mirfield 39. **d** 41 **p** 42 Sarum. C of St Paul Weymouth 41-43; St Geo-in-the-E 43-48; Res Chap of Guy's Hosp Lon 48-55; R of Binbrook and of Swinhope w Thorganby 55-61; Chap Eastbourne Hosps Dio Chich from 61; Can and Preb of Chich Cathl from 78. *Chaplain's Office, St Mary's Hospital, Eastbourne, Sussex, BN21 1QL.* (Eastbourne 20662)

GIDDINGS, Howard William. b 30. K Coll Lon and Warm AKC 61. **d** 62 **p** 63 Dur. C of St Chad Stockton-on-Tees 62-65; Horsham (in c of St Leon) 65-67; Chap RAF from 67. *Ministry of Defence, Adastral House, WC1.*

GIDEON, Ndooh. **d** 76 **p** 77 Mt Kenya E. P Dio Mt Kenya E. *Sagana Parish, PO Box 8064, Sagana, Kenya.*

GIDNEY, Richard Conrad. Univ of Guelph Ont BA 71. Trin Coll Tor MDiv 74. **d** 73 Keew **p** 74 Qu'App. C of Big Country 73-76; St Paul's Pro-Cathl Regina 76-79; I of St Jas Regina Dio Qu'App from 79. *1105 Empress Street, Regina, Sask, Canada.*

GIDUDU, Methuselah Makibwe. Buwalasi Th Coll 64. **d** 66 **p** 67 Mbale. P Dio Mbale; Dioc Treas 73-77. *PO Box 473, Mbale, Uganda.*

GIFF, William Lee Mather. b 1900. QUB BSc 25, MSc 27. Lon Coll of Div 25. **d** 27 **p** 28 S'wark. C of St Thos Telford Pk Streatham 27-29; CMS Miss Dio U Nile 29-34; C-in-c of Dowra w Inishmagrath 34-35; I of Ballysodare U 35-47; Exam Chap to Bp of Tuam 46-48; Supt ICM and Chap Miss Ch Townsend Street Dub 47-51; C of Rathmolyon w Laracor 51-52; I of Clara 52-65; Killucan 65-69; Exam Chap to Bp of Meath 57-69; Can of Meath 58-69; Preb of Tassagard in St Patr Cathl Dub 59-69; RD of Ardnurcher and Clonmacnoise 60-64; Archd of Meath 64-69. *30 Fortwilliam Park, Belfast, 15 4AP.*

GIFFORD, Bruce Campbell. Univ of BC BA 52. Univ of Calif MA 56. Trin Coll Tor LTh 59. **d** 58 **p** 59 Niag. C of Ancaster 58-60; St Jas Vancouver 60-66; L to Offic Dio New Westmr 66-76; I of St Mark Vanc Dio New Westmr from 76. *1805 Larch Street, Vancouver, BC, V6K 3N9, Canada.*

GIFFORD, Douglas John. b 24. Qu Coll Ox MA 50, BLitt 54. **d** 80 **p** 81 St Andr (NSM). Chap St Andr Univ from 80. *3 Balfour Place, St Andrews, Fife, KY16 9RQ.* (0334 72742)

GIGABA, Thomas Jabulani. St Bede's Coll Umtata 65. **d** 67 **p** 68 Natal. C of Springvale 67-71; Kwa Mbusi Eshowe 71-72; P-in-c of St Thos Eshowe 72-74; R of St Phil Stanger Dio Natal from 74. *St Philip's Rectory, Stanger, Natal, S Africa.* (Stanger 454)

✠ **GIGGALL, Right Rev George Kenneth.** b 14. OBE 61. Univ of Man BA (2nd cl French) 37. St Chad's Coll Dur Dipl Th 38. **d** 39 **p** 40 Man. C of St Alb Cheetwood 39-41; St Elizabeth Reddish 41-45; Chap RN 45-69; Hon Chap to HM the Queen 67-69; Dean of Gibr 69-73; Cons Ld Bp of St Helena in Ch of St Sav E Lon CP 4 May 73 by Abp of Capetn; Bps of Natal, Grahmstn, Lesotho, Kimb K, Johann, Swaz, Port Eliz, Lebom, Pret, St John's and Bloemf; and others; res 79; Chap at San Remo and Bordighera and Asst Bp Gibr in Eur 79-81. *Fosbrooke House, 8 Clifton Drive, Lytham, Lancs, FY8 5RQ.* (0253-734100)

GILA, Dennis Dan. **d** 78 New Hebr **p** 80 Vanuatu. P Dio New Hebr 78-80; Dio Vanuatu from 80. *Big Bay, Santo, Vanuatu.*

GILBERD, Bruce Carlyle. Univ of Auckld BSc 60. St Jo Coll Auckld LTh 64. **d** 62 **p** 63 Auckld. C of Devonport Auckld 62-65; All SS Ponsonby Auckld 65; Panmure 65-68; V of Avondale 68-72; Dir Interchurch Trade and Industr Miss Dio Wel 73-80; Hon C of Lower Hutt 73-77; Waiwhetu 77-80; Lect St Jo Th Coll Auckld from 80. *150 St Johns Road, Auckland 5, NZ.*

GILBERT, Alan John. BD (Lon) 57. Ridley Hall Cam 65. **d** 66 **p** 67 B & W. C of St Jas Taunton 66-67; Asst Master Keynsham Gr Sch 67-68; Asst Chap Wellington Coll Oxon 68-72; Actg Chap Em Sch Wandsworth 72-73; Chap Wellington Sch Somt 73-74; Em Sch Wandsworth Dio S'wark from 74. *c/o Emanuel School, Wandsworth Common, SW11.* (01-870 4171)

GILBERT, Andrew. St Francis Coll Brisb ACT ThL 56. Seabury-Western Th Sem Ill MA 68. **d** 56 **p** 57 Bath. M of Bro of Good Shepherd 54-59; C of Dubbo 59-61; P-in-c of Stuart Town 61-62; R 62-67; in Amer Ch 67-68; Perm to Offic Dio Melb 69-70; Dio Brisb from 80; R of Blackall 70-72; Hopetoun 72-80. *3 Wyllie Street, Redcliffe, Queensld, Australia 4020.*

GILBERT, Arthur Armstrong. b 53. Federal Th Sem Natal Dipl Th 77. **d** 77 Kimb K. Succr of Cathl Ch of St Cypr Kimberley 77-79; R of St Mary-le-Bourne Kuruman Dio Kimb K from 79. *Box 48, Kuruman, S Africa.*

GILBERT, Barry. b 46. Univ of Leeds BA (3rd cl Th) 67. Coll of Resurr Mirfield 67. **d** 69 **p** 70 Worc. C of Malvern Link w Cowleigh 69-73; C-in-c of All SS Bromsgrove Dio Worc from 73. *All Saints' Vicarage, Bromsgrove, Worcs.* (Bromsgrove 72326)

GILBERT, Donald. b 30. St Aid Coll. **d** 65 **p** 66 Man. C of Failsworth 65-70; V of St Barn Oldham 70-74; Peel Hall Dio Man from 74. *St Richard's Vicarage, Lomond Road, Peel Hall, Manchester, M22 5JD.* (061-437 2022)

GILBERT, Frederick Herbert. b 14. Worc Ordin Coll. **d** 66 **p** 67 Ex. C of St Paul's Conv Distr Burnthouse Lane Ex 66-69; Paignton 69-73; Team V of Offwell (in c of Farway w Northleigh and Southleigh) 73-79; Perm to Offic Dio Ex from 80. *3 Mount Close, Honiton, Devon, EX14 8QZ.* (Honiton 3300)

GILBERT, Frederick Joseph. b 29. Lich Th Coll 58. **d** 59 Man **p** 60 Hulme for Man. [f in CA] C of Westoughton 59-62; V of Goodshaw 62-68; R of Crumpsall 68-75; RD of Cheetham (N Man from 74) 70-75; V of St Aid Sudden Rochdale 75-78; Team V of Rochdale 78-80; V of Westhoughton Dio Man from 80. *Westhoughton Vicarage, Market Street, Bolton, BL5 3AZ.* (Westhoughton 813280)

GILBERT, Godfrey. St Jo Coll Morpeth 29. ACT ThL 30. **d** 31 **p** 33 Graft. C of Grevillia 31-32; Liston 33-34; P-in-c 34; V of Coraki 35-38; Supt of St Paul Moa I 38-42; P-in-c of Lochinvar 42-46; Chap AIF 43-45; P-in-c of Prov Distr of Lambton 46-49; Lect in Psychology St Jo Coll Morpeth 48; R of Violet Town w Dookie 49-54; Corryong 54-68; Tallangatta 68-72; Hon Can of Wang 65-72; Perm to Offic Dio Syd from 74. *St Luke's Village, Dapto, NSW, Australia.*

GILBERT, John. b 18. SOC 61. **d** 64 **p** 65 S'wark. C of Cheam Dio S'wark 64-74; Hon C from 74; Hd Master Cheam Junior Boys' Sch from 64. *37 Devon Road, Cheam, Surrey.* (01-642 3373)

GILBERT, John Barton. St Mich Th Coll Crafers ACT ThL 53. **d** and **p** 53 Adel. C of Port Adel 53-55; Hawthorn 55-56; Elizabeth 56-57; LPr Dio Adel 57-58; C of St John Salisbury 58-59; P-in-c of Tailem Bend Miss 59-62; R of Balaklava 62-68; Kens Gardens 68-79; Enfield Dio Adel from 79. *1 St Clement's Street, Blair, Athol, S Australia 5084.* (262 2434)

GILBERT, John Edwin. b 28. FCA 62. Bp's Coll Cheshunt 54. **d** 57 **p** 58 St Alb. C of Ch Ch Luton 57-60; Gt Berkhamsted (in c of All SS) 60-64; P-in-c of Kamptee 65-68; Dioc Treas Nagp 65-70; Hon Chap All SS Cathl Nagp 68-70; Perm to Offic Dio St Alb 71-77; l to Offic from 78. *43 Cedar Road, Berkhamsted, Herts.* (Berkhamsted 3811)

GILBERT, John Michael. b 06. St Bonif Coll Warm 27. **d** 31 **p** 32 Truro. C of St Ives 31-34; Miss At Siota 34-35; C of All SS Shrewsbury 36-38; St Geo Cathl Windhoek 38-48; R of Luderitzbucht 38-45; VG Dio Damar 48 and 49; C-in-c of Tolpuddle Dorset 50-51; C of St Austell 51-52; R of Bethlehem S Afr 52-59; V of Davidstow w Otterham 59-63; C-in-c of Lesnewth 59-63; V of Porthleven 63-74; L to Offic Dio Truro 74-78; Perm to Offic Dio Geo from 78; Dom Chap to Bp of Geo from 78. *88 Victoria Street, George 6530, CP, S Africa.*

GILBERT, Joseph. b 12. Chich Th Coll 33. **d** 36 **p** 37 Man. C of St Mark Bolton 36-39; St Crispin Withington 39-43; R of St Matt Ardwick 43-49; St Mark Heyside 49-65; V of Lever Bridge 65-76. *159 Bolton Road, Edgworth, Bolton, Lancs, BL7 0AF.* (Bolton 852736)

GILBERT, Canon Leslie Charles. Univ of Dur LTh 43. **d** 43 Cant **p** 44 Dover for Cant. C of St Luke Woodside Croydon 43-46; Bearsted 46-49; Daramombe S Rhod 49-54; V of Wymynswold 54-56; Min of Aylesham Conv Distr 54-56; C of Umtali 56-58; R of Mabelreign 58-62; Marlborough 62-67; Marandellas Dio Mashon from 67; Archd of W Mashon 66-68; Marandellas 68-74; Can of Mashon from 68. *Rectory, Marandellas, Zimbabwe.*

GILBERT, Raymond. b 34. K Coll Lon and Warm AKC 61. **d** 62 **p** 63 Derby. C of Newbold 62-66; PV and Succr of S'wark Cathl 66-68; Prec and Sacr of Ely Cathl 68-74; P-in-c of Stuntney 68-74; Min Can and Prec of Cant Cathl 74-79; Hon Min Can from 79; P-in-c of Patrixbourne w Bridge and Bekesbourne Dio Cant 79-81; V from 81. *23 High Street, Bridge, Canterbury, Kent, CT4 5JZ.* (Bridge 830250)

GILBERT, Reginald Earl. b 54. Qu Univ Kingston Ont BA 76. Huron Coll Lon Ont MDiv 79. **d** 79 **p** 80 Ont. C of Elizabethtown Dio Ont 79. *PO Box 119, Lyn, Ont, Canada.* (613-345 3715)

GILBERT, Roger Charles. b 46. Ex Coll Ox BA (2nd cl Th) 69, MA 74, MEducn 81. St Steph Ho Ox 69. **d** 71 B & W **p** 72 Bp Wilson for B & W (APM). C of Bridgwater 71-74; Rugeley 74-81; St Luke Cannock Dio Lich from 81. *41 Stafford Road, Cannock, Staffs.* (Cannock 70531)

GILBERT, Roger Geoffrey. b 37. K Coll Lon BD and AKC 69. St Aug Coll Cant 69. **d** 70 Dorking for Guildf **p** 71 Guildf. C of Walton-on-Thames 70-74; R of St Mabyn 74-81; P-in-c of Helland 74-81; Madron w Morvah Dio Truro from 81. *Madron Vicarage, Penzance, Cornw, TR20 8SW.* (Penzance 3116)

GILBERT, Roy Alan. b 48. Univ of Birm BEducn 70. Ripon Coll Cudd 74. **d** 76 Birm **p** 77 Bp Aston for Birm. C of St Mary Moseley 76-82; Asst Chap St Pet Coll Adel from 82. *St Peter's College, Adelaide, S Australia 5069.*

GILBERT, Sidney Horace. b 34. Univ of Dur BA 58, MA 69. BD (Wales) 62. St Mich Coll Llan 58. **d** 61 **p** 62 St A. C of Colwyn Bay 61-63; Llanrhos 63-69; V of Penley and Bettisfield 69-78; Brymbo w Bwlchgwyn Dio St A from 78. *Brymbo Vicarage, Wrexham, Clwyd.* (Wrexham 758107)

GILBERT, Stephen Wilson Langton. Hur Coll Ont BA 45, LTh 45. **d** 45 **p** 46 Alg. C of Port Carling 45-47; I of Murillo 47-50; Espanola 50-53; R of St Thos Owen Sound 53-58; Kingsville 58-68; Meaford 68-77; Corunna Dio Hur from 77. *Box 1615, Corunna, Ont., Canada.*

GILBERT, Canon William Alexander. Univ of Tor BA 59. Trin Coll Tor STB 62. **d** 62 **p** 63 Ott. C of St Richard Ott 62-64; I of Petawawa 64-68; C of St Martin Ott 68-72; Dep Dir of Programme Ott 73-80; Dir from 80; Hon Can of Ott from 80. *71 Bronson Avenue, Ottawa, Ont., Canada.* (1-613-232-7124)

GILCHRIST, David John. b 51. Merton Coll Ox BA 75, MA 79. St Jo Coll Nottm 77. **d** 79 Barking for Chelmsf **p** 80 Chelmsf. C of St Andr Gt Ilford 79-81; Buckhurst Hill Dio Chelmsf from 81. *Glebe House, High Road, Buckhurst Hill, Essex.* (01-504 6652)

GILCHRIST, Fred. b 07. Univ of Dur BCom 48. BSc (Econ) Lon 51. Ripon Hall Ox 65. **d** 66 **p** 67 Newc T. C of St Pet Cowgate Newc T 66-68; Berwick-on-Tweed 69-76; Perm to Offic Dio Newc T from 76. *9 Ashtree Close, Rowlands Gill, T & W, NE39 1RA.*

GILCHRIST, Gavin Frank. b 53. AKC 74. Coll of Resurr 76. **d** 77 Repton for Derby **p** 78 Derby. C of Newbold 77-80; Addlestone Dio Guildf from 80. *217 Station Road, Addlestone, Surrey.* (0932-47587)

GILCHRIST, Canon James. b 10. CCC Ox BA 35, MA 50. Ely Th Coll 36. **d** 37 **p** 38 Ely. C of Downham Mkt w Bexwell 37-40; CF (EC) 40-46; Hon CF 46; PC of Chipping Sodbury 46-49; V of Hoxne w Denham St John 49-55; R of Denning-ton 55-66; Team V of Raveningham 66-78; RD of Loddon 68-71 and 75-78; Hon Can of Nor 73-78; Can (Emer) from 79. *19 The Close, Norwich, NR1 4DZ.* (Nor 613013)

GILCHRIST, Lawrence Edward. b 29. Univ of Liv BSc 52. N-W Ordin Course 74. **d** 76 **p** 77 Derby (APM). C of Buxton Dio Derby from 76. *5 Milldale Avenue, Buxton, Derbys, SK17 9BE.*

GILDING, James Peter. b 33. Univ of Leeds BA (Sociology) 64. Ely Th Coll 61. **d** 63 **p** 64 Blackb. C of St Pet Chorley 63-66; Pemberton 66-69; C-in-c of Terrington St John 69-74; Walpole St Andr 69-74; V of Elm 73-81; Team R of Stanground w Farcet Dio Ely from 81. *Rectory, Mace Road, Stanground, Peterborough, PE2 8RQ.* (Peterborough 63662)

GILDING, Richard Herbert. b 11. St Jo Coll Dur LTh 46, BA 47. ALCD 35. **d** 35 **p** 36 Lon. C of St Pet Staines 35-39; Chap RNVR 38-52; V of Aldbourne 48-56; Studley 56-75. *2 Church Corner, Potterne, Devizes, Wilts.*

GILES, Barry James. b 35. Kelham Th Coll 54. **d** 59 **p** 60 Chelmsf. C of St Marg w St Columba Leytonstone 59-62; Prec of Gibr Cathl 62-66; V of St Geo Over Darwen 66-69; St Edm Forest Gate w St Steph Upton Pk 69-73; R of St Pet Jersey Dio Win from 73. *St Peter's Rectory, Jersey, CI.* (Jersey 81805)

GILES, David Michael Peryer. b 34. K Coll Lon and Warm AKC 66. **d** 67 **p** 68 Roch. C of H Trin Twydall Gillingham 67-71; Leatherhead 71-75; V of Meopham 75-79; R of Meopham w Nurstead Dio Roch from 79; RD of Cobham from 79. *Rectory, Shipley Hills Road, Meopham, DA13 0AD.* (Meopham 813106)

GILES, Edward Alban. b 34. Bps' Coll Cheshunt. **d** 58 Blackb **p** 59 Lanc for Blackb. C of Colne 58-61; St Paul Warrington 61-63; Knysna 63-66; R of Eersterus w Silverton 66-70; Asst Chap HM Pris Wandsworth 70; Chap HM Pris Camp Hill 70-75; Stafford from 75. *9 Lawn Road, Rowley Park, Stafford.* (Stafford 3774)

GILES, Eric Francis. b 34. Sarum Th Coll 61. **d** 63 **p** 64 Ex. C of Plympton 63-71; R of Dumbleton w Wormington (and Toddington with Stanley Portlarge from 77) 71-79; P-in-c of Toddington w Stanley Pontlarge 71-77; V of St Jo Evang Churchdown Dio Glouc from 79. *St John's Vicarage, Churchdown, Gloucester, GL3 2DA.* (Churchdown 713421)

GILES, Francis Alec. b 09. K Coll Lon 28. **d** 36 **p** 37 Glouc. C of Pebworth w Marston Sicca and Dorsington 36-38; St Lawr Stroud 38-40; CF (EC) 40-45; R of Haselton w Compton Abdale (w Cold Salperton from 46) 45-47; V of Bisley 47-49; Chap Gordon Boys' Sch Woking and L to Offic Dio Guildf 49-74; Perm to Offic Dio Guildf from 74. *c/o Gordon Boys' School, West End, Woking, Surrey, GU24 9PT.*

GILES, Frank Edwin. St Aid Coll 50. **d** 53 **p** 54 Dur. C of Chester-le-Street 53-56; PC of Sariston 56-70; V of St Paul, Hook 70-80; Langley Dio Birm from 80. *33 Moat Road, Oldbury, Warley, Worcs.* (021-552 1809)

GILES, John Robert. b 36. Em Coll Cam 2nd cl Hist Trip pt i 58, BA (3rd cl Th Trip pt ii) 60, MA 65. Ripon Hall Ox 60. **d** 61 **p** 62 Nor. C of Lowestoft 61-65; Chap Univ of E Anglia 65-72; R of Kidbrooke 72-79; Sub-Dean of Greenwich 74-79; V of St Mark City and Dio Sheff from 79. *Vicarage, Broomhill, Sheffield, S10 2SG.* (Sheffield 663613)

GILES, Kevin Norman. BD (Lon) 68. Moore Coll Syd ACT ThL (1st cl) 67. **d** 68 **p** 69 Syd. C of St Clem Mosman 68-69; St Mich Wollongong 69; Chap Wollongong Univ Coll 70-72; on leave 72-74; Chap Univ of New Engl Armid 75-81; R of Kens Dio Adel from 81. *146 Kensington Road, Maryatville, S Australia 5068.*

GILES, Maurice Alfred Douglas. b 15. Bps' Coll Cheshunt. **d** 66 **p** 67 Lon. C of H Trin E Finchley 66-69; St Andr Southgate 69-71; V of St Paul New Southgate 71-75; C of Friern Barnet 75-80; Perm to Offic Dio Lon from 80. *66 Granville Road, N12 0HT.* (01-346 0214)

GILES, Canon Michael Faraday. b 1894. St Jo Coll Ox BA 18. Ridley Hall Cam 19. **d** 20 **p** 21 Newc T. C of St Aid Elswick 20-24; Gedling 24-29; V of Arnold 29-43; R of Wollaton (w Cossall to 53) 43-64; Hon Can of Southw 56-65; Can (Emer) from 65. *7 Derbyshire Crescent, Wollaton Road, Wollaton, Notts.*

GILES, Richard Stephen. b 40. Univ of Dur BA 63. MRTPI 71. Cudd Coll 64. **d** 65 **p** 66 Pet. C of Higham Ferrers 65-68; Perm to Offic Dio Ox 69; C of Oakengates 70; St Geo Stevenage 71-75; P-in-c of Howdon Panns 75-76; Team V of Willington 76-79; V of St Jude City and Dio Pet from 79; Bp of Pet Adv for Planning from 79. *49 Atherstone Avenue, Peterborough.* (Pet 264169)

GILES, Robert Medwin. b 37. Univ of Man BA (Econ) 58. Ripon Hall Ox 64. **d** 66 Hulme for Man **p** 67 Man. C of Peel 66-68; Alverstoke 68-71; P-in-c of Edale 71-79; Warden Champion House Dioc Youth Centre Edale 71-79; Sen Dioc Youth Officer Dio York from 79. *398 Huntington Road, York, YO3 9HU.*

GILKES, Donald Martin. b 47. St Jo Coll Nottm 78. **d** 80 **p** 81 Sheff. C of Conisbrough Dio Sheff from 80. *18b Church Street, Conisbrough, S Yorks.*

GILKES, Overton Weldon. Codr Coll Barb. **d** 56 **p** 57 Barb. C of St Mich Cathl Barb 57-60; Friern Barnet 60-63; Kingstown Cathl 63-66; Montego Bay 67-68; Asst Master Cornwall Coll 67-70; R of Falmouth 70-75; St D Dio Barb from 76. *St David's Rectory, Christ Church, Barbados, WI.*

GILL, Alan Gordon. b 42. Sarum Wells Th Coll 73. **d** 75 **p** 76 Sarum. C of Wimborne Minster 75-78; R of Winterbourne Stickland w Turnworth, Winterbourne Houghton, Winterbourne Whitechurch and Winterbourne Clenston Dio Sarum from 78. *Winterbourne Stickland Rectory, Blandford, Dorset, DT11 0NL.* (Milton Abbas 880482)

GILL, Ven Arthur Charles. b 1898. Trin Coll Dub BA 23, MA 27. **d** 27 **p** 29 Oss. C of Maryborough and Dysart Enos 27-32; C-in-c of Preban w Moyne 32-38; I of Schull 38-40; Ballydehob 40-49; Templebreedy (w Nohoval and Tracton from 59) 49-75; Treas of Cloyne and Can of Cahirlag in Cork Cathl 59-65; Prec of Cloyne and Can of Killuspugmullane in Cork Cathl 65-67; Treas of Cork Cathl 67-68; Archd of Cloyne and Preb of Liscleary in Cork Cathl from 68. *Moyne, Forge Cross, Crosshaven, Co Cork, Irish Republic.*

GILL, Arthur John Colin Burke. Late Scho of Ex Coll Ox 23. St Steph Ho Ox 27. **d** 28 **p** 29 St E. C of All SS Ipswich 28-31; Perm to Offic at St Alb Holborn 31-41; V of St Martin Brighton 41-60; Commiss Nass 46-63; R of St Magnus Mart City and Dio Lon from 60; Master Coll of Guardians of Our Lady of Walsingham from 73. *St Magnus the Martyr, The Vestry, Lower Thames Street, EC3.* (01-626 4481)

GILL, Brian Alvan. b 35. Codr Coll Barb 59. **d** 62 **p** 63 Windw Is. C of Kingstown 62-64; P-in-c of Marriaqua 64-69; R 69-73; Calliaqua 73-74; C of Clun 74-77; P-in-c of Bucknell w Buckton Dio Heref 77-78; V (w Llanfair-Waterdine and Stowe) from 79. *Vicarage, Bucknell, Salop, SY7 0AD.* (Bucknell 340)

GILL, Christopher John Sutherland. b 28. Selw Coll Cam 2nd cl Mod Lang Trip (French) pt i 51, BA (2nd cl Th Trip pt ia) 52, MA 70. Ely Th Coll 52. **d** 54 **p** 55 Chich. C of Portslade 54-58; Goring 58-60; Chap St Edm's Sch Cant 60-76; Bennett Mem C E Girls' Sch Tunbridge Wells from 76. *Flat 1, Hurstleigh, Hurstwood Lane, Tunbridge Wells, TN4 8YA.* (0892-28409)

GILL, David. b 38. Univ of St Andr MB, ChB 63. E Midl Min Tr Course 79. **d** 81 Sherwood for Southw. C of St Jo Evang Carrington Dio Southw from 81. *1 Malvern Court, 29 Mapperley Road, Nottingham, WG3 5AG.*

GILL, Donald Maule Harvell. Keble Coll Ox BA 33, MA 39. Wells Th Coll 34. **d** 35 **p** 36 Win. C of St Andr Bournemouth 35-38; Min of Epiph Conv Distr Moordown Bournemouth 38-45; V of Micheldever 45-70; Insp of Schs Dio Win 45-64; R of Minstead 70-80. *23 Rodbourne Close, Newlands Manor Estate, Everton, Lymington, Hants.*

GILL, Douglas Henry John. **d** 57 Bp Snell for Tor **p** 60 Tor. C of St Luke Tor 59-60; R of Creemore 60-80. *Box 275, Creemore, Ont, Canada.*

GILL, Frank Emanuel. b 34. Oak Hill Coll 73. **d** 75 Kens for Lon **p** 76 Lon. C of St Steph w St Thos Uxbridge Rd Hammersmith 75-79; Dioc Commun and Race Relns Officer from 77; P-in-c of St Thos Kensal Town Dio Lon from 79. *231 Kensal Road, W10 5DB.* (01-969 1684)

GILL, Geoffrey Fitzell. b 17. Selw Coll Cam BA 39, MA 43. Linc Th Coll 39. **d** 41 **p** 42 Pet. C of All SS Wellingborough 41-46; St Jo Bapt Knighton Leic 46-51; V of Enderby w Lubbesthorpe Dio Leic from 51; RD of Guthlaxton i 63-74. *Enderby Vicarage, Leics.* (Leic 863220)

✠ **GILL, Right Rev Kenneth Edward.** b 32. [Methodist Min]. In Ch of S India 58-72; Cons Ld Bp in Karnataka Centr (Ch of S India) in St Mark's Cathl Bangalore 19 Oct 72; res 80; Asst Bp of Newc T from 80. *4 Grainger Park Road, Newcastle-upon-Tyne, NE4 8DP.*

GILL, Canon Lewis Frank. Em Coll Sktn 61. **d** 61 **p** 62 Sktn. I of Cut Knife 61-69; Watson Dio Sktn from 69; I of Pathlow 69-72; Lashburn 72-76; Hon Can of Sktn from 72; R of Parkland 76-77; Biggar Dio Sktn from 77. *Box 551, Biggar, Sask, Canada.*

GILL, Michael Harvey. b 52. St Pail's Th Coll Grahmstn 78. **d** 80 Bp Ndwandwe for Johann. C of Lichtenburg Dio Johann from 80. *PO Box 262, Lichtenburg, S Africa 2740.*

GILL, Neil Raymond. St Francis Coll Brisb 66. **d** 68 **p** 69 Brisb. C of All SS Chermside Brisb 68-72; Perm to Offic Dio Brisb from 72. *12 Mole Street, Teneriffe, Queensland, Australia 4005.* (52 8046)

GILL, Noel Charles. St Francis Coll Brisb 65. **d** 69 Brisb. C of Warwick 69-70; Miss at Mitchell River 70-73; Chap Aerial Miss Dio Carp 73; P-in-c of Richmond Par Distr Dio N Queensld from 74. *PO Box 51, Richmond, Queensland, Australia 4822.*

GILL, Paul Joseph. b 45. Ridley Coll Melb 73. **d** and **p** 74 Perth. C of Applecross 74-76; St Martin Birm 77-80; V of St Mary Pype Hayes, Erdington Dio Birm from 80. *St Mary's Vicarage, Tyburn Road, Pype Hayes, Birmingham, B24 0TB.* (021-373 3534)

GILL, Richard Ward. b 26. Univ of Lon BD 53. Oak Hill Th Coll 53. **d** 54 **p** 55 Ely. C of St Andr L Cam 54-56; w CMS 56-64; Prin Bp Gwynne Coll Mundri 61-64; C of Dagenham 64-65; V of St Paul City and Dio St Alb from 65. *9 Brampton Road, St Albans, Herts, AL1 4PN.* (St Albans 54619)

GILL, Canon Robert Henry. b 01. AKC 29. **d** 29 **p** 30 Lon. C of St Sav Warwick Avenue Paddington 29-35; LDHM of St Aug of Cant Whitton 35-47; Chap RAFVR 40-45; Gen Sec C of E Youth Coun 47-52; L to Offic at St Sav Paddington 49-52; R of St Andr w St Nich and St Mary Hertford 52-70; RD of Hertford 64-70; Hon Can of St Alb 66-70; Can (Emer) from 70. *25 North Road Avenue, Hertford.* (Hertford 52108)

GILL, Robin Morton. b 44. K Coll Lon and Warm AKC and BD (2nd cl) 66. Univ of Lon PhD 69. Univ of Birm MSocSc 72. **d** 68 Bp McKie for Cov **p** 69 Cov. C of Rugby 68-71; Lect Newton Th Coll Papua 71-72; New Coll Edin Univ from 72; C-in-c of St Phil Edin 73-75; Ford w Etal Dio Newc T from 75. *Old Vicarage, Branxton, Cornhill-on-Tweed, Northumb.* (Crookham 248)

GILL, Stanley. b 34. Sarum Th Coll 66. **d** 68 **p** 69 St E. C of St Mary Stoke Ipswich 68-73; V of St Geo Bury St Edms 73-78; C of St Mary Stoke Ipswich Dio St E 78-80; Team V from 80. *Church House, Stoke Park, Ipswich, Suff.*

GILL, Thomas. b 21. St Aid Coll 62. **d** 63 **p** 64 York. C of St Aug Newland 63-67; V of Burstwick w Thorngumbald 67-78; RD of S Holderness 74-78; R of Brandesburton Dio York from 78; RD of N Holderness from 80. *Brandesburton Rectory, Driffield, Yorks.* (0401 42350)

GILL, William. b 08. St Aid Coll 59. **d** 60 **p** 61 Bradf. C of Menston in Wharfedale 60-63; V of Cowling 63-68; Austwick 68-78; Perm to Offic Dio Bradf from 79. *4 Studdley Crescent, Gilstead, Bingley, W Yorks, BD16 3NF.* (Bradford 568549)

GILL, William Booth. St Francis Coll Brisb 50. ACT ThL 50. **d** 51 **p** 52 New Guinea. C of Dogura 51-52; P-in-c of Port Moresby 52-54; C of All SS Hobart 54-56; P-in-c of Boianai 56-59; Perm to Offic Dio Melb 60-62 and from 67; C of Ch Ch Essendon and of Strathmore 62-67. *19 Clan Brae Avenue, Burwood, Vic, Australia 3125.* (03-288 6624)

GILLA, Nikodemo Girima. Bp Gwynne Coll Mundri 57. **d** 59 **p** 61 Sudan. P Dio Sudan 59-76; Dio Rumbek from 76. *ECS, Wandi, Sudan.*

GILLAN, Ian Thomson. b 15. Univ of Aber MA 37, BD 40. Univ of Edin PhD 43. **d** 52 RC Abp of Paris **p** 53 RC Abp of St Andr & Edin. In RC Ch 52-72; Rec into Angl Commun 73 by Bp of Moray; Perm to Offic Dio Moray 73; C of Aber Cathl 73-74; P-in-c of Gordon Chapel Fochabers 74-75; Aberlour 74-75; Prec of St Andr Cathl Inverness 75; P-in-c of St Clem Aber 76-78; Perm to Offic Dio Aber from 78. *297 Union Grove, Aberdeen, AB1 6TD.* (Aber 324046)

GILLARD, Brian Roy. b 49. Bp's Univ Lennoxville BA 72. Trin Coll Tor MDiv 75. **d** and **p** 75 Ott. C of St John Smiths Falls 75-79; I of Maberley-Lanark 79-81; on leave. *28a George Street North, Smiths Falls, Ont, Canada.*

GILLARD, Geoffrey Vernon. b 48. Univ of Man BA 70. Univ of Nottm MPhil 80. St Jo Coll Nottm 74. **d** 78 **p** 79 Liv. C of Ch Ch Aughton 78-81; V of Ch Ch Kowloon Tong Dio Hong from 81. *Christ Church Vicarage, Kowloon Tong, Hong Kong.*

GILLARD, Reginald Philip Thompson. Em Coll Sktn 49. **d** 54 **p** 55 Sktn. R of Macklin 54-58; P-in-c of Lamerton Miss 59-61; I of All SS w Transfig Calg 61-65; CF (Canad) 65-68; I of Wawota 68-69; Assiniboia 75-79; Oxbow Dio Qu'App from 79. *Box 732, Oxbow, Sask, Canada.*

GILLESPIE, Albert Joseph. Trin Coll Dub BA and Higher Dipl Educn 35. **d** 35 **p** 36 Down. C of Bangor 35-37; Galway 37-38; St Thos St Annes-on-the-Sea 38-40; Chap RAFVR 40-46; C of Blackpool 46-49; V of H Trin Blackb 49-56; Asst Dioc Insp of Schs Dio Blackb from 50; R of Heysham 56-77; P-in-c of Leck 77-79. *Leodest Road, Andreas, IM.* (Kirk Andreas 662)

GILLESPIE, Canon Arthur Leonard. St Francis Coll Brisb ACT ThL 41. **d** 41 **p** 43 Brisb. C of H Trin Fortitude Valley 41-44; M of Bush Bro of St Paul Dio Brisb 44-56; R of Dalby 56-65; Bundaberg 65-73; Charleville 73-78; Laidley Dio Brisb from 78; Hon Can of Brisb from 73. *Rectory, Ambrose Street, Laidley, Queensland, Australia 4341.* (Laidley 253)

GILLESPIE, George Henry. b 20. Late Scho of SS Coll Cam BA 46, MA 55. Cudd Coll 46. **d** 48 **p** 49 Liv. C of Wigan 48-53; Ashbourne w Mapleton (in c of Clifton) 53-55; PC of Allenton 56-68; V 68-71; Chap Derby High Sch for Girls 58-71; V of Ascen Bath 71-78; C-in-c of Norton St Phil w Hemington, Hardington and Laverton Dio B & W 78-81; R from 81. *Norton St Philip Rectory, Bath, Avon, BA3 6LY.* (Faulkland 447)

GILLETT, David Keith. b 45. Univ of Leeds BA 65, MPhil 68. Oak Hill Th Coll 66. **d** 68 **p** 69 St Alb. C of St Luke's Eccles Distr Watford 68-71; Sec Pathfinders and CYFA N Area 71-74; Lect St Jo Coll Nottm 74-77; Dir of Ex Stud

77-80; Publ Pr Dio Southw 74-80; Dio Down from 80. *Christian Renewal Centre, Shore Road, Rostrevor, Co Down, BT34 3AB.* (Rostrevor 492)

GILLETT, James. b 01. Pemb Coll Ox BA (3rd cl Mod Hist) 23, MA 26. Wycl Hall, Ox 24. **d** 25 **p** 26 Southw. Asst Master Trent Coll Derbys 23-28; LPr Dio S'wark 25-27; C of St John Long Eaton 27-28; Asst Master and Chap Prince of Wales Sch Nairobi 28-31; Hd Master Nairobi Scho 31-49; L to Offic Dio Momb 28-53; Hon Chap to Bp of Momb 37-53; Hon Chap to Kenya Regmt 36-45 and 50-53; R of Stockton Warws 53-56; Chap of the Isles of Scilly and V of St Mary's 56-66; L to Offic Dio Truro from 66. *11 Marlborough Crescent, Falmouth, Cornw, TR11 2RJ.* (Falmouth 312849)

GILLETT, Victor Henry John. b 31. Clifton Th Coll 59. **d** 62 Warrington for Liv **p** 63 Liv. C of Walton Breck 62-65; Heath Town 65-68; V of St Paul Tipton 68-76; Moulton Dio Pet from 76. *Moulton Vicarage, Northampton.* (Northn 491060)

GILLETT, Vincent. b 30. Univ of Lon BSc (Chem) 55. Univ of E Anglia MSc 72. Chich Th Coll 59. **d** 61 **p** 62 Blackb. C of St Mich AA Blackpool 61-63; Chap Adisadel Coll 63-66; Chap Kumasi Univ 66-72; L to Offic Dio Accra 63-72; Asst Master St Marg High Sch for Boys Liv 72-75; Halewood Comprehensive Sch Liv 75-79; L to Offic Dio Liv 72-79; Dio Ex from 79; Hd Master St Wilfrid's Sch Ex from 79. *25 St David's Hill, Exeter, Devon.*

GILLETT, William Charles. b 05. Sarum Th Coll 28. **d** 31 Win **p** 32 Southn for Win. C of H Trin Southn 31-37; Sunningdale 37-40; Tiverton 40-44; R of Uplowman 44-49; Blackborough w Sheldon 49-51; E Anstey w W Anstey 51-78; Publ Pr Dio Ex from 78. *Sarum, East Anstey, Tiverton, Devon.*

GILLHAM, Martin John. b 45. Qu Coll Birm 72. **d** 75 **p** 76 Reading for Ox. [f CA]. C of Ch Ch Reading 75-78; Team V of Crowmarsh Gifford w Newnham Murren 78-79; Wallingford w Crowmarsh Gifford and Newnham Murren Dio Ox from 79. *Vicarage, Crowmarsh, Wallingford.* (Wallingford 37626)

GILLHESPEY, Clive. b 28. Dipl Th (Lon) 66. BD (Lon) 73. Cranmer Hall Dur 63. **d** 65 **p** 66 Carl. C of St Luke Barrow-F 65-69; V of Flookburgh 69-74; St Geo w St Luke Barrow-F Dio Carl 74-80 Team R from 80. *Rectory, Roose Road, Barrow-in-Furness, Cumb, CA13 9RL.* (Barrow-in-Furness 21641)

GILLIAT, John Howard George. b 07. ALCD 33. **d** 33 **p** 34 Roch. C of St Pet Tunbridge Wells 33-36; St Pet w Ch Ch Southborough 36-40; V of Ch Ch Ware 40-48; Chorley Wood 48-69. *1 Nethercote Drive, Bourton-on-the-Water, Glos.* (Bourton 20168)

GILLIAT, Canon Patrick Nevile. b 10. G and C Coll Cam BA (2nd cl Hist Trip pt ii) 32, MA 36. Tyndale Hall, Bris 32. **d** 34 **p** 35 Ox. C of St Pet-le-Bailey Ox 34-36; St Paul S Harrow 36-38; LDHM of St Thos Oakwood 38-41; V 41-48; V of H Trin Brompton 49-69; CF (EC) 44-46; Chap Chelsea Hosp for Women 50-54; Commiss U Nile 53-61; Mbale from 61; Preb of Holbourn in St Paul's Cathl 58-69; RD of Kens 60-65; Can Res and Succr of Sheff Cathl 69-76; Can (Emer) from 76; Perm to Offic Dio B & W from 76. *20 Henrietta Gardens, Bath, BA2 6NA.* (Bath 61828)

GILLIES, Canon Eric Robert. b 19. Worc Ordin Coll 61. **d** 63 **p** 64 Chich. C of Bexhill 63-67; R of Aldrington 67-82; RD of Hove 77-82; Can and Preb of Chich Cathl from 81; Surr 81-82; V of Findon Dio Chich from 82. *Vicarage, Findon, Worthing, W Sussex, BN14 0TR.* (Findon 2309)

GILLIES, Robert Arthur. b 51. Univ of Edin BD 77. Edin Th Coll 73. **d** 77 **p** 78 Edin. C of Falkirk 77-80; Ch Ch Morningside City and Dio Edin from 80. *6 Morningside Road, Edinburgh, EH10 4DD.* (031-228 6553)

GILLIGAN, Harry. b 07. Univ of Dur 56. **d** 58 Portsm **p** 59 Bp Robin for Cant. [f in CA] C of St Pet Southsea 58-66; V of St Polycarp Everton 66-68; Chap RADD Portsm 59-66; Walsall 68-71; Chap to the Deaf Southport 71-79; Perm to Offic Dio Portsm from 80. *4 Lampeter Avenue, East Cosham, Portsmouth, Hants.* (Portsm 324710)

GILLING, John Reginald. b 25. Trin Hall and Down Coll Cam BA 49, MA 51, MLitt 55. Cudd Coll 53. **d** 55 **p** 56 Chelmsf. C of Romford 55-58; St Mary L Cam 58-62; Coll Chap Ch Ch Ox 62-71; V of St Mary Pimlico Dio Lon from 71; Area Dean of Westmr (St Marg) from 80. *St Mary's Presbytery, Graham Terrace, SW1.* (01-730 2423)

GILLING, Very Rev Walter Joseph. MBE 46. Trin Coll Tor LTh 35, Hon DD 61. **d** 35 Hur for Tor **p** 36 Tor. C of St John Pet 35-36; St Simon Tor 36-37; Chap Trin Coll Tor 37-39; Chap CASF 39-46; Men in Disp 45; R of St Luke Pet 46-56; Can of Tor 52-53; Archd of Pet 53-56; Archd without territorial jurisd and Dir of Ch Ext Dio Tor 56-61; Hon C of St Jas Cathl Tor 57-61; Dean and R 61-74; Dean (Emer) from 75. *3 Nanton Avenue, Toronto, Ont., Canada.*

GILLINGHAM, John Bruce. b 48. Ch Ch Ox BA 69, MA 73. Univ of Nottm BA 73. St Jo Coll Nottm 70. **d** 73 Crediton for Ex **p** 74 Ex. C of St Andr Plymouth 73-77; St Aldate City and Dio Ox and Chap Jes Coll Ox from 78. *14 Walton Street, Oxford, OX1 2HG.* (Oxford 52849)

GILLINGHAM, Kenneth John. b 18. Keble Coll Ox 3rd cl Th 39, BA 40. Chich Th Coll. **d** 40 **p** 42 Swan B. C of St Paul Landore 40-50 and (in c of Treboeth) 53-56; St Jas Wednesbury 50-52; Noviciate Nashdom Abbey 52-53; C-in-c of St Alb Conv Distr Treboeth 56-63; V of St Mary Virg Cardiff 63-73; Gilfach Goch w Llandyfodwg 73-79; Llwynypia w Clydach Vale Dio Llan from 79; C-in-c of St Steph Cardiff 67-73; RD of the Rhondda 78-80. *Vicarage, Tonypandy, Mid Glam.*

GILLINGHAM, Michael John. b 46. Chich Th Coll 68. **d** 71 Swan B for Llan **p** 72 Llan. C of Llanharan w Peterstone super Monten Llan 71-73; Skewen 73-76; Team V of Kirkby Dio Liv from 76. *12 Melling Way, Kirkby, Liverpool, L32 1TP.* (051-546 5303)

GILLINGHAM, Canon Peter Llewellyn. b 14. MVO 55. Or Coll Ox BA (2nd cl Phil Pol and Econ) 35, Dipl Th 36, MA 39. Wycl Hall Ox 35. **d** 37 **p** 38 Roch. C of Tonbridge 37-40; C-in-c of St Geo Conv Distr Oakdale 40-43; Chap RNVR 43-46; Blundells School Tiverton 46-49; R Chap Windsor Gt Pk 49-55; Chap to HM the King 49-52; to HM The Queen from 52; V of St Mildred Addiscombe 55-59; Horsham 59-77; Can and Preb of Chich Cathl 69-77; Can (Emer) from 77; RD of Horsham 74-77; Chap and Libr Sherborne Sch for Girls from 78. *Kenelm House, Sherborne School for Girls, Sherborne, Dorset.*

GILLINGS, Richard John. b 45. St Chad's Coll Dur BA 67. Linc Th Coll 68. **d** 70 **p** 71 Ches. C of Altrincham 70-75; P-in-c of St Thos Stockport Dio Ches 75-77; R from 77; P-in-c of St Pet Stockport Dio Ches from 78; M Gen Syn from 80. *25 Heath Road, Stockport, Gtr Man.* (061-483 2483)

GILLION, Canon Frederick Arthur. b 08. St Jo Coll Dur LTh 30, BA 31, MA 34. ALCD 30. **d** 31 **p** 32 Nor. C of Gorleston 31-34; St John Tunbridge Wells 34-35; PC of St Cath Mile Cross 35-50; V of Docking 50-54; Sec Nor Dioc Youth Coun 43-50; Chairman 50-55; Bp's Chap for Youth Work Dio Nor 44-47; RD of Heacham 52-53; V of Sprowston 54-62; R of St Andr Beeston 54-62; Hon Can of Nor from 59; Surr from 50; Dir Relig Educn Dio Nor 62-70; R of Beeston Regis 69-75; RD of Repps 69-75; Bps's Chap to Retired Cl Dio Nor from 76. *66 The Street, Ingworth, Norwich, NR11 6AE.* (Aylsham 2583)

GILLIS, Roderick Joseph. b 54. St Francis Xavier Univ NS BA 75. Atlantic Sch of Th Halifax NS MDiv 78. **d** 77 NS **p** 78 Bp Hatfield for NS. C of Bridgewater 78-79; R of Neil's Harbour Dio NS from 79. *Box 21, Neil's Harbour, NS, Canada.*

GILLMAN, Noel Francis. b 26. St D Dioc Course 78. **d** 79 **p** 80 St D (NSM). C of Llanelli Dio St D from 79. *4 Oaklands, Swiss Valley, Felinfoel, Llandelli, Dyfed.*

GILLMAN, Richard Bernard Stewart. b 09. St Pet Coll Ox BA (3rd cl Engl Lang and Lit) 31, Dipl Th 32, MA 35. Wycl Hall Ox 31. **d** 33 Win **p** 34 Southn for Win. C of St Jo Evang Boscombe 33-37; Ch Ch Croydon 37-38; V of Ch Ch Portsdown 38-48; St Sav Stoke-next-Guildford 48-56; St Jo Evang W St Steph Reading 56-67; R of Newc L w Butterton 67-77; RD of Newc L 67-77; Surr 70-77. *47 Airdale Road, Stone, Staffs.* (Stone 5848)

GILLMOR, Samuel Frederick. b 29. St Aid Coll. **d** 62 **p** 63 Oss. C of Carlow U 62-64; R of Fenagh U 64-68; Maryborough w Dysart Enos 68-79; Preb of Oss and Leigh Cathls 78-79; I of Clane w Donadea Dio Kild from 79. *St Michael's Vicarage, Sallins, Co Kildare, Irish Republic.* (Naas 68276)

GILMAN, Charles Philip. b 12. Tyndale Hall Bris 39. **d** 41 **p** 42 Liv. C of St Mary Kirkdale 41-43; All SS Wellington 43-46; Org Sec CPAS for SW Area 46-50; Perm to Offic Dio Mon 47-50; Dio Ex 50; V of St Cath Leyton 50-64; Chap Whipps Cross Hosp 59-63; R of Mark's Tey 64-74; Aldham 64-74; V of St Bart Leigh 74-81. *10 Alswitha Terrace, Winchester, Hants, SO23 7DQ.*

GILMORE, Henry. b 51. Univ of Man BA 72. TCD 73. **d** 75 Armagh. C of Armagh & Aghavilly 75-78; St Patr Nat Cathl Group Min 78-81; R of Stranorlar w Meenglass and Kilteevogue Dio Raph from 81. *Rectory, Stranorlar, Co Donegal, Irish Republic.* (Ballybofey 81)

GILMORE, Kenneth Clarence. Moore Th Coll Syd 52. **d** 56 **p** 57 Syd. C of St Phil Syd 56-57; Lithgow 58-59; R of Denham Court 59-62; C-in-c of Croydon Pk 62-67; Harbord Dio Syd 67-74; R from 74. *30 Dowling Street, Harbord, NSW, Australia 2096.* (93-3531)

GILMORE, Canon Norman. b 16. Univ of Leeds BA 38. Coll of Resurr Mirfield, 38. **d** 40 **p** 41 Dur. C of Brandon 40-42; St Mary Blyth 42-46; Orlando Miss Distr Dio Johann 46-47; Temp Prin of St Mich Sch Bremersdorp Swaz 47-48; Dir of Kambula Miss 48-52; St Aug Miss 52-60; Archd of W

Zulu 58-60; E Zulu 60-63; Dir of Kwa Magwaza Miss, Chap St Mary's Hosp and P-in-c of All SS Melmoth 60-63; Hon Can of Zulu from 63; R of Friern Barnet 63-78; Commiss Zulu from 64; Swaz from 70; Argent from 76; RD of Centr Barnet 72-78; V of Mortimer W End w Padworth Dio Ox from 78. *Vicarage, Mortimer West End, Reading, Berks, RG7 2HU.* (0734-701017)

GILMOUR, David William. b 48. Univ of Syd BSc 68. BD (Lon) 76. Moore Th Coll Syd ACT ThL 75. **d** 77 Bp Dain for Syd **p** 77 Syd. C of St Alb French's Forest 77-79; Ch Ch St Ives 79-81; R of St Luke Northmead Dio Syd from 81. *7 Thomas Street, Northmead, NSW, Australia 2152.* (630-4098)

GILMOUR, George Henry. b 26. Univ of Glas MA 56. Edin Th Coll 67. **d** and **p** 69 Edin. C of St Mich and All SS Edin 69-71; R of St Mary Dalmahov 71-75; Selkirk Dio Edin from 75. *St John's Rectory, Viewfield Park, Selkirk.* (Selkirk 21364)

GILMOUR, John Douglas. Univ of W Ont BA 35. Hur Coll Ont LTh 35. **d** 35 **p** 36 Hur. C of St Pet Lucknow 35-36; I of Thamesford w Lakeside and Crumlin 36-38; Canon Davis Mem Ch Sarnia 38-41; I of St Andr Windsor 41-51; St Jo Evang Hamilton 51-59; Exam Chap to Bp of Niag 56-61; R of St Thos Hamilton 59-76; Hon Can of Niag 65-76; Chap Hamilton and Henderson Hosps Ont 76. *Apt 510, 100 Bay Street South, Hamilton, Ont, Canada.* (416-529 4763)

GILMOUR, John Logan. Cudd Coll 46. **d** 48 **p** 49 Ox. C of St Mary Virg Reading 48-51; Miss of St Barn Conv Distr Reading 51-55; Chap at Bangkok 55-58; V of Ellel Lancs 58-60; P-in-c of Ascen Capetn 60-72; R of Goodwood Dio Capetn from 72. *31 Fisher Street, Goodwood, CP, S Africa.* (984703)

GILMOUR, Thomas Calum. NZ BD of Th Stud LTh (2nd cl) 59. Univ of Auckld BA 74, MA 76. St Jo Coll Auckld 56. **d** 59 **p** 60 Auckld. C of Papatoetoe 59-62; N Wairoa 62-64; V of Hauraki Plains 64-70; P-in-c of Mangere Bridge 70-71; Team V of Mangere Miss Distr 71-74; V of Sandringham 74-80; Prec of H Trin Cathl Auckld from 80. *429 Parnell Road, Parnell, Auckland 1, NZ.*

GILPIN, John. b 25. St Mich Coll Llan. **d** 61 **p** 62 St A. C of Llangollen 61-64; Asst Chap United Sheff Hosps 64-70; Chap from 70. *40 Barholm Road, Sheffield, S10 5RS.*

GILPIN, Richard John. b 45. BSc (2nd cl Econ) (Lon) 66. Univ of Bris Dipl Th 69. Wells Th Coll 67. **d** 70 **p** 71 Man. C of Ch Ch Davyhulme Dio Man 70-74; in Prot Ch of Germany 74-77; R of Ch w All SS Heaton Norris Dio Man from 77. *Rectory, Manchester Road, Heaton Norris, Stockport, SK4 1NL.* (061-480 2282)

GILPIN, Richard Thomas. b 39. Lich Th Coll 60. **d** 63 **p** 64 Ex. C of Whipton 63-66; Tavistock w Gulworthy 66-69; V of Swimbridge w Traveller's Rest and Gunn 69-73; Tavistock w Gulworthy Dio Ex from 73; C-in-c of St Pet Tavy Dio Ex from 73; Surr from 74. *Vicarage, Tavistock, Devon, PL19 8AU.* (Tavistock 2162)

✠ **GILPIN, Right Rev William Percy.** b 02. Keble Coll Ox 3rd cl Cl Mods 23, BA (1st cl Th) 25, MA 28. **d** 25 **p** 26 Birm. C of Solihull 25-28; Vice-Prin of St Paul's Miss Coll Burgh and Gen Pr Dio Linc 28-29; Chap Storrington Coll 29-30; C of St Bart Chich and Chap Chich Th Coll 30;33; V of Manaccan w St Anthony-in-Meneage 33-36; St Mary Penzance 36-44; Exam Chap to Bp of Truro 34-44; Dioc Insp of Schs Dio Glouc 44-48; Dir of Relig Educn Dio Glouc 44-49; Exam Chap to Bp of Glouc 46-52; Can Missr of Glouc 47-52; Archd of S'wark 52-55; Cons Ld Bp Suffr of Kingston T in S'wark Cathl 22 May 52 by Abp of Cant; Bps of S'wark; Nor; Birm; Glouc; Bps Suffr of Woolwich and Tewkesbury; res 70; Perm to Offic Dio Heref from 70. *50 Lower Broad Street, Ludlow, Salop.* (Ludlow 3376)

GILROY, Paul. b 50. Univ of Leic BSc 72. St Steph Ho Ox 72. **d** 76 **p** 77 St A. C of Shotton 76-78; Hawarden 78-81; USPG Miss Dio Lusaka from 82. *c/o USPG, 15 Tufton Street, SW1P 3QQ.*

GILSON, Cecil Henry. b 02. Lich Th Coll 24. **d** 27 Chelmsf for St Alb **p** 28 St Alb. C of Woburn Sands 27-29; St Alb Bournemouth 29-30; Christchurch 30-38; V of E Boldre 38-45; R of Morestead 45-57; V of Owslebury (w Morestead from 57) 45-61; E Stratton w Woodmancote and Popham 61-70. *51 Blenheim Drive, Oxford.* (Ox 56559)

GILTRAP, Stanley William. Lon Coll of Div. **d** 64 Willesden for Lon for Syd **p** 64 Syd. Federal Financial and Admin Sec CMS Austr 64-67; Regional Sec for Afr 64-73; for Aborigines from 67; C of St Paul Chatswood 64-67; L to Offic Dio Syd from 64; Dio N Terr from 71. *CMS, 93 Bathurst Street, Sydney, NSW, Australia 2000.* (61-9487)

GILU, Francis Mesach. St Pet Coll Siota 63. **d** 66 **p** 68 Melan. P Dio Melan 66-75; Dio New Hebr 75-80; Dio Vanuatu from 80. *Box 221, Vila, Vanuatu.*

GIMBLETT, Dennis. b 11. Qu Coll Birm. **d** 47 **p** 48 Chich. C of Eastbourne 47-50; V of Paulton 50-54; St Jo Evang Brighton 54-60; Putaruru NZ 60-61; St Wilfrid Brighton 61-71; V of Washington 71-73; C of St Luke Toowoomba 73-74; P-in-c of Allora 74-76; Perm to Offic Dio Chich 77-79; P-in-c of St Mark Woody Point, Redcliffe 79-80. *86 Arthur Street, Woody Point, Queensld, Australia 4019.*

GINEVER, Geoffrey James. Univ of Auckld BA 60, MA 62. Univ of Otago BD 67. St Jo Coll Auckld 66. **d** 67 **p** 68 Waik. C of New Plymouth 67-69; Claudelands 69-71; V of Putaruru Dio Waik 71-76; Min 77-79; C of New Plymouth 79-81; Perm to Offic Dio Waik from 81. *Box 807, New Plymouth, NZ.* (88-216)

GINEVER, Preb John Haynes. b 20. St Jo Coll Dur Westcott Ho Cam. **d** 43 **p** 44 Lon. C of Ch of Ascen Preston Wembley 43-46; Min of Conv Distr of Ascen Preston Wembley 46-50; PC of All H N Greenford 50-63; V of John Keble Ch Mill Hill 63-70; RD of W Barnet 67-70; Wolverhampton from 70; R (Team R from 78) of Wolverhampton Dio Lich from 70; P-in-c of All SS and St Geo Wolverhampton 70-78; Preb of Lich Cathl from 75; P-in-c of St Mark Wolverhampton 75-78; St Chad Wolverhampton 76-78; Selector ACCM from 78; M Gen Syn from 80. *42 Park Road East, Wolverhampton, Staffs.* (Wolverhampton 23140)

GINEVER, Paul Michael John. b 49. AKC 71. St Aug Coll Cant 71. **d** 72 **p** 73 Man. C of Davyhulme 72-75; Mt Lawley Inglewood Perth 76-77; Tettenhall Wood 77-80; Team V of Halesowen w Hasbury and Lapal Dio Worc from 80. *19 Lapal Lane North, Halesowen, W Midl.*

GINGELL, John Lawrence. b 27. Univ of Lon BD 55. Lon Coll of Div ALCD 54. **d** 55 **p** 56 Derby. C of Normanton-by-Derby 55-58; Ilkeston (in c of St Bart Hallam Fields) 58-60; Toc H Area Padre SE Lon 61-66; N Region 67-70; Asst Chap S Lon Industr Miss 61-64; L to Offic Dio S'wark 61-66; Dio Liv 67-70; V of Somercotes 70-72; Bp's Industr Adviser Derby Area from 72. *9 Hartington Street, Derby, DE3 5CA.* (Derby 361305)

GINGO, Kezekia. b 21. **d** 77 Nam. d Dio Nam. *Balitta Church of Uganda, PO Luweero, Uganda.*

GINN, Richard John. b 51. BD (Lon) 77. Univ of Dur Dipl Th 78. Cranmer Hall Dur 77. **d** 79 Edmon for Lon **p** 80 Lon. C of Ch Ch Crouch End Hornsey Dio Lon from 79. *1 Monkridge, Crouch End Hill, N8 8DE.*

GINNEVER, John Buckley. b 20. Univ of Man BA 42. Ridley Hall, Cam 46. **d** 48 **p** 49 Man. C of Tyldesley 48-51; C-in-c of Limeside Conv Distr Oldham 51-57; R of St Mark Levenshulme 57-76; V of St Matt Chadderton Dio Man from 76. *St Matthew's Vicarage, Chadderton, Oldham, OL1 2RT.* (061-624 8600)

GINNO, Albert Charles. Lon Coll of Div 66. **d** 68 **p** 69 Chich. C of St Mark w St Matt Kemp Town Brighton 68-72; C-in-c of E Hoathly Dio Chich from 72. *East Hoathly Rectory, Lewes, E Sussex, BN8 6EG.* (Halland 270)

GINNS, Raymond William. St Jo Coll Morpeth 61. **d** 62 **p** 63 River. C of Leeton 63-64; P-in-c of Lake Cargelligo 65-68; R of Tocumwal 68-74; P-in-c of Tennant Creek 75-79; R of Hay Dio River from 80. *St Paul's Rectory, Hay, NSW, Australia 2711.*

GIOVETTI, William James Belford. St Chad's Coll Regina, LTh 52. **d** 52 New Westmr for Sask **p** 53 Sask. I of Spiritwood 52-54; Madoc 54-59; V of Whalley 59-63; R of St Mich Regina 63-65; P-in-c of St Alb Regina 64-65; R of St Phil Regina 65-67; I of Wadena 67-70; in Amer Ch 70-77; C of Aborfield 77-79; I of Neepawa Dio Bran from 79. *Box 448, Neepawa, Manit, Canada.*

GIPPSLAND, Lord Bishop of. *See* Chynoweth, Right Rev Neville James.

GIRARD, William Nicholas Charles. b 35. Coll of Resurr Mirfield 65. **d** 67 **p** 68 Tewkesbury for Glouc. C of Yate 67-70; St Alb Westbury Pk Bris 70-73; Chap K Sch Ely 73-76; Min Can Ely Cathl 73; V of Fenstanton Dio Ely from 76; St Mary Magd Hilton Dio Ely from 76. *Vicarage, Fenstanton, Huntingdon, Cambs, PE18 9JL.* (St Ives 63334)

GIRDWOOD, James Brown. b 43. Ex Coll Ox BA 67, MA 69. BD (Lon) 69. Oak Hill Th Coll 66. **d** 69 Lon **p** 70 Stepney for Lon. C of Islington Dio Lon 69-74; St Mary Southgate Crawley (in c of St Andr Furnace Green) 74-79; Team V 79-81; Beccles Dio St E from 81. *c/o 55 Rigbourne Hill, Beccles, Suff.*

GIRDWOOD, Richard John. b 43. Univ of Natal BA 77. St Paul's Th Coll Grahmstn 77. **d** 79 Bp Ndwandwe for Johann **p** 80 Johann. C of Orchards Dio Johann from 79. *c/o 18 High Road, Orchards, S Africa 2192.*

GIRDWOOD, William McLeod. Univ of Lon BD 15. Wells Th Coll 40. **d** and **p** 41 Carl. [f Congregational Min] C of Wigton 41-42; P-in-c of St Aid Clarkston Glas 42-46; R 46-54; Coupar Angus 54-67. *361 Main Street, Wellington, Ont, Canada.*

GIRISINI, Very Rev Yotoma Fandasi. Bp Gwynne Coll Mundri 58. **d** 57 **p** 61 Sudan. P Dio Sudan 61-76; Dio Yambio from Hon Can Khartoum Cathl 71-76; Provost of Yambio from 76. from 71. *ECS, Yambio, Sudan.*

GIRLING, Andrew Martin. b 40. Em Coll Cam 2nd cl Th Trip pt 1 61, BA (3rd cl Th Trip pt ii) 63, MA 67. Wycl Hall Ox 63. **d** 65 **p** 66 St Alb. C of St Mary Luton 65-69; Chap Univ of Hull 69-75; V of Dringhouses City and Dio York from 75. *Vicarage, Dringhouses, York, YO2 2QG.* (York 706120)

GIRLING, David Frederick Charles. b 33. Edin Th Coll 58. **d** 61 **p** 62 Nor. C of Caister 61-65; Leigh-on-Sea 65-66; CF from 66. *c/o Ministry of Defence, Bagshot Park, Bagshot, Surrey.*

GIRLING, (Vincent) Francis Richard. b 28. Worc Coll Ox BA (2nd cl Engl) 52, MA 56. BD (3rd cl) Lon 65. Coll of Resurr Mirfield 55. M CR 57. **d** 57 **p** 59 Wakef. *House of the Resurrection, Mirfield, Yorks.*

GIRLING, Gordon Francis Hulbert. b 15. TD 61. C de L'O de Leopold II avec Palme, Croix de Guerre (Belgian) avec Palme 45. Men in Disp 45. Univ Coll Ox BA 37, MA 41. Wells Th Coll 39. **d** 46 **p** 47 S'wark. C of St Luke w St Paul Old Charlton 46-49; CF (TA) 48-66; CF (TARO) 66-70; Hon CF from 70; C of St Mary-at-Finchley 49-51; V of St Geo Enfield 51-59; Kingsbury 59-79; Perm to Offic Dio Chich from 80. *212 Coast Road, Pevensey Bay, E Sussex, BN24 6NR.* (0323-66359)

GIRLING, Timothy Havelock. b 43. St Aid Coll 63. **d** 67 Barking for Chelmsf **p** 68 Chelmsf. C of Wickford 67-70; Luton 70-74; All SS (w St Pet from 76) Luton 74-80; R of Northill w Moggerhanger Dio St Alb from 80. *Northill Rectory, Biggleswade, Beds, SG18 9AH.* (Northill 262)

GIRLING, William Havelock. b 18. Late Scho of Ex Coll Ox 2nd cl Cl Mods 39, BA and MA 46, 2nd cl Th 47. Ridley Hall Cam. **d** 49 **p** 50 Portsm. C of Alverstoke 49-54; Asst Chap Bradfield Coll 54-70; C-in-c of Stanford Dingley Dio Ox from 71. *Oakthorpe, Southend Road, Bradfield, Reading, Berks, RG7 6EY.*

GIRVAN, Ven Henry Hugh. ACT ThL 52. **d** 50 **p** 51 Gippsld. C-in-c of St John Neerim S 50-52; Commiss Gippsld 51-56; Asst Master Syd Gr Scho 52-54; C of St Andr Cathl Syd 53-54; Prec of St Paul's Cathl Melb 54-57; Chap Cranbrook Gr Scho Edgecliffe 57-59; R of Burwood 60-61; Prec and Min Can of St Paul's Cathl Melb 61-64; R of Mildura 64-68; Ch Ch Cathl St Arn Dio St Arn 68-70; Asst Chap O of St John of Jer from 64; Archd of Mildura 64-68; St Arn 68-70; Can Res 68-70; R of St Jo Launceston 70-74; St Paul Bend 74-77; Can of Bend 74-77; I of Ch Ch Geelong Dio Melb from 77; Archd of Geelong from 78. *57 McKillop Street, Geelong, Vic, Australia 3220.* (052-21 4507)

GIRVAN, Wesley David. Moore Th Coll Syd 59. **d** 60 **p** 61 Syd. C of St Matt Manly 60-61; C-in-c of Baulkham Hills 61-67; R of Kiama 67-74; Can of St Mich Prov Cathl Wollongong 73-78; R of Dapto 74-78; Vic Sec Bible S in Austr and L to Offic Dio Melb from 78. *16 Maude Street, Box Hill North, Vic., Australia 3129.* (63 1896)

GISI, Gibson. Newton Th Coll Papua 55. **d** 59 **p** 62 New Guinea. P Dio New Guinea 59-71; Dio Papua from 71. *Nindewari, PO Box 304, Lae, New Guinea.*

GISSING, Sydney William. Moore Th Coll Syd ACT ThL 52. **d** and **p** 53 Syd. C of Dee Why 53-54; C-in-c of Forestville 54-58; R of Oatley W 58-60; Lithgow 60-65; W Ryde 65-74; Petersham 74-81; Oatley W Dio Syd from 81. *Rectory, Oatley West, NSW, Australia 2223.*

GITAHI, Paul Ngure. b 42. **d** 76 **p** 77 Nak. P Dio Nak. *PO Box 325, Nakuru, Kenya.*

✠ **GITARI, Right Rev David Mukuba.** b 38. BA (Lon) 64, Dipl Th (Lon) 69, BD (Lon) 71. Tyndale Hall Bris 70. **d** 71 Nai **p** 72 Mt Kenya. P Dio Nai 71-72; Gen Sec Bible S Kenya 72-75; Cons Ld Bp of Mt Kenya E in Em Ch Kigari 20 July 75 by Abp of Kenya; Bps of Momb, Mt Kenya S, Maseno N and Maseno S; and others. *Box 189, Embu, Kenya.* (Embu 218)

GITHINJI, Ven Eshban Gitura. St Paul's Dioc Div Sch Limuru, 50. **d** 52 **p** 54 Momb. P Dio Momb 52-61; Dio Mt Kenya 61-75; Dio Mt Kenya S from 75; Exam Chap to Bp of Mt Kenya 61-75; to Bp of Mt Kenya S from 75; Archd of Centr Distr Mt Kenya 71-75; Centr and N Distr Mt Kenya S from 75; Provost of Mt Kenya S 75-77. *Box 121, Murang'a, Kenya.* (Murang'a 53)

GITHITU, James Peter. b 40. St Paul's Coll Limuru 69. **d** 72 **p** 74 Mt Kenya. P Dio Mt Kenya 72-74; Dio Mt Kenya S from 75. *Box 8, Thika, Kenya.*

GITOGO, Samuel. **d** 77 **p** 78 Nak. P Dio Nak. *Box 171, Molo, Kenya.*

GITTINGS, Graham. b 46. Qu Coll Birm 75. **d** 78 **p** 79 Lich. C of Caverswall 78-81; St Matt Wolverhampton Dio Lich from 81. *29 Denmore Gardens, Heath Town, Wolverhampton. W Midl.* (Wolverhampton 54408)

GITTINS, Thomas Raymond. b 06. St Aid Coll. **d** 50 **p** 51 St A. C of Wrexham 50-71; Team V 72-73. *29 Elm Grove, Acton Park, Wrexham, Clwyd.*

GIVAN, Canon Desmond George. b 11. Worc Coll Ox BA 34, MA 38. Wycl Hall Ox 34. **d** 36 **p** 37 Wakef. C of H Trin Huddersfield 36-39; Prin Buxton Sch Momb 39-40; CMS Miss at Butere 41-48; CMS Miss at Momb and RD of Coast 48-51; Sub-Dean of Momb Cathl 49-51; CMS Dioc Sec Sier L 52-58; Can Missr of Sier L 53-58; Exam Chap to Abp of Sier L 53-58; Hon Can of Sier L 58-63; V of Port Loko 60-63; V of Trans Nzoia 64-71; Hon Can of Nak from 64; Provost of Momb Cathl 71-75; C of St Jo Evang Huddersfield 75-76; L to Offic Dio Wakef from 77. *1 Dingley Road, Lindley, Huddersfield.*

GIVEN, Harold Richard. b 54. Oak Hill Th Coll 73. **d** 78 **p** 79 Down. C of St Clem Belf Dio Down from 78. *77 Ardenlee Avenue, Belfast, BT6.*

GIVEN, John Thornton. Trin Coll Dub BA 36, Wall Bibl Scho and Div Test 38, MA 45. **d** 40 Bp Kennedy for Dub for Oss **p** 41 Oss. C of Kells U 40-43; St John Malone Belfast 43-46; C-in-c of Preben w Moyne 46-50; R of Wau 50-55; Ingham 55-60; Mirani 60-67; R of Oakey 67-74; Home Hill Dio N Queensld from 74. *Rectory, Home Hill, Qld, Australia 4806.* (077-821624)

GIZAMBA, Joseph. **d** 77 Nam. d Dio Nam. *Bombo Church of Uganda, PO Box 166, Bombo, Uganda.*

GLADSTONE, William Edward. b 03. OBE 42. SS Coll Cam BA 28, MA 32. St Steph Ho Ox 28. **d** 29 **p** 30 S'wark. C of Mortlake w E Sheen 29-33; CF 33-53; R of Codford 53-62; R of Upton Lovell 53-62; Bourton-on-the-Hill 62-68. *9 Hillands Drive, Leckhampton, Cheltenham, Glos.* (Cheltenham 31024)

GLADWIN, John Warren. b 42. Churchill Coll Cam 2nd cl Hist Trip pt i 63, BA (2nd cl Th Trip pt ii) 65, MA 68. Univ of Dur Dipl Th (w distinc) 66. Cranmer, Hall Dur 65. **d** 67 Pontefract for Wakef **p** 68 Wakef. C of Kirkheaton 67-71; Tutor St Jo Coll Dur 71-77; Dir Shaftesbury Project Nottm and Publ Pr Dio Southw from 77. *5 Grange Road, Woodthorpe, Nottingham.* (0602-606324)

GLADWIN, Thomas William. b 35. St Alb Min Tr Scheme 78. **d** 81 St Alb. C of St Andr Hertf Dio St Alb from 81. *99 Warren Way, Digswell, Nr Welwyn, Herts, AL6 0DL.*

GLADWIN, William Philip Wright. b 19. TD 54. St Deiniol's Libr Hawarden 70. **d** 72 **p** 73 Ban. C of Aberdovey Dio Ban from 72. *12 Penhelig Terrace, Aberdovey, Gwyn, LL35 0PS.* (Aberdovey 220)

GLAISYER, Hugh. b 30. Or Coll Ox BA 51, MA 55. St Steph Ho Ox 51. **d** and **p** 56 Man. C of Tonge Moor 56-62; Sidcup 62-64; V of Ch Ch Milton-next-Gravesend 64-81; Leader of E Gravesend Group Min 74-77; RD of Gravesend 74-81; V of Hove Dio Chich from 81. *Vicarage, Wilbury Road, Hove, Sussex, BN3 3PB.* (Brighton 73331)

GLANFIELD, Canon Douglas Frederick Hall. b 13. AKC 39. **d** 39 **p** 40 Roch. C of St Jas Elmers End 39-40; Northfleet 40-45; CF 45-52; V of Northfleet 52-81; Hon Can of Roch Cathl 75-81; Can (Emer) from 81. *c/o Vicarage, Northfleet, Kent.* (Gravesend 66400)

GLANVILLE-SMITH, Michael Raymond. b 38. K Coll Lon and Warm AKC 61. **d** 62 **p** 63 Lon. C of St Mark w St Luke St Marylebone 62-64; St Mary Penzance 64-68; R of All SS w St Andr St Helen St Alb and St Mich Worc 68-74; Youth Chap Dio Worc 68-74; Hon Min Can of Worc Cathl from 70; V of Catshill 74-80; P-in-c of St Martin w St Pet Worc 80-81; Team R of St Martin w St Pet, St Mark and Norton w Whittington City and Dio Worc from 81. *6 St Catherine's Hill, Worcester, WR5 2EA.* (Worc 355119)

GLARE, Michael Francis. b 28. Univ of Southn BA 54. St Steph Ho Ox 56. **d** 57 **p** 58 Ex. C of Withycombe Raleigh w Exmouth 57-62; C-in-c of St Geo Conv Distr Goodrington 62-65; C of Tamerton Foliot 65-70; R of Weare Giffard w Landcross 70-76; RD of Hartland 74-76; P-in-c of Babbacombe Dio Ex 76-79; V from 79. *Babbacombe Vicarage, Cary Avenue, Torquay, Devon, TQ1 3QT.* (Torquay 33002)

GLASBY, Alan Langland. b 46. Univ of Nottm LTh 77. St Jo Coll Nottm 74. **d** 77 **p** 78 Roch. C of St Paul Erith 77-80; Moor Allerton Dio Ripon 80-81; Team V from 81. *79 The Avenue, Alwoodley, Leeds, LS17 7NP.* (Leeds 678487)

GLASCOTT, Leslie Evan. K Coll Lon. **d** 34 **p** 35 Lon. C of St Alb N Harrow 34-38; St Barn Mitcham 38-40; Actg C of Iver 40-41; C 41-44; V of Lannarth (or Lanner) 44-47; St Hilary 47-66. *Miles Court, Hereford Street, Brighton, BN2 1JT.*

GLASGOW and GALLOWAY, Lord Bishop of. *See* Rawcliffe, Right Rev Derek Alec.

GLASGOW and GALLOWAY, Dean of. *See* Singer, Very Rev Samuel Stanfield.

GLASGOW, Provost of. *See* Grant, Very Rev Malcolm Etheridge.

GLASS, Ven Edward Brown. b 13. St Jo Coll Dur BA 35, MA 38. **d** 37 **p** 38 Man. C of St Mary Wardleworth 37; St Jas Gorton 37-42; V of St Jo Evang Hopwood 42-51; Ramsey IoM 51-55; Castletown 55-64; Proc Conv S & M 59-64;

Archd of Man 64-78; Archd (Emer) from 78; R of Andreas 64-78; M Gen Syn from 70; Exam Chap to Bp of S & M from 75. *Balholm, Lhen Bridge, Kirk Andreas, IOM.* (Kirk Andreas 568)

GLASS, Edward Eric Ivor. Rhodes Univ Grahmstn BA 56. Univ of Natal BA (Hons Div) 62. St Aug Coll Cant 62. **d** 63 Cant for Natal **p** 63 Natal. C of St Sav Cathl Pietermaritzburg 63-64; St Jas Dundee 65; St Jo Bapt Ixopo 66-68; St Martin Maidstone (in c of Parkwood) 76-77; Asst Master Durban High Sch 70-75; Glenwood High Sch Durban 77-82. *1 Nicolson Road, Durban 4001, S Africa.*

GLASS, Geoffrey Norman. b 34. Ridley Coll Melb 75. **d** 76 Melb **p** 77 Bp Muston for Melb. C of St Luke Frankston E 76-80; I of Lancefield Dio Melb from 80. *Vicarage, Lancefield, Vic, Australia 3435.*

GLASS, Kenneth William. b 23. **d** 57 **p** 58 St E. C of St Matt Ipswich 57-59; R of Glemsford 59-63; C-in-c of Somerton 59-63; V of St Nich Ipswich 63-73; Asst Dioc Dir of Relig Educn 63-68; Bp's Press Officer from 69; C-in-c of St Helen Ipswich 73; R of Sproughton w Burstall 73-76; Perm to Offic Dio St E from 76. *247 Henley Road, Ipswich, IP1 6RL.*

GLASS, Thomas Oswald Welch. b 08. Magd Coll Cam BA 32, MA 36. Westcott Ho Cam. **d** 48 **p** 49 Nor. C of Sprowston 48-51; V of Stoke H Cross w Dunston 51-59; Dersingham 59-71; RD of Rising 63-69; R of Tasburgh and V of Tharston 71-79. *Baynards, Bell Rope Lane, Roydon, Diss, IP22 3RG.*

GLASSOCK, Geoffrey Thomas. Wayne State Univ MEducn 63. Ridley Coll Melb ACT ThL 57. **d** 58 **p** 59 Melb. C of Bentleigh 58-60; Merrow Surrey 60-62; V of St Silas Geelong 63-68; Chap R Melb Inst of Technology 68-70; L to Offic Dio Syd from 71; Lect Syd Teachers Coll from 74. *27 William Edward Street, Longueville, NSW, Australia 2066.* (42-6074)

GLASSWELL, Mark Errol. Late Exhib St Chad's Coll Dur BA (2nd cl Th) 60, PhD 65. Westcott Ho Cam. **d** 66 Jarrow for York for Sier L **p** 67 Dur. Lect in Th Fourah Bay Coll Sier L 65-74; Hon C of Kissy 66-69; H Trin Freetown 69-74; Exam Chap to Bp of Sier L 69-74; L to Offic Dio Dur 74-75; Lect Univ of Dur 75; Sen Lect Univ of Nigeria from 75; L to Offic Dio Enugu from 75; Chap Ch Ch Nsukka 78-80. *c/o University of Nigeria, Nsukka, Nigeria.*

GLAZEBROOK, Ronald Victor. Keble Coll Ox BA (Th) 41, MA 48. St Steph Ho Ox 41. **d** 43 **p** 44 Lon. C of St Cuthb Kensngton 43-48; Chap Ashford Res Sch Dio Lon 48-52; Asst Master All SS Cathl Coll Bath NSW 52-55; Hd Master Karachi Gr Sch 55-64; Bernard Mizeki Coll Mashon 65-66; Chap and Asst Master Greycoat Sch Lon 64-65; Perm to Offic Dio Cant 64-65; C of St John U Norwood 66-70; St Barn Beckenham 72-75; Hd of St Marg Ho Bethnal Green from 76; L to Offic Dio Lon from 77. *The Athenaeum, Pall Mall, SW1Y 5ER.*

GLAZEBROOK, William Leng. b 29. Edin Th Coll 76. **d** 76 **p** 77 Andr (APM). C of Dollar Dio Dunb from 76. *12 Harviestoun Road, Dollar, Clackmannanshire, FK14 7HF.* (Dollar 2494)

GLEADALL, John Frederick. b 39. Sarum Th Coll 69. **d** 70 **p** 71 Cant. C of Ch Ch (in c of St Francis from 73) S Ashford 70-76; P-in-c of Hothfield Dio Cant from 76; Westwell Dio Cant from 81; Boughton Aluph Dio Cant from 81. *Vicarage, Westwell, Ashford, Kent.* (Charing 2576)

GLEAVE, Charles Haughton. b 03. Fitzw Hall Cam BA 25, MA 33. Ridley Hall Cam 26. **d** 27 **p** 28 York. C of St Steph Hull 27-29; Bedworth 29-32; Attleborough Warws 32-35; R of Whitnash 35-67; V of Offchurch 67-75; RD of Leamington 59-69; Surr 59-75. *Station House, Grange Court, Westbury-on-Severn, Glos.* (W-on-S 417)

GLEDHILL, Alfred Gavan. b 21. FCA 60. SOC 67. **d** 70 **p** 71 Bp White for Guildf. C of Cuddington 70-74; Haywards Heath 74-79; R of Horsted Keynes Dio Chich from 79. *Horsted Keynes Rectory, Haywards Heath, Sussex.* (Danehill 790317)

GLEDHILL, James William. b 27. Late Scho Univ of Dur BA (2nd cl Phil) 52. Westcott Ho Cam 52. **d** 56 **p** 57 Sheff. C of Mexborough 56-59; CF 59-61; C of Bywell St Pet 61-65; V of Warden Dio Newc T from 65; RD of Hexham from 78. *Warden Vicarage, Hexham, Northumb.* (Hexham 3910)

GLEDHILL, Jonathan Michael. b 49. Univ of Keele BA 72. Univ of Bris MA 75. Trin Coll Bris 72. **d** 75 **p** 76 Ches. C of Marple 75-78; H Trin w Ch Ch Folkestone Dio Cant from 78. *St George's Parsonage, Shorncliffe Road, Folkestone, CT20 3PB.* (Folkestone 55907)

GLEDHILL, Norman. b 09. St Jo Coll Dur LTh 40, BA 41. St Aid Coll 37. **d** 41 **p** 42 Lich. C of St Leon Bilston 41-44; V of St Thos Stafford 44-61; Hilderstone 61-80. *20 Wissage Lane, Lichfield, Staffs.*

GLEDHILL, Peter. b 29. Late Scho of Ball Coll Ox BA (1st cl Lit Hum) 53, MA 54, 2nd cl Th 55. Cudd Coll 54. **d** 56 **p** 57 S'wark. C of Balham 56-58; Loughton 58-63; Dir of Relig Educn Dio Ja 63-66; Tutor Codr Coll Barb 66-67; Asst Master Cheadle Grammar Sch 68-70; L to Offic Dio Lich 70-71; P-in-c of Kingstone w Gratwich Dio Lich from 71. *Gratwich Rectory, Uttoxeter, Staffs, ST4 8SE.* (Field 218)

GLEDHILL, Rolf. b 04. Univ of Wales BA 25. CCC Cam BA (2nd cl Th Trip pt i) 28, MA 32. Univ of Lon BD 43. Wells Th Coll. **d** 29 **p** 30 Swan B. C of St Mary Swansea 29-31; Rhyl 31-34; St John Sparkhill 34-35; V of St Clem Nechells 35-39; St Germain Edgbaston 39-45; R of Norton 45-73; Surr 47-73; RD of Staveley 49-61 and 73; Exam Chap to Bp of Derby 53-61; Hon Can of Derby 60-73; Perm to Offic Dio Sheff from 78. *39 Glebe Rise, Mickleover, Derby, D3 6GX.*

GLEED, Keith William. Montr Dioc Th Coll LTh 59. **d** 59 **p** 60 Tor. C of St Mark Parkdale Tor 59-60; Chap Trin Coll Sch Port Hope 60-63; St Jas Cathl Tor 63-65; I of St Barn Halton Tor 65-68; St Alb Hamilton 68-74; Chap Lakefield Coll Ont 75-81. *333 Meadows Boulevard, Unit 87, Mississauga, Ont., Canada.*

GLEED, Roy Edward. b 19. Linc Coll Ox BA (3rd cl Th) 48, MA 53. Chich Th Coll. **d** 50 **p** 51 Ripon. C of Ch Ch U Armley 50-52; Chap Kiambu and Limuru 53-57; Eldoret 57-62; Exam Chap to Bp of Nak 61-62; R of Shipton-Oliffe w Shipton-Sollars, Haselton and Cold Salperton 63-74; C-in-c of Dowdeswell 69-74; R of Avening (w Cherington from 75) Dio Glouc from 74. *Avening Rectory, Tetbury, Glos.* (Nailsworth 2098)

GLEN, Robert Marshall. Univ of NZ MA 53. Fitzw Ho Cam BA 57, MA 62. **d** 58 **p** 59 Ch Ch for Centr Tang. C of Woolston NZ 58-60; Asst Master Alliance Secondary Sch Dodoma 60-62; Miss Dio Vic Nyan 62-65; Lect St Phil Th Coll Kongwa 65-69; Prin 69-73; L to Offic Dio Centr Tang 65-73; Dio Ch Ch 73-74; Perm to Offic Dio Auckld from 75; Lect Bible Coll of NZ from 75. *Bible College of NZ, Henderson, Auckland, NZ.* (71-989)

GLEN, Robert Sawers. b 25. Qu Coll Cam BA 49, MA 56. Sarum Wells Th Coll 79. **d** 81 Sarum (NSM). Chap Sherborne Sch Dorset from 81. *Abbeylands, Sherborne, Dorset.*

GLENCROSS, Bruce Robert. b 53. McGill Univ Montr BA 76. Montr Dioc Th Coll 80. **d** 81 Montr. C of St Pet Mt R Dio Montr from 81. *900 Laird Boulevard, Montreal, Que, Canada, H3R 1Y8.*

GLENDALOUGH, Bishop of. *See* Dublin.

GLENDINING, Canon Alan. b 24. MVO 79. Westcott Ho Cam 58. **d** 60 **p** 61 Linc. C of S Ormsby 60-63; R of Raveningham Group 63-70; C-in-c of Raveningham 63-70; C-in-c of Hales w Heckingham 63-70; R of Thurlton w Thorpe 63-70; V of Norton Subcourse 63-70; C-in-c of Aldeby w Burgh St Pet and Wheateacre 66-70; Haddiscoe w Toft Monks 68-70; R of Sandringham (and R of Sandringham Group) 70-79; Dom Chap to HM the Queen 70-79; Hon Chap from 79; RD of Heacham and Rising 72-76; Hon Can of Nor from 77; R of Lowestoft Group (R of St Marg) Dio Nor from 79. *16 Corton Road, Lowestoft, Suff.* (Lowestoft 3046)

GLENN, Michael David. b 37. Lich Th Coll 67. **d** 70 **p** 71 Hulme for York. C of Ch Ch Denton Man 70-74; Chap of Oldham Hosps & L to Offic Dio Man 74-77; C-in-c of Moss Side 77-78; Dir of Stewardship Promotion Dio Lich from 78; C of Hints Dio Lich from 78; Drayton Bassett and Fazeley Dio Lich from 78. *Hints Vicarage, School Lane, Tamworth, Staffs.* (Shenston 480210)

GLENNIE, Canon Charles. b 08. Edin Th Coll 28. **d** 30 **p** 31 Edin. C of Ch Ch Falkirk (in c of St Mary Grangemouth) 30-35; Chap HM Borstal Polmont 31-35; HM Pris Peterhead 37-40; HM Pris Aber 42-67; R of St Jas Cruden 35-42; St Pet Torry Aberdeen and St Mary Cove Bay 42-67; CF (TA - R of O) 48-50; CF (TA) from 50; R of Coupar Angus 67-73; Can of St Paul's Cathl Dundee 57-67; Hon Can from 73; Hon Super Dio St Andr from 73. *An Oisinn, Newton Street, Blairgowrie, Perthshire, PH10 6HZ.* (Blairgowrie 2293)

GLENNON, Alfred James. Moore Th Coll Syd ACT ThL 50. **d** and **p** 51 Syd. C of Haberfield 51; St John Darlinghurst Syd 52; on leave 54-55; C of St Andr Cathl Syd 55-56 and from 62; Prec 56-62; Min Can from 68; Chap St Geo Hosp Syd 62-66. *59 Boundary Street, Clovelly, NSW, Australia 2031.* (665-1526)

GLENNY, William Richard Harcourt Raeburn. b 21. Bps' Coll Cheshunt 54. **d** 56 **p** 57 Chelmsf. C of Gidea Park 56-59; Buckhurst Hill 59-61; V of All SS Forest Gate 61-68; Chap St Gabr Conv Sch Newbury and CJGS Community Sandleford Priory 68-74; Downe Ho Sch Cold Ash 73-74; V of St Andr City and Dio Chelmsf from 74. *88 Chignall Road, Chelmsford, Essex.* (Chelmsf 52097)

GLEW, George William. b 24. Oak Hill Th Coll 64. **d** 66 **p** 67 Cant. C of St Mary Bredin Cant 66-69; CF (R of O) from 67; C of Willesborough 69-73; V of Burlingham w Lingwood Dio Nor from 73. *Lingwood Vicarage, Norwich, NR13 4TW.*

GLOUCESTER, Lord Bishop of. *See* Yates, Right Rev John.

GLOUCESTER, Archdeacon of. (vacant)

GLOUCESTER, Dean of. *See* Thurlow, Very Rev Alfred Gilbert Goddard.

GLOVER, Arthur Anderson. b 15. NOC 79. **d** 80 Wakef for York for Bradf **p** 81 Bradf (APM). Hon C of Idle Dio Bradf from 80. *16 Thackley View, Thackley, Bradford, W Yorks, BD10 0RU.*

GLOVER, Brian Reginald. b 38. St D Coll Lamp BA 60. Sarum Th Coll 60. **d** 62 Bp Stuart for Worc **p** 63 Worc. C of Redditch 62-68; V of St Geo Redditch 68-74; Ellistown 74-77; St Aid New Parks Leic 77-82; Fleckney Dio Leic from 82. *Vicarage, Saddington Road, Fleckney, Leic, LE8 0AW.* (Leicester 402215)

GLOVER, David. b 50. Coll of the Resurr Mirfield 77. **d** 80 **p** 81 Man. C of St Jas Hope Salford Dio Man from 80. *Flat 7, 93 Eccles Old Road, Hope, Salford 6, Gtr Man.*

GLOVER, Elistan Patrick. b 44. Rhodes Univ BA 63. Keble Coll Ox BA 66. St Paul Th Coll Grahmstn 69. **d** 69 Bp Carter for Johann **p** 70 Johann. C of St Pet Krugersdorp 70-71; Rosebank 71-74; R of Bramley Dio Johann from 74. *Box 39063, Bramley, Transvaal, S Africa.* (011-786 7682)

GLOVER, Frederick. Selw Coll Dun 64. NZ Bd of Th Stud LTh 66. **d** 64 **p** 65 Dun. C of NE Valley 64-67; P-in-c of Mornington 67; V of Wakatipu 67-71; V of Bluff w Stewart Island 71-73; Riverton 73-78; Maniototo 78-79; St Martins Dio Ch Ch from 79. *9 Wilson's Road, Christchurch 2, NZ.* (327 195)

GLOVER, Henry Arthur. b 32. BSc (Lon) 58. Wycl Hall Ox. **d** 61 **p** 62 Portsm. C of St Jo Evang Fareham 61-63. *15 Thorncliffe Road, Wallasey, Cheshire.*

GLOVER, John. b 48. Kelham Th Coll 67. **d** 71 **p** 72 Worc. C of H Innoc Kidderminster 71-75; Team V of Sutton 75-79; P-in-c of Churchill-in-Halfshire w Blakedown Dio Worc from 79. *Churchill Rectory, Blakedown, Kidderminster, Worcs.*

GLOVER, John Trevor. b 25. Clifton Th Coll 52. **d** 56 **p** 57 Derby. C of St Chad Derby 56-59; Skellingthorpe w Swallowbeck 60-64; PC of Swallowbeck 64-69; Miss CMS 69-79; V of H Trin W Bromwich Dio Lich from 79. *Holy Trinity Vicarage, West Bromwich, Staffs.* (W Bromwich 0172)

GLOVER, Michael John Myers. b 28. BSc (2nd cl Eng) Lon 48. Cudd Coll 54. **d** 56 **p** 57 Leic. C of St Pet Leic 56-60; Isandhlwana 60-61; R of Nongoma 61-73; Bp's Chap E Area Northn Dio Pet 73-74; Team R of Em Northn Dio Pet from 74. *The Lakes, Billing Park, Northampton, NN3 4BQ.* (Northn 408123)

GLOVER, Neil Reheiri. Ridley Coll Melb ACT ThL 45. **d** 46 **p** 47 Melb. C of St Thos Essendon 46-47; Min of Whittlesea 47-49; Wallan 49-52; V of N Richmond 52-58; I of Kilsyth 58-62; C of Burwood 62-64; I of Newport 64-67; Perm to Offic Dio Melb 73-79; P-in-c of Preston W Dio Melb from 79. *122 Morton Road, Ashwood, Vic, Australia 3147.* (03-25 8306)

GLOVER, Peter Ronald. b 45. Qu Coll Birm. **d** 77 Worc **p** 80 Leic. C of St Steph Redditch 77-79; Birstall Dio Leic from 80. *11 Fieldgate Crescent, Birstall, Leicester, LE4 3JE.* (Leic 675822)

GLOVER, Richard John. b 47. Univ of Nottm BTh 77. Linc Th Coll 73. **d** 77 Penrith for Carl **p** 78 Carl. C of Barrow-F 77-79; Netherton 79-80; P-in-c of Addingham w Gamblesby Dio Carl from 80; Edenhall w Langwathby and Culgaith Dio Carl from 80. *Vicarage, Langwathby, Penrith, Cumb.* (Langwathby 212)

GNOKORO, Eric. St Luke's Coll Siota 33. **d** 34 **p** 38 Melan. P Dio Melan. *Melanesian Mission, British Solomon Islands.*

GOAD, Reginald Edwin. b 1896. Cudd Coll 51. **d** 51 **p** 52 Blackb. C of St Geo Chorley 51-53; Bridlington 53-55; V of Boosbeck w Moorsholme 55-57; R of Potter Hanworth 57-59; V of Morton 59-63; V of E Stockwith w Walkerith 59-63; R of Warter w Huggate 63-67. *Meadowville, Glebe Drive, Bowness-on-Windermere, Cumb.*

GOALBY, George Christian. b 55. Univ of Leeds BA 77. St Jo Coll Nottm 79. **d** 81 Wakef. C of St Andr w St Mary City and Dio Wakef from 81. *10 St Mark's Street, Wakefield, W Yorks.*

GOATER, Very Rev Noel Leslie. Em Coll Sktn. **d** 65 **p** 66 Qu'App. Prin of Gordon's Ind Sch 65-68; Admin of Shingwauk Hall Sault Ste Marie 68-70; C of St Luke's Cathl Sault Ste Marie 70-71; R of Copper Cliff 71-74; I of St John N Bay 74-80; Exam Chap to Bp of Alg 76-80; to Bp of Bran from 80; Dean and R of St Matt Cathl City and Dio Bran from 80. *403 13th Street, Brandon, Manit, Canada.*

GOATER, William Arthur. b 12. Chich Th Coll 33. **d** 36 **p** 37 Lich. C of St Mary and St Chad Longton 36-39; St Kath Rotherhithe 39-46; V 46-53; PC of N Nibley w The Ridge 53-68; V 68-77; V of Stinchcombe 55-77; RD of Dursley 73-77; Perm to Offic Dio Glouc from 77. *Church Cottage, Stinchcombe, Dursley, Glos.* (Dursley 2116)

GOBLE, Clifford David. b 41. Oak Hill Th Coll 69. **d** 72 **p** 73 Roch. C of St Paul Northumberland Heath Erith 72-76; St Jas Tunbridge Wells 76-79; R of Southfleet Dio Roch from 79. *Rectory, Southfleet, Kent.* (Southfleet 3252)

GOBODO, Wilberforce Tukela. b 26. **d** 79 St John's (APM). d Dio St John's. *Umtata Street, Cala, Transkei.*

GODBER, Francis Giles. b 48. Ridley Hall Cam 72. **d** 75 **p** 76 Birm. C of St Paul Blackheath 75-78; St Matt Wolverhampton 78-80; Team V of Exe Valley Team Min Dio Ex from 80. *Vicarage, Chevithorne, Tiverton, Devon.* (Tiverton 252357)

GODDARD, Charles Douglas James. b 47. Div Hostel Dub 67. **d** 70 **p** 71 Down. C of St Jo Evang Orangefield 70-73; Stormont Belf 73-75; Chap Miss to Seamen Belf 75-77; Sen Chap and Sec N Ireland from 77. *15 Thirlmere Gardens, Belfast, BT15 5EF.* (Belfast 778095)

GODDARD, Christopher. b 45. Sarum Wells Th Coll 79. **d** 81 Carl. C of Whitehaven Dio Carl from 81. *5 Earls Road, Whitehaven, Cumbria, CA28 6BB.*

GODDARD, Christopher Robert Wynn. b 08. Trin Coll Cam BA 30. Cudd Coll 32. **d** 33 **p** 34 Lon. C of John Keble Ch Mill Hill 33-37; C-in-c of St Edm Conv Distr Allenton Derby 37-46; Ch Ch St Marylebone 46-47; R 47-50; C-in-c of St Barn St Marylebone 48-50; V of Headstone 50-55; Tillingham 55-63; R of Dengie w Asheldham 55-63; V of St Jo Bapt w Winnall Win 63-68; Kersey w Lindsey 68-73; Perm to Offic Dio St E from 74. *Ship Cottage, Dunwich, Saxmundham, Suff.*

GODDARD, David Ivan. b 26. Oak Hill Th Coll 58. **d** 60 **p** 61 Win. C of St Jo Evang Boscombe Bournemouth 60-63; V of E Boldre w S Baddesley 63-78; Shirley Dio Win from 78. *Vicarage, Wordsworth Road, Shirley, Southampton, SO1 5LX.* (Southn 771755)

GODDARD, Canon Frederick Paul Preston. b 24. Jes Coll Cam BA 49, MA 51. Westcott Ho Cam 49. **d** 51 **p** 52 St Alb. C of Bp's Hatfield 51-57; Chap Univ of Cant NZ 57-61; Cathl Gr Sch Ch Ch 60-61; V of Abbots Langley 61-68; Sherborne w Castleton and Lillington Dio Sarum from 68; Commis Nel from 69; RD of Sherborne 73-77; Can and Preb of Sarum Cathl from 75. *Vicarage, Sherborne, Dorset.* (Sherborne 2452)

GODDARD, Harold Frederick. b 42. Keble Coll Ox BA (2nd cl Hist) 63, Dipl Th 65, MA 69. Cudd Coll 64. **d** 66 **p** 67 Birm. C of St Pet Birm 66-70; Alverstoke 70-72; P-in-c of St Geo Conv Distr Portsea 72-76; Hon Chap Portsm Cathl 73-76; P-in-c of Stoke Prior 76-78; V (w Wychbold and Upton Warren) 78-80; P-in-c of Wychbold w Upton Warren 77-78; Chap R Marsden Hosp Fulham and Sutton from 80; L to Offic Dio Lon from 80; Perm to Offic Dio S'wark from 80. *27 Holland Avenue, Cheam, Sutton, Surrey, SM2 6HW.* (01-642 0833)

GODDARD, Hubert George. b 07. Dorch Miss Coll 37. **d** 40 **p** 41 Glouc. C of St Jas Dursley 40-44; All SS Glouc 44-47; All SS Cheltm 47; C-in-c of St Mich Conv Distr Lynworth 47-53; V 53-60; PC of Bussage 60-65. *18 St Ledgers Road, Bournemouth, Hants.*

GODDARD, John. b 09. K Coll Lon and Warm 57. **d** 58 **p** 59 Ox. C of Banbury 58-61; R of Heyford Warren w Lower Heyford and Rousham 61-66; Launton 66-76; RD of Bicester w Islip 74-76; Perm to Offic Dio Pet from 76. *61 Stanwell Lea, Middleton Cheney, Banbury, Oxon.*

GODDARD, John William. b 47. St Chad Coll Dur BA (2nd cl Th) 69, Dipl Th 70. **d** 70 **p** 71 York. C of S Bank 70-74; Cayton w Eastfield 74-75; V of Ascen Middlesbrough 75-81; All SS Middlesbrough Dio York from 81. *All Saints Centre, Church House, Grange Road, Middlesbrough TS1 2LR.* (Middlesbrough 245035)

GODDARD, Leslie Arthur. b 20. Commun of Resurr Mirfield 60. **d** 61 Bp Graham for Carl **p** 62 Carl. C of Egremont 61-65; V of Lamplugh w Ennerdale 65-75; C-in-c of Arlecdon 74-75; V of Pennington 75-77; P-in-c of Farlam 77-80; Nether Denton 77-80; V of Farlam w Nether Denton 80-81. *Hinksfield, Bogmuchals, Banff.*

GODDARD, Matthew Francis. b 45. Dipl Th (Lon) 69. Kelham Th Coll 65. **d** 69 Sherwood for Southw **p** 70 Southw. C of St Mark Mansfield 69-72; St Barn Northolt Pk 72-78; P-in-c of St Pet Acton Green Dio Lon from 78. *206 St Alban's Avenue, W4 5JU.* (01-994 5735)

GODDARD, Morse Anson-Cartwright Minet. Univ of W Ont BA 60. Hur Coll LTh 60. **d** 60 **p** 61 Tor. C of Trin Ch Port Credit 60-61; St Simon Ap Tor 61-64; Apsley 64-66; I of St Sav Orono Newc 66-69; Hon C of Cobourg 69-71; on leave from 71. *PO Box 566, Grafton, Ont., Canada.*

GODDARD, Canon Sydney Thomas. b 16. St Aid Coll 46. **d** 49 **p** 50 Liv. C of St Jo Evang Ravenhead 49-52; St Helens (in c of St Andr) 52-55; V of St Ambrose Widnes and Chap of Crow Wood Hosp 55-59; V of St Sav Liv 59-71; Warden World Friendship Ho and Chap Liv Maternity Hosp from 59; Hon Can of Liv from 69. *World Friendship House, 2-10 Falkner Square, Liverpool, L8 7NX.* (051-709 9398)

GODDARD, Canon William. b 09. Kelham Th Coll 29. **d** 34 **p** 35 Wakef. C of Wrangbrook 34-37; St Aid Small Heath 37-39; Bathwick w Woolley 39-42; Chap RAFVR 42-46; V of Paulton 46-50; St Barn Swindon 50-52; St Agnes (w St Simon from 56) Bris 52-59; R of St Nicolas Guildf 59-74; RD of Guildf 67-73; Hon Can of Guildf 71-74; Can (Emer) from 77; R of Tilbrook 74-77; Covington 74-77; Gt Catworth 74-77; Perm to Offic Dio Glouc from 77. *8 Gallops Lane, Noverton Park, Prestbury, Cheltenham, GL52 5SD.* (Cheltenham 28849)

GODDARD, William Edwin George. b 14. Clifton Th Coll 66. **d** 68 **p** 69 Bris. C of Rodbourne Cheney 68-71; Beaford w Roborough 71-78; R (w St Giles-in-the-Wood) 78-79. *The Manse, High Street, Purton, Swindon, SN5 9BB.*

GODDEN, Graham Russell. **d** 57 C & Goulb. Hon C of Albury 57-60; W Tamworth Dio Armid from 61. *72 Panorama Road, Calala, Tamworth, NSW, Australia 2340.*

GODDEN, Ven Max Leon. b 23. Worc Coll Ox BA (3rd cl Mod Hist) 50, MA 54. Chich Th Coll 50. **d** 52 **p** 53 Chich. C of Cuckfield 52; Brighton 53-57; PC of Hangleton 57-62; V of Glynde and W Firle w Beddingham 62-82; m gen syn from 70; Archd of Lewes 72-75; Lewes and Hastings from 75. *c/o Glynde Vicarage, Lewes, Sussex.*

GODDEN, Walter Henry. **d** 51 Dub for Moos **p** 52 Moos. I of Hornepayne 51-54; Bourlamaque 54-58; R of Geraldtown 58-62; Mitchell 62-65; St Mark Windsor Dio Hur from 65. *1661 Leduc Street, Windsor, Ont., Canada.* (519-256 7081)

GODDING, William Ronald. b 09. Univ of Wales, BSc 35. St Aid Coll 36. **d** 39 **p** 40 Sheff. C of St Jas Clifton Rotherham 39-40; C of Eccleshall Sheff 40-47; V of Stainforth (in C of Dunscroft) 47-61; All SS 61-72; R of Harthill 72-75. *223 Ellesmere Road, Sheffield, S Yorks.*

GODECK, John William George. b 30. Chich Th Coll 57. **d** 60 **p** 61 Chich. C of Wadhurst and of Tidebrook 60-62; Eastbourne 62-63; R of Zeal Monachorum 63-77; Bondleigh 63-78; C-in-c of Broadwoodkelly 65-67; R 67-78; R of Dunchideock w Shillingford St Geo and Ide Dio Ex from 78. *Shillingford St George Rectory, Exeter, Devon.* (Kennford 832589)

GODFREY, Brian Ernest Searles. b 37. Univ of Lon BSc 60, MSc 63, PhD 72. SOC 78. **d** 81 Roch. Hon C of St Mary Virg Hayes Dio Roch from 81. *23 Kechill Gardens, Hayes, Bromley, Kent, BR2 7NQ.*

GODFREY, David Samuel George. b 35. **d** 66 **p** 67 Derry. C of Ch Ch Londonderry 66-68; I of Tomregan w Drumlane 68-71; Manorhamilton 71-79; Templebreedy Dio Cork from 79. *Rectory, Crosshaven, Co Cork, Irish Republic.* (021-831236)

GODFREY, Edward Colin. b 30. Wells Th Coll 63. **d** 65 **p** 66 Win. C of Lyndhurst 65-69; Paignton (in c of St Bonif) 69-73; V of Stockland w Dalwood 73-77; Asst Chap HM Pris Strangeways Man 77-78; HM Pris Cant from 78. *c/o HM Prison, Canterbury, Kent.*

GODFREY, Frederick Hodgson. KCNS BA 32. **d** 33 **p** 34 NS. C of Rawdon 33-43; Chap RCN 43-63; R of Hantsport 63-77; Exam Chap to Bp of NS 65-71. *Hantsport, NS, Canada.* (634-3875)

GODFREY, Canon Frederick Lindesay. b 02. Mert Coll Ox 3rd cl Mod Hist 24, BA 26, MA 28. Wycl Hall Ox 26. **d** 27 **p** 28 Leic. C of H Ap Leic 27-29; St Mark Leic 29-32; St Dunstan Stepney 32-35; V of St Matt Stepney 35-43; St Pet St Helier 43-54; R of Cole Orton 54-57; Hon Can of Leic 57-68; Can Res 68-72; Can (Emer) from 72; Warden Leic Dioc Retreat Ho Launde Abbey 57-63; C-in-c of Loddington 58-63; Surr from 59; Proc Conv Leic from 62; Dioc Missr Dio Leic 63-72; Chap Groby Road Hosp Leic 64-70; L to Offic Dio Leic from 72. *38 Main Street, Swithland, Loughborough, LE12 8TH.* (Woodhouse Eaves 890531)

GODFREY, Harold William. b 48. AKC 71. St Aug Coll Cant 71. **d** 72 Sherwood for Southw **p** 73 Southw. C of Warsop w Sookholme 72-75; Team V of Hucknall Torkard Dio Southw from 75; Ecumen Officer to Bp of Southw from 81. *Vicarage, Ruffs Drive, Hucknall, Nottingham, NG15 6JG.* (Nottm 633640)

GODFREY, John Frederick. b 31. Univ of Lon LLB 53. AKC 54. Cudd Coll 59. **d** 61 **p** 62 S'wark. [f Solicitor] C of St Luke Battersea 61-65; Min of St Phil Conv Distr Reigate 65-72; Publ Pr Dio St Alb from 73. *Thicketts, Theobald Street, Radlett, Herts.* (Radlett 5558)

GODFREY, Michael. b 49. AKC 72, BD 70. St Aug Coll Cant 71. **d** 72 Jarrow for Dur **p** 73 Dur. C of St Jo Evang Birtley 72-75; Industr Chap in Gateshead Dio Dur 76-79; P-in-c of St Mary Bilston Dio Lich 79-80; Team V from 80; Industr Chap Black Country Urban Miss from 81. *43 Willenhall Road, Bilston, W Midl, WV14 6WW.*

GODFREY, Nigel Philip. b 51. M RTPI 76. Univ of Ox BA 78. Ripon Coll Cudd 77. **d** 79 **p** 80 S'wark. C of St Jo Div Kennington Dio S'wark from 79. *96 Vassall Road, SW9 6JA.* (01-582 2126)

GODFREY, Canon Robert Bernard. b 16. Wells Th Coll 55. **d** 56 **p** 57 Roch. C of Meopham 56-58; R of Wouldham 58-62; R of St Mary Stoke Ipswich 62-76; C-in-c of St Pet (to 73) w St Mary at Quay Ipswich 65-76; Wherstead 68-76; Hon Can of St E Cathl from 73; RD of Stamford from 75; R of Sproughton w Burstall 76-81. *c/o Sproughton Rectory, Ipswich, Suff.* (Ipswich 41106)

GODFREY, Robert John. Sarum Th Coll 52. **d** 54 **p** 55 Ripon. C of St Edm Roundhay 54-57; Gt Marlow 57-59; V of Long Crendon 59-61; Chap RAF 61-63; Crookham Court Sch 63-79; P-in-c of Yattendon w Frilsham 79-81; Team V of Hermitage and Hampstead Norreys, Cold Ash and Yattendon w Frilsham Dio Ox from 81. *Rectory, Yattendon, Nr Newbury, Berks, RG16 0UR.* (Hermitage 201213)

GODFREY, Canon Rupert Christopher Race. b 12. Qu Coll Ox BA (2nd cl Mod Hist) 34, Dipl Th 35, MA 38. Ridley Hall Cam 35. **d** 36 Chelmsf for St E **p** 37 St E. C of St Helen Ipswich 36-38; St Geo Edgbaston 38-46; CF (EC) 40-46; Hon CF 46; V of Aldeburgh w Hazelwood 46-59; RD of Saxmundham 54-59; Hon Can of St E 57-77; Can (Emer) from 77; V of St Mary Bury St Edms 59-77; Proc Conv St E 59-69; RD of Thingoe 67-70; Perm to Offic Dio St E from 77. *Archway House, Pytches Road, Woodbridge, Suff, IP12 1EY.* (Woodbridge 2816)

GODFREY, Simon. b 43. Kelham Th Coll 60. **d** 69 Bp Daly for Cov **p** 70 Cov. C of Styvechale 69-74; Wyken 74-76; Team V of Caludon Cov 76-80; P-in-c of St Paul Warwick Dio Cov from 80. *33 Stratford Road, Warwick, CV34 6AS.*

GODFREY, Simon Henry Martin. b 55. AKC and BD 80. St Steph Ho Ox 80. **d** 81 Pet. C of SS Pet and Paul Kettering Dio Pet from 81. *27 Bow Hill, Kettering, Northants.*

GODFREY, Stanley William. b 24. M IEE CEng 67. Qu Coll Birm 71. **d** and **p** 74 Birm. C of St Chad Sutton Coldfield 74-78; St Andr Handsworth 78-81. *Address temp unknown.*

GODFREY, William Thomas. b 12. ACP 67. K Coll Lon and Warm. **d** 69 **p** 70 Win. C of All SS Southbourne Bournemouth 69-72; V of S Petherwyn w Trewen 72-77; Chap U Chine Sch Shanklin 77-78. *3 Lincoln Close, Bembridge, IW, PO35 5RP.* (Bembridge 3774)

GODFREY-THOMAS, Cecil Stephens Godfrey. b 09. St D Coll Lamp BA 31. St Cath Coll Cam BA 45, MA 48. **d** 32 **p** 33 St A. C of Colwyn Bay 32-35; Widcombe 35-37; Harborne 37-39; CF (TA R of O) 39-54; Hon CF 54; R of E Donyland 45-52; V of Castle Hedingham 52-67; R of Woodham Mortimer w Hazeleigh 67-79; Woodham Walter 67-79. *38 Bathurst Road, Ilford, Essex.* (01-554 4485)

GODKIN, Nehemiah John. Em Coll Sktn BA and LTh 39, BD 49. **d** 39 Edmon **p** 40 Rupld for Edmon. C of St John Cadomin 39-40; H Trin Edmon 41-42; Chap RCAF 42-46; V of St Paul Edmon 46-47; R of Royal Oak 47-56; St Cath N Vancouver 56-70; R of St Lawr Coquitlam 70-73; I of St Hilda Sechelt 73-78. *RR1 Halfmoon Bay, BC, Canada.*

GODLEY, Denis John. K Coll NS. **d** 61 Bp W W Davis for NS **p** 63 NS. I of Aylesford 61-66; Westphal Dio NS from 66; R of Port Wallis 66-72; P-in-c of Westphal Dio NS from 72. *30 Raymoor Drive, Dartmouth, NS, Canada.* (434-1760)

GODMAN, Canon Cyril John Philip. b 16. St Aid Coll 43. **d** 45 **p** 46 Roch. C of H Trin Beckenham 45-47; Keston 47-48; All SS Alton 48-52; V of St Luke Bournemouth 52-71; V of St Kath w St Nich Southbourne 71-81; Hon Can of Win Cathl from 79. *62 Ulwell Road, Swanage, Dorset, BH19 1LN.* (Swanage 42335)

GODSALL, Ralph Charles. b 48. Qu Coll Cam BA 71, MA 75. Cudd Coll 73. **d** 75 Nor **p** 76 Lynn for Nor. C of Sprowston 75-78; Chap Trin Coll Cam from 78. *Trinity College, Cambridge, CB2 1TQ.* (0223-358201)

GODSELL, Arthur Norman. b 22. St D Coll Lamp BA 47. **d** 49 **p** 50 St D. C of Tenby w Gumfreston 49-62; V of Heybridge w Langford 62-73; RD of Maldon from 70; R of Rochford Dio Chelmsf from 73. *Rectory, Hall Road, Rochford, Essex, SS4 1NT.* (Southend-on-Sea 544304)

GODSELL, David Brian. b 40. Univ of Lon BA (2nd cl Mod Hist) 62. Coll of Resurr Mirfield 65. **d** 67 **p** 68 York. C of All SS Middlesbrough 67-72; Stainton-in-Cleveland 72-75; V of St Anthony Byker City and Dio Newc T from 75. *Vicarage, Enslin Gardens, Newcastle-on-Tyne, NE6 3ST.* (Newc T 651605)

GODSELL, Kenneth James Rowland. b 22. Qu Coll Birm Dipl Th 50. **d** 76 **p** 77 Birm (nsm). Hon C of Selly Hill Dio Birm from 76; Sen Lect Westhill Coll Birm from 76. *7 Farquhar Road East, Edgbaston, Birmingham, B15 3RD.* (021-454 3737)

GODSON, Alan. b 31. Ch Coll Cam BA 61, MA 65. Clifton Th Coll 61. **d** 63 Burnley for Blackb **p** 64 Blackb. C of All SS Preston 63-66; LPr Dio Man 66-69; Asst Chap Emb Ch Paris 69; Dioc Evang Dio Liv from 69; C-in-c of St Mary

Edge Hill Dio Liv 72-78; V from 78. *St Mary's Vicarage, Towerlands Street, Liverpool, L7 8TT.* (051-709 6710)

GODWIN, Aubrey Eric Walter. Bp's Univ Lennox. **d** and **p** 35 Queb. C of Peninsula 35-40; I of Sawyerville 40-44; L to Offic Dio Edmon 44-45; Miss at Fitch Bay 45-47; R of Clayton 47-50; Prin of Wabasca Ind Sch 50-56; V of Burquitlam 56-63; Whalley 63-67; St Mary Virg Vancouver 67-71; I of Pemberton St Geo w Squamish St Jo 71-75. *19707 Poplar Drive, Pott Meadows, BC, Canada.*

GODWIN, David Harold. b 45. Dipl Th (Lon) 71. Kelham Th Coll. **d** 71 **p** 72 S'wark. C of St Phil and St Mark Camberwell 71-75; Asst Chap Lon Hosp 75-79; Hosp Chap Hastings from 79. *c/o Royal East Sussex Hospital, Cambridge Road, Hastings, Sussex.* (0424-434513)

GODWIN, Michael Francis Harold. b 35. Univ of Nottm BSc (2nd cl Chem) 57. Ely Th Coll 59. **d** 61 **p** 62 Guildf. C of Farnborough 61-65; V of St Barn Epsom Dio Guildf from 66. *St Barnabas's Vicarage, Epsom, Surrey.* (Epsom 22874)

GODWIN, Noel. b 29. Qu Coll Ox BA 52, MA 57. St Steph Ho Ox 52. **d** 54 **p** 55 S'wark. C of St Pet Streatham 54-57; Chap Adisadel Coll Accra 58-63; V of St Edw Holbeck 63-65; Sub Warden (Warden 73-78) Commun of All H Ditchingham and L to Offic Dio Nor 65-77; Commiss Accra 72-74; RD of Depwade 76-77; R of Attleborough (w Besthorpe from 80) 77-82; P-in-c of Besthorpe 78-80; Hon Can of Nor Cathl 81; V of St Mich AA w St Jas Croydon Dio Cant from 82. *Vicarage, Oakfield Road, Poplar Walk, Croydon, Surrey, CR0 2UX.* (01-688 0694)

GODWIN, Peter. b 19. MBE 77. Ridley Hall Cam 77. **d** 77 Guildf for Argent & E S Amer. C of All SS Headley Guildf 77-78; H Trin Lomas de Zamora Buenos Aires Dio Argent & E S Amer from 78. *Ave Almirante Brown 2577, 1832 Lomas de Zamora, Pcia de Buenos Aires, Argentina.*

GOETZ, Grevis. OBE 51. **d** 58 **p** 59 Auckld. C of St Andr Epsom Auckld 58-61; V of Henderson 61-65; St Andr Epsom Auckld 65-74; Hon C of Tamaki Dio Auckld from 74. *116 Allum Street, Kohimarama, Auckland 5, NZ.* (589-552)

GOFF, Brian Ernest. St Jo Coll Morpeth. **d** 61 **p** 62 Bath. C of Mudgee 61-65; Condobolin 65-66; R of Coolah 66-69; Milthorpe 69-75; Molong Dio Bath from 75. *Rectory, Molong, NSW, Australia 2866.* (6932 89)

GOFF, Philip Francis Michael. b 52. AKC and BD 73. St Aug Coll Cant 74. **d** 75 Willesden for Lon **p** 76 Lon. C of Ruislip 75-79; Chap Aldenham Sch Elstree from 79. *Chaplain's Lodge, Aldenham School, Elstree, Herts. WD6 3AJ.* (Radlett 3360)

GOFTON, William Alder. b 31. Univ of Dur BA (2nd cl Mod Hist) 54. Coll of Resurr Mirfield 59. **d** 61 **p** 62 Newc T. C of St Aid Newc T 61-64; N Gosforth 64-69; V of Seaton Hirst 69-77; H Cross Fenham Dio Newc T from 77. *16 Whittington Grove, Newcastle upon Tyne, NE5 2QP.* (Newc T 744476)

GOGAN, Vincent. b 40. **d** and **p** 79 New Guinea Is. P Dio New Guinea Is. *PO Box 159, Rabaul, E.N.B.P., Papua New Guinea.*

GOIANE, Jaime. d and **p** 75 Lebom. P Dio Lebom 75-79; Dio Niassa from 79. *Lago, Niassa, Mozambique.*

GOING, William Ray. b 53. Univ of Nottm BTh 81. St Jo Coll Nottm LTh 81. **d** 81 Birm. C of St Paul Blackheath Dio Birm from 81. *33 Hope Street, Halesowen, W Midl, B62 8LU.*

GOJELA, Ndabankulu Christopher. b 51. St Bede's Coll Umtata Dipl Th 79. **d** 79 **p** 80 Port Eliz. C of St Pet Uitenhage Dio Port Eliz from 79. *c/o 25-3rd Avenue, Xaba, Uitenhage 6233, S Africa.*

GOLBOURNE, Winston George. b 30. Sarum Wells Th Coll 71. **d** 73 Southn for Win **p** 74 Win. C of Bitterne Pk 73-76; R of St D Snowdon, Ja 76-79; C of St Andr Handsworth (in c of St Francis) Dio Birm from 79. *c/o Vicarage, Laurel Road, Handsworth, Birmingham, B21 9PB.*

GOLD, Guy Alastair Whitmore. b 16. TD 50. Trin Coll Cam 3rd cl Geog Trip pt i 37, BA (3rd cl Econ Trip pt ii) 38, MA 48. Qu Coll Birm 55. **d** 55 **p** 56 Chelmsf. C of St Pet Prittlewell 55-57; Dom Chap to Bp of Chelmsf 58-61; R of Wickham Bishops 62-69; Hasketon 69-76; Sec St E Dioc Syn 70-76; Perm to Offic Dio St E from 76. *45 Ipswich Road, Woodbridge, Suff, IP12 4BT.*

GOLDER, Stacey Mortimer. b 11. **d** 74 **p** 75 Nel. Hon C of Picton 74-78; Offg Min Dio Nel from 78. *65 Broadway, Picton, NZ.* (Picton 523)

GOLDIE, David. b 46. Univ of Glas MA 68. Fitzw Coll Cam BA (2nd cl Th Trip pt ii) 70. Westcott Ho Cam. **d** 70 **p** 71 Bris. C of Swindon 70-73; Troon (in c of Irvine New Town) 73-75; R of Ardrossan Dio Glas from 75; Irvine New Town Dio Glas from 75. *133 Bank Street, Irvine, Ayrshire, KA12 0NH.* (Irvine 71529)

GOLDIE, Canon David Campbell. b 23. Edin Th Coll 50. **d** 52 **p** 53 Glas. C of St Marg Newlands Glas 52-55; C-in-c of E Kilbride 55-60; St Clem Aber 60-65; R of Clydebank 65-75; St Aid Clarkston City and Dio Glas from 75; Can of St Mary's Cathl Glas from 80. *8 Golf Road, Clarkston, Glasgow, G76 7LZ.* (041-638 2860)

GOLDIE, Donald Norwood. b 14. St Chad's Coll Dur BA and De Bury Exhib 36. Dipl Th (w distinc) 37, MA 39. **d** 37 **p** 38 Dur. C of Tudhoe Grange 37-39; Ch Ch Bp Wearmouth 39-41; Offg C-in-c of St Mark Darlington 41-44; V of St Luke W Hartlepool 44-49; Archd in Cyprus and Chap at Nicosia w Kyrenia 49-55; V of H Trin Darlington and Chap Darlington Mem Hosp 55-62; R of Bp Wearmouth 62-70; C-in-c of St Hilda Millfield Bp Wearmouth 66-70; Chap Sunderland R Infirm; Surr 63-70; Hon Can of Dur 65-70; V of Bedlington T 70-80; Chap St Vincent's Algarve Portugal Dio Gibr in Eur from 80. *Pula da Lebre, Caldus de Monchique, Algarve, Portugal.*

GOLDING, Calvin Alphonso. St Pet Coll Ja. **d** 59 Ja **p** 60 Kingston for Ja. C of Christiana 59-61; P-in-c Mile Gully 61-62; V of Southfield 62-70; R of Savanna la Mar Dio Ja from 70. *Rectory, Savanna-la-Mar, Jamaica, W Indies.* (095-52731)

GOLDING, Cecil Eric Bernard. b 24. **d** 76 **p** 77 Capetn (APM). C of St Marg Fish Hoek Cape Dio Capetn from 76. *147 Highway, Fish Hoek 7975, CP, S Africa.* (82-1496)

GOLDING, George Charles. b 11. Univ Coll Dur Th Exhib and LTh 38, BA 39. St Aug Coll Cant 35. **d** and **p** 39 Cant. C of St Pet Croydon 39-42; Ox Miss Calc 42-67; Barisal from 67. *c/o Oxford Mission, 35 Great Peter Street, SW1.*

GOLDING, James Ward. K Coll NS LTh 64. **d** 63 **p** 64 Fred. C of Stanley 63-64; R 64-67; St Jas St John Fred 67-71; Chap Rothesay Colleg Sch Dio Fred from 71. *Rothesay Collegiate School, Rothesay, NB, Canada.*

GOLDING, Piers Edwin Hugh. b 26. St Aug Coll Cant 48. Edin Th Coll 50. **d** 53 **p** 54 Guildf. C of Ch Ch Guildf 53-55; Enfield 55-58; Chap RN 58-62; RNR from 62; V of St Aug of Hippo S Bermondsey Dio S'wark from 62. *Vicarage, Lynton Road, SE1.* (Bermondsey 1446)

GOLDING, Simon Jefferies. b 46. Linc Th Coll 72. **d** 74 **p** 75 York. C of Wilton-in-Cleveland 74-77; Chap RN from 77. *c/o Chaplain of the Fleet, Lacon House, Theobalds Road, WC1X 8RY.*

GOLDINGAY, John Edgar. b 42. Keble Coll Ox BA 64. Clifton Th Coll 64. **d** 66 **p** 67 Lon. C of Ch Ch Finchley 66-69; Lect St Jo Coll Nottm 70-75; Dir of Stud 76-79; Regr from 79; Hon C of Chilwell Dio Southw from 71. *St John's College, Bramcote, Nottingham, NG9 3DS.* (Nottm 251114)

GOLDSCHMIDT, Otto. St Francis Coll Brisb. **d** 65 Brisb. Hon C of Caloundra 66-68; Perm to Offic Dio Brisb 68-79. *c/o PO Box 29, Yandina, Queensland, Australia 4561.* (Yandina 192)

GOLDSMID, Peter Edward. b 13. Ely Th Coll 46. **d** 48 Dover for Cant **p** 49 Cant. C of All SS Westbrook Margate 48-51; Buckland in Dover 51-54; R of Aldington 54-59; Chap of Aldington Pris Camp 54-59; C of Ashford (in c of Ch Ch S Ashford) 59-60; V of Ch Ch S Ashford 60-65; Reculver 65-74; Chap at Marseilles 74-77; C of St Mary Ashford 77-78; L to Offic Dio Cant from 78. *Mill House, Mill Lane, Monk's Horton, Ashford, Kent, TN25 6AS.* (Sellindge 3586)

GOLDSMITH, Brian Derek. b 36. Univ of Leeds, BA (3rd cl Geog and Sociology) 64. Coll of Resurr Mirfield 64. **d** 66 **p** 67 Chich. C of Littlehampton 66-69; St Nicolas Guildf 69-73; V of St Aug Aldershot Dio Guildf from 73. *St Augustine's Vicarage, Holly Road, Aldershot, Hants, GU12 4SE.* (Aldershot 20840)

GOLDSMITH, Charles James. Ch Ch Coll 57. **d** 58 **p** 59 Ch Ch. C of Fendalton 58-60; P-in-c 61; V of W Lyttelton 61-63; Timaru 63-68; Kaiapoi 68-73; Leeston 73-78; Southbridge 76-78; Hon C of Highfield Dio Ch Ch from 78. *47 Broadway Avenue, Timaru, NZ.* (7326)

GOLDSMITH, John Oliver. b 46. K Coll Lon BD and AKC 69. St Aug Coll Cant 69. **d** 70 Repton for Derby **p** 71 Derby. C of Dronfield 70-73; Ellesmere Port 73-74; Team V 74-81; P-in-c of Pleasley w New Houghton Dio Derby from 81. *57 Newboundmill Lane, leasley, Mansfield, Notts, NG19 7PT.* (Mansfield 810278)

GOLDSMITH, Malcolm Clive. b 39. Univ of Birm B Social Sc (2nd cl) 60. Ripon Hall Ox 60. **d** 62 **p** 63 Birm. C of Balsall Heath 62-64; Chap Univ of Aston in Birm and Publ Pr Dio Birm 64-72; Bp of Southw's Adv on Industr S 72-78; Chap C of E Men's S Dio Southw 73-78; C of Sherwood 78-79; Chairman Bd of Social Responsibility Dio Southw from 79; R of St Pet w St Jas Nottm Dio Southw from 79. *3 King Charles Street, Standard Hill, Nottingham. NG1 6GB.* (Nottm 44891)

GOLDSMITH, Stephen. b 32. **d** 76 **p** 77 Edin (APM). C of Penicuik 76-81; St Nich Newport City and Dio Linc from 81. *Cantilupe Chantry North, Minster Yard, Lincoln, LN2 1PX.* (0522-24171)

GOLDSPINK, David. b 35. Lon Coll of Div. **d** 65 **p** 66 Nor. C of Mile Cross 65-68; St Austell 68-70; V in Bramerton

Group 70-73; C of Gunton 73-75; R of Mutford w Rushmere, Gisleham and North Cove w Barnby 75-81; Asst Chap HM Pris Man from 81. *c/o Chaplain's Office, HM Prison, Southall Street, Manchester, M60 9AH.*

GOLDSPINK, Robert William. b 23. Fitzw Coll Cam BA 52, MA 56. Trin Coll Bris 47. **d** 52 Lancaster for Blackb **p** 53 Blackb. C of St Mark Blackpool 52-56; V of St Paul Erith 56-64; St Jas Tunbridge Wells Dio Roch from 64. *12 Shandon Close, Tunbridge Wells, Kent, TN2 3RE.* (Tunbridge Wells 30687)

GOLDSTRAW, William Henry. b 15. Lich Th Coll 60. **d** 61 **p** 62 Lich. C of Stone 61-68; V of Alton Dio Lich from 68; Bradley-le-Moors Dio Lich from 68. *Alton Vicarage, Stoke-on-Trent, Staffs, ST10 4AR.* (Oakamoor 702469)

✠ **GOLDSWORTHY, Right Rev Arthur Stanley.** St Columb's Hall, Wang ThL 50. **d** 51 **p** 52 Wang. C-in-c of Bethanga 51-52; R of Chiltern 52-55; Kens 55-59; Yarrawonga 59-68; Lect St Columb's Hall Wang 68-72; Archd Dio Wang 72-77; R of Shepparton 72-76; Wodonga 77; Cons Ld Bp of Bunb in St Geo Cathl Perth 18 Oct 77 by Abps of Perth and Adel; Bps of NW Austr and Wang; Bp Coadj of Bunb; and Bps Macdonald, Bryant, Hawkins, Muschamp and Strong. *15 Cross Street, Bunbury, W Australia 6230.* (097-21 2163)

GOLDSWORTHY, Graeme Lister. Univ of Syd BA 55. BD (2nd cl) Lon 59. Clare Coll Cam BA (3rd cl Th Trip pt iii) 61. Moore Th Coll Syd ACT ThL (2nd cl) 57. **d** 58 Syd **p** 58 Bp Hilliard for Syd. Tutor Moore Th Coll Syd 58-59 and 63-68; on leave 69-72; R of Yagoona 72-75; Perm to Offic Dio Brisb from 75. *23 Orsan Street, Wynnum West, Queensland, Australia 4178.*

GOLDSWORTHY, John Lawler. **d** 60 **p** 61 Tas. C of St John Launceston 60-62; R of Cullenswood 62-65; C of St Jas w St John's Miss Distr Melb 65-72; I of Ch Ch Hawthorn 72-76; St Luke Springvale N Dio Melb from 76. *59-61 Police Road, Springvale North, Vic, Australia 3170.* (03-546 6533)

GOLDSWORTHY, Canon Warren Kenneth Lewis. Qu Coll Newfld. **d** 47 **p** 48 Newfld. C of Herring Neck 47-48; R of Greenspond 48-53; I of Brooklyn 53-55; Bay St Geo 55-59; R of Pouch Cove 59-63; Chap of St John's Cathl St John's 63-68; I of Carbonear 68-75; Heart's Content Dio Newfld (E Newfld from 76) from 75; Can of E Newfld from 81. *PO Box 56, Heart's Content, Trinity Bay, Newfoundland, Canada.*

GOLDTHORPE, Peter Martin. b 36. K Coll Lon and Warm 58. **d** 62 **p** 63 Chelmsf. C of St Barn L Ilford 62-66; Wickford 66-68; Luton 68-78; P-in-c of Linby w Papplewick Dio Southw from 78. *Rectory, Linby, Nottingham, NG15 8AE.* (Nottm 632346)

GOLIATH, John. b 44. St Pet Coll Alice Dipl Th 68. **d** 68 **p** 69 Geo. C of St Andr Riversdale 68-72; P-in-c of Albertinia 72-77; R of Mossel Bay 77-80; Macassar Dio Capetn from 80. *28 Angelo Street, Marvin Park, Macassar 7110, CP, S Africa.*

GOLIGHTLY, William Michael. b 43. Chich Th Coll 67. **d** 70 Bp Ramsbotham for Newc T **p** 74 Newc T. C of St John Sleekburn 70-71; St Luke Wallsend 71; Shiremoor Tynemouth 74-77; Delaval (in c of St Mich AA New Hartley) 77-81; Team V of Bellingham-Otterburn Group Dio Newc T from 81. *Rectory, West Woodburn, Hexham, NE48 2SG.*

GOLLEDGE, Leonard. b 09. St Jo Coll Dur BA and LTh 36. Lon Coll of Div 33. **d** 36 **p** 37 Bris. C of Ch Ch Swindon 36-39; C of St Paul Chippenham 39-45; CF (EC) 45-48; C of Stoke Bishop 48-49; V of All SS Swindon 49-57; St Cuthb Brislington 57-63; Merriott 63-76; Perm to Offic Dio B & W from 79. *2 Wyke Road, Ansford, Castle Cary, BA7 7LL.* (Castle Cary 50854)

GOLLMER, Alfred William Inches. **d** 28 **p** 29 Qu'App. C of Cereal 28-29; I of Tuberose 29-31; R of Broadview 31-36; I of Outlook 36-41; Lumsden 41-46; Kamsack 46-47; Stoughton 47-53; C of Nanaimo 53-55; L to Offic Dio BC from 55. *1635 Cook Street, apt 109, Victoria, BC, Canada.*

GOMERSALL, Clarence Edgar. St Francis Coll Brisb 64. **d** 66 **p** 67 Graft. C of Lismore 66-70; V of Mid-clarence 70-73; Copmanhurst 70-73; Chap Wolston Pk Hosp, Wacol 73-78; R of Ch Ch Milton City and Dio Brisb from 78. *Rectory, Chippendall Street, Milton, Queensland, Australia 4064.* (36 2797)

GOMERSALL, Ian Douglass. b 56. Univ of Birm BSc 77. Fitzw Coll Cam BA 80. Westcott Ho Cam 78. **d** 81 Dur. C of St Mark w St Paul Darlington Dio Dur from 81. *96 Thompson Street West, Darlington, DL3 0HQ.* (Darlington 64207)

GOMEZ, Cyprien Scipio. b 04. **d** 74 Gambia. d Dio Gambia 74-78. *Eglise de la Toussaint, Mission Anglicane, Box 105, Conakry, Guinea, W Africa.*

✠ **GOMEZ, Right Rev Drexel Wellington.** b 37. St Chad Coll Dur BA 59. Codr Coll Barb 55. **d** 59 Barb **p** 61 Nass. C of St Barn and St Agnes Nass 60-62; R of Eleuthera 62-64; Tutor Codr Coll Barb 64-68; R of Grand Bahamas 68-70; Treas Dio Nass 70-72; Exam Chap to Bp of Nass 71-72; Cons Ld Bp of Barb in St Mich Cathl Bridgetown 24 June 72 by Bp of Ja; Bp of Windw Is; and Bp Suffr of Stabroek. *Bishop's Court, St Michael 16, Barbados, W Indies.* (93139)

GOMEZ, Lorenzo. **d** and **p** 74 N Argent. P Dio N Argent. *Parsonage, Misión La Paz, N Argentina.*

GOMEZ, Raul. b 34. **d** 71 **p** 72 Parag for Argent. P Dio Argent 71-73; N Argent from 73. *Parsonage, Embarcación, N Argentina.*

GOMPERTZ, Peter Alan Martin. b 40. ALCD (2nd cl) 63. **d** 64 Warrington for Liv **p** 65 Liv. C of St Luke Eccleston 64-69; on staff Script U 69-73; C of Yeovil 73-75; V of St Giles Northn Dio Pet from 75. *St Giles's Vicarage, Northampton.* (Northn 34060)

✠ **GONAHASA, Right Rev Alupakusadi Lucas.** Buwalasi Th Coll. **d** 57 **p** 58 U Nile. P Dio U Nile 58-60; Dio Ankole-K 60-67; SCF Dio Ank 67-77; Cons Asst Bp of Bukedi in St Pet Pro-Cathl Tororo 19 March 78 by Abp of Ugan; Bps of Ruw, Busoga, Bunyoro, Soroti, Mbale, Mityana, W Ank and W Bugan; and others. *Box 170, Tororo, Uganda.*

GONIN, Christopher Willett. b 33. K Coll Lon and Warm AKC 59. **d** 60 **p** 61 S'wark. C of St Geo Camberwell 60-64; Stevenage (in c of St Hugh Chells) 64-70; Bletchley (in c of St Frideswide) 70-73; R of Newington 73-76; Hon C of Horfield Dio Bris from 77. *51 Falmouth Road, Bristol, BS7 8PY.* (Bristol 423951)

GONZALEZ, David. b 22. **d** and **p** 66 Argent. P Dio Argent 66-73; N Argent from 73. *Parsonage, Misión La Paz, N Argentina.*

GONZALEZ, Felipe. **d** and **p** 74 N Argent. P Dio N Argent. *Parsonage, Misión La Paz, N Argentina.*

GOOCH, Canon Francis Nelson. Bp's Univ Lennox BA 48. **d** 48 **p** 49 Ott. C of Smith's Falls 48-50; I of Petawawa 50-58; R of Bearbrook 58-64; N Gower 64-70; R of St Paul Ott 70-74; Morrisburg Dio Ott from 74; Can of Ott from 77. *Box 615, Morrisburg, Ont, Canada.* (1-613-543-2867)

GOOCH, Robert Frank. b 27. **d** 72 **p** 79 Bal. C of Warrnambool 72-78; Perm to Offic Dio Bal from 78. *44 Hickford Parade, Warrnambool, Vic, Australia 3280.* (055-62 2649)

GOOD, Anthony Ernest. b 28. ARIBA 51. Heriot-Watt Univ MSc 73. Wells Th Coll 54. **d** 56 **p** 57 Cant. C of Maidstone 56-60; St Mary Virg (in c of All SS) Reading 60-62; R of Sandhurst 62-70; Perm to Offic Dio Ex from 71; Lect Plymouth Poly 71-72; Sen Lect from 72. *Chapel Cottage, Cotts, Bere Alston, Yelverton, Devon.*

GOOD, Claude Wilfrid. b 1891. Qu Coll Cam BA 14, MA 19. Ridley Hall Cam. **d** 19 **p** 20 Southw. C of Basford Nottm 19-23; V of Tibshelf 23-25; CF (TA) 21-35; R of Gotham 25-30; V of Old Radford 30-47; Surr 31-47; V of Shorne 47-55; Totland Bay 55-60; Perm to Offic Dio Win from 60; Sarum 60-64. *Langham Hotel, Valley Drive, Harrogate, N Yorks.*

GOOD, Ernest Charles. St Jo Th Coll Auckld LTh 36. **d** 34 **p** 36 Auckld. C of Ellerslie 34-37; P-in-c of Avondale 37-39; L to Offic Dio Auckld from 39. *21 Fontenoy Street, Mount Albert, Auckland, NZ.* (866-872)

GOOD, Geoffrey. b 27. St Aid Coll. **d** 61 Warrington for Liv **p** 62 Liv. C of Roby 61-65; V of Staincliffe 65-79; Thornes Dio Wakef from 79. *Thornes Vicarage, Wakefield, Yorks, WF2 8DW.* (Wakef 374009)

GOOD, Very Rev George Fitzgerald. b 19. Trin Coll Dub BA 41. Div Test (1st cl) 42. **d** 42 **p** 43 Arm. C of Drumglass 42-45; Cler V of Ch Ch Cathl Dub 45-49; R of Inniskeel w Lettermacaward 49-60; Raph w Reymochy 60-67; Can of Raph 60-62; RD of Raph 60-64; Dean of Raph 62-67; Derry from 67; Priv Chap to Bp of Derry 60-69; I of Templemore Dio Derry from 67. *Deanery, Londonderry, N Ireland.* (Londonderry 2746)

GOOD, Canon James. b 06. MBE 40. Trin Coll Dub BA 30, MA 46. **d** 30 **p** 31 Derry. C of Ch Ch Derry 30-32; C-in-c of Moville Upper 32-35; CF 35-54; ACG 54-61; Hon Chap to HM the Queen 59-61; R of Lutterworth w Cotesbach 61-77; RD of Guthlaxton ii 61-77; Surr 64-77; Hon Can of Leic Cathl 71-77; Can (Emer) from 77. *17a Quarter Mile Road, Godalming, Surrey, GU7 1TG.* (Godalming 29836)

GOOD, Very Rev James Herbert Rosmond. b 19. Trin Coll Dub BA 41, MA 51. **d** 42 **p** 43 Connor. C of Carrickfergus 42-46; St Anne's Cathl Belf 46-53; V Cho 49-53; I of Loughinisland 53-59; RD of Lecale W 56-59; Min Can of Down Cathl from 58; Belf Cathl from 63; C of Ballymacarrett 59-60; C-in-c of Killaney w Carryduff Dio Down 60-71; R from 72; Regr Dios Down and Drom 64-81; Can of St Anne's Cathl Belf 76-78; Preb of Down Cathl 78-81; Dean from 81. *Carryduff Rectory, Belfast, N Ireland.* (Carryduff 812342)

GOOD, John Hobart. b 43. Coll of Resurr Mirfield 68. **d** 69 **p** 70 Ex. C of St Jas Ex 69-73; Cockington w Chelston 73-75;

Wolborough 75-78; P-in-c of Exminster Dio Ex 78-80; V (w Kenn) from 80; P-in-c of Kenn 78-80. *Vicarage, Exminster, Exeter, EX6 8AD.* (Exeter 832283)

GOOD, Joseph Kevin Ross. Univ of Melb BA 54. LLCM 53. ACT ThL 64. Trin Coll Melb 63. **d** 64 **p** 65 Melb. C of Hampton 64-65; Murrumbeena 65-67; P-in-c of Milawa 67-69; Lect and Tutor St Columb's Hall 67-69; Chap Melb Gr Sch 69-73; St Mich Gr Sch Melb 73-74; P-in-c of St Jas E St Kilda 74-77; Perm to Offic Dio Melb 77-80. *c/o 43 Bennett Street, N Fitzroy, Vic, Australia 3068.*

GOOD, Kenneth Raymond. b 52. Univ of Dub BA 74. Univ of Nottm BA 76. St Jo Coll Nottm 75. **d** 77 **p** 78 Down. C of Willowfield 77-79; Chap Ashton Sch Cork from 79. *Ashton School, Cork, Irish Republic.*

GOOD, Kenneth Roy. b 41. K Coll Lon and Warm BD and AKC (2nd cl) 66. **d** 67 **p** 68 Dur. C of St Pet Stockton-on-Tees 67-70; Chap Miss to Seamen Antwerp 70-74; Kobe 74-79; Asst Gen Sec Miss to Seamen from 79. *St Michael Paternoster Royal, College Hill, EC4R 2RL.*

GOOD, Canon Raymond Thomas William. Trin Coll Dub BA 39, MA 45. **d** 39 **p** 40 Oss C of Castlecomer 39-43; I of Kilnagross 45-52; Dioc C Dio Cork 43-45; I of Castleventry w Kilmean 52-60; Rathcooney 60-73; Can of Cloyne 67-69; Prec from 69; Can of Cork from 67. *c/o Rectory, Carrighohanne, Cork, Irish Republic.* (Cork 871106)

GOOD, Robert Stanley. b 24. TCD BA 45, Th Exhib 47, BD 55. **d** 47 Down **p** 48 Connor. C of Shankill 47-49; CMS Miss Dio Momb 50-60; Prin of St Paul's Dioc Div Sch Limuru 51-55; Prin Maseno Bible Sch 56-60; Exam Chap to Bp of Momb 55-60; Sen Div Master Maidstone Gr Sch 62-64; Sen Lect Relig Stud Ch Ch Coll Cant 64-78. *44 Ivanhoe Road, Herne Bay, Kent, CT6 6EG.* (Herne Bay 63561)

GOOD, Stuart Eric Clifford. b 37. Wycl Hall Ox 63. **d** 64 **p** 65 Ox. [f Congregational Min] C of H Trin Aylesbury 64-66; Nedlands 66-67; R of Mundaring 67-71; R of Bassendean 71-78; Como Dio Perth from 78. *58 Park Street, Como, W Australia 6152.* (450 4683)

GOOD, Thomas Harvey. d 49 **p** 51 Ont. Miss at Madoc 49-53; R of St Paul Kingston Dio Ont from 53; R of Wolfe I 57-58; R of St Barn Danforth Avenue Tor 67-73; Port Credit Dio Tor from 73. *21 Park Street East, Port Credit, Ont., Canada.*

GOODACRE, David Leighton. b 36. K Coll Lon and Warm AKC 59. **d** 60 **p** 61 Dur. C of St Chad Stockton-on-Tees 60-63; Birtley 63-68; Chap Sunderland Gen Hosp 69-74; P-in-c of Ryhope 75-81; V of Ovingham Dio Newc T from 81. *Vicarage, Ovingham, Prudhoe, Northumb, NE42 6BS.* (Prudhoe 32273)

GOODACRE, Norman William. b 07. Univ of Liv BArch 31, MA 33. ARIBA 32. Westcott Ho Cam 32. **d** 33 **p** 34 Liv. C of Ch Ch Toxt Pk 33-35; Gt Budworth (in c of Arley and Tabley) 35-36; Otley 36-38; V of St Marg Thornbury 38-45; Coniston Cold 45-58; RD of Settle 52-58; Chap Qu Ethelburga Sch Harrogate 58-69; L to Offic Dio Ripon 58-78; Dio Liv from 79. *81 Holmefield Road, Liverpool, L19 3PF.* (051-724 4176)

GOODALL, Canon Herbert Geoffrey. b 06. St Cath Coll Cam 2nd cl Hist Trip pt i 27, BA (2nd cl Hist Trip pt ii) 28, MA 32. Coll of Resurr Mirfield, 28. **d** 30 Derby for Cov **p** 31 Cov. C of St John Leamington Spa 30-33; Perm to Offic at Folkestone 33-34; C of Warminster w St Laur and St John Boreham 34-38; St Mich (in c of H Rood) Southampton 38-41; V of Farley w Pitton 41-47; R of St Edm Sarum 47-59; Chap Sarum Gen Infirm 48-50; R of Blandford Forum 59-72; R of Langton Long 59-72; Can and Preb of Sarum Cathl 61-74; Can (Emer) from 74; RD of Blandford 63-69. *7 Barrack Street, Bridport, Dorset, DT6 3LX.* (Bridport 24459)

GOODALL, John Llewellyn. b 17. Univ of Leeds BA 41. Dipl Th (Lambeth) 59. Sarum Wells Th Coll 78. **d** 78 **p** 79 Ex. C of Kentisbeare Dio Ex from 78. *Old School House, Kentisbeare, Cullompton, Devon, EX15 2AA.*

GOODALL, John William. b 45. Univ of Hull BA (2nd cl Th and Soc) 69. Ripon Hall Ox 69. **d** 71 **p** 72 Leic. C of Em, Loughborough 71-74; Dorchester (in c of Berinsfield) 74-78; Team V (in c of Berinsfield and Drayton St Leonard) 78-80; P-in-c of Wishford Magna Dio Sarum from 80; Asst Dir S Dios Ministerial Tr Scheme Sarum from 80. *Rectory, Great Wishford, Salisbury, Wilts, SP2 0PQ.* (Stapleford 363)

GOODALL, Maurice John. MBE 74. Cant Coll Univ of NZ BA 50. **d** 51 **p** 52 Ch Ch. C of St Alb 51-54; V of Waikari 54-59; Shirley 59-67; Chap Kingslea Girls' Tr Centre 67-69; City Missr and Assoc P of St Jo Bapt Ch Ch 69-76; Perm to Offic Dio Ch Ch from 76. *151 Waimairi Road, Christchurch 4, NZ.* (584-840)

GOODBURN, David Henry. b 41. SOC 73. **d** 76 Lon **p** 77 Edmon for Lon. C of SS Pet & Paul Enfield Lock Dio Lon from 76. *226 Ordnance Road, Enfield Lock, EN3 6HE.* (Lea Valley 762542)

GOODCHILD, Canon Charles Frank. St Aid Coll 42. **d** 44 **p** 45 Bradf. C of St Mary-le-Gill Barnoldswick 44-47; Lightcliffe 47-49; V of Tosside 49-51; Youth Chap Dio Bradf 49-60; V of Settle 51-58; Tong w Holme Wood 58-68; Waddington w W Bradford Dio Bradf from 68; RD of Bowling 64-68; Hon Can of Bradf from 64; RD of Bolland 72-78. *Waddington Vicarage, Clitheroe, Lancs.* (Clitheroe 23589)

GOODCHILD, James Brian. b 08. AKC 42. **d** 42 **p** 43 Roch. C of Aylesford 42-44; All SS Chatham 44-46 St Jas Bury St Edms 46-51; V of Isleham 51-76; Perm to Offic Dio St E from 77. *6 Sun Street, Isleham, Cambs, CB7 5RT.* (Isleham 244)

GOODCHILD, Canon John McKillip. b 42. Clare Coll Cam 3rd cl Math Trip pt i 62, BA (1st cl Th Trip pt ii) 64, MA 68. Wycl Hall Cam 67. **d** 69 Warrington for Liv **p** 70 Liv. C of Clubmoor 69-72; w CMS Nigeria (Trin Coll Umuahia) from 72; Exam Chap to Bp of Aba from 72; Hon Can of Aba from 75. *Trinity College, PO Box 97, Umuahia, Nigeria.*

✠ **GOODCHILD, Right Rev Ronald Cedric Osbourne.** b 10. Trin Coll Cam 2nd cl Hist Trip pt i 30, BA (2nd cl Hist Trip pt ii) and Dealtry Exhib 31, 3rd cl Th Trip pt i 32, MA 35. Bps' Coll Cheshunt 34. **d** 34 **p** 35 Lon. C of St Mary EAling 34-37; Chap of Oakham Sch 37-42; Chap RAFVR 42-46; Men in Disp 44 and 45; Warden of St Mich House Hamburg 46-49; Gen Sec SCM in Schs 49-53; C-in-c of St Helen Bishopsgate w St Martin Outwich Lon 51-53; V of Horsham 53-59; RD of Horsham 55-59; Surr 55-59; Archd of Northn 59-64; R of Ecton 59-64; Exam Chap to Bp of Pet 59-64; Can (Non-res) of Pet 62-64; Cons Ld Bp Suffr of Kens in St Paul's Cathl 1 May 64 by Abp of Cant; Bps of Lon, Pet, St Alb, Chich, Nor, B & W, Roch, and Ely; Bps Suffr of Willesden, Stepney and Maidstone; and others; res 80. *Star Cottage, Welcombe, Nr Bideford, N Devon.*

GOODCHILD, Roy John. b 30. Wycl Hall, Ox 60. **d** 61 **p** 62 Roch. C of Hayes 61-64; S w N Bersted 64-68; R of Birdham w W Itchenor 68-73; V of Saltdean Dio Chich from 74. *Vicarage, Saltdean Vale, Brighton, BN2 8HE.* (Brighton 32345)

GOODCHILD, Roy Theodore Scovel. b 06. Univ of Lon MB BS 31. FRCS (Edin) 45. Oak Hill Th Coll 63. **d** 66 Colchester for Chelmsf **p** 67 Chelmsf. C of Coopersale 66-70; Cockfosters (in c of St Paul Hadley Wood) 70-75. *49 Offington Avenue, Worthing, W Sussex, BN14 4PJ.* (Worthing 68821)

GOODDEN, John Maurice Phelips. b 34. Sarum Wells Th Coll 70. **d** 72 Sherborne for Sarum **p** 75 Chelmsf. C of H Trin Weymouth 72-74; St Paul Harlow New Tn 74-78; Industr Chap and Chap Princess Alexandra Hosp Harlow from 78. *45 Sayesbury Road, Sawbridgeworth, Herts, CM21 0EB.*

GOODE, Allan Kenneth. b 37. SOC. **d** 72 **p** 73 Willesden for Lon. C of Belmont Stanmore 72-74; V of St Bride w St Sav Liv 74-78; Eccleston Park Dio Liv from 78. *St James Vicarage, St Helens Road, Prescot, Liverpool, L34 2QB.* (051-426 6421)

GOODE, Anthony Thomas Ryall. b 42. Ex Coll Ox BA 64, MA 71. Cudd Coll 65. **d** 67 **p** 68 Ox. C of Wolvercote 67-71; Chap RAF from 71; C-in-c of Edith Weston w Normanton 72-74. *c/o Ministry of Defence, Adastral House, WC1.*

GOODE, Colin. b 37. Univ of Nottm BTh 79. St Jo Coll Nottm LTh 79. **d** 79 Bp Barron for Capetn **p** 80 Capetn. C of St John Wynberg Dio Capetn from 79. *St Luke's Cottage, Annandale Road, Diep River 7800, Cape, S AFrica.*

GOODE, Graham Steven. b 46. Wycl Coll Tor LTh 76. **d** and **p** 76 Calg. I of Lamerton Miss 76-81; C of St Steph City and Dio Calg from 81. *1121-14th Avenue SW, Calgary, Alta, Canada.*

GOODE, Leonard Stanley. b 1893. **d** and **p** 66 Bris. C of H Trin Hotwells w St Pet Clifton Wood and St Andr L Clifton 66-73. *5 Haberfield, Hotwells, Bristol 8.* (Bristol 298457)

GOODE, Leslie Patrick. d and **p** 80 Perth. C of Nedlands 80-; Chap Angl Homes Dio Perth from 80. *14 Camden Street, Wembley Downs, W Australia 6019.* (271-9633)

GOODE, Michael Arthur John. b 40. K Coll Lon and Warm BD and AKC 63. **d** 64 **p** 65 Dur. C of St Mary Virg w St Pet Bp Wearmouth 64-68; Solihull 68-70; R of Fladbury w Wyre Piddle and Moor 70-75; P-in-c of H Innoc Kidderminster Dio Worc from 75; RD of Kidderminster from 81; M Gen Syn from 80. *Holy Innocents Vicarage, Foley Park, Kidderminster, Worcs.* (Kidderminster 2186)

GOODE, Peter William Herbert. b 23. Oak Hill Th Coll 60. **d** 62 **p** 63 Chelmsf. C of All SS Woodford Wells 62-65; Min of St Paul Eccles Distr Harold Hill Romford 65-72; V of St Paul Harold Hill 72-76; Ch Ch Gt Warley Dio Chelmsf from 76. *79 Mount Crescent, Warley, Brentwood, Essex, CM14 5DD.* (Brentwood 220428)

GOODE, William Aubrey. b 08. Bps' Coll Cheshunt, 63. **d** 65 **p** 66 York. C of Hessle 65-67; V of Kirk Fenton 67-77; C-in-c of Ryther 72-75; Perm to Offic Dio York from 76. *135 Clifton, York, YO3 6BL.* (York 55199)

GOODER, Martin Lee. b 37. Univ of Sheff BSc (2nd cl Gen) 58. Oak Hill Th Coll 59. **d** 60 **p** 61 Carl. C of St Mark Barrow F 60-63; St Pet Halliwell 63-66; R of St Sav Chorlton-on-Medlock 66-71; Brunswick Dio Man from 71. *Rectory, Brunswick Street, Manchester, M13 9TP.* (061-273 2470)

GOODERHAM, Daniel Charles. b 24. St Francis Coll Brisb ACT ThL 51. **d** 52 **p** 53 Brisb. C of St Andr Lutwyche Brisb 52-54; C-in-c of Moorooka Brisb 54-56; V 56-58; R of Biggenden Dio Brisb 58-60; C of Staveley 60-61; St Thos Ipswich 61-64; V of St Bart Ipswich 64-71; R of Rattlesden 71-78; R of Drinkstone 71-78; RD of Lavenham 75-78; V of St Mich AA w St Aug Beckenham Dio Roch from 78. *St Michael's Vicarage, Birkbeck Road, Beckenham, Kent, BR3 4SS.* (01-778 6569)

GOODERHAM, Peter Hugh Daking. b 16. AKC (1st cl) 37. Univ of Lon BD 37, MTh 43. **d** 39 **p** 40 Chich. C of Arundel w S Stoke and Tortington 39-43; Eastbourne 43-48; Chap St Mary's Hosp Eastbourne 47-48; R of Plumpton w E Chiltington and Novington 48-53; V of St Aug Brighton 53-62; R of Rotherfield 62-70; Proc Conv Chich from 62; V of St Andr (Old Ch) Hove 70-81; P-in-c of Clymping Dio Chich from 81. *St Mary's Vicarage, Clymping, Littlehampton, W Sussex.* (Littlehampton 5882)

GOODERHAM, Raymond Frederick. d 63 Bp Snell for Tor **p** 64 Tor. C of H Trin City and Dio Tor from 63. *50 Four Oaks Gate, Toronto 6, Ont, Canada.*

GOODERICK, Peter Handley. b 26. Down Coll Cam 2nd cl Mod Langs Trip BA 50, (2nd cl Th Trip pt ia 51), MA 52. Linc Th Coll 51. **d** 53 **p** 54 Wakef. C of Brighouse 53-56; Prec of H Trin Cathl Gibr 56-58; Chap Izmir Turkey 58-59; C of Wimbledon (in c of St Jo Bapt) 59-63; CF (TAVR) 59-74; V of St Paul Furzedown Streatham 63-68; St Jas Merton 68-80; P-in-c of Stoneleigh w Ashow Dio Cov 80-81; V (w Baginton) from 81; Baginton 80-81. *Stoneleigh Parsonage, Coventry, CV8 3DN.* (Cov 414598)

GOODERIDGE, Roy Douglas. b 42. Univ of Wales, BA (Bibl Stud) 65. Coll of Resurr Mirfield. **d** 67 Bp T M Hughes for Llan **p** 68 Llan. C of Ystrad-Mynach 67-70; St Sav Roath 70-74; V of Hirwaun 74-77; R of Bettws Newydd w Trostrey and Kemeys Commander Dio Mon from 77. *Bettws Newydd Rectory, Usk, Gwent.* (Nantydeny 880258)

GOODERSON, Canon William Dennis. b 09. St Pet Hall Ox BA (1st cl Th) 35, MA 39. Wycl Hall, Ox 35. **d** 36 **p** 37 Ches. Tutor St Aid Coll Birkenhead 36-41; C-in-c of St Pet Rugby 41-44; Warden of Melville Hall Ibad 45-56; Hon Can of Lagos 49-55; Can (Emer) from 55; Chap St Pet Hall Ox 56-57; V of Norton-juxta-Kempsey 57-60; C-in-c of Whittington Worc 58-60; Vice-Prin of Wycl Hall Ox 60-65; V of Cumnor 66-77; RD of Abingdon 69-76. *18 Arnold's Way, Cumnor Hill, Oxford, OX2 9JB.*

GOODES, William John. Univ of Adel BSc 57. St Jo Coll Morpeth ACT ThL 59. **d** 60 **p** 61 Adel. C of Burnside 60-62; P-in-c of Kangaroo I Miss 62-66; Berri w Barmera 66-70; R of Mt Barker 70-75; Hon Can of The Murray 74-75; Hawthorn Dio Adel from 75. *2 Kent Street, Hawthorn, S Australia 5062.* (08-71 3418)

GOODFELLOW, Ian. b 37. St Cath Coll Cam 2nd cl Geog Trip pt i, 60, BA (2nd cl Hist Trip pt ii) 61, MA 65. Wells Th Coll 61. **d** 63 **p** 64 St Alb. C of Dunstable 63-67; Chap Haileybury and Imperial Service Coll 67-71; Lect (and Asst Chap to 74) Bede Coll Dur 71-75; Sen Lect Coll of St Hild and St Bede Dur 75-78; Sen Counsellor Open Univ SW Region from 79; Perm to Offic Dio Ex from 80. *The Open University, South Side Street, The Barbican, Plymouth, PL1 2LA.* (Plymouth 28321)

GOODFELLOW, Robert Francis. Moore Th Coll Syd ThL 66. **d** 66 Bp Loane for Syd **p** 67 Syd. C of Peakhurst 66-68; Guildf Dio Syd 68-70; C-in-c of Berowra 70-75; R of St Thos Auburn Dio Syd from 75. *3a Provincial Street, Auburn, NSW, Australia 2144.* (649-7016)

GOODFIELD, Dudley Francis. b 40. K Coll Lon and Warm AKC 65. **d** 66 **p** 67 B & W. C of Twerton-on-Avon 66-69; Lache w Saltney Ferry 69-71; Portishead 71-76; V of Bournville Weston-super-Mare Dio B & W from 76. *Vicarage, Bournville, Weston-super-Mare, Avon, BS23 3RX.* (W-s-M 23837)

GOODHEW, Ven Richard Henry. ACT ThL (2nd cl) 57. Moore Th Coll Syd. **d** 58 Syd **p** 58 Bp Hilliard for Syd. C of Bondi 58-59; C-in-c of Beverly Hills 59-63; Ceduna 63-66; R of Carlingford 66-71; Coorparoo 71-76; St Mich Wollongong 76-79; Can of St Mich Prov Cathl Wollongong 76-79; Archd of Wollongong and Camden from 79. *49 Market Street, Wollongong, NSW, Australia 2500.* (042-28 4816)

GOODIER, Canon Cyril. Bp's Univ Lennox LST 31. **d** 23 Queb for Alg **p** 24 Alg. Miss at Kirkland Lake 23-26; on leave 26-28; R of Milford Bay 28-31; I of Gravenhurst 31-36; Sturgeon Falls 36-46; R of Haileybury 46-58; Hon Can of Alg from 50. *St Joseph Villa, Suite 9, Dundas, Ont., Canada.*

GOODIER, Sidney Arthur Richmond. b 17. Kelham Th Coll 34. **d** 41 **p** 42 Newc T. C of St Phil Newc T 41-43; All S Leeds 43-47; H Sav Hitchin (in c of St Faith Walsworth) 47-48; Filton Bris 48-50; H Nativ Knowle 50-52; L to Offic Dio Bris 52-55; Min of Lawrence Weston Conv Distr 55-58; C of St Martin Knowle 58-62; V of S Leigh 62-69; Perm to Offic Worc 69-73; Dio Sarum from 73. *The Friary, Hilfield, Dorchester, Dorset.*

GOODING, Gregston Sylvester. b 45. Univ of WI BA 76. Codr Coll Barb 73. **d** 76 Barb **p** 76 Nass. P-in-c of St John & St Geo Grand Turk 76-78; R of St Patr Eleuthera 78-80; St D Ch Ch Dio Barb from 80. *St David's Rectory, Christ Church, Barbados, W Indies.*

GOODING, Ian Eric. b 42. Univ of Leeds BSc 63, BComm 65. CEng 69. ALCD 72 (LTh from 74). St Jo Coll Nottm 70. **d** 73 **p** 74 S'wark. C of Wandsworth 73-77; P-in-c of Stanton-by-Dale w Dale Abbey Dio Derby from 77; Adv to Bp of Derby on Industr Relns from 77. *Stanton-by-Dale Rectory, Ilkeston, Derbys, DE7 4QA.* (Ilkeston 324584)

GOODING, Ludwick Eugene. b 33. AIB. St Steph Ho Ox 76. **d** 79 Ox **p** 80 Dorchester for Ox (NSM). C of St Giles Reading Dio Ox from 79. *15 Lesford Road, Coley Park, Reading, RG1 6DX.* (Reading 56065)

✠ **GOODINGS, Right Rev Allen.** Sir Geo Williams Univ Montr BA 58. McGill Univ Montr BD 59. Montr Dioc Th Coll LTh 59; Hon DD 78. **d** and **p** 59 Montr. C of Trin Mem Ch Montr 59-61; I of St Ignatius Montr 61-65; R of Ascen Ch Montr 65-69; Dean and R of H Trin Cathl Queb 69-77; Cons Bp Coadj of Queb in St Pet Ch Sherbrooke 18 Sept 77 by Abp of Prov of Canada, Bps of Queb, NS, Fred, Montr, Rupld and Ott; and others; Apptd Bp of Queb 77. *36 rue des Jardines, Quebec, PQ, Canada G1R 4L5.* (418-692 3858)

GOODISSON, Kenneth Paul. St Aid Th Coll Bal ACT Th L (1st cl) 24, Th Scho 27. **d** 24 **p** 25 Bal. C of Mildura 24-25; P-in-c of Merbein 25-27; V 27-29; P-in-c of Dunolly 29; V of Rupanyup 29-31; C of Sedgley Staffs 31-32; Perm to Offic at St Mich Aldershot 32-33; C of Ch Ch Cathl Bal 34-35; V of Merino 35-37; Dimboola 37-41; Chap RAAF 41-46; Chap Bal Boys' Gr Sch 46-48; Perm to Offic Dio Melb 48; I of Flinders 48-52; Hawksburn 52-57; Murrumbeena 57-66; Glenhuntly 66-70; Perm to Offic Dio Melb from 70. *16 Harris Avenue, Gardiner, Vic, Australia 3146.* (03-20 2717)

GOODLAD, Martin Randall. b 39. Linc Th Coll 63. **d** 66 Ripon **p** 67 Knaresborough for Ripon. C of Bramley 66-69; Team V of Daventry 69-71; Asst Dir of Educn Wakef 71-74; Dioc Liaison Officer for C of E Gen Syn Bd of Educn from 74. *Church House, Dean's Yard, Westminster, SW1P 3NZ.* (01-222 9011)

GOODLEY, Christopher Ronald. b 47. AKC and BD 72. St Aug Coll Cant 72. **d** 73 **p** 74 Chelmsf. C of Shenfield 73-77; Hanley Dio Lich 77-78; Team V from 78. *Cobridge Vicarage, Emery Street, Stoke-on-Trent, ST6 2JJ.* (Stoke-on-T 22639)

GOODLUCK, Michael Douglas. b 55. Ridley Coll Melb 75. **d** 79 **p** 80 Melb. C of St Mary Caulfield 79-81; Thomastown-Epping Dio Melb from 81. *789 High Street, Epping, Vic, Australia 3076.*

GOODMAN, Alan Edward. b 05. Late Stewart of Rannoch Scho of G and C Coll Cam, 1st cl Or Lang Trip pt i 26, pt ii 27, BA 27, Tyrwhitt Hebr Scho and Mason Pri 28, MA 31. Ely Th Coll 28. **d** 29 **p** 30 Lon. C of St Pancras 29-33; Lect Univ of Cam 33-72; C-in-c of St Mark Cam 40-43; CF (EC) 43-46; L to Offic at St Luke Chesterton 50-53; R of Rampton 53-63; Perm to Offic Dio Ely from 63; Fell Univ Coll Cam 65-72. *23 The Coppice, Impington, Cambridge.*

GOODMAN, Denys Charles. b 24. Selw Coll Cam BA 49, MA 56. Linc Th Coll 49. **d** 51 **p** 52 Man. C of St Mary Virg Leigh 51-54; St Aug Pendlebury 54-57; V of Hollinwood 57-70; R of St Mary (w St Jo Bapt from 78) Bathwick Bath Dio B & W from 70; C-in-c of St Jo Bapt Bathwick 76-78; M Gen Syn from 79; RD of Bath from 81. *St Mary's Rectory, Sham Castle Lane, Bathwick, Bath, BA2 6JL.* (Bath 60052)

GOODMAN, Derek George. b 34. Keble Coll Ox BA 57, MA 60. Ridley Hall Cam 59. **d** 61 **p** 62 Southw. C of Attenborough w Bramcote and Chilwell 61-65; R of Eastwood Dio Southw from 65; Insp of Schs Dio Southw from 65; Surr from 69. *Eastwood Rectory, Nottingham.* (Langley Mill 2395)

GOODMAN, Ernest Edwin. b 14. BNC Ox BA 49, MA 53. Chich Th Coll 53. **d** 54 **p** 55 Pet. C of Kettering 54-57; R of Stoke Bruerne w Grafton Regis and Alderton 57-61; Chap Barnes Sch Deolali 61-63; USPG Sec Dio Nasik 63-67; Perm to Offic Dio Pet 67-70; R of Clayton w Keymer 71-79. *52 Roche Way, Harrowdene Heights, Wellingborough, Northants.* (Wellingborough 677801)

GOODMAN, Frank. b 10. Univ of Liv BSc 32. **d** 75 Ox **p** 76 Buckingham for Ox (APM). C of Beaconsfield 75-80. *7 Wycombe End, Beaconsfield, Bucks.*

GOODMAN, James Joseph. Moore Th Coll Syd. **d** 49 **p** 50

Syd. C of St Luke Liv 49-52; R of Rockley 52-56; Wauchope 56-65; P-in-c of Aiome Miss Distr New Guinea 65-67; C of Jandowae 67-72; V of Norman Pk Brisb 72-76; L to Offic Dio Armid from 76. *c/o Box 198, Armidale, NSW, Australia.*

GOODMAN, John. b 20. Selw Coll Cam BA 42, MA 46. Linc Th Coll 47. **d** 49 **p** 50 Worc. C of St Jo Bapt Kidderminster 49-53; Marlborough 54-56; V of Wootton Bassett 56-65; PC of Broad Town 56-65; St Mark City and Dio Sarum 65-68; V from 68. *21 Bourne Avenue, Salisbury, Wilts, SP1 1LP.* (Salisbury 6453)

GOODMAN, John Badams. Univ of Syd BA 50. St Francis Coll Brisb ACT ThL (2nd cl) 52. Melb Coll of Div Dipl Relig Educn 63. **d** 53 **p** 54 Bath. C of Dubbo 53-55; Chap of Lockhart Riv Miss 55-58; R of Violet Tn 58-62; V of Edenhope 62-67; R 67-69; V of Sebastopol 69-72; Timboon 72-76; R of Elliston, Lock and Wudinna Dio Willoch from 76. *Box 28, Elliston, S Australia 5670.* (Elliston 24)

GOODMAN, John Dennis Julian. b 35. FCA 68. Sarum Wells Th Coll 74. **d** 76 Repton for Derby **p** 77 Derby. C of Cotmanhay & Shipley 76-79; Team V of Old Brampton and Loundsley Green Dio Derby from 79. *Church House, Arden Close, Loundsley Green Chesterfield, Derbys, S40 4NE.* (Chesterfield 76805)

GOODMAN, John Henry. b 08. Chich Th Coll 35. **d** 37 **p** 38 Lon. C of St Pet Fulham 37-39; St Mich Beckenham 39-42; Tewkesbury Abbey 42-43; St Martin Brighton 43-52; R of St Pet Parmentergate w St Julian Nor 52-56; Org Sec UMCA 56-58; V of St Mich AA Ladbroke Grove w Ch Ch Notting Hill Kens 58-74. *21a Woodlea Road, Worthing, Sussex, BN13 1BP.* (0903 200289)

✠ **GOODMAN, Right Rev Morse Lamb.** Univ of Tor BA 40. Trin Coll Tor LTh 42, DD 61. Em Coll Sktn Hon DD 68. **d** 42 **p** 43 Alg. C of St Paul Fort William 42-43; I of Murillo 43-46; R of St Thos Fort William 46-53; St Jas Winnipeg 53-60; Dean and R of St Matt Cathl Brandon 60-65; Exam Chap to Bp of Bran 60-65; R of Ch Ch Edmon 65-68; Cons Ld Bp of Calg in Cathl Ch of Redeemer Calg 6 Jan 68 by Abp of Rupld; Bps of Sktn; Athab; Qu'App; Edmon; Bran; Sask; Montana. *3015 Glencoe Road South West, Calgary 6, Alta, Canada.* (243 3673)

GOODMAN, Richard George. Moore Th Coll Syd ACT ThL 61. **d** and **p** 61 Bend. C of All SS Cathl Bend 61-63; V of Mooroopna Dio Bend from 63. *Vicarage, Elizabeth Street, Mooroopna, Vic, Australia.* (058-25 2031)

GOODMAN, Canon Sidney William. b 10. Kelham Th Coll 27. **d** 33 **p** 34 Liv. C of St Mich AA Wigan 33-36; Gt Grimsby (in c of St Hugh) 36-39; V of Fulstow 39-44; Offg C-in-c of N Thoresby 40-44; V of Habrough (w Immingham to 55) 44-71; C-in-c of Killingholme and of E Halton 54-55; V of Killingholme 55-71; V of E Halton 55-71; RD of Grimsby N 57-69; Haverstoe 69-78; Can and Preb of Linc 69-79; Can (Emer) from 79; P-in-c of Wold Newton w Hawerby and Beesby 71-78. *Rectory Cottage, Wold Newton, Lincoln.* (Binbrook 328)

GOODRICH, Canon Alec Thorpe. b 14. Ch Coll Cam BA 37, 3rd cl Th Trip pt i 38, MA 41. Men in Disp 44. Westcott Ho Cam 37. **d** 39 **p** 40 Ripon. C of St Andr Starbeck 39-43; Chap RAFVR 43-46; V of Hampsthwaite w Felliscliffe 46-52; CF(TA) 49-52; Chap RAF 52-64; V of Aylesford 64-79; Surr 64-79; RD of Malling 66-79; Hon Can of Roch from 70. *c/o Aylesford Vicarage, Maidstone, Kent.* (Maidstone 77434)

GOODRICH, Ven Derek Hugh. Selw Coll Cam 2nd cl Hist Trip pt i 47, BA (2nd cl Hist Trip pt ii) 48, MA 54. St Steph Ho Ox 50. **d** 52 **p** 53 Lon. C of St Andr Willesden Green 52-57; St Phil Georgetn 57; V of Lodge 57-67; Port Mourant 67-71; Can of Guy from 66; Exam Chap to Bp of Guy from 69; R of New Amsterdam Dio Guy from 71; Archd Dio Guy from 80. *All Saints' Rectory, New Amsterdam, Berbice, Guyana.* (03-2717)

GOODRICH, Peter. b 36. Univ of Dur BA (2nd cl Mod Hist) 58. Cudd Coll 60. **d** 62 Warrington for Liv **p** 63 Liv. C of St Jo Evang Walton-on-the-Hill 62-66; Prescot (in c of St Paul Bryer Estate) 66-68; V of St Marg Anfield 68-72; St Faith Gt Crosby Dio Liv from 72; P-in-c of St Thos Seaforth 76-80; RD of Bootle from 78. *St Faith's Vicarage, Crosby Road North, Liverpool, L22 4RE.* (051-928 3342)

✠ **GOODRICH, Right Rev Philip Harold Ernest.** b 29. St Jo Coll Cam BA 52, MA 56. Cudd Coll 52. **d** 54 **p** 55 Cov. C of Rugby 54-57; Chap St Jo Coll Cam 57-61; R of S Ormsby w Ketsby, Calceby and Driby 61-68; Harrington w Brinkhill 61-68; Oxcombe 61-68; Ruckland w Farforth and Maidenwell 61-68; Somersby w Bag Enderby 61-68; Tetford w Salmonby 61-68; V of Bromley 68-73; Cons Ld Bp Suffr of Tonbridge in Cant Cathl 7 April 73 by Abp of Cant; Bps of Roch, Linc and Carl; Bps Suffr of Dover, Maidstone, Grantham and Warrington; and Bps Warner, J K Russell and Betts; Trld to Worc 82; Dir of Ordins Dio Roch 74-82. *Bishop's House, Hartlebury Castle, Kidderminster, Worcs, DY11 7XX.* (Hartlebury 214)

GOODRICKE, Guy Alwyn. Keble Coll Ox BA 33, MA 49. St Steph Ho Ox 33. **d** 34 **p** 35 Newc T. C of St Gabr Heaton (in c of St Francis High Heaton from 35) 34-36; Perm to Offic Dio Roch 48-49; P-in-c of Georgetown Tas 50-52 *145 Talbot Road, Launceston, Tasmania.*

GOODRIDGE, Fitz Winfield. Codr Coll Barb 59. **d** 62 **p** 63 Nass. C of Long Island 62-66; P-in-c of Abaco 66-71; R of St Steph w St Mary Magd Grand Bahama Dio Nass from 71. *Box 7, West End, Grand Bahama, W Indies.*

GOODRIDGE, Jack Amos. Ridley Coll Melb ACT ThL 59. **d** 60 **p** 61 Melb. C of H Trin Kew 60-63; Dandenong 63-64; St Paul's Cathl Melb and Home Sec CMS Vic 64-67; V of Bacchus Marsh 67-72; I of St Geo Bentleigh 73-80; H Trin Oakleigh Dio Melb from 80. *810 Warrigal Road, Oakleigh, Vic, Australia 3166.*

GOODRIDGE, Laurence Raymond. b 17. ACIS 64. **d** 65 **p** 72 Bunb. C of Albany Dio Bunb 65-78 and from 79; Perm to Offic Dio Bunb 78-79. *Box 440, Albany, W Australia 6330.*

GOODRIDGE, Peter David. b 32. K Coll Lon and Warm AKC 57. **d** 58 **p** 59 Lon. C of Eastcote 58-64; V of St Phil Tottenham 64-71; W Drayton Dio Lon from 71. *191 Station Road, West Drayton, Middx, UB7 7NQ.* (West Drayton 42194)

GOODRIDGE, Ray Laurence. **d** 65 Bunb. C of Albany Dio Bunb from 65. *28 Wylie Crescent, Albany, W Australia.* (098-41 2904)

GOODRIDGE, Canon Sehon Sylvester. b 37. BD (Lon) 66. Huron Coll Lon Ont Hon DD 77. Codr Coll Barb. **d** 63 **p** 64 Windw Is. C of H Trin Castries St Lucia 63-66; Chap Univ Coll of WI Kingston 67-69; Tutor United Th Coll of WI 69-71; Prin Codr Coll Barb and Exam Chap to Bp of Windw Is from 71; to Bp of Bel from 72; Antig from 74; Hon Can of Barb from 76. *Codrington College, St John, Barbados, W Indies.* (31274)

GOODSELL, Patrick. b 32. Linc Th Coll 62. **d** 64 **p** 65 Cant. C of St Jude Thornton Heath 64-66; Croydon (in c of St Geo) 66-70; V of St Mich AA Tenterden 70-78; P-in-c of Sellindge w Monks-Horton and Stowting Dio Cant from 78. *Sellindge Vicarage, Ashford, Kent.* (Sellindge 3168)

GOODSHIP, Robert George. b 14. BSc (Econ) (Lon) 47. **d** 69 Sarum **p** 70 Bp MacInnes for Sarum. C of St Mich AA Sarum 69-75; Bemerton Dio Sarum from 75. *326 Devizes Road, Salisbury, Wilts.* (Sarum 5687)

GOODSON, Paul Frederick. b 34. Univ of Birm Dipl Th 61. Qu Coll Birm. **d** 62 **p** 63 Lon. C of H Trin Stepney 62-65; Our Lady and St Nich Liv 65-68; V of Skerton 68-74; Poulton-le-Fylde Dio Blackb from 74. *Vicarage, Poulton-le-Fylde, Lancs.* (Poulton 883086)

GOODSWAN, William James. Wycl Coll Tor. **d** 58 **p** 59 Tor. C of Creemore 58-59; Ch Ch Oshawa 59-63; I of Minden 63-64; P-in-c of Malton 64-67; on leave 67-79. *RR2, Picton, Ont, Canada.*

GOODWIN, Ven Clive Andrew. MBE 68. Moore Th Coll Syd 32. **d** 32 Syd **p** 33 Bp Kirby for Syd. C of St John Shoalhaven 33-34; St Geo Hobart 34-36; Rockdale 36-37; R of St Mary w Rooty Hill 37-40; Kembla 40-43; Chap Miss to Seamen Syd 43-50; R of St Mark Darling Point Syd 50-64; Hon Can of Syd 60-62; Can from 67; Archd of Syd 62-73; Archd (Emer) from 73; R of St Phil Ch Hill 64-80; Dir of Syd C of E Homes for Aged 64-77; Vice-Pres from 77; L to Offic Dio Syd from 80. *1/33a Mona Road, Darling Point, NSW, Australia 2027.* (32-2547)

GOODWIN, Deryck William. b 27. Univ of Birm BSc 48, MSc 49, PhD 51. N-W Ordin Course 74. **d** 77 **p** 78 York. Hon C of Elvington w Sutton Derwent Dio York from 77; Sen Lect Univ of York from 77. *5 Beech Close, Elvington, York, YO4 5AN.*

GOODWIN, Florence Ann. b 34. Mt St Vincent Univ Halifax NS BNursing 75. Wycl Coll Tor MDiv 78. **d** 78 **p** 79 Rupld. C of St Paul Winnipeg 78-81; Chap Health Sciences Centre and Hon C of St Paul Winnipeg Dio Rupld from 81. *77 University Crescent, Winnipeg, Manit, R3T 3N8, Canada.*

GOODWIN, Canon John Fletcher Beckles. b 20. Late Exhib and Scho of Jes Coll Cam, 2nd cl Cl Trip pt i 41, BA (2nd cl Th Trip pt ii) 43, MA 46. Ridley Hall Cam 42. **d** 45 Stepney for Lon **p** 46 Lon. C of H Trin Southall 45-48; St Andr Drypool 48-49; Tutor Trin Coll Umuahia 50-52; Tutor St Paul's Coll Awka 52-57; Vice-Prin Ripon Hall Ox 57-62; V of Merton 62-70; Gen Ed *World Christian Books* 62-70; V of Heanor 70-74; Hazelwood Dio Derby from 74; Turnditch Dio Derby from 74; Commiss Aba from 73; Hon Can of Derby Cathl from 81. *Hazelwood Vicarage, Duffield, Derby, DE6 4AL.* (Derby 840161)

GOODWIN, Rodney Keith. b 47. St Jo Coll Morpeth 72. **d** 72 Newc. C of New Lambton 72-75; Griffith 75-76. *Box 1239, Griffith, NSW, Australia 2680.* (069-62 3204)

GOODWIN, Thomas Jenkins. St D Coll Lamp BA 13. **d** 13 **p** 14 St D. C of St Paul Llanelly 13-20; Felinfoel 20-24; V of Llangynnog or Llangunnock 24-32; St Jos Cwmaman 32-34; Tylorstown 34-42; R of Dowlais w Pant and Pengarnddu 42-52; Llangan 52-64; V of St Mary Hill 52-64; Surr 42-64. *58 Eustace Drive, Bryncethyn, Bridgend, Mid Glam.*

GOODWINS, Christopher William Hedley. b 36. Late Cho Stud of St Jo Coll Cam BA 58, MA 62. Linc Th Coll 62. **d** 64 **p** 65 Nor. C of Lowestoft 64-69; V of Tamerton Foliot Dio Ex from 69; P-in-c of H Spirit Southway Plymouth Dio Ex from 78. *124 Beverston Way, Roborough, Plymouth, PL6 7EG.* (Plymouth 771938)

GOODYER, Canon Edward Arthur. Univ of Witwatersrand, BA 64. SS Coll Cam BA (2nd cl Th Trip pt ii) 67. St Pet Coll Grahmstn. **d** 68 Bp Carter for Johann **p** 69 Johann. C of Rosebank 68-73; Chap St Jo Coll Houghton 73-76; R of Stellenbosch Dio Capetn from 76; Exam Chap to Abp of Capetn from 78; Can of Capetn from 81. *8 Helderberg Street, Stellenbosch, CP, S Africa.* (Stellenbosch 3125)

GOODYER, Howard Edward Jay. St Paul's Coll Grahmstn S Afr LTh 36. **d** 36 **p** 37 Johann. C of Ch Ch Mayfair Johann 36-39; R of Bloemhof 39-45; CF (S Afr) 45-46; C of St Paul Durban 46-47; P-in-c of St Raph Durban 47-52; Bulwer w Himerville 52-55; V of Drakensberg 55-57; Sydenham 57-78; R of Umkomaas 78-80. *Box 53, Umkomaas, Natal, S Africa.* (Umkomaas 56)

GOOK, Bernard William James. Oak Hill Th Coll 40. **d** 43 **p** 44 Lon. C of St Luke W Kilburn 43-45; Cheadle 45-48; Sec Young Churchmen's Movement and Hon C St Jo Bapt Beckenham 48-50; V of St Luke Walthamstow 50-55; Missr Dio Syd 55-56; R of St Bart Syd 56-58; R of St Barn (w St Bart from 65) Syd 59-67; St John Darlinghurst City and Dio Syd from 67; Abp's Chap to Univ of Syd 59-67; Actg R of Flinders Street Dio Syd from 78. *120 Darlinghurst Road, Darlinghurst, Sydney, NSW, Australia 2010.* (31-6412)

GOOLD, Peter John. b 44. Univ of Lon BD 74. St Steph Ho Ox 67. **d** 70 **p** 71 Lon. C of Chiswick Lon 70-73; Asst Chap R Masonic Hosp Lon 73-74; Basingstoke Distr Hosp 74-77; Chap R Marsden Hosp Lon 77-80; Sen Chap Basingstoke Distr Hosp from 80. *The Lodge, Park Prewett, Aldermaston Road, Basingstoke, Hants.* (Basingstoke 3202)

GOORAHOO, Ephraim Basant. b 08. Codr Coll Barb 54. **d** 57 **p** 58 Barb for Gui. C of St Geo Cathl Georgetn 57-61; R of St Jos Port Mourant 61-67; E Bank Demarara 67-73. *417 Elton Street, Brooklyn, NY 11208, USA.*

GORDON, Alan Bacchus. b 1898. Ripon Hall Ox. 1 26 **p** 27 Bradf. C of St Steph W Bowling Bradf 26-29; Chap (CCCS) of Mt Kenya Distr 29-36; V of Parklands Kenya 36-38; R of Clowne 38-51; V of Old Brampton 51-68; RD of Chesterfield 57-67. *Queenhythe, Long Compton, Warws.*

GORDON, Alan Rex. b 19. Bps' Coll Cheshunt, 51. **d** 53 **p** 54 Lon. C of St Luke Old Street Lon 53-54; St Matt Bethnal Green 54-57; Edenbridge 57-60; V of All SS Perry Str Northfleet Dio Roch from 60. *All Saints' Vicarage, Perry Street, Northfleet, Gravesend, Kent.* (Gravesend 534398)

GORDON, Alexander. b 49. Univ of Nottm BPharm 71. Univ of Leeds Dipl Th 76. Coll of Resurr Mirfield 74. **d** 77 **p** 78 Ripon. C of St Mich AA Headingley 77-80; SS Pet & Paul Fareham Dio Portsm from 80. *Manor Cottage, Church Path, Fareham, PO16 7DT.* (Fareham 280226)

GORDON, Alexander Thomson. Univ of Edin MA (1st cl Semitic Lang) and Vans Dunlop Semitic Scho 31. Jes Coll Ox BA and Nubar Pasha Armenian Scho 34, MA 38. Edin Th Coll 34. **d** 36 **p** 37 Glas. C of St John Dumfries 36-38; Prof Amer Univ Cairo 38-40; Contr of Educn MELF 48-50. *Box 359,Bapco, Awali, Bahrain, Arabian Gulf.*

✠ **GORDON, Right Rev Archibald Ronald McDonald.** b 27. Late Scho of Ball Coll Ox BA 50, MA 52. Cudd Coll 50. **d** 52 **p** 53 Lon. C of Stepney 52-55; Chap Cudd Coll Ox 55-59; L to Offic Dio Ox 57-59; V of St Pet Birm 59-67; Lect Qu Coll Birm 60-62; Proc Conv Birm 65-71; Can Res of Birm 67-71; L to Offic Dio Malawi 70; V of St Mary Virg w St Cross and St Pet-in-the-E Ox 71-75; Commiss Lake Malawi from 75; Cons Ld Bp of Portsm in Westmr Abbey 23 Sep 75 by Abp of Cant; Bps of Lon, Ox, Birm, Derby, St Alb, Nor, Chich, Heref, Guildf, Ely and S & M; Bps Suffr of Willesden, Stepney, Kingston, Southn, Ramsbury, Aston, Basingstoke, Reading, Buckingham, Grantham and Tonbridge; and others; Chairman ACCM from 76. *Bishopswood, Fareham, Hants, PO14 1NT.* (Fareham 280247)

GORDON, Arthur. b 10. Trin Coll Dub BA 41, MA 44. **d** 41 **p** 42 Cork. C of Kinsale w Rincurran 41-43; I of Kilmeen 43-47; Carrigaline U 47-62; Can of I in Ross Cathl and of Dromdaleague in Cork Cathl 59-64; I of Clonmel U 62-68; Prec of Ross Cathl 64-67; Can of Inniskenny in Cork Cathl 64-67; Liscleary in Cork Cathl and Archd of Cloyne 67-68; Dean and I of Ross and Can of H Trin in Cork Cathl 68-78; Chan of Cork 76-78. *13 Farranlea Park, Model Farm Road, Cork, Irish Republic.*

GORDON, Bruce Harold Clark. b 40. Cranmer Hall Dur 65. **d** 68 **p** 69 Edin. C of St Jas L Leith 68-71; St Jo Evang Blackheath 71-74; R of Ch Ch Duns Dio Edin from 74. *Rectory, Duns, Berwick.* (Duns 2209)

GORDON, Donald Ian. b 30. Univ of Nottm BA 52, PhD 64. Westcott Ho Cam 71. **d** 71 Chelmsf **p** 72 Colchester for Chelmsf (NSM). C of Newport 71-75; Asst Master St Pet Sch Burnham-on-Crouch from 76; Hon C of Cricksea w Althorne 76-81; Latchingdon and N Fambridge 76-81; Cricksea w Althorne and Latchingdon w N Fambridge Dio Chelmsf from 81. *Holden House, Steeple Road, Latchingdon, Chelmsford, CM3 6JX.* (Maldon 740296)

GORDON, Donald McAuley. Univ of BC BSc (Eng) 50. Angl Th Coll Vancouver LTh 61. **d** 61 **p** 62 New Westmr. C of Maple Ridge 60-63; I 63-67; V of Port Moody 70-74; on leave 74-78; I of Ladner Dio New Westmr from 78. *4755 Arthur Drive, Delta, BC, Canada.*

GORDON, Edward John. b 32. Univ of Wales BA (2nd cl Hist) 52. St Mich Coll Llan 52. **d** 55 **p** 56 Llan. C of Baglan 55-61; Newcastle w Laleston and Tythegston 61-65; V of Ynyshir 65-69; C of Bramhall 69-72; V of Cheadle Hulme 72-79; St Paul w St Luke Tranmere Dio Ches from 79. *St Paul's Vicarage, Old Chester Road, Rock Ferry, Birkenhead, Mer.* (051-645 3547)

GORDON, Ernest Leopold Henry. b 09. Qu Coll Birm 39. **d** and **p** 40 S'wark. C of Ch Ch Battersea 40-45; C-in-c 45-51; CF (EC) 44-45; V of Ch Ch Battersea 51-66; Chap and Asst Master Greycoat Hosp Westmr 66-68; R of Gt Chart 68-77. *3 Sunley Close, Broome, Bungay, Suff, NR35 2RR.*

GORDON, Ernle Patrick. St Pet Th Coll Ja. **d** 66 **p** 67 Ja. C of Mona Heights 66-68; Stony Hill 68-69; C-in-c of St Mary's Maverley 69-70; R from 72; Chap St Jago High Sch from 71. *5 Cowper Drive, Kingston 10, Jamaica.*

GORDON, Ewart Hastings. St Pet Th Coll Ja 59. **d** 62 **p** 63 Ja. C of St Mich Kingston 62-67; R of Balaclava 67-73; May Pen Dio Ja from 73. *Rectory, May Pen, Jamaica.*

GORDON, Ezie Hardie. b 37. Codr Coll Barb 71. **d** 71 Br Hond **p** 81 Bel. C of St John's Cathl Bel Dio Br Hond (Bel from 73) from 71. *29 Albert Street West, Belize City, Belize.*

✠ **GORDON, Right Rev George Eric.** b 05. Late Exhib of St Cath Coll Cam 2nd cl Cl Trip pt i 26, BA (2nd cl Anthrop Trip) 27, 2nd cl Th Trip pt i and Jeremie LXX Pri 28, MA 31. Wycl Hall Ox 27. **d** 29 Leic **p** 30 Pet for Leic. C of H Trin Leic 29-31; Vice-Prin Bp Wilson Th Coll IM 31-35; Prin and Dom Chap to Bp of S & M 35-42; R of St Paul Kersal 42-45; Exam Chap to Bp of Man 42-51; R of Middleton 45-51; RD of Middleton 45-51; Proc Conv Man 48-51; Provost and R of the Cathl Ch of St Mary Virg St Pet and St Cedd Chelmsf 51-66; Proc Conv Chelmsf 51-66; Cons Ld Bp of S & M in York Minster 29 Sept 66 by Abp of York; Bps of Man; Sheff; Liv; Leic; and Chelmsf; Bps Suffr of Hulme; Burnley; Penrith; Whitby; Pontefract; Selby; Jarrow; Knaresborough; and Stockport; and Bp Gerard; res 74; Dean of St German's Cathl Peel 66-74. *Cobden, Queen Street, Eynsham, Oxon.* (Oxford 881378)

GORDON, John Beauchamp. b 08. Selw Coll Cam BA 30, MA 34. BC Coll Bris 30. Clifton Th Coll Bris 32. **d** 32 **p** 33 Ex. C of St Mark Ex 32-34; St Geo Mart Deal 34-36; Maidenhead 36-37; R of Vange 37-40; Keinton-Mandeville 40-49; V of Freethorpe w Wickhampton 49-55; R of Ashwellthorpe w Wreningham 55-61; Whitewell 62-73. *134 Tarring Road, Worthing, Sussex.*

GORDON, John Scott. b 17. Trin Coll Dub MA 63. **d** 64 **p** 66 Connor. C of St Geo Belf 64-66; St Mary Belf 66-75; Hon C of Hilborough Dio Nor from 75. *The Old Laundry, Dicklington, Thetford, Norf, IP26 5AT.* (Mundford 286)

GORDON, Canon Kenneth Davidson. b 35. Univ of Edin MA 57. Tyndale Hall Bris 58. **d** 60 **p** 61 Liv. C of St Helens 60-66; V of St Geo Mart Daubhill Bolton 66-71; R of St Devenick Bieldside Dio Aber from 71; Exam Chap to Bp of Aber from 78; Can of St Andr Cathl Aber from 81. *Rectory, Bieldside, Aberdeen, AB1 9AP.* (Aberdeen 861352)

GORDON, Neil Albert Oniyide. Fourah Bay Coll 61. **d** 65 **p** 66 Sier L. P Dio Sier L from 65. *Vicarage, Gloucester, Sierra Leone, W Africa.*

GORDON, Canon Weeville McHervin. St Pet Coll Kingston, 49. **d** 52 **p** 53 Ja. C of Stony Hill 52-53; P-in-c of L London w Negril 53-62; Grange Hill 56-62; R of St Matt Kingston Dio Ja from 62; Can of Ja from 76. *13 Kings Drive, Kingston 6, Jamaica, W Indies.* (093-75467)

GORDON CLARK, Charles Philip. b 36. Late Scho and Pri of Worc Coll Ox BA (2nd cl Mod Hist) and Liddon Stud 59, 2nd cl Th 61, Ellerton Pri 62. Cudd Coll 61. **d** 62 **p** 63 Guildf. C of Haslemere 62-65; Chap Tonbridge Sch 65-68; R of Keston 68-74; V of King Chas Mart Tunbridge Wells Dio

Roch from 74. *King Charles Vicarage, Frant Road, Tunbridge Wells, Kent, TN2 5SB.* (Tunbridge Wells 25455)

GORDON CLARK, John Vincent Michael. b 29. SOC 73. **d** 76 **p** 77 Guildf (APM). C of H Trin City and Dio Guildf from 76. *1 Shalford Road, Guildford, GU1 3XL.*

GORDON-CUMMING, Henry Ian. b 28. Oak Hill Th Coll 54. **d** 57 **p** 58 Portsm. C of St Jude Portsea 57-60; CMS 60-61; Chap to Bp of Ankole-K 61-65; Ntare Sch 65-67; V of Virginia Water 68-78; R of Busbridge Dio Guildf from 78. *Busbridge Rectory, Godalming, Surrey, GU7 1XA.* (Godalming 21267)

GORDON-KERR, Francis Alexander. b 39. Univ of Dur BA 64, MA 67. Univ of Hull PhD 81. Wycl Hall Ox 65. **d** 67 **p** 68 Dur. C of Heworth 67-70; Chap Newc T Poly 70-75; Sen Chap Univ of Hull from 75. *13 Arlington Avenue, Cottingham, N Humb, HU16 4DP.* (Hull 842891)

GORE, Canon John Charles. b 29. Univ of Leeds BA 52. Coll of Resurr Mirfield 52. **d** 54 **p** 55 York. C of St Jo Evang Middlesbrough 54-59; Msoro N Rhod 59-64; Zam 64-70; P-in-c of Chipata Lusaka 71-75; Can of Lusaka 70-75; Can (Emer) from 75; R of Elland Dio Wakef from 75; RD of Brighouse and Elland from 77. *75 Victoria Road, Elland, W Yorks, HX5 0QA.* (Elland 72133)

GORE, John Harrington. b 24. Em Coll Cam BA 49, MA 52. Westcott Ho Cam 49. **d** 51 **p** 52 Man. C of Deane Lancs 51-54; Whitstable 54-59; CF (TA) 57-59; CF 59-62; V of Wymynswold 62-67; Min of Aylesham Conv Distr 62-67; R of Deal (w Sholden from 75) 67-80; Surr from 67; RD of Sandwich 70-78; C-in-c of Sholden 74-75; R of Southchurch Dio Chelmsf from 80. *Southchurch Rectory, Southend-on-Sea, Essex.* (Southend-on-Sea 66423)

GORHAM, Andrew Arthur. b 51. Univ of Bris BA 73. Qu Coll Birm 77. **d** 79 **p** 80 Roch. C of St Mary Plaistow Dio Roch from 79. *Curates Flat, Church House, 61 College Road, Bromley, Kent.*

GORHAM, William Robert. b 46. **d** 72 **p** 74 Newfld. C of Flower's Cove 72-74; R of Cartwright 74-77; Trin Dio Centr Newfld from 77. *Rectory, Trinity, Trinity Bay, Newfoundland, Canada.*

GORIN, Walter. b 10. Univ of Lon BA (3rd cl French) 32. AKC 32. Lich Th Coll 39. **d** 41 **p** 42 Grimsby for Linc. C of St Martin w St Pet at Arches Linc 41-43; Chap RNVR 43-46; R of St Andr Edin 47-49; St Mary Dunblane 40-53; Chap RN 53-57; R of Campsea Ashe 57-69; R of Marlesford 57-69; Gt w L Saxham and Westley 69-79; Perm to Offic Dio St E from 79. *16 Samuel Street Walk, Bury St Edmunds, Suff.*

GORING, Vincent Ingham. McGill Univ BSc 47, BD 50. Montr Dioc Th Coll. **d** 50 **p** 51 Montr. C of St Clem Verdun Montr 50-54; Gen Sec Stud Christian Movement Canada 54-57; Assoc Sec 57-62; Miss Angl Ch of Canada 62-72; R of St Barn City and Dio Tor from 72. *20 Bowden Street, Toronto, Ont., Canada.* (416-463 1344)

GORMANDY, Canon Lionel Courtney. Univ of Dur LTh 47. Codr Coll Barb. **d** 47 Barb **p** 47 Gui. C of St Matt E Bank Demerara 47-50; St Geo Cathl Georgetn 50-52; R of Fort Wellington 52-56; V of St Simon Barb 56-58; St Clem w Swith Barb 58-63; St Matt Barb 63-66; P-in-c of Mayaro w Rio Claro 66-68; Hon Can of Trinid 69-78; Guy from 80; R of Belmont Trinid 68-78; V of Lodge Dio Guy from 78. *St Sidwell's Vicarage, Lodge, Guyana.*

GORNALL, William Brian. b 36. Ely Th Coll 61. **d** 64 Blackb **p** 65 Burnley for Blackb. C of St Mich AA Eccles Distr Blackpool 64-67; Cheshunt 67-69; P-in-c of St Pet (w All SS from 75) Blackb 69-75; V 75-79; Chap and Lect Blackb Coll of Tech 71-79; M Lancs Industr Miss from 75; V of St Mich AA Blackpool Dio Blackb from 79. *St Michael's Vicarage, Staining Road, Blackpool, FY3 0AG.* (Blackpool 33928)

GOROA, Richard. Bp Patterson Th Centre. **d** 71 Melan. d Dio Melan 71-75; Dio Ysabel from 75. *Vulavu, Bugotu, Santa Ysabel, Solomon Islands.*

GORRIE, Reginald James. St Jo Coll Morpeth. ACT ThL 53. **d** 52 **p** 53 Armid. C of St Pet Cathl Armidale 52-53; Tamworth 53-54 and 56-57; V of Delungra 54-56; Chap R Melb Hosp 57; AMF from 57; C of Melb Dioc Centre 56-61; V of Flinders 61-65; R of Red Cliffs 65-69; Perm to Offic Dio Adel 69-81; L to Offic from 81; Dio St Arn 69-76. *23 Clinton Avenue, Myrtlebank, S Australia 5064.* (08-79 4865)

GORRIE, Richard Bingham. b 27. Late Exhib of Univ Coll Ox BA (1st cl Mod Hist) 49, MA 53. Ridley Hall, Cam 49. **d** 51 **p** 52 Ox. C of St Clem Ox 51-54; Morden Surrey 54-56; Scottish Rep Script U from 56; Chap Fettes Coll Edin 60-74; Dir Inter-Sch Chr Fellowship Scotland from 74. *280 St Vincent Street, Glasgow, G2 5RT.*

GORRING, Neville. St Francis Coll Brisb 72. **d** 73 Bp Hudson for Brisb. C of Holland Pk 73-74; St Andr Lutwyche Brisb 74-75; V of Tara 75-79; R of Ch of Annunc Camp Hill City and Dio Brisb from 79. *101 Watson Street, Camp Hill, Queensland, Australia 4152.* (398 2106)

GORSE, Henry John Lancelot. b 03. Late Exhib of Ball Coll Ox BA 25, MA 46. Westcott Ho Cam 40. **d** 40 **p** 41 Lon. Asst Master Harrow Sch 31-68; Sen Sc Master 58-66. *8 Cambridge Road, Coton, Cambridge, CB3 7PJ.* (Madingley 210344)

GORSUCH, Frank Austin. b 14. Qu Coll Birm 49. **d** 51 **p** 53 Cov. C of St Jo Bapt Leamington 51-53; Bedworth 53-55; R of Gt Houghton Dio Pet from 55. *Great Houghton Rectory, Northampton.* (Northampton 61708)

GORTON, Anthony David Trevor. b 39. Univ of Lon BSc 65. Oak Hill Coll 78. **d** 81 St Alb. C of Colney Heath Dio St Alb from 81. *Waterdell, Lane End, Hatfield, Herts, AL10 9DU.*

GOSDEN, Timothy John. b 50. Chich Th Coll 74. **d** 77 **p** 78 Cant. C of All SS Cant 77-81; Asst Chap of Loughborough Univ from 81. *1 Holywell Drive, Loughborough, Leics, LE11 3TU.* (Loughborough 32790)

GOSLIN, Charles Percy. b 07. AKC (1st cl) and Knowling Pri 34. **d** 34 Pet for Cov **p** 35 Cov. C of Atherstone 34-36; Leominster and Eyton 36-39; Stoke 39-44; R of Corley 44-56; Hon Ed of Cov Dioc Gazette 50-59; PC of Binley w Coombe Fields 56-62; V of St Luke Hammersmith 62-75; Perm to Offic Dio S'wark from 75. *17 Cambray Road, SW12 0DX.* (01-673 4261)

GOSLING, Arthur Henderson. St Paul's Th Coll Grahmstn 60. **d** 62 **p** 63 Natal. C of Kloof 62-64; Mobeni 64-68; R of St Barn Bluff Durban 68-73; St Mary Greyville Durban 73; Greenwood Pk Durban Dio Natal from 74. *Rectory, Greenwood Park, Durban, Natal, S Africa.* (Durban 833419)

GOSLING, David Lagourie. b 39. Univ of Man MSc 63. Fitzw Coll Cam 2nd cl Th Trip pt ii BA 65, MA 69. M Inst Phys 72. Lanc Univ PhD 74. Ridley Hall Cam 63. **d** 73 Blackb **p** 74 York. Hon C of Lancaster 73-74; St Matt Hull 74-77; Tutorial Fell of Relig Stud Univ of Lanc from 73; Lect Univ of Hull from 74; LPr Dio York 77-79; Hon C of Cottingham Dio York from 78. *266 Northgate, Cottingham, N Humb, HU16 5RN.*

GOSLING, John William Fraser. b 34. Univ of Dur BA 58, Dipl Th 60, MA 71. Univ of Ex PhD 78. Cranmer Hall Dur 58. **d** 60 Crediton for Ex **p** 61 Ex. C of Plympton 60-68; V of Newport 68-78; P-in-c of Bp's Tawton 77-78; Org Sec CECS Dios Ox and St Alb from 78. *31 Abbotts Road, Aylesbury, Bucks, HP20 1HY.* (Aylesbury 26366)

GOSS, Arthur John Knill. b 10. Late Exhib of St Jo Coll Dur BA and Van Mildert Scho 34. Capel Cure Pri 35, MA and Dipl Th (w distinc) 37. **d** 35 **p** 36 Bris. C of Brislington 35-36; St Mich Bournemouth 36-41; V of Old Radnor w Kinnerton 41-52; R of Knill 41-52; CF (EC) 40-42; Proc Conv Heref 50-69; V of St Jo Bapt Southend-on-Sea 52-54; Surr 52-54; V of St Pet w St Owen Heref 54-65; St Geo Worthing 66-71; Chap Co Hosp Heref 56-65; R of Buxted 71-76; Perm to Offic Dio Bris from 77; Dio Glouc from 78; Dio Ex from 79. *6 Westbourne Terrace, Budleigh Salterton, Devon.*

GOSS, Michael John. b 37. Chich Th Coll 62. **d** 65 **p** 66 S'wark. C of Angell Town 65-68; Catford Dio S'wark 68-71; V of St Swith Hither Green 71-81; St Jo Evang Redhill Dio S'wark from 81. *St John's Vicarage, Church Road, Redhill, Surrey.* (Redhill 66562)

GOSS, Very Rev Thomas Ashworth. b 12. Univ of St Andr MA 36. Ridley Hall Cam 35. **d** 37 **p** 38 Linc. C of Frodingham 37-41; Chap RAFVR 41-47; V of Sutton-le-Marsh 47-51; Chap RAF 51-67; Hon Chap to HM the Queen from 66; R of St Sav Jersey 67-71; Dean of Jersey and R of St Helier Jersey Dio Win from 71; Hon Can of Win from 71. *Deanery, St Helier, Jersey, CI.* (20001)

GOSSE, John Frederick. Mem Univ Newfld BA 62. Qu Coll Newfld LTh 63. **d** 61 **p** 63 Newfld. on leave 61-63; C of Corner Brook 63-64; R of Antigonish 64-65; P-in-c of Country Harbour 64-65; on leave 65-69; Chap Kingston Penit 69-73; I of Stirling 74-77; R of St Paul Kingston Dio Ont from 77; Barriefield w Pittsburgh 77-80. *832 Ludgate Crescent, Kingston, Ont, Canada.*

GOSSE, Canon Stephen Baxter Gordon. **d** 53 **p** 54 Alg. C of Sturgeon Falls 53-56; R of St Brice North Bay 56-72; Hon Can of St Luke's Cathl Ch Sault Ste Marie from 69; I of Sturgeon Falls Dio Alg from 72. *210 Fourth Avenue West, North Bay, Ont., Canada.* (705-472 6146)

GOSSET, George Allen. St Pet Hall, Ox BA 48, MA 51. Ridley Hall, Cam. **d** 50 **p** 51 Sarum. C of St Luke Parkstone 50-53; Lenton (in c of Priory Ch) 53-56; R of E Bilney w Beetley 57-66. *8 Lloyd Road, Walmer, Port Elizabeth, S Africa.*

GOSSWINN, Nicholas Simon. b 50. St D Coll Lamp Dipl Th 73. Bp Burgess Hall Lamp 72. **d** 73 **p** 77 Mon. C of St Mary Abergavenny 73-74; Bassaleg 77-80; Team V of St Geo w St Luke Barrow-F Dio Carl from 81. *28 St Luke's Avenue, Barrow-in-Furness, Cumb.*

GOSWELL, Geoffrey. b 34. **d** 71 **p** 72 Glouc. C of Em, Cheltenham 71-73; Lydney w Aylburton 73-76; P-in-c of Falfield w Rockptn and Chap Eastwood Pk Detention Centre 76-79; CMS Area Sec for Dios Linc, Pet and Huntingdon and Archd of Dio Ely from 79. *88 Bourne Road, Spalding, Lincs.*

GOTA, Lamek Yona. St Phil Coll Kongwa. **d** 60 Bp Omari for Centr Tang **p** 60 Bp Wiggins for Centr Tang. P Dio Centr Tang 60-66; Dio W Tang 66-73. *Kibondo, Tanzania.*

GOTELEE, Peter Douglas. b 28. K Coll Lon and Warm 50. **d** 54 Croydon for Cant **p** 55 Cant. C of St Pet Croydon 54-57; St Paul w St Mary Camberley 57-65; C-in-c of St Geo Conv Distr Badshot Lea 65-75; V of West End Chobham 75-76; C-in-c of Bisley Dio Guildf 75-76; R (w West End) from 76. *Rectory, Clews Lane, Bisley, Surrey.* (Brookwood 3377)

GOTO, Elia. St Jo Sem Lusaka, 56. **d** 58 **p** 60 Mashon. P Dio Mashon 58-81; Dio Mutare from 81. *Avondale, Zimbabwe.*

GOTT, Joseph Desmond. b 26. Ch Ch Ox BA 47, MA 51. St Chad's Coll Dur Dipl Th 52. **d** 52 Jarrow for Dur **p** 53 Dur. C of Horden 52-55; Bp Wearmouth (in c of St Hilda Millfield) 55-58; PC of St Hilda Millfield Bp Wearmouth 58-66; Prin Argyle Ho Scho Sunderland 59-65; Poulton 66-72; V of Down Ampney 66-72; St Steph Cheltm Dio Glouc from 72. *St Stephen's Vicarage, Cheltenham, GL51 5AD.* (Cheltm 22467)

GOTT, Wayne Thomas. b 53. Univ of New Engl Armidale BEcon. Moore Th Coll BD, ThL. **d** 81 Syd. C of St John Camden Dio Syd from 81. *10 View Street, Camden, NSW, Australia 2570.*

GOTTO, Erunato. Bp Tucker Coll Mukono 55. **d** 56 Ugan **p** 58 Bp Balya for Ugan. P Dio Ugan 56-60; Dio Nam 60-65; Dio W Bugan 65-68. *Kiteregga, PO Bukuya, Mityana, Uganda.*

GOUDKAMP, Maarten. Univ of Utrecht, BD 35, BA (Th) 38. **d** 65 Graft. C of Murwillumbah 65-66; R of Woodenbong w Liston 66-70; C of Ch Ch Cathl City and Dio Graft from 73. *38 Victoria Street, Grafton, NSW, Australia 2460.* (42 1602)

GOUGE, Canon Frank. b 16. St Pet Hall Ox BA (3rd cl Hist) 38, MA 45. Wycl Hall Ox 38. **d** 40 **p** 41 Sheff. C of Wadsley 40-42; St Mary Sheff 42-44; Chap RNVR 44-47; V of Chapeltown 47-67; Hall Green Dio Birm from 67; Chap of Hallamshire Maternity Home Chapeltown 51-67; RD of Tankersley 58-67; Solihull 68-79; Hon Can of Birm from 73. *592 Fox Hollies Road, Hall Green, Birmingham, B28 9DX.* (021-777 3689)

GOUGH, Anthony Jobson. b 39. Ridley Hall Cam 75. **d** 77 **p** 78 Pet. C of Rushden w Newton Bromswold 77-81; V of Lyddington w Stoke Dry and Seaton Dio Pet from 81. *Lyddington Vicarage, Uppingham, Leics, LE15 9LR.* (Uppingham 2221)

GOUGH, Anthony Walter. b 31. Chicago Th Sem DMin 81. Dipl Th (Lon) 68. Univ of Leic MA 76. Chicago Th Sem DMin 81. Oak Hill Th Coll 57. **d** 60 **p** 61 Portsm. C of St Simon Southsea 60-64; R of Peldon 64-71; V of Rothley 71-80; Chap St John's Hosp Stone Aylesbury from 81. *c/o St John's Hospital, Stone, Aylesbury, Bucks, HP17 8PP.*

GOUGH, Colin Richard. b 47. St Chad's Coll Dur BA 69. Cudd Coll 73. **d** 75 Stafford for Lich **p** 76 Lich. C of St Chad Lich 75-78; Codsall Dio Lich from 78. *Church House, Bilbrook, Wolverhampton, WV8 1EU.* (Codsall 2912)

GOUGH, David Norman. b 42. Oak Hill Th Coll Lon 70. **d** 70 **p** 71 Lich. C of Penn Fields 70-73; Stapenhill 73-76; V of Heath Dio Derby from 77. *Heath Vicarage, Chesterfield, Derbys, S44 5RX.* (Chesterfield 850339)

GOUGH, Derek William. b 31. Pemb Coll Cam BA 55, MA 59. St Steph Ho Ox 55. **d** 57 **p** 58 Lon. C of All SS Finchley 57-60; St Andr Roxbourne Harrow 60-66; V of St Mary w St Jo Evang U Edmon Dio Lon from 66. *St John's Vicarage, Dyson's Road, N18 2DS.* (01-807 2767)

GOUGH, Ernest Hubert. Trin Coll Dub BA 53, MA 57. **d** 54 **p** 55 Connor. C of Glenavy 54-57; Ch Ch Lisburn 57-61; C-in-c of St Ninian Belf 61-62; I 62-71; I of St Bart Belf Dio Connor from 71. *St Bartholomew's Rectory, Mount Pleasant, Stranmillis, Belfast, BT9 5DS.* (Belfast 669995)

GOUGH, Frank Peter. b 32. Lon Coll Div 66. **d** 68 **p** 69 Sarum. C of St Mary Weymouth 68-70; Attenborough w Chilwell 70-73; R of Barrow 73-77; V of St Mary Summerstown Dio S'wark from 77; RD of Tooting from 80. *St Mary's Vicarage, Wimbledon Road, SW17 0UQ.* (01-946 9853)

✠ **GOUGH, Right Rev Hugh Rowlands.** b 05. CMG 65. OBE (Mil) 45. TD 50. Trin Coll Cam 3rd cl Hist Trip pt i 26, BA (2nd cl Geog Trip pt i) 27, MA 31. DD (Lambeth) 59. ACT Hon ThD 59. Wycl Coll Tor Hon DD 63. Lon Coll of Div 28. **d** 28 **p** 29 Lon. C of St Mary Isl 28-31; PC of St Paul Walcot Bath 31-34; V of St Jas Carl 34-39; St Matt Bayswater 39-46; CF (TA) 39-45; Hon CF (2nd cl) 45; Men in Disp 45; V of Isl 46-48; Preb of St Paul's Cathl 48; RD of Islington 46-48; Archd of W Ham 48-58; Cons Ld Bp Suffr of Barking in St Paul's Cathl Lon 1 Nov 48 by Abp of Cant; Bps of Lon; S'wark; Chelmsf; Roch; Nel; and Momb; Bps Suffr of Colchester; Stepney; Kens; and Willesden; Trld to Syd 58; elected Primate of Austr 59; res 66; Sub-Prelate O of St John of Jer 59-72; Golden Lect (Haberdashers' Co) 53 and 56; R of Freshford 67-72. *Forge House, Over Wallop, Stockbridge, Hants, SO20 8JF.* (Wallop 315)

GOUGH, Stephen William Cyprian. b 50. Univ of Alberta BSc 71. Cudd Coll BA (Th) 80. **d** 79 **p** 80 Liv. C of Walton-on-the-Hill Dio Liv from 79. *c/o Walton Rectory, Liverpool, L4 6TJ.*

GOULBURN, *See* Canberra and Goulburn

GOULBURN, Dean of. (Vacant)

GOULD, Alan Charles. b 26. Univ of Lon Dipl Th 53. **d** 62 **p** 63 Ches. C of Bromborough 62-67; V of Audlem (w Burleydam from 68) 67-80; Knowbury Dio Heref from 80; P-in-c of Coreley Dio Heref from 80. *Knowbury Vicarage, Clee Hill, Ludlow, Salop, SY8 3JG.* (Ludlow 890223)

GOULD, Douglas Walter. b 35. St Jo Coll Cam BA 59, 3rd cl Th Trip pt ii 60, MA 63. Ridley Hall Cam. **d** 61 **p** 62 York. C of St Phil and St Jas Clifton York 61-64; Bridgnorth w Tasley 64-67; R of Acton-Burnell w Pitchford 67-73; P-in-c of Cound 68-73; Frodesley 69-73; V of Bromyard Dio Heref from 73; RD from 73; P-in-c of Stanford Bp Dio Heref from 73; Stoke Lacy w Much Cowarne and Moreton Jeffries 76-78; Ocle Pychard and Ullingswick Dio Heref from 76. *Vicarage, 28 Church Lane, Bromyard, Herefs.* (Bromyard 82438)

GOULD, Frederick Leslie. b 02. Linc Th Coll. **d** 29 **p** 30 Southw. C of St Mich AA Radford Notts 29-32; St Mary Magd Millfield Sunderland 32-35; V of Hovingham 35-40; PC of St Paul Low Team Gateshead 40-56; St Mary Sculcoates 56-66; V of St Anthony Byker Newc T 66-75; Chap St Wilfrid Conv Selsey 75-81. *Address temp unknown.*

GOULD, Canon Jack. b 15. **d** 45 **p** 47 Argent. Asst Chap St Geo Coll Chap Quilmes 45-47; Chap at Pernambuco 48-53; Port Stanley Falkland Is 53-57; V of H Trin Lomas de Zamora Buenos Aires 57-67; Dom Chap to Bp of Argent 57-67; Archd in Republics of the River Plate 64-71; Hon Can of St Jo Bapt Cathl Buenos Aires 64-71; Ch Ch Cathl Port Stanley Falkland Is from 71; V of Kingswear Dio Ex from 71. *Kingswear Vicarage, Dartmouth, TQ6 0BX.* (Kingswear 338)

GOULD, John Barry. b 38. M ICE 68. SOC 77. **d** 77 **p** 78 S'wark. C of St Leon Streatham 77-80; V of H Trin U Tooting Dio S'wark from 80. *14 Upper Tooting Park, SW17 7SW.* (01-672 4790)

GOULD, Maxwell Selwyn. d 63 Bp McKenzie for Wel **p** 64 Wel. Hon C of Ruapehu 63-67; Wainuiarua 67-68; L to Offic Dio Wel 69-71; Perm to Offic Dio Auckld from 72. *103 Korora Road, Oneroa, Waiheke, NZ.* (Waiheke 8462)

GOULD, Peter Richard. b 34. Univ of Wales BA (Phil) 57. Univ of Birm Dipl Th 62. Qu Coll Birm 60. **d** 62 Ripon **p** 63 Knaresborough for Ripon. C of Rothwell 62-68; Chap and Asst Master Agnes Stewart C of E Sch Leeds 65-68; V of Allerton Bywater 68-73; Asst Master Southw Minster Gr Sch 73-76; Chap and Asst Master L Victuallers Sch Slough from 76. *The Licensed Victuallers School, Slough, Berks, SL1 1XP.* (Slough 22958/23781)

GOULD, Robert Douglas. b 21. MBE (Mil) 46. Wells Th Coll 58. **d** 60 **p** 61 Lon. M OGS. C of St Mich Wood Green 60-65; V of St Matt U Clapton Dio Lon from 68; St Thos Clapton Common 70-80; Chap to Commun of St Jo Bapt Clewer from 80. *53 Hatch Lane, Clewer, Windsor, Berks, SL4 3QY.* (Windsor 63060)

GOULD, Robert Ozburn. b 38. Williams Coll Mass USA BA 59. Univ of St Andrews PhD 63. **d** 78 Edin. Hon C of St Columba Edin 78-80; Hon Super Dio Edin from 80. *33 Charterhall Road, Edinburgh, EH9 3HS.*

GOULD, Thomas Cyril Powell. b 1891. St Edm Hall Ox BA 14, MA 19. Leeds Cl Scho 14. **d** 14 **p** 16 Birm. C of King's Norton 14-15; TCF 18-19; C of St Mary Bearwood Smethwick 15-21; Min Can of Worc Cathl 21-25; Chap Berkeley Hosp Worc 22-28; V of Cotheridge w Crown E 25-47; R of Shrawley 48-59. *The Ferns, Brent Road, E Brent, Somt.*

GOULD, Tom. b 12. Sarum Th Coll 34. **d** 37 Wakef **p** 38 Pontefract for Wakef. C of Grimethorpe 37-40; E Barnet 40-46; PC of St Pet Arkley 46-68; V 68-78; Perm to Offic Dio St Alb from 78. *7 Whitefriars Court, Friern Park, N12.*

GOULDEN, Joseph Notley. b 19. TCD BA 41, MA 50. **d** 42 Arm for Down **p** 43 Down. C of St Paul Belf 42-44; Warrenpoint and Clonallon 44-50; Hd of Trin Coll Miss Belf 50-54; R of Romoan 54-77; RD of Carey 61-77. *13 Clare Road, Ballycastle, Co Antrim, N Ireland.* (Ballycastle 62778)

GOULDING, Charles John. Sarum Th Coll 56. **d** 58 **p** 59 S'wark. C of St Mich AA S Beddington 58-61; Horsell 61-63;

V of Ardleigh 63-72; Shrub End Dio Chelmsf from 72; Surr from 77; RD of Colchester from 81. *Shrub End Vicarage, Colchester, Essex.* (Colchester 74178)

GOULDING, Edward William. b 23. St Aid Coll 54. **d** 56 **p** 57 Heref. C of Ross-on-Wye 56-60; V of St Chad w Ch Ch Everton 60-64; Knotty Ash 64-65; Llangarron w Llangrove 65-69; Asst Chap HM Pris Liv 69; Chap HM Pris Birm 69-72; V of Gt Harwood 72-76; L to Offic Dio Blackb 76-78; V of Wray w Tatham Fells Dio Blackb from 78. *Vicarage, Knott Hill, Tatham, Lancaster, LA2 8PS.* (Bentham 61877)

GOULDING, Leonard William. b 08. OBE 73. St Aug Coll Cant 30. Univ of Dur LTh 34. **d** 34 Knaresborough for Ripon **p** 35 Ripon. C of St Matt Holbeck 34-37; Barton-on-Humber 37-42; V of Ulceby 42-55; Chap RAFVR 43-47; R of Croxton w Kirmington 49-55; Thorpe-on-the-Hill 55-63; R of N Scarle 55-63; V of Eagle 55-63; RD of Graffoe 58-64; V of Canwick 63-75; Asst Chap O of St Jo of Jer from 63; RD of Longobody 64-69. *Address temp unknown.*

GOULDSTONE, Timothy Maxwell. b 46. Univ of Ex BSc 68, MSc 76. Trin Coll Bris 76. **d** 78 **p** 79 St Alb. C of Ch Ch Ware 78-81; P-in-c of Ansley Dio Cov from 81. *Vicarage, Birmingham Road, Ansley, CV10 9PS.* (Chapel End 392240)

GOULSTONE, Thomas Richard Kerry. b 36. St D Coll Lamp BA 58. St Mich Coll Llan. **d** 59 **p** 60 St D. C of Llanbadarn-Fawr 59-61; St Pet Carmarthen 61-64; V of Whitchurch w Solva and St Elvis 64-67; Gorslas 67-76; Surr from 75; V of Burry Port w Pwll Dio St D from 76. *Vicarage, Church Road, Burry Port, Dyfed.* (Burry Port 2475)

GOUNDRY, Ralph Walter. b 31. St Chad's Coll Dur BA 56, Dipl Th 58. **d** 58 **p** 59 Dur. C of W Harton 58-62; C and Prec of St Nich Cathl Newc T 62-65; V of Seghill 65-73; Long Benton Dio Newc T from 73. *3 Station Road, Denton, Newcastle-upon-Tyne, NE12 8AN.* (Newcastle 662015)

GOURDIE, Rona McLeod. St Jo Coll Auckld Bd Th Studies, NZ LTh 39. DSO 45. **d** 39 Aotearoa for Wel **p** 40 Wel C of Petone 39-46; CF (NZ) 41-46; V of Mangatainoka w Pongaroa 46-47; Pongaroa 47-52; Manaia 52-59; Shannon 59-66; Greytown 66-72; L to Offic Dio Wel from 72. *2a Norton Street, Foxton Beach, NZ.*

GOURLEY, William Robert Joseph. b 48. K Coll Lon BD 74. Div Hostel Dub 68. **d** 75 **p** 76 Down. C of Newtownards 75-78; R of Currin w Drum and Newbliss 78-81; Dioc Youth Adv Dio Clogh 78-81; R of St Geo and St Thos City and Dio Dub from 81. *St George's Rectory, Lower Drumcondra Road, Dublin, 9.* (Dublin 305289)

GOVER, Michael Sydney Richard. b 41. Chich Th Coll 67. **d** 71 **p** 72 Portsm. Asst Master Ryde Sch 69-75; C of Ryde 71-75; Waterlooville Dio Portsm from 75. *5 Warfield Avenue, Waterlooville, Hants.* (Waterlooville 52350)

GOVO, Simon. St Barn Coll Westwood. **d** 80 Matab. d Dio Matab 80-81; Dio Lundi from 81. *Box 28, Gokwe, Zimbabwe.*

GOW, Canon William Connell. b 09. Univ of Dur LTh 36. Edin Th Coll 34. **d** 36 **p** 37 Brech. C of St Mary Magd Dundee 36-40; R of St Jas Dingwall w St Anne Strathpeffer 40-77; Hon Can of St Andr Cathl Inverness 53-61 and from 77; Dean of Moray Ross and Caithness 60-77. *14 Mackenzie Place, Maryburgh, Ross-shire, IV7 8DY.*

GOW, William Masterton. **d** 32 **p** 33 Newc T. C of Berwick-on-Tweed 32-35; L to Offic Dio Llan (Dioc Messenger) 35-37; C-in-c of St Mark Conv Distr Shiremoor 37-43; V of Byker St Anthony Newc T 43-52; Stamfordham 52-76; Ed Newc T Dioc Cal 68-76. *32 Castleway, Dinnington, Newcastle-upon-Tyne, NE13 7LS.* (Ponteland 25562)

GOWDEY, Canon Alan Lawrence. b 25. Trin Coll Tor BA 50. Ridley Hall, Cam. **d** 52 Malmesbury for Bris **p** 53 Bris. C of St Aug Swindon 52-55; Marshfield w Cold Ashton 55-57; L to Offic Dio Bris 57-62; Asst to Social and Industr Adv to Bp of Bris 57-62; Hon C of H Trin Dartford 62-66; St Geo Gravesend 66-75; Industr Chap Dio Roch 62-75; Chap Heathrow Airport from 75; Hon Can of H Trin Cathl Gibr from 80. *Room 309e, Control Tower Building, Heathrow Airport, Hounslow, Middx.* (01-759 7685)

GOWDEY, Michael Cragg. b 32. Or Coll Ox BA (2nd cl Th) 56, MA 58. Qu Coll Birm Dipl Th 57. **d** 58 Derby **p** 59 Bp Sinker for Derby. C of Ashbourne (in c of H Trin Clifton from 60) 58-63; PC of Chellaston 63-69; Asst Chap Ellesmere Coll 69-74; L to Offic Dio Lich 70-74; Dio Derby 74-81; Chap Trent Coll 74-81; Ecumen Educn Chap Stourbridge Deanery and Coun of Chs from 81. *26 Croftwood Road, Wollescote, Stourbridge, Worcs, DY9 7EX.* (Lye 6796)

GOWER, Archdeacon of. *Vacant* Hughes, Ven Hubert Benjamin William.

GOWER, Christopher Raymond. b 45. Univ of Nottm BA (Th) 73. St Jo Coll Nottm 70. **d** 73 Kens for Lon **p** 74 Lon. C of Hounslow 73-76; All H Greenford 76-77; P-in-c of St Gabr Willesden Dio Lon from 77; St Anne Brondesbury Dio Lon from 81. *St Gabriel's Vicarage, Walm Lane, NW2 4RX.* (01-452 1758)

GOWER, Frank Charles. b 36. Wycl Coll Tor 75. **d** 77 **p** 78 Alg. C of St Luke's Cathl Sault Ste Marie 77-78; I of New Liskeard Dio Alg from 78. *Box 8, New Liskeard, Ont, Canada.*

✠ **GOWER, Most Rev Godfrey Philip.** St Jo Coll Manit BA 29, LTh 30, DD 54. **d** 30 **p** 31 Edmon. C of Sedgewick 30-32; R and RD of Camrose 32-35; R of Ch Ch Edmon 35-41; Exam Chap to Bp of Edmon 38-41; Can of Edmon 40-44; Chap RCAF 41-44; R of St Paul Vancouver 44-51; Cons Ld Bp of New Westmr in Ch Ch Cathl Vancouver 25 Jan 51 by Abp of Yukon; Bps of Br Columb; Carib; Caled; Koot; Oregon; Olympia; Bps Heathcote and Sovereign; elected Abp and Metrop of Prov of BC 68; res 71; Chan Vanc Sch of Th 70-74. *1522 Everall Street, White Rock, BC, Canada.*

GOWER, John Byron. b 25. St D Coll Lamp BA 48. St Mich Coll Llan 50. **d** 52 **p** 53 Llan. C of St Jo Evang Canton 52-55; Llangynwyd w Maesteg and Troedshiw Garth 55-60; Hd of Soc and Relig Stud Wolverhampton Educn Authority from 60. *51 Pinfold Lane, Penn, Wolverhampton, Staffs.*

GOWER, Nigel Plested. SS Coll Cam BA 62, MA 65. Ridley Hall, Cam 61. **d** 63 **p** 64 Chelmsf. C of St Jo Evang Walthamstow 63-66; CMS Miss Nigeria 67-78; P-in-c of Loscoe Dio Derby from 78. *Loscoe Vicarage, Derby.* (Langley Mill 3392)

GOWER, Peter Charles Gwynne. b 24. St D Coll Lamp 61. **d** 63 **p** 64 Mon. C of Llanfihangel-Llantarnam 63-69; CF (TA) 65-67; (TAVR) 67-72; (RARO) 72-79; C-in-c of Fairwater in Rectorial Benef of Cwmbran 69-70; V 71-75; Raglan w Llandenny and Llansoy Dio Mon from 75; Ed Mon Dioc Directory from 81. *Vicarage, Primrose Green, Raglan, Gwent.* (Raglan 690330)

GOWER-JONES, Alfred. b 08. Univ of Man BA 30. Coll of Resurr Mirfield, 32. **d** 34 **p** 35 Man. C of Our Lady of Mercy and St Thos of Cant Gorton 34-37; St Mark Swindon (in c of St Luke) 37-44; R of Our Lady of Mercy and St Thos of Cant Gorton 44-74. *11 Fosbrooke House, 8 Clifton Drive, Lytham, Lancs, FY8 5RE.* (0253-734100)

GOWER-JONES, [vn] geoffre. b 10. BNC Ox BA (3rd cl Th) 33, MA 37. Wells Th Coll 33. **d** 34 **p** 35 Man. C of St Paul Royton 34-39; Prestwich 39-43; V of Belfield 43-50; St Steph Blackpool 50-81; Proc Conv Man 46-50; Surr 50-81; Proc Conv Blackb 60-67; Can of Blackb 62-67; RD of Fylde 62; Blackpool 63-66; Commiss Damar 63-70; Hon Sec Blackb Dioc Conf 65-70; Archd of Lanc 66-81; Archd (Emer) from 81. *7 Egerton Drive, Hale, Chesh.* (061-980 3886)

GOWER-SMITH, Frederick Richard. b 1898. Wycl Hall Ox 40. **d** 41 Bp Mann for Roch **p** 42 Roch. C of Yalding 41-43; V of Bredhurst 43-47; Monkton, Cant 47-72; Perm to Offic Dio Cant from 79. *Downe House, Meare, Glastonbury, Somt.*

GOWER REES, Cecil Roy. b 06. St D Coll Lamp BA 28. **d** 29 **p** 30 St A. C of Newtown 29-30; St Jas Tredegar 30-33; St Mary Abergavenny 33-40; OCF 40-45; V of Llanarth w Clytha and Llansantffraed (w Bryngwyn R from 49) 40-52; St Mellons 52-76; Surr from 41; Perm to Offic Dio Llan from 76. *16 Ty-Pica Drive, Wenvoe, Cardiff, CF5 6BS.* (Cardiff 593646)

GOWING, Arthur Frederick. b 30. Em Coll Sktn LTh 70. **d** 70 **p** 71 BC. C of St Jo Victoria 70-72; I of Alert Bay 72-77; Perm to Offic Dio New Westmr from 81. *2040 York Street, Vancouver, BC, Canada.*

GOWING, Donald Boyd. Moore Th Coll Syd 64. **d** 67 Graft. C of Kempsey 67-69; Murwillumbah 69-70; P-in-c of Nimbin 71-73; V of Werris Creek 74-78; Guyra Dio Armid from 78. *Vicarage, Guyra, NSW, Australia 2365.*

GOWING, Ven Frederick William. b 18. TCD BA 40, Div Test (2nd cl) 41. **d** 41 **p** 42 Arm. C of Portadown 41-47; R of Woods Chapel 47-56; Mullavilly Dio Arm from 56; Preb of Arm Cathl 73-75; Treas 75-79; Archd of Arm from 79. *89 Mullavilly Road, Tandragee, Craigavon, Co Armagh, N Ireland BT62 2LX.* (Tandragee 840221)

GOWING, John Ellis. b 18. Magd Coll Ox BA (3rd cl Mod Hist) 40, MA 45. Westcott Ho Cam 40. **d** 41 **p** 42 Chich. C of Horsham 41-45; H Trin Hastings 45-48; St Barn Bexhill 48-51; C-in-c of St Richard Conv Distr N Aldrington 51-53; Cler Publicity Sec St Pancras Housing S 53-64; Hon C of St Mary Virg Somers Tn 53-73; Chap of Highgate Sch 65-66; Lect Barnet Coll of Further Educn 67-79; L to Offic Dio Lon 73-79; Perm to Offic Dio Ox from 79. *7 Thurne Cloe, Newport Pagnell, Bucks, MK16 9DY.* (0908-611500)

GOWING, Leslie Edward. b 1899. Lich Th Coll. **d** 23 Bp Baynes for Birm **p** 24 Birm. C of St D Birm 23-26; Dagenham 26-29; W Thurrock (in c of Purfleet) 29-31; I of St Paul New Cross w St Mich and St Thos Red Bank Man 31-59; V of Macclesfield Forest w Wildboarclough 59-66. *10 Poulton Avenue, Lytham St Annes, Lancs, FY8 3JR.* (St Annes 22354)

GOWLLAND, Geoffrey. b 03. St Geo Windsor 56. **d** 56 **p** 57 Win. C of Hartley Wintney w Elvetham 56-59; R of

Exbury 59-62; V of Longstock w Leckford 62-69. *Bell Cottage, Tilshead, Salisbury, Wilts.* (0980-620220)

GOWTY, Richard Newton. St Francis Coll Brisb. **d** and **p** 72 Brisb. C of St Luke Toowoomba 72-75; P-in-c of Gatton 76-77; R 77-80; St Andr Indooroopilly Dio Brisb from 80. *St Andrew's Rectory, Indooroopilly, Qld, Australia 4068.* (370-7263)

GOYMOUR, Michael Edwyn. b 29. Selw Coll Cam 2nd cl Eng Lit Trip pt i 49, BA (2nd cl Th Trip pt ii) 51. McGill Univ Montr BD 53. Wells Th Coll 53. **d** 53 Dunwich for Cant **p** 54 St E. C of St Jo Evang Bury St Edms 53-56; St Bart Ipswich 56-60; R of Gamlingay 60-68; Asst Master Pet Co Gr Sch for Girls from 68. *56 Church Drive, Orton Waterville, Peterborough.*

GQWABAZA, Waddleton Zalisile Victor. St Bede's Coll Umtata, 63. **d** 64 St John's **p** 66 Johann for St John's. O of Ethiopia. P Dio St John's from 64. *Private Bag 405, Qumbu, Transkei, S Africa.*

GRACE, Blair Sydney. ACT ThL 63. Melb Coll of Div Dipl Relig Educn 66. Moore Th Coll Syd 62. **d** 63 **p** 64 Syd. C of Dee Why 63-64; Mascot 65-67; R of Norseman 67-70; P-in-c of Rosebery-Zeehan-Savage River 71-74; Sec Bush Ch Aid S Dio Adel 74-78; C of Norwood 74-78. *c/o Diocesan Registry, 23 Raymond Street, Sale, Vic, Australia 3850.*

GRACE, John Edward. b 34. **d** 77 **p** 78 Bal. Perm to Offic Dio Bal 77-78; C of Warrnambool Dio Bal from 78. *Box 331, Warrnambool, Vic, Australia 3280.*

GRACE, Kenneth. b 24. Univ of Leeds, BA (2nd cl French) 49. Wycl Hall, Ox 62. **d** 63 Middleton for Man **p** 64 Man. C of Tonge w Alkrington 63-66; R of Thwing 66-70; V of Wold Newton 66-70; Chap St Andr Sch Worthing 70-76; R of Berwick w Selmeston and Alciston 77-81; P-in-c of Kingston Buci Dio Chich from 81. *Kingston Buci Rectory, Rectory Road, Shoreham-by-Sea, W Sussex.* (Brighton 592591)

GRACE, Richard Maurice. b 29. St Chad's Coll Dur BA 53. Chich Th Coll 53. **d** 55 **p** 56 Liv. C of St Agnes Toxt Pk 55-58; St Pet Wolverhampton 58-62; V of St Francis Friar Park W Bromwich 62-78; P-in-c of Salt Dio Lich from 78. *Salt Vicarage, Stafford.* (Sandon 341)

GRACE, Sidney Edmund. LTh S Afr 53. **d** 52 **p** 53 Grahmstn. C of St Sav E Lon 53-55; R of St Pet E Lon 55-60; Middelburg 60-68; St Sav Walmer 70-74; Somerset E 75-77. *Box 5154, Port Elizabeth 6065, CP, S Africa.*

GRACE, Wilfrid Windsor. b 15. ACA 39, FCA 60. Westcott Ho Cam 52. **d** 53 **p** 54 Bris. C of St Andr Chippenham 53-57; V of Minety w Oaksey 57-71; Oldland w Longwell Green 71-76; Abbots Leigh w Leigh Woods 76-80; Chap Ham Green Hosp Avon from 79; Cheshire Home Axbridge from 81. *Cornerways, Bristol Road, Sidcot, Avon.*

GRACIE, Anthony Johnstone. b 25. Ch Coll Cam BA 48, MA 51. Linc Th Coll 57. **d** 59 **p** 60 Birm. C of St Geo Edgbaston 59-62; R of Lyndon w Manton Martinsthorpe and Gunthorpe 62-76; C-in-c of N Luffenham 63-66; R 66-76; RD of Oakham 69-70; V of Odiham and S Warnborough w Long Sutton Dio Win from 76. *Odiham Vicarage, Basingstoke, Hants.* (Odiham 2112)

GRACIE, Bryan John. b 45. Open Univ BA 81. K Coll Lon and Warm AKC 67. **d** 68 **p** 69 Ex. C of Whipton 68-72; Chap St John's Sch Tiffield 72-73; Asst Chap HM Pris Liv 74; Chap HM Borstal Stoke Heath 74-78; Feltham from 78. *HM Borstal, Bedfont Road, Feltham, Middx.* (01-890 0061)

GRACIE, Thomas. Wycl Coll Tor. **d** 60 **p** 61 Tor. C-in-c of Minden 60-63; I of Beeton 63-68; R of Bowmanville 68-81; Archd of Dur 77-81; I of Ch of Messiah City and Dio Tor from 81. *240 Avenue Road, Toronto, M5R 2J4, Ont, Canada.*

GRACO, Warren Charles. Ridley Coll Melb 59. **d** 61 **p** 62 St Arn. C of Tresco 61-63; V of Quambatook 63-69; R of Rushworth and Murchison 69-74; H Trin Roch 74-77; Dunolly Dio Bend from 77. *Vicarage, Thompson Street, Dunolly, Vic, Australia 3472.*

GRAEBE, Denys Redford. b 26. Qu Coll Cam BA 48, MA 51. Westcott Ho Cam 50. **d** 51 **p** 52 St Alb. C of Hitchin 51-57; R of Gt Parndon 57-72; V of Norton Dio St Alb from 72. *17 Norton Way North, Letchworth, Herts.* (Letchworth 5059)

GRAESSER, Adrian Stewart. b 42. Tyndale Hall, Bris 63. **d** 67 Sherwood for Southw **p** 68 Southw. C of St Jude Mapperly Nottm 67-69; Slaithwaite 69-72; CF 72-75; V of Earlsheaton 75-81; R of Norton Fitzwarren Dio B & W from 81. *Norton Fitzwarren Rectory, Rectory Road, Taunton, Somt, TA2 6SE.* (Taunton 72570)

GRAFTON, Lord Bishop of. *See* Shearman, Right Rev Donald Norman.

GRAFTON, Dean of. *See* Schultz, Very Rev Bruce Allan.

GRAHAM, Alan Robert. b 44. St Edm Hall Ox BA (2nd cl Geog) 67, (2nd cl Th) 69, MA 71. St Steph Ho Ox 67. **d** 70 **p** 71 Malmesbury for Bris. C of All SS Clifton 70-74; Tadley (in c of St Luke) 74-77; P-in-c of U Clatford w Goodworth Clatford 77-79; R of Abbotts Ann and U Clatford w Goodworth Clatford Dio Win from 79. *Upper Clatford Rectory, Andover, Hants.* (Andover 52906)

GRAHAM, Alfred. b 34. Univ of Bris BA (2nd cl Th) 57. Tyndale Hall Bris. **d** 58 Derby **p** 59 Bp Sinker for Derby. C of Chaddesden 58-61; Bickenhill w Elmdon 61-64; V of St Lawr Kirkdale 64-70; Stapleford Dio Southw from 70. *Stapleford Vicarage, Nottingham.* (Sandiacre 397333)

✠ GRAHAM, Right Rev Andrew Alexander Kenny. b 29. Late Scho of St Jo Coll Ox BA (2nd cl Mod Lang) 52, Dipl Th (w distinc) 53, Heath Harrison Travelling Scho (German) 51, Ellerton Pri 55, MA 57. Ely Th Coll 53. **d** 55 **p** 56 Chich. C of Hove 55-58; Chap and Tutor in Th Worc Coll Ox 58-70; Fell 60-70; Hon Fell from 81; Exam Chap to Bp of Carl 67-77; M Gen Syn Univ of Ox 69-70; Linc 75-77; Warden of Linc Th Coll 70-77; Preb and Can of Linc Cathl 70-77; Exam Chap to Bp of Bradf 72-77; Bp of Linc 73-77; Select Pr Univ of Ox 74; Cons Ld Bp Suffr of Bedford in Westmr Abbey 31 March 77 by Abp of Cant; Bps of Lon, St Alb, Linc, Bradf, Ely, Glouc, Guildf, Lich, Portsm, Roch and Worc; Bps Suffr of Buckingham, Dorch, Edmon, Grimsby, Hertf, Horsham, Huntingdon, Jarrow, Kingston, Knaresborough, Malmesbury, Selby, Sherborne, Shrewsbury, Stafford, Tonbridge and Willesden; and others; Trld to Newc T 81. *Bishop's House, 29 Moor Road South, Newcastle-on-Tyne, NE3 1PA.* (Gosforth 852220)

GRAHAM, Anthony Nigel. b 40. Univ of Wales BA (Hist) 62. Ripon Hall, Ox 62. **d** 64 **p** 65 Heref. C of H Trin Heref 64-67; St Martin's Birm 67-69; Asst Master Mt Pleasant Comprehensive Sch Birm 70-73; C of Selly Oak 71-75; V of St Mary and St Ambrose Edgbaston Dio Birm from 75. *15 Raglan Road, Birmingham, B5 7RA.* (021-440-2196)

GRAHAM, Anthony Stanley David. b 34. SS Coll Cam BA (2nd cl Mod Lang Trip pt ii) 56, 2nd cl Th Trip pt ia 57, MA 60. Cudd Coll 58. **d** 60 **p** 61 St Alb. C of Welwyn Garden City 60-64; Asst Chap Ipswich Sch 64-65; C of Margate 65-68; Area Sec (and Reg Co-ordinator from 74) Chr Aid and L to Offic Dio Chich from 68. *48 Springfield Road, Southgate, Crawley, RH11 8AH.* (Crawley 26279)

GRAHAM, Carole Rose-Mary. b 43. Univ of Cant NZ BA 66. St Jo Coll Auckld LTh 72. **d** 72 **p** 78 Ch Ch. C of Cashmere Hills 72-74; Riccarton St Pet 74-78; V of Ellesmere Dio Ch Ch from 78. *St John's Vicarage, 28 Selwyn Street, Leeston, NZ.* (801)

GRAHAM, Douglas Leslie. Late Scho of Trin Coll Dub BA 31, MA 34. **d** 37 **p** 38 Ox. Asst Master Eton Coll and L to Offic Dio Ox 37-41; Chap RNVR 41-45; Hd Master of Portora R Sch 45-54; Dean Close Sch Cheltm 54-68; Select Pr Univ of Ox 56-57. *Forest Cottage, West Woods, Lockeridge, Wilts, SN8 4EG.* (Lockeridge 432)

GRAHAM, Preb Douglas Wrixon. b 13. Trin Coll Dub BA 39. **d** 41 Down **p** 43 Dub for Oss. C of Donaghcloney 41-42; Dundrum 42-43; New Ross 43-50; I of Killegney U 50-66; Roscommon U Dio Elph from 66; Preb of Elph Cathl from 79. *Rectory, Abbey Town, Roscommon, Irish Republic.* (Roscommon 6230)

GRAHAM, Duncan Claire MacRae. b 49. Trent Univ Ont BA 73. Trin Coll Tor 74. **d** 76 Hur for Niag. C of St Geo St Catharines 76-77. *Box 893, Catharines, Ont, Canada, L2R 6Z4.*

GRAHAM, Edgar George. b 55. Sarum Wells Th Coll 74. **d** 78 **p** 79 Connor. C of Ch Ch Lisburn Dio Connor from 78. *4 Llewellyn Avenue, Lisburn, Co Antrim, N Ireland.*

GRAHAM, Frederick Lawrence. b 35. TCD BA 65, Div Test 66. **d** 66 **p** 67 Connor. C of St Matt Shankill Belf 66-69; Team V of Chelmsley Wood 69-73; Ch of Ireland Youth Officer 73-78; C of Ballymacash (in c of Stoneyford) Dio Connor from 78. *Stoneyford Vicarage, Lisburn, Co Antrim, N Ireland.* (Stoneyford 203)

GRAHAM, Frederick Louis Roth. b 20. Selw Coll Cam BA 47, MA 49. Ridley Hall Cam. **d** 50 **p** 51 Win. C of Shirley 50-53; R of St Jo Evang Old Trafford 53-61; Wombwell 61-71; V of Thorne 71-77; C-in-c of Chilton Polden w Edington Dio B & W from 77; Catcott Dio B & W from 77. *Chilton Polden Vicarage, Bridgwater, Somt.* (Chilton Polden 722454)

GRAHAM, Geoffrey Noel. b 02. Univ of Lon Dipl Th 41. St Andr Coll Pampisford, 41. **d** 41 **p** 42 Lich. C of Hartshill 41-44; C-in-c St Mich AA Cross Heath Conv Distr 44-46; R of Farmington 46-50; V of Turkdean 47-50; R of Upton St Leon 50-55; Chief Insp of Schs Dio Glouc 50-55; L to Offic Dio Bradf 55-60; V of Cowling 60-63; Austwick 63-68; Perm to Offic Dio Glouc from 74. *84 Roman Way, Bourton-on-the-Water, GL54 2HD.* (Bourton-on-the-Water 21355)

GRAHAM, George David. b 42. Jes Coll Cam BA 64, MA 68. Lon Coll Div 66. **d** 71 **p** 72 Pet. C of St Columba Corby 71-74; St John Deptford 74-77; V of St Pet Brockley Dio S'wark from 77. *St Peter's Vicarage, Wickham Road, SE4 1LT.* (01-692 4248)

GRAHAM, George Gordon. St Chad's Coll Dur BA 48, Dipl Th 50, MSc 71. **d** 50 Bedford for St Alb **p** 51 St Alb. C of Ch Ch Luton 50-53; Bakewell (in c of St Ann-over-Haddon) 53-56; PC of Wheatley Hill 56-69; V of Hunwick Dio Dur from 69. *Hunwick Vicarage, Crook, Co Durham, DL15 0JU.* (Bishop Auckland 604456)

GRAHAM, Gordon Cecil. b 31. Late Tancred Stud of Ch Coll Cam BA 53, MA 57 . Ripon Hall, Ox 53. **d** 55 **p** 56 Man. C of Em Didsbury 55-58; Rochdale 58-60; R of Heaton Mersey 60-67; Chap and Asst Master Hulme Gr Sch Oldham 67-74; L to Offic Dio Man 67-73; Dio Ches from 73. *21 The Crescent, Davenport, Stockport, Chesh.* (061-483 6011)

GRAHAM, Canon Harold Alexander Vermont. St Pet Coll Ja. **d** 22 **p** 23. C of Spanish Town Cathl 22-25; R of Kings w Bluefields 25-27; Harewood 27-31; Balaclava 31-35; Annotto Bay 35-43; Morant Bay 43-69; Can of Ja 57-69; Can (Emer) from 69. *Duncans PO, Jamaica, W Indies.*

GRAHAM, Ven Harold Alfred Douglas. St Columb's Hall Wang ThL 36. **d** 37 Wang **p** 38 Bath. C of Wang 37-38; Junee 38; Forbes 38-39; Isivita 39-41; R of Nagambie 41-42; Chap AIF 42-43; R of Wellington Dio Bath from 43; Archd of Marsden 54-61 and 65-68; Barker 61-65; and from 71; Long 68-71; Exam Chap to Bp of Bath from 75. *Rectory, Wellington, NSW, Australia 2820.* (068-62 1868)

GRAHAM, Canon Ian Hamilton. St Jo Coll Auckld LTh 64. **d** 56 **p** 57 Waik. C of Te Awamutu 56-58; V of Kawhia 58-59; Chap to HM Pris Te Awamutu 59-61; V of Inglewood 61-65; Otorohanga 65-71; Forest Lake Dio Waik from 71; Can of Waik from 80. *Box 5496, Frankton, Hamilton, NZ.* (76-581)

GRAHAM, Canon Isaac Wilson. b 34. Em Coll Sask. **d** 58 **p** 59 Sask. I of Meadow Lake 58-63; St Geo Prince Albert E 63-69; Leask 69-73; Shellbrook 69-77; Hon Can of Sask 71-77; Athab from 80; R of Fairview Dio Athab from 77. *Box 727, Fairview, Alta, TOH 1LO., Canada.*

GRAHAM, John Francis Ottiwell Skelton. b 15. G and C Coll Cam BA 37, MA 48. Wells Th Coll 37. **d** 39 **p** 40 Liv. C of Walton-on-the-Hill (in c of St Aid) 39-48; V of Speke 48-58; Winterbourne Earls w Winterbourne Dauntsey and Winterbourne Gunner 58-72; R of Bincombe w Broadwey 72-80. *57 Southampton Road, Lymington, Hants. SO4 9GH.*

GRAHAM, Llewellyn Charles Edwards. Univ of W Ont BA 38. Hur Coll Ont LTh 39. **d** 39 Hur for NS **p** 40 NS. C of All SS Cathl Halifax 39-41; I of Delhi w Lyndoch 41-43; C of Ch Ch Ott 43-50; R of Almonte 50-56; St Aug Coll Cant 56-58; R of Perth Ott 58-62; C of Grace Ch-on-the-Hill Tor 63-65; R of St Chris Ott 65-72; St Alb Ott 72-77. *4-344 Daly Avenue, Ottawa, Ont, Canada.*

GRAHAM, Very Rev Malcolm Frederick. b 15. TCD BA 37. **d** 40 **p** 41 Down. C of St Martin Ballymacarret 40-45; Templemore 45-47; C-in-c of Clondehorkey 47-48; R 48-53; St Luke w Lower Falls Belf 53-60; I of Kilbroney 60-79; RD of Kilbroney 61-79; Newry and Mourne 61-79; Preb of St Patr Cathl Dub 69-72; Dean of Killala from 79; Bp's C of Kilmoremoy Dio Killala from 79. *Rectory, Crossmolina, Co Mayo, Irish Republic.*

GRAHAM, Matthew. b 30. Univ Coll Dur BSc 54. Univ of K Coll Halifax BD 71. Ridley Hall Cam 54. **d** 56 **p** 57 Derby. C of Littleover 56-59; C of Em Fazakerley 59-61; V of St Geo Huyton 61-65; R of Sackville Dio Fred 65-71; R of Dorchester Dio Fred 65-71; V of St Columba Sutton Coldfield Dio Birm from 71. *280 Chester Road North, Sutton Coldfield, W Midl, B73 6RR.* (021-354 5873)

GRAHAM, Michael. b 30. Westcott Ho Cam. **d** 61 **p** 62 Man. C of Withington 61-64; V of St Mich AA Lawton Moor Dio Man from 64. *Vicarage, Orton Road, Wythenshawe, Manchester 23.* (061-998 2461)

GRAHAM, Michael Alastair. b 47. Div Hostel Dub 67. **d** 70 **p** 71 Dub. C of Clontarf 71-75; St Mich Ox 76-78; P-in-c of St Jo Evang Sandymount Dio Dub from 80. *18 Trimleston Drive, Booterstown, Co Dublin, Irish Republic.* (Dublin 692704)

GRAHAM, Canon Peter Bartlemy. b 23. K Coll Cam BA (2nd cl Med and Mod Lang Trip pt i) 47, 2nd cl Med and Mod Lang pt ii 48, MA 52. Ely Th Coll. **d** 52 **p** 53 St Alb. C of St Alb Abbey 52-55; V of Eaton Bray 55-64; R of Harpenden 64-73; Surr 65-73; V of Aylesbury 72-82; Surr 73-82; Hon Can of Ch Ch Ox 79-82; R of Elford Dio Lich from 82; Adv in Pastoral Care & Counselling Dio Lich from 82. *Rectory, Elford, Tamworth, Staffs.*

GRAHAM, Reginald Edgar. b 09. Univ of Lon BA 33. AKC 34. MRCS LRCP 50. DA FFARCS 61. Ely Th Coll 32. **d** 34 **p** 35 S'wark C of St Phil Cheam Common 34-38; H Spirit Clapham 38-41; St Luke Glas 41-46; R 46-51. *11 Lambton Crescent, Sedgefield, Co Durham.*

GRAHAM, Canon Robert John. b 15. BD (Lon) 54. Bp Wilson Th Coll IM. **d** 42 **p** 43 Wakef. C of Ravensthorpe 42-44; Ch Ch Skipton 44-47; C-in-c of St Martin's Conv Distr Heaton 47-49; V of Grimethorpe 49-55; Asst Synodal Sec Conv of York 51-67; Sec and Treas from 67; Ed *York Journal of Convocation* from 58; V of Beeston Hill 55-58; Howden 58-78; Wressell 62-78; Barmby-Marsh 62-78; Proc Conv York 65-70; RD of Howden 70-78; Can and Preb of York Minster 74-78; Can (Emer) from 78. *The Old Parsonage Flat, Clumber Park, Worksop, Notts, S80 3BE.* (0909-472045)

GRAHAM, Ronald Fleming. b 33. Edin Th Coll 67. **d** and **p** 69 Aber. Chap St Andr Cathl Aber 69-73; R of Ch of Good Shepherd Hillington Glas 73-75; Ascen Moss Park Glas 75-76; Peterhead 76-80; Itin P and Bp's Chap Dio Arg Is from 80. *St Adamnan's Rectory, Duror of Appin, Argyll, PA38 4BS.* (Duror 218)

GRAHAM, Roy Richard Arthur. b 39. ALCD (1st cl) 62. BD (Lon) 63. Open Univ BA 78. **d** 63 **p** 64 Portsm. C of St Jude Southsea 63-66; Morden (in c of Em) 66-70; V of Tittensor 70-79; R of Hurworth Dio Dur from 79; Dinsdale w Sockburn Dio Dur from 79. *Rectory, Croft Road, Hurworth, Darlington, DL2 2HD.* (Darlington 720362)

GRAHAM, Thomas Edward. b 31. Univ of Nebraska BA 53. Univ of Iowa MA 69, PhD 75. Lutheran Sch of Th Chicago MDiv 57. **d** 80 **p** 81 Rupld. Hon C of St Luke Winnipeg Dio Rupld from 80. *276 Harvard Avenue, Winnipeg, Manit, Canada, R3M 0K7.*

GRAHAM, William Andrew. Em Coll Sktn. **d** 56 **p** 57 Arctic. Miss Pangnirtung 56-61; Port Harrison 62-75; Hon Can of St Jude's Pro-Cathl Frobisher Bay 66-75; I of Milford Bay Dio Alg from 75. *Milford Bay, Ont., Canada.*

GRAHAM, William Eadington. b 1894. **d** 61 **p** 62 Sktn. R of St Luke Sktn 61-68; Perm to Offic Dio Newc T from 73. *18 Northumberland Avenue, Gosforth, Newcastle, NE3 4XE.* (Newc 853790)

GRAHAM, William Harold. Univ of Melb BA 43, ACT ThL 44. **d** 44 **p** 45 Gippsld. C of Drouin 44-45; P-in-c of Rosedale 45-46; Sub-Warden of St Geo Coll Perth 46-49; Chap Grimwade Ho Melb 49-54; P-in-c of Sunbury 54-56; Chap Kew and RP Ment Hosps 56-61; R Melb Hosp 61-66; Exam Chap to Abp of Melb 61; I of Kooyong 66-69; Archd of Kew 66-69; Chap Yarra Valley C of E Sch 69-75; Perm to Offic Dio Tas 76-79; C in Dept of Chap Dio Melb from 79. *161 Lincoln Road, Croydon, Vic, Australia 3136.* (723 3051)

GRAHAM, William James. ACT ThL 62. Moore Th Coll Syd 62. **d** 62 **p** 63 Syd. C of St Barn Syd 62-64; H Trin Adel 64-68; CMS Miss Dio Chile 69-74; Prec of Syd Cathl 74-77; R of St Mark Avalon Dio Syd from 77. *4 Kevin Street, Avalon Beach, NSW, Australia 2107.* (918-2829)

GRAHAM, William Victor. Hur Coll. **d** 62 **p** 63 Hur. C of St Barn Windsor Ont 63-64; R of Harrow Ont 64-70; I of Trin Sarnia 70-76; St Aid Windsor Dio Hur from 76. *264 Jefferson Boulevard, Windsor, Ont., Canada.* (519-948 0625)

GRAHAM-BROWN, John George Francis. b 34. CA (Scotld) 60. Wycl Hall Ox 60. **d** 63 **p** 64 Dur. C of Darlington 63-67; Rufforth w Moor Monkton 67-73; Hon C St Barn City and Dio York from 73; Sec York Redundant Chs Uses Committee from 69. *204 Mount Vale, York, YO2 2DL.* (0904-55466)

GRAHAM-HARRISON, Evelyn Cyril Arthur. b 01. Magd Coll Ox 3rd cl Hist 23, BA and MA 26. Ely Th Coll 25. **d** 26 Stepney for Lon **p** 27 Lon. C of St Columba Haggerston 26-34; St Mich Shoreditch (in c of St Agatha Finsbury) 35-37; V of St Bart L Lon 37-40; Hosp of St Bart's Hosp 37-40; R of The Lea 41-46; Chap RNVR 44-46; V of Minster Lovell 46-53; R of Lamport w Faxton 53-66; Perm to Offic Dio Cant from 66; Dio Chich from 66. *Glyndes, Wittersham, Tenterden, Kent.* (Wittersham 398)

GRAHAM-ORLEBAR, Ian Henry Gaunt. b 26. New Coll Ox BA (2nd cl Jurispr) 49, MA 56. Cudd Coll 60. **d** 62 **p** 63 St Alb. [f Solicitor] C of Hemel Hempstead 62-70; R of Barton-le-Cley (w Higham Gobion and Hexton from 80) Dio St Alb from 70; R of Higham Gobion 70-80. *Barton-le-Cley Rectory, Bedford, MK45 4LA.* (Luton 881226)

GRAHAMSTOWN, Lord Bishop of. *See* Oram, Right Rev Kenneth Cyril.

GRAHAMSTOWN, Assistant Bishop of. *See* Sobukwe, Right Rev Ernest Archibald.

GRAHAMSTOWN, Dean of. *See* Barker, Very Rev Roy Thomas.

GRAIN, Anthony Ernest. CCC Cam BA 31, MA 35. Ely Th Coll 31. **d** 32 **p** 33 Lon. C of St Clem Fulham 32-34; Cheshunt 35-41; C-in-c of Eversholt 41-43; V of Stotfold 43-48; Chap CCG 48-52; Chap at Marseilles 52-55; P-in-c of St Barn Miss Edin 55-58; Chap de Carteret Sch Mandeville Jamaica 61-62; Springvale Sch Dio Mashon 63-70; L to Offic Dio Mashon from 71. *c/o Box UA7, Salisbury, Zimbabwe.*

GRAIN, Canon Keith Charles. b 27. K Coll Lon and Warm AKC 51. **d** 52 **p** 53 Wakef. C of Liversedge 52-55; Barnsley 55-60; V of Hanging Heaton 60-70; Heckmondwike Dio Wakef from 70; Hon Can of Wakef Cathl from 74; RD of Birstall from 79. *Vicarage, Heckmondwike, Yorks, WF16 0AX.* (Heckmondwike 405881)

GRAINGE, Alan Herbert. b 16. Univ Coll Dur BA 49, MA 53. Sarum Th Coll 49. M SSJE 76. **d** 51 **p** 52 Linc. C of St Jo Div Gainsborough Lincs 51-54; P-in-c of St Mary's Pro-Cathl Bath 54-60; Hon Can of Bath Cathl 56-60; P-in-c of Fajara w Serekunda 58-60; Archd of Gambia 58-60; V of Immingham 61-70; Perm to Offic Dio Ox 70-74; L to Offic Dio Ox from 74; Leic from 80. *St John's House, 2 Woodland Avenue, Leicester.*

GRAINGER, Bruce. b 37. Univ of Nottm BA (2nd cl Th) 62. Cudd Coll 62. **d** 64 **p** 65 Bradf. C of Bingley 64-67; Chap and Asst Master K Sch Cant and L to Offic Dio Cant 67-72; Hon Min Can of Cant 69-72; V of Baildon Dio Bradf from 72; M Gen Syn from 82. *Baildon Vicarage, Shipley, W Yorks, BD17 6BY.* (Bradford 594941)

GRAINGER, George Thomas. b 13. Nottm Th Coll. **d** 57 **p** 58 Lon. C of St Helen Kens 57-59; C-in-c of Ch Ch Conv Distr Southall w H Redeemer Gt Greenford 59-64; V of Ch the Redeemer Southall Dio Lon from 64. *Vicarage, Allenby Road, Southall, Middx.* (01-578 2711)

GRAINGER, Roger Beckett. b 34. Univ of Birm MA 70. Univ of Leeds PhD 79. Univ of Lon BA 80. Lich Th Coll 64. **d** 66 **p** 69 Lich. C of W Bromwich 66-68; Walsall 69-73; Chap Stanley Royd Hosp Wakef from 73. *Stanley Royd Hospital, Wakefield, WF1 4DQ.* (Wakef 375217)

GRAINGER, William David. b 10. **d** and **p** 79 S'wark. Hon C of St Jo Evang Waterloo Rd Lambeth Dio S'wark from 79. *36 Dulwich Village, SE21 7AL.* (01-693 2171)

GRAMLEY, John Cyrus. Lycoming Coll USA BA 53. St Paul's Coll Grahmstn 64. **d** 65 **p** 67 Damar. C of Windhoek 65-67; R of Luderitz 67-73. *PO Box 401, Luderitz, SW Africa.*

GRANCHELLI, Gordon Francis. Dalhousie Univ BA 66. K Coll NS BST 68. **d** 66 **p** 67 NS. I of Falmouth 66-72; on leave. *115 Patric Avenue, Sydney, NS, Canada.* (539-5484)

GRANGE, Tom Wilkinson. b 01. St Cath Coll Cam 2nd cl Hist Trip pt i 24, BA (2nd cl Hist Trip pt ii) 25, MA 29. Ridley Hall Cam 25. **d** 27 **p** 28 Bradf. C of Pudsey 27-29; Lanc 29-32; V of St Anne Lanc 32-36; St Barn Morecambe 36-41; St Lawr Barton 41-48; Melling (w Tatham from 56) 48-66. *14 Haverbreaks Place, Lancaster, LA1 5BH.* (Lancaster 65405)

GRANGER, Arthur Charles. b 1899. St Paul's Coll Burgh 22. **d** 25 **p** 26 Truro. C of Kenwyn 25-27; St Jo Cathl Antig 27-30; R of St Phil Antig 30-39; C of Hugglescote 39-41; V of Donisthorpe 41-56; R of H Trin Jersey 56-76. *Springfield House, Trinity, Jersey, CI.*

GRANGER, Canon Ronald Harry. b 22. Selw Coll Cam BA 49, MA 53. Cudd Coll 49. **d** 51 **p** 52 Portsm. C of St Mary Portsea 51-57; V of St Jo Evang Sandown IW 57-63; Ryde 63-70; Petersfield w Sheet Dio Portsm from 70; RD of E Wight 65-70; Petersfield 75-80; Hon Can of Portsm from 67; P-in-c of Buriton Dio Portsm from 79. *Vicarage, Swan Street, Petersfield, Hants, GU32 3AJ.* (Petersfield 4138)

GRANGER, Thomas Leigh. Univ of W Ont BA 62. Trin Coll Tor STB 65. **d** and **p** 65 Tor for Moos. I of Long Lac 67-74; C of Geraldton Dio Moos from 74. *Box 872, Geraldton, Ont., Canada.* (807-854 1433)

GRANGER, Very Rev William James. b 1891. Codr Coll Barb. **d** 49 **p** 50 Nass. C of St Agnes Nass 49-50; P-in-c of St Sav Cat I 50-61; Chap Foxhill Pris and Boys' Sch Nass 61-72; Can of Nass 67-72; Dean and R of Ch Ch Cathl Nass Dio Nass from 72; VG Dio Nass from 78. *PO Box N-653, Nassau, Bahamas, W Indies.* (21523)

GRANT, Alastair Sims. SS Coll Cam BA 49, MA 53. Sarum Th Coll 49. **d** 51 **p** 52 Pet. C of St Jas Northn 51-54; Conisborough 54-57; Org Sec CECS for E Anglia 57-58; V of Haddenham 58-65. *9 Manor Avenue, Penwortham, Preston, Lancs.*

GRANT, Andrew Richard. b 40. Univ of Wales BA 62. Chich Th Coll 63. **d** 65 **p** 66 S'wark. C of St Jo Div Kennington 65-69; Hon C 70-72; Stockwell Green 69-70; V of St Antony Nunhead 72-79; R of N Lambeth Dio S'wark from 79. *St Anselm's Vicarage, Kennington Road, SE11.* (01-735 3415)

GRANT, Antony Richard Charles. b 34. Ch Ch Coll Ox BA 59, MA 64. Coll of Resurr Mirfield 72. **d** 74 **p** 75 Lon. C of St John's Wood 74-77; Novice CR Mirfield 77-79; M from 79; L to Offic Dio Wakef from 80. *House of The Resurrection Mirfield, W Yorks, WF14 0BN.*

GRANT, Arthur Glyndwr Webber. Wells Th Coll 52. **d** 54 **p** 55 Lich. C of Cannock 54-57; St Aug Miss Penhalonga 57-63; Paignton (in c of St Bonif) 63-68; Good Shepherd Preston 68-76; Moulsecoomb 76-80; P-in-c of Wartling Dio Chich from 80; Chap HM Pris Northeye from 80. *Wartling Vicarage, Boreham Street, Nr Hailsham, E Sussex, BN27 4SD.* (Hurstmonceux 2506)

GRANT, Daniel Ian. Sir Geo Williams Univ Montr BA 62. Montr Dioc Tr Coll LTh 65. **d** 64 Montr. C of Trin Mem Ch Montr 64-67; Ch Ch Cathl Vancouver 67-70; R of St Cath N Vanc Dio New Westmr from 70. *1062 Ridgewood Drive, North Vancouver, BC, Canada.*

GRANT, David Francis. Chich Th Coll. **d** 60 Lon **p** 61 Kens for Lon. C of St Pet Acton Green 60-63; Ruislip 63-68; V of Oving w Merston 68-75; Dom Chap to Bp of Chich 68-75; R of Graffham w Woolavington Dio Chich from 75. *Graffham Rectory, Petworth, W Sussex.* (Graffham 247)

GRANT, David Rogers Ogilvie. b 25. K Coll Lon and Warm AKC 52. **d** 53 **p** 54 Lon. C of St Geo-in-the-East Lon 53-54; Belmont Middx 54-57; Ch Ch St Pancras 57-60; V of Ainstable w Armathwaite 60-68; Ireleth w Askam 68-74; Haverthwaite (w Finsthwaite from 75) 74-77; P-in-c of Finsthwaite 74-75; Pastoral Care of Staveley-in-Cartmel 76-77; V of Leven Valley Dio Carl from 77. *Leven Valley Vicarage, Haverthwaite, Ulverston, Cumb, LA12 8AJ.* (Newby Bridge 476)

GRANT, Douglas George. Lich Th Coll 37. **d** 40 **p** 41 Newc T. C of All SS Gosforth 40-45; St Andr Newc T 45-48; V of St Hilda Jesmond Newc T 48-79; Master of St Mary Magd Hosp Newc T from 79. *c/o 46 Sanderson Road, Jesmond, Newcastle-upon-Tyne.* (Newc T 813130)

GRANT, Douglas Wyndham Maling. b 22. Trin Coll Cam BA 48, MA 52. Edin Th Coll 53. **d** 55 **p** 56 Moray. Prec of St Andr Cathl Inverness 55-58; R of St Andr Banff and of St Jo Bapt Portsoy 58-61; P-in-c of St Columba Grantown-on-Spey w Rothiemurcus 61-65; R of Lenzie 65-70; Alyth 70-78; Blairgowrie 70-78; Inverurie Dio Aber from 78; Alford Dio Aber from 78; Auchindoir Dio Aber from 78; P-in-c of Kemnay Dio Aber from 78. *Rectory, St Mary's Place, Inverurie, Aberdeen, AB5 9QN.* (Inverurie 20470)

GRANT, Prec Edward Francis. Trin Coll Dub BA 37. **d** 40 **p** 41 Oss. C of New Ross 40-43; C-in-c of Preban w Moyne 43-46; I of Eethard U 46-56; RD of Carnew 54-60; C-in-c of Ardcolm 56-70; I of Wexford w Ardcolm Dio Ferns from 70; Preb of Kilrane and Taghmon in Ferns Cathl 57-63; Treas 64-65; Chan 65-69; Prec from 69; RD of New Ross from 60. *Rectory, Wexford, Irish Republic.*

GRANT, Evert Ronald. b 09. K Coll Lon BA 32, BD 34, AKC (1st cl) 34. **d** 36 **p** 37 Lich. C of Cheadle Staffs 36-39; V of Oakamoor w Cotton 39-48; Cauldon 48-56; V of Waterfall 48-56; Cheswardine 56-71. *17 Naish Road, Barton-on-Sea, Hants, BH25 7PT.*

GRANT, Geoffrey. b 27. Lich Th Coll 55. **d** 58 **p** 59 Bris. C of St Mark Swindon 58-62; V of St Thos Ap Eastville Bris 62-67; Sherston Magna w Pinkney and Easton-Grey 67-75; C-in-c of Luckington w Alderton 71-75; Publ Pr 75-76; V of St Mary Cotham 76-78; St Sav w St Mary Cotham 78-80; R of Yate New Town Dio Bris from 80. *Yate Rectory, Bristol.* (Chipping Sodbury 313105)

GRANT, Geoffrey Leslie. b 33. Trin Coll Cam BA 57, MA 61. Ridley Hall, Cam. **d** 59 **p** 60 Lon. C of Chelsea 59-64; R of Nacton and Levington (w Bucklesham and Foxhall from 78) Dio St E from 64; P-in-c of Bucklesham w Brightwell and Foxhall 75-76; Chap Orwell Park Sch Nacton from 64. *Nacton Rectory, Ipswich, Suff, IP10 0HY.* (Nacton 232)

✠ **GRANT, Right Rev James Alexander.** Univ of Melb BA (2nd cl Hist) 54. Trin Coll Melb ACT ThL (1st cl) 58. Melb Coll of Div BD 69. **d** 59 **p** 60 Melb. C of Murrumbeena 59-60; Dioc Task Force w Heidelberg 60; Broadmeadows 61-66; Dom and Exam Chap to Abp of Melb 66-70; Chap Trin Coll Melb 70; Hon Chap 71; Cons Bp Coadj of Melb 21 Dec 70 in St Paul's Cathl Melb by Abp of Melb; Bps of St Arn; Bend; Gippsld; Wang; Bps Strong and Dann; Chairman Dioc Dept of Chr Educn from 71; Res Fell Trin Coll Melb from 75. *8 Stanley Grove, Canterbury, Vic., Australia 3126.* (82 6714)

GRANT, John Peter. b 19. TD 50. Wycl Hall, Ox. **d** 62 **p** 63 Chich. C of St Paul w St Bart Chich 62-64; R of Adwell w S Weston 64-67; V of Lewknor 64-67; Chap Warneford Hosp Ox 67-71; R of Hartley Rhodesia 71-80; CF 74-80; V of Gayton Dio Nor from 80; P-in-c of Westacre Dio Nor from 80; Gayton Thorpe w E Walton Dio Nor from 80. *Gayton Vicarage, King's Lynn, Norf.* (Gayton 227)

GRANT, Kenneth Gordon. ARCM 54. K Coll Lon and Warm. **d** 55 **p** 56 Glouc. C of Wotton-under-Edge 55-58; R of Charfield Dio Glouc from 58. *Charfield Rectory, Wotton-under-Edge, Glos.* (Falfield 260489)

GRANT, Kenneth Wallace Walmsley. b 30. Moore Coll Syd 77. **d** 78 Graft. Hon C of Coffs Harbour Dio Graft from 78. *c/o PO Box 163, Coffs Harbour, NSW, Australia 2450.*

GRANT, Very Rev Malcolm Etheridge. b 44. Univ of Edin BSc (2nd cl Chem) 66, BD (2nd cl) 69. Edin Th Coll 66. **d** 69 **p** 70 Glas. C of St Mary's Cathl Glas 69-72; Grantham (in c of Epiph Earlesfield) 72; Team V 72-78; P-in-c of St Ninian Invergordon 78-81; Exam Chap to Bp of Moray 79-81; Provost and R of St Mary's Cathl Glas from 81. *45 Rowallan Gardens, Glasgow, G11 7LH.* (041-339 4956)

GRANT, Murray William. b 36. Chich Th Coll 64. **d** 66 Warrington for Liv **p** 67 Liv. C of St Anne Stanley 66-70; St

Mary Magd Munster Sq St Pancras 70-74; St Sav w St Jas L Westmr Dio Lon from 74. *3 Moreton Place, SW1.* (01-828 8404)

GRANT, Rodney Arthur. b 26. K Coll Lon and Warm AKC 52. **d** 53 **p** 54 Edin. C of St Jas Leith 53-56; Musselburgh (in c of Prestonpans) 56-59; P-in-c 59-60; St Aid Miss Niddrie Mains 60-72; R of Ch Ch Trinity Road Leith 72-80; St Jas Inverleith Row (and Ch Ch Trinity Road Leith from 80) City and Dio Edin from 72. *5 Wardie Road, Edinburgh, EH5 3QE.* (031-552 4300)

GRANT, Roy Malcolm. d and **p** 55 Perth. C of Wembley 55-57; P-in-c of Hilton Pk 57-60; Sag Sag 63-68; C of St Jas Toowoomba 68-69; R of Goondiwindi 69-74; Nambour Dio Brisb from 74. *174 Currie Street, Nambour, Queensland, Australia 4560.* (Nambour 41 1018)

GRANT, Stephen Laurence. d 41 **p** 42 RC Bp of Portsm. Rec into C of E by Bp of Croydon 49. C of St Nich Guildf 50-52; CF 52-60; R of Downton w Burrington Aston and Elton 60-66; Etton w Helpston 66-79. *24 Goodwood Avenue, Bridgnorth, Salop.*

GRANT, Stuart David. b 51. Univ of Syd BA. Moore Th Coll Syd BTh. **d** 81 Syd. C of St Andr Dundas Dio Syd from 81. *Unit 9, 13-15 Robert Street, Telopea, NSW, Australia 2117.*

GRANT, William Ainslie Macintosh. BC Coll Bris 39. **d** 41 **p** 42 St E. C of Grundisburgh and Hasketon 41-43; CF (EC) 43-46; Hon CF 46; R of Finningham 46-50; Douglas w Campbell Griquatown and Hopetown 50-52; R of Letton w Willersley and Staunton-on-Wye 52-54; C of St Mich St Alb 54-56; R of Clophill 56-62; R of Morcott w S Luffenham 62-64; V of St Steph Colchester 64-70; R of Tendring 70-75; Frating w Thorrington 75-79. *1 Cinque Port Road, Brightlingsea, Nr Colchester, Essex.*

GRANT, William Frederick. b 23. Fitzw Ho Cam BA 48, MA 50. Wycl Hall, Ox 51. **d** 53 Lon **p** 54 Kens for Lon. C of St Paul Canonbury 53-57; CF (R of O) from 56; V of All SS Caledonian Road Isl 57-60; Asst Master Leatherhead Co Secondary Sch from 60; Perm to Offic Dio Guildf from 66. *50 Hillside Gardens, Brockham, Betchworth, Surrey.*

GRANT, Very Rev William James. b 29. **d** 58 **p** 59 Down. C of S Miss Ballymacarrett 58-60; St Geo Belf 60-63; I of Grand Falls 63-66; Asst Chap Miss to Seamen Dub 66-70; I of Fethard w Tintern and Killesk 70-77; Cong U 77-81; Dom Chap to Bp of Tuam from 77; Archd of Tuam from 80; Dean and R of Tuam Cathl from 81; Warden of Lay Readers from 81. *Deanery, Tuam, Co Galway,* (Tuam 24180)

GRANTHAM, Bishop Suffragan of. *See* Hawker, Right Rev Dennis Gascoyne.

GRASON, Philip Charles. b 24. **d** 79 **p** 80 Wai. Hon C of Opotiki Dio Wai from 79. *114 Bridge Street, Opotiki, NZ.*

GRATTON, Donald Peter. Wycl Coll Tor 54. **d** 55 Tor for Amrit **p** 56 Amrit. I of St Paul Amrit 55-58; CMS Miss Srinager 58-63; R of Erindale 64-74; St Timothy City and Dio Tor from 74. *40 Ridley Boulevard, Toronto, Ont., Canada.* (416-481 0587)

GRATY, Canon John Thomas. b 33. Univ Coll Ox BA 58, MA 60. Coll of Resurr Mirfield 58. **d** 60 **p** 61 Cov. C of St Mark Cov 60-63; St Mary Hitchin (in c of St Mark) 63-67; V of St Alb Stoke Heath 67-75; C-in-c of Warmington w Shotteswell Dio Cov 75-77; R (w Radway and Ratley) from 77; P-in-c of Radway w Ratley 75-77; RD of Dassett Magna 76-79; Hon Can of Cov Cathl from 80. *Warmington Rectory, Banbury, Oxon.* (Farnborough Warws 213)

GRAVELL, David Ernald. b 1898. St D Coll Lamp Phillips Scho 18, BA 19, BD 27. **d** 21 **p** 22 St D. C of Abergwili 21-24; Eglwys Newydd 24-27; Mynyddisllwyn 27-30; R of Wolves Newton w Kilgwrrwg 31-57; V of Llanddewi Rhydderch and R of Llanwapley 57-68. *Bryn Hyfryd, Bancffos-Felen, Pontyberem, Llanelli, Dyfed.*

GRAVELL, John Hilary. b 45. Univ of Wales, BA (2nd cl Geog) 65. St D Coll Lamp 66. **d** 68 **p** 69 St D. C of Abth 68-72; R of Llangeitho w Blaenpennal (w Betws Leiki from 73) 72-81; V of Llannon Dio St D from 81. *Y Ficerdy, Llan-Non, Llanelli, Dyfed.* (Crosshands 841358)

GRAVELLE, John Elmer. b 25. St Jo Coll Dur BA 50, Dipl in Th 51. **d** 51 **p** 52 St Alb. C of Luton Beds 51-54; CF 54-58; R of Toddington 58-64; V of Hatfield Hyde 64-71; C-in-c of Great Munden 71-74; Dep Dir Clinical Th Assoc 71-80; Perm to Offic 74-80; P-in-c of Fryerning (w Margaretting from 81) Dio Chelmsf from 80; Margaretting 80-81. *Fryerning Rectory, Ingatestone, Essex.* (Ingatestone 3034)

GRAVELLE, Paul Lynton. b 31. St Jo Coll Auckld. **d** 75 **p** 77 Auckld. Hon C of New Lynn 75-77; Coromandel 77-81; Massey E Dio Auckld from 81. *21 Gardiner Avenue, New Lynn, Auckland 7, NZ.*

GRAVEN, Canon James Harold. KCNS BA 34, MA and LTh 37. **d** 37 **p** 38 NS. C of Pugwash 37-41; Chap RCN 41-45; R of Cornwallis 45-49; Bridgwater 49-55; Truro 55-62; Hon Can of NS from 61; R of Lunenberg 62-68; Archd of S Shore 62-68; Exam Chap to Bp of NS 65-70; R of Jollimore Dio NS from 70; Hon Can of NS 70-72; Can from 72. *Rectory, Jollimore, Halifax, NS, Canada.* (477-5242)

GRAVES, Barry Ashby. b 45. St Jo Th Coll 67. **d** 70 Monteith for Auckld **p** 71 Auckld. C of Henderson 70-73; St Aid Remuera 73-75; V of Clevedon 75-80; St Barn Mt Eden City and Dio Auckld from 80. *St Barnabas Vicarage, Mount Eden, Auckland, NZ.* (600-411)

GRAVES, Canon Eric Arthur. b 13. Univ of Leeds, BA (2nd cl Hist) 34. Coll of Resurr Mirfield, 34. **d** 36 **p** 37 Blackb. C of St Luke Skerton 36-39; Rugby (in c of St John) 39-46; V of Haverhill 46-81; Surr 63-81; Hon Can of St E from 70; RD of Clare 72-81; P-in-c of L Wratting 78-81. *20 Saxon Rise, Bury St Edmunds, Suff.*

GRAVES, Peter. b 33. E Midl Min Tr Course 78. **d** 81 Chich (NSM). C of Roffey Dio Chich from 81. *2 Coniston Close, Roffey, Horsham, RH12 2PE.* (Horsham 58363)

GRAVES, Stanwood Eugene. b 34. E Tennessee Univ BS 68. Episc Th Sem Lexington USA. **d** 68 **p** 68 Lexington. C of Long Island Dio Nass from 68. *Rectory, St Paul's Clarence Town, Long Island, Bahamas.*

GRAVES, William Herbert. b 1895. Wells Th Coll. **d** 47 **p** 48 Ex. C of St Phil Weston Mill Devonport 47-48; R of Bratton Clovelly (w Germansweek from 52) 48-54; C-in-c of Germansweek 50-52; R of Longborough w Sezincote and Condictoe 54-58. *Thicket House, Elm Grove, Southsea, Hants, PO5 1LW.* (Portsmouth 824269)

GRAY, Alan. b 25. Qu Coll Birm 51. LRAM 52. **d** 54 **p** 55 Newc T. C of St Pet Monkseaton 54-56; Seghill (in c of Seaton Delaval) 56-61; C-in-c of St Pet Conv Distr Balkwell 61-66; R of Callander w Lochearnhead and Killin 66-74; P-in-c of Alloa 74-77. *Address temp unknown.*

GRAY, Albert Alan. b 10. **d** 75 **p** 76 Cov (APM). C of Bulkington Dio Cov from 75. *4 Arundel Road, Bulkington, via Nuneaton, Warwicks.*

GRAY, Albert Robert William. AKC 33. **d** 33 **p** 34 S'wark. C of H Redeemer Streatham Vale 33-37; Iver 37-39; CF (TA) 39-45; Hon CF 45 R of Gayton-Thorpe w E Walton V 39-45; Southacre w Westacre 45-47; St Mich Penkevil w Lamorran and Merther Dio Truro from 47. *Tresillian Rectory, Truro, Cornw.* (Tresilian 272)

GRAY, Arthur Alan Western. Late Rustat Scho of Jes Coll Cam 1st cl Cl Trip pt i 25, Carus Gr Test Pri and Wordsworth Stud 26, BA (2nd cl Th Trip pt ii) 27, MA 31. Ridley Hall, Cam 27. **d** 29 **p** 30 S'wark. C of H Trin Richmond 29-31; Chap St Lawr Coll Ramsgate 31-32; Tutor Oak Hill Th Coll 32-35; Warden St Andr CMS Hostel Stoke Newington 35-39; V of H Trin Weston-s-Mare 39-43; Metrop Sec CMS 43-49; Warden Ch Coll Hobart 49-53; SCM Chap Vic Univ Coll Wel 55-61; Hon C of Wel Cathl 55-61; L to Offic Dio Adel from 62. *43 Inverness Avenue, St Georges, S Australia 5066.* (08-79 7932)

GRAY, Arthur Joseph. d 34 **p** 39 St Arn. C of Maryborough 35-36; Murrayville 36-40; V of Merbein 40-42; Chap RAAF 42-46; V of Mooroopna 47-49; R of Linton 49-52; V of Mortlake 52-53; Warracknabeal 54-59; Chap to Bp of Bal 57-61; P-in-c of All SS Bal 59-61; Can of Bal 57-61; I of Kingsville w Spotswood 61-66; V of Kallista 66-69; R of Donald 69-71; Regr Dio St Arn 69; C of Maryborough 72-76; Perm to Offic Dio Bal from 76. *27 Hotham Street, Ballarat, Vic, Australia 3350.* (053-32 1350)

GRAY, Bernard Reginald. b 1898. Ridley Coll Melb 33. ACT ThL 37. **d** 36 **p** 38 Bend. C of Murrabit 36-37; Koondrook 37-38; V 38-39; C of Summertown 39-41; RNVR 41-46; V of Gt w L Tew 47-49; Dropmore St Anne 49-54; Chap at Berne Neuchâtel and Stuttgart 54-68; Asst Chap 68-74. *Ramsay Hall, Byron Road, Worthing, Sussex.*

GRAY, Charles Malcolm. b 38. Lich Th Coll 67. **d** 69 Stepney for Lon **p** 70 Lon. C of St Mary Cable Str Whitechapel 69-72; St Mark Bush Hill Park Lon 72-75; V of H Trin Winchmore Hill Dio Lon from 75. *Holy Trinity Vicarage, King's Avenue, Winchmore Hill, N21 3NA.* (01-360 2947)

GRAY, Christopher John. b 46. Univ of Ex BA (Th) 68. Ripon Hall Ox 71. **d** 73 **p** 74 S'wark. C of Putney 73-76; V of St Andr S Wimbledon 76-81. *c/o 47 Wilton Grove, SW19.*

GRAY, Cyril Samuel. b 08. AKC 40. **d** 40 **p** 41 S'wark. C of St Steph Walworth Common 40-44; Chap RNVR 44-47; C of Potters Bar 47-51; R of Bridford 51-63; V of St Jas L Ham Plymouth 63-74. *16 Lockyer Terrace, Saltash, Cornw, PL12 6DF.* (Saltash 6393)

GRAY, David. d 64 **p** 65 Fred. I of St Martin's w Black River 64-68; R of Salisbury w Havelock 68-71; St Jas St John 71-80; Grand Manan Dio Fred from 81. *Grand Harbour, Grand Mandan, NB, Canada.*

GRAY, David Bryan. b 28. Roch Th Coll 59. **d** 61 **p** 62 Linc. C of St Giles Linc 61-65; V of Thurlby 65-67; C-in-c of Ropsley w L Humby 67-75; Sapperton w Braceby 67-75; Somerby w Gt Humby 67-75; R of Trimley Dio St E from 75. *Trimley Rectory, Ipswich, Suff.* (Felixstowe 6188)

GRAY, David Kenneth. b 22. Sarum Th Coll 53. **d** 55 Kens for Lon **p** 56 Lon. C of Hillingdon 55-60; V of St Pet Edmon 60-65; St Paul Hounslow Heath Dio Lon from 65. *285 Bath Road, Hounslow, Middx, TW3 3DB.* (01-570 1806)

GRAY, Canon Donald Cecil. b 24. Linc Th Coll 49. **d** 50 **p** 51 Pet. C of Abington 50-53; St Paul Bedford and Chap Bedford Gen Hosp 53-56; C of St Paul Knightsbridge 56-59; V of N Holmwood 59-67; RD of Dorking 63-67; Farnham 69-74; R of Farnham Surrey Dio Guildf from 67; Surr from 67; Hon Can of Guildf from 71. *Rectory, Farnham, Surrey.* (Farnham 716119)

GRAY, Donald Clifford. b 30. TD 70. K Coll Lon and Warm AKC 55. Univ of Liv MPhil 80. **d** 56 **p** 57 Man. C of Leigh Lancs 56-60; CF (TA) 58-67; CF (TAVR) 67-77; V of St Pet Westleigh 60-67; All SS Elton Bury Man 67-74; Proc Conv Man 64-74; R of Our Lady and St Nich City and Dio Liv from 74; RD of Liverpool 75-81; Hon Chap to HM the Queen 74-77; M Gen Syn from 80. *Parish Church, Old Church Yard, Liverpool, L2 8TZ.* (051-236 5287)

GRAY, Frank Harold Castell. b 14. ALCD 41 (LTh from 74). **d** 41 **p** 42 Lon. C of Em Northwood 41-45; C-in-c of St Ann Nottm 45-47; V of St Paul Gatten Shanklin 47-53; Prestonville 53-66; St Luke Watford 66-79. *9 Southwell Close, Trull, Taunton, Somt.*

GRAY, Geoffrey Thomas. b 23. Oak Hill Th Coll. **d** 46 **p** 47 Chelmsf. C of Havering-atte-Bower (in c of Calvary Miss) 46-48; Dovercourt 48-49; St Mich Chester Square Lon 49-51; V of Good Shepherd Lee 51-56; C-in-c of St Pet Lee Eltham 52-56; Chap Sir Robert Geffrey's Homes Mottingham 54-56; Hon Sec S'wark Dioc Coun for Work Amongst Men 55-59; Chap to Bermondsey Med Miss 56-59; R of Bermondsey 56-59; C-in-c of St Luke Bermondsey 57-59; V of Yalding 59-66; Gillingham 66-75; RD of Malling 64-66; Gillingham 66-75; Surr 66-75; Ed Roch Dioc Directory 64-70; Perm to Offic Dio Roch 75-80; V of St Nich w St Mary Strood Dio Roch from 80. *Vicarage, Central Road, Strood, Kent.*

GRAY, George Donald Allan. Univ of W Ont BA 60. Hur Coll BTh 62. **d** 62 Bp Appleyard for Hur **p** 63 Hur. C of St Jo Evang Kitchener 63-66; R of Port Dover 66-68; I of St Aid Lon 68-77; Exam Chap to Bp of Hur 70-77; L to Offic Dio Calg from 77. *3803 24th Street NW, Calgary, Alta, Canada.*

GRAY, George Francis Selby. b 03. Late Scho of Trin Coll Cam 1st cl Cl Trip pt i 23, BA (1st cl Cl Trip pt ii) 25, 2nd cl Th Trip pt ii 26, Evans Pri 27, Hulsean Pri 28, MA 29. Westcott Ho Cam 25. **d** 27 **p** 28 Newc T. C of St Luke Newc T 27-29; CMS Miss at Kweilin 30-32; P-in-c 32-34; Lect Centr Th Sch Nanking 34-45; Prof of Ch Hist Huachung Univ 47-51; Exam Chap to Bp of Hankow 49-51; V of Bottisham 51-53; C-in-c of Six Mile Bottom 51-53; Fell of St Aug Coll Cant 53-57; L Pr Dio Cant 53-57; R of Fakenham 57-69; C-in-c of Kettlestone 59-61; RD of Burnham 68-69; V of Over 69-79; Perm to Offic Dios Ely and Chelmsf from 79. *22 Rookery Close, Great Chesterford, Saffron Walden, Essex, CB10 1QA.* (Saffron Walden 30730)

GRAY, George Samuel. b 03. Worc Ordin Coll 60. **d** 62 **p** 63 Sarum. C of Melksham 62-65; R of Owermoigne w Warmwell 65-69; Chap HM Pris Dorch 69-78. *53 Glenferness Avenue, Bournemouth, Dorset, BH3 7EU.*

GRAY, Gerald. **d** 81 Fred (APM). Perm to Offic Dio Fred from 81. *Salisbury, NB, Canada, E0A 3E0.*

GRAY, Harold Reginald St George. b 16. Trin Coll Dub BA and Div Test 40. **d** 40 **p** 41 Liv. C of St Nich Blundellsands 40-43; Chap RN 43-71; R of Slindon w Eartham 71-81. *2 School Terrace, The Street, Walberton, Arundel, W Sussex.*

GRAY, Chan Hugh Henry James. b 21. Trin Coll Dub BA 48, MA 64. **d** 49 **p** 50 Ferns. C of Enniscorthy 49-51; I of Fenagh w Myshall 51-60; Clonenagh U Dio Leigh from 60; RD of Dunleckney from 62; Preb of Oss and Leigh Cathls 70-78; Treas 78-80; Chan from 80; Sec Dioc Bd of Relig Educn from 78; I of Offerlane Dio Oss from 80. *St Peter's Rectory, Mountrath, Leix, Irish Republic.* (0502 32146)

GRAY, John Howard. b 39. St Aid Coll. **d** 65 **p** 66 Man. C of St Cuthb Trafford Pk 65-68; Urmston 68-74; V of St Thos Moorside Dio Man from 74. *Moorside Vicarage, Oldham, Lancs.* (061-624 4311)

GRAY, Joseph William. b 1898. Univ of Dur LTh 31. St Aid Coll 26. **d** 30 **p** 31 Wakef. C of Normanton 30-36; V of St Cath Sandal Magna 36-45; Ch Ch Mt Pellon 45-67. *31 Barnsley Road, Cawthorne, Barnsley, Yorks.*

GRAY, Kenneth Amphlett. b 11. St Jo Coll Dur BA 34, MA and Dipl in Th 37. **d** 35 **p** 36 Guildf. C of St Paul Dorking 35-38; Walcot 38-41; V of Ch Ch Croydon 41-47; R of Clapham w Patching 47-53; BFBS Sec Devon and Cornw 53-56; NW Engl 56-62; Dorset Wilts and N Berks 62-72; Dorset Wilts and SE Somt 72-73; Dorset and Wilts 73-75. *Windwhistle, Triple Plea Road, Woodton, Bungay, Suff NR35 2NS.* (Woodton 395)

GRAY, Kenneth Charles. b 15. **d** 78 Perth. C of Kelmscott Dio Perth from 78. *26 Ecko Road, Kelmscott, W Australia 6111.*

GRAY, Kenneth Rowland. b 20. Worc Ordin Coll 60. **d** 62 **p** 63 Ex. C of St Mary Magd Torquay 62-67; V of Wembury 67-76; P-in-c of Broadhempston w Woodland 76-77; Perm to Offic Dio Ex from 78. *26 Ash Hill Road, Torquay, Devon, TQ1 3HZ.* (Torquay 22221)

GRAY, Martin Clifford. b 44. Westcott Ho Cam 78. **d** 80 **p** 81 Nor. C of Gaywood Dio Nor from 80. *5 Gayton Road, Gaywood, King's Lynn, Norfolk.*

GRAY, Maurice William Halcro. b 27. Hertf Coll Ox BA 48, MA 60. Coll of Resurr Mirfield. **d** 60 **p** 61 Bris. C of Cricklade w Latton 60-63; Chap Ellesmere Coll from 63; L to Offic Dio Lich from 63. *Ellesmere College, Ellesmere, Salop.* (Ellesmere 2321)

GRAY, Michael Frederick Henry. b 36. Lich Th Coll 62. **d** 65 Barking for Chelmsf **p** 66 Chelmsf. C of Ascen Vic Dks 65-67; Plaistow 67-70; Chap RN 70-72. *67 Windsor Road, Chichester, W Sussex, PO19 2XG.*

GRAY, Neil Kenneth. b 48. Kelham Th Coll 67. **d** 71 Blackb **p** 72 Lanc for Blackb. C of Chorley Blackb 71-73; H Trin Blackpool 74-78; P-in-c of St Osw Preston Dio Blackb from 78. *St Oswald's Vicarage, Preston, Lancs, PR1 6XE.* (Preston 795395)

GRAY, Norman. ACT ThL 58. St Mich Th Coll Crafers 53. **d** 58 **p** 59 N Queensld. C of Atherton 58-59; Ingham 59-61; Cairns 61-63; R of Mareeba 63-67; Charters Towers 67-73; Innisfail 73-77; C in Dept of Chap Dio Melb from 77. *Chaplain's Residence, Royal Park Hospital, Parkville, Vic., Australia 3052.* (380 5151)

GRAY, Patrick Trevor Robert. Univ of Tor BA 62. Trin Coll Tor STB 65. Yale Univ STM 66. **d** 65 Bp Snell for Tor **p** 66 Tor. Hon C of St Simon Tor 65-69; C 69-72; on leave 72-78; Hon C of St Marg Hamilton 78-80; St John Ancaster Dio Niag from 80. *Green Knoll, RR2, Lynden, Ont, Canada.*

GRAY, Percy. b 28. TD 71. Univ of Lon BA 53. St Cath S Ox BA (3rd cl Th) 55, MA 59. Wycl Hall Ox 53. **d** 55 **p** 56 Liv. C of Sutton 55-58; Ch Ch Chelsea 58-59; V of St Crispin w Ch Ch Bermondsey Dio S'wark from 59; CF (TA) 59-67; CF (TAVR) from 67. *St Crispin's Vicarage, Southwark Park Road, SE16 2HU.*

GRAY, Philip Thomas. BA (Lon) 65. Chich Th Coll 66. **d** 68 Bradwell for Chelmsf **p** 69 Chelmsf. C of Leigh 68-74; V of Mendlesham Dio St E from 74. *Mendlesham Vicarage, Stowmarket, Suff, IP14 5RS.* (Mendlesham 359)

GRAY, Canon Roy Francis. Univ of Syd BA 52. Moore Th Coll Syd. **d** 47 **p** 48 Syd. C of St Barn Syd 48-49; C-in-c of Provisional Distr of St Anne Hammondville 49-50; R of Cook's River 50-52; St Geo Hurstville 52-57; W Wollongong 57-65; Five Dock 65-73; Cronulla Dio Syd from 73; Can of St Mich Prov Cathl Wollongong from 73. *1 St Andrew's Place, Cronulla, NSW, Australia 2230.* (523-5124)

GRAY, Sidney Patrick. Worc Ordin Coll. **d** and **p** 63 Linc. C of Skegness 63-65; V of Dunholme 65-71; R of Cliffe-at-Hoo w Cooling 71-78; V of St Aug Gillingham Dio Roch from 78. *Vicarage, Rock Avenue, Gillingham, Kent.* (Medway 50288)

GRAY, Stanley. b 23. **d** 69 Bp Russell for Capetn **p** 70 Capetn. Dom Chap to Abp of Capetn 70-72; C of Good Shepherd Maitland 72-76; R of St Mark City and Dio Capetn from 77. *35 Beresford Road, University Estate, Cape Town, S Africa.* (55-1006)

GRAY, Stephen Hatley. b 42. St Jo Coll Morpeth 72. **d** 74 Graft. C of Lismore 74-80; V of Kavina Dio Bal from 80. *Vicarage, Kaniva, Vic, Australia 3419.*

GRAY, Thomas John. b 1899. Lon Coll of Div 31. **d** 33 **p** 34 Down. C of St Phil (Drew Mem) Belf 33-38; C of St Anne's Cathl (in C of Miss Distr) Belf 38-41; C-in-c of St Silas Belfast 41-45; R 45-52; Kilbride 52-55; Tyrella w Rathmullen 55-62; I of Mucknoe w Broomfield (and Clontibret from 63) 62-74. *6 Shimnavale, Newcastle, Co Down, N Ireland.*

GRAY, Timothy Francis de Langley. b 49. St Paul's Coll Grahmstn 75. **d** 77 **p** 78 Johann. C of Vereeniging 77-79; Benoni Dio Johann from 79. *38 O'Reilly Merry Street, North Mead, Benoni 1500, S Africa.*

GRAY, William Christopher. St Barn Coll Adel ACT ThL (2nd cl) 32. **d** 32 **p** 33 Adel. C of St John Adel 32-33; Miss Chap Pinnaroo 34-36; P-in-c of Tailem Bend w Meningie 37-39; R of Burra 39-42; Renmark 42-49; P-in-c of Berri 42-46; Loxton Miss 42-49; R of Hindmarsh 49-56; Mt Barker 56-63; Org Sec ABM and L to Offic Dio Adel 63-67 and from 74; Commiss Kuch 63-68; P-in-c of Tea Tree Gully Miss Distr 67-73; Hon Can of Adel 67-73. *109 Glengyle Terrace, Plympton, Australia 5038.* (297-4871)

GRAY-STACK (formerly STACK), Very Rev Charles Maurice. b 12. Trin Coll Dub BA 34, MA 37. Univ Coll Dur Dipl Th 36. **d** 37 Killaloe **p** 39 Oss. C of Birr w Eglish 37-38; Ardamine 38-40; C-in-c of Kilnahue w Kilpipe 40-41; L to Offic at Instioge 41-44; C of Killarney and Dioc C of Ardf and Agh 44-49; Rathkeale and Nantenan 49-53; I of Kilgobbin 53-61; Kenmare U Dio Ardf from 61; Preb of Ballycahane in St Mary's Cathl Lim 62-63; Prec 63-66; Exam Chap to Bp of Lim 62-70; RD of Listowel 62-65; Kilcolman from 65; Dean of Ardf from 66; Chan of Lim from 66. *St Patrick's Parsonage, Kenmare, Co Kerry, Irish Republic.*

GRAYSHON, Matthew Richard. b 47. St Jo Coll Nottm BTh 81. **d** 81 York. C of St Jo & St Martin Beverley Minster Dio York from 81. *16 The Leases, Beverley, N Humb, HU17 8LG.* (0482 881324)

GRAYSON, Ven Lester William. St Francis Coll Brisb ACT ThL 44. **d** and **p** 44 Brisb. C of St Paul Ipswich 44-45; St Aug Hamilton 45-46; M Bush Bro of St Paul Charleville 46-50; R of All SS chermside 51-61; St Paul Maryborough Dio Brisb from 61; Hon Can of Brisb 63-70; Archd of Wide Bay and Burnett from 70. *21 Churchill Street, Maryborough, Queensland, Australia 4650.* (21 3385)

GRAYSON, Canon Robert William. b 24. Worc Coll Ox BA (2nd cl Mod Hist) 48, MA 49, Dipl Th 50. Wycl Hall Ox 49. **d** 50 Warrington for Liv **p** 51 Liv. C of N Meols 50-53; CMS Miss at Barharwa Dio Bhag 53-55; P-in-c of Ch Ch Bhagalpur and Chap to Bp 55-57; C-in-c of St Paul Litherland 57-61; V of Knowsley 61-66; Stanwix 66-79; RD of Carl 71-79; Hon Can of Carl Cathl from 76; V of Appleby Dio Carl from 79; P-in-c of Ormside Dio Carl 81-82; R from 82. *Vicarage, Appleby, Cumb, CA16 6QW.* (Appleby 51461)

GRAYSTON, Donald Edward. b 39. Univ of BC BA 60. Gen Th Sem NY STB 63. Trin Coll Tor ThM 74. Coll of Resurr Mirfield 60. **d** 63 **p** 64 Koot. C of Trail 63-67; on leave 67-69; Staff P of Boundary Region Par (in c of St Geo Rossland) 70-72; Chap Selkirk Coll Castlegar 70-72; Hon C of St Mark Parkdale 72-74; Tutor Trin Coll Tor 72-77; I of All SS Burnaby Dio New Westmr from 77. *7405 Royal Oak Avenue, Burnaby, BC, Canada.*

GRAZEBROOK, Francis Michael. b 08. Ch Ch Ox BA 30, MA 56. St Aug Coll Cant. **d** 57 **p** 58 Cov. C of St Nich Warw 57-61; V of Wolverley 61-71; Perm to Offic Dio Heref 72-80; Hon C of Tenbury Dio Heref from 80. *Lions Den, Oldwood Common, Tenbury Wells, Worcs.*

GRAZETTE, Canon Cyril Bernard. Codr Coll Barb. **d** 51 **p** 54 Trinid. C of St Paul San Fernando 51-66; R of Gracechurch 66-68; Pembroke Dio Trinid from 68; Hon Can of H Trin Cathl Port of Spain from 74. *Rectory, Pembroke, Tobago, WI.*

GREADY, Canon Leslie. b 33. Univ of Southn BA (2nd cl Engl) 54. Univ of Sheff MEd 81. Wells Th Coll 54. **d** 56 **p** 57 Liv. C of Walton 56-59; Isandhlwana 59-60; Dir of Kambula 60-63; Kwamagwaza 63-65; Dom Chap to Bp of Matab 65-66; Dir of Training Matab 65-73; Archd of Bembesi 66-69; Matab 69-73; Exam Chap to Bp of Matab 69-73; to Bp of Sheff from 73; Can Res of Sheff from 73; Commiss Matab from 73; Adult Educn Adv Dio Sheff 75-81; Dir of Post-Ordin Tr Dio Sheff from 78; M Gen Syn from 80; Dioc Dir of Ordins Dio Sheff from 81. *393 Fulwood Road, Sheffield, S10 3GE.* (Sheff 305707)

GREANY, Richard Andrew Hugh. b 44. Late Exhib of Qu Coll Ox 2nd cl Cl 65, BA (1st cl Th) 67. Coll of Resurr Mirfield 67. **d** 69 Dur **p** 70 Dur. C of St Osw Hartlepool 69-72; All SS Clifton w St Mary Virg Tyndall's Park Bris 72-75; Sen Tutor Coll of Resurr Mirfield 75-78; V of Whitworth w Spennymoor Dio Dur from 78; P-in-c of Byers Green 78-79. *St Paul's Vicarage, Spennymoor, Co Durham, DL16 7AA.* (Spennymoor 814522)

GREASLEY, James Kenneth. b 39. K Coll Lon and Warm BD and AKC 66. **d** 67 **p** 68 Lich. C of Stoke-on-Trent 67-70; P-in-c of St Pet Lusaka 70-76; V of Gt Staughton 76-81; Melbourn and of Meldreth Dio Ely from 81; Chap HM Borstal Gaynes Hall 76-81. *Vicarage, Vicarage Close, Melbourn, Royston, Herts, SG8 6DY.* (Royston 60295)

GREATHEAD, Edwin Bateson. b 24. Univ of Man BA 49. Wycl Hall, Ox 49. **d** 51 **p** 52 Sheff. C of Goole 51-56; V of Bramley 56-61; Hatfield 61-78; Frodingham Dio Linc from 78; Chap HM Borstal Hatfield 75-78. *Frodingham Vicarage, Scunthorpe, Lincs, DN15 7AZ.* (Scunthorpe 2726)

GREATREX, Warren Robert. Qu Univ Kingston Ont BCom 41. Trin Coll Tor LTh 50, BD 51. **d** 49 **p** 50 Ott. Miss at Mattawa 49-52; C of St John Ott 52-55; R of Wetaskiwin 55-58; Sec-Treas Dio Rupld 58-63; Chap RCN 63-66; Hon Can of Rupld 63-66; Perm to Offic Dio Ott from 70. *85 Grange Road, Ottawa, Ont., Canada.*

GREAVES, Anthony Victor. b 31. **d** 72 Bp McKenzie for Wel **p** 73 Wel. C of All SS Palmerston N 72-78; P-in-c of Wanganui Par Distr Dio Wel from 78. *34 Maxwell Avenue, Wanganui, NZ.* (57-432)

GREAVES, Arthur Roy Hurst. b 15. Univ of Man BA (3rd cl Lat) 38. Ridley Hall Cam 38. **d** 40 **p** 41 Man. C of St Jas New Bury 40-43; St Mich AA Lawton Moor 43-45; St Jas Heywood 45-47; St Geo Stockport 47-50; Ch Ch Denton 50-52; V of Goodshaw 52-56; R of S Cross W Austr 56-59; and 60-64; Bayswater 59-60; R of Bluff Point 64-68; V of Diseworth Dio Leic 69-78; R (w Long Whatton) from 78. *2 Mill Lane, Long Whatton, Loughborough, LE12 5BD.* (Loughborough 842285)

GREAVES, Barry John. Univ of Queensld BA 59. St Francis Coll Bris ACT ThL (2nd cl) 62. **d** 61 **p** 62 Brisb. C of All SS Chermside Brisb 61-64; Ch Ch Bundaberg 64-65; Chap St Jo Coll St Lucia 65-68; M of Bush Bro St Paul Brisb 68-72; Hd Master St Barn Sch Ravenshoe 72-73; R of Chermside Brisb 73-80; Ch Ch Boonah Dio Brisb from 80. *Box 55, Boonah, Queensland, Australia 4310.* (63-1014)

GREAVES, David Reginald. b 19. ALCD (2nd cl) 49. **d** 49 Kens for Lon **p** 50 Lon. C of St Matt Bayswater 49-52; Bromley Kent 52-55; V of Green Street Green 55-61; Billericay 61-77; R (w L Burstead) 77-79; Surr from 61; P-in-c of L Burstead Dio Chelmsf 62-69 and 75-77; RD of Barstable (or Brentwood) 69-76; P-in-c of Langdon Hills Dio Chelmsf from 79. *Langdon Hills Rectory, Basildon, Essex, SS16 6HZ.* (Basildon 42156)

GREAVES, Gerald Raymond. b 32. ACT ThDip 70. St Francis Coll Brisb 68. **d** 69 **p** 70 Brisb. C of Toowoomba 69-70; V of Taroom 71-74; R of Nanango 74-77. *18 Burnett Street, Nanango, Queensland, Australia 4315.* (Nanango 156)

GREAVES, Herbert Alan. b 22. BA (Lon) 47. Sarum Wells Th Coll 75. **d** 77 Ex **p** 77 Plymouth for Ex. C of Tavistock 77-81; R of Northlew w Ashbury Dio Ex from 81; Bratton Clovelly w Germansweek Dio Ex from 81. *Northlew Rectory, Okehampton, Devon, EX20 3NJ.* (Beaworthy 418)

GREAVES, John Dawson. b 04. Cudd Coll. **d** 58 **p** 59 Ox. C of Thame 58-61; V of Wotton Underwood w Ashendon 61-74; C of Chilton w Dorton 71-74; Perm to Offic Dio Ox 74-78. *103 Milford Avenue, Stony Stratford, Milton Keynes, Bucks.*

GREAVES, John Neville. b 29. Dipl Th (Lon) 60. St Aid Coll 58. **d** 61 **p** 62 Man. C of St Ambrose Pendleton 61-63; Benchill (in c of All SS Peel Hall) 63-65; C-in-c of St Richard Wythenshawe (f All SS) 65-69; Min 69-71; V 71-73; R of Sadberge 73-78; V of St Cuthb City and Dio Dur from 78; Chap New Coll Dur from 78; RD of Durham from 80. *St Cuthbert's Vicarage, Western Hill, Durham, DH1 4RJ.* (Durham 64526)

GREAVES, Peter William Campbell. St Jo Coll Morpeth. **d** 56 **p** 57 Newc. C of Muswellbrook 56-57; Hamilton 57-61; R of Wollombi 61-66; Williamtn 66-72; Scone 72-78; on leave. *c/o Rectory, Scone, NSW, Australia 2337.*

GREAVES, Robert Bond Handley. b 26. St Jo Coll Dur 49. **d** 52 **p** 53 Sheff. C of Goole 52-55; C-in-c of Elsecar 55-56; V 56-62; Thorne 62-71; Surr from 64; R of Kirk Bramwith 71-74; C-in-c of Fenwick 71-74; R of Brightwalton w Catmore, Chaddlesworth, Leckhampstead and Fawley Dio Ox from 74. *Chaddleworth Rectory, Newbury, Berks.* (Chaddleworth 566)

GREED, Frederick John. b 44. Trin Coll Bris 79. **d** 81 Win. C of Yateley Dio Win from 81. *27 Bartons Drive, Yateley, Camberley, Surrey, GU17 7DW.*

GREEDY, Tegryd Joseph. St D Coll Lamp 59. **d** 61 **p** 62 Mon. C of Newbridge 61-64; Bassaleg 64-66; V of St Teilo Newport 66-74. *Address temp unknown.*

GREEN, Adrian Linsley. Rhodes Univ BCom 65, BA 67. St Paul's Coll Grahmstn 67. **d** 68 **p** 69 Grahmstn. C of St Pet Cradock 68-72; St John Walmer 72-74; R of Middelburg and Colesburg Dio Port Eliz from 74. *Rectory, Middelburg, CP, S Africa.* (0020 49)

GREEN, Canon Alan Thomas. b 21. **d** 64 **p** 65 Leic. C of Loughborough 64-67; V of Oaks-in-Charnwood 67-70; St Pet Braunstone 70-74; Warden Launde Abbey Dioc Retreat Ho from 74; C-in-c of Loddington Dio Leic from 74; Hon Can of Leic from 78; P-in-c of Knossington w Cold Overton Dio Leic from 81; Owston and Withcote Dio Leic from 81. *Launde Abbey, East Norton, Leicester.* (Belton 254)

GREEN, Alfred. b 06. St Aid Coll 47. **d** 48 Pontefract for Wakef **p** 49 Wakef. C of Birkenshaw w Hunsworth 48-51; C-in-c of Lundwood 51-52; V of St Steph Newc T 52-55; Cullingworth 55-60; St Matt Blackb 60-66; Holme-in-Cliviger 66-73. *40 Richmond Avenue, Cliviger, Burnley, Lancs.* (Burnley 38429)

GREEN, Arthur Edward. b 27. Chich Th Coll 58. **d** 59 **p** 60 S'wark. C of St Jas New Malden 59-62; Caterham 62-67; R of Burgh Parva w Briston 67-75; V of Middleton (w E Winch from 76) Dio Nor from 75; E Winch 75-76. *Middleton Vicarage, King's Lynn, Norf.* (King's Lynn 840252)

GREEN, Canon Arthur John Ernest. b 09. Kelham Th Coll 26. **d** 33 **p** 34 S'wark. C of Richmond 33-38; Dom Chap to Bp of Johann 38-39; C of St Paul Herne Hill 39-40; Chap RNVR 40-46; C-in-c of St Bart Battersea 46-50; V of H Spirit Clapham 50-57; Cheshunt 57-65; RD of Ware 61-65; Surr 61-65; V of Ascen Mitcham 65-76; PV of Westmr Abbey 74-80; Hon Can of S'wark Cathl 76; Can (Emer) from 76; Hon Min Can of Cant from 80. *19 Thirlmere, Kennington, Ashford, Kent, TN24 9BD.* (Ashford 24674)

GREEN, Barrie. b 51. SS Coll Cam BA 72, MA 76. Wycl Hall Ox 75. **d** 78 **p** 79 Birm. C of Castle Vale 78-81; V of St Anne W Heath Dio Birm from 81. *Vicarage, Lilley Lane, West Heath, Birmingham, B31 3JJ.* (021-475 4487)

GREEN, Barry Warren. d 61 Bp Arthur for C & Goulb **p** 63 C & Goulb. C of All SS Canberra 61-63; Cooma 63-65; P-in-c of Kununurra 65-70; R of Gunning 70-71; Sec Bush Ch Aid S Vic 71-78; I of Bulleen Dio Melb from 78. *31 Lillian Street, Bulleen, Vic, Australia 3105.* (850 2393)

GREEN, Brian Robert. b 31. Univ of Bris BA (2nd cl Th) 55. Tyndale Hall, Bris 52. **d** 56 **p** 57 Liv. C of St Philemon Toxt Pk 56-58; V (in c of Toxt Team Min) of St Philemon w St Silas Toxt Pk 58-69; C-in-c of St Gabr Toxt Pk 64-69; St Jo Bapt Toxt Pk 64-69; St Jas Toxt Pk 68-69; V of Henham Dio Chelmsf from 69; V of Elsenham Dio Chelmsf from 69. *Henham Vicarage, Bishop's Stortford, Herts.* (Bp's Stortford 850281)

GREEN, Canon Bryan Stuart Westmacott. b 01. Univ of Lon BD 22. St Jo Coll Winnipeg DD (*hon causa*) 61. Lon Coll of Div 19. **d** 24 **p** 25 S'wark. C of New Malden w Coombe 24-28; Missr Children's SS Miss and Perm to Offic Dio S'wark 28-31; Chap Ox Pastorate and L to Offic Dio Ox 31-34; V of Ch Ch Crouch End 34-38; H Trin Brompton 38-48; Proc Conv Lon 45-48; R of St Martin Birm 48-70; Hon Can of Birm 50-70; Can (Emer) from 70; Proc Conv Birm 50-51; C of Thame Dio Ox from 71. *West Field, Southern Road, Thame, Oxon, OX9 2EP.* (Thame 2026)

GREEN, Canon Cecil Frederick. MBE 56. St Jo Coll Dur LTh 31, Capel Cure Pri 32, BA (2nd cl Th) 33, BD 35, MA 36. Tyndale Hall Bris 29. **d** 33 Bris for Col **p** 35 Sier L. BCMS Miss Morocco Dio N Afr 34-67; Dio Jer from 67; Asst Chap St Jo Evang Casablanca 34-39; Chap from 39; Field Sec BCMS N Afr 39-66; Field Chairman from 67; Exam Chap to Bp in N Afr 49-54; Hon Can of All SS Cathl Cairo from 73. *33 Boulevard d'anfa, Casablanca, Morrocco.*

GREEN, Charles. Mem Univ Newfld BA 67. Qu Coll Newfld LTh 67. **d** 55 **p** 56 Newfld. R of Burgeo 55-60; P-in-c of Trinity E 61-69; R of Meadows 69-74; Bonavista Dio Newfld (Centr Newfld from 76) from 74. *Box 267, Bonavista, Newfoundland, Canada.* (709-468-7357)

GREEN, Canon Charles Beauchamp Griffith. Keble Coll Ox BA (2nd cl Th) 25, MA 32. Ely Th Coll 26. **d** 26 **p** 27 Ex. C of St Pet Plymouth 26-29; Queenstown CGH 29-31; St Aug Masiyeni 31-33; R of O'Okiep 33-35; Robertson 35-39; H Redeemer Sea Point 39-42; CF (S Afr) 42-45; R of H Trin Paarl 45-50; Caledon 50-52; Archd of Caledon 52-65; R of Somerset W 55-61; Caledon 61-64; Commiss St Hel 61-69; R of Strand 64-72; Can of St Geo Cathl Capetn 65-72; Can (Emer) from 73; P-in-c of Gordon's Bay 74-78; Perm to Offic Dio Capetn from 78. *Box 5, Gordon's Bay, CP, S Africa.*

GREEN, Charles Clisby. b 11. St Aid Coll. **d** 48 **p** 49 Chelmsf. C of Plaistow 48-50; Lymington 50-53; R of Northn W Austr 53-56; V of Chandler's Ford 56-68; Eling 68-73; Testwood 68-73; C-in-c of Marchwood 71-73; Surr 68-75; R of Eling w Testwood and Marchwood (Totton Team Min) 73-75; Perm to Offic Dio Man 77-79; Dio Win from 79. *18 Oxburgh Close, Woodlands, Boyatt Wood, Eastleigh, Hants.*

GREEN, Christopher Frederick. b 46. Univ of Nottm BTh 75. Linc Th Coll 71. **d** 75 **p** 76 Birm. C of Hodge Hill 75-78; S Lafford Group Sleaford 78-79; Dines Green Dio Worc from 79. *Vicarage, Burleigh Road, Dines Green, Worcester.* (Worc 421986)

GREEN, Clifford. b 28. Univ of Leeds BA 51. Coll of Resurr Mirfield 51. **d** 53 Bp Linton for Cant **p** 54 Birm. C of Solihull 53-56; M CR from 58; L to Offic Dio Wakef 59-62 and from 67; Dio Grahmstn 63-66; Dio Ripon 75-76. *House of the Resurrection, Mirfield, Yorks.*

GREEN, David Elliot Walton. d 45 **p** 46 Gippsld. C of Mirboo N 45-46; P-in-c 46-47; V of Rosedale 47-54; Trafalgar 54-59; Chap Manager Bro of St Laur Dio Melb 59-64; C of Melb Dioc Centre 59-64; V of Mt Duneed 64-71; Miss at Kumbun 71; Perm to Offic Dio Melb from 72. *2 Sheringham Drive, Glen Waverley, Vic, Australia 3149.*

GREEN, David John. b 32. Sarum Th Coll 63. **d** 64 **p** 65 Sarum. C of H Trin Trowbridge and Asst Master Trowbridge High Sch 64-68; V of St Francis Bournemouth 68-70; St Paul Weymouth Dio Sarum from 70; Chap S Dorset Tech Coll from 80. *St Paul's Vicarage, Abbotsbury Road, Weymouth, Dorset, DT4 0BJ.* (Weymouth 71217)

GREEN, David Mitchell. b 20. Univ of St Andr MB ChB 47, MD 56. **d** 79 **p** 80 Brech. Hon C of St Marg Lochee, Dundee Dio Brech from 79. *3 Coupar Angus Road, Dundee, DD2 3HG.*

GREEN, David Norman. b 37. Magd Coll Cam 3rd cl Law Trip pt i, 59, BA (3rd cl Law Trip pt ii) 60. Clifton Th Coll 60. **d** 62 **p** 63 Lon. C of Islington 62-65; Burley 65-68; Thika 70-74; V of St Mark Nai 75-81; P-in-c of Brimscombe 81; R of Woodchester and Brimscombe Dio Glouc from 81. *Brimscombe Vicarage, Stroud, Glos, GL5 2PA.* (Brimscombe 882204)

GREEN, Canon Dennis John. b 45. Lich Th Coll 69. **d** 72 **p** 73 Kens for Lon. C of All SS Hampton 72-74; C-in-c of Leverington 75-76; R 76-80; Can Res of Ely and Dioc Development Officer from 80. *The Black Hostelry, The College, Ely, Cambs, CB7 4DL.* (Ely 2612)

GREEN, Canon Derek George Wilson. b 27. Univ of Bris BA (2nd cl Th) 53, MA 58. Tyndale Hall, Bris 48. **d** 53 Bris for Sarum **p** 54 Sarum. C of Weymouth 53-55; Chap RAF 55-58; R of N Pickenham w Houghton-on-the-Hill Dio Nor from 58; S Pickenham Dio Nor from 58; M Gen Syn Nor 70-75; RD of Breckland from 70; Hon Can of Nor Cathl from 78; Field Co-ordinator Script U from 80. *South Pickenham Rectory, Swaffham, Norf.* (Great Cressingham 292)

GREEN, Donald Pentney. b 25. Univ of Leeds BA 50. Coll of Resurr Mirfield 50. **d** 52 **p** 53 Man. C of St Benedict Ardwick 52-55; M SSF from 55; L to Offic Dio Chelmsf 58-60; Papua New Guinea 60-63; Chelmsf 69-72; Chap HM Pris Kingston Portsm 72-76; L to Offic Dio Edin 76-77; Org Sec Catholic Renewal 77-78; Sec for Miss SSF from 78. *42 Balaam Street, Plaistow, E13 8AQ.* (01-476 5189)

GREEN, Douglas Edward. b 17. Sarum Th Coll 47. **d** 50 **p** 51 Glouc. C of St Paul Glouc 50-53; Malvern Link 53-56; V of Ch Ch Eccles Distr Tolladine Worc 56-58; Bosbury 58-80; R of Coddington 59-78; V of Wellington Heath 59-78; C of Minsterley 78-80. *2 The Hollies, Minsterley, Shropshire.*

GREEN, Edward Bankes. St D Coll Lamp BA 07. **d** 08 Thetford for Nor **p** 09 Nor. C of Wymondham 08-11; St Barn Bexhill 11-14; Banbury w St Paul Neithrop 15-26; R of Shenington w Alkerton 26-58. *Wellfield, Temple Street, Llandrindod Wells, Powys.*

GREEN, Edward Eugene. Trin Coll Tor. **d** and **p** 53 Qu'App. C of Weyburn and of Radville 53-54; I of Raymore 54-58; C of St Paul's Pro-Cathl Regina 58-60; R of St Agnes Tor 60-63; All SS Westboro Ott 63-69; Chap Ashbury Coll City and Dio Ott from 69. *577 Windermere Avenue, Ottawa 13, Ont, Canada.*

GREEN, Edward John. b 35. Lich Th Coll. **d** 59 **p** 60 Cov. C of Longford 59-61; Wigston Magna 61-65; V of Ellistown 65-73; Wigston Magna Dio Leic from 73. *Wigston Magna Vicarage, Leicester, LE8 2BA.* (Leic 883419)

GREEN, Canon Edward Michael Bankes. b 30. Late Exhib and Scho of Ex Coll Ox 2nd cl Cl Mods 51, BA (1st cl Lit Hum) 53, MA 56. Late Found Scho of Qu Coll Cam BA (1st cl Th Trip pt 111) and Carus Gr Test Pri 57, MA 61, BD 66. Ridley Hall, Cam 55. **d** 57 **p** 58 Chich. C of H Trin Eastbourne 57-60; Tutor Lon Coll of Div (St Jo Coll Nottm from 70) 60-69; Prin 69-75; Can Th of Cov 70-78; Can Th (Emer) from 78; R of St Aldate w H Trin City and Dio Ox from 75. *St Aldate's Rectory, Pembroke Street, Oxford, OX1 1BP.* (Oxford 44713)

GREEN, Edward Wallace. b 11. K Coll Lon BA (2nd cl Cl) 32, AKC 33. Ripon Hall Ox 33. **d** 35 **p** 36 Glouc. C of Coln St Aldwyn w Hatherop and Quenington 35-39; C-in-c 39-45; Asst Master Hawtreys Sch Savernake 45-46; Chap and Asst Master The Abbey Ashurst Wood 46-52; Asst Master St Edm Sch Hindhead 52-54; Chap Oakham Sch 54-58; Asst Master Alleyn Court Sch Westcliff-on-Sea 58-79; Perm to Offic Dio Chelmsf from 61. *Alleyn Court, Westcliff-on-Sea, Essex, SSO.*

GREEN, Canon Edwin Arthur. b 1892. Wycl Coll Tor LTh 16. Ch Coll Cam BA 21, MA 25. **d** 16 Tor for Fred **p** 17 Fred. C of St Luke St John NB 16-18; TCF 18-20; C of St Andr L Cam 20-22; St Mary Magd Peckham 22-26; V of St Barn York 26-30; St John Worksop and Chap of Worksop Inst 30-37; St Mary Rushden 37-54; Can (Emer) of Pet from 54; Surr 40-54; V of Ch Ch Tunbridge Wells 54-67. *77 Queen's Road, Tunbridge Wells, Kent.*

GREEN, Eric Kenneth. b 18. Tyndale Hall Bris 40. **d** 45 **p** 47 Sarum. C of St John Parkstone 45-48; Radipole 48-49; Bucknall Stoke-on-Trent 49-50; V of Halwell w Moreleigh 50-53; St Mary Wakef 53-55; R of Peldon 55-57; Aythorpe Roding (w High Roding from 60) 57-63; C-in-c of High Roding 57-58; C-in-c of Leaden Roding 57-58; R 58-63; All Cannings w Etchilhampton 63-75; V of Over Kellett Dio Blackb from 75. *Vicarage, Over Kellett, Carnforth, Lancs.* (Carnforth 2454)

GREEN, Preb Ernest James. b 31. Pemb Coll Cam BA 55, MA 62. Linc Th Coll 55. **d** 57 **p** 58 Sheff. C of Rawmarsh 57-60; Sec Th Coll Dept SCM 60-62; Perm to Offic Dio Lon 60-62; Prec Sacr and Min Can of Bris Cathl 62-65; V of Churchill (w Burrington from 78) Dio B & W from 65; RD of Locking 72-78; Preb of Wells Cathl from 81. *The Parsonage, Langford, Bristol, BS18 7JE.*

GREEN, Ernest Swinfen. b 12. Wells Th Coll 66. **d** 67 Chich **p** 67 Lewes for Chich. C of Eastbourne 67-70; V of

Lower Beeding 70-77. *Upper Benacre, Hammerpond Road, Plummer's Plain, Horsham, W Sussex RH13 6PE.*

GREEN, Floyd Elvin. Sir Geo Williams Univ Montr BA 58. McGill Univ Montr BD 61. Montr Dioc Th Coll 61. **d** 60 **p** 61 Ont. C of Brockville 60-61; St Jo Evang Montr 61-62; R of Newboro 62-68; Chap St Thos Hosp St Thos 70-79; Qu Street Mental Health Centre Tor from 80. *1001 Queen Street West, Toronto, M6J 1H4, Ont, Canada.*

GREEN, Francis James. b 13. Univ of Lon BD 38. ALCD 38. **d** 39 **p** 40 Bradf. C of Eastwood 39-41; Ch Ch Watford 41-43; Cf (EC) 43-47; V of Silsden 47-51; Chap of Toc H 52-63; Miss to Seamen Port Sudan 63-69; Lagos 69-70; Swansea 71-72; C of Grays 73-79; Hon C of Bearsted Dio Cant from 79. *32 The Grove, Bearsted, Maidstone, Kent.* (Maidstone 37980)

GREEN, Frank Gilbert. Kelham Th Coll, 46. **d** 50 **p** 51 Sheff. C of St Cecilia Parson Cross Sheff 50-56; St Geo w St Jo Bapt Nottm 56-58; Asst P Teyateyaneng 58-62; Dir of Welkom Miss 62-65; Modderpoort 65-69; R of Teyateyaneng 69-76; C of St Barn Masite Dio Les from 76. *Masite Priory, PO Maseru, Lesotho.* (Teyateyaneng 244)

GREEN, Frederick George. b 40. Univ of Nottm BA (2nd cl Th) 62, MA 67. Linc Th Coll 64. **d** 66 **p** 67 Southw. C of Warsop w Sookholme 66-70; V of Clipstone 70-76; R of Warsop w Sookholme Dio Southw from 76. *Warsop Rectory, Mansfield, Notts.* (Mansfield 843290)

GREEN, Gary Francis Malcolm. b 48. St Barn Coll Belair 78. **d** 80 River. C of Broken Hill Dio River from 80. *337 Lane Street, Broken Hill, NSW, Australia 2880.* (080 881756)

GREEN, George Henry Langston. b 12. St Aug Coll Cant 38. **d** 41 **p** 42 Liv. C of St Chris Norris Green 41-43; St Mich Garston 43-44; St Pet Aintree w St Giles 44-46; CF (EC) 46-47; V of Neen Savage 47-50; V of Kinlet 47-50; R of Ironbridge 50-55; V of Frodsham 55-78; Perm to Offic Dio Ches from 78; Chap of Merit to Bp of Ches from 78. *River View, Gwespyr, Holywell, Clwyd.* (07456 7489)

GREEN, George James. b 26. Cudd Coll 69. **d** 69 Aston for Birm **p** 70 Birm. C of Handsworth 69-76; R of Croughton w Evenley Dio Pet from 76. *Rectory, Broad Lane, Evenley, Brackley, Northants.* (Brackley 702650)

GREEN, Gordon Sydney. b 33. Ridley Hall Cam 77. **d** 79 **p** 80 St E. C of St Marg Ipswich Dio St E from 79. *15 Bolton Lane, Ipswich, Suffolk, IP4 2BX.*

GREEN, Graham Herbert. b 53. City Univ Lon BSc 74. Westcott Ho Cam 75. **d** 78 **p** 79 S'wark. C of St Cath Hatcham Dio S'wark from 78. *61 Erlanger Road, New Cross, SE14.* (01-639 3733)

GREEN, Graham Reginald. b 48. Sarum Wells Th Coll 71. **d** 74 Lanc for Blackb **p** 75 Blackb. C of Chorley 74-76; Padiham 76-79; V of Osmondthorpe Leeds Dio Ripon from 79. *Vicarage, Osmondthorpe Lane, Leeds, LS9 9EF.* (Leeds 497371)

GREEN, Canon Harry George. b 04. Univ of Lon BA (1st cl Hist) and Barry Pri (Arts) 25. AKC 27. Wells Th Coll 28. **d** 29 **p** 30 Carl. C of St Mary Walney I 29-31; Penrith 31-35; Min of Kells Distr Whitehaven 35-39; V 39-43; V of Ch Ch Warminster 43-65; C-in-c of Bishopstrow 53-56; Exam Chap to Bp of Sarum 58-71; Can and Preb of Sarum Cathl 61-71; Can (Emer) from 71; V of Abbotsbury 65-71; Perm to Offic Dios Sarum and B & W from 72. *The Old School House, Lopen, South Petherton, Somt.* (S Petherton 40077)

GREEN, Howard Edward. Univ of Tor BA 51. Univ of Michigan, MA 65. Wycl Coll Tor. **d** 54 Tor **p** 54 Coadj Bp for Tor. C of Ch of Messiah Tor 54-56; in Ch in Japan 57-75; R of Melfort Dio Sask from 75. *Rectory, Melfort, Sask, Canada.*

GREEN, Howard Vernon. b 11. Univ of Leeds, BA 35. Coll of Resurr Mirfield 35. **d** 38 **p** 39 Cant. C of St Mich Croydon 38-41; St Andr Buckland-in-Dover 41-46; R of Croyland (or Crowland) 46-54; V of West End Southn 54-77. *58 Telegraph Road, West End, Southampton.*

GREEN, (Benedict) Humphrey Christian. b 24. Late Postmaster of Mert Coll Ox 1st cl Cl Mods 43, BA (2nd cl Lit Hum and 2nd cl Th) 49, MA 52. Cudd Coll 50. **d** 51 **p** 52 Lon. C of Northolt 51-56; Lect in Th K Coll Lon 56-60; Sub-Warden Th Hostel 57-60; L to Offic Dio Wakef from 61; M CR from 62; Vice-Prin Coll of Resurr Mirfield 65-75; Prin from 75; Exam Chap to Bp of Wakef from 77. *College of the Resurrection, Mirfield, Yorks, WF14 0BW.* (Mirfield 493362)

GREEN, James Hardman. b 19. Open Univ BA 74. **d** 52 **p** 53 Dur. C of St Paul Darlington 52-54; St Hilda Darlington 54-57; V of Hunwick 57-60; Chap R Assoc for Deaf and Dumb and L to Offic Dio Lon 60-65 and 75-77; R of Morcott w S Luffenham 65-75; V of St Geo E Boldon Dio Dur from 77. *2 Ashleigh Villas, East Boldon, T & W, NE36 0LA.* (Boldon 362557)

GREEN, Jeffrey. b 43. Chich Th Coll 76. **d** 78 B & W **p** 79 Taunton for B & W. C of Crewkerne 78-81; Cockington w Chelston Dio Ex from 81. *c/o Cockington Vicarage, Torquay, Devon.* (Torquay 65177)

GREEN, John. b 28. K Coll Lon and Warm AKC 54. **d** 55 **p** 56 Blackb. C of Poulton-le-Fylde 55-57; St Annes-on-Sea (in c of St Marg) 57-63; V of Inskip 63-75; Fairhaven Dio Blackb from 75. *83 Clifton Drive, Lytham St Anne's, Lancs, FY8 1BZ.* (Lytham 734562)

GREEN, Ven John. St Jo Coll Morpeth 63. **d** 66 **p** 67 Adel. C of Gawler 66-69; P-in-c of O'Halloran Hill 69-75; R of Port Lincoln Dio Willoch from 75; Archd of Eyre Peninsula from 80. *Box 73, Port Lincoln, S Australia 5606.* (086-82 1119)

GREEN, John Baines. St Francis Coll Brisb. **d** 55 **p** 56 Bath. M Bro of Good Shepherd Dubbo 55-63; C of Bourke 57-58; P-in-c of Gilgandra 59-63; C of Petersham w Enmore 63-67; H Trin Fortitude Valley Brisb 67; R of St John Hendra City and Dio Brisb from 67. *12 Burilda Street, Hendra, Queensland, Australia 4011.* (268 3092)

GREEN, John David. b 29. Roch Th Coll 63. BD (Lon) 66. **d** 66 Bp Stannard for Roch **p** 66 Roch. C of St Pet w St Marg Roch 66; V of Oxshott Dio Guildf from 72. *Vicarage, Steel's Lane, Oxshott, Leatherhead, Surrey.* (Oxshott 2071)

GREEN, John Henry. b 44. AKC and BD 72. St Aug Coll Cant 72. **d** 73 **p** 74 Heref. C of Tupsley 73-77; Asst Chap Univ of Newc T 77-79; V of Chells Stevenage Dio St Alb from 79. *St Hugh's House, Mobbsbury Way, Chells, Stevenage.* (Stevenage 54307)

GREEN, John Herbert Gardner-Waterman. b 21. Trin Hall, Cam BA (3rd cl Mod Lang Trip pt ii) 48, MA 58. Wells Th Coll 58. **d** 59 Bp Rose for Cant **p** 60 Cant. C of New Romney 59-63; V of Hartlip 63-68; R of Sandhurst w Newenden Dio Cant from 68; RD of W Charing 74-81. *Sandhurst Rectory, Hawkhurst, Kent.* (Sandhurst 213)

GREEN, Preb John Stanley. Keble Coll Ox BA (3rd cl Th) 33, MA 37. Wells Th Coll 33. **d** 35 **p** 36 Ches. C of St Matt Stockport 35-39; St Mary Bournemouth 39-46; PV of Ex Cathl 46-49; Dep PV 49-77; R of St Jas w St Anne's Chap Ex 49-77; Preb of Ex Cathl from 69. *2 Whiteway Drive, Exeter, Devon, EX1 3AN.* (Ex 37291)

GREEN, Joseph Hudson. b 28. TD 76. Kelham Th Coll 48. **d** 53 **p** 54 Dur. C of St Mich AA Norton Co Dur 53-56; Heworth (in c of St Andr from 60) 56-62; V of W Harton 62-69; Chap S Shields Gen Hosp 62-69; CF (TA) 63-67; CF (TAVR) 67-77; V of Leadgate 69-78; Criftins-by-Ellesmere Dio Lich from 78; Dudleston Dio Lich from 78. *Vicarage, Criftins-by-Ellesmere, Salop.* (Duddleston Heath 212)

GREEN, Laurence Alexander. b 45. AKC and BD 68. NY Th Sem STM 69. St Aug Cant 70. **d** 70 **p** 71 Birm. C of St Mark, Kingstanding 70-73; V of St Chad Erdington Dio Birm from 73. *10 Shepherd's Green Road, Erdington, Birmingham, B24 8EX.* (021-373 3915)

GREEN, Lawrence Victor. Ridley Coll Melb 53. **d** 56 **p** 57 Melb. C of Bentleigh 56-58; CMS Miss Dio Sing 58-59; Dio Borneo 59-62; Dio Jess 62-68; R of Mirboo N w Mardan S 68-72; St Aug Moreland 72-79; I of Geelong E Dio Melb from 79. *230 McKillop Street, Geelong East, Vic, Australia 3219.* (052-21 5412)

GREEN, Leslie James. b 31. K Coll Lon and Warm BD 53, AKC 54. **d** 56 **p** 57 S'wark. C of St Andr Catford 56-60; R of St Osw K Pk Glas 60-70; L to Offic Dio Dur 71-73; V of Oxclose Dio Dur from 73. *37 Brancepeth Road, Oxclose, Washington, T & W NE38 0LA.* (Washington 462561)

✠ **GREEN, Right Rev Mark.** b 17. MC 45. Linc Coll Ox BA (3rd cl Th) 40, MA 44. Univ of Aston Hon DSc 80. Cudd Coll 40. **d** 40 **p** 41 Glouc. C of St Cath Glouc 40-42; CF (EC) 43-46; Men in Disp 45; Dir of Service Ordinands 47-48; V of St John Newland 48-53; CF 53-56; V of S Bank 56-58; R of Cottingham 58-64; Can and Preb of Holme in York Minster 63-72; V of Bishopthorpe 64-72; V of Acaster Malbis 64-72; RD of Ainsty 64-68; Hon Chap to Abp of York 64-72; Cons Ld Bp Suffr of Aston in S'wark Cathl 11 May 72 by Abps of Cant and York; Bps of Lon; Ely; Bris; Heref; Derby; Birm; Portsm; Nor; and others; Res 82; Dioc Dir of Ordinands Dio Birm 80-82. *13 Archery Court, Archery Road, St Leonards-on-Sea, E Sussex, TN38 0HZ.*

GREEN, Martyn. b 41. FCA. Ridley Hall Cam 78. **d** 80 **p** 81 Ripon. C of Wetherby Dio Ripon from 80. *53 Barleyfields Road, Wetherby, W Yorks, LS22 4PT.*

GREEN, Maurice Fernley. ACT ThL 36. **d** 33 **p** 35 Bend. C of Ch Ch Echuca 33-34; V of Koondrook 34-37; R of Milloo w Mitiamo 37-41; St Pet Elmore 41-45; Asst Sec CMS for Victoria 45-47; R of Orbost 47-51; Lang Lang 52-55; Dom Chap to Bp of Gippsld 52-60; R of Lakes Entrance 55-60; Min of Kallista 60-62. *2 Berwick Street, Camberwell, Vic, Australia 3124.*

GREEN, Maurice Paul. b 34. Wells Th Coll 68. **d** 70 **p** 71 Lynn for Nor. C of Eaton 70-74; R of N w S Wootton Dio Nor from 74. *Wootton Rectory, Castle Rising Road, South Wootton, King's Lynn, n 671381)*

GREEN, Nicholas Eliot. b 54. Univ of Leeds BA 76. AKC and BD 78. Westcott Ho Cam 78. **d** 79 Edmon for Lon **p** 80 Lon. C of Ch Ch Southgate Dio Lon from 79. *62 Oakfield Road, Southgate, N14.* (01-886 3346)

GREEN, Norman. Wycl Coll Tor BA 41, LTh 44. **d** 43 **p** 44 Tor. C of St Phil Tor 43-44; I of Fenelon Falls 44-47; Palmerston 47-52; R of Milton 52-55; Beamsville 55-60; Field Sec Wycl Coll Tor 60-69; on leave 70-78; Hon C of St Mark Niag-on-the-lake Dio Niag from 80. *Box 1377, Niagara-on-the-Lake, Ont, Canada.* (416-468 3669)

GREEN, Paul. b 25. Sarum Wells Th Coll 72. **d** 74 **p** 75 Ex. C of Pinhoe Dio Ex 74-77; P-in-c 77-79; V from 79. *Pinhoe Vicarage, Exeter, Devon.* (Ex 67541)

GREEN, Paul Francis. b 48. St Jo Coll Dur BA 78. Cranmer Hall Dur 75. **d** 79 **p** 80 Glouc. C of Cirencester w Watermoor Dio Glouc from 79. *59 North Home Road, Cirencester, Glos.* (Cirencester 4779)

GREEN, Paul John. b 48. Sarum Wells Th Coll 72. **d** 73 **p** 74 Glouc. C of St Barn Tuffley Glouc 73-76; Prestbury 76-82; P-in-c of Highnam w Lassington and Rudford Dio Glouc from 82. *Highnam Rectory, Gloucester.* (Glouc 25567)

GREEN, Peter. b 38. Univ of Ex BSc (2nd cl Math) 59. Sarum Th Coll 59. **d** 61 **p** 62 Chelmsf. C of Romford 61-66; Chap Trin Coll Kandy 66-70; V of Darnall 71-80; Team V of Stantonbury Dio Ox from 80. *44 Farrier Place, Downs Barn, Milton Keynes, MK14 7PL.* (M Keynes 663346)

GREEN, Peter Edwin. Lich Th Coll. **d** 62 **p** 63 Nor. C of Sprowston 62-65; Min of St Francis's Conv Distr Heartsease Sprowston 65-73; V of Loddon w Sisland Dio Nor from 73. *Loddon Vicarage, Norwich, Norfolk.* (Loddon 251)

GREEN, Canon Philip Harry. b 19. ALCD 50. **d** 50 **p** 51 Bradf. C of St Andr Keighley 50-53; V of St Sav Everton 53-57; Barnoldswick w Bracewell 57-64; Shipley 64-77; Gargrave Dio Bradf from 77; Hon Can of Bradf Cathl from 77. *Kirkfell, Kirkhead Road, Kent's Bank, Grange-over-Sands, Cumbria.* (Grange-over-Sands 2931)

GREEN, Philip John. b 53. Rhodes Univ BSocSc 76. St Paul's Coll Grahmstn Dipl Th 80. **d** 79 **p** 80 Capetn. C of All SS Plumstead Dio Capetn from 79. *6 Brent Road, Plumstead, Cape Town 7800, S Africa.*

GREEN, Richard Charles. b 49. St Aug Coll Cant 73. **d** 74 **p** 75 Heref. C of Broseley w Benthall 74-80; St Martin City and Dio Heref from 80. *c/o St Martin's Vicarage, Hereford.*

GREEN, Robert Stanley. b 42. Univ of Dur BA 65. Wells Th Coll 65. **d** 67 **p** 68 Cant. C of Ashford 67-73; R of Otham 73-79; V of Bethersden w High Halden Dio Cant from 79. *Bethersden Vicarage, Ashford, Kent.* (Bethersden 266)

GREEN, Robin Christopher William. b 43. Univ of Leeds BA (2nd cl Engl and Fine Art) 64. Fitzw Ho Cam BA (2nd cl Th) 67. Ridley Hall Cam 65. **d** 68 **p** 69 S'wark. C of H Trin S'wark 68-71; Englefield Green 71-73; Chap Whitelands Coll of Educn 73-78; Publ Pr Dio S'wark from 77; M Gen Syn from 80. *115 St George's Road, SE1 6HY.* (01-928 5765)

GREEN, Roger Thomas. b 43. Oakhill Th Coll Dipl Higher Educn 79. **d** 79 **p** 80 Roch. C of Paddock Wood Dio Roch from 79. *3 Ashcroft Road, Paddock Wood, Kent.*

GREEN, Preb Ronald Henry. b 27. Bps' Coll Cheshunt, 53. **d** 55 Kens for Lon **p** 56 Lon. C of Ch Ch w St Barn St Marylebone 55-58; R 58-62; C of St Andr Holborn Lon and Youth Tr Officer Dio Lon 62-64; Hon Youth Chap and RE Adv Dio Lon 63-73; V of St Steph Hampstead 64-73; RD of N Camden 67-73; V of Heston 73-79; Preb of St Paul's Cathl Lon from 75; Jt Dir of Educn Dios Lon and S'wark from 79. *60 North Road, N6.* (01-348 9989)

GREEN, Sidney Leonard. b 44. BD (Lon) 72. Oak Hill Th Coll 69. **d** 72 Warrington for Liv **p** 73 Liv. C of Skelmersdale 72-74; St Jas Denton Holme Carl 74-77. *6 Herbert Road, Sherwood Rise, Nottingham, NG5 1BT.* (Nottm 624495)

GREEN, Thomas. b 28. St Aid Coll 65. **d** 67 **p** 68 Blackb. C of Scotforth 67-70; H Trin S Shore Blackpool (in c of St Nich Marton Moss) 70-72; V of Chipping 72-80; Pilling Dio Blackb from 80. *Vicarage, Pilling, Preston, Lancs, PR3 6AA.* (Pilling 231)

GREEN, Thomas George. St Jo Coll Morpeth ACT ThL 69. **d** 66 Bal **p** 71 Melb. C of Warrnambool 66-67; C of St John Bentleigh 67-71; St Andr Brighton 71-72; Dandenong 72-73; P-in-c of St Mary Magd Dallas 73-75; C in Dept of Chap Dio Melb from 75; Chap HM Pris Pentridge from 78. *HM Prison, Pentridge, Coburg, Vic, Australia 3058.* (350 1322)

GREEN, Canon Titus Tamuno-omoni. St Paul's Tr Coll Awka 48. Dipl Th (Lon) 54. Univ of Dur BA 61. **d** 53 Nig Delta **p** 55 Niger for Nig Delta. P Dio Nig Delta from 53; Synod Sec Dio Nig Delta 63-65; Exam Chap to Bp on Niger Delta from 64; Can of Nig Delta from 72; Dean of Port Harcourt Chr Coun Project Nigeria from 75. *PO Box 592, Port Harcourt, Nigeria.*

GREEN, Trevor Howard. b 37. Sarum Wells Th Coll 72. **d** 74 **p** 75 Lich. C of Bloxwich 74-77; St Steph Willenhall Dio Lich 77-79; P-in-c 79-80; V from 80. *St Stephen's Vicarage, Wolverhampton Street, Willenhall, W Mid, WV13 2PS.* (Willenhall 65239)

GREEN, Vivian Hubert Howard. b 15. Late Scho and Exhib of Trin Hall Cam 1st cl Hist Trip pt i and Scho 36, BA (1st cl Hist Trip pt ii) 37, Lightfoot Scho 38, MA 41, Thirlwall Pri 41, BD 45, DD 58. Linc Coll Ox MA 51, BD 51, DD 58. **d** 39 Cant **p** 40 Ex. Fell of St Aug Coll Cant and L to Offic Dio Cant 39-47; Perm to Offic Dio B & W 40; Asst Chap and Lect St Luke's Tr Coll Ex 40-42; Asst Master and Offg Asst Chap Sherborne Sch 42-46; Chap 46-51; Perm to Offic Dio Sarum 42-51; Fell, Chap (to 69) and Tutor in Mod Hist Linc Coll Ox from 51; Sen Tutor 53-62 and 74-77; Sub-Rector from 70; Select Pr Univ of Ox 59-60. *Lincoln College, Oxford.* (Oxford 43658)

GREEN, Warren. b 20. Trin Coll Melb. **d** and **p** 81 Dun. Hon C of E Otago Dio Dun from 81. *117 Ronaldsay Street, Palmerston, Otago, NZ.*

GREEN, William John. b 23. Univ of Birm BSc 43. Roch Th Coll. **d** 66 **p** 67 gloucc. C of Minchinhampton 66-68; Standish w Hardwicke and Haresfield 68-70; R of Eastington w Frocester 70-80; V of S Cerney w Cerney Wick Dio Glouc from 80. *South Cerney Vicarage, Cirencester, Glos, GL7 5TP.* (Cirencester 860221)

GREEN, William Lewis. Late Drury Exhib of St Cath Coll Cam 1st cl Math Trip pt i 32, BA (2nd cl Th Trip pt i) 34, MA 39. Cudd Coll 34. **d** 35 **p** 36 Lon. C of St Mary of Eton Hackney Wick 35-46; Perm to Offic at Desborough Rothwell and Arthingworth 39-41; Vice-Prin of Old Rectory Coll Hawarden 46-47; Chap and Lect St Mary's Coll Ban and L to Offic Dio Ban 47-62; Prin Thogoto Coll Kikuyu 62-68; Kagwno Coll Nyeri 68-70; Nana Coll Warri 70-73; St Mich Coll Oleh 73-76; L to Offic Dio Ft Hall 62-64; Dio Mt Kenya 64-70; Dio Benin 70-76; Dio Aba 76-78; Tutor Trin Th Coll Umuahia 76-78; Perm to Offic Dio Ches 78-79; Dioc Sec Dio Zanz T from 79; Dom Chap to Bp of Zanz T from 80. *c/o Box 35, Korogwe, Tanga, Tanzania.*

GREENACRE, Canon Roger Tagent. b 30. Late Exhib of Clare Coll Cam 2nd cl Hist Trip pt i 51, BA (2nd cl Th Trip pt ia) 52, MA 56. Coll of Resurr Mirfield, 52. **d** 54 Kens for Lon **p** 55 Lon. C of All SS Hanworth 54-59; Chap Ely Th Coll 59-60; Chap and Asst Master Summerfields Sch Ox 60-61; Abp's P-Stud Louvain Univ 61-62; C of St Mark N Audley Street Lon 62-63; Chap Liddon Ho 63-65; St Geo Paris 65-75; RD of France 70-75; Chan and Can Res of Chich Cathl from 75; M Gen Syn from 80; M Bd for Miss and Unity from 81. *4 Vicars' Close, Chichester, Sussex.* (Chichester 784244)

GREENALL, Ronald Gilbert. b 41. St Aid Coll 61. **d** 64 Blackb **p** 65 Burnley for Blackb. C of Adlington 64-67; Ribbleton (in c of St Anne Moor Nook) 67-69; V of St Jo Div Coppull Dio Blackb from 69. *St John's Vicarage, Coppull, Chorley, Lancs.* (Coppull 791258)

GREENAWAY, Alwyn Lawrence. b 13. Univ of Syd BA 35. **d** 69 **p** 70 Melb. C of St Jo Toorak 69-73; Dioc Chap Dio Melb from 73. *64 Stanley Street, Frankston, Vic, Australia 3199.* (03-783 5927)

GREENAWAY, Ven James Bruce. St Jo Coll Auckld LTh 67. **d** 67 **p** 68 Wai. C of Tauranga 68-70; Washington Durham 70-71; Banbury (in c of St Paul) 71-72; V of Rotorua 72-80; Can of Wai 78-80; Hon C of St John Campbells Bay 80; Dir of Social Services Dio Auckld from 80; Archd of Hauraki from 81. *Box 6611, Auckland, NZ.*

GREENE, Charles Fenton. b 28. **d** 51 **p** 52 Sask. Dio Keewatin 51-57; Hon C of St Luke Winnipeg 71-73; St Geo Transcona Dio 73-76; St Geo Crescentwood Winnipeg 76-79; I of H Nativ City and Dio Calg from 79. *13844 Parkland Boulevard SE, Calgary, Alta, Canada, T2J 3X4.*

GREENE, Colin John David. b 50. Qu Univ Belf BA 73. Fitzw Coll Cam MA (Th) 75. St Jo Coll Nottm 78. **d** 80 Derby **p** 81 Bp Markham for Leic. C of Sandiacre 80-81; Em Ch Loughborough Dio Leic from 81. *46 Forest Road, Loughborough, Leicester, LE11 3NW.* (Loughborough 61581)

GREENE, David Arthur Kirsopp. b 36. St Pet Coll Ox BA 60, MA 64. Tyndale Hall, Bris 61. **d** 63 **p** 64 Chich. C of St Mary Southgate Crawley 63-66; Kirby Grindalythe 66-69; C of N Grimstone w Wharram Percy and Wharram-le-Street 66-69; R of Folke, N Wootton and Haydon (w Long Burton to 81 and Caundle Purse from 75) 69-81; P-in-c of Thornford w Beer Hackett Dio Sarum from 81; C-in-c of High Stoy Dio Sarum from 81. *c/o Folke Rectory, Sherborne, Dorset, DT9 5HP.*

GREENE, John Howe. b 22. K Coll Lon and Warm AKC (2nd cl) and Jelf Pri 48, BD 49. **d** 49 **p** 50 Lich. C of Drayton-in-Hales 49-52; Stoke-on-Trent 52-56; V of Wilnecote 56-62; Lodsworth 62-69; R of Selham w S Ambersham 62-69; Burwash 69-75; Petworth Dio Chich from 75; P-in-c of Egdean Dio Chich 76-79; R from 79; RD of Petworth from 76. *Rectory, Petworth, W Sussex, GU28 0DB.* (Petworth 42505)

GREENE, Robert Stuart Harvey. Univ of Tor BA 49. Trin Coll Tor LTh 54. **d** 53 Niag **p** 54 Athab. C of St Paul Tor 53-54; I of Lac la Biche 54-59; Fairview 59-65; Ch of Good Shepherd Calg 65-72; Can of Athab 59-65; R of St Bede Winnipeg 72-77; St Bart City and Dio Tor from 77. *70 Pashler Avenue, Toronto, Ont., Canada.*

GREENE, Thomas Michael. b 42. W Ont Univ BA 65. Late Scho of Linacre Coll Ox BA 69, MA 73. Trin Coll Tor STB 70. **d** 70 Bp Wilkinson for Niag **p** 70 Niag. C of Kitchener 70-71; St Geo, St Catharine's 71-73; in Amer Ch 73-77; I of Markham Dio Tor from 77. *30 Maple Street, Markham, Ont, L3P 2TA, Canada.*

GREENFIELD, Anthony Philip. b 48. Qu Coll Birm 74. **d** 77 **p** 78 Dur. C of Southwick 77-79; Hodge Hill Dio Birm from 79. *95 Hodge Hill Road, Birmingham, B34 6DX.*

GREENFIELD, George Halstead. b 1892. St Jo Coll Dur BA 24, Dipl in Th 25, MA 27. **d** 25 **p** 26 Pet. C of The Martyrs Leic 25-27; C-in-c of St Chris Leic 27-34; V of Brandon Dur 34-49; Herriard w Lasham R 49-53; Denmead 53-67; Perm to Offic Dio Chich 68; Dio Ox 69; Dio Ex from 70. *Woodcot, Cliff Road, Salcombe, Devon, TQ8 8JU.*

GREENFIELD, Martin Richard. b 54. Em Coll Cam MA 75. Wycl Hall Ox BA (Th) 78. **d** 79 Lon **p** 80 Edmon for Lon. C of Ch Ch Cockfosters Dio Lon from 79. *2 Chalk Lane, Cockfosters, Barnet, Herts.*

GREENFIELD, Norman John Charles. b 27. Univ of Leeds BA 51. Chich Th Coll 51. **d** 53 **p** 54 Portsm. C of St Cuthb Copnor 53-56; Ch Ch Reading 56-60; V of Moor Ends 60-65; Littleworth 65-71; New Marston Ox 71-79; Dioc Stewardship Adv and P-in-c of Amberley Dio Chich from 79. *Amberley Vicarage, Arundel, W Sussex.*

GREENFIELD, Canon Walter. b 16. TD 67. Selw Coll Cam BA 49, MA 53. Ridley Hall, Cam 48. **d** 50 **p** 51 Ripon. C of Richmond Yorks 50-52; C-in-c of Bentley Conv Distr 52-53; V of Waterfoot 53-58; CF (TA) 55-67; V of Ch Ch Blacklands Hastings 58-63; Willingdon 63-72; Hove 72-78; P-in-c of St Agnes Hove 73-77; RD of Hove 72-77; Surr from 73; Can and Preb of Chich Cathl from 74; V of W Wittering Dio Chich from 78. *West Wittering Vicarage, Cakeham Road, Chichester, Sussex.* (W Wittering 2057)

GREENHALGH, David Murray. b 13. Jes Coll Cam 3rd cl Engl Trip pt i 33, BA and Corrie Pr 34, 2nd cl Th Trip pt i 35, MA 38. Univ of Lon BD 47. Ridley Hall, Cam 34. **d** 36 **p** 37 Man. C of St Mark Worsley 36-38; Ch Ch Pennington 38-43; R of St Anne Newton Heath 43-49; V of Guilden Morden 49-55; Terrington St Clem 55-59; Shirley 59-78; Surr 69-78; Perm to Offic Dio B & W from 78; Dio Sarum from 80. *8 Kippax Avenue, Wells, Somt, BA5 2TT.* (Wells 74869)

GREENHALGH, Eric. b 26. Late Jenkyns Scho of St Jo Coll Dur BA 51, Dipl Th 53. **d** 53 **p** 54 Man. C of Tyldesley 53-55; St Pet Blackley 55-56; V of Rhodes Dio Man from 56; V of Birch-in-Hopwood Dio Man from 63. *Rhodes Vicarage, Middleton, Manchester, M24 4PU.* (061-643 3224)

GREENHALGH, Eric. b 20. Tyndale Hall, Bris. **d** 63 Burnley for Blackb **p** 64 Blackb. C of St Mary Preston 63-66; C-in-c 66-68; V 68-72; V of Partington w Carrington 72-80; Inskip Dio Blackb from 80. *St Peter's Vicarage, Inskip, Preston, Lancs, PR4 0TT.* (Catforth 690316)

GREENHALGH, Ven George Henry. Em Coll Sktn LTh 39. **d** 39 **p** 40 Sktn. C of Denholm and of Delishe 39-40; Charlottetown 41-42; I of Colwood 42-46; Port Alberni 47-57; Nanaimo 57-71; St Paul Vic 71-80; Hon Can of BC 59-75; Archd of Esquimalt 75-80; Archd (Emer) from 80; Perm to Offic Dio BC from 80. *1242 Rockcrest Avenue, Victoria, BC, Canada.* (604-382 3087)

GREENHALGH, Ian Frank. b 49. Wycl Hall Ox 74. **d** 77 **p** 78 Liv. C of Parr 77-80; V of St Barn Marsh Green, Wigan Dio Liv from 80. *St Barnabas Vicarage, Lancaster Road, Marsh Green, Wigan, Gtr Man, WN5 0PT.* (Wigan 222092)

GREENHALGH, Canon Jonathan Alfred. St Jo Coll WInnipeg BA 60. Angl Th Coll BC LTh 64. **d** 64 **p** 65 Koot. C of Vernon 64-67; R of Revelstoke 67-73; Exam Chap to Bp of Koot from 73; I of Kelowna Dio Koot from 73; Hon Can of Koot from 75. *608 Sutherland Avenue, Kelowna, BC, Canada.* (765-5131)

GREENHALGH, Philip Adrian. b 52. Wycl Hall Ox 76. **d** 79 Colchester for Chelmsf **p** 80 Chelmsf. C of Gt Clacton Dio Chelmsf from 79. *112 Woodlands Close, Great Clacton, Essex, CO15 4RY.*

GREENHALGH, Robert John. Wollaston Coll W Austr 60. **d** 65 **p** 68 Perth. Dioc Sec Perth 66-70; Regr 70-71; R of Graylands 71-73; Trayning 74-77; Lynwood Dio Perth from 77. *Rectory, Tavistock Crescent, Lynwood, W Australia 6155.* (458 8648)

GREENHALGH, Stephen. b 53. Trin Coll Bris 77. London Bible Coll BA 80. **d** 81 Man. C of H Trin Horwich Dio Man from 81. *27 Brownlow Road, Horwich, Bolton, Gtr Manchester.*

GREENHALGH, Ven William Edward. Em Coll Sktn LTh 42. **d** 42 Arctic for Sktn **p** 43 Sktn. C of Paynton 42-44; I of Radisson 44-45; Ladysmith w Cedar Distr 45-50; St Alb Vic 50-57; V of Quamichan 57-66; R of Royal Oak 66-72; St Matthias Vic Dio BC from 72; Hon Can of Ch Ch Cathl Vic BC from 76; Archd Dio BC from 81. *1670 Richardson Street, Victoria, BC, Canada.* (604-592 1048)

GREENHALL, Leonard William. Ridley Coll Melb ACT ThL 64. **d** and **p** 64 Melb. C of Ivanhoe 64-65; St Thos Essendon 65-66; I of Dampier 66-69; Perm to Offic Dio Melb 69-76; C of Lara Dio Melb from 76. *5 Cortland Road, Highton, Vic., Australia 3216.* (052-75 1158)

GREENHILL, Anthony David. b 39. Univ of Bris BSc 59. Tyndale Hall, Bris 61. **d** 63 **p** 64 Portsm. C of St Jude Southsea 63-65; w Bible and Med Miss Fellowship India 65-78; C of Kinson 78-81; V of St Phil Girlington Dio Bradf from 81. *St Philip's Vicarage, Baslow Grove, Bradford, BD9 5JA.* (Bradf 44987)

GREENHOUGH, Alan Kenneth. b 40. St D Coll Lamp Dipl Th 66. **d** 66 Repton for Derby **p** 67 Derby. C of Allestree 66-70; Ilkeston 70-73; V of Bradwell Dio Derby from 73. *Bradwell Vicarage, Sheffield, S30 2HJ.* (Hope Valley 20485)

GREENHOUGH, Arthur George. b 30. Fitzw Ho Cam BA (Math Trip Jun Opt) 52, MA 56. Tyndale Hall, Bris. **d** 57 **p** 58 Wakef. C of St Andr Wakef 57-63; R of Birkin w Haddlesey Dio York from 63; RD of Selby from 77. *Haddesley Rectory, Selby, N Yorks.* (Burn 245)

GREENHOUGH, Geoffrey Herman. b 36. Univ of Sheff BA 57. BD (Lon) 71. St Jo Coll Nottm 74. **d** 75 **p** 76 Ches. C of St Andr Cheadle Hulme 75-78; R of Tilston Dio Ches from 78; V of Shocklach Dio Ches from 78. *Rectory, Inveresk Road, Tilston, Malpas, Chesh.* (Tilston 289)

GREENING, Gilbert Royden. b 03. Lon Coll of Div 37. **d** 38 **p** 39 B & W. C of St Paul Walcot 38-40; CF (EC) 40-45; Hon CF 45; R of Dowdeswell 45-51; Chap RAF 51-52; V of Ruyton-XI-Towns 52-57; Meole-Brace 57-68; R of Sutton Salop 57-68. *Ashbrook Crescent, Church Stretton, Salop.*

GREENLAND, Clifford James Gomm. b 09. Clifton Th Coll 63. **d** 64 **p** 65 Guildf. C of Woking 64-67; V of St Mary Magd Wiggenhall 67-75; Perm to Offic Dio Chelmsf from 75. *6 Sunset Avenue, Woodford Green, Essex.*

GREENLAND, Robin Anthony Clive. b 31. Univ of Dur BA 53. MRTPI 57. Linc Th Coll 59. **d** 61 **p** 62 Wakef. C of Marsden 61-63; Cleethorpes 63-65; V of Holton-le-Clay 65-70; Tetney 65-70; Embsay w Eastby 70-78; Earby Dio Bradf from 78. *Vicarage, Skipton Road, Earby, Colne, Lancs, BB8 6JL.*

GREENLAND, Roy Wilfred. b 37. St Steph Ho Ox 71. **d** 73 **p** 74 Barking for Chelmsf. C of Wanstead 73-76; V of St Mary Magd Harlow Dio Chelmsf from 76. *Vicarage, Harlow Common, Essex, CM17 9ND.* (Harlow 22681)

GREENLEES, Geoffrey Ian Loudon. b 20. Sarum Th Coll 70. **d** 71 Sherborne for Sarum **p** 72 Sarum. C of Wilton Dio Sarum 71-74; R of Woodchurch Dio Cant from 75. *Woodchurch Rectory, Ashford, Kent.* (Woodchurch 257)

GREENMAN, David John. b 35. BA (Lon) 59. Oak Hill Th Coll 57. **d** 61 **p** 62 S'wark. C of St Steph Wandsworth 61-63; St Gabr Bp Wearmouth 63-66; P Missr of H Spirit Conv Distr Bedgrove, Aylesbury 66-74; Ch Ch Macclesfield 74; P-in-c 74-77; V 77-81; V of St Jas City and Dio Glouc 81; P-in-c of All SS City and Dio Glouc from 81. *St James Vicarage, Upton Street, Gloucester, GL1 4LA.* (0452-422349)

GREENSHIELDS, James Alenson. St Columb's Hall Wang 62. **d** 64 Wang **p** 66 St Arn for Wang. C of Shepparton 64-66; Maryborough 66-67; CF (Austr) 67-72; R of Corryong 72-74; L to Offic Dio Wang 74-80; C of Seymour Dio Wang from 80. *PO Box 107, Seymour, Vic, Australia 3707.*

GREENSIDES, Leonard. b 17. Kelham Th Coll 38. **d** 43 **p** 44 Sheff. C of St Leon Norwood 43-46; St John Balby Sheff 46-50; Chap at Patterson Settlement Suva 50-59; Prec of H Trin Pro-Cathl and Supt Melan Miss Suva 52-59; V of Worsborough 59-62; Ashmansworth w Crux Easton and woodcott 62-66; Yateley 66-70; Abbotskerswell Dio Ex from 70. *Abbotskerswell Vicarage, Newton Abbott, Devon.* (Newton 61911)

GREENSLADE, John McDonald. b 34. St Jo Coll Auckld LTh 70. **d** 65 Nel for Kar **p** 66 Kar. Tutor Bible Tr Inst Hyderabad 65-70; C of Cashmere Hills 70; Bryndwr-Burnside 70-73; V of Burnside Dio Ch Ch from 73. *40 Kendal Avenue, Christchurch 5, NZ.* (588-174)

GREENSLADE, Keith James Inglis. b 27. St Mich Coll Llan 60. **d** 62 **p** 63 Bris. C of Bishopsworth 62-65; St Paul Chippenham 65-68; V of U Stratton Dio Bris from 68. *Vicarage, Beechcroft Road, Upper Stratton, Swindon, Wilts SN2 6RE.* (Swindon 723095)

GREENSLADE, Peter Michael. b 37. Bp Burgess Th Hall 69. **d** 71 St D **p** 74 Liv. C of Llanwnda w Manorowen 71-73; Lydiate 73-75; V of St Cath Wigan 75-76; Chap Newsham Gen Hosp 76-78; C of Lache-cum-Saltney Ferry 78-80; V of

Barnton Dio Ches from 80. *Barnton Vicarage, Northwich, Chesh, CW8 4JH.* (Northwich 74358)

GREENSLADE, Ronald. b 09. GOC 73. **d** and **p** 76 Glouc. C of St Steph Cheltm 76-79; P-in-c of Tibberton w Taynton Dio Glouc from 80. *Rectory, Tibberton, Gloucester, GL19 3AG.* (Tibberton 286)

GREENTREE, David Lindsay. b 49. Univ of Syd BE 71, MEngSc 76. Moore Th Coll Syd ThL 78. **d** and **p** 79 Gippsld. P-in-c of Lang Lang Dio Gippsld from 79. *Rectory, Lang Lang, Vic, Australia 3984.*

GREENUP, Basil William. b 08. Late Exhib of St Jo Coll Cam BA 30, MA 37. Bps' Coll Cheshunt 38. **d** and **p** 39 S'wark. C of St Luke Richmond 39-40; Conduct Eton Coll 40-64; Master of the Choristers Eton Coll 40-64; Perm to Offic Dio Win 43-61; Dio Truro from 68. *Clouds, Rock, Wadebridge, Cornw.*

GREENUP, Geoffrey Frederick. b 02. Late Scho of Keble Coll Ox BA (2nd cl Hist) 24, MA 28. Wells Th Coll 26. **d** 26 **p** 27 Bris. C of St Jo Evang Clifton 26-31; V of St Agnes Bris 31-36; R of Frenchay 36-56; CF (EC) 40-45; V of Sandon 56-75. *5 Oxford Road, Thame, Oxon, OX9 2AG.*

GREENWAY, John. b 32. Qu Coll Birm 68. **d** 69 **p** 70 St Alb. C of Ch Ch Luton 69-74; Pulloxhill w Flitton 74-76; P-in-c of Marston Morteyne 76-81; Lidlington 77-81; R of Marston Morteyne w Lidlington Dio St Alb from 81. *Marston Morteyne Rectory, Bedford, MK43 0NF.* (Lower Shelton 248)

GREENWAY, John Waller Harry Kelynge. b 07. Cudd Coll. **d** 49 **p** 50 St E. C of Creeting St Mary w St Olave and All SS 49-50; C-in-c Stonham Aspal 50-51; R 51-54; Theberton 54-63; Middleton w Fordley 59-63; Itchen-Abbas w Avington 63-72; Hon Chap of Win Cathl from 65. *16 Bereweeke Way, Winchester, Hants.* (Winchester 63200)

GREENWAY, Lionel Edward. b 05. Coll of Resurr Mirfield 24. **d** 31 **p** 32 Truro. C of Redruth 31-37; St Teath (in c of Delabole) 37-44; V of Downside 44-80; RD of Midsomer Norton 51-71; Preb of Wells Cathl 54-80. *Longcroft, Churcham, Glos, GL2 8AW.*

GREENWELL, Christopher. b 49. Linc Th Coll 79. **d** 81 York. C of St Martin Scarborough Dio York from 81. *136 Filey Road, Scarborough, N Yorks, YO11 3AA.*

GREENWOOD, Frank Braithwaite. b 1885. Magd Coll Cam BA 06. Leeds Cl Scho 07. **d** 08 **p** 09 Wakef. C of St Mary Barnsley 08-11; C-in-c of Hebden Bridge 11-14; V of New Hanover Natal 14-17; TCF 18-19; C of Karkloof 20-22; V 22-30; V of Cawthorne 30-44; Flookburgh 44-53; Field Broughton 53-59. *Woodlands, Queens Road, Kendal, Cumb.*

GREENWOOD, Gordon Edwin. b 44. Trin Coll Bris 78. **d** 80 Liv **p** 81 Warrington for Liv. C of St Matt Bootle Dio Liv from 80. *St Andrew's House, St Andrew's Road, Litherland, Mer.*

GREENWOOD, Canon Gerald. b 33. Univ of Leeds, BA 57. Linc Th Coll 57. **d** 59 **p** 60 Sheff. C of Rotherham 59-62; V of Elsecar 62-69; Wales 69-77; P-in-c of Thorpe Salvin 74-77; Hooton Roberts Dio Sheff 77-78; R from 78; P-in-c of Ravenfield 77-78; Dioc Schs Officer 77-81; Dioc Dir of Educn from 81; Hon Can of Sheff Cathl from 80. *Hooton Roberts Rectory, Rotherham, S65 4PF.* (Rotherham 850217)

GREENWOOD, Hilary Peter Frank. b 29. Univ of Nottm BA 57. M SSM 54. Kelham Th Coll. **d** 57 **p** 58 Southw. C of Modderpoort Miss 59-60; Tutor SSM Austr Th Coll and L to Offic Dio Adel 60-67; Warden Kelham Th Coll and Publ Pr Dio Southw 70-74; Asst Chap Madrid 74-76; L to Offic Dio Blackb 76-80; Dio Man from 80; Hon Chap Hulme Hall Univ of Man from 81. *11 Upper Lloyd Street, Moss Side, Manchester, M14 4HY.* (061-226 5961)

GREENWOOD, John. **d** and **p** 53 Bal. C-in-c of Ballan 53-56; Hopetoun 56-58; P-in-c of Mukawa 58-59; V of Rupanyup 60-63. *83 Cox Street, Port Fairy, Ballarat, Vic, Australia.*

GREENWOOD, John Newton. b 44. St Chad's Coll Dur BA 69, Dipl Th 70. **d** 70 **p** 71 Dur. C of H Trin Hartlepool 70-72; Asst Master Billingham S Jun Sch 72-75; Billingham C of E Jun Sch 76-78; Marton Grove Jun Sch Middlesbrough from 78; L to Offic Dio Dur from 72. *1 Brae Head, Eaglescliffe, Stockton-on-Tees, Cleveland.*

GREENWOOD, John Robert. Moore Th Coll Syd ACT ThL 43. **d** and **p** 43 Syd. C of St Clem Mosman 43-44; Bush Ch Aid Miss at Ceduna 44-45; Minnipa 45-50; Sydney 50-62; L to Offic Dio Syd 50-63; Org Sec Bush Ch Aid S Dio Syd 59-63; R of St Steph Coorparoo 63-71; P-in-c of Chester Hill 71-72; R 72-74; Randwick 74-78; Chap Toowoomba Hosp Dio Brisb from 79. *98 Long Street, Toowoomba, Queensland, Australia 4350.* (32 7414)

GREENWOOD, Leslie. Univ of Dur BA 59, Dipl Th 61. Cranmer Hall Dur. **d** 61 **p** 62 Wakef C of Birstall 61-63; St Mary Virg Illingworth Halifax 64-70; Chap H Trin Secondary Sch Halifax from 64; V of St Thos Halifax Dio Wakef from 70. *St Thomas's Vicarage, Claremont, Halifax, Yorks.*

GREENWOOD, Michael Eric. b 44. Oak Hill Coll 78. **d** 80 Liv **p** 81 Warrington for Liv. C of Clubmoor Dio Liv from 80. *9 Bellefield Avenue, West Derby.*

GREENWOOD, Norman David. b 52. Univ of Edin BMus 74. Univ of Lon BD 78. Oak Hill Coll 76. **d** 78 **p** 79 Nor. C of Gorleston 78-81; Miss w SAMS in Paraguay from 81. *Casilla 1124, Asuncion, Paraguay.*

GREENWOOD, Robert John Teale. b 28. Univ of Leeds, BA 53. Coll of Resurr Mirfield, 53. **d** 55 **p** 56 Wakef. C of S Kirkby w N Elmsall 55-60; St Mary (in c of St Mark) Hitchin 60-63; C-in-c of St Mich Arch Wakef 63-64; V 64-68; Asst Chap HM Pris Man 68-69; Chap 71-77; Chap HM Pris Holloway 69-70; L to Offic Dio Man 71-77; Dio Ches from 77; Chap HM Pris Styal Wilmslow from 77. *Chaplain's Office, HM Prison, Styal, Wilmslow, Cheshire, SK9 4HR.* (Wilmslow 532141)

GREENWOOD, Robin Patrick. b 47. St Chad's Coll Dur BA 68, Dipl Th 69, MA 71. **d** 70 **p** 71 Ripon. C of Adel 70-73; Min Can and Succr of Ripon Cathl 73-78; V of Halton Dio Ripon from 78. *Halton Vicarage, Selby Road, Leeds, LS15 7NP.* (Leeds 647000)

GREENWOOD, Roy Douglas. b 27. Tyndale Hall, Bris 58. **d** 60 **p** 61 Ox. C of St Matt Ox 60-62; V of Ulpha (w Seathwaite 63-72) 62-72; C-in-c of Haverthwaite 72-74; C of Ulverston 74-76; Lect 76-78; V of Egton w Newland Dio Carl from 78. *Vicarage, Penny Bridge, Ulverston, Cumb, LA12 7RQ.* (0229 86285)

GREER, John Edmund. b 32. Qu Univ Belf BSc 53, BAgr (1st cl) 54, PhD 56. Trin Coll Dub BD 65. Univ of Ulster MPhil 72. Bps' Coll Cheshunt 56. **d** 58 **p** 59 Connor. C of St Paul Belf 58-61; Tutor Bps' Coll Cheshunt 61-64; Chap 64; Educn Org for Ch of Ireland 65-68; Chap Univ of Ulster 68-72; Lect from 72. *Seacon Road, Ballymoney, Co Antrim, N Ireland.* (Ballymoney 62368)

GREER, John Edward. Selw Coll Dun LTh 65. **d** 55 **p** 56 Dun. C of Roslyn 55-58; V of Waimea Plains 58-62; N Invercargill 62-71; Fitzroy 71-80; Frenkton Dio Waik from 80. *8 Vincent Place, Hamilton, NZ.* (76-053)

GREER, Robert Ferguson. b 34. TCD BA (3rd cl Mod Hist) 56, MA 59. **d** 60 **p** 61 Down. C of Dundela 60-65; I of Castlewellan (w Kilcoo from 78) Dio Drom from 65. *Rectory, Castlewellan, Co Down, BT31 9NB. N Ireland.* (Castlewellan 306)

GREETHAM, William Frederick. b 40. Cranmer Hall Dur 63. **d** 66 Lanc for Blackb **p** 67 Blackb. C of St Annes-on-the-Sea 66-69; St Andr Ashton-on-Ribble 69-71; Chap Aysgarth Sch Bedale 71-75; C of Bedale 72-75; V of Patr Brompton w Hunton 75-81; Crakehall w Langthorne 75-81; Hornby 75-81; Kirkby-Stephen w Mallerstang Dio Carl from 81. *Vicarage, Vicarage Lane, Kirkby Stephen, Cumb, CA17 4QX.* (Kirkby Stephen 71204)

GREG, John Kennedy. b 24. Trin Coll Cam BA (3rd cl Hist) 46, MA 61. Chich Th Coll 46. **d** 49 **p** 50 Man. C of Ch Ch Walmsley 49-51; H Trin Carl 51-55; V of Lanercost w Kirkcambeck 55-62; Cumwhitton 62-75; Team V of St Barn (w H Trin from 80) City and Dio Carl from 75. *3 Housesteads Road, Carlisle, CA2 7XF.* (Carlisle 36710)

GREGG, Arthur Willard Richey. Sir Geo Williams Univ BA 61. Montr Dioc Th Coll LTh 65. **d** and **p** 65 Fred. I of Canterbury w Benton 65-71; R of McAdam 70-74; Douglas Dio Fred from 74. *106 Summer Street, Fredericton, NB, Canada.*

GREGG, David William Austin. b 37. BD (2nd cl) Lon 66. MA (Bris) 69. Tyndale Hall, Bris 63. **d** 68 Penrith for Carl **p** 69 Carl. C of St Mark Barrow-F 68-71; C-in-c of Lindal-in-Furness w Marton 71-75; Communications Sec Bd for Miss and Unity of Gen Syn 76-81; Prin Romsey Ho Cam from 81. *Romsey House Theological College, 274 Mill Road, Cambridge, CB1 3NQ.* (0223-248224)

GREGG, Peter Michael Damien. **d** 80 N Queensld (NSM). C of St Geo Mareeba Dio N Queensld from 80. *14 Quill Street, Mareeba, Qld, Australia 4880.*

GREGOROWSKI, Anthony Peter. St Paul's Coll Grahmstn 66. **d** 68 **p** 69 Capetn. C of St Sav Claremont 68-74; R of St Mark and St Phil Capetn 74-76. *Box 187, Bredasdorp, CP, S Africa.*

GREGOROWSKI, Canon Christopher John. Univ of Capetn BA 60. Cudd Coll 61. **d** 63 Bp Thorne for Capetn **p** 64 Capetn. C of St Sav Claremont 63-67; Clydesdale w Umzimkulu 67-68; P-in-c of St Cuthbert's 68-74; R of St Thos Rondebosch Dio Capetn from 74; Can of Capetn from 80. *Rectory, Camp Ground Road, Rondebosch, CP, S Africa.* (65-6752)

GREGORY, Alan Paul Roy. b 55. AKC and BD 77, MTh 78. Ripon Coll Cudd, 78. **d** 79 **p** 80 Guildf. C of Walton-on-Thames Dio Guildf from 79. *39 Winchester Road, Walton-on-Thames, Surrey.*

GREGORY, Anthony Lawrence. b 43. Dipl Th 69, BD 71 (Lon). Tyndale Hall Bris 67. **d** 71 **p** 72 Sarum. C of St Clem

Parkstone 71-74; SAMS Miss Dio Chile from 74. *Casilla 561, Vina Del Mar, Chile.*

GREGORY, Canon Charles George. TCD BA 30, MA 33. CBE 59. **d** 31 **p** 32 Dub. C of Donnybrook 31-33; Treas V in St Patr Cathl Dub 32-33; CF 33-59; Hon chap to HM the Queen 57-59; V of Okewood 59-63; R of Kilcummin Dio Tuam from 63; Can of Tuam Cathl 73-75; C-in-c of Aasleagh Dio Tuam from 74. *Kilcummin Rectory, Oughterard, Co Galway, Irish Republic.* (Oughterard 73)

GREGORY, Canon Douglas Alexander. Sir Geo Williams Univ BA 42. BC Th Coll 47. **d** 49 New Westmr **p** 51 Sktn. C of St Jas (in c of H Trin Miss) Sktn 49-50; I of Watrous 50-55; Tisdale 55-61; Can Missr Dio Sask 61-68; Regr 62-68; Dir of St Luke's Ho Meadow Lake Dio Sask 65-68; R of St Jude Winnipeg 68-73; I of St Steph Winnipeg Dio Rupld from 73; Can of Rupld from 80. *220 Helmsdale Avenue, Winnipeg, Manit, Canada.*

GREGORY, Graham. b 36. Open Univ BA 78. Dipl Th (Lon) 65. Tyndale Hall Bris 63. **d** 66 **p** 67 S'wark. C of St Mich AA Southfields 66-71; Em Hastings 71-74; V of St Ninian Douglas Dio S & M from 75; Dioc Youth Officer Dio S & M from 78. *St Ninian's Vicarage, Douglas, IM.* (Douglas 21694)

GREGORY, Howard Kingsley Ainsworth. b 50. Univ of WI Ja BA 73. Virginia Th Sem 73. **d** 73 **p** 74 Ja. Chap Univ of WI Ja 73 and from 73, on leave 73-74. *PO Box 30, Kingston 7, Jamaica.*

GREGORY, Ian Peter. b 45. Chich Th Coll 67. **d** 70 **p** 71 Lich. C of Tettenhall Regis 70-73; H Cross Shrewsbury 73-76; P-in-c of St Mary and All SS Palfrey Walsall 76-80; R of Petrockstowe w Petersmarland, Merton, Meeth and Huish Dio Ex from 80. *Petrockstowe Rectory, Okehampton, Devon, EX20 3HQ.* (Hatherleigh 336)

GREGORY, Ivan Henry. b 31. Univ of Leeds BA 52. Ely Th Coll 58. **d** 60 Bp Wand for Lon **p** 60 Lon. C of St Faith w St Matthias and All SS Stoke Newington 60-63; Withycombe Raleigh 63-67; V of Braunton w Saunton and Knowle 67-77; Tintagel Dio Truro from 77. *Vicarage, Tintagel, Cornwall.* (Camelford 770315)

GREGORY, John Benjamin Evans. b 1895. Lon Coll of Div. **d** 24 **p** 26 Oss. C of Maryborough 24-27; I of Timahoe U 27-31; Clonenagh (Mountrath) 31-34; Stradbally 34-61. *The Chalet, Greystones, Co Wicklow, Irish Republic.*

GREGORY, John Edwin. b 15. Univ of Birm BSc 37, PhD 49. **d** and **p** 77 Birm (APM). C of St Pet Maney Dio Birm from 77. *5 Silvermead Road, Sutton Coldfield, W Midl, B73 5SR.* (021-354 3263)

GREGORY, John Frederick. b 33. **d** and **p** 78 Glouc. Hon C of S Cerney w Cerney Wick 78-82; Coates, Rodmarton and Sapperton w Frampton Mansell Dio Glouc from 82. *Brynbeth, Frampton Mansell, Stroud, Glos, GL6 8JE.*

GREGORY, Kenneth. Wycl Hall, Ox 45. **d** and **p** 46 Roch. C of Gravesend 46-48; V of Wairau Valley 48-50; Brightwater and Dioc Missr Dio Nel 50-55; St Matt Dun 55-59; H Trin Karachi 59-61; L to Offic Dio Nel 61-63 and from 66; V of Suburban N 63-66. *Pilgrim's Rest, Coastal Highway, RD1, Richmond, Nelson, NZ.* (Nel 20-897)

GREGORY, Neil Thomas. b 44. Em & St Chad Coll Sktn 79. **d** 81 Sktn. C of Lloydminster Dio Sktn from 81. *Box 98, Kitscoty, Alta, Canada.*

GREGORY, Peter. b 35. Cranmer Hall Dur 59. **d** 62 **p** 63 Man. C of Pennington 62-65; N Ferriby 65-68; V of Tonge Fold 68-72; Hollym w Welwick and Holmpton 72-77; P-in-c of Foston w Flaxton 77-80; Crambe w Whitwell and Huttons Ambo 77-80; R of Whitwell w Crambe, Flaxton, Foston and Huttons Ambo Dio York from 80. *Flaxton Rectory, York.* (Flaxton Moor 243)

GREGORY, Raymond William. Univ of Melb MA 49. Ridley Coll Melb ACT ThL 59. **d** 60 **p** 61 Melb. Asst Master Brighton Gr Sch 51-61; Chap 63-68; C of Sandringham 60-61; Hampton 61-63; Dean of Trin Coll Univ of Melb 69-72; Hd Master All S School Charters Towers Queensld 72-78; Perm to Offic Dio Melb 78-81; Dio C & Goulb from 81. *9 Adam Place, Farrer, ACT, Australia 2607.*

GREGORY, Richard. b 11. Lich Th Coll 39. **d** 43 **p** 44 Lich. C of St Thos Wednesfield 43-45; St Mich AA Walsall 45-47; Gt Yarmouth (in c of St Jas) 47-50; V of Westcott 50-56; Ide and Chap R Devon and Ex Hosp 56-63; R of W w E Lydford (and Wheathill to 72) 63-76; Alford w Hornblotton 63-76; Perm to Offic Dio Ex from 76-81; Hon C of St Marychurch Dio Ex from 81. *Madeira Villa, 100 Westhill Road, St Marychurch, Torquay, Devon, TQ1 4NT.* (0803-35048)

GREGORY, Canon Richard Branson. b 33. Fitzw Ho Cam BA 58, MA 62. Ridley Hall Cam 59. **d** 60 **p** 61 Sheff. C of St Cuthb Firvale Sheff 60-62; Asst Chap Univ of Leeds 62-64; V of Yeadon 64-71; Exam Chap to Bp of Bradf 66-80; R of Keighley (w Lawkholme from 74) Dio Bradf from 71; RD of S Craven 71-73 and from 78; Hon Can of Bradf from 71. *Rectory, Woodville Road, Keighley, Yorks.* (Keighley 7001)

GREGORY, Roger. b 1889. St Jo Coll Dur LTh 14, BA 23. St Aid Coll. **d** 14 **p** 15 Liv. C of St Cypr Edge Hill Liv 14-17; St Andr Southport 17-24; Cler Supt Liv Scrip Readers' S 24-27; V of St Simon and St Jude Anfield 27-30; St Paul Jersey 30-40; C-in-c of Crossens 40-42; V of St John Silverdale 42-48; R of Cold Norton w N Fambridge 48-53; Horseheath 53-64; R of Bartlow 53-64. *Fitzpatrick House, Ely Road, Waterbeach, Cambridge.*

GREGORY, Stephen Simpson. b 40. Univ of Nottm BA (Th) 62. St Steph Ho Ox. **d** 68 **p** 69 Guildf. C of Aldershot Guildf 68-71; Chap St Mary Sch Wantage 71-74; R of Holt Dio Nor from 74; Edgefield Dio Nor from 74; RD of Holt from 80. *Rectory, Holt, Norf.* (Holt 3173)

GREGORY, Thomas. b 1899. Lon Coll Of Div 31. **d** 33 **p** 34 Man. C of Ch Ch Bradford 33-35; St Mary Deane 35-38; V of St Jas Ashton L 38-45; Urmston 45-56; Belmont 56-64; V of Bp Wilton 64-71; LPr Dios York and Ripon from 71. *Flat 2, 4 St George's Road, Harrogate, N Yorks.*

GREGORY, William. b 11. LRAM 55. Linc Th Coll 42. **d** 44 **p** 45 Dur. C of Chester-le-Street 44-48; St Nich Bishopwearmouth 48-50; C-in-c of St Mary's Conv Distr Humbledon 50-53; V of Boulton 53-67; Ticehurst 67-70; R of Breadsall 70-76. *The Old Boys School, School Square, West Hallam, Derbys.*

GREGORY, William Herbert. **d** 56 **p** 57 Wai. C of Gisborne 56-57; V of Woodville 57-64; Te Puke Par Distr 64-75; C of St Pet Palmerston N 76-77; Perm to Offic Dio Wel from 77. *53 Lincoln Terrace, Palmerston North, NZ.*

GREGORY, William Thomas. Moore Th Coll Syd. **d** and **p** 59 Nel. C of Surburban N 59-60; V 60-62; Chap Miss to Seamen and Chap Nelson Hosp 59-62; R of Gymea w Gymea Bay 62-67; C-in-c of W Pennant Hills Dio Syd 67-74; R from 74. *64 Castle Hill Road, West Pennant Hill, NSW, Australia 2120.* (84-2937)

GREGORY-SMITH (formerly SMITH), Thomas Gregory. b 08. Late Scho of St Jo Coll Cam BA (2nd cl Mech Sc Trip) 30, MA 34. Lon Coll of Div 33. **d** 34 **p** 35 Lon. C of St Jude Mildmay Pk 34-36; Em S Croydon 36-38; CMS Miss at Kabale 38-47 and 52-62; Fort Portal 62-63; L to Offic at St Jas Shirley Hants 48; Financial Sec Ruanda Miss 49-52; Asst Sec 64-71; L to Offic Dio S'wark 65-71; Perm to Offic Dio Guildf 65-71; Dio Win from 77; Min of Em Chap Wimbledon 71-76. *46 Sea Road, Barton-on-Sea, New Milton, BH25 7NG.*

GREGSON, Ernest. b 06. St Aid Coll 50. **d** 52 **p** 53 Derby. C of Church Gresley 52-56; PC of Ch Ch Chesterfield 56-71; L to Offic Dio Blackb from 79. *31 Highfield Road South, Chorley, Lancs, PR7 1RH.* (Chorley 76403)

GREGSON, Peter John. b 36. Univ Coll Dur BSc 61. Ripon Hall Ox 61. **d** 63 **p** 64 Man. C of St Thos Radcliffe 63-65; Brooklands 65-67; Chap RN from 68. *c/o Ministry of Defence, Lacon House, Theobalds Road, WC1X 8RY.*

GREGSON, Roger Granville. Moore Th Coll Syd ACT ThL 63. **d** 63 **p** 64 Syd. C of Punchbowl 63-65; Nowra 65-67; Chap Norf I 68-69; C-in-c of Merrylands W Provisional Distr 69-76; C of Gunnedah 76-77; V of Tambar Springs Dio Armid from 77. *Vicarage, Tambar Springs, NSW, Australia 2381.*

GREIG, Frederick Robert. Ch Ch Th Coll 58. NZ BD of Th Stud LTh 65. **d** 60 **p** 61 Nel. C of Blenheim 60-63; Collingwood 63-64; V of Havelock and of The Sounds 64-72; S CMS Miss Kenya 73-76; V of Awatere Dio Nel from 77. *Vicarage, Seddon, NZ.*

GREIG, George Malcolm. b 28. **d** 81 Brech (NSM). C of St Mary Magd Dundee Dio Brech from 81; St Jo Bapt Dundee Dio Brech from 81. *61 Charleston Drive, Dundee, DD2 2HE.*

GREIG, John Kenneth. Univ of Natal BA 57. St Paul's Th Coll Grahmstn LTh 60. **d** 61 **p** 62 Natal. C of St Thos Durban 61-65; Sheldon 65-66; Friern Barnet 66-69; St Mary Virg (in c of H Spirit) Kenton 69-71; Asst Chap Dioc Coll Rondebosch 71-76; Chap 76-78; Whitelands Coll Putney from 78. *Whitelands College, West Hill, SW15.* (01-788 8268)

GREIG, Martin David Sandford. b 45. Univ of Bris BSc 67. St Jo Coll Nottm 72. **d** 75 **p** 76 Cov. C of Keresley 75-79; St Andr Rugby Dio Cov from 79. *St George's House, St John's Avenue, Rugby, CV22 5HR.*

GRELLIER, Brian Rodolph. b 34. K Coll Lon and Warm AKC 61. **d** 62 **p** 63 S'wark. C of St Paul Wimbledon Pk 62-66; Chap Miss to Seamen Kobe 66-72; Gravesend 72-76; V of Freiston w Butterwick Dio Linc from 76. *Pinchbeck House, Butterwick, Boston, Lincs, PE22 0HZ.* (Boston 760550)

GRESHAM, Eric Clifford. b 15. Univ of Lon BA (French) 37. K Coll Lon & Warm. **d** and **p** 60 Matab. C of St Jo Bapt Bulawayo 60-62; Gwelo 62; Ascen Bulawayo 63-65; V of St Aid Bamber Bridge 65-71; Dir Relig Educn Dio Bloemf 71-72; R of Bethlehem OFS 72-73; Prin St Jo Sch Chikwaka Mashon 73-75; P-in-c of Cranborne & Hatfield Mashon 75-77; Min of Keele Dio Lich from 78. *3 Quarry Bank Road, Keele, Staffs, ST5 5AF.*

GRESSWELL, George Gilbert. b 03. Univ of Lon BA (3rd cl German) 38. Hartley Coll Man. **d** 43 **p** 44 S and M. C of Kirk Braddan 43-48; V of Rushen 48-59; RD of Castletown from 56; V of Laxey 59-70. *Ballafletcher Farm House, Cronkbourne, Braddan, IM.* (Douglas 22778)

GRETTON, Tony Butler. b 29. St Jo Coll Dur BA 53. **d** 54 B & W for Ex **p** 55 Ex. C of W Teignmouth 54-57; R of Norton Fitzwarren 57-68; Perm to Offic Dio B & W 68-72; Dio Glouc 72-73; Chap Mariners' Ch Dio Glouc from 73; P-in-c of Brookthorpe w Whaddon Dio Glouc from 79. *26 Lansdown Road, Gloucester, GL1 3JD.*

GREW, Richard Lewis. b 32. Clare Coll Cam BA (Nat Sc) 54, MA 58. Wycl Hall, Ox 67. **d** 68 Repton for Derby **p** 70 Derby. C of Repton 68-73; L to Offic Dio Derby from 73. *Brook House, Repton, Derbys, DE6 6ES.*

GREW, Timothy Alexander. K Coll NS BA 64. **d** 65 **p** 66 NS. R of Antigonish 66-68; P-in-c of Country Harbour 66-68; P-in-c of Puerto la Cruz Venezuela 69-72; on leave. *84 Deerwood Drive, Thompson, Manit., Canada.*

GREWCOCK, Peter Joseph. b 28. Sarum Th Coll. **d** 58 **p** 59 S'wark. C of St Barn Mitcham 58-60; Kingswood 60-62; V of Howe Bridge 62-72; St Chad's Leic 73-76; P-in-c of Werrington 72-73; St Giles-in-the-Heath w Virginstowe 72-73; Trotton w Chithurst 76-80; C of Broadstone Dio Sarum from 80. *c/o Vicarage, Macaulay Road, Broadstone, Dorset.*

GREY, Bruce Edwin. Ridley Coll Melb ACT ThL 75. **d** 76 **p** 77 Melb. C of St Mark Camberwell 76-78; St Steph Richmond 78-79; P-in-c of Marshall-Grovedale Dio Melb from 79. *112 Burdoo Drive, Grovedale, Vic, Australia 3216.* (052-43 3238)

GREY, Canon Edward Alwyn. b 23. Univ of Wales (Swansea) BA 48. St D Coll Lamp. **d** 50 Swan B for St A **p** 51 St A. C of Wrexham 50-58; R of Llanfynydd 58-69; Flint Dio St A from 69; RD of Holywell from 73; Cursal Can of St A Cathl from 76. *Rectory, Flint, Clwyd.* (Flint 3274)

GREY, Edwin Charles. b 03. Men in Disp 46. Wycl Coll Tor 46. **d** 48 **p** 49 Moos. I of Virginiatown 48-50; R of Geraldton 50-56; Nor Ont 56-60; Oldcastle 60-70; C of Bowdon 70-76; Asst Chap at Santa Cruz 77-79; Perm to Offic Dio Glouc from 79. *Pike's Cottage, 166 Washpool Lane, Kemble, Cirencester, Glos.*

GREY, Eric Myrddin. b 16. St D Coll Lamp BA 40. Lich Th Coll. **d** 47 **p** 48 St D. C of Henfynyw 47-50; Cwmaman 50-55; R of Capel Cynon w Talgarreg 55-60; Brechfa w Abergorlech and Llanfihangel-Rhos-y-corn Dio St D from 60. *Brechfa Rectory, Carmarthen, Dyfed.* (026 789-248)

GREY, Richard Thomas. b 50. St D Coll Lamp BA 73. Ripon Hall Ox 75. **d** 75 **p** 76 Mon. C of Blaenavon 75-77; St Paul Newport 77-80; Industr Chap Newport and Gwent from 77; CF (TAVR) from 78; R of Bedwellty Dio Mon from 80. *Bedwellty Rectory, Blackwood, Gwent, NP2 0BE.* (Bargoed 831078)

GREY, Roger Derrick Masson. K Coll Lon and Warm AKC 61. **d** 62 **p** 63 Dur. C of H Trin Darlington 62-63; Bp Wearmouth 63-67; Dioc Youth Chap and V of Mabe Dio Truro 67-70; Youth Chap Dio Glouc 70-76; Hon Dom Chap to Bp of Glouc 70-76; Hon Min Can of Glouc from 70; M Gen Syn from 75; V of H Trin Stroud Dio Glouc from 77. *10 Bowbridge Lane, Stroud, Glos, GL5 2JW.* (Stroud 4551)

GREY, Canon Thomas Hilton. b 18. St D Coll Lamp BA 39. Keble Coll Ox BA 41, MA 46. St Mich Coll Llan 41. **d** 42 **p** 43 St D. C of H Trin Aberystwyth 42-49; R of Ludchurch w Templeton 49-64; St Thos Haverfordwest w St Issell Haroldston Dio St D from 64; Can of St D from 73; RD of Roose from 75; V of St Mary Haverfordwest Dio St D from 77; Treas of St D Cathl from 80. *Rectory, Scarrowscant Lane, Haverfordwest, Dyfed, SA61 1EP.* (Haverfordwest 3170)

GREY-SMITH, Donald Edward. St Mich Coll Crafers ACT ThL 64. **d** 64 **p** 65 Adel. C of Gawler 64-66; P-in-c of Elliston 66-68; C of Weeke Hants 69-71; R of Ceduna Miss Distr 71-75; Broadview Dio Adel from 75; P-in-c of Northfield Dio Adel from 81. *19 Staffa Street, Broadview, S Australia 5083.* (08-44 5255)

GRIBBEN, John Gibson. b 44. Dipl Th (Lon) 73. K Coll Lon BD 75. Queen's Univ Belf MTh 81. Div Hostel Dub 73. **d** 75 **p** 76 Connor. C of Dunmurry 75-78. *c/o Community of the Resurrection, Mirfield, Yorks.*

GRIBBIN, Bernard Byron. b 35. St Aid Coll 58. **d** 60 **p** 61 Liv. C of Maghull 60-63; Prescot (in c of St Paul) 63-65; V of Denholme 65-71; Bankfoot 71-79; Chr Stewardship Adv Dios Bradf, Ripon and Wakef 78-79; Dio Bradf from 79; L to Offic Dio Bradf from 79. *398 Halifax Road, Wibsey, Bradford, W Yorks, BD6 2JR.* (Bradf 679062)

GRIBBLE, Canon Arthur Stanley. b 04. Qu Coll Cam 2nd cl Th Trip sect a, pt i, 26, BA (2nd cl Th Trip sect b, pt i) 27, 1st cl Th Trip pt ii and Burney Stud 29, MA 31. Westcott Ho Cam 27. **d** 30 **p** 31 Carl. C of St Mary Windermere 30-33; Almondbury 33-36; Chap Sarum Th Coll 36-38; R of Shepton Mallet 38-54; Exam Chap to Bp of B & W 47-54; Proc Conv B & W 47-54; RD of Shepton Mallet 49-54; Preb of Wiveliscombe in Wells Cathl 49-54; Prin of Qu Coll Birm and Lect Univ of Birm 54-67; Hon Can of Birm 54-67; Commiss Kimb K 61-66; Can Res, Chan and Libr of Pet Cathl 67-79; Can (Emer) from 79; Exam Chap to Bp of Pet from 68. *2 Princes Road, Stamford, Lincs.* (Stamford 55838)

GRIBBLE, David George. St Jo Coll Auckld LTh 66. **d** 67 **p** 68 Nel. C of Greymouth 67-69; V of Cobden-Runanga 69-72; Hon C of Motueka 72; V of Havelock 72-76; Cheviot Dio Nel from 76. *Vicarage, Cheviot, NZ.*

GRIBBLE, Howard Frank. b 27. Magd Coll Cam BA 50, MA 56. Ely Th Coll 50. **d** 52 **p** 53 Chelmsf. C of St Marg Leytonstone 52-56; R of Mufulira 56-59; L to Offic Dio Lon 59-62; Metrop Area Sec UMCA 59-62; V of St Mary Magd Harlow 62-70; R of Lezant 70-81; Lawhitton 70-81; RD of Trigg Maj 75-81; P-in-c of S Petherwyn w Trewen 77-81; Angl Chap R Cornw Hosps Treliske City & St Clem Truro from 81. *c/o Royal Cornwall Hospital* (Treliske), *Truro, Cornwall.* (Truro 74242)

GRIBBLE, Malcolm George. b 44. Churchill Coll Cam BA 67, MA 71. Linc Th Coll 79. **d** 81 Roch. C of St Giles Farnborough Dio Roch from 81. *Church House, Leamington Avenue, Orpington, Kent, BR6 9QB.* (Farnborough 52843)

GRIBBLE, Paul Anthony Bousfield. St Francis Coll Brisb ACT ThL 60. **d** 60 **p** 61 Rockptn. C of Emerald 60-62; St Luke Wandal 62-63; V of Baralaba 63-66; Dawson Valley 66-69; V of S Gladstone w Miriam Vale 69-70; Chap Miss to Seamen Port Hedland 71-74; Supt St Geo Homes for Children Parkhurst Dio Rockptn from 75. *St George's Homes for Children, Parkhurst, Queensland, Australia 4702.* (079-36 1133)

GRICE, Charles. b 24. **d** 58 **p** 59 Sheff. C of Stocksbridge 58-61; R of Armthorpe 61-66; Industr Missr Dio Sheff 66-69; Industr Chap from 69; V of Tinsley 69-73; Oughtibridge 73-76; Gen Sec CLB from 77. *Church Lads' and Church Girls' Brigade, 15 Etchingham Park Road, N3 2DU.* (01-349 2616)

GRICE, David Richard. b 32. Keble Coll Ox BA 55, MA 59. St Steph Ho Ox 55. **d** 57 **p** 58 Ripon. C of St Aid Leeds 57-61; St Mary Virg Middleton 61-62; V of Woodlesford 62-69; St Wilfrid Leeds 69-78; R of Seacroft Dio Ripon from 78. *Seacroft Rectory, St James Approach, Leeds, LS14 6JJ.* (Leeds 732390)

GRICE-HUTCHINSON, Canon George Arthur Claude. b 12. Bps' Coll Cheshunt 39. **d** 39 **p** 40 Lon. C of St Leon Shoreditch 39-40; Seaton Hirst 40-41 and 43-46; Asst Chap Charterhouse Miss S'wark 41-43; C of Pershore (in c of St Mary Wick) 46-47; C-in-c of Holywell 47-49; V of St Cuthb (w All SS from 55) Newc T 49-56; V of All SS Newc T 50-55; St Mary Blyth 56-63; St Jas Benwell Newc T 63-74; N Sunderland and Warden Newc and Dur Youth Hostel 74-79; Sec Newc T Dioc Advisory C'tte from 74; Hon Can of Newc T 77-80; Can (Emer) from 80. *17 Westacres Crescent, Newcastle-upon-Tyne 5.* (0632-747975)

GRIERSON, Peter Stanley. b 42. BD (Lon) 68. Univ of Leeds MPhil 74. Linc Th Coll 68. **d** 69 **p** 70 Blackb. C of Clitheroe 69-71; Aston w Aughton 72-75; V of St Jude (w St Paul from 75) Preston Dio Blackb from 75. *115 Watling Street Road, Fulwood, Preston, PR2 4BQ.* (Preston 700563)

GRIEVE, David Campbell. b 51. St Jo Coll Dur BA 74. Wycl Hall Ox 74. **d** 76 **p** 77 Ches. C of Overchurch (or Upton) 76-80; Selston Dio Southw from 80. *26 Wilde Crescent, Selston, Notts, NG16 6EG.*

GRIEVE, Ian Alastair. Univ of Lon BSc 50. **d** 65 **p** 68 Niag. Hon C of Oakville 75-79; P-in-c of St John Burlington Dio Niag from 79. *216 Third Line, Oakville, Ont, Canada.* (416-827 2350)

GRIEVE, Canon Malcolm Douglas. b 1899. St Edm Hall, Ox BA 21, MA 29. Westcott Ho Cam. **d** 22 **p** 23 Carl. C of St Aid Carl 22-24; Ch Ch Whitehaven 25-26; Dalton-F 26-29; V of Satterthwaite 29-32; Dearham 32-45; Urswick 45-69; Hon Can of Carl 62-69; Can (Emer) from 69; RD of Ulverston 65-69; L to Offic Dio Carl from 69. *Valley Howe, Cartmel, Grange-over-Sands, Lancs.* (Cartmel 357)

GRIEVE, Robert Andrew Cameron. b 33. ACP 65. Edin Th Coll 69. **d** 71 **p** 72 Man. C of Leigh 71-73; Hon C of Chedburgh w Depden and Rede 73-75; L to Offic Dio St E 75-77; V of Assington 77-79; P-in-c of Newton 77-79; L Cornard 77-79; R of Fraserburgh Dio Aber from 79; New Pitsligo Dio Aber from 79. *39 Victoria Street, Fraserburgh, Aberdeen, AB4 5PJ.* (Fraserburgh 2158)

GRIFFIN, Alan Howard Foster. b 44. TCD BA 66, MA 69. Peterho Cam PhD 71. Sarum Wells Th Coll 75. **d** 78 **p** 79 Ex. Lect Univ of Ex from 78; Asst to the Lazenby Chap Ex Univ from 78. *Duryard House, Duryard Halls, University, Exeter. EX4 4RE.* (Ex 77911)

GRIFFIN, Catherine Ann. b 39. Univ of Tor BA 65, BSW 68. Trin Coll Tor MDiv 79. **d** 78 **p** 79 Rupld. C of Emerson

Area Dio Rupld from 78. *Box 29, Emerson, Manitoba, Canada. R0A 0L0.*

GRIFFIN, Ven Charles Whittaker. b 02. TCD BA 23, Div Test 25, Elrington Th Pri 28, MA 41. **d** 25 **p** 26 Lim. PV Cho and C of St Mary's Cathl Lim 25-27; Succr 26-27; C of Kilnamanagh 27-29; I of Castle-island w Ballycushlane 29-35; Tralee 35-62; Exam Chap to Bp of Lim 41-62; Preb of Ballycahane in Lim Cathl 41-47; Treas of St Mary's Cathl Lim 47-52; RD of Tralee 47-54; Sec to Dioc Counc and to Glebes C'tee 50-54; Archd of Ardf and Agh and Preb of Effin in St Mary's Cathl Lim 52-62. *56 Crannagh Park, Rathfarnham, Dublin 14, Irish Republic.*

GRIFFIN, David Leslie. Ridley Coll Melb 73. **d** 75 Bp Dann for Melb **p** 76 Melb. C of Greensborough 75-77; Kerang 77; V of Collarenebri 78; C of Port Kemba 78-80; R of H Trin Erskineville Dio Syd from 80. *2 Rochford Street, Erskineville, NSW, Australia 2043.* (51-1796)

GRIFFIN, Dennis Gordon. b 24. Worc Ordin Coll 66. **d** 68 **p** 69 Worc. C of Cradley 68-69; St Barn Rainbow Hill Worc 69-74; R of St Jo Evang Broughton Salford 74-79; V of Pendlebury Dio Man from 79. *Christ Church Vicarage, Pendlebury, Manchester, M27 1AZ.* (061-794 2962)

GRIFFIN, Gerald Albert Francis. b 31. Qu Coll Birm 74. **d** 77 **p** 78 Lich (APM). C of Bushbury Dio Lich from 77. *92 Fifth Avenue, Low Hill, Wolverhampton.*

GRIFFIN, Harold Rodan Bristow. b 12. Jes Coll Cam BA 33, LLB 34, MA 43. Ridley Hall Cam 43. **d** 45 **p** 46 York. C of Kirbymoorside and Edston 45-49; St Barn Linthorpe (in c of St Jas) 49-52; Boylestone 52; R of Atlow 52-54; R of Hulland (w Atlow and Bradley from 54) 52-61; Helmingham 61-71; V of Framsden 61-71. *Address temp unknown.*

GRIFFIN, John Harry Travis. late Exhib of St Chad's Coll Dur BA 25, Dipl Th 26, MA 28. **d** 26 **p** 28 Lich. C of All SS Wolverhampton 26-28; St Mary Virg Shrewsbury 28-34; Asst Org Sec SPG Ludlow 34-59; V of Sibdon Carwood w Halford Dio Heref from 34. *Halford Vicarage, Craven Arms, Shropshire, SY7 9BT.* (05882 3307)

GRIFFIN, Canon John Henry Hugh. b 13. St Cath Coll Cam BA 35, MA 39. Linc Th Coll 35. **d** 38 **p** 39 St E. C of Bramford w Burstall 38-42; L to Offic as C-in-c of Halesworth 42-46; R of Stratford St Mary 46-72; V of Higham St Mary 46-72; C of Hadleigh Suff 72-74; P-in-c of Gt and L Glemham 73-79; Blaxhall w Stratford St Andr and Farnham 73-79; Hon Can of St E Cathl 78-79; Can (Emer) from 79; Perm to Offic Dio St E from 79. *3 Church Street, Hadleigh, Suffolk.*

GRIFFIN, Joseph William. b 48. Univ of Wales (Cardiff) Dipl Th 73. St Mich AA Llan 70. **d** 74 **p** 75 Swan B. C of Killay 74-78; St Thos Kilvey 78-81; V of Troedrhiwgarth Dio Llan from 81. *Garth Vicarage, Bridgend Road, Maesteg, Mid Glam, CF34 0NL.* (0656-732441)

GRIFFIN, Kenneth Francis. b 21. BSc (Lon) 64. St Jo Coll Nottm 72. **d** 73 **p** 74 Roch. C of Bexleyheath 73-76; R of Kingsdown w Mappiscombe Dio Roch from 76. *Rectory, West Kingsdown, Sevenoaks, Kent.* (W Kingsdown 2265)

GRIFFIN, Canon Leslie Jack. b 09. St Jo Coll Dur BA 36, Dipl in Th 37, MA 39. **d** 37 **p** 38 Man. C of St Mark Cheetham 37-39; Ch Ch W Didsbury 39-42; R of St Luke Miles Platting 42-46; St Paul Withington 46-82; Hon Can of Man from 59; RD of Heaton 61-65; Withington 65-72; Chap Christie Hosp Man 61-71. *491 Wilmslow Road, Manchester 20.* (061-445 3781)

GRIFFIN, Malcolm Neil. b 36. Univ of Leeds, BA (2nd cl Hist) 57. Coll of Resurr Mirfield 57. **d** 59 **p** 60 Lich. C of Cheadle 59-61; Bloxwich 61-64; C-in-c of St Anne Willenhall 64-69; V of Stretton w Claymills 69-75; Berkswich w Walton Dio Lich from 75. *Berkswich Vicarage, Baswich Lane, Stafford, ST17 0BN.* (Stafford 51057)

GRIFFIN, Canon Michael Richard. BC Coll Bris 43. **d** and **p** 44 Roch. C of St Steph Tonbridge 44-45; Ch Ch Tunbridge Wells 45-47; V of St Pet Hindley 47-51; I of Kirkton Ont 52-54; St Steph Brantford 54-56; Trin Ch St Thomas 56-61; R of St Jas Stratford Dio Hur from 61; Can of Hur from 64; SB of St John of Jer from 67. *108 Mornington Street, Stratford, Ont., Canada.* (519-271 3572)

GRIFFIN, Niall Paul. b 37. TCD BA 61. **d** 61 **p** 62 Down. C of Newtownards 61-63; Armagh 63-64; Cross Roads Jamaica 64-66; Shankill Lurgan 66-69; Chap RAF from 69. *c/o Ministry of Defence, Adastral House, WC1.*

GRIFFIN, Nigel Charles. b 48. Univ of Leic BSc 71. Cudd Coll Dipl Th 73. **d** 74 **p** 75 S'wark. C of St Anne Wandsworth 74-77; V of Good Shepherd Tadworth Dio S'wark from 77. *Vicarage, The Avenue, Tadworth, Surrey, KT20 5AS.* (Tadworth 3152)

GRIFFIN, Nigel Robert. b 50. St D Coll Lamp BA 72. Ripon Hall Ox 71. **d** 73 **p** 74 St D. C of Burry Port 73-77; Carmarthen 77-80; Dioc Youth Chap from 79; V of Whitland w Kiffig Dio St D from 80. *Vicarage, Whitland, Dyfed.* (Whitland 494)

GRIFFIN, Robert Maurice. b 13. Tyndale Hall, Bris 52. **d** 54 **p** 55 Lich. C of Heath Town 54-57; V of Bayston Hill 57-66; C-in-c of St Chrys Everton 66-70; C-in-c of St Jo Evang Everton 69-71; N Area Sec BCMS 70-75; Perm to Offic in Dios of N Provs 70-75; V of Withnell 75-79; L to Offic Dio Blackb from 79. *86 Runshaw Lane, Euxton, Chorley, Lancs.*

GRIFFIN, Canon Roger Thomas Kynaston. Univ of Lon ALCD (2nd cl) 41. **d** 41 **p** 42 S'wark. C of St Pet Norbiton (in c of St Steph) 41-45; V of Good Easter 45-55; V of Berners Roding 45-55; R of Abbess Roding w Beauchamp Roding 49-55; Surr from 51; V of Becontree 55-61; W Ham Dio Chelmsf from 61; C-in-c of St Mary Plaistow 71-72; Chairman RADD from 73; Hon Can of Chelmsf from 80. *West Ham Vicarage, Devenay Road, E15 4AZ.* (01-519 0955)

GRIFFIN, Canon Rutland Basil. b 16. ALCD (1st cl) 41. **d** 41 **p** 42 Ox. C of Aylesbury and Chap Tindall Hosp 41-45; Bp's Hatfield (in c of St Mich AA Birchwood) 45-50; V of Biggleswade 50-61; Surr from 51; Chap Biggleswade Hosp 51-61; RD of Biggleswade 57-61; Dartford from 64; Surr from 61; V of Dartford Dio Roch from 61; C-in-c of St Edm Dartford 67-70; Hon Can of Roch from 70; Asst Sec Dioc Syn 70-73. *Vicarage, Dartford, Kent.* (Dartford 22782)

GRIFFIN, Samuel St John George. b 1899. FIMarE CEng. St Bonif Coll Warm. **d** 49 **p** 50 Bris. C of Hengrove 49-54; V of St Bede Bris 54-61; Wendron 61-69; L to Offic Dio Truro from 69. *Talybont, Rinsey Lane, Ashton, Helston, Cornw.*

GRIFFIN, Thomas Arthur. Hur Coll Ont. **d** 57 **p** 59 Hur. I of Ilderton 57-62; St Alb Lon 62-68; H Trin Lon 68-71; R of Lambeth 71-75; Ingersoll Dio Hur from 75. *60 Frances Street, Ingersoll, Ont., Canada.* (519-485 0502)

GRIFFIN, Very Rev Victor Gilbert Benjamin. b 24. Late Scho of TCD BA 46, Div Test 47, MA 57. **d** 47 **p** 48 Derry. C of St Aug Derry 47-51; Ch Ch Londonderry 51-57; I 57-68; RD of Londonderry 60-62; Lect Magee Univ Coll Londonderry 60-68; Preb of Howth in St Patr Cathl Dub 62-68; Dean of St Patr Cathl Dub from 68. *Deanery, St Patrick's Close, Dublin 8, Irish Republic.* (Dublin 752451)

GRIFFIN, Wilfred Gordon. b 04. AKC 35. **d** 35 **p** 36 Glouc. C of St Mary Thornbury Glos 35-37; Bp's Lavington w Cheverell Parva 37-39; C-in-c Surlingham 39; V of Tilshead 39-45; PC of Dundry 45-52; V of Othery 52-57; Middlezoy 52-57; C-in-c of Angersleigh 58-69; Dioc Insp of Schs 58-66; L to Offic Dio B & W from 69; C of Walton-in-Gordano 72-76. *34 Tennyson Avenue, Clevedon, Avon.*

GRIFFIN, William George. Late Scho of St Pet, Hall Ox 3rd cl Cl Mods 34, BA (2nd cl Th) 36, MA 45. Wycl Hall, Ox 36. **d** 37 **p** 38 Roch. C of St Paul Chatham 37-41; C-in-c of St Francis Temple Farm Conv Distr Strood 41-45; V of St Paul Lozells 45-51; Bp Ryder Ch Birm 51-56; All SS Burton-on-Trent 56-59; Bretby w Newton Solney 59-66; Ch Broughton w Barton and Sutton-on-the-Hill 66-72; R of Brington w Whilton 72-78. *6 Riverside Drive, Weedon, Northampton.*

GRIFFITH, Arthur Leonard. b 20. McGill Univ Montr BA 42. Queens Univ at Kingston Ont MDiv 58. United Th Coll Montr Hon DD 62. **d** 75 Bp Read for Tor **p** 76 Tor. C of St Paul Bloor Street City and Dio Tor from 75. *102 Arjay Crest, Willowdale, Ont, Canada, M2L 1C7.*

GRIFFITH, Bernard Macfarren. Univ of the WI BA (Th) 76. Codr Coll Barb 73. **d** and **p** 76 Barb. C of H Cross I and Dio Barb from 76. *Holy Cross Rectory, Massiah Street, St John, Barbados.*

GRIFFITH, Clive Leslie. Laurentian Univ of Sudbury Ont BA 77. Codr Coll Barb 70. **d** 71 **p** 72 Trinid. C of All SS Port of Spain 71-74; R of St Chris Siparia 74-77; St Clem Naparima Dio Trinid from 78. *St Clement's Rectory, Naparima, Via San Fernando, Trinidad.*

GRIFFITH, David Vaughan. b 36. St D Coll Lamp BA 60. Lich Th Coll 60. **d** 62 **p** 63 Ban. C of Llanfairfechan 62-66; Dolgelley 66-70; R of Llanfair-Talhaiarn Dio St A from 70; P-in-c of Llangernyw w Llanddewi and Gwytherin Dio St A from 77. *Llanfair-Talhaiarn Rectory, Abergele, Clwyd.* (Llanfair-Talhaiarn 273)

GRIFFITH, David Wellesley. Bps' Coll Cheshunt, 63. **d** 65 **p** 66 Guy. C of E Bank Demerara 65-67; Kitty 67-70; R of Plaisance 70-75; Beterverwagting 70-75; V of Meten-meer-Zorg 75-79. *675 East 219th street, Bronx, NY 10467, USA.*

GRIFFITH, Preb Dermot George Wallace. b 13. TCD BA 35. **d** 36 **p** 37 Down. C of Ballymacarrett 36-40; St Mark Ballysillan 40-42; C-in-c of Ardoyne 42-47; R of Killyman Dio Arm from 47; RD of Dungannon from 67; Preb of Arm Cathl from 73. *Killyman Rectory, Dungannon, Co Tyrone, N Ireland.* (Dungannon 22500)

GRIFFITH, Donald Bennet. b 17. Univ of Dur LTh 40. St Aid Coll 36. **d** 40 **p** 41 Man. C of St Osw Collyhurst 40-43; St John Pendlebury 43-45; C-in-c of St Ambrose Pendleton 45-47; V of St Cuthb Everton 47-52; Lathom 52-58; R of Frating w Thorington 58-66; Lawford 66-73; Theydon Garnon 73-77; Insp of Schs Dio Chelmsf 58-82; C-in-c of Bradfield 77-82. *Porto Cristo, Mill Lane, Thorpe-le-Soken, Clacton-on-Sea, Essex.* (Clacton-on-Sea 861766)

GRIFFITH, Eric William. b 42. St Jo Coll Morpeth ACT ThL 70. **d** 69 **p** 70 Newc. C of Mayfield 69-71; Cardiff 71-72; Wallsend 72-74; Murwillumbah 74-76; R of Bonalbo 76-79; Bellingen Dio Graft from 79. *Box 13, Bellingen, NSW, Australia 2454.*

GRIFFITH, Frank Michael. b 24. Univ of Bris BSc 50. Dipl Th (Lon) 60. St Aid Coll 58. **d** 60 **p** 61 Cov. [f Miss in Dio Momb] C of H Trin Leamington 60-63; Stratford-on-Avon w Bishopton 63-67; V of Rounds Green 67-70; Wasperton 70-78; R of Barford (w Wasperton and Sherbourne from 78) Dio Cov from 70; RD of Stratford-on-Avon 77-79; Fosse from 79. *Barford Rectory, Warwick, Coventry.* (Barford 624238)

GRIFFITH, Canon Geoffrey Grenville. b 17. Linc Coll Ox BA (3rd cl Th) 48. Chich Th Coll. **d** 50 **p** 51 York. C of St Aug Newland Hull 50-53; R of Waddington 53-57; Chap of Univ Coll and of Hatf Coll Univ of Dur and L to Offic Dio Dur 57-66; V of Chapel-en-le-Frith Dio Derby from 66; RD of Buxton 71-78; Hon Can of Derby Cathl from 80. *23 High Street, Chapel-en-le-Frith. Stockport, Chesh, SK12 6HD.* (029 8812134)

GRIFFITH, Glyn Keble Gethin. b 37. St D Coll Lamp BA 59. Ridley Hall Cam 67. **d** 69 Bp Parfitt for Cant **p** 70 Derby. C of St Aug Derby 69-72; Coity w Nolton 72-75; P-in-c of Heage 75-81; V of St Nich Allestree Dio Derby from 81. *Vicarage, Lawn Avenue, Allestree, Derby.* (Derby 50224)

GRIFFITH, Hugh Emrys. b 24. St D Coll Lamp BA 53. **d** 54 **p** 55 St A. C of Welshpool 54-56; Abergele 56-58; R of Llanfair Talhaiarn 58-61; Llangeinwen w Llangaffo and Llanfair-yn-y-Cwmwd 61-75; Llanllyfni w Talysarn and Penygroes 75-81; Team R of Almwch Dio Ban from 81. *Rectory, Amlwch, Anglesey, Gwyn, LL68 9EA.* (Amlwch 830740)

GRIFFITH, John Laurence Powell. b 30. Univ of Tor BA 53. Coll of Resurr Mirfield 69. **d** 71 **p** 72 St Alb. C of Gt Berkhamsted 71-79; P-in-c of Wilden w Colmworth and Ravensden Dio St Alb 80-81; R from 81. *Wilden Rectory, Bedford, MK44 2PB.* (Bedf 771434)

GRIFFITH, John Vaughan. b 33. St D Coll Lamp LTh 57. **d** 58 **p** 59 Ban. C of Holyhead 58-63; R of Trawsfynydd (w Maentwrog from 67) 63-68; Chap RAF 68-72; V of St Luke and H Trin Northwich 72-81; Sandiway Dio Ches from 81. *Sandiway Vicarage, Northwich, Chesh.* (Sandiway 883286)

GRIFFITH, Joseph Harry Cyril Wheldon. b 08. Jesus Coll Ox 27. Lich Th Coll 29. **d** 31 **p** 32 St A. C of Cerrig-y-druidion w Llanfihangel Glyn Myfr 31-38; V of Llanuwchllyn 38-48; Llangedwin 48-55; Northop 55-68; R of Llanfwrog w Efenechtyd 68-75. *6 Parc y Llan, Llanfair DC, Ruthin, Clwyd.*

GRIFFITH, Samuel Rhys. Late Exhib and Scho of St D Coll Lamp BA 53. CCC Cam BA 55, MA 60. St Mich Coll Llan 56. **d** 57 **p** 58 Swan B. C of Sketty 57-60; L to Offic Dio Swan B 60-62; Asst Master Craig-y-Nos Sch 60-62; C of Portsm Cathl 62-64; Asst Master Portsm Gr Sch 62-64; Chap 64-67; Wellingborough Sch 67-77. *c/o Wellingborough School, Northants.*

GRIFFITH, William Graham Allix. b 1898. St Jo Coll Cam 3rd cl Cl Trip pt i 21, BA (2nd cl Cl Trip pt ii) 22, MA 26. Bps' Coll Cheshunt 26. **d** 26 **p** 27 York. C of Beverley Minster 26-29; Scarborough 29-34; CF (TA) from 35; V of St Jo Evang Drypool 34-42; Rudby-in-Cleveland w Middleton 42-47; Aldborough w Dunsforth 47-50; St Columb Scarborough 50-62; St Olave w St Giles York 62-69. *28 Lang Road, Bishopthorpe, York, YO2 1QL.*

GRIFFITH, William Stephen. b 50. Univ of Wales (Bangor) BA 71. Westcott Ho Cam 71. **d** 73 Bp Vaughan for Ban **p** 74 Ban. C of Llandudno 73-76; Calne 76-78; P-in-c of Broadwindsor w Burstock and Seaborough 78-79; Team V of Beaminster Area 79-81; L to Offic from 81. *St Francis School, Hooke, Beaminster, Dorset, DT8 3NY.* (0249-860260)

GRIFFITH-MALLEY, John Rodney. b 40. **d** 66 **p** 67 Down. C of St Molua Stormont Belf 66-69; Carrickfergus 69-71; CF from 71. *c/o Ministry of Defence, Bagshot Park, Bagshot, Surrey.*

GRIFFITHS, Alan Charles. b 46. Univ of Dur BA 67, Dipl Th 69. Cranmer Hall Dur 66. **d** 69 **p** 70 Leic. C of H Ap Leic 69-72; L to Offic Dio York 73-77; V of St Richard Lea Hall Dio Birm from 77. *Vicarage, Hallmoor Road, Birmingham, B33 9QY.* (021-783 2319)

GRIFFITHS, Alec. b 42. St Chad's Coll Dur BA 63, Dipl Th 65. **d** 65 **p** 66 Glas. C of St Ninian Glas 65-68; St Jo Evang Greenock 68-72; R of H Cross Knightswood Glas 72-79; V of Birchencliffe Dio Wakef from 79. *Birchencliffe Vicarage, Marling Road, Fixby, Huddersfield, Yorks, HO2 2EE.* (Elland 72679)

GRIFFITHS, Alwyn Geoffrey. ACT ThL 62. **d** 61 **p** 62 Gippsld. C of Wonthaggi 61-63; St Barn Punchbowl 64-65; R of Erskineville 65-68; St Barn Punchbowl (w Greenacre from 79) 68-81; P-in-c of Greenacre 75-77; R of Dulwich Hill Dio Syd from 81. *11 Herbert Street, Dulwich Hill, NSW, Australia 2203.* (569-1290)

GRIFFITHS, Arthur Evan. b 27. ACP 66. St Deiniol's Libr Hawarden. **d** 69 Bp Partridge for Sheff **p** 70 Heref. C of Cleobury Mortimer Dio Heref from 69. *Maryn, Catherton Road, Cleobury Mortimer, Kidderminster, Worcs.*

GRIFFITHS, Benjamin Denyil Mortimer. K Coll Lon. **d** 47 **p** 48 St D. C of Laugharne w Llansadyrnen and Llandawke 47-48; Narberth w Robeston-Wathen and Mounton 48-51; R of Morfil w Pontfaen and Llanychllwydog 51-59; V of Llandefeilog 59-81. *5 St David's Avenue, Carmarthen, Dyfed.*

GRIFFITHS, Bernard Frederick David. Wollaston Coll W Austr 64. **d** 66 **p** 67 Kalg. C of St Jo Bapt Cathl Kalg 66-67; R of Esperance 68-73; Innaloo w Karrinyup 73-80; Chap St Jo of God Suciaco Dio Perth from 80. *73 Selby Street, Daglish, W Australia 6008.* (381-5050)

GRIFFITHS, Colin Lindsay. b 50. SSM Th Coll Adel 75. **d** 79 **p** 80 Adel. M SSM. C of St John Adel 79-80; L to Offic Dio Adel from 81. *St Michael's House, Summit Road, Crafers, S Australia 5152.*

GRIFFITHS, Canon Conrad Daniel Lynn. b 16. St D Coll Lamp BA 38, LTh 41. **d** 41 **p** 42 St D. C of St Issell Sandersfoot 41-44; Chap RNVR 44-48; C of Tenby 48-49; R of Burton 49-57 and 58-59; Exchange R of Anoka Minnesota USA 57-58; V of Dale 59-75; RD of Roose 72-75; V of Llanwnda w Manorowen and Goodwick (w Llanstinan from 78) Dio St D from 75; Can of St D Cathl from 78. *Vicarage, Goodwick, Dyfed.* (Fishguard 873251)

GRIFFITHS, Cyril. **d** 49 **p** 50 St Arn. C of Murrayville 49-50; V of Wedderburn 50-53; R of Birchip 53-54; V of Carisbrooke 54-56; Nyah 56-57; Natimuk 57-60; Coleraine 60-64; L to Offic Dio Bal 65-73. *PO Box 128, Esperence, W Australia 6450.*

GRIFFITHS, David. b 38. Univ of Wales (Cardiff) Dipl Th 67. St Mich Coll Llan. **d** 67 **p** 68 St A. C of Llangollen 67-71; Rhyl 71-74; V of Kerry (w Llanmerewig from 77) Dio St A from 74. *Kerry Vicarage, Newtown, Powys.* (Kerry 688)

GRIFFITHS, David Nigel. b 27. RD 77. Worc Coll Ox Gladstone Mem Pri and BA (3rd cl Phil Pol and Econ) 52, MA 56. Arnold Hist Essay Pri 59. Linc Th Coll 56. **d** 58 **p** 59 Pet. C of St Matt Northn 58-61; SPCK HQ Staff 61-67; Hon C of St Andr Bromley 65-67; Chap RNR 63-77; R of St Mary Magd w St Paul-in-the-Bail Linc 67-73; V of St Mich-on-the-Mt Linc 67-73; Vice-Chan and Libr Linc Cathl 67-73; R of New Windsor Dio Ox 73-81; Team R from 81; Surr from 73; Chap to HM the Queen from 77; RD of Maidenhead from 77. *Rectory, Park Street, Windsor, Berks, SL4 1LU.* (Windsor 64572)

GRIFFITHS, David Percy Douglas. **d** 78 **p** 79 St D. St Mich Coll Llan 77. C of Bettws w Ammanford 78-80; Llanarth Dio St D from 80; Capel Cynon w Talgarreg Dio St D from 80. *Vicarage, Llanarth, Dyfed.*

GRIFFITHS, David Rowson Hopkin. Oak Hill Th Coll 59. **d** 62 Penrith for Carl **p** 63 Carl. C of St Mark Barrow-F 62-65. *Overseas Missionary Fellowship, Kawabata Cho, 1 Jo 7 Chome, Asahikawa, Hokkaido, Japan.*

GRIFFITHS, David Wynne. b 47. Univ of Wales (Cardiff) BD 73. St Mich Coll Llan 69. **d** 73 **p** 74 Llan. C of Gabalfa 73-76; L to Offic Dio Llan 77-79; Hon C of Llwynypia w Clydach Vale 79-80; Pontypridd Dio Llan from 80. *2 Brynheulog, Porth, Mid Glam, CF39 9YB.*

GRIFFITHS, Edward Pitt. Univ of Liv BSc (Chem) 23. St Chad's Coll Regina. **d** and **p** 29 Qu'App. C of Waldeck 29; I of Mossbank 29-33; V of Kaslo 33-36; R of Revelstoke 36-43; Kamloops 43-50; Can of St Paul Kamloops 45-50; I of White Rock 50-69. *1475 Blackwood Street, White Rock, BC, Canada.*

GRIFFITHS, Evan David. b 32. Open Univ BA 77. St D Coll Lamp 64. **d** 66 **p** 67 St D. C of Betws w Ammanford 66-72; V of Newchurch w Merthyr 72-80; Llanybydder and Llanwenog w Llanwnnen Dio St D from 80. *Vicarage, Llanybydder, Dyfed, SA40 9QE.* (Llanybydder 480483)

GRIFFITHS, Frank Wall Griffith. b 07. Late Scho of St Cath Coll Cam 1st cl Geog Trip pt i, 27, BA (1st cl Geog Trip pt ii) 29, MA 33. Coll of Resurr Mirfield, 33. **d** 35 **p** 36 Llan. C of Merthyr Tydfil 35-37; St German Roath 37-39; St Luke Canton Cardiff 39-40; V of St Julian Newport 40-43; St Dyfrig Cardiff 43-50; R of Llanfrynach w Cantref 50-55; Exam Chap to Bp of Swan B 54-65; V of Ch Ch Swansea and Chap HM Pris Swansea 55-58; R of Llanelwedd w Llanfaredd 58-65; RD of Elwell 59-64; V of Padbury w Adstock 65-72. *Nutshell Cottage, Llangunllo, Knighton, Powys.*

GRIFFITHS, Frederick Cyril Aubrey Comber. b 10. St Bonif Coll Warm 39. 1 41 **p** 42 Sarum. C of Sherborne w Castleton and Lillington 41-44; Norton St Phil 44-45; L to Offic at Fordington St Geo 45-46; R of W Parley 46-47; V of Holt 47-51; R of Hinton Parva 48-51; CF (TA) 50-53; V of S

Baddesley 51-53; Perm to Offic Dio Win 53-61; Asst Master Ch Ch Cathl Sch Ox and Chap Ch Ch Cathl Ox 61-62; Org Sec CECS and Perm to Offic Dios Sarum Win and Portsm 62-67; Asst Master Qu Eliz Gr Sch Wimborne 67-68; Perm to Offic Dio Sarum from 75. *c/o 4 Boundary View, Blandford Forum, Dorset.*

GRIFFITHS, Garrie Charles. b 53. St Jo Coll Nottm LTh 77. **d** 77 Ches for Arctic **p** 78 Ches. C of Gt Whale River 77-78; H Trin & Ch Ch Castle Hall Stalybridge 78-81; Moreton Dio Ches from 81. *441 Hoylake Road, Moreton, Wirral, Merseyside, L46 6DQ.* (051-678 1646)

GRIFFITHS, Geoffrey Ernest. b 28. K Coll Lon and Warm AKC 52. **d** 53 **p** 54 Bris. C of Shirehampton 53-59; Sec SCM W Engl Schs 58-61; L to Offic Dio Bris 59-63; Chap Colston's Girls' Sch Bris 59-75; St Brandon's Sch Clevedon 60-63; V of Atworth Dio Sarum from 63; Chap Stonar Sch 63-66; C-in-c of Shaw Dio Sarum 69-72; V from 73. *Atworth Vicarage, Melksham, Wilts, SN12 8JA.* (Melksham 703357)

GRIFFITHS, George Brian. b 25. Kelham Th Coll 46. **d** 51 **p** 52 Bloemf. Miss St Patr Miss Bloemf 51-60; R of Teyateyaneng 60-63; C of Amersham 64-65; C-in-c of St Mich AA Conv Distr Amersham-on-the-Hill 66-73; V of Amersham-on-the-Hill Dio Ox from 73; M Gen Syn Ox 75-80. *70 Sycamore Road, Amersham, Bucks, HP6 5DR.* (Amersham 7553)

GRIFFITHS, Canon George Francis. b 09. Edin Th Coll. **d** 42 Hull for York **p** 43 York. C of Heworth and St Mary Castlegate w St Mich Spuriergate 42-45; Hessle 45-46; V of St Matt Hull 46-54; St Sav Denmark Pk 54-60; Ch Ch w St Andr and St Mich E Greenwich 60-65; R of Gt w L Weldon (w Deene from 67) 65-77; RD of Weldon 67-69; Corby 69-76; Can (Non-Res) of Pet 74-77; Can (Emer) from 77. *324 Bowthorpe Road, Norwich.*

GRIFFITHS, Gordon John. b 31. Univ of Wales (Cardiff) BA 53. SOC 72. **d** 75 **p** 76 S'wark (APM). Hon C of St Nich Sutton 75-78; Asst Chap Eastbourne Coll 78-81; L to Offic Dio Chich from 81. *15 Buckhurst Close, Eastbourne, E Sussex.* (Eastbourne 55547)

GRIFFITHS, Harvey Stephen. b 35. Linc Coll Ox BA (3rd cl Phil Pol and Econ) 58, MA 62. Linc Th Coll 60. **d** 62 **p** 63 Linc. C of Frodingham 62-65; Darlington (in c of All SS Blackwell) 65-70; Chap RN from 70. *c/o Ministry of defence, Lacon House, Theobalds Road, WC1X 8RY.*

GRIFFITHS, Hugh. b 44. Univ of Nottm BEducn 78. Clifton Th Coll Bris 69. **d** 71 **p** 72 Southw. C of Mansfield 71-77. *129 Chatsworth Drive, Southlands, Mansfield.* (Mansfield 642585)

GRIFFITHS, Hugh Peregrine. b 1890. Late Exhib of St Jo Coll Cam BA 12, MA 18. Ridley Hall, Cam 12. **d** 13 St Alb **p** 14 Chelmsf. C of Braintree 13-18; St Pet Clerkenwell 18-21; H Trin Richmond Surrey 21-23; Chap and Dir Allen Gardiner Mem Inst Los Cocos (SAMS) 23-29; C of St Paul St Alb 29-30; V of St Minver w St Mich and St Enodoc 30-46; Axmouth 46-70; Proc Conv Ex 50-51. *1 Manor House, The Street, Charmouth, Dorset.*

GRIFFITHS, Jack. b 16. St D Coll Lamp BA 39. **d** 42 **p** 43 Swan B. C of Cefn Coed w Nantddu 42-45; Llansantffraed-juxta-Usk w Llanthettyard Glyncollwng 45-50; Shirley Birm 50-51; V of Water Orton 51-60; Ward End 60-80; Asst Chap Eastbourne Coll from 80. *14a Grange Road, Eastbourne, BN21 4HJ.* (Eastbourne 73411)

GRIFFITHS, John Gareth. b 44. Lich Th Coll 68. **d** 71 **p** 72 St A. C of Shotton 71-73; Rhyl 73-76; V of Llanasa Dio St A from 76. *Vicarage, Llanasa Road, Gronant, Prestatyn, Clwyd, LL19 9TL.* (Prestatyn 3512)

GRIFFITHS, John Handel Wood. b 08. Late Exhib of St D Coll Lamp BA (3rd cl Hist) 31. St Mich Coll Lan 31. **d** 33 **p** 34 Ban. C of Llanfaethlu 33-35; Pwllheli 35-38; V of Llanfihangel-y-Pennant (or Abergynolwyn) 38-41; Llanfihangel-Aberbythick 41-58; Penllergaer 58-74. *6 Princess Street, Gorseinon, Swansea, W Glam.*

GRIFFITHS, John Herbert. St Francis Coll Brisb 59. **d** 62 **p** 63 Rockptn. C of Clermont 62-64; Longreach 64-66; V of Springsure 66-68; R of St Matt Pk Avenue Rockptn 68-72; Young 72-76; S Wagga Wagga Dio C & Goulb from 76. *31 Fernleigh Road, Turvey Park, NSW, Australia 2650.* (069-25 1707)

GRIFFITHS, John Medwyn. b 20. Univ of Leeds, BA 50. M CR 58-74. Coll of Resurr Mirfield. **d** 52 **p** 53 St D. C of St Paul Llanelli 52-55; L to Offic Dio Wakef 57-62; Dio Lon 62-63 and 71-75; Dio Ripon 63-66; Warden Hostel of the Resurr Leeds 64-66; Publ Pr Dio Win 75-81; P-in-c of H and Undivided Trin Halifax Dio Wakef from 81; St Jas w St Mary Virg Halifax Dio Wakef from 81. *9 Love Lane, Halifax, HX1 2BQ.* (0422-52446)

GRIFFITHS, John Trevor. BD (Lon) 62. Moore Th Coll Syd ACT ThL 62. **d** 62 **p** 63 Bp Hudson for Syd. C of Penrith 62-64; C-in-c of Narraweena w Ox Falls and Beacon Hill 64-69; R of E Willoughby 69-79; Dep Dir Angl Retirement Villages Dio Syd from 79. *132 Comenarra Parkway, Wahroonga, NSW, Australia 2076.* (48-1679)

GRIFFITHS, John Whitmore. AKC (2nd cl) 38. **d** 38 **p** 39 Guildf. C of St Paul The Hythe Egham 38-41; Ch Ch St Marylebone 41-44; V of H Trin Latimer Road 44-48; St Aug Fulham 48-56; C-in-c of St Osw Fulham 55-56; V of St Osw w St Aug Fulham 56-59; Chap St Mary's Hosp Paddington 59-66; R of Bow w Bromley St Leon 66-72; V of H Trin Stepney 66-72; V of St Paul w St Steph Old Ford 66-72; C-in-c of St Barn Bethnal Green 67-72; Chap W Pk Hosp Epsom 72-77; Perm to Offic Dio Ex from 77. *3 Kerri House, The Square, North Tawton, Devon, EX20 2ER.* (N Tawton 530)

GRIFFITHS, Leonard Lewis Rees. b 09. St Jo Coll Dur BA and LTh 31, MA 43. Lon Coll of Div 27. **d** 32 St Alb for Cov **p** 33 Cov. C of St Paul Leamington 32-35; V of Styvechale w Green Lanes Conv Distr 35-38; PC of Finham 38-39; Chap RN 39-64; Chap and Asst Master St Luke's Secondary Sch for Girls Portsm 64-67; R Sch for Daughters of Officers of RN and RM Haslemere 67-75; and 77-81; L to Offic Dio Antig 75-76; Guildf from 76. *Angle Cottage, Polecat Valley, Hindhead, Surrey, G26 6BE.* (Hindhead 5508)

GRIFFITHS, Lewis Eric Holroyd. b 05. Univ Coll Dur BA 29. **d** 29 **p** 30 Liv. C of St Andr Litherland 29-32; St Paul Ches 32-35; St Aug Wisbech 35-37; V of Gt w L Witchingham R 37-42; St Phil Heigham 42-58; Chap Hellesdon Hosp Nor 45-59; V of Bawburgh 58-59; V of L Melton 58-59; R of Tendring 59-70; Perm to Offic Dio Chelmsf from 70. *12 The Cedars, Adelaide Road, Teddington, Middx, TW11 0AX.*

GRIFFITHS, Martyn Robert. b 51. Univ of Nottm BTh 74. Kelham Th Coll 70. **d** 74 **p** 75 Birm. C of King's Heath 74-77; Solihull (in c of St Francis Elmdon Heath) 77-79; Team V 79-81; Asst Admin Shrine of Our Lady of Walsingham from 81. *The College, Shrine of Our Lady of Walsingham, Walsingham, Norf, NR22 6EF.* (032 872 266)

GRIFFITHS, Matthew Morgan. b 15. St D Coll Lamp BA 37. K Coll Lon Teaching Dipl 49. **d** 38 **p** 39 Wakef. C of St Edw Barnsley 38-41; Lampeter and Asst Master St D Coll Sch 41-44; Chap RNVR 44-47; Chap Qu Mary's Hosp Carshalton 47-51; Chap and Asst Master Em Sch Wandsworth 51-63; C-in-c of St D Welsh Ch Paddington 55-63; V of Llanrhystyd w Llanddeiniol 63-67; Chap and Asst Master Sandbach Sch and L to Offic Dio Ches 67-73; R of Newport w Cilgwyn Dio St D from 73. *Rectory, Newport, Dyfed.* (Newport 820380)

GRIFFITHS, Meirion. Clifton Th Coll 63. **d** 66 **p** 67 Stepney for Lon. C of St Pet U Holloway 66-68; St Jas Taunton 68-70; Radipole 70-74; R of St Pancras w St Jo Evang City and Dio Chich from 74. *St Pancras Rectory, St John Street, Chichester, W Sussex, PO19 1UR.* (Chich 782124)

GRIFFITHS, Mervyn Harrington. b 15. Ripon Hall, Ox 53. **d** 54 Liv **p** 55 Warrington for Liv. C of Aigburth 54-56; Grassendale 56-58; Findon 58-59; V of Bp's Sutton 59-74; R of Bighton (w Bp's Sutton from 74) 59-78; Perm to Offic Dio Ex from 80. *Kimberley, Clapps Lane, Beer, Nr Seaton, Devon.*

GRIFFITHS, Morgan Emlyn. b 17. St D Coll Lamp BA 38. St Mich Th Coll Llan 39. **d** 43 **p** 44 Swan B. C of Loughor 43-45; Devynock w Rhydybriw 45-47; St Matthias and St Lawr Barb 47; V 48-59; C of St Barn Swansea 60; R of Cwmdu w Tretower (w Crickhowell from 78) Dio Swan B from 60. *Rectory, Rectory Lane, Crickhowell, Powys.* (Crickhowell 811224)

GRIFFITHS, Neville. b 39. Univ of Wales, BA 63. St D Coll Lamp LTh 66. **d** 66 **p** 67 Mon. C of St Mark Newport 66-68; St Jo Bapt Cardiff 68-70; Greystoke 70-76; Team V 76; Chap and Tutor Greystoke Th Tr Coll 70-76; Chap Grey Coll Dur 76-81; C of Croxdale 76-81; R of Ch Ch W Didsbury Dio Man from 81. *Rectory, Darley Avenue, West Didsbury, Manchester.* (061-445 4152)

GRIFFITHS, Norman. b 12. Late Organ Scho of St D Coll Lamp BA 36. **d** 36 **p** 37 Llan. C of Ch Ch Cyfarthfa 36-37; Cymmer w Porth 37-42; St Martin Roath 42-48; V of St Matt Pontypridd 48-64; R of Penarth w Lavernock 64-77; Perm to Offic Dio Llan from 79. *52 Coed Mawr, Highlight Park, Barry, S Glam.* (Barry 743778)

GRIFFITHS, Richard Barré Maw. b 43. CCC Ox BA 65, MA 69. Cranmer Hall Dur Dipl Th 71, BA 71. **d** 71 **p** 72 Sheff. C of Fulwood Sheff 71-74; Univ of Sheff Research Fell and Hon C of St Jo Evang Park Sheff 74-76; C of St Matt Fulham Dio Lon 76-78; P-in-c from 78. *2 Clancarty Road, SW6 3AB.* (01-736 4452)

GRIFFITHS, Robert Arthur. b 25. St D Coll Lamp BA (2nd cl Phil) 50, LTh 52. **d** 52 **p** 53 St A. C of Eglwys-Rhos (in c of Duke of Clarence Ch) 52-57; V of St Pet Hindley 57-71; Charlesworth 71-77; Perm to Offic Dio Derby from 77. *47 Sheffield Road, Glossop, Derbys, SK13 8QJ.* (Glossop 61816)

GRIFFITHS, Robert Herbert. b 53. Univ Coll of N Wales (Bangor) Dipl Th 75. Chich Th Coll 75. **d** 76 **p** 77 St A. C of Holywell 76-80; CF (TAVR) from 79; V of Llanfair-

Dyffryn-Clwyd Dio St A from 80. *Llanfair-Dyffryn-Clwyd Vicarage, Ruthin, Clwyd, LL15 2SA.* (Ruthin 4551)

GRIFFITHS, Robert Rhys. Univ of BC BA 55. Angl Th Coll of BC LTh 55. **d** 58 **p** 59 Calg. C of St Mich AA Calg 58-60; I of Okotoks 60-64; Exam Chap to Bp of Calg 61-68; C of Redeemer Cathl Calg 64-67; I of H Nativ Calg 67-69; Foothills Miss 69-74; Exam Chap to Bp of Calg 71-74 and from 79; I of Castlegar 74-76; Oyama 76-78; C of Ch Ch City and Dio Calg from 78. *3602-8th Street SW, Calgary, Alta, Canada.*

GRIFFITHS, Roger. b 46. Trin Coll Bris 70. **d** 74 **p** 75 Derby. C of Normanton-by-Derby 74-77; Bucknall Dio Lich 77-80; Team V from 80. *28 Greasley Road, Abbey Hulton, Stoke-on-Trent, ST2 8JE.* (Stoke-on-T 542861)

GRIFFITHS, Rowland Powell. b 07. Worc Coll Ox BA (2nd cl Th) 29, MA 33. Westcott Ho Cam 29. **d** 31 Win **p** 32 Southn for Win. C of Romsey 31-38; St Jas Milton Portsm 38-40; Newland w Redbrook 40-43; Bishop's Lavington w Little Cheverell and Gt Cheverell 43-49; V of Chedworth 49-53; Heytesbury w Tytherington and Knook 53-59; Perm to Offic Dio Portsm from 60; Dio Chich 65-70; Dio Win from 66. *Pennymarsh, Abbotts Ann, Andover, Hants.*

GRIFFITHS, Russell Howard. b 22. GOC 75. **d** 77 **p** 78 Heref (APM). Hon C of Fownhope w Fawley and of Brockhampton 77-80; P-in-c of Bridstow w Peterstow 80-82; Team V of Ross-on-Wye Dio Heref from 82. *Bridstow Vicarage, Ross-on-Wye, Herefs, HR9 6QE.* (Ross-on-Wye 5805)

GRIFFITHS, Canon Stanley Arthur. b 17. Univ of Lon BSc (Hons) 38. Cudd Coll 46. **d** 47 **p** 48 Portsm. C of St Matt Southsea 47-48; H Spirit Southsea 48-51; Cowley St Jas Ox 51-55; V of Northbourne 55-65; St Neots 65-77; Hon Can of Ely from 76; RD of St Neots 76-82; V of Buckden 77-82. *c/o Vicarage, Church Street, Buckden, Huntingdon, Cambs, PE18 9TL.* (Huntingdon 810371)

GRIFFITHS, Thomas. b 31. K Coll Lon and Warm AKC 57. **d** 58 **p** 59 Ches. C of Cheadle Hulme 58-61; Oxton 61-63; V of Micklehurst 63-72; Ringway Dio Ches from 73. *Ringway Vicarage, Altrincham, Chesh.*

GRIFFITHS, Thomas Elwyn. b 12. Univ of Wales, BA (1st cl Phil 35). Or Coll Ox BA (3rd cl Th) 38, MA 45. St Steph Ho Ox 37. **d** 38 **p** 39 St D. C of Carmarthen 38-40; Min Can of Brecon Cathl 41-47; C-in-c of Llandegley 48-53; R of New Radnor w Llanfihangel Nantmelan 53-66; Dir of Educn Dio Swan B 56-78; RD of Knighton 58-66; Can of Brecon from 61; V of Bronllys w Llanvillo and Llandefaelog Tre'r-graig 66-70; Archd of Brecon 69-78. *27 Parc Pendre, Brecon, Powys.* (Brecon 5756)

GRIFFITHS, Thomas Wailes. b 02. Wadh Coll Ox 3rd cl Engl Lit 24, BA 25, MA 33. St D Coll Lamp. **d** 25 **p** 26 St D. C of Pemb Dk 25-27; St Luke W Norwood 27-29; Ch Ch Swansea 29-33; V of H Trin Abergavenny 33-37; R of St Bride w Marloes 37-49; C-in-c of Dale 39-43; V of Southill 49-52; Combe-Longa 52-57; Gt w L Tew 57-68; C-in-c of Over w Nether Worton 58-67; P-in-c of St Andr Innerpleithen 68-71; Perm to Offic Dios Newc T and Carl 72-73; Dio Sarum 73-79; Dio B & W 76-79; P-in-c of Lerwick and of Burravoe 78-79; Perm to Offic Dio Newc T from 79. *5 Raise Hamlet, Alston, Cumbria, CA9 3AS.* (Alston 81756)

GRIFFITHS, Trevor Bryce. Moore Th Coll Syd 55. **d** 55 **p** 56 Armid. C of Gunnedah 55-57; V of Mungindi 57-61; C-in-c of Villawood 61-62; R of Rozelle 62-64; Actg R of Balmain 62-64; R of Guildf 64-70; Pagewood 70-80; Coogee Dio Syd from 80. *123 Brook Street, Coogee, NSW, Australia 2034.* (665-5409)

GRIFFITHS, Tudor Francis Lloyd. b 54. Jes Coll Ox BA 76, BA (Th) 78, MA 81. Wycl Hall Ox 76. **d** 79 **p** 80 Swan B. Min Can Brecon Cathl 79-81; C of Swansea Dio Swan B from 81. *63 Walter Road, Swansea, SA1 4PT.* (0792-474088)

GRIFFITHS, Vyrnach Morgan. b 24. St D Coll Lamp BA 50. St Mich Coll Llan 52. **d** 54 **p** 55 Llan. C of Llantrisant 54-56; Ystradyfodwg 56-60; Cwmavon 60-61; V of Clydach Vale 61-63; R of Llanfair-Talhaiarn 63-69; V of Dinas and Penygraig 69-74; R of Llanddulas (and Llysfaen from 81) Dio St A from 74; Hon Chap Miss to Seamen from 78. *Rectory, Rhodfa Wen, Llysfaew, Colwyn Bay, Clwyd.* (Colwyn Bay 516728)

GRIFFITHS, William Bevan. b 13. AKC 37. **d** 37 **p** 38 Swan B. C of Llangyfelach w Morriston 37-50; R of Llanbadarn Fawr w Llandegley 50-59; R of Braunston 59-79. *73 Glannant Way, Cimla Neath, W Glam.*

GRIFFITHS, William David Maldwyn. b 23. St D Coll Lamp BA 47. **d** 50 St D **p** 51 Bp R W Jones for Wales. C of St Mary Cardigan 50-54; Henfynyw w Aberayron 54-56; C-in-c of Llechryd 56-59; V of Mathry w St Edrens and Llanrheithan 59-67; Llanfihangel-Geneu'r-Glyn w Talybont Dio St D from 67. *Vicarage, Llandre, Bow Street, Dyfed.* (Aberystwyth 828298)

GRIFFITHS, Preb William Reginald. b 1896. MBE 44. Qu Coll Cam BA 26, MA 30. Westcott Ho Cam 26. **d** 26 **p** 27 Heref. C of Ch Stretton 26-29; V of Stokesay w Craven Arms 29-34; Lydbury N 34-38; R of Onibury 38-49; CF (TA - R of O) 39-60; Hon CF 46; TD 51; R of Eardisley w Bollingham 49-59; Proc Conv Heref 55-64; RD of Weobley 56-64; Preb of Bullinghope in Heref Cathl from 57; V of Brilley w Michaelchurch 59-64; R of Aylton w Pixley and Munsley (w Putley from 67) 64-68; L to Offic Dio Heref from 68. *7 Pilley Road, Tupsley, Hereford.*

GRIFFITHS, William Thomas Gordon. b 48. Univ of York BA 70. Fitzw Coll Cam BA 79. Ridley Hall Cam 78. **d** 80 **p** 81 S'wark. C of St Barn Dulwich Village Dio S'wark from 80. *18 Calton Avenue, Dulwich, SE21 7DQ.* (01-693 5492)

GRIFFITHS, Preb William Vaughan George. b 10. St D Coll Lamp. Jes Coll Ox BA (3rd cl Th) 33, MA 37. **d** 33 **p** 34 Llan. C of Treherbert 33-35; St Woolos Newport 35-39; CF 39-45; R of Hodnet w Weston-under-Redcastle and Peplow 45-61; V of Burton-on-Trent 61-69; Surr 62-76; RD of Tutbury 64-69; Lich 69-76; V of L Aston 69-76; Preb of Lich Cathl 74-76; Preb (Emer) from 76. *35 Valley Road, Bude, Cornw.* (Bude 2679)

GRIGG, Ven Robert Stanley Cutler. McMaster Univ BA 50. Qu Univ Kingston MA 61. Trin Coll Tor LTh 58, STB 59. **d** 57 **p** 58 Niag. C of Erin 57-58; Dundas 58-61; R of St Jas Guelph 61-65; All SS Hamilton 65-71; Ancaster Dio Niag from 71; Can of Ch Ch Cathl Hamilton 67-74; Archd of Wentworth and Haldimand from 74. *21 Halson Street, Ancaster, Ont., Canada.* (416-648 6038)

GRIGG, Ronald Henderson. St Francis Coll Brisb ThDip 79. **d** 79 **p** 80 Brisb. C of St Andr Lutwyche Dio Brisb from 79. *54 Khartoum Street, Gordon Park, Queensld, Australia 4031.* (57 2793)

GRIGG, Terence George. b 34. Kelham Th Coll 54. **d** 59 **p** 60 Lon. C of St Anne Brookfield St Pancras 59-62; Chap of Lee Abbey 63-66; Chap and Lect St Luke's Coll Ex 66-70; V of Stainton-in-Cleveland Dio York from 70; M Gen Syn from 80. *Vicarage, Thornton Road, Middlesbrough, Cleve, TS8 9BS.* (Middlesbrough 590423)

GRIGG, William John Frank. b 27. Ripon Hall Ox. **d** 66 Warrington for Liv **p** 67 Liv. C of Wigan 66-67; St Luke Leek 67-69; Fenton 69-71; St Steph-by-Saltash 73-75; Team V of Redruth 76-79; C-in-c of Laneast w St Clether and Tresmere 79-81; P-in-c of Wendron Dio Truro from 81. *Wendron Vicarage, Helston, Cornwall.* (Helston 2169)

GRIGGS, Alan Sheward. b 33. Trin Hall, Cam BA 56, MA 60. Westcott Ho Cam 58. **d** 60 **p** 61 Southw. C of Arnold 60-63; PV and Succr of S'wark Cathl 63-66; Industr Chap Dio S'wark 66-71; Soc and Industr Adv Dio Ripon from 71; C of H Trin Leeds Dio Ripon 71-81; V from 81. *23 Harrowby Road, Leeds, LS16 5HX.* (Leeds 758100)

GRIGGS, Canon Charles David. St Jo Th Coll Winnipeg LTh 62. **d** 61 **p** 62 Rupld. C of All SS Winnipeg 61-63; V of St Chrys Winnipeg 64-67; St Barn Winnipeg 64-70; St Geo Transcona 70-76; on leave 76-78; I of St Bede Winnipeg Dio Rupld from 78; Can of Rupld from 80. *99 Turner Avenue, Winnipeg, Manit., Canada.*

GRIGGS, Douglas William. b 16. SOC 65. **d** 68 Kens for Lon **p** 69 Lon. C of Gt Greenford 68-76; Battersea 76-79; C-in-c of St Mary-le-Park Battersea Dio S'wark from 79. *48 Parkgate Road, Battersea, SW11.* (01-228 4818)

GRIGGS, Frederick John. b 20. Peterho Cam BA 48, MA 53. Linc Th Coll. **d** 50 **p** 51 Man. C of All SS Stand 50-53; Writtle 53-55; C-in-c of Chignal St Jas w Mashbury 55-58; V of St Andr Chelmsf 58-62; R of Colne Engaine 62-80; P-in-c of Frating w Thorington Dio Chelmsf from 80. *Rectory, Salmons Lane, Thorington, Colchester, CO7 8HQ.* (Gt Bentley 251158)

GRIGGS, Canon Ian Macdonald. b 28. Trin Hall Cam 2nd cl Eng Trip 51, 2nd cl Hist Trip BA 52, MA 56. Westcott Ho Cam. **d** 54 **p** 55 Portsm. C of St Cuthb Copnor 54-59; Chap to Bp of Sheff 59-62; Youth Chap Dio Sheff 59-64; V of St Cuthb Firvale 64-71; Kidderminster Dio Worc from 71; Hon Can of Worc from 77. *Vicarage, Roden Avenue, Kidderminster, Worcs.* (Kidderminster 3265)

GRIGGS, Kenneth Courtenay. b 13. Worc Ordin Coll 56. **d** 58 **p** 59 Worc. C of St Jas Gt Dudley 58-60; St Geo Kidderminster 60-64; V of Dodford 64-79. *81 Golden Vale, Churchdown, Gloucester, GL3 2LX.* (Churchdown 856285)

GRIGGS, Thomas Herbert Samuel. **d** 42 **p** 43 Arctic. C-in-c St Mary Sioux Lookout 42-44; R 44-48; St Matt Boissevain 48-53; Comforter Ch Tor 53-63; I of Apsley 63-64; on leave. *770 Wilton Crescent, Woodstock, Ont, Canada.*

GRIGOR, David Alexander. b 29. Dipl Th (Lon) 54. St Aid Coll 51. **d** 54 **p** 55 Bris. C of Hengrove 54-57; Marshfield 57-60; V of Newport Devon 60-67; St Paul Preston Ex 67-73; R of Ch Ch Rio de Janeiro 73-74; Chap Ex Sch & C of St Mich AA Heavitree Ex 74-77; Chap Brighton Coll from 77. *8 Clarendon Place, Brighton, BN2 4AL.*

GRIMASON, Alistair John. b 57. Div Hostel Dub 76. **d** 79

Connor. C of H Trin Belf Dio Connor fom 79. *11 Cliftondene Gardens, Belfast, BT14 7PF.*

GRIME, Arthur Michael. b 28. Kelham Th Coll 48. **d** 52 **p** 53 Basuto. LPr Dio Basuto 52-55; C of St Barn Ealing 55-57; St Gabr Westmr 57-59; H Cross (in c of St Edw) Gt Greenford 59-62; V of St Pet Fulham 62-66; St Paul Grove Pk Chiswick Dio Lon from 66. *64 Grove Park Road, W4 3SB.* (01-994 0625)

GRIME, William John Peter. b 39. St Jo Coll Ox BA (Mod Hist) 60, (Th) 70, MA 66. Cudd Coll 69. **d** 70 **p** 71 Blackb. C of St Jas Blackb 70-74; Chap St Martin's Coll Lanc 74-77; V of Seascale (w Drigg from 78) Dio Carl from 77; Drigg 77-78. *Vicarage, The Banks, Seascale, Cumb., CA20 1QT.* (Seascale 217)

GRIMES, Geoffrey William. BD Lon 64. Moore Th Coll Syd. ACT ThL 64. **d** 64 **p** 65 Syd. C of St John Parramatta 64-68; Chap and Asst Master The K Sch (Prep) from 68. *The King's Preparatory School, Parramatta, NSW, Australia 2150.*

GRIMES, William Geoffrey. b 33. Cranmer Hall, Dur 59. **d** 62 **p** 63 Blackb. C of St John Preston 62-65; Ribbleton 65-68; V of New Longton 68-77; Adv on Services for the Deaf Sefton Mer from 77. *20 South Avenue, New Longton, Preston, PR4 4BB.* (Longton 616849)

GRIMLEY, Robert William. b 43. Ch Coll Cam BA (2nd cl Th Trip pt ii) 66, MA 70. Wadh Coll Ox BA (2nd cl Or Stud) 68. Ripon Hall Ox 66. **d** 68 St Alb **p** 69 Hertford for Cant. C of Radlett 68-72; Hon C of Moseley Dio Birm from 72; Chap K Edw Sch Birm from 72. *34 Elmfield Crescent, Moseley, Birmingham, B13 9TN.* (021-449 3568)

GRIMMER, Howard Melville. Univ of Acadia BA 28. **d** 39 **p** 40 Fred. I of Canterbury 39-44; All SS St John 44-49; Miss Canning and Chipman 49-58; R of Andover NB 58-64. *422 Raymond Avenue, Santa Monica, California, USA.*

GRIMSBY, Lord Bishop Suffragan of. *See* Tustin, Right Rev David.

GRIMSHAW, Ven Arthur John. Univ of Melb BA 57. St Jo Coll Morpeth ACT ThL (2nd cl) 56. **d** 57 **p** 58 Melb. C of Surrey Hills 57-58; Asst Chap Geelong Gr Sch 59-61; V of Romsey w Sunbury and Lancefield 61-64; Prec of St Geo Cathl Perth 64-68; R of H Trin Fortitude Valley Brisb 68-75; St Paul Ipswich 75-80; St Aug Hamilton City and Dio Brisb from 80; Archd of Moreton from 75. *9 Charlton Street, Hamilton, Queensland, Australia 4007.* (71 1051)

GRIMSHAW, Eric Fenton Hall. b 34. Univ of Bris BA 57. Tyndale Hall Bris 54. **d** 58 **p** 59 Man. C of St Jas Moss Side 58-61; Leyland 61-64; V of St Mark Preston Blackb 64-72; St Andr Mirehouse Whitehaven Dio Carl from 72. *Vicarage, Hollins Close, Mirehouse, Whitehaven, Cumb, CA28 8EX.* (Whitehaven 3565)

GRIMSHAW, Gilbert. b 1896. Univ of Man BSc 25. Wells Th Coll 31. **d** 31 **p** 32 Liv. C of H Trin Wavertree 31-34; Stoke-on-Trent (in c of All SS Boothen) 34-38; V of Ipstones 38-42; R of Thornton-in-Craven 42-55; Rode w Rode Hill and Woolverton 55-59; Min of Gurnard Conv Distr 59-62. *20 Place Road, Cowes, IW.*

GRIMSTER, Barry John. b 49. Univ of Ex BA 70. Trin Coll Bris 72. **d** 74 **p** 75 S'wark. C of St Steph S Lambeth 74-78; New Malden w Coombe Dio S'wark from 78. *89 Clarence Avenue, New Malden, Surrey.* (01-942 0544)

GRIMWADE, Eric Peter. b 14. AKC 37. **d** 37 **p** 38 S'wark. C of St Silas Nunhead 37-39; St Mark Camberwell 39-40; Chap RAFVR 40-46; C of Redruth 46-48; R of St Enoder 48-52; V of St Clement 52-62; Chap R Cornwall Infirm 52-62; St Lawr Hosp Bodmin 62-69; Cane Hill Hosp Coulsdon 69-78; Publ Pr Dio Truro 62-69; C of Lee-on-the-Solent Dio Portsm 77-79; Hon C 79-81. *50 Brookway, Lindfield, W Sussex.* (Haywards Heath 414761)

GRIMWADE, Canon John Girling. b 20. Keble Coll Ox BA (3rd cl Pol Phil and Econ) 48, MA 52. Cudd Coll. **d** 50 **p** 51 S'wark. C of Kingston-upon-Thames 50-53; St Mary Virg Ox and Sec Ox Univ SCM 53-56; PC of Londonderry Staffs 56-62; R of Caversham (and Mapledurham from 81) Dio Ox from 62; C-in-c of Mapledurham 68-81; Hon Can of Ch Ch Cathl Ox from 73; Chap to HM the Queen from 80. *20 Church Road, Caversham, Reading, RG4 7AD.* (Reading 471703)

GRIMWADE, Leslie Frank. b 24. Trin Coll Bris 74. **d** 77 Taunton for B & W **p** 78 B & W C of St Jas Taunton 77-80; Polegate (in C of St Wilfrid) Dio Chich from 80. *90 Broad Road, Lower Willingdon, E Sussex, BN20 9RA.* (Polegate 2088)

GRIMWOOD, David Walter. b 48. Univ of Lon BA 70. K Coll Lon AKC and BD 73. St Aug Coll Cant 73. **d** 74 **p** 75 Newc T. C of St Geo Jesmond Newc T 74-78; Whorlton 78-80; Team V of Totton Dio Win from 80. *Eling Vicarage, Totton, Southampton, SO4 4HF.* (Totton 866426)

GRIMWOOD, Peter Stuart. b 18. Lich Th Coll 39. **d** 44 **p** 45 Lich. C of St Edw Leek 44-47; Chap RAF 47-68; Reg Dir Lon & SE Miss to Seamen 68-72; R of Basildon w Laindon 72-76; Widdington Dio Chelmsf from 76; RD of Basildon 72-76. *Widdington Rectory, Saffron Walden, Essex, CB11 3SB.* (Saffron Walden 40270)

GRIMWOOD, William. b 11. St Cath S Ox BA 36, MA 39. Ripon Hall, Ox 35. **d** 36 **p** 37 Liv. C of St John Birkdale 36-38; Old Ch Smethwick 38-40; Actg C of Gatley (in c of St Cath Heald Green) 40-45; V of Tilstone Fearnall 45-56; Surr from 49; R of Burbage w Aston Flamville Dio Leic from 56. *Rectory, New Road, Burbage, Hinckley, Leics.* (0455 39534)

GRINDELL, James Mark. b 43. Univ of Nottm BA (2nd cl Th) 66. Univ of Bris MA 69. Wells Th Coll 66. **d** 68 **p** 69 St Alb. C of Bushey Heath 68-72; St D w St Mich AA Ex 72-74; Chap St Audries Sch W Quantoxhead from 74. *Williton Lodge, St Audries, W Quantoxhead, Taunton, Somt, TA4 4DL.* (Williton 33115)

✠ **GRINDROD, Most Rev John Basil Rowland.** Qu Coll Ox BA (Th) 49, MA 53. Linc Th Coll 49. **d** 51 **p** 52 Man. C of St Mich Hulme 51-54; Bundaberg Queensld 54-56; R of All S Ancoats Man 56-60; Emerald Queensld 60-61; St Barn N Rockptn 61-65; Archd of Rockptn 60-65; V of S Yarra 65-66; Cons Ld Bp of River in St Andr Cathl Syd 24 Aug 66 by Abp of Syd; Abps of Melb; and Brisb (actg Primate); Bps of Bath; C & Goulb; Newc; and Wang; Bps Coadj (Hulme-Moir and Dain) of Syd; Asst Bps of Newc; and C & Goulb; and Bp Moyes; Trld to Rockhampton 71; to Brisb (Metrop of Prov of Queensld) 80. *Bishopsbourne, 39 Eldernell Avenue, Hamilton, Queensland, Australia 4007.* (268 2706)

GRINHAM, Garth Clews. b 36. Oak Hill Th Coll 61. **d** 64 **p** 65 Roch. C of Ch Ch Beckenham 64-68; Wallington (in c of St Patr) 68-71; V of St Paul Erith 71-76; Cler Asst Sec CPAS 76-81; Hon C of Knockholt 76-81; V of Ch Ch Southport Dio Liv from 81. *12 Gloucester Road, Southport, Mer, PR8 2AU.* (Southport 65120)

GRINHAM, Julian Clive. b 39. Univ of Lon BA 65. Oak Hill Coll 79. **d** 81 Blackb. C of Ch Ch w St Matt City and Dio Blackb from 81. *21 Sunnybank Road, Blackburn, Lancs, BB2 3ND.*

GRINHAM, Canon Robert. OBE 56. Keble Coll Ox BA (*sc* Engl Lit w distinc) 21, MA 25. Wells Th Coll 21. **d** 23 **p** 24 Win. C of St Mary Extra Southampton 23-25; LPr Dio Johann 25-27; Hd Master Ruzawi Dioc Prep Sch for Boys 27-50; Chap 56-58; Hd Master Springvale Dioc Prep Sch 50-56; Hon Can of Mashon from 54; L to Offic Dio Mashon from 58. *PO Box 129, Marandellas, Zimbabwe.*

GRINSTED, Richard Anthony. b 43. Univ of Leic BSc 65. Oak Hill Th Coll Lon 67. **d** 70 **p** 71 Dorking for Guildf. C of Egham 70-73; Woodford Wells 73-76; P-in-c of Havering-atte-Bower Dio Chelmsf 76-81; V from 81. *Havering-atte-Bower Vicarage, Romford, Essex, RM4 1PP.* (Romford 43330)

GRISDALE, Keith Noel. Moore Coll Syd ThL 50. **d** and **p** 50 Syd. C of Summer Hill 50; St Anne Ryde 50-52; Asst Chap Miss to Seamen Syd 52-53; C-in-c of S Granville 53-58; Toongabbie w Seven Hills 58-60; R of Corrimal 60-65; Kensington 65-79; Ch Ch Bexley Dio Syd from 79. *Box 82, Bexley, NSW, Australia 2207.* (59-1800)

GRISDALE, Robert Eric. Wycl Coll Tor LTh 65. **d** 64 Bp Snell for Tor **p** 65 Tor. C of Ch K Etobicoke Tor 64-69; R of St Bede Scarborough Tor 69-76; Thornhill Dio Tor from 76. *Box 185, Thornhill, Ont., Canada.*

GRIST, Anthony John. b 51. Univ of Kent at Cant BA 72. Westcott Ho Cam 73. **d** 76 Man **p** 77 Middleton for Man. C of Wythenshawe 76-79; Reddish Dio Man from 79. *Rectory Flat, St Elisabeth's Way, Reddish, Stockport, SK5 6BL.*

GRIST, Peter Arthur. b 42. Sarum Wells Th Coll 71. **d** and **p** 74 Nass. P-in-c of St Andr Nass 74-76; St John Harbour I 76-79; St Mary I and Dio Nass from 79. *Box N-3178, Nassau, Bahamas.*

GRIST, Robert Frederick. b 19. Chich Th Coll 51. **d** 53 **p** 54 Newc T. C of Bywell St Pet 53-58; V of St Mich Byker Newc T 58-64; R of Petrockstowe w Petersmarland (w Merton and Meeth w Huish from 71) 64-79; P-in-c of Cheriton Bp Dio Ex from 79. *Cheriton Bishop Rectory, Exeter, Devon.* (Cheriton Bp 517)

GRISWELL, Herbert Henry. b 01. St Aid Coll 28. **d** 30 **p** 31 Chelmsf. C of All SS Goodmayes 30-32; St Matt Hull 32-33; St Pet and St Paul Grays Thurrock 33-36; V of Ch Ch Stratford 36-38; PC of Alvaston 38-42; V of St Thos-by-Launceston w St Mary Tregadillet 42-45; Org Sec Miss to Seamen NW Area 45-46; C of Stanhope 46-47; R of L Bentley 47-50; Wivenhoe 50-55; Bratton Clovelly w Germansweek 55-60; L Burstead 60-63; Croscombe 63-71; Perm to Offic Dios Chelmsf, Ex and Truro 73-78; Dios Chelmsf and Truro from 79. *30 Belgrave Road, Billericay, Essex.* (Billericay 3215)

GRITTEN, Desmond Digby. b 17. ALCD 54. **d** 54 **p** 55 S'wark. C of St Jo Evang Blackheath 54-58; V of St Jo Evang

Kenilworth Dio Cov from 58; RD of Kenilworth 63-73. *St John's Vicarage, Kenilworth, Warws, CV8 1HX.* (Kenilworth 53203)

GROBECKER, Ven Geoffrey Frank. b 22. MBE 59. Qu Coll Cam BA 49, MA 53. Ridley Hall, Cam. **d** 50 **p** 51 S'wark. C of Morden 50-52; CF from 52; Sen Chap RMA Sandhurst 66-69; DACG 69-72; ACG 72-77; Hon Chap to HM the Queen 73-77; V of Swaffham 77-80; Archd of Lynn from 80; Bp's Adv for Hosp Chaps Dio Nor from 81. *Lynn House, Scarning, Dereham, Norf, NR19 2PF.*

GROENEWALD, Peter. St Pet Coll Alice 66. **d** 68 **p** 69 Geo. C of St Andr Riversdale 68-69; St Paul City and Dio George from 69. *Box 182, George, CP, S Africa.* (3932)

GROEPE, Thomas Matthew Karl. b 51. St Pet Coll Natal 76. **d** 78 **p** 79 Capetn. C of Ch the Mediator Portland Dio Capetn from 78. *c/o Wall Street & Westminster Close, Portland 7785, CP, S Africa.*

GROSE, Charles Frederick. b 01. K Coll Lon 43. **d** 45 Barking for Chelmsf **p** 46 Chelmsf. C of Chadwell Hth 45-46; Stow Maries 46-47; Lenton (in c of St Barn Lenton Abbey) 47-49; V of St Paul Burslem 49-52; Childs Ercall 52-55; Wrangthorn 55-59; Dunton Green 59-66. *20 Glebelands, Biddenden, Ashford, Kent, TN27 8EA.* (0580 291533)

GROSE, Reginald Ewart. b 06. Lich Th Coll 58. **d** 58 **p** 59 Man. C of Crumpsall 58-60; V of St Jas Thornham 60-71. *Portland Cottage, Northfield End, Henley-on-Thames, Oxon.* (Henley 3130)

GROSSE, Anthony Charles Bain. b 30. Oak Hill Th Coll 58. **d** 61 **p** 62 Roch. C of Ch Ch Chislehurst 61-65; Washfield 65-71; Team V in Exe Valley Group 71-73; R of Hemyock w Culm Davy (and Clayhidon from 76) Dio Ex from 73. *Hemyock Rectory, Cullompton, Devon.* (Hemyock 244)

GROSVENOR, Royston Johannes Martin. b 47. AKC and BD 70. St Aug Coll Cant 70. **d** 71 **p** 72 Heref. C of Pontesbury w Cruckton 71-75; Bishopston 75-79; P-in-c of St Pet Croydon Dio Cant 79-81; V from 81. *Vicarage, St Peter's Road, Croydon, Surrey.* (01-688 2823)

GROUNDWATER, Keith. b 34. Canberra Coll of Min. **d** 79 **p** 80 C & Goulb. Hon C of H Cross Hackett Dio C & Goulb from 79. *17 Dunlop Street, Hackett, ACT, Australia 2602.*

GROVE, Brian Douglas. Open Univ BA 73. Chich Th Coll 51. **d** 53 **p** 54 Worc. C of St Jo Bapt Kidderminster 53-55; St Luke Torquay 55-58; V of St Matt Southn 58-66; R of Nursling w Rownhams 66-78; P-in-c of St Alb Bournemouth Dio Win from 78. *St Alban's Vicarage, Linwood Road, Bournemouth, Hants, BH8 9DL.* (Bournemouth 522452)

GROVE, Canon John Montgomery. b 13. Late Exhib of Magd Coll Cam BA (1st cl Cl Trip pt ii) 35, MA 39. Westcott Ho Cam 39. **d** 39 **p** 40 Cant. Chap Dover Coll 39-43; Clifton Coll 43-57; Hd Master Chorister Sch Dur 57-78; L to Offic Dio Dur from 58; Hon Can of Dur from 74. *22 South Street, Durham.* (Dur 44787)

GROVE, Ronald Edward. Oak Hill Th Coll 60. **d** 63 **p** 64 Roch. C of St Jo Evang Bromley 63-66; V of St Paul Stratford Dio Chelmsf from 66. *St Paul's Vicarage, Maryland Road, Stratford, E15.* (01-534 3640)

GROVER, Wilfrid John. b 29. Lich Th Coll 55. **d** 58 **p** 59 Pet. C of St Alb Mart Northn 58-61; All SS Boyne Hill Maidenhead 61-65; V of Cookham Dio Ox from 65. *Vicarage, Cookham, Berks.* (Bourne End 23969)

GROVES, Gerald William Norris. b 08. OBE 53. Keble Coll Ox 34. ALCD 31. **d** 31 **p** 32 Ox. C of St Matt Ox 31-34; Chap RAF 34-59; Men in Disp 41; Asst Chap-in-Chief 44-59; Commandant RAF Chaplains' Scho 50-51; Prin 51-52; Hon Chap to HM The Queen 54-59; Res Chap St Clem Danes Lon 58-59; V of W Hoathly 59-74. *Lilac Cottage, Norton Green, Freshwater, IW.* (Freshwater 753625)

GROVES, James Alan. b 32. CCC Cam 2nd cl Hist Trip pt i, 57, BA (2nd cl Th Trip pt ia) 58, MA 62. Wells Th Coll 58. **d** 60 **p** 61 Roch. C of Ch Ch Gravesend 60-64; St Jas Beckenham 64-66; V of St Andr Orpington Dio Roch from 66. *Vicarage, Anglesea Road, Orpington, Kent.* (Orpington 23775)

GROVES, Robert John. b 42. Trin Coll Bris 74. **d** 76 **p** 77 S'wark. C of St Luke W Norwood 76-79; V of Clapham Pk Dio S'wark from 79. *250 Lyham Road, SW2 5NP.* (01-674 4994)

GROWNS, John Huntley. Chich Th Coll 57. **d** 60 Lon **p** 61 Kens for Lon. C of Hayes 60-64; Addlestone (in c of St Aug) 64-67; C-in-c of Transfig Conv Distr Kempston 67-74; R of St Geo Stevenage 74-82; Felpham w Middleton Dio Chich from 82. *Rectory, Limmer Lane, Felpham, Bognor Regis, W Sussex.* (Bognor Regis 821155)

GRUBB, Frederick Henry. b 16. K Coll Lon. **d** 66 **p** 67 Cant. C of St Phil Norbury 66-70; Faversham 70; V of Bredgar w Bicknor (and Huckinge to 74) 72-78; P-in-c of Milstead 74-78. *20 Oaken Hill Place, Canterbury, Kent, CT1 3HJ.*

GRUBB, Greville Alexander. b 36. St Jo Coll Nottm 72. **d** 74 **p** 75 Pet. C of Rushden w Newton Bromswold Dio Pet from 74; Chap St D Coll Llandudno from 77. *c/o St David's College, Llandudno, LL30 1RD.* (Llandudno 76702)

GRUBB, Philip Herbert Watkins. b 12. St Pet Hall, Ox BA 34, MA 38. Westcott Ho Cam 35. **d** 36 Cant for Portsm **p** 37 Portsm. C of St Mary Portsea 36-43; R of Bedhampton 43-53; Shillingstone 53-65; RD of Milton 61-65; R of Barford St Martin 65-70; R of Baverstock 65-70; Custos of St John's Hosp Heytesbury 70-74; Publ Pr Dio Sarum 71-74; C of Milford 74-77; Chap Hordle Ho Sch Milford from 74. *3 Canon's Walk, Milford-on-Sea, Lymington, Hants, SO4 0SH.* (Milford 3893)

GRUCHY, George. Qu Coll Newfld. **d** 33 **p** 34 Newfld. P-in-c of Salmon Cove and Brigus 34-38; I 38-42; Brooklyn Newfld 42-49; R of Trinity 49-50; Catalina 50-57; I of Deer Lake 57-64; C of St Thos St John's 64-73. *Pine Bud Apts., 5 Churchill Square, St John's, Newfoundland, Canada.*

GRUNDY, Anthony Brian. b 36. Pemb Coll Cam 2nd cl Econ Trip pt i, 59, BA (2nd cl Th Trip pt ii) 62. Ridley Hall, Cam 61. **d** 63 **p** 64 S'wark. C of Hatcham 63-66; H Trin Margate 66-68; Brixton Hill 68-70; V of Assington 70-76; C of Cornard Parva and of All SS Newton 70-76; Much Wenlock w Bourton 76-81; Team V of Wenlock Dio Heref from 81. *Priory Cottage, The Bull Ring, Much Wenlock, Shropshire.* (Much Wen 727310)

GRUNDY, Christopher John. b 49. Trin Coll Bris 74. **d** 77 **p** 78 Cant. C of St Luke Maidstone 77-81; SAMS Miss Dio Argent from 81. *Iglesia Anglicana, Casilla 187, 4400, Salta, Argentina.*

GRUNDY, Harold. b 02. Egerton Hall, Man 37. **d** 39 **p** 40 Man. C of St Agnes Birch-in-Rusholme 39-42; Offg C-in-c of St Ambrose Pendleton 42-45; V of St Thos Radcliffe 45-49; R of Toft Newton 49-51; V of Sutton-le-Marsh 51-62; R of Gt Ponton 62-67; C-in-c of L Ponton 62-66; R 66-67; L to Offic Dio Linc from 67. *Rosemary Cottage, 22 Moor Lane, Leasingham, Sleaford, Lincs, NG34 8JN.* (Sleaford 303201)

GRUNDY, Jocelyn Pratchitt. b 22. Trin Coll Cam MA. Westcott Ho Cam 64. **d** 66 **p** 67 Guildf. C of Guildf 66-68; R of Shere w Peasleake 68-73; V of Fleet Dio Guildf from 73. *Vicarage, Fleet, Hants.* (Fleet 6361)

GRUNDY, Malcolm Leslie. b 44. Open Univ BA 76. K Coll Lon and Warm AKC 68. **d** 69 Sheff **p** 70 Bp Gerard for Sheff. C of Doncaster 69-72; Industr Chap Sheff 72-80; Sen Chap 74-80; Dir of Educn and Commun Dept Lon Dioc Bd of Educn from 80. *7 St Andrew Street, EC4A 3AB.* (01-353 5337)

GRUNDY, Paul. b 55. AKC and BD 77. Linc Th Coll 79. **d** 80 **p** 81 Dir. C of Ryhope Dio Dur from 80. *11 Williams Terrace, Ryhope, Sunderland, SR2 0HT.*

GRUNDY, Thomas Philip. St Jo Coll Ox BA 55, MA 58. Wells Th Coll 55. **d** 57 **p** 58 Pet. C of Kettering 57-60; All S Cathl Bath 60-63; R of Nyngan 63-68; Field Officer in Evangelism Dio C & Goulb from 68. *88 Finiss Crescent, Narrabundah, ACT 2604, Australia.*

GRUNEBERG, Alan Conrad. Univ of Lon BSc (2nd cl Chem) 34. Oak Hill Th Coll 67. **d** 68 **p** 69 Lich. C of St Phil Penn Fields 68-73; R of Leaden Roding w Aythorpe Roding and High Roding 73-79; Perm to Offic Dio St E from 79. *3 Manor Park Road, Southwold, Suff.*

GRYLLS, Michael John. b 38. Qu Coll Cam BA 62, MA 66. Linc Th Coll 62. **d** 64 **p** 65 Sheff. C of St Silas Sheff 64-67; C-in-c of Ch Ch Conv Distr Dunscroft 67-70; V of Herringthorpe 70-78; Amport and Grateley and Monxton and Quarley Dio Win from 78. *Amport Vicarage, Andover, Hants.* (Weyhill 2950)

GUBBINS, Lionel Alfred Nelson. St Bonif Coll Warm 31. **d** 45 **p** 46 Sarum. C of St Denys Warm 45-49; St Jo Bapt Kingsthorpe 49-50; V of Ch Ch W Green Tottenham 50-59; St Anne Brondesbury w H Trin Kilburn Lon 59-72; L to Offic Dio Argent from 77. *Rieja 2995, 1636 Olivos, Buenos Aires, Argentina.*

GUDGEON, Michael John. b 40. Qu Coll Cam BA 63, MA 67. Chich Th Coll 65. **d** 66 **p** 67 Birm. C of King's Heath 66-72; Asst Chap K Edw Sch Birm 69-72; Tutor Cudd Th Coll Ox 72-75; V of Hawley 75-80; Minley 75-80; Adult Educn Adv Dio Chich from 80. *293 South Farm Road, Worthing, BN14 7TL.* (Worthing 36348)

GUDWIN, Mark Alan. b 46. Univ of Michigan BA 68. Univ of Tor MA 69. Coll of Resurr Mirfield 73. **d** 75 Asst Bp of Wakef for Tor **p** 76 Tor. C of St Jude Wexford Tor 75-78; V of Ch Ch Cathl Montr 78-81 P-in-c of Eglise du Redempteur City and Dio Montr from 81. *243 Avenue Querbes, Montreal, PQ, Canada.*

GUERNSEY, Dean of. (Vacant)

GUERNSEY, Hugh Crawford. b 1900. Westcott Ho Cam. **d** 50 **p** 51 Portsm. C of Carisbrooke 50-52; C-in-c of Leigh Pk Conv Distr Bedhampton 52-54; I of Kilmallock 55-71; Dom Chap to Bp of Lim from 61; RD of Newcastle 61-63; St

Mary's 63-71. *RR 1, Ganges vos IEO, BC, Canada.*

GUERRERO, Orlando Jesus. **d** 79 **p** 80 Venez. P Dio Venez. *Apartado 4538, Puerto la Cruz, Venezuela.*

GUEST, David. b 41. Univ of Dur BA 62. Coll of Resurr Mirfield 70. **d** 72 **p** 73 Ripon. C of Horsforth 72-75; Richmond 75-78; R of Middleham (and Coverham w Horsehouse from 81) Dio Ripon from 78. *Deanery, Middleham, Leyburn, N Yorks, DL8 4PN.* (Wensleydale 22276)

GUEST, Frederick William. St Aug Coll Cant 27. **d** 32 **p** 33 Chelmsf. C of St Jo Bapt Tilbury Dks 32-34; R of Bruce Rock 34-39; Mundaring 39-45; Chap AMF 41-44; R of St Mary S Perth 45-64; Can of Perth 51-73; Commiss Melan 54-70; Archd of Canning 61-67; Perth 67-73. *30 Renwick Street, South Perth, W Australia 6151.* (67 5058)

GUEST, John. Clifton Th Coll 58. **d** 61 **p** 62 Bris. C of St Luke w Ch Ch Bris 61-64; St Sav Liv 65-66. *840 Carpenter Lane, Philadelphia, Pa 19119, USA.*

GUEST, John Andrew Kenneth. b 55. St D Coll Lamp BA 78. Wycl Hall Ox 78. **d** 80 **p** 81 Southw. C of St Mary Eastwood Dio Southw from 80. *2 Church Walk, Eastwood, Nottingham, NG16 3BG.*

GUEST, Leslie Leonard. b 15. Ripon Hall, Ox 62. **d** 63 **p** 64 Worc. C of Ch Ch w St Andr Malvern 63-66; V of Norton and Lenchwick 66-77; Inkberrow w Cookhill and Kington w Dormston Dio Worc from 77. *Inkberrow Vicarage, Worcester, WR7 4DU.* (Inkberrow 792222)

GUEST, Canon Stephen Arthur Ravely. b 10. Late Exhib of St Edm Hall Ox Abbott Scho 30, 2nd cl Cl Mods 31, BA (3rd cl Lit Hum) 33, MA 36, Dipl in Th 34. Wycl Hall, Ox 33. **d** 35 **p** 36 S'wark. C of H Trin Redhill 35-39; St Luke Manningham Bradf 39-45; Chap of Is of Scilly 45-53; V of St Steph-by-Saltash 53-76; RD of E Wivelshire 67-71; Hon Can of Truro from 69. *Arnewood, Creed Lane, Grampound, Truro, Cornw.*

GUIBUNDA, Jose Joad. **d** 79 **p** 80 Lebom. P Dio Lebom. *CP 57, Maputo, Mozambique.*

GUILD, Canon Frederick Goodwin. Harvard Univ AB 50. Nashotah Ho Wisconsin BD 53. **d** 52 **p** 53 Nass. C of St Matt Naa 54-55; P-in-c of St Mary Magd Eleuthera Dio Nass from 55; Can of Nass from 73. *St Luke's Rectory, Rock Sound, Eleuthera, Bahamas, W Indies.* (3342070)

GUILDFORD, Lord Bishop of. *See* Brown, Right Rev David Alan.

GUILDFORD, Assistant Bishop of. *See* Pike, Right Rev St John Surridge.

GUILDFORD, Dean of. *See* Bridge, Very Rev Anthony Cyprian.

GUILLE, John Arthur. b 49. Univ of Southn BTh 79. Srum Wells Th Coll 73. **d** 76 **p** 77 Win. C of Chandler's Ford 76-79; P-in-c of St Jo Evang Bournemouth Dio Win from 79. *Vicarage, Surrey Road, Bournemouth, Dorset.*

GUILLOTEAU, Claude. b 32. Ripon Coll Cudd 77. **d** 57 RC Bp of Rome **p** 57 RC Bp of Angers. In RC Ch 57-76; Rec into Angl Commun 78 by Bp of Ox. C of Warmsworth 78-80; Goole Dio Sheff from 80. *St Mary's Church House, Swinefleet Road, Goole, Humberside, DN14 5YL.* (Goole 69186)

GUIMEI, Peter. Newton Coll Dogura 70. **d** 73 Bp Meredith for Papua **p** 74 Papua. P Dio Papua 73-77; Dio Aipo 77-78; Dio New Guinea Is from 78. *Leiama, via Kandrian, Papua New Guinea.*

GUINNESS, Christopher Paul. b 43. Lon Coll of Div 64. **d** 67 **p** 68 Guildf. C of Farnborough Hants 67-70; Tulse Hill 70-74; Worting 74-78; V of St Steph S Lambeth Dio S'wark from 78. *Vicarage, St Stephen's Terrace, S Lambeth, SW8 1DH.* (01-735 8461)

GUINNESS, Garry Grattan. b 40. Em Coll Cam 2nd cl Th Trip pt i, 62, BA (2nd cl Th Trip pt ii) 64. Ridley Hall, Cam 64. **d** 66 **p** 67 S'wark. C of Wallington 66-69; All S Langham Place St Marylebone 69-72; P-in-c of H Trin Hotwells w St Andr L and St Pet Clifton 72-79; V of St Luke Watford Dio St Alb from 79. *Vicarage, Devereux Drive, Watford, Herts, WD1 3DD.* (Watford 31205)

GUINNESS, Paul Grattan. Northwestern Univ Evanston Ill BSc 35. Dallas Th Sem Texas BD 36. Lon Coll of Div 36. **d** 36 Lewes for Chich **p** 37 Chich. C of Bp Hannington Mem Distr W Hove 36-38; Perm to Offic at St Eliz Eastbourne 38-39; All SS Sanderstead 39-40; CF (EC) 40-45; Hon CF 45; World's C'ttee YMCA Geneva 45-58; V of Ch Ch Ashton L 58-65; LPr Dio Man 66-71; L to Offic Dio Gibr 71-73. *Apartado 184, San Antonio Abad, Ibiza, Baleares, Spain.*

GUINNESS, Robert Desmond. Ch Coll Cam BA 27, MA 30. Ridley Hall, Cam. **d** 28 **p** 29 Sarum. C of St John Weymouth 28-31; CIM Miss E Szechwan 32-38; R of Hartshorne 40-43; V of St Martin-at-Oak Nor 43-46; R of St Mich-at-Coslany Nor 43-46; St Jo Bapt Bedford 46-52; V of Laleham 52-77. *110 Penton Road, Staines, Middx.*

GUINNESS, Robin Gordon. St Jo Coll Cam BA 60, 3rd cl Th Trip pt ii, 61, MA 64. Ridley Hall, Cam 62. **d** 63 Bp McKie for Cov **p** 64 Cov. C of Bedworth 63-66; CMS Miss 66-68; w Canad IVF 68-72; P-in-c of Lakefield 73-75; R of St Steph Westmount Dio Montr from 75. *47 Prospect Street, Westmount, PQ, Canada.* (514-931 6796)

GUIVER, Paul Alfred. b 45. St Chad Coll Dur BA 68. Cudd Coll 71. **d** 73 **p** 74 St Alb. C of Mill End w Heronsgate 73-76; P-in-c of Castle Frome Dio Heref from 76; Acton Beauchamp and Evesbatch Dio Heref from 76; Bp's Frome Dio Heref from 76. *Vicarage, Bishops Frome, Worcester.*

GULL, John. **d** 48 **p** 66 Moos. Miss at Waswanapi Dio Moos from 48. *Waswanapi River, Coniagas Mine, Demaraisville, PQ, Canada.*

GULL, William John. b 42. Ripon Hall, Ox 63. **d** 65 **p** 66 Southw. C of Worksop 65-69; Newark-on-Trent 69-71; P-in-c of St Lawr Mansfield 71-77; V 77-78; R of Lambley Dio Southw from 78. *Lambley Rectory, Nottingham, NG4 4BE.* (Burton Joyce 3531)

GULLEY, Hubert Edward Raymond. b 06. Univ of Bris BA (1st cl Hist) 27. Sarum Th Coll 27. **d** 29 **p** 30 Bris. C of St John Bedminster 29-31; Horfield 31-35; St Aldhelm Branksome 36-41; C-in-c of St John's Conv Distr Boreham Warm 41-44; V of Idmiston w Porton 44-53; Bedwyn Magna 53-57; V of Bedwyn Parva 54-57; P-in-c of Dalry 57-75. *College of St Barnabas, Blackberry Lane, Lingfield, Surrey.* (Domans 430)

GULOBA, Sadulaka. Buwalasi Th Coll 57. **d** 59 **p** 60 U Nile. P Dio U Nile 59-61; Dio Mbale 61-72; Dio Bukedi from 72. *Church of Uganda, Kakora, Post-Box 963, Mbale, Uganda.*

GUMA, Canon Michael Ndleleni. St Bede's Coll Umtata. **d** 39 **p** 42 St Jo Kaffr. P Dio St John's 39-79; Hon Can of St John's from 76. *PO Tsolo, Transkei, S Africa.* (Umtata 2924)

GUMA, Mongezi David. b 53. St Pet Coll Alice Dipl Th 74. **d** 75 **p** 77 Capetn. P-in-c of H Cross Nyanga 75-77; C of St Mich Miss Herschel 77-79; R of Bethal Dio Johann from 79. *Box 611, Bethal, Johannesburg, S Africa.*

GUMBULI, Michael. **d** and **p** 73 N Terr. R of Nqukurr Roper River Dio N Terr from 73. *Free Bag, Nqukurr, Roper River, via Darwin, NT, Australia.*

GUMEDE, Enoch. St Bede's Coll Umtata, 51. **d** 51 **p** 53 Natal. P Dio Natal. *Box 135, Howick, Natal, S Africa.*

GUMEDE, Matthew Matthias Thokozani. St Bede's Coll Umtata, 62. **d** 63 Zulu **p** 65 Bp Cullen for Zulu. P Dio Zulu 65-70; Dio Johann from 70. *10484 Qupe Street, Phirima, Tvl, S Africa.* (011-989 186)

GUMEDE, Ven Patrick Simon Phiwayinkosi. St Bede's Coll Umtata, 62. **d** 63 Zulu **p** 65 Bp Cullen for Zulu. P Dio Zulu; Archd of N Zulu from 77. *PB 39, Mahlabatini, Zululand.*

GUMMER, Dudley Harrison. b 28. Roch Th Coll 61. **d** 63 **p** 64 S'wark. C of St Paul w St Mark Deptford 63-65; Melton Mowbray 65-68; C-in-c of St Hilda's Conv Distr E Goscote 68-75; V of E Goscote 75-78; St Anne Luton Dio St Alb from 78. *7 Blaydon Road, Luton, LU2 0RP.* (Luton 20052)

GUMMER, Selwyn. b 07. Univ of Wales, BA 34. Wycl Hall, Ox 39. **d** 39 Ches **p** 40 Bp Tubbs for Ches. C of St Thos Norbury 39-41; Bexley 41-44; V of H Trin Brompton Gillingham 44-53; Ed 'The Pulpit Monthly' from 49; R of Gravesend 53-65; RD of Gravesend 53-65; Surr 54-65; Hon Can of Roch 56-65; V of St Pet w St John Preston Brighton 65-70. *Shandwick House, 17 Cobham Street, Gravesend, Kent.*

GUNDRY, Canon Dudley William. b 16. K Coll Lon BD (1st cl) 39, AKC (1st cl) 39, MTh 41. **d** 39 **p** 40 S'wark. C of St Matt Surbiton 39-44; Lect Univ Coll of N Wales Ban 44-60; M of Senate and Warden of Reichel Hall Bangor 47-60; Dean of Faculty of Th 56-59; Exam in Th Univ of Leeds 50-53 and 56; St D Coll Lamp 50-60; Univ of Lon 61-65; Univ of Keele 76-79; Exam Chap to Bp of Ban 54-60; to Bp of St D 57-60; to Bp of Leic 63-78; Select Pr Trin Coll Dub 57; Prof of Relig Stud and M of Senate Univ Coll of Ibad 60-63; Can Res and Chan of Leic Cathl from 63; Commiss N Nig 63-69; Surr from 64; RD of Christianity 66-74; Proc Conv Leic 70-80. *3 Morland Avenue, Leicester.* (Leicester 704133)

GUNDRY, Ven Ernest Arthur Clement. AKC (2nd cl). **d** 41 **p** 42 Sheff. C of St Jo Evang Park 41-42; St Aid Sheff 42-44; Mexborough 44-47; Ranmoor 47-53; Chap Rivelin Hosp 47-53; V of St Hilda Shiregreen Sheff 53-56; R of Carlisle W Austr 56-62; Beaconsfield (w Spearwood and Hilton Pk from 65) 62-68; Swanbourne 68-74; Can of Perth 67-78; R of Como 74-78; Archd of Fremantle 74-78; Perth 79-80; Archd (Emer) from 80; Dioc Regr Dio Perth 79-80; Perm to Offic Dio Perth from 80. *103 Riley House, 20 Excelsior Street, Shenton Park, W Australia 6008.* (381-3728)

GUNDUZAH, Jonah. **d** 73 **p** 75 Mashon. P Dio Mashon. *St Clare's Mission District, Box 122, Mtoko, Zimbabwe.*

GUNN, Eric James. b 24. Kelham Th Coll 47. **d** 52 Lich **p** 53 Stafford for Cant. C of St Mary Kingswinford 52-55; Tettenhall Regis 55-59; PC of New Mills 59-69; Surr from 68;

R of Eckington w Renishaw 69-74; P-in-c of Ridgeway 72-74; R of Eckington & Handley w Renishaw & Ridgeway 74-78; V of Hornsea w Atwick Dio York from 78. *Vicarage, Hornsea, Yorks.* (Hornsea 2531)

GUNN, Frederick Craig. Edin Th Coll 27. **d** 32 **p** 33 Newc T. C of Ashington 32-38; Amble 38-46; Perm to Offic at Norham 46; Wylam-on-Tyne 46-47; St Thos Newc T 47; Ingram w Ilderton 47-48; C of St Jas Benwell Newc T 48-56; PC of Newton Hall 56-79. *31 Glebelands, Corbridge, Northumb, NE45 5DS.* (Corbridge 2588)

GUNN, Frederick George. b 11. **d** and **p** 51 Bradf. C of H Trin Bingley 51-53; King's Lynn (in c of St Nich) 53-55; R of Sculthorpe w Dunton and Doughton 55-64; C-in-c of Tatterford 56-60; R 60-64; Witton w Brundall and Bradeston 64-80; RD of Blofield 74-79. *18 Thirlby Road, North Walsham, Norfolk, NR28 9BA.* (N Walsham 403948)

GUNN, Geoffrey Charles. Kelham Th Coll 28. **d** 36 **p** 37 York. C of St Olave and St Mich-le-Belfrey York 36-39; St Geo Cathl Kingstown 39-40; P-in-c of Georgetown St Vincent 40-45; Min Can and Sacr of Carl Cathl 45-48; C of Romsey 48-51; V of St Cuthb Holme Cultram 51-56; R of Shotesham and Chap Trin Hosp Shotesham 56-77; Hon Min Can of Nor Cathl from 57; Chap from 59. *Shepherds Close, Priory Lane, Shotesham, Norwich.*

GUNN, George West. b 02. Edin Th Coll 28. **d** 30 **p** 31 Glas. C of St Geo Maryhill 30-33; St Marg Newlands Glas (in c of St D Pollokshaws) 33-36; St Mary's Cathl Glas (in c of Gartcosh Miss) 36-43; R of St Vincent Edin 43-47; St Jo Evang New Pitsligo 47-55; P-in-c of St Luke Downfield Dundee 55-60; R 60-71. *59c Douglas House, Allanfauld Road, Cumbernauld, Glasgow, G67 1HB.* (Cumbernauld 26263)

GUNN, Jeffery Thomas. b 47. St Chad's Coll Dur BA 77. Coll of the Resurr Mirfield 77. **d** 79 **p** 80 Glouc. C of Prestbury Dio Glouc from 79. *Oak Cottage, Blacksmith's Lane, Prestbury, Cheltenham, Glos.*

GUNN, Robert. b 35. Oak Hill Th Coll 59. **d** 62 **p** 63 Lon. C of St John U Holloway 62-66; St John Woking (in c of St Sav Brookwood) 66-69; w Script U 69-71; R of Necton w Holme Hale 71-76; St Jo Bapt Tottenham Dio Lon from 76. *113 Creighton Road, N17 8JS.* (01-808 4077)

GUNN, Walter Frederick. b 13. **d** and **p** 74 Bp Stopford for Jer for Jordan (APM). Chap at Amman 74-76; Limassol, Paphos and Troodos 76-78; P-in-c of St Paul Rothesay 78-80. *St Paul's Rectory, Auchinacloich Road, Rothesay, Bute, PA20 0EB.*

GUNN-JOHNSON, David Allan. b 49. St Steph Ho Ox 79. **d** 81 St Alb. C of St Matt Oxhey Dio St Alb from 81. *25 Silk Mill Road, Oxhey, Herts, WD1 4JW.*

GUNNER, Laurence Francois Pascal. b 36. Keble Coll Ox BA (3rd cl Jurispr) 59, MA 63. Wells Th Coll 59. **d** 61 Glouc **p** 62 Tewkesbury for Glouc. C of Charlton Kings 61-65; Hemel Hempstead (in c of St Barn) 65-69; Chap Bloxham Sch from 69. *Courtington House, Bloxham, Banbury, OX15 4PQ.* (Banbury 720626)

GUNNING, Peter Leslie. b 50. Univ of Rhodes BA 72. St Paul's Coll Grahmstn 74. **d** 74 **p** 75 Johann. C of Vereeniging 74-77; Lect St Paul's Coll Grahmstn 78-81; Dir of Th Educn Dio Johann from 81; R of Turffontein Dio Johann from 81. *Box 74138, Turffontein 2140, S Africa.*

GUNSTONE, Canon John Thomas Arthur. b 27. St Chad's Coll Dur BA (2nd cl Mod Hist) 48, MA 55. Coll of Resurr Mirfield 50. **d** 52 **p** 53 Chelmsf. C of St Jas Greater Walthamstow 52-53; St Edm Forest Gate 53-58; C-in-c of St Aug Conv Distr Rush Green Romford 58-71; Chap Whatcombe House Blandford 71-75; Tutor Sarum and Wells Th Coll 71-75; Publ Pr Dio Man from 75; Sec Gtr Man Co Ecumen Coun from 75; Hon Can of Man Cathl from 80. *719 Burnage Lane, Manchester, M19 1RR.* (061-432 2729)

GUNTER, Timothy Wilson. b 37. Univ of Leeds, BA (2nd cl Engl) 59. St Jo Coll Cam BA (3rd cl Th Trip pt ii) 62, MA 66. Ridley Hall, Cam 59. **d** 62 **p** 63 York. C of Beverley Minster 62-65; Hornsea w Goxhill (in c of Mappleton) 65-70; V of Silsden 70-80; Sunninghill Dio Ox from 80; Chap St George's Sch Ascot from 80. *Sunninghill Vicarage, Ascot, Berks, SL5 7DD.* (Ascot 20727)

GUNTER, Canon William Aston. b 05. Wycl Hall, Ox. **d** 41 **p** 42 Bradf. C of St Mary Eastwood 41-43; All SS Bradf 43-45; V of St Sav Harden 45-49; Bingley 49-62; Surr from 50; Hon Can of Bradf 59-66; Can (Emer) from 66; V of St Luke Manningham 63-66; L to Offic Dio Ches 67-71; Dio Bradf from 71. *12 Hawber Cote Drive, Silsden, Yorks, BD20 0JN.* (Steeton 52060)

GUNTHORPES, Alexander. b 48. Univ of WI LTh 75. Codr Coll Barb 74. **d** and **p** 75 Antig. C of St Geo St Kitts 75-76; R of St Geo Montserrat 76-80; Ch Ch Saba Dio Antig from 80. *Rectory, The Bottom, Saba, W Indies.*

GUNULA, Sezi. d 39 **p** 41 Ugan. P Dio Ugan 39-60; Dio Ankole-K 60-67; Dio Ank 67-74. *Box 14, Mbarara, Uganda.*

GUNYAU, James. Ho of Epiph Kuch 52. **d** 55 **p** 56 Borneo. P Dio Borneo 55-62; Dio Kuch from 62. *St John's Mission, Tai-i, Sarawak.*

GUNYON, Stephen Francis. b 14. Selw Coll Cam 2nd cl Hist Trip pt i, 37, BA (3rd cl Hist Trip pt ii), 38, MA 48. Linc Th Coll 38. **d** 40 **p** 41 Lon. C of St Jo Bapt Greenhill Harrow 40-43; SSF Cerne Abbas 43-44; CF (EC) 44-48; C of St Steph Rochester Row w St Mary Virg Westmr 48-50; V of Thornaby-on-Tees and Surr 50-57; Chap Middx Hosp 57-66; V of Hinchley Wood 66-71; Hindhead 71-80. *18 Waverley Road, Kettering, Northants, NN15 6NT.* (83885)

GUPPY, Kenneth Henry Stanley. b 29. St D Coll Lamp BA 54. St Mich Coll Llan 54. **d** 56 **p** 57 Mon. C of Rumney 56-61; Chap Shirley House Sch Watford 61-63; V of Llangwm Uchaf w Llangwm Isaf w Gwernesney and Llangeview (and Wolvesnewton from 81) Dio Mon from 63. *Gwernesney Rectory, Usk, NP5 1HF.* (Usk 2518)

GURD, (Simon) Brian Charles. b 44. M OSP 67. Sarum Wells Th Coll 72. **d** 74 Southn for Cant for Win **p** 75 Win. L to Offic Dio Win from 74; Prior OSB from 77. *The Abbey, Alton, Hants, GU34 4AP.* (Alton 62145)

GURNEY, Dennis Albert John. b 31. Lon Coll of Div. **d** 67 Bp Cornwall for Win **p** 68 Win. C of St Jo Evang Boscombe 67-69; V of Hurstbourne Tarrant w Faccombe 69-77; M Gen Syn Win from 75; R of St Ouen Jersey Dio Win from 77. *Rectory, St Ouen, Jersey, CI.* (0534 82461)

GURNEY, Edgar Albert. b 1898. St Paul's Th Coll Burgh, 31. **d** 33 **p** 34 York. C of Hinderwell w Roxby 33-34; Dairycoates 34-36; St Mary Magd Bradf 36-39; V of Hawsker 39-45; St Chad Eccles Distr Middlesborough 45-52; R of Barley 52-66. *Ramsay Hall, Byron Road, Worthing, Sussex.*

GURNEY, Richmond Harptree. b 24. Worc Coll Ox BA and Ma 48. Cudd Coll. **d** 50 **p** 51 Dur. C of Bishopwearmouth 50-53; Beamish 53-55; PC of Silksworth 55-66; R of Gateshead 66-75; P-in-c of Eskdale w Irton, Muncaster and Waberthwaite Dio Carl 75-78; V of Eskdale, Irton, Muncaster and Waberthwaite Dio Carl from 78; Commiss Bal from 75. *Eskdale Vicarage, Boot, Holmrook, Cumb, CA19 1TF.* (Eskdale 242)

GURNEY, Stanley Noel. Kelham Th Coll 30. M SSM 36. **d** 38 **p** 39 Bloemf. Miss Kroonstad 38-44; Wepener 46-48; C of St Kath Uitenhage 48-50; R of Alexandria 50-53; Dir of Ovamboland Miss 53-59; Archd of Ovamboland 54-59; Chap and Dir St Phil Miss Grahmstn 59-60; R of St Jo Evang E Lon 60-65; Molteno 65-66; Cathcart Dio Grahmstn from 66; Archd of Queenstn 65-70; K William's Town 71-80; R of K William's Town Dio Grahmstn from 72. *Holy Trinity Rectory, King William's Town, CP, S Africa.* (3145)

GURR, Ralph Sydney. b 27. K Coll Lon and Warm AKC 55. **d** 57 **p** 58 S'wark. C of Lewisham 57-63; Chap Lewisham Hosp 61-63; Cheam (in c of St Osw) 63-69; V of Wyke Bradf 69-72; V of St Mich Edmon Lon 72-79; Fordingbridge w Ibsley Dio Win from 79. *Vicarage, Fordingbridge, Hants, SP6 1BB.* (Fordingbridge 53163)

GURRIER-JONES, Paul. Moore Th Coll Syd ACT ThL 62. **d** 62 **p** 63 Syd. C of Eastwood 62-64; Blacktown 64-67; R of Milton Syd 67-72; Numbulwar 72-74; C of Jamberoo 74-76; R of Denham Court w Rossmore Dio Syd from 76. *100 Oxford Road, Ingleburn, NSW, Australia 2565.* (605-1247)

GUSH, Laurence Langley. b 23. Univ of Lon BSc 44. ARIC 47. M ICE CEng 52. N-W Ordin Course 73. **d** 76 Doncaster for Sheff **p** 77 Sheff (APM). C of St Matt City and Dio Sheff from 76. *11 Brentwood Road, Sheffield, S Yorks, S11 9BU.*

GUSSMAN, Robert William Spencer Lockhart. b 50. Ch Ch Ox BA 72, MA 76. Univ of Leeds BA (Th) 74. Coll of the Resurr Mirfield 72. **d** 75 Willesden for Lon **p** 76 Lon. C of Pinner 75-79; St Jos Northolt 79-81; P-in-c of Sutton Dio Ely from 81; Witcham & Mepal Dio Ely from 81. *Sutton Vicarage, Ely, Cambs.* (Ely 778645)

GUSTERSON, Preb Charles John. b 10. AKC 37. Cudd Coll 37. **d** 38 **p** 39 S'wark. C of St Andr Catford 38-41; Eltham 41-44; C-in-c of St Jas Conv Distr Merton 44-45; CF (EC) 45-48; Jt Metrop Sec SPG and L to Offic Dio S'wark 48-53; V of All SS Sydenham 53-62; Stokesay 62-76; C-in-c of Hopesay 62-66; Holdgate w Tugford 66-73; Dir of Relig Educn Dio Heref 64-76; Preb of Heref Cathl 66-76; Preb (Emer) from 76; RD of Stokesay 69-72; C-in-c of Acton-Scott 73-75; Pastoral Care of Acton-Scott from 75. *45 Back Lane, Onibury, Craven Arms, Salop.* (Bromfield 389)

GUTAKA, Gidion. Buwalasi Th Coll 60. **d** 62 **p** 63 Mbale. P Dio Mbale. *Box 297, Bumasobo, Mbale, Uganda.*

GUTCH, John Pitt. b 14. St Edm Hall, Ox BA (3rd cl Th) 36, MA 42. Cudd Coll Ox 37. **d** 38 **p** 39 S'wark. C of St Mich AA Camberwell 38-41; Cheshunt 41-43; Miss Dio Bloemf 43; P-in-c of St Mark w St Francis Port Eliz 43-58; St Francis

Port Eliz 58-59; Can Grahmstn 57-59; PC of St Jas Derby 59-67; R of Elton 67-80; C-in-c of Folksworth 69-73; RD of Yaxley Dio Ely 72-79; P-in-c of Stibbington 75-80; Water Newton 76-80; Perm to Offic Dio Chelmsf from 80. *52 St Marys Road, Frinton-on-Sea, Essex.* (Frinton 78374)

GUTHRIE, Arthur. b 12. MC 44. Trin Coll Dub BA 38, MA 41. **d** 39 **p** 40 Down. C of St Patr Coleraine 39-41; CF 41-46; C of Stoneyford 46-48; I of Killead w Gartree 48-82; RD of Antrim 57-74. *114 Belfast Road, Antrim, N Ireland.*

GUTHRIE, David Alexander. b 44. Univ of Sask BA 66. Trin Coll Tor STB 70. **d** 68 **p** 69 Qu'App. C of St Paul's Pro-Cathl Regina 68-72; I of Craik 73-74; St Phil Regina 74-79; Estevan Dio Qu'App from 79; Exam Chap to Bp of Qu'App from 78. *1133 Third Street, Estevan, Sask, Canada.* (634 2260)

GUTHRIE, David Ian. Univ of Auckld LLB 63. NZ Bd of Th Stud LTh (1st cl) 66. St Jo Coll Auckld 63. **d** 66 **p** 67 Auckld. C of Pukekohe 66-70; N Wairoa 70-71; V of New Lynn 71-78; C of St Mark Remuera Auckld 78-79; Hon C of St Paul Auckld 79-80; P-in-c of Clevedon 80-81; Chap Kingseat and Raventhorpe Hosps Dio Auckld from 81. *Magnolia Avenue, Papakura, NZ.*

GUTHRIE, Donald Angus. b 31. Trin Coll Ox BA 54, MA 58. Westcott Ho Cam 56. **d** 58 Lich **p** 59 Stafford for Lich. C of Rugeley 58-61; Penn 61-63; R of Selkirk 63-69; Vice Prin Edin Th Coll 69-74; C-in-c of Whitburn 74-76; Ecumen Officer Dio Dur 75-76; Provost of St Paul's Cathl Dundee 76-77; Episc Chap to Univ of Montana 77-80; I of Estevan Dio Qu'App from 80. *1133-3rd Street, Estevan, Sask, Canada.*

GUTHRIE, Edward John. Trin Coll Tor LTh 63. **d** 62 Bp Snell for Tor **p** 63 Tor. C of Ch Ch Deer Pk Tor 62-66; R of Lakefield 66-68; R of Warsaw 66-68; on leave. *Site 10, Comp 30, Penetanguishene, Ont, Canada.*

GUTHRIE, George Alexander. b 08. Trin Coll Dub BA 32, MA 41. **d** 33 **p** 34 Down. C of St Aid Belf 33-37; St Mary Belf 37-40; C-in-c of Ardmore Dio Drom 40-52; I 52-77; Dom Chap to Bp of Down 70-77. *120 Kingsway, Dunmurry, Belfast, BT17 9NP.* (Belf 622284)

GUTHRIE, William. b 49. Univ of WI LTh 72, BA 74. Codr Coll Barb 69. **d** 73 **p** 74 Guy. C of St Geo Cathl Georgetn 73-77; R of Canje w Berbice River 77-79; in Amer Ch. *1042 Preston Ave, Charlottesville, VA 22901, USA.*

GUTIERREZ, Delfo. d and **p** 66 Argent. P Dio Argent 66-73. N Argent from 73. *Parsonage, Misión Chaque£na, N Argentina.*

GUTIERREZ, Felipe. b 31. **d** 68 **p** 69 Argent. P Dio Argent 68-73. N Argent from 73. *Parsonage, Yuto, N Argentina.*

GUTSELL, David Leonard Nicholas. b 35. Univ of Sheff BA 59. ALCD 61 (LTh from 74). **d** 61 **p** 62 S'wark. C of St Barn Clapham Common Battersea 61-65; V of St Matthias U Tulse Hill 65-75; RD of Clapham and Brixton 74-75; V of Patcham Dio Chich from 75. *Vicarage, Church Hill, Brighton, BN1 8YE.* (B'ton 552157)

GUTTERIDGE, John. b 34. Oak Hill Th Coll 60. **d** 63 **p** 64 S'wark. C of St Luke Deptford 63-66; St Mary Southgate Crawley (in c of H Trin Tilgate) 66-70; P-in-c of Ch Ch Brixton 70-73; Manuden w Berden 73-76; Distr Sec N Lon Herts and Essex BFBS 76-81; Ex Sec from 81; Hon C of St Gabr Walthamstow Dio Chelmsf from 79. *25 Palmerston Road, Buckhurst Hill, Essex, IG9 5PA.* (01-504 2046)

GUTTERIDGE, John Philip. b 52. Qu Univ Belf BA 74. Chich Th Coll 75. **d** 78 Knaresborough for Ripon **p** 79 Ripon. C of St Aid Leeds Dio Ripon from 78. *Vicarage Flat, St Aidan's Vicarage, Vicar's Road, Shepherd's Lane,*

GUTTERIDGE, Richard Joseph Cooke. b 11. Trin Hall, Cam 2nd cl Hist Trip pt i, 31, BA (2nd cl Th Trip pt i) 32, MA 36. Wells Th Coll 34. **d** 35 **p** 36 Birm. Tutor Qu Coll Birm 35-37; C of St Bart Edgbaston and Asst Chap Qu Coll Birm 35-38; Lect 37-38; C of St Pet Bexhill 38-40; Temple Balsall (in c of St Pet Balsall Common) 40-41; Prin of Blue Coat Sch Birm and LPr Dio Birm 41-45; R of Brampton 45-52; Chap RAF 52-68; Bampton Fell Univ of Ox 69-72; C-in-c of Longstowe 72-73. *10 Archway Court, Cambridge CB3 9LW.* (Cambridge 352626)

GUTTRIDGE, John Arthur. b 26. Trin Hall Cam 2nd cl Hist Trip pt i 50, BA 51, 2nd cl Th Trip pt ii 52, MA 55. Westcott Ho Cam 51. **d** 53 **p** 54 Cov. C of Rugby 53-59; Lect Wells Th Coll 59-61; Chap 61-63; Vice-Prin 63-66; Dir of Post-Ordin Tr and Dom Chap to Bp of Wakef 66-68; Dir of Further Tr Dio Dur 68-74; Dir of Stud Sarum & Wells Th Coll 74-78; C of Bilston (in c of St Chad) Dio Lich 78-80; Team V from 80. *The Corner House, Claremont Street, Bilston, W Midl, WV14 6BA.* (Bilston 44786)

GUY, Chan Francis George. Trin Coll Dub BA 32, MA 46. **d** 33 **p** 34 Down. C of Trin Coll Dub Miss Belf 33-35; I of Ballyfin 35-42; CF (EC) 42-46; C of St Martin Birm 46-68; St Jas Belf 48-49; I of Dunluce Dio Connor from 49; Can and Preb of Connor Cathl 73-78; Chan from 78. *Dunluce Rectory, Bushmills, Co Antrim, N Ireland.* (Bushmills 221)

GUY, Gordon Ernest Scott. Montr Dioc Th Coll. **d** 65 **p** 66 Montr. I of Mascouche 65-68; R of Otterburn Heights 68-76; Dorval Dio Montr from 76. *2210 Swallow Avenue, Montreal, Canada.* (514-631 1379)

GUY, Gordon Frank. St Francis Coll Brisb. **d** 39 **p** 40 Brisb. C of St Andr Indooroopilly 39-41; M of Bush Bro of St Paul Charleville 41-43; V of Taringa 43-46; R of Darwin 46-48; Chelmer w Graceville 48-51; Chap RAAF 51-54; R of Goondiwindi 54-57; Roma 57-62; Charters Towers 63-67; Mackay Dio N Queensld from 67; Exam Chap to Bp of N Queensld 66-71; Hon Can of N Queensld 68-72; Archd of Mackay 72-76. *Box 234, Mackay, Queensland, Australia.* (079-573341)

GUY, Henderson Birchmore. Univ of WI LTh 72. Codr Coll Barb 69. **d** 71 **p** 73 Windw Is. C of St Geo Grenada 73-77; R of Carriacou 77-79. *c/o Diocesan Registry, Bridgetown, Barbados, W Indies.*

GUY, John Richard. b 44. St D Coll Lamp BA (2nd cl Hist) 65. St Steph Ho Ox 65. **d** 67 **p** 68 Llan. C of St Cath Canton 67-68; St Sav Roath 68-70; Bp's Messenger Llan 70-71; C of Machen (in c of Rudry) 71-74; R of Wolves-Newton w Kilgwrwg and Devauden 74-81; Perm to Offic Dio B & W from 81. *Selden End, Ash, Martock, Somt, TA12 6NS.* (Martock 3457)

GUY, Simon Edward Walrond. b 39. Univ of St Andr MA 61. St D Coll Lamp LTh 67. **d** 67 Malmesbury for Bris **p** 68 Bris. C of St Mary Redcliffe Bedminster 67-68; St Martin Knowle 68-71; Bishopston 71-75; C-in-c of Westwood 75; V 75-81; Team V of Melksham Dio Sarum from 81. *Vicarage, 5 Brampton Court, Bowerhill, Melksham, Wilts, SN12 6TH.* (Melksham 702037)

GUY, Walter. b 19. Univ of Man BA 52. St Cath S Ox BA 54, MA 58. Wycl Hall, Ox 52. **d** 54 **p** 55 Man. C of St Paul Withington 54-58; R of St Anne Newton Heath 58-68; V of Ellel Dio Blackb from 68. *Ellel Vicarage, Galgate, Lancaster.* (Galgate 751254)

GUYANA, Lord Bishop of. *See* George, Right Rev Randolph Oswald.

GUYANA, Lord Bishop Suffragan of. *See* Stabroek.

GUYANA, Dean of. *See* Clement, Very Rev James Orlando.

GUYER, Alan James. Moore Th Coll Syd ACT ThL (2nd cl) 65. **d** 65 Syd **p** 66 Bp Loane for Syd. C of Sans Souci 65-67; Wahroonga 68-71; Min of St Mark Sadleir and St Clem Busby 71-73; P-in-c of Kangaroo Valley 73-76. *Rectory, Kangaroo Valley, NSW, Australia 2577.*

GUYMER, Ernest William Rendell. Qu Coll Cam BA 31, MA 35. Ridley Hall, Cam 31. **d** 32 **p** 33 S'wark. C of St Alb Streatham Pk 32-35; Org Sec Dr Barnardo's Homes Dios B & W Bris and Glouc 35-36; R of Stanton St Quintin 36-45; Offg Chap RAF 37-39; Chap RAFVR 39-46; Sec SCm 46-47; Chap Iraq Petrol Co and L to Offic Dio Jer 47-58; V of Tolaga Bay 59-60; R of St Martin Jersey 60-61; Dean and V of St Jo Evang Cathl Napier 61-64. *3a Audrey Road, Auckland 9, NZ.*

GUYMER, Raymond John. b 41. K Coll Lon and Warm AKC 64. **d** 65 **p** 66 Lich. C of W Bromwich 65-70; Chap HM Borstal Portland 70-78; L to Offic Dio St E from 78; Chap HM Detention Centre Borstal Hollesley Bay Colony Woodbridge from 78. *50 Oak Hill, Hollesley Bay, Woodbridge, Suff, IP12 3JS.* (0394 411741)

GWAJA, Gideon. b 38. St Cypr Coll Rondo 69. **d** 72 **p** 73 Abp Sepeku for Masasi. P Dio Masasi. *PO Box 34, Lindi, Tanzania.*

GWASSA, Edwin Peter. St Paul's Th Coll Limuru, 61. **d** and **p** 63 Vic Nyan. P Dio Vic Nyan 63-65; Dio Dar S 65-72. *Box 2537, Dar-es-Salaam, Tanzania.*

GWATIDZO, Cyprian Mapayiwa. St John's Sem Lusaka. **d** 68 Mashon. d Dio Mashon 68-81; Dio Mutare from 81. *c/o 115 Main Street, Umtali, Zimbabwe.*

GWAYAKA, Patrick. b 41. **d** 74 **p** 75 Nam. P Dio Nam. *Kiwoko, Box 824, Luweero, Uganda.*

GWEKWERERE, Junius Garikayi. St John's Sem Lusaka. **d** 68 **p** 70 Matab. P Dio Matab 68-81; Dio Lundi from 81. *PO Box 172, Selukwe, Zimbabwe.* (Selukwe 28622)

GWETU, Ernest George. St Jo Coll Lusaka. **d** 58 **p** 60 Matab. P Dio Matab. *Holy Cross Mission, PO Luveve, Zimbabwe.*

GWETU, Canon Paul. St Aug Coll Penhalonga. **d** 34 **p** 39 S Rhod. P Dio S Rhod 34-52; Dio Matab 52-64; Hon Can of Matab from 64. *Box 98, Que Que, Zimbabwe.*

GWILLIAM, Christopher. b 44. St Chad's Coll Dur BA 65, Dipl Th 67. **d** 67 **p** 68 Mon. C of Chepstow 67-70; Risca 70-72; V of Cwmtillery 72-75; St Osw Hartlepool 75-82; Relig Affairs Producer Radio Tees from 82; C of Stockton-on-Tees Dio Dur from 82. *c/o Radio Tees, Dovecot Street, Stockton-on-Tees, Cleveland, TS18 1HB.*

GWILLIAM, Canon Oswald Noel. b 03. Late Exhib of St Chad's Coll Dur BA (3rd cl Th) and De Bury Scho 24. **d** 26 **p** 27 Dur. C of Gateshead 26-32; V of H Trin S Shields 32-41; Seaham w Seaham Harbour 41-48; R of Houghton-le-Spring 48-71; RD of Houghton-le-Spring 51-71; Hon Can of Dur 53-71; Can (Emer) from 71. *c/o Sacriston Vicarage, Durham, DH7 6LD.* (Sacriston 710294)

GWILYM-JONES, David Brinley. Wycl Hall Ox 58. **d** 58 Warrington for Liv **p** 59 Liv. C of St Mark Newtown 58-60; V of Parr Mt 60-64; R of Carlton Curlieu w Shangton and Ilston 64-70; V of Clodock w Longtown Craswall and Llanveynoe 70-77. *Castell Rhingyll, Llansteffan, Caerfyrddin, Dyfed, SA33 5JH.*

GWINGUZYE, John. **d** 68 **p** 69 W Tang. P Dio W Tang 68-76. *Box 13, Kasulu, Tanzania.*

GWOK, Canon Kwo Mwo. **d** 42 **p** 43 Sing. P Dio Sing 42-55; Hon Can of Sing from 55. *Jalan Besar, Singapore.*

GWYNNE, Robert Durham. b 44. Univ of Birm Dipl Th 70. Qu Coll Birm 67. **d** 70 **p** 72 Kens for Lon. C of St Kath, N Hammersmith 70-75; Ramsey 75-77; Team V of Old Brumby 77-81; P-in-c of St Matt Fairfield Conv Dist Scartho 81; Goxhill Dio Linc from 81; Thornton Curtis Dio Linc from 81. *Goxhill Vicarage, Barrow-on-Humber, Humb.* (Barrow H 30407)

GWYTHER, Geoffrey David. b 51. St D Coll Lamp Dipl Th 73. **d** 74 **p** 75 St D. C of Pembroke Dock 74-77; Milford Haven 77-81; V of Llawhaden w Bletherston Dio St D from 81. *Llawhaden Vicarage, Narberth, Dyfed.* (Llawhaden 225)

GWYTHER, Ronald Lloyd. b 23. St Francis Coll Brisb ACT ThL 47. **d** 47 **p** 48 Brisb. C of St Luke Toowoomba 48-49; H Trin Fortitude Valley 49; Perm to Offic Dio Ox 50-51; P-in-c of St Mark Mundubbera w Eidsvold 51-53; R of Sarina 53-56; C of Broadstairs 56-60; R of Pinxton 60-73; V of St Mary Swanley Dio Roch from 73. *St Mary's Vicarage, Swanley, Kent.* (Swanley 62201)

GYTON, Robert Wilfred. b 21. **d** 78 **p** 79 Nor (APM). Hon C of Gimingham Dio Nor from 78. *Trunch Rectory, North Walsham, Norfolk, NR28 0QE.* (0263 720420)

H

HA, John Sang-ho. b 10. **d** 66 **p** 67 Taejon. P Dio Taejon 66-74. *Box 19, Ch'ongju 310, Korea.*

HA, Ven Luke. St Mich Sem Oryudong 61. **d** and **p** 64 Korea. P Dio Korea 64-65; P Dio Taejon from 65; Dioc Treas Dio Taejon from 70; VG from 76; Archd Dio Taejon from 76. *Anglican Church, PO Box 19, Chongju 310, Korea.*

HABBERTON, Benjamin Walter. b 12. Qu Coll Birm 46. **d** 48 **p** 49 Cov. C of New Milverton 48-50; CF 50-55; R of Benoni 55-67; V of Springfield 67-81; Perm to Offic Dio Ex from 81. *11 Third Avenue, Teignmouth, Devon TQ14 9DW.* (062-67 5211)

HABERMEHL, Canon Kenneth Charles. b 22. Em Coll Cam 2nd cl Hist Trip pt i 42, 2nd cl pt ii 47, BA 46, MA 48. Chich Th Coll 47. **d** 49 Bedford for St Alb **p** 50 St Alb. C of St Chris Conv Distr Round Green 49-53; Ch Ch (in c of St Pet) Luton 53-56; V of Caddington 56-65; Kempston Dio St Alb from 65; Hon Can of St Alb Cathl from 81. *Kempston Vicarage, Bedford.* (Bedford 852241)

HABERSHON, Arthur Willoughby. b 1896. Or Coll Ox BA (*sc* Mod Hist w distinc) 21, Dipl in Th w distinc 22, MA 25. Wycl Hall Ox 22. **d** 23 **p** 24 Roch. C of Sevenoaks 23-26; V of St Jo Evang Blackheath 26-28; Prin Oak Hill Coll Southgate 28-32; Publ Pr Dio St Alb 30-32; V of H Trin Cheltenham 33-35; New Malden w Coombe 35-44; Ch Ch Chislehurst 44-53; H Trin Tunbridge Wells 53-66. *Flat 4, 105 Grandfield Avenue, Watford, Herts, WD1 3XD.*

HABERSHON, Kenneth Willoughby. b 35. New Coll Ox 2nd cl Cl Mods 55, BA (3rd cl Mod Hist) 57, Dipl Th 58, MA 60. Wycl Hall Ox 57. **d** 59 **p** 60 Lon. C of Ch Ch Finchley 59-66; Sec Ch Youth Fellowships Assoc 66-74; Staff Mem CPAS from 74; Hon C of St Andr Chorley Wood 71-77; Reigate Dio S'wark from 78. *7 High Trees Road, Reigate, Surrey, RH2 7EH.*

HABGOOD, John Gerald Peace. b 18 St Cath Coll Ox BA 40, MA 45. Cudd Coll 45. **d** 47 **p** 48 Glouc. C of Stonehouse 47-49; Parkend (in c of Yorkley) 49-51; V of Selsley 51-56; R of Warsop w Sookholme 56-65; St Anne (w All SS, St Mich and St Thos from 75) Lewes, Dio Chich from 65; St Thos w All SS, Lewes 68-75; Surr from 65. *Rectory, St Anne's Crescent, Lewes, Sussex, BN7 1SD.* (Lewes 2545)

✠ **HABGOOD, Right Rev John Stapylton.** b 27. K Coll Cam 1st cl Nat Sc Trip pt i 47, BA (1st cl Nat Sc Trip pt ii) 48, MA 51, PhD and Fell 52, Univ of Dur Hon DD 75. Cudd Coll 53. **d** 54 **p** 55 Lon. C of St Mary Abbots Kens 54-56; Vice-Prin Westcott Ho Cam 56-62; Select Pr Univ of Cam 59 and 77; Select Pr Univ of Ox 77; Exam Chap to Bp of Worc 60-73; to Bp of Edin 62-67; Perm to Offic Dio Ely 61-62; R of St Jo Evang Jedburgh 62-67; Prin Qu Coll Birm 67-73; Hon Can of Birm Cathl 71-73; Cons Ld Bp of Dur in York Minster 1 May 73 by Abp of York; Bps of Ches, Liv, Wakef, Man, Southw, Sheff, Blackb, Bradf, Newc T, Worc, Birm and Edin; Bps Suffr of Jarrow, Hull, Stockport, Selby, Burnley, Penrith, Pontefract, Whitby, Knaresborough and Doncaster; and others. *Auckland Castle, Bishop Auckland, Co Durham, DL14 7NR.* (Bp Auckland 602576)

HABIMANA, Samuel. **d** 66 **p** 67 Vic Nyan. P Dio Vic Nyan. *Katoke College, PO Katoke, Bukoba, Tanzania.*

HABIMANA, William Baker. b 47. **d** 77 **p** 78 W Ank. P Dio W Ank. *PO Mitooma-Ruhinda, Uganda.*

HABYARA, Chrysostom. **d** 58 **p** 59 Bp Brazier for Ugan. P Dio Ugan 58-60; Dio Rwanda B 60-66; P Dio Bur 66-68; Dio Rwa 68-75; Dio Kiga from 75. *BP 51, Byumba, Rwanda.*

HACK, Rex Hereward. b 28. Pemb Coll Cam BA 50, MA 56. ACA 56, FCA 67. Ripon Hall Ox 58. **d** 59 **p** 60 Ches. C of St Mary Magd Ashton-on-Mersey 59-62; Ellesmere Port 62-65; V of Norton-Cuckney w Welbeck and Holbeck 65-69; V of Bramhall Dio Chesh from 69. *Bramhall Vicarage, Stockport, Chesh.* (Bramhall 2254)

✠ **HACKER, Right Rev George Lanyon.** b 28. Ex Coll Ox BA (2nd cl Th) 52, MA 56. Cudd Coll 52. **d** 54 **p** 55 Bris. C of St Mary Redcliffe Bedminster 54-59; Chap St Bonif Coll Warm and L to Offic Dio Sarum 59-64; PC of Ch of Good Shepherd, Bp Wearmouth 64-71; R of Tilehurst 71-79; Cons Ld Bp Suffr of Penrith in York Minster 10 Oct 79 by Abps of York and the Indian Ocean; Bps of Dur, Carl, Bradf, Brech, Chich, Ripon and S & M; Bps Suffr of Reading, Kingston T, Tonbridge, Plymouth, Doncaster, Whitby, Lanc, Stockport, Warrington, Hull, Sherwood, Jarrow and Edmon; and others. *Great Salkeld Rectory, Penrith, Cumb, CA11 9NA.* (Lazonby 273)

HACKETT, Frank James. b 33. Univ of Birm MA 77. Bps' Coll Cheshunt 62. **d** 64 **p** 65 Lon. C of Feltham 64-69; Industr Chap to Bp of Lich 69-73; L to Offic Dio Lich 69-73; Dio Lon 73-79; Perm to Offic from 79; Industr chap to Port of Lon from 73; Perm to Offic Dio Chelmsf 73-79; P-in-c of N Ockendon Dio Chelmsf from 79. *51 Courtnay Gardens, Upminster, Essex, RM14 1DH.* (Upminster 21461)

HACKETT, Geoffrey. Kelham Th Coll 26. **d** 33 **p** 34 Wakef. C of Sowerby Bridge w Norland 33-37; Heckmondwike 37-42; Monk Bretton 42-44; V of Scholes 44-55; PC of E Rainton 55-60; Lumley 60-64; Perm to Offic Dio Dur from 64. *9 Egerton Terrace, Greatham, Hartlepool, Co Durham.*

HACKETT, John. b 38. Late Exhib of Selw Coll Cam 2nd cl Hist Trip pt i 59, BA 60, 2nd cl Th Trip pt ii 61, MA 65. Linc Th Coll 61. **d** 63 Middleton for Man **p** 64 S'wark. C of Newton Heath 63-64; Merton 64-70; Hon C of St Matt Redhill 70-72; S-E Sec of Ch Chr Educn Movement from 70; Tutor SOC from 72; V of Ch Ch Sutton Dio S'wark from 74. *14 Christchurch Park, Sutton, Surrey.* (01-642 2757)

HACKETT, John Nigel. b 32. Trin Hall Cam BA 55, MA 59. Ely Th Coll. **d** 59 **p** 60 Birm. C of Handsworth 59-66; V of St Jas Handsworth Dio Birm from 66. *Vicarage, Austin Road, Birmingham 21.* (021-554 4151)

HACKETT, Peter Edward. b 25. Late Acad Clk of Magd Coll Ox BA 48, MA 51. ALCD 60. **d** 60 **p** 61 Southw. C of Lenton 60-62; Attenborough w Bramcote and Chilwell 62-63; V of St Barn Lenton Abbey 63-67; R of Acton Beauchamp and Evesbatch w Stanford Bp 67-71; V Chor and Chap Heref Cathl 72-76; P-in-c of St Weonards w Orcop 76-79; Tretire w Michaelchurch 76-79; Garway 76-79; Welsh Newton w Llanrothal 77-79; V of Rounds Green Dio Birm from 79. *Vicarage, Shelsley Avenue, Oldbury, Warley, W Midl, B69 1BG.* (021-552 2822)

HACKETT, Ronald Glyndwr. b 47. Hatfield Coll Dur BA (3rd cl Th) 70. Cudd Coll 70. **d** 72 **p** 73 St D. C of Pembroke 72-75; Bassaleg 75-78; V of Blaenavon w Capel Newydd Dio Mon from 78. *Vicarage, Blaenavon, Gwent.* (Blaenavon 790292)

HACKING, Philip Henry. b 31. St Pet Hall Ox BA (2nd cl Mod Hist) 53, MA 57. Oak Hill Th Coll 53. **d** 55 **p** 56 Liv. C of St Helens 55-58; Chap of St Thos Edin 58-68; V of Fulwood City and Dio Sheff from 68. *2 Chorley Drive, Sheffield, S10 3RR.* (0742 301911)

HACKING, Richard. b 06. Tyndale Hall Bris 31. **d** 36 **p** 39 Momb. BCMS Miss Dio Momb from 36; Marsabit 36-40; CF (E Afr) 40-46; Miss Samburu 48-54; Perm to Offic (Col Cl Act) at All H Bispham Blackpool 46-47; at St John Harborne Birm 55; Perm to Offic Dio Momb 55-59; V of St Pancras

Pennycross Plymouth 59-72; V of Barston 72-76; Perm to Offic Dio Cov from 76. *33 Braemar Road, Lillington, Leamington Spa.* (Leamington Spa 28855)

HACKING, Rodney Douglas. b 53. AKC and BD 74. St Aug Coll Cant 75. **d** 76 Newc T **p** 78 S'wark. C of St Mich Byker Newc T 76-77; St John Eltham 77-80; Industr Chap Leeds Dio Ripon from 80. *23 Harrowby Road, Leeds, LS16 5HZ.* (Leeds 758100)

HACKNEY, Archdeacon of. *See* Sharpley, Ven Roger Ernest Dion.

HACKNEY, Bryan William George. b 41. Linc Th Coll 65. **d** 68 **p** 69 Bradf. C of Baildon 68-71; R of Gt Casterton w Pickworth Tickencote and L Casterton 71-74; L to Offic Dio Linc 74-77; V of Barnetby-le-Wold 77-81; P-in-c of Bigby and Somerby 77-81; Bp's Adv for Industr Work in the Derby Area from 81. *c/o Diocesan Registrar, 35 St Mary's Gate, Derby.*

HACKSHALL, Brian Leonard. b 33. K Coll Lon and Warm BD and AKC 53. **d** 57 **p** 58 Portsm. C of St Mary Portsea 57-62; St Alb Westbury Pk Clifton 62-64; V of Avonmouth 64-71; Chap Miss to Seamen Shoreham 71-77; Mer 77-79; Perm to Offic Dio Ches 78-79; Team V of Crawley Dio Chich from 79. *7 The Parade, Northgate, Crawley, W Sussex, RH10 2DT.* (Crawley 20621)

✠ **HADDAD, Right Rev Faiq Ibrahim.** Amer Univ Beirut BA 38. Near E Sch of Th Beirut. **d** 39 **p** 40 Jer. C of Acre 39-44; Jaffa 44-49; Amman 49-59; Nablus 60-65; V of Her 65-71; Can Res of St Geo Colleg Ch Jer 71-74; Cons Bp Coadj in Jer and Jordan, Lebanon and Syria in St Geo Colleg Ch Jer 29 Aug 74 by Bp Stopford (VG in Jer), Bps in Jordan and Iran; and Bps Ashton abd A MacInnes; Apptd Bp in Jer 76. *Bishop's House, PO Box 1248, Jerusalem.*

HADDAD, Joseph Said. b 23. **d** and **p** 78 Jer. Dir of Stud St Geo Coll Jer from 78. *c/o The Registrar, American University, Beirut, Lebanon.*

HADDAD, Wadi Zaydan. Amer Univ Beirut BA 58. Episc Th Sch Cam USA BD 58. Near East Sch of Th Beirut Dipl Th 58. **d** 58 **p** 59 Jordan. C of Zerka 58-67; Beirut Dio Jordan from 67. *Beirut, Lebanon.*

HADDELSEY, Charles Vincent Bernard. b 03. Lich Th Coll 22. **d** 26 **p** 27 Southw. C of Long Eaton 26-28; St Anne 78-80. St Agnes Kennington Pk 30-33; Godshill (in c of St Alb) 33-38; V of St Olave Mitcham 38-50; CF (EC) 41-46; V of Syston 50-59; CF (TA) 53-59; Hon CF 59; R of Stratton Audley w Godington 59-63; V of S Ascot 63-68; Warden Launde Abbey Dioc Retreat Ho 68-74; C-in-c of Loddington 68-74. *6 Shepherds Way, Uppingham, LE15 9PW.* (Uppingham 3698)

HADDELSEY, Stephen Andrew. b 36. Late Pri of Ch Ch Ox BA (3rd cl Mod Hist) and Squire Scho 58, 2nd cl Th 60, MA 62. Coll of Resurr Mirfield 60. **d** 62 **p** 63 Lon. C of Pinner 62-66; S Ascot 66-68; Dean of Students Ch Ch Coll Ch Ch NZ 68-70; C of Oakham 70; V of St Luke Stocking Farm Leic 70-78; Asst Master Prince Rupert Sch W Germany 78-80; P-in-c of Claybrooke w Wibtoft and of Frolesworth Dio Leic 80; V from 80. *Claybrooke Vicarage, Lutterworth, Leics.*

HADDEN, Geoffrey Paddock. b 05. Kelham Th Coll 26. **d** 31 **p** 32 Ches. C of Coppenhall 31-35; P-in-c of Franklin Harbour Miss Dio Willoch 35-37; R of St Thos Port Lincoln 37-39; P-in-c of St James Waikerie 39-41; Victor Harbour 41-45 (w St Jude Port Elliot from 42); Chap RAAF 44-45; V of St Luke L Tranmere 46-51; New Bilton 51-56; St Barn Hove 56-65; R of Horsted Keynes 65-73; Perm Offic Dio Cov from 73. *100 Kingsley Road, Bishop's Tachbrook, Leamington Spa, Warws.*

HADDEN, Henry Richards. b 10. AKC 33. **d** 33 Sarum **p** 40 York. C of H Trin Bradford-on-Avon 33-35; Perm to Offic at St Clem Parkstone 36-37; Fordington St Geo 37-38; Asst Master Orleton Sch Scarborough 38-40; C of Redcar 40-41; Perm to Offic at Clun w Chapel Lawn 41-43; C of St Pet Heref 43-47; Kington w Huntington 47-48; V of L Dewchurch w Aconbury 48-50; R of Chipstable w Raddington 50-55; Camerton 55-59; V of Stoke St Greg 59-66; Alderholt 66-77. *252 Station Road, West Moors, Wimborne, Dorset, BH22 0JF.*

HADDLETON, Peter Gordon. b 53. Univ of E Anglia BA 74. Sarum Wells Th Coll 76. **d** 79 **p** 80 S'wark. C of Thamesmead Dio S'wark from 79. *508 Besant Court, Titmuss Avenue, Thamesmead, SE28 8BL.*

HADDOCK, Malcolm George. b 27. Univ Coll Cardiff Dipl Th 53, BA 56. **d** 80 Mon **p** 81 Llan for Mon. C of H Trin Christchurch Dio Mon from 80. *164a Christchurch Road, Newport, Gwent.*

HADDOCK, Canon Norman. St D Coll Lamp BA 41, BD 51. **d** 42 **p** 43 Llan. C of Llanwonno 42-46; Porthkerry w Barry 46-59; PC of St Luke Cheltm Dio Glouc 59-60; V (w St John from 67) from 60; C-in-c of St John Cheltm 66-67; Hon Can of Glouc from 74; Surr from 75; RD of Cheltm from 77. *St Luke's Vicarage, College Road, Cheltenham, Glos.* (Cheltenham 53940)

HADDON, Ven Ernest Roy. Em Coll Sktn 40. **d** 41 **p** 42 Sask. C of Sturgeon Valley Lake and Briarlea 41-42; Hudson's Bay Junction 42-45; I of Nipawin 45-48; R of Spirit River 48-50; Chapleau 50-53; St Thos Thunder Bay Dio Alg from 53; Hon Can of Alg 62-71; Archd of Thunder Bay from 71. *1408 Edward Street, Thunder Bay, Ont., Canada.* (807-622 4980)

HADFIELD, Christopher. b 39. Jes Coll Cam BA 61. Wells Th Coll 63. **d** 65 **p** 66 Penrith for Carl. C of Wigton 65-68. *Newlands School, Seaford, E Sussex, BN25 4NP.*

HADFIELD, Graham Francis. b 48. Univ of Bris BSc 69. St Jo Coll Dur Dipl Th 71. **d** 73 **p** 74 Blackb. C of St Thos Blackpool 73-76; CF from 76. *c/o Ministry of Defence, Bagshot Park, Bagshot, Surrey, GU19 5PL.*

HADFIELD, Ven John Collingwood. b 12. Late Exhib of Jes Coll Cam 2nd cl Cl Trip pt i 33, BA (1st cl Cl Trip pt ii) 34, MA 38. Wells Th Coll 34. **d** 35 **p** 36 Man. C of St Chad Ladybarn (in c from 40) 35-44; V of St Mark Bolton 44-50; Belfield 50-62; Surr 44-62; Proc Conv Man 50-62; R of St Paul Rothesay 62-64; Itin P Dio Arg Is 64-77; Can of St John's Cathl Oban 65-77; Insp of Schs Dio Arg Is 66-77; Syn Clk Dio Arg Is 73-77; R of Wick Dio Moray from 77; P-in-c of Thurso Dio Moray from 77; Hon Archd of Caithness from 77. *4 Sir Archibald Road, Thurso, Caithness, KW14 8HN.* (Thurso 2047)

HADFIELD, Jonathan Benedict Philip John. b 43. Univ of Lon BA (1st cl Cl) 64. Jes Coll Cam BA (2nd cl Th Trip pt ii) 67, MA 72. Edin Th Coll 66. **d** 68 **p** 69 Arg Is. C of Fort William 68-70; Chap K Sch Glouc from 70. *Dulverton House, King's School, Pitt Street, Gloucester, GL1 2BE.*

HADIDO, Gershom Samuel. b 46. Bp Tucker Coll Mukono 69. **d** 73 Bukedi. d Dio Bukedi 73-74; Dio Kamp from 74. *20012, Kampala, Uganda.*

HADKINSON, Frank. Chich Th Coll 36. **d** 38 **p** 39 Lon. C of St Aug Whitton 38-43; Folkstone 43-46; C-in-c 46-48; V of H Trin Winchmore Hill 48-75; Chap to Highlands Hosp 48-75. *Brookfield, Clun Road, Craven Arms, Salop, SY7 9QW.*

HADLEY, Charles Adrian. b 50. Trin Coll Cam BA 71, MA 75. Cudd Coll 73. **d** 75 **p** 76 St E. C of Hadleigh 75-78; Bracknell Dio Ox 78-80. *Address temp unknown.*

HADLEY, Donald Thomas. b 30. Lich Th Coll 55. **d** 58 Aston for Birm **p** 59 Birm. C of Saltley 58-61; Min of St Mich AA Eccles Distr S Yardley 61-66; V 66-70; V of Tonge Moor Dio Man from 70. *St Augustine's Vicarage, Tonge Moor, Bolton, Lancs.* (Bolton 23899)

HADLEY, Steven Frank. b 50. Univ of Wales (Bangor) BA 73, BD 76. St Mich AA Llan 75. **d** 76 **p** 77 Llan. C of St Andrew's Major w Michaelston-le-Pit 76-80; Chap of Bryn-y-Don Approved Sch 76-80; R of Llanfyllin Dio St A from 80; Bwlch-y-Cibau Dio St A from 80. *Rectory, Llanfyllin, Powys, SY22 5BW.* (Llanfyllin 306)

HADLEY, Stuart James. b 55. AKC and BD 76. St Steph Ho Ox 77. **d** 78 **p** 79 Southw. C of St Mark Mansfield Dio Southw from 78. *26 Berry Hill Lane, Mansfield, Notts, NG18 4BW.*

HADLOW, Gerald James John Austin. St Jo Coll Auckld 63. **d** 65 **p** 66 Auckld. C of St Matt, Auckld 65-69; V of Tuakau 69-73; Morrinsville 73-80; Archd of Piako 77-80; V of Rotorua Dio Wai from 80. *Vicarage, Rutland Street, Rotorua, NZ.* (89-383)

HADLOW, Selwyn Sidney. St Jo Coll Morpeth 52. **d** 52 **p** 53 Armid. C of Quirindi 52-53; C-in-c of Tambar Springs 53-56; V of Walgett 56-59; Walcha 59-63; Chap Miss to Seamen Fremantle 64-66; Madras 66-69; Wellington 69-74; Perm to Offic Dio Auckld 74-80; Chap RNZN from 74; V of Seatoun Dio Wel from 80. *40 Ferry Street, Seatoun, Wellington, NZ.* (886-882)

HADRILL, Hugh Francis. Univ of Tas BA 49. Ch Coll Tas ACT ThL 53. **d** 50 **p** 51 Tas. C of All SS Hobart 50-51; St Paul Launceston Tas 51-52; Eastleigh Hants 53-54; R of Avoca w Fingal Tas 54-57; Cygnet 57-61; R of Franklin 61-64; St Jas New Town Tas 64-77; Perm to Offic Dio Tas from 77. *28 Seaview Avenue, Taroona, Tasmania 7006.* (002-27 8995)

HAFFENDEN, Eric Vivian. Em Coll Sktn LTh 62. **d** 62 **p** 63 Calg. I of Delia w Byemoor 62-65; Pike Lake 65-69; All SS Calg 71-74; L to Offic Dio Calg from 74. *2340 Paliswood Road SW, Calgary, Alta., Canada.* (281-4812)

HAGAN, Kenneth Raymond. b 40. St Jo Coll Morpeth. **d** 64 **p** 65 Newc. C of Charlestown 64-69; Cessnock 69-70; R of E Pilbara 70-75; C of St Mary Portsea (in C of St Faith) 75-78; P-in-c of Wolvey w Burton Hastings and Stretton Baskerville Dio Cov from 78; Withybrook w Copston Magna Dio Cov from 78; Ansty w Shilton Dio Cov from 78. *Wolvey Vicarage, Hinckley, Leics.* (Hinckley 220385)

HAGERIA, Benjamin. **d** 21 **p** 24 Melan. P Dio Melan. *Melanesian Mission, Honiara, British Solomon Islands.*

HAGESI, Robert. St Pet Coll Siota 64. **d** 68 **p** 70 Melan. P Dio Melan 68-73; Tutor Bp Patteson Th Centre Honiara from 73; L to Offic Dio Centr Melan from 75. *PO Box 19, Honiara, British Solomon Islands.*

HAGGARD, Amyand Richard. b 21. Jes Coll Ox MA 57. Ripon Hall Ox 56. **d** 58 **p** 59 S'wark. C of St Luke Battersea 58-61; V of St Phil Battersea 61-68. *78 Eland Road, Battersea Park Road, SW11.* (01-228 8166)

✠ **HAGGART, Most Rev Alastair Iain Macdonald.** b 15. Univ of Dur LTh 41, BA 42, MA 45. Edin Th Coll 38. Univ of Dundee Hon LLD 70. **d** 41 **p** 42 Glas. C of St Mary's Cathl Glas 41-45; Hendon Lon 45-48; Prec of St Ninian's Cathl Perth 48-51; R of St Osw King's Pk Glas 51-59; Synod Clk and Can of Glas 58-59; Provost of St Paul's Cathl, Dundee 59-70; Exam Chap to Bp of Brech 64-75; Prin Edin Th Coll 70-75; Can of St Mary's Cathl Edin 71-75; Cons Ld Bp of Edin in St Mary's Cathl Edin 4 Dec 75 by Bp of Arg Is (Primus); Bps of St Andr, Moray, Aber, Glas, Brech, Carl and Man; Bp Suffr of Bedford; and Bps Easson, Sprott, Moncreiff, Carey and Russell; Elected Primus of Episc Ch in Scotld 77. *19 Eglinton Crescent, Edinburgh, EH12 5BY.* (031-337 8948)*; and Diocesan Centre, Walpole Hall, Chester Street, Edinburgh, EH3 7EN.* (031-226 3358)

HAGUE, Arthur Cyril. b 13. Univ Coll Dur BA 24. **d** 24 Dur **p** 25 Jarrow for Dur. C of Shadforth 24-28; St Helen Low Fell Gateshead 28-30; Bp Auckland 30-33; V of H Trin Hartlepool 33-46; Chap RNVR 41-48; Chap Sunderland Hosps 48-61; R of Byers Green 61-66. *Homelands Hospital, Crook, Co Durham.*

HAGUE, Eric. b 13. Univ of Lon BA (2nd cl Mod Chinese) 52. St Aid Coll 36. **d** 39 **p** 40 Liv. C of St Cypr Edge Hill 39-43; CMS Miss Dio Kwangsi-H 43-52; Dio Hong 52-56; V of St Andr Kowloon 55-56; Ch Ch Woking 57-62; High Wycombe 62-69; R of L Shelford w Newton 69-76; C-in-c of Parr Mount 76; V 77-79. *47 North Parade, Hoylake, Wirral, Mer, L47 3AL.* (051-632 2535)

HAGUE, John Rayson. St Jo Coll Manit 28. **d** 37 **p** 38 Calg. Miss at Coutts 37-38; I of Coleman w Blairmore 38-44; R of Innisfail 44-52; I of Revelstoke 52-59; C-in-c of Armstrong 59-68; V of Shuswap Lakes 68-71. *3408 Spruce Drive, Lethbridge, Alta, Canada.*

HAHN, Leslie William. St Jo Coll Morpeth ACT ThL 49. **d** 49 **p** 50 Perth. C of St Geo Cathl Perth 49-51; Forrest River Miss 51-53; R of Wongan Hills 53-56; Hosp Chap in Dio Melb 56-60; Dio Bal 58-60; on leave 60-63; Chap Monash Univ 66-69; Perm to Offic Dio Brisb 68-78 and from 80; Chap St Hilda Sch Southport 78-80. *33 Tamarind Street, Maleny, Queensland, Australia 4552.*

HAIG, Alistair Matthew. b 39. Univ of Lon BD and AKC 63. **d** 64 **p** 65 Chelmsf. C of St Edm Forest Gate 64-67; Laindon w Basildon 67-71; V of S Woodham Ferrers 71-78; P-in-c of H Trin City and Dio Bath from 78. *Holy Trinity Rectory, Marlborough Lane, Bath, Avon, BA1 2NQ.* (Bath 22311)

HAIG, Andrew Livingstone. b 45. Keble Coll Ox BA (Th) 67. Coll of Resurr Mirfield 67. **d** 69 Hulme for Man **p** 70 Man. C of All SS Elton Bury 69-75; R of Brantham (w Stutton from 76) Dio St E from 75; RD of Samford from 81. *Brantham Rectory, Manningtree, Essex.* (Manningtree 2646)

HAIG, Brian Douglas. b 40. Univ of Melb BComm 63. St Barn Th Coll Belair. **d** 69 Bp Porter for Bal **p** 70 Bal. C of Warrnambool 70-73; R of Rupanyup 73-75; Chr Educn Officer 75-78; Executive Officer Ch Comm on Educn Dio Perth 78-80; Chap Perth Coll from 80. *23 Derrington Crescent, Balga, W Australia 6061.* (342 2291)

HAIG, John Alastair. b 30. Univ of Tor BD 58. Mt Allison Univ NB BA 58. Andover Newton Th Coll Mass STM 60. **d** and **p** 77 Ont. Hd Master Grenville Chr Coll Dio Ont from 77. *Grenville Christian College, Box 610, Brockville, Ont, Canada, K6V 5V8.*

HAIG, Murray Nigel Francis. b 39. St D Coll Lamp BA 62. Kelham Th Coll 62. **d** 66 **p** 67 St E. C of St Jo Bapt Felixstowe 66-72; C of Morpeth 72-74; V of St Mich (w St Lawr from 78) Byker Newc T 74-81; St Jas Benwell City and Dio Newc T from 81. *Benwell Vicarage, Newcastle upon Tyne, NE15 6RS.* (Newc T 35021)

HAIG-BROWN, William John. Univ of Dur LTh 39. St Aug Coll Cant 34. **d** 39 **p** 40 Guildf. C of Thames Ditton 39-42; Asst Chap Miss to Seamen Middlesbrough and L to Offic Dios York and Dur 42-45; Chap Miss to Seamen Ports of Antwerp and Ghent 45-48; Belf 48; Hong Kong 49-57; C of Harborne 57-58; PC of St Pet Tile Cross Yardley 58-63; Chap Moor Pk Coll Farnham 63-67; C of Portsea 67-70; Waterlooville 70-75; Milton (in c of St Patr Southsea) 75-80. *21 The Avenue, Fareham, Hants.*

HAIGH, Colin. b 15. St Chad's Coll Dur BA 40. Dipl in Th 41, MA 43. **d** 41 **p** 42 Wakef. C of Linthwaite 41-44; Featherstone 44-45; St Pet Streatham 45-48; All SS Benhilton 48-50; St Bart Ipswich 50-52; Leigh Essex 52-56; R of Fobbing 56-64; Publ Pr Dio Chelmsf 64-68; C-in-c of Rawreth 64-68; V of St Alb Romford 68-80. *93 Egremont Street, Glemsford, Sudbury, Suff, CO10 7SG.* (Glemsford 281173)

HAIGH, Gordon Thomas. Univ of Dur LTh 33, BA 34, MA 40, MLitt 44. Qu Coll Birm 30. **d** 34 **p** 35 Glouc. C of Winchcombe w Gretton and Sudeley Manor 34-39; V of Oakridge 39-59; Castle Morton 59-62; L to Offic Dio Worc from 76. *Church Road, Castlemorton, Malvern, Worcs.*

HAIGH, Maurice. b 22. St Cath Coll Cam. BA 46, MA 48. Univ of Lon BD 60. **d** 60 Burnley for York **p** 61 Blackb. Hon C of Marton Dio Blackb from 60. *11 Beechfield Avenue, Blackpool, Lancs.*

HAIGH, Norman. b 02. Dorch Miss Coll 27. **d** 30 **p** 31 Lon. C of St John Stamford Hill 30-31; St Matt Oakley Sq 31-34; Old St Pancras 34-36; Slaugham 36-39; Findon 39-42; CF (EC) 42-46; V of Ripponden w Rishworth Yorks 46-50; P-in-c of Likwenu 50-52; Chap at Blantyre and Zomba Nyasa 52-54; V of All SS Pontefract 54-57; C of St Mich Stonebridge Willesden 58-59; St Mich Wood Green 60-62; V of Childs Wickham 62-72; R of Aston Somerville 62-72; Perm to Offic Dio Cov 72-77. *32 Willes Road, Leamington Spa, Warws, CV31 1BN.* (Leamington Spa 36597)

HAIGH, Owen Quentin. b 15. St Chad's Coll Dur BA 43, MA 46. **d** 43 **p** 44 Dur. C of Birtley 43-47; Billingham 47-50; Min of St Mark's Eccles Distr Darlington 50-55; R of Wiston 55-75; R of Ashington w Buncton 55-75; Seq of Worminghurst 56-60; RD of Storrington 70-76; C-in-c and Seq of Stedham w Iping Dio Chich from 75; P-in-c of Trotton w Chithurst Dio Chich from 80. *Stedham Rectory, Midhurst, W Sussex, GU29 0NQ.* (Midhurst 3342)

HAIGH, Richard Michael Fisher. b 30. Univ of Dur BA 57, Dipl Th 59. Cranmer Hall Dur 57. **d** 59 **p** 60 Carl. C of Stanwix 59-62; CMS Miss Srinagar Dio Amrit 63-67 and 68-70; R of St Clem w St Cypr Ordsall Salford 71-75; Em Holcombe Dio Man from 75. *Holcombe Rectory, Carrwood Hey, Ramsbottom, Lancs, BL0 9QT.* (Ramsbottom 2312)

HAIHAMBO, Canon Lazarus Siisu. **d** 36 **p** 37 Damar. P Dio Damar 37-80; Dio Namibia from 80; Can of Damar 65-72; Hon Can from 72; R of Ch K Onekuaja 67-71; L to Offic Dio Damar 71-80; Dio Namibia from 80. *c/o St Mary's Church, Odibo, PO Oshikango, Ovamboland, SW Africa.* (Oshikango 5)

HAIHAMBO, Polycarp Lazarus. **d** 68 **p** 72 Damar. C of Odibo 68-71; L to Offic Dio Damar 71-72; C of Tsumeb Dio Damar (Namibia from 80) from 72. *Box 527, Tsumeb, SW Africa.* (0671-27122)

HAILEY, Maurice James. b 10. Lon Coll of Div 63. **d** 64 **p** 65 St Alb. C of Ch Ch Ware 64-66; R of Palgrave 66-77; Perm to Offic Dio St Alb from 77. *29 New Road, Ware, Herts, SG12 7BS.*

HAILS, Brian. b 33. N-E Ordin Course. **d** 81 Dur (NSM). C of Harton Dio Dur from 81. *5 Hepscott Terrace, South Shields, Tyne & Wear, NE33 4TH.*

HAINES, Maurice Humphrey Colton. b 06. St Cath Coll Cam BA 32, MA 36. **d** 35 **p** 36 Newc T. C of Chevington 35-37; Ch Ch (in c of St Faith and St Osw) Tynemouth 37-40; C-in-c of H Cross Newc T 40-42; V of St Paul Choppington 42-51; Thorney Abbey w Wrydecroft Knarr Fen and Willow Hall 51-63; R of Glatton 63-72. *Holmrook, Kirkhead Road, Grange-over-Sands, Cumb, LA11 7DD.* (Grange-o-S 2729)

HAINES, Reginald. b 15. Wycl Hall Ox 60. **d** 61 **p** 62 Win. C of Highcliffe w Hinton Admiral 61-64; R of Newnham Nately Scures and Mapledurwell w Up Nately 64-80. *7 Crow Lane, Ringwood, Hants, BH24 3DZ.* (Ringwood 6349)

HAINES, Richard Sharsted. b 18. Bp's Coll Cheshunt. **d** 44 Bp Heywood for St Alb **p** 45 St Alb. C of H Trin Bp's Stortford 44-47; Chap Wellington Ho Prep Sch 47-48; L to Offic at St Luke Guildf and Asst Chap of St Luke's Hosp Guildf 48-50; C of Ilford (in c of St Alb) 50-54; Chieveley (in c of All SS Curridge) 54-59; R of Middleton Stoney 59-64; PC of Gosberton Clough 64-69; Hon C of H Trin Win 70-73; Perm to Offic Dio Chich 73; Hon C of All SS Ryde Dio Portsm from 75. *Flat 4c, 4 Spencer Road, Ryde, IW, PO33 2NZ.*

HAINES, Robert Melvin. b 31. Coll of Resurr Mirfield 71. **d** 73 **p** 74 Selby for York. C of Ch of Ascen Derringham Bank Hull 73-76; Howden Dio York 76-79; Team V from 79. *Vicarage, Thimble Hall, Newport, Nr Brough, N Humb.* (0430-40546)

HAINES, Robert Melvin. b 57. Univ of Leeds BA 79. St Steph Ho Ox 80. **d** 81 Lich. C of Rushall Dio Lich from 81. *61 Daw End Lane, Rushall, Walsall, W Midl.* (Walsall 35116)

HAINES, Ronald Frederick. Mem Univ Newfld BA 58, LTh 59. **d** 57 **p** 58 Newfld. C of Change Is 57-61; R of Burgeo 61-65; Brooklyn 65-66; C of St Thos St John's 66-68. *152 Signal Hill Road, St John's, Newfoundland, Canada.*

HAINES, Stephen Decatur. b 42. Univ of Freiburg MA 68.

Fitzw Coll Cam BA 70, MA 74. **d** 71 **p** 72 Kens for Lon. C of St Dionis Parson's Green Fulham 71-75; St Mary Finchley Dio Lon from 75. *28 Hendon Lane, Finchley, N3 1TR.* (01-346 7573)

HAIR, James Eric. b 48. BA (Lon) 69. St Steph Ho Ox 69. **d** 72 **p** 73 Bris. C of St Jo Div Fishponds 72-75; Bushey 75-79; P-in-c of St Sav-on-the-Cliff Shanklin Dio Portsm from 79; Lake Dio Portsm from 79. *Good Shepherd Vicarage, Lake, IW.* (Sandown 405666)

HAIRE, Alan Jackson. b 50. Qu Coll Birm 74. **d** 77 **p** 78 Connor. C of St Aid Belf 77-79; Armagh 79-80; CF from 80. *SOQ 7, Queens Avenue, Falling Bostel 3032, W Germany.*

HAIRE, Reginald Alfred William. **d** 59 **p** 62 Adel. C of St Barn Croydon 59-60; St Luke Adel 60-61; Payneham 61-63; Hillcrest 63-64; P-in-c of Minnipa Miss 64-65; Port Elliot 65-72; L to Offic Dio Adel 72-77 and 80-81; Perm to Offic Dio Murray 72-77; P-in-c of St Luke Adel 77-78; R 78-80; Perm to Offic Dio Newc from 81. *Rectory, Paterson, NSW, Australia 2421.*

HAKE, Andrew Augustus Gordon. b 25. Trin Coll Cam BA (1st cl Th Trip pt i) 49, 2nd cl Th Trip pt iii 50. Wells Th Coll 50. **d** 51 **p** 52 Bris. C of H Cross Filwood Park Bris 51-54; St Thos Bedminster 54-57; Industr Adv to Chr Coun of Kenya 57-69; Perm to Offic Dio Bris from 72. *70 Bath Road, Swindon, Wilts, SN1 4AY.* (Swindon 35772)

HAKES, Leslie John. Roch Th Coll 60. **d** 62 Bp T M Hughes for Llan **p** 63 Llan for Swan B. C of Cockett Swansea 62-67; V of St Phil Griffin Blackb 67-71; V of Dolphinholme (w Quernmore from 74) Dio Blackb from 71. *Vicarage, Dolphinholme, Lancaster, LA2 9AH.* (Forton 791300)

HALA'API'API, Ven Viliami Maelivaki. St Jo Bapt Th Coll Suva 62. **d** 65 **p** 67 Polyn. P Dio Polyn 65-70 and from 72; C of Mt Waverley 71-72; Archd in Polyn from 75. *PO Box 29, Labasa, Fiji.*

HALAHAN, Maxwell Crosby. b 30. BSc (2nd cl Eng) Lon 52. Westcott Ho Cam 54. **d** 56 **p** 57 Portsm. C of Forton 56-60; Our Lady and St Nich Liv 60-62; Dom Chap to Bp of Nass 62-64; Asst Master St Anne's Sch Nass 62-64; Gen Miss Nass 63-64; Perm to Offic at St Pet Wymering 64-66; C-in-c of St Faith's Conv Portchester Sch from 79. Distr Cowes 66-71; V of St Faith's Cowes 71-77; Hon C of St Sav Portsea Dio Portsm from 77; Asst Master Littlemead Sch Oving 78-79; Portchester Sch from 79. *11 Bertie Road, Milton, Portsmouth, PO4 8JX.*

✠ **HALAPUA, Right Rev Fine Tenga'ila.** **d** 53 **p** 56 Polyn. P Dio Polyn 56-67; Hon Can of Suva Cathl 62-67; L to Offic Dio Melb 64-66; Cons Asst Bp in Polyn (Bp Suffr of Nuku-'alofa) in St Paul's Ch Nuku'alofa 27 Aug 67 by Abp of NZ; Bps of Polyn; Auckld; Asst Bps of Melan; Los Angeles; res 77; Can of H Trin Cathl Suva from 73. *Bishop's House, PO Box 157, Nuku'alofa, Tonga.*

HALAPUA, Winston. b 45. Pacific Th Coll Suva BD 71. **d** 71 Bp Halapua for Polyn **p** 72 Polyn. C of Viti Levu W 71-74; on leave 74-76; P-in-c of St Luke Par Distr Suva Dio Polyn from 77. *Box 199, Suva, Fiji.*

HALDANE-STEVENSON, James Patrick. TD and clasp 50. St Cath S Ox 3rd cl Hist BA 33, MA 41. Bps' Coll cheshunt 35. **d** 35 **p** 37 S'wark. C of St Mary L Lambeth 35-38; St Jas Pokesdown Bournemouth 38-39; R of Hillington 39-46; Commiss Moos 39-43; CF (TA) 37-45; CF 45-55; R of Cockburn Sound 55-56; Wongan Hills 56-59; V of St Silas N Balwyn 59-80; Perm to Offic Dio Melb from 80. *19 Morris Street, North Balwyn, Vic, Australia 3104.*

HALDENBY, Allan Edward. Univ of Tor BA 46. Wycl Coll Tor LTh 49. **d** 48 **p** 49 Alg. I of Emsdale w Sprucedale 49-51; Little Current 51-54; Dawson 54-63; Archd of the Klondike 60-63; C of St Wilfrid Tor 63-65; R of Innisfil 65-69; St Agnes Tor 69-77; Newcastle Dio Tor from 77. *Box 248, Newcastle, Ont, Canada.* (416-987 4745)

HALE, Dennis Ernest. b 26. Univ of Southn MA (Educn) 66. Sarum Wells Th Coll 74. **d** 77 Win **p** 78 Basingstoke for Win (NSM). Hon C of N Stoneham w Bassett Dio Win from 77. *12 Field Close, Bassett Green Road, Southampton, SO2 3DY.*

HALE, Francis Norman. St Jo Coll Ox BA 26, MA 30. Wells Th Coll 27. **d** 28 Lon **p** 29 Chelmsf. C of St Mary Virg Primrose Hill 28; Dovercourt 28-31; E Ham 31-33; Woodford Essex 34-36; Pontesbury (1st and 2nd portion) 36-38; V of Middleton-in-Chirbury 38-52; R of Stretton Sugwas 52-69. *Somerville Hotel, Bodenham Road, Hereford.*

HALE, Herbert. b 10. Univ of Liv BA 36. Lich Th Coll 36. **d** 38 **p** 39 Liv. C of Farnworth 38-43; St Chad Over w Winsford 43-47; V of Moulton 47-64; Norley 64-75. *59 Hillside Road, Frodsham, Chesh.*

HALE, John. b 37. St D Coll Lamp Dipl Th 66. **d** 66 **p** 67 St D. C of Tenby w Gumfreston 66-71. R of Burton Dio St D from 71; V of Rosemarket Dio St D from 78. *Burton Rectory, Milford Haven, Dyfed.* (Neyland 600275)

HALE, John Frederick. b 29. Fitzw Ho Cam BA 54, MA 58. Tyndale Hall Bris. **d** 55 **p** 56 Nor. C of H Trin Heigham 55-58; St Jas Paddington 58-61; V of St Ethelburga St Leonards-on-Sea 61-79; C of St Luke Prestonville Brighton Dio Chich from 79. *42 Stafford Road, Brighton, BN1 5PF.* (Brighton 557208)

HALE, Peter Raymond Latham. b 30. St Pet Hall Ox BA 54, MA 58. Linc Th Coll 54. **d** 56 **p** 57 Linc. C of Old Brumby 56-59; Prec and Chap of Gibr Cathl 59-62; V of St Aid New Cleethorpes 62-67; Chap Sebright Sch Wolverley 67-70; V of St Jas Gt Dudley 70-76; Crowthorne Dio Ox from 76; RD of Sonning from 81. *56 Duke's Ride, Crowthorne, Berks, RG11 6ND.* (Crowthorne 2413)

HALE, Richard Laurence. b 13. Jes Coll Cam 1st cl Hist Trip pt i 34. BA (1st cl Hist Trip pt ii) 35, MA 39. Westcott Ho Cam 42. **d** 43 **p** 44 Sheff. C of Attercliffe 43-47; St Paul Arbourthorne Sheff 47-48; Chap of Ely Th Coll 48-50; R of Long Stanton 50-56; V of St Cecilia Parson Cross Sheff 56-59; Sheff Dioc Educn Sec 59-61; Can of Sheff 59-61; V of Gt Shelford 61-78; Perm to Offic Dio Nor from 78. *5 Hare Road, Great Plumstead, Norwich.* (Norwich 721062)

HALE, Roger Anthony. b 41. Oak Hill Th Coll 72. **d** 72 **p** 73 Blackb. C of Ch of the Sav Blackb 72-75; St Pet Burnley 75-77; V of Fence-in-Pendle Dio Blackb from 77; Industr Chap Lancs Industr Miss from 78. *12 Wheatcroft Avenue, Fence, Burnley, BB12 9QL.* (Nelson 67316)

HALES, Edward Taylor. b 49. York Univ Ont BA 72. Trin Coll Tor MDiv 75. **d** 75 Bp Read for Tor **p** 76 Tor. C of St John Pet 75-79; R of The Atonement Alderwood City and Dio Tor from 79. *256 Sheldon Avenue, Islington, Ont, M8W 4L9, Canada.*

HALES, George Frederick. b 01. MC 43. Jes Coll Cam BA 23, MA 33. Westcott Ho Cam. **d** 25 **p** 26 Win. C of Petersfield 25-28; Asst Chap St Mary Cairo 28-30; R of Willey w Barrow 30-33; Chap Shirlet Sanat 30-33; Chap of Port Said 33-37; V of Netheravon 37-50; R of Fittleton 37-50; St Mary Southn 50-54; C-in-c of H Trin Southn 50-54; CF (EC) 39-45; CF (TA) 46-56; RD of Enford 48-49; R of Green's Norton w Bradden 54-66. *The Laurels, Bradden, Towcester, Northants.* (Blakesley 541)

HALES, Leonard John. Univ of Sask BA 51. Em Coll Sktn LTh 26, BD 58. **d** 26 **p** 27 Sask. C-in-c of Runciman 26-27; I 27-28; Miss at Vanderhoot 28-29; I of Smithers and Telkwa 29-37; Sec of Caled Synod 32-37; RD of Hazelton 36-37; Miss Wells (Barkerville Miss) 38-39; I of Kinistino 40-52; RD of Melfort 48-52; R of Minnedosa 52-55; Bethany 55-59; Flin Flon 59-60; Deloraine 60-64; R of Melita 61-64. *419 10th Street, Brandon, Manit., Canada.*

HALES, Robert Russell. Montr Dioc Th Coll LTh 67. **d** 67 **p** 68 Sask. I of Star City 67-69; Macklin 74-75; Adolphustown 76-79; St Thos Kingston Dio Ont from 79. *4 Knightsbridge Road, Kingston, Ont, Canada.* (613-389 5643)

HALEY, Albert Naunton. Melb Coll of Div LTh 45. **d** 46 **p** 47 Melb. C of St John Heidelberg 46-48; N Essendon 48; Min of St Mary Warburton 48-50; Dir of Torres Straits Miss 50-52; R of Darwin 52-55; C of Cooma 55-57; R of Crookwell 57-59; P-in-c of Rabaul 59-68; Org Sec ABM Queensld 68-73; L to Offic Dio N Terr 71-73; R of Warwick 73-75; All SS City and Dio Brisb from 75. *39 Isaac Street. Spring Hill, Brisbane, Australia 4000.* (31 1135)

HALFORD, Harry William. b 20. Qu Coll Birm 47. **d** 50 **p** 51 Sheff. C of Rotherham 50-52; Maltby 52-55; V of New Rossington 55-60; Kimberworth Dio Sheff from 60. *Vicarage, Church Street, Kimberworth, Rotherham, S Yorks.* (Rotherham 554441)

HALFORD, Philip John. b 27. Bps' Coll Cheshunt 54. **d** 56 **p** 57 Lon. C of St Alphege Edmonton 56-59; St Matt Willesden 59-60; Overton w Laverstoke and Freefolk 60-61; Sudbury Middx 65-66; All SS Falmouth 66-68; St Andr Liswerry Newport 68-69; V of Garndiffaith w Varteg 69-73; C of W Drayton 73-74; St Jo Bapt Spalding 74-76; Leckhampton 76-79; Perm to Offic Dio Glouc 79-81; C of St Steph Cheltm Dio Glouc from 81. *222 Gloucester Road, Cheltenham, GL51 8NR.* (Cheltm 516326)

HALFPENNY, Brian Norman. b 36. St Jo Coll Ox BA 60, MA 64. Wells Th Coll 60. **d** 62 **p** 63 Sarum. C of Melksham 62-65; Chap RAF from 65. *c/o Ministry of Defence, Adastral House, WC 1.*

HALIFAX, Dean of. *See* Munroe, Very Rev John Austin.

HALKETT, Charles. b 19. **d** 70 **p** 71 Sask. C of Montreal Lake 70-71; I of Cumberland House 71-74; Dom Chap to Bp of Sask from 71; Miss at Lac La Ronge Dio Sask from 74. *Box 96, La Ronge, Sask, Canada.*

HALL, Adrian Charles. b 45. St Mich AA Llan 76. **d** 78 Bp Reece for Llan. C of Pontlottyn w Fochriw 78-80. *c/o 15 Reform Street, Pontlottyn, Bargoed, Mid Glam. CF8 9RB.*

HALL, Canon Albert Peter. b 30. St Jo Coll Cam BA 53, MA 56. Ridley Hall Cam 53. **d** 55 **p** 56 Birm. C of St Martin Birm 55-60; Asst P of Avondale Dio Mashon 61-63; R 63-70;

Can of St Mary and All SS Cathl Salisbury Rhodesia 68-70; Hon Can from 70; R of St Martin City and Dio Birm from 70; Hon Can of Birm from 75; M Gen Syn from 80. *37 Barlows Road, Birmingham, B15 2PN.* (021-454 0119)

HALL, Canon Alfred Christopher. b 35. Trin Coll Ox 3rd cl Cl Mods 56, BA (2nd cl Lit Hum) 58, MA 61. Westcott Ho Cam 58. **d** 61 **p** 62 Derby. C of Frecheville 61-64; Dronfield w Unstone 64-67; V of St Matt (w St Chad from 70) Smethwick 67-75; M Gen Syn Birm 72-75; Dio Man from 75; Can Res of Man from 75; Adult Educn Officer from 75. *2 Deanery Gardens, Bury New Road, Salford, M7 0WT.* (061-792 4030)

HALL, Andrew Stanford. Qu Coll St John's Newfld 54. **d** 59 **p** 60 Newfld. L to Offic Dio Newfld 59-60; C of Channel 60-61; R of Rose Blanche 61-66; C of St Mich AA, St John's 66-69; I of Brooklyn 69-76; Spaniard's Bay Dio E Newfld from 76. *Rectory, Spaniard's Bay, Newfoundland, Canada.*

HALL, Arthur John. b 23. Univ of Bris BSc 48. **d** 76 Taunton for B & W **p** 77 B & W. C of Portishead Dio B & W from 76. *34 Beechwood Road, Portishead, Bristol, BS20 8EP.*

HALL, Barry George. b 38. Oak Hill Coll 78. **d** 81 Bradwell for Chelmsf (NSM). Hon C of Stock Harvard Dio Chelmsf from 81. *7 Juniper Close, Norsey Road, Billericay, Essex.* (Billericay 25874)

HALL, Basil. b 15. Univ of Dur BA 36, MA 40. Fitzw Coll Cam BA 39, MA 42, PhD 70. FRHistS 66. Univ of Man MA (Th) 72. Univ of St Andr DD 75. **d** 70 **p** 71 Ches. Lect Univ of Wales 49-56; Univ of Cam 56-68; Select Pr Univ of Cam 56 and 62; Fell Fitzw Coll Cam 63-68; Prof Eccles Hist Univ of Man 68-75; Hon C of Bramhall 70-75; Select Pr Univ of Ox 75 and 78; Dean and Fell of St John's Coll Cam 75-80; Birkbeck Lect in Eccles Hist Univ of Cam 75. *2 Newton House, Newton Street, Cyres, Devon, EX5 5BL.*

HALL, Benjamin Stanley. **d** 58 **p** 60 Hur. R of Paisley 58-60; I of Walter's Falls 60-63; Miss at Hay River Dio Arctic 63-66; Dio Athab 66-70; on leave 71-74; I of Gleichen 74-76; Teslin 76-79. *St Philip's Church, Teslin, Yukon Territory, Canada.*

HALL, Brian Arthur. b 48. Univ of Ex BEd 70. Cudd Coll 73. **d** 75 **p** 76 Birm. C of Hob's Moat 75-79; V of Smethwick Dio Birm from 79. *Old Church Vicarage, Church Road, Smethwick, Warley, W Midlands.* (021-558 1763)

HALL, Brian Patrick. Univ of BC BA 62. Hur Coll BTh 65. **d** 65 Niag **p** 65 Costa Rica for Niag. MSCC Miss 65-69; in Amer Ch. *1706 Russell Place, Pomona, California 91767, USA.*

HALL, Bruce Jonathan. Univ of Melb BSc 69. Moore Coll Syd ACT ThL 74. BD (Lon) 75. **d** and **p** 76 Syd. C of St Paul Wahroonga 76-78; on leave. *c/o 4 Ingram Road, Wahroonga, NSW, Australia 2076.*

HALL, Bryan Francis. **d** 54 Perth **p** 57 Melb. C of Northam 54-55; Victoria Pk 55-56; Kew 56-58; I of Cranbourne 58-60; CF (Austr) 60-64; R of St Alb Highgate Perth 64-77; Balcatta w Hamersley Dio Perth from 77; Commiss Centr Tang from 69. *30 Eversley Street, Balcatta, W Australia 6021. 349 1070)*

HALL, Charles Bryan. Univ of Liv BA 59. St Mich Coll Llan 59. **d** 62 **p** 63 St A. C of Prestatyn 62-64; St Mary Virg Cardiff 64-67; Hawarden 67-72; V 72-73; St Mary Virg (and St Steph from 76) Cardiff 73-81; Penycae Dio St A from 81; C-in-c of St Steph Cardiff 73-76. *Vicarage, Penycae, Wrexham, Clwyd, LL14 2RL.* (Rhos 840878)

HALL, Charles John. b 13. **d** 62 **p** 63 Leic. C of St Steph N Evington 62-66; R of Newbold de Verdun Dio Leic from 66. *Newbold de Verdun Rectory, Leicester.* (Desford 2528)

HALL, Charles John. b 40. ALCD 68 (LTh from 74). **d** 68 **p** 69 Ches. C of Upton (Overchurch) 68-72; Morden (in c of St Geo) 72-76; V of Hyson Green Dio Southw from 76. *St Paul's Vicarage, 18 Russell Road, Forest Fields, Nottingham, NG7 6HB.*

HALL, Cyril Raymond. b 1898. **d** 62 Southw **p** 63 Bp Gelsthorpe for Southw. Publ Pr Dio Southw from 62. *89 Cow Lane, Bramcote, Nottingham.*

HALL, David Anthony. b 43. Univ of Reading BA 66. Qu Coll Birm 79. **d** 81 St Alb. C of Norton Dio St Alb from 81. *8 Eastholm Green, Letchworth, Herts, SG6 4TW.*

HALL, David Everson. St Jo Coll Auckld LTh 67. **d** 67 **p** 68 Waik. C of Cambridge 67-69; St Pet Cathl Hamilton 69-71; V of Brooklands 71-75; Min 75-77; V of Dannevirke Dio Wai from 77. *Vicarage, High Street, Dannevirke, NZ.* (7407)

HALL, Denis. b 43. Lon Coll of Div 65. **d** 69 Warrington for Liv **p** 70 Liv. C of St Osw Netherton 69-71; Roby 72-75; V of St Steph Wigan Dio Liv from 75. *St Stephen's Vicarage, Wigan, Lancs, WN2 1BL.* (Wigan 42579)

HALL, Derek Guy. b 26. Tyndale Hall Bris 50. **d** 51 **p** 52 Blackb. C of All SS Preston Lancs 51-54; St Pet Halliwell 54-56; C-in-c of Trin Chap Buxton 56-58; V of St Jude Blackb 58-67; Fazakerley 67-74; R 74-81; V of Langdale Dio Carl from 81. *Langdale Vicarage, Ambleside, Cumb, LA22 9JG.* (Langdale 267)

HALL, Desmond. b 27. St Cuthb Soc Dur BSc 54, PhD 58. N-E Ordin Course 78. **d** 81 Dur. C of St Mich AA Bp Wearmouth Dio Dur from 81. *95 Nursery Road, Sunderland, Tyne & Wear, SR3 1NU.*

HALL, Douglas Warren. b 1883. St Chad's Coll Dur BLitt 05, Van Mildert Scho and BA 08, MA 23. **d** 09 **p** 10 Man. C of H Trin Shaw 09-11; St Mary Rochdale 11-12; St Gabr Hulme 13-16; St Jas Oldham 16-21; TCF 18-20; V of St Pet Westleigh Lancs 21-31; H Angels Claremont Pendleton 31-58. *Palatine House, Church Street, Durham.*

HALL, Douglas Wilfred. **d** 63 Bp Snell for Tor. **p** 64 Tor. C of St Andr Scarborough Tor 63-65; Cobourg 65-67; R of St Dunstan Tor 67-78. *26 Underhill Drive, Don Mills, Ont, Canada.*

HALL, Ven Edgar Francis. b 1888. Late Scho of Jes Coll Ox 2nd cl Math Mods 09, BA (3rd cl Math) 11, MA 19. **d** 14 **p** 15 Ex. C of St Jas Ex (w St Anne from 19) 14-21; Asst Master Ex Sch 11-15; Chap 17-21; Dioc Insp Dio Ex 15-34; V of Leusden 21-34; Dir of Relig Educn Dio Ex 34-62; Can Res of Ex Cathl 34-47; Treas 51-62; Gen Sec Nat S 43-47; Hon Sec C of E Coun for Educn 47-49; Chairman 49-58; Proc Conv Ex 44-50; Archd of Totnes 47-62; Archd (Emer) from 62. *Leusden Vicarage, Newton Abbot, Devon.* (Poundsgate 329)

HALL, Ven Enoch Margrave. St Chad's Coll Regina 37. **d** 37 **p** 38 Qu'App. C-in-c of Hemaruka 37-39; I 39-40; Alsask 40-43; Milden 43-44; Kindersley 44-56; Swift Current 56-68; Maple Creek 68-79; Can of Qu'App 56-73; Hon Can 73; Archd of Swift Current 68-79; Archd (Emer) from 79. *Box 880, Maple Creek, Sask., Canada.* (667-2311)

HALL, Eric Richard. b 06. Linc Th Coll 52. **d** 53 **p** 54 Ex. C of Okehampton 53-55; V of St Day 55-75; C-in-c of Launcells 75-76. *10 Weston Lane, Funtington, Chichester, Sussex, PO18 9LG.* (West Ashling 779)

HALL, Ernest. b 10. AKC 36. **d** 36 **p** 37 Lon. C of Kingsbury 36-40; St Mich Highgate 40-44; V of St Mich AA Enfield 44-49; Kingsbury 49-59; R of Clifton Beds 59-69; RD of Shefford 66-69; V of Osmotherley 69-75. *1 Crowood Avenue, Stokesley, Cleveland, TS9 5HY.*

HALL, Everard. b 1892. Sarum Th Coll 14. **d** 16 **p** 17 Bris. C of Corsham 16-19; Burghfield 19-20; Pewsey 20-28; R of Huish w Oare 28-44; V of Frampton 44-52; V of Sydling St Nich 46-52. *15 Highdown Road, Lewes, Sussex.* (Lewes 3779)

HALL, Everest Evans Daniel. Codr Coll Barb 62. **d** 65 **p** 66 Trinid. C of San Fernando 65-67; R of Couva Dio Trinid from 67. *St Andrew's Rectory, Couva, Trinidad, W Indies.*

HALL, Francis George. **d** 24 **p** 26 Fred. Miss at Grand Falls 25-26; V of St Jude Barb 27-28; St Patr Barb 28-43; H Innoc Barb 43-64; L to Offic Dio Barb from 64. *Clermont Park, Barbados, W Indies.*

HALL, Francis Henry. b 14. Univ of Leeds BA 36. Coll of Resurr Mirfield 36. **d** 38 **p** 39 St D. C of St Paul Llanelli 38-48; St Mary Virg Reading 48-52; V of Williton 52-62; St Barn Twerton Hill Bath 62-70; V of Castle Cary w Ansford 70-79; RD of Cary 71-79. *8 Erw Non, Llannon, Llanelli, Dyfed, SA14 6BH.* (Cross Hands 843578)

HALL, Francis James Thomas. b 07. AKC 35. **d** 33 **p** 34 Chelmsf. C of All SS w St Pet Maldon 33-34; St Steph S Kens 35-36; St Mich and St Geo Fulwell 36-38; LDHM of Ch of Ascen Hanger Hill 38-48; V of St Phil Earl's Court Kens 48-59; Hampstead 59-74; C-in-c of Deopham 74-75; C of Twickenham Dio Lon from 76. *Ground Floor Flat, 15 Cambridge Park, Twickenham, Middx.* (01-891 2797)

HALL, Frederick George. Univ of Tor BA 53. Wycl Coll Tor BTh and LTh 56. **d** 55 Newfld for Tor **p** 56 Tor. C-in-c of L'Amoureux 55-56; C of St Geo Winnipeg 56-58; I of St Hugh Malton Tor 58-60; R of St Richard Tor 60-68; Aurora 68-80; Ch Ch Brampton Dio Tor from 80. *4 Elizabeth Street North, Brampton, Ont, Canada.*

HALL, Geoffrey Hedley. b 33. Univ of Bris BA (2nd cl Gen) 55. St Steph Ho Ox 63. **d** 65 **p** 66 B & W. C of H Trin Taunton 65-67; CF from 67; SCF from 80; C-in-c of Ambrosden 72-75. *c/o Ministry of Defence, Bagshot Park, Bagshot, Surrey.*

HALL, George. b 06. Dioc Th Coll Montr LTh 33. **d** 31 **p** 33 Montr. I of River Desert 31-33; Aylwin 33-38; C of Thorpe Episcopi 38-41; V of St Geo, Tombland w St Simon and St Jude, Nor 41-71. *43 St Clement's Hill, Norwich, NOR 15O.*

HALL, George Bertram. b 14. Late Scho of St Jo Coll Ox, Hall Houghton Syriac Pri 36, BA 37, MA 44. Wycl Hall Ox 37. **d** 38 **p** 39 Sarum. C of Kinson 38-42; V of St Jude Mildmay Park Lon 42-49; R of Sherfield English 49-56; V of St Luke Ramsgate 56-68; Perm to Offic Dio Bradf 68-71; V of St Paul Clacton-on-Sea 71-79; Perm to Offic Dio Sarum from 80. *Halstock, Clappentail Lane, Lyme Regis, Dorset.* (02974-3773)

HALL, George Richard Wyndham. b 49. Univ of Ex LLB 71. Wycl Hall Ox BA (Th) 74, MA 78. **d** 75 Buckingham for Ox **p** 76 Ox. C of H Trin Walton Aylesbury 75-79; Farnborough Dio Guildf from 79. *45 Sand Hill, Farnborough, Hants.* (Farnborough 43789)

HALL, George Rumney. b 37. Westcott Ho Cam 60. **d** 62 **p** 63 S'wark. C of St Phil Camberwell 62-65; Waltham Cross 65-67; R of Buckenham w Hassingham and Strumpshaw 67-74; V of Wymondham Dio Nor from 74. *Vicarage, Wymondham, Norf.* (Wymondham 602269)

HALL, George Stanley. Trin Coll Melb ACT ThL 30. **d** 30 **p** 31 Melb. C of Miss Distr of St Jas and St John Melb 30-32; C-in-c 34-39; C of St Aug Moreland 32-34; Prin St Paul's Tr Home for Boys Newhaven 39-50; V of Mornington 50-58; Kooyong 58-66; Min of Wattle Pk 66-71; Perm to Offic Dio Melb from 71. *Wembley Road, Kallista, Vic, Australia 3791.* (750-1068)

HALL, Godfrey Charles. b 43. Linc Coll Ox BA (4th cl Th) 66, MA 72. Cudd Coll 66. **d** 68 S'wark **p** 69 Stepney for S'wark. C of St Helier 68-72; Asst Chap Ch Hosp Horsham from 72; Ho Master from 77. *The Housemaster's House, Leigh Hunt 'A', Christ's Hospital, Horsham, Sussex.* (Horsham 63311)

HALL, Halsey Charles. b 31. Univ of Lon BSc 53, MSc 57. Sarum Wells Th Coll 76. **d** 78 **p** 79 Win. C of St Chris Thornhill Southn 78-81; Team V of Southn (City Centre) Dio Win from 81. *46 Byron Road, Thornhill, Southampton, SO2 6FQ.*

HALL, Harold Henry Stanley Lawson. Qu Coll Birm 56. **d** 58 **p** 59 Dur. C of Ch Ch Bp Wearmouth 58-61; Winlaton (in c of St Patr High Spen) 61-65; V of Cockerton 65-69; V of Newton Aycliffe 69-76; Surr from 76; C-in-c of Whitburn Dio Dur from 76. *51 Front Street, Whitburn, Sunderland, T & W, SR6 7JD.* (Whitburn 2232)

HALL, Herbert Alexander. b 05. **d** 61 **p** 62 York. C of Elloughton 61-64; V of Burton Pidsea w Humbleton and Elsternwick 64-70; R of Sigglesthorne (w Nunkeeling and Bewholme from 72 and Rise from 74) 70-76; Hon C of St Mary Beverley Dio York from 81. *19 Manor Close, Beverley, Yorks, HU17 7BP.* (0482-867889)

HALL, Horace Alphonso. ACT ThL 38. **d** 36 **p** 39 St Arn. C of Talbot 36-37; Tempy 37-39; V of Manangatang 39-41; Nyah w Woorinen 41-45; R of Red Cliffs 45-51; V of Dunolly 51-56; Can of St Arn 53-56; Min of Flinders 56-61; Highett 61-72; V of Golden Square 72-75; Perm to Offic Dio Bend from 75. *47 Raglan Street, White Hills, Bendigo, Vic, Australia.*

HALL, Hubert William Peter. b 35. Ely Th Coll 58. **d** 60 **p** 61 Linc. C of Louth 60-62; Gt Grimsby (in c of St Hugh) 62-71; V of Immingham Dio Linc from 71. *344 Pelham Road, Immingham, Grimsby, S Humb, DN40 1PU.* (Immingham 72560)

HALL, James. TCD 55. **d** 56 **p** 57 Connor. C of St Mich Belf 56-59; I of Cleenish 59-62; R of Openshaw 63-68; C of Chatswood 68; C-in-c of Figtree Provisional Distr 68-71; R 72-81; L to Offic Dio Syd from 81. *15 Taronga Avenue, Mangerton, NSW, Australia 2500.*

HALL, James Robert. b 24. TCD BA 48, MA 54. **d** 49 **p** 50 Down. C of Seagoe 49-51; Ch Ch Lisburn 51-59; I of St Mich Belf 59-66; Finaghy Dio Connor from 66. *104 Upper Lisburn Road, Belfast 10, N Ireland.* (Belfast 611050)

HALL, Jeffrey Ernest. b 42. Linc Th Coll 73. **d** 75 Repton for Derby **p** 76 Derby. C of St Thos Brampton 75-78; New Whittington 78-81; Team V of Riverside and Industr Chap Burnham Dio Ox from 81. *Vicarage, Colnbrook, Slough, SL3 0JY.* (Colnbrook 2156)

HALL, Jesse Alexander. b 05. **d** 51 **p** 52 Newc T. C of Walker 51-54; Benwell (in c of Ven Bede) 54-57; V of Howdon Panns 57-63; St Pet Cowgate, Newc T 63-68; Lesbury 68-75. *East House, Howick, Alnwick, Northumb, NE66 3LE.* (Longhoughton 301)

HALL, John Bellamy. b 10. Ridley Hall Cam 55. **d** and **p** 57 Roch. C of Tonbridge 57-59; V of Ickleton 59-66; R of Daglingworth w Duntisbourne Rous and Duntisbourne Abbots (and Winstone from 72) 66-74; C-in-c of Kempley w Oxenhall 74-77. *22 Collington Lane East, Bexhill-on-Sea, Sussex.*

HALL, John Bruce. b 33. ALCD 60 (LTh from 74). **d** 60 **p** 61 York. C of Hull 60-67; Beverley Minster 67-68; V of St Steph Clapham Pk 68-76; M Gen Syn S'wark from 75; R of Tooting Graveney Dio S'wark from 76. *Rectory, Rectory Lane, SW17 9QJ.* (01-672 7691)

HALL, John Charles. b 46. Univ of Hull BA (Th) 71. Ridley Hall Cam 71. **d** 73 **p** 74 Roch. C of Bromley Common 73-76; Perm to Offic Dio Lon 76-77; C of St Alb Westbury Pk 77-80; Chap at Ruwi, Oman Dio Cyprus from 80. *Box 4982, Ruwi, Sultanate of Oman.*

HALL, John Derek. St Cuthb S Dur BA 50. Linc Th Coll 50. **d** 52 **p** 53 York. C of Redcar 52-54; St John Newland Hull 54-57; V of Boosbeck w Moorsholm 57-61; St Osw Middlesbrough 61-68; St Chad City and Dio York from 68. *Vicarage, Campleshon Road, York, YO2 1EY.* (York 54707)

HALL, John Henness Vine. b 12. AKC 34. Univ of Lon BD 35. **d** 35 **p** 36 Lon. C of H Cross w St Jude St Pancras 35-38; St John Workington 38-40; Kirkby Lonsdale w Mansergh 40-43; V of St Pet Kells Whitehaven 43-51; Hutton Roof w Lupton 51-62; R of Threlkeld 62-77. *3 The Green, Melmerby, Penrith, Cumb, CA10 1HE.* (Langwathby 509)

HALL, John Kenneth. b 32. Qu Coll Birm 61. **d** 63 Taunton for B & W **p** 64 B & W. C of Ilminster w Whitelackington 63-66; St Francis Mackworth 66-69; R of Allerton 69-76; V of Blackford 69-76; W New Plymouth Dio Waik from 77. *188c Tukapa Street, New Plymouth, NZ.* (34-306)

HALL, John Michael. b 47. Oak Hill Coll 68. **d** 73 **p** 74 Barking for Chelmsf. C of Walthamstow 73-76; Rainham 76-79; P-in-c of Woodham Mortimer w Hazeleigh Dio Chelmsf from 79; Woodham Walter Dio Chelmsf from 79. *Woodham Mortimer Rectory, Maldon, Essex.* (Maldon 53778)

HALL, John Robert. b 49. St Chad's Coll Dur BA 71. Cudd Coll 73. **d** 75 **p** 76 S'wark. C of St Jo Div Kennington 75-78; V of All SS Wimbledon Dio S'wark from 78. *Vicarage, De Burgh Road, SW19 1DX.* (01-542 5514)

HALL, John Selwyn. b 43. Lich Th Coll 64. **d** 67 **p** 68 Sheff. C of Ch Ch Doncaster 67-70; C of Barnsley 70-73; V of Staincross 73-77; Athersley Dio Wakef from 77. *27 Laithes Lane, Athersley, Barnsley, S71 3AF.* (Barnsley 45361)

HALL, John Wintour. b 17. Univ of Leeds BA (3rd cl Gen Hons) 39. Coll of Resurr Mirfield 39. **d** and **p** 41 Glouc. C of Cirencester w H Trin Watermoor 41-43; CF (EC) 43-47; C of Henley-on-Thames 47-49; V of H Trin Forest of Dean 49-53; Chap to Prince Rupert Sch Wilhelmshaven 53-56; Merchant Taylors' Sch Rickmansworth 56-82. *19 Scutts Close, Lytchett Matravers, Nr Poole, Dorset.*

HALL, Joseph Hayes. TD 71. St Jo Coll Dur BSc 53, Dipl Th 55. Univ of Liv MA 73. Wycl Hall Ox 53. **d** 55 **p** 56 Ches. C of Wallasey 55-59; Macclesfield 59-60; CF (TA) from 59; V of Barnton 60-67; All SS New Brighton 67-81; Woodford Dio Ches from 81. *Vicarage, Wilmslow Road, Woodford, Stockport, Chesh.* (061-439 2286)

HALL, Kenneth David. BSc (2nd cl Phys) Lon 49, PhD 52. ACT ThL (2nd cl) 67. St Barn Th Coll Adel 66. **d** 68 **p** 69 Adel. C of Unley 68-70; P-in-c of Morphettville 70-77; R of Alberton Dio Adel from 77. *St George's Place, Alberton, S Australia 5014.* (08-47 1217)

HALL, Kenneth Stephen. b 25. Late Scho of SS Coll Cam BA 47, MA 51. PhD (Lon) 71. MIEE 66. Oak Hill Th Coll 49. **d** 51 **p** 52 S'wark. C of All SS Shooters Hill Plumstead 51-54; Asst Lect NW Kent Coll of Techn Dartford 54-58; Lect Willesden Tech Coll 58-60; Northampton Coll of Adv Techn Lon 60-66; City Univ from 66. *23 Bromley Grove, Shortlands, Bromley, Kent.* (01-460 2306)

HALL, Kevin Edward. St Mich Th Coll Crafers 56, ACT ThL 61. **d** 59 **p** 61 Perth. C of Canning 61-62; Northam 62-64; Chap Forrest River Miss 64-65; P-in-c of Spearwood w Hilton 65-68; R of Dalwallinu 68-72; Port Hedland 72-77; Guildford Dio Perth from 78. *219 James Street, Guildford, W Australia 6055.* (279 1141)

HALL, Keven Neil. d 79 **p** 80 Auckld. C of St Aid Remuera City and Dio Auckld from 79. *c/o 8 Ascot Avenue, Remuera, Auckland, NZ.*

HALL, Leonard Charles. b 1899. Oak Hill Th Coll 59. **d** 60 **p** 61 Lon. C of All SS Tufnell Pk 60-62; V of Mayfield 62-68. *Address temp unknown.*

HALL, Levi E. d 77 Ja (APM). C of Snowdon Dio Ja from 77. *Ellen Street, PO., Jamaica, W Indies.*

HALL, Ven Michael Anthony. St Paul's Coll Grahmstn LTh (SAfr) 64. **d** 64 **p** 65 Grahmstn. C of Vincent 64-67; St Mich AA Queenstown 67-69; R of All SS Port Eliz 70-78; Orange Grove E Lon 78-81; St Mich AA Queenstn and St Mary Tarkastad Dio Grahmstn from 81; Archd of Queenstn from 81. *Box 119, Queenstown 5320, CP, S Africa.*

HALL, Michael Arthur Paxton. *See* Paxton-Hall, Michael Arthur Paxton.

HALL, Michael Edward. b 32. Fitzw Ho Cam BA 57, MA 61. Ridley Hall Cam 68. **d** 69 Southw **p** 70 Sherwood for Southw. C of Aspley 69-73; P-in-c of St Jo Div Bulwell 73-75; V 75-81; P-in-c of Tyler's Green Dio Ox from 81. *Tyler's Green Vicarage, High Wycombe, Bucks.* (Penn 3367)

HALL, Murray. b 34. K Coll Lon and Warm 57. **d** 61 **p** 62 Nor. C of Eaton 61-64; Shalford 64-67; V of Oxshott 67-72; R of Filby w Thrigby and Mautby (w Stokesby, Herringby and Runham from 81) Dio Nor from 72; C-in-c of Runham 72-81; Stokesby w Herringby 72-81. *Filby Rectory, Great Yarmouth, Norf.* (Fleggburgh 237)

HALL, Nigel David. b 46. Univ of Wales (Cardiff) BA 67, BD 76. St Mich Coll Llan 73. **d** 76 **p** 77 Llan. C of St Jo Bapt Cardiff 76-81; R of Llandbadarn-Fawr w Llandegley &

Llanfihangel Rhydithon Dio Swan B from 81. *Rectory, Llanbadarn-Fawr, Crossgates, Llandrindod Wells, Powys, LD1 5TT.* (Penybont 204)

HALL, Philip Edward Robin. b 36. Oak Hill Th Coll 64. **d** 67 **p** 68 St Alb. C of Ch Ch, Ware 67-70; Rayleigh 70-73; R of Leven w Catwick Dio York from 73. *Rectory, Leven, Hull, N Humb, HU11 5PA.* (Leven 42456)

HALL, Canon Philip Humphrey. b 1900. Sarum Th Coll 26. **d** 29 **p** 30 Sarum. C of Blandford Forum 29-31; R of Wongan Hills 31-35; S Perth 35-38; V of Ramsbury w Axford 38-47; Commiss Dio Perth 41; CF (EC) 43-45; R of Clifton Beds 47-51; Bishopstone w Stratford Tony 51-65; RD of Chalke 55-64; Hon Chap to Bp of Sarum 59-62; Can and Preb of Sarum Cathl 60-80; Can (Emer) from 80; Chap Newbridge Hosp 65-70; V of The Close 68-80. *c/o 23 St Nicholas Hospital, Salisbury, Wilts.* (Salisbury 27203)

HALL, Reginald William. b 34. St Jo Coll Auckld LTh 77. **d** 77 **p** 78 Ch Ch. C of Fendalton Dio Ch Ch from 77. *139 Fendalton Road, Christchurch 4, NZ.* (517-392)

HALL, Richard Ian Voss. b 40. St Paul's Coll Grahmstn Dipl Th 72. **d** 72 **p** 73 Capetn. C of St John Evang Wynberg 72-76; R of Malmesbury Dio Capetn from 76. *Box 100, Malmesbury, CP, S Africa.* (0224-22545)

HALL, Richard Panton. b 45. Univ of Reading BSc 68. Univ of Bris Dipl Th 72. Trin Coll Bris 70. **d** 73 Chich **p** 74 Lewes for Chich. C of H Trin Eastbourne 73-76. *Flat 1, 10 Trinity Trees, Eastbourne, BN21 3LD.* (Eastbourne 37743)

HALL, Robert Arthur. b 35. BSc (Lon) 66. N-W Ordin Course 74. **d** 77 **p** 78 York. C of St Paul York 77-79; R of Elvington and Sutton-on-Derwent w E Cottingwith Dio York from 79. *Elvington Rectory, York.* (Elvington 462)

HALL, Robert Henry Cuthbert. b 11. Univ of Dur LTh 45. Edin Th Coll 34. **d** 37 **p** 38 Glas. C of St Marg Newlands Glas 37-38; Miss at Chanda 38-48; R of St Francis Kirkcudbright 48-51; SPG Miss Dio Nasik 51-62; R of Kirklington w Hethersgill 62-69; V of Urswick 69-74; RD of Ulverston 69-70; Furness 70-74; P-in-c of Bardsea 72-74; Watermillock 74-78. *Old Rectory, West Linton, Peeblesshire.* (West Linton 288)

HALL, Ronald Cecil. b 20. St Aid Coll 63. **d** 65 **p** 66 Lich. C of Tamworth 65-69; R of Talke 69-73; V of Birstwith Dio Ripon from 73; P-in-c of Thornthwaite w Darley and Thruscross 76-78. *Birstwith Vicarage, Harrogate, N Yorks, HG3 2QF.* (Harrogate 770348)

HALL, Stephen Clarence. Kelham Th Coll 46. **d** 51 **p** 52 Newc T. C of Killingworth 51-53; H Cross Fenham Newc T 53-56; R of Makoni 56-59; P-in-c of Bonda 59-62; R of Mabelreign 62-68; Chap Univ Coll of Rhod 68-77; Michaelho Sch and L to Offic Dio Natal from 77. *Michaelhouse, Balgowan, Natal, S Africa.*

HALL, Stuart George. b 28. New Coll Ox 2nd cl Cl Mods 50, BA (1st cl Lit Hum) 52, 2nd cl Th 54. BD 73. Ripon Hall Ox 53. **d** 54 **p** 55 Southw. C of Newark 54-58; Tutor Qu Coll Birm 58-62; Lect (Sen Lect 73-78; Reader 78) in Th Univ of Nottm 62-78; Exam Chap to Bp of Pet from 73; Prof of Eccles Hist Univ of Lon from 78. *16 Abbey Avenue, St Albans, Herts, AL3 4A7.* (St Albans 56358)

HALL, Thomas. b 10. Lich Th Coll 51. **d** 53 **p** 54 Carl. C of St Pet Kells Whitehaven 53-56; V of Broughton Moor 56-62; R of Newbiggin w Milburn 62-70; Seq of Dufton 62-70; R of Bewcastle 70-76; Seq of Stapleton 74-76. *c/o Dyke Nook, Wilton, Egremont, Cumb.*

HALL (formerly MATTHEWS), Thomas Bartholomew Hall. b 39. St Francis Coll Brisb 63. **d** 65 **p** 66 Rockptn. C of St Jas Cathl Townsville 65-66; St Paul's Cathl Rockptn 66-69; P-in-c of Emerald 69-70; R 70-75; P-in-c of Whitehawk Dio Chich from 75. *44 Fletching Road, Brighton, BN2 5LG.* (Brighton 692576)

HALL, Thomas Ward. Qu Coll Ox BA 11, MA 15. **d** 13 **p** 14 Birm. C of St John Sparkhill 13-18; TCF 18-19; C of Sherborne Dorset 20-22; Miss to Seamen Chap at Shanghai 22-31; furlough 26; Asst Supt Miss to Seamen and Publ Pr Dio St Alb 31-32; Miss to Seamen Chap at Buenos Aires 32-47; Chap of Hurlingham and Devoto 40-62; Hon Can of St John's Pro-Cathl Buenos Aires 38-62; Archd in Repubs of River Plate 49-62. *304 West Queen's Road, North Vancouver, BC, Canada.*

HALL, Walter Kenneth. b 19. Wycl Hall Ox 64. **d** 66 Colchester for Chelmsf **p** 67 Chelmsf. C of Barking 66-68; Marton-in-Cleveland 68-70; Filey 70-71; C-in-c of St Cuthb Middlesbrough 71-78; V of Glaisdale Dio York from 78. *Glaisdale Vicarage, Whitby, YO21 2PL.* (Whitby 87214)

HALL, Warren Ernest. Melb Coll of Div LTh and Dipl Relig Educn 55, ACT ThL 60. **d** and **p** 60 C & Goulb. C of Wagga Wagga 60-61; Albury 61-62; R of Bribbaree 62-64; Moruya 64-72; St Luke City and Dio Bend from 73. *492 Napier Street, White Hills, Bendigo, Vic, Australia.* (054-43 6396)

HALL, William Cameron. b 40. K Coll Lon and Warm 60. **d** 65 **p** 66 York. C of Thornaby-on-Tees 65-68; Chap to Arts and Recreation in NE Engl from 68; V of Grindon 71-80. *59 Western Hill, Durham, DH1 4RJ.* (Durham 63177)

HALL, William Nawton Sinclair. Kelham Th Coll 35. **d** 41 **p** 42 Dur. C of St Cuthb Gateshead 41-43; All SS Notting Hill 43-46; Clewer (in c of All SS Dedworth) 46-50; V of St Aid Gateshead 50-55; R of Witton Gilbert 55-61; Lowther w Askham Dio Carl from 61. *Askham Rectory, Penrith, Cumb.* (Hackthorpe 221)

HALL, William Norman. b 30. TCD BA (2nd cl Mod) 52, Div Test (1st cl) 54, MA 64, BD 65. ARIC 74. **d** 54 **p** 55 Down. C of Dundela 54-58; Holywood 58-63; R of Drumgooland w Kilcoo 63-66; Chap St Jas Choir Sch Grimsby 66-70; Asst Master Hautlieu Sch Jersey 70-73; V of St Mark Evang Jersey Dio Win from 73. *Vicarage, Springfield Road, St Helier, Jersey C.I.* (0534-20595)

HALL-CARPENTER (formerly CARPENTER), Canon Leslie Thomas Frank. b 19. Lich Th Coll 55. **d** 57 **p** 58 Ripon. C of Methley 57-59; V of Kirkby Ravensworth w Dalton 59-61; Chap at Dibrugarh 61-63; Hon Can of Shillong Cathl from 63; Commiss Assam from 63; V of Ellingham 63-67; Horsford and of Horsham St Faith 67-69; R of Ch Ch Lochgilphead 69-70; Area Sec USPG York 70-73; V of Kirk Hammerton w Nun Monkton and Hunsingore 74-77; P-in-c of Hackness w Harwood Dale 77-79; V of Muker w Melbecks Dio Ripon from 79. *Muker Vicarage, Richmond, Yorks.* (Richmond 86276)

HALL-MATTHEWS, John Cuthbert Berners. b 33. Univ of Queensld BA (2nd cl Hist) 55. Coll of Resurr Mirfield 58. **d** 60 **p** 61 Ox. C of Woodley 60-63; Ch Ch w St John and St Luke Isle of Dogs Poplar 63-65; Asst Chap Ch Hosp Horsham 65-72; Chap R Hosp Sch Ipswich 72-75; V of Tupsley Dio Heref from 75; Commiss Dio Carp from 75; P-in-c of Hampton Bp Dio Heref from 77. *107 Church Road, Hereford, HR1 1RT.* (Hereford 274490)

HALLAM, Lawrence Gordon. b 31. Lich Th Coll 61. **d** 63 **p** 64 Chich. C of St Martin Brighton 63-68; R of Cocking w Bepton 68-71; V of Ch Ch Eastbourne Dio Chich from 71. *Christ Church Vicarage, Eastbourne, Sussex.* (Eastbourne 21952)

HALLAM, Peter Hubert. b 33. Trin Hall Cam BA 56, MA 60. Westcott Ho 56. **d** 58 Blackb **p** 59 Lanc for Blackb. C of St Anne St Annes-on-the-Sea 58-62; Asst Chap and Tutor Bede Coll and L to Offic Dio Dur 62-67; V of Briercliffe Dio Blackb from 67. *Briercliffe Vicarage, Burnley, Lancs, BB10 2HU.* (Burnley 23700)

HALLAM, Stanley Bywater. b 16. Wells Th Coll 71. **d** 71 Dur **p** 72 Jarrow for Dur. C of Haughton-le-Skerne 72-74; R of Stanhope Dio Dur from 74. *Stanhope Rectory, Bishop Auckland, Co Durham, DL13 2UE.* (Stanhope 308)

HALLATT, David Marrison. b 37. Univ of Southn BA (2nd cl Geog) 59. St Cath Coll Ox BA (3rd cl Th) 62, MA 66. Wycl Hall Ox 59. **d** 63 Warrington for Liv **p** 64 Liv. C of Maghull 63-67; V of Totley 67-75; R of Didsbury Dio Man 75-80; Team R (w Em) from 80; R of Em Didsbury 76-80. *9 Didsbury Park, Manchester, M20 0LH.* (061-434 2178)

HALLATT, John Leighton. b 34. St Pet Coll Ox BA (2nd cl Geog) 58, MA 62. Wycl Hall Ox 58. **d** 60 **p** 61 St E. C of St Jo Bapt Ipswich 60-63; St Paul Warrington 63-66; V of Wadsley 66-72; V of St Pet, Hindley 72-75; CMS Area Sec for Scotland and Dios Newc T and Dur from 75; Asst Home Sec Prov of York 78-81; Asst Reg Sec Prov of York from 81. *2a Chapel House Drive, West Denton, Newcastle-on-Tyne, NE5 1AB.*

HALLETT, Howard Adrian. Oak Hill Coll BA 81. **d** 81 Man. C of Ch Ch Walshaw Dio Man from 81. *52 Sycamore Road, Tottington, Bury, Manchester, BL8 3EG.*

HALLETT, Keith Philip. b 37. Tyndale Hall Bris 64. **d** 64 Middleton for Man **p** 65 Man. C of St Clem Higher Openshaw 64-68; Bushbury 68-71; V of Fazeley Dio Lich from 71; C-in-c of Drayton Bassett Dio Lich 71-72; R from 72; P-in-c of Hints Dio Lich from 78; Canwell Dio Lich from 78; RD of Tamworth from 81. *St Paul's Vicarage, West Drive, Bonehill, Tamworth, Staffs, B78 3HR.* (Tamworth 67424)

HALLETT, Peter. b 49. Univ of Bath BSc 72. Oak Hill Coll 73. **d** 76 **p** 77 Sheff. C of Brinsworth 76-80; P-in-c of St Jas Doncaster Dio Sheff 80-81; V from 81. *54 Littlemoor Lane, Doncaster, S Yorks, DN4 0LB.* (Doncaster 65544)

HALLETT, Peter Duncan. b 43. CCC Cam BA 66, MA 68. Westcott Ho Cam 69. **d** 71 Huntingdon for Ely **p** 72 Ely. C of Sawston 71-73; Lyndhurst w Emery Down 73-78; Skegness and Winthorpe 78-80; P-in-c of Samlesbury and Asst Dir of Relig Educn Dio Blackb from 80. *Vicarage, Potters Lane, Samlesbury, Preston, Lancs.* (Samlesbury 229)

HALLETT, Ronald Walter. b 13. Univ of Lon BD 36. **d** 36 **p** 37 S'wark. C of All SS Sydenham 36-41; Chap RNVR 41-45; C of St Jo Bapt Sevenoaks 45-49; Chap of Worksop Coll 49-51; Publ Pr Dio Birm and Chap Solihull Sch 51-53; V of St Osw Bordesley 53-59; Chap Lausanne 59-63; in Amer

Ch 64-80; Chap Commun of St Denys Warm from 80. *St Denys Lodge, Warminster, Wilts, BA12 8PG.* (0985-213292)

HALLETT, Roy. b 17. St D Coll Lamp BA 48. **d** 49 **p** 50 Mon. C of Llanfihangel Llantarnam 49-52; Llanfrechfa 52-58; V of Caldicot 58-71; Rumney Dio Mon from 71. *702 Newport Road, Rumney, Cardiff, CF3 8DF.* (Cardiff 77882)

HALLIBURTON, Canon Robert John. b 35. Selw Coll Cam BA 56, MA 60. Keble Coll Ox BA 58. Sen Denyer and Johnson Scho 60, DPhil 61, MA 71. St Steph Ho Ox 58. **d** 61 **p** 62 Lon. C of Stepney 61-67; Lect St Steph Ho Ox 67-71; Vice-Prin 71-75; Lect Linc Coll Ox 73-75; Prin Chich Th Coll from 75; Can and Preb of Chich Cathl from 76. *Theological College, Chichester.* (Chichester 783369)

HALLIDAY, Edwin James. b 35. N-W Ordin Course 70. **d** 73 Man **p** 74 Hulme for Man. C of St Jas New Bury Farnworth 73-76; V of St Phil Bolton Dio Man from 76. *St Philip's Vicarage, Bridgeman Street, Bolton, Gtr Man, BL3 6TH.* (Bolton 61533)

HALLIDAY, Geoffrey Lewis. b 40. Lon Coll of Div ALCD 66 (LTh from 74). **d** 66 **p** 67 Southw. C of W Bridgford 66-71; V of Woodborough 71-78; C of St Geo Berm (in c of St D) 78-80; P-in-c of St D Conv Distr Berm 80; Laneham 80-81; Treswell w Cottam 80-81; V of Rampton Dio Southw 80-81; R (w Laneham, Treswell and Cottam Dio Southw from 81). *Rectory, Rampton, Retford, Notts.* (Rampton 375)

HALLIDAY, Canon Robert Taylor. b 32. Univ of Glas MA 54, BD 57. Edin Th Coll 55. **d** 57 **p** 58 St Andr. C of St Andr 57-60; St Marg Newlands Glas 60-63; R of H Cross Davidson's Mains Dio Edin from 63; Lect in NT Edin Th Coll 63-74; Exam Chap to Bp of Edin 67-73; Can of Edin from 73. *18 Barnton Gardens, Edinburgh, EH4 6AF.* (031-336 2311)

HALLIDAY, Sydney Lang. St Columb's Hall Wang ACT ThL. **d** 17 **p** 19 Wang. C of Springhurst 17; C-in-c of Walwa 18-21; C of Petersham 22-24; Deputn duty 24-25; R of Weston w Abermain 26-28; Chap of Asansol 28-32; Chap (Ind Eccles Est) 32-47; Hon CF 47; Ed Ind Ch Directory 35-37; Perm to Offic Dio Lon 48-49; V of Birchencliffe 50-53; Ermington Dio Ex 53-54; Perm to Offic Dio Natal 55-57. *c/o 57 Dickson Street, Morningside, Brisbane, Queensland, Australia.*

HALLIDIE SMITH, Andrew. b 31. Pemb Coll Cam BA 54, 2nd cl Th Trip pt iii 55, MA 58. Ely Th Coll 55. **d** 56 **p** 57 Birm. C of St Mary Pype Hayes 56-58; Sec Albany Trust Lon 58-60; R of Carmacks Yukon 60-63; V of Elmstead 63-67; I of Port Edward 67-68; Stewart 68-70; R of Alresford 70-79; Midlakes, Sask, 79-81; V of Elsecar Dio Sheff from 81. *23 Armroyd Lane, Elsecar, Barnsley, S74 8ES.* (Barnsley 742149)

HALLIDIE SMITH, William. Pemb Coll Cam BA 58, 2nd cl Th Trip pt ii 59, MA 62. Coll of Resurr Mirfield 59. **d** 60 **p** 62 Lon. C of Poplar 60-67. *7 Earlham Road, Norwich, Norf.*

HALLING, William Laurence. b 43. Linc Coll Ox BA 64, Dipl Th 66, MA 68. BD (Lon) 68. Tyndale Hall Bris 66. **d** 68 **p** 69 Roch. C of St Jo Bapt, Beckenham 68-72; H Trin Aylesbury (in c of Good Shepherd) 72-78; V of St Mark Barrow-F Dio Carl from 78. *St Mark's Vicarage, Rawlinson Street, Barrow-in-Furness, Cumb.* (Barrow-F 20405)

HALLIWELL, Ivor George. b 33. St Cath Coll Cam 2nd cl Hist Trip pt i 56, 2nd cl Hist Trip pt ii 57, BA 57 2nd cl Th Trip pt ia 58, MA 61. Wells Th Coll 58. **d** and **p** 60 Lon. C of Hanworth 60-62; Willenhall w Whitley 62-65; Min of St Jas Eccles Distr Whitley 65-72; V of Corton 72-77; C-in-c of Hopton 72-74; V 74-77; Asst Chap HM Pris Pentonville 77; Chap HM Pris Ex from 77. *60 Velwell Road, Exeter.*

HALLIWELL, Michael Arthur. b 28. St Edm Hall Ox BA 50, MA 53. Ely Th Coll 52. **d** 54 **p** 55 S'wark. C of St Mary Virg Welling 54-57; St Alb Bournemouth 57-59; Asst Gen Sec C of E Coun on Foreign Relations 59-62; C of St Dunstan-in-the-W Lon 60-62; Chap to Br Embassy Bonn and All SS Cologne 62-67; Chap RAF 66-67; V of St Andr Croydon 67-71; R of St Brelade Jersey Dio Win from 71; Chap HM Pris Jersey 75-80. *St Brelade's Rectory, Jersey, CI.* (0534 42302)

HALLIWELL, Thomas. b 1900. Univ of Man BA (2nd cl Engl Lang and Lit) 23, MA 44. Univ of Wales Hon LLD 66. Ridley Hall Cam 24. **d** 25 **p** 26 Birm. C of Aston 25-27; Chap and Tutor Trin Coll Carmarthen 27-31; V of St Geo Wigan 31-36; St Pet Chorley and Chap Chorley Inst 36-40; Prin of Trin Coll Carm 40-65; Publ Pr Dio St D from 40; Can of Llangan in St D Cathl 46-56; Can of Llandyssilio-gogo and Treas 56-70. *Way Side, St Davids, Haverfordwest, Dyfed, SA62 6PE.* (St Davids 267)

✠ **HALLOWES, Right Rev Kenneth Bernard.** St Edm Hall Ox BA 46. Westcott Ho Cam 46. MA 47. **d** 46 Guildf for Natal **p** 47 Natal. Vice-Prin St Chad's Coll Ladysmith 47-52; P-in-c of Springvale 52-64; R 65; St Mark Pmbg 66-69; Can of St Sav Cathl Pmbg from 65; Cons Ld Bp Suffr of Natal in St Sav Cathl Pmbg 13 July 69 by Abp of Capetn; Bps of Zulu; and Swaz; and Bps Paget and Pickard; res 80; L to Offic Dio Natal from 80. *Rustling Pines, Winterskloof 3240, S Africa.*

HALLS, James Walter. b 1899. **d** 37 **p** 38 York. C of St Jo Bapt Newington Yorks 37-39; St Thos York 39-44; C-in-c of Carlin How Conv Distr w Skinningrove 44-50; V of Ugthorpe 50-54; PC of Trimdon Grange 54-63; W Pelton 64-68. *71 Hylton Road, Hartlepool, Cleve, TS26 0AH.* (Hartlepool 68095)

HALLS, Peter Ernest. b 38. Univ of Bris BA (2nd cl Th) 62. Tyndale Hall Bris 59. **d** 64 **p** 65 Blackb. C of St Barn Blackb 64-67; Ch Ch Bromley 67-70; V of Freethorpe w Wickhampton 70-79; Halvergate w Tunstall 70-79; P-in-c of Beighton w Moulton 77-79; V of Tuckswood Dio Nor from 79. *22 Little John Road, Tuckswood, Norwich, NR4 6BH.* (Norwich 53739)

HALLS, Canon Ronald Stanley. Kelham Th Coll 33. **d** 40 **p** 41 Aber. Chap of St Andr Cathl Aber 40-43; P-in-c of St Ninian Comely Bank Edin 43-46; R of St Pet Kirkcaldy 46-51; St Mark Portobello 51-57; Can Res and R of St Arn Cathl 57-62; Can Res Sub-Dean and R of All SS Cathl, Bend 62-72; R of Colac 72-81; Can of Bal 73-81; Can (Emer) from 81; Perm to Offic Dios Melb and Bal from 81. *24 View Court, Shoreham, Vic, Australia 3916.*

HALLS, Thomas James. Moore Coll Syd ThL 68. **d** and **p** 71 Syd. C of Carlingford 71; Peakhurst 72-74; C-in-c of McCallum's Hill 74-77; R 77-80; St Pet Cook's River Dio Syd from 81. *187 Princes Highway, St Peters, NSW, Australia 2044.* (51-2332)

HALONGO, Ven Ham. Bp Tucker Coll Mukono. **d** 61 **p** 63 Nam. P Dio Nam; Archd of Ndeeba from 78. *PO Box 30896, Kampala, Uganda.*

HALSALL, James Campbell. b 18. FCP 73. N-W Ordin Course 76. **d** 79 **p** 80 Bradf. Hon C of St Paul & St Jude Manningham Dio Bradf 79-81; P-in-c from 81. *School House, Low Moor, Bradford, W Yorks.*

HALSE, Raymond Stafford. b 19. BA (Lon) 49. Oak Hill Th Coll 46. **d** 50 **p** 51 Bris. C of Rodbourne Cheney 50-52; Farnborough Hants 52-54; V of St Jude Mildmay Pk Islington 54-59; Over Stowey w Aisholt 59-68; St Luke Ramsgate Dio Cant from 68. *St Luke's Vicarage, St Luke's Avenue, Ramsgate, Kent, CT11 7JY.* (Thanet 52562)

HALSEY, Anthony Michael James. b 35. K Coll Cam BA 56, MA 62. St Jo Coll Nottm 73. **d** 75 Repton for Derby **p** 76 Derby. C of St Werburgh Derby 75-77; Chap Canford Sch Wimborne from 78. *c/o Canford School, Wimborne, Dorset.*

HALSEY, George John. b 16. Univ of Lon BSc 36. Wycl Hall Ox 38. **d** 39 Ox **p** 40 Dorch for Ox. C of St Andr w St Mary Magd Maidenhead 39-43; H Trin Brompton 43-47; V of H Trin Southall 47-51; R of Ashtead 51-66; V of Radcliffe-on-Trent 66-68; Shelford 66-68; L to Offic Dio S'wark 73-81; Dio Guildf from 81. *70 Ashcombe Road, Dorking, Surrey.*

✠ **HALSEY, Right Rev Henry David.** b 19. Univ of Lon BA 38, 2nd cl Engl 40. Sarum Th Coll 40. **d** 42 **p** 43 Portsm. C of Petersfield 42-45; Chap RNVR 46-47; C of Plymouth 47-50; V of Netheravon 50-53; R of Fittleton 50-53; Min of St Steph Eccles Distr Chatham 53-59; V 59-62; Bromley 62-68; Hon Can of Roch 64-68; RD of Bromley 65-66; Archd of Bromley 66-68; Cons Ld Bp Suffr of Tonbridge in Cant Cathl 2 Feb 68 by Abp of Cant; Bps of St Alb; and Roch; Bps Suffr of Croydon; Hertford; and Dover; and Bps Anderson, Warner, Boys, Clark, Russell, Betts and White; Trld to Carl 72. *Rose Castle, Carlisle, Cumb.* (Raughton Head 274)

HALSEY, John Walter Brooke. b 33. Magd Coll Cam 3rd cl Nat Sc Trip pt i 56, BA (3rd cl Nat Sc Trip pt ii) 57. Westcott Ho Cam 58. **d** 61 Sheff **p** 62 Bp Gerard for York. C of Stocksbridge 61-65; Commun of Transfig from 65. *26A George Street, Millport, Isle of Cumbrae.*

HALSON, Bryan Richard. b 32. Jes Coll Cam 2nd cl Hist Trip pt i 56 BA (2nd cl Hist Trip pt ii) and Lady Kay Scho 56, 2nd cl Th Trip pt ii 58, MA 60. Univ of Liv MA 72. Ridley Hall Cam. **d** 59 **p** 60 S'wark. C of St Andr Coulsdon 59-62; Tutor St Aid Coll Birkenhead 62-65; Sen Tutor 65-68; Vice-Prin 68-69; L to Offic Dio Ches from 63; Lect Alsager Coll 69-74; Prin Lect from 74; Exam Chap to Bp of Ches 69-76. *c/o Crewe and Alsager College of Higher Educn, Alsager, Chesh, ST7 2HL.*

HALSTEAD, Leonard. b 13. St Andr Th Coll Pampisford 44. **d** 46 **p** 47 Man. C of H Trin Littleborough 46-48; Castleford 48-51; V of Silkstone 51-56; Crosland Moor 56-65; R of Partney w Dalby 65-69; R of Ashby-by-Partney 65-69; V of Skendleby 65-69; Markington w S Stainley 69-73; Bishop Thornton 72-73; Southowram 73-78. *c/o Southowram Vicarage, Halifax, Yorks.*

HALTON, Joseph Henry. Univ of Leeds BA (2nd cl Gen) 58, Wells Th Coll 58. **d** 60 **p** 61 Lich. C of St Giles Willenhall 60-62; Friern Barnet 62-64. *52 Slades Hill, Enfield, Middx.*

HALUCHISU, Michael. d 41 p 43 N Rhod. Miss P Dio N Rhod 41-64; Dio Zam from 64. *USPG, Mapanza, Zambia.*

HALUMANE, Joshua. Patteson Th Centre Kohimarama. d 72 p 74 Melan. P Dio Melan 72-75; Dio Malaita from 75. *Liwi, Malaita, Solomon Islands.*

HAM, Fraser Charles. St Francis Coll Brisb ACT ThL (2nd cl) 40. d 39 p 41 Brisb. C of St Jas Toowoomba 39-44; R of St John Inglewood 44-46; V of Clifton 46-49; R 49-53; Rosewood 53-54; CF (Austr) 54-59; RAAF from 59; Hon Miss Chap Dio Brisb 54-68; Perm to Offic Dio C & Goulb 68-71; Dio Newc from 71. *Riverden, Woolooma, NSW, Australia 2337.*

HAMATY, Michael Llewellyn. Moore Th Coll Syd ACT ThL 69. d 70 p 71 Syd. C of St Sav Punchbowl 70-72; Guildford 72-73; C-in-c of Prov Distr Canley Heights 73-78; R of St Mark Sylvania Dio Syd from 78. *46 Princes Highway, Sylvania, NSW, Australia 2224.* (522 7648)

✠ **HAMBIDGE, Most Rev Douglas Walter.** BD (Lon) 58. ALCD 53. Angl Th Coll BC DD 70. d 53 Lon p 54 Kens for Lon. C of St Mark w St Bart Dalston 53-56; R of Cassiar 56-58; Smithers 58-64; Fort St John 64-69; Can of St Andr Cathl Prince Rupert 65-69; Cons Ld Bp of Caled at Prince Rupert BC 11 May 69 by Abp of BC; Bp of Yukon; Bp Coadj of New Westmr; and Asst Bp of Carib; Trld to New Westmr 80; Elected Abp and Metrop of Prov of BC 81. *101-325 Howe Street, Vancouver, BC, V6C 1Z7.* (604-684 6306)

HAMBIDGE, John Robert. b 29. Sarum Th Coll. d 55 p 56 Newc T. C of H Trin Tynemouth 55-57; St Jo Evang Middlesbrough 58-63; H Redeemer Clerkenwell 63-64; St Jo Div Richmond 64-66; V 66-75; R of Swanscombe Dio Roch from 75. *The Rectory, Swanscombe, Kent, DA10 0JZ.* (Greenhithe 843160)

HAMBLEN, John William Frederick. b 24. Sarum Th Coll 64. d 65 p 66 Sarum. C of H Trin Weymouth 66-68; Marlborough 68-70; V of St Andr w All SS Chardstock 70-77; P-in-c of Lytchett Matravers Dio Sarum from 77. *Rectory, Jenny's Lane, Lytchett Matravers, Poole, Dorset, BH16 6BP.*

HAMBLETON, Ronald Dalzell. b 27. Ripon Hall Ox 61. d 62 p 63 Heref. C of Stokesay 62-65; V of Knowbury 65-75; P-in-c of Weston-under-Penyard Dio Heref 75-80; R (w Hope Mansel and The Lea) from 80; P-in-c of Hope Mansel 75-80; C-in-c of The Lea 78-80. *Rectory, Weston-under-Penyard, Ross-on-Wye, Herefs, HR9 7QA.* (Ross-on-Wye 62926)

HAMBLIN, Gary Wayne. Univ of Sask BA 60. Angl Th Coll Vanc 64. d 64 p 65 Qu'App. Hon C of St Luke Winnipeg 65-70; L to Offic Dio Rupld 71-75; on leave. *14115-59a Avenue, Surrey, BC, Canada.*

HAMBLIN, John Talbot. b 38. St Steph Ho Ox 64. d 66 p 67 Newc T. C of St Jo Bapt Newc T 66-70; St Paul, Covent Garden 70-71; Ch Ch w St Paul St Marylebone 71-73; Hendon 73-76; V of Ch Ch W Green (w St Pet from 77) Tottenham Dio Lon from 76; C-in-c of St Pet Hornsey 76-77. *Christ Church Vicarage, Waldeck Road, West Green, N15 3EP.* (01-889 9677)

HAMBLIN, Roger Noel. b 42. Ripon Hall Ox 67. d 70 Lanc for Blackb p 71 Blackb. C of Scotforth 70-73; Altham w Clayton-le-Moors 73-76; V of Cockerham w Winmarleigh Dio Blackb from 76. *Vicarage, Cockerham, Lancaster, LA2 0EB.* (Forton 791390)

HAMBLY, Richard Arthur William. b 11. Kelham Th Coll 28. d 34 p 35 Bris. C of Horfield 34-42; CF (EC) 42-45; CF 45-71; DACG 60-68; Chap R Hosp Chelsea 68-72; R of Compton Guildf 72-80. *Mauley House, Kempsford, Glos.*

HAMBORG, Graham Richard. b 52. Univ of Bris BSc 73. Univ of Nottm BA 76, MTh 77. St Jo Coll Nottm 74. d 77 p 78 Birm. C of St Pet Tile Cross 77-80; Upton-cum-Chalvey (in c of St Pet) Slough Dio Ox from 80. *52 Montem Lane, Slough, SL1 2QJ.* (Slough 20725)

HAMBREY, Canon Frank Bernard. b 14. Univ of Leeds BA (3rd cl Pol and Econ Sc) 42. Coll of Resurr Mirfield 43. d 44 p 45 Lich. C of St Andr W Bromwich 44-46; Edgmond 46-51; V of St Thos Bury 51-57; SPG Area Sec Dios Man and Liv 57-64; USPG 65-68; V of Colton Ulverston 68-70; Can Res of Berm 70-75; Can (Emer) from 76. *Bully Cottage, Embleton, Cockermouth, Cumb.*

HAMBREY, Frederick Charles. b 19. Univ of Leeds BA (2nd cl Cl) 41. Coll of Resurr Mirfield 41. d 43 p 45 Lich. C of Bloxwich 43-45; St Giles Willenhall 45-49; Hednesford 49-54; V of Good Shepherd W Bromwich 54-59; Hanbury 59-70; Colton w Satterthwaite and Rusland Dio Carl from 70. *Colton Vicarage, Ulverston, Cumb, LA12 8HF.* (Greenodd 361)

HAMEL, Peter John. b 40. McMaster Univ Ont BA 62. Wycl Coll Tor BTh 65. Trin Coll Cam BA (3rd cl Th Trip pt iii) 68. d 64 Bp Snell for Tor p 65 Tor. C of St John W Tor 64-66; C of Grace Ch Tor 68-69; Tutor Bp Tucker Th Coll Mukono 70-72; Chap and Lect Carleton Univ Ott 73-77; Consultant Nat Affairs Angl Ch of Canada from 77. *600 Jarvis Street, Toronto, Canada.*

HAMER, Andrew Frank. b 07. Wycl Hall Ox 65. d 66 Colchester for Chelmsf p 67 Chelmsf. C of Buckhurst Hill 66-71; V of Wethersfield 71-77. *9 High Green, Easton, Wells, Somt.*

HAMER, Charles Athelstan. b 20. Vanc Sch of Th 73. d and p 75 BC. I of St John Port Alice 75-78; St Pet Vic Dio BC from 78. *3937 St Peter's Road, Victoria, BC, Canada.*

HAMER, David Handel. b 41. Univ of Capetn BA (1st cl Cl) 61. Trin Coll Ox BA (2nd cl Th) 66. Coll of Resurr Mirfield 62. d 66 p 67 Capetn. C of Claremont 66-70; Chap St Paul's Coll Grahmstn 70-73; Publ Pr Dio Ex from 73; Chap Blundells Sch Dio Ex from 73. *2 Tidcombe Lane, Tiverton, Devon.* (Tiverton 253098)

HAMER, Frank. b 01. Bp Wilson Coll IM 41. d 43 p 44 S & M. C of Rushen 43-46; St Leon Middleton 46-47; V of Laxey 47-49; Tipton 49-55; St Ninian Douglas 55-65; Snettisham 65-69. *54 Harbour Road, Onchan, IM.*

HAMER, Joseph. b 09. St Jo Coll Dur BA 37, Capel Cure Pri 38, MA 41, Dipl in Th 41. d 38 p 39 Man. C of St Jas Heywood 38-40; H Trin Horwich 40-42; Marton 42-46; V of St Barn Oldham 46-51; Rhodes 51-56; Thornham w Gravelhole 56-58; Asst Master Fleetwood Gr Sch 58-61; V of St Anne Copp (or Gt Eccleston) 61-67. *59 Meadows Avenue, Thornton-Cleveleys, Blackpool, Lancs.* (Cleveleys 855022)

HAMER, Roderick John Andrew. b 44. K Coll Lon. Ridley Hall Cam 67. d 68 Stockport for Ches p 69 Ches. C of Timperley 68-72; Brewood 72-74; V of Chesterton 74-80; C of S Gillingham Dio Roch from 80. *60 Parkwood Green, Rainham, Gillingham, Kent, MR8 9PP.* (Medway 35837)

HAMER, Canon Thomas. b 15. Univ of Wales BA 37. St Mich Coll Llan 37. d 38 p 39 St D. C of Llanllwchaiarn 38-41; Llandefeilog 41-47; V of Maenclochog w Llanycefn (w Henry's Moat from 52) 47-80; Hon Can of St D Cathl from 79. *Bryngwyn, The Crescent, Narberth, Dyfed.*

HAMERSTON, Leslie Thomas. ACT ThL 53. d 51 p 52 St Arn. C of Tresco 51-52; V 52-54; R of Birchip 54-73; Chap to Bp of St Arn 64-76; Can of Ch Ch Cathl, St Arn 65-76; R of Tyrrell Dio St Arn (Dio Bend from 77) from 73. *St Paul's Rectory, Birchip, Vic, Australia 3483.* (Birchip 40)

HAMERTON, Thomas Patrick. b 13. St Edm Hall Ox BA (2nd cl Mod Hist) 35, MA 50. Dipl in Th 36. Cudd Coll Ox 37. d 38 p 39 Man. C of Bury 38-40; Southbourne 40-42; Miss SPG Industr Settlement Hubli Dio Bom 42-44; C of St Pet Parkstone (in C of H Angels) 44-52; V of Lois-Weedon w Plumpton (and Moreton Pinkney from 58) 52-63; V of Abthorpe 52-58; R of Slapton 52-58; R of Abington 63-76; V of Welton w Ashby St Ledgers Dio Pet from 76. *Welton Vicarage, Daventry, Northants.* (Daventry 2664)

HAMEY, Geoffrey Allan. b 25. Univ of Lon BSc 47. SOC 75. d 78 Willesden for Lon p 79 Lon. C of St Jo Bapt Pinner Dio Lon from 78. *20 Holmdene Avenue, N Harrow, Middx, HA2 6HR.*

HAMID, David. b 55. McMaster Univ Hamilton Ont BSc 78. Trin Coll Tor MDiv 81. d 81 Bp CM Mitchell for Niag. C of St Chris Burlington Dio Niag from 81. *c/o St Christopher's Church, 662 Guelph Line, Burlington, Ont, Canada L7R 2V1.* (416-634 4778)

HAMILL-STEWART, Simon Francis. b 32. Pemb Coll Camb BA 56. N Ordin Course 77. d 80 Ches p 81 Birkenhead for Ches (NSM). C of Neston Dio Ches from 80. *Mill Dene, Leighton Road, Neston, Cheshire.*

HAMILTON, Dean of (Dio Waikato). *See* Palmer, Very Rev Clifford George.

HAMILTON, Alan Edward. Moore Coll Syd ThL 70. d and p 71 Syd. C of Beecroft 71-74; C-in-c of Prov Par S Granville Dio Syd from 74. *104 Farnell Street, Merrylands, NSW, Australia 2160.* (637-2184)

✠ **HAMILTON, Right Rev Alexander Kenneth.** b 15. Trin Hall Cam 2nd cl Hist Trip Pt i 36, BA 37, 3rd cl Th Trip pt i 38, MA 41. Westcott Ho Cam 37. d 39 Bp Willis for Leic p 40 Leic. C of Birstall 39-41; Whitworth w Spennymoor 41-45; Chap RNVR 45-47; V of St Francis Ashton Gate Bedminster 47-58; St Jo Bapt Newc T 58-65; RD of Centr Newc 62-65; Cons Ld Bp Suffr of Jarrow in York Minster 24 Feb 65 by Abp of York; Bps of Dur; Edin; Newc T; Ripon; Bradf; and Sheff; Bps Suffr of Hull; Whitby; Pontefract; and Selby; and Bps Gerard and Hudson; res 80; Exam Chap to Bp of Dur 65-66. *3 Ash Tree Road, Burnham-on-Sea, Somt, TA8 2LB.* (Burnham 783823)

HAMILTON, Andrew Robert. New Coll Ox BA 60, MA 64. Ripon Hall Ox 60. d 64 Bp Parfitt for Derby p 65 Derby. C of St Bart Derby 64-67; Bakewell 67-69. *11 Holcon Court, London Road, Redhill, Surrey, RH1 2JZ.*

HAMILTON, Brian John. b 46. Univ of Auckld BA 70, LTh 72. St Jo Coll Auckld 72. d and p 72 Wai. C of Havelock N 72-75; Tauraga 76; V of Wairoa-Mohaka Past 76-81;

Edgecumbe-Kawerau Dio Wai from 81. *Galway Street, Kawerau, NZ.*

HAMILTON, Charles Robert. b 42. St Jo Coll Auckld LTh 67. **d** 65 **p** 66 Auckld. C of Sandringham Auckld 65-68; Asst P Maori Miss Auckld 69-73. *St Michael's House, Crafers, S Australia 5152.*

HAMILTON, David Alexander. St Paul's Th Coll Grahmstn 58. **d** 61 **p** 62 St John's. C of Clydesdale 61-65; P-in-c of St Mark's Dio St John's 65-74; C of Orange Grove 74-76; R of Malvern Dio Johann from 76. *14 Bartle Street, Malvern, Johannesburg, S Africa.* (011-25 1354)

HAMILTON, David Ashbury. b 31. Trin Coll Tor LTh 77. **d** 77 **p** 78 Niag. C of St Mark Orangeville 77-80; R of St Paul Shelburne w Dundalk and Whitfield Dio Niag from 80. *304 Owen Sound Street, Shelburne, Ont, Canada.* (519-925 2923)

HAMILTON, Edgar Reid. b 27. TCD BA (2nd cl Mod Mental and Mor Sc) 49, Div Test (2nd cl) 51, MA 52. **d** 51 **p** 52 Down. C of St Donard Belf 51-55; Dean's V of St Anne's Cathl Belf 55-59; Min Can from 64; C-in-c of Stormont Belf Dio Down 60-64; R from 64; RD of Dundonald from 77; Exam Chap to Bp of Down from 80. *64 Wandsworth Road, Belfast 4, N Ireland.* (Belfast 657667)

HAMILTON, George Alan. Univ of W Ont Hur Th Coll LTh 53. **d** 53 **p** 54 Hur. I of Lion's Head 53-56; C of St Jo Div Verdun 56-57; I of Old Crow 57-61; Miss at Fort Simpson 61-66; I of Warwick 66-68; R of Pelee I 68-73; Glencoe Dio Hur from 73. *Box 578, Glencoe, Ont., Canada.* (519-287 2541)

HAMILTON, George Nairne Gordon. Univ of Glas DSc 38. **d** 60 **p** 61 St John's. C of St John's Cathl Umtata 60-65; R of Port Shepstone 66-69; P-in-c of Port St John's 69-72; L to Offic Dio Grahmstn from 75. *4 Ivon Court, Elton Street, East London, CP, S Africa.*

HAMILTON, Gerald Murray Percival. b 14. Ch Coll Cam 2nd cl Econ Trip pt i 35, BA (3rd cl Th Trip pt i) 37, 3rd cl Th Trip pt ii 38, MA 41. Ridley Hall Cam 37. **d** 39 **p** 40 Win. C of Shirley 39-40; Offg Sec to Win Dioc Coun for Youth and Dom Chap to Bp of Win 40-41; C of Odiham 41-44; Leeds 44-46; V of St Mary Magd Ashton-upon-Mersey 46-51; Surr from 47; Proc Conv Ches 50-55; Relig Broadcasting Org N Region BBC 52-65; L to Offic Dio Ches 51-65; Dio York from 67; Can Res of Newc T 65-67; Industr and Commun Adv to Bp of Newc T 65-67; Prin Lect St John's Coll of Educn York (Coll of Ripon and York St John from 75) 67-79; P-in-c of Crayke w Brandsby and Yearsley 78-80; R 80-82. *Tanglewood Cottage, Newton on Ouse, York, YO6 2BN.* (L-on-O 219)

HAMILTON, Henry. b 05. Clifton Th Coll 38. **d** 40 Truro **p** 41 Ex for Truro. C of Callington w South Hill Truro 40-42; CF (EC) 42-46; C of Penkridge (in c of Stretton) 46-48; V of Malins Lee 48-51; Dawley Magna 51-60; Wrockwardine 60-63; Marston-on-Dove 63-73. *Address temp unknown.*

HAMILTON, Henry Fowler Hew. b 08. ACA 34, FCA 40. Ripon Hall Ox 54. **d** 55 **p** 56 Roch. C of All SS Chatham 55-57; V of Burham 57-61; R of Horsmonden 61-66. *64 Farmcombe Road, Tunbridge Wells, Kent.* (Tunbridge Wells 24281)

HAMILTON, James. Trin Coll Dub BA (Resp) 31, Downes Comp Pri (1st) 32, MA 35. **d** 32 Derry for Down **p** 33 Down. C of Donaghcloney 32-36; Bangor (in c of Bangor Abbey) 36-41; I of Bangor Abbey 41-79; Can and Preb of Talpestone in Down Cathl 58-79; Prec 68-79. *34 Bryansburn Road, Bangor, Co Down, N Ireland.* (Bangor 5976)

HAMILTON, Canon James. b 22. Univ of Dur LTh 48. Tyndale Hall Bris 41. **d** 49 **p** 50 Carl. C of St Jo Evang Carl 49-52; N Area Rep BCMS 52-55; V of St Simon and St Jude Southport 55-66; Ch Ch Eccleston Dio Liv from 66; Can of Liv Cathl from 76. *Eccleston Vicarage, Chapel Lane, St Helen's, Lancs.* (St Helen's 22698)

HAMILTON, James Davy. Hatf Coll Dur 38. Edin Th Coll 40. **d** 43 **p** 45 St Andr. C of St Pet Kirkcaldy 43-46; St Paul Wokingham 46-49; Chap RAF 49-55; St Athan 49-50; Boscombe Down 50-52; MEAF 52-55; C of Amersham (in c of St Geo) 55-62; R of Sandford w Upton Hellions 62-79; P-in-c of Ashprington 79-81; Cornworthy 79-81; V of Ashprington, Cornworthy and Dittisham Dio Ex from 81. *Ashprington Rectory, Totnes, Devon.* (Harbertonford 403)

HAMILTON, John Frederick. b 57. Univ of Leeds BA 78. Edin Th Coll 78. **d** 80 Ripon **p** 81 Knaresborough for Ripon. C of Whitkirk Dio Ripon from 80. *32 Woodland Road, Whitkirk, Leeds, LS15 7SF.* (Leeds 609704)

HAMILTON, John Gordon. Perry Hall Melb ACT ThL 66. **d** 65 **p** 66 Melb. C of St Osw Glen Iris 65-68; St John Croydon Melb 68-69; CF (Austr) from 70; Perm to Offic Dio Brisb from 74. *16 Rifle Range Road, Toowoomba, Queensld, Australia 4350.*

HAMILTON, John Hans Patrick. K Coll Lon and Warm BD and AKC 66. **d** 67 **p** 68 Heref. C of Cleobury Mortimer w Hopton Wafers Dio Heref from 67-69; C of Sanderstead (in c of St Antony Hamsey Green) 69-72; V of St Mary-le-Park Battersea 72-76. *Address temp unknown.*

HAMILTON, John Nicholas. b 49. Trin Coll Cam BA 71, MA 75. Ridley Hall Cam 72. **d** 75 **p** 76 Willesden for Lon. C of St John W Ealing 75-79; Em Stoughton Dio Guildf from 79. *12 Grange Close, Stoughton, Guildford, Surrey.*

HAMILTON, Lennox Thomas Newton. See Newton-hamilton, Lennox Thomas.

HAMILTON, Nigel John. b 53. Univ Coll of N Wales (Bangor) BA 75. Qu Coll Birm Dipl Th 76. Ch Div Sch of the Pacific Berkeley Calif 77. **d** 78 S'wark. C of Ch Ch W Wimbledon 78-80. *Address temp unknown.*

HAMILTON, Noble Holton. b 1898. Trin Coll Dub BA 20, Div Test 21, MA 22. **d** 21 **p** 22 Dub. C of Drumcondra 21-23; Zion Ch Rathgar 23-26; Min Can of St Patr Cathl Dub 24-29; C of Ch Ch Leeson Pk 26-29; I of St Jude 29-32; Ch Ch Kingstown 32-39; R of Ch Ch Leeson Pk Dub 39-50; Dean of Waterf Cathl and R of H Trin w St Olaf, St Patr and Ballinakill 50-67; Surr 52-67; Can and Preb of Newcastle in St Patr Cathl Dub 57-65. *64 Wandoford Road, Belfast 4, N Ireland.*

HAMILTON, Prec Noble Ridgeway. b 23. TD 66. Trin Coll Dub BA (Mod Hist and Pol Sci Mod) 45, MA 49. **d** 47 **p** 48 Down. C of Dundela 47-51; Holywood 51-55; R of St Clem Belf 55-61; Seapatrick Dio Drom from 61; RD of Aghaderg from 64; Preb of Drom Cathl 66-75; Prec from 75. *Seapatrick Rectory, Banbridge, Co Down, N Ireland.* (Banbridge 22612)

HAMILTON, O'Brien. b 13. Pemb Coll Ox BA 37, MA 40. Cudd Coll 37. **d** 39 Dorch for Ox **p** 40 Ox. C of All SS Wokingham 39-42; St Mich E Wickham 42-46; St Aug Whitton 46-48; V of St Jo Evang (w St Simon Zelotes and St Anthony from 51) Bethnal Green 48-58; St Sav Paddington 58-77. *Chez Madame Fumero, Place Bellevue, 06440 Berre les Alpes, France.*

HAMILTON, Peter Napier. b 24. Late Scho of Trin Coll Cam 1st cl Math Trip pt ii 48, BA 49, MA 53, PhD 71. Wells Th Coll 57. **d** 59 **p** 60 Portsm. C of St Mark Portsea 59-61; Petersfield (in c of Sheet) 61-63; Asst Chap Marlb Coll 63-66; Chap Girton Coll Cam 67-69; Brighton Coll 69-77; L to Offic Dio Chich 69-77; R of Frant (w Eridge from 78) Dio Chich from 77. *Frant Rectory, Tunbridge Wells, TN3 9DX.* (Frant 208)

HAMILTON, Prince Albert. d 50 **p** 51 Sudan. Agent of BFBS and C of All SS Cathl Khartoum 50-66. *P.O. Box 588, Asmara, Eritrea, Ethiopia.*

HAMILTON, Raymond. b 11. Trin Coll Dub BA 36, MA 41. **d** 37 **p** 38 Down. C of St Luke Belf 37-40; Asst Chap Miss to Seamen 40-41; Chap Orkneys 41-45; Grimsby and Immingham 45-46; Immingham 46-49; LPr Dio Linc 45-49; Chap Miss to Seamen Capetn 49-52; C of S Bersted (in c of N Bersted) 52-53; Eastleigh 53-59; Chap RNR from 58; C of Ch Ch Eastbourne 59-61; Hounslow 61-67; Poplar 67-71; St Mich Wood Green 71-77; Perm to Offic Dio Chich from 80. *1 Manor Court, Barnsite Close, Rustington, Littlehampton, BN16 3QQ.* (Rustington 2244)

HAMILTON, Robert. b 52. Keble Coll Ox BA 74, MA 78. Ripon Coll Cudd 78. **d** 81 Ches. C of Neston Dio Ches from 81. *Hillcrest, Marshlands Road, Little Neston, S Wirral, L64 4AD.*

HAMILTON, Robert Hair. b 26. Oak Hill Coll 75. **d** 76 **p** 77 Liv. C of St Matt Bootle 76-78; Horwich 78-81; R of Whalley Range Dio Man from 81. *St Margaret's Rectory, Rufford Road, Manchester, M16 8AE.* (061-226 1289)

HAMILTON, Samuel Derek. b 34. Univ of Bris BA 58. Tyn Hall Bris 54. **d** 59 **p** 60 Dub. C of St Cath Dub 59-61; Booterstown 61-63; R of Drumcliffe w Lissadell 63-69; Cahir 69-78; C of Willowfield Dio Down from 78. *57 Blenheim Drive, Belfast, BT6 9GD, N Ireland.* (Belfast 56967)

HAMILTON, Stephen Heysham. b 10. **d** 48 Bp Curzon for Cant **p** 49 Ex. C of Honiton 48-51; Berkeley (in c of Sharpness) 51-56; R of Awliscombe Dio Ex from 56; Chap Honiton Hosp from 60. *Awliscombe Rectory, Honiton, Devon.* (Honiton 2983)

HAMILTON-BROWN, James John. b 35. Univ of Lon BSc 59. Ridley Hall Cam 59. **d** 61 **p** 62 Southw. C of Attenborough w Bramcote and Chilwell (in c of Bramcote 62-67) 61-67; V of Bramcote 67-76; Research and Development Officer Abp's Coun on Evang from 76; Publ Pr Dio Sarum 76-81; Team R of Dorchester Dio Sarum from 81. *17 Edward Road, Dorchester, Dorset, DT1 2HL.* (0305-68837)

HAMISI, Evans. b 49. St Cypr Th Coll Rondo 73. **d** and **p** 76 Masasi. P Dio Masasi. *KJT Nanguruwe, PO Box 92, Newala, Mtwara Region, Tanzania.*

HAMLET, Paul Manning. b 42. Open Univ BA 81. Kelham Th Coll 61. **d** 66 **p** 67 Chich. C of Rumboldswyke Chich 66-69; H Trin w St Mary Ely 69-73; St Bart Ipswich Dio St E from 73. *17 Broadmere Road, Ipswich, Suff, IP1 5BU.* (Ipswich 41956)

HAMLETT, Leslie. b 26. St Aid Coll 60. **d** 62 **p** 63 Lich. C of Porthill 62-64; C-in-c of Grindon 64-66; C-in-c of Butterton 64-66; V of Alsagers Bank Dio Lich from 66. *Alsagers Bank Vicarage, Stoke-on-Trent, Staffs.* (Stoke-on-Trent 720624)

HAMLEY, William. Linc Th Coll. **d** 61 **p** 62 Linc. C of Swinderby and of Thurlby w Norton Disney 61-64; V of Cornwood 64-70; Perm to Offic Dio Adel from 71. *Flat 9, Carlisle Street, Northfield, S Australia 5085.* (08-62 2177)

HAMLIN, Keith Allan. b 50. Univ of K Coll Halifax NS BA 71. Atlantic Sch of Th Halifax NS MDiv 76. Trin Coll Tor MTh 78. **d** 75 **p** 76 NS. On study leave 75-80; R of Antigonish Dio NS from 81; Country Harbour Dio NS from 81; Chap St Francis Xavier Univ from 81. *Box 169, Antigonish, NS, B2G 1C0, Canada.*

HAMLYN, Eric Crawford. b 37. Univ of Dur BA 60, Dipl Th 62. Cranmer Hall Dur 60. **d** 62 **p** 63 Lich. C of Bushbury 62-64; Whitchurch 64-67; V of St Paul Burslem 67-72; Forebridge 72-77; Trentham Dio Lich from 77. *Trentham Vicarage, Stoke-on-Trent, ST4 8AE.* (S-on-T 658194)

HAMMER, Canon Raymond Jack. b 20. St Pet Hall Ox 3rd cl Cl Mods 40, BA (2nd cl Lit Hum) 42, Dipl Th (w distinc) 43, MA 45. Univ of Lon BD (1st cl) 45, MTh 55, PhD 61. Wycl Hall Ox 42. **d** 43 **p** 44 Liv. C of St Mark St Helens 43-46; Tutor St Jo Coll Dur 46-47; Sen Tutor 47-49; Lect in Th Univ of Dur 46-49; Prof at Nippon Sei Ko Kwai Centr Th Coll Tokyo 50-64; Hon Chap to Br Embassy Tokyo 54-64; Lect in Chr Doctrine St Paul's Univ Tokyo 57-58; Prof 58-64; Hon Can of Kobe from 64; Lect in Th Univ of Birm 65-77; Exam Chap to Bp of Liv from 65; L to Offic Dio Birm 65-77; Exam Chap to Bp of Birm 73-78; Dir Bible Reading Fellowship from 77; Publ Pr Dio Lon from 77. *Bible Reading Fellowship, 2 Elizabeth Street, SW1W 9RQ.* (01-730 9181)

HAMMERSLEY, Preb John Goodwin. b 34. Keble Coll Ox 3rd cl Cl Mods 55, BA (3rd cl Lit Hum) 57, MA 60. Westcott Ho Cam 57. **d** 60 **p** 61 Sheff. C of St Swith Sheff 60-67; Sec 'Parish and People' 67-70; P-in-c of St Mary-le-Wigford and St Mark Linc 70-78; Team V of Tettenhall Regis Dio Lich from 78; Preb of Lich Cathl from 81. *15 Grotto Lane, Wolverhampton, W Midl, WV6 9LP.*

HAMMERSLEY, Peter. b 41. BD (Lon) 79. Kelham Th Coll 60. **d** 65 **p** 66 Leic. C of Oadby 65-69; R of Linstead w Bog Walk 69-73; Chap DeCarteret Coll Mandeville 73-77; Min Can of Worc from 77; Chap K Sch Worc from 77. *77 Woolhope Road, Worcester, WR5 2AR.* (Worc 356880)

HAMMERSLEY, Peter Angus Ragsdale. b 35. Linc Th Coll 74. **d** 76 **p** 77 Lich. C of S Mary Stafford 76-79; P-in-c of St Andr W Bromwich Dio Lich from 79. *St Andrew's Vicarage, Oakwood Street, West Bromwich, W Midl.* (021-525 5836)

HAMMERTON, Canon Howard Jaggar. b 14. Univ of Man BA (2nd cl Engl Lang and Lit) 36. Univ of Leeds MA (Phil and Hist Relig w distinc) 44. Ridley Hall Cam 36. **d** 38 **p** 39 Ripon. C of Beeston 38-39; St Bart Armley 39-42; Kippax (in c of St Aid Gt Preston) 42-46; V of Hunslet 46-53; Surr 46-81; C-in-c of St Silas Hunslet 47-53; Chap Rothwell Hosp 46-53; R of Garforth 53-59; Exam Chap to Bp of Ripon 58-81; Lect of H Trin Leeds 59-65; Hon Can of Ripon 63-81; Can (Emer) from 81; V of (St Jo Evang to 75) w H Trin Leeds 65-81; M Gen Syn 71-75. *4 Bramhope Manor, Bramhope, Leeds.*

HAMMERTON, Raymond Keith. b 15. Univ of Lon BD (2nd cl) 40. ALCD (1st cl) 40, MTh 43. **d** 40 **p** 41 S'wark. C of All SS Shooters Hill 40-42; Lee 42-46; V of St Pet Paddington 46-53; Chap to Paddington Hosp 46-53; V of St Mary Priory Road Hampstead 53-60; Chap St Columba's Hosp Swiss Cottage 54-56; V of Harmondsworth Dio Lon from 61. *Vicarage, Harmondsworth, Middx, UB7 0AQ.* (01-759 1652)

HAMMETT, Barry Keith. b 47. Magd Coll Ox BA 71, MA 74. St Steph Ho Ox 71. **d** 74 **p** 75 Ex. C of St Pet Plymouth 74-77; Chap RN from 77. *c/o Ministry of Defence, Lacon House, Theobald's Road, WC1X 8RY.*

HAMMETT, Walter Leslie. **d** 60 **p** 61 Edmon. I of Tofield 60-67. *201 1764 Oak Bay Avenue, Victoria, BC., Canada.*

HAMMOND, Brian Leonard. Univ of Bris BSc (2nd cl Biol-Chem) 54. Wells Th Coll 56. **d** 58 **p** 59 S'wark. C of Clapham 58-62; V of All SS and St Steph Walworth 62-72; S Merstham Dio S'wark from 72; RD of Reigate from 80. *All Saints Vicarage, Battlebridge Lane, South Merstham, Surrey, RH1 3LH.* (Merstham 2722)

HAMMOND, Charles Kemble. Late Scho and Exhib of Trin Coll Dub 31, 1st cl Mod (Ment and Mor Sc) 32, BA 33, Div Test (1st cl) 34, MA 37. **d** 34 Arm for Down **p** 35 Down. C of Willowfield 34-36; St Donard Belf 36-37; St Andr Summer Hill 37-38; C-in-c of St Alb Golden Grove 38-40; Dir of Educn Dio Syd 40-52; Asst Min H Trin Miller's Point 41-49; R of Carlingford 49-52; Heyfield 52-58; Exam Chap to Bp of Gippsld 50-58; C of Melb Dioc Centre 58-64; Chap Parramatta Psychiatric Hosp 64-66; R Melb Hosp 66-78; Dir Dept of Chaps Dio Melb 66-78; L to Offic Dio Melb from 81. *36 William Street, Avalon Beach, NSW, Australia 2107.* (918-8025)

HAMMOND, Edward Guy. b 02. Em Coll Cam BA 26, MA 30. Ridley Hall Cam 26. **d** 27 **p** 28 Ex. C of St Andr Plymouth 27-31; Bath Abbey 31-34; V of St Jas Bath 34-39; R of St Leon Ex 39-51; V of Cullompton 51-60; Surr from 53; R of Nailsea 60-66; Keinton Mandeville 66-72. *28 Severn Avenue, Weston-super-Mare, Avon.*

HAMMOND, Eric Penharwood. b 08. Van Mildert Scho of St Chad's Coll Dur BA 31, Dipl in Th (w distinc) 32, MA 47. **d** 32 **p** 33 Newc T. C of N Gosforth 32-36; St Martin Knowle 36-42; H Trin Bath 42-43; C-in-c of St Martin Stubton 43-47; R (w Fenton from 48) 47-50; R of Westborough w Dry Doddington and Stubton 47-52; V of Mickleton 52-74. *St Francis, Outlands Lane, Curdridge, Southampton, SO3 2HD.*

HAMMOND, Frank. b 49. Linc Th Coll 75. **d** 77 **p** 78 Liv. C of Sutton 77-80; Blundellsands Dio Liv from 80. *13 Leicester Avenue, Crosby, Liverpool, LL2 2BA.*

HAMMOND, Frederick Walter. Qu Coll St John's Newfld 54. **d** 59 **p** 60 Newfld. C of Pouch Cove 59; I of Brigus w Salmon Cove 61-68; Smith's Sound Dio Newfld (Centr Newfld from 76) from 68. *Box 207, Clarenville, Trinity Bay, Newfoundland, Canada.* (709-466-2177)

HAMMOND, James Francis. b 48. Div Hostel Dub 69. **d** 72 **p** 73 Abp of Dub. C of Ch Ch Leeson Park w St Bart Clyde Road Dub 72-76; Monkstown 76-79; I of Dunboyne w Moyglare, Maynooth and Dunshaughlin Dio Meath from 79. *Rectory, Ballygoran, Maynooth, Co Kildare, Irish Republic.*

HAMMOND, John Hugh. b 11. Chich Th Coll 39. **d** 41 **p** 42 Ox. C of St Pet Chalfont 41-43; St Marg Ox 43-45; Cowley St John 45-48; Shrewsbury 48-50; St Mark Swindon 50-55; C-in-c of St Luke's Conv Distr Milber 55-63; V 63-77; C of Dawlish (in c of Holcombe) Dio Ex from 77. *Ash Park, Holcombe, Dawlish, Devon, EX7 0LH.* (Dawlish 862678)

HAMMOND, Michael John. b 36. St Jo Coll Dur BA 57, MA 65. N-W Ordin Course 73. **d** 76 Liv. C of St Pet Formby Dio Liv from 76. *14 Dunes Drive, Freshfield, Merseyside, L37 1NE.*

HAMMOND, Peter. Mert Coll Ox BA (2nd cl Mod Hist) 48, MA 52. Univ of Salonica 48. Cudd Coll 50. **d** 51 **p** 52 Ox. C of Summertown Ox 51-53; St Anne w St Thos Regent Street and St Pet Soho Lon 53-55; Gen Sec Angl and Eastern Chs Assn 53-55; V of Stowe 55-56; R of Radclive w Chackmore 55-56; Bagendon 56-61; L to Offic Dio York from 62. *Norfolk Cottage, Elloughton, N Humb.* (0482-667475)

HAMMOND, Peter Clark. b 27. Linc Coll Ox BA (2nd cl Hist) 49, MA 53. Wells Th Coll 51. **d** 52 Dover for Cant **p** 53 Cant. C of Willesborough 52-55; Croydon 55-59; R of Barham 60-66; V of Walmer Dio Cant from 66. *Vicarage, St Clare Road, Walmer, Kent.* (Deal 4645)

HAMMOND, Richard John. b 45. Clare Coll Cam BA 67, MA 71. St Steph Ho Ox 70. **d** 74 **p** 75 Ex. C of St D Ex 74-79; V of Docking Dio Nor from 79; P-in-c of Gt Bircham w Bircham Newton and Bircham Tofts Dio Nor from 79. *Vicarage, Docking, Kings Lynn, Norf.* (Docking 247)

HAMMONDS, Paul Edward Russell. b 39. Univ of Cant BCom 62. NZ Bd of Th Stud LTh 68. Ch Ch Coll 61. **d** 64 **p** 65 Ch Ch. C of Burwood 64-67; Hornby 67-69; Miss at Mwanza Town Vic Nyan 69-74; V of Hoon Hay 74-78; Bryndwr Dio Ch Ch from 78. *63 Brookside Terrace, Christchurch 5, NZ.* (518-075)

HAMNETT, Herbert Arnold. K Coll Lon BSc 49. Qu Coll Birm 49. **d** 51 **p** 52 Lon. C of St Jo Bapt Greenhill Harrow 51-54; Horsham 55-60; V of Yapton w Ford Dio Chich from 60. *Yapton Vicarage, Arundel, Sussex.* (Yapton 319)

HAMONET, Noel Clive. St Jo Coll Morpeth. **d** 62 **p** 63 Newc. C of E Maitland 62-63; Waratah 63-65; Belmont 65-66; R of Clarencetown 66-71; C of Waratah 71-80. *46 Branxton Street, Waratah, NSW, Australia 2298.* (68-2466)

HAMPSON, Claude Eric. b 35. Univ of S Afr BA 48, LTh 50. St Paul's Coll Grahmstn 49. **d** 50 **p** 51 Natal. C of St Sav Cathl Maritz 50-54; C of Greenford 54-58; Sec Fellowship of St Alb and St Sergius 58-60; M Bro of St Barn Dio N Queensld 60-66; R of Mt Isa 67-74; Archd of the West 67-74; V of St Aug w St John Kilburn 75-77; R of Branxton Dio Newc from 77. *Rectory, Drinan Street, Branxton, NSW, Australia 2330.* (38-1235)

HAMPSON, David. b 46. Chich Th Coll 69. **d** 72 **p** 73 Carl. C of Penrith 72-78; V of Crosscrake Dio Carl from 78. *Crosscrake Vicarage, Kendal, Cumb, LA8 0AB.* (Sedgwick 60333)

HAMPSTEAD, Archdeacon of. *See* Pickering, Ven Fred.

HAMPTON, Alastair Terence Godfrey Macpherson. b 38. ALCD (1st cl) 63. BD (Lon) 68. **d** 64 **p** 65 Bris. C of Ch Ch w Em Clifton 64-66; Ickenham 66-67; Patchway 67-73; Team V of St Brelade (in c of St Aubin) Jersey Dio Win from 73. *Vicarage, High Street, St Aubin, Jersey, CI.* (0534 44009)

HAMPTON, Allen Christian. Moore Th Coll Syd 59, ACT ThL (2nd cl) 62. BD (Lon) 68. **d** 60 **p** 61 Armid. C of Narrabri 61; Tamworth 62-63; P-in-c of Delungra 64-68; Nundle 68-72; L to Offic Dio Armid from 72. *c/o Diocesan Registry, Box 198, Armidale, NSW, Australia.*

HAMPTON, Cyril Herbert. b 1897. BC Coll Bris. **d** 49 **p** 50 Roch. C of St Steph, Tonbridge 49-51; Southborough 51-54; V of Biddulph 54-57; St Sav Forest Gate 57-64; R of Piddlehinton 64-70. *84 Dudsbury Road, Ferndown, Dorset.*

HAMPTON, John Stanley. b 13. Chich Th Coll 46. **d** 48 **p** 49 S'wark. C of Old Malden 48-52; St Pet Vauxhall 52-54; UMCA Area Sec for N Midlds 54-56; V of St Mary Magd (w St Mich AA from 59) Manningham 56-79; Healaugh w Wighill and Bilbrough 79-81. *St Bernard, Dudwell St Mary, Burwash, Etchingham, Sussex, TN19 7BE.* (Burwash 882359)

HAMPTON, John Waller. b 28. Linc Coll Ox BA 51, MA 58. Westcott Ho Cam 51. **d** 53 **p** 54 Cov. C of Rugby 53-56; Chap of St Paul's Sch Kens 56-65; V of Gaydon and Chadshunt 65-69; C-in-c of St Nich Warwick 69-75; Asst Dir of Relig Educn Cov 65-70; Research Fell Qu Coll Birm 75-76; P-in-c of Alstonfield Dio Lich from 76; Wetton Dio Lich from 76; Sheen 76-80; Butterton Dio Lich from 80; Warslow w Elkstone Dio Lich from 80; RD of Alstonfield from 80. *Alstonfield Vicarage, Ashbourne, Derbys.* (Alstonfield 216)

HAMPTON-SMITH, David Charles. Ch Ch Ox 2nd cl Mods 42, BA (2nd cl Th) and MA 48, Cudd Coll 48. **d** 50 **p** 51 Lich. C of St Chad Shrewsbury 50-53; Kingswood (in c of Ch of Wisdom of God Lower Kingswood) 53-56; V of Howe Bridge 56-62; Chap and Asst Master Woodbridge Sch Suff 62-65; St Pet Colleg Sch Adel 65-69; R of Prospect Dio Adel from 69. *2 Ballville Street, Prospect, S Australia 5082.* (08-44 1627)

HAMSINI, Zephaniah. St Andr Th Coll Likoma 50. **d** 52 SW Tang **p** 55 Nyasa. P Dio Nyasa 52-61; Dio Lebom 61-66; and from 71; Dio Malawi 66-71. *St George's Church, Beira, Mozambique.*

HAMUTUMBANGELA, Teofilusa Hingasikuka. St Bede's Th Coll Umtata 44. **d** 46 **p** 47 Damar. P Dio Damar 46-80; Dio Namibia from 80. *c/o St Mary's Mission, Odibo, PO Oshikango, Ovamboland, SW Africa.* (Oshikango 5)

HAN, Paul Ho. St Mich Sem Seoul 76. **d** 76 Taejon. d Dio Taejon. *Anglican Diocese of Taejon, PO Box 22, Taejon, S Korea.*

HAN TIN, b 41. **d** 74 **p** 75 Pa-an. P Dio Pa-an. *Khupyaung Village, Thandaung Township, Karen State, Burma.*

HANBIDGE, Kenneth Robert. b 51. TCD 72. **d** 75 Arm. C of Derryloran 75-78. *115a North King Street, Dublin 7, Irish Republic.*

HANCOCK, Alfred John. b 28. BSc (Lon) 52. **d** 77 **p** 78 Truro. C of Phillack w Gwithian & Gwinear 77-78; Hon C of Camborne Dio Truro from 78. *Redlands, Rosewarne Downs, Camborne, TR14 0BD.* (Camborne 713527)

HANCOCK, Arnold Elliott. Univ of W Ont BA 59. Trin Coll Tor 58, STB 61. **d** 61 Tor **p** 61 Bp Snell for Tor. C of St Geo Willowdale Tor 61-64; I of Ch Ch Bridgnorth Pet 64-67; R of St Monica City and Dio Tor from 67. *75 Normandy Boulevard, Toronto 8, Ont., Canada.* (416-466 3415)

HANCOCK, Bernard. b 13. Wycl Hall Ox 61. **d** 62 **p** 63 Worc. C of Gt Malvern 62-65; R of Peopleton w Naunton-Beauchamp 65-69; Hagley 69-76. *Old Post Office, Birlingham, Pershore, Worcs.*

HANCOCK, Bertram Edgar. Moore Th Coll 38, ACT ThL 40. **d** 40 **p** 41 Syd. C of Manly 40-43; Chap RAAF 43-44; P-in-c of Coolamon 44-46; Barham 46-49; V of Mooroopna 49-52; R of Milloo w Mitiamo 52-59; Sec ABM S Austr 59-64; L to Offic Dio Adel 60-62; Dioc Sec Dio N Queensld 62-64; R of Wau w Bulolo 64-67; Oatlands 68-71; Perm to Offic Dio Melb from 71. *17 Keilor Avenue, Reservoir, Vic. 3073, Australia.*

HANCOCK, Douglas. b 25. SOC 63. **d** 67 Lon **p** 68 Kensington for Lon. C of St Steph, Hounslow 67-70; Highcliffe and Hinton Admiral 70-72; R of Newton-in-the-Isle 72-78; C-in-c of Gorefield 72-74; V 74-78; R of Tydd St Giles 74-78; P-in-c of Chirton w Marden, Patney, Charlton and Wilsford Dio Sarum 78-79; R from 79. *Chirton Rectory, Devizes, Wilts.* (Chirton 271)

HANCOCK, Douglas Charles. b 16. Univ of Lon BSc (2nd cl Chem) 39, PhD 52. Wycl Hall Ox 59. **d** 60 Win **p** 61 Southn for Cant. C of St Alb Bournemouth 60-64; R of Baughurst w Ramsdale 64-70; V of St Andr, Bournemouth 70-79; R of Hinton Ampner w Bramdean and Kilmeston Dio Win from 79; RD of Alresford from 80. *Rectory, Wood Lane, Bramdean, Alresford, Hants, SO24 0JN.* (Bramdean 223)

HANCOCK, George Alfred. Univ of Adel BA 01, MA 09. **d** 28 **p** 29 Bal. Hd Master CE Gr Sch Ararat and C of Ararat 28-30; Chap Lake Tyers Aboriginal Station 31-43; Actg R of Heyfield 43-46. Perm to Offic Dio Melb from 47. *Claremont, High Street, Healesville, Vic. 3777, Australia.*

HANCOCK, Canon Herbert. b 07. St Jo Coll Dur BA and Van Mildert Scho 35. Dipl Th (w distinc) 36, MA 38. **d** 36 **p** 37 Dur. C of Chester-le-Street 36-40; PC of Eighton Banks 40-45; V of Stranton 45-61; Surr from 45; RD of Hartlepool 58-61; Hon Can of Dur 59-72; Can (Emer) from 72; R of Sedgefield 61-72; Perm to Offic Dio Dur and York from 73. *22 Admiral's Court, Sowerby, Thirsk, N Yorks.* (Thirsk 23035)

HANCOCK, Ivor Michael. b 31. BD (Lon) 60. Linc Th Coll 65. **d** 66 **p** 67 Portsm. C of Havant 66-69; V of Ch Ch Gosport 69-76; Team V of Southend-on-Sea 76-80; C-in-c of St Alb Mart Westcliff-on-Sea 76-80; V of Hawley Dio Guildf from 80; Minley Dio Guildf from 80. *Hawley Vicarage, Blackwater, Camberley, Surrey, GU17 9BN.* (Camberley 35287)

HANCOCK, John Clayton. b 36. Univ of Dur BA 58, Dipl Th 60. Cranmer Hall Dur 58. **d** 60 Penrith for Carl **p** 61 Carl. C of St Paul Newbarns w Hawcoat Barrow-F 60-65; V of Ch Coniston 65-76; R of Torver 65-76; P-in-c of Heversham Dio Carl 76-77; V from 77. *Heversham Vicarage, Milnthorpe, Cumb, LA7 7EW.* (Milnthorpe 3125)

HANCOCK, John King. St Steph Ho Ox 79. **d** 81 Lich. C of St Jo Evang Tipton Dio Lich from 81. *4 Hickman Road, Tipton, W Midl, DY4 9QB.*

HANCOCK, John Mervyn. b 38. St Jo Coll Dur BA 61, Dipl Th (w distinc) 64, MA 70. Hertf Coll Ox BA (2nd cl Th) 63, MA 66. Cranmer Hall Dur 63. **d** 64 **p** 65 Dur. C of St Gabr Bp Wearmouth 64-67; V of St Jo Evang Hebburn Dio Dur from 67. *St John's Vicarage, St John's Avenue, Hebburn, T & W, NE31 2TZ.* (0632 832054)

HANCOCK, John Raymond. b 11. FBOA 32. St Bonif Coll Warm. **d** 62 **p** 63 Win. C of Andover 62-65; R of St Michel du Valle Guernsey 65-79. *Kingsomborne, The Broadway, Totland Bay, IW. PO39 0BL.*

HANCOCK, Leonard George Edward. b 28. Open Univ BA 81. ALCD 52. **d** 52 Lich **p** 56 Sheff. C of Bilston 52-53; St Swith Sheff 56-58; Ecclesfield 58; C-in-c of St Paul's Conv Distr Ecclesfield 58-63; V of St Mary w St Simon and St Matthias Sheff 63-72; Kirk Michael 72-76; R of Loughborough Dio Leic from 76. *Rectory, Loughborough, Leics.* (Loughborough 212780)

HANCOCK, Michael John. b 33. Lich Th Coll 55. **d** 58 Chich **p** 59 Lewes for Chich. C of Rumboldswyke 58-62; Perm to Offic at St Jo Evang U Norwood 62-63; C of St Jude Hampstead Garden Suburb 63-66; V of Cinderford 66-67; C of Brockworth 67-69; Romsey 69-72; Moordown 72-75; Christchurch w Mudeford 75-78; V of St Jo Evang Guernsey Dio Win from 78. *St John's Vicarage, Guernsey, CI.* (Guernsey 20879)

HANCOCK, Paul. b 43. K Coll Lon and Warm AKC (2nd cl) 66. **d** 67 **p** 68 Lich. C of St Paul Wednesbury 67-70; Rugeley 70-73; V of St Pet Rickerscote Stafford 73-75; R of Blisland w St Breward 75-78; V of St Lawr Mansfield Dio Southw from 78. *Vicarage, Shaw Street, Mansfield, Notts.* (Mansfield 23698)

HANCOCK, Paul Byron. b 51. Univ of Bris BA 71, MA 73. Ripon Hall Ox 72. **d** 75 Cant **p** 76 Croydon for Cant. C of Croydon 75-79; in Amer Ch. *806 Terrell Road, San Antonio, Texas, USA.*

HANCOCK, Peter. b 55. Selw Coll Cam BA 76. MA 79. Oak Hill Coll BA 80. **d** 80 **p** 81 Portsm. C of Portsdown Dio Portsm from 80. *159 The Dale, Widley, Portsmouth, Hants, PO7 5JH.*

HANCOCK, Peter Ernest. b 33. Univ of Man BA (Th) 54. Qu Coll Birm 54. **d** 56 **p** 57 Leic. C of Wigston Magna 56-59; Hucknall 59-61; V of St Mich AA Sutton-in-Ashfield 61-65; Youth Officer Portsm 65-73; R of Broughton Astley Dio Leic from 73. *Broughton Astley Rectory, Leicester.* (Sutton Elms 282261)

HANCOCK, Peter Thompson. b 31. G & C Coll Cam BA 54, MA 58. Ridley Hall Cam 54. **d** 56 **p** 57 Roch. C of Ch Ch Beckenham 56-59; Chap St Lawr Coll Ramsgate 59-62; Stowe Sch Bucks 62-67; Asst Chap and Lect Embassy Ch Paris 67-70; V of H Trin Aylesbury 70-80; R of St Pet Mt Royal City and Dio Montr from 80. *900 Laird Boulevard, Montreal, PQ, Canada H3R 1Y8.* (514-739 4776)

HANCOCK, Reginald Legassicke. b 28. Trin Coll Cam BA 51, MA 57. Clifton Th Coll 60. **d** 61 Kens for Lon **p** 62 Lon. C of Ch Ch Finchley 61-63; CF from 63. *c/o Ministry of Defence, Bagshot Park, Bagshot, Surrey, GU19 5PL.*

HANCOCK, Richard. Univ of Auckld BA 65. Univ of Otago BD 68. St Jo Coll Auckld 65. **d** 67 Auckld **p** 68 Bp Monteith for Auckld. C of St Mary's Cathl Auckld 67-71; Chap St Francis Coll Brisb 71-72; Prec of St Jo Evang Cathl Brisb 73-75; C of Mt Isa 75-76; V of Bombay 76-80; N Wairoa Dio Auckld from 80. *Box 378, Dargaville, NZ.* (Dargaville 253)

HANCOCK, Ronald Edward. b 24. MRCS 49, LRCP 49. **d** 78 Bp Howell for Lon **p** 79 Lon. C of Ch Ch Highbury Dio Lon from 78. *47 Aberdeen Park, Highbury, N5.*

HANCOCK, Canon Ronald James. St Francis Coll Queensld 46. **d** 48 **p** 49 Graft. C of Murwillumbah 48-52; R of Dorrigo 52-54; Woodburn 54-56; Ballina 56-66; Dunoon 69-70; Hon Can of Graft from 64; R of All SS Kempsey 70-81. *Clevedon, Clunes, NSW, Australia 2480.*

HANCOCK, Roy Stanley. b 33. AKC 65. **d** 66 Warrington for Liv **p** 67 Liv. C of Kirkby 66-71; V of St Mark Stockland Green 71-79. *c/o Vicarage, Bleak Hill Road, Birmingham, B23 7EL.* (021-373 0130)

HANCOCK, Canon Thomas Cyril John. Keble Coll Ox BA (2nd cl Th) 28, MA 47. Ely Th Coll 29. **d** 29 Lon **p** 30 N Queensld. C of St Mark Marylebone Rd 29-30; Mackay 30-33; M of St Barn Bush Bro Dio N Queensld 33-38; V of All SS Southend 38-44; R of Charlcombe 44-56; Langridge 53-56; V of Pukekohe 56-62; Sen Hosp Chap Auckld 62-71; Hon Can of Auckld 67-78; Can (Emer) from 78; Offg Min Dio Auckld from 71. *PO Box 334, Thames, NZ.* (Thames 1244)

HANCOCK, Walter Bruce. **d** 63 **p** 65 C and Goulb. C of Temora 63-65; Cooma 65-67; R of Tarcutta 67-70; W Goulb 70-81; N Albury Dio C & Goulb from 81. *328 Gulpha Street, Albury, NSW, Australia 2640.*

HANCOCK, William Russell. b 07. Lich Th Coll 29. **d** 31 **p** 32 Worc. C of St Edm Dudley 31-34; King's Norton (in c of W Heath and Longbridge to 37) 34-40; V of Vowchurch w Turnastone 40-48; CF (EC) 42-46; Hon CF 46 ; V of H Trin Ashton L 48-55; St Mich AA Lawton Moor 55-64; St Gabr Prestwich 64-72. *Norden, Ford Lane, Northenden, Manchester, M22 4NQ.* (061-998 8742)

HANCOCKS, Graeme. b 58. Univ of N Wales (Bangor) BD 79. Linc Th Coll 79. **d** 81 Ban for St A. C of Denbigh Dio St A from 81. *34 Trewen, Denbigh, Vale of Clwyd, Clwyd, LL16 3HF.*

HANCOX, Granville Leonard. b 32. Lich Th Coll 67. **d** 70 **p** 71 Lich. C of Caverswall 70-73; Norton-le-Moors 73-76; P-in-c of St Luke Leek Dio Lich 76-79; Team V from 79. *St Luke's Vicarage, Novi Lane, Leek, Staffs.* (Leek 373306)

HAND, Canon Charles. b 08. Univ of Birm BA (3rd cl Engl) 29. Wycl Hall Ox 42. **d** 43 **p** 44 Worc. C of Lower Mitton 43-47; Belbroughton (in c of Fairfield) 47-49; V of Wribbenhall 49-61; St Barn Rainbow Hill Worc 61-64; R of Upton-on-Severn 64-73; Hon Can of Worc Cathl 73; Can (Emer) from 74. *23 Scafell Close, Warndon, Worcester.* (Worcester 23371)

HAND, David Maxwell Cowley. St Mich Coll Crafers 61. **d** 67 **p** 68 Adel. C of Mt Gambier 67-69; P-in-c of Seacliff 69-74; R of Minlaton 74-79; P-in-c of Glenelg N Dio Adel from 79. *27 David Avenue, Glenelg North, S Australia 5045.* (295 6992)

✠ **HAND, Most Rev Geoffrey David.** CBE 75. Or Coll Ox BA (2nd cl Mod Hist) 41, MA 46. Cudd Coll 40. **d** 42 **p** 43 Wakef. C of Heckmondwike 42-46; Missr Dio New Guinea from 46; P-in-c of Sefoa 47-48; Sangara 48-50; Archd of N New Guinea 50-63; Cons Bp Coadj of New Guinea 29 June 50 in Dogura Cathl by Abp of Brisb; Bps of New Guinea; Rockptn; Adel; and Graft; Apptd Bp of Papua New Guinea 63; Port Moresby (Apptd Abp and Metrop of Prov of Papua New Guinea) 77. *Box 806, Port Moresby, Papua New Guinea.* (214648)

HAND, (Simon) Peter Jowett. Univ of Leeds BA 34. Or Coll Ox BA 37, 3rd cl Th 37, MA 40. Ely Th Coll 37. **d** 38 Ox **p** 39 Dorch for Ox. C of All SS Boyne Hill 38-41; St Sav w St Pet S'wark and Succr of S'wark Cathl 41-45; Sub-Warden of Bp Cotton Sch Bangalore Dio Madr 46-53; Ch of S India 47-53; V of St Barn Southfields Surrey 54-59; Prin of St Paul's Th Coll Moa I 59-69; P-in-c of Moa I 59-69; Can of Carp 63-69; Exam Chap to Bp of Carp 64-69; M SSF from 69; Perm to Offic Dio Brisb 69-70; Dio Newc from 78; w SSF Jegarata 70-77. *SSF Friary, Sheddon Street, Islington, NSW, Australia 2296.*

HAND, Peter Michael. b 42. Univ Coll Ox BA 63. BSc (Lon) 75. Sarum Wells Th Coll 77. **d** 80 Sarum **p** 81 Sherborne for Sarum (NSM). C of Shaston 80-81; Team V of Tisbury Dio Sarum from 81. *Melbury, Wardour, Tisbury, Salisbury.* (Tisbury 870625)

HANDFORD, Ven George Clive. Univ of Dur BA (2nd cl Arabic) 61. Univ of Birm Dipl Th 63. Qu Coll Birm 61. **d** 63 Bp Gelsthorpe for Southw **p** 64 Southw. C of Mansfield 63-67; Chap All SS Beirut 67-74; Dean of St Geo Colleg Ch Jer 74-78; Chap at Abu Dhabi and Archd of the Gulf Dio Cyprus from 78. *Box 262, Abu Dhabi, United Arab Emirates, Arabian Gulf.* (Abu Dhabi 361531)

HANDFORD, John Richard. b 32. Univ of Syd BSc 53. Univ of Lon MSc 58. Dipl Th (Lon) 67. Lon Coll of Div 68. **d** 69 **p** 70 Ox. Asst to Chap and Asst Master Wel Coll Crowthorne from 69. *Wellington College, Crowthorne, Berks.*

HANDFORD, Maurice. b 25. Oak Hill Th Coll 48. **d** 52 **p** 53 Dub. C of Mission Ch Townsend Street Dub 52-55; Org and Deputn Sec ICM for N and Midlds from 55; Min of Trin Chap Buxton Dio Derby from 58. *Trinity Parsonage, Buxton, Derbys.* (Buxton 3461)

HANDFORTH, Richard Brereton. b 31. St Pet Coll Ox BA 55, MA 60. Westcott Ho Cam 63. **d** 64 Chelmsf **p** 65 Colchester for Chelmsf. C of Hornchurch 64-65; Warden St Steph Coll Hong Kong 65-73; L to Offic Dio Hong 65-73; Chap CMS Fellowship House Foxbury Chislehurst 73-75; C of Chislehurst 73-75; Home Educn Sec CMS from 75; L to Offic Dio Roch from 76. *CMS, 157 Waterloo Road, SE1 8UU.* (01-928 8681)

HANDISYDE, Canon George Henry. b 02. Late Scho of Pemb Coll Cam 1st cl Hist Trip pt i, 23, BA (1st cl Hist Trip pt ii) 24, Lightfoot Scho 25, MA 28. Cudd Coll 32. Fell of St Aug Coll Cant 27-30. **d** 32 Chich **p** 33 Bp Southwell for Chich. C of Ch Ch Eastbourne 32-37; C-in-c of Camelsdale Conv Distr 37-38; Min 38-44; R and V of Selsey 44-66; R of Fittleworth 66-73; Exam Chap to Bp of Chich from 42; RD of Chich 52-56; Can and Preb of Chich Cathl 57-77; Can (Emer) from 77; Actg RD of Petworth 74-77; Perm to Offic Dio St Alb from 77. *4 Langdon Street, Tring, Herts, HP23 6AZ.* (Tring 4881)

HANDLEY, Ven Anthony Michael. b 36. Selw Coll Cam 3rd cl Th Trip pt i 58, BA (3rd cl Th Trip pt ii) 60, MA 64. Chich Th Coll 60. **d** 62 **p** 63 Nor. C of Thorpe Episcopi 62-66; Gaywood 66-72; V of Hellesdon 72-81; RD of Nor N 80-81; M Gen Syn from 80; Archd of Nor from 81; Chairman Youth Comm Dio Nor from 81. *40 Heigham Road, Norwich, NR2 3AU.*

HANDLEY, Douglas Walter. Univ of Hull, BA 60. Linc Th Coll 60. **d** 62 Man. C of St Phil w St Steph Salford 62-63. *112 Kendal Drive, Halton Moor Estate, Leeds 12.*

HANDLEY, Harold. b 14. ACIS 42. AACCA 44. Bps' Coll Cheshunt, 62. **d** 63 **p** 64 St Alb. C of Hitchin 63-65; V of Totternhoe 65-79; C of Ringwood 79-80. *16 Barton Court Avenue, Barton-on-Sea, Hants, BH25 7HD.* (New Milton 611771)

HANDLEY, Neil. b 40. St Aid Coll 64. **d** 67 **p** 68 Man. C of Ch Ch Ashton L 67-70; All SS Stretford 70-73; Tonge w Breightmet 73; C-in-c of St Jo Evang Breightmet Conv Distr 74-79; V of St John Top O' Th' Moss Bolton-le-Moors 79-80; R of St John Broughton Salford Dio Man from 80. *237 Great Clowes Street, Salford, Lancs, M7 9DZ.* (061-792 9161)

HANDS, Graeme. b 35. Cranmer Hall Dur. **d** 61 **p** 62 Cov. C of Atherstone 61-63; Chap Aldwickbury Sch Harpenden 63-66; C of St Alb Stoke Heath 66-68; P-in-c of St Paul Warw 68-80; V of St Nich Radford City and Dio Cov from 80. *21 Tulliver Street, Coventry, CV6 3BY.* (Cov 598449)

HANDS, Leonard Paul. b 41. **d** 73 Keew. I of Red Lake and Ear Falls 73-77; C of St Alb Cathl Kenora and St Jas Keew Dio Keew 77-80; P-in-c from 80. *Box 398, Keewatin, Ont, Canada.*

HANDSCOMBE, Richard John. b 23. Cudd Coll 58. **d** 60 **p** 61 Chelmsf. C of All SS Shrub End 60-63; V of Fingringhoe Dio Chelmsf from 63; C-in-c of E Donyland 75-77. *Fingringhoe Vicarage, Colchester, Essex.* (Rowhedge 383)

HANDY, Maurice Arthur. b 04. TCD BA (Resp) Downes Oratory Pri 26, MA 34. **d** 27 **p** 28 Dub. C of St Steph Dub 27-36; Hd of Trin Coll Dub Miss Belf 36-39; C of St Mary Donnybrook 40-41; C-in-c of Whitechurch 41-55; I 55-65; RD of Taney 52-65; Can of Ch Ch Cathl Dub 63-72; Warden of Ch's Ministry of Healing in Ireland 65-72; I of Hacketstown 72-76. *55 Marley Avenue, Rathfarnham, Dublin 16, Irish Republic.*

HANES, Hubert Stanley. **d** 66 **p** 67 Tor. C of St Matt Islington Tor 66-70; R of St Paul Rexdale Tor 70-75; Fort McPherson 76-77; Tuktoyaktuk 77-78; Hinton Dio Edmon from 80. *Box 2099, Hinton, Alta, T0E 1B0, Canada.*

HANFORD, Canon William Richard. b 38. Late Exhib of Keble Coll Ox BA (2nd cl Mod Hist) and Squire Scho 60, 3rd cl Th 62, MA 64. BD (2nd cl) Lon 66. Trin Coll Dub MA (by incorp) 67. St Steph Ho Ox 60. **d** 63 Llan **p** 64 Bp T M Hughes for Llan. C of St Martin Roath 63-66; Perm to Offic Dio Llan 66-67; C of Llantwit Major w St Donats 67-68; PV of Llan Cathl 68-72; Chap RN 72-76; L to Offic Dio Gibr 74-76; Hon Chap Gibr Cathl 74-76; Perm to Offic Dio Chich 76-77; Hon C of St Sav w St Pet Eastbourne 76-77; C of Brighton 77-78; Can Res and Prec of Guildf Cathl from 78. *5 Cathedral Close, Guildford, Surrey, GU2 5TL.* (Guildf 31693)

HANGO, Harold Joseph. St Phil Th Coll Kongwa. **d** 64 **p** 65 Centr Tang. P Dio Centr Tang 64-77; Dio Vic Nyan from 78. *Box 26, Tarime, Tanzania.*

HANGO, Petero. St Phil Th Coll Kongwa. **d** 57 Centr Tang **p** 58 Bp Omari for Centr Tang. P Dio Centr Tang. *PO Kikombo, Tanzania.*

HANGULA, Abraham Mwelija. b 31. **d** 71 **p** 72 Damar. P Dio Damar 71-80; Dio Namibia from 80. *PO Box 11, Oshakati, SW Africa.* (Oshakati 187)

HANK, Christopher James. b 32. **d** 74 **p** 75 Johann. C of

Kliptown Dio Johann from 74. *Box 6, Miday Tvl 1816, S Africa.* (011-22 2673)

HANKEY, John Duncan. AKC 33. Cudd Coll 34. **d** 34 **p** 35 Lon. C of St Andr Stockwell Green 34-35; St Matt Westmr 35-38; St Barn Wood End 38-43; All SS Clifton 43-49; Hd Master of Ullenwood Manor Sch and Perm to Offic Dio Glouc 49-64; Perm to Offic Dio Chich 66-70. *Pitt House, Bovey Tracey, Newton Abbot, Devon.*

HANKEY, Simon. b 26. CCC Cam BA 48, MA 53. Cudd Coll 48. **d** 50 **p** 51 Pet. C of Wellingborough 50-52; St Giles Cam 52-54; C-in-c of Berwick Hills Middlesbrough 54-60; PC of All SS Scarborough 60-71; V of Earls (or Long) Wittenham w Abbotts (or Little) Wittenham 71-78; R of Ashingdon w S Fambridge Dio Chelmsf from 81. *Rectory, Church Road, Ashingdon, Essex, SS4 3HY.* (Southend 544327)

HANKEY, Wayne John. b 44. Dalhousie Univ BA 65. Trin Coll Tor MA 69. **d** 70 **p** 71 NS. C of Parkdale Tor 69-72; I of Petite Riviere 72-76; Lect York Univ Tor 71-72; K Coll Halifax 72-78 and from 82; Hon C of St Jas Armdale 76-78; and from 82; Libr Pusey Ho Ox 79-81. *King's College, Halifax, NS, Canada.*

HANKIN, Gayai. St Columb's Hall Wang ACT ThL 68. **d** 69 **p** 70 Carp. P Dio New Guinea 69-71; Dio Papua 71-74; Dio Carp from 74. *c/o Box 79, Thursday Island, Queensld, Australia 4875.*

HANKIN, Jack. **d** 73 Carp. C of Murray Island Dio Carp from 73. *c/o Box 79, Thursday Island 4875, Qld., Australia.*

HANKINS, Clifford James. b 24. Chich Th Coll 70. **d** 72 **p** 73 Chich. C of Henfield 72-76; V of Fernhurst Dio Chich from 76. *Fernhurst Vicarage, Haslemere, Surrey, GU27 3EA.* (0428-52229)

HANKINSON, Michael Roderic. Univ of Manit BA 49. St Jo Coll Winnipeg, LTh 52. **d** 51 Rupld **p** 56 Qu'App. I of Fairford 51-53; C of Moose Jaw 54-55; I of Rockglen 55-58; Cabri 58-63; Garden River 63-70; Blind River 70-75; Ascen Sudbury Dio Alg from 75; Garson Dio Alg from 75. *1162 Rinfret Street, Sudbury, Ont., Canada.* (705-566 2761)

HANLEY, Ian David. b 46. **d** 79 Bp Wiggins for Wel **p** 80 Wel. Hon C of Tawa-Linden Dio Wel from 79. *16 Duncan Street, Tawa, Wellington, NZ.*

HANLIN, Philip Sydney. St Jo Coll Morpeth 73. **d** and **p** 74 Bath. C of Parkes 74-77; Alice Springs 77-78. *c/o Cathedral Buildings, Bathurst, NSW, Australia 2795.*

HANLON, CN Reginald William. Moore Th Coll Syd ACT ThL 54. **d** & **p** 55 Syd. C-in-c of St Paul Oatley 55-59; R of Mittagong 59-61; S Kinangop Miss Distr 62-65; Chatswood 65-75; St Mark W Wollongong Dio Syd from 75; Can of St Mich Prov Cathl Wollongong from 77. *429 Crown Street, West Wollongong, NSW, Australia 2500.* (042-29 2914)

HANLON, Robert Irwin. b 17. Trin Coll Dub BA (2nd cl Mod) 40, BD 55. **d** 41 **p** 42 Down. C of Glenavy 41-44; C-in-c of Garrison and Slavin 44-47; Tempo 47-54; CF 54-58; V of Sproxton w Saltby and Coston 58-63; Croxton Kerrial w Branston-by-Belvoir (and Knipton w Harston from 74) Dio Leic from 63. *Knipton Rectory, Grantham, Lincs.* (Knipton 274)

HANMER, Richard John. b 38. Peterho Cam BA 61, MA 65. Linc Th Coll 62. **d** 64 **p** 65 Sheff. C of St Swith Sheff 64-69; Dom Chap to Bp of Nor 69-73; V of Cinderhill 73-81; Eaton Dio Nor from 81. *210 Newmarket Road, Norwich, NR4 7LA.* (Nor 52837)

HANNA, Canon Aziz. Bp's Coll Calc. **d** 42 **p** 43 Egypt. P at Menouf 42-44; I 44-60; Giza Dio Egypt from 60; Hon Can of All SS Cathl Cairo from 65. *CMS, Giza, Egypt.*

HANNA, Canon Charles Patrick. b 16. Ex Coll Ox BA 37, MA 41. Sarum Th Coll 37. **d** 39 Sherborne for Sarum **p** 40 Sarum. C of Wareham 39-43; Chap RNVR 43-47; C of Warminster (in c of St John Boreham) 47-49; R of Hilperton w Whaddon 49-55; V of E w W Harnham 55-65; Bp's Lavington 65-79; R of L Cheverell 66-81; Hon Can of Sarum Cathl from 78; P-in-c of Gt Cheverell and Erlestoke 79-81. *16 Wolds View, Fotherby, Louth, Lincs.*

HANNA, Desmond Haldane. b 41. TCD BA 63, Div Test 64, MA 67. **d** 64 Tuam for Down **p** 65 Down. C of Shankill (Lurgan) 64-70; Cregagh 70-72; R of St Chris Belf 72-80; Belvoir Dio Down from 80. *3 Brerton Crescent, Belfast, BT8 4QD.* (Belfast 643777)

HANNA, Robert Charles. b 46. Oak Hill Coll 75. **d** 77 **p** 78 Connor. C of Coleraine 77-82; I of Convoy and Donaghmore w Monellan Dio Raph from 82. *Rectory, Main Street, Convoy, Lifford, Co Donegal, Irish Republic.*

HANNA, Samuel James. Wycl Coll Tor BA 56, BTh 59. **d** 58 **p** 59 Hur. C of St Aid Riverside 58-60; Fort Simpson 60-63; CF (Canad) 63-68; Hon C of St Aid City and Dio Tor from 69. *609 Milverton Boulevard, Toronto 13, Canada.*

HANNAFORD, John Alfred Victor. b 46. Moore Th Coll Syd ACT ThL 75. **d** 76 **p** 77 Adel. C of St Martin Campbelltown 76-77; P-in-c of Morphettville Dio Adel from 77. *129 Morphett Road, Morphettville, S Australia 5043.* (295 4759)

HANNAFORD, Robert. b 53. Univ of Ex BEducn 76, MA 78. St Steph Ho Ox 78. **d** 80 **p** 81 Ex. C of St Jas City and Dio Ex from 80. *32 Sylvan Road, Exeter, EX4 6EU.* (Exeter 58631)

HANNAH, John Douglas. St Paul's Coll Grahmstn Dipl Th 71. **d** 71 **p** 72 Pret. C of Ch Ch Pietersburg 72-75; R of Waterberg 75-76; R of Cullinan and C of St Alb Cathl Pret 76-78; R of St Wilfrid Hillcrest City and Dio Pret from 78. *92 Duxbury Road, Hillcrest, Pretoria 0083, S Africa.*

HANNAH, Canon John Maitland Charles. b 05. Univ of Edin MA 28. Edin Th Coll 31. **d** 33 **p** 34 Glas. C of St Geo Glas 33-36; Chap of St Mary's Cathl Edin 36-40; P-in-c of St Ebba Eyemouth 40-48; R of St Jo Evang Selkirk 48-58; St Jo Evang Alloa 58-70; Can of St Ninian's Cathl Perth 67-70; Hon Can from 72; Hon Asst Super Edin from 74. *Caddonmill, Clovenfords, Selkirkshire, TD1 3LZ.*

HANNAH, Richard. b 24. CCC Ox BA 49, MA 53. St Mich Coll Llan 49. **d** 51 **p** 52 Llan. C of St Jo Bapt Cardiff 51-55; Usk U 55-58; V of Llanfihangel Crucorney w Oldcastle 58-63; R of Shenington w Alkerton (w Shutford from 69) 63-78; P-in-c of Deddington w Clifton and Hempton Dio Ox 78-81; V (w Barford) from 81; RD of Deddington from 78. *Deddington Vicarage, Oxford, OX5 4TJ.* (Deddington 38329)

HANNAM, Duncan Chisholm. b 18. Univ of Dur BA (2nd cl Th) 42, MA 45. Linc Th Coll 45. **d** 45 **p** 46 Dur. C of St Hilda S Shields 45-51; Harton 52-55; R of Hetton-le-Hole 55-60; C-in-c of Hutton Henry Conv Distr 60; C of Gateshead 60-64; Camberwell 64-76; P-in-c of Eldon Dio Dur 76-81; V from 81; C of Shildon 76-81. *4 Eldon Bank, Eldon, Bishop Auckland, Co Durham, DL14 8DX.* (Shildon 2397)

HANNANT, John McRuer. **d** 62 **p** 63 Tor. C of St Clem Eglinton Tor 62-65; Sec Dioc Coun for Social Service Tor from 65; on leave. *362 Manor Road East, Toronto, Ont., Canada.*

HANNAY, Robert Fleming. b 23. Ch Ch Ox MA 49. Cudd Coll 63. **d** 65 **p** 66 Heref. C of Ch Stretton 65-69; R of Garsington 69-79; R of The Claydons Dio Ox from 79. *Rectory, Queen Catherine Road, Steeple Claydon, Buckingham.*

✠ **HANNEN, Right Rev John Edward.** McGill Univ Montr BA 59. Coll of Resurr Mirfield, 59. **d** 61 Aston for Birm **p** 62 Birm. C of Solihull 61-64; Chetwynd 65-67; Greenville 67-68; I of Port Edward 68-71; Kincolith 71-81; Hon Can of Caled 76-81; Cons Ld Bp of Caled at Sen Sec Sch Prince Rupert 15 Feb 81 by Bp of New Wetmr (Actg Metrop); Bps of Carib, Koot and BC; and Bp Frame. *Bishop's Lodge, 208 West Fourth Avenue, Prince Rupert, BC, Canada.* (604-624 6044)

HANNEN, Peter Douglas. Bp's Univ Lennox BA 56. K Coll Lon and Warm AKC 58. McGill Univ BD 66, MA 71. **d** 59 Lon for Niag **p** 59 Niag. C of Thorold 59-61; R of Stanbridge E 61-67; St Aid Montr 67-71; St Columba City & Dio Montr from 71. *4040 Hingston Avenue, Montreal, PQ, Canada.* (514-484 3202)

HANNON, Brian Christopher. Mem Univ Newfld BA 77. Atlantic Sch of Th MDiv 81. **d** 80 E Newfld. d Dio Newfld 80-81; C of Channel Dio W Newfld from 81. *Channel, Newfoundland, Canada, A0M 1C0.*

HANNON, Brian Desmond Anthony. b 36. Trin Coll Dub BA (2nd cl Ancient and Mod Lang Mod) 59, MA 63. **d** 61 **p** 62 Derry. C of All SS Clooney 61-64; I of Desertmartin 64-69; R of Ch Ch Londonderry Dio Derry from 69; Dir of Ordinands Dio Derry 73-79; RD of Londonderry from 78. *80 Northland Road, Londonderry, BT48 0AL, N Ireland.* (Londonderry 63279)

HANNON, Canon James Sherwood. b 18. Univ of Liv BA (1st cl Hist) 40, MA 60. St Cath S Ox BA (2nd cl Th) 42, MA 47. Ripon Hall Ox. **d** 42 **p** 43 Ely. C of St Benedict Cam and Sec SCM Cam 42-44; LPr Dio Ely 44; Dio Lon 44-46; Asst Gen Sec SCM 44-46; C of Huddersfield 46-49; Chap of Chich Th Coll 49-55; Asst PV of Chich Cathl 54-55; V of St Mary Magd Winton 55-60; Swinton 60-80; Team R 80-81; Chap Swinton Hosp 60-81; Proc Conv Man 64-75; RD of Eccles 67-81; Hon Can of Man 69-81; Surr 70-81; V of Coniscliffe Dio Dur from 81; Piercebridge Dio Dur from 81. *Coniscliffe Vicarage, Darlington, Co Durham, DL2 2LR.* (Piercebridge 510)

HANNON, John Frederick. b 27. St Jo Coll Morpeth ACT ThL 55. **d** 54 **p** 55 C & Goulb. C of Wagga Wagga 54-56; R of Adelong 56-59; Chap St Vinc Hosp 59-64; V of Niddrie 65-70; Min of Moorabbin 70-73; C of St Alb Dartford 73-74; I of Ferntree Gully 75-79; C in Dept of Industr Miss Dio Melb from 79. *Lot 79 Bellbird Crescent, Emerald, Vic, Australia 3782.* (059-68 4100)

HANSCOMBE, Derek George. b 33. Chich Th Coll 60. **d** 62 Pontefract for Wakef **p** 63 Wakef. C of St Mary Virg Illingworth (in c of Holmfield Conv Distr from 67) Halifax

62-68; Youth Chap Dio Lich 68-73; V of St Chad Coseley 73-78; Tr Officer for USPG from 78. *12 Madeley Road, Ironbridge, Telford, Salop, TF8 7PP.*

HANSEN, Ernest Paul. b 46. Linc Th Coll 78. **d** 80 **p** 81 Dur. C of Greenside Dio Dur from 80. *22 Clifford Terrace, Crawcrook, Ryton T & W, NE40 4UA.*

HANSEN, Harold Percy. b 05. St Chad's Coll Dur BA 29, Dipl in Th 30, MA 32. **d** 30 **p** 31 Ripon. C of St Aid Leeds 30-32; Keighley (in c of All SS) 32-35; St Cuthb Stella 35-38; V of Cassop w Quarrington 38-50; CF (EC) 41-46; R of Croxdale 50-58; V of Studham w Whipsnade 58-66; R of Campton 66-70; V of Shefford 66-70; Perm to Offic Dio St Alb from 77. *58 High Street, Roxton, Bedford.* (Bedford 870810)

HANSEN, Canon Karl Augustus. Seager Hall Ont Dipl Th 64. **d** 63 **p** 64 Hur. I of Six Nations Reserve 63-75; Can of Hur 73-79; Can (Emer) from 79; I of Watford 75-79. *RR1, Tichborne, Ont, Canada.*

HANSEN, Kevin Roy. Ridley Coll Melb. **d** 68 Armid. C of Moree 68-69; Tambar Springs 69-70; P-in-c 71-73; V of Bingara Dio Armid from 73. *Vicarage, Bingara, NSW, Australia 2404.* (Bingara 68)

HANSEN, Ven Neil Bertram. Univ of NZ BA 51. St Steph Ho Ox 52. **d** 53 **p** 54 Ex. C of St Pet Plymouth 53-55; V of Bluff w Stewart I 55-58; Dunstan 58-66; St Kilda 66-71; N Invercargill 71-73; Andersons Bay 73-77; St John Invercargill Dio Dun from 77; Archd of Southland from 77. *182 Leet Street, Invercargill, NZ.* (Invercargill 86-845)

HANSEN, Robert. St Jo Coll Auckld 57. **d** 58 **p** 59 Auckld. C of Whangarei 58-61; V of Islands 61-64; Chap Middlemore Hosp Auckld 64-81; V of Waiuku Dio Auckld from 81. *40 Queen Street, Waiuku, NZ.*

HANSFORD, Bruce Euan. b 44. BD (Lon) 71. ACT ThL 71. Ridley Coll Melb 68. **d** 72 **p** 73 Melb. C of St Thos Essendon 72-73; St John Blackburn 73-75; P-in-c of Lilydale 75-79; Alyangula Dio N Terr from 79. *PO Groote Eylandt, NT, Australia 5791.*

HANSFORD, Gordon John. b 40. Univ of Southn BSc 61. Trin Coll Bris 77. **d** 79 **p** 80 Ex. C of St Leon City and Dio Ex from 79. *27 Barnado Road, Exeter, Devon, EX2 4ND.*

HANSFORD, Hartley Grahame. St Jo Coll Morpeth, 66. **d** 66 **p** 67 Bath. Bro of Good Shepherd Bourke 66-68; Tennant Creek 68-71; P-in-c 71-72; C of Mt Isa 72-74; V of St Osw Banyo Brisb 74-80; R of Goondiwindi Dio Brisb from 80. *Box 37, Goondiwindi, Queensland, Australia 4390.* (71 1051)

HANSON, Canon Anthony Tyrrell. b 16. Trin Coll Dub BA (1st cl Cl Mod) 38. (1st cl Ment and Moral Sc) 38. DD 53. **d** 41 **p** 42 Down. C of Bangor Abbey 41-43; Th Colls Asst Study Sec SCM and LPr Dio Lon 43-47; Tutor Dorn Div Sch 47-55; United Th Coll Bangalore 55-59; Can Th of Belf Cathl 59-62; Exam Chap to Bp of Dorn 50-55; to Bp of Connor 60-62; to Abp of York from 63; Prof of Th Hull Univ from 63; Prov Can of York from 69. *197 Victoria Avenue, Hull, Yorks.*

HANSON, Fred Gordon. Moore Th Coll Syd, ACT ThL 64. **d** 64 **p** 65 Syd. C of Wentworthville 64-65; C-in-c of Wilberforce 65-66; C of Katoomba 66-70; C-in-c of Provisional Distr of Waitara Dio Syd from 71. *34 Palmerston Road, Waitara, NSW, Australia 2077.* (48-4793)

HANSON, Canon John Westland. OBE 74. St Jo Coll Dur BA (2nd cl Hist) 41, MA 44, Dipl in Th 43. **d** 43 **p** 44 Linc. C of Louth (in c of Withcall) 43-50; R of Grimoldby w Manby 50-76; Chap RAF Flying Coll Manby 50-59; Chap and Lect from 59; RD of E Louthesk 60-68; Louthesk 68-77; Can and Preb of Linc Cathl from 67; V of Woodhall Spa Dio Linc from 76. *Vicarage, Woodhall Spa, Lincs, LN10 6SL.* (Woodhall Spa 52554)

HANSON, Peter Richard. b 45. Chich Th Coll 72. **d** 75 Chelmsf **p** 76 Barking for Chelmsf. C of St Edm Forest Gate 75-79; Chingford 79-81; V of Harrow Green Dio Chelmsf from 81. *4 Holloway Road, E11 4LD.*

HANSON, Richard. b 14. Wells Th Coll 40. **d** 42 **p** 43 Carl. C of Penrith 42-45; Ludlow 45-48; Chap Control Comm Germany 48-50; Chap at Geneva 50-56; V of Goole 56-60; RD of Snaith 56-60; V of Ecclesall 60-67; Chap Milan 67-72; V of Harrow Weald 72-77; P-in-c of Alfrick and Lulsley and Suckley Dio Worc 77-78; R (w Leigh and Bransford) from 78; P-in-c of Leigh w Bransford 77-78. *Rectory, Leigh, Worcester, WR6 5LF.* (Leigh Sinton 32355)

✠ **HANSON, Right Rev Richard Patrick Crosland.** b 16. Late Scho of TCD BA (1st cl Cl and 1st cl Ancient Hist Mod) 38, Div Test (1st cl) 40, BD 41, DD 50, MA 61, M RIA 71. Univ of Man MA 77. **d** 41 **p** 42 Dub. C of St Mary Donnybrook 41-44; Holy Trin Seapatrick 44-45; Vice-Prin Qu Th Coll Birm 45-50; LPr Dio Birm 46-50; V of Shuttleworth 50-52; Lect in Th Univ of Nottm and L to Offic Dio Southw 52-62; Exam Chap to Bp of Wakef 61-64; to Bp of Man 62-70; to Bp of Dur 62-64; to Bp of Southw 67-70; Lightfoot Prof of Div Univ of Dur 62-64; Can Res of Dur 62-64; Prof of Christian Th Univ of Nottm 64-70; Hon Can of Southw 64-70; Can Th of Cov 67-70; Cons Ld Bp of Clogh 17 March 70 in Arm Cathl by Abp of Arm; Abp of Dub; Bps of Cashel; Connor; Derry; Down; Killaloe; Kilmore; Meath; Tuam; and Dur; res 73; Asst Bp of Man from 73; Prof of Hist and Contemporary Th Univ of Man from 73. *Faculty of Theology, University of Manchester, Manchester, M13 9PL.*

HANSON, Robert Arthur. b 35. Univ of Keele BA (2nd cl Phil) 57. St Mich Coll Llan 59. **d** 60 **p** 61 Lich. C of St Mary and St Chad Longton 60-65; Chap St Mary's Cathl Edin 65-69; R of St Matt Possilpark Glas 69-79; H Trin Paisley Dio Glas from 79. *9 Townhead Terrace, Paisley, Renfrew, PA1 3AU.* (041-889 4022)

HANSON, Robert Frank. St Jo Coll Morpeth. ACT Dipl Th 72. **d** and **p** 73 Perth. L to Offic Dio Perth 73-74; C of Spearwood-Willagee 74-77; R of Kambalda-Norseman 77-79; Gosnells-Maddington 79-80; Gosnells Dio Perth from 80. *34 Dorothy Street, Gosnells, W Australia 6110.* (398-4668)

HARADUN, George Francis Gabriel. **d** 56 Maur. d Dio Maur from 56. *16 Willoughby Street, Rose Hill, Mauritius.*

HARARA, Caspar Lonsdale. St Pet Coll Siota 59. **d** 62 **p** 64 Melan. P Dio Melan 62-75; Dio Centr Melan from 75. *Pamua, Makira Region, Solomon Islands.*

HARAWERA, Frederick. b 03. **d** 77 Aotearoa for Wai. C of Whakatane Ruatoki Past Dio Wai from 77. *RD 1, Whakatane, NZ.*

HARAWIRA, Frederick. b 03. **d** 77 **p** 78 Wai. Hon C of Ruatoki-Whakatane Maori Past Dio Wai from 77. *RD1, Whakatane, Bay of Plenty, NZ.*

HARBIDGE, Adrian Guy. b 48. St Jo Coll Dur BA 70. Cudd Coll 73. **d** 75 **p** 76 Southn for Win. C of Romsey 75-80; V of St Andr Bournemouth Dio Win from 80. *53 Bennett Road, Bournemouth, BH8 8QQ.* (Bournemouth 36022)

HARBORD, Charles Derek. b 02. St Mich Coll Llan 24. Barrister (Gray's Inn) 25. **d** 25 **p** 26 S'wark. C of St Luke W Norwood 25-27; St Leon Streatham 27-29; V of Stoke Lyne 29; CF Aldershot 29-30; V of Hindolvestone 30-33; Ch of the Good Shepherd Bromwich 33-35; in RC Ch 35-59; Readmitted into Angl Ch by Bp of Accra and L to Offic Dio Accra 59-61; C of Caterham (in c of St Paul) 61-62; R of St Botolph without Aldgate w H Trin Minories Lon 62-74. *Winterslow, Bayley's Hill, Sevenoaks, Kent.*

HARBORD, Charles Richard Llewellyn. St Jo Coll Manit. **d** 41 **p** 42 Keew. C of St Mark's Miss Norway Ho 41-45; Thompson River Miss 45-47. *Wilson Creek, BC, Canada.*

HARBORD, Philip James. b 56. St Cath Coll Ox BA (Th) 77. St Jo Coll Dur 78. **d** 80 **p** 81 Edmonton for Lon. C of St Andr Enfield Dio Lon from 80. *41 Fir Tree Walk, Enfield, Middx, EN1 3TZ.*

HARBOTTLE, Anthony Hall Harrison. b 25. MVO 79. Ch Coll Cam BA 50, MA 53. Wycl Hall, Ox 50. **d** 52 Dover for Cant **p** 53 Cant. C of Boxley 52-54; St Pet-in-Thanet 54-60; R of Sandhurst w Newenden 60-68; Chap R Chap Windsor Gt Pk 68-81; Chap to HM the Queen from 68; R of E Dean w Friston and Jevington Dio Chich from 81. *East Dean Rectory, Eastbourne, E Sussex.* (E Dean 2366)

HARBOUR, Richard Brian Lindsay. CCC Cam BA 53, MA 57. Ridley Hall Cam 53. **d** 56 **p** 57 Man. C of Harpurhey 56-59; All SS Wel Dio Lich 59-63. *c/o Overseas Missionary Fellowship, PO Box 2217, Manila, Philippines.*

HARBOUR, Ven William Leslie Scott. Univ of NZ BA 49. St Jo Coll NZ, Bd of Th Stud LTh 35. **d** 35 **p** 37 Dun. C of All SS Dun 35-37; V of Winton 37-43; Anderson Bay w Peninsula 43-54; Roslyn 54-65; Hon Can of Dun 54-66; Commiss Melan 63-74; V of St John Invercargill 65-77; Archd of Southland 66-77; Archd (Emer) from 77; P-in-c of Hampden-Maheno-Palmerston 77-78; Hon C of E Otago 78; Chap Cherry Farm Hosp 78-80. *Worcester Street, Hampden, NZ.* (896)

HARCOURT, Giles Sidford. b 36. Westcott Ho Cam 68. **d** 71 **p** 72 Dur. C of Bishopwearmouth 71-73; Fishponds 73-75; Dom Chap to Bp of S'wark 75-78; Publ Pr Dio S'wark 76-79; V of H Trin w St Pet S Wimbledon Dio S'wark from 79. *234 The Broadway, SW19 1SB.* (01-542-7098)

HARCOURT-NORTON, Michael Clive. Selw Coll Cam 2nd cl Law Trip pt i 55, BA (2nd cl Law Trip pt ii) 56, MA 60. Wells Th Coll 56. **d** 58 **p** 59 Chelmsf. C of St Jo Evang Gt Ilford 58-62; NSW State Sec for Austr Coun of Chs 62-68; L to Offic Dio Syd 62-68; Dios Armid, Bath, C & Goulb, Graft, Newc and River 63-66; on leave 68-69; C-in-c of Mortdale Provisional Distr Dio Syd 69-77; R from 77. *112 Morts Road, Mortdale, NSW, Australia 2223.* (57-6852)

HARCUS, Arthur Reginald. b 38. Univ of Lon BD 71, MPhil 78. Kelham Th Coll 58. **d** 63 **p** 64 S'wark. C of Old Charlton 63-69; Warden St Luke's Tr Ho 69-71; Asst Master Price's Coll Fareham 72-78; C of Felpham w Middleton

78-80; P-in-c of Donnington Dio Chich from 80. *65 Stockbridge Road, Chichester, Sussex, PO19 2QE.* (Chich 776395)

HARD, Carl Alfred. **d** 62 Bunb. C of Denmark Dio Bunb from 62. *Denmark, W Australia.*

HARD, Laurence John Hereward. b 13. TD 51. Jes Coll Cam BA 35, MA 45. Westcott Ho Cam 35. **d** 36 Bp Nickson for Heref **p** 37 Heref. C of Ludlow 36-39; Reader 37-39; CF (TA) 39-45; V of All SS Cam 45-73; L to Offic Dio Ely from 73. *58 Radegund Buildings, 58 Jesus Lane, Cambridge, CB5 8BS.* (Cam 55292)

HARDAKER, Ian Alexander. b 32. K Coll Lon and Warm BD and AKC 59. **d** 60 **p** 61 Roch. C of Beckenham 60-65; V of Eynsford w Lullingstone 65-70; St Steph Chatham Dio Roch from 70; RD of Roch from 78. *181 Maidstone Road, Chatham, Kent.* (Medway 49791)

HARDAKER, Leonard. b 24. K Coll Lon and Warm AKC 54. **d** 54 **p** 55 Bradf. C of Menston 54-58; C-in-c of St Martin's Conv Distr Heaton 58-59; V 59-68; Bolney 68-81; Hooe Dio Chich from 81; R of Ninfield Dio Chich from 81. *Ninfield Rectory, Battle, E Sussex, TN33 9JW.*

HARDCASTLE, Frank Rata. b 05. Univ of Lon BA (1st cl Hist) 24, BD 30. King's Coll Lon Collins Pri 29, AKC (1st cl) and Plumptre Pri 30. **d** 30 **p** 31 S'wark. C of H Trin Wimbledon 30-32; St Luke W Norwood (in c of St Paul) 32-38; St Andr (in c of St Francis) Coulsdon 38-47; CF (EC) 44-46; Hon CF 46; V of St Cuthb Firvale Sheff 47-48; PC of St Mich AA Watford 48-69, Chap Holywell Hosp Watford 49-69, Surr 51-69; C of Welwyn (in c of St Mich Woolmer Green) 69-71; Perm to Offic Dio Ex from 71. *30 Ashleigh Road, Exmouth, Devon.* (Exmouth 4491)

HARDCASTLE, Nigel John. b 47. Univ of Reading BSc (Phys) 68. Qu Coll Birm Dipl Th 71. **d** 72 **p** 73 Birm. C of Weoley Castle 72-75; St Andr Handsworth (in c of St Francis) 77-78; V of Garretts Green Dio Birm from 78. *Vicarage, Rotherfield Road, Garretts Green, Birmingham, B26 2SH.* (021-743 2971)

HARDCASTLE, Richard. Univ of Leeds BA 29, MA 31. Coll of Resurr Mirfield, 26. **d** 35 **p** 36 Wakef. C of St Aug Halifax 35-38; St Giles Pontefract 39-43; C-in-c of Gildersome 43-45; V of Gawber 45-54; Batley Carr 54-60; R of Bilsdale Priory 60-75; R of Bilsdale Midcable 60-75; C-in-c of Hawnby 63-75. *c/o St John's Vicarage, Chop Gate, Middlesbrough, Yorks.*

HARDCASTLE, Roger Clive. b 52. Univ of Southn BSc 73. Univ of Birm Dipl Th 77. Qu Coll Birm 75. **d** 78 **p** 79 Liv. C of Walton-on-the-Hill Dio Liv from 78. *Rectory, Walton Village, Liverpool, L4 6TJ.*

HARDIE, Archibald George. b 08. Trin Coll Cam 3rd cl Hist Trip pt i, 29, BA 3rd cl Hist Trip pt ii, 30, MA 35. Westcott Ho Cam 30. **d** 34 **p** 35 Lon. C of All H Lombard Street and Lon Sec SCM 34-36; Commiss Jamaica 50-68; Chap Repton Sch and Publ Pr Dio Derby 36-38; V of St Alb Golders Green 38-44; R of Hexham 44-62; Mercer's Lect 44-62; Surr from 44; Commiss W Indies 45-49; V of Halifax 62-70; RD of Halifax 62-70; Hon Can of Wakef 63-70; V of Haile 70-79; Archd of W Cumb 70-79; Hon Can of Carl 71-79. *c/o Haile Vicarage, Egremont, Cumb, CA22 2PD.* (Beckermet 336)

HARDIE, David John. Edin Th Coll 63. **d** 66 Aber. C of St Mary Aber 66-67; Hon C of Old St Paul Edin 68-70; C of St Pet Lutton Place edin 71-73; P-in-c of St Columba Bathgate 73-76. *c/o Parsonage, Muir Road, Bathgate, West Lothian.* (Bathgate 2292)

HARDIE, John Blair. b 16. MBE 46. Edin Th Coll 73. **d** and **p** 76 Brech (APM). C of St Paul's Cathl Dundee Dio Brech from 76. *4 Lammerton Terrace, Dundee, DD4 7BW.*

HARDIE, Stephen. b 41. K Coll Lon and Warm AKC 67. **d** 68 Lon **p** 69 Willesden for Lon. C of St Andr Roxbourne Harrow 68-73; St Mary Virg-at-Walls Colchester 73-76; R of Wivenhoe Dio Chelmsf from 76. *Wivenhoe Rectory, Colchester, Essex.* (Wivenhoe 5174)

HARDING, Canon Anthony William. b 36. **d** 73 **p** 75 Carib (APM). C of Lillooet 73-74; Lytton 74-80; Dom Chap to Bp of Carib from 80; Can of Carib from 80. *Box 62, Lytton, BC, Canada.* (455-2336)

HARDING, Brian Arthur Carey. Ridley Coll Melb ACT ThL 62. **d** 61 **p** 62 Bal. C of Warrnambool 61-63; Alphington 63; P-in-c of Balmoral 64-66; R 66-69; V of All SS Bal 69; Chap of Bal Gen Hosp 69-77; R of Kyneton Dio Bend from 77. *Rectory, Yaldwin Street, Kyneton, Vic., Australia.* (059-22 1025)

HARDING, Brian Edward. b 38. ALCD 65. **d** 65 **p** 66 Roch. C of Ch Ch Chislehurst 65-68; C-in-c of Baxenden Accrington Dio Blackb 68-70; V from 70. *Vicarage, Langford Street, Baxenden, Lancs, BB5 2RF.* (Accrington 32471)

HARDING, Charles Leslie. Wycl Coll Tor. **d** 30 **p** 31 Ont. I of Pittsburg 30-32; R of Kitley 32-40; Frankford w Stirling 40-43; Actg R of St Mary Magd Picton 43; Chap CASF 43-46; I of Westport 46-48; Chap RCAF 48-58; P-in-c of Walkerville 58-59; R of St Pet Scarborough Tor 59-73. *Apt 604, 2185 Lawrence Avenue East, Scarborough, Ont., Canada.*

HARDING, Charles Wyatt Cater Freeman. Pemb Coll Ox BA 24, MA 28, Cudd Coll 24. **d** 25 **p** 26 Bris. C of St Jo Bapt Bedminster 25-28; St Steph Bournemouth 28-31; St Mary Bournemouth 31-34; V of St Mary W Fordington 34-54; Perm to Offic Dio Bris 59-72; Dio Sarum 63-64. *c/o Messrs Bush & Bush, 9 Whiteladies Road, Clifton, Bristol.*

HARDING, Clifford Maurice. b 22. Univ of Leeds, BA 47. Coll of Resurr Mirfield, 46. **d** 48 **p** 49 Man. C of St Aug Tonge Moor 48-54; Asst P at Blantyre Dio Nyasa 54-56; CF 56-59; V of St John Werneth Oldham 59-65; L to Offic Dio Blackb from 65. *31 Riley Avenue, St Annes, Lytham St Annes, Lancs.* (St Annes 725138)

HARDING, David Anthony. b 30. St Edm Hall, Ox BA (2nd cl Mod Hist) 54, MA 58. Ely Th Coll 54. **d** 56 **p** 57 Lon. C of Fulham 56-59; Lect Armenian Sem Istanbul 59-62; Chap K Sch Cant 63-68; Westmr Sch 68-74; Bede Coll Dur 74-75; Coll of St Hild and St Bede 75-80; Worksop Coll, Worksop from 80. *Worksop College, Worksop, Notts.*

HARDING, Ernest Osbourne. Moore Coll Syd. **d** 42 Syd for Nel **p** 43 Nel. C of Cobden w Runanga 42-44; V 44-47; Picton 47-56; Takaka 56-58; R of Hartley 58-59; Carlton 59-66; St Nich Coogee 66-80; L to Offic Dio Syd from 80. *44 Wideview Road, Berowra Heights, NSW, Australia 2082.* (456-1728)

HARDING, Frederick Arthur. b 16. OOC 75. **d** 77 **p** 78 S'wark. C of Oxted Dio S'wark from 77. *76 Central Way, Oxted, Surrey, RH8 0LY.*

HARDING, Geoffrey Clarence. b 09. MC 44. Late Scho of St Jo Coll Ox BA (2nd cl Lit Hum) 31, 2nd cl Th 32, MA 35. Bps' Coll Cheshunt 32. **d** 32 **p** 33 Lon. C of St Jo Evang Smith Sq Westmr 32-34; St Mark N Audley Street 35-37; Perm to Offic at Hanworth 39-40; V of St Erkenwald Southend 40-43; Chap RAFVR 43-46; L to Offic Dio Sarum 47; Perm to Offic Dio St Alb 50-51; R of Inkpen 51-54; V of Kilmeston w Beauworth 54-57; Perm to Offic Dio Cant 57-60; St Antholin Lect at St Mary Woolnoth Lon 59-62; L to Offic Dio Cant from 60; Dir Chs' Coun of Healing 59-73; C of St Mich Cornhill 70-74; Bp's Chap for Health and Healing Dio Lon from 73; V of St Mary Woolnoth City and Dio Lon from 74. *St Mary Woolnoth, Lombard Street, EC3V 9AN.* (01-626 9701)

HARDING, George Alfred. b 38. Fourah Bay Coll. **d** and **p** 70 Sier L. P Dio Sier L. *92a Kissy Road, Freetown, Sierre Leone.*

HARDING, Herbert Collison. b 1895. **d** and **p** 51 Cov. C of Chilvers-Coton 51-55; V of St Mary Leamington 55-64; Perm to Offic Dio Cov 64-70 and from 74; Dio Ox 71-74. *2 Bridge House, 1 Leam Terrace, Leamington Spa, Warws.*

HARDING, Canon John Ambrose. b 1894. Keble Coll Ox BA 19, MA 20. Ripon Hall, Ox 19. **d** 21 Dover for Cant **p** 22 Cant. C of St Luke Woodside Croydon 21-24; Chipping Barnet 25-26; Chap (Eccles Est) at Kirkee 26-28 and 33-35; Colaba 28-29; Steamer Point Aden 29-31; Ahmedabad 31-33; Ahmednagar 36-38; Mingaladon 38-41; Hon Can of Rangoon 40-49; Can (Emer) from 49; Ch Ch Canton Rangoon 41-42; St D Allahabad 42-45; Agra 45-46; Ranikhet 46; St John Meerut 46-47; Hon CF 47; C of Kingston Jamaica 47-48; Halfway Tree 48-49; L to Offic Dio Jamaica 49-50; Dio Tas 50-52; C of Newtown 52-53; R of Belmont 53-55; Chap at Tangier 55-56; R of St Phil de Torteval Guernsey 56-65; Perm to Offic Dio Win from 66. *Plympton Cottage, Rohais, Guernsey, CI.*

HARDING, John James. b 08. Worc Ordin Coll 60. **d** 62 **p** 63 Ex. C of Highweek 62-64; Blandford Forum and of Langton Long 64-66; V of Stourpaine 66-71; C-in-c of Bockleton w Leysters 71-76. *Address temp unknown.*

HARDING, John Stuart Michael. b 45. St Jo Coll Nottm 79. **d** 81 Southw. C of St Mary Clifton Dio Southw from 81. *6 Myrtus Close, Barton Green, Clifton, Nottingham.*

HARDING, John William Christopher. b 31. St Jo Coll Dur BA (3rd cl Th) 55. **d** 58 Warrington for Liv **p** 59 Liv. C of St Cath Wigan 58-60; St Pet Woolton 60-63; V of Whiston 63-73; St John Birkdale Dio Liv from 73. *17 Kirkstall Road, Birkdale, Southport, Lancs, PR8 4RA.* (Southport 68318)

HARDING, Lyman Nelson. Univ of W Ont BA 60. Bps Univ Lennox LST 63. **d** 63 Niag for Fred **p** 64 Fred. I of Bright 63-66; R of Madawaska 66-71; Ch Ch St Steph 71-74; Exam Chap to Bp of Fred from 72; I of Woodstock Dio Fred from 74. *Box 677, Woodstock, NB, Canada.*

HARDING, Canon Malcolm Alfred Warden. Univ of W Ont BA 59. Hur Coll LTh 62. **d** & **p** 62 Bp Appleyard for Hur for Fred. I of Richibucto and Rexton 62-64; L to Offic Dio Bran 71-73; R of Birtle 73-78; St Geo City and Dio Bran from 78; Can of Bran from 80. *79 Ashgrove Boulevard, Brandon, Manit, Canada.*

HARDING, Mark. Univ of Tas BA 73. Moore Coll Syd ACT BTh 78. BD (Lon) 79. **d** 80 Syd **p** 80 Bp Short for Syd.

C of St Steph Port Kembla Dio Syd from 80. *52 Kelly Street, Berkeley, NSW, Australia 2506.* (71-1289)

HARDING, Michael Anthony John. b 37. Sarum Th Coll 68. **d** 71 **p** 72 S'wark. C of Forest Hill 71-72; Catford 72-74; Leominster 74-77; V of Ditton Priors Dio Heref from 77; R of Neenton Dio Heref from 77; P-in-c of Burwarton w Cleobury N Dio Heref from 77; Aston Botterell w Wheathill and Loughton Dio Heref from 77. *Ditton Priors Vicarage, Bridgnorth, Salop.* (Ditton Priors 636)

HARDING, Michael David. b 38. Univ of Man BA (2nd cl Russian) 61. Lich Th Coll 61. **d** 63 **p** 64 Lich. C of Hednesford 63-67; Blurton 67-70; V of St Paul Newc L Dio Lich from 70. *St Paul's Vicarage, Newcastle-under-Lyme, Staffs, ST5 1HT.* (Newcastle 617913)

HARDING, Michael John. b 48. Selw Coll Cam BA 77. Westcott Ho Cam 76. **d** 78 **p** 79 S'wark. C of St Mich AA Abbey Wood 78-81; St Jo w St Bart Bethnal Green Dio Lon from 81. *Vicarage, Buckhurst Street, Bethnal Green, E1 5QT.* (01-247 8013)

HARDING, Peter Edward. b 39. Univ Coll Ox BA (2nd cl Geol) 61, MA 69. Wycl Hall Ox 62. **d** 64 **p** 65 Lich. C of St Andr Conv Distr Westlands Newc L 64-67; H Trin Hinckley 67-69; R of Sutton w Duckmanton 69-75; C-in-c of Shardlow w Gt Wilne, Elvaston, Thulston and Ambaston Dio Derby from 75. *Elvaston Vicarage, Thulston, Derby, DE7 3EQ.* (Derby 71790)

HARDING, Peter Gordon. b 45. BA (Lon) 70. St Jo Coll Dur Dipl Th 79. **d** 79 **p** 80 Wakef. C of Kirkheaton Dio Wakef from 79. *423 Wakefield Road, Dalton, Huddersfield, W Yorks.*

HARDING, Peter Richard. b 46. K Coll Lon AKC 69. St Aug Coll Cant 69. **d** 70 **p** 71 Lanc for Blackb. C of St Pet, Chorley 70-73; Ribbleton (in c of St Anne) 73-74; St Marylebone w H Trin 74-80; P-in-c of St Cypr Clarence Gate Dio Lon from 80. *16 Clarence Gate Gardens, Glentworth Street, NW1 6AY.* (01-262 0781)

HARDING, Raymond Edgar Charles. b 21. Keble Coll Ox BA 48, MA 53. Wells Th Coll 52. **d** 54 B & W **p** 55 Taunton for B & W. C of H Trin Yeovil 54-57; R of N w S Barrow 57-68; V of Lovington 57-68; V of St Mary Virg Frome Selwood Dio B & W from 68. *St Mary's Vicarage, Innox Hill, Frome, Somt.* (Frome 2737)

HARDING, Roderick Osbourne. b 46. Moore Coll Syd ThL 71. **d** and **p** 73 Syd. C of St Matt Manley 73-74; Gladesville 74-76; R of Campsie Dio Syd from 77. *71 Angelo Road, Campsie, NSW, Australia 2194.* (78-2879)

HARDING, Rolf John. b 22. Lon Coll Div 46. **d** 49 **p** 50 S'wark. C of H Trin Sydenham 49-52; St Pet Harold Wood 52-53; Min of Legal Distr of St Paul Harold Hill Hornchurch 53-61; V of Coopersale Dio Chelmsf from 61. *Coopersale Vicarage, Epping, Essex.* (Epping 2188)

HARDING, Warren John. Univ of Tor BA 64. Trin Coll Tor STB 67. **d** 67 **p** 68 Alg. C of Huntsville 67-69; on leave. *Apt 1401, 50 Hillsboro Avenue, Toronto, Ont., Canada.*

HARDING, William Douglas. Univ of NZ MA 40. NZ Bd of Th Studies LTh 41. **d** 41 **p** 42 Ch Ch. C of Ashburton 41-45; P-in-c of Kumara 45-46; V 46-47; Little River 47-53; Prebbleton 53-56; Hornby 57-59; Asst Hosps Chap Dio Ch Ch 59-65; Sen Chap from 65. *141 Rose Street, Christchurch 2, NZ.* (326-572)

HARDINGHAM, Paul David. b 52. Univ of Lon BSc 74. Fitzwm Coll Cam BA 77. Ridley Hall Cam 75. **d** 78 Ely **p** 79 Huntingdon for Ely. C of St Martin Cam 78-81; Clayton Mem Ch Jesmond City and Dio Newc T from 81. *2 Otterburn Villas North, Otterburn Terrace, Newcastle-upon-Tyne, NE2 3AS.* (Newc T 810491)

HARDMAN, Bryan Edwin. Selw Coll Cam PhD 64. BD (1st cl) Lon 60. Moore Th Coll Syd ACT ThL 54. **d** and 55 Syd. C of Hurstville 55-57; Summer Hill 57; Hurstville 57-60; Perm to Offic Dio Ely 60-65; V of St Andr L Cam 65-68; Perm to Offic Dio Adel 68-69 and from 80; Dio Murray 69-79. *176 Wattle Street, Malvern, S Australi 5061.*

HARDMAN, Edward Foster. b 02. St Chad's Coll Dur BA 23, Dipl in Th 24, MA 27. **d** 26 **p** 28 Ripon. C of St Luke Beeston Hill Leeds 26-30; St Pet Barcaldine 31-33; Actg R 33-34; R 34-35; C of Chapel Allerton 36-37; St Luke Conv Distr Scarborough 37-38; C-in-c 38-42; V of St Luke York 42-49; C of Whitby (in c of St Ninian) 49-57; C of Blantyre 57-64; Chap All SS Conv Lon Colney 65-68. *8 Clifton Drive, Lytham, Lancs, FY8 5RE.*

HARDMAN, Frank. b 09. Lon Coll Div 51. **d** 53 **p** 54 Man. C of Urmston 53-56; V of St Aug Bradf 56-62; Eston w Normanby 62-73; R of Rowley 73-76. *68 Wrenbeck Drive, Otley, W Yorks.* (Otley 463624)

HARDMAN, Geoffrey James. b 41. Univ of Birm BA 63. N Ordin Course 77. **d** 80 Ches **p** 81 Birkenhead for Ches. C of St Jas Latchford Dio Ches from 80. *43 Chester Road, Stockton Heath, Warrington, Cheshire.*

HARDMAN, Harry. b 10. Egerton Hall, Man 36. **d** 38 **p** 39 Blackb. C of St Paul Scotforth 38-40; St Pet Burnley 40-43; Actg C of Preston 43-44; C of Fleetwood (in c of St Nich) 44-49; V of St Cath Burnley 49-54; Chatburn 54-59; Chap City Sherwood St Francis and Firs Hosps Nottm 59-68; V of Fence-in-Pendle 68-75; Publ Pr Dio Blackb from 75. *30 Red Lees Avenue, Burnley, Lancs, BB10 4JE.* (Burnley 21149)

HARDMAN, Maurice Alvin Edward. Univ of Manit BA 45, MA 52. St Jo Coll Manit LTh 48, BD 49. **d** 48 **p** 49 Rupld. C of St Geo Winnipeg 48-50; R of Stonewall 50-53; LPr Dio Rupld 53-59; C of St John's Cathl Winnipeg 59-67; Hon C of St Mich AA Winnipeg Dio Rupld from 67. *889 Warsaw Avenue, Winnipeg 9, Manit, Canada.*

HARDMAN, Peter George. b 35. Univ of Man BSc 56. Ridley Hall, Cam 58. **d** 60 **p** 61 Man. C of St Paul Oldham 60-63; NW Area Sec SCM in Schs 63-64; CEM 64-67; LPr Dio Man 63-67; Asst Chap Marlborough Coll 67-72; Chap 72-79; P-in-c of Wareham Dio Sarum 79-80; Team R from 80. *Rectory, Wareham, Dorset BH20 4LQ.* (Wareham 2684)

HARDWICK, Alfred Robert. Univ of New Engl BA 69. St Jo Coll Morpeth ACT ThL 57. **d** 58 **p** 60 Graft. C-in-c of Wyan Rappville 58-59; C of Lismore 59-61; V of Lower Macleay 61-65; Mallanganee 65-70; R of Dorrigo 70-73; Kingscliff Dio Graft from 73. *Rectory, Kingscliff, NSW, Australia 2413.* (74 1513)

HARDWICK, Graham John. b 42. Qu Coll Birm 68. **d** 70 **p** 71 St Alb. C of St Mich AA Watford 70-73; N Mymms 73-75; Cathl Youth Chap Dio Cov 75-81; Chap Lanchester Poly 76-81; V of Nuneaton Dio Cov from 81. *61 Ambleside Way, Nuneaton, Warws, CV11 6AU.* (Nuneaton 346900)

HARDWICK, John Audley. b 28. Em Coll Cam BA 51, MA 55. Westcott Ho Cam 51. **d** 53 **p** 54 York. C of Selby 53-56; Chap and Asst Master St Edm Sch Hindhead 56-60 and 63-64; Ho Master 64-74; Asst Hd Master from 71; Aysgarth Sch Bedale 60-63. *St Edmund's School, Hindhead, Surrey.*

HARDWICK, Canon William George. b 16. Lich Th Coll 40. **d** 44 **p** 45 Pet. C of Ch Ch Northampton 44-46; St Paul Leic 46-49; Dir of Tsikoane Miss and R of Leribe 49-52; R of Mtubatuba 52-72; Can of Zulu 69-72; Can (Emer) from 73; R of Umkomaas w Scottsburg 73-76; St Jas Greytown 76-78; V of Brigstock w Stanion 78-79; Bellair 79-81; Verulam Dio Natal from 81. *Box 9, Maidstone 4380, Natal, S Africa.*

HARDWICKE, Paul Anthony. b 49. Linc Th Coll 74. **d** 77 **p** 78 Lich. C of St Pet Rickerscote Stafford 77-79; Tamworth Dio Lich from 79. *The Parsonage, Masefield Drive, Leyfields, Tamworth, Staffs.* (Tamworth 4918)

HARDY, Bertram Frank. b 08. Lich Th Coll 51. **d** and **p** 52 Pet. [f Bapt Ch] C of Isham 52; Kettering 52-54; V of Mears Ashby 54-57; R of Hardwycke 54-57; Pingelly W Austr 57-61; Kojonup W Austr 61-64; Morchard Bp 64-69; C-in-c of N w S Barrow 69-74; Lovington 69-74; Perm to Offic Dio B & W from 74. *7 Churchill Avenue, Wells, Somt, BA5 3JE.* (Wells 74696)

HARDY, Preb Brian Albert. b 31. St Jo Coll Ox BA 54, Dipl in Th 55, MA 58. Westcott Ho Cam. **d** 57 **p** 58 Lich. C of Rugeley 57-62; Chap Down Coll Cam and Perm to Offic Dio Ely 62-66; C-in-c of Livingston Miss Edin 66-74; Chs Planning Officer for Telford 74-78; Preb of Heref Cathl from 74; RD of Telford Severn Gorge 75-78; Chap Edin Th Coll from 78; R of St Columba City and Dio Edin from 82. *9 Ramsay Garden, Edinburgh, EH1 2NA.* (031-225 1634)

HARDY, Donald William. Trin Coll Melb BA 50, ACT ThL 51, Th Scho 66. **d** 51 **p** 52 Bal. C of Horsham 51; P-in-c of Hopetoun 52-56; Wendouree 56-62; Belmont w Marshall 62-69; St Geo E Ivanhoe 69-74; I of St Andr Brighton 74-79; St Faith Burwood Dio Melb from 79. *4 Charles Street, Burwood, Vic, Australia 3125.*

HARDY, Ian Alexander. Ridley Coll Melb. Moore Th Coll Syd 64, ACT ThL 67. **d** 67 Willoch **p** 68 Adel for Willoch. C of Port Pirie 67-74; Assoc R 74-75; R of Auburn-Riverton Dio Willoch from 75. *Box 45, Riverton, S Australia 5412.*

HARDY, John Charles. b 22. Univ of Sheff BA (2nd cl Hist) 48. Dipl Th (Lon) 53. **d** 67 **p** 68 Blackb. Hon C of Chorley Dio Blackb from 67. *4 Glamis Drive, Chorley, Lancs, PR7 1LX.* (Chorley 65743)

HARDY, John Lewis Daniel. b 26. St Chad's Coll Dur BA 51, Dipl Th 52. **d** 52 **p** 53 Southw. C of Hucknall Torkard 52-58; V of Harworth 58-65; Sutton-in-Ashfield Dio Southw from 65; Surr from 69. *Vicarage, Sutton-in-Ashfield, Notts.* (Mansfield 54509)

HARDY, Michael Frederick Bryan. b 36. Selw Coll Cam 2nd cl Th Trip pt i 58, BA (2nd cl Th Trip pt ii) 60. Linc Th Coll 60. **d** 62 Wakef **p** 63 Pontefract for Wakef. C of Pontefract 62-66; Lightcliffe 66-69; V of Hightown 69-77; St Cuthb Birkby Huddersfield Dio Wakef from 77. *5 Grimscar Avenue, Birkby, Huddersfield, HD2 2TY.* (Huddersfield 24071)

HARDY, Michael John. b 35. Keble Coll Ox BA 58, MA 66. Cudd Coll Ox 59. **d** 61 Penrith for Carl **p** 62 Carl. C of Dalton-in-Furness 61-64; Harborne 64-68; Min Can of Ripon Cathl 68-73; C of Ripon w Littlethorpe 68-73; Appointment and Tr Sec USPG 73-80; Perm to Offic Dio S'wark 73-80; R of St Pet Stretford Dio Man from 80. *24 Canute Road, Stretford, Manchester, M32 0RJ.* (061-865 1802)

HARDY, Michael Wilfred. St Chads Coll Dur BA 52. Coll of Resurr Mirfield. **d** 54 **p** 55 Newc T. C of St Geo Cullercoats 54-57; R of Qacha's Nek 58-62; C of All SS Gosforth 66-69; Bush Bro of St Barn Collinsville 69-70; Chap Cloncurry Dio N Queensld from 70. *Cloncurry, Queensland, Australia.*

HARDY, Canon Paul Richard. K Coll Cam 2nd cl Nat Sc Trip pt i, 51, BA (2nd cl Nat Sc Trip pt ii) 52, MA 56. St Steph Ho Ox 57. **d** 59 **p** 60. Chelmsf. C of Corringham 59-61; All SS Southend-on-Sea 61-64; Chap Univ Coll Dar-es-Salaam and L to Offic Dio Zanz 64-65; Dio Dar-S 65-77; Admin Sec Dio Dar-S from 69; Can of Dar-S from 74; P-in-c of St Alb City and Dio Dar-S from 77. *PO Box 2184, Dar-es-Salaam, Tanzania.* (051-63151)

HARDY, Reginald Robert. d 61 **p** 62 Newc. R of Gundy (w Aberdeen from 66) 62-69; Kendall 69-70; Malmsbury 70-73; Perm to Offic Dio Newc from 73. *29 Princess Street, Cundletown, NSW, Australia 2430.*

✠ **HARDY, Right Rev Robert Maynard.** b 36. Clare Coll Cam 1st cl Hist Trip pt i, 59, BA (2nd cl Th Trip pt ia) 60, MA 64. Cudd Coll 60. **d** 62 Hulme for Man **p** 63 Man. C of St Aid Conv Distr Langley 62-64; All SS and Marts Langley 64-65; Fell, Chap and Lect in Th Selw Coll Cam 65-72; V of Borehamwood 72-75; C-in-c of Aspley Guise 75-80; R (w Husborne Crawley and Ridgmont) 80; C-in-c of Husborne Crawley 76-80; Cons Bp Suffr of Maidstone in Cant Cathl 29 Nov 80 by Abp of Cant; Bps of St Alb and Roch; Bps Suffr of Dover, Hertf, Bedford, Tonbridge and Croydon; and Bps Hook, Isherwood, J Hughes and Warner; Chairman C of E Nat Coun for Social Aid from 81. *Bishop's House, Egerton, Ashford, Kent, TN27 9DJ.* (Egerton 431)

HARDY, Thomas Woodburn. b 26. Bps' Univ Lennox BA 48. **d** 49 **p** 50 Queb. C of Sherbrooke 49-52; P-in-c of Shigawake w Port Daniel 52-54; Miss at Magd Is 54-57; C of Gt Bookham Surrey 57-59; R of E Angus PQ 59-62; C of St Osw w St Aug Fulham 62-68; C-in-c 68-73; V of St Aug of Hippo Fulham Dio Lon from 73. *257 Lillie Road, SW6.* (01-385 5760)

HARDY, William Dalrymple. b 07. Pemb Coll Cam 3rd cl Engl Trip pt i, 34, pt ii, 35, BA 36, MA 39. Westcott Ho Cam 36. **d** 37 **p** 38 Bris. C of Horfield 37-40; Chippenham 40-41; V of Bucklebury w Marlston 41-58; R of Gatcombe 58-60; V of Sunningdale 60-66; R of Horne 66-72; P-in-c of Arlington 79-80; Perm to Offic Dio Chich from 80. *Little Lions, Arlington, Polegate, Sussex, BN26 6SE.* (Alfriston 807864)

HARDY, William Marshall Conyers. b 25. Linc Th Coll 55. **d** 56 **p** 57 Newc T. C of H Cross Fenham Newc T 56-60; Wooler 60-62; V of Belford 62-77; RD of Bamburgh and Glendale 71-77; V of Riding Mill Dio Newc T from 77. *Vicarage, Riding Mill, Northumb, NE44 6AB.* (Riding Mill 240)

HARE, Christopher Henry. b 10. CCC Ox 3rd cl Lit Hum 33, BA 34, MA 39. Wells Th Coll 36. **d** 37 **p** 38 Chelmsf. C of Hornchurch 37-39; Min Can and Sacr of Ely Cathl and Asst Master Cathl Choir Sch 39-41; Prec of Ely Cathl and PC of Chettisham 41-43; Chap RNVR 42-44; Min Can St Geo Chap Windsor 44-54; C of Eton 45-54; R of Taplow 54-77; P-in-c Dropmore 69-77; Chap Canad Red Cross Mem Hosp Taplow from 54. *5 Bannard Road, Maidenhead, Berks, SL6 4NG.* (Maidenhead 27368)

HARE, Frank Richard Knight. b 22. Trin Hall Cam BA (2nd cl Hist Trip pt i) 46, MA 48. Cudd Coll 46. **d** 48 **p** 49 St E. C of Dennington and Badingham 48-51; Eastbourne 51-54; R of Rotherfield 54-62; V of Steyning 62-70; R of Ashurst 62-70; V in Raveningham Group 70-71; R of Barnham Broom Group 71-79; V of Buxton w Oxnead Dio Nor from 79; R of Lammas w L Hautbois Dio Nor from 79. *Buxton Vicarage, Norwich, NR10 5HD.* (Buxton 225)

HARE, George Harry. b 15. Qu Coll Birm. **d** 63 **p** 64 Cant. C of St Lawr-in-I-of-Thanet 63-68; Minster-in-Sheppey 68-71; V of Thurnham w Detling 71-77; Perm to Offic Dio Cant form 79. *24 Ulcombe Gardens, Canterbury, Kent, CT2 7QY.* (Canterbury 69236)

HARE, Stanley Thomas. b 23. Roch Th Coll. **d** 62 **p** 63 York. C of St Lawr York 62; Newland (in c of St Faith Miss) 63-65; R of Sutton w Duckmanton 65-69; V of St Barn Sheff 69-73; Chap Farnborough and Orpington Hosps from 73. *15 Warren Gardens, Chelsfield, Kent.* (Farnborough 51751)

✠ **HARE, Right Rev Thomas Richard.** b 22. Trin Coll Ox BA 48, MA 53. Westcott Ho Cam 48. **d** 50 **p** 51 Newc T. C of Haltwhistle 50-52; Dom Chap to Bp of Man and LPr Dio Man 52-59; Can Res of Carl 59-65; Hon Can 65-71; Exam Chap to Bp of Man 59-66; Archd of Westmorland and Furness 65-71; V of St Geo w St Luke Barrow-F 65-69; Winster 69-71; Cons Ld Bp Suffr of Pontefract in York Minster 21 Sept 71 by Abp of York; Bps of Blackb; Bradf; Sheff; Carl; Liv; Wakef; Man; Southw; Bps Suffr of Whitby; Selby; Hull; Burnley; Penrith; Bps Bevan; Gerard; Ramsbotham; Shearburn; Bloomer; Skelton. *306 Barnsley Road, Wakefield, WF2 6AX.* (Wakefield 256935)

✠ **HARE DUKE, Right Rev Michael Geoffrey.** b 25. Trin Coll Ox 2nd cl Lit Hum 49, BA (2nd cl Th) 50, MA 51. Westcott Ho Cam **d** 52 **p** 53 Lon. C of St John's Wood Ch (f St Steph St Marylebone) 52-56; V of St Mark Bury 56-62; Pastoral Dir Clinical Th Centre Nottm 62-64; Consultant 64-69; V of Daybrook 64-69; C-in-c of Bestwood Pk 68-69; Cons Ld Bp of St Andr, Dunk and Dunbl in St Ninian's Cathl Perth 16 Sept 69 by Bp of Glas (Primus); Bps of Moray; Aber; Brech; Edin; and Southw; Asst Bps of Edin; and Newc T. *Bishop's House, Fairmount Road, Perth.* (Perth 21580)

HARES, David Ronald Walter. b 40. Qu Coll Cam BA 63, MA 67. Westcott Ho Cam 64. **d** 66 **p** 67 Lich. C of Cannock 66-69; Chap of Peterho Cam 69-72; Asst Master Chesterton Sch Cam 72-74; V of Kesgrave Dio St E from 74. *Kesgrave Vicarage, Ipswich, Suff.* (Ipswich 622181)

HARES, Canon Walter Ronald Frederick. b 10. Em Coll Cam BA 33, MA 37. Ridley Hall, Cam 33. Lon Coll of Div 35. **d** 35 **p** 36 Roch. C of St Paul Chatham 35-37; St Nich N Walsham 37-38; Chap (Eccles Est) St Paul's Cathl Calc 38; Quetta 38-39; Razmak 39-40; Risalpur 40-42 and 44-45; Field Service Irak and Burma 42-44; Ambala w Sabuthu 45-46; furlough 46; Karachi 46-47; R of Boddington 48-50; Beccles 5o-63; RD of Beccles 53-63; Hon Can of St E 58-63. R of St Pet Port Guernsey 63-76; Hon Can of Win 73-76; Can (Emer) from 76; Perm to Offic Dio St E from 76. *45 Bredfield Road, Woodbridge, Suff.* (Woodbridge 2875)

HAREWOOD, Ivan Henderson. b 40. **d** 76 Derby **p** 77 Southw. C of All SS Mickleover 76-77; Radcliffe-on-Trent Dio Southw from 77. *19 Cropwell Road, Radcliffe-on-Trent, Nottingham.*

HAREWOOD, John Rupert. b 24. Univ of Man BA 48. Sarum Wells Th Coll 76. **d** 79 **p** 80 B & W (APM). C of St Jas Taunton Dio B & W from 79. *59 Parmin Way, Taunton, Somerset, TA1 2JX.*

HARFIELD, William Charles. b 04. **d** 36 **p** 36 Perth. C of Northam 36-37; R of Narembeen and Corrigin 37-39; Pinjarra and Chap AMF 39-41; Chap AIF 41-45; Perm to Offic Dio Perth 43-45; R of York 45-47; C of Davenham 47-49; V of Turner's Hill 49-52; CF 52-55; Hon CF 55; R of Denton w S Heighton and Tarring Neville 55-58; V of St Elis Eastbourne 58-64; R of Lurgashall w Roundhurst 64-68; Stedham w Iping 68-75. *Briarwood, Vanzell Road, Easebourne, Midhurst, W Sussex.* (Midhurst 3810)

HARFORD, Canon Christopher Edward Audley. b 07. Late Scho of Magd Coll Cam 2nd Cl Trip pt i, 28, BA (2nd cl Th Trip pt i) 30, MA 34. Wells Th Coll 30. **d** 31 **p** 32 Cant. C of All SS Maidstone 31-36; Walmer 36-40; V of Bramford w Burstall 40-48; R of Chipstead 48-72; Hon Can of S'wark 72; (Emer from 72); Publ Pr Dio S'wark from 73. *43 Watermill Close, Ham, Richmond, Surrey, TW10 7UJ.* (01-940 8489)

HARFORD, John Murray. St Jo Coll Auckld LTh 65. **d** 65 **p** 66 Auckld. C of St Mark Remuera Auckld 65-68; Kaitaia 69-71; V of Coromandel 71-73; CF (NZ) from 73; Hon C of Taihape 73-77. *22 Cameron Street, Papakura, NZ.* (299-9370)

HARFORD, Julian Gray. Univ Coll Ox BA (3rd cl Mod Lang) 52, MA 59. Univ of Birm Dipl Th 64. Qu Coll Birm. **d** 64 Southn for Win **p** 65 Win. C of West End 64-67; C-in-c Chearsley w Nether Winchendon 67-77; C of Chilton 72-77; V of Westbury w Turweston, Shalstone and Biddlesden Dio Ox from 77. *Westbury Vicarage, Brackley, Northants, NN13 5JT.* (Brackley 704964)

HARFORD, Michael Rivers Dundas. Trin Coll Cam BA (3rd cl Th Trip) 49, MA 51. Westcott Ho Cam 50. **d** 52 **p** 53 Blackb. C of Ashton-on-Ribble 52-55; Perm to Offic Dio Edin 55-56; C of St Andr Cathl Sing and Chap Univ of Malaya 56-60; C of St Mary Kuala Lumpur Selangor 60-62; V 62-66; St D Childwall 66-71; R of Katanning 71-76; Albany 76-79; Exam Chap to Bp of Bunb 73-79; Archd of Albany 76-79; R of Bicton-Attadale Dio Perth from 79. *118 Waddell Road, Bicton, W Australia 6157.* (330 4938)

HARGER, Robin Charles Nicholas. b 49. Sarum Wells Th Coll 78. **d** 81 Glouc. C of St Mary Charlton Kings Dio Glouc from 81. *3 Copt Elm Road, Charlton Kings, Cheltenham, Glos.* (Cheltm 519095)

HARGRAVE, William Stallard Lawrence. b 01. G and C Coll Cam BA 27, MA 31. **d** and **p** 42 Worc. C of St Anne Bewdley 42-45; R of Salwarpe 45-48; PC of Wilden 48-50; R of Abberley 50-55; Bincombe w Broadwey 55-66; RD of Weymouth 62-64; L to Offic Dio Sarum from 66. *2 King Street, Wilton, Salisbury, Wilts.*

HARGREAVE, James David. b 44. Univ of Lon BA 66.

Univ of Leeds Dipl Th 72. Coll of Resurr Mirfield 70. **d** 73 **p** 74 Dur. C of Houghton-le-Spring 73-77; St Cuthb w St Paul Gateshead 77-79; V of Trimdon Dio Dur from 79. *Vicarage, Trimdon Village, Co Durham.* (Trimdon 880430)

HARGREAVES, Arthur Cecil Monsarrat. b 19. Trin Hall Cam BA 42, MA 46, 1st cl Th Trip pt i 47. Westcott Ho Cam 47. **d** 49 **p** 50 Lon. C of Wembley 49-52; Lect Bps' Coll Calc 52-58; Vice-Prin 58-61; Asia Sec CMS from 61-69; Nat Chr Coun India 70-72; Lect United Th Coll Bangalore 72-76; Gen Sec Conf of Br Miss Societies 76-79; C of St Aug Croydon 79-81; V of Marden Dio Cant from 81. *Marden Vicarage, Tonbridge, Kent, TN12 9DR.* (Maidstone 831379)

HARGREAVES, Gordon Russell. Ridley Coll Melb ACT ThL 75. **d** 76 **p** 77 Melb. C of St Bart Ferntree Gully 76-78; P-in-c of Healesville Dio Melb from 78. *Vicarage, Symons Street, Healesville, Vic, Australia 3777.* (059-62 4105)

HARGREAVES, Herbert Price. b 1890. MC 18. Pemb Coll Cam 3rd cl Math Trip pt i, 10, BA 12, MA 16. Ridley Hall Cam 12. **d** 14 **p** 15 Ripon. C of Bradf Yorks 14-17; TCF 17-19; C of W Ham 19-20; Min at Owo 21 and 23-24; Actg Vic-Prin of St Andr Coll Oyo 21-22 and 24-25; CMS Supt at Ado Ekiti 24-27; Warden of Melville Hall Oyo 27; Supervisor of CMS Schs Dio Lagos 28-29; Chap Wellington Coll 29-34; L to Offic Dio Ox 31-34; PC of Ripley 34-49; V of Newtown Linford 49-68; RD of Sparkenhoe iii 54-59; L to Offic Dio Win from 68. *Langdale, Fairfield Road, Shawford, Winchester, Hants.* (Twyford 712201)

HARGREAVES, James Ronald. b 33. BD (Lon) 60. Oak Hill Th Coll 57. **d** 61 **p** 62 Man. C of Rusholme 61-64; New Malden 64-67; V of St Barn Cray 67-75; Egham Dio Guildf from 75; RD of Runnymede from 78. *Vicarage, Vicarage Road, Egham, Surrey.* (Egham 32066)

HARGREAVES, Canon John Henry Monsarrat. b 11. Trin Coll Cam 3rd cl Cl Trip pt i, 32, BA (2nd cl Th Trip pt i) 33, MA 37. Westcott Ho Cam 35. **d** 37 **p** 38 Dur. C of Bp Wearmouth 37-39; Hunslet (in c of St Chad) 39-43; CMS Miss at Oyo 43-49; Tutor at Union Th Coll Dio Niger 49-51; Melville Hall Ibad 51-54; Sec CMS Dio N Nig 54-57; C of Kens Lon 57-58; St Mich w Childwick St Alb 58-60; Warden Buwalasi Th Coll Ugan 61-63; w CMS Lon 63-65; Min of St Luke's Conv Distr Sevenoaks Dio Roch from 65; RD of Sevenoaks 74-79; Hon Can of Roch Cathl from 81. *St Luke's Parsonage, Eardley Road, Sevenoaks, Kent.* (Sevenoaks 52462)

HARGREAVES, John Rodney. b 36. Open Univ BA 74. St Deiniol's Libr Hawarden 74. **d** 74 **p** 75 Mon. [f Methodist Min] C of Pontypool 75-77; Llanedeyrn 77-79; Chap HM Pris Aylesbury from 79. *c/o HM Prison, Aylesbury, Bucks.* (0296-24435)

HARGREAVES, Raymond. b 41. Open Univ BA 79. Ripon Hall Ox 72. **d** 73 **p** 74 Carl. C of Stanwix 73-78; Chap St Pet Sch York from 78. *32 Forest Gate, Haxby, York, YO3 8WT.* (York 763127)

HARGREAVES, Reginald Cecil Collwyn. King's Coll Cam BA 23, MA 27. Cudd Coll 23. **d** 24 **p** 25 Glouc. C of Cheltm 24-29; R of Springfield 29-47; Chap RNVR 41-46; V of Beverley Minster 47-58; RD of Beverley 53-58; R of Batsford w Morton-in-Marsh 58-66; C-in-c of Bp Burton 58. *Bridge End Cottage, Walhampton, Lymington, Hants.*

HARGREAVES-STEAD, Terence Desmond. Edin Th Coll 60. **d** 63 Penrith for Carl **p** 64 Carl. C of Walney I 63-66; Chap Withington Hosp Man 66-72; V of St Paul Westleigh Leigh Dio Man from 72. *Vicarage, Westleigh Lane, Leigh, Lancs.* (0942-882883)

HARIKIPA, Patrick Piriri. Newton Coll Dogura 69. **d** 75 Bp Ambo for Papua. d Dio Papua. *c/o Box 304, Lae, Papua New Guinea.*

HARINGTON, Roger John Urquhart. b 48. Trin Hall Cam BA 70, MA 74. Coll of Resurr Mirfield 72. **d** 75 Warrington for Liv **p** 76 Liv. C of Our Lady & St Nich Liv 75-78; Asst Chap Leeds Univ and Poly 78-81; Team V of Moor Allerton Dio Ripon from 81. *St Stephen's House, Cranmer Road, Leeds, LS17 5DR.* (Leeds 687338)

HARKER, Brian Douglas. Moore Th Coll Syd ACT ThL 55. **d** 55 **p** 58 Armid. C of Quirindi 55-56; Gunnedah 56-59; P-in-c of Boggabilla 60-61; C of St Paul Islington 62; St Mich AA Sydenham 63-65; Perm to Offic Dio Adel 65-66; Dio Syd from 72; C of Hawthorn 66-68; P-in-c of Glenelg N 68-72. *2/23b Albert Parade, Ashfield, NSW, Australia 2192.*

HARKER, Donald Frederick. b 45. St Pet Coll Alice Dipl Th 69. **d** 69 **p** 70 Geo. C of All SS Mossel Bay 69-74; P-in-c of Beaufort W 74-77; Albertinia Dio Geo from 77. *Box 7, Albertinia, CP, S Africa.* (Albertinia 127)

HARKER, Hugh Alfred. Univ of Leeds BA (2nd cl Hist) 37. Coll of Resurr Mirfield 37. **d** 39 Willesden for Lon **p** 40 Lon. C of H Cross Greenford 39-44; Chap RNVR 44-46; Chap St Andr Coll Grahmstn 47-62; Dir of Usuthu Miss 62-63; Chap St Andr Sch Bloemf 63-67; C of Rosebank 67-71; R of Parkmore 71-80; Tugela Rivers Dio Natal from 80. *PO Box 94, Bergville, Natal, S Africa.*

HARKER, Ian. b 39. Univ of Dur BA (2nd cl Hist) 61. Lich Th Coll. **d** 63 **p** 64 Wakef. C of Knottingley 63-66; Youth Worker 66-70; Perm to Offic Dio Wakef 66-70; Dir Blenheim Project Lon (attached Notting Hill Group Min) 70-75; Master St Thos Mart City and Dio Newc T from 75; Chap Univ of Newc T 75-79. *14 Summer Hill Street, Newcastle-upon-Tyne.* (Newc T 736749)

HARKER, Ven Peter. Univ of Leeds BA 49. Coll of Resurr Mirfield 49. **d** 51 **p** 52 Natal. C of St Jas Durban 51-54; St Aug Miss 55-57; Dir Isandhlwana Miss 57-65; Can of St Mich Pro-Cathl Eshowe 62; Archd of W Zulu 63-65; E Zulu 65-67; S Zulu 67-79; E Zulu from 79; R of Kwamagwaza 65-69; Melmoth 69-70; H Cross Empangeni Dio Zulu from 70. *Rectory, PO Box 55, Empangeni, Zululand.* (Empangeni 82)

HARKER, Stephan John. b 47. Em Coll Cam 2nd cl Nat Sc Trip pt ia 66, pt ib 67, 3rd cl pt ii BA 68, 2nd cl Th Trip pt ia 69, MA 72. Westcott Ho Cam 70. **d** 72 Lanc for Blackb **p** 73 Blackb. C of Marton 72-76; St Matt Preston 76-79; Fleetwood 79-81. *Charterhouse, Godalming, Surrey.*

HARKNESS, Verney Austin Barnett. b 19. BA (Lon) 40, Dipl Th (Lon) 63. Ridley Hall Cam 46. **d** 47 **p** 48 Carl. C of Cockermouth 47-50; Chap of Kabwangasi Vernacular Teacher Tr Centre Dio U Nile 50-53; R of The Shelsleys 53-56; V of H Trin Bris 56-60; Lect at St Osyth's Tr Coll Clacton-on-Sea 60-63; Publ Pr Dio Chelmsf 60-63; R of Stoke-next-Guildf 63-72; Chap Trin Coll Kandy 73-77; P-in-c of Walkington 78-79; Bp Burton 78-79; R of Bishop Burton w Walkington Dio York from 79. *Walkington Rectory, Beverley, N Humb, HU17 8SP.* (0482-868379)

HARLAND, Albert Henry. b 17. Oak Hill Th Coll 57. **d** 59 Argent **p** 61 Newc T. SAMS Miss 59-60; C of Jesmond 61-63; C-in-c of Dowdeswell 63-68; V of Renhold 69-80. *123 Putnoe Lane, Bedford, MK41 8LB.* (Bedford 45831)

HARLAND, Frederick Campbell. Univ of Tas BA 68. ACT ThDip 70. Ch Coll Hobart 60. **d** 68 **p** 69 Tas. C of H Trin Hobart 68-73; Hon C of Sandy Bay Dio Tas from 73. *42 Wellesley Street, South Hobart, Tasmania 7000.* (002-23 1485)

HARLAND, Harold William James. b 35. Hertf Coll Ox BA 59, MA 63. Clifton Th Coll 59. **d** 61 **p** 62 S'wark. C of Reigate 61-64; Farnborough 64-68; V of Walmley 68-74; Ch Ch Bromley Dio Roch from 74. *18 Highland Road, Bromley, Kent, BR1 4AD.* (01-460 4864)

HARLAND, Ven Ian. b 32. Peterho Cam BA 56, MA 60. Wycl Hall Ox 58. **d** 60 Bp Maxwell for Leic **p** 61 Leic. C of Melton Mowbray 60-63; V of Oughtibridge 63-72; St Cuthb Firvale 72-75; C-in-c of All SS Brightside Sheff 72-75; RD of Ecclesfield 73-75; Rotherham 76-79; V of Rotherham 75-79; M Gen Syn from 75; Archd of Doncaster from 79; C-in-c of Dunscroft Dio Sheff from 81. *2 Durham Road, Dunscroft, Doncaster, DN7 4NQ.* (Doncaster 841769)

✠ **HARLAND, Right Rev Maurice Henry.** b 1896. Ex Coll Ox BA (*sc* Mod Hist) 21, MA 36, Hon Fell 50. DD (Lambeth) 48. Univ of Dur Hon DD 56. Leeds Cl Sch 21. **d** 22 **p** 23 Pet. C of St Pet Leic 22-27; C-in-c of St Anne's Conv Distr Leic 27-33; PC of St Matt Holbeck 33-38; V of St Mary Windermere 38-42; RD of Ambleside 38-42; Cons Ld Bp Suffr of Croydon in Croydon Parish Ch 25 July 42 by Abp of Cant; Bps of Lon; Guildf; and Carl; Bps Suffr of Barking; Kingston T; Lewes; Woolwich; and Kens; and Bps de Labillière, Golding-Bird, and Roberts; V of Croydon 42-47; Hon Can of Cant 43-47; Archd of Croydon 46-47; Catechist Ex Coll Ox and Select Pr Univ of Ox 49-50; Trld to Linc 47; to Dur 56; res 66. *White Chimneys, West Wittering, N Chichester, Sussex, PO20 8LT.* (West Wittering 2351)

HARLAND, Robert Peirson. G and C Coll Cam 3rd cl Mod Lang Trip pt 1, 38, BA (2nd cl Archael and Anthrop Trip Sect A) 39, MA 43. Tyndale Hall Bris 39. **d** and **p** 41 Kingston T for S'wark. C of H Trin Redhill 41-43; Miss at Mirzapur 44-45 and 50-55; Chap at Kachhwa 45-49; Varanas 58-68; Allahabad 68-78; Archd of Luckn 66-78; S W Area Org Sec for BCMS 56-58 and from 79; L to Offic Dio S'wark from 79. *3 Seale Hill, Reigate, Surrey, RH2 8HZ.* (Reigate 42600)

HARLAND, Canon Samuel James. b 1898. OBE 75. AKC (1st cl) and McCaul Hebr Jun Pri 30, Trench Gr Test Pri 29 Univ of Lon BD 30. **d** 29 **p** 30 Chelmsf. C of St Martin Dagenham 29-30; St Mich AA Westcliff-on-Sea 30-31; R of Stathern 31-36; TCF Aldershot 36-37; Chelsea 37-39; R of Knossington w Cold Overton 39-47; CF (EC) 39-45; RD of Goscote (1st Deanery) 45-47; R of Asfordby Dio Leic 47-51; Chap at Maisons Laffitte 51-54; Central Field Sec CCCS 54-56; Chap at Versailles 56-58; Can of Centr Tang from 58; Gen Sec CCCS 58-61; Chap at Moshi 62-64; Ch Ch Amsterdam 64-66; L to Offic Dio Sheff from 66; Commiss Centr

Tang from 77. *2 Durham Road, Dunscroft, Doncaster, DN7 4NQ.* (Doncaster 841769)

HARLEY, Brian Mortimer. K Coll Lon and Warm 48. M SSF 57. **d** 53 **p** 54 Bris. C of St Agnes Bris 53-56; L to Offic Dio Sarum 56-62; P-in-c of St Francis Koke Miss Port Moresby 62-63; Prin St Francis Evangelists' Coll Jegaratta 63-67; Guardian St Francis Friary Jegaratta Dio New Guinea 67-71; Dio Papua from 71. *Friary, Box 78, Popondetta, New Guinea.*

HARLEY, Canon Brian Nigel. b 30. Clare Coll Cam BA 53, MA 57. Cudd Coll 53. **d** 55 **p** 56 Win. C of Basingstoke 55-60; W End Southn (in c of Thornhill) 60-61; C-in-c of St Chris Conv Distr Thornhill 61-71; Team V of Basingstoke 71-73; R 73-80; Hon Can of Win Cathl from 75; V of Eastleigh Dio Win from 80. *Vicarage, 1 Cedar Road, Eastleigh, Hants, SO5 5DB.* (Eastleigh 612073)

HARLEY, Christopher David. b 41. Selw Coll Cam 3rd cl Cl Trip pt i 62, BA (2nd cl Th Trip pt ia) 63, MA 69. Clifton Th Coll 64. **d** 66 **p** 67 Lon. C of Ch Ch Finchley 66-69 and 75-78; CMJ Miss Ethiopia 70-75; Hd of UK Miss CMJ from 75; Lect All Nations Chr Coll Ware from 78. *All Nations Christian College, Easneye, Ware, Herts, SG12 8LX.* (Ware 61243)

HARLEY, David Bertram. b 22. Down Coll Cam BA 50, MA 55. Westcott Ho Cam. **d** 56 **p** 58 St Alb. Asst Master Bedford Sch 50-58; C of Biddenham 56-58; Chap of Stamford Sch from 58; L to Offic Dio Linc from 59. *Beggars' Roost, Priory Road, Stamford, Lincs.* (Stamford 3403)

HARLEY, John William. b 35. ACT ThL 69. **d** 66 **p** 69 St Arn. Hon C of Sea Lake 66-69; V of Quambatook 69-71; C of Swan Hill 71-74; V of Tyrrell Dio St Arn (Dio Bend from 77) from 74. *PO Box 160, Sea Lake, Vic., Australia 3533.* (Sea Lake 114)

HARLEY, Michael. b 50. AKC 73. St Aug Coll Cant 74. **d** 75 Tonbridge for Roch **p** 76 Roch. C of St Wm Chatham 75-78; Weeke (in c of St Barn) 78-81; V of St Mary Extra (Pear Tree) Southn Dio Win from 81. *Vicarage, Pear Tree Avenue, Southampton.* (Southn 448353)

HARLEY, Percival Howard. b 1900. Selw Coll Cam BA 26, MA 30. Ridley Hall, Cam 26. **d** 26 **p** 28 St Alb. C of St Andr Watford 26-29; St Mary Luton 29-34; V of St Jo Bapt Hoxton 34-43; Downend 43-62; L to Offic Dio Bris from 62. *Pinewood, Kingsdown, Chippenham, Wilts, SN14 9BD.* (Box 420)

HARLEY, Roger Newcomb. b 38. Ely Th Coll 61. **d** 64 **p** 65 Ex. C of St Pet Plymouth 64-66; Heston 66-69; Maidstone 69-73; R of Temple Ewell w Lydden 73-79; V of St Geo Shirley Dio Cant from 79. *St George's Vicarage, The Glade, Shirley, Croydon, CR0 7QJ.* (01-654 8747)

HARLEY, William Ernest. b 08. St Pet Coll Ox BA 32, MA 37. Wycl Hall, Ox. **d** 33 **p** 34 Liv. C of Garston 33-35; Asst Chap Mersey Miss to Seamen Liv 35-38; C of St Jo Bapt Claines 38-41; Chap of Watt's Naval Tr Sch Elmham 41-43; Offg C-in-c of Wribbenhall 43-44; C of Tardebigge w Webheath 44-47; V of Selsley 47-50; PC of St Jas Glouc 50-54; R of Meysey-Hampton w Marston Meysey 54-60; PC of Oakridge 60-72; V of Leck 72-75; L to Offic Dio Blackb from 79. *1 Nutter Crescent, Higham, Burnley, Lancs, BB12 9BQ.* (Padiham 73732)

HARLOW, Derrick Peter. b 30. St Jo Coll Cam BA 53, MA 57. Ridley Hall, Cam 53. **d** 55 **p** 56 Chelmsf. C of Barking 55-58; V of Em Leyton 58-63; All SS Goodmayes 63-75; R of Thundersley Dio Chelmsf from 75. *Thundersley Rectory, Benfleet, Essex.* (S Benfleet 2235)

HARMAN, Preb John Gordon Kitchener. b 14. Qu Coll Cam BA 36, MA 40. Lon Coll Div 36. **d** 37 **p** 38 Lon. C of All S Langham Place 37-38; Edgware (in c of St Andr) 38-42; Travelling Sec of Univs and Colls Chr Fellowship 42-45; Miss CIM Dio E Szech 45-48; Dio W Szech 49-52; Chap of Holy Light Sch Soochow 48-49; R of Cheadle 52-60; Edgware 60-75; Preb of St Paul's Cathl Lon 65-75; Preb (Emer) from 75; Min of Ch Ch Westbourne Bournemouth 75-81. *32 Lansdowne Road, Shepshed, Leics, LE12 9RS.* (05095-2865)

HARMAN, Leslie Davies. b 46. Univ of Nottm BTh 76. St Jo Coll Nottm 72. **d** 76 **p** 77 S'wark. C of All SS w H Trin Wandsworth 76-78; Godstone Dio S'wark from 78. *16 Lagham Road, South Godstone, Surrey, RH9 8HB.* (South Godstone 3155)

HARMAN, Leslie Wallace. b 10. St Cath S Ox 29. **d** 43 **p** 44 Reading for Ox. C of St Giles Reading 43-47; V of St Luke Reading 47-60; Chap HM Pris Reading 46-60; R of Shellingford 60-63; C-in-c of Longcot w Fernham 60-62; V 62-63; C of Limpsfield w Titsey and Dir of Relig Sociology Dio S'wark 63-69; V of Hardingstone 69-75; Development Adv Dio Pet 69-75; Churches Commun Development Consultancy 75-81. *72 Westmount Road, Eltham Park, SE9 1JE.*

HARMAN, Michael John. b 48. Chich Th Coll 71. **d** 74 Lanc for Blackb **p** 75 Blackb. C of St Steph Blackpool Dio Blackb from 74. *St Anne's Parsonage, Salmesbury Avenue, Blackpool, FY2 0PR.* (Blackpool 53900)

HARMAN, Robert Desmond. b 41. Trin Coll Dub BA (Hebr and Or Lang Mod) 65, Div Test 67, MA 71. **d** 67 **p** 68 Dub. C of Taney 67-73; I of Santry and Glasnevin Dio Dub from 73. *Rectory, Santry, Co Dublin, Irish Republic.* (Dublin 373518)

HARMAN, Theodore Allan. b 27. Linc Coll Ox BA 52, MA 56. Wells Th Coll 52. **d** 54 **p** 55 Carl. C of Hawkshead 54-55; Kirby Stephen 55-57; Asst Master and Asst Chap Sedbergh Sch from 57; L to Offic Dio Bradf from 57. *2a The Leyes, Sedbergh, Cumb, LA10 5DJ.* (Sedbergh 20770)

HARMER, Canon Gerald William Sinden. b 04. Univ of Reading Dipl Educn 23. Sarum Th Coll 26. **d** 28 Win for Sarum **p** 29 Sarum. C of Gillingham Dorset 28-31; PV of Truro Cathl Chap of Cathl Sch and C of St Mary Truro 31-34; C of Bp's Hatfield 36-37; Chap of Toc H NW Area 34-36; Chap Toc H Lon and C of St Swith Lon Stone 37-40; PV of Truro Cathl and C of St Mary Truro 40-44; Succr of Truro Cathl 44-46; Hon Can of Truro from 45; V of Bodmin (w Nanstallon to 58) 46-71; R of Helland 46-67; Chap E Cornwall Hosp 48-72; Surr 48-71; RD of Bodmin 56-59; L to Offic Dio Truro from 71. *The South Flat, Lanhydrock, Bodmin, Cornw.* (Bodmin 2767)

HARMER, Leslie Guy. Ridley Coll Melb LTh 49. **d** 45 **p** 46 Gippsld. C of Poowong w Loch 45; V 46-47; Mirboo N 47-49; Home Sec CMS Melb 49-52; Min of Winchelsea 52-55; Essendon 55-61; I of St Jas Old Cathl and Missr St Jas and St John Miss Melb 61-78; Can of Melb 64-80; L to Offic Dio Melb 78-80; Perm to Offic Dio Melb from 80. *10 Edith Court, Doncaster, Vic, Australia 3108.* (848 2610)

HARMER, Wilfred Lancelot. Brisb Th Coll ACT ThL 28. **d** 28 **p** 29 Brisb. C of St Jas Toowoomba 28-30; M of Bush Bro of St Paul Charleville Queensld 30-36; Perm to Offic (Col Cl Act) at St Osmund Parkstone 36-37; V of Mary Valley 37-38; R of O'Connell 38-40; C of D Cathl Hobart 40-42; Min CAn and Prec Tas Cathl 42-45; V of Camp Hill 45-63; Commiss (in Austr) N Queensld 53-69; R of All SS Brisb 63-69; Dean and R of St Jas Cathl Townsville 69-73; Perm to Offic Dio Brisb from 73. *7 Bishop Street, Nundah, Queensland, Australia 4012.* (266-7792)

HARNOTT, Ronald Robert. **d** 57 **p** 58 Johann. C of Malvern Johann 57-59; St Mary's Cathl Johann 59-61; R of Rosettenville Dio Johann from 61. *Rectory, Rosettenville, Johannesburg, S Africa.* (011-26 4075)

HAROLD, Stephen Roland. b 37. Linc Th Coll 74. **d** 78 **p** 79 St E (APM). C of Kirton w Falkenham Dio St E from 78; Trimley 78-80. *196 Kirton Road, Trimley, Ipswich, IP10 0QL.*

HARPAUL, Canon Joseph Wortley. St Pet Coll Ja 34. **d** 34 **p** 35 Ja. L to Offic Dio Ja 34-38; C of Swallowfield 38-45; R of Pedro Plains 45-53; P-in-c of Kew Pk 53-58; R of Woodford Craigton and Clifton Dio Ja from 58; Can of Ja from 76. *Gordon Town PO, Jamaica, W Indies.* (092-78847)

HARPER, Alan Edwin Thomas. b 44. Univ of Leeds BA 65. Div Hostel Dub 75. **d** 78 **p** 79 Connor. C of Ballywillan 78-80; I of Moville U Dio Derry from 80. *Moville Rectory, Co Donegal, Irish Republic.* (Moville 18)

HARPER, Alfred Geoffrey. b 09. Lich Th Coll 32. **d** 35 **p** 36 Ripon. C of St Pet Bramley 35-39; (in c 39-40); CF (EC) 40-46; Hon CF from 46; Dom Chap to Bp of Ripon and L to Offic Dio Ripon 46-49; V of Pateley Bridge 49-59; C-in-c of Greenhow Hill 49-53; V 53-59; Surr 49-59; C of All SS Alton 60-67; St Mich Southn 68-70; Perm to Offic Dio Win from 70. *8 Queen's Road, Alton, Hants, GU34 1HU.* (Alton 82614)

HARPER, David Laurence. b 51. Qu Coll Cam BA 73, MA 77, PhD 78. Univ of Ox BA 80. Wycl Hall Ox 79. **d** 80 **p** 81 Southw. C of SS Pet & Paul Mansfield Dio Southw from 80. *1 Pinewood Drive, Mansfield, Notts, NG18 4PG.* (Mansfield 29177)

HARPER, David Richardson. NZ Bd of Th Stud LTh 63, St Jo Coll Auckld. **d** 63 **p** 64 Ch Ch. C of Fendalton 63-66; Hokitika 66-68; P-in-c of Kumara 66-68; Belfast-Styx 68-69; C of Sumner-Heathcote 69-71; V of Heathcote-Mt Pleasant 71-75; Rangiora Dio Ch Ch from 75. *155 High Street, Rangiora, NZ.* (Ran 6148)

HARPER, Donald Morrison. Qu Coll Cam BA 36, MA 41. Ridley Hall Cam 36. **d** 38 Lon **p** 39 Willesden for Lon. C of St Paul S Harrow 38-39; Chap Bancroft's Sch Woodford Green and Perm to Offic Dio Chelms 39-40; Chap RAFVR 40-46; RAF 46-65; Actg C of Brompton Lon 46; C-in-c of St Geo Brighton 65-70; Exam and Dom Chap to Bp of Lagos 70-72; Chap at All SS Ibadan 72; H Trin Madeira 72-76; Marbella 76-77; San Pedro de Alcantara Dio Gibr (Gibr in Eur from 80) from 77. *Apartado 106, Calle Los Naraigos 169, San Pedro de Alcantara, Spain.* (811972)

HARPER, Geoffrey. b 32. Hertf Coll Ox BA 55, MA 59. Coll of Resurr Mirfield. **d** 57 **p** 58 Cov. C of St Pet Cov 57-60; St Mich Handsworth 60-62; C-in-c of St Mark's Conv Distr Kingstanding 62-67; Min 67-71; V 71-73; R of Sheviock 73-80; C-in-c of Antony Dio Truro 76-80; R (w Sheviock) from 80. *Sheviock Rectory, Torpoint, Cornw, PL11 3EH.* (St Germans 477)

HARPER, Gordon. b 32. Oak Hill Th Coll 64. **d** 66 **p** 67 Man. C of St Pet Halliwell 66-71; P-in-c of Brinsworth 71-75; V (w Catcliffe) from 75. *Brinsworth Vicarage, Rotherham, Yorks, S60 5JR.* (Rotherham 63850)

HARPER, Gordon William Robert. b 48. Vic Univ of Wel NZ BA 70. St Chad's Coll Dur BA (Th) 74. Coll of the Resurr Mirfield 74. **d** 75 Pontefract for Wakef **p** 76 Wel. C of Battyeford 75-76; St Paul's Cathl Wel 76-78; Chap Vic Univ of Wel 78-80; P-in-c of Byers Green Dio Dur from 80. *Byers Green Rectory, Spennymoor, Co Durham, DL16 7NW.* (Bp Auckland 602646)

HARPER, Henry Samuel Braughall. Univ of Manit BA 34. Bp's Univ Lennox LST 36. **d** 36 **p** 37 Queb. C of Ireland 36-37; Cathl Ch Quebec 37-39; St Clem Miss Labrador 39-41; Kenogami 41-42; Chap CASF from 42; C of H Trin Cathl Queb 46-47; St Aid Tor 47-48; R of St Sav Tor 48-58; P-in-c of N Essa 58-64; R of Lakeview 64-68; Port Credit 68-78. *Apt 203, 2345 Confederation Parkway, Mississauga, Ont, Canada.*

HARPER, Horace Frederic. b 37. Lich Th Coll 58. **d** 60 **p** 61 Lich. C of Stoke-upon-Trent Fenton 63-66; PC of Coseley 66-68; V 68-75; Trent Vale Dio Lich from 75. *Trent Vale Vicarage, Stoke-on-Trent, Staffs, ST4 6QB.* (Stoke-on-Trent 48076)

HARPER, Ian. b 54. AKC 78. Oak Hill Coll 79. **d** 80 **p** 81 Roch. C of St Jo Evang Sidcup Dio Roch from 80. *22 Hamilton Road, Sidcup, Kent, DA15 7HB.*

HARPER, John Alexander. b 17. Worc Ordin Coll 61. **d** 63 **p** 64 Worc. C of St Jo Bapt-in-Bedwardine Worc 63-65; V of Clifton-on-Teme 65-72; R of Lower Sapey 65-72; Miserden w Edgeworth and Cranham Dio Glouc from 72. *Miserden Rectory, Stroud, Glos.* (Miserden 254)

HARPER, John Anthony. b 46. K Coll Lon AKC 69. St Aug Coll Cant 69. **d** 70 **p** 71 Pet. C of St Mary Pet 70-73; Abington 73-75; V of Grendon w Castle Ashby Dio Pet from 75; Asst Dioc Youth Chap from 75. *Grendon Vicarage, Northampton, NN7 1JF.* (Wellingborough 663227)

HARPER, John Hugh. b 34. Hertf Coll Ox BA (2nd cl Th) 57, MA 61. Wells Th Coll 57. **d** 59 Taunton for B & W **p** 60 Taunton for Cant. C of Twerton-on-Avon 59-62; R of Allerton 62-69; PC of Blackford 62-69; V of Halsetown Dio Truro from 69. *St John-in-the-Fields Vicarage, Higher Stennack, St Ives, Cornw, TR26 2HG.* (Penzance 796035)

HARPER, Joseph Frank. b 38. Univ of Hull BA 60. Linc Th Coll 80. **d** 81 Burnley for Blackb. C of St Cuthb Preston Dio Blackb from 81. *72 Lytham Road, Fulwood, Preston, PR2 3AQ.*

HARPER, Canon Kenneth. b 13. Hatf Coll Dur Hatf and Th Exhibs and L Th 36, BA (w distinc) 37, MA 40, M Litt 47. Edin Th Coll 33. **d** 37 **p** 38 Ripon. C of St Marg Horsforth 37-38; Leeds 38-39; St Mich AA Norton 39-41; St Jas Darlington 41-44; Actg C of Windermere 44-45; C of Geo Mart w Haverigg Millom (in c of St Luke) 45-47; V of Ainstable 47-51; PC of Armathwaite 47-51; Carl Dioc Insp of Schs 49-75; Ed Carl Dioc Year Book 50-74; V of Brampton 51-60; Walton 60-75; C-in-c 75-78; Exam Chap to Bp of Carl 65-75; Hon Can of Carl 66-75; Can (Emer) from 75; Proc Conv Carl 67-75. *Culreoch, Aaronstown Lonning, Brampton, Cumb CA8 1QR.* (Brampton 2353)

HARPER, Malcolm Barry. b 37. Univ of Dur BSc 59. Wycl Hall Ox 59. **d** 61 **p** 62 Chelmsf. C of Harold Wood Hornchurch 61-65; Madeley Salop 65-68; V of Slaithwaite w E Scammonden 68-75; Walmley Dio Birm from 75. *Walmley Vicarage, Sutton Coldfield, W Midl.* (021-351 1030)

HARPER, Maurice. b 20. St Steph Ho Ox 60. **d** 62 **p** 63 Chelmsf. C of Upminster 62-67; V of St Mary Virg Gt Ilford 67-71; Surr from 67; R of Upminster Dio Chelmsf from 71; RD of Havering from 80. *Rectory, Gridiron Place, Upminster, Essex.* (Upminster 20174)

HARPER, Michael Claude. b 31. Em Coll Cam 2nd cl Law Trip pt i, 52, BA (2nd cl Th Trip pt ii) 54, MA 57. Ridley Hall, Cam 53. **d** 55 **p** 56 S'wark. C of St Barn Clapham Common 55-58; All S Langham Place St Marylebone and Chap to Ox Street Stores 58-64; Perm to Offic Dio Lon 65-75; Gen Sec Fountain Trust 64-72; Dir 72-75; Perm to Offic Dio Guildf from 72; Exam Chap to Bp of Guildf from 74; C of Hounslow 75-81; Commiss Port Eliz from 75; St John's from 80; L to Offic Dio Chich from 81. *27 Muster Green, Haywards Heath, W Sussex, RH16 4AL.*

HARPER, Paul. b 11. Pemb Coll Ox BA 34, MA 38 Clifton Th Coll 35. **d** 35 **p** 36 Ox. C of St Mich Ox 35-38; Chap of St Mark Parklands Nairobi 38-39; CF (EC) 39-46; Hd Master St Goar Sch Bris 46-61; Colston Prep Sch Bris 61-68. *4 The Square, Lydd, Kent.*

HARPER, Richard Michael. b 53. Univ of Lon BSc 75. Univ of Wales PhD 78. St Steph Ho Ox BA (Th) 80. **d** 81 Nor. C of Holt Dio Nor from 81; Edgefield Dio Nor from 81. *28 Pearsons Road, Holt, Norfolk, NR25 6EJ.* (Holt 2823)

HARPER, Thomas Reginald. b 31. Univ of Dur BA 57, MA 67. **d** 58 **p** 59 Newc T. C of Corbridge 58-60; St Mich Byker Newc T 60-62; V of Ushaw Moor 62-67; N Area Sec CMS 67-74; Commiss Ja 70-77; V of Thornthwaite cum Braithwaite (and Newlands from 76) Dio Carl from 74. *Thornthwaite Vicarage, Braithwaite, Keswick, Cumb, CA12 5RY.* (Braithwaite 243)

HARPER, Victor Selkirk. b 12. Cranmer Hall, Dur 64. **d** 65 **p** 66 Penrith for Carl. C of St Paul Newbarns w Hawcoat Barrow-F 65-68; R of Asby w Ormside 68-72; V of Blawith w Lowick 72-77. *8 Canberra, Stonehouse, Glouc, GL10 2PR.* (Stonehouse 4322)

HARPER-HOLDCROFT, Reginald Norman. b 08. MBE 46. St Chad's Coll Dur BA 39. **d** 39 Lich **p** 40 Stafford for Lich. C of St Giles Willenhall 39-40; CF (EC) 40-47; Hon CF 47; C of Boston (in c of St Jas) 47-48; Henley-on-Thames 49; R of Rawmarsh 50-54; Chap Warlingham Pk Hosp 54-55; R of Breamore 55-58; Chap Holloway Sanat Virginia Water 58-65; R of Gt Brickhill 65-70; C of St John Moulsham 70-71; C-in-c of Downham 71-72. *Bockleton Vicarage, Tenbury Wells, Worcs.*

HARPUR, Robert Alexander. b 15. OBE 63. BNC Ox BA 38, MA 42. Westcott Ho Cam 39. **d** 40 **p** 41 Blackb. C of Lancaster 40-43; CF 43-67; V of Whalley 67-80. *34 Knowlys Road, Heysham, Morecambe, Lancs, LA3 2PF.* (Heysham 54841)

HARRADENCE, Peter John. Ridley Coll Melb ACT ThL 57. **d** 58 **p** 59 Melb. C of Hawthorn 58-59; Melb Dioc Centre 59; P-in-c of St Jude Carlton 60-64; V of St Aid Parkdale 64-70; Niddrie 70-78; Highton Dio Melb from 78. *269 Roslyn Road, Highton, Vic, Australia 3216.* (052-43 3561)

HARRADINE, Eric Stafford. d 65 **p** 66 Melb. C of All SS E St Kilda 65-67; C in Angl Inner-City Min (in c of St Alb N Melb and St Geo Flemington) 67-70; I of H Trin Hastings 70-72; Perm to Offic Dio Melb 73-75. *30 Katrina Drive, Tullamarine, Vic., Australia 3043.*

HARRADINE, Canon John Candy Williamson. b 16. Keble Coll Ox BA (2nd cl Hist) 38, MA 42. St Steph Ho Ox 38. **d** 40 Worc **p** 41 Bp Duppuy for Worc. C of St Thos Stourbridge 40-42; St Luke Bournemouth 42-46; St Pet and St Paul Ringwood 46-51; V of Nempnett Thrubwell and R of Butcombe 51-57; V of Harptree W 57-65; R of Biabou St Vincent 65-71; H Trin St Lucia 71-75; Hon Can of Windw Is from 75; C-in-c of Halse 75-81; Ash Priors 75-81. *c/o Halse Rectory, Taunton, Somt.*

HARRAP, William Charles. b 32. **d** 72 **p** 74 Stepney for Lon. C of St Jas L Bethnal Green Dio Lon from 72. *4 Trevelyan House, Morpeth Street, E2 0PY.* (01-980 6887)

HARRIES, Alfred Egerton. b 1891. Prelim TE (1st cl) 14. **d** 14 **p** 15 Chich. C of Hartfield 14-17; and 21-27; St Mary Magd Brighton 18-21; Bexhill 27-34; V of Compton w Up Marden 34-69; Seq of N Marden 42-69; E Marden 42-62; R 62-69. *c/o 45 Warrenside, South Harting, Petersfield, Hants.*

HARRIES, Gwilym David. b 41. St D Coll Lamp BA (2nd cl Hist) 63. St Mich Coll Llan 63. **d** 65 **p** 66 Swan B. C of Llanguicke 65-68; Llangyfelach w Morriston 68-71; Team V of Aberystwyth 71-76; R of Hubberston Dio St D from 76. *Hubberston Rectory, Milford Haven, Dyfed.* (Milford Haven 2251)

HARRIES, Henry Rayner Mackintosh. b 30. MBE 67. Chich Th Coll 53. **d** 55 **p** 56 Chich. C of H Trin Hastings 55-58; Chap RAF from 58. *c/o Ministry of Defence, Adastral House, WC1.*

HARRIES, Lewis John. b 27. Univ of Wales BA 52. St Mich Coll Llan 51. **d** 53 **p** 54 Mon. C of Maindee 53-58; V of Whitson w Goldcliffe and Nash 58-64; Tredegar Dio Mon from 64; RD of Bedwellty from 78; Surr from 78. *St George's Vicarage, Tredegar, Gwent.* (Tredegar 2672)

HARRIES, Canon Raymond John. b 17. OBE 72. Oak Hill Th Coll 40. **d** 42 Glouc **p** 43 Tewkesbury for Glouc. C of H Trin Cheltenham 42-45; St Jas Shirley 45-50; V of Bitterne 50-55; Chap Kampala and Entebbe 55-61; Provost of All SS Cathl Nairobi 61-71; Commiss of Nai 62-71; Hon Can of Nai from 71; V of St Jo Bapt Halifax Dio Wakef from 71; RD of Halifax from 71; Surr from 72; Hon Can of Wakef from 75. *Halifax Vicarage, Skircoat Green Road, Halifax, Yorks, HX3 0BQ.* (Halifax 65477)

HARRIES, Richard Douglas. b 36. Selw Coll Cam 2nd cl Th Trip pt i 60, BA (2nd cl Th Trip pt ii) 61, MA 65. Cudd Coll 61. **d** 63 **p** 64 Lon. C of Hampstead 63-69; Chap Westfield Coll 67-69; Tutor Wells Th Coll 69-71; Warden of Wells, Salisbury and Wells Th Coll 71-72; V of Fulham 72-81; Dean of K Coll Lon from 81. *King's College, Strand, WC2R 2LS.*

HARRIMAN, John Walter. Edin Th Coll 19. Univ of Dur LTh 21. **d** 22 **p** 23 Glas. C of St Mary's Cathl Glas 22-26; R of St Martin Polmadie Glas 26-31; V of St Cuthb Hebburn 31-37; R of Inverurie 37-52; Kelso 52-58; V of Birkenhead

NZ 59-64; Hon C of Devonport Dio Auckld from 65. *38 Onepoto Road, Takapuna, Auckland, NZ.* (494 929)

HARRINGTON, Charles William. b 04. Linc Th Coll. **d** 42 **p** 43 Southw. [f Baptist Min] C of Gedling 42-44; Cler Dir of ICF for W Midlands and Perm to Offic Dios Southw, Heref and Worc 44-47; Chap HM Pris Nottm 47-50; V of Woodborough 47-50 and 57-63; All SS Nottm 50-55; R of Harrismith OFS and Dir of Harrismith Miss 55-57; Chap HM Borstal Inst Roch 63-65; V of Horley w Hornton 65-70; C-in-c of Hanwell 65-70; V of Letcombe Regis w Letcombe Bassett 70-73; Hon Chap of Cant Cathl from 74. *50 Bridgedown, Bridge, Canterbury, CT4 5BA.* (Bridge 830783)

HARRINGTON, Graham Anthony. b 20. Linc Coll Ox BA (2nd cl Th) 48, MA 52. Wells Th Coll 48. **d** 49 **p** 50 S'wark. C of Bermondsey 49-52; CF (TA) 51-55 and 63-67; (TA-R of O) 55-63; V of Merrington 52-54; R of Wolviston 54-62; V of St Andr Wakef 62-68; V of St Mary Wakef 62-68; St Mich Blundellsands Dio Liv from 68. *41 Dowhills Road, Liverpool, L23 8SJ.* (051-924 3424)

HARRINGTON, John Christopher. b 43. Qu Coll Birm 71. **d** 74 **p** 75 Pet. C of St Mich AA Northampton 74-76; Paston 76-79; CF (TA) 75-82; R of Doddington Dio Ely from 79; Benwick Dio Ely from 79. *Rectory, Ingles Lane, Doddington, Cambs.* (March 740161)

HARRINGTON, Peter Anthony Saunders. b 30. Fitzw Ho Cam BA 52, Th Trip pt ii 53, MA 58. Ely Th Coll 53. **d** 55 Croydon for Cant **p** 56 Cant. C of St Mich AA Croydon 55-59; M Bro of Good Shepherd Dubbo 59-62; C of W Wycombe (in c of St Mary and St Geo) 63-66; L to Offic Dio Ox 67-78; L to Offic Dio St Alb from 78; Perm to Offic Dio Ox from 78. *5 Linfields, Little Chalfont, Amersham, Bucks, HP7 9QH.* (Little Chalfont 3471)

HARRINGTON, William Harry. K Coll Lon and Warm AKC 57. **d** 58 **p** 59 Liv. C of Childwall 58-60; Sutton Lancs (in c of All SS) 60-64; V of Ditton Liv 64-75; St Barn Mossley Hill Dio Liv from 76. *St Barnabas's Vicarage, Mossley Hill, Liverpol 18.* (051-733 1432)

HARRIS, Albert Edward. b 16. St Aid Coll 50. **d** 52 **p** 53 Worc. C of St Clem Worc 52-55; V of Partington (w Carrington from 63) 56-71; Ashley Dio Ches from 72. *Ashley Vicarage, Altrincham, Cheshire.* (061-928 0063)

HARRIS, Alfred Burgy. Univ Coll Dur BA 06, LTh 07, MA 10. **d** 07 **p** 08 Man. C of Failsworth 07-11; Blackpool 11-15; C-in-c of St Gabr Conv Distr Blackb 15-23; V of St Steph Haslingden Grane 23-28; All S Bolton 28-33; Surr 29-52; R of Broughton Lance 33-37; St Andr Blackley 37-45; Perm to Offic Dio Blackb 45-52; Dio Sarum 52-55. *Berkeley Hotel, Clifton Drive North, Lytham St Annes, Lancs.*

HARRIS, Ven Arnold William. St Jo Coll Morpeth, ACT ThL 26, Th Scho 32. **d** 27 **p** 29 Goulb. C of Cathl Ch Goulb 27-28; Wagga 29-30; P-in-c of Adelong 30-34; R of Berridale 34-42; Cootamundra 42-56; Can of Goulb 50-57; Dioc Regr C & Goulb 56-71; Archd of Goulb 57-71; Archd (Emer) and L to Offic Dio C & Goulb from 71; Exam Chap to Bp of C & Goulb 64-71. *110 Macarthur Avenue, O'Connor, ACT, Australia.*

HARRIS, Barry William. b 40. St Jo Coll Morpeth 70. **d** 71 **p** 72 Graft. C of Murwillumbah 71-72; V of Woolgoolga Dio Graft from 72. *PO Box 49, Woolgoolga, NSW, Australia 2450.* (54 1370)

HARRIS, Basil George. b 17. St Mich Coll Llan 59. **d** 61 **p** 62 Man. C of St Benedict Ardwick 61-62; Farnworth and of Kearsley 62-63; Chap at Ghana 64; Perm to Offic Dio Llan 65-71; C of St Sav St Alb 71-74; V of St Cross Middleton 74-79; R of Helpringham w Hale Dio Linc from 79. *Helpringham Vicarage, Sleaford, Lincs.* (Swaton 306)

HARRIS, Bernard Malcolm. b 29. Univ of Leeds, BA 54. Coll of Resurr Mirfield, 54. **d** 56 **p** 57 Lich. C of St Chad Shrewsbury 56-60; Porthill 60-61; V of Birches Head 61-66; St Jas W Bromwich 66-78; Sedgley Dio Lich from 78. *All Saints Vicarage, Vicar Street, Sedgley, Dudley, W Midl, DY3 3SD.* (Sedgley 3255)

HARRIS, Brian. Univ of Man BSc. Qu Coll Birm 79. **d** 80 **p** 81 Lich. C of St Chad City and Dio Lich from 80. *5 Ashmole House, Bloomfield Crescent, Lichfield, Staffs.* (Lich 51009)

HARRIS, Brian Ronald. b 39. K Coll Lon and Warm AKC 64. **d** 65 **p** 66 Portsm. C of All SS Portsea 65-71; Chap HM Borstal Portsm 66-69; HM Pris Portsm 69-71; R of Aldington and Chap HM Detention Centre Aldington 71-79; P-in-c of Bonnington (w Bilsington from 79) 73-79; Falconhurst 73-79; V of Minster-in-Sheppey Dio Cant from 79. *Minster-in-Sheppey Vicarage, Sheerness, Kent, ME12 2HE.* (Minster 873185)

HARRIS, Brian William. b 38. K Coll Lon and Warm BD (2nd cl) and AKC (2nd cl) 61. **d** 62 **p** 63 Wakef. C of Liversedge 62-65; St Martin Southdene Kirkby 65-70; V of St Mich AA Dalton 70-79; Aberford w Saxton Dio York from 79. *Vicarage, Greystones Park, Aberford, Leeds, W Yorks, LS25 3AS.* (Leeds 813623)

HARRIS, Cedric Herbert. b 13. Univ of Lon 34. AKC 37. Wycl Hall, Ox 37. **d** 37 Pontefract for Wakef **p** 38 Wakef. C of Normanton 37-42; Brighouse 42-44; V of Barkisland w W Scammonden 44-49; Thornes (w Ch Ch Wakef from 57) 49-73; V of Ch Ch Wakef 50-57; Shepley 73-78. *44 Rayner Street, Horbury, Wakefield, W Yorks, WF4 5BD.*

HARRIS, Charles Edward. b 20. Roch Th Coll 63. **d** 65 **p** 66 St Alb. C of St Andr w St Nich and St Mary Hertford 65-70; R of Sywell w Overstone Dio Pet from 71. *Sywell Rectory, Northampton, NN6 0BA.* (Northampton 44658)

HARRIS, Charles Edwin Laurence. b 1896. Ridley Hall Cam. **d** 47 **p** 48 Sarum. C of H Trin Dorchester 47-50; V of Burbage 50-65. *Church House, Sutton-by-Dover, Kent, CT15 5DF.* (Deal 4809)

HARRIS, Charles Frederick. **d** 54 Newc **p** 57 C & Goulb. C of Adamstown 54-57; Wagga Wagga 57-59; R of Thuddungra 59-61; Bungendore 61-64; N Goulburn 64-70; Tehora 70-74; Perm to Offic Dios C & Goulb and Newc from 74. *3 Ruskin Row, Killarney Vale, NSW, Australia 2262.*

HARRIS, Charles William. b 27. **d** 78 **p** 79 Capetn. C of Wellington Dio Capetn from 78. *2 Herbert Street, Paalzicht, Paarl 7646, S Africa.*

HARRIS, Claude Anthony. b 16. Univ of Dur LTh 39. Oak Hill Th Coll 36. **d** 39 **p** 40 Lich. C of St Lawr Darlaston 39-45; St Matt Walsall (in c of St Luke) 45-48; V of Wombridge 48-53; St Matt Tipton 53-60; R of Stone 60-82; V of Aston w Burston 60-82; Surr 60-82. *c/o Rectory, Lichfield Road, Staffs, ST15 8PG.* (Stone 2747)

HARRIS, Cyril Evans. b 30. Linc Th Coll 61. **d** 63 **p** 64 Ox. C of Beaconsfield 63-68; V of Stoke Poges Dio Ox from 68. *Stoke Poges Vicarage, Slough, Bucks.* (Farnham Common 4177)

HARRIS, David. b 52. AKC 76. St Steph Ho Ox 76. **d** 77 **p** 78 S'wark. C of St Mary Wimbledon 77-80; Coalbrookdale w Ironbridge and L Wenlock Dio Heref from 80. *22 Madeley Road, Iron-Bridge, Telford, Salop.*

HARRIS, David Frederick Leonard. Oak Hill Th Coll. **d** and **p** 54 Syd. C of Kembla 54; Eastwood 54-56; Chap RAAF 56-60; R of Eastergate 60-63; Distr Sec BFBS S Yorks 63-68; State Gen Sec in S Austr from 68; Perm to Offic Dio Adel from 68. *Bible House, 133 Rundle Street, Adelaide, S Australia, 5000.* (08-223 3833)

HARRIS, David James. Westcott Ho Cam. **d** 69 Bp T M Hughes for Llan **p** 70 Llan. C of Cymmer w Abercregan 69-70; Llangynwydd w Maesteg 70-74; V of Michaelstone-super-Avon 74-77; Perm to Offic Dio Llan from 78. *The Mill House, Rhiw Saeson, Pontyclun, Mid Glam.*

HARRIS, David Rowland. b 46. Ch Ch Ox BA 69, MA 72, Dipl Th 71. Wycl Hall Ox 70. **d** 73 Dorking for Guildf **p** 74 Guildf. C of Virginia Water 73-76; Ch Ch Clifton 76-79; Perm to Offic Dio Ox from 79. *49 Barnsdale Road, Reading Berks, RG2 7JN.* (Reading 862706)

HARRIS, Denis Francis. **d** 58 **p** 59 New Westmr. I of Gibsons 58-64; Squamish w Woodfibre 64-67; Maple Ridge 67-78. *11604 Laity Street, Maple Ridge, BC, Canada.*

HARRIS, Derrick William. b 21. **d** 63 Warrington for Liv **p** 64 Liv. C of St John Birkdale 63-67; V of Billinge 67-81; Walton Dio Ches from 81. *Vicarage, Chester Road, Higher Walton, Warrington, WA4 6TJ.* (Warrington 62939)

HARRIS, Donald Bertram. b 04. Late Cho Scho of K Coll Cam BA 25, MA 29. Cudd Coll 26. **d** 27 **p** 28 Derby. C of St Mary and All SS Chesterfield 27-31; St Mary L Cam 31-36; Chap K Coll Cam 32-33; Exam Chap to Bp of Wakef 32-36; R of Gt Greenford 36-45; St Mary Bedford 45-55; C-in-c of St John Bedford 52-54; Commiss Zanz 44-68; Capetn 48-58; Archd of Bedford 46-55; Select Pr Univ of Cam 51; V of St Paul Knightsbridge 55-77; Proc Conv Lon 57-59. *105 Marsham Court, Westminster, SW1P 4LU.* (01-828 1132)

HARRIS, Emery Gordon. K Coll Halifax NS BA 52, BS Litt 54, BD 68. **d** 54 **p** 55 NS. R of Maitland 54-59; C of Dartmouth 59-65; R of Spryfield 65-70; R of H Spirit Dartmouth 70-76; Dir of Programme Dio NS from 76. *5732 College Street, Halifax, NS, Canada.*

HARRIS, Ernest Edward. St Jo Coll Morpeth, ACT ThL 66. **d** 66 Rockptn **p** 67 Brisb for Rockptn. C of St Thos Toowong Brisb 66-68; V of Springsure 68-72; R of Blackall 72-76; Emerald Dio Rockptn from 76. *PO Box 18, Emerald, Queensland, Australia 4720.* (Blackall 54)

HARRIS, Ernest John. b 46. Qu Univ Belf Dipl Th 74, BD 75. Div Hostel Dub 67. **d** 75 **p** 76 Connor. C of Ch Ch Lisburn 75-78; Coleraine Dio Connor from 78. *1F Elms Park, Ballysally, Coleraine, Co Londonderry, N Ireland.*

HARRIS, Evan Rufus. b 21. St D Coll Lamp BA 49. **d** 50 **p** 51 Linc. C of St Luke Gt Grimsby 50-52; Gainsborough and Chap John Coupland Mem Hosp and Co Maternity Home 52-54; R of Gate-Burton 54-57; V of Marton 54-57; R of Barrowby Dio Linc from 57; RD of Grantham 69-78; Offg

Chap RAF 70-76. *Barrowby Rectory, Grantham, Lincs.* (Grantham 3791)

HARRIS, Frank Edward. b 33. St Francis Coll Brisb 66. ACT ThL 68. **d** 68 **p** 69 N Queensld. C of Mundingburra 68-71; Plymstock 71-72; Perm to Offic Dio Lon 72-73; P-in-c of Pingelly 73-75; C of St Bonif Cathl Bunb 75-76; Bodmin 76-77; P-in-c of Menheniot w Merrymeet 77-79; V of Winton Dio Man from 79. *Vicarage, Albany Road, Winton, Eccles, Manchester, M30 8DE.* (061-788 8991)

HARRIS, Frank Henry. Lon Coll of Div 39. **d** 40 Lon for E Szech **p** 42 E Szech. CIM Miss Dio E Szech 43-51; West Borneo 51-58. *Wheaton College, Wheaton, Illinois, 60187, USA.*

HARRIS, Frederick John. b 17. Worc Ordin Coll 67. **d** 68 Sheff **p** 70 Bp Gerard for Sheff. C of Bolton-upon-Dearne 68-69; St Nathaniel Crookesmoor Sheff 69-71; Aston-juxta-Birm 71-73; R of St Steph Lyttelton 73-75; Sabie w Lydenburg 75-76; Perm to Offic Dio Portsm 77; C of St Mary Portsea 77; Clun 77-79; St Aid Hartlepool 79-80; V of Trimdon Station (f Trimdon Grange) Dio Dur from 80. *Vicarage, Trimdon Grange, Co Durham, TS29 6EX.* (Trimdon 880872)

HARRIS, Geoffrey Daryl. b 39. Dipl Th (Lon) 66. St Aid Coll 63. **d** 66 **p** 67 York. C of Eston w Normanby 66-70; Iffley 70-75; V of Bubwith (w Ellerton and Aughton from 79) 75-79; C-in-c of Ellerton Priory w Aughton and E Cottingwith 75-79; P-in-c of Stillingfleet w Naburn 79-80; R of Escrick and Stillingfleet w Naburn Dio York from 80. *Escrick Rectory, N Yorks, YO4 6EX.* (Escrick 406)

HARRIS, Geoffrey Fuller. b 20. OBE 66. Or Coll Ox MA 46, BM BCh 49. MRCP (Edin) 56. Wycl Hall Ox 65. **d** 65 **p** 66 S'wark (APM). C of St Swith Purley Surrey Dio S'wark from 65. *167 Chaldon Road, Caterham, Surrey, CR3 5PL.* (Caterham 47172)

HARRIS, George. b 36. Sarum Th Coll 66. **d** 68 **p** 69 Dur. C. of Shildon 68-70; CF 70-74; C-in-c of Doddington 74-75; R 75-78; R of Benwick 74-78; V of Shotton Dio Dur from 78. *Vicarage, Shotton Colliery, Durham.* (Hetton-le-Hole 261156)

HARRIS, Canon George Richmond. MBE 66. Moore Th Coll Syd. **d** and **p** 54 Syd. R of Pitt Town 54-58; Miss CMS Dio Carp 58-60; Actg Supt Oenpelli Miss Dio Carp 60-62; Chap 62-65; C of Pitt Town 66-70; Hon Can of N Terr from 71; Perm to Offic Dio N Terr from 72. *11 Coolong Street, Castle Hill, NSW, Australia 2154.*

HARRIS, Gilbert Andrew. Codr Coll Barb. **d** 68 Barb for Guy **p** 68 Guy. C of E Bank Demarara 68-69; CF 69-70; V of NE La Penitence Dio Guy from 70; Dioc Dir of Publicity and Radio Dio Guy from 70. *522 NE La Penitence, Gtr Georgetown, Guyana.* (02-61878)

HARRIS, Ven Harold Mayo. OBE 49. **d** 27 **p** 28 Wel. C of St Pet Wel 27-30; V of Taihape 30-34; Suva 34; Dioc Sec Dio Polyn 34-37; VG 34-41; Archd of Fiji 35-41; Archd (Emer) 45; serving w RAN 41-45; Perm to Offic Dio Melb 45-46; Chap RNZN 46-54; V of Clevedon 54-58; Devonport 58-61; Archd of Hauraki 58-64; Archd (Emer) from 64; Hon C of Clevedon 64-80; Perm to Offic Dio Waik from 80. *67 Williams Street, Cambridge, NZ.*

HARRIS, Herbert Edgar. Angl Th Coll BC. **d** 53 **p** 54 New Westmr. V of Port Coquittam 53-61; R 61-68; Ocean Pk w Crescent Dio New Westmr from 68. *12989 24th Avenue, Surrey, BC, Canada.*

HARRIS, Herbert Lewis. b 05. Late Scho of Jes Coll Cam 2nd cl Cl Trip pt i 26, BA (2nd cl Cl Trip pt ii) 27, MA 31. Westcott Ho Cam 38. **d** 38 Lon **p** 39 Willesden for Lon. Asst Master Harrow Sch 36-70. *19 High Street, Harrow Hill, Middx.* (01-422 3792)

HARRIS, James Nigel Kingsley. b 37. St D Coll Lamp BA 60. Sarum Th Coll. **d** 62 Tewkesbury for Glouc **p** 63 Glouc. C of Painswick 62-65; St Paul Glouc 65-67; V of Uplands w Slad 67-77; Cam (w Stinchcombe from 78) Dio Glouc from 77; P-in-c of Stinchcombe 77-78. *Vicarage, Church Road, Cam, Dursley, Glos, G11 5PQ.* (Dursley 2084)

HARRIS, John. b 32. Late Scho of St D Coll Lamp BA 55. Sarum Th Coll. **d** 57 **p** 58 Mon. C of Pontnewynydd 57-60; Bassaleg 60-63; V of Penmaen 63-69; St Paul Newport Dio Mon from 69; RD of Newport from 77; Surr from 77. *St Paul's Vicarage, Newport, Gwent, NPT 4EA.* (Newport 64722)

HARRIS, John. St Steph Ho Ox 72. **d** 75 **p** 76 Chelmsf. C of St Mary w Ch Ch Wanstead Dio Chelmsf from 75. *13 Wanstead Place, Wanstead, E 11.*

HARRIS, John Peter. b 33. St D Coll Lamp BA 57. **d** 58 **p** 59 Mon. C of Newport 58-60; Chap St Woolos Hosp 58-63; St Woolos Cathl Newport 60-63; CF from 63. *c/o Ministry of Defence, Bagshot Park, Bagshot, Surrey, GU19 5PL.*

HARRIS, John Stuart. b 29. Hertf Coll Ox BA 52, MA 56. Wells Th Coll 52. **d** 54 **p** 55 Guildf. C of Epsom 54-58; Guildf 58-63; R of Bentley 63-72; V of Milford Dio Guildf from 72. *Vicarage, Milford, Godalming, Surrey, GU8 5BX.* (Godalming 4710)

HARRIS, John Sydney Etheridge. b 13. BNC Ox BA (2nd cl Mod Hist) 35, MA 40. Cudd Coll 37. **d** 38 Bp Allen for Ox **p** 39 Buckingham for Ox. C of Wantage 38-42; St Alb Teddington 42-44; Abingdon (in c of St Mich) 44-50; PC of St Pet Stockport 50-59; V of H Nativ Knowle 59-70; R of Southery 70-79; RD of Fincham 73-75; Perm to Offic Dio Chich from 80. *10 St Michael's Road, Worthing, W Sussex.* (Worthing 30982)

HARRIS, Kenneth. b 28. NW Ord Course 70. **d** 72 Ches **p** 73 Stockport for Ches. C of H Ascen Upton 72-77; Eccleston and Pulford 77-80; P-in-c of Hargrave Dio Ches 80-81; V from 81. *Hargrave Vicarage, Chester, CH3 7RN.* (Huxley 378)

HARRIS, Lawrence Rex Rowland. b 35. St Cath Coll Cam BA 59, MA 63. Ely Th Coll. **d** 61 **p** 62 Southw. C of Carrington 61-63; Chap Rampton Hosp 63-66; V of Bole w Saundby Dio Southw from 66; V of Sturton-le-Steeple w Littleborough 66-71; R of Clowne Dio Derby from 71; RD of Bolsover and Staveley from 81. *Clowne Rectory, Chesterfield, Derbys.* (Clowne 810387)

HARRIS, Leonard John. Moore Th Coll Syd 32. **d** 37 **p** 38 Syd. C of Berrima w Moss Vale 37-38; Manly 38-39; Chap (CMS) at Groote Eylandt 39-44; Oenpelli 44-46; I of Prospect Seven Hills and Blacktown 46-50; Asst Gen Sec of BFBS in NSW 50-52; R of Liverpool 52-56; Lidcombe 56-60; Chap R Prince Alfred Hosp Syd 60-64; L to Offic Dio Syd 63-64; R of Croydon 64-70; Chap Lidcombe Hosp 71-73; C of Kiama 73-74; L to Offic Dio Syd from 75. *Marrow Lane, Gerringong, NSW, Australia 2543.* (042-34 1561)

HARRIS, Leslie Ernest. b 08. Kelham Th Coll 31. **d** 31 **p** 32 Southw. C of St Swith E Retford 31-35; St Mark Bury 35-40; CF (EC) 40-46; C of St Cuthb Fir Vale Sheff 46-47; C-in-c of Herringthorpe 47-50; V 50-58; Northfield 58-65; Swinton 65-76. *23 Griffiths Avenue, Lancing, Sussex.* (Lancing 5291)

HARRIS, Leslie Gerald Conley. b 44. Wycl Hall Ox 71. **d** 75 **p** 76 Nai. Chap Banda Sch and Hon C of St Francis Karen Dio Nai from 75. *Box 43798, Nairobi, Kenya.*

HARRIS, Leslie Owen. b 29. St Mich Coll Llan 61. **d** 63 **p** 64 Bris. C of Horfield 63-71; R of Winterton w E Somerton Dio Nor from 71; P-in-c of Horsey Dio Nor from 77. *Winterton-on-Sea Rectory, Great Yarmouth, Norf, NR29 4AW.* (Winterton-on-Sea 227)

HARRIS, Mark Hugh. Univ of California, BSc 59. Cudd Coll 63. **d** 64 **p** 65 Kimb K. C of St Cypr Cathl Kimberley 64-67. *c/o PO Box 45, Kimberley, CP, S Africa.*

HARRIS, Michael Andrew. b 53. Trin Coll Bris. **d** 78 **p** 79 Roch. C of St Barn Cray Dio Roch from 78. *2 Church House, Rushet Road, St Paul's Cray, Orpington, Kent BR5 2PU* (Orpington 33706)

HARRIS, Michael William Henry. b 42. Codr Coll Barb 66. **d** 70 Barb for Guy **p** 70 Guy. C of St Matt Demerara 70-73; V of Meten-Meer-Zorg 73-75. *Address temp unknown.*

✠ **HARRIS, Right Rev Patrick Burnet.** b 34. Keble Coll Ox BA 58, MA 63. Clifton Th Coll 58. **d** 60 **p** 61 Ox. C of St Ebbe Ox 60-63; w SAMS from 63; Archd of N Argent 70-73; Cons Ld Bp of N Argent at Misión Chaque£na, Padre Lozano, Salta 27 May 73 by Bp of Parag; Bps Flagg and Leake; res 80; Asst Bp of Wakef from 81; R of Kirkheaton Dio Wakef from 81; Commiss N Argent from 81. *Kirkheaton Rectory, Huddersfield, Yorks, HD5 0JR.* (Huddersfield 31449)

HARRIS, Peter Malcolm. b 52. Em Coll Cam BA 74, MA 79. Trin Coll Bris 78. **d** 80 Ches **p** 81 Birkenhead for Ches. C of Upton (or Overchurch) Dio Ches from 80. *20 Oakland Drive, Upton Wirral, Merseyside.*

HARRIS, Peter Wright. b 45. Dalhousie Univ Halifax NS BA 68. Kings Coll Halifax NS MSLitt 72. 1 71 NS **p** 72 Bp Arnold for NS. Tutor Trin Coll Tor 71-75; R of Tangier Dio NS from 76. *Rectory, Tangier, NS, Canada.* (Tangier 12)

HARRIS, Raymond. b 36. Univ of Nottm BA (3rd cl Lat) 58. Lich Th Coll 58. **d** 60 **p** 61 Southw. C of St Francis New Clifton 60-63; Davyhulme 63-65; V of Ch Ch Bacup Dio Man from 65. *Christ Church Vicarage, Bacup, Lancs, OL13 9DQ.* (Bacup 874628)

HARRIS, Canon Raymond John. b 29. Univ of Leeds, BA 51. Coll of Resurr Mirfield 51. **d** 53 **p** 54 Carl. C of Workington 53-59; V of St Barn Swindon Dio Bris from 59; Surr from 74; Hon Can of Bris Cathl from 80. *Vicarage, Ferndale Road, Swindon, Wilts, SN2 1EX.* (Swindon 23648)

HARRIS, Ven Reginald Brian. b 34. Ch Coll Cam BA 58, MA 61. Ridley Hall Cam. **d** 59 Stafford for Lich **p** 60 Lich. C of St Bart Wednesbury 59-61; Uttoxeter 61-64; V of St Pet Bury 64-70; Ed Man Dioc Directory 69-75; V of Ch Ch Walmsley 70-80; RD of Walmsley 70-80; Archd of Man and Can Res of Man Cathl from 80. *4 Victoria Avenue, Eccles, Manchester, M30 9HA.* (061-707 6444)

HARRIS, Robert Austin Meire. b 1895. Late Exhib of Ch Ch Ox BA (*sc* Nat Sc) 20, MA 27. Westcott Ho Cam 35. **d** 35 **p** 36 St Andr. Asst Master Trin Coll Glenalmond 35-37; V of Casterton 37-45; Knutsford 45-68; V of Toft 57-68. *32 Coppice Road, Willaston, Nantwich, Chesh.* (Crewe 67583)

HARRIS, Robert James. b 45. ALCD 73. St Jo Coll Nottm 69. **d** 72 Doncaster for Sheff **p** 73 Sheff. C of St Jo Evang Park Sheff 72-75; Goole 75-78; V of Bramley and Ravenfield Dio Sheff from 78. *Bramley Vicarage, Rotherham, S Yorks.* (Wickersley 542028)

HARRIS, Ven Robert James. St Pauls' Coll Grahmstn 65. **d** 65 **p** 66 Kimb K. C of St Jo Evang Mafeking 65-68; St Alb Cathl Pret 68-71; R of Tzaneen w Duiwelskloof and Phalaborwa Dio Pret from 71; Archd of N Transvaal from 78. *PO Box 612, Tzaneen, Transvaal, S Africa.* (Tzaneen 21894)

HARRIS, Robert William. b 26. Roch Th Coll 64. **d** 66 Dover for Cant **p** 67 Cant. C of Herne Bay 66-70; V of Nonington (w Barfreystone from 74) 70-77; C-in-c of Barfreystone 72-74; C of Herne Bay Dio Cant from 77. *10 Cecil Park, Herne Bay, Kent.* (Herne Bay 3020)

HARRIS, Ronald Edward. Univ of K Coll NS BA 55, LTh 58. **d** 57 **p** 58 Bp W W Davis for NS. R of Blandford 57-61; Pugwash 61-64; R of River John 61-64; C of All SS Cathl Halifax 64-67; R of Bridgewater 67-75; St Jas Halifax Dio NS from 76. *16 Dutch Village Road, Halifax, NS, Canada.*

HARRIS, Ronald Wilfred. b 15. Roch Th Coll 64. **d** 66 Linc **p** 66 Grimsby for Linc. C of L Coates 66-68; St Laur-in-Thanet 68-73; P-in-c of Bishopsbourne w Kingston 73-77; R of Barham (w Bishopsbourne and Kingston from 77) 75-80. *1 Woodford Court, Birchington-on-Sea, Thanet, Kent, CT7 9DR.* (Thanet 41707)

HARRIS, Roy Edward. b 24. St Jo Coll Dur BA and Van Mildert Scho 47, Dipl Th (w Distinc) 49, MA 59. **d** 49 **p** 50 Ex. C of St Andr w St Cath Plymouth 49-52; Chipping Barnet 52-53; PC of St Geo w St Paul Stonehouse 53-58; V of Wadsley 58-65; PC (V from 69) of Em Plymouth 65-73; Totnes w Bridgetown Dio Ex from 73; Surr from 74. *Vicarage, Totnes, Devon.* (Totnes 863191)

HARRIS, Roy Stanley Henry. b 29. St Paul's Coll Grahmstn 71. **d** 73 **p** 74 Johann. C of Benoni Dio Johann from 73. *104 Cranbourne Avenue, Benoni, Transvaal 1500, S Africa.* (011-849 5111)

HARRIS, Rupert Gustavus Musgrave. b 13. Trin Coll Dub BA 36, MA 56. **d** 37 **p** 38 Down. C of Shankill (Lurgan) 37-40; CF (EC) 40-46; I of Cloone and Chap of Lough Rynn 46-52; Castlebar 52-56; Galway 56-80; Athenry w Monivea 56-80; Dom Chap to Bp of Tuam 57-80; Provost of Tuam 60-70; Archd 70-80; Can and Preb 60-80; Exam Chap to Bp of Tuam 70-80. *c/o Rectory, Taylors Hill, Galway, Irish Republic.*

HARRIS, Seymour David. b 40 SOC 73. **d** 75 Lon **p** 76 Kens for Lon. C of St Jas Hampton Hill 75-79; P-in-c of Fulwell Dio Lon from 79. *Vicarage, Clonmell Road, Teddington, TW11 0ST.* (01-977 2853)

HARRIS, Silas Morgan. b 1888. St D Coll Lamp Bates Pri and Eldon Scho 11, Butler Scho 12, W D Llewellyn (Sen) Scho 13, Engl Essay Pri and Creaton Pri 12 & 13, BA (1st cl Welsh Mods and Finals) 14. Powis Exhib Keble Coll Ox BA (2nd cl Th) 16, MA 20. **d** 16 **p** 17 Llan. C of St Mary Virg Cardiff 16-18; St Steph Birm 18-19; Perm to Offic as Chap of H Cross Retreat Ho Limpsfield 21-22; Chap Conv of Good Shepherd Canvey I 23-24; P-in-c of St Columba Newton w Cambuslang 24-26; V of Egmanton 27-56; L to Offic Dio Heref 57-68; Perm to Offic Dio Llan from 68. *4 Park View Court, Coldstream Terrace, Cardiff, CF1 8LY.*

HARRIS, Thomas. b 1900. Univ of Wales BSc 26. St Mich Coll Llan 29. **d** 30 **p** 31 St D. C of Yspytty Ystwyth w Ystrad Meurig and Asst Master at St Jo Coll Ystrad Meurig 30-34; C of St Deiniol Cathl and St Jas Ban 34-38; St Jas Ban 38-40; V of Caerdeon w Bontddu 40-56; Amlwch 56-69. *29 Penrhos Road, Bangor, Gwyn, LL57 2AX.* (Bangor 53922)

HARRIS, Thomas. Univ Coll Tor 45. Wycl Th Coll. Columb Univ MA 50. **d** 45 NS. C of St Paul Halifax 45-46; St Paul Runnymede Tor 48-50; E Field Sec Bd Relig Educn Ch of Engl in Canada 52-55; Prof of Relig Educn and Dir of Field Work Hur Coll Lon Ont from 55. *Huron College, London, 72, Ont, Canada.*

HARRIS, Thomas Eric. Angl Th Coll Vancouver LTh 36. **d** 36 Koot for New Westmr **p** 38 New Westmr. C of St Helen Vancouver 36-40; I of Langley Prairie (w Fort Langley 40-55) and Otter 40-63; Hon Can of New Westmr 59-75; I of St Marg of Scotld Burnaby 63-75. *3594 East 22nd Avenue, Vancouver, BC, Canada.*

HARRIS, Canon Thomas Heywood. Em Coll Cam BA 41, MA 45. St Paul's Coll Grahmstn 45. **d** 46 **p** 47 Natal. C of St Pet Maritzburg 46-51; V of Mooi River 51-55; Durban S 55-58; York w Ravensworth 58-61; St Martin Durban N 61-65; C of St Paul Durban 65-66; R of Kloof 66-73; Archd of Pinetown 66-73; Hon Can of Natal from 73; R of Greyville 74-76; L to Offic Dio Natal 76-79; R of Umzinto Dio Natal from 79. *Box 615, Umzinto, Natal, S Africa.*

HARRIS, Thomas William. b 54. AKC 76. Linc Th Coll 77. **d** 78 Doncaster for Sheff **p** 79 Sheff. C of St Chad Norton Woodseats Sheff 78-81; V of Barnby Dun Dio Sheff from 81; P-in-c of Kirk Bramwith Dio Sheff from 81; Fenwick from 81. *Vicarage, Barnby Dun, Doncaster, S Yorks, DN3 1AA.* (Doncaster 882835)

HARRIS, Canon Wallace George. b 03. Wycl Hall Ox 44. **d** 45 Stepney for Lon **p** 46 Lon. [f Baptist Min] C of St Jas Alperton 45-47; St Mary Virg Reading (in c of All SS) 47-51; CF 51-59; Dir of Chr Stewardship Dio S'wark 60-78; Publ Pr Dio S'wark from 61; Commiss Barb from 65; Hon Can of S'wark Cathl 72-80; Can (Emer) from 80. *3 High Street, Cranborne, Dorset.*

HARRIS, Walter Ruggles. K Coll NS BA 38. **d** 40 **p** 41 NS. C of H Trin Liv NS 40-41; I of Petite Riviere 41-47; Musquodoboit Harbour 47-55; R of Bedford 55-64; St Matthias Halifax 64-77; Truro Dio NS from 77; Hon Can of NS 73-76. *Box 83, Truro, NS, Canada.* (893-2173)

HARRIS, William Edgar. b 1890. **d** 52 **p** 53 St E. C of Troston w Gt Livermere 52-53; C-in-c of Honington w Sapiston 53-54; R 54-70; C-in-c of Thorpe-by-Ixworth 53-58. *Rye House, Downham-in-the-Isle, Ely, Cambs, CB6 2TR.*

HARRIS, William Eric Mackenzie. b 46. Sarum Wells Th Coll 72. **d** 75 **p** 76 Chich. C of St Richard Langney Eastbourne 75-79; Moulsecoomb Dio Chich 80-81; Team V from 81. *Barn Lodge, Norwich Drive, Brighton, BN2 4LA.*

HARRIS, William Ernest. b 21. TCD BA 48, MA 57. **d** 48 **p** 49 Connor. C of St Matt Belf 48-51; St Thos Belf 51-53; Hd of S Ch Miss Ballymacarrett 53-59; I of Annahilt 59-63; Regr Dios Down and Drom 59-63; R of St Pet Belf Dio Connor from 63; Dioc Dir of Ordinands and Stewardship Adv from 63. *697 Antrim Road, Belfast, N Ireland.* (Belfast 777053)

HARRIS, William Fergus. b 36. CCC Cam BA 59, MA 63. Westcott Ho Cam 60. **d** 62 **p** 63 St Andr. C of St Andr St Andr 62-64; Chap Univ of Edin 64-71; R of St Pet Lutton Place City and Dio Edin from 71. *3 Bright's Crescent, Edinburgh, EH9 2DB.* (031-667 6224)

HARRIS, William Joseph Kenneth. b 10. Sarum Th Coll 31. **d** 33 **p** 34 Southw. C of St Mich AA Radford 33-37; Redruth 37-43; Withycombe Raleigh (in c of All SS Exmouth) 43-49; PC of St John Torquay 49; V of Burlescombe 49-52; Mullion 52-75; Perm to Offic Dio Ex from 77. *1 Beacon Court, Louisa Terrace, Exmouth, Devon, EX8 2AQ.* (Exmouth 6460)

HARRIS, William Murray. Ridley Coll Melb ACT ThL 63. **d** 64 **p** 65 Tas. C of New Norf 64-66; R of Macquarie Plains 66-69; Deloraine 69-76. *c/o Holdsworthy Military Camp, NSW, Australia 2173.*

HARRIS-DOUGLAS, John Douglas. b 36. Ripon Hall Ox 65. **d** 66 Win **p** 67 Lich. C of Ringwood 66-67; Berkswich w Walton 67-71; R of St Tudy (w Michaelstow from 74) 71-76; Fiskerton 76-79; V of Brafferton w Pilmoor & Myton-on-Swale Dale York from 79; P-in-c of Thormanby Dio York from 79. *Brafferton Vicarage, Helperby, York, YO6 2QB.* (Helperby 244)

HARRIS-EVANS, Canon Francis Douglas Harris. b 07. Keble Coll Ox BA 32, MA 39. Linc Th Coll 32. **d** 35 **p** 36 Leic. C of Birstall 35-39; Ashby-de-la-Zouch 39-40; St Jo Bapt Knighton 40-41; Ashby-de-la-Zouch 41-45; Ashe Lect 40 and 42-45; V of Horninghold w Blaston 45-51; C-in-c 51-54; RD of Gartree iii 49-57; R of Medbourne w Holt 51-57; Cler Sec of Leic Dio Conf 51-62; Hon Can of Leic 54-74; Can (Emer) from 74; Surr 56-74; Asst RD of Christianity 60-62; RD 62-66; V of St Jo Bapt Knighton 57-68; Newtown Linford 68-74; Proc Conv Leic 63-64; Commiss Brisb 71-80; Perm to Offic Dios Leic and Pet from 74. *2 Castle Close, Uppingham, Leics, LE15 9PN.* (Uppingham 3699)

HARRIS-EVANS, William Giles. b 46. K Coll Lon and Warm AKC 68. U Th Coll Bangalore Dipl Th 70. **d** 70 **p** 71 S'wark. C of Clapham 70-74; Miss P Kandy 75-78; V of Benhilton Dio S'wark from 78. *Benhilton Vicarage, All Saints' Road, Sutton, Surrey.* (01-644 9070)

HARRISON, Alan George. b 20. Univ of Leeds BA (2nd cl Phil) 49. Coll of Resurr Mirfield 49. **d** 51 **p** 52 Pet. C of St Mary Wellingborough 51-55; R of Corozal Br Hond 55-61; V of St Francis Bournemouth 61-68; Eastleigh 68-72; Commiss Br Hond (Bel from 73) from 61; Chap Guild of Health Lon 72-76; Chap St Mich Conv Ham from 73; Sec Coun for Relig Commun from 76. *St Anselm's House, 43 Ham Common, Richmond, Surrey, TW10 7JG.* (01-948 0775)

HARRISON, Alan William. b 16. Lich Th Coll 38. **d** 41 **p** 42 Cant. C of St Osw Thornton Heath 41-43; St Cuthb Fir Vale Sheff 43-49; V of Orton-on-the-Hill w Twycross 49-55; R and V of Somerby w Burrough-on-the-Hill and Pickwell 55-72; R of Boxford w Hadleigh Hamlet 72-82. *70 Woolpit, Suffolk.*

HARRISON, Alastair Lee. b 22. ALCD 51. **d** 51 **p** 52 Ex. C of Stoke Damerel 51-54; Chap RAF 54-67; Miss to Seamen

Anglesey 69-72; Dublin 72-77; L to Offic Dios Dub and Glendal and Meath and Kild from 77. *2 Church Avenue, Rathmines, Dublin 6.*

HARRISON, Albert Arthur. b 01. **d** 63 Knaresborough for Ripon **p** 64 Ripon. C of Richmond 63-65; Perm to Offic Dio Ripon 65-67; Chap at Aske from 65; P-in-c of Rokeby w Brignall Dio Ripon from 67. *16 Ronaldshay Drive, Richmond, Yorks.* (Richmond 3072)

HARRISON, Alfred Tuke Priestman. b 21. Ch Ch Ox 1st Cl Mods 40, BA 43, 2nd cl Lit Hum 47, MA 47, Dipl Th 49. Wells Th Coll 48. **d** 49 **p** 50 B & W. C of St Andr Taunton 49-55; C-in-c of St Pet Conv Distr Lyngford Taunton 55-58; V 58; V of La Brea 59-66; In Amer Ch 66-68; Dean and R of H Trin Cathl Port of Spain 69-73; V of Leesfield Dio Man from 73. *St Thomas Vicarage, Thomas Street, Lees, Oldham, Lancs OL4 5DA.* (061-624 3731)

HARRISON, Bernard Charles. b 37. st Mich Coll Llan 61. **d** 64 Warrington for Liv **p** 65 Liv. C of St Marg Toxt Pk 64-69; Hindley 69-71; V of St Geo Wigan Dio Liv from 71. *6 Wrightington Street, Wigan, Lancs.* (Wigan 44500)

HARRISON, Bruce Mosman. St Jo Coll Morpeth ACT ThL 49. **d** 47 **p** 48 Bath. C of Cobar 47-51; P-in-c 51-58; Nyngan 58-59; E Orange 59-62; Oberon 62-64; E Orange, Kilmore, and Yackandanah 65; Cohuna 66-72; Loddon w Raywood 72-73; Bridgewater 73-76; Golden Square 76-77; R of Daylesford Dio Bend from 77. *Rectory, Daylesford, Vic, Australia 3460.*

HARRISON, Bruce Mountford. b 49. AKC 71. St Aug Coll Cant 71. **d** 72 Bp Skelton for Dur **p** 73 Dur. C of St Cuthb Hebburn 72-75; St Jo Evang Bethnal Green 75-77; P-in-c of St Bart Bethnal Green 77-78; Team V of St Jo Evang and St Simon Zelotes w St Bart Bethnal Green 78-80; P-in-c of St Thos Conv Distr Pennywell Bp Wearmouth Dio Dur from 80. *Parsonage, Pennywell, Sunderland, Co Durham.* (Hylton 2100)

HARRISON, Cecil Marriott. b 11. Trin Coll Cam BA 32, MA 36. Westcott Ho Cam. **d** 66 **p** 67 Pet. Hd Master K Sch Pet 51-69; V of Aislaby 69-79. *4 Rosedale Abbey, Pickering, N Yorks, YO18 8RA.* (Lastingham 569)

HARRISON, Cecil Paul. b 19. Keble Coll Ox BA 41, MA 46. Westcott Ho Cam 42. **d** 43 **p** 44 Ches. C of All SS Cheadle Hulme 43-44; Broadheath 44-47; Knutsford 47-52; V of Whitegate 52-61; Ed Ches Dioc Leaflet 55-61; The Pilot from 63; R of St Clem Jersey Dio Win from 61. *St Clement's Rectory, Jersey, CI.* (0534-51992)

HARRISON, Charles Haydn. b 32. Lich Th Coll 57. **d** 60 **p** 61 Ripon. C of All H w St Simon Leeds 60-64; Barwick-in-Elmet 64-66; V of Swine 66-73; Sen Dioc Youth Officer York from 73; V of Osbaldwick w Murton Dio York from 78; Actg RD of Bulmer from 80. *Osbaldwick Vicarage, York, YO1 3AX.* (York 411901)

HARRISON, Christopher Joseph. b 38. Univ of Bris BEducn 75. K Coll Lon and Warm AKC 61. **d** 62 **p** 63 Linc. C of Bottesford w Ashby 62-67; Elloughton 67-68; C-in-c of Farmington 69-74; C of Tewkesbury Dio Glouc from 74; C-in-c of Tredington w Stoke Orchard Dio Glouc from 74. *Vicarage, Tredington, Tewkesbury, Glos.*

HARRISON, Colin Charles. b 32. Univ of Nottm BA (3rd cl Th) 59. Ripon Hall Ox 59. **d** 61 **p** 62 Liv. C of St Chad w Ch Ch Everton 61-64; Chap Miss to Seamen and R of Ch Ch Yokohama 64-66; Asst Chap Glas and C-in-c of St Gabr Govan 66-71; R of St Aid Clarkston 71-74; Area Sec Chr Aid Inner Lon from 74; Hon C of St Nich Cole Abbey Lon 74-78; St Botolph-without-Bishopsgate City and Dio Lon from 78. *32 Mayow Road, SE26 4JA.* (01-778 0244)

HARRISON, David Henry. b 40. Dipl Th (Lon) 67. Tyndale Hall, Bris 65. **d** 68 **p** 69 Man. C of St Paul Bolton 68-72; V of Birtle (or Bircle) Dio Man from 72. *Birtle Vicarage, Bury, Lancs.* (061-764 3853)

HARRISON, David Robert. b 31. Univ of Bris BSc 52. Oak Hill Th Coll 56. **d** 58 **p** 59 S'wark. C of Brixton Hill 58-60; Harpurphey 60-62; Overseas Miss Fellowship of CIM Sing 62-67; V of Greenfield 67-78; Tonge Fold Dio Man from 78. *St Chad's Vicarage, Tonge Fold, Bolton, BL2 6AW.* (Bolton 25809)

HARRISON, David Samuel. b 44. Univ of Wales (Bangor) BSc 67. St Mich Th Coll Llan 67. **d** 70 **p** 71 Llan. C of Canton 70-74; Witton 74-78; V of Sutton Dio Ches from 78. *St George's Vicarage, Byrons Lane, Macclesfield, Chesh.* (Macclesfield 23209)

HARRISON, David Shirley. **d** 61 **p** 62 Wel. C of Hawera 61-66; Chap RNZAF 67-74; Perm to Offic Dio Auckld 67-69; Dio Wel 69-71; Hon C of Te Atatu 71-74; V of Pongaroa 74-81; L to Offic Dio Waik from 81. *21 Hori Street, New Plymouth, NZ.*

HARRISON, Ernest Wilfrid. St Edm Hall Ox BA (2nd cl Engl Lang and Lit) 38, MA 56. Univ of Tor MA 69. Sarum Th Coll 38. **d** 40 **p** 41 Liv. C of St Bart Roby 40-43; C-in-c of St D Huyton w Roby 43-45; C of Coulsdon 45-47; Min of Conv Distr of St Barn Coulsdon 47-50; Asst Missr Dio S'wark 50-51; M and Missr of St Sav Coll S'wark and Ed S'wark Dioc Leaflet 51-52; I of Waterville PQ 52-56; Sillery 56-62; Exam Chap to Bp of Queb 57-62; Dom Chap 60-62; Assoc Ed Sec GBRE 62-66; Lect Ryerson Polytechnical Inst Tor from 66. *72 Shippigan Crescent, Willowdale, Ont, Canada.*

HARRISON, Francis. Coll Ho Ch Ch 53. **d** 58 **p** 59 Auckld. C of Kawakawa 58-60; Waimate N 60-64; Pukekohe 64-66; CF (NZ) from 66; L to Offic Dio Wel 66-71; Hon C of Phillipstown Ch Ch 72-74; P-in-c of N Hokianga Distr 77-80; V of Bombay Dio Auckld from 80. *Box 6, Bombay, S Auckland, NZ.* (870)

HARRISON, Fred. St Aid Coll. **d** 59 **p** 60 Liv. C of Prescot 59-62; V of St Andr Litherland 62-76; Hon C of Kirkham Dio Blackb from 76. *St Michael's Cottage, Kirkham, Nr Preston, PR4 2SL.*

HARRISON, Frederick Charles. Univ of Lon BD 36. AKC (1st cl) 36. Linc Th Coll 36. **d** 37 **p** 38 Southw. C of E Retford 37-38; St Mary Bulwell 38-39; Chap RAFVR 39-45; C of Sunninghill 45-48; V of All SS Dun 48-63; P-in-c of Ravensbourne 51-63; Exam Chap to Bp of Dun 50-55; Lect Selw Coll Dun 56-63; Chap Otago Univ SCM 59-63; Dir Relig Broadcasting and Television Prov of NZ from 63; Hon C of St Paul's Cathl Wel from 64. *37 Moana Road, Kelburn, Wellington, NZ.* (757-351)

HARRISON, Graham Leslie. BD Lon 76. Moore Th Coll Syd ACT ThL (2nd cl) 59. **d** and **p** 60 Syd. C of Marrickville 60-61; Liverpool 61-63; BFBS and L to Offic Dios C & Goulb and River 63-65; Dio Syd 63-66; C of Katoomba 66; C-in-c of Wilberforce 66-74; R 74-75; Enfield Dio Syd from 75. *53 Coronation Parade, Enfield, NSW, Australia 2136.* (642 3171)

HARRISON, Guy Airy. Clare Coll Cam BA 29, MA 33. Wycl Hall, Ox 48. **d** 49 **p** 50 Roch. C of St Jo Evang Bromley 49-51; St Mark Lyncombe 51-52; V of North Stoke w Ipsden and Mongewell 52-57; R of Channell Tas 57-58; Chap Launceston Gr Sch 58-62; Asst Master Canberra Gr Sch 63-73; Perm to Offic Dio Melb 73-79; Dio Chich from 79. *Ramsay Hall, Bryon Road, Worthing, BN11 3HN.* (Worthing 36880)

HARRISON, Harold Vernon. Coll Ho Ch Ch 59. NZ Bd of Th Stud LTh 66. **d** 59 Ch Ch **p** 60 Dun for Ch Ch. C of Riccarton 59; Ashburton 59-63; V of Kumara and C of Hokitika 63; V of Ross w S Westland 63-66; Waikari 66-70; Temuka 70-74; P-in-c of N Brighton Dio Ch Ch from 74. *103 Marriott's Road, Christchurch 7, NZ.* (889-032)

HARRISON, Herbert Gerald. b 29. Oak Hill Th Coll 53. **d** 56 **p** 57 Derby. C of H Trin Chesterfield 56-59; St Andr L Cam (in c of St Steph) 59-64; Chap Miss to Seamen Momb 64-68; Port Chap Ipswich 68-74; V of All SS Ipswich 74-81; P-in-c of Elmsett w Aldham Dio St E from 81; Kersey Dio St E from 81. *Rectory, Hadleigh Road, Elmsett, Ipswich, Suff, IP7 6ND.* (Offton 219)

HARRISON, Ian Wetherby. b 39. Kelham Th Coll 59. **d** 64 **p** 65 S'wark. C of St Agnes Kennington Pk 64-67; East Ham 67-71; V of St Mich AA Walthamstow 71-78; P-in-c of U Hopton Dio Wakef from 78; Dioc Ecumen Officer Dio Wakef from 78. *Upper Hopton Vicarage, Mirfield, W Yorks, WF14 8EL.* (Mirfield 493569)

HARRISON, Jack. b 08. Ripon Hall Ox 64. **d** 65 **p** 66 Roch. C of St Francis Conv Distr Strood 65-69; V of Downe 69-76. *Jolly Cottage, Langham Road, Robertsbridge, Sussex.*

HARRISON, James Taute. b 32. **d** 81 Auckld. C of Parengarenga Ahipara Peria Dio Auckld from 81. *Oruru, R.D. 3, Kaitaia, NZ.*

HARRISON, John. b 49. Fitzw Coll Cam BA 71, MA 74. Westcott Ho Cam 74. **d** 77 **p** 78 York. C of Nunthorpe-in-Cleveland 77-81; St Steph Acomb Dio York from 81. *12 Askham Lane, Acomb, York, YO2 3HA.* (York 791511)

HARRISON, John Gilbert. St Francis Coll Nundah. **d** 31 **p** 33 N Queensld. C of St Jas Cathl Townsville 31-34; M of Bro of St Barn 33-39; C of Mackay 40-41; Chap AMF 41-46; Chap C of E Gr Sch Brisb 46-51; C of St Andr S Brisb 51-52; V of St Matt Holland Pk 52-56; R 56-63; Chap Wolston Pk Hosp Bris 63-72; Perm to Offic Dio Brisb from 73. *103 Highland Terrace, St Lucia, Queensland, Australia 4067.* (370 9639)

HARRISON, Canon John Gordon. b 13. Trin Coll Bris 32. Wadh Coll Ox BA (2nd cl Th) 48, MA 52. **d** 36 Lon for Col **p** 38 Egypt. Miss at Kapoeta 36-39; Opari 39-40; Kapoeta 40-41; CMS Nugent Sch Loka S Sudan 41-45; C of St John Reading 45-46; L to Offic Dio Ox 46-48; V of Weald 48-52; Gerrard's Cross Dio Ox from 52; RD of Amersham 71-78: Hon Can of Ch Ch Cathl Ox from 75. *Vicarage, Vicarage Way, Gerrard's Cross, Bucks, SL9 8AS.* (Gerrard's Cross 83301)

HARRISON, John Northcott. b 31. St Jo Coll Cam 2nd cl Hist Trip pt i, 53, BA (3rd cl Th Trip pt i) 54. Westcott Ho

Cam 54. **d** 56 **p** 57 Ripon. C of Moor Allerton 56-59; Bedale 59-61; V of Hudswell w Downholme 61-64; Youth Chap Dio Dur 64-68; V of Bp Auckland 68-75; Commun Chap Stockton-on-Tees Dio Dur from 75. *3 Darlington Lane, Norton, Stockton-on-Tees, Cleve.*

HARRISON, Joseph. b 05. Univ Coll Dur BA (2nd cl Engl Lang and Lit) and Van Mildert Scho 28, Dipl in Th 30, MA 31. LGSM (Eloc) 34. **d** 30 **p** 31 Dur. C of S Westoe 30-37; PC of St Osw Hebburn 37-47; PC of St Paul Stockton-on-Tees 47-61; Chap Stockton Children's Hosp 57-61; Surr from 60; V of Grindon 61-71; L to Offic Dio Dur from 71. *Sheep Dene, Wynyard Park, Thorpe Thewles, Stockton-on-Tees, TS21 3JH.*

HARRISON, Joseph Benson. b 11. OBE 74. **d** 49 **p** 50 S & M. C of Rushen 49-52; CF (TA) 52-55; St Geo Douglas 52-53; V of Marown 53-55; Gen Sec C of E Coun for Social Aid and Gen Perm to Offic 55-75. *The Beehive, Chipping Campden, Glos, GL55 6DE.* (0386-840420)

HARRISON, Leslie John. b 12. Univ of Lon (2nd cl Econ) 33, Dipl Educn 34. Wells Th Coll 63. **d** 64 **p** 65 Bris. C of St Alb Westbury Pk Clifton 64-67; V of St Anne Greenbank Bris 67-73; V of Caxton 73-80; R of Longstowe 73-80. *55 Long Lane, Willingham, Cambridge, CB4 5LD.*

HARRISON, Canon Lorenzo Bancroft. St Pet Th Coll Ja 47. Dipl in Th (St Aug Cant) 55. **d** 48 Kingston for Ja **p** 49 Ja. C of St Mich Kingston 49-51; Spanish Town Cathl 51-52; R of St Ann's Bay 52-62; Montego Bay 62-68; Commiss Br Hond 67-68; C of St Geo St Catharine's 68-70; R of St Cuthb Oakville 70-76; Commiss Ja 70-77; Antig from 71; Hon Can of Niag from 74; P-in-c of Woodburn 76-78; Exam Chap to Bp Suffr of Niag 76-79; R of St Aug Hamilton Dio Niag from 78. *2017 Kingsbridge Court, Burlington, Ont, Canada.* (416-335 4213)

HARRISON, (Crispin) Michael Burt. b 36. Univ of Leeds BA (2nd cl Phil) 59. Trin Coll Ox BA (2nd cl Th) 62, MA 66. Coll of Resurr Mirfield 62. M CR 68. **d** 63 **p** 64 Dur. C of St Aid W Hartlepool 63-64; All SS Middlesbrough 64-66; L to Offic Dio Wakef from 67; St Pet Coll Federal Th Sem S Afr 69-77; Regr Coll of Resurr Mirfield from 78. *House of the Resurrection, Mirfield, W Yorks, WF14 0BN.* (Mirfield 493362)

HARRISON, Michael Vibert. b 19. Ex Coll Ox BA 42, MA 45. Linc Th Coll 42. **d** 44 **p** 45 Guildf. C of Merrow 44-47; Woodstock Capetn 47-50; R of Clanwilliam 50-55; P-in-c of Matroosfontein 55-59; R of Bredasdorp 59-62; Robertson 62-67; Prec and C of St Nich Cathl Newc T 67-69; C-in-c of St Cuthb Conv Distr Southwick 69-71; R of St Mary Jersey Dio Win from 72. *St Mary's Rectory, Jersey, CI.* (Jersey 81410)

HARRISON, Noel Milburn. St Aid Coll 54. Dipl Th (Lon) 56. Univ of Leeds MPhil 75. **d** 57 **p** 58 Sheff. C of St Jas Doncaster 57-60; Chap Yorks Residential Sch for Deaf Doncaster and Hon Chap to Deaf and Dumb Dio Sheff 60-68; C of Woodlands 60-62; Hd Master Elmete Hall Sch for Deaf Leeds from 68. *Elmete Hall School, Elmete Lane, Leeds, 8.* (Leeds 656666)

HARRISON, Paul Graham. b 53. Sarum Wells Th Coll 76. **d** 79 **p** 80 Ex. C of Brixham w Churston Ferrers Dio Ex from 79. *5a Heath Road, Brixham, Devon, TQ5 9BL.*

HARRISON, Peter George Stanley. b 22. St Jo Coll Dur BA (Hons Th) 49, Dipl Th (w distinc) 50. **d** 50 **p** 51 Birm. C of St Martin Birm 50-55; Chap of St Jo Coll Dur 56-59; V of St Jas W Derby 59-68; Beverley Minster w Tickton Dio York from 68; C-in-c of Routh Dio York from 68; RD of Beverley from 73. *Minster Vicarage, Beverley, N Humb, HU17 0DN.* (Beverley 881434)

HARRISON, Peter Graham. Ch Ch Ox BA (3rd cl Phil Pol and Econ) 34, MA 38. Westcott Ho Cam 34. **d** 35 **p** 36 Cant. C of St Pet-in-Thanet 35-38; St Sav Croydon 38-41; Chap RNVR 41-46; V of St Jas Westgate 45-52; R of Hawkinge 52-58; R of Acrise 52-58; C-in-c of Swingfield 52-56; V of Gt Torrington 58-78; R of L Torrington 59-78; RD of Torrington 66-77; P-in-c of Holne Dio Ex from 78. *Holne Vicarage, Newton Abbot, Devon TQ13 9QD.* (Poundsgate 382)

HARRISON, Peter John. b 40. K Coll Lon and Warm AKC 62. **d** 63 **p** 64 Southw. C of Hucknall Torkard 63-66; Ordsall 66-70; Carlton 70-74; Colwick 70-74; P-in-c of Overton w Fyfield and E Kennett 74-75; Team V of Upper Kennet 75-80; R of Hickling w Broughton Sulney and Kinoulton Dio Southw from 80. *Rectory, Newbold Way, Kinoulton, Notts.* (Kinoulton 657)

HARRISON, Peter Keith. b 44. St Aid Coll 65. **d** 68 **p** 69 Ches. C of Higher Bebington 68-71; Walmsley 71-74; V of Lumb-in-Rossendale 74-79; C-in-c of St Marg Heywood Dio Man 79; V from 79. *St Margaret's Vicarage, Heys Lane, Heywood, Gtr Man, OL10 3RD.* (Heywood 68053)

HARRISON, Peter Leonard. b 43. Wollaston Coll Perth ACT Dipl Th 71. **d** & **p** 72 NW Austr. C of Ch Ch Cathl Darwin 72-74; Chap Miss to Seamen Port Hedland W Austr 74-75; R of S Cross 75-78; Bayswater Dio Perth from 78. *7 Murray Street, Bayswater, W Australia 6053.* (271-1906)

HARRISON, Peter Reginald Wallace. b 39. Selw Coll Cam BA 62. Ridley Hall Cam 62. **d** 64 **p** 65 Bris. C of St Luke w Ch Ch Bris 64-69; Chap to Greenhouse Trust 69-77; Dir of Northorpe Hall Trust from 77. *Northorpe Cottage, Mirfield, W Yorks.* (0924-492183)

HARRISON, Philip Hubert. b 37. Sarum Wells Th Coll 77. **d** 79 **p** 80 Nor. C of Wymondham Dio Nor from 79. *43 Ashleigh Gardens, Wymondham, Norfolk.* (Wymondham 604342)

HARRISON, Raymond Harold. b 16. Keble Coll Ox BA 41, MA 45. St Aug Coll Cant. **d** 42 **p** 43 Newc T. C of St Pet Balkwell 42-45; Henfield 45-46; Wisbech 46-49; V of Stow-Bardolph w Wimbotsham 49-56; R of Fen Ditton 56-75; RD of Quy 73-75; V of W Wratting Dio Ely from 75; C-in-c of Weston Colville Dio Ely 75-76; R from 76. *West Wratting Vicarage, Cambridge, CB1 5NA.* (West Wratting 377)

HARRISON, Robert Peter. b 28. Chich Th Coll. **d** 60 Lon **p** 61 Kens for Lon. C of Ch Sav Ealing 60-64; St Mich and St Geo Conv Distr White City Hammersmith 64-66; C-in-c of St Pet Fulham Dio Lon 66-73; V from 73. *St Peter's Vicarage, Fulham, SW6.* (01-385 2045)

HARRISON, Roland Kenneth. ALCD 43. Univ of Lon BD (2nd cl) 43, M Th 47, PhD (Th) Lon 52. Hur Coll Hon DD 63. **d** 43 **p** 44 Blackb. C of St Mark Preston Blackb 43-45; All SS Marple 45-47; Chap Clifton Th Coll 47-49; Prof of Bibl Gr and NT at Hur Coll 49-52; OT and Hebr at Univ of W Ont 52-60; OT at Wycl Coll Tor from 60; Hon C of Ch of Transfig City and Dio Tor from 64. *Wycliffe College, Toronto, 5, Ont, Canada.*

HARRISON, Ronald Eric. b 47. Univ of BC BA 68. Espic Th Sch Cam Mass BD 71. **d** 71 New Westmr. C of St Phil Vanc 72-76; I of St Aug Vanc Dio New Westmr from 76. *Box 304, 2168 West 2nd Avenue, Vancouver 9, BC, Canada.*

HARRISON, Roy. K Coll Lon and Warm AKC 58. **d** 59 Stafford for Lich **p** 60 Lich. C of St Andr W Bromwich 59-60; Brierley Hill 60-63; H Cross Shrewsbury 63; Coseley 64-66; Wednesfield 66-68; P-in-c of Maer 68-80; Chap Chorlton 68-80; Commiss Damar 70-75; V of High Offley Dio Lich from 80. *High Offley Vicarage, Newport Road, Woodseaves, Stafford ST20 0NP.* (Woodseaves 392)

HARRISON, Thomas David Coleman. b 07. St Chad's Coll Regina, 38. **d** 38 **p** 39 Qu'App. C of Canora 38-39; Rocanville 39-43; R of Saltcoats 43-45; St Pet Williams Lake 45-46; C of Davenham 46; V of Wharton 47-52; R of Pulford 52-73. *5 Holly Field, Gresford, Clwyd.*

HARRISON, Thomas Henry. b 05. Keble Coll Ox BA (3rd cl Th) 28, MA 32. St Steph Ho Ox 31. **d** 31 **p** 32 Chelmsf. C of St Pet Upton Cross 31-33; Bp's Cleeve w Stoke Orchard 33-34; S w New Hinksey 34-36; L to Offic Dio Ox 36-41; and from 44; C of St Thos Ox 41-43. *67 Lonsdale Road, Oxford.* (Oxford 58102)

HARRISON, Walter Edward. b 1900. Em Coll Sktn. **d** and **p** 26 Athab. P-in-c of Fort Vermilion 26-30; Peace River 30-38; Hon Can of Athab and Sec of Dioc Synod 33-38; Org Sec CCCS for SW Distr 38-41; R of St Bride Old Trafford 41-49; V of Monton 49-55; Surr 42-68; V of St Cath Horwich 55-58; R of Healing 58-64; V of Stallingborough 58-64; Mossley 64-68. *Axford, Ford Lane, Northenden, Manchester, M22 4NQ.*

HARRISON, Walter William. b 28. St Jo Coll Nottm. **d** 71 **p** 72 Southw. C of Lenton Nottm 71-74; R of Carlton-in-the-Willows Dio Southw from 74. *St Paul's Rectory, Church Street, Carlton, Nottingham.* (Nottm 248555)

HARRISON, Very Rev William Edward. MBE 45. St Jo Coll Manit BA 40, LTh 41, DD (*jure dig*) 53. **d** and **p** 43 Bp Robins for Nor for Col Bp. Chap CASF 43-46; (Men in Disp 45) V of St John Edmon 46-52; Dean and R of Calg 52-58; Dean and R of St John's Cathl Winnipeg Dio Rupld from 58; Exam Chap to Abp of Rupld 62-79. *64 St Cross Street, Winnipwg, Manit, Canada.*

HARRISON, William Roy. b 34. Univ of Dur BA (2nd cl Th) 58, Dipl Th 59. Cranmer Hall 57. **d** 59 **p** 60 Bris. C of Kingswood 59-62; Tutor at St Paul's Th Coll Limuru and L to Offic Dio Ft Hall 62-65; P-in-c Gt w L Somerford and Seagry 66; V of Soundwell Dio Bris from 66. *Soundwell Vicarage, Sweets Road, Kingswood, Bristol.* (Bristol 671511)

HARRISSON, John Anthony Lomax. b 47. Univ of Ex BA 72. Qu Coll Birm 72. **d** 74 **p** 75 Chelmsf. C of Loughton 74-81; V of St Anne Chingford Dio Chelmsf from 81. *200a Larkshall Road, E4 6NP.* (01-529 4740)

HARROD, Victor Ralph. b 33. Oak Hill Coll 76. **d** 79 **p** 80 Bradwell for Chelmsf. Hon C of N Fambridge 79-81; Cricksea w Althorne and Latchingdon w N Fambridge Dio Chelmsf from 81. *Noak Vuni, The Avenue, North Fambridge, Chelmsford, Essex, CM3 6LZ.*

HARROLD, Jeremy Robin. b 31. Hertf Coll Ox BA 54, BSc 56, MA 58, Dipl Th 59. Wycl Hall, Ox. **d** 59 **p** 60 Pet. C of Rushden 59-61; Dom Chap to Bp of Lon 61-64; to Abp of Perth 64-67; Dioc Regr Dio Perth 66-67; V of St Mark Harlesden 67-72; St Paul Mill Hill Dio Lon from 72. *Vicarage, Hammers Lane, NW7.* (01-959 1856)

HARROLD, Keith Martin. **d** 74 **p** 75 Worc. C of Stourport Dio Worc from 74. *Church Cottage, Church Avenue, Stourport-on-Severn, Worcs, DY13 9DD.* (Stourport 4954)

HARROLD, Robert George. b 43. Em & St Chad Coll Sktn 78. **d** 79 **p** 80 Sktn. I of Watrous Dio Sktn from 79. *PO Box 244, Watrous, Sask, Canada, S0K 4T0.*

HARRON, James Alexander. b 37. St Aid Coll 63. **d** 65 **p** 66 Down. C of Willowfield 65-69; R of Desertmartin 69-80; Deputn Sec BCMS Ireland from 80. *c/o 12 Broughton Park, Belfast, BT6 0BD. N Ireland.* (Belfast 649762)

HARROP, Douglas. b 21. St Aid Coll 62. **d** 64 **p** 65 Sheff. C of Wombwell 64-67; St Leon and St Jude Doncaster (in c of St Luke Scawthorpe) 67-70; R of N Witham 70-76; S Witham 70-76; RD of Beltisloe 72-76; V of Kirkdale w Nawton Dio York from 76. *Kirkdale Vicarage, Nawton, York, YO6 5ST.* (Helmsley 71206)

HARROP, Joseph Blakemore. b 17. Qu Coll Birm 51. **d** 53 Lich for Sudan **p** 56 Shrewsbury for Lich. [f CMS Lay Miss] CMS Miss at Yei Dio Sudan 53-55; C of Stoke-upon-Trent 56-58; V of Foxt w Whiston Dio Lich from 58; P-in-c of Cotton Dio Lich from 78. *Foxt-Whiston Vicarage, Foxt, Stoke-on-Trent, ST10 2HN.* (Ipstones 315)

HARROP, Stephen Douglas. b 48. Edin Th Coll 77. **d** 79 York. C of St Martin and of St Cuthb Middlesbrough Dio York from 79. *24 Connaught Road, Middlesbrough, TS5 4AP.*

HARROW, Reginald Arthur. b 38. St D Coll Lamp BA 63. Univ of Birm Dipl Th 65. Qu Coll Birm 63. **d** 65 Bp McKie for Cov **p** 66 Cov. C of Rugby 65-70; Missr of St Mich Conv Distr Farnham R S 70-75; P-in-c of St Paul Foleshill 75-79; Loughton Dio Ox from 79; Shenley Dio Ox from 79. *Loughton Rectory, Pitcher Lane, Loughton, Milton Keynes, Bucks.* (Shenley Church End 275)

HART, Allen Sydney George. b 38. Chich Th Coll 64. **d** 67 Lon **p** 68 Willesden for Lon. C of St Cuthb N Wembley 67-71; W Bromwich 71-74; Team V of Hucknall Torkard 74-80; V of Annesley Dio Southw from 80. *Vicarage, Annesley Cutting, Annesley, Notts.* (Mansfield 759666)

HART, Anthony. b 35. St Mich AA Llan 77. **d** 79 **p** 80 Win (APM). Hon C of St Helier Jersey 79-81; C of All SS City and Dio Heref from 81. *Vicarage, Clehonger, Hereford.* (Belmont 224)

HART, Arthur Reginald. b 03. Worc Ordin Coll 63. **d** 64 **p** 65 Sarum. C of Trowbridge 64-67; R of S Tarrant 67-70; Broughton-Gifford w Gt Chalfield 70-73; Perm to Offic Dio Sarum from 73. *174 Frome Road, Trowbridge, Wilts.*

HART, Ven Arthur Stanley. K Coll (NS) S Th 39, AKC (NS) 54. Pine Hill Div Hall Halifax NS Hon DD 68. **d** 38 **p** 39 NS. R of Weymouth 39-42; New Ross 42-44; CF (Canad) 44-47; R of Pugwash 47-50; Em Dartmouth 50-70; Exam Chap to Bp of NS 52-70; Hon Can of NS 61-70; Archd of Halifax and E Shore 61-70; Archd (Emer) from 70; R of Terence Bay 70-75. *Site 6, Box 4, RR2 Armdale, NS, Canada.* (852-3382)

HART, Arthur Tindal. b 08. Late Scho of Em Coll Cam 2nd cl Hist Trip pt i, 30, BA (1st cl Hist Trip pt ii) 31, MA 36, BD 44, DD 52. Ripon Hall, Ox 31. **d** 32 **p** 33 Cant. C of Herne Bay 32-35; Lydd 35-37; V of St Paul Bordesley Green 37-46; Chap Birm City Sanat 37-46; R of Blatherwyke (w Laxton from 56) 46-59; Kynges Clyffe 46-55; RD 47-59; R of Appleton 59-66; Select Pr Univ of Ox 62; V of Selmeston w Alciston 66-73. *College of St Barnabas, Blackberry Lane, Lingfield, Surrey, RH7 6NJ.* (Dormans Park 585)

HART, Bernard Arthur. Univ of Sask BA 56. Em Coll Sktn LTh 56. **d** and **p** 56 Athab. I of Boyle 56-59; R of High Prairie 59-61; Vermilion 61-70; Prince Geo 70-74; Shaunavon Dio Qu'App from 74. *Box 658, Shaunavon, Sask, Canada.* (297-2536)

HART, Brian William. ACP 68. LCP 75. M OGS 75. **d** 76 **p** 77 Melb. C of St Steph Mt Waverley 76-77; St John Geelong 77-78; Chap Bal and Qu Angl Gr Sch Wendouree 78-81; Perm to Offic Dio Syd from 81. *2/38 Flood Street, Bondi, NSW, Australia 2026.* (389-7589)

HART, Colin Edwin. b 45. Univ of Leeds BA 66. Fitzw Coll Cam BA 73, MA 77. K Coll Lon MTh 76. Trin Coll Bris 74. **d** 74 **p** 75 St Alb. C of Ch Ch Ware 74-78; Team V of Sheff Manor 78-80; V of Wombridge Dio Lich from 80. *Vicarage, Wombridge Road, Wombridge, Telford, TF2 6HT.* (Telford 613334)

HART, David James. b 40. Univ of Lon AKC 66. Wells Th Coll. **d** 67 **p** 68 Lon. C of St Mich Highgate 67-69; Chap Univ of Birm 69-71. *5 The Hawthorns, Woodbridge Road, Moseley, Birmingham 13.*

HART, David Leonard. b 42. Ripon Hall Ox 68. **d** 71 **p** 72 Birm. C of Castle Vale 71-73; Chap All SS Hosp Birm from 73. *12 Dorchester Drive, Harborne, Birmingham, B17 0SW.* (021-427 7828)

HART, David Maurice. b 35. Univ Coll Dur BSc 57. Clifton Th Coll 59. **d** 61 **p** 62 Man. C of St Paul Bolton 61-64; Hamworthy 64-70; R of W Dean w E Grimstead Dio Sarum from 70; P-in-c of Farley w Pitton Dio Sarum from 81. *West Dean Rectory, Salisbury, Wilts, SP5 1JL.* (Lockerley 40271)

HART, Canon Dennis Daniel. b 22. Linc Th Coll 45. **d** 48 **p** 49 St Alb. C of Abbots Langley 48-49; St Paul Bedford 49-53; CF 53-55; PC of St Sav City and Dio St Alb 55-68; V from 68; Hon Can of St Alb from 74. *25 Sandpit Lane, St Albans, Herts.* (St Albans 51526)

HART, Dennis William. b 30. Open Univ BA. Oak Hill Th Coll 75. **d** 78 Chelmsf **p** 79 Colchester for Chelmsf. Hon C of Clacton-on-Sea Dio Chelmsf from 78. *Ogilvie School, Clacton-on-Sea, Essex.*

HART, Edwin Joseph. b 21. Oak Hill Th Coll 56. **d** 58 **p** 59 Chelmsf. C of St Paul Harlow New Town w St Mary L Parndon 58-60; Leyton 60-61; Min of St Luke's Eccles Distr Cranham Pk 61-69; V 69-71; R of Markfield w Stanton-under-Borden Dio Leic from 71. *Markfield Rectory, Leicester, LE6 0WE.* (Markfield 2844)

HART, Eric John. b 19. Univ of Lon BD 54. Bps' Coll Cheshunt 47. **d** 50 **p** 51 Lon. C of Paddington 50-55; V of All S w St Luke Willesden 55-63; St Mark w St Luke St Marylebone 63-72; Little Marlow w Flackwell Heath Dio Ox from 73. *9 Chapel Road, Flackwell Heath, High Wycombe, Bucks.* (Bourne End 22795)

HART, Ven Frederick. **d** 36 Waik (at L Bardfield) **p** 37 Waik. C of St Cath Milford Pembs Dom Chap to Bp of Waik 36-37; C of New Plymouth 37-40; Chap (NZ) EF 40-45; V of St John Whangamomona 45; R of Bluff Point and Chap Miss to Seamen at Geraldton 46-48; C of St Paul S Harrow 48-49; V of Epping Upland Essex 49-51; R of Kellerberrin W Austr 51-58; Chap CMF 53-60; R of Bridgetown 58-64; Narrogin 64-68; Manjimup Dio Bunb 68-70; Archd of Albany 64-68; Bunb 68-70; and 73-79; Dioc Archd 79-80; Sub Dean of St Boniface Cathl Bunb 70-72; R of Brunswick Junction 72-80; Bp's Commiss 79-80; Perm to Offic Dio Newc from 80. *Rectory, Stroud, NSW, Australia 2425.*

HART, Canon Frederick Arthur. St Jo Coll Morpeth. **d** 43 **p** 44 Goulb. C of Wagga 43-44; Canberra 44-46; at Univ of Melb 46-47; P-in-c of Pambula 49-54; R of Gundagai 54-63; Cooma 63-73; S Wagga Wagga 73-76; Good Shepherd Canberra Dio C & Goulb from 76; Can of St Sav Cathl Goulburn from 74. *18 Allan Street, Curtin, ACT, Australia 2605.* (062-81 2661)

HART, Canon Geoffrey William. b 27. Ex Coll Ox BA 51, MA 55. Ridley Hall, Cam 51. **d** 54 **p** 55 Lon. C of Islington 54-58; St Geo Leeds 58-59; V of St Pet Harold Wood 59-65; Chap Harold Wood Hosp 59-65; V of Ch Ch Southport 65-73; M Gen Syn 70-73; R of Cheltm 73-76; Team R of St Mary Virg w St Matt, H Trin and St Paul Cheltm Dio Glouc from 76; Hon Can of Glouc from 78. *Rectory, Park Place, Cheltenham, Glos, GL50 2QT.* (Cheltenham 512208)

HART, Gerald Hamilton Vickers. b 1900. RMC Sandhurst 18. AKC 35. Westcott Ho Cam 35. **d** 35 **p** 36 Cant. C of St Jo Bapt Croydon 35-39; Org Sec Miss to Seamen for E Distr and Publ Pr Dio St Alb 39-40; CF (EC) 40-46; Chap Miss to Seamen Hamburg 46-51; Dar-es-Salaam 51-55; Org Sec Miss to Seamen Dios St Alb, Pet and Ely 55-64; R of Westmill 64-70; Perm to Offic Dio Chelmsf 71-72; Dio St Alb from 78; in Amer Ch 72-75. *4 Pilgrims Close, West Mill, Buntingford, Herts, SG9 9LE.* (Royston 72836)

HART, Graham Merril. b 23. **d** and **p** 77 Vic Nyan. P Dio Vic Nyan. *PO Box 69, Musoma, Tanzania.*

HART, Henry St John. b 12. Late Scho of St Jo Coll Cam 1st cl Th Trip pt ia 33, BA (1st cl Th Trip pt ib) and Naden Div Stud 34, 1st cl Or Lang Trip pt i and Crosse Stud 35, Tyrwhitt Scho (1st) and Mason Pri 37. Qu Coll Cam MA 38, BD 54. **d** 36 **p** 37 Ely. Chap Qu Coll Cam 36-50; Fell from 36; Dean 40-50 and 55-72; Vice Pres 78-79; Select Pr Univ of Cam 43; Exam Chap to Abp of York 39-42; Asst Lect in Div Univ of Cam 38-43; Lect 43-72; Lady Marg Pr Univ of Cam 57; Reader in Hebr and Intertestamental Stud 72-79; Select Pr Univ of Ox 78; L to Offic Dio Nor from 80. *The Retreat, Felbrigg Hall, Norwich, Norf.* (W Runton 652)

HART, Canon John Arthur. Trin Coll Tor BA 49, LTh 53. **d** 52 **p** 53. **d** 52 **p** 53 Ont. R of Kitley 52-56; Cataraqui 56-65; R of Kemptville 71-75; Napanee Dio Ont from 71; Can of Ont from 79. *122 Bridge Street West, Napanee, Ont, Canada.*

HART, John Charles. b 11. Worc Coll Ox BA (4th cl Phil Pol and Econ) 34, MA 40. Wycl Hall, Ox 34. **d** 36 **p** 38 Chich. C of St Eliz Eastbourne 36-38; Chap Heritage Craft Sch 38-46; C of Chailey 42-46; V of Wartling 46-53; Seq of Bodle Street Green 47-53; R of Plumpton w E Chiltington 53-66; V of Rudgwick 66-77. *68 The Sheeplands, Sherborne, Dorset, DT9 4BS.* (Sherborne 3921)

HART, John Richard. b 16. **d** 75 **p** 76 Ox (APM). C of St Matt (Conv Distr to 76) Reading 75-77; Grazeley w Beech Hill Dio Ox from 77; Spencers Wood Dio Ox from 77. *59 Shepley Drive, Southcote, Reading, Berks, RG3 3HG.* (Reading 55559)

HART, Canon Kendrick Hopwood. b 11. Keble Coll Ox BA (2nd cl Th) 32, MA 39. Bps' Coll Cheshunt, 33. **d** 34 **p** 35 Blackb. C of St Pet Fleetwood 34-37; Stevenage 37-42; PC of All SS Bedford 42-51; V of Rickmansworth 51-60; Chap R Masonic Sch for Girls Rickmansworth 51-60; Surr 51-76; V of Pontefract 60-62; Apsley End 62-67; Aldenham 67-76; RD of Berkhamsted 65-67; Aldenham 70-75; Hon Can of St Alb 68-76; Can (Emer) from 76; Publ Pr Dio Bris from 80. *25 Milborne Park, Malmesbury, Wilts, SN16 9JE.* (Malmesbury 3888)

HART, Lionel Warren. b 1893. St Edm Hall Ox BA (*sc* Th) 21, MA 21. Cudd Coll 21. **d** 23 **p** 24 Win. C of St Denys Southampton 23-25; R of Meckering W Austr 25-26; C of St Pet Port Guernsey 26-27; St Steph Ealing 27-29; R of Smallburgh 29-30; E w W Harling 30-34; V of St Steph S Dulwich 34-54; St Geo Mart Deal 54-64; Perm to Offic Dio Cant 65-77. *Address temp unknown.*

HART, Michael Anthony. b 50. AKC 71. St Aug Coll Cant 72. **d** 73 **p** 74 Dur. C of St Columba Southwick Dur 73-76; St Alphage Hendon 76-78; V of St Luke Eltham Dio S'wark from 78. *107 Westmount Road, SE9.* (01-850 3030)

HART, Canon Michael Stuart. b 39. St D Coll Lamp BA (2nd cl Th) 61. Univ of Lanc MA 72. Wycl Hall Ox 61. **d** 63 **p** 64 Lich. C of St Jas W Bromwich 63-66; Tarrington w Stoke Edith 66-67; Putney 67-70; V of St Mary Magd Accrington Dio Blackb from 70; RD of Accrington from 76; Hon Can of Blackb from 81. *5 Queens Road, Accrington, Lancs.* (Accrington 33763)

HART, Noel Edward. Moore Th Coll Syd, ACT ThL 59. **d** and **p** 60 Syd. C of Penrith 60-62; R of Derby 62-65; Home Miss Soc and Court Chap Dio Syd from 65. *16 Phillip Crescent, Mangerton, NSW 2500, Australia.*

HART, Philip Gordon. K Coll Lon and Warm 57. **d** 61 **p** 62 Bris. C of St Mark Swindon 61-66; St Barn (in c of Ch the K) 66-67; St Marg Liguanea 67-70; R of Par Ch Kingston Dio Ja from 71. *70b King Street, Kingston, Jamaica, W Indies.* (092-26888)

HART, Rodney Tasman. b 42. St Jo Coll Morpeth 75. **d** 76 **p** 78 Graft. Hon C of Ballina 76-77; All SS Murwillumbah 77-78; Coffs Harbour 78-79; Port Macquarie 79-81; Graft Dio Graft from 81. *38 Victoria Street, Grafton, NSW, Australia 2460.*

✠ **HART, Right Rev Rogers Nathanael Bara.** St Andr Coll Oyo 21. St Aid Coll 52. **d** 29 **p** 31 Niger. P Dio Niger 29-52; Tutor CMS Coll Awka 38-44; Synod Sec Dio Nig Delta 52-60; Archd without Territorial Jurisdiction 54-60; Archd of Delta E 60-61; Cons Ld Bp on Nig Delta in All SS Cathl Onitsha 21 Dec 61 by Abp of W Afr; res 70. *c/o Box 3, Bonny, Port Harcourt, Nigeria.*

HART, Tony. b 36. CCC Cam 2nd cl Th Trip pt i, 57, BA (2nd cl Th Trip pt ii) 59, MA 63. Cudd Coll. **d** 61 **p** 62 York. C of All SS Middlesbrough 61-64; Dom Chap to Bp of Dur and L to Offic Dio Dur 64-67; C of St Jas Conv Distr Owton Manor Hartlepool 67-70; V of W Harton Dio Dur 70-71; R from 71; RD of Jarrow from 77. *All Saints Vicarage, Tyne Terrace, South Shields, T & W, NE34 0NF.* (South Shields 561851)

HART, Canon William Edward. K Coll (NS) BA 31. **d** 32 **p** 33 Fred. Miss in Ludlow w Blissfield 32-36; R of Norton and Springfield 36-76; Can of Ch Ch Cathl Fred 72-78; Hon Can from 78. *RR2, Clifton Royal, NB, Canada.*

HART, William Percy. MC 43. **d** 37 Graft **p** 38 Syd for Graft. C of Bowraville 38-40; Chap AIF 40-44; C of W Manly 44-47; R of Maroubra 47-67; Canowindra Dio Bath from 67. *Rectory, Canowindra, NSW, Australia 2804.* (4421 75)

HARTE, Frederick George. b 25. K Coll Lon and Warm AKC 53. **d** 54 **p** 55 S'wark. C of St Jo Bapt Southend Lewisham 54-57; H Trin Eltham 57-60; V of Bellingham 60-73; St Nich Plumstead Dio S'wark from 73. *64 Purrett Road, Plumstead, SE18 1JP.* (01-854 0461)

HARTE, Matthew Scott. b 46. Trin Coll Dub BA 70, Div Test 71. Div Hostel Dub 69. **d** 71 **p** 72 Down. C of Bangor Abbey 71-74; Ballynafeigh 74-76; I of Ardara w Glencolumbkille and Killybegs Dio Raph from 76; Dioc Youth Adv Dio Raph from 79. *Rectory, Ardara, Co Donegal, Irish Republic.*

HARTEL, William George. b 21. **d** 76 **p** 77 Capetn (APM). C of H Trin Paarl Dio Capetn from 76. *PO Box 19, Klapmuts 7625, CP, S Africa.* (Paarl 5257)

HARTIN, Prec James. b 30. Late Scho of Trin Coll Dub BA (1st cl Mod in Hist and Pol Sc) 52, Downes Comp and Oratory Pri (1st) and Bp Forster's Pri (1st) 53, Div Test (1st cl) 54, MA 60. **d** 54 **p** 55 Connor. C of Derriaghy 54-56; Finaghy 56-59; St Mark Dundela 59-60; I of Knocknagoney 60-62; Sub-Warden of Div Hostel Dub 63-80; Prin Th Coll from 80; Lect Trin Coll Dub from 64; Prof of Th from 80; M Inter Angl Doctrinal and Th Comm from 80; Chan of St Patr Cathl Dub 80; Prec from 80. *Theological College, Braemor Park, Rathgar, Dublin 14, Irish Republic.* (Dublin 975506)

HARTLAND, David Robson. b 33. Qu Coll Birm 64. **d** 66 **p** 67 Lich. C of Brierley Hill 66-71; V of Hartshill 71-76; Moxley Dio Lich from 76. *Moxley Vicarage, Sutton Road, Wednesbury, W Midl, WS10 8SG.* (Bilston 41807)

HARTLESS, Gordon Frederick James. b 13. LRAM 40. LTCL 42. **d** 55 Bp Stuart for Cant **p** 56 Worc. C of Malvern Link 55-59; Ilfracombe 59-62; Org Sec for CECS in Dios Bris and Glouc 62-69; R of Scawton w Cold Kirby 69-78; C-in-c of Old Byland 69-78. *Piper Cottage, Church Street, Castleton, Whitby, N Yorks, YO21 2EL.*

HARTLEY, Allan. b 25. **d** and **p** 74 Keew. C of St Pet Big Trout Lake Dio Keew from 74. *St Peter's Church, Big Trout Lake, via Central Patricia, Ont., Canada.*

HARTLEY, Cyril Seymour. St Bonif Coll Warm 57. **d** 58 **p** 59 Blackb. C of Thornton le Fylde 58-61; V of Woolley 61-78. *18 Hatchfields, Great Waltham, Chelmsford, Essex, CM3 1AJ.* (Chelmsford 360631)

HARTLEY, Godfrey. b 37. Cudd Coll. **d** 64 **p** 65 Southw. C of Balderton 64-67; Chap Miss to Seamen Lebom 67-73; R of Beira 67-73; C-in-c of St Gabr Govan City and Dio Glas from 73; Sen Chap and Sec Miss to Seamen Scotld and Chap Miss to Seamen Glas and Clyde from 73; Chap RNR from 74. *121 Southbrae Drive, Glasgow, G13 1TU.* (041-954 7968)

HARTLEY, Graham William Harrington. b 21. Ripon Hall Ox. **d** 62 Warrington for Liv **p** 63 Liv. C of N Meols 62-65; V of St Geo Kano 65-66; Knowsley 66-72; Langdale 72-81; Team V of Egremont w Haile Dio Carl from 81. *Vicarage, Fell View Drive, Egremont, Cumb, CA22 2JL.*

HARTLEY, Canon Harry. b 02. Univ of Birm BSc 28. Open Univ BA 76. St Steph Ho Ox 28. **d** 30 **p** 31 Wakef. C of S Elmsall 30-32; SSJE Miss P of St Cuthb Tsolo 33-34; C of Prestbury 34-35; V of Flockton w Denby Grange 35-44; Malvern Link 44-53; R of Solihull 53-70; Surr 54-70; Proc Conv Birm 55-70; Fell of Woodard Corp 55-68; Hon Can of Birm 64-70; Can (Emer) from 70. *Coulter Cottage, Prestbury, Cheltenham, Glos.*

HARTLEY, Herbert. b 28. K Coll Lon and Warm AKC 52. **d** 53 **p** 54 Blackb. C of H Cross Blackpool 53-55; St Giles Reading 55-58; PC of Ruscombe (w Twyford from 61) 58-66; CF (TA) 59-66; V of Twyford 58-61; Chap RN 66-73; C of Langley Marish 73-77; R of Hedsor w Bourne End Dio Ox from 77. *19 Southbourne Drive, Bourne End, Bucks, SL8 5RY.* (Bourne End 23046)

HARTLEY, John Arthur James. b 1898. Qu Coll Ox BA (3rd cl Mod Hist) 22, MA 25. Ripon Hall Ox. **d** 32 **p** 33 Sheff. C of Barnburgh 32-42; Oldbury 45-50; V of St Chrys Birm 50-70. *8 Whin Bank, Scarborough, Yorks.*

HARTLEY, John William. b 47. St Jo Coll Dur BA (2nd cl Gen Stud) 69. Linc Th Coll 70. **d** 72 **p** 73 Blackb. C of Poulton-le-Fylde 72-76; Lancaster 76-79; V of Barrowford Dio Blackb from 79. *St Thomas Vicarage, Wheatley Lane Road, Barrowford, Nr Nelson, BB9 6QS.*

HARTLEY, Peter. b 44. St Cath Coll Cam BA 66, MA 69. Sarum Wells Th Coll 77. **d** 78 Basingstoke for Win **p** 79 Win. Hon C of Freemantle 78-79; Asst Master K Edw Sch Southn 78-79; Chr Educn Officer Dio Pet 79-81; Dir of Educn from 81. *c/o Islip Rectory, Kettering, NN14 3LH.* (Thrapston 3695)

HARTLEY, Canon Peter Goodwin. b 19. Keble Coll Ox BA (3rd cl Th) 48, MA 52. Wells Th Coll 49. **d** 50 Bedford for Cant **p** 51 St Alb. C of Willian 50-53; V of Elstow 53-76; Can Res of Berm from 76. *POB 627, Hamilton 5, Bermuda.*

HARTLEY, Ven Peter Harold Trahair. b 09. Univ of Lon BSc (1st cl Zoology) 35. Qu Coll Ox MA 48 (*by decree*). Cudd Coll 52. **d** 53 Ely for St E **p** 54 St E. C of Dennington and of Badingham 53-55; R (P-in-c from 77) of Badingham (w Bruisyard from 60 and Cransford 73-77) Dio St E from 55; RD of Loes 67-70; Archd of Suff 70-75; Archd (Emer) from 75; P-in-c of Dennington Dio St E from 77. *Pollards, Badingham, Woodbridge, Suff.* (Badingham 217)

HARTLEY, Robert George. Qu Univ Ont BA 60. Wycl Coll Tor LTh and BTh 63. **d** 63 Bp Snell for Tor **p** 66 Bp Hunt for Tor. C of St Hilda Fairbank Tor 63-65; I of S Orillia 67-79; Lindsay Dio Tor from 79. *45 Russell Street West, Lindsay, Ont, K9V 2W8, Canada.*

HARTLEY, Stephen William Mark. b 50. St Chad's Coll Dur BA 71. Westcott Ho Cam 72. **d** 74 **p** 75 Bp Mackie for Cov. C of Holbrooks 74-76; Styvechale 76-79; V of Snitterfield w Brearley Dio Cov from 79. *Snitterfield Vicarage, Stratford-on-Avon, Warws.* (Stratford-on-Avon 731263)

HARTLEY, Stewart John Ridley. b 47. St Jo Coll Nottm 78. **d** 80 **p** 81 Blackb. C of Altham w Clayton-le-Moors Dio

Blackb from 80. *6 Brisbane Street, Clayton-le-Moors, Lancs, BB5 5LX.*

HARTLEY, Thomas. b 05. AKC 36. **d** 36 **p** 37 Chelmsf. C of Shenfield 36-38; Chingford 38-41; All SS Tooting 41-44; Dovercourt 44-47; L to Offic as C-in-c of St Paul Parkeston 47-50; V of St Martin Dagenham 50-57; Barling w Wakering 57-66; Min of St Marg Conv Distr Ilford 66-74; Perm to Offic Dio Chelmsf from 74. *145 Northbrook Road, Ilford, Essex, IG1 3BE.* (01-554 4324)

HARTLEY, William Henry Darien. **d** 40 **p** 41 Waik. C of St Andr Ohura 40-41; P-in-c 41-42; CF (NZ) 42-44; P-in-c of Manunui 44-48; V 48-50; Levuka 50-53; Waimea Plains 54-58; V of Bluff w Stewart I 58-61; C of Paraparaumu 61-64; V of Martinborough 64-67; Hosp Chap Dio Wel 67-76; Hon C of Kapiti Dio Wel from 76. *98 Rosetta Road, Raumati South, NZ.* (Paraparaumu 6328)

HARTLEY, Canon William Reginald. b 19. CCC Cam 2nd cl Mod and Med Lang Trip pt i, 39, BA (1st cl Th Trip pt i) 41, MA 45. Linc Th Coll 41. **d** 42 **p** 43 Worc. C of St Thos Stourbridge 42-46; Tutor CA Tr Coll and L to Offic Dio Ox 46-47; C of Tardebigge w Webheath (in c of Webheath) 47-50; V of White Ladies Aston w Churchill and Spetchley 50-53; St Barn Pendleton 53-59; Exam Chap to Bp of Man from 57; R of Birch-in-Rusholme 59-74; V of Atherton Dio Man from 74; Hon Can of Man from 76; RD of Leigh from 79. *Atherton Vicarage, Manchester, M29 0BL.* (Atherton 882892)

HARTNELL, Bruce John. b 42. Univ of Ex BA (2nd cl Cl) 64. Linacre Coll Ox BA (2nd cl Th) 66. Ripon Hall, Ox 64. **d** 66 Bp Cornwall for Win **p** 67 Win. C of S Stoneham 66-69; Chap and Tutor Ripon Hall Ox 69-74; V of Knowl Hill w Littlewick 74-78; Sen Angl Chap Univ of Southn from 78. *Chaplaincy Centre, The University, Southampton, SO9 5NH.* (Southn 559122)

HARTRY, David Robert. K Coll NS LTh 65. **d** 64 **p** 65 NS. C-in-c of Rosette 64-67; All SS Cathl Halifax 67-72; Youth Officer Dio Nass 72-75; Chap Renison Coll Waterloo Ont from 75. *Renison College, Waterloo, Ont., Canada.*

HARTSHORN, William Francis John. St Paul's Th Coll Grahmstn 60. **d** and **p** 61 Bloemf. C of Bloemf Cathl 61-63; Edenburg 63-64; R of Sasolburg 64-68; V of St Jo Evang Accrington 68-71; R of St Matt w Claremont 71-76; C of Hangleton 76-81. *Address temp unknown.*

HARTWIG, Frank. St Paul's Th Coll Grahmstn 62. **d** 64 **p** 65 Pret. C of St Marg Witbank 64-66; R of Waterberg 66-72; Dir of Relig Educn Dio Bloemf from 72; P-in-c of Springfontein 72; Tweespruit and Westmr 76-80; Archd of Modderpoort 74-80; R of St Alb Virginia Dio Bloemf from 81. *49 Dahlia Avenue, Virginia 9430, S Africa.*

HARTWIG, Vernon Desmond. ACT ThL 38. **d** 40 **p** 42 St Arn. C of Quambatook 40-42; R of Merbein 42-46; Broken Hill 46-55; Hon Can of St Paul's Pro Cathl Hay 49-55; R of Semaphore 55-59; Mudgee 59-63; Kapunda 63-66; P-in-c of Somerton Pk 66-81; L to Offic Dio Adel from 81. *5 Newcastle Street, Warradale, S Australia 5046.*

✠ **HARUNA, Right Rev Herbert.** Melville Hall, Ibad. **d** 52 **p** 53 Ondo-B. P Dio Ondo-B 52-58; C of St Mich Stoke Cov 58-59; P Dio N Nig 59-74; Exam Chap to Bp of N Nig 62-72; Cons Ld Bp of Kwara in St Jas Cathl Ibad 27 Oct 75 by Abp of W Afr; Bps of Ibad, Lagos, Ow, Accra, Gambia, Nig Delta, Ondo, Ekiti, Benin, Enugu, Aba and Kum. *Bishop's House, Box 21, Offa, Kwara State, Nigeria.*

HARVARD, John Tyler. b 47. **d** 79 Peru. d Dio Peru. *Apartado 1424, Arequipa, Peru.*

HARVEY, Alan Douglas. b 25. **d** 79 Tas. Hon C of New Norfolk Dio Tas from 79. *66 Sharland Avenue, New Norfolk, Tasmania 7450.*

HARVEY, Canon Anthony Ernest. b 30. Worc Coll Ox BA 53, MA 56. Westcott Ho Cam 56. **d** 58 **p** 59 Lon. C of Ch Ch Chelsea 58-62; Research Stud Ch Ch Ox 62-69; Warden St Aug Coll Cant 69-75; Exam Chap to Abp of Cant from 75; Lect Univ of Ox from 76; Fell of Wolfson Coll Ox from 76; Chap of Qu Coll Ox 77-82; Six Pr in Cant Cathl from 77; Bampton Lect 80; Can of Westmr from 82. *5 Little Cloister, Westminster Abbey, SW1.*

HARVEY, Anthony Peter. b 42. Univ of Birm BSc 63, MSc 64. Wycl Hall Ox 79. **d** 81 Ex. C of Stoke Damerel Dio Ex from 81. *37 Valletort Road, Stoke Damerel, Plymouth, Devon.*

HARVEY, Arthur Ernest. b 31. Dipl Th (Lon) 58. Co for Nat Acad Awards MSc 80. Oak Hill Th Coll 54. **d** 57 **p** 58 Chelmsf. C of Rayleigh 57-60; Morpeth 60-63; R of Pitsea 63-73; Bobbingworth (or Bovinger) 73-81; Industr Officer to Bp of Chelmsf 73-78; V of Warialda NSW 80-81; Chap St Nich Bordeaux Dio Gibr in Eur from 81. *5 Impasse Joseph, Anglade 31500, Toulouse, France.*

HARVEY, Very Rev Brian. b 16. Trin Coll Dub BA (1st cl Ment and Mor Sc) 38, BD 41. **d** 40 **p** 41 Dub. C of St Geo Dub 40-45; Min Can of St Patr Cathl Dub 42-45; Belf Cathl 45-48; Sec (Ireland) for SCM and Dean of Residences QUB 45-48; Miss Trin Coll Dub Miss to Chota N 48-51; and 55-63; Hd 51-55; Archd of Hazaribagh 60-63; Exam Chap to Bp of Chota N 61-63; Can Th of Belf Cathl 63-70; Exam Chap to Bp of Connor 63-70; Mem Gen Syn from 66; Dean of Oss from 70; Can of Leigh Cathl from 70; Exam Chap to Bp of Oss from 70; Dir of Ordinands Dio Oss from 70; I of Kilkenny Dio Oss from 70. *Deanery, Kilkenny, Irish Republic.* (Kilkenny 21516)

HARVEY, Charles Alma West. b 07. Univ of Glas MA 29. Edin Th Coll 29. **d** 31 **p** 32 Glas. C of Ch Ch Glas (in c of St Columba from 32) 31-35; Ch Ch Morningside Edin 35-37; R of Penicuik 37-57; CF (EC) 40-45; r of Gullane 57-75. *17 Yewlands Crescent, Edinburgh, EH16 6TB.*

HARVEY, Christopher John Alfred. b 41. SOC 66. **d** 69 **p** 70 Chelmsf. C of Grays 69-73; Gt Baddow (in c of St Paul's) 73-75; V of Berechurch Dio Chelmsf from 75. *348 Mersea Road, Colchester, Essex.* (Colchester 76859)

HARVEY, Cyril John. b 30. St D Coll Lamp BA 51. Coll of Resurr Mirfield 51. **d** 53 **p** 54 Llan. C of Caerau w Ely 53-57; Milford 57-61; V of Castlemartin w Warren 61-65; R of Begelly 65-73; V of St Martin Haverfordwest w Lambston Dio St D from 73. *St Martin's Vicarage, Haverfordwest, Dyfed, SA61 1TD.* (*Haverfordwest* 2509)

HARVEY, Dennis William. TCD BA 44, Div Test (2nd cl) 45, MA 48. **d** 46 **p** 47 Dub. C of Portarlington 46-48; Santry w Glasnevin 48-49; Chap RN 49-53; C of Seagoe 53-59; St Phil Belf 60; R of Claverton Dio B & W from 60. *93 Hantone Hill, Warminster Road, Bath, BA2 6XE, Avon.* (Bath 66841)

HARVEY, Donald Frederick. Qu Coll Newfld. **d** 63 **p** 64 Newfld. I of Portugal Cove 63-64; Twillingate 64-65; R of King's Cove 65-68; Happy Valley 68-73; Portugal Cove 73-77; St Mich AA St John's Dio E Newfld from 77. *150 LeMarchant Road, St John's Newfoundland, Canada.*

HARVEY, Edgar Arthur Calverley. ACT ThL (1st cl) 52. **d** 52 **p** 53 Bend. C of Kangaroo Flat 52-53; Bend Cathl 53-55; R of Rochester 55-61; V of Ch Ch Ormond 61-69; Ashburton 69-77; I of St Matt Cheltm Dio Melb from 77. *161 Park Road, Cheltenham, Vic., Australia 3192.* (03-93 2205)

HARVEY, Edwin. b 30. Virginia Th Sem BD 58, STM 59. Univ of Heidelberg DTh 65. **d** 58 **p** 59 Florida. Amer Ch 58-64 and from 74; Warden St Jo Bapt Coll Suva 65-69; Can of Polyn 65-73; Lect Pacific Th Coll Suva from 70; L to Offic Dio Polyn from 73. *4129 Oxford Avenue, Jacksonville, USA.*

HARVEY, Ven Francis William. b 30. Lich Th Coll 60. **d** 62 Warrington for Liv **p** 63 Liv. C of Rainhill 62-65; V of St Mark Liv 65-69; Planning Adv Dio Liv 67-71; L to Offic Dio Liv 69-71; Area Sec of the Lon Dioc Fund 71-75; Pastoral Sec 75-78; L to Offic Dio Lon 72-78; Preb of St Paul's Cathl Lon 75-78; Archd of Lon and Can of St Paul's Cathl from 78; Exam Chap to Bp of Lon from 81. *2 Amen Court, EC4M 7BU.* (01-248 3312)

HARVEY, Canon Frank Chivas. b 12. Edin Th Coll. **d** 49 **p** 50 Edin. Chap St Mary's Cathl Edin 49-51; Succr and Sen Chap 51-60; Prec St Ninian's Cathl Perth 60-61; R of St Jas Cupar 61-69; Dioc Chap Dio St Andr from 69; Chap HM Prison Perth from 69; Can of St Ninian's Cathl Perth from 77. *10 Pitcullen Terrace, Perth, PH2 7EQ.* (0738 28885)

HARVEY, George William. **d** 65 Bunb. C of St Bonif Cathl Bunb 65-68; Perm to Offic Dio Adel 69-70; P-in-c of Ravensthorpe 70-72; C of St Bonif Cathl Bunb 72-75; R of Boyanup Dio Bunb from 75. *Rectory, Boyanup, W Australia 6237.* (097-71 1015)

HARVEY, Gradon Johnson. b 56. Univ of Melb LTh 80. St Jo Coll Auckld 79. C of St Matt Masterton Dio Wel from 80. *54 Church Street, Masterton, NZ.*

HARVEY, Gregory Newton James. Univ of W Austr BA 68. Wollaston Coll W Austr 66. **d** 68 Perth **p** 69 Bp Macdonald for Perth. C of Claremont 68-69; Chap Ch Ch Gr Sch Claremont 70; Guildf Gr Sch 71-78; R of E Claremont w Graylands Dio Perth from 78. *60 Napier Street, Nedlands, W Australia 6009.* (386 1987)

HARVEY, James Edwin. Univ of Tor BA 45. Wycl Coll Tor. **d** 47 **p** 48 Tor. C of Medonte and Washago 47; St Anne Tor 47-50; I of Port Whitby 50-53; Ajax 53-56; St Pet Tor 56-73; St Matt Islington City and Dio Tor from 73. *94 Smithwood Drive, Islington, Toronto, Ont., Canada.* (416-231 4014)

HARVEY, John. b 30. SOC. **d** 65 **p** 66 S'wark. C of St John Southend Lewisham 65-73; V of Bellingham 73-78; Team V of Bourne Valley Dio Sarum 78-81; Team R from 81. *Rectory, High Street, Porton, Salisbury, Wilts SP4 0LH.* (Idmiston 610305)

HARVEY, John Coburn. b 07. Trin Coll Cam BA 28, MA 33. **d** 36 Swan B for St D **p** 37 Colom. Chap of Trin Coll Carmarthen 36; Vice-Prin Peradeniya Tr Coll Ceylon 36-41;

Prin 41-45; R of Long Ditton 45-55; Distr Sec BFBS for Middx Beds Bucks and Oxon 55-61; W Midls Regional Sec 61-72; Perm to Offic Dio Wakef from 72. *28 Thorpe Lane, Almondbury, Huddersfield, W Yorks, HD5 8TA.* (Huddersfield 24675)

HARVEY, John Diseworth. b 09. **d** 58 **p** 59 Wakef. C of Lindley 58-61; V of Cross Stone 61-63; St Paul Morley 63-65; Skipsea w Ulrome 65-66; Bilton-in-Holderness 66-68; St Mich Castleford 69-72; C of Fenton, Staffs 72-73; Hednesford 73-76; Hon C of St Mary Newington 77-78; V of Hutts Gate Dio St Hel from 78. *Vicarage, Hutts Gate, Island of St Helena, S Atlantic.*

HARVEY, John Ray. b 13. AKC 40. Ely Th Coll 40. **d** 40 **p** 41 Roch. C of All SS Belvedere 40-43; Plumstead 43-51; V of St Faith Wandsworth 51-57; H Spirit Clapham 57-72; R of Horne Dio S'wark from 72; P-in-c of Outwood Dio S'wark from 79. *Horne Rectory, Horley, Surrey.* (Smallfield 2054)

HARVEY, John Wilfred. b 05. Univ of Lon 33. Lon Coll of Div 37. **d** 39 **p** 40 Truro. C of St Mary Magd Launceston 39-45; V of Perranzabuloe w Perranporth 45-60; E w W Looe 60-70; RD of W Wivelshire 68-70; Publ Pr Dio Truro 70-77; C-in-c of Sheviock 71-72; P-in-c of St Martin-by-Looe 77-79. *c/o Chy Morvah, Marine Drive, Hannafore, Cornwall, PL13 2DJ.* (Looe 3327)

HARVEY, Lance Sydney Crockford. b 25. Ridley Hall Cam 67. **d** 69 Kingston T for S'wark **p** 70 S'wark. C of Mortlake w E Sheen 69-74; R of St Thos Woolwich Dio S'wark from 74. *80 Maryon Road, Charlton, SE7 8DL.* (01-854 1828)

HARVEY, Maurice. b 31. **d** 70 **p** 71 Connor. C of St Paul Lisburn 70-72; Ballymacarrett 72-77; R of Ballyphilip w Ardquin 77-79; Ardmore and Craigavon Dio Drom from 79. *Ardmore Rectory, Derryadd, Craigavon, Co Armagh, N Ireland, BT66 6QR.* (Craigavon 41557)

HARVEY, Michael John. b 52. AKC 76 BD 75. St Aug Coll Cant 75. **d** 76 Lon **p** 77 Stepney for Lon. C of St Matt U Clapton 76-79; Cuddington Dio Guildf from 79. *55 Thorndon Gardens, Ewell, Surrey.* (01-393 6748)

HARVEY, Norman Roy. b 43. Wycl Hall Ox 66. **d** 69 Bp Parfitt for Cant **p** 70 Derby. C of Clay Cross 69-72; Dronfield 72-76; Team V 76-79; Dioc Youth Officer Dio Derby from 79; P-in-c of Rowsley Dio Derby from 79. *Rowsley Vicarage, Matlock, Derbys.* (Darley Dale 3296)

HARVEY, Oliver Douglas. b 01. Magd Coll Ox BA (2nd cl Th) 25, MA 45. Wells Th Coll 25. **d** 25 **p** 26 Wakef. C of S Ossett 25-27; St Mary Barnsley 27-29; C-in-c of St Leon Conv Distr Norwood Yorks 29-31; PC of Mytholmroyd 31-34; R of Stanway 34-54; Tilehurst 54-62; V of Puddletown w Athelhampton and Burleston 62-69. *19 Orchard's Way, Highfield, Southampton, SO2 1RF.*

HARVEY, Oliver Paul. b 33. Magd Coll Ox BA (Eng Sc) 55, MA 59. Cudd Coll 57. **d** 59 Dover for Cant **p** 60 Cant. C of St Mark S Norwood 59-61; Hythe Kent 61-64; R of Bancroft (Chililebombwe from 67) 64-71; Lect Cant Tech Coll 71-77; Chap K Sch Roch and Hon P-V of Roch Cathl from 77. *King's School, Rochester, Kent.*

HARVEY, Patrick Roger. b 1900. St Chad's Coll Dur BA 22. **d** 29 **p** 30 Ox. Asst Chap King Alfred Sch Wantage 29-30; Chap Edgeborough Sch Guildf 31-32; Chap RN 33-37; V of Wymeswold 38-46; Chap RNVR 41-44; V of Yarnscombe 46-51; R of Horwood w Newton Tracey 46-51; Awliscombe 51-56; V of Aukborough w Whitton 56-61; R of Upton w Skilgate 61-71; C of Puxton w Hewish and Wick 71-75. *Humble Cottage, Buckland Saint Mary, Chard, Somt.*

HARVEY, Canon Peter Harold Noel. b 16. Univ of Wales BA 44. St Aug Coll Cant 39. **d** 40 **p** 41 Mon. C of St Geo Tredegar 40-46; Malvern Link (in c of Ch of the Ascen) 46-49; R of Ashchurch 49-56; V of Wilmington 56-63; R of Folkington 56-63; Ed *Church Illustrated* 55-66; *Anglican World* 60-68; *Sunday* 66-76; Hon Chap of St Bride Fleet Str from 57; V of Udimore 69-76; C-in-c of Brede 75-76; R of Brede w Udimore Dio Chich from 76; Can and Preb of Chich Cathl from 76. *Udimore Vicarage, Rye, E Sussex, TN31 6AY.* (Brede 882457)

HARVEY, Reginald. **d** 61 **p** 62 Berm. [f in CA] C of Pembroke 61-64; Sandys 64-65; R of Southn Dio Berm from 65. *St Anne's Rectory, Southampton, Bermuda.*

HARVEY, Richard Kenneth. ACT ThL 73. Moore Coll Syd 73. **d** and **p** 74 Syd. C of St Paul Redfern 74-76; Ch Ch St Ives 76-77; C-in-c of Lugarno w Illawong Dio Syd from 77. *10 Old Forest Road, Lugarno, NSW, Australia 2210.* (533-4271)

HARVEY, Robert James. b 18. Keble Coll Ox BA 39, MA 46. St Steph Ho Ox 40. **d** 41 **p** 42 Birm. C of Ch Ch Yardley Wood 41-43; H Trin Taunton 43-45; St Mary Virg Penzance 45-47; V of St Cury w St Gunwalloe 47-53; Much Marcle w Yatton 53-66; R of Edvin Ralph w Collington and Thornbury 66-71. *25 Nelson Street, Hereford, HR4 8LH.*

HARVEY, Robert Martin. b 30. SOC 69. **d** 70 **p** 71 S'wark. C of St Barn, Sutton 70-75; Leatherhead 75-78; V of Wadworth w Loversall Dio Sheff from 78. *Wadworth Vicarage, Wadworth, Doncaster, S Yorks.* (Doncaster 851974)

HARVEY, Stephen George Kay. b 06. Univ of Lon BD (2nd cl) 39. Ridley Coll Melb 32, ACT Th L (1st cl) 33. **d** 33 **p** 34 Melb. C of Diamond Creek 33-34; St Aug Moreland 34-36; Min of Phillip I 36-39; Perm to Offic (Col Cl Act) at Stoke Poges and at Addiscombe 39; C of Ropley (in c of Four Marks) 40-42; CF (EC) 42-46; V of St Thos Kensal Town (w St Andr and St Phil N Kens from 51) 47-55; St Mary Summerstown 55-60; R of Wath 60-72; Perm to Offic Dio Nor 72-73; Dio St E 73-74; Dio Sarum from 74. *11 Hannams Close, Lytchett Matravers, Poole, Dorset, BH16 6DN.*

HARVEY, Trevor John. b 43. Univ of Sheff BA 64. Coll of Resurr Mirfield, 64. **d** 66 **p** 67 Lich. C of St Mary Kingswinford 66-72; V of U Gornal 72-77; Meir Dio Lich from 77. *715 Uttoxeter Road, Meir, Stoke-on-Trent, ST3 5PY.* (S-on-T 313347)

HARVEY, Victor Llewellyn Tucker. b 16. Ch Coll Cam BA (3rd cl Th Trip pt i) 38, MA 42. Ridley Hall, Cam 38. **d** 39 **p** 40 Chelmsf. C of W Ham 39-41; CF (EC) 41-46; V of Em Forest Gate 46-50; St Nich w All SS Sutton Lancs 50-59; Surr from 50; Hon Sec Liv Dioc Bd of Missions 53-59; R of Sanderstead 59-63; St Mary Bryanston Square St Marylebone Dio Lon from 63. *73 Gloucester Place, W1.* (01-935 2200)

HARVEY, William Thomas. b 03. Univ of Man. **d** and **p** 61 Leic. C of St Pet Leic 61-63; V of Arnesby w Shearsby 63-72. *Willow Field, Castle Horneck Lane, Penzance, TR18 4LA.* (Penzance 2723)

HARVEY SUTTON, David. **d** 78 **p** 79 N Queensld. C of St Andr Cloncurry Dio N Queensld from 78; Hon Can of St Jas Cathl Townsville Dio N Queensld from 78. *PO Box 76, Cloncurry, Qld, Australia 4824.*

HARVEY-FULLER, Vernon Maurice. Oak Hill Th Coll 35. **d** 39 **p** 40 Linc. C of Scunthorpe 39-41; Porlock 41-43; Actg C of Northleach 43-44; C of Eyke w Bromeswell 44-47; R of Cransford w Bruisyard 47-58; R of Cooee Tas 58-66. *Amberley, Flowerdale, Tasmania 7321.*

HARVIE, Paul Johnston. Trin Coll Melb 61. **d** 62 **p** 63 Melb. C of Murrumbeena 62-64; St Silas Pentonville Islington Lon 64-66; Chap Melb C of E Gr Sch Caulfield 66-68; Prec of H Trin Cathl Wang 68-77; C of Ch Ch Brunswick Dio Melb from 77. *6 Glenlyon Road, Brunswick, Vic, Australia 3056.* (380 1905)

HARWOOD, Frederick Ronald. b 21. Wells Th Coll 61. **d** 63 Ex **p** 64 Crediton for Ex. C of St Mark Ford Devonport 63-66; PC of Hessenford 66-69; (V 69-71); V of St Elwyn Dio Truro from 71. *3 Harbour View, Hayle, Cornwall, TR27 4LB.* (Hayle 752258)

HARWOOD, John Rossiter. b 26. Selw Coll Cam BA 51, MA 55. Wycl Hall Ox 51. **d** 53 Bp Linton for Cant **p** 54 Birm. C of Handsworth 53-55; Tutor Trin Coll Umuahia 57-64; Exam Chap to Bp on the Niger 57-64; to Bp of Nig Delta 57-64; to Bp of Ow 60-64; Dom Chap to Bp of Sier L and Warden Ministerial Tr Centre Freetown 64-67; CMS Home Educn Sec 67-75; Commiss Sier L from 70; V of Ch Ch Cheltm Dio Glouc from 75. *Vicarage, Malvern Road, Cheltenham, Glos.* (Cheltenham 55983)

HARWOOD, Leslie Thomas Prosser. b 03. Trin Hall Cam 3rd cl Hist Trip pt i 24, BA 25, MA 30. Westcott Ho Cam 25. **d** 26 **p** 27 Chelmsf. C of St Jas Forest Gate 26-29; St Nich Harwich 29-31; L to Offic in St Luke Temple Mills Leyton 31-32; V 32-42; St Aug New Basford 42-52; R of Hickling 52-78; V of Kinoulton 52-78. *Glebe Farm Cottage, Hickling, Melton Mowbray, Leics.* (Melton Mowbray 822267)

HARWOOD, Thomas Smith. b 10. St Jo Coll Dur 38. **d** and **p** 41 York. C of St Barn Hull 41-43; Beverley Minster 43-47; Chap RAF 43-47; R of S Milford 47-50; V of St Lawr w St Nich and New Fulford York 50-55; Leake 55-59; V of Over w Nether Silton and Kepwick 55-59; Sec BFBS E Anglia and Perm to Offic Dio Ely 59-62; V of Middleton 62-75; E Winch 62-75; Asst RD of Lynn 66-68. *8 Beechwood Close, Watlington, Kings Lynn, Norf.*

HARWOOD, William George. b 07. Kelham Th Coll 24. **d** 30 **p** 31 Southampton for Win. C of Basing w Up Nateley and Mapledurwell w Andwell 30-33; St Mark Lakenham 33-40; H Trin w St Mary (in c of St Pet) Ely 40-47; R of Winterton w E Somerton 47-58; V of St Mich AA Walsall 58-76. *7 Mandeville Gardens, Jesson Road, Walsall, Staffs.* (Walsall 21047)

HARWOOD-JONES, John Anthony. McGill Univ Montr BA 62. Trin Coll Tor STB 65. **d** 65 Ott for Rupld **p** 66 Bp J O Anderson for Rupld. C of St Aid Winnipeg 65-67; All SS Winnipeg 67-71; on leave 72-74; I of St Patr Winnipeg Dio Rupld from 74. *612 Valour Road, Winnipeg, Manit, Canada.*

HASAHYA, Erifazi. **d** 64 **p** 65 Mbale. P Dio Mbale 64-72; Dio Bukedi from 72. *Church of Uganda, Busolwe, Uganda.*

HASELDEN, Canon Eugene John Charles. b 17. Em Coll

Cam BA 40, MA 44. Ridley Hall, Cam 40. **d** 42 **p** 43 S'wark. C of St Mary Magd Bermondsey 42-46; St Aldate Ox 46-49; Chap RNVR 48-58; Metrop Sec of CMS 49-52; V of H Trin Leic and Chap HM Pris Leic 52-58; Surr 56-58; V of H Trin Leamington 58-74; RD of Leamington 69-75; Hon Can of Cov 69-75; Can (Emer) from 75; V of Lymington Dio Win from 74; RD of Lyndhurst 78-81; Surr from 78. *Vicarage, Grove Road, Lymington, Hants, SO4 9RF.* (Lymington 73847)

HASELER, Hubert Leslie. b 1889. St Cath Coll Cam BA (3rd cl Th Trip) 12, MA 26. Cl Tr Sch Cam 12. **d** 13 **p** 15 Wakef. C of St Mary Halifax 13-18; Dewsbury 18-19; Asst Master and Chap Old Hall Sch Wellington 19-26; Chap Wellingborough Sch 26-39; V of Sutton w Upton 39-46; Gretton 46-58; R of Seaton w Harringworth 58-65. *3 Park Cottages, Glaston, Uppingham, Rutld.*

HASELL, Ven William Dacre. St Chad's Coll Regina, DD (*hon causa*) 46. **d** 17 **p** 22 Qu'App. C-in-c of Loverna w Coleville and Major Sask 17-22; I of Loverna Coleville and Hemaruka 22-60; RD of Kindersley 27-60; Hon Can of Qu'App 34-45; Archd of Kindersley 45-61; and 63-68; I of Alsask Dio Qu'App from 64; Archd (Emer) from 68. *Box 266, Alsask, Sask, Canada.*

HASKELL, Charles William. MBE 55. NZ Bd of Th Stud LTh 29. **d** 29 **p** 30 Ch Ch. C of Ashburton NZ 29-32; CMS Miss at Karachi 32-49; Prin of Karachi Gr Sch 40-55; Gen Sec NZ Ang Bd of Miss and Hon C of St Mark Wel 55-64; L to Offic Dio Ch Ch 55-64; V of Nae Nae 64-68; Waikanae 68-73; Hon C of Waikanae Dio Wel from 73. *7 Island View Terrace, Wainkanae, NZ.* (5396)

HASKINS, Thomas. b 41. Univ of Dub BA 72. TCD 71. **d** 73 **p** 74 Connor. C of Larne w Inver 73-78; Antrim Dio Connor from 78. *28 Steeple Green, Antrim, N Ireland.* (Antrim 2966)

HASLAM, David. b 31. St Chad's Coll Dur BA 57. Wells Th Coll 57. **d** 59 Knaresborough For York **p** 60 Ripon. C of Manston 59-62; St Pet Bournemouth 62-65; V of E Worldham w W Worldham and Hartley Mauditt (w Kingsley and Oakhanger from 67) 65-71; V of St Andr Boscombe Bournemouth Dio Win from 71; RD of Bournemouth from 80. *3 Wilfred Road, Bournemouth, BH5 1NB.* (Bournemouth 34575)

HASLAM, Canon Frank. b 26. Univ of Bris BA 50. Tyndale Hall, Bris 49. **d** 51 **p** 52 Man. C of St Paul Halliwell 51-55; Miss at Lotome Ugan 56-60; C of Heath Town 60-61; V of St Matt Wolverhampton 61-65; Ch Ch Blackpool 65-70; V of Macclesfield 70-80; M Gen Syn Ches 76-80; Hon Can of Ches from 81; Dir of Resources Dio Ches from 80. *17 Carrick Road, Curzon Park, Chester, Chesh.* (0244-671564)

HASLAM, James Alexander Gordon. b 1896. MC and DFC 18. CCC Cam BA 30, MA 34. St Geo Windsor. **d** 54 Malmesbury for Bris **p** 55 Bris. [f Fell of CCC Cam 49-52] C of St Paul Chippenham 54-57; R of Sutton Benger 57-64; R of Tytherton Kellaways 58-64; L to Offic Dio Ely from 65. *12 Marlborough Court, Cambridge, CB3 9BQ.* (Cam 355016)

HASLAM, James Robert. b 31. Open Univ BA 74. Bps' Coll Cheshunt 55. **d** 57 **p** 58 Blackb. C of Penwortham 57-63; V of Cockerham (w Winmarleigh from 74) 63-76; Chap Ellel Grange 63-76; V of Gt Harwood Dio Blackb from 76. *Vicarage, Church Lane, Great Harwood, Blackburn, Lancs, BB6 7PU.* (Gt Harwood 884039)

HASLAM, John Gordon. b 32. Univ of Birm LLB 53. Qu Coll Birm 75. **d** 77 Birm **p** 77 Bp Aston for Birm. C of Bartley Green 77-80; Hon C of Moseley Dio Birm from 80. *34 Amesbury Road, Moseley, Birmingham, B13 8LE.*

HASLAM, Robert John Alexander. b 34. CCC Cam BA 58. Coll of Resurr Mirfield 58. **d** 60 **p** 61 Sheff. C of Rawmarsh 60-66; Perm to Offic Dio Edin 66-73; Dio Carl 73-77; P-in-c of St Pet Peebles 77-81; V of Darnall Dio Sheff from 81. *66 Mather Road, Sheffield, S9 4GQ.* (Sheff 440167)

HASLAM-JONES, Christopher John. b 28. ALCD 53. **d** 53 **p** 54 Chelmsf. C of St Jo Evang Walthamstow 53-57; High Wycombe 57-62; V of Parkfield 62-68; St Andr Radcliffe Dio Man from 68. *Vicarage, Cannon Street, Radcliffe, Manchester, M26 0HE.* (061-723 2427)

HASSALL, William Edwin. b 41. St Jo Coll Nottm 75. **d** 77 **p** 78 Lich. C of All SS Wellington 77-80; Fairwell (or Farewell) Dio Lich 80-82; V from 82; C of Gentleshaw Dio Lich 80-82; V from 82. *Vicarage, Budds Road, Cannock Wood, Rugeley, Staffs, WS15 4NB.* (Burntwood 4329)

HASSAN, Levi. d 60 **p** 61 Sudan. P Dio Sudan 60-76; Dio Juba from 76. *Box 110, Juba, Sudan.*

HASSELL, Kenneth Frank. Codr Coll Barb. **d** 45 **p** 46 Antig. C of St Pet Antig 45-47; St Mich Cathl Barb 47-49; V of St Bart Barb 49-55; St Leon Barb 55-61; St Jo Bapt I and Dio Barb from 61. *St Johns Vicarage, Barbados, W Indies.*

HASSEN, Edward William. b 27. TCD 56. **d** 56 **p** 57 Connor. C of Larne 56-59; Derriaghy 59-61; Chap RAF 61-64; C-in-c of Muckamore Dio Connor 64-67; R from 67; RD of Antrim from 74. *Rectory, Muckamore, Co Antrim, N Ireland.*

HASSETT, Jack Richard. b 11. ALCD 36. **d** 36 **p** 37 Lon. C of H Trin Kilburn 36-38; Darfield (in c of Gt Houghton) 38-40; V of Bp Ryder Ch Birm 40-47; RD of Central Birmingham 43-47; V of Rodbourne Cheney 47-55; St John Worksop 55-62; Gen Sec CCCS 62-66; L to Offic Dio Lon 64-66; R of Stanford-le-Hope (w Mucking from 73) 66-77; C-in-c of Mucking 66-73; Surr 69-77; Perm to Offic Dio Southw from 77. *4 Landa Grove, Tuxford, Newark, Notts, NG22 0JG.* (Tuxford 870784)

HASSING, André Eugène. St Paul's Th Coll Maur LTh 64. **d** 64 **p** 65 Maur. C of St Paul Vacoas 64-66; Miss at Praslin 66-70; St Paul's Cathl Mahé 70-73; R of Vacoas 73; C of St Paul's Cathl Mahé Sey 74-76; Dean 76-77; C of Warrnambool 77-78; R of Corowa 78-80; St Pet Murrumbeena Dio Melb from 80. *371 Neerin Road, Murrumbeena, Vic, Australia 3163.*

HASSING, Georges Henry. St Paul's Th Coll Maur LTh 64. **d** 64 **p** 65 Maur. C of H Trin Rose Hill 64-69; R of Quatre Bornes 69-75; St Pet Cassis Port Louis 76-77; Donald Dio Bend from 77. *St George's Rectory, Donald, Vic., Australia 3480.*

HASTE, James Victor William. St Mich Th Coll Crafers ACT ThL 68. **d** 68 Melb **p** 70 S'wark for N Guinea. C of Ormond 68-69; C of Roehampton 70-72; P-in-c of Boroko 72-76; State Sec ABM Vic and L to Offic Dio Melb 76-81; I of Armadale w Hawksburn Dio Melb from 81. *27 Cromwell Road, South Yarra, Vic, Australia 3141.*

HASTE, Rowland Herbert. b 1896. Tyndale Coll Bris 26. **d** 47 **p** 48 St E. C of St Helen Ipswich 47-49; C-in-c of Raydon w Shelley 49-51; R of Raydon 51-69; R of Holton St Mary w Gt Wenham 51-69. *Cloud End, Windermere Crescent, Radipole Village, Weymouth, Dorset.*

HASTED, Canon John Arthur Ord. b 28. Keble Coll Ox BA 50, MA 54. Wells Th Coll 51. **d** 53 **p** 54 St Alb. C of Cheshunt 53-58; Prec of Birm Cathl 58-59; V of Bulkington 59-61; Styvechale 61-64; Yoxford 64-79; Sibton 64-78; RD of Saxmundham 74-79; Hon Can of St E Cathl 75-79; Can (Emer) from 79; Surr 77-79. *111 Kimbolton Road, Bedford.* (Bedford 66724)

HASTED, Marcus Arthur David. b 35. Qu Coll Birm 63. **d** 66 **p** 67 Ches. C of Woodchurch 66-69; W Kirby 69-72; V of Farndon (w Coddington from 76) 72-79. *Address temp unknown.*

HASTEY, Erle. b 44. St Mich Coll Llan 66. **d** 68 Wakef **p** 69 Pontefract for Wakef. C of Pontefract 68-71; Almondbury 71-74; V of St Andr Purlwell Batley 74-79; C-in-c of Batley Carr 76-79; V of Ynyshir Dio Llan from 79. *Vicarage, Ynyshir, Mid Glam.* (Porth 2450)

HASTIE, Canon Barry Winfield Victor. Trin Coll Dub BA and Div Test (2nd cl) 43. **d** 43 **p** 44 Down. C of Willowfield 43-52; Chap RAF 52-58; I of Derryvullan 58-73; R of Fivemiletown Dio Clogh from 73; Can of Clogh from 81. *Fivemiletown Rectory, Co Tyrone, N Ireland.* (Fivemiletown 224)

HASTIE, Ronald William. b 36. Moore Coll Syd 65. **d** 71 **p** 72 Graft. C of Ch Ch Cathl Graft 71-75; Collarenebri 75-78; V of Werris Creek Dio Armid from 78. *Vicarage, Werris Creek, NSW, Australia 2341.*

HASTIE-SMITH, Ruthven Carruthers. b 13. St Edm Hall Ox BA (3rd cl Engl) 36. Westcott Ho Cam 36. **d** 39 **p** 40 Carl. C of St Jas Barrow-F 39-42; CF (EC) 42-46; Chap and Asst Master Trin Coll Glenalmond 46-51; Chap Adisadel Coll Accra 51-54; R of Aboyne 54-58; Dioc Insp of Schs Dio Aber and Ork 56-58; Dio Edin 62-63; R of H Cross Davidson's Mains 58-63; Chap Bromsgrove Sch 63-68; R of St Jo Evang Forfar 68-72; St Andr Strathtay w St Marg Aberfeldy 72-75; Hon Super Dio St Andr 75-78. *The Milton, Comrie, Perthshire, PH6 2LS.* (Comrie 70510)

HASTROP, Paul. b 39. Wells Th Coll 70. **d** 72 **p** 73 Sarum. C of St Osmund Parkstone 72-76; St Mary w St Paul Penzance 76-79; V of St Blazey Dio Truro from 79. *Vicarage, St Blazey, Cornw.* (Par 2113)

HASTWELL, James Sydney. b 37. Roch Th Coll 67. **d** 69 **p** 70 Cant. C of St Aug Croydon 69-73; Hurstpierpoint 73-76; R of Albourne w Sayers Common and Twineham Dio Chich from 76. *Vicarage, Sayers Common, Hassocks, W Sussex, BN6 9HU.* (Hurstpierpoint 832129)

HATCH, George Andrew. Univ of Leeds, BA 51. Coll of Resurr Mirfield, 51. **d** 53 **p** 54 Guildf. C of St Mark S Farnborough 53-55; R of Bequia N Grenadines 55-57; St John Grenada 57-63; V of St Mary I and Dio Barb 63-69; R from 69. *St Mary's Rectory, Cave Hill, Bridgetown, Barbados, W Indies.*

HATCH, Canon George William. b 12. Univ of Lon BA 33. Clifton Th Coll 32. **d** 35 **p** 36 Newc T. C of St Mark Byker 35-39; Org Sec CPAS for NE Distr 39-42; V of St Andr Whitehall Park 42-51; Surr from 45; Chap Archway Hosp

48-51; V of Duffield 51-56; Surr from 52; R of Rayleigh Dio Chelmsf from 56; Surr from 57; Hon Sec Dioc Miss Coun 58-64; Chap HM Borstal Bullwood Hall 62-68 and from 75; Hon Can of Chelmsf from 76; RD of Rochford from 79. *Rectory, Rayleigh, Essex.* (Rayleigh 742151)

HATCH, Richard Francis. b 36. Qu Coll Cam 2nd cl Th Trip i 58, BA (2nd cl Th Trip pt ii) 60, MA 64. Cudd Coll 60. **d** 62 Hulme for Man **p** 63 Man. C of Leigh Lancs 62-66; V of Peel Green (w Barton-on-Irwell from 71) 66-75; R of Birch-in-Rusholme 75-78; Fallowfield 75-78; Publ Pr Dio Man from 78; Chs Radio Correspondent Gtr Man Ecumen Coun from 78. *24 Denison Road, Victoria Park, Manchester, M14 5RY.* (061-225 0799)

HATCHER, Reuben. Qu Coll Newfld 60. **d** 62 **p** 63 Newfld. C of Lamaline 62-64; R of Pushthrough 64-67; Grand Bank 67-71; Trin E 71-73; Petty Harbour 73-77; Hosp Chap St John's Dio E Newfld from 77. *39 Fox Avenue, St John's, Newfoundland, Canada.*

HATCHETT, Michael John. b 49. Enfield Coll of Tech BSc 72. AKC and BD 77. Linc Th Coll 77. **d** 78 Chelmsf **p** 79 Colchester for Chelmsf. C of St Andr w H Trin Halstead 78-81; St Jas Greenstead Green 78-81; Greenstead Dio Chelmsf from 81. *6 Patmore Road, Colchester, Essex.* (Colchester 860855)

HATCHLEY, Walter John. b 24. BA (Lon) 65. Coll of Resurr Mirfield. **d** 66 **p** 67 Newc T. C of St Pet Monkseaton 66-69; All SS Gosforth 69-72; St Geo Cullercoats 72; Team V 72-78; V of St Francis High Heaton City and Dio Newc T from 78. *St Francis's Vicarage, High Heaton, Newcastle upon Tyne, NE7 7RE.* (Newc T 661071)

HATCHMAN, Hugh Alleyne. b 28. Qu Coll Cam BA (2nd cl Mod Lang Trip pt ii) 52, MA 56. Ridley Hall Cam 52. **d** 54 **p** 55 Lon. C of St Steph E Twickenham 54-56; Morden 56-59; Org Sec CPAS in E Midls 59-63; Perm to Offic Dios Ely and Pet 59-63; V of St Luke New Catton 63-79; C-in-c of St Mich Coslany 65-67; Chap Bexley Hosp from 79. *Bexley Hospital, Dartford, Kent.*

HATCLIFFE, Charles John William Coombes. b 26. St Aid Coll 59. **d** 61 **p** 62 Man. C of Stowell Mem Ch Salford 61-64; V of St Phil Stubbins 64-71; C-in-c of Clifton Green 71-74; V 74-82; P-in-c of Condover Dio Heref from 82; Acton Burnell w Pitchford Dio Heref from 82; Frodesley Dio Heref from 82. *Condover Vicarage, Shrewsbury SY5 7AA.* (Bayston Hill 2251)

✠ HATENDI, Right Rev Ralph Peter. AKC 68. St Pet Coll Rosettenville, 55. **d** 57 **p** 58 Mashon. C of Bonda 57-62; Chap Bernard Mizeki Sch Marandellas 62-63; C of S Ormsby 63-65; Lect St Jo Sem Lusaka 68-76; United Bible S Consultant for Afr 76-79; Cons Bp Suffr of Mashon in All SS Cathl Salisbury 4 Feb 79 by Abp of Centr Afr; Bps of Mashon and Matab; and Bp Suffr of Johann; Apptd Bp of Mashon 81. *PO Box UA7, Salisbury, Zimbabwe.*

HATFIELD, Donald Aidan. Univ of BC BA 52. Angl Th Coll BC LTh 52. BD (Gen Syn) 53. Keble Coll Ox BA (2nd cl Th) 59, MA 63. **d** 52 **p** 53 New Westmr. C-in-c of S Westmr 52-56; I of Colwood 59-64; Chap RN (Canad) from 64. *CFB Petawawa, Ont., Canada.*

✠ HATFIELD, Right Rev Leonard Fraser. K Coll (NS) BA Div Test and LTh 42, MA 43, Hon DD 56. **d** 42 **p** 43 NS. C of All SS Cathl Halifax 42-46; R of Antigonish 46-52; Dominion Chap Angl Young Peoples' Assoc 53-54; Gen Sec Coun for Social Services of ACC 55-61; R of Ch Ch Dartmouth 61-71; Can of All SS Cathl Halifax 69-71; R of Truro 71-76; Archd of Northumb (NS) 71-76; Cons Bp Suffr of NS in All SS Cathl Halifax 17 Oct 76 by Abp of Prov of Canada and Abp Davis; Bps of NS, Fred, Montr, Queb and Centr Newfld; and Bp Maguire; Apptd Ld Bp of NS 80. *5732 College Street, Halifax, NS, Canada.* (423 8301)

HATHAWAY, David Alfred Gerald. b 48. Univ of Wales (Cardiff) Dipl Th 72. S Mich Coll Llan 69. **d** 72 **p** 73 Mon. C of St Julian Newport 72-74; Oakham w Hambleton and Egleton 74-77; V of St Matt Newport Dio Mon from 77. *9 Summerhill Avenue, Newport, Gwent.* (Newport 58127)

HATHAWAY, John Albert. b 24. Sarum Th Coll 59. **d** 60 Bp Dale for Cant **p** 61 Guildf. C of Fleet 60-64; Cowley (in c of St Jas) 64-66; V of St Mary Magd Holmwood 66-71; St Francis Westborough 71-74; All SS Newmarket Dio St E from 74. *All Saints Vicarage, Newmarket, Suff.* (Newmarket 2514)

HATHERLEY, Peter Graham. b 46. St Mich Coll Llan 70. **d** 72 **p** 73 Llan. C of Ystrad Mynach 72-75; Hon C of Tonyrefail from 75. *Plot 53, Tylcha Fach, Tonyrefail, W Glam.*

HATHERLEY, Victor Charles. b 17. St Aug Coll Cant 63. **d** and **p** 64 B & W. C of Crewkerne 64-68; R of E Harptree 68-72; V of E Harptree w W Harptree (and Hinton Blewett from 76) Dio B & W from 72; C-in-c of Hinton Blewett 75-76; Dioc Ecumen Officer Dio B & W 77-79. *East Harptree Rectory, Church Lane, Bristol, BS18 6BD.* (West Harptree 239)

HATHERLY, Brian Francis. St Jo Coll Morpeth ACT ThL 60. **d** 59 **p** 60 Armid. C of Inverell 59-61; W Tamworth 61-63; L to Offic Dio Syd 63-64; V of Levuka 64-70; R of Coonamble 70-76; Grenfell Dio Bath from 76. *Box 33, Grenfell, NSW, Australia 2810.* (43 1097)

HATHWAY, Richard Peter. b 17. Kelham Th Coll 34. **d** 41 **p** 42 Wakef. C of St Jo Evang Cleckheaton 41-44; C-in-c of Monk Bretton 44-46; CF 46-66; Perm to Offic Dio Momb 48-50; KRU Pusan Korea 50-51; Lichfield Staffs 52-53; MELF 53-56; Chatham 56-59; Sing 59-62; Plymouth 62-64; Chap Highgate Sch 66-81. *10 Station Road, Harleston, Norf.*

HATT, Michael John. b 34. Sarum Th Coll 67. **d** 69 **p** 70 Ex. C of St Mary Arches 70-73; Ex Centr Dio Ex from 73. *133 Topsham Road, Exeter, Devon.*

HATTAM, Morley. b 08. BSc (1st cl Math) Lon 28. Sarum Th Coll 62. **d** 63 **p** 64 Truro. C of St Paul Truro 63-68; V of St Crantock 68-79; RD of Pydar 71-73; Perm to Offic Dio Truro from 79. *St Rumon, North Pool Road, Illogan, Redruth, Cornw.* (0209-217912)

HATTAWAY, Robert. St Jo Coll Auckld. **d** 57 Auckld **p** 58 Bp Caulton for Auckld. C of St Mary's Cathl Auckld 57-59; V of Hauraki Plains 59-64; C of Takapuna 65; St Pet Onehunga Auckld 65-68; Manurewa 68-72; Hon C 73-76; Otara 76-79; Papakura Dio Auckld from 79. *Box 58-016, East Tamaki, Auckland, NZ.*

HATTER, David George. b 21. Lich Th Coll. **d** 57 **p** 58 Southw. C of Carrington 57-61; V of Clipstone 61-67; St Mark Mansfield 67-81; Carlton-on-Trent Dio Southw from 81; Sutton-on-Trent Dio Southw from 81; Normanton-on-Trent Dio Southw from 81; Marnham Dio Southw from 81. *Sutton-on-Trent Vicarage, North Road, Newark, Notts.* (Newark 821797)

HATTERS, Alvin Victor. Ridley Coll Melb ACT ThL 46. **d** 46 Bp Stephen for Rockptn **p** 48 Bp Cranswick for New Guinea. C of Glenhuntly 46-49; P-in-c of Mukawa 49-51; Arawe Kumbun 51-55; Taupota 55-61; Madang 61-68; Goroka 68-73; R of Smithton Dio Tas from 73. *Rectory, Smithton, Tasmania 7330.* (004-52 1066)

HATTERSLEY, John Martin. b 32. Univ of Cam 2nd cl Econ Trip pt i 53, BA (2nd cl Law Trip pt ii) LLB 56, MA 59. **d** 73 **p** 74 Edmon. Hon C of St Pet City and Dio Edmon from 73. *8112 - 144th Street, Edmonton, Alta., Canada.* (403-424 6151)

HATTON, George Arthur. K Coll (NS) 34. **d** 34 **p** 35 NS. C of Liscomb 34-38; R of Queensport 38-39; Canso 39-42; Chap CASF 42-46 and from 50; R of Port Greville 46-50; New Maryland 61-67; Hon C of Ch Ch Fred 67-71; Dioc Regr Dio Fred 71-76. *Box 66, Silverwood, RR6, Fredericton, NB, Canada.*

HATTON, George Ockleston. b 08. St Aid Coll 45. **d** 48 **p** 49 Ches. C of Grappenhall 48-51; Wilmslow 51-53; V of Nether Whitley 53-60; L Leigh w Nether Whitley 60-73; RD of Gt Budworth 61-71. *Clatterbrune Farm House, Presteigne, Powys.*

HATTON, George Russell. b 32. Univ of K Coll Halifax NS BA 56, LTh 58. Gen Th Sem NY STB 59. Yale Div Sch STM 63. Univ of Minn PhD 71. **d** 57 **p** 58 NS. C of All SS Cathl Halifax 57-62; I of Lantz 63-65; In Amer Ch 65-73; Consultant Nat Affairs Angl Ch of Canada 74-77; pres Atlantic Sch of Th from 80. *Atlantic School of Theology, Halifax, NS, Canada.*

HATTON, Jeffrey Charles. b 49. K Coll Lon BD 70. Univ of Bris MA 72. Westcott Ho Cam 73. **d** 74 **p** 75 Thetford for Nor. C of St Pet Mancroft Nor 74-78; St Anne Earlham 78-79; Relig Broadcasting Asst IBA and Perm to Offic Dio Lon from 79. *23c Addison Road, Kensington, W14 8LH.* (01-602 2210)

HATTON, Michael Samuel. b 44. St Jo Coll Dur BA 72, Dipl Th 74. **d** 74 **p** 75 Worc. C of St Jas Dudley 74-75; St Marg King's Lynn 75-76; Walsall Wood (in c of St Mark) Dio Lich from 78. *Church House, Green Lane, Shelfield, Walsall, WS4 1RN.*

HAUGH, John Colin. Ridley Coll Melb. **d** 57 **p** 58 Bal. C of Warrnambool 57-60; P-in-c of St Luke Bal 60-61; C of Colac 61-62; V of Heywood 62-66; Beech Forest 66-69; R of Otway 69-70; R of Terang Dio Bal from 70. *Rectory, Terang, Vic, Australia 3264.* (055-92 1085)

HAUGHAN, John Francis. b 28. Tyndale Hall, Bris 56. **d** 60 Tonbridge for Cant **p** 61 Roch. C of St Steph Tonbridge 60-63; St Mark Cheltm (in c of St Barn) 63-67; V of H Trin Tewkesbury Dio Glouc from 67. *Holy Trinity Vicarage, Tewkesbury, Glos.* (Tewkesbury 293233)

HAUGHTON, Thomas George. b 08. MBE 53. **d** 53 **p** 54 Down. C of St Donard Belf 53-58; Sec CMS Belf 58-61; I of St Jo Bapt U Falls Belf 61-79; RD of S Belf 73-79; Can of St

Anne's Cathl Belf 77-79. *47 Abbey Drive, Bangor, Co Down, N Ireland.* (61994)

HAUKONGO, Very Rev Lazarus Hiuanapo. **d** 66 **p** 67 Damar. P Dio Damar 66-80; Dio Namibia from 80; Archd of Ovamboland from 70. *c/o St Mary's Church, Odibo, PO Oshikango, SW Africa.* (Oshikango 5)

HAULANGI, Phallo. b 36. **d** 77 Aotearoa for Wai. C of Te Kaha Past Dio Wai from 77. *P Bag 59, Opotiki, NZ.*

HAULI, Julius. St Phil Th Coll Kongwa. **d** 58 Bp Omari for Centr Tang **p** 58 Centr Tang. P Dio Centr Tang. *PO Box 35, Mpwapwa, Tanzania.*

HAULI, Lazaro Augustino. **d** 57 **p** 60 SW Tang. P Dio SW Tang. *Milo, Njombe, Tanzania.*

HAUNDU, Birinus. St Jo Th Sem Lusaka, 60. **d** 61 **p** 63 N Rhod. P Dio N Rhod 61-64; Dio Zam 64-70; Dio Lusaka from 71. *Mpanza Mission, via Choma, Zambia.*

HAVARD, Alan Ernest. b 27. Qu Coll Birm 79. **d** 81 Cov. C of St Matt Rugby Dio Cov from 81. *16 Chaucer Road, Rugby, CV22 5RP.*

HAVELL, Edward Michael. b 38. Univ of Dur BA 65. Ridley Hall Cam 66. **d** 68 **p** 69 Sheff. C of All SS Ecclesall 68-71; C of St Justus Roch 71-74; C-in-c of Holbeach Hurn 74-75; C of St Jo Evang Hollington Dio Chich from 75. *208 St Helens Road, Hastings, Sussex.* (Hastings 426095)

HAVERGAL, Donald Ernest. St Edm Hall Ox BA (3rd cl Mod Hist) 25, MA 29. Linc Th Coll 40. **d** 40 **p** 41 Pet. C of St Jo Bapt Pet 40-47; R of Ashton w Hartwell 47-60; Morcott w S Luffenham 60-62; Wilby 62-78; Hon Min Can of Pet Cathl from 68. *91 Claverham Road, Yatton, Avon.* (Yatton 834752)

HAVERS, Thomas Lionel. b 1897. Chich Th Coll 21. **d** 23 **p** 24 Chich. C of Westbourne 23-25; All S Brighton 25-26; H Trin Win 26-27; Perm to Offic at Bracknell 28-29; C of Mayfield 29-31; St Barn Tunbridge Wells 31-35; St Alb Teddington 37-38; R of Rampton 38-41; Perm to Offic Dio Lon 41-47; Dio Guildf 45-61; Dio Chich 61-77; Dio Ex from 77. *Champerty, Dalwood, Axminster, Devon, EX13 7EA.*

HAVILAND, Douglas Thomas Archibald. K Coll (NS) BA 34. **d** 36 **p** 37 Fred. C of St Anne Fred 36-37; Miss at Gladstone 37-42; Chap RCAF 42-47; in Amer Ch 47-54; C of All SS Cathl Halifax 54-57; R of Bridgetown 57-60; Birch Cove 60-65; Chap Camp Hill Hosp Halifax from 65. *Camp Hill Hospital, Halifax, NS, Canada.*

HAVILAND, Edmund Selwyn. b 24. King's Coll Cam BA 49, MA 51. Wells Th Coll 49. **d** 51 **p** 52 S'wark. C of St Pet St Helier 51-55; Chap Charterho Miss and C-in-c of St Paul Bermondsey 55-56; Min of St Hugh's Conv Distr S'wark (Charterho Miss) 56-58; V of Ockbrook w Borrowash 58-68; E Peckham (w Nettlestead from 78) Dio Roch from 68; C-in-c of Nettlestead 77-78. *East Peckham Rectory, Tonbridge, Kent.* (0622 871278)

HAW, Reginald. b 15. DSC 45. St Chad's Coll Dur BA 37, Dipl Th 38, MA 40, BCL 46. **d** 38 **p** 39 York. C of N Ormesby 38-41; Skelton-in-Cleveland 41; Chap RNVR 41-46; V of Newington 46-49; Humberston 49-54; PC of Newland 54-66; V of All SS w St John Hertford Dio St Alb from 66; Surr from 70. *All Saints' Vicarage, Churchfields, Hertford, SG13 8AE.* (Hertford 52096)

HAWES, Canon Albert Emanuel. McGill Univ Montr BA 37. Montr Dioc Th Coll LTh 39. **d** 39 **p** 40 Montr. C of Maniwaki 39-41; R of Grenville 41-50; Valois 50-66; P-in-c of Lakeside Heights 55-58; Dir of Dioc Programming 66-69; Hon Can of Montr 66-77; Can (Emer) from 78; Admin Officer Dio Montr 69-77. *16-4200 Cavendish Boulevard, Apt 16, Montreal, PQ, Canada.*

HAWES, Andrew Thomas. b 54. Univ of Sheff BA 77. Em Coll Cam BA (Th) 79. Westcott Ho Cam 77. **d** 80 Grimsby for Linc **p** 81 Linc. C of Gt Grimsby Dio Linc from 80. *18 Lawrence Street, Grimsby, S Humb, DN31 2JF.*

HAWES, Arthur John. b 43. Chich Th Coll. **d** 68 **p** 69 Worc. C of St Jo Bapt Kidderminster 68-72; Droitwich (in c of St Richard) 72-76; R of Alderford w Attlebridge and Swannington Dio Nor from 76; Sen Chap of Hellesdon Hosp from 76; RD of Sparham from 81. *Attlebridge Rectory, Norwich, NR9 5SU.* (Norwich 860644)

HAWES, Clive. b 37. Univ of Wales BSc (Geog) 59. Coll of Resurr Mirfield 61. **d** 63 **p** 64 Llan. C of Ynyshir 63-65; Roath 65-72; V of Llanddewi-Rhondda 72-75; Chap Ch Coll Brecon from 75. *Christ's College, Brecon, Powys.*

HAWES, George Walter. b 10. Lon Coll of Div 39. **d** 41 **p** 42 Chelmsf. C of All SS Woodford Wells 41-48; Chap to Herts Sanat 43-46; V of St Paul E Ham 48-56; Archd of W Kenya 56-60; R of Rowner 60-78. *90 Kiln Road, Fareham, Hants.*

HAWES, Howard John Richard. **d** 73 Queb for Ruw **p** 74 Queb. [f in CA]. Miss in Tanzania 73-74; C of Harrington Harbour Queb 75-77; Valcartier 77-79; I of Richmond Dio Queb from 79. *Box 156, Richmond, PQ, Canada J0B 2H0.*

HAWES, Michael Rowell. b 31. K Coll Lon and Warm AKC 61. **d** 62 **p** 63 Guildf. C of Epsom 62-65; Chap RAF from 65. *c/o Ministry of Defence, Adastral House, WC1.*

HAWES, Stanley John. b 06. K Coll Lon 32. **d** 36 **p** 37 Sheff. C of Tinsley 36-39; Ch Ch Heeley 39-41; CF (EC) 41-46; CF (R of O) 46-54; Hon CF from 54; C of Ch Ch Fulwood Sheff 46-47; V of Worsborough Common 47-51; Chap to HM Pris Liv 51-56; V of Clareborough w Hayton 56-60; Bradley 60-69; Hoyland-Swaine 69-77; Perm to Offic Dio Wakef from 77. *58 Churchfields, Thurgoland, Sheffield, S30 4BH.*

HAWIRA, Thomas Turama. b 29. St Jo Coll Auckld 74. **d** 75 Aotearoa for Wel **p** 76 Wel. Hon C of Ruapehu & Wainuiarua Dio Wel from 75. *Parapara Road, Raehiti, NZ.* (Raehiti 4461)

HAWKEN, Russell. b 13. Ex Coll Ox BA 39, MA 40. Wycl Hall Ox 37. **d** 39 **p** 41 Portsm. C of St Jude Southsea 39-41; Portsdown 41-42; Chap RNVR 42-46; V of H Trin Ox 46-51; St Jo Bapt Folkestone 51-58; St Luke S Lyncombe 58-66; Chap St Martin's Hosp Bath 58-66; R of Holton w Waterperry 66-71; Perm to Offic Dio Syd from 77. *31 Milson Road, Cremorne Point, Sydney, NSW, Australia 2090.* (90-3050)

HAWKER, Alan Fort. b 44. Univ of Hull BA (2nd cl Social Stud) 65. Dipl Th (Lon) 68. Clifton Th Coll 65. **d** 68 Warrington for Liv **p** 69 Liv. C of St Leon Bootle 68-71; Em Fazakerley 71-73; V of St Paul Goose Green 73-81; Team R of St Mary Southgate, Crawley Dio Chich from 81. *Rectory, Forestry Road, Southgate, Crawley, Sussex, RH10 6EH.* (Crawley 23463)

HAWKER, Alan John. b 53. AKC and BD 76. Sarum Wells Th Coll 77. **d** 78 **p** 79 Glouc. C of St Jo Coleford 78-81; Up Hatherley Dio Glouc from 81. *68 Alma Road, Cheltenham, Glos, GL51 5NB.* (Cheltm 75601)

HAWKER, Brian Henry. b 34. K Coll Lon and Warm AKC 61. **d** 62 **p** 63 St Alb. C of Hemel Hempstead (in c of St Paul Highfield) 62-66; Chap Co Mental Hosp Stone 66-69; V of Hartwell w Stone and Bishopstone 66-69; W Wycombe 69-72; Pastoral Consultant Clin Th Assoc from 72; Perm to Offic Dio Southw 73-75; Publ Pr from 75; Perm to Offic Dio B & W from 76. *Huntham Cottage, Huntham Lane, Stoke St Gregory, Taunton, Somt.* (N Curry 490229)

✠ **HAWKER, Right Rev Dennis Gascoyne.** b 21. Qu Coll Cam BA 48, MA 53. Cudd Coll 48. **d** 50 Dover for Cant **p** 51 Cant. C of St Mary and St Eanswythe Folkestone 50-55; V of St Mark S Norwood 55-60; L to Offic and St Hugh's Missr Dio Linc 60-65; Can and Preb of Linc Cathl from 64; Proc Conv Linc 64-75; V of Gt Grimsby 65-72; Surr 65-72; Cons Ld Bp Suffr of Grantham in Westmr Abbey 29 Sept 72 by Abp of Cant; Bps of Linc; Ex; B & W; Ely; St Alb; Ox; and Nor; Bps Suffr of Southn; Crediton; Croydon; Malmesbury; Edmonton; Dover; Bedford; Grimsby and Huntingdon; and others; Dean of Stamford from 73; Hon Chap RNR from 78. *Fairacre, 243 Barrowby Road, Grantham, Lincs, NG31 8NP.* (Grantham 4722)

HAWKER, Gerald Wynne. b 03. Late Scho of Univ Coll Ox 1st cl Cl Mods 23, BA (2nd cl Lit Hum) 25, MA 28. Cudd Coll 26. **d** 27 **p** 28 St Alb. C of Ch Ch Luton Beds 27-29; Miss (OMC) Calc 29-34; Chap Westcott Ho Cam 34-35; C-in-c of St Chris Round Green Conv Distr Luton 35-41; V of Radlett 41-47; Chap to Control Comm Germany 47-52; V of Ch Ch w St Andr and St Mich E Greenwich 52-60; RD of Greenwich and Deptford 58-60; V of Caterham Valley 60-68; Warden Homes of St Barn Dormans 68-72. *71 Cantelupe Road, East Grinstead, Sussex, RH19 3BL.* (E Grinstead 23523)

HAWKER, Canon Peter Charles. b 17. Ch Coll Cam BA 39, MA 43. St Barn Coll Adel 40, ACT ThL 41. Univ of W Austr MA (*ad eund*) 43. FSA 67. **d** 43 Adel for Kalg **p** 44 Kalg. C of St John's Cathl Kalg 43-47; R of Leonora 47-48; C of St Steph Gloucester Road Lon 48-51; R of Gautby w Waddingworth 51-60; V of Minting 51-60; Sec Gen of Confraternity of the Blessed Sacrament from 56; V of Cherry Willingham w Greetwell 60-69; V of St Botolph City and Dio Linc from 69; Custos Thesauri of Linc Cathl from 60; Can and Preb of Linc Cathl from 77; M Gen Syn from 80. *84 Little Bargate Street, Lincoln, LN5 8JL.* (Linc 20469)

HAWKER, Peter John. b 37. Univ of Ex BA 59. Wycl Hall Ox 69. **d** 70 Fulham for Lon **p** 71 Lon. Asst Chap at St Ursula Berne Dio (Gibr in Eur from 80) Lon (N & C Eur) 70-75; Chap from 75. *Jubilaumsplatz 2, Berne, Switzerland.* (031-430343)

HAWKES, Canon Cyrus Alvin. K Coll (NS) STh 42. **d** 39 **p** 40 Fred. C of St David 40-43; R of Newcastle 43-45; McAdam 45-52; St Jas St John 52-56; Kingsclear 56-61; Douglas 61-74; Can of Ch Ch Cathl Fred from 71. *207 Cherry Avenue, Fredericton, NB, Canada.*

HAWKES, Francis George. b 23. St Barn Coll Adel 48, ACT ThL 50. **d** and **p** 51 Adel. C of Mt Gambier 51-53; Brighton 53-54; Miss Chap at Broadview 54-57; R of Tatiara

57-60; CF (Austr) 60-65; CF from 65. *c/o Ministry of Defence, Bagshot Park, Bagshot, GU19 5PL.*

HAWKES, Keith Andrew. b 28. Oak Hill Coll 72. **d** 74 **p** 75 Nor. C of St Nich Gt Yarmouth 74-77; Chap of Ch Ch Dusseldorf Dio (Gibr in Eur from 80) Lon (N and C Eur) from 77. *Vicarage, Rotterdamstrasse 135, 4000 Dusseldorf, W Germany.*

HAWKES, Peter John Edward Job. Pemb Coll Cam BA 37, MA 43. Linc Th Coll 38. **d** 39 **p** 40 Worc. C of Netherton 39-42; Asst Chap Miss to Seamen Cardiff 42-45; Chap Miss to Seamen Newport 45-51; Trinidad 51-56; R of King I Tas 56-59; Franklin 59-61; Chap Univ of Tas 61-62; Monash Univ Austr 62-65; Sen Teaching Fell 65-69; Lect Univ of NB from 69. *c/o University of New Brunswick, St John, NB, Canada.*

HAWKES, William Henry. b 09. St Deiniols Libr Hawarden 71. **d** 71 **p** 72 Blackb. C of St Laur Morecambe 71-81; H Trin Morecambe 73-81; H Trin Poulton-le-Sands w St Laur Morecambe Dio Blackb from 81. *50 Michaelson Avenue, Morecambe, Lancs.* (Morecambe 417659)

HAWKETT, Graham Kenneth. b 20. Bps' Coll Cheshunt 61. **d** 63 **p** 64 Guildf. C of Farncombe 63-67; V of Wyke Dio Guildf from 67. *Wyke Vicarage, Normandy, Guildford, Surrey.* (Guildf 811148)

✠ **HAWKEY, Right Rev Ernest Eric.** Moore Th Coll Syd 30. ACT ThL 35. **d** 33 **p** 36 Syd. C of St Alb Ultimo 33-34; St Paul Burwood 34-40; P-in-c of Kandos 40-46; R 46-47; Actg Org Sec ABM for Queensld 47-50; Org Sec 50-68; L to Offic Dio Carp 52-68; Can Res of Brisb 62-68; Cons Ld Bp of Carp in St Jo Evang Cathl Brisb 23 April 68 by Abp of Brisb; Abp of Syd; Bps of N Queensld; Rockptn; N Terr; Newc; Wang; Melan; and River; Bp Coadj of Brisb; Asst Bp of New Guinea (Meredith); Bps Matthews and Muschamp; and Abp Moline; res 74; Dean of All S Cathl Thursday I 68-74; Perm to Offic Dio Brisb from 74. *2-12 Wellington Street, Clayfield, Queensland, Australia 4011.* (262 2108)

HAWKINGS, Timothy Denison. b 55. Univ of Ex BA 78. Univ of Nottm BA (Th) 80. St Jo Coll Nottm 78. **d** 81 Lich. C of St Bart Penn Dio Lich from 81. *46 Brenton Road, Penn, Wolverhampton, W Midl, WV4 5NX.*

HAWKINS, Alec Borman. b 07. ACP. **d** 68 **p** 69 Birm. Hon C of Boldmere Dio Birm from 68. *312 Orphanage Road, Sutton Coldfield, W Midl.* (021-373 4028)

HAWKINS, Alfred Pryse. b 29. St Mich Coll Llan 57. **d** 59 **p** 60 Llan. C of Dowlais 59-62; Caerau w Ely 62-66; V of Aberaman w Abercwmboi 66-77; R of Ebbw Vale Dio Mon from 77. *Rectory, Eureka Place, Ebbw Vale, Gwent.* (Ebbw Vale 305268)

HAWKINS, Allan Raeburn Giles. b 34. Selw Coll Cam BA 58, MA 62. Cudd Coll 58. **d** 60 **p** 61 Pet. C of Wellingborough 60-63; Stevenage (in c of St Geo) 63-71; R of St Geo Stevenage 71-74; V of New Swindon 74-80; in Amer Ch. *Chaplains Office, Fort Hood, Texas, TX76544, USA.*

HAWKINS, Alun John. b 44. K Coll Lon AKC, BA 66. Univ of Wales (Bangor) BD 81. St Deiniol's Libr Hawarden 78. **d** 81 Ban. C of Penmaenmawr Dio Ban from 81. *Ty Gwynin Sant, Dwygwfylchai, Penmaenmawr, Gwynedd.*

HAWKINS, Andrew Robert. b 40. Univ of St Andr BSc 64. Univ of Dur BA (2nd cl Th) 68, Dipl Th 69. St Chad's Coll Dur 65. **d** 69 Stepney for S'wark **p** 70 S'wark. C of Sutton 69-73; Wimbledon 73-77; Team V of Cramlington 77-81; R of Clutton w Cameley and Temple Cloud Dio B & W from 81. *Rectory, Main Road, Temple Cloud, Bristol, BS18 5DA.* (0761-52296)

HAWKINS, Canon Arthur Herbert. b 06. Univ of Lon BD 33. Peache Scho and Lon Coll of Div 27. **d** 33 **p** 34 Guildf. C of Woking 33-37; Org Sec CPAS for NE Distr 37-38; SE Distr 38-41; V of H Trin Richmond 41-49; Ch Ch Bridlington 49-68; RD of Bridlington 62-68; R of Leven w Catwick 68-73; Can and Preb of York Minster 68-73; Can (Emer) from 76. *31 Beech Drive, Bridlington, E Yorks, YO16 5TP.* (Bridlington 78579)

HAWKINS, Canon Brinley Handel. b 13. Late Scho and Pri St D Coll Lamp BA (2nd cl Engl) 34. Chich Th Coll 35. **d** 36 **p** 37 Swan B. C of Devynock w Rhydybriw 36-40; Llangyfelach w Morriston 40-44; V of Elgwys-Oen-Duw 44-51; St Weonard's 51-58; V of Orcop 57-58; St Thos Ap Hanwell (exch w Trenton USA 61-62) 58-64; St Bart Sheff 64-66; Stocksbridge 66-79; RD of Tankersley 67-73; Surr 68-79; Hon Can of Sheff from 75. *26 Ralph Ellis Drive, Stocksbridge, Sheffield, S30 5EW.*

HAWKINS, Bruce Alexander. b 44. Qu Coll Ox BA 66, MA 71. Sarum Th Coll 66. **d** 68 **p** 69 Guildf. C of Epsom 68-71; Dioc Youth Chap Cant from 71; Hon Min Can of Cant Cathl from 75; Dep Dir of Educn Dio Cant from 81. *Diocesan House, Lady Wootton Green, Canterbury, Kent.* (Canterbury 59401)

HAWKINS, David Frederick Cox. b 17. Clare Coll Cam BA 38, MA 45. Westcott Ho Cam. **d** 48 Dur **p** 49 Niger. C of St Gabr Bishopwearmouth Co Dur 48-49; Tutor and Prin of St Paul's Coll Awka 49-62; Tutor Trin Coll Umuahia 63; Can of All SS Cathl Onitsha 64-69; C of St Phil and St Jas Leckhampton 69-73; Commiss Niger from 70; Nig Delta from 74; R of Clifford Chambers w Marston Sicca 73-79; Welford w Weston and Clifford Chambers 79-82. *Orchard Rise, Bradford-on-Tone, Taunton, Somt.* (B-on-T 331)

HAWKINS, David Geoffrey. Univ of Sask BA 59. Em Coll Sktn LTh 59. Univ of BC BD 65. **d** 59 **p** 60 Sask. I of Birch Hills 60-63; C of Ch Ch Cathl Vancouver 65-66; St Paul Vancouver 66-68; C of St Helen Vanc 70-71; Chap Vanc Gen Hosp Dio New Westmr from 73; P-in-c of St Geo Vanc Dio New Westmr from 80. *2950 Laurel Street, Vancouver 9, BC, Canada.*

HAWKINS, David John. St Mich Th Coll Crafers, ACT ThL 64. **d** 64 Bunb for Melb **p** 64 Melb. C of Reservoir 64-65; Chap Miss to Seamen and C of H Cross Cathl Geraldton 65-66; Asst Chap Miss to Seamen S Shields 66-67; Port Chap Sing 67-75; R of Gnowangerup 75-80; Assoc P of Albany Dio Bunb from 80. *St John's House, Albany, W Australia 6330.* (41-3360)

HAWKINS, David John Leader. b 49. Univ of Nottm BTh 73. ALCD 73. St Jo Coll Nottm 69. **d** 73 Stockport for Ches **p** 74 Ches. C of Bebington 73-76. *Box 14, Bida, Niger State, Nigeria.*

HAWKINS, David Kenneth Beaumont. Em Coll Sktn LTh 63. **d** 63 **p** 64 Sktn. I of Northminster 63-69; C of Ch Ch Belleville 69-71; I of Wellington (Kente from 73) 71-79; Barriefield w Pittsburgh Dio Ont from 80. *240 Nelson Street, Kingston, Ont, Canada.* (613-549 3853)

HAWKINS, David Sewell. b 33. Bps' Coll Cheshunt. **d** 58 Chelmsf **p** 59 York. C of St Anne Chingford 58-59; Ch Ch Bridlington 59-63; V of Rudston w Grindall and Ergham (w Boynton from 64) 63-68; C-in-c of Boynton 63-64; Chap RADD 68-77; R of Burton Agnes w Harpham Dio York from 77; P-in-c of Kilham and Lowthorpe w Ruston Parva Dio York from 77. *Burton Agnes Rectory, Driffield, Humb.* (Burton Agnes 293)

HAWKINS, Donald John. b 39. K Coll Lon and Warm BD and AKC 62. **d** 63 **p** 64 Dur. C of Winlaton 63-66; Gateshead 66-69; Ryhope 69-71; R of Cockfield 71-79; Chap N Staffs R Infirm and City Gen Hosp Stoke-on-Trent from 79. *Royal Infirmary, Princes Road, Hartshill, Stoke-on-Trent, ST4 7LN.* (S-o-T 49144)

HAWKINS, Canon Francis John. b 36. Ex Coll Ox BA (2nd cl Th) 61, MA 63. Chich Th Coll 59. **d** 61 **p** 62 Ex. C of Tavistock w Gulworthy 61-64; Lect and Tutor Chich Th Coll 64-73; Vice-Prin 73-75; V of St Mary Virg E Grinstead 75-81; Sidlesham Dio Chich from 81; Can and Treas of Chich Cathl from 81. *Sidlesham Vicarage, Chichester, Sussex.* (Sidlesham 237)

HAWKINS, Garth Stephen. b 45. Ch Coll Hobart 69. **d** 72 **p** 73 Tas. C of St Geo Launceston 72-73; P-in-c of Hamilton 73-78; R of E Devonport Dio Tas from 78. *St Paul's Rectory, 121 David Street, E Devonport, Tasmania 7310.* (004 27 8984)

HAWKINS, Ian Clinton. b 27. Roch Th Coll 63. **d** 65 **p** 66 Derby. C of Boulton 65-68; V of Cotmanhay w Shipley 68-77; Ospringe Dio Cant from 77; Eastling Dio Cant from 79. *Ospringe Vicarage, Faversham, Kent.* (Faversham 2438)

HAWKINS, James Reginald. b 39. Univ of Ex BA (2nd cl Th) 61. Westcott Ho Cam 61. **d** 63 **p** 64 Lich. C of Cannock w Chadsmoor 63-66; Wem 66-67; Cheddleton 67-69; R of Yoxall 69-77; The Quinton Dio Birm from 77. *773 Hagley Road West, Birmingham, B32 1AJ.* (021-422 2031)

HAWKINS, John Arthur. b 45. Dipl Th (Lon) 69. Kelham Th Coll 64. **d** 69 Bp McKie for Cov **p** 70 Cov. C of St Alb Stoke Heath 70-73; Fletchamstead 73-77; V of Whitley 77-81; Team V of Em Northn Dio Pet from 81. *17 Brittons Drive, Southfields, Northampton, NN3 5DP.*

HAWKINS, John Charles Lacey. b 18. Linc Th Coll 40. **d** 42 **p** 43 Carl. C of Dalton-in-Furness 42-44; Workington 44-48; V of Westnewton 48-53; Thornton w Allerthorpe and Melbourne 53-60; R of Stockton-on-the-Forest w Holtby and Warthill 60-77; Sigglesthorne and Rise w Nunkeeling and Bewholme Dio York from 77. *Sigglesthorne Rectory, Hull, Humb, HU11 5QA.* (Hornsea 3033)

HAWKINS, John Edward. Moore Th Coll Syd ACT ThL 62. **d** 64 **p** 65 Syd. C of St John Darlinghurst Syd 64-66; Port Kembla 66-68; C-in-c of W Cabramatta 68-72; C of St Mark Dalston 72-73; R of Lidcombe Dio Syd from 73. *1 Mark Street, Lidcombe, NSW, Australia 2141.* (649-7004)

HAWKINS, Canon John Henry. b 13. TCD BA (1st cl Mod) 35, Div Test (1st cl) 37, BD 51. **d** 37 **p** 38 Down. C of St Patr Ballymacarrett 37-39; Min Can and C of Down Cathl 39-44; R of Ballee w Bright 44-50; Dioc Insp of Schs Dio Down 46-50; V of Antrim (w Connor to 55) 50-67; R of

Agherton 67-78; Can of Connor Cathl from 76. *11 Carnreagh Avenue, Hillsborough, Co Down, N Ireland.* (Hillsborough 682565)

HAWKINS, Michael Neil. b 46. BD (Lon) 77. Moore Coll Syd 76. **d** 77 **p** 78 Ch Ch. C of Sydenham-Beckenham Dio Ch Ch from 77. *194 Colombo Street, Christchurch 2, NZ.*

HAWKINS, Paul Henry Whishaw. b 46. Ex Coll Ox BA (2nd cl Th) 68. St Steph Ho 70. **d** 72 **p** 73 Win. C of Fawley 72-75; St Steph W Ealing 75-77; P-in-c of Dorney 77-78; Team V of Riverside 78-81; Fell and Chap Sidney Sussex Coll Cam from 82. *c/o Sidney Sussex College, Cambridge.*

HAWKINS, Peter Edward. b 35. Univ of Leeds BA 60. Coll of Resurr Mirfield 60. **d** 62 **p** 63 Chelmsf. C of St Edm Forest Gate 62-65; St Jo Bapt Sevenoaks 65-68; Chap Metrop Police Cadet Corps Tr Sch 68-73; P-in-c of H Nativ Knowle 73-74; Team V of Knowle 74-79; V of Westbury-on-Trym Dio Bris from 79. *44 Eastfield Road, Westbury-on-Trym, Bristol, BS9 4AG.* (Bris 621536)

HAWKINS, Peter Michael. b 38. Kelham Th Coll 58. **d** 63 Dunwich for Calc **p** 64 Calc. Miss OMC 63-64; C of Calc Cathl 64-66; C-in-c of Kidderpore 66-68; V of Asansol w Burnpur 68-69; C of St Paul and St Jude Manningham Bradf 70-72; Bradf Cathl 72-75; Bp's Chap for Commun Relns Bradf from 72; V of Allerton Dio Bradf from 75. *Vicarage, Ley Top Lane, Allerton, Bradford, BD15 7LT.* (Bradf 41948)

✠ **HAWKINS, Right Rev Ralph Gordon.** CMG 77. Hatf Coll Dur BA and LTh 34. ACT DTh 60. St Bonif Coll Warm 29. **d** 35 **p** 36 Bris. C of St Anne Brislington 35-38; R of Morawa 38-44; Chap RAAF 43-45; R of Wembley 44-49; St Hilda Perth 49-57; Can of Perth 54-57; Archd of Perth 57; Cons Ld Bp of Bunb in St Geo Cathl Perth 6 Aug 57 by Abp of Perth; Abp of Syd; Bps of NW Austr; and Kalg; and Bps Freeth; Elsey; and Riley; res 77; Perm to Offic Dio Bunb from 78. *9 Cross Street, Bunbury, W Australia 6230.*

HAWKINS, Reginald Richard. Moore Th Coll Syd 18, ACT ThL 18. **d** 18 **p** 19 Syd. C of Drummoyne 18-20; R of Cobar 20-25; P-in-c of Canley Vale w Cabramatta 25-27; R of Waterloo 27-37; Riverstone 37-53; Kangaroo Valley 53-65; L to Offic Dio Syd from 65. *Unit 3, 15 Station Street West, Harris Park, NSW 2150, Australia.*

HAWKINS, Richard Randal. Univ of Natal BA 61. Ridley Hall Cam 63. **d** 65 **p** 66 Lich. C of Bushbury 65-68; Woodford 68-71; Asst Chap Michaelhouse Sch Natal 71-77. *Michaelhouse, Balgowan, Natal, S Africa.* (Balgowan 3)

HAWKINS, Ven Richard Stephen. b 39. Ex Coll Ox BA (2nd cl Th) 61, MA 65. Univ of Ex BPhil 76. St Steph Ho Ox 61. **d** 63 **p** 64 Ex. C of St Thos Ex 63-66; Clyst St Mary 66-75; Team V of Clyst Valley 75-78; Centr Ex 78-81; Bp's Officer for Min Dio Ex 78-81; Jt Dir Ex-Truro Min Tr Scheme 78-81; Dir of Ordin Tr 79-81; Archd of Totnes from 81; P-in-c of Whitestone w Oldridge Dio Ex from 81. *Whitestone Rectory, Exeter, Devon, EX4 2JT.* (Longdown 406)

HAWKINS, Robert Henry. b 1892. St Edm Hall Ox BA (2nd cl Th) 13, MA 19. **d** 19 **p** 20 Worc. C of St Thos Dudley 19-23; V of Maryport w Ch Ch 23-27; Surr from 23; V of St Geo Barrow-F 27-34; RD of Dalton 28-34; Dalston w Cumdivock 34-43; Proc Conv Carl 31-35; V and RD of Nottm 43-58; Hon Can of Southw 43-58; Can of St Geo Chap Windsor 58-70. *Manormead, Tilford Road, Hindhead, Surrey.* (Hindhead 6493)

HAWKINS, Roger David William. b 33. K Coll Lon and Warm BD and AKC 58. **d** 59 **p** 60 Lon. C of St Mary Twickenham 59-61; Heston 61-64; Dorking 64-65; V of St Mark Mitcham 65-74; St Matt Redhill Dio S'wark from 74. *St Matthew's Vicarage, Ridgeway Road, Redhill, Surrey, RH1 6PQ.* (Redhill 61568)

HAWKINS, Roger Julian. b 32. Ripon Hall Ox 59. **d** 61 **p** 62 Man. C of St Francis Conv Distr Wythenshawe 61-63; Chap RAF 63-67; R of Mawgan-in-Pydar 67-75; R of Lanteglos-by-Camelford w St Adwena 75-78; Newmarket w Exning Dio St E from 78. *St Mary's Rectory, Fordham Road, Newmarket, Suff, CB8 0JW.* (Newmarket 2448)

HAWKINS, Theodore Harold Jefferies. b 14. Univ of Man BA 37. St Aid Coll 37. **d** 39 **p** 40 Man. C of Ch Ch Moss Side 39-46; Asst Chap Man R Infirm 39-46; V of St Geo Heap Bridge 46-48; Waddington Yorks 48-62; Ed Bradf Dioc Year Book 54-62; RD of Bolland 60-62; V of Rawdon 62-71; Chap Woodlands Hosp Rawdon 63-71; C of Beverley Minster 71-75; V of Lastingham 75-80; C-in-c of Appleton-le-Moors 75-80. *St Wilfrid's Cottage, York Road, Harrogate, N Yorks, HG1 2QL.*

HAWKINS, William Arthur. b 18. Univ of Bris 49. Clifton Th Coll 50. **d** 53 **p** 54 Ex. C of Ellacombe 53-54; Totnes 54-58; R of Ashill w Broadway 58-74; Herstmonceux Dio Chich from 74. *Herstmonceux Rectory, Hailsham, East Sussex.* (Herstmonceux 3124)

HAWKSBEE, Canon Derek John. b 28. Univ of Lon BSc 49. SOC 70. **d** 71 **p** 72 S'wark. C of Norbiton 71-75; Cands' Sec, S Area Sec (and Overseas Sec from 73) SAMS 71-81; Dir of Tr SAMS in USA from 81; Hon Can of Parag from 73; Hon C of St John Tunbridge Wells 75-81. *Box 276, Union Mills, N Carolina 28167, USA.*

HAWLEY, Anthony Broughton. b 41. St Pet Coll Ox BA 67, MA 71. Westcott Ho Cam 67. **d** 69 **p** 70 Lich. C of Wolverhampton 69-72; St Sav (in c of All H) Borough and Dio S'wark from 73; C-in-c of St Hugh's Conv Distr and Dir of Charterhouse Borough and Dio S'wark from 73. *40 Tabard Street, SE1 4XZ.* (01-407 1123)

HAWLEY, George William. b 14. Worc Ordin Coll 64. **d** 66 Lon **p** 67 Willesden for Lon. C of St Andr Roxbourne Harrow 66-69; Queensbury 69-79; Perm to Offic Dio Lon from 79. *21 Crowshott Avenue, Stanmore, Middx.* (01-952 1873)

HAWLEY, John Andrew. b 50. AKC and BD 71. Wycl Hall Ox 72. **d** 74 **p** 75 York. C of Hull 74-77; Cathl Ch Bradf 77-80; V of Woodlands Dio Sheff from 80. *Woodlands Vicarage, Doncaster, S Yorks.* (Doncaster 723268)

HAWLEY, Nigel David. b 51. Coll of Resurr Mirfield 77. **d** 80 **p** 81 Man. C of Birch-in-Rusholme w Fallowfield Dio Man from 80. *13 Cawdor Road, Fallowfield, Manchester, M14 6LG.*

HAWNT, John Charles Frederick. b 30. **d** 75 **p** 76 Mashon. P Dio Mashon. *56 Palmer Road, Hilton Park, PO Belvedere, Salisbury, Rhodesia.*

HAWORTH, Gerald Nixon. Univ of BC BA 46. Trin Coll Tor LTh 49, BD 50. **d** 49 New Westmr for Calg **p** 50 Calg. C of Pro-Cathl Calg 49-51; I of Sylvan Lake 51-52; Elnora 52-54; C of St Thos Tor 54-56; R of St Martin Vancouver Dio New Westmr from 56. *3155 St George's Avenue, North Vancouver, BC, Canada.*

HAWORTH, Harry Cecil. b 1892. Univ of Man BSc 22. Egerton Hall, Man 22. **d** 24 **p** 25 Man. C of Ch Ch Patricroft 24-28; R of St Aug Newton Heath 28-62. *17 Marshside Road, Churchtown, Southport, Mer, PR9 9TJ.*

HAWORTH, John Luttrell. b 28. **d** 67 **p** 68 Kilm. C of Kilcommick 67-70; Ballymacelligot 70-71; Team V of Tralee 71-72; I of Kinneigh w Ballymoney 72-76; Easkey w Kilglass Dio Killala from 77. *Rectory, Easkey, Ballina, Irish Republic.* (Easkey 9)

HAWORTH, Very Rev Kenneth William. b 03. Late Scho of Clare Coll Cam Stewart of Rannoch Scho 22, 1st cl Cl Trip pt i 23, BA (1st cl Th Trip pt i) 24, MA 28. Wells Th Coll 25. **d** 26 **p** 27 Lich. C of St Giles Willenhall 26-28; SPG Chap at Montana 29-31; Dom and Dioc Chap to Bp of Lich and Lect Lich Th Coll 31-37; Exam Chap to Bp of Lich 38-48; B & W 47-60; Sarum 61-71; Chap Wells Th Coll 37-39; CF (R of O) 39-43; R of Stratton w Baunton 43-46; Vice-Prin Wells Th Coll 46-47; Prin 47-60; Preb of Combe ii in Wells Cathl 47-60; Proc Conv B & W 56-60; Dean of Sarum 60-71; Dean (Emer) from 71. *The Common, Woodgreen, Fordingbridge, Hants.* (Downton 22239)

HAWORTH, Paul. b 47. G and C Coll Cam BA 68, MA 72. Westcott Ho Cam 75. **d** 78 Chelmsf **p** 79 Barking for Chelmsf. C of Hornchurch 78-81; St Mary Loughton Dio Chelmsf from 81; P-in-c of High Beech Dio Chelmsf from 81. *Vicarage, Church Road, High Beech, Loughton, Essex.* (01-508 1791)

HAWORTH, Stanley Robert. b 48. St Jo Coll Dur BA 69. Sarum Wells Th Coll 71. **d** 73 **p** 74 Bradf. C of H Trin Skipton-in-Craven 73-76; St Pet Cathl Ch Bradf 76-78; Team V of Grantham Dio Linc from 78. *St John's Vicarage, London Road, Grantham, NG31 6ER.* (Grantham 72770)

HAWTHORN, Christopher John. b 36. Qu Coll Cam 3rd cl Math Trip pt i 58, BA (3rd cl Th Trip pt ii) 60, MA 64. Ripon Hall Ox 60. **d** 62 **p** 63 York. C of Sutton-in-Holderness 62-66; V of St Nich Hull 66-72; E Coatham 72-79; St Martin Scarborough Dio York from 79. *St Martin's Vicarage, Scarborough, N Yorks.* (0723-60437)

HAWTHORN, John Christopher. b 03. Late Exhib and Scho of G and C Coll Cam 2nd cl Hist Trip pt i 24, BA (1st cl Th Trip pt i) 25, MA 29. Westcott Ho Cam 25. **d** 26 **p** 27 Wakef. C of St Aug Halifax 26-29; Rugby (in c of St Pet) 29-31; Vice-Prin St Jo Coll Dur and L to Offic Dio Dur 31-33; V of St Gabr Bp Wearmouth 33-38; Chatteris 38-73. *2 Trinity Close, Ely, Cambs, CB6 1AX.* (Ely 2441)

HAWTHORN, Thomas Kenneth. Seager Hall, Ont 61. **d** 61 Hur **p** 62 Bp Townshend for Hur. I of Cainsville 61-63; St D Brantford 63-70; R of St Paul Wingham 70-77; Dorchester Dio Hur from 77. *Box 58, Dorchester, Ont., Canada.*

HAWTHORNE, John William. b 32. St Aug Coll Cant 74. **d** 77 **p** 78 Cant. C of Boxley and Detling 77-80; R of Otham Dio Cant from 80; Langley Dio Cant from 80. *Otham Rectory, Maidstone, Kent.* (Maidstone 861470)

HAWTHORNE, Noel David. b 30. BNC Ox BA (3rd cl Hist) 53, MA 58. Ridley Hall, Cam 53. **d** 55 **p** 56 Sheff. C of St Pet Abbeydale Sheff 55-58; Keighley (in c of Braithwaite and Newsholme) 58-61; V of H Trin Idle 61-70; R of Colne

Dio Blackb from 70. *Rectory, Colne, Lancs, BB8 0AE.* (Colne 863479)

HAWTHORNE, William James. b 46. TCD 66. **d** 69 **p** 70 Down. C of Gilnahirk 69-72; Asst Chap Miss to Seamen 72-76; C of Boultham 76-78; Bracebridge Heath Dio Linc from 78; Relig Programmes Producer BBC Radio Lincs from 80. *1 Churchill Avenue, Bracebridge Heath, Lincoln.* (Linc 22204)

HAWTIN, David Christopher. b 43. Keble Coll Ox BA (2nd cl Th) 65, MA 70. Cudd Coll 66. **d** 67 **p** 68 Dur. C of St Thos Conv Distr Pennywell Bp Wearmouth 67-71; St Pet Stockton-on-Tees 71-74; C-in-c of St Andr Conv Distr Leam Lane Heworth 74-79; R of Washington Dio Dur from 79. *Rectory, Washington Village, Washington, Tyne & Wear, NE38 7LE.* (Washington 463957)

HAWTIN, Ralph Hamilton. b 15. Worc Ordin Coll 59. **d** 61 Bp McKie for Cov **p** 62 Cov. C of Keresley w Coundon 61-66; R of Clifton Reynes w Newton Blossomville (and Emberton w Tyringham and Filgrave from 75) 66-81; C-in-c of Emberton w Tyringham and Filgrave 72-75. *Gazerdine Cottage, Munsley, Nr Ledbury, Herefs, HR8 2PZ.*

HAY, Canon Alexander Charles de Prudnik. b 10. St Jo Coll Cam 2nd cl Hist Trip pt i 31, BA (2nd cl Hist Trip pt ii) 32, MA 36. Westcott Ho Cam 33. **d** 34 **p** 35 Newc T. C of St Paul Cullercoats 34-36; St Nich Cathl Newc T 37-39; Hon C 39-48; Chap and Asst Master Dame Allan's Sch Newc T 39-54; Chap and Second Master 54-71; V of Healey 48-58; Heddon-on-the-Wall 58-63; Hon Can of Newc T 70-80; Can (Emer) from 80; V of Wooler 71-74; R (w Doddington, Ilderton, Ingram and Kirknewton) 74-78; P-in-c of Doddington, Ilderton and Ingram 71-74; Chatton w Chillingham 75-78; R of Wooler w Doddington, Ilderton, Ingram, Kirknewton, Chatton and Chillingham 78-80; L to Offic Dio Newc T from 80. *25 Ryecroft Way, Wooler, Northumb, NE71 6DY.* (Wooler 427)

HAY, Archibald MacAlister. b 1890. Qu Coll Ox BA 15, MA 19. **d** 42 **p** 43 Chelmsf. C of Braintree 42-46; R of St Mich-at-Coslany Nor 46-65; V of St Martin-at-Oak Nor 46-57. *3 Daleside, Riverdale Road, Sheffield, S10 3FA.*

HAY, Arthur Lincoln Baron. b 02. Jes Coll Cam BA 23, MA 28, St Steph Ho Ox 53. **d** 54 Reading for Cant **p** 55 Ox. C of Bucklebury 54-56; R of Stanford Dingley 56-66; Perm to Offic Dio Ox 66-78. *16 The Circus, Bath, BA1 2ET.*

HAY, Herbert Waldo St Aubyn. Univ of Dur BA 56. St Pet Coll Ja 57. **d** 57 **p** 58 Ja. Asst Master Kingston Coll 56; C of Vere 57-62; P-in-c of Blackstonedge Dio Ja from 77. *Blackstonedge PO, Jamaica, W Indies.*

HAY, Ian Gordon. b 52. Univ of Dundee MA 73. Univ of Edin BD 76. Edin Th Coll 73. **d** 76 **p** 77 Glas. C of Dumfries 76-79; Chap Dio Brech 79-81; R of St Andr Brechin Dio Brech from 81. *Rectory, Church Street, Brechin, DD9 6HB.* (Brechin 2708)

HAY, Jack Barr. b 31. Bps' Coll Cheshunt 57. **d** 60 **p** 61 Newc T. C of St Anthony Newc T 60-63; Killingworth (in c of St Paul Dudley) 63-68; V of St Pet Cowgate Newc T 68-77; Woodhorn w Newbiggin Dio Newc T from 77. *Vicarage, Front Street, Newbiggin-by-Sea, NE64 6PS.* (Ashington 817220)

HAY, John. b 45. Div Hostel Dub 77. **d** 79 **p** 80 Down. C of Newtownards 79-81; R of Galloon and Drummully Dio Clogh from 81. *Galloon Rectory, Newtownbutler, Co Fermanagh, N Ireland.* (Newtownbutler 245)

HAY, John. b 43. St D Coll Lamp 63. **d** 67 **p** 68 Bp Hughes for Llan. C of Ynyshir 67-70; St Mary Virg Cardiff 70-74; V of Llanwonno 74-78; P-in-c of All SS Weston-super-Mare 78-79; Team V of Weston-super-Mare Centr Pars (in c of All SS from 79) Dio B & W from 78. *Holy Trinity Vicarage, St Peter's Avenue, Weston-super-Mare, Avon.*

HAY, Kenneth Gordon. b 14. TD 50. Worc Ordin Coll 63. **d** 65 Barking for Chelmsf **p** 66 Chelmsf. C of St Sav Westcliffe-on-Sea 65-68; CF (TA) from 66; R of Kelvedon Hatch 68-73; P-in-c of St Steph Eccles Distr Prittlewell 73-78; V 78-79. *26 Warwick Road, Thorpe Bay, Essex.*

HAY, Raymond. b 38. QUB BSc (Econ) 60. TCD BD 68. Cranmer Hall Dur 60. **d** 62 **p** 63 down. C of Bangor Abbey 62-67; Tutor St Jo Coll Dur from 68; L to Offic Dio Dur 68-76; C-in-c of Bearpark 76-81. *c/o St John's College, Durham.* (Durham 2306)

HAYA, Ven James Mbokot 'Ebomvu. Coll of Resurr Rosettenville 48. **d** 50 **p** 52 Grahmstn. P Elizabeth, Grahmstn 50-70; R of H Spirit City and Dio Port Eliz from 70; Archd of Algoa from 80. *PO Box 42, Kwazakhele, Port Elizabeth, S Africa.* (041-62086)

HAYBALL, Douglas Reginald. b 18. Oak Hill Th Coll 66. **d** 68 **p** 69 Bradf. C of Ilkley 68-72; V of Parr-Mount 72-75; C-in-c of Sheepy Magna and Parva w Ratcliffe Culey 75-76; R of Sibson w Sheepy and Ratcliffe Culey Dio Leic from 76. *Sheepy Rectory, Atherstone, Warws.* (Tamworth 880301)

HAYCRAFT, Roger Brian Norman. b 43. Oak Hill Coll 69. **d** 73 **p** 74 Edmon for Lon. C of St Pet Belsize Pk 73-76; Yardley 76-79; V of H Cross Hornchurch Dio Chelmsf from 79. *Holy Cross Vicarage, Hornchurch Road, Hornchurch, Essex.* (Hornchurch 47976)

HAYDAY, Alan Geoffrey David. b 46. Kelham Th Coll 65. **d** 69 **p** 70 Leic. C of St Steph Evington 70-72; Spalding 72-78; V of Cherry Willingham Dio Linc from 78. *Vicarage, Cherry Willingham, Lincoln, LN3 4AB.*

HAYDEN, David Frank. b 47. Dipl Th (Lon) 69. BD (Lon) 71. Tyndale Hall Bris 67. **d** 71 **p** 72 Chich. C of St Matt Silverhill St Leon-on-Sea 71-75; Galleywood 75-79; R of Redgrave w Botesdale and Rickinghall Dio St E from 79; RD of Hartismere from 81. *Rectory, Botesdale, Nr Diss, Norf, IP22 1DT.* (Botesdale 685)

HAYDEN, Dennis Barry. Univ of W Ont BA 66. Hur Coll BTh 69. **d** 69 **p** 70 Hur. I of Six Nations Reserve 69-71; I of All SS Waterloo 71-74; H Trin Chatham Dio Hur from 74. *77 Selkirk Street, Chatham, Ont., Canada.* (519-884 8706)

HAYDEN, Eric Henry Ashmore. b 26. ACII 65. Sarum Wells Th Coll 71. **d** 73 Chich. **p** 74 Lewes for Chich. C of Horsham 73-78; V of Cuckfield Dio Chich from 78. *Cuckfield Vicarage, Haywards Heath, Sussex.* (Haywards Heath 54007)

HAYDEN, Eric Sidney. b 27. Sarum Th Coll. **d** 69 Portsm **p** 70 Bp Woolmer for Portsm. C of Havant 69-70; Hayling S w N 70-73; C-in-c of Calbourne w Newtown 73-74; R 74-81; V of Brading w Yaverland Dio Portsm from 81. *Brading Vicarage, Sandown, IW.* (Brading 262)

HAYDEN, John Carleton. Wayne State Univ BA 55. Univ of Detroit MA 62. St Chad's Coll Regina LTh 63. **d** 63 **p** 64 Qu'App. Univ Chap Regina 63-67; Hon C of St Jas Regina 67-69. *Box 503 Howard University, 2400 Sixth Street North-West, Washington, DC 20001, USA.*

HAYDEN, John Donald. b 40. BD (Lon) 62. Tyndale Hall Bris 63. **d** 65 **p** 66 Ches. C of Ch Ch Macclesfield 65-68; H Spirit Cathl Dodoma 68-69; V of St Marg Moshi 70-77; Home Sec United S for Chr Lit from 77. *c/o Luke House, Farnham Road, Guildford, Surrey, GU1 4XD.*

HAYDOCK, Alan. b 41. Kelham Th Coll 60. **d** 65 **p** 66 Southw. C of Rainworth 65-68; Hucknall Torkard 68-71; Team V 71-74; V of St Jo Bapt Bilborough 74-80; R of E Bridgford Dio Southw from 80; P-in-c of Kneeton Dio Southw from 80. *Rectory, East Bridgford, Nottingham, NG13 8PE.* (E Bridgford 20218)

HAYDOCK, Joseph William. b 11. Univ of Lon BSc 31. Bps' Coll Cheshunt, 32. **d** 34 Derby **p** 35 Bp Crick for Derby. C of Cotmanhay 34-37; Hasland 37-39; C-in-c of Pilsley 39-40; V of Stanley 40-50; Castleton Derby 50-57; Cranborne w Boveridge 57-76. *30 Oakhurst Road, West Moors, Wimborne, Dorset, BH22 0DS.*

HAYDON, Keith Frank. b 46. Cudd Coll 73. **d** 75 Stepney for Lon **p** 76 Lon. C of De Beauvoir Town 75-77; St Thos Wells w Horrington 77-80; Team V of Weston-super-Mare Dio B & W from 80. *St Saviour's Vicarage, Elmhyrst Road, Weston-super-Mare, Somt, BS23 2SJ.* (W-s-M 23230)

HAYES, Charles Gerald. **d** 37 Abp of Ratiara **p** 38 S'wark (RC). Received into Angl Ch by Bp of Adel 52. L to Offic Dio Adel 52-57; R of S Yorke Peninsula 57-61; Kadina 61-64; St Alb Largs 64-71; Perm to Offic Dio Adel from 71; L to Offic Dio Murray from 71. *11 Crittenden Road, Morphett Vale, S Australia 5162.* (08-382 3916)

HAYES, Cuthbert John. St D Coll Lamp 55. **d** 57 **p** 58 Mon. C of Machen w Rudry 57-59; R of Wolves-Newton w Kilgwrrwg and Devauden 59-60; V of Clifford 60-72; C-in-c of Brilley w Michaelchurch 66-71. *Longhope, Swainshill, Hereford.*

HAYES, Cuthbert Rowland James. b 02. Late Scho of Selw Coll Cam 1st cl Th Trip pt i, 32, BA (1st cl Th Trip pt ii) 33, MA 37. **d** 33 **p** 34 Man. C of Ch of the Sav Bolton 33-35; Tutor Oak Hill Th Coll Southgate 35-37; V of St Jo Evang Worksop 37-46; C-in-c of St Luke Shireoaks 43-46; Offg Chap Kilton Hill Co Hosp 37-46; V of Ecclesfield 46-64; Proc Conv Sheff 49-64; RD of Ecclesfield 61-64; PC of Hambleton 64-69; L to Offic Dio Blackb from 69. *25 Highgate Avenue, Fulwood, Preston, Lancs, PR2 4LL.* (Preston 719858)

HAYES, David Clifford. Moore Th Coll Syd. **d** 49 **p** 50 Syd. C of St Mark Darling Point 49-51; Marrickville 51-52; St Jas Syd 52-54; Chap Repatriation Hosp Concord Dio Syd from 62. *c/o Repatriation General Hospital, Concord, NSW, Australia 2139.* (73-0411)

HAYES, David Malcolm Hollingworth. b 42. K Coll Lon and Warm BD (2nd cl) and AKC (2nd cl) 68. **d** 69 Lon **p** 70 Kens for Lon. C of St Pet and St Paul Teddington 69-70; St Martin Ruislip 70-75; P-in-c of Ludford 75-80; Ashford Carbonell w Ashford Bowdler 75-80; V of Eastcote Dio Lon from 80. *Eastcote Vicarage, Bridle Road, Pinner, Middx, HA5 2SJ.* (01-866 1263)

HAYES, David Roland Payton. b 37. Hertf Coll Ox BA 62, MA 66. Coll of Resurr Mirfield 62. **d** 64 **p** 65 Ox. C of

Woodley 64-67; All SS Emscote Warwick 67-69; Farnham Royal (in c of Farnham Common) 69-75; P-in-c 75-78; Newport Pagnell 78-79; Lathbury 78-79; R of Newport Pagnell w Lathbury Dio Ox from 79; RD of Newport from 80. *Rectory, High Street, Newport Pagnell, Bucks, MK16 8AB.* (Newport Pagnell 611145)

HAYES, Very Rev Ernest. Univ Coll Dur LTh 30. Edin Th Coll 27. **d** 31 **p** 32 Glas. C of St Ninian Pollokshields 31-34; P-in-c of St Barn Dennistoun Glas 34-47; R of St John Ballachulish 47-50; Stonehaven 50-75; Catterline 50-75; R of Drumlithie Dio Brech from 53; Can of St Paul's Cathl Dundee from 64; Synod Clk Dio Brech from 65; Dean of Brech from 71. *West Newbigging Cottage, Drumlithie, Kincard, AB3 2YA.* (Drumlithie 622)

HAYES, Frederick William. **d** and **p** 58 BC. I of St Alb Vic Dio BC from 58. *1500 Holly Street, Victoria, BC, Canada.* (604-595 5339)

HAYES, John. **d** 78 N Queensld (NSM). Perm to Offic Dio N Queensld from 78. *c/o Racecourse Mill, Mackay, Qld, Australia, 4740.*

HAYES, Leslie. b 13. Kelham Th Coll 29. **d** 36 **p** 37 S'wark. C of All SS Newington 36-41; CF (EC) 41-46; Men in Disp 45; C of St Steph Walworth 46-48; Industr Chap Dio Sheff 48-51; V of St Swithun Sheff 51-55; R of Dinnington 55-62; V of St Thos w St Jas Worsborough 62-71; Surr 62-71; Chap at Qu Mary's Hosp for Children Carshalton and Henderson and Belmont Hosp Sutton 71-73; V of Jurby 73-74; Chap of St Jude Andreas 73-74; V of Kirk Braddan 74-78; Surr 74-78; Perm to Offic Dio Bradf 79-80; Dio Sheff from 80. *205 Westwick Road, Greenhill, Sheffield, S8 7BW.* (Sheff 377558)

HAYES, Michael Gordon William. b 48. St Cath Coll Cam BA 69, MA 73, PhD 73. Ridley Hall Cam 73. **d** 75 **p** 76 B & W. C of Combe Down w Monkton Combe 75-78; H Trin Cam 78-81; V of Bathampton Dio B & W from 81. *Bathampton Vicarage, Bath, Avon, BA2 6SW.* (Bath 63570)

HAYES, Michael John. b 52. Univ of Lanc BA 73. Coll of the Resurr Mirfield 75. **d** 78 Lon **p** 79 Kens for Lon. C of Notting Hill 78-81; P-in-c of St Mich & St Geo Conv Distr White City Hammersmith Dio Lon from 81. *1 Commonwealth Avenue, White City, W12.* (01-743 7100)

HAYES, Reginald Brian Michael. b 40. Univ of Wales (Cardiff) Dipl Th 71. St Mich Coll Llan 67. **d** 71 **p** 72 Llan. C of St Martin Roath 71-77; Commiss Masasi from 72; V of Brynmawr 77-80; CF (TA) 79; P-in-c of Porthleven Dio Truro 80-81; V (w Sithney) from 81; P-in-c of Sithney 80-81. *Porthleven Vicarage, Helston, Cornw, TR13 9LQ.* (Helston 62419)

HAYES, Richard. b 39. K Coll Lon and Warm BD and AKC 68. **d** 69 **p** 70 Roch. C of Dartford 69-72; St Steph Glouc Rd Kens 72-76; V of St Paul Ruislip Manor 76-82; St Pet Mount Park Ealing Dio Lon from 82. *St Peter's Vicarage, Mount Park Road, W5 2RU.* (01-997 1620)

HAYES, Stephen Tromp Wynn. Univ of Natal BA 65. St Chad's Coll Dur Dipl Th 68. **d** 68 Natal **p** 70 Damar. Asst Chap Miss to Seamen Durban 68-69; C of St Geo Cathl Windhoek 69-71; St Martin-in-the-Fields 72-77; R of Melmoth Dio Zulu from 77. *Box 96, Melmoth, Zululand, S Africa.*

HAYLES, Geoffrey Edwin. Moore Th Coll Syd ACT ThL 55. **d** 56 **p** 57 Syd for Perth. C of Bondi 56-57; R of Meckering 57-62; C of Broadwater 62-64; R of Berkley w Rodden 64-68; Kelmscott 68-75; Wembley 75-81; Hon Can of Perth 80-81; Oenpelli Dio N Terr from 81. *Rectory, Oenpelli, via Darwin, NT, Australia 5791.*

HAYLES, Graham David. b 39. Dipl Th (Lon) 66. Clifton Th Coll 64. **d** 67 **p** 68 S'wark. C of Ch Ch Gipsy Hill 67-70; St Jo Evang Heatherlands, Parkstone 70-74; V of St Jas W Streatham Dio S'wark from 74. *236 Mitcham Lane, Streatham, SW16 6NT.* (01-677 3947)

HAYLLAR, Bruce Sherwill. b 23. Trin Hall, Cam BA (2nd cl Hist Trip pt i) 47, MA 53. Cudd Coll 48. **d** 50 **p** 51 Wakef. C of Almondbury 50-53; Miss Dio Chota N 53-63; PC of Peacehaven Dio Chich 63-68; V 68-72; P-in-c of Kabwe 73-76; V of Moulsecoomb Dio Chich 76-81; Team R from 81. *St Andrew's Vicarage, Hillside, Moulsecoomb, Brighton, BN2 4TA.* (Brighton 680680)

HAYLLAR, Sidney Philip. b 10. Selw Coll Cam 3rd cl Hist Trip pt i, 33, BA (2nd cl Anthrop Trip) 34. Wells Th Coll 34. **d** 35 **p** 36 Bris. C of St Alb Westbury Pk Clifton 35-38; H Trin S Shore (in c of St Nich) Blackpool 38-43; Hd Master Chesterton Sch Glouc 43-46; C of St Helier 46-48; Hd Master Walhampton Sch Lymington 48-56; R of Uckfield 56-64; R of Isfield 56-64; R of Horsted Parva 56-64; RD of Uckfield 59-64; V of Eridge Green 64-68; Ringmer 69-75; P-in-c of Arlington 75-80. *c/o Dale Cottage, Eastport Lane, Lewes, E Sussex.* (Lewes 77192)

HAYMAN, Andrew William. Moore Th Coll Syd ACT ThL 51. **d** and **p** 52 Syd. C-in-c of Wilberforce 52-53; R of Pitt Town 53-54; C-in-c of St Barn Punchbowl 54-60; R of Naremburn 60-68; Austinmer 68-76; C-in-c of Jamberoo Dio Syd from 76. *Rectory, Churchill Street, Jamberoo, NSW, Australia 2533.* (042-36 0136)

HAYMAN, Arnolis. **d** 52 **p** 53 Syd. C of Willoughby 52-54; C-in-c of Flemington w Homebush 54-59; Berala 59-66; L to Offic Dio Syd from 66. *5 St Anne's Court, William Street, Ryde, NSW 2112, Australia.*

HAYMAN, Eric. b 17. Worc Ordin Coll 61. **d** 63 **p** 64 Ex. C of Em Plymouth 63-66; K Chas Mart w St Luke and St Matthias Plymouth 66-67; St Jo Bapt-in-Bedwardine Worc 67-72; Highweek w Abbotsbury 72-74; C-in-c of Wrabness Dio Chelmsf 74-75; R (w Wix) from 75. *Wrabness Rectory, Manningtree, Essex.* (Ramsey 880359)

HAYMAN, Canon Perceval Ecroyd Cobham. b 15. St Jo Coll Cam BA 37, MA 41. Linc Th Coll 48. **d** 50 **p** 51 Sarum. C of Marlborough 50-53; Chap of Marlborough Coll 53-63; V of Rogate 63-81; R of Terwick 63-81; RD of Midhurst 72-81; Can and Preb of Chich Cathl from 77. *Fiddler's Green, Cocking, Midhurst, W Sussex, GU29 0HU.* (Midhurst 3198)

HAYMAN, Theodore John. Moore Th Coll Syd ACT ThL 44. **d** and **p** 45 Syd for Armid. C of St John Willoughby 45-46; P-in-c of Streaky Bay 47-49; Ceduna 50-57; R of Streaky Bay 57; Kensington 57-66; V of W Tamworth 66-71; Can of Armid 68-71; L to Offic Dios Syd and N Terr 71-80; Federal Sec Bush Ch Aid S Syd 71-80; Perm to Offic Dio Newc 79-80; R of St Steph Willoughby Dio Syd from 80. *211 Mowbray Road, Chatswood, NSW, Australia 2067.* (412-1453)

HAYMAN, Canon William Samuel. b 03. Late Exhib of St Jo Coll Ox BA (3rd cl Th) 25, MA 28. Sarum Th Coll 25. **d** 26 **p** 27 S'wark. C of St Matt Brixton 26-32; Wimbledon (in c of St Mark) 32-34; V of Finstall 34-38; CF (TA) 37-39; R of Cheam 38-72; Hon Can of S'wark 52-60; Can (Emer) from 72; RD of Beddington 55-60; Archd of Lewisham 60-72; Chap to HM the Queen 61-73. *Wayside, Houghton, Stockbridge, Hants.* (King's Somborne 204)

HAYNE, Harold Robert. Univ of W Ont BA 61. Hur Coll LTh 64. **d** and **p** 64 Bp Snell for Tor. C of St Clem Eglington Tor 64-67; I of Newcastle 67-76; Six Nations Reserve W 76-80; St Mich and All SS Lon Dio Hur from 80. *412 Pinewood Drive, London, Ont, Canada N6J 3L2.*

HAYNE, Raymond Guy. b 32. Chich Th Coll 57. **d** 60 **p** 61 Birm. C of All SS K Heath 60-63; Clewer 63-67; V of Grimsbury 67-76; C-in-c of Wardington 71-74; R of Brightwell w Sotwell Dio Ox from 76; RD of Wallingford from 81. *Brightwell Rectory, Wallingford, Berks, OX10 0RX.* (Wallingford 37110)

HAYNES, Cyril Alphonza. b 30. **d** 80 **p** 81 Calg. Hon C of St Barn Sarcee Dio Calg from 80. *508 Lysander Drive SE, Calgary, Alta, Canada, T2C 1L7.*

HAYNES, Donald Irwin. b 28. Univ of Birm BA (2nd cl Geog) 51. Ripon Hall Ox 59. **d** 59 Roch **p** 60 Tonbridge for Cant. C of Chatham 59-66; Hon C of Gillingham 66-71; Asst Master Simon Digby Sch Chelmsley Wood and Publ Pr Dio Birm 71-81; P-in-c of Whittington Dio Derby from 82. *Whittington Rectory, Chesterfield, Derbys, S41 9QW.* (Chesterfield 450 651)

HAYNES, Frederick Charles Ronald. St D Coll Lamp BA 50. M CR 57. **d** 51 **p** 52 St E. C of St Bart Ipswich 51-55. *Priory of St Peter, Rosettenville, Johannesburg, S Africa.*

HAYNES, (Mark) James Dalrymple. Univ of Adel BA (2nd cl Hist) 50, ACT ThL 50. M SSM 56. St Mich Th Coll Crafers 50. **d** 53 **p** 54 Adel. L to Offic Dio Adel 53-60 and from 67; Chap and Tutor St Mich Th Coll Crafers 54-60 and 67-74; L to Offic Dio Perth 60-66; Chap Perth Coll 64-66; Chap and Tutor SSM Th Coll Austr 67-74; Hon C of Glenelg Dio Adel from 80. *59 Moseley Street, Glenelg South, S Australia 5045.*

HAYNES, John Edward. St Mich Coll Crafers ACT ThL 60. **d** 54 **p** 55 Adel. C of St Paul Adel 54-56; St Pet Glenelg 56-57; P-in-c of Koolunga 57-61; Liss Hants 61-62; St Pet Paddington 62-66. *Church Office, 18 King William Road, N Adelaide, S Australia 5006.*

HAYNES, John Richard. Ely Th Coll 60. **d** 63 **p** 64 Ches. C of St Jo Bapt Bollington 63-67; St Jo Bapt Ches 67-68; Davenham 68-70; R of St Luke Que Que 70-78; Sub-Dean of St Jo Bapt Cathl Bulawayo and Exam Chap to Bp of Matab from 78. *Box 2422, Bulawayo, Zimbabwe.* (62732)

HAYNES, Kenneth Gordon. b 09. Worc Ordin Coll. **d** 56 **p** 57 Ox. C of Earley 56-61; V of Burwell 61-70; R of Feltwell 70-75; RD of Fordham 66-70; Feltwell 70-75; C of Steeton 75-79. *44 Main Street, Yaxley, Cambs, PE7 3LU.*

HAYNES, Leonard Thomas. b 17. **d** 69 **p** 70 Leic. C of Lutterworth w Cotesbach 69-73; C-in-c of Stanford w Swinford and Catthorpe w Shawell Dio Leic 73-75; V from 75. *Swinford Vicarage, Lutterworth, Leics, LE17 6BQ.* (Swinford 221)

HAYNES, Michael Thomas Avery. b 32. K Coll Lon and Warm AKC 61. **d** 62 **p** 63 Wakef. C of Hebden Bridge 62-64;

Elland (in c of All SS) 64-68; V of Thornhill Lees w Savile Town Dio Wakef from 68. *Thornhill Lees Vicarage, Dewsbury, Yorks.* (0924-461269)

HAYNES, Canon Oliver Carrington. Univ of Dur Codr Coll Barb BA 36, MA 43. **d** 38 **p** 39 Barb. C of St Paul Barb 38-41; Chap Westbury Cem 41-43; V of St Barn I and Dio Barb from 43; Can of Barb from 75. *St Barnabas's Vicarage, Barbados, W Indies.*

HAYNES, Ven Peter. b 25. Selw Coll Cam BA 49, MA 54. Cudd Coll 50. **d** 52 **p** 53 York. C of Stokesley 52-54; Hessle 54-58; V of St John Drypool 58-63; Bp's Chap for Youth and Asst Dir of Relig Educn Dio B & W 63-70; V of Glastonbury (w Godney from 72) 70-74; Archd of Wells from 74; Can Res and Preb of Wells Cathl from 74; Surr from 74; M Gen Syn from 76. *6 The Liberty, Wells, Somt., BA5 2SU.* (Wells 72224)

HAYNES, Peter Nigel Stafford. b 39. Hertf Coll Ox BA (3rd cl Phil Pol and Econ) 62, MA 66. Cudd Coll 62. **d** 64 **p** 65 Cant. C of All SS U Norwood 64-68; St Mark N End Portsea (in c of St Francis) 68-72; Asst Chap H Trin Brussels 72-76; Team V of Banbury 76-80; Internat Affairs Specialist Bd for Social Responsibility from 80. *Church House Dean's Yard, SW1P 3NZ.* (01-222 9011)

HAYNES, Philip Mayo. b 25. St Edm Hall Ox BA and MA 50. Cudd Coll 50. **d** 54 **p** 55 S'wark. C of Richmond 54-58; Raynes Pk 58-63; Limpsfield w Titsey 63-70; V of Woodcote Surrey Dio S'wark from 70. *22 Peak's Hill, Purley, CR2 3JE.* (01-660 7204)

HAYNES, Ralph Douglas. Univ of Tor BA 56. Wycl Coll Tor LTh and BTh 59. **d** and **p** 59 Tor. C of St Barn Danforth Tor 59-61; I of Cloverdale 61-69. *c/o Synod Office, 818 837 West Hastings Street, Vancouver 1, BC, Canada.*

HAYNES, Robert John. Univ of Syd BA 69. Moore Coll Syd ACT ThL 74. BD (Lon) 76. **d** and **p** 76 Syd. C of St John Beecroft 76-78; St John Parramatta 78-79; R of St Martin Kens Dio Syd from 79. *103 Todman Avenue, Kensington, NSW, Australia 2033.* (663-1538)

HAYNES, Walter John. Ridley Coll Melb ACT ThL 42. **d** and **p** 43 Syd. C of St Clem Marrickville 43-45; CMS Miss Dio W Szech China 45-51; R of Lawson w Hazelbrook 51-54; LPr Dio Adel 56-60; R of St Sav Punchbowl 60-64; C-in-c of W Pennant Hills 64-67; Oatley 67-68; L to Offic Dio Syd from 68. *20 Tuckwell Road, Castle Hill, NSW, Australia 2154.* (634-1429)

HAYNES, William Beresford. b 11. Univ of Leeds BA 35. Coll of Resurr Mirfield, 35. **d** 37 Wakef **p** 38 Pontefract for Wakef. C of Ravensthorpe 37-40; C-in-c of Sharlston 40-41; CF (EC) 41-46; CF 46-51; Iraq 46; Oswestry 46-48; Duke of York's RM Sch Dover 48-51; SCF W Africa 51-54; Woolwich 54-57; 2nd Div BAOR 57-60; Plymouth 60-61; CF (R of O) 61-66; V of Breinton Dio Heref from 61. *Breinton Vicarage, Hereford, HR4 7PG.* (Hereford 3447)

HAYS, Michael John. Univ of Natal BA 62. St Paul's Coll Grahmstn LTh 64. **d** 65 **p** 66 Natal. C of Alphege Pietermaritzburg 65-71; R of Estcourt 71-80; Pinetown Dio Natal from 80; Archd of Ladysmith 75-80. *16 Padfield Road, Pinetown, Natal, S Africa.*

HAYSMORE, Frederick Charles. b 03. Bps' Coll Cheshunt 44. **d** 45 **p** 46 St Alb. C of Gt St Mary Sawbridgeworth 45-48; St Jo Evang Palmers Green 49-51; V of St Gabr Bounds Green 51-59; Chap Wood Green and Southgate Hosp 51-59; V of Ponders End 59-74; Perm to Offic Dio Chelmsf from 74. *21 Crossways, Chelmsford, Essex.* (0245 63773)

HAYSOM, Alan Challes. Brisb Th Coll ACT ThL 34, Th Scho 45. **d** 34 **p** 35 Brisb. C of St Paul Ipswich 34-37; M of Bro of St Paul Charleville 37-39; V of St Matt Holland Pk 39-42; Noosa 42-45; C of St Pet Gympie 45-46; R of Crow's Nest 46-49; Rosewood 49-53; Boonah 53-61; St Matt Groveley Brisb 61-65; Dalby 65-70; V of St Bart Bardon Bris 70-74; Perm to Offic Dio Brisb from 74. *7 Wharf Street, Woody Point, Queensland, Australia 4019.*

HAYTER, Canon John Charles Edwin. b 15. St Edm Hall Ox BA 37. MA 46. Westcott Ho Cam 37. **d** 38 **p** 39 Win. C of Romsey 38-41; Asst Chap of Sing Cathl 41-45; V of S Perak 46-49; C of Solihull 49-52; St Thos w St Clem and St Mich Win 52-54; Chap R Free Hosp Lon 54-55; V of Boldre 55-82; Hon Can of Win Cathl from 79. *4 St Thomas Park, Lymington, Hants.*

HAYTER, Canon Michael George. b 18. Ch Ch Ox BA 39, MA 43. Cudd Coll 40. **d** 41 **p** 42 York. C of St Mary Scarborough 41-46; R of Steeple Aston (w N Aston and Tackley from 77) Dio Ox from 46; RD of Woodstock 64-74; Hon Can of Ch Ch Cathl Ox from 75; P-in-c of Tackley 75-77. *Steeple Aston Rectory, Oxford, OX5 3SF.* (Steeple Aston 40317)

HAYTER, Raymond William. b 48. Oak Hill Coll 74. **d** 77 **p** 78 S'wark. C of St Jas w Ch Ch Bermondsey 77-80; H Trin Sydenham Dio S'wark from 81. *1 Sydenham Park Road, SE26 4DY.* (01-699 5303)

HAYTER, Ronald William Joseph. b 19. Keble Coll Ox BA 40, MA 44. Wells Th Coll 40. **d** 42 **p** 43 Ex. C of Honiton 42-45; St Mark Ex 44-47; St Thos Ex 47-51; Paignton (in c of St Mich) 51-55; V of Countess Wear Dio Ex from 55. *375 Topsham Road, Exeter, Devon.* (Topsham 3263)

HAYTER, Thomas Hugh Osman. b 1900. St Cath Coll Cam BA 22, MA 26. Ridley Hall Cam 21. **d** 23 **p** 24 Heref. Asst Master St MIch Coll Tenbury 22-24; C of St Mich AA near Tenbury 23-24; Ross 24-26; Fugglestone w Bemerton 26-31; R of Sutton Benger 31-35; Tytherton-Kelways 32-35; V of St Matt Moorfields Bris 35-41; Charlton All SS 41-45; Somerton 45-68. *Privet Cottage, Hartham, Corsham, Wilts, SN13 0PZ.* (Corsham 713285)

HAYTHORNTHWAITE, Alfred Parker. b 10. Wycl Hall Ox 29. **d** 35 **p** 36 Carl. C of Aspatria 35-38; Penrith 38-46; CF 39-45; Hon CF 45; R of Kirkby Thore w Temple Sowerby 46-57; V of Seascale 57-67; Allithwaite 67-76; Perm to Offic Dio Carl from 77. *The Rectory Cottage, Kirkby Lonsdale, Carnforth, Lancs.*

HAYTHORNTHWAITE, Robert Brendan. b 31. Trin Coll Dub BA 53, LLB 56, MA 64. Edin Th Coll 63. **d** 64 Tuam for Down **p** 65 Down. [f Solicitor] C of St John Laganbank and Orangefield 64-66; St Thos Belfast 66-68; L to Offic Dio Connor from 68; C of Malone Dio Connor from 75. *11 Windsor Avenue, Belfast, BT9 6EE.* (Belfast 665561)

HAYTHORNTHWAITE, William. b 1897. MBE 55. St Bonif Coll Warm 59. **d** 59 **p** 60 Crediton for Ex. C of Whipton 59-62; R of Huntsham 62-67; R of Clayhanger 62-67; PC of Petton 62-67; C of Christchurch 67-75; L to Offic Dio Win from 75. *1 Glebe Cottage, Church Lane, New Milton, Hants, BH25 6SL.* (New Milton 610354)

HAYWARD, Alan Richard. b 25. Wycl Hall Ox 54. Open Univ BA 72. **d** 56 **p** 57 Worc. C of St Francis Dudley 56-59; C-in-c of St Andr Conv Distr Wollescote Dio Worc 59-65; Min 65; V from 65. *St Andrew's Vicarage, Wollescote, Stourbridge, W Midl, DY9 9DG.* (Lye 2695)

HAYWARD, Alfred Ross. b 20. Clifton Th Coll 52. **d** 54 **p** 55 Southw. C of Attenborough w Bramcote and Chilwell 54-56; V of Friston w Snape 56-60; Willoughby-on-the-Wolds w Wysall 60-65; Woodborough 65-70; Warden Braithwaite Gospel Trust Stathern 73-77; V of Tugby w E Norton and Skeffington 77-81; R of Beeston Regis Dio Nor from 81. *All Saints Rectory, Cromer Road, Beeston Regis, NR27 9NG.* (Sheringham 822163)

HAYWARD, Christopher Joseph. b 38. Trin Coll Dub BA (2nd cl Ment and Moral Sc) 63, MA 67. Ridley Hall Cam 63. **d** 65 **p** 66 S'wark. C of Hatcham 65-69; Dep Warden Lee Abbey Internat Students' Club 69-71; Warden 71-74; Chap of Chelmsf Cathl 74-77; P-in-c of All SS Darlaston Dio Lich from 77; Industr Chap from 77. *All Saints Vicarage, Franchise Street, Wednesbury, WS10 9RE.* (021-526 4481)

HAYWARD, Clifford. b 08. St Paul's Coll Grahmstn 51. **d** 52 St Jo Kaffr for Lebom **p** 53 Lebom. C of St Cypr Lourenco Marques 52-53; P-in-c of S Miss Distr Lourenco Marques 54; N (Inhambane) Miss Distr 54-56; Dir of Miss Cathl Distr 56-57; C of St Cypr Cathl Kimberley 57-62; St Andr Coulsdon 63-64; C of St Jo Cathl Umtata 65-66; Humansdorp 66-67; R of St Alb Kimberley 68-73; C of St Mary Lewisham 73-78; hon C of St Jo Evang E Dulwich Dio S'wark from 78. *Charterhouse, Charterhouse Square, EC1M 6AN.*

HAYWARD, Preb Edwin Calland. b 11. ATCL 30. Univ of Lon BSc (2nd cl Phys) 32. Linc Th Coll 35. **d** 36 Bradf **p** 37 Bp Mounsey for Bradf. C of St Barn Heaton 36-41; C-in-c of St Martin Conv Distr Heaton Bradf 41-46; Chan's V of Lich Cathl 46-49; L to Offic Dio Lich 47-49; V of Riddlesden 49-52; St Francis Friar Pk W Bromwich 52-62; Pattingham 62-69; Burton-on-Trent 69-81; RD of Tutbury from 69; Preb of Lich Cathl 72-81; Preb (Emer) from 81; P-in-c of Ch Ch Burton-on-Trent 76-81. *19 Henhurst Hill, Burton-on-Trent, Staffs, DE13 9TB.* (0283-48735)

HAYWARD, Grant Clifton. b 45. St Jo Coll Auckld LTh 79. **d** 79 **p** 80 Waik. C of Cathl Ch of St Pet Hamilton Dio Waik from 79. *13a Howell Avenue, Hamilton, NZ.*

HAYWARD, Jeffrey Kenneth. b 47. Univ of Nottm BTh 74. St Jo Coll Nottm LTh 74. **d** 74 **p** 75 Worc. C of Stambermill 74-77; St Jo Bapt Woking Dio Guildf from 77. *13 Heath Drive, Brookwood, Woking, Surrey, GU24 0HG.* (Brookwood 2161)

HAYWARD, John David. b 40. K Coll Lon and Warm AKC 63. **d** 65 Hulme for Man **p** 66 Man. C of St Pet Westleigh 65-68; All SS Elton Bury 68-72; R of St Chad Moston 72-77; Team V of Stantonbury Dio Ox from 77. *New Vicarage, Bradwell Road, Bradville, Milton Keynes, Bucks.* (Milton Keynes 314224)

HAYWARD, Ven John Derek Risdon. b 23. Trin Coll Cam 1st cl Th Trip pt i 54, BA (2nd cl Th Trip pt ii) 56, MA 64. Westcott Ho Cam 56. **d** 57 **p** 58 Sheff. C of St Mary w St

Simon and St Matthias Sheff 57-59; V of St Silas Sheff 59-63; Isleworth Dio Lon from 64; Archd of Middx 74-75; Archd (Emer) from 75; Dioc Gen Sec Dio Lon from 75; M Gen Syn from 75. *61 Church Street, Isleworth, Middx, TW7 6BE.* (01-560 6662)

HAYWARD, Preb John Talbot. b 28. Selw Coll Cam BA 52, MA 56. Wells Th Coll 52. **d** 54 B & W **p** 55 Taunton for B & W. C of S Lyncombe 54-58; R of Lamyatt 58-71; V of Bruton w Wyke Champflower and Redlynch 58-71; RD of Bruton 62-71; R of Weston-super-Mare 71-75; Preb of Wells Cathl from 73; Team R of Weston-super-Mare Centr Pars Dio B & W from 75. *Rectory, Weston-super-Mare, Avon.* (W-s-M 25360)

HAYWARD, Maurice Arthur. St Francis Coll 59, ACT ThL 60. **d** 60 Bp Redding for Bal **p** 61 Bal. C of Horsham 61-62; L to Offic Dio Syd 63-64; Miss Papua 64-71; C of Indooroopilly 71-72; Chermside 72-73; V of Tara 73-75; C of Sunnybank Brisb 75-76; Kowanyama 76-79; All S and St Bart Cathl Thursday I Dio Carp from 79. *c/o All Souls' Cathedral, Thursday Island, Queensld, Australia 4875.*

HAYWARD, Peter Noel. b 26. Univ of Leeds BA 48, BD 78. Coll of Resurr Mirfield 48. **d** 50 **p** 51 Wakef. C of S Elmsall (in c of Moorthorpe from 51) 50-56; Chap of Sheldon (in c of Garretts Green) 56-60; C-in-c of Garretts Green Conv Distr Dio Birm 60-67; Min 67-69; V 69-70; N Cave w N and S Cliffe from 70; R of Hotham Dio York from 70; RD of Howden from 78. *North Cave Vicarage, Brough, N Humb.* (N Cave 2398)

HAYWARD, Roynon Albert Oscar James. b 25. **d** 67 **p** 68 Glouc. C of St Paul City and Dio Glouc from 67. *37 Forest View Road, Gloucester.* (Gloucester 21104)

HAYWARD, William Frank. Moore Th Coll Syd ACT ThL 51. **d** and **p** 52 Syd. C of Corrimal 52; C-in-c of Riverstone 53; R 53-57; C-in-c of Berowra 57-64; Belfield 64-73; R of Five Dock Dio Syd from 73. *173 Great North Road, Five Dock, NSW, Australia 2046.* (713-6840)

HAYWOOD, Frank. b 19. St Cath S Ox BA 40, MA 44. Cudd Coll 40. **d** 42 **p** 43 Pet. C of All SS Pet 42-46; K Norton 46-49; R of Orton Waterville 49-62; V of Challock w Molash Dio Cant from 62. *Challock Vicarage, Ashford, Kent, TN25 4BJ.* (Challock 263)

HAYWOOD, Frederick Arthur Edward. b 17. **d** 72 **p** 74 Rupld. C in the Selkirk Area 72-74; Hon C of St Phil Winnipeg Dio Rupld from 74. *91 Des Meurons Street, Winnipeg, Manitoba, Canada.*

HAYWOOD, James William. b 36. Chich Th Coll 69. **d** 73 **p** 74 Ripon. C of Halton 73-76; St John Workington 77-78; V of Clifton-in-Workington Dio Carl from 78. *Great Clifton Vicarage, Workington, Cumb.* (Workington 3886)

HAZELGROVE, Trevor John. b 42. SOC 71. **d** 74 **p** 75 S'wark. C of N Beddington 74-78; V of St Jo Div Merton and Industr Chap Dio S'wark from 78. *Vicarage, High Path, SW19.* (01-542 3283)

HAZELL, Ven Frederick Roy. b 30. Fitzw Ho Cam 2nd cl Hist Trip pt i 52, BA (2nd cl Hist Trip pt ii) 53. Cudd Coll 54. **d** 56 **p** 57 Derby. C of Ilkeston 56-59; Heanor (in c of All SS Marlpool) 59-62; PC of Marlpool Derbys 62-63; Chap to Univ of WI Ja 63-66; C of St Martin-in-the-Fields Westmr 66-68; V of St Sav Croydon Dio Cant from 68; RD of Croydon 72-78; Hon Can of Cant from 73; Archd of Croydon from 78. *96 Lodge Road, Croydon, Surrey, CRO 2PF.* (01-684 2526)

HAZELL, Maxwell Robert Thomas. ACT ThL 63. **d** 54 **p** 55 St Arn. C of Bealiba 54-55; V of Quambatook 55-58; Manangatang 58-60; Robinvale 60-64; R of Charlton 64-67; V of W Coburg 67-72; I of Preston 73-75; C in Dept of Chap Dio Melb from 75. *133 Cramer Street, Preston, Vic, Australia 3072.* (03-47 1437)

HAZELL, Thomas Jeremy. b 35. Univ of Bris LLB 56. St D Coll Lamp 56. **d** 58 **p** 59 Mon. C of St Paul Newport 58-61; St Jo Evang Derby 61-64; V of Arksey 64-69; Stud Counsellor Univ of Cardiff from 69. *c/o University College, Cathays Park, Cardiff.*

HAZELTON, Edwin Geoffrey. b 08. OBE 45. St Geo Windsor 50. **d** 51 **p** 52 Sheff. C of Rotherham 51-53; Ranmoor (in c of St Columba Crosspool) Sheff 53-56; V of Amesbury 56-67; RD of Avon 64-67; PC of Flushing 67-69; R of Wylye (w Stockton to 73) Fisherton Delamere (and The Langfords from 73) 69-76. *Streetly Cottage, Steeple Langford, Salisbury, Wilts.*

HAZELTON, John. b 35. St Cath Coll Cam BA 56, MA 60. Univ of Bris MLitt 74. Wells Th Coll. **d** 61 **p** 62 B & W. C of Twerton-on-Avon 61-65; V of Pitcombe w Shepton Montague 65-72; Lect St Hild's (and St Bede from 75) Coll Dur from 72. *36 Orchard Drive, Durham.* (Durham 63035)

HAZELTON, Robert Henry Peter. b 22. Wells Th Coll 65. **d** 67 **p** 68 B & W. C of St Jo Bapt Bridgwater 67-69; Milton Somt 69-76; V of Peasedown St John (W Wellow from 80) Dio B & W from 76. *Vicarage, Peasedown St John, Bath, Avon.* (Radstock 32293)

HAZELTON, Preb Robert John. b 10. Trin Coll Dub BA and Div Test 34, MA 43. **d** 34 **p** 35 Clogh. C of Monaghan w Tyholland 34-37; Mucknoe w Crossduff and Broomfield 37-38; C-in-c of Lack (or Colaghty) 38-41; Killenaule 41-43; I of Fethard 43-50; Fethard U 50-65; RD of Fethard 51-65; Can Treas of Cash Cathl 60-65; R of Fiddown Clonegam and Kilmeaden Dio Lism from 65; Preb and Treas of Lism Cathl from 69; Prec from 74; Preb and Treas of Waterf Cathl from 69; Prec from 74. *Fiddown Rectory, Piltown, Co Kilkenny, Irish Republic.* (Piltown 7)

HAZEN, Ford Harold. K Coll Halifax, BA 56, LTh 58. **d** 57 **p** 58 Fred. C of St Luke St John 57-58; R of Grand Manan 58-62; I of Maugerville w Marysville 62-70; R of Sussex Dio Fred from 70. *Box 227, Sussex, NB, Canada.*

HAZLEDINE, Basil William. b 18. St Pet Hall Ox BA 42, MA 45. Wycl Hall Ox 42. **d** 43 **p** 44 Ox. C of All SS Highfield Ox 43-46; Gerrards Cross 46-51; V of St Patr Barking 51-55; Sayers Common and R of Twineham 55-60; Em Stoughton 60-70; St Andr Westlands 70-77; P-in-c of Whatfield w Semer Dio St E 77-78; R from 78; P-in-c of Nedging w Naughton Dio St E 77-81; R from 81. *Whatfield Rectory, Ipswich, Suff, IP7 6QU.* (Hadleigh 822100)

HAZLEHURST, Anthony Robin. b 43. Univ of Man BSc (Engl) 64. Tyndale Hall Bris 65. **d** 68 **p** 69 Ches. C of Ch Ch Macclesfield 68-71; Bushbury 71-75; New Clee Dio Linc 75-77; Jt C-in-c 77-80. *Address temp unknown.*

HAZLEHURST, David. b 32. Univ of Liv BSc 54. St Steph Ho Ox 55. **d** 57 **p** 58 Sheff. C of Arbourthorne Sheff 57-59; Ch Ch Doncaster 59-61; W Wycombe 61-63; C-in-c of St Jas Collyhurst, Man 66-67; V of Blackrod 67-79; St Marg Halliwell Bolton Dio Man from 79. *1 Somerset Road, Halliwell, Bolton, Lancs.* (Bolton 40850)

HAZLEWOOD, David Paul. b 47. Univ of Sheff MB ChB 70. Univ of Ox BA 72. Wycl Hall Ox 70. **d** 73 **p** 74 Sheff. C of Chapeltown 73-76; Overseas Miss Fellowship Singapore from 76. *Overseas Missionary Fellowship, 2 Cluny Road, Singapore.*

HAZLEWOOD, George Ian. b 28. St Francis Coll Brisb. **d** 55 **p** 56 Brisb. C of St Colomb Clayfield Brisb 55-56; C (Col Cl Act) of All SS Poplar 56-62; Bp's Youth Chap Dio St Alb 62-67; V of H Trin Yeovil 67-74; Commiss Wang from 70; Bal from 75; RD of Merston 72-74; V of Prestbury Dio Glouc from 74. *Prestbury Vicarage, Cheltenham, Glos.* (Cheltenham 44373)

HAZLEWOOD, Canon Gordon Vivian Elton. Univ of Dur (Codr Coll Barb) LTh 31, BA 33, MA 38. **d** 32 **p** 33 Windw Is. C of St Geo Cathl Kingstown 32-33; Carriacou 33-34; R of Rivière Dorée 34-46; C of St Mich Cathl Barb 46-51; Prec 50-51; Dean 51-71; R of St Cypr I and Dio Barb from 72; Hon Can of Barb from 72. *Eleventh Avenue, Belleville, St Michael, Barbados, W Indies.*

✠ **HAZLEWOOD, Right Rev John.** K Coll Cam BA 48, MA 52. Cudd Coll 48. **d** 49 **p** 50 S'wark. C of St Mich Camberwell 49-50; Randwick Dio Syd 50-51; Dubbo Dio Bath 51-53; St Mich AA Camberwell 53-54; Vice-Prin St Francis Th Coll Brisb 54-60; Dean and R of St Paul's Cathl Rockptn 60-68; St Geo Cathl Perth 68-75; Exam Chap to Bp of Rockptn 64-69; Cons Ld Bp of Bal in St Paul's Cathl Melb 29 Sept 75 by Abps of Melb, Perth and Adel; Bps of Gippsld, St Arn, Bend, Newc, Graft and River; and others. *Bishopscourt, 454 Wendouree Parade, Ballarat, Vic, Australia 3350.* (053-39 2370)

HAZLEWOOD, Roy Maxwell. St Jo Coll Morpeth. **d** and **p** 54 Newc. C of Largs 54; New Lambton 54-58; R of Bullahdelah 58-64; Murrurundi 64-79; P-in-c of Toukley w Budgewoi Dio Newc from 79. *Rectory, Hammond Road, Toukley, NSW, Australia 2263.* (043-96 3859)

HEAD, David Nicholas. b 55. Pemb Coll Cam BA 77, MA 81. Westcott Ho Cam 78. **d** 81 S'wark. C of St Andr & St Mark Surbiton Dio S'wark from 81. *The Curate's Flat, St Andrew's Church Hall, Balaclava Road, Surbiton, Surrey KT6 5PN.*

HEAD, David Rodney. b 51. Monash Univ Melb BChemEng 72. ACT BTh 77. St Jo Coll Morpeth 77. **d** 78 **p** 79 Melb. C of St Geo Malvern 78-80. *1/296 Glenferrie Road, Malvern, Vic, Australia, 3144.*

HEAD, Derek Leonard Hamilton. b 34. ALCD 58. **d** 58 **p** 59 Roch. C of Ch Ch Bexleyheath 58-61; Wisley w Pyrford 61-66; P-in-c of St Paul's Conv Distr Howell Hill Ewell 66-73; R of All SS Headley Dio Guildf 73-81; Team R from 81; RD of Farnham from 79. *Headley Rectory, Bordon, Hants, GU35 8PW.* (Headley Down 3123)

HEAD, Graham Bruce. b 49. St Barn Th Coll Adel 77. **d** 80 **p** 81 Adel. C of H Cross Elizabeth Dio Adel from 80. *6 Easton Road, Elizabeth North West, S Australia 5113.*

HEAD, Ivan. Univ of W Austr BA 75. Melb Coll of Div

BD 78. **d** and **p** 79 Perth C of Mosman Pk Dio Perth from 79. *1 Willis Street, Mosman Park, W Australia 6012.* (384 5506)

HEAD, John Leslie. b 06. Univ of Dur LTh 31. Sarum Th Coll 29. **d** 31 **p** 32 Lon. C of St Barn Kentish Town 31-34; Perm to Offic at St Barn W Silvertown Vic Dks 34-36; C-in-c of St Mark Vic Dks 36-37; Min of St Aug Leytonstone 37-41; CF (EC) 41-46; Hon CF 46; Men in Disp 46; R of Black Notley and Chap of Black Notley Municipal Hosp 46-50; R of Leigh-on-Sea 50-72; Surr 50-72. *21 Selwyn Road, Southend-on-Sea, Essex.*

HEAD, Peter Ernest. b 38. BSc (Lon) 59. Ridley Hall, Cam 61. **d** 63 **p** 64 Sheff. C of Fulwood Sheff 63-66; Belper (in c of St Swith) 66-68; Hon C of St Mich AA Westcliff-on-Sea 69-73; Asst Master Shoeburyness High Sch 69-73; Sen Tutor Bilborough 6th Form Coll from 73; Publ Pr Dio Southw from 73. *51 Burnside Drive, Bramcote Hills, Beeston, Notts, NG9 3EF.* (Nottm 253799)

HEAD, Canon Ronald Edwin. Univ of Lon AKC 49, BD 50. Ex Coll Ox BLitt 59. St Bonif Coll Warm 49. **d** 49 **p** 50 S'wark. C of St Pet Vauxhall 49-52; Headington Quarry Ox 52-56; PC 56-68; V from 68; Chap Churchill Hosp Ox 55-72; Proc Conv Ox from 62; Hon Can of Ch Ch Cathl Ox from 80. *Headington Quarry Vicarage, Oxford.* (Oxford 62931)

HEAD, William Peter. St Edm Hall Ox BA 46, MA 51. Cudd Coll 46. **d** 48 **p** 49 Southw. C of St Jo Bapt Beeston 48-52; CF 52-56; V of St Barn Wellingborough 56-61; Chap Highfield Sch Liphook 61-74. *Little Kimble, Hollycombe Close, Liphook, Hants.*

HEADING, Richard Vaughan. b 43. Univ of Lon BSc and ARCS 65. Coll of Resurr Mirfield 66. **d** 68 **p** 69 Heref. C of St Martin Heref 68-75; P-in-c of Northwood 75-77; Birches Head 75-77; Team V of H Evang Hanley (in c of Birches Head and Northwood) Dio Lich from 77. *Vicarage, Cromer Road, Northwood, Hanley, Stoke-on-Trent ST1 6QN.* (Stoke-on-T 25499)

HEADLAND, James Frederick. b 20. Clifton Th Coll 51. **d** 53 Lon **p** 54 Kens for Lon. C of St Andr Thornhill Sq Islington 53-55; Spitalfields 55-57; V of St Matthias U Tulse Hill 57-65; R of Pulverbatch 65-80; Reedham (w Cantley, Limpenhoe and Southwood from 81) Dio Nor from 80; C-in-c of Smethcote (w Woolstaston from 69) 65-80; P-in-c of Cantley w Limpenhoe and Southwood 80-81. *Reedham Rectory, Norwich, Norf, NR13 3TZ.* (Gt Yarmouth 700268)

HEADLAND, John Edward. K Coll Lon and Warm AKC 60. **d** 61 **p** 62 Guildf. C of Oatlands 61-64; Kendal 64-66; St Alb Kimb 66-67. *c/o Diocesan Secretary, PO Box 45, Kimberley, CP, S Africa.*

HEADLEY, Lewis Victor. b 06. OBE 50. St D Coll Lamp BA 28. Ripon Hall Ox 28. **d** 29 **p** 30 Ban. C of Llanwnog 29-31; The Cotteridge 31-33; CF Aldershot 33-38; Singapore 38-45; Aldershot 46-47; SCF Bordon and Longmoor 47-48; DACG W Afr Commd 48-50; Aldershot 50-53; BTA Austria 53-55; Berlin 55-58; Antwerp 58-59; R Hosp Chelsea 59-67; R of E Tisted w Colmer 67-80. *c/o East Tisted Rectory, Alton, Hants.* (Tisted 412)

HEADS, William Dobson. b 28. Bps' Coll Cheshunt. **d** 61 **p** 62 Dur. C of Beamish 61-64; St Andr Monkwearmouth 64-65; St Chad Stockton-on-Tees 65-68; V 68-76; Chap of N Tees Hosp from 76; L to Offic Dio Dur from 76. *7 Ashville Avenue, Norton, Stockton, Cleveland, TS20 1PS.* (Stockton 553032)

HEAGERTY, Alistair John. b 42. Or Coll Ox BA 63, MA 67. BD (Lon) 68. Lon Coll of Div 65. **d** 68 **p** 69 Cant. C of H Trin Margate 68-72; CF from 72. *c/o Ministry of Defence, Bagshot Park, Bagshot, Surrey, GU19 5JP.*

HEAL, Geoffrey. b 28. Linc Th Coll 54. **d** 56 **p** 57 S'wark. C of Camberwell 56-59; St Mary (in c of Epiph) Rotherhithe 59-62; V of St Chrys and St Jude Peckham 62-66; St John Peckham 66-75; Hon Chap to Bp of S'wark from 64; V of St Barn Southfields Dio S'wark from 75. *St Barnabas's Vicarage, Merton Road, SW18.* (01-874 7768)

HEAL, Preb Guy Martin. b 13. Linc Th Coll 43. **d** 46 Chich for Gui **p** 46 Gui. C of All SS New Amsterdam 46-48; V of Wismar w Demerara River Miss 48-54; R of New Amsterdam Dio Gui 54-62; V of St Jo Bapt Sevenoaks 62-71; St Mary Magd Munster Square St Pancras Dio Lon from 71; Preb of St Paul's Cathl Lon from 79. *58 Osnaburgh Street, NW1 3BP.* (01-387 4929)

HEAL, Canon Harold Francis. b 10. Selw Coll Cam BA 37, MA 41. Sarum Th Coll 37. **d** 38 **p** 39 Liv. C of H Trin Formby 38-41; C-in-c of St Osw Conv Distr Netherton 41-43; V of Leebotwood w Longnor 43-47; TCF 44-47; V of St Briavels 47-54; V of Hewelsfield 47-54; CF (TA) 52-64; Hon CF from 64; V of Painswick 54-76; RD of Bisley 59-76; Hon Can of Glouc Cathl from 73. *The Old Malt Barn, Bourton-on-the-Water, Cheltenham, Glos.* (Bourton 21159)

HEALD, John Geoffrey. Em Coll Sktn 56. **d** 60 **p** 61 Bran. C of Snow Lake 60-62; R of Oak Lake 63-68; C of Cathl Ch of Redeemer City and Dio Calg from 68. *3013 Centre Street North, Calgary, Alta, Canada, T2E 2X2.* (277-7484)

HEALD, William Roland. St Jo Coll Auckld 71. **d** 74 **p** 75 Auckld. C of Howick 74-75; Kaitaia 76; St Paul Auckld 76-78; St Francis Bournville 78-79; V of Henderson Dio Auckld from 79. *425 Great North Road, Henderson, Auckland 8, NZ.* (83-68380)

HEALE, Walter James Grenville. b 40. Wycl Hall Ox 77. **d** 79 **p** 80 Lich. C of St Matt Walsall Dio Lich from 79. *164 Birmingham Road, Walsall, WS1 2NJ.* (Walsall 645445)

HEALES, John. b 48. AKC and BD 71. St Mich AA Llan 75. **d** 76 **p** 77 Mon. C of Cwmbran 76-78; Chap Rendcomb Coll and P-in-c of Rendcomb Dio Glouc from 78. *Rendcomb Rectory, Cirencester, Glos, GL7 7EZ.* (N Cerney 319)

HEALEY, Charles William. b 1897. MC 18. TD 36. Univ of Liv MD 26. Lich Th Coll 61. **d** 62 **p** 63 Lich. C of Tamworth 62-66; R of Draycott le Moors 66-77. *17 Norfolk Road, Harrogate, N Yorks.*

HEALEY, Edgar James. b 40. Univ of Windsor W Ont MSW 71. Hur Coll Ont MDiv 79. **d** 79 Bp Parke-Taylor for Hur **p** 80 Bp Robinson for Hur. I of Six Nations Reserve W Parish Dio Hur from 79. *Oshweken, Ont, Canada, N0A 1M0.*

HEALEY, Francis John. b 14. Wells Th Coll 64. **d** 65 B & W **p** 65 Taunton for B & W. C of H Trin Hendford Yeovil 65-68; R of Cucklington w Stoke Trister 68-79; Perm to Offic Dio Win from 79. *3a Rushton Crescent, Bournemouth, Dorset, BH3 7AF.* (0202-22229)

✠ **HEALEY, Right Rev Kenneth.** b 1899. MA (Lambeth) 58. Linc Th Coll 28. **d** 31 **p** 32 Linc. C of Grantham 31-35; R of Bloxholme w Digby 35-43; V of Ashby-de-la-Launde 39-43; RD of Lafford N 38-43; V of Nocton 43-50; Ch Comm 52-72; R of Algarkirk 50-58; Proc Conv Linc 45-55; Archd of Linc 51-58; Preb of Linc Cathl from 51; Cons Ld Bp Suffr of Grimsby in Cant Cathl 11 June 58 by Abp of Cant; Bps of Birm; Guildf; and Linc; Bps Suffr of Southn; Grantham; Maidstone; and Dover; and Bps Bell and Rose; res 65; Proc Conv Linc 58-70; Asst Bp of Linc from 65. *Little Needham, Gedney Dyke, Spalding, Lincs.*

HEANEY, Michael Roger. b 43. TCD BA 66, MA 69. Div Hostel Dub 74. **d** 76 **p** 77 Dub. Asst Chap St Columbas Coll Dub from 76. *Montana, Scholarstown Road, Templeogue, Dublin 14.*

HEAP, Daniel James MacDonell. Qu Univ Ont BA (1st cl) 48. McGill Univ Montr BD 51. Montr Dioc Th Coll 51. **d** 51 **p** 52 Montr. I of Kazabazua 51-55; C of St Matthias Tor 56-60; Hon C of St Matt Tor 60-65. *18 Bain Avenue, Toronto 6, Ont., Canada.*

HEAP, Edward Jocelyne Fortrey. b 07. OBE 49. RMA Woolwich 25. St Geo Windsor 53. **d** 54 Malmesbury for Sarum **p** 55 Sarum. C of Gillingham 54-57; R of Patney 57-63; V of Chirton w Marden 57-63; Horton w Chalbury 63-68. *1 Woodside Road, West Moors, Wimborne, Dorset, BH22 0LY.* (Ferndown 4778)

HEAP, Simon Robin Fortrey. b 36. K Coll Lon and Warm AKC 59. **d** 60 **p** 61 Sarum. C of Gillingham 60-64; Littleham-cum-Exmouth 71-77. *66 Foxholes Hill, Exmouth, Devon, EX8 2DH.* (Exmouth 75050)

HEAPS, Richard Peter. b 35. Qu Coll Birm 58. **d** 61 **p** 62 Birm. C of Castle Bromwich 61-65; C-in-c of St Chad's Conv Distr Erdington 65-68; Min 68-70; V of Nechells 70-81; Marston Green Dio Birm from 81; RD of Aston 75-81; Exam Chap to Bp of Birm from 78. *Vicarage, Elmdon Road, Marston Green, Birmingham, B37 7BY.* (021-779 2492)

HEARD, Arthur Robert Henderson. b 16. CCC Cam BA 41, MA 45. Linc Th Coll 41. **d** 42 **p** 43 Win. C of Ch Ch Portswood 42-44; St Sav Iford 44-47; Ascen Bitterne Pk Southn 47-51; V of Hedge End 51-60; R of Eversley 60-65; Perm to Offic Dio Lich 72-81; Team V of Wordsley Dio Lich from 81. *1 Denleigh Road, Kingswinford, Brierley Hill, W Midl, DY6 8QB.* (K'ford 279737)

HEARD, Charles. b 19. SOC 62. **d** 65 **p** 66 S'wark. C of St Nich Plumstead 65-71; All SS Blackheath 71-72; V of H Trin Barnes Dio S'wark from 72. *162 Castelnau, SW13 9ET.* (01-748 5744)

HEARD, Robert Donald Frederick. b 47. Trent Univ Ont BA 71. Trin Coll Tor MDiv 79. **d** and **p** 79 Ott. C of H Trin Pembroke 79-80; I of Buckingham Dio Ott from 80. *545 Georges Street, Buckingham, PQ, Canada.*

HEARD, Ross McPherson. b 11. Clifton Th Coll 38. **d** 41 B & W **p** 42 Pet. C of St Mark Lyncombe Bath 41-42; St Mary Rushden 42-44; Lect of St Mary Watford 44-47; V of St Pet Rushden 47-50; Amuri NZ 50-52; Hanmer NZ 52-54; PC of Colney Heath 54-57; R of Hatch Beauchamp w Beercrocombe 57-76; V of W Hatch 62-76. *235 Queen Edith's Way, Cambridge, CB1 4NJ.*

HEARDER, John Frederic. **d** 62 Bp Snell for Tor. C of

Mono Mills Dio Tor 62-67; Hon C from 67. *RR 1, Mono Mills, Ont., Canada.*

✠ **HEARN, Right Rev George Arthur.** ACT ThL 65. **d** 64 **p** 65 Gippsld. C of Traralgon 64-66; V of Omeo 66-69; Wonthaggi 69-73; R of Kyabram 73-77; Field Officer Dept of Chr Educn Dio Melb 77-78; L to Offic Dio Melb 77-81; Dir Gen Bd of Relig Educn 78-81; Cons Ld Bp of Rockptn in St John's Cathl 30 April 81 by Abp of Brisb, Bps of N Queensld, Carp, Graft, Armid, Bend and Bunb; and Bps Wicks, Shand, Walden, Housden and Hawkey. *Lis Escop, Athelstone Street, Rockhampton, Queensland, Australia 4700.* (079-23755)

HEARN, Peter Brian. b 31. St Jo Coll Dur 52. **d** 55 **p** 56 Linc. C of Frodingham 55-59; R of Belton 59-64; PC of Manthorpe w Londonthorpe 59-64; V of Billingborough 64-73; V of Sempringham w Pointon and Pointon Fen w Birthorpe 64-73; Burton-on-Stather w Normanby, thealby, Coleby and Flixborough Dio Linc from 73. *Burton-on-Stather Vicarage, Scunthorpe, S Humb.* (Scunthorpe 720276)

HEARN, Thomas Michael. b 12. Oak Hill Th Coll 55. **d** 57 **p** 58 Lon. C of St Jas L Bethnal Green 57-59; V of Ch Ch Camberwell 59-65; Tushingham (and Whitewell from 79) Dio Ches from 65; Chap High Sheriff of Chesh 68-69; C-in-c of Whitewell 73-79. *Tushingham Vicarage, Whitchurch, Salop, SY13 4QS.* (Hampton Heath 328)

HEARN, Thomas Peter. b 18. Selw Coll Cam BA 40, MA 45. Linc Th Coll 40. **d** 42 **p** 43 St Alb. C of St Matt Oxhey 42-45; St Jo Bapt Cirencester 45-52; V of Childswyckham 52-62; R of Aston Somerville 52-62; RD of Winchcombe 60-62; R of Stratton w Baunton 62-75; V of France Lynch Dio Glouc from 75. *Vicarage, Brantwood Road, Chalford Hill, Stroud, Glos, GL6 8BS.* (Brimscombe 883154)

HEARN, Trevor. b 36. Sarum Th Coll 61. **d** 64 **p** 65 Lon. C of St Steph Hounslow 64-67; Chap Miss to Seamen Momb 67-74; Port Chap Ipswich 74-80; Avonmouth from 80. *124 Portview Road, Avonmouth, Bristol, BS11 9JB.* (Avonmouth 822122)

HEARNE, James Russell. Seattle Pacific Coll BA 55. Evang Th Sem USA BD 62. **d** 62 **p** 63 Koot. C of Trail 62-64; I of Kokanee 64-68; C of St Sav Cathl Nelson 68-69; V of Golden 69-73; P-in-c 73-76; I of Lacombe Dio Calg from 76. *Box 1042, Lacombe, Alta, Canada.* (782-3173)

HEARSEY, Canon Henry William Moorcroft. OBE 64. Pemb Coll BA 31, MA 33. Sarum Th Coll 32. **d** 34 **p** 35 Win. C of All SS W Southbourne 34-38; St Pet Bournemouth 38-40; CF (EC) 40-49; DACG Austria 48; Men in Disp 45; Hon CF 48; Chap Ch Ch Vienna 45-48; Chap CCG 49; H Trin Nice 49-77; St Geo Cannes 49-63; Hon Can of Malta Cathl from 56; Archd of the Riviera 72-76. *c/o 19 Brunswick Gardens, W8 4AS.*

HEARTFIELD, Peter Reginald. b 27. Chich Th Coll 61. **d** 63 **p** 64 Chich. C of Hurstpierpoint 63-67; V of St Alb Preston Brighton 67-73; Chap Kent and Cant Hosp from 73. *7 Lime Kiln Road, Canterbury, Kent, CT1 3QH.* (Canterbury 65454)

HEASLETT, Samuel Johnson. TCD BA 31. **d** 32 **p** 33 Derry. C of Maghera 32-34; C-in-c of Glencolumbkille 34-45; U Molville 45-47; R of Balteagh 47-78. *c/o Limavady, Co Derry, N Ireland.*

HEASLIP, William John. b 44. TCD BA 66. Ch of Ireland Th Coll 79. **d** 80 **p** 81 Dub (APM). Chap Mt Temple Comprehensive Sch from 80. *1 Hoar Rock, Skerries, Co Dublin, Irish Republic.*

HEASMAN, Frank Richard. b 18. K Coll Lon and Warm AKC (2nd cl) 49. **d** 49 Bedford for St Alb **p** 50 St Alb. C of Sawbridgeworth 49-53; Kingsthorpe 53-56; Miss P Berbice River 56-57; V of Ch Ch Georgetn Guy 57-60; Woolavington 60-66; Westfield, Somt 66-73; Sparkwell Dio Ex from 73. *Vicarage, Sparkwell, Plymouth, Devon.* (Cornwood 218)

HEATH, Arthur Christopher. b 01. Qu Coll Ox BA 23, MA 27. Westcott Ho Cam 43. **d** 44 Lon **p** 45 Stepney for Lon. Chap and Asst Master St Paul's Sch Hammersmith 44-56; R of Barnes 56-63; Perm to Offic Dios Guildf and S'wark from 63. *38 Tattenham Grove, Epsom, Surrey.* (Burgh Heath 50336)

HEATH, Christopher John. b 51. Univ of Adel BEng 74. St Barn Coll Adel 74. **d** 77 **p** 78 Adel. C of St Mary S Road 77-79; Hawthorn 79-80; P-in-c of Kidman Pk w Flinders Pk Dio Adel from 80. *Rectory, Hart Street, Kidman Park, S Australia 5025.* (353 2563)

HEATH, Frank William. b 10. Univ of Liv BA 36. Tyndale Hall Bris 36. **d** 38 **p** 39 Liv. C of St Simon and St Jude Anfield 38-46; V of St Chrys Everton 46-51; H Trin Parr-Mount 51-55; Mansell Lacy w Yazor 55-61; PC of Wormesley 55-61; R of St Nich Heref 61-79. *16 Granby Road, Grange-over-Sands, Cumbria, LA11 7AU.* (04484 4388)

HEATH, George Nicholas. b 24. G and C Coll Cam BA 46, MA 50. Linc Th Coll 49. **d** 51 **p** 52 Linc. C of Spalding 51-55; Stevenage (in c of St Andr Bedwell) 55-60; V of St Alb Acton Green 60-70; St Steph Hounslow Dio Lon from 70. *Vicarage, Parkside Road, Hounslow, Middx.* (01-570 3056)

HEATH, Henry. b 40. FCII 77. Oakhill Coll 77. **d** 80 Chelmsf **p** 81 Colchester for Chelmsf. C of Lexden Dio Chelmsf from 80. *10 The Avenue, Colchester, CO3 3PA.*

HEATH, Canon John Gordon. Univ of Lon 25. AKC (2nd cl) 34. **d** 33 **p** 34 Guildf. C of Bramley Surrey 33-36; C of Cathl Ch Grahmstn 36-40; PV 37-40; CF (S Afr) 40-46; R of Queenstown 46-61; Archd and R of Cradock 61-73; Can of Port Eliz from 73. *32 Lange Street, Uitenhage, CP, S Africa.* (2-1342)

HEATH, John Gordon. St Jo Coll Auckld 33. **d** 35 **p** 36 Melan. Asst Master Maravovo Sch 35-38; Supervisor Distr Schs Dio Melan 38-39; C of Addington 39-40; V of Papakura 40-44; Waimate N 44-50; Howick 50-57; P-in-c of H Sepulchre Auckld 57-59; V 59-63; Orewa 63-66; E Coast Bays 66-72; St Geo Epsom Auckld 72-77; Offg Min Dio Auckld 77-78; Hon C of Waiuku Dio Auckld from 78. *27 Kaiwaka Road, Waiuku, NZ.* (59-361)

HEATH, John Henry. b 41. Chich Th Coll 69. **d** 71 **p** 72 Ex. C of Crediton 71-74; Tavistock w Gulworthy 74-76; Brixham 76-79; R of Bere Ferrers w Bere Alston Dio Ex from 79. *Bere Alston Rectory, Yelverton, Devon, PL20 7HH.* (Tavistock 840229)

HEATH, Maurice Dolbear. b 07. ALCD 39 (LTh from 74). **d** 39 **p** 40 Bris. C of St Gabr Bris 39-41; St Alb Westbury Pk Clifton 41-47; PC of St Mich Devonport 47-56; V of St Luke Kens 56-75. *South Hacketty, Hacketty Way, Porlock, Somt.*

HEATH, Peter Henry. b 24. Kelham Th Coll 40. **d** 47 **p** 48 Derby. C of St Anne Derby 47-49; Staveley 49-52; Brampton Derby 52-54; C-in-c of St Mark Conv Distr Brampton 54-59; PC of New Whittington 59-66; V of All SS Glossop Dio Derby from 66. *Vicarage, Old Glossop, Derbys.* (Glossop 2146)

HEATH, Raymond Walker. b 19. Cudd Coll 46. **d** 47 **p** 48 Cov. C of St Nich Radford Cov 47-50; St Mich Tilehurst 50-54; Org Sec Miss to Seamen Dios Ox and Guildf 54-56; Gtr Lon Area 56; Home Base Sec 57-58; V of Walmer 58-66; Rolvenden 66-75. *High Lodge, Kineton, Guiting Power, Cheltenham, Glos.* (Guiting Power 440)

HEATH, Robin Leslie. b 29. **d** 81 Pret. C of St Francis Waterkloof Dio Pret from 81. *31 Matroosberg Road, Ashlea Gardens 0181, S Africa.*

HEATH, Canon Thomas. Univ of Man BA 22. Wycl Hall Ox 22. **d** 24 **p** 25 Man. C of St Thos Werneth Oldham 24-27; Bickenhill 27-29; Sheldon (in c of St Leon Marston Green from 27) 29; King Wms Tn S Afr 29-32; St Jo Bapt Greenhill 32-33; R of Dordrecht 33-35; Vereeniging 35-42; Brakpan 42-48; Malvern Johann 48-53; Krugersdorp 53-68; Can of Johann 53-68; Hon Can from 68; C of Benoni 70-72; L to Offic Dio Johann from 72. *PO Box 1519, Benoni, Transvaal, S Africa.* (011-54 2813)

HEATH, William Walter. b 11. St Jo Coll Ox BA 32. **d** 72 **p** 73 Chich. C of Petworth Dio Chich from 72. *The Malt House, Lurgashall, Petworth, Sussex.*

HEATH-CALDWELL, Cuthbert Helsham. b 1889. Bps' Coll Cheshunt 35. **d** 37 **p** 38 Sarum. C of Longbridge Deverill w Crockerton and Hill Deverill 37-39; R of Kingston Deverill w Monkton Deverill 39-48; Brixton Deverill 39-48; Perm to Offic Dio Sarum 50-51. *The Pound House, Cattistock, Dorset.* (Maiden Newton 292)

HEATHCOCK, Douglas William. Bp's Coll Calc. **d** 37 **p** 38 Lah. Asst Chap St Andr Lah 37-39; Chap at Jhelum 39-42; Ind Eccl Est on active service 42-46; Hon CF 46; Chap at Razmak 46-47; Sialkot 47; Perm to Offic Dio Chich 48-50; C of St Paul Durban 50-54; V of Steep 55-57; Middleton Norf 57-60; Perm to Offic Dio Cant 60-81. *Address temp unknown.*

HEATHCOTE, Arthur Edwin. b 24. Sarum Th Coll 68. **d** 70 **p** 71 Roch. C of Chatham 70-74; Hon C of St Steph Chatham and Industr Chap Dio Roch 74-77; Warden Roch Dioc Conf and Retreat Ho 77-79; V of Aylesford Dio Roch from 79; Surr from 80. *Aylesford Vicarage, Maidstone, Kent.* (Maidstone 77434)

HEATHCOTE, Canon Clarence Frederick. Wycl Coll Tor LTh 30. **d** 28 **p** 29 Niag. C of Homer w Virgil and McNab 28-35; Palmerston 35-43; R of Burlington 43-67; Can of Niag 62-72; Can (Emer) from 72. *264 Kent Crescent, Burlington, Ont., Canada.*

HEATHCOTE, Edgar. b 15. Linc Th Coll 62. **d** 63 **p** 64 Linc. C of All SS Linc 63-66; Haslemere 66-69; R of Ashbrittle (w Bathealton, Stawley and Kittisford from 72) 69-78; C-in-c of Bathealton w Stawley and Kittisford 71-72; RD of Tone 76-78; Perm to Offic Dio B & W from 79. *23 Bath Place, Taunton, Somt, TA1 4ER.*

HEATHWOOD, Thomas Charles. BEM 82. ACT 60. **d** 73 **p** 74 Melb. C of Springvale N 73-74; Sunbury 74; P-in-c of Westmeadows 74-81; Perm to Offic Dio Melb from 81. *3 Vincent Street, Mulgrave, Vic, Australia 3170.*

HEATLEY, Henry Daniel. b 24. Trin Coll Dub 66. **d** 68 **p** 69 Connor. C of St Matt Shankill Belf 68-72; C-in-c of Layde w Cushendun 72-78; C of St Mary Belf 78-80; I of St Barn Belf Dio connor from 80. *102 Salisbury Avenue, Belfast, BT15 5ED.* (Belfast 779405)

HEATLEY, Leon. b 23. St Jo Coll Dur BA (Phil) Dipl Th (w distinc) 50, MA 51. **d** 50 **p** 51 York. C of St Mary Bridlington 50-53; Hull 53-56; V of St Andr Wakef and of St Mary Wakef 56-62; Stranton (w Ch Ch Hartlepool from 73) Dur 62-74; R of Greenstead Dio Chelmsf from 74. *Greenstead Rectory, Howe Close, Colchester, CO4 3XD.* (Colchester 865762)

HEATLEY, William Cecil. b 39. QUB BA (3rd cl Math) 61. Ridley Hall Cam 62. **d** 64 Tuam for Down **p** 65 Down. C of Ballymacarrett 64-69; Herne Hill 69-74; Team V (in c of St Antony Hamsey Green) of Sanderstead Dio S'wark from 75. *43 Clyde Avenue, South Croydon, Sanderstead, Surrey, CR2 9DN.* (01-657 7813)

HEATON, Alan. b 36. K Coll Lon and Warm BD (2nd cl) and AKC (1st cl) 64. Univ of Nottm MTh 76. **d** 65 **p** 66 Dur. C of St Chad Stockton-on-Tees 65-68; Englefield Green 68-70; Winlaton (in c of Rowland's Gill) 70-74; Chap Bp Lonsdale Coll Derby 74-79; V of Alfreton Dio Derby from 79; RD of Alfreton from 81. *Vicarage, Church Street, Alfreton, Derby, DE5 7AH.* (Alfreton 833280)

HEATON, Very Rev Eric William. b 20. Late Exhib Ch Coll Cam 2nd cl Engl Trip pt i 41, BA (1st cl Th Trip pt i) 44, MA 46. **d** 44 **p** 45 Dur. C of St Osw Dur 44-45; Sec of SCM Univ of Dur 44-45; Chap G and C Coll Cam 45-46; Dean and Fell 46-53; Tutor 51-53; Bp of Derby's Chap in Univ of Cam 46-53; Exam Chap to Bp of Portsm 47-74; to Bp of Sarum 49-63; to Abp of York 51-56; to Bp of Nor 60-71; to Bp of Wakef 61-74; to Bp of Roch 62-74; Can and Preb of Netherbury in Ecclesia and Can Res of Sarum 53-56; Can and Preb of Bricklesworth and Chan of Sarum 56-60; Select Pr Univ of Cam 48 and 58; Univ of Ox 59, 67 and 71; Fell and Chap St Jo Coll Ox 60-74; Sen Tutor 66-73; Lect Univ of Ox 61-74; Moderator Gen Ordin Exam 71-81; Dean of Dur 74-79; Ch Ch Ox from 79. *Deanery, Christ Church, Oxford, OX1 1DP.* (Oxford 47122)

HEATON, Thomas. b 05. Clifton Th Coll 40. **d** 42 **p** 43 Ches. C of Tarvin 42-53; R of Coddington 53-57; Loxton w Christon 57-79. *1 Tormyngton Road, Worle, Weston-super-Mare, BS22 9HU.*

HEATON-RENSHAW, Canon Squire Heaton. b 09. TD 50. Late Org Scho of Selw Coll Cam BA, MusB and John Stewart of Rannoch Scho 30, MA 34. Westcott Ho Cam 34. **d** 35 **p** 36 S'wark. C of Mortlake 35-39; CF (TA) 39-45; Men in Disp 45; V of Ch Ch (w St Andr and St Mich from 51) E Greenwich 45-52; C-in-c of St Andr and St Mich E Greenwich 45-51; V of Merton 52-75; RD of Wimbledon 60-65; Merton 65-75; Hon Can of S'wark 62-75; Can (Emer) from 75. *Paddock Cottage, Bentworth, Alton, Hants.*

HEAVEN, Edwin Boyd Gyde. McMaster Univ BA 54, MA 65. Trin Coll Tor LTh and STB 57. **d** 56 **p** 57 Niag. P-in-c of Grimsby Beach 57-58; R of Transfig St Cath 58-61; Chap McMaster Univ 62-68; Lect 70-75; Provost and Vice-Chan of Thoneloe Coll Ont from 76. *Thorneloe College, Ramsay Lake Road, Sudbury, Ont, Canada.*

✠ **HEAVENER, Right Rev Robert William.** b 05. Trin Coll Dub BA 28, Div Test 29. **d** 29 **p** 30 Clogh. C of Clones 29-31; Dioc C Dio Clogh 31-32; C-in-c of Lack (or Colaghty) 32-38; I of Derryvullan N 38-46; R of Monaghan (w Tyholland 46-51; w Tydavnet from 51) 46-73; RD of Monaghan 46-73; Exam Chap to Bp of Clogh and Can of Clogh 51-62; Can of St Patr Cathl Dub 62-68; Archd of Clogh 68-73; Exam Chap to Bp of Clogh 69-73; Cons Ld Bp of Clogh in St Patr Cathl Arm 29 June 73 by Abps of Arm and Dub; Bps of Meath, Kilmore, Connor, Down, Cork, Tuam and Lim; res 80. *Fardross, Clogher, Co Tyrone, N Ireland.*

HEAVER, Derek Cyril. b 47. St Jo Coll Nottm BTh 73. **d** 73 **p** 74 Win. C of Ch Ch Win 73-76; CF from 77. *c/o Ministry of Defence, Bagshot Park, Bagshot, Surrey, GU19 5PL.*

HEAVISIDES, Neil Cameron. b 50. Selw Coll Cam BA 72. Univ of Ox BA 74, MA 76. Ripon Hall Ox 72. **d** 75 **p** 76 Dur. C of St Pet Stockton-on-Tees 75-78; Succr of S'wark Cathl 78-81; V of Seaham w Seaham Harbour Dio Dur from 81. *Vicarage, Seaham, Co Durham.* (Seaham 813385)

HEAWOOD, Canon Alan Richard. b 32. G and C Coll Cam 2nd cl Hist Trip pt i 53, BA 54, 2nd cl Th Trip pt ii 55, MA 58. U Th Sem NY BD 56. Ripon Hall Ox 56. **d** 57 **p** 58 Man. C of Horwich 57-59; St Luke w All SS Weaste Salford 59-60; Beverley Minster w Tickton 60-62; Chap and Lect in Div St Pet Coll Saltley Birm 62-65; R of Hockwold w Wilton 65-72; R of Weeting 65-72; Dioc Insp of Sch Dio Ely from 66; V of Melbourn 72-80; Meldreth 72-80; Surr from 72; M Gen Syn Ely from 74; Dir of Educn Dio Ely from 80; P-in-c of Teversham Dio Ely from 80; Hon Can of Ely Cathl from 80. *Teversham Rectory, Cambridge, CB1 5AW.* (Teversham 2220)

HEAWOOD, Raymond Garth. b 02. G and C Coll Cam BA 27, MA 30. Ridley Hall, Cam 27. **d** 28 **p** 29 Cov. C of St Andr Rugby (in c of H Trin from 29) 28-30; Chap Toc H Rugby 30; Publ Pr Dio Derby and Chap Toc H House Derby 31-33; V of Ch Broughton w Barton Blount R 33-36; CCCS Chap Kampala and Entebbe 36-39; V of Water Orton 39-45; CF (EC) 40-45; V of Swaffham 45-50; RD of Swaffham 45-50; R of Hethersett w Canteloff 50-59; V of Ketteringham 55-59; Dore 59-67; L to Offic Dio Carl from 67. *Cooksons' Garth, Clappersgate, Ambleside, Cumb.* (Ambleside 3109)

HEBB, Cecil St Clair. K Coll Halifax NS BA 50, BSLitt 53. **d** 53 **p** 54 NS. I of Pugwash 53-57; R of Ship Harbour 57-63; I of Hubbards 63-70; R of Pictou Dio NS from 70. *Pictou, NS, Canada.* (485-4174)

HEBBLETHWAITE, Brian Leslie. b 39. Magd Coll Ox BA (2nd cl Lit Hum) 61 MA 67. Magd Coll Cam 1st cl Th Trip pt ia 62, BA (1st cl Th Trip pt iii) 63, MA 68. Burney Stud Univ of Heidelberg 64. Westcott Ho Cam 62. **d** 65 **p** 66 Man. C of All SS Elton Bury 65-68; Fell and Dean of Chap Qu Coll Cam from 69; Asst Lect 73-77; Lect from 77; Exam Chap to Bp of Man from 77. *Queens' College, Cambridge.* (Cam 65511)

HEBDEN, John Percy. b 18. St Aid Coll 58. **d** and **p** 60 Bradf. C of Skipton-in-Craven 60-62; Perm to Offic Dio Bradf 62-63; R of Kirby Misperton 63-67; V of Laxey Dio S & M from 70; Kirk Lonan Dio S & M from 80. *Vicarage, Laxey, IM.* (Laxey 666)

HEBDEN, William Francis. **d** 62 Tor for Fred **p** 63 Fred. C of Cam and Waterboro 62-64; I of Richibucto and Rexton 64-67; P-in-c of Grand Falls 67-72; R of Maitland Dio NS from 72. *Upper Kennetcook, Hants Co., NS., Canada.*

HEBDITCH, Ronald Edwin. b 08. SOC 61. **d** 64 **p** 65 S'wark. C of Warlingham w Chelsham and Farleigh 64-68; Castle Cary w Ansford 68-79; Perm to Offic Dio B & W from 79. *Outwood, Chapel Close, Castle Cary, Somt.*

HEBDITCH, Wilfrid Arthur. b 08. SOC 68. **d** 68 **p** 69 S'wark. C of St Barn Purley 68-76; Perm to Offic Dio Sarum 76-81. *1 St Osmund Close, Yetminster, Sherborne, Dorset.*

HEBER-PERCY, Christopher John. b 41. St Jo Coll Cam BA (2nd cl Th) 64, MA 68. Wells Th Coll 66. **d** 68 **p** 69 Man. C of Leigh 68-71; Asst Industr Chap Dio Man 71-79; C-in-c of St Andr Oldham 75-78; Team V of Oldham 78-80; Industr Chap S Hants Industr Miss Dio Win from 80. *26 Clifton Road, Shirley, Southampton, SO1 4GX.* (Southn 779605)

HECKINGBOTTOM, John Michael. b 33. Univ of Leeds BA (2nd cl Th) 55. St Steph Ho Ox 55. **d** 57 **p** 58 Liv. C of Wigan 57-59; Succr and Min Can of Ripon Cathl 59-63; C-in-c of St Luke Swarcliffe in Par of Seacroft 63-66; V of Menston-in-Wharfedale w Woodhead Dio Bradf from 66. *Vicarage, Fairfax Gardens, Menston, Ilkley, Yorks, LS29 6ET.* (Menston 72818)

HEDENI, John Mark. St Pet Coll Siota 54. **d** 56 **p** 59 Melan. P Dio Melan 56-75; Dio Ysabel 75-78. *Tirotonna, Santa Ysabel, Solomon Islands.*

HEDGCOCK, Walter Paul. b 09. Univ of Lon MB, BS 32, MD 34. SOC 69. **d** 72 **p** 73 Nor. C of Blakeney Group 72-73; P-in-c of Field Dalling w Saxlingham 73-76; L to Offic Dio Nor from 76; Bp's Adv Dio Nor from 76. *Fairstead Cottage, Cley-next-the-Sea, Nr Holt, Norfolk, NR25 7RJ.* (Cley 355)

HEDGES, Dennis Walter. b 29. Sarum Th Coll. **d** 62 **p** 63 Guildf. C of Walton-on-Thames 62-66; St Francis Westborough Guildf 66-69; V of Blackheath and Chilworth 69-79; R of Farncombe Dio Guildf from 79. *Farncombe Rectory, Farncombe Hill, Godalming, Surrey, GU7 2AU.* (Godalming 6091)

HEDGES, John Michael Peter. b 34. Univ of Leeds BA 60. Ripon Hall, 60. **d** 61 **p** 62 Man. C of St Luke w All SS Weaste Salford 61-65; V of St Pet Ashton L 65-74; Team V of Easthampstead Dio Ox from 74. *4 Qualitas, Roman Hill, Bracknell, Berks.*

HEDGES, Leslie Norman. b 26. Univ of Bris BA (2nd cl) 51. BD (Lon) 56. Clifton Th Coll 48. **d** 53 **p** 54 S'wark. C of Summerstown 53-55; St Luke Wolverhampton 55-56; Reigate 56-59; V of Clapham Pk 59-70; V of Willington Dio Derby from 70; Findern Dio Derby from 70. *Willington Vicarage, Derby.* (Burton-on-Trent 702203)

HEDLEY, Charles John Wykeham. b 47. Univ of Lon BSc 69, PhD 73. Fitzw Coll Cam BA 75, MA 79. Westcott Ho Cam 73. **d** 76 Chelmsf **p** 77 Barking for Chelmsf. C of St Anne S Chingford 76-79; St Martin-in-the-Fields, Trafalgar Square, Westmr Dio Lon from 79. *5 St Martin's Place, WC2.* (01-930 0089)

HEDLEY, Henry. St Edm Hall Ox BA 32, MA 43. Linc Th Coll 33. **d** 34 Carl **p** 35 Barrow-F for Carl. C of Kendal 34-38; H Trin S Shore (in c of St Mary) Blackpool 38-42; R of Lambeth (w St Mary w H Trin and Em from 51) 42-63; RD of Lambeth 56-63; R of Bletchley 63-80. *c/o Rectory, Bletchley, Bucks.* (Bletchley 3357)

HEDLEY, Ronald. Codr Coll Barb. **d** 64 **p** 65 Trinid. C of H Trin Cathl Port of Spain 64-68; V of Laventille Dio Trinid from 68. *Laventille, Trinidad, W Indies.*

HEDLEY, William Clifford. b 35. Tyndale Hall, Bris 65. **d** 67 **p** 68 Carl. C of Hensingham 67-69; Rainhill 69-71; St Helens 71-73; V of St Steph Low Elswick Newc T 73-81; St Aid Southcoates Drypool Hull Dio York from 81. *139 Southcoates Avenue, Hull, N Humb.* (Hull 74403)

HEENEY, William Brian Danford. Univ of Tor BA 54. St Jo Coll Ox DPhil 62. Episc Th Sch Mass USA BD 57. **d** 56 **p** 57 Edmon. Chap and Prof Univ of Alta 62-69; L to Offic Dio Edmon 65-73; Chap Univ of Trent Ont from 73. *Master's House, Champlain College, Trent University, Peterborough, Ont., Canada.*

HEERDEGEN, William George Murliss. Univ of NZ BA 35. St Jo Coll Auckld. **d** 36 **p** 37 Auckld. C of Mt Albert 36-38; St Matt Auckld 38-39; P-in-c of Bombay NZ 39-41; R of Milthorpe 41-44; Chap RAAF 43-44; Chap Miss to Seamen Bunbury 44-45; Chap Miss to Seamen Fremantle 45-48; V of Fairlie 48-51; Rangiora 51-58; City Miss at Wadestown Wel 58-63; L to Offic Dio Wel 63-64; V of Roseneath 64-78; Offg Min Dio Wel from 78. *52 Alexander Road, Wellington 3, NZ.* (861-787)

HEFFER, William John Gambrell. b 30. K Coll Lon and Warm AKC 55. **d** 56 **p** 57 St Alb. C of Biggleswade 56-59; St Jas Clacton-on-Sea 59-61; V of Langford 61-67; All SS Luton 67-73; C-in-c of Eaton Socon 73-75; V 75-77; Publ Pr Dio St Alb 78-81; V of Wingrave w Rowsham, Aston Abbots and Cublington Dio Ox from 81. *Wingrave Vicarage, Aylesbury, Bucks, HP22 4PA.* (Aston Abbots 623)

HEFFLER, Canon Foster Wesley Almon. Wycl Coll Tor BA 17. **d** 17 **p** 18 Tor. C of Grafton Ont 17-22; R of Stellarton 22-44; H Trin Halifax 44-67; Hon Can of NS from 51. *Apt 612, 1333 South Park Street, Halifax, NS, Canada.* (423-5987)

HEGGS, Thomas James. b 40. Inter Amer Univ of Puerto Rico BA 65. Linc Th Coll 75. **d** 77 **p** 78 Southw. C of Newark-on-Trent 77-80; R of Barwell w Stapleton & Potters Marston Dio Leic from 80. *Barwell Rectory, Leicester, LE9 8EB.* (Earl Shilton 43866)

HEIDT, John Harrison. b 32. Yale Univ BA 54. Nashotah Ho Wisc BD 57, MDiv 69. Univ of Ox BLitt 67, DPhil 75. **d** 56 **p** 57 Bp Hallock for Milwaukee (USA). in Amer Ch 56-75; C of St Mary Magd Ox 75-80; V of Up Hatherley Dio Glouc from 80. *Up Hatherley Vicarage, Cheltenham, Glos.* (Cheltm 516445)

HEIGHAM, John Lysley. b 07. Edin Th Coll 53. **d** 53 **p** 54 Ripon. C of Bedale 53-56; PC of Arkengarthdale 56-59; V of Weare 59-76. *Marston House, Union Street, Cheddar, Somt.* (Cheddar 743284)

HEIGHWAY, Thomas John Francis. St D Coll Lamp BA 47, BD 65. **d** 48 **p** 49 St D. C of St Paul Llanelly 48-51; Kidbrooke 51-54; V of St Mary-le-Park Battersea 54-58; Bradley Staffs 58-60; St Aug S Bermondsey 60-62; Asst Master Hertf Gr Sch 60-62; Perm to Offic Dio St Alb 61-62; Chap Stockton Gr Scho 62-66; L to Offic at Stockton-on-Tees 62-66; V of Heyhouses (or Sabden) 66-69; St Silas Blackb Dio Blackb from 69; Dioc Insp of Sch Dio Blackb from 66; RD of Blackb from 80. *Vicarage, Preston New Road, Blackburn, Lancs.* (Blackburn 51446)

HELEY, John. b 28. Bps' Coll Cheshunt 54. **d** 56 Lon for Capetn **p** 57 Capetn. C of Claremont 56-61; Wimborne Minster 61-62; V of Narborough w Narford 62-67; V of Pentney w W Bilney 62-67; V of Old Catton 67-69; L to Offic Dio Ox 69-72; V of E w W Rudham 72-74; C-in-c of Houghton-next-Harpley 72-74; V 74; V of St Edm Hunstanton Dio Nor from 75; P-in-c of Ringstead Dio Nor from 79. *St Edmund's Vicarage, Northgate, Hunstanton, Norf.* (Hunstanton 2157)

HELFT, Gunter. b 23. Univ of Lon BA 48. Ely Th Coll 46. **d** 48 **p** 49 Chelmsf. C of Ascen Chelmsf 48-49; Chap Essex Home Sch for Boys Chelmsf 48-52; C of Billesley Common 52-53; Chap Miss to Seamen Kobe 53-54; Yokohama 54-56; Port Sudan 57; Lit Sec HQ 57-62; Bp's Youth Officer Dio Ox 62-65; Tr Officer C of E Youth Coun 65-67; Hd Master Abp Temple's Sch Lambeth 67-71; Don Balley High Sch Yorks from 72. *7 Remple Avenue, Hatfield Woodhouse, Doncaster, Yorks.*

HELLABY, Victor Richard Douglas. b 10. TD 50. Ely Th Coll 45. **d** 46 Lewes for Chich **p** 47 Chich. C of St Elis Eastbourne 46-48; Chap Philanthr S Sch Redhill 48-50; V of Lady Marg Walworth 50-54; C-in-c of St Mary Magd S'wark 50-54; CF (TA) 50-60; V of St Andr Eastbourne 54-62; Portslade 62-69; Chap Mile Oak Sch 66-69; R of Brightling (w Dallington from 77) Dio Chich from 69; R of Dallington 69-77; RD of Dallington from 77. *Brightling Rectory, Robertsbridge, Sussex, TN32 5HE.* (Brightling 281)

HELLEUR, Lawrence Francis Morel. b 14. Late Exhib of Pemb Coll Ox BA (3rd cl Mod Hist) 36, MA 40. Wycl Hall, Ox 37. **d** 38 **p** 39 Heref. C of Madeley 38-41; Boldmere 41-51; R of Ryton 51-54; St Lawr Jersey 54-62; Perm to Offic Dio Win 62-71; L to Offic Dio Win from 71. *Glenbrook, Beach Road, St Saviour, Jersey, CI.* (0534- 30685)

HELLICAR, Arnold Hugh Gadsby. b 06. Univ of Lon BA (2nd cl Psychol) 30. Wells Th Coll 30. **d** 31 **p** 32 S'wark. C of St Paul Bermondsey 31-34; St Andr Kingsbury Middx 34-37; LDHM of St Chris Cuckoo Estate Hanwell 37-43; Actg C of All SS Pokesdown (in c of St Chris Southborne) 42-45; Gen Sec of Christian Aux Movement 45-48; Dir of Industr Christian Fellowship (E Midl Area) 48-51; C of St Jas Piccadilly 51-53; Chap at St Mary's Hosp Paddington 53-59; V of St Mary Magd Enfield 59-66; Chap at Malaga 66-71; Chap at Costa del Sol West 71-76; Perm to Offic Dio Chich 77-82. *1/14 Lewes Crescent, Brighton, Sussex.* (0273-695966)

HELLICAR, Hugh Christopher. b 37. Qu Coll Birm 69. **d** 70 **p** 71 Heref. C of Bromyard 70-73; Bp's Castle 73-75; Perm to Offic Dio S'wark from 77. *c/o Midland Bank, Winchester House, EC2.*

HELLIER, Jeremy Peter. b 53. AKC and BD 75. St Aug Coll Cant 75. **d** 76 St E **p** 77 Dunwich for St E. C of Walton 76-79; St Francis Ipswich 79-80; Wolborough 80-82; CF from 82. *Ministry of Defence, Bagshot Park, Bagshot, Surrey.*

HELMS, Charles Henry. Univ of Melb BA (2nd cl Phil) 61. ACT ThL 62. **d** 62 Bp Redding for Wang **p** 63 Wang. C of H Trin Cathl Wang 62-65; Sub-Warden St Columb's Hall Wang 65-69; Exam Chap to Bp of Wang 67-71; to Bp of Papua 71-75; Warden of Newton Coll Dogura 71-75; Perm to Offic Dio Wang 76-77; C of H Trin Cathl Wang 77-81. *c/o 59 Murdoch Road, Wangaratta, Vic, Australia 3677.*

HELYER, Patrick Joseph Peter. b 15. ALCD 39. Wycl Hall, Ox 38. **d** 38 **p** 39 Cant. C of St Paul Maidstone 38-41; Asst Chap Miss to Seamen Glasgow and the Clyde 41-42; Chap RNVR 42-46; V of St Nich-at-Wade w Sarre 46-50; Chap Miss to Seamen Fremantle 51-52; Chap RAN 52-61; V of Rolvenden 62-66; R of Evershot w Frome St Quintin and Melbury Bubb 66-71; R of Ch Ch Cathl Port Stanley Falkland Is 71-75; Hon Can of Ch Ch Cathl Port Stanley 72-75; R of Streat w Westmeston 75-78; P-in-c and USPG Miss at Tristan da Cunha Dio Capetn from 78. *Tristan da Cunha, South Atlantic.*

HEMANA, Raureti Lawrence. b 22. **d** 77 Aotearoa for Wai **p** 78 Wai. Hon C of Te Ngae Past Dio Wai from 77. *31 Ariari Te Ranci Street, Rotorua, NZ.*

HEMINGWAY, Peter. b 32. SOC 72. **d** 75 **p** 76 S'wark. C of Belmont 75-79; Herne Hill 79-81; V of St Geo Headstone Hatch End Dio Lon from 81. *96 Pinner View, Harrow, Middx, HA1 4RJ.* (01 427 1253)

HEMMING, Canon George Ratcliffe. MBE 60. Univ of Queensld BA 32, ACT ThL 34. **d** 34 **p** 35 Brisb. C of St Aug Hamilton 34-35; Fortitude Valley Brisb 35-40; Offg Min Dio Polyn 41-46; 49-61 and 63-65; Chap Hosp of Epiph Fanabu 46-49; L to Offic Dio Auckld 61-63 and 65-67; Can and Prec of H Trin Cathl Suva from 67; C of St Luke Suva Dio Polyn from 68. *Box 417, Suva, Fiji Islands.*

HEMMING, Robert William West. Moore Th Coll Syd 33, ACT ThL 35. **d** 36 **p** 37 Syd. C of St Paul Lithgow 36-37; St Clem Marrickville 37-39; R of Milton 39-42; C-in-c of Kogarah W 42-48; Prov Distr of St Thos Kingsgrove w Bexley N 42-47; R of Wentworthville 50-59; Annandale 59-70; L to Offic Dio Syd from 70. *Nigella, Glossop Road, Linden, NSW, Australia 2740.* (51-1428)

HEMMING CLARK, Stanley Charles. b 29. Peterho Cam 2nd cl Mod Lang Trip pt i 50, BA (2nd cl Th Trip pt ii) 52, 3rd cl Th Trip pt iii 53, MA 56. Ridley Hall Cam 52. **d** 54 **p** 55 S'wark. C of H Trin Redhill Surrey 54-56; St Jo Bapt Woking (in c of Knaphill) 56-59; V of Crocken Hill Dio Roch from 59. *Crockenhill Vicarage, Swanley, Kent, BR8 8JY.* (Swanley 62157)

HEMMINGS, William Edward. b 1899. **d** 62 **p** 63 Mon. C of Bedwellty 62-65; V of Crumlin 65-72. *2 The Retreat, Kings Fee, Overmonnow, Gwent.* (0600-2268)

HEMMONS, Laurence John. b 19. Worc Ordin Coll 64. **d** and **p** 66 B & W. C of St Jo Bapt Weston-s-Mare 66-69; R of Churchstanton Dio Ex 69-70; C-in-c of Otterford 69-70; R of Churchstanton w Otterford Dio B & W from 70; P-in-c of Buckland St Mary Dio B & W from 81. *Rectory, Churchstanton, Taunton, Somt, TA3 7QE.* (Churchstanton 228)

HEMPENSTALL, John Albert. b 43. Trin Coll Dub 64. **d** 67 **p** 68 Oss. C of Carlow U 67-70; Chap RN from 70. *c/o Ministry of Defence, Lacon House, Theobalds Road, WC1X 8RY.*

HEMPHILL, John James. b 44. TCD BA 68, MA 72. Oak Hill Coll 71. **d** 73 **p** 74 Down. C of Dundonald 73-78; I of Balteagh Dio Derry from 78. *115 Drumsurn Road, Limavady, Co Derry, N Ireland.* (Limavady 2718)

HEMPTON, Canon George Basil. Univ of Leeds BA 34. Coll of Resurr Mirfield, 34. **d** 36 **p** 37 Ches. C of St Paul

Tranmere 36-39; Audlem 39-42; Chap RNVR 42-48; V of Helsby 48-60; RD of Frodsham 55-60; Wirral S 69-78; Surr 59-78; V of Neston 60-78; Hon Can of Ches 62-78; Can (Emer) from 78. *45 Priory Avenue, Hastings, TN34 1UH.*

HEMS, Richard Brian. b 30. Univ of Lon BD 58. St Aug Coll Cant 58. **d** 59 **p** 60 Cov. C of Whitnash 59-63; C-in-c of Tuckswood Conv Distr 63-69; V of St Paul Tuckswood 69-78; R of Poringland w Howe Dio Nor from 78; Framingham Earl Dio Nor from 78. *Rectory, Rectory Lane, Poringland, Norwich, NR14 7SH.* (Framingham Earl 2215)

HEMSLEY, Canon Cecil Bernard. Kelham Th Coll 20. M SSM 25. **d** 25 **p** 26 York. C of St Sav Wilmington Hull 25-29; Miss P St Aug Modderpoort 29-31; Heilbron 31-40; R of Smithfield 40-45; Wepener 45-49; Warden of Modderpoort Sch 51-52; Miss P at St Francis Miss Kroonstad 52-56; Provincial SSM St Aug Miss Modderpoort 56-65; Can of Bloemf 56-71; Hon Can from 71; R of St Jas Ladybrand 61-65; C of St Patr Miss Bloemf 65-71; R of Teyateyaneng 71-73; C of St Andr and St Mich Cathl Bloemf 73; L to Offic Dio Bloemf from 73. *St Augustine's Priory, Modderpoort, OFS, S Africa.* (Modderpoort 1)

HEMSLEY, David Ridgway. b 36. K Coll Lon and Warm AKC 61. **d** 61 **p** 62 Bris. C of Penhill 61-64; Highworth w Sevenhampton, Inglesham and Hannington 64-66; St Andr Surbiton 67-70; C-in-c of Tingewick 70-75; Water-Stratford 70-75; Radclive w Chackmore 72-75; Priest Missr in N Marston w Granborough 75-81; Hardwicke w Weedon 75-81; Oving w Pitchcott 75-81; Quainton 75-81; Team V of Schorne Dio Ox from 81. *Rectory, Church Street, Quainton, Aylesbury, HP22 4AP.* (Quainton 237)

HENARE, Wiremu. b 16. **d** 77 Aotearoa for Wai. C of Hikurangi Past Dio Wai from 77. *PO Box 13, Waipiro Bay, NZ.*

HENCHER, John Bredon. b 31. Lich Th Coll 58. **d** 60 **p** 61 Worc. C of Pershore 60-62; Dom Chap to Bp of Worc 63-64; V of Amblecote 64-70; On study leave 70-72; Perm to Offic Dio Glouc 72-74; R Educn Adv Heref Archd from 74. *The Tank House, Weston, Pembridge, Leominster, HR6 9JE.* (Pembridge 540)

HENCKEN, Alfred David. b 15. AKC (2nd cl) 42. **d** 42 **p** 43 Lon. C of St Cath Coleman N Hammersmith 42-45; St Jo Evang Palmers Green Lon 45-48; V of St Paul Tottenham 48-55; St Sav Alexandra Pk 55-68; K Chas Mart S Mymms 68-80; Perm to Offic Dio Sarum from 80. *19 Lane Side, Shaftesbury, Dorset, SP7 8DY.* (Shaftesbury 4576)

HENDERSON, Canon Alastair Roy. b 27. BNC Ox BA 51, MA 54. Ridley Hall, Cam 52. **d** 54 Roch for Ex **p** 55 Ex. C of St Leon Ex 54-57; Trav Sec Inter-Varsity Fellowship and Perm to Offic Dio Lon 57-60; V of St Luke w Ch Ch Bris 60-67; P-in-c of St Phil and St Jacob w Em Bris 67-68; V of Stoke Bp Dio Bris from 68; Lect Clifton Th Coll 69-71; Trin Coll Bris 71-73; RD of Westbury and Severnside 73-79; Hon Can of Bris Cathl from 80; M Gen Syn from 80. *Stoke Bishop Vicarage, Mariners Drive, Bristol, BS9 1QJ.* (Bristol 681858)

HENDERSON, Andrew Douglas. b 36. Trin Coll Cam BA 60, MA 64. Dipl Publ and Soc Admin (Oxon) 63. Cudd Coll 60. **d** 62 **p** 63 S'wark. C of St Paul Newington 62-64; Hon C St Luke Camberwell Dio S'wark 65-80; Hon Chap to Bp of S'wark 74-80; Dir of Soc Services Kens & Chelsea from 76. *4 Ladbroke Square House, 2/3 Ladbroke Square, W11 3LX.*

HENDERSON, Andrew Johannes. b 33. Federal Th Sem Pmbg Dipl Th 77. **d** 77 **p** 78 Capetn. C of Bellville S 77-80; St Nich Matroosfontein Dio Capetn from 80. *St Faith's Rectory, Thor Street, Elsies River, CP, S Africa.* (7460)

HENDERSON, Charles Richard Wallace. Univ of W Ont BA 62. Hur Coll BTh 64. **d** 64 Bp Snell for Tor **p** 66 Tor. C of St Geo Willowdale Tor 64-66; Barrie (in c of St Pet Minesing) 66-69. *42 Melrose Avenue, Barrie, Ont., Canada.*

HENDERSON, Donald Stuart. Vic Coll Tor BA 53. Em Coll Tor BD 56. Trin Coll Tor MTh 63. **d** 78 Tor **p** 79 Bp Stiff for Tor. Hon C of St Jas Cathl City and Dio Tor from 78. *Rudon Productions Ltd., Suite 1505, 480 University Avenue, Toronto M5G 1V2, Canada.*

✠ **HENDERSON, Right Rev Edward Barry.** b 10. DSC 44. Trin Coll Cam BA 31, MA 42. DD (Lambeth) 69. Univ of Bath DLitt 75. Cudd Coll 32. **d** 34 **p** 35 Lon. C of St Gabr Warwick Square Westmr 34-35; C-in-c of All SS Grosvenor Rd Westmr 36-39; R of H Trin Ayr w St John Wallacetown and St Osw Maybole (and St Ninian Prestwick from 40) 39-47; Chap RNVR 43-44; V of St Paul Knightsbridge 47-55; Chap Hostel of St Luke 51-55; Commiss to Bp of N Rhod 52-55; RD of Westmr 52-55; Cons Ld Bp Suffr of Tewkesbury in St Paul's Cathl 11 June 55 by Abp of Cant; Bps of Lon; Guildf; Glouc; St E; and Lich; Bp Suffr of Kens; and Bps Moberley and Hamilton; Trld to B & W 60; res 75; Chairman C of E Youth Coun 61-69; Sub-Prelate O of St John of Jer 62-75. *Hill Cottage, Ryme Intrinseca, Sherborne, Dorset.* (Yetminster 872894)

HENDERSON, Edward Chance. b 16. Univ of Lon BD 39. ALCD 39. **d** 39 **p** 40 Newc T. C of St Steph Elswick Newc T 39-42; Org Sec CPAS for NE Distr 42-46; V of St Mary of Bethany New Wortley 46-52; C-in-c of Armley Hall 48-52; St Jo Bapt New Wortley 49-52; V of All S Halifax 52-59; Dewsbury 59-68; Darrington w Wentbridge 68-75; RD of Dewsbury 61-68; Proc Conv Wakef 63-64; Hon Can of Wakef 65-68; Archd of Pontefract 68-81; Exam Chap to Bp of Wakef 72-81. *c/o 12 Park Lane, Balne, Goole, N Humb, DN14 0EP.* (Goole 85284)

HENDERSON, Euan Russell Milne. b 42. St Steph Ho Ox (NSM) 75. **d** 80 **p** 81 Ox. C of Hambleden Valley Dio Ox from 80. *The Old Forge, Stonor, Henley-on-Thames, Oxon, RG9 6HE.*

HENDERSON, Francis Colin. b 35. St Cath Coll Cam 2nd cl Nat Sc Trip pt i 58, BA (2nd cl Nat Sc Trip pt ii) 59, 2nd cl Th Trip pt ia 60, MA 63. Cudd Coll 60. **d** 62 **p** 63 Cant. C of Croydon 62-67; V of Westwood 67-75; Chilvers Coton w Astley 75-80; P-in-c of Wolston Dio Cov 80; V (w Ch Lawford) from 80; P-in-c of Ch Lawford w K Newnham 80. *Wolston Vicarage, Coventry, CV8 3HD.* (0203-542722)

HENDERSON, George. b 07. ALCD 32. **d** 32 **p** 33 Carl. C of St Mary Ulverston 32-36; Dalton-in-Furness 36-38; V of Tebay 38-46; Whittingham 46-55; Farlam 55-71; L to Offic Dio Carl from 71. *11 Morton Close, Morton, Carlisle, Cumbria.*

✠ **HENDERSON, Right Rev George Kennedy Buchanan.** b 21. MBE 74. St Chad's Coll Dur LTh 43, BA 47. Edin Th Coll 40. **d** 43 **p** 45 Glas. C of Ch Ch Glas 43-48; P-in-c of St Bride Nether Lochaber w St Paul Kinlochleven 48-50; R of Fort William 50-77; Chap to Bp of Arg Is 48-50; Can of St John's Cathl Oban 60-77; Synod Clk Arg Is 64-73; Dean of Arg Is 73-77; Cons Ld Bp of Arg Is in St John's Cathl Oban 30 Nov 77 by Bp of Edin (Primus); Bps of St Andr, Moray, Glas and Brech; and Bps N Russell and R K Wimbush. *Bishop's House, Alma Road, Fort William, Inverness-shire, PH33 6HD.* (0397 4230)

HENDERSON, Ian Robert. b 29. SOC 64. **d** 67 **p** 69 Lon. C of St Pet Ealing 67-72; Hon Chap for Social Responsibility to Bp of Willesden from 72; Dir of Nat Elfrida Rathbone S 73-74; Hon C of St Gabr N Acton 72-74; V of Ch of Ascen Hanger Hill Dio Lon from 74. *100 Boileau Road, W5 3AJ.* (01-997 2845)

HENDERSON, James. b 22. Chich Th Coll 51. **d** 54 **p** 55 Man. C of St Nich Burnage 54-56; Prestwich 56-59; V of Waterfoot 59-61; C-in-c of Cloughfold 61-64; V of St Geo Bolton-le-Moors 64-70; Newhey Dio Man from 70. *Newhey Vicarage, Rochdale, Gtr Man.* (Shaw 845159)

HENDERSON, James Edward. Trin Coll Dub BA 58. **d** 59 **p** 60 Dub. C of Drumcondra 59-62; Monkstown 62-65; I of Donagh U Dio Derry from 65. *Rectory, Carndonagh, Co Donegal, Irish Republic.* (Carndonagh 86)

HENDERSON, Jean Graham. **d** 46 **p** 78 Ch Ch. C of Papanui 46-50; St Mary Portsea 51; Youth Officer Dio Ch Ch 52-56; C of Papanui 57-61; St Jas Riccarton 61-75; Winston Churchill Fellowship Chr Ed 65-66; Perm to Offic Dio Ch Ch from 75. *231 Pine Avenue, Christchurch 7, NZ.* (883-543)

HENDERSON, John Raymond. ACT ThL 60. Moore Th Coll Syd 58. **d** 61 Syd **p** 61 Bp Kerle for Syd. C of Kingsford 61-63; Chap CMF from 62; L to Offic Dio Syd 63-74; R of Greenwich Dio Syd from 74. *6 Greendale Street, Greenwich, NSW, Australia 2065.* (43-2134)

HENDERSON, John William. b 13. Late Exhib of K Coll Lon AKC 38. **d** 38 **p** 39 Roch. C of St John Welling 38-41; Orpington 41-44; R of Hartley 44-58; RD of Cobham 56-58; R of Cliffe at Hoo w Cooling 58-63; V of Wateringbury 63-78. *Cumloden, The Triangle, Somerton, Somt.*

HENDERSON, Julian Tudor. b 54. Keble Coll Ox BA 76, MA 81. Ridley Hall Cam 77. **d** 79 Lon **p** 80 Stepney for Lon. C of St Mary Isl Dio Lon from 79. *33 Barnsbury Street, Islington, N1.*

HENDERSON, Murray Balfour. b 46. Univ of Manit BA 67. McGill Univ Montr BD 70. **d** 70 Rupld **p** 71 Keew for Rupld. C of St Geo Transcona Winnipeg 71-72; Roxboro 72-75; I of St Mich AA Pierrefonds Dio Montr from 75. *15560 Cabot Street, Pierrefonds, PQ, Canada.* (514-626 4205)

HENDERSON, Nicholas Paul. b 48. Selw Coll Cam BA 73, MA 77. Ripon Hall Ox 73. **d** 75 **p** 76 St Alb. C of St Steph St Alb 75-78; Warden J F Kennedy Ho Cov Cathl 78-80; Team V of Bow Dio Lon from 80. *St Mary's House, Fairfield Road, E3.* (01-980 1721)

HENDERSON, Robert. b 43. Trin Coll Dub 66. **d** 69 **p** 70 Arm. C of Drumglass 69-72; Chap Miss to Seamen Belf 72-74; Sen Chap & Sec for N Ireland 74-77; Sen Chap Miss to Seamen Mombasa 77-78; R of Granard w Abbeylara, Drumlummon and Mostrim Dio Ard from 78; Clonbroney w Killoe Dio Ard from 78; Rathaspeck Streete & Kilglass Dio

Ard from 78. *Mostrim Rectory, Edgeworthstown, Co Longford, Irish Republic.* (Edgeworthstown 6)

HENDERSON, Robert McGregor. b 02. St Aid Coll 33. **d** 35 Liv **p** 36 Warrington for Liv. C of St Mark St Helens Liv 35-41; CF (EC) 41-45; C of Ch Ch Walker Newc T 46-48; PC of Hedworth 48-54; V of Walker 54-59; Greenhead 59-64; R of Bothal 64-75. *10 Castleway, Dinnington, Newcastle-on-Tyne, NE13 7LS.*

HENDERSON, Ronald James. b 42. Univ of Qld BA 75. Oriel Coll Ox BA 81. St Barn Th Coll Adel 66. **d** 67 **p** 69 Brisb. C of All SS Chermside Brisb 67-68; M of Bush Brotherhood St Paul 69-73; Hon Chap Univ of Qld 74-76; Chap St Jo Coll and Univ of Queensld 77-79; Perm to Offic Dio Ox 79-81; Chap St Jo Coll Brisb from 81. *St John's College, St Lucia, Qld, Australia 4067.* (370 8171)

HENDERSON, Samuel James Noel. b 16. Hertf Coll Ox BA 39, MA 42. **d** 42 **p** 43 Down. C of Seagoe 42-45; Donaghadee 45-46; C-in-c of St Marg Clabby 46-47; C of All SS Ipswich 47-48; Heacham and Ingoldisthorpe 48-49; R of E w W Lexham 49-53; Gt Dunham 49-53; St Aug Nor 53-56; V of St Mary Virg Coslany Nor 53-56; Ch Ch Eastbourne 56-65; Hickling 65-82; R of Hickling Group of Pars 65-70. *20 Ebbisham Drive, Eaton, Norwich, NR4 6HN.* (Norwich 54296)

HENDERSON, Terry James. b 45. St Deiniol's Libr Hawarden 76. **d** and **p** 77 St A. [in CA]. C of Wrexham Dio St A from 77. *160 Borras Road, Rhosnesni, Wrexham, Clwyd.*

HENDERSON, Wilfrid John Lys. Univ of Natal, BA (Th) 66. Westcott Ho Cam. **d** 67 Ely for Natal **p** 67 NY for Natal. d Dio Natal 67-68; C of St Jas Durban 68-69; R of Port Shepstone 69-74; Kloof Dio Natal from 74. *Rectory, Kloof, Natal, S Africa.* (Durban 742264)

HENDERSON, William Desmond. b 27. TCD BA and Div Test 56, MA 64. **d** 56 **p** 57 Arm. C of Derryloran (Cookstown) 56-59; Conwall 59-62; R of Killoughter 62-64; Kilrush 64-66; Tubbercurry w Kilmactigue 66-73. *Kingston Cottage, Mitchelstown, Co Cork.*

HENDERSON, William Ralph. b 32. Oak Hill Th Coll 65. **d** 67 Derby **p** 69 Southw. C of Littleover 67-68; St Sav Nottm 68-74; V of Alne w Aldwark Dio York from 74. *Alne Vicarage, Monk Green, York, YO6 2HY.* (Tollerton 450)

HENDERSON-BEGG, Robert John. b 11. Univ of Edin MA 32. Qu Coll Birm 37. **d** 37 **p** 39 Sarum. C of Bradford-on-Avon 37-40; CF (EC) 40-46; Asst Master All Hallows Sch 46-47; RAF (Educn Branch) 47-57; Perm to Offic Dio Ox and St Alb from 73; Asst Master Beds LEA 57-76. *Stone Cottage, Carlton, Bedford.* (Bedford 720366)

HENDERY, Alister Graeme. St Jo Coll Auckld 79. **d** 80 Bp Bennett for Wai. C of Tauranga Dio Wai from 80. *22 Third Avenue, Tauranga, NZ.*

HENDERY, Noel Arthur. b 45. **d** 77 Wai. C of Rotorua Dio Wai from 77. *8 Tumene Drive, Owhata, Rotorua, NZ.*

HENDERY, William George. Univ of NZ BA 49. **d** 61 **p** 62 Wel. C of Gonville 61-63; Chap Wanganui Colleg Sch 63-69; Prec St Paul's Cathl Wel 69-70; V of Gonville 70-73; Paraparaumu 73-80; Otane Distr Dio Wai from 80. *Vicarage, Henderson Street, Otane, NZ.* (68-246)

HENDEY, Clifford. K Coll Lon and Warm BD and AKC 53. **d** 54 **p** 55 S'wark. C of All SS S Wimbledon 54-58; V of Toco 58-65; R of St Jos w San Juan 65-66; Sangre Grande 66-71; V of Spratton 72-77; All S Leeds 77-80; Corringham w Springthorpe, Heapham, Willoughton and Blyborough 80-81; L to Offic Dio Trinid from 81. *c/o Diocesan Office, 21 Maraval Road, Port of Spain, Trinidad, W Indies.*

HENDRA, Ven Gordon Ernest. Vic Coll Tor BA 49. Wycl Coll Tor LTh 51. **d** 52 **p** 53 Tor. C of St Timothy Tor 52-55; V of Rimbey 55-57; R of St Mark Calg 57-65; H Trin Winnipeg 65-69; St Jas Kingston 69-78; Can of Ont 77-80; Dir of Programme Dio Ont from 78; Dioc Ecumen Officer from 80; Archd of Kingston from 80. *90 Johnson Street, Kingston, Ont., Canada.* (613-546 9993)

HENDRICKS, Fred Stuart. b 54. Univ of W Cape BA 75. St Paul Coll Grahmstn Dipl Th 78. **d** 78 **p** 79 Capetn. C of Plumstead Dio Capetn from 78. *6 Brent Road, Plumstead, CP, S Africa.*

HENDRICKSE, Clarence David. b 41. CEng, M IMechE 71. St Jo Coll Nottm 71. **d** 74 Warrington for Liv **p** 75 Liv. C of St Helens 74-76; Ch Ch Netherley Dio Liv 76-77; V from 77. *44 Brownbill Bank, Netherley, Liverpool, L27 7AE.* (051-487 7759)

HENDRY, Leonard John. b 34. St D Coll Lamp Dipl Th 68. **d** 68 **p** 69 Glouc. C of Minchinhampton 68-71; Bp's Cleeve 71-74; V of St Mich Cheltm 74-78; Horsley and Newington Bagpath w Kingscote Dio Glouc from 78. *Horsley Vicarage, Stroud, Glos.* (Nailsworth 3814)

HENDRY, Philip David. b 48. AKC and BD 72. St Aug Coll Cant 72. **d** 73 **p** 74 S'wark. C of Benhilton 73-78; Team V of Catford (Southend) and Downham (in c of St Barn Downham) Dio S'wark from 78. *1 Churchdown, Downham, Bromley, Kent.* (01-698 4851)

HENDY, Graham Alfred. b 45. St Jo Coll Dur BA 67 MA 75. Sarum Th Coll 67. **d** 70 Ox **p** 71 Buckingham for Ox. C of High Wycombe (in c of St John from 73) 70-75; Team V 75-78; R of Upton w Chalvey Dio Ox from 78. *18 Albert Street, Slough, Bucks, SL1 2BU.* (Slough 72472)

HENEY, Canon William Butler. b 22. TCD **d** 60 **p** 61 Down. C of Seagoe 60-63; I of Carrickmacross 64-73; Gt Connell w Carnalway and Kilcullen Dio Kild from 73; Ballysonnon w Ballysax Dio Kild from 74; Treas & Can Kild Cathl from 81. *Rectory, Newbridge, Co Kildare, Irish Republic.* (045-31306)

HENJEWELE, Stefano. St Paul's Coll Liuli. **d** 59 **p** 62 SW Tang. P Dio SW Tang 59-70 and from 75; Dio Ruv 71-75. *PO Manda, Njombe, Tanzania.*

HENLEY, Claud Michael. b 31. Keble Coll Ox BA (3rd cl Th) 55, MA 59. Chich Th Coll 55. **d** 57 **p** 58 Ox. C of St Jas Cowley Ox 57-60; Wetherby 60-63; Brighton 63-69; V of St Jo Evang Brighton 69-75; New Groombridge Dio Chich from 75. *Groombridge Vicarage, Tunbridge Wells, Kent, TN3 9SE.* (Groombridge 265)

HENLEY, David Edward. b 44. Sarum Wells Th Coll 69. **d** 72 **p** 73 Portsm. C of H Trin Fareham 72-76; P-in-c of St Clare Leigh Pk 76-78; R of Freshwater Dio Portsm from 78. *Freshwater Rectory, IW.* (Freshwater 2010)

HENLEY, Michael Harry George. b 38. ALCD 60 (LTh from 74). **d** 61 **p** 62 Willesden for Lon. C of St Marylebone 61-64; Chap RN 64-68; Chap Univ of St Andr 68-72; Asst Chap R Hosp Sch Holbrook 72-74; Chap RN from 74. *c/o Ministry of Defence, Lacon House, Theobald's Road, WC1X 8RY.*

HENLY, Francis Michael. b 25. Sarum Th Coll. **d** 67 **p** 68 Sarum. C of Harnham 67-70; P-in-c of Stower Provost w Stower Row and Todbere 70-75; rowde Dio Sarum 75-79; V from 79; P-in-c of Poulshot Dio Sarum 75-79; R from 79. *Rowde Vicarage, Devizes, Wilts.* (Devizes 2564)

HENN, Ven Wilfrid Elliott. b 03. Worc Coll Ox BA (3rd cl Th) 25, MA 29. Cudd Coll 25. **d** 26 **p** 27 Cov. C of St Paul Foleshill 26-29; W Wycombe (in c of St Mary Sands) 29-32; St Faith Wandsworth 32-34; R of Dalwallinu 34-38; Vic Pk 38-42; E Claremont 42-46; C of Chieveley (in c of Curridge) 47-48; Exam Chap to Abp of Perth 49-56; R of Queen's Pk 48-52; Can of Perth 51-56; Youth Org Dio Perth and Chap Le Fanu Ho 52-54; Chap Perth Coll 54-56; Asst Chap and Master Worksop Coll 57-58; R of Katanning 58-62; Exam Chap to Bp of Bunb 59-62 and 68-73; Commiss Bunb 62-68; V of Branscombe 62-68; Hon Can of Bunb 66-73; R of Boyanup 68-71; Dom Chap to Bp of Bunb 71-73; Archd in Bunb 71-73; Archd (Emer) from 73; Chap Bunb Cathl Gr Sch 72; Perm to Offic Dio Perth from 74. *Felicity Cottage, Lionel Road, Darlington, W Australia 6070.* (092-94 6770)

HENNELL, Canon Michael Murray. b 18. St Edm Hall, Ox BA (2nd cl Mod Hist) 40, Dipl in Th 41, MA 44. Qu Coll Cam MA (by incorp) 49. Wycl Hall Ox 40. **d** 42 **p** 43 Lon. C of St Steph w St Bart Isl 42-44; All SS Queensbury Lon 44-48; Tutor of Ridley Hall Cam 48-51; Senior Tutor of St Aid Coll 51; Vice-Prin 52-59; Prin 59-63; L to Offic Dio Ches 52-63; Prin Ridley Hall Cam 63-70; Exam Chap to Bp of Chelmsf 64-70; to Bp of Man from 65; to Bp of Liv 65-75; to Bp of Derby from 70; Can Res of Man from 70; Commiss Niger from 75. *21 Morville Road, Chorlton-cum-Hardy, Manchester, M21 1UG.* (061-881 9289)

HENNESSEY, David Brian. b 44. ACIS 69, FCIS 75. N-W Ordin Course 76. **d** 79 Bradf. Hon C of Ch Ch Skipton-in-Craven 79-80; Dioc Sec Dio Bradf 79-80; Dio St E from 80. *Diocesan House, Tower Street, Ipswich.*

HENNESSEY, Michael John. b 44. Univ of Leeds BSc 65. Ripon Hall Ox 65. **d** 67 **p** 68 York. C of Scarborough 67-70; Alverthorpe 70-72; Asst Master Helsby Co Gr Sch for Girls 72-78; Helsby High Sch from 78. *27 Porthleven Road, Brookvale, Runcorn, Chesh, WA7 6BE.*

HENNING, Reginald Cecil. b 18. St Aug Coll Cant 53. **d** and **p** 53 Aber. Super Dio Aber 53-54; R of Cuminestown 54-57; Kirkmanshulme 57-71; Ascencion Lower Broughton Salford Dio Man from 71. *Ascension Rectory, Duke Street, Lower Broughton, Salford, M7 9GX.* (061-834 4370)

HENNIS, Joseph Gabriel Lake. Dipl Th (Lon) 58. Codr Coll Barb. **d** 57 Barb for Antig **p** 58 Antig. C of St Ant Montserrat 58-59; R of St Geo Montserrat 59-65; All SS w St Anne Antig 65-71; Archd of Antig 68-71; Hon Can of Antig 71. *c/o Diocesan Registrar, Bridgetown, Barbados.*

HENRICKS, Tony Ernest. Ridley Coll Melb ACT ThL 66. **d** 67 **p** 68 Tas. C of St Steph Sandy Bay Hobart 67-71; P-in-c of Avoca w Fingal 71-76; R of Stanley 76-79; C of St John Launceston Dio Tas from 79. *39 Elizabeth Street, Launceston, Tasmania 7250.* (003 31 4896)

HENRY, Very Rev Bryan George. b 30. St D Coll Lamp BA 51. St Mich Coll Llan 51. **d** 53 **p** 54 Llan. C of St Fagan

Aberdare 53-57; All SS Penarth 57-63; Chap RAF 63-81; Provost of St Paul's Cathl Nicosia and Archd in Cyprus from 81. *2 Afxentiou Street, Box 2075, Nicosia, Cyprus.* (Nicosia 42241)

HENRY, Douglas Steele. Univ of W Ont BA 41. **d** 41 **p** 42 Hur. I of Port Burwell and Port Rowan 41-44; Ridgetown and Highgate 44-50; R of Amherstburg 50-68; Port Dover Dio Hur from 68. *Box 33, Port Dover, Ont., Canada.* (519-583 0323)

HENRY, Earl Fitzgerald. b 51. Codr Coll Barb 75. **d** 78 Bel **p** 79 Nass for Bel. L to Offic Dio Bel from 78. *c/o Bishopthorpe, PO Box 535, Belize City, Belize.*

HENRY, Leslie Victor. b 24. Trin Coll Dub BA 48, MA 65. **d** 48 **p** 49 Derry. C of Ch Ch Derry 48-51; C-in-c of Garrison 51-55; Chap RAF 55-79. *Tay's Gateway, The Bullring, Deddington, Oxford, OX5 4TT.*

HENRY, Lloyd. b 47. U Th Coll of WI 67. **d** 70 Ja for Br Hond **p** 71 Br Hond. C of St Jo Cathl Bel 70-72; Dioc Chap Dio Bel 72-74; V of Corozal 74-76; Cayo Dio Bel from 76. *San Ignacio, Garbutts Creek, Cayo, Belize.* (09-2108)

HENRY, Canon Maurice James Birks. b 14. Dorch Miss Coll 34. **d** 38 Pontefract for Wakef **p** 39 Wakef. C of St John Wakef 38-41; Dewsbury (in c of St Jas) 41-43; Bredbury (in c of St Barn) 43-47; R of Taxal w Kettleshulme 47-56; Davenham 56-60; Rode w Rode Hill and Woolverton 60-65; V of Chelford w Lower Withington 65-81; RD of Knutsford 73-80; Hon Can of Ches from 76. *56 Holly Tree Road, Plumley, Knutsford, Cheshire, WA16 0UJ.*

HENRY, Stephen Kenelm Malim. b 37. Bps' Coll Cheshunt 60. **d** 62 **p** 63 Leic. C of St Phil Leic 62-67; CF 67-70; V of Woodhouse Dio Wakef from 70. *Woodhouse Vicarage, Huddersfield, Yorks, HD2 1DH.* (Huddersfield 24669)

HENRY, Trevor. b 09. St Aid Coll 52. **d** 54 **p** 55 Leic. C of Kirby Muxloe 54-56; Kidderminster (in c of St Barn Franche) 56-63; V of Cookley 63-73. *Cherry Cottage, Trimpley Lane, Shatterford, Arley, Kidderminster Worcs.* (Arley 249)

HENSHALL, Edwin. b 1895. **d** 56 **p** 57 Ches. C of Bollington 56-59; V of Ashley 59-67; Hon C of Altrincham Dio Ches from 68. *12 Alstead Avenue, Hale, Chesh, WA15 8BS.* (061-980 2171)

✠ **HENSHALL, Right Rev Michael.** St Chad's Coll Dur BA 54, Dipl Th 56. **d** 56 **p** 57 York. C of H Trin Bridlington and of Sewerby 56-59; Min of All SS Conv Distr Micklehurst 59-62; V 62-63; St Geo Altrincham 63-76; Proc Conv Ches 64-76; Hon Can of Ches 72-76; Cons Ld Bp Suffr of Warrington in York Minster 27 Jan 76 by Abp of York; Bps of Blackb, Southw, Liv, Ches and Moray; Bps Suffr of Hull, Jarrow, Stockport, Burnley, Penrith, Pontefract, Selby, Knaresborough, Doncaster, Birkenhead, Sherwood and Hulme; and others. *Martinsfield, Elm Avenue, Great Crosby, Liverpool, L23 2SX.* (051-924 7004)

HENSHAW, George William. b 21. St Edm Hall, Ox BA (2nd cl Th) 48, MA 48. Qu Coll Birm 48. **d** 49 **p** 50 Lich. C of Stoke-on-Trent 49-51; Wednesbury 51-54; R of St John Longsight 54-63; St Paul New Cross Man 64-70; Prin PSW Univ Hosp of S Man 70-71; Stud Counsellor Man Polytechnic from 71. *16 Burford Drive, Manchester, M16 8FJ.* (061-881 9898)

HENSHAW, Nicholas Newell. b 49. Univ of Rhodes Grahmstn Ba 72. Cudd Coll 73. **d** 75 Buckingham for Ox **p** 76 Ox. C of Beaconsfield 75-78; Chap of Wellington Coll Crowthorne 78-80; C of St Pet Eaton Sq w Ch Ch Broadway Dio Lon from 80. *24 Lower Belgrave Street, SW1W 0NL.* (01-730 4454)

HENSON, John Arthur. b 21. Qu Coll Birm 68. **d** 69 **p** 70 B & W. C of Wellington w W Buckland 69-71; C of Nynehead 69-71; Romney Marsh Group 71-75; P-in-c of Steeple w Tyneham w Church Knowle and Kimmeridge 75-77; V of Alderholt Dio Sarum from 77. *Alderholt Vicarage, Fordingbridge, Hants.* (Fordingbridge 3179)

HENSON, John Richard. b 40. Selw Coll Cam 2nd cl Mod Lang Trip pt i 60, BA (3rd cl Th Trip pt ii) 62, MA 66. Ridley Hall Cam 62. **d** 65 **p** 66 Southw. C of Ollerton 65-68; Univs Sec CMS 68-73; Chap Scargill Ho Skipton 73-78; V of Shipley Dio Bradf from 78. *Vicarage, Kirkgate, Shipley, W Yks, BD18 3EH.* (0274-583652)

HENSTRIDGE, Edward John. b 31. Ex Coll Ox BA (2nd cl Psychology) 55, MA 59. Wells Th Coll 55. **d** 57 **p** 58 Portsm. C of St Jas Milton 57-62; V of Soberton w Newtown 62-69; L to Offic Dio Derby 69-71; Perm to Offic Dio Guildf from 72. *The White House, Thursley Road, Elstead, Godalming, Surrey GU8 6LW.*

HENTHORNE, Thomas Roger. b 30. E Anglian Min Tr Course. **d** 79 **p** 80 Ely. Hon C of St Neots Dio Ely from 79; Hdmaster St Mary's Sch St Neots from 79. *7 Chestnut Grove, Eynesbury, St Neots, Cambs, PE19 2DW.* (0480 72548)

HENTON, John Martin. b 48. AKC 71. St Aug Coll Cant 73. **d** 74 **p** 75 S'wark. C of Woolwich 74-77; St Mary Cotham 77-80; R of Filton Dio Bris from 80. *Filton Rectory, Bristol, BS12 7BX.* (Bristol 791128)

HENWOOD, Douglas Edward. b 22. **d** 79 Bp Stanage for Johann **p** 80 Johann (NSM). C of Orange Grove Dio Johann from 79. *29-6th Avenue, Edenvale, S Africa 1610.*

HENWOOD, Godfrey John. b 51. St Paul's Coll Grahmstn 74. **d** 75 Bp Carter for Johann **p** 76 Johann. C of Germiston 75-78; R of Standerton w Evander Dio Johann from 78. *1 Dublin Road, Evander, Transvaal, S Africa.* (013-63 3260)

HENWOOD, John Henry. b 08. Lich Th Coll 30. **d** 32 **p** 33 Sheff. C of Brinsworth 32-34; Chap S Afr Ch Rly Miss Dio S Rhod 34-35; Dio Pret 35-37; C of All H Tottenham 37-40; C-in-c of St Pet Walthamstow 40-41; PC of St John Stamford Hill 41-47; V of W Alvington 47-54; Metrop Sec SPCK and Gen Perm to Offic 54-56; V of St Luke Dukinfield 56-73. *35 Cross Way, Lewes, Sussex, BN7 1NE.* (079 162067)

HENWOOD, Peter Richard. b 32. St Edm Hall Ox BA (3rd cl Th) 55, MA 69. Cudd Coll 56. **d** 57 **p** 58 Cov. C of Rugby 57-62; C-in-c of Gleadless Valley Conv Distr 62-71; V of Plaistow Dio Roch from 71; RD of Bromley from 79; M Gen Syn from 81. *74 London Lane, Bromley, Kent.*

HENZELL, Bruce Edgell. Univ of Queensld BSurv 68, BDiv 71. St Francis Coll Brisb 68. **d** 70 Brisb **p** 71 New Guinea. C of St Andr Indooroopilly 70-71; Miss Dio Papua 71-74; C of St Lucia Brisb 75; Ipswich 76-78; R of Charleville Dio Brisb from 78. *Rectory, Alfred Street, Charleville, Queensland, Australia 4470.* (Charleville 43)

HEPEPAINE, Michael Davis. b 40. **d** 67 New Guinea **p** 68 Melan. P Dio Melan 67-75; Centr Melan from 75. *Patteson House, Honiara, Solomon Islands.*

HEPPENSTALL, Lewis David. b 1898. Late Scho of Jes Coll Ox 2nd cl Cl Mods 20, BA 21, MA 24. Coll of Resurr Mirfield 26. **d** 28 **p** 29 Lon. C of St Barn Pimlico 28-30; L to Offic Dio Wakef 30-31; C of St Sav Leeds 31-32; St Aug Queen's Gate 32-36; Chap Commun of H Name Malvern Link 36-38; Chap Gen 38-55; Chap S of Sacred Cross 55-57; Commun of H Cross Haywards Heath 57-65. *Holy Cross Guest House, Haywards Heath, Sussex.* (Haywards Heath 3714)

HEPPER, Samuel Robert. Wycl Hall Ox 57. **d** 57 **p** 58 Roch. C of St Paul Penge 57-58; Dartford 58-59; Perm to Offic at St Jo Bapt w St Wilfrid Bognor Dio Chich from 59. *8 Greenwood Avenue, Bognor Regis, Sussex.* (Bognor Regis 4133)

HEPPLE, Gordon. Edin Th Coll. **d** 63 **p** 68 Dur. C of Billingham 63-64; Ryhope 64; Perm to Offic Dio Dur 66-68; C of Wingate 68-69; Heworth 69; Gateshead 69-71; C-in-c of St Paul Gateshead 71-72; R of Lyons 72-79; V of St Aid Basford Dio Southw from 79. *St Aidan's Vicarage, Tewksbury Drive, Basford, Nottingham.* (Nottm 703483)

HEPWORTH, Ernest John Peter. b 42. K Coll Lon and Warm BD and AKC 65. **d** Ripon 66 **p** 67 Knaresborough for Ripon. C of Headingley 66-69; Asst Chap St Geo Hosp Lon 69-71; C of Gt Grimsby 71-72; Team V 72-74; V of Crosby 74-80; Barton-on-Humber Dio Linc from 80. *Vicarage, Barton-on-Humber, S Humb, DN18 5EY.* (B-on-H 32202)

HEPWORTH, James Stanley. b 09. ALCD 31. **d** 32 **p** 33 Blackb. C of All SS Preston 32-34; St Paul Kirkdale 34-36; R of Albert Mem Ch Man 36-42; V of St Thos Crookes 42-50; St Paul Bolton 50-54; Histon 54-60; St Jas Clapham Pk 60-65; St Steph Tonbridge 65-73; Hon C of Fulwood Dio Sheff from 74. *13 Hallamshire Road, Fulwood, Sheffield, S10 4FN.* (Sheff 306812)

HEPWORTH, John Anthony. d and **p** 68 RC Abp of Adel. Rec into Angl Commun 76. Perm to Offic Dio Bal 76-77; C of Colac 77-78; R of H Trin Sebastopol S Bal 78-80. *20 Chopin Road, Somerton Park, S Australia 5044.*

HEPWORTH, Michael David Albert. b 37. Em Coll Cam BA (Th Trip pts i & ii) 59, MA 63. Ridley Hall Cam 65. **d** 67 **p** 68 Chich. C of All SS Eastbourne 67-69; Asst Chap Bedford Sch 69-72; Chap from 72. *Bedford School, Bedford.* (Bedford 67775)

HEPWORTH, Michael Edward. b 29. Univ of Leeds BA 51. N-W Ordin Course 74. **d** 77 **p** 78 Ches. C of Timperley Dio Ches from 77. *51 Ridgway Road, Timperley, Altrincham, Cheshire, WA15 7HL.*

HERBERT, Alan. b 33. Open Univ BA 80. Coll of Resurr Mirfield. **d** and **p** 68 Carl. C of Cockermouth 68-71; V of Clifton-in-Workington 71-77; St Mary Westfield Workington Dio Carl from 77. *Westfield Vicarage, Workington, Cumb, CA14 3TR.* (Workington 3227)

HERBERT, Alfred William. d 57 **p** 58 Sask. I of Star City 57-67. *11 Heather Crescent, London, Ont., Canada.*

HERBERT, Anthony. b 19. Qu Coll Birm 46. **d** 48 **p** 49 Linc. C of Frodingham 48-51; Bp's Chap Univ of Liv SCM Sec and C of St Bride Liv 51-54; C of St Sav Liv 54-55; Stapleton Bris (in c of St Giles Begbrook) 55-58; V of All SS Hamer Rochdale 58-64; PC of St Cuthb Dur (V from 69) 64-78; Chap HM Remand Centre Low Newton 65-77; V of

Barrow-upon-Soar 78-82. *c/o Barrow-upon-Soar Vicarage, Loughborough, Leics.* (Quorn 42133)

HERBERT, Canon Arnold Cuthbert. Tyndale Hall, Bris 27. **d** 30 Bp Newnham for Moos **p** 34 Montr for Arctic. Miss (BCMS) Port Harrison 30-36; Pangnirtung 36-40; Eskimo Point 42-47; I of Creemore 47-49; Alliston and W 49-73; Bowmanville 55-63; Ajax 63-72; Can of Tor from 69; P-in-c of St Jo Bapt Norway Tor 74-75; C of Ch Mem Ch Oshawa Dio Tor from 75. *306-555 Mayfair Avenue, Oshawa, Ont, Canada.*

HERBERT, Canon Charles Robert Valentine. b 12. Bps' Coll Cheshunt 56. **d** 58 **p** 59 St E. C of St Jo Bapt Felixstowe 58-62; R of Long Melford 62-77; Suff 65-77; RD of Sudbury 67; Hon Can of St E 77; Can (Emer) from 77. *Farm House, Brundon, Sudbury, Suff.* (Sudbury 72273)

HERBERT, Canon Charles Vernon. b 18. St Jo Coll Dur BA and Van Mildert Scho 42, Dipl in Th 43, MA 45. **d** 43 **p** 44 Liv. C of Em Fazakerley 43-46; St Helens 46-49; V of Laister Dyke 49-55; CMS Area Sec Dios Liv; Man; and Ches 55-61; Perm to Offic Dio Man 55-61; V of Portsdown 61-79; RD of Havant 72-77; Hon Can of Portsm from 76; V of Hambledon Dio Portsm from 79. *Hambledon Vicarage, Portsmouth, Hants, PO7 6RT.* (Hambledon 717)

HERBERT, Christopher John. b 37. Univ of Dur BA 60, Dipl Th 62. Cranmer Hall, Dur 60. **d** 62 Warrington for Liv **p** 63 Liv. C of St Gabr Huyton Quarry 62-65; Rainford 65-68; V of Impington 68-78; Gt Shelford Dio Ely from 78; RD of N Stowe 76-78; Shelford from 80. *Great Shelford Vicarage, Cambridge.* (Shelford 3274)

HERBERT, Christopher William. b 44. St D Coll Lamp BA 65. Wells Th Coll 65. **d** 67 **p** 68 Heref. C of Tupsley 67-71; Adv in Relig Educn Dio Heref 71-76; Dir 76-81; Preb of Heref Cathl 76-81; V of The Bourne Dio Guildf from 81. *The Bourne Vicarage, Swingate Road, Farnham, Surrey.* (Farnham 715505)

HERBERT, Clair Geoffrey Thomas. b 36. Tyndale Hall, Bris 61. **d** 64 **p** 65 Southw. C of St Sav Nottm 64-67; Harwell and of Chilton 67-70; V of Bucklebury w Marlston 70-80; Chap Brighton Coll Jun Sch from 80. *Brighton College Junior School, 9 Elm Drive, Hove, BN3 7JS.* (Brighton 733249)

HERBERT, David Alexander Sellars. b 39. Univ of Bris BA (2nd cl Engl) 60. St Steph Ho Ox 65. **d** 67 **p** 68 Chich. C of Ch Ch St Leonards-on-Sea 67-81; V of St Geo Bickley Dio Roch from 81. *Vicarage, Bickley Park Road, Bromley, Kent, BR1 2BE.* (01-467 3809)

HERBERT, David Roy. b 51. AKC and BD 73. St Aug Coll Cant 73. **d** 74 **p** 75 Sheff. C of St Aid w St Luke Sheff 74-76; Sheff Manor 76-78; Team V of Gleadless Valley Dio Sheff from 78. *Holy Cross Vicarage, Spotswood Mount, Sheffield, S14 1LG.*

HERBERT, George Reginald. b 1896. St Chad's Coll Dur BA and Dipl in Th 20, MA 23. **d** 21 **p** 22 Dur. C of Brandon 21-24; Min of Easington Colliery 24-29; V 29-43; CF (EC) 41-47; Hon CF 47; R of Tretire w Michaelchurch (w Pencoyd from 48) 47-66; Ed Heref Dioc Year Book 56-65. *The Chantry, Monmouth, NP5 3PA.* (Monmouth 2713)

HERBERT, Graham Paul. b 54. Univ of Birm BA 75. Wycl Hall Ox BA (Th) 80. **d** 81 Chich. C of Crowborough Dio Chich from 81. *2 Woodland Way, Crowborough, Sussex, TN6 3BG.*

HERBERT, Henry Samuel. b 14. SOC 69. **d** 72 **p** 73 Barking for Chelmsf. SSF. C of St Andr Plaistow 72-73; St Phil and St Jas Plaistow 72-73; Aldersbrook 73-75; C-in-c of Gt Ilford 73-75; P-in-c 75-79; V 79-81; Wroxall Dio Portsm from 81. *Vicarage, Yarborough Road, Wroxall, IW.* (Ventnor 852744)

HERBERT, Canon Hugh Maurice. Univ of Wales, BA (2nd cl Cl) 22. Men in Disp 19. Wells Th Coll 22. **d** 23 **p** 24 Cant. C of Cranbrook 23-26; Kingston T 26-29; V of High Hurst Wood 29-34; St Phil Norbury 34-56; CF (R of O) 39-41; R of Coulsdon 56-70; Surr from 64; Can Emer Dio S'wark from 70; LPr Dio S'wark from 70. *25 Brighton Road, Coulsdon, Surrey, CR3 2BF.* (01-668 3535)

HERBERT, John William. b 42. Sarum Wells Th Coll 74. **d** 77 **p** 78 Worc. C of St Thos w St Luke Dudley 77-79; Team V of Malvern Link w Cowleigh Dio Worc from 79. *49 Yates Hay Road, Malvern, Worcs.* (Malvern 4041)

HERBERT, Kenneth Cyril. b 20. Univ of Wales, (Abth) BA (2nd cl Engl) 41. St D Coll Lamp LTh 43. **d** 43 **p** 44 St D. C of St Pet Carmathen 43-56; V of Llangorwen Dio St D from 56; RD of Llanbadarn Fawr from 80. *Llangorwen Vicarage, Clarach, Aberystwyth, Dyfed.* (Aberystwyth 828207)

HERBERT, Malcolm Francis. b 53. AKC & BD 74. Trin Coll Bris 76. **d** 77 Glouc **p** 78 Tewkesbury for Glouc. C of Wotton-under-Edge 77-80; Worle Dio B & W from 80. *2a St Mark's Road, Worle, Weston-super-Mare, BS22 0PW.* (W-s-M 512093)

HERBERT, Michael. b 35. Univ of Nottm BA (2nd cl French) 57. St D Coll Lamp. **d** 61 **p** 62 Pet. C of Paston 61-65; All SS Northn 65-67; V of Sutton w Upton 67-72; Asst Dioc Youth Chap Dio Pet 67-72; Industr Chap Dio Pet from 72; P-in-c of Pitsford Dio Pet from 79. *28 Clarence Avenue, Northampton, NN2 6NZ.* (Northn 711817)

HERBERT, Ronald. b 53. Worc Coll Ox BA 75, MA 80. BD (Lon) 78. Oak Hill Coll 75. **d** 79 **p** 80 Roch. C of Welling Dio Roch from 79. *52 Clifton Road, Welling, Kent, DA16 1QD.*

HERBERT, Ronald Walter. Univ of Queensld BSc 52. BD (Lon) 58. Moore Th Coll Syd ACT ThL 57. **d** 57 **p** 58 Adel. C of H Trin Adel 57-60; Chap C of E Gr Sch E Brisb 60-68; Perm to Offic Dio Brisb from 69. *69 Prospect Street, Wynnum North, Queensland, Australia 4178.* (396 4354)

HERBERT, Roy. b 22. St D Coll Lamp BA (2nd cl Th) 47. Jes Coll Ox BA (2nd cl Th) 49, MA 54. Wells Th Coll 50. **d** 50 **p** 51 Glouc. C of Cirencester 50-54; Bp's Chap for Youth Dio Glouc 55-61; Tr Tutor C of E Youth Coun 61-64; Sec 64-71; C-in-c of St Phil Lambeth 71-74; R of North Lambeth 74-78; RD of Lambeth 71-78; C of St Cuthb Copnor Dio Portsm from 78. *2 Lichfield Road, Portsmouth, PO3 6DE.* (Portsm 827071)

HERBERT, Timothy David. b 57. Univ of Man BA (Th) 78. Ridley Hall Cam 79. **d** 81 Ches. C of St Mich Macclesfield Dio Ches from 81. *57 Beech Farm Drive, Macclesfield, Cheshire.*

HERD, Kenneth. Qu Coll Cam BA (3rd cl Th Trip pt i) 47, MA 58. **d** 64 Bp G M McKenzie for Wel **p** 65 Wel. C of Wanganui E 64-69; V of Taita 69-73; Gonville 73-79; Perm to Offic Dio Wel from 79. *86 Jellicoe Street, Wanganui, NZ.*

✠ **HERD, Right Rev William Brian.** Clifton Th Coll 55. **d** 58 **p** 59 Lich. C of St Luke Wolverhampton 58-61; Miss of Lotome 61-64; I of Moroto 64-67; L to Offic Dio Soroti 67-75; Archd of Karamoja 70-75; Cons Ld Bp of Karamoja in St Paul's Cathl Nam 11 Jan 76 by Abp of Ugan; Bps of Bukedi, Nam, Ank, Bunyoro, Busoga, Mbale, N Ugan, Ruw, W Bugan, Buj and Buye; res 81; Deputn Sec BCMS from 77. *34 Clonlee Drive, Belfast, BT4.* (Belf 659593)

HERDE, Ronald Oscar. St Barn Coll Adel 49. ACT ThL 51. **d** and **p** 51 Adel. C of Brighton 51-52; Glenelg 52-54; P-in-c of Mt Pleasant 54-56; V of Koroit 56-59; Nhill 59-63; P-in-c of Wendouree 63-66; V 66-67; R of St Mary Adel 67-75; P-in-c of St Paul Adel 68-71; Perm to Offic Dio C & Goulb 75-76; Dio Adel 75-77; C of St Geo Goodwood 77; Chap Edw River Queensld 78; Actg P-in-c of Ingle Farm-Pooraka 78-79; Murray Bridge 79; P-in-c of Eliz Downs Dio Adel from 79. *111 York Town Road, Elizabeth Park, S Australia 5113.* (255 1530)

HEREFORD, Lord Bishop of. *See* Eastaugh, Right Rev John Richard Gordon.

HEREFORD, Assistant Bishop of. (Vacant).

HEREFORD, Archdeacon of. *See* Barfett, Ven Thomas.

HEREFORD, Dean of. *See* Rathbone, Very Rev Norman Stanley.

HERGETT, Douglas Harold. Dalhousie Univ BCom 61. K Coll NS. **d** 63 **p** 64 NS. d Dio NS 63-64; R of Maitland 64-67; Ch Ch Dartmouth 67-72; Horton Dio NS from 72. *106 Main Street, Wolfville, NS, Canada.* (542-2464)

HERITAGE, Barry. b 35. Clifton Th Coll 59. **d** 61 **p** 62 Lich. C of St Jude Wolverhampton 61-65; Chaddesden 65-67; V of Kidsgrove 67-76; NE Area Sec CPAS from 76; LPr Dio York from 76; Perm to Offic Dio Bradf from 79. *10 Ainsty Grove, Dringhouses, York, YO2 2HQ.* (York 706113)

HERITAGE, Henry Rymer. b 09. Univ of Leeds BSc 33. Lich Th Coll 33. **d** 35 **p** 36 Sheff. C of St Timothy Sheff 35-37; Miss in Shantung China 38-46; C of Blyth 46-49; V of Norwell 49-54; R of Finningley w Awkley 54-65; V of Harworth 65-74; Kirklington w Hockerton 74-77; P-in-c of Winkburn 74-77; Maplebeck 76-77; Perm to Offic Dio Southw from 77. *The Cottage, Galley Hill Road, Southwell, NG25 0PX.*

HERITAGE, Peter Bertram. b 30. Univ of Sask BMus 73. Em Coll Sktn LTh 57. **d** 57 **p** 58 Sktn. I of Northminster 57-59; Humboldt 59-63; R of Unity 63-70; I of Edgerton 76-78; Leduc 78-80; on leave. *Box 807, Devon, Alta, T0C 1E0, Canada.*

HERITAGE, Canon Thomas Charles. b 08. St Edm Hall, Ox BA (2nd cl Engl Lang and Lit) 29, MA 44. A Mus TCL 31. **d** 34 Derby **p** 38 Portsm. C of Ch Ch Chesterfield and Asst Master Chesterfield Gr Scho 34-38; C of St Mark Portsea 38-40; Asst Master Portsm Gr Sch 38-64; C of St Chris Bournemouth 40-44; Chap Portsm Cathl 45-64; Exam Chap to Bp of Portsm 56-60 and 65-75; Hon Can of Portsm 58-64; Can Res 64-76; Can (Emer) from 76. *117 The Close, Salisbury, Wilts, SP1 2EY.* (0722-29104)

HERIZ-SMITH, Eustace Edward Arthur. Pemb Coll Cam BA (1st cl Cl Trip and 2nd cl Hist Trip pt ii) 11, MA 19. Cudd Coll 15. **d** 15 **p** 16 Sarum. Asst Chap Sherborne Sch 15-17; TCF 18-20; C of St Pet Bournemouth 17-21; R of H Trin Win

21-25; Asst Chap Bedford Sch 25-29; Chap 29-34; Hd Master St Geo Coll Quilmes 35-37; Hon Can of St John's Pro-Cathl Buenos Aires 37; Chap Elstree Sch 37-39; V of Radley 39-41; Offg Chap Malvern Coll 41-47; Chap St Mich Sch Limpsfield 48-49; Asst Chap Tonbridge Sch and LPr Dio Roch 50-59. *Clock House Cottage, Bruisyard, Saxmundham, Suff.* (Rendham 512)

HERKLOTS, John Radu. b 31. Trin Hall Cam 2nd cl Hist Trip pt i 52, BA (2nd cl Th Trip pt ia) 53, MA 61. Westcott Ho Cam 54. **d** 55 **p** 56 Sheff. C of Attercliffe w Carbrook Sheff 55-60; Stoke Damerel Devonport 60-65; PC of St Bart Devonport Dio Ex 65-68; V 68-72; Denmead Dio Portsm from 72; Dioc Ecumen Officer Dio Portsm from 77. *Denmead Vicarage, Portsmouth, Hants, PO7 6NN.* (Waterlooville 55490)

HERMAN, Malcolm. b 26. Em Coll Sask. **d** 64 **p** 65 Athab. I of Fort Chipewyan 64-66; Lac La Biche 66-71; Boyle Dio Athab from 71. *Boyle, Alta, TOA OMO Canada.* (689 3616)

HERNIMAN, Ven Ronald George. b 23. Univ of Lon BA 51. Oak Hill Th Coll. **d** 54 **p** 55 Lon. C of Cockfosters 54-56; Tutor Oak Hill Th Coll 56-61; R of Washfield 61-72; C-in-c of Withleigh 61-72; Calverleigh 61-72; R of Stoodleigh 62-72; C-in-c of Oakford 63-72; Morebath 63-72; Rackenford 65-72; Templeton w Loxbeare 66-72; R of Shirwell w Loxhore Dio Ex from 72; Archd of Barnstaple from 70. *Shirwell Rectory, Barnstaple, Devon.* (Shirwell 371)

HERON, Alexander Francis. b 28. Univ of BC BA 60. Angl Th Coll Vanc LTh 53. **d** 52 **p** 53 Edmon. C of St Mark Edmon 52-53; I of St Barn Edmon 53-54; C of St Barn Beckenham Kent 54-55; R of Vegreville Alta 55-58; C of St Paul Vanc 58-62; Chap RAF 62-77; R of St John Brantford 77-79; St Mary Magd City and Dio Tor from 79. *479 Manning Avenue, Toronto, Ont, M6G 2V8, Canada.*

HERON, David George. b 49. AKC 72. St Aug Coll Cant 72. **d** 73 **p** 74 Dur. C of St Chad Stockton-on-Tees 73-77; Beamish 77-80; R of Willington and Sunnybrow Dio Dur from 80. *Willington Rectory, Crook, Co Durham, DL15 0DE.* (Willington 6242)

HERON, George Dobson. b 34. Cranmer Hall, Dur. **d** 61 Jarrow for Dur **p** 62 Dur. C of Benfieldside 61-65; Winlaton 65-68; V of St Nich (w Ch Ch from 77) Dunston Dio Dur from 68; P-in-c of Ch Ch Dunston 74-77. *1 Bracken Drive, Dunston, Gateshead-on-Tyne, T & W.* (Dunston 604659)

HERRETT, Graham. b 40. Sarum Wells Th Coll 75. **d** 77 Repton for Derby **p** 78 Derby. C of St Mary Virg Ilkeston 77-80; Team V of Hucknall Torkard Dio Southw from 80. *St John's Parsonage, Hucknall, Notts.*

HERRING, George Gilbert. b 04. Chich Th Coll 61. **d** 61 **p** 64 Chich. C of Midhurst 61-64; Easebourne 64-72; L to Offic Dio Chich from 72. *11 Derby Road, Haslemere, Surrey.* (Haslemere 2275)

HERRING, Herbert Douglas. Hur Coll. **d** 58 **p** 60 Hur. I of Chatsworth 58-61; R of Port Rowan 61-71; I of Norwich 70-79. *Box 427, Norwich, Ont., Canada.* (519-863 2519)

HERRING, Canon Ian Napier. Ridley Coll Melb ACT ThL 61. **d** 62 Bp Redding for Melb **p** 63 Melb. C of St John Croydon 62-64; St Geo Malvern 64-66; Dioc Centre Melb 66-70; R of Ch Ch Cathl St Arn 70-76; Exam Chap to Bp of St Arn and Can Res 70-76; R of Ararat Dio Bal from 77; Can of Bal from 80. *Rectory, Ararat, Vic, Australia 3377.* (053-52 1109)

HERRING, Ven Nigel Denzil. Trin Coll Melb 1897. **d** 1900 **p** 01 Melb. C of Kyneton Vic 1900-01; Werribee Vic 01-02; V of Broken Hill NSW 02-09; St Aug Shepparton Vic 09-19; R of Benalla 19-28; Can of H Trin Cathl Wang 24-28; Archd of Bend VG Dioc Regr and Org Sec Bend Dioc Centr Fund 28-49; Admin Dio Bend 38; 40-41; and 43-44; Archd of Kyneton 49-64; Archd (Emer) from 64; VG 57-62. *Bethlehem Home for Aged, Specimen Hill, Golden Square, Vic, Australia.*

HERRINGTON, Fred. b 09. Kelham Th Coll 29. **d** 34 **p** 35 Wakef. C of Chapelthorpe 34-37; Conisborough 37-44; C-in-c of Moor Ends Conv Distr 44-51; V of Worsborough Common 51-57; Denaby Main 57-61; Wincobank Dio Sheff from 61. *Vicarage, Wincobank, Sheffield, S9 1LN.* (Sheffield 386507)

HERRINGTON, Henry George. b 05. AKC 35. **d** 35 **p** 36 Lon. C of St Matt Oakley Sq 35-38; H Cross w St Jude St Pancras 38-41; C-in-c of Swineshead 41-45; V of Middle Rasen Drax w Middle Rasen Tupholme 45-51; C-in-c of W Rasen 45-52; V of Nettleham 51-81. *11 Ash Tree Avenue, Nettleham, Lincoln, LN2 2TQ.* (0522 754003)

HERRINGTON, Wilfrid Spencer. b 17. Chich Th Coll 72. **d** & **p** 72 Portsm. C of Bedhampton 72-77; P-in-c of Raydon Dio St E from 77; Holton St Mary w Gt Wenham Dio St E from 77. *Rectory, Raydon, Ipswich, Suff.* (Gt Wenham 310332)

HERRON, Robert Gordon John. b 36. Wycl Hall Ox 65. **d** 77 **p** 78 Liv. C of St Mich Ditton 77-80; W Kirby Dio Ches from 80. *St Michael's House, Queensbury, Newton, W Kirby.* (061-625 8517)

HERRON, Warren Alfred. Univ of Tor BA 56. Wycl Coll Tor BTh 59. **d** 59 Tor. C of Eatonville 59; on leave from 59. *14 Tunbridge Crescent, Etobicoke, Ont., Canada.*

HERTFORD, Lord Bishop Suffragan of. *See* Pillar, Right Rev Kenneth Harold.

HERTZLER, Harold Leopold. Univ of Pennsylvania BA (Hist) 31. Gen Th Sem New York STB 44. **d** 44 Rhode I **p** 45 Long I. In Amer Ch 44-49; Dean of Residence and Lect in Liturgics and Ch Hist at Montr Dioc Th Coll 49-51; R of St Jo Evang Montr 51-62; Hon Can of Montr 60-62; Chap at Copenhagen 62-67; C of St Thos Tor 67-73; R of St Mich AA Winnipeg 73-76; Hon Can of Rupld 75; L to Offic Dio Moray 76-79. *c/o Rectory, Seafield Avenue, Keith, Banffshire, AB5 3BS.* (Keith 2782)

HERVE, Charles. b 08. AKC 31. St Steph Ho Ox 31. **d** 31 **p** 32 Derby. C of Langley Mill 31-34; Spondon 34-39; V of St Mark Derby 39-46; Chap RAFVR 43-46; PC of Wormhill 46-51; V of Baddesley Ensor 51-55; St Chad Smethwick 55-60; St Wulstan Selly Oak 60-78; C of Kingsbury (in c of Hurley) 78-81. *St Andrew's Vicarage, Handsworth, Birmingham, B21 9PB.* (021-551 2097)

HERVE, John Anthony. b 49. Open Univ BA 80. Qu Coll Birm 72. **d** 73 Selby for York **p** 74 York. C of All SS Middlesbrough 73-76; CF 76-81; P-in-c of St Andr Handsworth Dio Birm from 81. *Vicarage, Laurel Road, Handsworth, Birmingham, B21 9PB.* (021-551 2097)

HERVEY, Frederick Alan Romaine. b 1899. Sarum Th Coll 28. **d** 30 **p** 31 Chich. C of Wadhurst 30-32; V of Woburn 32-37; Langcliffe w Stainforth 37-46; R of Whicham 46-55; V of Whitbeck 46-55; R of Inkpen 55-66. *6 Millfield, Beaminster, Dorset.* (Beaminster 862868)

HERYET, Dudley. b 18. AKC 42. **d** 42 Southampton for Win **p** 43 Win. C of St Alb Southampton 42-45; St Thos Finsbury Pk Lon 45-48; St Mary of Eton Hackney Wick 48-50; C-in-c of St Mary Stepney 50-53; V 53-58; V of St Mich Edmon 58-62; Blean 62-73; Kennington, Kent Dio Cant from 73. *St Mary's Vicarage, Faversham Road, Ashford, Kent.* (Ashford 20500)

HESELTON, Peter Rodolphus. b 30. Em Coll Cam 2nd cl Cl Trip pt i 52, BA 53, 2nd cl Th Trip pt ii 54, MA 57. Qu Coll Birm 53. **d** 55 **p** 56 Lich. C of St Matt Walsall 55-59; V of Moxley 59-64; Castlechurch 64-73; Asst Master Taunton Manor Sch Old Coulsdon 73; Blue Coat Sec Sch Walsall from 74; L to Offic Dio Lich from 73. *29 Mendip Aveue, Hillcroft Park, Stafford, ST17 0PF.* (Stafford 64220)

HESKETH, Canon Douglas Campbell. b 09. St Pet Hall Ox BA (2nd cl Th) 37, MA 44. Wycl Hall Ox 37. **d** 38 **p** 39 Liv. C of Em Fazakerley 38-42; C-in-c of St Mich Liverpool 42-44; V of St Aug Halifax 44-53; St Barn Mossley Hill 53-75; RD of Childwall 69-75; Can of Liv from 73. *52 Skipton Avenue, Crossens, Southport.*

HESKETH, Canon Harold. Wycl Coll Tor LTh 15. **d** and **p** 15 Athab. I of St Jas Peace River Crossing Alta 15-19; R of Hardwicke 19-23; C of St Olave Swansea Tor 24-25; R of Chapleau 25-38; RD of Chapleau 28-38; R of Trin Queb 38-41; Chap CAAF 41-42; I of Cannington w Beaverton and Sunderland 42-48; R of Lindsay 48-61; Can of Tor from 56. *369 Aberdeen Avenue, Peterborough, Ont., Canada.*

HESKETH, John Arthur. b 14. Lich Th Coll 54. **d** 56 **p** 57 Ches. C of Stockport 56-60; V of Millbrook 60-76; C of St Jas w St Bede Birkenhead Dio Ches from 76. *3 Buckingham Avenue, Claughton, Birkenhead, L43 8TD.* (051-652 9180)

HESKETH, Canon John Talbot. Univ Coll Tor BA 52. Wycl Th Coll Tor BTh 66. **d** 52 **p** 53 Tor. C of Ch of Redeemer Tor 52-53; R of Whitehorse 53-56; Chap Ridley Coll St Catharine's 56-61; R of St Thos St Catharine's 61-69; Ch Ch Niagara Falls 69-73; St D and St Patr Guelph 73-77; Grimsby Dio Niag from 77; Can of Ch Ch Hamilton from 67. *154 Main Street West, Grimsby, Ont, Canada.* (416-945 3254)

HESKETH, Robin Adams Lemprière. b 18. St Cath S Ox BA (3rd cl Th) 43, MA 47. St Steph Ho Ox 43. **d** 45 **p** 46 Ex. C of All SS Babbacombe 45-48; Perm to Offic Dio Ex 48-51; C of Dawlish 51-55; Brixham (in c of St Pet) 55-61; V of S Petherwyn w Trewen 61-72; Lewannick 62-71; P-in-c of Penponds Dio Truro 72-73; V from 73. *Penponds Vicarage, Camborne, Cornw, TR14 0QH.* (Camborne 712329)

HESKETH, Ronald David. b 47. Bede Coll Dur BA 68. St Mich Coll Llan 69. **d** 71 Warrington for Liv **p** 72 Liv. C of H Trin, Southport 71-74; Asst Chap Miss to Seamen Liv 74-75; Chap RAF from 75. *Ministry of Defence, Adastral House, WC1.*

HESKETH, William Ritchie Harrison. b 08. Chich Th Coll 43. **d** 44 **p** 45 Pet. C of St Mich AA Northn 44-46; R of St Paul Rothesay 46-49; C of Sudbury (in c of St Cuthb Miss Ch) Middx 49-50; Min of St Cuthb Conv Distr Sudbury 50-53; V of St Steph w St Luke Westbourne Pk Paddington 53-55;

CMS Area Sec Dios Heref Lich and Worc 55-62; V of Shelton w Oxon 62-66; Ogley Hay w Brownhills 67-71; Hints 71-77; R of Weeford 71-77; C-in-c of Canwell 71-77; C of Newborough w Needwood 77-79. *4 Winchester Close, Lichfield, Staffs.* (Lich 55941)

HESKINS, Jeffrey George. b 55. AKC 78. **d** 81 Edmon for Lon. C of St Mary Primrose Hill Hampstead Dio Lon from 81. *15 Elsworthy Rise, Primrose Hill, NW3.*

HESLEHURST, Raymond Errol. b 47. Moore Coll Syd ACT ThL 77. **d** and **p** 77 Armid. C of S Tamworth 77-79; Centennial Pk Dio Syd from 79. *4-54 Bishops Avenue, Randwick, NSW, Australia 2031.* (665-3000)

HESLOP, Harold William. b 40. Univ of Leeds BA 62. Open Univ BA 72. **d** 78 Reading for Cant for Ox **p** 79 Buckingham for Ox (APM). C of Stoke-Mandeville Dio Ox from 78. *7 Chiltern Road, Wendover, Bucks, HP22 6DB.*

HESLOP, James Alan. b 37. Codr Coll Barb 61. **d** 64 Barb for Gui **p** 65 Gui. C of Bartica 64-68; P-in-c of Long I Nass 68-71; C of Ch Ch Cathl Nass 71-72; Haxby w Wigginton 72-74; Team V 74-76; V of St Olave w St Giles City and Dio York from 76. *Vicarage, 52 Bootham, York.* (York 25186)

HESLOP, Michael Andrew. b 47. Trin Coll Bris 73. **d** 76 **p** 77 Ripon. C of Burmantofts 76-81; V of Thorpe Edge Dio Bradf from 81. *Vicarage, Northwood Crescent, Thorpe Edge, Bradford, W Yorks BD10 9HX.* (Bradf 613246)

HESS, Bernard Daniel. b 33. Univ of Capetn BA 56. **d** and **p** 77 Capetn (APM). C of St Mary Woodstock 77-80; Mitchells Plain Dio Capetn from 80. *3 Punt Street, Diep River 7800, CP, S Africa.* (72-9046)

HESS, John Peter. Bp Gray Th Coll Capetn 59. **d** 61 **p** 62 Capetn. C of Silvertown 61-68; R of Athlone Capetn 68-74; C of Alverstoke 74-76; P-in-c of All SS Conv Distr Gurnard 76-78; R of St Paul Capetn 78-80; H Nativ Athlone Dio Capetn from 80. *Rectory, Jonathan Road, Hazendal, Athlone 7764, CP, S Africa.* (638-2392)

HESSELGREAVES, Canon Arthur. b 16. Late Scho of Univ Coll Dur BA (3rd cl Math) 38, Dipl Th 40, MA 41. Qu Coll Birm 39. **d** 40 **p** 41 Wakef. C of Ossett 40-45; Knottingley w E Knottingley 45-49; V of St Andr Purlwell Batley 49-65; R of Cumberworth w Denby Dale 65-80; RD of Kirkburton 71-80; Surr 71-80; Hon Can of Wakef Cathl from 74. *1 Park Avenue, Denby Dale Road, Thornes, Wakefield, WF2 8DS.*

HESSEY, Stanley John. St Francis Coll Brisb. **d** 53 **p** 55 Bath. C of Wellington 53-55; E Orange 55-56; Mackay 56-57; R of Proserpine 57-60; Aramac 60-63; V of Keppel 64-68; CF (Austr) from 68. *Barracks, Samford Road, Enoggerd, Queensland 4051, Australia.*

HESTER, Donald Rackstrow. Wycl Coll Tor STh 52. **d** 53 **p** 53 Qu'App. I of Broadview 53-58; Kenaston 58-63; R of Lashburn 63-69; I of Belmont 69-70; Melita w Deloraine and Napinka 70-75; L to Offic Dio Sktn from 77. *General Delivery, Naicam, Sask, Canada.*

HESTER, Canon John Frear. b 27. Late Exhib of St Edm Hall, Ox BA 48, MA 52. Cudd Coll 51. **d** 52 **p** 53 Lon. C of St Geo Southall 52-55; H Redeemer Clerkenwell 55-58; Sec Actors' Ch U 58-63; Chap S of Sisters of Bethany Lloyd Square 59-62; Dep Min Can of St Paul's Cathl Lon 62-75; R of St Anne w St Thos and St Pet Soho Lon 63-75; P-in-c of St Paul Covent Gdn Westmr 69-75; Sen Chap Actors' Ch U 70-75; V of Brighton (w Chap R from 78 and St Jo Evang from 80) Dio Chich from 75; Surr from 75; P-in-c of St Jo Evang Brighton 75-80; Canon and Preb of Chich Cathl from 76; RD of Brighton from 76; Kemp Town from 76; Preston from 76; P-in-c of The Chap R Brighton 77-78. *Brighton Vicarage, London Road, Brighton, BN1 4JF.* (Brighton 682960)

HETHERINGTON, Andrew. b 50. Univ of Sheff BSc 71. Wycl Hall Ox 71. **d** 74 **p** 75 Leic. C of Trin Leic 74-78; H Ap Leic 78-82; V of St Mary w St Paul Bootle Dio Liv from 82. *Vicarage, Merton Road, Bootle, Mer.* (051-922 1315)

HETHERINGTON, Dermot Hugh. b 42. **d** 78 **p** 79 Nor. C of Raveningham Dio Nor from 78. *1 Whiteways Church, Wheatacre, Beccles, Suffolk.*

HETHERINGTON, Frank Walter. St Jo Coll Morpeth 73. **d** 74 **p** 75 Bath. Hon C of Bath Dio Bath from 74. *Church Street, Bathurst, NSW, Australia 2795.*

HETHERINGTON, John Edward. b 10. Sarum Wells Th Coll 75. **d** 76 **p** 77 Sarum (APM). C of Owermoigne w Warmwell 76-78; Chap Torbay Hosp from 78. *69 Swedwell Road, Barton, Torquay, Devon.* (Torquay 312077)

HETHERINGTON, Preb Richard Nevill. b 08. Lich Th Coll 30. **d** 32 **p** 33 Lon. C of St Luke Uxbridge Rd 32-34; St Barn Ealing 34-43; Chap RNVR 43-46; V of St Jas Gt Bethnal Green 46-51; St Barn Ealing 51-76; Preb of St Paul's Cathl Lon from 71. *30 Glencairn Drive, W5.*

HETLING, William Maurice. b 37. K Coll Lon and Warm AKC 61. **d** 62 **p** 63 S'wark. C of St Barn Eltham 62-66; Horley S'wark 66-71; Kingston Ja 71-72; R of Highgate 73-74; P-in-c of Porus Ja 74-75; Missr of St Mich Conv Distr Farnham Royal S 75-78; Team V of W Slough Dio Ox 78-80; Team R from 80. *298 Stoke Poges Lane, Slough, SL1 3LL.* (0753-39062)

HEUSSLER, David Nicholson. b 48. St Jo Coll Morpeth ACT ThL 76. **d** 76 **p** 77 Graft. C of Tweed Heads 76-79; Lismore 79-80; Casino Dio Graft from 80. *39 West Street, Casino, NSW, Australia 2470.*

HEUSTON, Canon Keith John. St Jo Coll Morpeth, NSW ThL 39. **d** 41 **p** 42 Newc. C of Terrigal 41-43; Actg I of Terrigal 43-44; P-in-c of Aberdare 44-46; R of Jerry's Plains 46-48; Cardiff 48-54; Chap CMF from 53; R of Waratah 54-64; Gosford Dio Newc from 64; Can of Newc from 71. *3 Mann Street, Gosford, NSW, Australia 2250.* (043-25 2051)

HEWAT, Patrick Duxbury. b 13. Late Found Scho of CCC Cam BA (1st cl Mod Lang Trip pt ii) 35, MA 55. K Coll Lon and Warm 48. **d** 49 **p** 50 Cov. C of St Mary Virg Nuneaton 49-51; V of Binley w Coombe Fields 51-55; Grantchester 55-70; Counsellor Westmr Pastoral Found 71; L to Offic Dio Ely from 70. *39 Edgecombe, Cambridge, CB4 2LN.*

HEWAT, Robert Anthony. b 32. St Jo Coll Auckld 70. **d** 71 **p** 72 Waik. C of Matamata 71-74; V of Pio Pio w Aria 74-75; Min 75-80; C of Fitzroy w Bell Block Dio Waik from 80. *30 Murray Street, Bell Block, New Plymouth, NZ.* (71-027)

HEWER, Sidney Eric. **d** 78 **p** 79 Nor (APM). Hon C of Grimston w Congham Dio Nor from 78; Roydon Dio Nor from 78. *Sunnymead, Vong Lane, Pott Row, Grimston, Norf.*

HEWES, John. b 29. Univ. of Nottm BA 50. Chich Th Coll 79. **d** 81 Cant. C of Buckland-in-Dover Dio Cant from 81. *35 Hillside Road, Dover, Kent, CT17 0JQ.* (0304 206994)

HEWETSON, Christopher. b 37. Trin Coll Ox BA 60, MA 64. Chich Th Coll 67. **d** 69 **p** 70 Glouc. C of Leckhampton 69-71; Wokingham 71-73; V of St Pet Didcot 73-82; R of Ascot Heath Dio Ox from 82. *Ascot Heath Rectory, Ascot, Berks.* (Ascot 21200)

HEWETSON, David Milroy. Moore Th Coll Syd ACT ThL 52. **d** and **p** 53 Syd. C of Bondi 53-55; R of Emu Plains 55-57; H Trin Miller's Point Syd 57-59; Dioc Miss Dio Syd 59-60; CMS Miss Tanzania 61-65; Actg Prin St Phil Th Coll Kongwa 63-65; Educn Sec CMS in NSW 65-71; Gen Sec 71-74; C-in-c of Provisional Par Turramurra S Dio Syd from 74. *5 Parkinson Avenue, Turramurra, NSW, Australia 2074.* (44-7989)

HEWETSON, Geoffrey David. b 31. SOC 71. **d** 74 Lewes for Chich **p** 75 Chich (APM). C of St Mich AA Brighton Dio Chich from 74. *3 Clifton Hill, Brighton, BN1 3HL.* (Brighton 27637)

HEWETSON, Robin Jervis. b 39. K Coll Lon and Warm AKC (2nd cl) 63. **d** 64 **p** 65 Nor. C of Thorpe Episcopi 64-67; E Dereham 67-69; V in Dereham Group (in c of Mattishall; Mattishall Burgh; and Welborne) 69-72; R of Ingham w Sutton 72-78; Catfield 75-78; Taverham w Ringland Dio Nor from 78. *Taverham Rectory, Norwich, NR8 6TE.* (Nor 868217)

HEWETT, John Reginald. b 07. **d** 71 Koot. C of Koot Lake 71-75; L to Offic Dio Calg from 76. *1205-18th Street North, Lethbridge, Alta, Canada.*

HEWETT, Maurice Gordon. b 28. Univ of Lon BA 53. Oak Hill Th Coll 49. **d** 54 **p** 55 S'wark. C of Gipsy Hill 54-57; St Faith Maidstone 57-60; R of Chevening Dio Roch from 60. *Chevening Rectory, Sevenoaks, Kent.* (Sevenoaks 53555)

HEWETT, Paul Clayton. b 48. Temple Univ Philadelphia BA 70. Phil Div Sch MDiv 73. **d** 73 Penn **p** 74 S'wark. C of St Faith Wandsworth 73-76; In Amer Ch from 76. *1111 County Line Road, Rosemont, Pa 19010, USA.*

HEWETT, Ven Robert John. Moore Th Coll Syd 21, ACT ThL 21. **d** 21 **p** 22 Syd. C of Marrickville 21-24; L to Offic Dio Syd 24-28; Asst Gen Sec CMS of Austr and Tas 24-25; Dep Gen Sec 25-28; R of St Paul Wahroonga 28-31; Asst Min St Andr Cathl Syd 31-36 and 45-47; L to Offic Dio Syd 31-36; R of St Paul Chatswood 36-37; St Clem Mosman 37-45; Hon Can of Syd 49-56; Archd of Ryde 56-60; Archd (Emer) from 60; Chap to Abp of Syd (for Lay Readers) 60-65; L to Offic Dio Syd from 60. *Phillip Lodge, Kilvington Village, Castle Hill, NSW, Australia 2154.* (634-3423)

HEWINS, Geoffrey Shaw. b 1889. Univ of Wales (Abth) BA 13. Lich Th Coll 13. **d** 14 **p** 15 Southw. C of Stanley (in c of All SS) 14-24; Perm to Offic at Hodnet (in c of Weston-under-Redcastle) 25-30; C of Hanmer (in c of Tallarn Green) 31-34; R of Hamstall-Ridware w Pipe-Ridware 34-39; V of Easton Maudit 39-40; R of Oxhill w Whatcote 40-44; Exhall w Wixford 44-50; V of Cleeton w Silvington 50-71. *Address temp unknown.*

HEWISON, Alan Stuart. b 30. K Coll Lon and Warm. **d** 57 **p** 58 Lon. C of K Chas Mart S Mymms 57-60; St Thos-on-the-Bourne 60-63; Chap RN from 63. *c/o Ministry of Defence, Lacon House, Theobald's Road, WC1X 8RY.*

HEWITSON, Canon Gordon Frank. Univ of Adel BA 50. St Barn Coll Adel ACT ThL 47. **d** and **p** 48 Adel. C of

Woodville 48; Asst Chap and Master St Pet Colleg Sch Adel 48-54; Hd Master St Aug Gr Sch Unley and C of Unley 54-58; R of Coromandel Valley 58-65; Kadina 65-68; R of H Trin Whyalla Dio Willoch from 68; Can of Willoch from 76. *PO Box 2056, Whyalla, Norrie, S Australia 5068.* (086-45 7559)

HEWITSON, John Kenneth. b 48. St Mich Ho Crafers 67. ACT ThL 70. **d** 71 Willochra for NW Aust **p** 72 Bris. C of Swindon 71-74; Spearwood-Willagee 74-76; R of Balga 76-77; on leave 77-79; Assoc Chap R Perth Hosp from 79. *33 Manolas Way, Girrawheen, W Australia 6064.* (342 4700)

HEWITT, Alexander John. b 43. Waterloo Lutheran Univ BA 65. **d** 75 **p** 76 Niag. C of St Chris Burlington 75-78; R of Fergus Dio Niag from 78; Exam Chap to Bp of Niag from 81. *320 Union Street East, Fergus, Ont, Canada.* (519-843 2024)

HEWITT, Brian. Univ of Liv BSc (2nd cl Botany) 51. Westcott Ho Cam 53. **d** 55 **p** 56 Liv. C of Roby 55-60; V of St Jo Evang Dukinfield Dio Ches from 60. *St John's Vicarage, Dukinfield, Chesh.* (Stalybridge 2036)

HEWITT, Charles David. b 38. Or Coll Ox 3rd cl Cl Mods 58, BA (3rd cl Lit Hum) 60, MA 63. Clifton Th Coll 63. **d** 66 Warrington for Liv **p** 67 Liv. C of St Simon and St Jude Southport 66-70; St Mark Vic Pk Bethnal Green 70-76; Hon C of St Paul Old Ford Bow Dio Lon from 76. *98 Cadogan Terrace, E9 5HP.* (01-985 7797)

HEWITT, Christopher James Chichele. b 45. Univ of the Witwatersrand BSc 67. Univ of S Africa BA 77. St Paul's Th Coll Grahmstn 77. **d** 78 Bp Ndwandwe for Johann **p** 79 Johann. C of Vanderbijl Park Dio Johann from 78. *PO Box 470, Vanderbijl Park, S Africa 1900.*

HEWITT, David. b 44. Mem Univ of Newfld BA 74. **d** and **p** 76 E Newfld. C of Random 76-80; Hearts Delight Dio E Newfld from 80. *Box 59, Hearts Delight, Newfoundland, Canada.*

HEWITT, David John. b 40. Wells Th Coll 65. **d** 68 **p** 69 Portsm. C of H Spirit Southsea 68-70; Bramshott 70-72; Much Wenlock 72-74; CF 74-78; V of Tibberton w Bredicot and Hadzor w Oddingley Dio Worc from 78. *Parsonage, Church Lane, Tibberton, Droitwich, Worcs.* (Spetchley 449)

HEWITT, David Warner. b 33. Late Exhib Selw Coll Cam 2nd cl Hist Trip pt i, 55, BA (2nd cl Hist Trip pt ii) 56, MA 60. Wells Th Coll 57. **d** 59 **p** 60 Birm. C of Longbridge 59-61; Sheldon 61-64; V of Smethwick 64-78; Littlehampton Dio Chich from 78; P-in-c of St Jas Littlehampton Dio Chich from 78; All SS Wick Dio Chich from 78. *34 Fitzalan Road, Littlehampton, Sussex.* (Littlehampton 5479)

HEWITT, Francis John Adam. b 42. St Chad's Coll Dur BA 64, Dipl Th 66. **d** 66 Wakef **p** 67 Pontefract for Wakef. C of Dewsbury Moor 66-69; St Jo Evang Huddersfield 69-73; V of St Paul King Cross Halifax 73-81; Lastingham w Appleton-le-Moors Dio York from 81; P-in-c of Appleton-le-Moors 81. *Lastingham Vicarage, York.* (Lastingham 344)

HEWITT, Garth Bruce. b 46. St Jo Coll Dur BA 68. ALCD 70. **d** 70 **p** 71 Cant. C of St Luke, Maidstone 70-75; Hon C of St John w Ealing Dio Lon from 75. *37 Queen's Gardens, W5 1SE.* (01-998 1094)

HEWITT, Geoffrey Williams. b 48. Univ of Leeds BA (3rd cl Th) 69. Wells Th Coll 70. **d** 72 Man **p** 73 Middleton for Man. C of Heywood 72-74; Industr Chap and C-in-c of St Geo Hulme Man 74-77; Industr Chap and R of Mamhilad w Llanfihangel Pontymoile 77-80; V of Arthog w Fairbourne Dio Ban from 80. *Vicarage, Arthog, Gwyn, LL39 1YU.* (Fairbourne 250389)

HEWITT, Canon George Herbert. Fitzw Hall Cam BA 13, MA 20. MBE 59. Westcott Ho Cam. **d** 13 **p** 14 S'wark. C of Rotherhithe 13-16; UMCA Miss P Dio N Rhod 16-24; P-in-c of Fiwila 24-33; Warden Teachers' Tr Coll Fiwila 28-29; Dioc Th Coll Fiwila 31-33; C of St Jo Evang Watford 33-35; V of St Ippolyt w Gt Wymondley 35-39; St Sav St Alb 39-45; Proc Conv St Alb 39-45; P-in-c of Lusaka 45-50; Mapanza 50-53; Luanshya 53-56; Fiwila 56-59; Can of N Rhod 53-64; Zam 64-70; Lusaka from 71. *St Francis Hospital, PO Box 16, Katete, Zambia.*

HEWITT, George William Henry. b 08. K Coll Dur BA (2nd cl Engl Lit and Phil) 29, MA 32. Coll of Resurr Mirfield 29. **d** 31 **p** 32 Dur. C of St Ignatius Mart Sunderland 31-37; Matatiele 37-38; R of Beaconsfield S Afr 38-44; Perm to Offic at Henfield 44-45; R of Usworth 45-52; N Area Sec UMCA 52-60; L to Offic Dio Newc T and Perm to Offic Dios Dur Blackb and Carl 52-60; Dio York 54-60; V of St Geo Barrow-F 60-64; Chap Killingbeck and Seacroft Hosps Leeds 64-75; Meanwood Park Hosp 64-78; Perm to Offic Dio Ripon from 78. *1 Hollin Crescent, Leeds, LS16 5ND.* (Leeds 785748)

HEWITT, Harold William. b 12. Fitzw Ho Cam 2nd cl Hist Trip pt i, 34, BA (2nd cl Hist Trip pt ii) 35, MA 39. Wycl Hall, Ox 36. **d** 38 **p** 39 Man. C of St Bart Westhoughton 38-40; St Paul Kersal 40-43; V of St Paul Oldham 43-52; R of St Mary Droylsden 52-66; Proc Conv Man 55-64; Surr 55-66; V of Gt Bowden w Welham 66-77; Perm to Offic Dio Ches from 77. *25 Brereton Drive, Nantwich, Ches, CW5 6HE.* (Nantwich 626660)

HEWITT, Henry Alexander Chichele. Keble Coll Ox BA 03, MA 05. Ely Th Coll 01. **d** 03 **p** 04 Ox. C of All SS Ascot 03-08; Graaff Reinet Cape Col 08-09; R of Tarkastad 09-12; St Pet E Lon 12-38; Warden Commun of Resurr and Chap of St Pet Home Grahmstn 38-48; P-in-c of Ch Ch Grahmstn 40-44; R of Sidbury 40-49; L to Offic Dio Grahmstn 49-66; Archd of K William's Tn 50-57; Can of Grahmstn 50-60. *16 Donkin Street, Grahamstown, CP, S Africa.*

HEWITT, Henry Thomas Maxwell. Trin Coll Dub BA 44, MA 63. **d** 44 **p** 45 Oss. C of Ardamine w Kiltennel 44-48; I of Glasscarrig, Monamolin and Kilmuckridge 48-54; C of St Jas Alperton 54-61; V of Em Paddington 61-72; I of Abbeyleix Dio Leigh from 72. *Vicarage, Abbeyleix, Irish Republic.*

HEWITT, James Herbert. b 17. Ch Coll Cam 2nd cl Hist Trip 38, BA 39, 3rd cl Th Trip 40 MA 42. Ridley Hall, Cam 40. **d** 41 **p** 42 York. C of Heworth & St Mary Castlegate w St Mich Spurriergate York 41-43; H Trin Tulse Hill 43-45; V of H Trin Lah 47-49; Cathl Ch of Resurr Lah 49-52; Abbottabad and St John Peshawar 52-55; Murree 56-60; Vice-Prin CMS Men's Tr Coll Chislehurst 61-65; C of Ch Ch Spitalfields 64-65; V of St Paul Beckenham 65-71; Commiss Lah 68-80; R of Mereworth w West Peckham 71-75; V of St Aug Bradf 75-82; Commun Relns Chap Bradf 75-82. *49 Barnton Road, Dumfries, DG1 4HN.* (Dumfries 63973)

HEWITT, John Kaffrell. b 34. St Aid Coll 60. **d** 63 **p** 64 Guildf. C of Ch Ch Woking 63-66; C-in-c of All SS Sudbury w Ballingdon and Brundon 66-70; V 70-80; Portsdown Dio Portsm from 80. *Portsdown Vicarage, Cosham, Portsmouth, Hants, PO6 1BE.* (Cosham 375360)

HEWITT, Kenneth Victor. b 30. Univ of Lon BSc (2nd cl Gen) 49, Certif Educn 51, MSc 53. Cudd Coll 60. **d** 62 **p** 63 Cant. C of St Martin Maidstone 62-64; St Mich AA Croydon 64-67; Asst Chap Univ of Lon 67-73; C-in-c of St Aug Queen's Gate Kens Dio Lon 67-73; V from 73. *117 Queen's Gate, SW7 5LW.* (01-581 1877)

HEWITT, Michael David. b 49. AKC and BD 79. Qu Coll Birm 79. **d** 80 **p** 81 Roch. C of Ch Ch Bexleyheath Dio Roch from 80. *50 Martin Dene, Bexleyheath, Kent, DA6 8NA.* (01-303 3551)

HEWITT, Norman Leslie. b 09. **d** 56 **p** 57 Leic. C of Broughton Astley 56-58; V of Arnesby w Shearsby 58-63; R of Broughton Astley 63-73; L to Offic Dio Leic from 73. *3 Lawyers Lane, Oadby, Leicester.* (Leic 719207)

HEWITT, Robert Marlow. b 88. Pemb Coll Ox BA (2nd Cl Mod Hist) and MA 21. **d** 41 Penrith for Carl **p** 42 Carl. C of Wigton 41-45; Asst Chap St Marg Conv E Grinstead 45-52; Chap St Mary's Conv Chiswick 52-60; Hon C of St Jo Bapt Holland Rd Kens 60-69. *Address temp unknown.*

HEWITT, Robert Samuel. b 51. Qu Univ of Belf BSc 73. Div Hostel Dub 77. **d** 80 **p** 81 Down. C of Dundela Dio Down from 80. *217 Holywood Road, Belfast, BT4 2DH.*

HEWITT, Thomas Peter James. b 24. Univ of St Andr MA 50. St Steph Ho Ox 50. **d** 52 **p** 53 Bp Tubbs for Ches. C of Ellesmere Port 52-56; St Marg Leytonstone 56-60; V of Barlby 60-65; Godshill Dio Portsm from 65. *Godshill Vicarage, IW.* (Godshill 272)

HEWITT, William. Open Univ BA 73. Tyndale Hall Bris 42. **d** 44 **p** 45 Lich. C of St John Burslem 44-47; St Andr Bebington 47-50; V of St Thos Wavertree Dio Liv from 50; Surr from 50. *25 Dudlow Lane, Liverpool, L18 2EX.* (051-722 2707)

HEWITT, William Charles. Univ of Sask BA 38. Em Coll Sktn LTh 37. **d** 37 **p** 38 Bran. C of Pilot Mound 37-38; I of Deloraine 38-40; RCAF 40-46; C of Ascen Ch Montr 46-48; in Amer Ch 48-51; Chap RCAF 51-63; Hon C of St Olave City and Dio Tor from 63. *1835 Yonge Street, Toronto, Ont, Canada.*

HEWITT, William Patrick. b 48. Univ of Nottm BTh 79. Linc Th Coll 75. **d** 79 Penrith for Carl **p** 80 Carl. C of St John Workington Dio Carl from 79. *3 Bank Road, Workington, Cumbria, CA14 3YN.*

HEWLETT, Charles Michael. b 30. St D Coll Lamp BA 58. **d** 59 **p** 60 Mon. C of Ch Ch Ebbw Vale 59-60; St Mark Newport 60-63; Bp's Messenger Dio Mon 63-66; V of New Tredegar 66-70; R of Llanddewi Skirrid and Llanvetherine and Llangattock Lingoed w Llanfair Chap 70-74; V of Pontypool 74-78. *18 Syr David's Avenue, Pencisely, Cardiff.*

HEWLETT, David Bryan. b 49. Univ of Bris BEducn 72. Qu Coll Birm 77. **d** 79 **p** 80 Heref. C of Ludlow 79-81; V of Ashford Carbonell w Ashford Bowdler Dio Heref from 81; Caynham Dio Heref from 81; Richard's Castle Dio Heref from 81. *Vicarage, Ashford Carbonell, Ludlow, Shropshire.* (Richard's Castle 205)

HEWLETT, Frank Mayne. b 13. **d** 63 **p** 64 S'wark. C of All SS Shooter's Hill 63-67; V of St Luke Walthamstow 67-80. *Nepenthe, Thorington Road, Bramfield, Halesworth, Suff, IP19 9JD.* (Bramfield 424)

HEWLETT, John Allan Dalrymple. b 14. **d** 72 **p** 73 Antig (APM). C of St John's Cathl Antig 73-78. *Bishopgate Street, St John's, Antigua.*

HEWLETT, John Oswald. Moore Th Coll Syd. **d** and **p** 55 Nel. C of All SS 55-58; Miss Lower Perak 58-66; V of All SS Taiping 66-75; Perm to Offic Dio Auckld from 75; Hon C of Ellerslie Dio Auckld from 77. *427 Queen Street, Auckland, NZ.* (37-2551)

HEWLETT, Kenneth James. b 44. St Mich Th Coll Crafers 67. **d** 72 **p** 73 Melb. C of Glenroy 72-74; St Jas Syd 74-76; in Dept of Chap Dio Melb 76-81; I of St John Bentleigh Dio Melb from 81. *624 Centre Road, Bentleigh, Vic, Australia 3165.*

HEWLETT, Michael Edward. b 16. Mert Coll Ox BA 39, MA 46. Qu Coll Birm 46. **d** 48 **p** 49 Chich. C of Good Shepherd Preston 48-51; Crawley (in c of St Pet W Crawley) 51-56; V of Malden 56-69; C of Kennerleigh 69-72; Team V of Woolfardisworthy E, Kennerleigh, Washford Pyne, Puddington and Poughill Dio Ex from 72. *Poughill Vicarage, Crediton, Devon, EX17 4LA.* (Cheriton Fitzpaine 426)

HEWSON, Alan Douglas. Univ of NZ BCom 50. ACA 46. ACIS 47. St Jo Coll Auckld 64. **d** 64 **p** 65 Ch Ch. C of Merivale 64-68; V of Waihoo Downs 68-70; Tinwald-Hinds 70-73; Kaiapoi 73-77; Avonside 77-79; Perm to Offic Dio Ch Ch from 79. *86a Winchester Street, Christchurch 1, NZ.*

HEWSON, George Edmund. b 03. St Cath Coll Cam BA 25, MA 29. Westcott Ho Cam 25. **d** 26 Southw **p** 27 Derby. C of St John Derby 26-28; Stokesley 28-36; V of E w W Looe 37-45; St Geo Mart Truro 45-64. *63 Daniell Road, Truro, Cornw.* (Truro 3169)

HEWSON, John Patrick. b 19. M RCS, LRCP 57. **d** 72 Bunb. Hon C of Albany 72-77; Perm to Offic Dio Nor from 79. *Address temp unknown.*

HEWTON, William Douglas. McMaster Univ Ont BA 61. Wycl Coll Tor BTh 64. **d** 63 **p** 64 Tor. C of St Pet Oshawa 63-64; I of N Essa 64-67; St Ninian Tor 67-76; Woodbridge 76-81; St Paul L'amoreaux City and Dio Tor from 81. *333 Finch Avenue East, Agincourt, Toronto, Ont, Canada.*

HEYDON, Francis Garland William Woodard. K Coll Lon Sambrooke Exhib 34, AKC 36. **d** 36 **p** 37 Lon. C of St Geo Mart w H Trin Holborn 36-37; Hayes (in c of St Nich Grange Pk) 37-39; St Pet Port Guernsey 39-40; All SS (in c of St Chris) W Southbourne 40-42; Dioc Insp of Schs Dio Win 41-42; Chap RAFVR 42-44; C-in-c of St Paul Paddington 45-52; V of H Trin Paddington (w St Paul from 52) 45-62; Asst Dioc Insp of Schs Dio Lon 48-62; R of Nuthurst 62-78. *Flat 26, Bromley College, London Road, Bromley, Kent, BR1 1PE.* (01-290 1731)

HEYDON, Lawrence. St Mich Th Coll Crafers 48. **d** 53 Adel **p** 54 River. C of Corowa 53-54; Griffith 54-59; R of Ariah Pk 59-62; Deniliquin 62-67; C of Gulliver Townsville 69-70; St Jas Cathl Townsville 70-71; CF (Austr) from 71; Perm to Offic Dio Syd 71-73; Dios Murray and Adel 73-77; Dio Newc from 77. *Infantry Centre, Singleton, NSW, Australia 2330.*

HEYES, Canon Rupert Lionel. Ch Coll Hobart 66. ACT ThL 68. **d** 68 **p** 69 Tas. R of Furneaux Is 68-71; Scottsdale 71-74; Devonport Dio Tas from 74; Can of Tas from 80. *3 Newton Street, Devonport, Tasmania 7310.* (004-24 2161)

HEYGATE, Jack Lincoln. b 11. CCC Cam 3rd cl Hist Trip pt i 31, BA (3rd cl Th Trip pt i) 33, MA 36. Cudd Coll 35. **d** 36 **p** 37 Win. C of St Ambrose Bournemouth 36-40; St Luke Pallion 40-44; R of Stibbington w Sibson 44-54; Water Newton 44-54; Hougham w Marston 54-65; V of Hough-on-the-Hill w Brandon and Gelston 55-65; R of Warbleton 65-69. *Windrush, Leafield, Oxford, OX8 5NP.* (Asthall Leigh 659)

HEYHOE, Jonathan Peter. b 53. Univ of Man BA 75. Trin Coll Bris 77. **d** 80 Guildf **p** 81 Dorking for Guildf. C of St Pet Woking Dio Guildf from 80. *12 Vicarage Road, Kingfield, Woking, Surrey, GU22 9BP.*

HEYL, Henry Albertus. b 18. **d** 75 Bp Carter for Johann **p** 76 Johann. C of St Pet Brakpan Dio Johann from 75. *305 St Andrew's Building, Prince George Avenue, Brakpan 1540, S Africa.*

✠ **HEYWARD, Right Rev Oliver Spencer.** Univ of Tas BA (Hons) 49. Late Rhodes Scho of Or Coll Ox BA 52, MA 56. Cudd Coll 51. **d** 53 **p** 54 Chich. C of Brighton 53-56; R of Sorell 56-60; Richmond 60-62; Prec St D Cathl Hobart 62-63; Warden Ch Coll Hobart 63-75; Cons Ld Bp of Bend in St Paul's Cathl Melb 1 Feb 75 by Abp of Melb; Bps of Wang, St Arn, Tas and River; and others. *Bishopscourt, Forest Street, Bendigo, Vic, Australia 3550.* (054-43 4668)

HEYWOOD, Geoffrey Thomas. b 26. St Mich Coll Llan 60. **d** 62 **p** 63 Ban. C of Portmadoc 62-64; Llandudno 64-67; V of Caerhun w Llangelynin 67-74; Asst Chap HM Pris Walton 74-75; Chap HM Pris Ex 75-77; HM Pris Wakef 77-79; HM Pris Leyhill Glouc from 79; HM Detention Centre Eastwood Pk & Officers Tr Sch Leyhill from 79. *Leyhill Prison, Wotton-under-Edge, Glos.*

HEYWOOD, Very Rev Hugh Christopher Lemprière. b 1896. Late Exhib and Scho of Trin Coll Cam 1st cl Th Trip pt i and Carus Gr Test Pri 24, BA (1st cl Th Trip pt i w distinc) and Stanton Stud 25, 1st cl Th Trip pt ii w distinc 27, MA 29. Westcott Ho Cam 25. **d** 26 **p** 27 Ely. [f in Army] C of St Andr Gt Cam 26-27; Greenford 27-28; CF (R of O) 28-37; Exam Chap to Bp of S'wark 32-42; Select Pr Univ of Cam 32, 33, 38, 40, 45, and 49; Ox 42, 43, 44, and 63; Pro-Proctor Univ of Cam 33-34 and 41-42; Jun Proctor 34-35 and 42-43; Addl Pro-Proctor 35-37; Lect in Div 37-45; Fell and Dean of G and C Coll Cam 28-45; Exam Chap to Bp of Southw 41-69; Provost of Southw and R of St Mary Virg Southw 45-69; Provost (Emer) from 76; Proc Conv Southw 45-69; RD of Southw 45-56; Hulsean Pr Univ of Cam 56-57; Ch Comm 62-68; C-in-c of Upton 69-76. *26 Lyndewode Road, Cambridge.*

HEYWOOD, John. Egerton Hall, Man 35. **d** 35 **p** 36 Man. C of St Clem Chorlton-cum-Hardy 35-37; St Matt Stretford 37-41; Davenham 41-46; C-in-c of St Marg Dunham Massey 46-47; V of Seacombe 47-53; Dunham Massey 53-75. *Dumbreck, Sylvan Grove, Altrincham, Ches.*

HEYWOOD, Michael Herbert. b 41. Univ of Liv BSc 63. Clifton Th Coll 63. **d** 65 **p** 66 Newc T. C of St Steph Newc T 65-68; St Mark St Helens 68-75; NE Area & Cumbria Org Leprosy Miss 75-78; L to Offic Dio Dur from 75. *72 Station Road, Hetton-le-Hole, T & W, DH5 9JB.* (Hetton 263180)

HEYWOOD, Peter. b 29. K Coll Lon and Warm AKC 54. **d** 55 **p** 56 Newc T. C of Tynemouth 55-59; Seaton Hirst 59-63; V of St John Sleekburn 63-71; St Luke Wallsend Dio Newc T from 71; M Gen Syn from 80. *St Luke's Vicarage, Wallsend, T & W.* (Wallsend 623723)

HEYWOOD, Peter. b 46. Cranmer Hall Dur 72. **d** 75 **p** 76 Man. C of St Andr Blackley 75-78; Ch Ch Denton 78-80; V of Constable Lee Dio Man from 80. *76 Burnley Road, Rawtenstall, Rossendale, Lancs, BB4 8EW.* (Rossendale 228634)

HEYWOOD, Samuel Frank Bruce. b 30. Oak Hill Coll 79. **d** 81 Buckingham for Ox. C of Chenies w L Chalfont Dio Ox from 81. *St George's Parsonage, White Lion Road, Amersham Common, Amersham, Bucks HP7 9LW.*

HEYWOOD-WADDINGTON, Roger. b 23. Bps' Coll Cheshunt 58. **d** 58 **p** 59 Heref. C of Leominster 58-61; V of Neen Savage w Kinlet Dio Heref from 61; C-in-c of Cleeton w Silvington Dio Heref from 76. *Neen Savage Vicarage, Kidderminster, Worcs.* (Cleobury Mortimer 278)

HEZEL, Adrian. b 43. Univ of Lon BSc 64, PhD 67. NOC 78. **d** 81 Pontefract for Wakef (NSM). C of St Mary Mirfield Dio Wakef from 81; Lect Leeds Poly from 81. *1 Blake Hall Road, Mirfield, W Yorks, WF14 9NN.*

HEZRONA, Rahova. **d** 77 Diego S. d Dio Diego S. *Eklesia Episkopaly Malagasy, Ambahatra, Bemanevika, Ambanja, Malagasy Republic.*

HIBBERD, Brian Jeffery. b 35. Fitzw Ho Cam 2nd cl Th Trip pt i, 56, BA (2nd cl Th Trip pt ii) 58, MA 62. Ridley Hall, Cam 58. **d** 60 **p** 61 Ely. C of H Trin Cam 60-63; St Mary Doncaster 63-66; Asst Master Price's Sch Fareham 66-69; Warblington Sch Havant 69-73; Carisbrooke High Sch from 73. *10 Wray Street, Ryde, IW.*

HIBBERD, John Charles. b 38. Chich Th Coll 63. **d** 66 Kens for Lon **p** 67 Lon. C of W Drayton 66-70; St Mark Wood Green 70-72; St Steph W Ealing 72-75; V of St Jas Gunnersbury Dio Lon from 75. *St James's Vicarage, Chiswick High Road, Gunnersbury, W4 5QQ.* (01-994 0936)

HIBBERT, Charles Dennis. b 24. Linc Th Coll 69. **d** 70 **p** 71 Southn. C of Radcliffe-on-Trent Dio Southw 70-73; C-in-c of St Mary Ladybrook Mansfield 73-77; V 77-79; Ollerton Dio Southw from 79; Boughton Dio Southw from 79. *New Ollerton Vicarage, Newark, Notts.* (Mansfield 860323)

HIBBERT, James Raymond. b 10. St Pet Coll Ox BA (2nd cl Engl Lang and Lit) 32, MA 36. Wycl Hall, Ox 32. **d** 34 **p** 35 Liv. C of Em Southport 34-37; Lanc Priory 38-45; CF (TA-R of O) 39-56; Active Service 40-45; V of Fulwood 45-75; Chap Sharoe Green Hosp 47-71; Ed Blackb Dioc Mag 49-64; L to Offic Dio Blackb from 75. *39 Harrison Road, Fulwood, Preston, PR2 4QJ.* (Preston 719113)

HIBBERT, Roy Trevor. b 30. K Coll Lon and Warm AKC (2nd cl) 54. **d** 55 **p** 56 Lich. C of St Francis Friar Pk W Bromwich 55-58; Cannock (in c of St John Heath Hayes) 58-60; Min of Sneyd Green Eccles Distr 60-62; V 62-67; Harlescott 67-81; Surr from 68; R of Newport w Longford and Chetwynd Dio Lich from 81. *Rectory, Newport, Shropshire.* (0952-810089)

HIBBITTS, John Bernard. Dalhousie Univ Halifax NS BA (Hons Engl) 45, MA 46. Univ of K Coll Halifax, BSLitt w distinc 48. Gen Th Sem NY STB 49, STM 51. Univ Coll Ox DPhil 54. **d** 47 NS **p** 48 Bp Suffr of NY for NS. On leave 48-55; Fell and Tutor Gen Th Sem NY 49-51; Actg Chap

Univ Coll Ox 52; Assoc Prof in Div K Coll Halifax NS from 55; Prof of Bibl Stud from 60; Dean of Div from 63. *640 Francklyn Street, Halifax, NS, Canada.* (423-6939)

HIBBS, Canon Lawrence Winston. b 14. Kelham Th Coll 31. **d** 37 **p** 38 S'wark. C of St John Walworth 37-39; St Alphage Hendon 39-46; R of H Trin Jersey 46-55; Chap Jersey Gen Hosp 50-55; V of St Alb Bournemouth 55-68; Chandler's Ford 68-75; Chap R Vic Hosp Bournemouth 65-68; Proc Conv Win 68-70; R of Grouville Jersey Dio Win from 75; Hon Can of Win Cathl from 76. *Grouville Rectory, Jersey, CI.* (Central 53073)

HICHENS, Anthony. b 29. K Coll Lon and Warm AKC 59. **d** 60 Lon **p** 61 Kens for Lon. C of St Hilda Ashford 60-64; St Wilfrid Leeds 64-66; V of Waramuri 67-75; P-in-c of Stratton Audley w Goddington Dio Ox from 76; Finmere w Mixbury Dio Ox from 76; Stoke Lyne Dio Ox from 76; Fringford w Hethe and Newton Purcell Dio Ox from 76. *Manor Cottage, Stratton Audley, Bicester, Oxon, OX6 9BW.* (Stratton Audley 238)

HICHENS, Thomas Sikes. b 11. Wells Th Coll 48. **d** 50 **p** 51 St E. C of St Marg Ipswich 50-51; R of Westerfield 51-62; V of Zennor 62-69; PC of Towednack 62-69; R of Stoke Climsland 69-76; Perm to Offic Dio Truro from 76; Chap St Mich's Mount Marazion from 77. *Perch Cottage, Lamorna Cove, Penzance, Cornw.* (Mousehole 395)

HICK, Geoffrey Lockwood Allanson. b 07. Qu Coll Cam BA 31, MA 35. Wycl Hall Ox 31. **d** 33 **p** 34 Sheff. C of St Pet Bentley 33-37; Ecclesall 37-40; V of Campsall 40-53; R of Brechin 53-78; R of Lochlee 54-78. *Balloch View, Church Street, Edzell, DD9 7TQ.* (Edzell 219)

HICKES, Roy Edward. b 31. Dipl Th (Lon) 60. St Aid Coll 56. **d** 59 **p** 60 Man. C of St Jas New Bury Farnworth 59-63; Ven Bede Wyther Leeds 63-65; V of St Andr Oldham 65-69; Smallbridge 69-79; R of Winford Dio B & W from 79; V of Felton Common Dio B & W from 80. *Rectory, Winford, Bristol.* (Lulsgate 2526)

HICKEY, Canon Francis Joseph. b 20. AKC 49. St Bonif Coll Warm 49. **d** 50 **p** 51 Portsm. C of St Mary Portsea 50-58; V of Tilbury Dks Dio Chelmsf from 58; Chap Tilbury Seamen's Hosp from 58; Surr from 58; RD of Orsett and Grays from 70; Hon Can of Chelmsf Cathl from 79. *Vicarage, Dock Road, Tilbury, Essex.* (Tilbury 2417)

HICKIN, Leonard Charles. b 05. Late Scho of Magd Coll Cam 1st cl Cl Trip pt i 25, BA (2nd cl Cl Trip pt ii) 26, 2nd cl Th Trip pt i 27, MA 30. Ridley Hall Cam 26. **d** 28 **p** 29 S'wark. C of St Mary Magd Peckham 28-30; CMS Miss Old Cairo 30-33; Dio Lagos 34-38; CMS Sec N Nigeria Miss 38-43; Tutor at Oak Hill Th Coll 43-44; V of St Jo Bapt Folkestone 44-51; Selly Hill 51-64; RD of Moseley 62-64; Hon Can of Birm 64-67; R of Chesham Bois 64-73. *7 Nelson Close, Winchmore Hill, Amersham, Bucks, HP7 0PB.* (Amersham 5004)

HICKIN, Maurice Whitehouse. St Cath Coll Cam 2nd cl Eng Trip pt i, 30, BA (2nd cl Or Lang Trip pt i) 32, MA 38. Univ of Bonn 32. Ely Th Coll 33. **d** 34 **p** 35 Lon. C of St Andr W Kens 34-35; St Pet Lon Dks 35-36; Miss P St Aug Coll Kumasi 36-38; C of St Mary Magd Paddington 40-46; St Mich AA Beckenham 46-48; St Andr Worthing 48-51; Clewer (in c of St Agnes Spital) 51-55; Perm to Offic Dio Ox 55-58; C of Kirkley 58-61; R of Runwell 61-75. *Casa de Nuestra, Senora, Benidoleig, Alicante, Spain.*

HICKIN, Ronald Arrowsmith. BA (Syd) 65. **d** and **p** 44 Syd. C of Provisional Distr of Kingsgrove w Bexley North 44-45; I of All SS Cammeray 45-48; R of St Paul Syd 48-56; on leave 56-57; R of Sans Souci 57-60; Dep Sec BFBS in Austr from 60; L to Offic Dio Syd from 60; Dio C & Goulb from 69. *223 Phillip Lodge, Kilvington Village, Castle Hill, NSW, Australia 2154.* (680-2421)

HICKINBOTHAM, James Peter. b 14. Exhib of Magd Coll Ox BA (1st cl Mod Hist) 35, 1st cl Th 37, MA 42. DD (Lambeth) 79. Wycl Hall Ox 35. **d** 37 **p** 38 Leic. C of St Jo Bapt Knighton 37-39; Perm to Offic at H Trin Brompton 39-40; C of St Paul S Harrow 40-42; Chap of Wycl Hall Ox 42-45; Actg Chap of Wadham Coll Ox 42-45; LPr Dio Ox 44-50; Vice-Prin Wycl Hall Ox 45-50; Exam Chap to Bp of Man 47-50; to Bp of Leic 48-54; Prof of Th at Univ Coll of Gold Coast 50-54; Prin St Jo Coll (and Cranmer Hall from 58) Dur and L to Offic Dio Dur 54-70; Exam Chap to Bp of Dur 55-66 and 68-70; Proc Conv Dur from 58-70; Hon Can of Dur 59-70; Commiss Sier L 59-61; Ibad 60-72; Port Eliz from 75; Prin Wycl Hall Ox 70-79; Hon C of Ch Ch Downend Dio Bris from 81. *46 Chesterfield Road, Downend, Bristol, BS16 5RQ.* (Bris 562054)

HICKLEY, Peter Michael. b 28. Ely Th Coll 56. **d** 59 **p** 60 Lon. C of St Steph Shepherd's Bush Hammersmith 59-62; Good Shepherd w St Pet Lee 62-66; V of Carlton Yorks 66-68; C of Ch of Ch and St John w St Luke Poplar 68-70; R of St John of Jer w Ch Ch S Hackney 70-77; Euston w Barnham and Fakenham Magna 77-80; R of Fenny Stratford w Water Eaton Dio Ox from 80. *Fenny Stratford Vicarage, Manor Road, Bletchley, Milton Keynes, Bucks, 2825)*

HICKLING, Colin John Anderson. b 31. K Coll Cam BA 53, MA 57. Chich Th Coll 56. **d** 57 **p** 58 Dur. C of St Luke Pallion Bp Wearmouth 57-61; Asst Tutor Chich Th Coll 61-65; Asst PV of Chich Cathl 64-65; Asst Lect K Coll Lon 65-68; Lect from 68; Hon C of St Mary Magd Munster Square 68-69; St John E Dulwich from 70; Dep Min Can of St Paul's Cathl Lon 69-78; Dep P in Ord to HM the Queen 71-74; P in Ord from 74; Sub-Warden K Coll Hall 69-78; Warden K Coll Hostel 78-81. *44 Westminster Place Gardens, Artillery Row, SW1P 1RR.* (01-222 1832)

HICKLING, Frank William. b 08. Linc Th Coll 41. **d** and **p** 41 Linc. C of Clee w Cleethorpes 41-44; PC of Barlings w Langworth 44-49; V of Stainton-by-Langworth w Newball Coldstead and Reasby 44-49; Coalbrookdale 49-57; R of Wetheral w Warw 57-60; V of Hartshill 60-71; Ruyton-XI-towns 71-75; Perm to Offic Dio Lich from 75. *52 Walford Road, Oswestry, Salop, SY11 2LE.* (Oswestry 5729)

HICKLING, John. b 34. **d** 69 **p** 70 Leic. C of Melton Mowbray 69-71; Team V 71-75; R of Waltham-on-the-Wolds w Stonesby and Saltby Dio Leic from 75. *Rectory, Waltham-on-the-Wolds, Melton Mowbray, Leics, LE14 4AJ.* (Waltham 233)

HICKMAN, Geoffrey Donald. Univ of Auckld BA 64. St Jo Coll Auckld NZ Bd of Th Stud LTh (2nd cl) 66. **d** 66 **p** 67 Auckld. C of New Lynn 66-70; Panmure 70-71; V of Kamo-Hikurangi 71-80; Archd of Waimate 77-81; V of Takapuna Dio Auckld from 80. *Vicarage, Killarney Street, Takapuna, Auckland, NZ.*

HICKMAN, George May. b 11. AKC 33. **d** 35 **p** 36 Lon. C of Hayes 35-36; St Paul Bow Common 36-39; Bray 39-41; V of Beedon 41-45; St Barn Rotherhithe 45-50; R of Nettlecombe 50-68; Withycombe w Rodhuish Dio B & W from 68. *Withycombe Rectory, Minehead, Somt.* (Washford 227)

HICKOX, Sidney Edwin. b 13. AKC 36. **d** 36 **p** 37 Ox. C of St Luke Maidenhead 36-40; Leatherhead (in c of All SS) 40-42; V of Stokenchurch 42-55; Cadmore End 49-55; Wooburn 55-72; R of Hedsor 55-72; V of Bisham Dio Ox from 72. *Bisham Vicarage, Marlow, Bucks.* (Marlow 2743)

HICKS, Bradley Charles Alfred. b 56. Univ of Sherbrooke PQ BTh 80. **d** 79 **p** 80 Queb. C of Saguenay Dio Queb from 79. *182 Radin Road, Arvida, Que, Canada, G7S 2M1.*

HICKS, Francis Fuller. b 28. Sarum Wells Th Coll 71. **d** 74 Sarum **p** 75 Sherborne for Sarum. C of Broadstone 74-77; P-in-c of Kington Magna and Buckhorn Weston 77-79; Team V of Gillingham Dio Sarum from 79. *Buckhorn Weston Rectory, Gillingham, Dorset, SP8 5HG.* (0963-70215)

HICKS, Henry Edward. Univ of NZ BA 57. St Jo Coll Auckld LTh 59. **d** 60 Bp Rich for Wel **p** 61 Wel. C of All SS Palmerston N 60-65; V of Eketahuna 65-69; Featherston 69-73; Marton 73-78; St Pet Palmerston N Dio Wel from 78. *225 Ruahine Street, Palmerston North, NZ.* (85-403)

HICKS, Herbert. b 10. Bede Coll Dur BA 32, MA 47. Ridley Hall Cam 34. **d** 36 **p** 37 Leic. C of Humberstone 36-38; Knighton 38-43; V of St Andr Starbeck 43-55; Bramhope 55-75. *2 Larkfield Drive, Harrogate, N Yorks.*

HICKS, Michael Keith. Univ of Tor BA 49, MA 50. Gen Th Sem NY STB 60. **d** 60 **p** 61 Ott. C of Smith's Falls 60-61; Div Tutor Trin Coll Tor 61-63; Angl Chap Univ of Manit 63-67; Asst Prof Pol Sc from 67; P-in-c of Grace Ch Winnipeg 68-71; on leave. *256 First Avenue, Ottawa, Ont., Canada.*

HICKS, Peter John. b 27. Keble Coll Ox BA 50, MA 64. Coll of Resurr Mirfield. **d** 67 Pontefract for Wakef **p** 68 Wakef. C of Huddersfield 67-70; V of Hanging Heaton 70-78; Stanley Dio Wakef from 78. *Stanley Vicarage, Aberford Road, Wakefield, Yorks, WF3 4HE.* (Wakef 822143)

HICKS, Richard Barry. b 32. Univ of Dur BA 55. Sarum Th Coll 59. **d** 61 **p** 62 Newc T. C of St Luke Wallsend 61-64; Tynemouth 64-69; V of St Jo Evang Percy Tynemouth 69-75; Prudhoe Dio Newc T from 75. *Vicarage, Prudhoe, Northumb, NE42 5HH.* (Prudhoe 32595)

HICKS, Stuart Knox. b 34. Univ of W Ont BA 56. Hur Coll LTh 59. **d** 58 **p** 60 Sktn. C of St Jo Evang Lon Ont 58-59; I of Endeavour 59-62; R of St Geo w Sarcee Calg 62-65; C of Allerton 65-66; Asst Master Enfield Gr Sch 67-72; Hon C of Rye Pk Hoddesdon 68-72; Asst Master Beechen Cliff Sch Bath from 72; Sec Bath Coun of Chr Chs 75-77; Actg Chap St Mary Magd Chap Holloway Bath from 80. *16 Kensington Place, Bath, BA1 6AP.* (Bath 313023)

HICKS, William Trevor. b 47. Univ of Hull BA (2nd cl Th) 68. Fitzw Coll Cam BA (Th Trip pt 3) 70, MA 74. Westcott Ho Cam 68. **d** 70 **p** 71 York. C of Cottingham 70-73; Elland (in c of All SS) 73-76; V of Walsden 76-81; Knottingley Dio Wakef from 81. *Vicarage, Knottingley, W Yorks, WF11 9AN.* (Knottingley 82267)

HIGDON, Lewis George. b 36. Univ of Dur BA (2nd cl Psychology) 58, Dipl Th 60. Cranmer Hall, Dur 58. **d** 60 **p** 61 Ripon. C of Leeds 60-65; Shipley 65-66; V of Esholt w

Hawksworth 67-75; Kirkstall 75-79; Stanwix Dio Carl from 79. *Stanwix Vicarage, St Georges Crescent, Carlisle, Cumb.* (Carlisle 24978)

HIGGINBOTHAM, Brian Gordon. ACT ThL 60. Moore Th Coll Syd 58. **d** 61 Syd **p** 61 Bp Kerle for Syd. C of Parramatta 61-62; CMS Miss Mwanza 63-66; Katoke 66-69; Oenpelli 69-70; C-in-c of Dundas 70-78; R 78-79; St Bede Drummoyne Dio Syd from 79. *19 College Street, Drummoyne, NSW, Australia 2047.* (81-1653)

HIGGINBOTTOM, Richard. b 48. Univ of Lon Dipl Th (Extra-Mural) 72, BD (Lon) 74. Oak Hill Coll 70. **d** 74 Cov **p** 75 Bp McKie for Cov. C of St Jo Evang Kenilworth 74-77; St Martin-in-the-Fields Finham 77-79; V of Attleborough Dio Cov from 79. *Attleborough Vicarage, Nuneaton, Warws, CV11 4JW.* (Nuneaton 382926)

HIGGINS, Alexander George Maclennan Pearce. b 1900. Ch Coll Cam BA 22, MA 26, Seatonian Pr 52, 56 and 61. **d** 38 **p** 39 Cov. C of Stockingford 38-40; R of Croxton 40-46; V of Eltisley 40-46; R of Holywell w Needingworth 46-60; Boxford w Hadleigh Hamlet 60-65; V of Madingley 65-70. *19 Thornton Court, Girton, Cambridge.*

HIGGINS, Angus John Brockhurst. b 11. Univ of Wales, BA 34, MA 37. Univ of Man BD 39, PhD 45, DD 65. **d** 56 **p** 57 Bradf. Lect in NT Univ of Leeds 56-61; Sen Lect 61-66; Reader 66-70; C of St Marg Ilkley 56-70; Prof of Th St D Univ Coll Lamp 70-76. *Cwm, North Road, Lampeter, Dyfed.*

HIGGINS, Bernard George. b 27. Wycl Hall Ox 68. **d** 70 **p** 72 S'wark. C of St Matt Surbiton 70-72; St Mary Battersea 72-76; Warblington w Emsworth 77-81; Milton (in c of St Patr) Dio Portsm from 81. *Parsonage, Empshott Road, Southsea, PO4 8BY.* (Portsm 32943)

HIGGINS, Frank Roylance. b 34. Open Univ BA 74. Bps' Coll Cheshunt 59. **d** 62 **p** 63 Dur. C of Sunderland 62-64; S Westoe 64-66; C-in-c of St Mich AA Smethwick Dio Birm 66-67; V 67-70; Garretts Green 70-75; L to Offic Dio Worc from 76. *Warden's Flat, The Polytechnic, King Edmund Street, Dudley, W Midl, DY1 3HU.*

HIGGINS, Frank William. b 17. Sarum Th Coll 67. **d** 69 Bp MacInnes for Sarum **p** 70 Sarum. C of Trowbridge 69-72; Perm to Offic Dio Sarum from 72. *39 West Ashton Road, Trowbridge, Wilts, BA14 7BL.*

HIGGINS, Geoffrey Minta. b 27. New Coll Ox BA (2nd cl Th) 52, MA 56. Cudd Coll 52. **d** 54 **p** 55 Pet. C of St Mary Pet 54-56; CF 56-77. *Flat H 18th Floor, Far East Consortium Building, Main Road, Yuen)*

HIGGINS, Godfrey. b 39. St Chad's Coll Dur BA 61, Dipl Th 62. **d** 63 **p** 64 Wakef. C of Brighouse 63-66; St Jo Evang Huddersfield 66-68; R of High Hoyland 68-75; V of Marsden Dio Wakef from 75. *Marsden Vicarage, Huddersfield, HD7 6DG.* (Huddersfield 844174)

HIGGINS, James Alroy. Montr Dioc Th Coll LTh 66. **d** 65 **p** 66 Sask. I of Paddockwood 65-69; Arborfield 69-70. *Box 62, Tisdale, Sask., Canada.*

HIGGINS, John. b 44. Trin Coll Bris 71. **d** 73 **p** 74 S'wark. C of St Jas Clapham Park 73-74; St Sav w St Matt Ruskin Park 74-76; Hamworthy 76-80; V of Bordesley Dio Birm from 80. *117 Green Lane, Birmingham, B9 5BW.* (021-772 1533)

HIGGINS, John Leslie. b 43. Lich Th Coll 64. **d** 66 **p** 67 Ches. C of St Anne Sale 66-69; Bredbury 69-72; V of Wharton 72-74; Hon C of Lockerbie 75-79; Annan 75-79; V of Coseley Dio Lich from 79. *Christ Church Vicarage, Coseley, Bilston, Staffs, WV14 8YB.* (Bilston 42178)

HIGGINS, Canon John Norman. b 14. Em Coll Cam 2nd cl Mod Lang Trip pt i, 34, BA (3rd cl Th Trip pt i) 36, MA 40. Wells Th Coll 39. **d** 40 **p** 41 York. C of St Paul Thornaby-on-Tees 40-42; Chap RNVR 42-46 C of All SS Fulham 46-47; V of Wilton 47-51; Twerton-on-Avon 51-58; Greenwich 58-64; Redcar 64-67; V of Kirkleatham 64-67; RD of Guisborough 64-67; R of Sutton Surrey 67-77; Exam Chap to Bp of S'wark from 72; Hon Can of S'wark Cathl from 76; R of Limpsfield w Titsey Dio S'wark from 77. *Limpsfield Rectory, Oxted, Surrey.* (Oxted 2512)

HIGGINS, Leslie. b 07. **d** 65 **p** 66 Ches. C of Northwich 65-68; V of Lostock Gralam 68-75; C of Over w Winsford 75-81. *170 Middlewich Road, Clive, Winsford, Chesh.* (Winsford 4357)

HIGGINS, Michael John. b 35. Univ of Birm LLB 57. G and C Coll Cam LLB 59, PHD 62. Ridley Hall, Cam 63. **d** and **p** 65 Warrington for Liv. C of Ormskirk 65-67; Selection Sec ACCM 67-74; Hon C of St Mark Marylebone Road 69-74; V of Frome Selwood 74-80; C-in-c of Woodlands 74-80; Team R of Preston Dio Blackb from 80. *13 Ribblesdale Place, Preston, Lancs.* (Preston 52528)

HIGGINS, Timothy John. b 45. Univ of Bris BEduc 70. Univ of Lanc MA 74. St Jo Coll Dur Dipl Th 79. **d** 79 **p** 80 Pet. C of All SS Northn Dio Pet from 79. *5 Woodland Avenue, Northampton, NN3 2BY.* (Northn 713335)

HIGGINSON, Alexander Boyd. Trin Coll Tor BA 1898, MA 1899. **d** 00 **p** 01 Niag. Miss at Smithville Ont 00-03; I of Waterdown Ont 03-05; C of St Pet Sherbrooke PQ 05-07; Ascen Hamilton Ont 07-09; R of Georgetown w Glenwilliams 09-16; Port Dalhousie 16-20; Fergus 22-23; Hagersville 23-27; on leave 27-28; I of Aldershot 28-32; Glanford w Tapleytown Woodburn and Rymal 32-41. *Apt 806, 160 Hughson Street, Hamilton, Ont, Canada.*

HIGGINSON, Arthur Rothwell. b 14. Edin Th Coll 48. **d** 51 **p** 52 Glas. C of Ch Ch Glas 51-52; St Mary's Cathl Glas 52-54; R of Weldon 55-64; RD of Weldon 62-64; V of Ch Ch Northn 64-74; St Mich Whitewell 74-79; P-in-c of Hurst Green 76-79; Mytton 76-79. *24 Moorlands, 103 Garstang Road, Preston, Lancs PR1 1NN.* (0772 51660)

HIGGINSON, Christopher Paul Aubrey. b 38. St Steph Ho Ox. **d** 67 Bp T M Hughes for Llan **p** 68 Llan. C of Merthyr Dyfan 67-71. *Clarebrook, St Clears, Carms.*

HIGGINSON, Gerald Scott. b 29. Univ of Keele BA 54. Univ of Birm PhD 57. N-W Ordin Course 73. **d** 76 **p** 77 York. Hon C of St Mary Bishophill Jun w All SS N Street City and Dio York from 76. *The Provost's House, Vanbrugh College, The University, York, YO1 5DD.* (York 413149)

HIGGINSON, Richard Edwin. b 15. St Jo Coll Dur BA 39, MA 42. Univ of Lon BD (2nd cl) 51. Tyndale Hall, Bris 35. **d** 39 **p** 40 Blackb. C of All SS Preston 39-42; Ch Ch Chadderton 42-44; V of Em Chadderton 44-47; St Pet Halliwell 47-56; Redland 56-69; Em S Croydon 69-78; P-in-c of Weeton 78-80. *30 Pennine Way, Great Eccleston, Nr Preston, Lancs.* (9294-70634)

HIGGS, Allan Herbert Morris. b 22. St Jo Coll Dur BA 48, Dipl Th (w distinc) 50. **d** 50 **p** 51 Newc T. C of Morpeth 50-54; V of Amble 54-61; St Jas and St Basil Newc T 61-75; Adv in Adult Educn Dio Linc 75-80; V of Stamfordham w Matfen Dio Newc T from 80. *Stamfordham Vicarage, Newcastle upon Tyne, NE18 0QQ.* (Stamfordham 456)

HIGGS, David Allan. **d** 72 **p** 73 Edmon. Hon C of St Mich AA Edmon 72-75; St Paul Edmon 75-79; St Luke Regina Dio Qu'App from 79. *1730 Uhrich Avenue, Regina, Sask, Canada.*

✠ **HIGGS, Right Rev Hubert Laurence.** b 11. Late Scho of Ch Coll Cam 1st cl Cl Trip pt i 32 BA (1st cl Th Trip pt i) 34, MA 37. Ridley Hall Cam 34. **d** 35 S'wark **p** 36 Lon. C of H Trin Richmond 35-36; St Luke Redcliffe Square S Kens 36-38; St John Boscombe and Jt Sec Win Dioc Coun of Youth 38-39; V of H Trin Aldershot 39-45; Ed Sec CMS 45-52; V of St Jo Bapt Woking w Knaphill and Brookwood 52-57; Proc Conv Guildf 55-57; RD of Woking 56-57; Can Res of Bradf 57-65; Archd of Bradf 57-65; Cons Ld Bp Suffr of Hull in York Minster 27 May 65 by Abp of York; Bps of Dur; Carl; Bradf; Sheff; Chelmsf; and Roch; Bps Suffr of Warrington; Whitby; Pontefract; Selby; and Jarrow; and Bp Townley; res 76; RD of Hull 72-76; Perm to Offic Dio St E from 76. *The Farmstead, Chediston, Halesworth, Suff.*

HIGGS, Hubert Richard. Keble Coll Ox BA (2nd cl Th) 14, MA 20. **d** 14 **p** 15 Ox. Hebr Lect Cudd Coll and C of Cuddesdon 14-20; TCF 18-20; C of St Mary Johann 20-22; Chap of Pro-Cathl Lourenco Marques 22-23; V of Clifton w Vrededorp 23-27; Modderfontein 27-29; Exam Chap to Bp of Johann 26-49; Dioc SS Org and Missr 29-31; P-in-c of W Transvaal 31-35; E Rand Miss 35-40; R of St Gabr Boksburg N 36-40; Randfontein 40-46; Bezuidenhout Valley 46-47; Potchefstroom 47-49; L to Offic Dio Natal from 49. *PO Kloof, Natal, S Africa.*

HIGGS, Michael John. b 53. Sarum Wells Th Coll 76. **d** 80 **p** 81 Cant. C of St Martin w St Paul City and Dio Cant from 80. *16 Love Lane, Canterbury, Kent.*

HIGGS, Stanley Eaton. Univ of Dur LTh 27. St Aug Coll Cant 23. **d** 27 Cant for Col **p** 28 Carib. Miss among N-Amer Indians 27-33; Bonaparte Miss 33-35; Quesnel 35-37; Lytton Ind Miss 37-41; Chap CASF 41-46; C of Ch Ch Cathl Vanc 46-49; R of St Mich Vanc 49-60; Hon Can of New Westmr 57-74; Chap Haney Correctional Inst 60-68; Dir Centr City Miss Vanc 69-74. *209-4775 Valley Drive, Vancouver, BC, Canada.*

HIGH, Gordon Maurice Verdun. b 16. Keble Coll Ox BA (2nd cl Th) 48, MA 52. St Steph Ho Ox 48. **d** 50 **p** 51 Ox. C of Kidlington and Hampton Poyle 50-52; H Cross Miss E Pondoland 52-54; C-in-c of Somerset E 54-56; PC of Claydon w Mollington 56-61; R of Charwelton w Fawsley and Preston Capes 61-81. *2 Spring Close, Daventry, Northants.* (Daventry 77749)

HIGHAM, Gerald Norman. b 40. St Aid Coll 64. **d** 68 Warrington for Liv **p** 69 Liv. C of St Mich Garston 68-71; Blundellsands 71-73; V of All S w St Jas Bolton-le-Moors 73-78; Tonge w Alkrington Dio Man from 78. *Tonge Vicarage, Townley Street, Middleton, Manchester, M24 1BT.* (061-643 2891)

HIGHAM, Jack. b 33. Late Scho and Pri of Linc Coll Ox

BA (2nd cl Mod Lang) 56, 2nd cl Th 58, MA and Ellerton Pri 60. Univ of Birm Dipl Th 59. U Th Sem NY STM (*summa cum laude*) 61. Qu Coll Birm 58. **d** 60 **p** 61 Sheff. C of Handsworth 60-64; Ecumenical Fell U Th Sem NY 60-61; Stephenson Fell Univ of Sheff 63-64; V of Handsworth-Woodhouse 64-70; in Amer Ch 70-78; R of Stoke Bruerne w Grafton Regis and Alderton Dio Pet from 78. *Stoke Bruerne Rectory, Towcester, Northants, NN12 7SD.* (Roade 862352)

HIGHAM, John Leonard. b 39. Wycl Hall Ox 62. **d** 65 Warrington for Liv **p** 66 Liv. C of Prescot (in c of St Paul Bryer Estate from 68) 65-71; V of Hollinfare 71-74; Adult and Youth Service Adv Knowsley 75-76; Team V of Padgate Dio Liv from 76. *Birchwood Vicarage, Birchwood, Warrington.* (Padgate 811906)

HIGHMORE, Geoffrey William. b 1897. Wells Th Coll 22. **d** 24 **p** 25 York. C of St John Newland 24-27; St Mary (in c of St Nich) Beverley 27-32; V of Newport Yorks 32-37; Stonehouse 37-49; R of Stonegrave w Nunnington 49-58; Chap Standish Ho Sanat 42-45; RD of Stonehouse 47-49; Helmsley 53-58; V of Welton w Melton 58-65; Perm to Offic Dio Nor 65-66; C-in-c of Merton Nor 66-69; Tottington w Tompson and Sturston 66-69; Hon C of Watton 71-81. *Guild House, Denmark Road, Gloucester.*

HIGTON, Anthony Raymond. b 42. BD (Lon) 65. Oak Hill Th Coll 65. **d** 67 **p** 68 Southw. C of Ch Ch Newark-on-Trent 67-69; St Mark Cheltenham 70-75; R of Hawkwell Dio Chelmsf from 75. *Hawkwell Rectory, Hockley, Essex.* (Southend-on-Sea 203870)

HIINI, Pateriki. b 12. **d** 77 Aotearoa for Wai. **p** 78 Wai. C of Te Puke Maori Past Dio Wai from 77. *RD 6, Te Puke, NZ.*

HILBORNE, Douglas Eric. b 27. Wycl Hall Ox 65. **d** 66 **p** 67 Sheff. C of St Paul Norton Lees Sheff 66-68; Thrybergh (in c of Whinney Hill) 68-71; R of Byers Green 71-75; P-in-c of All SS Monk Wearmouth 75-81; R of Ebchester Dio Dur from 81. *Ebchester Rectory, Consett, Co Durham.* (Ebchester 301)

HILCHEY, Ven Harry St Clair. Univ of Dalhousie, NS BA 41. Univ of Tor MA 45. Wycl Coll Tor LTh 44, BD 51, DD 72. **d** 44 **p** 45 Tor. I of Stanhope Miss 44-46; Alderwood and Queensway 46-51; St Eliz Queensway Tor 51-55; R of St Paul Halifax 55-64; Hon Can of NS 59-64; R of St Jas Ap Montr 64-79; Hon Can of Montr 67-74; Prin Montr Dioc Th Coll 74-78; Dioc Archd Dio Montr from 74; Gen Sec Gen Syn of Canada from 79. *600 Jarvis Street, Toronto, Ont, Canada, M4Y 2J6.*

HILDAGE, James Francis. Univ of Wales, BA 44. Coll of Resurr Mirfield. **d** 46 **p** 47 Derby. C of Long Eaton 46-51; Chesterfield 51-54; PC of Monyash 54-56; C-in-c of Earl Sterndale Dio Derby 54-56; V (w Monyash from 56) from 56; P-in-c of Taddington w Chelmorton and Flagg Dio Derby from 80. *Monyash Vicarage, Bakewell, Derbys.* (Bakewell 2234)

HILDEBRAND, Alton Roy. Moore Th Coll ACT ThL 54. **d** and **p** 55 Syd. C of Sutherland 55; C-in-c of Hammondville 56-57; Botany and Enmore 57; Chap Dioc Bd of Educn 58-61; Norf I 61-62; C-in-c of Wilberforce 62-65; McCallum's Hill 65-70; R of Wentworth Falls Dio Syd from 70. *17 Armstrong Street, Wentworth Falls, NSW, Australia 2782.* (047-57 1516)

HILDER, Geoffrey Frank. b 06. Late Scho of Linc Coll Ox BA (2nd cl Mod Hist) 28, MA 32. Ely Th Coll 30. [Called to the Bar 30] **d** 31 **p** 32 S'wark. C of St Jo Evang E Dulwich 31-34; Goldthorpe 35-37; R of Ruardean 37-41; V of St Steph Cheltm 41-48; L to Offic Dio Truro 48; PC of Hambridge w Earnshill 48-59; Dir of Moral Welfare Dio B & W 49-54; Proc Conv B & W 50-51; Archd of Taunton 51-71; Preb of Wells Cathl 51-73; Prolocutor of Lower Ho of Conv 55-70; Provost of W Div Woodard Corp 60-70. *4 Falcon Terrace, Bude, Cornwall, EX23 8LJ.*

HILDYARD, Christopher. Magd Coll Cam BA 23, MA 28. MVO 66. Cudd Coll 24. **d** 25 York **p** 26 York for Wakef. C of Glass Houghton 25-27; Guisborough 27-28; Asst Min Can of Westmr Abbey 28-32; Min Can 32-74; Sacr 59-74. *c/o 2 The Cloisters, Westminster, SW1.*

HILES, Douglas Arthur. b 18. St Deiniol's Libr Hawarden 78. **d** 80 **p** 81 Man. C of Ch Ch Heaton Dio Man from 80. *1 Thorncliffe Road, Sharples, Bolton, BL1 7ER.*

HILES, John Michael. b 32. Qu Coll Cam BA 57, MA 61. Sarum Th Coll 57. **d** 59 **p** 60 Sheff. C of Clifton 59-62; V of Bramley 62-69; Asst Master Honley High Sch Huddersfield from 70; L to Offic Dio Wakef from 69. *Rosehill, Parkhead Lane, Holmfirth, Huddersfield, HD7 1LB.* (Holmfirth 3045)

HILEY, Edgar William. b 07. Univ of Queensld BA 60. **d** 73 Brisb **p** 74 Bp Wicks for Brisb. Hon C of St Bart Mt Gravatt 73-75; V of Moorooka Brisb 75-78; Perm to Offic Dio Brisb from 78. *88 Tarragindi Road, Tarragindi, Queensland, Australia 4121.* (48 3947)

HILL, Adrian Ray. b 37. St Francis Coll Brisb 59. **d** and **p** 63 Bal. C of Portland 63; Colac 63-67; P-in-c of Merino 67-69; R of Coleraine 69-70; Miss at Santa Ysabel 70-74; R of Otway 74-77; Kenainj 77-78; St Geo Launceston Dio Tas from 78. *98 Invermay Road, Launceston, Tasmania 7250.* (003 26 1052)

HILL, Alfred Richard. b 1899. Bps' Coll Cheshunt 28. **d** 30 **p** 31 Man. C of St Jas Gorton 30-34; St Jo Evang Boxmoor 34-37; Chap HM Pris Lewes and L to Offic Dio Chich 37-40; Chap HM Pris Win 40-45; V of Vernham Dean w Linkenholt 45-65. *Duncliffe View, 31 Breach Lane, Shaftesbury, Dorset.*

HILL, Arthur Edward. b 31. Lich Th Coll 62. **d** 64 **p** 65 York. C of Elloughton 64-65; Ascen Derringham Bank Newington 65-68; V of Skidby Dio York from 68. *32 Main Street, Skidby, Cottingham, N Humb, HU16 5TG.* (0482 847652)

HILL, Canon Bernard. b 18. St D Coll Lamp BA 39. **d** 41 **p** 42 Southw. C of Mansfield Woodhouse 41-47; C-in-c of St Aug Bull Farm Conv Distr Pleasley Hill Mansfield 47-51; V of St Leon Newark 51-55; Sutton-in-Ashfield 55-65; R of Bulwell 65-70; RD of Bulwell 69-70; V of Thurgarton w Hoveringham Dio Southw from 70; C-in-c of Bleasby w Halloughton Dio Southw from 70; Hon Can of Southw from 71; RD of Southw from 72; C-in-c of Morton 76-80. *Thurgarton Vicarage, Nottingham.* (Newark 830234)

HILL, Brian John. b 43. Univ of Capetn BSc (Chem Eng) 64. ALCD 70. **d** 70 **p** 71 Capetn. C of Wynberg 70-78; P-in-c of Bothasig w Edgemead Dio Capetn 78-80; R from 80. *Rectory, De Hoop, Edgemead 7405, CP, S Africa.* (58-4139)

HILL, Charles Merrick. b 52. Univ of Strathclyde BA 74. Univ of Birm Dipl Th 79. Qu Coll Birm 77. **d** 80 **p** 81 Dur. C of Silksworth Dio Dur from 80. *22 Frobisher Court, Doxford Park, Sunderland, SR3 2LT.*

HILL, Christopher Glynn. b 43. Tyndale Hall Bris 66. **d** 70 **p** 71 Sarum. C of Longfleet 70-74; Warden Fellowship Ho Brentwood and L to Offic Dio Chelmsf from 74. *Lamb of God Community, Pilgrims' Hall, Brentwood, Essex.*

HILL, Christopher John. b 45. Univ of Lon BD 67, MTh 68. AKC 67. **d** 69 **p** 70 Lich. C of St Mich Tividale Tipton 69-73; Codsall 73-74; Asst Chap to Abp of Cant (Foreign Relns) and Sec Angl-RC Internat Comm 74-81; Abp of Cant Asst for Ecumen Affairs from 82. *Lambeth Palace, SE1 7JU.* (01-928 4880)

HILL, Christopher Matthias. Vic Univ of Wel BA 68. St Jo Coll Auckld. **d** 70 **p** 71 Wel. C of Karori 70-74; V of Foxton 74-79; Northland-Wilton Dio Wel from 79. *14 Farm Road, Wellington 5, NZ.* (759-085)

HILL, Colin. b 42. Univ of Leic BSc (2nd cl) 64. Ripon Hall Ox 64. **d** 66 **p** 67 Leic. C of The Martyrs, Leic 66-69; Braunstone 69-71; Lect Ecumen Inst Thornaby Teesside 71-72; V of St Thos w St Jas Worsbrough 72-78; Planning Officer Telford Dios Lich and Heref from 78; RD of Telford and of Telford Severn Gorge from 80. *Pakfield, Park Avenue, Madeley, Telford, Salop, TF7 5AB.* (0952-585731)

HILL, Canon Colin Arnold Clifford. b 29. Univ of Bris 52. Ripon Hall Ox 55. **d** 57 **p** 58 Sheff. C of Rotherham (in c of St Barn Broom Valley) 57-61; V of Brightside w Grimesthorpe Sheff 61-64; R of Easthampstead 64-73; Chap RAF Coll Bracknell 68-73; Proc in Conv Ox 70-73; M Gen Syn 70-73; and from 80; V of Croydon Dio cant from 73; Hon Can of Cant from 75. *22 Bramley Hill, South Croydon, Surrey, CR2 6LT.* (01-688 1387)

HILL, Canon David. b 25. K Coll Lon and Warm AKC 54. **d** 55 **p** 56 Lon. C of H Innoc Kingsbury 55-58; Putney (In c of All SS) 58-62; V of St Mich Wandsworth Common Dio S'wark from 62; RD of Battersea 69-76; Hon Can of S'wark from 74. *93 Bolingbroke Grove, SW11 6HA.* (01-228 1990)

HILL, David Michael. St Jo Coll Morpeth ThDip 72. **d** 71 **p** 72 C & Goulb. C of Manuka 71-73; Albury 74-75; S Wagga Wagga 75-76; Chap RAN from 76. *Preston Point Road, Fremantle, W Australia 6160.* (39 1522)

HILL, David Rowland. b 34. Univ of Lon BSc (Econ) 55. Qu Coll Birm. **d** 59 **p** 60 S'wark. C of H Trin U Tooting 59-61; Cheam 61-63; Richmond 63-68; V of Lutton w Gedney Drove End (and Holbeach Bank to 75) Dio Linc from 68. *Lutton Vicarage, Spalding, Lincs, PE12 9HP.* (Holbeach 362386)

HILL, Canon Derek Bertram. K Coll Lon BD 57. LTCL 44. St Paul's Coll Grahmstn LTh 48. **d** 48 **p** 49 Johann. C of Vereeniging 48-50; Springs 50-51; P-in-c of St Paul Parkhurst Johann 51-54; C of St Alb Mart Holborn 54-60; V of St Aug w St Phil Stepney 60-68; Chap Lon Hosp 66-68; Vice-Provost and R of St Mary's Colleg Ch Port Eliz Dio Grahmstn 68-70; Dio Port Eliz from 70; Can of Port Eliz from 75. *PO Box 566, Port Elizabeth, CP, S Africa.* (041-29773)

HILL, Canon Derek Ingram. b 12. Trin Coll Ox BA (2nd cl Mod Hist) 34, MA 38. Wells Th Coll 34. **d** 35 **p** 36 Cant. C of Buckland-in-Dover 35-39; St Andr Croydon 39-43; Min of H Innoc Conv Distr S Norwood 43-49; V 49-57; St Greg Gt

Cant 57-65; Chap St John's Hosp Cant 57-65; Six Pr in Cant Cathl 64-70; Proc Conv Cant 64-75; R of St Alphege w St Marg and St Pet (and St Mildred w St Mary de Castro from 74) Cant 65-76; Master of Eastbridge Hosp 65-76; RD of Cant 69-76; Hon Can of Cant 70-75; Can (Res) from 75; C-in-c of St Mildred w St Mary de Castro Cant 73-74; Prior St John's Hosp Cant from 76. *15 The Precincts, Canterbury.* (Cant 61954)

HILL, Derek Stanley. b 28. K Coll Lon and Warm AKC 53. **d** 53 St E **p** 54 Bp H A Wilson for St E. C of St Andr Rushmere 53-55; Kimb Cathl 55-57; Boreham Wood 57-59; V of Crowfield 59-67; C-in-c of Stonham Aspal 59-61; R 61-67; V of St Geo Bury St Edms 67-73; C-in-c of Ampton 68-73; V of Gazeley with Dalham (and Moulton from 74) 73-78; C-in-c of Lydgate w Ousden 73-74; Gt Bradley 74-78; V of Gt Barton Dio St E from 78. *Great Barton Vicarage, Bury St Edmunds, Suff.* (Gt Barton 274)

HILL, Donald Rupert. b 21. Fitzw Ho Cam 3rd cl Hist Trip pt i 50, BA (2nd cl Hist Trip pt ii) 51, MA 55. Univ of Dur LTh 45. Oak Hill Th Coll. **d** 45 **p** 46 Roch. C of St Steph Tonbridge 45; Asst Master Eversfield Sch Solihull 47-56; Chap St John's Sch Pinner 56-65; Hd Master The Mall Sch 65-69; Hd Master The Prep Sch Twickenham from 69; Perm to Offic Dio Ely from 48; Dio Lon 56-59; L to Offic Dio Lon from 59; Perm to Offic Dio Guildf from 70. *86 Blinco Grove, Cambridge CB1 4TS.* (Cambridge 46025); *and The Cross Road, The Green, Twickenham, Middx.* (01-898 0849)

HILL, Dudley Joseph. b 13. Univ of Leeds BA (2nd cl Cl) 35, MA 40. Coll of Resurr Mirfield 35. ARCO 34. **d** 37 **p** 38 Pet. C of St Mary Wellingborough 37-40; All SS Leamington 40-43; CF (EC) 43-47; L to Offic as Chap of Butlin's Camp Filey 47-49; V of Lythe 49-56; Thirsk w S Kilvington 56-68; Fulford York 68-78; Surr 56-68; RD of Thirsk 60-68; Hon Chap to Bp of Kimb K 61-65. *26 Curlew Glebe, Dunnington, York, YO1 5PQ.* (York 488370)

HILL, Preb Eric Claude Combe. b 11. Late Scho of Selw Coll Cam 1st cl Cl Trip Pt i 32, BA (1st Cl Th Trip pt i) 33, 1st cl Th Trip pt ii 35, Jeremie Sept Pri 35, MA 37. Wells Th Coll 35. **d** 35 Bp Baynes for Birm **p** 36 Birm. C of St Marg Ward End 35-38; Coleshill 38-39; Offg C-in-c of Perry Beeches Conv Distr 39-42; V of Em Wylde Green Birm 42-48; St Agatha Sparkbrook 48-55; Chap Dioc Home for Girls 51-55; C-in-c of St Mich AA Conv Distr S Yardley 55-56; Min 56-60; R of Blymhill w Weston-under-Lizard 60-72; Exam Chap to Bp of Lich from 61; RD of Penkridge 66-72; Preb of Lich Cathl 67-81; Preb (Emer) from 81; R of Elford 72-80; P-in-c of Harlaston 77-80; Edingale 77-80. *61 The Leasowe, Lichfield, Staffs, WS13 7HA.*

HILL, Eugene Mark. b 48. Late Scho of St D Coll Lamp BA 71. Sarum Th Coll 71. **d** 73 **p** 74 S'wark. C of Sutton Dio S'wark 73-77; Hon C from 77; Asst Chap Em Sch Battersea Rise from 77. *2a Dempster Road, SW18 1AT.* (01-870 9876)

HILL, Everett Ethen. **d** 59 **p** 60 NS. R of Port Medway 59-65; Newport 65-74; Windsor Dio NS from 74. *531 King Street, Windsor, NS, Canada.* (798-2454)

HILL, Frederick Allen. Univ of W Ont BA 35. Hur Coll LTh 35. **d** 35 **p** 36 Niag. C of St Geo Lowville w St John Nassagaweya 35-41; I of Hagersville 41-44; R of Grace Ch St Catharines 44-50; St Jas Dundas 50-60; Hon Can of Ch Ch Cathl Hamilton 49-61; R of H Trin Welland 61-75; Archd of Erie 61-74; Brock 75; Assoc P of St Geo Guelph Dio Niag from 75. *67 College Avenue West, Guelph, Ont, Canada.* (519-823 5939)

HILL, Frederick Ashton. b 13. Late Scho of Ch Coll Cam 1st cl Nat Sc Trip pt i 33, BA (2nd cl Nat Sc Trip pt ii) 34, MA 38. Chich Th Coll 36. **d** 38 **p** 39 Roch. C of St Barn Beckenham 38-44; St Mark Swindon 44-50; R of Letchworth 50-69; Gt w L Ryburgh Gateley and Testerton Dio Nor from 69; R of Stibbard Dio Nor from 69. *Great Ryburgh Rectory, Fakenham, Norf, NR21 0EB.* (Great Ryburgh 234)

HILL, Geoffrey Dennison. b 31. Dipl Th (Lon) 55. Tyndale Hall Bris 52. **d** 56 **p** 57 Carl. C of St Jas Carl 56-59; R of Asby w Ormside 59-63; Arthuret 63-71; V of Arnside 71-76; Ch Coniston 76-80; P-in-c of Torver 76-80. *c/o Vicarage, Coniston, Cumb, LA21 8DB.* (Coniston 262)

HILL, Ven George Walter. Univ of S Afr BA 48, LTh (w distinc) 50. St Paul's Coll Grahmstn 49. **d** 50 **p** 51 Grahmstn. C of St Kath Uitenhage 50-53; Herschel 53-54; Miss at Bolotwa 54-61; R of Komgha 61-68; P-in-c of St Phil 68-70; R of St Bart Grahmstn 70-78; Cathcart Dio Grahmstn from 78; Archd Dio Grahmstn from 81. *Box 54, Cathcart, CP, S Africa.* (Grahmstn 2786)

HILL, Harold Gordon Haynes. b 15. Tyndale Hall Bris 36. **d** 39 **p** 40 Lich. C of Aldridge 39-42; Org Sec S for ICM for N and Midls 42-46; Centr Sec S for ICM and L to Offic Dio S'wark 46-48; R of Whinburgh w Westfield 48-81; Reymerston 48-81; P-in-c of Cranworth w Letton and Southbergh 79-81; Perm to Offic Dio Nor from 81. *c/o The English Churchman, PO Box 217, SE5 8NP.* (01-701 0380)

HILL, Harry Baxter. b 19. **d** 79 St Alb **p** 80 Hertf for St Alb. C of Mill End w Heronsgate and W Hyde Dio St Alb from 79. *Eston, Shire Lane, Chorleywood, Herts.* (Chorleywood 2309)

✠ **HILL, Right Rev Henry Gordon.** Qu Univ Ont BA 45. St Jo Coll Cam BA 50, MA 54. Trin Coll Tor LTh 48. Univ of Windsor Hon DD 76. **d** 48 Ont **p** 50 Ely for Ont. C of Belleville 50-51; R of Adolphustown 51-52; Chap St Jo Coll Cam 52-55; C of Wisbech 55-56; R of Reddendale 57-62; Prof Cant Coll Windsor 62-64; Asst Prof 64-68; Vice-Prin 65-68; Asst Prof Univ of Windsor 68-75; Cons Bp Coadj of Ont in St Geo Cathl Kingston Ont 6 Jan 75 by Abp of Moos; Bps of Tor, Hur, Niag, BC, Ott and Rupld; Bps Suffr of Moos and Tor; and others; Apptd Bp of Ont 75; res 81; Chairman Angl-Orthodox Jt Doctrinal Comm from 80; Asst Bp of Montr from 81. *c/o Benedictine Priory, 1475 Pine Avenue West, Montreal, Quebec H3G 1B3, Canada.* (514-849 2728)

HILL, Herbert. b 1898. St Aid Coll. **d** 49 **p** 50 Cov. C of Foleshill 49-53; V of Grandborough w Willoughby 53-56; Burton Dassett 56-63. *12 Holland Close, Bidford-on-Avon, Warws.*

HILL, James Arthur. b 47. Div Hostel Dub 69. **d** 72 **p** 73 Connor. C of Ballymena 72-74; Armagh 74-78; Derg U 78-79; I of Inver w Mt Charles Dio Raph from 79; Killaghtee Dio Raph from 79. *Rectory, Inver, Co Donegal, Irish Republic.*

HILL, James Carthew. b 15. Linc Th Coll 37. **d** 40 Bp Willis for Leic **p** 41 Leic. C of St Pet Leic 40-41; Missr Shrewsbury Sch Miss Liv 42-53; C-in-c of St Timothy Everton 49-57; V of St Ambrose w St Pet and All SS Everton 53-57; V of St Ambrose w St Timothy Everton 57-61; R of Newport w Longford (and Chetwynd from 81) 61-81; C-in-c of Chetwynd 66-81; Surr 69-81; RD of Edgmond 71-81. *10 Helmeth Road, Church Stretton, Salop, SY6 7AS.* (0694 722067)

HILL, James Reginald. b 06. Univ of Man BA 29. SOC. **d** 69 **p** 70 S'wark. C of Purley 69-77. *Chantry Lane Cottage, Highland Croft, Steyning, Sussex.*

HILL, John Cyril. b 05. Late Exhib of Jes Coll Ox 2nd cl Cl Mods 26. BA (1st cl Th) and Jun Gk Test Pri 28, MA 34. **d** 28 **p** 29 St D. C of Tenby w Gumfreston 28-31; Chap of Brecon Cathl and C of St Mary Brecon w Battle 31-40; Exam Chap (Readers) to Bp of Swan B 39-40; CF (EC) 40-45; C-in-c of St Barn Carl 45-46; V of Sketty 46-50; C of Caverswall 50-52; Gt Bookham 52-56. *24 Pelham Road, Wimbledon, SW19.*

HILL, John Paul. b 07. Univ of Dur BA 30. Lich Th Coll 26. **d** 30 **p** 31 Lich. C of St Mary Tunstall 30-32; St Benedict Ardwick 33-35; St Andr Walsall 35-36; Byker St Anthony Newc T 36-37; V of Healey 37-41; C of St Mary Virg Newc T 41-42; V of Holy I 42-44; C of St Jas w Pockthorpe Nor 44-47; St Mark Lakenham 47-52; C-in-c of Nether Lochaber w Kinlochleven 52-53; R of Muchalls 53-59; Woodhead 59-62; Chap Ty Mawr Conv and L to Offic Dio Mon 62-65; V of Scredington 65-72; V of Burton Pedwardine 66-72; Perm to Offic Dio Lon from 72. *50 Lansdowne Road, W 11.*

HILL, John William Barnabas. b 44. Univ of Tor BASc 66. St Jo Coll Nottm BA 72, MTh 73. **d** 73 **p** 74 Bp Read for Tor. C of All SS Pet Tor 73-76; I of Bolton Dio Tor from 76; Exam Chap to Bp of Tor from 77. *Box 567, Bolton, Ont., L0P 1A0, Canada.* (416-857 1575)

HILL, Kathleen Muriel. b 12. **d** 71 **p** 77 Bran. C of St Faith's Miss The Pas 71-80. *Box 480, The Pas, Manitoba, R9A 1K6, Canada.*

HILL, Kenneth. b 27. Wycl Coll Tor LTh. **d** 58 **p** 59 Tor. C of St Jas Cathl Tor 59-61; St Matt Newc T 61-62; Novice SSF 62-64; St Werburgh Burslem 64-67; St Gabr Fullbrook Walsall 67-70; P-in-c of St Jude Hanley 70-79; P-in-c of Chacewater Dio Truro from 79. *Chacewater Vicarage, Truro, Cornw.* (Truro 560225)

HILL, Kenneth James. b 43. Univ of Leic BA (2nd cl Hist) 64. BD (Lon) 68. Oak Hill Th Coll 65. **d** 69 Kens for Lon **p** 70 Willesden for Lon. C of St Jo Evang Southall 69-72; St Mich AA Blackheath Pk 72-75; C-in-c of St Mich w St Paul Bath Dio B & W from 75; C of Bath Abbey Dio B & W from 75. *41 St James Square, Bath, BA1 2TU.* (Bath 313454)

HILL, Laurence Bruce. b 43. K Coll Lon and Warm AKC 67. **d** 69 Lon **p** 70 Kens for Lon. C of Feltham 69-72; Hampstead 72-76; St Steph Hampstead 72-76; V of H Trin E Finchley Dio Lon from 76. *Holy Trinity Vicarage, Church Lane, N2 0TH.* (01-883 8720)

HILL, Leonard Jonathan. b 27. Univ of Leeds BA (2nd cl Latin) 48. Coll of Resurr Mirfield 48. **d** 50 **p** 51 Chelmsf. C of Upminster 50-53; St Marg Leigh-on-Sea 53-61; V of St Cedd Canning Town 61-65; R of Corringham Dio Chelmsf from 65. *Corringham Rectory, Stanford-le-Hope, Essex, SS17 9AP.* (Stanford-le-Hope 3074)

HILL, Leslie Hugh. b 23. Westcott Ho Cam 73. **d** 73 **p** 74 Derby (APM). C of Holbrook and L Eaton 73-78; St Luke

Loscoe Dio Derby from 79. *1 Hunter Drive, Kilburn, Derbys.*

HILL, Malcolm Crawford. b 43. Dipl Th (Lon) 70. Oak Hill Th Coll 68. **d** 71 **p** 72 Cant. C of St Luke Maidstone 71-74; Longfleet 74-79; V of St Pet Bexleyheath Dio Roch from 79. *St Peter's Vicarage, Bristow Road, Bexleyheath, Kent, DA7 4QA.* (01-303 8713)

HILL, Malcolm John. b 26. Bps' Coll Cheshunt 64. **d** 65 **p** 66 St Alb. C of Ch Ch Luton 65-70; V of Wilstead 70-78; P-in-c of Westoning w Tingrith Dio St Alb 78-80; V from 80. *Westoning Vicarage, Bedford, MK45 5JW.* (Flitwick 3703)

HILL, Michael. b 32. TD 77. K Coll Lon and Warm AKC 55. **d** 56 **p** 57 Newc T. C of Cullercoats 56-59; Mkt Drayton 59-61; V of Milton 61-64; Leaton (w Preston Gobalds from 73) 64-76; Preston Gobalds 64-73; CF (TA) 65-67; CF (TAVR) from 67; V of Oswestry Dio Lich from 76; Surr from 77; P-in-c of Trefonen Dio Lich from 80. *Vicarage, Oswestry, Salop, SY11 2AN.* (Oswestry 3467)

HILL, Michael. b 42. Moore Th Coll Syd ACT ThL 69. **d** 70 **p** 71 Armid. C of St Cypr Narrabri 70-72; St Pet Cathl Armid 72-74; Chap Univ of New Engl Armid 74-75; C of Turramurra 75-76; Lect Moore Th and L to Offic Dio Syd from 76. *c/o Moore Theological College, Carillon Avenue, Newtown, NSW, Australia 2042.* (51-1103)

HILL, Michael Arthur. b 49. Ridley Hall Cam 74. **d** 77 **p** 78 Cant. C of St Mary Magd Addiscombe 77-81; C-in-c of Slough Dio Ox from 81. *205 Rochford Gardens, Slough, Berks.* (Slough 21508)

HILL, Norman. b 20. St Chad's Coll Dur LTh 48. Linc Th Coll 45. **d** 49 **p** 50 Sheff. C of Swinton 49-59; V of Mosborough 59-72; C-in-c of Codnor Dio Derby 72-79; V from 79. *Codnor Vicarage, Derby, DE5 4SN.* (Ripley 2516)

HILL, Canon Norman Leslie George. Selw Coll Cam BA 49, MA 53. Cudd Coll 49. **d** 51 **p** 52 Portsm. C of St Mary Portsea 51-55; St Mary Gt Cam 55-58; Wimbledon (in c of St Mark) 58-62; V of St Matt Brixton 62-69; C-in-c of Crowhurst Dio S'wark from 69; Ecumen Officer Dio S'wark from 69; Hon Can of S'wark Cathl from 78. *Crowhurst Vicarage, Lingfield, Surrey, RH7 6LR.* (Lingfield 833733)

HILL, Norman William. b 14. Ch Coll Cam BA 36, MA 40. Linc Th Coll. **d** 45 **p** 46 St Alb. C of St Mary Hitchin 45-49; St Alb Cathl 49-60; V of Rickmansworth 60-74; P-in-c of Northill 75-78; R (w Moggerhanger) 78-79; Moggerhanger 75-78. *West Sillywrea, Langley-on-Tyne, Hexham, Northumb, NE47 5NE.* (Haydon Bridge 635)

HILL, Oliver Jestyn. b 13. St D Coll Lamp BA (Aegr) 34. St Mich Coll Llan 34. **d** 36 **p** 37 St A. C of Eglwys Rhos (or Llanrhos) 36-39; C-in-c of Penrhyn Llanrhos 39-47; V of Mochdre 47-52; R of Llanfyllin 52-60; Surr from 52; V of Shotton 60-69; Gresford 69-75. *School House, Clappers Lane, Gresford, Nr Wrexham, Clwyd.* (Gresford 4210)

HILL, Percival Albert James. Kelham Th Coll. **d** 41 Dorchester for Ox **p** 41 Ox. C of Banbury 41-47; R of Gt w L Hampden Dio Ox from 47. *Great Hampden Rectory, Great Missenden, Bucks.*

HILL, Percy William. b 1890. St Bonif Coll Warm 12. Univ of Dur LTh 18. **d** 15 **p** 16 Chelmsf. C of St Barn L Ilford 15-18; All SS Middlesbrough 18-25; V 25-35; R of Brede 35-75. *St Anthony's Nursing Home, Wilbury Villas, Hove.*

HILL, Peter. b 36. K Coll Lon and Warm AKC 60. **d** 61 **p** 62 St Alb. C of Gt Berkhamsted 61-67; R of St Mary Bedford Dio St Alb 67-69; C-in-c 69-70; V of Goldington 69-79; Biggleswade Dio St Alb from 79; RD of Biggleswade from 80. *Vicarage, Shortmead Street, Biggleswade, Beds, SG18 0AT.* (Biggleswade 312243)

HILL, Peter Allen. McMaster Univ BA 62. Hur Coll BTh 65. **d** 65 Niag for Alg **p** 66 Alg. C of Port Arthur 65-69; I of St Jos I 69-77; Chap Trin Coll Sch Port Hope from 76. *Trinity College School, Port Hope, Ont., Canada.*

HILL, Peter John. St Jo Coll Morpeth 75. **d** 76 **p** 77 Melb. C of St Andr Brighton 76-77; Glenroy 77-79; P-in-c of Kilsyth Dio Melb from 79. *686 Mount Dandenong Road, Kilsyth, Vic, Australia 3137.* (728 2696)

HILL, Peter Thomas. Perry Hall Melb. **d** 66 **p** 67 Melb. C of St Mark E Brighton 66-68; Morwell 68-69; V of Werribee 69-76; E Doncaster 76-79; Hampton Dio Melb from 79. *10 Thames Street, Hampton, Vic, Australia 3188.* (598 1707)

HILL, Ralph Jasper. b 15. Tyndale Hall Bris 38. **d** 41 **p** 42 Worc. C of Stambermill 41-44; Harmondsworth 44-45; St Steph Wandsworth 45-48; Org Sec SAMS and Perm to Offic Dios Lon St Alb Ox Guildf and S'wark 49-59; Asst Master Hillcroft Boys' Sch Balham 60-65; Hove Gr Sch 65-78. *29 Gorham Way, Telscombe Cliffs, Newhaven, Sussex.* (Peacehaven 3729)

HILL, Raymond John Walter. b 09. AKC 34. **d** 34 **p** 35 Bris. C of Bishopston 34-36; St Pet Henleaze 36-37; St Luke Cross Roads Ja 37-38; Chertsey 38-41; Pontesbury i and ii 41-45; Ludlow 45-47; V of Elmsted w Hastingleigh 47-50; R of Adisham 50-54; Kingsnorth 54-65; R of Shadoxhurst 54-65; V of Westbury w Turweston 65-77; C-in-c of Shalstone w Biddlesden 68-77. *15 Shepherd's Way, Stow-on-the-Wold, Glos.*

HILL, Raymond William. b 17. SOC **d** 63 **p** 64 S'wark. C of All SS Shooter's Hill 63-66; St Faith Virg and Mart Maidstone 66-69; V of Oulton Broad Dio Nor from 69. *Oulton Broad Vicarage, Lowestoft, Suff.* (Lowestoft 2563)

HILL, Richard Brian. b 47. Univ of Dur BA 68, Dipl Th 70. Westcott Ho Cam 70. **d** 71 **p** 72 Carl. C of Cockermouth 71-74; SS Geo & Luke Barrow-F 74-76; V of Walney I Dio Carl from 76. *Walney Island Vicarage, Barrow-in-Furness, Cumb, LA14 3QU.* (Barrow-F 41268)

HILL, Preb Richard Hebert. b 11. Linc Th Coll 34. **d** 36 **p** 37 Ripon. C of St John Moor Allerton 36-39; CF (R of O) 39-45; R of Berrington w Betton-Strange 45-61; V of Bromyard 61-72; RD 61-72; Preb of Heref Cathl 65-78; Preb (Emer) from 78; C-in-c of Pencombe 69-72; R of Ledbury 72-78; RD 72-78; C-in-c of Eastnor 73-78. *4 Old School, Henley Road, Ludlow, Salop, SY8 1RA.*

HILL, Richard Hugh Oldham. b 52. CCC Ox BA (Jurispr) 74, BA (Th) 77. Wycl Hall Ox 75. **d** 78 Barking for Chelmsf **p** 79 Chelmsf. C of St Pet Harold Wood Romford 78-81; Hampreston Dio Sarum from 81. *101 Wimborne Road West, Wimborne, Dorset, BH21 2DH.* (Wimborne 884796)

HILL, Richard Owen. b 40. Univ of Liv BA 63, MA 65. Cudd Coll 65. **d** 68 **p** 69 Ox. C of St Luke, Reading 68-72; Towcester w Easton Neston 72-73; SS Mary and John Ox 73-75; Walker 75-78; P-in-c of H Trin Tynemouth Dio Newc T from 78. *Holy Trinity Vicarage, Waterville Road, North Shields.* (N Shields 70937)

HILL, Robert Joseph. b 45. Oak Hill Coll BA 81. **d** 81 Warrington for Liv. C of St Luke W Derby Dio Liv from 81. *4 South Cantril Avenue, West Derby, Liverpool, L12 6QZ.* (051-220 1173)

HILL, Robin. b 35. Cranmer Hall Dur. **d** 62 Southw **p** 63 Bp Gelsthorpe for Southw. C of Aspley 62-65; V of St Aug Mansfield 65-71; R of Hulland w Atlow and Bradley 71-76; C-in-c of Hognaston 73-76; R of Nollamara Dio Perth from 76. *18 Nanson Way, Nollamara, W Australia 6061.* (349 1125)

HILL, Roger Anthony John. b 45. Univ of Liv BA 67. Linacre Coll Ox BA 69. Ripon Hall Ox 67. **d** 70 **p** 71 S'wark. C of St Helier 70-74; Dawley Parva and at Lawley and at Malins Lee and at Stirchley 74-75; Centr Telford Dio Lich 75-76; Team V 77-80; Team R from 81. *Rectory, Church Road, Dawley, Telford, Shropshire.* (Telford 501655)

HILL, Ven Roland. Wycl Coll Tor DD (*hon causa*) 50. **d** 43 **p** 44 Tor. C of Agincourt 43-44; St Paul Tor 44-47; R of St Jas Cathl Peace River 47-51; Dean 49-51; Exam Chap to Bp of Athab 47-51; R of St Barn Danforth Avenue Tor 52-60; Dom Chap to Bp of Tor 55-77; R of St Geo-on-the-Hill Tor 60-74; Can of St Jas Cathl Tor 64-77; Dir of Ch Development 74-81; Dioc Archd Dio Tor 77-81. *85 Cumberland Drive, Mississauga, Ont, Canada.*

HILL, Sidney John. b 16. MBE (Mil) 45. Oak Hill Th Coll 46. **d** 48 **p** 49 Guildf. C of Woking 48-52; R of Hatch Beauchamp w Beercrocombe 52-57; St Nich Nottm 57-63; V of Wembdon 63-74; Chap CCCS at Rouen Chantilly and Le Havre 74-78; R of Gressenhall w Longham and Bittering Parva 78-81; P-in-c of Chawleigh w Cheldon Dio Ex from 81. *Chawleigh Rectory, Chumleigh, Devon.* (Chumleigh 285)

HILL, Thomas. b 31. Lich Th Coll 63. **d** 65 **p** 66 Lich. C of Brewood 65-68; V of Coven 68-74; Temuka 74-78; New Brighton Dio Ch Ch from 78. *36 Howe Street, Christchurch 7, NZ.* (889-118)

HILL, Thomas Duncan. NZ Bd of Th Stud LTh 66. **d** 64 **p** 65 Nel. C of Blenheim 64-67; V of Cobden w Runanga 67-69; Chap K Sch Remuera 69; Chap RNZN 70-80; Sen Chap from 80; Hon C of One Tree Hill 71-80; Devenport Dio Auckld from 80. *113 Calliope Road, Devonport, Auckland, NZ.*

HILL, Canon Thomas Henry. b 19. Univ of Wales BA 41, BD (w distinc) 45. **d** 66 **p** 67 Llan. [f Bapt Min]. C of Roath 66-67; C-in-c of Cymmer w Abercregan 67-71; Glyncorrwg 67-71; Avan Vale 67-71; R of Glyncorrwg w Afan Vale and Cymer Afan 71-74; Ed *Welsh Churchman* 66-72; V of Pembroke Dio St D from 74; Can of St D Cathl from 80. *Vicarage, Westgate Hill, Pembroke, Dyfed.* (Pembroke 2710)

HILL, Timothy Frank. b 42. Hur Coll Lon BA, MDiv 73. **d** 73 **p** 74 Hur. C of Trin Ch Cambridge 73-75; R of Delhi and Scotland 75-80; Thedford Dio Hur from 80. *Box 159, Thedford, Ont, Canada.*

HILL, Trevor Walton. Univ of Leeds BA (2nd cl Gen Stud) 57. Coll of Resurr Mirfield. **d** 59 **p** 60 Ches. C of St John Bollington 59-62; Woodchurch 62-64; V of Addingham w Gamblesby 64-67; H Trin Carlisle 67-71; V of Wetheral w Warwick 71-80; Doddington w Wychling Dio Cant from 80. *Doddington Vicarage, Sittingbourne, Kent.* (Doddington 265)

HILL, Victor Rowland. b 1891. Univ Coll Dur BA 23, Dipl

Th 25, MA 27. Wells Th Coll. **d** 24 **p** 25 Dur. C of Cuthb Hebburn 24-27; St Nich Cathl Newc T 27-31; V of Matfen 31-57; Perm to Offic Dio Carl from 57. *Brockleside, Keswick, Cumb.* (Keswick 190)

HILL, William Charles. b 07. BSc (2nd cl Gen) Lon 27. Ripon Hall Ox 62. **d** 63 **p** 64 Win. Hd Master Gr Sch for Boys Guernsey 48-67; C of H Trin Guernsey 63-67; V of Appleshaw 67-73. *4 Broadhurst Gardens, Reigate, Surrey.* (Reigate 42644)

HILL, Canon William Henderson. St Pet Th Coll Ja 47. Univ of Lon BA 50. **d** 50 **p** 51 Ja. C of St Geo Kingston 51-53; R of Black River and Lacovia 53-56; Linstead 56-59; Stony Hill 59-62; on leave and in Amer Ch 62-68; I of Northminster Dio Sktn from 68; I of Lashburn 69-72; Lloydminster Dio Sktn from 72; Hon Can of Sktn from 75; Commiss Ja from 77. *Box 1082, Lloydminster, Sask., Canada.*

HILL, William Henry George. b 21. SOC 66. **d** 69 **p** 70 S'wark. C of St Mary Welling 69-73; St Luke Reigate (in c of St Pet Doversgreen) 73-76; V of Lynsted w Kingsdown Dio Cant from 76; R of Norton Dio Cant from 76. *Lynsted Vicarage, Sittingbourne, Kent.* (Teynham 521371)

HILL, Ven William James. St Chad's Coll Regina 46. **d** 49 Qu'App **p** 50 Edmon for Qu'App. V of Hodgeville 49-52; I of Saltcoats 52-56; Melville 56-65; Chemainus 65-72; St Mich AA Vic Dio BC from 72; Hon Can of BC from 79; Archd Dio BC from 81. *4733 West Saanich Road, Victoria, BC, Canada.* (604-479 4198)

HILL, William James. b 13. Ripon Hall Ox 60. **d** 61 **p** 62 Derby. C of Breaston 61-63; Darley w S Darley (in c of St Mary S Darley) 63-66; PC of Chinley w Buxworth 66-68; V 68-74; Surr from 70; R of Whitwell 74-77; P-in-c of Denby 77-79. *15 Harewood Road, Allestree, Derby, DE3 2JP.* (Derby 556135)

HILL-TOUT, Mark Laurence. b 50. AKC 73. St Aug Coll Cant 73. **d** 74 Lewes for Chich **p** 75 Chich. C of Resurr Brighton 74-77; Old and New Shoreham 77-79; Dioc Stewardship Adv Lewes and Hastings and P-in-c of Stonegate Dio Chich from 79. *Stonegate Vicarage, Wadhurst, E Sussex, TN5 7EJ.* (Ticehurst 200515)

HILLARY, George William. St Chad's Coll Regina. **d** 35 **p** 36 Qu'App. C of Kelliher 35-36; I 36-37; I of Foam Lake 37-41; Balgonie 41-43; Arcola 43-44; R of Grenfell 44-50; Melville 50-54; I of St Thos Whalley 55-59; C of Ch Ch Cathl 59-60; R of St Mich Vanc 60-76. *141b-8635 120th Street, Delta, BC, Canada.*

HILLEBRAND, Frank David. b 46. K Coll Lon and Warm AKC 68. **d** 69 Willesden for Lon **p** 70 Lon; C of St Mich, Wood Green 69-72; Evesham 72-75; V of H Trin w St Matt Ronkswood Worc 75-81; St Jo Bapt Kidderminster Dio Worc from 81. *33 Lea Bank Avenue, Kidderminster, Worcs.* (Kidderminster 2649)

HILLIARD, Denis Robert Coote. b 11. Trin Coll Dub BA 34, MA 44. **d** 35 **p** 36 Down. C of St Columba Knock Belf 35-38; S Ch Miss Ballymacarrett 38-40; Asst Chap Miss to Seamen Dub 40-45; Chap from 45; I of St John Monkstown 45-54; Zion Ch Rathgar 54-71; RD of Killiney 65-68; Preb of St Patr Cathl Dub 67-76; I of Geashill 71-80; Can and Preb of Kild Cathl 71-80. *37 Newcourt Road, Bray, Co Wicklow, Irish Republic.*

HILLIARD, George Percival St John. b 45. Trin Coll Dub BA 67. **d** 69 **p** 70 Down. C of Seapatrick 69-73; St Nich Carrickfergus 73-76; R of Fanlobbus U Dio Cork from 76. *Rectory, Dunmanway, Co Cork, Irish Republic.* (Bandon 45151)

HILLIARD, John William Richard. b 19. St Jo Coll Morpeth. **d** 55 Bp Storrs for Graft **p** 56 Graft. R of Mallanganee 55-59; Coramba 59-61; Nimbin 61-62; Dunolly 62-64; Langfield U 64-68; Carbury 68-72; C of W Bridgford (in c of St Luke's) 72-78; V of St Aug Mansfield Dio Southw from 78. *Vicarage, Abbott Road, Mansfield, Notts.* (Mansfield 21247)

HILLIARD, Robert Godfrey. b 52. Univ of Wales (Cardiff) Dipl Th 75. St Mich AA Llan 72. **d** 75 **p** 76 Llan. C of Whitchurch 75-80; Chap (RNR) 77-80; Chap (RN) from 80. *c/o Ministry of Defence, Lacon House, Theobalds Road, WC1X 8RY.*

HILLIER, Derek John. b 30. Sarum Th Coll 61. **d** 63 **p** 64 Sarum. C of St Mark Sarum 63-65; H Trin Weymouth 65-66; R of Caundle Bp w Caundle Marsh and Holwell 66-75; The Caundles & Holwell Dio Sarum from 75; P-in-c of Pulham 70-78; Folke Dio Sarum from 81. *Rectory, Bishop's Caundle, Sherborne, Dorset, DT9 5ND.* (Bishop's Caundle 243)

HILLIER, Horace William. **d** and **p** 65 Perth. C of Victoria Pk 65-66; Northam 66-68; R of Belmont 68-70; Dongara-Greenough 71-75. *Rectory, Dongara, W Australia 6525.* (271164)

HILLIER, Michael Bruce. b 49. St Barn Coll Adel 71. **d** 74 Adel **p** 75 Bp Renfrey for Adel. C of Plympton 74-76; Assoc P of Walkerville 76-80; on leave. *c/o 1 Reece Avenue, Klemzig, S Australia 5086.* (261 2768)

HILLMAN, Donald. b 02. **d** and **p** 31 Dun. C of Oamaru 31-34; V of Balclutha 34-37; C of St Pet Henleaze Bris 37-40; St Clem Parkstone 41-43 and 49-56; Ch Ch Swindon 43-48; Broadstone 57; Downend 58-63; V of Pilning w Severn Beach and Northwick 63-67; Perm to Offic Dio B & W from 68. *503 Locking Road, Weston-super-Mare, Avon, BS22 8QT.*

HILLMAN, Gary Walter. b 46. St Barn Coll Adel 70. **d** and **p** 72 Bal. C of Horsham 72-74; Warrnambool 75; R of Willaura 74-78; Edwardstown w Ascot Pk Dio Adel from 78. *11 Dinwoodie Avenue, Edwardstown, S Australia 5039.* (293 3027)

HILLMAN, John Anthony. St Chad's Coll Dur BA 54. St Mich Coll Llan 54. **d** 56 **p** 57 St A. C of Llangollen 56-60; Silvertown 60-64; P-in-c of Matroosfontein 63-72; R of Noorder Paarl 72-75; Durbanville 75-80; All SS Somerset W Dio Capetn from 80. *Rectory, Oak Street, Somerset West 7130, CP, S Africa.*

HILLS, Arthur Philip. **d** 58 **p** 59 Kimb K. C of St Cypr Cathl Kimb 58-60; Warden of Bp's Hostel and Dom Chap to Bp of Kimb K 58-60; Dir of St Paul's Miss Beaconsfield Kimb 60-62; R of St Aug Kimb 61-62; Hon Chap to Bp of Kimb K 62-65; R of H Trin Upington and Dir Upington Miss 62-66; W Suburbs Pret 66-67; Pris Chap Pret 67-72; L to Offic Dio Pret 71-72; Dio Natal from 81; R of Irene 72-76; P-in-c of All SS Barberton 76-81. *30 Oakleigh Drive, Howick 3290, Natal, S Africa.*

HILLS, Kenneth Hugh. b 30. Univ of NZ BCom 54. Ripon Hall Ox 55. **d** 57 **p** 58 Birm. C of Handsworth 57-59; V of Wanganui Par Distr 59-61; Porirua 61-67; Exam Chap to Bp of Wel 62-67; Industr Chap Dio Birm 67-74; Chap Univ of Aston Birm from 74. *3 Jaffray Court, 52 Gravelly Hill North, Erdington, Birmingham B23 6BB.* (021-382 2055)

HILLS, Leslie. b 1897. Q Coll Cam BA 20, MA 26. Ridley Hall Cam. MC 19. **d** 21 **p** 22 Liv. C of St Mary St Helens 21-24; Chap in the Sudan 24-25; CMS Miss at Juba 25-27; C of Luton 27-29; St Jas Paddington 29-30; V of Ch Ch Rotherhithe 30-35; Ch of Good Shepherd Lee 35-36; CF (R of O) from 39; V of Seal 45-60; W Malling 60-66; Warden Angl Conf Centre Stella Carmel Israel 66-67. *The Little House, Winchelsea, Sussex.*

HILLS, Mervyn Hyde. Ch Coll Cam 3rd cl Math Trip pt i 38, BA (3rd cl Th Trip pt i) 40, MA 44. Westcott Ho Cam 40. **d** 42 **p** 43 Cant. C of St Sav Croydon 42-44; All SS Boyne Hill 44-49; Ch Ch Reading (in c of St Agnes Whitley) 49-53; V of Bourn Dio Ely from 53; R of Kingston Dio Ely from 53 *Bourn Vicarage, Cambridge.* (Caxton 256)

HILLS, Philip Vaughan. b 16. ACIS 48. Cudd Coll 69. **d** 69 Shrewsbury for Lich **p** 70 Lich. C of Walsall 69-72; Kenwyn w Tregavethan 72-77; P-in-c of St Steph-by-Saltash Dio Truro 77-81; V from 81. *St Stephen's Vicarage, Saltash, Cornw, PL12 4AR.* (Saltash 2323)

HILLS, Rowland Jonathan. b 12. Late Stud of Selw Coll Cam 2nd cl Cl Trip pt i 34, BA 35, 1st cl Th Trip pt i 36, MA 39. Cudd Coll 36. **d** 37 **p** 38 Lon. C of All SS Hampton 37-39; Forest Row 39-40; C-in-c 40-44; V 44-48; Good Shepherd, Preston Brighton 48-59; Iffley Ox 59-75; Perm to Offic Dios Ox and St D 76-80; Chap of St Geo Venice Dio Gibr in Eur from 80. *Dorsoduro 870, 30123 Venice, Italy.* (29195)

HILLS, Stanley Brassington. **d** 57 **p** 58 Qu'App. I of Wadena 57-59; Hillsdale Regina 59-62; St Aug Hamilton 62-78; P Assoc of H Trin Welland Dio Niag from 78; I of All SS Welland (w St Paul Port Robinson from 81) Dio Niag from 79. *14 Crescent Drive, Welland, Ont, Canada.* (416-735 2857)

HILLS-HARROP, George Douglas. b 16. Late Scho of Trin Hall Cam, Mod Lang Trip pt i 35, BA (2nd cl Mod Lang Trip pt ii) 37, MA 41. Univ of Birm Dipl Educn (1st cl) 38. Sarum Th Coll 50. **d** 52 **p** 53 Win. C of Newnham w Nately Scures 52-54; V of Fair Oak 54-58; Higher Bebington 58-61; Asst Master Chich High Sch for Girls 61-64; Bp Blackall Sch Ex 64-73; Perm to Offic Dio Ex 65-79; Lect Ex Coll of Further Educn 73-79; Perm to Offic Dio Swan B from 79; Dio Heref from 80. *Anchorage Caravan Park, Bronllys, Brecon, Powys.*

HILLYER, Charles Norman. b 21. Univ of Lon BD 48. STh (Lambeth) 67. ALCD 48. **d** 48 Lon **p** 49 Stepney for Lon. C of Ch Ch Finchley 48-51; Ch Ch New Malden (in c of St John) 51-54; V of St Sav w St Paul Holloway 54-59; Chap City of Lon Mat Hosp 54-59; V of Ponsbourne 59-70; Warden of Ponsbourne Coll 59-70; Chap Tolmers Pk Hosp 59-70; Libr Tyndale Ho Cam 70-73; Perm to Offic Dio Ely 70-79; Dio Sarum 75-79; Dio Guildf 75-79; Sec Tyndale Fellowship Bibl Research Cam 73-75; Organizing Ed Univs and Colls Chr Fellowship 73-79; P-in-c of Hatherleigh Dio Ex 79-81; V from 81. *Hatherleigh Vicarage, Okehampton, Devon, EX20 3JY.* (Hatherleigh 314)

HILTON, Clive. b 30. K Coll Lon 54. **d** 58 **p** 59 Man. C of

Woodhouse Pk Conv Distr 58-61; Newton Heath 61-62; C-in-c of St Chad's Conv Distr Limeside Oldham Dio Man 62-65; V 65-70; C-in-c Ch of the H Family Milton Gravesend 70-71; R of Killamarsh Dio Derby from 71. *Killamarsh Rectory, Sheffield.* (Sheff 482769)

HILTON, Grant Adams. b 54. St Jo Coll Morpeth. **d** and **p** 79 Bunb. C of Busselton Dio Bunb from 79. *90 Marine Terrace, Busselton, W Australia 6280.*

HILTON, John. b 49. Univ of Ex BA 70. Cuddesdon Coll 71. **d** 73 **p** 74 Warrington for Liv. C of Tue Brook 73-79; V of St Andr Orford Dio Liv from 79. *St Andrew's, Poplars Avenue, Orford, Warrington, Chesh, WA2 9UE.* (Warrington 31903)

HILTON, John Gordon. Bp's Univ Lennox BA 59. Nashota Ho USA BD 62. **d** 62 **p** 63 Ott. C of St Matthias Ott 62-65; I of Navan 65-68; Chap Univ of Ott 68-77; P-in-c of Combermere 77-78; R of Quyon Dio Ott from 78. *Box 24, Quyon, PQ, Canada.*

HILTON, John Read. b 41. K Coll Lon and Warm BD 63, AKC 65. **d** 65 Bp McKie for Cov **p** 66 Cov. C of H Trin Cov 65-69; Hemel Hempstead 69-70; Hon C of St Andr Catford Dio S'wark from 70. *89 Arngask Road, Catford, SE6 1XZ.* (01-698 1965)

HILTON, Roger John Denyer. b 42. ACT ThDip 78. St Barn Coll Adel 75. **d** 77 **p** 78 Murray. C of Murray Bridge 77-79; P-in-c of Bordertown Dio Murray 79; R from 79. *67 McLeod Street, Bordertown, S Australia 5268.* (087-521151)

HILTON-TURVEY, Geoffrey Michael. b 34. Oak Hill Coll 80. **d** 81 Burnley for Blackb. C of Bispham Dio Blackb from 81. *Church Villa, All Hallows Road, Bispham, Blackpool, Lancs, FY2 0AY.* (0253 53648)

HILTZ, Frederick James. b 53. Dalhousie Univ NS BSc 75. Atlantic Sch of Th Halifax NS MDiv 78. **d** 77 Bp Hatfield for NS **p** 78 NS. C of St Luke Dartmouth 77-78; Ch Ch Syd Dio NS from 78. *195 Hospital Street, Sydney, NS, Canada.*

HINCHEY, Peter John. b 30. Chich Th Coll 55. **d** 58 **p** 59 S'wark. C of St Jo Bapt Malden 58-61; V of Rosherville 61-67; St Aug Gillingham 67-72; St Andr Bromley 72-74; Hon Chap to Bp of Roch 74-78; Hon C of H Redeemer Lamorbey 76-78; R of Foots Cray Dio Roch from 78. *Foots Cray Rectory, Sidcup, Kent.* (01-300 7096)

HINCHLIFF, George Victor. b 19. TCD BA (Mod Ment and Mor Sc) 41. Div Test 42. **d** 42 Arm for Down **p** 43 Connor. C of St Patr Coleraine 42-48; I of Tamlaghtard w Aghanloo 48-54; R of Newtownhamilton w Ballymoyer U 54-59; I of Ballinderry w Tamlaght 59-64; Clonfeacle w Derrygortreavey Dio Arm from 64. *Benburb Rectory, Dungannon, Co Tyrone, N Ireland.* (Benburb 239)

HINCHLIFF, Canon Peter Bingham. b 29. Rhodes Univ Grahmstn BA 48, PhD 58. Trin Coll Ox BA (2nd cl Th) 50, MA 54, BD 62, DD 64. St Paul's Coll Grahmstn 51. **d** 52 **p** 53 Grahmstn. C of St Kath Uitenhage 52-55; Sub-Warden St Paul's Coll Grahmstn 55-59; Prov Can of Capetn from 60; Prof Eccles Hist Rhodes Univ 60-69; L to Offic Dio Grahmstn 60-64; Exam Chap to Bp of Geo 60-68; to Bp of Kimb K 62-68; to Bp of Grahmstn 64-68; Chan of Grahmstn Cathl 64-69; Can 64-69; Hon Can from 69; Sec Ch Assembly Miss and Ecumen Coun 69-72; Fell and Chap Ball Coll Ox from 72; Can Th of Cov from 72; Prov Commiss to Abp of Capetn 73-76; Exam Chap to Bp of Newc T from 73; to Bp of Ox 74-78; Hulsean Lect Univ of Cam 75-76; bampton lect univ of ox from 82. *Balliol College, Oxford.*

HINCHLIFFE, Canon James Fletcher. Trin Coll Tor BA 34. **d** and **p** 36 Niag. C of Ch Ch Niag Falls 36-40; I of Wainfleet w Welland and Dainville 40-43; Copper Cliff 43-48; R of Huntsville 48-54; St Paul Fort William 54-71; Archd of Thunder Bay 57-71; Exam Chap to Bp of Alg 59-76; R of Lively 71-75; Hon Can of Alg from 71. *Box 235, Port Sydney, Ont., Canada.*

HIND, Clarence Hedley. b 1898. **d** 62 **p** 63 Southw. C of Bulwell 62-65; C-in-c of Bestwood Pk 65-67. *Address temp unknown.*

HIND, John William. b 45. Univ of Leeds BA (Th) 66. Cudd Coll 70. **d** 72 **p** 73 S'wark. C of Southend, Lewisham 72-76; V of Ch Ch Forest Hill Dio S'wark from 76; P-in-c of St Paul Forest Hill Dio S'wark from 81. *Vicarage, Sunderland Road, SE23 2PY.* (01-699 6538)

HIND, Stanley Maurice. b 29. K Coll Lon and Warm AKC (2nd cl) 53. **d** 54 Warrington for Liv **p** 55 Liv. C of Haydock 54-57; Elland (in c of All SS) 57-60; V of St Paul Eastthorpe Mirfield 60-67; Carleton (w E Hardwick from 72) 67-78; Morley w Churwell Dio Wakef from 78. *Vicarage, Rooms Lane, Morley, Leeds, W Yorks, LS27 9PA.* (Morley 532052)

HINDE, Lano Ross. Em Coll Sktn LTh 61. **d** 61 **p** 62 Sktn. I of Carragana 61-69; Gillam 69-70; Pikwitonei 69-70; Lynn Lake 70-75; Ch Ch The Pas 75-80; Devon Miss The Pas Dio Bran from 80. *Box 1075, The Pas, Manit., Canada.*

HINDE, Richard Standish Elphinstone. b 12. Peterho Cam BA 34, MA 38. St Pet Hall Ox MA (by incorp) 39, BLitt 48, MLitt 79. Trin Coll Dub MA (*ad eund*) 62. Wycl Hall Ox 34. **d** 35 **p** 36 Leic. C of H Trin Leic 35-39; Offg C-in-c of St Matt Grandpont Ox 39-43; Chap HM Pris Ox 39-43; Chap RAF-VR 43-46; Chap BNC Ox 46-47; Hertf Coll Ox 47-61; Sen Tutor 48-61; Fell 51-61; L to Offic Dio Ox 48-61; Select Pr Univ of Ox 58-60; Univ of Dub 63; C-in-c of St Andr Dub 61-65; Commiss Argent 63-66 and from 74; Hon Cler V of Ch Ch Cathl Dub 63-66; and 73-74; Sub-Dean, Can and R of St Jo Bapt Cathl Buenos Aires 66-68; Home Sec JEM 68-69; LPr Dio Cov 69-72; Perm to Offic Dio Lon 69-72; Cler V of Ch Ch Cathl Dub & L to Offic Dios Dub & Glendal 74-81. *17 St Stephen's Green, Dublin 2, Irish Republic.* (Dublin 000162975)

HINDLEY, Anthony Talbot. Oak Hill Th Coll 62. **d** 66 **p** 67 Guildf. C of Stoke-next-Guildf 66-71; Eldoret 71-72; V of Menengai Nak 72-79; All S Eastbourne Dio Chich from 79. *53 Susan Road, Eastbourne, BN21 3TH.* (Eastbourne 31366)

HINDLEY, Godfrey Talbot. b 09. Ch Coll Cam BA 31, BChir 34, MB 35, MA 46. **d** 66 **p** 67 Vic Nyan. Asst P Bushubi 66-70; V of St Francis Nai 70-75. *Karibu, Lower Park, Umberleigh, N Devon, EX37 9DA.* (Chittlehamholt 468)

HINDLEY, Roger Dennis. b 48. Univ of Birm BA 70. Univ of Ox BA (Th) 77. Ripon Coll Cudd 75. **d** 78 **p** 79 Birm. C of Rubery 78-81; Henbury Dio Bris from 81. *Church Flat, 188 Okebourne Road, Brentry, Bristol, BS10 6QY.* (0272 503850)

HINDLEY, Thomas Richard. b 31. Univ of Sheff BA (Architecture) 53. BD (Lon) 66. Clifton Th Coll 61. **d** 63 Bp McKie for Cov **p** 64 Cov. C of St Jo Evang Kenilworth 63-67; Cheadle (in c of St Phil) 67-70; R of Ch Ch Harpurhey Dio Man from 70; St Steph Harpurhey Dio Man from 72. *Rectory, Church Lane, Harpurhey, Manchester, M9 1BG.* (061-205 4020)

HINDS, Dallas Joseph. LTh (Melb) 53. St Jo Coll Morpeth 59. **d** and **p** 59 Newc. C of St Pet E Maitland 59; St Phil Waratah 59-61; P-in-c of Boolaroo 61-64; R of Aberdeen 64-66; C of W Wyalong 66-67; R of Stuart Town 67-68; Gulgong 68-72; Warracknabeal 72-77; V of All SS Bal 77-81; in Dept of Chap Dio Melb from 81. *10 Darling Street, Burwood, Vic, Australia 3125.*

HINDS, Denzil Ivelaw Granville. b 48. Codr Coll Barb 72. **d** and **p** 76 Guy. C of Lodge Dio Guy from 76. *St Barnabas Vicarage, Bourda, Georgetown, Guyana.* (02-61728)

HINDS, Kenneth Arthur Lancelot. b 30. Bps' Coll Cheshunt. **d** 64 **p** 65 St Alb. C of Sawbridgeworth 64-67; Gt Berkhamsted (in c of All SS) 67-71; V of St Mich AA Borehamwood 71-75; R of Princes Town, Trinid 75-79; P-in-c of St Luke Gt Ilford Dio Chelmsf 79-81; V from 81. *St Luke's Vicarage, Ilford, Essex.* (01-478 1104)

HINE, John Timothy Matusch. b 27. TCD BA (3rd cl Mod Lang) 51, MA 54. **d** 55 **p** 56 Linc. C of Boston 55-57; PV, Sacr and Succr of Linc Cathl 57-60; Min Can of St Geo Chap Windsor 60-62; C of Bray w Braywood 60-61; V of Laneast w St Clether 62-65; V of Tresmere 62-65; H Trin Fareham 65-67; Asthall and Swinbrook w Widford Dio Ox from 67; Hon Ed Ox Dioc Year Book 75-79; RD of Witney 76-81. *Swinbrook Vicarage, Burford, Oxford, OX8 4DY.* (Burford 3200)

HINE, Rupert Francis Henry. b 22. Oak Hill Th Coll 62. **d** 63 **p** 64 Lon. C of H Trin Southall 63-67; Southborough (in c of St Matt High Brooms) 67-73; C-in-c of Farmborough (w Priston from 76) Dio B & W 73-77; R from 77. *Rectory, Church Lane, Farmborough, Bath, Avon.* (Timsbury 70727)

HINES, Bruce David. b 36. Westcott Ho Cam 71. **d** 72 **p** 73 St E. C of Woodbridge 72-76; Whitton Dio St E from 76. *Richmond, Burgh, Woodbridge, Suffolk, IP13 6SU.*

HINES, Canon Frank. b 13. Tyndale Hall Bris 36. **d** 39 **p** 40 Man. C of St Geo Mart Daubhill 39-42; Perm to Offic at Penn Fields 42-43; Actg C of Iver 44-46; R of Ashby St Mary w Thurton 46-51; V of Barston 51-57; PC of H Trin Skirbeck 57-68; V 68-71; Surr 65-71; Can and Preb of Decem Librarum in Linc Cathl 67-71; Can Emer from 71; RD of Holland E 68-71; V of Claybrooke w Wibtoft 71-78. *28 Overdale Road, Bayston Hill, Shrewsbury.*

HINETT, Canon James France. b 06. Univ of Lon BA (2nd cl Engl) 27, BD 44. Ripon Hall Ox 28. **d** 29 **p** 30 Birm. C of All SS Birm 29-33; St John Sparkhill 33-36; V of H Trin Bordesley 36-41; Ch Ch Summerfield Birm 41-60; RD of Edgbaston 49-60; Sutton Coldfield 66-71; Hon Can of Birm 54-71; Can (Emer) from 71; V of St Pet Maney 60-71. *Brockley Combe, Bleadon Hill, Weston-s-Mare, Avon, BS24 9JN.* (Bleadon 812514)

HINEY, Thomas Bernard Felix. b 35. MC 61. Ridley Hall Cam 67. **d** 69 **p** 70 Birm. C of St Aug Edgbaston 69-71; CF from 71. *c/o Ministry of Defence, Lansdowne House, Berkeley Square, W1.*

HING'AMBIRE, Paul. Buwalasi Th Coll 64. **d** 66 **p** 67 Mbale. P Dio Mbale 64-72; Dio Bukedi from 72. *Church of Uganda, Kachonga, Uganda.*

HINGE, David Gerald Francis. b 30. Wells Th Coll 64. **d** 66 Lon **p** 67 Willesden for Lon. C of St Anne Brookfield 66-69; All H N Greenford 69-71; V of Winton 71-78; R of Etherley Dio Dur from 78. *Rectory, Etherley, Bishop Auckland, Co Durham.* (Bp Auckld 832350)

HINGLEY, Christopher James Howard. b 48. Trin Coll Ox BA 69, MA 71. Wycl Hall Ox 81. **d** 80 **p** 81 Matab. C of St John's Cathl Bulawayo 80-81; on study leave. *c/o Wycliffe Hall, Oxford.*

HINGLEY, Robert Charles. b 46. Ball Coll Ox BA 69, MA 74. Univ of Birm Dipl Th 72. Qu Coll Birm 70. **d** 73 **p** 74 S'wark. C of Old Charlton 73-76; Asst Warden The Abbey Iona 76-77; Team V of Langley Marish Dio Ox from 77. *Christ the Worker House, Parlaunt Road, Langley, Slough, Berks.* (Slough 45167)

HINGLEY, Roderick Stanley Plant. b 51. St Chad's Coll Dur BA 72. St Steph Ho Ox 74. **d** 75 **p** 76 Lich. C of Lower Gornal 75-79; St Mich Tividale Dio Lich from 79. *Holy Cross House, Ashleigh Road, Tividale, Warley, W Midl, B69 1LL.* (Dudley 57060)

HINGSTON, Augustus Shodekeh. d 66 **p** 67 Sier L. P Dio Sier L. *46b Syke Street, Freetown, Sierra Leone, W Africa.* (Freetown 40505)

HINGSTON, John Hamilton Noel. b 1888. Keble Coll Ox BA 19, MA 20. St Steph Ho Ox 19. **d** 21 **p** 22 Lon. C of St Matthias Earl's Court 21-23; St Andr W Kens 23-31; All SS Babbacombe 31-36; H. Cross St Pancras 36-40; C-in-c of St Matt Westminster 40-46; Actg C 46-58; Asst Chap of Westmr Hosp 46-58. *Three Ways Nursing Home, Beacon Road, Seaford, E Sussex, BN25 2LT.*

HINKES, Sidney George Stuart. b 25. Univ of Lon BA 50. BD 70. St Steph Ho Ox 50. **d** 52 Lich **p** 53 Stafford for Cant. C of St Paul Burton-on-Trent 52-54; St Clem Leigh-on-Sea 54-58; Upton w Chalvey 58-66; Priest-Missr of St Mary's Conv Distr Bayswater City and Dio Ox from 66. *St Mary's Church House, Bayswater Road, Headington, Oxford, OX3 9EY.* (Oxford 61886)

HINKLEY, Canon William Taylor. Late Scho of St Jo Coll Dur BA (3rd cl Th) 34, MA 38. **d** 35 **p** 36 Dur. C of St Hilda Hartlepool 35-38; S Westoe 38-40; V of H Trin Jesmond 40-44; Walker 44-53; Bywell St Andr w Riding Mill 53-66; RD of Corbridge 60-66; Alnwick 67-81; Hon Can of Newc T from 64; P-in-c of St Paul Alnwick 73-74; Edlingham w Bolton 73-74; Alnwick (w St Paul Alnwick & Edlingham w Bolton from 74) 66-80. *Woodlea, Denwick, Alnwick, Northumb, NE66 3RE.* (Alnwick 602237)

HINKSMAN, Barrie Lawrence James. b 41. K Coll Lon and Warm BD and AKC 64. **d** 65 **p** 66 Linc. C of Crosby 65-69; Frodingham 67-69; Ecumen Development Officer Scunthorpe 67-69; Chelmsley Wood 69-72; Team V 72-74; C-in-c of Offchurch 75-80; Dioc Tr Officer Dio Cov 75-79. *57 Ashby Close, Coventry, CV3 2LN.* (0203 449739)

HINTON, Alfred Richard. b 05. AKC 35. **d** 35 **p** 36 Lon. C of St Thos Acton-Vale 35-38; St Anne Brookfield 38-41; C-in-c of Ermington 41-43; C of St Alban Holborn 43-44; CF (EC) 44-47; Perm to Offic Dio Lon 47-49; V of St Columba Haggerston 49-75; CF (TA) from 54. *25 McKinlay Court, The Parade, Birchington, Kent, CT17 9QE.*

HINTON, Bertram George. b 17. Qu Coll Birm 76. **d** 79 **p** 80 Worc. (NSM). C of St Geo Kidderminster Dio Worc from 79. *22 Drake Crescent, Habberley Estate, Kidderminster, Worcs, DY11 6EE.*

HINTON, David Hugh. b 31. Tyndale Hall Bris. **d** 63 **p** 64 Derby. C of Belper 63-67; St Steph Bowling 67-71; V of Denholme 71-79; P-in-c of Morton Dio Bradf 79-80; V from 80. *Morton Vicarage, Keighley, W Yorks, BD20 5RS.* (Bingley 3829)

HINTON, Geoffrey. b 34. Univ of Dur BA 56. Em Coll Cam BA (2nd cl Archit and Fine Arts Trip pt ii) 67, MA 72. Ridley Hall Cam 58. **d** 60 Glouc **p** 61 York. C of Cheltm 60-61; Beverley Minster 61-65; Newark-on-Trent 70-71. *c/o 16 Keith Road, Bournemouth, BH3 7DU.*

HINTON, Harold Arthur. McGill Univ BEng 52. Trin Coll Tor STB 64. **d** 64 **p** 65 Newfld. C of Corner Brook 64-67; R of Bay L'Argent 67-71; Stephenville 71-76; New Harbour Dio E Newfld from 76. *New Harbour, Trinity Bay, Newfoundland, Canada.*

HINTON, Harold Herbert. Moore Th Coll Syd ACT ThL 67. **d** 68 **p** 69 Syd. C of Hunters Hill 68-69; Kangaroo Valley Dio Syd from 69. *Rectory, Kangaroo Valley, NSW 2577, Australia.*

HINTON, John Dorsett Owen. b 21. Wells Th Coll 59. **d** 61 **p** 62 Ex. C of Littleham w Exmouth 61-66; V of Pucklechurch w Abson and Dyrham Dio Bris from 67. *Pucklechurch Vicarage, Bristol, BS17 3RD.* (Abson 2260)

HINTON, Canon John Percy. b 07. St Pet Coll Ox BA 33 MA 43. Westcott Ho Cam 33. **d** 34 **p** 35 Liv. C of St Simon and St Jude Anfield 34-36; Calne 36-40; Tottenham 40-41; V of Westbury w Dilton and Westbury Leigh 41-55; R of Bridport 55-74; Can and Preb of Sarum Cathl 65-75; Can (Emer) from 75. *52 Bratton Road, Westbury, Wilts, BA13 3ES.* (0373 823848)

HINTON, Michael Ernest. b 33. K Coll Lon and Warm. **d** 57 **p** 58 Ex. C of Babbacombe 57-60; H Redeemer Sea Point CP 60-62; R of Goodwood CP 62-66; C-in-c of St Pet Limehouse 66-68; R of Felmingham 68-72; R of Suffield 68-72; C-in-c of Colby w Banningham and Tuttington 68-72; P-in-c of Abaco 72-76; V of Mylor w Flushing 76-80. *c/o Mylor Vicarage, Falmouth, TR11 5UD.* (Penryn 74408)

HINTON, Roger Amos. b 33. Keble Coll Ox BA 56, MA 60. Ridley Hall Cam 56. **d** 58 **p** 59 York. C of Drypool 58-61; CMS Miss Patna 62-66; on Tr Coll Staff 67-69; V of Kar Cathl 69-76; V of Coalville (w Bardon Hill from 78) Dio Leic from 76; RD of Akeley S from 81. *Christ Church Vicarage, Coalville, Leicester, LE6 2JA.* (Coalville 38287)

HINTSA, Headman Mbovane Lizo. St Pet Coll Alice 63. **d** 65 **p** 66 Grahmstn. O of Ethiopia. P Dio Grahmstn 65-68 and from 75; Dio St John's 68-75. *c/o 96 High Street, Grahamstown, S Africa.*

HINXMAN, Frederic William. b 32. Episc Th Sem Kentucky LTh 74. **d** 74 Lexington for NS **p** 74 Bp Arnold for NS. C of Port Dufferin Dio NS from 74. *The Rectory, Port Dufferin, NS, Canada.*

HINYURA, Meshak. b 54. **d** 79 W Tang. d Dio W Tang. *DWT Mulela, c/o PO Box 175, Kigoma, Tanzania.*

HIPKIN, Canon Frederick William. ACT ThL 32. **d** 30 **p** 32 Bend. C of Pyramid Hill 30-32; V 32-33; R of St Matt Long Gully and Chap Bendigo Base Hosp 33-35; Cohuna 35-37; C of Bp's Castle w Mainstone 37-39; V of Foster 39-41; R of Orbost 41-47; Maffra 47-52; Dir of Relig Educn Dio Gippsld 47-52 and from 60; Chap of Yarrabah 52-59; V of Rosedale 59-63; Can of St Paul's Cathl Sale 61-71; Can (Emer) from 74; R of Yarram 63-71; Archd of S Gippsld 64-71; VG of Gipplsd 66-71; Perm to Offic Dio Gippsld from 71. *Kathleen Taylor Memorial Homes, Rosedale, Vic., Australia.* (051-99 2526)

HIPKIN, Howard Stockdale. b 1899. **d** 35 **p** 36 Melan. Commiss Dio Melan 35-39; Perm to Offic (Col Cl Act) At St Steph Paddington 40-43; Home Sec Melan Miss 41-43; C of St Mich Wood Green 43-45; V of St Andr Southgate 45-69. *43 Highcroft Crescent, Bognor Regis, Sussex.*

HIPKIN, Peter William. b 37. Univ of Witwatersrand BA 57. Westcott Ho Cam 58. **d** 61 Bp Reeves for Johann **p** 62 Johann. C of St Mary Virg Cathl Johann 61-66; P-in-c of Kliptown 66-72; Formosa 72-73; Masite Miss 73-74; L to Offic Dio Capetn 74-76; P-in-c of Mitchell's Plain Capetn 77-80; V of St Greg Gt Small Heath Dio Birm from 80. *22 Tennyson Road, Smallheath, Birmingham 10.* (021-772 7673)

HIPKINS, John Malcolm. b 33. Qu Coll Birm 78. **d** 80 Lich **p** 81 Derby. Perm to Offic Dio Lich 80-81; C of St Luke City and Dio Derby from 81. *28 Hindscarth Crescent, Mickleover, Derby, DE3 5NN.*

HIPKINS, Leslie Michael. b 35. Univ of Dur BA 57. ACIS 60. Oak Hill Coll 78. **d** 81 Colchester for Chelmsf (NSM). C of Halstead Dio Chelmsf from 81. *Pentire, Great Maplestead, Essex, CO9 2RH.*

HIPP, Thomas Leo. St Jo Coll Armid 22. ACT ThL 24. **d** 30 New Westmr for Br Columb **p** 31 Br Columb. C of Cumberland w Denman I 30-36; V of Chemainus w Westholme 36-42; CF (Canad) 42-46; Chap of Fairbridge Farm Sch Cowichan 46-50; R of St Nich N Burnaby 50-68. *Apt 106, 7272 Salisbury Avenue, Burnaby 1, BC, Canada.*

HIPWELL, Preb Trevor Senior. Trin Coll Dub BA 47. **d** 47 **p** 48 Lim. C of St Mary's Cathl Lim 47-49; Taney 49-56; Min Can of St Patr Cathl Dub 49-56 and from 64; R of St Thos Mt Merrion City and Dio Dub from 56; Preb of St Patr Cathl Dub from 75. *Rectory, Foster Avenue, Mount Merrion, Blackrock, Co Dublin, Irish Republic.*

HIRD, Edward Allen. b 54. Vanc Sch of Th MDiv. **d** 80 Abp Somerville for New Westmr **p** 81 Abp Hambidge for New Westmr. C of St Phil Vanc Dio New Westmr from 80. *3741 West 27th Avenue, Vancouver, BC, Canada, V6S 1R2.*

HIRI, Moffatt. b 50. Bp Patteson Th Centre Kohimarama 70. **d** 73 **p** 74 Melan. P Dio Melan 73-75; Centr Melan from 75. *Noranora, Bauro, Solomon Islands.*

HIRONS, Malcolm Percy. b 36. Or Coll Ox 2nd cl Cl 57, BA 2nd cl Th 59, MA 62. Wycl Hall Ox 59. **d** 61 **p** 62 Birm. C of St Aug of Hippo Edgbaston 61-64; Chap of Warwick Sch 64-65; C of Beverley Minster 65-69; V of Barnby Dun 69-80; C-in-c of Kirk Bramwith 75-80; Fenwick 75-80; V of St Paul Norton Lees City and Dio Sheff from 80. *Vicarage, Norton Lees Lane, Sheffield, S8 9BD.* (Sheff 51945)

HIRST, Alan. Linc Th Coll 79. **d** 81 Man. C of Newton Heath Dio Man from 81. *7 Leng Road, Newton Heath, Manchester.*

HIRST, Anthony Melville. b 50. Univ of Keele BA 73. Cudd Coll 74. **d** 77 **p** 78 Roch. C of S Gillingham 77-80; Coity w Nolton Dio Llan from 80; Oblate OSB W Malling Abbey from 81. *Y Lletty, School Road, Coity, Bridgend, Mid Glam, CF35 6BL.*

HIRST, David William. b 37. Univ of Man BA (Psychol) 78. St Aid Coll 61. **d** 63 Middleton for Man **p** 64 Man. C of St Cross Clayton 63-64; St John Bury 64-66; Perm to Offic Dio Ripon 66-67; C of Woodhouse Pk 67-70; V of St Chad's Limeside Oldham 70-79; Friezland Dio Man from 79. *Friezland Vicarage, Greenfield, Oldham, Lancs.* (Saddleworth 2507)

HIRST, Godfrey Ian. b 41. St D Coll Lamp BA 63. Chich Th Coll. **d** 65 Blackb **p** 66 Lanc for Blackb. C of Brierfield 65-68; Industr Chap Kirkby 68-71; P-in-c of St Chad Kirkby 71; Team V 71-75; P-in-c of Treales and Industr Co-Ordinator Dio Blackb from 75; Sen Chap Lancs Industr Miss from 78. *Treales Vicarage, Kirkham, Lancs.* (0772 682219)

HIRST, John Adrian. b 49. Univ of Nottm BTh 78. St Jo Coll Nottm 75. **d** 78 **p** 79 Glouc. C of St Mark Cheltenham Dio Glouc from 78. *33 Farmington Road, Benhall, Cheltenham, Glos, GL51 6AG.*

HIRST, Martin Bertram. b 07. Late Exhib of Keble Coll Ox BA (3rd cl Mod Hist) 29, MA 57. Bps' Coll Cheshunt 29. **d** 31 **p** 32 Lich. C of All SS Wolverhampton 31-32; St Mary Sedgley 32-34; Bognor Regis 34-36; St Mich Newquay 36-39; V of Cabacaburi w Pomeroon R 39-43; P-in-c of Rupununi Missions 44-45; V of Cabacaburi 45-52; R of Anna Regina 52-55; V of Morwenstow 55-60; Probus w Cornelly 60-72. *St Morwenna, Devoran Lane, Devoran, Truro.* (Devoran 862962)

HIRST, Peter Thornton. b 34. Univ of Leeds BA (2nd cl Gen) 59. Ely Th Coll 59. **d** 61 **p** 62 Lich. C of Brierley Hill 61-64; Wednesfield 64-66; R of St Bart, Salford 66-71; V of St Mary Sedgley 71-77; R of St Aid Billingham Team Min Dio Dur from 77. *12a Tintern Avenue, Billingham, TS23 2DE.* (Stockton 531740)

HIRST, Reginald Arnold Archer. St Paul's Coll Grahmstn. **d** 60 **p** 61 Capetn. C of Stellenbosch 60-64; St Sav Claremont 64-66; St Martin Durban 68-72; R 72-76; Parktown Dio Johann from 76. *8 Eton Road, Parktown, Johannesburg, S Africa.* (011-31 2998)

HIRST, Roland Geoffrey. b 42. St Cath Coll Cam BA 63, MA 68. N-W Ordin Course 74. **d** 77 **p** 78 York. C of St Mary Beverley 77-81; P-in-c of Flamborough and of Bempton Dio York from 81. *Flamborough Vicarage, Bridlington, E Yorks, YO15 1PE.* (Bridlington 850336)

HIRST, Wilfrid. b 11. Roch Th Coll 65. **d** 66 **p** 67 S'wark. C of Woodmansterne 66-69; Shere w Peaslake 69-71; R of Lifton 71-74; Kelly w Bradstone 71-74; Exbourne w Jacobstowe 74-77. *3 Park Drive, Felpham, Bognor Regis, Sussex.* (Middleton-on-Sea 4058)

HIRST, William John. b 15. St Pet Coll Ox BA (4th cl Th) 38, MA 41. Wycl Hall Ox 38. **d** 40 **p** 41 Ripon. C of Ch Ch U Armley 40-43; Ch Ch Harrogate 43-47; V of Kettlewell w Conistone 47-55; Hoo All Hallows w Stoke 55-76; Hon C of St Pet Harrogate Dio Ripon from 77. *52 Unity Grove, Harrogate, N Yorks, HG1 2AQ.* (0423 504990)

HISCOCK, Charles William. Qu Coll Newfld LTh 65. **d** 64 **p** 65 Newfld. C of St Mich AA St John's 64-65; R of Greenspond 65-72; C of St Thos, St John's 72-77; I of St Mark, St John's Dio E Newfld from 78. *7 Poles Crescent, St John's, Newfoundland, Canada.*

HISCOCK, Donald Henry. St Mich Th Coll Crafers 50. ACT ThL 56. **d** 53 **p** 54 Adel. M SSM from 54; L to Offic Dio Adel 53; C of Averham w Kelham 56-58; Ho of SSM Kelham 58-59; L to Offic Dio Southw 58-59; C of Modderpoort 59-60; St Jas Miss Mantsonyane 60-61; Sub-Prior St Mich Ho Crafers and Novice Master 65-73; Prior 73-76; Dio Perth 76-80; R of Girrawheen w Koondoola Dio Perth from 76. *Nelligan Avenue, Girrawheen, W Australia 6064.* (42 4076)

HISCOCK, Edward Percy. Univ of Sheff BA 22. Leeds Cl Scho 22. **d** 23 **p** 24 Newfld. C of Trinity 23-24; R 24-29; R of Burin 29-33; Perm to Offic (Col Cl Act) at Winshill 33-35; C 35-37; PC of St Bart Derby 37-39; R of St Mary Belize and Sec of Synod Dio Br Hond 39-42; C of St Marg Fredericton 42-44; Corner Brook 45-48; R of Pouch Cove 48-59; Jacobstow w Warbstow 59-60; C-in-c of Treneglos 59-60; R of Milverton Ont 60-64. *20 Edinburgh Drive, Mount Pearl, Newfoundland, Canada.*

HISCOCK, Hollis Robert Nathanael. Mem Univ Newfld BA 64. Qu Coll Newfld. **d** 64 **p** 65 Newfld. C of Flower's Cove 64-65; I of Cow Head 65-69; on leave 70-71; C of St Thos, St John's 72-75; Hon C of Corner Brook 76-77; C of St Thos, St John's Dio E Newfld 78-80; R from 80. *26 Empire Avenue, St John's, Newfoundland, Canada.*

HISCOCK, Peter George Harold. b 31. Wadh Coll Ox BA 54, MA 66. Ely Th Coll 54. **d** 58 Liv **p** 59 Warrington for Liv. C of St Dunstan Edge Hill 58-61; Kirkby 61-64; St Luke Southport 64-66; Asst Dean of Residence Trin Coll Dub 66-68; Dean 68-73; Min Can of St Patr Cathl Dub 67-70; Chap and Lect St Steph Coll Delhi 73-76; Team V of Jarrow Dio Dur from 77. *St Paul's House, Borough Road, Jarrow, T & W.* (Jarrow 897402)

HISCOX, Edward. St D Coll Lamp BA 54. Wells Th Coll 54. **d** 56 **p** 57 Swan B. C of St Gabr Swansea 56-59; Llanguicke (Pontardawe) 59-64; V of Drybrook 64-74; R of Daglingworth w Duntisbourne Rous and Duntisbourne Abbots and Winstone Dio Glouc from 74. *Daglingworth Rectory, Cirencester, Glos.* (Miserden 301)

HISLOP, John. b 40. Melb Univ ACT ThL 74. St Jo Coll Auckld 75. **d** 75 **p** 76 Auckld. C of Papakura 75-78; Ellerslie 79; St Hilary Kew Dio Melb from 79. *St Hilary's Vicarage, John Street, Kew, Vic, Australia 3101.*

HISLOP, William Maxwell. St Bonif Coll Warm 27. **d** 30 **p** 31 York. C of Thornton-le-Street and N Otterington w Thornton-le-Moor and Thornton-le-Beans 30-33; Ash w Ash Vale 33-35; Fordingbridge w Ibsley 35-39; Actg C of St Ambrose Bournemouth 40-42; R of Godmanstone 42-51; V of Nether Cerne 42-51; PC of Cudworth w Chillington Dio B & W from 52. *Vicarage, Cudworth, Ilminster, Somt.* (Ilminster 180)

HITCH, Allen Thomas. b 34. Univ of Windsor Ont BA 62. Trin Coll Tor STB 65. **d** and **p** 68 Queb. C of St Jo Evang Montr 68; P-in-c of Magdalen Is 68-69; on leave 70-75; R of Ch Ch Kitchener Dio Hur from 76. *187 Carson Drive, Kitchener, Ont, Canada, N2B 2Z3.*

HITCH, Kim William. b 54. Univ of Leic BSc 75. Trin Coll Bris 76. **d** 78 **p** 79 Chelmsf. C of St Mary Becontree 78-80; Huyton Quarry Dio Liv from 80. *51a Darwick Drive, Huyton, Liverpool, L36 0SP.* (051-489 2412)

HITCHCOCK, David. b 37. SOC 70. **d** 73 **p** 74 Roch (APM). C of Ch Ch Milton-next-Gravesend Dio Roch from 73. *148 Old Road East, Gravesend, Kent.* (Gravesend 61091)

HITCHINSON, Preb William Henry. b 12. Chich Th Coll 51. **d** 53 **p** 54 Lon. C of Twickenham 53-56; V of Eastcote 56-80; Preb of St Paul's Cathl Lon 76-80; Preb (Emer) from 80. *66 Waller Drive, Northwood, Middx, HA6 1BW.* (Northwood 29778)

HITOKALAPO, Stephen Ndemongela. **d** 71 Damar **p** 72 Bp Wade for Capetn for Damar. P Dio Damar 71-80; Dio Namibia from 80. *PO Box 11, Oshakati, SW Africa.* (Oshakati 187)

HITSMAN, Anthomy William. b 49. Trent Univ Ont BA 77. Trin Coll Tor MDiv 80. **d** 81 Alg. C of St Mich AA Thunder Bay Dio Alg from 81. *2 Ryde Avenue, Thunder Bay, Ont, Canada, P7B 4M2.*

HIVES, Arthur Royston. Angl Th Coll BC LTh 59. **d** and **p** 59 New Westmr. R of Miss City 59-65; Regional Rep BC Div of Broadcasting from 65. *690 Burrard Street, Vancouver 1, BC, Canada.*

HJORTH, Rolf Gunnar Leer. b 25. St Jo Coll Ox BA 46, MA 50. Wycl Hall Ox 61. **d** 62 **p** 63 Ox. C of Cumnor 62-65; V of Bramfield w Walpole 65-69; Oulton 69-78; Chap at Ostend, Knokke and Bruges Dio (Gibr in Eur from 80) Lon (N & C Eur) from 78. *101 Langestraat, 8400 Ostend, Belgium.* (511731)

HKA MAW, Gam. **d** 38 **p** 39 Rang. P Dio Rang 38-70; Dio Mand 70-72. *Jedung, Burma.*

HLA AUNG, Andrew. Em Div Sch Mohnyin. **d** 62 Rang. d Dio Rang 62-70; Dio Mand from 70. *St George's Church, Taunggyi, Burma.*

HLA AUNG, Lay Wee. H Cross Coll Rang. **d** 59 Rang. d Dio Rang 59-70; Dio Pa-an from 70. *c/o St Luke's Compound, Toungoo, Burma.*

✠ **HLA GYAW, Most Rev Gregory.** **d** 70 **p** 71 Rang. C of All SS Thingangyun 70-73; Chap Miss to Seamen Rang 72-73; Cons Ld Bp of Pa-an in H Trin Cathl Rang 25 Feb 73 by Abp of Burma and Abp Ah Mya; Bps of Mand and Akyab; and Bp Ta Preh Paw; Trld to Rang (Abp and Metrop of Prov of Burma) 79. *140 Pyidaungsu, Yeiktha Road, Rangoon, Burma.* (Rangoon 12668)

HLA GYAW, Ven John. **d** and **p** 31 Rang. St Pet Miss 31-45; Archd of Toungoo 45-48 and 53-70; Rang 48-53; Pa-an 70-73. *St Peter's Mission, Toungoo, Burma.*

HLA MAUNG, Peter. St Aug Coll Cant. **d** 63 Cant for Rang. d Dio Rang. *St John's Church, Rangoon, Burma.*

HLANYA, Williard Clement. St Jo Sem Lusaka. **d** 63 N Rhod **p** 65 Zam. P Dio Zam 65-70; Dio N Zam from 71; Dean of St Mary's Pro-Cathl Mufulira Dio N Zam 71-76; VG Dio N Zam from 74. *PO Box 838, Mufulira, Zambia.* (024-4775)

HLAULA, Canon Silas. St Pet Coll Rosettenville. **d** 42 **p** 43 Grahmstn. Asst Miss St Matt Miss Grahmstn 42-44; St Steph Port Eliz 44-45; St Pet Peddie 45-49; Miss St Steph Port Elizabeth 49-56; St Matt Miss Grahmstn 56-62; Bolotwa 62-73; Hon Can of Port Eliz from 81. *Box 55, Somerset East, CP, S Africa.*

HLOAHLOA, James Qhezi. Coll of Resurr Rosettenville 51. **d** 53 **p** 54 Johann. C of St Cypr Miss Distr Vereeniging 53-58; R of Ventersdorp 58-62; Lichtenburg 62-66; Jouberton

66-69; P-in-c of Evaton w Sebokeng 69-76; C of Fobane 76-79; Perm to Offic Dio Johann from 79. *Box 5, Sebokeng 1982, S Africa.*

HLOMA, Austin. **d** 79 Matab. d Dio Matab. *PO Mpopoma, Bulawayo, Zimbabwe.*

HO, Allan Hin-Ming. U Th Coll Hong Kong. **d** 66 **p** 67 Hong. P Dio Hong. *St Luke's Church, Kennedy Town, Hong Kong.* (5-977881)

HO, Simon Sai-ming. Ming Hua Coll Hong. **d** 55 **p** 57 Hong. P Dio Hong. *St Luke's Church, Kennedy Town, Hong Kong.* (3-678031)

HOAD, Ven Edward John Idenden. Univ of Manit BA 35. St Jo Coll Manit LTh 37, Hon DD 75. **d** 37 **p** 38 Calg. Miss of Blackie Miss 37-39; I of Claresholm w Nanton 39-42; Strathmore 42-43; R of St Pet Okotoks 43-45; Stonewall 45-49; RD of Selkirk 46-49; R of St Anne Winnipeg 49-60; St Phil Winnipeg Dio Rupld 60-71; Hon Can of Rupld 60-63; Exam Chap to Abp of Rupld 62-71; Can of Rupld 63-71; Archd of Selkirk 71-78; Archd (Emer) from 78; I of Ch Ch Selkirk 71-78; Perm to Offic Dio New Westmr from 81. *113-1509 Martin Street, White Rock, BC, Canada.*

HOAR, George Stanley. b 20. Chich Th Coll 47. **d** 50 Newc T **p** 53 Linc. C of St Geo Cullercoats 50-52; Old Brumby 53-56; PC of Alvingham w N and S Cockerington 56-60; V of Leake 60-71; V of Castle Bytham Dio Linc from 71; R of Bytham Parva Dio Linc from 71; Careby w Holywell and Aunby Dio Linc from 71. *Castle Bytham Vicarage, Grantham, Lincs, NG33 4SG.* (Castle Bytham 308)

HOARE, Bruce John. b 47. St Jo Coll Morpeth 71. **d** and **p** 73 River. C of Griffith 73-76; Chap Miss to Seamen Syd 76-78; Perm to Offic Dio Syd 77-78; P-in-c of Lockhart Dio River from 78. *Box 49, Lockhart, NSW, Australia 2656.* (205549)

HOARE, David Marlyn. b 33. Bps' Coll Cheshunt 60. **d** 63 **p** 64 St Alb. C of Ampthill w Millbrook and Steppingley 63-67; Bushey 67-70; V of Harlington 70-76; All SS Oxhey 76-81; Hellesdon Dio Nor from 81. *6 Wensum Crescent, Hellesdon, Norwich, NR6 5DL.* (Norwich 46902)

HOARE, Canon Kenneth Gerard. b 03. Trin Coll Cam BA 25, MA 29. Wells Th Coll. **d** 27 Bris **p** 28 Malmesbury for Bris. C of St Paul Swindon 27-31; St Aug Bermondsey 31-32; Putney (in c of All SS) 32-36; C-in-c of St Edw Conv Distr Mottingham 36-43; V of Betchworth 43-55; R of Godstone 55-65; Elsing w Bylaugh 65-71; RD of Sparham 67-69; Perm to Offic Dio S'wark from 72; Hon Can of S'wark 72; Can (Emer) from 72. *Walkingstead, Godstone, Surrey.* (Godstone 842274)

HOARE, Patrick Reginald Andrew Reid. b 47. TD 80. Wycl Hall Ox 77. **d** 80 **p** 81 York. C of Guisborough Dio York from 80. *38 Cobble Carr, Guisborough, Cleve, TS14 6NR.* (0287 35873)

HOARE, Roger John. b 38. Tyndale Hall Bris 63. **d** 66 **p** 67 Guildf. C of Em Stoughton 66-70; Chesham 70-73; V of St Bart Bath Dio B & W from 73. *5 Oldfield Road, Bath, Avon, BA2 3ND.* (Bath 22070)

HOARE, Canon Rupert William Noel. b 40. Trin Coll Ox BA (1st cl Th) 61, MA 66. Fitzw Ho Cam BA (1st cl Th Trip pt iii) 64. Univ of Birm PhD 73. Westcott Ho Cam 62. **d** 64 Middleton for Man **p** 65 Man. C of Oldham 64-67; Lect Qu Coll Birm 68-72; Can Th of Cov 70-76; R of The Resurr Man 72-78; Can Res of Birm Cathl 78-81; Prin Westcott Ho Cam from 81. *Westcott House, Cambridge.* (Cambridge 350074)

HOARE, Simon Gerard. b 37. K Coll Lon and Warm AKC 61. **d** 62 **p** 63 Ripon. C of Headingley 62-65; Adel 65-68; R of Spofforth w Follifoot (and Kirk-Deighton from 71) 68-76; V of Rawdon Dio Bradf from 76. *Vicarage, Rawdon, Leeds, LS19 6QQ.* (Rawdon 503263)

HOARE, William Albert George. St John's Coll Morpeth ACT ThL 45. **d** 44 **p** 45 Newc. C of New Lambton 44-45; P-in-c of Clarencetown 45-49; R of Bulahdelah 49-50; C-in-c of Belmont 50-53; R 53-58; Branxton 58-62; Wyong 62-72; Perm to Offic Dio Newc from 72. *60 Karingal Crescent, French's Forest, NSW, Australia 2086.*

HOARE, William Gilbert David. **d** 67 **p** 73 NW Austr. C of Carnarvon 67-68; Kwinana 69-73; R of Murchison 74-80; Harvey Dio Bunb from 80. *Rectory, Young Street, Harvey, W Australia.* (29-1041)

HOBAN, John. St Aid Coll 37. **d** 40 **p** 41 Blackb. C of St Phil Blackb 40-43; St Jo Bapt Bapt Earlestown 43-46; Ch Ch Mt Pellon 46-48; V of Stonefold 48-52; Sunnybrow 52-55; Ch Ch Bacup 55-60; V of Over Kellet 60-63; Rishton 63-70; Glasson 70-72; L to Offic Dio Blackb from 79. *14 Broad Oak Road, Accrington, Lancs, BB5 2BP.* (Accrington 33808)

HOBART, Dean of. *See* Parsons, Very Rev Jeffrey Michael Langdon.

HOBBS, Antony Ewan Talbot. Ripon Hall Ox 58. **d** 60 **p** 61 Chich. C of Cuckfield Hosp from 62; V of Staplefield Dio Chich from 64. *Staplefield Vicarage, Haywards Heath, Sussex, RH17 6EN.* (Handcross 241)

HOBBS, Basil Ernest William. b 22. St Chad's Coll Dur BA (Hons Th) 49. Dipl in Th 50. **d** 51 **p** 52 S'wark. C of St Mark, Mitcham 51-54; CF 54-68; Asst Chap St Mary's Hosp Lon 69-72; L to Offic H Trin Paddington 70-72; Novice CR 72-74; Publ Pr Dio Southw from 74; Pastoral Consultant Clinical Th Assoc from 74; Chap HM Pris Nottm from 81. *7 Weston Avenue, Nottingham, NG7 4BA.* (Nottm 785475)

HOBBS, David Stanley. b 20. St D Coll Lamp BA (2nd cl Hist) and LTh 44. **d** 44 **p** 45 St D. C of St Issell 44-52; Asst Master St Paul's Cathl Choir Sch Lon and C of All H St Pancras 52-56; V of Martlewy U 56-58; R of Crunwere (w Amroth from 70) 58-78. *Hill Top, St Bride's Lane, Saundersfoot, Dyfed, SA69 9HL.*

HOBBS, Everett Macklin. b 36. Mem Univ Newfld BA 60. Qu Coll Newfld LTh 61. Univ of Lon BD (2nd cl) 68. **d** 61 **p** 62 Newfld. C of Foxtrap 61-66; Hon C of St Mary Primrose Hill Hampstead 66-67; Chap Qu Coll Newfld 68-69; R of Trin E Newfld 69-71; Hon C of St Aug Qu Gate Kens 72-78; C of St Mich AA St Johns 78-80; Hosp Chap Dio E Newfld from 80. *23a King's Bridge Road, St John's, Newfoundland, Canada.*

HOBBS, Frank. b 07. St D Coll Lamp BA 34. **d** 35 **p** 36 St D. C of Laugharne 35-37; Chap RAF 37-46; R of Rhoscrowther w Pwllcrochan 46-54; V of Lamphey w Hodgeston 54-72. *5 Penllwyn Park, Carmarthen, Dyfed.*

HOBBS, James. b 42. Linc Th Coll 66. **d** 68 Aston for Birm **p** 69 Birm. C of St Mary Moseley 68-73; V of St Mark Kingstanding 73-77; R of Bradfield St Geo (w Bradfield St Clare and Felsham w Gedding from 80) Dio St E from 77; R of Rushbrooke 77-78; P-in-c of Bradfield St Clare 77-80; Felsham w Gedding 77-80. *Bradfield St George Rectory, Bury St Edmunds, Suff.* (Sicklesmere 347)

HOBBS, John Graham. b 29. Univ of Bris BA (2nd cl) 52. Wells Th Coll 52. **d** 54 **p** 55 Win. C of Maybush Peel Distr Shirley 54-59; C-in-c of St Ives and St Leon Conv Distr Ringwood 59-66; V of Hythe Win 66-72; Eastleigh 72-79; Surr 73-79; P-in-c of Ampfield Dio Win from 79. *Ampfield Vicarage, Romsey, Hants.* (Braishfield 68291)

HOBBS, Ven Keith. b 25. Ex Coll Ox BA 46, MA 51. Wells Th Coll 56. **d** 58 **p** 59 Ox. C of St Steph, Clewer 58-60; Perm to Offic Dio Lon 60-71; Hon C St Steph Gloucester Rd, Kens 62-71; C 71-78; Actg Gen Sec Ch U 78; Dom Chap to Bp of Chich 78-81; Archd of Chich from 81. *4 Canon Lane, Chichester, W Sussex, PO19 1PX.* (0243-784260)

HOBBS, Kenneth Brian. b 22. AKC 49. St Bonif Coll Warm 49. **d** 50 **p** 51 Glouc. C of Cainscross 50-51; All SS Cheltenham 51-55; Grantham 55-58; Area Sec for UMCA in SE Engl 58-62; V of Ch Ch Milton Gravesend 62-64; C of All SS Cheltm 64-71; V of Em Cheltm Dio Glouc. *98 Leckhampton Road, Cheltenham, Glos.* (Cheltenham 23674)

HOBBS, Kenneth Ian. b 50. Oak Hill Coll 74. **d** 77 **p** 78 Roch. C of Southborough 77-80; Hoole Dio Ches from 80. *44 Ullswater Crescent, Newton, Chester.* (0244-319677)

HOBBS, Michael Bedo. b 30. Fitzw Ho Cam BA 58, MA 62. Clifton Th Coll 58. **d** 60 **p** 61 Portsm. C of St Jude Southsea Portsea 60-63; Chap at Asuncion Paraguay 63-65; Salta 65-67; PC of Potters Green 68-69; V 69-74; Distr Sec BFBS Kent, Surrey and S Lon 75-81; Ex Sec from 81. *95 London Road, Tonbridge, Kent, TN10 3AJ.* (Tonbridge 353739)

HOBBS, Canon Philip Bertram. b 20. MBE 81. Wells Th Coll 46. **d** 48 **p** 49 Glouc. C of Ch Ch Glouc 48-51; R of Boxwell w Leighterton 51-60; C-in-c of Ozleworth 58-60; C-in-c of Newington Bagpath w Kingscote 58-60; V of St Jas Glouc 60-74; Chap of HM Pris Glouc from 61; V of Sevenhampton w Charlton Abbots and Hawling (w Whittington from 75) Dio Glouc from 74; C-in-c of Whittington 74-75; Hon Can of Glouc Cathl from 77. *Vicarage, Sevenhampton, Cheltenham, Glos.* (Andoversford 246)

HOBBS, William Ebert. Bp's Univ Lennox BA 51. BD (Gen Synod) 61. **d** 51 **p** 52 Ott. C-in-c of Stafford 51-53; CF (Canad) 53-56; R of St Richard 56-60; Hon Can of NS 60-72; Dioc Comm Dio NS 60-62; Supervisor of Stewardship Gen Synod 62-63; Dir of Information and Stewardship 63-66; in Amer Ch. *412 Sycamore, Cincinnati, OH45202, USA.*

HOBBY, Ronald Joseph. St Jo Coll Morpeth. **d** 42 **p** 43 Perth. C of Mosman Pk 42-44; P-in-c of Bruce Rock 44-50; Carnarvon 50-54; R of Kelmscott-Armadale 55-58; St Phil Cottesloe 59-64; CF (Austr) 64-69; L to Offic Dio Perth 66-69; R of N Beach 70-73; Chap Shenton Pk Centre and St Jo Hosp Subiaco 73-80; Repat Gen Hosp from 80. *35 Whitfield Street, Floreat Park, W Australia 6014.* (387 2319)

HOBCROFT, John. Trin Coll Dub BA 32, MA 39. **d** 32 **p** 33 Connor. C of St Bart Belf 32-39; I of Tartaraghan 39-55; Drogheda 55-59; RD of Athirdee and Drogheda 58-61; Creggan 61-63; Mullabrack from 63; I of Loughgilly w Clare 59-63; R of Kilmore w Diamond 63-79; Hon V Cho of Arm Cathl 61-73; Preb of Arm Cathl 73-79; RD of Kilmore 75-79.

16 Alexandra Park, Holywood, Co Down, N Ireland. (Holywood 4975)

HOBDAY, Walter William Henry. b 10. Ely Th Coll 56. **d** 57 Lon **p** 58 Kens for Lon. C of Perivale 57-59; R 59-72; C-in-c of Lichborough w Maidford 72-74; R (w Farthingstone from 76) 74-79; Blakesley w Adstone 72-74; C-in-c of Farthingstone 74-76. *20 The Vale, Northampton, NN1 4ST.* (Northn 712714)

HOBDEN, Brian Charles. b 38. Oak Hill Th Coll 63. **d** 66 **p** 67 S'wark. C of St Steph S Lambeth 66-70; Cheadle 70-76; in Amer Ch from 76. *Box 75, Disputanta, Virginia 23842, USA.*

HOBDEN, David Nicholas. b 54. AKC and BD 76. Ripon Coll Cudd 77. **d** 78 Sarum **p** 79 Ramsbury for Sarum. C of Marlborough 78-81; St Thos of Cant and St Edm of Abingdon City and Dio Sarum from 81. *21 Wyndham Terrace, Salisbury, Wilts.* (0772-25863)

HOBSON, Anthony John. b 42. Univ of Wales (Abth) BSc 64. Univ of Birm MSc 65. Qu Coll Birm 79. **d** 81 **p** 82 Cov (NSM) Sen Lect Cov Poly from 75; C of St Mark Bilton Dio Cov from 81. *4 Juliet Drive, Bilton, Rugby, CV22 6LY.*

HOBSON, Anthony Peter. b 53. St Jo Coll Cam BA 74. St Jo Coll Nottm 75. **d** 77 Man **p** 78 Bp Hulme for Man. C of Brunswick Dio Man from 77. *7 Pedley Walk, Brunswick, Manchester, M13 9XA.* (061-273 5651)

HOBSON, George Douglas. b 06. Trin Coll Dub BA 29, Div Test and Comp Pri 32, MA 34. **d** 32 **p** 33 Dub. C of St Michan and St Paul Dub 32-37; Taney 37-41; Cler V Ch Ch Cathl Dub 39-55; I of St Mark Dub 41-57; Chap to Actors' Ch U 47-76; RD of St Werburgh 54-76; I of St Michan w St Paul (w St Mary from 62) Dub 57-76; Can of Ch Ch Cathl Dub 65-76; Chap Damer Home Dub from 76. *22 Casimir Road, Harold's Cross, Dublin 6, Irish Republic.*

HOBSON, George Ernest. **d** 62 **p** 63 Tor. C of Ch of Transfig Tor 62-64; R of Uxbridge 64-66; Exec Sec of Synod Dio Qu'App 66-71; Archd Dio Qu'App 69-71; Hon Archd 71-77; Dir of Pensions Gen Syn of Canada from 71. *600 Jarvis Street, Toronto, Ont., Canada.*

HOBSON, Herbert Leslie. b 09. St Aid Coll 37. **d** 39 **p** 40 Southw. C of Ch Ch Newark 39-42; Bulwell (in c of St Alb Bulwell Hall Estate) 42-47; PC of Awsworth (in c of Cossall) 47-53; Awsworth w Cossall 53-59; Chap Mansfield Gen Hosp 59-68; V of St Jo Evang Mansfield 59-68; Heath 68-75; Perm to Offic Dio Derby from 75; Dio Southw from 76. *40 High Tor, Skegby, Sutton-in-Ashfield, Notts, NG17 3EX.* (Mansfield 557083)

HOBSON, John Philip Hilary. b 20. Keble Coll Ox BA 42, MA 46. Ripon Hall Ox 42. **d** 43 Roch **p** 45 Liv for Roch. C of St Mary Shortlands 43-44; Prescot 44-46; Chap and Ho Master St Mary's Sch Melrose and Perm to Offic Dio Edin 46-50; Hd Master St Mary's Sch Reigate from 50; Publ Pr Dio S'wark from 50; Perm to Offic Dio Chich from 56. *St Mary's School, Reigate, Surrey, RH2 7RN.* (Reigate 44880)

HOBSON, Patrick John Bogan. b 33. MC 53. Magd Coll Cam BA 56, MA 60. Qu Coll Birm 77. **d** 79 **p** 80 Worc. C of St John in Bedwardine Worc 79-81; R of Clifton-on-Teme, Lower Sapey and the Shelsleys Dio Worc from 81. *Rectory, Church Road, Clifton-on-Teme, Worcester, WR6 6DJ.* (Shelsley Beauchamp 483)

HOBSON, Philip Charles. b 53. Univ of Tor BA 75, MA 76. Trin Coll Tor MDiv 80. **d** 80 Bp Read for Tor **p** 81 Bp Hunt for Tor. C of All SS Whitby Dio Tor from 80. *534 Mary Street E, RR 216, Whitby, Ont, Canada, L1N 2R1.*

HOBSON, Stephen Newton. b 50. Univ of Nottm BTh 79. Linc Th Coll 75. **d** 79 **p** 80 Bradf. C of H Trin Skipton-in-Craven Dio Bradf from 79. *4 Ash Grove, Skipton, Yorks, BD23 1QP.* (Skipton 3747)

HOBSON, Walter John Graham. b 1894. Em Coll Cam BA 16, MA 20. Ridley Hall Cam 19. **d** 19 **p** 20 Lon. C of St John Ealing 19-22; St Jo Evang (in c of St Steph) Reading 22-24; Missr CSSM 24-27; R of Radipole 27-36; Org Sec CPAS for E Distr 36-38; Org Sec (Evacuation) Campaigners 39-40; Chap and Jt-Sec 40-44; Perm to Offic at H Sepulchre Ch Cam 42-44; V of St Steph Tonbridge 44-55; Min of Ch Ch Westbourne Bournemouth 55-65; Perm to Offic Dio Ex 66-68; Dio Ox 68-69; Dios Sarum and Win from 70. *51 Poole Road, Wimborne, Dorset.*

HOCKIN, William Joseph. Em Coll Sktn LTh 64. **d** 62 Bp Appleyard for Hur **p** 63 Hur. C of All SS Windsor 62-66; I of All SS Waterloo 66-71; R of Tillsonburg 71-75; St Geo Lon Dio Hur from 75. *227 Warncliffe Road North, London, Ont., Canada.* (519-438 8991)

HOCKING, Canon Hugh Michael Warwick. b 12. Ch Coll Cam 2nd cl Engl Trip pt i 33, BA 34, (3rd cl Th Trip pt i 35), MA 38. Westcott Ho Cam 34. VRD 54. **d** 36 **p** 37 Lon. C of St John-at-Hackney 36-37; Stoke Damerel 37-39; Chap RNVR 39-46; V of Madron w Morvah 46-54; Chap Poltair Hosp 50-54; V of St Ambrose Bris 54-62; R of H Trin w St Mary Guildf 62-77; Chap St Luke's Hosp Guildf 63-77; Proc Conv Guildf 64-75; Hon Can of Guildf 68-77; Can (Emer) from 77; Exam Chap to Bp of Guildf from 74; Chap W Cornw Hosp Penzance from 78. *2 Clarence Place, Penzance, Cornw, TR18 2QA.* (Penzance 3229)

HOCKING, John Theodore. b 28. Oak Hill Th Coll 61. **d** 63 **p** 64 Chelmsf. C of Woodford Wells 63-67; N Area Sec BCMS 67-71; Hon C of All SS Preston 67-71; V of Hoghton 71-78; Blawith w Lowick Dio Carl from 78. *Lowick Vicarage, Ulverston, Lancs.* (Lowick Bridge 248)

HOCKLEY, Paul William. b 47. Churchill Coll Cam BA 68, MA 72. Univ of Nottm BA (Th) 73. St Jo Coll Nottm 71. **d** 74 **p** 75 Roch. C of St Phil & St Jas Chatham 74-78; St John Tunbridge Wells 78-81; V of Penketh Dio Liv from 81. *5 Beadnell Drive, Penketh, Warrington, WA5 2EG.* (Penketh 3492)

HOCKLEY, Canon Raymond Alan. b 29. LRAM 53. Em Coll Cam MA (by incorp) 71. Westcott Ho Cam 56. **d** 58 **p** 59 Sheff. C of St Aug Sheff 58-61; C-in-c of H Trin Wicker w Neepsend Sheff 61-63; Chap Westcott Ho Cam 63-68; Fell and Chap Em Coll Cam 68-76; Can Res, Prec and Chamberlain of York Minster from 76. *2 Minster Court, York, YO1 2JJ.* (York 24965)

HOCKLEY, Robert Edward. Univ of NSW BEng 62. BD (Lon) 68. Moore Th Coll Syd ACT ThL 68. **d** 68 **p** 69 Syd. C of St John Parramatta 68-69; Beverly Hills 69-72; Chap Kenmore Hosp Dio C & Goulb 76-81; Perm to Offic Dio Syd from 81. *8 River Road, West Lane, Cove, NSW, Australia 2066.* (427-4664)

HODDER, Hayward Garland. K Coll NS STh 42. Bp's Univ Lennox BA 55. Qu Coll Newfld. **d** 35 **p** 36 Newfld. C of St Mary St John's 35-36; P-in-c of Burgeo 36-38; R 38-40; R of Port Greville 42-45; Port Morien 45-50; N Syd 50-59; St Geo Halifax 59-77. *2647 Windsor Street, Halifax, NS, Canada.* (454-1014)

HODDER, John Kenneth. b 45. Univ of Edin MA 68. Cudd Coll 71. **d** 73 **p** 74 Leic. C of Kibworth 73-76; Whittlesey 76-80; R of L Downham w Pymoor Dio Ely from 80; P-in-c of Coveney Dio Ely 80-81; R from 81. *Little Downham Rectory, Ely, Cambs, CB6 2ST.* (Pymoor 237)

HODDER, Trevor Valentine. b 31. Bps' Coll Cheshunt 65. **d** 67 **p** 68 St Alb. C of All SS, Oxhey 67-70; Digswell 70-73; V of Colchester Dio Chelmsf from 73. *St Anne's Vicarage, Compton Road, Colchester, Essex.* (Colchester 5931)

HODGE, Anthony Charles. b 43. K Coll Lon and Warm AKC 66. **d** 67 **p** 68 Southw. C of Carrington Notts 67-69; Bawtry w Austerfield and of Misson 69-72; R of St D w St Paul Grenada 72-74; Scarborough Tobago 74-76; V of Tuckingmill 76-78; St Paul Manton Worksop 78-81; P-in-c of Patrington w Winestead Dio York from 81; Hollym w Welwick and Holmpton Dio York from 81. *Patrington Rectory, Hull, HU12 0RJ.* (Patrington 30327)

HODGE, Canon Bernard Garfield. Codr Coll Barb 63. **d** 67 Antig. C of St Pet Montserrat 67-68; St Geo, Basseterre, St Kitts 68-71; Dom Chap to Bp of Antig 71-73 and 74-79; P-in-c of St Steph I and Dio Antig from 73; Can of Antig from 80. *St Stephen's Rectory, Glanville's, Antigua, WI.* (32034)

HODGE, Darrel Eric John. b 07. Linc Th Coll 28. **d** 31 **p** 32 Ches. C of Ch ch Ellesmere Port 31-33; S Hill w Callington 33-35; Asst Chap St Andr Cathl Sing 35-36; Actg Chap N Perak 37; Asst Chap St Andr Cathl Sing 37-40; I of Bandarawela and Chap of Haputale and Diyitalawa 41-44; V of Alfred County 44-48; Teynham 48-55; Seq of Buckland 48-49; R 49-55; Adisham 55-61; V of Offley w Lilley 61-63; Albury 63-72. *20 Newcroft, Warton, Carnforth, Lancs.*

HODGE, Denis Ian Dermott. b 32. Univ of Bris MB ChB 56. Cudd Coll 68. **d** 69 **p** 70 B & W. C of Westbury-sub-Mendip 69-72; V of Alcombe 72-76; Chap Dunstan Hosp and L to Offic Dio Dun from 76. *Box 44, Clyde, Central Otago, NZ.* (651)

HODGE, Preb Francis Vere. b 19. Worc Coll Ox BA 46, MA 46. MC 43. Cudd Coll 46. **d** 48 **p** 49 Chich. C of Battle 48-54; R of Iping w Chithurst 54-58; Seq and C-in-c of Linch 54-56; R 56-58; V of Kingswood Surrey 58-65; Moorlinch w Stawell and Sutton Mallet 65-80; R of Greinton 68-80; Lydeard St Lawr w Coombe Florey and Tolland Dio B & W from 80; RD of Glastonbury 75-79; Preb of Wells Cathl from 80. *Rectory, Lydeard St Lawrence, Taunton, Somt, TA4 3SF.* (Lydeard St Lawr 220)

HODGE, Graham Anthony. b 49. STh (Lambeth) 82. Linc Th Coll 79. **d** 80 **p** 81 Guildf. C of Hale 80-82; The Bourne Dio Guildf from 82. *3 South Avenue, Heath End, Farnham, Surrey, GU9 0QY.* (Farnham 715695)

HODGE, Canon Herbert Alfred. b 1890. Univ of Bris BA (Hons Hist) 22. Wells Th Coll 25. **d** 25 **p** 26 Bris. C of St Andr Montpelier Bris 25-29; Chap HMS *Worcester* and Publ Pr Dio Roch 29-33; Chap Kent Co Mental Hosp Barming 33-44; V of Brookland w Fairfield 44-49; R of Wittersham 49-60; RD of Lympne S 53-60; Hon Can of Cant 58-62; Can (Emer) from 62; C-in-c of Wambrook 62-67. *Address temp unknown.*

HODGE, Hugh Peter Vere. St Barn Coll Adel 37. ACT ThL 38. **d** 38 Bunb for Perth **p** 39 Perth. C of Cottesloe 38-40; R of Bencubbin 40-42; Wiluna 42-44; Chap AIF 44-46; C of Ch Ch Claremont 46-47; P-in-c of S Road w Edwardstown and O'Halloran Hill 47-52; Edwardstown w Ascot Pk 52-57; Chap Fairbridge Farm Sch Pinjarra 57-60; R of Midl Junction 60-66; Dir and Chap St Bart Ho E Perth 66-74; Perm to Offic Dio Perth from 74. *PO Box 167, Midland, W Australia 6056.* (94 1745)

HODGE, John Shaw. b 30. Chich Th Coll 78. **d** 80 Dorchester for Ox **p** 81 Ox. C of St Pet Maidenhead Dio Ox from 80. *7 Camley Gardens, Maidenhead, Berks, SL6 5JW.*

HODGE, Leonard Cameron. b 09. St Jo Coll Dur BA 30, Dipl Th 31, MA 35. **p** 33 Linc. C of Boston (in c of St Jas from 36) 32-38; PC of Eastville w Midville 38-44; R of Stickney 44-72; V of Stickford 44-72; RD of Bolingbroke 52-64. *17 Linley Drive, Boston, Lincs.* (Boston 61590)

HODGE, Canon Michael Robert. b 34. Pemb Coll Cam BA 57, MA 61. Ridley Hall Cam 57. **d** 59 Man **p** 60 Burnley for York. C of Harpurhey 59; St Mark Layton Blackpool 59-62; V of Old St Geo Stalybridge 62-67; Cobham w Luddesdowne 67-81; M Gen Syn Dio Roch from 70; Surr from 79; Hon Can of Roch Cathl from 81; R of Bidborough Dio Roch from 81. *Rectory, Rectory Drive, Bidborough, Tunbridge Wells, Kent, TN3 0UL.* (Tunbridge Wells 28081)

HODGE, Canon Raymond John. Wells Th Coll 63. **d** 64 **p** 65 Ex. C of Churston Ferrers w Goodrington 64-66; Bunb Cathl 67-68; R of Carey Park 68-70; Manjimup 70-80; Boyup Brook Dio Bunb from 80; Can of Bunb from 80. *Rectory, Boyup Brook, W Australia 6244.* (65-1350)

HODGE, Valentine Bernard. b 45. Univ of WI BA 73. Codr Coll Barb 69. **d** 72 **p** 73 Antig. P-in-c of St Anne w St Thos St Kitts 73-76; R 77-79; St Phil I and Dio Antig from 79; Exam Chap to Bp of Antig from 79. *St Philip's Rectory, Antigua, W Indies.*

HODGE, Warren Harry Theodore. b 43. St Jo Coll Auckld 70. **d** 72 **p** 73 Nel. C of Greymouth 72-76; V of Ahaura-Brunnerton (w Reefton from 77) 76-79; Motueka Dio Nel from 79. *Vicarage, Motueka, NZ,* (204)

HODGES, Barrie Edward. b 34. Chich Th Coll 58. **d** 61 **p** 62 Southw. C of Worksop 61-64; Daybrook 64-66; Min of St Pet Conv Distr Larch Farm Blidworth 66-71; V of Ravenshead 71-78; Ashford Dio Lon from 78. *Vicarage, Ashford, Middx.* (Ashford 52459)

HODGES, Canon Dudley Alban. b 09. Selw Coll Cam BA 30, MA 34. Cudd Coll 30. **d** 32 **p** 33 S'wark. C of St Sav w St Pet S'wark 32-40; PV of S'wark Cathl 33-40; Succr 35-40; Sacr 37-39; Offg Chap Guy's Hosp 36-40; V of H Spirit Clapham 40-50; Eltham 50-55; RD of Clapham and Brixton 47-50; Surr from 51; R of Stafford 55-65; RD of Stafford 61-65; Preb of Bishopshull in Lich Cathl 63-65; Can Res and Prec of Lich Cathl 65-76; Can (Emer) from 76; Dir of Ordins 65-76; Can and Preb of Sarum Cathl from 80; V of The Close Dio Sarum from 80. *31 The Close, Salisbury, Wilts, SP1 2EJ.* (Salisbury 20041)

HODGES, Eric Henry. b 16. AKC 39. **d** 39 Willesden for Lon **p** 40 Lon. C of St Pet Paddington 39-40; St Matt Ponders End 40-41; Harlington 41-43; CF (EC) 43-47; Hon CF 47; C of St Andr Boscombe 47-50; V of St Luke Hackney 50-56; CF (TA) from 53; R of Landewednack Dio Truro from 56; Ruan Major 56-63. *Rectory, The Lizard, Helston, Cornw, TR12 7PQ.* (The Lizard 290713)

HODGES, Francis Reginald. b 26. Selw Coll Cam 2nd cl Hist Trip pt i 47, BA 48, MA 61. Chich Th Coll 48. **d** 50 **p** 51 Portsm. C of St Alb Copnor Portsea 50-56; Ho of Resurr Mirfield 56-58; C of All SS Heref 58-61; R of St Breoke Wadebridge 61-76; C of St Kew 77-78; P-in-c 78-80. *c/o Lands, Chapel Amble, Wadebridge, Cornw.*

HODGES, Canon Joseph Percy. b 1899. Down Coll Cam BA (1st cl Hist Trip pt ii) 24, 2nd cl Th Trip pt i 25, MA 28. Ripon Hall Ox 24. **d** 25 **p** 26 Ox. C of Caversham 25-29; St Martin Birm 29-32; V of St Luke Liv 32-37; St Andr Bournemouth 37-46; R of Falmouth 46-55; Hon Can of Truro 47-55; RD of Carnmarth S 48-51; Proc Conv Truro 51-55; R of Streatham 55-64; RD of Streatham and Mitcham 57-64; Hon Can of S'wark 60-64; Can (Emer) from 64. *Rose Cottage, Brudenell Road, Canford Cliffs, Poole, Dorset.* (Canford Cliffs 709270)

HODGES, Keith Michael. b 53. Chich Th Coll 77. **d** 80 **p** 81 S'wark. C of St Phil Sydenham 80-81; All SS Sydenham Dio S'wark from 81. *41 Trewsbury Road, Sydenham, SE26.* (01-778 5838)

HODGES, Lawrence John. Univ of Melb BSc 55. ACT ThL (2nd cl) 57. St Francis Coll Brisb. **d** and **p** 57 Bal. C of Milton 57; Warrnambool 57-59; V of Lismore 59-62; Warracknabeal 62-71; R of Coleraine Dio Bal from 71. *Holy Trinity Rectory, Coleraine, Vic., Australia 3315.* (055-75 2152)

HODGES, Lionel Charles. b 09. Univ of Birm BA 32. Lich Th Coll 33. **d** 35 **p** 36 Lich. C of Hednesford 35-38; Berkeley w Sharpness 38-44; V of Coaley 44-52; Horsley 52-72. *48 Althorp Close, Tuffley, Gloucester.*

HODGES, Murray Knowles. b 02. K Coll Cam 2nd cl Hist Trip pt i 23, BA (2nd cl Hist. Trip pt ii) 24, MA 29. **d** 25 Barrow-F for Carl **p** 26 Carl. C of Ch Ch Cockermouth 25-26; St Wilfrid Newton Heath 26-27; H Trin Kendal 27-31; V of Mungrisdale 31-34; Loweswater 34-45; Muncaster (w Waberthwaite from 57) 45-75. *Eskside, Ravenglass, Cumb.* (Ravenglass 259)

HODGETTS, Colin William John. b 1940. St D Coll Lamp BA 61. Ripon Hall Ox 61. **d** 63 **p** 64 Lon. C of Hackney 63-68; Gen Sec Inverliever Lodge Trust 68; Dir Chr Action from 70; Hon C St Martins-in-the-Fields Trafalgar Sq Dio Lon from 70; Creeksea and Althorne Dio Chelmsf from 75. *c/o 5 St Martin's Place, WC2 4JJ.*

HODGETTS, Harry Samuel. b 30. Chich Th Coll 63. **d** 65 Dur **p** 66 Jarrow for Dur. C of W Harton 65-68; St Mary Penzance 68-70; V of Penwerris 70-79; St Mary Kettering Dio Pet from 79. *St Mary's Vicarage, Kettering, Northants, NN16 9SU.* (Kettering 512736)

HODGINS, George Eric. b 12. ALCD 39. **d** 39 **p** 40 Chelmsf. C of St Botolph Colchester 39-40; St Mich Gidea Pk 40-42; Offg C-in-c of H Trin Springfield 42-45; C of St Samson Guernsey 46-50; V of All SS Forest Gate 50-54; R of Highnam w Lassington 54-56; Wivenhoe 56-59; V of White Ladies Aston w Churchill and Spetchley 59-60; Wakes Colne w Chappel 60-63; R of L Easton 63-73; C-in-c of Alphamstone w Lamarsh 73; R (w Pebmarsh from 75) 74-77; Perm to Offic Dio B & W from 79. *14 Pretoria Road, Halstead, Essex, CO 9 2EG.*

HODGINS, John Henry. b 21. Trin Coll Dub BA (1st cl Mod) 43, Abp King's Pri and Bp Forster's Pri 42, Downes Pri 43, Th Exhib 45, BD 48. **d** 45 **p** 46 Down. C of Shankill 45-49; Miss at Bp Tucker Mem Coll Mukono 50-61; N Ireland Area Sec CMS 61-64; R of Aghalee 64-69; Educn Org Ch of Ireland 69-71; Can Th of St Anne's Cathl Belf 71-76; Exam Chap to Bp of Connor 71-79; Dean of Killala 76-79; I of Killala 76-79; Area Sec CMS Dios York and Ripon from 79. *23 Wetherby Road, York, YO2 5BS.* (0904-79 2496)

HODGINS, John Joseph Albert. b 09. Trin Coll Dub, Abp King's Div Pri (1st), Bp Forster's Pri (1st), Ryan Pri and Bedell Scho 32, BA and Div Test (2nd cl) 33, Elrington Th Pri 34, MA 48. **d** 33 **p** 34 Worc. C of Pershore (in c of Pinvin) 33-36; St Dunstan Stepney 36-37; CF 37-65; Men in Disp 44; ACG 59-65; Hon Chap to HM the Queen 62-65; V of Helsby 65-66; Perm to Offic Dio Ches 66-68; V of Eaton 68-75; C-in-c of Scalford w Wycombe & Chadwell 74-75. *41 North Parade, Grantham, Lincs.* (Grantham 66655)

HODGINS, Ven Michael Minden. b 12. Hon MA (Lambeth) 60. Cudd Coll 38. **d** 39 **p** 40 Lon. C of St Barn Wood End Northolt 39-43; Asst Sec Lon Dioc Fund 43-46; Sec 46-74; L to Offic Dio Lon 47-51 and 71-77; Proc Conv Lon 50-51; Archd of Hackney 51-71; Archd (Emer) from 71; Exam Chap to Bp of Lon 51-71. *2 Pottery Close, Brede, Nr Rye, E Sussex.* (Brede 882224)

HODGKINSON, Arthur Douglas. b 41. Univ of Manit BA 62. Univ of BC MA 73. St Jo Coll Winnipeg BTh 66. **d** 66 **p** 67 Koot. P-in-c of Lumby 66-68; C of Penticton 69-71; on leave. *600 Jarvis Street, Toronto, Ont, Canada.*

HODGKINSON, Canon Arthur Edward. b 13. Edin Th Coll 36. Univ of Dur LTh 42. **d** 39 **p** 40 Glas. C of St Geo Maryhill Glas 39-43; Choir Chap St Ninian's Cathl Perth 43-44; Prec 44-47; P-in-c of Lochgelly 47-52; R 52-54; R of Motherwell 54-65; Can of Glas 63-65; Provost of St Andr Cathl Aber 65-78; Hon Can of Ch Ch Cathl Hartford Conn 65-78; Commiss for New Guinea 67-70; Papua from 71; Sec USPG S Wales from 78; Hon Can of St Andr Cathl Aber from 81. *4 Aquilla Court, Conway Road, Cardiff, CF1 9PA.*

HODGKINSON, Frank Cyril. b 18. Univ of Lon BA 50. Oak Hill Th Coll 46. **d** 51 **p** 52 Nor. C of Gaywood 51-53; Hall Green 53-55; V of St Paul W Bromwich 55-57; Donington 57-65; R of Aldham 65-68; R of Elmsett 65-68; V of Barkby 68-74; St Chris Leic 74-77; Ryhall w Essendine Dio Pet from 77. *Ryhall Vicarage, Stamford, Lincs, PE9 4HR.* (Stamford 2398)

HODGKINSON, Harry. b 11. ACP 47. Qu Coll Birm. **d** 62 **p** 63 Worc. C of Kidderminster Dio Worc from 62. *24 St John's Avenue, Kidderminster, Worcs.* (Kidderminster 61840)

HODGKINSON, John. b 27. Trin Hall Cam BA 51, MA 55. Linc Th Coll 51. **d** 53 **p** 54 Carl. C of Penrith 53-56; St Nich w St John Linc 56-58; C-in-c of St Jo Bapt Conv Distr Ermine Estate Linc 58-60; Min 60-63; PC 63-66; V of Old Brumby 66-71; V of Kendal Dio Carl from 71. *33 Sedbergh Road, Kendal, Cumbria, LA9 6AD.* (Kendal 21248)

HODGKINSON, John David. b 09. Fitzw Ho Cam 2nd cl Med and Mod Lang Trip pt i 29, BA (2nd cl Med and Mod Lang Trip pt ii) 31, MA 35. Bps' Coll Cheshunt 38. **d** 38 **p** 39 Lon. C of St Andr Enfield 38-40; St Jas L Westmr 40-43; St Sav Denmark Pk 43-44; St Pancras 44-47; Epping 47; Asst Master Badingham Coll Leatherhead 47-52; C of St Vedast Foster Lane Lon 52-54; Asst Master Lon Schs of Engl and Foreign Lang from 54; Perm to Offic Dio Lon from 54. *106 Earls Court Road, W 8.* (Western 4916)

HODGKINSON, John Graeme. Moore Coll Syd ThL 71. **d** 72 **p** 73 Brisb. C of St Steph Coorparoo Brisb 72-75; Booval 75-77; P-in-c of Goodna 77-78; R of Mt Gravatt City and Dio Brisb from 78. *Box 275, Mount Gravatt, Brisbane, Queensland, Australia.* (349 1964)

HODGKINSON, Oswald Merchant. b 21. Qu Coll Birm 68. **d** 69 **p** 70 Birm. C of Shard End 69-74; V 74-80; Team V of Wrexham Dio St A from 80. *160 Borras Road, Wrexham, Clwyd.*

HODGSON, Canon Alfred. b 04. Bps's Coll Cheshunt 32. **d** 34 **p** 35 Blackb. C of St Bart Gt Harwood 34-37; V of Brierfield 37-44; Adlington 44-62; Surr from 45; RD of Leyland 55-62; Garstang 63-73; Proc Conv Blackb 58-64; Can of Blackb 60-73; Can (Emer) from 73; V of Goosnargh 62-73. *33 Birks Drive, Tottington, Bury, Lancs.* (061-764 9588)

HODGSON, Andrew. b 13. Mert Coll Ox BA 36, MA 45. TD 63. Westcott Ho Cam 45. **d** 47 **p** 48 Ripon. C of Bedale 47-49; Harewood (in c of E Keswick) 49-52; CF (TA) 50-64; (TA-R of O) 64-68; V of Killinghall 52-58; Honingham w E Tuddenham 58-81. *10 Brook Street, Heage, Derbys, DE5 2AG.* (Ambergate 2759)

HODGSON, Anthony Owen Langlois. b 35. Ripon Hall Ox 60. **d** 62 **p** 63 Nor. C of Blakeney and of Stiffkey w Morston 62-65; Ch Ch Lanc Gate Paddington 66-70; Chr Aid Area Sec for Beds, Cambs, Herts and Hunts 70-73; Beds, Cambs, Rutland and Northants 73-74; V of Gt w L and Steeple Gidding 77-81; Warden Dovedale Ho and P-in-c of Ilam w Blore Ray Dio Lich from 81. *Dovedale House, Ilam, Ashbourne, Derbys, DE6 2AZ.* (Thorpe Cloud 365)

HODGSON, Anthony William. b 35. Univ of Dur BSc 56. Wells Th Coll 58. **d** 60 **p** 61 Dur. C of St Mary Gateshead 60-62; All SS w St Alb Leeds 62-66; V of St Osw Hartlepool 66-75; P-in-c of St Jas Conv Distr Stockton-on-Tees 75-81; V of Easington Colliery Dio Dur from 81. *Vicarage, Easington Colliery, Co Durham, SR8 3PJ.* (Sunderland 270272)

HODGSON, Archibald Edward. Moore Th Coll ACT ThL 25. **d** 25 **p** 26 Syd. C of Leichhardt 25-27; P-in-c of Far West Miss 27-30; R of George Town 30-31; Cullenswood 31; Channel 31-35; Richmond Tas 35-36; St John Wallerawang 36-37; V of Dee Why w Brookvale 37-40; Chap AIF 40-41; R of St Paul Castle Hill 41-47; Penrith 47-60; Blackheath 60-61; L to Offic Dio Syd 61-67. *21 Davies Road, Ashgrove, Queensland 4060, Australia.*

HODGSON, Arthur Douglas. b 1889. Late Cl Scho of Selw Coll Cam BA (3rd cl Cl Trip) 11, MA 20. Wells Th Coll 13. **d** 13 Win **p** 14 Southampton for Win. C of Aldershot 13-19; TCF 17-19; Hon CF 20; Asst Chap at St Mark Alex 19-21; C of St Pet-in-Thanet 21-29; V of Rainham 29-39; St Jo Evang Bromley 39-54; Hon Chap to Bp of Roch 54-60; Chap Morden Coll Blackheath 54-75. *33 Kidbrooke Grove, Blackheath, SE3 0LE.* (01-853 3675)

HODGSON, Cecil Mervyn. **d** and **p** 59 Perth. C of Claremont 59-60; R of Narembeen 61-65; L to Offic Dio Bunb 65-72; Perm to Offic Dio Perth 73-79; C of Albany 79. *c/o Box 440, Albany, W Australia 6330.* (407 5361)

HODGSON, Canon Charles. b 16. St Jo Coll Dur LTh 42, BA (w distinc) 43, MA 46. St Aid Coll 39. **d** 43 **p** 44 Blackb. C of St Lawr Chorley 43-46; Preston 46-49; C-in-c of St Geo Preston 49-50; V of St Thos Preston 50-55; Idle 55-61; Middleton 61-71; R of Wishaw 61-71; Adult Educn Officer Dio Birm 61-71; Tr Officer and Missr Dio Ox from 71; C-in-c of S Leigh 71-72; Hon Can of Ch Ch Cathl Ox from 81, RD of Witney from 81. *4 Wychwood View, Minster Lovell, Oxford.* (Witney 75030)

HODGSON, Christopher. b 24. Or Coll Ox BA 49, MA 54. Qu Coll Birm 50. **d** 52 **p** 53 Glouc. C of Ch Ch Cheltm 52-55; Our Lady and St Nich Liv 55-57; V of St Columba Anfield 57-64; Pembury Dio Roch from 64; Chap Pembury Hosp from 66. *Pembury Vicarage, Tunbridge Wells, Kent.* (Pembury 2204)

HODGSON, Derek Cyril. b 29. Late Wansbrough Scho of Hatf Coll Dur BA (2nd cl Cl) 50, Dipl Th 54. St Chad Dur 52. **d** 54 **p** 55 Wakef. C of Lindley w Quarmby 54-58; C-in-c of H Nativ Conv Distr Mixenden Halifax 58-62; V of Thurlstone 62-75; Mytholmroyd Dio Wakef from 75. *Mytholmroyd Vicarage, Hebden Bridge, HX7 5EG.* (Halifax 883130)

HODGSON, George. b 36. Qu Coll Birm 75. **d** 78 Lich **p** 79 Wolverhampton for Lich. C of Wordsley Dio Lich from 78. *1 Newfield Drive, Kingswinford, W Midl, DY6 8HY.* (Kingswinford 292543)

HODGSON, John. b 35. St Jo Coll Cam MA 62. Univ of Lon BD 61. St Deiniol's Libr Hawarden 80. **d** 81 Burnley for Blackb. C of Padiham Dio Blackb from 81. *13 Harewood Avenue, Simonstone, Burnley, BB12 7JB.*

HODGSON, John Daniel Garner. NZ Bd of Th Stud LTh 31. **d** 29 **p** 30 Wai. C of Wairoa 30-31; V of Tolaga Bay 31-34; Te Karaka 35-43; Takapau 43-48; Woodville 48-52; St Kilda NZ 52-59; R of Cubley w Marston Montgomery 59-62; V of Wickhambrook 62-70; L to Offic Dio Waik 70-74; Perm to Offic 74-77; Dio Wai from 77. *Flat 6, 5 Danvers Street, Havelock North, NZ.*

HODGSON, Canon John Derek. b 31. Univ of Dur BA (3rd cl Hist) and De Bury Scho 53, Dipl Th 59. Cranmer Hall Dur 57. **d** 59 **p** 60 Dur. C of Stranton 59-62; St Andr Monkwearmouth 62-64; PC of Stillington 64-66; V of Consett 66-75; R of Gateshead Dio Dur from 75; RD of Gateshead from 76; Hon Can of Dur Cathl from 78; M Gen Syn from 80. *91 Old Durham Road, Gateshead, T & W, NE8 4BS.* (Gateshead 773990)

HODGSON, John Eric. b 11. Hur Coll Lon Dipl Th 65. **d** 65 Keew **p** 76 Bp Robinson for Hur. C of Rainy River 65-66; on leave 66-76; Hon C of St Geo Sarnia Dio Hur from 76. *2399 Lakeshore Road, Route 1, Bright's Cove, Ont, Canada, N0N 1C0.*

HODGSON, Kenneth Jonah. b 36. Oak Hill Th Coll 66. **d** 69 Warrington for Liv **p** 70 Liv. C of Rainford 69-72; Fazakerley (in c of St George) 72-74; Team V 74-79. *72 Stopgate Lane, Sparrow Hall, Liverpool, L9 6AR.* (051-523 1536)

HODGSON, Kenneth Russell Stephen. Univ of Melb BA 50, MA 60. ACT ThL 45. **d** 49 **p** 50 Bp James for St Arn. C of Mildura 49-52; C (Col Cl Act) of St Cypr St Marylebone 52-55; Chap All SS Coll City and Dio Bath 55-56; Perm to Offic Dio Melb 69-70; C-in-c of Middle Park Dio Melb from 70. *39 Park Road, Middle Park, Vic 3206, Australia.*

HODGSON, Matthew William. b 13. Lich Th Coll 40. **d** 44 **p** 45 Newc T. C of St Columba N Gosforth 44-47; St Luke Wallsend-on-Tyne 47-49; Haltwhistle 49-50; Winlaton (in c of St Barn Rowlands Gill) 50-51; Chap and Sub-Warden of Aberlour Orph 52-53; R of Ch Ch Jarrow and Chap Palmer Mem Hosp 54-60; R of St Columba Nairn 60-64; V of St Laur Byker 64-71; Woodhorn w Newbiggin 71-77. *Address temp unknown.*

HODGSON, Peter Richard. b 23. Univ Coll Dur BA 50. Bps' Coll Cheshunt 49. **d** 52 **p** 53 York. C of Redcar 52-55; Beverley Minster 55-57; V of Lythe 57-61; Bolsterstone 61-80; Kirton-in-Holland Dio Linc from 80. *Vicarage, Lime Tree House, Willington Road, Kirton, Boston, Lincs, PE20 1EH.* (Boston 722380)

HODGSON, Robert Edward Stephen. b 14. St Aid Coll 38. **d** 39 **p** 40 Liv. C of St Luke Evang Walton-on-the-Hill 39-42; Actg C of St Chad Kirkby and Chap Kirkby Fields Hostel 42-43; Offg C-in-c of St Pet Aintree 43-45; V of St Chad Everton 45-48; Chap Liv Stanley Hosp 46-48; V of St Paul Wigan 48-56; St Matt, Blackb 56-59; R of St Aid Clarkston Glas 59-63; V of Astley Bridge 63-71; Chap Wilkinson Hosp Astley Bridge 63-71; V of Shuttleworth 71-79. *17 Simpsons Way, Broughton, Chester, CH4 0RA.* (Hawarden 536217)

HODGSON, Roger Vaughan. b 27. Magd Coll Cam BA 49, MA 54. Cudd Coll 55. **d** 56 **p** 57 Lon. C of St Matt, Westmr 56-59; St Pet Eaton Square Westmr 59-65; R of L Hadham 65-78; Chap at St Jas Oporto 78-80; Chap & Lect St Deiniol's Libr Hawarden from 81. *St Deiniol's Library, Hawarden, Clwyd.*

HODGSON, Ven Thomas Richard Burnham. b 26. St Jo Hall Lon BD 52. ALCD 52. **d** 52 **p** 53 Carl. C of Crosthwaite 52-55; Stanwix 55-59; V of St Nich Whitehaven 59-65; R of Aikton 65-67; Surr from 62; V of Raughton Head w Gatesgill 67-73; Grange-over-Sands 73-79; Mosser Dio Carl from 79; Dom Chap to Bp of Carl 67-73; Hon Can of Carl from 72; Hon Chap to Bp of Carl 73-79; Dioc Dir of Ordins 70-73; RD of Windermere 76-79; Archd of W Cumb from 79. *Mosser Vicarage, Cockermouth, Cumbria, CA13 0RX.* (Cockermouth 822479)

HODGSON, William Tempest. b 21. St Aid Coll 47. **d** 50 **p** 51 Blackb. C of St Jo Evang Blackb 50-53; C-in-c of St Wilfrid's Conv Distr Mereside Blackpool 53-61; Chap RAF 61-63; V of Northcote NZ 63-68; R of Upwell-Christchurch (w Welney from 69) 68-74; V of Littleport 74-78; C-in-c of St Matt Littleport 74-78. *68 Green Park, Chatteris, Cambs.* (Chatteris 3642)

HODKIN, Canon Hedley. b 02. Univ of Sheff MA 23. Ch Coll Cam BA 25, MA 31. Westcott Ho Cam 35. **d** 35 **p** 36 Newc T. C of Morpeth 35-38; St Geo Jesmond 38-40; V of St Luke Newc T 40-47; Exam Chap to Bp of Newc T 39-47; V of H Trin Millhouses Sheff 47-57; Exam Chap to Bp of Sheff 50-61; to Bp of Man 57-70; Hon Can of Sheff 55-57; Can Res of Man 57-70; Sub-Dean 66-70; Can (Emer) from 70; Select

Pr Cam 68; Perm to Offic Dio Sheff from 70. *79 Folds Crescent, Sheffield 8.* (Sheff 362155)

HODSON, Bernard Cyril. St Chad's Coll Regina 52. **d** 53 **p** 54 Qu'App. I of Lumsden 53-57; Rocanville 57-60; Oxbow 60-67; St Paul Regina 67-68; L to Offic Dio Qu'App 68-73; Dio Sask from 74. *Box 1174, Melfort, Sask, Canada.*

HODSON, Gordon George. b 35. St Chad's Coll Dur BA 59, Dipl Th 60. **d** 60 **p** 61 Lich. C of Tettenhall 60-64; Rugeley 64-68; V of St Mich Shrewsbury 68-74; Kinnerley w Melverley Dio Lich from 74; P-in-c of Knockin w Maesbrook Dio Lich from 75. *c/o Kinnerley Vicarage, Oswestry, Salop.* (Knochin 233)

HODSON, Howard Arthur. b 03. **d** 31 **p** 32 Roch. [f Methodist Min] C of Ch Ch Bexleyheath 31-34; Abbots Langley 34-36; R of Dordrecht 36-39; C of St Paul Durban 39-46; CF (S Afr) 42-46; V of St Mary Durban 46-52; Umhlatuzana 52-64; R of St Luke Pietermaritzburg 64-70; L to Offic Dio Natal from 70. *Victoria Memorial Home, 257 Retief Street, Pietermaritzburg, Natal, S Africa.*

HODSON, Canon John Henry. St Edm Hall Ox BA 35, MA 45. Cudd Coll 36. **d** 37 **p** 38 S'wark. C of St Jo Div Kennington 37-40; C-in-c of St Francis Friar Pk W Bromwich 41-43; Chap RNVR 43-46; V of Helmsley w Sproxton, Carlton and Rievaulx 46-53; Pockley w Eastmoors 46-53; Chap Duncombe Pk Sch 46-53; RD of Helmsley 49-53; Dean and R of Grahmstn Cathl and Archd of Grahmstn 53-64; Hon Can of Grahmstn from 64; R of St Sav Claremont 64-72; Constantia 72-81; Perm to Offic Dio Capetn from 81. *44 Kendall Road, Meadowridge, Cape Town, 7800, S Africa.*

HODSON, Keith. b 53. Hatf Coll Dur BA 74. Wycl Hall Ox 77. **d** 80 Ches **p** 81 Stockport for Ches. C of St Mary Magd Ashton-on-Mersey Dio Ches from 80. *12 Willoughby Close, Sale, Cheshire, M33 1PJ.*

✠ **HODSON, Right Rev Mark Allin.** b 07. Univ of Lon BA 29. Wells Th Coll 30. **d** 31 **p** 32 Lon. C of St Dunstan Stepney 31-35; LDHM of St Nich Perivale 35-40; R of Poplar (w St Frideswide from 52) Chap of St Andr Hosp Bromley-by-Bow 40-55; Chap of Poplar Hosp 41-55; Offg C-in-c of All Hallows E Ind Dks 42-52; St Steph Poplar 43-52; C-in-c of St Frideswide Poplar 47-52; Preb of Newington in St Paul's Cathl Lon 51-55; Surr 40-55; Cons Ld Bp Suffr of Taunton in St Paul's Cathl Lon 6 Jan 56 by Abp of Cant; Bps of B & W; S'wark; Heref; St Alb; Glouc; Truro; and Antig; Bp Suffr of Stepney; and Bps Wand; Roberts; and Moberly; Preb of Dinder in Wells Cathl 56-61; R of Dinder 56-61; Trld to Heref 61; res 73; Asst Bp of Lon from 73; Exam Chap to Bp of Lon 74-81; Fell Univ Coll Lon from 74. *150 Marsham Court, Marsham Street, London, SW1P 4LB.*

HODSON, Raymond Leslie. b 42. St Chad's Coll Dur BSc (2nd cl Math and Physics) 64, Dipl Th 66. **d** 66 Lanc for Blackb **p** 67 Blackb. C of Adlington 66-68; St Andr Cleveleys 68-72; V of St Bart Ewood Blackb 72-77; Nazeing Dio Chelmsf from 77. *Nazeing Vicarage, Waltham Abbey, Essex, EN9 2DB.* (Nazeing 3167)

HOETA, Bruce Ogaita. Newton Coll Dogura 70. **d** 73 **p** 74 Papua. P Dio Papua. *Box 26, Popondota, Papua New Guinea.*

HOEY, David Paul. b 57. Qu Univ Belf BD 79. Ch of Ireland Th Coll 79. **d** 81 Connor. C of Whiterock Dio Connor from 81. *35 Westway Park, Belfast, BT13 3NW.*

HOEY, Raymond George. b 46. TCD BA (Gen Stud) 70. Div Hostel Dub 70. **d** 72 **p** 73 Armagh. C of Portadown 72-78; R of Camlough w Mullaglass Dio Armagh from 78. *Rectory, Bessbrook, Co Armagh, N Ireland.*

HOEY, (Augustine) Thomas Kenneth. b 15. St Edm Hall Ox BA (3rd cl Hist) 38, MA 44. Cudd Coll 39. **d** 40 **p** 41 Lon. C of St Mary of Eton Hackney Wick 40-48; M CR from 50; Prior St Francis's Priory Sekhukhuniland 58-61; Ho of Resurr Mirfield 61-66; St Paul's Priory Lon 66-68; Master R Found of St Kath in Ratcliffe 68-72; Publ Pr Dio Man 73-76. *542 John Nash Crescent, Manchester, M15 5DS.*

HOEY, William Thomas. b 32. Div Hostel Dub 64. **d** 66 **p** 67 Connor. C of St Mary Belf 66-68; Ch Ch Lisburn 69-72; I of Ballinderry 72-78; St Simon w St Phil Belf Dio Connor from 78. *11 Rugby Road, Belfast, BT7 1PT, N Ireland.* (Belfast 31901)

HOFFMAN, George Conrad. b 33. Univ of Bris BA 59. Tyndale Hall Bris. **d** 61 **p** 62 S'wark. C of St Luke Wimbledon 61-66; Edgware 66-68; Asst Sec Evang Alliance 68-70; Dir The Evang Alliance Relief Fund from 70; Perm to Offic Dio Lon from 70; Commiss Chile from 77. *11 Station Road, Teddington, Middx, TW11 9AA.*

HOFFMAN, Canon Stanley Harold. b 17. St Edm Hall Ox BA 39, MA 43. Linc Th Coll 40. **d** 41 **p** 42 Ox. C of St John w All SS Windsor 41-44; All SS Weston Somt 44-47; Chertsey (in c of All SS) 47-51; V of Shottermill 51-65; Dioc Dir of Relig Educn Dio Roch 65-80; Hon Can of Roch 65-80; Can (Emer) from 80; Proc Conv Dio Roch 69-70; Exam Chap to Bp of Roch 73-80; Warden of Readers 74-80; Chap to HM the Queen from 76. *Cedarwood, Holly Close, Headley Down, Bordon, Hants, GU35 8JN.* (0428-713128)

HOFFMANN, Kevin Douglas. **d** 59 **p** 61 Willoch. C of Melrose 59-62; P-in-c 62-64; L to Offic Dio Wang 66-68; Perm to Offic Dio Melb 71-74; Dio C & Goulb 74-80; R of Woomera 80-81; L to Offic Dio Willoch from 81. *24 Pine Street, Peterborough, S Australia 5422.*

HOFLAND, John William. Em Coll Sktn 53. **d** 57 **p** 58 Arctic. Miss at Hay River 57-62; C of Grace Ch Brantford 62-64; I of Dundalk 64-67; Shelburne 67-73; Lucan 73-80; Watford and Kerwood Dio Hur from 80. *Box 36, Watford, Ont, Canada.*

HOFMEESTER, Adrian Sidney. Trin Coll Dub BA 50, MA 53. **d** 51 Dub for Centr Tang **p** 52 Centr Tang. Miss at Katoke Dio Centr Tang 51-56; C of St Bart Belf 56-58; St Mary, Belf 58-61; I of Connor Dio Connor from 61; RD of Ballymena from 74. *Connor Rectory, Kells, Ballymena, Co Antrim, N Ireland.* (Kells 891254)

HOGAN, John James. b 24. St Edm Hall Ox BA 51, MA 56. Wells Th Coll 51. **d** 53 Stafford for Cant **p** 54 Lich. C of Cannock 53-55; Market Drayton 55-58; V of Woore Dio Lich from 58. *Woore Vicarage, Crewe, Chesh.* (Pipe Gate 316)

HOGAN, William Riddell. b 22. Qu Coll Birm 48. **d** 51 **p** 52 Wakef. C of Brighouse 51-54; P-in-c of St Hilda Katong Sing 55-58; V of Greetland (and W Vale from 73) 59-80; Kellington w Whitley Dio Wakef from 80. *Kellington Vicarage, Goole, Yorks, DN14 0NE.* (Whitley Bridge 662876)

HOGARTH, Foley James Myddelton. Ch Ch Ox BA (3rd cl Th) 38, MA 42. Wells Th Coll 38. **d** 39 **p** 40 Worc. C of St Barn Worc 39-41; H Ap Charlton Kings 41-42; CF (EC) 42-46; Hon CF 46; V of St Pet Fordcombe 47-52; Asst Hd Master of Holmewood Ho Sch Tunbridge Wells 52-53; Chap St Pet Coll Prep Sch City and Dio Adel from 53. *9 Northumberland Street, Heathpool, S Australia 5068.* (08-31 6318)

HOGARTH, John Oswald Vereker. b 13. Selw Coll Cam BA 36, MA 45. Wycl Hall Ox 36. **d** 38 **p** 39 Worc. C of Upton-on-Severn 38-40; St Andr Bournemouth 40-43; CF (EC) 43-47; Hon CF 47; V of Hartpury (w Ashleworth 66-73; and Corse w Staunton from 73) 47-78; C-in-c of Ashleworth 51-66; RD of Glouc N 74-78. *Clifton, Bromsberrow Heath, Ledbury, Herefs, HR8 1NX.* (Bromsberrow 223)

HOGARTH, Jonathan Foley Stewart. b 46. Ridley Coll Melb ThL 73. **d** 74 Adel **p** 75 Bp Renfrey for Adel. C of Kens 74-75; Perm to Offic Dio Melb 76-79; Dio Moro from 80. *Box 113, Morogoro, Tanzania.*

HOGARTH, Joseph. b 32. Edin Th Coll 65. **d** and **p** 67 Carl. C of Walney I 67-71; V of St Jas Whitehaven 71-75; H Trin and The Hill Chapel Millom Dio Carl from 75; Thwaites Dio Carl from 75. *Holy Trinity Vicarage, Millom, Cumb, LA18 5AD.* (Millom 2889)

HOGBEN, Canon Peter Graham. b 25. Bps' Coll Cheshunt 60. **d** 61 **p** 62 Guildf. C of Hale 61-64; V of St Francis Westborough 64-71; V of St Mary Virg Ewell Dio Guildf from 71; Hon Can of Guildf from 79; RD of Epsom from 80. *Vicarage, Church Street, Ewell, Surrey.* (01-393 2643)

HOGBEN, Stephen Edward. b 51. AKC 75, BD 73. St Aug Coll Cant 74. **d** 75 Lon **p** 76 Willesden for Lon. C of SS Pet and Paul Harlington 75-79; Christchurch w Mudeford Dio Win from 79. *5 Foxwood Avenue, Mudeford, Christchurch, Dorset, BH23 3JZ.* (Christchurch 5889)

HOGBO, Paul. **d** 72 **p** 73 Sudan. P Dio Sudan 72-76; Dio Yambio from 76. *ECS, Ezo, Sudan.*

HOGG, Anthony. b 42. St D Coll Lamp BA 63. Linc Th Coll 64. **d** 78 Bp Bulley for Ox **p** 79 Ox (APM). Hon C of Ridgeway 78-81; East Challow Dio Ox from 81; Hd of Middle Sch King Alfred's Wantage from 81. *Eight Belmont, Wantage, Oxon.* (Wantage 65537)

HOGG, George Smith. b 10. TCD BA 32. **d** 33 **p** 34 Clogh. C of Mucknoe Broomfield and Crossduff 33-36; Dioc C Dio Clogh 36-37; C-in-c of Sallaghy 37-41; R of Clonoulty w Ardmayle 41-47; I of Tipperary (w Cullen 47-62) 47-80; Surr 52-80; Dom Chap to Bp of Cash 55-80; Can and Chan of Cash Cathl 60-65; Archd 65-80; RD of Tipperary and Duntryleague 61-80. *Sunnyhome, Love Lane, Tramore, Co Waterford, Irish Republic.*

HOGG, Peter Stuart. b 42. Ch Coll Cam BA 65, MA 68. N-W Ordin Course 74. **d** 77 **p** 78 Ches (APM). C of Bollington Dio Ches from 77. *3 Fairfield Avenue, Bollington, Macclesfield, Cheshire.* (0625-74310)

HOGG, William Ritson. b 47. Univ of Leeds BSc 69. Univ of Birm Dipl Th 71. Qu Coll Birm 69. **d** 72 Bp Skelton for Birm **p** 73 Birm. C of St Osw Bordesley 72-76; Team V of Seacroft Dio Ripon from 76. *St Luke's Vicarage, Stanks Lane North, Leeds LS14 5AS.* (Leeds 735837)

HOGGETT, Robert William John. b 13. **d** 67 **p** 68 Worc. C of Bromsgrove 67-71; V of Keelby Dio Linc from 71; Riby Dio Linc from 71; Aylesby Dio Linc from 77; RD of Haverstoe from 81. *Keelby Vicarage, Grimsby, Humb, DN37 8EH.* (Roxton 60251)

HOGWOOD, Charles Thomas. b 05. Lon Coll of Div 29. **d** 34 **p** 35 Lon. C of H Trin Isl 34-36; St Paul Canonbury 36-38; St Mich Southfields 38-39; W Thurrock (in c of St Steph Purfleet) 39-43; R of St Mary Chadwell 43-64; Tunstall w Dunningworth 64-76; R of Iken 64-76; Perm to Offic Dio St E from 80. *6 The Harbourage, Beccles, Suff, NR34 9RN.* (Beccles 714561)

HOHUA, William King. b 37. **d** 77 **p** 79 Aotearoa for Wai. C of Te Kaha Past Dio Wai from 77. *PO Box 322, Opotiki, NZ.*

HOI KYIN, Daniel. St Francis Coll Brisb 62. **d** 63 Bp Hudson for Brisb for Rang. d Dio Rang 63-70 and from 72; Dio Pa-an 70-71. *43 Maha Bandoola Street, Rangoon, Burma.*

HOKOSENI, David. St Pet Coll Siota 62. **d** 64 **p** 65 Melan. P Dio Melan 64-75; Dio Centr Melan from 75. *Longu, Guadalcanal, Solomon Islands.*

HOLBECK, Very Rev James Evans. BD (Lon) 68. ACT ThL (2nd cl) 66, Th Scho 68. Ridley Coll Melb 64. **d** 68 **p** 69 Brisb. C of St Steph Coorparoo 68-72; R of St Bart Mt Gravatt Brisb 72-78; Dean and V of St Pet Cathl City and Dio Armid from 78. *Deanery, Armidale, NSW, Australia 2350.* (72-2269)

HOLBROOK, Colin Eric Basford. b 42. St Steph Ho Ox 73. **d** 75 **p** 76 Liv. C of Dovecot 75-79; V of St Helen's Hollinfare Dio Liv from 79. *Hollinfare Vicarage, Warrington, Chesh.* (061-775 2160)

HOLBROOKE-JONES, Stanley Charles William. Univ of Dur BA 58, Dipl Th 60, MA 77. Cranmer Hall Dur 58. **d** 60 Tonbridge for Cant **p** 61 Roch. C of Gravesend 60-63; Im w St Anselm Streatham 63-66; V of H Trin W Bromwich 66-79; St Paul Tiverton Dio Ex from 79. *St Paul's Vicarage, Baker's Hill, Tiverton, Devon, EX16 5NE.* (Tiverton 256369)

HOLCOMBE, Graham William Arthur. b 50. Univ of Wales (Cardiff) Dipl Th 80. St Mich AA Coll Llan 77. **d** 80 **p** 81 Llan. C of Neath w Llantwit Dio Llan from 80. *35 Trevallen Avenue, Cimla, Neath, W Glam, SA11 3US.* (Neath 4014)

HOLDAWAY, Graham Michael. b 51. Univ of Southn BSc 73. Sarum Wells Th Coll 74. **d** 77 **p** 78 Guildf. C of Walton-on-Thames 77-81; Team V of Westborough Dio Guildf from 81. *St Clare's Vicarage, Cabell Road, Park Barn, Guildford, Surrey.*

HOLDAWAY, Simon Douglas. b 47. Univ of Lanc BA 73. Univ of Sheff PhD 81. NOC 78. **d** 81 Doncaster for Sheff (APM). C of Ch Ch Gleadless Dio Sheff from 81; Lect Univ of Sheff from 81. *57 Endowood Road, Millhouses, Sheffield, S7 2LY.*

HOLDAWAY, Stephen Douglas. b 45. Univ of Hull BA (2nd cl Th) 67. Ridley Hall Cam 67. **d** 70 **p** 71 Win. C of St Chris Thornhill Southn 70-73; Tardebigge (in c of Webheath) 73-78; Industr Chap in Redditch 73-78; in City of Linc from 78. *Rectory, Station Road, Potterhanworth, Lincoln.* (Linc 791320)

HOLDCROFT, Ian Thomas. b 46. St Jo Coll Cam 1st cl Cl Trip pt i 66, BA (1st cl Th Trip pt ii) 68, MA 71. Westcott Ho Cam 72. **d** 73 **p** 74 Bris. C of St Mary Redcliffe 73-76; Th Educn Sec Chr Aid 76-80; Executive Sec 80-82; Hon C of Battersea Dio S'wark from 79; Dep Sec Bd for Miss and Unity Gen Syn from 82. *113 Bolingbroke Grove, SW11 1DA.* (01-228 9060)

HOLDEN, Canon Arthur Stuart James. b 23. ALCD 51. **d** 51 **p** 52 Chelmsf. C of Barking 51-54; C-in-c of Berechurch 54-55; V 55-61; Earls Colne Dio Chelmsf from 61; C-in-c of White Colne Dio Chelmsf 66-67; V from 67; Hon Can of Chelmsf from 80. *Vicarage, High Street, Earls Colne, Colchester, CO6 2RB.* (Earls Colne 2262)

HOLDEN, Colin Peter. b 51. Univ of Melb BA 74, MA 76. Trin Coll Melb 75. **d** and **p** 76 Wang. C of Wodonga 76-78; St Bonif Cathl and Carey Pk Dio Bunb from 78. *82 Beach Road, Bunbury, W Australia 6230.*

HOLDEN, Geoffrey. b 26. FCII 54. Oak Hill Th Coll 57. **d** 59 **p** 60 Sheff. C of St Thos Crookes Sheff 59-61; St Pet Belper (in c of St Mark Openwoodgate) 61-63; St John Woking (in c of St Sav Brookwood) 63-66; R of St Mich w St Paul Bath 66-73; Chap Bath Group of Hosps from 73. *10 Marlborough Lane, Bath, Avon.* (Bath 27933)

HOLDEN, Geoffrey Ralph. b 25. Ripon Hall Ox 64. **d** 65 Aston for Birm **p** 66 Birm. C of Sparkhill 65-68; Walsall 68-71; R of Longton 71-75. *Craft Supplies, Church Street, Barmouth, Gwynedd.*

HOLDEN, Hyla Rose. Sarum Th Coll. **d** 30 **p** 31 Man. C of St Jo Bapt Atherton 30-36; St Jas Cowley 36-37; Caversham (in c of St Andr) 37-43; CF (RA-R of O) 39-56; R of St Laur Upminster 44-70; Surr 55-70. *15 Ashdown Crescent, Hadleigh, Essex.*

HOLDEN, (Simon) Jack Crawford. b 30. Univ of Leeds BA (2nd cl Engl) 59. Coll of Resurr Mirfield 59. **d** 61 **p** 62 York. C of All SS Middlesbrough 61-64; M CR from 67; Asst Chap Univ Coll Lon 69-74; L to Offic Dio Lon from 70. *House of the Resurrection, Mirfield, W Yorks.*

HOLDEN, Canon Jack Hatherley. b 12. MBE 65. St Aug Coll Cant 40. **d** 41 Bp Kitching for Portsm **p** 42 Portsm. C of St Marg Eastney 41-44; V of St Mary Yupukari w Rupununi Distr 45-50; Morawhanna 50-55; V of Cacababuri 53-64; P-in-c of Rupununi Miss 56-64; Can of Guy 63-65 and from 81; V of St Andr, Stoke Newington 65-79; Commiss to Bp of Guy from 77; P-in-c of St Jas w St Phil Isl 80-82; St Pet Isl 80-82. *2 Bishop Street, Islington, N1.* (01-226 2769)

HOLDEN, James Alexander. b 13. Bps' Coll Cheshunt 64. **d** 65 **p** 66 St Alb. C of Hitchin 65-70; R of Holwell 70-79. *11c The Cloisters, Radcliffe Road, Hitchin, Herts.* (Hitchin 59534)

HOLDEN, John. b 33. MBE 76. Ridley Hall Cam 65. **d** 67 **p** 68 Man. C of St John's Conv Distr Flixton 67-71; V of Jinja 71-75; Aston-juxta-Birm Dio Birm from 75. *Aston Vicarage, Sycamore Road, Birmingham, B6 5UH.* (021-327 5856)

HOLDEN, Philip Giffard. b 1886. Linc Coll Ox BA (3rd cl Th) 09, MA 13. OBE 19. **d** 12 **p** 13 Ches. C of All SS Runcorn 12-19; TCF 15-19; C of Portsea 19-24; Wimbledon 24-30; V of Witley 30-64; Hon Chap to Bp of Guildf 62-64. *1 The Wilderness, Sherborne, Dorset, DT9 3AE.*

HOLDEN, Ralph William. Univ of Adel BTech 58. Melb Coll of Div BD (Hons) 60. ACT ThL (2nd cl) 60. Ridley Coll Melb 58. **d** 61 **p** 62 Adel. C of Toorak Gardens 61-63; P-in-c of Cummins 63-67; P-in-c of Tumby Bay 64-67; R of Minlaton 67-74; Plympton 74-78; P-in-c of Mile End w Richmond Dio Adel from 78. *10 Falcon Avenue, Mile End, S Australia 5031.* (43 4701)

HOLDEN, Richard Davis. b 03. St Aid Coll 33. **d** 36 Warrington for Liv **p** 37 Liv. C of St Phil Litherland 36-39; Berry-Pomeroy w Bridgetown 39-44; R of Bridestowe 44-50; V of Newport 50-60; V of Sidbury w Sidford 60-70. *Greystones, Harpford, Sidmouth, Devon, EX10 0NJ.* (Colaton Raleigh 68534)

HOLDER, Eric Thomas. Univ of Capetn BA 48. St Paul's Coll Grahmstn LTh 50. **d** 50 **p** 51 Capetn. C of St Geo Cathl Capetn 50-53; Claremont 53-56; R of Namaqualand 56-61; Elgin 61-64; Ceres 64-67; Bergvliet 67-80; Camps Bay Dio Capetn from 80. *Rectory, Park Avenue, Camps Bay 8001, CP, S Africa.* (48-9254)

HOLDER, Frank. b 13. Univ of Dur BA 35, MA 45. **d** 45 **p** 46 Dur. L to Offic Dio Dur from 45; Chap Miss to Deaf and Dumb for Northumb and Dur 45-80; Perm to Offic Dio Newc T from 52. *84a Trajan Walk, Heddon-on-the-Wall, Newcastle upon Tyne, NE15 0BL.* (Wylam 3414)

HOLDER, John Walder Dunlop. b 48. Univ of WI BA (Th) 75. Codr Coll Barb 73. **d** 74 **p** 75 Windw Is. C of St Geo Cathl St Vinc 74-77; Tutor Codrington Coll Barb from 77. *Codrington College, St John, Barbados, W Indies.* (31226)

HOLDER, Kenneth William. b 29. Sarum Th Coll 60. **d** 61 **p** 62 Chich. C of Crawley 61-65; C-in-c of All SS Conv Distr Wick Dio Chich 65-73; V of Hangleton 73-79; R of Rotherfield (w Mark Cross from 81) Dio Chich from 79. *Rectory, Rotherfield, Crowborough, TN6 3LU.* (Rotherfield 2536)

HOLDER, Michael Rawle. b 44. Codr Coll Barb Dipl Th 75. **d** and **p** 75 Barb. C of St Mich Cathl I and Dio Barb from 75. *Cathedral Curate's House, 7th Avenue, Bellevue, St Michael, Barbados, WI.*

✠ **HOLDERNESS, Right Rev George Edward.** b 13. ERD (with 2 clasps) 55. Late Exhib of Keble Coll Ox Henry Oliver Becket Mem Pri 34, BA (1st cl Geog) 35, MA 39. Westcott Ho Cam 35. **d** 36 **p** 37 Ripon. C of Bedale 36-38; L to Offic Dio Ripon 38-47; Chap and Asst Master Aysgarth Sch 39-47; CF (RARO) 39-46; Hon CF 46; CF (TA) 46-55; V of Darlington 47-55; Hon Can of Dur and Sec of Dur Dioc Conf 54-55; Cons Ld Bp Suffr of Burnley in York Minster 2 Feb 55 by Abp of York; Bps of Dur; Blackb; Ripon; Man; Wakef; Brech; and Guildf; Bps Suffr of Selby; Warrington; Jarrow; Stockport; Middleton; Pontefract; Whitby; and Sherborne; Res 70; R of Burnley 55-70; Can of Blackb 55-70; Commiss Tor 67-72; Dean of Lich 70-79; Dean (Emer) from 79; Asst Bp in Dio York from 80. *Riseborough Cottages, Marton, Sinnington, York, YO6 6RD.* (Kirbymoorside 31593)

HOLDERNESS, Richard Hardwicke. Rhodes Univ Grahmstn BA 31. St Paul's Th Coll Grahmstn LTh 35. **d** 35 **p** 36 S Rhod. C of Gwelo 35-36; St Patr Miss Gwelo 36-37; P-in-c of St D Miss Bonda 37-43; R of Fort Victoria w Shabani 43-47; Asst Master Prince Edw Sch Salisbury S Rhod 47-52; Highlands Sch 54-60; Oriel Boys' Sch 61-62; C of Highlands 55-61; L to Offic Dio Mashon 55-61; C of Salisbury Cathl 62-63 and 66-67; Chap Ruzawi Sch Marandellas 63-66; R of Borrowdale Dio Mashon from 67. *Christchurch Rectory, Crowhill Road, Borrowdale, Salisbury, Rhodesia.*

HOLDING, Kenneth George Frank. b 27. Sarum Wells Th

Coll 75. **d** 77 **p** 78 Roch. C of St Mary Bexley 77-80; Min in Conv Distr of St Barn Joydens Wood Bexley Dio Roch from 80. *St Barnabas Church House, Tile Kiln Lane, Bexley, Kent, DA5 2BD.* (0322-528923)

HOLDRIDGE, Bernard Lee. b 35. Lich Th Coll 64. **d** 67 **p** 68 Sheff. C of Swinton 67-71; V of St Jude Hexthorpe Doncaster 71-81; R of Rawmarsh w Parkgate Dio Sheff from 81. *Rawmarsh Rectory, Rotherham, S Yorks, S62 6LT.* (Rotherham 522596)

HOLDROYD, James Malcolm. b 35. Univ of Lon LLB (2nd cl) 56, LLM 58. Cudd Coll 58. **d** 60 **p** 61 Wakf. C of Brighouse 60-66; V of Staincross 66-72; Marsden 72-75; St Bart Brighton Dio Chich from 75. *16 Richmond Terrace, Brighton, BN2 2SA.* (Brighton 685142)

HOLDSTOCK, Godfrey. b 48. St Jo Coll Cam BA 69, MA 72. Univ of Ox BA (Th) 77. St Steph Ho Ox 76. **d** 78 **p** 79 Roch. C of Ch of the Annunc W Chislehurst Dio Roch from 78. *47 Holmdale Road, Chislehurst, Kent.*

HOLDSWORTH, Desmond Maurice. b 29. **d** and **p** 77 Capetn (APM). C of St Pet Mowbray Dio Capetn from 77. *13 Hampstead Road, Claremont 7700, CP, S Africa.* (61-7885)

HOLDSWORTH, Ian Scott. b 52. Sheff Poly BA 75, BA (Th) 81. Oak Hill Coll 79. **d** 81 Reading for Ox. C of St Mary Denham Dio Ox from 81. *St Mark's House, Green Tiles Lane, Denham, Bucks.*

HOLDSWORTH, John Alexander Philip. b 22. St Jo Coll Cam BA 47, MA 49. Wells Th Coll 52. **d** 53 **p** 54 Liv. C of All SS Wigan 53-56; St Phil, Norbury 56-59; V of Tovil 59-66; St Alb S Norwood Dio Cant from 66. *6 Dagmar Road, SE 25.* (01-653 6092)

HOLDSWORTH, John Ivor. b 49. Univ of Wales (Abth) BA 70. Univ of Wales (Cardiff) BD 73, MTh 75. St Mich Coll Llan 70. **d** 73 **p** 74 Mon. C of St Paul Newport 73-77; V of Abercraf and Callwen Dio Swan B from 77. *Abercraf Vicarage, Swansea, SA9 1TJ.* (Abercraf 640)

HOLE, Derek Norman. b 33. Linc Th Coll 57. **d** 60 Bp Maxwell for Leic **p** 61 Leic. C of Knighton 60-62; Dom Chap to Abp of Capetn 62-64; C of Kenilworth 64-67; R of Burton Latimer 67-73; V of St Jas Gtr City and Dio Leic from 73. *St James The Greater Vicarage, London Road, Leicester, LE2 1NE.* (Leicester 542111)

HOLE, Herbert Oliver. St Jo Coll Armid ACT ThL 20. **d** 20 Bath **p** 22 Syd. C of Orange NSW 20-21; Ashfield 21-26; R of Springwood 26-30; Prec and Min Can of Ch Ch Cathl Newc 30-36; Prec of St Paul's Cathl Melb 36-42; I of St Pet Box Hill 42-51; P-in-c of Merlynston 51-71; Perm to Offic Dio Melb from 71. *2 Churchill Avenue, Glenroy, Vic, Australia 3058.* (306-5578)

HOLE, Herbert Oliver. ACT ThL 20. St Jo Coll Armid. **d** 20 Bath **p** 22 Syd. C of Orange NSW 20-21; Ashfield 21-26; R of Springwood 26-30; Prec and Min Can of Ch Ch Cathl Newc 30-36; Prec of St Paul's Cathl Melb 36-42; I of St Pet Box Hill 42-51; P-in-c of Merlynston 51-71; Perm to Offic Dio Melb from 71. *19 Glyndon Avenue, Merlynston, Vic. 3058, Australia.*

HOLEHOUSE, Ernest William. b 15. St Aid Coll 38. **d** 41 **p** Man. C of St Clem Urmston and Chap Urmston Cottage Hosp 41-45; St Bride Old Trafford 45-46; R of St Mark Newton Heath 46-49; PC of Hayfield 49-57; C-in-c of Claxby w Normanby-le-Wold 59-64; C of Wickenby w Friesthorpe of Lissington w Holton-le-Beckering and of Snelland w Snarford 64-80; Faldingworth and Buslingthorpe 73-80. *12 Ridgeway, Nettleham, Lincoln, LN2 2TL.*

HOLETON, David Ralph. b 48. Univ of BC BA 70. Nashotah Ho Wisc USA MDiv 73. STM 74. **d** 73 Bp of Milwaukee for New Westmr **p** 73 New Westmr. Asst Teacher Nashotah Ho Wisc 73-74; I of St Richard N Vanc 74-77; on study leave. *22 rue du Champ de l'Alouette, 75013 Paris, France.*

HOLFORD, John Alexander. b 40. Chich Th Coll 65. **d** 67 **p** 68 Bradf. C of Cottingley 67-71; Baildon 71-73; C-in-c of H Trin Bingley Dio Bradf 73-74; V from 74. *Vicarage, Oak Avenue, Bingley, Yorks, BD16 1ES.* (Bingley 3909)

✠ **HOLLAND, Right Rev Alfred Charles.** St Chad's Coll Dur BA 50, Dipl Th (w distinc) 52. **d** 52 **p** 53 Lon. C of W Hackney 52-54; R of Scarborough Perth 54-70; Archd of Coast 67-70; Cons Asst Bp of Perth in St Geo Cathl Perth 6 Aug 70 by Abp of Perth; Bps of Bunb; Kalg; and NW Austr; Bp Coadj of Bunb; and Bp Riley; Apptd Ld Bp of Newc 78; Archd of Northam 70-72; Stirling 75-78. *Bishopscourt, Brown Street, Newcastle, NSW, Australia 2300.* (049-23027)

HOLLAND, Bruce. Moore Th Coll Syd. **d** 56 **p** 57 Armid. C of W Tamworth 56-59; P-in-c of Delungra 59-63; V of Bundarra 63-68; Werris Creek 68-74; Tenterfield 74-81; Perm to Offic Dio Newc from 81. *12 Greenoaks Road, Narara, NSW, Australia 2250.*

HOLLAND, Desmond William. BD (Lon) 65. Moore Th Coll Syd ACT ThL 66. **d** 67 **p** 68 Syd. C of Yagoona 67-70; Castle Hill 70-71; C-in-c of Allambie Heights w Manly Vale Provisional Distr 71-74; R of Robertson 74-78; St Mary Magd St Mary's Dio Syd from 78. *24 King Street, St Mary's NSW, Australia 2760.* (623-1653)

HOLLAND, Edward. b 36. K Coll Lon and Warm AKC 64. **d** 65 **p** 66 Roch. C of H Trin Dartford 65-69; John Keble Ch Mill Hill 69-72; Prec of H Trin Cathl Gibr 72-74; Chap of Ch Ch Naples 74-79; V of St Mark Bromley Dio Roch from 79. *51 Hayes Road, Bromley, Kent, BR2 9AE.* (01-460 6220)

HOLLAND, Geoffrey. b 04. K Coll Cam BA 26, MA 35. **d** 36 **p** 37 S'wark. C of St Jo Evang Caterham Valley 36-40; CF (EC) 40-45; R of Exbourne w Jacobstowe 45-48; Chap and Asst Master Eton Coll 48-53; C of St Martin-in-the-Fields Westmr 53-58; Chap Luxborough Lodge and Nat Heart Hosp 58-65. *32 Endsleigh Road, W Ealing, W13 0RE.*

HOLLAND, Jack Newton Charles. b 08. OBE 57. St Edm Hall Ox BA 30, MA 47. Westcott Ho Cam. **d** 31 **p** 32 Cant. C of St Sav Westgate-on-Sea 31-34; Chap RN 35-59; R Hosp Sch Holbrook 59-69; R of St Mabyn 69-74; C-in-c of Helland 69-74; Perm to Offic Dio B & W from 75. *9 Playfield Close, Hemstridge, Templecombe, Somt.* (Stalbridge 62128)

HOLLAND, James Ernest. K Coll Lon and Warm AKC 50. **d** 51 **p** 52 Leic. C of Braunstone 51-53; Maidstone 53-55; V of Newington Kent 55-61; St Columb Minor 61-71; V of St Colan 69-71; RD of Pydar 69-71; R of Denmark 71; Boyanup 71-74; Mt Barker 74-79; L to Offic Dio Bunb from 79. *Box 256, Denmark, W Australia 6333.*

HOLLAND, Jan Petrus Fourie. b 29. **d** 74 **p** 75 Pret. C of Pret N w Brits & Hercules Dio Pret from 74. *720 Hanny Street, Pretoria Gardens 0002, S Africa.* (77-2005)

HOLLAND, John Harley. Ch Coll Hobart ACT ThL 62. **d** 63 **p** 64 Tas. Hon C of Clarence 63-65; R of Buckland 65-67; Perm to Offic Dio Melb 70-73; C of Morwell 73-74. *24 Fran Street, Glenroy, Vic., Australia 3046.*

HOLLAND, John Stuart. b 52. Sarum Wells Th Coll 77. **d** 80 **p** 81 Birm. C of Wylde Green Dio Birm from 80. *236 Orphanage Road, Erdington, Birmingham, B24 0BE.*

✠ **HOLLAND, Right Rev John Tristram.** b 12. CBE 75. Univ Coll Ox BA (2nd cl Engl Lang and Lit) 33, MA 37. Westcott Ho Cam 33. **d** 35 **p** 36 Wakef. C of St Pet Huddersfield 35-37; Commiss Wel 36-37; V of Featherston 38-41; CF (2 NZEF) 41-45; V of St Pet Riccarton 45-49; New Plymouth 49-51; Cons Ld Bp of Waik in St Pet Cathl Hamilton NZ 1 May 51 by Abp of NZ; Bps of Nel; Auckld; Wel; Dun; and Wai; Trld to Polyn 69; res 75; L to Offic Dio Cant 75-76; Perm to Offic Dio Waik from 79. *8 Short Street, Otumoetai, Tauranga, NZ.*

HOLLAND, Matthew Francis. b 52. Univ of Lon BA 73. Univ of Birm Dipl Th 78. Qu Coll Birm 76. **d** 79 **p** 80 Sheff. C of Ecclesall Dio Sheff from 79. *2 Dobbin Hill, Sheffield, S11 7JB.*

HOLLAND, Paul William. b 55. Coll of the Resurr Mirfield 78. **d** 80 **p** 81 Sarum. C of St Pet and St Osmond Parkstone Dio Sarum from 80. *79 Church Road, Parkstone, Poole, Dorset.*

HOLLAND, Peter Christie. Univ of St Andr BSc 60. Univ of Dur Dipl Th 62. Cranmer Hall, Dur 60. **d** 62 **p** 63 Dur. C of St Jo Evang Darlington 62-64; Ch Ch Bp Wearmouth 64-69; V of Tudhoe 69-77; New Seaham Dio Dur from 77. *Vicarage, Station Road, New Seaham, Co Durham, SR7 0BH.* (Seaham 813270)

HOLLAND, Robert Douglas. Univ of Melb BA 67. Trin Coll Melb ACT ThL (2nd cl) 69. **d** and **p** 69 Melb. C of Moorabin 69-70; Darwin 70-72; R of Manning 72-74; C of St Mary S Perth 75-76; Perm to Offic Dio Perth from 76. *44 Ashburton Street, Bentley, W Australia 6102.* (51 1940)

HOLLAND, Simon Paul. b 56. Univ of Lon LLB 77. Called to Bar Gray's Inn 78. Qu Coll Cam BA 80. Westcott Ho Cam 79. **d** 81 Chich. C of Uckfield Dio Chich from 81. *School House, Belmont Road, Uckfield, E Sussex.* (Uckfield 61373)

HOLLAND, Thomas Reginald. b 13. Univ of Reading BA 37. MA 49. **d** 78 **p** 79 Huntingdon for Ely (NSM). Hon C of Haddenham 78-81; Sutton Dio Ely from 81; Witcham w Mepal Dio Ely from 81. *59 High Street, Sutton, Ely, Cambs, CB6 2RA.* (Ely 778579)

HOLLAND, William Geoffrey Bretton. b 36. Magd Coll Cam BA 59, MA 63. Westcott Ho Cam 61. **d** 63 **p** 64 Lich. C of Cannock 63-66; Ch Ch Lancaster Gate 66-69; Chap Magd Coll Cam 69-73; V of Twyford (and Owslebury w Morestead from 78) Dio Win from 73. *Twyford Vicarage, Winchester, Hants.* (Twyford 712208)

HOLLAND, William Michael Tristram. b 26. Jes Coll Cam BA 50, MA 52. St Steph Ho Ox 79. **d** 81 Ox. C of High Wycombe Dio Ox from 81. *21 The Haystacks, High Wycombe, HP13 6PY.* (0494 23333)

HOLLANDS, Albert William. b 17. Roch Th Coll 60. **d** 62 **p** 63 Nor. C of Aylsham 62-66; R of Syderstone w Barmer (and Bagthorpe from 79) Dio Nor from 66; Tattersett Dio Nor from 66; P-in-c of Bagthorpe 66-79; Tatterford Dio Nor from 75. *Hephzibah, Dunton Road, Tatterford, Fakenham, NR21 7AX.* (East Rudham 250)

HOLLANDS, Derek Gordon. b 45. Chich Th Coll 72. **d** 74 **p** 75 Guildf. C of Banstead 74-77; Cranleigh 77-79; Haywards Heath (in c of Good Shepherd) Dio Chich 79-80; Team V from 80. *Good Shepherd Vicarage, Franklands Village, Haywards Heath, W Sussex, RH16 3RL.* (H Heath 56894)

HOLLANDS, Canon Edwin James. b 07. Univ of Aber MA 31. Edin Th Coll 31. **d** 33 **p** 34 Glas. C of St John Greenock 33-36; St Pet Torry (in c of St Ternan Muchalls) 36-38; R of H Trin Keith 38-45; St Columba Clydebank 45-52; H Trin Kilmarnock 52-57; St Geo Oldham Road (w St Barn from 59) Man 57-60; St Congan Turriff 60-75; Cuminestown 60-75; Can of Aber 69-75; Hon Can from 75; R of Banff 71-75. *Address temp unknown.*

HOLLANDS, Percival Edwin Macaulay. Edin Th Coll 57. **d** 60 **p** 61 Glas. C of St Jo Evang Greenock 60-64; St Mary Aber 64-65; P-in-c of St Clem Aber 65-68; R of Cruden 68-70; CF from 70. *c/o Ministry of Defence, Lansdowne House, Berkeley Square, W1.*

HOLLANDS, Ray Leonard. b 42. SOC 68. **d** 71 **p** 72 Kens for Lon. C of All SS, Hanworth 71-77; St Geo Hanworth Dio Lon from 77. *2 Woodlawn Drive, Hanworth, Middx, TW13 5HX.* (01-894 9040)

HOLLE, John. ACT ThL 57, Moore Th Coll Syd. **d** 58 Syd **p** 58 Bp Hilliard for Syd. C of Epping 58-60; Chap and Supt St Geo's Homes for Children Rockptn 60-64; Chap Ho of Epiph Syd 64-69; Warden 70-74; L to Offic Dio Syd from 64-75; C of Hunter's Hill 75-76; R of Burwood Dio Syd from 77. *207 Burwood Road, Burwood, NSW, Australia 2134.* (747 4327)

HOLLEY, Canon Geoffrey Raymond. b 28. K Coll Lon and Warm AKC 51. **d** 52 **p** 53 Chelmsf. C of Gt Ilford 52-53; Gt Burstead 53-56; V 56-75; Bp of Chelmsf's Ecumen Officer from 72; R of Loughton Dio Chelmsf from 75; Hon Can of Chelmsf from 78. *48 Hilltop, Loughton, Essex.* (01-508 1224)

HOLLEY, Graham Albert. Ridley Coll Melb 55. **d** 57 **p** 58 St Arn. [f in CA] C of Maryborough St Arn 57-58; V of Woomelang 58-60; P-in-c of Penola 60-64; V of Bend N 64-70; R of Woodend 70-73; Perm to Offic Dio Bal 73-75; and from 79; Hon Chap to Bp of Bal from 75. *314 Landsborough Street, Ballarat, Vic., Australia 3350.* (053-32 6015)

HOLLEY, Graham Frank. b 29. Sarum Th Coll. **d** 61 Bp Sara for Heref **p** 62 Heref. C of All SS Heref 61-63; W Wycombe (in c of St Jas Downley) 63-67; V of Much Marcle w Yatton Dio Heref from 67. *Much Marcle Vicarage, Ledbury, Herefs, HR8 2NL.* (Much Marcle 643)

HOLLIDAY, Arthur. b 22. St Jo Coll Dur 80. **d** 81 Bradf. Hon C of Allerton Dio Bradf from 81. *9 Alston Close, Bradford, BD9 6AN.*

HOLLIDAY, Eric Hedley. b 13. Univ of Lon BSc 35, ARCS 34. Ridley Hall Cam 35. **d** 37 **p** 38 S'wark. C of St Luke Deptford 37-40; St Jo Bapt Woking (in c of St Sav Brookwood) 40-44; V of W Thurrock w Purfleet 44-55; St Paul Canonbury 55-78; Perm to Offic Dio Ely from 78. *4 George Place, Eynesbury, St Neots, Huntingdon, Cambs, PE19 2QG.* (0480-215703)

HOLLIDAY, William. b 33. Qu Coll Cam BA 56, MA 60. McGill Univ Montr BD and LTh 58. Linc Th Coll 58. **d** 58 **p** 59 Ripon. C of Stanningley 58-63; Romaldkirk 63-64; In Ch of India 64-70; N India 70-77; V of Thwaites Brow Dio Bradf from 77. *St Barnabas Vicarage, Thwaites Brow, Keighley, BD21 4TA.* (Keighley 604666)

HOLLIER, Francis Samuel. b 43. St Paul's Coll Grahmstn Dipl Th 78 **p** 79 Pret. C of St Marg Witbank 78-80; All SS Barberton Dio Pret from 80. *PO Box 149, Barberton 1300, S Africa.*

HOLLIER, George Peter Emmanuel. b 30. **d** 80 Pret. C of Ch the K Voortrekkerhoogte Dio Pret from 80. *4 Maximoff Road, General Kemphill, Voortrekkerhoogte 0143, S Africa.*

HOLLIMAN, John James. b 44. St D Coll Lamp BA 66. **d** 67 Repton for Derby **p** 68 Derby. C of Tideswell 67-71; CF from 71. *c/o Ministry of Defence, Bagshot Park, Bagshot, Surrey.*

HOLLIN, Ian. b 40. Open Univ BA 76. Sarum Th Coll 67. **d** 70 **p** 71 Blackb. C of Ch Ch Lanc 70-72; H Trin (in c of St Nich Marton Moss) Blackpool 72-75; V of St Laur Morecambe 75-78; St Mary Blackpool Dio Blackb from 78. *59 Stony Hill Avenue, South Shore, Blackpool, FY4 1PR.* (Blackpool 42713)

HOLLINGHURST, Ronald. b 26. St Mich Coll Llan 62. **d** 64 Blackb **p** 65 Burnley for Blackb. C of St Matt Preston 64-67; Broughton 67-70; V of St Jas Ap Leyland Dio Blacb from 70. *St James's Vicarage, Slater Lane, Leyland, Preston, Lancs PR5 3SH.*

HOLLINGSHURST, Robert Peter. b 38. Ridley Hall, Cam 64. **d** 67 **p** 68 Lon. C of Ch Ch Roxeth Harrow 67-70; Attenborough w Chilwell 70-73; St Luke Ramsgate 74-75; Chap to the Deaf Cant Dioc Assoc 78-80; Team V of Louth Dio Linc from 80. *Holy Trinity Vicarage, Eastgate, Louth, LN11 8DT.*

HOLLINGSWORTH, Canon Gerald Frank Lee. b 26. Univ of Lon BA 53. Oak Hill Th Coll. **d** 54 Warrington for Liv **p** 55 Liv. C of Sutton 54-57; All H Ipswich 57-59; V of Yoxford 59-64; C-in-c of Sibton 59-62; V 62-64; Dioc Youth Chap Dio St E 60-62; V of H Trin Ipswich 64-72; Adv for Industry to Bp of St E from 64; R of St Clem and H Trin Ipswich 72-75; Gt and L Bealings w Playford and Culpho Dio St E from 75; RD of Woodbridge from 76; Hon Can of St E Cathl from 76. *Bealings Rectory, Woodbridge, Suff.* (0473 623884)

HOLLINGWORTH, Harold Procter Petitjean. b 10. St Aid Coll 38. **d** 41 **p** 42 Lich. C of Hednesford 41-43; St Pet Belper 43-47; V of Kingston w Gratwich 47-51; Dunston w Coppenhall 51-62; L Horkesley 62-80. *Meadow View, Oaklands, Harrow Street, Colchester, Essex.*

HOLLINGWORTH, Martin Douglas. b 50. R Man Coll of Mus GRSM 73. Trin Coll Bris 74. **d** 77 **p** 78 Ches. C of Hartford Dio Ches from 77. *71 School Lane, Hartford, Northwich, Cheshire.*

HOLLINGWORTH, Canon Peter John. OBE 76. Univ of Melb BA 58. Trin Coll Melb ACT ThL (2nd cl) 59. **d** 60 **p** 61 Melb. C of Dioc Centre 60; P-in-c of St Mary N Melb 60-64; C of St Silas N Balwyn 64-66; St Faith Burwood 67-70; C-in-c of Fitzroy Dio Melb from 70; Assoc Dir Bro of St Laur Dio Melb from 70; Can of Melb from 80. *15 Gore Street, Fitzroy, Vic, Australia 3065.* (03-41 4720)

HOLLINS, John Edgar. b 35. St Jo Coll Cam BA (2nd cl Math Trip pt ii) 58, MA 62. Oak Hill Th Coll 58. **d** 60 **p** 61 Man. C of St Edm Whalley Range 60-63; Highbury 63-66; St Paul (in c of St Luke) St Alb 66-71; Hon C of St Paul's Halliwell 71-72; C of St John Ravenhill 72-73; on Study Leave 73-78; Perm to Offic Dio Birm 79-81; V of Millbrook Dio Ches from 81. *28 Buckton Vale Road, Carrbrook, Stalybridge, Chesh, SK15 3LW.* (Mossley 3295)

HOLLINS, Peter Charles. b 31. Wycl Hall Ox 61. **d** 62 **p** 63 Leic. C of St Hugh's Conv Distr Eyres Monsell Leic 62-65; Westwood 65-67; L to Offic Dio Roch 72-77; Perm to Offic Dio Worc from 80. *Landkey, Holly Green, Upton-on-Severn, Worcester.*

HOLLINSHEAD, Cyril Wyndham. b 09. Linc Th Coll 45. **d** 47 **p** 48 B & W. C of St Mich AA Yeovil 47-54; V of Peasedown St John 54-76. *65 Ridgeway, Sherborne, Dorset.* (Sherborne 4232)

HOLLINSHEAD, John Woodhouse. b 02. AKC (2nd cl Hons) 37. **d** 37 **p** 38 Lon. C of Greenhill 37-40; C-in-c of Bowdon 40-41; V of Braunstone 41-46; Hayling S w Hayling N 46-59; R of Spetisbury w Charlton Marshall 59-65; Perm to Offic Dio Chich 65-79; Dio Sarum from 79. *Grey Stones, Spetisbury, Blandford, Dorset, DT11 9DL.* (Sturminster Marshall 857403)

HOLLIS, Arnold Thaddeus. b 33. Stockton State Coll NJ USA BA 74. NY Th Sem STM 76, DMin 78. Codr Coll Barb. **d** 59 Barb for Berm **p** 60 Wakef for Berm. C of St John Bapt Wakef 60-62; R of St Mich Berbice Guy 62-64; C of Horbury (in c of Horbury Bridge) 64-66; Loughton 66-69; in Amer Ch 69-77; R of St Jas Sandys Dio Berm from 77; Chap HM Pris Casemates Berm from 77. *Box 74, Somerset 9, Bermuda.* (809-4 0834)

✠ **HOLLIS, Right Rev Arthur Michael.** b 1899. Late Scho of Trin Coll Ox BA (2nd cl Cl Mods) 20, 1st cl Lit Hum 22, MA 24, Sen Denyer and Johnson Scho 25, BD 31. Leeds Cl Sch 22. **d** 23 **p** 24 Wakef. C of St Andr Huddersfield 23-24; Chap and Lect of Hertf Coll Ox 24-31; Fell 26-31; Exam Chap to Bp of Ripon 26-31; Lect of St Pet Leeds 31; SPG Miss Bp's Th Sem Nazareth Tinn 31-37; furlough 36-37; PC of Charlton Kings 37-42; CF (R of O) from 39; Cons Ld Bp of Madras in Madras Cathl 27 Sept 42 by Bp of Calc; Bps of Nagp; Tinn; Trav and Bp Pakenham-Walsh; Prof of Ch Hist United Th Coll Bangalore 55-60; Visiting Prof Vanderbilt Div Sch Nashville Tennessee 60; Luce Prof of World Christianity U Th Sem NY 61; R of Todwick 61-64; Asst Bp of Sheff 63-66; of St E 66-75; Hon Can of St E 66-75; Can (Emer) from 75. *Flat 6, Manor Mead, Tilford Road, Hindhead, Guildford, GU26 6RA.* (Hindhead 6951)

HOLLIS, Canon Christopher Barnsley. b 28. Clare Coll Cam BA 52, MA 59. Wells Th Coll 60. **d** 62 **p** 63 Bradf. C of Baildon 62-64; V of Esholt w Hawksworth 64-66; St Barn Heaton Dio Bradf from 66; RD of Airedale from 73; Hon Can of Bradf Cathl from 77. *Vicarage, Ashwell Road, Bradford, W Yorks, BD9 4AU.* (Bradford 47355)

HOLLIS, Ven Gerald. b 19. Ch Ch Ox BA 42, MA 45. Wells Th Coll 45. **d** 47 Lon **p** 48 Stepney for Lon. C of St Dunstan Stepney 47-50; Rossington (in c of St Luke) 50-54;

R of Armthorpe 54-60; V of Rotherham 60-74; RD of Rotherham 60-74; Proc Conv Sheff 67-74; Hon Can of Sheff from 70; Archd of Birm from 74; M Gen Syn from 74. *59 Salisbury Road, Moseley, Birmingham, B13 8LB.* (021-449 1642)

HOLLIS, Howard Charles. b 16. Univ of Melb MusBac 40. Trin Coll Melb ThL 43. **d** 45 **p** 46 Melb. C and Organist of Ch Ch S Yarra 45-47; C of St Luke Woodside 47-49; St Steph S Kens (Organist) Lon 49-51; Min Can of Westmr Abbey 51-59; Dep P-in-ord to HM the Queen 54-59; Chap Westmr Sch 57-59; Geelong Gr Sch 59-65; Exam Chap and Dom Chap to Abp of Melb 64-65; V of St Mary Virg Primrose Hill w St Paul Hampstead 65-76; Commiss Melb 68-76; R of St Jas City and Dio Syd from 76. *51 Bradley's Head Road, Mosman, NSW, Australia 2088.* (969 6872)

HOLLIS, Jeffrey Norman. b 30. Qu Coll Birm 71. **d** 74 **p** 75 Worc. C of Inkberrow 74-76; Eastleigh 76-79; V of St Jas Jersey Dio Win from 79; St Luke Jersey Dio Win from 79. *St James Vicarage, St James Street, St Helier, Jersey, CI.* (Jersey 73980)

HOLLIS, Peter. b 20. Jes Coll Cam BA (2nd cl Hist) 49. Wells Th Coll 49. **d** 51 **p** 52 Birm. C of Yardley 51-55; Coleshill 55-57; V of Kingshurst 57-67; R of St Greg w St Pet Sudbury (and Chilton from 81) Dio St E from 67; P-in-c of Chilton 67-81. *19 Gainsborough Street, Sudbury, Suff.* (Sudbury 72611)

✠ **HOLLIS, Right Rev Reginald.** Selw Coll Cam BA 54, MA 58. McGill Univ Montr BD 56. Montr Dioc Th Coll Hon DD 75. Univ of the S Tenn Hon DD 77. **d** 56 Lich for Montr **p** 56 Montr. Chap Montr Dioc Th Coll and McGill Univ 56-59; C of St Matthias Montr 60-63; R of Roxboro Pierrefonds 63-71; Ch Ch Beaurepaire 71-75; Dir of Dioc Services Montr 74-75; Cons Ld Bp of Montr in Ch Ch Cathl Montr 25 Jan 75 by Abp of Prov of Canada; Bps of Newfld, Fred, Ott and Albany (USA); Bp Suffr of NS (Arnold); and others. *1444 Union Avenue, Montreal, PQ, H3A 2B8, Canada.* (514-845 6211)

HOLLIS, Timothy Knowles. b 28. St Steph Ho Ox 54. **d** 58 Kingston T for Guildf **p** 59 Guildf. C of Oatlands 58-60; Crawley (in c of St Eliz Northgate) 60-63; Wrentham w Benacre, Covehithe and Henstead 63-69; C of Sotterley w Willingham and Shadingfield 63-69; R (w Ellough w Weston and Henstead) 69-76; Perm to Offic Dio St E from 77. *14 London Road, Beccles, Suff.*

HOLLOWAY, Canon Alan James. b 23. BD (2nd cl) Lon 58, MTh (Lon) 67. Oak Hill Coll 53. **d** 56 **p** 57 Roch. C of St Steph Tonbridge 56-58; Chalk 58-59; V 59-62; Tutor Oak Hill Th Coll Southgate and Publ Pr Dio St Alb 62-68; Chap and Lect St Paul's Coll Cheltm 69-73; V of Maisemore 73-76; Can Res of Glouc Cathl from 74; Dir of Educn Dio Glouc from 74. *Church House, College Green, Gloucester, GL1 2LY.*

HOLLOWAY, Alfred Edwin Jon. Em Coll Sktn. **d** 61 **p** 62 Sask. C of Hines Miss 61-63; I of Birch Hills 63-66; R of Mayo Dio Yukon from 66. *Elsa, Yukon, Canada.*

HOLLOWAY, Charles Turley. Ridley Coll Melb 46, ACT ThL 47. **d** 47 **p** 48 St Arn. C of Quambatook 47; V 48-50; R of Birchip 50-52; P-in-c of Phillip I and Prin St Paul's Home Newhaven 52-54; Perm to Offic Dio St Arn 55-57; R of Boort 57-63; V of Chelsea 63-69; Strathmore 69-73; C in Dept of Industr Miss Dio Melb from 73. *Lot 27, French Road, Greenvale, Vic, Australia 3047.* (03-30 7034)

HOLLOWAY, Cyril Edgar. b 11. Lich Th Coll 54. **d** 55 **p** 56 Lich. C of Gt Barr (in c of St Chad from 57) 55-61; V of Halwell w Moreleigh 61-72. *Sea Glimpse, Wadstray, Blackawton, Totnes, Devon.* (Blackawton 264)

HOLLOWAY, David Dennis. b 43. Lich Th Coll 65. **d** 68 **p** 69 Bris. C of Cricklade w Latton 68-71; St Agnes w St Simon Bris 71-74; V of Bitton 74-78; Team V of E Bristol 78-80; Publ Pr Dio Bris from 80; Chap HM Remand Centre Pucklechurch from 80. *Tormarton Rectory, Badminton, Wilts, GL9 1HU.* (Badminton 277)

HOLLOWAY, David Maxwell. b 45. St Mich Ho Crafers ACT ThL 71. **d** 72 **p** 73 Wang. C of Wodonga 72-75; Shepparton 75-76; P-in-c of Moyhu Dio Wang from 76. *Rectory, Moyhu, Vic, Australia 3732.*

HOLLOWAY, David Ronald James. b 39. Univ Coll Ox BA 62, MA 66. Ridley Hall Cam 65. **d** 67 Knaresborough for Ripon **p** 68 Ripon. C of St Geo Leeds 67-71; Tutor Wycl Hall Ox 71-72; V of Jesmond Dio Newc T from 73; M Gen Syn from 75. *7 Otterburn Terrace, Newcastle-upon-Tyne, NE2 3AP.* (0632-812001)

HOLLOWAY, Graham Edward. b 45. Chich Th Coll 69. **d** 72 **p** 73 Willesden for Lon. C of West Drayton 72-75; P-in-c of Cotham 75-80; Hawton 75-80; Shelton 75-80; V of St Mary Ladybrook, Mansfield Dio Southw from 80. *St Mary's Vicarage, Ladybrook, Mansfield, Notts, NG18 5LZ.* (Mansfield 21709)

HOLLOWAY, Howard Robinett. Keble Coll Ox BA (4th cl Th) 27, MA 31. Wells Th Coll 27. **d** 29 **p** 30 Mon. C of St Paul Newport 29-32; Cathl Ch Birm 32-38; V of Bedfont 38-48; St Paul Hounslow Heath 48-65; Treleigh 65-70; R of Perranuthnoe 70-72. *Storm Crest, Downderry, Torpoint, Cornw, PL11 3JA.*

HOLLOWAY, Keith Graham. b 45. Linc Coll Ox BA 67. Univ of Dur Dipl Th 72. St Jo Coll Dur 70. **d** 73 **p** 74 Barking for Chelmsf. C of St Andr Gt Ilford 73-78; Hon C of Squirrels Heath 78-80; Min of Conv Distr of Chelmer Village E Springfield Dio Chelmsf from 80. *11 Murrell Lock, Barlows Reach, Chelmer Village, Chelmsford, CM2 6QA.*

HOLLOWAY, Richard Frederick. b 33. BD (Lon) 63. Union Th Sem NY STM 68. Edin Th Coll 58. **d** 59 **p** 60 Glas. C of St Ninian Glas 59-63; P-in-c of St Marg and St Mungo Glas 63-68; R of Old St Paul Edin 68-80; in Amer Ch. *30 Brimmer, Boston, MA02108, USA.*

HOLLOWAY, Roger Graham. b 33. Selw Coll Cam BA 58, MA 61, SOC 74. **d** 78 S'wark for Hong **p** 80 Cant for Hong. Hon C of St John's Cathl Dio Hong from 78. *c/o Jardine Matheson & Co Ltd., World Trade Centre, Hong Kong.*

HOLLOWAY, Simon Anthony. b 50. Univ of Sussex BSc 72. Trin Coll Bris 76. **d** 79 Wolverhampton for Lich **p** 81 Lich. C of Bushbury 79-81; Castle Church Dio Lich from 81. *10 Lovelace Close, Stafford, ST17 9JB.* (Stafford 41011)

HOLLOWELL, Barry Craig Bates. b 48. Univ of Valparaiso BA 70. Univ of Cam Engl BA 72, MA 76. Episc Th Sch Cam Mass MDiv 73. **d** 73 N Ind **p** 74 Suffr Bp of Mass. In Amer Ch 73-74; P at Ch Ch Cathl Fred 74-75; Chap Univ of NB Fred from 75. *377 St John Street, Fredericton, NB, Canada.*

HOLLOWOOD, Lewis William Rye. b 17. Edin Th Coll 37. **d** 40 **p** 41 Brech. C of St Paul's Cathl Dundee 40-41; Chap 41-43; C of St Jo Bapt Chester 43-44; R of St Andr Fortrose 44-46; PC of Cromarty 44-46; R of H Trin Paisley w St Marg Renfrew and H Spirit Barrhead 46-47; H Rood Carnoustie 47-49; Chap King's Coll Hosp Lon 49-50; V of Markbeech 50-59; Groombridge 59-67; Hadlow Down 67-74; St Mary Buxted 72-74; St Barn Bexhill 75-81; Chap of Commun of the Servants of the Cross Lindfield from 81. *Chaplain's Lodge, Convent of the Holy Rood, Lindfield, Haywards Heath, W Sussex, RH16 2RA* (Lindfield 2090)

HOLMAN, Francis Noel. b 37. Sarum Th Coll 62. **d** 65 **p** 66 Pet. C of Weston Favell 65-68; Eckington w Renishaw 68-71; Chap in St Thos Hosp Group Lon 72-77; Hope, Salford R and Ladywell Hosps Man from 78. *90 Rocky Lane, Monton, Eccles, Manchester, M30 9LY.* (061-707 1180)

HOLMAN, Geoffrey Gladstone. b 32. AKC 56. **d** 57 **p** 58 S'wark. C of St Barn Eltham 57-60; CF from 60; DACG 73-80; ACG from 80. *c/o Williams and Glyn's Bank Ltd, Holt's Farnborough Branch, 31-37 GU14 7PA.*

HOLMAN, Hamish Urquhart. b 34. St Paul's Coll Grahmstn 68. **d** 69 St John's **p** 70 Bp Sobukwe for St John's. C of St Jo Cathl Umtata 69-75; Dir Youth Work Dio St John's 75-76; R of Queensburgh 76-79; Hosp Chap Dio Natal from 79. *Box 2393, Pietermaritzburg 3200, S Africa.*

HOLMAN, Michael. K Coll NS LTh 63. **d** 63 **p** 64 Qu'app. I of St Phil Regina 63-65; Broadview 65-67; Ogema 67-70; Gull Lake w Cabri 70-73; Kamsack 73-76; Hazelton Dio Caled from 76. *Box 94, Hazelton, BC, Canada.*

HOLME, Arthur. b 18. St Aid Coll 67. **d** 69 Warrington for Liv **p** 70 Liv. C of St Mark Newtown Pemberton 69-73; V of St Phil Nelson Dio Blackb from 74. *St Phillip's Vicarage, Nelson, Lancs.* (Nelson 63941)

HOLME, Thomas Edmund. b 49. Selw Coll Cam 2nd cl Th Trip pt 1 69, BA (2nd cl Th Trip pt ii) 71. Coll of Resurr Mirfield 71. **d** 73 **p** 74 Ripon. C of Ven Bede Wyther Leeds 73-76; Wimbledon 76-78; V of St Anne Bermondsey 78-81. *Cedar House, 91c High Street, Caterham, Surrey, CR3 5UH.* (Caterham 48087)

HOLMES, Anthony David Robert. b 38. Oak Hill Th Coll 75. **d** 77 Buckingham for Ox **p** 78 Reading for Ox. C of Iver 77-81; V of Bucklebury Dio Ox from 81. *Bucklebury Vicarage, Reading, Berks.* (Woolhampton 3193)

HOLMES, Arthur William Seddon. b 09. St Chad's Coll Dur 28. Bps' Coll Cheshunt 31. **d** 33 **p** 34 Lon. C of St Mary of Eton Hackney Wick 33-37; R of St Kiaran Campbeltown 37-39; C-in-c of St Cuthb Millwall 39-40; Chap RNVR 40-46; Chap HM Pris Birm 46-48; R of Sarsden w Churchill 48-63; V of Etwall w Egginton 63-74. *44 Catherine Street, Gatehouse-of-Fleet, Kirkcudbrights, DG7 2JB.* (Gatehouse 313)

HOLMES, Charles Derek. Dipl Th (Lon) 52. Wycl Hall Ox 63. **d** 65 **p** 66 Lich. C of St Leon Bilston 65-67; Downend 67-70; R of Claremont and Chigwell 70-74; Lindisfarne 74-77; St Jas New Town Dio Tas from 77. *29 Augusta Road, New Town, Tasmania 7008.* (002-281214)

HOLMES, Christopher Kelly. b 44. St Paul's Coll Grahmstn 67. **d** 69 Grahmstn **p** 70 Port Eliz. C of St Paul,

Port Eliz 70-77; R of St Nich Redhouse w Swartkops 77-80; Bluewater Bay and Amsterdam Hoek 77-80; St Mark Humansdorp Dio Port Eliz from 80; P-in-c of St Patr Humansdorp Dio Port Eliz from 80. *Box 66, Humansdorp, CP, S Africa.*

HOLMES, Derek de Lacy. b 04. Late Scho of Univ of Leeds BA (1st cl Hist) 26. Sarum Th Coll 29. **d** 30 **p** 31 Wakef. C of Lightcliffe 30-33; Todmorden 33-36; V of St Andr Huddersfield 36-43; Cragg Vale 43-49; Barkisland w W Scammonden 49-55; Osmotherley 55-69; Bilton-in-Holderness 69-70. *1 Old Deanery Close, Ripon, N Yorks.* (Ripon 3314)

HOLMES, Canon Edward Wilmot Graham. MBE 73. St Chad's Coll Dur BA 25, Dipl in Th 26, MA 28. **d** 26 Willesden for Lon **p** 27 Lon. C of St Mary Stratford Bow 26-31; R of St Mary Nass 31-73; Dioc Sec and Regr Dio Nass 32-47; Can of Nass 45-73; Hon Can from 73; Sub-Dean 52-73. *PO Box N-877, Nassau, Bahamas, W Indies.* (51481)

HOLMES, Frank. b 22. N-W Ordin Course 75. **d** 78 **p** 79 Ches. C of Hyde 78-81; Poynton Dio Ches from 81. *11 Deva Close, Chester Road, Poynton, Cheshire.* (Poynton 871958)

HOLMES, Frederick William. b 03. AKC 32. ACP 38. Lich Th Coll 26. **d** 38 **p** 39 Lon. C of Yiewsley 38-40; St Cath Coleman Hammersmith 40-41; Whixall 41-42; Tamworth (in c of Glascote) 42-46; V of Milwich 46-54; Chelmarsh 54-63; R of Cheddington w Mentmore 63-68; Perm to Offic Dio Ches 68-78; Dio Lich 73-78. *Chapel House, Agden, Whitchurch, Salop, SY13 4RG.* (Whitchurch 2005)

HOLMES, George Henry. b 07. ATCL 34. **d** 42 **p** 44 Bradf. C of St Luke Eccleshill 42-43; Offg C of St Jude Bradf 43-45; C of St Jo Div Gainsborough 45-47; St Andr Langton or Woodhall Spa (in c of Thornton and Martin-by-Horncastle) 47-50; V of N Kelsey 50-63. *Lupin Cottage, Withern, Alford, Lincs, LN13 0NB.*

HOLMES, Gerald Paul. McMaster Univ BA 57. Hur Th Coll LTh 60. **d** 59 **p** 60 Niag. C of H Trin Welland 59-63; R of Hagersville w Cheapside 63-67; St Eliz Burlington 67-70; on leave 70-76; C of St Matt Burlington Dio Niag from 76. *537 Stillwater Crescent, Burlington, Ont., Canada.* (416-639 0770)

HOLMES, Grant Wenlock. b 54. St Steph Ho Ox BA (Th) 78. **d** 79 **p** 80 S'wark. C of Benhilton Dio S'wark from 79. *3 Aylesbury Court, Benhill Wood Road, Sutton, Surrey.* (01-644 4475)

HOLMES, James William. Moore Th Coll Syd ACT. **d** 45 Syd **p** 46 Bp Pilcher for Syd. C of St Steph Kembla 45-47; St Faith Narrabeen 47-48; Chap of Norfolk I 48-52; C-in-c of Abbotsford w Russell Lea 52-54; R of Corrimal 54-60; Botany 60-71; Croydon Dio Syd from 71. *Rectory, Highbury Street, Croydon, NSW, Australia 2132.* (798-6102)

HOLMES, John Arthur Ellis. b 11. Lich Th Coll 65. **d** 66 **p** 67 Nor. C of N Walsham 66-69; V in Wells Group C-in-c of Warham 69-77. *4 Heath Rise, Norwich Road, Fakenham, Norf.*

HOLMES, John Robin. b 42. Univ of Leeds, BA (2nd cl Politics and Phil) 64. Linc Th Coll 64. **d** 66 **p** 67 Ripon. C of Ven Bede Wyther Leeds 66-69; Adel 69-73; V of Beeston Hill (Holbeck from 76) Dio Ripon from 73. *St Luke's Vicarage, Malvern View, Leeds, LS11 8SG.* (Leeds 717996)

HOLMES, Leslie Gregory. St Jo Coll Morpeth. **d** 62 **p** 63 Newc. C of Cardiff 62-63; Mayfield 64-67; Hamilton 67-68; Chap Ch Ch Cathl Newc 68-72; P-in-c of Kotara S 72-79; R of E Maitland Dio Newc from 79. *Rectory, William Street, East Maitland, NSW, Australia 2323.* (33 7475)

HOLMES, Melville Edward. St Jo Coll Auckld LTh 46. **d** 30 **p** 31 Wel. C of Karori 30-32; Tauranga 32-35; Perm to Offic (Col Cl Act) at St Mich Tividale 35-36; C 36-42; Chap RAFVR and RNZAF 42-46; C of Tauranga 46-48; V of Papakura 48-51; Mount Albert 51-57; Howick 57-67; Islands 67-71; L to Offic Dio Auckld 71-79; Perm to Offic from 80. *60 Craig Road, Maraetai, NZ.* (72-6537)

HOLMES, Nigel Ernest Hartley. b 37. Em Coll Cam BA 58, BChir 61, MB 62, MA 64. Ridley Hall Cam 62. **d** 64 **p** 65 Ely. C of St Phil Cam 64-68; Min of St Paul Jersey 68-77; C of Cam 77-80; Perm to Offic Dio Ely from 80; Dio St E from 80. *1 Pretoria Road, Cambridge, CB4 1HD.* (Cam 55165)

HOLMES, Nigel Peter. b 48. BTh (Nottm) 72. BD (Lon) 76. Kelham Th Coll. **d** 72 Penrith for Carl **p** 73 Carl. C of St Matt Barrow-F 72-75; St Bart Derby 75-78; P-in-c of Gt Barlow Dio Derby from 78. *Barlow Vicarage, Sheffield, S18 5TR.* (Sheff 890269)

HOLMES, Noel Edwin. St Jo Coll Auckld 48. NZ Bd of Th Stud LTh 65. **d** 51 **p** 52 Auckld. C of St Andr Epsom Auckld 51-54; Takapuna 54-56; on leave 56-58; Ellerslie 58-59; V of Orewa 59-63; Ruawai 63-69; Palmerston N 69-70; Milford Dio Auckld from 71. *Vicarage, Milford, Auckland, NZ.* (491-010)

HOLMES, Percival Ernest. b 06. **d** 42 **p** 43 Ja. C of St Thos ye Vale 42-45; R of Vere 45-46; Annotto Bay 46-49; C of Ch Gresley 49-51; Blakenall Heath 51-53; V of Edstaston 53-58; Betley 58-62; R of Pitney 62-69; R of Aller 62-69. *10 Greenhill Gardens, Greenhill, Evesham, Worcs, WR11 4ND.* (Evesham 3016)

HOLMES, Peter Geoffrey. b 32. Univ of Bris BSc 59, MSc 69. Univ of Leic PhD 74. St Deiniol's Libr Hawarden 74. **d** 76 **p** 77 Leic (APM). Hon C of Glen Parva Dio Leic from 76; Lect Univ of Leic from 76. *19 Windsor Avenue, Glen Parva, Leicester, LE2 9TQ.*

HOLMES, Robert James. b 12. Kelham Th Coll 29. **d** 36 **p** 37 Linc. C of St Steph Grimsby 36-38; St Alb Hull 38-40; CF (EC) 40-46; V of Osmotherley 46-50; CF 50-67; MELF 50-67; PC of Breamore 67-71; Chap St Jas Oporto 71-74; Chap at St Bonif Antwerp Dio Lon (N & C Eur) 74-77; Perm to Offic Dio B & W from 78. *Little Bridge, Stoke Trister, Wincanton, Somt.* (Wincanton 32768)

HOLMES, Robert John Geoffrey. b 28. Trin Coll Dub BA (2nd cl Mod Hist and Pol Sc) 53, MA 57. Ely Th Coll 56. **d** 57 **p** 58 Lon. C of St Aug of Cant Eccles Distr Whitton 57-59; St Pancras 59-63; Stepney 63-66; St Aug w St Phil Stepney 66-68; Chap Lon Hosp 63-68; R of Middelburg, Steynsburg and Colesburg 68-74; Perm to Offic Dio Ely 74; Dio Chich 74-76; R of Telscombe w Piddinghoe and Southease Dio Chich from 76. *Elderberry House, Piddinghoe, E Sussex.* (Newhaven 5530)

HOLMES, Robert Nowell Roland. Univ of Manit BA 34. St Jo Coll Winnipeg 36. **d** 38 **p** 39 Calg. C of Foremost 38-39; I 39-42; Red Deer 40-43 Chap R Canad N 43-45; R of Macleod 45-47; Gen Miss Dio Rupld 47-50; Archd of Selkirk 48-55; R of Selkirk 50-55; Steveston 55-57; South Westmr 57-65; I of St Sav Vancouver 66-69; R of Mission 69-71; Perm to Offic Dio BC from 72. *155 South Turner Street, Victoria, BC, Canada.*

HOLMES, Stanley Thomas. b 11. Selw Coll Cam BA 34, MA 46. St Steph Ho Ox 34. **d** 36 **p** 37 Ox. C of Headington 36-48; V of Goring Dio Ox from 48. *Vicarage, Goring-on-Thames, Oxon.* (Goring 872196)

HOLMES, Stephen William. Univ of Syd BA 50, ACT ThL 52. **d** 50 **p** 51 C & Goulb. C of Goulb Cathl 50-51; R of Koorawatha 51-54; Murrumburrah 54-57; Young 57-68; St Phil Canberra 68-72; Albury 72-78; Archd of Albury 73-78. *PO Box 682, Albury, NSW, Australia 2640.*

HOLMES, William Ernest. b 32. St Barn Th Coll Adel 67. **d** 70 Adel **p** 70 Murray. C of Mt Gambier 70-72; Albany 72-73; R of Kojonup 73-75; Latrobe 76-79. *c/o Rectory, Last Street, Latrobe, Tasmania 7307.* (004-261104)

HOLNESS, Edwin Geoffrey Nicholas. b 39. Sarum Th Coll 68. **d** 71 **p** 72 Chich. C of U Beeding and of Bramber w Botolphs 71-74; St Mary Magd Munster Sq St Pancras 74-75; Annunc Brighton 75-76 Perm to Offic Dio Chich from 77; Chap E Sussex Hosps from 77. *Chaplains Office, Brighton General Hospital, Brighton, BN2 3EW.* (0273-606444)

HOLROYD, Gordon Eric. b 31. **d** 76 Lanc for Blackb **p** 76 Blackb. M SSM. Asst Chap St Martin's Coll Lancaster 76-77; Chap 77-78; C of St Matt Sheff 78-80; L to Offic Dio Man 80-81; P-in-c of Willen Dio Ox from 81. *Willen Priory, Milton Keynes, Bucks, MK15 9AA.* (0908-611749)

HOLROYD, John Richard. b 54. Univ of Liv BA 75. Wycl Hall Ox 78. **d** 81 Willesden for Lon. C of Gt Stanmore Dio Lon from 81. *11 Elm Park, Stanmore, Middx.* (01-954 4616)

HOLROYD, Thomas Arthur Wulstan. b 13. **d** 51 **p** 52 Ox. Nashdom Abbey 51-58; C of St Gabr Walsall 58-59; St Mary Magd Paddington 59-61; Chap Centr Middx and Neasden Hosps 61-66; V of St Dunstan E Acton 67-78; Perm to Offic Dio Nor from 78. *20 Hale Road, Bradenham, Thetford, Norf.*

HOLT, Alan Leonard. b 12. Univ of Dur LTh 42. Edin Th Coll 39. **d** 42 **p** 43 Carl. C of Ulverston 42-44; St Aid Carl 44-46; All SS W Bromwich 46-50; PC (V from 68) of Streetly 50-77. *The Old Vicarage, Rectory Way, Lympsham, Avon, BS24 0EW.*

HOLT, Brian. b 30. Huron Coll BMin 73. **d** 70 **p** 71 Hur. C of Bp Cronyn Mem Ch Lon 71-74; R of Tyrconnell 74-76; St Alb Lon Ont 77-78; V of St Mark w Ch Ch Glodwick Oldham Dio Man from 78. *Vicarage, Alexandra Road, Glodwick, Oldham, Lancs.* (061-624 4964)

HOLT, David. b 44. St Jo Coll Dur BSc 67, Dipl Th 69. **d** 70 **p** 71 Hulme for York. C of St Pet, Blackley 70-73; St Thos Radcliffe 73-75; V of St Pet Ashton L 75-79; Dioc Youth Officer Dio Guildf from 79. *Diocesan House, Quarry Street, Guildford, Surrey, GU1 3XG.* (0483-71826)

HOLT, Desmond David. Angl Th Coll Vanc 49. **d** 51 **p** 52 Koot. C of Vernon 51-54; V of Enderby 54-62; Creston 62-71; R of Okanagan Dio Koot from 71; Hon Can of Koot 75-78. *Box 348, Oliver, BC, Canada.* (498-2559)

HOLT, Canon Donald. b 13. St D Coll Lamp BA 37. **d** 37 Lich **p** 38 Stafford for Lich. C of St Alkmund Shrewsbury 37-46; St Aug Edgbaston 46-49; Wimbledon (in c of Ch Ch) 49-56; V of St Pet Croydon 56-64; Gt Yarmouth 64-78; Surr

65-78; Hon Can of Nor from 70. *West Croft, Rectory Close, Rollesby, Norfolk, NR29 5HW.* (Gt Yarmouth 740546)

HOLT, Francis Thomas. b 38. Edin Th Coll 79. **d** 81 Bp Gill for Newc T. C of St Geo Cullercoats Dio Newc T from 81. *22 St Oswin's Avenue, Cullercoats, North Shields, T & W, NE30 4PH.*

HOLT, Canon Frederick Albert. Univ of Dur LTh 15. St Aid Coll Exhib 13. **d** 15 **p** 16 Liv. C of St Clem Toxt Pk Liv 15-19; C of St Jo Bapt (in c of St Phil Distr) Earlestown 19-23; C-in-c of St Phil Conv Distr Newton Common Earlestown 23-24; C of Em Ch Hastings 24-26; R of Botus Fleming 26-33; Ludborough 33-79; C-in-c of North Ormsby w Wyham and Cadeby 45-51; R 51-79; RD of Ludborough 47-67; Surr 53-79; Can and Preb of Linc Cathl from 55; V of Fotherby w Utterby and L Grimsby 66-79. *c/o Ludborough Rectory, Grimsby, Lincs.* (North Thoresby 252)

HOLT, Harold. b 20. **d** and **p** 52 Aber and Ork. Asst Super Dio Aber 52; P-in-c of Burravoe 52-56; R of Strichen w Boyndlie 56-60; V of Stonefold 60-72; St Aid City and Dio Blackb from 72. *St Aidan's Vicarage, Blackburn, Lancs, BB2 4EA.* (Blackburn 53519)

HOLT, Ivan Edmund. b 16. Univ of Leeds, BA 37, MA 57. Coll of Resurr Mirfield, 39. **d** 39 **p** 40 B & W. C of Street 39-40; St Cuthb Wells 40-42; St John Leamington 42-43; Coleford w Staunton 43-46; Ch Ch Frome 46-52; R of Halse w Heathfield 52-57; V of Stowey w Bp's Sutton 57-76. *40 Windsor Crescent, Frome, Somt.*

HOLT, Jack Derek. b 38. Trin Coll Bris 71. **d** 73 **p** 74 Man. C of St Geo Mart Daubhill Bolton 73-76; C-in-c of Thornham Dio Man 76-79; V from 79. *1177 Manchester Road, Castleton, Rochdale, Gtr Man, OL11 2XZ.* (Rochdale 31825)

HOLT, John Owen. Univ of Liv BA and Pri 26. St Steph Ho Ox 26. **d** 27 Man for Ches **p** 28 Ches. C of All SS w St Bede Birkenhead 27-29; St Jas Ch Kirk 29-31; St Aug Tonge Moor 31-33; PC of Kentmere 33-42; V of Preston Patrick 42-53; St Jo Evang Windermere 53-66; C of Gt Ness (in c of L Ness) 66-72; Perm to Offic Dio Lich from 73. *11 The Oval, Bicton, Shrewsbury, Shropshire.* (Shrewsbury 850572)

HOLT, Joseph. 1891. St D Coll Lamp LDiv 22. **d** 23 **p** 24 Man. C of St Anne Longsight Oldham 23-27; Adlington 27-31; C-in-c of St Osw Conv Distr Preesall 31-34; V 34-61; Surr 50-61. *241 Tixall Road, Stafford.*

HOLT, Michael. Late Scho and Pri of St D Coll Lamp BA 61, Dipl Th (w distinc) 63. **d** 63 Hulme for Man **p** 64 Man. C of All SS Stand 63-69; V of Bacup Dio Man from 69. *St John's Vicarage, Bacup, Lancs.* (Bacup 275)

HOLT, Norman Botterill. Worc Ordin Coll. **d** 60 **p** 61 Worc. C-in-c of Dines Green Conv Distr 60-62; R of Earl's Croome w Hill Croome and Strensham Dio Worc from 62. *Earl's Croome Rectory, Worcester.* (Upton-on-Severn 2141)

HOLT, Paul William Charles. b 53. St Jo Coll Dur BA (Th) 75. Ridley Hall Cam 76. **d** 77 **p** 78 Roch. C of Bexleyheath 77-80; Frimley Dio Guildf from 80. *4 Warren Rise, Frimley, Camberley, Surrey, GU16 5SH.* (0276-66740)

HOLT, Canon Wilfrid. Univ of Melb Dipl Com 41, BA 55. ACT ThL 41. **d** 42 Geelong for Melb **p** 43 Melb. C of H Trin Coburg 42-44; AIF 44-46; Min of Ch Ch Whittlesea 46-47; Dioc C Melb 47-49; V of St Silas N Geelong 49-52; Balwyn 52-61; I of St Mark Camberwell Dio Melb from 61; Can of Melb from 62. *1 Canterbury Road, Camberwell, Vic., Australia 3124.* (03-82 6511)

HOLTAM, Nicholas Roderick. b 54. Univ of Dur BA 75. AKC and BD 78. Westcott Ho Cam 78. **d** 79 Lon **p** 80 Stepney for Lon. C of Stepney Dio Lon from 79. *Flat 2, Stepney Rectory, White Horse Lane, E1 3NE.*

HOLTAM, Canon Ralph. b 16. Univ of Wales BA 40. St Mich Coll Llan 40. **d** 42 **p** 43 Llan. C of Merthyr Tydfil 42-49; Org Sec of Prov Youth Coun of Ch in Wales 49-55; Gen Sec Ch in Wales Prov Coun for Educn 50-55; V of Ynyshir 55-65; Surr from 56; SB O of St John of Jer from 56; V of Roath 65-76; R of Sully Dio Llan from 76; Can of Llan from 81. *Rectory, South Road, Sully, Penarth, S Glam.* (Sully 530221)

HOLTBY, Very Rev Robert Tinsley. b 21. St Edm Hall Ox BA (2nd cl Mod Hist) 43, MA 46, BD 57. Late Cho Scho K Coll Cam 45, BA (2nd cl Th Trip pt ii) 47, MA 52. Cudd Coll 43. Westcott Ho Cam 1944. **d** 46 **p** 47 York. C of Pocklington w Yapham and Kilnwick Percy 46-48; CF 48-52; P-in-c Johore Bahru 50-52; Hon CF 52; Chap and Asst Master Malvern College and L to Offic Dio Worc 52-54; Chap and Asst Master St Edw Sch Ox 54-59; L to Offic Dio Ox 55-59; Can Res of Carl 59-67; Can (Emer) from 67; Dir of Relig Educn Dio Carl 59-67; Gen Sec NS 67-77; Sec C of E Schs Coun 67-74; L to Offic Dio S'wark 68-77; Gen Sec Gen Syn Bd of Educn 74-77; Dean of Chich from 77. *Deanery, Chichester, Sussex, PO19 1PX.* (Chichester 783286)

HOLTH, Öystein Johan. b 31. Open Univ BA 75. K Coll Lon and Warm AKC 54. **d** 54 **p** 55 Lon. C of Gt Greenford 54-56; L to Offic Dio Borneo 56-58; P-in-c of Kudat 58-61; St Columba's Miss Miri 61-66; Labuan 66-67; Chap O of the H Paraclete and St Hilda's Sch Whitby 67-75; C-in-c of St Barn Pimlico Dio Lon and Industr Chap W Lon from 75. *Clergy House, St Barnabas' Street, SW1W 8PF.* (01-730 5054)

HOLTH, Canon Sverre. **d** and **p** 42 Shensi. Dean Ching-feng Th Coll Sian 42-44; Lect Th Coll Chengtu 44-50; Dean 48-50; V of St John Chengtu 44-50; Archd of W Szech and Sec CMS W China Miss 50-53; Warden St Pet Hall Sing and Exam Chap to Bp of Sing 53-64; Hon Can of Sing 56-64; Can (Emer) from 64. *Tao Fong Shan Christian Institute, Shatin, Hong Kong.*

HOLTON, David Ralph. b 48. **d** 73 Milwaukee for New Westmr; on leave 73-74; I of St Richard Vanc 74-77; on leave. *1351 West 15th Street, N Vancouver, BC, Canada.*

HOLYER, Vincent Alfred Douglas. b 28. Univ of Ex BA (Lon) 54. Oak Hill Th Coll 54. **d** 56 **p** 57 Lon. C of St Jas L Bethnal Green 56-58; Braintree 58-61; V of All SS Islington 61-65; R of St Ruan w St Grade Dio Truro from 65. *Rectory, Ruan Minor, Helston, Cornw, TR12 7JS.* (0326-290540)

HOLYHEAD, Rex Noel Humphrey. b 32. **d** 68 **p** 69 Glouc. C of St Mary-de-Lode w St Nich Glouc 68-70; Christchurch w Mudeford 70-77; R of St Jo Bapt w Winnall Win 77-81; P-in-c of Millbrook Dio Win from 81. *Millbrook Rectory, Regents Park Road, Southampton, SO1 3NZ.* (Southn 773417)

HOLZ, Michael Thomas. b 39. Moore Coll Syd ThL 71. **d** 73 Syd **p** 73 Bp Robinson for Syd. C of St John Parramatta 73-77; Chap RAN from 78. *Chaplain's Office, HMAS Cerebus, Western Port, Vic., Australia 3920.* (059-83 9403)

HOMAN, Richard Arthur. b 18. Late Scho of Em Coll Cam 2nd cl Hist Trip pt i 39, BA (2nd cl Hist Trip pt ii) 40, MA 44. Ridley Hall Cam 40. **d** 42 **p** 43 Birm. C of St Mary Pype Hayes 42-47; Chap Thos Coram Schs Berkhamsted 47-49; Chap and Asst Master Cranleigh Sch 50-53; Birkenhead Sch and L to Offic Dio Ches from 54. *58 Claremount Road, Wallasey, Merseyside.* (051-638 6770)

HOMER, Alan Fellows. b 30. Ridley Hall, Cam 61. **d** 63 **p** 64 Heref. C of St Jas Heref 63-66; Hon CF 63-66; V of St Sav Brixton Hill 66-73; CF (TAVR) 70-73; CF 73-76; V of Heeley City and Dio Sheff from 75. *Heeley Vicarage, Gleadless Road, Sheffield, S2 3AE.* (0742-57718)

HOMEWOOD, Michael John. b 33. Wells Th Coll 69. **d** 71 **p** 72 Ex. C of Ilfracombe 71-75; P-in-c of Woolacombe 75-78; Team V of Ilfracombe Dio Ex from 78. *Vicarage, Woolacombe, Devon.* (Woolacombe 870467)

HOMFRAY, John Bax Tayler. b 29. Keble Coll Ox BA (3rd cl Hist) 52. Ridley Hall Cam 52. **d** 54 Malmesbury for Bris **p** 55 Bris. C of H Trin Kingswood 54-57; Leckhampton 57-64; V of Staverton w Boddington Dio Glouc from 64. *Staverton Vicarage, Cheltenham, Glos.* (Coombe Hill 307)

HONE, Canon Frank Leslie. b 11. Kelham Th Coll 32. **d** 38 **p** 39 Sheff. C of St Paul Arbourthorne Sheff 38-40; CF (EC) 40-45; C of St Phil and St Anne Sheff 45-46; Rotherham 46-49; V of St Thos Brightside Sheff 49-53; Attercliffe w Carbrook 53-60; Proc Conv Sheff 59-66; C-in-c of St Swith Manor Sheff 60-66; V of Frodingham 66-78; RD of Manlake 69-76; Can and Preb of Linc Cathl 72-78; Can (Emer) from 78. *Vicarage, Wragby, Wakefield, W Yorks.* (Wakef 862246)

HONES, Simon Anthony. b 54. Univ of Sussex BSc 75. Qu Coll Birm Dipl Th 78. **d** 79 **p** 80 Win. C of Ch Ch City and Dio Win from 79. *18 Sparkford Close, Winchester, Hants.*

HONEY, Canon Frederick Bernard. b 22. Selw Coll Cam BA (2nd cl Th) 48, MA 72. Wells Th Coll 48. **d** 50 **p** 51 S'wark. C of St Geo Mart S'wark 50-52; St Jo Bapt Claines Worc 52-55; V of Wollaston Dio Worc from 55; RD of Stourbridge from 72; Hon Can of Worc Cathl from 75. *Wollaston Vicarage, Stourbridge, W Midl, DY8 4NP.* (Stourbridge 5674)

HONEYBALL, Mark George. b 56. Ch Coll Cam BA (Th) 78. Westcott Ho Cam 79. **d** 81 Colchester for Chelmsf. C of Witham Dio Chelmsf from 81. *99 Hatfield Road, Witham, Essex, CM8 1EF.* (Witham 511571)

HONEYGOLD, Thomas Felix. Qu Coll Newfld. **d** and **p** 37 Newfld. C of Port de Grave 37; P-in-c of Trin 37-38; I of Cow Head and Coast Miss 38-45; I of Sandwich Bay Labrador 46-50; R of Burgeo 50-55; Belle I 55-56; St Mich AA St John's 56-76; Can of Newfld 72-76. *St Luke's Homes, Topsail Road, St John's, Newfoundland, Canada.*

HONG, Derek Tack Weng. b 47. **d** 75 **p** 76 Sing. P Dio Sing from 75. *Church of Our Saviour, 2 Prince Charles Crescent, Singapore 3.*

HONG, Ignatios Sung Man. b 49. St Mich Sem Seoul 77. **d** 77 Taejon. d Dio Taejon. *226 Osanri, Taesomyon, Umsungkun 312-15, Chungbuk, Korea.*

HONG, Ven John. Yonse Univ BTh 66. **d** 68 **p** 69 Seoul. P Dio Seoul; Arch P of Seoul from 77. *256 Anjung, Osong Myon, P'yongt'aek, Kun 180, Korea.* (Anjung 167)

HONG KONG, Lord Bishop of. *See* Kwong, Right Rev

Peter.

HONG KONG, Assistant Bishop of. (Vacant)

HONG KONG, Dean of. *See* Sidebotham, Very Rev Stephen Francis.

HONNER, Canon Robert Ralph. b 15. St Chad's Coll Dur BA 37, Dipl Th 38, MA 40. **d** 38 **p** 39 Liv. C of St Faith Gt Crosby 38-41; C-in-c of St Andr Wigan 41-44; C of Rugby (in c of H Trin) 44-49; PC of St Barn Derby 49-53; V of Melbourne, Derby 53-72; RD of Melbourne 54-67; Exam Chap to Bp of Derby 56-60; Hon Can of Derby 58-80; Can (Emer) from 80; Surr 66-80; V of Beeley w Edensor 72-80; RD of Bakewell and Eyam 73-78. *Amber Rigg, Pentrich, Ripley, Derbys, DE5 3RE.* (Ripley 43226)

HONORE, Christopher Grant. b 52. St Jo Coll Auckld 77. **d** 79 **p** 80 Auckld. C of Pakuronga Dio Auckld from 79. *33 Riverhills Avenue, Pakuronga, Auckland, NZ.*

HONOUR, George Spencer. Hur Coll LTh 45. **d** 42 **p** 44 Hur. C of St Jas Westmr Lon 42-43; Bervie 43-45; I of Wiarton and Lion's Head 45-49; Merlin 49-51; Thessalon 51-52; Sudbury 53-59; R of Marathon 59-66; I of Central Patricia 66-73; Leask w Shell Lake and Mt Nebo 73-76; Big River (w Paddockwood to 80) Dio Sask from 76. *Box 188, Big River, Sask, Canada.*

HOOD, Allan Donald. b 46. Waterloo Lutheran Univ Ont BA 70. Trin Coll Tor MDiv 73. **d** and **p** 77 Ont. I of Lansdowne Front 77-80; C of St Matt Ott 80-81; P-in-c of Trin Ott 81; Chap Carleton Univ 81; Bp's Missr Dio Ott from 81. *71 Bronson Avenue, Ottawa, Ont, Canada.*

HOOD, Donald McKenzie. Univ of Syd BA 54. **d** 59 **p** 61 Bp in Medak. [f in Ch of S India] C of Pymble 67-68; Asst Master Barker Coll Hornsby from 68; Longueville 68-69; Turramurra 69-70; L to Offic Dio Syd from 73. *Barker College, Pacific Highway, Hornsby, NSW, Australia 2077.* (47-1456)

HOOD, Douglas Edward. St Paul's Coll Burgh, 27. **d** 31 **p** 32 Ripon. C of St Sav Leeds 31-34; St Mary Penzance 34-36; Babbacombe 36-37; St D (in c of St Mich AA) Ex 37-47; Chap RAFVR 41-45; Chap HM Pris Ex 39-41; V of St Mich E Teignmouth 47-65; W Hill 65-74; Publ Pr Dio Ex from 75. *Winsford, Ridgeway, Ottery St Mary, Devon.*

HOOD, Eric James. Clifton Th Coll 39. **d** 40 **p** 41 B & W. C of St Luke S Lyncombe 40-42; V of Locking 42-46; R of Worting 46-53; Area Chap Reading Hosps 53-59; V of Thorncombe 59-64. *3 Coppershell, Gastard, Corsham, Wilts.* (Corsham 713307)

HOOD, Kenneth Ernest. b 14. Univ of Lon BSc 33. Em Coll Cam BA (2nd cl Mor Sc Trip pt ii) 36, MA 41. Westcott Ho Cam 36. **d** and **p** 38 S'wark. C of All SS S Lambeth 38-41; St Bart Edgbaston 41-45; V of St Barn Balsall Heath 45-52; Hazelwell 52-68; Kingsbury w Hurley 68-80. *78 Goodere Drive, Polesworth, Tamworth, Staffs, B78 1BZ.*

HOOD, Norman Arthur. b 24. Kelham Th Coll 48. **d** 52 **p** 53 Ex. C of St Gabr Plymouth 52-55; Chap RN 55-59; V of St Hilda Prestwich 59-62; Dir of Stud ICF and C of St Kath Cree Lon 62-63; V of Outwood 63-79; Press Officer Dio S'wark 63-79; Dio Truro from 79; P-in-c of St Erme 79-81; Press Sec to Bp of Lon from 81. *2a Fairby Road, Lee, SE12 8JL.* (01-318 4669)

HOOD, Peter Michael. b 47. Univ of Sheff BSc 68. St Pet Coll Ox Dipl Th 72. Wycl Hall Ox 70. **d** 73 **p** 74 Bris. C of Soundwell 73-76; P-in-c of St Andr Conv Distr Walcot Swindon 76-77; Team V of St Jo Bapt and St Andr Swindon 77-80; V of Esh Dio Dur from 80; Hamsteels Dio Dur from 80. *Vicarage, Church Street, Langley Park, Durham, DH7 9TZ.* (Dur 731344)

HOOD, Robert Ernest Nathaniel. b 12. TCD BA 34, MA 42. **d** 37 **p** 38 Down. C of St Aid Belf 37-39; Org Sec ICM 39-41; C of Ch Ch Brixton Road 41-42; V of Skellingthorpe 42-46; St Steph Lambeth 46-57; Em w St Barn Holloway 57-77; Perm to Offic Dio Cant from 79. *78 Poplar Drive, Herne Bay, Kent.* (Herne Bay 66317)

HOOD, Thomas Henry Havelock. Chich Th Coll 51. **d** 54 **p** 55 Dur. C of Stella 54-57; M Bush Bro of St Paul Brisb 58-64; R of Killarney 64-65; V of Surfer's Paradise Dio Brisb 65-67; R 67-71; St Matt Sherwood City and Dio Brisb from 71. *St Matthew's Rectory, Quarry Road, Corrinda, Brisbane, Australia 4075.* (379 9472)

HOOG, Canon John Austin. St Francis Coll Brisb. **d** 66 Brisb for N Queensld **p** 68 N Queensld. C of St Matt Mundingburra Townsville 66-70; R of Sarina 70-73; Heatley, Townsville Dio N Queensld from 73; Can of N Queensld from 81. *Rectory, Heatley, Townsville, Qld, Australia.* (077-792434)

HOOG, Ven William. St Francis Coll Nundah ACT ThL 20. **d** 20 Coadj Bp of Brisb for Rockptn **p** 21 Rockptn. C of St Paul's Cathl Rockptn 20-21; Gladstone 21-26; V of Par Distr of Keppel 26-27; R of Blackall 27-30; St Alb Wilston Brisb 30-32; Chap Miss to Seamen Brisb 32-47; serving w AMF 40-47; R of Warwick 47-62; Hon Can of Brisb 49-63; Archd of W Area 56-61; Downs 61-62; L to Offic Dio Brisb 62-71; Dio N Queensld from 71. *c/o St Luke's Rectory, Sarina, Queensland, Australia.*

HOOK, Gilbert Alexander. BC Coll Bris 27. **d** 30 **p** 31 Lon. C of St John U Holloway 30-31; Miss Dio Vic 31-41; R of St Jas Croydon Syd 41-45; Chap Western Suburbs Hosp Syd 41-45; St Steph Willoughby 45-47; V of Scottow w Lammas and L Hautbois Norf 47-50; R of Bowral 50-58; and 66-73; Lindfield 58-65; Can of St Mich Pro Cathl Wollongong 69-73; L to Offic Dio Syd from 73; Chap Tudor Ho Sch Moss Vale from 73. *Osborne Road, Burradoo, NSW, Australia 2576.* (048-61 1904)

HOOK, Canon Herbert. Univ of NZ BA 36, MA 37. Selw Coll Dun. **d** 37 **p** 38 Dun. C of All SS Dun 37-40; V of Waitaki 40-41; Milton 41-47; Gore 47-60; Hon Can of St Paul's Cathl Dun 56-74; Can (Emer) from 74; V of Oamaru 60-66; Dunstan 66-74; L to Offic Dio Dun from 74. *Box 21, Hawea Flat, Central Otago, NZ.*

HOOK, Ronald Arthur. b 10. Or Coll Ox BA (2nd cl Th) 33, MA 46. Sarum Th Coll 33. **d** 34 **p** 35 Ox. C of Cowley Ox 34-39 and 45-46; CF (R of O) 39-45; PC of St Andr Luton 46-54; R of St Anne Lewes 54-65; Surr 60-75; R of Hurstpierpoint 65-75; Albourne 71-75. *Headley Cottage, Goring Road, Steyning, W Sussex, BN4 3GF.* (Steyning 814762)

✠ **HOOK, Right Rev Ross Sydney.** b 17. MC 45. Peterho Cam 2nd cl Hist Trip pt i 38, BA 39, 3rd cl Th Trip pt i 40, MA 43. Univ of Bradf Hon DLitt 81. Ridley Hall Cam 39. **d** 41 **p** 42 Win. C of Milton 41-43; Chap RNVR 43-46; Chap Ridley Hall Cam 46-48; Select Pr Univ of Cam 48; R of Chorlton-cum-Hardy 48-52; St Luke Chelsea 52-61; RD of Chelsea 52-61; Surr 53-61; Chap Chelsea Hosp for Women 54-61; St Luke's Hosp Chelsea 57-61; Can of Roch 61-65; Exam Chap to Bp of Roch 61-65; to Bp of Linc 66-72; Dir of Post Ordin Tr 61-65; Preb of Linc Cathl 66-72; Dean of Stamford 72; Cons Ld Bp Suffr of Grantham in Westmr Abbey 30 Nov 65 by Abp of Cant; Bps of Lon; Linc; Roch; Win; and Pet; Bps Suffr of Southn; Grimsby; Tonbridge; and Buckingham; Bps Montgomery; Campbell; Mann; Otter; J K Russell; and others; Trld to Bradford 72; res 80; Chief of Staff to Abp of Cant from 80. *Lambeth Palace, SE1 7JU.* (01-928 8282)

HOOKER, Kenneth Howard. b 06. Ch Coll Cam BA 28, MA 32. Wycl Hall Ox 30. **d** 33 **p** 34 Roch. C of Sevenoaks 33-36; All S Langham Place 36-39; V of St Matt Fulham 39-45; St Phil w St Jacob Bris 45-48; St Paul Cam 48-58; Cockfosters 58-73. *2 Old Pound Yard, High Street, Great Shelford, Cambs.* (Cam 842712)

HOOKER, Roger Hardham. b 34. St Edm Hall Ox BA 58. Wycl Hall Ox 58. **d** 60 **p** 61 Dur. C of Stockton-on-Tees 60-63; CMS Miss Dio Luckn 65-78; C of Agra 67-69; in Ch of N India 70-78; Tutor Crowther Hall Selly Oak Coll from 79. *Crowther Hall, Weoley Park Road, Selly Oak, Birmingham, B29 6QT.*

HOOLE, Charles. b 33. St Aid Coll 61. **d** 63 **p** 64 Blackb. C of St Luke Skerton 63-65; C-in-c of St Jas Ap Preston 65-69; V of St Jas Lostock Hall Preston 69-73; Chap HM Prison Eastchurch Kent 74-75; V of St Marg St Annes-on-Sea 75-81; St Pet Blackpool Dio Blackb from 81. *26 Ullswater Road, Blackpool, Lancs, FY4 2BZ.* (Blackpool 41231)

HOOLEY, John Philip. b 45. St Deiniol's Libr Hawarden 78. **d** and **p** 79 Heref. C of St Martin Heref 79-81; CF from 81. *Ministry of Defence, Bagshot Park, Bagshot, Surrey, GU19 5PL.*

HOOPER, Alfred John. b 10. **d** 80 Stepney for Lon. C of St John Hackney Dio Lon from 80. *4b Southborough Road, Hackney, E9.*

HOOPER, Aubrey William. b 1889. MC 17. Em Coll Cam BA 11, MA 20. Wells Th Coll 12. **d** 25 Sarum **p** 37 Win. C of Sherborne 25-29; Hd Master Sherborne Prep Sch 23-29; L to Offic Dio Win and Hd Master St Neot's Sch Eversley, Hants 29-56; PC of Ebbesbourne Wake w Fifield Bavant 56-63; PC of Alvediston 56-63. *2 Moulsham Copse Lane, Yateley, Camberley, Surrey.*

HOOPER, Canon Charles. Univ of Witwatersrand Johann BA (Hons) 48. Coll of Resurr Mirfield, 49. **d** 51 **p** 52 Johann. C of St Mary's Cathl Johann 51-54; R of Zeerust and P-in-c of Miss Distr Johann 55-58; Chap St John's Conv Pietermaritzburg 58-60; St Mich Sch Manzini Dio Zulu 60-68; Dio Swaz from 68; Can of Swaz from 71. *PO Box 15, Manzini, Swaziland, S Africa.* (Manzini 2771)

HOOPER, Ven Charles German. b 11. Linc Coll Ox BA 32, MA 49. St Aug Coll Cant. **d** 34 **p** 35 Bris. C of Corsham 34-36; St Sav Claremont 36-39; C-in-c of St Aug w St Geo Bris 39-40; R of Castle Combe 40-46; Chap RAFVR 42-46; R of Sandy 46-53; V of Bp's Stortford 53-63; RD of Bp's Stortford 54-61 and 62-63; Surr from 54; R of Bildeston 63-67; V of Wattisham 63-67; R of St Lawr w St Steph Ipswich 67-74; Archd of Ipswich 63-75; Archd (Emer) from 76; Hon Can of

St E from 63; P-in-c of Kelsale w Carlton 74-76; L to Offic Dio St E from 76. *East Green Cottage, Kelsale, Saxmundham, Suff.* (Saxmundham 2702)

HOOPER, Derek Royston. b 33. St Edm Hall, Ox BA (2nd cl Engl) 57, MA 65. Cudd Coll 57. **d** 59 Thetford for Cant **p** 60 Nor. C of Walsingham 59-62; Dartmouth w Townstal 62-65; V of Lynton w Brendon 65-69; C of Littleham w Exmouth 70-72; Team V 72-79; R of Wrington w Butcombe Dio B & W from 79. *Wrington Rectory, Bristol.* (Wrington 862201)

HOOPER, Geoffrey Michael. b 39. K Coll Lon and Warm 61. **d** 66 **p** 67 Derby. C of Chesterfield 66-69; Chap RAF 69-74; P-in-c of Hook Norton, Swerford and Wigginton 74-81; Gt Rollright 75-81; R of Hook Norton w Gt Rollright, Swerford and Wigginton Dio Ox from 81. *Hook Norton Rectory, Banbury, Oxon, OX15 5QQ.* (Hook Norton 737223)

HOOPER, Geoffrey Neil. St Barn Coll Adel 39. ACT ThL 41, Th Scho 55. Metrop Univ California BTh (1st cl) 59, MTh 62. **d** 41 **p** 42 Adel. C of St Pet Glenelg 41-44 Chap RAAF 43-44; Miss Chap Penola Miss 44-47; P-in-c of St Luke w St Steph Bal 47; V of Colac and Warden of St Cuthbert's Home for Boys Colac 47-53; V of Skipton 53-59; L to Offic Dio Melb 60; Chap and Master Mentone Gr Sch Dio Melb 61-78; Perm to Offic Dio Melb from 78. *20 Cromer Road, Beaumaris, Vic, Australia 3193.* (93 4443)

HOOPER, Kevin John. b 56. St Cath Coll Cam BA 77, MA 81. Coll of Resurr Mirfield 78. **d** 80 Bp McKie for Cov **p** 81 Cov. C of Holbrooks Dio Cov from 80. *25 Deerhurst Road, Whitmore Park, Holbrooks, Coventry, CV6 4EJ.*

HOOPER, Preb Michael Wrenford. b 41. St D Coll Lamp BA (2nd cl Ancient Hist and Lit) 63. St Steph Ho Ox 63. **d** 65 **p** 66 Heref. C of St Mary Magd Bridgnorth 65-70; V of Minsterley 70-81; P-in-c of Habberley Heref 70-78; R 78-81; RD of Pontesbury 75-81; Leominster from 81; V of Leominster Dio Heref from 81; P-in-c of Eyton Dio Heref from 81; Preb of Heref Cathl from 81. *Vicarage, Leominster, Herefs.* (Leominster 2124)

HOOPER, Paul Denis Gregory. b 52. Univ of Man BA 75. Univ of Ox BA 80. Wycl Hall Ox 78. **d** 81 Knaresborough for Ripon. C of St Geo Leeds Dio Ripon from 81. *45 Clarendon Road, Leeds, LS2 9NZ.* (0532 444609)

HOOPER, Peter Guy. b 30. K Coll Lon and Warm 51. **d** 55 **p** 56 Wakef. C of Huddersfield 55-60; H Trin Brompton Kens 60-67; R of Hazelbury Bryan w Stoke Wake Fifehead Neville and Mappowder Dio Sarum from 72. *Hazelbury Bryan Rectory, Sturminster Newton, Dorset, DT10 2ED.* (Hazelbury Bryan 251)

HOOPER, Robert George Gregory. b 10. Univ of Lon BD (2nd cl) 42. ALCD (1st cl) 42. Em Coll Cam BA (2nd cl Th pt i) 44, MA 49. **d** 42 **p** 43 Ely. C of St Barn Cam 42-45; Tutor Oak Hill Th Coll Southgate 44-46; L Pr Dio St Alb 45-46; Tutor London Coll Div 46-47; Chap 47-52; V of Midhurst 52-59; Surr 52-59; RD of Midhurst 54-59; Lewes 61-65; R of Newhaven 59-65; V of St Jo Evang Meads Eastbourne 65-72; Perm to Offic Dio Ex from 72. *Nethercleave, Withleigh, Tiverton, Devon.* (Tiverton 253644)

HOOPER, Stanley Frederick. b 16. St Jo Coll Dur BA 47. Ridley Hall Cam 49. **d** 51 Dover for Cant **p** 52 Cant. C of St Paul Cliftonville Margate 51-53; V of Bexley 53-62; Ch Ch Woking 62-70; Grayshott 70-79; R of Barningham w Matlaske and Baconsthorpe, Plumstead and Hempstead Dio Nor from 79. *Matlaske Rectory, Norwich, Norf, NR11 7JB.* (Matlaske 420)

HOOPER, Walter McGehee. b 31. Univ of N Carolina BA 54, MA 58. St Steph Ho Ox. **d** 64 **p** 65 Ox. Hon C of Headington Quarry Ox 64-65; Chap Wadh Coll Ox 65-67; Asst Chap Jes Coll Ox 67-70; Perm to Offic Dio Ox from 70. *19 Beaumont Street, Oxford, OX1 2NA.* (Oxford 44442)

HOOPES, David Bryan. b 43. Findlay Coll Ohio BA 66. Andover Newton Th Sch Mass BDiv 70. **d** 75 **p** 76 Nass. C of Ch Ch Cathl Nass 75-80; in Amer Ch. *Order of the Holy Cross, West Park, NY 12493, USA.*

HOORE, Donald Henry. ACT ThL 57. St Jo Coll Morpeth. **d** 57 **p** 58 River. C of Broken Hill 57-58; Leeton 58-63; P-in-c of Balranald 61-63; R 63-67; P-in-c of Mulwala Par Distr 67-69; Urana 69-70; Coolamon 70-74; Eliz S Adel 74-75; R of Barellan-Weethalle 75-80; Perm to Offic Dio Syd from 80; Dio River from 81. *3 Prince Edward Street, Carlton, NSW, Australia 2218.* (587-2299)

HOOSANG, Leslie. **d** 75 **p** 76 Ja. C of St Luke Cross Roads Dio Ja from 75. *7 Aberdeen Drive, Kingston 8, Jamaica, W Indies.*

HOOTON, Arthur Russell. Moore Th Coll Syd ACT ThL 51. **d** and **p** 52 Syd. C of Wollongong 52-53; C-in-c of Normanhurst 53-57; R of Bowraville 57-61; C of Styvechale Warws 62-63; R of Eureka w Clunes NSW 63-65; V of Stockingford Dio Cov from 65. *Stockingford Vicarage, Nuneaton, Warws, CV10 8LG.* (Nuneaton 383024)

HOOTON, James William Edward. b 1890. Can Scho Linc 11. Chich Th Coll 13. **d** 15 **p** 17 Chelmsf. C of St Sav Walthamstow 15-18; St Simon Bris 19-20; Perm to Offic Dio Ex 21-22; C of Annunc Brighton 22-24; H Trin Hoxton 25-29; V of Poundstock 29-33; Perm to Offic Dio Lon 34-69; Dio Chich from 59; V of Huncote 43-44. *151 Goldstone Crescent, Hove, Sussex, BN3 6BB.* (Brighton 555432)

HOPA, Canon Ephraim Mzamo. St Bede's Coll Umtata 38. **d** 40 St Jo Kaffr for Grahmstn **p** 43 Grahmstn. P Dio Grahmstn 40-44; CF (S Afr) 44-46; Miss O of Ethiopia at St Barn E Lon 46-55; Uitenhage 55-62; Senaoane Dio Johann 63-70; Prov of O of Ethiopia Bernard Mizeki Miss Dio Port Eliz from 70; Can of Port Eliz from 77. *PO Box 50, Kwazakele, Port Elizabeth, CP, S Africa.* (041-61895)

HOPCRAFT, Jonathan Richard. b 34. Or Coll Ox BA (3rd cl Mod Hist) 55, Dipl Educn 66, MA 66. Westcott Ho Cam 57. **d** 59 **p** 60 Lich. C of Cannock 59-63; Msoro 63-64; St Mary and All SS Cathl Salisbury 64-65; Hon C of Olton 67-68; R of St Geo Antig 68-72; C of Gt Grimsby (in c of St Hugh's) 72-73; Team V 73-76; V of Blyton w Pilham Dio Linc from 76; P-in-c of Laughton w Wildsworth Dio Linc from 76; E Stockwith w Walkerith Dio Linc from 76. *Blyton Vicarage, Gainsborough, Lincs, DN21 3JZ.* (Laughton 216)

HOPE, Colin Frederick. b 49. Univ Coll Cardiff Dipl Th 76. St Mich AA Llan 73. **d** 76 **p** 77 Liv. C of St Elphin Warrington 76-80; V of All SS Newton-in-Makerfield Dio Liv from 80. *All Saints Vicarage, Cross Lane, Newton-le-Willows, Merseyside, WA12*

HOPE, Cyril Sackett. b 24. St Edm Hall Ox BA (2nd cl Th) 49, MA 54. Ely Th Coll 50. **d** 51 **p** 52 Leic. C of Wigston Magna 51-55; Hawley w Blackwater and Minley 55-58; R of Clayhidon 58-63; Dunchideock w Shillingford St Geo 63-77; Asst Dir of Relig Educn Dio Ex from 73; P-in-c of Stockland w Dalwood Dio Ex 77-79; V from 79. *Stockland Vicarage, Honiton, Devon.* (Stockland 401)

HOPE, David Michael. b 40. Univ of Nottm BA (2nd cl Th) 62. Linacre Ho Ox DPhil 65. St Steph Ho Ox 62. **d** 65 Warrington for Liv **p** 66 Liv. C of Tue Brook 65-67 and 68-70; Chap Ch of Resurr Bucharest 67-68; V of St Andr Orford 70-74; Prin St Steph Ho Ox from 74; Warden Commun of St Mary Virg Wantage from 80; Exam Chap to Bp of Nor from 81. *St Stephen's House, OX4 1JX.* (Ox 47874)

HOPE, George Edward. b 08. AKC 34. St Steph Ho Ox 34. **d** 34 **p** 35 Guildf. C of Gt Bookham 34-37; Cathl Ch Guildf 37-39; CF (R of O) 39-45; CF 45-62; R of Upton Lovell 62-71; Codford 63-71; Cholderton 71-73; Newton Tony 71-73. *16 Upton Lovell, Warminster, Wilts.* (Codford St Mary 249)

HOPE, James Cotton. **d** 59 **p** 60 Tas. C of St Steph Hobart 59-61; V of Castra 61-64; C of Queenstown 64-65; R of Ringarooma w Derby 65-68; Sheffield 68-70; Lang Lang 72-75; Perm to Offic Dio Tas 75-78. *40 Percy Street, Devonport, Tasmania 7310.* (004-24 2257)

HOPE, John. OBE 56. St Jo Coll Melb. **d** 14 **p** 15 Syd. C of St Jude Randwick NSW 14-16; St Lawr Syd 16-19; V of All SS Clifton Queensld 19-25; R of Ch Ch St Lawr Syd 26-64. *Unit 66, 441 Alfred Street, North Sydney, NSW, Australia.*

HOPE, Montague Henry. b 12. Univ of Chicago BD 71. K Coll Lon. **d** 58 **p** 59 Atlanta USA. In Amer ch 58-74; C of St Martin Maidstone 74-78; Perm to Offic Dio Cant from 79; Chap HM Pris Maidstone from 81. *26 The Woodcut, Sandling Lane, Maidstone, Kent, ME14 2EQ.* (Maidstone 677661)

HOPE, Richard Earwaker. b 15. Linc Th Coll 70. **d** and **p** 57 RC Bp of Menevia. In RC Ch 57-70; Rec into Angl Commun 70 by Bp of Linc; C of Highters Heath 70-73; Gt Grimsby 73-80. *60 The Limes, Milson Road, Keelby, Grimsby, DN37 8HA.*

HOPE, Robert. b 36. Univ of Dur BSc 61. Clifton Th Coll 61. **d** 63 **p** 64 Guildf. C of St Mary of Bethany Woking 63-66; Ch Ch Surbiton Hill (in c of Em) 66-68; Hon C of Wallington 69-71; C of St Ebbes Ox 71-74; V of Walshaw Dio Man from 74. *Christ Church Vicarage, Walshaw, Bury, Lancs, BL8 3AG.* (061-764 2035)

HOPE, William. b 08. St Chad's Coll Dur BA (2nd cl Mod Hist) 30, MA 34. **d** 31 **p** 32 Blackb. C of Haslingden 31-33; St Paul w Ch Ch Adlington 33-37; V of Baxenden 37-47; Euxton 47-73; Sen Lect Edge Hill Coll of Further Educn 60-73; Exam Chap to Bp of Blackb from 70; L to Offic Dio Blackb from 79. *45 Church Walk, Euxton, Chorley, Lancs.* (Chorley 73178)

HOPES, Alan Stephen. b 44. K Coll Lon and Warm BD and AKC 66. **d** 67 **p** 68 Lon. C of All SS E Finchley 67-72; St Alphage Hendon 72-77; V of St Paul Tottenham Dio Lon from 77; Area Dean of E Haringey from 81. *60 Park Lane, N17 0JR.* (01-808 7297)

HOPKIN, Gerallt. b 12. Univ of Wales BA (Econ and Pol Sc) 36. Sarum Th Coll 37. **d** 38 Swan B for Llan **p** 39 Llan. C of St Fagan Aberdare 38-40; St Cynfelyn Caerau 40-44; Gellygaer 44-50; V of Penrhiwceiber (w Tyntetown and Ynysboeth 55-68) 50-68; Surr 65; R of St Fagan's w

Michaelston-super-Ely 68-77; Perm to Offic Dio Llan from 79. *25 Tangmere Drive, Fairwood Chase, Llandaff, Cardiff, CF5 2PP.* (Cardiff 553985)

HOPKIN, Watkin William Lynn. b 16. St D Coll Lamp BA 50. **d** 51 **p** 52 Swan B. C of Gorseinon 51-54; Neath 55-58; St Marg Toxt Pk 59-60; Ystalyfera 61-64; Llansamlet Dio Swan B from 72. *c/o 61 Church Road, Llansamlet, Swansea.*

HOPKINS, Aubrey Lionel Evan. b 06. Late Rustat Scho of Jes Coll Cam 1st cl Math Trip pt i 26 BA (2nd cl Th Trip pt i) 28, MA 32. Ridley Hall, Cam 28. **d** 30 Dover for Cant **p** 31 Cant. C of Ch Ch Croydon 30-33; Gerrard's Cross 33-35; Watford 35-37; V of St Luke Wimbledon Pk 37-41; Kew 41-50; High Wycombe 50-62; Surr 51-62; RD of Wycombe 57-62; Proc Conv Ox 59-64; V of H Trin w Ch Ch Folkestone 62-74; RD of Elham 70-74. *38 Worcester Road, Chipping Norton, Oxon.*

HOPKINS, Canon Charles Henry Gordon. b 09. Mert Coll Ox BA 30, MA 63. Cudd Coll 31. **d** 32 **p** 33 Ches. C of St Luke Lower Tranmere 32-39; V of St Luke Pallion Bp Wearmouth 39-70; Proc Conv Dur from 50; Hon Can of Dur 57-69; Can Res 70-78; Can (Emer) from 78; RD of Wearmouth 62-70; Chap to HM the Queen 64-80. *Prebend's Gate Cottage, Quarry Heads Lane, Durham, DH1 3DZ.*

HOPKINS, Christopher Freeman. Univ of Dur BA 63. Wells Th Coll 63. **d** 65 Cant **p** 66 Dover for Cant. C of All SS Spring Pk Croydon 65-69; St Jo Evang Mafeking 69-70; R of Potchefstroom 70-78; L to Offic Dio Botswana 78-81; R of Beckley and Peasmarsh Dio Chich from 81. *Rectory, School Lane, Peasmarsh, Rye, E Sussex, TN31 6UW.* (Peasmarsh 255)

HOPKINS, Douglas Roy. **d** 62 NS. d Dio NS from 62. *777 Tower Road, Halifax, NS, Canada.* (422-4745)

HOPKINS, Canon Douglass. b 04. Keble Coll Ox BA (2nd Cl Engl Lit) 25, Dipl Th w distinc 26, MA 30. Wycl Hall Ox 25. **d** 27 **p** 28 Sheff. C of St Mark Sheff 27-32; V of H Trin Millhouses 32-40; Chap RNVR 40-46; R of Weston Favell 46-62; V of Ketton 62-73; RD of Barnack 63-73; Can (Non-res) of Pet 67-73; Can (Emer) from 73. *Spring Cottage, Dunsby, Bourne, Lincs.*

HOPKINS, Ernest. b 16. Tyndale Hall Bris 68. **d** 69 Warrington for Liv **p** 70 Liv. C of Walton Breck 69-70; C-in-c of Em Ch Everton 70-74; St Chrys Everton 70-74; St Jo Evang Everton 70-74; V of St Jo Chrys Everton 74-79; St Luke Eccleston Dio Liv from 79; RD of Walton 76-79. *St Luke's Vicarage, Mulberry Avenue, St Helen's Mer, WA10 4DE.* (St Helens 22456)

HOPKINS, Henry Charles. Edin Th Coll 66. **d** 71 **p** 72 Brech. C of St Martin Dundee 71-74; R of Monifieth 74-78; Chap Miss to Seamen Momb from 78. *Box 80424, Mombasa, Kenya.*

HOPKINS, Canon Henry Ivor. OBE 76. Univ of NZ BA 30. **d** 31 **p** 32 Ch Ch. C of Ragiora 31-34; V of Chatham Is 34-37; St Pet Kensington w Otipua 37-40; CF (NZ) 39-45; C of Addington 45; V of Temuka 46-52; Addington 52-59; Pris Chap Ch Ch 59-73; L to Offic Dio Ch Ch from 73; Hon Can of Ch Ch 72-75; Can (Emer) from 75. *97 Sullivan Avenue, Christchurch 2, NZ.* (891-077)

HOPKINS, Hugh. b 33. **d** 62 **p** 63 Connor. C of Ballymena 62-64; Ch Ch Belf 64-67; R of Ballintoy 67-72; I of St Ninian Belf 72-81; R of Mossley Dio Connor from 81. *Rectory, Mossley, Co Antrim, N Ireland.*

HOPKINS, Canon Hugh Alexander Evan. b 07. Em Coll Cam BA 30, MA 34. OBE 55. Ridley Hall Cam 30. **d** 31 Lon for Col **p** 32 Tinn. M of Dohnavur Fellowship 32-37; Travelling Sec to Inter-Varsity Fellowship 37-39; V of H Trin Redhill 40-44; St Nich Dur 44-47; Prov Can (Dioc) and R of all SS Cathl Nairobi 47-55; Archd of Nairobi 54-55; R of St Mary-le-Bow Lon 55-58; Cheltm 58-73; Proc Conv Glouc 59-70; Hon Can of Glouc 61-73; Can (Emer) from 73. *138 Thornton Road, Cambridge.*

HOPKINS, Canon Hugh Graham Beynon. b 18. Jes Coll Ox BA (3rd cl Hist) 40, MA 45. St Mich Coll Llan 40. **d** 42 **p** 43 St D. C of St Mary Cardigan 42-45; St Jo Evang Canton Cardiff 45-52; R of Dowlais 52-59; V of Aberavon Dio Llan from 59; RD of Margam from 81; Can of Llan Cathl from 81. *68 Pentyla, Port Talbot, W Glam.* (Port Talbot 883824)

HOPKINS, John Allan. b 33. St D Coll Lamp BA 55. St Steph Ho Ox 55. **d** 57 **p** 58 St D. C of Aberystwyth 57-59; St Paul Llanelli 59-62; R of Eglwys Cummin w Marros 62-76; V of St Paul Llanelli Dio St D from 76. *St Paul's Vicarage, Llanelli, Dyfed, SA15 1BY.* (Llanelli 3865)

HOPKINS, John Edgar Alexander. b 19. Jes Coll Cam BA 46, MA 48. TD 65. Wells Th Coll. **d** 48 **p** 49 Chelmsf. C of Forest Gate 48-50; Min of Maybush Peel Conv Distr Shirley 50-59; V 59-65; C-in-c of Nursling 50-55; V of Holdenhurst w Throop 65-71; C-in-c of St Barn Conv Distr Queen's Pk 65-71; Chap Stonar Sch Melksham 71-80; P-in-c of Broad Town 80-81; Clyffe Pypard and Tockenham 80-81; V of Clyffe Pypard, Tockenham and Broad Town Dio Sarum from 81. *Clyffe Pypard Vicarage, Swindon, Wilts, SN4 7PY.* (Broad Hinton 623)

HOPKINS, Canon John Howard Edgar Beynon. b 14. Univ Coll Ox BA (3rd cl Th) 36, MA 39. St Mich Coll Llan 36. **d** 37 **p** 38 St D. C of Pontyberem 37-39; Llanedy 39-41; CF (EC) 41-46; C of All SS Pontardawe 46-49; R of All SS Jordanhill (w St D Scotstoun 49-51 and 57-62; Glas 49-62; Kilmalcolm w Bridge of Weir 62-75; R of St Marg Newlands City and Dio Glas from 75; Can of Glas from 79. *22 Monreith Road, Newlands, Glasgow, G43 2NY.* (041-632 3292)

HOPKINS, John Llewelyn. **d** 29 **p** 30 Llan. C of Treorchy 29-30; St Theo Port Talbot 30-35; V of Bedlinog 35-42; Pontrhydfen 42-55. *242 Margam Road, Port Talbot, W Glam.*

HOPKINS, Joseph Jonas. b 50. St Jo Coll Morpeth 74. **d** 75 **p** 76 Bunb. C of St Bonif Cathl Bunb 75-78; Busselton 78-79; R of Jerramungup Dio Bunb from 79. *Rectory, Jerramungup, W Australia 6337.*

HOPKINS, Kenneth Victor John. b 45. Univ of Lon BA 66, BD 69. Tyndale Hall Bris 66. **d** 69 **p** 70 Lon. C of Ch Ch Mymms Barnet 69-72; St Clement Parkstone 72-75; C-in-c of St Thos Trowbridge 75-76; V 76-81; C-in-c of Wingfield 75-76; R 76-81; Chap and Lect N-E Surrey Coll of Tech Ewell from 81. *Chaplain's Office, North-East Surrey College of Technology, Reigate Road, 394 1731)*

HOPKINS, Canon Leslie Freeman. b 14. Late Exhib and Squire Scho of Ex Coll Ox 2nd cl Cl Mods 35, BA (2nd cl Th) 37, MA 40, BD 53. Wells Th Coll 37. **d** 38 **p** 39 Roch. C of Crayford 38-40; Uley w Owlpen (in c of Nympsfield) 40-42; St Thos (in c of H Trin) Old Charlton 42-45; V of St Chrys Peckham 45-56; C-in-c of St Jude Peckham 48-56; Surr 49-62; Chap of Camberwell Ho Mental Hosp 50-54; Chief Insp of Schs Dio S'wark 54-62; V of All SS Battersea Pk 56-62; Sec Dioc Bd of Educn Dio Liv and Dir of Relig Educn Liv 62-72; Chap and Lect JB Coll 62-72; Can Res and Treas of Liv Cathl 64-79; Can (Emer) from 79. *Laurel Cottage, Peasmarsh, Rye, E Sussex, TN31 6SX.*

HOPKINS, Lionel. b 48. Bp Burgess Hall Lamp 67. **d** 71 **p** 72 Swan B. C of Llandeilo-Talybont 71-74; Morriston 74-78; P-in-c of Waunarlwydd Dio Swan B 78-80; V from 80. *St Barnabas Parsonage, Victoria Road, Waunarlwydd, Swansea, SA5 4SY.* (Swansea 872251)

HOPKINS, Ven Ormond Archibald. Bp's Univ Lennox BA and LST 49. **d** 49 **p** 50 Ott. C of St Matthias Ott 49-53; CF (Canad) from 53; Archd from 74. *c/o Chaplain's Department, War Office, Ottawa, Ont, Canada.*

HOPKINS, Reginald Evan. b 10. Jes Coll Cam BA 33, MA 43. Wycl Hall Ox 46. **d** 47 Kens for Lon **p** 48 Ugan. CMS Miss Dio Ugan 47-57; V of Billingshurst 57-73; Commiss Ondo-B 56-60; V of Compton w Up Marden 73-79; R of E Marden and of N Marden 73-79; V of Compton, The Mardens, Stoughton, Racton and Lordington 79-81. *Mardens, Myrtle Road, Crowborough, E Sussex, TN6 1EX.*

HOPKINS, Robert James Gardner. **d** 79 St Alb. Hon C of Ch Ch Chorley Wood Dio St Alb from 79. *Woodlow, Solesbridge Lane, Chorleywood, Herts.*

HOPKINS, Thomas Clifford Millward. St Cath Coll Cam BA (3rd cl Hist Trip pt ii) 37, MA 41. St Mich Coll Llan 37. **d** 38 **p** 41 St A. C of Wrexham 38-52; V of Penley 52-56; Hanmer (w Bronington from 66 and Bettisfield from 80) Dio St A from 56; RD of Bangor-Is-y-Coed 63-80. *Merehead House, Hanmer, Whitchurch, Salop.*

HOPKINS, Thomas Edward. Edin Th Coll 32. **d** 35 Argyll for Aber **p** 36 Aber. C of Bucksburn (in c of All SS Miss Hilton) 35-38; St Andr Miss Lusikisiki 38-41; P-in-c of Indawana 41-44; C of H Cross Miss East Pondoland 44-45; R of Clydesdale 45-49; St Marnan Aberchirder 49-51; Fersfield 51-52; P-in-c of Estcourt 52-60; St John's Native Miss Ladysmith 60-65; St Barn Bluff Durban 65-68; Estcourt 68-71; Archd of Ladysmith 68-71; R of St D Pietermaritzburg 71-72; Hon Can of Natal 71-75; R of Girvan 72-75; St Mich AA Queenstn 75-80; P-in-c of St D Queenstn and St Mary Tarkastad 75-80; Archd of Queenstown 77-80; C of St Thos Berea Dio Natal from 81. *191 Musgrave Road, Durban 4001, S Africa.*

HOPKINS, Timothy Alban. **d** 79 Kens for Lon. C of Teddington Dio Lon from 79. *c/o The Vicarage, Kingston Road, Teddington, Middx, TW11 9HX.*

HOPKINS, William. Univ of Wales BA 30. St Mich Th Coll Llan 28. **d** 29 Llan **p** 30 Malmesbury for Llan. C of St Gwladys Bargoed 29-33; C-in-c of Ynyscynon Conv Distr 33-39; C of Withycombe Raleigh (in c of St John in the Wilderness) 39-41; Llangelynin (in c of Fairbourne) 41-47; V of Llanwnog (w Penstrowed from 50) 47-57; R of Llanmerewig 57-75. *c/o Llanmerewig Rectory, Aburmule, Powys.*

HOPKINSON, Alfred Stephan. b 08. Late Scho of Wadh Coll Ox 2nd cl Cl Mods 29, BA 30, MA 35. Linc Th Coll 34. **d** 35 **p** 36 S'wark. C of Putney 35-39; V of St Jo Evang Barrow-F 39-43; Battersea 43-52; RD of Battersea 48-52;

C-in-c of St Mary Woolnoth w St Mary Woolchurch Lon 52-54; RNR 53-62; V of St Mary Woolnoth Lon 54-59; C-in-c of St Anne Holloway 55-56; Gen Dir of ICF 58-63; V of St Kath Cree Lon 59-63; Proc Conv Lon 59-64; Preb of Caddington Minor in St Paul's Cathl Lon 60-63; R of Bobbingworth (or Bovinger) 63-73; Angl Adv ATV 60-68; Industr Adv to Bp of Chelmsf 63-73; Counsellor of Win Coll from 73; Asst Chap from 79; Publ Pr Dio Win from 73. *The College, Winchester, Hants.*

HOPKINSON, Barnabas John. b 39. Trin Coll Cam 2nd cl Th Trip pt i 61, BA (2nd cl Th Trip pt ii) 63, MA 67. Linc Th Coll 63. **d** 65 **p** 66 Man. C of All SS and Marts Langley 65-67; St Mary Gt Cam 67-71; Asst Chap of Charterhouse Sch Godalming 71-75; P-in-c of Preshute 75-76; Team V of Marlborough 76-81; RD of Marlborough 77-81; Team R of Wimborne Minster w Holt Dio Sarum from 81. *Rectory, King Street, Wimborne, Dorset.* (Wimborne 882340)

HOPKINSON, Benjamin Alaric. b 36. Trin Coll Ox BA (2nd cl Mod Hist) 59. Chich Th Coll 59. **d** 61 **p** 62 Dur. C of St Luke Pallion Bp Wearmouth 61-66; Hillside Bulawayo 66-67; P-in-c of Mmadinare 67-70; L to Offic Dio Matab 70-74; Dio Botswana 72-74; Dio Southw 74; P Missr of Carrington 74-77; Sherwood 74-77; V of Lowdham w Gunthorpe and Caythorpe Dio Southw from 77; M Gen Syn from 80; Overseas Adv to Bp of Southw from 80. *Lowdham Vicarage, Nottingham, NG14 7BU.* (Lowdham 2269)

HOPKINSON, David John. b 47. **d** 79 Ox **p** 80 Buckingham for Ox (APM). C of Wardington 79-80; St Pet Didcot Dio Ox from 80. *18 Fleetway, Didcot, Oxon.* (Didcot 817247)

HOPKINSON, Edward Alban Ernest. b 01. **d** 29 **p** 30 Keew. C of Emo w Barwick and Stratton Ont 29-32; Perm to Offic (Col Cl Act) at Ch Ch Burton on Trent 32-33; C 33-36; V of St Paul N Shore Kirkdale 36-44; St Luke Halliwell 44-49; R of Blisworth 49-51; V of Ch Ch Burton-on-Trent 51-66; Perm to Offic Dio Glouc from 66. *5 Brooklyn Road, Cheltenham, Glos.* (Cheltenham 21089)

HOPKINSON, William Deighton. b 14. Univ of Leeds BA 33. Kelham Th Coll 33. **d** 39 **p** 40 Man. C of Ch Ch Walmersley 39-42; Farnham Guildf 42-45; Stevenage 45-47; Distr Sec BFBS Staffs and Salop 47-49; V of Short Heath 49-56; C-in-c of St Aid Ernesettle Plymouth 57-59; V 59-62; Brixham 62-68; Aldbrough w Colden Parva Dio York 68-70; C of Hornsea 70-75. *Flat 2, Willow Drive, Newbiggin, Hornsea, Yorks.*

HOPKINSON, William Humphrey. b 48. Univ of Lon BSc 69. ARIC 73. Univ of Dur MA 78. St Jo Coll Dur Dipl Th 76. **d** 77 Repton for Derby **p** 78 Derby. C of Normanton-by-Derby 77-80; Sawley Dio Derby from 80. *681 Tamworth Road, Long Eaton, Nottingham, NG10 3AB.*

HOPLEY, David. b 37. Wells Th Coll 62. **d** 65 **p** 66 B & W. C of Frome Selwood 65-68; V of Staunton-on-Arrow w Byton and Kinsham 68-81; P-in-c of Lingen 68-81; Aymestrey and Leinthall Earles 72-81; R of Buckland Newton Dio Sarum from 81; Long Burton Dio Sarum from 81; Pulham Dio Sarum from 81; Wootton Glanville w Holnest Dio Sarum from 81. *Vicarage, Buckland Newton, Dorchester, Dorset, DT2 7BY.* (Buckland Newton 456)

HOPLEY, Gilbert. b 40. Univ of Wales (Ban) BA (2nd cl Hist) 62. St D Coll Lamp LTh 65. **d** 65 **p** 66 St A. C and V Cho of St A Cathl 65-73; Warden Ch Hostel Ban 73-76; Chap Univ Coll of N Wales 73-76; V of Meifod w Llangynyw 76-79; Chap St Marg Sch Bushey from 79. *Chaplain's House, St Margaret's School, Bushey, Watford, WD2 1DT.* (01-950 4616)

HOPLEY, William James Christopher. b 50. AKC 74. St Aug Coll Cant 74. **d** 75 **p** 76 Worc. C of St Jo Bapt Kidderminster 75-78; Industr Chap Kidderminster from 78. *15 St John's Avenue, Kidderminster, Worcs.* (Kidderminster 3929)

HOPPER, Bernard. b 20. Univ of Leeds BA (3rd cl Lat) 42. Coll of Resurr Mirfield. **d** 44 Lon **p** 45 Stepney for Lon. C of St Pet Fulham 44-46; St Mary and St John Ox 46-48; St Steph Clewer 48-50; Chap of Sandleford Priory and of St Gabr Sch Newbury 50-55; V of St Agatha Sparkbrook 55-67; St Mich AA w All SS Brighton Dio Chich from 67. *13 Windlesham Gardens, Brighton 1, Sussex, BN1 3AJ.*

HOPPER, Geoffrey Oliver. b 22. **d** and **p** 74 Sask. Chap Prince Albert Stud Ho Sask 73-80; I of Paddockwood Dio Sask from 80. *General Delivery, Paddockwood, Sask, Canada.*

HOPPER, Robert Keith. b 45. St Jo Coll Dur 74. **d** 77 **p** 78 Dur. C of Oxclose 77-80; St John Evang Hebburn Dio Dur from 80. *Marley Munro Villas, Hebburn, T & W, NE31 2UP.* (Hebburn 832053)

HOPPERTON, Thomas. b 33. Chich Th Coll 71. **d** 73 **p** 74 S'wark. C of Cheam (in c of St Alb from 76) Dio S'wark from 73. *4 Tudor Close, Cheam, Surrey.* (01-644 7280)

HOPTON, Francis John. St Mich Th Coll Crafers 49. ACT ThL 54. **d** and **p** 53 Adel. C of Ch Ch N Adel 53-54; Miss Chap Somerton Pk 54-56; P-in-c of Koolunga 56-57; C of Melb Dioc Centre 57-59; I of Riverton 59-63; Minlaton 63-66; R of Crafers 67-80; Kens Gardens Dio Adel from 80. *17 East Terrace, Kensington Gardens, S Australia 5068.* (31 8079)

HOPTON, Peter Philip Adrian. DFC 43. Univ of Adel BA 47. Cudd Coll 47. **d** 48 **p** 49 Lon. C of Fulham 48-51; C-in-c of Berri w Barmera 51-61; R of Brighton 61-74; Kapunda 74-77; L to Offic Dio Murray from 77. *Trotts Road, McLaren Flat, S Australia 5171.* (08-3830214)

✠ **HORAN, Right Rev Forbes Trevor.** b 05. Trin Hall Cam BA 32, MA 36. Westcott Ho Cam 33. **d** 33 **p** 34 Newc T. C of St Luke Newc T 33-36; St Geo Jesmond Newc T 36-38; C-in-c of Balkwell Conv Distr N Shields 38-40; Chap RNVR 40-45; V of St Chad Shrewsbury 45-52; V and RD of Huddersfield 52-60; Surr 53-60; Hon Can of Wakef 55-60; Proc Conv Wakef 55-60; Cons Ld Bp Suffr of Tewkesbury in St Paul's Cathl 18 Oct 60 by Abp of Cant; Bps of Lon; Ely; Glouc; Wakef; Heref; Chich; and Man; Bps Suffr of Willesden; Dunwich; Malmesbury; and Pontefract; and Bps Vibert; Jackson; Sinker; Chase; Craske; and others; res 73. *79 Naunton Lane, Cheltenham, Glos, GL53 7AZ.* (Cheltm 27313)

HORBURY, William. b 42. Late Exhib of Or Coll Ox 2nd cl Cl Mods 62, BA (2nd cl Or Stud) 64, Mew Hebr Pri 66, MA 67. Clare Coll Cam BA (1st cl Th Trip pt II and Hebr Pri 66, MA (by incorp) 68, PhD 71. Westcott Ho Cam 64. **d** 69 Ely **p** 70 Huntingdon for Ely. Fell of Clare Coll Cam 68-72; L to Offic Dio Ely 69-72; V of Gt and R of L Gransden 72-78; Exam Chap to Bp of Pet from 73; Fell and Dean of Chap CCC Cam from 78. *Corpus Christi College, Cambridge, CB2 1RH.* (Cam 59418)

HORDERN, Cyril Calveley. b 06. Keble Coll Ox BA 30, MA 49. Cudd Coll 29. **d** 30 **p** 31 Lon. C of St Mich Shoreditch 30-36; Perm to Offic at St Andr Hillingdon (in c of St Pet) 36-37; V of St Pet Limehouse 37-53; St Jo Bapt Holland Road Kens 53-72. *36 Sutton Road, Seaford, Sussex, BN25 1SG.*

HORDERN, Peter John Calveley. Jes Coll Cam BA 59, MA 64. Linc Th Coll. **d** 61 **p** 62 Dur. C of St Aid Conv Distr Billingham 61-63; Hon C of All SS Hamilton 71-74; L to Offic Dio Bran from 74. *624 16th Street, Brandon, Manit., Canada.*

HORE, Michael John. b 50. Univ of Man BSc 71. Linc Th Coll 75. **d** 78 **p** 79 Cant. C of St Mart Maidstone 78-81; St Peter in Thanet Dio Cant from 81. *2 Ranelagh Gardens, St Peter's, Broadstairs, Kent, CT10 2TJ.*

HORLOCK, Ven Brian William. OBE 78. St D Coll Lamp BA 55. Chich Th Coll 55. **d** 57 **p** 58 Lon. C of St Nich Chiswick 57-61; Witney 61-62; V of St Gabr N Acton 62-68; Chap of St Edm Oslo Dio (Gibr in Eur from 80) Lon (N and C Eur) from 68; RD of Scandinavia 75-79; Archd in Scandinavia from 79; Hon Can of H Trin Cathl Brussels from 81. *British Embassy, Heftyes Gt 8, Oslo 2, Norway.* (565201)

HORN, Michael Leonard. b 32. Oak Hill Coll 56. **d** 59 **p** 60 Lon. C of Ealing 59-62; L to Offic Dio Luckn 62-64; Chap to Bp of Luckn and Dioc Youth Adv 64-67; on leave 67-69; P-in-c of St Andr w Ch Ch Gorakhpur and Gondo Dio Luckn 69-75; V of Par Distr of Pohangine Dio Wel from 77. *Vicarage, Ashhurst, NZ.*

HORNBURG, Doreen Marianne Goodman. b 52. Chapman Coll Calif BA 73. St Jo Coll Auckld LTh 78. **d** 78 **p** 79 Auckld. C of Clevedon 78-81; Hosp Chap Dio Auckld from 81. *130 Ladies Miles, Ellerslie, Auckland 5, NZ.*

HORNBURG, Robert Dana. b 52. St Jo Coll Auckld LTh 77. **d** 77 Bp Spence for Auckld **p** 78 Auckld. C of Howick 77-80; Mt Albert Dio Auckld from 80. *4 Grande Avenue, Mount Albert, Auckland 4, NZ.*

HORNBY, John Hulme. b 24. AKC 47. Qu Coll Birm 48. **d** 49 Kens for Lon **p** 50 Lon. C of St Alb N Harrow 49-51; St John at Hackney (in c of All SS Clapton) 51-53; V of St Paul Old Ford 53-57; Amer Ch 57-58; R of Croydon w Clopton 59-66; V of Tadlow w E Hatley 59-66; R of Hatley St Geo 59-66; Stretham w L Thetford 66-74; P-in-c of Bratton Fleming Dio Ex from 74; Stoke-Rivers Dio Ex from 74; Challacombe Dio Ex from 75; RD of Shirwell 77-80. *Rectory, Bratton Fleming, Devon.* (Brayford 253)

HORNBY, Raymond Sefton. b 1898. **d** 21 **p** 23 Queb. Miss at Kingsey 21-23; Magdalen Is 23-26; C of H Trin Cathl Queb 26-27; in Amer Ch 27-34; Perm to Offic (Col Cl Act) at St John Jersey 34-38; R 38-47; St Clem Jersey 47-57; Hinton Ampner w Bramdean 57-68. *Les Deux Demis, La Mielle Clemont, St Brelade, Jersey, CI.*

HORNE, Anthony Cedric. b 26. MIMechE 61. MIEE 67. **d** 77 **p** 78 Bris (APM). C of St Matt Kingsdown City and Dio Bris from 77. *24 Somerset Street, Kingsdown, Bristol, BS2 8LZ.*

HORNE, Brian Lawrence. b 39. Univ of Natal BA (1st cl Engl) 60. Univ of Dur Dipl Th 62, MLitt 68. Gen Th Sem NY MDiv 63. Univ of Lon PhD 71. St Chad's Coll Dur 60. **d** 62 Wakef for Natal **p** 63 Natal. Jun Research Fell and Tutor St

Chad's Coll Dur 63-66; Lect K Coll Lon from 66; Sub-Warden K Coll Th Hostel Vincent Sq 66-78. *11b Roland Gardens, SW7.* (01-373 5579)

HORNE, Edmund Walter. b 41. Ridley Coll Melb 79. **d** 81 Willoch. C of Ceduna Dio Willoch from 81. *PO Box 162, Ceduna, S Australia 5690.*

HORNE, Graham Philip. b 48. St Jo Coll Auckld 71. **d** 73 Bp Monteith for Auckld **p** 74 Auckld. C of Papakura 73-76; Te Amamutu 76-77; V of Orakau 77-81; C of Te Awamutu Dio Waik from 81. *5 Young Street, Te Awamutu, NZ.* (6081)

HORNE, Jack Kenneth. b 20. Linc Th Coll 68. **d** 70 **p** 71 Chelmsf. C of Danbury 70-75; V of Frampton Dio Linc from 75. *Frampton Vicarage, Boston, Lincs, PE20 1AE.* (Boston 722294)

HORNE, James Robert. Univ of W Ont BA 54, MA 58. Hur Coll BTh 58. Columb Univ NY PhD 64. **d** 58 **p** 59 Hur. C of St Jo Evang Kitchener 60-63; Asst Prof of Phil and Relig Renison Coll 63-66; Univ of Waterloo 66-69. *499 Forest Hill Drive, Kitchener, Ont., Canada.*

HORNE, Robin Godolphin Hastings. b 21. Peterho Cam BA (Hist) 42, MA 46. St Cath S Ox BA (2nd cl Th) 48, MA 53. Wycl Hall Ox 46. **d** 48 **p** 49 Glouc. C of St Cath Glouc 48-51; Chipping Campden 51-53; Lect Bexley Hall USA 53-54; R of Barton Bendish 54-57; Beachamwell w Shingham 54-57; Herstmonceux 57-74; V of Lynchmere Dio Chich from 74. *Lynchmere Vicarage, Haslemere, Surrey, GU27 3NF.* (Liphook 723197)

HORNE, Roger Harry. b 30. ACP 52. Cudd Coll 65. **d** 67 Lon **p** 68 Willesden for Lon. C of St Andr Willesden 67-69; Chap Cottesmore Sch Crawley and L to Offic Dio Chich 69-75; St Mich Sch Tawstock and L to Offic Dio Ex 76-77; Chap at Br Embassy Ankara 77-80; Strasbourg and Stuttgart Dio Gibr in Eur from 80. *10 Rue des Ypres, 67000 Strasbourg, France.* (88-611928)

HORNE, Sidney Gordon. CD 68. St Chad's Coll Regina 47. **d** 50 Niag **p** 52 Qu'App. C of Alsask 50-53; R of St Mich AA Moose Jaw 53-56; CF (Canad) 56-80; C of Kente Dio Ont from 80. *18 Marmora Street, Trenton, Ont, Canada, K8V 2H5.*

HORNER, George Shillito. b 06. Didsbury Th Coll 25. St Aug Coll Cant 56. **d** 57 **p** 58 Sheff. [f Methodist Min] C of Heeley Sheff 57-59; Div Master Aston Woodho High Sch from 59. *Northfield, Treeton Lane, Aughton, Sheffield.* (Aston Common 424)

HORNER, John Henry. b 40. Univ of Leeds BA 62. Oakhill Coll 76. **d** 79 **p** 80 St Alb. Hon C of Datchworth w Tewin Dio St Alb from 79; Asst Master Simon Balle Sch Hertford from 79. *41 St Leonards Road, Bengeo, Hertford.* (Hertford 551696)

HORNER, Kenneth George. b 14. Late Scho of Ch Coll Cam Tancred Div Stud 33, 1st cl Cl Trip pt i 35, BA (1st cl Th Trip pt i) 36, MA 40. Wells Th Coll 36. **d** 37 **p** 38 S'wark. C of St Jo Evang E Dulwich 37-39; Beckenham 39-43; V of St Jas Oldham 43-45; PC of St Mark Conv Distr Biggin Hill 45-49; V of Ch Ch Erith 49-55; St Jas Elmers End Beckenham 55-62; RD of Beckenham 62; Chap Chich Th Coll 62-64; Vice-Prin 64-69; Exam Chap to Bp of Roch 63-71; Hon Chap from 71; Chap St Mary's Home Buxted 69-71. *The Quadrangle, Morden College, Blackheath, SE3.* (01-853 3369)

HORNER, Peter. b 27. Jes Coll Ox BA 51, MA 55. Kelham Th Coll 52. M SSM 58. **d** 54 **p** 55 Southw. Tutor Kelham Th Coll from 54; Chap from 58; C of Averham w Kelham 54-56; Publ Pr Dio Southw from 56. *SSM Priory, Willen, Milton Keynes, Bucks, MK15 9AA.* (0908-611749)

HORNER, Philip David Forster. b 30. Tyndale Hall Bris. **d** 67 **p** 68 Carl. C of Ulverston 67-71; Princes Risborough 71-76; C-in-c of Ellesborough Dio Ox from 76; C of Wendover Dio Ox from 76. *Ellesborough Rectory, Butlers Cross, Aylesbury, Bucks. HP17 0XA.* (Wendover 622110)

HORNER, Robert William. b 17. RD 73. St Pet Hall Ox BA 38, MA 46. Ripon Hall Ox. **d** 57 **p** 58 Ex. C of Ch Ch Paignton 57-60; V of W Bickleigh 60-66; Chap RNR 63-73; R of Chinnor (w Emmington and Sydenham from 73) Dio Ox from 66; Emmington 66-73; C-in-c of Sydenham 66-73. *Chinnor Rectory, Oxford.* (Kingston Blount 51309)

HORNETT, Charles Albert Victor. **d** 62 **p** 65 Moos. C of St Matt Cathl Timmins 62-64; Dioc Sec and Treas Dio Moos 62-64; on leave 64-65; R of Malartic 65-67; Calstock and of Hearst 67-69; Bourlamaque 69-73; I of Thessalon Dio Alg from 73. *Box 88, Thessalon, Ont., Canada.* (705-842 3148)

HORNSBY, Edgar. b 23. AKC (2nd cl) 50. **d** 51 **p** 52 Portsm. C of St Mary Portsea 51-55; Chap RAF 55-69; Chap St Mary's Hall and Brighton College 69-74; St Swith Sch Win and Hon Chap of Win Cathl from 74. *37 Park Road, Hayling Island, Hants.* (Hayling Island 5518)

HOROBIN, Hector Stanley. b 09. Edin Th Coll 46. **d** 46 **p** 47 St Andr. C of St Serf Burntisland 46-47; Winlaton w Rowland's Gill and High Spen 47-50; V of Coundon 50-57; PC of Birtley 57-62; V of Petts Wood Dio Roch from 62. *Vicarage, Willett Way, Petts Wood, Orpington, Kent.* (Orpington 29971)

HORREX, Arthur Hugh. Moore Th Coll Syd 62. ACT ThL (2nd cl) 63. **d** 63 **p** 64 Syd. C of Dapto 63; Parramatta 63-64; Rozelle 64-67; St Mary Balmain 64-67; R 67-69; R of Robertson 69-74; Kambalda 74-76; Rockdale Dio Syd from 77. *429 Princes Highway, Rockdale, NSW, Australia 2216.* (59-2350)

HORROCKS, Canon Joseph Barnes. b 01. Late Scho of Univ of Man BSc 22, BD (w distinc) 45. Fitzw Hall Cam BA 26, MA 30. Wesley Ho Cam 23. **d** 28 **p** 29 Man. C of St Mark Glodwick 28-30; Weaverham 30-35; V of Sandiway 35-61; Exam Chap to Bp of Ches 50-61; RD of Middlewich 57-61; Hon Can of Ches 59-61; Can (Emer) from 61; R of Taynton 61-69; Tibberton 61-69. *The Spinney, Harcombe Road, Raymonds Hill, Axminster, EX13 5TB.*

HORROCKS, Oliver John. b 30. Clare Coll Cam BA 53, MA 57. Westcott Ho Cam 53. **d** 55 **p** 56 Man. C of Moss Side 55-58; Arnold 58-60; R of All S w St Andr Ancoats Man 60-67; Barthomley Dio Ches from 67. *Barthomley Rectory, Crewe, Chesh.* (Alsager 2479)

HORROCKS, Raymond. St Paul's Coll Grahmstn LTh 66. **d** 65 **p** 66 Natal. C of St Jas Durban 65-67; Asst Chap Michaelhouse 67-71; R of Amanzimtoti Dio Natal from 71. *PO Box 104, Amanzimioti, Natal, S Africa.* (Durban 941895)

HORROCKS, Stanley. b 22. Univ of Man BA (Th) 76. Coll of the Resurr Mirfield 77. **d** 78 **p** 79 Man. Hon C of St Cuthb Miles Platting Man 78-81; C-in-c of St Clem w St Matthias Salford Dio Man from 81. *80 Northumberland Street, Salford, Lancs, M7 0DG.*

HORSEFIELD, Raymond Bell. Univ of Sask BA 26. Em Coll Sktn DD (*hon causa*) 63. **d** 26 **p** 27 Sask. C of Grand Rapids 26-27; I 27-31; Miss Devon Ind Miss 31-42; R of Flin Flon 42-57; Hon Can of Bran 49-51; Archd of Dauphin and Exam Chap to Bp of Bran 51-60; R of Pilot Mound 57-60; Prin Ind Tr Coll Dauphin 58-62; R of Cowichan Lake 60-64; I of Salt Spring I 64-72; Perm to Offic Dio BC from 73. *2370 Amelia Street, Sidney, BC, Canada.*

HORSEMAN, Colin. b 46. BD (Lon) 70. ALCD 69. STh 75. **d** 70 **p** 71 Man. C of St Clem Higher Openshaw 70-74; Darfield 74-78; V of Stainforth Dio Sheff from 78. *Stainforth Vicarage, Doncaster, S Yorks.* (Doncaster 841295)

HORSEY, Herbert Anglin. McGill Univ Montr BSc 58. Hur Coll LTh 62. **d** 62 **p** 63 Ott. C of St Jas Carleton Place 62-65; Ch Ch Cathl Ott 65-67; R of Clayton 67-71; Huntley 71-75; on leave. *Box 848, Stratford, Ottawa, Ont, Canada.*

HORSEY, Stanley Desmond. b 20. Ely Th Coll 46. **d** 49 **p** 50 B & W. C of St Jo Evang Clevedon 49-51; St Marg Leigh-on-Sea 51-53; St Steph Barbourne Worc 53-55; V of St Jas Edgbaston 55-60; St Martin Brighton 60-67; St Barn (and St Agnes from 77) Hove Dio Chich from 67. *88 Sackville Road, Hove, Sussex, BN3 3HE.* (Brighton 732427)

HORSFALL, Keith. b 39. Tyndale Hall Bris 62. **d** 65 Warrington for Liv **p** 66 Liv. C of Walton Breck 65-68; Em Fazakerley 68-70; Mile Cross 70-73; V of Gayton 73-80; P-in-c of Westacre 80; Gayton Thorpe w E Walton 80. *c/o Gayton Vicarage, King's Lynn, Norf.* (Gayton 227)

HORSFIELD, Alan Peter. Angl Th Coll Vancouver, LTh 49. **d** 49 New Westmr **p** 50 Br Columb. I of Mayne Is 49-52; Alberni 52-60; Terrace 61-71; on leave 71-75; Perm to offic Dio BC from 76. *RR1 Seagirt Road, Gabriola Island, BC, Canada.*

HORSFIELD, Allan. b 48. Univ of Nottm BA 70. Sarum Wells Th Coll 70. **d** 72 Wakef **p** 73 Pontefract for Wakef. C of Airedale w Fryston 72-74; Howden 74-76; P-in-c of Rudston w Boynton Dio York from 77. *Rudston Vicarage, Driffield, Yorks, YO25 0XA.* (Kilham 663)

HORSFIELD, Robert Alan. b 38. Univ of Leeds, BA (2nd cl Mod Hist) 60, MA 66. Coll of Resurr Mirfield 61. **d** 63 **p** 64 Lich. C of Lower Gornal 63-66; H Trin Bridlington and of Sewerby w Marton 66-68; C-in-c of St Matt Fairfield Conv Distr Scartho 68-73; R of Scartho 73-79; V of Cleobury Mortimer w Hopton Wafers Dio Heref from 79; P-in-c of Doddington Dio Heref from 79; Neen Sollars w Milson Dio Heref from 81. *Cleobury Mortimer Vicarage, Kidderminster, Worcs.* (Cleobury Mortimer 270264)

HORSFORD, David Dennis O'Bryen. Ridley Coll Melb ACT ThL 54. **d** 55 **p** 56 Melb. C of St Thos Essendon 55-57; Min of Belgrave 57-62; St Geo Bentleigh 62-72; I of Rosanna 73-78; Williamstown Dio Melb from 78. *2 Pascoe Street, Williamstown, Vic, Australia 3016.* (397 5330)

HORSHAM, Lord Bishop Suffragan of. *See* Docker, Right Rev Ivor Colin.

HORSHAM, Archdeacon of. *See* Kerr-Dineen, Ven Frederick George.

HORSINGTON, Timothy Frederick. b 44. Univ of Dur BA (3rd cl Th) 66. Wycl Hall Ox 67. **d** 69 Warrington for Liv **p** 70 Liv. C of Halewood 69-72; Farnworth (in c of St Jo Bapt

Widnes) 72-75; P-in-c of Llangarron w Llangrove Dio Heref from 75; Whitchurch w Ganarew Dio Heref from 77. *Llangarron Vicarage, Ross-on-Wye, Herefs, HR9 6NN.* (Llangarron 341)

HORSLEY, Canon Alan Avery. b 36. St Chad's Coll Dur BA 58. Qu Coll Birm. **d** 60 **p** 61 Pet. C of Daventry 60-63; St Giles Reading 63-64; St Paul Wokingham 64-66; V of St Andr Yeadon 66-71; R of Heyford w Stowe Nine Churches 71-78; RD of Daventry 76-78; V of Oakham w Hambleton and Egleton Dio Pet from 78; Surr from 78; Can (Non-Res) of Pet Cathl from 79; V of Braunston w Brooke Dio Pet from 81. *Vicarage, Oakham, Leics, LE15 6EG.* (Oakham 2108)

HORSLEY, Canon Boyce Rowley. Univ of Syd BA 41. Univ of Lon BD 51. Moore Th Coll Syd ACT ThL 35. **d** 36 **p** 37 Syd. C of St Pet Cooks River 36-37; St Paul Syd 37-40; St Mich Vaucluse Syd 40-41; Chap RAN 43-46; R of Eastwood 46-56; Exam Chap to Abp of Syd 54-70; on leave 56-58; R of Bowral 58-65; Ch Ch N Syd 65-77; Chap to Abp of Syd 63-77; Hon Can of Syd from 68; Dioc Archivist and L to Offic Dio Syd from 77. *St Andrew's House, Sydney Square, NSW, Australia 2000.* (269-0642)

HORSLEY, Hugh Reginald. b 10. Knutsford Test Sch 32. Bps' Coll Cheshunt 33. **d** 37 **p** 38 Cant. C of St Paul Thornton Heath 37-39; Chap (Indian Eccles Est) Jubbulpore 39-40; Pachmarhi 40-41; Nasirabad 41-46; R of Stutterheim 46-51; Kingsnorth 51-54; R of Shadoxhurst 51-54; V of Lowdham w Gunthorpe 54-58; Chap of Lakhimpur Assam 58-60; R of Sabie w Lydenburg, Pilgrim's Rest and Graskop 60-66; USPG Area Sec Dio Chich 66-78. *11 Charmandean Road, Worthing, Sussex.* (Worthing 36901)

HORSMAN, Andrew Alan. b 49. Univ of Otago BA 70, Univ of Man MA (Econ) 72, PhD 75. St Steph Ho Ox BA 80. **d** 81 Willesden for Lon **p** 82 Lon. C of All SS Hillingdon Dio Lon from 81. *19 Denecroft Crescent, Hillingdon, Middx, UB10 9HU.* (Uxbridge 54975)

HORSMAN, Clifford. St Paul's Th Coll Grahmstn 66. **d** 68 Bp Carter for Johann **p** 69 Johann. C of Linden 68-70; Springs 70-72; R of Westonaria 72-77; CF (S Afr) from 77; L to Offic Dio Pret from 77. *14 Second Street, Waterkloof Base, Transvaal, S Africa.*

✠ **HORSTEAD, Right Rev James Lawrence Cecil.** b 1898. CMG 62. CBE 56. Late Found Scho of Univ Coll Dur BA (2nd cl Math) 21, Lightfoot Scho 21, 2nd cl Th 23, MA 24, Hon DD 56. **d** 23 **p** 24 Dur. C of St Marg Dur 23-26; Prin of Fourah Bay Coll and CMS Sec Dio Sier L 26-36; Can Missr Dio Sier L 28-36; Exam Chap to Bp of Sier L 29-36; Bp's Commiss 33-36; Cons Ld Bp of Sier L in St Paul's Cathl 24 June 36 by Abp of Cant; Bps of Lon; St Alb; Roch; St E; Pet; Linc; Derby; Gibr; and N Afr; Bps Suffr of Stepney and Willesden; res 61; Dean of St Geo Cathl Freetown and Visitor of Fourah Bay Coll Freetown 36-61; Provincial Sec to Abp of W Afr 53-55; Abp and Metrop of W Africa 55-61; Asst Bp in Dio Leic 62-77; R of Appleby Magna 62-68; Commiss Lagos 64-74; L to Offic Dio Leic 68-77; Can (Emer) of Leic Cathl from 77; Perm to Offic Dio Nor from 78. *37 Albany Court, Cromer, Norf, NR27 9AZ.* (0263-513795)

HORTH, Ernest Edmund. Ridley Coll Melb 62, ACT ThL (2nd cl) 65. **d** 65 **p** 66 Gippsld. C of St Paul's Cathl Sale 65-66; Moe 66-67; Narrabeen 67-68; CF (Austr) 68-74; Perm to Offic Dio Melb 73-74; I of Parkdale 74-79; Sec Bush Ch Aid S Vic 79-81; R of St John Launceston Dio Tas from 81. *157 St John Street, Launceston, Tasmania 7250.*

HORTON, Andrew Charles. b 50. Univ of Ex BA 71. Sarum Wells Th Coll 71. **d** 73 **p** 74 Bris. C of St Alb Westbury Pk, Clifton 73-76; in Amer Ch from 76. *St Peter's Rectory, Westfield, NY, USA.*

HORTON, Bruce Robert. Moore Th Coll Syd ACT ThL (2nd cl) 63. **d** 63 **p** 64 Syd. C of Pittwater 63-67; C-in-c of St Mich Provisional Distr Newport 67-70; Ermington 70-72; Perm to Offic Dio Wang 72-74; Dio C & Goulb from 74; CF (Austr) from 72. *1 Fraser Road, Duntroon, NSW, Australia 2600.* (062-663453)

HORTON, Christopher Peter. b 26. Univ of Leeds, BA 49. Coll of Resurr Mirfield 49. **d** 51 **p** 52 Newc T. C of St Mary Blyth 51-55; Delaval 55-59; V of Grangetown Dio York from 59. *Vicarage, Clynes Road, Grangetown, Middlesbrough, Cleve, TS6 7LY.* (Eston Grange 453704)

HORTON, Ernest Patrick. b 06. St Steph Ho Ox 31. **d** 33 **p** 34 Lon. C of St Andr Bethnal Green 33; St Aug Haggerston 33-35; L to Offic Dio Ox 35-37; R of Hedsor 37-53; Asst Sec Ox Dioc Counc of Educn 48; Sec 49-55; V of St Paul Ox 53-59; Perm to Offic Dios Ox and Guildf from 59. *79 Brighton Road, Godalming, Surrey, GU7 1NX.*

HORTON, Frederick Tom. b 21. **d** 78 Graft. Hon C of Bellingen Dio Graft from 78. *c/o PO Bellingen, NSW, Australia 2454.*

HORTON, Jeremy Nicholas Orkney. b 44. Cranmer Hall, Dur 64. **d** 68 Penrith for Carl **p** 69 Carl. C of Dalton-in-Furness 68-70; Penrith 70-73; V of Hudswell w Downholme and Marske 73-75; Middleton Tyas (w Melsonby 75-78) 75-81; P-in-c of Croft 78-81; Eryholme 78-81; V of Wortley-de-Leeds Dio Ripon from 81. *Wortley Vicarage, Dixon Lane Road, Leeds, LS12 4RU.* (Leeds 638867)

HORTON, John Ward. b 27. Univ of Leeds BA 50. Coll of Resurr Mirfield 50. **d** 52 **p** 53 Newc T. C of St Pet Conv Distr Balkwell 52-55; E Coatham 55-58; C-in-c of Acomb Moor Conv Distr City and Dio York 58-68; Min 68-71; V from 71. *Vicarage, Thanet Road, Dringhouses, York, YO2 2PE.* (York 706047)

HORTON, Ralph Edward. b 41. SOC 75. **d** 78 **p** 79 S'wark. C of St Leon Streatham 78-81; Team V of Catford (Southend) and Downham Dio S'wark from 81. *c/o 353 Bromley Road, SE6 2RP.*

HORTON, Ronald Harcourt. Lich Th Coll 23. **d** 25 Stafford for Ja **p** 26 Lich. C of Kingston Ja 25; St John West Bromwich 26-27; CF Aldershot 27-28; RAF Manston 28-29; Cranwell 29-30; C-in-c of St Mary Conv Distr Unstone 31-32; PC of Mosbrough 32-36; R of Pinxton 36-57; Commiss Windw Is 36-58; Surr 48-57; R of Cold Higham 57-60; V of Pattishall (w Cold Higham from 60) 57-75. *Rockville, Chesterfield Road, Alfreton, Derbys.* (Alfreton 833117)

HORTON, Silas Alfred. Moore Th Coll ACT ThL 54. **d** and **p** 55 Syd. C of St Clem Mosman 55-56; Chap of Norf I 56-58; C-in-c of Regent's Park Provisional Distr 58-63; Beverly Hills 63-69; R 69-71; Roseville Dio Syd from 71. *3 Bancroft Avenue, Roseville, NSW, Australia 2069.* (412-2553)

HORWOOD, Brian. St Jo Coll Morpeth, 66. **d** and **p** 67 Tas. C of Avoca-Fingal 67-69; R of Evandale 69-71; Dir of Overseas Dept 71-72; L to Offic Dio Tas 71-72; R of St John New Town 72-79; Longford & Perth Dio Tas from 79. *Rectory, Longford, Tasmania 7301.* (003 91 1307)

HORWOOD, Graham Frederick. Univ of Wales, BA 55. Coll of Resurr Mirfield 55. **d** 57 Mon **p** 58 Llan. C of Llantrisant 57-61; St Sav Roath 61-62; Roath 62-66; V of Clydach Vale 66-77; St Luke Canton Cardiff Dio Llan from 77; Commiss Matab from 80. *12 Thompson Avenue, Victoria Park, Cardiff, CF5 1EY.* (Cardiff 562022)

HORWOOD, Thomas Gilbert. b 15. Univ of Man BA 41. Westcott Ho Cam 45. **d** 46 **p** 47 Blackb. C of St Thos Blackb 46-48; Whitby 48-49; PC of Cornholme 49-51; R of Everingham w Seaton Ross and Harswell 51-55; C-in-c of Beilby 51-55; Org Sec Miss to Seamen NE Area 54-62; Area Sec Gtr Lon 62-67; SE Regional Sec 67-68; L to Offic Dio Ripon 55-62; Publ Pr Dio Chelmsf 62-67; V of Brompton w Snainton 68-80; RD of Pickering 73-75. *Cravenlea, David Avenue, Pontesbury, Shrewsbury, SY5 0QB.* (0743-790554)

HOSBAND, Eliot Arnold. b 1895. Late Choral Scho of St Cathl Coll Cam BA 19, MA 22. Cl Tr Sch Cam 19. **d** 19 Dur **p** 20 Jarrow for Dur. C of St Ignatius Hendon Bp Wearmouth 19-21; Putney (in c of St John 22-27) 21-27; Succr of Ripon Cathl 27-30; Min Can and Jt-V of Ripon Cathl 30-37; R of Wath 37-60; Chap and Lect in Div Ripon Tr Coll 43-45. *28 Mallorie Park Drive, Ripon, Yorks.*

HOSEASON, Kenneth Edward Malcolm. b 16. **d** 71 **p** 72 Mashon (APM). C of Waterfalls Dio Mashon from 71. *50 Parkway, Parktown, Waterfalls, Salisbury, Rhodesia.*

HOSFORD, William Popham. b 16. MBE 55. Kt O Oranje-Nassau 70. OBE 71. TCD BA and Div Test (2nd cl) 39, MA 48. **d** 39 **p** 40 Arm. C of Derryloran 39-42; St Luke Belfast 42-44; Chap Miss to Seamen S Shields and L to Offic Dio Dur 44-45; Chap of St Mary Rotterdam and Chap Miss to Seamen Rotterdam Dio Lon (N and C Eur) 45-70; RD of the Netherlands 49-70; V of St Geo Brighton 70-77; Chap Miss to Seamen Dub and L to Offic Dio Dub 77-81. *287 South Coast Road, Peacehaven, Sussex, BN9 7HX.* (079-14 6929)

HOSIE, David Graham. K Coll Lon and Warm AKC 62. **d** 62 **p** 63 Ches. C of H Trin Ches 62-65; Melksham 65-67; V of St Aid Buttershaw 67-70; C-in-c of Winterbourne St Martin 70-75; V 71-75; C-in-c of Winterbourne Monkton 70; V 71-75; V of The Winterbournes and Compton Valence Dio Sarum from 75. *Vicarage, Martinstown, Dorchester.* (Martinstown 241)

HOSKEN, Harold Wesley. Univ of Witwatersrand BSc (2nd cl Chem and 1st cl Geog) 32. Coll of Resurr Mirfield 33. **d** 35 **p** 36 S'wark. C of Clapham 35-40. St Thos St Annes-on-the-Sea 40-44; V of All SS Habergham 44-49; Prin of Pret Dioc Tr Coll Pietersburg 49-53; L Pr Dio Johann 54-79; Dir of Th Educn Dio Johann 78-79; *9 22nd Street, Parkhurst, Johannesburg, S Africa.* (011-47 2172)

HOSKIN, Alan Stanley. Ridley Coll Melb ThL 68. **d** 68 **p** 69 Melb. C of Blackburn 68-70; Toorak 70-71; R of Nightcliff 71-75; I of Langwarrin Dio Melb from 75. *Vicarage, Warrandyte Road, Langwarrin, Vic, Australia 3910.* (059-78 2302)

HOSKIN, Andrew James Erskine. b 49. Univ of Alta BA 72. Wycl Coll Tor LTh 76. **d** 76 **p** 77 Athab. C of Fort McMurray w Chipewyan 76-78; I of Manning Dio Athab from 78. *Box 395, Manning, Alta, Canada, T0H 2M0.*

HOSKIN, David William. b 49. Hatf Coll Dur BSc 71. Wycl Hall Ox 72. **d** 75 **p** 76 York. C of Bridlington 75-79; Rodbourne-Cheney 79-80; Bebington Dio Ches from 80. *49 Dibbins Hey, Poulton, Bebington, Wirral, L63 9JU.* (051-334 6780)

HOSKIN, Derek Balfour Erskine. b 43. Univ of Tor LTh 72. Linc Th Coll 72. **d** 72 Tor **p** 73 Calg. C of St Aug Calg 72-75; I of Fort Macleod Dio Calg from 75. *Box 335, Fort Macleod, Alta, Canada.*

HOSKIN, Canon Eric James. b 28. St Chad's Coll Dur BA 50, Dipl Th 52. **d** 52 **p** 53 Glouc. C of St Osw Coney Hill Glouc 52-54; Stroud 54-57; R of Ruardean 57-63; C-in-c of Lydbrook 61-63; V of Em Cheltm 63-70; R of Dursley w Woodmancote Dio Glouc from 70; RD of Dursley from 78; Hon Can of Glouc Cathl from 81. *Rectory, Kingshill Road, Dursley, Glos.* (Dursley 2053)

HOSKIN, Henry Brian. b 32. N-W Ordin Course 72. **d** 75 **p** 76 Derby. C of SS Aug Chesterfield 75-79; Bolsover Dio Derby from 79. *St Mary's House, Castle Street, Bolsover, Chesterfield, S44 6PP.* (Chesterfield 823471)

HOSKIN, Very Rev James Alfred Erskine. b 11. St Jo Coll Winnipeg 46. **d** 48 **p** 49 Rupld. I of Carman 48-61; High Prairie 62-69; Hon Can of Athab 65-69; Dean and R of St Jas Cathl Peace River Dio Athab 70-79; Dean (Emer) from 79; P-in-c of St Paul's McLennan Dio Athab from 79. *Box 457, McLennan, Alta, T0H 2X0, Canada.* (403-624 2743)

HOSKING, Ven Alfred James. Univ of Alta BA 49, B Educn 51. Carleton Univ Ott B Journ 53. St Jo Coll Winnipeg LTh 63. **d** 63 Bp Anderson for Rupld. C of All SS Winnipeg 63-65; I of Emerson 65-69; Ponoka 69-74; Prince Geo Dio Carib from 74; Archd of Carib from 78. *193 Nicholson Street North, Prince George, BC, Canada.* (562-6194)

HOSKING, Canon Harold Ernest. b 19. Lich Th Coll 51. **d** 53 **p** 54 Truro. C of Penwerris 53-56; R of St Mawgan-in-Pydar 56-61; PC of St Pet Newlyn 61-69; V of Newquay 69-74; R of Redruth (w Lanner from 80) Dio Truro from 74; Hon Can of Truro Cathl from 78. *Rectory, Clinton Road, Redruth, Cornw.* (Redruth 215258)

HOSKINS, Hubert Henry. b 21. BNC Ox BA (1st cl Engl Lang and Lit) 43, MA 47. Westcott Ho Cam 43. **d** 45 Stepney for Lon **p** 46 Lon. C of Em Northwood 45-47; Wm Hulme Sen Scho BNC Ox 47-49; Lect Univ of Groningen Holland 49-52; Chap R Masonic Sch Bushey and L to Offic Dio St Alb 52-56; Producer Relig Broadcasting Dept BBC Lon from 57. *587 Rayners Lane, Pinner, Middx.* (01-866 9640)

HOSKINS, Ian David. b 41. St Chad's Coll Dur BA 63, Dipl Th 65. **d** 65 Dur **p** 66 Jarrow for Dur. C of St Cuthb Conv Distr Southwick 65-68; Beamish 68-72; V of S Moor 72-77; Dep Chap HM Pris Dur 76-80; R of Witton Gilbert Dio Dur from 77; Chap Earls Ho Hosp for Mentally Handicapped Durham from 80. *Rectory, Witton Gilbert, Durham.* (Sacrison 710376)

HOSKINS, Canon James Paul. b 07. Univ of Lon BA (2nd cl Hist) 27. Wells Th Coll 30. **d** 31 **p** 32 Ex. C of St Mark Ford Devonport 31-33; Spalding 33-37; R of St John w St Clem Stamford 37-39; St Mary Stamford 40-58; Dom Chap to Marq of Ex 39-42; Proc Conv Linc 45-50; Surr from 50; Vice-Dean of Stamford 50-58; Chap Browne's Hosp Stamford 52-58; Can of Linc Cathl 53-58; Can (Emer from 74); V of Budleigh Salterton 58-62; St Jo Bapt Spalding 62-67; Malborough w S Huish 67-77; Publ Pr Dio Ex from 77. *Brigadoon, Church Road, Colaton Raleigh, Sidmouth, Devon.* (Colaton Raleigh 68643)

HOSKINS, Joseph Thomas. b 1899. AKC 22. **d** 23 **p** 24 York. C of St Barn Hull 23-28; Gorleston 28-30; V of St Steph Sheff 30-41; Dio Chap 40-41; Chap RAFVR 41-49; C of Doncaster 49-52; V of St Paul Penge 52-69. *72 South Croxted Road, SE21.* (01-670 0681)

HOSKYNS, John Algernon Peyton. b 20. Pemb Coll Cam BA (2nd cl Hist Trip pt i) 41, MA 45. Westcott Ho Cam 47. **d** 49 **p** 50 Win. C of Eastleigh 49-52; H Trin Brompton 52-54; V of Hartley Wintney w Elvetham 54-62; R of Worplesdon 62-72; L to Offic Dio Heref 72-76; P-in-c of Linton w Upton Bp 76-78; How Caple w Sollers Hope Dio Heref from 76; K Caple Dio Heref from 81. *Riverknoll, Hoarwithy, Hereford, HR2 6QF.* (Carey 282)

✠ **HOSKYNS-ABRAHALL, Right Rev Anthony Leigh Egerton.** b 03. Westcott Ho Cam 30. **d** 31 **p** 32 Portsm. C of St Mary Portsea 31-33; Chap Shrewsbury Sch 33-36; C of St Wilfrid Harrogate 36-39; Offg Min to Troops in Tower of Lon 39; Chap RNVR 39-45; V of Aldershot 45-55; RD of Aldershot 49-55; Proc Conv Guildf 51-55; Cons Ld Bp Suffr of Lanc in York Minster 2 Feb 55 by Abp of York; Bps of Dur; Blackb; Ripon; Man; Wakef; Brech; and Guildf; Bps Suffr of Selby; Warrington; Jarrow; Stockport; Middleton; Pontefract; Whitby; and Sherborne; res 74; Provost of N Div Woodard Corp 64-77; Hon Asst Bp of Blackb from 75. *14 Riversmead Drive, Garstang, Preston, Lancs.* (Garstang 2300)

HOSSENT, George William Thomas. b 14. Wycl Hall Ox 61. **d** 63 **p** 64 Sheff. C of Goole 63-67; V of St Bart Sheff 67-75; Arksey 75-80. *19 Sunnyvale Avenue, Totley, Sheffield, S Yorks, S17 4FD.* (Sheff 363676)

HOUGH, Arthur John Bates. Univ of W Ont BA 50, MA 55. St Jo Coll Manit LTh 39. **d** 39 **p** 40 Keew. Miss at Red Lake 39-41; on Active Service 41-47; I of Can Davis Mem Ch Sarnia 47-50; Ch of Redeemer Lon 50-55; Assoc Prof of Psychol Univ of Alta Edmon from 55; L to Offic Dio Edmon 55-60; Hon C of St Jo Evang Edmon 60-76; Exam Chap to Bp of Edmon 60-69. *885 Forestbrook Drive, Penticton, BC, Canada.*

HOUGH, Edward Lewis. St D Coll Lamp BA 60. St Mich Coll Llan 60. **d** 62 **p** 63 Llan. C of Baglan 62-69; Industr Chap Hull 69-72; R of Cilybebyll Dio Llan from 72. *Rectory, Cilybebyll, Pontardawe, W Glam.* (Pontardawe 2118)

HOUGH, Canon John Francis. b 06. Late Scho of St Jo Coll Ox 3rd cl Cl Mods 27, BA (2nd cl Th) 29, MA 32. Westcott Ho Cam 29. **d** 30 **p** 31 Ripon. C of St Matt Holbeck 30-34; Moor Allerton 34-36; V of Kirkstall 36-46; R of W Wickham 46-55; V of Folkestone 55-66; Tenterden w Small Hythe 66-74; Chap R Vic Hosp Folkestone 55-66; Hon Can of Cant 58-79; Can (Emer) from 79. *1 The Mercers, Hawkhurst, Kent, TN18 4LH.* (Hawkhurst 2575)

HOUGH, Norman Stanley. b 1898. AKC (2nd cl Hons) 22. **d** 22 **p** 23 Newc T. C of St Mark Byker Newc T 22-24; St Sav Raynes Pk 25-28; St Luke W Norwood 28-31; R of H Trin S'wark 31-41; V of St Barn Sutton Surrey 41-51; All SS Tooting Graveney 51-67. *The Bungalow, Churchfield Road, Walton-on-the-Naze, Essex, CO14 8BL.* (025-56 5615)

HOUGH, Peter George. b 40. Univ of Dur BA (3rd cl Th) 62. Wells Th Coll 62. **d** 64 **p** 65 Leic. C of St Luke's Conv Distr Stocking Farm Leic 64-68; V of St Aid New Parks Leic 68-76; Knutton Dio Lich from 76. *Knutton Vicarage, Newcastle, Staffs, ST5 6DU.* (Newcastle 624282)

HOUGH, Sidney Stephen Valentine. G and C Coll Cam BA 50, MA 54. Ripon Hall Ox 55. **d** 57 **p** 58 Chelmsf. C of Goodmayes 57-60; St Mary Warw 60-62; V of Messing (w Inworth from 72) 62-78; R of Inworth 62-72; Chap Warley Hosp Brentwood 78-79; R of Alphamstone w Lamarsh and Pebmarsh Dio Chelmsf from 79. *74 Alphamstone Rectory, Bures, Suff, CO8 5HH.* (Twinstead 262)

HOUGHAM, Canon Ernest George Reginald. b 1899. AKC (1st cl) 31. **d** 31 **p** 32 Roch. C of Crayford 31-34; Perm to Offic at Orpington 34-35; V of St Andr Orpington 35-38; All SS Perry Street Northfleet 38-44; C of Shere 44-47; V of W Byfleet 47-50; R of Shere w Peaslake 50-68; Rd of Cranleigh 59-64; Hon Can of Guildf 65-69; Can (Emer) from 69. *22 Charts Close, Cranleigh, Surrey.* (Cranleigh 272936)

HOUGHTBY, Frank. b 12. Chich Th Coll 41. **d** 41 **p** 42 Pet. C of Daventry 41-44; Chap RAFVR 43-47; C of Daventry 46-47; R of Wittering Thornhaugh w Wansford 47-56; Carlton E 57-58; C of Leamington Priors (in c of St Alb) 58-59; R of N Runcton (w Hardwick and Setchey) Dio Nor from 59. *North Runcton Rectory, King's Lynn, Norf.* (King's Lynn 840271)

HOUGHTON, Canon Alfred Thomas. b 1896. Univ Coll Dur LTh and Long Reading Pri 22, BA 23, MA 29. Lon Coll of Div. **d** 21 **p** 22 Roch. C of H Trin Tunbridge Wells 21-24; BCMS Field Sec at Mohnyin Dio Rang 24-39; LPr (in c of H Sepulchre Cam) Dio Ely 44; Gen Sec BCMS 45-66; Perm to Offic Dio Lon from 45; Commiss Momb 53-66; Hon Can of Moro from 65. *14 Alston Court, St Albans Road, Barnet, Herts, EN5 4LJ.* (01-449 1741)

HOUGHTON, Bernard Frank. b 15. Linc Coll Ox BA 37, MA 73. Cudd Coll 40. **d** 41 **p** 42 York. C of St John Middlesbrough 41-44; Northallerton 44-47; E Retford 47-50; R of Winthorpe 50-61; V of Langford w Holme 50-61; PC of Lacey Green 61-68; V 68-81. *19 Bathurst Road, Chesterton, Cirencester, Glos.*

HOUGHTON, David Bradley. Univ of BC BA (1st cl Phil) 33. Angl Th Coll BC LTh 34. **d** 33 **p** 34 New Westmr. C of Maple Ridge w Whonnock and Haney 33-34; R 34-39; Perm to Offic (Col Cl Act) at St Mich Hamworthy 39-42; Perm to Offic Dio Win 42-44; R of Ellisfield 44-47; C-in-c of Bradley 45-47; V of St Aug Ogden Calg 47-50; Strathmore 50-51; R of St Jo Evang Calg 51-54; Lockeport 54-55; Ladysmith 55-67; I of Cumberland 67-70. *Maple Acres, Watts Road, RR2, Ladysmith, BC, Canada.*

HOUGHTON, David John. b 47. Univ of Edin BSc 68. Cudd Coll 69. **d** 71 **p** 72 Glouc. C of St Mary, Prestbury 71-74 Prec Gibr Cathl 74-76; Chap at St Geo Madrid 76-78; C of St John Croydon 78-80; Chap Warw Sch from 80. *Warwick School, Myton Road, Warwick.* (0926-862092)

HOUGHTON, Edward Johnson. b 23. Keble Coll Ox BA and MA 48. Linc Th Coll 48. **d** 50 **p** 51 Blackb. C of Nelson-in-Marsden 50-52; Lancaster 52-55; Chap R Albert

Hosp (and Ripley Sch 52-56) Lancaster 52-61; R of Quernmore 55-61; CF (TA) 56-62; Chap Hellingly and Amberstone Hosps from 61. *Chaplain's House, Hellingly Hospital, Hailsham, Sussex.* (Hailsham 844391)

HOUGHTON, Canon James Edward Gordon. Hur Th Coll LTh 46. **d** 45 **p** 46 Hur. C of Huntingford w Zorra 45-47; R of Kerrwood 47-50; Grand Bend 51-55; Oldcastle 55-60; St D Lon Hur 60-71; Ch of Transfig Lon Hur 71-75; Can of Hur 72-79; Can (Emer) from 79; I of Tillsonburg 75-79. *Box 665, Forest, Ont, Canada.*

HOUGHTON, James Robert. b 44. K Coll Lon and Warm AKC 67. **d** 68 **p** 69 Dur. C of Herrington 68-70; Asst Dioc Youth Chap and Warden Legge Ho Swindon 70-72; Perm to Offic Dio Ex 73-74; C of Heavitree Ex 74-78; Perm to Offic Dio Lon 78-80; Hon C of W Drayton Dio Lon from 80. *6 Copse Wood, Iver Heath, Bucks, SL0 0PT.*

HOUGHTON, Canon John Caswell. b 16. Univ of Dur BA LTh and Th Exhib 38. St Bonif Coll Warm 34. **d** 39 Buckingham for Ox **p** 40 Ox. C of St Geo Wolverton 39-42; UMCA Miss at Mapanza 42-47; Warden Dioc Th Sem Dio N Rhod 47-52; P-in-c of St Pet Miss Distr Lusaka 52-62; Can of N Rhod 60-62; Archd of N Rhod 62-64; S Zam 64-70; P-in-c of S Midlds, Zam 67-70; Dio Lusaka 71-74; Can of Lusaka 71-74; Can (Emer) from 74; Promotions Sec Feed the Minds 74-81. *18 Cornelia Close, Bletchley, Milton Keynes, MK2 3LX.* (0908-70526)

HOUGHTON, Canon John Cuthbert. b 20. Selw Coll Cam BA 41, MA 45. Linc Th Coll 41. **d** 43 **p** 44 St Alb. C of St Sav St Alb 43-47; St Pet Plymouth 47-51; Univ Miss Centr Afr 51-54; C-in-c of St Chris Crownhill Plymouth 54; V of St Hilda Leeds 55-63; C-in-c of St Sav Leeds 55-63; V of St Sav w St Hilda Cross Green 63-74; Proc Conv Ripon 64-70; Hon Can of Ripon 69-75; Can (Emer) from 75; R of Halton w Aughton Dio Blackb from 75. *Halton Rectory, Lancaster, LA2 6PU.* (Halton-on-Lune 811370)

HOUGHTON, Michael Alan. b 49. Univ of Lanc BA 70. Chich Th Coll 78. **d** 80 **p** 81 Pet. C of All H Wellingborough Dio Pet from 80. *27 Church Street, Wellingborough, Northants*

HOUGHTON, Ven Michael Richard. CCC Cam BA 52, MA 56. Cudd Coll 52. **d** 54 **p** 55 Portsm. C of St Mark Portsea 54-57; Ponsonby NZ 57-60; Chap for Youth Work Dio Auckld 60-63; V of Glen Innes 63-67; Howick 67-79; St Helier's Bay Dio Auckld from 79; Archd of Tamaki from 77. *Vicarage, Tuhimata Street, St Helier's, Auckland 5, NZ.* (585-288)

HOUGHTON, Ralph Edward Cunliffe. b 1896. Late Scho of Ch Ch Ox 1st cl Cl Mods 17, BA (2nd cl Lit Hum) 21, MA and Matthew Arnold Essay Pri 23. Westcott Ho Cam 24. **d** 24 **p** 26 Cant. Asst Master of St Pet Coll Westmr 21-25 and 26-28; Tutor of St Pet Coll Ox 28-63; Fell 49-63; Fell (Emer) from 63; Lect Or Coll Ox 39-56; R of Hanborough 40-45; L to Offic Dio Ox from 47. *2 Belbroughton Road, Oxford.*

HOUGHTON, Reginald Leighton. b 10. St Chad's Coll Dur BA 33, Dipl in Th 34, MA 36. **d** 34 **p** 35 Dur. C of Billingham 34-38; Hunslet 38-42; V of S Benfleet 42-50; Bassingbourne 50-60; C-in-c of Whaddon 52-54; V 54-60; V of Bartley Green 60-75. *73 Hollies Drive, Bayston Hill, Salop.* (Bayston Hill 2172)

HOUGHTON, Robert Sherwood. Trin Coll Melb BA 48, LLB 59. Clare Coll Cam BA 51, MA 56. Wells Th Coll 51. **d** 52 **p** 53 Man. C of St Mich AA Howe Bridge 52-54; Min of St Albans w E Sunshine and Braybrook 54-59; Chap Grimwade House C of E Gr Sch Melb 60-65; Sub-Warden St Barn Th Coll Belair 65-69; C-in-c St Mary N Melb 70-77; I of Ashburton Dio Melb from 77. *334 High Street, Ashburton, Vic, Australia 3147.* (25 3701)

HOUGHTON, Stephen Moseley. Selw Coll Cam BA 54, MA 58. Tyndale Hall Bris 55. **d** 57 **p** 58 Chelmsf. C of Dagenham 57-60; Miss at Marsabit 60-77; Prin St Andr Bible Sch Embu from 77. *Box 189, Embu, Kenya, E Africa.*

HOUGHTON, Thomas. b 17. N-W Ordin Course 71. **d** 74 **p** 75 Lich. C of Newc-u-Lyme Dio Lich from 74. *Fernyhough, Little Madeley, via Crewe, Cheshire, CW3 9JT.*

HOUGHTON, William. ACT ThL. St Francis Coll Brisb 59. **d** 62 New Guinea **p** 63 Rockptn. C of St Paul's Cathl Rockptn 62-64; Koeno 65-66; P-in-c of Managalas w Musa 66-73; Simbai 74; Warden Goroka Teachers Tr Coll from 75; Hon C of Goroka Dio Papua (Dio Aipo from 77) from 75. *Box 1078, Goroka, Papua New Guinea.*

HOUGHTON, Canon William Reginald. b 10. St Jo Coll Dur BA 40, Dipl in Th 41, MA 43. Westcott Ho Cam 41. **d** 41 **p** 42 Ripon. C of St Clem Sheepscar Leeds 41-43; C and Clk O of Leeds 43-47; PC of St Mary Beeston 47-54; Surr 49-54; Asst Sec S Lon Ch Fund and S'wark Dioc Bd of Finance 54-56; Dep Sec 56-60; Sec 60-61; Sec S'wark Dioc Dilapidations Bd 56-60; Publ Pr Dio S'wark 55-62; Ed S'wark Dioc Directory 56-62; Can and Treas of S'wark 59-62; R of St Mary de Crypt w St Jo Bapt Glouc 62-69; Can Res of Glouc 69-78; Can (Emer) from 78. *Church Cottage, Diddlebury, Craven Arms, Shropshire, SY7 9DH.* (Munslow 208)

HOUKAMAU, Huna Pore Te Ua. b 37. **d** 77 **p** 78 Aotearoa for Wai. C of Wairoa-Mohaka Past Dio Wai from 77. *55a Black Street, Wairoa, NZ.*

HOULDEN, James Leslie. b 29. Late Scho of Qu Coll Ox BA (2nd cl Mod Hist) and Holwell Stud 52, Liddon Stud 53, 1st cl Th 54, MA 56. Cudd Coll 53. **d** 55 **p** 56 Ripon. C of St Mary Hunslet 55-58; Tutor Chich Th Coll 58-59; Chap 59-60; Chap and Fell of Trin Coll Ox 60-70; Prin Cudd Coll 70-75; Ripon Coll Cudd 75-77; V of Cudd 70-77; Hon Can of Ch Ch 76-77; Lect K Coll Lon from 77. *33 Raleigh Court, Lymer Avenue, SE19.* (01-670 6648)

HOULDEN, Kenneth Harry. b 10. Ridley Hall Cam 53. **d** 55 **p** 56 Chelmsf. C of Chadwell Heath 55-57; Southn 57-60; R of Stockbridge 60-67; Commiss Auckld 61-67; Surr 67; V of Bramley 67-75. *3 Kingfisher Court, Highfield Road, Southampton, SO2 1UN.* (Southn 554199)

HOULDING, David Nigel Christopher. b 53. AKC 76. St Aug Coll Cant 75. **d** 77 Lon **p** 78 Willesden for Lon. C of All SS Hillingdon 77-81; St Alb Mart Holborn w St Pet Saffron Hill Dio Lon from 81. *c/o St Alban's Clergy House, Brooke Street, EC1N 7RD.*

HOULDSWORTH, Raymond Clifford. Bps' Coll Cheshunt, 64. **d** 66 **p** 67 Guildf. C of St Paul The Hythe Egham 66-70; Cranbrook 70-76; V of Hernhill Dio Cant from 76. *Hernhill Vicarage, Faversham, Kent.* (Claypits 362)

HOULT, Edward Ingham. Clifton Th Coll 36. **d** 38 **p** 39 York. C of Kirby Moorside and Gt Edston 38-42; V of Bettws-y-Crwyn w Newcastle 42-46; R of Clungunford 46-53; V of Paraparaumu 53-64; Ngaio 64-70; L to Offic Dio Wel from 71. *53 Haunui Road, Pukerua Bay, Wellington.* (Pukerua Bay 419)

HOULT, Roy Anthony. K Coll Lon and Warm AKC 58. **d** 59 **p** 60 Liv. C of St Mary Walton-on-the-Hill 59-63; Ch Ch Cathl Vic 63-71; R of Vernon 71-79; St Thos City and Dio Tor from 79; Hon Can of Koot 75-79. *381 Huron Street, Toronto, Ont, M5S 2G5, Canada.*

HOUMAESIUGI, Malachi. St Pet Coll Maka. **d** 37 **p** 59 Melan. P Dio Melan 37-75; Dio Malaita 75-77. *Maniade, Malaita, Solomon Islands.*

HOUNDLE, Edward Henry Garvock. **d** 51 **p** 52 Athab. R of Beaver Lodge 51-58; I of St Matt Vancouver 58-61. *620 East 63rd Avenue, Vancouver 15, BC, Canada.*

HOUNSFIELD, Thomas Paul. b 15. Lon Coll of Div 46. **d** 47 **p** 48 Lich. C of St Phil Penn Fields 47-50; R of Treeton 50-61; Donington 61-80. *6 Pear Tree Road, Dibden Purlieu, Hythe, Hants.*

HOUNSOME, Allan George. b 32. SOC 70. **d** 72 **p** 73 S'wark. C of All SS New Eltham 72-75; Goldthorpe 75-78; V of St Hilda Thurnscoe E from 78. *Vicarage, Hanover Street, Thurnscoe, Rotherham, S Yorks.* (Rotherham 893259)

HOUSANAU, John Still. St Pet Coll Melan. **d** 46 **p** 53 Melan. P Dio Melan. *Atta, Malaita, British Solomon Islands.*

✠ **HOUSDEN, Right Rev James Alan George.** Univ of Queensld BA (1st cl Ment and Mor Phil) 28. St Jo Th Coll Brisb 28. ACT ThL (1st cl) 29, ThD 47. **d** 28 **p** 29 Brisb. C of St Paul Ipswich 28-30; Chap of Mitchell River Miss 30-32; C of All S Cathl Thursday I 32-33; R of Ch Darwin 33-37; V of Coolangatta 37-40; R of St Mark Warwick 40-46; Chap AMF 40-44; RD of Warwick 44-45; V of Ch S Yarra 46-47; Cons Ld Bp of Rockptn in St Jo Cathl Brisb 28 Oct 47 by Abp of Brisb; Bp of Carpentaria; and Bps Cranswick Halford and Dixon; Trld to Newc 58; res 72; Perm to Offic Dio Brisb from 73. *38 Maltman Street, Caloundra, Queensland, Australia 4551.* (91 2762)

HOUSE, Edward Emmanuel Lovell. Mem Univ Newfld BA 62. **d** and **p** 62 Newfld. P-in-c of U I Cove 62-63; Harbour Buffett 63-70; R of Barronallie 70-73; Trin E Dio Newfld (Centr Newfld from 76) from 73. *Trinity, Trinity East, Newfoundland, Canada.* (709-464-3658)

HOUSE, Ven Francis Harry. b 08. OBE 55. Wadh Coll Ox BA (2nd cl Mod Hist) 30, 2nd cl Phil Pol and Econ 31, MA 34. Cudd Coll 34. **d** 35 **p** 36 S'wark. L to Offic in Pemb Coll Miss Newington 35-37; Sec World Stud Christian Federation Geneva and L to Offic Dio Gibr 38-40; C of Leeds 40-42; Sec Youth Dept World Coun of Chs Geneva 46-47; Relig Broadcasting Dept BBC and L to Offic Dio Lon 42-44 and 47-55; Hon C of St Jude-on-the-Hill Hampstead 47-55; Select Pr Univ of Cam 49; Assoc Gen Sec World Coun of Chs Geneva 55-62; Asst Ed *Ecumenical Review* 60-62; V of Pontefract 62-67; R of Gawsworth 67-78; Archd of Macclesfield 67-78; Archd (Emer) from 78; Ecumen Officer 67-74; M Gen Syn 70-78. *11 Drummond Court, Leeds, LS16 5QE.* (Leeds 783646)

HOUSE, George Ernest. Hur Coll 61. **d** 63 **p** 64 Bran. I of Gladstone 63-66; R of Gilbert Plains 66-71; I of Gold River

71-73; R of Virden 73-77; Shoal Lake Dio Bran from 77. *Box 296. Shoal Lake, Manit., Canada.*

HOUSE, Graham Ivor. b 44. Coun for Nat Acad Awards BA 80. Oak Hill Coll 77. **d** 80 **p** 81 St E. C of St Jo Bapt Ipswich Dio St E from 80. *443 Woodbridge Road, Ipswich, Suffolk.*

HOUSE, Jack Carl. d 62 **p** 63 Tor. C of St Mich AA Tor 62-64; I of Stoney Lake 64-73; Bradford 73-80. *General Del, Kincardine, N0G 2G0, Ont, Canada.*

HOUSE, Jack Francis. b 35. Univ of Bris BEducn 70. Univ of Lon MA 80. **d** 80 **p** 81 Malmesbury for Bris (NSM). Hon C of Bedminster Dio Bris from 80. *48 Hendre Road, Ashton, Bristol, BS3 2LR.* (Bris 661144)

HOUSE, Simon Hutchinson. b 30. Peterho Cam BA 65, MA 67. Cudd Coll 61. **d** 64 **p** 65 York. C of St Jas Sutton-in-Holderness 64-67; St Steph Acomb York 67-69; V of St Nich Allestree 69-81; Bitterne Pk Dio Win from 81; RD of Duffield 74-81. *Vicarage, Thorold Road, Bitterne Park, Southampton, Hants.* (Southn 55814)

HOUSE, Vickery Willis. b 45. Kelham Th Coll. **d** 69 **p** 70 Ex. C of Crediton 69-76; Team V of Sampford Peverell 76-81; R of Berwick w Selmeston and Alciston Dio Chich from 81. *Berwick Parsonage, Polegate, E Sussex.* (Alfriston 870512)

HOUSTON, John Kenneth. QUB MB and BCh 38. **d** 61 New Guinea. Miss at Dogura 61-69. *Anglican Mission, Dogura, via Samarai, Papua.*

HOUSTON, William Paul. b 54. Qu Univ Belf BSSc 76. Ch of Ireland Th Coll Dub 78. **d** 81 Connor. C of Carrickfergus Dio Connor from 81. *19 Oakland Drive, Carrickfergus, Co Antrim, N Ireland.*

HOVENDEN, Gerald Eric. b 53. Univ of York BA 75. Univ of Ox BA 80. Wycl Hall Ox 78. **d** 81 Doncaster for Sheff. C of Pitsmoor Dio Sheff from 81. *76 Andover Street, Pitsmoor, Sheffield, S3 9EH.* (Sheff 750826)

HOVIL, Richard Guy. b 29. Ex Coll Ox BA 51, MA 57. Ridley Hall Cam. **d** 55 **p** 56 Lon. C of Ch Ch N Finchley 55-58; Hon C of Wimbledon 58-71; Chap of Monkton Combe Sch from 71. *Shaft House, Monkton Combe, Bath, Avon.*

HOVSEPIAN, John. b 12. Wycl Hall Ox 64. **d** 65 **p** 66 Iran. C of St Paul Tehran 64-72; Perm to Offic Dio St Alb from 72. *99 Sherwood Avenue, St Albans, AL4 9PW.* (St Alb 50534)

HOW, Charles Geoffrey. b 1900. St Steph Ho Ox 28. **d** 30 **p** 31 S'wark. C of St Chrys Peckham 30-33; H Cross and Warden Tonbridge Sch Clubs Cromer Str St Pancras 33-38; Chap Wel Coll 38-43; Chap RNVR 43-46; V of Offley 46-49; Chap of Bloxham Sch 49-57; C-in-c of St Andr Bethnal Green 57-58; St Jas Gt Bethnal Green 57-68; R of St Matt Bethnal Green 58-68; RD of Bethnal Green 58-66; R of St Vedast *alias* Foster Lon 68-74. *Charterhouse, EC1.*

HOW, John Douglas. b 05. Or Coll Ox BA (2nd cl Th) 27, MA 31. Sarum Th Coll 27. **d** 28 **p** 29 S'wark. C of St Laur Catford 28-31; Chap Sarum Th Coll and C of St Martin Sarum 31-33; Vice-Prin of Sarum Th Coll 33-36; Publ Pr Dio Sarum 35-36; M of Bro of St Paul Charleville 36-41; Chap AIF 41-45; Chap St Geo Coll Perth 45-46; Actg C of Wimbledon (in c of St Jo Bapt) 46-47; C 47-48; Parson Cross 49-52; R of All SS Port of Spain and Exam Chap to Bp of Trinid 52-67; Hon Can of H Trin Cathl Trinid 59-67; P-in-c of St Lawr Barb 67-74; Perm to Offic Dios Bris and Glouc from 74. *64 Parklands, Wotton-under-Edge, Glos, GL12 7NR.*

HOW, Canon John Maxloe. b 15. Late Exhib of Magd Coll Cam BA 37, MA 49. Westcott Ho Cam 39. **d** 39 **p** 40 Dur. C of Norton 39-44; Offg C-in-c of W Pelton 44-45; C-in-c of Stella 46-47; V of Thornley 47-51; PC of St Andr Monkwearmouth 51-59; V of Barton w Pooley Bridge 59-73; Kirkby Lonsdale w Mansergh Dio Carl 73-76; R 76-81; RD of Penrith 60-73; Hon Can of Carl 72-81; Can (Emer) from 81; Perm to Offic Dio Carl from 81. *4 Kilmidyke Drive, Grange-over-Sands, Cumbria, LA11 7AL.*

HOW, Percy Frederick Harold. b 1898. AKC 26. **d** 26 **p** 27 Chelmsf. C of St Barn W Silvertown and Asst Chap St Andr Waterside Ch Miss to Sailors 26-28; St Mary Bocking 28-30; Littleham w Exmouth (in c of St Andr Exmouth) 30-39; V of Bushley 39-45; Chap Runwell Hosp Essex 45-55; V of Woolfardisworthy w Bucks Mills 55-64; C of St Gabr Plymouth 64-68; L to Offic Dio Ex 68-72; Dio Chich from 72. *Ramsay Hall, Byron Road, Worthing, Sussex, BN11 3HW.* (Worthing 36880)

HOWARD, Alan James. b 45. Univ of Bris BA (2nd cl Th) 69. Clifton Th Coll. **d** 71 **p** 72 Roch. C of Welling 71-74; Cromer 74-78; V of St Andr Sidcup Dio Roch from 78. *Vicarage, St Andrew's Road, Sidcup, Kent.* (01-300 4712)

HOWARD, Alban Caldicott Morton. b 13. Keble Coll Ox BA (3rd cl Jurispr) 35, MA 43. Ely Th Coll 36. **d** 37 **p** 38 York. C of St Sav Scarborough 37-43; Clewer 43-45; V of Clifford 45-54; Barlby 54-60; St Mary Bishophill Jun w All SS N Street City and Dio York from 60. *Old Rectory, Tanner Row, York YO1 1JB.* (York 54316)

HOWARD, Alfred William. St Jo Coll Auckld LTh 65. **d** 64 **p** 65 Auckld. C of Avondale 65-68; Manurewa 68-70; Team V of Linstead w Chediston and Halesworth 70-73; C of Hastings 74-76; P-in-c 76-77; V of Clive 77-78; Offg Min Dio Wai from 79. *918 Gordon Road, Hastings, NZ.* (83-405)

HOWARD, Charles Stanley Allan. Univ of Dur LTh 12, BA 20, MA 22. Moore Th Coll Syd 05. **d** 05 **p** 06 Syd. C of St Jo Evang Gordon NSW 05-07; Miss at Oba New Hebrides 07-10; Bugotu Br Solomon Is 10-11; C of St Jude Randwick 11-12; St Phil Syd 12-13; Travelling Sec ABM 13-14; C of Ch Ch Lumley 14-15; TCF 15-19; Hon CF 21; C of St Jas Birkdale 19-20; All SS Weaste 20-23; St Geo Hurstville 23-25; R of Pitt Town (w Wilberforce and Sackville Reach to 36) 25-37; Kangaroo Valley 37-40; Gen L Dio Syd from 40. *3 Elm Street, Bowral, NSW, Australia.*

HOWARD, Charles William Wykeham. b 52. Sarum Wells Th Coll 76. **d** 79 Chelmsf **p** 80 Barking for Chelmsf. C of Latton Dio Chelmsf from 79. *43 Blackbush Spring, Harlow, Essex, CM20 3DY.* (Harlow 411670)

HOWARD, David Edward. b 34. Ridley Hall Cam 77. **d** 79 **p** 80 Aber. C of Bieldside 79-81; P-in-c of Berrington w Betton Strange Dio Heref from 81; Cound Dio Heref from 81. *Berrington Rectory, Shrewsbury, Salop.* (Cross Houses 214)

HOWARD, David John. b 51. Univ of Lon BSc 73. Oak Hill Coll 74. **d** 77 **p** 78 Sarum. C of Radipole & Melcombe Regis Dio Sarum from 77. *74 Field Barn Drive, Southill, Weymouth, Dorset, DT4 0EF.* (Weymouth 782426)

HOWARD, David John. b 47. Ripon Hall Ox 70. **d** 72 Man **p** 73 Middleton for Man. C of Benchill 72-75; Sedgley 75-77; C-in-c of Lostock Conv Distr Bolton Dio Man from 77. *120 Regent Road, Lostock, Bolton, BL6 4DE.* (Bolton 43559)

HOWARD, David William. K Coll Lon and Warm 63. **d** 67 **p** 68 Linc. C of Skegness 67-69; Gainsborough 69-72; R of St Mich Kew Dio Ja from 72. *St Michael, Kew Park, Jamaica.*

HOWARD, Very Rev Donald. b 27. K Coll Lon and Warm BD and AKC 58. **d** 59 **p** 60 York. C of Saltburn-by-the-Sea 59-62; R of Warrenton w Hartswater 62-65; Dir of S Bechuanaland Miss 62-65; Chap Bp's Hostel Kimb 63-64; R of St Jo Evang E Lon 65-71; R of H Trin Haddington 72-78; Provost of St Andr Cathl Aber from 78; Hon Can of Ch Ch Cathl Connecticut USA from 78. *145 Gray Street, Aberdeen, AB1 6JJ.*

HOWARD, Donald Owen. Moore Th Coll Syd ACT ThL (2nd cl) 65. **d** 65 Syd **p** 66 Bp Loane for Syd. C of Balgowlah w Manly Vale 65-66; Croydon 66-67; R of E Burwood 67-78; Asst Missr Dept of Evang and L to Offic Dio Syd from 78. *St Andrew's House, Sydney Square, Sydney, Australia 2000.* (2-0642)

HOWARD, Francis Curzon. Dipl Th (Lon) 57. St Aid Coll 55. **d** 57 **p** 58 Ches. C of Claughton w Grange 57-60; St Paul Cheltm 60-62; V of St Barn Sheff 62-65; R of Sandys Berm 65-71; in Amer Ch from 72. *Church of the Atonement, Westfield, Mass, USA.*

HOWARD, Frank John. b 05. Clifton Th Coll 63. **d** 64 **p** 65 Win. Hon C of Freemantle 64-66; R of Shermanbury 66-69; Perm to Offic Dio Guildf from 69. *Flat 1, Rapallo Close, Rectory Road, Farnborough, Hants.*

HOWARD, Frank Thomas. b 36. Univ of Lon BSc (Econ) 57. Bps' Coll Cheshunt 59. **d** 61 **p** 62 Ches. C of Macclesfield 61-64; Claughton w Grange 64-66; V of Lache-cum-Saltney 66-76; R of Stanton Dio St E from 76; RD of Ixworth from 79. *Stanton Rectory, Bury St Edmunds, Suff, IP31 2DQ.* (Stanton 50239)

HOWARD, Geoffrey. b 45. St Jo Coll Dur BA 68, Dipl Th 70. Cranmer Hall Dur 67. **d** 71 Man **p** 72 Hulme for Man. C of St Luke Cheetham 71-74; Ch Ch Denton 75-77; V of St Ambrose Pendleton Dio Man from 77. *92 Fitzwarren Street, Salford, M6 5RS.* (06-736 3855)

HOWARD, George Joseph. Univ of Bangalore BD 42. St Bonif Coll Warm 30. **d** 34 **p** 35 Liv. C of St Pet Aintree 34-36; Chap of Coimbatore 36-37; Chap (Eccles Est) Mysore and Mercara 37-40; Garrison Chap H Trin Bangalore 40-43; St George Wellington Dio Madr 43-44; Ordination Candidates Sec Ind Command 44-46; CF (India) 46-47; Hon CF from 47; V of Balderstone 48-49; Chap and Sch Prin of Kolar Gold Field Mysore State 50-56; R of Mayfair Johann 56-57; V of Hoddlesden 57-58; Wankie 58-75. *Flat 103, Umdoni Heights, Scottborough, Natal, S Africa.*

HOWARD, Henry. b 1883. **d** 45 **p** 46 Liv. C of Ch Ch Norris Green 45-49; Litherland (in c of St Paul Hatton Hill) 49-54; Perm to Offic Dio St Alb from 55. *15 Barnfield Road, Harpenden, Herts.* (Harpenden 4033)

HOWARD, John Alexander. Univ of Tor BASc 48. Wycl Coll Tor LTh 63, BTh 65. **d** 62 **p** 63 Tor. P-in-c of Cookstown 62-68; I of Hastings 68-73; R of Drummondville 73-76; Marmora Dio Ont from 76. *Box 329, Marmora, Ont., Canada.* (613-472 2331)

HOWARD, John Alexander. b 27. Coll of Resurr Mirfield 66. **d** 67 Pontefract for Wakef **p** 68 Wakf. [f Methodist Min]

C of Almondbury 67-70; V of Skelmanthorpe 71-80; R of Fortrose w Cromarty Dio Ross from 80. *1 Deans Road, Fortrose, Ross, IV10 8TJ.* (Fortrose 20255)

HOWARD, John Liddon. b 13. G and C Coll Cam BA 3rd cl Th Trip pt i 48, MA 56. AKC 36. Wells Th Coll 36. **d** 37 **p** 38 Southw. C of Newark w Coddington 37-39; Yarm 40-42; Newark-on-Trent (in c of E Stoke and Syerston) 42-47; V of E Stoke w Syerston 47-52; CF 52-55; Hon CF from 55; R of Lamplugh 55-57; Emerson Manit 57-58; V of Addingham w Gamblesby 58-63; Westward, Rosley-w-Woodside (and Welton from 76) 63-79. *4 Park Terrace, Maryport, Cumb, CA15 6HS.*

HOWARD, Lloyd Melville. **d** 48 **p** 49 Moos. I of Foleyet 48-50; Virginiatown 50-56; Itin Miss Dio Moos 56-58; R of Claremont and Moneague Ja 58-62; Geraldton 62-67; Noranda 67-70; Chapelton 70-74; Linstead 74-77; N Essa Dio Tor from 77. *RR3, Thornton, Ont, LOL 2NO, Canada.*

HOWARD, Malcolm. b 29. St Deiniol's Libr Hawarden. **d** 73 Bp Mort for Leic **p** 74 Leic (APM). C of Birstall Dio Leic from 73. *65 Fielding Road, Birstall, Leicester.*

HOWARD, Canon Michael Charles. b 35. Selw Coll Cam BA (3rd cl Th Trip pt ii) 58, MA 63. Wycl Hall, Ox 58. **d** 60 **p** 61 St E. C of Stowmarket 60-64; Exam Chap to Bp of Ondo and Dioc Youth Chap 64-71; Hon Can of Ondo 70-71; (Emer) from 71; Commiss Ondo 71-76; Hon C of Southborough Dio Roch from 72; L to Offic Dio Ox from 73. *17 Milton Road, Bloxham, Oxon.*

HOWARD, Michael Paul Penrose. b 40. Univ of Keele BA 62. BD (Lon) 69. Lon Coll of Div 66. **d** 69 Southw **p** 70 Sherwood for Southw. C of St Nich Nottm 69-72; St Aldate Ox 72-77; Chap Ox Past 72-77; Actg Chap CCC Coll Ox 75-77; V of Ch Ch Dartford Dio Roch from 77. *67 Shepherd's Lane, Dartford, Kent.* (Dartford 20036)

HOWARD, Patrick Stirling Wykeham. b 05. Chich Th Coll 25. **d** 28 **p** 29 Sheff. C of Ecclesfield 28-32; Haslemere (in c of St Chris from 34) 32-39; CF (Temp) 39-43; CF 43-52; L to Offic Dio St E 53-56; Asst Hd Master Upland Hall Bungay 54-56; Tutor and Chap Edgarley Hall Glastonbury 56-60; Perm to Offic Dio B & W 60-70; Dio Sarum 61-70; Dio Win from 70. *10 Courtenay Place, Lymington, Hants, SO4 9NQ.* (Lymington 75698)

HOWARD, Paul David. b 47. Lanchester Poly Cov BA 69. St Jo Coll Nottm 74. **d** 77 Bp McKie for Cov **p** 78 Cov. C of Bedworth Dio Cov from 77. *Curate's House, Smorrall Lane, Bedworth, Nuneaton, CV12 0JN.* (Cov 363322)

HOWARD, Peter Leslie. b 48. Univ of Nottm BTh 77. Univ of Birm MA 80. St Jo Coll Nottm LTh 77. **d** 77 **p** 78 Birm. C of Gospel Lane 77-81; P-in-c of Nechells Dio Birm from 81. *c/o 8 Stanley Road, Nechells, Birmingham, B7 5QS.* (021-327 1044)

HOWARD, Reginald James. b 33. K Coll Lon and Warm AKC 60. **d** 61 **p** 62 Dur. C of Shildon 61-64; Hurworth 64-66; V of St Paul Morley 66-75; St Mich Arch City and Dio Wakef from 75. *3 Ashleigh Avenue, Dewsbury Road, Wakefield, W Yorks, WF2 9DA.* (Wakef 373020)

HOWARD, Richard Leonard. b 03. St Paul's Coll Burgh, 26. **d** 30 **p** 31 Linc. C of St Faith Linc 30-33; Frodingham (in c of Old Brumby) 33-36; Min of Old Brumby 36-39; PC 39-45; C of Bp's Hatfield (in c of St Mich) 45-49 PC of St Mich AA New Southgate 49-56; V of Henlow 56-68; C of U w Lower Stondon 57-60; V of Markyate 68-73. *90 High Street South, Stewkley, Leighton Buzzard, Beds.* (Stewkley 220)

HOWARD, Canon Robert Weston. b 28. Pemb Coll Cam 1st cl Math Trip pt i 47 BA (3rd cl Mech Sch Trip pt i) 49, MA 53. Westcott Ho Cam 51. **d** 53 **p** 54 Dur. C of Bp Wearmouth 53-56; St Mary Gt Cam 56-60; V of Ch Ch Kowloon 60-66; Prenton 66-75; RD of Frodsham from 74; V of Helsby (w Dunham-on-the-Hill from 78) Dio Ches from 75; Ince (w Thornton-in-the-Moors and Elton from 77) 75-78; C-in-c of Dunham-on-the-Hill 75-78; Hon Can of Ches Cathl from 78. *Vicarage, Helsby, Warrington, Chesh, WA6 9AB.* (Helsby 2151)

HOWARD, Canon Ronald Claude. b 02. SS Coll Cam 3rd cl Engl Trip BA 24, MA 28. Westcott Ho Cam 24. **d** 26 Lewes for Chich **p** 27 Bp Southwell for Chich. C of Eastbourne 26-28; Chap Bradfield Coll and L to Offic Dio Ox 28-30; Asst Chap and Asst Master Tonbridge Sch 30-37; Marlborough Coll 37-43; Chap at Marlborough Coll 38-43; Chap and Asst Master Radley Coll 43-45; L to Offic Dio Chich from 46; Hd Master Hurstpierpoint Coll 45-64; Can and Preb of Chich Cathl 57-69; Can (Emer) from 69. *3 Adelaide Crescent, Hove, E Sussex.*

HOWARD, Ronald Roland Rupert Cave. St Cath Coll Cam BA 22, MA 26. St Bonif Coll Warm 56. **d** 56 **p** 57 S'wark. C of Redhill 56-58; R of South Tarrant 58-67; Perm to Offic Dio Sarum from 67. *59 Upton Way, Broadstone, Dorset.* (Broadstone 4124)

HOWARD, Canon Ronald Trevor. b 19. Pemb Coll Cam BA 41, MA 45. Wells Th Coll 52. **d** 54 **p** 55 Chelmsf. C of Moulsham 54-59; R of Belchamp Otten w Belchamp Walter and Bulmer Dio Chelmsf from 59; RD of Belchamp from 74; Hon Can of Chelmsf Cathl from 79. *Belchamp Otten Rectory, Sudbury, Suff.* (Clare 277318)

HOWARD, Sidney. b 23. Univ of Dur BA and MA 47. Linc Th Coll 47. **d** 49 **p** 50 Newc T. C of St Pet Conv Distr Balkwell 49-52; Queenstown 52-54; Salisbury Cathl 54-55; St Alb Cathl Pret 55-58; M OGS from 56; Perm to Offic Dio Ely 59; C of St Geo Cullercoats 59-60; Min of Ch Ch Eccles Distr Hackenthorpe Beighton 60-66; R of Auchterarder 66-68; Chap HM Pris Perth 66-68; P-in-c of Bo'ness w Linlithgow 68-76; Egglestone 76-79; Chap HM Borstal Deerbolt Barnard Castle from 76. *38 Woodside, Barnard Castle, Co Durham, DL12 8DX.* (Teesdale 37561)

HOWARD, Stanley Reginald Kekewich. b 10. St Pet Hall Ox BA 31, MA 35. Ridley Hall Cam 31. **d** 33 **p** 34 S'wark. C of St Mich Wandsworth Common 33-36; St Andr Watford 36-39; H Trin Margate 39-40; R of Cuxton 40-51; Offg Chap No 4 RAF Reserve Station Rochester 48-51; V of St Paul Cheltm 51-76; Chap St Cath Ho 51-68; Cheltm Boys' Home 51-56; Cheltm Maternity and St Paul's Hosps 61-76; L to Offic Dio Win from 76. *3 Montague Road, Southbourne, Bournemouth, BH5 2EW.* (Bournemouth 427376)

HOWARD, Thomas Norman. b 40. St Aid Coll 64. **d** 67 **p** 68 Man. C of Farnworth 67-70; St Marg Prestwich 70-73; V of Heyside Dio Man from 73. *St Mark's Vicarage, Heyside, Royton, Oldham, Lancs.* (Shaw 47177)

HOWARD, Wilfred. b 06. Clifton Th Coll 36. **d** 38 **p** 39 Chelmsf. C of Chadwell Heath 38-40; St Thos Becontree 40-42; V of St Edw and St Nich Birm 42-45; Tibshelf 45-49; Newburn 49-55; R of Darfield 55-72; C-in-c of Luccombe 72-77; Perm to Offic Dio B & W from 79. *Cumbria, Carhampton, Minehead, Somt.* (Dunster 214)

HOWARD, William Alfred. b 47. St Jo Coll Dur BA 69. Wycl Hall Cam 74. **d** 77 Kingston T for S'wark **p** 79 S'wark. C of Norbiton 77-80; St Cath Mile Cross City and Dio Nor from 80. *140 Mile Cross Road, Norwich, NR3 2LD.* (Nor 45493)

HOWARD JONES, Preb Raymond Vernon. b 31. K Coll Lon and Warm AKC 54. **d** 55 **p** 56 Chelmsf. C of Hutton 55-58; CF 58-62; V of Walpole St Andr 62-64; Chap St Crispin Hosp Duston 64-70; V of Fownhope (w Fawley to 80) Dio Heref from 70; Brockhampton (w Fawley from 80) Dio Heref from 70; RD of Hereford Rural from 77; Preb of Heref Cathl from 81. *Fownhope Vicarage, Hereford.* (Fownhope 365)

HOWARTH, Albert. b 08. Bp Wilson Th Coll IM 36. **d** 39 **p** 40 Wakef. C of St Geo Ovenden 39-42; Lightcliffe 42-43; Slaithwaite St Jas Huddersfield 43-44; Ripponden (in c of St Jo Div Rishworth) 44-48; V of St Jo Evang Birkenhead 48-71; R of Byley w Lees 71-73. *50 Albert Road, Levenshulme, Manchester M19 2AB.*

HOWARTH, Arthur. Univ of Dur 36. **d** 37 **p** 38 Ox. C of Aylesbury 37-40; Perm to Offic Dio Lon 39-41; L to Offic Dio Ox 40-41; C of W Wycombe (in c of St Jas Downley) 41-42; St Thos Ap Acton Vale 42-43; All SS Fulham 43-44; Hornsey 44-46; Commiss Windw Is 43-46; R of Georgetown St Vincent 46-51; Perm to Offic Dio Ox 51-54; Dio Guildf 54; Lect in Bibl Stud St Paul's Coll Awka 55-56; L to Offic Dio Niger 55-56; Dio Accra 56-66; Sub-Warden and Tutor Bp's Ho Accra 56-58; Chap Ridge Ch Accra 58-60; Dean and Chap Sch of Administration Univ of Ghana Achimota 60-66; Fell Univ of Ghana from 65; Chap and Tutor Bp Lasbrey Coll Ow 66-68; in Amer Ch (Liberia) from 68; Chap to British Embassy Monrovia from 72. *Box 277, Monrovia, Liberia, W Africa.*

HOWARTH, Benjamin Wrigley. b 20. AKC 43. **d** 43 **p** 44 Man. C of Ch Ch Moss Side 43-49; CF 49-78; DACG 67-70 and 73-75; ACG 75-78; Hon Chap to HM the Queen 73-78; R of Chew Stoke w Nempnett Thrubwell Dio B & W from 78; Norton Malreward Dio B & W from 78. *Chew Stoke Rectory, Bristol.* (Chew Magna 2554)

HOWARTH, Geoffrey Gifford. b 21. Oak Hill Th Coll 65. **d** 66 Barking for Chelmsf **p** 67 Chelmsf. C of Woodford Wells 66-69; C-in-c of St Mary w St John Bootle 69-73; V of Newburn w Throckley Dio Newc T from 73. *Newburn Vicarage, Newcastle upon Tyne, NE15 8LQ.* (Lemington 670958)

HOWARTH, Canon Gerald Simeon. b 10. AKC 35. **d** 35 Liv **p** 36 Warrington for Liv. C of St Ann Stanley 35-37; St Faith Gt Crosby 37-39; C of Eckington 39-43; C-in-c of St Mark Derby 43-47; PC of St Barn New Whittington 47-55; Milford 55-75; Ed Derby Dioc Yr Bk 55-69; Hon Can of Derby 63-75; Can (Emer) from 75. *12 Langton Avenue, Ewell, Surrey.*

HOWARTH, Jack Raymond. b 13. Univ of Leeds BSc 34. Coll of Resurr Mirfield 34. **d** 36 **p** 37 Liv. C of St Columba Anfield 36-39 and 46-47; St Mary Illingworth (in c of St Andr Holmfield) 39-43; Chap RAFVR 43-46; C of Birstall 47-48;

V of Harley Wood 48-52; St Jude Manningham 52-63; RD of Bradf 58-63; R of Elland 63-75; RD of Brighouse and Elland 72-74; V of Cragg Vale 75-78; Hon C of Haydock Dio Liv from 78. *36 Rectory Road, Ashton-in-Makerfield, Wigan.*

HOWARTH, Leslie John. b 22. Sarum Wells Th Coll 75. **d** 78 **p** 79 Ex (APM). C of St Gabr Plymouth Dio Ex from 78. *1 Wardlow Gardens, Trevannion Park, Crownhill, Plymouth, Devon, PL6 5PU.* (Plymouth 773641)

HOWARTH, Robert Francis Harvey. b 31. SOC 71. **d** 72 Lon **p** 73 Kens for Lon. C of All S Langham Place 72-73; St Helen Bishopsgate w St Martin Outwich Lon 73-78; V of Harlow Dio Chelmsf from 78. *Vicarage, Staffords, Old Harlow, Essex, CM17 0JR.* (Harlow 27295)

HOWARTH, Ronald. Trin Coll Dub BA 51, MA 54. Linc Th Coll 52. **d** 52 **p** 53; Blackb. C of Gannow 52-55; Chap Victory Coll Ikare 55-60; St Paul's Teacher Tr Coll Abeokuta 60-66; Egbado Coll Ilaro from 66; L to Offic Dio Lagos 70-76; Dio Egba from 76; Exam Chap to Bp of Egba from 76. *Egbado College, Ilaro, Egbado District, Nigeria.*

HOWARTH, Wilfred Alan. b 09. Univ of Lon Knowling Pri, AKC and BD 37, MTh 45. **d** 37 **p** 38 S'wark. C of Em W Dulwich 37-41; H Trin S Wimbledon 41-44; St Mich Gidea Pk 44-46; V of Matching Dio Chelmsf from 46. *Matching Vicarage, Harlow, Essex.* (Matching 259)

HOWARTH, William. Moore Th Coll Syd 56, ACT ThL 58. **d** 59 Bp Hilliard for Syd **p** 59 Syd. C of Lithgow 59-60; C-in-c of Sefton 60-66; R of Carlton 66-70; Chap Armid Sch Dio Armid from 74. *Armidale School, Armidale, NSW, Australia 2350.* (72 6087)

HOWAT, Jeremy Noel Thomas. b 35. Em Coll Cam BA 59, MA 63. Ridley Hall Cam 59. **d** 63 Warrington for Liv **p** 64 Liv. C of Sutton 63-65; Kirk Ella 65-66; Ch Ch Bridlington 66-69; R of Wheldrake 69-78; Asst Dioc Youth Officer 70-74; V of Hurlingham and Devoto 78-81. *Address Temp Unknown.*

HOWDEN, Canon Arthur Travis. b 11. Clare Coll Cam Th Exhib and 3rd cl Cl Trip pt i 32, BA (2nd cl Th Trip pt i) 33, MA 37. Wycl Hall, Ox 33. **d** 34 Chelmsf for St Alb **p** 35 St Alb. C of St Paul St Alb 34-37; CMS Miss Dio Iran Kerman 37-44; Yezd 44-45; Chap Clare Coll Cam 45-46; R of Sundridge 46-53; V of H Trin Beckenham 53-61; RD of Beckenham 55-61; Hon Can of Roch 57-61; Can (Emer) from 62; Commiss Iran 61-67; and from 71; Home Sec Ch Assembly Overseas Coun 62-63; Asst Sec Miss and Ecumenical Coun Ch Assembly 64-66; Asst to Bp in Iran 67-71; R of Wortham and Redgrave w Botesdale 71-76; RD of Hartismere 73-76; Perm to Offic Dio St E from 76. *Little Thatch, Oak Lane, Rougham, Bury St Edmunds, Suff.*

HOWDEN, Ven Herbert Reginald. Univ of Tor BA 34. Trin Coll Tor LTh 36. **d** 37 Tor **p** 37 Bp Beverley for Tor. C of St Clem N Tor 37-39; R of St John Lakefield and Chap Grove Sch Lakefield 38-41; R of Barrie 41-48; St Mich AA Tor 48-53; in Amer Ch 53-61; R of Thornhill 61-76; Can of Tor 69-74; Archd of Scarborough 74-76; Archd (Emer) from 76; P Assoc of St Thos St Catharines Dio Niag from 76. *324 Victoria Street, Niagara-on-the-Lake, Ont., Canada.* (416-468 2887)

HOWDEN, John Travis. b 40. Sarum Th Coll 66. **d** 69 **p** 70 Roch. C of St Matt Gillingham 69-72; Banbury 72-73; L to Offic Dio York 73-74; C of Newland Hull 74-81; Hon C of Stock Harvard Dio Chelmsf from 82. *44 High Street, Stock, Ingatestone, Essex.* (Stock 840594)

HOWE, Alan Raymond. b 52. Univ of Nottm BTh 79. St Jo Coll Nottm 76. **d** 80 **p** 81 Portsm. C of St Simon Southsea Portsea Dio Portsm from 80. *31 Gains Road, Southsea, Hants, PO4 0PJ.*

HOWE, Alfred William. Late Welsh Ch Scho of St D Coll Lamp 2nd cl Engl Hons 32, BA 32. **d** 33 **p** 34 St D. C of Gorslas 33-35; Llanedy 35-39; V of Llanycrwys 39-51; Whitchurch w Solva and St Elvis 51-59; Forthampton w Chaceley 59-79. *1 Masons Court, Barton Street, Tewkesbury, Glos.*

HOWE, Bruce Herbert Warren. b 47. Univ of K Coll NS BA 67, MSLitt 70. **d** 69 NS **p** 71 Bp Arnold for NS. On leave 69-74; R of Glace Bay Dio NS from 75. *171a Main Street, Glace Bay, NS, Canada.*

HOWE, Charles. b 30. BD (Lon) 65. Open Univ BA 79. Tyndale Hall, Bris 58. **d** 58 **p** 59 Down. C of Willowfield 58-60; Derryloran 60-64; St Bart Belf 64-65; I of Tullyaughnish U 65-72; St Aug City and Dio Derry from 73; Dom Chap to Bp of Derry from 76; Dioc Regr Dio Derry and Raph from 78. *25 Bishop Street, Londonderry, N Ireland.* (Londonderry 62773)

HOWE, Cypriani Nathaniel. Em Coll Sktn. **d** and **p** 67 Trinid. C of Belmont 67-72; St Mich Diego Martin Dio Trinid from 72. *St Michael's Rectory, Diego Martin, Trinidad, W Indies.*

HOWE, David Randall. b 24. St Jo Coll Cam BA 51, MA 55. Wells Th Coll 51. **d** 53 **p** 54 Win. C of Basingstoke 53-59; R of Rotherwick w Hook and Greywell 59-70; Broughton w Bossington (and Mottisfont from 81) Dio Win from 70. *Broughton Rectory, Stockbridge, Hants.* (Broughton 287)

HOWE, Earle Dixon. NZ Bd of Th Stud LTh (2nd cl) 68. St Jo Coll Auckld 65. **d** 67 **p** 68 Waik. C of Tokoroa 67-68; Taumarunui 68-71; P-in-c 71-72; V of Okato 73-80; Matamata Dio Waik from 80; Exam Chap to Bp of Waik from 79. *12 Hohaia Street, Matamata, NZ.* (7001)

HOWE, George Alexander. b 52. St Jo Coll Dur BA 73. Westcott Ho Cam 73. **d** 75 **p** 76 Dur. C of Peterlee 75-79; St Mary Norton 79-81; V of Hart w Elwick Hall Dio Dur from 81. *Hart Vicarage, Hartlepool, Cleve, TS27 3AP.* (Hartlepool 62340)

HOWE, George Reginald. b 13. TCD BA 37, MA 51. **d** 39 **p** 40 Down. C of St Clem Belf 39-43; C-in-c of Drumkeeran 43-44; R 44-57; RD of Kesh 51-57; I of Rossory 57-80; Dom Chap to Bp of Clogh 63-65; Preb of Clogh Cathl 67-79; Preb of St Patr Cathl Dub 70-79; Chan of Clogh Cathl 79-80. *Johnston Ville, Chanterhill, Enniskillen, Co Fermanagh, N Ireland.* (Enniskillen 22389)

HOWE, Harry Norman. b 10. St Paul's Coll Limuru 72. **d** 73 **p** 74 Nai. P Dio Nai 73-74; C of Fringford 75-76; Perm to Offic Dio York 76-80; Dio Linc from 80. *14 Avenue B, Upton, Gainsborough, Lincs, DN12 5NT.* (Corringham 262)

HOWE, John. b 36. Ex Coll Ox BA (3rd cl Jurispr) 58, MA 63. St Steph Ho Ox 58. **d** 61 **p** 62 Lich. C of Horninglow 61-64; Sedgley 64-66; V of St Mark Evang Ocker Hill Tipton 66-73; Gnosall (w Knightley to 74) 73-79; Surr from 74; P-in-c of Hoar Cross Dio Lich from 79. *Hoar Cross Vicarage, Burton-on-Trent, DE13 8QR.* (Hoar Cross 263)

✠ **HOWE, Right Rev John William Alexander.** b 20. St Chad's Coll Dur BA (2nd cl Th) 43, MA 48, BD 48. Gen Th Sem NY Hon DD 74. DD (Lambeth) 78. **d** 43 Hull for York **p** 44 York. C of All SS Scarborough 43-46; Chap Adisadel Coll Accra 46-50; Vice-Prin Edin Th Coll 50-55; Hon Chap of St Mary's Cathl Edin 51-55; Cons Ld Bp of St Andr in St Ninian's Cathl Perth 18 Oct 55 by Bp of Arg Is (Primus); Bps of Aber; Brech; Edin; Glas; Moray; and Dur; and Bp P H Wilson; res 69; Executive Officer Angl Communion 69-71; Sec-Gen Angl Consultative Coun from 71; Hon Can of Glas from 69; Episc Can of St Geo Jer from 76; Sec Lambeth Conf 78. *14 Great Peter Street, London, SW1P 3NQ.* (01-222 2851)

HOWE, Canon Rex Alan. b 29. Ch Coll Cam 3rd cl Th Trip pt i 52, BA (3rd cl Th Trip pt ii) 53, MA 57. Coll of Resurr Mirfield 53. **d** 55 **p** 56 Wakef. C of St Pet Barnsley 55-57; Helmsley 57-60; V of St Martin Middlesbrough 60-67; Redcar 67-73; V of Kirkleatham 67-73; RD of Guisborough 67-73; Dean of Hong Kong 73-76; Archd 75-76; R of Grantham Dio Linc from 77; RD of Grantham from 78; Can and Preb of Linc Cathl from 81. *Rectory, Grantham, Lincs, NG31 6RR.* (Grantham 3710)

HOWE, Ronald Douglas. b 38. K Coll Lon and Warm BD and AKC 62. Lon Sch Econ Dipl Soc Admin 63. **d** 64 **p** 65 Lon. C of All SS Child's Hill 64-67; St Mary Virg Northn 67-69; V of Potterspury w Furtho and Yardley Gobion 69-81; R of Corby Dio Pet from 81; RD of Corby from 81. *Rectory, Argyll Street, Corby, Northants, NN17 1RU.* (Corby 3314)

HOWE, Roy William. ALCD 66. **d** 66 **p** 67 Bradf. C of St Pet Cathl Ch Bradf 66-70; Barnoldswick w Bracewell 70-72; V of Yeadon 72-79; P-in-c of Middleton-on-the-Wolds Dio York from 79; Bainton Dio York from 79; N Dalton Dio York from 79; RD of Harthill from 81. *The New Rectory, Bainton, Driffield, N Humberside, YO25 9NR.*

HOWE, William Ernest. b 25. ARICS 51. Westcott Ho Cam 68. **d** 70 Bp Gerard for Sheff **p** 71 Sheff. C of Anston and of Woodsetts 70-73; V of Greasbrough Dio Sheff from 73. *16 Church Street, Greasbrough, Rotherham, S Yorks, S61 4DX.* (Rotherham 551288)

HOWELL, Alfred. Wells Th Coll 57. **d** 59 **p** 60 Dur. C of Ferryhill 59-61; Tankersley 61-63; V of New Edlington 63-66; Sparkbrook 66-73; Publ Pr Dio Chelmsf from 73. *40 Ravenscourt Drive, Vange, Basildon, Essex.*

HOWELL, Andrew John. b 44. Clifton Th Coll 68. **d** 71 Man **p** 72 Hulme for Man. C of St Pet Halliwell 71-77; V of Facit Dio Man from 77. *Facit Vicarage, Shawforth, Rochdale, OL12 8LT.* (Whitworth 3931)

HOWELL, Canon Basil Rayson. b 20. St Pet Hall Ox BA 49, MA 53. Wycl Hall Ox 49. **d** 51 **p** 52 Southw. C of St John Worksop 51-54; C-in-c of St Paul's Conv Distr Manton 54-61; V of St Nich Blundellsands 61-81; RD of Bootle 69-78; Hon Can of Liv Cathl from 78. *9 Arlington Court, Arlington Avenue, Leamington Spa, Warws, CV32 5HR.* (0926-314746)

HOWELL, Canon Charles Ernest. b 09. MBE (Mil) 46. ALCD 36. **d** 36 **p** 37 Blackb. C of St Thos Preston 36-38; St Pet w St Greg Sudbury 38-39; CF (R of O) 39-46; CF 46-50; R of Beeston St Lawr w Ashmanhaugh and Hoveton St Pet 50-56; V of Tunstead w Ruston Sco 50-56; N Walsham w

Antingham 56-69; Old Catton 69-76; RD of Tunstead 61-64; Hon Can of Nor from 66. *3 Fairview Close, Drayton, Norwich.*

HOWELL, Christopher Alfred. b 1886. St Cath S Ox BA (3rd cl Th) 10, MA 14. Ely Th Coll 11. **d** 11 **p** 12 Wakef. C of St Mary Barnsley 11-19; All S (Hook Mem) Leeds 19-24; PC of St Mary Virg Ilford 24-39; R of Willingale w Shellow 39-58; C-in-c of Berners Roding 55-58; R of Willingale w Shellow Bowells and Berners Roding 58-60; Perm to Offic Dio Sarum from 60. *Kites Nest Cottage, Bourton, Gillingham, Dorset.* (Bourton 840396)

HOWELL, David. b 29. Clifton Th Coll 56. **d** 59 **p** 60 Lich. C of Tipton 59-62; V of St Paul W Bromwich 62-71; St John Deptford 71-81; Chap to Div Healing Miss Crowhurst from 81. *The Old Rectory, Crowhurst, Near Battle, Sussex, TN33 9AD.*

HOWELL, Deryck King. b 45. Moore Coll Syd ACT ThL 69. **d** 70 Syd **p** 71 Bp Begbie for Syd. C of St Jo Pro-Cathl Parramatta 70-72; Manly 73-74; R of Hurstville Grove Dio Syd from 75. *127 Hillcrest Road, Hurstville Grove, NSW, Australia 2220.* (57-4090)

HOWELL, Garnet Hughes. b 16. Late Welsh Ch Exhib and Griffiths Scho of St D Coll Lamp BA (2nd cl Engl) 37. **d** 39 **p** 40 Llan. C of Aberdare 39-41; Penydarren 41-43; Talybont-on-Usk 43-44. *16 College Street, Lampeter, Dyfed.*

HOWELL, John Anthony Neil Belville. b 39. Univ of Man BA 64. St Deiniol's Libr Hawarden 77. **d** 79 **p** 81 Ches. C of Wistaston Dio Ches from 79. *6 Arundel Close, Wistaston, Crewe, Cheshire, CW2 8EY.*

HOWELL, John Oliver Nicholas. b 37. Ch Ch Ox BA (Th) 61, MA 64. Wells Th Coll 60. **d** 62 **p** 63 Lon. C of Ch of Ascen Wembley 62-67; Bp's Youth Officer Dio Ox 67-72. *Address temp unknown.*

✠ **HOWELL, Right Rev Kenneth Walter.** b 09. St Pet Hall Ox BA 32, MA 36. Wycl Hall Ox 32. **d** 33 **p** 34 S'wark. C of St Mary Magd Peckham 33-37; Chap SAMS Paraguay 37-38; Quepe (Chile) 38-47; Supt Araucanian Miss Chile 40-47; V of Wandsworth 48-63; RD of Wandsworth 57-63; Chap R Hosp and Home for Incurables Putney 57-63; Hon Can of S'wark 62-63; Cons Ld Bp in Chile, Bolivia and Peru in Westmr Abbey 18 Oct 63 by Abp of Cant; Bps of Lon; Win; Ely; Leic; and S'wark; Bps Suffr of Kingston T; Maidstone; Stepney; and Tonbridge; Bp Simpson and others; res 71; Min of St John Downshire Hill, Hampstead 72-79; Asst Bp in Dio Lon 76-79; Perm to Offic Dio St E from 80. *147 Southgate Street, Bury St Edmunds, Suff.*

HOWELL, Lindsay Momber. Trin Coll Melb BA 57. St Aid Th Coll Bal 32. St Columb's Hall, Wang 33. ACT ThL 33. **d** and **p** 37 Bal. C of St Pet Bal 37-38; P-in-c of Natimuk 38-39; Hopetoun w Beulah Rainbow and Jeparit 39-40; Edenhope 40-44; Chap RAAF 42-43; Actg I of St Pet Bal 44-45; P-in-c of Bunninyong 46; V of Ararat 46-51; St Pet Bal 52-62; Can of Bal 59-62; I of St John E Malvern 62-77; Perm to Offic Dio Melb from 77. *95 Claremont Avenue, The Basin, Vic, Australia 3154.* (762-6618)

HOWELL, Martin John Hope. b 38. Univ of Bris BA (3rd cl Th) 62. Tyndale Hall Bris 59 **d** 64 Middleton for Man **p** 65 Man. C of St Paul Bolton 64-67; Bishopsworth 67-70; V of St Aug Swindon 70-81; R of Stratton St Marg w S Marston and Stanton Fitzwarren Dio Bris from 81. *Vicarage, Church Street, Stratton St Margaret, Swindon, SN3 4NB.* (Swindon 822793)

HOWELL, Robert Price. b 44. St Jo Coll Morpeth ThL 71. **d** 71 **p** 72 Newc. C of Merewether 71-72; Mayfield 72-74; Wallsend 75-77; R of Camden Haven Dio Newc from 77. *Rectory, Laurie Street, Laurieton, NSW, Australia 2443.* (065-599107)

HOWELL, Roger Brian. b 43. ALCD 67. **d** 67 **p** 68 S'wark. C of St Sav Battersea Pk 67-71; St Mary Crawley 71-76; V of Pendeen 76-81; Bedgrove Aylesbury Dio Ox from 81; P-in-c of Sancreed 76-81. *Bedgrove Vicarage, Camborne Avenue, Aylesbury, Bucks, HP21 7UE.* (Aylesbury 22214)

HOWELL, Ronald William Fullerton. b 51. Univ of Man BA 72. Univ of Ox BA 78. Ripon Coll Cudd 76. **d** 79 **p** 80 Newc T. C of St Francis High Heaton Newc T 79-81; Warmsworth Dio Sheff from 81. *23 Wrightson Avenue, Warmsworth, Doncaster, S Yorks.* (0302-854597)

HOWELL, Preb Walter Ernest. b 17. St D Coll Lamp BA 49. **d** 50 **p** 51 Lon. C of St Mich AA Bromley-by-Bow 50-56; V of St Mary Virg St Pancras 56-68; St Benet and All SS St Pancras 68-79; St Sav Alexandra Pk Dio Lon from 79; Preb of St Paul's Cathl Lon from 78. *268 Alexandra Park Road, N22 4BG.* (01-888 5683)

HOWELL-EVERSON, Douglas Norman. b 19. TD 53. Ripon Hall Ox 59. **d** 60 **p** 61 Southw. C of Bulwell 60-62; PC of Stanton-in-Peak w Birchover 62-68; V 68-75; R of Bamford-in-the-Peak Dio Derby from 75. *Bamford Rectory, Sheffield, S30 2AY.* (Hope Valley 51375)

HOWELLS, Alun. b 24. St D Coll Lamp. **d** 64 **p** 65 St D. C of St D w Ch Ch Carmarthen 64-70; V of Llandyssilio w Egremont and Llanglydwen w Cilymaenllwyd 70-71; Meidrim w Llanboidy (and Merthyr from 81) Dio St D from 71. *Meidrim Vicarage, Carmarthen, Dyfed.* (St Clears 230506)

HOWELLS, Canon Arthur Glyn. b 32. St D Coll Lamp BA 54. St Mich Coll Llan. **d** 56 **p** 57 Swan B. C of Oystermouth 56-58; Llangyfelach w Morriston 58-64; R of Llandefalle w Llyswen Boughrood and Llanstephan 64-70; Youth Chap Dio Swan B 67-71; V of Landore 70-80; Can of Brecon Cathl from 80. *104 West Cross Lane, West Cross, Swansea.* (Swansea 402464)

HOWELLS, David. b 55. Grey Coll Dur BA (Th) 78. Ripon Coll Cudd 79. **d** 81 Dur. C of Birtley Dio Dur from 81. *13 Scafell, Vigo, Birtley, Co Durham.*

HOWELLS, David Morgan. b 23. Qu Coll Birm 72. **d** 75 Bp Parker for Cov **p** 76 Bp McKie for Cov (APM). C of St Nich Radford City and Dio Cov from 75. *7 Middlemarch, Radford, Coventry, CV6 3GE.*

HOWELLS, Canon Donald Lockwood. b 20. Univ of Lon BA 43. Oak Hill Th Coll 39. **d** 43 **p** 44 S'wark. C of St Mich AA Southfields S'wark 43-45; St Jo Bapt Folkestone 45-48; Watford 48-49; V of Weston 49-54; C of Stevenage (in c of St Mary Shephall) 54-57; R of Knebworth 57-66; V of Tring Dio St Alb 66-80; Team R from 80; Surr from 70; P-in-c of Aldbury 78-80; Puttenham w Long Marston and Wilstone 79-80; RD of Berkhamsted from 80; Hon Can of St Alb Cathl from 80. *Rectory, Church Yard, Tring, Herts.* (Tring 2170)

HOWELLS, Garfield Edwin. Univ of Man. K Coll Lon and Warm. **d** 54 **p** 55 S'wark. C of Sanderstead 54-57; CF 57-60; R of Kingsdown w Mappiscombe 60-64; Gnowangerup 64-67; Como 66-74; Swanbourne 74-79; Kojonup Dio Bunb from 79. *Rectory, Kojonup, W Australia 6395.*

HOWELLS, John Conrad. Univ of Melb BSc 54, BA and B Educn 62. Trin Coll Melb 59, ACT ThL 62. **d** 60 **p** 61 Melb. C of St John E Malvern 60-61; Mitcham 61-62; Min of Nunawading w Donvale 62-66; V of W Footscray 66-70; C of St Geo E Ivanhoe Dio Melb from 70. *55 Exhibition Street, Melbourne, Vic, Australia 3000.* (03-49 6698)

HOWELLS, John St Quentin. Univ of Melb BA 58. St Mich Coll Crafers 58, ACT ThL (1st cl) 63. **d** 62 Bp Redding for Melb **p** 63 Melb. C of Melb Dioc Task Force 62-63; Coburg 63-65; V of Braybrook 65-70; I of Cheltenham 70-77; All SS Geelong Dio Melb from 77. *15 Talbot Street, Geelong, Vic, Australia 3220.* (052-21 1994)

HOWELLS, Meredydd. Univ of Wales, BA 36. St Mich Coll Llan 37. **d** 40 **p** 41 Swan B. C of Llanelly (Brecons) 40-45; Sketty 45-54; R of Llanmadoc w Cheriton 54-58; V of St Thos Blackb 58-76; L to Offic Dio Blackb from 79. *35 Ramsgreave Drive, Blackburn, Lancs.* (Blackb 47056)

HOWELLS, Neil. b 23. Qu Mary Coll Univ of Lon BSc (Phys) 48. Bps' Coll Cheshunt 48. **d** 50 **p** 51 Ox. C of St Jas Cowley Ox 50-54; Forest Hill Ox (in c of St Mary Sandhills) 54-56; Min of St Mary Conv Distr Bayswater Headington Ox 56-60; V of St Luke Maidenhead 60-68; Surr 60-68; Chap Maidenhead Hosp 60-68; R of Welford w Wickham (and Gt Shefford from 72) 68-77; RD of Newbury 73-77; V of Bray Dio Ox from 77; Surr from 77. *Bray Vicarage, Maidenhead, Berks, SL6 2AB.* (Maidenhead 21527)

HOWELLS, Roger Douglas. b 45. St Chad's Coll Dur BA (1st cl Gen) 67. Univ of Leeds Dipl Th 69. Coll of Resurr Mirfield 67. **d** 70 **p** 71 Llan. C of St German, Roath 70-75; St Fagan Aberdare 75-77; V of Porth Dio Llan from 77. *St Paul's Vicarage, Porth, Rhondda, Mid Glam, CF39 9UU.* (Porth 2401)

HOWELLS, William Gordon. b 26. **d** 61 Bp T M Hughes for Llan **p** 62 Llan. C of Aberdare 61-64; Coity w Nolton 64-67; Northam w Westward Ho 67-71; V of Bp's Tawton 71-76; Cofton w Starcross 76-80; Modbury w Brownston Dio Ex from 80; Aveton Gifford Dio Ex from 80. *Vicarage, Modbury, Ivybridge, Devon, PL21 0TA.* (Modbury 250)

HOWES, Alan. b 49. Chich Th Coll 76. **d** 79 **p** 80 Southw. C of St Jo Bapt Bilborough Dio Southw from 79. *44 Darnhall Crescent, Bilborough, Nottingham, NG8 4PZ.*

HOWES, David. b 30. Open Univ BA 75. Roch Th Coll 62. **d** 64 **p** 65 Ex. C of Highweek w Abbotsbury 64-67; Clyst St Geo 67-71; C-in-c of E Woolfardisworthy w Kennerleigh and of Washford Pyne w Puddington 71-72; R of E Woolfardisworthy, Cheriton-Fitzpaine, Kennerleigh, Washford Pyne, Puddington, Poughill and Stockleigh English 72-73; Perm to Offic Dio Ex 74-77; C of Walworth 77-79; Min of Roundshaw Conv Distr Wallington Dio S'wark from 79. *32 Waterer Rise, Wallington, Surrey.*

HOWES, Edward Horace. b 18. Coll of Resurr Mirfield 56. **d** 58 **p** 59 Llan. C of Newton Nottage 58-60; St Gabr Swansea 60-62; All SS Clifton w St Mary Tyndalls Pk 62-65; V of St Steph w St Cath Liv 65-72; C-in-c of All SS Sculcoates 72-73;

St Jude w St Steph Hull 72-73; V of St Steph Sculcoates Hull 73-80; Allerton Bywater Dio Ripon from 80. *Vicarage, Allerton Bywater, Castleford, W Yorks, WF10 2DJ.* (Castleford 554186)

HOWES, Eric James. b 45. Trent Univ Ont BA 69. Waterloo Lutheran Sem MDiv 73. **d** 72 **p** 73 Ont. C of St Jas Kingston 72-76; R of St Thos Hamilton Dio Niag from 76. *186 St Clair Boulevard, Hamilton, Ont, Canada.* (545 2281)

HOWES, Michael John Norton. b 43. Univ of Hull BA (3rd cl Th) 66. Linc Th Coll 66. **d** 68 **p** 69 St Alb. C of Gt Berkhamsted 68-71; Ampthill Dio St Alb from 71; Chap RAF from 72. *c/o RAF Chaplains, Adastral House, Theobalds Road, WC1X 8RU.*

HOWES, Norman Vincent. b 36. K Coll Lon and Warm AKC 61. **d** 62 Bp McKie for Cov **p** 63 Cov. C of St Nich Radford Cov 62-66; V of Napton-on-the-Hill 66-72; Exhall Dio Cov from 72. *Exhall Vicarage, Ash Green, Coventry, Warws.* (Coventry 362997)

✠ **HOWES, Right Rev Peter Henry Herbert.** OBE 61. Kelham Th Coll 29. **d** 34 **p** 35 Dur. C of St Mich AA Norton Dur 34-37; Miss of St Aug Miss Betong 37-38; Hd Master St Mich Sch Sandakan 38-40; P-in-c of Quop 40-50; Tai-i 50-52; Prin of Ho of Epiph Th Sch Kuch 52-56; Can of Borneo 55-62; Kuch 62-71; L to Offic Dio Borneo 56-60; Archd of Sarawak 61-62; Kuch 62-65; Brunei and N Sarawak 65-71; Archd (Emer) from 71; Can Missr 61-71; Warden of Dioc Th Coll Ho of Epiph Kuch 71-76; Cons Asst Bp of Kuch in St Thos Cathl Kuch 6 Aug 76 by Bp of Kuch; Bps of Sabah and W Mal; res 81. *Diocesan Centre, Kuching, Sarawak, Malaysia.*

HOWES, Canon Roger Hylton. b 24. Linc Th Coll 56. **d** 58 **p** 59 Worc. C of Kidderminster 58-60; Industr Chap of Kidderminster 60-64; Industr Adv to Bp of Worc from 64; Hon Can of Worc from 69; Dir of Worc Industr Miss 70-79; V of Defford w Besford Dio Worc from 79; Eckington Dio Worc from 79. *Eckington Vicarage, Pershore, Worcs, WR10 3AX.* (Evesham 750203)

HOWITT, Canon Alan John. b 26. Univ of Leeds BA 50. Coll of Resurr Mirfield 50. **d** 53 **p** 54 Chelmsf. C of Wanstead 53-57; Chap and Ho Master at St Jo Approved Sch Tiffield 57-64; V of St Mary Virg Northn 64-75; RD of Wootton 70-74; V of St Jo Bapt City and Dio Pet from 75; Can (Non-Res) of Pet from 75; RD of Pet from 76. *Vicarage, Thorpe Road, Peterborough, PE3 6AN.* (Pet 64899)

HOWITT, John Leslie. b 28. Lon Coll of Div 60. **d** 62 Southw **p** 63 Bp Gelsthorpe for Southw. C of Chilwell 62-66; Chap Rampton Hosp 66-71; C-in-c of Treswell w Cottam 68-71; Chap HM Pris Cardiff 71-75; HM Borstal Dover 75-79; HM Pris Dartmoor from 79. *Chaplain's House, Princetown, Yelverton, Devon.* (Princetown 309)

HOWLDEN, Paul Wilfrid. b 41. Trin Coll Cam 1st cl Hist Trip pt i, 62 BA (2nd cl Hist Trip pt ii) 63, MA 67. Cudd Coll 64. **d** 66 **p** 67 Portsm. C of Paulsgrove 66-73; Hon C of Ascen Hanger Hill Dio Lon from 75. *4 Denbigh Road, West Ealing, W13.*

HOWLETT, Ernest Carl. K Coll NS STh 63. **d** 61 **p** 63 Fred. I of Aber w Brighton 61-71; R of Kingston Fred 70-80. *c/o Trinity Rectory, Kingston, NB, Canada.*

HOWLETT, Robert Keith. b 50. Univ of NB BA 72. Atlantic Sch of Th Halifax NS MDiv 75. **d** 74 **p** 76 Fred. C of Kingston 74-75; I of Canterbury 75-80; Hillsborough w Riverside Dio Fred from 80. *Box 52, Hillsborough, NB, Canada.*

HOWLETT, Roy William Patrick. b 23. Sarum Th Coll 57. **d** 59 **p** 60 Ex. C of Northam w Westward Ho 59-64; V of Tremaine Dio Truro from 64; PC (V from 68) of Egloskerry Dio Truro from 64; V of N Petherwyn Dio Truro from 68. *Egloskerry Vicarage, Launceston, Cornw, PL15 8RX.* (N Petherwin 365)

HOWORTH, John Hamer. St Francis Coll Brisb 53. **d** 54 **p** 55 Rockptn. V of Emerald 54-60; Edenhope 60-62; C of St Pet Kells Whitehaven 62-63; R of Drayton 64-73; Perm to Offic Dio Brisb 73-74; C of St Jas Toowoomba Dio Brisb from 75. *Boundary Street, Toowoomba, Queensland, Australia, 4350.* (076-34 3522)

HOWSE, Preb Jesse. b 1890. Kelham Th Coll 06. **d** 13 **p** 15 Lich. C of Blakenall Heath 13-15; TCF 15-17; C of Stoke-on-Trent 17-20; V of Hanford 20-26; PC of St Andr Porthill 26-37; V of Fenton 37-43; Tunstall Staffs 43-53; Preb of Lich Cathl 43-71; Preb (Emer) from 71; Dioc Insp of Schs 43-57; Proc Conv Lich 45-50; RD of Stoke-on-Trent 52-59; V of Sneyd 53-60; PC of St Werburgh Burslem 56-60; V of Warslow w Elkstone 60-70; RD of Alstonfield 63-70. *Manifold, Hinton Martell, Wimborne, Dorset.*

HOWSON, David James. b 34. Kelham Th Coll 54. **d** 58 Blackb **p** 59 Burnley for Blackb. C of St Barn Morecambe 58-61; Burnley 61-63; C-in-c of St Leon Conv Distr Penwortham and Dioc Sch Insp 63-65; Bp's Youth Officer Dio Ox 65-67; V of Whitworth 67-71; R of St Mary Virg Rufford 71-78; V of Mellor Dio Blackb from 78. *Vicarage, Mellor, Blackburn, Lancs, BB2 7JL.* (Mellor 2324)

HOWSON, Canon George. b 15. Univ of Man BA 46. Sarum Th Coll 47. **d** 49 **p** 50 Ches. C of Liscard 49-52; Astbury 52-53; V of Seacombe 53-60; Over 60-80; RD of Middlewich 74-80; Hon Can of Ches Cathl 75-80; Can (Emer) from 80. *58 Mount Drive, Nantwich, Cheshire, CW5 6JQ.* (0270-627870)

HOWSON, Robert Henry. Em Coll Sktn LTh 44. **d** 44 **p** 45 Sktn. Miss at Unity 44-46; I of Kerrobert w Luseland and Salvador 46-47; Miss at Macklin 47-49; C of Oakville 49-50; R of Hagersville 50-51; Bolton w Tullamore 51-53; Campbellford 53-54; Chap RCAF from 54-70; L to Offic Dio Calg 62-71; R of Cobble Hill 71-79; Perm to Offic Dio BC from 79. *957 Oliver Street, Victoria, BC, Canada.*

HOY, Michael John. b 30. Univ of Reading BSc 52. Oak Hill Th Coll 57. **d** 59 Lewes for Chich **p** 60 Chich. C of St Geo Worthing 59-62; Tulse Hill 62-66; R of Danby Wiske w Yafforth and Hutton Bonville 66-76; V of Camelsdale Dio Chich from 76. *Vicarage, School Road, Camelsdale, Haslemere, GU27 3RN.*

HOYAL, Richard Dunstan. b 47. Ch Ch Ox BA 67, MA 71, BA (Th) 78. Ripon Coll Cudd 76. **d** 79 **p** 80 St Alb. C of St Geo Stevenage Dio St Alb from 79. *19 Poppy Mead, Stevenage, Herts.* (Stevenage 67654)

HOYE, Reginald George. b 16. Tyndale Hall Bris 58. **d** 60 **p** 61 Lich. C of Penn Fields 60-62; V of St Sav Nottm Dio Southw from 62. *St Saviour's Vicarage, Arkwright Walk, Nottingham, NG2 2JU.* (Nottm 864046)

HOYLAND, John Gregory. b 50. Univ of Sussex BEducn 73. Wycl Hall Ox 75. **d** 78 **p** 79 Bradf. C of Pudsey 78-81; P-in-c of Long Preston Dio Bradf from 81; Tosside Dio Bradf from 81. *Vicarage, Long Preston, Skipton, BD23 4NJ.* (Long Preston 242)

HOYLE, Ven Frederick James. b 18. St Jo Coll Dur BA 47, Dipl Th 49, MA 58. **d** 49 **p** 50 Man. C of St Paul Withington 49-52; C-in-c of St Martin's Conv Distr Wythenshawe 52-61; V 61-65; Vice-Chairman and Exec Officer Man Dioc Pastoral C'tte from 65; L to Offic Dio Man 65-70; Hon Can of Man from 67; V of Rochdale 70-78; RD of Rochdale 70-82; Archd of Bolton from 82. *c/o 90 Deansgate, Manchester, M3 2QH.*

HOYLE, Ian Leslie. b 33. Heriot-Watt Coll Edin BSc 66. Westcott Ho Cam 70. **d** 72 Lynn for Nor **p** 73 Nor. C of Eaton 72-76; St Nich Gt Yarmouth Dio Nor from 76. *208 Palgrave Road, Gt Yarmouth, Norf.* (Gt Yarmouth 4735)

HOYLE, James Clifton. St Paul's Coll Grahmstn. **d** 66 Zam **p** 67 Bp Mataka for Zam. C of St Mich AA Kitwe 67-68; P-in-c of Luanshya 68-70; R of Molteno 70-75; St John E Lon Dio Grahmstn from 75. *3 Hill View Road, Beach, East London, CP, S Africa.* (27021)

HOYLE, Lawrence. b 27. St Aid Coll 52. **d** 55 **p** 56 Wakef. C of All S Halifax 55-57; Bromley 57-59; V of St Ambrose Widnes 59-61; R of Lanteglos-by-Camelford w St Adwena 61-66; V of St Cuthb Wrose 66-70; R of Thwing 70-81; V of Wold Newton 70-81; Warden Lamplugh Ho Conf Centre from 72; Co-ordinator of Angl Renewal Ministries from 81. *Lamplugh House, Thwing, Driffield, Yorks, YO25 0DY.* (0262 87282)

HOYLE, Thomas Oldland. b 22. St Edm Hall Ox 2nd cl Engl Lang and Lit 48, BA 49, MA 53. Chich Th Coll 49. **d** 50 Bedford for St Alb **p** 51 St Alb. C of All SS Luton 50-53; Winchmore Hill 53-56; V of Calverton Dio Southw from 56. *Calverton Vicarage, Nottingham.* (Nottingham 652552)

HOYT, Harold Hammond. **d** 27 Queb for Fred **p** 28 Fred. Miss of Richmond 27-31; R of Dalhousie 27-37; Miss at East St John 37-40; CF (Canad) 40-47; Miss at Renforth and Coldbrook 47-64. *RR1, Hampton, NB, Canada.*

HOYT, Canon Herbert James. Bp's Univ Lennox LST 28. **d** 28 **p** 29 Fred. Miss at Burton and Maugerville 28-31; Salisbury w Havelock 31-33; Gagetown 33-52; R of St George w Pennfield 52-58; Sussex 58-69; Can of Ch Ch Cathl Fred from 64. *Sussex, NB, Canada.*

HPA EH, b 32. **d** 74 **p** 75 Pa-an. P Dio Pa-an. *c/o Bishopkone, Pa-an, Karen State, Burma.*

HRYNIEWICZ, Marian. b 42. Univ of Rome BA 72. York Univ Tor BA 77. **d** and **p** 73 RC Abp of Tor. In RC Ch 73-77; Rec into Angl Commun 78 by Bp of Tor. Hon C of All H City and Dio Tor from 79. *7 George Webster Road, Toronto, Canada, M4B 3K9.*

HSER EE, b 46. **d** 74 **p** 75 Pa-an. P Dio Pa-an. *St Mark's Church, New Thandaung, Thandaung Township, Karen State, Burma.*

HSI, Walter Yu Mou. St Jo Coll Shanghai BA 45. **d** 54 Hong. d Dio Hong. *51 Kimberley Road, Kowloon, Hong Kong.*

HTAUNG OKE, Samuel. Univ of Rang BA 79. **d** 81 Akyab. d Dio Akyab. *St Mark's Church, Akyab, Burma.*

HTOO KHOO, Paul. **d** 36 **p** 37 Rang. P Dio Rang 36-70; Dio Pa-an 70-80. *Thaya Gone, Toungoo, Burma.*

HU, Ronald Toh Tong. b 47. Univ of W Aus BSc 69. Fitzwm Coll Cam MA 75. Ridley Hall Cam 73. **d** 76 **p** 77 Sing. C of St Andr Cathl Sing 76-81; P-in-c of St Jas City and Dio Sing from 81. *1 Leedon Road, Singapore 1026.*

HUAHUATI, Jasper. b 48. Bp Patteson Th Coll 71. **d** 73 melan **p** 74 Bp Dudley for Melan. P Dio Melan 73-74; Dio Ysabel 75-76; Dio Centr Melan from 77. *Church of Melanesia, Siarana, Gela Is, Ysabel, Solomon Islands.*

HUANG, Canon Tung Hsi. Centr Th Sch Nanking. **d** 27 Fukien **p** 28 Bp Ding for Fukien. P Dio Fukien 27-36; Dio Sing from 36; Can of Sing 52-71; Can (Emer) from 71; L to Offic Dio Sing 59-71. *St Paul's Mission, 56 MacAlister Road, Penang, Malaya.*

HUARD, Geoffrey Robert. b 43. Dipl Th (Lon) 71. Clifton Th Coll 69. **d** 70 **p** 71 Barking for Chelmsf. C of Barking 70-73; St Ambrose w St Timothy Everton 73-74; St Pet Everton 74-76; R of St Sav S Sydney Dio Syd from 76. *119 Young Street, Redfern, NSW, Australia 2016.* (Sydney 698-9497)

HUATA, Canon Wi Te Tau. Te Aute Coll MC 45. **d** 39 **p** 40 Wai. C of Motio and Waipatu Pastorates 40-50; CF 43-46; V of Te Ngae Maori Distr 50-52; P-in-c of Waik Maori Past and Dioc Maori Missr Dio Waik 52-60; Supt 60-70; Can of Waik 54-73; Hon Can from 73; P-in-c of Hamilton Maori Past 70-73; Chap to Bp of Waik 70-73; V of Wairoa-Mohaka Maori Past Dio Wai from 73. *43 Hunter Brown Street, Wairoa, NZ.*

HUBAND, Eric Bob. b 27. Univ of Bris BSc 50. Sarum Th Coll 50. **d** 52 **p** 53 Bris. C of Conv Distr of St Mary and St Francis Lockleaze 52-56; Bishopsworth 56-60; V of St Anne Greenbank Bris 60-67; Hengrove 67-77; R of E Horsley Dio Guildf from 77. *East Horsley Rectory, Ockham Road South, Leatherhead, Surrey, KT24 6RL.* (E Horsley 2359)

HUBAND, Richard William. b 39. Trin Coll Cam BA 62, MA 66. Qu Coll Birm 76. **d** 78 **p** 79 St Alb. C of St Geo Norton 78-81; R of Aspley Guise w Husborne Crawley and Ridgmont Dio St Alb from 81. *Aspley Guise Rectory, Milton Keynes, Bucks, MK17 8HN.* (Milton Keynes 583169)

HUBBARD, Alfred Francis. **d** 61 **p** 62 Waik. C of Te Aroha 61-62; Stratford 62-63; V of Kawhia 63-66; Katikati 66-68; Ngaruawahia 68-73; C of St Jo Bapt Kidderminster 73-74; Perm to Offic Dio Waik from 74. *11 Leo Street, Waihi Beach, NZ.* (Waihi Beach 703)

HUBBARD, Christopher Maurice. b 25. Trin Coll Cam BA 49, MA 69. Chich Th Coll 51. **d** 53 **p** 54 Win. C of Ringwood 53-56; Ch Ch Cathl Vic BC 56-60; Holdenhurst (in c of St Barn Qu Pk) 60; Min of St Barn Qu Pk Conv Distr Bournemouth 61-65; V of Wymeswold 65-72; R of Lambley 72-77; Chap HM Borstal Inst Lowdham Grange 74-77; P-in-c of Chilbolton and Wherwell Dio Win 77-79; R from 79. *Chilbolton Rectory, Stockbridge, Hants.* (Chilbolton 258)

HUBBARD, David Harris. b 33. St Pet Hall Ox BA (2nd cl Th) 57. MA 61. Ridley Hall Cam 59. **d** 60 **p** 61 Lon. C of St Mark w St Bart Dalston 60-63; Woodberry Down 63-67; Hon C 67-68; Asst Master Dalston Sch 67-75; Hon C of Ch Ch Crouch End Hornsey Dio Lon 69-70; V from 70; Area D of W Haringey from 78. *Christ Church Vicarage, 32 Crescent Road, N8 8AX.* (01-340 1566)

HUBBARD, Ian Maxwell. b 43. Sarum Wells Th Coll 69. **d** 74 **p** 75 S'wark. C of H Trin w St Matt S'wark 74-78; St Mich AA w All S and Em Camberwell Dio S'wark from 78. *22 Orlwin Street, Camberwell, SE5.*

HUBBARD, John Waddington. b 1896. Qu Coll Cam BA 21, MA 24. Univ of Lon BSc 23. Ridley Hall Cam 27. **d** 28 Lon for Col **p** 29 Niger. CMS Miss Warri Province Nigeria 29-35; R of Cusop 35-38; V of Ch Ch St Alb 38-48; Offg Chap St Alb Inst 38-48; R of St Lawr w St Mary S Walsham 48-63. *19 West View Road, Blofield, Norwich, NR13 4JR.*

HUBBARD, Julian Richard Hawes. b 55. Em Coll Cam BA 76, MA 80. Wycl Hall Ox BA (Th) 80. **d** 81 Kens for Lon. C of St Dionis Parsons Green Fulham Dio Lon from 81. *16 Parsons Green, SW6 4TS.* (01-736 4849)

HUBBARD, Laurence Arthur. b 36. Qu Coll Cam BA 60, MA 64. Wycl Hall Ox 60. **d** 62 **p** 63 B & W. C of Widcombe 62-65; V of Nyeri Kenya 66-70; C of Nanyuki Kenya 70-72; V 72-73; V of St Mary Pype Hayes Erdington 73-79; P-in-c of St Aug City and Dio Nor from 79; St Geo Colegate City and Dio Nor from 79. *1 Mill Lane, Magdalen Road, Norwich, NR3 4LD.* (Nor 618612)

HUBBARD, Roy Oswald. b 32. Lich Th Coll 62. **d** 64 **p** 65 Lich. C of Berkswich w Walton 64-68; C-in-c of Ash 68-70; V of St Pet Broadwater Stevenage 70-78; Flitwick Dio St Alb from 78. *Flitwick Vicarage, Dunstable Road, Flitwick, Beds, MK45 1HT.* (Flitwick 712369)

HUBBARD, Canon Royston Percy. **d** 53 **p** 54 Bran. R of Elkhorn 53-55; Hamiota and Shoal Lake 55-59; Miss Moose Lake 59-72; I of Grand Rapids 72-78; Hon Can of Bran 76-78; Can (Emer) from 78. *Box 363, Elkhorn, Manit, Canada.*

HUBBARD, Simon Timothy. **d** and **p** 78 Syd. C of Gladesville 78-79; Chap RAN from 80. *RAN College, Jervis Bay, ACT, Australia 2540.*

HUBBLE, Raymond Carr. b 30. Wm Temple Coll 60. **d** 61 **p** 62 Derby. C of Newbold w Dunstan 61-64; Chap RAF from 64; Asst Chap-in-Chief from 80. *c/o Ministry of Defence, Adastral House, WC1.*

HUBBLE, Ronald Ernest Breward. **d** 71 **p** 72 Johann. C of Nigel 71-81; Jeppe Dio Johann from 81. *55 Jules Street, Jeppestown, Johannsburg, S Africa.*

HUBBLE, Trevor Ernest. b 46. Chich Th Coll 70. **d** 76 **p** 77 S'wark. C of St Barn Eltham 76-80; Asst P of St Barn Masite Dio Les from 80. *St Barnabas Rectory, Masite, PO Maseru, Lesotho.*

HUCKETT, Andrew William. b 50. AKC 72. St Aug Coll Cant 72. **d** 73 **p** 74 Glouc. C of Chipping Sodbury w Old Sodbury 73-76; Chap Miss to Seamen at Flushing 76-79. *c/o Missions to Seamen, Scheldepoort, Flushing, Holland.* (24029)

HUCKLE, Stephen Leslie. b 48. ch Ch Ox BA (Hist) 70, BA (Th) 72, MA 74. Coll of the Resurr Mirfield 73. **d** 75 **p** 76 Lich. C of St Paul Wednesbury 75-78; Aylesbury (in c of St Pet Quarrendon) Dio Ox from 78. *35 Abbey Road, Aylesbury, Bucks, HP19 3NP.* (Aylesbury 24869)

HUCKLE, Sydney George. b 16. Oak Hill Coll 76. **d** 79 **p** 80 Colchester for Chelmsf. C of Wakes Colne w Chappel 79-80; Aldham Dio Chelmsf from 80; Marks Tey Dio Chelmsf from 80. *Oaklea, Swan Street, Chappel, Colchester, Essex.*

HUDDLESON, Robert Roulston. b 32. QUB BA 55. TCD Div Test 57. **d** 57 **p** 58 Connor. C of Ballymena 57-59; St Jas Belf 59-63; Asst Dir Inter Ch Aid Ethiopia 65-69; Exec Asst World Coun of Chs Geneva 69-75; Dep Sec Bd for Miss and Unity of Gen Syn 75-81; Admin Secr Dio Dur from 81. *Diocesan Office, Auckland Castle, Bishop Auckland, Co Durham DL14 7QJ.* (Bp Auckland 604515)

✠ **HUDDLESTON, Most Rev Ernest Urban Trevor.** b 13. Ch Ch Ox BA 34, MA 38. Univ of Aber Hon DD 56. Univ of Lanc Hon DLitt 72. Wells Th Coll 35. **d** 36 **p** 37 Bris. C of St Mark Swindon 36-39; M CR from 41; P-in-c of Sophiatown and Orlando Miss Johann 43-49; Prov CR S Afr 49-56; Commiss N Rhod 52-60; Novice Guardian Mirfield 56-58; Prior of Lon Ho of CR 58-60; Cons Ld Bp of Masasi in St Nich Ch Dar-es-Salaam 30 Nov 60 by Abp of E Afr, Bps of Zanz, SW Tang, Bps Omari, Kariuki, and Olang'; res 68; Apptd Bp Suffr of Stepney 68; BP of Maur 78; Elected Abp of Prov of the Indian Ocean 78; Commiss Masasi 69-78; Commiss Damar 70-78. *Bishop's House, Phoenix, Mauritius.*

HUDDLESTON, Geoffrey Roger. b 36. Trin Coll Dub BA (3rd cl Hebr Mod) 63, MA 67. Ridley Hall Cam 63. **d** 65 **p** 66 Roch. C of Tonbridge 65-69; Chap RAF from 69. *c/o Ministry of Defence, Adastral House, WC1.*

HUDSON, Allen. St Barn Th Coll Adel 66. **d** 69 **p** 70 Adel. C of Edwardstown w Ascot Pk 69-72; Tea Tree Gully 72-74; St Jas Paddington Lon 74-76; Perm to Offic Dio Adel 76-77 and from 80; P-in-c of St Paul Adel 77-80. *186 Military Road, Semaphore, S Australia 5019.* (49-6497)

✠ **HUDSON, Right Rev Arthur William Goodwin.** Lon Coll of Div 39. ACT ThD 61. **d** 40 **p** 41 Roch. C of St Paul Chatham 40-42; V of Good Easter 42-45; Hon CF 42-45; Dioc Miss Dio Chelmsf 43-45; Hd Master Windsor Sch Santiago 45-48; Chap at Santiago Chile 45-48; V of St Mary Magd Holloway (w St Jas from 53) 48-55; Hon Gen Sec S Amer MS 49-60; V of All SS Woodford Wells 55-60; Cons Bp Coadj of Syd in Westmr Abbey 25 Mar 60 by Abp of Cant; Bps of Lon; Win; Ely; Heref; B & W; Chich; Nor; St E; Chelmsf; Leic; Pet; and Southw; Bps Suffr of Kens; Fulham; Tonbridge; Barking; and Whitby; Bps Cowdry; Carpenter-Garnier; Kitching; Simpson; Wand; Robin; Cockin; Chase; Bayne; and Craske; and Abp of Utrecht and Bp of Deventer; res 65; also Dean of Syd 62-65; V of St Paul Portman Square St Marylebone 65-78; Chairman Temperance Coun of Chr Chs from 74; Asst Bp of Derby from 81. *14 Newton Park, Newton Solney, Derby.*

HUDSON, Brainerd Peter de-Wirtz Goodwin. b 34. K Coll Lon BD and AKC 57. Westcott Ho Cam 57. **d** 59 **p** 60 S'wark. C of Morden 59; Asst Chap for Youth and Dir C of E Boys' S Dio Syd 61-65; L to Offic Dio Syd 61-65; Asst Sec CCCS and L to Offic Dio Lon 65-68; Chap St Lawr Coll Ramsgate and L to Offic Dio Cant 68-74; Chap Repton Sch Derbys and L to Offic Dio Derby from 74. *11 The Cross, Repton, Derbys.* (Burton-on-Trent 703250)

HUDSON, Christopher John. b 45. Univ of Lon BSc 68. Cranmer Hall Dur Dipl Th 77. **d** 77 Taunton for B & W **p** 78 B & W. C of St Jo Evang Weston Bath 77-80; P-in-c of Baltonsborough and Butleigh Dio B & W from 80; W Bradley

& Lottisham Dio B & W from 81. *Vicarage, Church Close, Butleigh, Glastonbury, Somerset, BA6 8SH.* (0458 50409)

HUDSON, Edmund John. b 21. Late Exhib of Qu Coll Cam BA 46, MA 48. Cudd Coll 47. **d** 49 **p** 50 Dur. C of St Andr Monkwearmouth 49-52; CF 52-55; V of St Hilda City and Dio York from 56. *Vicarage, Tang Hall Lane, York.* (York 23150)

HUDSON, Canon Edward Freeman. b 06. St Jo Coll Dur Capel Cure Pri 36, BA (2nd cl Th) 37, MA 40. **d** 37 **p** 38 Chelmsf. C of Barking 37-47; RAFVR 42-46; Dir of Relig Educn Dio Chelmsf 47-55; LPr Dio Chelmsf 47-49; R of Dengie w Asheldham 49-52; Ingatestone w Buttsbury Dio Chelmsf from 52; Hon Can of Chelmsf from 62; C-in-c of Mountnessing 63-69; Hon Chap to Bp of Chelmsf from 77. *Rectory, Ingatestone, Essex, CM4 0DD.* (Ingatestone 3106)

HUDSON, Frederic Cecil Willis. b 01. Keble Coll Ox BA (3rd cl Mod Hist) and Gladstone Hist Pri 23, MA 27. Cudd Coll 23. **d** 24 Southw **p** 25 Derby for Southw. C of St Mary Virg Nottm 24-27; Chap Bp's Hostel Linc 27-33; LPr Dio Linc 28-33; R of Partney w Dalby 33-39; V of Quadring 39-48; R of Aisthorpe w Scampton 48-61; R of Brattleby 48-61; RD of Lawres West 49-61; V of Askrigg w Stalling Busk 61-67; L to Offic Dio Carl from 68. *29 Balmoral Drive, Holmes Chapel, Chesh, CW4 7JQ.*

HUDSON, Canon Gerald Ernest. b 20. Ex Coll Ox BA (2nd cl Th) 42, MA 46. Westcott Ho Cam 42. **d** 43 Kingston T for S'wark **p** 44 S'wark. C of St Paul w St Mark Deptford 43-47; St Sav Raynes Park (in c of H Cross Miss) 47-51; V of Catford 51-60; Roehampton 60-71; Hon Can of S'wark 68-80; Can (Emer) from 80; Exam Chap to Bp of S'wark 69-80; Prin SOC 71-80; R of St Mary-le-Bow City and Dio Lon from 80. *Rector's Lodgings, St Mary-le-Bow, Cheapside, EC2V 6AU.* (01-248 5139)

HUDSON, Harold Paige. b 05. New Coll Ox 2nd cl Hist 27, BA 28, MA 32. Westcott Ho Cam 32. **d** 34 **p** 35 Lon. C of Em Maida Hill 34-36; St Mary Handsworth 36-39; V of Ashby Magna 39-45; Kirby Muxloe 45-50; Perm to Offic Dio Glouc 51-53. *La Mouette, Pontac, St Clement, Jersey, CI.*

HUDSON, James W.. b 45. Ridley Coll Melb 75. **d** 76 Gippsld. C of Toora 76-79; Austrn Bush Ch-Aid Society 79-81; C of Wallamba Dio Newc from 81. *Rectory, Bent Street, Tuncurry, NSW, Australia 2428.*

HUDSON, Canon John Cecil. b 22. Late Exhib of Selw Coll Cam BA (3rd cl Cl Trip pt i) 46, MA 48. Qu Coll Birm BD 51. **d** 48 **p** 49 Dur. C of Darlington 48-53; CF (TA) 50-57; R of Usworth 53-57; V of Padiham w Higham 57-68; Clitheroe Dio Blackb from 68; RD of Burnley 65-68; Whalley from 68; Hon Can of Blackb Cathl from 79. *St Mary's Vicarage, Clitheroe, Lancs.* (Clitheroe 23317)

HUDSON, John Leonard. b 44. K Coll Lon and Warm AKC 66. **d** 67 **p** 68 Wakef. C of Dodworth Dio Wakef 67-70; Prec of Wakef Cathl 70-73; V of Ravensthorpe 73-80; Royston Dio Wakef from 80. *Royston Vicarage, Barnsley, S Yorks S71 4QZ.* (Barnsley 722410)

HUDSON, John Peter. b 42. K Coll Lon and Warm AKC and Jelf Pri 64. **d** 65 **p** 66 Dur. C of S Shields 65-68; Chap RN from 68. *c/o Ministry of Defence, Lacon House, Theobalds Road, WC1X 8RY.*

HUDSON, John Richard Keith. b 35. Late Exhib of St Pet Coll Ox BA (2nd cl Engl) 60, MA 64. Linc Th Coll 60. **d** 62 **p** 63 Lich. C of Tettenhall Wood 62-65; Chap Linc Dioc Tr Coll and L Pr Dio Linc 65-72; w C of E Bd of Educn 72-73. *PO Box 588, Wagga Wagga, NSW, Australia 2650.*

HUDSON, John Stuart. b 34. K Coll Lon and Warm AKC 59. **d** 60 **p** 61 Cov. C of St Pet Cov 60-63; Rugby 63-64; C-in-c of H Trin Rugby 64-67; V of Willenhall Dio Cov from 67. *Willenhall Vicarage, Coventry, W Midl.* (Coventry 303266)

HUDSON, Leslie William George. b 11. Em Coll Sktn 34. **d** 39 **p** 40 Calg. Miss Rocky Mountain Ho 39-41; I of Delburne w Elnora 41-42; Lacombe w Rimbey 42-46; C of St Jas Milton 46-50; PC of Derry Hill 50-69; V of Frampton 69-77; V of Sydling 69-77; Perm to Offic Dios Ex, Sarum and B & W from 77. *Melness, New Road, Combe St Nicholas, Chard, Somt.* (Chard 3447)

HUDSON, Canon Raymond Mansfield Harry. Univ of Melb BA 30. Ridley Coll Melb ACT ThL 23. **d** 23 **p** 24 Melb. C of St Steph Richmond 23-26; Priv Chap to Bp of Wang Warden of St Columb's Hall Wang and R of Milawa 26-29; C of St Jas and St John Miss Melb 29-34; I of St Matt Geelong 35-37; St Steph Richmond 37-49; V of Ivanhoe 49-64; Can of Melb 49-69; Can (Emer) from 70; V of Deepdene 64-69. *4 Carlyle Street, Hawthorne East, Vic, Australia 3123.* (03-82 5304)

HUDSON, Thomas Bernard. b 16. Late Scho of Ch Coll Cam BA 38, MA 42. Chich Th Coll 38. **d** 40 **p** 41 Chelmsf. C of St Edm Forest Gate 40-42; St Matt Sheff 42-49; St Paul Arbourthorne Sheff 49-50; L to Offic Dio Madag 50-68; Dioc Chan Madag 52-68; Tam 69-76; Regr 70-76; Prin of St Paul's Coll Ambat 52-66; P-in-c of Ampahomanitra 67-72; Sahavato 67-72; Exam Chap to Bp of Tam 70-76; Chan of Diego S 70-76; C of St Jas Conv Distr Owton Manor Hartlepool 77-81; Hon C of Lavender Hill Dio S'wark from 81. *The Ascension Clergy House, Pountney Road, SW11 5TU.* (01-228 5340)

HUDSON, Thomas George. b 32. Trin Coll Dub BA and Div Test 54. **d** 55 **p** 56 Connor. C of St Matt Belf 55-58; Ch Ch Belf 58-60; Carlow 60-61; I of Hackestown Dio 61-69; Kinneigh U 69-72; Monasterevan Dio Kild from 72. *Rectory, Monasterevan, Co Kildare, Irish Republic.*

HUDSON, Trevor. b 32. Univ of Dur BA 56. Cranmer Hall, Dur. **d** 58 **p** 59 Sheff. C of St Mary Doncaster 58-62; Attercliffe w Carbrook Sheff (in c of St Alb Darnall) 62-64; V of Stannington 64-78; St Jo Evang Abbeydale Dio Sheff from 78. *Abbeydale Vicarage, Dore, Sheffield, S17 3LA.* (Sheff 360786)

HUDSON, Wilfred. b 23. St Jo Coll Dur BA 49. **d** 51 **p** 52 Sheff. C of St Mary Doncaster 51-56; V of Brampton Bierlow 56-64; Anston 64-74; V of Woodsetts 64-74; St Andr Sharrow City and Dio Sheff from 74. *45 St Andrew's Road, Sheffield, S11 9AL.* (Sheffield 550533)

HUDSON, Wilfrid. b 14. St Jo Coll Dur BA 36, Dipl Th 37, MA 39. **d** 37 **p** 39 Newc T. C of Cramlington 37-41; C-in-c 41-44; C-in-c of St Oswald's Conv Distr Newc T 44-49; CMS Area Sec Dios Liv Man and S & M 49-54; Ches 51-54; Gen Perm to Offic 49-67; Asst Home Sec CMS N Prov 54-67; Area Sec Dio Sheff 54-67; Wakef 54-62; Southw 62-67; L to Offic Dio Sheff 63-67; V of Goole 67-79; RD of Snaith 67-79; Hon Can of Sheff 67-79; Can (Emer) from 79. *11 Dale Grove, Leyburn, N Yorks, DL8 5JG.* (Wensleydale 23466)

HUDSON, Wilfrid Reginald. Clifton Th Coll 48. St Aid Coll 49. **d** 51 **p** 52 Liv. C of Em Fazakerley 51-55; St Jo Evang Heatherlands Parkstone 55-58; V of Hatherleigh 58-63; St Mark Scarisbrick 63-78; Chap New Hall Hosp 63-78; Surr 63-78; P-in-c of Witheridge 78-79; Thelbridge 78-79; Creacombe 78-79; Meshaw 78-79; W w E Worlington 78-79; V of Witheridge, Thelbridge, Creacombe, Meshaw and E and W Worlington Dio Ex from 79. *Witheridge Vicarage, Tiverton, Devon, EX16 8AE.* (Witheridge 535)

HUDSPITH, Edward. St Jo Coll Dur BA 33, MA 36. **d** 34 **p** 35 Newc T. C of St Silas Byker 34-36; Wellington w Eyton 36-40; C-in-c of St Andr Whitehall Pk 41-42; V of St Thos Kensal Town 42-47; Asst Master St Aubyn's Sch Tiverton 47-48; Scunthorpe Gr Sch 49-56; R of Gaulby w K Norton and L Stretton 56-62; Eastling 62-77. *38 All Saints Close, Whitstable, Kent, CT5 1SD.* (Whitstable 264814)

HUDSPITH, Ernest. b 26. Univ of Birm Dipl Th 64. Qu Coll Birm 61. **d** 64 **p** 65 Southw. PV of St Mary Virg Cathl Southw 64-67; Prec Gibr Cathl 67-68; C of Twickenham Dio Lon from 69. *St Mary's Flat, Riverside, Twickenham, Middx.* (01-892 6012)

HUELIN, Gordon. b 19. Univ of Lon BD 42, MTh 47, PhD 55. FKC 78. **d** 42 **p** 43 Lon. C of All SS Fulham 42-44; St Luke Battersea 44-50; All H Barking-by-the-Tower 50-52; C-in-c of St Bart Gray's Inn Road Lon and Chap Lon Ho 52-59; Dep Min Can of St Paul's Cathl Lon 55-63; External Lect Univ of Lon from 56; St Antholin Lect Lon 57-60; Commiss Windw Is 58-79; Lect K Coll Lon from 59; M of Senate Univ of Lon 60-80; Prof of Div Gresham Coll 62-67; V of St Marg Pattens City and Dio Lon from 63; Exam Chap to Bp of Lon 76-81. *2 South Square, Gray's Inn, WC1.* (01-242 4018 and 01-623 6630)

HUENCHUNIR, Alberto. **d** 67 **p** 72 Chile. P Dio Chile. *Casilla 4, Cholchol, Chile, S America.*

HUETHER, Canon David Gilbert. Univ of Tor BA 36, Wycl Coll Tor Lth 38. **d** 38 Bp Beverley for Tor **p** 39 Athab. C of Goldfields 38; R 38-41; C of Ascen Hamilton 41-43; I of Palmerston w Rothesay and Drayton 43-47; R of Port Dalhousie 47-49; H Trin Hamilton 49-65; Dunnville 65-73; Hon Can of Ch Ch Cathl Hamilton Ont from 65; R of Ch Ch Niagara Falls 73-78; P Assoc of St Mary Hamilton Dio Niag from 78. *771 Hyde Road, Burlington, Ont, Canada.* (416-634 8301)

HUETT, Basil George Pringle. b 19. Univ of Lon BA 39. Univ of Man BD 42. Roch Th Coll. **d** and **p** 62 Roch. Industr Chap Dio Roch and C of Erith 62-72. *c/o Hazelcroft, Stonehouse Road, Halstead, Kent.*

HUFFAM, Edward Valentine. **d** 68 **p** 71 Perth. L to Offic Dio Perth 68-71; Chap at Dharan Dio Jer 71-74; R of E Claremont w Graylands and Mt Claremont 74-78; L to Offic Dio Murray from 79. *35 Woodside Road, Nairne, S Australia 5252.*

HUFFTON, Harry Valentine. Univ of Rang BA (2nd cl Phil) 26. Bp's Coll 27. Serampore Coll BD 31. **d** and **p** 30 Rang. Asst Chap Rang Cathl 30; Maymyo 30-31; St Phil E Rang 31-34; C of St Mary Newington 34-36; Rly Chap Dio Rang 36-42; Chap Sialkot 44; Lahore Cantonment w Ferozapore 45; Sialkot w Jheleun 46; Razmak 47; Hon CF 47; St John Rang 50-52; Prin St John's Sch 48-52; Regr Dio Rang

49-56; V of H Trin Cathl Rang 52-67; Hon Can of Rang 54-67. *42 Tamwe Road, Kyaukmyaung, Rangoon, Burma.*

HUGGETT, Barry David. Moore Th Coll Syd ACT ThL 62. **d** 62 **p** 63 Syd. C of Panania Provisonal Distr 62; Baulkham Hills 63-64; R of Port Hedland 64-65; NSW Sec Bush Ch Aid S 66-72; L to Offic Dio Syd 66-72; Dioc Dir of Information Melb from 72. *46 Mortimore Street, Moorabbin, Vic, Australia 3189.* (03-97 4463)

HUGGETT, David John. b 34. Univ of Lon BSc (1st cl Eng) 56. Univ of Southn PhD 59. Clifton Th Coll 64. **d** 67 Sarum **p** 68 Sherborne for Sarum. C of St Jo Evang Heatherlands Parkstone 67-70; H Sepulchre Cam 70-73; R of St Nich Nottm Dio Southw from 73. *30 Barrack Lane, The Park, Nottingham, NG7 1AN.* (nottm 411383)

HUGGETT, John Victor James. b 39. Univ of Dur BA (2nd cl Gen) 64. Tyndale Hall, Bris 64. **d** 66 **p** 67 Chich. C of Hailsham 66-69; St Geo Worthing 69-71; Woking 71-73; Buckhurst Hill 73-76; V of Meltham Mills 76-79; Wilshaw 76-79; Hon C Skelmanthorpe 79-81. *88 Woodlands Way, Southwater, Horsham RH13 7DR.* (Southwater 731819)

HUGGILL, Cyril Howard. b 20. St Cath S Ox BA (3rd cl Engl Lang and Lit) 42, MA 46. AKC (1st cl) 44. **d** 44 **p** 45 Ches. C of Macclesfield 44-47; Chap RNVR 47-49; C of St Steph Prenton 49-51; R of Delamere 51-66; RD of Middlewich 61-65; Exam Chap to Bp of Ches 63-65; to Bp of Derby 66-70; Proc Conv Ches 64-66; Chap and Lect bp Lonsdale Coll of Educn Derby 66-70; V of Hartington 70-76; Biggin 70-76; Goostrey Dio Derby from 76. *Goostrey Vicarage, Crewe, Chesh.* (Holmes Chapel 32109)

HUGGILL, Ven Geoffrey Richard. Univ of Sask BA 56, Em Coll Sktn LTh 56 BD 64. **d** 56 **p** 57 Sktn. I of Meota 56-58; St Mark Sktn 58-65; Rosthern 62-65; Dioc Sec and Treas Dio Skin from 65; Hon Can of Sktn 67-70; I of Rosthern 69-71; Pike Lake 69-71; Archd of Sktn from 70. *1406-11th Street East, Saskatoon, Sask, Canada.* (244-5651)

HUGGINS, Canon Allan Thomas. d 67 **p** 68 Gippsld. C of Leongatha 67-69; Warragul Dio Gippsld from 69; P-in-c of Neerim S 69-72; R of Orbost 72-74; Prec of St Paul's Cathl Sale 74-76; Dioc Educn Officer Dio Gippsld 74-79; R of Traralgon Gippsld from 79; Can of Gippsld from 81. *7 Burns Street, Traralgon, Vic, Australia 3844.*

HUGGINS, Ven Arthur Hoskins. Codr Coll Barb 54. **d** 57 Barb for Windw Is **p** 58 Windw Is. C of St Geo Grenada 57-60; P-in-c of St Andr Grenada 60-61; R of H Trin Georgetn 61-66; St Patr Grenada 66-70; Dean of Kingstown Cathl St Vincent 70-73; Archd of Grenada from 73; R of St Geo Grenada and VG Dio Windw Is from 73; Can of Kingstown Cathl from 73. *St George's Rectory, Grenada, W Indies.* (2169)

HUGGINS, Philip James. b 48. Monash Univ Vic BEcon 70. **d** 77 Melb. C of Ch Ch Maryborough 77-81; Perm to Offic Dio Melb from 81. *Olsen Road, Nar Nar Goon North, Vic, Australia 3812.*

HUGGINS, Robert William Lynton. b 01. St Jo Coll Dur BA 34, MA 37. **d** 34 **p** 35 Man. C of Facit 34-36; Haslingden 37-40; V of H Trin Colne 40-58; Stalmine 58-68; Perm to Offic Dio Lich from 68. *Black and White House, Blymhill, Shifnal, Shropshire.*

HUGH, Very Rev Fabian Woolcott. b 32. Em & St Chad Sktn LTh 69. **d** and **p** 69 Edmon. I of Barrhead 69-73; R of St Mary Edmon 73-79; Dean and R of St Jas Cathl Peace River Dio Athab from 79; Abp's Commiss from 79. *Box 545, Peace River, Alta, Canada.* (624 2743)

HUGH, Hope. d 36 **p** 37 Lab. C of St Thos Cathl Kuching 36-37; P-in-c of Lundu 37-56. *c/o Bishop's House, Kuching, Sarawak.*

HUGHBOY, Sam. b 17. **d** 74 **p** 75 Moos. C of St Mark East Main Dio Moos from 74. *St Mark's Church, East Main PQ, via Moosonee, Ont., Canada.*

HUGHES, Alan. b 46. Edin Th Coll 71. **d** 74 **p** 75 Edin. C of St Cuthb Colinton Edin 74-76; P-in-c of Wester Hailes and Baberton 76-78; C of Marske-in-Cleveland 78-81; V of New Marske Dio York from 81. *10 Allendale Tee, New Marske, Cleve, TS11 8HN.* (0642 484833)

HUGHES, Alan. b 34. St D Coll Lamp BA 54. St Mich Coll Llan 58. **d** 60 **p** 61 Llan. C of Aberavon 60-62; Chap RAF 62-66; CF from 66. *Address temp unknown.*

HUGHES, Albert Ashbden. b 10. Univ of Wales, BA 37. St Mich Coll Llan 38. **d** 39 Bp Wentworth-Shields for Ban **p** 40 Ban. C of Llangeinwen w Llangaffo 39-42; TCF 43-44; C of Llanfachraeth 42-45; Llandegai 45-49; R of Blaina 49-55; V of Harlech 55-58; H Trin Coldhurst Oldham 58-64; Chap Oldham and Distr Gen Hosp 57-64; PC of Goostrey 64-68; V 68-76; Perm to Offic Dio Ches from 76. *12 Park Mount Drive, Macclesfield, Chesh, SK11 8NT.* (Macclesfield 24483)

HUGHES, Andrew Terrell. b 29. Univ of Bris BA (2nd cl) 56. Coll of Resurr Mirfield, 64. **d** 66 **p** 67 B & W. C of St Sav Weston-s-Mare 66-70; Yeovil Dio B & W 70-76; Team V from 76. *97 Preston Road, Yeovil, Somt.* (Yeovil 5771)

HUGHES, Arnold Geoffrey. b 25. St Jo Coll Auckld 77. **d** 78 **p** 79 Dun. Hon C of Gore 78-81; C of All SS w Port Chalmers Dio Dun from 81. *9 Scotia Street, Port Chalmers, NZ.* (8187)

HUGHES, Arthur Lewis. b 36. **d** 68 **p** 69 St A. C of Holywell 68-71; Lect St Mary Watford 71-75; V of Thornton-in-Lonsdale w Burton-in-Lonsdale Dio Bradf from 75. *Vicarage, Burton-in-Lonsdale, Carnforth, Lancs, LA6 3JZ.* (Bentham 61579)

HUGHES, Arthur William Ronald. b 14. Ch Coll Cam (3rd cl Engl Trip pt 1) 35, BA 36 (3rd cl Eng Trip pt 2) MA 40. St Mich Coll Llan 37. **d** 39 **p** 41 St A. C of Rhosddu 39-40; Minera 40-42; Wrexham 42-49; R of Llangynyw 49-53; St John Moston 53-57; V of Coalbrookdale 57-67; Arthog 67-74; R of Machynlleth w Llanwrin 74-77. *2 Erw Goch, Waun Fawr, Aberystwyth, Dyfed, SY23 3AZ.* (0970 3779)

HUGHES, Bernard Patrick. b 35. Dipl Th (Lon) 64. Oak Hill Th Coll 62. **d** 65 **p** 66 Lon. C of St Matt Fulham Dio Lon 65-69; Hon C from 69; Chap St Steph Chelsea, St Mary Abbots Kens and W Fever Hosps Fulham 69-81. *9 Walham Grove, SW6.* (01-385 1348)

HUGHES, Bertram Arthur Edwin. b 23. Clifton Th Coll 64. **d** 66 **p** 67 B & W. C of St Jas Taunton 66-68; St Luke Ramsgate 68-70; R of Belmont Perth 70-75; P-in-c of Swanton Abbot w Skeyton Nor 75-80; Scottow Nor 75-80; R of Franklin Dio Tas from 80. *Rectory, Ranelagh, Tasmania 7108.* (002 64 1017)

HUGHES, Christopher Clarke. b 40. ALCD 65 (LTh from 74). **d** 65 **p** 66 Ex. C of Broadclyst 65-68; Chenies w L Chalfont 68-70; Team V in Lyd Valley Team 70-74; V of Buckland Monachorum Dio Ex from 74. *Buckland Monachorum Vicarage, Yelverton, Devon.* (Yelverton 2227)

HUGHES, David Anthony. b 25. Trin Coll Cam BA 48, MA 55. Linc Th Coll 74. **d** 76 **p** 77 Linc. C of St Botolph Boston 76-78; R of Graffoe Dio Linc from 78. *Wellingore Vicarage, Lincoln, LN5 0JF.* (Linc 810246)

HUGHES, David Frederick. b 38. St Francis Coll Brisb 77. **d** 78 **p** 79 Brisb. C of St Luke Toowoomba 78-80; V of Jandowae Dio Brisb from 80. *Vicarage, Market Street, Jandowae, Queensland, Australia 4410.* (074-68 5383)

HUGHES, David Harwood. b 09. Univ of Wales BA (2nd cl Engl Hons) 30. St Mich Th Coll Llan 31. **d** 32 **p** 33 Llan. C of St D Ton Pentre 32-36; Llantrisant Glam 36-40; CF (EC) 40-46; V of Penrhiwceiber 47-50; Winterbourne St Martin 50-69; Chap HM Pris Dorchester 51-69; R of Winterbourne Monkton 55-69; V of Thorncombe 69-75. *54 Newstead Road, Bournemouth, BH6 3HL.*

HUGHES, David Howard. d 79 **p** 80 St A. C of Llanrhos Dio St A from 79. *36 Llandudno Road, Penrhyn Bay, Llandudno, Gwynedd, LL30 3HA.*

HUGHES, David Michael. b 41. BD (Lon) 67. Oak Hill Th Coll 63. **d** 68 **p** 69 Roch. C of St John Tunbridge Wells 68-73; St Thos Crookes Sheff 73-81; V of Normanton Dio Wakef from 81. *Vicarage, High Street, Normanton, W Yorks.* (Wakefield 893100)

HUGHES, David Robert. Univ of Wales BA 29. St Mich Th Coll Llan 29. **d** 31 Ban **p** 33 St A for Ban. C of Maentwrog w Festiniog 31-39; R of Aberffraw w Llangwyfan 39-60; V of Llanerchymedd w Rhodogeidio and Gwredog 60-70; V of Llangwyllog w Coedana 67-71. *98 Fferam Estate, Benllech, Anglesey, L74 8RP.* (Tynygongl 2554)

HUGHES, Donald John Michael. McGill Univ Montr BA 48, BD 63. Montr Dioc Th Coll LTh 63. **d** 62 **p** 63 Montr. C of Ch of Ascen Montr 62; Bp's Miss S Shore PQ 63-64; I of Arundel 64-66; Hon C of St Barn Ott 66-67; St Matt City and Dio Queb from 67; Hd Relig Services Dept of Educn Quebec from 67. *1585 Mgr Taché, Sainte Foy, Quebec 10, Canada.*

HUGHES, Douglas. b 25. Univ of Lon BD and ALCD 54. **d** 54 **p** 55 Liv. C of Ravenhead 54-57; Bunbury 57-60; V of Cotmanhay and Shipley 60-68; R of Risley 68-77; P-in-c of Horsley Dio Derby from 77. *Horsley Vicarage, Derby, DE2 5BR.* (Derby 880284)

HUGHES, Earl James. Moore Th Coll Syd ACT ThL (2nd cl) 53. **d** and **p** 54 Syd. C of W Manly 54-55; R of Wallerawang 55-57; Chap Rose River Miss 57-69; Numbulwar Miss 69-72; L to Offic Dio Armid 72-73. *c/o Diocesan Registry, Box 198, Armidale, NSW, Australia.*

HUGHES, Edward Marshall. b 13. Univ of Lon Wordsworth Pri 33, BD and AKC (1st cl) 35, MTh 49, PhD (Th) 53. Cudd Coll 35. **d** 36 **p** 37 Cant. C of St Martin w St Paul Cant 36-41; Chap RAFVR 41; Bearsted 41-46; V of Woodnesborough 46-52; Chap St Bart Hosp Sandwich 47-52; Warden St Pet Th Coll Kingston Ja 52-61; Exam Chap to Bp of Ja 53-61; Can Missr of Ja 55-61; Ed *Jamaica Churchman* 55-61; Visiting Lect McGill Univ Montr 57; Fell St Aug Coll Cant 61-65; L to Offic Dio Cant 61-65; V of St Aug Croydon 65-71; Proc Conv Cant 66-75; Exam Chap to Abp of Cant 67-75; Commiss Ja from 68; V of Dover Dio Cant from 71; Surr from 71; Chap to HM the Queen from 73; RD of Dover

74-81. *Vicarage, Taswell Street, Dover, Kent, CT16 1SE.* (Dover 206842)

HUGHES, Elfed. b 53. Univ Coll Cardiff BD 75. St Mich AA Llan 71. **d** 77 Llan **p** 78 Bp Reece for Llan. C of Skewen 77-80; V of Ystradyfodwg 80-81; P-in-c of Conv Distr of Pentre Dio Llan from 81. *St Peter's Vicarage, 1 Maindy Grove, Ton Pentre, Rhondda, Mid Glam.*

HUGHES, Canon Elias Edgar. b 22. Univ of Wales BA 49. Coll of Resurr Mirfield. **d** 51 **p** 52 Ban. C of Dolgelley 51-56; V of Blaenau Ffestiniog 56-64; RD of Ardudwy 62-64; R of Llanfairmathafarneithaf w Llanbedrgoch 64-76; Dolgellau w Llanfachraeth and Brithdir w Bryncoedifor (w Llanelltud from 77) Dio Ban from 76; Can of Ban Cathl from 78; Surr from 80; RD of Ystumaner from 81. *Rectory, Dolgellau, Gwyn, LL40 2YW.* (Dolgellau 422225)

HUGHES, Canon Evan Arthur Bertram. b 25. St D Coll Lamp BA (2nd cl Hist) 48 LTh 50. **d** 50 St D **p** 51 Bp R W Jones for Llan. C of Abergwili w Llanfihangel-uwch-Gwili 50-53; Llanelly 53-58; CMS Tr Coll 58-59; CMS Miss at Taljhari 59-62; Bhag 63-69; Archd of Bhag 65-66; Patna 66-69; C of Llanstadwell CMS Miss Lahore 73; V of Johnston w Steynton 74-80; Newcastle Emlyn (w Llandyfriog and Troedyraur from 81) Dio St D from 80; Can of St D Cathl from 80. *Vicarage, Newcastle Emlyn, Dyfed, SA38 9LL.* (Emlyn 710385)

HUGHES, Evan Emrys. b 05. St D Coll Lamp BA 37. **d** 37 **p** 38 Llan. C of Dowlais 37-40; CF (EC) 40-45; C-in-c of St Jos Cwmaman 46-48; PC of Garw Valley 48-53; R of Llanwern w Bishton 53-57; Huntsham 57-62; R of Clayhanger 57-62; PC of Petton Chap 57-62; RD of Cullompton 61-62; V of Coxley 62-71; V of Godney 62-71; Perm to Offic Dio Heref from 76. *9 Alton Close, Ross-on-Wye, Herefs, HR9 5LP.*

HUGHES, Evan Thomas. b 08. Univ of Lon BD 50. FCII 36. **d** 47 **p** 48 Chelmsf. C of St Mary Becontree 47-50; V of St Pet Rushden 50-55; St Giles Northn 55-64; Chap Northn Gen Hosp 55-64; Can (Non-res) of Pet 57-64; Sen Lect and Chap St Mary's Coll Cheltm 64-71; Perm to Offic Dio Derby from 73. *197 Allestree Lane, Allestree, Derby, DE3 2PF.* (Derby 556602)

HUGHES, George Edward. Univ of Glas MA (1st cl Phil) 40, 1st cl Post-graduate Ment Phil 41. **d** 49 **p** 50 Ban. L to Offic at Glanadda w Penrhosgarnedd 49-51; Lect in Phil at Univ Coll of N Wales 49-51; Prof of Phil Vic Univ Wel from 51; L to Offic Dio Wel from 51. *Victoria University, Wellington, NZ.*

HUGHES, Geraint Morgan Hugh. b 34. Keble Coll Ox BA 58, MA 62. St Mich Coll Llan. **d** 59 **p** 60 Swan B. C of Gorseinon 59-63; Oystermouth 63-68; R of Llanbadarn Fawr w Llandegley and Llanfihangel Rhydithon 68-76; Llandrindod w Cefnllys Dio Swan B from 76. *Rectory, Llandrindod Wells, Powys.* (Llandrindod Wells 2043)

HUGHES, Gerald Thomas. b 30. BD (Lon) 63. Qu Coll Birm 72. **d** 72 **p** 73 Cov. Dir of Relig Stud Rugby Sch 72-79; Ho Master 78-80; P-in-c of Leamington Hastings and Birdingbury Dio Cov from 80; Dioc Educn Officer Dio Cov from 80. *Leamington Hastings Vicarage, Rugby, Warws, CV23 8DY.* (Marton 632455)

HUGHES, Gwilym Berw. b 42. St Mich Coll Llan 65. **d** 68 **p** 69 Ban. C of Conway w Gyffin 68-71; V of Llandinorwic 71-75; Team V of Llandudno 75-80; V of Dwygyfylchi Dio Ban from 80. *Vicarage, Penmaenmawr, Gwyn, LL34 6BN.* (Penmaenmawr 3300)

HUGHES, Gwilym Evans. b 24. **d** 66 St A **p** 67 Swan B for St A. C of Denbigh 66-69; V of Llawr-y-Bettws w Bettws-Gwerfil-Goch and Dinmael 69-72; V of Brymbo and Bwlchgwyn 72-77; Dyserth and Trelawnyd and Cwm 77-80; Perm to Offic Dio St A from 80. *Bryn Haul, Castle Road, Chirk, Wrexham.* (Chirk 773236)

HUGHES, Gwilym Frank. b 13. St D Coll Lamp BA 35. **d** 39 **p** 40 Ban. C of Llanengan w Llangian 39-42; Abergele 42-49; R of Pont Robert (w Pont Dolanog from 53) 49-57; Llanrwst 57-67; V of Prestatyn 67-78; Can of St A Cathl 74-78; RD of St Asaph 76-78. *59 Moel Gron, Mynydd Isa, Mold, Clwyd.*

HUGHES, Gwilym Thomas. b 09. Late Exhib and Scho of St D Coll Lamp BA (2nd cl Hist) 33. Linc Th Coll 33. **d** 35 Llan for Ban **p** 36 Ban. C of St D Glanadda w Penrhosgarnedd 35-37; Llanengan w Llangian 37-41; V of Llandrygarn w Bodwrog 41-44; R of Llangynhafal w Llangwyfan 44-67; RD of Dyffryn Clwyd 66-70; Warden and R of Ruthin w Llanrhydd 67-70; V of Llantysilio 70-72; Llanarmon-Dyffryn-Ceiriog w Llansantffraid-Glyn-Ceiriog and Pontfadog 72-79. *23 Penycae, Gobowen, Oswestry, Salop.* (Oswestry 62142)

HUGHES, Gwyndaf Morris. b 36. St D Coll Lamp BA 57. St Mich Coll Llan. **d** 59 St A for Ban. **p** 60 Ban. C of Glanogwen 59-62; Chap RN 62-78; R of Llanfair-Pwllgwyngyll w Penmynydd Dio Ban from 78. *Rectory, Llanfair-PG, Gwyn, LL61 5YH.* (Llanfairpwll 714244)

HUGHES, Canon Harold Mervyn. b 13. St D Coll Lamp BA 34. **d** 37 Glouc **p** 38 Tewkesbury for Glouc. C of St Cath Glouc 37-40; C-in-c of Churchdown 40; CF (EC) 40-46; V of Hucclecote 46-78; Hon Can of Glouc from 72. *13 Woodland Close, Upton St Leonards, Gloucester.*

HUGHES, Canon Henry. b 18. Kelham Th Coll 35. **d** 41 **p** 42 Man. C of St Aug Tonge Moor 41-45; All SS Wigston Magna 45-50; V of St Luke Holbrooks Dio Cov from 50; Hon Can of Cov from 73; M Gen Syn Cov 75-80. *St Luke's Vicarage, Rotherham Road, Holbrooks, Coventry, Warws.* (Coventry 88604)

HUGHES, Henry Charles William. b 30. Roch Th Coll 59. **d** 61 **p** 62 Chelmsf. C of Em Forest Gate w St Pet Upton Cross 61-64; St Barn Woodford 64-72; Publ Pr Dio Chelmsf from 72. *99 St Anthony's Drive, Chelmsford, Essex, CM2 9EH.* (Chelmsford 65230)

HUGHES, Henry James Cecil. **d** 34 Lon for Col **p** 35 Willoch. M of Bush Bro Quorn 34-36; Perm to Offic Dio Adel 36-37; C of Unley 37-38; P-in-c of Kangaroo I 38-41; Mid Yorke Peninsula Miss 41-43; R of Willunga 43-54; N Benfleet w Nevendon Essex 55-59; Balhanna S Austr 59-65; V of Ford End 65-66; P-in-c of Norton Summit 66-67; R of Angaston 67-70; L to Offic Dio Adel from 70. *115 Military Road, Tennyson, S Australia 5022.* (356-9487)

HUGHES, Ven Hubert Benjamin William. b 13. St D Coll Lamp BA (2nd cl Hist) 37. **d** 38 **p** 39 Lon. C of St Mary Hornsey 38-40; Devynock w Rhydybriw 40-42; CF (EC) 42-47; C-in-c of Llandefalle 47-52; C-in-c of Llyswen 50-52; V of St Thos Swansea 52-58; Llangyfelach w Morriston Dio Swan B 58-71; Morriston 71-79; Can of Crickhowell in Brecon Cathl from 69; RD of Cwmtawe 75-79; Prec of Brecon Cathl 76-79; V of St Mark Swansea 79; Archd of Gower from 79. *31 Pantygwydr Road, Uplands, Swansea, W Glam.* (Swansea 298306)

HUGHES, Hugh. b 13. St D Coll Lamp BA 35. St Mich Coll Llan 35. **d** 36 Llan for Ban **p** 37 Ban. C of Llanfaethlu w Llanfwrog 36-41; Holyhead 41-45; V of Dolwyddelan 45-56; R of Llanbeulan w Llangaelog and Talyllyn 56-69; Llaneugrad w Llanallgo and Penrhosilugwy w Llanfihangel Tre'r Beirdd Dio Ban from 73; RD of Twrcelyn from 80. *Rectory, Moelfre, Anglesey, Gwynedd.* (Moelfre 654)

HUGHES, Canon Hywel Maldwyn. b 20. Univ of Wales BA (2nd cl Hons Welsh) 42. St Mich Coll Llan 42. **d** 44 **p** 45 Swan B. C of Llangyfelach w Morriston 44-46; Builth Wells w Alltmaur 46-48; Chap and Min Can of Brec Cathl 48-53; R of Llanveigan w Llanddetty and Glyncollwng 53-59; Ystradgynlais 59-68; Surr from 62; V of Killay Dio Swan B from 68; Can of Brecon from 75; Treas from 81; RD of Clyne from 79. *30 Goetre Fach Road, Killay, Swansea, W Glam.* (Swansea 24233)

HUGHES, Canon Ieuan Delvin Powell. b 10. Univ of Wales BA (2nd cl Phil) 33. St Mich Coll Llan 33. Ripon Hall, Ox 34. **d** 35 **p** 36 Llan. C of Cymmer w Porth 35-38; H Trin Hinckley 38-40; V of Hedworth 40-48; Min of St Chris Conv Distr (Park Estate) Leic 48-51; V of Oadby 51-64; R of Harby 64-74; Surr 56-74; Hon Can of Leic 60-76; Can (Emer) from 76; L to Offic Dio Leic from 75. *1 Hawthorn Close, Old Dalby, Leics.*

HUGHES, Ivor Gordon. b 45. Ripon Coll Cudd 75. **d** 77 **p** 78 Lich. C of Newport 77-79; Children's Educn Adv CMS from 79. *c/o 157 Waterloo Road, SE1 8UU.*

HUGHES, Jack Griffiths. b 15. St Jo Coll Dur BA 37. Oak Hill Th Coll 33. **d** 38 **p** 39 Man. C of Ch Ch Salford 38-42; Brierley Hill 42-45; R of Ch Ch Salford (w St Paul from 65) 45-67; Heaton Mersey 67-80; C-in-c of St Paul Paddington Salford 61-65. *4 Brook Avenue, Heaton Chapel, Stockport, Chesh.*

HUGHES, James Edmund Crowden. b 11. St D Coll Lamp BA 32. St Mich Coll Llan 33. **d** 35 **p** 36 Llan. C of St Mary Seven Sisters 35-37; St Theo Port Talbot 37-44; CF (EC) 44-46; Hon CF 47; V of Llangenny 46-54; Oystermouth 54-80; Can of Brecon Cathl 72-80. *6 Myrtle Terrace, Mumbles, Swansea, SA3 4DT.* (Swansea 66710)

HUGHES, James Webb. b 05. Worc OTC 56. **d** 57 **p** 58 Glouc. C of Bisley w Lypiatt and Eastcombe 57-59; V of Cold Aston w Notgrove (and Turkdean from 67) Dio Glouc from 59. *Cold Aston Vicarage, Cheltenham, Glos, GL54 3BW.* (Bourton-on-the Water 20287)

HUGHES, Canon John Bernard Wyn. b 08. Univ of Lon BA 28, MA 31. St Steph Ho Ox. **d** 32 **p** 33 Southw. C of St Leon Newark 32; Ordsall 32-36; Rusthall 36-41; V of St Jas Elmers End Beckenham 41-55; RD of Beckenham 53-55; R of Northchurch 55-75; Asst RD of Berkhamsted 67-68; RD 68-73; Hon Can of St Alb 72-75; Can (Emer) from 75; Perm to Offic Dio Truro from 75; Dio Ex from 76. *The Shielan, Trekenner, Launceston, Cornw, PL15 9PH.* (Stoke Climsland 580)

HUGHES, John Chester. b 24. St Jo Coll Dur BA 48 (w Distinc), Dipl in Th (w Distinc) 50, Jenkyns Scho 49-50, MA

51. **d** 50 **p** 51 Chelmsf. C of St Sav Westcliff 50-53; Succr of Chelmsf Cathl 53-55; V of St Barn New Humberstone Leic and Chap Towers Hosp Leic 55-61; Croxton Kerrial w Branston-by-Belvoir 61-63; Provost and V of St Martin's Cathl Leic 63-78; Surr from 74; Chap Order of St John of Jer from 74; V of Bringhurst w Gt Easton and Drayton Dio Leic from 78. *Great Easton Vicarage, Market Harborough, Leics, LE16 8SX.* (Rockingham 770279)

HUGHES, John David. St Francis Coll Brisb. **d** 60 **p** 61 Brisb. C of Gympie 61-62; St Luke Toowoomba 62-63; Warwick 63-65; V of Texas 65-68; R of Kilcoy 68-71; St Hilda Perth 71-73; Chap All S Sch Charters Towers Queensld 74-77; R of St John Bulimba City and Dio Brisb from 77. *171 Oxford Street, Bulimba, Queensland, Australia 4171.* (399 1508)

HUGHES, Canon John George. b 35. Late Exhib of Qu Coll Cam 2nd cl Hist Trip pt i 56, BA (2nd cl Hist Trip pt ii) 57, Th Trip pt iii 58 (cl 2 div 1), MA 61. Univ of Leeds PhD 80. Cudd Coll 58. **d** 60 61 Wakef. C of Brighouse 60-63; V of Clifton 63-70; Selection Sec ACCM 70-73; Sen Selection Sec 73-76; Warden St Mich Coll Llan from 76; Lect Univ of Wales 76; Hon Can of Llan Cathl from 80. *St Michael's College, Llandaff, Cardiff, S Glam.* (Cardiff 563379)

HUGHES, John Herbert Vivian. b 28. Late Scho St D Coll Lamp BA (Hist) 51, LTh 53. **d** 53 **p** 54 St D. C of Abergwili w Llanfihangel-uwch-Gwili 53-58; Llanelly 58-62; V of Newchurch w Merthyr 62-71; Abergwili w Llanfihangel-uwch-Gwili Dio St D from 71; Surr from 74. *Abergwili Vicarage, Carmarthen, Dyfed.* (Carmarthen 7239)

HUGHES, John Malcolm. b 47. Univ of Man BSc (2nd cl Phys) 68. Univ of Leeds Dipl Th 70. Coll of Resurr Mirfield. **d** 71 **p** 72 Llan. C of Newton-Nottage 71-78; V of Llanwonno w Ynysybwl Dio Llan from 78. *Vicarage, Heol-y-Plwyf, Ynysybwl, Pontypridd, CF37 3HU.* (Ynysybwl 790340)

HUGHES, John Neville. Jes Coll Ox BA (Mod Hist) 35, MA 40. St D Coll Lamp 35. **d** 38 **p** 40 St D. C of Castlemartin w Warren and St Twynnell 38-41; Bettws w Ammanford 41-44; L Pr Dio St D 44-74; Asst Master Llandovery Coll 44-74; V of Llangadog (w Gwynfe w Llanddeusant from 75) Dio St D from 74. *Vicarage, Llangadog, Dyfed.* (Llangadog 239)

HUGHES, John Patrick. b 41. Oak Hill Th Coll Dipl Th (Lon) 66. **d** 67 **p** 68 St Alb. C of St Andr Eccles Distr Chorley Wood 67-71; St Steph E Twickenham 71-76; Team V of High Wycombe Dio Ox from 76. *St Andrew's House, Hatters Lane, High Wycombe, Bucks.* (H Wycombe 29668)

HUGHES, John Richard Dutton. b 40. Fitzw Ho Cam BA 61, MA 66. Linc Th Coll 62. **d** 64 **p** 65 Chelmsf. C of Tye Green w Netteswell 64-67; L to Offic Dio Liv 68-70; C of Farnworth 70-71; L to Offic Dio Ches 71-73; C of Sandbach Dio Ches from 73. *The View, Clay Lane, Haslington, Crewe, CW1 1SE.* (Crewe 582732)

HUGHES, John Stunt Dickson. b 01. Keble Coll Ox BA 25, MA 48. Cudd Coll. **d** 26 **p** 27 Ox. C of Burnham Bucks 26-31; Shoreham 31-42; V of Washington 42-70. *3 Wye House, Down View Road, W Worthing, Sussex.*

✠ **HUGHES, Right Rev John Taylor.** b 08. CBE 75. Bede Coll Dur BA 31, Dipl in Th (w distinc) 32, MA 35. **d** 31 **p** 32 Dur. Tutor and Asst Chap Bede Coll Dur and L to Offic Dio Dur 31-34; Lect Bede Coll Dur 34-35; C of St John Shildon 34-37; V of St Jas W Hartlepool 37-48; Can Miss of S'wark, Warden of S'wark Dioc Ho Blackheath and of St Sav Coll 48-56; Cons Ld Bp Suffr of Croydon in Westmr Abbey 21 Sept 56 by Abp of Cant; Bps of S'wark; Win; and Cov; Bps Suffr of Woolwich; Dover; Kens; and Kingston T; Bps Hawkes; Leslie; Lang; and Roberts; res 77; Abp's Rep w HM Forces 66-75; Archd of Croydon 67-77. *1 Burgate House, Burgate, Canterbury, Kent, CT1 2HB.*

HUGHES, John William George. b 48. Univ of Wales (Cardiff) Dipl Th 72. St Mich Llan 69. **d** 72 **p** 73 Swan B. C of St Pet Cockett Swansea (in c of St Illtyd's) 72-76; V of Cwmdeuddwr w Nantgwyllt, St Harmon and Llanwrthwl 78-79; St Teilo Caereithin Swansea Dio Swan B from 79. *c/o Caereithin Vicarage, 64 Cheriton Crescent, Portmead, Swansea SA5 5LA.* (0792 583646)

HUGHES, Canon Llewelyn. b 06. Univ of Wales, BA 26. Linc Th Coll 28. **d** 29 **p** 30 Ban. C of Llandysilio 29-31; St Mary Ban 31-34; Chap S Afr Ch Rwy Miss Dio N Rhod 34-37; V of Llanerchymedd w Rhodogeidio and Gwredog 37-47; Chap RNVR 41-46; R of Machynlleth (w Llanwrin from 50) 47-55; V of Abergele 55-56; Wrexham Dio St A 66-71; R 71-73; Cursal Can of St A Cathl 69-74; Can (Emer) from 74. *21 Monmouth Road, Borras Park, Wrexham, Clwyd.*

HUGHES, Canon Malcolm Albert. Bp's Univ Lennox BA 50, LST 60. **d** 60 **p** 61 Ott. C of St Matthias Ott 60-62; R of St Thos Grand Turk 62-65; Dioc Cler Sec Nass 65-66; R of Sandakan 67-71; C of Vaudreuil 70-74; R of Pointe Claire 74-77; Admin Officer Dio Montr from 78; Hon Can of Montr from 78. *1444 Union Avenue, Montreal, PQ, Canada.* (514-845 6211)

HUGHES, Martin Conway. b 40. Ex Coll Ox BA (3rd cl Th) 61, MA 67. Chich Th Coll. **d** 63 **p** 64 S'wark. C of Roehampton 63-67; Addlestone 67-71; V of Burpham Dio Guildf from 71. *Burpham Vicarage, Guildford, Surrey, GU4 7LZ.* (Guildf 68494)

HUGHES, Martyn Lawrence. b 19. Magd Coll Ox BA 42, MA 46. Cho Scho K Coll Cam BA 43, MA 52. Westcott Ho Cam. **d** 44 **p** 45 S'wark. C of St Jo Bapt Eltham 44-46; Chap Yenching Univ Peking 47-50; Warden Student Movement Ho 51-53; Chap of K Coll Cam 53-56; Asst Chap Uppingham Sch 56-61; Chap Harrow Sch 61-73; Hd Relig Stud Coll of Richard Collyer Horsham from 73. *Perriley, Amberley, Arundel, Sussex.*

HUGHES, Michael John Minto. b 50. Univ of Liv MB, ChB 74. Wycl Hall Ox 76. **d** 79 **p** 80 Dur. C of Stranton w W Hartlepool Dio Dur from 79. *41 Arncliffe Gardens, Stranton, Hartlepool, Cleve.*

HUGHES, Owen. b 17. Univ of Wales BA (3rd cl Welsh) 39. St Mich Coll Llan 39. **d** 40 **p** 41 Ban. C of Heneglwys w Trewalchmai 40-42; Llanfairisgaer 42-45; Chap RNVR 45-47; C of Llandudno 47-50; Halsall 50-53; V of St Ann Stanley Liv 53-57; Lydiate 57-62; Wesham 62-70; R of Llanbeulan w Llanfaelog and Talyllyn 70-71; Church Kirk 71-73; V of All SS Oswaldtwistle Dio Blackb from 73. *All Saints' Vicarage, Oswaldtwistle, Accrington, Lancs, BB5 4QA.* (Accr 34755)

HUGHES, Peter John. b 43. Univ of Melb BA 67. ACT Th Scho 70. Trin Coll Melb 64. Ch Ch Ox BPhil 77. **d** and **p** 70 Melb. C of Warrnambool 70-72; St John Croydon 72-74; C of Angl Inner-City Min Melb 74; Perm to Offic Dio Ox 75-77; Chap & Tutor Ripon Coll Cudd 77-79; L to Offic Dio Ox 77-79; Chap Univ of Lon from 79. *2 The Cloisters, Gordon Square, WC1H 0AG.* (01-387 0670)

HUGHES, Philip. b 47. St Jo Coll Nottm 79. **d** 81 Ban. C of Dolgellau Dio Ban from 81. *Ty'r Ficer, Pencefn Road, Dolgellau, Gwyn.* (Dolgellau 123323)

HUGHES, Philip Edgcumbe. Univ of Capetn BA 37, MA 39. DLitt 56. Univ of Lon BD 46. ACT ThD 64. Tyndale Hall Bris 40. **d** 41 **p** 42 S'wark. C of St John Deptford 41-43; in S Afr Ch 43-47; Tutor Tyndale Hall Bris 47-51; Vice-Prin 51-53; Sec Ch S 53-56; C of Mortlake w E Sheen 58-60; in Amer Ch; Commiss Chile from 75. *1565 Cherry Lane, Rydal, PA 19046, USA.*

HUGHES, Philip Stephen. b 34. Univ of Dur BA (2nd cl Th) 59. Coll of Resurr Mirfield, 59. **d** 62 **p** 63 Bris. C of St Greg Horfield 62-66; St Mich AA Bedminster 66-69; P-in-c of St Pet Chippenham Dio Bris 69-71; V from 71. *Vicarage, Lord's Mead, Chippenham, Wilts.* (Chippenham 4835)

HUGHES, Richard Clifford. Pemb Coll Cam BA (2nd cl Hist Trip pt i) 47. **d** 50 **p** 51 S'wark. C of St Anne Wandsworth 50-53; Miss at SA Ch Rly Miss Bulawayo 53-56; Asst P Salisbury Cathl 56-57; Bulawayo Cathl 57-61; R of Que Que 61-65; St Jas Dundee 65-69; St D Pmbg 69-71; Westville Dio Natal from 71; Archd of Pinetown 73-78. *45 Salisbury Avenue, Westville, Natal, S Africa.* (Durban 856149)

HUGHES, Richard Evan. b 1892. Lich Th Coll 26. **d** 28 **p** 29 St A. C of Brymbo 28-30; Llawr-y-Bettws 32-36; V of Rhos-y-Gwalia 36-47; Cilcain 46-53; Llanrhaiadr-ym-Mochnant w Llanarmon Mynydd Mawr 53-61; R of Llanbedr-Dyffryn-Clwyd 61-63; L to Offic Dio St A from 63. *26 Roe Parc, St Asaph, Clwyd.* (St A 583389)

HUGHES, Richard Jeffrey. b 47. St Mich Coll Llan 74. **d** 76 **p** 77 Ban. C of Llanbeblig w Caernarfon 76-78; Team V of Holyhead Dio Ban from 78. *Vicarage, Gors Avenue, Holyhead, Gwyn.*

HUGHES, Richard Millree. b 33. Univ of Wales, BA 56, MA 79. St Mich Coll Llan 56. **d** 58 **p** 59 St A. C of Mold 58-61; V Cho and C of St A Cathl 61-64; V of Towyn 64-67; Asst Master Marlborough Sch Woodstock 77-79; R of Whitchurch Dio Ox from 79. *Rectory, Whitchurch on Thames, Reading, RG8 7DF.* (Pangbourne 3219)

HUGHES, Ven Robert Daniel Pakenham. Coll Ho Ch Ch LTh 52. **d** and **p** 49 Nel. C of All SS Nelson 49-50; V of Ahaura 50-57; Kaikoura 57-64; Stoke 64-77; Greymouth Dio Nel from 77; Archd of Mawhera from 77. *Vicarage, Greymouth, NZ.* (7508)

HUGHES, Robert Elistan-Glodrydd. b 32. Trin Coll Ox BA (2nd cl Th) 54, MA 58. Westcott Ho Cam 55. **d** 57 **p** 58 Cov. C of St Mich Stoke Cov 57-61; Industr Chap at St Mary Woolwich 61-64; Chap Univ of Birm and Publ Pr Dio Birm 64-69; Lodgings Warden and Stud Welfare Adviser Univ of Birm from 69. *32 Kensington Road, Birmingham 29.* (021-472 0686)

HUGHES, Robert Stewart. St Jo Coll Morpeth. **d** 59 **p** 60 Newc. C of Merewether 59-62; Singleton 62-64; Woy Woy 64-66; Adamstown 67; Charlestown 68; Perm to Offic Dio

Newc from 70. *6 Victoria Street, New Lambton, NSW, Australia 2305.*

HUGHES, Rodney Thomas. b 39. Univ of Dur BA 60. St Cath Coll Ox Dipl Th 61. Wycl Hall Ox 60. **d** 62 **p** 63 Edin. C of St Thos Edin 62-65; Harlow New Town w L Parndon 65-67; R of Haworth 67-74; W Knighton w Broadmayne (w Overmoigne and Warmwell and Holworth from 77) Dio Sarum from 74. *Broadmayne Rectory, Dorchester, Dorset.* (Warmwell 852435)

HUGHES, Ven Thomas Bayley. b 16. Univ of Wales, BA 39. St D Coll Lamp 39. **d** 41 **p** 42 Ban. C of St Mich Llanrug 41-43; Llanberis 43-50; R of Llangwnadl w Penllech (and Bryncroes from 51) 50-55; Llanllechid 55-62; Asst Sec Ban Dioc Bd of Finance 59; Sec 60-64; R of Llangefni w Tregaean 62-76; Llanbedr w Llandanwg 76-78; Surr from 67; Can Res of Ban Cathl 71-76; Hon Sec Ban Dioc Conf and Patr Bd 73-76; Archd of Merioneth from 76; R of Maentwrog w Trawsfynydd Dio Ban from 78. *Rectory, Trawsfynydd, Gwyn, LL41 4RY.* (076687-472)

HUGHES, Thomas Ernest. b 10. Edin Th Coll 47. **d** 50 **p** 51 St Andr. C of St Pet Kirkcaldy 50-52; P-in-c of St D Scotstoun Glas 52-56; P-in-c of St John Cranstonhill Glas 53-56; R 56-59; R of St Andr-by-the-Green Glas 56-61; H Trin Paisley 61-69; C of St Steph Acomb York 69-74; V of Stillington and Marton w Moxby and Farlington 74-81. *28 Haxby Road, York, YO3 7JX.* (York 32818)

HUGHES, Canon Thomas Melville. Angl Th Coll of BC LTh 17. **d** 16 Columb for New Westmr **p** 17 New Westmr. C of St Paul Vancouver BC 16-17; Ch Ch Cathl Vic BC 17-21; Wolborough w Newton Abbot 21-22; R of N Saanich w Sidney 22-36; Quamichan w Cowichan 36-49; Hon Can of Ch Ch Cathl Vic 38-62. *1355 Victoria Avenue, Victoria, BC, Canada.*

HUGHES, Timothy Griffith Richard. b 18. AKC and Whichelow Pri 42. **d** 42 **p** 43 Chelmsf. C of St Elisabeth Becontree 42-45; Offic C-in-c of St Nich Elm Pk w S Hornchurch 45-46; V of W Mersea 46-57; R of E Mersea 52-57; Chap Miss to Seamen 57-67; V of Longhorsley 67-81; Perm to Offic Dio Newc from 81. *1 Sedbergh Road, Marden Estate, Tynemouth, T & W.* (Whitley Bay 511052)

HUGHES, Tudor Owen. St D Coll Lamp BA 14. **d** 14 **p** 15 St D. C of St Paul Llanelly 14-18; Llanedy 19-27; V of Llanfihangel-y-Creuddyn w Llantrisant 27-33; Cwmamman 33-49; Surr from 34; V of Llandeilo Fawr w Llandefeisant 49-64; 3rd Cursal Can of St D Cathl 50-64 *The Walk, Llandilo, Dyfed.*

HUGHES, Walter Robin John. b 40. St Francis Coll Brisb 77. **d** 78 **p** 79 Brisb. C of St Luke Ekibin 78-80; V of St Luke Miles Dio Brisb from 80. *Box 80, Miles, Queensld, Australia 4415.*

HUGHES, William James. St Jo Coll Auckld LTh 46. **d** 44 **p** 45 Auckld. C of St Aid Remuera 44-48; V of Kamo Hikurangi 48-55; Helensville 55-60; L to Offic Dio Auckld 60-62; C of New Lynn 62-65; Avondale 65-66; P-in-c of Marsden Miss Distr Dio Auckld 66-71; L to Offic Dio Auckld 71-75; Perm to Offic from 80; Chap N Shore Hosp Auckld 76-80. *12a James Evans Drive, Northcote, Auckland, NZ.*

HUGHES, Canon William Rowland. b 10. St D Coll Lamp BA 35. **d** 35 **p** 36 Llan. C of Michaelston-super-Avon 35-40; Aberdare 40-46; C-in-c of Cwmbach 46-49; V of Clydach Vale 49-51; Pontlottyn 51-63; Llanegryn w Rhoslefain 63-69; Almwch 69-70; R of Amlwch and Rhosybol w Llandyfrydog (w Llanwenllwyfo from 72, Llaneilian from 74, w Llangwyllog w Coedana w Llannerchymedd w Rhodogeidio w Gwredog from 78) 70-80; RD of Twrcelyn 73-80; Hon Can of Ban Cathl from 78. *12 Upper Breeze Hill, Benllech, Anglesey, Gwyn.*

HUGILL, Fred. b 24. St Paul's Coll Grahmstn Dipl Th 78. **d** 78 Pret **p** 79 Bp Stevenson for Pret. C of St Alb Cathl Pret 78-80; R of Ch Ch Pietersburg Dio Pret from 80. *PO Box 343, Pietersburg 0700, S Africa.*

HUGO, Keith Alan. b 41. Univ of Nottm BA 62. Chich Th Coll 62. **d** 64 **p** 65 Wakef. C of Pontefract 64-68; Chesterfield 68-71; V of Allenton and Shelton Lock 71-77; Ed Derby Dioc News 73-77; V of Potterne Dio Sarum from 77; Worton Dio Sarum from 77; Dioc Communications Officer from 77. *Vicarage, Rookes Lane, Potterne, Devizes, Wilts, SN10 5NF.* (0380-3189)

HUHUGU, Harper. St Pet Coll Siota. **d** 53 **p** 57 Melan. P Dio Melan 53-75; Dio Ysabel 75-78. *Marulaon, Russell Islands, Solomon Islands.*

HUI, To Kan. St Pet Hall, Sing 55. **d** 58 **p** 59 Borneo. P Dio Borneo 58-62; Dio Kuch 62-65; Dio Sing from 66. *1716-G Jalan Bukit Merah, Block 113, Singapore 3.*

HUITSON, Christopher Philip. b 45. Keble Coll Ox BA (2nd cl Th) 66, MA 70. Cudd Coll 67. **d** 69 **p** 70 Cant. C of St Sav Croydon 69-71; Social Service Unit St Martin-in-the-Fields Lon 71-73; C of St Pet St Alb 73-77; V of Cople (w Willington from 78) Dio St Alb from 77; P-in-c of Willington 77-78. *Cople Vicarage, Bedford.* (Cardington 431)

HULANA, Ishmael. St Pet Coll Siota 59. **d** 62 **p** 64 Melan. P Dio Melan 62-75; Dio Malaita from 75. *Maarou, Malaita, Solomon Islands.*

HULBERT, Charles Donald. b 09. Linc Th Coll 37. **d** 38 **p** 39 St E. C of Beccles 38-40; R of Halesworth 40-56; Chap RAFVR 42-46; Hon Chap to Bp of St E 54-57; Area Sec BFBS Dios Nor; Ely; and St E 56-58; V of Norton Subcourse 58-62; R of Thurlton w Thorpe next Haddiscoe 58-62; Plaxtol 62-74; Perm to Offic Dio Nor from 75. *31 Holt Road, Weybourne, Holt, Norfolk, NR25 7SU.*

HULBERT, Hugh Forfar. b 22. Univ of Bris BA 49. Tyndale Hall, Bris 46. **d** 50 **p** 51 S'wark. C of Summerstown 50-53; Felixstowe 53-55; Min of St Jas Eccles Distr Collier Row Romford 55-59; Org Sec in SW for CPAS 59-63; V of St Luke Portsea 63-75; H Trin Worthing 75-81; P-in-c of H Trin Conv Distr Hove Dio Chich from 81. *Holy Trinity Parsonage, Blatchington Road, Hove, BN3 3TA.* (Brighton 739870)

HULBERT, John Anthony Lovett. b 40. Trin Coll Cam 2nd cl Hist Trip pt i, 62, BA (2nd cl Hist Trip pt ii) 63, MA 67. Wells Th Coll 64. **d** 66 **p** 67 Portsm. C of H Trin Fareham 66-70; R of St Nich Wickham 70-79; RD of Bp's Waltham 74-79; V of St Andr Bedford Dio St Alb from 79. *Vicarage, St Edmond Road, Bedford, MK40 2NQ.* (Bedford 54234)

HULBERT, Martin Francis Harrington. b 37. Univ of Dur BSc (2nd cl Agr) 58, MA 62. Ripon Hall, Ox 58. **d** 60 **p** 61 Derby. C of Buxton 60-63; Eglingham 63-67; C-in-c of Ascen Loundsley Green Conv Distr 67-71; Frecheville 71-73; Team R (w Hackenthorpe) 73-77; P-in-c of Hathersage Dio Derby from 77; Surr from 80; RD of Bakewell & Eyam from 81. *Hathersage Vicarage, Sheffield, S30 1AB.* (Hope Valley 50215)

HULBURD, Ivan Mitchell. b 13. Worc Coll Ox MA 38. **d** 54 **p** 55 Worc. C of Old Swinford 54-57; Belbroughton (in c of Fairfield) 57-60; V of Bretforton 60-67; R of Hindlip w Martin Hussingtree 67-78. *14 Camp Hill Road, Worcester, WR5 2HE.* (Worc 356192)

HULETT, Peter. b 31. CEng MIMechE 62. Wycl Hall Ox 75. **d** 77 **p** 78 Southw. C of Eastwood 77-80; Tythby w Cropwell Butler Dio Southw from 80. *Granby Vicarage, Nottingham, NG13 9PY.* (Whatton 50774)

HULFORD, Edward John. Univ of BC BA 46. Trin Coll Tor LTh 49. **d** 49 **p** 50 BC. C of Ch Ch Cathl Vic 49-51; St Jas Vancouver 51-57; Chap Haney Correctional Inst 57-60; R of St Jas Vancouver 60-65; Chap Oakalla Pris Farm Dio New Westmr from 65. *5700 Royal Oak Avenue, Burnaby 1, BC, Canada.*

HULL, Lord Bishop Suffragan of. *See* Snelgrove, Right Rev Donald George.

HULL, John Hammond. b 36. Sarum Th Coll 60. **d** 61 Colchester for Chelmsf **p** 62 Chelmsf. C of Gt Clacton w L Holland 61-66; Area Chap Toc H, E Anglia 66-70; Midl Region 70-75; Publ Pr Dio Chelmsf 66-76; Dio Ox from 75; Chap of Toc H HQ Wendover from 75. *Toc H, 1 Forest Close, Wendover, Bucks, HP22 6BT.* (0296-623911)

HULL, Maxwell Stanley. b 38. **d** 76 **p** 77 Armid. C of Ashford, Delungra & Tingha 76-81; Perm to Offic Dio Armid from 81. *Box 40, Inverell, NSW, Australia 2360.*

HULL, Canon Robert Edward Davison. St Chad's Coll Dur BA 40, Dipl Th 41, MA 44. **d** 41 **p** 42 S'wark. C of St Geo Mart Camberwell 41-43; St Bart Brighton 43-45; CF (EC) 45-47; Bp's Chap for Youth Dio Chich 48-50; V of Portfield 50-57; Burgess Hill 57-59; R of Beechworth 59-76; Lect St Columb's Hall Wang from 65; Exam Chap to Bp of Wang from 71; Hon Can of Wang from 72; R of Yackandandah and Kiewa Dio Wang from 76. *Rectory, Yackandandah, Vic, Australia 3749.*

HULL, Russell Medway. St Francis Coll Brisb ACT ThL 60. **d** 59 **p** 60 Bath. C of Cobar 59-61; P-in-c of Tottenham 61-62; R of Tennant Creek 62-64; P-in-c of Brewarrina 64-65; C of Parkes 65-66; R of Trundle 66-69; E Orange 69-72; Perm to Offic Dio Bath from 72. *2 Rhyana Court, Dubbo, NSW, Australia 2783.*

HULLAH, Peter Fearnley. b 49. AKC and BD 71. Cudd Coll 73. **d** 74 Dorchester for Ox **p** 75 Ox. C of Summertown (w Wolvercote from 76) 74-77; Asst Chap St Edw Sch Ox 74-77; Chap Sevenoaks Sch Kent from 77; C of Sevenoaks Dio Roch from 77. *Orchards, Solefields Road, Sevenoaks, Kent.* (Sevenoaks 56710)

HULLETT, Frederick Graham. Univ of Leeds, BA 58. Coll of Resurr Mirfield. **d** 60 Lon **p** 61 Kens for Lon. C of St Pet Acton Green 60-61; W Hackney 61-64; Paddington Green 64-67; Hon C 67-69; Youth worker 67-71; C-in-c of St Aug w St Steph Haggerston 69-73; L to Offic Dio Lon from 73; Tutor Warden Pimlico Youth Centre from 71. *65 St George's Drive, SW1V 4DD.* (01-828 3817)

HULLEY, Frank. b 18. **d** 73 **p** 74 Johann. C of Rosebank Dio Johann from 73. *Box 52139, Saxonwold, Johannesburg 2132, S Africa.* (011-47 3211)

HULME, Lord Bishop Suffragan of. *See* Galliford, Right Rev David George.

HULME, Norman. Kelham Th Coll 50. **d** 54 **p** 55 Blackb. C of St Pet Blackb 54-57; Blakenall Heath 57-59; V of Gannow 59-64; Anwick 64-73; PC of S w N Kyme Dio Linc 64-69; V 69-74; Moulton Dio Linc from 74. *Moulton Vicarage, Spalding, Lincs.* (Holbeach 370203)

HULSE, Arthur. b 20. Univ of Dur BSc 42. Linc Th Coll 46. **d** 47 **p** 48 Lich. C of Cannock (in c of Heath Hayes from 49) 47-54; Dep Chap RAF Hednesford 53-54; V of St John Bury 54-77; Surr 54-77; V of Gt and L Ness Dio Lich from 77. *The Nesses Vicarage, Little Ness, Shrewsbury, SY4 2LG.* (Baschurch 260474)

HULSE, Canon Robert Edgar. Univ of Tor BA 58, MA 63. Wycl Coll Tor BTh 61. **d** 60 Bp Hunt for Tor **p** 62 Tor. C of St Marg Tor 60-64; R of Elora Dio Niag from 64; Hon Can of Niag from 77. *The Rectory, Box 384, Elora, Ont., Canada.* (519-846 9666)

HULSE, William John. Univ of Dur BA 65. Linc Th Coll 65. **d** 67 **p** 68 Dur. C of S Westoe S Shields 67-70; L to Offic Dio Newc T 70-72; C of Far Headingley 72; R of Swillington Dio Ripon from 76. *Swillington Rectory, Leeds, LS26 8DS.* (Leeds 860172)

HUM, Walter. b 08. Univ of Lon BSc (2nd cl Econ) 33. Bps' Coll Cheshunt, 34. MRST 31. **d** 35 **p** 36 Chelmsf. C of Barking (in c of Ascen Eastbury from 36) 35-38; St Ives w Oldhurst and Woodhurst 38-42; V of St Matt Littleport 42-47; Proc Conv Ely 45-47; V of St Edw Holbeck 47-54; All S Leeds 54-74; Perm to Offic Dio Nor 74-77 and from 79; P-in-c of Ringstead 77-79. *9 Peddar's Drive, Hunstanton, Norf.* (Hunstanton 2871)

HUMBLE, Joseph Francis. b 24. Univ Coll Ox BA (3rd cl Th) 54, MA 57. Cudd Coll 54. **d** 56 **p** 57 Cov. C of Rugby 56-61; V of Thurcroft 61-66; Lillington 66-78; CF (TA) 63-67; RD of Leamington 74-78; Chap Miss to Seamen Kowloon Dio Hong from 78. *Missions to Seamen, Middle Road, Kowloon, Hong Kong.* (3-688261)

HUME, Cecil. b 13. Cudd Coll. **d** 55 Dur **p** 56 Jarrow for Dur. C of St Helen Bp Auckland 55-59; V of Newport Yorks 59-67; R of Middleton-on-the-Wolds 67-75; C-in-c of N Dalton 67-70; V 70-75; Kirkby-in-Cleveland 75-78. *100 Weaponess Valley Road, Scarborough, N Yorks.* (Scarborough 70258)

HUME, Ernest. b 45. Linc Th Coll 77. **d** 79 **p** 80 Derby. C of Ilkeston 79-81; Sheff Manor Team Min City and Dio Sheff 81-82; Team V from 82. *St Paul's Vicarage, East Bank Road, Sheffield, S2 2AD.* (Sheff 398533)

HUME, Leslie Paul. b 09. Kelham Th Coll 27. M SSM 32. **d** 32 **p** 33 Liv. C of St Nich Liv 32-37; Chap Kelham Th Coll 37-41; St Geo Nottm 41-43; Kroonstad Miss 43-47; Modderpoort and Warden SSM 47-49; Dir of Teyateyaneng Miss 50-51; Modderpoort Miss 51-52; Commiss Basuto 52-62; Bloemf 53-62; Melan 56-62; Dir of S of Sacred Miss and L to Offic Dio Southw 52-62; Teyateyaneng Miss 62-66; R of St Phil Bloemf 66-73; P-in-c of St Jas Ladybrand 73-76; Warden of Commun of St Laur Belper from 78. *SSM Priory, Willen, Milton Keynes, Bucks, MK15 9AA.*

HUME, Paul Morton. b 53. ACT ThDipl 77. Ridley Coll Melb 76. **d** and **p** 78 Perth. C of Applecross 78-80; R of Lockridge Dio Perth from 80. *31 Woolgar Way, Lockridge, W Australia 6054* (279-4883)

HUMMERSTONE, Jeremy David. Merton Coll Ox BA 65, MA 70. Wells Th Coll 70. **d** 72 **p** 73 York. C of Helmsley w Sproxton, Carlton and Rievaulx 72-75; Pockley w Eastmoors 72-75; C-in-c of Manningford Bruce w Manningford Abbas 75; Team V of Swanborough 75-79; C-in-c of Gt Torrington Dio Ex 79-81; R (w L Torrington and Frithelstock) from 81; L Torrington 79-81; Frithelstock 79-81. *Vicarage, Torrington, Devon.* (Torrington 2166)

HUMPHREY, Albert Thomas. b 1886. AKC 13. **d** 13 **p** 14 Lon. C of St Steph Hounslow 13-15; Lect St Steph Coll Delhi 17-19; C of Stratton St Marg 19-21; V of Galle 23-31; C of Aylesbury (in c of St John) 31-34; PC of Grimsbury 34-45; R of Hartley Wespall w Stratfield Turgis 45-64; C-in-c of Stratfieldsaye 50-51; R 51-64; C of Westbourne and of Forest Side w Stansted 64-78; Perm to Offic Dio B & W from 79. *Carters, Stretcholt, Bridgwater, TA6 4SR.* (Puriton 683266)

HUMPHREY, Derek Hollis. b 37. Chich Th Coll 69. **d** 72 **p** 73 Portsm. C of Havant 72-75; H Spirit Southsea 75-78; V of St Thos Finsbury Pk Dio Lon from 78. *194 Drayton Park, Highbury, N5 1LU.* (01-226 3115)

HUMPHREY, Edward John. Univ of W Ont BA 62. Trin Coll Tor STB 65. **d** 65 **p** 66 Hur. C of Bp Cronyn Mem Ch Lon Ont 65-70; St Mary Windsor 70-72; R of Ch of Epiph Lon Dio Hur from 72. *19 Holborn Avenue, London, Ont., Canada.* (519-432 2837)

HUMPHREY, George Edward. b 28. **d** 66 **p** 67. In C of E SA 66-75; C of Cathl Ch of St John Evang Umtata 75-77; P-in-c of St Steph Metatiele Dio St John's from 77. *Box 33, Matatiele 4730, S Africa.*

HUMPHREY, George William. b 38. BD (Lon) 61. Oak Hill Th Coll. **d** 62 **p** 63 Nor. C of H Trin Heigham 62-64; P-in-c of Buckenham w Hassingham and Strumpshaw 64-67; Asst Master Mexborough Gr Sch 67-69; Cheadle Co Gr Sch 69-76; Hon C of St Andr Cheadle Hulme Ches 70-76; Asst Master Thurnscoe Sch 76-80; Perm to Offic Dio Wakef 77-78; P-in-c of Kellington w Whitley 78-80; Relig Educn Adv Co and Dio Glouc from 80. *c/o Church House, College Green, Gloucester.*

HUMPHREY, Howard Jack. b 38. Ridley Coll Melb ThL 69. **d** 69 **p** 70 Melb. C of St Columb, Hawthorn 69-70; St Jas, Dandenong 70-72; P-in-c of St Martin Airport W 72-75; I 75-76; Abp's Consultant on Evang Dio Melb 76-77; I of St Steph Richmond 77-81; St Luke Vermont Dio Melb from 81. *551 Mitcham Road, Vermont, Vic, Australia 3133.*

HUMPHREYS, Benjamin Thomas. b 12. Trin Coll Dub BA 35. **d** 35 **p** 36 Derry. C of Baronscourt w Drumclamph 35-38; Drumachose w Carrick 38-40; C-in-c of Dunfanaghy 40-48; I 48-53; Muff 53-77; Priv Chap to Bp of Derry 61-69; Dioc Regr Dio Derry and Raph 64-77; RD of Londonderry 69-77; Can of Derry Cathl 71-77; Dom Chap to Bp of Derry 75-77. *21 Castle Park, Eglinton, Londonderry, N Ireland, BT48 8JW.* (Eglinton 641)

HUMPHREYS, Canon Bernard Bramley. Linc Th Coll 55. **d** 57 **p** 58 Linc. C of St Giles Linc 57-59; R of Fiskerton 60-70; Ed Linc Dioc Directory from 59; V of Middle Rasen Dio Linc from 70; R of W Rasen Dio Linc from 70; P-in-c of Toft w Newton Dio Linc from 73; Surr from 78; Can and Preb of Linc Cathl from 81. *Middle Rasen Vicarage, Market Rasen, Lincs, LN8 3TS.* (Market Rasen 842249)

HUMPHREYS, Frederic William Ivor. b 1899. Em Coll Cam BA 25, MA 29. Cudd Coll 25. **d** 26 **p** 27 S'wark. C of St Barn Southfields 26-30; Perm to Offic at Stoke-on-Trent 30-31; C of Chalfont St Pet 32-37; V of Grazeley 37-47; PC of Embleton w Wythop 47-54; V of Levens 54-63; Soulby w Crosby Garrett 63-70. *78 Meadow Park, Galgate, Lancs.* (Galgate 751627)

HUMPHREYS, George Bernard. b 10. AKC 36. **d** 36 **p** 37 Man. C of St Mary Virg Leigh 36-38; St Pet Streatham 38-41; Actg C of Syston 41-42; C of Tarporley 42-48; R of Moreton Corbet 48-53; V of Dawley Parva 53-65; R of Fobbing 65-78; Perm to Offic Dio Ex from 78. *Homelea, Christow, Exeter, Devon.*

HUMPHREYS, James Graham. b 36. Univ of Liv BEng 57, PhD 60. Tyndale Hall, Bris 61. **d** 63 **p** 64 Carl. C of St Jas Denton Holme Carl 63-66; St Mark St Helens 66-68; V of Houghton 68-79; Bramcote Dio Southw from 79. *Vicarage, Bramcote, Nottingham, NG9 3HH.* (Nottm 254306)

HUMPHREYS, Canon John Elwyn Price. b 15. OBE 77. Univ of Wales BA 37. St Mich Coll Llan 37. **d** 39 **p** 41 St A. C of Newtown 39-42; Rhosymedre 42-43; Chap RNVR 43-46; Chap RN 46-51; Hon Chap Santa Cruz 51-52; Chap and Asst Master Reed's Sch Cobham and L to Offic Dio Guildf 53-57; Chap at St Paul Estoril 57-80; Commiss Lebom 63-80; Can of Gibr 67-80; Hon Can from 80. *Casa Contente, 2675 Monte Estoril, Portugal.*

HUMPHREYS, John Louis. b 51. Jes Coll Cam BA 72, MA 76. Univ of Nottm BA (Th) 75. St Jo Coll Nottm 73. **d** 76 **p** 77 Lich. C of Good Shepherd w St Jo Evang W Bromwich 76-79; Woodford Wells Dio Chelmsf from 79. *7 Marion Grove, Woodford Green, Essex, IG8 9TA.* (01-505 1431)

HUMPHREYS, John Robin. b 46. BSc (Eng) (Lon) 68. St Steph Ho Ox 73. **d** 76 B & W **p** 77 Taunton for B & W. C of St Mary Bathwick 76-78; Elland (in c of All SS) 78-81; V of St Jude Hexthorpe Doncaster Dio Sheff from 81. *132 Shadyside, Hexthorpe, Doncaster, DN4 0DG.* (0302 852057)

HUMPHREYS, Kenneth Glyn. b 28. Bps' Coll Cheshunt 64. **d** 66 **p** 67 Ox. C of Windsor 66-67; Ch Ch Reading 67-70; V of Compton Parva (w E Ilsley from 74) 70-75; R of E Ilsley 74; C of Wokingham 75-77; Chap Lucas Hosp Wokingham 77-81; V of California Dio Ox from 81. *145a Nine Mile Drive, Finchampstead, Berks, RG11 4HY.* (Eversley 730030)

HUMPHREYS, Canon Neil Edgar. b 20. St Pet Hall, Ox BA (2nd cl Geog) 48, MA 52. Linc Th Coll 48. **d** 50 **p** 51 Liv. C of St Geo Wigan 50-53; Our Lady and St Nich Liv 53-56; V of Dalston w Cumdivock 56-64; Hon Chap to Bp of Carl 61-64; Chap Achimota Sch and L to Offic Dio Accra 64-69; Asst Chap Univ of Liv 69-78; Dioc Planning Adv Dio Liv 72-78; Bp's Planning Adv 78-79; Hon Can of Liv from 78; V of Croxteth Pk (W Derby Team Min) Dio Liv from 79. *19 Huntsman Wood, Croxteth Park, Liverpool, L12 0HY.* (051-220 7944)

HUMPHREYS, Owen Gwilym. b 11. St D Coll Lamp BA 33. St Mich Coll Llan 33. **d** 35 Bp Wentworth Shields for Ban **p** 36 Ban. C of Amlwch 35-38; Llanbedr-y-cennin 38-43; CF 44-47 and 49-59; V of St Ann Llandegai 47-49; PC (V from 69) of Chilton-super-Polden w Edington 59-76; RD of Glastonbury 69-75; C-in-c of Catcott 75-76. *31 Fairfield Road, Caerleon, Newport, Gwent, NP6 1DQ.*

HUMPHREYS, Philip Noel. b 34. Bps' Coll Cheshunt, 62. **d** 64 **p** 65 Ex. C of St Andr Plymouth 64-68; Chap Lee Abbey 68-73; V of St Jas Porchester Nottm 73-82; R of W Bridgford Dio Southw from 82; RD of W Bingham from 82. *Rectory, Church Drive, West Bridgford, Nottingham, NG2 6AY.* (Nottm 811112)

HUMPHREYS, Robert Allan. ACT ThL 72. Moore Coll Syd 72. **d** and **p** 74 Syd. C of St Paul Wahroonga 74-75; Eastwood 76-77; on leave. *8a Clanwilliam Street, Eastwood, NSW, Australia 2122.* (85-1827)

HUMPHREYS, Stephen Robert Beresford. b 52. St Aug Coll Cant 74. **d** 76 Lon **p** 77 Willesden for Lon. C of St Edm Northwood Hills Pinner 76-79; St Mary Magd w St Mich AA Manningham Dio Bradf from 79. *St Mary Magdalene's Vicarage, White's View, Bradford, BD8 8NN.* (Bradford 42886)

HUMPHREYS, William Alfred. b 18. Lich Th Coll 54. **d** 56 **p** 57 Lich. C of Stone 56-60; V of Fazeley 60-65; Prees Dio Lich from 65; C-in-c of Fauls Dio Lich 66-69; V from 69; RD of Wem and Whitchurch from 80. *Prees Vicarage, Whitchurch, Salop.* (Prees 243)

HUMPHREYS, William Haydn. b 09. AKC 36. St D Coll Lamp 29. **d** 36 **p** 37 Wakef. C of Kirkheaton 36-43; CF (EC) 43-47; PC of St Mark Dewsbury Dio Wakef 48-68; (V 69-78); Chap Dewsbury Gen Hosp 50-78. *24 Marion Court, Lisvane Road, Cardiff.*

HUMPHRIES, Andrew Pamment Norton. K Coll Lon 72. **d** 72 **p** 73 Roch. C of H Trin Dartford 72-75; Sacr of Cant Cathl 75-78; P-in-c of Bradpole 78-79. *c/o The Vicarage, Newport, Essex.*

HUMPHRIES, Anthony John. Moore Th Coll Syd ACT ThL 62. **d** 62 **p** 63 Bp Hudson for Syd. C of Burwood 62-67; R of Stanmore 67-68; Enmore (w Stanmore from 68) 67-72; St John Balmain Dio Syd from 72. *Birchgrove Road, Balmain, NSW, Australia 2041.* (82-1396)

HUMPHRIES, Arthur William. b 1892. AKC 31. **d** 31 **p** 32 Lon. C of Ch Ch S Hackney 31-33; W Hackney 33-36; St Faith Wandsworth 36-41; R of Churchstanton 41-63; Perm to Offic Dio Ex from 64. *16 Dillons Road, Creech St Michael, Taunton, Somt, TA3 5DS.*

HUMPHRIES, Christopher William. b 52. St Jo Coll Cam BA 73. MA 77. St Jo Coll Nottm 76. **d** 79 **p** 80 Bradf. C of Eccleshill Dio Bradf from 79. *95 Pullan Avenue, Eccleshill, Bradford, BD2 3RL.* (Bradf 638878)

HUMPHRIES, David Graham. b 48. Univ of Wales (Cardiff) Dipl Th 70. St Mich Coll Llan 67. **d** 71 **p** 72 Llan. C of Neath 71-72; Bp's Cleeve Dio Glouc from 81. *2a Orchard Road, Bishop's Cleeve, Cheltenham, Glos.*

HUMPHRIES, Donald. b 43. Univ of Bris BA (2nd cl Th) 66. Clifton Th Coll 66. **d** 68 Bp Sinker for Birm **p** 69 Birm. C of Selly Hill 68-74; Chap Warw Univ 74-79; V of Ch Ch Bedford Dio St Alb from 79; M Gen Syn from 80; M BCC from 80. *115 Denmark Street, Bedford, MK40 3TJ.* (Bedford 59342)

HUMPHRIES, Frank Charles. b 40. St Chad's Coll Dur BA 61, Dipl Th 63. **d** 63 **p** 64 Lon. C of Tottenham 63-66; St Paul S Harrow 66-71; V of All SS Hillingdon 71-80; Ascen Wembley Dio Lon from 80. *319 Preston Road, Kenton, Harrow, Middx, HA3 0QQ.* (01-904 4062)

HUMPHRIES, Grahame Leslie. b 44. ALCD 70 (LTh from 74). **d** 71 **p** 72 S'wark. C of St Mich AA, Southfields 71-74; St Paul (in c of Ch Ch) Slough 74-77; P-in-c of Arley Dio Cov from 77. *Arley Rectory, Coventry, CV7 8FL.* (Fillongley 40378)

HUMPHRIES, Harold Joseph. b 14. MIEE 52. Dipl Bibl and Relig Stud (Lon) 70. SOC 70. **d** 70 S'wark **p** 71 Glouc. C of Merton 70-71; All SS Glouc 71-75; St Jas Glouc 75-77; Hon Min Can of Glouc Cathl from 77; C of All SS City and Dio Glouc from 78. *Monument House, St Mary's Street, Gloucester, GL1 2QR.* (Glouc 20449)

HUMPHRIES, John. b 49. Univ of Wales (Cardiff) Dipl Th 76. St Mich AA Llan 73. **d** 76 **p** 77 Mon. C of Pontynewynydd 76-78; Ebbw Vale 78-81; V of Ch The Carpenter City and Dio Pet from 81. *Vicarage, Chestnut Avenue, Peterborough, PE1 4PE.* (Pet 67140)

HUMPHRIES, Canon Reginald Norton. AKC 43. **d** 43 **p** 44 Chelmsf. C of H Cross Hornchurch 43-46; in c 45-46; Saffron Walden 46-49; V of Newport Dio Chelmsf from 49; V of Ugley Dio Chelmsf from 55; Dioc Insp of Schs Dio Chelmsf from 57; RD of Newport and Stansted from 61; Hon Can of Chelmsf Cathl from 75. *Newport Vicarage, Saffron Walden, Essex.*

HUMPHRIES, Warwick Arthur. St Jo Coll Morpeth. **d** 64 Newc **p** 69 Tas. C of Adamstown 64-66; St Jas New Town 68-69; P-in-c of Geeveston w Port Esperance 69-74; R of Queenstown 74-76; Sorell-Richmond 76-80; St Aid Launceston Dio Tas from 80. *Rectory, Lanoma Street, Launceston, Tasmania 7250.* (003 31 1627)

HUMPHRIS, Richard. b 44. Sarum Wells Th Coll 69. 43751) 72 **p** 73 Glouc. C of St Luke w St Jo Cheltenham 72-77; Lydney w Aylburton Dio Glouc from 77. *The Parsonage, Aylburton, Lydney, GL15 6DF.* (Dean 43751)

HUMPHRISS, Reginald George. b 36. Kelham Th Coll 56. **d** 61 **p** 62 Birm. C of Londonderry 61-63; Abp's Chap for Youth and Asst Dir of Relig Educn Dio Cant 63-66; V of Preston-next-Faversham 66-72; C-in-c of Goodnestone w Graveney 71-72; V of All SS Spring Pk Croydon 72-76; R of St Martin and St Paul City and Dio Cant from 76. *13 Ersham Road, Canterbury, Kent.* (Canterbury 62686)

HUMPLEBY, Peter. b 40. Open Univ BA 76. Linc Th Coll 75. **d** 77 **p** 78 Wakef. C of Todmorden 77-80; V of Bruntcliffe Dio Wakef from 80. *4 Lewisham Street, Bruntcliffe, Morley, Leeds, LS27 0LA.* (Morley 523783)

HUNG, Frank Yu-Chi. b 45. Univ of Birm BSc 68, BA 75. Univ of Liv MSc 71. Univ of Ox Dipl Th 77. Wycl Hall Ox 76. **d** 78 Buckingham for Ox **p** 79 Ox. C of H Trin Aylesbury Dio Ox from 78. *32 Westmorland Avenue, Aylesbury, Bucks, HP21 7HW.*

HUNGWE, Richard. St Pet Coll Siota 59. **d** 62 **p** 63 melan. P Dio Melan 62-75; Dio New Hebr from 75. *Duindui, Aoba, New Hebrides.*

HUNKIN, Andrew Wellington. b 22. G & C Coll Cam BA 45, MA 48. Ridley Hall Cam 45. **d** 47 **p** 48 S'wark. C of Woolwich 47-50; Chilvers Coton 53-55; Iffley 56-58; St Aug Chesterfield 76-77; St Alb Dartford 79-80; Eckington Dio Derby from 80. *1b Church Street, Eckington, Derby.* (Eckington 432275)

HUNKIN, Oliver John Wellington. G and C Coll Cam BA 38, MA 53. Wycl Hall, Ox 52. **d** 53 **p** 54 Pet. C of St Jo Bapt Pet 53-56; Asst Hd of Relig Broadcasting (TV) BBC 56-67; Hd 67-73. L to Offic Dio S'wark from 57. *31 Leyborne Park, Kew, Surrey.* (Richmond 4601)

HUNNISETT, John Bernard. b 47. AKC 73. St Aug Coll Cant 72. **d** 73 **p** 74 Glouc. C of Charlton Kings 73-77; St Mary Portsea (in c of St Wilfrid's) 77-80; V of Badgeworth w Shurdington Dio Glouc from 80. *Vicarage, Shurdington, Cheltenham, Glos, GL51 5TQ.* (Cheltm 862241)

HUNNYBUN, Martin Wilfrid. b 44. Oak Hill Th Coll 67. **d** 70 **p** 71 St Alb. C of Ch Ch Ware 70-74; Exe Valley Team Min 74-75; Team V 75-80; R of Braunston Dio Pet from 80. *Braunston Rectory, Daventry, Northants, NN11 7HS.* (Rugby 890235)

HUNT, Alan. b 31. St Mich Coll Llan 65. **d** 67 **p** 68 Blackb. C of Standish 67-72; V of St Paul Low Moor Clitheroe 72-77; L to Offic Dio Blackb from 79. *12 Tennyson Place, Walton-le-Dale, Preston, Lancs.* (Preston 39554)

HUNT, Andrew Horton Colin. Ball Coll Ox 2nd cl Cl Mods 34, BA (2nd cl Lit Hum) 36. Westcott Ho Cam 38. **d** 39 **p** 40 Lon. C of All SS Queensbury 39-43; Bp's Chap for Youth Dio Leic 43-53; V of Shepshed 46-53; R of Gatooma 53-60; Hatfield S Rhod 60-66; Hd Master Bernard Mizeki Coll Dio Mashon (Dio Mutare from 81) from 66. *Box 790, Marandellas, Zimbabwe.*

HUNT, Bruce Allan. b 32. Univ of Nottm BA (2nd cl Hist) 54, ALCD (1st cl) 59. **d** 61 **p** 62 St Alb. C of Watford 61-64; Rayleigh 64-69; V of Lepton 69-81; St Jo Evang Worksop Dio Southw from 81. *St John's Vicarage, Shepherds Avenue, Worksop, Notts, S81 0JD.* (0909 472595)

HUNT, Charles Evans. b 13. Univ of Dur LTh 44. ALCD 37. **d** 37 **p** 38 Sheff. C of St Jude Doncaster 37-41; Wadsley 41-47; Doncaster 47-49; V of St Paul Masbrough 49-73; C-in-c of St John Masbrough 56-73; V of Wentworth 73-79; L to Offic Dio Ely from 80. *1 Vicarage Lane, Whittlesford, Cambridge, CB2 4NT.* (Cam 833402)

HUNT, Christopher Paul Colin. b 38. Ch Coll Cam 2nd cl Hist Trip pt i 61, BA (2nd cl Th Trip pt ia) 62. Clifton Th Coll 63. **d** 65 Warrington for Liv **p** 66 Liv. C of St Paul Widnes 65-68; St Paul Petaling Jaya Sing 68-70; W Mal 70-71; Dom Chap to Bp of Iran 74-78; Exam Chap 77-80; Overseas Service Adv CMS from 81. *c/o CMS, 157 Waterloo Road, SE1 8UU.*

HUNT, David John. b 35. Kelham Th Coll 60. **d** 65 **p** 66 Lon. C of St Jo Evang w St Simon Bethnal Green 65-69; St Mich AA Mill Hill 69-73; R of Staple Fitzpaine w Orchard Portman, Thurlbear and Stoke St Mary 73-79; P-in-c of E Coker w Sutton Bingham Dio B & W from 79; C of Yeovil (in c of Closworth) Dio B & W from 80. *Vicarage, East Coker, Yeovil, Somt.* (W Coker 2125)

HUNT, Derek Henry. b 38. ALCD (2nd cl) 61. **d** 62 **p** 63 Lon. C of Ch Ch Roxeth 62-66; Radipole 66-70; C-in-c of Shalbourne w Bagshot, Ham and Buttermere 70-72; V of Burbage (w Savernake Christchurch 73-75) from 72-78; Savernake 72-75; R of Cranfield Dio St Alb from 78; P-in-c of Hulcote w Salford Dio St Alb from 78. *Cranfield Rectory, Bedford, MK43 0DR.* (Bedford 750214)

✠ **HUNT, Right Rev Desmond Charles.** Univ of Tor BA 39. Wycl Coll Tor LTh 42, Hon DD 77. **d** 42 **p** 43 Tor. C of All SS Tor 42-43; R of Trin Queb 43-50; in Amer Ch 50-53; R of St Jas Kingston 53-69; Archd of Kingston 59-69; R of Ch of Messiah Tor 69-81; Can of Tor 77-81; Cons Ld Bp Suffr of Tor in St Paul's Ch Bloor Street E, Tor by Abp of Tor; Bps of Alg, Carib, Hur, Moos, Ott and W New York (USA); Bps Suffr of Tor, Niag, Hur and The Artic; and others. *135 Adelaide Street East, Toronto, Ont, M5C 1L8, Canada.* (416-363 6021)

HUNT, Donald Philip. Trin Coll Tor BA 50. **d** 52 **p** 53 Tor. C of Ch of Transfig Tor 52-54; R of New Tor 54-60; St Aid Oakville 60-61; Chap Ridley Coll St Catharines 61-76; Hd Master Lower Sch Ridley Coll St Catharines from 76. *Ridley College, St Catharines, Ont, Canada.* (416-682 5152)

HUNT, Edward Trebble. b 31. St Mich Coll Llan 56. **d** 58 **p** 59 Swan B. C of St Thos Swansea 58-62; St Mary Swansea 62-65; C-in-c of Glantawe Conv Distr 66-72; V of Glantawe 72-75; Ch Ch Swansea Dio Swan B from 76; Chap HM Pris Swansea from 76. *Christ Church Vicarage, Swansea, W Glam, SA1 3UH.* (Swansea 52606)

HUNT, Ernest William. b 09. St Jo Coll Dur BA (2nd Class Hist) Gladstone Mem Pri and Van Mildert Exhib 31, MA 34. Univ of Birm BD 46. St Cath S Ox BLitt 51. **d** 32 **p** 33 Dur. C of Gateshead Fell 32-37; V of Dunston 37-43; C and Succr of Birm Cathl and Lect of Qu Coll Birm 43-51; Vice-Prin Lich Th Coll 51-57; Perm to Offic Dio Birm 51-54; L to Offic Dio Lich 51-57; Prof of Th and Hebr at St D Coll Lamp 57-69; Exam Chap to Bp of St D 58-69. *Address temp unknown.*

HUNT, Frank Edward Peter. b 25. St Jo Coll Morpeth 78. **d** and **p** 79 River. C of Narrandera 79-80; P-in-c of Barellan Dio River from 80. *St Clement's Rectory, Barellan, NSW, Australia 2665.*

HUNT, Giles Butler. b 28. Trin Hall Cam BA (2nd cl Hist Trip) 51, MA 55. Cudd Coll 51. **d** 53 **p** 54 Leic. C of St Steph N Evington 53-56; Northolt 56-58; Dom Chap to Bp of Portsm 58-59; to Bp of Nor 59-62; R of Holt 62-67; R of Kelling w Salthouse 63-67; C of St Pet Eaton Square 67-72; V of Barkway w Reed and Buckland 72-79; Preston-next-Faversham and Goodnestone w Graveney Dio Cant from 79. *Preston Vicarage, Faversham, Kent.* (Faversham 6801)

HUNT, Harold Richard. Em Coll Sktn. **d** and **p** 57 Calg. I of Stettler 57-64; R of Williams Lake 64-73; R of Chilcoten 64-67; Can of Carib 66-73; R of Campbell River Dio BC from 73. *812 8th Avenue, Campbell River, BC, Canada.* (604-287-3911)

HUNT, Hubert de Jersey. b 12. Chich Th Coll 36. **d** 38 **p** 39 Lon. C of W Hackney 38-40 (in c 40-41); Malvern Link 41-46; Chap RNVR 42-46; V of St Jas Jersey 46-50; St Mich Edmon 50-58; R of Marston Magna w Rimpton 58-79; C-in-c of Corton Denham 72-79; Hon Inland Chap Miss to Seamen from 79. *West House, Dinder, Wells, Somt, BA5 3PL.* (0749-75251)

HUNT, Canon Ian Carter. b 34. Chich Th Coll 61. **d** 64 **p** 65 Plymouth for Ex. C of St Pet Plymouth 64-67; Daventry 67-70; V of St Paul Northn Dio Pet from 70; Can (Non-res) of Pet Cathl from 81. *St Paul's Vicarage, 104 Semilong Road, Northampton, NN2 6EX.* (Northampton 712688)

HUNT, James Edward. Trin Coll Tor BA 59, STB 62. **d** 62 Bran for Rupld **p** 63 Rupld. C of St Jas Winnipeg 62-64; R of St Chad Winnipeg 64-65. C of St Paul Lachine Montr 65-69; C of St Timothy Tor 76-80; Hon C of St Jas Cathl City and Dio Tor from 80. *405-540 Russell Hill Road, Toronto, Ont, Canada.*

HUNT, John Stewart. b 37. **d** 78 **p** 79 Nor (APM). Hon C of St Edm Hunstanton 78-81; St Mary Hunstanton Dio Nor from 81. *10 Peddars Drive, Hunstanton, Norfolk, PE36 6HF.* (Hunstanton 33424)

HUNT, John Barry. b 46. Qu Coll Birm 72. **d** 73 **p** 74 Dur. C of Bp Auckland 73-77; Consett 77-79; R of Lyons Dio Dur from 79. *Lyons Rectory, High Street, Easington Lane, Houghton-le-Spring, T & ole 265505)*

HUNT, John Edwin. b 38. Univ Coll Dur BA 60. E Midl Min Tr Course 78. **d** 81 Repton for Derby. C of St Jo Evang Newbold Dio Derby from 81. *4 Ardsley Road, Ashgate, Chesterfield, S40 4DG.*

HUNT, Leslie Pfeilitzer. Univ of Tor BA 30, DD 60. Wycl Coll Tor LTh 34, BD 37, MTh 54, DD 59. **d** 32 Niag for Tor **p** 34 Tor. C of Ch of Messiah Tor 32-33; Ch of Epiph Tor 33-35; R of Ch of Resurr Tor 35-38; C of St Paul Tor 38-41; R of St Alb Tor 41-45; Ch of Epiph Tor 49-59; Exam Chap to Bp of Tor 55-59; Can of Tor 56-75; Prin Wycl Coll Tor 59-75; Prof of New Test from 76; Hon C of St Paul Bloor St Tor 64-75; Warden of Garden Tomb Jer 75-76; CA Canada from 79. *Wycliffe College, Toronto, Ont., Canada.*

HUNT, Martin Howard. b 39. Univ of Dur BA (2nd cl Engl) 60. Univ of Lon BD (2nd cl) 62. Tyndale Hall, Bris 60. **d** 63 **p** 64 York. C of Hull 63-66; St Jas Sutton-in-Holderness 66-67; V of Walshaw Man 67-74; Ch Ch Southport 74-80; St Luke W Derby Dio Liv from 80. *Vicarage, Princess Drive, Liverpool, L14 8XG.* (051-228 6025)

HUNT, Michael Francis. b 26. Wadh Coll Ox BA 49, MA 50. St Steph Ho Ox 49. **d** 51 **p** 52 B & W. C of All SS Clevedon 51-55; C-in-c of St Martha's Conv Distr Broxtowe 56-62; R of Auchterader 62-66; Dumfries 66-73; Arbroath 73-78; St Jo Evang w St Mich AA Inverness 78-80; P-in-c of Koinambe 80; R of Mt Hagen Dio Aipo from 80. *c/o Box 182, Mount Hagen, Papua New Guinea.*

HUNT, Montague Laban. b 1897 Leeds Cl Scho 20. **d** 23 **p** 24 Pet. C of Lutterworth 23-26; H Trin Cov 26-30; R of Whitchurch w Preston-on-Stour 30-53; CF 44-47; R of St Ferriby 53-66; Hon CF from 54; V of Horkstow 57-66; RD of Yarborough N 60-64. *186 Nettleham Road, Lincoln, LN2 4DQ.* (Lincoln 28551)

HUNT, Nicholas James Irwin. Univ of NZ BA 48 (2nd cl Phil) MA 50. St Jo Coll Auckld NZ Bd of Th Stud LTh (2nd cl) 51. **d** 51 **p** 52 Auckld. C of Onehunga 51-52; Whangarei 52-54; Tutor Th Coll Siota 54-56; Hd Master Vureas Sch 56-63; St Paul's Sch Lolowai 63-70; L to Offic Dio Auckld 66; Hd Master All H Sch Pawa 70-74; Chap St Steph Sch Auckld and Hon C of Bombay Dio Auckld from 74. *St Stephen's School, Private Bag, Auckland 1, NZ.* (Bombay 864)

HUNT, Peter John. b 35. K Coll Lon and Warm AKC 58. **d** 59 Bp Sinker for Derby **p** 60 Derby. C of Chesterfield 59-61; Matlock w Tansley 61-63; Lect Matlock Tech Coll 61-63; CF (TA) 65-67; CF from 75; V of Tottington 63-69; Bollington 69-76; R of Wilmslow Dio Ches from 76. *12 Broadway, Wilmslow, Chesh.* (061-95 23127)

HUNT, Philip Edgar. b 11. **d** 68 Bp Horstead for Leic **p** 69 Leic. C of Blaby 68-72; V of Whitwick St Geo (w Swannington and Cole Orton from 75) 72-78; L to Offic Dio Leic from 78. *13 Sapcote Drive, Melton Mowbray, Leics.*

HUNT, Philip Lacey Winter. b 09. St Steph Ho Ox. **d** 68 **p** 69 Ox. Chap to the Deaf Dio Ox from 68; Hon C of St Barn City and Dio Ox from 76. *47 Cardigan Street, Oxford.*

HUNT, Richard William. b 46. G and C Coll Cam 2nd cl Math Trip pt ia 65, 2nd cl pt ib 66, BA (Jun Opt pt ii) 67, 2nd cl Th Trip pt ii 69, MA 71. Westcott Ho Cam 68. **d** 72 **p** 73 Bris. C of St Agnes and St Simon w St Werburgh Bris 72-77; Fell Chap and Prec Selwyn Coll Cam from 77; Perm to Offic Dio Antig 78. *Selwyn College, Cambridge, CB3 9DQ.* (Cambridge 62381)

HUNT, Ronald Arliss. Univ of W Ont BA 56. Hur Coll. **d** 58 **p** 59 Hur. C of Simcoe 58-60; I of Dundalk 60-64; C of St Jas Westmr Lon Ont 64-65; I of St Barn Sktn 65-67 C of St Steph Calg 67-70; I of Fort Macleod w Brochet 70-75; All SS Miss Dio New Westmr from 75. *7369 James Street, Mission, BC, V2V 3V7, Canada.*

HUNT, Ronald Horace. Bp's Univ Lennox BA 62, LST 63. Wycl Coll Tor BTh 65. **d** and **p** 63 Niag. C of St Geo St Catharines 63-65; Chap Ont Tr Sch for Girls 65-66; for Boys 66-68; P-in-c of Merlin Dio Hur 71-74; R from 74. *Box 164, Merlin, Ont., Canada.* (519-689 4916)

HUNT, Russell Barrett. b 35. NY Univ MAnaes 61. Westcott Ho Cam 73. **d** 75 **p** 76 Leic. C of St Mary de Castro Leic 75-78; V of St Gabr City and Dio Leic from 78. *20 Kerrysdale Avenue, Leicester, LE4 7GH.* (Leic 61452)

HUNT, William de Vere Angus. b 02. St Jo Coll Manit BA 30. **d** 30 **p** 31 Edmon. C of Barrhead 30-31; I of St Luke Mayerthorpe 31-43; R of Edson 43-47; Hon Can of Edmon 45-47; I of St Patr Guelph 47-55; R of Oare w Culbone 55-58; Seaborough 58-61; R of Wayford 58-61; Bathealton w Stawley and Kittisford 61-71; Perm to offic Dio Ex 71-73; Dio B & W 73-75. *West House, Dinder, Wells, BA5 3PL.* (0749 75251)

✠ **HUNT, Right Rev William Warren.** b 09. Late Exhib of Keble Coll Ox BA (2nd cl Mod Hist) 31, MA 35. Cudd Coll 31. **d** 32 **p** 33 Carl. C of Kendal 32-35; St Martin-in-the-Fields 35-40; CF (EC) 40-44; V of St Nich Radford Cov 44-48; H Trin Leamington 48-57; RD of Leamington 53-57; V and RD of Croydon 57-65; Hon Can of Cant 57-65; Cons Ld Bp Suffr of Repton in Westmr Abbey 30 Nov 65 by Abp of Cant; Bps of Lon; Linc; Roch; Win; Pet; Derby; and Cov; Bps Suffr of Southn; Grimsby; Tonbridge; and Buckingham; and Bps Montgomery; Campbell; Mann; Otter; Russell; and others; res 77; Hon Asst Bp of Portsm from 77; Chich from 78. *15 Lynch Down,Funtington, Nr Chichester, W Sussex, PO18 9LR.* (West Ashling 536)

HUNTER, (George) Alan George. Univ of Tor BA 52. St Chad's Coll Sask LTh 50. M SSF 57. **d** 51 **p** 52 Qu'App. C of Shaunavon 51-52; I of Major 52-53; Ogema 53-55; C of Assiniboia 55-56; I of St Mich Moose Jaw 56-57; Perm to Offic Dio Brisb 67-73; P-in-c of Quilpie Distr 73-75; Hon C of Glen Innes 77-79; Perm to Offic Dio Auckld from 79. *132 Taniwha Street, Glen Innes, Auckland, NZ.*

HUNTER, Allan Davies. b 36. St D Coll Lamp BA 57. Coll of Resurr Mirfield. **d** 59 **p** 60 Llan. C of St Jo Bapt Cardiff

59-68; V of Llansawel (w Briton Ferry from 76) 68-79; St Cath Canton Dio Llan from 79; Dioc Youth Chap Llan 71-77. *St Catherine's Vicarage, Rumilly Crescent, Canton, Cardiff, CF1 9NR.* (Cardiff 22796)

✠ **HUNTER, Right Rev Anthony George Weaver.** b 16. Univ of Leeds BA 39. Coll of Resurr Mirfield 39. **d** 41 **p** 42 Newc T. C of St Geo Jesmond Newc T 41-43 and 48-49; Orlando Miss Distr 43-47; St Alb Miss Distr Johann 47-48; V of Ashington 49-60; Proc Conv Newc T 49-60; Wakef 62-68; V of Huddersfield 60-68; RD of Huddersfield 60-68; Commiss Zulu 60-68; Hon Can of Wakef 62-68; Cons Ld Bp of Swaz in St Paul's Ch Durban 17 Nov 68 by Abp of Capetn; Bps of Geo; Lebom; Johann; Les; Bloemf; Pret; Kimb K; St John's; Grahmstn; Natal; and Zulu; Bps Suffr of Capetn; and Les; Asst Bps of Grahmstn; Johann; and Natal; and Bps Stainton and Fosseys (Lutheran Ch); res 75; R of Hexham 75-78; Asst Bp of Newc T 76-81; Commiss Swaz from 76. *Knocklaw Cottage, Rothbury, Northumb.*

HUNTER, Archibald. b 36. Montr Dioc Th Coll LTh 78. **d** 77 **p** 78 Ott. I of Combermere Dio Ott from 77. *Box 14, Combermere, Ont, Canada.*

✠ **HUNTER, Right Rev Barry Russell.** St Francis Coll Brisb ACT ThL 52. **d** and **p** 53 Brisb. C of St Matt Sherwood Brisb 53-56; M of Bush Bro of St Paul 56-61; R of Chinchilla 61-66; Callide Valley 66-71; Archd of The East 69-71; Cons Ld Bp of Riverina in St Andr Cathl Syd 30 Nov 71 by Abp of Syd; Bps of Newc; Bath; and Wang; Bps Strong; Hulme-Moir; Begbie; Delbridge; Stibbard and Shearman. *Bishop's Lodge, 127 Audley Street, Narrandera, NSW, Australia 2700.* (069-59 1177)

HUNTER, Cyril Stanley Maurice. b 18. Worc Ordin Coll 67. **d** 69 Whitby for York **p** 70 York. C of Guisborough w Commondale 69-72; Northallerton w Kirby Sigston and Romanby 72-75; C-in-c of Thornton-le-Street w Thornton-le-Moor and Thornton-le-Beans 75-79; V of Thornton-le-Street w N Otterington, Thornton-le-Moor, Thornton-le-Beans and S Otterington Dio York from 79. *Thornton-le-Moor Vicarage, Northallerton, N Yorks.* (Northallerton 4232)

HUNTER, David. b 30. Edin Th Coll 60. **d** 64 **p** 65 Glas. C of Ch Ch Glas 64-67; R 67-70 and 75-78; R of Coatbridge 70-73; Chap HM Pris Barlinnie from 72; P-in-c of H Trin Riddrie Dio Glas from 73. *1014 Cumbernauld Road, Glasgow, G33.* (041-770 5393)

HUNTER, David Hilliard Cowan. St Jo Coll Auckld 72. **d** 73 **p** 74 Nel. C of Stoke 73-75; Ch Ch Cathl Nel 75-77; V of Reefton 77; Waimea 78-79; Chap Tongariro Pris Farm and Perm to Offic Dio Wai from 79. *26 Hautu Village, Turangi, NZ.* (8627)

HUNTER, David Matheson. b 46. AKC and BD 69. St Aug Coll Cant 72. **d** 76 **p** 77 Ex. C of St Bonif Paignton 76-79; Plymstock Dio Ex from 79. *15 Goosewell Terrace, Plymstock, Plymouth, PL9 9HW.* (Plymouth 47788)

HUNTER, Frank Geoffrey. b 34. Keble Coll Ox BA (3rd cl Phil Pol and Econ) 56, MA 60. Fitzw Ho Cam BA (2nd cl Th Trip pt ii) 58, MA 62. Ridley Hall, Cam 57. **d** 59 **p** 60 Man. C of Bircle 59-62; Ch Ch Jarrow Grange 62-65; V of St Martin Hull 65-72; St Barn Linthorpe 72-76; R of Heslington Dio York from 76; RD of Escrick 78-81; Derwent from 81. *Heslington Rectory, York, YO1 5EE.* (York 410389)

HUNTER, Harold Hamilton. b 23. Univ of Dur BSc 48. Cranmer Hall Dur 76. **d** 79 **p** 80 Newc T. C of Corbridge Dio Newc T from 79. *8 Aydon Drive, Corbridge, Northumberland, NE45 5ED.*

HUNTER, Henry. b 07. Tyndale Hall Bris 32. **d** 45 **p** 46 Man. [f BCMS Miss in S China] C of St Pet Halliwell 45-47; Felixstowe 47-50; V of St Geo Mart Daubhill 50-57; St Edm Burlingham w Lingwood (w St Andr and St Pet Burlingham from 62) 57-73; C-in-c of St Andr w St Pet Burlingham 57-62. *1 Johnspool, Fulwood, Preston, Lancs, PR2 3FY.*

HUNTER, Canon Hugh. b 1893. Univ of Man BA 18, Bp Lee Gk Test Pri Jun 20, Sen 21 BD 21. **d** 34 **p** 35 Bradf. C of Clayton 34-36; V of Riddlesden 36-44; H Trin Bingley 44-54; Hon Can of Bradf 48-64; Can (Emer) from 64; Exam Chap to Bp of Bradf 48-57; R of Bolton Abbey w Barden 54-61; RD of Skipton 56-64; V of Hubberholme 61-64. *Sherburn House, Durham, DH1 2SE.*

HUNTER, Ian Nason. St Francis Coll Brisb 65. **d** 68 **p** 69 Brisb. C of St Thos Toowong Brisb 68-69; St Luke Toowoomba 69-72; V of Inala 72-74; C of Ch Ch St Lucia 74-75; P-in-c 75; Chap R Melb Inst of Tech 76-80; I of Glenhuntly Dio Melb from 80. *116 Booran Road, Glenhuntly, Vic, Australia 3163.*

HUNTER, Ian Paton. b 20. Em Coll Cam 3rd cl Hist Trip pt I 45, BA (3rd cl Hist Trip pt ii) 46, MA 50. Tyndale Hall, Bris. **d** 43 **p** 47 Pet. C of Harrington 43-47; St Paul Portman Sq Lon 47-50; V of Furneux Pelham w Stocking Pelham 50-54; Moulton 54-60; Danehill 60-67; R of Plumpton w E Chiltington 67-77; V of Burwash Weald Dio Chich from 77. *Burwash Weald Vicarage, Burwash Common, Etchingham, TN19 7NA.* (West Burwash 287)

HUNTER, Jack Dudley. b 09. Univ of Queensld BA 37. St Francis Th Coll Brisb ACT ThL 38. **d** 38 **p** 39 Brisb. C of St Alb Auchenflower Brisb 38-41; M of Bush Bro of St Paul Dio Brisb 41-46; C of Dalby 46-49; Poplar Lon 49-50; Cricklade 50-52; H Trin w St Mary Ely 52-54; V of Impington 54-68; Cler Sec Ely Dioc Conf 57-64; Commiss Brisb 61-71; RD of N Stowe 64-68; Camps 69-76; R of Balsham 68-78. *Address temp unknown.*

HUNTER, Canon John Gaunt. Late Gisborne Scho of St Jo Coll Dur BA (2nd cl Pol and Econ) 49. Ridley Hall, Cam 49. **d** 51 **p** 52 Bradf. C of Bradf Cathl 51-54; Em Plymouth 54-56; V of St Matt Bootle 56-62; Warden Bp Tucker Coll Mukono 62-65; V of Altcar 65-78; Dioc Missr Dio Liv 65-71; M Gen Syn 70; Abp York Adv in Miss 71-78; Hon Can of Liv Cathl from 71; R of Buckhurst Hill Dio Chelmsf from 78. *Rectory, High Road, Buckhurst Hill, Essex, IG9 5RX.* (01-504 1931)

HUNTER, John Richard. Univ of Melb BA 73, BD 76. Trin Coll Melb 73. **d** 76 **p** 77 Melb. C of St Thos Essendon 76-77; St Matt Cheltenham Dio Melb from 77. *15-17 Cameron Street, Cheltenham, Vic, Australia 3192.* (93 8109)

HUNTER, Lemuel Lahai. b 25. Fourah Bay Coll. **d** 70 Sier L. C of St Mich, Waterloo Dio Sier L from 70. *SLC Mission, Bauya, Sierra Leone.*

✠ **HUNTER, Right Rev Leslie Stannard.** b 1890. New Coll Ox BA (2nd cl Th) 12, MA 17. Univ of Dur Hon DCL 40. DD (Lambeth) 49. Univ of Sheff Hon LLD 53. Trin Coll Tor Hon DD 54. Commdr of O of the Dannebrog 52. **d** 15 **p** 16 S'wark. Asst Sec SCM 13-20; C of St Pet Brockley 15-18; St Martin-in-the-Fields and Chap of Charing Cross Hosp 21-22; Can of St Benedict Biscop in Newc T Cathl 22-26; V of Barking 26-30; Select Pr Univ of Glas 33; Cam 36-37 and 61; Aber 38 and 47; Ox 29-31; 39-41; 56; and 66; St Andr 40 and 57; Edin 47; Archd of Northumb Can of Newc T Cathl and Exam Chap to Bp of Newc T 31-39; Chap to HM the King 36-39; Cons Ld Bp of Sheff in York Minster 29 Sept 39 by Abp of York; Bps of Dur; Carl; S'wark; Newc T; Southw; and Wakef; Bps Suffr of Burnley; Knaresborough; Jarrow; Penrith; and Pontefract; and Bps Hudson and Mounsey; res 62. *545 Fulwood Road, Sheffield, S10 3QG.*

HUNTER, Lionel Lawledge Gleave. b 24. ALCD 53. **d** 53 Bp Hollis for Cant **p** 54 Leic. C of H Trin Leic 53-56; St Giles Northn 56-58; St Chrys Everton 58-59; C-in-c of St Mich Liv 59-61; SAMS Miss Chile 61-72; V of Diddlebury w Bouldon and Munslow 72-75; C-in-c of Holdgate w Tugford 73-75; Heath 73-75; Abdon 73-75; R of Kitwanga 75-77; I of Smithers Dio Caled from 77. *Box 147, Smithers, BC, Canada.* (604-847 9271)

HUNTER, Michael John. b 45. CCC BA 67, MA 71, PhD 71. Univ of Ox BA (Th) 75. Wycl Hall Ox 73. **d** 76 **p** 77 Ches. C of Patrington w Carrington Dio Ches from 76. *Beechfield, Chapel Lane, Partington, Urmston, Gtr Man M31.*

HUNTER, Michael Oram. b 40. K Coll Lon and Warm BD and AKC 64. **d** 65 **p** 66 Lich. C of St Mich Tividale Tipton 65-68; St Wilfrid Harrogate 68-70; V of Hawksworth Wood w Moor Grange 70-78; Whitkirk Dio Ripon from 78; M Gen Syn from 81. *Whitkirk Vicarage, Selby Road, Leeds, LS15 0AA.* (Leeds 645790)

HUNTER, Peterson Campbell. St Jo Coll Morpeth ACT ThL (2nd cl) 63. **d** 63 **p** 64 Adel. C of Ch Ch N Adel 63-64; Plympton 64-65; Chap of Woodville Gdns Miss 65-68; CF (Austr) 68-72; L to Offic Dio C & Goulb 69-72; Dio Brisb 71-72; P-in-c of Mile End, Hindmarsh and Bowden 73-78; R of Port Adel L to Offic Dio Parag from 80. *Casilla 98, Concepcion, Paraguay.*

HUNTER, Robert. b 36. Univ of Man BSc (2nd cl Physics) 60. Clifton Th Coll 61. **d** 63 Hulme for Man **p** 64 Man. C of Ch Ch Chadderton 63-65; St Mary Balderstone Rochdale 65-69; Newburn (in c of Throckley) 69-73; Team V of Sutton-in-Holderness w Wawne 73-81; V of Bilton-in-Holderness Dio York from 81. *Bilton-in-Holderness Vicarage, Hull, Humb, HU11 4AD.* (0482-811441)

HUNTER, Robert Arthur Butler. b 21. **d** 79 **p** 80 Auckld. C of Waimaite N Dio Auckld from 79. *PO Box 60, Okaihau, Northland, NZ.*

HUNTER, Robert Clifford. b 09. St Pet Th Coll Ja 38. **d** 42 **p** 43 Ja. C of St Jas Cathl Spanish Town 42-43; St Luke Cross Roads Ja 43; CF 43-51; Hon CF 51; C of Lee 51-53; V of St Mich AA Sydenham 53-60; S Nutfield 60-73; C of Gt and L Ness 73-77. *16 Lower Mill Street, Ludlow, Salop SY8 1BH.* (Ludlow 2989)

HUNTER, Very Rev Rodney Squire. Ex Coll Ox BA (Th) 56, MA 61. Coll of Resurr Mirfield. **d** 58 **p** 59 Chelmsf. C of St Edm Forest Gate 58-61; Libr Pusey Ho Ox 61-65; Chap Wadh Coll Ox 62-65; Sub Warden St Jo Bapt Th Sem Lusaka

65-73; Kachebere Sem Dio Lake Malawi 73-81; Dean of Lake Malawi from 81. *Box 1, Likoma Island, Malawi.*

HUNTER, William Barrell. ACT ThL 41. **d** 42 Geelong for Melb **p** 43 Melb. C of St Pet Melb 42-49; V of E Thornbury Dio Melb 49-51; Perm to Offic (Col Cl Act) at H Redeem Clerkenwell Lon 52-54; P-in-c of E Brunswick 54-58; I 58-66; C of St Geo Reservoir 57-68; H Trin Coburg 68-71; P-in-c of Merlynston 71-74; Perm to Offic Dio Melb from 74; Dio Bal from 80. *Box 111, Camperdown, Vic, Australia 3260.*

HUNTER-BAILEY, James Ralph. b 11. Univ of Poitiers BL 47. Ripon Hall Ox 55. **d** 56 **p** 57 Worc. C of St Jo Bapt-in-Bedwardine Worc 56-58; St Pet Ealing 58-59; Pershore 59-61; V of Skegby 61-64; Wychbold w Upton Warren 64-71; L to Offic Dio Sarum 71-78. *Eyeworth Lawn, West Cliff Gardens, Bournemouth, Dorset.*

HUNTING, Raymond John. b 18. St Aid Coll 47. **d** 49 **p** 50 Man. C of Ch Ch Pennington 49-52; St Marg Whalley Range 52-53; V of H Trin Waterhead Oldham 53-56; Sileby Dio Leic from 56. *Sileby Vicarage, Loughborough, Leics.* (Sileby 2493)

HUNTINGDON, Lord Bishop Suffragan of. *See* Roe, Right Rev William Gordon.

HUNTINGDON, Archdeacon of. *See* Sledge, Ven Richard Kitson.

HUNTLEY, David Anthony. BA (Lon) 60. **d** and **p** 65 Sing. Miss Overseas Miss Fellowship 65-68; C of Good Shepherd Sing 68-77; Chap Overseas Miss Fellowship Kowloon from 77. *Overseas Missionary Fellowship, 15-D-9/F Mt Sterling Mall, Meifoo Sun* (3-720974)

HUNTLEY, Denis Anthony. b 56. Qu Coll Birm 77. **d** 80 **p** 81 Llan. C of Llanblethian w Cowbridge & Llandough w St Mary Church Dio Llan from 80. *12 Grays Walk, Cowbridge, S Glam.*

HUNTRESS, Franklin Elias. b 33. Colby Coll Maine BA 56. Berkeley Div Sch 59.**d** 62 Bp Stokes **p** 63 Bp Lawrence. In Amer Ch 62-65; C of St Mary Chester 65-67; Waltham Abbey 67-74; V of St Gabr Leic 75-78. *Spring Hill Road, Easy Sandwich, Massachusetts, USA.*

HUNTRISS, John Charles. b 49. Worc Coll Ox BA 71, MA 74. St Steph Ho Ox 71. **d** 74 **p** 75 Tewkesbury for Glouc. C of Badgeworth w Shurdington 74-77; Asst Univ Chap Cardiff 77-79; P-in-c of Mickleton Dio Glouc from 79. *Mickleton Vicarage, Chipping Campden, Glos.* (Mickleton 279)

HUNWICKE, John William. b 41. Late Scho of Hertf Coll Ox 2nd cl Cl Mods 62, BA (3rd cl Lit Hum) 64, 2nd cl Th 66, MA 67. St Steph Ho Ox. **d** 67 **p** 68 Ox. C of Beaconsfield 67-70; St Paul Newington Dio S'wark 70-73; Chap of Lancing Coll from 73. *Hoe Court House, Lancing, Sussex, BN15 0QX.* (Lancing 2145)

HURCOMBE, Thomas William. b 45. AKC 76 and BD 74. St Aug Coll Cant 74. **d** 76 Lon **p** 77 Edmon for Lon. C of All S Hampstead 76-80; Team V of Ch of Ch & St John w St Luke Isle of Dogs Poplar Dio Lon from 80. *St Luke's House, Strafford Street, E14 8LT.* (01-515 9888)

HURD, Arthur Edward Stanley. St Jo Coll Dur LTh 41, BA 42, MA 45. Tyndale Hall Bris 38. **d** 42 S'wark for Chich **p** 43 Chich. C of Broadwater 42-45; BCMS Miss Ethiopia 45-57; Archd of Maralal 59-63; Sec BCMS Kenya Miss 57-62; VG of Nak and Exam Chap to Bp of Nak 61-62; R of St Jo Bapt Southover Lewes 63-77; Commiss Nak from 63. *10 Rectory Close, East Hoathly, Sussex, BN8 6EG.* (Halland 543)

HURD, John Coolidge. b 28. Episc Th Sch Cam Mass BD 52. Yale Univ MA 57, PhD 61. **d** 52 **p** 53 Mass. In Amer Ch 52-57; Prof of NT and Chap on Staff Trin Coll Tor from 67. *49 Wanless Avenue, Toronto 12, Ont, Canada.*

HURD, John Patrick. b 37. Open Univ BA 73. Chich Th Coll 77. **d** 80 Chich **p** 81 Horsham for Chich (NSM). C of Billingshurst Dio Chich from 80. *Groomsland Cottage, Parbrook, Billingshurst, Sussex, RH14 9EU.*

HURD, Very Rev Michael John. b 44. Univ of Otago BA 65. St Jo Coll Auckld LTh 67. **d** 67 **p** 68 Dun. C of Anderson's Bay 67-70; Tauranga 70-72; V of Tapanui 72-77; Andersons Bay 77-81; Dean and V of Ch Ch Cathl City and Dio Nel from 81. *Deanery, Trafalgar Street, Nelson, NZ.* (88-574)

HURDLE, Canon Thomas Vivian. b 15. Late Exhib of St Cath Coll Cam 1st cl Nat Sc Trip pt i 36, BA 37, 2nd cl Th Trip pt i 38, MA 40. Ely Th Coll 38. **d** 39 **p** 40 S'wark. C of St Luke Camberwell 39-42; Soham w Barway 42-45; R of Buckworth 45-50; R of Upton 45-50; V of Lowdham w Gunthorpe 50-54; R of Upwell-Christchurch 54-60; Chap Derby Dioc Tr Coll 60-65; L to Offic Dio Derby from 60; V of Gt w L Gransden 65-70; Dioc Dir Relig Educn 65-80; Hon Can of Ely from 67; V of Madingley 70-80. *The Old Post Office, West Wratting Road, Balsham, Cambridge.*

HURDMAN, William Richard. b 40. K Coll Lon and Warm AKC 66. **d** 67 Portsm **p** 72 Thetford for Nor. C of St Mary Portsea 67-68; N Walsham 71-74; V of Friskney 74-81; Team R of Bottesford w Ashby Dio Linc from 81. *Rectory, Ashby, Scunthorpe, S Humb, DN16 3OL.*

HURFORD, Colin Osborne. Qu Coll Ox 2nd cl Math Mods 53, BA (3rd cl Th) 55, MA 59. Wells Th Coll 55. **d** 57 **p** 58 Bradf. C of Barnoldswick w Bracewell 57-61; Warrington 61-63; Asst Master and Chap St Paul's Sch Beaufort Sabah 63-68; Prin 68-70; C-in-c of Annscroft 71-79; Pontesbury 3rd Portion w Longden 71-79; R of Longden and Annscroft Dio Heref from 79; P-in-c of Pulverbatch Dio Heref from 81. *Rectory, Longden, Shrewsbury, Salop.*

HURFORD, Richard Warwick. b 44. St Jo Coll Morpeth ACT Dipl Th 70. **d** 69 **p** 70 Graft; Prec Graft Cathl 69-71; C-in-c of Tisbury 71-73; V (w Swallowcliffe and Ansty from 75) 73-76; R (w Chilmark) 76-77; Prec of Ch Ch Cathl Graft 77-78; R of Coffs Harbour Dio Graft from 78. *Box 163, Coffs Harbour, NSW, Australia.*

HURLEY, Ven Alfred Vincent. b 1896. OBE (Mil) 44, CBE (Mil) 45. TD 46. Keble Coll Ox BA 21, MA 27. Cudd Coll 21. **d** 22 **p** 23 Ripon. C of St Bart Armley 22-24; Chap HM Prison Leeds 23-24; HM Borstal Inst Portland 24-28 and 34-42; Dep Gov 28-31; R of Portland w Southwell (w St Pet Portland 33) 31-48; RD of Weymouth 37-43; Surr and CF (TA) 32-46; (R of O) 46-53; ACG 8th Army 44-45; DCG SE Asia 45-46; Men in Disp 44; Can and Preb of Chisenbury and Chute in Sarum Cathl 39-48; Can (Emer) from 48; R of Old Swinford 48-64; Archd of Dudley 51-68; Archd (Emer) from 68; Hon Can of Worc 51-67; Exam Chap to Bp of Worc 51-68. *Belbroughton Road, Halesowen, W Midl, B63 4LS.* (021-550 3575)

HURLEY, Daniel Timothy. b 37. St Mich Coll Llan 68. **d** 70 **p** 71 Bp Hughes for Llan. C of Llanfabon 70-73; CF 73-79; R of W Walton Dio Ely from 79. *West Walton Rectory, Wisbech, Cambs, PE14 7EU.* (Wisbech 3913)

HURLEY, Canon Joseph James. **d** 29 **p** 31 Fred. C of St Luke St John 29-31; R of Westfield 32-33; Master of Wiggins Orph for Boys St John Dio Fred from 33; C of St Paul St John NB 33-45; R of St Anne Ketepec St John 45-72; Can of Ch Ch Cathl Fred 71-72; Hon Can from 72. *Box 921, Saint John, NB, Canada.*

HURLOW, Canon Winston Gordon. b 14. Univ of Wales BA 35. St Jo Coll Ox BA 37, MA 47. St Mich Coll Llan 37. **d** 38 Swan B for Llan **p** 39 Llan. C of Neath w Llantwit 38-43; Chap RNVR 43-48; C-in-c of St Donats Llantwit 48-52; R of Eccleston 52-57; V of Sale 57-65; Chap Sale Brooklands Hosp 62-65; R of St Mary City and Dio Ches from 65; C-in-c of St Bridget w St Martin Ches 66-72; Ed Ches Dioc Leaflet 67-76; Dioc Information Officer 69-78; Hon Can of Ches from 69. *St Mary's Rectory, Chester, CH4 7HL.* (0244 671202)

HURON, Lord Bishop of. *See* Ragg, Right Rev Theodore David Butler.

HURON, Suffragan Bishop of. *See* Robinson, Right Rev Morse Cyril.

HURON, Dean of. *See* O'Driscoll, Very Rev Percival Richard.

HURRELL, John William. b 25. Ripon Hall, Ox 65. **d** 66 **p** 67 Glouc. C of Painswick 66-68; St Geo Glouc 68-70; Thornbury 70-73; V of St Steph City and Dio Glouc from 73. *St Stephen's Vicarage, Frampton Road, Gloucester.* (Glouc 24694)

HURRELL, Lionel Rex. b 41. Univ of Southn BA (3rd cl Hist) 64. Coll of Resurr Mirfield 64. **d** 66 Ex **p** 67 Crediton for Ex. C of Marychurch 66-69; Dawlish 69-71; Cathl Youth Officer Dio Cov 71-75; V of Porthleven 75-80; RD of Kerrier 78-80; P-in-c of St Sithney 78-80; V of Swindon New Town Dio Bris from 80. *St Marks Vicarage, Church Place, Swindon, Wilts, SN1 5EH.* (Swindon 22546)

HURST, Alan Greaves. b 17. Coll of Resurr Mirfield. **d** 49 Kens for Lon **p** 50 Lon. C of H Trin Paddington 49-53; St Marg Swinton 53-57; V of St Andr Hoyland Dio Sheff from 57. *St Andrew's Vicarage, Hoyland, Barnsley, Yorks, S74 0ET.* (Barnsley 742126)

HURST, Geoffrey. b 30. St Aid Coll 59. **d** 64 **p** 65 Sheff. C of St Cecilia Parson Cross Sheff 64-69; V of St Mark Wellingborough 69-77; P-in-c of St Mark City and Dio Leic and Industr Liaison Officer from 77. *3 Hoylake Close, Leicester.* (Leic 707743)

HURST, George Herbert. b 07. St Jo Coll Dur Barry Scho 32, BA (2nd cl Th), Univ Hebr Scho and Capel Cure Pri 33, MA 37. **d** 33 **p** 34 Blackb. C of Ch Ch Thornton 33-36; Adlington (in c of Ch Ch) 36-37; V of St Sav Preston 37-42; Em Preston 42-47; All SS Blackpool 47-49; R of Hockering w Mattishall Burgh 49-55; Reepham w Hackford Whitwell and Kerdiston 55-67; Kirstead w Langhale and Brooke 67-72; RD of Sparham 56-67. *The Place, Sharrington, Melton Constable, Norf, NR24 2PG.*

HURST, Jeremy Richard. b 40. Trin Coll Cam BA (2nd cl Th) 61. Linc Th Coll 62. **d** 64 **p** 65 S'wark. C of Woolwich 64-69; Perm to Offic Dio Ex 69-76; Dio Ox from 79. *110 Grenfell Road, Maidenhead, Berks.*

HURST, John. b 31. N-W Ordin Course 76. **d** 79 **p** 80 Man.

C of Flixton Dio Man from 79. *81 Derwent Road, Flixton, Manchester, M32 2UJ.* (061-747 8557)

HURST, John Cecil. b 08. Trin Coll Cam BA (2nd cl Hist Trip) 30, MA 37. Westcott Ho Cam 31. **d** 32 **p** 33 S'wark. C of St Geo Camberwell 32-36; Perm to Offic at Hinckley 36-37; C of Rye 37-41; R of Yoxall 41-50; W Meon (w Warnford from 63) 50-73; RD of Petersfield 57-62. *Middle Butts, Rectory Lane, Meonstoke, Southampton SO3 1NF.*

HURST, John Wilton. b 22. Univ of Kent Dipl Th 80. Tyndale Hall Bris 45. **d** 48 **p** 49 Blackb. C of St Thos Blackpool 48-51; St Pet Halliwell 51-54; Org Sec CPAS in SW Distr and Publ Pr Dio Bris 54-59; V of St Pet Tunbridge Wells Dio Roch from 59; Chap Pembury Hosp 60-65. *129 Forest Road, Tunbridge Wells, Kent.* (Tunbridge Wells 30384)

HURST, Joseph Bennett. Univ of Man BA 54. Ripon Hall, Ox 54. **d** 56 **p** 57 Man. C of St Jas Farnworth 56-59; Whitfield 59-61; R of Sawley 61-69; V of Dethick w Lea and Holloway Dio Derby from 69; P-in-c of Tansley Dio Derby from 79. *Lea Vicarage, Matlock, Derbys.* (Dethick 275)

HURST, Very Rev Walter Edmund Wilmshurst. CBE 76. Trin Coll Dub BA 34, MA 38. **d** 35 **p** 36 Derry. C of Drumachose 35-38; Lower Hutt 38-46; CF (NZ) 40-45; V of Waiwhetu 46-48; Stratford 48-51; R of New Plymouth and Can of Waik 51-56; Dean of Dun 56-63; Dean and V of St Paul's Cathl Wel 63-77; Dean (Emer) from 77; Perm to Offic Dio Wai from 77. *112 Grace Road, Tauranga, NZ.*

HURST-BANNISTER, Michael Barnabas St Leger. b 19. Dorch Miss Coll 41. **d** 44 **p** 45 Mon. LPr Dio Mon 44-45; C of Machen 45-46; Actg C of W Wycombe 46-47; C 47-48; H Trin Hendford Yeovil 48-49; V of Pilton 49-56; R of Fuglestone w Bemerton 56-63; Wishford Magna 63-67; R of L Langford 63-67; CECS Cler Org Sec Dios Win, Sarum and Portsm 67-78; LPr Dio Sarum 72-78; Sen Chap Actors Ch U from 75; P-in-c of St Anne Soho Dio Lon from 78. *57 Dean Street, W1V 5HH.* (01-437 5006)

HURT, Arnold Herbert. b 04. Univ of Man BSc 1st cl Eng 24. Cudd Coll 28. **d** 28 **p** 29 Blackb. C of St Mark Witton 28-31; St John Sunderland 31-36; PC of Shirebrook 37-45; V of Woodville 45-53; PC of St Aid New Cleethorpes 53-62; Hd Master St Mich Coll Belize 62-68; V of Resurr Berkeley Scunthorpe 69-71; P-in-c of Innerleithen 75-77. *29 Heliers Road, Liverpool, L13 4DH.*

HUSBAND, Terence. b 26. N-W Ordin Course 72. **d** 75 Man **p** 76 Hulme for Man. C of St Luke w All SS Weaste Salford 75-78; R of St Phil Gorton 78-82; V of Belford Dio Newc T from 82. *Vicarage, Belford, Northumb.* (Belford 545)

HUSBANDS, Canon Norman. b 03. AKC 32. St Steph Ho Ox 32. **d** 32 **p** 33 Pet. C of St Edm Northn 32-37; St Jo Div Richmond 37-41; V of Roade 41-76; C-in-c of Courteenhall 47-54; Surr 63-76; RD of Wotton 63-69; Can (Non-res) of Pet 67-76; Can (Emer) from 76. *47 Ridge Way, Weston Favell, Northampton, NN3 3AP.* (0604-408024)

HUSBANDS, Preb Philip Harold. b 09. Univ of Leeds BA (2nd cl Hist) 33. Coll of Resurr Mirfield 30. **d** 35 **p** 36 Newc T. C of St Mary Newc T 35-39; St Aug Tonge Moor 39-41; Chap RNVR 41-46; R of St Jas Wednesbury 46-80; Proc Conv Lich 64-80; Preb of Lich Cathl 69-80; Preb (Emer) from 80. *Charterhouse, EC1M 6AN.*

HUSSELL, Thomas Stanley. b 13. Univ of Wales BSc (2nd cl Math) 34, 2nd cl Physics 35. Sarum Th Coll 35. **d** 37 Wakef **p** 38 Pontefract for Wakef. C of St Paul Morley 37-42; Liversedge w Hightown 42-44; V of West Vale 44-50; St Marg Thornbury 50-57; C of All SS Cathl Wakef 57-61; Asst Master Qu Eliz Gr Sch Wakef 57-78; V of Wragby 61-71; L to Offic Dio Wakef from 71. *22 St John's Grove, Wakefield, Yorks, WF1 3SA.* (Wakef 377891)

HUSSEY, Very Rev John Walter Atherton. b 09. Keble Coll Ox BA (Phil Pol and Econ) 30, MA 34. Hon FRIBA 76. Univ of Sussex Hon DLitt 77. Cudd Coll 31. **d** 32 **p** 33 Lon. C of St Mary Abbots Kens (in c of St Paul 35-36) 32-37; V of St Matt Northn 37-55; Can (non-resid) of Pet 49-55; Master of St Jo Hosp Northn 48-55; RD of Northn 50-55; Surr 50-55; Proc Conv Pet 54-55; Dean of Chich 55-77; Dean (Emer) from 77. *5 Trevor Street, SW7 1DU.* (01-581 1819)

HUSSEY, William Kenneth Alfred. b 27. St Jo Coll Ox BA 48, Dipl Educn 49, MA 52. Wycl Hall, Ox. **d** 52 Bris **p** 53 Malmesbury for Bris. Asst Master Cathl Sch Bris 49-55; Asst Chap and Asst Master Wrekin Coll 55-60; Chap Ipswich Sch and L to Offic Dio St E 60-72; Hon Chap to Bp of St E 67-72; Hd Master Ches Cathl Choir Sch 72-74; P-in-c of Rendcomb 74-78; Chap Rendcomb Coll 74-78; Berkhamsted Sch from 78. *131 High Street, Berkhamsted, Herts, HP4 2DJ.* (Berkhamsted 73008)

HUSTON, Dale Rupert. Univ of Sask BA 64. Trin Coll Tor STB 66. **d** 66 **p** 67 Qu'App. I of St Phil Regina 66-73; Univ Chap Regina 66-73; C of St Paul's Cathl Lon Ont 73-77; R of Meaford 77-81; All SS Regina Dio Qu'App from 81. *3007 Westgate Avenue, Regina, Sask, Canada.*

HUTCHEON, Harold. b 14. Late Scho and Exhib of St D Coll Lamp BA 41. **d** 41 **p** 42 Llan. C of Seven Sisters 41-44; St Marg Hollinwood 44-47; V of Friezland 47-79. *7 April Grove, Tuebrook, Liverpool 6.*

HUTCHESON, Charles William James. d 67 Moos **p** 68 Bp Clarke for Moos. C of Foleyet 67-71; R of Hornepayne 71-76; Matheson Dio Moos from 76. *Box 370, Matheson, Ont, Canada.* (705-273 2212)

HUTCHINGS, Cecil Laurence Gifford. b 11. Mert Coll Ox BA (2nd cl Jurispr) 33, 3rd cl Th 35, MA 37. Cudd Coll 35. **d** 36 **p** 37 Linc. C of Grantham 36-40; Wendover 40-48; R of Nash w Thornton and Beachampton 48-51; RD of Wolverton 51-67; PC of Stony Stratford 51-67; R of Brightwell w Sotwell 67-76; Perm to Offic Dio Ox from 77. *17 East Saint Helen Street, Abingdon, Oxon, Ox14 5EE.* (Abingdon 26949)

HUTCHINGS, Colin Michael. Clifton Th Coll 66. **d** 68 **p** 69 Southw. C of St Jo Evang Worksop 68-71; Hampreston 71-76; Team V of Tisbury Dio Sarum from 76. *Chilmark Vicarage, Salisbury, Wilts, SP3 5AH.* (072-287 307)

HUTCHINGS, Evan David. b 09. Univ of Leeds BA (2nd cl Cl) 31. Coll of Resurr Mirfield 28. **d** 33 **p** 34 Llan. C of Merthyr Tydfil 33-35; St Geo Georgetown 35-38; R of St Mich Fort Wellington w Belladrum 38-41; C of Roath 41-43; CF (EC) 43-47; C of Ash 47-49; CF 49-52; PC (V from 69) of Dundry 52-74; Perm to Offic Dio B & W from 78. *Anglebury, Warren's Close, Cheddar, Somt.*

HUTCHINGS, Ian James. b 49. Dipl Th (Lon) 72. Trin Coll Bris 72. **d** 73 **p** 74 Warrington for Liv. C of Parr 73-77; Timperley 77-81; V of Partington and Carrington Dio Ches from 81. *Partington Vicarage, Urmston, Manchester, M31 4FB.* (061-775 3542)

HUTCHINGS, John Denis Arthur. b 29. Keble Coll Ox BA 53, MA and BSc 59. Chich Th Coll 58. **d** 60 Lon **p** 61 Kens for Lon. C of St Pancras 60-63; Asst Chap Denstone Coll Staffs 63-67; C of Stepney 67-78; Asst Master Sir John Cass Found and Red Coat Sch Stepney 67-78; Hon C of St Jas New Malden Dio S'wark from 70; Asst Master and Chap Denstone Coll Staffs from 79. *Denstone College, Uttoxeter, Staffs, ST14 5HN.*

HUTCHINGS, Leslie Bloom. b 10. OBE (Mil) 51. Late Scho of Magd Coll Cam 2nd cl Cl Trip pt i 31, BA (2nd cl Cl Trip pt ii) 32, MA 36. Univ of Birm Dipl Th 59. **d** 60 Birm **p** 61 Aston for Birm. Asst Master Solihull Sch 32-67; Asst Chap 60-67; C of Knowle 60-67; V of Modbury w Brownston 67-79; P-in-c of Aveton Gifford 75-77; R 77-79; Publ Pr Dio Ex from 80. *Morleigh Cottage, Morleigh Road, Harbertonford, Totnes, Devon TQ9 7TS.*

HUTCHINGS, Norman Leslie. Wycl Hall Ox 42. **d** and **p** 43 Roch. [f REC Min] C of Tonbridge 43-46; V of St Steph w St Bart and St Matt Islington 46-53; Oxgate 53-62; Ch Ch Ore 62-77. *6 Sunnyside Road, Rusthall Common, Tunbridge Wells, Kent.* (Tunbridge Wells 33264)

HUTCHINS, Alfred Cuthbert le Gassick. d 46 **p** 48 Sktn. Miss at Carragana 46-49; I of Lashburn 49-52; R of All SS Sktn 52-58; I of Hanley 54-58; St Faith Vanc 58-66; C of St Jas Vanc 66-68; I of All SS Vanc 68-76; I of St Sav Vanc 68-76; R of St D Vanc 68-76; Perm to Offic Dio BC from 78. *2848 George View Drive, Vancouver, BC, Canada.*

HUTCHINS, Charles Henry. b 37. Univ of Leeds BA (2nd cl Th) 60, BD 67. Ridley Hall, Cam 60. **d** 62 **p** 63 Wakef. C of Kirkheaton 62-65; R of Arthingworth w Kelmarsh and Harrington 65-68; V of Ch Ch U Armley 68-79; RD of Armley 75-79; Prin CA Wilson Carlile Coll of Evang Blackheath from 79. *103 Mycenae Road, SE3.*

HUTCHINS, Edgar Brian. b 46. Univ of K Coll Halifax NS BA 72. Atlantic Sch of Th 72. **d** 74 **p** 76 NS; on leave 74-75; R of Pugwash and River John 76-78. *Rectory, Pugwash, NS, Canada.*

HUTCHINSON, Charles William Aldersey. b 10. SS Coll Cam BA 32, MA 37. Ely Th Coll 33. **d** 33 **p** 34 Chelmsf. C of St Barn L Ilford 33-35; Saffron Walden 35-37; R of Washingborough w Heighington Dio Linc from 37; Chap RNVR 43-46. *The Old Rectory, Washingborough, Lincoln.* (Linc 790379)

HUTCHINSON, Cyril Peter. b 37. Univ of Dur BA 61. **d** 63 **p** 64 Birm. C of St Paul w St Mark Birm 63-67; Perm to Offic Dio Birm from 67; Dio Bradf 69-75; Hon C of Manningham 75-76; V of St Jo Bapt Clayton Dio Bradf from 76; RD of Bowling and Horton from 80. *vicarage, Clayton Lane, Clayton, Bradford, BD14 6AX.* (Bradford 880373)

HUTCHINSON, David Bamford. b 29. QUB BSc 53. TCD Div Test 55. **d** 55 **p** 56 Connor. C of Ch Ch Lisburn 55-57; BCMS Dio Soroti 57-63; Chap Teso Coll Soroti 63-65; Div Master Annandale Gr Sch Belf 65-66; I of Kilkeel 66-75; Willowfield Dio Down from 75. *Willowfield Rectory, Belfast 6, N Ireland.* (Belfast 57654)

HUTCHINSON, Hugh Edward. b 27. Bps' Coll Cheshunt. **d** 61 **p** 62 Lon. C of St Anne Limehouse 61-64; Dartmouth w Townstal 64-67; V of St Mark Ex 67-75; R of Beeford w

Lissett and Dunnington 75-80; C-in-c of Foston-on-the-Wolds 75-77; R 77-80; C-in-c of N Frodingham 75-77; R 77-80; RD of N Holderness 79-80; P-in-c of Appleton Roebuck w Acaster Selby Dio York from 80; Sec Dioc Advisory C'tte Dio York from 80. *Vicarage, Appleton Roebuck, York, YO5 7DG.* (Appleton Roebuck 327)

HUTCHINSON, Jeremy Olpherts. b 32. Or Coll Ox BA 55, MA 60. St Jo Coll Dur Dipl Th 57. **d** 57 **p** 58 Lon. C of Shoreditch 57-60; V of Hoxton 60-78; Co-ordinator Huddleston Centre for Handicapped Children in St Jas Clapton from 78. *56 Rushmore Road, E5.* (01-985 7115)

HUTCHINSON, John Charles. b 44. K Coll Lon and Warm 64. **d** 69 Portsm **p** 70 Bp Woolmer for Portsm. C of All SS Portsea 69-73; Team V of H Trin Fareham 73-78; P-in-c of Pangbourne Dio Ox from 78. *Rectory, St James Close, Pangbourne, Reading, Berks.* (Pangbourne 2928)

HUTCHINSON, Ven John Desmond. b 17. Trin Coll Dub BA (1st cl Mod) 39, Div Test (1st cl) Wall Bibl Scho and Downes Pri (2nd) 40, MA 46. Univ of Lon BD 48, MTh 56. **d** 40 **p** 41 Oss. C of Maryborough 40-42; Asst Chap Miss to Seamen Belf 42-43; Chap Miss to Seamen Port of Spain Trinid 44-46; R of Rathcormac 47-49; C-in-c of Rushbrooke 49-50; R of Clonmel w Rushbrooke 50-58; Exam Chap to Bp of Cork from 52; RD of Castleyons and of Cloyne 53-60; Kerricurrihy and Kinalea 60-67; Treas of Cloyne and Can of Cahirlag in Cork Cathl 58-60; R of St Mich Blackrock 58-75; Prec of Cloyne Cathl 60-65; Can of Killaspugmullane in Cork Cathl 60-65; Preb of St Patr Cathl Dub 64-81; Archd of Cloyne 65-67; Can of Liscleary in Cork Cathl 65-67 and from 76; Archd of Cork (w Ross from 72 and Cloyne from 73) from 67; Chap Univ Coll Cork from 67; I of Moviddy w Kilmurry Dio Cork from 75. *Moviddy Rectory, Aherla, Cork, Irish Republic.* (Aherla 80)

HUTCHINSON, Canon John Lewen Fernand. Trin Coll Tor LTh 28. **d** 27 **p** 28 Bran. C of Makinak and Winnipegosis 27-28; R of Holmfield 28-32; Oak Lake 32-35; I of Pittsburg 35-40; Actg V of Trenton 40-44; Chap RCN 44-45; I of Madoc 46-47; R of St Pet Brockville 47-59; Can of Ont from 56; Exam Chap to Bp of Ont 56-72; Sec Information and Stewardship Comm 59-72. *1206 Peden Boulevard, Brockville, Ont, Canada.* (613-342 5131)

HUTCHINSON, Keith. b 40. Keble Coll Ox 2nd cl Nat Sc Mods 61, BA (2nd cl Nat Sc) 63, Liddon Stud 63, 2nd cl Th 65, MA 68. St Steph Ho Ox 63. **d** 66 **p** 67 Wakef. C of Brighouse 66-72; R of Workington Dio Carl from 72. *Rectory, Parsons Court, Workington, Cumb, CA14 2EZ.* (Workington 2311)

HUTCHINSON, Paul Edward. b 33. K Coll Lon and Warm. **d** 59 **p** 60 Lon. C of St Mich AA Bromley-by-Bow 59-63; St Mich AA Mill Hill 63-66; Sandridge (in c of St Mary Marshalswick) 66-72; V of St Mary Marshalswick St Alb 72-80; Tunstall Dio Lich from 80. *26 Stanley Street, Tunstall, Stoke-on-Trent, ST6 6BW.* (S-on-T 88288)

HUTCHINSON, Philip. b 14. St Jo Coll Dur BA (2nd cl Th) 37, MA 40. BD (Lon) 60. **d** 37 **p** 38 Dur. C of Blackhill 37-40; Stranton 40-46; V of St Thos Westoe 46-56; W Hartlepool 56-61; St Paul Stockton-on-Tees 61-75; Bp Middleham 75-79. *20 Woodvale Road, Darlington, Co Durham, DL3 8EZ.*

HUTCHINSON, Philip Sheldon. Pemb Coll Cam BA 56, MA 59. Chich Th Coll 56. **d** 58 **p** 59 S'wark. C of St Nich Plumstead 58-60; Roehampton 60-64; R of St Thos Old Charlton Woolwich 65-69; P-in-c of Marysville 69-70; R of Alexandra 70-73; Exam Chap to Bp of Wang 71-73; I of St Mark Leopold 73-77; Ch Ch St Kilda Dio Melb from 77. *14 Acland Street, St Kilda, Vic, Australia 3182.* (534 3892)

HUTCHINSON, Raymond. b 30. Univ of Lon Dipl Th 59. Richmond Coll 53. **d** 56 **p** 58 Mysore. In Ch of S India 56-60; C of Wooburn 60-63; Caversham (in c of St Barn Emmer Green) 63-65; R of Duror w Portnacrois and Glencreran 65-70; R of Partney w Dalby 70-73; Ashby-by-Partney 70-73; V of Skendleby 70-73; R of Candlesby w Scremby 72-73; Arundel Dio Montr from 78. *Box 67, Arundel, PQ, Canada.* (819-687 3776)

HUTCHINSON, Raymond John. b 51. Univ of Liv BSc 73. Westcott Ho Cam 73. **d** 76 **p** 77 S'wark. C of St Jo Peckham 76-79; Prescot (in c of St Paul) 79-81; V of St Dunstan Edge Hill Dio Liv from 81. *St Dunstan's Vicarage, Earle Road, Liverpool, L7 6HD.* (051-733 4385)

HUTCHINSON, Roland Louis. b 29. Trin Coll Dub BA 51, MA 61. **d** 52 **p** 53 Arm. C of Mullabrack w Kilcluney 52-54; Dromore Cathl 54-62; C-in-c of Tyrella w Rathmullen 62-65; R 65-74; Magheralin Dio Drom from 74. *New Forge Road, Magheralin, Co Armagh, N Ireland.* (Moira 611273)

HUTCHINSON, Stephen. b 38. St Chad's Coll Dur BA 60, Dipl Th 62. **d** 62 **p** 63 Lich. C of St Mich Tividale Tipton 62-68; V of St Andr Walsall 68-73; R of Headless Cross 73-81; Team R of The Ridge, Redditch Dio Worc from 81. *69 Evesham Road, Redditch, Worcs, B97 4JX.* (Redditch 45521)

HUTCHINSON, Stephen Theodore. b 04. Keble Coll Ox BA 29, MA 31. **d** and **p** 72 Brech. C of Arbroath 72-75; St Salvador Dundee 75-77; P-in-c of Muchalls Dio Brech from 77. *Rectory, Muchalls, Stonehaven, AB3.*

HUTCHINSON, William. b 03. Wycl Hall Ox 57. **d** and **p** 58 Roch. C of Isle of Grain Dio Roch 58-60; V (w Stoke from 76) 60-82; RD of Strood 73-79. *Address temp unknown.*

HUTCHINSON, William David. b 27. Wycl Hall, Ox 55. **d** 57 **p** 58 St E. C of St Jo Bapt Ipswich 57-60; R of Combs 60-65; V of St Aug of Hippo Ipswich 65-76; R of Ewhurst 76-81; V of Aldeburgh w Hazlewood Dio St E from 81. *Vicarage, Church Walk, Aldeburgh, Suff.* (Aldeburgh 2223)

HUTCHISON, Alfred Powell. b 07. St Aug Coll Cant 35. **d** 38 **p** 39 Lon. C of St Mich AA Harrow Weald 38-40; Asst Chap Miss to Seamen Tyne and L to Offic Dio Dur 40-41; Glas and the Clyde and Oban 41; Chap Miss to Seamen Port of Spain Trinidad 42-44; Org Sec Miss to Seamen and L Pr Dio Guildf 45-48; Chap Miss to Seamen Fremantle 48-51; Org Sec Miss to Seamen and LPr Dios Ox and Guildf 51-54 and 57-64; Dio Ex 54-57; Chap Miss to Seamen Walvis Bay 64-65; Staff Chap Miss to Seamen from 65; Sec Lightships Committee 69-72; Hon Liaison Chap from 72; Hon C of Banstead Dio Guildf from 74. *47 Diceland Road, Banstead, Surrey.* (Burgh Heath 52369)

HUTCHISON, Andrew Sandford. b 38. York Univ Tor. **d** and **p** 69 Tor. C of Ch Ch Deer Pk Tor 69-71; R of Minden and Kinmount 71-74; St Francis Meadowvale 74-81; St Luke City and Dio Tor from 81. *904 Coxwell Avenue, Toronto, M4C 3G3, Ont, Canada.*

HUTCHISON, Brian Bridger. Ch Coll Hobart ACT ThL 61. **d** 67 **p** 68 Tas. C of Devonport 67-68; Beaconsfield w Exeter 68-69; P-in-c 69-72; R of Buckland 72-79; sheff Dio Tas from 79. *Rectory, Sheffield, tasmania 7306.* (004 91 1119)

HUTCHISON, Eric William. b 21. McGill Univ Montr BA 42. U Th Sem NY BD 55, **d** and **p** 55 NY. In Amer Ch 55-59; Tutor Buwalasi Th Coll Mbale 59-63; Lect Makerere Univ Kamp 63-69; Hon C of St Jas Cam Dio Ely from 80. *77 Long Road, Cambridge, CB2 2HE.*

HUTCHISON, Geoffrey John. b 52. Trin Hall Cam BA 75, MA 78. Ridley Hall Cam 77. **d** 79 Chelmsf **p** 80 Barking for Chelmsf. C of St Pet Harold Wood Dio Chelmsf from 79. *48 Harold Court Road, Romford, RM3 0YX.*

HUTCHISON, George Malcolm. Hur Coll. **d** 55 Hur **p** 57 NS. C of Centreville 55-56; St Jas Stratford 56-57; St Paul Halifax 57-58; R of Westville 58-60; Valcartier 60-69; I of Fitch Bay Dio Queb from 69. *Fitch Bay, PQ, Canada.*

HUTCHISON, Henry Peter. b 20. CCC Ox MA 49. TCD MA 52. SS Coll Cam MA 55. FIChemE. Linc Th Coll 80. **d** 81 Ely (APM). C of St Barn Cam Dio Ely from 81. *Browning House, Great Shelford, Cambridge, CB2 5LJ.*

HUTT, David Handley. b 38. K Coll Lon and Warm AKC 68. **d** 69 Lon **p** 70 Kens for Lon. C of St Mich AA Bedford Pk 69-70; St Matt Westmr 70-73; PV and Succr of S'wark Cathl 73-78; Sen Chap of K Coll Taunton 78-82; V of St Alb w St Patr Bordesley Dio Birm from 82. *St Alban's Clergy House, Stanhope Street, Birmingham, B12 0XB.* (021-440 4605)

HUTT, Mountain Coulter De Witt. Trin Coll Tor BA 41, LTh 50. **d** 50 Bp Wells for Tor **p** 50 Tor. R of Holland Landing 50-51; Iroquois Falls 51-61; St Monica Tor 61-66; St Mary Magd Tor 66-79. *114 Delamere Avenue, Stratford, Ont, N5A 4Z5, Canada.*

HUTTON, Brian Allan. b 40. Bps' Coll Cheshunt. **d** 69 Bp Ramsbotham for Newc T **p** 70 Newc T. C of St Matt w St Mary Virg Newc T 69-72; St Mary Blyth 72-75; V of St Cath Woodthorpe City and Dio Sheff from 75. *300 Hastilar Road South, Sheffield, S13 8EJ.* (Sheffield 399598)

HUTTON, David James. b 40. Univ of Dur BA 64. Univ of Kent MA 79. Coll of Resurr Mirfield 64. **d** 66 Warrington for Liv **p** 67 Liv. C of Kirkby 66-70; Asst Chap Univ of Kent 70-73; Chap 73-78; Hon Min Can of Cant Cathl from 71; Six Pr Cant Cathl 74-80; Chap The Lon Hosp Whitechapel from 78. *Chaplain's Office, The London Hospital, Whitechapel, E1.* (01-247 5454)

HUTTON, Griffith Arthur Jeremy. b 31. Trin Hall, Cam 3rd cl Th Trip pt i 53, BA 56, MA 59. Linc Th Coll 56. **d** 58 **p** 59 Newc T. C of Hexham 58-60; All SS Gosforth (in c of Regent Farm from 62) 60-65; V of Whitegate (w L Budworth from 71) 65-78; R of Dowdeswell and Andoversford w The Shiptons and Cold Salperton Dio Glouc from 78. *Shipton Oliffe Rectory, Cheltenham, Glos.* (Andoversford 230)

HUTTON, Henry John. b 12. **d** 71 **p** 72 Swaz. C of St Anne Pigg's Peak (in c of Bulembu and Havelock) 71-73; Hd Master Herbert Stanley Sch Bulembu 71-73; St Mark's Sch Mbabane and C of All SS Mbabane and Malambanyati 73-75; C of Ellesmere Port Dio Ches 75-79; Team V from 79. *Vicarage, Denbigh Gardens, Ellesmere Port, Chesh, L65 9BG.* (051-355 5661)

HUTTON, John Alexander. b 26. **d** 77 **p** 78 Edin (APM). C of Cathl Ch of St Mary Dio Edin from 77. *7 Carberry Place, Edinburgh, EH12 5HY.*

HUTTON, Joseph Charles. b 21. DFC 41. Westcott Ho Cam 63. **d** 65 **p** 66 Ex. C of Marychurch 65-67; PC of Warborough 67-68; V 69-70; V of Earley 70-75; R of Ludgvan 75-79; Perm to Offic Dio Truro from 79. *13 Rosevale, Alexandra Road, Penzance, Cornwall.* (Penzance 61868)

HUTTON, Patrick George. Chich Th Coll 65. **d** 68 Willesden for Lon **p** 69 Lon. C of St Jo Evang Palmers Green 68-71; St Geo Cathl Georgetn 71-73; R of Anna Regina 73-75; V of Yupukari 75-80; P-in-c of Rupununi 75-80; Stow Bardolph w Wimbotsham Dio Ely from 80; Nordelph Dio Ely from 80. *34 Church Road, Wimbotsham, King's Lynn, Norf, PE34 3QG.* (Downham Market 387854)

HUTTON, Peter George. St Jo Coll Auckld LTh 53. **d** 54 **p** 55 Auckld. C of St Andr Epsom Auckld 54-55; Chap St Pet Th Coll Siota 55-57; C of Rotorua 57-60; L to Offic Dio Auckld 61-70; Chap RNZAF 64-67; RNZN from 67; Hon C of H Trin Devonport 71-73. *HMNZS Philomel, Devonport, Auckland, NZ.*

HUTTON, Canon Stanley Peart. b 15. St Jo Coll Dur BA (1st cl Mod Hist) 37, Jenkyns Scho 37, Dipl Th 38, MA 40. **d** 38 **p** 39 Dur. C of Beamish 38-40; St Paul Jarrow 40-42; Chap RAFVR 42-46; V of New Malton 47-54; Hessle 54-62; R of Stevenage 62-69; Hon Can of St Alb 66-80; Can (Emer) from 80; V of Sharnbrook 69-80; R of Knotting w Souldrop 69-80; Perm to Offic Dio Ex from 80. *Flat 2, Coly House, Rosemary Lane, Colyton, Devon, EX13 6LS.* (Colyton 52744)

HUTTON, William John. Univ of W Ont BA 55. Univ of Tor BEducn 62, MEducn 63. Hur Coll LTh 57. **d** 59 **p** 60 Tor. C of St Leon Tor 59-62; L to Offic Dio Rupld from 62; Hon C of St Mark Winnipeg Dio Rupld from 70. *177 Egerton Road, Winnipeg 8, Manit., Canada.*

HUXHAM, Hector Hubert. b 29. Univ of Bris BA 55. Tyndale Hall, Bris. **d** 56 Liv **p** 57 Warrington for Liv. C of St Luke Eccleston 56-58; H Trin Heworth York 59-60; V of Burley 61-66; Chap St Jas Hosp Leeds from 67. *Chaplain's Office, St James's University Hospital, Leeds, LS9 7TF.* (Leeds 33144)

HUXHAM, Peter Richard. b 38. Worc Coll Ox BA (2nd cl Th) 61. St Steph Ho Ox 61. **d** 63 **p** 64 Sarum. C of St Mary Gillingham Dorset 63-67; St Phil Osmondthorpe Leeds 67-70; V of Parkstone (St Osmund) 70-75; V of Parkstone St Pet w Branksea I & St Osmond Dio Sarum from 75. *19 Springfield Road, Parkstone, Poole, Dorset, BH14 0LG.* (0202-748860)

HUXLEY, Keith. b 33. Late Tancred Stud of Ch Coll Cam 2nd cl Geog Trip pt i 56, BA (2nd cl Geog Trip pt ii) 57, MA 61. Cudd Coll 57. **d** 59 **p** 60 Ches. C of Bowdon 59-61; Ch Ch Crewe 61-62; St Pet and St Mich Ches 62-64; Dioc Youth Chap Dio Ches 62-68; Asst Chap Ches Cathl 65-68; V of St Andr Grange Runcorn 68-73; R of E Runcorn w Halton Team Min 73-77; Home Sec Bd of Miss and Unity Gen Syn from 77; Chap to HM the Queen from 81. *Board for Mission & Unity, Church House, Dean's Yard, SW1P 3NZ.* (01-222 9011)

HUXLEY, Stephen Scott. b 30. Linc Th Coll 53. **d** 56 **p** 57 Newc T. C of St Geo Cullercoats 56-59; Eglingham 59-60; N Gosforth 60-63; V of Hartburn w Meldon 63-65; V of Netherwitton 63-65; H Sav Priory Ch Tynemouth 65-74; Warkworth 74-78; Acklington 74-78; P-in-c of St Jo Evang Percy Tynemouth Dio Newc T 78-82; V from 82. *Percy Main Vicarage, North Shields, T & W, NE29 6HS.* (N Shields 571819)

HUXLEY, William Thomas. b 31. Oak Hill Th Coll 60. **d** 63 **p** 64 Chelmsf. C of Rainham 63-66; H Trin Heworth York 66-67; R of The Chignals w Mashbury Dio Chelmsf from 67. *Chignal Smealey Rectory, Chelmsford, Essex. CM1 4SZ.*

HUYTON, Stuart. b 37. St D Coll Lamp BA 62, Dipl Th 63. **d** 63 **p** 64 Lich. C of Kingswinford 63-66; Leek 66-69; V of Wigginton 69-76; Wombourne Dio Lich from 76; RD of Trysull from 79. *Wombourne Vicarage, Wolverhampton, Staffs, WV5 9ED.* (Wombourne 892234)

HUZZEY, Peter George. b 48. Trin Coll Bris 74. **d** 76 **p** 77 Bris. C of Bishopsworth 76-79; Downend 79-80; Team V of Kings Norton Dio Birm from 80. *372 Shannon Road, Hawkesley, Birmingham, B38 9TR.*

HWANG, Jane Hsien Yuin. b 17. Hua Chung Univ China BA 43. Columbia Univ NY MA 48. U Th Sem Yunan 39. **d** 58 **p** 71 Hong. V of H Trin Kowloon 71-76; P-in-c of St Thos Kowloon Dio Hong from 76. *43 Berwick Street, Kowloon, Hong Kong.* (3-785544)

HWANG, Ven Joseph Jeong-ki. St Mich Sem Oryudong. **d** 68 **p** 69 Taejon. P Dio Taejon 68-73 and from 76; Perm to Offic Dio Pet 74-76; Archd of Chungchong from 76. *335-4 Kyohyundong, Chung Jusi 380, Chungbuk, Korea.*

HYALO, Very Rev Dawson. b 41. Bp Tucker Coll Mukono Dipl Th 76. **d** and **p** 66 Mbali. P Dio Mbali 66-72; Dio Bukedi 72-77; Dean of Bukedi from 78; Archd of Budaka from 81. *Saint Peter's Cathedral, PO Box 170, Tororo, Uganda.*

HYATT, Robert Keith. b 34. Em Coll Cam 3rd cl Geog Trip pt i 57, BA (3rd cl Th Trip pt ii) Ridley 59, MA 63. Ridley Hall Cam 58. **d** 60 **p** 61 Glouc. C of Cheltm 60-63; Asst Chap K Edw Sch Witley 63-65; C of Godalming 65-69; V of St Andr Kowloon 69-78; V of Claygate Dio Guildf from 78. *Vicarage, Church Road, Claygate, Surrey, KT10 0JP.* (Esher 63603)

HYDE, Alan. b 09. Univ of Liv BSc 33. St Aid Coll 46. **d** 48 Ches **p** 51 Lon. C of Seacombe 48-49; St Chris Conv Distr Hanwell 49-51; St Barn Ealing 51-52; Asst Master St Olave's Gr Sch Tower Bridge Lon 51-56; Acton Co Sch 56-70; Hon C of H Cross Greenford 52-54; Perm to Offic Dio Lon 56-70; V of Satley 70-77. *6 Pilling Lane, Lydiate, Merseyside, L31 4HF.* (051 5318561)

HYDE, Alfred Cecil. b 1895. **d** 62 **p** 63 Win. C of Basingstoke 62-64; St Chris Conv Distr Thornhill 64-72. *Address temp unknown.*

HYDE, Dennis Hugh. b 23. Univ of Leeds, BA (2nd cl Th) 56. Sarum Th Coll 60. **d** 60 Bp Dale for Cant **p** 61 Guildf. C of Farncombe 60-62; Burgh Heath 62-65; V of Shottermill 65-74; Pastoral Consultant Clinical Th Assoc from 74. *21 Pinewood Park, New Haw, Weybridge, Surrey.*

HYDE, Edgar Bonsor. b 29. Clifton Th Coll 59. **d** 61 **p** 62 B & W. C of Ch Ch Weston-s-Mare 61-66; Chipping Campden 66-70; R of Longborough w Sezincote and Condicote (and the Swells from 78) Dio Glouc from 70. *Longborough Rectory, Moreton-in-Marsh, Glos.* (Stow-on-the-Wold 30447)

HYDE, Vyvian Donald Wingfield. b 10. Univ of Dur LTh 33. Sarum Th Coll 30. **d** 33 **p** 34 Ox. C of Aylesbury 33-35; Publ Pr Dio S'wark 35-38; C of St Jo Bapt (in c of St Aug) Margate 38-40; R of St Ignatius Salford 40-41; C of St Pet Croydon 42-43; R of St Andr Deal 43-56; V of St Bart Dover 56-68; Hon C of St Geo Ramsgate Dio Cant from 68. *27 Albert Road, Ramsgate, Kent.*

HYDE-DUNN, Keith. b 43. Sarum Th Coll. **d** 69 Sarum **p** 70 Matab. C of St Athan Selukwe 70-72; Horsham 73-77; P-in-c of Fittleworth Dio Chich from 77. *Fittleworth Rectory, Pulborough, Sussex.* (Fittleworth 455)

HYDE-LINAKER, John Etheridge. b 28. St Deiniol's Libr Hawarden 74. **d** 76 **p** 77 St A. C of Bistre 76-78; Denbigh 78-80; R of Cerrigydrudion w Llangwm, Llanfihangel Glyn-Myfyr, Ysbyty Ifan, Pentrefoelas, Bettws Gwerfil Goch and Dinmael Dio St A from 80. *Rectory, Cerrigydrudion, Corwen, Clwyd, LL21 0RU.* (049-082 313)

HYDER, Geoffrey Frank. b 28. St Jo Coll Dur 49. **d** 53 **p** 54 York. C of H Trin Hull 53-56; St Sav Westcliff-on-Sea 56-59; V of All SS Haggerston 59-65; St Pet w St Mary Southwick 65-68; Chr Aid Reg Org Greater Lon and Publ Pr Dio S'wark 68-74; R of Keston Dio Roch from 74. *Rectory, Commonside, Keston, Kent, BR2 6BP.* (Farnborough 53186)

HYETT, Canon Edgar Henry. **d** 49 **p** 50 Bran. C-in-c of Bethany 49-50; R 50-52; Neepawa and Gladstone 52-54; Miss at Fort Simpson 54-56; Fort MacPherson 56-61; R of Oak Lake 61-63; I of Russell 63-72; Hon Can of Bran 65-73; Can (Emer) from 75. *Box 811, Russell, Manit., Canada.*

HYLAND, Cecil George. b 38. TCD BA 62, Bp Forster Prem (2nd) 62, Downes Oratory Pri 63, MA 78. **d** 63 **p** 64 Connor. C of St Nich Belf 63-66; Monkstown 66-68; Ch of Ireland Youth Officer 68-73; Chap of TCD 73-79; R of Tullow Dio Dub from 79. *Tullow Rectory, Brighton Road, Carrickmines, Dublin, Irish Republic.* (Dub 893135)

HYMAS, John Thomas. b 09. St Andr Coll Pampisford, 46. **d** 47 **p** 48 Ripon. C of St Mich AA Headingley 47-52; V of Ormesby 52-58; Sowerby 58-77; C-in-c of Sessay 63-77. *The School House, Sharow, Ripon, N Yorks, HG4 5BJ.* (Ripon 2402)

HYNARD, Grahame William. Moore Th Coll Syd 62. **d** 63 **p** 64 Syd. C of Lithgow 63-64; C-in-c of Mulgoa w Greendale and Luddenham 64-65; R 65-67; C-in-c of Engadine Dio Syd from 67-74; R from 74. *63 Cambrai Avenue, Engadine, NSW, Australia 2233.* (520-8965)

HYSLOP, James. b 09. Edin Th Coll 60. **d** 62 **p** 63 Brech. C of St Mary Arbroath 62-65; St Mich and All SS Edin 65-68; C-in-c of St Ninian Dundee 68-69; R of Galashiels 69-76; Perm to Offic Dio St Andr from 76; Dio Edin from 81. *17 North Street, St Andrews, Fife, KY16 9PW.*

HYSLOP, Robert Henry. b 07. St Aid Coll 46. **d** 48 **p** 49 Liv. C of Maghull 48-50; Prescot 50-51; CF (TA) 50-57; CF (TA - R of O) 57-62; C of Heanor (in c of Marlpool) 51-55; Luton (in c of St Anne) 55-57; Chap Rampton Hosp 57-62; Broadmoor Hosp 62-64; R of St Geo Berm 64-76; Perm to Offic Dio Ex from 77. *The Parsonage House, Burrington, Umberleigh, EX37 9LA.* (Ashreigney 231)

HYSLOP, Thomas. b 10. Worc Coll Ox BA 33, MA 36. Ripon Hall, Ox 33. **d** 35 **p** 36 Lon. C of St Steph Ealing 35-41; C-in-c of Ch Ch Chelsea 42-44; Perm to Offic Dio Ox 44-48; R of Salford w L Rollright 48-75; C-in-c of Gt Rollright

64-75; Cornwell 79-75. *36 Webb Crescent, Chipping Norton, Oxon, OX7 5HU.* (Chipping Norton 3506)

HYSLOP, Thomas James. b 54. Univ of St Andr Fife BD 76. Edin Th Coll 76. **d** 78 Penrith for Carl **p** 79 Carl. C of Whitehaven 78-81; Walney I Dio Carl from 81. *35 Vengeance Street, Walney Island, Barrow-in-Furness, LA14 3BY.*

I

IAGORO, Damien Sawaraba. Newton Coll Dogura 63. **d** 65 **p** 67 New Guinea. P Dio New Guinea 65-70; Dio Papua from 71. *Box 36, Popondota, Papua New Guinea.*

IANI, Grayden. St Aid Coll Dogura. **d** 57 **p** 70 New Guinea. P Dio Guinea 57-71; Dio Papua from 71. *Anglican Church, Huhuru, via Popondetta, Papua.*

IASSINE, Fernando. **d** and **p** 75 Lebom. P Dio Lebom. *CP 120, Maputo, Mozambique.*

IBADAN, Lord Bishop of. *See* Olufosoye, Most Rev Timothy Omotayo.

IBADAN, Provost of. (Vacant)

IBALL, Canon Charles Herbert. b 12. Univ of Leeds BA (2nd cl Hist) 34. Coll of Resurr Mirfield 34. **d** 36 **p** 37 Ches. C of St Thos Stockport 36-39; St Thos Dudley 39-41; Netherton (in c of Dudley Wood) 41-44; V of St Jo Bapt Barnsley 44-47; St Geo Redditch 47-53; Acock's Green 53-70; RD of Yardley 65-70; Surr 65-70; R of Curdworth 70-77; Hon Can of Birm 72-77; Can (Emer) from 77; Perm to Offic Dio Ches from 77. *89a High Street, Tarporley, Chesh, CW6 0AB.* (Tarporley 2169)

IBALL, Charles Martin John. b 40. Lich Th Coll 67. **d** 69 **p** 70 Worc. C of St Edm Dudley 69-73; St Jas W Bromwich 73-76; V of Oxley 76-80. *c/o Vicarage, Lymer Road, Oxley, Wolverhampton.* (Wolverhampton 783342)

IBALL, Glyn. b 41. Univ of Wales, BSc 63. St Mich Coll Llan 63. **d** 65 **p** 66 St A. C of Ruabon w Penylan 65-71; Chap Latymer U Sch Hammersmith Dio Lon from 71; L to Offic at St Mich and AA Bedford Pk Dio Lon from 71. *106 Woodstock Road, W4.* (01-994 4351)

IBARRA, Guilfredo. **d** and **p** 66 Argent. P Dio Argent 66-73; N Argent from 73. *Parsonage, Misión Chaque£na, N Argentina.*

IBBOTSON, Alick. St Aid Coll 49. **d** 51 **p** 52 Ripon. C of Wetherby 51-56; V of Bp Monkton w Burton Leonard 56-81. *c/o Bishop Monkton Vicarage, Harrogate, Yorks.* (Bishop Monkton 372)

IBBOTT, James Donald Shand. **d** 59 **p** 60 Ott. I of Combermere 59-63; Ingleside w Newington 63-67; R of Deep River 67-72; St Columba City and Dio Ott from 72. *24 Sandridge Road, Ottawa, Ont., Canada.* (1-613-745-6528)

IBE, Justice Bennett Chukwendu. b 37. Trin Coll Umuahia 71. **d** 74 Ow. d Dio Ow. *Box 7, Nkwerre, Imo State, Nigeria.*

IBEADUA, Alfred Emenike. b 29. Trin Coll Umuahia 66. **d** 68 **p** 70 Niger. P Dio Niger from 70. *Chirst Church, Onitsha, Nigeria.*

IBIAYEMIE, Jeremiah Kalabukien Dick. b 28. **d** 77 Nig Delta. d Dio Nig Delta. *St Peter's Parsonage, PO Box 11, Okrika, via Port Harcourt, Rivers State, Nigeria.*

IBILOLA, Festus Folorunso. b 36. **d** 73 **p** 75 Ondo. P Dio Ondo. *Vicarage, Ute, via Ondo, Nigeria.*

IBIRONKE, Titus Adegoroye. b 32. **d** 76 Ijebu. d Dio Ijebu. *St Philip's Church, Isanga-Ogbo, PA Ogbo, via Ijebu-Ode, Nigeria.*

IBRAHIM, Ven Bulus Idris. Bp Gwynne Coll Mundri. **d** 64 **p** 65 Sudan. P Dio Sudan 64-76; Dio Omdurman from 76; Archd of Omdurman from 76. *ECS, Box 258, Wad Medani, Sudan.*

IBULA, Erieza. Bp Tucker Mem Coll Mukono. **d** 21 **p** 22 Ugan. P Dio Ugan 21-48; Can of Ugan 48-61. *Kiyanga, Uganda.*

ICELY, Lawrence Valentine. b 07. Cudd Coll 40. **d** 40 **p** 41 Wakef. C of Penistone w Midhope 40-41; Chap Mersey Miss to Seamen at Runcorn 41-46; Min of Four Marks Conv Distr 47-48; C of Wybunbury 48-51; V of Ch Ch Dukinfield 51-56; Hargrave 56-74; Perm to Offic Dio Ches from 74. *61 Oxford Road, Runcorn, Chesh.* (Runcorn 77147)

✠ **IDAHOSA, Right Rev John Wilfred Izeobokun.** Melville Hall, Ibad 46. **d** 48 **p** 49 Lagos. P Dio Lagos 48-52; Dio Ondo-B 52-62; Dio Benin 62-67; Archd 67-77; Provost 76-77; Cons Ld Bp of Benin in St Matt Cathl Benin City 6 Aug 77 by Abp of W Afr; Bps of Lagos, Niger, Gambia, Nig Delta, Ibad, Ondo, N Nig, Ow, Ekiti, Enugu, Aba, Kum, Kwara, Ilesha, Egba-Egbado and Ijebu. *Bishopscourt, PO Box 82, Benin City, Nigeria.*

IDLE, Christopher Martin. b 38. St Pet Coll Ox BA (2nd cl Engl) 62. Clifton Th Coll. **d** 65 Penrith for Carl **p** 66 Carl. C of St Mark Barrow-F 65-68; Ch Ch Camberwell 68-71; C-in-c of St Matthias Poplar Lon 71-76; R of Limehouse Dio Lon from 76. *5 Newell Street, E14 7HP.* (01-987 1502)

✠ **IDOWU, Right Rev Emmanuel Olawale.** ACP 37. Im Coll Ibad Dipl Th 53. **d** 44 **p** 45 Lagos. P Dio Lagos 44-52; Dio Ibad 52-71; Tutor Im Coll Ibad 52-71; Can of Ibad 61; Archd of Ilesha 61-71; Exam Chap to Bp of Ibad 61-71; Cons Ld Bp of Ondo in Onitsha Cathl 29 Sept 71 by Abp of Sier L; Bps of Accra, Benin, Ekiti, Enugu, Ibad, Niger and Owerri; and Asst Bp of Nig Delta. *Bishopscourt, PO Box 25, Ondo, Nigeria.* (Ondo 2218)

IDOWU, Canon Jacob Titus Laseinde. Melville Hall Ibad. **d** 50 **p** 51 Lagos. P Dio Lagos from 50; Can of Lagos from 68. *PO Box 262, Yaba, Lagos, Nigeria.*

IDOWU, Josiah. b 49. Im Coll Ibad Dipl Th 71. **d** 71 **p** 72 N Nig. P Dio N Nig 71-80; Dio Kaduna from 81. *Diocesan Training Centre, Zaria, Nigeria.*

IDOWU, Kolawole Oladapo. Im Coll Ibad 64. **d** 66 **p** 67 Lagos. P Dio Lagos. *St James's Church, Otta, Lagos, Nigeria.*

IDOWU, Michael Oluwanwo. Im Coll Ibad 59. **d** 61 Ibad **p** 62 Lagos. P Dio Lagos 62-76; Dio Egba from 76. *Box 220, Abeokuta, Nigeria.*

IDUMA, Joshua Augustine. **d** 81 Benin. d Dio Benin. *St John's, Enwan, via Auchi, Nigeria.*

IDUME, James Lagos Akpovigwerie. b 30. Im Coll Ibad Dipl Th 70. **d** 69 **p** 70 Benin. P Dio Benin 70-77; Dio Asaba from 77; Exam Chap to Bp of Asaba from 78. *Anglican Parsonage, Igbodo, Nigeria.*

IENT, Peter. b 25. Univ of Leeds BA 49. Coll of Resurr Mirfield 49. **d** 51 **p** 52 Wakef. C of St Paul Halifax 51-55; Helmsley 55-57; Seamer (in c of Eastfield) 57-60; V of Batley Carr 60-64; St Columba Horton (w St Andr Listerhills from 66) Bradf 64-69; Chap HM Remand Centre Warrington 69-74; HM Pris Albany IW 74-80; HM Pris Winson Green from 80. *c/o HM Prison, Winson Green, Birmingham, B18 4AS.* (021-554 3838)

IFARAJIMI, Lawrence Oluwafemi. **d** 77 Ondo. d Dio Ondo. *Vicarage, Igbokoda, via Okitipupa, Ondo, Nigeria.*

IFEADI, Alexander Okolie. Trin Coll Umuahia, 55. **d** 57 **p** 58 Niger. P Dio Niger 57-62; Dio Benin from 62; Can of Benin 69-74; Archd 74-77. *Box 69, Asaba, Nigeria.*

IFEMELUDIKE, Wilfred Chukwudumogu. Trin Coll Umuahia, 62. **d** 63 **p** 64 Niger. P Dio Niger from 63. *St Simon's Parsonage, Ichida, Nigeria.*

IGBALAJOBI, Abel Olorunsomo. b 37. Im Coll Ibad 68. **d** 71 **p** 72 Lagos. P Dio Lagos. *Holy Trinity Vicarage, Aiyepe, Ijebu, Nigeria.*

IGBANUGO, Abel Chukunwike. St Paul's Coll Awka, 60. **d** 60 Niger. d Dio Niger. *Ufuma, Box 45, Ajalli, Nigeria.*

IGBEGIRI, Sylvanus Okpara. United Th Sem Dayton Ohio Dipl Th 75, MDiv 75. Centr State Univ Ohio BA 75. Trin Coll Umuahia 68. **d** 71 Ow **p** 72 Nig Delta. P Dio Nig Delta from 72. *College of Education, PMB 5047, Port Harcourt, Nigeria.*

IGE, Gabriel. b 36. **d** 76 **p** 77 Ilesha. P Dio Ilesha. *St John's Vicarage, Oke-Bode, Ilesha, Nigeria.*

IGE, Joseph Abodunrin. b 44. Im Coll Ibad 75. **d** 78 Ondo. d Dio Ondo. *St Andrew's Vicarage, Idimoge, Ondo, Nigeria.*

IGHODARO, Samuel Osarenkhoe. b 21. **d** 73 **p** 74 Benin. P Dio Benin; Dom Chap to Bp of Benin from 79. *St Paul's Vicarage, Box 369, Benin, Nigeria.*

IGIE, Ven Samuel Orhue. Melville Hall, Ibad 55. **d** 56 **p** 57 Ondo-B. P Dio Ondo-B 56-62; Dio Benin from 62; Can of Benin 75-77; Archd from 77; Exam Chap to Bp of Benin from 79. *St Peter's Vicarage, Benin City, Nigeria.*

IGILIGE, Ven Bernard Chukwuma Nwoye. Trin Coll Umuahia 57. **d** 59 **p** 60 Niger. P Dio Niger; Hon Can of Niger 76-80; Archd of Aguata from 80. *St John's Parsonage, Ekwulopia, Nigeria.*

IGO, Paul James. Chich Th Coll 78. **d** 79 **p** 80 Man. C of Hollinwood 79-81; St Ignatius Hendon Dio Dur from 81. *Clergy House, Bramwell Road, Hendon, Sunderland, T & W, SR2 8EW.* (Sunderland 75575)

IGWE, Canon Christopher Obiyo. Trin Coll Umuahia, 55. **d** 57 **p** 58 Nig Delta. P Dio Nig Delta 57-69; Dio Niger from 70; Hon Can of Niger from 80. *St Paul's Parsonage, Alor, Nigeria.*

IHAKA, Ven Kingi Matutaera. MBE 70. St John's Coll Auckld 47. **d** 49 **p** 50 Wel. C of Masterton 49-52; Maori P at Wanganui 52-58; at Maori Past Wel 58-66; Maori Missr Dio Auckld 66-75; Dir of Maori Miss from 75; Archd of Taitokerau from 76. *9 Piccadilly Place, Auckland 5, NZ.* (71-989)

IHEANACHO, Daniel Onwumere Brown. b 29. St Paul's Coll Awka. **d** 74 **p** 76 Nig Delta. P Dio Nig Delta. *PMB 5311, Port Harcourt, Nigeria.*

IHIM, Joseph Amaechi. St Paul's Coll Awka. **d** 62 **p** 63 Ow. P Dio Ow 62-75. *Box 6, Nkwerre, Nigeria.*

IJEBU, Lord Bishop of. *See* Akintemi, Right Rev Isaac Bamidele Omowaiye.

IJEBU, Provost of. *See* Talabi, Very Rev Samuel Bolaji.

IKAMUKUBA, Canon Musa. d 64 Ankole K. d Dio Ankole K 64-67; Dio Ank 67-77; Can of Ank 74-77; Dio E Ank from 77. *PO Ntungamo, Uganda.*

IKE, Jacob Onuegbune Chukwumalueze. b 22. St Paul's Coll Awka. **d** 76 **p** 77 Enugu. P Dio Enugu. *All Saints Parsonage, PO Box 112, Abakaliki, Enugu, Nigeria.*

IKEH, Dennis. d 75 **p** 76 Niger. P Dio Niger. *c/o Box 361, Onitsha, Nigeria.*

IKEJIANI, Jeremiah Ekemezie. d 38 Niger **p** 39 Bp Vining for Niger. P Dio Niger 38-59; Dio Ow 59-62. *Agukwu Nri, Awka, Nigeria.*

IKENYI, John. d 78 Nak. d Dio Nak. *c/o Box 244, Nakuru, Kenya.*

IKEONWU, Michael Onwukwo. d 43 **p** 45 Bp Patterson for Niger. P Dio Niger 43-63. *c/o St Mark's Church, Ogbunike, Onitsha, Nigeria.*

IKIN, Gordon Mitchell. b 30. K Coll Lon and Warm AKC 57. **d** 58 **p** 59 Man. C of Leigh 58-61; V of St Paul Westleigh, Leigh 61-72; St Jas Thornham Dio Man from 72. *Vicarage, Shaw Road, Thornham, Rochdale, Lancs.* (Rochdale 45256)

IKIOA, Barnabas. Patteson Th Centre Kohimarama. **d** 71 Melan. d Dio Melan 71-75; Dio Malaita from 75. *Oloha, S Malaita, Solomon Islands.*

IKOBO, Enoch Danfa Ekieri. St Paul's Coll Awka 60. **d** 61 Nig Delta. d Dio Nig Delta 61-73. *St Peter's Parsonage, Yenagoa, via Ahoada, Nigeria.*

IKPEZE, George Ibegbunam. d 50 **p** 51 Niger. P Dio Niger from 50. *Parsonage, Eziowelle, Nigeria.*

IKPRIRI, Clement Oghenekparobo Edafetano. b 32. **d** 73 **p** 74 Benin. P Dio Benin. *Okugbe Primary School, Ikipidiama-Kenan, c/o PA Ikpidiama, via Ughelli, Nigeria.*

ILECHUKU, Herbert Okoli. St Paul's Coll Awka. **d** 55 **p** 57 Nig Delta. P Dio Nig Delta. *Egwanga, Opobo, Nigeria.*

ILECHUKWU, Michael Madukejiaka. b 38. Trin Coll Umuahia 66. **d** 68 **p** 70 Niger. P Dio Niger from 70. *c/o Box 42, Onitsha, Nigeria.*

ILES, Francis John England. b 08. **d** 79 Tas. Hon C of The Huon Dio Tas from 79. *Esplanade Road, Cygnet, Tasmania 7112.*

ILES, Paul Robert. b 37. Fitzw Coll Cam 2nd cl Mus Trip pt i, 58, BA (2nd cl Th Trip pt ia) 59, MA 64. FRCO 65. Sarum Th Coll 59. **d** 61 **p** 62 Sarum. C of St Mich AA Sarum 61-64; Chap Bp Wordsworth Sch Sarum 61-67; Asst Master 64-67; V Cho Sarum Cathl 64-67; C of Bournemouth 67-72; R of Filton 72-79; V of St Phil and St Jas w St Marg City and Dio Ox from 79. *Vicarage, Church Walk, Oxford, OX2 6LY.* (Oxford 50460)

ILESHA, Lord Bishop of. *See* Olajide, Right Rev Gideon Isaac Oladipo.

ILETT, Louis Donald. St Pet Coll Rosettenville, 62. **d** 64 **p** 65 Johann. C of St Alb Johann 64-67; R of Riverlea Dio Johann from 67. *PO Box 43164, Industria, Johannesburg, Transvaal, S Africa.* (011-35 7911)

ILEVBARE, George Aradion Jonathan. Im Coll Ibad. **d** and **p** 66 Benin. P Dio Benin 66-71. *Afuze, Nigeria.*

ILIFF, Hugh Graham. b 07. Trin Hall Cam BA 31, MA 35. **d** 32 **p** 33 B & W. C of St Paul Bath 32-36; CIM Miss at Chuhsien 37-38; Kaihsien 38-45; V of Poughill 45; CIM Miss at Shanghai 46-48; Chap-in-c of H Trin Cathl Shanghai 47-48; CIM Miss at Kwangyuan 48-52; Gen Dir Br Syrian Miss 53-55; V of St Steph Newc T 55-60; in Ch of S India 60-72; Chap at Le Touquet, 73-76; Perm to Offic Dio Chich from 76; Dio Roch from 77. *Flat 24, Bromley College, Bromley, Kent, BR1 1PE.*

ILIFFE, Walter Richard. b 17. ALCD 41. St Andr Coll Pampisford. **d** 44 **p** 45 Sheff. C of St Mary Sheff 44-46; St Dunstan E Acton 46-48; Org Sec S Amer MS 48-50; C of Hagley 50-52; V of Broadwaters 52-56; St Pet Worc 56-68; R of Broome Dio Worc from 68. *Broome Rectory, Clent, Stourbridge, Worcs.* (Kidderminster 700292)

ILLING, Eric James. b 33. Kelham Th Coll 54. Chich Th Coll 55. **d** 57 **p** 58 Ripon. C of St Aid Leeds 57-60; All SS w St Alb Leeds 60-62; E Grinstead 62-65; V of Middleton Leeds 65-74; Felpham w Middleton 74-76; R 76-81; Team R of Heavitree w St Paul City and Dio Ex from 81. *Heavitree Rectory, Exeter, Devon, EX2 5DU.* (Ex 74489)

ILLINGWORTH, John Patrick Paul. New Coll Ox BA 59, Dipl Th 61, MA 63. Chich Th Coll 61. **d** 63 **p** 64 Wakef. C of Brighouse 63-66; St Andr Willesden 66-70; Chap at Gothenburg 70-74; C-in-c of St Bart Brighton 74; V of Ryhill 74-82; R of Weston Longville w Morton-on-the-Hill w Gt and Little Witchingham Dio Nor from 82. *Weston Longville Rectory, Norwich, NR9 5JU.* (Gt Witchingham 263)

ILLINGWORTH, William. b 23. E Midl Min Tr Course 80. **d** 81 Repton for Derby. C of St Edm Allestree Dio Derby from 81. *6 Gisborne Crescent, Allestree, Derby, DE3 2FL.*

ILOABA, George Adu. d 52 **p** 62 Niger. d Dio Niger 52-59; Dio Ow 59-62; P Dio Niger from 62. *St Jude's Parsonage, Oraifite, via Nnewi, Nigeria.*

ILOGU, Canon Edmund Christopher Onyedum. ALCD 53. Union Th Sem NY STM 58. Columb Univ MA 59. **d** 49 **p** 50 Lagos. P Dio Lagos 49-52; Dio N Nig 52-53; Dio Ibad 53-57; L to Offic Dio Ibad 57-66; Chap Nig Coll of Arts and Technology 55-59; on leave 59-61; Lect in Th Univ of Ibad 61-66; Univ of Nig from 70; Hon Can of Enugu from 73. *University of Nigeria, Nsukka, Nigeria.* (Nsukka 48)

ILONUBA, Jonah Chukwuemeka. b 38. Dipl Th (Lon) 73. Trin Coll Umuahia 72. **d** 73 **p** 74 Enugu. P Dio Enugu. *St Bartholomew's Cathedral, Asata, Box 444, Enugu, ECS, Nigeria.*

ILORI, Benjamin Oluwole. b 29. **d** 72 **p** 74 Lagos. P Dio Lagos 72-76; Dio Egba from 76. *St James Church, Orile, Ibadan Road, Orile Ilugun, Nigeria.*

ILORI, John Afolabi. b 20. Melville Hall, Ibad. **d** 57 **p** 58 Lagos. P Dio Lagos 57-76; Dio Egba from 76. *PO Box 90, Abeokuta, Nigeria.*

ILOTT, Philip Edwin. b 36. Roch Th Coll 66. **d** 68 **p** 69 St Alb. C of Leavesden 68-71; C-in-c of St Alb Conv Distr Godshill IW 71-77; V of Mayfield 77-81; St Barn Bexhill Dio Chich from 81. *Vicarage, Cantelupe Road, Bexhill-on-Sea, E Sussex.* (Bexhill 212036)

ILSON, John Robert. b 37. Univ of Leeds BSc 59. BD (Lon) 64, Certif Educn (Lon) 65. ALCD 63. **d** 64 **p** 65 S'wark. C of St Mark Kennington 64-67; H Trin Sydenham 67-70; Asst Dir Relig Educn Dio Sheff from 70; R of Hooton Roberts 70-77; V of Ravenfield 75-77; St Geo Kidderminster Dio Worc from 77. *30 Leswell Street, Kidderminster, Worcs, DY10 1RP.* (Kidderminster 2131)

✠ **ILUKOR, Right Rev Geresom.** Buwalasi Th Coll. **d** 64 **p** 65 Soroti. P Dio Soroti 64-75; Dioc Regr and Sec Dio Soroti 72-75; Cons Ld Bp of Soroti in St Paul's Cathl Nam 11 Jan 76 by Abp of Ugan; Bps of Ank, Bukedi, Bunyoro, Mbale, Busoga, Nam, N Ugan, Ruw, W Bugan, Buj and Buye. *Box 107, Soroti, Uganda.*

ILUYOMADE, Canon Jonathan Abiodun. Univ of Lon BA 51. **d** 58 **p** 59 Ondo-B. P Dio Ondo-B 58-62; Dio Ondo from 62; Prin of Ondo Boys' High Sch 58-62; Hon Can of Ondo from 67. *University of Ibadan, Oyo State, Nigeria.*

IM, Paul. St Mich Sem Oryudong, 61. **d** and **p** 64 Korea. P-in-c of Anjung Korea 64-70; Kang Wha 70-78; Archd of Seoul 72-73; V of Yongdungp'o 78-81. *6128 Yucca Street, Hollywood, CA 90028, USA.*

IMAGIE, Stephen Chakuam. St Paul's Coll Awka. **d** 47 Niger. d Dio Niger 47-52; and 60-75; Nig Delta 52-57; N Nig 57-60. *St Mary's Church, Awka-Etiti, Nigeria.*

IMAI, Canon Paul Ken. St Paul's Univ Tokyo BA 36. Gen Th Sem NY STB 41. Trin Coll Tor MTh 58. Centr Th Coll Tokyo 37. **d** 37 **p** 40 Bp Binsted for Tohoku. In Ch of Japan 39-53; P-in-c of St Andr Tor 53-77; Can of Tor from 75; V of H Cross Hamilton Dio Niag from 78. *Holy Cross Vicarage, Hamilton, Ont, Canada.*

IMISIDES, John Elvethon. Moore Th Coll ACT ThL (2nd cl) 57, Th Scho 66. **d** 58 Syd **p** 59 Bp Hilliard for Syd. C of W Wollongong 58; R of Wallerawang 59-61; C of St Geo Hurstville 61-62; C-in-c of Shellharbour w Warilla 62-74; on leave 74-75; L to Office Dio Syd from 75. *40 Mary Street, Shellharbour, NSW, Australia 2529.*

IMMS, William George Law. b 11. Lich Th Coll 64. **d** 64 Malmesbury for Bris **p** 65 Bris. C of Penhill 64-69; New Swindon (in c of St Sav) 69-76; Publ Pr Dio Bris from 76; Hon C of Cricklade 76-81. *24 Pauls Croft, Cricklade, Wilts, SN6 6AH.* (Swindon 750552)

IMORUA, Canon Gabriel Uzinigbe. Im Coll Ibad. **d** 61 **p** 62 Benin. P Dio Benin; Can of Benin from 78. *St Matthew's Cathedral, Benin, Nigeria.*

IMPEY, Richard. b 41. Em Coll Cam 2nd cl Nat Sc Trip pt i 62, BA 63, 2nd cl Th Trip pt ii 64, 2nd cl Th Trip pt iii 65, MA 67. Harvard Univ ThM 67. Ridley Hall Cam 67. **d** 68 Bp Sinker for Birm **p** 69 Birm. C of St Martin Birm 68-72; Bp's Chap for Study and In-Service Training Dio B & W 72-79; Dioc Dir of Ordin Dio B & W 76-79; V of Blackpool Dio Blackb from 79. *64 Park Road, Blackpool, FY1 4HT.* (Blackpool 20626)

IMRAY, Frederick Stanley James. Trin Coll Melb BA (1st cl) 46, MA 60. ACT ThL 41. **d** 48 **p** 49 Melb. C of St Paul Malvern 48-49; V of Black Rock 49-54; Chap Wadhurst Sch 54-61; Melb C of E Gr Sch 62-74; Perm to Offic Dio Melb

74-79; Dio Brisb from 80. *12 Lochiel Street, Kenmore, Brisbane, Australia 4069.* (378 3619)

INCE, David Malcolm. b 28. Bp's Coll Calc. **d** 51 **p** 52 Kurun. C of St Paul Kandy 51-55; Chap Dickoya-Dimbulla 55; C of Hangleton 55-60; Chap Miss to Seamen Rang 60-64; C of Odiham w S Warnborough 65-70; V of Simanggang 70-74; V of Newhall 74-80; Upton Grey w Weston Patrick, Tunworth, Herriard and Winslade Dio Win from 80. *Upton Grey Vicarage, Basingstoke, Hants.* (Long sutton 469)

INCE, Edgar Kenelm Peter. b 16. DFC 45. Wells Th Coll 54. **d** 56 **p** 57 Ex. C of Littleham w Exmouth 56-58; R of Burghclere w Newtown 58-66; Ashwater (and Halwill w Beaworthy from 73) Dio Ex from 66; RD of Holsworthy 74-80. *Ashwater Rectory, Beaworthy, Devon.* (Ashwater 205)

INCE, Gordon Bourchier. b 1896. **d** 21 **p** 22 Lon. C of St Gabr Poplar (Ardingly Coll Missr 22) 21-26; Percy (in c of Shiremoor) 26-28; R of Gt Sutton and V of Shopland 28-29; C of St Jas Gt Keyham (Kelly Coll Miss in c of St Chad) Devonport 29-32; St John New Clee 32-33; R of Long Melford 33-38; C of St Mary Norwood 38-47; CF (EC) 40-47; V of Croxley Green 47-53; Pirton 53-59; Misterton 59-63. *20 Whitecross Road, Weston-super-Mare, Somt, BS23 1EW.* (W-s-M 21318)

INCE, Peter Reginald. b 26. **d** 51 **p** 52 Calc. C of St Jas Calc 51-52; V 52-53; Chap at Khargpur 53-54; Asansol 54-55; C of St Luke Leek 55-57; Milton Staffs 57-59; St Luke Downham 59-62; R of Loddington w Cransley 62-75; V of Snibston 75-79; R of Mickleham Dio Guildf from 79. *Mickleham Rectory, Dorking, Surrey, RH5 6EE.* (Leatherhead 78335)

INCHLEY, John. b 06. Oak Hill Th Coll 50. **d** 50 Southn for Win **p** 51 Win. C of St Jo Evang Boscombe 50-52; V of H Trin Tewkesbury 52-55; Over-Stowey w Aisholt 55-58; Missr CSSM 59-72; Hon Chap Bath Abbey Dio B & W 72-77; Missr TTC from 72; Perm to Offic Dio B & W from 79. *5 Hare Knapp, Bradford-on-Avon, Wilts, BA15 1PJ.* (Bradford-on-Avon 2389)

IND, Philip William David. b 35. Cranmer Hall Dur. **d** 65 Dunwich for St E **p** 66 St E. C of St Jo Bapt Ipswich 65-67; Charlton Kings 67-71; R of Woolstone w Oxenton and Gotherington 71-74; on leave 74-76; Chap Alleyn's Sch Dulwich from 76. *160a East Dulwich Grove, SE22 8TB.* (01-693 4252)

IND, William. b 42. Univ of Leeds, BA (2nd cl Engl and Hist) 64. Coll of Resurr Mirfield 64. **d** 66 Kens for Lon **p** 67 Lon. C of Feltham 66-71; Northolt (in c of St Jos the Worker) 71-73; Team V of Basingstoke Dio Win from 73; Exam Chap to Bp of Win from 76; Vice Prin Aston Tr Scheme from 79; *539 Abbey Road, Popley, Basingstoke, Hants.*

INDALO, Peter Albert. b 45. St Paul's Coll Limuru 70. **d** 72 **p** 73 Maseno S. P Dio Maseno S. *Box 35, Ng'iya, Ramula, Maseno, Kenya.*

INDER, Patrick John. b 30. K Coll Lon and Warm BD and AKC (2nd cl) 54. **d** 55 **p** 56 Lon. C of St Marg-on-Thames 55-57; Golders Green 57-61; V of St Mellitus Hanwell 61-76; R of Rawmarsh w Parkgate 76-81. *Address temp unknown.*

INDER, Robert William Jack. b 15. AKC 38. **d** 38 **p** 39 York. C of St Andr Drypool 38-42; St Jo Evang Carlisle 42-43; R of Stapleton 43-51; V of Sinnington Dio York from 51. *Vicarage, Sinnington, York.* (Kirby Moorside 31422)

INDIAN OCEAN, Metropolitan of Province of. *See* Huddleston, Most Rev Ernest Urban Trevor.

INESON, David Antony. b 36. ALCD 62. **d** 62 **p** 63 Wakef. C of Sandal Magna w Newmillerdam 62-65; St Geo Birm 66-71; V of All SS Horton Bradf 71-80; Sedbergh w Cautley and Gardsdale Dio Bradf from 80; RD of Bowling and Horton 78-80. *Vicarage, Sedbergh, Cumb, LA10 5SQ.* (Sedbergh 20283)

INGALL, Heber Doveton. b 18. Univ of Lon ALCD 43. **d** 43 **p** 44 Chelmsf. C of Gt Clacton w L Holland 43-46; Ch Ch Brixton 46-49; Aylesford 49-51; Rusthall 51-52; R of Coates 52-56; Benefield 56-70; C-in-c of Stoke Doyle 63-67. *4 Casburn Lane, Burwell, Cambridge.*

INGALL, Michael John Frederick. St Mich Th Coll Crafers. **d** 63 **p** 64 Bal. C of Portland 63-65; Horsham 65-67; R of Timboon 67-72; Edenhope 72-77; Mortlake Dio Bal from 77. *Rectory, Mortlake, Vic, Australia 3272.* (055-991211)

INGAMELLS, Harold Frankish. b 34. Codr Coll Barb. **d** 59 **p** 60 Barb. C of St Mich Cathl Bridgetown Barb 59-66; C-in-c of Horbury Bridge 66-68; V of Horbury Junction 68-75; Monk Bretton Dio Wakef from 75. *Monk Bretton Vicarage, Barnsley, S Yorks, S71 2HQ.* (Barnsley 203159)

INGAMELLS, Ronald Sidney. b 32. K Coll Lon and Warm AKC 56. **d** 57 **p** 58 Ripon. C of Ch of Epiph Gipton Leeds 57-59; Gt Yarmouth (in c of St John) 59-64; Youth Officer Dio Nor 64-79; C of St Pet Mancroft Nor 64-79; P-in-c of Lemsford Dio St Alb from 79. *7 High Oaks Road, Welwyn Garden City, Herts.* (Welwyn Garden 27621)

INGE, Lawrence Gane. b 05. St Aid Coll 48. **d** 48 **p** 49 York. C of Stokesley 48-52; R of Sangre Grande 52-54; R of Pembroke Tobago 54-58; Plymouth Tobago 59; Orcheston 59-65; Stourton Caundle w Caundle Purse 65-72; Chap Westmr Mem Hosp Shaftesbury from 78. *11 St James Street, Shaftesbury, Dorset.* (Shaftesbury 3571)

INGHAM, Ernest Walter Patrick. b 04. AKC (1st cl) 29. **d** 29 **p** 30 Wakef. C of St John Carlinghow 29-31; H Trin Hoxton 31-35; R of Peatling Parva 35-47; Org Sec C of E Children's S Dios Pet and Leic 38-39; Min of Conv Distr of St Gabr Leic 47-54; Chap St Andr Hosp Northn 54-63; R of Capel St Mary w L Wenham 63-75; Perm to Offic Dio St E from 76. *Russet House, Capel Road, Bentley, Ipswich.* (Gt Wenham 310403)

INGHAM, John Barrie. b 34. [f in CA] **d** 73 **p** 74 Wai. V of Murupara-Reporoa 74-78; Waipatu Moteo Past 78-81; Opotiki Distr Dio Wai from 81; Ruatoki-Whakatane Past Dio Wai from 81. *Vicarage, Richards Street, Opotiki, NZ.*

INGHAM, John Edmund. b 34. Univ of Reading, BA (3rd cl Pol Econ) 56. Clifton Th Coll 58. **d** 60 **p** 61 Bris. C of Rodbourne Cheney 60-63; St Jo Div Tunbridge Wells 63-67; V of Weald Dio Roch from 67. *Weald Vicarage, Sevenoaks, Kent.* (Weald 291)

INGHAM, Michael Colin. b 49. Univ of Edin MA 70, BD 73. **d** and **p** 74 Ott. C of St John Ott 74-76; I of Ch K Burnaby 76-80; St Francis-in-the-Woods W Vanc Dio New Westmr from 80. *4767 South Piccadilly, West Vancouver, Canada.*

INGHAM, Russell Edward. b 39. Univ of Glas MA (2nd cl Hist) 61. Keble Coll Ox BA 63, MA 67. Cudd Coll 63. **d** 64 **p** 65 Glas. C of St Mary's Cathl Glas 64-69; Warden St John's Youth Centre Tuebrook 69-71; R of St Mary Virg Port Glas 71-77; All SS City and Dio St Andr from 77. *All Saints' Rectory, North Street, St Andrews, Fife.* (St Andrews 73193)

INGHAM, Stephen Charles. b 49. SOC 75. **d** 78 **p** 79 S'wark. C of St Aug Grove Park Lee Dio S'wark from 78. *9 Luffman Road, Grove Park, SE12 9SZ.*

INGLEDEW, Peter David Gordon. b 48. AKC 77. St Steph Ho Ox 77. **d** 78 **p** 79 Newc T. C of Whorlton Dio Newc T 78-81; All SS Poplar Dio Lon from 81. *St Michael's Vicarage, St Leonard's Road, Poplar, E14.* (01-987 1795)

INGLESON, David James. Wollaston Coll W Austr 64. **d** 66 **p** 67 Perth. C of Nollamara 66-68; P-in-c of Woodlands w Wembley Downs 68-69; Perm to Offic Dio Perth 70-80; R of Belmont Dio Perth from 80. *123 Arlunya Avenue, Cloverdale, W Australia 6105.* (277-4338)

INGLIS, Canon Angus. b 08. TD 46. Men in Disp 45. St Jo Coll Ox BA (2nd cl Th) 30, MA 34. Westcott Ho Cam 30. **d** 31 **p** 32 Pet. C of St Jo Bapt Pet 31-34; St Mary Nottm 34-37; PC of St Faith N Wilford 37-45; CF (TA) 38-46; R of Cotgrave 45-48; St Pet w St Jas Nottm 48-79; Hon Can of Southw 55-79; Can (Emer) from 80; Surr 58-79. *The Old Rectory, Belton, Nr Grantham, Lincs, NG32 2LW.* (Grantham 74545)

INGLIS, William Arnold. b 44. Univ of BC BA 67. Episc Th Sch Cam Mass BD 70. **d** 70 Caled. C of St Andrew Cathl Caled 70-72. *1800 East 6th Avenue, Prince Rupert, BC, Canada.*

INGOLDSBY, Frederick Searle. Moore Th Coll Syd ACT ThL 50. **d** 51 **p** 53 Syd. C of Kiama w Gerringong 51-53; R of Wentworth Falls 53-58; Normanhurst 58-59; Swansea 59-62; Chap Hutchins Sch Hobart 62-64; V of Claremont w Chigwell 64-69; BFBS Rep Dio Melb from 69; Perm to Offic Dio Melb 70-76. *38 Breakwater Road, East Geelong, Vic, Australia 3219.* (052-93 779)

INGRAHAM, William Eric. K Coll Halifax NS BA 51, LTh 52. **d** 52 **p** 53 NS. C of Glace Bay 52-53; I of New London 53-60; R of St Marg of Scotld Halifax 60-68; Yarmouth 68-75; Bridgewater Dio NS from 75. *78 Alexandra Avenue, Bridgewater, NS, Canada.*

INGRAM, Bernard Richard. b 40. Lon Coll of Div. **d** 66 **p** 67 Roch. C of St Aug Bromley 66-70; Gravesend 70-74; V of St Edm Dartford Dio Roch from 75. *St Edmund's Vicarage, Dartford, Kent.* (Dartford 25335)

INGRAM, Donald Drury. b 21. **d** 74 **p** 75 Johann. C of Primrose 74-80; Alberton Dio Johann from 80. *36 Barnard Street, Hazeldene 1401, S Africa.*

INGRAM, Edward George Cecil Brett. b 20. Late Pri of Trin Coll Dub BA 44, BD 54. **d** 45 **p** 47 Meath. C of Dunboyne U 45-46; Athlone 46-47; Bangor 47-52; I of Drumbanagher 52-60; Errigal-Keerogue Dio Arm from 60; Exam Chap to Abp of Arm from 72. *Richmond Rectory, Ballygawley, Dungannon, N Ireland.* (Ballygawley 670)

INGRAM, Gordon Earl. Em Coll Sktn LTh 60. **d** 58 **p** 59 Edmon. I of Edgerton 59-62; R of Drayton Valley (w evansburg from 66) 62-70; St Phil Edmon 70-79; Chap R Alex Hosp Edmon from 79. *10240 Kingsway, Edmonton, Alta, Canada.*

INGRAM, James Gordon. Em Coll Sktn. **d** and **p** 63 Edmon. I of Edgerton 63-64; St Jas Edmon 64-65; L to Offic Dio BC from 69. *305 1180 View Street, Victoria, BC, Canada*

INGRAM, Michael. b 28. St Jo Coll Dur 49. **d** 53 **p** 54 Chelmsf. C of St Sav Westcliff-on-Sea 53-56; Stoke Damerel Devonport 56-60; Chap RAF 60-76; C-in-c of St Enoder 76-80. *c/o St Enoder Rectory, Summercourt, Newquay, cornw.*

INGRAM, Walter Robert Moresby. b 1900. Univ of Lon Dipl Th 30. Bps' Coll Cheshunt 32. **d** 32 **p** 33 S'wark. C of Clapham 32-37; Lymington (in c of All SS) 37-40; CF (EC) 40-45; C of Witham 46-48; Cockington 48-50; V of Bp's Teignton 50-70; Perm to Offic Dio Ex from 72. *14 Travershes Close, Exmouth, Devon, EX8 3LH.* (Exmouth 71437) *12040, 139th Street, Edmonton, Alta, Canada.*

INKPEN, Richard John. b 28. K Coll Lon and Warm AKC 56. **d** 58 **p** 59 Lon. C of Willesden 58-61; Hendon (in c of St Mary Magd Holders Hill) 61-66; C-in-c of Annunc Conv Distr S Kenton 66-69; Chap St Jo Evang Montreux 69-70; V of Blackmoor Dio Portsm from 70; RD of Petersfield from 80. *Blackmoor Vicarage, Liss, Hants.* (Bordon 3548)

INMAN, Gordon Harold. K Coll Lon and Warm 54. **d** 58 Pontefract for York for Wakef **p** 59 Wakef. C of Marsden 58-60; Mt Pellon 60-62; V of St Phil Dewsbury 62-64; Arthington 64-69; M Tr Officer C of E Youth Coun from 69. *Church House, Dean's Yard, SW1.* (01-222 9011)

INMAN, John Phillips. b 12. St Jo Coll Dur BA (2nd cl Mod Hist) and De Bury Scho 35, Dipl in Th 36, MA 38. **d** 36 **p** 37 Dur. C of Crook 36-39; St Andr Monkwearmouth 39-40; Esh (in c of Langley Park) 40-43; V of Cleadon 43-50; St John-in-Weardale 50-56; C-in-c of Westgate-in-Weardale 50-56; V of Grindon 56-60; Hist Lect Charlotte Mason Coll Ambleside 60-73; L to Offic Dio Carl from 60. *Balla Wray Cottage, High Wray, Ambleside, Cumb.*

INMAN, Malcolm Gordon. Edin Th Coll 58. **d** 60 **p** 61 Wakef. C of Lundwood 60-63; Heckmondwike 63-70; V of Wrenthorpe 70-75; V of St Jo Evang Cleckheaton Dio Wakef from 75. *St John's Vicarage, Cleckheaton, W Yorks, BD19 3RN.* (Cleckheaton 874896)

INMAN, Martin. b 50. AKC 73 BD 72. St Aug Coll Cant 72. **d** 73 **p** 74 Heref. C of St Mary Magd Bridgnorth 73-77; Parkstone w Branksea I 77-79; V of St Anne Willenhall Dio Lich from 79. *St Anne's Vicarage, Ann Street, Willenhall, W Midl, WV13 1EN.* (Willenhall 66516)

✠ **INMAN, Right Rev Thomas George Vernon.** Selw Coll Cam 3rd cl Hist Trip pt i 27, BA (3rd cl Th Trip Pt i) MA 32. Hon DD Univ of the S Tenn USA 58. St Aug Coll Cant 26. **d** 30 **p** 31 S'wark. C of St Mark East Street Walworth and Asst Missr Wel Coll Miss Walworth 30-33; C of Estcourt 33; St Paul Durban 33-37; V 37-51; Can of Natal 44-51; Archd of Durban 50-51; Cons Ld Bp of Natal in St Paul's Ch Durban 18 Oct 51 by Abp of Capetn; Bps of S Rhod; Grahmstn; Basuto; and Zulu; and Bps T W Stainton and Ferguson-Davie; res 74; Sub-Prelate of the O of St John of Jer from 53; Dean of St Sav Cathl Pietermaritzburg 51-68; Perm to Offic Dio Syd from 78. *74 Ray Road, Epping, NSW, Australia 2121.* (869-2050)

INMAN, Thomas Jeremy. b 45. Rhodes Univ BA 67. St Steph Ho Ox 67. **d** 69 S'wark **p** 70 Natal for S'wark. C of St Paul w St Mark Deptford 69-72; Bellville Capetn 72-73; R of Malmesbury 73-76; P-in-c of Donnington 76-80; V of Hangleton Dio Chich from 80. *127 Hangleton Way, Hove, E Sussex, BN3 8ER.* (Hove 419409)

INNES, Alan Henry. St Francis Th Coll Brisb ACT ThL 36. **d** 38 **p** 39 N Queensld. C of St Matt Mundingburra 38-41; H Trin Ingham 41-42; P-in-c 42-43; P-in-c of Sarina Distr 43-45; R 45-46; R of Home Hill 47-52. *Innesfree, Bohlane, Townsville, Queensland, Australia.*

INNES, Donald John. b 32. St Jo Coll Ox BA (3rd cl Hist) 54, MA 58. Westcott Ho Cam 54. **d** 56 **p** 57 Lon. C of St Mark St John's Wood 56-58; Walton-on-Thames 58-67; Farnham 67-76; Chap Moor Pk Coll Farnham 67-76; P-in-c of Tilford Dio Guildf from 76. *Tilford Vicarage, Farnham, Surrey.* (Frensham 2333)

INNES, Donald Keith. b 33. St Jo Coll Ox BA (3rd cl Th) 56, MA 60. BD (2nd cl) Lon 58. Clifton Th Coll 56. **d** 58 **p** 59 Chelmsf. C of St Paul Harold Hill 58-61; St John Ealing Dean 61-65; V of Westacre 65-70; R of Gayton Thorpe w E Walton 65-70; V of St Paul Woking 70-78; R of Alfold and Loxwood Dio Guildf from 78. *Rectory, Loxwood, Billingshurst, W Sussex, RH14 0RG.* (Loxwood 752320)

INNES, Ven James Harold Roy. St Jo Coll Armid ACT ThL 23. **d** 24 **p** 26 Bath. M of Bro of Good Shepherd Dubbo 24-29; Vice-Prin 29; R of Proserpine 29-31; Ayr 31-51; Can of St Jas Cathl Townsville 47-51; R of Mackay 51-67; Archd of Mackay 51-67; Archd (Emer) from 69; V of Wondai 69. *St Mary's Vicarage, Wondai, Queensland 4606, Australia.*

INNES, James Michael. b 32. Univ of Lon BA (2nd cl Russian) 56, BD (2nd cl) 59. Clifton Th Coll Bris. **d** 59 Lanc for Blackb **p** 60 Burnley for Blackb. C of St Thos Blackpool 59-62; Tutor Clifton Th Coll Bris 62-65; V of All SS Burton-on-Trent 65-73; St Mary Magd Ashton-on-Mersey Dio Ches from 73. *20 Beeston Road, Sale, Chesh, M33 5AG.* (061-973 5118)

INNISS, Kyle Darrell. Codr Coll Barb. **d** 64 **p** 65 Barb. C of St Mich Cathl I and Dio Barb from 64. *Tweedside Road, Bridgetown, Barbados, W Indies.*

INOUE, Stephen Shunichi. b 45. Vanc Sch of Th MDiv 75. **d** 76 **p** 77 Caled. C of Terrace Dio Caled from 77. *3411 Eby Street, Terrace, B.C. V8G 2Y6, Canada.*

INSHAW, Reginald John Seymour. Wycl Coll Tor. **d** 51 **p** 52 Alg. C of Emsdale w Sprucedale 51-53; I of Rosseau 53-56; R of Schreiber 56-67; Nipigon 67-74; Onaping 74-76. *Dorion, Ont., Canada.*

INSLEY, Edgar John. Hur Coll LTh 65. **d** 64 **p** 65 Hur. C-in-c of Thorndale and of Nissouri 64-67; R of Thedford 67-71; St Pet Windsor Dio Hur from 71. *2337 Rossini Boulevard, Windsor, Ont., Canada.* (519-948 4612)

INSLEY, Harold Mourant. b 1899. St Cath S Ox BA 31. Linc Th Coll 32. **d** 32 Bp Hine for Linc **p** 33 Linc. C of Grantham 32-36; H Trin Guildf 36-37; Miss S Afr Ch Rly Miss Naauwpoort 37-41; Port Eliz (w St Aug Miss Walmer) 41-44; C of H Trin w St Mary Guildf 44-45; R of Ash w Ash Vale 45-64; Gt w L Kimble 64-67. *Mayfield, Avenue Road, Bovey Tracey, Devon, TQ13 9BQ.* (Bovey Tracey 833493)

INSLEY, Michael George Pitron. b 47. Trin Coll Ox BA (2nd cl Lit Hum) 69, 2nd cl Th 71, MA 72. Wycl Hall Ox 69. **d** 72 **p** 73 Roch. C of Ch Ch Beckenham 72-76; P-in-c of Cowden 76-79; Lect St Jo Coll Nottm and Publ Pr Dio Southw from 80. *St John's College, Chilwell Lane, Bramcote, Notts.*

INSULL, Francis. b 07. Linc Th Coll 46. **d** 48 **p** 49 Lich. C of St Francis Friar Park W Bromwich 48-50; I of Suez Egypt 50-53; C-in-c of Conv Distr of Em Bentley 53-57; V of Hibaldstow 57-63; R of Lympstone 63-72. *Gwernyrefail Fach, Cross Inn, Llandysul, Dyfed. SA44 6NH.* (New Quay 560236)

INVERNESS, Provost of (Dio Moray). *See* Wheatley, Very Rev Arthur.

INWOOD, Richard Neil. b 46. Univ Coll Ox BSc 70, MA 73. Univ of Nottm BA 73. St Jo Coll Nottm 71. **d** 74 Doncaster for Sheff **p** 75 Sheff. C of Ch Ch Fulwood Sheff 74-78; All S w St Pet and St Jo Evang, St Marylebone 78-81; V of St Luke Bath Dio B & W from 81. *St Luke's Vicarage, Hatfield Road, Bath, Avon, BA2 2BD.* (0225-311904)

ION, Robert Henry. b 18. Late Scho of Pemb Coll Ox 2nd cl Cl Mods 39, BA (3rd cl Lit Hum) 41, MA 44, BD 47. Ripon Hall Ox 41. **d** 42 Liv **p** 49 Ches. C of All H Allerton 42-43; Bromborough 49-52; V of Tintwistle 52-53; Crewe Green 53-59; Div Lect Chesh Co Tr Coll Crewe from 56; Sen Lect 62-73; R of Church Lawton 73-78; Perm to Offic Dio Ches from 78. *School House, Church Road, Alsager, Stoke-on-Trent, ST7 2HS.* (Alsager 6653)

IORNS, Derrick John. b 11. AKC 33. **d** 34 **p** 35 Cant. C of Rainham 34-38; C-in-c of St Paul's Conv Distr Bentley Common 38-51; V 51-53; Maldon 53-71; RD of Maldon 56-70; R of Gt Warley 71-72; C-in-c of Childerditch w L Warley 71-72; R of Gt Warley w Childerditch 72-81; P-in-c of Ingrave 79-81. *c/o Rectory, Great Warley, Essex.* (Brentwood 777)

IPEMA, Theo. b 47. Univ of Calgary BA 72. Trin Coll Tor MDiv 75. **d** 75 Bp Read for Tor **p** 76 Tor. C of St Jas Cathl Tor 75-80; I of Shanty Bay Dio Tor from 80. *Rectory, Shanty Bay, Ont, Canada.*

IPINMOROTI, Samuel Olorunleke. b 32. **d** 74 Lagos **p** 76 Ijebu. d Dio Lagos 74-76; P Dio Ijebu from 76. *St Peter's Vicarage, Box 11, Imagbon, Ijebu-Ode, Nigeria.*

IPINMOYE, Joseph Ibikunle. **d** 58 **p** 59 Lagos. P Dio Lagos 58-72; Dio Ekiti from 72; Prin Isonyin Gr Sch 67-72. *All Saints Vicarage, Iyin-Ekiti, Nigeria.*

IPINMOYE, Michael Omojoyegbe. b 46. Im Coll Ibad 74. **d** 77 **p** 78 Ibad. P Dio Ibad; Dom Chap to Bp of Ibad from 80. *c/o Box 3075, Ibadan, Nigeria.*

IPO, William. St Pet Coll Siota. **d** 54 **p** 60 Melan. P Dio Melan 54-75. *Ugi, Solomon Islands.*

IPSWICH, Archdeacon of. *See* Walsh, Ven Geoffrey David Jeremy.

IPSWICH, *See* St Edmundsbury and Ipswich.

IRAN, Lord Bishop in. *See* Dehqani-Tafti, Right Rev Hassan Barnaba.

IRELAND, Ven Anthony John. **d** 61 **p** 63 C & Goulb. C of Temora 61-63; Albury 63-66; R of St Geo Downer Canberra 66-68; Berridale 68-71; State Sec ABM in NSW from 71; Perm to Offic Dio C & Goulb 71-78; Dios Newc and Graft from 71; Dio Syd 71-77; Dio Wang from 78; R of N Albury 78-81; Wagga Wagga Dio C & Goulb from 81; Archd of Wagga Wagga from 81. *Rectory, Church Street, Wagga Wagga, NSW, Australia 2650.*

IRELAND, David Arthur. b 45. Mert Coll Ox BA 67, MA 71. Cudd Coll 67. **d** 69 **p** 70 Ripon. C of Chapel Allerton

69-72; St Nich Harpenden (in c of St Mary Kinsbourne Green) 72-76; R of Clifton Beds Dio St Alb from 76. *Rectory, Clifton, Shefford, Beds, SG17 5EL.* (Hitchin 812295)

IRELAND, Robert. b 48. Univ of Syd BA 69. ACT BTh 77. Ridley Coll Melb 75. **d** 77 Graft for Melb **p** 78 Graft. C of E Bentleigh 77-79; Kempsey Dio Graft from 80. *Box 45, West Kempsey, NSW, Australia 2440.*

IRELAND, William Herbert. b 1890. **d** 55 **p** 56 Birm. C of St Martin Birm 55-59; C-in-c of Deritend 59-63; C of St Faith w St Laur Harborne 63-69. *23 London Road, Stroud, Glos.*

IRERI, Ven Bedan. St Paul's Th Coll Limuru, 56. **d** 57 **p** 59 Momb. P Dio Momb 57-61; Dio Ft Hall 61-64; Mt Kenya 64-75; Dio Mt Kenya E from 75; Exam Chap to Bp of Mt Kenya 66-75; Mt Kenya E from 75; Archd of N Distr Mt Kenya 72-75; Mt Kenya E from 75; Hon Can from 78. *PO Box 345, Embu, Kenya.*

IRERI, Donald. b 48. **d** 78 **p** 79 Mt Kenya E. P Dio Mt Kenya E. *Box 652, Embu, Kenya.*

IRESON, Arthur Stanley. b 05. St Cath Coll Cam BA 30, MA 34. Ridley Hall Cam 29. Lich Th Coll 30. Men in Disp 45. **d** 30 **p** 31 Cov. C of St Nich Radford Cov 30-32; Bp's Hatfield (in c of St Mark) 32-36; V of St Jas Watford 36-42; Chap Watford Inst 37-45; Chap RAFVR 40-46; Res Can of Cov Cathl and Dir of Relig Educn Dio Cov 46-50; Chap and Private Sec to Bp of Cov 46-47; Relig Adviser to Nat Assoc of Boys' Clubs and Gen Perm to Offic 47-69; Proc Conv Cov 50-53; Asst Master Wyggeston Boys' Sch Leic 55-72; L to Offic Dio Leic from 69; Hd Master Laurels Coll Leic 72-79. *348 Victoria Park Road, Leicester, LE2 1XF.* (Leic 704715)

IRESON, Canon Gordon Worley. b 06. Hatf Coll Dur LTh Univ Th Exhib and Hatfield Exhib 32, BA 33. Edin Th Coll 29. **d** 33 **p** 34 Nor. C of Sheringham 33-36; Chap of St Mary's Cathl (in c of H Trin Dean Bridge) Edin 36-37; P Lect Nat S 37-39; L to Offic Dio Lon 38-39; Dioc Missr Dio Ex 39-46; Dio Newc T 46-58; Hon Chap to Bp of Ex and Sec Ex Dioc Youth Conv 43-47; Can of Newc T Cathl 46-58; Exam Chap to Bp of Newc T 49-73; St Alb 58-73; Can Res Dio St Alb 58-73; (Emer) from 73; Dioc Missr 58-73; Warden Commun of the H Name from 74. *11 Ranelagh Road, Malvern Link, Worcs.* (Malvern 63535)

IRESON, Richard Henry. b 46. Linc Th Coll 69. **d** 71 **p** 72 Linc. C of Spilsby 71-74; Team V of Grantham 74-76; R of N w S Claypole 76-79; P-in-c of Westborough w Dry Doddington and Stubton 76-77; R 77-79; V of Burgh-le-Marsh Dio Linc from 79; Orby Dio Linc from 79; Welton-le-Marsh w Gunby Dio Linc from 79; R of Bratoft w Irby Dio Linc from 79. *Burgh-le-Marsh Vicarage, Skegness, Lincs.*

IRIWIN, David Richard James. b 49. ACT ThL 76. Moore Coll Syd 75. **d** 77 **p** 78 Armid. C of Gunnedah Dio Armid from 77. *The Curatage, Jensen Street, Gunnedah, NSW, Australia 2380.*

IROEGBU, Joshua Chikezie. b 24. Trin Coll Umuahia 64. **d** 66 **p** 67 Nig Delta. P Dio Nig Delta 67-72; Dio Aba from 72. *St Peter's Parsonage, Ekenobizi, Umuopara, Umuahia, Nigeria.*

IRONSIDE, John Edmund. b 31. Peterho Cam BA 55, MA 59. Qu Coll Birm 55. **d** 57 **p** 58 Cant. C of All SS Spring Pk Croydon 57-60; St Simpson Guernsey and Asst Master Eliz Coll 60-63; V of Bangkok 63-66; St Jo Evang Guernsey 66-72; Sholing Dio Win from 72. *41 Station Road, Southampton, SO2 8FN.* (Southn 448337)

IRUMBA, Wilson. **d** 78 **p** 79 Ruw. P Dio Ruw. *c/o Box 497, Fort Portal, Uganda.*

IRUNGU, Sylvester. **d** 65 **p** 66 Ruw. P Dio Ruw. *Bubandi, Uganda.*

IRVINE, Christopher Paul. b 51. Univ of Nottm BTh 75. Univ of Lanc MA 76. Kelham Th Coll 73. **d** 76 Lanc for Blackb **p** 76 Blackb. Asst Chap Univ of Lanc 76-77; C of St Mary Stoke Newington Lon 77-80; Chap Univ of Sheff from 80. *36 Roslin Road, Sheffield, S10 1FA.* (Sheff 669243)

IRVINE, Donald Frederick. Univ of W Ont BA 60. Hur Coll BTh 62. **d** 62 Bp Appleyard for Hur **p** 63 Hur. C of St Aid Riverside 62-64; Ch of H Sav Waterloo 64-67; on leave 67-69; Prof Hur Coll from 69; Dean of Faculty of Th from 77. *c/o Huron College, London 72, Ont, Canada.*

IRVINE, Gerard Philip. b 30. QUB BA 52. Edin Th Coll 56. **d** 56 **p** 57 Aber. Chap of St Andr Cathl Aber 56-58; Prec 58-59; C of St John Malone Belf 61-66; Chap Commun of St Jo Evang Dublin 67-77; C of St Jo Evang City and Dio Dub from 77. *32 Mitchel House, Appian Way, Dublin 6, Irish Republic.* (760450)

IRVINE, James Clyde. b 35. QUB BA 57. TCD Higher Dipl Educn and Div Test (1st cl) 59. **d** 59 **p** 60 Connor. C of St Luke Belf 59-62; Ch Ch Cathl Lisburn 62-65; I of Duneane w Ballyscullion 65-69; Kilbride Connor 69-74; Asst Master (Relig Educn) Ballyclare High Sch from 73; L to Offic Dio Connor from 73. *1a Rathmena Avenue, Ballyclare, Co Antrim, N Ireland.* (Ballyclare 22933)

IRVINE, James Theodore. b 45. K Coll NS BA 69, STB 71. **d** 70 **p** 72 Fred. C of Trin St John 70-71; I of Ludlow w Blissfield 71-74; C of St Paul St John 74-77; I of Vic St John Dio Fred from 77. *325 St James's Street, Saint John, NB, Canada.*

IRVINE, John Dudley. b 49. Univ of Sussex BA 70. Univ of Ox BA (Th) 80. Wycl Hall Ox 78. **d** 81 Lon. C of H Trin Brompton Kens Dio Lon from 81. *Flat 1, Holy Trinity Church House, Ennismore Gardens Mews, SW7 1JA.*

IRVINE, John Graham Gerard Charles. b 20. Late Postmaster of Mert Coll Ox BA (2nd cl Lit Hum) 42, MA 46, 1st cl Th 44. St Steph Ho Ox 42. **d** 45 Bris **p** 46 B & W for Bris. C of H Nativ Knowle 45-48; St Mary and St Chad Longton 48-51; St Thos Regent Street 51-53; LDHM of H Angels Cranford 53-61; V of St Cuthb w St Matthias Earls Court Kens 61-69; St Matt Gt Peter Str Westmr Dio Lon from 69. *20 Great Peter Street, SW1.* (01-222 3704)

IRVINE, Very Rev John Murray. b 24. Late Scho of Magd Coll Cam 1st Cl Trip pt i 44, BA (2nd cl Cl Trip pt ii) 45, MA 49. Ely Th Coll 46. **d** 48 **p** 49 Stepney for Lon. C of Poplar 48-53; Chap SS Coll Cam and L to Offic Dio Ely 53-60; Select Pr Univ of Cam 59; Sec CACTM 60-65; L to Offic Dio Lon 61-65; Res Can and Preb of Hunderton; Chan and Libr of Heref Cathl 65-78; Dir of Ordin Tr Dio Heref 65-78; Provost and R of Southw Minster from 78; Exam Chap to Bp of Southw from 78; P-in-c of Edingley w Halam Dio Southw from 78. *The Residence, Southwell, Notts, NG25 0HP.* (Southwell 812593)

IRVINE, Michael. b 47. St Jo Coll Morpeth ThDip 79. **d** 79 **p** 80 Graft. C of Tweed Heads Dio Graft from 79. *48 Thompson Street, Tweed Heads, NSW 2485, Australia.*

IRVINE, Roderick David. Univ of Syd BSc, PhD. Moore Coll Syd ThL 79. **d** 79 **p** 80 Brisb. C of All SS Booval Dio Brisb from 79. *15 Horton Street, Bundamba, Queensland, Australia 4304.*

IRVINE, Very Rev Thomas Thurstan. b 13. Magd Coll Ox BA (2nd cl Hist) 34, Dipl in Th 35, MA 38. Cudd Coll 37. **d** 38 Bedford for St Alb **p** 39 St Alb. C of All SS w St John Hertford 38-40; Prec of St Ninian's Cathl Perth (in c of St Kath Newburgh) 40-43; (in c of Ch of the Ascension Leslie) 42-43; Dioc Chap of St Andr 43-45; C of H Trin Dunfermline (in c of St Finnian Lochgelly) 45; R of St Sav Bridge of Allan 45-47; St Andr Callander w St Angus Lochernhead and Killin 47-66; R of St Mary Aberfoyle 47-53; St Jo Bapt Perth Dio St Andr from 66; Exam Chap to Bp of St Andr from 50; Dean of St Andr from 59; Can of St Ninian's Cathl Perth from 59. *St John's Rectory, Dupplin Terrace, Perth.* (Perth 21379)

IRVINE, William Barry. b 48. Qu Univ Coll Belf BD 75. St Jo Coll Nottm 75. **d** 76 **p** 77 Connor. C of St Mich Belf 76-80; Mansfield Dio Southw from 80. *85 Delamere Drive, Mansfield, Notts.*

IRVING, Andrew. b 27. **d** 65 **p** 66 Newc T. C of St Jas Benwell Newc T 65-69; Langley Marish 69-73; V of Moulsford 73-81. *c/o Moulsford Vicarage, Wallingford, Berks.*

IRVING, Donald Richard. b 31. Univ of Lon BSc 55. Lon Coll of Div 66. **d** 68 Bp Horstead for Leic **p** 69 Leic. C of H Trin Leic 68-71; Trav Sec Ch Youth Fellowships Assoc and Pathfinders 71-75; Chap Leic Poly 70; Gen Sec of Ch S 75-82; CCCS from 82; Sec of C of E Evang Co 76-81. *10 Nevill Avenue, Hove, Sussex, BN3 7NA.* (0273-779858)

IRVING, Leslie. b 09. Keble Coll Ox BA 30, Dipl Th 31, MA 46. Wycl Hall Ox 30. **d** 32 **p** 33 Ches. C of Neston 32-35; Hawarden 35-36; Asst Master Dioc Coll Rondebosch 36-56; Chap 43-56; Exam Chap to Abp of Capetn 49-56; V of Aldborough w Dunsforth 56-57; Commiss Geo 56-66; Chap and Asst Master Dover Coll 57-63; L to Offic Dio Cant 57-63; R of Risby 63-65; L to Offic Dio Guildf 65-67; Chap St Cath Sch Bramley 67-74; Perm to Offic Dio Chich from 74. *c/o Lloyd's Bank, Terminus Road, Eastbourne, E Sussex.*

IRVING, Michael John Derek. b 43. Coun for Nat Acad Awards BEducn 80. Qu Coll Birm 80. **d** 81 Tewkesbury for Glouc. C of Coleford w Staunton Dio Glouc from 81. *7 Highfield Place, Coalway, Coleford, Glos, GL16 7JX.* (0594 32017)

IRWIN, Albert Samuel. b 14. Trin Coll Dub BA and Div Test 38, MA 44. **d** 38 **p** 39 Man. C of St Pet Bury 38-42; St Pet Bolton 42-45; Lect of Bolton 45-47; Chap RNVR 47-48; C of Gillingham 48-49; St John's Pro-Cathl Buenos Aires 49-52; Chap and Asst Master St Geo Coll Quilmes 52-54; V of Woodnewton w Apethorpe 54-59; R of Clyst St Mary and of Clyst St Geo 59-61; V of St Martin Stamford Baron 61-81; P-in-c of Tinwell 77-81. *22 St Martin's, Stamford, Lincs, PE9 2LF.*

IRWIN, Alexander John. b 14. Westcott Ho Cam 71. **d** 71 Chelmsf **p** 72 Bradwell for Chelmsf. C of South Weald 71-75; P-in-c of Shalford 75-77; V of Wethersfield w Shalford Dio Chelmsf from 77. *Vicarage, Wethersfield, Braintree, Essex.* (Gt Dunmow 850245)

IRWIN, David John. b 44. K Coll Lon and Warm AKC 66. **d** 67 **p** 68 S'wark. C of All SS Sydenham 67-70; Ch the Sav

Ealing 70-76; V of St Francis of Assisi Gladstone Pk Dio Lon from 76; P-in-c of St Andr Willesden Dio Lon from 76. *110 Ellesmere Road, NW10 1JS.* (01-452 7939)

IRWIN, Eric Clifford. Bp's Univ Lennox BA 54, LST 55. **d** 55 **p** 56 NS. C of Glace Bay 55-57; R of Weymouth 57-62; Chap RCAF from 63. *c/o Canadian Forces Headquarters, Ottawa 4, Ont., Canada.*

IRWIN, Francis William. b 29. Late Lightfoot Scho of St Chad's Coll Dur BA (2nd cl Mod Hist) 52, Dipl Th (w distinc) 54, MA 56. **d** 54 **p** 55 Liv. C of Warrington 54-58; V of Staincross 58-66; R of Aldborough w Thurgarton (w Gunton and Hanworth and Bessingham from 80) 66-80; C-in-c of Hanworth (w Gunton from 76) 66-80; Bessingham 75-80; R of Shipdham (w E and W Bradenham from 81) Dio Nor from 80; P-in-c of E w W Bradenham 80-81. *Shipdham Rectory, Thetford, Norf, IP25 7LX.* (Dereham 820234)

IRWIN, Frederick Leslie. Selw Th Coll 30, NZ Bd of Th Stud LTh 33. **d** 31 **p** 32 Dun. C of St Paul's Cathl Dun 32-33; Coll Distr Dun 33-34; St Paul Rockptn 34-35; V of Riverton 35-39; Tuapeka 39-47; Bluff w Stewart I 47-50; Helensville 50-55; St Thos Auckld 55-58; C of Mt Roskill 58-61; Northcote 61-66; Whangarei 66-73; P-in-c of Glenfield 73-74; Hon C of Whangarei 74-75; Marsden-Waipu Miss Distr Dio Auckld from 75. *76 Hatea Drive, Whangarei, NZ.*

IRWIN, George Thomas Gorton. St Jo Coll Morpeth. **d** 64 **p** 65 Graft. C of Kempsey 64-65; V of U Macleay 65-69; C of Wyong 69-70; Taree 70-71; L to Offic Dio Graft from 72. *65 Broughton Street, Kempsey Heights, NSW, Australia 2440.*

IRWIN, John Edward Gilmour. b 30. Univ of NZ BSc 54, BD 58, LTh 68. Gen Th Sem NY STM 68. Drew Univ NJ PhD 74. Selw Coll Dun. **d** 57 **p** 58 Ch Ch. C of Highfield 57-58; Papanui 58-60; in Amer Ch 61-80; V of All SS Dun w Port Chalmers Dio Dun from 80; Exam Chap to Bp of Dun from 80. *786 Cumberland Street, Dunedin, NZ.*

IRWIN, Paul William. b 29. Sarum Wells Th Coll 72. **d** 74 Ex. C of St Matt Ex 74-75; Cockington 75-81; Team V of Centr Torquay Dio Ex from 81. *1a Lower Ellacombe Church Road, Torquay, Devon.* (Torquay 23441)

IRWIN, Ven Philip Sidney. Bp's Coll Lennox BA 49, BD 63. **d** 49 **p** 50 Ott. I of Beachburg 49-53; C-in-c of Stafford 53-56; R of St Luke Ott 56-66; Smith's Falls 66-72; Can of Ott 67-77; R of Trin Ch Cornw 72-77; Manotick Dio Ott from 77; Archd of Cornw from 77; Dom Chap to Bp of Ott from 79. *Box 221, Manotick, Ont, Canada.* (1-613 692 3467)

IRWIN, Robert George. St Jo Coll Morpeth. **d** 66 Bath. C of Parkes 66-69; E Orange 69-70; Perm to Offic Dio Brisb from 71. *c/o 417 Ann Street, Brisbane, Queensland, Australia.*

IRWIN, Victor. b 32. Lon Coll of Div 64. **d** 66 **p** 67 Leic. C of H Trin Leic 66-68; CF 68-72; V of Quarry Bank 72-81; Lydbury N Dio Heref from 81; P-in-c of Hopesay w Edgton Dio Heref from 81. *Vicarage, Lydbury North, Salop.*

IRWIN, Canon William Basil. Bp's Univ Lennox LST 28. **d** 27 Carib **p** 28 Queb for Carib. C of All SS E Finchley 29-30; I of Lillooet 30-33; C of Ch of the Advent Westmount 34-36; I of Enderby 36-41; Lowville w Nassagaweya 41-44; St Mary Bartonville 44-49; R of Fort Erie 50-68; Hon Can of Ch Ch Cathl Hamilton 64-72; Can (Emer) from 72. *250 Highland Avenue, Fort Erie, Ont., Canada.*

IRWIN, William George. b 53. Qu Univ Belf BSc 77. Div Hostel Dub 80. **d** 80 **p** 81 Connor. C of St Paul Lisburn Dio Connor from 80. *12 Belvoir Crescent, Lisburn, Co Antrim, BT28 1UA.*

IRWIN-CLARK, Peter Elliot. b 49. Univ Coll Lon LLB 71. St Jo Coll Dur BA 81. [f Barrister]. **d** 81 Pontefract for Wakef. C of St Jo Bapt Kirkheaton Dio Wakef from 81. *29 Regent Road, Kirkheaton, Huddersfield, HD5 0LW.*

ISAAC, Arthur Kenneth. b 12. St Aug Coll Cant. **d** 62 **p** 63 B & W. C of Combe Down 62-65; R of Rode w Rode Hill and Woolverton 65-72; Hutton 72-77; Perm to Offic Dio Ex from 77. *Forge Cottage, Bratton Clovelly, Okehampton, Devon, EX20 4JW.*

ISAAC, Bryan Raymund. b 09. MBE (Mil) 46. Ch Coll Cam BA 31, MA 35. Wycl Hall, Ox 31. **d** 33 **p** 34 Lon. C of St John Ealing Dean 33-36; Walcot 36-38; V of St Sav Battersea Pk 38-43; CF (EC) 43-46; Home Sec Ruanda Miss CMS 46-62; Perm to Offic Dio S'wark 48-62; V of Cudham 62-73; S Area Sec CMS Ruanda Miss 73-75. *2 Pear Tree Cottage, West Milton, Bridport, Dorset, DT6 3SH.*

ISAAC, David Thomas. b 43. Univ of Wales BA (2nd cl Hist) 65. Cudd Coll 65. **d** 67 Bp Hughes for Llan **p** 68 Llan. C of Llan 67-71; Swansea Dio 71-73; Chap Ch of Wales Youth Coun 73-77; V of Llanguicke (Pontardawe) 77-79; Youth Chap Dio Ripon from 79. *7 Loxley Grove, Wetherby, LS22 4YG.* (Wetherby 65606)

ISAAC, Edward Henry. b 20. Qu Coll Cam BA 42, MA 46. Ridley Hall, Cam 45. **d** 47 **p** 48 Lich. C of St Bart Wednesbury 47-51; V of St Phil Liv 51-56; Knowsley 56-61; St Mich Garston 61-66; St Geo Millom Dio Carl from 66. *St George's Vicarage, Millom, Cumb.* (Millom 2332)

ISAAC, Canon Philip Davies. b 16. St D Coll Lamp BA 37. Chich Th Coll 38. **d** 42 Grimsby for Linc **p** 43 Linc. C of Bilsby w Farlesthorpe Meeby w Fordington and Haugh 42-45; All SS Holbeach 45-48; St Thos Derby 48-53; R of Turriff 53-58; St Paul Aber 58-64; Ellon 64-72; Cruden 70-72; P-in-c of St Pet Stornoway 72-75; R of H Trin Dunoon 75-78; Can of St John's Cathl Oban 78-81; Hon Can of Cumbrae from 81; P-in-c of St Pet Stornoway 78-81. *21 Dores Road, Inverness, IV2 4RF.*

ISAAC, Wayne Erskine. b 52. Univ of WI BA 78. Codr Coll Barb 75. **d** 78 **p** 79 Windw Is. C of St Geo Grenada Dio Windw Is from 78. *PO Box 104, Canterbury Cottage, St George's, Grenada.*

ISAACHSEN, Robert John. b 43. Univ of Adel BChemEng 66. Univ of Nottm BA 72. St Jo Coll Nottm 70. **d** 73 Bp Muston for Melb **p** 74 Bp Dann for Melb. C of Dandenong 73-76; P-in-c of Dingley Dio Melb from 76. *Old Dandenong Road, Dingley, Vic, Australia 3172.* (551-1510)

ISAACS, Hubert John. Qu Coll Newfld. **d** 42 **p** 43 Newfld. C of St Mary St John's 42-45; White Bay Miss 45-47; on leave 47-49; R of St Jas St John 49-52; Dean of Resid of St Chad's Coll Regina 52-54; R of New Germany 54-55; on leave 55-56; I of Dunham and St Armand 57-59; R of St Steph Lachine Montr 59-63; Strathmore 63-69; Dorval 69-70; St Simon Highland Creek Tor 70-80. *c/o 1438 Military Trail, Highland Creek, West Hill, Ont., Canada.*

ISAACS, Frederick Perumuhad. b 43. **d** 77 **p** 78 Natal. C of St Gabr Wentworth 77-80; Durban N Dio Natal from 80. *c/o 12 Chelsea Drive, Durban North, 4051, S Africa.*

ISAACS, Tudor Llewellyn. Lon Coll of Div 25. **d** 28 **p** 29 Lon. C of St Martin Edmon 28-30; Chap of Quilmes 30-32; Chap Miss to Seamen Rosario 32-37; Camp Chap W and N Provinces 37-38; Chap H Trin Montevideo 38-67. *c/o 25 de Mayo 282, Buenos Aires, Argentina.*

ISAACS, Winston Lionel. b 40. St Pet Coll Alice 73. **d** 75 **p** 76 Capetn. C of Ch of Resurr Bonteheuwel 75-77; R of Woodstock 77-81; Miss at Kabwe Dio Centr Zam from 81. *Box 80042, Kabwe, Zambia.*

ISAACS-SODEYE, William Akintunde. b 34. Univ of Ox BA 60, MA 64, BM 64, BCh 64, DM 71. MRCS 63. Im Coll Ibad 76. **d** 76 **p** 77 Ibad. P Dio Ibad. *St Paul's Church, Aiyegbaju, Ile-Ife, Nigeria.*

ISAACSON, Cecil James. b 17. Sarum Th Coll. **d** 53 **p** 54 Nor. C of Gaywood w Bawsey 53-55; PC of Hellesdon 56-62; R of Burnham Thorpe w Burnham Overy Dio Nor from 62; C-in-c of Burnham Sutton w Burnham Ulph, Burnham Westgate and Burnham Norton Dio Nor 67-69; R from 69. *Burnham Sutton Rectory, King's Lynn, Norf.* (Burnham Market 317)

ISABIRYE, Amosi. **d** 52 Ugan. d Dio Ugan 52-62; Dio Nam from 62. *PO Namutumba, Busiki, Uganda.*

ISABIRYE, Eria Kesi. Bp Tucker Coll Mukono. **d** 53 **p** 56 Ugan. P Dio Ugan 53-61; Dio Nam from 61. *Kiyunga, PO Box 4533, Bulopa, Uganda.*

ISBISTER, Charles. b 27. Chich Th Coll 58. **d** 60 **p** 61 Newc T. C of Tynemouth 60-64; All SS Boyne Hill Maidenhead 64-67; V of H Trin Cookridge Dio Ripon from 67. *53 Green Lane, Leeds, LS16 7LW.* (Leeds 674921)

ISDELL-CARPENTER, Philip Wynn Howard. b 11. St Jo Coll Ox BA (3rd cl Jurispr) 33, MA 37. Westcott Ho Cam 35. **d** 36 **p** 37 Guildf. C of Leatherhead 36-39; Frimley (in c of St Andr Frimley Green) 39-44; R of Winterslow 44-48; V of Preston w Sutton Poyntz 48-60; Ed Sarum Dioc Gazette 49-56; R of Frimley 60-72. *Furze Quarry, Durrus, Bantry, Co Cork, Irish Republic.*

ISHERWOOD, David Owen. b 46. Coun for Nat Academic Awards BA 75. Ridley Hall Cam 76. **d** 78 **p** 79 S'wark. C of All SS Sanderstead 78-82; St Bart (in c of St Wilfrid) Horley Dio S'wark from 82. *St Wilfrid's House, Horley Row, Horley, Surrey, RH6 8DF.* (Horley 3332)

✠ **ISHERWOOD, Right Rev Harold.** b 07. MVO (4th cl) 55. OBE 59. Selw Coll Cam BA 38, MA 46. Ely Th Coll 38. **d** 39 **p** 40 Southw. C of Beeston 39-43; Chap Nat Nautical Sch Portishead 43-51; Helsinki and Moscow 51-54; Oslo 54-59; H Trin [f Ch Ch and Ch of Resurr) Brussels 59-70; V Gen N and C Eur (in the Jurisd of Fulham) and Gibr from 70; Can of Gibr 71-74; Cons Asst Bp of Gibr in Lambeth Palace Chap 15 Feb 74 by Abp of Cant; Bps of Lon, Win, Truro and Leic; Bps Suffr of Edmon, Colchester and Fulham; and others; res 77; Asst Bp in Dio Cant from 79; Asst Bp of Dio Gibr in Eur from 80. *16a Burgate, Canterbury, Kent, CT1 2HG.* (0227) 52790

ISHERWOOD, Marmaduke. b 1900. St Aug Coll Cant 37. **d** 39 **p** 40 Lon. C of St Andr Sudbury 39-41; R of Tumby Bay 41-43; Whyalla Willoch 43-46; Hon Can Willoch 44-46; Min Can Roch Cathl and Chap to St Bart's Hosp Roch 46-49; Sen

Chap to Hackney Hosps Group No 6 49-60; R of H Trin Ex 60-67; Musbury, Devon 67-73; Perm to Offic Dio Ex 73-80. *Address temp unknown.*

ISHERWOOD, Samuel Peter. b 34. ALCD 62 (LTh from 74). **d** 62 **p** 63 Man. C of St Sav Bacup 62-65; Albert Mem Ch Man 65-67; V of St Andr Livesey Blackb 67-79; Handforth Dio Ches from 79. *36 Sagars Road, Handforth, Wilmslow, Chesh, SK9 3EE.* (Wilmslow 524119)

ISHERWOOD, Stanley Thomas. Dalhousie Univ BA 63. Wycl Coll Tor BTh 66. **d** 69 Edmon. L to Offic Dio Edmon 69-77; on leave 77-79; I of St John Whitby Dio Tor from 79. *1604 Dufferin Street, Whitby, Alta, Canada.*

ISHIKAWA, Timothy Katsumoto. Rikkyo Univ, Tokyo BA 55. Centr Th Sem Tokyo 60. **d** 61 **p** 62 Yokohama. In Ch of Japan 61-68; Asst Chap Miss to Seamen Dio Syd from 68. *100 George Street, Sydney 2000, Australia.*

ISHUNGISA, Edward. d 76 **p** 77 Ank. P Dio Ank 76-77; Dio W Ank from 77. *PO Rubaare, Rwashamaire, Uganda.*

ISINGOMA, Yafesi Lwakabwa. Bp Tucker Coll Mukono. **d** 51 **p** 55 Ugan. P Dio Ugan 51-61; Dio Ruw 61-77. *PO Box 497, Fort Portal, Uganda.*

ISITT, Canon David Edgar Reid. b 28. K Coll Cam 2nd cl Cl Trip pt i 48, BA (2nd cl Cl Trip pt ii) 49, MA 53. Wells Th Coll 51. **d** 53 **p** 54 Malmesbury for Bris. C of Westbury-on-Trym 53-56; Chap K Coll Cam 56-60; V of Haslingfield 60-68; R of Harlton 60-68; Select Pr Univ of Cam 61 and 71; Chap St Edw K and Mart Cam 68-77; Asst Chap Trin Hall Cam 68-77; Can Res of Bris Cathl from 77; Dir Bris Sch of Min from 81; Exam Chap to Bp of Bris from 81. *18 Percival Road, Bristol, BS8 3LN.* (Bristol 37969)

ISITT, Norman. b 34. Univ of Dur BA 56, Dipl Th 59. Cranmer Hall, Dur 57. **d** 59 **p** 60 Chelmsf. C of St Mary Virg Loughton 59-62; Moulsham Chelmsf (in c of St Luke) 62-64; Asst Master Billericay Co Sch 64-65; Squirrels Heath Jun Sch Romford 65-66; Althorpe and Keadby Co Primary Sch from 66. *21 Cambridge Avenue, Bottesford, Scunthorpe, S Humb.*

ISLES, Peter William Richard. Em Coll Sktn 58. **d** 58 **p** 59 Sktn. I of Colonsay 58-60; R of Maidstone Sask 60-64; R of Colwood w Langford 64-68; St Mark Vic Dio BC from 68; R of St Chris Vic Dio BC from 68. *4171 Oakridge Crescent, Victoria, BC, Canada.* (604-479 5546)

ISOKE, Zaburoni Eyahura. Dioc Coll Momb 30. **d** 32 **p** 34 U Nile. P Dio U Nile. *CMS, Kitgum, Uganda.*

ISON, David John. b 54. Univ of Leic BA 76. Univ of Nottm BA (Th) 78. St Jo Coll Nottm 76. **d** 79 **p** 80 S'wark. C of St Luke w St Nich Deptford Dio S'wark from 79. *11 Evelyn Street, Deptford, SE8.*

ISON, Canon Francis James. St Jo Coll Manit BA 27, MA 33. **d** 27 **p** 28 Bran. C of Reston 27; R of Boissevain 27-31; St Mary Virg Bran 31-34; Chap at Utrecht 34-36; R of St Thos Winnipeg 36-38; St Steph Winnipeg 38-61; Hon Can of Rupld from 78. *Box 31, Sandy Hook, Manit, Canada.*

ISOROEMBO, Ambrose. b 20. St Aidan Coll Dogura. **d** 64 **p** 70 New Guinea. d Dio New Guinea 64-70; P Dio Papua from 71. *Anglican Church, Pongani, Papua New Guinea.*

ISRAEL, Martin Spencer. b 27. Univ of Witwatersrand MB 49, MRCP 52. **d** 74 **p** 75 Lon. C of St Mich Cornhill Lon 74-77; H Trin w All SS S Kens Dio Lon from 77. *Flat 2, 26 Tregunter Road, SW10 9LS.*

ISSBERNER, Norman Gunther Erich. b 34. Fitzw Ho Cam Engl and Th Trip. BA 58, MA 61. Clifton Th Coll. **d** 59 S'wark for Cant **p** 60 Cant. C of Ch Ch Croydon 59-61; Ch Ch Surbiton Hill (in c of Em Tolworth) 61-66; V of Egham 66-74; Wallington Dio S'wark from 75; Chairman AIM from 77. *Vicarage, Maldon Road, Wallington, Surrey.* (01-647 7605)

ITALY, Archdeacon of. (Vacant)

ITAMAKINDE, Christopher Folowosene. Im Coll Ibad 62. **d** 64 **p** 65 Ondo. P Dio Ondo. *Vicarage, Erusu-Akoko, Ondo, Nigeria.*

ITHAKA, Ithaca Eru. b 30. **d** 81 Auckld. C of Auckld Angl Maori Miss Dio Auckld from 81. *108 Mount Albert Road, Mount Albert, Auckland 3, NZ.*

ITIMA, Ven Burasiyo. Bp Tucker Coll Mukono, 60. **d** 60 **p** 62 Ankole-K. P Dio Ankole-K 60-67; Dio Ank 67-76; Dio W Ank from 77; Can of Ank 70-76; W Ank from 77; Archd from 78. *PO Mitoomba, Ruhinda, Uganda.*

ITUMELENG, Johannes Mosimanethebe. St Bede's Coll Umtata, 60. **d** 62 **p** 64 Kimb K. P Dio Kimb K from 62. *PO Box 925, Kuruman, CP, S Africa.*

ITUMU, Marclus Maringa. St Paul's Th Coll Limuru 64. **d** 67 **p** 68 Mt Kenya. P Dio Mt Kenya 67-75; Dio Mt Kenya E from 75; Exam Chap to Bp of Mt Kenya E from 75. *Box 48, Kerugoya, Kenya.*

IVANY, Canon Randall Eugene. McMaster Univ BEng 57. Wycl Coll Tor LTh 60, BTh 61, Hon DD 73. **d** 60 **p** 61 Calg. Univ of Alta Hon LLD 81. C of St Paul Tor 60; I of Bowness w Montgomery 61-63; R of Red Deer 63-68; in Amer Ch 68-69; Can Pastor of All SS Cathl Edmon 69; Dean and R 70-74; Exam Chap to Bp of Edmon 70-76; Hon Can of Edmon from 74; Ombudsman Prov of Alta from 74; Hon C of Ch Ch Edmon 75-80; St Mich AA City and Dio Edmon from 81; Hebrew Univ of Jer Hon Fell from 81. *Suite 401, 12207 Jasper Avenue, Edmonton, Alta, Canada, T5N 3K2.* (403-488 8889)

IVENS, Edmund Masters. Edin Th Coll 37. **d** 37 **p** 38 Arg Is. C of St Andr Fort William 37-39; St Pet Kirkcaldy 39-44; R of St Paul Kinross 44-52; St Anne Dunbar 52-79. *Drylaw Hill, East Linton, E Lothian.* (E Linton 860283)

IVES, David. Matab Ordin Course. **d** 80 Matab. d Dio Matab. *Bulawayo, Zimbabwe.*

IVES, George Rodney. K Coll Halifax NS BA and LTh 65. **d** 64 **p** 65 NS. C of Dartmouth 64-67; CF (Canad) from 67. *c/o CFH, Dept National Defence, Ottawa 4, Ont, Canada.*

IVES, John Edward. K Coll Lon BD 74, AKC 75, MTh 76. Chich Th Coll 78. **d** 79 Willesden for Lon **p** 80 Lon. C of St Edm Northwood Hills Pinner Dio Lon from 79. *103 Rickmansworth Road, HA5 3TT.* (01-866 9734)

IVES, Leonard. Edin Th Coll 25. **d** 27 **p** 28 Nel. C of Wairau Valley 27-28; V 28-34; V of Collingwood 34-36; Eketahuna 36-41; St Paul Okato 41-48; St Luke Te Kuiti 48-50; Forest Lake 51-52; Perm to Offic Dio Auckld 52-56; LPr Dio Wai 56-60; P-in-c of Apia W Samoa Dio Polyn from 60. *Apia, W Samoa.*

IVES, William. b 15. Linc Th Coll 47. **d** 48 **p** 49 Nor. C of N Walsham 48-51; CF 51-54; R of Kirstead w Langhale and Brooke 54-67; V of St Thos Heigham Dio Nor from 67. *St Thomas's Vicarage, Norwich, NR2 3RL.* (Norwich 24390)

IVEY, Edward Harold Scott. Wollaston Coll W Austr 65. **d** 67 Perth. C of Applecross 67-70; Perm to Offic Dio Perth from 70. *19 Sussex Street, Nollamara, W Australia 6061.*

IVEY, William Phineas. Univ of Manit BSc 66. Huron Coll Ont MDiv 74. **d** 74 Alg. I of Chapleau Dio Alg from 74. *Box 756, Chapleau, Ont., Canada.* (705-864 1056)

IVORY, Christopher James. b 54. Univ of Reading BSc 76. Univ of Birm Dipl Th 80. Qu Coll Birm 78. **d** 81 St Alb. C of Waltham Cross Dio St Alb from 81. *103 Northfield Road, Waltham Cross, Herts, EN8 7RD.* (Waltham Cross 38897)

IWAYEMI, Stephen Albert Olarewaju. Melville Hall Ibad 54. **d** 55 **p** 56 Ibad. P Dio Ibad 55-80; Can of Ibad 75-80. *St David's Vicarage, Ode-Omu, via Ede, Nigeria.*

✠ **IWE, Right Rev Agori.** MBE 57. St Andr Coll Oyo 24. **d** 38 Niger **p** 39 Bp Vining for Niger. P Dio Niger 38-52; Hon Can of Niger 52-53; Archd of Warri 53-61; Cons Ld Bp of Benin in St Andr Ch Warri 30 Nov 61 by Abp of Niger; Bps of Ibadan; Nig Delta; Owerri; and Bps Nkemena; Uzodike; Dimieari; and Awosika; res 77. *c/o PO Box 18, Ughelli, Nigeria.*

IWENOFU, Nelson Emeka.. b 44. Trin Coll Umuahia 66. **d** 68 **p** 70 Niger. P Dio Niger from 70. *St John's Parsonage, Ekwulobia-Aguata, via Awka, East Central State, Nigeria.*

IWO, Edwin Osigoboka. Trin Coll Umuahia, 58. **d** 59 **p** 60 Nig Delta. P Dio Nig Delta. *PO Box 11, Port Harcourt, Nigeria.*

IWUAGWU, Canon Augustine Onyiyirichuku. Univ of Ibad BD 63. Trin Coll Umuahia. **d** 63 **p** 64 Ow. P Dio Ow; Exam Chap to Bp of Ow from 71; Can of Ow from 75. *Alvan Ikoku College, Owerri, Nigeria.*

IWUAGWU, Vincent Agbanye Chukuemeka. Trin Coll Umuahia, 62. **d** 64 Ow. d Dio Ow. *Parsonage, Obollo, via Okigwe, Nigeria.*

IWUNO, Ven Christopher Obiefuna. Trin Coll Umuahia, 55. **d** 57 **p** 58 Niger. P Dio Ow 57-60; Dio Niger from 60; Hon Can of Niger 69-80; Archd of Nnewi from 80. *St Mary's Parsonage, Nnewi, Nigeria.*

IWUORA, Jeremiah Agbadebelumonwu. d 45 Bp Patterson for Niger **p** 47 Niger. P Dio Niger 45-72. *c/o St Philip's Church, Ogidi, Nigeria.*

J

JABU, Francis. St Cypr Coll Lindi 71. **d** 74 **p** 75 Masasi. P Dio Masasi. *c/o St Cyprian's College, Box 212, Lindi, Tanzania.*

JACK, Alexander Richard. b 30. Univ of Leeds BSc 55, MSc 66. Oak Hill Th Coll 69. **d** 71 **p** 72 Lich. C of Penn Fields (in c of St Joseph from 78) Dio Lich from 71. *100 Bellencroft Gardens, Merry Hill, Wolverhampton, WV3 8DU.*

JACK, Henry Graham. b 21. K Coll Lon AKC 48, BD 49. St Bonif Coll Warm. **d** 49 **p** 50 Lon. C of Ch Ch Crouch End

49-50; Steyning 52-56; R of Warbleton 56-61; V of Alfriston w Lullington 61-65; RD of Seaford 64-65; Sub-Dean and R of St Andr Cathl Santiago 65-74; Hon Can of Chile 66-74; R of Trowbridge Dio Sarum from 74. *Rectory, Trowbridge, Wilts.* (Trowbridge 5121)

JACK, Walter George Andrew. Trin Coll Melb 45, BA 46. Ridley Coll Melb ThL 41. **d** 46 Bal **p** 46 Bend for Bal. C of Warrnambool 46; P-in-c of Panmure and Allansford 46-48; Edenhope 48-51; Wendouree and Chap C of E Gr Sch Dio Bal 51-56; C of Ch Ch Doncaster 56-57; St Andr Willesden Green 57-60; Croydon Vic 60-61; Melb Dioc Centre 61-64; St Pet Melb 64-66; C in Dept of Chaps Dio Melb from 67. *24 Spray Street, Merricks, Vic, Australia 3916.* (059-89 5474)

JACKLIN, John Frederick. b 30. Oak Hill Th Coll 72. **d** & **p** 72 Chile. C of Santiago 72-75; Ch Ch Roxeth 75-78; V of Selston w Westwood Dio Southw from 78. *Selston Vicarage, Nottingham, NG16 6EW.* (Ripley 810247)

JACKLIN, Leonard. Em Coll Sktn L Th 34. BA (Sask) 57. **d** 31 **p** 32 Sask. C of Rosthern 31-32; Carragana 32-35; Marshall 35-37; I of Colonsay 37-42; Dundalk w Melancthon and Maxwell 42-44; Forest w Thedford and Kettle Point 44-46; Ch Ch Forest 46-50; St Mary's w Ch Ch Lakeside 50-60; R of Hyde Pk Hur 60-71. *RR3, Ilderton, Ont, Canada.*

JACKSON, Alan. b 44. Univ of Newc T BA 68, MEducn 78. N-E Ordin Course 80. **d** 81 Bp Gill for Newc T (NSM). Hon C of H Trin Jesmond City and Dio Newc T from 81. *7 Selborne Gardens, Newcastle upon Tyne, NE2 1EY.*

JACKSON, Canon Albert John. Wycl Coll Tor BA 27, MA 28. **d** 29 **p** 30 Tor. C of St D Tor 29-30; St Pet Cobourg 30-34; R of St Hilda Fairbank Tor 34-57 and 62-72; Chap RCAF 41-44; Can of Tor from 56; C of St Paul Bloor Street City and Dio Tor from 72. *2353 Dufferin Street, Toronto 10, Ont, Canada.*

JACKSON, Alexander. b 1897. Jes Coll Cam BA 20, MA 23. TD 37. Qu Coll Birm 55. **d** and **p** 57 Birm. C of Moseley 57-61; V of Shuttington w Amington 61-67; Perm to Offic Dio Birm from 67. *Bryony House, Selly Oak, Birmingham, B29 4BX.* (021-475 2996)

JACKSON, Arthur. b 10. **d** 78 Graft. C of Ballina Dio Graft from 78. *12 Greenhalgh Street, Ballina, NSW, Australia 2478.*

JACKSON, Arthur Malcolm. b 31. TCD BA and Div Test 54, MA 60. **d** 54 **p** 55 Connor. C of Templecorran U 54-57; Santry U 57-58; Bp's V and Libr of St Canice's Cathl Kilk and Regr Dios Oss, Ferns and Leigh 58-61; I of Monastereevan 61-68; Narraghmore and Fontstown w Timolin Dio Glendal from 68. *Ballytore Rectory, Athy, Co Kildare, Irish Republic.* (Athy 23114)

JACKSON, Arthur Samuel. Hatf Coll Dur LTh 23. St Paul's Miss Coll Burgh. **d** 24 **p** 25 Linc. C of Owston w E Ferry 24; St Pet w All SS Stamford 27-29; P-in-c of Wyalkatchem 29-31; V of Mt Hawthorn 31-32; C of Sandal Magna (in c of Walton) 32-35; V of Horbury Junc 35-56; R of Shottesbrooke w White Waltham 56-72. *75 The Promenade, Peacehaven, Sussex, BN9 8LY.*

JACKSON, Barry. b 30. Late Scho of St Jo Coll Cam BA (2nd cl Cl Trip) 53, Dipl Educn 54, MA 57. Westcott Ho Cam 63. **d** 65 **p** 66 Ches. C of St Geo Stockport 65-68; Bridgwater w Chilton Trinity 68-70; C-in-c of Thurloxton 70-75; Asst Master Bp Fox Gr Sch Taunton 70-75; Chap Wycl Coll from 75. *Ivy Grove, Bath Road, Stonehouse, Glos.*

JACKSON, Very Rev Brandon Donald. b 34. Univ of Liv LLB 56. St Cath S Ox Dipl Th 59. Wycl Hall Ox 57. **d** 58 Woolwich for Cant **p** 59 S'wark. C of New Malden w Coombe 58-61; St Geo Leeds 61-65; V of St Pet Shipley 65-77; M Gen Syn Dio Bradf from 70; Ch Comm 71-73; Exam Chap to Bp of Bradf from 74; Provost and V of Cathl Ch City and Dio Bradf from 77. *Provost's House, Cathedral Close, Bradford, Yorks, BD1 4EG.* (Bradford 32023)

JACKSON, Brian Walter. b 46. Univ of Natal BComm 70. Wycl Hall Ox 74. **d** 77 **p** 78 Port Eliz. C of St Kath Uitenhage 77-81. *PO Box 486, Uitenhage, CP, S Africa.*

JACKSON, Canon Cecil Thomas. b 09. TCD BA 30, Div Test 31, MA 37. **d** 32 Derry for Down **p** 33 Down. C of Carnmoney 32-37; I of Ballywater 37-74; RD of Ards 55-73; Can of Down from 68. *Tanglewood Cottage, Lisbane Road, Kircubbin, Co Down, N Ireland.* (Kircubbin 449)

JACKSON, Christopher John Wilson. b 45. St Pet Coll Ox BA (Mod Hist) 67. Ridley Hall Cam 69. **d** 72 **p** 73 S'wark. C of St Marg Putney 72-76; St Pet w St Paul Battersea 76-79; Team V of Preston Dio Blackb from 79. *St Stephen's Vicarage, Broadgate, Preston, Lancs, PR1 8DU.* (Preston 55762)

JACKSON, Christopher William. b 47. K Coll Lon AKC 69. St Aug Coll Cant 69. **d** 70 Jarrow for Dur **p** 71 Dur. C of Newton Aycliffe 70-73; St Jas Conv Distr Owton Manor Hartlepool 73-76; Novice CGA 77; Team V of W Harton 77-79; R of Hemsworth Dio Wakef from 79. *Hemsworth Rectory, Pontefract, W Yorks.* (Hemsworth 610507)

JACKSON, Canon David. b 33. Univ of Leeds, BA (1st cl Gen) 60. Coll of Resurr Mirfield 60. **d** 62 **p** 63 S'wark. C of St Steph Lewisham 62-65; C-in-c of New Charlton 65-69; Sub-R of St Luke w St Paul Old Charlton 69-72; Sen Tutor Coll of the Resurr Mirfield 72-75; R of Clapham Dio S'wark from 75-78; Team R of Clapham Old Town Dio S'wark from 78; C-in-c of St Pet Clapham 76-78; Hon Can of S'wark Cathl from 80. *20 North Side, Clapham Common, SW4 0RQ.* (01-622 7505)

JACKSON, David Bryans. St Jo Coll Winnipeg BA and BTh 65. **d** 64 Bp Anderson for Rupld **p** 65 Rupld. I of Rathwell 64-68; Manitou 68-73; Wicklow w Wilmot and Peel Dio Fred from 74. *Box 54, Florenceville, NB, Canada.*

JACKSON, David Michael. Univ of Tor BA 62, MA 66. **d** 77 Qu'App. C of St Paul's Cathl Regina Dio Qu'App from 77. *2768 McAra Street, Regina, Sask, Canada.*

JACKSON, David Reginald Estcourt. OBE. Qu Coll Cam BA 45, MA 49. St Jo Coll Dur 80. **d** 81 Blackb. C of Douglas from 81. *64 The Common, Parbold, Wigan, Lancs, WN8 7EA.*

JACKSON, Derek. b 26. Ex Coll Ox BA 51, MA 55. Westcott Ho Cam 51. **d** 53 **p** 54 Southw. C of Radcliffe-on-Trent 53-56; Frome Selwood 56-57; V of Eaton Socon 57-63; Boxmoor 63-74; Bp's Stortford Dio St Alb from 74. *Vicarage, Church Street, Bishop's Stortford, Herts.* (Bp's Stortford 54416)

JACKSON, Derek Reginald. b 49. AKC and BD 72. St Aug Coll Cant 72. **d** 73 **p** 74 Man. C of Westhoughton 73-75; Kendal 75-78; V of Pennington Dio Carl from 78; Lindal-in-Furness w Marton Dio Carl from 78. *Pennington Vicarage, Ulverston, Cumb, LA12 0JW.* (Ulverston 53174)

JACKSON, Derrick Raymond. Worc Ordin Coll 63. **d** 65 **p** 66 Worc. C of Old Swinford 65-68; Headless Cross 68-70; R of Mamble w Bayton 70; V in Shinghay Group 71-80; V of Hunningham Dio Cov from 80; Wappenbury w Weston-under-Wetherley Dio Cov from 80. *Hunningham Vicarage, Leamington Spa, Warws, CV33 9DS.* (Marton 632382)

JACKSON, Douglas George. Wycl Coll Tor. **d** 58 **p** 59 Tor. C of Washago 58-60; St Cuthb Tor 60-62; I of St Pet Oshawa 62-63; Brooks 63-67; High River 67-76; Cochrane Dio Moos from 76. *Box 429, Cochrane, Ont, Canada.*

JACKSON, Frederick Charles. **d** 60 **p** 62 Tor. C-in-c of Richvale 60-63; Thornhill 63-65; Hon C of Richmond Hill Dio Tor from 66. *194 Hillsview Drive, Richmond Hill, Ont, Canada.*

JACKSON, Frederick George. b 43. Univ of Leeds BA (2nd cl Engl and Th) 70. Cudd Coll 70. **d** 72 **p** 73 Glouc. C of Cirencester 72-74; St Aug Kilburn, Paddington 74-77; St Mary Pimlico 77-81; Dom Chap to Bp of Chich from 81. *c/o The Palace, Chichester, Sussex.*

JACKSON, Frederick John. AKC 37. **d** 37 **p** 38 Chelmsf. C of St John Walthamstow 37-40; Woodford 40-43; CF (EC) 43-47; Hon CF 47; R of Little Thurrock 43-53; V of St Paul (w St Bart from 59) Chich 53-80; Chap RW Sussex Hosp 54-80. *Upalong, The Drive, Chichester, W Sussex, PO19 4QQ.*

JACKSON, George. b 10. St Jo Coll Dur LTh 33, BA (3rd cl Th) 35, MA 39. St Aid Coll 30. **d** 35 **p** 36 Blackb. C of St Cuthb Fulwood 35-37; St Jas Accrington 38-40; V of Stonefold 40-43; St Mich Blackb 43-53; PC of Woodplumpton 53-69; V 69-74; C of Broughton 74-77. *37 Stanley Croft, Woodplumpton, Preston, PR4 0BS.*

✠ **JACKSON, Most Rev George Frederic Clarence.** Univ of Tor BA 32, LTh 33. Wycl Coll Tor Hon DD 59. St Chad Coll Regina DD (*hon causa*) 63. Em Coll Sktn DD (*hon causa*) 63. St Jo Coll Winnipeg Hon DCnL 75. **d** 34 **p** 35 Niag. C of Erin 34-35; I of Hornby Stewarttown and Norval 35-37; C of H Trin Tor 37-38; Perm to Offic (Col Cl Act) Dio Ches 38-42; V of St John Egremont 42-47; I of Lowville 47-48; Oakville 48-58; Can of Niag 52-58; Dean and R of St Paul's Pro-Cathl Regina 58-60; Cons Ld Bp of Qu'App in St Paul's Pro-Cathl Regina 21 Aug 60 by Abp of Rupld; Abp of Edmon (Primate); Bps of Bran; Sktn; Calg; and Sask; Bp Suffr of Edmon; Bp of N Dakota (USA); and Bp Knowles; Elected Metrop of the Prov of Rupld 70; res 77; Hon C of Fort Qu'App Dio Qu'App from 77. *Box 519, Fort Qu'Appelle, Sask, SOG 1SO, Canada.*

JACKSON, Graham Robert. St Mich Th Coll Crafers 64. ACT ThL 68. **d** 69 **p** 70 Adel. C of Eliz N 69-73; Missr St Pet Coll Miss Eliz 73-77; P-in-c of Northfield 77-80; Admin Angl Child Care Services Dio Adel from 80. *9 Tennyson Street, Clearview, S Australia 5085.*

JACKSON, Harry Francis. b 30. K Coll Lon BD and AKC 61. Sarum Th Coll 61. **d** and **p** 62 Berm. C of Devonshire and of H Trin Cathl Hamilton 62-65; Cobham 65-69; R of Ash

Dio Guildf from 69. *Rectory, Church Road, Ash, Aldershot, Hants, GU12 6LU.* (Aldershot 21517)

JACKSON, Hilary Walton. b 17. St Chad's Coll Dur Lindsay Cl Scho 36, Univ Hebr Scho 38, BA (3rd cl Th) 40, MA 48. **d** 46 Selby for York **p** 47 York. C of Selby Abbey 46-49; All SS Middlesbrough 49-51; V of Thornley 51-56; PC of Beamish 56-66; Surr from 59; V of Heighington w Bolam Dio Dur from 66. *Heighington Vicarage, Darlington, Co Durham.* (Aycliffe 312134)

JACKSON, Hubert Edwyn Alston. b 08. M IEE 67. Ripon Hall Ox Dipl Th 56. **d** 58 B & W **p** 59 Taunton for B & W. c of Yeovil 58-61; V of Ilton 61-79; C-in-c of Ile Abbotts 61-62; V 62-79. *c/o Ilton Vicarage, Ilminster, Somt.* (Ilminster 2860)

JACKSON, Ian. b 53. Jes Coll Ox BA 75. Linc Th Coll 76. **d** 78 **p** 79 Linc. C of Holbeach Dio Linc from 78. *5 Church Walk, Holbeach, Spalding, Lincs, PE12 7DT.* (Holbeach 24037)

JACKSON, Canon James Alan. St Chad's Coll Regina. **d** 34 **p** 44 Qu'App. C of Weyburn 43-46; I of Oxbow w Gainsborough 46-47; R 48-52; I of Assiniboia 52-61; R of Woodsdale 61-63; Rossland 63-64; Chap Univ of BC 65-67; P-in-c of Grand Forks 66-70; L to Offic Dio Koot 71-72; C of Kelowna 72-73; Dean and R of St Sav Cathl Nelson 73-80; Can of Koot from 80. *723 Ward Street, Nelson, BC, Canada.* (352-6844)

JACKSON, James Gordon. Univ of Tor BA 62. Univ of Manit BSW 63. Trin Coll Tor STB 66. **d** 65 Ont for Rupld **p** 66 Rupld. C of St Luke Winnipeg 65-67; Port Edward 67-69; I of Kitkatla 69-71; Smithers 71-77; Executive Asst Dio Koot 77-79; P-in-c of St Geo City and Dio Calg from 79. *1727 42nd Street NE, Calg, Alta, Canada, T1Y 2L6.* (280-4991)

JACKSON, James Henry. Univ of Tor BA 49. Wycl Tor Coll LTh 52, BD 55. **d** 51 Tor for Alg **p** 52 Alg. I of Port Carling 52-55; CF (Canad) from 55; I of Redeemer Kingston w Storrington Dio Ont from 75. *11 Lyons Street, Kingston, Ont, Canada.*

JACKSON, Ven James Marcus Neville. Univ of Tor BSA 34. BA 49. Univ of W Ont MA 36. Trin Coll Tor. **d** 39 **p** 40 Tor. C of St Alb Tor 39-41; St Thos Tor 41-47; R of St Mark Parkdale Tor 47-56; St Martin-in-the-Fields Tor 56-80; Can of Tor 72-73; Archd of Tor W 73-80. *705-236 Dixon Road, Weston, Ont, Canada.*

JACKSON, John. b 20. G and C Coll Cam BA 48, MA 50. BD (Lon) 58. St Aug Coll Cant. **d** 57 **p** 58 Blackb. C of St Pet Burnley 57-60; L to Offic Dio Blackb 61-67; Perm to Offic Dio Bradf from 68. *8 Aireville Drive, Shipley, W Yorks, BD18 3AD.* (Bradford 487892)

JACKSON, John. b 1891. **d** 59 **p** 60 Dub. C of Rathfarnham 60-65; C-in-c of Edenderry w Ballyburley Dio Kild 65-68; R 68-69; Edenderry, Clonbulloge and Rathangan 69-72. *122 Loughbollard Estate, Clane, Co Kildare, Irish Republic.*

JACKSON, John Benedict. b 07. **d** 67 **p** 68 Newc T. C of Denton Newc T 67-70; St Gabr Heaton Newc T 70-73; P-in-c of Simonburn Dio Newc T from 73. *Simonburn Rectory, Hexham, Northumb, NE48 3AR.* (Humshaugh 220)

JACKSON, John Edward. b 29. K Coll Lon and Warm AKC and BD 57. **d** 58 **p** 59 S'wark. C of Crofton Pk 58-61; V of Bremhill w Foxham 61-69; Netheravon w Fittleton (and Enford from 73) Dio Sarum from 69. *Netheravon Vicarage, Salisbury, Wilts, SP4 9QP.* (Netheravon 353)

JACKSON, John Reginald. b 25. Selw Coll Cam BA 45, MA 49. Ridley Hall, Cam. **d** 48 **p** 49 Sheff. C of St Jas Doncaster 48-50; Walcot 50-53; St Mark Cheltenham 53-56; R of Clannaborough 56-67; R of Down 56-67; Georgeham 67-73; V of Waresley 73-79; Abbotsley 73-79; Everton w Tetworth 73-79; P-in-c of St Weonards w Orcop Dio Heref from 79; Tretire w Michaelchurch and Pencoyd Dio Heref from 79; Garway Dio Heref from 79; Welsh Newton w Llanrothal Dio Heref from 79. *Vicarage, St Weonards, Hereford.*

JACKSON, John Thomas. St Aid Coll 49. **d** 51 Whitby for York **p** 52 York. C of St Steph Acomb York 51-56; St Mary w St Nich Beverley 56; R of Stretton w Clipsham 56-58; C-in-c of Greetham 56-58; R of Norseman 59-60. *Norseman, W Australia.*

JACKSON, Preb John Wilson. b 14. St Jo Coll Dur BA 38. Wycl Hall, Ox 38. **d** 40 **p** 41 Birm. C of H Trin Bordesley 40-41; St John Sparkhill 41-44; St Matt Walsall 44-46; R of All SS Birm 46-50; PC of St Aug Bromley Common 50-52; V of Sparkhill and Chap Women's Hosp Birm 52-64; Surr 57-64; Hon Can of Birm 61-64; V of Swindon and Chap Swindon Hosps 64-68; V of Walsall 68-81; RD of Walsall 68-81; Surr 68-81; Preb of Lich Cathl 72-81; Preb (Emer) from 81. *6 Arnold Grove, Shirley, Solihull, W Midl.* (021-744 1288)

JACKSON, Kenneth Allan. St Francis Coll Brisb 52. ACT ThL 56. **d** and **p** 56 Brisb. C of Gympie 56-58; St Jas Toowoomba 58; Beenleigh 59; P-in-c of Tully 62-65; Perm to Offic Dio Brisb 67-69; Dio Rockptn from 69. *124 Kariboe Street, Biloela, Queensland, Australia 4715.* (Biloela 22545)

JACKSON, Kenneth Evans. Kelham Th Coll 50. **d** 54 Stockport for Ches **p** 55 Ches. C of St Mich Coppenhall 54-57; St Alb Stockport 57-60; CF 60-67; R of Lew-Trenchard w Thrushelton 67-77; P-in-c of Stowford 73-77; Malborough w S Huish Dio Ex from 77; W Alvington Dio Ex from 82. *Malborough Vicarage, Kingsbridge, Devon, TQ7 3RR,* (Kingsbridge 561234)

JACKSON, Kenneth Herbert. b 14. Coll of Resurr Mirfield. **d** 45 **p** 46 Ox. C of Beaconsfield 45-49; R of Kimpton w Thruxton and Fyfield 49-59; V of Wootton 59-60; R of Ch Oakley w Wotton 60-72; V of St Ambrose Bournemouth 72-81. *12 Traherne Close, Deer Park, Ledbury, Herefs, HR8 2RF.*

JACKSON, Kenneth William. b 30. Chich Th Coll 70. **d** 72 **p** 73 Portsm. C of Eastney 72-74; Portchester 74-79; V of Elson Dio Portsm from 79. *Elson Vicarage, Gosport, Hants, PO12 4BL.* (Gosport 82824)

JACKSON, Very Rev Lawrence. b 26. K Coll Lon and Warm AKC 50. **d** 51 **p** 52 Leic. C of St Marg Leic 51-55; V of Wymeswold 55-59; St Jas Gtr Leic 59-65; H Trin Cov 65-73; Hon Can of Cov 67-73; RD of Cov N 68-73; Provost and V of Blackb from 73. *Provost's House, Preston New Road, Blackburn, Lancs.* (Blackburn 52502)

JACKSON, Martin. b 56. Clare Coll Cam BA 77, MA 81. St Jo Coll Dur BA (Th) 80. Cranmer Hall Dur 78. **d** 81 Dur. C of Houghton-le-Spring Dio Dur from 81. *The Kepier Flat, Houghton-le-Spring, T & W, DH4 4DN.* (Houghton 848970)

JACKSON, Mark Harding. b 51. Sarum Wells Th Coll 76. **d** 79 **p** 80 Birm. C of Hob's Moat Dio Birm from 79. *29 Jillcot Road, Solihull, Birmingham, W Midl.*

JACKSON, Canon Michael James. b 25. Late Scho and Exhib of Trin Hall, Cam BA 50, MA 58. Wells Th Coll 51. **d** 55 **p** 57 Sheff. Industr Miss Dio Sheff and C of Tinsley 55-59; Sen Chap Sheff Industr Miss 59-69; Exam Chap to Bp of Sheff 67-73; V of Doncaster 69-73; Asst RD of Doncaster 69-73; Surr 69-73; and from 75; Hon Can of Sheff 71-73; V of Nottm Dio Southw from 73; RD of Nottm from 73; Hon Can of Southw from 73; C-in-c of St Cath Nottm 75-78; N Wilford Dio Southw from 76. *St Mary's Vicarage, Nottingham, NG1 6GA.* (Nottm 42476)

JACKSON, Michael Richard. b 31. Selw Coll Cam BA (2nd cl Th) 54, MA 58. Westcott Ho Cam 54. **d** 56 **p** 57 Newc T. C of All SS Gosforth 56-62; R of Dinnington 62-76; V of Swinton Dio Sheff from 76. *Swinton Vicarage, Golden Smithies Lane, Mexborough, S Yorks, S64 8DL.* (Mexborough 582259)

JACKSON, Neil Lawrence. b 35. BD 71 (Lon). St Jo Coll Nottm 70. **d** 71 **p** 72 Willesden for Lon. C of Wealdstone 71-75; H Trin w St Matt Worthing 75-78; V of St Steph Bowling Dio Bradf from 78. *48 Newton Street, Bradford, Yorks, BD5 7BH.* (Bradford 720784)

JACKSON, Noel Benjamin. b 26. Trin Coll Dub BA 50, MA 55. **d** 51 Derry **p** 52 Raph. C of Conwall U 51-55; I of Laghey 55-59; Dromore 59-66; Epiph U Malone Belf Dio Connor from 66; RD of S Belf from 79. *480 Lisburn Road, Belfast 9, N Ireland.* (Belfast 667843)

JACKSON, Noel George. Late Scho of Em Coll Cam BA 33, MA 37. K Coll Lon 33. **d** 35 **p** 36 Bradf. C of St Aug Bradf 35-38; Gt Malvern 38-40; Lenton (in c of St Barn Lenton Abbey) 40-43; Todmorden (in c of St Mary) 43; V of St John Bowling 44-47; Lect Folkestone Tr Coll 47-50; Asst Master Sir Roger Manwood's Sch Sandwich 50-52; Southlands Sch New Romney 52-59; Perm to Offic Dio Cant 53-59. *3 Grange Park Road, Ripon, Yorks.*

JACKSON, Norman. b 20. CEng MIMechE 54. SOC 74. **d** 77 **p** 78 Roch (APM). C of Ch Ch Erith Dio Roch from 77. *6 Bramble Croft, Erith, Kent, DA8 1BX.* (Erith 32279)

JACKSON, Norman. b 14. St Jo Coll Dur BA 39, Dipl in Th 40, MA 42. **d** 40 **p** 41 Blackb. C of St Geo Chorley 40-42; Poulton-le-Fylde 42-45; Distr Sec for BFBS in Man Area 45-49; Perm to Offic Dio Blackb 46-48; V of H Trin Bolton 49-53; Surr 49-80; V of Norden and Ashworth 53-69; R of St Mewan 69-80. *Address temp unknown.*

JACKSON, Patrick Neville. St Francis Coll Brisb 66. **d** 67 **p** 68 Brisb. C of St Matt Sherwood 67-71; Perm to Offic Dio Brisb 71-74; R of St Barn Ithaca City and Dio Brisb from 74. *286 Waterworks Road, Ashgrave, Queensland, Australia 4060.* (38 2320)

JACKSON, Paul Alexander. Montr Dioc Th Coll. **d** 65 **p** 66 Ont. C of St Geo Cathl Kingston Ont 65-68; Dundas 68-70; R of Wainfleet 70-76; R of St Cuthb Oakville Dio Niag from 76. *229 Albion Avenue, Oakville, Ont, Canada.* (416-842 0353)

JACKSON, Peter. Sarum Th Coll 67. **d** 68 **p** 69 York. C of Skelton-in-Cleveland 68-69; C of Upleatham 68-70; Chap

RN from 71. *c/o Ministry of Defence, Lacon House, Theobalds Road, WC1X 8RY.*

JACKSON, Peter Jonathan Edward. b 53. St Pet Coll Ox BA 74, MA 78. St Steph Ho Ox 79. **d** 79 **p** 80 Worc. C of Malvern Link Dio Worc. from 79. *2 Leigh Sinton Road, Malvern Link, Worcs.* (Malvern 5531)

JACKSON, Peter Lewis. b 34. Bps' Coll Cheshunt 63. **d** 66 Bp McKie for Cov **p** 67 Cov. C of Stockingford 66-67; Kenilworth 67-72; P-in-c of Napton-on-the-Hill Dio Cov 72-75; V from 75; Lower Shuckburgh Dio Cov from 75. *Vicarage, Napton, Rugby, Warws.* (Southam 2383)

JACKSON, Canon Ralph Boyes. b 1900. CBE 58. Qu Coll Cam 3rd cl Hist Trip pt i 21, BA (3rd cl Hist Trip pt ii) 22, MA 26. Westcott Ho Cam 22. **d** 24 **p** 25 Wakef. C of Liversedge 24-27; Dioc Chap Dio Argent 27-28; Chap at San Isidro 28-29; Chap Toc H Dio Argent 29-32; Asst Master St Geo Coll Quilmes 32-40; Hd Master 40-62; Hon Can of St John's Pro-Cathl Buenos Aires 47-62; Can (Emer) from 68; P-in-c of All SS Quilmes Buenos Aires 51-52; R of Langton w Birdsall 62-76; RD of Buckrose 63-75; Commiss Argent from 63. *41 Hunters Way, Dringhouses, York, YO2 2JL.*

JACKSON, Reginald. b 05. Lon Coll Div. **d** 45 **p** 46 Cant. C of St Faith Maidstone 45-48; St Jo Bapt Woking (in c of St Sav Brookwood) 48-52; R of St Pet Thetford 52-58; V of Sissinghurst 58-70; Master of St Jo Hosp Bath 70-75; C of Sturminster Newton Dio Sarum from 79. *10 Marnhull Road, Hinton St Mary, Sturminster Newton, Dorset.*

JACKSON, Reginald Grant. Univ of Birm BA (2nd cl Phil) 29. Ripon Hall, Ox 28. **d** 29 **p** 30 Birm. C of St Andr Bordesley 29-31; St Mary Moseley 31-32; Keston 32-35; V of Saul (w Whitminster from 37) 35-43; Painswick 43-54; R of Dur Ont 54-58; I of Alvinston 58-62; R of Ailsa Craig 62-67; Thorndale 67-70; R of Parkhill 71-72. *200 Main Street, Ailsa Craig, Ont., Canada.*

JACKSON, Robert Fielden. b 35. St D Coll Lamp BA 57. Sarum Th Coll 57. **d** 59 Blackb **p** 60 Lanc for York. C of Clayton-le-Moors 59-62; Lytham 62-64; V of St Chad Skerton 64-69; Preesall Dio Blackb from 69. *St Oswald's Vicarage, Knott End, Blackpool, Lancs, FY6 0DU.* (Knott End 810297)

JACKSON, Preb Robert Stewart. b 29. Trin Coll Dub BA 53, Div Test 54, MA 56. ALCM 48. **d** 54 **p** 55 Down. C of Aghalee 54-57; I of Derrybrusk 57-61; Magheracross 61-68; Lisnaskea Dio Clogh from 68; Dom Chap to Bp of Clogh from 73; Preb of Clogh Cathl from 79. *Lisnaskea, Co Fermanagh, N Ireland.* (Lisnaskea 21237)

JACKSON, Robert William. b 49. K Coll Cam MA 73. Univ of Man MA 73. St Jo Coll Nottm 78. **d** 81 Sheff. C of Ch Ch Fulwood City and Dio Sheff from 81. *1 Silver Birch Avenue, Sheffield 10.*

JACKSON, Roger Brumby. b 31. Univ of Dur BSc 53, Dipl Educn 54. Ridley Hall, Cam 57. **d** 59 **p** 60 Portsm. C of Rowner 59-61; Drypool 61-64; Asst Chap HM Pris Hull 61-64; V of St Jo Bapt w St Jas (and St Paul from 68) Plumstead 65-74; Deane Dio Man 74-80; Team R from 80; C-in-c of St Paul Plumstead 65-68; Sub Dean of Woolwich 71-74; RD of Deane from 80. *Deane Vicarage, Wigan Road, Bolton, BL3 5QE.* (Bolton 61819)

JACKSON, Roland Francis. b 20. St D Coll Lamp BA. St Mich Coll Llan 42. **d** 44 **p** 45 Mon. C of Risca 44-49; Chepstow w St Arvans 49-54; R of Haughton Staffs 54-61; V of St Paul Forebridge 61-72; Surr from 68; V of Eccleshall Dio Lich from 72; RD of Eccleshall from 72. *Church Street, Eccleshall, Stafford, ST21 6BY.* (Eccleshall 850351)

JACKSON, Ronald William. b 37. Lon Coll of Div 67. **d** 69 **p** 70 Portsm. C of Crofton 69-74; V of St Matt Wolverhampton Dio Lich from 74. *14 Sydenham Road, Wolverhampton, Staffs.* (Wolverhampton 53300)

JACKSON, Canon Stanley. b 21. St Cath S Ox BA 48, MA 52. Linc Th Coll. **d** 50 **p** 51 Man. C of Swinton 50-52; Skegness 52-56; CF 56-68; V of L Coates 68-73; R 73-78; Ruskington Dio Linc from 78; V of Dorrington Dio Linc from 78; Can and Preb of Linc Cathl from 79. *Ruskington Rectory, Sleaford, Lincs.* (Ruskington 832463)

JACKSON, Canon Stephen Alexander. b 18. Keble Coll Ox BA (3rd cl Mod Hist) 40, MA 44. Cudd Coll 40. **d** 42 **p** 43 St Alb. C of Bp's Hatfield 42-45; St Francis Welwyn Garden City 45-49; Leic Dioc Youth Chap and L to Offic Dio Leic 49-52; R of Asfordby 52-58; C-in-c of Frisby-on-Wreake w Kirby Bellars 52-54; V of Quorn 58-65; R of St Andr Aylestone City and Dio Leic from 65; Surr from 67; Hon Can of Leic Cathl from 74; RD of Christianity S 74-81. *Aylestone Rectory, Leicester, LE2 8ND.* (Leic 832458)

JACKSON, Thomas Peter. St D Coll Lamp BA 50. St Mich Coll Llan 50. **d** 52 **p** 53 Swan B. C of St Mary Swansea 52-58; UMCA Area Sec for S Midl and S Wales 58-60; PC (V from 69) of St Steph Glouc 60-73; R of Upton St Leon Dio Glouc from 73. *Rectory, Upton St Leonards, Gloucester.* (Gloucester 66171)

JACKSON, Verne Ernest. b 47. **d** 78 Caled. C of St Pet Kitkatla Dio Caled from 78. *Kitkatla, BC, Canada, V0V 1C0.*

JACKSON, Wilfrid Hall. b 1900. St Chad's Coll Dur BA 26, Dipl in Th 28, MA 29. ATCL 42. **d** 28 **p** 29 York. C of Cottingham 28-30; St Geo Gateshead 30-34; V of Lesbury 34-55; C of Skelton-in-Cleveland 55-64; V of Old Malton 64-70. *136 Micklow Close, Redcar, Cleve.*

JACKSON, William. Edin Th Coll. **d** 66 **p** 67 Newc T. C of Willington-on-Tyne 66-69; Haltwhistle 69-71; R of All SS Buckie 71-80; Portsoy 71-80. *c/o All Saints Rectory, Buckie, Banff, AB5 1HA.*

JACKSON, William Stanley Peter. b 39. Univ of Wales, Dipl Th 66. St Mich Coll Llan 63. **d** 66 **p** 67 Swan B. C of Llandrindod w Cefnllys 66-69; Gowerton w Waunarlwydd 69-73; V of Crickadarn w Gwenddwr and Alltmawr 73-79; R of Llanfeugan w Llanddetty and Llansantyffraed- Justa-Usk Dio Swan B from 79. *Rectory, Talybont-on-Usk, Brecon, Powys, LD3 7UX.*

JACKSON-STEVENS, Nigel. b 42. St Steph Ho Ox. **d** 68 **p** 69 Ex. C of Babbacombe 68-73; V of Swimbridge w Gunn (and W Buckland from 75) Dio Ex from 73; C-in-c of Buckland 73-75. *Swimbridge Vicarage, Barnstaple, Devon.* (Swimbridge 257)

JACOB, Ven Bernard Victor. b 21. St Pet Hall Ox BA 48, MA 52. Wycl Hall Ox 49. **d** 50 **p** 51 Man. C of Middleton (Lancs) 50-54; V of H Trin Ulverston 54-59; Bilston 59-65; Mortlake w E Sheen 68-76; R 76-77; Warden Scargill Ho 65-68; RD of Richmond and Barnes 75-77; Archd of Kingston-T from 77. *7 Cornwall Road, Sutton, Surrey, SM2 6DT.* (01-661 9038)

JACOB, John Lionel Andrew. b 26. Selw Coll Cam 2nd cl Hist Trip pt i 49, BA 50, 2nd cl Th Trip pt ii 51, MA 54. Westcott Ho Cam 50. **d** 52 **p** 53 Sheff. C of St Thos Brightside Sheff 52-55; Maltby 55-58; V of Intake 58-67; St Aid w St Luke Sheff 67-75; Leader Manor Par Group Sheff 71-75; R of Sheff Manor 75-81; Waddington Dio Linc from 81. *Rectory, Rectory Lane, Waddington, Lincoln, LN5 3RS.* (0522 720323)

JACOB, Joseph. b 38. Trin Coll Dub 65. **d** 68 **p** 69 Connor. C of St Aid Belf 68-70; Dom Chap to Bp of Connor 70-71; V of Kilscoran 71-80; R of Geashill Dio Kild from 80. *Rectory, Geashill, Co Offaly, Irish Republic.*

JACOB, William Mungo. b 44. Univ of Hull LLB 66. Linacre Coll Ox BA (2nd cl Th) 69, MA 73. St Steph Ho Ox 70. **d** 70 **p** 71 Thetford for Nor. C of Wymondham 70-73; Asst Lazenby Chap Univ of Ex 73-75; Dir of Pastoral Stud Sarum Wells Th Coll 75-80; Vice-Prin 77-80; Selection Sec and Sec C'tte for Th Educn ACCM from 80. *Church House, Dean's Yard, SW1P 3NZ.* (01-222 9011)

JACOB, William Ungoed. b 10. Late Exhib of Jes Coll Ox BA (2nd cl Hist) 32, 2nd cl Th 33, MA 37. Wycl Hall Ox 32. **d** 34 **p** 35 St D. C of H Trin Aberystwyth 34-36; Lampeter 36-40; V of Blaenau Festiniog 40-51; R of Hubberston w Hakin 51-55; Surr from 53; V of Carmarthen 55-67; Can of St D 57-60; RD of Carmarthen 58-60; Archd of Carmarthen 60-67; Dean of Brecon Cathl and V of Brecon w Battle 67-78; Gen Sec Prov Coun for Mission & Unity 67-73. *110 Sketty Road, Swansea, W Glam.*

JACOBS, Abraham William. b 19. **d** 72 **p** 73 Geo (APM). C of St Paul City and Dio Geo from 72. *PO Zebra Dist, George, CP, S Africa.* (Zebra 7)

JACOBS, Adrian John. b 44. Univ of Reading BA (2nd cl Engl) 65. St Chad's Coll Dur BA (2nd cl Th) 68, Dipl Th (w Distinc) 69. K Coll Lon MTh 72. **d** 69 **p** 70 Cant. C of St Jo Evang U Norwood 69-72; Addington Cant 72-76; St Botolph without Bishopsgate Lon 77-79; R of Wilsford Dio Linc from 79. *Wilsford Rectory, Grantham, Lincs, NG32 3NP.* (Loveden 30224)

JACOBS, Alvin Francis. b 47. Coll of Em & St Chad LTh 76. **d** 76 **p** 77 Bran. C of Devon Miss 76-78; I of Rivers and Rapid City and Dio Bran from 78. *Box 279, Rivers, Manit, Canada.*

JACOBS, Charles W.. **d** 78 **p** 79 Kimb K. P Dio Kimb K. *35 Lynch Road, Kimberley, CP, S Africa.*

JACOBS, Dennis Reginald. St Pet Coll Alice, 66. **d** 68 **p** 69 Kimb K for Grahmstn. C of St Mich AA Port Eliz 68-70; Ch K Port Eliz 70-73; R of Kliptown Dio Johann from 74. *Box 37, Kliptown, Transvaal, S Africa.* (011-980 158)

JACOBS, Laverne Valentino Burton. b 42. Univ of Windsor Ont BA 71. Hur Coll Ont MDiv 74. **d** 74 **p** 75 Hur. C of All SS Windsor 74-75; Walpole Island 75-81; I of Forest and Kettle Point Dio Hur from 81. *Box 402, Forest, Ont, Canada.*

JACOBS, Lentor Patrick. **d** 78 **p** 79 Geo. C of All SS Mossel Bay Dio Geo from 78. *6 Gardenia Avenue, New Sunnyside, Mossel Bay, CP, S Africa 6500.*

JACOBS, Michael David. b 41. Late Scho of Ex Coll Ox BA 63, MA 67. Chich Th Coll 63. **d** 65 Barking for Chelmsf

p 66 Chelmsf. C of St Pet Walthamstow 65-68; Chap Univ of Sussex 68-72; Counsellor Univ of Leic from 72. *33 Holme Drive, Oadby, Leics, LE2 4HF.* (Leic 713771)

JACOBS, Neville Robertson Eynesford. b 32. ALCD 59 (LTh from 74). **d** 59 **p** 60 Ox. C of Chesham 59-62; CMS Miss 62-67; Keynsham 68-71; R of Croscombe and Dinder 72-80; V of Pilton w Croscombe, N Wootton and Dinder Dio B & W from 80. *Croscombe Rectory, Wells, Somt, BA5 3QN.* (Shepton Mallet 2242)

JACOBS, Ralph Leonard. d 65 **p** 66 Bran. I of Shoal River 65-69; R of Birtle 69-73; Minnedosa 73-80; Hon Can of Bran 76-80. *Box 776, Grand Forks, BC, Canada.*

JACOBS, Walter George Henson. Univ of Dur (Codr Coll Barb) LTh 37, BA 39. **d** 39 **p** 40 Windw Is. C of St Geo Grenada 39-43; R of Cedros 43-45; V of St Mary Pembroke 45-54. *Pembroke, Tobago, W Indies.*

JACOBSEN, Kenneth Ian. d 63 Bp McKenzie for Wel **p** 64 Wel. C of Tawa-Linden 63-64; Nae Nae 64-68; Masterton 68-70; V of Masterton S 70-76; Chap Palmerston N Hosps 75-80; Perm to Offic Dio Wel from 80. *33 Hedges Street, Sanson, NZ.*

JACOBSEN, Noel David. St Paul's Coll Grahmstn Dipl Th. **d** 78 **p** 79 Capetn. C of Bellville 78-80; St Osw Wilnerton Dio Capetn from 80. *18 Dreyer Street, Rugby 7405, CP, S Africa.*

JACOBSON, Norman. b 47. Chich Th Coll 73. **d** 76 **p** 77 York. C of St Thos Middlesbrough 76-79; Team V of Thornaby-on-Tees (in c of St Paul) Dio York from 79. *Vicarage, Lanehouse Road, Thornaby-on-Tees, Cleve, TS17 8EA.* (Stockton 69661)

JACOBSON, William Walter. b 24. Cant Coll NZ 41, LTh (2nd Cl) 51. **d** 51 **p** 52 Ch Ch. C of Papanui 51-54; V of Hororata 54-58; C-in-c of Poughill w Stockleigh English 58-59; PC of Shiphay Collaton 59-69; V 69-76; Team V of Clyst Valley Dio Ex 76-79 and from 81; C of Ottery 79-81. *Vicarage, Clyst Valley Road, Clyst St Mary, Exeter, Devon.* (Topsham 4363)

JACQUES, Edwin Douglas. Wycl Coll Tor. **d** 60 **p** 61 Tor. C of St Geo-on-the-Hill Tor 60-65; I of Coldwater 65-67; Campbellford 67-72; St Luke Pet 72-79; Malton Dio Tor from 79. *7520 Darcel Avenue, Mississauga, Ont, Canada.*

JACQUES, Humphrey James Kynaston. MBE 45. TD 57. Wells Th Coll 46. **d** 47 **p** 48 B & W. C of Beckington 47-53; Orchardleigh w Lullington 47-53; C-in-c 53; V of Portesham (w Langton Herring from 68 and Abbotsbury from 80) Dio Sarum from 53; RD of Abbotsbury from 59; C-in-c of Langton Herring 67-68; P-in-c of Abbotsbury 78-80. *Portesham Vicarage, Weymouth, Dorset.* (Abbotsbury 217)

JACQUES, Canon John Herbert. b 12. Trin Coll Ox BA (2nd cl Phil, Pol and Econ) 35, MA 39. Univ of Lon Dipl Th 46. Trin Coll Dub BLitt 51. St Aid Coll 36. **d** 37 **p** 38 St A. C of Welshpool 37-42; Hawarden 42-46; R of S Witham 46-62; R of N Witham 48-62; Lect Kesteven Tr Coll 49-56; RD of Beltisloe 60-62; N Hill 62-65; S Hill 62-65; Exam Chap to Bp of Linc 61-74; Surr from 62; V of Spilsby w Hundleby 62-69; R of Aswardby w Sausthorpe 68-69; R of Langton-by-Partney w Sutterby 68-69; Ed Linc Dioc Mag 66-75; Can and Preb of Linc Cathl from 66; R of Thoresway w Croxby 70-79; Rothwell w Cuxwold 70-79; M Gen Syn 70-75. *St Mary's, Mulberry Road, Claxby, Market Rasen, Lincs, LN8 3YS.* (Owersby Moor 435)

JACSON, Edward Shallcross Owen. b 38. St Steph Ho Ox 61. **d** 64 **p** 65 Glouc. C of Yate 64-67; Churchdown 67-71; P-in-c of Sandhurst 71-75; V of Sherborne w Windrush and Gt w L Barrington (Aldsworth from 76) 75-80; Team V of Shaston (in c of Motcombe) Dio Sarum from 80. *Vicarage, Motcombe, Shaftesbury, Dorset, SP7 9NX.*

JADORE, Daniel Parongwa. d 71 Sudan. d Dio Sudan 71-76; Dio Juba from 76. *PO Box 110, Juba, Equatoria Province, Sudan.*

JAGER, George. b 10. SS Coll Cam BA 32, MA 36. Westcott Ho Cam 37. **d** 38 **p** 39 Man. C of Swinton 38-41; V of Billesley Common 41-48; CF 48-49; V of St Leon Leic 49-54; Chap of Leic Cathl and Chap of Christian Industr Coun Leic 54-56; V of Earl Shilton w Elmesthorpe 56-68; Sutton Courtenay w Appleford 68-75. *The Dixons, Welford Road, South Kilworth, Lutterworth, LE17 6DY.* (Welford 475)

JAGGARD, Alan Lionel. Codr Coll Barb. **d** 58 **p** 59 Barb. C of St Mary Barb 58-59; St Phil Barb 59-60; St Matthias Barb 60-64; Em Forest Gate w St Pet Upton Cross Dio Chelmsf from 64. *Given Wilson Institute, Church Lodge, St Mary's Road, Plaistow, E13.* (01-470 1954)

JAGGER, Peter John. b 38. MA (Lambeth) 71. Univ of Leeds MPhil 76. FRHistS 78. Coll of Resurr Mirfield 67. **d** 68 **p** 69 Ripon. C of All SS w St Alb Leeds 68-71; V of Bolton cum Redmire 71-77; Dir of NSM, Warden and Chief Libr of St Deiniol's Libr Hawarden from 77; L to Offic Dio St A from 77; Perm to Offic Dio Ches from 78. *St Deiniol's Library, Hawarden, Clwyd, CH5 3DF.* (0244-532350)

JAGGS, William Kenneth. b 29. Univ of W Ont BA 57. Hur Coll LTh 58. **d** 57 **p** 58 Hur. C of Walkerville 57-58; R of Brussels 58-60; C of Grace Ch Brantford 61-62; I of St Geo Walkerville 62-67. *Box 1148, Essex, Ont, Canada.*

JAGO, Alfred Douglas James. b 08. Univ of Leeds, BA (2nd cl Hist) 30. Coll of Resurr Mirfield, 30. **d** 32 **p** 33 Ex. C of St Pet Plymouth 32-42; C-in-c of Honicknowle Conv Distr 42-57; V 57; PC of Penwerris 57-65; RD of S Carnmarth 63-65; R of St Steph-in-Brannel 65-76; RD of St Austell 71-76; Hon C of Charlestown Dio Truro from 76. *22 Fairbourne Road, St Austell, Cornw.* (St Austell 5208)

JAGO, Kenneth Bruce. Univ of Syd BA 50. Univ of Melb BEducn 55. **d** 55 **p** 56 Armid. C of St Pet Cathl Armid and Asst Master Armid Sch 55-57; Tamworth 57-60; Exec Sec Gen Bd of Relig Educn 60-63; Dir 68-71; Dir Dept Chr Educn Dio Melb 63-67; Hd Master Yarra Valley Sch and L to Offic Dio Melb 71-75; Perm to Offic Dio Melb from 76; Hd Master St Paul's Sch Frankston from 80. *Lot 1, Robinsons Road, Langwarrin, Vic, Australia 3910.*

JAGOE, John Edward Ellis. b 51. Univ of NB BSc 75. Atlantic Sch of Th NS MDiv 78. **d** 78 **p** 79 Fred. C of Hammond River 78-80; I of Musquash Dio Fred from 80. *RR1, Lepreau, NB, Canada E0G 2H0.*

JAGOE, Joh Francis Henry. b 24. Univ of Natal BSc 47. **d** 76 Bp Carter for Johann **p** 77 Johann. C of Benoni Dio Johann from 76. *20 Ambleside Avenue, Lakefield, Benoni 1500, S Africa.*

JAISINGH, Samuel Carlton. b 13. **d** 70 **p** 80 Guy. C of St Jos, Port Mourant 70-78; Beterverwagting 78-80; P-in-c of Belladrum Dio Guy from 80. *Rectory, Belladrum, Berbice, Guyana.*

JAIYEOBA, Canon John. Im Coll Ibad. **d** 58 **p** 59 Ondo-B. P Dio Ondo-B 58-62; Dio Ondo from 62; Perm to Offic Dio Guildf 70-71; Hon Can of Ondo from 77. *Vicarage, Arigidi-Akoko, Nigeria.*

JAIYEOBA, Joseph Oluwatayo. Im Coll Ibad 63. **d** 65 **p** 66 Ondo. P Dio Ondo. *St David's Vicarage, Akure, Nigeria.*

JAIYEOLA, David Olarewaju Oladipo. b 38. Im Coll Ibad. **d** 72 **p** 76 Ibad. P Dio Ibad. *Bishopscourt, Bodija Estate, Ibadan, Nigeria.*

JAIYEOLA, Thomas Olaniran. Melville Hall, Ibad 55. **d** 57 **p** 58 Ibad. P Dio Ibad 57-75; Dio Kwara 75-77; Hon Can of Kwara 75-77. *c/o Box 324, Ilorin, Nigeria.*

JAJA, Festus Dienye. Awka Th Coll 30. **d** 31 Niger **p** 33 Bp Howells for Niger. P Dio Niger 31-52; Dio Nig Delta 52-56. *c/o St Paul's Church, Opobo Town, Nigeria.*

JAKEMAN, Canon Derek Graham. Selw Coll Cam BA 42, MA 46. Cudd Coll. **d** 43 Cant **p** 45 Dover for Cant. C of St Steph Norbury 43-46; P-in-c of H Cross Aruba 46-52; PC of Old Brumby 52-59; V of Spalding Dio Linc from 59; Surr from 64; Can and Preb of Linc Cathl from 69. *Parsonage, Spalding, Lincs.* (Spalding 2772)

JAKEMAN, Francis David. b 47. Univ of Leeds BSc 69. Cudd Coll 71. **d** 74 **p** 75 Linc. C of St Jas Gt Grimsby 74-77; Industr Chap (NW Lon) Dio Lon from 77. *128 Pinner View, Harrow, Middx, HA1 4RN.* (01-427 8678)

JAKOBSSON, Maurice Leslie Jeans. ALCD 35. Univ of Dur LTh 35. **d** 35 **p** 36 S'wark. C of St Sav Herne Hill Road 35-41; Hilton w Melcombe Horsey and Cheselborne 41-44; C-in-c of St Cath Leyton 44-47; V of Mayfield 47-52; C of St Pet Woking 52-55; R of Fyfield 55-72. *Teglan, Ongar Road, Stondon Massey, Brentwood, Essex CM15 0EQ.*

JALASI, Canon Alexander Sheldon Nindi. MBE 62. **d** 41 **p** 43 N Rhod. Miss P Dio N Rhod 41-62; Can of N Rhod 62-64; Archd of Nkhotakota 64-65; Ntchisi 65-70; P Dio Lusaka 71-72; Dio Lake Malawi from 72; Can of Lusaka 71-72; Can (Emer) from 75. *Anglican Church, PO Chipoka, Malawi.*

JALI, Mikael. St Cypr Th Coll Tunduru. **d** 57 Masasi. d Dio Masasi from 57. *Box 92, Newala, Tanzania.*

JALI, Wilmot Bransby Lushington. St Bede's Coll Umtata. **d** 50 **p** 51 Zulu. P Dio Zulu from 50; Can of Zulu 62-70. *St Paul's Church, Nkwenkwe, PO Nkwaleni, Zululand.*

JALLAND, Hilary Gervase Alexander. b 50. Univ of Ex BA 72. Coll of Resurr Mirfield 74. **d** 76 **p** 77 Ex. C of St Thos Ex 76-80; Portsea (in C of St Wilfrid) Dio Portsm from 80. *166 Shearer Road, Portsmouth, Hants.* (Portsmouth 820486)

JAMAICA, Lord Bishop of. *See* De Souza, Right Rev Neville Wordsworth.

JAMAL, Khalil Sany Shukry. b 15. Amer Univ of Beirut, BA 36. Wycl Hall, Ox 38. **d** 39 **p** 40 Jer. C of St Andr Ramallah 39-41; V 41-42; Ch Ch Nazareth 42-56; Secr Palestine Ch Coun 46-56; P-in-c of St Mary Dalkeith 56-60; Asst-Lect in Arabic Univ of Edin 58-60; V of Kirtling 60-65; R of Fletton Dio Ely from 65; Commiss Jordan 73-76; Jer from 76. *Fletton Rectory, Peterborough, PE2 8DF.* (Peterborough 62783)

JAMBABA, Benson Basada. Newton Coll Dogura 68. **d** 73

p 74 Papua. P Dio Papua. *Anglican Church, Sakarina, via Popondota, Papua New Guinea.*

JAMBAN, Barnabas. d 38 **p** 47 Lab. C Dio Lab 38-49; Dio Borneo 49-56. *c/o Bishop's House, Kuching, Sarawak.*

JAMBUNATHAN, Kiramathypathy. Serampore Coll BD 62. Bp's Coll Calc. **d** 55 **p** 56 Sing. P Dio Sing 55-70; Dio W Mal from 70; Archd of W Mal 75-79; Exam Chap to Bp of W Mal 75-79. *St Barnabas' Church, 4 Jalan Sultan, Kelang, Malaysia.*

JAMES, Alan Frederick. b 20. Coll of Resurr Mirfield. **d** 50 **p** 51 Newc T. C of H Trin N Shields 50-55; Milo Dio SW Tang 55-58; V of Horton Dio Newc T from 58. *Horton Vicarage, Blyth, Northumb, NE24 4HH.* (Bedlington 823297)

JAMES, Alan Raymond. b 30. Roch Th Coll 65. **d** 66 **p** 67 Ex. C of St Matt Ex 66-70; V of King's Kerswell Dio Ex from 70. *King's Kerswell Vicarage, Newton Abbot, Devon, TQ12 5DW.* (King's Kerswell 2305)

JAMES, Andrew Nicholas. b 54. Coun for Nat Acad Awards BSc 76. Trin Coll Bris 77. **d** 80 **p** 81 Liv. C of Prescot Dio Liv from 80. *St Mary's House, West Street, Prescot, Merseyside, L34 1LQ.*

JAMES, Arthur Kenneth. b 14. St Chad's Coll Dur BA and Dipl in Th 35, MA 38. **d** 37 **p** 38 Mon. C of Bedwas 37-39; St Paul Newport Mon 39-42; CF (EC) 42-46; CF 46-64; V of Marshfield w Peterstone Wentloog and R of Coedkernew w St Bride Wentloog 64-79. *c/o 8 Marshfield Vicarage, Cardiff, CF3 8UF.* (Castleton 257)

JAMES, Billie. b 24. St D Coll Lamp BA 50, LTh 52. **d** 52 **p** 53 Southw. C of Ordsall 52-56; V of Rainworth 56-61; Scrooby w Ranskill 61-74; Norwell dio Southw from 74; P-in-c of Kneesall Dio Southw from 74; Ossington Dio Southw 74; Laxton 77-78. *Norwell Vicarage, Newark, Notts.* (Caunton 329)

JAMES, Brian Percival Harold. b 26. Univ of Southn BSc (3rd cl Chem) 53. Wycl Hall Ox. **d** 64 Southn for Win **p** 65 Win. C of Hartley Wintney w Elvetham 64-66; Shelf 66-71; V of St Ambrose Oldham Dio Man from 71. *St Ambrose's Vicarage, Oldham, Lancs.* (061-624 7122)

JAMES, Canon Charles Hubert. Univ of W Ont BA 27, BD 31. Hur Coll LTh 27. **d** 28 **p** 29 Hur. I of Ripley and Pine River 28-30; St Luke Yarmouth Heights St Thomas 30-32; C of St Gabr Bris 32-35; I of Thedford Arkona and Kettle Point 35-38; Kirkton w Saitsbury 38-42; R of St John St Thomas 42-50; Trillsonburg and Culloden 50-58; St Paul Stratford Hur 58-72; Can of Hur 64-72; Can (Emer) from 72. *105 Cherry Hill Boulevard, Apt 704, London, Ont., Canada.*

JAMES, Christmas. b 1896. **d** 51 **p** 52 Bradf. Bp's Chap to Deaf and Dumb Bradf 51-72; Perm to Offic at St Jude (w St Paul from 69) Manningham 52-72; L to Offic Dio Bris from 72. *11 Lea Croft, Molesworth Drive, Withywood, Bristol, BS13 9BX.* (0272-640960)

✠ **JAMES, Right Rev Colin Clement Walter.** b 26. K Coll Cam BA (2nd cl Hist) 49, MA 51. Cudd Coll 50. **d** 52 **p** 53 Lon. C of St Dunstan Stepney 52-55; Asst Chap and Asst Master Stowe Sch 55-56; Chap 56-59; Perm to Offic Dio Ox 55-59; Asst Relig Broadcasting Dept BBC 59-60; L to Offic Dio Lon 59-60; Relig Broadcasting Org W Region BBC 60-67; L to Offic Dio Bris 64-67; V of Bournemouth 67-73; C-in-c of St Steph Bournemouth 70-73; Dir of Ordin Tr Dio Win 72-77; Can Res of Win 73-77; Cons Ld Bp Suffr of Basingstoke in St Paul's Cathl 2 Feb 73 by Abp of Cant; Bps of Win, Glas, Linc, Glouc, Ely, Nor; Bps Suffr of Grantham, Huntingdon, Maidstone, Thetford, Willesden and others; Trld to Wakef 77; Chairman C of E Information C'tte 77-79; Centr Relig Advisory Coun for BBC and IBA from 79. *Bishop's Lodge, Woodthorpe Lane, Wakefield, W Yorks.* (Wakefield 255349)

JAMES, Cyril George. b 06. Late Scho of St D Coll Lamp BA (Hist) 27. **d** 29 **p** 30 St D. C of Pemb Dk 29-34; UMCA Miss Lulindi 34-37; P-in-c of Mindu w Lumesule 37-39; Namasakata 39-40; Tunduru 40-45; L to Offic Dio Heref 46-47; Org Sec UMCA in Wales and W Midlands 45-47; C of Pemb Dk Dio St D 47 and 53-57 (in c of St Patr); V of Wiston 47-53; R of Crickhowell 57-76; Commiss SW Tang 62-76; L to Offic Dios Swan B & Mon from 76. *Bank House, Crickhowell, Powys.* (Crickhowell 81034)

JAMES, Cyril Henry. b 18. Univ of Wales, BA (2nd cl Gr) 40. St Mich Coll Llan 39. **d** 41 **p** 42 Llan. C of Cadoxton-juxta-Neath 41-43; Bedlinog 43-48; St Cath Canton 48-51; P-in-c of St John's Conv Distr Graig Pontypridd 51-56; V of Treharris 56-63; Pontlottyn 63-75; Ystrad-Mynach Dio Llan from 75. *Ystrad Mynach Vicarage, Hengoed, Mid Glam.* (Hengoed 813246)

JAMES, David. b 38. Univ of Southn BEducn 74. **d** 77 Win **p** 78 Basingstoke for Win (APM). C of Headbourne Worthy & K Worthy Dio Win from 77. *11 Alresford Road, Winchester, Hants.*

JAMES, David Brian. b 30. Univ of Wales, BA (3rd cl Phil) 63. FCA 52. St Mich Coll Llan 55. **d** 57 **p** 58 Swan B. C of Llandilo-Talybont 57-59; Ch Ch Swansea 59-63; R of Bryngwyn w Newchurch and Llanbedr-Painscastle 63-70; Llanfeugan w Llanthetty and Llansantffraed-juxta-Usk 71-79; Dioc Insp of Schs 77-79; V of Ilston w Pennard Dio Swan B from 79. *88 Pennard Road, Pennard, Swansea, W Glam, SA3 2AD.* (Bishopston 2928)

JAMES, David Charles. b 45. Univ of Ex BSc 66, PhD 71. Univ of Nottm BA 73. St Jo Coll Nottm 70. **d** 73 **p** 74 Win. C of Ch Ch Portswood (or Highfield) Southn 73-76; Goring 76-78; Chap Univ of E Anglia 78-82; V of Ecclesfield Dio Sheff from 82. *45 Church Street, Sheffield, S30 3WE.* (0742-467569)

JAMES, David Clive. b 40. Univ of Bris BA (2nd cl Cl) 61. St Steph Ho Ox 64. **d** 65 **p** 66 Chich. C of Portslade 65-68; Haywards Heath 68-71; Chap Brighton Poly 71-75. *19 Grange Road, Lewes, E Sussex, BN7 1TS.*

JAMES, David Walter Skyrme. b 36. Univ of Nottm BA (1st cl Th) 61. Wells Th Coll 61. **d** 63 **p** 64 Southw. C of St Cypr Carlton Hill Sneinton 63-66; Newark-on-Trent 66-69; V of St Thos Kirkby-in-Ashfield 69-76; R of E Leake Dio Southw from 76; C-in-c of Rempstone, Costock and of Stanford-on-Soar Dio Southw from 76. *Rectory, Bateman Road, East Leake, Loughborough, Leics.* (E Leake 2228)

JAMES, Derek George. b 27. Sarum Wells Th Coll 72. **d** 74 **p** 75 Portsm. C of Petersfield 74-77; P-in-c of Ch Ch Gosport Dio Portsm 77-81; V From 81. *Christ Church Vicarage, Elmhurst Road, Gosport, Hants, PO12 1PG.* (Gosport 81609)

JAMES, Douglas Gordon. b 22. Univ Coll of Wales (Abth) BA 47. [f Solicitor]. Qu Coll Birm 45. **d** 75 Bp Poole-Hughes for Llan **p** 76 Llan. C of Cwmbach Dio Llan from 75. *31 Abernant Road, Aberdare, Mid Glam.* (Aberdare 2559)

JAMES, Edmund Pollard. b 10. MBE 70. St D Coll Lamp LDiv 37. **d** 37 **p** 38 Llan. C of Seven Sisters 37-39; Colyton 39-46; R of Pyworthy (w Pancraswyke from 60) 46-77; RD of Holsworthy 56-59; Preb of Ex 60-77. *St Agnes, All Saints Lane, Clevedon, Avon.*

JAMES, Canon Eric Arthur. b 25. K Coll Lon and Warm AKC 50, BD 51. Trin Coll Cam MA 55. **d** 51 **p** 52 Lon. C of St Steph w St John Westmr 51-55; Chap of Trin Coll Cam 55-59; Select Pr Univ of Cam 59-60; V of St Geo Camberwell and Warden Trin Coll Cam Miss 59-64; Dir 'Parish and People' 64-69; Proc Conv S'wark 64-72; Commiss Kimb K 65-67; Melan from 69; Can Res and Prec of S'wark Cathl 66-73; Can Res and Missr Dio St Alb from 73; Exam Chap to Bp of St Alb from 73; Pr to Gray's Inn from 78; Dir 'Chr Action' from 79. *43 Holywell Hill, St Albans, Herts.* (St Albans 54832)

JAMES, Frederick David Blakey. d 59 **p** 60 St Arn. C-in-c of Bealiba 59-60; V of Wedderburn 60-67; Whittlesea 67-74; Perm to Offic Dio Melb from 74. *59 Valley Fair Drive, Narre Warren, Vic, Australia 3805.* (704-6548)

JAMES, Frederick George. Univ of W Ont BA 59. Hur Coll BTh 65. **d** 65 **p** 66 Hur. I of Wheatley 65-68; R of Parkhill 68-71; on leave 72-73; Dir Sorrento Centre Dio Koot 73-76; Perm to Offic Dio Edmon 76-70; Hon C of All SS Cathl City and Dio Edmon from 79. *14519-84th Avenue, Edmonton, Alta, Canada.*

JAMES, Frederick Trevellyan. d 49 **p** 50 Hur. C of Morpeth, Clearville and Howard 49-51; I of Ch of Resurr Lon 51-68. *617 Ridgewood Crescent East, London 63, Ont, Canada.*

JAMES, Gareth Hugh. b 40. Dipl Th (Wales) 66. St D Coll Lamp 65. **d** 66 **p** 67 Llan. C of All SS Llan 66-68; Whitchurch 68-71; Chap Cathl Sch Llan from 71. *The Cathedral School, Llandaff, S Glam.*

JAMES, Garfield Hughes. b 12. Univ of Wales, BA (2nd cl Phil) 34. St Mich Coll Llan 35. **d** 35 **p** 36 Swan B. C of St Mary Swansea 35-40; CF (EC) 40-46; C of St Jude Swansea 46-47; Chap of Butlin's Holiday Camp Pwllheli 47-48; L to Offic Dio Ban 47-48; Bp's Messenger Dio Swan B 48-51; Exam Chap to Bp of Swan B 49-79; V of Manselton Swansea 51-58; Sketty 58-79; Can of Brecon Cathl 59-71; Chan 71-79; Perm to Offic Dio Guildf from 79. *6 Oatlands Court, St Mary's Road, Weybridge, Surrey.*

JAMES, George Gwynfryn. b 09. Lon Coll of Div 56. **d** 58 **p** 59 Lon. C of All SS Queensbury 58-63; V of Kinnerley w Melverley 63-74. *39 Hazel Grove, The Paddocks, Oswestry, Salop.*

JAMES, Godfrey Walter. b 36. St D Coll Lamp BA 58. Univ Coll of S Wales & Mon MA 60. St Pet Coll Ox BA 63, MA 67. St Mich Coll Llan. **d** 64 Bp Hughes for Llan **p** 65 Llan. C of St Jo Evang Canton 64-71; V of Williamstown Dio Llan from 71. *Vicarage, Williamstown, Tonypandy, Mid Glam.* (Tonypandy 433010)

JAMES, Gordon Cecil. b 35. Sarum Th Coll 66. **d** 67 **p** 68 S'wark. C of Kew 67-72; P-in-c of Weston Longville w Morton-on-the-Hill w Gt and L Witchingham 72-81; R of Diss Dio Nor from 81. *26 Mount Street, Diss, Norf, IP22 3QG.* (Diss 2072)

JAMES, Graham Richard. b 51. Univ of Lanc BA (Hist) 72. Univ of Ox Dipl Th 74. Cudd Coll 72. **d** 75 **p** 76 Pet. C of Ch the Carpenter Pet 75-78; Digswell Dio St Alb from 79. *71 Haldens, Welwyn Garden City, Herts, AL7 1DH.* (Welwyn Gdn 35537)

JAMES, Henley George. b 31. Sarum Wells Th Coll 79. **d** 81 Edmon for Lon. C of H Trin Tottenham Dio Lon from 81. *Rectory, Priory Road, Hornsey, N8 7QT.*

JAMES, Henry Anthony. b 14. St Pet Hall, Ox BA (3rd cl Hist) 36, MA 43. St Mich Coll Llan 36. **d** 37 **p** 38 Swan B for Llan. C of St Mary Virg Cardiff 37-40; Merthyr Tydfil 40-44; Newcastle w Laleston and Tythegston 44-49; St Bride's Major 49-79. *Bryn-y-Fro, Lon Yr Eglwys, St Brides Major, Bridgend, Mid Glam.*

JAMES, Henry Desmond. b 21. St Cath S Ox BA (2nd cl Th) 47, MA 47. St Mich Llan 48. **d** 49 **p** 50 Llan. C of Coity w Nolton 49-50; Pontypridd 50-53; Newbury 53-55; C-in-c of St Barn Conv Distr Reading 55-57; C of Heacham 57-59; R of Gt Bircham w Newton and Bircham Tofts 59-61; Chap RAF 61-65; V of Long Wittenham w Abbots or L Wittenham 65-70; Doddington (Chesh) 70-76; Aston-by-Sutton 76-77; Perm to Offic Dio Ches from 77. *Church Cottage, Crewe Green, Crewe, Chesh.*

JAMES, Henry Glyn. b 26. Keble Coll Ox BA (2nd cl Mod Lang) 50, Dipl Th (w Distinc) 51, MA 62. Univ of Tor MEducn 74. Wycl Hall Ox 50. **d** 52 Birm **p** 53 Bp Linton for Cant. C of St Aug Edgbaston 52-54; St Matt Surbiton 54-57; Ho Master Kingham Hill Sch 57-62; Chap St Lawr Coll Ramsgate 62-68; Ashbury Coll Ott 68-69; Trin Coll Sch Port Hope Tor 69-73; C of Kidmore End 74-77; Hon C of Remenham Dio Ox from 77; Ho Master K Jas Coll of Henley from 74. *1 Harcourt Close, Henley-on-Thames, Oxon, RG9 1UZ.* (04912-4245)

JAMES, Herbert Royston Joseph. b 22. Sarum Th Coll 65. **d** 67 **p** 68 Ex. C of Whipton 67-75; V of Shaugh Prior Dio Ex from 75. *St Edward's Vicarage, Shaugh Prior, Plymouth, Devon.* (Shaugh Prior 247)

JAMES, Idris Frank. b 20. St D Coll Lamp 53. **d** 55 Llan **p** 60 Chelmsf. C of Llangynwyd w Maesteg 55-59; St Andr Plaistow 59-60; Chadwell Heath 60-62; R of Dunton Waylett 62-77; C-in-c of Bulphan 62-64; R 64-77. *Address temp unknown.*

JAMES, James Thomas Lawrence. b 33. Univ of Tor BA 55. Trin Coll Tor LTh 59, STB 60. **d** 58 **p** 59 Alg. I of Lake of Bays 58-62; All SS Windsor 62-64; Prof at Cant Coll Windsor 64-66; Hon C of St John's Cathl Winnipeg 67-68; Chap Manit Custodial Insts 68-70; Hon C of St Bede Winnipeg 70-72; River N 72-76; Perm to Offic Dio Edmon from 77; Program Dir Dio Edmon from 78. *8127 80th Avenue, Edmonton, Alta, Canada, T6C 0S7.* (465-5829)

JAMES, John. Univ of Wales BA 39, MA 41, BD 42. St Mich Coll Llan 43. **d** 44 Mon **p** 45 Llan for Wales. C of St Mark Newport 44-45; Bedwellty w Aberbargoed and Markham 45-52; Machen w Rudry 52-55; V of Llangattock-Vibon-Avel U 55-63; L to Offic Dio Mon from 63. *Avelon, Newcastle, Monmouth, Gwent.*

JAMES, John Ashley Norman. St Barn Coll Adel 36. ACT ThL 38. **d** and **p** 39 Adel. C of St Cuthb Prospect 39-40; P-in-c of Tailem 40-41; Miss Chap Tatiara 41-44; R of Auburn 44-52; Tumby Bay 52-58; P-in-c of Seacliff 58-64; R of Payneham 64-78; L to Offic Dio Adel from 78. *585 Brighton Road, Seacliff, S Australia 5049.*

JAMES, John Charles. b 35. Keble Coll Ox BA (2nd cl Hist) 59. Linc Th Coll 68. **d** 70 Jarrow for Dur **p** 71 Dur. C of S Shields 70-77; P-in-c of St Mary Tyne Dock S Shields 77-79; S Mahe Dio Sey from 79. *Rectory, Anse Royale, Mahe, Seychelles.*

JAMES, John David. b 23. CCC Cam Th Trip pt i, 48. Wells Th Coll. **d** 50 **p** 51 Chelmsf. C of St Edw Romford 50-54; Cannock (in c of St Thos) 54-56; R of Wickham Bishops 56-61; V of Stansted 61-71; St Jas Clacton-on-Sea Dio Chelmsf from 71. *St James's Vicarage, Clacton-on-Sea, Essex.* (Clacton-on-Sea 22007)

JAMES, John Emlyn. b 09. AKC 35. Bps' Coll Cheshunt 36. **d** 36 **p** 37 Sarum. C of Mere w W Knoyle 36-39; Perm to Office at Devizes 39-41; C of St Mark Torquay 41-43; C-in-c of St Andr Cranleigh 43-49; R of Gt w L Kimble 49-64; Woodstock w Bladon 64-79. *Tyrhibin, Newport, Dyfed, SA42 0NT.*

JAMES, John Frank. b 33. Univ of Madr MA 57. Coll of Resurr Mirfield, 60. **d** 62 **p** 63 Portsm. C of St Mark N End Portsea 62-64; Hartcliffe 64-65; St Agnes w St Simon Bris 65-68; V of St Sav Portsea 68-74; Youth Sec USPG from 74. *USPG, 15 Tufton Street, SW1P 3QQ.* (01-222 4222)

JAMES, John Hugh. b 56. St Jo Coll Dur BA 78. St Mich AA Coll Llan Dipl Th 81. **d** 81 Llan. C of Newton-Nottage Dio Llan from 81. *18 Picton Avenue, Porthcawl, Mid Glam.* (Porthcawl 3762)

JAMES, John Morgan. b 21. Univ of Lon BD (1st cl) 43, MTh 45, ALCD 43. **d** 44 **p** 45 Chelmsf. C of St Mary Virg Leyton 44-47; St Sav Westcliff 47-50; C and Prec of Chelmsf Cathl 50-53; PC of St Mark Kemp Town Brighton 53-65; RD of Kemp Town 55-65; Surr from 55; R of Balcombe 65-67; V of Sunbury-on-Thames 67-77; Dir Coll of Prs from 77; LPr Dios Lon & Guildf from 77. *c/o The College of Preachers, St Margaret Pattens Church, Eastcheap, EC3M 1HS.*

JAMES, Very Rev John Paul. Sarum Th Coll 58. **d** 60 **p** 61 Portsm. C of St Jas Milton 60-65; Moulsecoombe w Stanmer and Falmer (in c of H Nativ Lower Bevendean) 65-69; PC of H Trin Brighton 69-71; R of Saguenay 71-77; Dean and R of H Trin Cathl City and Dio Queb from 77. *Deanery, 1410 des Gouverneurs, Quebec, PQ, G1T 2G5, Canada.*

JAMES, John William. b 1889. Late Dur Univ Th Scho St Chad's Hall, Dur 09, BA (1st cl Th) and Univ Hebr Scho 12, MA 15, BD (distinc) 24, DD 31. **d** 12 Ban for Llan **p** 13 Llan. C of Llangynwyd 12-16; Dinas w Penygraig 16-19; C-in-c of Conv Distr of Cwmcarn 19-22; V of Cwmcarn 22-25; R of Portskewett w Sudbrook and St Pierre 25-30; Dolgelley 30-45; V of Aberdovey 45-52; Surr 32-74; Exam Chap to Bp of Ban 37-72; Chan of Ban Cathl 40-64; R of Aber 52-59. *23 Coolhurst Road, Crouch End, Hornsey, N8.*

JAMES, Joshua John Gerwyn. b 31. St D Coll Lamp BA 52. **d** 54 **p** 55 St D. C of Haverfordwest 54-56; Barmouth w Bontddu 56-57; CF 57-76; V of Tidenham w Beachley and Lancaut 76-80; Aberdovey Dio Ban from 80. *Vicarage, Aberdovey, Gwyn.* (Aberdovey 302)

JAMES, Lawson John. St Jo Coll Morpeth. **d** and **p** 56 C & Goulb. C of St Paul Canberra 56-59; R of Kameruka 59-63; Tumbarumba 63-73; N Goulb 73-75. *10 Franklin Street, Bundaberg, Queensland, Australia 4670.*

JAMES, Lettie. b 24. Univ of Dur BA 42, DTh 48. K Coll Lon PhD 51. **d** 76 **p** 78 Montr. C of St Phil Montr W 78; P-in-c of Delson 78-81; R of St Steph Lachine w St D Delson Dio Montr from 81. *91 Ballantyne Avenue North, Montreal, Queb, Canada, H3A 2B8.*

JAMES, Lewis John. St D Coll Lamp BA 42. **d** 48 **p** 49 Swan B. C of Llanguicke 48-55; Clydach 55-57; R of Whitton w Pilleth 57-60; PC (V from 69) of Smalley Dio Derby from 60; P-in-c of Morley 72-81. *Smalley Vicarage, Derby.* (Horsley 380)

JAMES, Lionel Dennis. b 07. Qu Coll Birm. **d** 62 **p** 63 Pet. C of Kingsthorpe 62-65; V of Weedon-Bec 65-74; C-in-c of Dodford w Brockhall 65-66; V 66-74. *7 Springfield Park, Mylor Bridge, Falmouth, Cornw.* (Penryn 73743)

JAMES, Maurice. Late Exhib of St Chad's Coll Dur LTh 37, BA 38. St Aug Coll Cant 34. **d** 38 **p** 39 Dur. C of St John Sunderland 38-41; Miss at Matatiele 41-45; P-in-c of St Barn W Pondoland 45-52; Mohales Hoek 52-56; Archd of S Basuto 55-65; P-in-c of Masite 56-67; R of St John Maseru 68-73; Groot Drakenstein 73-78; Perm to Offic Dio Ex from 78. *10 Croft Road, East Ogwell, Newton Abbot, TQ12 6BD.* (Newton Abbot 68168)

JAMES, Michael Henry Clarke. b 38. Wells Th Coll 68. **d** 71 **p** 72 Bris. C of St Mich AA Bishopston 71-75; Kingswood 75-76; St Mary Cotham 76-77. *11 North View, Bristol, BS6 7PT.*

JAMES, Canon Ninian Shelby. St D Coll Lamp BA 34. **d** 34 Lon for Col **p** 35 Willoch. M of Bush Bro Quorn 34-37; P-in-c of Tumby Bay 38-39; Master St Pet Coll Adel 39-41; Served in RAAF 41-45; I of Port Elliston 46-49; Jamestown (w Gladstone and Laura from 71) 49-76; Can of Willoch 58-76; Can (Emer) from 76; Dioc Regr Dio Willoch 65-67; L to Offic Dio Willoch 76-77; R of S Yorke Peninsula Dio Willoch from 77. *44 Edithburgh Road, Yorketown, S Australia 5576.* (Yorketown 50)

JAMES, Noel Beddoe Walters. b 39. Dipl Th (Wales) 68. St Mich Coll Llan. **d** 68 **p** 69 Swan B. C of St Nich-on-the-Hill Swansea 68-70; St Pet Cockett Swansea 70-72; Chap RAF from 72. *c/o Ministry of Defence, Adastral House, Theobalds Road, WC1.*

JAMES, Paul Dominic Denis. b 48. AKC 71. St Aug Coll Cant 71. **d** 72 **p** 73 Barking for Chelmsf. C of St Marg w St Columba Leytonstone 72-74; St Marg Leigh 74-79; V of St Sav Walthamstow Dio Chelmsf from 79. *210 Markhouse Road, E17 8EP.* (01-520 2036)

JAMES, Paul Maynard. b 31. Univ Coll Ban BA (2nd cl Hist) 52. Fitzw Ho Cam BA (Th Tri pt ii) 54, MA 58. Ridley Hall Cam 56. **d** 57 **p** 58 Chich. C of Newhaven 57-60; Chap at Mt Kenya 60-62; V 62-65; SW Area Sec CCCS 65-68; V of St Julian Shrewsbury 68-76; C-in-c of H Trin Shrewsbury Dio Lich 75; V (w St Julian) from 76. *Holy Trinity Vicarage, Greyfriars Road, Shrewsbury, SY3 7EP.* (Shrewsbury 51165)

JAMES, Paulding. b 30. Wesleyan Univ Conn BA 54. Ch Div Sch of the Pacific Calif MDiv 66. **d** 66 Calif **p** 66 Bp Millard (USA). In Amer Ch 66-68; Tutor Bp Tucker Coll Mukono from 68; Exam Chap to Bp of Soroti 68-72. *Bishop Tucker College, PO Box 4, Mukono, Uganda.*

JAMES, Peter David. b 42. Keble Coll Ox BA (2nd cl Mod

Hist) 63. BD (2nd cl) Lon 67. Tyndale Hall, Bris 64. **d** 67 Warrington for Liv **p** 68 Liv. C of St Mark Haydock 67-69; St Thos Ashton-in-Makerfield 69-74; V of Whiston 74-80; Harlech w Llanfair Harlech, Llanfihangel-y-Traethau and Llandecwyn Dio Ban from 80. *Y Ficerdy, Harlech, Gwyn.* (Harlech 780383)

JAMES, Peter Heppell. b 19. Tyndale Hall, Bris 39. **d** 42 **p** 43 Lich. C of St Thos Stafford 42-44; Chap RAFVR 44-47; C of Bucknall (in c of St John Abbey Hulton) 47-49; Watford (in c of St Luke) 49-51; V of Braintree 51-60; R of L Leighs 60-70. *62 Main Street, Asfordby, Melton Mowbray, Leics, LE14 3SA.* (0664 812384)

JAMES, Raymond Victor. b 31. Ripon Hall Ox 60. **d** and **p** 62 Leic. C of All SS Loughborough 62-64; V of St Mich AA Knighton 64-68; Industr Chap and L to Offic Dio Leic 68-73; C-in-c of N w S Carlton 73-77; Burton-by-Linc 73-77; V of Halton Dio Ches from 80. *Halton Vicarage, Runcorn, Chesh.* (Runcorn 63636)

JAMES, Reg. b 27. **d** 77 **p** 78 Johann. C of Parkmore Dio Johann from 77. *PO Box 4561, Johannesburg 2000, S Africa.*

JAMES, Richard Andrew. b 44. Mert Coll Ox BA 67, MA 70. Univ of Bris Dipl Th 69. Tyndale Hall Bris 67. **d** 70 **p** 71 Ches. C of Bebington 70-73; Histon 73-77; Chap Guildf Co Coll of Tech from 77; C of St Sav w Stoke Guildf 77-80; Chap Bedford Coll from 80. *Bedford College, Inner Circle, Regent's Park, NW1 4NS.*

JAMES, Richard David. b 45. Lon Coll Div. **d** 70 **p** 71 Grantham for Linc. C of Boultham 70-74; P-in-c of New Waltham 74-77; Team V of Cleethorpes Dio Linc from 77. *St Aidan's Vicarage, Cleethorpes, Lincs.* (Cleethorpes 62989)

JAMES, Richard William. b 47. Bp Burgess Hall Lamp 72. **d** 75 **p** 76 St D. C of Hubberston 75-78; R of Pendine Dio St D from 78; Eglwys Gymin w Marros Dio St D from 78. *Rectory, Pendine, Dyfed.*

JAMES, Robert Leslie. b 44. Canberra Coll of Min 71. **d** 71 **p** 72 C & Goulb. C of S Wagga Wagga 71-74; St Paul Canberra 74; R of Batlow 74-76; Binda 76-80; C of St Anne Strathfield Dio Syd from 80. *42 Homebush Road, Strathfield, NSW, Australia 2135.* (764-2559)

JAMES, Roger Michael. b 44. K Coll Lon and Warm BD and AKC 66. **d** 69 **p** 70 Roch. C of Frindsbury w Upnor 69-72; L to Offic Dio St Alb 73-78; C of Digswell 78-81; R of Knebworth Dio St Alb from 81. *Rectory, St Martin's Road, Knebworth, Herts.* (Stevenage 812101)

JAMES, Stuart McFarlane. b 26. St Francis Coll Brisb 74. **d** 76 **p** 77 Brisb. Hon C of Kingaroy Dio Brisb from 76. *36 James Street, Kingaroy, Queensland, Australia 4610.*

JAMES, Canon Thomas Llewellyn Emlyn. b 09. Univ of Wales BA 35. St Mich Coll Llan. **d** 36 **p** 38 Llan. C of Tylorstown 36-40; Caerphilly 40-44; St Mark Swansea 44-51; CF 51-58; V of Talgarth w Llanelieu 58-77; RD of Brecon 1 72-77; Hon Can of Brecon Cathl from 72. *Monmouth House, Maendu Street, Brecon, Powys, LD3 9HD.* (Brecon 4570)

JAMES, Canon Thomas Rees Walters. b 05. Late Exhib of St D Coll Lamp BA 27. **d** 28 **p** 29 Swan B. C of Llansamlet 28-30; St Pet Cockett 30-31; Llansamlet 31-35; V of L Llanstephan w Boughrood 35-42; Cwmbwrla 42-51; Surr 50-75; CF (TA) 50-58; V of Llanguicke (Pontardawe) 51-75; RD of E Gower (Cwmtawe from 73) 58-75; Hon Can of Brecon 60-61; Can of Brecon Cathl 61-75. *21 Primrose Lane, Rhos, Pontardawe, W Glam.*

JAMES, Walter Trevor Grattan. b 47. Vic Univ of Wel BA 71. BD (Melb) 75. St Jo Coll Auckld 72. **d** 73 **p** 74 Wel. C of Karori 73-75; on leave 75-77; V of Murupara-Reporoa 78-80; Perm to Offic Dio Waik from 80. *173 Peachgrove Road, Hamilton, NZ.*

JAMES, William Arthur. b 10. Univ of Wales BA 40. St Mich Coll Llan 40. **d** 42 **p** 43 St D. C of Steynton w Johnston 42-44; Llanstephan 44-45; Llanybri (w Llandilo-Abercowin) 45-46; Maindee 46-54; R of Bedwas 54-77. *5 St Benedict Court, Caerphilly Road, Bassaleg, Newport, NP1 9LY.*

JAMES, William Geraint Lewis. b 21. Clifton Th Coll 51. **d** 53 Stafford for Cant **p** 54 Lich. C of Bucknall w Bagnall 53-56; Bedworth 56-58; R of Biddulph Moor 58-65; V of Ch Ch City and Dio Cov from 65. *Vicarage, Frankpledge Road, Coventry, W Midl, CV3 5GT.* (0203-502770)

JAMESON, Bert Desmond. Moore Th Coll Syd ACT ThL 47. **d** 45 **p** 46 Nel. C of Westport 45-46; Ch Ch Cathl Nel 46-48; V of Ahaura w Brunnerton 48-50; Westport 50-58; Takaka 58-66; Waimea 66-78; Can of Nel 58-62; Archd of Mawhera 61-70; Waimea 71-78; Perm to Offic Dio Nel from 78. *67 Neale Avenue, Stoke, NZ.*

JAMESON, David Kingsbury. b 28. Mert Coll Ox BA 50, MA 55. Qu Coll Birm 50. **d** 53 **p** 54 Heref. C of Leominster 53-56; Portsm Cathl 56-60; Dioc Youth Chap Dio Portsm 58-61; V of Ch Ch Gosport 60-65; St Cuthb Copnor 65-70; Jesus Ch Forty Hill Enfield 70-74; Nuneaton 74-80; RD of Nuneaton 74-79; Cler Org CECS Leics & Northants from 80; Perm to Offic Dios Leic and Pet from 80. *c/o Church of England Children's Society, Old Town Hall, Kennington Road, SE11 4QD.*

JAMESON, Preb Dermot Christopher Ledgard. b 27. Trin Coll Dub BA (2nd cl Mods Phil) 49, Div Test (2nd cl) 49, MA 54. **d** 50 **p** 51 Down. C of Seagoe 50-53; Holywood 53-57; I of Kilkeel 57-62; Donaghcloney w Waringstown 62-79; Preb of Drom Cathl from 77; Treas from 81. *Vicarage, Rostrevor, Co Down, N Ireland.* (Rostrevor 293)

JAMESON, Geoffrey Vaughan. b 27. Wycl Hall Ox 68. **d** 70 **p** 71 Ox. C of Buckingham 70-73; V of Exton and Horn w Whitwell Dio Pet from 73. *Whitwell Rectory, Oakham, Leics. LE15 8BW.* (Empingham 210)

JAMESON, Canon John Edward. b 16. Kelham Th Coll 34. **d** 39 **p** 40 Newc T. C of Haltwhistle 39-47; Seaton Hirst (in c of St Andr) 47-52; V of Sugley 52-62; Surr from 58; V of All SS Gosforth 62-76; RD of Newc Centr 65-75; Hon Can of Newc T from 72; R of Rothbury Dio Newc T from 76. *Rectory, Rothbury, Morpeth, Northumb, NE65 7TL.* (Rothbury 20482)

JAMESON, Peter. b 31. Trin Coll Cam BA 54, MA 60. Linc Th Coll. **d** 62 **p** 63 Lon. C of St Cuthb w St Matthias Kens 62-68; St Clem Notting Dale Kens 68-72; St Clem and St Mark Notting Hill Kens 72-75; Team V 75-77; V of Woodberry Down Dio Lon from 77. *St Olave's Vicarage, Woodberry Down, N4.* (01-800 1374)

JAMIESON, David Stanger. b 06. Man Bapt Th Coll 28. **d** 66 **p** 67 Ches. [F Bapt Min] C of Hyde 66-69; St Geo Stockport 69-72; P-in-c of St Aug Brinksway Stockport 72-74; C of Claughton w Grange 74-78; Perm to Offic Dio Ches 78-80. *Address temp unknown.*

✠ **JAMIESON, Right Rev Hamish Thomas Umphelby.** ACT ThL 56. Univ of New Engl NSW BA 74. St Mich Ho Crafers, 56. **d** 55 **p** 56 Bath. C of Bro of Good Shepherd Dubbo 55-56; Gilgandra 56-57; Katherine 57-62; R of Darwin 62-67; Can of Carp 63-67; Chap Ran 67-74; Cons Ld Bp of Carp in St Jo Evang Cathl Brisb 1 Nov 74 by Abps of Brisb and Melb (Primate); Bps of Rockptn, Papua, N Terr, N Queensld, Newc and Graft; and others. *Bishop's House, PO Box 79, Thursday Island, Queensland, Australia 4875.* (96)

JAMIESON, Hugh Gollan. b 20. Trin Coll Dub BA 49, Div Test 49. **d** 49 **p** 50 Lim. C of St Laur w H Trin and St John Lim 49-51; I of Ballinaclough U 51-53; Sec BCMS and L to Offic Dio Dub 53-56; R of Murragh U 56-60; Birkin w Haddlesey 60-63; I of Derralossary 63-69; Mothel 69-76; R of U w Lower Badoney 76-78; I of Donagh w Tyholland Dio Clogh from 78; Errigal-Trough w Errigal-Shanco Dio Clogh from 78. *Rectory, Glaslough, Co Monaghan, Irish Republic.* (Glaslough 28)

JAMIESON, Kenneth Euan Oram. b 24. Dipl Th (Lon) 68. Roch Th Coll 60. **d** 62 **p** 63 Roch. C of Bromley 62-66; R of St Mary Magd Colchester 66-71; V of St Pet Bexleyheath 71-78; P-in-c of St Faith Maidstone Dio Cant from 78; St Paul Maidstone Dio Cant from 78. *130 Boxley Road, Maidstone, Kent, ME14 2AH.* (Maidstone 54618)

JAMIESON, Thomas Lindsay. b 53. N Lon Poly BSc 74. Cranmer Hall Dur Dipl Th 76. **d** 77 **p** 78 Dur. C of St John Gateshead Fell 77-80; Gateshead Dio Dur from 80. *Church House, Wordsworth Street, Gateshead, T & W.* (Gateshead 782730)

JAMIESON, William Douglas. b 38. Oak Hill Th Coll 63. **d** 66 **p** 67 Lich. C of St Julian Shrewsbury 66-68; Bucknall w Bagnall 68-70; Otley Yorks 70-74; Team V of Keighley (in c of St Mark Utley) 74-81; V of St Mark Utley Dio Bradf from 81. *Vicarage, Greenhead Road, Utley, Keighley, Yorks, BD20 6ED.* (Keighley 607003)

JANDA, Clement Guya. Makerere Univ Kamp BA. Episc Sem of the SW Texas MA. Bp Tucker Coll Mukono Dipl Th 68. **d** 69 Nam. d Dio Nam 69-77; Dio Nai from 77. *PO Box 14205, Nairobi, Kenya.*

JANGMAN, Hpung. **d** 60 Rang. d Dio Rang 60-70; Dio Mand from 70. *St Paul's Church, Sahman, Burma.*

JANKE, Harry Edward. Univ of W Ont BA 49. Huron Coll LTh 49. **d** 49 **p** 50 Hur. C of Pelee Is 49-53; I of St Pet Windsor 53-57; R of Tillsonberg 57-64; I of St Andr Kitchener Dio Hur from 64. *30 Sycamore Place, Kitchener, Ont., Canada.* (519-743 0911)

JANSZ, Preb Basil Edward Toussaint. Selw Coll Cam 3rd cl Th Trip pt i 24, BA (3rd cl Th Trip pt i) 25, MA 32. St Steph Ho Ox 25. **d** 26 Willesden for Lon **p** 27 Lon. C of S Hackney 26-29; St Pet De Beauvoir Town 29-39; R of St Paul Shadwell (w St Jas Ratcliffe from 51) 39-75; RD of Stepney 64-66; Preb of St Paul's Cathl Lon 56-75; Preb (Emer) from 75; Perm to Offic Dio York from 75. *166 Huntington Road, York, YO3 7RT.*

JANTJIES, Andrew John. b 44. St Pet Coll Alice Dipl Th 76. **d** 76 **p** 77 Port Eliz. C of St Mary Salt Lake Dio Port Eliz from 76. *55 Martin Street, Gelvandale, Port Elizabeth 6016, CP, S Africa.*

JAONA, Bartolomeo. **d** 77 **p** 78 Diego S. P Dio Diego S 77-79; Dio Antsir from 79. *Eklesia Episkopaly Malagasy, Marodimaka, Ambilobe Antsiranana, Malagasy Republic.*

JAONA, Lehibe. b 48. **d** 75 **p** 77 Diego S. P Dio Diego S 75-79; Antsir from 79. *Misiona Anglikana, Sambava, Antsiranana, Madagascar.*

JAOVITA, Theogene. b 53. Chich Th Coll 74. **d** 77 Diego S for Antan **p** 79 Antan. P Dio Antan; Tutor St Paul's Th Coll Ambatoharanana from 77. *St Paul's College, Ambatoharanana, Merimandroso, Ambohidratrimo, Malagasy Republic.*

JAOZANDRY, Paul Bert. b 52. **d** 78 **p** Diego S. d Diego S 78-79; Antsir from 79. *Misiona Anglikana, Antsahampano, Daraina, Vohemar, Antsiranana, Madagascar.*

JAQUET, Peter Michael. b 23. ARIBA 51. Wells Th Coll 56. **d** 57 Dover for Cant **p** 58 Cant. C of Hythe 57-60; R of Stowting 60-62; V of Sellindge (w Monks-Horton and Stowting from 62) 60-78; C of Drypool Dio York 78-80; Team V from 80. *Leconfield Rectory, Beverley, N Humb, HU17 7NP.* (Leconfield 50188)

JAQUIERY, Canon Alan Victor. **d** and **p** 47 Dun. C of Caversham 47-51; P-in-c of Tapanui 51-54; V 54-57; Winton 57-59; St Kilda 59-66; Riverton 66-70; Gore Dio Dun from 70; Hon Can of Dun from 74. *15 Trafford Street, Gore, NZ.* (Gore 7366)

JARDIN, Kenneth. b 35. TCD 67. **d** 69 **p** 70 Arm. C of Armagh and Chap R Sch Armagh 69-72; Chap RAF 72-78; V of Sudbrooke 78; Barlings Dio Linc from 78. *Vicarage, Langworth, Lincoln, LN3 5BB.* (Scothern 233)

JARDINE, Anthony. b 38. Dipl Th (Lon) 70. Qu Coll Birm 64. **d** 67 **p** 68 St Alb. C of Baldock w Bygrave and Clothall 67-71; N Stoneham w Bassett 71-73; P-in-c of Ecchinswell w Sydmonton 73-79; Burghclere w Newtown Dio Win 78-79; R (w Ecchinswell and Sydmonton) from 79. *Rectory, Burghclere, Newbury, Berks.* (Burghclere 470)

JARDINE, David Eric Cranswick. b 30. CCC Ox BA (2nd cl Mod Hist) 53, Dipl Th 54, MA 57. Wycl Hall Ox. **d** 55 Warrington for Liv **p** 56 Liv. C of St Mary Wavertree 55-58; All S Springwood Liv 58-62; Horley Surrey (in c of St Wilfrid) 62-65; V of Ch Ch Mitcham 65-72; St Sav Iford Dio Win from 72. *Vicarage, Colemore Road, Iford, Bournemouth, Dorset, BH7 6RZ.* (Bournemouth 425978)

JARDINE, David John. b 42. QUB BA (Spanish) 65. TCD Div Test 67. **d** 67 **p** 68 Down. C of Ballymacarrett 67-70; Asst Chap QUB 70-73; SSF from 73; Chap from 79. Asst Chap Cromlin Road Pris Belf 75-79; Chap from 79. *Friary, Deer Park Road, Belfast, BT14 7PW.* (Belfast 743480)

JARDINE, Norman. b 47. Qu Univ Belf BSc 72. Trin Coll Bris 74. **d** 76 **p** 77 Down & Drom. C of Magheralin 76-78; Dundonald 78-80; Bp's C of Ballybeen Dio Down from 80. *149 Comber Road, Dundonald, Co Down, N Ireland.* (Dundonald 5491)

JARED, Arthur Henry. Hur Coll Ont LTh 39. **d** 39 **p** 42 Hur. C of St Mark Windsor 39-42; St Paul's Cathl London 42;45; R of Wallaceburg 45-50; St John London Township 50-74; Dom Chap to Bp of Hur 52-70. *31 Northcrest Drive, London, Ont., Canada.*

JARMAN, Christopher. b 38. QUB BA 63. Wells Th Coll 69. **d** 71 **p** 72 Glouc. C of St Phil and St Jas Leckhampton 71-73; Chap RN from 73. *c/o Ministry of Defence, Lacon House, Theobalds Road, WC1X 8RY.*

JARMAN, John Geoffrey. b 31. SOC 75. **d** 78 Barking for Chelmsf **p** 79 Chelmsf. C of Chigwell Dio Chelmsf from 78. *20 Stevens Way, Chigwell, Essex, IG7 6HR.*

JARMAN, Thomas Morris. Univ of Ox Dipl in Econ and Pol Sc 27. Chich Th Coll 31. **d** 33 **p** 34 Llan. C of St Anne Ynyshir 33-38; V of Tyntetown w Ynysboeth 38-54; R of Coychurch 54-67. *14 St Mary View, Coychurch, Bridgend, Mid Glam.* (Pencoed 307)

JARMY, David Michael. b 49. Chich Th Coll 76. **d** 79 Chich **p** 80 Lewes for Chich. C of Ch Ch St Leonards-on-Sea Dio Chich from 79. *17 Alfred Street, St Leonards-on-Sea, E Sussex, TN38 0HD.*

JARRATT, Robert Michael. b 39. K Coll Lon and Warm BD and AKC 62. **d** 63 **p** 64 Pet. C of St Columba Corby 63-67; Lay Training Officer The Manor Par Sheff 67-72; LPr Dio S'wark 72-75; Chap S Lon Industr Miss 72-80; V of Betchworth 75-80; Ranmoor Dio Sheff from 80. *Ranmoor Vicarage, Sheffield, S10 3GX.* (Sheff 301671)

JARRATT, Stephen. b 51. Univ of Edin BD 76. Edin Th Coll 74. **d** 78 **p** 79 Ripon. C of Horsforth 78-81; Stanningley Dio Ripon from 81. *27 Wellstone Gardens, Swinnow, Leeds, LS13 4EF.* (Leeds 566535)

JARRETT, Keith Charles. b 37. Wycl Hall Ox 69. **d** 71 **p** 72 Carl. C of Stanwix 71-73; C of Erdington 73-75; V 75-78; Temple Balsall and Master of Lady Katherine Leveson Hosp Dio Birm from 78. *Master's House, Temple Balsall, Knowle, Solihull, Warws.* (021-560 2415)

JARRETT, Martyn William. b 44. K Coll Lon and Warm BD and AKC 67. **d** 68 **p** 69 Bris. C of St Geo Bris 68-70; New Swindon 70-74; Northolt (in c of St Jos) 74-76; V of St Jos Northolt 76-81; St Andr Uxbridge Dio Lon from 81. *St Andrew's Vicarage, Uxbridge, Middx, UB8 1AH.* (Uxbridge 35025)

JARRETT, Spencer Churchill. **d** 22 **p** 23 Tor. C of W Mono 22-25; I of Port Perry w Brooklin 25-28; R of S Oshawa 28-40; Chap CASF 40-46; R of St Dunstan Tor 46-64. *Apt 401, Sheldon Towers, 270 Sheldon Avenue, Toronto 14, Ont, Canada.*

JARRETT-KERR, William Robert. b 12. BNC Ox BA (2nd cl Engl Lang and Lit) 34, Dipl Th 35, MA 38. Westcott Ho Cam 35. **d** 36 **p** 37 York. C of St Paul Thornaby-on-Tees 36-44; M CR from 43; L to Offic Dio Llan 46-49; and 59-63; Vice-Prin Coll of Resurr Mirfield 49-52; Coll of Resurr Rosettenville Johann 52-59; Hosp Chap Johann 58-61; Exam Chap to Bp of Sheff from 62; L to Offic Dio Lon 63-67; Select Pr Univ of Ox 66-67; Assoc Lect Univ of Leeds 67-79; L to Offic Dio Ripon 67-76; Dio Wakef from 67; Consultant Lambeth Conf 68-78. *c/o House of The Resurrection, Mirfield, W Yorks, WF14 0BN.*

JARROLD, George Edward. b 11. Tyndale Hall, Bris 34. **d** 37 **p** 38 Man. C of St Marg Burnage 37-41; Ch Ch Chadderton 41-43; R of St Sav Chorlton-on-Medlock 43-50; Ellingham 50-60; Chap of St Jas Hostel Shipmeadow 50-54; R of Rougham 60-75; Perm to Offic Dio Nor from 75. *Suffield Park Lodge, Station Road, Cromer, NR27 0DX.* (Cromer 513010)

JARROW, Lord Bishop Suffragan of. *See* Ball, Right Rev Michael Thomas.

JARVIE, Alexander Michael Milne. b 40. Em Coll Cam BA 63, MA 66. Linc Th Coll 63. **d** 65 Knaresborough for Ripon **p** 66 Ripon. C of St Aid Leeds 65-68; Fleetwood 68-70; N Gosforth 70-73; C-in-c of Copley 73-76; Chap Derby City Manor and Women's Hosps from 76. *4 South Drive, Mickleover, Derby, DE3 5AN.* (Derby 514154)

JARVIS, David Thomas. b 15. Late Scho and Exhib of St D Coll Lamp BA 36. **d** 38 **p** 39 Nor. C of Sheringham 38-39; Reepham w Hackford Whitwell and Kerdiston 39-41; St Steph Westbourne Pk 41-42; St Marylebone 42-45; R of Gt w L Bealings 45-53; V of Ch Ch Hampstead 53-69; JEM Pilgrimage Chap 69-71; V of Ch Ch Turnham Green Dio Lon from 72. *Vicarage, Wellesley Road, W4.* (01-994 1617)

JARVIS, Canon Eric Thomas Noel. Qu Coll Cam BA 52, MA 54. Ridley Hall Cam 52. **d** 54 **p** 55 Chelmsf. C of Stratford 54-57; V of Ansley 57-64; St Jo Evang Woodbridge 64-68; St Edm Roundhay Dio Ripon from 68; RD of Allerton from 79; Hon Can Ripon Cathl from 81. *St Edmund's Vicarage, Lidgett Park Avenue, Leeds, LS8 1EU.* (Leeds 662550)

JARVIS, Geoffrey Thomas Henry. b 21. Bps' Cheshunt 61. **d** 62 **p** 63 St Alb. C of Mill End w Heronsgate 62-68; Abbots Langley 68-70; Chap to the Deaf Dio St Alb from 70; C-in-c of Sandridge Dio St Alb 76-79; V from 79. *Vicarage, Anson Close, House Lane, Sandridge, Herts.* (St Albans 66089)

JARVIS, Ian Frederick Rodger. b 38. Univ of Bris BA (2nd cl Th) 60. Tyndale Hall, Bris 61. **d** 63 **p** 64 Roch. C of Ch Ch w H Trin Penge 63-67; Bilston 67-71; V of St Silas Lozells 71-76; Chaddesden Dio Derby from 76. *Chaddesden Vicarage, Chaddesden Lane, Derby, DE2 6LL.* (Derby 672336)

JARVIS, Jeffrey Wallace. b 45. Sarum Wells Th Coll 73. **d** 75 Huntingdon for Ely **p** 76 Ely. C of Cherry Hinton 75-77; St Marg Virg Nottm 77-78; R of Greenwood 78-79; Chap Ch Ch Gr Sch from 80. *9 Marita Road, Nedlands, W Australia 6009.* (386 7081)

JARVIS, Kenneth Eric. b 06. AKC and Barry Div Pri 33. **d** 33 **p** 35 Chelmsf. C of Chingford 33-38; Asst Chap at Montreux 38-39; C of Portsea 40-45; Stansted 45-48; Chap to Bryanston Sch 48-60; V of Beaulieu 60-77. *4 Bramwell Lodge, Terry's Cross, Henfield, Sussex.* (Henfield 2735)

JARVIS, Lawrence Richard William. b 16. Worc Ordin Coll. **d** 68 Bp McKie for Cov **p** 69 Cov. C of Alcester w Arrow Oversley and Weethley 68-72; R of Barmston w Fraisthorpe 72-76; V of Hutton Cranswick w Skerne Dio York from 76. *Hutton Cranswick Vicarage, Driffield, N Humb, YO25 9QA.* (Driffield 70402)

JARVIS, Stanley Henry Frank. Bp's Coll Prince Albert 30. **d** 33 Sask **p** 34 Sktn for Sask. C of Christopher Lake 33-34; Meadow Lake 34-38; I of Birch Hills 38-42; R of Tisdale 42-54; Hon Can of Sask 50-54; R of Fort Sask 54-57; V of Cobble Hill 57-65; L to Offic Dio BC from 65. *1612 Myrtle Street, Victoria BC, Canada.*

JARVIS, Walter Whitehead. **d** 34 **p** 35 Alg. C of Purbrook 34-35; I of Gore Bay 36-39; RD of Manitoulin 39-47; R of St John N Bay 39-51; RD of Nipissing 47-51; R of St Paul Fort William 51-54; Archd of Thunder Bay 53-54; R of St Thos Tor 54-64. *2696 Bloor Street West, Toronto 18, Ont, Canada.*

JARVIS, Wilfrid Harry. b 20. Univ of Leeds BA 43. Coll of Resurr Mirfield 43. **d** 45 **p** 46 Ox. C of St Marg Ox 45-48; Asst Master Summer Fields Sch 48-58; Chap 49-58; C of Worksop 60-64; Southwell Minster 64-65; V of New Basford Dio Southw from 65. *14 Claremont Road, Nottingham.* (Nottingham 605427)

JARVIS, William Arthur Walter. b 16. St Edm Hall, Ox BA (1st cl Engl Lang and Lit) 38, MA 42. Sarum Th Coll 38. **d** 40 **p** 41 Bradf. C of Guiseley 40-46; Chap and Lect St Steph Coll Delhi 46-62; Asst Chap Sherborne Sch 62-63; R of Allington w Boscombe 63-72; C of Thatcham 72-81; Perm to Offic Dio Ox from 81. *14 The Green, Charlbury, Oxon.*

JARVIS, William Grantham. b 13. **d** 66 Bp McKie for Cov **p** 67 Cov. C of St Mich Stoke 66-67; Binley 67-71; V of Clifton-on-Dunsmore w Brownsover and Newton Dio Cov from 71. *Clifton Vicarage, Rugby, Warws.* (Rugby 2328)

JASPER, Arthur Thomas Mclean. b 15. Oak Hill Th Coll 36. **d** 39 Taunton for B & W **p** 40 B & W. C of widcombe 39-43; Weston-s-Mare 43-45; Otley (in c of Denton and Weston) 45-46; 80; of Weston 46-50; Denton 46-50; R of Marhamchurch 50-57; Chap Miss to Seamen 57-67; V of St Gulval 67-73; Publ Pr Dio Truro from 73; Perm to Offic Dio Ex from 78. *4 Coryton Close, Dawlish, Devon.* (Dawlish 863735)

JASPER, David. b 51. Jes Coll Cam BA 72, MA 76. St Steph Ho Ox BA (Th) 75, MA 79. Keble Coll Ox BD 80. **d** 76 Dorchester for Ox **p** 77 Ox. C of Buckingham 76-80; St Osw City and Dio Dur from 80; Chap Hatfield Coll Dur from 80. *10 Mount Joy Crescent, Durham, DH1 3BA.* (Dur 49495)

JASPER, David Julian McLean. b 44. Univ of Dur BA (2nd cl French) 66. Dipl Th (Nottm) 68. Linc Th Coll 66. **d** 68 **p** 69 Truro. C of Redruth 68-72; V 72-74; Team V 74-75; V of St Just-in-Penwith Dio Truro from 75. *Vicarage, St Just-in-Penwith, Cornw.* (St Just-in-Penwith 672)

JASPER, Jonathan Ernest Farley. b 50. AKC 72. St Aug Coll Cant 72. **d** 73 **p** 74 St Alb. C of Cheshunt 73-75; St Paul and of St Pet de Merton w St Cuthb Bedford 75-77; Asst Chap of Southn Univ 77-80; Chap Univ of Lon Medical Schs from 80. *14 Rokeby House, Lambs Conduit Street, WC1N 3LX.* (01-242 6261)

JASPER, Very Rev Ronald Claud Dudley. b 17. CBE 81. Univ of Leeds BA (2nd cl Hist) 38, MA (w distinc) 40, BD 50, DD 61. FRHistS 54. Coll of Resurr Mirfield 38. **d** 40 **p** 41 Dur. C of Ryhope 40-42; St Osw Dur 42-43; Esh (in c of Langley Pk) 43-44; C-in-c of Esh w Langley Pk 44-45; St Giles Dur 45-46; Chap of Univ and Hatfield Coll Dur 46-48; L to Offic Dio Dur 46-48; V of Stillington 48-55; Succr of Ex Cathl 55-60; Lect K Coll Lon 60-67; Reader 67-68; L to Offic Dio S'wark 61-68; Chairman Liturgical Comm 64-80; Hon Can of Derby 65-75; Proc Conv Univ of Lon 65-70; Can of Westmr 68-75; Lect RSCM 64-70; M Gen Syn Dio Lon 70-80; Archd of Westmr 74-75; Dean of York from 75. *Deanery, York, YO1 2JD.* (York 23608)

JAUREGUI ESPINOZA, Pedro. b 44. **d** 79 **p** 81 Peru. P Dio Peru. *Apartado 1424, Arequipa, Peru.*

JAWAI, Waiaka. d 51 **p** 55 Carp. C of Torres Strait Miss 51-56 and 66-69; Yorke I 56-60; Warraber I 60; Mabuiag I 69-74; Perm to Offic Dio Carp 74-77; C of Bamaga Dio Carp from 77. *Bamaga Post Office, Queensland, Australia 4875.*

JAY, Edmund Arthur. b 41. St Chad's Coll Dur BA 63. **d** 65 Dur **p** 66 Jarrow for Dur. C of Good Shepherd Bp Wearmouth 65-69; St Columba Southwick 69-70; Hon C of Westbury-on-Trym 72-73; P-in-c of St Francis S Shields 73-77; Hon C of St Hilda S Shields Dio Dur from 77; Chap S Shields Gen and Deans Hosps from 78. *40 Lawe Road, South Shields, T & W.* (S Shields 569650)

JAY, Canon Eric George. Univ of Leeds BA (1st cl Cl) 29, MA 30. Univ of Lon BD 37, MTh 40, PhD 51. Montr Dioc Th Coll Hon DD 64. Coll of Resurr Mirfield 29. **d** 31 **p** 32 Ches. C of St Aug Brinksway Stockport 31-34; Asst Lect King's Coll Lon 34; Lect 35-47; Fell of King's Coll Lon from 48; C of St Andr Undershaft Lon 35-40; Exam Chap to Bp of Leic 44-48; and 51-53; Chap RAFVR 40-45; R of St Mary-le-Strand and C-in-c of St Clement Danes 45-47; Dean of Nass and R of Ch Ch Cathl Nass 48-51; Sen Chap to Abp of Cant 51-58; Commis Nass from 52; Antig 53-68; St Antolin Lect at St Mary Aldermary Lon 54-57; Prin Montr Dioc Th Coll 58-64; Exam Chap to Bp of Montr 58-76; Prof of Hist Th McGill Univ 58-75; Dean of Div 63-70; Hon Can of Montr 60-75; Can (Emer) from 76. *Apt 15, 570 Milton Street, Montreal 130, PQ, Canada.* (514-844 8322)

JAY, Idris Owen. Late Exhib of St D Coll Lamp BA 26, BD 35. **d** 26 **p** 27 S'wark. C of Em Camberwell 26-30; St Luke Woodside Croydon 30-32; Whitstable 32-34; All SS Castleford 36-40; V of Purston w S Featherstone 40-67; R of Burghwallis w Skelbrooke 67-74. *c/o Church of England Nursing Home, Knutsford, Chesh.*

JAY, Richard Hylton Michael. b 31. Univ of Bris BEducn 75. Sarum Wells Th Coll 77. **d** 79 B & W **p** 80 Taunton for B & W (APM). C of St Barn Twerton Hill Bath Dio B & W from 79. *Homeland, Padleigh Hill, Bath, BA2 9DP.*

JAY, Stanley Ernest. Univ of W Ont BA 56. Hur Coll BD 60, LTh 55. **d** 54 **p** 56 Hur. C-in-c of Warwick 54-55; I of Walter's Falls 55-57; St D Windsor 57-60; R of Blenheim 60-65; Lucknow 65-69; St John St Thomas 69-76; La Salle 76-81; Mitchell and Sebringville Dio Hur from 81. *Box 184, Mitchell, Ont, Canada.*

JEACOCK, Roland Newport. b 07. Worc Ordin Coll. **d** 54 Stockport for Ches **p** 55 Ches. C of Moreton 54-57; L to Offic Dio Ches 57-58; Min of St Chad Eccles Distr Leasowe Wallasey 58-67; V 67-74. *21 The Woodlands, Upton, Wirral, Mer, L49 6NQ.*

JEANES, Dennis. b 32. K Coll Lon and Warm AKC 58. **d** 59 **p** 60 Birm. C of H Trin Smethwick 59-61; Aston 61-62; St Geo Becontree 62-67; V of St Pet Westleigh 67-71. *55 Marlborough Road, Atherton, Lancs.*

JEANS, Richard. b 23. St Edm Hall Ox (3rd cl Th) BA 48, MA 53. Ely Th Coll. **d** 49 **p** 50 Dur. C of St Aid W Hartlepool 49-52; Weston Surrey 52-54; Dorking 54-56; V of Westcott 56-59; Chipping Norton w Over Norton 59-65; R of Heythrop 59-64; Surr from 59; Chap Chipping Norton War Mem Hosp and Cotshill Hosp 59-65; RD of Chipping Norton 61-65; R of Upwell St Pet 65-72; V of Cherry Hinton 72-81; R of W Woodhay, Enborne w Hamstead Marshall, Inkpen and Combe Dio Ox from 81. *Enborne Rectory, Newbury, Berks, RG15 0HD.* (Newbury 34427)

JEANS, Thomas Jeffery. b 01. Keble Coll Ox BA 23, MA 39. Egerton Hall, Man 25. **d** 26 **p** 27 Man. C of St Mary Hulme 26-29; St Chad Ladybarn 29-31; R of St Ignatius Salford 31-40; St Elisabeth Reddish 40-45; Asst Master Maltby Gr Sch 45-68; L to Offic Dio Sheff from 45. *35 Parkstone Crescent, Hellaby, Maltby, Rotherham, S Yorks S66 8HQ.*

JEAVONS, Maurice. b 32. Ely Th Coll 60. **d** 62 **p** 63 Lich. C of St Jo Bapt Longton 62-68; V of St Greg Gt Wednesfield 68-81; Lower Gornal Dio Lich from 81. *Lower Gornal Vicarage, Dudley, W Midl, DY3 2PF.* (Sedgeley 2023)

JEAVONS, Richard Antony. b 52. St Jo Coll Cam BA 73. MA 77. Univ of W Indies Trinid MSc 75. Wycliffe Hall Ox 75. **d** 78 **p** 79 Liv. C of St Luke W Derby 78; Allerton Dio Liv from 78. *7 Wyndcote Road, Liverpool, L18 2EB.* (051-722 7696)

JEBI, Setepano Jesu. d 71 Sudan. d Dio Sudan 71-76; Dio Juba from 76. *PO Box 110, Juba, Equatoria Province, Sudan.*

JEE, Colin Scott. b 32. Worc Coll Ox BA (2nd cl Th) 55, MA 59. Clifton Th Coll 55. **d** 57 **p** 58 Lon. C of Spitalfields 57-62; New Malden w Coombe 62-66; R of Ludgershall (w Wotton Underwood and Ashendon from 78) Dio Ox from 66; RD of Waddesdon 73-78; P-in-c of Wotton Underwood w Ashendon 74-78; Oakley Dio Ox from 73. *Ludgershall Rectory, Aylesbury, Bucks, HP18 9PG.* (Brill 238335)

JEFF, Gordon Henry. b 32. Late Scho of St Edm Hall Ox BA (2nd cl Engl) 56, MA 60. Wells Th Coll 59. **d** 61 **p** 62 S'wark. C of St Bart Sydenham 61-64; Kidbrooke 64-66; V of St Paul Clapham 66-72; Raynes Pk 73-79; RD of Merton 77-79; V of Good Shepherd Carshalton Dio S'wark from 79. *38 Beeches Avenue, Carshalton, Surrey, SM5 3LW.* (01-647 6056)

JEFFERIES, Cecil Arthur. b 11. **d** 69 **p** 70 Glouc. C of Caincross Dio Glouc from 76. *Daytona, Upper Church Road, Cainscross, Stroud, Glos.*

JEFFERIES, Phillip John. b 42. St Chad Coll Dur BA 65, Dipl Th 67. **d** 67 **p** 68 Lich. C of Tunstall 67-71; St Pet Wolverhampton 71-74; P-in-c of Oakengates 74-82; Ketley 78-82; V of Horninglow Dio Lich from 82. *Vicarage, Rolleston Road, Burton-on-Trent, Staffs DE13 0JZ.* (0283-68613)

JEFFERSON, Charles Dudley. b 55. St Pet Coll Ox BA 78, MA 81. Ridley Hall Cam 79. **d** 81 Stockport for Ches. C of St Chad Chadkirk Dio Ches from 81. *21 Guywood Lane, Romiley, Nr Stockport, Cheshire, SK6 4AN.*

JEFFERSON, David Charles. b 33. Univ of Leeds BA (3rd cl Gen) 57. Coll of Resurr Mirfield 57. **d** 59 **p** 60 S'wark. C of Kennington Cross 59-62; Richmond Surrey 62-64; Chap Wilson's Gr Sch Camberwell 64-74; Wilson's Sch Sutton from 75; Publ Pr Dio S'wark from 65. *Wilson's School, Mollison Drive, Wallington, Surrey, SM5 9JW.* (01-647 9530)

JEFFERSON, Canon Philip Clarke. Univ of Tor MEducn 70. K Coll NS BA 51, BD 57, MDiv 75. U Th Sem NY STM 58. **d** and **p** 52 NS. R of Ship Harbour 52-57; Ed Sec Dept Relig Educn Gen Synod of Canada 58-73; Gen Sec 66-73; Hon Can of NS 65-74; I of Dundas Dio Niag from 73; Hon Can of Niag from 80. *141 Melville Street, Dundas, Ont., Canada.* (416-628 8170)

JEFFERY, Ven Alfred Edwin. Codr Coll Barb 57. **d** 60 **p** 61 Antig. C of St Jo Cathl St John's 60-63; St Pet Montserrat 63-66; Dir Chr Family Centres Kingston 70-73; R of All SS I and Dio Antig from 73; Exam Chap to Bp of Antig from 76;

Archd of Antig from 78. *Box 1023, Antigua, W Indies.* (31095)

JEFFERY, Alfred Stephen. b 1891. St Steph Ho Ox 31. **d** 31 **p** 32 Chelmsf. C of St Edm Forest Gate 31-33; H Trin Barkingside 33-34; Perm to Offic at St Steph Bournemouth 34-35; R of Lound 36-43; Min of St Pet Becontree 43-45; Perm to Offic at St Greg Horfield 45-47; C 47-49; Withycombe Raleigh 49-56; R of E Allington 56-61; Perm to Offic Dio Ox 61-67; Dio Ex from 67. *11 Gussiford Lane, Exmouth, Devon, EX8 2SD.* (Exmouth 6761)

JEFFERY, Arthur Francis. b 11. St D Coll Lamp BA 33. St Mich Coll Llan 33. **d** 35 **p** 36 Llan. C of Penydarren 35-39; Eglwysilan 39-40; St Aug Penarth w Lavernock 40-44; Llanharan 44-50; Garw Valley and Blaengarw 50-53; V of Buttington 53-68; Rhydymwyn 68-78; Perm to Offic Dio St A from 78. *36 Llys Alyn, Rhydymwym, Mold, Clwyd, CH7 5HW.* (Hendre 435)

JEFFERY, Graham. b 35. Qu Coll Cam BA 58. Wells Th Coll 58. **d** 60 **p** 61 Win. C of St Pet Maybush 60-63; M Bush Bro of St Barn Dio N Queensld 63-66; C of E Grinstead 66-68; C-in-c of St Pet Conv Distr Hydneye, Hampden Pk 68-74; All SS Wick 74-76; C of Hove 76-78; P-in-c of Newtimber w Pyecombe Dio Chich from 78. *Pyecombe Rectory, Brighton, Sussex, BN4 7FE.* (Hassocks 2464)

JEFFERY, Graham Derrick. b 36. St Paul's Coll Grahmstn 76. **d** 77 **p** 78 Natal. C of St Thos Durban Dio Natal from 77-81; R of Howick Dio Natal from 81. *Box 88, Howick, Natal, S Africa.*

JEFFERY, Kenneth Charles. Univ of Wales, BA (2nd cl Bibl Stud) 64. Linacre Coll Ox BA 67, MA 70. St Steph Ho Ox 64. **d** 67 Malmesbury for Bris **p** 68 Ox. C of New Swindon 67-68; Summertown 68-71; St Pet Brighton 71-77; V of Ditchling Dio Chich from 77. *Ditchling Vicarage, Hassocks, BN6 8TS.* (Hassocks 3165)

JEFFERY, Leonard Herbert. **d** 59 **p** 60 Wang. C of Shepparton Dio Wang 59-61 and from 69; Violet Tn 61-65; P-in-c of Marysville 65-69; R of Yackandandah 73-76; L to Offic Dio C & Goulb 78-80; Perm to Offic Dio Wang from 80. *55 Salisbury Street, Benalla, Vic, Australia 3672.*

JEFFERY, Michael Frank. b 48. Linc Th Coll 74. **d** 76 **p** 77 S'wark. C of Caterham Valley 76-79; Tupsley Dio Heref from 79; Hampton Bp Dio Heref from 79. *2 Litley Close, Tupsley, Hereford, HR1 1TN.*

JEFFERY, Norman. b 42. Bps' Coll Cheshunt. **d** 67 **p** 68 S'wark. C of St Marg Putney 67-71; St Paul Hoddesdon 71-74; C-in-c of Roxton w Gt Barford Dio St Alb 74-78; V from 78. *Great Barford Vicarage, Bedford.* (Bedford 870363)

JEFFERY, Peter James. b 41. Univ of Leeds, BSc 63. Oak Hill Th Coll 64. **d** 66 **p** 67 S'wark. C of St Alb Streatham Pk 66-70; St Giles Northn 70-73; St Pet Rushden 73-77; V of St Mark Siddal Dio Wakef from 77. *St Mark's Vicarage, Siddal, Halifax, HX3 9AD.* (Halifax 69538)

JEFFERY, Peter Noel. b 37. Late Scho of Pemb Coll Ox BA 60, MA 64. Linc Th Coll 60. **d** 62 **p** 63 Birm. C of St Paul W Smethwick 62-64; C-in-c of St Andr w St Giles Bordesley 64-69; R of Turvey Dio St Alb from 69; P-in-c of Stevington Dio St Alb from 79. *Turvey Rectory, Bedford.* (Turvey 210)

JEFFERY, Peter Richard. b 48. St Pet Coll Ox BA 70, MA 75. St Jo Coll Nottm Dipl Th 80. **d** 81 Liv. C of St Nich Halewood Dio Liv from 81. *The Old School House, Church Road, Halewood, Liverpool, L26 6LA.*

JEFFERY, Richard William Christopher. b 43. Univ of Ex BA (2nd cl Th) 65. Coll of Resurr Mirfield 66. **d** 68 **p** 69 Portsm. C of Wymering w Widley 68-71; St Mich AA Sarum 71-74; Team V of Ridgeway 74-80; V of Stanford-in-the-Vale w Goosey and Hatford Dio Ox from 80. *Stanford-in-the-Vale Vicarage, Faringdon, Oxon, SN7 8HU.* (Stanford-in-the-Vale 267)

JEFFERY, Ven Robert Martin Colquhoun. b 35. K Coll Lon and Warm BD and AKC 58. **d** 59 **p** 60 Dur. C of Grangetown 59-61; Barnes 61-63; Asst Sec Miss and Ecumen Coun Ch Assembly 64-68; Sec Dept of Miss and Unity Br Coun of Chs 68-71; Perm to Offic Dio S'wark 64-65; Publ Pr 65-71; V of St Andr Headington Ox 71-78; RD of Cowley 73-78; P-in-c of Tong and Dioc Missr Dio Lich from 78; Hon Can of Lich Cathl from 80; Archd of Salop from 80. *Tong Vicarage, Shifnal, Salop, TF11 8PW.* (Albrighton 2622)

JEFFERY, Canon Robert Michael. b 17. Selw Coll Cam 2nd cl Engl Trip pt i 38, BA 39, 2nd cl Th Trip pt i 40, MA 43. Westcott Ho Cam 39. **d** 41 **p** 42 Ex. C of Ilfracombe 41-44; Chap and Asst Master Portsm Gr Sch 44-46; Chap Khaiso Sch Pietersburg 46-55; Vice-Prin 46-52; Prin 52-55; Prov Commiss S Afr 55-57; Dir of S Afr Ch Inst 55-57; C of St Geo Hanover Square Lon 56; Prin Grâce Dieu Sch Pietersburg 58-59; Warden Zonnebloem Coll Capetn 59-69; Prin Bp Gray Th Coll Capetn 59-63; Exam Chap to Abp of Capetn 61-69; Can of Capetn Cathl 62-69; Actg Dep Executive Officer Angl Communion 69-72; Sen Chap to Abp of Capetn 72-74; Prov Can of Capetn from 70; R of Woodstock 75-76; Chap Prestfelde Sch Shrewsbury from 77. *Prestfelde School, Shrewsbury, Salop.*

JEFFERY-MACHIN (formerly MACHIN), Canon Ivor William John. b 09. Univ of Lon BA (1st cl Engl) 29, MA 32, PhD 39. Bps' Coll Cheshunt 39. **d** 39 **p** 40 Portsm. C of St Jas Milton 39-43; V of Westend 43-52; Andover 52-67; H Trin Bournemouth 67-75; Team V (w St Pet St Swith and St Steph) 73-75; Surr 52-75; Hon Can of Win 64-75; Can (Emer) from 75; RD of Andover 65-67. *1 Hadley Court, St Catherine's Road, Southbourne, Bournemouth.* (0202-422 423)

JEFFERYES, Neil. b 37. Univ of St Andr BSc (2nd cl Math) 60. BD (Lon) 62. Tyndale Hall, Bris 60. **d** 63 Warrington for Liv **p** 64 Liv. C of St Helens (in c of St Mary) 63-68; V of St Mark Barrow-F 68-77; RD of Furness 74-77; Aston from 81; P-in-c of S Weston w Adwell 77-81; Stoke Talmage w Wheatfield 77-81; Tetsworth Dio Ox 77-81; R (w Adwell, S Weston, Lewknor, Stoke-Talmage and Wheatfield) from 81. *Tetsworth Rectory, Oxford, OX9 7AL.* (Tetsworth 267)

JEFFERYS, Graham. Moore Th Coll Syd ACT ThL 66. **d** 67 **p** 68 Syd. C of Roseville E 67-68; Wollongong 68-69; St Andr Wahroonga 70-71; Res Min New Housing Distr Tregear 71-74; SAMS Miss 74-80; C of Marrickville Dio Syd from 81. *220 Illawarra Road, Marrickville, NSW, Australia 2204.*

JEFFORD, Brian Harrison. b 30. S Dioc Min Tr Scheme. **d** 81 Chich (NSM). C of St Jo Evang Meads Eastbourne Dio Chich from 81. *14 Derwent Road, Eastbourne, BN20 7PH.*

JEFFORD, Peter Ernest. b 29. K Coll Lon and Warm AKC 53. **d** 54 Bp Barkway for Cant **p** 55 Glouc. C of Berkeley w Sharpness 54-57; Petersfield (in c of Sheet) 57-61; R of Rollesby (w Burgh and Billockby from 62) 61-71; V of Watton Dio Nor from 71; P-in-c of Carbrook w Ovington Dio Nor from 80. *Watton Vicarage, Thetford, Norf, IP25 6DB.* (Watton 881439)

JEFFREE, Robin. K Coll Lon and Warm AKC 54. **d** 55 **p** 56 Lon. C of St Alb Harrow 55-59; Hendon 59-62; V of Manea 62-67; Hartford Dio Ely from 67. *Hartford Vicarage, Huntingdon.*

JEFFREY, Michael David. b 30. Sarum Th Coll 63. **d** 65 Sherborne for Sarum **p** 66 Sarum. C of St Mark Sarum 65-68; Melksham 68-70; R of Durrington 70-82; V of Colehill Dio Sarum from 82. *Vicarage, Smugglers Lane, Colehill, Wimborne, Dorset BH21 2RY.* (0202-883721)

JEFFRIES, John. Wycl Coll Tor. **d** 45 Tor for Sask **p** 46 Sask. Miss at Onion Lake 45-47; Mattagami 47-62; Calstock 52-63; Prin John Smith Sch Kinistino 63-65; Miss Lac La Ronge 65-69; Hon Can of Moos 57-63; Sask 67-76; I of Nipawin 70-76; P-in-c of Native Min Vanc Dio New Westmr from 76. *3316 West 14th Avenue, Vancouver, BC, Canada.*

JEFFRIES, Peter George Charles. b 28. Qu Coll Birm 54. **d** 56 **p** 57 Glouc. C of Slad w Uplands 56-59; St Barn Tuffley 59-62; V of Clearwell 62-69; R of Ampney w Ampney Crucis, Harnhill and Driffield Dio Glouc from 69. *Ampney St Peter Rectory, Cirencester, Glos.* (Poulton 240)

JEFFRIES, Walter Ernest Phillip. **d** 33 **p** 34 Sheff. C of Goole 33-35; Handsworth (in c of St Cath Woodthorpe) 35-37; Perm to Offic at St Nich Hull 37; C-in-c of Upper and Gate Helmsley w Holtby and Warthill 38-39; C of Ch Ch Stepney 40-42; CF (TA-R of O) from 39; R of Shardlow w Gt Wilne 42-54; PC (V from 69) of Tottenhill w Wormegay 54-74. *11 Southside, Wimbotsham, King's Lynn, Norf.* (Downham Market 3835)

JEFFROY, William George. b 05. Univ of Serampur BD 44. **d** and **p** 46 Bom. C of Ch Ch Bom 46; St Paul Poona 49-52; Bandra and St Mary Parel Bom 52-61; C of Highworth w Sevenhampton, Inglesham and Hannington 61-64; C-in-c of Sharpness w Purton 64-69; Toddington w Stanley Pontlarge 69-71; V of Kempley w Oxenhall 71-73. *21 Randwick Road, Lower Tuffley, Gloucester, GL4 0NH.*

JEFFS, George Hyndman. b 09. **d** 65 **p** 66 Leic. Hon C of St Pet Belgrave Dio Leic from 65. *14 Lynmouth Drive, Wigston, Leics, LE8 1BP.*

JEFFS, Noel Thomas. b 50. Univ of Melb BA 71. St Barn Coll Adel 73. **d** 75 **p** 76 Bal. C of Ararat 75-77; Horsham 77-79; Perm to Offic Dio Brisb from 79. *131 Brookfield Road, Brookfield, Queensland, Australia 4069.* (378 2160)

JEGA, Samson. Newton Coll Dogura 72. **d** 74 Bp Ambo for Papua. d Dio Papua 74-77; Dio Aipo 77-78 and from 80; Dio Popondota 78-80. *Anglican Church, Simbai, via Madang, Papua New Guinea.*

JEGEDE, Canon Julius Oluwatayo. Melville Hall, Ibad. **d** 50 **p** 51 Lagos. P Dio Lagos 50-52; Dio Ondo-B 52-59; and 60-62; Dio Ondo from 62; C of Northenden 59-60; Hon Can of Ondo from 67. *Box 14, Oka-Akoko, Nigeria.*

JEGEDE, Samuel Ojo. Im Coll Ibad 61. **d** 63 Ibad. d Dio Ibad 63-74; Dio Ilesha from 74. *Vicarage, Ikeji-Ile, via Ilesha, Nigeria.*

JELBART, Alexander Parismas. b 21. Oak Hill Th Coll 51. Univ of Lon Dipl Th 53. **d** 53 Stafford for Cant **p** 54 Lich. C of Bucknall 53-56; V of St Steph Walthamstow 56-62; PC of Chell 62-67; V 68-70; V of Madeley 70-78; St Mark St Helens Dio Liv from 78. *Vicarage, North Road, St Helens, Mer, WA10 2TZ.* (St Helens 23806)

JELLEY, James Dudley. b 46. Linc Th Coll 78. **d** 80 **p** 81 S'wark. C of Stockwell Green Dio S'wark from 80. *77 Tasman Road, SW9 9LY.*

JELLIE, Wilfred Raymond. b 1899. K Coll Lon 27. **d** 29 **p** 30 Lon. C of All S Harlesden 29-31; Org Sec CMS Dios Liv, Ches and S & M and L to Offic Dio Liv 31-36; V of St Paul Birkenhead 36-41; Chap of Giggleswick Sch Settle 41-43; L to Offic Dio Bradf 41-43; V of St Thos Pendleton 43-52; St Cath Barton-on-Irwell 52-59; R of Benwick 59-68; Croxton 68-71; V of Eltisley 68-71; C-in-c of Toseland 68-71; Perm to Offic Dio Chich 72-80. *Address temp unknown.*

JELLY, James Hugh. b 08. Selw Coll Cam 3rd cl Th Trip pt ia, 30, BA (3rd cl Th Trip pt ib) 31, MA 36. Wells Th Coll 31. **d** 32 **p** 33 S'wark. C of St Marg Streatham Hill 32-36; St Mary Lewisham 36-39; V of St Mark Lewisham 39-47; Churchstoke 47-55; Seq of Hyssington w Snead 47-52; V of Hyssington 52-55; R of Credenhill 55-58; V of Brinsop 55-58; S Petherton 58-74; PC of Lopen 58-60; C of Malborough w S Huish (in c of H Trin Galmpton and St Clem Hope Cove) 74-78; Perm to Offic Dio B & W from 79. *53 Hillview Road, Minehead, Somt, TA24 8EF.* (Minehead 2041)

JEMBA, Yosiya. **d** 44 **p** 45 Ugan. P Dio Ugan 44-61; Dio Nam 61-64; Can of Nam 63-74. *Box 14297, Kampala, Uganda.*

JEMMOTT, Anthony Gordon Edwin. Univ of WI BA (Th) 73. Codr Coll Barb 73. **d** 73 **p** 75 Barb C of Ch the K I and Dio Barb from 73. *The Lodge, Millbank, Cave Hill, St Michael, Barbados, WI.*

JENKIN, Christopher Cameron. b 36. Late Exhib of BNC Ox BA (1st cl Forestry) 61, MA 64. Clifton Th Coll 61. **d** 63 **p** 64 Chelmsf. C of Walthamstow 63-68; Ch Ch Surbiton Hill (in c of Em Tolworth) 68-78; V of St Jo Bapt Carisbrooke Dio Portsm from 78. *St John's Vicarage, 1 Watergate Road, Newport, PO30 1XN, IW.* (Newport 522148)

JENKIN, Edward George. **d** 73 Carp. C of Mossman Dio Carp from 73. *c/o PO Box 79, Thursday Island 4875, Australia.*

JENKINS, Allan Kenneth. b 40. Univ of Lon BD and AKC 63. MTh (Lon) 69. St Mich Coll Llan 63. **d** 64 Bp Hughes for Llan **p** 65 Llan. C of Llanblethian w Cowbridge 64-70; Lect Serampore Coll W Bengal 70-76; V of Llanarth w Clytha, Llansantffraed and Bryngwyn 76-78; Dir of Stud Chich Th Coll from 78. *The Theological College, Chichester, PO19 3ES.*

JENKINS, Brian Téychenné. Univ of NZ BA 55, MA 63. St Jo Coll Auckld LTh (2nd cl) 59. **d** 59 **p** 60 Auckld. C of Otahuhu 59-62; Paparoa 62-64; V of Birkenhead 64-71; Mt Roskill 71-76; Devonport Auckld 76-81; Archd of Hauraki 76-81; Exam Chap to Bp of Auckld and Dir CA from 81. *782 Remuera Road, Auckland 5, NZ.*

JENKINS, Clifford Thomas. b 38. Sarum Wells Th Coll 74. **d** 77 Taunton for B & W **p** 78 B & W (NSM). C of Yeovil and Chap Yeovil Coll Dio B & W from 77. *10 Grove Avenue, Yeovil, Somt, BA20 2BB.* (0935-5043)

JENKINS, Cyril. b 27. St D Coll Lamp BA (2nd cl Engl) 53. Wells Th Coll 53. **d** 55 **p** 56 Lich. C of Uttoxeter 55-57; St Alkmund Shrewsbury 57-60; V of Essington 60-69; Gnosall w Knightley 69-72; Chap St Alb Sch Chorley 72-74; Asst Master Runshan Coll Leyland from 74; L to Offic Dio Blackb from 79. *10 Casterton, Church Park, Euxton, Chorley, Lancs.* (Chorley 79195)

JENKINS, David Charles. St Mich Coll Llan 55. **d** 56 St A for Ban **p** 57 Ban. C of Llandegai w Tregarth 56-58; Llangelynin (in c of Fairbourne) 58-61; R of Cemmaes (Monts) 61-70; Llangristiolus w Cerrig-Ceinwen and Trewalchmai 70-73; Garthbeibio w Llanerfyl and Llangadfan 73-75. *Aeronfa, Llangrannog, Llandyssul, Dyfed.*

JENKINS, Canon David Edward. b 25. Qu Coll Ox 2nd cl Cl 49, BA (2nd cl Lit Hum) 51, 1st cl Th 52, MA 54. Linc Th Coll 52. **d** 53 Bp Linton for Cant **p** 54 Birm. C of St Phil Cathl and Lect Qu Coll Birm 53-54; Fell, Chap and Praelector in Th Qu Coll Ox 54-69; Lect in Th Univ of Ox 55-69; Exam Chap to Bp of Lich 56-69; Newc T 57-69; Bris from 59; Wakef from 77; Bradf from 78; Select Pr Univ of Ox 61; Bampton Lect 66; L to Offic Dio Ox 56-69; Can Th of Leic from 66; Dir in World Coun of Chs Study Dept 69-73; William Temple Found Man 73-78; Jt Dir from 79; Lindsay Lect Univ of Keele 75; Publ Pr Dio Man 73-80; Hulsean Pr Univ of Cam 72; Prof of Th and Relig Studs Univ of Leeds from 79; Heslington Lect Univ of York 80; Drummond Lect Univ of Stirling 81; L to Offic Dio Ripon from 81. *Department of Theology, The University, Leeds, LS2 9JT.* (0532-31751)

JENKINS, Canon David Ernest. Univ of Witwatersrand BA 50. St Paul's Th Coll Grahmstn LTh 51. **d** 51 **p** 52 S Rhod. C of St Patr Miss Gwelo 51-52; Melfort 52-54; R of Salisbury E 54-63; Dir of Relig Broadcasting Rhod Television 60-64; Dir Publ Relations Dept Prov of Centr Africa 63-65; Hon Can of Mashon 63-66; R of Somerset W 66-70; Chap St Andr Sch Grahamstn 70-71; R of St Alphege Pmbg 71-77; Hon Can of Natal from 76; L to Offic Dio Natal from 78. *201 Medical Centre, Burger Street, Pietermaritzburg, Natal, S Africa.*

JENKINS, David Myrddin. b 30. St Mich Coll Llan 59. **d** 61 **p** 62 St D. C of St Mary w St Thos Haverfordwest 61-63; Pembroke Dock 63-67; R of Ch Ch Yokohama 67-69; Chap Miss to Seamen Yokohama 67-69; Port of Lon 69-71; V of Llansteffan w Llan-y-bri and Llandeilo Abercywyn 71-78; Llantwit Major w St Donats Dio Llan from 78. *Vicarage, Llantwit Major, S Glam.* (Llantwit Major 2324)

JENKINS, David Noble. b 25. CCC Cam BA 47, MA 50. Cudd Coll Ox 48. **d** 50 **p** 51 Pet. C of St Matt Northn 50-54; Chap Hurstpierpoint Coll 54-59; Home Staff SPG 60-65; Chap Eastbourne Coll 66-74; V of Jarvis Brook Dio Chich from 75. *Jarvis Brook Vicarage, Tubwell Lane, Crowborough, E Sussex.* (Crowborough 2639)

JENKINS, David Roland. Kelham Th Coll 55. **d** 59 **p** 60 York. C of St John Middlesbrough 59-60; St Alb Hull 60-64; Roehampton 64-68; V of St Jerome Dawley Hillingdon 68-73; R of Harlington Dio Lon from 73. *Rectory, St Peter's Way, Harlington, Middx, UB3 5AB.* (01-759 9569)

JENKINS, David Ronald. Univ of Wales, BA 38. St Mich Coll Llan 39. **d** 40 **p** 41 St D. C of Henfynyw 40-43; C-in-c of Lampeter Velfrey 43-46; C of Eglwysnewydd 46-47; R of Llangynllo (w Troedyraur from 52) 47-56; Pendine w Llanmiloe 56-78; RD of St Clears 67-77; R of Eglwys Gymin w Marros 77-78. *c/o Rectory. Pendine, Dyfed.*

JENKINS, David Thomas. b 43. Dipl Th (Lon) 79. soc 76. **d** 79 **p** 80 Llan. Hon C of Merthyr Tydfil & Cyfarthfa Dio Llan from 79. *1 King Edward Villas, Merthyr Tydfil, Mid Glam, CF47 8SH.*

JENKINS, Canon David Thomas Ivor. b 29. K Coll Lon and Warm BD and AKC 52. Univ of Birm MA 63. **d** 53 **p** 54 Cov. C of Bilton 53-56 V of Wolston 56-61; L to Offic Dio Carl 61-63; Asst Dir of Relig Educn Dio Carl 61-63; V of St Barn Carl 63-72; St Cuthb (w St Mary from 76) City and Dio Carl from 72; C-in-c of St Mary w St Paul Carl 72-76; Sec of Carl Dioc Synod and of Bp's Council from 72; Hon Can of Carl Cathl from 75. *St Cuthbert's Vicarage, Carlisle, Cumb, CA3 8UF.* (Carlisle 21982)

JENKINS, Delme. b 18. St D Coll Lamp BA 41. St Mich Coll Llan 41. **d** 43 **p** 44 St D. C of Llanwnda w Manorowen 43-46; St Paul Llanelly 46-49; Chap of Llan Cathl 49-58; V of Penyfai 58-69; All SS Llan Dio Llan from 70. *59 Station Road, Llandaff, North Cardiff, CF4 2FB.* (Cardiff 564096)

JENKINS, Edward Morgan. b 09. St D Coll Lamp BA 35. **d** 35 **p** 36 Chelmsf. C of St Mary Plaistow 35-38; St Dionis Parson's Green 38-40; C-in-c of Ch Ch Chelsea 40-41; Asst Chap St Luke's Hosp Chelsea 40-41; C of Isleworth (in c of St Jo Bapt) 41-45; V of St Jo Bapt Isleworth 45-53; R of S Shoebury (or Shoeburyness) 53-75; Chap Shoeburyness Hosp 54-75. *11 The Circus, Eastbourne, BN23 6LL.* (Eastbourne 37464)

JENKINS, Eric Coronwy. **d** 58 **p** 59 Geo. C of All SS Mossel Bay 58-61; Oudtshoorn 62-65; St Mark's Cathl Geo 66-67; R of Formosa 67-72; L to Offic Dio Geo 72-77; Dio Natal from 79. *Box 119, Hilton, Natal, S Africa.*

JENKINS, Eric Neil. b 23. Univ of Wales BSc (1st cl) 43, MSc 47. Wycl Hall Ox 60. **d** 62 Warrington for Liv **p** 63 Liv. C of Allerton 62-65; V of Hale 65-73; St Steph Hightown and Bp's Adv on Social and Scientific Affairs Dio Liv from 73. *St Stephen's Vicarage, Hightown, Liverpool 38.* (051-929 2469)

JENKINS, Very Rev Frank Graham. b 23. St D Coll Lamp BA (2nd cl Hist) 47. Jes Coll Ox BA (2nd cl Th) 49, MA 53. **d** 50 Bp Jones for Llan **p** 51 Llan. C of Llangeinor 50-53; Chap Llan Cathl 53-60; V of Abertillery 60-64; Risca 64-74; Can of Mon from 67; V of Llangattock-juxta-Caerleon 75-76; Dean of Mon and V of St Woolos Cathl Ch Newport Dio Mon from 76; Surr from 76. *The Deanery, Stow Hill, Newport, Gwent.* (Newport 63338)

JENKINS, Frederick Llewellyn. b 14. St D Coll Lamp BA (2nd cl Engl Hons) 35. St Mich Coll Llan 36. **d** 37 **p** 38 Llan. C of Gilfach Goch 37-40; Bp's Castle w Mainstone 40-45; CF 45-64; CF (R of O) 64-69; Chap R Masonic Sch Bushey 64-77; Perm to Offic Dio Lich from 77. *Plas Uchaf, Trefonen, Oswestry, Shropshire, SY10 9DT.* (Oswestry 3918)

JENKINS, Garry Frederick. b 48. Univ of Southn BTh (extra mural) 79. Chich Th Coll 75. **d** 79 Willesden for Lon **p** 80 Lon. C of St Andr Kingsbury Dio Lon from 79. *32a Wells Drive, NW9 8DG.* (01-200 5709)

JENKINS, George Patrick. St D Coll Lamp BA 61. Lich Th Coll 61. **d** 63 **p** 64 Glouc. C of Dursley 63-66; H Trin

Stroud 66-69; V of Churcham w Bulley (and Minsterworth from 81) Dio Glouc from 69; RD of Forest N from 79. *Vicarage, Church Lane, Churcham, Gloucester, GL2 8AF.* (Minsterworth 252)

JENKINS, Canon Henry Maurice. b 13. AKC (2nd cl) 36. Sambrooke Exhib 35. **d** 36 **p** 37 Southw. C of Mansfield Woodhouse 36-39; Daybrook 39-42; Dir Southw Dioc Youth Comm 42-45; Dioc Educn Officer 44-46; Org Insp Sch 47-51; PC of St Cath Nottm 45-54; Dir of Educn and Chief Insp of Schs Dio Southw 50-54; V of Ch Ch w St Pet Luton 54-71; Industr Adviser to Bp of St Alb 55-78; Hon Can of St Alb 60-78; Can (Emer) from 78; RD of Luton 60-67; Proc Conv St Alb 63-64; V of Southill 71-78. *New House, Skinners Green, Metfield, Harleston, Norf.* (Fressingfield 478)

JENKINS, Canon Illtyd Stephen. b 1893. Qu Coll Ox BA 16, MA 18. Cudd Coll 19. **d** 20 **p** 21 Truro. C of St Mich Newquay 20-24; R of Landulph 24-29; Calstock 29-36; PC of St Ives 36-63; RD of Penwith 48-50; Hon Can of Truro 54-63; Can (Emer) from 63. *32 Cavell Road, Oxford.*

JENKINS, Islwyn. b 12. Univ of Wales BA 37, Dipl Educn 49, MA 57. St Mich Coll Llan 37. **d** 38 Swan B for Llan **p** 39 Llan. C of Llangynwyd 38-41; Whitchurch 41-44; CF (EC) 44-47; Hon CF 47; C of St Sav Roath Cardiff 47-50; Perm to Offic Dios Ely and Llan 50-53; L to Offic Dios Llan and Mon from 53; Dio St D from 66; Asst Master Gr Sch Wisbech 50-53; Cathays Sch for Boys Cardiff 53-66; Lect Trin Coll Carmarthen 66-77. *15 Courtlands Park, Carmarthen, Dyfed.*

JENKINS, John Alfred Morgan. St D Coll Lamp BA 58. St Cath Coll Ox BA 60, MA 64. Wycl Hall Ox. **d** 61 **p** 62 Swan B. C of Sketty 61-69; R of All SS Belize 69-72; Dioc Chap Br Hond 70-72; Exam Chap to Bp of Br Hond 71-72; Asst Master St Hilda's Coll Belize 70-72; V of St Jo Bapt W Byfleet Dio Guildf from 73. *5 Dartnell Avenue, West Byfleet, Weybridge, Surrey, KT14 6PJ.* (093-23 45270)

JENKINS, John Francis. b 46. Ripon Coll Cudd 75. **d** 77 **p** 78 Bris. C of Filton Dio Bris from 77. *16 Branksome Drive, Filton, Bristol, BS12 7EP.* (Bris 697004)

JENKINS, John Frederick. St D Coll Lamp BA 35. **d** 39 **p** 40 Sheff. C of St Chad Norton Woodseats Sheff 39-42; Stocksbridge 42-45; Llanengan w Llangian 45-46; Portmadoc 46-48; Treherbert 48-54; V of Llanfair-Orllwyn 54-60; Gartheli w 60-72; R of Capel Cynon w Talgarreg Dio St D from 72-80. *Address temp unknown.*

JENKINS, John Howard David. b 51. Univ of Birm BA (Th) 72. St Steph Ho Ox 72. **d** 74 **p** 75 St D. C of Milford Haven 74-77; PV Llan Cathl 77-81; V Cho of St A Cathl and Chap Lowther Coll from 81. *Groesffordd, Mount Road, St Asaph, Clwyd.*

JENKINS, John Lewis. b 1889. MBE 36. St Edm Hall Ox BA and MA 25. Can Sch Linc 20. **d** 22 **p** 23 Ches. C of St John Egremont 22-25; Chap Miss to Seamen Calc 25-45; furlough 33 and 36; St Nich Calc 35; R of Melbury Abbas 46-53; C-in-c of Fontmell Magna 51-53; R of Ch Knowle 53-59; R of Steeple w Tyneham 53-59; PC of Kimmeridge 53-59. *8 Battle Mead, Swanage, Dorset, BH19 1PH.* (Swanage 2860)

JENKINS, John Michael. b 36. Or Coll Ox BA (3rd cl Th) 60, MA 64. St Steph Ho Ox 60. **d** 62 **p** 63 Birm. C of Solihull (in c of St Mary Hob's Moat) 62-65; Lect Qu Coll Birm 64-65; Chap Radley Coll from 65. *Radley College, Abingdon, Berks, OX14 2HR.* (Abingdon 20294)

JENKINS, John Owen. b 06. St D Coll Lamp BA (1st cl Hist) 26, Powis Exhib 28. Jes Coll Ox BA and MA 57. St Mich Coll Llan 29. **d** 29 **p** 30 St D. C of Cwmamman 29-33; Llanelly 33-39; R of Treffgarn w Spittal 39-49; V of Llangadock 49-60; CF (EC) 43-46; Cler Sec St D Dioc Conf and Sec Dioc Bd of Patr 51-63; Ed St D Dioc Year Book 54-63; Can of Clydey in St D Cathl 58-62; R of Newport 60-67; Archd of Cardigan and Preb of Llandyfriog in St D Cathl 62-67; Archd of Carmarthen and Preb of St D Cathl 67-74; V of Llanfihangel Aberbythick 67-74. *Morfa Gwyn, Aberporth, Dyfed.*

JENKINS, John Raymond. K Coll Lon and Warm Whichelow Pri 52. **d** 53 **p** 54 St A. C of Wrexham 53-56; Welshpool 56-57; V of Mochdre 57-65; Llandyssul 65-67; Llanfair Caereinion w Llanllugan 67-70; Asst Master Bryn Offa Wrexham 72-74; St D Sch Wrexham from 75; Hon C of Wrexham Dio St A from 77. *Bersham Bank, Bersham, Wrexham, Clwyd.* (Wrexham 55821)

JENKINS, Kenneth Thomas. St D Coll Lamp BA (2nd cl Hist) 36. Ripon Hall Ox 36. **d** 38 Bp Allen for Ox **p** 39 Buckingham for Ox. C of St Mich Ox 38-39; Chap RAFVR 39-44; C-in-c of Cuddesdon 44-45; R of Ewelme 45-52; Britwell-Salome w Britwell-Prior 47-52; Chap at Qatar 52-57; R Masonic Sch Bushey 57-59; St Pet Coll Sch Adel 59-62. *Walkerville Terrace, Walkerville, S Australia.*

JENKINS, Lawrence Clifford. b 45. AKC 70. Open Univ BA 77. St Aug Coll Cant. **d** 71 **p** 72 Ripon. C of St Phil Osmondthorpe Leeds 71-74; Monkseaton 74-78; V of Shiremoor Dio Newc T from 78. *St Marks Vicarage, Brenkley Avenue, Shiremoor, Newcastle upon Tyne, NE27*

JENKINS, Llewelyn. b 1898. St Mich Coll Llan 26. **d** 28 **p** 29 Llan. C of St Andr Llwynpia 28-30; Kenilworth 30-31; Perm to Offic at St Mary Maidenhead 31-32; C of Walker 32-35; R of Nettleton 35-42; Hadstock 42-49; V of Newbiggin-on-Lune 49-54; Perm to Offic Dio Dur from 55; Dio York from 60. *173 Prospect Road, Scarborough, Yorks.*

JENKINS, Paul Morgan. b 44. Univ of Sussex BEducn 68. Fitzw Coll Cam BA 73, MA 76. Westcott Ho Cam 71. **d** 74 Barking for Chelmsf **p** 75 Chelmsf. C of St Edm Forest Gate 74-77; Chap and Asst Master Bryanston Sch from 77; P-in-c of Durweston Dio Sarum from 77. *Bryanston School, Blandford Forum, Dorset.* (Blandford 2411)

JENKINS, Canon Raymond Gordon Finney. b 1898. Late Sen Exhib of Trin Coll Dub Scho Sen Mod and BA 23, Wall Bibl Scho Aramaic, Syriac, and Hebr Pri 24, 1st cl Or Lang Mod 26, Div Test (1st cl) 28, MA 32, BD 36. **d** 30 **p** 31 Dub. C of St Thos Dub 30-33; St Bart Dub 33-34; Asst To Abp King's Prof of Div TCD 31-40; Warden of Div Hostel Dub 34-39; Dean of Res TCD 35-40; Lect 39-67; Hon Cler V of Ch Ch Cathl Dub from 31; I of All SS Grangegorman Dub 39-76; Chap St Brendan's Hosp 39-76; Treas of St Patr Cathl Dub 52-62; Chan 62-77; Exam Chap to Bp of Cork 52-56; to Abp of Dub from 54; Hon Cler Sec Gen Synod 54-75; Lect in Or Lang TCD 58-69; Archd of Dub 61-74; Can (Emer) of Ch Ch Cathl Dub from 74. *14 Woodlawn Park, Upper Mount Town, Dunlaoghaire, Co Dublin, Irish Republic.* (Dublin 802441)

JENKINS, Richard David. b 33. Magd Coll Cam 2nd cl Th Trip pt i 56, BA (3rd cl Th Trip pt ii) 58. Westcott Ho Cam 59. **d** 61 **p** 62 Derby. C of Staveley 61-64; St Aid Billingham (in c of St Luke) 64-68; V of St John The Pleck and Bescot Walsall 68-73; R of Whitchurch Dio Lich from 73. *Rectory, Church Street, Whitchurch, Salop, SY13 1LB.* (Whitchurch 2342)

JENKINS, Richard Morvan. b 44. Univ of Wales (Cardiff) Dipl Th 68. St Mich Coll Llan 65. **d** 69 **p** 70 St D. C of Tenby w Gumfreston and Penally 69-73; V of Llanrhian w Llanhowell and Carnhedryn (w Llanrhethan from 77) 73-80; Johnston w Steynton Dio St D from 80. *Steynton Vicarage, Milford Haven, Dyfed.* (Milford Haven 2867)

JENKINS, Robert Francis. b 33. BNC Ox BA 57, MA 59. Wycl Hall Ox 57. **d** 59 **p** 60 Birm. C of Hall Green 59-63; PC of Dosthill w Wood End 63-67; V 68-71; V of St Bede's Brandwood Dio Birm from 71. *77 Doversley Road, Brandwood, Birmingham, B14 6NN.* (021-444 4631)

JENKINS, Thomas Dryden. b 1900. Keble Coll Ox BA 20, MA 25. Wells Th Coll 24. **d** 25 **p** 26 S'wark. C of St Steph Battersea 25-27; Tidenham 27-33; Standish w Hardwicke 33-37; V of Brookthorpe w Whaddon 37-71; CF (EC) 40-45; RD of S Glouc 52-68; C-in-c of Harescombe 54-65. *St Jude, 1a Park Avenue, Longlevens, Gloucester.* (Glos 24815)

JENKINS, Thomas Edward. b 02. Late Scho of St D Coll Lamp BA 22, Powis Exhib 24, BD 32. Wycl Hall Ox 24. **d** 25 **p** 26 St D. C of Llanelly 25-34; R of Begelly w E Williamston 34-38; V of Ch Ch Llanelly 38-46; Lampeter-Pont-Stephen 46-56; Can and Preb of 6th Cursal in St D Cathl 51-57; RD of Lampeter 49-54; Surr from 53; V of Cardigan 56; V of Verwick w Mount 56-57; Dean and V of St D 57-72; RD of Dewisland 61-65. *18 North Road, Cardigan, Dyfed.*

JENKINS, Thomas Glennard Owen. b 22. St Jo Coll Ox BA (3rd cl Th) 48. MA 52. Wells Th Coll Wycl Hall, Ox. **d** 50 **p** 51 Bp R W Jones for Llan. Min Can of St D Cathl 50-54; Chap RN 54-58; Prec and Sacr of Worc Cathl 58-60; L to Offic Dio Worc 59-60; V of Hailey w Crawley 60-79; Penbryn w Blaenporth Dio St D from 79; Betws Evan w Brongwyn Dio St D from 79. *Vicarage, Sarnau, Llandyssul, Dyfed, SA44 6QR.*

JENKINS, Thomas William. Univ of Wales BA (1st cl Music) 40. St Mich Coll Llan 40. **d** 42 **p** 43 Mon. C of St Mark Newport Mon 42-46; St Mary and All SS Kidderminster 46-48; V of St John The Pleck and Bescot Walsall 48-67; H Trin Shrewsbury 67-75; Chap Manor Hosp and St John's Hosp 48-67; R of Ruyton-XI-Towns 75-81. *c/o Ruyton-XI-Towns Vicarage, Shrewsbury, Salop.* (Baschurch 254)

JENKINS, Trevor Illtyd. b 03. Chich Th Coll 26. **d** 27 **p** 29 Swan B. C of Ystradgynlais 27-30; Oystermouth 30-41; R of Bishopston 41-49; V of St Gabr Swansea 49-73; Surr 49-73; Hon Can of Brecon 69-73; Perm to Offic Dio Swan B from 73. *5 Ffynone Close, Swansea, Glam.* (Swansea 472799)

JENKINS, William David. b 42. Univ of Birm BA (2nd cl Hist) 63. St D Coll Lamp LTh 65. **d** 65 **p** 66 Swan B. C of Gorseinon 65-67; Llanelli 67-72; V of Clydach 72-82; Llanrhos Dio St A from 82. *Llanrhos Vicarage, Vicarage Road, Llandudno, Gwyn.* (Llandudno 76152)

JENKINS, William Frederick. b 08. St Jo Coll Dur BA 33, MA 38. **d** 35 **p** 36 Blackb. C of The Sav Blackb 35-38; Ch Ch Chadderton 38-40; V of Ch Ch Dover 40-44; Ch of the Sav Blackb 44-53; St Paul Hyson Green Nottm 53-60; V of Histon

60-75; L to Offic Dio Blackb from 75. *6 Warwick Drive, Clitheroe, Lancs.* (Clitheroe 22460)

JENKINS, William Morgan. b 13. Univ of Wales, BA 36, 2nd cl Welsh 37. St D Coll Lamp 37. **d** 39 **p** 40 St D. C of Pontyberem 39-42; Llandyssul 42-46; R of Capel Cynon w Talgarreg 46-54; V of Llanpumpsaint 54-67; Llanrhystyd w Llanddeiniol Dio St D from 67. *3 Pentre Isaf, Llanrhystud, Dyfed.* (Llanon 448)

JENKINSON, James Anthony. St Jo Coll Morpeth, 40. **d** and **p** 41 River. C of Hay 41-44; R of Berrigan 44-46; C (Col Cl Act) of Epsom 51-52; Ludlow 52-53; St Kilda Vic 53; I of E Thornbury 53-61; Perm to Offic Dio Melb from 61. *21 Chambers Street, South Yarra, Vic 3141, Australia.*

JENKS, Gregory Charles. b 52. St Francis Coll Brisb 77. **d** 78 **p** 79 Brisb. C of St Matthias Zillmere and of St Matt Grovely 78-80; P-in-c of Deception Bay Dio Brisb from 80. *7 Oxley Street, Deception Bay, Queensland, Australia 4508.*

JENKS, Canon Raymond Barry. Angl Th Coll BC. **d** 64 **p** 65 New Westmr. C of St Jo Evang N Vancouver 64-66; I of Sechelt 66-70; Departure Bay and Lantzville 71-75; St Geo Mart Vic 75-79; Hon Can of BC from 79; Dir of Programme Dio BC from 79; Exam Chap to Bp of BC from 79. *912 Vancouver Street, Victoria, BC, Canada.* (604-386 7781)

JENKYNS, Henry Derrik George. b 30. Sarum Th Coll 57. **d** 60 **p** 61 Pet. C of St Pet and St Paul Kettering 60-64; V of St Geo Shrewsbury 64-71; St Paul's Wood Green Wednesbury 71-76; Stokesay Dio Heref from 76; P-in-c of Acton-Scott Dio Heref from 76; RD of Condover from 80. *Stokesay Vicarage, Clun Road, Craven Arms, Shropshire, SY7 9QY.* (058-82 2797)

JENKYNS, John Thomas William Basil. Late Scho of St D Coll Lamp BA 54. St Cath S Ox BA 57, MA 62. Wycl Hall, Ox 54. **d** 57 **p** 58 Lon. C of Neasden 57-60; S Lyncombe (in c of St Phil and St Jas) 60-64; V of Gt Harwood 64-66; R of Colne 66-69; Surr from 66; V of Chard Dio B & W from 69. *Vicarage, Chard, Somt.* (Chard 2320)

JENKYNS, Percy. b 1899. St D Coll Lamp BA 26. **d** 26 Swan B **p** 27 St D. C of St Jude Swansea 26-27; Conwil Gaio 27-29; Llandingat 29-32; Clun 32-35; V of Bettws-y-Crwyn w Newcastle 35-42; Dioc Insp of Schs 35-47; R of Jackfield 42-47; Tacolneston 47-56; V of Fundenhall 47-56; Gt w L Hockham, Wretham and Illington 56-69. *10 Trinity Hospital, Clun, Craven Arms, SY7 8LE.*

JENKYNS, Thomas John Blackwell. b 31. St D Coll Lamp BA 52. **d** 54 St D **p** 55 Llan for St D. C of St Paul Llanelly 54-58; Windsor 58-64; Chap RAF from 64. *c/o Ministry of Defence, Adastral House, Theobalds Road, WC1.*

JENNER, John Peter. b 52. Univ of New Engl BEcon 73, BA, BD. Moore Th Coll Syd ThL 77. **d** 79 **p** 80 Armid. C of Gunnedah Dio Armid from 79. *12 Jensen Street, Gunnedah, NSW, Australia 2380.*

JENNER, Leonard David. Bp's Univ Lennox BA 61. **d** and **p** 61 Niag. C of St Geo Guelph 61-64; I of Lillooet 64-66; St Phil Vancouver 66-67; St John Vic, BC 67-70; R of St Alb Port Alberni 70-74; on leave. *RR2, Wentworth Road, Courtenay, BC, Canada.*

JENNER, Michael Albert. b 37. Oak Hill Coll 75. **d** 77 **p** 78 Nor. C of St Cath Mile Cross Nor 77-80; P-in-c of Ellington Dio Ely from 80; Grafham Dio Ely from 80; Spaldwick w Barham and Woolley Dio Ely from 80; Easton Dio Ely from 80. *Ellington Vicarage, Huntingdon, PE18 0AB.* (Huntingdon 890118)

JENNER, William Jack. b 06. AKC (2nd cl) 32. **d** 32 **p** 33 Chelmsf. C of St Columba Wanstead Slip 32-34; St Pet Limehouse 34-37; Leigh-on-Sea 37-40; Chap HM Pris Birm 40-42; V of St Jude w St Matthias Bris 42-50; St Geo Southall 50-58; St Silas Pentonville Islington 58-63; Can Missr Dio Br Hond 63-64; V of St Mich AA Bedford Pk 65-78; Perm to Offic Dios Portsm and Lon from 79. *5 Brooklands Cottage, Sheet, Petersfield, GU32 2AG.*

JENNETT, Maurice Arthur. b 34. Univ of Dur BA 60. Cranmer Hall, Dur 60. **d** 62 **p** 63 Ches. C of Marple 62-67; V of Withnell 67-75; Stranton w W Hartlepool Dio Dur from 75; Surr from 78. *34 Westbourne Road, Hartlepool, Cleve.* (Hartlepool 63190)

JENNINGS, David. b 48. K Coll Lon AKC, BD 73. St Aug Coll Cant 73. **d** 74 **p** 75 Worc. C of Halesowen w Hasbury and Lapal 74-77; Perm to Offic Dio Leic 78-81; Dio Birm from 79; Commun Relns Officer Dio Leic from 81; P-in-c of Snibston dio Leic from 81. *Vicarage, Highfield Street, Coalville, Leicester.*

JENNINGS, David Willfred Michael. b 44. K Coll Lon and Warm AKC 66. **d** 67 Warrington for Liv **p** 68 Liv. C of Walton-on-the-Hill 67-69; Christchurch w Mudeford 69-73; V of Hythe 73-80; Romford Dio Chelmsf from 80; Exam Chap to Bp of Win 76-80. *15 Oaklands Avenue, Romford, Essex.* (Romford 40385)

JENNINGS, Eric Parry. b 1893. Qu Coll Cam BA and LLB 14, MA 20. Ridley Hall, Cam. **d** 21 **p** 22 Win. C of St Jas Shirley 21-23; St Luke Hampstead 23-24; Org Sec CMS Dios Chelmsf and St E 24-28; CMS Sec for Miss Service League 28-31; V of St Mich AA Blackheath 31-33; Ch Ch Croydon 33-41; C of Pulborough 41-42; V of Chapel Royal Brighton 42-60; C-in-c of St Jo Bapt Conv Distr Hove 60-65. *Elizabeth Cottage, New Road, Keyhaven, Lymington, Hants.*

JENNINGS, Francis Kingston. b 16. Trin Coll Dub BA 39. **d** and **p** 41 Clogh. C of Mucknoe w Crossduff and Broomfield 41-52; I of Kilmore w Drumsnatt 52-57; R of Charlestown w Ardee Dio Arm from 57; Collon w Tullyallen Dio Arm from 64; RD of Athirdee and Drogheda from 62; Dundalk from 62. *Rectory, Ardee, Co Louth, Irish Republic.* (Ardee 4320)

JENNINGS, George. b 20. BD (Lon) 64. Oak Hill Th Coll 46. **d** 51 **p** 52 Bradf. C of Laister Dyke 51-53; Morden 53-56; V of Houghton 56-66; St Mark Haydock 66-77; Newburgh Dio Liv from 77. *Newburg Vicarage, Parbold, Wigan, Lancs, WN8 7XB.* (Parbold 3267)

JENNINGS, Harold Andrew. b 15. FTCL 37. St Deiniol's Libr Hawarden 63. **d** 63 **p** 64 Swan B. C of St Gabr Swansea 63-67; R of Aberedw w Llandilo-Graban and Llanbadarn-y-Garreg 67-79; V of Knighton and Norton Dio Swan B from 79. *Vicarage, Knighton, Powys, LD7 1AG.* (Knighton 566)

JENNINGS, Henry Allan. b 17. St Edm Hall Ox BA (3rd cl Or Stud) 39, MA 45. St Steph Ho Ox 40. **d** 41 Linc **p** 42 Grimsby for Linc. C of Holbeach 41-44; St Mich AA Summertown 44-46; Skegness 46-49; PC of Wildmore w Langrick and Thornton-le-Fen 49-56; R of Skirbeck 56-68; Chap City of Linc Hosps 68-78; V of Bicker Dio Linc from 78. *Bicker Vicarage, Boston, Lincs, PE20 3BX.* (Spalding 820574)

JENNINGS, Henry Leonard. Univ of W Ont BA 35, LTh 36. Hur Coll Ont. **d** 35 **p** 36 Hur for Athab. C of Ch of Redeemer Lon 35-36; Miss of Fort Norman 36-40; Fort Smith 40-41; I of Thedford 41-42; Morpeth 42-48; RD of Kent from 46; I of Brantford 48-52; Lucknow 52-60; Brussels 60-66; Huntingford 66-68. *Box 733, Wingham, Ont, Canada.*

JENNINGS, Kenneth Neal. b 30. CCC Cam 2nd cl Hist Trip pt i 53, BA (2nd cl Th Trip pt ia) 54, MA 58. Cudd Coll 54. **d** 56 Dover for Cant **p** 57 Cant. C of H Trin Ramsgate 56-59; Lect Bp's Coll Calc 59-61; Vice-Prin 61-66; Vice-Prin Cudd Coll Ox 67-73; V of Hitchin Dio St Alb 73-76; R from 77. *21 West Hill, Hitchin, Herts, SG5 2HZ.* (Hitchin 4017)

JENNINGS, Paul Warwick. b 55. Univ of Birm BSc 77. Coll of Resurr Mirfield 77. **d** 80 **p** 81 Worc. C of St Jas Dudley Dio Worc from 80. *11 Kew Drive, Dudley, W Midlands.*

JENNINGS, Peter Harold Charles. Qu Coll Cam 2nd cl Math Trip pt i 50, BA (3rd cl pt ii) 52, MA 56. Chich Th Coll 54. **d** 56 Bp Hawkes for Cant **p** 57 Guildf. C of Shalford 56-58; Netteswell 58-59; Caversham NZ 60-61; V of Wakatipu 61-64; Bluff w Stewart I 64-68; L to Offic Dio Wel 68-70; Chap Vic Univ Wel 68-72; Hon C of Kelburn 70-72; Brooklyn Wel 72-76. *49 Hicks Close, Whitby, Paremata, NZ.*

JENNINGS, Peter James. b 28. St D Coll Lamp BA 56. **d** 57 **p** 58 Worc. C of St John Dudley 57-60; Dudley (in c of St Jas Gt) 61-64; Chap HM Borstal Portland 64-66; HM Pris Wakef 66-70; HM Pris Liv 70-76; HM Pris Styal Wilmslow from 76; RD of Walton 75-76. *2 Clifton Drive, Meadow Way, Wilmslow, Ches.* (Alderley Edge 584415)

JENNINGS, Robert Charles. b 31. St Edm Hall Ox BA 56. St Steph Ho Ox 55. **d** 57 **p** 58 Lich. C of St Mary and St Chad Longton 57-60; Ascot Heath 60-62; K Chas Mart S Mymms 62-64; C-in-c of St Jo Div Vartry Road Tottenham 64-70; Chap to Bp of Willesden 66-73; L to Offic Dio Lon 70-73; C-in-c of Perivale 73; R of Letchworth 73-78; Hayes Dio Lon from 78; Surr 73-78. *170 Church Road, Hayes, Middx, UB3 2LR.* (01-573 2470)

JENNINGS, Robert Henry. b 46. St Jo Coll Dur BA (2nd cl Th) 69, MA 79. Qu Coll Birm Dipl Th 71. **d** 72 **p** 73 Glouc. C of Dursley 72-74; Coleford 75-78; Team V of Bottesford w Ashby Dio Linc from 78. *Riddings Vicarage, Enderby Road, Scunthorpe, S Humb, DN17 2JX.*

JENNINGS, Canon Ronald Osmund. Univ of Leeds BA (2nd cl Hist) 42. BD (Lon) 56. Bps' Coll Cheshunt 42. **d** 44 **p** 45 Worc. C of St Edm Dudley 44-47; Chap RAFVR 47-49; V of St Mich Handsworth 49-61; Commiss River 49-61 from 69-77; Archd of Gambia 61-63; V of St Ives (w Oldhurst and Woodhurst to 68) Dio Ely from 63; Surr from 63; RD of St Ives 69-72; Hon Can of Gambia from 70. *Vicarage, St Ives, Cambs, PE17 4DH.* (St Ives 63254)

JENNINGS, Thomas Robert. Trin Coll Dub BA 47, MA 51. **d** 48 **p** 49 Derry. C of Drumragh 48-51; CF 51-67; I of Killeshandra 67-70; Newcastle Dio Glendal from 70. *Newcastle, Co Wicklow, Irish Republic.* (Newc 819255)

JENNINGS, Walter James. b 37. Univ of Birm BMus 60. Qu Coll Birm 77. **d** 80 **p** 81 Birm. Hon C of Hampton-in-Arden Dio Birm from 80. *46 Winterbourne Road, Solihull, W Midl, B91 1LX.*

JENNISON, Ronald Bernard. b 27. Chich Th Coll 57. **d** 59 **p** 60 York. C of Thornaby-on-Tees 59-62; V of St Mich AA

Hull 62-69; H Trin Bridlington (and Sewerby w Marton from 77) 69-79; Sewerby w Marton 69-77; Chap at Marseille and St Raphael Dio Gibr (Gibr in Eur from 80) from 79. *52 rue Raphael, Saint Giniez, Marseille, France.* (91-771280)

JENNO, Charles Henry. b 25. Wells Th Coll 65. **d** 66 **p** 67 Bris. C of Shirehampton 66-69; Fishponds 69-73; V of Thornes 73-78; Carleton Dio Wakef from E Hardwick Dio Wakef from 78. *Carleton Vicarage, Pontefract, W Yorks, WF8 3RW.* (Pontefract 702478)

JENSEN, Clarence Colin. d 47 **p** 48 Queb. C of Sherbrooke 47-49; Miss P Dio Queb 49-52; CF (Canad) from 52. *Department of National Defence, Ottawa 4, Canada.*

JENSEN, Daniel Irwin. St Jo Coll Auckld 62. NZ BD of Th Stud LTh (1st cl) 65. **d** 65 **p** 66 Dun. C of Invercargill 65-69; Gisborne 69-75; V of Opotiki 75-81; St Aug Napier Dio Wai from 81. *46 Riverbend Road, Napier, NZ.* (437-823)

JENSEN, Erik Henning. b 33. Univ of Copenhagen BPhil 51. Univ of Harvard STM 54. Worc Coll Ox BLitt 58, DPhil 69. Ripon Hall Ox 56. **d** 58 **p** 59 Chelmsf for Lon. C of Highwood 58-59; C of Simanggang 59-61; L to Offic Dio Borneo 61-62; Dio Kuch 62-66. *c/o USPG, 15 Tufton Street SW1.*

JENSEN, Peter Frederick. Univ of Lon BD 70. Univ of Syd MA 76. Univ of Ox DPhil 80. Moore Th Coll Syd ACT ThL 69. **d** 69 **p** 70 Syd. C of St Barn Syd 69-76; Lect Moore Th Coll Syd 73-76 and from 80; Perm to Offic Dio Ox 76-79. *40 Carillon Avenue, Newtown, NSW, Australia 2042.* (51-5787)

JENSEN, Phillip David. b 45. Univ of Syd BA 67. Moore Coll Syd ACT ThL 69. Univ of Lon BD 70. **d** 70 **p** 71 Syd. C of St Matt Manly 70-73; Asst Dioc Missr Syd 73-75; Chap Univ of NSW from 75; R of Centennial Pk Dio Syd from 78. *59 Garden Street, Maroubra, NSW, Australia.* (349-2763)

JENSEN, Raymond Ernest. Bp's Univ Lennox BA 50. Univ of Montr MA 57. **d** 59 **p** 60 Queb. Chap Lower Canada Coll Montr 60-69; Baron Byng High Sch Montr 69-72; Hon C of H Trin Cathl Queb 72-80; La Tuque Dio Queb from 80. *929 Valcartier Boulevard, Loretteville, PQ, Canada.*

JENSON, Francis William. St Thos Coll Colom 35. **d** 37 **p** 39 Antig. C of St John's Cathl Antig 37-40; P-in-c St Pet Montserrat 40; R of St Mary Antig 40-43; Ch Ch w H Trin Saba 43-52; P-in-c of Aruba and Curacao 43-45; V of St Sav Barb 52-54; St Silas and St Alb Barb 54-71; R of H Trin I and Dio Barb from 71. *Holy Trinity Rectory, St Philip, Barbados, W Indies.*

JEPHSON, Douglas Ronald Shipstone. b 17. St Jo Coll Dur BA 38, MA 43. **d** 40 **p** 41 Ripon. C of St Jo Evang Wortley 40-43; Armley 43-45; St Mark Woodhouse 45-47; PC of Riddings 47-54; V of Elmton w Creswell 54-70; Tysoe w Compton-Wynyates and Oxhill Dio Cov from 70; Whatcote Dio Cov from 76. *Tysoe Vicarage, Warwick.* (Tysoe 201)

JEPPS, Philip Anthony. b 34. BNC Ox BA (2nd cl Mod Lang) 58, MA 68. Wycl Hall Ox 58. **d** 60 Man **p** 73 Pet. C of All SS, Elton 60-61; Perm to Offic Dio Pet 70-73; R of Ch Brampton w Chap Brampton 73-80; P-in-c of Harlestone 79-80; V of St Andr Kettering Dio Pet from 80. *St Andrew's Vicarage, Kettering, Northants.* (Kettering 2754)

JEREMIAH, Francis Roy. b 11. St D Coll Lamp Th Sch 30, Hebr Scho 31, BA (2nd cl Th) and Hebr Pri 33. **d** 34 **p** 35 Man. C of St Bride Stretford 34-37; St Geo Altrincham 37-39; St Sampson Guernsey 39-40; St Geo Mossley 41-43; R of Ch Ch Bradford 43-45; V of H Trin Guernsey 45-54; LPr Dio S'wark and Deputn Sec Miss to Lepers 54-62; Warden Home of Div Healing Kearnsey Natal 62-64; Chap Lon Healing Miss 65-77. *20 Dawson Place, W2 4TL.*

JERMAN, Cecil Maldwyn. b 13. Late Exhib of St D Coll Lamp BA (2nd cl Hist Hons) 34. St Mich Coll Llan 34. **d** 36 Swan B for Ban **p** 37 Ban. C of Harlech 36-37; Llanfechell 37-38; Llandegai 38-41; C-in-c of Llandegai w Tregarth 41-44; C of Hoylake 45-48; V of St Barn Crewe 48-55; Surr from 49; V of St Jas New Brighton 55-74; L to Offic Dio Ban from 75. *Bryn Haul, Llaneilian, Amlwch, Anglesey.*

JERMY, Jack. ACP 65. Ripon Hall, Ox 64. **d** 65 **p** 66 Man. C of SS Simon and Jude Bolton 65-74 C-in-c of Rivington Dio Man from 74. *Vicarage, Rivington Lane, Horwich, Bolton, BL6 7SL.* (Horwich 66198)

JERMYN, Peter. b 20. Chich Th Coll 65. **d** 67 Lon **p** 68 Willesden for Lon. C of St Mary Virg Primrose Hill Hampstead 67-70; R of Gunthorpe w Bale 70-73; C-in-c of Sharrington 70-73; V of St Mary Virg Kenton Dio Lon from 73. *St Mary's Vicarage, Kenton, Harrow, Middx, HA3 8EJ.* (01-907 2914)

JEROME, Charles Stephen. b 17. Linc Th Coll 48. **d** 50 **p** 51 Leic. C of Birstall and Wanlip 50-52; CF 52-55; Min of Eccles Distr St Chad Leic 55-59; V of St Aid w St Luke Sheff 59-66; Dir Chr Stewardship Dio Derby 66-71; R of Shardlow w Gt Wilne 66-68; C-in-c of Elvaston w Thulston and Ambaston (V 67) 66-68; V of Denby 69-71; Dir Chr Stewardship Dio Ely from 71; P-in-c of Holywell w Needingworth 71-78; V of Impington Dio Ely from 78. *Vicarage, Impington Lane, Cambridge, CB4 4NJ.* (Histon 2826)

JERRAM, Herbert Lennox Jenner. Down Coll Cam 3rd cl Engl Trip pt i 33, BA (3rd cl Arch and Anth Trip Sect B) 34, MA 38. Westcott Ho Cam 34. **d** 36 **p** 37 Ox. C of Beaconsfield 36-42; V of Barton St D (w Kingweston R) 42-48; R of Milton 48-66; Perm to Offic Dios Ox and Chich from 66. *Fluellen, Maudlyn Close, Steyning, Sussex, BN4 3PQ.* (Steyning 812654)

✠ **JERRIM, Right Rev Henry Allingham.** ACT ThL (2nd cl) 39. **d** 40 **p** 41 Tas. C of H Trin Hobart 40-41; P-in-c of Smithton 41-43 Chap AIF 43-45; R of Cullenswood 45-46; Cygnet 47-49; Devonport 49-58; St Steph Hobart 58-61; St John Launceston 61-70; Can of St D Cathl Hobart 65-66; Chan 66-67; Archd of Launceston 67-70; R of St Jo Bapt Hobart 70-74; Archd of Hobart from 70; Cons Asst Bp of Tas in St D Cathl Hobart 21 Dec 74 by Abp of Melb; Bp of Tas; and Bps G B Muston and G F Cranswick. *72 Augusta Road, Lenah Valley, Hobart, Tasmania 7008.* (002-28 3819)

JERRY-COOPER, Herbert Alfred. AKC (NS) 62. Sarum Th Coll 52. **d** 56 **p** 57 Bran. I of Holland 56-58; R of St Mary Virg Bran 58-75; Hon Can of Bran 65-75; Synod Sec 72-75; Chap Lakehead Hosp from 75. *Lakehead Psychiatric Hospital, Thunder Bay, Ont., Canada.*

JERSEY, Dean of (Dio Win). *See* Goss, Very Rev Thomas Asworth.

JERUSALEM, Lord Bishop in. *See* Haddad, Right Rev Faik Ibrahim.

JERUSALEM, Assistant Bishop in. *See* Khoury, Right Rev Elia Khader.

JERUSALEM, Dean of. *See* Elliott, Very Rev David.

JERVIS, Clement Frank Cooper. b 16. St Jo Coll Dur LTh 39, BA 40, MA 45. St Aid Coll 36. **d** 40 **p** 41 Lich. C of St Matt Wolverhampton 40-43; LPr Dio Lich 43-46; V of Wilnecote 46-56; Pensnett 56-80. *Address temp unknown.*

JERVIS, Preb Horace Roland. b 14. St Jo Coll Dur LTh 38, BA 39. St Aid Coll 35. **d** 39 **p** 40 Lich. C of St Luke Cannock 39-43; C-in-c of St John Heath Hayes Cannock 43-49; V of Donnington Wood 49-79; Preb of Lich Cathl 77-79; Preb (Emer) from 79. *27a Kilnbank Road, Market Drayton, Salop, TF9 1LB.*

JERVIS, Canon John William. b 17. Univ of Dur LTh 42, BA 45. St Aid Coll 39. **d** 42 **p** 43 Chelmsf. C of St Jo Evang Walthamstow 42-44; St Matt Preston 45-48; V of St Ann Warrington 48-51; St Sav Preston Lancs 51-55; St John Idle 55-65; St Mark Low Moor Dio Bradf from 65; RD of Bowling (and Horton from 73) 68-78; Hon Can of Bradf from 72. *St Mark's Vicarage, Low Moor, Bradford, Yorks.* (Bradford 677754)

JERVIS, William Edward. b 47. ARICS 74. Linc Th Coll 74. **d** 77 **p** 78 Lich. C of All SS W Bromwich 77-80; Horsham Dio Chich from 80. *Trinity House, Blunts Way, Horsham, RH12 2BJ.* (Horsham 65401)

JERVIS-READ, Canon Robert Shellard. Bp's Coll Lennox BA 49, MA 53, BD 59. **d** 50 **p** 51 Ott. C of Cornwall 50-51; I of Cobden 51-57; W Sherbrooke (w E Sherbrooke from 60) 57-64; R of Coaticook 64-71; Exam Chap to Bp of Queb 67-76; I of Cookshire Dio Queb from 71; Sand Hill Dio Queb from 71; Can of Queb from 78. *RR1, Martinville, PQ, Canada.*

JERWOOD, Bernard Ellery. b 1892. SS Coll Cam BA 14, MA 20, BChir 22, MD 24. MRCS and LRCP 16. **d** 49 **p** 50 Nor. C of St Anne Earlham 49-53; LPr Dio Nor 53-70; Perm to Offic Dio Chich 70-72. *c/o 15 Highland Road, Chichester, Sussex.*

JESSETT, David Charles. b 55. AKC and BD 77. Westcott Ho Cam 78. **d** 79 Bradwell for Chelmsf **p** 80 Chelmsf. C of Aveley Dio Chelmsf from 79. *184 Centurion Way, Purfleet, Essex.*

JESSINGHOUSE, D.E.. d 76 E Newfld. Perm to Offic Dio E Newfld from 76. *c/o 68 Queen's Road, St John's, Newfoundland, Canada.*

JESSOP, Gilbert Laird Osborne. b 06. Ch Coll Cam BA 29, MA 34. Ridley Hall Cam 29. **d** 31 **p** 32 Portsm. C of Havant 31-34; Chap Qu Coll Cam and Cam Pastorate and C of St Andr Gt Cam 34-36; V of Fordington St Geo 36-56; Surr 36-56; Chap RNVR 40-46; V of Tacarigua Trinid 56-58; Perm to Offic Dio Syd 58-61; Prin Boys' Home Newhaven Phillip I 61-64; Supt Boy's Home Clifton Ja 64-65; P-in-c of Kew Pk 65-66; R of Annotto Bay 66-68; Kegworth 68-71; L to Offic Dio B & W from 72; Master of St Jo Hosp Bath Dio B & W from 75. *Master's Lodge, St John's Hospital, Bath, BA1 1SL.* (0225-64972)

JESSUP, Edmund Francis. b 14. Univ of Dur LTh 39. St Aug Coll Cant 36. **d** 39 **p** 40 Sheff. C of Goole 39-42; CF (EC) 42-50; CF (TA) from 50; Hon CF 50; R of Babworth Dio

Southw from 50. *Babworth Rectory, Retford, Notts.* (Retford 703253)

JESSUP, Gordon Ernest. b 36. BA (Lon) 59. Oak Hill Th Coll 57. **d** 61 **p** 62 Roch. C of Barnehurst 61-64; St Pet Rushden 64-67; SE Sec CMJ 67-76; Youth Sec 68-78; Tr Officer CMJ from 78; SE Secr CMJ from 80; Hon C of St Barn Woodside Park 78-80. *83 Brampton Road, Bexleyheath, Kent, DA7 4SH.*

JESSUP, William Roy. b 27. BSc (Lon) 48. Ridley Hall Cam. **d** 61 **p** 62 St E. C of Walton 61-64; R of Tuddenham w Cavenham Dio St E from 64; C-in-c of Eriswell 75-78. *Rectory, Eriswell, Suff.*

JESUTHASAN, Samuel Sebenesan. St Pet Hall Sing BTh 60. Trin Th Coll Sing. **d** 60 **p** 61 Sing. P 60-70; Dioc Sec Dio W Mal 70-72. *2-b Pesiaran Gurney, Kuala Lumpur, Malaya.*

JEVONS, Alan Neil. b 56. Univ of Ex BA 77. Selw Coll Cam BA (Th) 80. Ridley Hall Cam 78. **d** 81 Worc. C of Halesowen Dio Worc from 81. *48 Tenbury House, Highfield Lane, Halesowen, W Midl, B63 4RN.*

JEWELL, Charles John. b 15. Bps' Coll Cheshunt, 46. **d** 49 **p** 50 Bris. C of St Aug Swindon 49-52; CF 52-58; C-in-c of St Chad's Conv Distr Patchway 58-61; Chap Tristan da Cunha 61; USPG Area Sec N Ireland 62-69; Dios Ex and Truro 69-71; L to Offic Dios Ex and truro 69-71; Chap Tristan da Cunha 71-75; R of St Raph Durban 75-78; Sydenham Dio Natal from 78. *80 Rippon Road, Durban, S Africa.* (Durban 331873)

JEWELL, Frederick Elmer. Bps' Univ Lennox LST 29. **d** 29 **p** 31 Alg. C of Nipigon 29-30; I of Gore Bay 30-32; Englehart 32-37; Sheguiandah 37-43; Espanola 43-47; Burk's Falls and Magnetawan 47-56; R of Brussels 56-58; I of Walpole I 58-64; Portneuf 64-69. *10a-59 Ridout Street, London, Ont, Canada.*

JEWELL, Thomas Sydney. b 47. St Jo Coll Morpeth ThL 75. **d** 75 **p** 76 Newc. C of New Lambton 75-78; Charlestown 78-80; R of Williamtown Dio Newc from 80. *Rectory, Tomaree Street, Nelson Bay, NSW, Australia 2315.* (81-1839)

JEWETT, Thomas John. b 27. Moore Th Coll Syd ACT ThL 68. **d** 68 Bp Warren for C & Goulb **p** 69 C & Goulb. C of All SS Canberra 68-69; C of Tumut 69-70; Gilgandra 71-72; R of Gulgong 72-77; Hon C of St John Glebe Syd 77-79; Res Chap Lon Healing Miss and L to Offic Dios Cant and Lon from 79. *20 Dawson Place, Bayswater, W2 4TL.* (01-229 3349)

JEWISS, Brian James. b 37. ALCD (L Th from 74) 66. **d** 66 **p** 67 Roch. C of Chatham 66-70; St Aug Bromley Common 70-72; V of Wilmington 72-79; Rochester Dio Roch from 79. *Vicarage, Delce Road, Rochester, Kent.* (Medway 45122)

JEWITT, Martin Paul Noel. b 44. K Coll Lon AKC 69. St Aug Coll Cant. **d** 70 Jarrow for Dur **p** 71 Dur. C of Usworth 70-74; Tutor Newton Coll Dogura 74-77; Team V of Usworth 77-78; V of Ascen Balham Hill Dio S'wark from 78. *22 Malwood Road, SW12 8EN.* (01-673 7666)

JEWRAM, Alan Ramlagan. b 29. **d** 70 Guy. C of St Marg, Skeldon Dio Guy from 70. *c/o St Margaret's Vicarage, Skeldon, Corentyne, Guyana.*

JEYNES, Anthony James. b 44. K Coll Lon and Warm AKC 68. **d** 69 **p** 70 Ches. C of Ellesmere Port 69-73; St Pet w St Matt Birkenhead 73-75; R of Oughtrington 75-80; C of Timperley (in c of St D Hale) Dio Ches from 80. *56 Grove Lane, Hale, Altrincham, Chesh.* (061-980 3649)

JHUBOO, Philip. Coll of Resurr Mirfield 46. **d** 48 **p** 49 Maur. C of St Paul Vacoas 48-50; Port Mathurin 50-53; Praslin 54-60; St Jas and St Paul Vacoas 60-62; R of Souillac w Rose Bell 62-74; Dom Chap to Bp of Maur 74; R of Curepipe Dio Maur from 74. *Rectory, Dupin Street, Curepipe, Mauritius.* (Curepipe 2250)

JIGNASU, Nallinkumar Hiralal. Univ of Bom BA 48. Bp Tucker Coll Mukono 68. **d** 68 Soroti **p** 69 W Bugan. P Dio Soroti 68-69; W Bugan 69-70; Dio Nam 70-73; C of St Mary Leamington 73-75; Chap St Jo Coll Port Harcourt 75-80; P-in-c of St Barn City and Dio Leic from 80. *St Barnabas Vicarage, Leicester, LE5 4BD.* (Leic 766054)

JIJI, James Ekeke. b 38. **d** 73 **p** 74 Aba. P Dio Aba. *St Silas Parsonage, Box 69, Umuahia, Nigeria.*

JINADU, Very Rev Samuel Adedayo. Melville Hall Ibad 51. **d** 52 **p** 53 Ibad. P Dio Ibad 52-75; Archd of Ibad 72-75; Provost of St John's Cathl Ilesha from 76; Exam Chap to Bp of Ilesha from 80. *St John's Cathedral, Iloro-Ilesha, Nigeria.*

JINMAN, Cecil Alfred Keith. b 20. Keble Coll Ox BA (2nd cl Th) 48. MA 51. Wycl Hall Ox. **d** 50 **p** 51 Lon. C of H Trin Southall 50-52; St Marylebone Lon 52-54; R of Bruntingthorpe 54-56; Min of St Mich AA Eccles Distr Norton 57-59; V of Claines St Geo Worc 59-76. *11 Diglis Avenue, Worcester.*

JIYA, Daniel Tsado. **d** 60 **p** 61 N Nig. P Dio N Nig. *Christ Church, Fagge, PO Box 26, Kano, Nigeria.*

JOAD, Albert Howard. b 10. LCP 54. **d** 71 **p** 72 Kens for Lon. C of SS Pet & Paul Teddington 71-76; P-in-c of All H Twickenham 76-78; L to Offic Dio Lon from 77. *84 Sussex Avenue, Isleworth, Middx, TW7 6LB.* (01-560 7898)

JOB, Canon Evan Roger Gould. b 36. Late Exhib of Magd Coll Ox BA 60, MA 64. ARCM 55. Cudd Coll 60. **d** 62 Warrington for Liv **p** 63 Liv. C of Our Lady and St Nich Liv 62-65; V of New Springs Wigan 65-70; Minor Can and Prec of Man Cathl 70-74; Prec and Sacr of Westmr Abbey 74-79; Can Res, Prec and Sacr of Win Cathl from 79. *8 The Close, Winchester, Hants.* (Win 4771)

JOB, Frederick. **d** and **p** 53 Koot. I of Windermere 53-56; L to Offic Dio Koot 56-64. *Box 212, Enderby, BC, Canada.*

JOB, Ganamoney Swamidoss Moses. St Pet Hall Sing BTh 62. Trin Th Coll Sing. **d** 60 Kuala Lumpur for Sing. **p** 62 Sing. P Dio Sing from 60. *42 Woo Mon Chew Road, Singapore 16.*

JOBBER, Barry William. b 38. Cudd Coll 73. **d** 75 **p** 76 Lich. C of Fenton 75-79; V of Goldenhill 79-80. *c/o Goldenhill Vicarage, Stoke-on-Trent, Staffs.* (Kidsgrove 2736)

JOBBINS, Boak Alexander. Univ of Syd BA 68. BD (Lon) 71. Moore Coll Syd ThL 70. **d** 71 **p** 72 Syd. C of Dural 71-74; H Trin Adel 74-77; R of Mowbray Dio Syd from 77. *44 Beaconsfield Road, Chatswood, NSW, Australia 2067.* (419-3893)

JOBLIN, Ven Vernon William. St Jo Coll Auckld LTh 40. **d** 39 Aotearoa for Wel **p** 40 Wel. C of Masterton 39-42; C-in-c of Ohakune w Raetihi 42-43; Chap RNZAF 44-46; V of Miramar Wel 46-51; Marton and Chap Dioc Sch 51-59; Levin 59-71; Hon Can of Wel 63-73; V of Kelburn Wel 71-78; Archd of Wel 73-78; Archd (Emer) from 78; Perm to Offic Dio Wel from 78. *15 Beach Road, Foxton Beach, NZ.* (7406)

JOBLING, Michael John. b 39. Perry Hall Melb 67. **d** 69 **p** 70 Melb. C of St Andr, Brighton 69-71; Dept of Evangelism and Ex and C-in-c of Croydon S 71-74; I 74-77; C in Home Miss Dept Dio Melb from 77. *4 Mimosa Court, South Croydon, Vic., Australia 3136.* (870-6507)

JOBLING, Raymond. b 23. Oak Hill Th Coll 67. **d** 67 Lon **p** 68 Kens for Lon. C of H Trin Southall 67-70; St Mary Beeston 70-72; Felixstowe 72-75; R of Thorndon w Rishangles (w Bedingfield from 78) 75-80; C-in-c of Bedingfield 75-78; R of Gt and L Glemham, Blaxhall w Stratford St Andr and Farnham Dio St E from 80. *little Glemham Rectory, Woodbridge, Suff.* (Wickham Market 746301)

JOBLING, Robert Edminston. b 45. St Paul's Th Coll Grahmstn 77. **d** 79 Bp Ndwandwe for Johann **p** 80 Johann. C of Standerton w Evander Dio Johann from 79. *PO Box 1403, Kriel, S Africa 2271.*

JOBLING, William Jeffree. ACT ThL 64. Univ of Syd BA 65, MA 70, PhD 75. Moore Th Coll Syd 62. **d** 64 **p** 65 Syd. C of St Anne Strathfield 65-66; w Bush Ch Aid S 67; P-in-c of Outer Mt Isa 67-68; Asst Master Cranbrook Sch Bellevue Hill 68-76; L to Offic Dio Syd from 68; Lect Univ of Syd from 77. *14 Violet Street, Croydon Park, NSW, Australai 2133.* (74-9430)

JOBSON, Clifford Hedley. b 31. Late Exhib of St Jo Coll Dur BA 54, Dipl Th 56. **d** 56 **p** 57 Birm. C of Hall Green 56-59; Ambleside w Rydal 59-60; R of Arthuret 60-62; CF from 62; DACG 73-78; ACG from 78; Hon Chap to HM the Queen from 80. *c/o Barclay's Bank, Ambleside, Cumbria.*

JOBSON, John Xavier. Univ of Queensld BA (1st cl Hist) 60. St Jo Coll Morpeth ACT ThL (2nd cl) 56. **d** 60 **p** 61 Newc. C of Hamilton 60-65; Tutor St Jo Coll Morpeth 65-66. *c/o General Theological Seminary, 175 9th Avenue, New York, NY 10011, USA.*

JOBSON, Paul. b 39. Wells Th Coll 62. **d** 65 **p** 66 S'wark. C of Woolwich 65-68; Chap Culham Coll Abingdon 68-72; C-in-c of St Pet Walworth Dio S'wark 72-75; Team R from 75; All SS and St Steph Walworth 73-75. *Rectory, Liverpool Grove, SE17.* (01-703 3139)

JOCKEL, Alan Keith. b 25. St Pet Hall, Ox BA 50, MA 56. Wycl Hall, Ox. 50. **d** 53 **p** 54 Sheff. C of St Mary w St Simon and St Matthias Sheff 53-56; St Jo Evang Ranmoor Sheff 56-61; V of Hillsborough and Wadsley Bridge 61-75; Totley Dio Sheff from 76. *Totley Vicarage, Sunnyvale Road, Sheffield, S17 4FA.* (Sheff 362322)

JOCZ, Jakob. Univ of Edin PhD 45, DLitt 57. St Aid Coll 34. **d** 35 **p** 36 Fulham for Lon. CMJ Miss Warsaw 35-45; Hd of CMJ Lon Miss 45-48; Sel Pr and Lect Trin Coll Dub 48; C-in-c of St John Downshire Hill Hampstead 48-56; Supt Jewish Miss Tor 56-60; Prof at Wycl Coll Tor 60-76; Exam Chap to Bp of Tor 65-76; Hon C of St Alb Tor 69-76; Ch of Messiah City and Dio Tor from 78. *c/o 60 Kendall Avenue, Toronto, M5R IL9, Ont, Canada.*

JOHANNESBURG, Lord Bishop of. *See* Bavin, Right Rev Timothy John.

JOHANNESBURG, Bishops Suffragan of. *See* Stanage, Right Rev Thomas Shaun; and Ndwande, Right Rev Mfaniseni Sigisbert.

JOHANNESBURG, Assistant Bishops of. *See* Pickard, Right Rev Stanley Chapman; Tutu, Right Rev Desmond Mpilo.

JOHANNESBURG, Dean of. *See* Nkoane, Very Rev (Simeon) Joseph.

JOHANSEN, Peter Antony. AKC 58. **d** 59 **p** 60 Lon. C of St Thos Ap Hanwell 59-60; Stanwell 60-62; V of St Aid Sudden Rochdale 62-66; Asst Master Howard Sch Welwyn Garden City 66-81. *Address temp unknown.*

JOHN, Alexander Dominic. Episc Th Sem of SW Texas BD 63. **d** 63 **p** 64 Sheff. C of H Trin Millhouses 63-65; Asst Sec WCC Geneva 65-68; C of St Mark's Cathl Bangalore 68-72; Sec Chr Conf Asia 72-73; Gen Sec Chr Lit S of India 74-78; Org Sec Angl Miss Coun of WA from 79. *58 Castle Road, Woodlands, W Australia 6018.* (446 7417)

JOHN, Canon Arthur Gwynne. b 06. St D Coll Lamp BA 31. **d** 31 **p** 32 Wakef. C of St Edw Barnsley 31-36; Todmorden 36-40; CF (EC) 40-46; V of Morley w Churwell 46-76; Surr 46-76; Hon Can of Wakef 72-76; Can (Emer) from 77. *37 Bradford Road, Drighlington, W Yorks.* (Drigh 852676)

JOHN, Arthur Wyndham. d 59 **p** 60 Bp Morris. C of Wynberg Dio Capetn 61-63; and from 67. *98 Southfield Road, Plumstead, CP, S Africa.* (77-0482)

JOHN, Benjamin Ruati. b 36. **d** 64 **p** 67 Bp Dotiro for Sudan. P Dio Sudan 64-76; Dio Yambio from 76. *ECS Ngara, West Equatorial Province, Sudan.*

JOHN, Daniel Francis. b 09. AKC 36. **d** 36 **p** 37 Heref. C of Bromyard 36-39; CF 39-41; Kington w Huntington 41-42; R of Stoke Lacy (w Much Cowarne and Moreton Jeffries from 53) 42-76; R of Ullingswick w L Cowarne 45-53; C-in-c of Pencombe w Marston Stannett and Little Cowarne 68-76; Perm to Offic Dio Heref from 76. *Winslow Croft, Bromyard, HR7 4SE.*

JOHN, David Michael. b 36. St D Coll Lamp BA 57. St Mich Coll Llan 57. **d** 59 **p** 60 Mon. C of Pontypool 59-61; Roath 61-66; Asst Chap HM Pris Walton Liv 66-67; Chap HM Pris Ex 67-68; V of Ystrad Rhondda 68-76; Pontyclun w Talygarn Dio Llan from 76. *Vicarage, Pontyclun, Mid-Glam, CF7 9AJ.* (Pontyclun 477)

JOHN, Elwyn Crebey. b 36. St D Coll Lamp BA 57. St Mich Coll Llan 57. **d** 59 **p** 60 Swan B. C of Llanguicke and Pontardawe 59-62; Llandrindod w Cefnllys 62-66; V of Beguildy w Crugbyddor and Heyope 66-79; Builth and Llanddewir Cwm w Maesmynis, Llanynys and Alltmaur Dio Swan B from 79. *Vicarage, Builth Wells, Powys.* (Builth 2355)

JOHN, Canon Gwynfor. b 08. St D Coll Lamp BA 33. **d** 33 **p** 34 Worc. C of Cradley Heath 33-36; Kidderminster 36-43; V of Clent 44-75; RD of Swinford (Stourbridge from 72) 62-72; Surr 65-75; Hon Can of Worc 69-75; Can (Emer) from 75. *5 Summervale Road, W Hagley, Stourbridge, W Midl.* (Hagley 5718)

JOHN, Islwyn David. St D Coll Lamp BA 56. **d** 58 **p** 59 St D. C of Brynamman 58-61; St D Carmarthen 61-64; V of Penbryn w Blaenporth 64-68; Llandyssul Dio St D from 68. *Vicarage, Llandyssul, Dyfed.* (Llandyssul 2277)

JOHN, James Emrys. Univ of Wales BA 34. Clifton Th Coll 35. **d** 36 **p** 37 St A. C of Holywell 36-41; Newtown (Monts) 41-44; R of Pont Robert 44-49; V of Broughton 49-74; Surr from 55. *11 Burton Drive, Little Acton, Wrexham, Clwyd.*

JOHN, James Richard. b 21. Ch Coll Cam BA 47, MA 49. Cudd Coll 47. **d** 49 **p** 50 Roch. C of Sidcup 49-52; V of Gillingham w Upberry 52-66; RD of Gillingham 60-66; Surr from 60; V of St Jas Bolton w St Chrys Bradf 66-78; R of Guiseley Dio Bradf from 78; Surr from 78; RD of Otley from 80. *Rectory, The Green, Guiseley, Leeds.* (Guiseley 74321)

JOHN, Jeffrey Philip Hywel. b 52. Hertf Coll Ox BA 75, BA (Th) 77, MA 78. St Steph Ho Ox 75. **d** 78 Bp Reece for Llan **p** 79 Llan. C of Penarth w Lavernock 78-80. *c/o Holy Nativity Church House, Windsor Road, Penarth, S Glam.* (0222-701144)

JOHN, Meurig Hywel. b 46. St D Coll Lamp 69. **d** 71 **p** 72 St D. C of Ch Ch Llanelli 71-74; V of Penrhyncoch w Elerch 74-79; Llanfihangel Aberbythick 79-81; R of Cilgerran w Bridell Dio St D from 81. *Rectory, Cilgerran, Dyfed.*

JOHN, Robert Michael. b 46. Univ of Edin BSc 67. Univ of Man MSc 68, PhD 70. Univ of Otago BD 78. St Jo Coll Auckld. **d** 78 Wai. C of Tauranga 78-80; Hastings Dio Wai from 80. *502 Southampton Street West, Hastings, NZ.* (88-967)

JOHN, Samuel. b 52. **d** 79 **p** 81 Mal. P Dio W Mal. *c/o St John's Church, Jalan St John, Ipoh, Perak, Malaysia.*

JOHN, Sidney Arthur Charles Bernard. b 13. Late Exhib of Jes Coll Ox BA (Chem) 35, MA 39. **d** 38 **p** 39 S'wark. C of St Paul Newington 38-40; St Barn Rotherhithe 40; St Olave Mitcham 41-44; PV of Wells Cathl 44-47; C of Landore (in c of St Alb Treboeth) 47-49; St Aug Belvedere 49-50; H Trin Eltham 51; St Clem E Dulwich 51-55; V of St Phil Sydenham 55-58; R of Syderstone w Tattersett 58-65; C-in-c of Barmer 58-65; PC (V from 69) of Gt Barlow 65-78; Chap R Hosp Chesterfield from 80. *15 Avondale Road, Chesterfield, Derbys, S40 4TF.* (Chesterfield 72768)

JOHN, William Glyndwr. b 21. Roch Th Coll. **d** 60 **p** 61 S'wark. C of Streatham 60-64; V of Castleton Derbys 64-69; Frizinghall 69-73; Long Preston 73-80; Sutton-in-Craven Dio Bradf from 80; C-in-c of Rathmell-in-Craven w Wigglesworth 74-80. *Sutton-in-Craven Vicarage, Keighley, W Yorks.* (Cross Hills 33372)

JOHNS, Adam Aubrey. b 34. Trin Coll Dub BA 57, Div Test 58. New Univ of Ulster BA 75. **d** 58 **p** 59 Down. C of Aghalee 58-61; Derriaghy 61-63; I of Billy (w Derrykeighan from 77) Dio Connor from 63. *Derrykeighan Rectory, Dervock, Co Antrim, N Ireland.* (Dervock 241)

JOHNS, Alexander Anthony. b 27. St Barn Coll Adel 81. **d** 80 Bal. Perm to Offic Dio Bal from 80. *c/o St Barnabas College, Belair, SA 5052, Australia.*

JOHNS, (William) Andrew Peter Stabback. M SSF 51. St Francis Coll Brisb. **d** 67 **p** 68 Brisb. Perm to Offic Dio Brisb 67-69 and from 75. *131 Brookfield Road, Brookfield, Brisbane, Queensland, Australia 4069.* (378 2160)

JOHNS, Bernard Thomas. b 36. Univ of Birm BSc (3rd cl Phys) 58. St Mich Coll Llan 61. **d** 63 Llan **p** 64 Bp Hughes for Llan. C of Aberavon 63-65; St Andr Maj w Dinas Powis and Michaelston-le-Pit 65-70; V of St Andr w St Teilo Cardiff 70-76; Roath Dio Llan from 76. *Roath Vicarage, Waterloo Road, Cardiff, CF2 5AD.* (Cardiff 484808)

JOHNS, Courtney. Codr Coll Barb 50. **d** 52 **p** 53 Barb. C of St Leon Barb 52-53; Ch Ch Barb 53; V of St Phil L Barb 53-56; St Ambrose Barb 56-59; R of Black Torrington 59-63; V of Princetown w Postbridge and Huccaby 63-75; Chap HM Pris Dartmoor 63-75; Perm to Offic Dio Ex from 76. *2 Brookside Close, Kilmington, Axminster, Devon.*

JOHNS, James Dudley. b 09. Selw Coll Cam 2nd cl Hist Trip pt i 33, BA 34, 3rd cl Th Trip pt i 35, MA 38. Ridley Hall Cam 34. **d** 36 **p** 37 Chelmsf. C of Moulsham 36-39; Grays Thurrock 39-41; V of All SS Forest Gate 41-49; Chelmsf Dioc Insp of Schs 46-53; Res Chap Butlin's Camp Clacton 47-48; Chap of Selw Coll Cam 49-53; Dean 51-53; Staff Sec to SCM for Univ of Cam 49-51; Chap and Asst Master Barnard Castle Sch 53-64; St Geo Sch Harpenden 64-69; L to Offic Dio Dur 53-64; Dio St Alb 64-69; Perm to Offic Dio Chelmsf 49-69; V of Gt w L Wymondley (w Graveley and Chivesfield from 80) 69-81. *Apple Tree Cottage, Hales Street, Tivetshall St Margaret, Norwich, NR15 2EE.* (T St M 357)

JOHNS, Richard Gray. b 28. Whitman Coll Wasington BA 49. Ch Div Sch of the Pacific Calif MDiv 55. **d** and **p** 55 Calif. In Amer Ch 55-72; Dir of Resources Angl Ch of Canada from 72. *600 Jarvis Street, Toronto, Ont, Canada.*

JOHNS, Robert Mills. b 36. Trin Coll Dub BA 59, Abp King Pri (1st) 59, Div Test (2nd cl) 60, MA 69. **d** 60 **p** 61 Connor. C of Larne 60-64; Ballymena 64-65; R of Aghavilly w Derrynoose 65-72; Moy w Charlemont 72-80. *Address temp unknown.*

JOHNS, Ronald Charles. b 37. Univ of Dur BA 59. Wells Th Coll 59. **d** 61 **p** 62 Liv. C of Wigan 61-66; Kirkby (in c of St Mark Northwood) 66-70; Ho Master Ruffwood Sch Kirkby 70-75; C of Kirkby 70-75; CF (TAVR) from 72; Dep Hd Master Old Hall High Sch Maghull 75-79; C of Maghull 75-79; P-in-c of Borrowdale and Grange Dio Carl from 79; RD of Derwent from 81. *Borrowdale Vicarage, Keswick, Cumb.* (Borrowdale 238)

JOHNS, Thomas Morton. b 43. Oak Hill Th Coll 67. **d** 70 Warrington for Liv **p** 71 Liv. C of N Meols 70-73; Farnborough 73-76; P-in-c of St Geo Conv Distr Badshot Lea Dio Guildf from 76. *St George's Parsonage, Badshot Lea, Farnham, GU9 9LD.* (Aldershot 21939)

JOHNS, Trevor Charles. b 33. St D Coll Lamp BA 57. **d** 58 **p** 59 St D. C of Pembroke 58-61; R of Walwyn's Castle w Robeston W 61-67; CF 67-75; V of Spittal w Treffgarn 75-79; C of Tring Dio St Alb 79-80; Team V from 80. *Vicarage, Watery Lane, Wilstone, Tring, Herts.* (Tring 3008)

JOHNS, Canon Vernon. b 12. St D Coll Lamp BA 33. St Mich Coll Llan 34. **d** 35 St D **p** 36 Swan B for St D. C of Llanstadwell 35-38; Pemb D 38-40; C-in-c of Freystrop w Haroldstone 40-41; R of Cosheston 41-52; CF (EC) 43-46; V of Llanwnda w Manorowen 52-67; RD of Fishguard 59-65; Dewisland and Fishguard 65-67; Dungleddy 68-73; R of Prendergast (w Rudbaxton from 69) 67-73; Tenby w Gumfreston and Penally 73-78; Can of St D from 70; Surr 73-78. *1 Hop Gardens Road, Carew Park, Sageston, Dyfed, SA70 8SF.*

JOHNS, William Price. b 28. Keble Coll Ox BA (2nd cl Engl) 51, Dipl Th 52, MA 56. St Mich Coll Llan 52. **d** 53 **p** 54 Llan. C of Whitchurch 53-56; Pontypridd 56-59; Min Can of Brecon Cathl 59-62; V of Wel (w Moreton-on-Lugg w Pipe and Lyde from 78) Dio Heref from 62; P-in-c of Ford Dio Heref from 63. *Wellington Vicarage, Hereford.* (Canon Pyon 228)

JOHNSON, Alban Ernest Mackenzie. Keble Coll Ox BA

(2nd cl Th) 31. Ely Th Coll 31. **d** 32 **p** 33 York. C of All SS Scarborough 32-35; St Aid w St Alb Middlesbrough 35-37; St Silas Penton Street w All SS Miss Lon 37-46; V 46-47; C of All SS Middlesbrough 47-49; V of Northfleet 49-52; CF 52-57; R of Toft w Newton 57-62; R of Faldingworth w Buslingthorpe 57-62; Chap St Martin's Sch Johann 63-70; Chap St Anne's Sch Nass 70-72; P-in-c of St Pet Long Is 72-76; St Aug San Salvador Dio Nass from 76. *Rectory, San Salvador, Bahamas, W Indies.*

JOHNSON, Canon Alfred Henry. b 08. Hatf Coll Dur BA 34. Ely Th Coll 34. **d** 35 **p** 36 Chelmsf. C of St Jo Div Becontree 35-38; St Mary Magd E Ham 38-40; V of Bradfield 40-49; Dovercourt 49-75; Surr 50-75; Chap RNVR 43-46; Chap Harwich and Distr Hosp 57-75; Hon Can of Chelmsf 65-75; Can (Emer) from 75; RD of Harwich 68-75; Perm to Offic Dios St E and Chelmsf from 76. *Woodford, Stanningfield Road, Great Welnetham, Bury St Edmunds, Suff.* (Sicklesmere 430)

JOHNSON, Alonzo Irwin. MBE 56. Codr Coll Barb 37. **d** 39 **p** 41 Barb. C of Ch Ch Barb 39-42; V of St D Barb 42-54; R of Ch Ch Barb 54-75; C of Hockerill Dio St Alb from 80. *2 Green Road, Bishops Stortford, Herts.* (Bp's Stortford 57479)

JOHNSON, Anthony Arthur Derry. b 15. Kelham Th Coll 31. **d** 39 Willesden for Lon **p** 40 Lon. C of Pinner 39-42; St Andr Willesden Green 42-44; H Trin Winchmore Hill 44-49; V of St Anne Brookfield Highgate 49-60; St Mich AA Mill Hill 60-73; R of Chalfont St Giles 73-80. *Garden Close, Long Street, Sherborne, DT9 3DD.* (Sherborne 3469)

JOHNSON, Anthony Peter. b 45. Dipl Th (Lon) 71. AKC, BD 76, mth 79. Wells Th Coll 67. **d** 70 **p** 71 St Alb. C of Goldington 70-73; Hainault 73-76; Team V St Mary Virg Loughton 76-81; V of All SS Scunthorpe Dio Linc from 81. *All Saints Vicarage, Warwick Road, Scunthorpe, S Humb, DN16 1HH.* (Scunthorpe 69081)

JOHNSON, Canon Anthony Trevor. b 27. CCC Ox BA 51, MA 55. Cudd Coll 51. **d** 53 **p** 54 Sarum. C of Wareham 53-57; Melksham 57-60; R of Tarrant Gunville 60-67; R of Tarrant Hinton 60-67; V of Tarrant Monkton w Tarrant Launceston 60-67; Warminster Dio Sarum from 67; R of Upton Scudamore Dio Sarum from 67; Surr 68; RD of Heytesbury 71-76; Can and Preb of Sarum Cathl from 75; P-in-c of Horningsham Dio Sarum from 76. *Vicarage, Church Street, Warminster, Wilts, BA12 8PG.* (Warminster 213456)

JOHNSON, Arnold Georges. Univ of Manit BA 60. St Jo Coll Winnipeg. **d** and **p** 58 Rupld. V of Morden 58-62; Snowflake 62-63; R of Neepawa 63-67; L to Offic Dio Rupld 71-73; Hon C of All SS Winnipeg Dio Rupld from 73. *385 Brandon Avenue, Winnipeg, Manit., Canada.*

JOHNSON, Arthur Ernest. St Francis Coll Brisb 46. **d** 48 **p** 50 Brisb. C of Warwick 48-52; St Columba Clayfield Brisb 52-53; H Trin Fortitude Valley 53-54; V of Chinchilla 54-60; R of Nambour 60-67; Pittsworth 67-71; Stanthorpe 71-75; St Colomb Clayfield City and Dio Brisb from 75. *Rectory, Victoria Street, Clayfield, Brisbane, Australia 4011.* (262 2648)

JOHNSON, Arthur Victor. b 19. St Aid Coll 62. **d** 64 Lanc for Blackb **p** 65 Blackb. C of Kirkham 64-66; Padiham w Higham 66-69; V of All SS Oswaldtwistle 69-73; St Jo Evang w St Anne Lanc 73-79; Out Rawcliffe Dio Blackb from 79. *Vicarage, School Lane, Out Rawcliffe, Preston, Lancs PR3 6BH.* (Hambleton 700351)

JOHNSON, Beverley Charles. b 35. Bp Gray Th Coll Capetn 59. **d** 61 **p** 62 Capetn. C of Woodstock 61-64; Clanwilliam 64-65; Plumstead 65-67; St Pet Southsea 68-69; St Cuthb Southwick 70-71; P-in-c of Waterhouses 71-80; R of Burnmoor Dio Dur from 80. *Burnmoor Rectory, Houghton-le-Spring, Co Durham, DH4 6EX.* (Fence Houses 2695)

JOHNSON, Brian Braithwaite. b 08. St Aug Coll Cant 65. **d** 66 **p** 67 York. C of St Mark Newby Scarborough 66-69; V of Baldersby 69-76; V of Skipton-on-Swale 69-76; Perm to Offic Dio York from 76. *School House, Baldersby St James, Thirsk, Yorks.* (Melmerby 241)

JOHNSON, Brian Keith. Moore Th Coll Syd ACT ThL (2nd cl) 64. **d** 64 **p** 65 Syd. C of Dee Why 64-66; C-in-c of Allambie Heights w Manly Vale Provis Distr 66-71; R of Wentworthville Dio Syd from 71. *18 Pritchard Street, Wentworthville, NSW, Australia 2145.* (631-8407)

JOHNSON, Brian Robert. b 18. ARIBA 48. Univ of Lon Dipl Architecture 48. **d** 67 **p** 69 Cork. Bp's C of Brigown Dio Cloyne from 67; Chap Kingston Coll Mitchelstown from 67; RD in Dio Cork from 69. *Chaplaincy, Kingston College, Mitchelstown, Co Cork, Irish Republic.* (Mitchelstown 280)

JOHNSON, Charles Allan. Univ of Tor BA 21. **d** 37 Bp Beverley for Tor **p** 38 Tor. C of St Matt Tor 37-40; R of Perrytown 40-42; Brampton 42-60; St D Donlands Tor 60-72. *Box 17, RRI, Gore's Landing, Ont., Canada.*

JOHNSON, Charles Edmund. b 15. Em Coll Cam (2nd cl Hist Trip pt i) 39, BA (2nd cl Hist Trip pt ii) 40, MA 42. Ridley Hall Cam 40. **d** 42 **p** 43 Guildf. C of Ch Ch Woking 42-44; Hd Master Seaford Coll from 44; L to Offic Dio Chich from 44. *Seaford College, Lavington Park, Petworth, Sussex.* (Graffham 392)

JOHNSON, Charles Frank. Wycl Coll Tor. **d** 26 **p** 29 NS. C of Milton w Rustico 26-30; Dresden 30-34; Burford w Cathcart, Princeton and Drumbo 34-39; R of St Geo Lon Ont 39-45; Owen Sound 45-56; Wingham 56-66. *145 Patrick Street East, Wingham, Ont, Canada.*

JOHNSON, Christopher Dudley. b 26. Worc Coll Ox BA (3rd cl Th) 44, MA 51. Cudd Coll 53. **d** 56 **p** 57 Win. C of Basingstoke 56-61; V of St Barn Bethnal Green 61-67; Eton w Eton Wick and Boveney Dio Ox from 67. *Vicarage, Eton, Windsor, Berks.* (Windsor 60726)

JOHNSON, Christopher Frederick. b 43. ARICS 67. Ripon Hall Ox 71. **d** 74 Roch **p** 75 Tonbridge for Roch. C of St Steph Chatham 74-78; V of Slade Green Dio Roch from 78. *Vicarage, Slade Green, Erith, Kent.* (Erith 33970)

JOHNSON, Christopher Paul. b 47. Univ of Nottm BTh 74. St Jo Coll Nottm 71. **d** 74 Pontefract for Wakef **p** 75 Wakef. C of Normanton 74-78; P-in-c of St Mark Dewsbury Dio Wakef from 78. *St Mark's Vicarage, West Park Street, Dewsbury, W Yorks.* (Dewsbury 465789)

JOHNSON, Christopher Percival. b 1900. Qu Coll Birm 51. Lich Th Coll 52. **d** and **p** 52 Worc. C of St Jas Gt Dudley 52-54; C-in-c of Birchen Coppice Conv Distr Kidderminster 54-57; R of Harvington 57-68; L to Offic Dio Worc from 68. *30 The Close, Cleeve Prior, Evesham, Worcs.* (Bidford-on-Avon 773745)

JOHNSON, Christopher Robert. b 43. Lon Coll Div 66. **d** 70 **p** 71 Warrington for Liv. C of St Geo Everton 70-71; Childwall 71-75; Team V of Gateacre 75-76; C of Bushbury Dio Lich 76-77; Team V from 77. *17 Goodyear Avenue, Low Hill, Wolverhampton, WV10 9JX.* (Wolverhampton 731713)

JOHNSON, Colin Gawman. b 32. Univ of Leeds, BA (3rd cl Gen) 59. Coll of Resurr Mirfield, 59. **d** 61 Bp Graham for Carl **p** 62 Carl. C of St Matt Barrow-F 61-67; V of Addingham w Gamblesby 67-71; H Trin Carl 71-79; Wigton Dio Carl from 79. *Vicarage, Wigton, Carlisle, CA7 9PU.* (Wigton 2337)

JOHNSON, Colin Robert. b 52. Univ of W Ont BA 74. Trin Coll Tor MDiv 77. **d** 77 Bp Read for Tor **p** 78 Tor. C of St Simon Ap Tor 77-80; R of Georgina Dio Tor from 80. *Box 88, Main Street, Sutton West, Ont, Canada.* (416-722 3726)

JOHNSON, Cyril Francis. b 22. St Cath Coll Cam BA 49, MA 54. Ely Th Coll 50. **d** 52 **p** 53 Lon. C of All H Twickenham 52-56; Kingsthorpe 56-61; R of Harpole Dio Pet from 61. *Harpole Rectory, Northampton, NN7 4DR.* (Northn 830322)

JOHNSON, David Alan. b 43. Univ of Lon BSc 63, PhD 67. Trin Coll Bris 78. **d** 80 **p** 81 St Alb. C of St Mary Watford Dio St Alb from 80. *8a Lammas Road, Watford, Herts, WD1 8BA.*

JOHNSON, David Bryan Alfred. b 36. Kelham Th Coll 56. **d** 61 **p** 62 S'wark. C of St Paul Furzedown Streatham 61-63; St Thos Cathl Kuch 63-66; V of Sibu 66-71; Dines Green 71-74; Warden Lee Abbey Internat Studs Club S Kens 74-77; V of Plumstead Dio S'wark from 77. *11 Old Mill Road, Plumstead Common, SE18 1QE.* (01-854 2973)

JOHNSON, David Clark. b 15. Tyndale Hall, Bris 61. **d** 62 **p** 63 Bris. C of St Paul Chippenham 62-65; V of Bishopsworth 65-74; Stratton St Marg Dio Bris 75-78; R (w S Marston and Stanton Fitzwarren) 78-80. *13 High Kingsdown, Bristol.*

JOHNSON, David Francis. b 32. Univ Coll Ox BA 55, MA 59. Westcott Ho Cam 55. **d** 57 **p** 58 Cov. C of St Barbara Earlsdon Cov 57-59; Willenhall w Whitley 59-61; Attenborough w Bramcote and Chilwell 61-62; V of Ravenstone w Weston Underwood 62-66; Ch Ch Crewe 66-70; C-in-c of St Pet Crewe 67-70; V of Thornton w Allerthorpe and Melbourne 70-79; St Mich AA Hull 79-81; Leyburn w Bellerby Dio Ripon from 81. *Vicarage, Leyburn, N Yorks, DL8 5JF.* (Wensleydale 22251)

JOHNSON, David George. St Francis Th Coll Brisb 52. **d** 55 **p** 56 Brisb. C of Ch Ch Milton Brisb 55-56; M of Bush Bro of St Paul 56-57; C of St Matt Sherwood Brisb 57-58; R of Castra 58-61; Bothwell 61-65; P-in-c of the Channel w Bruny I 65-66; R of Geeveston 66-68; Queenstown 68-74; St Paul Launceston Dio Tas from 74. *13 Granville Street, W Launceston, Tasmania 7250.* (003-31 5367)

JOHNSON, David John. b 49. Univ of Lanc BA 72. Linc Th Coll 78. **d** 81 Ches. C of St Thos Stockport Dio Ches from 81. *90 Richardson Street, Hillgate, Stockport, Gtr Man, SK1 3JL.*

JOHNSON, David William. b 40. BD (Lon) 64. Oak Hill Th Coll 60. **d** 65 **p** 66 Roch. C of St Jas Tunbridge Wells 65-68; Kirby Muxloe 68-72; V of Burton Joyce w Bulcote Dio

Southw from 72. *Vicarage, Chestnut Grove, Burton Joyce, Nottingham, NG14 5DP.*

JOHNSON, David William. b 53. Selw Coll Cam BA 76. Ripon Coll Cudd 76. **d** 78 Lon **p** 79 Kens for Lon. C of St Etheldreda w St Clem Fulham Dio Lon from 78. *29 Ellerby Street, SW6 6EX.* (01-736 2398)

JOHNSON, Dennis George Hampton. d and **p** 50 Syd. C of Bankstown 50-51; C-in-c of Padstow 51-52; R of Dural 53-56; Kensington 56-60; Police Court Chap Syd 60-62; CF (Aust) R Mil Col Duntroon 62-67; R of Longueville 67-74; Perm to Offic Dio C & Goulb 74-76; P-in-c of Yass 76; H Covenant Canberra 77-80; Perm to Offic Dio C & Goulb from 80. *27 Fellowes Street, Latham, ACT, Australia 2615.*

JOHNSON, Derek John. b 36. St Aid Coll 65. **d** 68 **p** 69 Lich. C of Eccleshall 68-73; Stafford 73-75; Chap New Cross Hosp Wolverhampton from 75. *New Cross Hospital, Wolverhampton.* (Wolverhampton 732255)

JOHNSON, Donald Arnold. Linc Coll Ox BA (Th) 51, MA 59. Cudd Coll 51. **d** 53 **p** 54 Chich. C of Henfield 53-55; Horsham 55-59; Dom Chap to Bp of Chich 59-69; V of Oving w Merston 59-68; Hellingly 68-78; U Dicker 68-78; Funtington w Sennicotts Dio Chich from 78; R of W Stoke Dio Chich from 78. *Funtington Vicarage, Chichester, Sussex.* (West Ashling 257)

JOHNSON, Douglas Leonard. b 45. Trin Coll Bris 70. **d** 73 **p** 74 S'wark. C of New Malden w Coombe 73-76; V of St Matthias U Tulse Hill Dio S'wark from 76. *107 Upper Tulse Hill, SW2.* (01-674 6835)

JOHNSON, Edward Anthony. b 32. Univ of Wales (Swansea) BSc 54. St Steph Ho Ox 79. **d** 81 Reading for Ox. C of Wolvercote City and Dio Ox from 81. *2 Osborne Close, Wolvercote, Oxford, OX2 8BQ.*

JOHNSON, Edward Arthur. b 1891. AKC 14. **d** 14 **p** 15 S'wark. C of St Aug S Bermondsey 14-18; All SS w St Thos Ipswich 18-22; St Barn Dover 22-40; Drayton (in c of Hellesdon) 40-42; St Jas Nor 42-44; R of Buckenham w Hassingham 44-48; Alby w Thwaite 48-65; Perm to Offic Dio S'wark from 65. *33a Fife Road, Kingston-on-Thames, Surrey.*

JOHNSON, Edward Frederick. b 14. MC 44. Late Exhib of St Jo Coll Dur LTh 37, BA 38, MA 50. St Aid Coll 34. **d** 38 **p** 39 Liv. C of St John and St Jas Litherland 38-41; CF (EC) 41-46; R of N Cray 46-50; Milton-next-Gravesend 50-54; Chap and Asst Master Carn Brea Sch Bromley 54-61; C of St Jo Evang Bromley 55-57; Chap St Cecilia's Home Bromley 57-61; C of St Luke Bromley Common 57-61; Chap St Edm Sch Hindhead 61-62; R of Cranleigh 62-75; RD of Cranleigh 63-68. *Tormere, Downs Road, Witney, Oxon, OX8 7SH.* (Standlake 469)

JOHNSON, Eric. b 38. Univ of Nottm BSc 60. Qu Coll Birm 74. **d** 77 Bp McKie for Cov **p** 78 Cov (APM). Hon C of St Barbara Earlsdon City and Dio Cov from 77. *54 Styvechale Avenue, Earlsdon, Coventry, CV5 6DX.*

JOHNSON, Ernest. b 03. Kelham Th Coll 26. **d** 31 **p** 32 Dur. C of St Mary Tyne Dock 31-37; Whitburn (in c of St Andr Marsden) 37-39; R of St Steph S Shields 39-52; V of Ferryhill 52-61; Surr from 41; V of Satley 61-70; Perm to Offic Dio Dur from 70. *4 Park Terrace, Castleside, Consett, Co Durham, DH8 9QK.*

JOHNSON, Evan George Agbogay. Fourah Bay Coll. **d** 65 **p** 67 Sier L. P Dio Sier L. *18b Hamilton Lane, Freetown, Sierra Leone.*

JOHNSON, Geoffrey Kemble. b 22. RD 71. Roch Th Coll 62. **d** 64 **p** 65 Roch. C of Hayes 64-68; R of Worlingham Dio St E from 68. *Worlingham Rectory, Beccles, Suff, NR34 7DZ.* (Beccles 712018)

JOHNSON, Geoffrey Stuart. b 39. ALCD 65. **d** 65 **p** 66 Southw. C of St Jo Evang Worksop 65-68; C of St Andr Cathl Sing 71-76; P-in-c of Our Sav Sing 71-76; Perm to Offic Dio Heref from 78. *Baysham Court Cottage, Sellack, Ross-on-Wye, H & W.*

JOHNSON, Geoffrey Victor. b 39. **d** 80 **p** 81 Capetn. C of Bellville N Dio Capetn from 80. *52 Gainsborough Road, de la Haye, Bellville 7530, S Africa.*

JOHNSON, Ven George Harold. Univ of Tor BA 30, MA 32, BD 37, DD 44. **d** 32 Niag for Tor **p** 33 Tor. C of St Clem Eglinton Tor 32-36; R of Omemee 37-42; Newmarket 42-45; St Chad Tor 45-62; Exam Chap to Bp of Tor 55; Archd of Tor W 56-62; Urban Parishes 62-66; Tor 66-77; Archd (Emer) from 78. *Box 1027, Bracebridge, Ont, Canada*

JOHNSON, George William. b 03. SOC 67. **d** 68 Roch **p** 69 Tonbridge for Roch. C of Farnborough Kent Dio Roch from 68; Chap Farnborough Hosp 72-73. *64 Felstead Road, Orpington, Kent, BR6 9AE.* (Orpington 24804)

JOHNSON, Gerald Cecil. Univ of W Ont BA 62. Hur Th Coll. **d** 65 **p** 66 Hur. I of Ox Centre 65-68; R of Ilderton Dio Hur from 68. *Box 34, Ilderton, Ont., Canada.* (519-666 0125)

JOHNSON, Gordon. b 20. **d** 43 **p** 44 Glouc. C of St Steph Glouc and Asst Chap to HM Pris Glouc 43-46; C of Halifax and Chap to Halifax Gen Hosp 46-48; C-in-c of Seacroft Conv Distr Leeds 48-52; V of N Grimston w Wharram-le-Street and Wharram Percy 52-54; CF 54-59; V of Finchingfield 59-62; Perm to Offic Dio Ely 62-64; R of Horseheath 64-71; R of Bartlow 65-71; Perm to Offic St Aug Kens Dio Lon from 79; Rural Deanery of Linton Dio Ely from 79. *HQ Voluntary Social Aid, 117 London Road, Peterborough, Cambs.* (Peterborough 41360)

JOHNSON, Gordon Edward. b 27. Oak Hill Coll 76. **d** 77 **p** 78 York. C of St Mary Scarborough Dio York from 77. *20 Moorland Road, Scarborough, N Yorks, YO12 7RB.*

JOHNSON, Graham. b 37. Westcott Ho Cam 66. **d** 68 **p** 69 Lich. C of Stafford 68-71; Wombourn 71-74; Dioc Youth Chap Lich 74-77; P-in-c of Tong 76-77; Team V of Wednesfield Dio Lich from 77. *157 Stubby Lane, Wednesfield, Wolverhampton, WV11 3NE.* (Wolverhampton 732763)

JOHNSON, Graham James. b 43. Univ of Leeds BA 67, Dipl Th 69. Coll of Resurr Mirfield 67. **d** 70 Pontefract for Wakef, **p** 71 Wakef. C of Heckmondwyke 70-73; St Jude Pet 73-76; V of Gt w L Harrowden and Orlingbury Dio Pet from 76. *Vicarage, Kings Lane, Little Harrowden, Wellingborough, Northants.* (Wellingborough 678225)

JOHNSON, Harold. b 24. Dipl Th (Lon) 56. St Aid Coll 54. **d** 57 **p** 58 Ches. C of Barnston 57-61; V of Lindow 61-63; Alvaston 63-74; Etwall w Eggington Dio Derby from 74. *Etwall Vicarage, Derby, DE6 6LP.* (Etwal 2349)

JOHNSON, Harold. b 1899. **d** 62 Southw **p** 63 Bp Gelsthorpe For Southw. C of Attenborough 62-63; Win And Porstm Dioc Cler Regis From 63. *94 Ferndale, Waterlooville, Hants, PO7 7PQ.* (Waterlooville 52682)

JOHNSON, Harold Barnett. Ex Coll Ox BA 34, MA 37. Cudd Coll 34. **d** 35 Ox **p** 36 Cov. C of St Geo Wolverton 35-36; St Marg Cov 36-40; Wimbledon (in c of St Mark) 40-47; V of Southwick w Glapthorne 47-60; Hon Sec Pet Dioc Miss Coun 51-60; R of Waldron 60-75; Hon C of St Sav Eastbourne Dio Chich from 75. *17 Willingdon Park Drive, Eastbourne, E Sussex, BN22 0BS.*

JOHNSON, Harold Everard. b 14. TCD BA 36, Div Test 38, MA 40, BD 46. **d** 38 Down **p** 39 Bp Kennedy for Down. C of St Nich Belf 38-41; Whitehouse 41-43; R of Ballymartle 43-45; I of Drimoleague (w Caheragh from 47) 45-50; St Nich Cork 50-58; V of St Andr Eccles 58-80; Perm to Offic Dio Man from 80. *368 New Church Road, Stacksteads, Bacup, Lancs.* (Bacup 4922)

JOHNSON, Ven Hayman. b 12. New Coll Ox BA (3rd cl Mod Hist) 34, MA 38. Bps' Coll Cheshunt, 35. **d** 36 **p** 37 S'wark. C of Bermondsey 36-38; Perm to Offic at Immanuel Streatham 38-40; C 40-46; Chap RAFVR 41-46; V of St Pet Harold Wood 46-51; H Trin Aldershot 51-53; Chap and V Temporal of Hornchurch 53-61; Surr 55-61; R of Middleton 61-63; Tankersley 63-67; Exam Chap to Bp of Sheff 62-78; Select Pr Edin 68; Archd of Sheff 63-78; Archd (Emer) from 78; Chap to HM the Queen from 69; M Gen Syn 70-75; Can Res of Sheff Cathl 75-78. *8 Regency Green, Prittlewell, Southend-on-Sea, Essex.*

JOHNSON, Canon Hedley Wilson. b 10. Late Scho of Peterho Cam 2nd cl Cl Trip pt i 31, BA (3rd cl Cl Trip pt ii) 32, MA 36. **d** 40 **p** 41 Ex. C of St Matthias Ilsham Torquay 40-43; St Jo Bapt Woking 43; V of H Trin Torquay 43-53; R of Witnesham (w Swilland and Ashbocking from 61) 53-78; C-in-c of Swilland w Ashbocking 56-61; RD of Claydon 60-73; Hon Can of St E Cathl 75-78; Can (Emer) from 78; Perm to Offic Dio St E from 79. *45 Aldeburgh Road, Leiston, Suffolk, IP16 4PN.* (Leiston 830884)

JOHNSON, Henry James. b 11. St Aug Coll Cant 64. **d** 65 **p** 66 Lon. C of St Mary Stoke Newington 65-69; C-in-c 69-70; V of St Pet Paddington 70-81. *Flat 5, 61 Elgin Avenue, W9 2DB.* (01-286 9599)

JOHNSON, Herbert Allinson. b 04. Edin Th Coll. **d** 47 **p** 48 Brech. Chap of St Paul's Cathl Dundee and P-in-c of St Roque's 47-54; R of Lochgelly 54-60; V of Tolpuddle 60-77; V of Affpuddle w Tonerspuddle 60-77. *Church View, Hill Farm Lane, Lytchett Minster, Poole, Dorset.*

JOHNSON, Ian Lawrence. b 44. Wells Th Coll 68. **d** 71 **p** 72 S'wark. C of Benhilton 71-73; H Trin w St Nich Weymouth 73-75; R of Pewsey 75-81; P-in-c of Maiden Newton w Frome Vauchurch 81; Compton Abbas W w Wynford Eagle and Toller Fratrum 81; R of Maiden Newton and Valleys Dio Sarum from 81. *Maiden Newton Rectory, Dorchester, Dorset.* (Maiden Newton 20284)

JOHNSON, Canon James Bovell. St Chad's Hall Dur LTh 11, BA 12. St Bonif Coll Warm 07. **d** 14 **p** 15 S'wark. C of St Pet Vauxhall 14-17; TCF 18-19; Miss St Matt Miss Keiskama CGH 20-25; St Jo Miss Bolotwa 25-40; R of Kingwilliamstown 40-55; Hon Can Grahmstn Cathl from 52; R of Cradock 55-60; C of Vincent E Lon 60-72. *3 Prior Crescent, Beach, East London, CP, S Africa.* (2-8979)

JOHNSON, Canon James Nathaniel. b 32. Wells Th Coll 63. **d** 64 Malmesbury for Bris for St Hel **p** 65 Bris. C of

Lawrence Weston 64-66; P-in-c of St Paul's Cathl St Hel 66-69; V 69-71; Dom Chap to Bp of St Hel 67-71; Publ Pr Dio Ex 72-74; Perm to Offic Dio Truro 72-74; USPG Area Sec for Dios Ex and Truro 72-74; R of Combe Martin 74-80; Hon Can of St Hel from 75; V of Thorpe Bay Dio Chelmsf from 80. *86 Tyrone Road, Thorpe Bay, Essex, SS1 3HB.* (Southend-on-Sea 587597)

JOHNSON, James Raphael. St Paul's Th Coll Maur. **d** and **p** 64 Maur. R of St Sav Anse Royale S Sey 64-73; St Matt Praslin 73-75; C of Quatre Bornes 75-76; R of Mahebourg and Souillac Dio Maur from 76. *Rectory, Stanley Avenue, Quatre Bornes, Mauritius.*

JOHNSON, John Alan. b 51. Ripon Coll Cudd 75. **d** 77 **p** 78 St Alb. C of Borehamwood 77-80; Team V of Dunstable Dio St Alb from 80. *St Augustine's Vicarage, Sundown Avenue, Dunstable, Beds.* (Dunstable 68019)

JOHNSON, John Anthony. b 18. Selw Coll Cam BA 48, MA 53. St Jo Coll Dur Dipl Th 51. **d** 51 **p** 52 S'wark. C of Battersea 51-54; Merton 54-56; V of Balderton 56-60; Mansfield Woodhouse 60-70; Beeston Dio Southw from 70; RD of Beeston from 81. *Beeston Vicarage, Nottingham.* (Nottm 254571)

JOHNSON, John Cecil. b 23. Peterho Cam BA 48. Ely Th Coll 57. **d** 59 **p** 60 Lon. C of Whitton 59-70; C-in-c of St Andr Fulham Dio Lon 70-73; V from 73. *Vicarage, St Andrew's Road, W14 9SX.* (01-385 5578)

JOHNSON, John David. b 38. St Deiniol's Hawarden 71. **d** 71 **p** 72 Heref. C of St Martin Heref 71-73; P-in-c of Ewyas Harold w Dulas 73-79; Kenderchurch 73-79; Kilpeck 73-81; St Devereux w Wormbridge 73-81; Team R of Ewyas Harold w Dulas, Rowlestone, Llancillo, Waterstone, Kentchurch w Llangua, Kenderchurch, Abbey Dore and Bacton 79-81; Hosp Chap of Napsbury Hosp St Alb from 81. *c/o Napsbury Hospital, 2 East Drive, Shenley Lane, St Albans, AL2 1AA.*

JOHNSON, Joseph. b 11. Lon Coll Div 43. **d** 45 Stepney for Lon **p** 46 Lon. C of St Simon Hammersmith 45-47; Org Sec CPAS 47-50; R of All SS Birm 50-61; PC (V from 69) of Alperton 61-79; Perm to Offic Dio Ely from 79. *16 Gloucester Way, Sawtry, Huntingdon, Cambs.*

JOHNSON, Joseph Clarke. b 10. Bps' Coll Cheshunt 46. **d** 48 **p** 49 Carl. C of H Trin Carl 48-50; V of St John-in-the-Vale w Wythburn 50-57; Beckermet or Calderbridge w Ponsonby 57-78. *High Moss, Calderbridge, Seascale, Cumb.*

JOHNSON, Keith Winton Thomas William. b 37. K Coll Lon and Warm BD and AKC 63. **d** 64 **p** 65 Roch. C of Dartford 64-69; Chap at Kuwait 69-73; V of Erith 73-80; St Jo Evang Bexley Dio Roch from 80. *St John's Vicarage, Parkhill Road, Bexley, Kent, DA5 1HX.* (Crayford 521786)

JOHNSON, Kenneth Reginald. b 06. Univ of Leeds BA 27. Coll of Resurr Mirfield 24. **d** 29 **p** 30 Lon. C of St Mark Bush Hill Pk 29-31; Chap of St John Wei-hai-wei 31-32; Miss at Taian 32-37; Pingyin 38-45; C of St Alb Bournemouth 47-49; SPCK Port Chap Southn 49-54; R of Yattendon w Frilsham 54-60; V of St Luke Southn 60-71. *Milton Cottage, Church Street, Mere, Wilts.*

JOHNSON, Kevin Frederic. b 46. Univ of NSW BA 74. Univ of Queensld BD 76. St Mich Ho Crafers 66. **d** 75 **p** 76 Graft. C of Ch Ch Cathl Graft 75-79; Ch Ch St Lucia City and Dio Brisb from 79. *c/o 3 Baty Street, St Lucia, Queensland, Australia 4067.*

JOHNSON, Kevin Robert. Moore Coll Syd ThL 72. **d** 71 Syd **p** 73 Bp Dain for Syd. C of St Phil Syd 72-74; Denham Court 74-75; R of Wilberforce Dio Syd from 75. *Macquarie Road, Wilberforce, NSW, Australia 2756.* (045-75 1417)

JOHNSON, Malcolm Arthur. b 36. Univ Coll Dur BA 60, MA 64. Cudd Coll 60. **d** 62 **p** 63 Portsm. C of St Mark Portsea 62-67; Chap Univ of Lon 67-74; R of St Botolph without Aldgate w H Trin Minories City and Dio Lon from 74. *St Botolph's Vestry, Aldgate, EC3N 1AB.* (01-283 1670)

JOHNSON, Malcolm Stuart. b 35. K Coll Lon and Warm AKC 60. **d** 61 **p** 62 S'wark. C of Catford 61-64; St Cath Hatcham 66-76; C-in-c of Kingstanding Dio Birm 76-77; V from 77. *49 Caversham Road, Birmingham, B44 0LW.* (021-354 3281)

JOHNSON, Michael. b 42. Univ of Birm BSc 63. SOC 68. **d** 71 **p** 72 S'wark. C of Kidbrooke 71-74; Hon C of Eynsford w Farningham and Lullingstone Dio Roch from 74; Asst Master Swanley Sch from 74. *Yew Trees, Beechenlea Lane, Swanley, Kent, BR8 8DP.* (Swanley 65490)

JOHNSON, Michael Anthony. b 51. Univ of Ex BA (Th) 76. Ch Div Sch of the Pacific Berkeley Calif 78. **d** 78 Edmon for Lon **p** 79 Lon. C of St Mary Primrose Hill Hampstead 78-81; St John Hampstead Dio Lon from 81. *1 Holly Bush Vale, Hampstead, NW3 6TX.* (01-794 6838)

JOHNSON, Michael Colin. b 37. SOC 77. **d** 80 **p** 81 S'wark. C of New Eltham Dio S'wark from 80. *All Saints Vicarage, Bercta Road, New Eltham, SE9 3TZ.*

JOHNSON, Michael Earl. b 50. Waterloo Univ Ont BA 76. Hur Coll Lon Ont MDiv 79. **d** 79 Bp Robinson for Hur **p** 80 Hur. C of St Jo Evang Kitchener Dio Hur from 79. *23 Water Street N, Kitchener, Ont, Canada, N2H 5A4.*

JOHNSON, Michael Gordon. b 45. Kelham Th Coll 64. Dipl Th (Lon) 68. **d** 68 Bp McKie for Cov **p** 69 Cov. C of St Luke Holbrooks 68-72; Cannock 72-75; V of Coseley 75-79; P-in-c of Sneyd Dio Lich from 79. *Sneyd Vicarage, Burslem, Stoke-on-Trent, ST6 7BT.* (S-o-T 85060)

JOHNSON, Moses. b 44. St Paul's Coll Grahmstn Dipl Th 80. **d** 79 **p** 80 Kimb K. P Dio Kimb K. *Box 113, De Aar, S Africa.*

JOHNSON, Murray George. BD (Lon) 72. Ridley Coll Melb ACT ThL 65, Th Scho 67. **d** 68 **p** 69 Tas. C of St John Launceston 68-70; R of Buckland 70-72; Perm to Offic Dio Melb 72-74; Asst Sec World Chr Action Vic 72-74; Sec 74-80; L to Offic Dio N Terr from 80. *Nungalinya College, Casuarina, NT, Australia 5792.*

JOHNSON, Nigel Edwin. b 41. K Coll Lon and Warm AKC 64. **d** 65 Burnley for Blackb **p** 66 Blackb. C of Morecambe w Poulton-le-Sands 65-68; Chap RN from 68. *c/o Ministry of Defence, Lacon House, Theobalds Road, WC1X 8RY.*

JOHNSON, Norman Ernest Stephen. b 04. AKC 27. Bps' Coll Cheshunt 27. **d** 27 **p** 28 S'wark. C of St John Southend Lewisham 27-33; Kingston T 33-36; V of Ch Ch Battersea 36-43; Eaton Socon 43-56; R of L Barford 47-56; RD of Biggleswade 50-56; R of Shenley 56-67; V of King's Walden 67-72. *Whitehall Cottage, King's Walden, Hitchin, Herts.* (Whitwell 353)

JOHNSON, Patrick Innis. Angl Th Coll BC 59. **d** 62 New Westmr **p** 63 Ont. C of H Trin Brockville 62-67; Ch Ch Cathl Hamilton 67-72; R of All SS Hamilton Dio Niag from 72; Dir Miss to Seamen Hamilton from 78. *15 Queens Street South, Hamilton 12, Ont., Canada.* (416-529 7296)

JOHNSON, Paul Henry. b 08. Ch Coll Cam BA 36, MA 40. Wycl Hall Ox. **d** and **p** 38 Lon. C of St John Southall 38-41; CMS Miss at Lusadia 41-63; Archd of Ahmedabad 54-59; R of Ahmedabad and of Lusadia 60-63; V of St Geo Newc L 63-72; C of Welwyn Garden City Dio St Alb from 72. *39 High Oaks Road, Welwyn Garden City, Herts, AL8 7BT.* (Welwyn Garden 26457)

JOHNSON, Peter Frederick. b 41. Univ of Melb BA (1st cl Math) 63. Ch Ch Ox BA (2nd cl th) 68, Ellerton Pri 70, MA 72. St Steph Ho Ox. **d** 69 **p** 70 Ox for Melb. C of Banbury w Neithrop 69-71; Tutor St Steph Ho Ox 71-74; L to Offic Dio Ox 71-74; Dio Dur 74-80; Chap St Chad's Coll Dur 74-80; Vice-Prin 78-80; Asst Master K Sch Cant and perm to Offic Dio Cant from 80; Hon Min Can of Cant Cathl from 80. *27 Monastery Street, Canterbury, CT1 1NJ.*

JOHNSON, Philip. b 41. Univ of Lon BA (2nd cl Engl) and AKC 63. ARCM 62. Coll of Resurr Mirfield. **d** 65 Dur **p** 66 Jarrow for Dur. C of St Ignatius Mart Hendon 65-69; Eastleigh 69-75; Liaison Officer for Secondary Schs Dio Win 75-80; Asst Master Barton Peveril Coll Eastleigh from 80. *5 Justinian Close, Chandler's Ford, Eastleigh, Hants, SO5 2NW.* (Chandler's Ford 66679)

JOHNSON, Richard Le Bas. b 22. TCD BA 50, MA 58. Sarum Th Coll 50. **d** 52 **p** 53 Leic. C of Hugglescote w Donington 52-55; Hinckley 55-57; Prec and Sacr of Pet Cathl 57-62; R of Hartley Mashon 62-67; P-in-c of Lowveld, Mashon 67-72; C of Kings Worthy and Headbourne Worthy 72-74; R of Crawley w Littleton Dio Win from 74. *Rectory, Church Lane, Littleton, Winchester, Hants, SO22 6QY.* (Win 881898)

JOHNSON, Richard Nasmyth. **d** 68 Perth. L to Offic Dio Perth 68-73. *Grieve Place, Moora, W Australia 6510.*

JOHNSON, Canon Robert Dunmore. b 18. Pemb Coll Ox BA and MA 45. Westcott Ho Cam 46. **d** and **p** 48 Roch. C of H Trin Dartford 48-50; St John Bexley 50-53; R of Offham and C-in-c of Addington 53-59; V of Langton Green 59-73; R of Ashurst 59-63; R of Sundridge w Ide Hill Dio Roch from 73; Hon Can of Roch Cathl from 81. *Sundridge Rectory, Sevenoaks, Kent.* (Westerham 63749)

JOHNSON, Robert Francis Hamilton. **d** 23 **p** 25 Capetn. C of St Sav Claremont 23-28; R of Constantia 28-37; Paarl 37-44; Somerset Strand 44-49; C of St Geo Cathl (in c of Ch of Ascension) Capetn 49-53; I of Ch Ch Grahmstn 54-59. *c/o Greenoaks, College Road, Rondesbosch CP, S Africa.*

JOHNSON, Robert Henry. Univ of Tor BA 53. Wycl Coll Tor LTh 56. **d** 55 **p** 56 Calg. C of St Barn Calg 55-56; I of Vulcan 56-61; R of Taber 61-64; V of Okotoks 64-66; I of Sherwood Pk 67-70; St Andr Winnipeg Dio Rupld from 70. *2700 Portage Avenue, Winnipeg 12, Manit, Canada.*

JOHNSON, Robin Edward Hobbs. b 39. Fitzw Ho Cam 2nd cl Th Trip pt i 59, BA (2nd cl Th Trip pt ii) 61, 2nd cl Th Trip pt iii 63, MA 65. Ripon Hall Ox 61. **d** 63 Hulme for Man **p** 64 Man. C of Tyldesley 63-66; Lect Loughborough Coll and L to Offic Dio Leic 66-71; V of Castleton Moor 71-76; St Gabr Prestwich 76-81; Ch Ch Heaton Dio Man from 81; Bp of Man Chap for Ordins 76-81. *Heaton Vicarage, Bolton, Lancs, BL1 5EW.* (Bolton 40430)

JOHNSON, Ronald. b 40. Wycl Hall Ox 69. **d** 72 Man **p** 73 Middleton for Man. C of Deane 72-74; N Meols 74-75; Chap St John's Sch Tiffield from 75. *St John's School, Tiffield, Towcester, Northants.*

JOHNSON, Ronald Arthur. Moore Th Coll Syd ACT ThL 31. **d** 31 **p** 32 Goulb. C of Junee 31-33; Hornsby 33-34; Asst St John Darlinghurst 34; Supt Oenpelli Miss 34-36; R of Sutton Forest 36-43; Chap RAAF from 43; Chap to Abp of Syd 54-58 and from 73; R of Randwick 56-74; L to Offic Dio Syd from 74; Perm to Offic Dio Newc from 79. *32 Priestman Avenue, Umina, NSW, Australia 2516.* (043-41 5125)

JOHNSON, Ronald George. b 33. Chich Th Coll 75. **d** 76 Chich **p** 77 Horsham for Chich. C of St Mary Shipley 76-79; St Matthias Preston 79-82; P-in-c of Sutton w Bignor Dio Chich from 82; Barlavington Dio Chich from 82; Burton w Coates Dio Chich from 82. *Rectory, Pulborough, W Sussex, RH20 1PS.* (Sutton 220)

JOHNSON, Ronald Raymond. d and **p** 80 Syd. C of St Mich Flinders Street Dio Syd 80-81; R from 81. *196 Albion Street, Surry Hills, NSW, Australia 2010.* (31-2865)

JOHNSON, Ruthell Anthony. b 48. **d** 80 **p** 81 Port Eliz. C of St Hugh Newton Park Dio Port Eliz form 80. *32 Thames Road, Fern Glen, Port Elizabeth 6001, S Africa.*

JOHNSON, Very Rev Samuel Hugh Stowell Akinsope. Univ of Lon BD 61. Lich Th Coll 52. **d** 55 Kens for Lon **p** 56 Lon. C of Whitechapel 55-58; Sunbury-on-Thames 58-59; St Paul Lisson Grove 59-60; St Martin-in-the-Fields Westmr 60-62; Hd of Relig Broadcasting Nigeria and L to Offic Dio Lagos 63-70; Provost of Ch Ch Cathl Lagos from 70. *Provost's House, Box 726, Lagos, Nigeria.* (Lagos 20863)

JOHNSON, Solomon Ethelbert. b 54. Trin Coll Umuahia Dipl Th 80. **d** 79 **p** 80 Gambia. P Dio Gambia. *Anglican Mission, PO Box 51, Banjul, The Gambia, W Africa.*

JOHNSON, Stephen Winston. Univ of Auckld BA 68. St Jo Coll Auckld LTh 68. **d** 68 **p** 69 Auckld. C of All SS Ponsonby 68-72; P-in-c of St Patr & St Bart Barb 72-77; Meadowbank 77-78; Chap St Francis Coll Brisb 78-79; V of Orewa Dio Auckld from 79. *117 Centreway Road, Orewa, NZ.*

JOHNSON, Sylvanus Nargbay. Fourah Bay Coll 56. **d** 58 Sier L **p** 60 Bp Jones for Sier L. P Dio Sier L. *10 Steward Street, Freetown, Sierra Leone.*

JOHNSON, Terence John. b 44. ALCD 70 (LTh from 74). **d** 69 **p** 70 Ripon. C of Woodside 69-72; St Geo Leeds 72-76; H Trin Heworth York 76-81; V of Budbrooke w Hampton on the Hill Dio Cov from 81. *Budbrooke Vicarage, Warwick, CV35 8QL.* (Warwick 494002)

JOHNSON, Canon Thomas Wyndham Page. b 11. BNC Ox BA (3rd cl Hist) 33. Cudd Coll 34 **d** 36 **p** 37 Liv. C of St Dunstan Edge Hill 36-39; St Sav Oxton 39-41; Offg Chap Mersey Miss to Seamen 39-41; Chap to War Factories Dio Ches 41-44; Dio Lich 44-45; V of Kilndown Dio Cant from 45; Hon Can of Cant Cathl from 79. *Kilndown Vicarage, Cranbrook, Kent.* (Lamberhurst 890305)

JOHNSON, Verrall Cuthbert Broughton. St Jo Th Coll Lusaka. **d** and **p** 63 N Rhod. C of St Geo Luanshya 63-67; Mufulira 67-68; Komgha Dio Grahmstn 68-70; R of St Raph Durban 71-74; Margate Dio Natal from 74. *Box 266, Margate, Natal, S Africa.* (Margate 20415)

JOHNSON, Walter. b 21. St Aid Coll. **d** 59 **p** 60 Southw. C of W Bridgford 59-62; V of Bracebridge 62-73; R of Weston-sub-Edge w Ashton-sub-Edge (w Willersey and Saintbury from 77) Dio Glouc from 73. *Weston-sub-Edge Rectory, Chipping Campden, Glos.* (Evesham 840292)

JOHNSON, Walter Sidney. Wycl Coll Tor. **d** 50 **p** 51 Tor. C of St John W Tor 50-51; I of Cannington w Beavertown 51-53; Bradford 53-57; R of St Bede and P-in-c of Incarnation Tor 57-63; R of Caledon E 63-65. *Port Sydney, Ont., Canada.* (705-385 2769)

JOHNSON, William Courtnay Saunders. Univ of Adel BA 34. St Barn Coll Adel 34. **d** and **p** 36 Adel. C of St Columba Hawthorn 36-39; P-in-c of Murray Bridge 39-42; LPr Dio Adel 41-46; Chap AIF 42-46; Asst Chap Melb Gr Sch 46-48; I of St Luke N Brighton 48-56; R of Port Adelaide 56-68; Victor Harbour 68-72; L to Offic Dio Murray from 73. *23 Kent Drive, Victor Harbour, S Australia 5211.* (085-52 2405)

JOHNSON, William John. b 16. Oriel Coll Ox BA (2nd cl PPE) 38, MA 43, Dipl Th 47. Wycl Hall, Ox 46. **d** 48 Roch **p** 49 Colom. C of Ch Ch Galle Face Colom and Asst Master Christian Coll Kotte 48-50; Prin of Ch Ch Coll Kurun 50-52; C of Crewkerne w Hewish 52-54; V of Westleton w Dunwich 54-61; H Trin Darwen 61-64; Twerton-on-Avon Bath 64-77; C-in-c of Priston w Englishcombe 75-77; Hutton 77-81. *7 Bronel Close, Bleadon Hill, Weston-super-Mare, Avon, BS24 9SL.* (Bleadon 812982)

JOHNSTON, Alan Beere. Univ of Leeds, BA 36. Coll of Resurr Mirfield, 36. **d** 38 **p** 39 Bradf. C of St Chad Manningham 38-40; St Paul Middlesbrough 40-43; Perm to Offic Dio York 43-45; C of Crawley 45-47; Perm to Offic at St Mark Portsm 47-48; C of Marske-in-Cleveland (in c of St Thos New Marske) 48-50; C-in-c of Carlin How w Skinningrove 50-52; V 52-57; Clifton 57-62; St Mary Virg Lowgate Hull 62-68; Asst Master Sir Henry Cooper High Sch Kingston upon Hull 68-70; Waltham Toll Bar Sch Waltham 70-71; Tutor Workers' Educl Assoc 71-81. *6 Arlington Close, Goring-by-Sea, W Sussex, BN12 4ST.* (0903-46590)

JOHNSTON, Canon Albert Richard. b 06. K Coll Lon 37. **d** 41 **p** 42 Chelmsf. C of St Jo Bapt Tilbury Dks 41-43; Chap RAFVR 43-46; Men in Disp 45; R of St Leon Colchester 46-50; V and Lect Dedham 50-75; RD of Dedham 53-74; Hon Can of Chelmsf 64-75; Can (Emer) from 75; Perm to Offic Dio St E from 76. *The Old Manse, Swan Street, Boxford, Suff.*

JOHNSTON, Alexander Irvine. b 47. Univ of Keele BA 70. St Alb Ministerial Tr Scheme 77. **d** 80 **p** 81 St Alb (APM). C of Hockerill Dio St Alb from 80. *2 Maze Green Road, The College, Bishop's Stortford, Herts, CM23 2QZ.* (0279 57479)

✠ **JOHNSTON, Most Rev Allen Howard.** CMG 78. St Jo Coll Auckld LTh 36. Univ of Otago Hon LLD 69. **d** 35 **p** 36 Auckld. C of St Mark Remuera 35-37; V of Dargaville 37-42; N Wairoa 42-44; Otahuhu 44-49; Whangarei 49-53; Archd of Waimate 49-53; Cons Ld Bp of Dun 24 Feb 53 in St Paul's Cathl Dun by Abp of Wel (Primate); Bps of Auckld; Nel; Wai; Waik; Ch Ch; and Melan; Bp Suffr of Aotearoa; and Bp Rich; Trld to Waik 69; res 80; Fell of St Jo coll Auckld 70; Elected Primate and Abp of NZ 72; res 80; Perm to Offic Dio Waik from 80. *3 Wymer Terrace, Hamilton, NZ.* (53-238)

JOHNSTON, Cecil Macaulay. b 08. Univ of Bris BA (2nd cl Hist) 30. Univ of Dur LTh 32. Trin Coll Bris 30. **d** 32 **p** 33 S'Wark. C of St Steph Clapham Pk 32-34; BCMS Miss in Burma 34-42; CF (EC) 42-45; Hon CF 46; Travelling Sec IVF 45-47; Gen Supt Scripture U (CSSM) India 47-65; Reg Sec S Asia 66-72; C of All SS Eastbourne Dio Chich from 72. *4 Silverdale Road, Eastbourne, E Sussex.*

JOHNSTON, Charles Walter Barr. b 38. BSc (Lon) 61. Oak Hill Th Coll 62. **d** 64 Lon **p** 65 Stepney for Lon. C of St Mark Holloway 64-68; L to Offic Dio Argent 68-70; SAMS Miss Dio N Argent from 70. *Centro Anglicano, Casilla 19, Ing Juarez, Prov de Formosa, Argentina.*

JOHNSTON, Dana Carr. b 49. Univ of Ott BA 73. Carleton Univ Ont MA 74. Trin Coll Tor MDiv 81. **d** 81 Ott. C of St Steph City and Dio Ott from 81. *c/o 930 Watson Street, Ottawa, Ont, Canada, K2B 6B9.*

JOHNSTON, David Charles. b 39. Trin Coll Dub BA 62, Div Test 63, BD 69, MA 70. **d** 63 **p** 64 Dub. C of St Cath and St Jas Dub 63-68; St Mary Donnybrook Dub 68-71; Hon Cler V of Ch Ch Cathl Dub 64-71; Asst Master Bangor Gr Sch Co Down 71-72; K Sch Pet 72-76; Ashton Middle Comprehensive Sch Dunstable 76-81; Publ Pr Dio St Alb from 77; Asst Chap Highgate Sch Lon from 81. *Highgate School, Highgate, N6.*

JOHNSTON, Donald Walter. Univ of Melb BA 51. Em Coll Cam BA 63, MA 67. Ridley Hall Cam. **d** 64 **p** 65 York for Melb. C of Cottingham 64-66; V of Nunawading 67-69; Chap Brighton Gr Sch 70-74; Melb C of E Gr Sch from 74. *Church of England Grammar School, Domain Road, S Yarra, Vic, Australia 3141.* (26-2231)

JOHNSTON, Edward Alexander. Univ of NZ MA 53. St Jo Coll Auckld LTh (1st cl) 55. Princeton Th Sem ThM 64. **d** 56 **p** 57 Auckld. C of Devonport Auckld 56-58; V of Hokianga 58-62; Paparoa 62-66; Sub-Dean of Auckld 66-70; Prin Ch Ch Coll Ch Ch 70-74; Hon Can of Ch Ch 70-74; Dean and V of St Pet Cathl Hamilton 74-78; Exam Chap to Bp of Waik 74-78; Ecumen Chap to Ch Ch Hosp from 79. *108 Park Terrace, Christchurch 1, NZ.* (759-168)

JOHNSTON, Edwin Owen. Trin Coll Tor. **d** and **p** 48 Niag. C of Guelph 49-50; in Amer Ch 50-53; R of Bancroft (and of Maynorth 53-57;) 53-58; Kitley 58-66; St Pet Takhini Whitehorse 66-67; Squamish 75-77; on leave. *Box 236, Garibaldi, Highlands, BC, Canada.*

JOHNSTON, Frederick Mervyn Kieran. b 11. Trin Coll Dub BA 33, MA 52. **d** 34 **p** 36 Oss. C of Castlecomer 34-36; St Luke Cork 36-38; I of Kilmeen 38-40; Drimoleague 40-45; R of Blackrock 45-58; Can of St Mich in Cork Cathl 55-59; Brigown in Cloyne Cathl 55-59; R of Bandon 58-67; Treas of Ross Cathl 59-60; Can of Killanully in Cork Cathl 59-60; Archd of Cork 59-67; Dean 67-71; Exam Chap to Bp of Cork 60-78. *1 Pembroke Wood, Passage West, Co Cork, Irish Republic.* (021-841822)

JOHNSTON, Geoffrey Stanley. b 44. Dipl Th (Lon) 68. Univ of Aston MBA 81. Kelham Th Coll 64. **d** 68 Stafford for Lich. **p** 69 Shrewsbury for Lich. C of Blakenhall Heath 68-72; St Buryan St Levan and Sennen Dio Truro 72-73; Blakenall Heath 73-75; St Steph Willenhall 75-76; All SS W Bromwich

76-77; Lect W Bromwich Coll of Com and Tech from 78. *20 Culmore Close, Furlongs Estate, Willenhall, W Midl, WU12 4TP.* (Willenhall 634735)

JOHNSTON, George Ralph Harden. b 23. Trin Coll Dub BA 44, Div Test 45, MA 47. **d** 45 Bp Hind for Down **p** 47 Down. C of St Mark Dundela 45-56; Jordanstown (in c of Greenisland) 56-57; C-in-c of Greenisland Dio Connor 57-64; R from 64. *109 Station Road, Greenisland, Carrickfergus, Co Antrim, N Ireland BT38 8UW.* (Whiteabbey 63421)

JOHNSTON, Herbert Pearcey. b 03. Qu Coll Birm 54. **d** 54 **p** 55 Dur. C of Leadgate 54-57; Seaton Carew (in c of St Jas Owton Manor) 57-61; V of All SS Monk Wearmouth 61-74. *167 Belfast Road, Muckamore, Co Antrim, N Ireland.*

JOHNSTON, John George. St Aid Coll Bal ThL 37. **d** 27 **p** 29 St Arn. C of Wycheproof 27-29; Manangatang 29-31; M of Bush Bro Collinsville 31-33; C of St John Cairns 33-35 and 36-38; All SS Brisb 36; R of Proserpine 38-39; Mundingburra 39-40; Chap RAAF 40-44; R of St Phil Thompson Estate Brisb 50-74; Perm to Offic Dio Brisb from 74. *246 Gladstone Road, Dutton Park, Queensland, Australia 4102.* (44 2893)

JOHNSTON, John Martin. Moore Th Coll Syd ACT ThL 47. **d** 47 **p** 48 Syd. C of St Paul Wahroonga 47-49; R of St Leon Denmark 50-53; Wallerawang 53-54; Milton 54-57; Merrylands (w Holroyd and Greystanes 57-62) 57-77; L to Offic Dio Syd from 77. *8 Boynton Street, Blaxland, NSW, Australia 2774.* (047-39 1507)

JOHNSTON, Lance Andrew. Univ of Syd BA 56. Univ of Edin BD 68. **d** 68 Bp Warren for C & Goulb **p** 69 C & Goulb. C of H Cross Canberra 68-70; Young 70; Prin St Andr Sch Brunei and LPr Dio Kuch 70-73; Sub-Warden and Chap St Geo Coll Univ of W Austr 73-74; Warden St Jo Coll Morpeth 75-79; Prin Chr Commun Coll Maryborough from 79. *21 Kars Street, Maryborough, Vic, Australia 3465.*

JOHNSTON, Ralph Herbert George. b 16. Linc Th Coll 46. **d** 48 **p** 49 Chich. C of St Aug Preston Brighton 48-51; Rottingdean 51-56; V of St Jo Evang Hollington Dio Chich from 56; RD of Hastings 66-71 and 76-78; Surr from 68. *94 Lower Glen Road, St Leonards-on-Sea, Sussex, TN37 7Ar.* (Hastings 751103)

JOHNSTON, Randal William Douglas. Univ of Tor BA 64. Trin Coll Tor STB 67. **d** 67 **p** 68 Tor. C of St Jas Orillia 67-69; R of Caledon E 70-73; St Leon City and Dio Tor from 73. *25 Wanless Avenue, Toronto, Ont., Canada.* (416-485 7278)

JOHNSTON, Preb Rauceby Peter Pope. b 10. Oak Hill Th Coll 32. Men in Disp 42. **d** 35 Sarum **p** 36 Sherborne for Sarum. C of St Mary Weymouth 35-36; H Trin Tunbridge Wells 36; Seaford w Sutton 37-45; Chap RAFVR 39-45; V of St Matt Fulham 45-50; St Phil and St Jas Ilfracombe 50-53; St Jo Evang Heatherlands Parkstone 53-62; Proc Conv Sarum 55-64; RD of Poole 59-62; Isl 67-80; V of Isl 62-80; Proc Conv Lon 64-75; C-in-c of St Jo Bapt Isl 67-71; St Jas Ap w St Phil Isl 71-80; Preb of St Paul's Cathl Lon from 70; Commiss Gippsld from 76; Perm to Offic Dio Bris from 80. *8 Oakfield Road, Clifton, Bristol, BS8 2AL.*

JOHNSTON, Robert Hallam O'Hanlon. Trin Coll Dub BA (2nd cl Ment and Mor Sc Mod) 61, Div Test 62, BD 68. **d** 62 **p** 63 Down. C of Holywood Co Down 62-65; St John Ott 65-66; Univ Chap Ott 66-72; on leave. *160 Holland Avenue, Ottawa, Ont., Canada.*

JOHNSTON, Robert John. b 31. Oak Hill Th Coll 64. **d** 64 **p** 65 Ches. C of Bebington 64-68; R of Lack Dio Clogh from 68. *Rectory, Lack, Co Fermanagh, N Ireland.*

JOHNSTON, Thomas Cosbey. Em Coll Cam BA 40, MA 44. Ridley Hall, Cam 40. **d** 42 **p** 43 Birm. C of St Mary Handsworth 42-48; V of Malvern 48-51; Sumner-Heathcote 51-63; C of Linwood-Aranui 63-65; Asst Hosps Chap Dio Ch Ch from 65. *100 Chapter Street, Christchurch 5, NZ.*

JOHNSTON, Walter Barr. b 09. Univ of Lon MB BS 33, MRCS LRCP 32. Oak Hill Th Coll. **d** 67 Barking for Chelmsf **p** 68 Chelmsf. C of Dagenham 67-70; C-in-c of Burton Fleming w Forden Dio York 70; V from 71; V of Grindale and Ergham Dio York from 71. *Burton Fleming Vicarage, Driffield, Yorks, YO25 0PT.* (Thwing 668)

JOHNSTON, Wilfred Brian. b 44. Trin Coll Dub BA 67, MA 70. **d** 68 Down **p** 70 Drom. C of Seagoe 68-73; I of Iniskeel Dio Raph from 73. *Portnoo, Lifford, Co Donegal, Irish Republic.*

✠ **JOHNSTON, Right Rev William.** b 14. Selw Coll Cam 2nd cl Geog Trip pt i 36, BA (3rd cl Geog Trip pt ii) 37, MA 41. Westcott Ho Cam 37. **d** 39 Ripon **p** 40 Selby for York for Ripon. C of St Mich Headingley 39-43; St Jo Bapt Knaresborough 43-45; V of Stourton 45-49; PC of Armley 49-56; Surr from 49; V of St Chad Shrewsbury 56-64; Archd of Bradf 65-77; Dioc Missr Dio Bradf 65-74; Dir of Ordinands 65-77; Cons Ld Bp Suffr of Dunwich in S'wark Cathl 6 Jan 77 by Abp of Cant; Bps of St E, Bradf, Pet, Ely, Ox, Nor, S'wark and S & M; Bps Suffr of Edmonton, Huntingdon, Jarrow, Knaresborough, Lynn, Shrewsbury and Tonbridge; and others; res 80. *40 Shrewsbury Road, Church Stretton, Shrewsbury, SY6 6EU.* (Church Stretton 722687)

JOHNSTON, William Derek. b 40. TCD 68. **d** 68 Derry **p** 69 Clogh for Derry. V Cho of St Columb Cathl Derry 68-73; I of Killinkere w Mullagh Dio Kilm from 73; Lurgan w Munterconnaught and Loughan Dio Kilm from 73; Billis U Dio Kilm from 73. *Killinkere, Virginia, Co Cavan, Irish Republic.*

JOHNSTON, Ven William Francis. b 30 Trin Coll Dub BA 55, MA 69. **d** 55 **p** 56 Down. C of Orangefield 55-59; CF from 59; ACG 77-80; Chap-Gen from 80. *c/o Williams & Glyns Bank Ltd, Whitehall SW1.*

JOHNSTON, William John. b 35. Univ of Lon Dipl Th (Extra Mural Stud) 72. Div Hostel Dub 67. **d** 70 **p** 71 Down. C of St Donard Belf 70-72; Derg 72-78; R of Drumclamph w Drumquin Dio Derry from 78. *Drumclamph Rectory, Castlederg, Co Tyrone, N Ireland.* (Castlederg 71433)

JOHNSTON, Very Rev William McConnell. TCD BA 57. **d** 58 **p** 61 Connor. C of Ballymena 58-61; St Thos Belf 61-63; Finaghy 63-66; R of Kambula 66-74; Dean and R of St Mich AA Cathl Eshowe Dio Zulu from 74. *PO Box 207, Eshowe, Zululand.* (Eshowe 15)

JOHNSTON-HUBBOLD, Clifford Johnston. b 19. BA (Lon) 76. St Aid Coll 49. **d** 52 **p** 53 Carl. C of Stanwix 52-55; V of Gt Broughton 55-59; R of Sedgeberrow (w Hinton-on-the-Green from 73) Dio Worc from 59; C-in-c of Hinton-on-the-Green 72-73. *Sedgeberrow Rectory, Evesham, Worcs, WR11 6UE.* (Evesham 881291)

JOHNSTONE, David. Moore Th Coll Syd ACT ThL (2nd cl) 59. **d** and **p** 60 Syd. C of All SS N Parramatta 60-62; St Andr Willesden 63-66; Prec of St Jas Cathl Townsville 66-69; Chap CMF 69; RAAF Townsville 69-74; Dioc Sec Dio N Queensld 70-74; Hon Can of N Queensld 70-74; Chap Mentone Girls Gr Sch Melb 74-78; Asst Chap Southport Sch Dio Brisb from 79. *7 Truda Street, Southport, Queensland, Australia 4215.* (32 2506)

JOHNSTONE, Canon Frederic St. George Harden. b 12. TCD BA 34, MA 43. **d** 35 **p** 36 Derry. C of Conwall (Letterkenny) 35-40; C-in-c of U Moville 40-44; R of Lower Moville 44-55; Killenaule 55-65; Templemore w Kilfithmone Thurles and Loughmoe Dio Cash from 65; Can and Prec of Cash Cathl from 75. *Rectory, Templemore, Co Tipperary, Irish Republic.* (Templemore 65)

JOHNSTONE, Ian Douglas. b 42. St John Coll Morpeth. **d** 70 **p** 71 Bath. C of St Barn Orange 70-72; Dubbo 72-74; R of Natimuk 74-75; V of Fawkner 75-79; I of Bayswater Dio Melb from 79. *Vicarage, Warruga Avenue, Bayswater, Vic, Australia 3153.* (729 2092)

JOHNSTONE, John Howard Lindsay. b 45. Univ of Syd BA 66. Univ of Lon BD 70. Moore Th Coll Syd ACT ThL 69. **d** 70 **p** 71 Syd. C of St Andr Sans Souci 70-73; St Mark Darlington Point Syd 73-75; CMS Miss Tanzania 75-78; Field Officer Dioc Bd of Educn Syd from 79. *St Andrew's House, Sydney Square, Sydney, NSW, Australia 2000.* (269-0642)

JOHNSTONE, John James Thornton. Em Coll Sktn. **d** 58 **p** 59 Qu'App. Prin Gordon's Ind Sch Punnichy 58-65; Hon C of St Chad Winnipeg Dio Rupld from 70. *14 Canoe Bay, Winnipeg 22, Manit, Canada.*

JOHNSTONE, Canon John Roderic Lindsay. Univ of Syd LLB 38. Moore Th Coll Syd 39. ACT ThL 46. **d** 39 **p** 40 Syd. C of St Clem Mosman 39-41; C-in-c of Carlingford 41-42; R of Beecroft and Cheltm Dio Syd from 42; Hon Can of Syd 63-68; Can from 68. *9 Chapman Avenue, Beecroft, NSW, Australia 2119.* (84-1143)

JOHNSTONE, Leslie William. b 20. ALCD 49. **d** 49 **p** 50 Ches. C of Ch Ch Claughton w Grange 49-52; Crawley (in c of Three Bridges) 52-56; R of St Mark Bexhill Dio Chich from 56. *Rectory, Meads Road, Bexhill, Sussex.* (Cooden 3733)

JOHNSTONE, Peter Verney Lovett. b 37. Trin Coll Cam 2nd cl Th Trip pt i, 59, BA (3rd cl Th Trip pt ii) 61, MA 65. Cudd Coll 61. **d** 63 **p** 64 S'wark. C of St Jo Div Kennington 63-66; Asst Chap Univ of Southn 66-70; P-in-c of St Jo Div Earlsfield 70-79; V of Eltham Dio S'wark from 79. *Eltham Vicarage, Sowerby Close, SE9 6HB.* (01-850 2731)

JOHNSTONE, Robert William. b 49. ACT ThL 76. Ridley Coll Melb 74. **d** 77 **p** 78 Melb. C of St Andr Rosanna 77-80; I of All SS Northcote Dio Melb from 80. *Vicarage, High Street, Northcote, Vic, Australia 3070.*

JOHNSTONE, Canon Thomas John. St Jo Coll Morpeth ACT ThL 50. **d** 50 **p** 52 Newc. C of Cessnock 50-53; Mayfield 53; Taree 54; P-in-c of Charlestown 55-57; C of Ch Ch Cathl Newc 57-59; Home Miss Chap 59-69; L to Offic Dio Newc 59-69; R of Taree Dio Newc from 69; Hon Can of Newc 79. *St John's Rectory, Taree, NSW, Australia 2430.* (065-52 1310)

JOHNSTONE, William John Richard. Univ of Leeds, BA

(3rd cl Phil) 48. Coll of Resurr Mirfield. **d** 50 **p** 51 Ex. C of Cockington w Chelston 50-54; Wolborough 54-57; V of St Mich Wakef 57-63; St Neot Cornw. 63-71; St Paul Ruislip 71-76; C of St Francis Honicknowle Plymouth 76-77. *19 Trelawney Road, Peverell, Plymouth.*

JOINT, Michael John. Sarum Wells Th Coll 79. **d** and **p** 79 Win. *in CA.* Dioc Youth Officer Dio Win from 79; Hon C of Chandlers Ford Dio Win from 79. *105 Belmont Road, Chandlers Ford, Hants.* (C/Ford 61420)

JOLLIFFE, John Gordon. b 53. Simon Fraser Univ BC BGenStuds 77. Em & St Chad's Coll Sktn MDiv 81. **d** and **p** 81 Carib. C of Carib and Kootenay Miss Dio Carib from 81. *135 Battle Street, Kamloops, BC, Canada, V2C 2L1.*

JOLLIFFE, Peter Sydney. Univ of Syd BA (1st cl Engl and Educn 55) MA (1st cl Engl) 58. Univ of Lon PhD 67. ACT ThL 58. **d** 57 Gippsld **p** 58 Bp Redding for Borneo. C of St Paul Sale 57-58; Prin St Columb Sch Miri Borneo 59-61; Lect St Jo Coll Morpeth 62-64; and 67-70; Perm to Offic Dio Lon 65-67; Dio Melb from 70; Chap Retreat Ho Dio Melb from 70. *44 Cavanagh Street, Cheltenham, Vic, Australia 3192.* (03-93 2076)

JOLLIFFE, Stanley Frederick. ALCD (2nd cl) 39. **d** 39 **p** 40 Liv. C of Em Everton 39-40; St Leon Bootle 40-41; Chesham 42-44; R of St Paul Hulme Man 44-46; Thorndon 46-49; Seq of Blakemere and V of Bredwardine w Brobury 49-54; Chap Toc H Man Area and Perm to Offic Dios Man, Ches, Lich, Blackb and Wakef 54-58; V of Garway 58-61; Org Sec CECS 61-62; Chap Prestwich Psychiatric Hosp 62-74. *Cheddleton Lodge, North Road, Prestwich, Manchester M25 7AD.* (Prestwich 2236)

JOLLY, Leslie Alfred Walter. b 16. AKC 40. **d** 40 **p** 41 Lon. C of St Mary Bow 40-42; St Phil Cheam Common 42-50; St Andr Mottingham 50-52; V of St Matt Newington 52-57; R of Chaldon Dio S'wark from 57. *28 Doctors Lane, Caterham, Surrey, CR3 5AF.* (Caterham 43668)

JOLLY, William James. b 41. Linc Th Coll 74. **d** 76 **p** 77 Melb for Brisb. C of St Paul Ipswich 76-77; St Nicolas Sandgate Brisb 77-78; St Aug Palmwoods Dio Brisb from 78. *Box 42, Palmwoods, Queensland, Australia 4555.*

JOLOBE, Richard Robert Sipho. b 56. St Pet Coll Natal. **d** 79 **p** 80 Grahmstn. C of St John Bolotwa Dio Grahmstn from 79. *The Mission House, PO Bolotwa 5325, CP, S Africa.*

JONAS, Alfred Velile. b 49. Univ of Fort Hare CP BTh 76. St Pet Coll Natal 76. **d** 77 **p** 78 Port Eliz. C of Ch Ascen Cradock Dio Port Eliz from 77. *PO Box 503, Cradock, CP, S Africa.*

JONATHAN, d 69 Rang **p** 71 Akyab. P Dio Rang 69-70; Dio Akyab from 70. *St Barnabas Church, Hmumtnu, Burma.*

JONATHAN, Canon George Edward. Univ of Capetn. **d** 47 **p** 49 Capetn. C of St Mark Athlone 47-50; St Matt Claremont 50-56; Prin of St Matt Sch Claremont from 51; P-in-c of Lansdowne 56-58; R of Athlone 58;68; Can of Capetn 61-65; Can (Emer) from 65. *5 Athlone Street, Athlone, CP, S Africa.*

JONATHAN, Ronald Edwin. b 40. St Pet Coll Natal Dipl Th 76. **d** 76 **p** 77 Capetn (APM). C of St Paul Bree 76-78; P-in-c of Lutus River Dio Capetn 78-80; R from 80. *Priest's House, Sixth Avenue, Lotus River, CP, S Africa.* (73 5597)

JONES, Adrian Alfred Burkett. b 37. St Aid Coll 61. **d** 64 **p** 65 Derby. C of St Aug Derby 64-68; Chap RAF from 68. *c/o Ministry of Defence, Adastral House WC 1.*

JONES, Alan David. b 32. ALCD 58 (LTh from 74). Dipl Th 70. **d** 58 Dunwich for St E **p** 59 St E. C of All SS Ipswich 58-60; CF (TA) 60-62; CF (TA R of O) 62-67; C of St Jo Bapt Southend-on-Sea (in c of St Mark) 60-64; V of St Cath Leyton 64-70; Hatfield Broad Oak 70-77; C-in-c of Bush End 70-77; V of Theydon Bois Dio Chelmsf from 76. *Theydon Bois Vicarage, Epping, Essex.*

JONES, Alan John. b 47. Univ of Nottm BA (Th) 71. Coll of Resurr Mirfield 71. **d** 73 **p** 74 Lich. C of St Mary Hurst Hill Sedgley 73-76; St John Bapt Cov 76-78; V of St Francis Friar Pk W Bromwich Dio Lich from 78. *Friar Park Vicarage, Wednesbury, W Midl, WS10 0HJ.* (021-556 5823)

JONES, Alan Peter. Ridley Coll Melb ACT ThL (2nd cl) 66. **d** 67 **p** 68 Melb. C of St Mary Caulfield 67-69; Glenroy 69-70; Youth Chap to St John's Homes 70-71; C in Dept of Industr Miss Dio Melb from 72. *38 Triton Drive, Noble Park, Vic, Australia 3174.* (03-789 2368)

JONES, Alban Vaughan. b 24. St D Coll Lamp BA 51. **d** 52 **p** 53 Swan B. C of Llandilo-Talybont 52-55; St Pet Cockett Swansea 55-59; R of Llangammarch 59-65; CMS Area Sec Dios ches, Ban, St A and S & M 65-73; V of Ventnor 73-79; H Trin Ventnor 73-79; Marshfield w Peterstone Wentloog, Coedkernew and St Bride Wentloog Dio Mon from 79. *Vicarage, Church Lane, Marshfield, Cardiff, CF3 8UF.* (Castleton 680257)

JONES, Albert. b 13. K Coll Lon 37. **d** 41 **p** 42 Man. C of St Jo Evang Farnworth and Kearsley 41-46; C-in-c 45-46; C of St Jo Bapt Felixstowe 46-47; St Geo Headstone 47-49; R of All SS Stretford Man 49-52; Scarborough and Plymouth Trinid 52-54; Tacarigua Trinid 54-56; V of St Pet Farnworth 56-58; SPG Area Sec Yorks 58-63; V of Tillingham 63-66; R of Dengie w Asheldham 63-66; Stifford 66-72; Doddinghurst 72-79; C-in-c of Stondon Massey 72-79. *2 Pyefleet Close, Brightlingsea, Essex, CO7 0LL.* (Brightlingsea 3994)

JONES, Albert. Worc OTC 55. **d** 56 **p** 57 Glouc. MRST 38. C of Coleford 56-58; V of Coaley 58-61; C of St John Bethnal Green 61; St Gabr Warwick Square Westmr 61-63; and 68-72; C-in-c of St Pet Bethnal Green 63-68; Chap Qu Eliz Hosp for Children 63-68; Perm to Offic Dio Pet from 77. *c/o St Alban's Vicarage, Broadmead Avenue, Northampton.*

JONES, Alec Frank. d and **p** 78 Syd. C of Beecroft Dio Syd from 78. *21 Hannah Street, Beecroft, Australia 2119.* (84-1571)

JONES, Alfred Albert. St D Coll Lamp BA 59. **d** 61 Llan **p** 62 Bp T M Hughes for Llan. C of Treherbert 61-64; Horsham (in c of St Mark) Dio Chich from 64. *St Mark's House, Corunna Drive, Horsham, Sussex.* (Horsham 4964)

JONES, Alfred Richard. Late Scho of Hatf Coll Dur BA 36. **d** 38 **p** 39 Cov. C of St Anne Cov 38-46; C-in-c of Galley Common 46-49; V of Monk's Kirby 49-59; C-in-c of Willey 53-59; V of Husthwaite w Carlton and Birdforth 59-62; St Lawr w St Nich and New Fulford City and Dio York from 62. *St Lawrence's Vicarage, York.* (York 24916)

JONES, Alfred William. Univ of Dur 1900. **d** 04 **p** 08 Llan. C of Mountain Ash 04-09; All SS Newport Mon 09-11; Marshfield w Peterstone Wentloog 11-14; R of Penrieth w Castellan Chap 14-25; Henry's Moat 25-32; Trefilan 32-39; Merthyr 39-49. *6 Portland Place, Aberayron, Dyfed.*

JONES, Allan Stewart. Moore Th Coll Syd 54. **d** 55 **p** 57 Syd. C of Herne Bay 55-56; Marrickville 56-57; Erskineville 57-60; C-in-c of St Barn Punchbowl 60-62; L to Offic Dio Syd from 64. *8 Leeds Place, Turramurra, NSW, Australia 2074.* (44-2499)

JONES, Canon Alun. b 17. Univ of Wales, BA 40. St Steph Ho Ox 40. **d** 42 Ban **p** 43 St A for Ban. C of Machynlleth 42-46; Min Can of Ban Cathl 46-48; C of Portmadoc 48-55; R of Llanberis Dio Ban from 55; Can of Ban Cathl from 70; RD of Arfon from 73. *Rectory, Llanberis, Gwyn, LL55 4TF.* (Llanberis 285)

JONES, Alun Glyn. b 38. CCC Cam BA (Econ and Law Trip) 59, MA 63. Bps' Coll Cheshunt, 60. **d** 61 **p** 62 Portsm. C of Portsea 61-65; Chap and Asst Master Hampton Gr Sch 65-76; Hd Master Abp Tenison Gr Sch Croydon from 76. *c/o Archbishop Tenison's School, Selborne Road, Croydon, Surrey.*

JONES, Alwyn Humphrey Griffith. b 30. Univ of Leeds BSc (3rd cl Chem) 51. Coll of Resurr Mirfield 53. **d** 55 **p** 56 Lon. C of St Barn w Hackney 55-58; C-in-c of St Thos Dacca 58-64; Miss OMC Calc 65-68; Chap R Bombay Seamen's S 68-73; C-in-c of St Francis Ashton Gate Bedminster 73-75; Team R of Bedminster Dio Bris from 75. *287 North Street, Bristol, BS3 1JP.* (Bris 664025)

JONES, Very Rev Alwyn Rice. b 34. Late Welsh Ch Scho and Pri of St D Coll Lamp BA (2nd cl Welsh) 55. Powis Exhib Fitzw Ho Cam BA (3rd cl Th Trip pt ii) 57, MA 61. St Mich Coll Llan 57. **d** 58 **p** 59 Ban. C of Llanfairisgaer 58-62; N Wales Area Sec SCM 60-62; Staff Sec 62-65; L to Offic Dio Ban 62-74; Dir Relig Educn Dio Ban 65-75; Youth Chap Dio Ban 66-72; Warden of Ordins Dio Ban 70-75; Exam Chap to Abp of Wales 71-78; Hon Can of Ban Cathl 74-78; Preb 78; V of Portmadoc 75-79; Dean of Brecon Cathl and V of Brecon w Battle Dio Swan B from 79. *The Almonry, Cathedral Close, Brecon.* (Brecon 4876)

JONES, Andrew Christopher. b 47. Univ of Southn BA 69, PhD 75. Ridley Hall Cam 78. **d** 80 **p** 81 Sarum. C of Wareham Dio Sarum from 80. *110 Northmoor Way, Wareham, Dorset, BH20 4ET.*

JONES, Andrew Theodore Hugh. b 22. St Cath S Ox BA (3rd cl Th) 49, MA 53. St Steph Ho Ox. **d** 50 **p** 51 Ex. C of Hartland 50-54; V 54-55; Welcombe w Hartland 55-66; Witheridge 66-77; R of Thelbridge 67-77; R of Creacombe 67-77; R of W w E Worlington 67-77; C-in-c of Meshaw 68-77; RD of S Molton 72-74; C-in-c of Ilchester w Northover 77-78; R (w Limington Yeovilton and Podimore) 78-79; Limington 77-78; Yeovilton 78; Podymore-Milton 78; V of Newport Dio Ex from 79; Bp's Tawton Dio Ex from 79; RD of Barnstaple from 81. *Newport Vicarage, Barnstaple, Devon, EX32 9EF.* (Barnstaple 72733)

JONES, Anthony Spacie. b 34. K Coll Lon and Warm AKC 58. **d** 59 **p** 60 St Alb. C of St Martin Bedford 59-63; Georgetn Cathl 63-66; V of Metenmeerzorg Guy 66-71; All H Ipswich 72-80; RD of Ipswich from 78; Dom Chap to Bp of St E from 80. *1b Park Road, Ipswich, Suff, IP1 3SS.* (Ipswich 221502)

JONES, Canon Arthur Alexander. b 10. Univ of Birm BA

35, MA 48. Univ of Lon BD 45, PhD 53. **d** 52 **p** 53 Cov. C of St Mich AA Cathl Cov and Div Master Bablake Sch Cov 53-57; PC of St Silas Nunhead 57-62; Prin Div Lect Avery Hill Tr Coll from 62; Can (Emer) of S'wark from 75. *16 Heath Road, Beaconsfield, Bucks, HP9 1DD.* (04946-6746)

JONES, Arthur Douglas. b 17. **d** 77 **p** 78 Wel. Hon C of Trentham 77-78; Offg Min Dio Wel from 78. *7 Iris Grove, Trentham, NZ.* (87-326)

JONES, Arthur Edward. b 02. St D Coll Lamp BA 27. **d** 27 **p** 28 St A. C of Rhyl 27-35; R of St George (or Kegidog) 35-48; Trefnant 48-71; L to Offic Dio St A from 71. *2 Maes Teg, Trefnant, Clwyd, LL16 4YA.*

JONES, Arthur Howard Glyn. b 07. Ripon Hall Ox 53. **d** 55 Bp N Davis for Cov **p** 56 Cov. C of Stoke Cov 55-57; V of Walsgrave-on-Sowe 57-63; R of Warkleigh w Satterleigh and Chittlehamholt 63-68; Drewsteignton 68-76; Spreyton 73-76; Hittisleigh 73-76; Hon C of Stoke Fleming 76-81; Perm to Offic Dio Ex from 81. *15 Fore Street, Bradninch, Exeter.*

JONES, Arthur Kenneth Hughes. b 14. Ch Coll Cam 2nd cl Hist Trip pt i 35, BA (2nd cl Hist Trip pt ii) 36, MA 46. Wycl Hall Ox. **d** 53 **p** 54 Roch. C of St Paul Chatham 53-54; Dartford 54-57; C-in-c of St Barn Conv Dist Reading 57-64; R of Welford w Wickham 64-68; V of St Pet Maidenhead 68-79. *107 Farm Road, Maidenhead, Berks, SL6 5JQ.*

JONES, Arthur Leslie. Univ of Wales, BA 36. Qu Coll Birm 36. **d** 38 Mon **p** 39 Llan for Mon. C of Bedwellty 38-43; Stoughton 43; Farnborough Hants 43-48; V of Wyke Surrey 48-54; R of Tockenham 54-60; V of Clyffe Pypard 54-60; R of Upwey 60-80; Buckland Ripers 75-80. *4 St George's Close, Lower Street, Harnham, Salisbury, Wilts.*

JONES, Arthur Llewellyn. b 18. St D Coll Lamp BA 40. St Mich Coll Llan 41. **d** 42 **p** 43 Llan. C of St Fagan Aberdare 42-45; H Trin Wealdstone 45-48; Cler Deputn Sec Dr Barnardo's Homes for Dios Pet, Chelmsf and St Alb from 48 and Dios Ely, Nor and St E from 54; V of Totternhoe 50-54; Guilden Morden 55-56; Min of St Pet Conv Distr Watford 56-61; V 61-64; Nettledon w Potten End Dio St Alb from 64. *Potten End Vicarage, Berkhamsted, Herts.* (Berkhamsted 5217)

JONES, Arthur Redvers. St Paul's Coll Grahmstn 55. **d** 57 **p** 58 Grahmstn. C of Uitenhage 57-60; St Sav E Lon 60-61; Walmer Dio Grahmstn from 61. *c/o 40 8th Avenue, Walmer, Port Elizabeth, S Africa.*

JONES, Arthur Vivian. St Jo Coll Morpeth ACT ThL (2nd cl) 66. **d** 66 Bath. C of H Trin Orange 66-73; R of E Orange Dio Bath from 73; Exam Chap to Bp of Bath from 75. *Rectory, 381 Summer Street, Orange, NSW, Australia 2800.* (62-7729)

JONES, Ashford Bannister. Univ of Dur LTh 49. **d** 49 Barb **p** 50 Nass. C of St Matt Nass 49-50; P-in-c of Long Cay 50-54; Long I 54-57; V of St Marg Barbados 57-58; P-in-c of Abaco Nass 58-62; V of St Sar I and Dio Barb from 63. *St Saviour's Vicarage, Barbados, W Indies.*

JONES, Barry Mervyn. b 46. St Chad Coll Dur BA 68, Dipl Th 69. **d** 70 **p** 71 Lich. C of Bloxwich 70-72; All SS Upper Norwood 72-76; New Addington 76-78; Hosp Chap from 78. *17 Woodcroft Road, Thornton Heath, Surrey.*

JONES, Basil Alban. b 06. Fitzw Ho Cam 3rd cl Cl Trip pt i, 29, BA (2nd cl Geo Trip pt i) 30, MA 36. Univ of Lon BD 43. St Mich Coll Llan 33. **d** 34 Llan for Ban for St A **p** 35 St A. C of Ruabon 34-37; Llanishen w Lisvane 37-44; C-in-c of Sully 44-46; R 46-76. *13 Elan Road, Llanishen, Cardiff, CF4 5NR.* (761 354)

JONES, Canon Basil Clinton. Univ of Dur LTh 36. St Pet Coll Ja. **d** 35 **p** 36 Ja. C of Cathl Ch Spanish Town 35-36; C-in-c of Old Harbour 36-38; H Trin Montego Bay 38-44; R of Port Antonio 44-55; R and Can of Spanish Town Cathl 55-76; Can (Emer) from 76; R of Old Harbour Dio Ja from 76. *Box 182, Spanish Town PO, Jamaica, W Indies.* (098-42300)

JONES, Basil Henry. b 26. Bps' Coll Cheshunt, 63. **d** 64 **p** 65 St Alb. C of Gt Berkhampsted 64-67; V of St Luke Leagrave 68-74; RD of Luton 71-74; Surr from 71; P-in-c of St Paul Bedford 74-75; V of Wigginton Dio St Alb from 75. *Wigginton Vicarage, Tring, Herts.* (Tring 3273)

JONES, Benjamin Jenkin Hywel. b 39. Univ of Wales, BA 61. St Mich Coll Llan 61. **d** 64 **p** 65 St D. C of Carmarthen 64-70; V of Conwyl Cayo w Llansawel and Talley 70-80; Llanbadarn Fawr Dio St D from 80. *Vicarage, Llanbadarn Fawr, Aberystwyth, Dyfed.* (Aberystwyth 3368)

JONES, Benjamin Lloyd. b 05. Univ of Wales BSc (Phil) 31. Univ of Liv MA 34. **d** 31 Maenan for St A **p** 32 St A. C of Brymbo 31-35; Llangollen 35-36; Gresford (in c of Llay) 36-40; V of Rhesycae 40-71; Llanynys and Llanychan 71-75. *60 Park Street, Denbigh, Clwyd.* (Denbigh 3069)

JONES, Benjamin Raymond. St Barn Coll Adel 42. ACT ThL 44. **d** and **p** 45 Adel. C of St Pet Glenelg 45-47; Port Lincoln 47-49; P-in-c of Tatiara Miss Bordertown 49-52; R of Balhannah w Woodside 52-59; Semaphore 59-80; Woodville Dio Adel from 80. *793 Port Road, Woodville, S Australia 5011.*

JONES, Benjamin Tecwyn. b 17. Univ of Wales BA (2nd cl Hist) 38. St Bonif Coll Warm 38. **d** 40 **p** 41 St A. C of Hawarden 40-45; Pleasley (in c of Ch Ch New Houghton) 45-46; Ormskirk 46-49; R of Rufford 49-55; V of St Pet Blackpool 55-65; C of St Mary Oldham 65-69; Hd Master and Chap St Mary's Sch Bexhill-on-Sea 69-71; V of St Luke (w St Phil from 72) City and Dio Blackb from 71; C-in-c of St Phil Griffin Blackb 71-72. *Vicarage, Dalby Lea, Blackburn, Lancs.* (Blackburn 29206)

JONES, Brian Howell. b 35. Univ of Wales, Dipl Th 61. St Mich Coll Llan 58. **d** 61 **p** 62 Swan B. C of Llanguicke 61-63; Swansea 63-70; R of New Radnor w Llanfihangel Nantmelan 70-75; V of Evancoyd 70-75; Llansamlet Dio Swan B from 75. *Vicarage, Llansamlet, Swansea, W Glam.* (Swansea 71420)

JONES, Brian Noel. b 32. Edin Th Coll 59. **d** 62 **p** 63 Newc T. C of Monkseaton 62-65; Saffron Walden 65-69; C-in-c of Swaffham Bulbeck 69-75; Youth Officer Dio Ely 69-75; V of Ramsey Dio Ely from 75; Upwood w Gt and L Raveley Dio Ely from 75; RD of St Ives from 75. *Vicarage, Hollow Lane, Ramsey, Cambs, PE17 1DE.* (Ramsey 813271)

JONES, Brinley Morgan. b 13. St D Coll Lamp BA 37. **d** 40 **p** 41 Llan. C of H Trin Tylorstown 40-43; All SS Penarth 43-47; M of Bro of St Barn Dio N Queensld 47-52; C of Llwywypia 53-54; V of Pwllgwaun 54-72; R of Eglwysbrewis w St Athan 72-78. *228 New Road, Porthcawl, Mid Glam.*

JONES, Bryan Maldwyn. b 32. Univ of Wales, Dipl Th 62. St Mich Coll Llan 59. **d** 62 **p** 63 Swan B. C of St Barn Swansea 62-69; V of Trallwng w Bettws Penpont Dio Swan B from 69; R of Aberyskir w Llanfihangel Nantbran Dio Swan B from 75; RD of Brecon II from 80. *Vicarage, Trallong, Brecon, Powys, LD3 8HP.* (Sennybridge 549)

JONES, Bryan William. b 30. Late Exhib of Selw Coll Cam BA 53, 2nd cl Hist Trip pt i, 2nd cl Th Trip pt ii 54, MA 57. Linc Th Coll 53. **d** 55 **p** 56 Bris. C of St Osw Bedminster Down 55-58; Filton 58-62; C-in-c of St Mich AA Bedminster 62-65; V 65-72; C-in-c of St Matt Moorfields Bris 72-75; Warden of Readers from 73; Team V of E Bristol Dio Bris from 75. *Vicarage, Victoria Avenue, Redfield, Bristol, BS5 9NH.* (Bristol 557350)

JONES, Brynmor Lewis. b 16. St D Coll Lamp BA 37. **d** 39 **p** 40 Cov. C of Westwood 39-42; on Active Service w RN 42-46; Asst Master Broadway Sch Cov 46-48; Churchfield High Sch 48-54; C of St Mich Stoke Cov 52-54; Chap and Asst Master Arusha Sch 54-63; Hd Master 64-69; R of Michaelston-y-Fedw 70-73; V of Rhymney Dio Mon from 73. *Vicarage, Rhymney, Gwent, NP2 5LL.* (Rhymney 840500)

JONES, Bryon. b 34. St D Coll Lamp. **d** 64 **p** 65 Llan. C of Port Talbot 64-68; Aberdare 68-69; Up Hatherley 69-71; Oystermouth 71-74; V of Camrhos Dio St D from 74; St Lawr w Ford Dio St D from 77. *Vicarage, Camrhos, Haverfordwest, Dyfed.* (Camrose 501)

JONES, Canon Cecil Llewellyn. St D Coll Lamp BA 27. **d** 27 **p** 28 St A. C of Rhosddu 27-36; V of Mochdre 36-47; R of Montgomery 47-59; RD of Pool 59; R of Newtown w Llanllwchaiarn and Aberhafesp 59-67; Can of Adam Bekensall in St A Cathl 65-70; V of Llandrillo-yn-Rhos 67-74; Prec of St A Cathl 70-74; Can (Emer) from 74. *Dyffryn Awel, Upper Denbigh Road, St Asaph, Clwyd.* (St A 582418)

JONES, Charles Derek. b 37. K Coll Lon and Warm BD and AKC 60. **d** 61 **p** 62 Dur. C of St Chad Roseworth Stockton-T 61-64; St Eliz Becontree 64-66; St Mich AA S Beddington 66-73; Ed *Parish and People* 67-69; Publ Pr Dio Ex 72-77; Perm to Offic Dio Liv from 77. *8 Millfield Close, Barton Park, Farndon, Ches.*

JONES, Charles Emerson Glynne. b 08. **d** 31 **p** 32 St A. C of Bistre 31-35; Broughton 35-36; Northop 36-40; Chap RAFVR 40-47; RAF 47-52; R of Middleton Cheney w Chacombe 52-75; C of N Huish w Avonwick Dio Ex from 75. *Parsonage, Avonwick, S Brent, Devon, TQ10 9NB.* (S Brent 3200)

JONES, Charles Eurwyn. b 27. Univ of Wales BSc 48. St Mich Coll Llan. **d** 55 Swan B **p** Swan B for Wales 56. C of St D Brecon 55-57; St D Carmarthen 57-61; Tutor Old Catholic Sem Bonn 61-64; Bps' Coll Cheshunt 64-67; V of St Jo Bapt Carlton 67-75; C-in-c of Colwick 69-75; Bunny w Bradmore Dio Southw from 75; Dioc Inspector of Ch Schs from 75. *Bunny Vicarage, Nottingham.* (Nottm 217805)

JONES, Charles Frederick. b 02. Univ of Wales BSc 27. St Mich Coll Llan 27. **d** 28 **p** 29 Llan. C of Dowlais 28-33; Newcastle w Laleston and Tythegston 33-38; V of Trealaw 38-41; Ch Ch Swansea and Chap HM Pris Swansea 41-55; R of Llanfrynach w Cantref (w Llanhamlach from 63) 55-72; RD of Brecon 1 59-72; R of Llansantffraed-juxta-Usk w Llanhamlach 62-63; Can of Brecon Cathl 63-69; Prec 69-72. *134 Montagu Street, Compstall, Stockport, Cheshire, SK6 5JE.*

JONES, Charles Harold Lloyd. b 08. St D Coll Lamp 57. **d** 59 **p** 60 St D. C of Henfynyw w Aberaeron and Llanddewi Aberarth 59-60; R of Llanfair Orllwyn 60-70; Llangynllo 62-70; V of Llanllawddog w Capel-y-Groes Dio St D from 70. *Llanllawddog Vicarage, Dyfed.* (Llanpumpsaint 212)

JONES, Charles John Llewelyn. b 11. Late Rustat Exhib Jes Coll Cam 2nd cl Hist Trip pt i, 31, BA (2nd cl Hist Trip pt ii) 32, MA 36. St Aug Coll Cant 56. **d** 56 **p** 57 Southw. C of Warsop w Sookholm 56-59; V of Bole w Saundby 59-65; V of Sturton-le-Steeple w Littleborough 59-65; Whittlesford Dio Ely from 65. *Whittlesford Vicarage, Cambridge CB2 4NZ.* (Cam 833382)

JONES, Canon Cheslyn Peter Montague. b 18. Late Acad Clk of New Coll Ox BA (1st cl Th) 39. Sen Demy Magd Coll Ox 40-41; MA 43. **d** 41 **p** 42 Newc T. C of St Pet Wallsend 41-43; St Barn Northolt Pk 43-46; at Nashdom Abbey 46-51; Chap Wells Th Coll 51-52; Libr of Pusey Ho Ox 52-56; Chap Ch Ch Cathl Ox 53-56; LPr Dio Ox 55-56; Can and Chan of Chich Cathl 56-70; Can (Emer) from 71; Perm to Offic Dio Ox from 56; Prin of Chich Th Coll 56-69; Libr of Chich Cathl 59-68; Select Pr Ox Univ 60, 77, 78 and 81; Cam Univ 62; Stephenson Fell Univ of Sheff 69; Bampton Lect Univ of Ox 70; Prin of Pusey Ho Ox 71-81; R of Lowick w Sudborough and slipton Dio Pet from 81; P-in-c of Islip Dio Pet from 81. *Lowick Rectory, Kettering, Northants, NN14 3BQ.* (Thrapston 3216)

JONES, Christopher John Stark. b 39. Univ of Lon BA 60, AKC 60. Wells Th Coll 63. **d** 65 **p** 66 Win. C of St Luke Stanmore Win 65-67; Bournemouth 67-71; West Wycombe (in c of Birinus) 71-75; Team V 75-77; V of St Sebastian Wokingham Dio Ox from 77. *St Sebastian's Vicarage, Nine Mile Road, Wokingham, Berks, RG11 3AT.*

JONES, Christopher Mark. b 54. St Pet Coll Ox BA 75, Dipl Th 77, MA 79. Selw Coll Cam MPhil 80. Ridley Hall Cam 77. **d** 80 **p** 81 S'wark. C of St Marg Putney Dio S'wark from 80. *168 Tildesley Road, SW15 3AT.*

JONES, Clifford Albert. Edin Th Coll. **d** 56 **p** 57 Brechin. C of St Salvador Dundee 56-58; St Swith Linc 58-59; Grantham 59-60; R of St Salvador Dundee 60-69; V of Bradf Somt 69-74; St Jo Bapt Bridgwater 74-78; R (w Chedzoy) 78-80; RD of Bridgwater 76-80; P-in-c of Timsbury Dio B & W from 80. *Rectory, Timsbury, Bath, Avon.* (Timsbury 70153)

JONES, Canon Clifford Stanley. BEM 63. **d** 57 **p** 63 Nass. C of Grand Turk 57-76; Can of Nass from 75; P-in-c of St Thos Grand Turk Dio Nass from 76. *PO Box 25, Grand Turk, Turks and Caicos Islands, W Indies.*

JONES, Clive Morlais Peter. b 40. Univ of Wales BA (2nd cl Mus) 63. Powys Exhib 64-66. Chich Th Coll 64. **d** 66 **p** 67 Llan. C of Llanfabon 66-70; PV of Llan Cathl 70-75; R of Gelligaer Dio Llan from 75; Dioc Sec ACS from 77. *Rectory, Church Road, Gelligaer, Mid Glam, CF8 8FW.* (Bargoed 830303)

JONES, Colin Vivian. b 50. St Pet Coll Alice 73. **d** 75 **p** 76 Capetn. C of Athlone 75-78; R of Hopefield Dio Capetn from 78. *Box 52, Hopefield, CP, S Africa.* (Hopefield 142)

JONES, Cyril. b 27. Linc Th Coll 67. **d** 69 Middleton for Man **p** 70 Middleton for York. C of Milnrow 69-71; St Werburgh Chorlton-cum-Hardy 71-73; V of St Mark Chadderton 73-75; R of Ch Ch W Didsbury 75-81; V of Farlam w Nether Denton Dio Carl from 81. *Farlam Vicarage, Halbank Gate, Brampton, Cumb, CA8 1JL.* (069 76231)

JONES, Cyril Ernest. b 29. St D Coll Lamp BA 54. **d** 56 Wales **p** 57 St D. C of Llanedy 56-60; Llanelly 60-63; V of Dihewyd w Mydroilyn 63-66; Llanybyther (and Llanwenog w Llanwnen from 73) 66-78; Bettws w Ammanford 78-81; Conwyl Gayo w Llansawel and Talley Dio St D from 81. *Vicarage, Gayo, Llanwrda, Dyfed.*

JONES, Cyril Gordon. b 21. AKC 48. St Bonif Coll Warm 48. **d** 49 **p** 50 B & W. C of St Sav Walcot 49-53; H Trin Kingswood (in c of Ascen) 53-59; R of Blunsdon Dio Bris from 59; Broad Blunsdon Dio Bris from 59. *Broad Blunsdon Rectory, Swindon, Wilts.* (Swindon 721229)

JONES, Canon Daniel William Ellis. b 10. Qu Coll Cam BA 32, MA 36. Ridley Hall, Cam 32. **d** 34 **p** 36 Chelmsf. C of Rayleigh 34-38; Chadwell Heath 38-39; All SS Cardiff 39-45; PC of Charsfield 45-62; R of Monewden w Hoo 45-62; C-in-c of Easton w Letheringham 48-49; RD of Loes 52-62; R of St Martin (w St Mary from 66) Trimley 62-74; Hon Can of St E 73-74; Can (Emer) from 74. *8 Old Kirton Road, Trimley, Ipswich, Suff, IP10 0QH.* (03942-75233)

JONES, David Anthony Emlyn. b 01. St D Coll Lamp BA 27. **d** 28 **p** 29 St D. C of Llanegwad 28-31; Llandilo Talybont 31-37; R of Disserth 37-43; V of St Harmon 43-71. *42 Brecon Road, Ystrad Gynlais, Swansea, W Glam.*

JONES, David Arthur. b 44. Univ of Liv BA 66. Univ of Sussex MA 68. Bp Burgess Hall Lamp LTh 74. **d** 74 **p** 75 St D. C of Tenby 74-76; Chepstow 76-78; P-in-c of Teversal Dio Southw 78-81; R from 81. *Teversal Parsonage, Sutton-in-Ashfield, Notts.* (Mansfield 56730)

JONES, David Charles. b 44. Univ of Syd BA 67. Univ of Cam BA (Th) 76. Ridley Hall Cam 74. **d** 77 **p** 78 Tas. C of St John Launceston 77-81; Kens Dio Adel from 81. *133 Gage Street, Firle, S Australia 5070.*

JONES, David Edward. Univ of BC BA 50. Angl Th Coll Vancouver, LTh 52. **d** and **p** 52 Edmon. C of All SS Cathl Edmon 52-54; I of Leduc 54-56; R of St D Edmon 56-61; I of St Bede and P-in-c of Ch of Incarnation Tor 61-63; Hon C of Aurora 63-67; R of Ch Ch Brampton 67-80; on leave. *Watson Crescent, Brampton, Ont, Canada.*

JONES, Preb David Elidyr Glynne. b 07. St Edm Hall Ox 4th Cl Th 29, BA 30, MA 34. St Mich Coll Llan 29. **d** 30 **p** 31 Ban. C of Aberdovey 30-34; St Mary Swansea (in c of St Jas) 34-37; R of Montgomery 37-46; V of Gresford 46-54; Wrexham 54-66; Berriew 66-76; Can of St A 58-65; Preb of Llannefydd from 65; RD of Wrexham 58-66; Chan of St A Cathl 65-66; Archd of Montgomery 66-76. *Tyn-y-Coed Lodge, Berriew, Powys.* (Berriew 514)

JONES, David Emrys. b 21. St D Coll Lamp BA 42, MA (Wales) 74. BD (Lon) 69. Ch Hostel Ban 46. **d** 47 **p** 48 Ban. C of Llandinorwic 47-50; Conway w St Agnes and Gyffin 50-57; V of Beddgelert 57-72; R of Llangystennin Dio St A from 72. *Rectory, Glyn-y-Marl Road, Llandudno Junction, Gwyn.* (Deganwy 83579)

JONES, David Emrys. St D Coll Lamp BA 49. **d** 51 Swan B for St D **p** 52 St D. C of Gorslas 51-57; R of Llangranog (w Llandyssilio Gogo from 73) Dio St D from 57. *Llangranog Rectory, Llandyssul, Dyfed.* (Llangranog 275)

JONES, Canon David Frederick Donald. b 19. Univ of Wales (Abth) BA (2nd cl Phil) 41. Westcott Ho Cam 41. **d** 43 **p** 44 St D. C of Henfynwy w Aberaeron 43-46; St Pet Carmarthen 46-53; V of Pencarreg 53-64; V of Bettws w Ammanford 64-78; RD of Dyffryn Aman 72-78; Surr from 64; Can of St D Cathl from 75; V of Felinfoel Dio St D from 78. *Felinfoel Vicarage, Llanelli, Dyfed.* (Llanelli 3559)

JONES, David Gwynfryn. b 18. St Mich Llan 71. **d** 71 **p** 72 Llan. C of Penyfai (w Tondu from 78) Dio Llan from 71. *16 Woodland Rise, Penyfai, Bridgend, Mid Glam.*

JONES, David Henry. b 10. St D Coll Lamp. **d** 62 **p** 63 St D. C of Brynamman 62-65; R of Capel Cynon w Talgarreg 65-71; V of Strata-Florida (and Ystradmeurig from 74) 71-77. *c/o Vicarage, Pontrhyd-Fendigaid, Ystradmeurig, Dyfed.* (Pontrhydfendigaid 235)

JONES, David Hugh. b 34. St D Coll Lamp BA 56. St Mich Coll Llan 56. **d** 58 **p** 59 Swan B. C of Swansea 58-61; Inter Colleg Sec SCM Liv 61-63; C of St Pet Cockett Swansea 63-69; V of Abbey-Cwmhir w Llanddewi Ystradenni 69-75; R of Port Eynon and Rhossili and Llanddewi w Knelston Swan B from 75. *Porteynon Rectory, Swansea, W Glam, SA3 1NL.* (Gower 456)

JONES, David Huw. b 34. Univ Coll of N Wales, BA (2nd cl Phil) 55. Univ Coll Ox BA (2nd cl Th) 58, MA 62. St Mich Coll Llan 58. **d** 59 **p** 60 Llan. C of Aberdare 59-61; Neath w Llantwit 61-65; V of Crynant 65-69; Michaelstone-super-Avon 69-74; Sub-Warden St Mich Coll Llan 74-78; Lect in Univ Coll of S Wales and Mon Cardiff 74-78; Asst Dean Faculty of Th 77-78; L to Offic Dio Llan 74-78; V of Prestatyn Dio St A from 78; Dioc Ecumen Officer 79; Sec Prov Unity C'tte from 80. *Vicarage, High Street, Prestatyn, Clwyd.* (Prestatyn 3780)

JONES, David Ian Stewart. b 34. Selw Coll Cam BA 57, MA 61. Westcott Ho Cam 57. **d** 59 **p** 60 Man. C of Oldham 59-63; V of All SS Elton Bury 63-66; Asst Conduct and Chap Eton Coll 66-70; Conduct and Sen Chap 70-74; Hd Master Bryanston Sch Dorset from 74. *Bryanston School, Blandford, Dorset.*

JONES, David James. b 05. Clifton Th Coll 35. **d** 36 **p** 37 St D. C of Fishguard 36-39; Llangynog 39-44; R of Llanddensant 44-50; V of Silian 50-71; R of Bettws Bledrws w Llangybi 64-71; Asst Chap at Brussels Dio Lon (N and C Eur) from 72. *17 Avenue Edouard Lacomblé, 1040 Brussels, Belgium.*

JONES, David James Hammond. b 45. Dipl Th (Lon) 69. Kelham Th Coll. **d** 70 Stafford for Lich **p** 70 Lich. C of Cheadle 70-73; Hon C of W Bromwich Dio Lich from 78. *45 Charlemont Crescent, West Bromwich, W Midl.* (021-588 2429)

JONES, David John. b 18. St D Coll Lamp BA 51. **d** 52 **p** 53 St D. C of Brynamman w E Cwmllynfell 52-54; H Trin Aberystwyth 54-58; Min Can of St D Cathl 58-60; R of Llangeitho w Blaenpennal 60-72; Llanllwchaearn 72-79; Surr from 72; V of Llanfihangel Ystrad Dio St D from 79. *Ystrad Vicarage, Felinfach, Lampeter, Dyfed, SA48 8AE.* (Aeron 470331)

JONES, David John. b 06. St D Coll Lamp 55. **d** 57 **p** 58 St D. C of Pembrey w Llandyry 57-59; V of Brawdy w Hayscastle and Llandeloy 59-71; RD of Dewisland and Fishguard 68-71; V of Llangyndeyrn 71-76. *73 Heol Morlais, Trimsaran, Kidwelly, Dyfed.*

JONES, David Jonathan. b 04. St D Coll Lamp BA 34. **d** 34 **p** 35 Ban. C of Llanllyfni 34-38; Min Can of Ban Cathl 38-42; R of Llanymawddwy 42-48; Cemmaes 48-55; Nevin (w Edern and Ceidio 55-59) 55-60; Nefyn w Carngiwch and Pistyll 60-72; Can and Prec of Ban Cathl 63-67. *Cae'r Onnen, Llangristiolus, Anglesey, Gwynedd, LL62 5PR.* (Llangefni 722162)

JONES, David Lloyd. St D Coll Lamp BA 32. **d** 32 **p** 33 Llan. C of Dowlais 32-37; Llangyfelach w Morriston 37-39; V of Gwynfe 39-51; Cilcennin w Llanbadarn-Trefeglwys Dio 50-70. *Roscivina, Henfynyw, Abervaenon, Dyfed.*

JONES, David Marcus. NZ Bd of Th Stud LTh 65. St Jo Coll Auckld. **d** 62 **p** 63 Auckld. C of Sandringham 62-65; St Heliers Bay Auckld 65-68; Grey Lynn 68-69; V of Murupara 69-73; L to Offic Dio Wel from 73. *17 Buxton Avenue, Wellington 5, NZ.* (764-073)

JONES, David Michael. b 48. Chich Th Coll 75. **d** 78 **p** 79 B & W. C of Yeovil (in c of Barwick from 81) Dio B & W from 78. *5 Chestnut Drive, Yeovil, Somt.* (Yeovil 20661)

JONES, David Noel. St Deiniol's Libr Hawarden 69. **d** 71 **p** 72 Ban. C of Llandegfan w Beaumaris and Llanfaes 71-74; Team V of Amlwch w Rhosybol w Llandyfrydog w Llanwenllwyfo w Llaneilan 74-77; R of Llanfairmathafarneithaf w Llanbedrgoch Dio Ban from 77. *Rectory, Tyngongl, Gwyn.* (Tyngongl 348)

JONES, David Oswald. b 02. Univ of Wales, BA 37. St Mich Coll Llan 39. **d** 41 **p** 43 Swan B. C of Ystradgynlais 41-45; Lydney w Aylburton and Primrose Hill 45-49; R of Garthbeibio 49-51; V of Llansantffraed-in-Elwell w Bettws Disserth 51-58; R of Gt Hanwood 58-71. *12 Abernant Road, Cwmgors, Ammanford, Dyfed, SA18 1RB.*

JONES, David Raymond. b 34. Late Scho of St D Coll Lamp BA 54. St Cath S Ox BA 57, MA 61. Wycl Hall, Ox 54. **d** 58 **p** 59 Ex. C of St D Ex 58-60; Tamerton Foliott 60-61; Bideford 61-63; Chap Grenville Coll Bideford 63-66; Chap RN from 66. *c/o Ministry of Defence, Lacon House, Theobalds Road, WC1X 8RY.*

JONES, David Rees. b 07. Univ of Wales, BA 37. St D Coll Lamp 37. **d** 39 Swan B for Llan **p** 40 Llan. C of Clydach Vale 39-43; Dowlais 43-49; V of Cwmaman 49-65; R of Llandow w Llysworney (w Colwinston from 70) 65-77; Perm to Offic Dio Llan from 79. *65 Ewenny Road, Bridgend, Mid Glam.*

JONES, David Robert. b 37. Univ of Dur BA 59, Dipl Th 69. Cranmer Hall Dur 67. **d** 69 Hulme for Man **p** 70 Middleton for York. C of Middleton 69-72; CF from 72. *c/o Ministry of Defence, Bagshot Park, Bagshot, Surrey, GU19 5PL.*

JONES, David Robert Deverell. b 50. Sarum Wells Th Coll 72. **d** 75 Ches **p** 78 Lich. C of Altrincham 75-76; Perm to Offic Dio Lich 76-77; C of Clayton Lich 77-80; P-in-c of Ch the K Carriacou Dio Windw Is from 80. *Church of Christ the King, Carriacou, W Indies.*

JONES, David Ronald. b 14. Ch Coll Cam 2nd cl Cl Trip pt i 36, BA (2nd cl Cl Trip pt ii) 37. Ridley Hall Cam 37. **d** 39 **p** 40 Man. C of Ch Ch Heaton Norris 39-42; St Marg Whalley Range 42-43; All SS Stand 43-46; R of St Jo Evang Broughton 46-51; St Mark W Gorton 51-54; C of St Pet Roch 54-55; Min of Eccles Distr of St Justus Roch 55-59; Lect Dudley Tr Coll 59-65; Asst Master Mather Coll Man from 65. *675 Kingsway, East Didsbury, Manchester.* (061-432 4396)

JONES, David Roy. b 47. Univ of Hull BA 74. N Ordin Course 77. **d** 80 **p** 81 Man. C of St Jas New Bury Farnworth Dio Man from 80. *101 St James Street, New Bury, Farnworth, Bolton, Lancs.*

JONES, David Sebastian. b 43. St Cath Coll Cam BA 67, MA 73. Linc Th Coll 66. **d** 68 **p** 69 Man. C of Brooklands 68-71; Bray 71-73; V of S Ascot Dio Ox from 73. *South Ascot Vicarage, Ascot, Berks, SL5 9BX.* (Ascot 22388)

JONES, Canon David Tudor. b 02. Late Scho of St D Coll Lamp BA 26. **d** 27 **p** 28 St A. C of Northop 27-36; V of Bickley and Priv Chap to Marq of Cholmondeley 36-70; Surr from 48; RD of Malpas 55-70; Hon Can of Ches 65-70; Can (Emer) from 70. *Moat Farm, Norbury, Whitchurch, Salop.*

JONES, David Vernon. b 19. St D Coll Lamp BA 48. **d** 49 **p** 50 St D. C of Kidwelly 49-52; Langley Marish 52-62; V of St Geo Wolverton (w H Trin from 73) Dio Ox 62-75; Team R from 75. *Rectory, Aylesbury Street, Wolverton, Milton Keynes, MK12 5HY.* (Milton Keynes 312501)

JONES, David Victor. b 37. Univ of Dur BA (2nd cl Th) 59, Dipl Th (w distinc) 60. Cranmer Hall, Dur 59. **d** 62 Warrington for Liv **p** 63 Liv. C of St Luke Farnworth 62-65; CF 65-68; Asst Master Hutton Gr Sch Preston from 68; L to Offic Dio Blackb from 79. *10 Houghton Close, Penwortham, Preston, Lancs.* (Preston 45306)

JONES, David Vincent. **d** 28 **p** 29 Man. C of St Geo Mossley 28-31; St Paul Withington 31-35; C-in-c of Lostock Conv Distr 35-42; PC of Alvaston 42-63. *The Anchorage, Looe, Cornw.*

JONES, Denys Halworth. Keble Coll Ox 2nd cl Th 34, BA 35, MA 46. Cudd Coll 35. **d** 36 **p** 37 Ox. C of Newbury 36-39; SPG Miss Ranchi 39; Murhu 40; Ranchi 40-42; Itki 42; Kamdara 43; Dhanbad 43; Manoharpur 43-45; Itki 45-46; C of St Mary Hemel Hempstead 46-47; H Trin Upper Tooting 47-49; V of Wotton Underwood 49-52; Edlesborough w Northall and Dagnall 52-60; C of Ifield 60-63; Chap at Chittagong 63-67; C of Wimborne Minster 67-68; PC (V from 69) of Verwood 68-77. *c/o Verwood Vicarage, Wimborne, Dorset.* (Verwood 2298)

JONES, Derek Melvyn. b 45. St Jo Coll Morpeth 70. **d** 73 **p** 74 melb. C of St Mary Caulfield 73-75; St John Geelong W 75-76; P-in-c of St Martin Airport W 76-81; St Francis Mooroolbark Dio Melb from 81. *224 Hull Road, Mooroolbark, Vic, Australia 3138.*

JONES, Ven Derwyn Dixon. Hur Coll BA 46, LTh 46. **d** 46 **p** 47 Alg. C of H Trin Winnipeg 46-48; All SS Windsor 48-49; Kitchener 49-50; R 51-53; C of St Paul's Cathl Lon 53-55; I of Can Davis Mem Ch Sarnia 55-58; R of St Barn Windsor 58-66; St Pet Brockville 66-69; Exam Chap to Bp of Hur 62-66; Can of St Geo Cathl Kingston 66-69; R of St Jas Lon Dio Hur from 69; Can of Hur 70-78; Archd of Middx from 78. *115 Askin Street, London 16, Ont., Canada.* (519-432 1915)

JONES, Dick Heath Remi. b 32. Jes Coll Cam 3rd cl Th Trip pt i, 54, BA (3rd cl Th Trip pt ii) 56. Linc Th Coll 56. **d** 58 Dunwich for St E **p** 59 St E. C of St Thos Ipswich 58-61; Putney 61-65; C-in-c of Lawley 65-75; Dawley Parva 65-75; Malins Lee 72-75; RD of Wrockwardine 70-72; Telford 72-80; Surr 70-80; C-in-c of Stirchley 74-75; R of Central Telford 75-80; Preb of Lich Cathl 76-80; Team R of Bournemouth Dio Win from 80. *St Peter's Rectory, Wimborne Road, Bournemouth, Dorset, BH2 6NT.* (Bournemouth 24058)

JONES, Canon Douglas Rawlinson. b 19. St Edm Hall Ox Squire Scho 38, BA (2nd cl Th) 41, MA 45. Wycl Hall Ox 41. **d** 42 **p** 43 Bris. C of St Mich AA Windmill Hill 42-45; Lect Wycl Hall Ox 45-50; Chap Wadh Coll Ox 45-50; Lect in Div 48-50; Lect in Th Univ of Dur 51-64; Lightfoot Prof of Div from 64; Can of Dur from 64; Prolocutor of York 75-80; *12 The College, Durham.* (Durham 4295)

JONES, E. Keith. b 11. Wycl Coll Tor. **d** 76 Tor **p** 77 Iran. P Dio Iran. *St Andrew's Church, Khiaban Shahpur, Kerman, Iran.*

JONES, Edgar John. St D Coll Lamp BA (2nd cl Welsh) 53. St Mich Coll Llan 53. **d** 55 **p** 56 Ban. C of Holyhead 55-61; V of Bodedern w Llechcynfarwy 61-70; R of Llechylched w Ceirchiog Llanfihangel-yn-Nhywyn and Caergeiliog 70-73. *5 Glan Llyn, Llanfachreth, Holyhead, Anglesey, Gwyn.*

JONES, Edgar Joseph Basil. b 14. Univ of Wales LLB (3rd cl) 37. St Jo Coll Ox BA (3rd cl Phil, Pol and Econ) 40, MA 43. Ripon Hall Ox 40. **d** 41 **p** 42 St A. C of Rhyl 41-49; V of Llanuwchllyn 49-53; St Jo Evang Altrincham 53-61; Sandiway 61-80. *29 Church Walks, Llandudno, Gwyn, LL30 2HL.* (0492-76125)

JONES, Edward. b 36. Univ of Dur BA (2nd cl Th) 60. Ely Th Coll 60. **d** 62 **p** 63 Dur. C of St Hilda S Shields 62-65; St Cuthb Cleadon Pk 65-68; V of Hebburn 68-79; Team R of Winlaton Dio Dur from 79. *Winlaton Rectory, Blaydon-on-Tyne, T & W, NE21 6PJ.* (Blaydon 443165)

JONES, Edward Gareth. b 36. St D Coll Lamp BA 59. **d** 61 **p** 62 St D. C of Llanbadarn Fawr 61-66; V of Dihewyd w Mydroilyn 66-69; Missr to Deaf and Dumb Dio Mon 69-70; V of Tregaron 70-75; Chap to Deaf and Dumb Dios Llan and Mon from 75. *55 Bishops Walk, Llandaff. Cardiff, S Glam.*

JONES, Edward Graham. b 25. **d** 64 Bp T M Hughes for Llan **p** 65 Llan. C of Bargoed 64-70; V of Caerau w Nantyffyllon Dio Llan from 70; Surr from 71. *Vicarage, Cymmer Road, Caerau, Maesteg, Bridgend CF34 0YR.* (Maesteg 734223)

JONES, Edward Harries. b 16. St D Coll Lamp BA 38. Ely Th Coll 38. **d** 39 **p** 40 St A. C of Rhyl 39-52; V of Ffynnon-Groyw 52-81. *16 Coed Pella Road, Colwyn Bay, Clwyd.* (Colwyn Bay 2997)

JONES, Edward Lanphier Brooke. b 1899. LCD 35. **d** 37 **p** 38 Roch. C of Sevenoaks 37-41; R of Luddesdowne w Dode (w Cobham from 46) 41-50; C-in-c of Cobham 44-46; V of St Paul Worthing 50-60; Surr 52-64; R of Jevington 60-64; Perm to Offic Dio Chich from 64. *19 Ratton Garden, Ratton Drive, Eastbourne, E Sussex, BN20 9BT.* (Eastbourne 51874)

JONES, Edward Melville Royds. b 1899. Univ of Lon BSc 20. ACGI 20. DIC 21, MICE 24. **d** 32 **p** 33 Lon. C of All H Barking-by-the-Tower Lon 32-35; Chap Blundell's Sch Tiverton 35-36; C of Chislehurst 36-38; Fareham 38-64; Locks Heath 64-71. *Grove House, Grove Road, Fareham, Hants.* (Fareham 232323)

JONES, Edward Wynn. b 11. Univ of Wales, BA (2nd cl Econ and Pol Sc) 32. Lich Th Coll 40. **d** 42 **p** 43 Llan. C of Pentrebach 42-43; Neath w Llantwit 43-48; Worplesdon (in c of St Alb) 48-53; C-in-c of Conv Distr of St Aug Aldershot 53-56; R of Tivetshall 56-59; Redenhall w Harleston and

Wortwell 59-79; Surr from 74. *11 Blenheim Way, Roydon, Diss, Norf.*

JONES, Edward Wynne. b 45. Univ of Wales (Abth) LLB 71. St Mich Coll Llan 72. **d** 74 **p** 75 Ban. C of Beaumaris w Llandegfan & Llanfaes 74-76; R of Aberffraw w Llangwyfan 76-78; Chap RN from 78. *c/o Ministry of Defence, Lacon House, Theobald's Road, WC1X 8RY.*

JONES, Edwin John. b 04. Univ of Wales BA 26. St Aug Coll Cant 64. **d** 65 **p** 66 B & W. C of Twerton-on-Avon 65-67; Chap and Sec Partis Coll Bath 67-72. *22 St James's Square, Bath, BA1 2TS.* (Bath 29204)

JONES, Elidyr Price. b 26. St D Coll Lamp BA 51. **d** 53 **p** 54 Swan B. C of Brecon 53-59; Min Can of Brecon Cathl 55-59; Chap St Pet Sch York 59-65; Kelly Coll Tavistock from 65. *Kelly College, Tavistock, Devon.*

JONES, Ellis Herbert. St D Coll Lamp BA 41. Ripon Hall, Ox 41 and 46. **d** 46 **p** 47 B & W. C of Widcombe 46-50; St Barn Dulwich 50-55; V of All SS N Beddington 55-67; L to Offic Dio S'wark 69-72. *c/o Midland Bank, Wallington, Surrey.*

JONES, Ellis Stanley. b 40. ACT ThL 70. St Mich Crafers 67. **d** 70 **p** 71 St Arn. d Dio St Arn 70-71; C of Ch Ch Cathl St Arn 71-72; Swan Hill 72-73; R of Donald 73-74; C of Ch Ch St Lawr Syd 75-76; R of Hay 76-79; Culcairn-Henty Dio River from 79. *Rectory, Culcairn, NSW, Australia 2660.* (29-8425)

JONES, Elwyn. Univ of Wales, BA 35. St Mich Coll Llan 35. **d** 36 Llan for Ban **p** 37 Ban. C of Towyn 36-39; Dwygyfylchi 39-46; V of Llanfihangel-y-Pennant (or Abergynolwyn) 46-53; Penycae 53-61; Rhos-y-Medre 71-72; Meliden 72-77. *5 Bodelwyddan Close, Bodelwyddan, Clwyd.*

JONES, Emmanuel Thomas. b 19. S Dioc Min Tr Scheme. **d** 81 Portsm. C of H Trin w St Columba Fareham Dio Portsm from 81. *24 Maylings Farm Road, Fareham, Hants, PO16 7QU.*

JONES, Erasmus David. b 11. St D Coll Lamp BA 36. St Mich Coll Llan 36. **d** 38 Bp Wentworth-Shields for Ban **p** 40 Ban. C of Llanllyfni 38-42; Llanbeblig w Caernarvon 42-48; C-in-c of Llandyfrydog w Llanfihangel Tre'r Beirdd 49-53; R of Llanbrynmair w Dylife 53-57; Llangristiolus w Cerrig Ceinwen 57-62; Pennal (w Corris from 72) 62-77. *7 Awel Dyfi, Bron y Mor, Tywyn, Gwyn.*

JONES, Eric Alexander. b 19. Trin Coll Dub BA 40, MA and BD 45. **d** 42 Tuam for Down **p** 43 Down. C of St Matt Belfast 42-45; St Jas Belfast 45-47; St Nich Belfast 47-48; St Matt Belfast (in c of St Columba Highfield) 48-51; R of Larne 51-59; I of Jordanstown 59-68; V of Carnmoney 68-76; RD of N Belf 65-70; V of Hensall w Heck Dio Sheff from 76; RD of Snaith from 80. *Hensall Vicarage, Goole, N Yorks, DN14 0QQ.* (Whitley Bridge 661206)

JONES, Canon Eric de Lande. b 18. Clifton Th Coll 51. **d** 53 **p** 54 Chelmsf. C of St Andr Gt Ilford 53-56; Min of St Luke's Eccles Distr Cranham Pk 56-61; V of Leytonstone 61-70; C-in-c of St Aug Miss Leytonstone 62-65; St Luke Leyton 64-67; Chap Leytonstone Ho Hosp 61-70; Surr from 61; Asst RD of Waltham Forest 68-70; R of Hutton 70-79; Hon Can of Chelmsf from 76; V of All SS Ardleigh Green, Hornchurch Dio Chelmsf from 79. *36 Ardleigh Green Road, Hornchurch, Essex, RM11 2LQ.* (Hornchurch 46571)

JONES, Canon Eric Vernon. b 26. Ely Th Coll 57. **d** 59 Lanc for Blackb **p** 60 Burnley for York. C of H Trin S Shore Blackpool 59-63; V of St Matt Preston 63-77; R of Chorley Dio Blackb from 77; Can of Blackb from 81. *Rectory, Chorley, Lancs, PR7 1QW.* (Chorley 63114)

JONES, Eric Walter Nathaniel. b 26. Wells Th Coll. **d** 61 **p** 62 Ex. C of Buckfastleigh 61-64; Warden Trin Youth Centre Ex 64-67; PV of Ex Cathl 64-67; L to Offic Dio Ex from 67. *Redmount, Old Totnes Road, Buckfastleigh, Devon, TQ11 0BY.* (Buckfastleigh 3260)

JONES, Canon Eric Wilfred. b 22. Linc Coll Ox BA (2nd cl Th) 48, MA 53. Cudd Coll. **d** 50 **p** 51 S'wark. C of St Jo Evang E Dulwich 50-56; V of St Pet Cov 56-65; Tutor Pacific Th Coll Suva and L to Offic Dio Polyn 65-68; Warden St Pet Th Coll Siota 69-70; Warden Patteson Th Centre Dio Melan 70-74; Exam Chap to Bp of Melan 70-73; V of Binley w Coombe Fields Dio Cov from 74; RD of Cov E from 80; Hon Can of Cov Cathl from 80. *Binley Vicarage, Brinklow Road, Coventry, W Midl.* (Cov 458374)

JONES, Ernest Edward Stephen. b 39. St D Coll Lamp 63. Dipl Th 66. Univ of Lon BD 76. **d** 66 Warrington for Liv **p** 67 Liv. C of N Meols 66-69; Kirkby Liv 69-71; V of All SS Farnworth 71-74; C-in-c of Bempton 75-78; R of Rufford Dio Blackb from 78. *Rectory, Church Road, Rufford, Nr Ormskirk, Lancs, L40 1TA.* (07047 821261)

JONES, Eustan Ulric. b 41. Codr Coll Barb 74. **d** 76 **p** 77 Windw Is. C of St Mary Bequia 76-79; P-in-c of St Phil Mesopotamia Dio Windw Is from 79. *c/o St Philip's Rectory, Mesopotamia, St Vincent, W Indies.* (809-45 85235)

JONES, Evan Emrys. b 03. Univ of Wales BA 35. St D Coll Lamp 36. **d** 37 **p** 38 St D. C of Yspytty Ystwyth w Ystrad Meurig 37-40; Llandyssul 40-41; V of Llanfihangel Rhosycorn 41-48; Llandygwydd 48-69. *Tegfan, Verwig, Cardigan, Dyfed.* (Lechrydd 208)

JONES, Evan Hopkins. b 38. St Mich Th Coll 65. **d** 67 **p** 68 Ex. C of Churston Ferrers 67-70; Tavistock 70-73; R of Ashprington 73-78; V of Cornworthy 73-78; R of St John of Jer w Ch Ch S Hackney Dio Lon from 78. *Rectory, Church Crescent, E9 7DH.* (01-985 5145)

JONES, Evan John. b 12. St D Coll Lamp BA (2nd cl Th) 34. Hebr Scho 33. St Jo Coll Ox BA (3rd cl Th) 37, MA 41. St Mich Coll Llan 36. **d** 37 **p** 38 St A. C of Mold 37-48; V of Glyndyfrdwy 48-53; St Mary Ban w Eglwys-y-Groes 53-78; Dioc Insp of Schs 56-58; Can of Ban 68-78; Perm to Offic Dio Ban from 78. *Maesycoed, Bryn Coch Lane, Mold, Clwyd, CH7 1PS.* (0352-3476)

JONES, Evan Stephen. b 1899. St D Coll Lamp BA 20. **d** 22 Ban for St A **p** 23 St A. C of Llanrhaiadr-yn-Mochnant 22-27; R of Pont Robert 27-39; Llangystenyn 39-51; Llannefydd 51-66; C of Eglwys-Rhos 66-69. *Address temp unknown*

JONES, Evan Tawe. St Mich Coll Llan 28. **d** 28 **p** 29 Llan. C of Skewen 28-31; Llandygwydd 31-32; Brynamman 32-36; V of Llangwyryfon (w Llanfihangel-Lledrod from 53) 36-70. *Address temp unknown.*

JONES, Evan Trevor. Univ of Wales BA 40. St Mich Coll Llan 40. **d** 42 **p** 43 St D. C of Pontyberem 42-48; Llanedy 48-56; V of Nevern (w Cilgwyn 56-69) and Bayvil (w Moylgrove and Monington 69-77) Dio St D from 56; RD of Kemes and Sub-Aeron from 80. *Nevern Vicarage, Newport, Dyfed.* (Newport 427)

JONES, Evan Trevor. b 32. Univ of Wales BA 54, Coll of Resurr Mirfield. **d** 56 **p** 57 Ban. C of St Mary Ban 56-62; V of Llandinorwic 62-71; Team V of Llanbeblig w Caernarfon and Betws Garmon w Waunfawr Dio Ban from 71. *Vicarage, Maesincla, Caernarfon, LL55 1DD.* (Caernarfon 2742)

JONES, Canon Eynon Edryd Cyndeirne. b 06. Late Scho of St D Coll Lamp BA 27. Wycl Hall Ox 27. **d** 29 **p** 30 Swan B. C of St Jude Swansea 29-32; Chilvers Coton 32-38; Org Sec CMS Dios Birm Derby and Leic 38-43; V of Earl Shilton w Elmesthorpe R 43-48; Belgrave 48-60; Hon Can of Leic 58-73; (Emer) from 73; R of Mkt Bosworth 60-69; Appleby Magna 69-73; RD of Sparkenhoe I 60-69; Surr 60-73; L to Offic Dio Leic from 73. *19 Shenton Lane, Market Bosworth, Nuneaton, CV13 0LA.* (Market Bosworth 290382)

JONES, Francis Ernest Llewellyn. **d** 10 **p** 12 Llan. C of St Matt Pontypridd 10-11; Llowes 11-14; L to Offic Dio Worc 16-19; Dio Heref 19-20; Perm to Offic at Penydarren 21-25; St Mary Cardiff 25-26; Dio Heref 33-37; V of Kenderchurch 37-42; R of Ballingham w Bolstone 42-60. *c/o Barclays Bank, 50 Broad Street, Hereford.*

JONES, Frank Llewellyn. b 12. St Pet Hall Ox BA (3rd cl Engl) 36. Dipl Th 37. Wycl Hall Ox 36. **d** 37 **p** 38 Cant. C of St Geo Mart Deal 37-40; St Sav Stoke-next-Guildf 40-43; V of Wick 43-45; Org Sec CMS Dios Bradf, Blackb and Carl 45-49; V of St Pet Parr 49-56; St Phil Liv 56-69; St Paul Widnes 69-77. *14 Stigands Gate, East Dereham, Norf, NR19 2HF.*

JONES, Fred Leslie. b 12. St D Coll Lamp BA 34. St Mich Coll Llan **d** 35 **p** 36 Mon. C of Llanfrechfa Upper 35-37; New Tredegar 37-44; R of Bettws Newydd w Trostrey and Kemeys Commander 44-51; V of Mynyddyslwyn 51-67; St Mark Newport 67-77; Surr from 52; Can of Mon 67-79. *4 Stirling Court, 20 Portarlington Road, Bournemouth, Dorset.*

JONES, Frederick. b 33. Univ of Man BA (2nd cl Mod Hist) 54. Selw Coll Cam PhD 72. FRHistS 76. St Steph Ho Ox 56. **d** 58 Man **p** 59 Lon. C of St Ann Belfield 58-59; St Matt Gt Peter Street Westmr 59-60; Perm to Offic at St Mary L Cam Dio Ely 71-72; Dio Win 72-74; L to Offic from 74. *4a Castlemain Avenue, Southbourne, Bournemouth, Dorset.* (Bournemouth 426184)

JONES, Frederick John. Wells Th Coll 57. **d** 60 **p** 61 Man. C of St Anne Tottington 60-63; H Trin Horwich 63-65; R of All SS (w Ch Ch from 76) Heaton Norris 65-77; V of Castleton Moor Dio Man from 77. *Castleton Vicarage, Rochdale, OL11 2TE.* (Rochdale 32353)

JONES, Frederick Morgan. b 19. St D Coll Lamp BA 40, BD 49. St Mich Coll Llan 42. **d** 42 **p** 43 St D. C of St Paul Llanelly 42-50; Publ Pr Dio St D 50-52; ICF Org Dir for Wales from 50; C-in-c of Llwynhendy Conv Distr 52-56; C of Llanelly 56-57; V of Penrhyncoch w Elerch 57-61; R of Llanbedrog (w Penrhos to 74) Dio Ban from 61; Llannor w Llanfihangel Bachellaeth and Bodfuan Dio Ban from 77. *Ty'n Llan, Llanbedrog, Pwllheli, LL53 7TU.* (Llanbedrog 275)

JONES, Gareth. b 35. St Aid Coll 59. **d** 61 Sheff **p** 62 Bp Gerard for Sheff. C of Ch Ch Doncaster 61-65; Min Can and C of Ripon Cathl 65-68; Chap RAF from 68. *c/o Ministry of Defence, Adastral House, WC1.*

JONES, Gareth Lewis. b 42. K Coll Lon and Warm BD

and AKC 64, **d** 65 **p** 66 Mon. C of Risca 65-70; Perm to Offic Dio Win 70-74; Newc T 74-75; Sarum 75; C of Pontesbury w Cruckton 75-77; P-in-c of Presteigne w Discoyd 77-79; Team V of Hemel Hempstead Dio St Alb from 79. *22 Solway, Highfield, Hemel Hempstead, Herts, HP2 5QN.* (Hemel Hempstead 54904)

JONES, Gareth Lloyd. b 38. Univ of Wales BA 61. Selw Coll Cam BA 63, MA 67. Univ of Ox MA (By Incorp) 74. Yale Univ STM 69. Univ of Dub BD 70. Univ of Lon PhD 75. Westcott Ho Cam 62. **d** 65 **p** 66 Ban. C of Holyhead w Rhoscolyn 65-68; in Amer Ch 68-70; C-in-c of Merton Ox 70-72; Tutor Ripon Hall Ox 72; Sen Tutor 73-75; Tutor and Libr Ripon Coll Cudd 75-77; Lect Ex Coll Ox 73-77; Univ Coll Ban from 77; Exam Chap to Abp of Wales from 78; L to Offic Dio Ban from 78. *Nettuno, Mount Street, Menai Bridge, Anglesey, Gwyn.* (Menai Bridge 712786)

JONES, Gareth Thomas. b 14. Clifton Th Coll 32. Open Univ BA 75. **d** 37 **p** 38 Chelmsf. C of Em Leyton 37-39; C-in-c 39-43; C of Wetherby 43-45; RAChD 46-52; PC of Arkengarthdale 52-56; V of Mickley Dio Ripon from 56; V of Grewelthorpe Dio Ripon from 56; C-in-c of N Stainley Dio Ripon from 77. *Grewelthorpe Vicarage, Ripon, N Yorks.* (Kirkby Malzeard 233)

JONES, George Roscoe. b 12. Univ of Liv BA (2nd cl Cl) 34. Qu Coll Birm 64. **d** 64 **p** 65 Bradf. Hon C of Baildon Dio Bradf from 64. *32 Jenny Lane, Baildon, Shipley, W Yorks, BD17 6RJ.* (Bradford 56126)

JONES, George William Arthur. Late Exhib of St D Coll Lamp BA 27. St Mich Coll Llan 28. **d** 29 **p** 30 Ban. C of Llanllechid 29-31; Denbigh 31-37; St Jas Cathl Bury St Edms 37-40; V of Gt Finborough 40-73; R of Onehouse w Harleston 45-73; Perm to Offic Dio St E from 73. *21 Fircroft Road, Ipswich, Suffolk.*

JONES, Glyn Evan. b 44. ALCD 67. **d** 67 **p** 68 Bradf. C of St Jo Evang Gt Horton 67-70; Miss at Salta Argent 71-78; V of Idle Dio Bradf from 78. *480 Leeds Road, Thackley, Bradford, BD10 9AA.* (Bradford 613300)

JONES, Preb Glyn Owen. b 16. St D Coll Lamp BA (Hons Th) 37. St Mich Coll Llan 38. **d** 39 **p** 40 St A. C of Wrexham 39-47; CF (EC) 44-47; C of Connah's Quay 47-49; V of Whixall 49-53; Hengoed w Gobowen 53-75; Preb of Lich Cathl 73-81; Preb (Emer) from 81; V of Baschurch 75-81. *6 Larkhill Road, Park Hall, Oswestry, Salop, S711 4AW.*

JONES, Glyndwr. b 35. Univ of Wales Dipl Th 62. St Mich Coll Llan 59. **d** 62 **p** 63 Swan B. C of Clydach 62-64; Llangyfelach 64-67; Sketty 67-70; R of Bryngwyn w Newchurch Llanbedr-Painscastle and Llanddewi Fach 70-72; Port Chap Swan (Miss to Seamen) 72-76; Sen Chap Miss to Seamen Port of Lon 76-81; Publ Pr Dio Chelmsf from 76. *5 The Close, Grays, Essex.* (Grays Thurrock 5053)

JONES, Godfrey Caine. b 36. St Jo Coll Dur BA 59. Univ of Birm MEducn 71. St Deiniol's Libr Hawarden 76. **d** 78 **p** 79 St A (APM). C of Ruthin & Llanrhydd Dio St A from 78; Sen Lect Matlock Coll of Higher Educn from 81. *Bronorwen, Stanley Road, Ruthin, Clwyd, LL15 1PT.*

JONES, Gordon Howlett. b 26. G and C Coll Cam BA 47, MA 51. Westcott Ho Cam 49. **d** 51 **p** 52 Win. C of St Mary Magd Milton 51-54; St Helen Bishopsgate Lon and Study Sec SCM in Schs 54-58; V of H Angels Claremont Pendleton 58-63; R of Northenden 63-79; P-in-c of Hilmarton w Highway Dio Sarum from 79. *Hilmarton Vicarage, Calne, Wilts.* (Hilmarton 675)

JONES, Gordon Michael Campbell. b 33. St D Coll Lamp BA 56. St Jo Coll Dur 56. **d** 58 **p** 59 Mon. C of Maindee 58-61; Penhow 61-64; V of Magor w Redwick 64-68; R of S Cross Kalg 68-70; C of Wembley-Floreat Pk 70-72; R of Kirkby Thore w Temple Sowerby (and Newbiggin from 73) 72-80; P-in-c of St Jas Accrington 80-81; St Andr Accrington Dio Blackb from 80. *356 Blackburn Road, Accrington, Lancs, BB5 1RZ.* (Accrington 33770)

JONES, Gordon Rowland. b 24. Oak Hill Th Coll 56. **d** 58 **p** 59 S'wark. C of St Mich AA Southfields 58-61; St Paul Portman Square St Marylebone 61-63; R of Walcot 63-70; Dir of Past Tr St Jo Coll Nottm 70-73; V of Ch Ch Orpington 73-78; Sec for Chr Educn Tr CPAS from 78. *c/o Church Pastoral Aid Society, 32 Fleet Street, EC4Y 1DB.*

JONES, Graham Frederick. b 37. Univ of Leeds BA (2nd cl Gen) 60. Lon Coll of Div 64. **d** 66 Repton for Derby **p** 67 Derby. C of H Trin Chesterfield 66-70; St Geo Leeds 70-73; C-in-c of St Geo Newc L Dio Lich from 73. *Vicarage, Hempstalls Lane, Newcastle, Staffs, ST5 0SS.*

JONES, Gregory Alan. b 47. Ridley Coll Melb ACT ThL 75. **d** 76 **p** 77 Tas. C of Howrah 76-77; Burnie 77-78; P-in-c of Derby-Ringarooma 78-80; R of Beaconsfield & Ex Dio Tas from 80. *Rectory, Beaconsfield, Tasmania 7251.* (003 83 1174)

JONES, Griffith Bernard. b 20. St D Coll Lamp BA 42. St Mich Coll Llan 42. **d** 44 **p** 45 Llan. C of Ynyshir Rhondda 44-51; St Jas Handsworth 51-56; V of St Matt Smethwick 56-60; Swalcliffe w Shutford 60-64; Perm to Offic Dio Pet from 64; Dio St Alb from 74. *49 Beech Crescent, Irchester, Wellingborough, Northants.* (Rushden 4409)

JONES, Griffith Pugh. Univ of Bris BA (2nd cl Hist) 32. St Cath S Ox 3rd cl Th 36, BA 37, MA 40. Wells Th Coll 36. **d** 37 **p** 38 S'wark. C of St Mark Kennington 37-42; Presteigne w Discoyd 42-46; R of L Marcle 46-80; R of Preston 59-80. *109 Barncliffe Crescent, Fulwood, Sheffield 10.*

JONES, Preb Griffith Walter Hywyn. b 24. St Mich Coll Llan 47. **d** 50 **p** 51 Ban. C of Llanaber w Barmouth 50-52; Chap RAF 52-67; V of Betws-y-Coed (w Capel Curig from 70) 67-78; R of Holyhead Dio Ban from 78; Preb of Ban Cathl from 78; RD of Llifon and Talybolin from 80. *Rectory, Holyhead, Gwyn.* (Holyhead 2593)

JONES, Griffith William. b 31. St D Coll Lamp BA 53, LTh 55. **d** 55 **p** 56 St A. C of Llanycil w Bala and Frongoch 55-58; V of Llandrillo yn Edeyrnion (w Llandderfel from 66) Dio St A from 58. *Vicarage, Llandrillo, Corwen, Clwyd.* (Llandrillo 224)

JONES, Gwyn Harris. St D Coll Lamp BA 42. K Coll Lon 42. **d** 43 **p** 44 St D. C of St Jo Evang Pembroke Dk 43-44; Letterston 44-46; P Dio Ugan 46-53; C of Llanelly (Carms) 53-54; V of St Paul Wolverhampton 54-56; St Chad Burton-on-Trent 56-79; St Geo Shrewsbury Dio Lich from 79. *St George's Vicarage, Shrewsbury, Salop.* (Shrewsbury 53286)

JONES, Gwyn Sproule. b 05. St Mich Coll Llan 49. **d** 51 **p** 52 Mon. C of Blaina 51-53; St Woolos Newport 53-56; C-in-c of Llanbadoc and Llanllowel 56-57; V and R 57-75. *4 The Retreat, Kings Fee, Monmouth, Gwent.*

JONES, Gwynfryn Lloyd. St D Coll Lamp BA 59. St Mich Coll Llan 59. **d** 61 **p** 62 St A. C of Rhyl 61-64; Prestatyn 64-67; V of Whitford 67-75; Llay Dio St A from 75. *Llay Vicarage, Wrexham, Clwyd.* (Gresford 2262)

JONES, Gwynn Rees. b 32. St D Coll Lamp BA 55. **d** 57 **p** 58 St A. C of Llangystenyn 57-59; Eglwys Rhos 59-64; R of Cefn 64-68; Llanfyllin 68-80; V of Bistre Dio St A from 80. *Bistre Vicarage, Mold Road, Buckley, CH7 2NH.* (0244 542947)

JONES, Gwynne Ifor. b 10. Jes Coll Ox BA 36, MA 38. **d** 70 **p** 71 Ban. C of Llangefni w Tregaean 70-81. *Bryn Horton, Greenfield Avenue, Llangefni, Anglesey.* (Llangefni 723295)

JONES, Canon Harold Austin Earp. St Paul's Hostel Grahmstn 06. **d** 06 Capetn **p** 08 Bp Coadj for Capetn. C of St Paul's Miss Capetn 06-11; Asst P Cathl Capetn 11-14; P-in-c of Port Nolloth 14-16; Chap Miss to Seamen for Capetn 16-27; R of Caledon 27-45; Archd of Caledon 32-45; R of St Jas Sea Point 45-53; Hon Can of Capetn 32-61; Can (Emer) from 61; L to Offic Dio Capetn from 54. *216 High Level Road, Sea Point, CP, S Africa.* (44-8187)

JONES, Canon Harold Desmond. b 22. Sarum Th Coll 52. **d** 55 **p** 56 St Alb. C of Bushey Heath 55-58; Stevenage 58-64; V of Milton Ernest 64-80; V of Thurleigh 64-80; RD of Sharnbrook 70-81; Hon Can of St Alb from 78; V of Sharnbrook Dio St Alb from 80; P-in-c of Knotting w Souldrop Dio St A from 80. *Sharnbrook Vicarage, Bedford.* (Bedford 781444)

JONES, Harry Gordon. b 18. Bps' Coll Cheshunt, 49. **d** 52 **p** 53 St Alb. C of Goldington 52-56; CMS Miss 56-64; V of Hurley 64-70; Salcombe 70-79; P-in-c of Abbotsham Dio Ex from 79. *Abbotsham Vicarage, Bideford, Devon, EX39 5AP.* (Bideford 3487)

✠ **JONES, Right Rev Haydn Harold.** b 20. Bro of Barton Yorks 45. **d** 47 **p** 48 Bradf. C of St Barn Heaton 47-49; Tor Mohun Torquay 49-51; Chap RN 51-53; L to Offic Dio Lon 54-62; Dio Cov 62-63; C of St Pet Cov 63-64; R of Clutton (w Cameley from 75) 64-76; Surr 72-76; Cons Ld Bp of Venez in Pro-Cathl Ch of St Mary Caracas 6 June 76 by Abp of W Indies; Bps of Trinid, Antig, Ecuador and Colombia; Dean of St Mary Pro-Cathl from 76. *Bishop's House, Plaza Urape, San Roman, Las Mercedes, Caracas, Venezuela.* (91-4727)

JONES, Haydn Llewelyn. b 42. Edin Th Coll 63. **d** 65 **p** 66 Pet. C of Towcester w Easton Neston 65-68; St Matt Northn 68-72; CF from 72. *c/o Ministry of Defence, Bagshot Park, Bagshot, Surrey.*

JONES, Haydn Price. b 17. MBE 60. St D Coll Lamp BA 38. St Mich Coll Llan 39. **d** 40 **p** 41 Swan B. C of Knighton 40-43; St Aug Penarth w Lavernock 43-47; St Gabr Swansea 47-48; C-in-c of Ringshall w Battisford and Finborough Parva 48-50; R 50-65; Offg Chap RAF 49-65; R of Horringer w Ickworth 65-81; Chap W Suff Hosps 81; P-in-c of Aberedw w Llandilo-Graban Dio Swan B from 81. *Aberedw Rectory, Builth Wells, Powys.* (Erwood 267)

JONES, Herbert. ACT ThL 29. **d** 29 **p** 30 Bend. C of Kangaroo Flat 29-31; V of Raywood 31-34; R of Tatura 34-45; Kyneton 45-68; Can of Bend 49-68; L to Offic Dio Bend 68-73. *St Laurence Court, Upper Road, Cal Gully, Eaglehawk, Vic, Australia.*

JONES, Herbert Frederick. b 12. Univ of Dur LTh 36. St Aug Coll Cant 31. **d** 36 Jarrow for Dur **p** 37 Dur. C of Silksworth 36-39; Miss Madagascar 39-44; C of Sprowston 45-48; V of Horsham St Faith 48-53; CF 53-59; R of Byfleet 59-78. *29 The Verne, Church Crookham, Aldershot, Hants.* (Fleet 20943)

JONES, Canon Hugh Evans. **d** 43 Swan B for St A **p** 45 St A. C of Corwen 43-53; R of Garthbeibio (w Llanerfyl and Llangadfan from 58) 53-63; Llanycil w Bala and Frongoch Dio St A from 63; Surr from 64; RD of Penllyn from 69; Hon Can of St A Cathl from 76. *Rectory, Bala, Gwyn.* (Bala 296)

JONES, Hugh Owen. Coates Hall Edin 45. **d** 47 **p** 48 Brech. C of St Mary Magd Dundee 47-50; P-in-c of St Paul Airdrie 50-52; CF 52-58; R of Hope w Shelve 58-63; Bodenham w Hope-under-Dinmore (and Felton and Preston Wynne from 78) 63-80; P-in-c of Felton w Preston Wynne and Ullingswick 76-78. *4 Minster Court, Leominster, Hereford, HR6 8LJ.* (0568 3354)

JONES, Humphrey Ingham. b 20. St Pet Coll Ox BA (3rd cl Mod Hist) 42, MA 46. Cudd Coll 42. **d** 43 **p** 44 Newc T. C of St Phil Newc T 43-47; Haltwhistle 47-49; St Geo Cullercoats 49-50; C-in-c of St Francis's Conv Dist High Heaton Newc T 50-55; V 55-61; Monkseaton 61-67; Proc Conv Newc T 65-67; Regr and Tutor Richmond Fellowship from 68; Hon C of Bermondsey 73-78; Perm to Offic in Kens Area Dio Lon from 79. *Richmond Fellowship, 8 Addison Road, W14 8DL.* (01-603 6373)

✠ **JONES, Right Rev Hywel James.** Em Coll Sktn LTh 42. **d** and **p** Edmon. C of Tofield 42-43; Miss of Wabamun 43-44; Parksville 44-47; I of Colwood and Langford 47-56; R of Oak Bay 56-80; Hon Can of BC 59-68; Archd without jurisd BC 68-71; Archd of Vic 71-77; Archd (Emer) from 77; Cons Ld Bp of BC in Ch Ch Cathl Vic BC 1 May 80 by Abp of BC; Bps of Koot, Carib, Caled and Yukon; and Abp Gower and Bps Gartrell, Burch Wilkinson and Steer. *912 Vancouver Street, Victoria, BC, Canada.* (604-477 3293)

JONES, Hywel Tudur. b 13. St D Coll Lamp BA 38. **d** 40 **p** 41 St D. C of Yspytty Ystwyth w Ystradmeurig 40-44; C-in-c of Henllan Amgoed and Llangan 44-51; V of Llanafan-y-Trawscoed w Gwnnws 51-63; Dafen 63-73; R of Aberporth w Tremaen 74-78. *c/o Aberporth Rectory, Dyfed.* (Aberporth 810217)

JONES, Idris. b 43. St D Coll Lamp BA 64. Univ of Edin LTh 67. **d** 67 **p** 68 Lich. C of Stafford 67-70; Prec of Dundee Cathl 70-73; C of All SS Gosforth (in c of St Hugh) 73-79; Team V of The Ephiph Newc T 79-80; R of Montrose w Inverbervie Dio Brech from 80. *Rectory, Montrose, Angus, DD10 8ER.* (Montrose 2212)

JONES, Idris Lynworth. Wollaston Coll W Austr 62. **d** 64 **p** 65 Perth. C of Scarborough 65-67; P-in-c of Mingenew 67-69; R 69-72; Rockingham w Safety Bay 72-79; Bassendean Dio Perth from 79. *4 Wilson Street, Bassendean, W Australia 6054.* (279 1254)

JONES, Canon Idwal. Univ of Wales, BA 36. St Mich Coll Llan 36. **d** 38 Ban **p** 39 Bp Wentworth-Sheilds for Ban. C of Llanllyfni 38-40; Colwyn Bay 40-44; CF (EC) 44-47; CF 47-50; Hon CF 50; V of Cuddington 50-63; Leamington 63-79; Hon Can of Cov Cathl from 72. *30 Main Street, Birdingbury, Nr Rugby, Warws, CV23 8EL.*

JONES, Iorwerth Owen. b 24. St D Coll Lamp BA 51. **d** 53 **p** 55 St A. C of Rhos-y-Medre 53-57; Prestatyn 57-59; R of Nantglyn 59-63; Adwick-le-Street 63-68; V of Tickhill w Stainton 68-80; Elworth w Warmingham Dio Ches from 80. *38 Roman Way, Elworth, Sandbach, Chesh, CW11 9EW.* (Sandbach 2415)

JONES, Preb Ivor Brynmor. b 08. Univ of Wales, BA 31. St Mich Coll Llan. **d** 36 **p** 37 Llan. C of St Marg Aberaman 36-40; St Marg Mountain Ash 40-48; V of Tylorstown 48-53; R of Darlaston 53-78; Surr 60-78; RD of Wednesbury 60-78; Preb of Lich Cathl from 65-78; Preb (Emer) from 78. *25 Holifast Road, Wylde Green, Sutton Coldfield, W Midl, B72 1AP* (021-373 8454)

JONES, Canon Ivor McKinley. Univ of Dur BA 41. **d** 41 **p** 42 Barb. C of St Pet 41-42; Ch Ch Barb 42-43; V of St Clem and St Swith Barb 43-46; Hd Master Bp's High Sch Scarborough Tobago 46-55; LPr Dio Barb from 55; Can of Barb from 75. *Oistins, Christchurch, Barbados, W Indies.*

JONES, James Ernest. b 07. Late Exhib of St D Coll Lamp BA 30. **d** 30 **p** 31 St D. C of Dafen 30-33; St D Carmarthen 33-37; R of Llangynllo 37-46; V of Llanfihangel Ystrad 46-57; Cardigan Dio St D 57-73; Surr 57-73. *11 Preseli View, Llechryd, Dyfed.*

JONES, James Morgan. b 07. TD 47. **d** 57 Llan for Wales **p** 58 Swan B. C of Abercrave w Callwen 57-60; V of Garth 60-67; R of Coychurch 67-77; Llangan w St Mary Hill 67-77; Perm to Offic Dio Llan from 79. *4 Woodlands Rise, Bridgend, Mid-Glam, CF31 4SW.*

JONES, Jenkin David. b 15. ALCD 38. **d** 38 Llan **p** 39 Ban for Llan. C of St Tyfaelog Pontlottyn 38-42; Ch Ch Ferndale 42-51; C-in-c of Clydach Vale 51-59; V of Cynwyl Elfed Dio St D from 59; Newchurch Dio St D from 81. *Vicarage, Cynwyl Elfed, Dyfed.* (Conwil Elfed 350)

JONES, Jenkin Lloyd. b 09. St D Coll Lamp BA 37. **d** 37 **p** 38 Sheff. C of Attercliffe 37-42; All SS Woodlands 42-45; V of Swinefleet 45-53; Laughton-en-le-Morthen w Thorpe Dio Sheff from 53. *Laughton Vicarage, Sheffield.* (Dinnington 562300)

JONES, Jenkin Thomas Vivian. **d** 38 Mon **p** 39 Llan for Mon. C of Fleur-de-Lys 38-40; St Basil Bassaleg 40-43; St Phil Norbury 43-44; Birkenshaw (in c of Hunsworth) 44-47; St Andr Watford 47-51; V of Orleton Dio Heref from 51; R of Brimfield 52. *Orleton Vicarage, Ludlow, Salop.* (Yarpole 258)

JONES, John Arthur. b 19. Univ of Wales (Cardiff) BA 42. BD (Lon) 55. Qu Coll Birm 54. **d** 54 **p** 55 Man. C of Walkden 54-56; R of St Clem Ordsall Salford 56-58; V of Scouthead 58-65; Hopwood Dio Man from 65. *Hopwood Vicarage, Heywood, Lancs.* (Heywood 69324)

JONES, John Brynmor. b 14. Univ of Wales BA 36. St Bonif Coll Warm 37. **d** 39 **p** 40 St D. C of Tenby 39-42; Chap RAF 42-69; Perm to Offic Dio St D from 69. *Briarcroft, Serpentine Road, Tenby, Dyfed.* (Tenby 3246)

JONES, John Clifford. b 20. **d** 77 **p** 78 St D (NSM). C of St Mary Haverfordwest w St Thos Dio St D from 77. *5 Castle View, Simpson Cross, Haverfordwest, Dyfed, SA62 6EN.*

JONES, John Daniel. b 14. Univ of Wales (Aberystwyth), BSc 36. St Mich Coll Llan. **d** 48 **p** 49 St D. C of Milford Haven 48-51; Llangystenyn 51-53; V of Wiston 53-67; R of Narberth w Robeston Wathen and Mounton (and Crinow from 74) 67-79. *c/o Rectory, Narberth, Dyfed.* (Narberth 860370)

JONES, John David. b 35. Late Exhib of Jes Coll Ox BA (3rd cl Mod Hist) 56, Dipl Th 57, MA 60. St Mich Coll Llan 57. **d** 58 **p** 59 Llan. C of Merthyr Tydfil 58-60; PV of Llan Cathl 60-68; Super Lect St Mich Th Coll Llan 65-68. *c/o 57 Talbot Road, Port Talbot, W Glam.*

JONES, Canon John Dillwyn Llewellyn. b 10. Univ of Wales, BA (2nd cl Gk Hons) 31. St Cath S Ox BA (2nd cl Th) 33, MA 39. Ripon Hall, Ox 31. **d** 33 **p** 34 Llan. C of St John Penydarren 33-35; L to Offic Dio Llan 35-37; C of Merthyr Tydfil 37-39; C-in-c of St Agnes's Conv Distr Port Talbot 39-46; V of Baglan 46-61; Llantwit Major w St Donat Dio Llan 61-78; Hon Can of Llan Cathl 77-78. *2 St Paul's Court, Llandaff, S Glam.*

JONES, John Douglas Mathias. Clare Coll Cam BA (3rd cl Engl Lit pt i) 49, MA 51. Chich Th Coll 49. **d** 51 **p** 52 S'wark. C of All SS Battersea Pk 51-54; Caversham (in c of St John) 54-59; Chap RAF 59-66; Cranwell 59-60; Christmas I 60-61; Bridgnorth 61-63; Chaps Sch 63-64; Berlin 65-66; C of St Wilfrid Harrogate 66-67; PC of Cross Stone 67-68; V 68-76; Hepworth Yorks Dio Wakef from 76. *Vicarage, Hepworth, Huddersfield, HD7 1TF.* (Holmfirth 3466)

JONES, John Edward. St Jo Coll Auckld NZ BD of Th Stud LTh 36. **d** 34 **p** 35 Wel. C of Masterton NZ 34-37; CMS Miss Chapra 37-48; CMS NZ 48-50; V of Patea 50-53; Eltham 53-59; Chap Palmerston N Hosp 63-64; V of Katikati 64-66; Waitara 66-68; L to Offic Dio Nel 68-78; Dio Wel from 78. *15 Arthur Street, Paraparaumu Beach, NZ.*

JONES, Ven John Elliott. Moore Th Coll ACT ThL (2nd cl) 57. BD (Lon) 63. **d** 58 Syd **p** 58 Bp Hilliard for Syd. C of Gladesville 58-59; C-in-c of Canley Vale 59-63; Harbord 63-65; CMS Miss Dio Jess 65-66; Chap RAN from 67; Sen Chap 80; Command Chap Office Garden Is from 81. *48 Quirk Road, Manly Vale, NSW, Australia 2093.* (94-4929)

JONES, John Elwyn. b 14. St D Coll Lamp BA 38. **d** 40 **p** 41 St A. C of Colwyn Bay 40-42; St Mary Flint 42-46; Llangollen (in c of St D Vroncyyllte) 46-50; V of Bettisfield (w Bronington from 53) 50-59; Penrhyndeudraeth and Llanfrothen 59-67; R of Llanfairfechan (w Aber from 75) Dio Ban from 67. *Rectory, Llanfairfechan, Gwyn.* (Llanfairfechan 680 591)

JONES, John Emlyn. b 17. St Mich Coll Llan. **d** 59 **p** 60 St A. C of Rhosllanerchrugog 59-63; V of Llawr-y-Bettws w Bettws-Gwerfil-Goch and Dinmael 63-67; Llanrhaeadr-yn-Mochnant w Llanarmon Mynydd Mawr 67-79. *c/o Llanrhaeadr Vicarage, Oswestry, Salop.* (Llanrhaeadr 247)

JONES, John Emrys. St Andr Coll Pampisford 46. **d** 46 **p** 47 Cov. C of Chilvers Coton 46-48; V of Temple Grafton w Binton 48-54; R of Alcester w Arrow Oversley and Weethley 54-65; V of Thames Ditton 66-75; Perm to Offic Dio Cov from 75. *32 College Street, Old Town, Stratford-on-Avon, Warws.* (Stratford-on-Avon 66784)

JONES, John Evans (Sinnett). St Mich Coll Llan. **d** 28 **p** 29 St A. C of Rhosllanerchrugog 28-33; V of Llanuwchllyn 33-38; Rhydymwyn 38-68; RD of Mold 54-68. *Dol Hyfryd, Parc Bychan, Mold, Clwyd.*

JONES, Ven John Francis Nantlais. **d** 48 Centr Tang **p** 49 Fred. C of St Marg Fredericton 48-50; Miss at Prince William

50-54; R of Westfield 54-61; St Andrew's Dio Fred from 61; Can of Ch Ch Cathl Fred 71-74; Archd of St Andr from 74. *St Andrew's, NB, Canada.*

JONES, Canon John Francis Williams. St D Coll Lamp 48. **d** 52 St A for Ban **p** 53 Ban. C of Glanadda w Penrhosgarnedd 52-55; Portmadoc 55-57; V of Llandrygarn w Bodwrog (and Hen Eglwys from 62 w Trewalchmai from 74) Dio Ban from 57; RD of Menai and Malltraeth from 75; Surr from 76; Hon Can of Ban from 81. *Llandrygarn Vicarage, Tynlon, Holyhead, Anglesey, LL65 3AZ.* (Gwalchmai 234)

JONES, John Harries. b 11. **d** 60 **p** 61 Ban. C of Dwygyfylchi 60-64; C-in-c of Tudweiliog w Llandudwen w Edeyrn and Ceidio 64-67; R of Llanbedry-y-Cennin w Dolgarrog (w Trefriw w Llanrhychwyn 71-74) 67-74; Llanbeulan w Llanfaerlog and Talyllyn 74-81. *1 Carreg-y-Gad, Llanfair PG, Anglesey, Gwyn.*

JONES, John Hellyer. b 20. Univ of Birm LDS 43. Westcott Ho Cam 65. **d** 67 **p** 68 Ely. C of Haddenham 67-70; R of Lolworth 70-79; C-in-c of Conington 75-79; R of Houghton w Wyton 79; P-in-c of Lolworth & Conington Dio Ely from 81. *Lolworth Rectory, Cambridge, CB3 8HH.* (Crafts Hill 81001)

JONES, John Henry. b 26. Chich Th Coll. **d** 56 **p** 57 B & W. C of Ilminster 56-58; St Andr Taunton 58-60; Harpenden 60-66; V of St Mary Magd Thetford 66-70; V in Thetford Team Min 70-75; R of Poringland w Howe 75-78; Framingham Earl 75-78; V of Twerton-on-Avon Bath 78-81; Team R of Marlbrook, Bath Dio B & W from 81. *Twerton-on-Avon Vicarage, Bath, Avon.* (Bath 21438)

JONES, John Howard. b 48. New Coll Ox BA 69, MA 73. Sarum Wells Th Coll 76. **d** 77 **p** 78 Swan B. C of Morriston 77-80; Warden of Ordinands Dio Swan B from 80; V of Gowerton Dio Swan B from 80. *Vicarage, Gowerton, Swansea, W Glam.* (Gowerton 872266)

JONES, John Idris. b 16. St D Coll Lamp BA 41. **d** 43 **p** 44 Ban. C of Towyn w Bryncrug 43-45; Llanaber w Barmouth 45-48; Blaenau Festiniog 48-50; V Cho of St A Cathl 50-54; V of Kerry 54-66; Llay 66-75. *14 Acton Park Way, Wrexham, Clwyd, LL12 7LD.*

JONES, Ven John Jenkin. b 15. Univ Coll Dur BA 39, Dipl Th 40, MA 42. **d** 40 **p** 41 St A. C of Denbigh 40-43; Colwyn 43-46; Northop 45-51; V of Eglwysbach 51-60; Holywell 60-71; Surr from 60; RD of Holywell 69-71; Can of St A Cathl 70-74; V of Llanrhos 71-76; Archd of St A from 74; V of Whitford 76-80. *Dorlan, Pentre Llanrhaeadr, Denbigh, LL16 4YN.*

JONES, John Lewis. St D Coll Lamp BA 15. **d** 17 **p** 18 Llan. C of Cymmer w Porth 17-20; St Mary Magd Barnstaple 20-21; Pilton 21-26; St Mary Bury St Edms 26-29; R of Hawstead (w Nowton from 37) 29-71. *2 George Gibson Close, Exning, Newmarket, Suff.*

JONES, John Milton Granville. b 07. Late Exhib and Scho of St D Coll Lamp BA 29. **d** 30 **p** 31 St D. C of Pembrey w Llandyry 30-32; St Matt Blackb 32-35; All SS Bingley 35-38; V of Thornton-in-Lonsdale 38-46; Morton 46-50; Allerton Yorks 50-58; Steeton w Eastburn 58-66; W Harptree 66-72; Perm to Offic Dio B & W from 72. *9 Becket Place, Wells, Somt.*

JONES, John Morgan. b 17. Univ of Wales BA 39. Ely Th Coll 39. **d** 40 **p** 41 St A. C of Chirk 40-43; Colwyn Bay 43-46; Brymbo 46-50; R of Pontfadog 50-59; C of Rawmarsh 59-60; R of Adwick-le-Street 60-63; Asst Master Bentley Sch 63-65; Hatfield Sch from 66. *15 Strathmore Road, Doncaster, Yorks.*

JONES, John Owen. b 03. **d** 59 **p** 60 St A. C of Mold 59-63; R of Garthbeibio w Llanerfyl and Llangadfan 63-73; L to Offic Dio St A from 75. *Rectory, Trelawnyd, Rhyl, Clwyd.*

JONES, Canon John Philip. b 09. St Bonif Coll Warm 36. **d** 39 **p** 40 Newc T. C of Howden Panns 39-41; Ch Ch Newc T 41-47; V of St Aug Newc T 48-74; Hon Can of Newc T 72-74; Can (Emer) from 74. *20 Nuns Moor Crescent, Newcastle upon Tyne, NE4 9BE.* (Newcastle-upon-Tyne 733775)

JONES, John Samuel. b 11. Univ of Wales BA 36. St D Coll Lamp 36. **d** 38 **p** 40 St A. C of Llawr-y-Bettws 38-43; P-in-c of Llanarmon Dyffryn Ceiriog 43-57; R of Pont Robert w Pont Dolanog 57-66; C of Hoylake 66-69; R of Llanfihangel-yng-Ngwynfa w Llwydiarth 69-72; V of Llanfair-Dyffryn-Clwyd 72-79. *19 Egerton Walk, Garden Village, Wrexham, Clwyd.*

JONES, Ven John Samuel. b 16. St D Coll Lamp BA 37, BD 45. St Mich Coll Llan 38. **d** 39 **p** 40 St D. C of Llandyssul 39-42; Llandebie 42-49; V of Llanllwni Dio St D from 49; RD of Lampeter (w Ultra Aeron from 68) 64-82; Can of St D Cathl from 72; Chan 78-82; Archd of Cardigan from 82. *Vicarage, Maesycrugiau, Pencader, Dyfed.* (Maesycrugiau 254)

JONES, Preb John Stephen Langton. Jes Coll Cam BA 13. Wells Th Coll 13. **d** 14 **p** 15 Wakef. C of Halifax 14-16; Hambledon Bucks 19-21; V of St Matt Yiewsley 21-38; L to Offic Dio B & W 38-39; R of W Lydford 39-47; Proc Conv B & W 46-50; Can and Prec of Wells Cathl 47-67; Preb from 68. *25 Irnham Road, Minehead, Somt.*

JONES, John Trevor. b 14. St D Coll Lamp BA 42. **d** 43 **p** 44 St A. C of Rhosddu 43-52; Timperley 52-53; V of Barnton 53-60; St Luke Poulton Wallasey 60-81. *21 Sandy Lane, Wallasey, Mer.*

JONES, Canon John Williams. b 06. Univ of Wales, BA 31. St Mich Th Coll Llan 31. **d** 34 **p** 35 Ban. C of Llanfechell 34-37; Eglwysnewydd 37-39; R of Pennal 39-45; Llanllechid 45-55; V of Rhosllanerchrugog 55-65; Rhyl 65-74; Can of St A Cathl 70-74; Can (Emer) from 74. *24 Bryn Llys, Meliden, Prestatyn, Clwyd.* (Prestatyn 3161)

JONES, Joseph Henry. b 1894. OBE 57. MM 17. Univ of Liv Hon MA 58. **d** 59 **p** 60 Ches. C of St Paul S Tranmere 59-64; Perm to Offic Dio Ches 64-67; Dio Liv from 67. *36 Bushbys Park, Formby, Formby, Liverpool, L37 2EF.* (051-367 4965)

JONES, Joseph Howell. St D Coll Lamp BA 46. **d** 49 **p** 50 Llan. C of Whitchurch 49-51; Chap Romsey Coll 51-53; Hd Master Brookland Hall Sch 53-64; L to Offic Dio St A 53-64. *c/o Royal Dorset Yacht Club, 6 Charlotte Row, Weymouth, Dorset.*

JONES, Keith Brynmor. b 44. Selw Coll Cam 2nd cl Engl Trip pt i 64, BA (2nd cl Engl Trip pt ii) 65, 2nd cl Th Trip pt ii 67, MA 69. Cudd Coll 67. **d** 69 **p** 70 S'wark. C of Limpsfield w Titsey 69-72; Dean's V of Cathl and Abbey Ch St Alb 72-76; C-in-c of St Mich Borehamwood 76-79; Team V of Borehamwood Dio St Alb from 79. *Vicarage, Brook Road, Borehamwood, Herts, WD6 5EQ.* (01-953 2362)

JONES, Keith Ellison. b 47. Wycl Hall Ox 72. **d** 75 Warrington for Liv **p** 76 Liv. C of St Jo Chrys Everton 75-79; Buckhurst Hill Dio Chelmsf 79-81; Team V from 81. *18 Victoria Road, Buckhurst Hill, Essex, IG9 5ES.* (01-504 6698)

JONES, Kenneth John. b 26. ALCD 53. **d** 53 Lon **p** 54 Kens for Lon. C of Ch Ch Roxeth Harrow 53-57; St Jo Bapt Woking (in c of Brookwood) 57-59; R of S Normanton 59-65; V of Creech St Mich Dio B & W from 65. *Creech Vicarage, Taunton, Somt.* (Henlade 442237)

JONES, Canon Kenneth William. b 15. St D Coll Lamp BA (2nd cl Engl) 36. TD 61. St Mich Coll Llan 36. **d** 38 Stafford for Lich **p** 39 Lich. C of H Trin Oswestry 38-40; CF (EC) 40-47; CF (TA) 49-65; CF (TA-R of O) from 65; R of Birdsall w Langton 47-53; Trowell 53-58; Publ Pr Dio Roch 58-63; Bp's Chap to Industry 58-63; Ed *Roch Review* 59-63; Dir Adult Relig Educn Dio Roch 60-63; Dir Chr Stewardship Dio Chich 63-66; V of Wilmington 63-66; R of Folkington 63-66; PC of St Jo Bapt Hove 66-68; V 68-77; Hon Can of Albuquerque Cathl New Mexico from 69; R of Buxted Dio Chich from 77; P-in-c of High Hurstwood Dio Chich from 78; Commiss Benin from 78. *Buxted Rectory, Uckfield, Sussex.* (Buxted 2541)

JONES, Kingsley Charles. b 45. Univ of Birm BSc (Phys) 66. Open Univ BA 75. Sarum Th Coll 66. **d** 69 Blackb **p** 70 Lanc for Blackb. C of Penwortham 69-72; Broughton 72-74; P-in-c of Gt Wollaston 74-77; Chap RAF from 77. *c/o Adastral House, WC1X 8RU.*

JONES, Leonard. Clifton Th Coll 51. **d** 52 **p** 53 Bradf. [F Lay Miss in Afr]. C of St Lawr Pudsey 52-54; Thornham w Gravel Hole 54-55; V of Rufforth 55-57; R of Markfield w Stanton-under-Bardon 57-61; V of St Paul Elswick Newc T 61-63; R of Knodishall w Buxlow 63-73; C of Gt Crosby 73-74; St Mary w St John Bootle 74-78; L to Offic Dio Liv from 78. *7 Stuart Avenue, Hunts Cross, Liverpool, L25 0NH.* (051-486 0086)

JONES, Leonard Parry. b 29. Univ Coll of N Wales, BA 52. St Mich Coll Llan 52. **d** 54 **p** 55 St A. C of Newtown 54-58; Abergele 58-60; V of Pennant 60-65; Llanynys w Llanychan 65-71; Trofarth w Brynymaen Dio St A from 71; RD of Rhos from 77. *Brynymaen Vicarage, Colwyn Bay, Clwyd.* (Colwyn Bay 2567)

JONES, Leslie Cecil John Gruffydd. b 11. St D Coll Lamp BA (3rd cl Hist) 34. St Mich Coll Llan 35. **d** 36 **p** 37 Llan. C of Skewen 36-44; Cadoxton-juxta-Barry 44-49; R of Llansannor and V of Llanfrynach w Penllyne 49-55; V of Pentyrch 55-64; Caerwent w Dinham 64-77; R of Llanvair Discoed 64-77; Shirenewton 77-82; V of Newchurch 77-82. *4 St Stephen's Close, Caerwent, Newport, Gwent.* (Caldicot 421951)

JONES, Leslie Joseph. b 23. Linc Th Coll. **d** 57 Malmesbury for Bris **p** 58 Bris. C of Penhill 57-60; C-in-c of St Mary Magd Conv Distr Lockleaze 60-62; V (w St Francis) 62-69; St Aldhelm Bedminster 69-74; Team V of Bedminster 74-80; V of Abbots Leigh w Leigh Woods Dio Bris from 80. *Abbots Leigh Vicarage, Bristol, BS8 3QU.* (Pill 3996)

JONES, Leslie Lloyd. b 13. OBE 72. St D Coll Lamp BA 35. **d** 39 Swan B **p** 41 Llan. C of St Tyfaelog Pontlottyn 39-42; CF 42-73; DACG 62-73; V of Yarcombe w Membury Dio Ex from 73; P-in-c of Upottery Dio Ex from 81. *Yarcombe Vicarage, Honiton, Devon, EX14 9BD.* (Upottery 244)

JONES, Leslie Morgan. b 23. Welsh Ch Scho and Scho of St D Coll Lamp BA (2nd cl Hist) 46. St Mich Coll Llan. **d** 48 **p** 49 St D. C of Pembroke Dk 48-52; Burry Port 52-54; R of New Moat w Clarbeston (w Llysyfran from 79) Dio St D from 54; C-in-c of Mynachlogddu w Llangolman 57-77; V 77-79. *New Moat Rectory, Clarbeston Road, Haverfordwest, Dyfed.* (09913 238)

JONES, Llewellyn. Univ of Capetn BA 58. Coll of Resurr Mirfield. **d** 61 **p** 62 Capetn. C of Caledon 61-65; Bellville 65-67; R of Robertson 67-71; Namaqualand 71-74; Wanneroo-Greenwood 74-77; Greenwood 77-78; City Beach Dio Perth from 79. *17 Yalgun Road, City Beach, W Australia 6015.* (385 8393)

JONES, Malcolm Francis. b 44. Chich Th Coll 67. **d** 70 **p** 71 Ches. C of Prestbury 70-73; Chap RAF 73-81; R of Heaton Reddish Dio Man from 81. *Rectory, St Mary's Drive, South Reddish, Stockport, SK5 7AX.* (061-477 6702)

JONES, Malcolm Stuart. b 41. Univ of Sheff BA 62. Linc Th Coll 64. **d** 66 **p** 67 Newc T. C of St Mary Virg Monkseaton 66-69; Ponteland 69-72; Chap at Lake Maracaibo Venez 73-75; C of Hexham 75-77; P-in-c of Killingworth Dio Newc T from 77. *Killingworth Vicarage, Newcastle upon Tyne, NE12 0BL.* (Newc T 683242)

JONES, Maldwyn Lloyd. b 17. St D Coll Lamp BA 39. **d** 40 **p** 41 Swan B. C of Gorseinon 40-43; L to Offic Dio Ox 43-46; Chap of All SS Nichteroy Brazil 46-48; Hd Master St Paul's Sch S£ao Paulo Brazil 48-50; Chap of Ch Ch Cathl Port Stanley 50-51; Chap RN 52-68; Shattuck Sch Minn 68-70; Lon Nautical Sch 71-72; L to Offic Dio Ban from 72. *c/o Barclays Bank, Chipping Norton, Oxford.*

JONES, Maurice Hughes Rowlestone. b 06. **d** 47 **p** 48 Ox. C of St Matt Ox 47-50; CMS Area Sec Dios Derby, Linc and Southw and LPr Dio Linc 50-55; Dios Birm, Cov, Leic and Pet 55-62; LPr Dio Cov and Perm to Offic Dios Birm, Leic and Pet 55-62; CMS Sec Midl Region 55-62; V of H Trin Southall 62-75; Chap Mt Pleasant Hosp 62-75; Perm to Offic Dio Glouc from 75. *75 Medoc Close, Cheltenham, Glos, GL50 4SP.* (0242 30328)

JONES, Maurice Maxwell Hughes. b 32. Dipl Th (Lon) 58. Clifton Th Coll 56. **d** 60 Lon **p** 61 Kens for Lon. C of St Andr Islington Lon 60-63; Miss Dio Argent 63-69; Dio Parag w N Argentina 69-71; L to Offic Dio Llan 71-72; C of Whitchurch 72-73; NW Area Sec SAMS 73-77; V of St Mark Haydock Dio Liv from 78. *St Mark's Vicarage, Haydock, St Helens, Mer, WA11 0UL.* (St Helens 23957)

JONES, Max. b 24. **d** 79 **p** 81 Tas. Chap Inter-Ch Trade & Industry Miss Dio Tas from 79. *Goldwen Lodge, Briggs Road, Old Beach, Tasmania 7402.*

JONES, Maxwell Cleophas Marks. Qu Coll Newfld. **d** 38 **p** 39 Newfld. C of Bell I 39-41; Exploits 41-45; I of Random 45-52; Twillingate 52-54; Elizabethtown 54-60; Lanark 60-65; Bury 65-77. *RR3, Spring Road, Lennoxville, PQ, Canada.*

JONES, Melville Kenneth. b 40. Open Univ BA 82. St D Coll Lamp Dipl Th 66. **d** 66 **p** 67 Llan. C of Aberdare 66-71; Caerau w Ely 71-72; V of Graig Pontypridd Dio Llan from 72. *St John's Vicarage, The Graig, Pontypridd, Mid Glam, CF37 1LW.* (Pontypridd 402436)

JONES, Michael David. St Jo Coll Auckld LTh 69. **d** 68 **p** 70 Waik. C of Tokoroa 68-70; Te Awamutu 70-72; V of Orakau 72-77; on leave 77-79; V of Putaruru 79-81. *Box 31-050, Lower Hutt, NZ.*

JONES, Michael Denis Dyson. b 39. CCC BA 62, MA 66. Univ of Lon MSc 73. Wycl Hall Ox Dipl Th 75. **d** 76 **p** 77 Ex. C of St Andr w St Geo & St Paul Plymouth 76-81; V of St Budeaux Devonport Dio Ex from 81. *Vicarage, Agaton Road, Plymouth, Devon, PL5 2EW.* (Plymouth 361019)

JONES, Michael Emlyn. b 47. **d** and **p** 79 Centr Tang. P Dio Centr Tang. *Box 306, Moshi, Tanzania.*

JONES, Neil Crawford. b 42. Univ of Wales, BA (2nd cl Engl) 63. K Coll Lon and Warm BD (2nd cl) and AKC 66. **d** 67 Swan B for St A **p** 68 St A. C of Holywell 67-69; Rhyl 69-73; Christchurch w Mudeford 73-77; V of St Luke Stanmore City and Dio Win from77. *St Luke's Vicarage, Mildmay Street, Winchester.* (Winchester 65240)

JONES, Canon Neville Charles. b 29. Selw Coll Cam BA 52, MA 57. Linc Th Coll 52. **d** 54 **p** 55 Dur. C of Grangetown 54-58; Norton 58-60; V of Greenside 60-69; H Trin Stockton-on-Tees 69-73; R of Central Stockton 73-75; Longnewton (w Elton from 76) Dio Dur from 75; C-in-c of Elton 75-76; RD of Stockton from 77; Hon Can of Dur Cathl from 81. *Longnewton Rectory, Stockton, Cleve, TS21 1BX.* (Stockton 582932)

JONES, Neville George. b 36. Univ of Wales, BA 59. St Mich Coll Llan. **d** 61 **p** 62 St A. C of Broughton 61-65; Newc w Laleston and Tythegston 65-68; V of Laleston w Tythegston Dio Llan from 68. *Laleston Vicarage, Bridgend, Mid Glam.* (Bridgend 4254)

JONES, Nicholas Newman. b 51. St Aug Coll Cant 74. **d** 75 **p** 76 York. C of Derringham Bank Hull 75-78; Stokesley 78-81; P-in-c of Kirby Misperton Dio York from 81. *Kirby Misperton Rectory, Malton, N Yorks, YO17 OXP.* (Kirby Misperton 206)

JONES, Noel. b 26. St D Coll Lamp BA 49. St Deiniols Libr Hawarden 70. **d** 72 **p** 73 St A (APM). C of Rhosymedre Dio St A from 72. *Ty Cerrig, Smith Street, Rhos, Wrexham, Clwyd.* (Rhos 840138)

JONES, Noel Debroy. b 32. St D Coll Lamp BA 53. Wells Th Coll 53. **d** 55 **p** 56 Mon. C of St Jas Tredegar 55-57; St Mark Newport Mon 57-60; V of Kano N Nig 60-62; Chap RN from 62. *c/o Ministry of Defence, Lacon House, Theobalds Road, WC1X 8RY.*

JONES, Norman Foster. b 12. Keble Coll Ox 3rd cl Mod Hist 34, BA 37, MA 62. Chich Th Coll 37. **d** 39 **p** 40 Chich. C of Horsham 39-41; CF (EC) 42-49; CF 49-62; R of Michelmersh w Eldon and Timsbury 62-71; Burley Ville 71-78. *Harriet's Cottage, Sackmore Lane, Marnhull, Dorset.*

JONES, Oswald Everton. Univ of Dur Codr Coll Barb BA and Dipl Th 34, MA 43. **d** 34 **p** 35 Barb. C of St Steph and Chap of Westbury Barb 34-41; V of St Phil L Barb 41-49; H Trin Barb 49-67; Asst Master Lodge Sch St John Barb 67; Can of St Mich Cathl Barb 66-67; L to Offic Dio Barb from 67. *Home Cob, St Philip, Barbados, W Indies.*

JONES, Oswin Ralph Ifor. b 04. Keble Coll Ox BA 29, MA 40. St Steph Ho Ox 29. **d** 31 Bp Palmer for Glouc for Worc **p** 32 Worc. C of Upton-on-Severn 31-35; Chap RN 35; RAF 36-46; CF 47-54; Hon CF 54; R of Herriard w Lasham 54-75; Perm to Offic Dio Win from 75. *15 Complins, Holybourne, Alton, Hants.* (Alton 82638)

JONES, Ven Owain William. b 21. Late Scho of Selw Coll Cam BA (1st cl Th Trip pt i) 48, MA 53. St D Coll Lamp BA 46. St Mich Coll Llan 48. **d** 49 **p** 50 Llan. C of Roath 49-53; Chap St Mich Coll Llan 53-57; Warden Ch Hostel Ban 57-62; V of Builth (w Alltmawr and Llanynys to 62; and Llanddewi'r Cwm from 62) 62-78; Can of Brecon Cathl from 69; RD of Builth-Elwell 70-78; Prec of Brecon Cathl 75-76; Treas from 76; Archd of Brecon from 78; V of Newbridge-on-Wye w Llanfihangel-Bryn-Pabuan Dio Swan B from 79. *Vicarage, Newbridge-on-Wye, Powys.* (N-on-Wye 270)

JONES, Owen Lloyd. b 04. **d** 59 St A for Ban **p** 60 Ban. C of Rhosybol w Llandyfrydog 59-60; Llanaber w Barmouth and Bontddu 60-62; Llangelynin 62-65; R of Llanllyfni w Talysarn and Penygroes 65-69; Llandanwg w Llanbedr 69-74. *Dylife, Pen y Bonc, Amlwch, Gwynedd, LL68 9DU.* (Amlwch 830184)

JONES, Patrick George. b 42. Lich Th Coll 69. **d** 72 Ely **p** 73 Huntingdon for Ely. C of St Geo Chesterton 72-75; C-in-c of Waterbeach 75-78; R of St Pet and St Paul Charlton-in-Dover Dio Cant from 78. *Rectory, St Alphege Road, Dover, Kent.* (Dover 201143)

JONES, Paul Harwood. b 20. Qu Coll Birm. **d** 53 **p** 54 Lon. C of Queensbury 53-57; Jes Ch Forty-Hill Enfield (in c of St Giles Bullsmoor Lane) 57-59; V of St Steph U Holloway 59-68; White Notley w Faulkbourne 68-80; P-in-c of Cressing 75-80; V of Finchingfield w Cornish Hall End Dio Chelmsf from 80. *Finchingfield Vicarage, Braintree, Essex, CM7 4JR.* (Gt Dunmow 810309)

JONES, Paul Terence. b 35. Univ of Dur BA 60. Qu Coll Birm 60. **d** 62 **p** 63 Liv. C of Rainford 62-65; Skelmersdale 65-68; V of St Gabr Huyton Quarry 68-78; St Ambrose Widnes Dio Liv from 78. *St Ambrose Vicarage, Hargreaves Court, Widnes, Ches, WA8 0QA.* (051-420 8044)

✠ **JONES, Right Rev Percy John.** Fourah Bay Coll BA (Dur) 22, MA 40. **d** 29 **p** 32 Sier L. C of St Phil Freetown 29-30; H Trin Freetown 30-35; St Geo Cathl Freetown 35-42; Tutor CMS Gr Sch Dio Sier L 30-46; Vice-Prin 46-48; P of Bp Crowther Mem Ch Freetown 43-47; Cons Asst Bp of Sier L in Cant Cathl 11 June 48 by Abp of Cant; Bp of Sier L; Bp Suffr of Dover; and Bp Wright; res 69; Archd of Protectorate 48-57; Colony 54-59; Freetown 59-66; Dean of Sier L 66-69. *14 Pultney Street, Freetown, Sierra Leone.*

JONES, Peter Anthony Watson. b 53. AKC 75. Sarum Wells Th Coll 76. **d** 77 **p** 78 York. C of Hessle Dio York from 77. *Top Flat, 28 Ferriby Road, Hessle, N Humb.*

JONES, Peter Russell. b 48. St Jo Coll Cam BA 71, MA 75. Wycl Hall Ox Dipl Th 72. **d** 75 **p** 76 Pet. C of Northampton 75-79; Min Can of Ban Cathl 79-81; R of Pentraeth w Llanddyfynan Dio Ban from 81. *Rectory, Nant y Felin, Pentraeth, Anglesey, Gwyn.* (Pentreath 450)

JONES, Philip Smith. b 53. St Mich AA Coll Llan 75. **d** 79 **p** 80 St D. C of Milford Haven Dio St D from 79. *St Peter's House, Starbuck Road, Milford Haven, Dyfed, SA73 2BA.*

JONES, Philip Suttill. b 02. St Aug Coll Cant 60. **d** 61 Lon **p** 62 Willesden for Lon. [f Solicitor]. C of St John's Wood Ch 61-63; Commiss Kuch 63-76; Chap Lon Ho Mecklenburgh Sq and C of St Pancras 63-70; Perm to Offic Dio Chich from

70. *College of St Barnabas, Dormans, Lingfield, RH7 6NJ.*

JONES, Philip Thomas Henry. Qu Coll Birm 58. **d** 60 **p** 61 Birm. C of Castle Bromwich 60-67; St Mary Virg Reading (in c of All SS) 67-72; Missr All SS Conv Distr Reading 72-75; V of All SS Reading Dio Ox from 75. *All Saints Vicarage, Downshire Square, Reading, Berks, RG1 6NH.* (Reading 52000)

JONES, Phillip Bryan. b 34. Univ of Wales, Dipl Th 61. St Mich Coll Llan 58. **d** 61 **p** 62 St A. C of Hope 61-64; Eglwys-Rhos 64-67; V of Kerry 67-74; R of Newtown w Llanllwchaiarn and Aberhafesp Dio St A from 74; RD of Cedewain from 76; Surr from 76. *Rectory, Newtown, Powys, SY16 1BP.* (0686 25795)

JONES, Raymond. b 34. Chich Th Coll 64. **d** 67 **p** 68 Lich. C of St Mark Ocker Hill Tipton 67-70; St Paul Truro 70-71; Chap Selly Oak Hosp Birm 71-76; R of St Pet Abaco 76; St Paul Long I 77; St Thos Grand Turk 78-79; Chap Hospice of Our Lady and St John Willen from 80. *Hospice of Our Lady and St John, Willen, Milton Keynes, Bucks.*

JONES, Raymond Blake. b 29. K Coll Lon and Warm BD and AKC (2nd cl) 54. **d** 55 **p** 56 Ox. C of Fenny Stratford and L Brickhill 55-58; Wooburn 58-60; St Kath Southbourne 60-66; V of Eye 66-77; Braiseworth 66-77; Surr 67-77; C-in-c of Yaxley 74-77; RD of Hartismere 76-77; R of Ufford 77-82; Chap St Audry's Ment Hosp Melton 77-82; V of St Kath w St Nich Southbourne Dio Win from 82. *3 Wollaston Road, Southbourne, Bournemouth, Dorset, BH6 4AR.* (Bournemouth 423986)

JONES, Raymond John. b 33. Univ of Lon BD 57. Univ of Reading MA 61. St Aug Coll Cant 76. **d** 76 Lon **p** 76 Edmon for Lon. C of Ch Ch Southgate 76-79; P-in-c of St Pet w St Martin Lower Edmon Dio Lon from 79. *Vicarage, St Peter's Road, N9 8JP.* (01-807 2974)

JONES, Raymond Morgan. b 06. Chich Th Coll. **d** 32 **p** 33 Carl. C of Stanwix 32-35; Felpham w Middleton 35-39; Chap RN 39-58; R of W Chiltington 58-71. *Pine Lodge, Warren Road, Liss Forest, Hants.*

JONES, Reginald Tudor. **d** 55 **p** 56 Ban. C of Llanllyfni 55-60; V of Llanidan w Llanedwen and Llanddaniel-fab 60-76. *Farm Lodge, Llanedwen, Llanfairpwll, Anglesey.*

JONES, Richard. b 28. St D Coll Lamp 54. **d** 56 **p** 57 Ban. C of Llanaber 56-61; R of Aberffraw 61-73; V of Llanfairisgaer (w Llanddeiniolen from 80) Dio Ban from 73. *Vicarage, Portdinorwic, Caerns, LL56 4SQ.* (Portdinorwic 245)

JONES, Richard. b 36. Ely Th Coll 61. **d** 64 **p** 65 Newc T. C of St Mary Blyth 64-67; Wallsend 67-69; R of H Trin Paisley 69-78; Monifieth Dio Brech from 78. *29 Princes Street, Monifieth, Angus, DD5 4AW.* (Monifieth 532266)

JONES, Richard. b 23. St Deiniol's Libr Hawarden 74. **d** 76 **p** 77 St A (NSM). C of Welshpool and Castle Caereinion Dio St A from 76. *Sherwood, Rhos Common, Four Crosses, Llanymynech, Powys, SY22 6RN.*

JONES, Richard. b 42. Univ of Lon BSc 64. Westcott Ho Cam 65. **d** 68 **p** 69 Cant. C of Ch Ch S Ashford 68-74; V of St Mich Tokyngton Wembley Dio Lon from 74. *Vicarage, St Michael's Avenue, Wembley, Middx, HA9 6SL.* (01-902 3290)

JONES, Richard Anthony. b 55. Univ of Tor BSc 78. Wycl Coll Tor MDiv 81. **d** 81 Tor. C of Ch Mem Ch Oshawa Dio Tor from 81. *Unit 41, 1330 Tronbridge Drive, Oshawa, Ont, Canada, L1G 7L1.*

JONES, Richard Clifford. b 08. K Coll Lon 37. **d** 42 **p** 43 Chelmsf. C of Grays Thurrock 42-46; L to Offic In Conv Distr of St Martin Plaistow 46-50; C-in-c of St Nich Elm Pk (w Hornchurch S Conv Distr to 54) 50-57; V 57-68; Surr 62; Publ Pr Dio Chelmsf 68-71; P-in-c of St Cedd Becontree Dio Chelmsf from 71. *St Cedd's Vicarage, Lodge Avenue, Dagenham, RM8 2HQ.* (01-592 5900)

JONES, Richard Keith. Wycl Hall Ox 61. **d** 63 **p** 64 Mon. C of Blaenavon w Capel Newydd 63-67; Mynyddyslwyn 67-71; Pontypool 71; V of Abercarn 71-81; R of Penhow w St Bride's, Netherwent, Llanvaches and Llandevaud Dio Mon from 81. *Penhow Rectory, Newport, Gwent, NP6 3AD.* (Penhow 245)

JONES, Richard Martin Hugh. b 31. St D Coll Lamp. **d** 58 **p** 59 Swan B. C of St Pet Cockett Swansea 58-63; V of Llangynllo w Bleddfa 63-70; R of Llandefalle w Llyswen Boughrood and Llanstephan Dio Swan B from 70. *Llyswen Rectory, Powys.* (Llyswen 255)

JONES, Richard Meirion. b 08. **d** 70 **p** 71 Ban. Hon C of Llanfairisgaer 70-77; Perm to Offic Dio Ban from 77. *Coed Menai, Caernarvon Road, Port Dinorwic, Gwyn.* (Portdinorwic 670297)

JONES, Robert. b 55. Div Hostel Dub 77. **d** 79 **p** 80 Down. C of Seapatrick Dio Down from 79. *8 Church Street, Banbridge, Co Down, BT32 4AA.* (Banbridge 23528)

JONES, Robert. b 26. Univ of Lon BA 51. K Coll Lon BD 65. St Deiniol's Libr Hawarden 79. **d** 80 **p** 81 Sheff (APM). C of St Mary Wheatley Doncaster 80-81; Halifax Dio Wakef from 81. *92 Godfrey Road, Halifax, W Yorks, HX3 0ST.*

JONES, Robert. b 40. Chich Th Coll 78. **d** 80 **p** 81 Cant. C of St Laurence-in-Thanet Dio Cant from 80. *76 Southwood Gardens, Ramsgate, Kent.*

JONES, Robert Alan. Moore Coll Syd ThL 71. **d** and **p** 72 Syd. C of St Alb Lindfield 72-74; St Clem Mosman 74-76; R of Earlwood 76-81; Denistone E w Marsfield Dio Syd from 81. *132 North Road, Eastwood, NSW, Australia 2122.* (88-3188)

JONES, Robert Bernard. b 24. St Jo Coll Dur BA (Hons Th) 48. Wycl Hall Ox. **d** 50 **p** 51 Sheff. C of Ecclesall-Bierlow 50-53; Apsley End 53-58; Christchurch (in c of Mudeford) 58-61; V of Ringwood 61-75; Surr from 62; R of N Stoneham w Bassett Dio Win from 75. *62 Glen Eyre Road, Bassett, Southampton, SO2 3NL.* (0703-768123)

JONES, Canon Robert Dwyfor. b 20. Univ of Wales, (Bangor) BA 41. St Mich Coll Llan 46. **d** 47 Ban **p** 48 St A For Ban. C of Llandudno 47-55; R of Cemais 55-58; Llanenddwyn w Llanddwywe 58-65; V of Glanogwen 65-69; Conwy w Gyffin Dio Ban from 69; Can of Ban Cathl from 76. *Vicarage, Conwy, LL32 8LD.* (Conwy 3402)

JONES, Robert Edward. b 01. Bp's Coll Sktn 30. **d** 30 **p** 33 Sask. Miss at Ridgeview 30-33; Arborfield 33; Big River 33-35 (all in Sask) Perm to Offic (Col Cl Act) at Ogley Hay w Brownhills 35-37; C of Hednesford (in c of St Sav) 37-40; Cf (EC) 40-45; V of Fulford-in-Stone 45-54; Chap Stallington Hall Inst 49-54; V of Bicton 54-70; Perm to Offic Dio Ches from 70. *25 Green Acres Road, Congleton, Chesh.*

JONES, Robert Eifion. b 07. Linc Th Coll 53. **d** 53 **p** 55 Ban. C of Penstrowed w Llanwnog 53-55; C-in-c of Trefeglwys 55-59; V of Tudweiliog w Llandudwen Edern and Ceidio 59-64; R of Llangadwaladr 64-77; Perm to Offic Dio Ban from 77. *25 Belmont Road, Bangor, Gwyn.*

JONES, Robert George. b 55. Hatf Coll Dur BA 77. Univ of Ox BA 79. Ripon Coll Cudd 77. **d** 80 **p** 81 Worc. C of H Innoc Kidderminster Dio Worc from 80. *33 Beauchamp Avenue, Kidderminster, Worcs.*

JONES, Robert Hugh. St D Coll Lamp BA 41. **d** 42 **p** 43 Ban. C of Llanllechid 42-44; Llanfaethlu w Llanfurog 44-46; Glanadda (St D) w Penrhosgarnedd 46-48; Victoria Pk (in c of St D's Welsh Ch) Man 48-52; P-in-c of Middleton-by-Wirksworth 52-55; V of St Steph Newton Flowery Field 55-66. *9 Elan Road, Llandudno, Gwyn.*

JONES, Robert William Aplin. b 32. Univ of Wales BSC (Chem) 52, MSC 65, C Chem, FRIC (FRSC from 81) 72. St Deiniol's Libr Hawarden 72. **d** 73 **p** 74 Mon. C of Bassaleg Dio 73-77; V of Nantyglo 77-81; Cwmcarn Dio Mon from 81. *Vicarage, Park Street, Cwmcarn, NP1 7EL.*

JONES, Canon Robin Lang Wilson. b 07. Late Exhib of Worc Coll Ox BA (2nd cl Cl Mods) 28, 3rd cl Lit Hum 30, MA 33. St Mich Coll Llan 41. **d** 41 **p** 42 Mon. C of St Mary Mon 41-44; V of Kenaston Dio Qu'App 44-46; Milestone 46-47; Sub-Warden St Chad's Coll Regina 47; Warden 47-48; C of St Woolos Cathl Newport Mon 48-49; Chap of St Woolos Hosp 48-49; C of Risca 49-50; R of Caldbeck (w Castle Sowerby from 58) 50-59; RD of Wigton 55-59; V of Warcop w Musgrave 59-72; RD of Appleby and Kirkby Steph 60-66; Hon Can of Carl 64-72; Can (Emer) from 72; Perm to Offic Dio Carl from 72. *Fell End, Mungrisdale, Penrith, Cumb, CA11 0XR.*

JONES, Roderick. b 48. Univ of Leeds BA (Th) 70. Oak Hill Coll 74. **d** 76 **p** 77 Roch. C of Ch Ch Beckenham 76-80; Uphill Dio B & W from 80. *2 Westbury Crescent, Weston-super-Mare, Avon.* (W-s-M 23195)

JONES, Canon Ronald Albert. b 15. Em Coll Cam BA 37, MA 41. Qu Coll Birm 37. **d** 39 Mon **p** 40 Llan for Mon. C of St Pet Blaenavon 39-42; St Woolos Newport 42-48; Chap Wooloston Ho and Inf 42-48; R of Pontesbury (3rd Portion) 48-55; PC of Longden 48-55; V of Annscroft 54-55; R of Ribbesford w Bewdley 55-59; Loughborough 59-76; Chap Loughborough Gen Hosp 59-76; Surr 60-76; Hon Can of Leic from 63; RD of Akeley E 64-76; Woodstock from 80; P-in-c of Stonesfield 76-82. *c/o Stonesfield Rectory, Oxford, OX7 2PR.* (Stonesfield 664)

JONES, Ronald Elvet Lewis. b 14. Univ of Bris BA 38. Lich Th Coll 38. **d** 40 Llan for Mon **p** 41 Mon. C of Bassaleg 40-43; V of Marshfield w Peterstone Wentloog 43-64; R of Coedkernew w St Bride Wentloog 49-64; V of Newbridge 64-73; R of Penhow U 73-80. *1 The Retreat, Kings Fee, Monmouth, Gwent.* (Mon 6263)

JONES, Ronald Stanley. b 20. Sarum Wells Th Coll 71. **d** 72 **p** 73 B & W (APM). C of Street 72-73; Moorlinch w Stawell and Sutton Mallet 73-81. Greinton 73-81. *19 Manor House Road, Glastonbury, Somt.* (Glastonbury 32253)

JONES, Ronald Thomas. Univ of Wales BA (2nd cl Phil) 41. Westcott Ho Cam 41. **d** 43 **p** 44 St D. C of Bettws w Ammanford 43-48; Asst Master and Chap Oakham Sch 48-51; Ipswich Sch and Perm to Offic Dio St E 51-60; Lect Nor Tr Coll and L to Offic Dio Nor from 60. *3 Tungate Crescent, Cringleford, Norwich, NOR 60D.* (Nor 52166)

JONES, Rupert Sugg. b 35. Selw Coll Cam BA 59, MA 63. Wells Th Coll 59. **d** 61 **p** 62 Man. C of All SS Hamer Rochdale 61-64; V 64-77; Asst Master Agnes Stewart C of E High Sch Leeds and LPr Dio Man from 77. *Watch Hall Cottage, Millgate, Rochdale, Gtr Man, OL16 2NU.*

JONES, Samuel Leslie. Qu Coll Newfld 59. **d** 61 **p** 62 Newfld. I of White Bay 61-68; R of Fogo 68-72; Heart's Delight 72-77; Arnold's Cove Dio E Newfld from 77. *Box 9, Arnold's Cove, Newfoundland, Canada.* (709-463 2425)

JONES, Samuel Wynne Evans. b 06. Jes Coll Ox BA and MA 36. Wycl Hall Ox 28. **d** 30 **p** 32 York. C of Beverley Minster 30-37; Min Can of Heref Cathl 37-51; R of Thruxton (w Kingstone to 56) Dio Heref from 51; V of Allensmore Dio Heref from 57. *Thruxton Rectory, Hereford.* (Wormbridge 214)

JONES, Canon Selwyn Hugh. St Jo Coll Auckld LTh (1st cl) 68. **d** and **p** 68 Wai. C of Havelock N 68-72; V of Whakatane 72-77; Te Puke 77-80; Gisborne Dio Wai from 80; Can of Wai from 80. *34 Cobden Street, Gisborne, NZ.* (6284)

JONES, Stephen Edgar. Pemb Coll Ox BA 29, MA 32. Moore Th Coll Syd 21. **d** 21 **p** 23 Syd. C of Hornsby 21-24; St Ebbe (in c of St Pet-le-Bailey from 26) Ox 24-27; Chap HM Pris Ox 25-27; C of Summer Hill NSW 27-28; Ch Ch Chelsea 29-30; Hd Master Heiban Boys' Sch Egypt 30-32; Chap HM Borstal Inst Roch 32-37; Asst Chap and Asst Master C of E Gr Sch Geelong 37-43; Chap 44-58. *48 Skene Street, Newtown, Geelong, Vic, Australia 3220.* (052-2666)

JONES, Stephen Frederick. b 43. Wells Th Coll 68. **d** 71 **p** 72 Dur. C of St Jas Conv Distr Stockton-on-Tees 71-74; Asst Chap St Ebba's Hospital Epsom 74-79; Chap Warley Hosp from 79. *Warley Hospital, Brentwood, Essex.*

JONES, Stephen Richard. b 49. Oak Hill Coll 72. **d** 75 **p** 76 Roch. C of Welling 75-79; St Mark Cheltenham Dio Glouc from 79. *50 Shakespeare Road, Cheltenham, Glos.*

JONES, Stephen William. b 46. AKC and BD 70. St Aug Coll Cant 70. **d** 71 **p** 72 S'wark. C of St Pet Streatham 71-76; Leeds 76-79; P-in-c of St Sav w St Hilda Cross Green Leeds Dio Ripon from 79; Succr from 76. *c/o Clergy House, 70* (0978 780319) *Lane, Leeds 9.* (Leeds 33547)

JONES, Sydney Clarence. b 21. St Cath S Ox BA 42, MA 46. Linc Th Coll 43. **d** 44 **p** 45 Sarum. C of H Trin Weymouth 44-50; C-in-c of Wrangbook Conv Distr w N Elmsall 50-52; V of St Mary Sowerby 52-56; Drighlington 56-63; V of Dewsbury Moor 63-67; Field Officer Children's Coun C of E Bd of Educn from 67; Perm to Offic Dio Ox 67-69; Lect Marg McMillan Mem Coll of Educn Bradf 69-71; L to Offic Dio Bradf 69-71; V of Sharow w Copt Hewick 71-74; Chap Dame Alan's Schools 74-79; P-in-c of Chollerton w Thockrington and Dioc Schs Adv Dio Newc T 79-80; V of Scholes Dio Wakef from 80. *Scholes Vicarage, Cleckheaton, W Yorks, BD19 6PA.* (Cleckheaton 873024)

JONES, Tegid Owen. b 27. Univ of Wales LLB 47. **d** 68 **p** 69 St A. C of Rhosddu 68-71; Wrexham 71-75; R of Marchwiel Dio St A from 75. *Marchwiel Rectory, Wrexham, Clwyd.* (0978 780319)

JONES, Theodore Garnett. b 1899. Westcott Ho Cam 24. **d** 26 **p** 27 Ripon. C of St Wilfrid's Miss Ch Harehills Leeds 26-29; St Andr Starbeck 29-31; Pateley Bridge (to Offic at Greenhow Hill) 31-34; V of Well and Chap of Neville's Hosp and St Mary Snape 34-39; V of Winksley w Grantley 39-50; C-in-c of Aldfield w Studley 46-50; Chap United Cambridge Hosps 50-66; L to Offic Dio Ely 50-68; Hon Can of Ely 63-68; Perm to Offic Dio Ripon from 68. *3 The Raikes, Wilsill, Pately Bridge, Harrogate, N Yorks, HG3 5EG.* (Harrogate 711533)

JONES, Thomas Aelwyn. b 08. St D Coll Lamp BA 32. **d** 32 **p** 33 St D. C of Llandilo Fawr w Llandyfeisant 32-36; Pembrey (in c of St Mary Burry Port) 36-40; V of Whitchurch w St Elvis and Solva 40-51; Pembrey w Llandyry (and Burry Port 51-52) 51-73. *6 St Anne's Avenue, Cwmffrwd, Dyfed.*

JONES, Thomas Benjamin. b 05. Late Exhib of St D Coll Lamp BA 28. **d** 28 **p** 29 St D. C of Henfynyw 28-31; Min Can of St D Cathl 31-32; C of Lampeter-pont-Stephan 32-34; R of Llangrannog 34-45; V of Llansadwrn w Llanwrda and Capel Dewi Sant 45-52; R of Aberporth (w Tremaen from 64) 52-73; RD of Sub-Aeron 62-65; Kemes and Sub-Aeron 65-73; Can of Llangan in St D Cathl 64-73. *Richmond, Napier Street, Cardigan, SA43 1ED.* (Cardigan 613476)

JONES, Thomas Dale. Em Coll Sktn 34. **d** 34 Sktn **p** 35 Athab. C of Kerrobert 34; I of Colinton 34-48; R of Ch Ch Grande Prairie 38-42; Kamloops 42-43; Chap RCAF 43-49; R of Seaforth 49-51; C of St Paul's Cathl Lon Ont 51-52; R of Aylmer Ont 52-58; St Paul Cote des Neiges 66-73. *16 Adswood Place, London, Ont, Canada, N6E 1W7.*

JONES, Thomas Edward. b 23. Bps' Coll Cheshunt, 64. **d** 65 Bp Otter for Linc **p** 66 Linc. C of Swineshead 65-69; Ch Ch w Didsbury 69-72; R of St Wilfrid (and St Anne from 73) Newton Heath 72-75; Dioc Adv for Social Responsibility Dio Derby from 75; P-in-c of Ambergate Dio Derby from 79. *Ambergate Vicarage, Derby, DE5 2GD.* (Ambergate 2072)

JONES, Thomas Elias. St D Coll Lamp BA 32. **d** 32 **p** 33 Llan. C of Gilfach Goch 32-35; Chap Co Hosp and Medway Children's Home Chatham 35-41; V of Tysoe w Compton Wynyates 45-56; CF 41-46; and 56-63. *20 Cemetery Road, Porth, Mid Glam.*

JONES, Canon Thomas Glover. b 09. ALCD 34. **d** 33 **p** 34 Ches. C of St Mary Birkenhead 33-35; St Paul Brixton 35-38; St Luke Ramsgate 38-40; V of St Andr Thornhill Square Islington Lon 40-49; PC of Littleover 49-53; V of St Sav Herne Hill Road (w St Matt Ruskin Pk from 56) 53-80; C-in-c of St Matt Denmark Hill 53-56; Hon Can of S'wark Cathl from 80; L to Offic Dio Cant from 81. *155 Shirley Church Road, Shirley, Croydon, CR0 5HJ.* (01-777 3572)

JONES, Thomas Graham. b 33. St D Coll Lamp BA 57. **d** 59 **p** 60 St D. C of Llanelli 59-64; V of Ysbyty Cynfyn 64-72; Ch Ch Llanelli Dio St D from 72. *Christ Church Vicarage, New Dock Road, Llanelli, Dyfed.* (Llanelli 4264)

JONES, Thomas Hughie. b 27. Univ of Wales BA 49. BD (Lon) 53. Univ of Leic MA 72. **d** 66 **p** 67 Leic. Hon C of Evington 66-76; Kirby Muxloe 77-80; Prin Hind Leys Coll Shepshed Loughborough 75-81; L to Offic Dio Leic 77-80; R of Ch Langton w Tur Langton and Thorpe Langton Dio Leic from 80; Dioc Adult Educn Officer Dio Leic from 81. *Church Langton Rectory, Market Harborough, Leics.* (East Langton 217)

JONES, Thomas James. St D Coll Lamp BA 33. St Mich Th Coll Llan 34. **d** 35 St D **p** 36 Swan B for St D. C of Llandilofawr 35-38; Pembrey 38-41; V of Llanerchaeron w Ciliau-Aeron 41-53; Llanllwch 53-72; RD of Carmarthen 66-72. *Vicarage, Llanllwch, Dyfed.*

JONES, Thomas Jenkin. b 19. St Mich Coll Llan. **d** 49 **p** 50 Llan. C of St Luke Canton 49-51; Gellygaer 51-52; CF 52-68; V of Stokenham w Sherford Dio Ex from 68. *Stokenham Vicarage, Kingsbridge, Devon.* (Kingsbridge 580385)

JONES, Thomas Lloyd. b 20. Univ Coll Ox BA (2nd cl Lit Hum) 41, 3rd cl Th 42. Coll of Resurr Mirfield 42. **d** 44 **p** 45 Swan B. C of St Gabr Swansea 44-51; St Pet Acton Green 51-53; Ruislip 53-55; Kemptson Beds 55-58; V of Flamstead 58-63; H Trin Bp's Stortford 63-69; Welwyn Garden City Dio St Alb from 69. *Vicarage, Parkway, Welwyn Garden City, Herts.* (Welwyn Garden 23316)

JONES, Thomas Madoc. b 06. Late Scho of St D Coll Lamp BA 27. **d** 29 **p** 30 Swan B. C of St Mary Builth Wells 29; St Jo Bapt-juxta-Swansea 29-31; St Edm Crickhowell 31-33; Oystermouth 33-39; V of Llanddew w Talachddu 39-63; Dioc Insp of Schs Dio Swan B 43-61; Chief Insp 61-63; V of Awre w Blakeney 63-66; Kempley w Oxenhall 66-71. *Beacon Lodge, Battle, Brecon, Powys.* (Brecon 3517)

JONES, Thomas Percy Norman Devonshire. b 34. St Jo Coll Ox BA 58, MA 61. Cudd Coll 58. **d** 60 **p** 61 Portsm. C of St Cuthb Copnor 60-61; St Mark Portsea 61-67; Lect and Asst Chap Portsm Coll of Tech 67-70; Chap Portsm Poly 70-75; Trin Coll Hartford Connecticut 73-74; V of St Sav Folkestone 75-81; St Mark Prince Albert Road St Pancras Dio Lon from 81. *4 Regents Park Road, NW1 7TX.* (01-485 3077)

JONES, Canon Thomas Peter. b 20. Late Exhib of Ex Coll Ox BA 43, MA 46. St Mich Th Coll Llan 43. **d** 45 St A **p** 46 Ban for St A. C of Wrexham 45-48; Llandrillo yn Rhos 48-57; R of Overton w Erbistock Dio St A from 57; Cursal Can of St A Cathl from 78; RD of Bangor-Is-y-Coed from 80. *Overton Rectory, Wrexham, Clwyd, LL13 0ED.* (Overton on Dee 229)

JONES, Thomas Trevor. d 31 **p** 32 St D. C of Pembroke Dk 31-33; H Trin Abergavenny 33-35; Newtown 35-38; Llanfihangel Geneu'r Glyn 38-39; R of Burton 39-44; St Florence w Redberth 44-56; St Michaelston-u-Fedw 56-69. *Blaenblodau, Bridge Street, Lampeter, Dyfed.*

JONES, Thomas Vincent. Moore Th Coll ACT ThL 54. **d** 55 Syd for Adel **p** 55 Adel. C of H Trin Adel 55-57; P-in-c Ceduna Miss 57-62; P-in-c of Kingston w Robe 62-66; R of Naracoorte 66-69; Magill 69-78; Walkerville Dio Adel from 78; P-in-c of Hillcrest Dio Adel from 78. *41 Church Terrace, Walkerville, S Australia 5081.* (44 1304)

JONES, Thomas William Warren. b 25. Trin Coll Dub Div Test (1st cl) 49. **d** 49 **p** 50 Drom. C of Shankill Lurgan 49-54; Derriaghy 54-56; I of Ballintoy 56-60; C-in-c of Ardoyne 60-63; R 63-70; I of Ballymacash (w Stoneyford from 78) Dio Connor from 70. *97 Antrim Road, Lisburn, Co Antrim, N Ireland.* (Lisburn 2393)

JONES, Timothy Morgan. b 1896. Univ of Wales BA 21. St Mich Th Coll Llan 21. **d** 22 St A **p** 23 Ban for St A. C of Colwyn Bay 22-28; Minera 28-31; V of Pentrevoelas 31-47. *Llysdewi, Aberarth, Aberayron, Dyfed, SA46 0LP.*

JONES, Chan Trefor Thornley. b 05. Univ of Wales, BA (2nd cl Eng) 26, Univ Stud and 1st cl Phil 27, MA 29. Or Coll Ox 2nd cl Th 30, BA and MA 35. **d** 30 **p** 31 Swan B. C of H Trin Swansea 30-32; Builth w Alltmawr 32-38; V of

Cwmdauddwr w Nantgwyllt 38-70; Exam Chap (Readers) to Bp of Swan B 40-67; Dioc Insp of Schs 43-62; Can of Elwell in Brecon Cathl 49-54; Chan 54-70; Bp's Chap for Post Ordin Tr 65-70. *Llanerch, Trefecca, Brecon, LD3 0PR, Powys.*

JONES, Trevor. b 12. Univ of Wales, BA 36. St Mich Coll Llan 36. **d** 37 **p** 39 Bp Wentworth-Sheilds for Ban. C of Llanrug 37-41; Llandegfan w Beaumaris 41-43; Llandysilio 43-47; R of Llanaelhaiarn 47-54; Llanllyfni w Talysarn and Penygroes 54-58; Llanfaethlu 58-67; Llanfachraeth w Llanynghenedl Llanfigail and Valley (w Llanddeusant w Llanbabo Llantrisant and Llanllibio from 77) 67-80; RD of Llifon and Talybolion 75-80; Surr 77-80. *1 Maeshyfryd, Dwyran, Anglesey, Gwyn.*

JONES, Trevor Barnard. Late Exhib of St D Coll Lamp BA (2nd cl Hist) 28. Powis Exhib Jes Coll Ox BA (3rd cl Th) 31, MA 35. **d** 31 **p** 32 St D. C of St Paul Llanelly 31-35; C-in-c of Uzmaston w Boulston 35-41; V of Llanstadwell Dio St D 41-72; Surr 41-72; RD of Roose 55-72; Can and Preb of St D Cathl 60-72; Can Treas 70-72. *3 St Margaret's Road, Whitchurch, Cardiff, S Glam.*

JONES, Trevor Blandon. b 43. Oak Hill Coll 77. **d** 80 **p** 81 Stepney for Lon. C of St Barn w St Paul Homerton Dio Lon from 80. *49 Trehurst Street, Clapton, E5 0EB.* (01-986 0910)

JONES, Trevor Edwin. b 49. Ripon Coll Cudd 74. **d** 76 **p** 77 Lich. C of St Luke Cannock 76-79; Ascen Berwick Hills, Middlesbrough 79-81; V of St Steph and All Marts Oldham Dio Man from 81. *33 Scafell Close, Shaw Road, Oldham, OL1 3JR.* (061-624 2598)

JONES, Trevor Evans. b 07. Univ of Tor BA 30, BD 46. **d** 32 Niag for Moos **p** 32 Moos. Miss at Fort George 32-37; C of St John W Tor 37-38; Miss-in-c of Aklavik 38-44; Can of Arctic 39-44; C of Grace Ch Tor 44-47; St Jas Cathl in c of St Andr Centre I Tor 47-50; R of St Andr 50-53; Asst Sec Gen Bd of Relig Educn 53-61; Assoc Gen Sec 61-62; Dir of MSCC 63-69; Can of Ott 63-69; Hon C of St Geo Willowdale Tor 69-72, P-in-c of St Paul Dunbarton Tor 72-73; Hon C 73-79; Riverhead Dio Roch from 80. *42 Pontoise Close, Seven Oaks, Kent, TN13 3ET.*

JONES, Trevor Glyn. b 47. Trin Coll Cam BA 69, MA 73. Montr Dioc Th Coll MDiv 78. **d** 78 **p** 79 Montr. C of St Pet Montr 78-80; R of Lachute Dio Montr from 80. *715 Meikle Street, Lachute, Queb, Canada, J8H 1V4.* (54-562 2917)

JONES, Trevor Pryce. b 48. Univ of Southn BEducn 76, BTh 79. Sarum Wells Th Coll 73. **d** 76 **p** 77 Glouc. C of St Geo Lower Tuffley Glouc 76-79; Warden Bp Mascall Centre Ludlow from 79; M of Dioc Educn & Communications Officer from 80. *Hamlet House, Henley Road, Ludlow, SY8 1QE.* (0584 3979)

JONES, Tudor Howell. b 39. Univ of Wales Dipl Th 67. St Mich Coll Llan 64. **d** 68 **p** 69 Swan B. C of Clydach 68-72; St Pet Cockett Swansea 72-75; V of Ystradfellte w Pontneath-vaughan 75-79; Llanguicke Dio Swan B from 79. *Vicarage, The Uplands, Pontardawe, W Glam.* (Pontardawe 862003)

JONES, Victor Harvey. b 25. St D Coll Lamp BA 53. Coll of Resurr Mirfield. **d** 55 **p** 56 Llan. C of St Luke Canton 55-57; Caerau w Ely 57-61; Chap RN 62-76; Perm to Offic Dio Truro 77-80; C of St Pet Portishead Dio B & W from 80. *7 Channel View Road, Portishead, Bristol, BS20 9LZ.* (Portishead 849389)

JONES, Canon Victor Howell. Univ of Wales BA 41. St Mich Coll Llan. **d** 43 St D **p** 45 Llan for St D. C of St Paul Llanelly 43-46; C and PV of St D Cathl 46-54; V of Laugharne w Llansadwrnen and Llandawke 54-72; Llanllwch Dio St D from 72; Can of St D Cathl from 80. *Vicarage, Llanllwch, Dyfed.*

JONES, Vincent Gower. b 04. Jes Coll Ox BA (2nd cl Th) 29, MA 34. **d** 29 **p** 30 Swan B. C of Sketty 29-32; St Alb Westbury Pk Clifton 32-35; V of Caverswall 35-53; R of Myddle (or Middle) 53-59; V of Broughton 53-59; R of Scartho 59-73. *65 Sandbeck Avenue, Skegness, Lincs.*

JONES, Walter. b 14. TCD 63. **d** 65 **p** 66 Clogh. C of Monaghan 65-71; Chaddesden 71-72; Ch Ch Bootle 72-75; St Thos Ashton-in-Makerfield (in c of St Luke) 75-77; V in R Benef of Ebbw Vale Dio Mon from 77. *St Mary's Vicarage, Waunlwyd, Ebbw Vale, Gwent, NP3 6QY.* (Cwm 294)

JONES, Walter Frederick. b 04. ALCD 28 (LTh from 74). **d** 28 **p** 29 Lon. C of H Trin Dalston 28-30; St Mary Beeston Yorks 30-33; Rochford 33-38; V of High Beach 38-44; L to Offic Dio Cant 44-51; Metrop Sec (S) CMS 44-51; V of St Jas Hatcham 51-59; PC of St Barn Devonport 59-66; R of Pattiswick 66-68; Bradwell-juxta-Coggeshall 66-68; V of Wethersfield 68-71. *51a Downview Road, Worthing, Sussex, BN11 4QH.*

JONES, Preb Wilfred David. b 22. Keble Coll Ox BA (2nd cl Th) 47, MA 48. St Mich Coll Llan 47. **d** 48 **p** 49 Llan. C of Aberman 48-50; St Jo Bapt Cardiff 50-55; Chap Kelly Coll Tavistock 55-62; V of St Decuman 62-75; Ilminster w Whitelackington Dio B & W from 75; RD of Ilminster from 78; Preb of Wells Cathl from 81. *Vicarage, Ilminster, Somt.* (Ilminster 2610)

JONES, Wilfred Lovell. b 39. St D Coll Lamp Dipl Th 63. BD (Lon) 71. **d** 63 Ban. C of Llanllyfni 63-65; Llanbeblig w Caernarvon 65-68; V of Penstrowed w Llanwnog 68-73; Llanwnog w Carno 73-75; Asst Chap Dover Coll from 76. *123 London Road, Temple Ewell, Dover.* (Kearsney 2385)

JONES, William. Univ of Wales Ban Dipl Th 54. St Mich Coll Llan 54. **d** 55 **p** 56 Ban. C of Pwllheli 55-60; V of Aberdaron w Bodferin 60-66; Llandwrog w Groeslon 66-71; R of Llanystumdwy w Llangybi and Llanarmon (and Dolbenmaen from 74) Dio Ban from 71; Llanfihangel-y-Pennant Dio Ban from 74; RD of Eifionydd from 75. *Llanystumdwy Rectory, Cricieth, Gwyn, LL52 0SS.* (Cricieth 2325)

JONES, Canon William Alan. Univ of W Ont BA 47. Hur Th Coll LTh 49. **d** 49 **p** 50 Hur. C of Lion's Head 49-51; R of Seaforth 51-53; Kitchener 53-59; Can Davis Mem Ch Sarnia Dio Hur from 59; Can of Hur from 72. *378 North Russell Street, Sarnia Ont., Canada.* (519-344 9531)

JONES, William Alexander. Univ of Wales BA (1st cl Latin) 35. **d** 69 **p** 70 Ban. Hon C of Llandegfan w Beaumaris and Llanfaes 69-75; C 75-76; C-in-c of Penmon w Llangoed and Llanfihangel-Din-Silwy Dio Ban 76-77; Team V (w Llandegfan w Beaumaris and Llanfaes) from 77. *4 Coedwig Terrace, Penmon, Gwyn.* (Llangoed 509)

JONES, William Alfred Edward. b 03. Sarum Th Coll 57. **d** 57 **p** 58 Chich. C of Seaford 57-60; St John Invercargill 60-61; R of Balcombe 61-65; V of St Mich AA Lancing 65-73; C of Rumboldswhyke 73-81; Whyke w Rumboldswhyke Dio Chich from 81. *106 Whyke Lane, Chichester, Sussex, PO19 2AT.* (Chich 785610)

JONES, William David. b 28. Late Scho of St D Coll Lamp BA 48, BD (2nd cl) Lon 57. Univ of Leeds MA 73. St Mich Coll Llan 49. **d** 51 **p** 52 Mon. C of Risca 51-54; Chepstow w St Arvans and Penterry 54-55; St Geo-in-the-E 55-59; Farnham Royal 59-65; Lect in Div Culham Coll 65-67; Lect Doncaster Coll of Educn and L to Offic Dio Sheff 67-74; Vice-Prin Bede Coll Dur 74; Coll of St Hild and St Jude Dur from 75. *Easdale, St Hild's Lane, Durham.* (Durham 69501)

JONES, William Dearden. Wycl Coll Tor STh 65. **d** and **p** 65 Athab. I of Boyle 65-70; Beaverlodge 70-75. *RR1, Wyebridge, Ont., Canada.*

JONES, William Douglas. b 28. St Francis Coll Brisb ThL 56. **d** 56 Brisb for New Guinea **p** 58 New Guinea. C of Warwick 57-58; P Dio New Guinea 58-72: C of Manston 72-75; V of Middleton Leeds Dio Ripon from 75. *Middleton Vicarage, Town Street, Leeds, LS10 3TJ.* (Leeds 705689)

JONES, William Edward Benjamin. b 19. Trin Coll Dub BA 43, Div Test 44, MA 53. **d** 44 Down **p** 45 Connor. C of St Thos Belf 44-47; Sudbury 47-50; CF 50-54; V of St Pet Edmon 54-59; St Cuthb N Wembley 59-81; Ripley Dio Guildf from 81. *Vicarage, High Street, Ripley, Surrey, GU23 6AE.* (Guildf 225234)

JONES, William Ffrangcon. Univ of Wales (Bangor), BA 39. Late Scho of St D Coll Lamp 37. **d** 39 **p** 40 Ban. C of Llangelynin 39-40; Llanidan w Llanddaniel and Llanedwen 40-42; Chap Leatherhead Hosp 42-44; C-in-c of Middlewich 44-45; Chap RAF 45-49; V of Bredbury and Surr 49-53; Prin of Cyrene Miss Westacre S Rhod 53-58; Hd Master Peka High Sch 58-60; V of Tugela River 60-61; Chap Guinea Fowl Sch 61-65; L to Offic Dio Matab 61-65; Chap and Tutor Kabulonga High Sch Lusaka 65-67; Hon Chap St Mary Magd Woodlands Lusaka 67-69; R of Kabwe Zam 69-71. *PO Box 42, Kabwe, Zambia.*

JONES, William Glyndwr. b 17. St D Coll Lamp BA 39. **d** 42 **p** 43 St D. C of Monkton 42-48; Bettws w Ammanford 48-51; R of Grandston w St Nicholas 51-69; V of Mathry w St Edrens Grandston and St Nicholas (and Jordanston from 78) Dio St D from 69. *Rectory, St Nicholas, Goodwick, Dyfed.* (St Nich 230)

JONES, William Hugh. b 13. Univ of Wales BA (3rd cl Latin) 35. St Mich Coll Llan 35. **d** 38 **p** 39 St A. C of Flint 38-42; C-in-c of All SS Deganwy 42-46; C of Aylesford 46-49; V of Chearsley w Nether Winchendon 49-54; R of Princes Risborough (w Ilmer from 73) Dio Ox from 54; Surr from 60; C-in-c of Ilmer 70-73; RD of Aylesbury 77-80. *Rectory, Princes Risborough, Bucks.* (Princes Risborough 5670)

JONES, William John. Univ of Wales Clifton Th Coll. **d** 40 **p** 41 St D. C of Llanfihangel-ar-Arth 40-43; St Ishmael w Llansaint and Ferryside 43-49; R of Puncheston w L Newcastle (and Castle Bigh from 52) 49-59; V of Eglwyswrw w Meline Dio St D from 59. *Eglwyswrw Vicarage, Crymmych, Dyfed.* (Crosswell 641)

JONES, William Lincoln. b 19. Late Scho of St D Coll Lamp BA (2nd cl Eng) 41. St Mich Coll Llan. **d** 43 **p** 44 Llan. C of Roath 43-47; Wooburn 47-50; Bridgwater 50-55; V of Langford Budville w Runnington 55-60; Winscombe (w Sandford 60-64) 60-71; Bps Lydeard (w Cothelstone from 73 and Bagborough from 80) Dio B & W from 71; P-in-c of W

Bagborough 78-80. *Vicarage, Bishops Lydeard, Taunton, Somt, TA4 3AT.* (Bishops Lydeard 432414)

JONES, William Llewellyn. b 07. St Jo Coll Dur LTh 40, BA 41. Peterho Cam BA (3rd cl Th Trip pt i) 43, MA 47. Clifton Th Coll 35. **d** 38 Ex for Truro **p** 40 Truro. C of Padstow 38-40; St Andr L Cam 41-43; St Jude Thornton Heath 43-44; Em Plymouth 44-47; C-in-c of St Pancras Pennycross Plymouth 47-53; V 53-58; R of Hemyock w Culm Davy 58-72; RD of Cullompton 70-71. *Sycamore Close, Hemyock, Cullompton, Devon.* (Hemyock 680592)

JONES, William Lloyd. b 36. St D Coll Lamp BA (2nd cl Hist) 59. Wycl Hall Ox 59. **d** 61 **p** 62 Ban. C of Holyhead w Rhoscolyn and Llanfair-yn-Neubwll 61-65; Portmadoc 65-67; R of Llanfaethlu w Llanfwrog, Llanrhyddlad, Llanfairynghornwy and Llanrhwydrus 67-74; Llanengan w Llangian and Abersoch Dio Ban from 74. *Rectory, Abersoch, Pwllheli, Gwynedd, LL53 7EA.* (Abersoch 2871)

JONES, William Richard. b 15. Univ of Wales (Bangor) BA 38. St Bonif Coll Warm 38. **d** 40 **p** 41 Ban. C of Glanadda w Penrhos Garnedd 40-43; Chap RNVR 44-47; C of Llanfaes and Penmon and Llangoed w Llanfihangel 47-50; Llanor w Llanfihangel Bachellaeth w Bodfean 50-51; R of Penmachno Dio Ban from 51; RD of Arllechwedd 68-73; V of Dolwyddelan Dio Ban from 78. *Penmachno Rectory, Betws-y-Coed, Gwynedd.* (Penmachno 229)

JONES, [illegible] [illegible] Coll Llan 34. **d** 35 **p** 36 St D. C of Henfynyw 35-40; Llangathen w Llanfihangel Cilfargen (in c of Court Henry) 40-43; V of St Dogmael's (w Llantood 61-74) 43-74; RD of Kemes 60-65. *Randir Mwyn, 15 Heol Helyg, Cardigan, Dyfed.*

JONES, Wynne Martin Alban. b 02. BA (Lon) 29. **d** 56 **p** 57 Lim. C of Kilfinane and Kilflyn 56-59; C-in-c 59-60; I of Aney 60-76. *The Bungalow, Brookfield, College Road, Cork, Irish Republic.* (021-41990)

JONES-EVANS, Thomas Dewi Theodore. b 04. MBE (Mil) 54. TD 50. Lon Coll of Div 26. **d** 27 **p** 28 Mon. C of Blaenavon 27-29; St Mary Abergavenny 29-33; R of Brookton W Austr 33-37; Llanddewi Fach w Llandegveth 37-47; CF (TA-R of O) 39-47; Hon CF 47; SCF (TA) 51-56; C-in-c of Michaelston-y-Fedw 47-49; R 49-53; Chap Cafn Mably Sanat 47-53; R of Lurgashall 53-57; Chap St Francis Mental Hosp 57-63; W Pk Hosp Epsom 63-72; L to Offic Dio Mon from 75. *Knotty Pine, Mount Pleasant Road, Pontnewydd, Cwmbran, Gwent, NP4 1BD.*

JORDAN, LEBANON and SYRIA, Diocese of. Part of Diocese of Jerusalem from 76.

JORDAN, Arthur Edward. St Francis Coll Brisb ACT ThL 67. **d** 65 **p** 66 Brisb. C of Maryborough 65-68; Ch of Annunc Camp Hill Brisb 68-69; Cunnamulla 69-70; R of Brewarrina 70-74; Chap Mitchell Coll of Advanced Educn Bath 74-76; R of Gayndah 76-80; St Jas Kelvin Grove City and Dio Brisb from 80. *58 Enoggera Road, Newmarket, Queensland, Australia 4051.* (356 3794)

JORDAN, Canon Frederick William. b 05. St Aid Coll 27. **d** 30 **p** 31 Roch. C of Dartford 30-36; V of Rosherville 36-38; Ch Ch Dartford 38-44; Chap of S Hosp Dartford 38-44; V of Rainham 44-55; Min Can and Sacr of Roch 55-57; Sec and Surveyor Dioc Dilapidations Bd and Proc Conv Roch 55-59; L to Offic Dio Roch 55-61; Hon Chap to Bp of Roch 58-60; Hon Can of Roch 61-70; Can (Emer) from 70; C-in-c of St Nich w St Clem Roch 62-65; Succr Roch Cathl 65-67; PV from 67. *Ravenscourt Lodge, Brent Hill, Faversham, Kent.* (Faversham 3710)

JORDAN, Preb Hugh. b 06. TCD BA 30, Div Test (1st cl) 32, MA and BD (2nd cl) 35. **d** 32 **p** 33 Dub. C of St Kevin Dub 32-34; Gen Sec City of Dub YMCA 34-39; V of St Luke Eccleston 39-45; St Phil Penn Fields 45-49; Redland 49-56; Lect Tyndale Hall Bris 49-56; Prin Lon Coll of Div 56-69; Preb of Brownswood in St Paul's Cathl Lon 63-69; Preb (Emer) from 69; Asst Master Heref High Sch 69-72; L to Offic Dio Heref from 72. *Boylefield Cottage, Clehonger, Hereford, HR2 9SW.* (0981-250579)

JORDAN, John Edward. Bp's Univ Lennox BA 53. **d** and **p** 53 Alg. C of St John N Bay 53-54; I of cobalt 54-57; R of St Mich Port Arthur 57-68; on leave. *180 Woodside Street, Thunder Bay, Ont, Canada.*

JORDAN, Kenneth John. b 31. K Coll Lon. **d** 69 Stabroek for Guy **p** 70 Guy. C of St Jas L Kitty 69-70; St Phil and St Sav Georgetn 70-72; V 72-74; P-in-c of St Phil Georgetn 73; Lect Teacher's Tr Coll Georgetn 71-73; Dioc Communications Officer 72-74; C of Roath 74-76; V of Nantymoel w Wyndham 76-81; St Mary Virg and St Steph Cardiff Dio Llan from 81. *St Mary's Clergy House, Bute Street, Cardiff, S Glam, CF1 5HE.* (Cardiff 27402)

JORDAN, Peter Harry. b 42. Univ of Leeds BA 64. Cranmer Hall Dur 70. **d** 73 **p** 74 Southw. C of St Ann w Em Nottm 73-77; Edgware (in c of St Pet) Dio Lon from 77. *St Peter's Parsonage, Stonegrove, Edgware, Middx, HA8 8AB.* (01-958 5791)

JORDAN, Robert Brian. b 43. Qu Coll Birm 68. **d** 69 Dur. **p** 70 Jarrow for Dur. C of St Mich AA Norton 69-73; St Clem w All SS Hastings 73-74; All SS Carshalton 74-81; V of St Andr Catford Dio S'wark from 81. *135 Wellmeadow Road, Catford, SE6 1HP.* (01-697 2600)

JORDAN, Ronald Henry. b 30. K Coll Lon and Warm. **d** 57 **p** 58 Lon. C of H Redeemer Clerkenwell 57-58; Southgate 58-59; St Mary w St Jo Evang U Edmonton 62-69; V of St Mich-at-Bowes Bowes Pk 69-73; C of H Trin E Finchley Dio Lon from 80. *120 Church Lane, East Finchley, N2.* (01-883 7828)

JORDAN, Thomas. b 36. N-W Ordin Course. **d** 79 **p** 80 Ches. C of Prenton Dio Ches from 79. *7 Kindale Road, Prenton, Birkenhead, Mer, L43 3AU.*

JORGENSEN, Drew Ronald. b 43. Moore Coll Syd ACT ThL 68. **d** 69 **p** 70 Brisb. C of St Luke Ekibin 69-72; V of Mary Valley 72-76; R of St Geo Crow's Nest Dio Brisb from 76. *St George's Rectory, Thallon Street, Crow's Nest, Queensland, Australia 4355.* (076-98 1403)

JORY, Joseph Nicholls. b 07. Univ of Lon Dipl Th 31. St Andr Coll Whittlesford 40. **d** 40 **p** 41 Ripon. C of St Pet Harrogate 40-42; Chap RNVR 42-46; R of Spennithorne 46-66; R of Finghall 54-66; C-in-c of Hauxwell 59-64; R 64-66; Perm to Offic Dio Ex from 79. *Shilstone, Chagford, Devon, TQ13 8JX.*

JOS, Lord Bishop of. *See* Ebo, Right Rev Samuel Chukuma Nwokorie.

JOSELYN, Reginald Alfred. Bp's Coll Sktn 23. **d** 30 Sask **p** 32 Moos. C of Meadow Lake 30-31; Missr of Albany 32-45; R of Cochrane 45; I of Lucknow w Dungannon Port Albert and Ripley 45-48; R of Hyde Park 48-52; Byron 52-60; St Ann Lon 60-62; St Hilda St Thos 62-64; Lambeth 64-71. *270 Ridout Street South, London 16, Ont., Canada.*

JOSEPH, Augustine. Univ of WI LTh 73. Codr Coll Barb 70. **d** 73 Trinid. C of St Paul San Fernando 73-80. *c/o St Paul's Church, San Fernando, Trinidad.*

JOSEPH, Eric Arthur. b 40. Codr Coll Barb 72. **d** and **p** 74 Antig. C of St Kitts 74; P-in-c of St Geo Dominica Dio Antig 75-76; R from 76. *St George's Rectory, Box 66, Roseau, Dominica, WI.* (2100)

JOSEPH, Canon Ernest Elisha. Bp's Th Coll Calc 44. **d** 44 **p** 45 Calc. C of St Jas Calc 45-58; I of Kharagpur 58-61; St John Calc 61-63; Asanol 63-68; R of Lake Cargelligo 68-71; Ariah Pk 71-74; Coolamon 74-75; Tocumwal-Finley Dio River from 75; Hon Can of River from 75. *PO Box 196, Finley, NSW, Australia 2713.* (058-83 1262)

JOSEPH, Hugh Stephen. b 17. St Cath Coll Cam BA (2nd cl Th Trip pt i) 39 (2nd cl Th Trip pt ii) 40, MA 43. Ripon Hall Ox 39. **d** 40 **p** 41 Birm. C of Erdington (in c of Short Heath from 41) 40-54; H Trin w St Mary Ely 54-55; R of Tydd St Giles 55-62; C-in-c of Gorefield 59-62; Dioc Insp of Schs Dio Ely 61-79; V of Elm 62-73; R of Woodton Dio Ely from 73. *Woodston Rectory, Peterborough, Cambs.* (Peterborough 62786)

JOSEPH, John Franklin. b 43. **d** 76 **p** 77 Geo. C of St Paul Geo Dio Geo from 76. *PO Box 182, George, CP, S Africa.*

JOSEPH, Stefana. St Paul's Coll Ambat. **d** 54 **p** 55 Madag. P Dio Madag 54-69; Dio Diego S from 69. *Marodimaka, Anaborana, Ambilobe, Madagascar.*

JOSEPH, Winston. Univ of WI BA 73. Codr Coll Barb 68. **d** 73 Trinid. C of All SS Port of Spain Dio Trinid from 73. *c/o All Saints Rectory, Port of Spain, Trinidad.*

JOSEPHS, Isaac. St Pet Coll Natal 77. **d** 81 Geo. C of Plettenberg Bay Dio Geo from 81. *c/o PO Box 18, Plettenberg Bay 6600, S Africa.*

JOSEPHS, Joseph. b 19. Or Coll Ox BA 49, MA 54. **d** 59 **p** 60 Leic. C of Oadby 59-63; V of Billesdon w Rolleston and Goadby 63-65; St Jas Gtr Leic 65-73; L to Offic Dio Leic from 73; Hd Master Stoneygate Sch 73-82. *62 Stoneygate Court, London Road, Leicester.* (Leic 703236)

✠ **JOSOA, Right Rev Gabriel.** St Paul's Coll Ambatoharanana. **d** 44 **p** 45 Madag. Asst C of Betamboho 44-49; P-in-c of Diego Suarez Dio Madag and Tutor Marodimaka Tr Coll 49-61; Prin St Andr Past Coll Dio Madag 61-67; Archd of N Madag 57-67; Cons Asst Bp in Madag in St Laur Cathl Antananarivo 2nd Apr 67 by Bp of Madag; Bps of Maur; and Dar-S; Asst Bp in Madag; and Bp O'Ferrall; Trld to Diego S (Antsir from 79) 69. *Anglican Church, Post Box 278, Antsiranana, Malagasy Republic.*

JOSOA, Sola. St Andr Coll Marodimaka 53. St Paul's Coll Ambatoharanana 60. **d** 59 **p** 60 Madag. P Dio Madag 60-69; Dio Diego S 69-79; Dio Antsir from 79. *Mission Anglicane, Antsiranana, Malagasy Republic.*

JOURDAIN, Canon Ernest Edward. Selw Coll Cam BA 38, MA 42. Wells Th Coll 38. **d** 40 **p** 41 Linc. C of St Jo

Evang-in-Spitalgate Grantham 40-43; CF (EC) 43-47; C of St Mary and St Jas Grimsby 47-50; PC of St Anne Grantham 50-55; Chap of L Aden and Somaliland 56-61; St Chris Kaduna 61-66; V of St Piran Jos 66-69; Gedney 69-71; Hon Can of St Mich Cathl Kaduna 68-69; Can (Emer) from 69; V of Frisby-on-the-Wreake w Kirby Bellars 71-78; C of Braughing Dio St Alb from 78. *Albury Vicarage, Parsonage Lane, Ware, Herts, SG11 2HU.*

JOURDAIN, Canon Reginald Theodore. b 12. Late Scho and Cho Exhib of Peterho Cam 2nd cl Cl Trip pt i 33, BA (2nd cl Th Trip pt i) 34, MA 38. Chich Th Coll 37. **d** and **p** 38 S'wark. C of St Paul Newington 38-40; PV Lich Cathl 40-42; C of St Mich and Tutor Lich Th Coll 40-42; Chap RAFVR 42-47; SPCK Port Chap Lon Org Sec Port of Lon Area and LPr Dio Chelmsf 47-51; P Dir SPCK in S and E Afr and LPr Dio Zanz 51-56; Home Sec Overseas Coun of Ch Assembly 56-62; Research Sec 62-64; C of St Nich Cole Abbey Lon 56-64; V of Abbots Leigh 64-71; Dir Dioc Educn C'tee Bris 64-70; Hon Can of Bris 67-70; Can (Emer) from 70. *Calle Rector Llompart 25, La Cabaneta, Majorca.*

JOURDAN, Philip Drew. St Paul's Coll Grahmstn LTh 42. **d** 45 **p** 46 Johann. C of St Mary's Cathl Johann 45-47; Yeoville Johann 47-49; St Marg of Antioch Witbank 49-53; R of Swellendam 52-56; St Marg Bloemf 56-62; Can of Bloemf 60-64; R of St Geo Kroonstad 62-64; St Mich AA Port Eliz 64-66; Ch K Port Eliz 66-67; St Barn Port Eliz 68-73; Hosp Chap Dio Capetn 73-81; R of Westville Dio Natal from 81. *c/o 45 Salisbury Avenue, Westville, Natal, S Africa.*

JOWETT, Very Rev Alfred. b 14. CBE 72. St Cath Coll Cam 2nd cl Engl Trip pt i 34, BA (2nd cl Engl Trip pt ii) 35, MA 59. Linc Th Coll 43. **d** 44 **p** 45 Sheff. C of St Jo Evang Goole 44-47; Sec Sheff Angl and Free Ch Coun and Marriage Guidance Coun 47-51; V of St Geo w St Steph Sheff 51-60; Doncaster 60-64; Hon Can of Sheff 60-64; Select Pr Univ of Ox 64-65 and 78-79; O of St Jo of Jer from 79; Dean and R of Man Cathl from 64; Ch Comm 78-80. *Deanery, Prestwich, Manchester, M25 8QF.* (061-773 4301)

JOWETT, Nicholas Peter Alfred. b 44. St Cath Coll Cam 2nd cl Cl Trip pt i 65, 2nd cl Cl Trip pt ii 66, BA 66. Qu Coll Birm 72. **d** 75 **p** 76 Sheff. C of Wales 75-78; Team V of Sheff Manor Dio Sheff from 78. *225 Prince of Wales Road, Sheffield, S2 1FB.* (Sheffield 398202)

JOWITT, Canon David Arthur Benson. b 25. St Jo Coll Ox BA (2nd cl Th) 49, MA 53. Sarum Th Coll 49. **d** 51 **p** 52 Wakef. C of Heckmondwike 51-56; St Wilfrid Harrogate 56-59; V of Kirkby Fleetham w Fencote 60-69; R of Langton-on-Swale 60-69; P-in-c of St Ninian Edin 69-77; Commiss N Terr from 74; Supr OGS 75-81; Syn Clk Dio Edin from 77; Can of St Mary's Cathl Edin from 77; Chap Edin R Infirm and Super 77-80; Vice-Provost of St Mary's Cathl Edin from 81. *19 Coates Gardens, Edinburgh, EH12 5LG.* (031-346 0137)

JOWITT, John Frederick Benson. b 23. Oak Hill Th Coll 57. **d** 59 U Nile **p** 59 Bp Russell for U Nile. Miss Dio Ugan 59-63; CF 63-73; R of Stuston w Thrandeston, Brome and Oakley Dio St E from 73. *Oakley Rectory, Diss, Norfolk.* (Scole 322)

JOY, Canon Leslie John Clifton. b 09. AKC (2nd cl) 33. St Steph Ho Ox 33. **d** 33 **p** 34 Newc T. C of St Lawr Newc T 33-40; C-in-c of St Pet Conv Dist Balkwell N Shields 40-48; V of St Matt (w St Mary Virg from 61) Newc T 48-64; C-in-c of St Mary Virg Newc T 60-61; Chap Newc T Ear Nose and Throat Hosp 60-64; V of St Mary Blyth Dio Newc T from 64; Surr from 66; RD of Bedlington from 69; Hon Can of Newc T from 70. *St Mary's Vicarage, Blyth, Northumb, NE24 1BY.* (Blyth 3417)

JOY, Matthew Osmund Clifton. b 40. St Edm Hall, Ox BA 62, MA 66. St Steph Ho Ox 62. **d** 64 **p** 65 Ches. C of St Aug Brinksway 64-66; St Columba Southwick 66-69; V of H Trin Hartlepool Dio Dur from 69. *Vicarage, Davison Drive, Hartlepool, Cleve.* (Hartlepool 67618)

JOYCE, Anthony Owen. b 35. Selw Coll Cam 2nd cl Th Trip pt i 58, BA (2nd cl Th Trip pt ii) 60, MA 64. Wycl Hall Ox 60. **d** 62 **p** 63 Birm. C of St Martin Birm 62-67; Chap Falcon Coll Essexvale Matab 67-70; V of St Luke w St Thos Birm 70-79; Downend Dio Bris from 79. *Vicarage, Downend Road, Downend, Bristol, BS16 5UF.* (0272-568064)

JOYCE, David Richard. b 33. Univ of Mich BSc (Eng) 55. **d** 75 Hur. d Dio Hur. *1084 Fairlane Avenue, Sarnia, Ont., Canada.*

JOYCE, Ernest Thomas Chancellor. b 16. LLB (Lon) 67. Chich Th Coll 68. **d** 70 **p** 71 Portsm. C of H Spirit, Southsea 70-75; V of St Paul New Southgate 75-77; Chantry P for Chap of St Mich and H Souls Walsingham from 77. *20 Cleaves Drive, Walsingham, Norfolk.*

JOYCE, Henry Robert. b 12. St Chad's Coll Dur BA 37, MA 49. **d** 38 **p** 39 Blackb. C of St Matt Preston 38-42; Newbold w Dunston 42-46; St Thos Brampton (in c of St Pet Holymoorside) 46-50; PC of Calow 50-58; St Thos Ap Derby 58-67; Surr 62-77; V of Hathersage 67-77; RD of Eyam 67-73. *146 Watery Lane, Newent, Glos, GL18 1QE.* (Newent 821218)

JOYCE, John Barnabas Altham. b 47. St Chad's Coll Dur BA 69. St Steph Ho Ox 72. **d** 74 Dorchester for Ox **p** 75 Ox. C of St Giles Reading 74-77; Cowley St John (in c of St Alb Mart) Ox 77-80; Youth and Commun Officer Archd of Ox from 80. *c/o Diocesan Church House, North Hinksey, Oxford, OX2 0NB.*

JOYCE, Kingsley Reginald. b 49. Univ of Man BSc 70. Cudd Coll 70. **d** 73 Ox **p** 74 Dorchester for Ox. C of High Wycombe 73-76; P-in-c of Turville 76-79; C of Hambleden w Frieth and Skirmett 77-79; P-in-c of Hambleden Valley Dio Ox 79-80; R from 80. *Turville Vicarage, Henley-on-Thames, RG9 6QU.* (Turville Heath 240)

JOYCE, Martin Ernest Chancellor. K Coll Lon 69. **d** 73 **p** 74 Portsm. C of Leigh Park 73-77; Milton (in c of St Andr) Dio Portsm from 77. *51 Goldsmith Avenue, Milton, Southsea, Hants, PO4 8DU.* (0705-731024)

JOYCE, Melville Henry Bushell. b 14. St Coll Lamp BA 39. Univ of Bris MB and ChB 52, DPM 54. M RCPsych 71. Ely Th Coll 40. **d** 41 **p** 42 Mon. C of H Trin Abergavenny 41-43; St Winnow (in c of Bridgend) 43-45; Westbury-on-Trym 45-46; St Pet Henleaze 46-52; Publ Pr Dio Bris 52-69; Perm to Offic Dio Lon 55-69; L to Offic from 69. *7 Stanhope Terrace, W2 2UB.* (01-262 3718)

JOYCE, Canon Norman. b 14. St Jo Coll Dur BA 35, MA 38, Dipl Th 38. **d** 37 **p** 38 Dur. C of All SS Monk Wearmouth 37-40; St Paul West Hartlepool 40-43; PC of All SS Monk Wearmouth 43-53; R of Bowness-on-Solway 53-57; N Wingfield (w Pilsley and Tupton from 73) 57-80; Hon Can of Derby Cathl 77-80; Can (Emer) from 80. *Fell View, Thurstonfield, Carlisle, Cumb.* (Burgh-by-Sands 471)

JOYCE, Peter Donald. b 43. Carleton Univ Ott BA 65. Em Coll Tor BD 70. **d** 79 **p** 80 Queb. C of Ch Ch Valcartier Dio Queb from 79. *1752 Valcartier Boulevard, Valcartier Village, Que, Canada, G0A 4S0.*

JOYCE, Philip Rupert. b 38. Selw Coll Cam BA 68, MA 72. Univ of Dur Dipl Th 69. Cranmer Hall Dur 68. **d** 70 **p** 71 York. C of Newlands 70-73; Woolwich 73-77; Chap to Poly of the S Bank 77-79. *88 Pretoria Road, Ilford, Essex, IG1 2HW.*

JOYCE, Raymond. b 37. Univ of Keele BA 60, MA 67. Linc Coll Ox BA (Th) 62, MA 68. St Steph Ho Ox 78. **d** 80 Repton for Derby **p** 81 Derby (NSM). C of Normanton-by-Derby Dio Derby from 80. *9 Datchet Close, Derby, DE3 7SQ.* (Derby 516588)

JOYCE, Robert Leonard. b 40. Ridley Coll Melb 71. **d** 71 **p** 72 Melb. C of St John Camberwell 71-73; P-in-c of Wantirna S w Vermont Dio Melb 73-76; I from 76. *Vicarage, Burwood Highway, Wantirna, Vic, Australia 3152.* (03-231 2165)

JOYCE, Russell Stewart. b 49. La Trobe Univ Vic BA 72. Univ of Melb BD 75. Trin Coll Melb 72. **d** 75 Melb. C of Belmont 75-77; St Pet Box Hill 77-78; V of E Otago 78-80; Flagstaff-Brockville 80-81. *88 Tiverton Street, Palmerston, Otago, NZ.* (205)

JOYNER, Kevin Vincent. **d** 55 **p** 56 Bath. C of Orange 55-58; R of Dunedoo 59-63; C of All SS Cathl Bath 63-67; Chap HM Pris Bath 64-67; R of Rylstone 67-76; V of Birregurra Dio Bal from 77; Hon Chap to Bp of Bal from 80. *Vicarage, Birregurra, Vic., Australia 3242.* (052-362011)

JUBA, Lord Bishop of. *See* Ngalamu, Right Rev Elinana Jabi.

JUBB, William Arthur. b 21. Kelham Th Coll 39. **d** 45 **p** 46 Wakef. C of Whitwood Mere 45-47; Royston Yorks 47-52; V of Monk Bretton 52-74. *c/o Vicarage, Monk Bretton, Barnsley, Yorks, S71 2HQ.* (Barnsley 3159)

JUCKES, Nigel Patrick. b 49. St Jo Coll Nottm Dipl Th 75. **d** 77 **p** 78 Natal. C of Westville 77-80; R of Addington Dio Natal from 80. *Box 38088, Point 4069, Natal, S Africa.*

JUDD, Bernard George. MBE 73. Moore Th Coll Syd ACT ThL 41. **d** 42 **p** 43 Syd. C of St Clem Marrickville 42; C-in-c of Prov Distr of Flemington and Homebush 43-45; Par Distr of Abbotsford w Russell Lea 45-47; R of St Pet City and Dio Syd from 47. *188 Forbes Street, Darlinghurst, NSW, Australia 2010.* (33-4158)

JUDD, Colin Ivor. b 35. Univ of Dur BA 61. Ridley Hall Cam 61. **d** 63 **p** 64 Chelmsf. C of St John w Ch Ch Stratford 63-66; Kimberworth 66-68; CMS Area Sec Dios Bradf and Wakef 68-80; V of St Columba Horton w St Andr Listerhills City and Dio Bradf from 80. *163 Horton Grange Road, Bradford, BD7 2DN.* (0274-571975)

JUDD, Eric Sinclair Alderton. b 04. **d** 43 **p** 44 Lich. C of Gt Barr 43-45; Prec and C of Bridlington 45-47; C-in-c of East Keswick 47-49; R of Hinderclay w Wattisfield 49-55; Belleau w Aby 55-60; Muckton w Burwell and Walmsgate 57-60; V of Anwick 60-64; N Willingham w Legsby 64-73. *5 Baildon Crescent, North Hykeham, Lincoln.*

JUDD, Jack Lewis. b 09. Open Univ BA 79. Ripon Coll Cudd 80. [f Solicitor]. **d** 80 **p** 81 Glouc (APM). C of Berkeley w Wick, Breadstone & Newport Dio Glouc from 80. *Tintock House, Abwell, Berkeley, Glos, GL13 9RN.*

JUDD, Peter Somerset. b 49. Trin Hall Cam BA 71. Cudd Coll Ox 71. **d** 74 Man **p** 75 Middleton for Man. C of St Phil w St Steph Salford 74-76; Chap Clare Coll Cam 76-81; Fell & Actg Dean 80-81; Team V of Hitcham Dio Ox from 82. *Hitcham Parsonage, 1 The Precincts, Burnham, Slough, SL1 7HU.* (Burnham 2881)

JUDD, Sydney Joseph. St Francis Coll Brisb 53. **d** and **p** 54 Brisb. C of Toowoomba 55-56; R of Inglewood 56-60; Ch Ch Milton Brisb 60-78. *20 Dart Street, Toowong, Queensland, Australia 4066.* (370 9837)

JUDGE, James Arthur. b 20. Univ of Lon BD 50. ALCD (2nd cl) 50. **d** 50 **p** 51 Portsm. C of St Jude Southsea 50-52; R of Boyup Brook Dio Bunb 52-55; Chap Bal Mental Hosp 55-58; C of Melb Dioc Centre 55-58; Chap RMC Duntroon ACT 58-62; R of Street 62-77; V of Banwell Dio B & W from 77. *St Andrew's Vicarage, East Street, Banwell, Weston-super-Mare, Avon,*

JUDGE, Michael Charles. b 42. Univ of Southn 79. Chich Th Coll 71. **d** 74 Lewes for Chich **p** 75 Horsham for Chich. C of Eastbourne 74-79; Seaford w Chyngton 79-81; R of Hurstpierpoint Dio Chich from 81. *Rectory, Hurstpierpoint, Hassocks, Sussex.* (Hurstpierpoint 832203)

JUDGE, Patrick Russel. Sir Geo Williams Univ BA 52. McGill Univ BD 55. Montr Dioc Th Coll LTh 55. **d** 55 **p** 56 Montr. C of St Pet Mt Royal Montr 55-57; Ch Ch Calg 57-59; I of St Andr Calg 59-63; Univ Chap Calg 63-65. *3327 Barrett Place NW, Calgary, Alta., Canada.* (289-7832)

JUDGE, Ralph Stanley. Trin Coll Dub BA 35, MA 59, **d** 36 **p** 37 Cash. C of Clonmel w Innislonagh 36-39; I of Kiltullagh 39-45; Castlebar 45-51; R of Dalwallinu 52-55; Kalgoorlie 55-58; Woodville 58-64; Chap Qu Eliz Hosp Woodville Dio Adel from 64. *11 Troon Avenue, Seaton, S Australia 5023.* (08-356 5131)

JUKES, Henry Augustus Lloyd. b 13. Keble Coll Ox BA (3rd cl Th) 37, MA 41. FRHistS 58. STh (Lambeth) 76. **d** and **p** 38 S'wark. C of All SS Battersea Pk 38-39; Cathl Ch (in c of St Mich Portsea) Portsm 39-41; Okehampton 41-42; Chap RNVR 42-46; V of Stockland-Bristol 46-47; Tingewick 47-51; Melbourn 52-61; C-in-c of Meldreth 52-54; V 54-61; Dullingham 61-68; Tilney 68-78. *1 St Mary's Court, Ely, Cambs.*

JUKES, Keith Michael. b 54. Univ of Leeds BA 76. Linc Th Coll 77. **d** 78 **p** 79 Lich. C of Wordsley 78-81; Wolverhampton Dio Lich from 81. *The Flat, St Peter's House, Exchange Street, Wolverhampton, WV1 1PS.* (Wolverhampton 28491)

JUKO, Bulasiyo. Bp Tucker Coll Mukono. **d** 63 **p** 64 Nam. P Dio Nam. *Church of Uganda, Katikamu, PO Wobulenzi, Bombo, Uganda.*

JULIAN, Victor Ivor. b 21. K Coll Lon and Warm 48. **d** 51 **p** 52 Ripon. C of Chapel-Allerton 51-55; V of St Phil Osmondthorpe Leeds 55-64; V of St Mary Sanderstead Dio S'wark from 64. *85 Purley Oaks Road, Sanderstead, Surrey.* (Sanderstead 1725)

JULIEN, Canon Vivian Hilder. St Columb's Hall, Wang ACT ThL 39. **d** 40 **p** 41 Wang. C of Milawa 40-42; Shepparton 42; Chap RAAF 42-46; P-in-c of Lismore 46-52; V of Hamilton Dio Bal 52-67; R 67-81; Can of Bal 62-81; Can (Emer) from 81; Perm to Offic Dio Bal from 81. *90 Griffith Street, Port Fairy, Vic, Australia 3284.*

JULL, Alfred Stephen. OBE 78. St Francis Coll Brisb ACT ThL 38. **d** 39 Brisb **p** 40 Bp Dixon for Brisb. C of Bundaberg 39-44; R of Kilkivan 44-46; R of Woolloongabba 46-49; Kingaroy 49-51; Redcliffe 52-77; Hon Can of Brisb 72-77; Perm to Offic Dio Brisb from 78. *Cnr Lancewood and Morell Streets, Victoria Point, Queensland, Australia 4163.* (207 7638)

JUM TANG, Andrew. **d** 67 **p** 68 Rang. P Dio Rang 68-70; Dio Mand from 70. *St Andrew's Church, Tanai, Kachin State, Burma.*

JUMA, Albert Edward. **d** 24 Momb. d Dio Momb. *Nakuru, kenya.*

JUMA, Clement. **d** 79 Zanz T **p** 80 Bp Russell for Zanz T. P Dio Zanz T. *c/o Box 35, Korogwe, Tanzania.*

✠ **JUMAA, Right Rev Yohanna Samwil Edmund.** Hegongo Th Coll 43. **d** 44 **p** 48 Zanz. P Dio Zanz 44-63; Archd of Korogwe 63-68; Cons Ld Bp of Zanz T in Ch of St Mich AA Korogwe 25 April 68 by Asst Bp of Zanz T (Russell) for Abp of E Afr; Bp of Dar-S; Asst Bp of Zanz T (Lukindo); and Bp Baker; res 79. *PO Box 35, Korogwe, Tanzania.* (Korogwe 22)

JUMAA, Jonathan. **d** 75 **p** 76 Zanz T. P Dio Zanz T. *PO Bombani, Muheza, Tanzania.*

JUMBO, Samuel Biebara. Awka Coll Niger. **d** 36 Bp Gelsthorpe for Niger **p** 38 Niger. P Dio Niger 36-52; Dio Nig Delta 52-62; Can of Nig Delta 60-62. *PO Box 3, Bonny, Nigeria.*

JUMBO, Silvanus Abel. b 41. Trin Coll Umuahia 72. **d** 74 **p** 75 Nig Delta. P Dio Nig Delta. *Box 15, Buguma, Nigeria.*

JUPE, Derek Robert. b 26. Trin Coll Dub BA 53, Div Test (2nd cl) 54, Downes Oratory Pri (2nd cl) 54, MA 67. **d** 54 **p** 55 Down. C of Shankill Lurgan 54-57; Harolds Cross Dub 57-60; R of Easkey U 60-65; Deptn Sec BCMS Ireland 65-72; R of St Jerome w St Silas Ardwick Man 72-78; V of Ardsley Dio Sheff from 78. *Ardsley Vicarage, Doncaster Road, Barnsley, S Yorks, S71 5EF.* (Barnsley 203784)

JUPE, Martin Roy. b 27. Univ of Man 48. BD (Lon) 63. **d** 61 **p** 62 Truro. C of Camborne 61-64; V of St Jo Bapt Penzance Dio Truro from 64; RD of Penwith 73-76. *St John's Vicarage, Penzance, Cornw.* (Penzance 3620)

JUPP, Laurence Richard David Barry. Univ of W Austr BA 35. St Barn Coll Adel ACT ThL 36. **d** 36 **p** 37 Perth. C of Cottesloe 36-38; Chap Forrest River Miss 38-39; C of St John Fremantle 39-41; Chap AMF 41-43; Hd Master Ch Ch Gr Sch Claremont 43-48; R of Nedlands 48-53; Asst Chap St Pet Coll Adel 54-57; Dioc Insp of Schs 57-62; R of St Pet Adel 57-73; R of St Thos Balhannah 73-78; L to Offic Dio Adel from 78. *58 High Street, Grange, S Australia 5022.*

JUPP, Roger Alan. b 56. St Edm Hall Ox BA 78. Chich Th Coll 79. **d** 80 **p** 81 Derby. C of Newbold w Dunston Dio Derby from 80. *27 Willowgarth Road, Chesterfield, Derbys.* (Chesterfield 75236)

JUPP, Thomas Henry. b 1900. Univ of Lon BCom 24. Univ of Bris MA 35. **d** 28 **p** 30 Killaloe. C of Roscrea 28-31; St Jas w St Jo Bapt Bris 31-32; Org Sec CMJ SW Distr and Publ Pr Dio Bris 32-35; V of Churchdown 35-50; RNVR 40-42; V of St Pet Belsize Pk 50-61; R of St Mewan 61-69. *20 Raleigh Road, Exmouth, Devon.* (Exmouth 72766)

JUSTICE, Peter John Michael. b 37. Chich Th Coll 60. **d** 63 **p** 64 St Alb. C of Digswell 63-67; St Nich Guildf 67-68; Mill End w Heronsgate Rickmansworth 68-70; V of Eaton Bray 70-73; L to Offic Dio Ox from 80; Hon C of H Trin Prestwood Dio Ox from 80. *32 Copperkins Lane, Amersham, Bucks, HP6 5QF.* (Amersham 4555)

JUSTIN, George Leslie. Trin Coll Dub BA 51, Div Test 52, MA 54. **d** 52 Kilm for Connor **p** 53 Connor. C of St Aid Belf 52-55; Maralin 55-58; Dundonald 58-60; Shirley (in c of St John) 60-61; R of Keinton Mandeville 61-66; C of St Clem Ispwich 66-69; C-in-c 69-70; C of St Mich Ipswich 66-69; C-in-c 69-70; R of Raydon 70-76; Holton St Mary w Gt Wenham 70-76. *11 Harold Road, Frinton-on-Sea, Essex.* (Frinton 2496)

JUVIA, Clement. St Pet Coll Siota 66. **d** 68 Bp Alufurai for Melan **p** 70 Melan. P Dio Melan 68-75; Dio Centr Melan from 75. *Balo, Moli, Guadalcanal, Solomon Islands.*

JUWAI, Wesley. Newton Coll Dogura 72. **d** 74 Bp Ambo for Papua **p** 75 Bp Kendall for Papua. P Dio Papua. *PO Box 36, Popondota, Papua New Guinea.*

K

KAA, Gordon Hope. **d** 66 **p** 68 Waik. C of Piako Maori Past Dio Waik 66-68; P-in-c 68-71; P-in-c of Waitomo Maori Past 71-78; Hikurangi Past 78-81; Perm to Offic Dio Waik from 81. *Coronation Street, Paeroa, NZ.* (6057)

KAA, Canon Hone Te Kauru O Te Rangi. St Jo Coll Auckld LTh 67. **d** 65 **p** 66 Wai. C of Taupo Maori Distr 65-68; V of Waipawa Maori Past 68-72; on leave 73-74; C of Maori Miss Dio Auckld 75-76; Missr from 77; Can of Auckld from 81. *10 Burleigh Street, Auckland 3, NZ.* (75-400)

KAATZE, Alan William. b 32. **d** 74 **p** 75 Matab. P Dio Matab. *139 Matopos Road, Hillside, Bulawayo, Zimbabwe.* (19-88048)

KABA, Welsh Mandilakhe. St Bede's Coll Umtata 63. **d** 66 **p** 68 Grahmstn. P Dio Grahmstn 66-70 and from 79; Dio Port Eliz 70-72; Dio Kimb K 72-79. *24 Victoria Road, Grahamstown 6140, CP, S Africa.*

KABAHIKYEHO, Jack. Bp Tucker Coll 68. **d** 70 **p** 71 Kig. P Dio Kig from 71. *Rubiriizi, Box 2005, Kigezi, Uganda.*

KABANO, Canon Gideon. **d** 54 Bp Brazier for Ugan **p** 55 Ugan. P Dio Ugan 54-60; Dio Rwanda B 60-66; Dio Bur 66-67; Dio Vic Nyan from 67; Can of Bur 66-67; Vic Nyan from 68. *Box 946, Mwanza, Tanzania.*

KABAROLE, Baguma. b 42. **d** and **p** 77 Boga-Z. P Dio Boga-Z. *BP 154, Bunia, Zaire.*

KABAROLE, Munige. b 39. Bp Tucker Coll Mukono 72.

d 74 p 75 Boga-Z. P Dio Boga-Z. *BP 154, Bunia, Zaire.*

KABASO, Thomas. b 41. **d** 79 **p** 81 N Zam. P Dio N Zam. *St Mary's Cathedral, PO Box 159, Mufulira, Zambia.*

KABEBE, Papias. d 68 **p** 69 Bur. P Dio Bur 68-75; Dio Buye from 75. *D/S 127, Bujumbura, Burundi.*

KABIGI, Joel. d and **p** 65 Centr Tang. P Dio Centr Tang. *Box 9121, Dar-es-Salaam, Tanzania.*

KABIGUMIRA, Ven Elinasani. Bp Tucker Coll Mukono, 60. **d** 61 **p** 63 Ankole-K. P Dio Ankole-K 61-67; Dio Ank 67-71; Dio Kig from 71; Can of Kig from 75; Archd from 76. *Nyaruhanga, PO Mulore, Kigezi, Uganda.*

KABUDI, Aidan Mwaluko. St Phil Coll Longwa, 65. **d** and **p** 67 Centr Tang. P Dio Centr Tang. *Myumi, PO Dodoma, Tanzania.*

KABUGI, Johnson Kigotho. b 43. St Paul's Coll Limuru 72. **d** 74 Mt Kenya **p** 76 Mt Kenya S. P Dio Mt Kenya 74-75; Mt Kenya S from 75. *Box 279, Nanyuki, Kenya.*

KABUI, Geoffrey Koomu. St Paul's Coll Limuru 70. **d** 72 **p** 73 Nak. P Dio Nak. *Box 159, Naivasha, Kenya.*

KABUYE, Jeremiah. d 54 Bp Brazier for Ugan **p** 55 Ugan. P Dio Ugan 54-60; Dio Rwanda B 60-66; Dio Bur 66-75; Can of Bur 66-75; Buye 75-76. *Eglise Anglicane Au Burundi, Ibuye, Ngozi, Burundi, E Africa.*

KABWAINE, Byaruhanga. b 36. **d** 80 Boga-Z. d Dio Boga-Z. *E.A.Z. Kasenyi, BP 154, Bunia, Haut-Zaire.*

KABWEINE, James. d and **p** 75 Bunyoro. P Dio Bunyoro. *POB 910, Kabiso, Mabale, Hoima, Uganda.*

KADALI, Ven Abuneri Mugoloza. Bp Tucker Coll Mukono. **d** 53 **p** 54 Ugan. P Dio Ugan 53-61; Dio Nam 61-67; Archd of Iganga from 67. *Church of Uganda, PO Box 19, Iganga, Uganda.*

KADDU, Eriyasayn. Bp Tucker Coll Mukono. **d** 61 **p** 63 W Bugan. P Dio W Bugan. *Mitete, PO Box 696, Masaka, Uganda.*

KADEGE, Richard Azgad. St Paul's Th Coll Limuru 58. **d** 59 **p** 60 Centr Tang. P Dio Centr Tang 59-67; Dio Moro from 67; Chap Dar-s Univ from 80. *c/o Dar-es-Salaam University, Tanzania.*

KADER, Victor Herbert. St Pet Coll Alice, 66. **d** 68 **p** 69 Kimb K. C of St Matt Upington Kimb K 68-72; R 72-81; R of St Matt Kimberley Dio Kimb K from 81. *127 Barkly Road, Kimberley, S Africa.*

KADUNA, Lord Bishop of. *See* Ogbonyomi, Right Rev Titus Eyiolorunsefunmi.

KAENEL, Brian Herbert. b 19. Coll of Resurr Mirfield 57. **d** 59 **p** 60 S'wark. C of Nunhead 59-61; M Bro of St Barn Dio N Queensld 61-63; Asst Chap Southport Sch Queensld 63; Chap Slade Sch Warw Queensld 64-67; Asst Master Eccles Hall Sch Quidenham 67-69; St Aug Secondary Sch Kilburn 69-70; Ravensbourne Sec Sch Bromley 71-79; Perm to Offic Dio Roch from 72. *19 Graham Court, Cooden Close, Bromley, BR1 3TT.* (01-290 5728)

KAFERO, Yobu. Bp Tucker Coll Mukono. **d** 53 **p** 56 Ugan. P Dio Ugan 53-60; Dio W Bugan from 60. *Bukomero, PO Katera-Kampala, Uganda.*

KAFITY, Ven Samir. Univ of Beirut BA 57. Near E Sch of Th Dipl Th 57. **d** 57 Jer **p** 58 Jordan. P Dio Jer 57-59 and from 76; Dio Jordan 59-75; Archd in Beirut 74-77; Jer from 80; Gen Sec Centr Syn of Episc Ch in Jer and the Middle East from 77. *PO Box 19122, Jerusalem.* (Jer 282096)

KAFUUZI, Eryeza. d and **p** 79 W Ank. P Dio W Ank. *PO Mitooma, Ruhinda, Uganda.*

KAGERO, Raymond Robert. b 42. **d** 76 **p** 77 Vic Nyan. P Dio Vic Nyan. *PO Box 70, Ngara, West Lake, Tanzania.*

KAGO, John. St Paul's Th Coll Limuru. **d** 60 Momb **p** 61 Ft Hall. P Dio Ft Hall 60-64; Dio Mt Kenya 64-75; Dio Mt Kenya S from 75; Archd of S Distr Mt Kenya 71-75; Without Terr Jurisd 75-76; Exam Chap to Bp of Mt Kenya 72-75; Mt Kenya S 75-76; Prov Sec Kenya from 77. *Box 40502, Nairobi, Kenya.* (Nairobi 25027)

KAGO, Solomon. d 61 **p** 62 Ft Hall. P Dio Ft Hall 61-63; Dio Nak 63-67; Dio Mt Kenya 67-75; Dio Mt Kenya S from 75. *Box 70, Kagongo, Othaya, Kenya.*

KAGOLO, Apolo. Bp Tucker Coll Mukono. **d** 31 **p** 33 U Nile. P Dio U Nile 31-61; Dio Mbale from 61. *c/o PO Box 614, Mbale, Uganda.*

KAGULI, Robert. St Phil Coll Kongwa 75. **d** and **p** 77 Centr Tang. P Dio Centr Tang. *Box 587, Dodoma, Tanzania.*

KAGWA, Kezekiya. d 09 **p** 11 Ugan. P Dio Ugan 09-22; RD of Bulemezi 22-61; Can of Ugan 33-60. *Nangabo, PO Kasangate, Uganda.*

KAGWA, Nasanairi. d 44 Ugan. d Dio Ugan 44-60; Dio Nam 60-64. *Bombo, Uganda.*

KAGYENDERA, Eliasaph. d and **p** 79 W Ank. P Dio W Ank. *PO Kabwohe, Uganda.*

KAHEWANGA, John Emmanuel. d 74 **p** 75 SW Tang. P Dio SW Tang 74-78 and from 81. *PO Box 95, Mufindi, Tanzania.*

KAHINDO, Ezira. d 65 **p** 66 Ruw. P Dio Ruw. *Church of Uganda, Kyarumba, Uganda.*

✠ **KAHURANANGA, Most Rev Musa.** Bp Tucker Coll Mukoro. **d** 52 **p** 53 Centr Tang. Asst Prin St Phil Tr Coll Kongwa 52-54; P Dio Centr Tang 54-62; Can of Dodoma Cath 62-63; Cons Asst Bp in Centr Tang in St Andr Ch Kasulu 24 Aug 62 by Abp of E Afr; Bps of Centr Tang; and Nak; Asst Bps in Centr Tang (Omare and Wiggins) and Bp in Bukoba (Lutheran Ch of Sweden); Apptd Bp of W Tang 66; Archd of Western 63-66; Elected Abp and Metrop of Prov of Tanzania 79. *Box 13, Kasula, Tanzania.*

KAIAE, Ronald. Newtown Th Coll 55. **d** 59 **p** 64 New Guinea. P Dio New Guinea 64-71; Dio Papua from 71. *Gadovisu, Dogura, Papua, New Guinea.*

KAIB, Edwy. d 57 New Guinea. d Dio New Guinea 57-71; Dio Papua from 71. *Wanigela Anglican Mission, Samarai, Papua, New Guinea.*

KAICHE, Mattiya. St Cypr Th Coll Tunduru. **d** 57 **p** 60 Masasi. P Dio Masasi. *Nanyindwa Masasi, Tanzania.*

KAIJA, Benezeri. d 74 **p** 76 Ruw. P Dio Ruw. *c/o Box 201, Fort Portal, Uganda.*

KAIJUKA, Matiya. d 63 **p** 64 Rwanda B. P Dio Rwanda B 63-64; Dio Ankole-K 64-67; Dio Kig from 67. *Kitooma, PO Rubaya, Uganda.*

KAIKA, Tikitiki-O-Rangi. b 31. **d** 74 **p** 75 Wai (APM). Hon C of Waiapu Maori Past Dio Wai from 74. *The Vicarage, Tikitiki, E Coast, NZ.*

KAIKMATA, Thomas. b 41. **d** 78 **p** 79 New Guinea Is. P Dio New Guinea Is. *Menpa Private Bag, PO Kimbe, WNBP, Papua New Guinea.*

KAINES, Graeme David Proctor. St Barn Coll Adel ACT ThL 69. **d** 69 **p** 70 Adel. C of Hawthorn 69-71; Plymouth 71-73; P-in-c of Hillcrest 73-76; C of Ch Ch St Laur City and Dio Syd from 76. *507 Pitt Street, Sydney, Australia 2000.* (211-4868)

KAINEY, John Richard. Ridley Coll Melb ACT ThL 55. **d** 56 **p** 57 Melb. C of Ivanhoe 56-58; Dandenong 58-60; Min of Clayton 60-62; Tr Officer Dept Chr Educn Dio Melb 62-64; Sec Youth Div Gen Bd of Relig Educn Dio Melb 64-69; I of Belmont 69-76; Mulgrave Dio Melb from 76. *33 Ferndale Crescent, Mulgrave, Vic., Australia 3170.* (560-3701)

KAITA, Isaka. Buwalasi Th Coll. **d** 58 **p** 60 Soroti. P Dio Soroti. *PO Kobwin, Soroti, Uganda.*

KAJORO, Wilson. St Paul's Dioc Div Sch Frere Town 28. **d** 29 **p** 35 Momb. P Dio Momb 30-47; Perm to Offic Dio Momb from 48. *AAC, Jilore, PO Malindi, Kenya.*

KAJUGA, Canon Eustace. d 60 **p** 61 Rwanda B. P Dio Rwanda B 60-66; Rwa 66-75; Dio Kiga from 75; Can of Rwa 74-75; Kiga from 75. *BP 54, Byumba, Rwanda.*

KAJUGIRO, Anasthase. b 50. Bp Tucker Coll Mukono 71. **d** 74 **p** 75 Buye. P Dio Buye. *BP 58 Ngozi, Burundi, E Africa.*

KAJWARIRE, Eliasaph. d 74 **p** 75 Ank. P Dio Ank 74-76; Dio E Ank from 76. *Box 282, Mbarara, Ankole, Uganda.*

KAKA, Azariel. MBE 66. St Pet Coll Rosettenville 44. **d** 46 **p** 48 Bloemf. P Dio Bloemf 47-49; Dio Basuto 49-66; Dio Les from 66; Can of Basuto 59-66; Les 66-77; Archd of S Les 66-72; N Les 72-77. *Masite, PO Maseru, Lesotho.*

KAKAESE, Casper. St Francis Coll Brisb. **d** 46 **p** 51 Brisb. P Dio Melan 46-75; Dio Malaita 75-77. *Luaniua, Lord Howe, Solomon Islands.*

KAKASIK, Paulosee. d 61 **p** 65 Arctic. C of River Clyde Dio Arctic from 61. *Anglican Mission, Clyde River, NWT, via Montreal AMF, Canada.*

KAKEKAYASH, Henry. b 19. **d** 77 **p** 78 Keew. C of St Pet Weagamow Lake Dio Keew from 77. *St Peter's Church, Weagamow Lake, via Sioux Lookout, Ont, POV 2YO, Canada.*

KAKIZA, Thomas. Warner Mem Th Coll Ibuye, 56. **d** 58 Bp Brazier for Ugan **p** 60 Ugan. P Dio Ugan 58-60; Dio Ankole-K 60-67; Dio Ank from 67. *Church of Uganda, Kebisoni, PO Rukungiri, Kigezi, Uganda.*

KAKOBE, Nasani. d and **p** 79 W Ank. P Dio W Ank. *PO Marembo, Mbarara, Uganda.*

KAKONGORO, Elisha. d and **p** 75 Bunyoro. P Dio Bunyoro. *Box 20, Hoima, Uganda.*

KAKONGWE, Canon Arthur Samuel. St Cypr Th Coll Ngala, 60. **d** 62 **p** 64 SW Tang. P Dio SW Tang 62-71; Dio Ruv from 71; Can of Ruv from 77. *Ng'Ombo, PO Mbamba Bay, Tanzania.*

KAKONGWE, Manuel. b 28. **d** 76 Centr Zam. d Dio Centr Zam. *PO Box 80042, Kabwe, Zambia.*

KAKUDDI, Edward. Bp Tucker Coll Mukono. **d** 61 **p** 63 Ankole-K. P Dio Ankole-K 61-67; Dio Ank 67-73. *PO Kazo, Mbarara, Uganda.*

KAKYENKYE, Edward. Buwalasi Th Coll 64. **d** 65 **p** 67 Ank. P Dio Ank 65-76; Dio W Ank from 77. *PO Kabwohe, Mbarara, Uganda.*

KALAGE, Canon Petro. Hegongo Th Coll 43. **d** 44 **p** 48

Zanz. P Dio Zanz 44-65; Dio Zanz T 65-78; Can of Zanz T from 72. *PO Box 80, Muheza, Tanzania.*

KALAI, Timothy. b 32. Arthur Turner Tr Sch Pangnirtung 70. **d** 72 Arctic **p** 73 Qu'App for Arctic. Miss at Baker Lake 72-75; Cape Dorset Dio Arctic from 75. *St John's Mission, Cape Dorset, NWT, Canada.*

KALALE, Emilius. St Cypr Th Coll Namasakata. **d** 51 Masasi. d Dio Masasi 51-62. *USPG, Liloya, Tanzania.*

KALANGIRIRE, Yekosafati. Bp Tucker Coll Mukono. **d** 56 **p** 58 Ugan. P Dio Ugan 58-60; Dio W Bugan from 60. *Bamusuta, PO Kiboga, Uganda.*

KALANGULA, Peter. St Bede's Coll Umtata. **d** 68 Damar. d Dio Damar. *St Bede's College, Umtata, CP, S Africa.*

✠ **KALE, Right Rev Seth Irunsewe.** MBE 51. Fourah Bay Coll BA 34, Dipl Th 36, MA 43. Nsukka Univ Hon DD 65. **d** 42 **p** 43 Lagos. Vice-Prin CMS Gr Sch Lagos 42-44; Prin 44-51; Hon Chap to Bp of Lagos 44-49; Prin St Andr Coll Oyo 52-63; Can of Ibad 54-63; Exam Chap to Bp of Ibad 58-63; Cons Ld Bp of Lagos in Ch Ch Cathl Lagos 30 Nov 63 by Abp of W Afr; Bps of Ibad; Ondo; Benin; Ow; Nig; Delta; Accra; and Sier L; Asst Bps of Sier L; Niger; and Nig Delta; and Bp Deimieari; res 74. *Usiba House, PO Box 1, Ijebu-Ode, Nigeria.*

KALEEBYA, Peter. b 23. **d** 64 **p** 66 Ank. P Dio Kig. *Box 2015, Kisiizi, Kigezi, Uganda.*

KALESHU, Simon. St Phil Coll Kongwa. **d** 60 Bp Wiggins for Centr Tang **p** 61 Centr Tang. P Dio Centr Tang 60-63, Dio Vic Nyan from 63. *PO Muleba, Bukoba, Tanzania.*

KALGOORLIE, Diocese of. Part of Diocese of Perth from 73.

KALIBWAMI, Lameck. d 78 W Tang. d Dio W Tang. *DWT Urambo, SLP 44, Urambo, Tanzania.*

KALIISA, Richard. d 75 **p** 77 Ruw. P Dio Ruw. *Box 37, Fort Portal, Uganda.*

KALIMBE, Ananias. b 37. **d** 74 **p** 75 S Malawi. P Dio S Malawi. *Box 54, Mangochi, Malawi.*

KALIMI, Eri. Bp Tucker Coll Mukono. **d** 63 **p** 64 W Bugan. P Dio W Bugan 63-68; Dio Nam from 68. *Namusaale, PO Kapeeka, Uganda.*

KALIMU, Omari. b 25. **d** 76 Boga-Z **p** 77 Bukavu. P Dio Bukavu. *Lusumba Parish, BP 220, Kindu, Maniema, Zaire.*

KALIMUKIZA, Yoweri. b 57. **d** 77 Nam. d Dio Nam. *Balitta Church of Uganda, PO Luweero, Uganda.*

KALINAKI, Nekeneya. Bp Tucker Coll Mukono, 41. **d** 44 Ugan. d Dio Ugan 44-60; Dio Nam from 60. *COU Busesa, Box 21, Ingaga, Uganda.*

KALINGADA, Michael. St Cypr Th Coll Tunduru 52. **d** 54 Zanz for Masasi **p** 57 Masasi. P Dio Masasi. *Box 19, Nachingwea, Tanzania.*

KALLES, David Lee. W Washington State Coll BA 62. Angl Th Coll BC LTh 65. **d** 65 **p** 66 Yukon. I of Teslin 65-69; Haines Junction 69-70; Watson Lake Dio Yukon 70-73; Hon C from 74. *Box 201, Watson Lake, Yukon, Canada.* (403-536 2206)

KALOA, Basil. Patteson Th Centre Kohimarama. **d** 72 **p** 74 Melan. P Dio Melan 72-75; Dio Malaita from 75; VG from 76. *Lede, Malaita, Solomon Islands.*

KALULE, Zefaniya. Bp Tucker Coll Mukono. **d** 53 **p** 56 Ugan. P Dio Ugan 53-60; Dio Nam 60-68; Dio W Bugan from 68. *PO Box 162, Mpigi, Uganda.*

KALUME, Johnson Thomas. St Paul's Th Coll Limuru. **d** 65 Nai **p** 67 Momb. d Dio Nai 65-67; P Dio Momb from 67. *PO Box 72, Mombasa, Kenya.*

KALYAHWALI, Fesito. Bp Tucker Coll Mukono. **d** 50 **p** 52 Ugan. P Dio Ugan 50-65; Dio Ank 65-76; Dio W Ank from 77; Archd of Ank 65-74; Can of Ank 70-76. *Box 140, Bushenyi, Uganda.*

KAMAGARA, Canon Samwiri. Bp Tucker Coll Mukono. **d** 63 **p** 65 Ankole-K. P Dio Ankole-K 63-67; Dio Kig from 67; Hon Can of Kig from 74. *PO Rukungiri, Kigezi, Uganda.*

KAMALIZA, Michael Robert. St Andr Th Coll Mponda 64. **d** 66 **p** 67 Malawi. P Dio Malawi 66-71; Dio S Malawi from 71. *Mkope Local Court, PO Monkey Bay, Malawi.*

KAMANGA, Godfrey. b 31. **d** 71 **p** 73 Lake Malawi. P Dio Lake Malawi. *Box 22, Ntchisi, Malawi.*

KAMANYIRE, Very Rev Erick. Bp Tucker Coll Mukono 67. **d** 68 **p** 69 Bp Rwakaikara for Ruw. P Dio Ruw 68-72; Dio Bunyoro from 72; Dean of Bunyoro from 73. *PO Box 20, Hoima, Uganda.*

✠ **KAMANYIRE, Right Rev Eustace.** Bp Tucker Coll Mukono 61. **d** 62 **p** 66 Ruw. P Dio ruw 62-74; Dio Soroti 75; Dio Ruw 79-81; Exam Chap to Bp of Soroti 75; Prin Bp Tucker Coll Mukono 75-78; on leave 78-79; Cons Ld Bp of Ruw 81. *Box 37, Fort Portal, Uganda.* (Fort Portal 2271)

KAMARA, Ven Azaliya. d 65 **p** 66 Ruw. P Dio Ruw; Archd of Bumadu from 75. *PO Box 37, Fort Portal, Uganda.*

KAMARA, Henry Nicholas Bollo. Fourah Bay Coll 52. **d** 55 **p** 57 Sier L. P Dio Sier L 55-68. *20 Malta Street, Freetown, Sierra Leone.*

KAMAU, Bernard. St Paul's Th Coll Limuru. **d** 64 Mt Kenya. d Dio Mt Kenya 64-75; Dio Mt Kenya S from 75. *Muthiria, Box 44, Maragua, Kenya.*

KAMAU, Ven Dedan. St Paul's Th Coll Limuru, 56. **d** 57 **p** 59 Momb. P Dio Momb 57-61; Dio Ft Hall 61-64; Dio Mt Kenya 64-75; Dio Mt Kenya S from 75; Exam Chap to Bp of Mt Kenya 65-75; Mt Kenya S from 75; Archd of N Distr Mt Kenya 71-72; E Distr Mt Kenya 72-75; S Distr Mt Kenya from 75; Can of Mt Kenya S from 75. *Box 23031, Lower Kabete, Kenya.* (Nairobi 68435)

KAMAU, James. Weithaga Bible Sch 60. **d** 61 **p** 62 Ft Hall. P Dio Ft Hall 61-64; Dio Mt Kenya 64-75; Dio Mt Kenya S from 75. *Gatura, Box 192, Thika, Kenya.*

KAMAU, Ven Laadan. St Paul's Dioc Div Sch Limuru, 46. **d** 48 **p** 49 Momb. Asst Gen Sec Afr Coun 48-50; P at Kahuhia 50-51; Kathukeini 51; Chap E Afr ChD 51-53; Ft Hall 53-61; C of W Aberdare 61-67; V of Nyandarua Dio Nak from 67; Can of Nak from 67; Exam Chap to Bp of Nak from 68; Archd of Nak from 69. *Box 48, Ol'Kalou, Kenya.*

KAMAU, Samuel. St Phil Coll Maseno. **d** 69 Maseno **p** 71 Nak. d Dio Maseno 69-71; P Dio Nak from 71. *PO Box 9, North Kinangop, Kenya.*

KAMAU, Solomon. d 76 **p** 77 Nak. P Dio Nak. *c/o Box 56, Nakuru, Kenya.*

KAMBELO, Canon James. St Cypr Th Coll Tunduru, 46. **d** 47 **p** 50 Masasi. P Dio Masasi 47-77, Can of Masasi 57-77, Hon Can from 77; Archd of Masasi 59-63. *PO Masasi, Mtwara Region, Tanzania.*

KAMBERE, Erifazi. d 75 **p** 77 Ruw. P Dio Ruw. *PO Kyegegwa, Kyaka, Uganda.*

KAMIRA, Efulaimu. Bp Tucker Coll Mukono, 58. **d** 59 Ugan **p** 61 Nam. d Dio Ugan 58-61; P Dio Nam from 61. *PO Box 510, Bugiri, Uganda.*

KAMIRA, Zebuluni. Bp Tucker Coll Mukono, 56. **d** 56 Ugan **p** 58 Bp Balya for Ugan. P Dio Ugan 56-60; Dio Nam from 60. *Nasuti, PO Box 148, Iganga, Uganda.*

KAMISURU, Enosa Aburasu. Bp Gwynne Coll Mundri 59. **d** 63 **p** 65 Bp Dotiro for Sudan. P Dio Sudan. *Ibba Parish, c/o ECS, Maridi, Equatoria Province, Sudan.*

KAMONDO, Ven Geresom. Bp Tucker Coll Mukono 70. **d** 72 **p** 73 Ank. d Dio Ank 72-73; P Dio Ank 73-76; Dio E Ank from 76; Archd Dio E Ank from 79; Can from 79. *PO Bwizibwera, Mbarara, Uganda.*

KAMPALA, Lord Archbishop of, and Metropolitan of Province of Uganda, e. *See* Wani, Most Rev Silvano Goi.

KAMPANGO, Richard Bateman. b 24. **d** 69 **p** 70 Bp Mataka for Zam. P Dio Lusaka. *Box 3457, Lusaka, Zambia.*

KAMUHANGIRE, Johnson. b 39. Bp Tucker Coll Mukono 62. **d** 67 **p** 68 Kig. P Dio Kig. *PO Rukungiri, Uganda.*

KAMUHIGI, Yosiya. d 07 **p** 09 Ugan. P Dio Ugan 07-60; Dio Ruw 60-63. *PO Box 37, Fort Portal, Uganda.*

KAMUJANDUZI, Eriakimu. Bp Tucker Coll Mukona. **d** 44 **p** 45 Ugan. P Dio Ugan 44-60; Dio Ankole-K 60-67; Dio Ank from 67. *Kakika, Kyamugorani, PO Box 102, Mbarara, Uganda.*

KAMULINDWA, Yonasani. d 75 **p** 77 Ruw. P Dio Ruw. *Box 1215, Butiiti, Uganda.*

KAMUNDE, Elipaza Akim. St Paul's Th Coll Limuru 66. **d** 69 **p** 70 Ruw. P Dio Ruw. *c/o PO Box 37, Fort Portal, Uganda.*

KAMUNGU, Leonard. b 21. St Mark's Coll Dar-S. **d** 79 Dar-S **p** 80 Bp R N Russell for Dar-S. P Dio Dar-S. *PO Box 25016, Dar es Salaam, Tanzania.*

KAMUNYE, Nataneli. St Phil Th Coll Kongwe, 64. **d** 66 Bp Madinda for W Tang **p** 67 W Tang. P Dio W Tang 66-69; Dio Centr Tang from 70. *Box 233, Dodoma, Tanzania.*

KAMWAGA, John Brighton. St Phil Th Coll Kongwa, 63. **d** 64 Centr Tang **p** 64 Vic Nyan. P Dio Vic Nyan. *Murgwanza, Ngara, Tanzania.*

KAMYA, Ven Ezera. d 46 Ugan **p** 60 Ruw. d Dio Ugan 46-60; P Dio Ruw 60-63; Can and Treas of W Bugan 63-68; Sub-Dean of W Bugan 64-68; Archd from 68. *PO Box 102, Mityana, Uganda.*

KAN, Peter Paul. Ridley Coll Melb 62. **d** 68 **p** 69 Melb. C of St John Camberwell 68-69; St Jo Croydon 69-71; C-in-c of St Jo Sorrento 71-75; I of St Geo Reservoir 75-80; Warden Avalon Comm 80-81. *c/o 30 Ralph Street, Reservoir, Vic, Australia 3073.* (03-46 1451)

KANAKULYA, George. b 14. Bp Tucker Coll Mukono 73. **d** 74 **p** 75 Nam. P Dio Nam. *Namulonge, Box 6561, Kampala, Uganda.*

KANANURA, Ven Matthew. d 65 Rwanda B **p** 66 Rwa. P Dio Rwa 65-77; Dio Kiga from 75; Can of Rwa 74-75; Kiga from 75; Archd Dio Kiga from 79. *BP 17, Kibungo, Rwanda, Centr Africa.*

KANDAMIZA, Emmanuel. St Phil Coll Kongwa 71. **d** and **p** 74 Centr Tang. P Dio Centr Tang. *PO Kibakwe, Tanzania.*

KANDUME, Ndeunjema Levi. **d** 58 Damar **p** 60 Bp Tobias for Damar. P Dio Damar 58-80; Dio Namibia from 80. *St Mary's Mission, Odibo, PO Oshikango, SW Africa.* (Oshikango 5)

KANDUSI, Emmanuel Job. St Phil Coll Kongwa 69. **d** and **p** 73 Centr Tang. P Dio Centr Tang 73-79. *Box 233, Dodoma, Tanzania.*

KANG, Aidan Joon Hwee. St Mich Sem Seoul 40. **d** 49 **p** 50 Korea. P Dio Korea 48-65; Dio Seoul 65-77; Archd of Seoul 65-73; VG 73-77. *11 Kyo Dong, Suwon 170, Korea.* (Suwon 6442)

KANG, John Myong-Sik. St Mich Sem Seoul. **d** 68 **p** 70 Taejon. P Dio Taejon. *Anglican Church, Pudaedong, Ch'onan 330, Korea.*

KANGA, John. St Paul's Th Coll Limuru, 60. **d** 63 **p** 64 Maseno. P Dio Maseno 63-67; Dio Nak 67-70; Dio Maseno N from 71. *PO Box 220, Maseno, Kenya.*

KANGANGI, Joseph. St Paul's Th Coll Limuru. **d** and **p** 66 Mt Kenya. P Dio Mt Kenya 66-75; Dio Mt Kenya S 75; Dio Mt Kenya E from 76; Relig Educn Adv from 80. *Box 169, Embu, Kenya.*

KANGETHE, John Kimani. Ch Tr Centre, Kapsabet, 62. **d** 63 **p** 65 Nak. P Dio Nak. *Box 27, Kinangop, Nyandura, Kenya.*

KANGUMBU, Kantamba. b 04. **d** 77 Bukavu. d Dio Bukavu. *Lubili Parish, BP 220, Kindu, Maniema, Zaire.*

KANGUNU, Wilson Kago. b 43. **d** 74 Mt Kenya **p** 76 Bp Ngaruiya for Mt Kenya S. P Dio Mt Kenya 74-75; Mt Kenya S from 75. *Box 123, Murang'a, Kenya.*

KANGURA, Simon. St Phil Th Coll Kongwa, 60. **d** 60 Bp Wiggins for Centr Tang **p** 61 Centr Tang. P Dio Centr Tang 60-62 and 64-66; Dio Vic Nyan 62-64; Dio W Tang from 66. *Kalinzi, Private Bag, Matiazo, Tanzania.*

KANHAI, George Eric. b 31. Codr Coll Barb 71. **d** 71 Stabroek for Guy **p** 72 Guy. C of St Joseph Port Mourant 71-75; Ch Ch Georgetn Dio Guy from 75. *54 Eccles, East Bank, Demerara, Guyana.*

KANI, Welile Alfred. b 46. St Pet Coll Natal Dipl Th 76. **d** 77 **p** 78 Port Eliz. C of St Steph Port Eliz Dio Port Eliz from 77. *PO Box 9139, Estadeal, Port Elizabeth, S Africa 6012.*

KANIKE, Eriabu Gasalaire. Bp Tucker Coll Mukono. **d** 53 **p** 56 Ugan. P Dio Ugan 53-60; Dio Nam from 60. *Kiringa, Uganda.*

KANJEMA, Ackworth. St Andr Dioc Coll Nkwazi 30. **d** 31 Nyasa. d Dio Nyasa. *USPG, Mpondas, Fort Johnston, Malawi.*

KANNIAH, Joseph. Univ of Lon BA 74. Univ of Man MEducn 76. **d** and **p** 80 Sing. C of St Andr Cathl Sing 80-81; V of Ch of the Ascen City and Dio Sing from 81. *Church of the Ascension, Graham White Drive, Singapore 1335.*

KANNYUNT, Daniel. H Cross Coll Rang. **d** 59 **p** 60 Rang. P Dio Rang. *Christ Church, Mandalay, Burma.*

KANO, Lord Bishop of. *See* Ayam, Right Rev Baima Bertram.

KANO, Provost of. *See* Faji, Very Rev Josiah Oladele.

KANSHEBA, Peter. b 47. **d** 71 **p** 72 Vic Nyan. P Dio Vic Nyan. *Box 1033, Bukoba, Tanzania.*

KANUNA, Philip. St Paul's Coll Limuru 68. **d** 71 **p** 72 Nai. P Dio Nai 71-75; Dio Mt Kenya E 75-76; Dio Nak from 76. *PO Narok, Kenya.*

KANUNGHA, Meshak. **d** 64 **p** 65 Centr Tang. P Dio Centr Tang. *Kilimatinde, PO Manyoni, Tanzania.*

KANUNGHA, Richard. b 56. St Phil Coll Kongwa 77. **d** 81 Centr Tang. d Dio Centr Tang. *PO Box 50, Mvumi, Tanzania.*

KANYAMA, Gerald Marko Joseph. St Cypr Coll Ngala 64. **d** 66 Bp Mlele for SW Tang **p** 70 SW Tang. d Dio SW Tang 66-70; P Dio Ruv from 71. *Box 7, Songea, Tanzania.*

KANYAMUBARI, Elijah. **d** 54 Bp Brazier for Ugan **p** 55 Ugan. P Dio Ugan 54-60; Dio Rwanda B 60-66; Dio Rwa 66-75; Dio Kiga 75-76; Can of Rwa 66-75; Kiga 75-76. *BP 22, Kigali, Rwanda, E Africa.*

KANYANGA, Marriott Geoffrey. St Cypr Th Coll Ngala, 59. **d** 60 **p** 63 SW Tang. P Dio SW Tang 60-76; Dio Ruv from 77. *PO Liuli, Mbinga, Tanzania.*

KANYIKWA, John Lasu. Bp Tucker Coll Mukono 64. **d** 66 Nam for Sudan **p** 68 Sudan. d Dio Nam 66-68; C of St Paul St Alb 68-69; P Dio Nam 69-76; Dio Juba from 77; Prov Sec Sudan from 77. *Box 110, Juba, Sudan.*

KANYIMA, Kezekia. Bp Tucker Coll Mukono. **d** 63 **p** 65 Ankole-K. P Dio Ankole-K 63-67; Dio Kig from 67. *Kihihi, PO Karuhinde, Kabale, Kigezi, Uganda.*

KAO, Peter. b 19. **d** 57 Hong **p** 59 Chelmsf for Cant for Col Bp. Chap Miss to Seamen Vic Dks Dio Chelmsf from 58. *The Missions to Seamen, Chinese Centre, 35 Ethel Road, Custom House, E16 3AT.* (01-476 2644)

KAOMA, Canon Christopher. **d** 52 **p** 53 N Rhod. P Dio N Rhod 52-64; Dio Zam 65-71; Dio N Zam from 71; Can of N Zam from 74. *Box 159, Mufulira, Zambia.*

KAPA, Piripi Tutangiora. NZ BD of Th Stud LTh 66. St Jo Coll Auckld 55. **d** 58 **p** 59 Waik. C of Te Awamutu 58-60; Tokora 60-62; V of Turanga Maori Past 62-71; Te Ngae Maori Past 70-74; Takapau 74-81; Wairoa Par Distr Dio Wai from 81. *Box 166, Wairoa, NZ.*

KAPAKASA, Henry. **d** 68 **p** 70 Malawi. d Dio Malawi 60-70; P Dio Lake Malawi from 71. *Holy Trinity Church, Chididi, PO Chia, via Nkhotakotu, Malawi.*

KAPALAKILA, Wilson Percival. St Cypr Th Coll Tunduru, 52. **d** 54 **p** 57 SW Tang. P Dio SW Tang. *Mlangali, Njombe, Tanzania.*

KAPANDA, Paterson. St Andr Coll Mpondas 64. **d** 66 Malawi. d Dio Malawi 66-71; Dio Lake Malawi from 71. *Box 206, Salima, Malawi.*

KAPANDE, Amos Tabitha. b 48. St Mark's Coll Dar-S 74. **d** 75 **p** 77 Centr Zam. P Dio Centr Zam. *P Bag 52XK, Kabwe, Zambia.*

KAPATA, Vincent. b 38. **d** 73 **p** 74 N Zam (APM). P Dio N Zam; Dioc Treas from 79. *Box 20173, Kitwe, Zambia.*

KAPENYA, Simon. **d** 72 **p** 73 Lusaka. P Dio Lusaka. *Chimwale, Mbampongwe, Chief Sandwe, Petauke, Zambia.*

KAPERE, Christopher Eriya Musoke. Bp Tucker Coll Mukono. **d** 69 **p** 70 Nam. P Dio Nam. *Ssese, PO Kalangala, Uganda.*

KAPERE, Yosamu Bagulaine. Bp Tucker Coll Mukono. **d** 49 **p** 51 Ugan. P Dio Ugan 49-60; Dio Nam from 60. *Teachers' Training College, Ndejje, Uganda.*

KAPETA, Canon Vohana Shadrach. St Andr Coll Lik 57. **d** 59 **p** 60 Nyasa. P Dio Nyasa 59-64; Dio Malawi 64-71; Dio Lake Malawi from 71; Hon Can of Lake Malawi from 80. *PO Malomo, Ntohisi, Malawi.*

KAPICHILA, Fanvel. b 30. St Jo Sem Lusaka 68. **d** 70 Bp Mataka for Zam **p** 71 Centr Zam. Dio Lusaka 70-71; Dio Centr Zam from 71. *PO Box 7, Mkushi Boma, Zambia.*

KAPONDA, Canon James. **d** 45 **p** 49 Nyasa. P Dio Nyasa 45-53; Dio SW Tang 53-75; Can of SW Tang 59-75; Hon Can from 76; Archd of Songea 61-71; Mbeya 71-75; P Dio Ruv from 76; Hon Can from 78. *Chiulu, PO Mbamba Bay, Tanzania.*

KAPU, Fraser. St Jo Coll Auckld 61. St Pet Coll Siota 62. **d** and **p** 64 Melan. P Dio Melan 64-75; Dio Ysabel 75-76; Dio Centr Melan from 76; Can of St Barn Cathl Honiara 69-72; Dean 76-79. *Box 19, Honiara, Solomon Islands.*

KAPUNGWE, Cecil. b 29. St Mark's Th Coll Dar-S 77. **d** 80 **p** 81 N Zam. P Dio N Zam. *Chipili Mission, PO Chipili, Mansa, Zambia.*

KARAARA, Charles. Bp Tucker Coll Mukono 70. **d** 72 Ank. d Dio Ank. *Kajaaho, Box 129, Mbarara, Uganda.*

KARABANI, Jairus. Bp Patteson Th Centre Kohimarama. **d** 72 Melan. d Dio Melan 72-75; Dio New Hebr from 75. *Longana, Aoba, New Hebrides.*

KARABELAS, Michael Louis. b 43. Pepperdine Coll USA BA 67. Angl Th Coll of BC STB 70. **d** 70 **p** 71 New Westmr. C of St Phil Vanc 71-72; R of St Agnes N Vanc Dio New Westmr from 72. *2016 Boulevard Crescent, North Vancouver, BC, Canada.*

KARAKA, Wharepouhuai. b 33. **d** 77 **p** 78 Aotearoa for Wai. C of Te Puke Past Dio Wai from 77. *Vicarage, Pah Road, Te Puke, NZ.*

KARAMOJA, Lord Bishop of. *See* Davies, Right Rev Howell Haydn.

KARANI, Amos. **d** 75 **p** 76 Mt Kenya E. P Dio Mt Kenya E. *Kagaari Parish, Box 6051, Runyenje, Embu, Kenya.*

KARANI, Edward. b 46. St Paul's Coll Limuru 72. **d** 74 Mt Kenya **p** 75 Mt Kenya E. d Dio Mt Kenya 74-75; V of Kiriari 75-78; Kiandangae Dio Mt Kenya E from 78. *Box 63, Kerugoya, Kenya.*

KARANI, Zakaria Nyaga. **d** 69 **p** 70 Mt Kenya. P Dio Mt Kenya 69-75; Dio Mt Kenya E from 75; Exam Chap to Bp of Mt Kenya E from 78. *Box 119, Embu, Kenya.*

KARANJA, Joseph Muthama. b 29. **d** 78 Mt Kenya S. d Dio Mt Kenya S. *PO Box 153, Maragwa, Kenya.*

KARANSA, Peter. b 46. **d** 78 **p** 79 Mt Kenya E. P Dio Mt Kenya E. *Box 36, Kerugoya, Kenya.*

KARASHANI, Yakobo Kagina. **d** 41 **p** 43 Centr Tang. P Dio Centr Tang. *Kigoma, Tanzania.*

KARAU, Alhamdu Peter. Im Coll Ibad 62. **d** 65 N Nig. d Dio N Nig. *St Bartholomew's Church, Wusasa, PA, Zaria, Nigeria.*

KAREBYA, Peter. **d** 64 Ankole-K. d Dio Ankole-K 64-67; Dio Kig from 67. *Burema, PO Karuhinda, Kabale, Kigezi, Uganda.*

KAREMERA, Leuben. **d** 80 Kiga. d Dio Kiga. *BP 18, Kibungo, Rwanda.*

KARENGA, William. b 44. **d** 80 E Ank. d Dio E Ank. *PO Box 14, Mbarara, Uganda.*

KARENZI, John. **d** 75 Kamp. d Dio Kamp. *c/o Box Kampala, Uganda.*

KARENZO, Joash. **d** 54 Bp Brazier for Ugan

P Dio Ugan 54-60; Dio Rwanda B 60-66; Dio Bur 66-75. *CMS, Matana, Usumbura, Burundi, Centr Africa.*

KARIMA, Emmanuel. b 30. **d** 73 **p** 74 S Malawi. P Dio S Malawi. *Box 30046, Chichiri, Blantyre 3, Malawi.* (30215)

KARIOKI, Peter. St Paul's Th Coll Limuru 68. **d** 71 Mt Kenya. d Dio Mt Kenya. *Box 121, CPK Murang'a, Kenya.*

KARIOKI, Rowland. b 37. **d** 71 **p** 72 Mt Kenya. P Dio Mt Kenya 71-75; Dio Mt Kenya E from 75. *Box 153, Embu, Kenya.*

KARIUKI, David Mwangi. d 70 **p** 71 Nak. P Dio Nak. *Berea Farm and Mission, Private Bag, PO Nakuru, Kenya.*

KARIUKI, John. d 79 Mt Kenya E. d Dio Mt Kenya E. *PO Box 6093, Runyenjes, Embu, Kenya.*

KARIUKI, Samson Kabari. b 19. **d** 78 Mt Kenya S. d Dio Mt Kenya S. *PO Box 4, Sabasaba via Thika, Kenya.*

KARIUKI, Simon. d 67 **p** 69 Mt Kenya. P Dio Mt Kenya 67-75; Dio Mt Kenya E from 75. *Box 130, Kerugoya, Kenya.*

KARNEY, Gilbert Henry Peter. b 09. Trin Coll Cam 2nd cl Hist Trip pt i, 30, BA (2nd cl Hist Trip pt ii) 31, MA 36. Cudd Coll 32. **d** 34 **p** 35 Newc T. C of St Nich Cathl Newc T 34-36; Exam Chap to Bp of Lon 36-38; Chap Trin Coll Cam 36-40; Chap RNVR 40-46; R of Godstone 46-54; V of Embleton w Craster and Newton 54-74; Dioc Warden of Readers 67-71; C-in-c of Rennington w Rock 73-74. *Darden House, East Hanney, Wantage, OX12 0HG.*

KARNIK, Sabi'. Evang Sem Cairo 58. **d** 63 **p** 66 Jordan. P Dio Jordan 63-75; Dio Jer from 76. *PO Box 73, Zerka, Jordan.* (82765)

KAROKI, Nathan. Ch Tr Centre Kapsabet 66. **d** 67 **p** 68 Nak. P Dio Nak; Exam Chap to Bp of Nak from 76. *Box 745, Eldoret, Kenya.*

KARUHIJE, Alphonse. b 50. **d** 79 Kiga. d Dio Kiga. *BP 489, Kigali, Rwanda.*

KARUNGANWA, Erieza. Bp Tucker Coll Mukono, 62. **d** 63 **p** 65 Ankole-K. P Dio Ankole-K 63-67; Dio Kig 67-70; Dio Ank from 70. *PO Kihenzi, Mbarara, Uganda.*

KASAGALA, Asphodel. d 42 Ugan **p** 60 W Bugan. d Dio Ugan 42-60; P Dio W Bugan from 60. *Church of Uganda, Rakai, PO Box 2520, Kyotera, Uganda.*

KASANO, Canon Gervas Biteteyi. d 41 **p** 43 Centr Tang. P Dio Centr Tang 41-63; Dio Vic Nyan 63-76; Hon Can of Vic Nyan from 68. *Box 12, Muleba, Tanzania.*

KASEMBE, Daudi. d 60 **p** 64 Masasi. P Dio Masasi. *Box 121, Lindi, Tanzania.*

KASEMBE, Ven Laurence. St Cypr Th Coll Tunduru. **d** 47 **p** 50 Masasi. P Dio Masasi 47-69; Can from 69; Archd of Luatala 69; Masasi from 69. *CPEA, PO Masasi, Mtwara Region, Tanzania.*

KASENYA, Semei. Bp Tucker Coll Mukono. **d** 24 **p** 26 Ugan. P Dio Ugan 24-60; Dio W Bugan 60-62; Dio Ankole-K 62-67; Can of Ankole-K 64-67; Dio Ank 67-70. *PO Box 14, Mbarara, Uganda.*

KASERUZI, Isaka. Bp Tucker Coll Mukono, 59. **d** 61 **p** 63 W Bugan. P Dio W Bugan. *PO Box 164, Mityana, Uganda.*

KASHAMBUZI, Samwiri. d 64 **p** 66 Ankole-K. P Dio Ankole-K 64-67; Dio Kig from 67. *PO Rukungiri, Kigezi, Uganda.*

KASHAYA, Zebuloni. b 24. **d** 76 E Ank. d Dio E Ank. *PO Rubundi, Mbarara, Uganda.*

KASIBOTO, Lumga Lungile Magqwagqwa. St Bede's Coll Umtata 78. **d** 79 **p** 80 St John's. P Dio St John's. *P/Bag X405, Qumbu, Transkei.*

KASICHI, Zebedayo. d and **p** 78 Centr Tang. P Dio Centr Tang. *PO Kintinku, Tanzania.*

KASIGARA, Benedict Newton Fataki. b 43. St Phil Coll Kongwa 70. **d** 72 **p** 73 W Tang. P Dio W Tang. *Box 175, Kigoma, Tanzania.*

KASISIRI, Kezekiya. d 41 **p** 52 Ugan. P Dio Ugan 41-60; Dio Ankole-K 60-67; Dio Kig from 67. *PO Box 1202, Mparo, Kigezi, Uganda.*

KASORO, Asafu. d and **p** 75 Bunyoro. P Dio Bunyoro. *Box 20, Hoima, Uganda.*

KASOYAGA, Canon Carmichael Francis. St Cypr Th Coll Tunduru. **d** 47 **p** 50 Masasi. P Dio Masasi; Archd of Masasi 63-74; Can of Masasi from 63. *PO Box 212, Lindi, Tanzania.*

KASOZI, Abuneri. d 49 **p** 51 Ugan. P Dio Ugan 49-60; Dio Nam 60-63; L to Offic Dio Nam from 63. *PO Box 6353, Kampala, Uganda.*

KASSELL, Colin George Henry. b 42. Ripon Coll Cudd 76. **d** 68 RC Abp of Valladolid Spain **p** RC Bp of Leeds. In RC Ch 69-75; Rec into Angl Commun 76 by Bp of Ox; Perm to Offic Dio Ox 76-77; C of St Mary Denham 77-80; V of Brotherton Dio Wakef from 80. *Brotherton Vicarage, Knottingley, Yorks.* (Knottingley 82370)

KATAAHA, Alexander. Buwalasi Th Coll. **d** and **p** 66 Mbale. P Dio Mbale 66-68; Dio Ruw 68-72; Dio Bunyoro from 72. *Box 2, Kigumba-Masindi, Uganda.*

KATABAZI, Canon Abel. b 37. **d** 69 **p** 70 Vic Nyan. P Dio Vic Nyan from 70; Can of Vic Nyan from 79. *Box 12, Muleba, Tanzania.*

KATAGIRA, Elieza. d 76 **p** 77 Ank. P Dio Ank 76-77; Dio W Ank from 77. *Box 187, Bushenyi, Uganda.*

KATAKA, Thomas. d 75 **p** 76 Papua. C of Rabaul 75-77; Lae (in C of Markham from 79) Dio Aipo from 78. *Box 31, Lae, Papua New Guinea.* (42-2583)

KATAKANYA, Canon Keith. Bp Tucker Coll Mukono, 61. **d** 62 **p** 64 Ankole-K. P Dio Ankole-K 62-67; Dio Ank 67-76; Dio E Ank from 76; Dioc Regr and Sec Dio Ank 73-76; Dio E Ank 76-79; Archd Dio E Ank 76-79; Can from 79. *PO Box 4039, Ntungamo, Uganda.*

KATALI, Latima Lule. Bp Tucker Coll Mukono. **d** 49 **p** 51 Ugan. P Dio Ugan 49-60; Dio Nam 60-74. *Box 39, Mukono, Uganda.*

KATALIHWA, Ven Dani. Bp Tucker Coll Mukono. **d** 63 Ankole-K **p** 67 Ruw. d Dio Ankole-K 63-65; Dio Tor 65-67; Dioc Sec 67-79; Archd of Kabarole from 73. *c/o PO Box 37, Fort Portal, Uganda.*

KATAMBA, Balaam. b 45. Bp Tucker Coll Mukono 70. **d** 72 Ank. d Dio Ank 72-76; Dio W Ank from 77. *Box 207, Rwashamaire, Uganda.*

KATANDULA, Manuel. b 46. **d** 75 **p** 77 Centr Zam. P Dio Centr Zam. *PO Box 70172, Ndola, Zambia.*

KATARA, Canon Samusoni. Bp Tucker Coll Mukono. **d** 56 **p** 58 Ugan. P Dio Ugan 56-60; Dio Ruw 60-72; Dio Boga-Z from 72; Hon Can of Boga-Z from 74. *BP 154, Bunia, Zaire.*

KATEBARIRWE, Alfred. Bp Tucker Coll Mukono, 57. **d** 58 Ugan. d Dio Ugan 58-60; Dio Ankole-K 60-67; Dio Ank 67-76; Dio W Ank 77-79. *Kyagaju, Kabwohe, Uganda.*

KATEBARIRWE, d 74 **p** 75 Ank. P Dio Ank. *Eliasaph PO Box 31, Bushenyi, Mbarara, Uganda.*

KATEBE, Boniface. St Jo Sem Lusaka 57. **d** 58 **p** 60 N Rhod. P Dio N Rhod 58-64; Dio Zam from 64. *USPG, Chipili, Fort Rosebery, Zambia.*

KATEEBARIRWE, Adonia. d 75 Ank. d Dio Ank 75-77; Dio W Ank from 77. *PO Mitooma, Ruhinda, Uganda.*

KATEEKYEZA, Aberi. d and **p** 79 W Ank. P Dio W Ank. *PO Mitoomba, Ruhinda, Uganda.*

KATEMA, Charles Paulo. b 45. St Phil Coll Kongwa 74. **d** and **p** 76 Centr Tang. P Dio Centr Tang. *Box 93, Mpwapwa, Tanzania.*

KATEMANA, Daudi. St Phil Coll Kongwa. **d** 80 Vic Nyan. d Dio Vic Nyan. *PO Box 87, Maswa, Tanzania.*

KATEMBA, Christopher. Bp Tucker Coll Mukono. **d** 68 **p** 70 Nam. P Dio Nam. *PO Box 1020, Nakaseke, Uganda.*

KATEMBEKA, Godfrey. Bp Tucker Coll Mukono 78. **d** 80 E Ank. d Dio E Ank. *Kanoni Parish, PO Ibanda, Uganda.*

KATENE, Rio Petera. b 31. **d** 77 **p** 78 Aotearoa for Wai. C of Te Ngae Past Dio Wai from 77. *Okere Falls, PO, Rotorua, NZ.*

KATHEMANE, Robert. Bp Patteson Th Centre Kohimarama. **d** 71 Melan. d Dio Melan 71-75; Dio Ysabel from 75. *Sepi, Bugotu, Santa Ysabel, Solomon Islands.*

KATIB, Very Rev Made. Univ of Leeds BA (3rd cl Gen) 66. Coll of Resurr Mirfield 66. **d** 68 **p** 69 Kuch. P Dio Kuch; Dean of St Thos Cathl Kuch from 81. *Box 347, Kuching, Sarawak, Malaysia.*

KATIKUZI, Stephen. Bp Tucker Coll Mukono. **d** 51 **p** 54 Ugan. P Dio Ugan 51-60; Dio Ankole-K 60-67; Dio Ank 67-77; Dio W Ank from 77. *PO Kabwohe, Mbarara, Uganda.*

KATO, Ven Benjamin Amgbo. Im Coll Ibad 58. **d** 60 **p** 61 Ondo B. P Dio Ondo B 60-62; Dio Ondo 62-70; C of St Steph Acomb 70-73; Hon Can of Ondo 71-74; Archd of Kabba and Exam Chap to Bp of Kwara from 77. *Box 3, Kabba, Nigeria.*

KATO, Eliasaph. d 74 **p** 75 Ank. P Dio Ank 74-76; Dio W Ank from 77. *PO Kabwohe, Mbarara, Uganda.*

KATOTO, Godwin Hamilton. St Phil Th Coll Kongwa, 65. **d** 67 Bp Madinda for Centr Tang. **p** 67 Centr Tang. P Dio Centr Tang. *Box 799, Moshi, Tanzania.*

KATSIMBAZI, Blasio. Bp Tucker Coll Mukono, 62. **d** 63 **p** 65 Ankole-K. P Dio Ankole-K 63-67; Dio Ank 67-77; Dio W Ank from 77. *Box 2018, Rwashamaire, Uganda.*

KATUGUGU, John. Bp Tucker Coll Mukono 78. **d** 80 E Ank. d Dio E Ank. *PO Box 631, Mbarara, Uganda.*

KATUGUGU, Samwiri. d 58 Bp Brazier for Ugan **p** 60 Ankole-K. P Dio Ugan 58-60; Dio Ankole-K 60-67; Dio Kig from 67. *PO Rukungiri, Kigezi, Uganda.*

KATUMBA, Blasio. d 45 Ugan. d Dio Ugan 45-60; Dio Nam 60-65; Dio W Bugan 65-67; Dio Nam from 67. *PO Box 4618, Lubanyi, Uganda.*

KATUNGU, Mika. d 60 Centr Tang **p** 60 Bp Wiggins for Centr Tang. P Dio Centr Tang. *Box 489, Dodoma, Tanzania.*

KATUNGUUKA, Samuel. d 74 **p** 75 Ank. P Dio Ank 74-76; Dio E Ank from 76. *PO Box 261, Mbarara, Uganda.*

KATUNGYEZA, William. Bp Tucker Coll Mukono 69. **d**

71 Ank. d Dio Ank 71-76; Dio W Ank from 77. *Box 140, Bushenyi, Mbarara, Uganda.*

KATURAMU, Ven Anatosi. Bp Tucker Coll Mukono 57. **d** 58 Ugan **p** 60 Ruw. P Dio Ugan 58-60; Dio Ruw 60-69 and from 80; Dio Nam 69-80; Archd Dio Ruw from 81. *Box 37, Fort Portal, Uganda.*

KATUURAMU, Eliasaph. b 44. Bp Tucker Coll Mukono 75. **d** 77 **p** 78 W Ank. P Dio W Ank. *St Peter's Cathedral, PO Box 140, Bushenyi, Uganda.*

KATWESIGYE, George. Bp Tucker Coll Mukono 70. **d** 72 Kamp. d Dio Kamp. *Box 6056, Kampala, Uganda.*

KATYEGA, Stanley. b 38. **d** 77 **p** 78 Morogoro. P Dio Morogoro. *Tindiga, PO Kilosa, Tanzania.*

✠ **KAULUMA, Right Rev James Hamupanda.** Trin Coll Tor BA 74. Univ of NY MA 75. **d** 75 Damar **p** 77 New York. on leave 75-77; Cons Ld Bp Suffr of Damar (Namibia from 80) in Westmr Abbey 15 Jan 78 by Bps of Guildf, Liv, Roch, St Alb and Damar; Bp Suffr of Stepney; and Bps Howe, Knapp-Fisher and R Wood; Elected Bp of Namibia 81. *Bishop's House, Box 57, Windhoek, Namibia, SW Africa.*

✠ **KAUMA, Right Rev Misaeri.** Bp Tucker Coll Mukono Dipl Th 64. **d** 64 Nam **p** 67 Jarrow for Dur for Nam. P Dio Nam 64-75; Cons Asst Bp of Nam in St Paul's Cathl Nam 29 June 75 by Abp of Ugan; Bps of Soroti, W Bugan, Busoga, Ruw, Bunyoro, Sudan, Mbale, Nam and N Ugan; and others. *PO Box 14297, Mmengo, Kampala, Uganda.* (Kampala 46208)

KAUNHOVEN, Anthony Peter. b 55. Univ of Leeds BA (Th) 78. Episc Th Coll Edin 79. **d** 81 Knaresborough for Ripon. C of St Aid Leeds Dio Ripon from 81. *2 Roundhay Gardens, Leeds, LS8.*

KAVANAGH, Graham George. b 47. Worc Coll Ox BA 73, MA 78. St Cath Coll Cam MA 73. Cudd Coll 71. **d** 74 Lon **p** 75 Kens for Lon. C of Shepperton 74-77; In Amer Ch from 77. *Box 829, Topeka, Kansas, USA.*

KAVANAGH, Nicholas James Marner. d 80 **p** 81 S'wark. C of Ch Ch Forest Hill Dio S'wark from 80. *3 Ashleigh Point, Dacres Road, Forest Hill, SE23.* (01-291 4029)

KAVULU, Erieza Kazudde. d 42 **p** 44 U Nile. P Dio U Nile 42-61; Tutor Buwalasi Th Coll 61-62; Hon Can of Mblae 61-63; P Dio Nam from 62. *Kasoga, c/o Box 14123, Kampala, Uganda.*

KAVWENJE, Leonard. d 71 **p** 72 Lake Malawi. P Dio Lake Malawi. *P/A Nkhunga, Nkhotakota, Malawi.*

KAWEESA, Obadiya. Bp Tucker Coll Mukono. **d** 51 **p** 55 Ugan. P Dio Ugan 50-60; Dio Nam from 60. *PO Box 39, Mukono, Uganda.*

KAXUXUENA, Isaiah. d 64 **p** 65 Damar. P Dio Damar 64-80; Dio Namibia from 80. *c/o St Mary's Mission, Odibo, PO Oshikango, Ovamboland, SW Africa.* (Oshikango 5)

KAY, Canon Cyril John. b 05. St Aid Coll 44. **d** 46 **p** 47 Wakef. C of St Geo Lupset 46-48; Portland and Chap HM Borstal Inst 48-54; V of Welland 54-74; RD of Upton 59-73; Hon Can of Worc 69-74; Can (Emer) from 74. *16 Kayte Close, Bishop's Cleeve, Cheltenham, GL52 4AX.* (Bp's Cleeve 4306)

KAY, David Alfred. b 43. St Mich Coll Llan 67. **d** 69 Warrington for Liv **p** 70 Liv. C of Kirkby Liv 69-71; St Marg & All H Orford 71-75; V of St Jas Latchford 75-81; R of H Trin Without-the-Walls City and Dio Ches from 81. *Holy Trinity Rectory, Norris Road, Blacon, Chester.* (Ches 372721)

KAY, George Ronald. b 24. Sarum Wells Th Coll 74. **d** 77 **p** 78 Sarum (APM). C of Bemerton Dio Sarum from 77. *157 Wilton Road, Salisbury, Wilts.*

KAY, James William. b 49. Univ of Glas BSc 71, PhD 77. Univ of Edin BD 78. Edin Th Coll 75. **d** 78 Dur. C of St Chad Stockton-on-Tees 78-81. *Address temp unknown.*

KAY, Keith Alfred. Moore Th Coll Syd ACT ThL 43. **d** and **p** 44 Syd. C of St Clem Mosman 44-45; St Geo Hobart 45-47; R of Zeehan 47-49; St Aid Launceston 49-58; Burnie 58-73; H Trin Hobart 73-81; Can of Tas 71-81; *8 Ellis Street, Devonport, Tasmania 7310.*

KAY, Ronald William. b 28. Univ of Liv BEng (2nd cl Civil Eng) 49, MEng 51. Tyndale Hall Bris 59. **d** 61 Aston for Birm **p** 62 Birm. C of Sparkbrook 61-65; V of Westcombe Pk 65-76; Skellingthorpe (w Doddington from 78) Dio Linc from 76; R of Doddington w Whisby 76-78. *Skellingthorpe Vicarage, Lincoln, LN6 0UY.* (Linc 62520)

KAY, Canon Thomas Kindon. b 17. Edin Th Coll 42. **d** 45 **p** 46 Glas. C of Ch of Good Shepherd Hillington 45-47; R of H Trin Paisley 47-55; St Cypr Lenzie 55-64; H Trin Dunfermline Dio St Andr from 65; Can of St Ninian's Cathl Perth from 69. *3 Transy Place, Dunfermline, Fife.* (Dunfermline 21127)

KAYAAYO, Jackson. Bp Tucker Coll Mukono 79. **d** 80 W Ank. d Dio W Ank. *Greater Bushenyi Parish, PO Box 280, Bushenyi, Uganda.*

KAYAGIRA, Festo. d 80 Kiga. d Dio Kiga. *BP 22, Kigali, Rwanda.*

KAYE, Bruce Norman. b 39. BD Lon 64. Univ of Syd BA 66. Moore Th Coll Syd ACT ThL 64. **d** 64 **p** 65 Syd. C of Dural 64-66; Perm to Offic Dio Dur 67-69; L to Offic from 69; Tutor St Jo Coll Dur 68-75; Sen Tutor from 75; Vice Prin from 79. *17 South Bailey, Durham.*

KAYE, David Henry. Univ of W Ont BA 60. Hur Coll BTh 62. **d** 62 **p** 63 Tor. C of Rexdale 62-64; I of Mono 64-70; St Geo Barrie Dio Tor from 70. *11 Granville Street, Barrie, Ont., Canada.* (705-726 8121)

KAYE, Gerald Trevor. Univ of Man BSc (Maths cl iii) 54. Oak Hill Th Coll. **d** 56 Warrington for Liv **p** 57 Liv. C of St Ambrose Widnes 56-58; St Mark St Helens 58-62; V of St Sav Brixton Hill 62-65; I of Lac Seul 65-76; Cat Lake 66-76; Sioux Lookout 76-78; Chap Pelican Lake Residential Sch 65-68; Hon Can of Keew 70-75; Archd of Patricia 75-78; I of Alert Bay Dio BC from 78. *Box 201, Alert Bay, BC, Canada.* (604-974 5498)

KAYE, Norman. b 15. St Chad's Coll Dur BA 47. **d** 49 **p** 50 Wakef. C of St Paul Morley 49-51; Mexborough 51-54; V of Dalton Rotherham 54-59; St Paul Stanley Liv 59-68; Leighton-under-the-Wrekin w Eaton Constantine 68-80; C-in-c of Wroxeter 68-80. *7 Rope Lane, Shavington, Crewe, CW2 5DT.* (Crewe 664170)

KAYE, Peter Alan. b 47. AKC and BD 71. St Aug Coll Cant 71. **d** 72 **p** 73 Kens for Lon. C of Fulham 72-74; Chap of Rubery Hill, John Conolly and Sheldon Hosps 74-80. *Address temp unknown.*

KAYE, Timothy Henry. b 52. Linc Th Coll 77. **d** 80 **p** 81 Southw. C of Warsop Dio Southw from 80. *19 Rufford Avenue, Meden Vale, Mansfield, NG20 9PL.* (Mansfield 845229)

KAYEGA, Yekosafati. Bp Tucker Coll Mukono. **d** 56 Ugan **p** 58 Bp Balya for Ugan. P Dio Ugan 56-60; Dio Nam from 60. *Anglican Church, Bugulumbya, Uganda.*

KAYEMBA, George Thomas. b 57. **d** 77 Nam. d Dio Nam. *Kasoga Church of Uganda, PO Box 206, Lugazi, Uganda.*

KAYIJAMAHE, Justin. b 18. **d** 76 **p** 77 Kiga. P Dio Kiga. *c/o BP 17 Byumba, Rwanda.*

KAYIJUKA, Matthias. Warner Mem Th Coll Ibuye 61. **d** 63 **p** 64 Rwanda B. P Dio Rwanda B 63-66; Dio Bur from 66. *Post Box 17, Byumba, Rwanda.*

KAYIRA, George. Bp Tucker Coll Mukono 59. **d** 62 **p** 64 w Bugan. P Dio W Bugan. *COU Kabale-Sanje, Box 2535, Kyotera, Uganda.*

KAYLL, Arthur Gregory. b 01. Univ of NZ 22. St Jo Coll Auckld NZ 23. SS Coll Cam BA 30, MA 36. **d** 26 Chelmsf for Roch **p** 26 Roch. C of St Jo Div Chatham 26-27; St Mary the Gt w St Mich AA Cam 27-30; St Mich AA Watford 31-32; Perm to Offic at All SS St John's Wood 32; All SS Highgate 33; Chap RAF 33-46; PC of St Leonard's Ox 46-68; V 68-79; Perm to Offic Dio Ox from 80. *Old School House, St Leonards, Tring, Herts.* (Cholesbury 219)

KAYODE, Daniel Smith. Melville Hall, Ibad. **d** 53 **p** 54 Ondo B. P Dio Ondo B 53-62; Dio Ondo from 62. *PO Box 59, Ijebu-Owo, Nigeria.* (Owo 2037)

KAYODE, Elijah Ayeni. Melville Hall, Ibad 59. **d** 53 **p** 54 W Afr. P Dio Lagos. *Holy Trinity Vicarage, Ifo, Okenla, Nigeria.*

KAYODE, Canon Joshua Olumide. Dipl Th (Lon) 63. Univ of Ife, BA (1st cl Phil and Relig Stud) 67. Im Coll Ibad 61. **d** 63 **p** 67 Ibad. P Dio Ibad from 63; Exam Chap to Bp of Ekiti 71-80; to Bp of Ilesha from 80; Hon Can of Ilesha from 80; Lect Univ of Ife from 80. *Univ of Ife, Ile-Ife, Nigeria.*

KAYONDO, Ezekiel. d 54 Bp Brazier for Ugan **p** 55 Ugan. P Dio Ugan 54-60; Dio Rwanda B 60-66; Dio Rwa 66-75; Dio Kiga 75-76; Can of Rwa 72-75; Kiga 75-76. *Gahima, BP 18, Kibungo, Rwanda.*

KAYONGO, George William. Bp Tucker Coll Mukono. **d** 63 **p** 64 Nam. P Dio Nam. *PO Box 22011, Nakifuma, Uganda.*

KAZENGA, Johnstone. b 43. **d** 79 **p** 80 W Tang. P Dio W Tang. *D.W.T. Mabamba, c/o PO Box 15, Kibondo, Tanzania, E Africa.*

KAZIBURE, Albano. St Cypr Coll Lindi 71. **d** 74 **p** 75 Masasi. P Dio Masasi. *c/o St Cyprian's College, Box 212, Lindi, Tanzania.*

KEABLE, Geoffrey. b 1900. Late Scho of St Jo Coll Ox 2nd cl Cl Mods 19, BA 22, 2nd cl Lit Hum 22, Dipl Th (w distinc) 23, MA 25. Cudd Coll 23. **d** 24 **p** 25 Cant. C of Buckland-in-Dover 24-26; Lect Bp's Coll Calc 27-32; Lect St Aug Coll Cant 32-33; R of St Geo Mart w St Mary Magd Cant 33-46; Perm to Offic as C-in-c of St Pet Harrow 43-46; V of Lower Halstow 46-49; Welwyn Garden City 49-59; RD of Welwyn 53-58; C-in-c of Hatfield Hyde 53-56; V of Barnham 59-68; C of St Luke Chesterton 68-69; Hon C 69-78. *The Coach House, Mortimer Hill, Mortimer, Reading, RG7 3PG.* (Mortimer 333390)

KEAL, Canon Robben Thomas. **d** 31 **p** 32 Qu'App. C of Kenaston 31-32; I 32-35; C of Ollerton 35-40; V of Sutton-on-Trent 40-71; Carlton-on-Trent 46-71; RD of Norwell 46-65; R of Weston 54-66; Hon Can of Southw 56-71; Can (Emer) from 76; Perm to Offic Dio Southw from 73. *Qu'Appelle, Carlton-on-Trent, Newark, Notts.*

KEANE, Edward Lionel. Trin Coll Dub BA 16, MA 23. **d** 17 Clogh **p** 18 Lim. C of Tydavnet 17; Dingle w Ventry 17-19; Ematris 19-22; C-in-c of Mullaghdun 22-24; Clontibret 24-26; R of Cathl Ch Clogh 26-42; Donagh 42-44; Altedesert 44-49; Preb of Devenish in Clogh Cathl 32-44; I of U Drogheda 49-55; Heynestown U 55-61. *10 Anglesey Park, Killiney, Co Dublin, Irish Republic.*

KEANE, Francis Norman. Linc Th Coll 27. **d** 29 **p** 30 Glouc. C of St Steph Glos 29-31; St Mary Bury St Edms 31-33; R of S Elmham 33-58; PC of Rumburgh (w All SS St Jas and St Nich S Elmham from 58) 53-68; V 68-73. *St Elmham, St James, Halesworth, Suff.*

KEANE, Canon James Goldsworthy. b 23. Selw Coll Cam BA 47, MA 49. Cudd Coll. **d** 49 **p** 50 Llan. C of Penarth w Lavernock 49-56; Org Sec Prov Youth Coun of Ch in Wales 56-65; L to Offic Dio Llan 56-79; Perm to Offic Dio 58-79; Gen Sec Ch in Wales Prov Counc Educn and Dir Ch in Wales Publications 65-79; Perm to Offic Dio Mon 69-79; Hon Can of Llan from 73; Chairman Coun for Wales Voluntary Youth Services 78-82; R of St Andr Major w Michaelston-le-Pit Dio Llan from 79. *Rectory, Dinas Powis, S Glam, CF6 4BY.* (Dinas Powis 512555)

KEAR, Francis Herbert. b 02. St Mich Coll Llan 49. **d** 51 **p** 52 Mon. C of St Jo Bapt Newport Mon 51-55; Penhow Dio Mon 55-57; R 57-73; RD of Netherwent 69-72. *8 Cherry Tree Close, Langstone, Newport, Gwent.*

KEARLEY, Edwin Rex. Qu Coll Newfld BA 55. Trin Coll Tor STB 62. **d** 54 **p** 55 Newfld. C of Channel 54-57; R of Meadows 57-61; I of Gambo 62-67; L to Offic Dio E Newfld from 79. *24 Belfast Street, St John's, Newfoundland, Canada.*

KEARNEY, Peter Adderley. b 45. Ch Coll Hobart 67. **d** 70 **p** 71 Tas. Hon C of St D Cathl Hobart 70-74; Perm to Offic Dio Tas from 79. *PO Box 86, Zeehan, Tasmania 7101.*

KEARON, Kenneth Arthur. b 53. TCD BA 76. MA 79. Div Test 78. **d** 81 Dub. C of Raheny w Coolock Dio Dub from 81. *55 Ayrfield Estate, Coolock, Dublin 13, Irish Republic.*

KEARSE, Eric Donald. St Jo Coll Auckld. **d** 68 **p** 69 Wel. C of Levin 68-70; Masterton 70-71; V of Pongaroa 71-74; Chap RNZAF from 74; Perm to Offic Dio Auckld 74-77; V of Wainuiomata 77-81; Chap Palmerston N Hosps from 81. *50 Heretaunga Street, Palmerston North, NZ.* (73-618)

KEAT, Roger Leslie Samuel. Wells Th Coll 64. **d** 66 **p** 67 Dur. C of St Chad Bosworth Stockton-on-Tees 66-68; H Spirit Clapham 70-73; Wimbledon 73-75; CF from 75. *c/o Ministry of Defence, Lansdowne House, Berkeley Square, W1X 6AA.*

KEATES, Frederick. Ball Coll Ox 2nd cl Cl Mods 29, 2nd cl Lit Hum 31, BA and MA 35. Ripon Hall Ox 35. **d** 36 **p** 37 Birm. C of St Jas Handsworth 36-42; Seale and Lullington 42-45; V of Bordesley 45-51; Exam Chap to Bp of Birm 50-70; V of Four Oaks 51-72. *49 Four Oaks Road, Four Oaks, Sutton Coldfield, W Midlands.*

KEATING, Christopher Robin. b 39. Sarum Th Coll 62. **d** 65 **p** 66 Bradf. C of Baildon 65-67; CF 67-71; V of St Paul Thornton Heath 71-80. *Address temp unknown.*

KEATING, William Edward. b 10. Trin Coll Ox BA 32. Lich Th Coll 33. **d** 33 **p** 34 Chelmsf. Asst Missr Trin Coll Ox Miss Stratford 33-35; C of Gt Yarmouth (in c of St Pet) 35-37; St Andr Battersea 37-40; L to Offic Dio Ox 40-41; V of Northbourne Berks 41-55; RD of Wallingford 53-55; R of Welford w Wickham 55-63; C-in-c of Gt Shefford 61-63; Chap St Francis and Hurstwood Pk Hosps 63-75. *4 Beverley Court, Western Road, E Finchley, N2 9HX.*

KEAY, Alfred David. b 26. Univ of Aston in Birm MSc 72. Qu Coll Birm. **d** 79 **p** 80 Lich. Hon C of Penkridge Dio Lich from 79. *Redwharf, Wolverhampton Road, Penkridge, Stafford, ST19 5DR.*

KEAY, David William Alexander. ACT ThDip 69. St Barn Coll Adel 65. **d** 67 **p** 68 Adel. C of Edwardstown w Ascot Pk 67-69; P-in-c of Port Noarlunga 69-72; R of Mannum 73-76; P-in-c of Findon-Seaton Dio Adel from 76. *12 Balcombe Avenue, Findon, S Australia 5023.* (45 4495)

KEBWEMI, George. **d** 75 **p** 76 Ruw. P Dio Ruw. *Box 368, Fort Portal, Uganda.*

KEDDIE, Tony. b 37. Qu Coll Birm. **d** 66 **p** 67 Bradf. C of Barnoldswick w Bracewell 66-69; New Bentley 69-71; Team V of Seacroft 71-79; V of Kippax Dio Ripon from 79. *Kippax Vicarage, Leeds, LS25 7HF.* (Leeds 862710)

KEE, David. b 04. Linc Th Coll 45. **d** 47 **p** 48 Win. [f in CA]. C of St Alb Southn 47-49; Eastleigh 49-50; V of New Clipstone 50-55; M OGS from 55; Metrop Sec SPG and LPr Dio Chelmsf and Perm to Offic Dios Lon, S'wark and Guildf 55-60; V of St Matt Willesden 60-63; Chap CECS Alveston Leys and L to Offic Dio Cov 63-64; V of Podington w Farndish 64-73; Perm to Offic Dio St Alb from 74; Dio Win from 75. *33 St Leonard's Road, Highcliffe, Winchester, Hants, SO23 8QD.* (Winchester 2156)

KEEFE, Kenneth Bernard. Angl Th Coll BC LTh 41. **d** 40 New Westmr **p** 42 Fred for Montr. C of Ascen Montr 41-44; CASF 44-46; C of Ch Ch Cathl Montr 46-48; R of Sutton 48-53; Sillery 53-55; St Matthias Montr 55-62; Dean and R of St Paul's Cathl Lon Dio Hur 62-80. *RR2, Sutton, PQ, Canada, J0E 2K0.*

KEEGAN, Canon Donald Leslie. b 37. ACII. Div Hostel Dub 65. **d** 68 Derry **p** 69 Clogh pcr Derry. C of Drumragh and of Mountfield 68-72; I of Birr Dio Killaloe from 72; Can of Killaloe Cathl from 80. *Birr Rectory, Offaly, Irish Republic.*

KEELAN, Apirana Hikitoa. b 27. **d** 77 Aotearoa for Wai. C of Tolaga Bay Dio Wai from 77. *PO Box 121, Tolaga Bay, NZ.*

KEELEY, John Robin. b 38. G and C Coll Cam 2nd cl Mod Lang Trip pt i, 60, BA (2nd cl Th Trip pt ii) 62. Clifton Th Coll 62. **d** 64 **p** 65 Lon. C of St Paul Onslow Square Kens 64-66; Bp Hannington Mem Ch w H Cross Hove 66-69; St Jo Bapt Harborne 69-72; V of H Trin (and St Jo Div from 74) Leic 72-80; C-in-c of St Jo Div Leic 72-74; Perm to Offic Dio St Alb from 81. *5 Coombe Gardens, Berkhamsted, Herts, HP4 3PA.* (Berkhamsted 2306)

KEELEY, Keith Morgan. Univ of Man BA 33, MA 36. **d** 49 **p** 51 Bradf. C of Shipley 49-52; Gt Barr 52-53; Blakenall Heath 53-55; V of St John Tipton 55-59; R of Hinstock 59-64. *c/o Linington, Westering, Watergate Road, Newport, IoW.*

KEELEY, Robert Bruce. b 48. Univ of Cant NZ BSc 70. St Jo Coll Auckld LTh 77. **d** 77 Wai. C of Hastings Dio Wai from 77. *506 Henry Street, Hastings, NZ.*

KEELEY, Roger. b 35. K Coll Lon and Warm AKC 59. **d** 60 **p** 61 Sarum. C of E & W Harnham 60-63; Marlborough 63-68; V of Whiteparish Dio Sarum from 68. *Whiteparish Vicarage, Salisbury, Wilts.* (Whiteparish 315)

KEELING, James Michael. b 33. Univ of Dur BA (1st cl Pol and Econ) 55, MA 61. Cudd Coll 57. **d** 59 **p** 60 Dur. C of St Luke Pallion Bp Wearmouth 59-64; V of Appleton Roebuck w Acaster Selby 65-69; Asst Dir WCC Ecumen Inst Céligny 69-72; Lect Univ of St Andr from 73. *The Great House, Pittenweem, Anstruther, Fife, KY10 2LJ.*

KEELING, Canon John Nevill. b 07. St Edm Hall Ox BA and MA 40. Trin Coll Dub MA (*ad eund*) 48. Bps' Coll Cheshunt 29. **d** 30 **p** 31 Man. C of St Luke Weaste 30-33; St Clem Urmston 33-35; V of Newhey 35-37; CF (TA) 36-37; Chap RAF 37-60; Hon Chap to HM the Queen 57-60; Prin RAF Chaps Sch Cheltm 59-60; V of Brighton 60-74; RD of Brighton 60-74; Can and Preb of Waltham in Chich Cathl 60-76; Can (Emer) from 76; Proc Conv Chich 65-70. *6 Hailsham Close, East Preston, Littlehampton, Sussex.* (Rustington 70577)

KEELING, Michael John. b 28. Chich Th Coll 57. **d** 60 **p** 61 Chich. C of Hurstpierpoint 60-63; Southwick Sussex 63-64; R of Mt Pleasant Perth WA 64-68; Perm to Offic Dio Perth WA 68-73; Dio Lon from 73; Dio S'wark from 75. *66 Crownstone Court, St Matthew's Road, SW2.*

KEELING, Peter Frank. b 34. Kelham Th Coll. **d** 58 **p** 59 Wakef. C of S Elmsall 58-63; Barnsley 63-67; V of Ravensthorpe 67-73; Cudworth Dio Wakef from 73. *Cudworth Vicarage, Barnsley, Yorks, S72 8DE.* (Barnsley 710279)

KEEN, Charles William Ernest. b 14. Chich Th Coll 48. **d** 51 **p** 52 S'wark. C of St Helier 51-53; Beddington 53-56; Kingswood 56-59; R of Mereworth w W Peckham 59-66; V of Ide Hill 66-73; Chap Sundridge Hosp 66-73; Perm to Offic Dio Cant from 73. *4 Godwyn Road, Deal, Kent.* (Deal 62187)

KEEN, Frederic Norman. Keble Coll Ox BA 28, MA 33. Lich Th Coll 29. **d** 30 **p** 31 Lich. C of Horninglow 30-35; C-in-c of St Chad's Conv Distr Tunstall 35-42; V of St Mary Bilston 42-48; Daybrook 48-62; Chap Cedars Hosp Nottm 53-64; Proc Conv Southw 62-64; V of Beeston 62-70; Bosley w N Rode Dio Ches from 70. *Bosley and North Rode Vicarage, Macclesfield, Chesh.* (N Rode 264)

KEEN, Michael Spencer. b 41. GRSM 62. Late Scho of St Pet Coll Ox BA 68, MA 72. Westoctt Ho Cam 68. **d** 73 Warrington for Liv **p** 74 Liv. Hon C of Tue Brook 73-74; St Anne Stanley Liv 74-76; Ch's Youth and Commun Officer in Telford Dio Lich from 77; L to Offic Dio Lich from 77; Perm to Offic Dio Heref from 78. *30 Smith Crescent, Wrockwardine Wood, Telford, Salop, TF2 7AK.* (Telford 612740)

KEEN, Canon Neville James. Moore Th Coll Syd ACT ThL 54. **d** and **p** 55 Syd. C of Haberfield 55-56; Actg R of Concord West 56-58; R of Pittwater 58-62; Asst Gen Sec Home Miss S 62-64; Gen Sec 64-75; L to Offic Dio Syd 62-75; C-in-c of St Matt w Pymble Dio Syd from 75; Hon Can of Syd from 76. *Eppleston Place, West Pymble, NSW, Australia 2073.* (498-8739)

KEENAINAK, Eliyah. b 19. Arthur Turner Tr Sch Pangnirtung 70. **d** 72 Arctic. Miss at Coral Harbour 72-81; Pangnirtung Dio Arctic from 81. *St Luke's Mission, Pangnirtung, NWT, Canada.*

KEENAN, Leslie Herbert. b 32. Cranmer Hall Dur. **d** 66 **p** 67 Sheff. [f CA] C of Anston and of Woodsetts 66-70; V of Pollington w Balne 70-78; Poughill Dio Truro from 78; Chap HM Borstal Pollington 70-78; *Poughill Vicarage, Bude, Cornw, EX23 9ER.* (Bude 2510)

KEENE, Canon David Peter. b 32. Trin Hall Cam BA 56, MA 60. Westcott Ho Cam. **d** 58 Southw **p** 59 Bp Gelsthorpe for Southw. C of Radcliffe-on-Trent 58-61; Mansfield 61-64; V of St Cath Nottm 64-71; R of Bingham 71-81; Surr from 72; Can Res of Southw Minster from 81; Dir of Ords from 81. *2 Vicars' Court, Southwell, Notts, NG25 OHP.* (813188)

KEENE, Stanley Holmes. b 08. K Coll Lon 30. **d** 48 Ex **p** 52 Ox. C of Hartland 48-50; Aylesbury (in c of St Pet from 52 and St Pet and St Jo Evang from 54) 52-56; V of N Marston 56-58; Lacey Green 58-60; C of Crawley (in c of Three Bridges) 60-64; V of Colgate 64-72; C-in-c of St Andr Conv Distr Bexhill 72-78. *2 Merivale, Chowns Hill, Hastings, E Sussex, TN35 4PA.* (0424 753956)

KEEP, Andrew James. b 55. Collingwood Coll Dur BA (Th) 77. Sarum Wells Th Coll 78. **d** 80 **p** 81 Guildf. C of Banstead Dio Guildf from 80. *14 Glenfield Road, Banstead, Surrey, SM7 2DG.* (Burgh Heath 53938)

KEEP, Michael John. b 45. Univ of Rhodes Grahmstn BA 71. St Paul's Coll Grahmstn Dipl Th 70. **d** 71 **p** 72 Natal. C of St Alphege Scottsville 72-73; R of Mooi River 73-76; Chap St Andr Sch Bloemf from 76. *St Andrew's School, Bloemfontein, OFS, S Africa.*

KEETON, Barry. b 40. Univ of Dur BA (Lat) 61, MA 69, MLitt 78. K Coll Lon and Warm BD and AKC 63. **d** 64 **p** 65 York. C of S Bank 64-67; St Cuthb Middlesbrough 67-69; WCC Scho Gregorian Univ Rome 69-70; C of St Alb Hull 70-71; V of Appleton-le-Street w Amotherby 71-74; R of Ampleforth w Oswaldkirk 74-78; Ecumen Adv Dio York 74-81; M Gen Syn from 75; V of Howden 78-79; P-in-c of Wressle 78-79; Barmby Marsh 78-79; Laxton w Blacktoft 78-79; R of The Howden Team Min Dio York from 80. *Minster Rectory, Howden, Goole, N Humb, DN14 7BL.* (Howden 30332)

KEEWATIN, Lord Bishop of. *See* Allan, Right Rev Hugh James Pearson.

KEEWATIN, Dean of. *See* Carr, Very Rev Paul Ashley.

KEEWAYAGABO, Titus. b 34. **d** and **p** 74 Keew. C of Cat Lake Dio Keew from 74. *St John's Church, Cat Lake, via Central Patricia, Ont., Canada.*

KEFFORD, Peter Charles. b 44. Univ of Nottm BTh 74. Linc Th Coll 70. **d** 74 **p** 75 S'wark. C of Ch Ch W Wimbledon 74-77; All H Barking-by-the-Tower w St Dunstan-in-E 77-81; P-in-c of St Barn Conv Distr Pound Hill Dio Chich from 81. *St Barnabas House, Crawley Lane, Pound Hill, Crawley, S Sussex, RH10 4EB.* (Crawley 513398)

KEGGIE, Michael John. Univ of the Witwatersrand BComm. **d** 78 **p** 79 Capetn. C of St John Wynberg (in-c of Em) Dio Capetn from 78. *30 Pluto Road, Plumstead, CP, S Africa.* (77-3523)

KEHINDE, Joseph Adetunji. Univ of Lon Dipl Th (Extra-Mural) 56. Melville Hall Ibad 54. **d** 56 **p** 57 Lagos. P Dio Lagos 57-69; L to Offic Dio Ibad from 69; Chap Oduduwa Coll Ile-Ife Dio Ibad from 71. *Oduduwa College, Ile-Ife, Nigeria.*

KEHINDE, Joshua Ibidapo. b 49. Im Coll Ibad 71. **d** 74 **p** 75 Lagos. P Dio Lagos 74-76; Dio Ijebu from 76. *Holy Trinity Church, Ibefun, Box 22, Ijebu-Ode, Nigeria.*

KEIGHLEY, Robert Arthur Spink. b 13. Univ of Leeds MB ChB 38. **d** 78 **p** 79 Bradf. Hon C to the Dean of Skipton from 78. *Chapel House Lodge, Kilnsey, Skipton, N Yorks, BD23 5PR.*

KEIGHTLEY, Canon Peter Edward. b 17. Univ of Leeds BA 41. Coll of Resurr Mirfield 41. **d** 43 **p** 44 Pet. C of All H Wellingborough 43-45; Solihull 45-49; Cirencester (in c of H Trin Watermoor) 50-53; V of St Paul Glouc 53-59; Wymering w Widley 59-67; H Spirit Southsea Portsea 67-76; Chap St Mary's Gen Hosp Portsm from 76; Hon Can of Portsm Cathl from 81. *St Mary's General Hospital, Portsmouth, Hants.* (Portsm 822331)

KEIGHTLEY, Thomas. b 44. Div Hostel Dub 79. **d** 79 **p** 80 Down. C of Seagoe Dio Down from 79. *39 Gilford Road, Portadown, Craigavon, BT63 5EF, N Ireland.*

✠ **KEILI, Right Rev Michael.** MBE 65. OBE Fourah Bay Coll. **d** 46 **p** 49 Sier L. Tutor Union Coll 46-51; P Dio Sier L 51-63; Archd of Bo 63-81; Cons Ld Bp of Bo in St Geo Cathl Freetown 16 Aug 81 by Abp of W Africa; and Bps of Gambia and Portsm. *PO Box 21, Bo, Sierra Leone.* (Bo 411)

KEIR, Trevor David. b 49. Sarum Wells Th Coll 75. **d** 78 **p** 79 Man. C of Stand 78-81; C-in-c of Saltfleetby w Skidbrooke Dio Linc from 81; Theddlethorpe Dio Linc from 81. *Rectory, Saltfleetby, Louth, Lincs.* (Saltfleetby 680)

KEITH, Andrew James Buchanan. b 47. Qu Coll Cam BA 69, MA 73. Wycl Hall Ox 71. **d** 74 Warrington for Liv **p** 75 Liv. C of Warrington 74-77; V of Crawley Broadfield Conv Distr Dio Chich from 78. *10 Colonsay Road, Crawley, RH11 9DF.*

KEITH, Canon Bliss Thorne. Bp's Univ Lennox BA 26, LST 28. **d** 28 Queb for Fred **p** 29 Fred. Miss of St Martin's 28-30; R of Grand Manan 30-33; St Geo w Pennfield 33-43; CASF 43-46; Miss at Hillsboro Harvey Hopewell 46-47; Gladstone and Blissville 47-49; R of Kingston 49-53; Miss at Salisbury w Havelock 53-59; R of Addington w Campbellton 59-65; Shediac 65-70; Can of Ch Ch Cathl Fred from 64; Dom Chap to Bp of Fred 64-76. *141 Emmerson Street, Moncton, NB, Canada.*

KEITH, David. b 35. Linc Th Coll 66. **d** 68 **p** 69 Sheff. C of Rotherham 68-72; Industr Chap Kirkby 72-74. *Address temp unknown.*

KEITH, John. b 25. ASGM 50. LRAM 50. Cudd Coll 60. **d** 62 **p** 63 Portsm. C of Lee-on-the-Solent 62-65; Raynes Pk 65-68. *c/o Post Office, Tayinloan, Tarbert, Argyll, PA29 6XG.*

KEITH, Canon John Frederick Butterfield. Trin Coll Cam 3rd cl Hist Trip pt 1, 33, BA (2nd cl Th Trip pt i) 35, MA 44. Cudd Coll 36. **d** 37 **p** 38 Lon. C of H Cross Greenford 37-41; CF (EC) 40-46; R of Ashwell 46-51; Fakenham w Alethorpe 51-57; Surr 51-57; C of Ashburton NZ 58-59; Merivale 59-60; V of Philipstown 60-63; St Pet U Riccarton 63-71; Waimate Dio Ch Ch from 71; Hon Can of Ch Ch from 71; P-in-c of Waihao Downs 74-77; V of Woodend Dio Ch Ch from 77. *144 Main North Road, Woodend, Canterbury, NZ.*

KEITH, Ven Peter Meredith. Ridley Hall, Cam 46. **d** 48 **p** 49 Portsm. C of Alverstoke 48-50; Lower Hutt 50-51; V of Miramar Wel 51-59; Gonville 59-61; Sub-Dean of Auckld 62-66; Archd of Nel 66-77; Archd (Emer) from 76; V of All SS Nel 66-76; Amuri 76-78; C of St Paul's Cathl Wel 78-79; Perm to Offic Dio Wel from 79. *159 Waerenga Road, Otaki, NZ.*

KEITH, Ronald Gordon Layard. Coll Ho Ch Ch. **d** 47 **p** 48 Wel. C of St Jas Lower Hutt 47-50; V of Waverley-Waitotara 50-53; Featherstone 53-61; Pahiatua 61-66; Pauatahanui 66-72; Greytown 72-76; L to Offic Dio Wel from 76. *95 Derby Street, Feilding, NZ.*

KEJOA, Alfred. St Pet Coll Melan. **d** 46 **p** 49 Melan. P Dio Melan 46-75; Dio Centr Melan from 76. *Isunauvara, Guadalcanal, Solomon Islands.*

KELCEY, Belsey. b 1893. Univ of Dur LTh 23. Sarum Th Coll. **d** 22 **p** 23 Bris for B & W. C of St Anne Brislington 22-26; St Matt Moorfields 26-29; V of All SS Swindon 29-49; Avonmouth 49-58; Wicklewood w Crownthorpe 58-60; R of Trunch w Swafield 60-65; RD of Tunstead 64-65. *The Sycamores, Norwich Road, Pulham St Mary, Norf.*

KELL, Frederick John. b 01. **d** 58 **p** 59 Bunb. C of Collie 58-60; Manjimup 60-62; R of Denmark 62-63; V of Compton Bp 64-70. *Beechlands, Paul's Causeway, Congresbury, Bristol.*

KELL, Sidney Chamberlain. St Jo Th Coll Perth, 26; ACT ThL 28. **d** 26 **p** 27 Perth. C of St Mary W Perth 26-28; R of Meckering 29-30; Mullewa 30-32; Chap of St Luke's Hosp Chelsea 32-34; C of Eastleigh (in c of All SS) 34; V of Watton w Beswick 34-37; Offg Chap RAF 36-37; Chap of S Perak 37-41; V of Hempnall 42-44; Exmoor 44-47; Chap RAF 47-54; R of Down-Hatherley w Twigworth 54-57; Parracombe (w Martinhoe from 60) 57-63; V of Staverton w Landscove 63-68; L to Offic Dio Ex from 68. *2 Tapley Gardens, Bishopsteighton, Teignmouth, Devon.*

KELLAM, Rodney Ian. Ridley Coll Melb ACT ThL (2nd cl) 63. **d** 64 **p** 65 Tas. C of St Steph Hobart 64-66; New Norfolk 66-67; P-in-c of Zeehan w Rosebery 67-68; R of Sorell w Tasman Peninsula 68-73; R of Wonthaggi Dio Gippsld from 73. *5 Hagelthorne Street, Wonthaggi, Vic., Australia 3955.* (056-72485)

KELLAND, Kenneth William Jerome. b 16. SOC 63. **d** 66 **p** 67 Guildf. C of Addlestone 66-69; Sholing 69-74; V of Weston Hants 74-82; P-in-c of Odiham & S Warnborough w Long Sutton Dio Win from 82. *The Parsonage, South Warnborough, Basingstoke, RG25 1RH.* (Long Sutton 611)

KELLEN, David. b 52. Univ Coll Cardiff Dipl Th 73. St Mich AA Coll Llan 70. **d** 75 **p** 76 Mon. C of Mynyddyslwyn 75-77; Risca 77-78; Malpas Dio Mon from 78. *1 Tone Close, Bettws, Newport, Gwent.*

KELLETT, Colin. b 25. Worc Ordin Coll 65. **d** 67 **p** 68 Wakef. C of E Ardsley 67-69; St Jo Evang Dewsbury Moor 69-72; V of Lundwood 72-77; Gawber Dio Wakef from 77. *St Thomas Vicarage, Gawber, Barnsley, Yorks, S75 2RL.* (Barnsley 203897)

KELLETT, Harold. b 20. St Jo Coll Dur BA 49, Dipl Th 51. **d** 51 **p** 52 Blackb. C of St Jas Preston 51-53; Standish Lancs 53-55 V of St Anne Lanc 55-58; St Jo Evang w St Anne

Lanc 58-72; Hornby w Claughton Dio Blackb from 72; RD of Tunstall from 75. *Hornby Vicarage, Lancaster.* (Hornby 21238)

KELLETT, John Frederick. b 01. Egerton Hall, Man 37. **d** 39 **p** 40 Man. C of St Mich AA Ashton L 39-41; St Steph Blackpool 41-42; Spotland 42-46; R of St Cross Clayton 46-60; V of Musbury 60-64; St Pet Preston 64-66; C of Skerton 66-68; Hon C St Laur Morecambe Dio Blackb from 68. *217 Heysham Road, Morecambe, Lancs.*

KELLETT, Neil. b 41. Bps' Coll Cheshunt, 64. **d** 66 Ex **p** 67 Crediton for Ex. C of St Thos Mart Ex 66-72; H Trin Win 72-74; P-in-c of St Geo Redditch 74-77; R of Fogo I Dio Centr Newfld from 78. *Box 190, Fogo Island, Newfoundland, Canada.* (709-266 2283)

KELLEY, Cecil Allen. Moore Th Coll Syd. **d** 58 Syd **p** 58 Bp Hilliard for Syd. C of St Luke Mosman 58-59; St Thos N Syd 59-62; R of Lakemba Dio Syd from 62. *177 Lakemba Street, Lakemba, NSW, Australia 2195.* (759-1574)

KELLEY, Christopher Pierce. b 46. Univ of Calif BA 68. Univ of S Calif MSEd 70. Gen Th Sem NY STM 73. **d** 73 Calif **p** 74 Cant. In Amer Ch 73-74; C of St Martin and St Paul Cant 74-77. *c/o 1 Longport, Canterbury, Kent, CT1 1PE.*

KELLEY, Norman Stanley. b 43. Canberra Coll of Min 78. **d** 80 C & Goulb. C of Temora-Barmedman Dio C & Goulb from 80. *113 Polaris Street, Temora, NSW, Australia 2666.*

KELLY, Canon Albert Norman. b 21. TCD BA (Mod) 43, Div Test 44, MA 63. **d** 44 **p** 45 Down. C of Donagh[illegible] 44-46; St Jo Evang Malone 46-55; I of Billy 55-63; C of Dorking w Ranmore 63-66; V of New Haw 66-78; St Paul Egham Hythe Dio Guildf from 78; RD of Chertsey (Runnymede from 75) 73-78; Hon Can of Guildf from 80. *214 Wendover Road, Staines, TW18 3DF.* (Staines 53625)

KELLY, Canon Brian Horace. b 34. Late Gisborne Scho of St Jo Coll Dur BA 57, Dipl Th 58, MA 69. **d** 58 **p** 59 S & M. C of St Geo and St Barn Douglas 58-61; V of Foxdale 61-64; Ed Manx Ch Magazine 62-64; V of All S (w St Jas from 66) Bolton-le-Moors 64-73; Kirk Maughold (and Chap of Ch Ch Dhoon) 73-77; Kirk German Dio S & M from 77; M Gen Syn from 75; Dir of Ordins Dio S & M from 76; Exam Chap to Bp of S & M from 76; Can and Prec of S & M from 80. *Vicarage, Albany Road, Peel, IM.* (Peel 2608)

KELLY, Christopher Augustine. b 15. Keble Coll Ox BA (3rd cl Hist 37, 3rd cl Th 39). Croix de Guerre 45. TD 65. Ripon Hall, Ox 37. **d** 45 **p** 46 Birm. C of Aston 45-51; V of H Trin Habergham Eaves Burnley 51-57; Knuzden 57-67; Tonge w Breightmet 67-74; Breightmet 74-76; Nelson-in-Marsden Dio Blackb from 76. *St Mary's Vicarage, Manchester Road, Nelson, BB9 7HB.* (Nelson 64919)

KELLY, Dennis Charles. b 31. Univ of Liv BA 52. Lich Th Coll. **d** 56 **p** 57 Ches. C of St Paul Tranmere 56-59; C-in-c of St Andr Conv Distr Grange Runcorn 59-63; Min 63-65; V 65-67; R of St Mich Coppenhall Crewe Dio Ches from 67; Surr from 72. *Coppenhall Rectory, Crewe, Ches.* (Crewe 215151)

KELLY, Canon Edward William Moncrieff. b 28. K Coll Lon and Warm AKC 57. **d** 57 **p** 58 Portsm. C of Petersfield w Sheet 57-60; Miss Dio New Guinea 60-65; V of Ch Ch Gosport 65-69; Org Sec New Guinea Miss 69-77; Papua Ch Partnership from 77; C of St Jo Bapt Eltham Dio S'wark from 69; Hon Prov Can of Papua from 78. *32 Kings Orchard, SE9 5TJ.* (01-850 5747)

KELLY, George Dorrington. St Jo Coll Manit BA 42, LTh 42. **d** 41 **p** 42 Rupld. C of St Mary Magd Winnipeg 41-44; Manitou 44-47; V of St Paul Edmon 47-54; R of H Trin Winnipeg 54-65; Can of Rupld 58-65; R of St Mary Kerrisdale Vanc 65-74; on leave. *14276 Marine Drive, White Rock, BC, Canada.*

KELLY, Godfrey Marmaduke. b 06. **d** 77 **p** 78 Caled. C of St John Masset Dio Caled 77-78; Assoc P from 78. *Box 163, Masset, BC, Canada.*

KELLY, James Ganly Marks. b 16. TCD BA Div Test 39, MA 50. **d** 39 **p** 40 Connor. C of Ballymoney 39-42; Chap RAFVR 42-46; Men in Disp 45; C-in-c of Aghancon w Kilcolman and Seir-Keiran 46-47; C-in-c of Clanabogan 47-49; CF 49-71; R of Siddington w Preston 71-81. *34 Henry Avenue, Rustington, W Sussex.* (Rustington 70635)

KELLY, John Adrian. b 49. Qu Coll Birm 70. **d** 73 Warrington for Liv **p** 74 Liv. C of Formby 73-77; Cler Org Secr C of E Children's Soc for Dios Liv, Blackb and S & M from 78. *C of E Children's Society, Millfield, Powder Works Lane, Melling, Liverpool.*

KELLY, John Bernal. b 35. K Coll Cam BA 57, MA 61. Qu Coll Birm 58. **d** 60 **p** 61 Warrington for Liv. C of Huyton 60-62; Gateshead Fell 64-68; R of Openshaw 68-75; V of Hey Dio Man from 75. *36 Stamford Road, Lees, Oldham, OL4 3LL.* (061-624 1182)

KELLY, John Dickinson. b 42. Univ of Nottm BA (3rd cl Th) 63. Ripon Hall, Ox 63. **d** 65 Penrith for Carl **p** 66 Carl. C of Egremont 65-67; Upperby Carl 67-70; V of Arlecdon 70-72; St Aid Barrow-F 72-79; Milnthorpe Dio Carl from 79. *Vicarage, Milnthorpe, Cumb.* (Milnthorpe 22441)

KELLY, John Henry. b 20. Angl Th Coll BC STh 65. **d** 55 Adel **p** 59 New Westmr. C of Whyalla and Chap Miss to Seamen Whyalla S Austr 55-58; Chap Miss to Seamen N Vancouver 59-64; I of Gibsons 64-68; Birm Area Sec Leprosy Miss from 68; C of St Pet Hall Green 69-70; V of St Mich AA Smethwick 70-78; P-in-c of St Steph Smethwick 72-78; V of St Wulstan Selly Oak 78-80; R of Over Whitacre w Shustoke Dio Birm from 80. *Rectory, Pound Lane, Over Whitacre, Coleshill, Birmingham, B46 2NU.* (Furnace End 81268)

KELLY, Canon John Norman Davidson. b 09. Late Bursar and Scho of Univ of Glas MA (1st cl Cl) and Ferguson Scho (Cl) Scotld 30, Logan Med 31. Late Scho of Qu Coll Ox 1st cl Mods and Hertf Scho 31, BA (1st cl Lit) and Liddon Stud 33, 1st cl Th 34, Sen Denyer and Johnson Scho 36, BD and DD 51. Univ of Glas Hon DD 58. Univ of Wales Hon DD 71. St Stephen Ho Ox 33. **d** 34 Pet **p** 35 Ox. C of St Lawr Northn 34-35; Chap St Edm Hall Ox 35-38; Tutor in Th and Phil 35-51; Fell and Trustee and Vice-Prin 38-51; Prin 51-79; L to Offic Dio Ox from 35; Exam Chap to Bp of Southw 37-64; to Bp of Carl 38-53; to Bp of Chich 39-58; Select Pr Univ of Ox 44-46 and 59; Speaker's Lect in Bibl Stud 45-48; Univ Lect in Patristic Stud from 48; Select Pr Univ of Glas 46; Can and Preb of Wightring in Chich Cathl and Th Lect 48-64; Can and Preb of Highleigh from 64; Sen Chap S Div Woodard Schs 50-65; Select Pr Univ of Cam 53; Proc Conv Univ of Ox 58-64; Chairman of Abp's Comm RC Relns 64-68. *7 Crick Road, Oxford.* (Oxford 512987)

KELLY, Leonard Eric. b 38. Rhodes Univ BA 60. Univ of Nottm MA 64. Kelham Th Coll 61. **d** 69 **p** 70 Les. Hd Master and Chap St Steph Sch Mohales Hoek 70-76; Chap Herschel Sch Claremont and L to Offic Dio Capetn 76-77; C of St Andr and St Mich Cathl Bloemf 77-80; R of St Geo Kroonstad Dio Bloemf from 80. *Church Street, Kroonstad, OFS, S Africa.*

KELLY, Malcolm Bernard. b 46. St Mich AA Llan 72. **d** 74 **p** 75 Ches. C of St Paul Tranmere 74-77; Barnston 78-80; R of Thurstaston Dio Ches from 80. *Thurstaston Rectory, Wirral, Mer, L61 0HQ.* (051-648 1816)

KELLY, Norman James. K Coll Lon Robertson Pri 35, AKC (1st cl), BD and Trench Pri 36. Wycl Hall Ox 36. **d** 36 **p** 37 S'wark. C of St Sav Denmark Pk 36-39; Newhaven 39-40; E Grinstead 40-46; V of Westfield 46-50; W Lyttleton NZ 50-57; V of Canewdon w Paglesham Dio Chelmsf from 57. *Canewdon Vicarage, Rochford, Essex.* (Canewdon 217)

KELLY, Paul Maitland Hillyard. b 24. Ball Coll Ox BA (2nd cl Mod Hist) 50, MA 54. Wells Th Coll 50. **d** 52 **p** 53 Guildf. C of St Martin Epsom 52-57; Min of New Cathl Conv Distr Guildf 57-61; R of Abinger w Coldharbour 61-67; Asst Dir Relig Educn Dio Guildf 61-67; C-in-c of St Pet Preston 67-70; V of Ottershaw 70-77; R of Ickenham Dio Lon from 77. *38 Swakeley's Road, Uxbridge, UB10 8BE.* (71-32803)

KELLY, Roger Farquhar. b 45. ACT ThL 70. Ridley Coll Melb 71. **d** 73 **p** 74 Melb. C of St Steph Belmont 73-75; Shepparton 75-77; P-in-c of St Jas Gt E St Kilda Dio Melb from 77. *435 Inkerman Street, East St Kilda, Vic, Australia 3182.* (527 1017)

KELLY, Stephen Paul. b 55. Keble Coll Ox BA 77. Linc Th Coll 77. **d** 79 **p** 80 Wakef. C of St Mary Illingworth Halifax 82; Knottingley Dio Wakef from 82. *c/o Vicarage, Knottingley, W Yorks, WF11 9AN.*

KELLY, Thomas Aubrey. b 14. Univ of Wales, BA 37. Ripon Hall Ox 37. **d** 39 **p** 40 Swan B. C of Llansamlet 39-41; CF 42-54; C of Ystalyfera 54-58; V of Garthbrengy w Llandefaelog-Fach and Llanfihangel Fechan 58-79. *Address temp unknown.*

KELLY, Canon William. b 25. Late Exhib and Scho of St Jo Coll Dur BA (1st cl Th) 51. Tyndale Hall, Bris 51. **d** 52 **p** 53 Carl. C of St Jo Evang Carl 52-55; V of Flimby 55-64; St Mark Barrow-F 64-67; Hensingham Dio Carl from 67; Hon Can of Carl from 75; RD of Calder from 75; Surr from 76. *St John's Vicarage, Egremont Road, Hensingham, Whitehaven, Cumb.* (Whitehaven 2822)

KELLY, Canon William. b 35. Univ of Dur BA 58. St Cath S Ox Dipl Th 59. Wycl Hall, Ox 58. STh (Lambeth) 75. **d** 60 **p** 61 Carl. C of Walney I 60-66; R of Distington 66-71; V of St Matt Barrow-F 71-81; Dalston w Cumvidock Dio Carl from 81; RD of Furness 77-81; Hon Can of Carl Cathl from 79; Dioc Dir of Ordinands Dio Carl from 81. *Dalston Vicarage, Carlisle, Cumb, CA5 7JF.* (Dalston 710215)

KELLY, William Edward. Late Scho and Exhib of St D Coll Lamp BA 57. St Cath S Ox BA (Th) 59, MA 63. St Steph Ho Ox 57. **d** 60 **p** 61 York. C of South Bank 60-63; Ingoldisthorpe and of Heacham 63-66; Chap RAF 66-82. *3 Drew Close, Bridport, Dorset, DT6 3JG.* (Bridport 56954)

KELLY, William Frederick Paul. b 12. Late Exhib of Ch Ch Ox BA 35, MA 49. Sarum Th Coll 63. **d** 64 Thetford for

Nor **p** 65 Nor. C of Barnham Broom w Bixton, Kimb & Carlton Forehoe 64-68; R of Reepham w Hackford Whitwell and Kerdiston 68-80; P-in-c of Salle 68-72; Thurning w Wood Dalling 80-81. *c/o Reepham Rectory, Norwich, NR10 4RA.* (Reepham 220)

KELLY, William Norman. b 21. **d** 64 **p** 65 Liv. Asst Chap Mersey Miss to Seamen 64-66; C of St Geo Douglas IM 66-69; V of Wingates 69-75; Perm to Offic Dio Man from 76. *16 Brazley Avenue, Horwich, Bolton, Lancs.*

KELLY, William Ralston. b 27. Trin Coll Dub BA (2nd cl Mod) 52, MA 55. Lich Th Coll 52. **d** 54 **p** 55 Ches. C of St Mary Magd Ashton-on-Mersey 54-60; Asst Master Bablake Sch Cov from 60; Perm to Offic Dio Cov 60-64; Dio Ches from 60; LPr Dio Cov from 64. *108 Duncroft Avenue, Coventry, Warws, CV6 2BW.*

KELLY, William Robert. b 28. QUB BSc 57. TCD Div Test 62. **d** 62 **p** 63 Down. C of Shankill Lurgan 62-66; I of Clondehorkey 66-70; Raheny w Coolock 70-75. *Apartado 5152, Lima 18, Peru.*

KELSEY, Henry George. b 1900. Selw Coll Cam 2nd cl Hist Trip pt i 21, BA (2nd Cl Th Trip pt i) 23, MA 26. Ridley Hall Cam 22. **d** 23 **p** 24 S'wark. C of All SS S Lambeth 23-25; W Ham 26-28; St Mich AA Bournemouth 28-30; V of Sutton St Nich (or Lutton) 30-32; St Pet Battersea 32-37; St Paul Barton 37-47; R of Evershot w Frome St Quintin and Melbury Bubb 47-53; C of St Marylebone 55-66. *Tuderly, West Tytherley, Salisbury, Wilts.*

KELSEY, John Robert. b 28. Wycl Coll Tor LTh 78. **d** and **p** 78 Alg. C of W Thunder Bay Dio Alg from 78. *Rosslyn Village, RR 5, Thunder Bay, Ont, Canada, P7C 5M9.*

KELSEY, Michael Ray. b 22. Wycl Hall Ox. **d** 62 **p** 63 Man. C of St Clem Broughton Salford 62-64; V of Ingleby Greenhow 64-68; St Jas Scarborough 68-71; Asst to Gen Sec of United S for Chr Lit 71-74; V of St Jo Evang Blackheath Dio S'wark from 74. *59 Hervey Road, SE3 8BX.* (01-856 4280)

KELSEY, Philip Alwyn. b 03. Hartley Coll Man 28. **d** 42 **p** 43 Carl. C of Crosthwaite 42-44; R of Grafton Flyford w N Piddle 44-47; Earl's Croome w Hill Croome 47-55; R of Strensham 49-55; V of Sibsey 55-61; R of Lydeard St Lawr w Combe Florey 61-65; Kilmington Wilts 65-69. *2 St Martin's Close, Tregurthen Road, Camborne, Cornw.* (Camborne 713948)

KELSEY, Thomas Grisdale. b 12. St Cath S Ox BA (3rd cl Th) 47, MA 52. Wycl Hall, Ox 46. **d** 48 **p** 49 Sheff. C of Goole 48-50; C-in-c of Marr 50-53; Dioc Youth Org 50-53; V of Moxley 53-59; Wednesbury 59-63; Barton-under-Needwood 63-76; Surr from 59; P-in-c of Chebsey 76-80; Ellenhall 76-80. *Address temp unknown.*

KELSHAW, Terence. b 36. Oak Hill Th Coll Dipl Th (Lon) 66. **d** 67 **p** 68 Bris. C of Ch Ch w Em Clifton 67-71; St Jo Bapt Woking 71-73; C-in-c of St Gabr w St Lawr Easton 73-75; V of H Trin (w St Gabr and St Lawr Easton from 75) Bris 73-80; C-in-c of St Luke w Ch Ch Bris 76-80; In Amer Ch. *Trinity Episcopal School for Ministry, 311 Eleventh Street, Ambridge, Penn, USA.*

KELSO, William Thomas Proctor. b 19. TCD BA 41, MA 45, Div Test (2nd cl) 43. **d** 43 **p** 44 Lon. C of St Mary Spring Grove 43-45; Gt Yarmouth (in c of St Luke 45-46; St John from 46) 45-48; V of W Twyford 48-53; St Jo Bapt Isleworth 53-63; R of Blendworth w Chalton and Idsworth 63-70; V of Ascen Balham Hill 70-78; Chap and Tutor Whittington Coll Felbridge from 78. *c/o Whittington College, Felbridge, E Grinstead, Sussex.*

KELWAY, Cyril Cuthbert. b 1898. Wells Th Coll 27. **d** 31 **p** 32 Ex. C of Budleigh Salterton 31-36; R of Shobrooke 36-50; Stockleigh Pomeroy 36-40; RD of Cadbury 48-50; V of Bampton Proper w Bampton Lew 50-57; Beenham Valence 57-81. *Devonia, St James Close, Pangbourne, Reading, Berks.*

KEMBO, Joshua Mulatya. St Paul's Coll Limuru 58. **d** 62 **p** 63 Momb. P Dio Momb 62-65 and from 66; C of Falkirk 65-66. *PO Box 34, Nairobi, Kenya.*

KEMISH, Albert Leonard Samuel. Univ of Qld BA 78. St Francis Coll Brisb 77. **d** and **p** 78 Brisb. C of St Paul Ipswich 78-80; P-in-c of St Lawr Caboolture Dio Brisb from 80. *Rectory, King Street, Caboolture, Queensld, Australia 4515.* (95 1042)

KEMM, William St John. b 39. Univ of Birm BA (2nd cl Th) 62, MA 65. Ridley Hall, Cam 62. **d** 64 **p** 65 Lich. C of Kingswinford 64-68; Hednesford 68-71; V of Hanbury 71-76; R of Berrow and Breane Dio B & W from 76. *Vicarage, Berrow, Burnham-on-Sea, Somt.* (Burnham 782301)

KEMMIS, Charles Maddison. Moore Th Coll Syd 26. **d** 30 **p** 31 Syd. C of Eastwood 31-32; P-in-c of Wilcannia 32-34; St Barn Syd 34-36; R of Balmain 36-38; Bulli 38-44; Emu w Castlereagh and Actg C-in-c of Mulgoa w Luddenham 44-47; R of Belmore w Moorefields 47-52; Naremburn 52-55; Chap R Prince Alfred Hosp Camperdown 55-60; RN Shore Hosp 60-69; L to Offic Dio Syd from 69. *16a Merrigang Street, Bowral, NSW, Australia 2576.* (048-613040)

KEMP, Albert Edward. b 09. K Coll Lon CD 55. **d** 46 **p** 47 Bran. C of Ind Miss Griswold 46-47; C-in-c of Oak Lake 47-49; R of Trin Ch Queb 49-53; Port Whitby 53-56; V of St Andr w St Matthias Islington 56-64; St Paul Bournemouth 64-70; St Sav Bacup 70-73; R of Gaulby w K Norton and L Stretton 73-80; Perm to Offic Dio Sarum from 80. *71 South Street, Warminster, Wilts, BA12 8ED.* (Warminster 216121)

KEMP, Allan. b 43. Oak Hill Th Coll 67. **d** 68 **p** 69 Roch. C of St Jas Tunbridge Wells 68-76; V of St Mary Becontree Dio Chelmsf from 76; RD of Barking from 81. *191 Valence Wood Road, Dagenham, Essex, RM8 3AH.* (01-592 2822)

KEMP, Allan James. Fitzw Ho Cam 2nd cl Hist Trip pt i 47, BA 48, 3rd cl Th Trip pt I, 49. Wells Th Coll 49. **d** 50 Warrington for Liv **p** 51 Liv. C of Speke 50-54; V of Askern 54-58; R of Kalg 58-66; Exam Chap to Bp of Kalg 60-66; Archd of the Goldfields 61-66; C of St Paul Auckld 66-70; Hon C of Grey Lynn Auckld 70-74; Henderson Dio Auckld from 74. *Bethells Road, Waitakere, Auckland, NZ.* (8109-571)

KEMP, Barry. b 48. St Edm Hall Ox BA 70. Linc Th Coll 71. **d** 74 **p** 75 Man. C of Ch Ch Ashton L 74-77; CF from 77. *c/o Ministry of Defence, Bagshot Park, Bagshot, Surrey, GU19 5PL.*

KEMP, Canon Bernard Henry. b 06. St Chad's Coll Dur BA 26, MA Dipl Th 46. **d** 29 **p** 30 S'wark. C of All SS Sydenham 29-32; Asst Missr of CCC Cam Miss Camberwell 32-35; C of St Mich AA Bedford Pk 35-41; CF (EC) 41-46; PC of St Francis Isleworth 46-50; Chap at Beau Bassin Maur 50-54; Quatre Bornes 54-63; Archd of Maur and Exam Chap to Bp of Maur 54-63; Hon Can of Maur from 63; V of St Steph Guernsey 63-81. *Carrefour, La Haye De Poits, Castel, Guernsey, CI.* (Guernsey 56081)

KEMP, Christopher Michael. b 48. AKC and BD 71. St Aug Coll Cant 75. **d** 76 **p** 77 Ches. C of Weaverham 76-79; St Jas Latchford Dio Ches from 79. *15 Fletcher Street, Warrington, Cheshire.*

KEMP, Clive Warren. b 36. Univ of Sheff BSc 60. Clifton Th Coll 62. **d** 64 **p** 65 S'wark. C of Wandsworth 64-67; Normanton 67-71; V of Sandal 71-77. *c/o 218 Doncaster Road, Wakefield, Yorks.* (Wakefield 74120)

KEMP, Preb Cyril Kenneth Alfred. b 01. St Chad's Coll Dur BA 22, Dipl Th 23, MA 26. **d** 24 **p** 25 Chelmsf. C of St Columba Wanstead Slip 24-25; St Barn Walthamstow 25-29; St Mich and St Geo Fulwell 29-34; St Mich AA Bedford Pk 34-35; Min of Wood End Conv Distr Northolt 35-38; V of St Etheldreda Fulham 38-45; R of St Mary Magd Bridgnorth 45-63; C-in-c and Seq of Oldbury 48-63; Surr 48-63; RD of Bridgnorth 59-63; Preb of Heref Cathl 59-74; Preb (Emer) from 74; Proc Conv Heref 59-70; V of Stottesdon 63-67; C-in-c of Farlow 63-67; Bp of Heref Chap for Spiritual Direction 67-72; Perm to Offic Dio Ox from 74. *9 Church View, Freeland, Oxford.* (Freeland 881734)

KEMP, Canon Dudley Fitch. St Jo Coll Manit. **d** 27 **p** 29 Calg. C of Vulcan 27-31; I of Okotoks 31-33; R of Ch Ch Calg 33-44; RD of Calg 40-44; Archd of Calg 43-44; R of St Mary Kerrisdale Vancouver 44-56; Can of New Westmr 51-56; R of St Geo Montr 56-67; Exam Chap to Bp of Montr 61-67; Hon Can of Montr 65-67; Can (Emer) from 67. *2427 Point Grey Road, Vancouver, BC, Canada.*

KEMP, Eric Nelson. b 05. Lich Th Coll 37. **d** 40 **p** 41 Newc T. C of Delaval 40-42; Dallington 42-43; E Midl Area Dir ICF and Publ Pr Dio Derby 43-44; PC of Bradwell 44-47; V of St Mary Somers Town 47-49; R of St Columba-by-the-Castle Edin 49-58; Dir of ICF Dio Edin 49-58; R of St Mark Brantford Ont 58-63; Morton Derbys 63-64; Kimberley 64-66; C of Koot Boundary Reg Par 66-68; in Amer Ch 68-70; C of Hawksworth w Scarrington 70-72; Perm to Offic Dio Derby 73-81; P-in-c of Morley dio Derby 81-82. *1 Ivy Cottage, Bakers Lane, Lea, Matlock, Derbys.*

✠ **KEMP, Right Rev Eric Waldram.** b 15. Ex Coll Ox BA (2nd cl Mod Hist) 36, 2nd cl Th 38, MA 40, BD 44, DD 61. FRHistS 51. St Steph Ho Ox 36. **d** 39 **p** 40 Win. C of St Luke Southampton 39-41; Libr of Pusey Ho Ox 41-46; Chap Ch Ch Ox 43-46; Chap, Fell and Lect of Ex Coll Ox 46-69; L to Offic Dio Ox 41-69; Exam Chap to Bp of Mon 42-45; to Bp of S'wark 46-50; to Bp of St Alb 46-69; to Bp of Ex 49-69; to Bp of Linc 50-69; Proc Conv Univ of Ox 49-69; Can and Preb of Linc Cathl from 52; Lect in Div in Lich Cathl 56; Bampton Lect Univ of Ox 60; Commiss St John's 66-80; Chap to HM the Queen 67-69; Dean of Worc 69-74; Exam Chap to Bp of Worc 69-74; Cons Ld Bp of Chich in S'wark Cathl 23 Oct 74 by Abp of Cant; Bps of Lon, Chelmsf, Derby, Guildf, Leic, Nor, Portsm, S'wark, St E, Truro and Worc; Bps Suffr of Fulham and Gibr, Horsham, Kingston T, Lewes, Woolwich and Grimsby; and Abp of Utrecht and Bp of Haarlem (Old

Catholic Ch) and others. *The Palace, Chichester, Sussex.* (Chichester 782161)

KEMP, Ernest Edward. b 03. SOC. **d** 68 **p** 69 S'wark. C of Streatham Dio S'wark from 68. *55 Becmead Avenue, SW16.* (01-769 5614)

KEMP, Geoffrey Bernard. b 20. ALCD 42. Univ of Lon BD 43. **d** 43 **p** 44 Chelmsf. C of All SS Leyton 43-46; St Mary Woodford 46-49; V of St Laur Barkingside 49-60; St Barn Hadleigh 60-78; Navestock Dio Chelmsf from 79; R of Kelvedon Hatch Dio Chelmsf from 79. *Rectory, Church Road, Kelvedon Hatch, Brentwood, Essex.* (Coxtie Green 72466)

KEMP, Jack Noel. b 14. Univ of Lon BA (1st cl Cl) 36. MA 38. Wycl Hall, Ox 55. **d** 55 **p** 56 Birm. C of St Jo Bapt Harborne 55-58; PC of St Edm Tyseley Birm 58-64; V of St Mary w St Paul Cray 64-68; Four Elms 68-80; Lect Brasted 67-74; Surr 77-80. *16 Church Street, Whitstable, Kent, CT5 1PJ.* (Whitstable 265379)

KEMP, Jack Raymond King. St Jo Coll Morpeth, ACT ThL 36. **d** 37 **p** 38 Newc. C of Wyong 37-39; E Maitland 39-40; St Pet Hamilton 40-41; R of Jerry's Plains 41-46; Gundy 46-50; Paterson 50-52; Nimbin 52-55; Maclean 55-60; Moong 60-68; L to Offic Dio Syd from 69. *42 Brown Street, Newtown, NSW 2042, Australia.*

KEMP, John Graham Edwin. b 29. Univ of Bris BA (2nd cl Phil) 51. BD (Lon) 65. Wells Th Coll 63. **d** 65 **p** 66 Ox. C of St Luke Maidenhead 65-70; R of Rotherfield Greys 70-78; V of Highmore 70-78; P-in-c of Taplow Dio Ox from 78; Dep Dir Tr Scheme for NSM Dio Ox from 78. *Taplow Rectory, Maidenhead, Berks.* (Burnham 61182)

KEMP, John Robert Deverall. b 42. City Univ Lon BSc (1st Cl) 65. BD (Lon) 69. Oak Hill Th Coll 66. **d** 70 **p** 71 Kens for Lon. C of Ch Ch Fulham 70-73; Widford 73-79; P-in-c of St Geo Thundersley Dio Chelmsf from 79. *St George's Vicarage, Rushbottom Lane, Benfleet, SS7 4DN.* (S Benfleet 2088)

KEMP, Michael Rouse. b 36. Called to Bar Gray's Inn 59. Sarum Wells Th Coll 70. **d** 72 **p** 73 Kens for Lon. C of H Trin Brompton w Brompton Chap 72-76; V of St Timothy Crookes Sheff 76-81; Norton Woodseats City and Dio Sheff from 81. *St Chad's Vicarage, Linden Avenue, Woodseats, Sheffield, S8 0GA.* (Sheff 745086)

KEMP, Peter Scott. Univ of Syd BA 62, MEducn 71, MA 76. Moore Th Coll Syd ACT ThL 60. **d** 62 **p** 63 Syd. C of St Paul Wahroonga 63-65; Asst Chap Barker Coll Hornsby 63-67; Chap Trin Gr Sch Sumner Hill 69-76; R of Sutherland Dio Syd from 76. *43a Belmont Street, Sutherland, NSW, Australia 2232.* (521-4314)

KEMP, William Frederick. b 13. St Aug Coll Cant 38. **d** 40 **p** 41 Lich. C of Wolverhampton 40-46; St Steph Norbury Lon 46-51; Stoke-on-Trent (in c of St Paul) 51-53; PC of Gosberton Clough 53-64; R of Denton w Wootton and Swingfield 64-79; Hon Min Can Cant Cathl from 80. *7 Burgate House, Burgate, Canterbury, Kent.*

KEMP-WELCH, Noel Henry. b 10. Late Choral Scho of K Coll Cam 3rd cl Hist Trip pt i 31, BA (3rd cl Th Trip pt ii) 33, MA 37. Cudd Coll 33. **d** 35 **p** 36 Liv. C of St Dunstan Edge Hill 35-37; Chap K Coll Cam 37-40; C of St Mich Tilehurst 40-45; V of Chaddleworth w Woolley 45-47; Fawley 45-47; PC of St Mich Tenbury and Warden of St Mich Coll Tenbury 47-56; Chap St Pet Sch York 56-76. *Moor Farm, Sutton Road, Wigginton, York, YO3 8RB.*

KEMPE, Albert Edward. b 09 K Coll Lon CD 55. **d** 46 **p** 47 Bran. C of Ind Miss Griswold 46-47; C-in-c of Oak Lake 47-49; R of Trin Ch Queb 49-53; Port Whitby 53-56; V of St Andr w St Matthias Islington 56-64; St Paul Bournemouth 64-70; St Sav Bacup 70-73; R of Gaulby w K Norton and L Stretton 73-80; Perm to Offic Dio Sarum from 80. *71 South Street, Warminster, Wilts, BA12 8ED.* (Warminster 216121)

KEMPSON, Ven Norman Clifford. St Jo Coll Morpeth ACT ThL 53. **d** 53 **p** 55 Adel. C of Mt Gambier 53-56; Cummins 56-60; R of Kapunda 60-63; Dir of Promotion Dio Bath 63-66; P-in-c of Eliz 66-73; R of Orange Dio Bath from 73; Archd of Marsden from 74. *Rectory, Anson Street, Orange, NSW, Australia 2800.* (62-1623)

KEMPSTER, Robert Alec. b 29. Selw Coll Cam BA 53, MA 57. Coll of Resurr Mirfield 53. **d** 55 **p** 56 Lon. C of St Barn W Hackney 55-57; PV of S'wark Cathl and C-in-c of All H S'wark 57-60; C-in-c of All H Conv Distr S'wark 60-70; Chap Guy's Hosp Lon 70-81; Nat Hosp for Nervous Diseases Lon from 81. *Hospital for Nervous Diseases, Queen Square, WC1 3BG.* (01-837 3611)

KEMPTHORNE, Renatus. b 39. Wadh Coll Ox BA (2nd cl Phil Pol and Econ) 60, Dipl Th 61, MA 64. Wycl Hall Ox 60. **d** 62 Bp McKie for Cov **p** 63 Cov. C of Stoke Cov 62-65; Lect St Jo Coll Auckld 65-68; Perm to Offic Dio Auckld 65-68; R of Wytham 68-75; L to Offic Dio Linc from 75; Chap Bp Grosseteste Coll Linc from 75; Sen Lect from 80; Hon Sec Linc Coun of Chs 77-81. *Chaplain's House, Bishop Grosseteste College, Lincoln, LN1 3DY.* (Linc 27347)

KEMSLEY, Douglas Sinclair. Univ of Melb BSc 49, MSc 54. Univ of W Austr BA 57. Austr Nat Univ PhD 60. Qu Coll Ox BA 61, MA 65. **d** 57 **p** 59 C & Goulb. C of St Jo Bapt Canberra 57-59; St Mary Virg Ox 59-61; in Amer Ch 61-62; C of St Jo Bapt Canberra 62-64; Res Tutor St Mark's Colleg Libr Canberra 64-66. *c/o University of NSW, PO Box 1, Kensington, NSW 2033, Australia.*

KENDAL, Gordon McGregor. b 46. Univ of Dundee MA 70. Mansfield Coll Ox BA 72. BA (Lon) 73. PhD (Lon) 79. Edin Th Coll 72. **d** 74 Dorchester for Ox **p** 75 Reading for Ox. C of Bracknell 74-77; All SS Wokingham 77-79; Chap Linc Coll Ox from 79. *Lincoln College, Oxford, OX1 3DR.* (Oxford 48098)

KENDAL, Stephen. b 35. Univ of Leeds BA (3rd cl Phil and Hist) 59. Coll of Resurr Mirfield. **d** 61 **p** 62 Newc T. C of Seaton Hirst 61-63; St Geo Jesmond Newc T 63-66; All SS Gosforth (in c of St Hugh Regent Farm Estate) 66-70; Industr Chap Dio Llan 70-78; Chap Northumb Industr Miss Dio Dur from 78. *Pierremont, Wallace Street, Houghton-le-Spring, T & W, DH4 5BQ.*

KENDALL, Canon Bartholomew John. b 09. Late Wightwick Scho of Pemb Coll Ox BA 32. Wycl Hall, Ox 33. **d** 35 **p** 36 Sheff. C of St John Pk Sheff 35-38; St Mary Magd Peckham 38-42; St Jas W Streatham 42-45; St Sav Battersea Pk 45-48; V of St Jude S'wark (w St Paul from 57) 48-75; Hon Can of S'wark 75; Can (Emer) from 75. *26 Fairview Road, Hungerford, Berks, RG17 0BT.* (048-86 2264)

KENDALL, Canon Cosmo Norman. b 13. Keble Coll Ox BA 38, MA 42. Cudd Coll 38. **d** 39 **p** 40 Cant. C of St Greg Gt Cant 39-42; Chap Cranbrook Sch 42-47; Prec of Newc T Cathl and Hd Master Choir Sch Newc T 47-49; R of Buxhall w Shelland Dio St E from 49; C-in-c of Brettenham 64-71; Hd Master Buxhall Prep Sch for Boys 50-54; Hon Can of St E Cathl from 77. *Buxhall Rectory, Stowmarket, Suff.* (Rattlesden 236)

KENDALL, Edgar Donald. Qu Th Coll Ont 49. St Chad's Coll Dur LTh 55, BA 56. MA 61. **d** 52 Newfld. I of Cow Head 52-54; C of St Thos St John's Newfld 56-60; Corner Brook 60-62; Vice-Prin Qu Coll St John's Newfld 62-64. *88 Newcastle Street, Dartmouth, NS, Canada.*

KENDALL, Edward Oliver Vaughan. b 33. Univ of Dur BA 59. Ridley Hall Cam. **d** 61 **p** 62 Bris. C of Corsham 61-64; St Mary Portsea 64-67; Asst Chap HM Pris Pentonville 67-68; Chap HM Borstal Portland 68-71; L to Offic Dio Bradf from 71. *Aldby House, Stackhouse, Settle, Yorks.* (Settle 3555)

KENDALL, Frank. b 40. CCC BA 62, MA 68. SOC 74. **d** 74 S'wark **p** 75 S'wark for Swan B. Hon C of Lingfield Dio S'wark 74-75; and from 78; Sketty 75-78. *Noel Villa, Mount Pleasant Road, Lingfield, Surrey, RH7 6BH.* (Lingfield 832414)

KENDALL, George Vincent. b 21. Edin Th Coll 46. **d** 48 **p** 49 Brech. C of Lochee 48-51; Good Shepherd Hillington Glas 51-53; P-in-c of St Serf Shettleston Glas 53-56; C-in-c of All SS Gretna and P-in-c of All SS Langholm Dio Glas from 56. *All Saints' Parsonage, Gretna, via Carlisle, CA6 5DH.* (Gretna 268)

KENDALL, Gordon Sydney. b 41. **d** 72 **p** 74 Stepney for Lon. C of St Mark Vic Pk Dio Lon from 72. *93 Cadogan Terrace, E9 5HT.* (01-985 7710)

KENDELL, George Douglas Foster. Univ Coll Tor BA 26, MA 28. **d** and **p** 40 Montr. C of St Matthias Westmount 40-41; P-in-c of St Thos Montr 41-43; CF (Canad) 43-46; I of St Sav Victoria West 46-62; Chap to Bp of BC 47-62; L to Offic Dio BC from 63. *2521 Sinclair Road, Victoria, BC, Canada.*

KENDRA, Kenneth Ernest. Univ of Leeds BA 41, MA 48. OBE 66. Linc Th Coll 40. **d** 42 Hull for York **p** 43 York. C of Pocklington and Kilnwick Percy 42-46; CF 46-71; Hon Chap to HM the Queen 70-71; V of Lee-on-the-Solent 71-80; RD of Alverstoke 77-79. *Highfields, Castle Hill Lane, Mere, Warminster, Wilts, BA12 6JB.* (Mere 860823)

KENDRA, Neil Stuart. b 46. Univ of Leeds, BA (Th) 67. Univ of Bradf MSc 80. Linc Th Coll 67. **d** 69 Warrington for Liv **p** 70 Liv. C of Allerton 69-72; Youth Worker Ripon 73-75; Youth Adv Dio Ripon 75-77; Sen Lect Ilkley Coll from 77. *77 Leeds Road, Ilkley, W Yorks.*

KENDREW, Geoffrey David. b 42. K Coll Lon and Warm BD and AKC 66. **d** 67 **p** 68 Guildf. C of St Thos-on-the-Bourne 67-70; Haslemere 70-76; V of St Barn City and Dio Derby from 76. *122 Radbourne Street, Derby.* (Derby 42553)

KENDRICK, Canon Desmond Max. b 22. Univ of Leeds, BA 47. Wycl Hall, Ox 50. **d** 52 **p** 53 Man. C of St Mark Glodwick Oldham 52-54; V of St Clem and Chap Leeds Road Hosp Bradf 54-76; RD of Bradf 63-73; Hon Can of Bradf from 64; V of Otley Dio Bradf from 76. *Vicarage, Otley, W Yorks, LS21 3HR.* (Otley 462240)

KENDRICK, Ven Grover Edward. Bp's Univ Lennox 55. **d** and **p** 56 Queb. I of Inverness 56-59; R of Coaticook 59-64;

Wakeham Dio Queb from 64; Can of Queb 72-78; Archd of Gaspé from 78. *Box 525, Gaspé, PQ, Canada.*

KENNA, William Keith. Trin Coll Melb 20. Ridley Coll Melb 23. **d** 25 **p** 26 Gippsld. C of Yarragon 25-27; Warragul 27-28; Lang Lang 28-29; R of Elmore 30-34; Perm to Offic Dio Bend 34-38; Dio Melb 38-48; C of E Malvern 47; Asst Sec CMS 47; I of Em w St Gabr East Oakleigh 48-49; Min of Mitcham 52-54; Emerald 57-58; Perm to Offic Dio Melb 54-57 and from 59. *42 Mullum Road, Ringwood, Vic, Australia 3134.* (03-870 8921)

KENNABY, Very Rev Noel Martin. b 05. Qu Coll Cam BA 28, MA 32. Westcott Ho Cam. **d** 29 **p** 30 Guildf. C of Epsom 29-32; Scarborough (in c of Ch Ch) 32-36; V of St Andr Handsworth 36-42; Tynemouth 42-47; Surr 42-62; RD of Tynemouth 43-47; Provost and V of Newc T Cathl 47-62; RD of Newc T 47-62; Commiss Ja 50-70; Sen Chap to Abp of Cant 62-64; Hon Can of Newc T 62-64; Dean and R of Cathl and Abbey Ch St Alb 64-73; Dean (Emer) from 73. *60 Alexandra Road, Bridport, Dorset.*

KENNARD, Ronald Malcolm. b 15. FCA 60. **d** 75 Chich **p** 76 Horsham for Chich. Hon C of H Trin Cuckfield 75-79; Elstead w Didling and Treyford Dio Chich from 79. *Elsted Rectory, Midhurst, W Sussex.* (Harting 231)

KENNAUGH, Canon Thomas Edward. b 17. Keble Coll Ox BA 40, MA 45. Dipl Th 41. Bp's Coll Cheshunt. **d** 41 **p** 42 Carl. C of St Paul Newbarns w Hawcoat Barrow-F 41-47; Min of St Herbert Distr Ch Currock Carl 47-52; R of H Innoc Fallowfield 52-68; Kirkby Thore w Temple Sowerby 68-73; Flixton Dio Man from 73; RD of Stretford from 77; Hon Can of Man from 79. *Rectory, Flixton, Manchester, M31 3HR.* (061-748 2884)

KENNAWAY, Mark Bevan. b 20. Wycl Hall Ox 69. **d** 70 **p** 71 Truro. C of Liskeard 70-72; P-in-c of Boconnoc w Bradoc 72-74; R of Cardynham and Warleggan Dio Truro from 74; P-in-c of Helland Dio Truro from 81. *Rectory, Cardynham, Bodmin, Cornw.* (Cardynham 302)

KENNEDY, Anthony Reeves. b 32. Roch Th Coll 64. Dipl Th (Lon) 67. **d** 67 **p** 68 Heref. C of Ross-on-Wye 67-69; Marfleet Dio York 69-71; Team V 72-76; V of Lightwater Dio Guildf from 76. *Vicarage, Broadway Road, Lightwater, Surrey, GU18 5SJ.* (Bagshot 72270)

KENNEDY, Treas Aubrey Coppleston. b 09. Late Sizar and Exhib of Trin Coll Dub Sen Exhib 30, BA (2nd cl Mod) 32. MA 39. **d** 34 **p** 35 Dub. C of Bray 34-44; C-in-c of Donabate 44-46; R 46-54; RD of Garristown 52-62; Malahide 59-62; Finglas 62-69; Killiney 69-77; R of St John Monkstown Dio Dub from 54; Can of Ch Ch Cathl Dub from 70; Preb from 74; Treas from 79. *8 Lower Mounttown Road, Dun Laoghaire, Co Dublin, Irish Republic.* (Dublin 807419)

KENNEDY, Brian McMahon. b 11. TCD BA 33, MA 38. **d** 34 **p** 35 Dub. C of Harold's Cross 34-38; Ch Ch Leeson Pk Dub 38-41; Min Can of St Patr Cathl Dub 39-41; I of Kiltegan and C-in-c of Stratford-on-Slaney 41-43; Chap RNVR 43-46; RN 46-61; Chap Miss to Seamen Dub 61-68; Cork from 68; I of Clonmel w Rushbrooke Dio Cloyne from 68; RD of Midleton 75-80. *Rectory, Cobh, Co Cork, Irish Republic.* (Cork 811790)

KENNEDY, David George. b 46. Univ of Hull BEducn 71, MA 76. Linc Th Coll 77. **d** 79 **p** 80 Linc. C of St Faith City and Dio Linc from 79. *160 West Parade, Lincoln.*

KENNEDY, David John. b 57. St Jo Coll Dur BA (Th) 78. St Jo Coll Nottm 79. **d** 81 Dur. C of Tudhoe Grange Dio Dur from 81. *27 Lindisfarne Road, Tudhoe Grange, Spennymoor, Co Durham, DL16 6EJ.*

KENNEDY, Francis Robert Dixon. b 14. Wadh Coll Ox BA (3rd cl Th) 38, MA 43. Wycl Hall Ox 43. **d** 43 **p** 44 Worc. C of Gt Malvern 43-47; Hd Master Lyttelton Sch Malvern 44-47; C of H Trin Stroud 48-49; Chap Shoreham Gr Sch and L to Offic Dio Chich 49-71; R of Caythorpe 71-81. *5 Chantry Road, Tarring, Worthing, W Sussex.*

KENNEDY, Hugh Dodgson. b 20. Ex Coll Ox BA 41, MA 45. Linc Th Coll 45. **d** 47 **p** 48 Swan B. C of St Gabr (in c of St Aug from 48) Swansea 47-49; Buxton (in c of St Mary) 50-53; V of Methwold 53-55; Chap Leavesden Hosp Group 55-69; V of Abbots Langley 69-79; R of Bramfield w Stapleford and Waterford Dio St Alb from 79. *Stapleford Rectory, Hertford, SG14 3NB.* (Hertford 551560)

KENNEDY, James Ernest. b 20. Trin Coll Dub BA 45, Div Test (2nd cl) 46, MA 51. **d** 46 **p** 47 Oss. C of Kilnamanagh U 46-48; Ahogill 48; C-in-c of Portglenone 48-51; R 51-60; I of Agherton 60-67; R of Errigal and Desertoghill 67-81. *52 Prospect Road, Portstewart, Co Derry, N Ireland.* (Portstewart 3434)

KENNEDY, John Wilkinson. b 20. Trin Coll Dub BA (Resp) 44, LLB 44, MA 50. Qu Coll Birm. **d** 50 **p** 51 Sheff. Succr of Sheff Cathl 50-52; Prec and Chap 52-55; V of Thurcroft 55-60; St Jas Doncaster 60-70; Anlaby 70-80; Cloughton Dio York from 80; P-in-c of Hackness w Harwood Dale Dio York from 81. *Cloughton Vicarage, Scarborough, N Yorks.* (Scarborough 870270)

KENNEDY, Michael Charles. b 39. Trin Coll Dub BA (2nd cl Hebr and Or Lang) and Div Test (1st cl) 63. **d** 63 **p** 64 Arm. C of Drumglass 63-66; I of Lisnadill Dio Arm from 66; Kildarton Dio Arm from 66; Exam Chap to Abp of Arm from 73; Warden of Dioc Guild of Lay Readers Dio Arm from 74; Hon V Cho of St Patr Cathl Arm from 75; Dom Chap to Abp of Arm from 80. *60 Newtownhamilton Road, Armagh, BT60 2PW, N Ireland.* (Armagh 52 3630)

KENNEDY, Robert Brock. Univ of Tor BASc 49. Hur Coll 62. **d** 64 Alg for Hur. L to Offic Dio Hur 64-67. *503 Colborne Street, London, Ont., Canada.*

KENNEDY, Ross Melville. b 44. BD (Lon) 77. Moore Th Coll Syd ACT ThL 76. **d** 77 Bp Dain for Syd **p** 77 Syd. C of S Andr Sans Souci 77-79; St Matt Manly 79-81; R of McCallum's Hill Dio Syd from 79. *129 Moorefields Road, Kinsgrove, NSW, Australia 2208.*

KENNEDY, Walter Howard Frere. Univ of Tor BA 46, LLB 48. Bp's Univ Lennox LST 56. Gen Synod BD 63. **d** 55 Queb **p** 56 Tor. C of St Pet Sherbrooke 56-57; St Geo Willowdale Tor 57-61; Ch Ch Cathl Montr 61-63; I of N Clarendon 63-68; Aylwin-River Desert 68-71; Fitzroy Harbour 71-78; on leave. *Box 660, Bracebridge, Ont, Canada.*

KENNEDY, William Edmund. QUB BA (3rd cl Cl) 43. Late Exhib of Univ of Dub BA and Bibl Gr Pri 45. Trin Coll Dub MA 48. **d** 45 **p** 46 Down. C of Seagoe 45-48; St Jude Ballynafeigh Belfast 48-57; I of Ballyculter w Kelclief Dio Down from 57; RD of Lecale E (w Lecale W from 80) from 71. *Rectory, Strangford, Co Down, N Ireland.*

KENNEDY-BELL, Preb Winnington Douglas. b 15. Keble Coll Ox BA (3rd cl Th) 38, MA 42. Wells Th Coll 38. **d** 39 **p** 40 S'wark. C of St Mich E Wickham 39-41; St Mary Richmond 41-44; St Martin-in-the-Fields 44-48; Overseas Relig Broadcasting Organizer BBC 48-75; Reader at Temple Ch Lon from 55; Preb of St Paul's Cathl Lon from 73; Dep P in Ord to HM the Queen from 76. *1 Victoria Cottages, Kew Gardens, Surrey, TW9 3NW.*

KENNEN, Harry. b 16. DSC 45. Univ of Sheff BA 38. Bps' Coll Cheshunt 38. **d** 40 **p** 41 Sheff. C of Rotherham 40-43; Chap RNVR 43-47; C of Stocksbridge (in c of Deepcar) 47-49; V of Whitgift w Adlingfleet 49-52; V of Stocksbridge 52-59; Chap W Buckland Sch from 59; C of E Buckland 60-63; R of Filleigh w E Buckland 63-70; R of W Buckland 64-70; V of Whitchurch 70-77; RD of Tavistock 74-77; R of Highweek w Abbotsbury and Teigngrace 77-81; L to Offic Dio Ex from 81. *11 Deer Park Crescent, Tavistock, Devon.* (Tavistock 2466)

KENNETT-ORPWOOD, Jason Robert. b 55. St Mich AA Coll Llan Dipl Th 77. **d** 78 Mon. Chap of Cathl Ch of St Wooles Newport Dio Mon from 78. *10 Clifton Road, Newport, Gwent, NPT 4EW.* (0633 64805)

KENNEY, Dixon. St Mich Th Coll Crafers. **d** 64 **p** 65 Graft. C of Coff's Harbour 64-66; Casino 66-67; St Anne Strathfield 67-70; St Matt Mundingburra Townsville 70-73; P-in-c of Tully 73-74; C of Gordonvale 74-77; Wodonga 77-78; Chap Avalon Commun Dio Melb 79-81. *Avalon Community, Lara, Vic, Australia 3212.*

KENNEY, Peter. b 50. Univ of Edin BD 75. Edin Th Coll 73. **d** 76 **p** 77 Newc T. C of St Geo Cullercoats 76-81; Team V of Whorlton Dio Newc T from 81. *St Wilfrid's House, Trevelyan Drive, Newbiggin Hall Estate, Newcastle-on-Tyne.*

KENNING, Michael Stephen. b 47. St Chad Coll Dur BA 68. Westcott Ho Cam 69. **d** 71 **p** 72 Cant. C of Hythe 71-75; Team V of Bow Lon 75-77; P-in-c of St Alb W Leigh Havant 77-81; V of Lee-on-the-Solent Dio Portsm from 81. *Vicarage, Victoria Square, Lee-on-the-Solent, Hants, PO13 9NF.* (Lee 550269)

KENNON, Marjorie Alice. b 19. Angl Women's Tr Coll Tor STh 54. **d** 71 **p** 77 Bran. C-in-c of Kelwood & McCreary 71-75; Carberry Dio Bran from 75. *Box 646, Carberry, Manit, R0K 0H0, Canada.*

KENNY, Anthony John. St Mich Th Coll Crafers 61. **d** 66 **p** 67 Melb. C of Em Oakleigh 66-68; St Geo Malvern 68-69; Perm to Offic Dio Melb from 70. *3/18 Peace Street, Glen Irish, Vic 3146, Australia.*

KENNY, Charles John. b 39. QUB BA 61, MEd 78. TCD Div Test 69. **d** 69 **p** 70 Connor. C of St Paul Belf 69-71; Asst Master Grosvenor High Sch Belf from 71. *45 Deramore Drive, Belfast, BT9 5JS.*

KENNY, Charles William. Ridley Coll Melb 62. ACT ThL 64, Th Scho 67. **d** 64 **p** 65 Gippsld. Hon C of Yarralumba 64; C of St Luke Deakin 64-65; Warragul 65-66; Leongatha 66-67; V of Cann River 67-71; C of H Cross Canberra 71-73; R of Neerim S 73-75; I of St John Sorrento Dio Melb from 75. *St John's Vicarage, Sorrento, Vic, Australia 3943.* (059-84 2027)

KENNY, Francis Raymond. ACT ThDip 69. St Jo Coll Morpeth 62. **d** 63 **p** 64 Melb. C of St John Camberwell 63-65;

Min of Bellarine Par Distr 65-70 I of Em Oakleigh 70-78; E Ringwood Dio Melb from 78. *49 Patterson Street, East Ringwood, Vic, Australia 3135.* (870 1000)

KENNY, Frederic William Bouvier. b 30. Trin Coll Dub BA (Hist and Pol Sc 3rd cl Mod) 53, H Dipl Educn 54, Div Test (2nd cl) and MA 56. **d** 56 **p** 57 Down. C of Ballymacarrett 56-58; St John Blackpool 58-61; V of St Paul Preston 61-66; Chap Preston R Infirm 61-66; Youth Adv CMS Lon 66-70; Youth Sec HCMS Ireland 70-75; R of St Clem Belf 75-80; V of St Cuthb Preston Dio Blackb from 80. *St Cuthbert's Vicarage, Black Bull Lane, Fulwood, Preston, Lancs.* (Preston 717346)

KENNY, Thomas Patrick Francis. b 49. Univ Coll Cardiff Dipl Th 76. St Mich AA Llan 73. **d** 76 **p** 77 Man. C of St Chad Rochdale 76-80; R of St Geo Abbey Hey Gorton Dio Man from 80. *Rectory, Abbey Hey, Gorton, Manchester, M18 8RB.* (061-223 1624)

KENNY, Thomas Percival Robert. b 27. Trin Coll Dub BA 48, Div Test 49, MA 52. **d** 50 **p** 51 Arm. C of Drumglass 50-53; R of Derrynoose w Middletown 53-56; Aghavilly and Derrynoose 56-62; I of St Sav Portadown 62-66; Magherafelt 66-74; Derryloran Dio Arm from 74. *13 Loy Street, Cookstown, Co Tyrone, N Ireland, BT80 8PZ.* (Cookstown 62261)

KENRICK, Kenneth David Norman. b 44. Ripon Hall Ox 70. **d** 77 Ches **p** 78 Stockport for Ches. C of St Geo Stockport Dio Ches from 77. *31 Heath Road, Cale Green, Stockport, SK2 6JJ.* (061-483 3350)

KENSINGTON, Lord Bishop Suffragan of. *See* Santer, Right Rev Mark.

KENT, Eric Deacon. Trin Coll Melb MA 23. ACT ThL 23. **d** 23 **p** 24 Melb. C of S Sassafras 23-24; St John E Malvern 24-27; Chap of Brighton Gr Sch Melb 27-34; C of Fairfield 34; Min of Moonee Ponds 34-41; I of Clifton Hill 41-42; Asst Chap C of E Gr Sch Geelong 42-45; C of Toorak 45-47; V of Sorrento 47-69; Perm to Offic Dio Melb from 69. *40 Rosalind Street, Blackburn, Vic, Australia 3130.* (03-878 0063)

KENT, Frederick Walter George. b 11. Lon Coll Div 44. **d** 46 **p** 47 S'wark. C of Morden 46-49; Reigate 49-52; R of Meckering W Austr 52-55; V of Westcombe Pk 55-65; Org Sec CECS Dios Cant Chich and Roch 65-76; Perm to Offic Dio Roch from 80. *36 Swan Street, West Malling, Maidstone, Kent, ME19 6LP.* (W Malling 842334)

KENT, Canon John Aldwyn Pelham. b 14. Trin Hall Cam 1st cl Nat Sc Trip pt i 35, BA (3rd cl Nat Sc Trip pt ii) 36, MA 40. Westcott Ho Cam 39. **d** 41 **p** 42 Win. C of Eastleigh 41-43; CF 43-48; Chap Sea School Aberdovey 48-49; Dom Chap to Abp of York 49-52; Hon Chap 52-55; LPr Dio York 49-52; V of Abbey Ch of St Mary and St German Selby 52-77; Surr from 52; RD of Selby 67-71; Can and Preb of York Minster from 76. *Clachan Geala, Duror, Appin, Argyll.*

KENT, Keith Meredith. b 32. St Aid Coll 55. Dipl Th (Lon) 57. **d** 58 Blackb **p** 58 Burnley for Blackb. C of Fulwood 58-60; St Chrys Everton 60-62; Litherland 64-68; C-in-c of St Polycarp Everton 68-74; V of All SS Springwood 74-78; St D Carr Mill Dio Liv from 78. *Vicarage, Eskdale Avenue, Carr Mill, St Helens, Mer, WA11 7EN.* (74-32330)

KENT, Leonard Owen. b 07. **d** 45 **p** 46 Chelmsf. Chap to Deaf and Dumb Dio Chelmsf 45-50; Croydon Distr 50-51; W Distr from 51; C-in-c of St Sav Old Oak Road Acton 52-57; Chap St Barn Ch for Deaf and Dumb Lewisham 57-76; Perm to Offic Dio Chelmsf from 80. *23 Royston Avenue, Prittlewell, Southend-on-Sea, Essex.*

KENT, Michael Patrick. b 27. St Edm Hall Ox BA 50, MA 52. Cudd Coll 50. **d** 52 Jarrow for Dur **p** 53 Dur. C of St Aid W Hartlepool 52-57; C-in-c of St Thos Conv Distr Pennywell Bp Wearmouth 57-70; V of Cockerton Dio Dur from 70; RD of Darlington from 79. *Cockerton Vicarage, Darlington, Co Durham, DL3 9EX.* (Darlington 63705)

KENT, Neville. b 40. Sarum Wells Th Coll 70. **d** 72 **p** 73 B & W. C of St Andr Taunton 72-77; R of Bradford w Oake, Hillfarrance and Heathfield Dio B & W from 77. *Bradford-on-Tone Rectory, Taunton, Somt.* (B-o-T 423)

KENT, Richard Hugh. b 38. Worc Coll Ox BA (3rd cl Th) 61, MA 65. Chich Th Coll 61. **d** 63 Bp McKie for Cov **p** 64 Cov. C of All SS Warw 63-66; Finham 66-70; V of Parkend 70-75; St Aldate City and Dio Glouc from 75. *St Aldate's Vicarage, Finlay Road, Gloucester.* (Glouc 23906)

KENT, Roger Anthony Edward. b 56. Univ of Kent at Cant BA (Th) 78. St Steph Ho Ox 79. **d** 81 St E. C of All H Ipswich Dio St E from 81. *43 Clapgate Lane, Ipswich, Suffolk, IP3 0RB.*

KENT, Ronald. b 21. St Jo Coll Dur BA (2nd cl Th) 43, MA 46. **d** 45 **p** 46 Dur. C of Norton 45-50; PC of Cassop w Quarrington 50-55; V of St Luke Darlington 55-65; Chap to Coll of Ripon and York St John 65-76; Lect from 77. *c/o The College, College Road, Ripon, N Yorks, HG4 2QX.* (Ripon 2691)

KENT, Vernon Glen. b 43. Dalhousie Univ BA 66. Univ of NB MA 69. **d** 70 NS. C of St Mary's Glace Bay 70-72; R of Port Morien Dio NS from 72. *Rectory, Port Morien, NS, Canada.* (737-2471)

KENTIGERN-FOX, William Poyntere Kentigern. b 38. K Coll Lon and Warm AKC 63. **d** 64 **p** 65 Lon. C of Potters Bar 64-67; C-in-c of St Pet Page Green Tottenham 67-70; R of Barrowden w Wakerley (w S Luffenham from 77) 70-79; P-in-c of Duddington w Tixover 70-76; S Luffenham 75-77; R of Byfield w Boddington Dio Pet from 79. *Byfield Rectory, Daventry, Northants, NN11 6XN.* (Byfield 60204)

KENWARD, Roger Nelson. b 34. Selw Coll Cam 3rd cl Engl Trip pt i 57, BA (3rd cl Th Trip pt i) 58, MA 62. Ripon Hall Ox 58. **d** 60 **p** 61 Lon. C of St Jas Paddington 60-63; Chap RAF from 64; Asst Chap-in-Chief from 82. *c/o Ministry of Defence, Adastral House, WC1.*

KENWARD, Ven Stephen Bertram. Bp's Univ Lennox BA 50. **d** 50 **p** 51 Ott. I of Newington 50-52; Combermere 52-57; R of N Gower 57-64; Good Shepherd Cornw 64-70; Pembroke Dio Ott from 70; Archd of Pembroke from 73. *68 Renfrew Street, Pembroke, Ont., Canada.* (1-613-732-8611)

KENWAY, Ian Michael. b 52. Univ of Leeds BA 74. Coll of Resurr Mirfield 76. **d** 76 Bp Daly for Cov **p** 77 Cov. C of Cov E Team Min 76-79; Southmead 79-81. *21 Brockley Close, Stoke Lodge, Patchway, Bristol BS12 6EZ.* (Almondsbury 613018)

KENWORTHY, Hon Jonathan Malcolm Athol. b 16. Pemb Coll Cam BA 38, MA 47. Ridley Hall Cam 39. **d** 41 **p** 42 Lon. C of St Mary Hornsey Rise 41-43; CF 44-47; R of St Clem Ox 47-54; V of Hoddesdon 54-63; All SS Burton-on-Trent 63-65; in Ch of S India 65-66; V of Ch Ch w H Trin Penge 66-75; R of Yelvertoft w Clay Coton and Lilbourne Dio Pet from 75. *Rectory, Yelvertoft, Northampton, NN6 7LF.* (Crick 822046)

KENYA, Metropolitan of Province of. *See* Kuria, Most Rev Manasses.

KENYI, Ven Abarayama. b 27. Bp Gwynne Coll Mundri 55. **d** 59 **p** 61 Sudan. P Dio Sudan 59-76; Dio Juba from 76; Can of Sudan 74-76; Archd Dio Juba from 77. *Box 110, Juba, Sudan.*

KENYON, Stanley Robert. Kelham Th Coll 51. **d** 55 **p** 57 Derby. C of Eckington w Renishaw 55-57; St Andr Derby 57-59; Lullington 59-61; Netherseale w Overseal 59-61; PC of St Steph Grimsby 61-71; V of Habrough Dio Linc from 71; E Halton Dio Linc from 71; Killingholme Dio Linc from 71. *Vicarage, Habrough, S Humb, DN40 3BB.* (Immingham 2876)

KEOGH, Anthony. b 35. St Mich Coll Llan 63. **d** 66 **p** 67 Llan. C of Aberaman 66-70; All SS Penarth 70-76; R of H Trin Jersey Dio Win from 76. *Holy Trinity Rectory, Jersey, CI.* (Jersey 61110)

KEOGH, Henry James. b 39. TCD BA 61. NUIBMus 65. **d** 62 **p** 63 Cork. C of St Fin Barre Cathl Cork 62-65; St Luke Belf 65-66; Drom Cathl 66-68; R of Castlecomer Dio Oss from 68. *Rectory, High Street, Castlecomer, Kilkenny, Irish Republic.* (056-41234)

KEOUGH, Lance. **d** 74 **p** 75 Bath. C of Wellington 74-75; Dubbo Dio Bath from 75. *Box 158, Dubbo, NSW, Australia 2830.*

KEPPEL, Oswald Francis Arnold. b 10. AKC 34. **d** 34 **p** 35 Lon. C of St Matt Fulham 34-37; Chorley Wood 37-40; Cuckfield 40-42; R of Woodsford w Tincleton 42-66; Perm to Offic Dio Sarum from 66. *28 Culliford Road, Dorchester, Dorset.* (Dorchester 3078)

KER, Desmond Agar-Ellis. Wells Th Coll 58. **d** 58 Cov **p** 60 Ex. C of Wyken 58-59; Dawlish 60-61; Cockington w Chelston 61-69; V of St Jo Evang Bovey Tracey 69-80. *Address temp unknown.*

KER-FOX, Roderick Hugo. b 43. St Paul's Coll Grahmstn. **d** and **p** 70 Grahmstn. C of K Wm's Town 69-73; R of Komga 73-76; L to Offic Dio Grahmstn from 76. *35 Buxton Street, Queenstown, CP, S Africa.*

KERBY, Brian William. Pemb Coll Cam BA 54, MA 60. Ely Th Coll. **d** 56 Bp Maxwell for Leic **p** 57 Leic. C of St Steph N Evington 56-61; St Paul Leic 62-67; V of Hugglescote w Donington Dio Leic from 67. *Vicarage, Grange Road, Hugglescote, Leicester, LE6 2SQ.* (Coalville 32557)

KERFOOT, Preb Thomas Phoebus. b 09. OBE 76. ALCD 33 (LTh from 74). **d** 33 **p** 34 Liv. C of St Thos Wigan 33-36; Farnworth 36-37; Asst Org Sec Miss to Seamen for NW Distr and Asst Chap for Port of Man and LPr Dio Man 37-38; Chap Miss to Seamen Yokohama 38; Actg Chap Miss to Seamen Kobe 40-41; Durban 41-42; Capetn 42-48; Supt Miss to Seamen 48-59; Dep Gen Sec 59-69; Gen Sec 69-76; LPr Dio S'wark 48-69; Lon from 69; Chap St Mich Paternoster Royal Lon 69-76; Preb of St Paul's Cathl Lon 72-76; Preb (Emer) from 76; Sec-Gen Internat Chr Maritime Assoc from 76. *30 Combemartin Road, SW18 5PR.* (01-788 5926)

✠ **KERINA, Right Rev Blake Tawaru.** Newton Coll Dogura 59. **d** 61 **p** 63 New Guinea. C of Menapi 61-62; Movi

62-67; P-in-c of Aiome 68-81; Archd of New Guinea Mainland 74-77; Aipo from 77; Cons Asst Bp of Aipo at Simbai 10 Aug 81 by Abp of Prov of Papua; Bps of Aipo, New Guinea Is, Popondota and Dogura; and Abp Strong. *Box 340, Madang, Papua New Guinea.*

✠ **KERLE, Right Rev Ronald Clive.** Univ of Syd BA 42. Moore Th Coll Syd ACT ThL 37. **d** 39 **p** 40 Syd. C of St Paul Syd 39; St Anne Ryde 39-41; R of Kangaroo Valley 41-43; St Steph Port Kembla 43-47; Chap AIF 45-47; Gen Sec CMS in NSW 47-54; Archd of Cumb 54-59; R of Summer Hill 54-57; Cons Bp Coadj of Syd in St Andr Cathl Syd 1 May 56 by Abp of Syd; Abp of Brisb; Bps of Newc; C & Goulb; Graft; and River; and Bps Hilliard, Pilcher, Storrs, Collins, and Barrett; Trld to Armid 65; res 76; R of St Swith Pymble Dio Syd from 76. *11 Merrivale Road, Pymble, NSW, Australia 2073.* (44-1720)

KERLEY, Brian Edwin. b 36. St Jo Coll Cam BA 57, MA 61. Linc Th Coll 59. **d** 61 **p** 62 Cant. C of Sheerness 61-64; St Lawr-in-I of Thanet 64-69; St Andr Coulsdon 69-76; C-in-c of Fulbourn Dio Ely 76-77; R from 77. *Fulbourn Rectory, Cambridge, CB1 5EY.* (0223-880337)

KERLY, Henry Joseph Martin. **d** 58 **p** 60 Tas. C of Burnie 59-60; P-in-c of Sorell 60-63; R of Ringarooma w Derby 63-65; Oatlands 65-68; C of St Matt Groveley Bris 68-70; L to Offic Dio Tas 70-71; R of Bothwell w Kempton 73-74; Geo Tn 74-80; W Hobart Dio Tas from 80. *Rectory, Goulburn Street, W Hobart, Tasmania 700.* (002 34 1269)

KERNEBONE, Richard Alan. BD (2nd cl) Lon 64. Moore Th Coll Syd 61. **d** and **p** 64 Armid. C of Tamworth 64-66; Moree 66-68; P-in-c of Tingha 68-70; V of Mungindi 70-71. *Vicarage, Mungindi, NSW, Australia.*

KERNOT, Frank George. b 35. St Barn Coll Adel ThDip 79. **d** 79 **p** 80 Adel. C of St Mary S Road 79-80; St Mich Mitcham Dio Adel from 80. *9 St Michael's Road, Mitcham, S Australia 5062.*

KERR, Andrew Harry Mayne. b 41. TCD BA (2nd cl Mod Hist and Pol Sc) 63. **d** 65 **p** 66 Connor. C of St Luke Belf 65-68; SCM Sec for Ireland 68-72; C of All SS Clooney 72-74; Chap Swinburne Coll of Tech Melb 74-80; I of St Mary Magd Dallas Dio Melb from 80. *15 Emerald Street, Broadmeadows, Vic, Australia 3047.*

KERR, Arthur Henry. Trin Coll Dub BA 48. LRAM 47. **d** 49 Derry **p** 50 Dub. C of Derry Cathl 49-50; Harold's Cross Dub 50-57; on Staff of ICM 57-60; Chap Rotunda Hosp Dub from 58; C of Raheny 61-63; St Jude City and Dio Dub from 63. *102 Terenure Road West, Dublin, Irish Republic.* (Dublin 906241)

KERR, Charles Alexander Gray. b 33. Open Univ BA 75. Edin Th Coll Bp Douglas Pri 67. **d** 67 **d** 68 **p** 68 Edin. C of St Cuthb Hawick 67-70; St Geo Edgbaston 70-72; V of St Bonif City and Dio Birm from 72. *Vicarage, Quinton Road West, Birmingham 32.* (021-427 1939)

KERR, David James. b 36. Trin Coll Dub BA (3rd cl Ment and Mor Sc Mod), Bp Forster Pri and Downes Comp Pri (1st) 58; Div Test (1st cl) and Downes Oratory Pri (2nd) 59; Th Exhib 60; MA, BD and Elrington Th Pri 61. **d** 60 **p** 61 Connor. C of Trin Coll Miss Belf 60-63; Dean's V St Patr Cathl Dub 63-66; Chap Beechwood Pk Sch Markyate from 66; L to Offic Dio St Alb 66-74; C of Flamstead Dio St Alb from 74. *Beechwood Park School, Markyate, St Albans, Herts, AL3 8AW.* (Luton 841191)

KERR, Very Rev Eric John. St Jo Coll Morpeth ACT ThL 63. **d** 62 **p** 63 Newc. C of Maitland 62-63; Taree 64-65; P-in-c of Brisb Water 65-71; R 71-74; Dean and R of H Cross Cathl Geraldton Dio NW Austr from 75. *Deanery, Geraldton, W Australia 6530.* (099-213052)

KERR, George Cecil. b 36. TCD BA (2nd cl Hebr and Or Lang Mod) and Div Test 60, MA 65. **d** 60 **p** 61 Connor. C of St Patr Coleraine 60-63; Div Master Annandale Gr Sch Belf 63-65; Dean of Residences QUB 65-74; L to Offic Dio Down from 75. *Christian Renewal Centre, Shore Road, Rostrevor, Co Down, BT34 3AB. N Ireland.* (Rostrevor 492)

KERR, Gilbert Allan. St Jo Coll Winnipeg. **d** 56 **p** 57 Bran. C of St Matt Cathl Bran 56-58; R of Lynn Lake 57-61; Minnedosa 61-66; Duncan 66-75; St Alb Burnaby Dio New Westmr from 75. *7717-19th Avenue, Burnaby, BC, Canada.*

KERR, John Maxwell. b 43. Univ of Tor BASc 66. Univ of Leeds MSc 70. Univ of Nottm Dipl Th 76. Linc Th Coll 75. **d** 77 Buckingham for Ox **p** 78 Reading for Ox. C of H Trin New Windsor 77-80; Asst Chap Cheltm Coll 80-81; Chap & Asst Master from 81. *c/o Cheltenham College, Glos.*

KERR, John Winston. McGill Univ Montr BA 36, STM 60. Montr Dioc Th Coll 33. **d** 37 **p** 38 Alg. Miss at Bracebridge 37-39; I of White River 40-43; C of St Jas Vancouver 43-47; Chap RCN 44-47; V of Arrow Lakes 47-48 C of Ch of Advent Westmount Montr 48-50; R of Ste Anne de Bellevue 50-66; Dean of Studs Lakehead Univ and Hon C of St Mich Port Arthur 66-77. *250 Heath Street West, Apt 293, Toronto, Ont, Canada.*

KERR, Joseph Reid. b 43. Lamar Univ Beaumont Texas BSc (Hist) 65. St Steph Ho Ox 70. **d** 72 Chicago for Ox. C of St Phil and St Jas Ox 72-74; Kingston Dio Ja from 75. *Rectory, King Street, Kingston, Jamaica, WI.* (092-26888)

KERR, Michael Henry. NZ Bd of Th Stud LTh 67. St Jo Coll Auckld 64. **d** 66 **p** 67 Ch Ch. C of Merivale 66-69; Hornby 69-71; V of Kens Otipua 71-76; Chap Timaru Hosp from 76. *Mountain View Road, Timaru, NZ.* (80-057)

KERR, Nicholas Ian. b 46. Em Coll Cam BA 68, MA 72. Westcott Ho Cam 74. **d** 77 **p** 78 S'wark. C of St Mary Merton 77-80; Rainham Dio Roch from 80. *50 Beverley Close, Rainham, Gillingham, Kent, ME8 9HQ.* (Medway 376232)

KERR, Paul Turner. b 47. Cranmer Hall 68. **d** 71 York **p** 72 Hull for York. C of St Martin Hull 71-72; St Barn Linthorpe Middlesbrough 72-76; St Jo Evang Cam and Chap Addenbrookes Hosp 76-78; C-in-c of St Pet Newbold Rochdale 78; Team V of Rochdale Dio Man from 78. *St Peter's Vicarage, Newbold, Rochdale, OL16 5NW.* (Rochdale 522291)

KERR, Peter Albert Calvin. b 09. Univ of Lon BD 30. St Cath Coll Ox BA 32, MA 37. LLB (Lon) 60; Barrister at Law Gray's Inn 62. Qu Coll Birm 37. **d** and **p** 37 Birm. C of Aston-juxta-Birm 37-39; CF (TA R of O) 39-59; L to Offic Dio Mon from 81. *Hillside, Llanishen, Chepstow, Gwent, NP6 6QD.*

KERR, Reginald John. Univ of Tor BA 38. Wycl Coll Tor. **d** 41 **p** 42 Tor. C of Ch of Epiph 41-42; I of Mulmur 42-44; Haliburton Tor 44-50; Creemore 50-53; on leave 53-54; Publ Inst Chap Dio Tor 54-62; Chief Chap and Dir Hosp Chap from 62. *790 Meadow Wood Road, Mississauga, Ont., Canada.*

KERR, Robert Andrew James. b 06. Univ of Dub BA 26, MA 62, Div Test 27. **d** 29 **p** 30 Down. C of Donaghcloney 29-31; St Columb's Cathl Derry 31-33; C-in-c of Convoy 33-42; Actg C of Newtownards 43-44; Dioc C Dio Clogh 44-46; I of Derryvullen N 46-79; Preb of Clogh Cathl 66-79. *12 Crichton Park, Tamlaght, Co Fermanagh, N Ireland.*

KERR, Stephen Peter. b 46. TCD BA 68, Univ of Edin BD 71, MPhil 80. **d** 71 **p** 72 Connor. C of H Trin Belf 72-76; Ballywillan (Portrush) 76-78; Lect Linc Th Coll from 78. *Lincoln Theological College, Lincoln, LN1 3BN.*

KERR, Thomas Aulay Morrison. Dalhousie Univ BA 61. K Coll NS LTh 67. **d** 66 **p** 67 NS. I of Terence Bay 66-68; R of Guysborough 68-70; I of Port Hill 70-74; Rawdon 74-75; Aylesford w Berwick Dio NS from 75. *Box 177, Berwick, NS, Canada.*

KERR, Ven Victor Leroy. Angl Th Coll BC Dipl Th 67. **d** and **p** 67 Bp Greenwood for Carib. C of Prince George 67-70; V of Westsyde 70-75; Archd of Carib 72-75; R of St Pet Edmon 75-81; H Trin City and Dio Edmon from 81; Archd of Yellowhead from 80. *10037-84th Avenue, Edmonton, Alta, T6E 2G6, Canada.*

KERR, William George. b 04. TCD BA 29, MA 31. **d** 29 **p** 31 Arm. C of Portadown 29-34; R of Mullabrack (w Kilcluney from 52) 34-62; Preb of Loughall in Arm Cathl 55-61; Treas of Arm Cathl 61-65; chan 65-72; I of Moy w Charlemont 62-72. *55 Ashley Park, Armagh, N Ireland.*

KERR-DINEEN, Ven Frederick George. b 15. Tyndale Hall Bris 38. St Jo Coll Dur LTh 42, BA 43, MA 46. **d** 41 **p** 42 Lon. C of St Paul Portman Square St Marylebone 41-44; St John Weymouth 44-46; V of St Mich AA Blackheath Pk 46-53; Lindfield 53-61; H Trin Eastbourne 61-73; M Gen Syn Chich 70-74; Archd of Chich 73-75; R of Stopham Dio Chich from 73; Hardham Dio Chich from 73; Can Res of Chich Cathl 73-75; Archd of Horsham from 75. *Stopham Rectory, Pulborough, Sussex, RH20 1EG.* (Fittleworth 333)

KERRELL, Malcolm Anthony. b 38. Em Coll Cam 1st cl Th Trip pt i 58, BA 60, MA 64. Ex Coll Ox Dipl Th 62. Wycl Hall, Ox 60. **d** 63 **p** 64 Birm. C of St Aug Edgbaston Birm 63-66; Chap K Edw Sch Birm 65-69; L to Offic Dio Birm 65-69; Dio Cant 69-72; Dio St Alb from 72; Dep Sec NS 69-72; Admin Dir Chs TV Centre 72-78. *9 Thrush Green, Rickmansworth, Herts.*

KERRIN, Albert Eric. b 26. Univ of Aber MA 51. Edin Th Coll 51. **d** 53 **p** 54 Glas. C of Dumfries 53-55; P-in-c of Newton w Cambuslang 55-57; R of Alford 57-69; C-in-c of Stranraer w Portpatrick Dio Glas from 70; Dep Hd Master Pk Sch Stranraer from 71. *15 London Road, Stranraer, Wigtownshire, DG9 8AF.* (Stranraer 2822)

KERRIN, Canon Richard Elual. b 1898. Univ of Aber MA 20. Edin Th Coll 20. **d** 22 **p** 23 Edin. C of Old St Paul Edin 22-25; R of Inverurie 25-37; H Trin Stirling 37-47; Fraserburgh 47-54; St John Aber 54-69; Can of Aber 54-69; Dean of Aber and Ork 56-69; Hon Can of St Andr Cathl Aber from 70. *Elora, St Bryde's Road, Kemnay, Aberdeens.*

KERRISON, Stanley. Trin Coll Tor. **d** 40 **p** 41 Ont. Miss at Frontenac w N Addington 40-46; I of Kitley 46-50; R of Kemptville 50-71; Can of St Geo Cathl Kingston 69-77; Hosp

Chap Kingston 71-77. *Apt 1005, 66 Greenview Drive, Ont, Canada.*

KERRUISH, John Robert Joughin. b 16. Magd Coll Ox BA (2nd cl Mod Hist) 38, MA 43, Dipl in Th 39. Wycl Hall Ox 39. **d** 40 **p** 41 Southw. C of St Andr Nottm 40-46; V of St John Worksop 47-55; Proc Conv Southw 50-55; PC of Branksome Pk Dio Sarum 55-68; V from 68. *All Saints' Vicarage, Branksome Park, Poole, Dorset.* (Canford Cliffs 708202)

KERRY, Josiah Ofili. d 64 **p** 66 Benin. P Dio Benin. *Idumuje Ugboko, Nigeria.*

KERSEY, Lloyd Francis. d 67 **p** 68 Montr. P-in-c of Arundel 67-70; R of Caledonia Dio Niag from 70. *PO Box 611, Caledonia, Ont., Canada.* (416-765 4676)

KERSWILL, Anthony John. b 39. Linc Th Coll 72. **d** 73 Linc **p** 73 Grantham for Linc. C of Boultham 73-76; P-in-c of N Kelsey Dio Linc from 76; Cadney w Howsham Dio Linc from 76. *Vicarage, North Kelsey, Lincoln, LN7 6EZ. Kelsey* (06527 205)

KESSEBEH, Humphrey Max. Fourah Bay Coll 52. **d** 55 **p** 57 Sier L. P Dio Sier L 55-66 and from 67; L to Offic Dio Leic 66-67. *Vicarage, Lunsar, Sierra Leone.*

KESSLER, Edward Scharps. b 26. Princeton Univ BA 47. Univ of Chicago, MA 51. St Chad's Coll Dur 64. **d** 66 Jarrow for Dur **p** 67 Dur. C of St Luke Pallion Bp Wearmouth 66-68; St Ignatius Hendon Bp Wearmouth 68-70; Planning Officer Dio Dur 70-75; Planning Consultant from 75; C-in-c of Kimblesworth 74-80. *c/o 210 Gilesgate, Durham.* (Dur 62246)

KESTELL-CORNISH, Geoffrey. b 03 Bp's Univ Lennox LST 32. **d** 32 Queb **p** 33 York. C of St Pet Redcar 32-34; St Andr Aysgarth 34-37; Honiton 37-40; Commiss Queb 32-35; CF (EC) 40-46; C of Barnstaple 46-48; V of Bp's Tawton 48-53; C of Ilfracombe 57-68; Perm to Offic Dio Ex from 68. *31 Ashleigh Road, Barnstaple, Devon.* (Barnstaple 2566)

KETLEY, Michael James. b 39. Oak Hill Coll 79. **d** 81 Portsm. C of St Thos Bedhampton Dio Portsm from 81. *23 Lester Avenue, Bedhampton, Havant, Hants, PO9 3HE.*

KETT, Paul David. b 45. McMaster Univ Ont BSc 67. Wycl Coll Tor MDiv 80. **d** 80 Bp Read for Tor **p** 81 Tor. C of St Clem Eglinton Dio Tor from 80. *59 Briar Hill Avenue, Toronto, Ont, Canada, M4R 1H8.*

KETTLE, Alan Marshall. b 51. Univ of Leeds BA 72. Univ of Ox BA (Th) 78. Wycl Hall Ox 74. **d** 78 **p** 79 Llan. C of Llantwit Fardre 78-81; Prov Adv in Relig Educn Ch in Wales from 81. *c/o Church in Wales Centre, Woodland Place, Penarth, S Glam, CF6 2EX.*

KETTLE, Arthur John Clare. b 05. ARCM 30. LTCL 39. Bps' Coll Cheshunt. **d** 65 **p** 66 Pet. C of Oakham 65-69; R of Wing w Pilton 69-75; Preston and Ridlington (w Wing and Pilton from 75) 74-76. *61 South Street, Oakham, Rutland, Leics.* (Oakham 56301)

KETTLE, Cyril. b 17. Univ of Dur LTh 40. Oak Hill Coll 37. **d** 40 **p** 41 Bradf. C of Slaidburn 40-43; Stanhope-in-Weardale 43-44; Otley 44-46; Killingworth 46-49; Asst Chap Miss to Seamen Port of Lon 49; S Shields 49-51; Tees Chap 51-60; L to Offic Dio York 51-60; R of Fonthill Bp w Berwick-in-Tisbury 60-65; R of Fonthill Gifford 60-65; V of E Harsley 65-75; V of Ingleby Arncliffe 65-75; Cler Org Sec CECS Dios Nor, Ely and St E 75-78; V of Ingleby Greenhow (w Bilsdale Priory from 81) Dio York from 78; P-in-c of Kildale Dio York from 78; Bilsdale Priory 78-81. *Ingleby Greenhow Vicarage, Middlesbrough, Teesside.* (Gt Ayton 2909)

KETTLE, David John. b 47. Univ of Bris BSc 69. Fitzw Coll Cam BA 75, MA 79. Westcott Ho Cam 73. **d** 76 **p** 77 Bris. C of Hartcliffe 76-79; St Jo Div Fishponds 79-81; P-in-c of All SS Fishponds Dio Bris from 81. *All Saints Vicarage, Grove Road, Fishponds, Bristol, BS16 2BW.* (Bris 654143)

KETTLE, Martin Drew. b 52. New Coll Ox BA 74. Selw Coll Cam BA 76. Ridley Hall Cam 74. **d** 77 Edmon for Lon **p** 78 Lon. C of St Andr Enfield 77-80; Chap Ridley Hall Cam from 80. *Ridley Hall, Cambridge, CB3 9HG.*

KETTLE, Peter. b 51. AKC and BD 74. St Aug Coll Cant 74. **d** 75 **p** 76 S'wark. C of Angell Town Brixton 75-78; Putney 78-80; V of Raynes Pk Dio S'wark from 80. *73 Grand Drive, SW20 9DW.* (01-542 2787)

KETTLEBOROUGH, Edward Graham. McGill Univ BA 38. Montr Dioc Th Coll LTh 41. **d** 41 **p** 42 Montr. C of Ascen 41-42; St Luke Rosemount Montr 42-45; I of Aylwin w River Desert 45-47; P-in-c of Valleyfield 47-50; I of St Marg and St Chad Montr 50-51; R of Stanbridge East 51-54; Chap of Ashbury Coll Ott 54-59; R of St Clem Verdun 60-71; I of Rosemere 71-78. *33 Gault Street, Valleyfield, PQ, Canada.*

KEVEY, Lance Edward. b 50. St Jo Coll Auckld 71. **d** 74 **p** 75 Auckld. C of Devonport 74-76; Kaitaia 76-78; St Helier's Bay 78-79; P-in-c 79; V of Wellsford Dio Auckld from 79. *Box 82, Wellsford, NZ.* (Wellsford 8250)

KEVILL-DAVIES, Christopher Charles. b 44. AKC 69. St Aug Coll Cant 70. **d** 70 **p** 71 Cant. C of St Sav Folkestone 70-75; V of Yaxley 75-78; R of Chevington w Hargrave and Whepstead w Brockley Dio St E from 78; *Chevington Rectory, Bury St Edmunds, Suff, IP29 5QL.* (Chevington 461)

KEW, William Richard. b 45. BD (Lon) 69. Lon Coll of Div ALCD 68. **d** 69 Willesden for Lon **p** 70 Lon. C of St Paul Finchley 69-72; Stoke Bishop 72-76; in Amer Ch from 76. *c/o Diocesan Office, 935 East Avenue, Rochester, NY 14607, USA.*

KEWAZA, Samwiri. Bp Tucker Coll Mukono. **d** 56 Ugan **p** 58 Bp Balya for Ugan. P Dio Ugan 56-60; Dio W Bugan from 60. *Makonzi, PO Kassanda, Uganda.*

KEY, Christopher Halstead. b 56. St Jo Coll Dur BA (Th) 77. K Coll Lon MTh 78. Ridley Hall Cam 79. **d** 81 Man. C of St Mary Balderstone Rochdale Dio Man from 81. *2 Delamere Road, Turf Hill, Rochdale, Lancs, OL16 4XD.* (Roch 355378)

KEY, John Christopher. b 36. Pemb Coll Cam 3rd cl Cl Trip pt i 59, BA (2nd cl Th Trip pt ia) 60, MA 65. **d** 62 Bp McKie for Cov **p** 63 Cov. C of Rugby 62-67; Sec Melanesian Coun of Chs Port Moresby Papua 68-71; V of St Geo Cov 71-76; RD of Cov N 73-76; V of Redditch 76-81; RD of Bromsgrove 77; Dioc Ecumen Officer Dio Worc 80-81. *PO Box 759, Chatswood, NSW 2067, Australia.*

✠ **KEY, Right Rev John Maurice.** b 05. Pem Coll Cam BA (Jun Opt) 27, MA 35. DD (Lambeth) 60. Westcott Ho Cam 27. **d** 28 **p** 29 Portsm. C of St Mary Portsea 28-32; V of Aylesbeare 32-34; R of Highweek w St Mary Newton Abbot 34-40; Surr 34-47; R of Stoke Damerel 40-47; RD of Three Towns 44-47; Preb of Fordington and Writhlington in Sarum Cathl 47-60; Cons Ld Bp Suffr of Sherborne in S'wark Cathl 1 Nov 47 by Abp of Cant; Bps of Lon; Sarum; S'wark; and Portsm; Bps Suffr of Plymouth; and Stepney; and Bp Lovett; Trld to Truro 60; res 73; Commiss New Guinea 64-71; Papua 71-74; P-in-c of Teigngrace 75-77; Asst Bp of Ex from 75. *Donkeys, Stover, Newton Abbot, Devon.* (Newton Abbot 3997)

KEY, Robert Frederick. b 52. Univ of Bris BA 73. Oak Hill Coll 74. **d** 76 Dorchester for Ox **p** 77 Ox. C of St Ebbe Ox 76-80; Wallington (in c of St Patr) Dio S'wark from 80. *St Patrick's House, 47 Park Hill Road, Wallington, Surrey, SM6 0RU.* (01-647 7551)

KEY, Roger Astley. b 49. Coll of Resurr Mirfield 73. **d** 74 Bp Wood for Damar **p** 75 Bp Winter for Damar. C of Katutura Dio Damar (Namibia from 80) from 75. *PO Box 57, Windhoek, Namibia, SW Africa, 9100.* (Windhoek 27122)

KEYES, Alfred Edward de Hault. Keble Coll Ox (2nd cl Th) 39. Lich Th Coll 40. **d** 41 **p** 42 York. C of St Aug Newland Hull 41-42; St Andr Drypool 42-47; St Mary Scarborough 47-48; St Mary w St Nich Beverley 48-53; V of Old Malton 53-63; Goathland 63-73; R of Rockbourne w Whitsbury Dio Win from 73. *Rockbourne Rectory, Fordingbridge, Hants.* (Rockbourne 461)

KEYNES, Ronald Philip. Moore Th Coll Syd ACT ThL (2nd cl) 61. Melb Coll of Div Dipl Relig Educn 64. **d** 61 Bp Kerle for Syd **p** 62 Syd. C of St Aug Bulli 61-63; P-in-c of Leigh Creek 63-66; Ceduna Miss Distr Dio Adel 66-67; Dio Willoch 67-71; R of Port Augusta 71-74; Jt and Assoc R 74-75; R of N Goulb Dio C & Goulb from 76. *17 Kinghorne Street, Goulburn, NSW, Australia 2580.* (048-21 3369)

KEYT, Fitzroy John. b 34. Linc Th Coll. **d** 67 Birm **p** 68 Aston for Birm. C of Highters Heath 67-70; Hon C of Sheldon 70-73; V of Miles 73-76; R of Drayton Dio Brisb from 76. *Rectory, Glennie Street, Drayton, Queensland, Australia 4350.* (30 1235)

KEYTE, Douglas Joseph Henry. b 18. Late Scho of St Jo Coll Cam BA 40, MA 46. St Cath S Ox 46. Wycl Hall, Ox 46. **d** 48 **p** 49 Man. C of St Paul Kersal 48-51; C-in-c of St Francis Conv Distr Newall Green Wythenshawe 51-54; Asst Chap K William's Coll Castletown IM 54-55; Chap 55-57; Asst Master Adisadel Coll 57-61; L to Offic Dio Accra 58-61; Asst Master Co Gr Sch for Girls Sale from 61; Hon C of St Geo w St Barn Charlestown Salford Dio Man from 75. *26 Heathfield Close, Sale Moor, Sale, Ches, M33 2PQ.* (061-973 2844)

KHABUSH, Phillip Abbas. Bp Gwynne Coll Mundri. **d** 56 **p** 57 Sudan. P Dio Sudan. *c/o PO Box 135, Khartoum, Sudan.*

KHAILE, Albert Thabo. St Bede's Coll Umtata. **d** 27 **p** 31 St Jo Kaffr. C of H Cross Kaffr 33-45; Matatiele 47-48; Idutywa 48-62; Lusikisiki 62-65; L to Offic Dio St John's from 65. *c/o St Andrew's Mission, Lusikisiki, Transkei, S Africa.*

KHALIL, Adeeb Mikhail. b 37. Coptic Evang Sem Cairo 67. **d** 70 Bp Cragg for Jer. C of All SS Cathl Cairo Dio Egypt from 71. *1113 Corniche el Nil, Box 1427, Cairo, Egypt.*

KHAMIS, Mubaraka. d 74 Sudan **p** 77 Omdurman. d Dio Sudan 74-76; Dio Omdurman 76-77; P Dio Omdurman from 77. *Box 65, Omdurman, Sudan.*

KHAMIS, Otaniele. d 74 Sudan. d Dio Sudan 74-76; Dio Omdurman from 76. *Box 65, Omdurman, Sudan.*

KHANG, Gabriel Joseph. St Bede's Coll Umtata, 63. **d** 64 Basuto **p** 65 Les. P Dio Les. *St John's Rectory, Pohane, PO Quthing, Lesotho.*

KHANYILE, Herculas. b 32. **d** 77 **p** 78 Zulu. C of All SS Msebe Dio Zulu 77-78; P-in-c from 78. *All Saints Parish, Private Bag 515, Nongoma 3950, Zululand, S Africa.*

KHARTOUM, Provost of. (Vacant)

KHATONDI, Alfred. Buwalasi Th Coll 61. **d** 64 **p** 65 Mbale. P Dio Mbale. *PO Bukalasi, Mbale, Uganda.*

KHEE KHE, Lebohang Naphthali. b 46. **d** and **p** 74 Les. P Dio Les. *St Stephen's Mission, PO Box MH22, Mohales Hoek, Lesotho, S Africa.*

KHIN, Andrew. H Cross Coll Rang. **d** 66 **p** 67 Rang. P Dio Rang. *St Paul's Church, Yelegyi, Burma.*

KHOO, Boo Wah. **d** 67 Sing. d Dio Sing 67-71; Dio W Mal 71-77. *St John's, Ipoh, S Perak, Malaya.*

KHOSROUI, Khudadad. U Th Sem Bangalore. **d** 61 **p** 62 Iran. P Dio Iran from 61. *Ahwaz, Iran.* (061-25756)

✠ **KHOURY, Right Rev Elia Khader.** Oak Hill Th Coll 52. **d** 53 **p** 54 Jer. P Dio Jer 53-58; Dio Jordan 58-75; Dio Jer from 76; Exam Chap to Bp of Jordan 59-75; Dioc Archd of Jordan 74-75; Jer 76-79; Cons Asst Bp in Jer at Ch of Redeemer Amman 21 Nov 79 by Bp of Iran (pres); Bps of Cyprus, Jer and Egypt; and Bp N Cuba'ln. *PO Box 598, Amman, Jordan.* (24853)

KHUMALO, Simon Fanyana. b 39. St Pet Coll Alice 72. **d** 74 **p** 75 Zulu. C of St Aug Nqutu 74-78; R of St John Blood River Dio Zulu from 78. *PO Mkhonjane, via Dundee, Natal, S Africa.*

KIAKA, Canon Yusuf. Hegongo Th Coll 43. **d** 44 **p** 48 Zanz. P at Lewa 44-53; Chap at Kiwanda Tr Coll Zanz 53-61; P-in-c of Msalabani 61-66; Can of Zanz T from 66; Archd of Magila 66-74. *Box 35, Korogwe, Tanga, Tanzania.* (Tanga 2330)

KIARA, Jephthah. b 48. **d** 74 Mt Kenya **p** 75 Mt Kenya E. d Dio Mt Kenya 74-75; V of Kagio 75-78; Admin Sec Dio Mt Kenya E from 78. *Box 189, Embu, Kenya.*

KIBBLEWHITE, David Frederick. Univ of Cant NZ BSc 61. Ch Ch Coll 61. **d** 62 **p** 63 Nel. C of Blenheim 62-65; Ch Ch Cathl Nel 65-67; L to Offic Dio Nel 67-72; Dio Wai from 72. *75 Main Road, Edgecumbe, NZ.*

KIBBLEWHITE, William Edington Gerald. b 42. Waterloo Lutheran Univ Ont BA 69, Wycl Coll Tor MDiv 72. **d** 72 **p** 73 Tor. C of St Mich AA Tor 72-74; I of Coldwater-Medonte 74-78; Ajax Dio Tor from 78. *62 Rideout Street, Ajax, Ont, Canada.* (416-683 3863)

KIBE, Very Rev James. St Paul's Th Coll Limuru 68. **d** and **p** 71 Mt Kenya. P Dio Mt Kenya 71-75; Dio Mt Kenya S from 76; Provost of Mt Kenya S from 78. *Box 121, Murang'a, Kenya.* (Murang'a 53)

KIBETE, Yoswa. Bp Tucker Coll Mukono. **d** 64 **p** 65 Mbale. P Dio Mbale. *Nabumali, PO Box 902, Mbali, Uganda.*

KIBIRIGE, Daudi. **d** 46 **p** 47 Ugan. P Dio Ugan 46-60; Dio W Bugan from 60; Can of W Bugan 62-69. *CMS, Bamasuto, Uganda.*

KIBIRIGE, Geoffrey. Bp Tucker Coll Mukono 74. **d** 76 **p** 77 Nam. P Dio Nam. *PO Box 14297, Mmengo, Kampala, Uganda.*

KIBIRIGE, Matayo. **d** 63 **p** 64 W Bugan. P Dio W Bugan. *Ndoddo, PO Box 822, Bulo, Uganda.*

KIBIRIGE, Yafesi. Bp Tucker Coll Mukono. **d** 35 **p** 37 Ugan. P Dio Ugan 35-61; Dio Nam 62-64. *Anglican Church, Nakanyonyi, PO Nakipuma, Uganda.*

KIBIRIGE, Yokana. Bp Tucker Coll Mukono. **d** 35 **p** 39 Ugan. P Dio Ugan 35-60; Dio W Bugan 60-67; Dio Nam from 67. *Mwererwe, PO Box 843, Kampala, Uganda.*

KIBUKA, Ven Ernest Buzinde. b 38. Bp Tucker Coll Mukono 66. **d** 68 **p** 69 Nam. P Dio Nam; Archd of Nateete from 78. *Box 14106, Kampala, Uganda.*

KIBUKA, Yese. **d** 37 **p** 39 Ugan. P Dio Ugan from 37; Can of Ugan 58-61. *Kako, Uganda.*

KIBUUKA, Kupuliano. b 16. Bp Tucker Coll Mukono 73. **d** 74 Nam **p** 76 Bp Kauma for Nam. P Dio Nam 74-76; Dioc Secr Dio Nam from 77. *PO Box 14297, Mmengo Kampala, Uganda.*

KIBWOTA, Nimlodi. **d** 61 **p** 62 N Ugan. P Dio N Ugan. *Palabek, Uganda.*

KIDAGA, Lazalo Gaigulo. Bp Tucker Coll Mukono. **d** 49 **p** 51 Ugan. P Dio Ugan 49-61; Dio Nam from 61. *Namalemba, PO Box 50, Busembatia, Uganda.*

KIDD, Donald Worcester. ALCD 34. **d** 39 **p** 40 Roch. C of Milton-next-Gravesend 39-40; Dartford 40-44; CF (EC) 44-48; I of Valcartier 48-51; CF (Canad) 51-52; R of New Carlisle 52-55; Dom Chap to Abp of Queb 52-60; R of Three Rivers 55-60; St Pet Mt Royal 60-70; Okanagan Dio Koot from 71. *4333 Hobson Road, Kelowna, BC, Canada.* (764-4270)

KIDD, Douglas James. St Jo Coll Auckld LTh 56. BD (Lon) 61. **d** 56 **p** 57 Wai. C of Gisborne 56-58; St Thos Werneth Oldham 59-60; Hollinwood Man 60-61; Perm to Offic Dio Ox 61; V of Edgecumbe 62-67; Mahora 67-72; Avondale 72-75; Chap Auckld Hosp from 75. *32 Leys Crescent, Remuera, Auckland, NZ.* (503-052)

KIDD, George Frederick. b 03. TCD BA 26. Div Test 27, MA 29. **d** 26 **p** 27 Down. C of St Mary Belf 26-30; CMS Miss Butere Kenya 31-35; furlough 35-36; Maseno 36-40; Chap of Nzoia 40-46; R of Ballyculter w Kilclief 46-57; I of Carrowdore 57-62; R of Collingbourne Ducis 62-71; C-in-c of Collingbourne Kingston 62-63; V 63-71. *17 The Waldrons, Thornford, Sherborne, Dorset, DT9 6PX.* (Yetminster 872527)

KIDD, George Harold. b 1900. Trin Coll Dub BA 28, Div Test 29, MA 44. **d** 29 **p** 30 Cash. C of Cathl Ch Waterf 29-33; C-in-c of Killegney w Rossdroit and Adamstown 33-45; I of Achill U 45-51; Walkerton Ont 52-53; Drumshambo U 53-55; Preban w Moyne 55-58; V of Coverham w Horsehouse 58-81. *c/o Coverham Vicarage, Leyburn, Yorks.*

KIDD, John Alan. b 32. Pemb Coll Cam BA 58, MA 61. Ridley Hall Cam 57. **d** 61 **p** 62 Lon. C of St Paul Onslow Square 61-65; R of Bloemhof 65-67; Chap Jinja 67-69; P-in-c of Ch Ch Down Street Westmr 69-75; V 75-79; Virginia Water Dio Guildf from 79. *Christ Church Vicarage, Virginia Water, Surrey, GU25 4LD.* (Wentworth 2374)

KIDD, Maurice Edward. b 26. ALCD 54. **d** 55 **p** 56 Lon. C of Wembley 55-58; Middleton 58-61; Chap Pastures Hosp Mickleover 61-69; Guild of Health Lon 69-72; R of St Geo Hanworth 72-82; Chartham Dio Cant from 82. *Chartham Rectory, Canterbury, Kent, CT4 7HS.* (Chartham 256)

KIDD, Timothy. b 24. St Chad's Coll Dur BA 48, Dipl Th 50, MA 53. Univ of Nottm MA 57; MPhil 71; MEducn 80. STh (Lambeth) 74. **d** 50 **p** 51 Sheff. C of Mexborough 50-52; Lect of Boston 52-56; PC of St Anne Grantham 56-65; Asst Dioc Youth Chap Dio Linc 59-65; Dioc Insp of Schs Dio Linc 61-65; Prin Lect Kesteven Coll of Educn Stoke Rochford 65-79; Univ of Nottm 79-80; C of Harlaxton, of Stroxton, and of L Ponton 66-80; in Amer Ch from 81. *University of Evansville, Evansville 47702, Indiana, USA.*

KIDDELL, James Albert. Univ of W Ont BA 58. Trin Coll Tor 58. **d** 61 **p** 62 Tor. C of St Andr Scarborough 61-63; I of Grafton 63-65; Colborne 63-65; R of St Steph Beverley Hills Tor 65-75; St Matthias Etobicoke City and Dio Tor from 76. *208 La Rose Avenue, Weston, Ont., Canada.*

KIDDELL, Keith Graham. Univ of W Ont BA 45. **d** 46 **p** 47 Niag. C of Glanford w Woodburn Tapleytown and Hannon 46-47; R 47-50; C of Ascen Ch Hamilton 50-52; R of Caledonia w York 52-56; St John Weston Tor 56-60; St Hilda Tor 60-64; Atonement Tor 64-70. *7 Norgrove Crescent, Weston, Ont., Canada.*

KIDDLE, Mark Brydges. ACP 61. Wycl Hall Ox. **d** 63 **p** 64 York. C of St Luke Scarborough 63-66; St Sav Walthamstow 66-71; V of St Bede Nelson-in-Marsden 71-76; Perry Common 76-79; Kirton-in-Lindsey Dio Linc from 79; R of Grayingham Dio Linc from 79; Manton Dio Linc from 79. *Vicarage, Kirton-in-Lindsey, Gainsborough, Lincs, DN21 4PP.* (Kirton Lindsey 648366)

KIDDLE, Martin John. b 42. Univ of Lon Dipl Th 75. Open Univ BA 80. St Jo Coll Nottm 74. **d** 76 Chelmsf **p** 77 Barking for Chelmsf. C of Gt Parndon 76-80; Asst Chap HM Pris Wakef from 80. *c/o HM Prison, Love Lane, Wakefield, Yorks, WF2 9AG.* (0924 378282)

KIDDLE, Canon Peter. b 22. Fitzw Ho Cam BA 50, MA 54. Clifton Th Coll 57. **d** 57 **p** 58 Momb. Tutor St Paul's Th Coll Limuru 57-62; P-in-c of St Andr Malindi 62-63; Warden Bible Sch Momb 63-64; Prin 64-67; V of Momb Cathl 67-69; Bp's Chap 64-69; Warden Trin Coll Nai 69-72; Exam Chap to Bp of Nai 69-72; Hon Can of Nai 72; Can (Emer) from 73; V of St Paul Worthing Dio Chich from 73. *5 Christ Church Road, Worthing, Sussex, BN11 1JH.* (Worthing 202433)

KIDIMU, Canon Misaki Drake. St Aug Coll Cant 53. **d** and **p** 56 U Nile. Chap and Tutor Kabwangasi Dio U Nile 56-61; Dio Mbale 61-72; Dio Bukedi 72-81; Hon Can of Mbale 69-72; Bukedi from 81. *Box 170, Tororo, Uganda.*

KIDNER, Frank Derek. b 13. ARCM 33. Late Scho and Exhib of Ch Coll Cam 1st cl Econ Trip pt i 38, BA (1st cl Th Trip pt i) 40, 2nd cl Th Trip pt ii 41, MA 44. Ridley Hall Cam 40. **d** 41 Bp Mann for Roch **p** 42 Roch. C of Sevenoaks 41-47; V of Felsted 47-51; Sen Tutor Oak Hill Th Coll 51-64; Select Pr Univ of Cam 57; Warden Tyndale Ho Cam 64-78; Perm to Offic Dio Ely from 79. *56 Manor Park, Histon, Cambridge, CB4 4JT.* (Histon 2579)

KIDNER, Harold Stuart. Ridley Coll Melb ACT ThL 29. **d** 28 **p** 29 Bend for Centr Tang. Asst Miss Berega Distr 29-32; Hd Master Dodoma Sch 32-33; Chap at Moshi 33-36; Miss at Berega 37-41; Dodoma 44-47; Archd of Ukaguru 41-48;

Prin of Kongwa Coll 47-49; Archd without terr jur Dio Melb 49-50; Gen Sec CMS Vic 50-58; I of Faifield 59-63; Chap Mowll Mem Village 63-67; L to Offic Dio Syd from 67. *66 Warina Village, Castle Hill, NSW, Australia 2154.* (634-1107)

KIDNEW, William George. Univ of W Ont BA 56. Hur Coll LTh 59. **d** 59 **p** 60 Hur. C of Brantford 59-60; R of Chelsey 60-64; C of All SS Windsor 64-67; R of Merlin 67-71; Chap Picton Heights Hosp Dio Ont from 71. *Box 440, Picton, Ont, Canada K0K 2T0* (613-476 3645).

KIDSON, Canon Norman Stanley. b 1893. Qu Coll Cam BA 16, MA 21. MC 17. Ridley Hall Cam 19. **d** 19 **p** 20 Heref. C of Kington 19-22; St Sav Everton 22-24; V of Ch Ch W Bromwich 24-31; Priors Lee 31-39; Bakewell w Over Haddon 39-55; Surr 40-63; RD of Bakewell 41-55; Hon Can of Derby 48-63; Can (Emer) from 63; V of Etwall w Egginton 55-63. *Moriglen Nursing Home, Salterton Road, Exmouth, Devon, EX8 2EJ.*

KIDU, Zakayo. Bp Tucker Coll Mukono. **d** 34 **p** 36 U Nile. CMSP Dio U Nile 34-54; Dio Ugan 54-60; Dio Nam from 60; Hon Can of U Nile 50-54; *Kabowa, Uganda.*

KIERSTEAD, David Edward. b 43. Univ of NB BSc 70. Univ of Nottm BTh 75. Kelham Th Coll 70. **d** 74 Southw for Fred **p** 76 Fred. On leave 74-75; R of Richmond Dio Fred from 75. *RR3, Woodstock, NB, Canada.*

KIFUNDA, Dominic. b 44. St Mark's Coll Dar-S 69. **d** 72 **p** 74 Zanz T. P Dio Zanz T. *Box 24, Amani, Tanzania.*

KIGALI, Lord Bishop of. *See* Sebununguri, Right Rev Adoniya.

KIGENYI, Isaka. d 42 U Nile. d Dio U Nile 42-61; Dio Mbale 61-72; Dio Bukedi from 72. *Church of Uganda, Busabi, PO Busolwe, Uganda.*

KIGEZI, Lord Bishop of. *See* Kigezi, South

KIGEZI, NORTH, Lord Bishop of. *See* Ruhindi, Right Rev Yustasi.

KIGEZI, SOUTH, Lord Bishop of. *See* Kivengere, Right Rev Festo.

KIGHTLEY, David John. b 39. K Coll Lon and Warm AKC 67. **d** 68 **p** 69 Ex. C of St Andr Plymouth 68-70; St D Ex 70-73; Chap Brook Gen Hosp Woolwich and Greenwich Distr Hosp 73-76; C-in-c of Isleham Dio Ely from 76; Chippenham Dio Ely from 76; Snailwell Dio Ely from 76. *Chippenham Vicarage, Ely, Cambs, CB7 5PP.* (Newmarket 720550)

KIGOZI, Canon Simon Peter. b 15. Bp Tucker Coll Mukono 68. **d** 68 **p** 69 Nam. P Dio Nam 68-72; Dio Kamp from 72; Archd of Kamp 72-75; Can Missr from 72. *Box 335, Kampala, Uganda.*

KIHALA, Edward. St Cypr Coll Namasakata. **d** 53 **p** 55 Zanz. P Dio Zanz 53-62; Dio Zanz T from 62. *Box 45, Tanga, Tanzania.*

KIHAMPA, Canon Paolo. Th Coll Hegongo 32. **d** 33 **p** 36 Zanz. P Dio Zanz 33-59; Synod Sec Dio Zanz T 59-68; Can of Zanz T from 63; P-in-c of Kiwanda 71-75; Hale 75-79. *Box 5, Muheza, Tanzania.*

KIHIKA, Denesi. d 75 **p** 77 Ruw. P Dio Ruw. *Box 1210, Butiiti, Uganda.*

KIHOMBO, Leonard. b 48. St Mark's Coll Dar-S 77. **d** 79 **p** 80 SW Tang. P Dio SW Tang. *PO Itunou, Njombe, Tanzania.*

KIIZA, Hosea. b 36. **d** 69 **p** 70 Ruw. P Dio Ruw. *Box 132, Kasese, Uganda.*

KIIZA, Kefa Sifasi. d 54 **p** 57 Ugan. P Dio Ugan 54-60; Dio W Bugan from 60. *Kako, PO Box 242, Masaka, Uganda.*

KIJAMBU, Canon Andereya. d 46 **p** 47 Ugan. P Dio Ugan 46-60; Dio Nam from 60; Can of Nam from 78. *Naguru Estate, PO Box 2183, Kampala, Uganda.*

KIJANJALI, Aaron. d 78 **p** 79 Vic Nyan. P Dio Vic Nyan. *Box 93, Ngara, Tanzania.*

KIKOSO, Tefiro. Buwalasi Th Coll 62. **d** 64 **p** 65 Mbale. P Dio Mbale. *Church of Uganda, Dunga Buyobo, Uganda.*

KILA, Simon. St Pet Coll Siota. **d** 53 Melan. d Dio Melan. *Aoba, New Hebrides.*

KILALO, John Shadrach Musigwa. Moore Th Coll Syd 66. **d** 69 Bp Madinda for W Tang **p** 69 Centr Tang for W Tang. P Dio W Tang. *Box 175, Kigoma, Tanzania.*

KILBOURN, Mary Elizabeth. b 26. Univ of Tor BA 48. Harvard Univ MA 49. Trin Coll Tor MDiv 77. **d** 77 Bp Read for Tor **p** 78 Tor. Co-ordinator of Chap Services Dio Tor from 77. *135 Adelaide Street East, Toronto, Ont, Canada, M5C 1L8.*

KILDARE, Archdeacon of. *See* Finney, Ven Charles William.

KILDARE, Lord Bishop of. *See* Meath.

KILDARE, Dean of. *See* Paterson, Very Rev John Thomas Farquhar.

KILFENORA, Lord Bishop of. *See* Limerick.

KILFORD, John Douglas. b 38. Oak Hill Coll 73. **d** 75 **p** 76 Roch. C of St Jo Beckenham 75-80; P-in-c of Sinfin Moor Dio Derby from 80. *c/o 72 Redwood Road, Sinfin, Derby, DE2 9LA.*

KILGORE, Gary Steven. b 48. Simon Fraser Univ BC MA 74. Vanc Sch of Th MDiv 81. **d** 81 New Westmr. C of St Agnes N Vanc Dio New Westmr from 81. *B-2120 Mathers Avenue, West Vancouver, BC, Canada, V7V 2H3.*

KILLALA and ACHONRY, Archdeacon of. *See* Ewart, Ven William James.

KILLALA, Lord Bishop of. *See* Tuam, Lord Bishop of.

KILLALA, Dean of. *See* Graham, Very Rev Malcolm Frederick

KILLALOE, Lord Bishop of. *See* Limerick.

KILLALOE and KILFENORA, Archdeacon of. *See* Stanley, Ven Eric William.

KILLALOE and KILFENORA, Dean of. *See* Bourke, Very Rev Francis Robert.

KILLE, Vivian Edwy. b 30. Tyndale Hall Bris 60. **d** 62 **p** 63 Dub. C of Miss Ch Dub 62-66; R of Emlaghfad 66-74; Aghadrumsee Dio Clogh from 74. *Sunshine Rectory, Roslea, Co Fermanagh, N Ireland.* (Roslea 206)

KILLER, Ernest William. b 15. Wycl Hall Ox 54. **d** 54 Worc for Col Bp **p** 55 N Nig. Miss N Nig 54-60; R of Boddington w Aston-le-Walls 60-65; Miss Dio N Nig 65-72; V of Packington w Normanton-le-Heath Dio Leic from 73. *Packington Vicarage, Ashby-de-la-Zouch, Leics.*

KILLICK, Brian Anthony Hugh. b 29. Sarum Th Coll 69. **d** 70 **p** 71 Lon. C of St Andrew Kingsbury 70-74; Selston w Westwood 74-76; P-in-c of Sutton w Duckmanton 77-80; V of Stanley Dio Derby from 80. *Vicarage, Stanley, Derby.* (Ilkeston 2942)

KILLINGBACK, Oliver Edwin. b 44. SOC 75. **d** 77 **p** 78 S'wark. C of Kingston-upon-Thames 77-80; Horley Dio S'wark from 80. *84 Balcombe Road, Horley, Surrey, RH6 9AY.*

KILLOCK, Alfred Kenneth. b 26. Cranmer Hall Dur 72. **d** 74 **p** 75 Ripon. C of Moor Allerton 74-80; L to Offic Dio Bradf from 80. *10 Armidale Way, Bradford, BD2 1EN.*

KILLWICK, Simon David Andrew. b 56. AKC and BD 80. St Steph Ho Ox 80. **d** 81 Man. C of Worsley Dio Man from 81. *Vicarage, Worsley, Manchester, M28 4WH.*

KILMACDUAGH, Lord Bishop of. *See* Limerick.

KILMACDUAGH, Dean of. *See* Champ, Very Rev Cyril Bruce.

KILMORE, ELPHIN and ARDAGH, Lord Bishop of. *See* Wilson, Right Rev William Gilbert.

KILMORE, Archdeacon of. *See* Cave, Ven Guy Newell.

KILMORE, Dean of. *See* Turkington, Very Rev Robert Christopher Howard.

KILNER, Frederick James. b 43. Qu Coll Cam BA 65, MA 69. Ridley Hall Cam 67. **d** 70 **p** 71 Barking for Chelmsf. C of Harlow New Town 70-74; St Andr L Cam 74-79; P-in-c of Milton Dio Ely from 79. *Rectory, Milton, Cambs.* (Cambridge 861511)

KILPATRICK, George Dunbar. b 10. Late Granville Scho of Univ Coll Lon BA (1st cl Cl) 32, Fell 67. Late Scho of Or Coll Ox BA (2nd cl Lit Hum) 34, 2nd cl Th and Jun Gr Test Pri 36, Sen Gr Test Pr 37, MA and Jun Denyer and Johnson Scho 38, BD 44, DD 48. St Steph Ho Ox 34. **d** 36 **p** 37 Guildf. C of St Mary Horsell 36-39; Tutor Qu Coll Birm and Publ Pr Dio Birm 39; C of St Mary Selly Oak 40-41; Actg Warden Coll of Ascen Selly Oak 41-42; Lect Lichfield Th Coll 42-44; R of Wishaw 42-46; Grinfield Lect Univ of Ox 45-49; Reader in Th Univ of Nottingham 46-49; Dean Ireland's Prof of Exegesis of Holy Scripture Univ of Ox 49-77; Fell of Qu Coll Ox 49-77. *27 Lathbury Road, Oxford.* (Ox 58909)

KILPATRICK, Robert William Thomas Howard. b 10. Trin Coll Dub BA and 2nd cl Div Test 37, MA 48. **d** 37 **p** 38 Down. C of St Mary Belf 37-40; St Kath Belf 40-44; R of Ardglass w Dunsford 44-48; Cathl Ch of Ch the Redeemer Drom 48-58; RD of Drom 49-60; Preb of Drom Cathl 51-54; Treas 54-57; Prec 57-59; I of Ballymacarrett 58-64; R of Down w Holly Mount 64-81; Prec of Down Cathl 64-68; Dean of Down 68-81. *The Old School, Ballyculter, Strangford, Co Down, N Ireland.*

KILPIN, Stanley Leonard. Worc Ordin Coll 67. **d** 69 Chich **p** 70 Lewes for Chich. C of Littlehampton 69-75; P-in-c of Cold Waltham 75-80. *20 Hurston Close, Findon Valley, Worthing, W Sussex.* (Worthing 62944)

KILSBY, Alfred Daniel Joseph. b 29. St Chad's Coll Dur BA (2nd cl Th) 54. Univ of Lon BA (Psychol) 68, MSc 75. Westcott Ho Cam 54. **d** 56 **p** 57 S'wark. C of St Mich E Wickham 56-58; H Trin U Tooting 58-62; L to Offic Dio St E 62-65; Dio Chich from 68; Asst Master Hornchurch Gr Scho 65-68; Lect Inst of Educn Lon Univ from 68. *Hammonds, East Street, Billingshurst, Sussex.*

KILVERT, Canon Robert Wynne. b 13. Or Coll Ox BA 38, MA 56. Cudd Coll 39. **d** 40 Bp Kitching for Portsm **p** 41 Portsm. C of St Matt Southsea 40-47; C-in-c of Paulsgrove Conv Distr 47-57; V 57-62; Proc Conv Portsm 51-64; Hon Sec

Portsm Dioc Conf 61-70; Dioc Syn from 70; V of Catherington w Clanfield Dio Portsm from 62; Hon Can of Portsm Cathl from 71. *Vicarage, Catherington, Portsmouth, Hants, PO8 0TD.* (Horndean 593139)

KIM, David Ang'gi. b 38. Univ of Chungang BA 66, MA 72. St Mich Sem Seoul 67. **d** and **p** 71 Taejon. P Dio Taejon 71-74; Dio Pusan from 74. *PO Box 441, Pusan 600, Korea.* (Pusan 42-5846)

KIM, Elia. St Mich Th Coll Chong Chu. **d** 53 Bp Chadwell for Korea **p** 54 Korea. P Dio Korea 53-65; Dio Taejon 65-68; VG 65-68;. *c/o Anglican Church, Chong Dong 3, Seoul, Korea.*

KIM, Gabriel Sap'ung. b 33. St Mich Sem Oryudong. **d** 66 **p** 67 Seoul. P Dio Seoul 66-69; Dio Taejon from 69. *329 Eupnaeri, Jinchonkun 330, Chungbuk, Korea.*

KIM, John Jae Youl. b 39. Univ of Dongkuk 64. St Mich Sem 69. **d** and **p** 69 Seoul. P Dio Seoul from 69. *PO Box 5, P'yongt'aek 180, Korea.* (P'yongt'aek 3583)

KIM, Ven John Pyonghun. b 35. St Mich Sem Oryudong 61. **d** and **p** 64 Korea. P Dio Korea 64-65; Dio Taejon 65-74; Dio Pusan from 74; Archd of Kyongsang from 70. *Anglican Church, Pyongni-dong 828-1, Sow-Ku, Daegu, Korea.* (Daegu 3-9316)

KIM, Jonah. b 33. St Mich Th Coll Oryudong. **d** 62 **p** 63 Korea. P Dio Korea 63-65; Dio Taejon from 65; Archd of Kyong-Sang 68-70. *St Gregory's Abbey, Route 3, Box 330, Three Rivers, Michigan, 49093, USA.*

KIM, Ninian. b 39. St Mich Sem Oryudong 70. **d** 70 Seoul. d Dio Seoul 70-79. in Amer Ch. *35-13 23rd Avenue, Astoria, Long Island, NY 11105, USA.*

KIM, Paul Kunsang. b 52. St Mich Sem Seoul 78. **d** 79 **p** 80 Seoul. C of St Patric Naeri Dio Seoul from 79. *639 Naeri, Hwado myon, Kanghwa, Kyonggi do 150-25, Korea.*

KIM, Shindok. b 10. St Mich Th Coll Korea. **d** 52 **p** 53 Bp Chadwell for Korea. P Dio Korea 52-65; Dio Taejon 65-74; VG Dio Taejon 73-74. *32 Yonggondong, Jonro, Seoul, Korea.*

KIM, Simon. St Mich Sem Oryudong 61. **d** and **p** 64 Korea. P Dio Korea 64-65; Dio Seoul from 65; Arch P Dio Seoul 73-77; Dioc Sec from 80. *Box 7, Oryu, Seoul 150-04, Korea.*

KIM, Stephen Yongchol. b 47. St Mich Sem Seoul 70. **d** 73 **p** 75 Seoul. P Dio Seoul. *c/o 3 Chong dong, Chung Ku, Seoul 100, Korea.*

KIM, Thomas Kyongdok. b 38. Kyung Hee Univ Seoul 64. St Mich Seoul 67. **d** and **p** 71 Taejon. P Dio Taejon from 71. *Maryong School, Maryungmyon, Chungbuk, Korea.*

KIM, Timothy C. d and **p** 76 Taejon. P Dio Taejon. *300 Mookbangri, Bukilmyon, Chungbuk, Korea.*

KIMANI, Bernard. St Phil Coll Maseno 69. **d** 69 Maseno **p** 71 Nak. d Dio Maseno 69-70; P Dio Nak from 71. *PO Box 9, North Kinangop, Kenya.*

KIMANI, Stephen Kagaca. b 32. **d** 78 Mt Kenya S. d Dio Mt Kenya S. *PO Box 31, Murang'a, Kenya.*

KIMBER, John Keith. b 45. Univ of Bris BSc (3rd cl Chem) 66. St Mich Coll Llan. **d** Nicholas **p** 70 Llan. C of Caerphilly 69-72; Chap to Guild of Students at Birm Univ 72-75; R of St Agnes w St Simon and St Werburgh City and Dio Bris from 75; P-in-c of St Paul w St Barn City and Dio Bris from 80. *112 Foredown Drive, Portslade, Brighton, BN4 2BE.*

KIMBER, Kenneth Arthur John. b 26. Bps' Coll Cheshunt 65. **d** 66 Ex **p** 67 Plymouth for Ex. C of Gt Torrington 66-68; Merthyr Tydfil 68-72; R of Falmouth, Ja 72-74; Long Lac 74-78; Battleford w Meota and Langmeade Dio Sktn from 78. *Box 537, Battleford, Sask, S0M 0E0, Canada.*

KIMBER, Stuart Francis. b 53. Univ of Lon BSc 74. Fitzw Coll Cam BA 79. Ridley Hall Cam 77. **d** 80 **p** 81 Edmonton for Lon. C of Edgware Dio Lon from 80. *50 Fairfield Crescent, Edgware, Middx, HA8 9AH.*

KIMBERLEY and KURUMAN, Lord Bishop of. *See* Chadwick, Right Rev Graham Charles.

KIMBERLEY, Dean of. *See* Snyman, Very Rev Robin Roy.

KIMBERLEY, John Harry. b 49. St Steph Ho Ox 74. **d** 76 **p** 77 Chich. C of W Tarring 76-79; St Nicolas Portslade Dio Chich from 79. *112 Foredown Drive, Portslade, Brighton, BN4 2BE.*

KIMBERLEY, Ven Owen Charles Lawrence. Univ of NZ BCom 53. Tyndale Hall Bris 57. **d** 59 **p** 60 Man. C of Higher Openshaw Man 59-62; All SS Nel 62-64; V of Motupiko 64-69; Kaikoura 69-76; Tahunanui Dio Nel from 76; Exam Chap to Bp of Nel from 75; Hon Can of Nel 77-78; Archd of Waimea from 78. *Vicarage, Tahunanui Drive, Nelson, NZ.* (86-065)

KIMBERLEY, Canon Wilfred Harry. b 19. St Steph Ho Ox 51. **d** 53 Ox **p** 54 Reading for Cant. C of St Mary and of St Leon Wallingford 53-55; St Jo Evang Newbury 55-57; PC of Highter's Heath 57-65; V of Marsworth 65-72; C-in-c of Slapton 65-72; C-in-c of Cheddington w Mentmore 68-72; V of Buckingham 72-78; RD of Buckingham 76-78; Team R of High Wycombe Dio Ox from 78; Hon Can of Ch Ch Ox from 79. *Vicarage, Priory Avenue, High Wycombe, HP13 6SH.* (H Wycombe 25602)

KIMBILI, Kinamina. b 32. **d** 77 Bukavu. d Dio Bakavu. *Kindu Parish, BP 220, Kindu, Maniema, Zaire.*

KIMBUGWE, Canon Ezekieri. Bp Tucker Coll Mukono. **d** 56 U Nile. d Dio U Nile 56-61; Dio Mbale 61-72; Hon Can of Mbale 69-72; Can of Bukedi from 72. *PO Box 170, Tororo, Uganda.*

KIME, Thomas Frederick. b 28. Linc Coll Ox BA 50, MA 53. Cudd Coll 54. **d** 56 **p** 57 Chelmsf. C of St Edm K and Mart Forest Gate 56-58; Chap and Asst Master Dioc Coll Rondebosch Capetn 58-65; R of Noorder Paarl 65-71; C of Rondebosch 72-74; R of Ellisfield w Farleigh Wallop and Dummer Dio Win from 74. *Ellisfield Rectory, Basingstoke, Hants, RG25 2QR.* (Herriard 217)

KIMENGICH, Daniel. Ch Tr Centre Kapsabet 66. **d** 67 **p** 68 Nak. P Dio Nak. *Box 28, Kipkabus, Kenya.*

KIMMITT, Richard Desmond Fitzgerald. Trin Coll Dub BA (2nd cl Mod Lit) 53, Downes Pri Comp and Oratory 55, Liturgy 56, Div Test (2nd cl) 56. **d** 56 **p** 57 Down. C of Holywood 56-58; I of Windermere BC 58-60; R of St Anselm Vanc 60-66 and 68-72; All SS Winnipeg 66-67; R of St Chris W Vanc 72-80; on leave. *1669 Jefferson Avenue, West Vancouver, BC, Canada.*

KIMMORLEY, Arthur Maxwell. Moore Coll Syd ThL 50. **d** and **p** 51 Syd. C of Willoughby 51; R of Pitt Town 52-53; CF (Austr) 53-57; R of Milton 58-60; L to Offic Dio Syd 60-61; C-in-c of N Ryde Dio Syd 62-73; R from 73. *152 Cox Road, North Ryde, NSW, Australia 2113.* (88-3974)

KIMONYO, Felix. Warner Mem Th Coll Ibuye 56. **d** 58 **p** 59 Bp Brazier for Ugan. P Dio Ugan 58-60; Dio Rwanda-B 60-66; Dio Rwa 66-75; Dio Kiga from 75. *BP 17, Byumba, Rwanda.*

KIMORI, Naftal. d 66 **p** 67 Momb. P Dio Momb. *Anglican Church, Kishamba, Kenya.*

KIMUTAI, Paulo. Maseno Bible Sch. **d** 59 Momb **p** 61 Maseno. d Dio Momb 59-61; P Dio Maseno 61-70; Dio S Maseno from 70. *PO Box 434, Kericho, Kenya.*

KIMWELE, Daniel. d 66 **p** 68 Nai. P Dio Nai. *PO Box 100, Kitui, Kenya.*

KIMWERI, John. St Mark's Coll Dar-S. **d** 79 Zanz T **p** 80 Bp Russell for Zanz T. P Dio Zanz T. *PO Box 5, Zanzibar, Tanzania.*

KIMWERI, William. d 53 **p** 55 Zanz. P Dio Zanz T. *Tongwe, Muheza, Tanzania.*

KINAHAN, Timothy Charles. b 53. Jes Coll Cam BA 75. Div Hostel Dub 77. **d** 78 **p** 79 Connor. C of Carrickfergus 78-81; Lect Newton Th Coll Papua from 81. *Newton Theological College, Dogura, Papua New Guinea.*

KING, Andrew Bernard. b 40. Ex Coll Ox BA 62, MA 66. Coll of Resurr Mirfield 62. **d** 64 **p** 65 Ox. C of St Mary Upton w Chalvey Slough 64-68; H Trin Reading 68-70; Basingstoke Dio Win from 75. *18 Fairfields Road, Basingstoke, Hants.* (Basingstoke 55837)

KING, Andrew Maxwell. b 47. SSM Adel 65. **d** 70 **p** 71 Adel. C of Glenelg 71-72; Burnside 72-74; Res Missr Point Pearce Miss 74-76; Port Augusta 76-77; C 78-80; R of Whyalla Dio Willoch from 81. *Box 244, Whyalla, S Australia 5600.*

KING, Anthony Richard. b 34. Trin Hall Cam BA 58. Linc Th Coll 61. **d** 62 **p** 63 Newc T. C of St Jas Benwell Newc T 62-64; Thirsk w S Kilvington 64-67; V of St Aug Halifax 67-74; R of Upton-on-Severn Dio Worc from 74. *Upton-on-Severn Rectory, Worcester, WR8 0JQ.* (Upton-on-Severn 2148)

KING, Canon Arthur. b 06. Late Scho of St Jo Coll Dur BA (1st cl Th) and Univ Hebr Pri 30, MA 33. Wycl Hall Ox 30. **d** 32 **p** 33 Sheff. C of St Mark Sheff 32-38; C-in-c of Thurcroft Conv Distr 38-42; R of Bradfield Yorks 42-59; Sec Sheff Dioc Youth Coun 43-45; Ed Sheff Dioc Year Bk 45-59; Hon Can of Sheff 53-73; Can (Emer) from 73; V of Wentworth 59-73; Exam Chap to Bp of Sheff 65-73; Chapter Clk Sheff Cathl 65-73; Perm to Offic Dio St E 73-75; Dio Ripon from 75. *Flat 2, 19 Tewit Well Road, Harrogate, N Yorks, HG2 8JE.* (Harrogate 69828)

KING, Brian Franklin Vernon. Univ of NSW BCom 62. BD (2nd cl) Lon 64. ACA 59. Moore Th Coll Syd ACT ThL (2nd cl) 64. **d** 64 **p** 65 Syd. C of Manly 64-67; R of Dural 67-73; Wahroonga Dio Syd from 73. *10 Seaton Avenue, Wahroonga, NSW, Australia 2076.* (48-2863)

KING, Brian Henry. b 39. Chich Th Coll 63. **d** 65 **p** 66 Birm. C of Castle Bromwich 65-67; Southwick Sussex 68-70; V of Southwater 70-73; C of St Alb Preston Brighton 73-74; Team V of the Resurr Brighton 74-75; V of St elis Eastbourne Dio Chich from 75. *266 Victoria Drive, Eastbourne, BN20 8QX.* (Eastbourne 20068)

KING, Campbell Phillip. Moore Th Coll Syd BTh 78. Univ of Newc BA 68. **d** 79 Syd **p** 79 Bp Short for Syd. C of St Mark

W Wollongong Dio Syd from 79. *3 Therry Street, W Wollongong, NSW, Australia 2500.* (29-7162)

KING, Cecil John. b 46. Selw Coll Cam BA (Th) 67, MA 71. Coll of the Ressurr Mirfield 81. **d** 81 N Zam. Programme Org Th Educn in Lusaka, N & C Zam from 81. *PO Box 23054, Kitwe, Zambia.*

KING, Charles John. b 14. Univ of Lon BSc 39. MIEE CEng 46. St Steph Ho Ox 73. **d** 76 **p** 77 Reading for Ox (NSM). C of Cudd 76-78; Wantage Downs Dio Ox from 78. *48 Ardington, Wantage, Oxon, OX12 8PY.*

KING, Charles Rupert. Qu Coll St John's Newfld 45. **d** 49 **p** 50 Newfld. I of Miss of White Bay 49-52; Bay de Verde 52-54; Botwood 54-57; R of Catalina 57-67; P-in-c of Ch of Advent Tor 67-80; I of Ch Ch Mimico City and Dio Tor from 80. *329 Royal York Road, Toronto, M8V 2V9, Ont, Canada.*

KING, Clive Collingwood. St Jo Coll Morpeth ACT ThL 66. **d** 66 **p** 67 C & Goulb. C of St Jo Bapt Canberra 66-72; Chap RAAF from 72. *10 Cole Street, Point Cook, Vic, Australia 3029.* (03-395 1322)

KING, Cuthbert. Ch Ch Ox BA 11, MA 20. CIE. **d** 49 Win **p** 50 Southn for Win. Hon C of St Clem Jersey 49-51; St Luke Jersey 51-65; Perm to Offic Dio Sarum from 65. *3 Canford House, Canford Cliffs, Poole, Dorset.*

KING, Cyril Rockton. Moore Th Coll Syd ACT ThL (1st cl) 18. **d** 18 Syd for Newc **p** 20 Bath for Newc. C of Cossnock 19-20; Singleton 20-21; St D Syd 21-22; Erskineville 22-26; Kurrajong 26-27; R of St Mary w Rooty Hill 27-31; St D Syd 31-44; LPr Dio Syd from 45. *Mornington, Falls Road, Wentworth Falls, NSW, Australia 2782.* (Wentworth Falls 2782)

KING, David Charles. b 52. Coll of the Resurr Mirfield 77. **d** 78 **p** 79 York. C of Saltburn-by-the-Sea 78-81; P-in-c of Crathorne and Dioc Youth Officer Dio York from 81. *Rectory, Crathorne, Yarm, N Yorks, TS15 0BB.* (Stokesley 701158)

KING, David Frederick. b 32. Sarum Th Coll 59. **d** 61 Lon **p** 72 Win. Hon C of St Mich AA Dio Win from 71. *158 Weyhill Road, Andover, Hants.* (Andover 65393)

KING, David Russell. b 42. St D Coll Lamp BA (3rd cl Th) 67, Dipl Th 68. **d** 68 Penrith for Carl **p** 69 Carl. C of St Geo w St Luke Barrow-F 68-72; V of Edenhall w Langwathby (w Culgaith from 73) 72-74; C-in-c of Culgaith 72-73; Kirkland 72-74; V of Flookburgh 75-79; St Jas Barrow-F Dio Carl from 79. *St James's Vicarage, Barrow-in-Furness, Cumb.* (Barrow 21475)

KING, Ven David William. Univ of NZ BA 56. NZ Bd of Th Stud LTh 64. Coll Ho Ch Ch. **d** 59 Wel **p** 60 Bp Rich for Wel. C of All SS Palmerston N 59-66; V of Kelburn 66-71; Havelock N 71-79; Cambridge Dio Waik from 79; Can of Wai 76-79; Archd of Piako from 81. *Vicarage, Hamilton Road, Cambridge, NZ.* (7127-6751)

KING, David William Anthony. b 42. Ch Ch Ox BA (3rd cl Mod Hist) 63, MA 68. Westcott Ho Cam 63. **d** 65 **p** 66 York. C of Cayton w Eastfield 65-68; Southbroom 68-71; V of St Jas Holt (w Hinton Parva 72-78; and Horton w Chalbury from 75) 71-78; R of Hinton Parva 71-72; C-in-c of Horton 73-75; Team V of Melton Mowbray Dio Leic from 78. *Vicarage, Palmerston Road, Melton Mowbray, Leics.* (Melton Mowbray 63146)

KING, Dennis. b 31. ACA 53. FCA 64. E Midl Jt Ordin Tr Scheme 73. **d** 76 Repton for Derby **p** 77 Derby (APM). C of Chesterfield Dio Derby from 76. *Hillcrest, Stubben Edge, Ashover, Chesterfield.*

KING, Dennis Charles. b 27. Chich Th Coll 53. **d** 55 **p** 56 St Alb. C of Ch Ch Luton Dio St. Alb 55-58; in Amer ch 58-59; C of Ch Ch (in c of St Pet) Luton 59-63; R of Ch K Freeport Grand Bahama 63-64; PV of Ch Ch Cathl Nass 64-65; Chap Princess Margaret Hosp and the Lazaretto Nass 64-65; C of St Geo w St Marg Nass 65-66; R of Lluidas Vale 66-69; H Trin Montego Bay 69-77; V of Bromham w Oakley Dio St Alb from 77. *10 Neville Crescent, Bromham, Bedford, MK43 8JE.* (Oakley 3268)

KING, Dennis Keppel. b 33. Lich Th Coll 63. **d** 65 Warrington for Liv **p** 66 Liv. C of St Thos Eccleston 65-68; W Derby 68-71; V of St Giles Aintree Dio Liv from 71. *132 Aintree Lane, Aintree, Mer, L10 8LE.* (051-526 7908)

KING, Denys Penkivil. b 1899. Trin Coll Ox BA 22, MA 25. Wells Th Coll 22. **d** 23 **p** 24 Wakef. C of St John Wakef 23-26; Missr Trin Coll Ox Miss Stratford 26-34; PC of St Mich Castleford 34-39; R of Grasmere 39-45; V of H Trin Millhouses 45-47; Asst to Ed Sec SPCK 48-51; C of St Nich Linc 51-53; V of Aslackby w Kirkby Underwood 53-58; R of E Ilsley 58-70; RD of Newbury 66-70. *15 St George's Road, Twickenham, Middx.*

KING, Edward. b 46. Mem Univ of Newfld BA 71. Qu Coll Newfld LTh 73. **d** and **p** 72 Newfld. R of Cartwright 72-74; C of Grand Falls 74-76; R of Burgeo Dio W Newfld from 76. *Box 250, Burgeo, Newfoundland, Canada.* (709-886 2289)

KING, Very Rev Edward Laurie. Univ of Wales, BA 43. St Mich Coll Llan 43. **d** 45 **p** 46 Mon. C of Risca 45-48; Germiston 48-50; R of Robertson 50-53; Stellenbosch 53-58; Dean and R of St Geo Cathl Capetn from 58; Exam Chap to Abp of Capetn 61-67. *Deanery, Upper Orange Street, Cape Town, S Africa.* (45-2609)

KING, Ernest Cuthbert. Univ of W Austr BA 33. Wells Th Coll 35. **d** 36 **p** 37 Pet. C of St Jas Dallington 36-46; CF (EC) 39-46; V of Desborough 46-49; R of Kojonup 49-53; Pinjarra 54-60; Archd of South-West 56-58; Dir SW Native Miss W Austr 60-67; L to Offic Dios Perth and Bunb 60-67; R of Mosman Pk 67-77; Perm to Offic Dio Perth from 77. *Cottage 113, 31 Williams Road, Nedlands, W Australia 6009.* (386 7022)

KING, Ernest Frederick. St Jo Coll Morpeth ACT ThL 65. **d** 65 River **p** 66 Bath for River. C of Broken Hill 65-69; P-in-c of Hillston 69-70; C of St Pet Melb 71-73; P-in-c of St Mark Fitzroy 73-75; I 75-80. *c/o 268 George Street, Fitzroy, Vic, Australia 3065.* (03-41 2751)

KING, Frederick William. b 24. Qu Coll Birm 49. **d** 50 **p** 51 Sheff. C of Kimberworth 50-52; Luton 52-55; Chap RAF 55-70; The Leas Sch Hoylake 70-72; Wirral Gr Sch 74-75; Summer Fields Sch Ox from 75. *15 Mayfield Road, Oxford.*

KING, Gene Walton. b 45. Univ of Tor BA 73. Wycl Coll Tor MDiv 75. **d** 75 Bp Read for Tor **p** 76 Tor. C of St Paul Bloor Street Tor 75-78; on leave. *87 Morse Street, Toronto, Ont, Canada.*

KING, George Henry. b 24. **d** 79 St Alb **p** 80 Bedford for St Alb. C of Flamstead Dio St Alb from 79. *Chad Lane Farm, Flamstead, St Albans, Herts, AL3 8HW.*

KING, Gordon Donald. Wycl Coll Tor. **d** 56 Suffr Bp for Tor **p** 57 Tor. C-in-c of Vespra 56-58; R of St Geo Cliffrest Tor 58-63; Comforter Ch Tor 63-73; St Pet Oshawa 73-77; Bay Ridges 77-80; P-in-c of St Ninian Scarborough City and Dio Tor from 80. *930 Bellamy Road North, Scarborough, Toronto, Ont, Canada.*

KING, Gordon John. Univ of NZ BA 57. **d** 48 **p** 50 Wel. C of All SS Palmerston N 48-51; V of Bulls 51-54; Chap RNZAF 54-57; V of New Lynn 57-63; Takapuna Auckld 63-76; Hon C of St Mark Remuera Dio Auckld from 77. *54 Clonburn Road, Remuera, Auckland, NZ.* (549-713)

KING, Gordon John Shannon. Moore Th Coll Syd ACT ThL 35. **d** 36 **p** 37 Syd. C of St Matt Bondi 36-37; C-in-c of Huskisson 37-38; R of Erskineville 38-40; St Pet Syd 40-47; C-in c of Golden Grove 47-48; R of Lidcombe 48-56; St Paul Syd 56-58; Katoomba 58-70; L to Offic Dio Syd from 70. *30 Valley Road, Wentworth Falls, NSW, Australia 2782.* (57-1644)

KING, Gordon Virgo. St Jo Coll Morpeth 47. **d** 53 **p** 54 Perth. C of Kelmscott 53-54; St Geo Cathl Perth 54-57; Gordonvale 57-58; P-in-c of Babinda 58-67; R of N Mackay 67-72; P-in-c of S Townsville 72-74; Charters Towers Dio N Queensld from 74. *Rectory, Charters Towers, Qld, Australia.* (077-805185)

KING, Harry William. b 15. Oak Hill Th Coll 38. **d** 41 **p** 42 Lon. C of St Jo Evang U Holloway 41-44; Tooting Graveney 44-46; Perm to Offic Dio Lon 46-64 and from 67; Dio St Alb 58-64 and from 67; Chap Buckingham Coll Harrow 56-64; V of Sandon 64-67; V of Wallington w Rushden 64-67; Asst Master Greenway Sch Hillingdon 72-80; Perm to Offic Dios Lon & St Alb from 80. *318 Hempstead Road, Watford, Herts, WD1 3NA.* (Watford 32360)

KING, Jeffrey Douglas Wallace. b 43. K Coll Lon and Warm AKC 67. **d** 68 Lon **p** 69 Willesden for Lon. C of St Paul S Harrow 68-71; Garforth 71-74; V of Potternewton Dio Ripon from 74. *Vicarage, Laurel Mount, Newton Park, Leeds, LS7 3JY.* (Leeds 624271)

KING, John. b 38. SOC 77. **d** 80 **p** 81 Roch. C of S Gillingham Dio Roch from 80. *2 Fir Tree Grove, Bredhurst, Nr Gillingham, Kent.*

KING, Canon John Alexander. CCC Cam BA (2nd cl Th) 37, MA 44. Cudd Coll 37. **d** 38 **p** 39 Portsm. C of Cuthb Copnor 38-40; C of St Barn W Pondoland 40-42; P-in-c of All SS Engcobo and Warden St Aug Tr Sch 42-53; R of Rock w Heightington 53-55; Archd of Lebom and Dir of S Mis Distr 55-59; P-in-c of Cala w Elliott 59-63; R of De Aar 63-66; St Aug Kimberley 66-73; R of St Alb Kimberley 66-73; Archd of De Aar 64-66; Kimberley 66-73; Bloemf 73-76; Exam Chap to Bp of Bloemf 69-76; Kimb K 69-76; Hon Can of Kimb K from 73; P-in-c of Douglas Miss 73-76; Warden and Chap St Mich Sch for Girls Bloemf 73-76; R of St Paul Port Alfred Dio Grahmstn from 76. *Rectory, Port Alfred, CP, S Africa.* (Port Alfred 49)

KING, John Andrew. b 50. Qu Coll Birm 72. **d** 75 **p** 76 Worc. C of Halesowen 75-77; Milford Dio Derby 78-81. *141 Breedon Street, Long Eaton, Notts.*

KING, John Charles. St Pet Hall ox BA (2nd cl Eng Lang and Lit) 51, MA 55. Oak Hill Th Coll 51. **d** 53 **p** 54 Roch for Ox. C of St Paul Slough 53-57; V of Ch Ch Ware 57-60; Ed 'C of E Newspaper' 60-68; L to Offic Dio St Alb 60-70; Asst

Master Boston Gr Sch Lincs and L to Offic Dio Linc from 74. *6 Somersby Way, Boston, Lincs, PE21 9PQ.* (0205 63061)

KING, John Colin. b 39. Cudd Coll 69. **d** 71 Reading for Ox **p** 72 Ox. C of Cookham 71-75; Asst Youth Chap Dio B & W from 75; C-in-c of Merriott Dio B & W 76-80; V (w Hinton, Dinnington and Lopen) from 80; P-in-c of Hinton St Geo w Dinnington 79-80. *Vicarage, Merriott, Somt.* (Crewkerne 3226)

KING, John David. b 37. Univ of Wales Dipl Th 63. St Aid Coll 67. **d** 69 **p** 70 Derby. C of Whitfield 69-71; St Laur in I of Thanet 71-76; V of Alkham w Capel-le-Ferne and Hougham-by-Dover Dio Cant from 76. *20 Alexandra Road, Capel-le-Fern, Folkestone, Kent.* (Folkestone 50252)

KING, John Godfrey. b 1900. Trin Coll Dub BA 23. **d** 29 **p** 30 Down. Hd of Trin Coll Dub Miss Belf 29-33; C of St Jude Belf 33-35; R of Derriaghy 35-46; I of Larne 46-51; R of St Matt Shankill Belf 51-61; C-in-c of Layde w Cushendun 61-71; Can of St Anne's Cathl Belf 57-71. *8 Quarry Hill, Portstewart, Co Derry, N Ireland.*

KING, John Gordon. b 38. Lewis & Clark Coll Oregon USA BA 65. Trin Coll Tor 75. **d** 77 Bp Read for Tor **p** 78 BC. I of Cumb & Fanny Bay 78-80; St Sav Vic Dio BC from 81. *512 Catherine Street, Victoria, BC, Canada.*

KING, Canon John Humphrey. b 08. K Coll Cam BA (3rd Engl Trip) and Winchester Reading Pri 30, MA 34. MBE (Mil) 46. Cudd Coll 31. **d** 33 **p** 34 Win. C of N Stoneham 33-36; All SS Heref 36-39; Prec, Sacr and Min Can of Dur Cathl; L to Offic Dio Dur and CF (TA) 39-45; R of Stevenage 45-54; RD of Hitchin 53-54; V of St Paul Bedford 54-69; Bp's Chap 55-69; Chap Bedford Gen Hosp 59-66; Chap HM Pris Bedford 61-69; Hon Can of St Alb from 66. *25 Abbey Mill Lane, St Albans, Herts.* (St Albans 62852)

KING, Canon John Kenneth. b 25. Univ of Lon BD 50. ALCD 50. **d** 50 **p** 51 Chelmsf. C of St Paul East Ham 50-54; Laindon w Basildon (in c of St Andr Basildon from 56) 54-57; Min of St Andr Eccles Distr Basildon 57-61; Exam and Dom Chap to Bp of Lagos and Succr Ch Ch Cathl Lagos 62-67; Can of Lagos 65-67; Can (Emer) from 67; R of Irthlingborough 67-75; RD of Higham 69-74; V of St Mark City and Dio Pet from 75; Non-Res Can of Pet from 77; Dioc Warden of Readers from 77. *St Mark's Vicarage, Peterborough, PE1 2SN.* (Pet 54516)

KING, John Michael Stuart. b 22. St Edm Hall, Ox BA 48, MA 52. Cudd Coll. **d** 50 **p** 51 Dur. C of Ryhope 50-53; Guisborough 53-56; V of High w Low Worsall and of Kirk Levington 56-60; R of Hinderwell w Roxby 60-71; V of Hibaldstow Dio Linc from 71. *Hibaldstow Vicarage, Brigg, Lincs, DN20 9PB.* (Brigg 54348)

KING, John Robert. Seager Hall Ont. **d** 62 Bp Appleyard for Hur **p** 63 Hur. C of Lucknow 62-65; I of Walkerton 65-68; St Clair Beach 68-73; Kincardine Dio Hur from 73. *Kincardine, Ont., Canada.* (519-396 2185)

KING, Joseph Stephen. b 39. St Chad's Coll Dur BA (2nd cl Th) 62, Dipl Th (w distinc) 63. **d** 64 **p** 65 S'wark. C of Lewisham 64-68; Hon C of Ch Ch Milton-next-Gravesend Dio Roch from 68; Lect Avery Hill Coll of Educn 68-73; Sen Lect from 73. *4 Elmfield Close, Gravesend, Kent.* (G'end 68074)

KING, Keith Malcolm. b 49. St Jo Coll Auckld. **d** 78 **p** 79 Auckld. C of St Mark Remuera 78-81; V of Coromandel Dio Auckld from 81. *Vicarage, Annette Place, Whitianga, NZ.*

KING, Kenneth Marion. Univ of Minnesota PhD 40. **d** 57 **p** 58 BC. C of St John Vic 57-58; I of St Pet Vic 58-65; L to Offic Dio BC from 65. *2560 Queenswood Drive, Victoria, BC, Canada.*

KING, Kenneth Roy. b 32. Sarum Th Coll 62. **d** 64 **p** 65 Glouc. C of St Barn Tuffley Glouc 64-67; Swanage 67-71; V of Broadstone 71-80; R of Abenhall w Mitcheldean Dio Glouc from 80. *St Michael's Rectory, Mitcheldean, Glos, GL17 0BS.* (0594 542434)

KING, Lawrence Norman. b 38. ARICS. St Deiniol's Libr Hawarden 78. **d** 80 Bp Mort for Leic **p** 81 Leic (APM). Hon C of St Hugh L Bowden Dio Leic from 80. *21 Hillcrest Avenue, Market Harborough, Leics, LE16 7AR.*

KING, Ven Leonard Mansfield. Univ of NZ BA 36. **d** and **p** 46 Wel. C of St Jas Lower Hutt 46-47; V of Naenae 47-50; Eltham 50-53; St Pet Palmerston N 53-61; V of St Andr Epsom Auckld 60-65; Archd of Hauraki 64-65; V of All SS Palmerston N 65-79; Hon Can of Wel 68-71; Archd of Rangitikei 71-79; Archd (Emer) from 79; Perm to Offic Dio Auckld from 79. *Box 97, Whangaparoa, Auckland, NZ.*

KING, Canon Leslie Richard. b 06. St Jo Coll Dur BA 29, MA 32. **d** 30 **p** 31 S'wark. C of St Jas Hatcham 30-33; St John Ealing Dean 33-34; V of H Trin Jesmond 34-40; H Trin Anerley 40-47; Surr from 46; Home Sec BFBS and Publ Pr Dio Roch 47-58; R of Chelsfield 58-73; RD of Orpington 64-73; Hon Can of Roch 69-73; Can (Emer) from 73; Perm to Offic Dio Ex from 73. *St Martin's, Gidcot Cross, Holsworthy, Devon, EX22 7AS.* (Shebbear 412)

KING, Malcolm Charles. Chich Th Coll 67. **d** 70 **p** 71 St Alb. C of St Pet Mill End Rickmansworth 70-72; Chap RAF 72-76; R of St Pet W Lynn, King's Lynn 76-81; V of Croxley Green Dio St Alb from 81. *All Saints Vicarage, Croxley Green, Rickmansworth, Herts, WD3 3HJ.* (Rmnwth 72109)

KING, Malcolm Stewart. b 56. Sarum Wells Th Coll 77. **d** 80 **p** 81 Guildf. C of Farnham Dio Guildf from 80. *20 Stephendale Road, Farnham, Surrey, GU9 9QP.*

KING, Martin Quartermain. b 39. Univ of Reading, BA (2nd cl Cl) 61. Cudd Coll 62. **d** 64 **p** 65 Dur. C of St Hilda w St Thos S Shields 64-66; Newton Aycliffe 66-71; V of Chilton Moor 71-78; R of Middleton-S-Geo Dio Dur from 78. *Rectory, Middleton-one-Row, Darlington, Co Durham, DL2 1AP.* (Dinsdale 332410)

KING, Maurice Charles Francis. b 32. Em Coll Cam BA 55, MA 59. ACP 58. Chich Th Coll 78. **d** 79 **p** 80 Blackb. C of St Alb w St Paul and of St Cath Burnley Dio Blackb from 79. *472 Brunshaw Road, Burnley, Lancs, BB10 3JB.* (Burnley 27670)

KING, Meyrick Vincent Bryan. Univ of NZ MSc 36. **d** 48 **p** 49 Dun. C of Invercargill 48-51; V of Riverton 51-55; Balclutha 55-61; C of Oamaru 61-66; P-in-c of Hampden w Maheno 66-69; C of Anderson's Bay Dio Dun from 69. *68 Greig Street, Broad Bay, Otago Peninsula, NZ.* (Portobello 554)

KING, Michael Charles. Worc Coll Ox BA 56, MA 60. Coll Resurr Mirfield. **d** 62 **p** 63 Lon. Hon C of All S Hampstead 62-65; C of Thorpe Episcopi 66-69; Ed Sec Bible Reading Fellowship from 69. *65 Brinkburn Gardens, Edgware, Middx.* (01-952 4966)

KING, Nicholas Bernard Paul. b 46. Wycl Hall Ox 72. **d** 75 Doncaster for Sheff **p** 76 Sheff. C of Pitsmoor w Wicker 75-78; Erdington 78-80; H Trin Sutton Coldfield Dio Birm from 80. *10 Midland Drive, Sutton Coldfield, W Midl.* (021-355 3352)

KING, Noel Quinton. St Pet Hall, Ox BA (2nd cl *sc* Mod Hist) 47, MA 48, 1st cl Th 49. Univ of Nottm PhD 54. Wycl Hall Ox. **d** 50 **p** 51 Southw. C of East Retford 50-51; St Pet w St Jas Nottm 51-53; Lect in Ch Hist Nottm Univ 51-55; C of Shelford 53-55; Prof of Div Univ Ghana and L to Offic Dio Accra 55-62; Hd of Dept Relig Stud Makerere Coll and L to Office Dio Nam 63-68. *c/o Makerere University College, PO Box 262, Kampala, Uganda.*

KING, Paul Derwent. b 39. Ball Coll Ox 2nd cl Cl Mods 60, BA (3rd cl Lit Hum) 62, MA 65. Cudd Coll 63. **d** 65 **p** 66 Portsm. C of St Mark N End Portsea 65-67; Iffley 67-70; Asst Chap Univ of Nottm 70-72; C of E Chap Univ of Southn 72-78; V of St Andr Headington City and Dio Ox from 78; RD of Cowley from 81. *Vicarage, St Andrew's Road, Headington, Oxford, OX3 9DL.* (Oxford 61094)

KING, Peter Duncan. b 48. AKC 70. K Coll Lon LLB 70. Called to Bar Gray's Inn 70. Fitzw Coll Cam BA (Th) 72, MA 77. Westcott Ho Cam 70. **d** 80 **p** 81 Kens for Lon. C of St John Notting Hill Dio Lon from 80. *44 Kensington Park Gardens, W11.* (01-229 9139)

KING, Peter George. b 24. Univ of Lon LLB 52. ALCD 55. **d** 55 **p** 56 Lon. [f Solicitor] C of St Cuthb Chitts Hill Wood Green 55-59; Woking 59-61; V of St Bede Toxt Pk 61-68; St Paul Leyton Dio Chelmsf from 68. *St Paul's Vicarage, Essex Road, E10 6EG.* (01-539 2250)

KING, Canon Philip David. b 35. Keble Coll Ox BA 57, MA 61. Tyndale Hall Bris 58. **d** 60 **p** 61 S'wark. C of H Trin Redhill 60-63; Wallington Surrey 63-67; V of Ch Ch Fulham 67-74; Gen Sec SAMS from 74; Hon Can of Chile from 77. *Allen Gardiner House, Pembury Road, Tunbridge Wells, Kent, TN2 3QU.*

KING, Rawlins Henry Pyne. b 16. ALCD 42. **d** 42 S'wark for Chich **p** 43 Chich. C of Bp Hannington Mem Ch Hove 42-44; St Pet (in c of Ch Ch) Southborough 44-47; R of Ore 47-55; Chap Fairlight Sanat 49-55; Osborne Ho 51-55; Metrop Org Sec CPAS 55-60; Perm to Offic Dios Lon; S'wark; Chelmsf; Ox and Chich 55-60; V of Virginia Water 60-68; Hailsham 68-81. *19 Truleigh Court, Truleigh Road, Upper Beeding, W Sussex, BN4 3JR.* (Steyning 815748)

KING, Canon Rendolph Olenthius Constantine. MBE 58. Univ of Dur LTh 29, BA 30. Univ of NY MA 45. **d** 28 **p** 29 Ja. C of All SS Kingston 28-30; Asst Master Kingston Coll 31-36; R of Morant Bay 36-42; Commiss to Bp of Ja in USA 43-45; Dom Chap to Abp of West Indies 45-46; R of St Geo Kingston 46-69; Exam Chap to Bp of Ja 51-76; Can of Ja from 51; Sec of Synod 52-59. *5 Cargill Avenue, Kingston 10, Jamaica, WI.* (092-68418)

KING, Canon Robert Victor. b 17. St Jo Coll Dur BA 48. Dipl Th 50. **d** 50 **p** 51 S'wark. C of St Mary Magd Peckham 50-52; Reigate 52-56; V of Ch Ch Richmond 56-60; Peckham Dio S'wark from 60; RD of Camberwell 70-75; Hon Can of S'wark from 74. *22 St Mary's Road, SE15 2DW.* (01-639 4596)

KING, Canon Stuart John Langley. b 33. Selw Coll Cam

BA 57, MA 61. **d** 59 Ex **p** 60 Crediton for Ex. C of Ascen Crownhill Plymouth 59-62; Horsham (in c of St Jo Evang) 62-67; V of St Mark Ford Devonport 67-77; RD of Plymouth 74-77; Can Res of Cov Cathl from 77. *18 Belvedere Road, Coventry, CV5 6PF.*

KING, Terence Reginald. St Steph Ho Ox 58. **d** 61 **p** 62 Wakef. C of Thornhill Lees w Savile Town 61-65; V of Glass Houghton 65-77; Woodkirk Dio Wakef from 77. *Woodkirk Vicarage, Dewsbury, W Yorks.* (Batley 472375)

KING, Ven Thomas Bandele. Fourah Bay Coll 40. **d** 44 **p** 47 Sier L. Missr Dio Sier L 44-47; C of St Geo Cathl Freetown 47-54; Prec 54-66; R of H Trin Freetown Dio Sier L from 66; Can of Sier L from 57; Archd of Freetown from 66. *Holy Trinity Vicarage, Freetown, Kissy Road, Sierra Leone.* (Freetown 23743)

KING, Canon Thomas George. b 10. OBE 67. Late Scho of St D Coll Lamp BA (3rd cl Hist) 32. Jes Coll Ox BA (Th) 34, MA 38. DD (Lambeth) 79. St Steph Ho Ox 34. **d** 34 **p** 35 Mon. C of Machen 34-36; St Jas Pontypool 36-46; R of Stoke Charity w Hunton Dio Win from 46; Hon Sec Win Dioc Coun of Youth 47-64; Warden of Readers Dio Win 47-74; Hon Sec Centr Readers Bd 56-80; ACCM Readers C'tee 77-80; Hon Can of Win from 58. *33 Western Road, Winchester, Hants, SO22 5AJ.* (Win 61415)

KING, Walter Raleigh. b 45. New Coll Ox BA 67, MA 74. Cudd Coll 71. **d** 74 **p** 75 Ely C of Wisbech 74-77; Barrow-in-Furness 77-79; P-in-c of Cusop and of Clifford and of Hardwicke Dio Heref from 79; Whitney w Winforton Dio Heref from 81. *Cusop Rectory, Hay-on-Wye, Hereford.* (Hay-on-Wye 820634)

KING-EDWARDS, William Bagot Ramsey. **d** 51 **p** 52 Moos. C of Schumacher Miss 51-52; Centr Patricia 52-53; I of Hearst 53-57; Garden River 57-63; White River 63-69; Manitouwadge 69-74. *526 McKellar Street, Peterborough, Ont., Canada.*

KING-SMITH, (Robert) Philip Hugh. CCC Cam BA 52, MA 56. Cudd Coll 52. **d** 54 **p** 55 Dur. C of St Pet Stockton-on-Tees 54-59; PC of Ch of Good Shepherd Bp Wearmouth 59-64; M SSF from 64; Novice Master Amer Prov SSF from 66. *Little Portion Friary, Mt Sinai, NY 11766, USA.*

KINGCOME, Andrew David. b 47. Univ of Lon Dipl Th (Extra-Mural) 72. Kelham Th Coll 66. **d** 71 Middleton for Man **p** 72 Man. C of Hollinwood 71-74; St Chad Limeside, Oldham 74-76; V of Kirkholt 76-81; R of St Pet W Lynn, King's Lynn Dio Nor from 81; Chap to Queen Elizabeth Hosp King's Lynn from 81. *West Lynn Rectory, King's Lynn, Norf, PE34 3JT.* (King's Lynn 5093)

KINGCOME, John Parken. b 18. M IMechE (CEng) 50. Sarum Th Coll 65. **d** 67 **p** 68 Sarum. C of Melksham 67-70; C-in-c of Woodborough w Manningford Bohune and Beechingstoke 70-74; V of Swanborough 72-74; R 74-79; RD of Pewsey from 75; Custos of St John's Hosp Heytesbury from 79. *St John's Hospital, Heytesbury, Warminster, Wilts, BA12 0HW.*

KINGDON, Henry Kent. Univ of Lon BA 39. Westcott Ho Cam 42. **d** 43 Plymouth for Ex **p** 44 Ex. C of Stoke Damerel 43-47; C-in-c of St Bart Stoke Damerel 47-50; C-in-c of Bridestowe 50-53; R 53-58; PC of Sourton 53-58; V of Mortehoe Dio Ex from 58. *Mortehoe Vicarage, Woolacombe, N Devon.* (Woolacombe 870598)

KINGDON, Henry Paul. b 07. Late Scho of CCC Ox 1st cl Cl Mod 28, BA (2nd cl Lit Hum) 30. Dipl Th (w distinc) 31, MA 33. Ripon Hall Ox 33. **d** 33 **p** 34 Ox. Chap and Lect Ex Coll Ox 33-45; Fell 34-45; Libr 40-45; Select Pr Univ of Ox 40-42; R of Great Somerford 45-51; C-in-c of Little Somerford 47-51; L to Offic Dio Win and Chap and Lect K Alfred's Coll Win 51-56; Hd of Evang Ch Section Relig Affairs Branch Control Commiss Germany 47-49; V of Chewton Mendip w Emborrow 56-64; Lect Wells Th Coll 56-58; Perm to Offic Dio Bris from 64; Hon C of Almondsbury Dio Bris from 74. *3 Knole Park, Almondsbury, Bristol, BS12 4BS.* (Almondsbury 613587)

KINGHAM, Derek Henry. b 29. Oak Hill Th Coll 56. **d** 58 **p** 59 S'wark. C of St John Deptford 58-60; Normanton-by-Derby 60-63; R of Gaulby w K Norton and L Stretton 63-73; V of St Sav Bacup from 73. *St Saviour's Vicarage, New Line, Bacup, Lancs, OL13 0BY.* (Bacup 873362)

KINGHAM, Canon John Arthur. b 14. Ch Coll Cam BA 36, 3rd cl Th Trip pt i 37, MA 40. Ridley Hall Cam 36. **d** 38 Lon **p** 39 Willesden for Lon. C of Roxeth 38-40; Fisherton Anger 40-43; R of Hamworthy 44-51; V of Gt Baddow 51-82; RD of Chelmsf 67-77; Hon Can of Chelmsf Cathl 75-82; Can (Emer) from 82. *63 Tensing Gardens, Billericay, CM12 9JY.*

KINGHORN, Richard. b 16. CCC Cam 2nd cl Mod Lang Trip pt i 36, BA (2nd cl Th Trip pt i) 38, MA 42. Linc Th Coll 39. **d** 40 Win **p** 46 Pet. C of Eastleigh 40-41; serving w the Army 41-46; Chap of Stamford Sch 46-58; C-in-c of Stamford Baron 46-47; Chap K Coll Sch Wimbledon 58-77; Tutor Open Univ from 77. *5 Edge Hill, SW19 4LR.* (01-946 0393)

KINGI, Romana Tautari. b 15. **d** 77 **p** 78 Aotearoa for Wai. C of Ruatoki Whakatane Past Dio Wai from 77. *Poro Poro, Whakatane, NZ.*

KINGS, Graham Ralph. b 53. Hertf Coll Ox BA 77, MA 80. Selw Coll Cam Dipl Th 80. Ridley Hall Cam 78. **d** 80 Willesden for Lon **p** 81 Lon. C of St Mark Harlesden Dio Lon from 80. *26 Ashburnham Road, NW10 5SE.*

KINGS, James Albert. Linc Th Coll 27. **d** 30 **p** 31 Wakef. C of Chapelthorpe 30-34; Barnsley (in c of St Paul) 34-37; V of Luddenden 37-68; Crambe w Whitwell and Huttons Ambo 68-77. *Address temp unknown.*

KINGS, Peter Robert. K Coll Lon and Warm AKC 61. **d** 62 **p** 63 Bris. C of St Matt Moorfields Bris 62-65; Dept of Educn Univ of Hull 65-66; Dep Dir Lon and S'wark Dioc Bds of Educn 66-70; Asst Master K Edw VII Sch K Lynn from 70; L to Offic Dio Nor from 79. *113 Gaywood Road, King's Lynn, Norf.* (K Lynn 2404)

KINGSBURY, Leslie Raymond. Linc Th Coll 42. **d** 43 **p** 44 Lon. C of All H Twickenham 43-45; C of St Thos (in c of St Phil) Ex 45-47; V of Clawton 47-49; R of Tansor w Cotterstock and Fotheringhay 49-53; Eye 53-57; PC of Verwood 57-63; V of Rowde 63-66; R of Hethersett w Canteloff 66-71; V of Ketteringham 66-71; RD of Humbleyard 69-71; R of L Massingham 71-73. *112 Pytchley Road, Kettering, Northants.*

KINGSBURY, Richard John. b 41. Univ of Lon BA (2nd cl Engl) 63. Linc Th Coll 65. **d** 67 **p** 68 Newc T. C of St Luke Wallsend 67-69; Monkseaton 69-70; Chap K Coll Lon 70-75; L to Offic Dio Lon 70-75; V of Hungerford Dio Ox from 75. *Vicarage, Hungerford, Berks, RG17 0JB.* (Hungerford 2844)

KINGSFORD, Maurice Rooke. Univ of Tor BA 15. G and C Coll Cam BA (3rd cl Hist Trip) 20, MA 25. St Jo Coll Ox MA (*ad eund*) 44, BLitt 46. McGill Univ Montr STM 53. FRHistS 48. **d** 23 **p** 24 Tor. C of St John Pet Ont 23-24; R of Courteenhall 26-28; Master and Asst Chap Lower Canada Coll and C of St Steph Westmount Montr 28-30; I of Perrytown 30-32; Chap and Asst Master K Coll Sch Windsor NS 32-33; V of Orton-on-the-Hill w Twycross 34-36; Barton 36-38; R of Helhoughton w Raynham St Martin 38-41; CF (EC) 41-43; V of Fyfield w Tubney 43-47; R of Nuneham Courtenay 47-68. *423 Elm Avenue, Westmount, Montreal 217, PQ, Canada.*

KINGSLAND, Desmond George. b 23. Sarum Wells Th Coll 75. **d** 78 **p** 79 Win. C of Epiph Moordown Bournemouth Dio Win from 78. *23 Granby Road, Bournemouth, BH9 3NZ.*

KINGSLEY, Brian St Clair. b 26. St Steph Ho Ox 56. **d** 59 **p** 60 Ox. C of Tilehurst 59-63. *Monastery, Crawley Down, Crawley, Sussex.*

KINGSLEY-SMITH, John Sydney. b 45. Ridley Hall Cam 78. **d** 80 Taunton for B & W **p** 81 B & W. C of H Trin Nailsea Dio B & W from 80. *12 Trinity Road, Nailsea, Avon.*

KINGSMILL-LUNN, Brooke. b 32. Trin Coll Dub BA (1st cl Mod) 62, MA 66. Chich Th Coll 62. **d** 64 **p** 65 Lon. C of St Barn Northolt 64-66; All H St Pancras 66-68; P-in-c of St Luke Hornsey Dio Lon from 68; V of H Trin Stroud Green Dio Lon from 79. *Vicarage, Granville Road, Stroud Green, N4 4EL.* (01-340 2051)

KINGSNORTH, Canon Eric John. b 11. Wells Th Coll 45. **d** 47 **p** 48 Cant. C of St Jo Evang Upper Norwood 47-50; Maidstone 50-53; V of H Trin Yeovil 53-63; Preb of Henstridge in Wells Cathl 61-63; Exam Chap to Bp of B & W 61-78; Commiss SW Tang from 62; V of Newark-on-Trent 63-74; RD of Newark 63-74; Surr 65-74; C-in-c of Cotham 64-74; Hawton 64-74; Shelton 64-74; Sibthorpe 65-66; Hon Can of Southw 66-74; Can (Emer) from 74; Proc Conv Southw 67-75; C-in-c of St Leon Newark 72-74; P-in-c of Bradpole 74-78; Perm to Offic Dio Win from 78. *3 De Mowbray Way, Lymington, Hants, SO4 9PD.* (Lymington 78397)

KINGSNORTH, Canon John Sydney. b 15. Keble Coll Ox BA (2nd cl Th) 39, MA 61. Cudd Coll 39. **d** 40 **p** 41 Ripon. C of All S Leeds 40-45; UMCA Miss at Fiwila Miss 45-53; P-in-c of Chipili 53-61; Archd of Rhod N 61-62; Commiss SW Tang 62-65; Masasi 62-65; N Rhod 62-64; Zam 64-67; Nyasa 62-64; Malawi from 64; Hon Can of Lusaka Cathl from 61; Gen Sec UMCA 61-64; Sen Dep Sec USPG 65-67; P-in-c of Chingola 67-70; Sec of Zam Angl Coun 71-72; Dep Sec USPG 73-80; Commiss Centr Zam 73-74; N Zam and Lusaka from 73; Hon C of Ascen Blackheath 75-80; St Mich AA Barnes Dio S'wark from 81. *41 Elm Bank Gardens, Barnes, SW13 0NX.*

KINGSTON (Jamaica), Lord Bishop Suffragan of. (Vacant)

KINGSTON, Albert Victor. AKC 35. OBE 58. **d** 35 Bp Crick for Derby **p** 36 Derby. C of Bolsover 35-37; CF 37-63; Hon Chap to HM the Queen 61-63; Dean and R of Bulawayo Cathl 63-66; Commiss Matab from 66; V of Folkestone

66-72; St Mary Virg Platt 72-79; Perm to Offic Dio Cant from 79. *381 London Road, Deal, CT14 9PS.* (Deal 66217)

KINGSTON, Bertie William. b 47. Oak Hill Th Coll 69. **d** 72 Cork for Liv **p** 73 Liv. C of Walton Breck 72-75; St Columb's Cathl Templemore 75-76; I of Kildallon w Newtowngore and Corrawallen Dio Kilm from 76. *Kildallon Rectory, Ardlogher, Ballyconnell, Co Cavan, Irish Republic.* (049 26255)

KINGSTON, Eric. b 24. **d** 69 **p** 70 Down. C of Ballymacarrett 69-72; St Columba Knock Belf 72-76; R of Annahilt Dio Drom from 76; Dioc C Dio Down from 77. *Annahilt Rectory, Hillsborough, Co Down, N Ireland.*

KINGSTON, Frederick Temple. Univ of Tor BA 47, MA 50, LTh 50, BD 52. Ch Ch Ox DPhil 54. **d** 49 **p** 50 NS. Chap RCN 49-51; Prof of Systematic Th at Angl Th Coll Vancouver 55-58; Prof of Phil Cant Coll Windsor Dio Hur 59-63; Vice-Prin 63-65; Prin from 65. *Canterbury College, University of Windsor, Windsor, Ont., Canada.*

KINGSTON, George. TCD BA 44. **d** 44 **p** 45 Lim. C of St Lawr St John and Trin Lim 44-46; I of Templeharry 46-48; C of Ch Ch Belfast 48-51; C-in-c of Magharahamlet 51-54; R of Denmark w Austria 54-56; Gosnells 56-60; Cockburn Sound 60-63; Boyup Brook 63-65; Swanlinbar w Templeport 65-71; I of Killeshandra 71-79; Derrylane 71-79. *c/o Killeshandra Rectory, Co Cavan, Irish Republic.* (Killeshandra 38)

KINGSTON, George Mervyn. b 47. Div Hostel Dub 70. **d** 73 **p** 74 Down. C of Comber 73-77; St Donard Belf Dio Down from 77; Min Can of Down Cathl from 79. *20 Sandford Avenue, Belfast, BT5 5NW, N Ireland.* (Belfast 655702)

KINGSTON, John Desmond George. b 40. Trin Coll Dub BA 63, Div Test (3rd cl) 64, MA 66. **d** 64 **p** 65 Arm. C of Armagh Dio Arm from 64; Hon V Cho of Arm Cathl from 69; Chap Portora R Sch from 70. *45 Old Rossorry Road, Enniskillen, Co. Fermanagh, BT74 7LF, N Ireland.* (Ennisk 4493)

KINGSTON, Kenneth Robert. b 42. TCD BA 65, MA 69. **d** 66 **p** 67 Oss. C of Enniscorthy 66-69; Ballymena 70-72; Drumragh and Mountfield 72-78; I of Badoney U Dio Derry from 78. *Rectory, Glen Park Road, Gortin, Co Tyrone, N Ireland.* (Gortin 227)

KINGSTON, Michael Joseph. b 51. AKC and BD 73. St Aug Coll Cant 73. **d** 74 Ox **p** 75 Reading for Ox. C of H Trin Reading 74-77; New Eltham Dio S'wark from 77. *7 Craybury End, New Eltham, SE9.*

KINGSTON, Peter Bradley. Bps' Univ Lennox BA 47. Dioc Th Coll Montr 50. **d** 51 **p** 52 Queb. Miss Magd Is 51-54; R of Danville 54-59; Grand' Mère 59-61; and 65-67; St Cuthb Montr 61-65; Master St Lawr Coll Cornw Ont 67-69; I of Valcartier 69. *Apt 1516, 235 Sherbrooke Street, Montreal 129, BC, Canada.*

KINGSTON, Richard Albert. TCD BA 34. **d** 36 **p** 37 Clogh. C of Newbliss w Killeevan and Aghabog 36-38; C-in-c of Mullaghdun 38-45; I of Aghavea 45-77; Priv Chap to Bp of Clogh 55-60; Preb of Clogh Cathl 60-73; Chan 73-77. *c/o Aghavea Rectory, Brookeborough, Co Fermanagh, N Ireland.*

KINGSTON, Robert George. b 46. TCD BA 68. **d** 69 Connor. C of St Thos Belf 69-74; Dean's V of St Canice Cathl Kilkenny 75-77; I of Creagh U 77-79; R of Maryborough Dio Leigh from 79. *Rectory, Portlaoise, Co Laois, Irish Republic.* (Portlaoise 21154)

KINGSTON, Roy William Henry. b 31. Chich Th Coll 60. **d** 62 **p** 63 Ripon. C of St Aid Leeds 62-66; St Mary Cathl Johann 66-69; R of Bramley Johann 69-73; V of Bramley Leeds 74-81; R of Hemel Hempstead Dio St Alb from 81. *Rectory, 40 High Street, Hemel Hempstead, Herts, HP1 3AF.* (H Hempstead 3838)

KINGSTON, Thomas Martyn Sibbald. Univ of W Ont BA 61. Hur Coll BTh 64. **d** 64 Hur for Montr **p** 65 Montr. C of St Mathias Montr 64-66; Roxboro 66-68; R of St John's Mont 68-73; P-in-c of Iberville 68-73; on leave. *600 Jarvis Street, Toronto, Ont., Canada.* (416-924 9192)

KINGSTON, Walter Henry Christopher. b 35. Univ of man BSc 55. Wells Th Coll. **d** 59 Blackb **p** 60 Lanc for York. C of Ribbleton 59-62; St Matt Ex 62-65; V of All SS Chorley 65-67; Chap St D Miss Bonda 67-71; V of St Aid Bamber Bridge 71-80; Padiham w Higham Dio Blackb from 80. *1 Arbory Drive, Padiham, Burnley, Lancs BB12 8JS.* (Padiham 72442)

KINGSTON, William Ypres. b 19. Trin Coll Dub BA 40, Abp King Pri 42, MA 43, King Mem Pri 43, BD 46, Div Test (1st cl) 43. **d** 43 **p** 44 Connor. C of H Trin Portrush 43-47; H Trin Brompton Lon 47-51; CF 51-54; V of Ch Ch St Pancras 55-81. *c/o 3 Chester Place, NW1.* (01-935 1572)

KINGSTON-UPON-THAMES, Lord Bishop Suffragan of. *See* Sutton, Right Rev Keith Norman.

KINGSTON-UPON-THAMES, Archdeacon of. *See* Jacob, Ven Bernard Victor.

KINGTON, David Bruce. b 45. Trin Coll Bris 72. **d** 72 **p** 73 Lich. C of Wellington w Eyton 72-77; St Jo Evang Boscombe, Bournemouth 77-81; R of Michelmersh and Timsbury and Farley-Chamberlayne and Braishfield Dio Win from 81. *Rectory, Braishfield, Romsey, Hants, SO5 0PR.* (Braishfield 68335)

KINKLEY, Gordon Robert. b 43. Univ of Ott BA 73, MA 76. Wycl Coll Tor LTh 70. **d** 70 **p** 71 Ont. C of Kente 70-71; R of Elizabethtown 71-72; on leave 72-74; I of Tweed-Roslin 74-78; St John St Catharines Dio Niag from 78. *80 Main Street, St Catharines, Ont, Canada.* (416-934 1020)

KINNAIRD, Keith. b 42. Chich Th Coll 72. **d** 75 Reading for Ox **p** 76 Ox. C of St Pet Didcot 75-78; Chap Abingdon Hosp from 79; Abingdon (in c of St Mich) 78-82; R of Sunningwell Dio Ox from 82. *St Leonards House, 38 Sugworth Lane, Radley, Abingdon, Oxon, OX14 2HY.* (0865 735984)

KINNS, Kenneth Herbert Frank. b 12. AKC 36. **d** 36 **p** 37 Sheff. C of Woodhouse 36-39; Swinton 39-42; CF (EC) 42-46; C-in-c of Thurcroft Conv Distr 46-48; V 48-55; C-in-c of Ulley 48-55; V of St Nath Crookesmoor Sheff 55-64; St Pet Abbeydale Sheff 64-76; C-in-c of Rockland St Pet w All SS and St Andr 76-81. *Address temp unknown.*

KINSELLA, Nigel John Andrew. b 37. Univ of Lanc BA (2nd cl Phil and Rel Stud) 70. Kelham Th Coll 57. **d** 62 **p** 63 Southw. M SSM 61-80; C of St Geo Nottm 62-64; Chap St Martin's C of E Coll of Educn Lanc 64-67 and 73-74; L to Offic Dio Blackb 65-70; Tutor Kelham Th Coll 70-73; WCC Stud 75-77; Sub-Warden St Deiniol's Libr Hawarden 77-80; V of St Marg High Bentham Dio Bradf from 80. *Vicarage, High Bentham, Lancaster, LA2 7LH.* (Bentham 61321)

KINSEY, Russell Frederick David. b 34. Sarum Th Coll 59. **d** 62 **p** 63 B & W. C of Twerton-on-Avon 62-66; N Cadbury 66-76; Yarlington 66-76; C-in-c of Compton Pauncefoot w Blackford 66-76; Maperton 66-76; N Cheriton 66-76; Team V of Camelot 76-79; V of Pill Dio B & W from 79; P-in-c of Easton-in-Gordano w Portbury Dio B & W from 80. *Vicarage, Pill, Bristol.* (Pill 2230)

KINSLEY, James. b 22. Univ of Edin MA 43, PhD 51, DLitt 59. Or Coll Ox BA (1st cl Engl) 47, MA 51. FRHistS 61. FBA 71. Kelham Th Coll. **d** 62 **p** 63 Southw. Prof of Engl Stud Univ of Nottm from 61; Dean Faculty of Arts 67-70; C of Beeston 62-64; L to Offic Dio Southw from 64. *Department of English, The University, Nottingham.*

KINSMAN, John Brailsford. ACT ThL 65. St Jo Coll Morpeth. 61. **d** 65 **p** 66 Adel. C of Mt Gambier 65-67; P-in-c of Tumby Bay-Cummins 67-73; R of Bordertown 73-78; Gawler Dio Adel from 78. *21 Cowan Street, Gawler, S Australia 5118.* (085-22 2534)

KINSMEN, Barry William. b 40. **d** 74 **p** 75 Truro (APM). C of Padstow 74-78; Adv in Relig Educn Dio Truro from 79; Publ Pr Dio Truro 79-80; P-in-c of L Petherick 80-81; St Issey Dio Truro 80-81; V (w L Petherick) from 81. *St Issey Vicarage, Wadebridge, Cornw, PL27 7QB.* (Rumford 314)

KINTU, Zakaliya. **d** 39 **p** 41 Ugan. P Dio Ugan. *Naminango, Busoga, Uganda.*

KINUKA, Yosiya. **d** 41 **p** 42 Ugan. CMS P Dio Ugan 41-60; Dio Ankole-K 60-67. *Church of Uganda, Nshungyezi, Isingiro, PO Mbarara, Uganda.*

KINUTHIA, Wilson. b 41. **d** and **p** 76 Mt Kenya S. P Dio Mt Kenya S. *PO Box 271, Lumuru, Kenya.*

KINYANJUI, David. **d** 78 Nak. d Dio Nak. *Box 665, Nakuru, Kenya.*

KINYANZA, Geoffrey. Warner Mem Th Coll Ibuye 56. **d** 58 **p** 59 Bp Brazier for Ugan. P Dio Ugan 58-60; Dio Rwanda-B 60-66; Dio Rwa 66-75; Kiga from 75. *BP 61, Kigale, Rwanda.*

KINYINA, Yokasi. Bp Tucker Coll Mukono, 61. **d** 62 Ruw. d Dio Ruw from 62. *Kiburara, Uganda.*

KINYOGOTE, Erasto. **d** 65 Rwanda B **p** 66 Rwa. P Dio Rwa 65-75; Dio Kiga from 75. *BP 22, Nyabisindu, Rwanda.*

KINYOGOTE, Nathaniel. **d** 65 Rwanda B **p** 66 Rwa. P Dio Rwa 65-75; Dio Kiga from 75. *Gahini, d/s Kigali, Rwanda.*

KIONDO, Vincent. Th Coll Tunduru, 54. **d** 55 **p** 58 Zanz. P Dio Zanz T. *Box 53, Mombo, Tanzania.*

KIPALAMOTO, Canon Nathan John. St Cypr Coll Ngala 62. **d** 66 **p** 68 SW Tang. P Dio SW Tang 66-72; Dio Dar-S from 72; Can of Dar-S from 78. *Box 16546, Dar-es-Salaam, Tanzania.*

KIPFIZI, William. **d** 68 **p** 69 W Tang. P Dio W Tang. *Box 12, Nguruka, Tanzania.*

KIPILI, Daniel. b 42. St Phil Th Coll Kongwa 67. **d** and **p** 70 Vic Nyan. P Dio Vic Nyan. *PO Box 278, Mwanza, Tanzania.*

KIPTONUI, Eliud. **d** 65 Maseno. d Dio Maseno 65-70. *PO Box 181, Kericho, Kenya.*

KIRAHWA, Ven Nabosi. **d** 44 **p** 45 Ugan. P Dio Ugan 44-61; Dio Ruw 61-72; Dio Bunyoro from 72; Can of Ruw 72; Bunyoro from 72; Archd of Bunyoro from 72. *Box 64, Masindi, Bunyoro, Uganda.*

KIRAMA, Andrew Mulindwa. Bp Tucker Coll Mukono 67.

d 69 **p** 70 W Bugan. P Dio W Bugan. *Matale, Box 84, Kalisizo, Uganda.*

KIRANGAMA, Azaria. d 76 **p** 77 Ank. P Dio Ank 76-77; Dio W Ank from 77. *Box 49, Bushenyi, Uganda.*

KIRBY, Edward Charles. b 22. **d** 80 Bp Parker for Newc. Hon C of Taree Dio Newc from 80. *44 River Street, Cundletown 2430, NSW, Australia.*

KIRBY, Harry Bernard. Univ of Melb BA 50. St Jo Coll Morpeth ACT ThL 52. **d** and **p** 53 Newc. C of Cessnock 53-55; I of Singleton 55-56; R of Jerry's Plains 56-58; Lang Lang 58-61; Yallourn 61-65; Chap Geelong Hosp and Pris 65-71; I of St John Geelong W 71-78; St Paul Geelong Dio Melb from 78. *236 Latrobe Terrace, Geelong, Vic, Australia 3218.* (052-9 5698)

KIRBY, John Charles. McGill Univ Montr BA 36, PhD 62. Montr Dioc Th Coll LTh 39. Gen Th Sem NY STB 40. **d** 39 **p** 40 Montr. C of St Columba Montr 40-44; R of St Steph Lachine 44-59; Assoc Prof of Relig Stud McGill Univ Montr 59-79. *291 35th Avenue, Lachine 610, PQ, Canada.* (514-637 6216)

KIRBY, John David. Trent Univ BA 72. Trin Coll Tor MDiv 75. **d** 75 **p** 76 Ont. C of Elizabethtown 75; R 76-79; Adolphustown Dio Ont from 79. *RR1, Bath, Ont, Canada.* (613-373 2209)

KIRBY, John Patrick. b 24. Univ of Leeds BA 50. Coll of Resurr Mirfield 50. **d** 52 Birm **p** 53 Bp Linton for Cant. C of St Aid Small Heath 52-55; C of Usuthu Miss Swaziland 55-59; Solihull (in c of St Francis) Birm 59-63; Miss of St Mary's Th Sch Odibo 63-68; V of Coalbrookdale 68-77; P-in-c of Buildwas 68-77; L Wenlock 68-77; C of S Gillingham (in c of All SS from 80) Dio Roch from 77. *37 Birch Grove, Hempstead, Gillingham, ME7 3RB.* (Medway 367518)

KIRBY, Maurice William Herbert. b 31. K Coll Lon and Warm 50. **d** 55 **p** 56 S'wark. C of St Luke Eltham 55-56; C of Horley 56-59; Westbury 59-62; R of Worton w Marston and Poulshot 62-66; C-in-c of Cheverell Magna 65; PC of Burcombe 66-68; V 68-70; V of St Mich AA Sarum 70-73; Chap St Helen and St Katherine Sch Abindgon 73-79; Wrekin Coll Wellington Salop from 79. *Wrekin College, Wellington, Telford, Salop.*

KIRBY, Neville John. b 30. Univ of Bris Dipl Educn 73. St Aid Coll Lich Th Coll. **d** 59 **p** 60 Bris. C of St Greg Horfield 59-62; C-in-c of All H Eaton Bris 63-65; Publ Pr Dio Bris 65; Asst Master Cotham Sch Bris 65-66; Hon C of St Steph w St Nich St Leon and All SS City and Dio Bris from 65; Educn Officer Dio Bris 67-74; Lect Univ of Bris Sch of Educn 73-75; Coll of St Matthias Fishponds Bris 74-76; Bris Poly from 76. *88 Parry's Lane, Bristol, BS9 1AJ.* (0272-681386)

KIRBY, Norborne George. d 71 **p** 72 Pret. C of Waterberg 71-78; P-in-c of Zoutpansberg Dio Pret from 78. *PO Box 86, Louis Trichardt, Transvaal 0920, S Africa.*

KIRBY, Paul Michael. b 51. Wycl Hall Ox 74. **d** 76 **p** 77 Liv. C of Gateacre 76-79; Barton Seagrave w Warkton Dio Pet from 79. *Millbrook Church House, Churchill Way, Kettering, Northants, NN15 5BZ.* (Kettering 512828)

KIRBY, Robert Flooks. St Aug Coll Cant ACT ThL 45. **d** 38 **p** 39 Rockptn. C of Cathl Ch Rockptn 38-39; R of Barcaldine 39-45; P-in-c of St Sav Gladstone 45-46; C of Armid Cathl 46-47; V of Guyra 47-57; Gunnedah 58-65; Tamworth 65-68; Walcha Dio Armid 68-72; Hon Can of Armid 61-72; Perm to Offic Dio Brisb from 72. *8 Klein Street, Toowoomba, Queensland, Australia 4350.* (35 1087)

KIRBY, Ronald George. Univ of NZ BA 56, Dipl Educn 63. **d** 65 Bp McKenzie for Wel **p** 66 Wel. Hon C of Pauatahanui 65-69; Waikanae 69-71; Hd Master of St Mark's Sch City and Dio Wel from 71. *177 Darlington Road, Wellington 3, NZ.* (883-302)

KIRBY, Stennett Roger. b 54. St Pet Coll Ox BA 75. Sarum Wells Th Coll 75. **d** 77 Edmon for Lon **p** 78 Lon. C of St Pet Hampstead Dio Lon from 77. *51 Tudor Close, Belsize Avenue, NW3 4AG.* (01-794 2415)

KIRCHER, Godfrey William August. St Jo Coll Armid ACT ThL 25. **d** and **p** 26 Bath. M of Bro of the Good Shepherd 26-31; C of St Paul Cobar 26-27; R 28-31; L to Offic (Col Cl Act) as C of Our Lady of Mercy and St Thos of Cant Gorton 31-34; Chap Toc H in S Austr 34-36; C of St Pet Cathl Adel 35-36; R of Kandos 36-46; Chap AIF 40-46; R of Oberon w O'Connell 46-51; R of Chelmer w Graceville 51-54; Chap R Melb Hosp and C of Melb Dioc Centre 54-57; Prec of Melb Cathl 57-61; I of St Paul Malvern 61-68; C of St Jas w St John Miss Distr Melb 68-74; Perm to Offic Dio Melb from 74. *44 Railway Parade, Seaford, Vic, Australia 3198.* (03-786 6019)

KIRIBIRABO, Canon Ernest. d 65 Rwanda B **p** 66 Rwa. P Dio Rwa 65-75; Dio Kiga from 75; Can of Rwa 74-75; Kiga from 75. *Post Box 46, Byumba, Rwanda, Centr Africa.*

KIRK, Geoffrey. b 45. Keble Coll Ox BA (2nd cl Engl) 67, 2nd cl Th 69. Coll of Resurr Mirfield 71. **d** 72 **p** 73 Ripon. C of St Aidan Leeds 72-74; St Mark w St Luke St Marylebone 74-77; St Jo Div Kennington 77-81; V of St Steph Lewisham Dio S'wark from 81. *Vicarage, Cressingham Road, SE13 5AG.* (01-318 1295)

KIRK, George. b 14. Kelham Th Coll 32. **d** 38 **p** 39 Cant. C of St Osw Norbury 38-41; St Cuthb Sheff and Chap City Gen Hosp 41-43; C-in-c St Thos Brightside Sheff 43-44; V 44-48; Bentley 48-56; R of Aston w Aughton 56-80; C-in-c of Ulley 57-65; V 65-80; RD of Laughton 72-79; Bp's Chap for retired Clergy Dio Sheff from 80. *12 Begonia Close, South Anston, Sheffield, S31 7HU.*

KIRK, Gordon. St Paul's Th Coll Grahmstn 59. **d** 60 **p** 61 Mashon. C of Marandellas 60-61; St Mary and All SS Cathl Salisbury 61-65; Umtali (in c of Chapinga and of Melsetter) 65-67; R of Lomagundi Dio Mashon from 67. *PO Box 19, Sinoia, Rhodesia.*

KIRK, John Allan. b 45. Univ of Tor MusBac 67. Trin Coll Tor MDiv 74. **d** 74 **p** 75 Tor. C of Lindsay 74-76; I of Elmvale 76-80; St Theo of Cant City and Dio Tor from 80. *129 Connaught Avenue, Willowdale, Toronto, Ont, Canada.*

KIRK, John Andrew. Univ of Lon BD and AKC 61. Fitzw Ho Cam BA 63. Ridley Hall, Cam 61. **d** 63 **p** 64 Lon. C of Ch Ch Finchley 63-66; L to Offic Dio Argent from 66. *Facultad Evangelica de Teologia, Camacua 282, Buenos Aires, Argentina, S America.*

KIRK, Sidney Alexander. Univ of Tor BPHE 54. Wycl Coll Tor BTh 58, BD 67. **d** 58 **p** 59 Tor. C of Trin E Tor 58-59; I of Cannington 60-64. *Box 425, East Hampstead, New Hampshire 03826, USA.*

KIRK-DUNCAN, Brian Andrew Campbell. Pemb Coll Ox Law Mods 38, BA 46, MA 47. TCD MA 59, PhD 64. Cudd Coll 39. **d** 41 **p** 42 Ox. C of Summertown 41-43; Headington Quarry 43-44; Asst Master Dragon Sch Ox 41-44; V of Sevenhampton w Charlton Abbotts (w Hawling from 46) 44-47; R of Bredon w Bredon's Norton 47-62 Surr 48-62; Commiss Br Hond 51-52; R of St Mary at Hill w St Andr Hubbard, St Geo Botolph Lane and St Botolph Billingsgate City and Dio Lon from 62; Prin Becket Coll Lon 63-67; Dep Min Can of St Paul's Cathl Lon from 69; Asst Chap O of St John of Jer 76-79; Sub Chap 79-81; Offg Chap from 81. *Rectory, St Mary at Hill, Eastcheap, EC3R 8EE.* (01-626 4184)

KIRK-SMITH, Harold. Univ of Sheff BA 39, MA 46, PhD 53. Lich Th Coll 39. **d** 41 **p** 42 Sheff. C of Ch Ch Heeley Sheff 41-43; Owlerton 43-46; V of St Bart Sheff 46-51; Wadsley 51-58; Chap and Asst Master Jun Sch Rossall 58-60; Asst Master Rossall Sch 60-72; Chap 65-72; Asst Master Qu Mary Sch Lytham from 72. *20 Lowick Drive, Hardhorn, Poulton-le-Fylde, Lancs.* (Poulton 886709)

KIRKALDY, Denis John. Univ of Syd BA 68. Moore Coll Syd 74. **d** 74 Syd. C of SS Jas & John Mt Druitt 74-77; Port Kembla 77-78; R of St Aid Annandale Dio Syd from 78. *74 Booth Street, Annandale, NSW, Australia 2038.* (660-3602)

KIRKBY, Geoffrey Richard. b 1899. Worc Ordin Coll. **d** 59 Bp Stannard for Roch **p** 60 Roch. C of St Edm K & Mart Dartford 59-62; V of Letcombe Regis w Letcombe Bassett 62-70. *Address temp unknown.*

KIRKBY, John Victor Michael. b 39. Univ of Lon BSc (Eng) 62, BD 73. Ridley Hall Cam 65. **d** 67 Lon **p** 68 Willesden for Lon. C of St Jas Muswell Hill 67-70; Chap Hatfield Poly 71-75; V of Wootton Dio St Alb from 75. *Vicarage, Wootton, Bedford, MK43 9HF.* (Bedford 768391)

KIRKBY, Reginald Gresham. b 16. Univ of Leeds BA 40. Coll of Resurr Mirfield, 40. **d** 42 **p** 43 Man. C of Our Lady of Mercy and St Thos of Cant Gorton 42-44; All SS Middlesbrough 44-46; St Peter Becontree 46-48; St Mich AA Ladbroke Grove (in c of St Francis Dalgarno Way) Lon 48-51; V of St Paul w St Luke Bow Common Dio Lon from 51. *St Paul's Vicarage, Leopold Street, E3 4LA.* (01-987 4941)

KIRKBY, William John. Keble Coll Ox BA 22, MA 32. Wells Th Coll 24. **d** 25 **p** 26 Lon. C of St Jas Fulham 25-53; St Barn Kens 33-39; Actg C of St Marg Mountain Ash 39-43; Bassaleg 43-46; C-in-c of Llanvaches w Llanvair Discoed 46-47; R of Panteg (w Llanddewi-Fach and Llandegveth from 53) 47-54; V of Astwood w Hardmead and R of N Crawley 54-60; Langton Herring w Buckland Ripers 60-68. *Parnham House, Beaminster, Dorset.*

KIRKER, Richard Ennis. b 51. Sarum Wells Th Coll 72. **d** 77 Hertf for St Alb. C of St Mary Hitchin 77-78. *St Botolphs Church, Aldgate, EC3N 1AB.*

KIRKHAM, Clifford Gerald Frank. b 34. Sarum Wells Th Coll 72. **d** 74 **p** 75 B & W. C of Worle 74-76; E Preston w Kingston 76-78; Goring 78-81; P-in-c of St Rich Conv Distr Maybridge, Goring Dio Chich from 81. *81 Palatine Road, Goring-by-Sea, W Sussex, BN12 6JR.* (Worthing 49463)

✠ **KIRKHAM, Right Rev John Dudley Galtrey.** b 35. Trin Coll Cam BA 59, MA 63. Westcott Ho Cam 60. **d** 62 **p** 63 St E. C of St Mary-le-Towe Ipswich 62-65; Res Chap to Bp of Nor 65-69; P-in-c of Rockland St Mary w Hellington 67-69;

Chap to Bp of New Guinea 69-70; C of St Martin-in-the-Fields Westmr 70-72; St Marg Westmr 70-72; Dom Chap to Abp of Cant 72-76; Chap to Thames Television Euston Studios 71-76; Cons Ld Bp Suffr of Sherborne in Cant Cathl 30 Nov 76 by Abp of Cant; Bps of Lon, Sarum, B & W, Birm, Chelmsf, Chich, Heref, Lich, Nor, Roch and Ely; Bps Suffr of Barking, Bradwell, Dover, Croydon, Dorchester, Grantham, Ramsbury, Shrewsbury, Southn and Tonbridge; and Abp of Utrecht and Bps Ramsey, Isherwood, and others; Can and Preb of Sarum Cathl from 77. *Little Bailie, Sturminster Marshall, Wimborne, Dorset, BH21 4AD.* (Sturminster Marshall 659)

KIRKHAM, Ven Paul. Moore Th Coll Syd ACT ThL 34. **d** 35 **p** 36 Nel. C of Blenheim 35-36; V of Collingwood 36-37; Motueka 37-41; Greymouth 41-47; Blenheim 47-66; Wakefield 66-71; Archd of Marlborough 49-66; Waimea 66-71; Exam Chap to Bp of Nel 54-71; VG of Nel 56-71; Commiss Nel 65-71; Archd (Emer) from 71; L to Offic Dio Ch Ch from 71. *16 Bentley Street, Christchurch 4, NZ.*

KIRKLAND, Richard John. b 53. Univ of Leic BA 75. St Jo Coll Dur 76. **d** 79 **p** 80 Ches. C of Knutsford w Toft Dio Ches from 79. *12 Hayton Street, Knutsford, Cheshire.* (0585 2892)

KIRKMAN, Canon Harold. b 11. Univ of Man BA 43, BD 47. Egerton Hall Man 35. **d** 36 **p** 37 Man. C of Ch Ch Moss Side 36-43; V of Roundthorn 43-47; St Thos Halliwell 47-55; Commiss Lebom 50-61; Exam Chap to Bp of Man 51-57; V of Oldham (w St Pet from 64) 55-72; Hon Can of Man 59-76; Can (Emer) from 76; Proc Conv Man 62-70; RD of Oldham 63-76. *3 Black Dyke, Mankinholes Bank, Todmorden, Lancs, OL14 6JA.* (Todmorden 3499)

KIRKPATRICK, Cecil Stanley. b 04. Dorch Miss Coll 25. **d** 28 **p** 29 Man. C of Ladybarn 28-31; St Luke Kingston T 31-41; Chap RAFVR 41-46; V of Bellingham S'wark 46-52; R of Woodrising w Scoulton 52-56; Cockley Cley w Gooderstone 56-60; Smithton Tas 60-64; C-in-c of Henlow 64-65; R of Hunsdon 65-73; R of Widford 65-73; Perm to Offic Dio Ex from 73. *The Lodge, Abbotsham Court, Abbotsham, Bideford, Devon, EX39 5BH.*

KIRKPATRICK, Errol Francis. b 28. Downes Oratory Pri (1st) 51, Bp Forster Pri (2nd) 51, Div Test (1st cl) 52. **d** 52 **p** 53 Ferns. C of Enniscorthy 52-55; Wexford and Dioc C Dio Ferns 55-56; C of Bridgwater 56-59; R of All H Devons Rd Bromley St Leon 59-66; V of Rowlestone w Llancillo 66-77; Walterstone 66-77; R of Kentchurch w Llangua 66-77; RD of Abbeydore 72-77; R of Porlock w Stoke Pero Dio B & W from 77. *Porlock Rectory, Minehead, Somt.* (Porlock 862208)

KIRKPATRICK, Ivan Ridley. Late Scho of Trin Coll Dub BA (2nd cl Mod Ment and Mor Phil) 28, Div Test 31. **d** 31 **p** 32 Kilm. C of St John Sligo w Knocknarea 31-33; I of Tubbercurry 33-37; Enniskeen w Ardagh (w Nobber from 41) 37-47; Tullamore w Lynally and Durrow 47-50; S Sec Hib CMS 50-53; I of Powerscourt 53-56; Cloughjordan 56-58; Ballinaclough 58-62; Kilnasoolagh w Quin 62-65; Kilmacduagh 65-71; RD of O'Mullod Lower 62-65; Preb of Killaloe Cathl 62-63; Can and Preb of St Patr Cathl Dub 70-77; I of Drumcliffe 71-78; Kilfenora 71-78; Kilnaboy 71-78; RD of Corkovasker and O'Mullod U 72-78. *c/o Rectory, Ennis, Co Clare, Irish Republic.*

KIRKPATRICK, James Michael. b 46. Chich Th Coll 70. **d** 73 **p** 74 Moray. C of Elgin w Lossiemouth 73-76; St Mark Ford Devonport 76-77; C-in-c 77-80; Team V of Ilfracombe Dio Ex from 80. *St Peter's Clergy House, Highfield Road, Ilfracombe, Devon, EX34 9LH.* (0271 62668)

KIRKPATRICK, Robert. b 14. TCD BA 43, BD 47, MA 52. **d** 55 **p** 56 Down. C of Down 55-58; L to Offic Dio Niger 58-68; R of Houghton 68-71; C-in-c of Stockbridge 68-69; R 69-71; Dioc Missr Dio Ow from 71; Can of Ow 71-77; Exam Chap to Bp of Ow 72-77; R of Weldon w Deene Dio Pet from 77. *Weldon Rectory, Corby, Northants.* (Corby 3671)

KIRKPATRICK, William John Ashley. b 29. Sarum Th Coll 66. **d** 68 **p** 70 Stepney for Lon. C of St Mary Bow 68-71; St Anne w St Thos and St Pet Soho 71-75. *11 Shuttleworth Street, Rishton, Blackburn, Lancs, BR1 4LY.*

KIRKUP, George Brooks. b 16. Worc Ordin Coll 59. [f in CA]. **d** 61 **p** 62 Southw. C of Mansfield Woodhouse 61-65; V of Langold 65-70; R of Armthorpe 70-74; V of All SS Lobley Hill Gateshead Dio Dur from 74. *Vicarage, Rowanwood Gardens, Lobley Hill, Gateshead, T & W, NE11 0DP.* (Dunston 604409)

KIRKUP, Nigel Norman. b 54. AKC and BD 74. **d** and **p** 80 S'wark. Hon C of Catford (Southend) & Downham Dio S'wark from 80. *233 Bellingham Road, SE6.*

KIRKWOOD, David Christopher. b 40. Pemb Coll Ox BA 63. Clifton Th Coll 63. **d** 65 **p** 66 Roch. C of Wilmington 65-68; Green Street Green (in c of Pratts Bottom) 68-72; Youth and SW Area Sec BCMS 72-73; Educn and Youth Sec 73-80; Hon C of Ch Ch Sidcup 74-80; V of Rothley Dio Leic from 80. *128 Hallfields Lane, Rothley, Leicester, LE7 7NG.* (Leic 302241)

KIRKWOOD, Jack. b 21. Worc Ordin Coll 62. **d** 63 **p** 64 Truro. C of Penwerris 63-66; V of Torpoint 66-73; Turton 73-81; P-in-c of All S Castleton Heywood Dio Man from 81. *Vicarage, Rochdale Road East, Heywood, Lancs, OL10 1QU.* (Heywood 69244)

KIRONDE, Blasio. **d** 45 **p** 47 Ugan. P Dio Ugan 45-60; Dio W Bugan from 60. *Kigalama, PO Box 159, Mityana, Uganda.*

KIRTON, Canon Harold Arthur. b 12. St Jo Coll Dur BA and Jenkyns Scho 36. Dipl Th and Capel Cure Pri 37, MA 39. **d** 37 **p** 38 Southw. C of St Chris Sneinton 37-40; Radcliffe-on-Trent 40-44; V of Balderton 44-48 Arnold 48-52; Ed Southw Dioc Mag 46-49; R of E Leake 52-63; Bingham 63-71; Surr from 64; Sec Southw Dioc Pastoral C'tte 65-77; Can Res of Southw 70-75; Hon Can 75-77, Can (Emer) from 77; V of Norwell 70-74; R of Wilford 74-77; Perm to Offic Dio Southw from 78. *66 Headley Grove, Tadworth, Surrey, KT20 5UF.* (Burgh Heath 61671)

KIRTON, Richard Arthur. b 43. Univ of Dur BA 67, MA 73. Dipl Th (w distinc) 68. Wycl Hall Ox 68. **d** 69 Southw **p** 70 Sherwood for Southw. C of Warsop w Sookholme 69-72; Newark-on-Trent 72-75. *21 Jalan Sultan Abdul Samas, Kuala Lumpur, W Malaysia.*

KISANGA, Kennedy Stephen. b 47. **d** 72 Moro. d Dio Moro. *Box 113, Morogor, Tanzania.*

KISANGANI, Lord Bishop of. *See* Mugera, Right Rev Tibafa Silivestre.

KISEU, Apolo. St Paul's Th Coll Limuru. **d** 67 **p** 68 Momb. P Dio Momb. *Anglican Church, Wenuga, PO Box 1015, Wundanyi, Kenya.*

KISHAKA, Enosi. **d** 74 **p** 75 Ank. P Dio Ank. *PO Box 4039, Ntungamo, Mbarara, Uganda.*

KISHINDO, Canon William Justus George. St Andr Th Coll Likoma 38. **d** 39 **p** 43 Nyasa. P Dio Nyasa 39-52; Dio SW Tang 52-71; Dio Ruv 71-80; Can of SW Tang 65-71; Ruv 71-80; Hon Can from 80. *Lundo, PO Liuli, Tanzania.*

KISHISHI, Onesimo. **d** 58 **p** 59 Centr Tang. P Dio Centr Tang 58-63; Dio Vic Nyan from 63. *PO Box 100, Bariadi, Tanzania.*

KISITU, Wilberforce. b 56. **d** 77 Nam. d Dio Nam. *Mpererwe Church of Uganda, PO Box 3652, Kampala, Uganda.*

KISSA, Canon John. Buwalasi Th Coll. **d** 59 **p** 60 U Nile. P Dio U Nile 59-61; Dio Mbale from 61; Dioc Can and Treas from 78. *Box 473, Mbale, Uganda.*

KISSA, Yona. **d** 64 **p** 65 Mbale. P Dio Mbale. *c/o Box 473, Mbale, Uganda.*

KISSACK, Albert Westby Grandin. b 12. **d** 76 **p** 77 S & M (APM). C of St Geo & St Barn w All SS Douglas Dio S & M from 76. *83 Ballabrooie Avenue, Douglas, Isle of Man.* (Douglas 5316)

KISSELL, Barrington John. b 38. Lon Coll of Div 64. **d** 67 **p** 68 Truro. C of Camborne 67-71; St Andr Chorleywood Dio St Alb from 71. *Wick Cottage, Quickley Lane, Chorleywood, Herts.* (Chorleywood 2188)

KISSICK, Peter Daryl. Ridley Coll Melb ACT ThL 53. **d** 54 **p** 55 Melb. C of Essendon N 54-56; Min of Pascoe Vale 56-59; V of Hastings 59-69; R of Tongala 69-75; Kangaroo Flat Dio Bend from 75. *Rectory, Melbourne Road, Kangaroo Flat, Vic, Australia.* (054-47 7427)

KITABA, Kandolo. b 25. **d** 77 Bukavu. d Dio Bukavu. *Kalima Parish, BP 220, Kindu, Maniema, Zaire.*

KITAMIRIKE, James. Bp Tucker Coll Mukono 63. **d** 65 **p** 67 Nam. P Dio Nam. *Box 88, Jinja, Uganda.*

KITCHEN, Alan. b 39. Coll of Resurr Mirfield 72. **d** 74 **p** 75 Bradf. C of Shelf 74-76; Team V of Tong Dio Bradf 76-78; P-in-c 78-79; V from 79. *Tong Rectory, Holmewood Road, Bradford, BD4 9BP.* (Bradford 682100)

KITCHEN, Harold. Tyndale Hall Bris 25. **d** 38 **p** 39 Blackb. C of St Thos Blackpool 38-40; Morden 40-44; V of St Paul Canonbury 44-54; PC of All SS Sidmouth 54-69; RD of Ottery 63-67; L to Offic Dio Ex from 69. *Green Acres, Venn Ottery Road, Ottery St Mary, Devon.*

KITCHEN, Harold Malcolm. b 33. Trin Coll Cam BA 57, MA 61. Tyndale Hall Bris 57. **d** 59 Bp Gelsthorpe for Southw **p** 60 Southw. C of St John Worksop 59-61; H Trin Heworth 61-63; Chap at Tororo Ugan 63-66; R of Burythorpe w E Acklam Leavening and Westow 66-71; V of Wollaton Pk Dio Southw from 71; P-in-c of St Barn Lenton Abbey Dio Southw from 77. *St Mary's Vicarage, Wollaton Park, Nottingham, NG8 1AF.* (Nottingham 786988)

KITCHEN, Leslie Wilson. b 16. Univ of Man BA (2nd cl Hist) 38, MA 39. Bps' Coll Cheshunt, 39. **d** 41 **p** 42 Ripon. C of St Matt Chapel Allerton 41-45; St Mary Barnsley (in c of St Paul) 45-50; V of Skelmanthorpe 50-55; Chap Wakef Hosps B Group 55-60; R of Garforth 60-72; R of Hilborough Group (Cockley Cley w Gooderstone, Oxburgh w Foulden,

Hilborough w Bodney, Gt w L Cressingham and Threxton, and Didlington) 72-78; V of Pool w Arthington Dio Ripon from 78. *Pool-in-Wharfedale Vicarage, Otley, Yorks, LS21 1LH.* (Arthington 842206)

KITCHEN, Martin. b 47. BA (Lon) 71. K Coll Lon BD 76. AKC 77. SOC 77. **d** 79 **p** 80 S'wark. Lect CA Tr Coll and Hon C of Kidbrooke Dio S'wark from 79. *9 Fentons, Vanbrugh Park Road, Blackheath, SE3 7NJ.* (01-858 6802)

KITCHEN, Canon Thomas Basil. b 05. St Aug Coll Cant 31. **d** 34 **p** 35 Lon. C of St Pet Bethnal Green 34-35; P-in-c of St D Bonda 35-37; R of Selukwe 37-39; V of Brayton 39-45; Chap at Dhanbad 45-47; V of Howden 47-56; Surr 47-56; RD of Howden 53-56; R of Drewsteignton 56-60; C-in-c of Spreyton 57-60; RD of Okehampton 58-60; PC of St John Torquay 60-61; L to Offic Dio Ex from 61; Chap at Menton 70-71; Asst Chap Madrid 71-72; Chap at Malaga 72-73; Tangier 73-75; Lisbon 76-77; Oporto 77-78; and 80-81; Madeira 79-80; Hon Can of Gibr from 76; L to Offic Dio York from 78. *6 Castlemount Avenue, Scalby, Scarborough, N Yorks, YO13 0PJ.* (0723-72613)

KITCHENER, Michael Anthony. b 45. Trin Coll Cam 1st cl Cl Trip pt i 65, BA (1st cl Th Trip pt ii) 67, MA 70. PhD 71. Cudd Coll 70. **d** 71 Horsham for Chich **p** 72 Chich. C of Aldwick 71-74; Caversham (in c of St Marg) 74-77; Tutor Coll of the Resurr Mirfield Yorks 77. *27 Crowther Road, Mirfield, W Yorks.*

KITCHIN, Philip Edward. Ridley Coll Melb 60. **d** 62 Melb **p** 63 Bp Hudson for Syd. C of St Silas N Geelong 62-63; L to Offic Dio Syd 63-65; Chap at Norf I 65-68; C-in-c of Greenacre Provisional Distr 68-71; R of Botany 71-73; Katoomba 73-77; Chap Norf I Dio Syd from 77. *Box 14, Norfolk Island, Australia 2899.*

KITCHING, Albert Ford. b 1883. Keble Coll Ox BA 05, MA 08. **d** 47 **p** 48 Glouc C of Chipping Campden 47-49; Jt-Sec BFBS 50-60; Perm to Offic Dio B & W from 50; Dios Bris and Sarum 50-63. *Waterhouse, Monkton Combe, Bath.*

KITCHINGMAN, Allan. St Jo Coll Morpeth. **d** 63 **p** 64 Newc. C of Singleton 63-66; Wallsend 66-69; Lismore 69-70; R of Eureka 70-73; V of Dunoon 70-73; C of Lismore 73-76; R of Mullumbimby 76-81; Tweed Heads Dio Graft from 81. *Box 108, Tweed Heads, NSw, Australia 2485.*

KITEERA, Eliasaph. d 74 **p** 75 Ank. P Dio Ank 74-77; Dio W Ank 77-78; Dio E Ank from 78. *Box 14, Mbarara, Uganda.*

KITETO, Ven Stephano Tito. St Paul's Div Sch Limuru 46. **d** 48 **p** 49 Momb. P Dio Momb 48-60; Can of Momb 60-69; Archd of Momb 64-74; and from 76; Dioc Regr Dio Momb from 77. *Box 80072, Mombasa, Kenya.*

KITLEY, David Buchan. b 53. St Jo Coll Dur BA. Trin Coll Bris 78. **d** 81 Roch. C of St Steph Tonbridge Dio Roch from 81. *35 Waterloo Road, Tonbridge, Kent, TN9 2SD.*

KITOGBERE, Erisa Makasi. Bp Gwynne Coll Mundri 59. **d** 63 **p** 64 Bp Dotiro for Sudan. P Dio Sudan 63-76; Dio Yambio from 76. *ECS, Yambio, Equatoria Province, Sudan.*

KITOLOLO, Salman Johnson. St Paul's Div Sch Limuru 49. **d** 49 **p** 51 Momb. P Dio Momb 51-61. *Kigombo, PO Voi, Kenya.*

KITSON-WALTERS (Formerly WALTERS), Edward Victor. St Pet Th Coll Ja. **d** 39 **p** 40 Ja. C of St Matt Kingston 39; Pedro Plains 40-44; R of Buff Bay w Birnam Wood 44-48; Black River 48-51; Golden Grove 51-55; in Amer Ch 55-62; R of Port Maria 62-68; CF (Ja) 68-78. *c/o Up Park Camp, Kingston 5, Jamaica, W Indies.* (093-68121)

KITSUALIK, Gideon. d 64 **p** 66 Arctic. Miss at Gjoa Haven Dio Arctic from 64. *Church of the Messiah, Gjoa Haven, Via Cambridge Bay, NWT, Canada.*

KITTERINGHAM, Ian. b 35. CCC Cam BA 59, MA 63. Westcott Ho Cam 59. **d** 61 Sheff **p** 62 Bp Gerard for Sheff. C of All SS Rotherham 61-64; H Trin Eltham 64-66; V of St Mary-le-Park Battersea 66-73; St Mark Reigate 73-80; Caterham Valley Dio S'wark from 80. *1 Clareville Road, Caterham, Surrey, CR3 6LA.* (Caterham 43188)

KITTS, Joseph. b 27. Tyndale Hall Bris 58. **d** 60 **p** 61 Liv. C of St Pet Parr 60-63; St Leon Bootle (in c of St Mary w St John) 63-66; V of St Simon and St Jude Southport 66-74; in Amer Ch from 74. *c/o Diocesan Office, 110 W Franklin, Richmond, VA 23220, USA.*

KITUNA, Canon Eriasafu. d 63 Ankole-K. d Dio Ankole-K 63-67; Dio Ank 67-77; Dio W Ank from 77; Can from 80. *N Yakwebundika, PO Kabwohe, Uganda.*

KITWOOD, Thomas Marris. K Coll Cam 2nd cl Nat Sc Trip pt i 59, BA (2nd cl Nat Sc Trip pt ii) 60, MA 64. Wycl Hall Ox 62. **d** 63 **p** 64 Sarum. Asst Chap Sherborne Sch 63-69; Chap Busoga Coll Mwiri Dio Nam from 69. *c/o Box 14123, Kampala, Uganda.*

KIVA, Edmund. MBE 79. St Pet Coll Siota. **d** 46 **p** 51 Melan. P Dio Melan 46-74; Dio Ysabel 75-76; Dio Centr Melan from 76; Can of Melan 56-64; Archd of E Solomons 64-67; Outer E Is 67-70. *Bunana, Gela, Solomon Islands.*

✠ **KIVENGERE, Right Rev Festo.** b 19. Pittsburgh Th Sem M Div 67. **d** 66 Bp Thomas for Pittsburgh **p** 67 Kig. P Dio Kig 67-72; Cons Ld Bp of Kigezi (Kigezi S from 81) in Nam Cathl 5 Nov 72 by Abp of Ugan; Bps of W Bugan, Nam, Mbale, N Ugan, M & W Nile, Ank, Bukedi, Ruw, Bunyoro and Soroti. *PO Box 65, Kabale, Uganda.* (Kabale 231)

KIVETT, Michael Stephen. b 50. Bethany Coll W Va USA BA 72. Chr Th Sem Indiana MDiv 76. Sarum Wells Th Coll 76. **d** 77 **p** 78 Sarum. C of Harnham 77-80; E Dereham Dio Nor from 80. *34 William Cowper Close, Dereham, Norf.* (Dereham 2617)

KIVOSYO KINGANGA, Isaiah. b 49. **d** 75 **p** 77 Nai. C of St Andr Ukia 75-77; V of Kithangathini Dio Nai from 77. *PO Box 7021, Kilome, via Machakos, Kenya.*

KIWAMU, Christopher Uwamali. Trin Coll Umuahia 55. **d** 57 **p** 58 Niger. P Dio Ow 57-61; Dio Niger 61-62; Dio Benin 62-77; Dio Asaba from 77; Exam Chap to Bp of Asaba from 80. *Holy Trinity Church, Asaba, Nigeria.*

KIWANUKA, John. Bp Tucker Coll Mukono. **d** 69 **p** 70 Nam. P Dio Nam. *PO Box 166, Bombo, Uganda.*

KIWANUKA, Labani. d 45 Ugan. d Dio Ugan 45-46; CF (E Afr) from 57; Perm to Offic Dio Momb from 57. *c/o EAA Chaplains' Dept, PO Box 3000, Nairobi, Kenya.*

KIWANUKA, Canon Musa. Bp Tucker Coll Mukono. **d** 36 **p** 37 Ugan. P Dio Ugan 36-61; Dio Nam from 61; Hon Can of Nam from 64. *Box 829, Luwero, Uganda.*

KIWINDA, Jeremiah. St Paul's Dioc Div Sch Momb 28. **d** 29 **p** 35 Momb. P Dio Momb; Hon Can of Momb 49-64; Can Res 64-76; Tutor Limuru Sch 55-59; Chap HM Pris Momb 59-74; Archd of Momb 74-76. *PO Box 80072, Mombasa, Kenya.*

KIZZA, Nikolawo Gerusomu. Bp Tucker Coll Mukono. **d** 62 **p** 64 Nam. P Dio Nam. *Lubanyi, PO Jinja, Uganda.*

KLASSEN, Arthur Michael Lloyd. b 45. McGill Univ Montr BA 67. Trin Coll Tor STB 69. **d** and **p** 70 Montr. C of St Columba Montr 70-74; R of Farnham-Rougemont 74-77; St Mich AA Winnipeg Dio Rupld from 77. *300 Hugo Street North, Winnipeg, Manit, Canada.*

KLEB, Eric William. St Paul's Coll Grahmstn 53. **d** 55 **p** 56 Grahmstn. C of Uitenhage 55-60; St Mich Queenstown 60-61; Bellville 62-64; V of Jamestown 64-66; C of St Jo Evang E Lon 66-67; R of St Pet E Lon 68-72; St Mich Nahoon E Lon Dio Grahmstn from 72. *52 Stanmore Road, Nahoon, East London, CP, S Africa.* (8-1206)

KLEE, Edward George. b 09. Keble Coll Ox 2nd cl Hist 31, BA 32, MA 36. Wycl Hall Ox 33. **d** 35 **p** 36 Worc. C of St Thos Stourbridge 35-38; High Wycombe (in c of St John) 38-44; R of Quainton 44-75; RD of Claydon 58-71. *11 St Andrew's Street, Leighton Buzzard, Beds, LU7 8DS.* (L Buzzard 370165)

KLEIN, Clifford George. Univ of New Engl NSW BA (2nd cl Hist) 58. **d** and **p** 59 Graft. C of St John Canberra 59-60; Ch Ch Cathl Graft 60-64; V of Coramba 64-65; L to Offic Dio Graft from 65. *7 High Street, Nambucca Heads, NSW, Australia* (6921 287)

KLIN, Kendu. b 44. Ho of Epiph Kuch 73. **d** and **p** 75 Kuch. P Dio Kuch. *St Mary's Church Abok, c/o Farmers Training Centre, Sg. Pinang, Serian, Sarawak, Malaysia.*

KLOSE, Albert. St Barn Coll Adel ThL 44. **d** and **p** 45 Adel. C of St Paul Port Adel 45-48; Assoc P-in-c St Jo Mt Pleasant 48-50; SSM 50-51; P-in-c of Morgan w Waikerie S Austr 51-58; Miss P Quop Borneo 58; C of St Geo Camberwell 58-59; Gateshead Dur 60-61. *35 California Street, Nailsworth, Adelaide, S Australia.*

KLUGE, Hugo. d 69 Kimb K. C of St Paul De Aar Dio Kimb K. *PO Box 113, De Aar, CP, S Africa.*

KLYBERG, Very Rev Charles John. b 31. ARICS 57. Linc Th Coll. **d** 60 **p** 61 S'wark. C of St Jo Evang E Dulwich 60-63; R of Ft Jameson Zam 63-67; V of St Steph Battersea 67-71; C-in-c (V from 72) of Ch Ch w St Steph Battersea 71-77; Dean and R of H Cross Cathl City and Dio Lusaka from 77; VG from 77. *Deanery, PO Box 30477, Lusaka, Zambia.* (250484)

KNACK, George Louis. St Francis Coll Brisb. **d** 67 **p** 68 N Queensld. C of Ingham 67-71; St Jas Cathl Townsville 71-72; Perm to Offic Dio Melb 72-73; C of Box Hill 73-75; I of Ch Ch Melton 75-79; Brighton Beach Dio Melb from 79. *1 Moffat Street, Brighton Beach, Vic, Australia 3186.* (92-2397)

KNAPMAN, Preb Hugh William Hartly. b 07. St D Coll Lamp BA 33. **d** 32 **p** 33 Bris. C of St Pet Henleaze 32-36; St Sav Woolcott Pk 36-38; CF (TA) 33-37; V of Long Ashton 38-55; Glastonbury 55-69; RD of Glastonbury 56-69; Surr 56-75; C-in-c of Greinton 60-68; Preb of Wells Cathl from 67; R of Charlton Adam w Charlton Mackrell 69-75. *Thimble Cottage, Wayford, Crewkerne, Somt.* (Crewkerne 72821)

✠ **KNAPP-FISHER, Right Rev Edward George.** b 15. Trin Coll Ox BA (1st cl Jurispr) 36, MA 40. Univ of Cam MA (by incorp) 49. Wells Th Coll 38. **d** 39 St Alb **p** 40 Wakef. Actg

Chap Wells Th Coll 39; C of Brighouse 40-42; Chap RNVR 42-46; Chap Cudd Coll 46-49; L to Offic Dio Ox 47-49; Chap St Jo Coll Cam 49-52; L to Offic Dio Ely 49-52; Prin Cudd Coll 52-60; V of Cuddesdon 52-60; RD of Cuddesdon 58-60; Commiss Capetn 58-60 and from 76; Cons Ld Bp of Pret in St Geo Cathl Capetn 19 June 60 by Abp of Capetn; Bps of Grahmstn; Geo; Natal; Bloemf; St Jo Kaffr; Zulu; and Basuto; and Bps Cowdry; Bayne; and A H H Browne; res 75; Can of Westmr from 75; Archd from 75; Asst Bp of S'wark from 75; in Dio Lon from 76. *1 Little Cloister, Westminster Abbey, SW1P 3PL.* (01-222 4027)

KNAPPER, Peter Charles. b 39. Univ of Lon BA (2nd cl French) 61. St Steph Ho Ox 61. **d** 63 **p** 64 Carl. C of H Trin Carl 63-68; V of St Mary Westfield Workington 68-76; Bridekirk Dio Carl from 76. *Bridekirk Vicarage, Cockermouth, Cumb, CA13 0PE.* (Cockermouth 822257)

KNAPPER, William George. b 13. St Aid Coll. **d** 50 **p** 51 Lon. C of H Innoc Kingsbury 50-53; V of All SS Haggerston 53-59; Kentish Tn Dio Lon from 59. *16 Burghley Road, NW5 1UE.* (01-485 4748)

KNARESBOROUGH, Lord Bishop Suffragan of. *See* Dennis, Right Rev John.

KNEEBONE, William Arnold. b 01. Sarum Th Coll 27. **d** 30 **p** 31 Truro. C of St Just-in-Penwith 30-36; V of Altarnon 36-67; PC of H Trin Bolventor 44-67; C-in-c of Temple 44-51; RD of Trigg Major 48-51; L to Offic Dio Truro from 68. *11 Briar's Ryn, Pillaton, Saltash, Cornw, PL12 6RA.* (St Dominick 50503)

✠ **KNELL, Right Rev Eric Henry.** b 03. Trin Coll Ox BA (2nd cl Th) 27, MA 31. Cudd Coll 27. **d** 28 **p** 29 S'wark. C of St Barn Southfields 28-33; Dom Chap to Bp of Linc 33-36; Missr Trin Coll Ox Miss Stratford 36-41; V of Em Forest Gate 41-45; Ch Ch Reading 45-61; Archd of Berks 54-67; Cons Ld Bp Suffr of Reading in S'wark Cathl 25 Jan 55 by Abp of Cant; Bps of S'wark; Roch; B & W; and Ox; Bps Suffr of Buckingham; Fulham; and Dorch; and Bps Howe; Brown; and Parham; res 72; Asst Bp in Dio Ox 72-75. *College of St Barnabas, Lingfield, Surrey, RH7 6NJ.*

KNELL, Raymond John. b 27. Qu Coll Cam BA 48, MA 52. Ridley Hall Cam 50. **d** 52 Jarrow for Dur **p** 53 Dur. C of St Gabr Bp Wearmouth 52-57; S Shields 57-58; PC of St Osw Hebburn-on-Tyne 58-67; V of Castleside 67-76; Heworth Dio Dur from 76. *Heworth Vicarage, High Heworth Lane, Gateshead, T & W, NE10 0PB.* (Felling 692111)

KNIBBS, Norman Vivian. b 27. Ely Th Coll 61. **d** 63 **p** 64 Ox. C of St Giles Reading 63-67; V of St D Northn Dio Pet 67-73; Team V (w Kingsthorpe) 73-79; R of Brington w Whilton and Norton Dio Pet from 79. *Rectory, Great Brington, Northampton, NN7 4JB.* (East Haddon 402)

KNICKLE, Canon William Morris. K Coll NS BA 17, MA 20. **d** 20 **p** 22 NS. C of New Germany 20-26; R of French Village 26-37; Springhill 37-67; Hon Can of NS from 59; C of Em Dartmouth 70-74. *c/o 5732 College Street, Halifax, NS, Canada, B3H 1X3.*

KNIFE, James Anthony. ACT ThL 46. **d** 46 **p** 47 Melb. C of St Chad Chelsea 46-48; Min 48-50; V of Burwood w Mt Waverley 50-54; R of Swan Hill and Exam Chap to Bp of St Arn 54-60; Can of St Arn 56-60; R of Morwell 60-70; Archd of Latrobe Valley 60-73; without Terr Jurisd 73-76; Hon C of St Paul's Cathl Sale 70-76; VG and Regr Dio Gippsld 71-76; Perm to Offic Dio S'wark from 76. *c/o 33 Hollingbourne Road, Herne Hill, SE24.*

KNIFTON, Roy. St Paul's Coll Grahmstn 64. **d** 66 **p** 67 Pret. C of Hillcrest 66-71; L to Offic Dio Pret 71-81; Dio Johann from 81. *Box 4849, Johannesburg 2000, S Africa.*

KNIGHT, Alan Keith. b 27. Ripon Coll Ox 75. **d** 76 **p** 77 Bris. C of Ch Ch Swindon 76-80; V of Mark w Allerton Dio B & W from 80. *Mark Vicarage, Highbridge, Somt.* (Mark Moor 258)

KNIGHT, Alexander Francis. b 39. St Cath Coll Cam BA 61, MA 65. Wells Th Coll. **d** 63 **p** 64 St Alb. C of Hemel Hempstead 63-68; Chap Taunton Sch 68-75; Dir Bloxham Project 75-81; Dir of Stud Aston Tr Scheme from 81. *Elm Cottage, Willow Lane, Rubgy, CV22 5LX.* (Rugby 2085)

KNIGHT, Andrew James. b 50. Grey Coll Dur BA 72. Univ of Ox 74, (Th) 74, MA 81. Wycl Hall Ox 72. **d** 75 **p** 76 Swan B. Min Can of Brecon Cathl 75-78; C of Morriston Dio Swan B from 78. *2 Monmouth Place, Parc Gwernfadog, Morriston, Swansea.* (Swansea 793197)

KNIGHT, Arthur Clifford Edwin. b 42. Univ of Wales BSc 64. Wells Th Coll 64. **d** 66 **p** 67 Swan B. C of Llangyfelach w Morriston 66-68; Oystermouth 68-73; Chap RAF from 73. *RAF, Odiham, Hants.*

KNIGHT, Benjamin Edward. b 10. St Cath Coll Cam BA 34, MA 38. Wells Th Coll 34. **d** 36 **p** 37 S'wark. C of St Marg Streatham Hill 36-39; Chap RAF 39-65; Asst Chap-in-Chief 53-65; Hon Chap to HM the Queen 60-65; R of Symondsbury w Eype and Broadoak 65-78; V of Chideock 72-78. *The Coachhouse, Botenhampton Old Rectory, Bridport, Dorset, DT6 4BT.* (Bridport 24909)

KNIGHT, Christopher Colson. b 52. Univ of Ex BSc 73. Univ of Man PhD 77. Sarum Wells Th Coll 79. **d** 81 Edin. Chap Edin Cathl from 81. *32 Manor Place, Edinburgh, EH3 7EB.*

KNIGHT, Clement Samuel. Coll Ho Ch Ch. **d** 38 **p** 39 Ch Ch. C of St Luke Ch Ch 38-41; P-in-c of St Chad Linwood 41-45; V of New Brighton 45-49; Chap St Sav Home Timaru 49-51; Belf w Burwood 51-60; V of Burwood 60-62; Glenmark 62-70; L to Offic Dio Ch Ch from 70. *55 Parkstone Avenue, Christchurch 4, NZ.* (41-074)

KNIGHT, David Charles. b 32. Clare Coll Cam BA 55, MA 59. Tyndale Hall Bris 55. **d** 57 **p** 58 Ely. C of St Paul Cam 57-58; C of Ch Ch St Alb 58-61; Min of Em Chap Wimbledon 61-67; Publications Sec BCMS 67-68; Ed Asst *The Christian* 68-69; V of Lannarth 69-75; RD of N Carnmarth 72-75; V of Fremington Dio Ex from 75. *Vicarage, Fremington, Devon, EX31 2NX.* (Barnstaple 73879)

KNIGHT, David Charles. b 45. Univ of Lon BA (2nd cl Russian w Mus) 66. St Edm Hall Ox BA (3rd cl Th) 68, MA 73. St Steph Ho Ox 68. **d** 70 **p** 71 Willesden for Lon. C of H Trin Northwood 70-73; St Francis (All S from 75) Stevenage 73-77; P Missr of St Andr Conv Distr Cippenham, Burnham 77-78; Team V of W Slough (in-c of St Andr Cippenham) Dio Ox from 78; Dep Min Can of St Geo Chap Windsor from 81. *St Andrew's House, Washington Drive, Cippenham, Slough, Berks, SL1 5RE.* (Burnham 61994)

KNIGHT, David Lansley. b 33. Em Coll Cam BA (2nd cl Hist Trip pt i) 56, 2nd cl Th Trip pt ii, 58, MA 61. Ridley Hall Cam 57. **d** 59 Roch **p** 60 Tonbridge for Cant. C of St Steph Chatham 59-63; St Andr Plymouth 63-65; V of St Aid Gravesend 65-71; Bexley Dio Roch from 71. *Vicarage, Hill Crescent, Bexley, Kent, DA5 2DA.* (Crayford 523457)

KNIGHT, Canon Donald Martin. b 13. Univ of Lon BSc (2nd cl Hons) 33, BSc (2nd cl Physics) 34. St Cath S Ox Dipl Th (w distinc) 39. Wycl Hall Ox 38. **d** 39 Dorch for Ox **p** 41 Jer. C of Chesham 39; Asst Master St Luke's Sch Haifa 39-41; Bp Gobat Sch Jer 41-42; C of H Trin Tulse Hill 42-43; Chap RAFVR 43-46; Vice-Prin CA Tr Coll 46-49; V of St Paul Beckenham and Chap for Evangelism Dio Roch 49-57; R of Harlow New Town w L Parndon Dio Chelmsf from 57; RD of Harlow 60-73; Surr from 61; Proc Conv Chelmsf 64-70; Chap Harlow Hosp 65-78; Hon Can of Chelmsf from 71; Vice-Chairman CMJ from 74; M Gen Syn 75-80; M Bd of Miss and Unity 76-81. *Rectory, Upper Park, Harlow, Essex, CM20 1TW.* (Harlow 24616)

KNIGHT, Edwin Caleb Wardle. b 06. Men in Disp 54. Lich Th Coll 26. **d** 30 **p** 31 Lon. C of St Jo Evang w St Sav Fitzroy Square 30-33; TCF 33-37; CF 38-61; R of Chiddingfold 61-73; Perm to Offic Dio Nor from 74. *86 Hall Street, Briston, Melton Constable, Norf.* (Melton Constable 653)

KNIGHT, Eric Frank Walter. St Paul's Coll Grahmstn. **d** 51 Lon for Geo **p** 52 Geo. C of Knysna 51-55; R of Victoria West w Carnarvon 55-57; Beaconsfield 57-59; St Jo Evang Wick 61-63; Girvan 63-68; V of All SS Charlton Dio Sarum from 68; C-in-c of Britford Dio Sarum from 68. *Charlton All Saints' Vicarage, Salisbury, Wilts, SP5 4HQ.* (Downton 20685)

KNIGHT, Canon Ernest Paul. b 12. K Coll Lon 48. **d** 49 **p** 50 Linc. C of St Pet-at-Gowts Linc 49-53; Chap Bracebridge Heath Hosp Linc 50-51; V of Sutton Bridge 53-61; Deeping St Jas 61-77; Tallington 61-64; C-in-c of W Deeping St Andr 65-66; R 66-77; RD of Ness 64-65; Aveland and Ness (w Stamford from 69) 65-72; Can and Preb of Linc Cathl 67-78; Can (Emer) from 78. *12 Warn Crescent, Oakham, Leics, LE15 6LZ.* (0572 56103)

KNIGHT, Francis George. ACT ThL (1st cl) 52. **d** and **p** 53 Brisb. C of Dalby 53-55; St Luke Toowoomba 55-56; R of Palmwoods 56-69; Crow's Nest 59-62; Childers w Howard 62-65; St Matt Groveley, Brisb 65-73; St Matt Holland Pk Brisb 73-78; V of St Jude Everton Pk City and Dio Brisb 78-79; R from 79. *15 Buller Street, Everton Park, Brisbane, Australia 4053.* (355 0713)

KNIGHT, George. b 20. OBE (Mil) 71. Late Exhib of St Cath Coll Ox BA (2nd cl Th) 42, MA 46. Sarum Th Coll 47. **d** 47 **p** 48 Win. C of St Jo Bapt Moordown 47-49; Chap RN 49-75; RN Coll Greenwich 72-75; R of Linton-in-Craven w Hebden Dio Bradf from 75. *Linton Rectory, Grassington, N Yorks, Bd23 5LA.* (Grassington 752575)

KNIGHT, George William. Codr Coll Barb. **d** 68 **p** 69 Barb. C of St John 68-69; St Lucy 70-71; R of St Silas w St Alban Barb 71-75. *c/o St Alban's Rectory, Carlton, St James, Barbados, WI.*

KNIGHT, Graham Stephen. Moore Th Coll Syd ACT ThL 67. **d** 68 **p** 69 Syd. C of Chatswood 68-71; H Trin Adel 71-75; C-in-c of Manly Vale 75-79; R of St Steph Mittagong Dio Syd from 79. *7 Queen Street, Mittagong, NSW, Australia 2575.* (048-71 1947)

KNIGHT, Henry Christian. Fitzw Ho Cam BA 62, MA 66. Ridley Hall Cam 62. **d** 63 **p** 64 Bradf. Succr of Bradf Cathl 63-64; Chap 64-66; Chap at Tel Aviv Dio Jer from 67. *12 Be'er Hofman Street, Tel Aviv, Israel.* (03-426802)

KNIGHT, Herbert Frank. b 09. Late Sizar and Exhib of Trin Coll Dub BA (3rd cl Mod) and Ryan Pri 31. Div Test 32. **d** 32 **p** 33 Down. C of Whitehouse 32-36; St Martin's Miss Ballymacarett 36-38; CMS Miss Siapu 39-44; Chap Trin Coll Foochow 47-51; Min of St Chris Conv Distr Leic 51-54; R of Stathern 54-58; V of St Pet Mountsorrel 58-64; R of Catthorpe 64-73; R of Shawell 64-73. *Beehive Cottage, High Street, Adderbury, Banbury, Oxon, OX17 3LS.*

KNIGHT, Herbert John. b 15. Univ of Wales, BA 38. Ely Th Coll 38. **d** 39 **p** 41 St A. C of Prestatyn 39-42; St Andr Westcliff-on-Sea 42-44; Chap RAFVR 44-48; V of St Andr Oldham 48-52; Chap RAF 52-58; R of Lea Dio Linc from 58; PC (V from 68) of Knaith Dio Linc from 58; C-in-c of Upton w Kexby Dio Linc 60-61; V from 61; RD of Corringham from 78; V of Gate Burton Dio Linc from 78. *Lea Rectory, Gainsborough, Lincs, DN21 5HZ.* (Gainsborough 3188)

KNIGHT, John Bernard. b 34. ACIS 60. Oak Hill Th Coll 61. **d** 65 **p** 66 S'wark. C of Morden 65-69; in Amer Ch 69-71; V of Summerfield City and Dio Birm from 71. *99 Gillott Road, Birmingham 16.* (021-454 0374)

KNIGHT, John Boughton. b 09. Kelham Th Coll 30. **d** 36 **p** 37 Derby. C of Chesterfield 36-39; St Phil Dalston 39-41; St Pancras 41-44; St Jude-on-the-Hill Hampstead Garden Suburb 44-48; St Nich Portslade 48-53; Hendon (in c of St Mary Magd Holders Hill) 53-58; V of St Jo Evang w St Simon Zelotes Bethnal Green 58-71; C of St Anne Soho Lon 72-75; P-in-c of St Anne w St Thos and St Pet Soho 75-78. *4 Bishop Street, Islington, N1.* (02-226 6672)

KNIGHT, Very Rev John Francis Alan Macdonald. Coll of Resurr Mirfield, 59. **d** 61 **p** 62 Matab. C of Gwelo 61-66; R of Melfort 66-68; C of Highlands Salisbury 68-70; P-in-c of Chikwaka 68-70; L to Offic Dio Mashon 70-75; R of Umtali 76-81; Dean of Mutare from 81. *115 Main Street, Umtali, Zimbabwe.*

KNIGHT, Keith Kenneth. b 36. Univ of Southn BSc (3rd cl Physics) 58. Wycl Hall Ox 59. **d** 62 **p** 63 Blackb. C of Lower Darwen 62-64; Leyland 64-68; P-in-c of All SS Blackb 68-71; Youth Chap Dio Blackb from 71; C of St Pet Burnley 71-74. *220 Todmorden Road, Burnley, Lancs.* (Burnley 27378)

KNIGHT, Kenneth William. b 15. TD 50. Wycl Hall Ox. **d** 61 **p** 62 Ex. C of Ch Ch Paignton 61-63; V of Holbeton Dio Ex from 63. *Holbeton Vicarage, Plymouth, Devon.*

KNIGHT, Very Rev Marcus. b 03. Univ of Lon BA (2nd cl Cl) 24, AKC (1st cl), Trench Pri and Relton Pri 27, BD (1st cl Phil of Relig) 29, Caldecott Pri 32, Fell 46. Univ of Ex Hon LLD 73. Union Th Sem NY Mills Fell STM 30. **d** 27 **p** 28 Lon. C of St Andr Stoke Newington 27-29; Ealing 30-33; PV of Ex Cathl 33-36; V of Cockington w St Matt Chelston 37-40; Nuneaton 40-44; RD of Atherstone 40-44; Exam Chap to Bp of Cov 43-44; Can of St Paul's Cathl Lon 44-60; Prec 44-54; Chan 54-60; Treas to Chapter 50-60; Sec C of E Counc for Educn 49-58; Vice-Chairman Nat S 52-66; Dean of Ex 60-72; Dean (Emer) from 72; Ch Comm 68-72. *1 Execliff, Trefusis Terrace, Exmouth, EX8 2AX.* (Exmouth 71153)

KNIGHT, Michael Richard. b 47. St Jo Coll Dur BA 69, MA 79. Fitzw Coll Cam BA 73, MA 77. Westcott Ho Cam 71. **d** 74 **p** 75 St Alb. C of Bp's Stortford 74-75; St Andr Bedford 75-79; Chap to Angl Studs in Glas from 79. *43 Oakfield Avenue, Glasgow, G12 8LL.* (041-339 6202)

KNIGHT, Peter John. b 51. AKC 73. Sarum Wells Th Coll 79. **d** 80 **p** 81 Willesden for Lon. C of H Cross Gt Greenford Dio Lon from 80. *177 Costons Lane, Greenford, Middx, UB6 9AD.* (01-578 1596)

KNIGHT, Philip Stephen. b 46. Oak Hill Th Coll 75. **d** 77 **p** 78 Ex. C of St Pancras Pennycross Plymouth 77-80; Epsom (in c of St Steph) Dio Guildf from 80. *82 Rosebery Road, Langley Vale, Epsom, Surrey, KT18 6AA.* (Ashtead 75823)

KNIGHT, Ralph Derek. b 28. SS Coll Cam BA 53, MA 57. Sarum Th Coll 53. **d** 55 **p** 56 Ex. C of Holsworthy 55-57; St Luke Wallsend 57-58; St Lawr Newc T 58-60; Yeovil 60-66; St Benet Fink Tottenham Dio Lon from 74. *57 De Quincey Road, N17.* (01-801 0641)

KNIGHT, Roger George. b 41. Linc Th Coll 65. **d** 67 **p** 68 Bris. C of Hartcliffe 67-69; L to Offic Dio Pet from 69; Hd Master Twywell Sch Kettering 69-74; V of Naseby 74-79; P-in-c of Haselbech 74-79; Clipston 78-79; R of Clipston w Naseby and Haselbech 79-82; P-in-c of Kelmarsh 79-82; Team R of Corby w Gt & L Oakley Dio Pet from 82. *Rectory, Boughton Close, Coldermeadow, Corby, Northants, NN18 9AB.* (Gt Oakley 743425)

KNIGHT, Roger Ivan. b 54. AKC and BD 79. Ripon Coll Cudd 79. **d** 80 **p** 81 Roch. C of All SS Orpington Dio Roch from 80. *62 Bark Hart Road, Orpington, Kent.*

KNIGHT, Samuel Theodore Josiah. Codr Coll Barb 60. **d** 63 **p** 64 Antig. C of St Anthony w St Patr Montserrat 64-66; R of St Paul w St John St Kitts 66-68; St Matt I and Dio Barb from 76. *St Matthew's Rectory, St Michael, Barbados, WI.*

KNIGHT, Stanley Richard. Tyndale Hall Bris 63. **d** 65 Warrington for Liv **p** 66 Liv. C of St Cuthb Everton 65-68; Hon C of Paddock Wood Dio Roch from 68. *8 Ashley Gardens, paddock Wood, Kent.*

KNIGHT, Sydney Frederick Harrold. Univ of Leeds, BA (3rd cl Hist) 29. Coll of Resurr Mirfield, 25. **d** 33 **p** 34 Liv. C of St Jas Haydock 33-37; St Barn Miss Ntlaza 37-40; CF (S Afr) 40-46; P-in-c of Matatiele 46-75; Can of St Jo Cathl Umtata from 49; Archd of Matatiele (E Griqualand from 75) 57-77; P-in-c of Kokstad Dio St John's from 75. *Box 358, Kokstad 4700, S Africa.* (Kokstad 216)

KNIGHT, Terence. b 38. Lich Th Coll 60. **d** 63 **p** 64 Portsm. C of St Alb Copnor 63-67; St Mich AA Basingstoke (in c of All SS) 67-72; C-in-c of Northwood 72-75; Birches Head 72-75; V of St Sav Portsea Dio Portsm from 75; M Gen Syn from 80. *St Saviour's House, Twyford Avenue, Stamshaw, Portsmouth, Hants, PO2 8PB.* (Portsm 663664)

KNIGHT, Thomas. b 20. OBE (Mil) 60. Linc Th Coll 69. **d** 71 **p** 72 Cov. C of St Barbara Cov 71-74; R of Southam (w Stockton from 77) Dio Cov from 74; RD of Southam from 77. *Southam Rectory, Leamington Spa, Warws.* (Southam 2413)

KNIGHT, William Lawrence. b 39. Univ of Lon BSc 61, PhD 65. Coll of the Resurr Mirfield 75. **d** 77 **p** 78 St Alb. C of Bp's Hatfield 77-81; Asst Chap at H Trin Cathl Brussels Dio Gibr in Eur from 81. *23 Rue Armand Swevers, 1160 Brussels, Belgium.* (02-660 6320)

KNIGHTS, James William. b 34. K Coll Lon and Warm AKC 66. **d** 67 **p** 68 Pet. C of St Andr Kettering 67-71; V of Braunston w Brooke 71-81; St John Dudley Dio Worc from 81. *8a New Rowley Road, Dudley, W Midl, DY2 8AS.* (Dudley 53807)

KNIGHTS, Percy Lionel Scott. **d** 35 **p** 36 Lon. C of St Matt U Clapton 35-38; All SS S Acton 38-40; Chap RAFVR 40-48; C of St Leon Deal 48-50; St Thos Durban 50-54; V of Alfred County 54-56; Port Shepstone 56-66; R of Pinetown 66-70; L to Offic Dio Natal from 70. *PO Umtentweni, Natal, S Africa.*

KNIGHTS, Timothy John. b 10. St Cath Coll Cam 3rd cl Th Trip pt i 62, BA (3rd cl Th Trip pt ii) 64, MA 68. St Steph Ho Ox 64. **d** 66 **p** 67 Bris. C of St Mark Swindon 66-70; St Anne Brookfield St Pancras 70-74; V of St Steph w St Luke Paddington Dio Lon from 74. *25 Talbot Road, W2.* (01-229 5731)

KNIGHTS JOHNSON, Anthony Nigel. b 52. Counc for Nat Acad Awards BA 75. Wycl Hall Ox 78. **d** 80 **p** 81 Roch. C of Ch Ch Beckenham Dio Roch from 80. *25 Rectory Road, Beckenham, Kent, BR3 1HL.*

KNIVETON, Burkett. Temple Univ Philadelphia BSc (Educn) 42. Nashotah Ho Wisconsin BD 43. **d** 43 Pennsylvania **p** 43 Vermont. In Amer Ch 43-47 and 50-56; P-in-c of St Andr Exuma 47-50 and 56-60; L to Offic Dio Nass from 60. *PO Box 726, Nassau, Bahamas, W Indies.*

KNOCK, Andrew Henry Drysdale. b 49. Univ of Lon BA 71. Univ of Stirling PhD 78. Univ of Edin BD 78. Edin Th Coll 75. **d** 78 **p** 79 St Andr. Chap of St Ninian's Cathl Perth 78-80; C of Bridge of Allan and of Alloa (and of Dollar from 81) Dio St Andr from 80; Chap Stirling Univ from 80. *5 The Sycamores, Tullibody, Alloa, Clack, FK10 2XH.*

KNOPP, Alexander Edward Robert. b 09. St Jo Coll Cam 2nd cl Hist Trip pt i 31, BA (2nd cl Th Trip pt i) 33, MA 37. Ridley Hall Cam 32. **d** 34 **p** 35 Chelmsf. C of St Mary Virg Loughton 34-38; Prittlewell 38-40; R of Nevendon (in c of N Benfleet) 40; Nevendon w N Benfleet 41-48; V of St Jo Evang Walthamstow 48-50; Pampisford 50-59; Babraham 50-59; R of Quendon w Rickling 59-68; Gt Yeldham 68-73; Gt w L Snoring 73-76; Perm to Offic Dio Ely from 77. *24 Green Street, Duxford, Cambridge, CB2 4RG.* (Cam 835894)

KNOS, Jan Börje. St Paul's Coll Grahmstn 64. **d** 66 **p** 68 Capetn. C of Simonstown 66-68; Bonteheuwel 68-70; H Trin Caledon 70-72; R of Hopefield 72-74; C of Plumstead 74-76; Perm to Offic Dio Capetn 77-78; P-in-c of Sasolburg w St Edw Parys 78-81; V of St Mich AA Hull Dio York from 82. *St Michael's Vicarage, Orchard Park Road, Hull, HU6 9BX.* (Hull 853252)

KNOTT, Christopher Rodney. b 42. Open Univ BA 77. Kelham Th Coll 64. **d** 68 **p** 69 Ex. C of Withycombe Raleigh w All SS Exmouth 68-72; Team V of Farringdon w Aylesbeare 72-75; Woodbury-Salterton 72-75; Team V of Clyst Valley 75-76; R of Lynton w Brendon, Countisbury, Lynmouth, Barbrook, Parracombe and Martinhoe 76-81; Highweek w Abbotsbury and Teigngrace Dio Ex from 81. *Highweek Rectory, Newton Abbot, Devon.* (Newton Abbot 4949)

KNOTT, Graham Keith. b 53. Oak Hill Coll 77. **d** 80 **p** 81

Derby. C of Normanton-by-Derby Dio Derby from 80. *211 Village Street, Derby, DE3 8DE.*

KNOTT, Montague Hardwick. b 05. Oak Hill Th Coll 54. **d** 55 **p** 56 Chelmsf. C of Walthamstow 55-57; V of Blackmore (w Stondon Massey from 81) Dio Chelmsf from 57; P-in-c of Stondon Massey 80-81. *Blackmore Vicarage, Ingatestone, Essex, CM4 0RN.* (Blackmore 821464)

KNOTT, Neville James. St Jo Coll Morpeth ACT ThL 65. **d** 65 **p** 66 Brisb. C of St Luke Ekibin Bris 65-69; Southport 69-71; St Matt Stretford 71; V of Morabah 72-75; R of H Trin Fortitude Valley City and Dio Brisb from 75. *141-149 Brookes Street, Fortitude Valley, Brisbane, Australia 4006.* (52-1653)

KNOTT, Robert Michael. b 35. Clifton Th Coll 67. **d** 70 Stafford for Lich **p** 70 Shrewsbury for Lich. C of Rolleston Staffs 70-72; Anslow 70-72; Uphill (in-c of St Barn) 73-75; Perm to Offic Dio B & W 77-79; P-in-c of Palgrave Dio St E from 79; Wortham Dio St E from 79; Burgate Dio St E from 79. *Rectory, Wortham, Diss, Norf.* (Diss 3904)

KNOWERS, Stephen John. b 49. AKC and BD 72. St Aug Coll Cant 72. **d** 73 **p** 74 St Alb. C of Bps Hatfield 73-77; Cheshunt 77-81; P-in-c of St Mark Barnet Vale Dio St Alb from 81. *56 Potters Road, Barnet, Herts, EN5 5HY.* (01-449 4265)

KNOWLES, Albert Francis. St Aid Coll 64. **d** 65 Hulme for Man **p** 66 Man. C of St Luke Heywood 65-68; V of Hurst Green 68-76; C-in-c (V from 69) of Mytton 68-76; Perm to Offic Dio Bradf from 77. *Fairhaven, The Croft, Back Lane, Grindleton, Lancs BB7 4RW.* (Clitheroe 41789)

KNOWLES, Andrew William Allen. b 46. St Cath Coll Cam BA 68, MA 72. St Jo Coll Nottm 69. **d** 71 **p** 72 Leic. C of H Trin Leic 71-74; H Trin Cam 74-77; St Jo Bapt Woking 77-81; V of Goldsworth Park Dio Guildf from 81. *1 Muirfield Road, Woking, Surrey, GU21 3PW.* (Woking 64523)

KNOWLES, Charles Howard. b 43. Univ of Sheff BSc (2nd cl Math) 65. Fitzw Coll Cam BA (3rd cl Th Trip pt ii) 69, MA 73. Westcott Ho Cam 67. **d** 69 Southw **p** 70 Sherwood for Southw. C of St Jo Bapt Bilborough 69-72; V Cho of Southw Minster from 72. *1 Fern Close, Southwell, Notts.* (Southwell 813767)

KNOWLES, Clifford. b 35. N-W Ordin Course 74. **d** 77 Man **p** 78 Bp Hulme for Man. C of Urmston 77-80; V of St Luke Chadderton Dio Man from 80. *Vicarage, Queens Road, Chadderton, Oldham, Lancs.* (061-624 3562)

KNOWLES, Frederick Bertram. b 06. Worc OTC. **d** 55 Glouc **p** 56 Tewkesbury for Glouc. C of Lydney 55-58; R of Swindon w Uckington and Elmstone Hardwicke 58-68; Pebworth w Dorsington 68-73. *2 Brookhill, Great Wolford, via Shipston-on-Stour, Warwicks.*

KNOWLES, Canon George Woods Atkin. b 21. Trin Coll Dub BA 44, MA 47. **d** 44 **p** 45 Connor. C of Ardoyne 44-46; Knockbreda 46-49; I of Ballyscullion 49-63; Drumachose Dio Derry from 63; Can of Derry from 75. *Rectory, Killane Road, Limavady, Co Derry, BT49 0DJ, N Ireland.* (Limavady 2680)

KNOWLES, Graeme Paul. b 51. AKC 73. St Aug Coll Cant 73. **d** 74 **p** 75 Cant. C of St Pet-in-I-of-Thanet 74-79; St Pet Leeds 79-81; Chap Portsm Cathl from 81. *c/o Cathedral House, St Thomas's Street, Portsmouth.*

KNOWLES, Howard Ian. b 34. **d** 76 Bath. Hon C of Condobolin Dio Bath from 76. *PO Box 18, Condobolin, NSW, Australia 2877.*

KNOWLES, Hylton. Univ of Natal, BA 57. St Paul's Th Coll Grahmstn LTh 60. **d** and **p** 60 Natal. C of St Pet Pietmaritzburg 60-61; R of Drakensberg 62-65; Asst Chap St Andr Coll Grahmstn 66-70; Chap from 70. *St Andrew's College, Somerset Street, Grahamstown, CP, S Africa.* (Grahmstn 4012)

KNOWLES, Preb Ivo Douglas West. b 07. Keble Coll Ox BA (3rd cl Eng Lang and Lit) 30, MA 34. Cudd Coll 30. **d** 31 **p** 33 Lich. C of St Paul Burton-on-Trent 31-33; Perm to Offic at St Jo Bapt Pet 33-34; St Giles Willenhall 34-36; C 36-38; PC of Longsdon 38-44; V of Trent Vale 44-65; R of Stafford 65-71; RD of Stafford 65-71; Preb of Lich Cathl 67-80; Preb (Emer) from 80; V of Sambrook 71-80. *Steward's Lodge, Hilderstone Road, Sandon, Stafford, ST18 0DX.* (Sandon 313)

KNOWLES, John. b 28. **d** 73 **p** 74 Mon (APM). L to Offic Dio Mon from 73. *Hillcrest, Llwynarthen, St Mellons, Nr Cardiff, CF3 9XH.* (Castleton 680251)

KNOWLES, John Arthur. **d** 55 **p** 56 Clogh. C of Enniskillen 55-57; I of Cooneen w Mullaghford 57-59; Templeharry w Borrisnafarney 59-61; Clonsast w Rathangan 61-62; Bourney 62-65; Creagh 65-67; Donagh w Tyholland 67-70; C of Rathaspeck 70-76; I of Mohill w Cloone Dio Ard from 76. *Rectory, Mohill, Co Leitrim, Irish Republic.* (Mohill 42)

KNOWLES, Melbourne Uriah Hilary. b 33. St Francis Coll Brisb 75. **d** 77 **p** 78 Brisb. C of St Jas Toowoomba 77-80; V of Bramble Bay Dio Brisb from 80. *59 Georgina Street, Woody Point, Queensld, Australia 4019.*

KNOWLES, Melvin Clay. b 43. Stetson Univ Fla USA BA 66. Univ of Ex MA 73. Ripon Coll Cudd Dipl Th 76. **d** 77 **p** 78 Glouc. C of Minchinhampton 77-80; V of St Paul's Cathl I and Dio St Hel from 80. *St Paul's Vicarage, St Helena, S Atlantic Ocean.*

KNOWLES, Philip John. b 48. TCD Div Test 76. **d** 76 **p** 77 Connor. C of St Paul Lisburn 76-79; I of Manorhamilton Dio Kilm from 79. *Rectory, Manorhamilton, Co Leitrim, Irish Republic.* (Manorhamilton 41)

KNOWLES, Walter Roy. b 51. Westmount Coll Calif BA 72. Trin Coll Tor MDiv 77. **d** 77 Tor for Calg **p** 78 Calg. P-in-c of Oyen 77-80. *c/o Box 265, Oyen, Alta, Canada, T0L 0Z0.*

KNOWLES-BROWN, John Henry. b 30. K Coll Lon and Warm AKC 53. **d** 54 **p** 55 St Alb. C of St Andr Hertford 54-58; St Jas Bushey 58-61; Chap RAF 61-65; Min of St Jo Bapt [f St Mich and St Geo] Eccles Distr Farley Hill Luton Dio St Alb 65-69; V 69-72; V of Totteridge Dio St Alb from 72; RD of Barnet from 79. *Vicarage, Totteridge, N20 8PR.* (01-445 6787)

KNOWLING, Richard Charles. b 46. K Coll Lon BSc 67. St Edm Hall Ox BA 70. St Steph Ho Ox 69. **d** 71 **p** 72 Birm. C of St Mary Hobs Moat Solihull 71-75; St Mary w All SS and St Mich Shrewsbury 75-77; V of St Martin Rough Hills Wolverhampton Dio Lich from 77. *St Martin's Vicarage, Dixon Street, Wolverhampton, WV2 2BG.* (Wolverhampton 341030)

KNOWLSON, George Cecil Vernon. b 10. Qu Coll Birm 32. **d** 35 Lon **p** 36 Man. C of St Luke Paddington 35-36; St Jas Heywood 36-38; St Mich AA Lawton Moor (in c of Royal Oak) 38-40; CF (EC) 40-45; V of Hadnall 45-49; R of Oudtshoorn CP 49-52; C of Walsall 52-53; V of Hollinfare 53-55; St Paul Sale 56-64; Lindow 64-76. *21 Wilton Crescent, Alderley Edge, Chesh, SK9 7RE.* (Alderley Edge 583754)

KNOX, Canon David Broughton. Univ of Syd BA 38. ALCD 41. Univ of Lon BD 41; MTh 49. Univ of Cam 42. St Cath Soc Ox DPhil 54. **d** 41 **p** 42 Ely. C of St Andr L Cam 41-45; Chap RNVR 43-47; Lect at Moore Th Coll Syd 47-53; C of St Andr Cathl Syd 47-51; St Aldate Ox 52-53; Tutor and Lect Wycl Hall Ox 51-53; Vice-Prin Moore Th Coll Syd 54-59; Prin from 59; Can of Syd from 60. *Moore Theological College, Newtown, NSW, Australia 2042.* (51-1136)

KNOX, Geoffrey Martin. b 44. Univ of Dur BA (2nd cl Th) 66, Dipl Th (w distinc) 67. St Chad's Coll Dur 63. **d** 67 Sherwood for Southw **p** 68 Southw. C of Newark-on-Trent 67-72; Publ Pr Dio Derby 74; V of Woodville 74-81; RD of Repton 79-81; V of Long Eaton Dio Derby from 81. *Vicarage, Regent Street, Long Eaton, Nottingham.* (Long Eaton 3154)

KNOX, Canon Ian Carroll. b 32. St Jo Coll Dur BA (Th) 54, Dipl Th 55. **d** 55 **p** 56 Wakef. C of St Mary Illingworth Halifax 55-58; Lightcliffe 58-60; V of Rastrick 60-77; Huddersfield Dio Wakef from 77; Hon Can of Wakef Cathl from 76; RD of Huddersfield from 77; M Gen Syn from 80. *Parish House, Venn Street, Huddersfield, W Yorks, HD1 2RL.* (Huddersfield 27964)

KNOX, Iain John Edward. b 46. Univ of Hull BPhil 76. TCD BA 70, Div Test 71, MA 74. **d** 71 **p** 72 Connor. C of Malone 71-74; Dom Chap to Bp of Connor 72-74; Perm to Offic Dio Derry 74-76; R of Gweedore U 76-80; Clonmel and of Cahir and of Fethard Dio Lism from 80. *St Mary's Rectory, Western Road, Clonmel, Co Tipperary, Irish Republic.* (Clonmel 21369)

KNOX, Norman Dennis. Univ of Tor BA 38. Trin Coll Tor. **d** 39 **p** 40 Tor. Min of Washago 39-42; I of Stoney Lake 42-43; Chap RCAF 43-46; C of St Mary Tor 46-47; Miss E Moos Miss 47-50; R of New Liskeard 50-54; Exeter 54-58; I of Lambeth 58-64; R of St Hilda St Thos 64-67; P-in-C of Glanworth 67-69. *510 Oxford Street West, London 74, Ont, Canada.*

KNOX, Thomas Anthony. b 31. Ely Th Coll. **d** 56 **p** 57 Lon. C of All SS Poplar 56-59; St Andr Eastbourne 59-61; Welwyn 61-66; V of St Mich AA Boreham Wood 66-71; Puttenham w Long Marston and Wilstone 71-79; R of Toddington Dio St Alb from 79. *Toddington Rectory, Leighton Road, Dunstable, Beds, LU5 6AL.* (Toddington 2298)

KOBOYI, Ven Israiri. Buwalasi Th Coll 59. **d** 60 **p** 61 U Nile. P Dio U Nile 60-61; Dio Mbale from 61; Dioc Sec 67-78; Can from 78; Archd Dio Mbale from 78. *PO Box 1267, Mbale, Uganda.*

KOBWISHO, Enosi. Bp Tucker Coll Mukono, 61. **d** 63 **p** 65 Ankole-K. P Dio Ankole-K 63-67; Dio Ank 67-77; Dio W Ank from 77. *PO Rubaare, Mbarara, Uganda.*

KODIWA, Horace Royston. Newton Coll Dogura 70. **d** 74 Bp Kendall for Papua **p** 78 Aipo. P Dio Papua 74-77; C of Aiome 78-79; Madang 79-81; Mt Hagen Dio Aipo from 81. *Box 182, Mount Hagen, Papua New Guinea.*

KOECH, Isaac. St Phil Sch Maseno 73. **d** and **p** 75 Maseno

S. P Dio Maseno S. *PO Box 181, Kericho, Kenya.*

KOECH, Nimrod. b 32. **d** 76 **p** 77 Nak. P Dio Nak. *PO Box 235, Eldoret, Kenya.*

KOEKEMOER, Gerald John. b 34. **d** 80 Pret. C of St Steph Lyttelton Dio Pret from 80. *c/o Rectory, Cradock Avenue, PO Box 1-4338, Verwoerdburg 0140, S Africa.*

KOETE, Charles. b 51. Bp Patteson Th Centre Kohimarama 71. **d** 74 Melan. d Dio Melan 74-75; Centr Melan from 75. *Oa, Guadalcanal, Solomon Islands.*

KOFORIDUA, Lord Bishop of. *See* Okine, Right Rev Robert Garshong Allotey.

KOGONYA, Zakoki. b 25. Bp Tucker Coll Mukono 73. **d** and **p** 74 Mbale. P Dio Mbale. *Bukhabusi, PO Box 984, Mbale, Uganda.*

KOH, Ernest Jin Chin. Sing Th Sem 52. **d** 61 **p** 62 Sing. P Dio Sing from 62; Exam Chap to Bp of Sing from 77. *25g Perak Road, Singapore 8.*

KOHLER, John Maxwell. b 44. St Jo Coll Morpeth 69. **d** 70 **p** 71 C & Goulb. C of Ch Ch Queanbeyan 71-73; Cooma 73-74; Kameruka 74-76; St Pet Hornsby 76-78; Hunters Hill 78-79; R of St Mark Granville Dio Syd from 79. *39 Jamieson Street, Granville, NSW, Australia 2142.* (637-1073)

KOHNER, Canon Jenö George. K Coll Lon BD and AKC 56. Westcott Ho Cam 56. **d** 57 **p** 58 Liv. C of St Thos Eccleston 57-60; St Jo Evang Montr 60-63; Miss Thorndale Miss Pierrefonds Dio Montr 63-66; I 66-70; Chateauguay 70-75; Dir of Dioc Services Dio Montr from 75; Hon Can of Montr from 75; Exam Chap to Bp of Montr from 76. *1444 Union Avenue, Montreal, PQ, Canada.* (514-845 6211)

KOIBUA, Japhet. St Aid Coll Dogura. **d** 46 **p** 51 New Guinea. P Dio New Guinea 46-71; Dio Papua 71-77. *Iaudari, Samarai, Papua, New Guinea.*

KOIEBA, Caedmon. **d** 66 **p** 68 New Guinea. P Dio New Guinea (Papua from 71) 66-68 and 69-74; C of Mt Hawthorn W Australia 68-69; Perm to Offic Dio Newc 74-75; Archd and R of Port Moresby 75-77; R of Hohola Dio Port Moresby from 77. *PO Box 5396, Boroko, Papua New Guinea.*

KOIN, Yona Aggrey. St Cypr Coll Lindi 71. **d** 74 **p** 75 Masasi. P Dio Masasi. *Box 74, Mikindani, Mtwara, Tanzania.*

KOK, Yu Kong. b 17. **d** 71 Kuch **p** 72 Sabah. P Dio Sabah 71-76. *Box 15, Kota Kinabalu, Sabah, Malaysia.*

KOKILI, Zephaniah Austin. St Pet Coll Melan. **d** 46 **p** 57 Melan. P Dio Melan 46-75; Dio Ysabel from 75. *Jejevo, Maringe, Santa Ysabel, Solomon Islands.*

KO KO, Canon Saw. **d** and **p** 51 Rang. P Dio Rang 51-70; Dio Pa-an from 70; Hon Can of St Pet Cathl Pa-an from 75. *St Paul's Church, Toungoo, Burma.*

KOKO, John. **d** 54 Bp Brazier for Ugan. d Dio Ugan 54-60; Dio Rwanda B 60-66; Dio Bur from 66. *CMS, Buhiga, Ngozi, Burundi, Uganda.*

KOKO, Lorenzo. St Cypr Th Coll Tunduru. **d** 54 **p** 57 Zanz. P Dio Zanz T. *Vugire, Tanga, Tanzania.*

KOKOALI, Christian Tumelo. St Pet Coll Alice 66. **d** 71 **p** 72 Bloemf. C of St Aug thaba 'Nchu 68-71; St Patr Bloemf 71-73; P-in-c of The Transfig Harrismith 73-75; St Clem Winburg 75-76; Kaya Mandi Dio Capetn from 76. *PO Mbekweni, CP, S Africa.* (Paarl 27865)

KO KO MAUNG, Joseph. **d** 75 **p** 77 Rang. P Dio Rang. *St Michael's Church, Kemmendine Road, Rangoon, Burma.*

KOKUMO, Daniel. **d** and **p** 78 Centr Tang. P Dio Centr Tang. *PO Langasa, Tanzania.*

KOLADE, Abraham Ojo. Melville Hall Oyo 37. **d** 38 **p** 40 Lagos. P Dio Lagos 38-52; Archd of N Prov 45-50; P Dio Ondo-B 52-55; Hon Can of Ondo-B 55-64; Ondo 64-66; Archd of Lokoja 61-68. *St James's Church, Erin-Oke, Ilesha, Nigeria.*

KOLAWOLE, Samuel Dada. **d** 41 **p** 43 Lagos. P Dio Lagos 41-52; Dio Ondo-B 52-56. *Usi-Ebiti, Nigeria.*

KO LIN, **d** 78 **p** 79 Akyab. P Dio Akyab. *St James's Church, Tlen Thang Vum, Burma.*

KOLINGO, Frederick. b 44. St Phil Coll Kongwa 79. **d** 80 **p** 81 Centr Tang. P Dio Centr Tang. *PO Box 604, Zanza, Dodoma, Tanzania.*

KOLO, Joseph Odogharo. **d** 69 Benin. d Dio Benin 69-77; Dio Asaba from 77. *Onicha Olona College, Onicha Olona, Nigeria.*

KOMAKECH, Canon Yose. **d** 43 **p** 44 U Nile. P Dio U Nile 43-61; Dio N Ugan from 61; Archd of Acholi 67-69; Hon Can of N Ugan from 69. *Awac, Gulu, Uganda.*

KOMBA, Very Rev Othniel Patrick. St Cypr Th Coll Ngala 69. **d** 72 **p** 73 SW Tang. P Dio SW Tang; Can of SW Tang from 78; VG from 80; Dean of St Andr Cathl Njombe from 80. *Box 32, Njombe, Tanzania.*

KOMBA, Robinson. b 43. St Mark's Coll Dar-S 77. **d** 79 Dar-S **p** 80 Bp R Wood for Dar-S. P Dio Dar-S. *PO Box 60111, Dar es Salaam, Tanzania.*

KOMBO, Joel. **d** 62 **p** 66 Momb. P Dio Momb from 62. *PO Box 8294, Mombasa, Kenya.*

KOMI, Habil. **d** 72 Sudan. d Dio Sudan 72-76; Dio Omdurman from 76. *Box 8, Kadugli, Sudan.*

KOMOLAFE, Israel Ojo. Im Coll Ibad 62. **d** 64 **p** 65 Ondo. P Dio Ondo. *Vicarage, Omuo-Ekiji, Ondo, Nigeria.*

KOMOLAFE, Samuel Adejumobi. b 32. **d** 73 **p** 75 Ondo. P Dio Ondo. *St John's Vicarage, Atosin, via Akure, Nigeria.*

KOMPASS, Paul Michael. b 42. McMaster Univ BSc 65. Trin Coll Tor STB 71. **d** and **p** 71 Niag. C of Welland 71-73; I of St Simon Oakville 73-79; Palermo 73-79; Madoc Dio Ont from 79. *Rectory, Madoc, Ont, Canada.* (613-473 4217)

KOMUNDA, Wilson. b 22. Bp Tucker Coll Mukono 58. **d** 64 **p** 66 Ankole-K. P Dio Kig. *PO Box 190, Kabale, Kigezi, Uganda.*

KONDO, Thompson Rubwa. **d** 67 **p** 68 W Tang. P Dio W Tang. *Box 646, Ujiji, Kigoma, Tanzania.*

KONING, Teunis. **d** and **p** 66 Alg. R of Manitowaning 66-70; Englehart 70-75; Oldcastle Dio Hur from 75. *RR1, Oldcastle, Ont., Canada.*

KOOMSON, Francis Ato. b 45. **d** 73 RC Abp of Cape Coast **p** 75 Accra. P Dio Accra. *Box 23, Sunyani B/A, Ghana.*

KOOTENAY, Lord Bishop of. *See* Scott, Right Rev Edward Walter.

KOOTENAY, Dean of. *See* Donald, Very Rev Walter James.

KOOZA, Yekoyasi Musanje. Bp Tucker Coll Mukono 74. **d** 76 **p** 77 Nam. P Dio Nam. *PO Box 22011, Nakifuma, Uganda.*

KOPADA, Edison. b 43. **d** 80 Port Moresby **p** 81 Popondota. C of St Martin Boroko Dio Port Moresby from 80. *Box 5845, Boroko, Papua New Guinea.*

KOPERQUALUK, Isa. **d** 69 Arctic. Miss Gt Whale River 69-71; Payne Bay 72-76. *Povungnituk, PQ, Canada.*

KOPSCH, Hartmut. b 41. Univ of Sheff BA 63. Univ of BC MA 66. Univ of Lon PhD 70. Trin Coll Bris 78. **d** 80 **p** 81 Barking for Chelmsf. C of Cranham Pk Dio Chelmsf from 80. *4 Laburnham Gardens, Cranham, Essex.* (Upminster 25170)

KORENEFF-DOMOGATZKY, Sidney. b 18. St Jo Coll Auckld LTh 66. **d** 66 **p** 78 Wel. C of All SS Palmerston N 66-71; Upper Hutt 71-73; Wel Maor Past from 74. *Vicarage, 31 Egmont Street, Patea, NZ.*

KORI, Ibrahim Al-Hadeed. b 47. **d** 81 Omdurman. d Dio Omdurman. *c/o PO Box 65, Omdurman, Sudan.*

KORINA, Gilchrist Egimbari. Newton Coll Dogura. **d** 61 **p** 64 New Guinea. P Dio New Guinea 61-71; Dio Papua from 71. *Movi PMB, via Goroka, Papua New Guinea.*

KORNACZEWSKI, Alexander. b 46. Univ of Melb BSc 69, MSc 73. Univ of Nottm Dipl Th 75. St Jo Coll Nottm 74. **d** 78 **p** 79 Melb. C of St Mark E Brighton 78-80; I of St Mark Camberwell 80-81; Airport W Dio Melb from 81. *54 Roberts Road, Airport West, Vic, Australia 3042.*

KORNAHRENS, Wallace Douglas. b 43. The Citadel Charleston SC BA 66. Gen Th Sem NY STB 69. **d** 69 **p** 70 S Carolina. In Amer Ch 69-72; C of Potters Green 72-75; Perm to Offic Dio Ox 75-76; P-in-c of St Andr Millport 76-78; R of Grantown-on-Spey Dio Moray from 78; Rothiemurchus Dio Moray from 78. *Rectory, Grant Road, Grantown-on-Spey, PH26 3ER.* (Grantown-on-Spey 2866)

KOTTA, Patrick Gqibintetho. Univ of S Afr BA 65. St Bede's Coll Umtata 58. **d** 65 **p** 66 St John's. C of H Cross Miss 67-70; P-in-c St Iguatins Tsomo 70-76; Chap St Jo Coll Umtata from 77; Gen Sec Transkei Coun of Chs from 81. *Box 65, Umtata, Transkei, S Africa.*

KOVILA, John Palmer. St Pet Coll Siota 49. **d** 52 **p** 60 Melan. P Dio Melan 52-75; Dio Ysabel 75-76. *Burunia, Gela, Solomon Islands.*

KOW, Noel Albert Edward. Bp Gray Th Coll Capetn 59. **d** 61 **p** 62 Kimb K. P Dio Kimb K 61-67; Dio Geo from 67. *PO Box 169, Swellendam, CP, S Africa.*

KOWOSI, Titus Adebayo. Im Coll Ibad 54. **d** 55 **p** 56 Bp Akinyele for Ibad. P Dio Ibad 55-69; Dio Ekiti from 69. *St Saviour's Vicarage, Ipoti, Ekiti, Nigeria.*

✠ **KRAFT, Right Rev Richard Austin.** Ripon Coll Wisconsin BA 58. Gen Th Sem NY STB 61. **d** 61 Chicago **p** 61 Natal. C of St Alphege Pietermaritzburg 61-63; Ladysmith 63-65; R of Klip River 65-67; Dir of Chr Educn Dio Zulu 68-74; L to Offic Dio Zulu 68-74; Dio Johann from 77; Can of Zulu 72-76; Hon Can 77-79; Can (Emer) from 79; R of Melmoth 74-76; Prov Dir of Chr Educn S Africa 77-79; Dean and R of St Alb Cathl Pret 79-82; Cons Ld Bp of Pret 82. *Bishop's House, 264 Celliers Street, Muckleneuk, Pretoria, S Africa.* (44-3163)

KREAGER, Henry Ross. Univ of Tor BA 58, STB 61. Trin Coll Tor 58. **d** 61 Alg **p** 61 Caled. C of Port Edw 61-65; I of Old Masset 65-71; Chap Thorneloe Coll Sudbury 71-76; C of Epiph Sudbury 71-76; Lect Bp Gwynne Coll Juba from 77. *Bishop Gwynne College, Juba, Sudan.*

KRIEL, Ven Anthony John. St Paul's Coll Grahmstn LTh

57. **d** 57 **p** 58 Kimb K. C of Mafeking 57-58; R 59-62; R and Dir of Prieska 62-64; C of All SS Huntington York 64-65; St Steph Cant 65-66; R and Dir Upington 66-70; P-in-c of Prieska 68-70; Hon Chap to Bp of Kimb K 68; Archd of Mafeking 70-75; Griqualand W 76-78; R of Vryburg 71-75; St Andr Douglas 76-78; Port Shepstone Dio Natal from 78; Archd of Pinetown from 81. *Box 147, Port Shepstone, Natal, S Africa.*

KRIM, Yawan Ninghru Zau. **d** 59 Rang. d Dio Rang. *St Matthew's Church, Namti, Myitkyina, Burma.*

KRONENBERG, Selwyn Thomas Denzil. b 32. Univ of Wales, BA (2nd cl Hist) 54. St Cath S Ox BA (3rd cl Th) 57, MA 60. Univ of Leic MA 73. Wycl Hall Ox. **d** 57 **p** 58 S'wark. C of St Matt Surbiton 57-60; Luton 60-62; PC of Loscoe 62-65; Lect Relig Educn Bulmershe Coll 65-67; Whitelands Coll of Educn Putney from 67; Perm to Offic Dio Guildf from 77. *58 Woodfield Lane, Ashtead, Surrey.*

KRUSE, Colin Graham. BD (Lon) 66. Moore Th Coll Syd ACT ThL 66. **d** 67 **p** 68 Syd. C of St Andr Summer Hill 67-68; St Andr Cronulla 68; CMS Miss 69-75; in Amer Ch 76-78; Lect Ridley Coll Melb and L to Offic Dio Melb from 79. *Ridley College, Parkville, Vic, Australia 3052.* (387 4975).

KRZEMINSKI, Stefan. b 51. Univ of Nottm BTh 77. Linc Th Coll 74. **d** 77 Repton for Derby **p** 78 Derby. C of Sawley 77-79; Asst Master & Chap Bluecoat Sch Nottm from 79; Perm to Offic Dio Southw from 80. *51 Summerfields Way, Ilkeston, Derbys.*

KUALI, Matthias. St Pet Th Coll Siota 59. **d** 62 **p** 64 Melan. P Dio Melan 62-75; Dio Ysabel 75-76; Dio Centr Melan from 76. *Tasimboko, Guadalcanal, Solomon Islands.*

KUBOKO, Canon Andreya. Th Coll Kongwa. **d** 57 **p** 58 Centr Tang. P Dio Centr Tang 58-63; Dio Vic Nyan from 73; Hon Can of Vic Nyan from 74. *PO Box 93, Ngara, Tanzania.*

KUCHING, Lord Bishop of. *See* Temengong, Right Rev Basil.

KUCHING, Assistant Bishop of. (Vacant).

KUCHING, Dean of. *See* Katib, Very Rev Made.

✠ **KUDO, Right Rev John Yoshio.** b 01. St Paul's Univ Tokyo BA 25. Centr Th Coll Tokyo 26. St Steph Ho Ox 28. **d** 30 **p** 32 Korea. C Dio Korea 30-34; P-in-c 34-42; VG for Japanese Congregations Dio Korea 40-42; Cons Asst Bp in Korea 1 March 42; res 45; P-in-c of Ch of Our Lady Kiyose Dio Tokyo from 47. *1-1-25, Umezono, Kiyose-shi, Tokyo, Japan.*

KUFORIJI, Ayoola Oludayo. b 38. Im Th Coll Ibad 60. **d** 62 **p** 63 Lagos. P Dio Lagos from 62. *69 Great Bridge Street, Lagos, Nigeria.* (21897)

KUFTA, Yeremaya. Div Sch Yei. **d** 47 Sudan. CMS d Dio Sudan. *CMS, Yambio via Juba, Southern Sudan.*

KUGELMAN, Brian Strong. Univ of Melb 39. BA 59. ACT Th Scho 46. **d** 40 **p** 41 Goulb. C of St Sav Cathl Goulb 40-41; St Luke Junee 41-42; R of Barmedman 42-45; Chap AIF 45-46; V of Keppel 46-50; R of St Matt Townsville 50-52 and 54-58; Perm to Offic Dio Ely 52-53; C of Epping Dio Chelmsf 53-54; Archd of Burdekin 56-58; Cairns 58-62; R of Cairns 58-62. *c/o State Library of South Australia, North Terrace, Adelaide, S Australia.*

KUHNE, Klaus Wilhelm. b 53. St Paul's Coll Grahmstn Dipl Th 79. **d** 79 **p** 80 Bloemf. C of Bloemf Cathl 79-81; St Matt Welkom Dio Bloemf from 81. *PO Box 231, Welkom, OFS, S Africa.*

KUHOGA, Ezekiel. Th Coll Kongwa. **d** 57 Centr Tang **p** 58 Bp Omari for Centr Tang. P Dio Centr Tang from 58. *Box 27, Kongwa, Tanzania.*

KUHRT, Gordon Wilfred. b 41. BD (3rd cl) Lon 63. Oak Hill Th Coll. **d** 67 **p** 68 Truro. C of St Illogan 67-70; H Trin Wallington 70-73; V of Shenstone 73-79; P-in-c of Em Croydon Dio Cant from 79; RD of Croydon Centr from 81. *Emmanuel Vicarage, South Croydon, Surrey, CR2 7BT.* (01-688 6676)

KUIPER, Jan Lionel. b 30. **d** 77 **p** 78 Capetn. C of Bergvliet Dio Capetn from 77. *Westridge Close, Soetvlei, Cape Town 7800, S Africa.*

KUKU, Absolom. **d** 39 **p** 41 Ugan. P Dio Ugan 39-61; Dio Ruw 61-62; Sub-Dean of Ruw 62-69; Can of Ruw 66-78. *Box 37, Fort Portal, Uganda.*

KUKU, Yacub Idris. **d** 69 Sudan. d Dio Sudan 69-76; Dio Omdurman from 76. *Box 8, Kadugli, Sudan.*

KUKU, Yusif Abdalla. **d** 69 Sudan. d Dio Sudan 69-76; Dio Omdurman from 76. *Box 8, Kadugli, Sudan.*

KUKUUBA, John. **d** and **p** 79 W Ank. P Dio W Ank. *Box 2008, Rwashamaire, Uganda.*

KULE, Yona. **d** 69 **p** 70 Ruw. P Dio Ruw. Archd Dio Ruw 78-80. *Box 200, Kilembe, Uganda.*

KUMALIRWA, Ven Kefa. Buwalasi Th Coll. **d** and **p** 58 Ugan. P Dio Ugan 58-60; Dio W Bugan 60-67; Dio Ruw 67-72; Dio Bunyoro from 72; Can and Archd of Bunyoro from 73. *PO Kabiso, Hoima, Bunyoro, Uganda.*

KUMALO, John. **d** 35 **p** 39 Zulu. P Dio Zulu. *Nqutu, via Dundee, Natal, S Africa.*

KUMASI, Lord Bishop of. *See* Arthur, Right Rev John Benjamin.

KUME, Cecil Zungulu. St Bede's Coll Umtata 76. **d** 79 **p** 80 Port Eliz. C of St Mark Kirkwood Dio Port Eliz from 79. *c/o St Peter's Mission, 25 - 3rd Avenue, Kabah, Uitenhage 6233, S Africa.*

KUMGU LA, David. H Cross Th Coll Rang. **d** 59 **p** 60 Rang. P Dio Rang. *St Simon's, Nawng Hkang, Sumprabum PO, Myitkyina District, Burma.*

KUMJI, Gumse. **d** 60 Rang. d Dio Rang 60-70; Dio Mand from 70. *Hopin, Myitkyina District, Burma.*

✠ **KUMSAUNG TU, Right Rev James.** H Cross Th Coll Rang. **d** 57 **p** 58 Rang. P Dio Rang 57-70; Dio Mand from 70; Archd of Myitkyina 63-70; Mand from 70; Cons Asst Bp of Mand in H Trin Cathl Rang 25 Feb 73 by Abp of Burma; Bps of Pa-an, Mand and Akyab. *Christ Church, Myitkyina, Kachin State, Burma.*

KUNENE, Bernard Ignatius. b 1899. **d** and **p** 77 Swaz. P Dio Swaz. *Box 356, Mbabane, Swaziland.*

KUNNUJI, Samuel Segbenu Oladipo. b 38. **d** 68 **p** 69 Lagos. P Dio Lagos. *Holy Trinity Church, Box 302, Mushin, Lagos, Nigeria.*

KUNONGA, Nolbert. **d** 79 **p** 80 Mashon. P Dio Mashon. *c/o Anglican Diocesan Offices, PO Box UA7, Salisbury, Zimbabwe.*

KUNYONGANA, Amon. St Jo Sem Lusaka 64. **d** 66 Mashon **p** 68 Matab for Mashon. P Dio Mashon. *Rectory, Chimvuri, Zimbabwe.*

KUOT, David Alak. Bp Gwynne Coll Mundri, 63. **d** 67 Sudan. d Dio Sudan. *PO Box 40, Malakal, Sudan.*

KUPA, Yosamu. Bp Tucker Coll Mukono 58. **d** 59 Ugan **p** 61 Ruw. d Dio Ugan 58-61; P Dio Ruw from 61. *Butara, Uganda.*

KUPFUWA, Ishmael. b 40. **d** 74 **p** 75 Matab. P Dio Matab 74-81; Dio Lundi from 81. *78/2 MB120, Que Que, Zimbabwe.*

KUPPAN, Michael Kistan. b 33. St Pet Coll Alice 68. **d** 70 Bp Hallowes for Natal **p** 71 Natal. C of Ch Ch Overport Dio Natal from 70; R of Ch of Epiph Chatsworth, Durban Dio Natal from 73. *Box 98, Mobeni, Natal, S Africa.* (Durban 431447)

KURIA, Gad Karanja Njoroge. b 36. **d** 76 Nak. d Dio Nak. *PO Box 183, Kapsabet, Kenya.*

✠ **KURIA, Most Rev Manasses.** St Paul's Th Coll Limuru, 54. **d** 55 **p** 57 Momb. P Dio Momb 55-61; Dio Nak from 61; Archd of Eldoret 65-70; Exam Chap to Bp of Nak 64-76; Cons Asst Bp of Nak in the Cathl Ch of the Good Shepherd Nak 25 April 70 by Abp of E Africa; Bps of Mt Kenya, Maseno and Nak; Apptd Bp of Nak 76; Trld to Nai 80; Elected Abp and Metrop of Prov of Kenya 80. *Bishopsbourne, Box 40502, Nairobi, Kenya.* (Nairobi 20207)

KURIAN, Randolph Andrew. Univ of Madr BA Bp's Coll Calc. **d** 41 **p** 42 Tinn. P Dio Tinn 41-43; Katni 43-44; Mandla 44-47; P-in-c of St Phil and St Jas Katni 47-49; Patpara 49-55; Marpha 52-55; Hon Can of Nagp 53-57; Dom Chap to Bp of Nagp 55-65; Dioc Treas 55-57; Archd of Jabalpur 57-58; P-in-c of St Mary Selangor 59-66; Wellesley and of Kedah 66-73. *c/o 9 Jalan Tengah, Kuala Lumpur, Malaysia.*

KURRLE, Canon Stanley Wynton. Univ of Melb BA 47. St Cath S Ox BA 50, MA 54. Wycl Hall, Ox 49. St Aid Coll 52. **d** 52 **p** 53 Liv. C of Sutton 52-54; Hd Master Caulfield Gr Sch 54-64; K Sch Parramatta Dio Syd from 65; Hon Can of Syd from 73. *King's School, Parramatta, Sydney, NSW, Australia 2150.* (630-0202)

KUSE, Wandile Francis. Univ Coll Of Ft Hare, S Afr BSc 57. St Paul's Th Coll Grahmstn. **d** 61 **p** 62 Johann. C of St Alb Johann 62-66. *c/o PO Box 1131, Johannesburg, Transvaal, S Africa.*

KUSENHA, Ainea. **d** 78 Centr Tang. d Dio Centr Tang. *Box 263, Arusha, Dodoma, Tanzania.*

KUTOANE, Gabriel. b 33. **d** 76 Les. d Dio Les. *St Saviour's Rectory, PO Box LR 38, Leribe, Lesotho, S Africa.*

KUTOKA, Petro. **d** 66 Bp Madinda for Centr Tang **p** 66 Centr Tang. P Dio Centr Tang. *Box 2, Mpwapwa, Tanzania.*

KUUSK, Carl Peter. b 54. Univ of Hull BA 76. St Jo Coll Dur 79. **d** 81 Dur. C of Usworth Dio Dur from 81. *130 Donvale Road, Donwell, Washington, T & W, NE37 1DW.*

KVAN, Erik. **d** 51 Hong **p** 52 Bp Roberts for Hong. Master St Jo Coll Univ of Hong Kong. *St John's College, University of Hong Kong, Hong Kong.* (5-468161)

KWACHE, Benson. **d** 69 Maseno **p** 73 Maseno N. P Dio Maseno 69-70; Dio Maseno N from 70. *PO Busia, Kenya.*

KWAI, Noel. **d** 70 Pa-an. d Dio Pa-an. *St Paul's Church, Toungoo, Burma.*

KWAMYA, Zakayo. Bp Tucker Coll Mukono. **d** 36 **p** 37 Ugan. P Dio Ugan 37-69. *c/o PO Box 20, Hoima, Uganda.*
KWARA, Lord Bishop of. *See* Haruna, Right Rev Herbert.
KWATIA, Albert Offei. St Aug Coll Kumasi. **d** 52 **p** 53 Accra. P Dio Accra. *PO Box 15, Odumase-Krobo, Ghana.*
KWEBIHA, Kezironi. Bp Tucker Coll Mukono 58. **d** 59 **p** 60 Ugan. P Dio Ugan 59-60; Dio W Bugan from 60. *Church of Uganda, Kasenyi, Box 23, Mubende, Uganda.*
KWEBIIHA, Yesamu. d 75 **p** 77 Ruw. P Dio Ruw. *Box 37, Fort Portal, Uganda.*
KWEDA, Enosa Banja. Bp Gwynne Coll Mundri. **d** 61 **p** 63 Sudan. P Dio Sudan. *ECS, Yei, Sudan.*
KWEYAMA, Simon. St Bede's Th Coll Umtata 49. **d** 51 **p** 52 Natal. P Dio Natal 51-76; Perm to Offic Dio Natal from 77. *Box 167, Edendale, Natal, S Africa.*
KWEYAMA, Ven Thokozani Samuel. St Pet Coll Rosettenville, LTh (S Afr) 57. **d** 56 **p** 57 Natal. P Dio Natal; Archd of Durban from 77; Synod Sec Dio Natal from 77. *PO Box 35, Redhill, Durban, Natal, S Africa.* (Kwa Mashu 16)
KWOK, Henry Hee-Leung. Qu Coll Hong Kong, 37. **d** 51 **p** 53 Hong. C of St John's Cathl Hong Kong 51-52; C-in-c of St Luke Kennedy Town 52-63; L to Offic Dio Hong from 63; Chap St Pet Sch Hong 64-65; Prin St Basil's Sch Hong from 65. *71 Chai Wan Road, Sahukiwan, Hong Kong.* (605677)
KWOK, Michael Chin King. d 80 Sing. C of St Andr Cathl City and Dio Sing from 80. *St Andrew's Cathedral, Coleman Street, Singapore 0617.*

✠ **KWONG, Right Rev Peter. d** 65 **p** 66 Hong. P Dio Hong 65-81; Dioc Sec 79-81; Can of Hong 79-81; Cons Ld Bp of Hong Kong in St John's Cathl Hong Kong 25 March 81 by Bps of Kuch, Sabah, Hong Kong, W Mal, Waik, Taiwan (Amer Ch), Multan (Pakistan), Dacca (Bangladesh); Bp Porfirio de la Cruz (Philippine Ind Ch) and others. *Bishop's House, 1 Lower Albert Road, Hong Kong* (5-265355).
KWULUNEBE, Nelson Chukwudum. b 40. Trin Coll Umuahia 74. **d** 76 Niger. d Dio Niger. *St Barnabas Church, Igboukwu, via Nnewi, Anambra State, Nigeria.*
KYABUTUABUBI, Njoloko. b 11. Trin Coll Nai 75. **d** 75 **p** 76 Boga-Z; P Dio Boga-Z. *BP 220, Kindu, Zaire.*
KYAGABA, Yosiya. d 50 **p** 52 Ugan. P Dio Ugan 50-61; Dio Nam 61-72; Dio Kamp from 72. *Central Prison, Private Bag, PO Kampala, Uganda.*
KYAK, Moses. b 44. Arthur Turner Tr Sch Pangnirtung 76. **d** 79 **p** 80 Arctic. P-in-c of St Matt Povungnituk Dio Arctic from 79. *St Matthew's Anglican Mission, Povungnituk, Que J0M 1P0, Canada.*
KYAKUTAKWIRE, Yafesi. d 77 E Ank. d Dio E Ank. *PO Box 3007, Ibanda, Mbarara, Uganda.*
KYALIGONZA, Erinadi. d 75 **p** 77 Ruw. P Dio Ruw. *Box 1017, Kyenjojo, Uganda.*
KYAMIZA, Yafesi. d 63 **p** 66 Ruw. P Dio Ruw 63-72; Dio Bunyoro from 72. *Box 20, Hoima, Uganda.*
KYASI, Paulo. Momb Dio Coll 30 **d** 32 **p** 34 U Nile. P Dio U Nile; CF (E Afr) 45-46; P Dio Ugan 47-61; P Dio W Bugan from 70. *Katende, PO Box 20, Mpigi, Uganda.*

✠ **KYAW MYA, Right Rev George.** H Cross Coll Rang. **d** 60 **p** 61 Rang. P Dio Rang 61-79; Cons Ld Bp of Pa-an in H Trin Cathl Rang 9 Sept 79 by Abp of Burma; Bp of Mand; and Bps Ah Mya and P Ta. *Bishop's Kone, Pa-an, Karen State, Burma.*
KYEGIMBO, Ignatius. d and **p** 75 Bunyoro. P Dio Bunyoro. *PO Kakumiro, Mubende, Uganda.*
KYLE, Laurence Arthur Nelson. b 14. SOC 64. **d** 67 Tonbridge for Roch **p** 68 Roch. C of St Luke Bromley Common 67-70; R of Hopton-by-Thetford w Mkt Weston (and Barningham w Coney Weston from 72) 70-79; RD of Ixworth 73-79; P-in-c of Bodham Dio Nor from 80. *15 Knowle Road, Sheringham, Norfolk, NR26 8PX.*
KYLE, Leicester Hugo. Ch Ch Coll LTh 64. **d** and **p** 63 Ch Ch. C of St Matt St Alb 63-64; P-in-c of Fairlie 64-65; Airedale w Fryston 65-66; Brighton N 66-71; V of Methven 71-72; Banks Peninsula 72-77; Addington Dio Ch Ch from 77. *21 Church Square, Addington, Christchurch 2, NZ.*
KYME, Ven Brian Robert. Ridley Coll Melb ACT ThL (2nd cl) 56. **d** 58 **p** 60 Melb. C of St John E Malvern 58-60; Glenroy 60-61; Morwell 61-63; I of Ashburton 63-69; Dean and R of H Cross Cathl Geraldton 69-74; Claremont Dio Perth from 74; Archd of Stirling from 77. *Box 121, Claremont, W Australia 6010.* (384 0539)
KYOBE, Samusoni Mikaeri Patrick. Bp Tucker Mem Coll Mukono. **d** 34 **p** 36 U Nile. P Dio U Nile 34-53; Dio Ugan 53-60; Dio Nam from 60. *Luzira, Uganda.*
KYONGYEREIRE, Nekemiya. Bp Tucker Coll Mukono, 60. **d** 61 **p** 63 Ankole-K. P Dio Ankole-K 61-67; Dio Kig 67-71. *Private Bag, Jinja, Uganda.*
KYRIACOU, Brian George. b 42. Univ of Lon LLB 64. Oak Hill Coll 79. **d** 81 Barking for Chelmsf. C of St Mary Becontree Dio Chelmsf from 81. *19 Bosworth Road, Dagenham, Essex.*
KYRIAKIDES, Anthony Paul Richard. b 48. AKC and BD 73. **d** 74 Lon **p** 75 Stepney for Lon. C of Dalston 74-80; St Pet Lon Dks w St John Wapping 80-81; Hon C of St Mary w St Aug Hackney Wick Dio Lon from 81. *20 Moravian Street, Bethnal Green, E2 0NJ.* (01-980 1177)
KYTE, Frederick George. St Columb's Hall Wang ThL 38. **d** 39 **p** 40 Wang. C of Bethanga 39-40; Shepparton 40-42; M Bro of Good Shepherd Bath 42-47; Chap RAN 47-62; L to Offic Dio Syd 50-76; Perm to Offic Dio Graft from 76. *1 Vendul Crescent, Port Macquarie, NSW, Australia 2444.*

L

La TOUCHE, Francis William Reginald. b 51. Linc Th Coll 73. **d** 76 **p** 77 Bris. C of Yate 76-79; Chap Miss to Seamen at Flushing Dio (Gibr in Eur from 80) Lon (N & C Eur) from 79. *Missions to Seamen, Scheldepoort, Flushing, Holland.*
LABAN, Deveraj Ramanna. b 31. St Pet Coll Alice 68. **d** 70 **p** 71 Natal. C of St Aid Durban 70-73; R of St Paul Pmbg Dio Natal from 73. *557 Longmarket Street, Pietermaritzburg, Natal, S Africa.* (Pmbg 26583)
LABAN, Shadrack. Coast Bible Sch Momb. **d** 63 Momb. d Dio Momb. *Anglican Church, Mbale, PO Voi, Kenya.*
LABANI, James Nathaniel. St Cypr Th Coll Ngala 69. **d** 72 **p** 73 Tang. P Dio SW Tang. *PO Box 32, Njombe, Tanzania.*
LABUJA, Jonathan Lepele. d 65 **p** 68 Ondo. P Dio Ondo. *Holy Trinity Church, PO Box 28, Lokoja, Nigeria.*
LACEY, Canon Clifford George. b 21. AKC 49. St Bonif Coll Warminster, 49. **d** 50 **p** 51 S'wark. C of St Hilda Crofton Pk 50-53; Kingston T 53-56; V of St Jas Merton 56-66; Eltham 66-79; Hon Can of S'wark from 74; Borough Dean of Greenwich from 79. *8 Shrewsbury Lane, Shooters Hill, SE18 3JF.* (01-856 3641)
LACEY, Cyril Charles John. b 09. Bps' Coll Cheshunt 56. **d** 58 Bris for Sarum **p** 59 Sarum. C of Broadstone 58-64; PC of St Edm Weymouth 64-68; V 68-78. *12 Spiller Road, Chickerell, Weymouth, Dorset.*
LACEY, Eric. b 33. Cranmer Hall Dur 69. **d** 71 **p** 72 Blackb. C of St Jo Evang Blackpool 71-75; V of Whittle-le-Woods Dio Blackb from 75. *Vicarage, Preston Road, Whittle-le-Woods, Chorley, Lancs, PR6 7PS.* (Chorley 3306)
LACEY, Canon Frank Gordon. Magd Coll Cam 2nd cl Hist Trip pt i 46, BA (2nd cl Hist Trip pt ii) 47, MA 51. Ely Th Coll 48. **d** 50 **p** 51 Southw. C of St Cath Nottm 50-53; Mansfield Woodhouse 53-56; V of Rubery 56-64; PC of Dethick w Lea and Holloway 64-69; V of Ockbrook w Borrowash 69-73; Birtles 73-81; Sen Tutor N-W Ordin Course 73-81; Can Res of Sheff Cathl from 82. *c/o 1 Silverdale Road, Sheffield, S11 9JJ.*
LACEY, Graeme Alexander Warner. b 15. Wycl Hall, Ox. **d** 63 **p** 64 Roch. C of Meopham 63-67; St Jo Evang Bexley 67-73; R of Cuxton (w Halling from 76) 73-80. *c/o Cuxton Rectory, Rochester, Kent, ME2 1AF.* (Medway 77134)
LACEY, Ronald Gordon. b 24. Qu Coll Birm Dipl Th 56. **d** 56 **p** 57 Southw. C of Radcliffe-on-Trent 56-58; Bawtry w Austerfield 58-59; E Retford 59-60; V of St Leon Newark 61-69; C-in-c of Rolleston w Fiskerton and Morton 69-72; V 72-75; Sec Southw Dioc Bd for Social Action 75-80; C of St

Mary Virg Nottm 75-80; V of St Andr Nottm Dio Southw from 80. *St Andrew's Vicarage, Chestnut Grove, Nottingham, NG3 5AD.* (0602-604961)

LACHARITE, Paul Alfred Lorne. b 46. Univ of Ott BA 71. McGill Univ Montr STM 76. **d** 75 **p** 76 Ott. C of All SS Westboro Ott 75-78; R of Buckingham 78-80; in Amer Ch. *62 S Swan, Albany, NY 12210, USA.*

LACK, Leonard James Westbrook. b 16. Ripon Hall, Ox 65. **d** 66 **p** 67 St Alb. C of Leighton Buzzard 66-81. *Gables Cottage, The Street, Castle Combe, Chippenham, Wilts SN14 7HU.* (0249-782865)

✠ **LACKEY, Right Rev Edwin Keith.** Bp's Univ Lennox BA 53. **d** 53 **p** 54 Ott. C of Cornwall 53-55; I of Russell 55-60; Vankleek Hill 60-63; R of St Mich AA Ott 63-72; Dir of Program Dio Ott 72-78; Hon Can of Ott 72-78; Dioc Archd 78-81; Cons Ld Bp of Ott 29 Sept 81 in the Civic Centre Ott by Abp of Tor and Abp Scott (Primate); Bps of Alg, Niag, Hur, Moos and Ont; and others. *71 Bronson Avenue, Ottawa, Ont, K1R 6G6, Canada.* (1-613-232-7124)

LACKEY, Michael Geoffrey Herbert. b 42. Oak Hill Coll 73. **d** 75 **p** 76 S'wark. C of St Jas Hatcham 75-82; V of New Barnet Dio St Alb from 82. *11 Park Road, New Barnet, Herts, EN4 9QA.* (01-449 4043)

LACY, Hubert Cottrill. b 1899. Bps' Coll Cheshunt, 63. **d** 64 **p** 65 Lon. C of Ch Ch Crouch End Hornsey 64-68; C-in-c of Pebmarsh 68-71. *Flat 2, 51 Wilbury Road, Hove, Sussex.* (Brighton 734901)

LACY, Norman Henry. ACT ThL 63. Ridley Coll Melb 61. **d** 64 **p** 65 Melb. C of St Mary Caulfield 64-67; Richmond 67-68; Min of Healesville Par Distr 68-73; Perm to Offic Dio Melb from 73. *39 Alice Street, Croydon, Vic, Australia 3136.* (03-725 7495)

LACY, Patrick Michael. b 33. Univ of Dur BA (2nd cl Th) and Lightfoot Scho 55, Dipl Th 58. Cranmer Hall Dur 57. **d** 58 **p** 59 Man. C of Newton Heath 58-61; Faversham 61-63; V of H Angels Claremont Pendleton 63-72; R of Stand 72-76; V of Wragby w Panton Dio Linc from 76; Langton-by-Wragby Dio Linc from 76; P-in-c of Rand Dio Linc 78; R (w Goltho) from 78; Chr Stewardship Adv Dio Linc from 76; RD of Horncastle from 80. *Wragby Vicarage, Lincoln, LN3 5QX.* (Wragby 858368)

LACY-JONES, Cledwyn. b 13. St Jo Coll Dur BA 35, MA 42, Dipl Th 36. **d** 36 **p** 37 Dur. C of St Andr Auckland 36-42; V of Sunnybrow 42-51; Monk Wearmouth 51-62; St Geo Barnsley 62-77; P-in-c of Hoylandswaine 69-81. *6 Highfield, Hoylandswaine, Sheffield, S30 6JP.* (Barnsley 762469)

LADA, Robert Barnaba. St Cypr Th Coll Tunduru 45. **d** 47 Masasi. d Dio Masasi 47-68. *Anglican Church, Masasi, Tanzania.*

LADD, George Whitman. b 36. Oberlin Coll Ohio BA 57. Univ of Wisc Madison MSc 59. Temple Univ Penn PhD 72. **d** 74 Milwaukee **p** 74 Rupld. C of St Luke Winnipeg 74-75; I of Hodgson-Peguis Area 76-80; Exam Chap to Bp of Rupld 75-81; R of St Mark Winnipeg. *19 St Mark's Place, Winnipeg, Manit, Canada.*

LADD, Raymond Albert. St Jo Coll Auckld NZ LTh 65. **d** 61 **p** 62 Wai. C of Rotorua 61-64; V of Murupara 64-69; Stokes Valley Dio Wel from 69. *Vicarage, Stokes Valley Road, Stokes Valley, Taita, NZ.* (Stokes Valley 8069)

LADDS, Ven Cyril Edmund. Univ of W Ont BA 53, LTh 55. **d** 54 **p** 55 Hur. C of Brantford 54-56; I of St Steph Stratford 56-59; R of St Andr Kitchener 59-64; St John Preston 64-68; St Geo Lon, Hur 68-74; Exam Chap to Bp of Hur 68-74; Hon Cler Sec 73-74; Archd of Perth from 74; R of St Jo Evang Kitchener Dio Hur from 74. *23 Water Street North, Kitchener, Ont., Canada.* (519-743 0228)

LADDS, Reginald. St D Coll Lamp. Westcott Ho Cam. **d** 60 Bp Hulme for Man **p** 61 Man. C of Bolton-le-Moors 60-62; All S Bolton 62-69; Asst Master Canon Slade Gr Sch Bolton from 58; Hon C of Farnworth 76-78; East Farnworth and Kearsley Dio Man from 78. *53 Hillside Avenue, Bromley Cross, Bolton, BL7 9NQ.* (Bolton 56271)

LADDS, Robert Sidney. b 41. Univ of Lon BEducn 71. Cant Sch of Min 79. **d** 80 **p** 81 Cant. C of Hythe Dio Cant from 80. *School House, St Leonards Road, Hythe, Kent.* (0303 66708)

LADIMEJI, Daniel Oluwatunwase. Melville Hall, Ibad 48. **d** 50 Bp Phillips for Lagos **p** 51 Lagos. P Dio Ibad. *Jago, Ibadan, Nigeria.*

LADIPO, Adeyemi Olalekan. Clifton Th Coll 63. **d** 66 Lich. C of Bilston 66-68. *PO Box 336, Yaba, Lagos, Nigeria.*

LADIPO, Emmanuel Olugboyega. Im Coll Ibad 64. **d** 67 **p** 68 Ibad. P Dio Ibad. *Iloro, Box 45, Ilesha, Nigeria.*

LADIPO, Canon Lapese. St D Coll Lamp BA 58. Univ of Reading, Dipl Educn 58. St Aug Coll Cant. **d** 59 Lagos **p** 61 Ibad. P Dio Lagos 59-79; Dio Ibad from 79; Hon Can of Ibad from 80. *Ibadan Grammar School, Ibadan, Nigeria.*

LAFFERTY, James Dawson. Trin Coll Tor BA 49. **d** 52 Bran. C of Russell w Binscarth 52-54; Oakville 54-56; R of St Matt Hamilton 56-61; Belmont 61-64; on leave 65-74; Hon C of Dundas Dio Niag from 74. *2 Cameron Crescent, Dundas, Ont., Canada.*

LAFFORD, Percival John. b 02. Launde Abbey Leic. **d** 58 **p** 59 Leic. [f CA]. C of St Chad Leic 58-59; Humberstone 59-62; Min of St Chad's Eccles Distr Leic 62-65; R of Smeeton-Westerby 65-73; L to Offic Dio Leic from 73. *30 Winchester Road, Blaby, Leicester, LE8 3HJ.* (Leic 771464)

LAGOS, Lord Bishop of. *See* Segun, Right Rev Festus Oluwole.

LAGOS, Assistant Bishop of. (Vacant)

LAGOS, Provost of. *See* Johnson, Very Rev Samuel Hugh Stowell Akinsope.

LAGUSU, Hudson. b 47. Bp Patteson Th Coll Kohimarama 70. **d** 73 Melan **p** 74 Bp Dudley for Melan. P Dio Melan 73-74; Dio Ysabel from 75. *Church of Melanesia, Gizo, Western District, Ysabel, Solomon Islands.*

LAHEY, Ivan Alford. St Francis Coll Brisb 52. ACT ThL 59. **d** 55 **p** 56 Brisb. C of Redcliffe 55-56; St Matt Sherwood 56-57; M of Bush Bro of St Paul Charleville 57-62; Miss P at Movi 62-67; Kumbun 67-68; R of Noosa 68-72; Beaudesert 72-78; St Alb Wilston City and Dio Brisb from 78. *Rectory, Inglis and Lovedale Streets, Wilston, Brisbane, Australia 4051.*

LAI, Wen Hwa. Trin Coll Sing 49. **d** 56 **p** 57 Sing. P Dio Sing from 56. *c/o Bishopsbourne, 4 Bishopsgate, Singapore.*

LAI, Wen-Kwang. Trin Coll Sing 64. **d** and **p** 65 Sing. P Dio Sing from 65. *c/o Holy Trinity Church, 1 Hamilton Road, Singapore 8.*

LAIDLAW, Hugh Fraser. b 54. Univ of BC BA 76. Trin Coll Tor MDiv 80. **d** and **p** 80 Ott. C of St Aid City and Dio Ott from 80. *c/o 955 Wingate Drive, Ottawa, Ont, Canada, K1G 1S9.*

LAIGHT, Frederick. b 04. MBE 66. **d** 31 **p** 32 Falkd Is. Asst Chap of Magallanes Dio Falkd Is 31-32; Chap 32-36; Miss to Seamen Chap Port of Lon 36-38; Penarth and Barry Dk 38-41; Chap Miss to Seamen on the Tyne 41-49; Cardiff 49-52; Chap for Miss to Seamen Ship *John Ashley* Tilbury and Publ Pr Dio Chelmsf 52-69. *36 Parkway, Armthorpe, Nr Doncaster, Yorks.*

LAIKO, Gidiona Lokosang. Juba Bible Inst. **d** 71 Sudan. d Dio Sudan. *c/o Church Office, Box 110, Juba, Equatoria Province, Sudan.*

LAILA, Yona Lu'Bang. Bp Gwynne Coll Mundri, 60. **d** 64 **p** 65 Sudan. P Dio Sudan. *c/o CMS, Juba, Equatoria, Sudan.*

LAIMANASA, Joseph. St Paul's Th Coll Ambat 49. **d** 52 **p** 54 Madag. P Dio Madag 52-69; Dio Tam from 70. *Anivorano, Tamatave, Madagascar.*

LAING, Alan Glanville. Moore Th Coll Syd 57. **d** 57 **p** 58 Nel. C of Blenheim 57-59; Collingwood 59-61; C-in-c of Engadine w Heathcote 61-64; Miss SUM 64-66; C of Woking Surrey 66-67; R of Pitt Town 67-74; L to Offic Dio Syd from 74. *16 Beaconsfield Avenue, Concord, NSW, Australia 2137.*

LAING, Alexander Burns. b 34. Edin Th Coll. **d** 60 **p** 61 Edin. C of Ch Ch Falkirk 60-62; Ch Ch Morningside Edin 62-70; Chap RNR 64; P-in-c of St Fillan Edin 70-74; Chap R Infirm Edin 74-77; Edin Dioc Super 77; R of St Mich AA Helensburgh Dio Glas from 77. *Rectory, William Street, Helensburgh, Dunbartonshire, G84 8BD.* (Helensburgh 2500)

LAING, James. b 18. AKC 49. St Bonif Coll Warm 49. **d** 50 **p** 51 Lon. C of S Acton 50-53; All SS Friern Barnet 53-57; V of St Mich-at-Bowes Bowes Pk 57-69; St Andr Southgate Dio Lon from 69. *184 Chase Side, N 14.* (01-886 7523)

LAING, William Alexander. b 02. **d** 40 **p** 41 Wakef. C of Hemsworth 40-42; Holmforth (in c of Thongsbridge) 42-46; Hinckley 46-47; R of Stoney Stanton 47-52; V of Thelwall 52-57; R of Coddington w Handley 58-72; C-in-c of Coddington Ches 72-76. *The Old Post Office, Churton, Chester, CH3 6LE.*

LAING, William Sydney. b 32. TCD BA 54, Div Test 55, MA 62. **d** 55 **p** 56 Dub. C of Crumlin 55-59; St Ann Dub 59-65; I of Carbury 65-68; R of Finglas 68-80; Tallaght Dio Dub from 80; Warden of Dioc Guild of Readers 71. *Rectory, Sally Park, Firhouse Road, Tallaght, Irish Republic.* (Dublin 965709)

LAIRD, John Charles. b 32. Univ of Sheff BA 2nd cl Cl 53, MA 54. St Cath Coll Ox BA 3rd cl Th 58, MA 62. Ripon Hall, Ox 56. **d** 58 **p** 59 St Alb. C of Cheshunt 58-62; Asst Lect Bps' Coll Cheshunt 59-62; Chap 62-64; Vice-Prin 64-69; V of Keysoe w Bolnhurst and L Staughton Dio St Alb from 69. *Keysoe Vicarage, Bedford, MK44 2HW.* (Riseley 251)

LAIRD, Robert George. b 40. Edin Th Coll 63. **d** 65 **p** 66 Derry. C of Drumragh 65-68; CF from 68. *c/o Ministry of Defence, Bagshot Park, Bagshot, Surrey, GU19 5PL.*

LAISTER, Peter. b 27. St D Coll Lamp BA 54. St Steph Ho Ox 54. **d** 56 **p** 57 Chelmsf. C of Ascen Vic Dks 56-60; Chap RN 60-65; C of St Mary Magd Munster Square St Pancras 65-66; Chap Middx Hosp 66-70; V of H Redeemer Clerkenwell Dio Lon from 70. *Holy Redeemer Clergy House, Exmouth Market, EC1.* (01-837 1861)

LAITHWAITE, Peter Robert Prescott. b 43. Univ of Georgia MBA 67. St Paul's Coll Grahmstn Dipl Th 78. **d** 78 **p** 79 Capetn. R of Hout Bay Dio Capetn from 78. *Rectory, Main Road, Hout Bay, S Africa 7800.*

LAITY, Alan Gordon. St Jo Coll Morpeth ACT ThL 48. **d** 48 **p** 49 Bath. C of Bro of the Good Shepherd Gilgandra 48-52; P-in-c of Tottenham and Nyngan 52-54; C of Glenhuntly 54-58; Min of W Footscray 58-66; I of Murrumbeena 66-80; H Trin Balaclava Dio Melb from 80. *11 Hennesey Avenue, Balaclava, Vic, Australia 3184.*

LAITY, Ronald James Ross. b 34. Ridley Coll Melb ACT ThL (2nd cl) 59. Monash Univ BA 67. **d** 60 Melb **p** 73 Jer. C of Pascoe Vale 60-61; St Mary Caulfield 61; Perm to Offic Dio Melb 61-63; C of Gardenvale 63-66; St James Glen Iris 67; Asst Chap Caulfield Gr Sch 67-69; C of Ch Ch Jer 70; Dom Chap to Abp in Jer 73; Dioc Regr Dio Jer 73-77; L to Offic Dio Jer 73-74. *3/55 Filbert Street, Caulfield South, Vic., Australia 3162.*

LAKAVUTU, Ilai. b 35. St Jo Bapt Th Coll Suva 66. **d** 69 **p** 70 Polyn. P Dio Polyn. *PA Kaliwaqa, Nabunikadamu, Wainunu, Bua, Fiji.*

LAKE, David Eurwyn. b 17. St D Coll Lamp BA 39. TD 60. **d** 40 **p** 41 Llan. C of St John Miskin 40-43; St Jo Bapt Cardiff 43-50; CF (TA) 48-67; C-in-c of St Mary Llansawel Briton Ferry 50-56; V 56-62; Skewen Dio Llan from 62; RD of Neath from 76. *Skewen Vicarage, Neath Abbey, Neath, Glam.* (Skewen 84116)

LAKE, David Stuart. b 45. Univ of Nottm BA (2nd cl Th) 66. Univ of Glas MTh 67, PhD 70. Linc Th Coll 70. **d** 71 Linc **p** 73 Stepney for Lon. C of St Mary-le-Wigford Linc 71-73; Hoxton Dio Lon from 73. *80 Bridport Place, N1.* (01-739 9576)

LAKE, Ernest Lloyd. Univ of West Ont BA 48. Hur Th Coll LTh 48. **d** 48 **p** 49 Hur. C of St Jas Lon Ont 48; R of Wyoming 49-51; Harrow Ont 51-53; CF (Canad) 53-59; R of Eganville 59-67; Wilmot w Wicklow and Peel 69-74; All SS E St John Dio Fred from 74. *40 Park Avenue, Saint John, NB, Canada.*

LAKE, Thomas Raphael. b 12. Codr Coll Barb 76. **d** and **p** 77 Antig. C of H Trin Barbuda Dio Antig from 77. *The Rectory, Codrington, Barbuda, W Indies.*

LAKE, William Vincent. b 47. Univ of WI BA 73. Codr Coll Barb 69. **d** 72 **p** 73 Antig. C of St Geo Montserrat 72-73; P-in-c 73-76; R of St Anthony Montserrat 76-79; H Cross Aruba Dio Antig from 79. *Rectory, San Nicholas, Aruba, Netherland Antilles.*

LAKE, Wynne Vaughan. b 34. St D Coll Lamp BA 55. St Mich Coll Llan 55. **d** 57 Mon for Llan **p** 58 Llan. C of Cadoxton-juxta-Barry 57-61; St Sav Roath 61-64; V of Oakwood (w Bryn 64-67) 64-72; R of Shirenewton 72-77; V of Newchurch 72-77. *c/o Rectory, Shirenewton, Chepstow, Gwent, NP6 6RQ.* (Shirenewton 243)

LAKE MALAWI, Lord Bishop of. *See* Nyanja, Right Rev Peter Nathaniel

LAKELAND, William. b 05. Edin Th Coll 45. **d** 47 **p** 48 Dur. C of St Steph Willington 47-50; R of Good Shepherd Hillington Glas 50-52; C of Stockport 52-55; V of St Jo Evang Macclesfield 55-74. *31 Arundel Drive, Carlton-in-Lindrick, Worksop, Notts.* (0909 731368)

LAKER, James Stephen. b 10. Chich Th Coll 57. **d** 58 **p** 59 Roch. C of St Barn Tunbridge Wells 58-62; C-in-c of Athersley and New Lodge Conv Distr 62-65; PC of All SS Kettering 65-70; L to Offic Dio Cant 71-72; Chap St Steph Coll Broadstairs 71-72; Team V of Coleford w Staunton 72-73; V of Clearwell 73-75; Perm to Offic Dio Cant from 75; Dio Roch from 78; Dio Chich from 81. *42 Woodbury Park Road, Tunbridge Wells, Kent.* (Tunbridge Wells 23004)

LAKER, Leopold Ernest. b 38. Sarum Wells Th Coll 77. **d** 77 **p** 78 Roch. C of Rainham 77-80; V of Horton Kirby Dio Roch from 80. *Horton Kirby Vicarage, Dartford, Kent.* (Farningham 862201)

LALL, Osmond Tressler. b 15. Univ of Agra BSc 39, MA 60. **d** 54 Luckn **p** 66 St Alb. C of Jhansi 54-61; Asst Master CMS Gr Sch Freetown Sier L 61-64; Hon C of Kempston 65-68; Gravesend 68-76; St Mary Gravesend Dio Roch from 76. *10 Ascot Road, Gravesend, Kent.* (Gravesend 66032)

LALLY, Robert Alexander. b 18. St Aid Coll 46. **d** 49 **p** 50 S & M. C of St Geo w All SS Douglas 49-52; Ripley Derbys 52-53; CF 53-58; V of Whiston 58-63; St Sav Everton 63-69; Lowton St Mary Dio Liv from 69. *17 Beech Avenue, Lowton St Mary, Warrington, Lancs, WA3 2BZ.* (Leigh 673703)

LAM, Canon Andrew. Univ of BC BA 44. Angl Th Coll BC LTh 41. **d** 41 **p** 42 New Westmr. C of Good Shepherd Miss Vanc 41-56; R of St Barn Winnipeg 56-62; St Jo Bapt Winnipeg 62-73; Dioc Dir of Min to Elderly Rupld 73-81; C of St Aid Winnipeg 73-75; St Luke Winnipeg 75-77; Hon Can of Rupld from 77. *334 Carpathia Road, Winnipeg, Manit., Canada.*

LAM, Ian Sau-Fung. b 48. Univ of Hong Kong BA 71. Ripon Hall Ox 71. **d** 73 **p** 74 Hong. C of St Steph Hong Kong 73-74; Chap St Jo Coll Hong Kong 73-75; St John's Cathl Hong Kong 75-78; on study leave. *c/o Nashotah House, Nashotah 53058, Wisc, USA.*

LAM, Peter. b 42. U Coll Hong 69. **d** 72 **p** 73 Hong. Youth Officer Dio Hong 73-75; P-in-c of Kindly Light 76; V of St Jas Hong Dio Hong from 77. *100 Kennedy Road, Hong Kong.* (5-721856)

La MARCHE, Ronald Douglas. Univ of Tor BA 64. Trin Coll Tor STB 67. **d** 67 **p** 68 Tor. C of St Nich Birch Cliff Tor 67-69; R of Fenelon Falls Dio Tor from 69; R of Coboconk 69-75; St Mark and Calvary City and Dio Tor from 75. *354a Silverthorne Avenue, Toronto, Ont., Canada.* (416-769 7144)

LAMB, Alan. St Francis Coll Brisb 63. **d** 65 **p** 66 Rockptn. C of Longreach 65-68; P-in-c 68-69; C of St Luke's Wandal 69-70; M of SSF from 70; Perm to Offic Dio Brisb 70-71 and from 75; P-in-c of Koke 71-75. *Friary, Brookfield, Queensland, Australia 4068.* (378 2160)

LAMB, Bruce. b 47. Keble Coll Ox BA 69, MA 73. Univ of Leeds Dipl Th 72. Coll of Resurr Mirfield 70. **d** 73 **p** 74 Barking for Chelmsf. C of Romford 73-76; St Cedd Canning Town 76-79; V of St Luke Gillingham Dio Roch from 79. *Vicarage, Sidney Road, Gillingham, Kent, ME7 1PA.* (Medway 53060)

LAMB, Bryan John Harry. b 35. Univ of Leeds, BA 60. Coll of Resurr Mirfield 60. **d** 62 **p** 63 Birm. C of Solihull 62-65; Northfield Worcs Dio Birm from 65; Asst Master Malvern Hall Sch Solihull 65-74; Alderbrook Sch Solihull from 74; Hd of Light Hall Adult Educn Centre Solihull from 74. *52 Ladbrook Road, Solihull, Warws.* (021-705 3977)

LAMB, Canon Charles Willoughby Mortimer. b 11. Angl Th Coll BC LTh 33. **d** 37 **p** 38 New Westmr. C of St Pet Vancouver 40-42; V of Quesnel 42-43; Chemainus 43-47; (all in BC); C of St Mark Woodcote Purley (in c of St Swith) 47-50; C-in-c of St Swith Conv Distr Purley 50-54; V of Boxley 54-65; Ch Ch Forest Hill 65-75; Hon Can of S'wark from 75. *Mile Cottage, Birdham, Chichester.* (Chich 512469)

LAMB, Christopher Avon. b 39. Qu Coll Ox BA (Hist) 61, 2nd cl Th 63, MA 65. Univ of Birm MA (Islamic Studies) 79. Wycl Hall Ox 61. **d** 63 **p** 64 Lon. C of Enfield 63-69; CMS Miss in Pakistan 69-75; Tutor CMS Tr Coll Birm 75-78; BCMS/CMS Other Faiths Project from 79. *69 Willow Road, Bournville, Birmingham, B30 2AT.* (021 472 6875)

LAMB, Francis Adam Johnstone. St Edm Hall, Ox BA 27, MA 31. Trin Coll Dub BA (*ad eund*) 27, Div Test (2nd cl) 29. **d** 29 **p** 30 Dub. C of Rathmines 29-33; St Nich Galway 33-37; C-in-c of Dunboyne w Moyglare 37-39; I of Julianstown w Colpe 39-64; Priv Chap to Bp of Meath 52-64; RD of Trim 54-58; Ratoath and Skyrne 58-64; Can of Meath 58-64. *Woodfield House, Clara, Offaly, Irish Republic.*

LAMB, Francis William Mason. Univ of Birm MD 28. Coll of Resurr Mirfield 54. **d** and **p** 56 Windw Is. C of St Geo Cathl St Vincent 56-58; R of Dominica 58-61; St Anthony Montserrat 61-64; L to Offic Dio Windw is 64-66. *118 Duke Street, Port of Spain, Trinidad, W Indies.*

LAMB, Canon George. b 05. St Chad's Coll Dur BA (2nd cl Th) 28, MA 31. Ely Th Coll 28. **d** 28 **p** 29 Dur. C of St Jude S Shields 28-30; St Pet Stockton 30-33; Brandon (in c of St Cath) 33-37; V of St Cuthb Bensham 37 48; Shildon 48-55; Proc Conv Dur 45-50; RD of Auckland 50-55; Hartlepool 56-58; Hon Can of Dur 53-71; Can (Emer) from 71; R of Castle Eden 55-58; Whickham 58-71; RD of Chester-le-Street 60-64; Sec Dur Dioc Conf from 65-70. *40 Borough Road, Redcar, Cleveland.* (Redcar 484760)

LAMB, John Romney. b 21. Ch Ch Ox BA 48, MA 53. Wells Th Coll 49. **d** 50 Dover for Cant **p** 51 Cant. C of Tenterden w Smallhythe 50-53; Hythe Kent 53-55; CF 55-70; V of Horsell 70-76; Dorking w Ranmore 76-80. *c/o St Martin's Vicarage, Dorking, Surrey.*

LAMB, Canon John William. b 1896. TCD BA 23, MA 26. Univ of Leeds MA 33, PhD 53. **d** 23 **p** 24 Worc. C of H Trin Old Hill 23-26; Perm to Offic at All SS Wellington Salop 26-27; C of St Luke Barton Hill Bris 27-28; V of St Paul Constable Lee 28-30; Heworth 30-44; R of St Mary Castlegate w St Mich Spurriergate York 35-44; Bridlington 44-62; Can and Preb of York Minster from 42; Chairman of Bridlington Charity Trustees 45-62; V of Bessingby 45-55; Surr from 44; RD of Bridlington 46-62; Proc Conv York 47-70; Chap Bridlington Hosps 44-62; C-in-c of Boynton 51-62; Carnaby 51-55; R of Leven w Catwick 62-68. *61 St James's Road, Bridlington, N Humb, YO15 3PQ.* (Bridlington 75052)

LAMB, Nicholas Henry. b 52. St Jo Coll Dur BA 74. St Jo Coll Nottm 76. **d** 79 **p** 80 St Alb. C of St Hugh Lewsey Luton Dio St Alb from 79. *8 Paddock Close, Lewsey, Luton, Beds, LU4 0TY.*

LAMB, Omar Herbert. Univ of Manit BA 50, BEducn 61.

St Jo Coll Winnipeg LTh 53, BPaed 56. **d** 53 **p** 54 Bran. R of Macgregor 53-56; Ch of Messiah and Ch of Redeemer The Pas 56-61; Chap MacKay Ind Res Sch Dauphin 61-63; Prin St Paul's Sch Blood Reserve 63-67; I of Birch River 67-71; L to Offic Dio Bran from 70. *Box 310, Birch River, Manit, Canada.*

LAMB, Peter Francis Charles. b 15. St Cath Coll Cam BA 37, MA 41. Wells Th Coll 37. **d** 38 **p** 39 Pet. C of St Barn Wellingborough 38-42; Somersham w Pidley and Colne 42-45; Chap RNVR 46-48; C of Sherborne w Castleton and Lillington 48-51; P Gambia Miss 51-53; P-in-c of Kristi Kunda 53-57; V of Winkleigh 57-70; RD of Chulmleigh 62-63; R of Mells w Vobster and Whatley w Chantry 70-77. *1 Long Sutton Farm Cottages, Long Sutton, Langport, Somt.*

LAMB, Canon Philip James. b 06. Late Exhib of Magd Coll Ox BA (2nd cl Th) Hall-Houghton Sept Pri and Gr Test Pri Jun 28, Sen 30, MA 34. Cudd Coll 29. **d** 29 **p** 30 Carl. C of H Trin Carl 29-32; St Matt Chapel Allerton 32-35; V of St Aid Leeds 35-45; Prin of St John's Coll York 45-71; Can and Preb of York Minster 57-71; Can (Emer) from 76. *37 Westbourne Avenue, Harrogate, HG2 9BD.* (Harrogate 62273)

LAMB, Richard Eglington. Moore Th Coll Syd ACT ThL (2nd cl) 59. BD (Lon) 61. **d** and **p** 60 Syd. C of Eastwood 60-61; Thornleigh 61; St John Parramatta 61-62; C-in-c of Westmead 62-66; R of Caringbah Dio Syd from 66. *12 Combara Avenue, Caringbah, NSW, Australia 2229.* (524-6112)

LAMBERT, Ven Charles Henry. b 1894. Univ of Leeds BA 16, MA 32. Cudd Coll 17. **d** 17 **p** 18 York. C of Redcar 17-20; Guisborough 20-22; R of St Denys w St Geo York 22-24; V of Royston Yorks 24-28; R of St Mary Bishophill Sen w St Clem York 28-34; Proc Conv York 29-34; Blackb 35-45; Warden of Whalley Abbey 34-45; Dir of Relig Educn Dio Blackb 34-46; Can of Blackb Cathl 35-46; RD of Whalley 42-45; Exam Chap to Bp of Blackb 46-64; Archd of Blackb 46-59; Lanc 59-66; Archd (Emer) from 66; V of Lytham 60-66. *71a Upper Church Road, Weston-super-Mare, Avon, BS23 2HX.* (Weston-super-Mare 27851)

LAMBERT, Christopher Hugo. b 27. Late Exhib of Pemb Coll Cam BA 49, 2nd cl Th Trip pt i 50, MA 54. Wells Th Coll 50. **d** 52 **p** 53 S'wark. C of St Chrys Peckham 52-55; St Nich Plumstead 55-57; R of Middelburg 57-61; Waterkloof 61-73; C of St Mildred Addiscombe and of St Martin Croydon 74-78. *25 Sandford Close, Wivenhoe, N Colchester, Essex, CO7 9NP.*

LAMBERT, David Francis. b 40. Oak Hill Coll 72. **d** 74 **p** 75 Ex. C of St Paul Preston Paignton 74-77; Chap to Woking Tn Centre Dio Guildf from 77. *4 Orchard Drive, Woking, Surrey, GU21 4BN.* (Woking 5593)

LAMBERT, David Hardy. b 44. K Coll Lon and Warm AKC 66. **d** 67 **p** 68 York. C of Marske-in-Cleveland 67-72; V of N Ormesby Dio York from 73. *North Ormesby Vicarage, Middlesbrough, TS3 6LD.* (Middlesbrough 246278)

LAMBERT, David Nathaniel. b 34. Linc Th Coll. **d** 66 **p** 67 Grantham for Linc. C of Canwick 66-68; C-in-c of St John's Conv Distr Bracebridge Heath 68-69; R of All SS (to 74) w St Pet Saltfleetby (and Skidbrooke from 74) 69-80; R of St Clem Saltfleetby 70-74; V of Skidbrooke w Saltfleet Haven 70-74; R of Theddlethorpe 74-80; RD of Louthesk 77-80; R of Fotherby Dio Linc from 80. *Vicarage, Peppin Lane, Fotherby, Louth, Lincs LN11 0UG.* (Louth 606403)

LAMBERT, Donald William. b 19. Keble Coll Ox BA (3rd cl Hist) 40, 3rd cl Th 42, MA 44. St Steph Ho Ox 40. **d** 43 **p** 44 Chich. C of St Andr Worthing 43-47; St Barn Ox 47-51; C of St Matt Nass 51; P-in-c of Harbour I 51-53; R of St Matt Nass 53-56; V of St Jo Bapt Bathwick 57-66; R of Digswell 66-70; C of St Sav St Alb 70; V of St Pet Acton Green 71-77; Commiss Nass from 72. *11 Elizabeth Road, Worthing, W Sussex, BN11 4EF.* (0903 206978)

LAMBERT, Eric Stephen. Westcott Ho Cam. **d** 40 **p** 41 S'wark. M SSF from 39. C of St Chrys Peckham 40-43; L Pr Dio Lon 43-48; C of All H by-the-Tower 45-46; L to Offic Dio Sarum 47-59; Miss P at SSF Koki 59-65; Fiwila Dio Zam 65-70; Dio Centr Zam 71-76; L to Offic Dio Lusaka from 76. *Box 16, Katete, Zambia.*

LAMBERT, Gordon. b 32. St D Coll Lamp BA 56. Wycl Hall, Ox 56. **d** 58 **p** 59 Carl. C of St Paul Newbarns w Hawcoat (in c of St Aid from 60) Barrow-F 58-63; C-in-c of St Aid Conv Distr Barrow-F 63-67; Min 67; V 67-68; R of Ousby w Melmerby 68-71; V of Farlam 71-76; Team V of Thirsk w S Kilvington, Carlton Miniott and Sand Hutton (and Baldersby and Skipton-on-Swale from 77) Dio York from 76; RD of Thirsk from 81. *Carlton Miniott Vicarage, Thirsk, Yorks, YO7 4NJ.* (Thirsk 22003)

LAMBERT, Ian Anderson. b 43. BA (Lon) 72. Ridley Hall, Cam 66. **d** 67 **p** 68 S'wark. C of Bermondsey 67-70; R of Lluidas Vale Dio Ja 71-75; Chap RAF from 75. *c/o Ministry of Defence, Adastral House, WC1.*

LAMBERT, John Clement Antony. b 28. St Cath Coll Cam BA 48, MA 52. Cudd Coll 50. **d** 52 **p** 53 York. C of Hornsea 52-55; Leeds 55-59; R of Carlton-in-Lindrick Dio Southw from 59. *Carlton-in-Lindrick Rectory, Worksop, Notts, S81 9EF.* (Worksop 730222)

LAMBERT, Laurence Taplin. Moore Th Coll Syd ACT ThL 32. **d** 32 Syd **p** 33 Bp Kirkby for Syd. C of St Paul Wahroonga 32-34; P-in-c Wilcannia 34-37; St Luke Mosman 37; C-in-c of St Mark Brighton-le-Sands 37-42; Chap AIF 42-46; R of Springwood 46-52; Artarmon 52-61 and 64-67; L to Offic Dio Syd 62-64 and from 67. *20b Western Road, Castle Hill, NSW, Australia 2154.*

LAMBERT, Leonard. b 1900. Kelham Th Coll 17. **d** 23 **p** 24 Linc. C of Grantham 23-26; All SS New Amsterdam 26-28; P-in-c of Beterverwagting 28; Miss of Demerara River Distr 28-31; C of St Nich w St John (in c of St Matthias) Newport Linc 31-32; R and V of Minting 32-45; C of Hinckley 42-45; V of Stoke Golding w Dadlington 45-57; Donisthorpe 57-76; C-in-c of Stretton-en-le-Field 57-61; R 61-76; Perm to Offic Dio Guildf from 76. *Runnymede, All Saints' Road, Lightwater, Surrey, GU18 5SQ.*

LAMBERT, Michael Roy. b 25. Univ Coll Dur BSc 49. Cudd Coll 52. **d** 52 **p** 53 York. C of St Osw Middlesbrough 52-56; Romsey 56-59; Abp of York's Chap Univ of Hull 59-64; C of Cottingham Yorks 59-64; V of Saltburn-by-the-Sea 64-72; C-in-c of H Trin Shaftesbury 72-73; R of Shaston 73-78; Corfe Mullen Dio Sarum from 78. *Corfe Mullen Rectory, Wimborne, Dorset.* (Broadstone 692129)

LAMBERT, Norman. b 39. ACP 66. Chich Th Coll 67. **d** 70 **p** 71 Lich. C of St Mark Ocker Hill Tipton 70-73; St Edm Dudley 73-76; P-in-c of St Pet Darby End Dudley Dio Worc 76-77; V from 77. *26 Morville Road, Netherton, Dudley, W Midl, DY2 9HR.* (Dudley 55189)

LAMBERT, Philip Charles. b 54. St Jo Coll Dur BA 75. Fitzw Coll Cam BA (Th) 77, MA (Th) 81. Ridley Hall Cam 75. **d** 78 **p** 79 S'wark. C of H Trin U Tooting 78-81; Whorlton Dio Newc T from 81. *7 West Garth, Westerhope, Newcastle upon Tyne, NE5 4NS.* (Newc T 711053)

LAMBERT, Robert John Harding. St Jo Coll Morpeth 49. **d** 50 Newc for River **p** 51 River. C-in-c of Urana 50-51; R 51-55; R of Berrigan 55-61; V of Mortlake 61-66; R of Kaniva 66-71; Perm to Offic Dio Bal 71; Dio River from 73. *73 Ross Crescent, Griffith, NSW, Australia 2680.*

LAMBERT, Sydney Thomas. b 17. Keble Coll Ox BA 39, MA 44. Wells Th Coll 40. **d** 41 **p** 42 Lon. C of All SS Poplar 41-44; St Barn Ox 44-45; Bp Cotton Boys' Sch Bangalore 45-49; in Amer Ch 49-50; CF 50-67; R of Rendcomb 67-73; Colesbourne 67-73; P-in-c of St Pet Cheltm 73-78; Bourton-on-the-Hill Dio Glouc from 78; Todenham w Lower Lemington Dio Glouc from 78. *Rectory, Bourton-on-the-Hill, Moreton-in-Marsh, Glos, GL56 9AF.* (Blockley 700347)

LAMBERT, Canon William Victor. b 1899. St Aug Coll Cant 22. **d** 25 Cant for Col Bp **p** 26 Madag. SPG Miss Mahanoro and Chap to Bp of Madag 26-37; C of St Jas Westend 37-39; V of Iford 39-46; Eastleigh 46-61; Surr 47-61; Hon Can of Win 58-61; Can (Emer) from 61; R of St Dennis 61-64; V of Lower Halstow 64-69; Commiss Dio Tam (Toa from 79) from 71. *The Old Forge, Sparsholt, Winchester, Hants.*

LAMBERT-SMITH, John Henry. St Aid Coll 53. **d** 54 York **p** 55 Whitby for York. C of Drypool 54-58; V of Silsden 58-63; C-in-c of Moor Monkton 63-67; Wheldrake 67-69; St Mich-le-Belfrey City and Dio York 69-73; Hon C from 73; C of H Trin Micklegate York 64-66; St Phil and St Jas Clifton York 69-72; Hon C of St Cuthb (w St Mich-le-Belfrey from 75) City and Dio York from 73; H Trin Heworth 73-75. *1 Mill Lane, York, YO3 7TF.* (York 53124)

LAMBETH, John Raymond. b 20. Keble Coll Ox BA 45, MA 49. St Steph Ho Ox 45. **d** 47 **p** 48 Win. C of St Luke Bournemouth 47-49; St Andr w St Mich West Bromwich 49-52; All SS E Finchley 52-54; Greenford (in c of H Redeemer) 54-57; Chap of Stacklands Retreat Ho W Kingsdown Kent 57-58; V of St Mary Magd Munster Square Lon 58-64; Chap Conv of St Mary at the Cross Edgware 64-79; C of Ch the Sav Ealing 79-80; P-in-c of St Pet and St Andr Portslade Dio Chich from 80. *St Peter's Vicarage, Gardner Road, Portslade, BN4 1PN.* (Brighton 592474)

LAMBLE, Gilbert Clark. Ridley Coll Melb. **d** 47 **p** 48 Melb. C of St Thos Essendon 48-49; Moonee Ponds w Moonee Ponds West 49; V of Mt Dandenong 49-53; I of N Carlton 53-55; C of Melb Dioc Centre 55-61; I of All SS Malvern 61-68; Perm to Offic Dio Melb from 68; Dio Gippsld from 73; L to Offic Dio Bend 68-73. *PO Ensay, Vic, Australia 3895.*

LAMBLE, Horace Walter. **d** and **p** 62 Niag. C of Stoney Creek 62-63; St Jo Evang Hamilton 63-66; R of W Flamboro 66-72; Russell 72-80; Huntley Dio Ott from 80. *Box 89, Carp, Ont, Canada.* (613-839 3216)

LAMBOURNE, John Brian. b 36. Chich Th Coll 62. **d** 65

Cant **p** 66 Dover for Cant. C of St Greg Gt Northgate Cant 65-67; St Mary-in-the-Marsh 67-68; E Grinstead (in c of St Luke) 68-70; Storrington 70-76; Sullington 70-76; V of Salehurst Dio Chich from 76. *St Mary's Vicarage, Robertsbridge, E Sussex.* (Robertsbridge 880408)

LAMBRECHTS, Desmond Johan. b 57. St Pet Coll Natal 77. **d** 80 **p** 81 Capetn. C of Belville Dio Capetn from 80. *12 Reute Street, Kuils River, Cape 7580, S Africa.*

LAMBSDORFF, Bernard William. Univ of Tor MA 63. **d** 53 RC Bp of Regina **p** 53 RC Bp of Winnipeg. Rec into Angl Communion by Bp of Tor 60. C of St Clem N Tor 60-63; R of St Jas the Ap Brampton 63-69; C of Port Credit 69-70. *568 Melrose Boulevard, Timmins, Ont., Canada.*

LAMBTON, Alfred Harbord. St Francis Coll Brisb. ACT ThL 12. **d** 12 **p** 13 N Queensld. C of St Jas Cathl Townsville 12-14; Mackay 14-18; TCF 18-19; C of Sarina 19-20; R of Innisfail 20-23; P-in-c of Dogura 23-33; Sefowa 33-36; R of Home Hill 36-41; C-in-c of St Matt Mundingburra 41-45; R of Charters Towers 45-51; Bowen 51-54; Chap Gen Hosp Townsville 56-68; *Alexandra Street, North Ward, Townsville, Queensland, Australia.*

LAMBURN, Roger George Patrick. MBE 55. Late Exhib of Trin Coll Cam 2nd cl Nat Sc Trip pt i 25, BA (3rd cl Nat Sc Trip pt ii) 26, MA 61. St Steph Ho Ox 26. **d** 27 **p** 28 Lon. C of St Geo Southall 27-30; UMCA Miss Dio Masasi 30-36; Warden St Cypr Th Coll Tunduru 36-48; Can of Masasi 44-68; Archd of Masasi 49-59; Educn Sec Dio Masasi 49-61; P-in-c of Rufiji Miss Dio Masasi 61-69; Dio Dar S 69-72; Perm to Offic Dio Dar-S from 72. *c/o PO Ikwiriri, Dar-es-Salaam, Tanzania.*

LAMERTON, Robert William. b 48. St Jo Coll Morpeth 74. **d** and **p** 77 C & Goulb. C of Albury 77; Cooma 77-80; R of Batlow 80-81; C of Tumut Dio C & Goulb from 81. *Tweedie Cottage, River Street, Tumut, NSW, Australia 2720.*

LAMIKANRA, Samuel Adediji. Div Hall, Oyo 23. **d** 23 **p** 24 Lagos. P Dio Lagos 23-53; Dio Ibad 53-68; Hon Can of Ibad 62-68. *c/o Vicarage, Igangan, Ilesha, Nigeria.*

LAMING, Canon Frank Fairbairn. b 08. Univ of Dur LTh 36. Edin Th Coll 33. **d** 36 **p** 37 Glas. C of Ch Ch Glas 36-39; H Trin Paisley (in c of St Marg Renfrew) 39-44; R of H Trin Motherwell 44-53; Provost and R of St Mary's Cathl Glas 53-66; Provost of St Andr Cathl Inverness 66-74; Hon Can from 74; P-in-c of Glenurquhart Dio Moray from 74. *St Ninian's House, Glenurquhart, Inverness, IV3 6TN.*

LAMONT, Canon Colin. b 1899. Trin Hall Cam 3rd cl Hist Trip pt i 22, BA (3rd cl Th Trip pt i) 23, MA 27. Wells Th Coll. **d** 24 **p** 25 Man. C of Rochdale 24-28; SPG Miss At Gatooma w Hartley S Rhod 28-34; C-in-c of St Luke Conv Distr Benchill 34-36; I 36-39; V 39-41; R of Ch Ch Heaton Norris 41-47; V of Worsley 47-53; Hon Can of Man 51-69; Canon (Emer) from 69; Surr 48-69; R of Ashton-under-Lyne 53-69; RD of Ashton-under-Lyne 55-69. *56 Richmond Road, Romiley, Stockport, Ches.* (061-430 2698)

LAMONT, Graham Strathmore. Univ of NZ BA 52. Coll Ho Ch Ch. **d** 54 **p** 55 Ch Ch. C of Timaru 54-56; Hokitika and P-in-c of Kumara 56-59; V of Waikari 59-62; Spreydon 62-69; Opawa 69-70; Hon C of Hillcrest 70-75; Claudelands 75-78; Offg Min Dio Waik from 78. *68 Wellington Street, Hamilton, NZ.* (67-952)

LAMONT, Roger. b 37. Jes Coll Ox BA 60, MA 62. St Steph Ho Ox 59. **d** 61 **p** 62 Pet. C of St Alb Northn 61-66; V of St Olave Mitcham 66-73; N Sheen Dio S'wark from 73. *70 Marksbury Avenue, Richmond, Surrey, TW9 4JF.* (01-876 5123)

LAMONT, Canon Winston Alexander. Codr Coll Barb. **d** 44 **p** 45 Antig. Asst C of St Jo Cathl Antig 44-46; P-in-c of St Pet w St John and St Jas Montserrat 46-50; St Paul San Fernando 50-52; V of Chaguanas 52-63; Hon Can of Trinid from 65; R of St Agnes Port of Spain 67-71; St Paul's San Fernando 71-77; Woodbrook Dio Trinid from 77; Exam Chap to Bp of Trinid 71-73. *St Crispin's Rectory, Rosalino Street, Woodbrook, Trinidad, W Indies.*

LAMPRELL, Laurence Henry. b 07. Selw Coll Cam 3rd cl Mor Sc Trip pt i, 28, BA (2nd cl Archaeol and Anthrop Trip pt i) 29. Westcott Ho Cam 30. **d** 31 **p** 32 Dur. C of Billingham 31-34; UMCA Miss Luatala 34-35; P-in-c of Namagono 35-42; C-in-c of Welwyn 42-43; C of Beckenham 43-45; V of St Luke Gillingham (f New Brompton) 45-57; St Marg Cov 57-69; R of Gt w L Wigborough 69-72; R of Salcott-Virley w Salcott Wigborough 69-72. *8 Merton Close, Fordingbridge, Hants.*

LANCASHIRE, Allan. b 32. Univ of Birm BA (3rd cl Th) 54. Lich Th Coll. **d** 63 **p** 64 Wakef. C of Birstall Yorks 63-67; V of Wrenthorpe 67-70; C-in-c of Wolverton 70-73; Team V 73-76; Educn Officer Dio Ox 73-76; Schs Officer Dioc Educn Coun Dio Lich from 76; L to Offic Dio Lich from 76. *Lawley Vicarage, Telford, TF4 2PD.* (Telford 505145)

LANCASHIRE, Douglas. b 26. BA (2nd cl Mod Chinese) Lon 50, BD (Lon) 55, MA (Lon) 58. **d** 61 Hong **p** 79 Auckld. Tutor U Th Coll Hong 61-62; Lect Univ of Melb and Perm to Offic Dio Melb 62-67; Prof Univ of Auckld and Perm to Offic Dio Auckld 67-81; R of Boxted w Langham Dio Chelmsf from 80. *Vicarage, Parsonage Road, Boxted, Colchester, CO4 5ST.* (Boxted 250)

LANCASTER, Lord Bishop Suffragan of. *See* Page, Right Rev Dennis Fountain.

LANCASTER, Archdeacon of. *See* Gibbons, Ven Kenneth Harry.

LANCASTER, Bruce Arthur. **d** 58 **p** 59 Armid. C of Inverell 58-60; Tamworth 60-61; V of Werris Creek 61-68; Guyra 68-77; Inverell Dio Armid from 77. *Vicarage, River Street, Inverell, NSW, Australia 2360.*

LANCASTER, Charles William. b 08. **d** and **p** 64 Linc. C of Folkingham w Laughton 64-65; V of Heydour w Culverthorpe 66-75; Londónthorpe 66-75; R of Welby 66-73. *102 High Street, Skelton, Cleve.*

LANCASTER, Ernest Osborne. Wycl Coll Tor. **d** 32 Niag for Tor **p** 34 NS. C of Advent Tor 32-33; Milton 33-38; I of Dundalk, Melancthon and Maxwell 38-40; Thamesville w Dresden and Moraviantown 40-47; R of Wingham 47-52; Woodstock 52-61; Lucan 61-69; Forest 69-74. *474 Ashland Avenue, London, Ont., Canada.*

LANCASTER, Frederick Charles Thomas. b 16. Bps' Coll Cheshunt 48. **d** 51 St Alb for Cov **p** 52 Cov. C of St Mary Nuneaton 51-54; Upton w Chalvey Slough 54-57; V of Drayton 57-67; R of Ascot Heath 67-81. *21 Withington Court, Abingdon, Oxon, OX14 3QA.* (Abingdon 25584)

LANCASTER, Howard Anthony. b 44. Rhodes Univ BA 69. St Paul's Coll Grahmstn Dipl Th 68. **d** 69 **p** 70 Grahmstn. C of St Sav E Lon 70-73; St Mich Queenstn 73-75; R of Molteno 75-78; Ch Ch Amalinda Dio Grahmstn from 78. *116 Main Road, Amalinda, East London, CP, S Africa.*

LANCASTER, Ven John. Univ of BC BA (Phil) 60. Univ of St Andr BPhil 78. Angl Th Coll BC STB 66. Princeton Th Sem ThM 69. **d** 63 **p** 64 BC. C of Sooke 63-64; I (w Jordan River) 64-68; C of Ch Ch Cathl Vic 69-81; Hon Can from 79; I of Courtenay Dio BC from 81; Archd Dio BC from 81. *579-5th Street, Courtenay, BC, Canada.*

LANCASTER, Lyonel Lewis. b 17. Univ of Leeds BA (2nd cl Engl) 39. Coll of Resurr Mirfield 40. **d** 41 Ripon **p** 42 Knaresborough for Ripon. C of Ch Ch Leeds 41-43; St Mary Whitkirk Leeds 43-44; St Wilfrid Harrogate 44-46; Chap at Asansol 46-50; St Thos Calc 50-60; Can of Calc 57-60; R of St Andr Deal Dio Cant from 60; RD of Sandwich from 78. *St Andrew's Rectory, St Andrew's Road, Deal, Kent.* (Deal 4354)

LANCASTER, Norman. b 13. Univ of Leeds BA 36. Coll of Resurr Mirfield 36. **d** 38 Grantham for Linc **p** 39 Linc. C of Skegness 38-41; St Aid New Cleethorpes 41-42; St Jas and St Martin Grimsby 42-47; V of Caistor w Holton-le-Moor and Clixby 47-52; C-in-c of Nettleton 48-52; PC of H Trin Louth 52-57; V of Keddington 52-57; Hogsthorpe 57-62; Chap Butlin's Holiday Camps 59-62; R of Panton w Wragby 62-70; V of Langton-by-Wragby 62-70; R of Gt Coates 70-77; V of Aylesby 70-77; Perm to Offic Dio Linc from 77. *3 Haigh Street, Cleethorpes, Humb, DN35 8LN.*

LANCASTER, Ronald. b 31. St Jo Coll Dur BA 53, MA 56. Cudd Coll 55. **d** 57 Wakef **p** 58 Pontefract for Wakef. C of St Pet Morley 57-60; St Pet Harrogate 60-63; Chap Kimbolton Sch Huntingdon from 63; Perm to Offic Dio Ely 63-65; L to Offic from 65. *7 High Street, Kimbolton, Huntingdon, Cambs, PE18 0HB.* (Kimbolton 498)

LANCE, Preb John Du Boulay. b 07. MC 45. Late Rustat Scho of Jes Coll Cam BA 29, MA 34. Cudd Coll 30. **d** 30 **p** 32 Lich. C of St Pet Wolverhampton 30-34; Missr Trin Coll (Ox) Miss Ch Stratford 34-36; V of Bp's Lydeard 36-47; CF (EC) 41-46; Men in Disp 44; V of St Andr Rowbarton Taunton 47-57; Preb of Dultingcote in Wells Cathl 51-63; R of Bathwick 57-63; Proc Conv B & W 59-64; Dioc Adv in Chr Stewardship Dio B & W 61-67; Archd of Wells and Can Res and Preb of Wells Cathl 63-73; Warden Abbey Retreat Ho Glastonbury from 65; Preb of Wells Cathl 74; Dir of Ordin Dio B & W 74-76. *14 Portway Avenue, Wells, Somt, BA5 2QF.* (0749-72756)

LANCE, John Edward. Moore Th Coll Syd ACT ThL 61, Th Scho 63. **d** 61 Bp Kerle for Syd **p** 62 Syd. C of Seven Hills Provisional Distr 61-64; Sans Souci 64-65; C-in-c of Putney Provisional Distr 65-71; Riverwood Dio Syd 71-77; R 77-80; St Mark Brighton-le-Sands Dio Syd from 80. *1 Trafalgar Street, Brighton-le-Sands, NSW, Australia 2216.* (59-4102)

LANCE, Raymond Sullivan Knox. b 10. Lich Th Coll 31. **d** 34 **p** 35 B & W. C of Wellington w W Buckland 34-38; R of St Columba Largs 38-43; PC of Frome-Woodlands 43-45; V of Longbridge Deverill w Crockerton and Hill Deverill 45-62; Chap Ld Weymouth Sch Warminster 62-72; Warminster Sch 72-77; Perm to Offic Dio Sarum from 77; Dio B & W from 78; OCF Warminster from 80. *27 Plants Green, Warminster, Wilts, BA12 9NN.* (Warminster 213236)

LANCELOT, Roland. b 1899. Late Scho of Keble Coll Ox 2nd cl Cl Mods 20, BA (3rd cl Lit Hum) and Philpotts Pri 22, MA 28. Ely Th Coll 30. **d** 31 **p** 32 Derby. C of Eyam 31-33; Buxton (in c of St Anne w St Jas) 33-37; St Matt Sheff 37-41; C-in-c 41; Perm to Offic at Goldthorpe 42-43; C of St Sav Pimlico 43-44; R of Plaxtol 44-50; V of St Andr Orpington 50-53; Asst Master West House Sch Birm 53-63; Hallfield Sch Birm 63-70; LPr Dio Birm 55-72; Perm to Offic Dio Linc from 72. *210 Nettleham Road, Lincoln.* (Linc 29176)

LAND, Michael Robert John. b 43. Ripon Hall Ox 70. **d** 72 Ox **p** 73 Reading for Ox. C of Newbury 72-75; Team V of Chigwell 75-80; V of St Andr Walthamstow Dio Chelmsf from 80. *Vicarage, Sutton Road, E17 5QA.* (01-527 3969)

LANDEN, Edgar Sydney. b 23. Late Organ Scho of St Jo Coll Dur BA (2nd cl Music) 54, BMus 55, Dipl Th 55. ARCM and FRCO 46. **d** 55 **p** 56 Ripon. Succr of Leeds 55-58; Prec of Chelmsf Cathl 58-60; V of Bathampton 60-65; Perm to Offic Dio Glouc 65-69; C of Cirencester 69-76; R of Wytham Dio Ox from 76; Min Can of Ch Ch Ox from 76. *Wytham Rectory, Oxford, OX2 8QA.* (Oxford 48337)

LANDER, Arthur Alexander. b 09. Open Univ BA 79. AKC 36. **d** 36 **p** 37 Lon. C of All SS Clapton 36-38; St Aug Wembley Pk (in c of Annunc S Kenton) 38-43; V of Coniston Cold 43-45; Min Can of Ripon Cathl (in c of Littlethorpe) 45-51; Succr of Leic Cathl 51-54; V of Birstall 54-72; R of Wanlip 55-72; Surr 56-72; Perm to Offic Dio St Alb from 74. *16 Shrublands Road, Berkhamsted, Herts.* (Berkhamsted 3260)

LANDON, Donald Mackenzie. Univ of Tor BA 53, MA 59, LLB 56. Trin Coll Tor LTh and STB 59. **d** 58 **p** 59 Alg. C of St Paul Fort William 59-62; R of H Trin Sault Ste Marie 62-71; Dioc Sec Dio Alg 65-71; R of St Paul Thunder Bay Dio Alg from 71. *St Paul's Rectory, Thunder Bay, Ont., Canada.* (807-622 4836)

LANDRETH, Canon Derek. b 20. TD 63. K Coll Cam BA (2nd cl Hist Trip pt i) 47, MA 52. Bps' Coll Cheshunt 47. **d** 48 **p** 49 S'wark. C of St Hilda Crofton Pk 48-49; St Geo Camberwell 49-52; CF (TA) 51-67; (TAVR) 67-75; C of H Trin Tulse Hill 52-53; V of St Mark Battersea Rise 53-59; Richmond Surrey 59-70; Hon Chap to Bp of S'wark 62-80; Hon Can of S'wark 68-76; Can Res from 77; R of Sanderstead 70-76; Vice-Chairman of Pastoral C'tte Dio S'wark from 77; Chap to HM the Queen from 80; M Gen Syn from 80. *39 Albert Bridge Road, SW11 4PX.* (01-622 4439)

LANDRETH, Canon Stanley. b 1899. Late Exhib of Ball Coll Ox BA (2nd cl Mod Hist), 21, Dipl in Th w distinc 22, MA 32. Cudd Coll 22. **d** 23 **p** 24 Dur. C of St Columba Southwick 23-30; Brandon (in c of St Cath Sleetburn) 30-33; PC of Ven Bede Monkwearmouth 33-46; St Chad Bensham Gateshead 46-60; Surr 33-46 and 52-69; Hon Can of Dur 56-69; Can (Emer) from 69; RD of Gateshead 56-60; PC of Trimdon 60-69; Perm to Offic Dio Dur from 69. *3 Hospital Close, Greatham, Hartlepool, Cleve, TS25 2HR.* (Hartlepool 870582)

LANE, Andrew Harry John. b 49. Univ of Lanc BA 71. Cudd Coll 71. **d** 73 **p** 74 Ox. C of Abingdon 73-78; Chap RAF from 78. *c/o 8 Crescent Road, Tilehurst, Reading, Berks, RG3 5AN.*

LANE, Anthony James. b 29. Univ of Leeds BA 53. Coll of Resurr Mirfield 53. **d** 55 **p** 56 Ox. C of Tilehurst 55-60; Min Can and Sacr of Win Cathl and L to Offic Dio Win 60-63; V of Handley w Pentridge 64-80; Thurmaston Dio Leic from 80. *Vicarage, Melton Road, Thurmaston, Leicester, LE4 8BE.* (0533-692555)

LANE, Clement Alec Frere. St Francis Coll Brisb 45. ACT ThL 47. **d** 47 **p** 48 Bris. C of St Francis Nundah Brisb 47-50; V of Monto 50-53; Millmerran 53-57; R of Kingaroy 57-68; St Luke Ekibin City and Dio Brisb from 68. *193 Ekibin Road East, Annerley, Queensland, Australia 4103.* (48 2123)

LANE, David John. b 35. Magd Coll Ox BA (2nd cl Th) 58, Pusey and Ellerton Hebr Scho 59, 2nd cl Or Stud 60, Houghton Syriac Pri 61, MA 62, Kennicott Hebr Fell 66. Coll of Resurr Mirfield 60. **d** and **p** 62 Barb. Lect Codr Coll Barb 61-63; Tutor 63-65; C of Wolvercote 65-66; Assoc Chap Pemb Coll Ox 66-68; Tutor St Steph Ho Ox 68-71; Asst Prof Near E Studies Univ of Tor 71-75; Assoc Prof from 75; Perm to Offic Dio Glas and Gall from 66; Dio Tor from 71. *c/o Clydesdale Bank, New Galloway, by Castle Douglas; and Trinity*

LANE, David Protheroe. Worc Coll Ox 3rd cl Hist BA 33, MA 46. Ripon Hall Ox 33. **d** 34 **p** 36 Lich. C of Bushbury 34-37; St Francis Friar Pk Conv Distr W Bromwich 37-38; Brixham w Churston Ferrers 38-43; LPr Dio Derby 44-46; Asst Master Trent Coll 43-46; C of Charlbury w Chadlington, Shorthampton and Chilston 47-61; V of Langford w L Faringdon Dio Ox from 61. *Langford Vicarage, Lechlade, Glos, GL7 3LF.* (Filkins 366)

LANE, Denis John Victor. Univ of Lon LLB 49, BD 55. Oak Hill Th Coll 50. **d** 53 **p** 54 S'wark. C of St John Deptford 53-56; St Steph Cam 56-59; Overseas Miss Fellowship S Perak 59-64; Dept Supt S Perak Miss Distr 64-66; Supt Dio Sing from 67. *Overseas Missionary Fellowship, 2 Cluny Road, Singapore 10.*

LANE, Dennis Charles William. b 17. Univ of Lon BD (2nd cl) 40. AKC (1st cl) 40. **d** 40 **p** 41 Glouc. C of Chipping Campden 40-43 and 47-49; Chap RNVR 43-47; R of Blaisdon w Flaxley 49-55; Woodmansterne 55-64; V of Tandridge Dio S'wark from 64; Dir of Ordinands 61-67; Asst Dir from 67; Exam Chap to Bp of S'wark from 61; RD of Godstone 71-76. *Tandridge Vicarage, Oxted, Surrey.* (Oxted 2432)

LANE, Gerald. b 29. Bede Coll Dur BA (2nd cl Mod Hist) 52. Sarum Th Coll 52. **d** 54 **p** 55 S'wark. C of Camberwell 54-58; St Aug Gillingham 58-59; V of St Phil Camberwell 59-67; C-in-c of St Mark Camberwell 62-67; V of St Nich Plumstead 67-73; St Aug Gillingham 73-78; Hadlow Dio Roch from 78. *Hadlow Vicarage, Tonbridge, Kent.* (Hadlow 850238)

LANE, Gerald Richard. b 10. Univ of Lon BSc (1st cl Math) 31. St Cath S Ox Dipl in Th 36. Wycl Hall Ox 35. **d** 36 **p** 37 Chelmsf. C of St Andr Westcliff 36-38; CMS Miss Dio Nasik 39-45; Chap of Nasik 39-43; Aurangabad 43-45; Dioc Treas Dio Nasik 42-45; Sec Dio Bd of Fin and Dioc Trust Assoc 43-44; V of Bp Latimer Mem Ch Birm 45-49; Chap Winson Green Hosp 45-49; St Alb City Hosp 49-53; V of Chipperfield 53-60; Commiss Nasik 51-71; R of Hunsdon 60-65; R of Widford Herts 60-65; V of Stretton w Wetmoor 65-69; C of Boxmoor 69-71; R of Pertenhall w Swineshead 71-74; Hon C of Witham Dio Chelmsf from 79. *2 Ferndown Way, Hatfield Peverel, Chelmsford, CM3 2JU.*

LANE, Canon Gordon George. b 10. St Cath Coll Cam BA 32, MA 36. Wycl Hall Ox 34. **d** 34 **p** 35 Bradf. C of St Luke Manningham 34-37; St Steph Bowling 37-39; V of Arncliffe w Halton Gill 39-50; Calverley Dio Bradf from 50; Surr from 51; Hon Can of Bradf from 72. *Calverley Vicarage, Pudsey, W Yorks, LS28 5NF* (Pudsey 577968)

LANE, Canon Harold. b 09. MBE 56. St Chad's Coll Dur BA and LTh 33, MA 47. St Paul's Miss Coll Burgh 27. **d** 33 **p** 35 Ripon. C of St Bart Armley 33-36; St Jo Cathl Antig 36-38; Asst Master Gr Sch Antig 38-39; R of St Phil Antig 39-46; furlough 46-48; R of St Geo Montserrat 48-49; SPG Rep 49-50; Prec of St Mich Cathl Barb 50-51; V of St Martin Barb 51-52; R of St Phil w St Steph Antig 52-62; Can of Antig 56-66; Can (Emer) from 66; Exam Chap to Bp of Antig 59-65; Dioc Regr 60-64; R of Dominica Antig 62-66; Archd of Antig 64-66; C of Howden 66-67; Dioc Missr Dio Nass 67-76; P-in-c of Harbour I 73-76; St Chris Lyford Cay w St Jas Adel Nass 76-81. *20 Mallard Way, Haxby, Yorks, YO3 8NG.* (York 763558)

LANE, John Ernest. b 39. Cranfield Inst of Tech MSc 80. **d** and **p** 80 S'wark. C of St John w St Andr Peckham Dio S'wark from 80. *38 Ravenscroft Road, Beckenham, Kent, BR3 4TR.*

LANE, John Philip. b 11. **d** 76 **p** 77 Bath. P-in-c of Kandos 76-81; Perm to Offic Dio Syd from 81. *3/41 The Esplanade, Balmoral Beach, NSW, Australia 2088.*

LANE, John Philip. St Jo Coll Morpeth ACT ThL 62. **d** 61 **p** 62 Armid. C of Gunnedah 61-63; Glen Innes 63-68; R of Rockley w Geo Plains 68-70; Cobar 70-73; Beresfield 73-75; Cardiff 75-79; New Lambton Dio Newc from 79. *Rectory, Birdwood Street, New Lambton, NSW, Australia 2305.* (57 1173)

LANE, Martin. b 45. Mem Univ of Newfld BA 71. Qu Coll Newfld LTh 71. **d** 71 Newfld **p** 72 Bp Legge for Newfld. C of Burin 71-73; I of Forteau Dio Newfld (W Newfld from 76) from 73. *Forteau, Labrador, Newfoundland, Canada.* (709-936)

LANE, Michael Godfrey Mace. b 26. Univ of S Africa BA 66. **d** 78 Bp Stanage for Johann **p** 79 Johann (NSM). C of Linden Dio Johann from 78. *51 - 10th Avenue, Parktown North, S Africa 2193.*

LANE, Peter Charles Griffin. **d** 64 **p** 65 Melb. C of Mt Waverley 64-67; Dioc Centre (in c of Kensington) Dio Melb 67-68; Perm to Offic Dio Melb 68-70; C of St Osw Glen Iris 70-72; Murrumbeena 72-77; Perm to Offic Dio Tas 77-81. *21 Mookara Street, Howrah, Tasmania 7018.* (002-47 7269)

LANE, Reginald Wilfrid. Wycl Coll Tor. **d** 25 **p** 26 Tor. C of Ch Ch St Catherines Ont 25-26; Ch of the Redeemer 26-29; R of Burford w Cathcarth 29-34; Norwich w Oxford 34-36; St Paul W St Jas Brantford 38-42; Chap CASF 42-46; R of Amherstburg (w Aderdon 46-49) 46-50; St John St Thomas 50-62; St Aid Lon Ont 62-64; Chap Sir Adam Beck Sanat Lon 64-66; C of Grace Ch Brantford 66-69; P-in-c of H Trin St George Dio Hur from 69. *Box 8, St George, Ont, Canada.*

LANE, Ronald Chester. K Coll NS 63. **d** 65 **p** 66 NS. C of Bedford 65-67; I of Waverley 67-74; on leave. *Waverley, PO, NS, Canada.* (861-2493)

LANE, Canon Stanley. b 1897. Late Exhib of Univ of Dur LTh 24. St Aid Coll 22. **d** 24 **p** 25 Man. C of Ashton-under-

Lyne 24-30; V of Audenshaw 30-42; CF (TA) 31-37; R of Newchurch-in-Rossendale 42-56; Proc Conv Man 44-46 and 50-56; RD of Rossendale 46-56; Hon Can of Man 50-56; Surr 50-56; Can (Emer) from 56; V of Heversham 56-64; RD of Kirkby Lonsdale 60-64. *Marthwaite, Casterton, Carnforth, Lancs, LA6 2SA.* (Kirkby Lonsdale 71383)

LANE, Stephen Toller. b 29. SS Coll Cam BA 52, MA 56. ALCD 54 (LTh from 74). **d** 54 York **p** 55 Selby for York. C of H Trin Heworth York 54-57; V of St Cuthb Everton 57-63; St Luke Eccleston 63-71; R of Bradfield w Buckhold and Southend Dio Ox from 71. *Bradfield Rectory, Reading, Berks, RG7 6EU.* (Bradfield 744333)

LANE, Stewart. d 76 S Malawi. d Dio S Malawi. *P/Bag 303, Chichiri, Blantyre, Malawi.*

LANE, Virginia Charlene. b 46. Hur Coll Lon BMin 76. **d** 76 **p** 77 Hur. C of St Aid Lon Ont 76-77; R of St Hilda, St Thos Dio Huron from 77. *6 Mandeville Road, St Thomas, Ont., Canada.* (519-631 0504)

LANE, Walter Richard. b 08. Ch Coll Cam BA 30, MA 34. Ridley Hall, Cam 30. **d** 32 **p** 33 York. C of Acomb 32-35; CMS Miss Dio Dorn 35-47; Ch of S India 47-49; R of Ashdon 49-73. *Riverside Cottage, Garthbrengy, Brecon, Powys, LD3 9TR.*

LANE, William Michael. b 19. BNC Ox MA 47. **d** 79 **p** 80 Bris. Asst Chap Clifton Coll Bris from 79. *42 Canynge Square, Bristol, BS8 3LB.*

LANE, William Thomas. St D Coll Lamp 54. **d** 54 St D **p** 55 Llan for St D. C of Johnston w Steynton 54-56; R of Wambrook 56-58; V of Cwmcarn 58-64. *2 Webbs Hill, Broad Haven, Haverfordwest, Dyfed.*

LANG, Canon Cyrus Robert. Dioc Th Coll Montr LTh 33. **d** 33 **p** 34 Mont. C of St Luke Montr 33-36; P-in-c of Mirror Landing 36-38; R of Colinton 38-44; Lachute 44-68; Ste Agathe des Monts 68-75; R of Ste Marguerite 68-75; Hon Can of Montr 74-75; Can (Emer) from 75. *413 6th Avenue, City of Two Mountains, Quebec, Canada.*

LANG, Edwin Siah. Ridley Coll Melb ACT ThL 75. **d** 76 Melb **p** 77 Adel. C of St Matt Kens 76-78; St Columb Hawthorn 78-79; P-in-c of Diamond Creek Dio Melb from 79. *Vicarage, Diamond Creek, Vic, Australia 3089.* (438 1264)

LANG, Geoffrey Wilfrid Francis. b 33. Late Scho of St Jo Coll Ox BA (3rd cl Engl) 56, MA 61. Cudd Coll 56. **d** 58 **p** 59 Linc. C of Spalding 58-61; Asst Chap Univ of Leeds 61-62; C of St Luke Chesterton (in c of Good Shepherd) 62-63; C-in-c of Good Shepherd Conv Distr Chesterton Cambs 63-69; V 69-72; R of Willian 72-76; Dioc Dir Educn and Training Dio St Alb 72-76; Exam Chap to Bp of St Alb 76; V of King's Lynn Dio Nor from 76. *St Margaret's Vicarage, King's Lynn, Norf.* (King's Lynn 2858)

LANG, George Warren. Univ of BC BA 33. Angl Th Coll BC LTh 35. **d** 35 New Westmr **p** 36 Calg. C of St Steph Calg 35-37; I of Strathmore 37-39; Okotoks 39-43; R of Red Deer 43-54; Calg Dioc Chap and Hon Can of Calg 52-54; V of St Paul Edmon 54; C of Ch Ch Cathl Vic 54-56; R of St Sav Pro-Cathl Nelson 56-63; Can of Koot 56-63; I of All SS Regina 63-69; R of Fort St John 69-73; Vanderhoof 73-75; Perm to Offic Dio BC from 75. *51 Dawson Heights, 3800 Cedar Hill Cross Road, Victoria, BC, Canada.*

LANG, Very Rev John Harley. b 27. Em Coll Cam MA 60. K Coll Lon and Warm AKC 49, BD 60. **d** 52 Bp Kitching for Portsm **p** 53 Portsm. C of St Mary Portsea 52-57; PV and Sacr of S'wark Cathl 57-60; Chap Em Coll Cam 60-64; Perm to Offic Dio Ely 60-64; Asst Hd of Relig Broadcasting BBC 64-67; Hd of Relig Programmes BBC Radio 67-71; Hd of Relig Broadcasting BBC 71-80; C of Sacombe 73-80; Chap to HM the Queen from 76; Dean of Lich from 80. *Deanery, Lichfield, Staffs, WS13 7LD.* (Lichfield 22044)

LANG, William David. b 51. AKC and BD 74. St Aug Coll Cant 74. **d** 75 **p** 76 Guildf. C of Fleet 75-79; All SS W Ewell and of St Francis Ewell 79-82; V of Holmwood Dio Guildf from 82. *South Holmwood Vicarage, Dorking, Surrey, RH5 4JX.* (Dorking 67118)

LANG, William Peter. b 43. Univ of Lon BD 68, AKC 67. Coll of Resurr Mirfield 67. **d** 69 **p** 70 Lon. C of St Mary Virg Primrose Hill 69-73; P-in-c of St Mark w St Luke St Marylebone 73-78; Dir Lon Dio Pastoral Support Group Scheme from 77; R of Ch Ch St Marylebone Dio Lon from 78. *255 Old Marylebone Road, NW1.* (01-723 7544)

LANGA, David Magaiza. d 79 **p** 81 Lebom. P Dio Lebom. *PP de Nhamavila, Chongoene, Mozambique.*

LANGA, Jo£ao. d 60 **p** 61 Lebom. P Dio Lebom. *Caixa Postal 57, Lourenço Marques, Moçambique.*

LANGDON, Canon Alan Arthur. Univ of Syd BA 47, BD 50, MA 77. Moore Coll Syd. **d** and **p** 50 Syd. Org Sec Syd Dioc Bd of Educn 50-51; Dir of Educn 52-76; C of St Andr Cathl Syd 50-67; Hon Can of Syd from 65; L to Offic Dio Syd 67-69; C of St Andr Cathl City and Dio Syd from 69; Chairman Dioc Educn Comm Dio Syd from 76. *29 Fullers Road, Chatswood, NSW, Australia 2067.* (419-4325)

LANGDON, Eric. b 07. St Chad's Coll Dur BA 31, Dipl in Th 33, MA 34. **d** 32 **p** 33 Carl. C of Aspatria 32-35; Corbridge-on-Tyne w Halton 35-39; V of Alwinton w Holystone and Kidland 39-41; CF (EC) 42-44; Master Hendon Prep Sch 44-46; C of St Mark Teddington 46-50; R of St Martin Polmadie Glas 50-52; St Paul Kinross 52-57; V of Watton w Beswick and Kilnwick Dio York from 57. *Watton Vicarage, Driffield, Yorks. YO25 9AJ.* (Watton 285)

LANGDON, John Bonsall. Linc Coll Ox BA 51, MA 55. Ripon Hall, Ox 52. **d** 54 **p** 55 Roch. C of Erith 54-57; Christchurch 57-60; C and Min Can of Ripon Cathl 60-63; R of Swillington 63-75; V of All H w St Simon (w Wrangthorn from 76) Leeds Dio Ripon from 75; C-in-c of Wrangthorn 75-76. *All Hallows Vicarage, Regent Terrace, Leeds, LS6 1NP.* (Leeds 454893)

LANGDON, Canon William Ancell Martin. b 14. Selw Coll Cam BA 36, MA 41. Wells Th Coll 36. **d** 38 **p** 39 S'wark. C of St Bart Sydenham 38-40; Putney 40-42; Worplesdon 42-45; Chap HM Borstal Inst Portland 45-49; R of All SS w St Pet Portland 48-51; Langton Matravers 51-61; Surr 48-51 and 61-69; Hon Chap to Bp of Sarum 53-62; V of Melksham 61-69; RD of Bradf 67-69; Can and Preb of Sarum Cathl 68-81; Can (Emer) from 81; V of Charminster 69-81. *3a Bon Accord Road, Swanage, Dorset.*

LANGDON-DAVIES, Roland Charles. b 03. Late Exhib of Ch Ch Ox BA (2nd cl Mod Hist) 25. Coll of Resurr mirfield 28. **d** 30 **p** 31 Dur. C of St Columba Southwick 30-35; L to Offic Dio Wakef 35-39; M CR from 37; Miss P Penhalonga Dio S Rhod 39-52; Dio Mashon 52-54; L to Offic Dio Johann 54-55; Miss P at Rosettenville Johann 55-58; L to Offic Dio Ripon 60-65; Dio Wakef from 65. *c/o House of the Resurrection, Mirfield, W Yorks.*

LANGENHOVEN, Anthony Alexander. b 48. St Pet Coll Natal Dipl Th 76. **d** 76 **p** 77 Capetn. C of Grassy Park 76-78; Fish Hoek 78-80; R of Ocean View Dio Capetn from 80. *Box 22, Ocean View, Fish Hoek 7975, CP, S Africa.* (83 1825)

LANGENHOVEN, Harold Joseph. b 20. **d** 76 Capetn (APM). C of St Nich Matroosfontein Dio Capetn from 76. *14 School Street, Bellville South 7530, CP, S Africa.* (94-3126)

LANGFORD, Bernard Leslie. d and **p** 56 Tas. C of Devonport 56-57; Sec Austr Coun Chs Queensld 57-72; L to Offic Dio Brisb from 57. *48 Durham Street, St Lucia, Queensland, Australia 4067.* (370 7939)

LANGFORD, Donald Arthur. Moore Th Coll Syd ACT ThL 47, Th Scho 57. **d** and **p** 47 Syd. C of St Matt Botany 47-48; Ryde 48; C-in-c of Northmead and Rydalmere 49-50; R of Picton 50-56; Min of Winchelsea 56-65; I of Port Melb Dio Melb from 65. *162 Bay Street, Port Melbourne, Vic, Australia 3207.* (03-64 3572)

LANGFORD, Herbert Walter. b 19. Univ of Lon BA (1st cl Hist) 50. Wells Th Coll 50. **d** 52 Jarrow for Dur **p** 53 Dur. C of Stella 52-54; Winlaton (in-c of High Spen) 54-56; PC of Trimdon 56-59; V of St Ignatius Hendon 59-63; Vice-Prin St Chad's Coll Dur and L to Offic Dio Dur 63-69; Regr and Examns Sec ACCM 69-71; L to Offic Dio Cant 70-71; R of Winthorpe Dio Southw from 71; V of Langford w Holme-by-Newark Dio Southw from 71. *Winthorpe Rectory, Newark, Notts.* (Newark 704985)

LANGFORD, James Michael. b 47. St Cuthb Coll BA 68. St Steph Ho Ox 70. **d** 73 **p** 74 Dur. C of Hedworth 73-76; S Shields 76-81; Industr Chap Northumb Industr Miss 78-81; P-in-c of St Jas Conv Distr Owton Manor Dio Dur from 81. *St James Clergy House, Rossmere Way, Hartlepool, Cleve. TS25 5EF.* (Hartlepool 73938)

LANGFORD, Michael John. New Coll Ox BA 54, MA 58, Univ of Cam MA (by incorp) 59. Univ of Lon PhD 66. Westcott Ho Cam. **d** 56 **p** 57 Bris. C of St Nath w St Kath Bris 56-59; Chap Qu Coll Cam 59-63; L to Offic Dio Ely 61-63; C of Hampstead 63-66; Asst Prof Mem Univ St John's Newfld from 67; Hon C of St Aug, St John's Dio E Newfld from 80. *5 March Street, St John's, Newfoundland, Canada.*

LANGFORD, Peter Francis. b 54. Sarum Wells Th Coll 76. **d** 79 **p** 80 York. C of N Ormesby Dio York from 79. *14 Grove Road, North Ormesby, Middlesbrough, Cleve, TS3 6EH.* (Middlesbrough 222996)

LANGFORD, Peter Julian. b 33. Selwyn Coll Cam BA 58. Westcott Ho Cam 59. **d** 60 Chelmsf **p** 61 Colchester for Chelmsf. C of E Ham Dio Chelmsf 60-67; Hon C 67-71; L to Offic Dio St E 71-77; Warden of Ringsfield Hall from 71; P-in-c of Ringsfield w Redisham 76-80. *Ringsfield Hall, Beccles, Suffolk.* (Beccles 713020)

✠ **LANGFORD-SMITH, Right Rev Neville Langford.** Univ of Syd BA 32, MA 47. **d** 35 Centr Tang **p** 37 Syd for Centr Tang. CMS Miss Dio Centr Tang 35-47; Dio Momb 48-60; Hd Master Katoke Sch 35-36; Dodoma Sch and P-in-c Dodoma 37-41; Marangu Sch and Chap Moshi 41-43; Kotake Sch and P-in-c Bukoba 44; Arusha Sch and Chap Arusha-Moshi 45-46; Supervisor of Schs N Highlands 48-53;

Archd of Nairobi 55-58; Archd of Centr Kenya and Exam Chap Bp of Momb 58-60; Cons Asst Bp of Momb in All SS Cathl Nairobi 24 Aug 60 by Abp of E Afr; Bps of Zanz; SW Tang; and Centra Tang; Asst Bps of Momb (Kariuki and Olang); and U Nile (Russell); Apptd Bp of Nak 61; res 75; Prov Sec for Miss Kenya 75-78; L to Offic Dio Syd from 78. *6 Snowden Place, St Ives, NSW, Australia 2075.* (44-6030)

LANGHAM, John Godfrey. Dipl Th (Lon) 60. Oak Hill Th Coll. **d** 60 **p** 61 Pet. C of St Pet Rushden 60-63; V of Burton 63-79. *61 Holmdale, Sidmouth, Devon, EX10 8DN.*

LANGHORNE, Edward Herbert. b 1890. St Chad's Coll Dur BA 20, MA 23. **d** 20 Lon for Cant **p** 21 Dover for Cant. C of Ashford 20-24; St Mich AA Maidstone (in c of St Andr Barming Heath Conv distr) 24-30; Min of St Andr Barming Heath 30-31; V of St Matt U Clapton w H Trin Lea Bridge 31-35; St Alb S Norwood 35-55; St Pet Maidstone 55-67. *Trenethick, June Lane, Midhurst, Sussex.*

LANGKAN, George. d 54 **p** 55 Borneo. P Dio Borneo 54-62; Dio Kuch 62-75. *c/o St Luke's Church, Simanggang, Sarawak, Malaysia.*

LANGLEY, Allan Douglas. d 64 **p** 65 Ja. C of St Mich Kingston Dio Ja from 64. *11 Latham Avenue, Kingston 6, Jamaica, W Indies.* (092-78896)

LANGLEY, Canon Robert. b 37. St Cath Coll Ox BA 61. St Steph Ho Ox. **d** 63 **p** 64 Sheff. C of Aston w Aughton 63-68; Midl Area Sec Chr Educn Movement and L to Offic Dio Cov 68-71; HQ Sec CEM 71-74; L to Offic Dio Lon 73-74; Prin Ian Ramsey Coll Brasted 74-77; Prin Ministerial Tr Scheme Dio St Alb from 77; Can Res of St Alb Cathl from 77. *44 Clarence Road, St Albans, Herts.* (St Albans 31915)

LANGLOIS, Reginald William Justin. d 68 **p** 76 Tas. Hon C of Bellerive 68-81; Perm to Offic Dio Tas from 81. *11 Cato Avenue, W Hobart, Tasmania 7000.*

LANGMORE, Edward Richard. St Aug Coll Cant. **d** 35 **p** 36 Capetn. C of St Luke Salt River 35-39; Chap RAFVR 39-46; C of St Sav Claremont 46-48; R of Roodebloem 48-54; H Redeemer Sea Point 54-57; Maitland 57-64; Wellington 64-67; C of Woodstock 67-68; Elgin 68-73; St Geo Cathl City and Dio Capetn from 73. *323 Pinelands Place, Lonsdale Road, Pinelands 7405, S Africa.* (53-4616)

LANGO, Lord Bishop of. *See* Otim, Right Rev Melkizedek.

LANGRELL, Gordon John. Univ of Cant BA 58. Ridley Hall, Cam 65. **d** 67 **p** 68 Roch. C of Tonbridge 67-71; Wanganui 71-73; V of Taita Dio Wel from 73. *16 Pearce Crescent, Taita, Wellington, NZ.* (677-665)

LANGRISH, Michael Laurence. b 46. Univ of Birm BSocSc 67. Fitzw Coll Cam BA 73, MA 77. Ridley Hall Cam 71. **d** 73 Bp McKie for Cov **p** 74 Cov. C of Stratford-on-Avon 73-76; Chap of Rugby Sch 76-81; Dioc Dir of Ordinands and P-in-c of Offchurch Dio Cov from 81. *Offchurch Vicarage, Leamington Spa, Warws, CV33 9AL.* (Leamington Spa 24401)

LANGSFORD, Robert Bentley. Univ of Adel BA 67. St Barn Coll Adel ACT ThL 68. **d** and **p** 69 Adel. C of Lockleys 69-70; St Aug Unley 70-71; Perm to Offic Dio Melb 72-73; C of St Mark Hamilton Terrace St John's Wood Lon 74-75. *142 Puckle Street, Moonee Ponds, Vic, Australia 3039.*

LANGSHAW, Donald Edward. Moore Th Coll Syd 44. ACT ThL 44. **d** and **p** 45 Syd. C of St Matt Manly 45; C-in-c of Mascot Distr 45-48; R of Harris Pk 48-55; Naremburn 55-60; Five Dock 60-65; Leichhardt 65-69; C-in-c of Mona Vale 69-72; R 72-76; Naremburn w Cammeray 76-81; Asst Chap Retirement Villages Dio Syd from 81. *4 Sexton Avenue, Castle Hill, NSW, Australia 2154.*

LANGSHAW, Reginald Norman. Moore Th Coll Syd ACT ThL 34. **d** 35 **p** 36 Syd. C of Chatswood 35-37; P-in-c of Wilcannia 37-39; C of Gladesville 39-40; R of Prospect w Seven Hills 40-44; Canley Vale w Cabramatta 44-45; Belmore w Moorefields 45-47; St Mich Syd 47-54; Ryde 54-63; Hurstville 63-74; Chap to Abp of Syd 63-74; Sec Bush Ch Aid S in NSW 74-76; L to Offic Dio Syd from 74. *4/33 Elizabeth Street, Allawah, NSW, Australia 2218.* (587-3178)

LANGSHAW, Stuart Neale. Moore Th Coll Syd ACT ThL 66. **d** 67 **p** 68 Syd. C of Dapto 67-70; St Ives 71-72; R of Earlwood 72-76; C of H Trin City and Dio Adel from 76; Gen Sec CMS S Austr from 76. *16 Oaklands Avenue, Royston Park, S Australia 5070.* (212-4838)

LANGSTAFF, James Henry. b 56. St Cath Coll Ox BA 77, MA 81. Univ of Nottm BA (Th) 80. St Jo Coll Nottm 78. **d** 81 Guildf. C of Farnborough Dio Guildf from 81. *22 Rectory Road, Farnborough, Hants.*

✠ **LANGSTONE, Right Rev John Arthur William.** Univ of Tor BA 36. Yale Univ BD 47. Trin Coll Tor LTh 38. **d** 38 **p** 39 Tor. C of St John Norway Tor 38-43; Chap CASF 43-46; C of H Trin Tor 46-50; R of Port Credit 50-57; St Geo Edmon 58-69; St Faith Edmon 69-71; Exam Chap to Bp of Edmon 60-76; Can of Edmon 63-65; Archd of Edmon 65-70; Executive Archd 70-76; Cons Ld Bp of Edmon in All SS Cathl Edmon 7 March 76 by Abp of Rupld; Bps of Calg, Keew, Sask, Alg, Sktn, Athab and Bran; res 79. *5112-109th Avenue, Edmonton, Alta, T6A 1S1. Canada.*

LANGTON, Ernest William. b 05. St Jo Coll Cam BA 44, MA 48. **d** 47 **p** 48 Cov. C of All SS Leamington Priors 47-49; Asst Master Beverley Gr Sch 49-58; R of Brandesburton 58-73; Perm to Offic Dio York from 73. *164 Sewerby Road, Bridlington, YO16 5UP.* (0262 74506)

LANGTON, Canon Kenneth. b 26. Open Univ BA 76. St Aid Coll 52. **d** 55 **p** 56 Man. C of St Paul Oldham 55-57; Ch Ch Ashton L 57-58; C-in-c 58; V of New St Geo Stalybridge 58-69; C-in-c of Old St Geo Stalybridge 67-69; V of St Geo Stalybridge 69-71; R of St Mary Radcliffe Dio Man from 71; Surr from 72; Co-Dir Clergy In-Service Training from 79; Hon Can of Man Cathl from 80. *Rectory, Rectory Close, Radcliffe, Manchester, M26 9PZ.* (061-723 2460)

LANGTON, Canon Maurice Charles. b 09. Late Scho of Trin Coll Cam Stewart of Rannoch Scho and 1st cl Cl Trip pt i 28, BA (2nd cl Cl Trip pt ii) 30, MA 34. Sarum Th Coll 33. **d** 34 **p** 35 Chich. C of Horsham 34-37; Tutor Bp's Th Coll Tirumaraiyur 37-40; Sub-Warden 40-42; SPG Miss Ramnad 42-45; Prin CMS Schs for the Blind Palamcottah Dio Tinn 45-52; Ch of S India 47-52; V of Billingshurst 52-56; Dir of Relig Educn and Tr of Ordin Cands Dio Chich and Dep Dioc Sec 56-77; Can and Preb of Chich Cathl from 63; Perm to Offic Dio Linc from 77. *3 Caithness Road, Stamford, Lincs, PE9 2TE.*

LANGTON-DURHAM (formerly DURHAM), Alaric John. b 14. Late Exhib of Univ Coll Ox BA (2nd cl Engl Lang and Lit) 36, 2nd cl Phil Pol and Econ 38, MA 45. St Aid Coll 39. **d** 39 **p** 40 Wakef. C of Sandal Magna 39-41; Crosthwaite Keswick 41-42; CF (EC) 42-43; C of St John Weston Bath 43-46 and 49-54; C-in-c of St Pet Twerton-on-Avon Bath 46-48; C of St Mich Chester Square 48-49; R of W Winch 54-59; V of Croxton 59-65; R of Kilverstone 59-65; Fairstead w Terling Dio Chelmsf from 65. *Terling Rectory, Chelmsford, Essex, CM3 2PL.* (Terling 256)

LANGTRY, Arthur Melvin. b 11. TCD BA 33, MA 40. **d** 36 **p** 37 Sheff. C of St Jas Doncaster 36-40; St Mary Handsworth 40-44; Tinsley 44-45; V of St Jo Bapt Pollington w Balne 45-61; C-in-c of Sykehouse 50-61; Chap HM Borstal Inst Pollington 50-56 and 57-61; HM Pris Pollington 56-57; R of Rossington 61-75. *21 Hallcroft Drive, Armthorpe, Doncaster, S Yorks, DN3 3RT.* (Doncaster 832991)

LANHAM, Frederick James. b 07. Univ of Lon BCom 33. Wycl Hall Ox 33. **d** 35 **p** 36 S'wark. C of H Trin Wallington 35-40; Actg C of St Jas Gerrard's Cross 40-43; V of H Trin Tewkesbury 43-47; R of Quedgeley 47-61; C-in-c of Elmore 47-53; Longney 52-53; Chap HM Pris Glouc 53-61 PC of Ch Ch City and Dio Glouc 61-68; V 68-72. *Puckeridge, Burwash Weald, Sussex.* (Burwash 882742)

LANHAM, Canon Gordon Joicey. Univ of Leeds BA (2nd cl Lat) 38. Univ of Lon BD 51. Coll of Resurr Mirfield 35. **d** 40 **p** 41 Linc. C of St Nich w St John Newport Linc 40-45; St Pet St Helier Morden (in c of Bp Andrewes Ch) 45-47; V of St Luke Holbeach Hurn 47-53; L Coates 53-60; Alford w Rigsby and Ailby 60-70; RD of Calcewaith S 61-67; Can and Preb of Linc Cath from 66; RD of Calcewaith w Candleshoe 67-70; C-in-c of Well 67-70; C-in-c of Saleby w Thoresthorpe and Beesby 69-70; C-in-c of Maltby 69-70; V of Bourne Dio Linc from 70; RD of Aveland and Ness w Stamford 72-77. *Vicarage, Bourne, Lincs.* (Bourne 2412)

LANHAM, Richard Paul White. b 42. Univ of Dur BA 64. Wycl Hall, Ox 65. **d** 67 Dorch for Ox **p** 68 Ox. C of Gerrard's Cross 67-69; Horwich 69-72; Worsley w Ellenbrook 72-74; V of St Andr Accrington 74-80; Shillington Dio St Alb from 80; U w Lower Gravenhurst Dio St Alb from 80. *Shillington Vicarage, Hitchin, Herts.* (Shillington 240)

LANKESTER, Joseph Posford. b 17. AKC 42. **d** 42 **p** 43 Chelmsf. C of St Pet Becontree 42-45; P-in-c of St Anne Sandy Pt St Kitts BWI 46-50; Anguilla 50-51; C of Brentwood 51-53; R of Rivenhall 53-59; V of All SS Bromsgrove 59-73; Chap HM Borstal Inst Hewell Grange 64-67; Bromsgrove Gen Hosp 67-73; RD of Bromsgrove 68-73; R of Stanford-on-Teme w Orleton and Stockton-on-Teme 73-78; P-in-c of Pensax 73-78; St Martin-in-the-Cornmarket (f St Swith) City and Dio Worc 78-81; R (w Paul) from 81. *81 Bath Road, Worcester, WR5 3AE.* (Worc 353767)

LANSDALE, Charles Roderick. b 38. Univ of Leeds, BA 59. Coll of Resurr Mirfield 59. **d** 61 **p** 62 S'wark. C of Nunhead 61-65; Usuthu 65-68; R 69-71; P-in-c of Ingwempisana 68-69; V of Benhilton 71-78; Team R of Catford (Southend) and Downham Dio S'wark from 78. *353 Bromley Road, SE6 2RP.* (01-698 3898)

LANSDOWN, Reginald Stanley. b 09. Univ of Leeds, BA (2nd cl Hist) 33. Coll of Resurr Mirfield 33. **d** 35 **p** 36 Sarum. C of St Paul Weymouth 35-37; St Luke Richmond 37-39; All SS Blackheath 39-40; Letchworth 40-43; Min of St Chris

Conv Distr Round Green 43-47; M CR 47-48; C of Ch Ch Luton (in c of St Pet) 50-53; V of Bierley 53-61; Chap to Blackb Hosps 61-63; C-in-c of St Bede Nelson-in-Marsden 63-65; V 65-68; Perm to Offic Dio Sarum 68-80. *8 St Barnabas, Newland, Malvern, Worcs, WR13 5AX.* (Malvern 5178)

LANSLEY, Paul Sanford. b 33. Trin Coll Cam BA 56, MA 61. St Steph Ho Ox 56. **d** 58 **p** 59 Lon. C of St Gabr N Acton 58-60; Asst Master Manningtree Co Secondary Sch from 61; Colne High Sch Brightlingsea from 72; Hon C of St Jas Colchester Dio Chelmsf from 69. *24 Worcester Road, Colchester, Essex.*

LANTEY, Paul Kipamet. St Paul's Th Coll Limuru. **d** 65 **p** 67 Nak. P Dio Nak 65-70; Dio Nai from 70. *c/o Station Master, Kiu, PO Ulu, Kenya.*

LANTSBERY, Colin. b 39. Chich Th Coll 70. **d** 72 **p** 73 Lich. C of Wednesfield 72-75; C of W Bromwich 75-77; V of Normacot Dio Lich from 77. *Vicarage, Upper Belgrave Road, Normacot, Stoke-on-Trent, ST3 4QJ.* (S-on-T 319695)

LANYON JONES, Keith. b 49. Univ of Southn BTh 79. Sarum Wells Th Coll 74. **d** 77 **p** 78 Glouc. C of Charlton Kings 77-81; Chap Rugby Sch from 81. *11 Horton Crescent, Rugby, Warws, CV22 5DJ.* (0788-4939)

LAPAGE, Michael Clement. b 23. Selw Coll Cam BA 47, MA 73. Clifton Th Coll 60. **d** 61 **p** 62 Ft Hall. Asst P of Weithaga 61-65; V of Nanyuki 65-72; Chap Bedford Sch 73-75; Commiss Mt Kenya E 75-77; Chap at Lyon w Grenoble 76-79; V of Walford w Bishopswood Dio Heref from 79. *Walford Vicarage, Ross-on-Wye, Herefs.* (Ross 2703)

LAPAGE, Canon Peter Reginald. b 17. Selw Coll Cam BA 41, MA 44. MC 45. Ridley Hall Cam. **d** 48 **p** 49 Ox. C of St John w St Steph Reading 48-50; CMS Miss Hausa Distr Zaria 51-54; St John Bida 54-58; Kaduna 59-61; V of St Andr Zaria 61-65; Miss CMS Maguzawa 61-65; Area Sec CMS Dios Lon and S'wark from 66; Perm to Offic Dio Lon from 66; L to Offic Dio S'wark from 66; SE Reg Co-ordinator CMS from 74; Commiss N Nig 75-80; Kaduna from 80; Can (Emer) of Kaduna Cathl from 81. *60 Queen's Road, SW19 8LR.* (01-946 1124)

LAPHAM, Fred. b 31. St D Coll Lamp BA 53. Angl Th Coll Vancouver L Th 55, BD 58. **d** and **p** 55 Yukon. C of Teslin 55-56; R 56-59; Hon Sec of Synod Dio Yukon 56-59; C of Wallasey 59-62; V of St Jo Evang Over 62-70; V of Upton Dio Ches from 70. *Upton Vicarage, Chester.* (Chester 383518)

LAPOK, Bolly. b 52. Ho of Epiph Kuch 71. **d** and **p** 75 Kuch. P Dio Kuch. *St John's Church, Queensway, Sibu, Sarawak, Malaysia.*

LARAMIE, Canon Orrence James. Seager Hall Ont. **d** 61 Hur **p** 62 Bp Townshend for Hur. C of St Jas Lon 61-64; R of Southn Ont 64-67; I of La Salle 67-71; St Jas Sarnia 71-77; Gorrie Dio Hur from 77; Can of Hur from 80. *Gorrie, Ont., Canada.* (519-335 3384)

LARCOMBE, David John. b 51. Univ of Natal BSc 73. St Paul's Coll Grahmstn 74. **d** 76 **p** 78 Zulu. C of Eshowe Dio Zulu from 76. *PO Box 147, Eshowe 3815, Zululand, S Africa.*

LARCOMBE, Leslie Duke. b 12. N-W Ordin Course 75. **d** 77 Middleton for Man **p** 78 Man. C of All SS Elton Bury Dio Man from 77. *152 Tottington Road, Bury, BL8 1RU.* (061-797 6676)

LAREWAJU, Julius Simeon Adebiyi. b 23. BA (Lon) 53. St Andr Coll Oyo. **d** 69 **p** 70 Ibad. P Dio Ibad 69-72; Dio Lagos from 73. *PM Bag 2007, Shagamu, Nigeria.*

LARGE, Canon Charles Frederick. **d** 38 **p** 40 Alg. Miss at Muskoka 38-40; I of Capreol 40-44; CF (Canad) 44-46; I of Nipigon and Red Rock 46-51; St John N Bay 51-73; Hon Can of Alg from 58. *1579 Hampshire Road, Victoria, BC, Canada.*

LARGE, Denis Henry. b 18. Sarum Th Coll 39. **d** 42 Sarum **p** 43 Sherborne for Sarum. C of Warminster 42-44; All SS Kingston 44-48; Min of St Jas Conv Distr Merton 48-51; V 51-56; R of Sandford w Upton Hellions 56-61; Clyst St Mary 61-75; Clyst St Geo (w Aylesbeare, Clyst Honiton, Clyst St Mary, Farringdon, Rockbeare, Sowton and Woodbury Salterton from 75) Dio Ex from 61; C-in-c of Woodbury Salterton 66-67; R 67-75; C-in-c of Rockbeare 66-67; R 67-75; C-in-c of Farringdon w Aylesbeare 66-67; R 67-75; Clyst Honiton 67-75; Sowton 67-75; RD of Aylesbeare 73-76. *Clyst St George Rectory, Exeter, Devon.* (Topsham 3295)

LARGE, John Edward. b 15. Keble Coll Ox BA (2nd cl Mod Hist) 37, MA 46. Westcott Ho Cam 38. **d** 39 **p** 40 Cov. C of Rugby 39-47; R of Walvis Bay Dio Damar 47-51; Asst P at Ovamboland Miss 51-52; R of Gt Ringstead 52-66; V of Holme-next-the-Sea 52-66; C-in-c of Sedgeford 64-66; RD of Heacham 64-65; Waxham 66-77; V of Happisburgh w Salcot 66-79. *Rectory, Hawkchurch, Axminster, Devon, EX13 5XD.*

LARGE, Richard Groves. b 32. Trin Coll Dub BA 52, BD 57. **d** 54 **p** 56 Dub. C of Monkstown 54-58; Taney 58-63; R of Killiney 63-71; Bray Dio Dub from 71. *Rectory, Bray, Co Wicklow, Irish Republic.* (Bray 862968)

LARK, William Donald Starling. b 35. Keble Coll Ox BA (2nd cl Th) 59, MA 63. Wells Th Coll 59. **d** 61 Bp McKie for Cov **p** 62 Cov. C of Wyken 61-64; Christchurch w Mudeford 64-66; V of St Mich AA Yeovil 66-75; Earley Dio Ox from 75. *129 Whiteknights Road, Reading, RG6 2BB.* (Reading 62009)

LARKIN, Peter John. b 39. ALCD (2nd cl) 62. **d** 62 Bp Lash for Truro **p** 63 Truro. C of Liskeard w St Keyne 62-65; Rugby 65-67; Sec Bp of Cov Call to Mission 67-68; V of St Kea 68-77; Sec of Truro Dioc Coun for Miss & Unity 70-76; V of Bromsgrove 77-81; R of St Matthias w St Mark and H Trin Torquay Dio Ex from 81. *Rectory, Asheldon Road, Torquay, Devon, TQ1 2QS.* (Torquay 23280)

LARNER, Gordon Edward Stanley. b 30. Oak Hill Th Coll 57. **d** 59 **p** 60 S'wark. C of Peckham 59-62; Luton w E Hyde (in c of St Anne) 62-68; V of St Mich AA Sydenham 68-73; Industr Chap Dio S'wark from 73. *39 Burghill Road, Lower Sydenham, SE26 4HJ.* (01-778 4225)

LARREA, Jess. b 49. Moore Th Coll Syd BTh. **d** 81 Syd. C of St Steph Port Kembla Dio Syd from 81. *1/28 Windang Road, Primbee, NSW, Australia 2504.*

LARSON, John Milton. b 35. N-W Univ Ill BMus 56. Seabury-W Th Coll Ill BD 59. **d** and **p** 59 Chicago. Amer Ch 57-63 and 66-70; C of St Barn Nass 63-66; P-in-c of St Patr Eleuthera Dio Nass from 70. *Rectory, Governor's Harbour, Eleuthera, Bahamas.*

LARTER, John William. b 29. Univ of Lon BSc 51. Coll of Resurr Mirfield. **d** 54 York **p** 55 Selby for York. C of Redcar 54-56; Thornaby-on-Tees 56-59; Boreham Wood (in c of H Cross) 59-62; Perm to Offic Dio Ox 62-65; R of Middleton Stoney 65-70; C-in-c of Bucknell 65-69; R 69-70; V of N Hinksey 70-77; Eye w Braiseworth and Yaxley Dio St E from 77; Surr from 77; RD of Hartismere 78-81; P-in-c of Occold w Redlingfield Dio St E from 80; Bedingfield Dio St E from 81. *Vicarage, Eye, Suff, IP23 7AW.* (Eye 870277)

LARTEY, Nicholas. **d** 66 Accra. d Dio Accra. *PO Box 491, Accra, Ghana.*

LASEBIKAN, Gabriel Ladokun. b 13. **d** 76 **p** 78 Ibad. P Dio Ibad. *St John's Church, Ilare, Ile-Ife, Nigeria.*

✠ **LASH, Right Rev William Quinlan.** b 05. Em Coll Cam 3rd cl Cl Trip 26, BA (2nd cl Engl Trip) 27, MA 32. Westcott Ho Cam 27. **d** 28 **p** 29 Portsm. C of St Mary Portsea 28-32; M CSS Poona 32-34; Acharya CPSS 34-47 and 50-61; Cons Ld Bp of Bom in St Thos Cathl Bom 10 Aug 47 by Bp of Calc (Metrop); Bps of Nasik; and Trav; and Asst Bp of Colom; res 61; Asst Bp of Truro 62-73; PC of Treslothan 62-63; V of St Clement 63-73; Commiss Bom 63-70. *The Friary, Hilfield, Dorchester, Dorset, DT2 7BE.* (Cerne Abbas 345)

LASHBROOK, Douglas Leonard. Moore Th Coll Syd 65. **d** 68 **p** 69 Armid. C of Wee Waa 68-80. *Curatage, Pilliga, NSW, Australia 2388.* (95-4236)

LASHBROOKE, John. b 28. Kelham Th Coll 49. **d** 53 **p** 54 S'wark. C of St Jo Div Kennington 53-57; P-in-c of St Jos Port Mourant Gui 57-59; V of St Phil Sydenham 59-69; Commiss Guy from 66; R of Epiph w St Jo Bapt Corby 69-80; Surr 78-80; V of Rubery Dio Birm from 80. *St Chad's Vicarage, 160a New Road, Rubery, Birmingham, B45 9JA.* (021-453 3255)

LASHFORD, Kenneth Allan. St Jo Coll Morpeth 38. **d** 40 **p** 41 Bath. Bro of Good Shepherd Dubbo 40-47; R of Warren 48-50; R of Rylstone 52-58; Port Moresby 58-64; Sub-Dean of Pro-Cathl Port Moresby 58-64; Can of New Guinea 62-64; V of St Geo Windsor Brisb 64-68; R of St Mich AA New Farm City and Dio Brisb from 68. *655 Brunswick Street, New Farm, Queensland, Australia 4005.* (358 1555)

LASHLEY, Paul Hyacinth. Codr Coll Barb 64. **d** 66 Barb **p** 67 Windw Is for Barb. C of St Phil 66-70; V of All SS Barb 70-74; R of St Phil I and Dio Barb from 74. *Rectory, St Philip, Barbados, W Indies.*

LASLETT, Christopher John. b 42. Univ of Leeds BA (2nd cl Latin) 64. Lich Th Coll 64. **d** 66 **p** 67 Bradf. C of St Clem Bradf 66-69; Ch Ch U Armley 69-70; Asst Master Hartlepool Gr Sch 70-73; Brinkburn Comprehensive Sch from 73; Hon C of Stranton 79-81. *12 Linden Grove, Hartlepool, Cleve, TS26 9PX.*

LAST, Eric Cyril. Oak Hill Th Coll 77. **d** 79 80 S'wark. C of All SS w H Trin Wandsworth Dio S'wark from 79. *48 Ringford Road, Wandsworth, SW18 1RR.*

LAST, Harold Wilfred. b 17. Late Scho of CCC Cam 2nd cl Econ Trip pt i, 36, BA (1st cl Th Trip pt i) 38, MA 42. ARCM 52. ARCO 53. Linc Th Coll 39. **d** 40 **p** 41 Bradf. C of St Jas Bolton Bradf 40-44; Lect Leeds Univ 42-44; C of Woodbridge 44-45; Lect in New Testament and Music K Coll Lon 45-50; Organist and Lect in Music 50-53; Dir of Music St

Bees Sch 53-55; St Olave's Sch 56-57; Felsted Sch 57-73. *81 Dales View Road, Ipswich, Suff.* (Ipswich 45135)

LATHAEN, William Alan. b 06. MBE 46 TD 49. St Jo Coll Dur BA 30, MA 33. **d** 31 **p** 32 Dur. C of All SS Stranton 31-35; Miss Dio Lagos 35-37; C of St Mich AA S Westoe 37-38; V of Thornley 38-47; CF (TA) 38-56; DACG N Commd 57-60; PC of S Westoe S Shields 47-60; Surr 48-77; PC of St Andr Roker Monkwearmouth 60-68; Hon Can of Dur 61; R of Shincliffe 68-77. *67 Woodside, Barnard Castle, Co Durham, DL12 8AR.* (Teesdale 37570)

LATHAM, John Alfred. b 37. Hur Coll Lon Ont BMin 78. **d** 78 Bp Parke-Taylor for Hur **p** 79 Hur. C-in-c of Parkhill Dio Hur from 78. *Box 481, Parkhill, Ont, Canada, N0K 2K0.*

LATHAM, John Montgomery. Univ of NZ BA 60. Westcott Ho Cam. **d** 62 **p** 63 S'wark. C of St Geo Camberwell 62-65; Chap Trin Coll Cam 65-71; Chap Wanganui Colleg Sch 71-79. *c/o Box 7040, Collegiate School, Wanganui, NZ.*

LATHAM, John Westwood. b 31. Ely Th Coll 57. **d** 60 **p** 61 Wakef. C of St Jo Evang Cleckheaton 60-63; Hemel Hempstead 63-65; C and Sacr of Wakef Cathl 65-67; V of Outwood 67-72; Team V of Daventry (w Norton from 73) 72-79; V of Flore w Dodford and Brockhall Dio Pet from 79. *Flore Vicarage, Northampton, NN7 4LZ.* (Weedon 40510)

LATHE, Anthony Charles Hudson. b 36. Jes Coll Ox BA (2nd cl Geog) 59, MA 64. Lich Th Coll. **d** 61 **p** 62 York. C of Selby Abbey 61-63; V in Hempnall Group 63-72; R of Quidenham Group Dio Nor from 72. *Quidenham Rectory, Norwich, Norf, NR16 2NY.*

LATIGO, Canon Alipayo. CMS Coll Buwalasi 38. **d** 39 **p** 41 U Nile. P Dio U Nile 39-61; Dio N Ugan from 61; Hon Can of U Nile 55-61; N Ugan from 61. *PO Bobi, Uganda.*

LATIMER, Canon Ralph Robertson. McMaster Univ BA 30, MA 33. Wycl Coll Tor Hon DD 65. Hur Coll Hon DD 65. **d** 30 **p** 31 Hur. I of Florence w Aughrim 30-35; on leave 35-38; Prof Hur Coll 38-40 and 45-50; I of H Trin Chatham 40-42; Chap RCAF 42-45; R of Cronyn Mem Ch Lon 45-50; St Jas Montr 50-64; Hon Can of Montr 55-73; Can (Emer) from 74; Gen Sec of Gen Synod of Canada 64-68; Exec Comm Ch U Montr 68-73. *457 Glengarry Avenue, Toronto, Ont., Canada.*

LATTIMER, Douglas Locke. Univ of Tor BA 51. **d** 56 Bp Snell for Tor **p** 57 Tor. C of Apsley 56-58; R of Uxbridge 58-64; I of St Mark Otonabee 64-65; St Alb Pet 64-65. *25 Village Drive, Belleville, Ont., Canada.*

LATTIMORE, Anthony Leigh. b 35. Univ of Dur BA (2nd cl Mod Hist) 57. Lich Th Coll 60. **d** 62 **p** 63 Leic. C of St Andr Aylestone Leic 62-66; Min of St Hugh Eccles Distr Eyres Monsell Leic 66-69; V of St Hugh Eyres Monsell Leic 69-73; Somerby w Burrough-on-the-Hill and Pickwell Dio Leic from 73; RD of Goscote 1 from 80. *Somerby Vicarage, Melton Mowbray, Leics, LE14 2QQ.* (Somerby 318)

LAU, Baldwin Wan. U Th Coll Hong Kong LTh 63. **d** 62 **p** 63 Hong. P Dio Hong. *Kwun Tong, Macao, Hong Kong.* (3-893942)

LAU, Gordon Kwong-sum. b 42. Calif Bapt Coll BSc 73. Ch Div Sch of the Pacific Calif 73. **d** 76 **p** 77 Hong. C of St Steph Hong Dio Hong from 76. *St Stephen's Church, Bonham Road, Hong Kong.*

LAU, Ven Teik Oon. Trin Coll Sing. **d** 55 **p** 56 Sing. P Dio Sing from 55; Hon Can of Sing from 65; Archd from 67; Chairman Bd of Chinese Work from 71; Commiss Sabah from 78. *St Andrew's Cathedral, Singapore 6.*

LAU, Thomas Kin Chi. Ming Hwa Coll Hong Kong 51. **d** 53 **p** 54 Hong. P Dio Hong 54-56; and from 60-78; P-in-c of Good Shepherd Miss Vanc 56-60. *c/o Bishop's House, 1 Lower Albert Road, Hong Kong.* (5-265355)

LAUDER, Allan William. McGill Univ BA 64, BD 65. Montr Th Coll LTh 65. **d** 65 **p** 66 Ont. C of Ch Ch Belleville 65-68; St Geo Cathl Kingston Ont 68-72; R of Lansdowne Rear 72-77; Stirling Dio Ont from 77. *Rectory, Stirling, Ont, Canada.* (613-395 3374)

LAUGHTON, Derek Basil. b 24. Worc Coll Ox BA 49, MA 52. Westcott Ho Cam 49. **d** 51 **p** 52 Sarum. C of Wareham 51-53; CF 53-56; C of Hemel Hempstead (in c of St Paul) 56-59; V of Stretton w Wetmoor 59-64; Chap Wel Sch and L to Offic Dio B & W 64-72; Chap Ardingley Coll and L to Offic Dio Chich 73-77; R of Plumpton and E Chiltington Dio Chich from 77. *Plumpton Rectory, Lewes, E Sussex.* (Plumpton 890275)

LAUGHTON, John Robert Carr. b 07. K Coll Cam BA 29, MA 33. Cudd Coll 29. **d** 30 **p** 31 S'wark. C of St Anne S Lambeth 30-32; PV of S'wark Cathl and C of St Sav w St Pet S'wark 32-35; Miss Dio Gambia 35-38; R of Dumbleton w Wormington 39-45; Chap RNVR 40-46; V of Barnwood 47-58; St Matt Hammersmith 58-69; Asst Master Rickmansworh Sch 70-74. *63 Sherborne Close, Stonehouse, Glos, GL10 2HR.*

LAURENCE, Canon Hugh Peter. b 02. Em Coll Sktn 24. **d** 28 **p** 29 Sask. C of Maidstone Sask 28-30; R of Tisdale Sask 30-32; Thimbleby 32-46; CF (R of O) from 39; CF (EC) 39-45; Men in Disp 40; C-in-c of Edlington w Wispington 45-46; V of Horncastle w Low Toynton 46-59; RD of Horncastle 46-57; Can and Preb of Liddington in Linc Cathl 50-77; Can (Emer) from 77; R of Martin w Thornton 51-59; V of Bourne 59-70. *Cresta, Thimbleby, Horncastle, Lincs.*

LAURENCE, John Harvard Christopher. b 29. Trin Hall, Cam BA 53, MA 57. Westcott Ho Cam 53. **d** 55 **p** 56 Linc. C of St Nich Linc 55-59; V of Crosby 59-74; Surr 62-79; Can and Preb of Linc Cathl 74-79; Can (Emer) from 80; St Hugh's Missr 74-79; Bp's Dir for Clergy Tr Dio Lon from 79. *4 Cambridge Place, W8 5PB.* (01-937 2560)

LAURENCE, Vere Deacon. b 11. Ex Coll Ox BA (3rd cl Chem) 33, BSc 34, MA 37. Sarum Th Coll 34. **d** 36 **p** 37 Bris. C of St Greg Gt Horfield 36-42; St Jo Div Fishponds 42-43; Sec Bris Dioc Reorg C'tte 42-43; C of St Barn Knowle (in c of St Giles Filwood Pk) 43-47; Chap HM Pris Horfield 46-47; Stafford 47-52; V of St Sav U Sunbury 53-74; R of Jacobstow w Warbstow and Treneglos Dio Truro from 74; RD of Stratton from 77. *Jacobstow Rectory, Bude, Cornw.* (St Gennys 206)

LAURENCE, William Gregory. b 10. St Andr Coll Whittlesford 40. **d** 40 **p** 41 Sheff. [f Congregational Min] C of Mexborough 40-44; C-in-c of New Maltby 44-47; V of Kimpton 47-51; L Pr Dio St Alb 51-65; R of Aynhoe 65-74; V of Newbottle w Charlton 65-74. *14 Rose Hill, Worcester.* (Worc 356210)

LAURENS, William John Peter. b 49. St Pet Coll Alice Dipl Th 72. **d** 72 **p** 73 Capetn. C of Bonteheuvel Dio Capetn from 72. *c/o The Priest's House, David Profit Street, Bonteheuvel, CP, S Africa.*

LAURIE, James Andrew Stewart. b 26. Selw Coll Cam BA (2nd cl Th Trip pts i and ii), 51, MA 55. Ridley Hall, Cam 51. **d** 53 **p** 54 Lon. C of Neasden w Kingsbury 53-56; C of Cricklewood 56-59; Lancing 59-61; V of Freehay 61-65; Alstonfield 65-71; V of Wetton 65-71; C-in-c of Blore Ray and Okeover 65-71; C-in-c of Calton 66-71. *Carrig, Hodge Lane, Marchington Woodlands, Uttoxeter, Staffs.*

LAUT, Graham Peter. b 37. Chich Th Coll 63. **d** 67 Barking for Chelmsf **p** 68 Chelmsf. C of Corringham 67-68; St Marg Leytonstone 68-71; P-in-c of St Andr Leytonstone 71-74; V 74-80; Ascen Collier Row, Romford Dio Chelmsf from 80. *Ascension Vicarage, Collier Row, Romford, Essex.* (Romford 41658)

LAVENDER, Arthur Roy Atto. b 11. Lich Th Coll 32. **d** 35 **p** 36 Lon. C of All S St Marg-on-Thames 35-38; All S Clapton Pk 38-39; St Jas w Pockthorpe Nor 39-42; R of Twyford w Guist V 42-50; C of Billborough w Strelley 50-53; V 53-58; R of Gt w L Ellingham 58-78. *157 Mundesley Road, N Walsham, Norfolk, NR28 0DD.*

LAVENDER, Cyril Norman. b 01. St Aug Coll Cant 32. **d** 35 Sarum for Col Bp **p** 35 Rockptn. M of Bro of St Andr Dio Rockptn 35-40; P-in-c of Dawson Valley 36-38; Biloela 38-40; Lakes Creek 40-42; R of St Barn N Rockptn 42-45; P-in-c of St Sav Gladstone 46-48; R of Hasland 48-57; PC of Temple Normanton 48-57; Commiss Rockptn from 52; PC of St Andr Derby 57-60; R of Warham (w Wighton from 61) 60-69; Chap Nor Gt Hosp from 73; C-in-c of St Helen City and Dio Nor from 74. *2 Cotman House, Palace Plain, Norwich, NR3 1RN.* (Norwich 27502)

LAVER, Douglas Edward. St Francis Coll Brisb. **d** 59 **p** 60 Brisb. C of St Luke Ekibin Brisb 59-62; St Pet Southport 62-64; V of Wondai 64-67; St Barn Sunnybank Brisb 67-74; R of Boonah Dio Brisb from 74. *Rectory, Church Street, Boonah, Queensland, Australia 4310.* (Boonah 63 1041)

LAVERGNE, Gerald Joseph. b 35. Univ of W Ont BMin 78. Hur Coll Lon 76. **d** 78 Hur for Koot. C of Vernon Dio Koot from 78. *PO Box 21, Armstrong, BC, V0E 1V0, Canada.*

LAVERICK, Frederick George. b 1892. Qu Coll Cam BA 16, MA 20. **d** 16 **p** 17 S'wark. C of St Jas Bermondsey 16-20; AIM Miss at Dungu 20-26; CMS Miss at Maridi 26-34; Prin Nugent Sch Loka 34-37; R of Aldham Essex 37-39; Org Sec CMS Dios Ex Truro and B & W 39-44; CMS Miss Dio Sudan 44-48; R of Littledean 48-57; Easton w Letheringham 57-61; L to Offic Dio St E from 62. *5 Dellwood Avenue, Felixstowe, Suff.*

LAVERTY, Walter Joseph Robert. b 49. Glouc Ordin Course 73. Div Hostel Dub 70. **d** 73 **p** 74 Down. C of St Donard Belf 73-77; Ballymacarrett Dio Down from 77. *111 Holywood Road, Belfast, N Ireland.* (Belf 653905)

LAVERY, Edward Robinson. Open Univ BA. Univ of Lon Dipl Th. St Aid Coll 65. **d** 67 **p** 68 Connor. C of Trin Coll Miss Belf 67-69; St Mary Magd Belf 69-71; CF (TA) from 70; I of St Phil Belf 71-74; Craigs w Dunaghy and Killagan Dio Connor from 74. *Craigs Rectory, Cullybackey, Co Antrim, N Ireland.* (Cullybackey 880248)

LAVERY, Leonard. b 06. St Aid Coll 49. **d** 50 **p** 51 Carl. C of Hensingham 50-53; R of Moresby 53-59; V of Treleigh

59-64; St John Truro 64-73; Publ Pr Dio Truro from 73. *Glan-Mor, Falmouth Road, Truro, Cornw.* (Truro 2895)

LAVILLE, Jocelyn Roger. b 30. Late Scho of Ball Coll Ox BA 53, MA 62. ALCD 64. **d** 64 **p** 65 Roch. C of St Mark Gillingham 64-69; Thorpe Edge 69-72; w Overseas Miss Fellowship in the Philippines from 72. *c/o Overseas Missionary Fellowship, Newington Green, N16 9QD.*

LAW, Brian Charles. b 36. Aston Univ in Birm BSc 67. N-W Ordin Course 78. **d** 78 **p** 79 Liv. C of SS John & Jas Litherland 78-81; V of St Ann Warrington Dio Liv from 81. *St Ann's Vicarage, Orford Avenue, Warrington, Cheshire.* (Warrington 31781)

LAW, Bryan. b 36. Univ of Leeds BA 59. BD (Lon) 76. Coll of Resurr Mirfield, 59. **d** 61 **p** 62 Derby. C of Winshill 61-64; R of St Phil Gorton 64-70; L to Offic Dio Man 70-71; Perm to Offic Dio Ox from 71; Hd Master Page Hill County Middle Sch Buckingham from 81. *7 Goran Avenue, Stony Stratford, Milton Keynes, Bucks, MK11 1HQ.* (Milton Keynes 565651)

LAW, Canon Donald Edward Boughton. b 22. Lon Coll of Div 67. **d** 69 Bp Horstead for Leic **p** 70 Leic. C of H Aps Leic 69-73; V of Cosby 73-81; Commiss Arctic from 74; RD of Guthlaxton I 75-81; R of Melton Mowbray Dio Leic from 81; Hon Can of Leic Cathl from 81. *67 Dalby Road, Melton Mowbray, Leics.* (Melton Mowbray 62417)

LAW, Frank Joseph. b 04. Lon Coll of Div 42. **d** and **p** 43 Roch. C of Milton-next-Gravesend 43-45; V of Sutton-on-the-Hill 45-46; R of Brailsford 46-51; V of Shirley 46-51; Ticehurst 51-66; RD of Etchingham 63-66; Surr from 64; PC of St Andr (Old Ch) Hove 66-70; Perm to Offic Dio Chich from 70. *Fairways, Westfield, Hastings, Sussex.* (Hastings 752868)

LAW, Geoffrey Arthur. b 04. Bps' Coll Cheshunt, 37. **d** 39 **p** 40 York. C of South Bank 39-47; St Mary Bedford 47-51; V of St Martin Middlesbrough 51-59; Whorlton 59-75; C of St Olave City and Dio York 75-80; Hon C from 80. *4 Precentor's Court, York, YO1 2EJ.* (York 30062)

LAW, Gordon James. b 19. Worc Ordin Coll 67. **d** 69 Lon **p** 70 Kens for Lon. C of Hillingdon 69-72; Brixham 72-76; R of Drewsteignton 76-79; Spreyton 76-79; Hittisleigh 76-79. Dio Ex from 76. *c/o Vicarage, Aldershot, Hants.*

LAW, Gordon Peter. b 35. Chich Th Coll 60. **d** 64 **p** 65 Chelmsf. C of St Barn w St Jas Gtr Walthamstow 64-67; H Trin Southchurch 67-68; St Andr Plaistow 68-69; C-in-c of All SS Forest Gate Dio Chelmsf 69-74; V from 74. *All Saints' Vicarage, Saints' Drive, Forest Gate, E7 0RF.* (01-472 0592)

LAW, Herbert James Wentworth. b 12. Univ of Dur BA and Dipl Th 39, MA 42. **d** 40 **p** 41 Dur. C of All SS Monkwearmouth 40-43; Actg C-in-c of Ch Ch Felling 43-46; C-in-c of All SS Conv Dist Lobley Hill 46-49; V 49-52; Stoke Ferry w Wretton 52-58; V of Whittington 52-58; R of Welney 58-69; V of Barton 69-78; RD of Barton 72-76. *37 Westlands, Comberton, Cambridge, CB3 7EH.* (Comerton 3406)

LAW, Jim. b 20. Lon Coll Div 49. **d** 52 **p** 53 Blackb. C of Altham w Clayton-le-Moors 52-55; Bispham 55-56; V of St Jas Darwen 56-61; Gt Singleton Dio Blackb from 61. *Vicarage, Great Singleton, Lancs., FY6 8LS.* (Poulton 882389)

LAW, John Francis. b 35. Bps' Coll Cheshunt 65. **d** 67 Bp McKie for Cov **p** 68 Cov. C of Styvechale 67-71; P-in-c of St Anne and All SS Cov 71-73; Team V of Cov E 73-77; P-in-c of Corley Dio Cov from 77; Fillongley Dio Cov from 77. *Fillongley Vicarage, Near Coventry.* (Fillongley 40320)

LAW, John Michael. b 43. Open Univ BA 79. Westcott Ho Cam 65. **d** 68 Ripon **p** 69 Knaresborough for Ripon. C of Chapel Allerton 68-72; Ryhope 72-73; Chap to Fulbourn and Ida Darwin Hosps Cam from 74. *1 The Maples, Fulbourn, Cambridge.* (Cam 48074)

LAW, John Richard. b 13. Univ of Leeds BA 35. Coll of Resurr Mirfield 35. **d** 37 **p** 38 Man. C of St Thos Bury 37-40; C-in-c 42-44; St Anne Tottington 40-42; V of St John Werneth Oldham 44-47; Surr 44-47; V of Ingham w Sutton 47-54; R of Carleton-Rode 54-58; Gt w L Moulton and Aslacton Dio Nor from 58. *Great Moulton Rectory, Norwich, NR15 2HH.* (Tivetshall 213)

LAW, Kenneth. b 16. St Jo Coll Dur LTh 39, BA 40, MA 43. St Aid Coll 36. **d** 40 **p** 41 Liv. C of St Matt Bootle 40-41; St Nich Blundellsands (in c of St Steph Hightown) 41-43; Keighley (in c of St Mark Utley) 43-47; V of Allerton Yorks 47-50; St Cath Horwich 50-54; Ossett 54-81; Surr 55-81; CF (TA-R of O) 48-64; CF (TA) 64-81. *Heathdene, Cromwell Place, Ossett, W Yorks.* (Ossett 262740)

LAW, Peter Leslie. b 25. Bede Coll Dur BA 48, Dipl in Educn 49. Qu Coll Birm 53. **d** 55 **p** 56 S'wark. C of All SS Tooting Graveney 55-57; Frome Selwood 57-59; V of St Mary-le-Park Battersea 59-65; R of Brampton Ash w Dingley 65-69; Chap St Luke C of E Comprehensive Sch Southsea 69-79; Hon Chap Portsm Cathl 69-79; V of Eastney Dio Portsm from 79. *Vicarage, Cousins Grove, Southsea, Hants.* (Portsmouth 731316)

LAW, Richard Lindsey. b 34. Univ Coll Ox BA 58, MA 62. Cudd Coll 58. **d** 60 **p** 61 St Alb. C of Leighton Buzzard 60-63; R of Chaguanas Trinid 63-67; V of Stottesdon 67-72; C-in-c of Farlow 67-72; Chap Framlingham Coll from 72. *c/o Framlingham College, Woodbridge, Suffolk.*

LAW, Robert Frederick. b 43. St Aid Coll 67. **d** 69 **p** 70 St Alb. C of Bengeo 69-72; Sandy 72-76; C-in-c of St Ippolyts 76-82; Hosp Chap Jersey from 81. *c/o General Hospital, St Helier, Jersey, CI.*

LAW, Robert James Kelway. b 31. Univ of Lon MB BS 55. Ridley Hall, Cam 62. **d** 64 **p** 65 Roch. C of Barnehurst 64-66; Edgware (in c of St Pet) 66-72; V of Halwell w Moreleigh Dio Ex from 72; P-in-c of Woodleigh w Loddiswell Dio Ex 77-78; R from 78. *Halwell Vicarage, Totnes, Devon.* (Blackawton 257)

LAW, William Charles. b 37. St Jo Coll Auckld LTh 77. **d** 77 Bp Spence for Auckld **p** 78 Auckld. C of Whangarei 77-80; V of Bay of Is Dio Auckld from 80. *Vicarage, Kerikeri, Bay of Islands, NZ.*

LAWAL, Alexander Babatunde. Im Coll Ibad 72. **d** 75 **p** 76 Ondo. P Dio Ondo. *Box 55, Ondo, Nigeria.*

LAWES, Arthur Frank. b 14. Roch Th Coll 61. **d** 63 **p** 64 Bradf. C of Barnoldswick w Bracewell 63-65; R of Lockington w Lund 65-71; Burythorpe, Acklam and Leavening w Westow 71-79. *16 Uppercroft, Haxby, York, YO3 8GD.* (York 763290)

LAWES, David Hyland. b 22. Univ of Dur BA 42, MA 48, Dipl in Th 48. **d** 48 **p** 49 Dur. C of Stranton 48-51; V of Yealand Conyers 51-57; PC of St Aid S Shields 57-68; V 68-80; Sacriston Dio Dur from 80. *Vicarage, Sacriston, Durham, DH7 6AD.* (Durham 711661)

LAWES, Geoffrey Hyland. b 37. St Jo Coll Dur BA 58, Dipl Th 62. Squire Scho Hertf Coll Ox BA (2nd cl Th) 60, MA 64. Univ of Newc T MEducn 79. Cranmer Hall Dur 61. **d** 63 Jarrow for Dur **p** 64 Dur. C of St Mark Millfield Bp Wearmouth 63-66; Ch Ch Jarrow Grange Dio Dur from 66; Asst Master Jarrow Croft Sch 68-71; Boldon Comprehensive Sch from 71. *7 Ashleigh Gardens, Cleadon, Sunderland, SR6 7QA.* (Boldon 367693)

LAWES, Preb Gordon. Ripon Hall, Ox. **d** 51 Bp Willis for Truro **p** 52 Truro. C of K Chas Mart Falmouth 51-54; R of Lanivet 54-80; V of Lanhydrock 59-80; Preb of Marneys in Preb Ch of St Endellion from 59. *c/o Lanivet Rectory, Bodmin, Cornw.* (Lanivet 202)

LAWIN, Lawrence. Trin Th Coll Sing 66. **d** 68 Sabah. d Dio Sabah. *Holy Cross Mission, Sapi, c/o SAIM Rep Sandakan, Sabah, Malaysia.* (3457)

LAWIRI, Ezera. Mori Div Sch. **d** 47 Sudan **p** 50 Bp Allison for Sudan. Miss Dio Sudan 47-76; Vice-Prin Bp Gwynne Coll Mundri Dio Sudan 57-64; Prin from 64; Hon Can of Sudan 60-76; Bp's Commiss Dio Rumbek from 76. *c/o Bishop Gwynne College, Mundri, Equatoria, Sudan.*

LAW LAY, d 77 **p** 79 Akyab. P Dio Akyab. *St Luke's Church, Pung Daw, Burma.*

LAWLER, Canon Frank Roberts. McGill Univ BA 46. Montr Dioc Th Coll LTh 49. **d** 49 **p** 50 Montr. C of l'Eglise du Redempteur Montr 49-52; I of Quyon w Eardley and P-in-c of Bristol Corners and Mines 52-55; C of St John Ott 55-57; R of St Marg Ott 57-72; Hawkesbury Dio Ott from 72; Can of Ott from 72. *433 McGill Street, Hawkesbury, Ont., Canada.* (1-613-632-2329)

LAWLESS, Norman Henry. Moore Th Coll. **d** and **p** 57 Syd. C of Wollongong 57-59; RAAF from 59; Perm to Offic Dio Newc from 72. *RAAF Base, Williamtown, NSW, Australia 2314.*

LAWLEY, John Bryan. Trin Coll Melb BCom 59. ACT ThL (2nd cl) 60. **d** 61 **p** 62 Melb. C of H Trin Cathl Wang 61-62; Niddrie 62-64; Melb Dioc Task Force 64-65; Perm to Offic Dio Cant 65-66; V of Altona 66-72; Perm to Offic Dio Melb 73-80. *1 Patterson Street, Ringwood East, Vic, Australia 3135.* (870-5569)

LAWLEY, Peter Gerald Fitch. b 52. Chich Th Coll 77. **d** 80 **p** 81 Pet. C of St Jo Bapt City and Dio Pet from 80. *14 Holdich Street, Peterborough, PE3 6DH.* (0733 43507)

LAWN, Canon Geoffrey. b 27. Jes Coll Cam BA 48, MA 52. BD (2nd cl) Lon 56. Ripon Hall, Ox 56. **d** 57 **p** 58 York. C of Selby Abbey 57-61; V of Huntington York 61-70; Ecumen Adv to Abp of York 69-74; R of Newton Kyme 70-74; M Gen Syn York 71-75; V of Doncaster Dio Sheff from 74; Surr from 74; Hon Can of Sheff from 75. *60 Thorne Road, Doncaster, S Yorks, DN1 2JW.* (Doncaster 23748)

LAWRANCE, David. b 26. Univ of Man BA 51, BD 66. St Cathl S Ox BA (3rd cl Th) 53, MA 57. Wycl Hall, Ox 51. **d** 53 **p** 54 Man. C of St Mary Oldham 53-55; Chap RAF 55-58; P-in-c of Jer and E Miss Amman 58-61; V of St Thos Moorside 61-73; Chap Strinesdale Hosp 61-73; Chap Sheff Industr

Miss from 73. *21 Clarence Drive, Harrogate, N Yorks, HG1 2QE.* (0423 504050)

✠ **LAWRENCE, Right Rev Caleb James.** K Coll NS BA 62, BST 64, Hon DD 80. **d** 63 NS **p** 65 Arctic. Miss Gt Whale River Dio Arctic from 65; Hon Can of St Jude's Cathl Frobisher Bay 74-75; Archd of Arctic Queb 75-80; Cons Bp Coadj of Moos in St Matt Cathl Timmins 6 Jan 80 by Abp of Tor; Bps of Moos, Hur, Alg, Ont, Ott, Niag and The Arctic; Bps Suffr of Tor, Hur and The Arctic; Apptd Bp of Moos 80. *Bishopstope, Box 830, Schumacher, Ont, Canada.* (705-264 0641)

LAWRENCE, Cecil Harold. d 48 **p** 54 Mysore (S India). [f in Ch of S India] L to Offic Dio Auckld 59-70. *Selwyn Village, Target Street, Point Chevalier, Auckland, NZ.*

LAWRENCE, Charles Anthony Edwin. b 53. AKC 75. St Aug Coll Cant 75. **d** 76 **p** 77 S'wark. C of St Mark Mitcham Dio S'wark from 76. *7 Graham Road, Mitcham, Surrey, CR4 2HB.*

LAWRENCE, Charles William. b 14. Lon Coll Div 46. **d** 48 Lon **p** 49 Stepney for Lon. C of St Jas Muswell Hill 48-52; C-in-c of St Mark Colney Heath 52-53; Conv Distr of St Mich AA Boreham Wood 53-57; Min 57-58; V of Kimpton 58-61; Chap Edge Grove Sch Aldenham 58-65; V of St Osw Croxley Green 61-65; Newland w Redbrook 65-73; Ch Ch Glouc 73-79; Newland Lect 65-73; Chap Glos R Hosp from 73. *2 Prospect Terrace, St Swithuns Road, Hempstead, Gloucester, GL2 6LJ.* (Glouc 415850)

LAWRENCE, David John. b 08. Univ of Liv BA 28. ARCO 51. ARCM 52. Ridley Hall Cam 28. **d** 31 **p** 32 Birm. C of St Francis Bournville 31-33; V of St Luke Kingstanding 33-42; Eaton Bray 42-55; PC of Shefford 55-66; R of Campton 55-66; RD of Shefford 59-66; R of Wormley 66-75; Perm to Offic Dio Aber from 75. *The Old Schoolhouse, Blairmaud, Banff, AB4 2EJ.*

LAWRENCE, Eric George. b 37. St Paul Coll Maur 66. **d** 71 **p** 72 Maur. C of St Jas Cathl Port Louis 71-74; Quatre Bornes Dio Maur from 74. *443 Guy Rozemont Street, Rose-Hill, Mauritius.*

LAWRENCE, Frank John. b 48. Univ of Waikato BSocSc 75. Ridley Coll Melb BTh 80. **d** 81 Auckld. C of Takapuna Dio Auckld from 81. *3/18 Westwell Road, Belmont, Auckland 9, NZ.*

LAWRENCE, George Leslie. b 11. Bp Wilson Coll IM 38. **d** 41 **p** 42 Dur. C of St Hilda Hartlepool 41-46; Darlington (in c of Blackwell) 46-48; R of Jarrow Grange 48-53; CF (TA) 49-64; V of Bradley 53-60; Newsome 60-69; R of Crofton 69-78. *702 Doncaster Road, Crofton, WF4 1PX.* (Crofton 862174)

LAWRENCE, Ven Graeme Russell. St Jo Coll Morpeth 63. ACT ThL 65. **d** 65 C & Goulb for River **p** 66 River. C of Griffith 65-69; P-in-c of Berrigan-Mulwala 70-73; R 73-75; Griffith Dio River from 75; Archd of River from 78; Admin and Commiss Dio River from 78. *Box 31, Griffith, NSW, Australia 2680.* (069-62 3204)

LAWRENCE, Canon Harold. Univ Coll Dur LTh 35, BA 36. St Aug Coll Cant 31. **d** 36 **p** 37 Lon. C of Gt Stanmore 36-38; Miss Solomon Is 39; R of Rabaul 39-41; Chap (AIF) 41-46; C of Bramley 46-48; V of St Thos Durban 48-61 Archd of Durban 61-74; R of St Paul Durban 61-74; Can of Natal 61; Hon Can from 74; R of Richmond w Byrne 74-77; Perm to Offic Dio Natal from 77. *Box 266, Richmond, Natal, S Africa.*

LAWRENCE, Henry James. d 60 Rockptn. Hon C of St Luke Wandal City and Dio Rockptn from 61. *29 McKelliget Street, Wandal, Rockhampton, Queensland, Australia.* (079-2 1546)

LAWRENCE, John Graham Clive. b 47. AIB 74. Trin Coll Bris Dipl Th 78. **d** 78 **p** 79 Roch. C of St Phil & St Jas Chatham Dio Roch from 78. *3a Kit Hill Avenue, Walderslade, Chatham, Kent, ME5 9ET.*

LAWRENCE, John Shaw. b 27. Qu Coll Birm 81. **d** 81 Birm (NSM). C of St Martin City and Dio Birm from 81. *1 Sycamore Road, Bournville, Birmingham, B30 2AA.*

LAWRENCE, Leonard Roy. b 31. Keble Coll Ox BA 56, MA 59. Westcott Ho Cam 56. **d** 58 **p** 59 Ches. C of St Geo Stockport 58-62; V of Thelwall 62-68; Hyde 68-75; Prenton Dio Ches from 75. *1 Reservoir Road, Birkenhead, L42 8LJ.* (051-608 1808)

LAWRENCE, Lionel Frank. b 03. Clifton Th Coll 34. **d** 36 **p** 37 Lon. C of St Jude Mildmay Pk 36-42; St Jas Teignmouth 42-45; PC of Sourton 45-52; R of Reedham 52-72. *Northfield, North Walsham Road, Bacton, Norwich, NR12 0LN.* (06926-50470)

LAWRENCE, Norman. b 45. Univ of Lon BEducn 75. SOC 77. **d** 80 **p** 81 Kens for Lon. C of H Trin Hounslow Dio Lon from 80; Asst Master Lampton Comprehensive Sch Hounslow from 80. *89 Bulstrode Avenue, Hounslow, TW3 3AE.*

LAWRENCE, Patrick Henry Andrew. b 51. TCD BA 81. Ch of Ireland Th Coll 76. **d** 81 Derry. C of Cathl Ch of Derry from 81. *4 St Columb's Court, Bishop Street, Derry, N Ireland.*

LAWRENCE, Peter Anthony. b 36. Lich Th Coll 67. **d** 69 **p** 70 Leic. C of Oadby 69-74; C-in-c of N Marston w Granborough 74-76; P Missr 76-81; C-in-c of Hardwicke 74-76; P Missr 76-81; Quainton 76-81; Oving w Pitchcott 76-81; Team R of Schorne Dio Ox from 81. *Vicarage, Church Street, North Marston, Buckingham, MK18 3PH.* (N Marston 298)

LAWRENCE, Peter Halliday. b 47. Univ of Nottm BTh 76. St Jo Coll Nottm 72. **d** 76 **p** 77 Birm. C of St Luke Birm 76-79; V of Ch Ch Ward End Dio Birm from 79. *Vicarage, Burney Lane, Birmingham, B8 2AS.* (021-783 7455)

LAWRENCE, Philip Sydney. Univ of Melb BA 30, MA 33. Ridley Coll Melb ACT ThL 31, Th Scho 54. **d** 31 **p** 32 Perth. C of W Perth 32-33; Asst Master Gr Sch Guildf 33; C of St Mary W Perth 33-35; R of Swan 35-40; St Phil Cottesloe 40-48; Commiss Centr Tang 46-48; Min of Clayton and Springvale 48-55; R of Maylands 55-73; Perm to Offic Dio Perth from 73. *42 Grand Promenade, Bayswater, W Australia 6053.* (71 6652)

LAWRENCE, Thomas Ian. St Jo Coll Morpeth 36. ACT ThL 38. **d** 38 **p** 39 Graft. C of Kempsey 38-39; Casino 39-41 and 46-48; V of U Maclesay 41-44; Copmanhurst 44-45; Chap AIF 45-46; V of Grevillia 48-50; C of Port Macquarie 52-54; R of Dorrigo 54-55; Dunoon 55-60; Chap at Edward River Miss 60-62; Lockhart River Miss 62-64; Palm I 64-66; R of Rockley 66-67; C of W Wyalong 67; Perm to Offic Dio Syd from 68; Dio Newc from 76. *7/36 Sproule Street, Lakemba, NSW, Australia 2195.*

LAWRENCE, Thomas Montagu. b 09. Hertf Coll Ox BA 31, MA 35. Ely Th Coll 33. **d** 34 **p** 35 Ely. C of H Trin w St Mary Ely 34-36; Thrumpton 36-38; Chap RAF Uxbridge 38-43; V of Ramsgill 43-47; Burton Leonard 47-55; C-in-c of Bp Monkton 49-52; V 52-55; Dir of Music Chipping Norton Gr Sch 56-59; Perm to Offic Dio Ox from 56; Asst Master Southam High Sch 60-64; Sibford Sch 64-81. *Ginger Bread Cottage, Hook Norton, Banbury, Oxon.* (Hook Norton 737321)

LAWRENCE, Timothy Hervey. b 25. Ripon Hall, Ox 58. **d** 60 **p** 61 St E. C of All SS Newmarket 60-62; V of Kentford w Higham Green Dio St E from 62; P-in-c of Herringswell Dio St E from 76. *Higham Vicarage, Bury St Edmunds, Suff.* (Bury St Edmunds 810308)

LAWRENSON, James Percival. b 12. Kelham Th Coll 30. **d** 36 **p** 37 Man. C of St Jo Bapt Atherton 36-39; Chap Toc H E Yorks Area 39-40; C of Portland 40-42; Actg Chap HM Borstal Inst Portland 40-42; Chap 42-45; Chap HM Borstal Inst Roch 45-50; Asst Sec Lon Police Court Miss 50-56; Hon C of St Anne Wandsworth 50-52; Publ Pr Dio S'wark 52-56; Chap Berkhamsted Sch 56-78; Perm to Offic Dio St Alb from 78. *Downside, Torrington Road, Berkhamsted, Herts.* (Berkhamsted 5999)

LAWRENSON, Michael. b 35. Univ of Leeds BA 60. Coll of Resurr Mirfield 60. **d** and **p** 74 St Andr. C of Glenrothes Fife Dio St Andr from 74. *5 Liquorstane, Falkland, Fife, KY7 7DQ.*

LAWRENSON, Ronald David. b 41. Div Hostel Dub 68. **d** 71 **p** 72 Down. C of Seapatrick 71-78; Min Can & Res Pr of Down Cathl 78-79; V Cho of St Anne's Cathl Belf from 79. *St Anne's Cathedral, Donegall Street, Belfast, BT1 2HB.*

LAWRIE, Paul Edward. b 12. Univ of Freiburg LLD 35. St Cath S Ox BA 48, MA 53. Wycl Hall Ox 46. **d** 48 **p** 49 Sheff. C of St Mary Walkley 48-51; Thrybergh 51-54; V of Drax 54-64; R of Todwick 64-78; Chap Rotherham Gen Hosp from 78. *51 Olive Close, Sheffield, Yorks, S31 0RR.* (Sheff 874864)

LAWRIE, Peter Sinclair. b 39. Clifton Th Coll 62. **d** 65 **p** 66 Derby. C of St Chad Derby 65-68; St Philemon Toxteth Pk (in c of St Gabr) 68-71; V of Ramsey St Mary w Pondsbridge 71-81; Whitwick Dio Leic from 81. *Whitwick Vicarage, North Street, Leicester, LE6 4EB.* (0530-36904)

LAWRY, Peter Raymond. d 80 **p** 81 Melb. C of St Pet Mornington Dio Melb from 80. *3 Queen Street, Mornington, Vic, Australia 3831.*

LAWRY, Samuel John Lockhart. b 11. CCC Cam BA 33, MA 38. Wells Th Coll 34. **d** 35 **p** 36 Pet. C of Abington 35-40; Chap RNVR 40-47; C of St Mary Portsea 47-48; V of St Cuthb Copnor 48-57; E Meon 57-68; Perm to Offic Dio Portsm from 68. *Broadlands House, Sheet, Petersfield, Hants, GU31 4BA.* (Petersfield 2134)

LAWS, Edwin Kingsley. b 06. MVO 53. Bps' Coll Cheshunt 56. **d** 57 **p** 58 Sarum. C of Shaftesbury 57-60; V of Winterbourne Whitchurch w Winterbourne Clenston (w Milton Abbas from 72) 60-74; RD of Milton 66-73; Custos St John's Hosp Heytesbury 74-79. *Tree Tops, East Horrington, Wells, Somt, BA5 3DP.*

LAWS, George Gordon. St Jo Th Coll Morpeth. **d** 46 **p** 47

Goulb. C of Koorawatha 46; P-in-c 47-49; R of Kameruka 49-54; Tarcutta 54-59; C of Yass 59-61; L to Offic Dio C & Goulb from 61. *Deakin, ACT, Australia.*

LAWS, Howard Stracey. b 13. Worc Ordin Coll. **d** 67 **p** 68 Glouc. C of Wotton or Longlevens 67-70; R of Aston-Ingram (w The Lea from 75) 70-78; C-in-c of Lea 70-78. *The Coachmans House, The Lea, Ross-on-Wye, Herefs, HR9 7JY.*

LAWSON, Arthur Charles. b 41. Univ of Tor BA 64, MEducn 73. Trin Coll Tor MDiv 80. **d** 80 Bp Read for Tor **p** 81 Bp A.D.Brown for Tor. C of H Trin Thornhill Dio Tor from 80. *Box 185, Thornhill, Ont, Canada, L3T 3N3.*

LAWSON, Cecil Vaughan. b 1895. Univ of Leeds, BA 20. Coll of Resurr Mirfield, 13. **d** 24 Nassau **p** 25 Truro. C of St Matt Nass 24-25; St Agnes 25-31; Lelant (in c of Carbis Bay) 31-33; V of Poundstock 33-44; RD of Stratton 40-44; V of St Jas Watford 44-47; R of Tempsford 47-50; St Jas Cupar Fife 50-52; St Tudy 52-59; St Buryan 59-63; L to Offic Dio Truro from 63. *Thayngeld, Kingweston Road, Charlton Mackrell, Somerton, Somt, TA11 6AH.*

LAWSON, Christopher Michael. b 32. Late Scho of New Coll Ox 1st cl Cl Mods 54, BA (1st cl Lit Hum) 56, MA 59, BLitt 62. Wells Th Coll 58. **d** 60 **p** 61 Lich. C of Cannock 60-64; Chap Qu Coll Cam 64-68; Tutor Ridley Hall Cam 68-69; C of St Aug of Hippo Ipswich 69-72; R of Glemsford Dio St E from 72. *Glemsford Rectory, Sudbury, Suffolk, CO10 7RF.* (Glemsford 280361)

LAWSON, Preb Clifford John. b 21. St Cath S Ox BA 45, MA 47. Qu Coll Birm 45. **d** 47 Lich **p** 48 Stafford for Lich. C of Gt Barr 47-50; Hednesford 50-52; V of St Mich Shrewsbury 52-57; Eccleshall 57-71; Chap HM Pris Drake Hall 58-71; Surr from 62; RD of Eccleshall 65-71; Preb of Lich Cathl from 70; R and RD of Stafford 72-77; C-in-c of St Chad Stafford 72-74; R of Rhydycroesau Dio Lich from 77; Selattyn Dio Lich from 77; RD of Oswestry from 77. *Selattyn Rectory, Oswestry, Salop, SY10 7DH.* (Oswestry 59755)

LAWSON, David McKenzie. b 47. Univ of Glas MA 69. Univ of Edin BD 76. Edin Th Coll 73. **d** 76 **p** 77 Glas. C of St Mary's Cathl 76-82; V of All SS Keighley Dio Bradf from 82. *All Saints' Vicarage, View Road, Keighley, W Yorks, BD20 6JU.* (Keighley 607002)

LAWSON, Henry Charles Naylor. b 07. Lich Th Coll 31. **d** 36 **p** 37 Liv. C of Upholland 36-38; St Agnes Toxteth Pk 38-40; C-in-c of Hollinfare 40-42; C of West Derby 42-43; C-in-c of St Jo Bapt New Springs 43-44; H Trin Wavertree 45-47; V of Orleton 47-51; R of Ninfield 51-64; V of Hooe Sussex 52-64; RD of Battle and Bexhill 59-64; V of Cuckfield 64-67; R of Elsted w Didling and Treyford 67-71. *2 The Lawn, Budleigh Salterton, Devon.*

LAWSON, Canon John Lawrence. b 11. Univ Coll Dur BA and Thorp Scho 33, Dipl in Th (w distinc) 34, MA 36. Wycl Hall Ox 35. **d** 35 **p** 36 Ripon. C of St Geo Leeds 35-38; Doncaster 38-43; L to Offic Dio Heref 43-48; Min Can Heref 43-47; Chap and Asst Master Heref Cathl Sch 44-47; Min Can and Prec of Ely Cathl and Hd Master of Cathl Choir Sch 47-54; PC of Chettisham 47-54; Sacr Ely Cathl 50-54; Sacr Cant Cathl 54-60; Min Can and Prec 54-61; V of Chilham 61-73; Hon Can of Cant 61-79; Can (Emer) from 79. *13 Crawford Gardens, Cliftonville, Margate, Kent, CT9 2PU.* (Thanet 28758)

LAWSON, Michael. b 47. Waterloo Lutheran Univ BA 70. Em & St Chad's Coll Sktn 70. **d** 73 **p** 74 Bran. I of Boissevain 73-76; C of Drypool York 76-79; I of Birtle Dio Bran from 79. *Birtle, Manit, Canada, R0M 0C0.*

LAWSON, Michael Charles. b 52. Univ of Sussex BA 75. Trin Coll Bris 75. **d** 78 **p** 79 Horsham for Chich. C of Horsham 78-81; Dir of Pastoring All S Langham Place w St Pet and St Jo Evang St Marylebone Dio Lon from 81. *25 Fitzroy Street, W1P 5AF.*

LAWSON-TANCRED, Christopher. b 24. Trin Coll Cam BA 49, MA 65. Chich Th Coll 63. **d** 65 **p** 66 Chich. C of Uckfield 65-70; R of Wrington w Redhill (w Butcombe from 73) 70-79; Perm to Offic Dio Chich from 80. *Luxford, Luxford Road, Crowborough, TN6 2PR.* (Crowborough 2073)

LAWTON, Donald John William. b 48. Huron Coll Lon Ont BMin 77. **d** 77 **p** 78 Yukon. I of Elsa Mayo 77-80; C of Ch Ch Cathl Whitehorse Dio Yukon from 80. *3 Laird Road, Whitehorse, Yukon, Canada.*

LAWTON, George. b 10. Univ of Lon Dipl Th 35. MA (Liv) 58. BD (Nottm) 64, PhD (Nottm) 70. Qu Coll Birm 48. **d** 49 Bp Sara for Heref **p** 50 Heref. C of Madeley 49-51; V of Gayton w Fradswell 51-56; All SS Princes Pk Toxt Pk 56-59; R of Checkley 59-77; Perm to Offic Dio Ex from 77. *7 Taw View Terrace, Bishops Tawton, Barnstaple, EX32 0AW.*

LAWTON, Jack Desmond. b 15. Glouc Sch for Min 78. **d** 79 Tewesbury for Glouc **p** 79 Glouc. C of Didbrook w Stanway & Hailes Dio Glouc from 79. *St Leonards Close, Stanway Road, Toddington, Nr Cheltenham, Glos GL54 5DT.*

LAWTON, John Arthur. b 13. Fitzw Ho Cam BA 35, MA 40. Cudd Coll 35. **d** 37 **p** 38 Liv. C of St Dunstan Edge Hill 37-40; C-in-c of St Anne's Conv Distr Wigan 40-47; V of St Anne Wigan 47-56; St Luke Southport 56-60; Kirby 60-69; Hon Can of Liv from 63; Proc Conv Liv 64-75; R of Winwick Dio Liv from 69; Archd of Warrington 70-81. *Rectory, Golborne Road, Winwick, Warrington, Chesh, WA2 8SZ.* (Warrington 32760)

LAWTON, Canon John Stewart. b 19. Keble Coll Ox BA (2nd cl Th) 40, MA and BD 44, DPhil 50. Univ of Cam MA (by incorp) 48. St Steph Ho Ox 40. **d** 42 **p** 43 Carl. C of Addingham 42-44; Actg C of Ch Ch Ches 45-46; Chap Selw Coll Cam 46-49; Fell 48-49; V of Padiham w Higham 49-53; Warton 53-62; Exam Chap to Bp of Blackb 50-71; Warden and Libr St Deiniol's Libr Hawarden 62-73; Exam Chap to Abp of Wales from 72; V of L Leigh and of Nether Whitley 73-75; Hon Can 74-75; Can Res from 75; Dir of Ministry from 74. *5 Abbey Street, Chester, CH1 2JF.* (Chester 25854)

LAWTON, Thomas Robert. St Jo Coll Morpeth. **d** 49 **p** 51 Graft. C of Kempsey 49-52; Ch Ch Cathl Graft 52-53; Casino 53-54; V of Woodenbong 54-59; Ulmarra 59-65; Coraki 65-70. *42 Edgar Street, Auburn, NSW 2144, Australia.*

LAWTON, William James. BD Lon 60. ACT ThL 57, Th Scho 62. Moore Th Coll Syd. **d** 58 Syd **p** 58 Bp Hilliard for Syd. C of Eastwood 58-59; Tutor and Lect Moore Th Coll Syd 59-64; C of Woollahra 60-64; R of Dural 64-67; Mullewa 67-69; Gladesville 69-76; Dean of Students Moore Th Coll and L to Offic Dio Syd from 76. *42 Carillon Avenue, Newtown, NSW, Australia 2042.* (519-5031)

LAWTON, Willis Hill. b 34. Univ of W Ont BA 59. Univ of Sask MD 72. Hur Coll LTh 63. **d** 63 Hur **p** 64 Sktn. I of Wilkie 64-67; L to Offic Dio Sktn 68-72; Dio Sask 72-76; Dio Athab from 76. *Box 1168, High Level, Alta, T0H 1Z0, Canada.*

LAXTON, Joseph Henry. b 13. Univ of Leeds, BA (2nd cl Hist) 36. Coll of Resurr Mirfield, 36. **d** 38 **p** 39 York. C of All SS Middlesbrough 38-42; Helmsley 42-44; Chap RNVR 44-47; V of Dairycoates Hull 47-52; Chap RN 52-57; Chap Nautical Coll Pangbourne 57-71; R of Tidmarsh w Sulham 71-78. *27 Charlton Rise, Sheet Road, Ludlow, Salop.*

LAY, Brian Robert. b 37. Chich Th Coll 60. **d** 63 **p** 64 Wakef. C of Battyeford 63-66; All SS Belhus Pk 66-73; P-in-c of St Jo Evang Sutton-on-Plym Dio Ex 73-80; V from 80. *St John's Vicarage, Alma Street, Cattedown, Plymouth, Devon, PL4 0NL.* (Plymouth 664191)

LAYBOURN, Christopher John MacKenzie. b 48. Ripon Hall Ox 73. **d** 75 **p** 76 St Alb. C of Rickmansworth Dio St Alb from 75. *c/o Westminster College, Oxford.*

LAYNE, Winston Frederick. b 43. Univ of WI BA (Th) 75. Codr Coll Barb 71. **d** and **p** 75 Barb. P-in-c of St Silas w St Alb I and Dio Barb from 75. *St Alban's Rectory, Lower Carlton, St James, Barbados, WI.*

LAYTON, Desmond. b 35. Univ of Leeds, BA (2nd cl Th) 60. BD (Lon) 63. Qu Coll Birm 62. **d** 63 **p** 64 Wakef. C of Dewsbury Moor 63-66; V of St Andr Purlwell Batley 66-68; Asst Master St Ivo Sch St Ives Hunts 68-71; Matthew Murray High Sch Leeds from 71. *Matthew Murray High School, Brown Lane, Leeds 11.*

LAYZELL, George Douglas. b 51. York Univ Tor BA 75. Hur Coll Lon Ont MDiv 78. **d** 80 Hur **p** 81 Bp Robinson for Hur. C of Bp Cronyn Mem Ch Lon Dio Hur from 80. *21 Palace Street, London, Ont, Canada, N6B 3A6.*

LAZARUS, Watson James. **d** 75 Ja (APM). C of St Mich Kingston 75-79; L to Offic Dio Calg from 80. *8037 25th Street SE, Calgary, Alta, Canada.* (279-6312)

LAZONBY, Canon Alan Frederick. b 19. Late Scho of St Jo Coll Dur BA 40, Dipl Th 41, MA 43. TD 64. **d** 42 **p** 43 Dur. C of St Helen Auckl (in c of Evenwood 44-46) 42-46; Horden 46-50; CF (TA) 49-63; SCF (TA) 63-67; CF (TAVR) 67-77; PC of Witton Pk 50-57; Chap to Bp of Dur 53-57; R of Haughton-le-Skerne Dio Dur from 57; Hon Chap to Bp of Dur 57-67; RD of Darlington 74-78; Hon Can of Dur Cathl from 75. *Haughton-le-Skerne Rectory, Darlington, Co Durham, DL1 2DD.* (Darlington 68142)

LEA, Arthur Blackwall. b 06. Em Coll Sktn 41. **d** 41 **p** 42 Sask. I of Fort Pitt 41-45; Meadow Lake 45-48; R of St Gabr Calgary w Crossfield-Balzac 48-52; C of Milton Ernest (Col Cl Act) 52-53; R of Anstey 53-57; V of Brent Pelham w Meesden 53-57; R of Miserden w Edgeworth 57-71; P-in-c of Breamore 71-81. *1 Hollows Close, Salisbury, Wilts.*

LEA, Canon John Maurice. b 04. MRCS 37. LRCP 37. LMSSA 36. **d** 55 **p** 56 U Nile. Med Supt Kumi Leprosy Centre 54-67; Hon Can of Soroti 67-69; P at Ch Ch Gulu N Ugan 67-71; Hon Can of N Ugan 69-71; Can (Emer) from 71; Perm to Offic Dio Truro from 72. *Zimmerman's Cottage, Newlyn, Penzance, TR18 5QH.* (Penzance 3764)

LEA, Montague Brian. b 34. St Jo Coll Cam BA 55. BD (Lon) 71. St Jo Coll Nottm 68. **d** 71 **p** 72 Willesden for Lon. C of Em, Northwood 71-74; CCCS Chap at Barcelona 74-79;

V of Bp Hannington Mem Ch w H Cross Hove Dio Chich from 79. *82 Holmes Avenue, Hove, Sussex, BN3 7LD.* (Brighton 732821)

LEA, Norman. b 42. St D Coll Lamp BA 67. Coll of Resurr Mirfield, 66. **d** 68 **p** 69 Swan B. C of Newton St Pet 68-71; Oystermouth 71-73; Min Can of Brecon Cathl from 73; C of St Mary Brecon w Battle 73-74; V of Croesyceiliog in R Benef of Cwmbran 74-77; Talgarth Dio Swan B from 77. *Vicarage, Talgarth, Brecon, Powys.* (Talgarth 249)

LEA, Richard John Rutland. b 40. Trin Hall Cam 3rd cl Mod Lang Trip pt i 61, BA (2nd cl Engl Trip pt i) 63, MA 67. Westcott Ho Cam 63. **d** 65 **p** 66 Roch. C of Edenbridge 65-68; Hayes Kent 68-71; V of Larkfield Dio Roch from 71; P-in-c of Leybourne Dio Roch from 76; RD of Malling from 79. *Larkfield Vicarage, Maidstone, Kent.* (W Malling 843349)

LEACH, Gerald. b 27. **d** 73 **p** 74 Mon (APM). L to Offic Dio Mon from 73. *1 Egremont Road, Cardiff, CF2 5LP.*

LEACH, John. b 52. AKC and BD 79. St Jo Coll Dur 79. **d** 81 Nor. C of N Walsham Dio Nor from 81. *52 Norwich Road, North Walsham, Norfolk, NR28 0DX.* (0692 402084)

LEACH, Joseph. b 04. Late Scho of St Jo Coll Dur, BA 32, MA 33. **d** 32 **p** 33 Bradf. C of St Aug Bradf 32-35; CMS Miss Yungchow 35-38; Kweilin 38-43; C of Ch Ch Mt Pellon 45; CMS Miss Kweilin 45-48; V of Firbank w Howgill 48-51; St Andr Bradf 51-59 Allerton 59-64; Oakenshaw w Woodlands 64-70. *10 Hopton Avenue, Burnham Avenue, Bierley, Bradford, W Yorks, BD4 6JL.*

LEACH, Canon Percy Murthwaite. b 04. Univ of Dur LTh 38. St Aug Coll Cant 25. **d** 29 **p** 30 Lon. C of St Matt Ponders End 29-32; SPG Miss Ranchi 32-37; C of St Mich AA Plumstead 40-46; CF (EC) 40-46; Hon CF 46; R of Castle Rising w Roydon 46-53; V of St Andr Peckham (w All SS from 56) 53-76; C-in-c of All SS N Peckham 55-56; Hon Can of S'wark Cathl from 76; Can (Emer) from 76. *37 Lauderdale Drive, Petersham, Richmond, Surrey, TW10 7BB.* (01-948 3952)

LEACH, Stephen Lance. b 42. St Steph Ho Ox 66. **d** 69 **p** 70 Pet. C of Higham Ferrers w Chelveston 69-72; Team V of Ilfracombe 72-74; V of Goodleigh 74-77; St Mary Magd Barnstaple 74-77; P-in-c of St Pet w H Trin Barnstaple 76-77; Team R of Barnstaple w Goodleigh (and Landkey from 79) Dio Ex from 77; P-in-c of Landkey 77-79. *Rectory, Goodleigh, Barnstaple, Devon.* (Barnstaple 72268)

LEACH, Stephen Windsor. b 47. St Chad's Coll Dur BSc 70. Linacre Coll Ox BA 72; MA 76. Ripon Hall Ox 70. **d** 73 **p** 74 Man. C of Swinton 73-76; St Chad Limeside Oldham 77-79; V of Shaw Dio Man from 79. *Vicarage, Church Road, Shaw, Oldham, Lancs, OL2 7AT.* (Shaw 847369)

LEACH, Thomas Edward. b 16. Univ of Bris BA 38. Sarum Th Coll 37. **d** 39 **p** 40 Southw. C of St Mark Mansfield 39-47; St Anne Brislington 47-49; St Matt Westmr 49-53; V of Good Shepherd Furnham Chard Dio B & W from 53. *Furnham Vicarage, Chard, Somt.* (Chard 3167)

LEACH, Timothy Edmund. b 41. Univ of Dur BA 63. Ridley Hall, Cam 63. **d** 65 **p** 66 Sheff. C of Ecclesfield 65-68; Stocksbridge 68-71; P-in-c of W Bessacarr Conv Distr Doncaster 71-80; V of Goole Dio Sheff from 80. *Vicarage, Goole, N Humb, DN14 6AR.* (Goole 4259)

LEACH, William Howard. b 07. Em Coll Cam BA (2nd cl Cl Trip pt ii) 29, 2nd cl Th Trip pt i, 30, MA 33. Ridley Hall, Cam 29. **d** 31 **p** 32 Ox. C of St John Reading 31-37; C-in-c of St Martin's Conv Distr Hull 37-38; Min 38-39; V 39-47; H Trin (w Ch Ch from 54) Folkestone 47-61; Ch Ch Folkestone 47-54; Surr 48-61; V of Lydney w Aylburton 61-75; Surr 71-75; L to Offic Dio Newc T from 75. *112 Chapel Lands, Alnwick, Northumb, NE66 1ER.*

LEACHMAN, James Garnett. b 47. Grey Coll Dur BSc (Botany) 68. Linacre Coll Ox BA (Th) 71, MA 76. St Steph Ho Ox 69. **d** 72 **p** 73 S'wark. M OSB from 68; C of Ch Ch and St Steph and of St Mary-le-Park Battersea 72-75; St Jo Bapt Eltham 75-78; L to Offic Dio Ox from 78. *Nashdom Abbey, Burnham, Bucks, SL1 8NL.*

LEADBEATER, Michael John. b 45. Univ of Nottm BTh 72. Kelham Th Coll 68. **d** 73 **p** 74 Ripon. C of Manston 73-76; Holbrooks 76-79; V of St Jo Evang Tipton Dio Lich from 79. *St John's Vicarage, Upper Church Lane, Tipton, W Midl, DY4 9ND.* (021-557 1793)

LEADBEATER, Nicolas James. b 20. Univ of Wales, BA 43. St Steph Ho Ox 43. **d** 45 **p** 46 Mon. C of H Trin Abergavenny 45-47; Coleford 47-55; PC of Moreton Valence w Whitminster 55-67; R of Westcote 67-72; C-in-c of Icomb 67-72; R of Westcote w Incomb (and Bledington from 79) Dio Glouc from 72. *Westcote Rectory, Church Westcote, Oxford, OX7 6SH.* (Shipton-under-Wychwood 830209)

LEADBEATER, Ven Thomas Loudon. St Chad's Coll Regina, LTh 38, BD and DD *jure dig* 50. Univ of Pittsburgh, USA BA 44, MEducn 45. **d** 38 **p** 39 Qu'App. C of St Geo Moose Jaw w Buffalo Lake 38-39; Weyburn 39-40; Sub-Warden St Chad's Coll Regina 40-44; in Amer Ch 44-45; C of Ch Ch Cathl Vic 46-48; Dioc Dir Relig Educn BC 47-48; R of St Sav Pro-Cathl Nelson and Dean of Koot 49-56; R of St Barn Calg 56-59; H Trin Edmon 59-81; Exam Chap to Bp of Edmon 60-76; Can of Edmon 63-75; Archd of Edmon 75-80; Archd (Emer) from 80. *15218-83rd Avenue, Edmonton, Alta, Canada T5R 3T4.*

LEADBEATER, Worral Reginald. b 13. MC 43. TCD BA 36, Div Test 36, MA 58. **d** 36 **p** 37 Kilm. C of St John Sligo w Knocknarea 36-39; CF (EC) 40-50; CF 50-52. *4 Highmore Road, SE3.*

LEADBEATTER, Christopher John Thomas. b 54. Ridley Coll Melb 75. **d** 79 **p** 80 Melb. C of St Andr Glen Waverley 79-81; St Columb Hawthorn Dio Melb from 81. *9a St Columb's Street, Hawthorn, Vic, Australia 3122.*

LEAFE, Maurice Stanley Damian. Chich Th Coll 72. **d** 74 **p** 75 Birm. C of Allen's Cross 74-76; Solihull (in c of St Catherine's) Dio Birm from 76. *3 St Alphege Close, Church Hill Road, Solihull, W Midl, B91 3RQ.* (021-705 7038)

LEAH, Michael Frederick. b 36. **d** 70 **p** 71 St Arn. Hon C of Swan Hill 70-74; V of Manangatang 74-76; R of Beaufort Dio Bal from 76. *St John's Rectory, Beaufort, Vic, Australia 3373.* (053-492080)

LEAH, William Albert. b 34. K Coll Lon BA (2nd cl Hist) 56, AKC 57. K Coll Cam MA 63. Ripon Hall Ox 60. **d** 62 **p** 63 Truro. C of Falmouth 62-63; Chap K Coll Cam 63-67; Min Can of Westmr Abbey 67-74; V of Hawkhurst Dio Cant from 74; Hon Min Can of Cant Cathl from 78. *Vicarage, Hawkhurst, Kent, TN18 4QB.* (Hawkhurst 3397)

LEAK, Adrian Scudamore. b 38. Ch Ch Ox BA (2nd cl Th) 60, MA 65. Cudd Coll 64. **d** 66 **p** 67 Cov. C of St Mark Cov 66-69; Dorchester w Berinsfield 69-73; V of Badsey 73-80; Wickhamford 73-80; P-in-c of St Pet Monkwearmouth 80-81; Archivist of York Minster and V Cho from 81. *5 Minster Yard, York, YO1 1JD.* (York 25540)

LEAK, David. b 42. St Jo Coll Nottm 76. **d** 79 **p** 80 Lich. C of Oswestry Dio Lich from 79. *13 Fitzalan Close, Babbinswood, Oswestry, Salop.*

LEAK, Harry Duncan. b 30. St Cath Coll Cam BA 53, MA 57. Ely Th Coll 53. **d** 54 **p** 55 Capetn. C of Plumstead 54-57; Supr of N Distr Dio Lebom 57-61; C of Eccleshall 62-64; V of Normacot 64-66; C of Stoke-on-Trent 66-68; V of All SS Hanley 68-71; R of Swynnerton 71-80; Perm to Offic Dio Lich from 80. *15 Sutherland Road, Tittensor, Stoke-on-Trent, ST16 9JQ.*

✠ **LEAKE, Right Rev David.** ALCD 59 (LTh from 74). **d** 59 **p** 60 St Alb. C of Watford 59-61; Lect 61-63; SAMS Miss Dio Argent 63-69; Cons Asst Bp of Parag 21 Dec 69 in St Jo Cathl Buenos Aires by Bps of Argent; Chile; and Bp Bazley; Asst Bp of N Argent 73-80; Apptd Bp of N Argent 80. *Casilla 187, 4400, Salta, Argentina.* (20370)

LEAKE, Canon William Alfred. b 02. Lon Coll of Div. **d** 38 Cant for Col **p** 39 Argent. SAMS Miss Dio Argent 38-58; Hon Can of St Jo Bapt Pro-Cathl Buenos Aires 54-58 and 68-71; Can (Emer) from 71; R of Twyford w Guist 58-62; SAMS Miss Dio Argent 62-71. *The Anchorage, Lower Common, East Runton, Cromer, Norf, NR27 9PG.* (Cromer 513536)

LEAKEY, Ian Ramond Arundell. b 24. K Coll Cam BA 47, MA 49. Ridley Hall, Cam 48. **d** 50 **p** 51 Liv. C of St John and St Jas Litherland 50-53; CMS Ruanda Miss 53-73; Prin Shyogwe Tr Coll 62-64; Can of Bur 66; CMS Rep and Dioc Adv Bur 65-69; Warner Th Coll 65-72; V of Cudham (and Downe from 76) Dio Roch from 73. *Cudham Vicarage, Sevenoaks, Kent.* (Biggin Hill 72445)

LEAKEY, Peter Wippell. b 39. BSc (Lon) 60. Trin Coll Bris 73. **d** 75 Lanc for Blackb **p** 76 Blackb. C of Colne 75-79; V of Copp Dio Blackb from 79. *St Anne's Vicarage, Copp, Great Eccleston, Preston, PR3 0ZN.* (Gt Eccleston 70231)

LEAL, Malcolm Colin. b 33. Chich Th Coll 72. **d** 75 **p** 76 Chich. C of St Giles Shoreham Dio Chich from 75. *8 West Park Lane, Goring-by-Sea, Sussex, BN12 4ER.*

LEAMING, Ralph Desmond. b 21. Ripon Coll Cudd 79. **d** 81 Dur. C of H Trin Darlington Dio Dur from 81. *79 Orchard Road, Darlington, Co Durham, DL3 6HR.*

LEAMY, Stuart Nigel. b 46. Pemb Coll Ox BA (2nd cl Th) 68, MA 73. Sarum Th Coll 68. **d** 70 Warrington for Liv **p** 71 Liv. Hon C of C of Ch the Servant Digmoor in Up Holland Team Min 72-78; L to Offic Dio Lon from 78. *28 Church Street, Hampton, Middx, TW12 2EG.* (01-941 3930)

LEAN, David Jonathan Rees. b 52. St D Coll Lamp Dipl Th 74. Coll of Resurr Mirfield 74. **d** 75 **p** 76 St D. C of Tenby 75-81; V of Llanrhian w Llanhowell and Llanrheithan Dio St D from 81. *Llanrhian Vicarage, Haverfordwest, Dyfed.* (Croesgoch) *354*

LEAN, Canon Ernest Vickery. Kelham Th Coll 24. **d** 29 **p** 30 Lon. C of St Pet Lon Dks 29-32; UMCA Miss Dio Nyasa 32-36; P-in-c of Milo 36-38; Lupa 38-41; Hd Master Mbeya Sch Tanganyika 41-42; CF (E Afr) 42-46; R of Maseru 47-51; P-in-c of Masapong Miss 50-51; R of St Andr w H Innoc Grenada 51-54; R of Port St Johns w Lusikisiki and P-in-c of

St Andr Miss 54-61; Archd of St Mark's 61-68; Kokstad 69-73; Can of St Jo Cathl Umtata 61-73; Can (Emer) from 73; P-in-c of All SS Engcobo 61-64; Idutywa 64-69; Kokstad 69-75; Harding Dio Natal from 75. *Rectory, Harding, Natal, S Africa.* (Harding 195)

LEANEY, Alfred Robert Clare. b 09. Late Exhib of Hertf Coll Ox 2nd cl Cl Mods 30, BA (2nd cl Lit Hum) 32, Dipl Th 33, MA 39, BD 52, DD 66. Ripon Hall, Ox 32. **d** 33 **p** 34 Birm. C of Oldbury 33-36; V of Mountfield 36-44; R of Eastwood 46-48; Wishaw 48-52; CF (R of O) from 39; Hon CF 46; CF (TA) 48-51; Lect Qu Coll Birm 50-52; Chap Ripon Hall Ox 52-54; Vice-Prin 54-56; L to Offic Dio Southw 56-74; Lect in Th Univ of Nottm 56-64; Reader 64-69; Prof from 69; Head of Th Dept 70-74; Select Pr Cam 63. *Dunelm, Pulteney Road, Bath, Avon, BA2 4HA.* (Bath 60363)

LEANING, Ven David. Lich Th Coll 58. **d** 60 **p** 61 Linc. C of Gainsborough 60-65; R of Warsop w Sookholme 65-76; V of Kington and R of Huntington 76-80; RD of Kington and Weobley 76-80; Archd of Newark from 80. *Eastfield House, Westgate, Southwell.* (Southwell) *812113*

LEARY, Thomas Glasbrook. b 42. K Coll Lon and Warm AKC 66. **d** 67 **p** 68 Lich. C of W Bromwich 67-70; Team V of St Geo Croydon 70-75; C of Limpsfield (in c of St Andr) Dio S'wark from 75; Sec of Bp of S'wark's Adv C'tte of Pastoral Care and Counselling from 78. *St Andrew's House, Limpsfield Chart, Oxted, Surrey.* (Limpsfield Chart 3153)

LEASK, Kenneth James. Moore Th Coll Syd ThL 57. **d** and **p** 53 Syd. C of Balmain 53; C-in-c of The Oaks 53-55; R of Cook's River 55-58; Dural 58-61; Port Kembla 61-67; Dulwich Hill 67-77; The Oaks Dio Syd from 77. *Rectory, Russell Street, The Oaks, NSW, Australia 2570.* (046-57 1163)

LEATHBRIDGE, William. Ridley Coll Melb ACT ThL 43. **d** 43 **p** 44 Gippsld. C of Drouin w Bunyip and Nar-Nar-Goon 44-45; V of Omeo 45-48; R of Toora 48-54; V of Rosedale 54-59; P-in-c of Newborough 59-62; R of Orbost 62-71. *Clifton Waters Village, Bairnsdale, Vic 3875, Australia.*

LEATHEM, Thomas Lindsay. b 24. Trin Coll Dub BA 46, Div Test 47, MA 61. **d** 47 **p** 48 Connor. C of Carrickfergus 47-50; Ballymacarrett 50-52; I of Lack 52-61; Dioc Insp Relig Educn Clogh 58-61; C of Blackpool 61-63; V of St Jo Evang Darwen 63-65; C of Ballywillan 65-66; Asst Master Omagh Acad 66-67. *Plas Lloyd, Sea Road, Castlerock, Co Derry, N Ireland.*

LEATHER, James Stanley. b 06. Lich Th Coll 30. **d** 32 **p** 33 Ches. C of St Jas Gatley 32-34; St Aug Brinksway 34-36; St Jo Evang W Bromwich 36-38; H Trin (in c of St Jas Willenhall) Cov 38-41; St Anne Sale 41-44; V of St Thos Hyde 44-52; St Jas Congleton 52-65. *Compostella, Cloudside, Congleton, Ches.*

LEATHERBARROW, Canon Joseph Stanley. b 08. Univ of Man BA (2nd cl Hist) 29, MA 40, PhD (Birm) 77. Wells Th Coll 30. **d** 31 **p** 32 Man. C of Prestwich 31-37; V of St Mark Bolton 37-44; R of Areley Kings 44-47; V of Swinton Lancs 47-59; Hon Can of Man 55-59; Can (Emer) from 59; R of Martley 59-72; RD of Martley 64-71; L to Offic Dio Worc from 72; M Gen Syn Dio Worc 70-75. *34 Highfield Road, Malvern Link, Worcs.* (Malvern 4821)

LEATHERBARROW, Ronald. b 35. N-W Ordin Course 71. **d** 75 **p** 76 Liv. C of Eccleston 75-80; St Thos Eccleston Dio Liv from 80. *6 Osborne Road, Eccleston, St Helens, WA10 5JS.* (St Helens 24617)

LEATHERDALE, Vincent William Storey. b 01. Wycl Hall Ox 53. **d** 54 Reading for Cant **p** 55 Ox. C of Highfield Ox 54-58; R of Hardwick w Tusmore 58-62; R of Cottisford 58-62; V of Thornborough 62-69. *31 Bertie Road, Cumnor, Oxford.* (Cumnor 2487)

LEATHERLAND, Brian. b 43. Univ of Nottm BTh 73. Kelham Th Coll 69. **d** 74 **p** 75 Pet. C of Higham Ferrers 74-76; St Paul Pet 76-78; V of King's Heath Northants Dio Pet from 78. *Vicarage, King's Heath, Northampton.* (Northampton 51778)

LEATHLEY, Hubert Brian. b 28. Linc Th Coll 79. **d** 81 Win. C of Basingstoke Dio Win from 81. *11 St Mary's Court, Eastrop Lane, Basingstoke, Hants Rg21 2AT.* (Basingstoke 69219)

LEATON, Martin John. b 46. Clifton Th Coll 68. **d** 71 **p** 72 Cov. C of St Jo Evang Kenilworth 71-74; Stratford-on-Avon 74-77; P-in-c of Meriden Dio Cov 77-81; R from 82; Gt w L Packington Dio Cov from 82. *Rectory, The Green, Meriden, Coventry, W Midl, CV7 7LN.*

LEAVER, Esmond Aylmer. ACT ThL 28. **d** 27 **p** 28 Wang. C of Tallygaroopna 27-28; Myrtleford 28-31; R of Wodonga 31-35; Violet Town 35-39; Alexandra 39-46; Seymour w Broadford 46-48; Victorian Sec of Austr Bd of Missions 48-54; Min of Ashburton 54-58; V of Burnley 58-65; R of Yallourn 65-73; Hon Can of Gippsld 71-73; Perm to Offic Dio Brisb from 73; Dio Melb from 74. *44 Sesame Street, Mount Waverley, Vic, Australia 3149.* (03-232 9246)

LEAVER, John Aylmer. St Jo Coll Morpeth ThDip 54. **d** 56 Bal for Melb **p** 58 Melb. C of E Maitland 56; Murrumbeena 57-58; V of Romsey 58-61; Chap ACMF from 59; R of Seymour 61-65; Maryborough 66-74; Can of St Arn 66-73; Archd of St Arn 73-74; I of Mt Eliza N Dio Melb from 74. *60 Brighton Street, Frankston, Vic, Australia 3199.* (03-787 2315)

LEAVER, John Francis. b 31. MPS 53. Dipl Th (Lon) 63. St Mich Coll Llan 64. **d** 66 **p** 67 Glouc. C of St Cath Glouc 66-68; Hon C of St Mary de Lode 68-69; Matson 69-76; St Mary de Crypt and St Jo Bapt City and Dio Glouc from 76. *143 Maidenhall, Highnam, Gloucester, GL2 8DJ.*

LEAVER, Robin Alan. b 39. Clifton Th Coll 62. **d** 64 **p** 65 S'wark. C of Ch Ch Gipsy Hill 64-67; Gt Baddow 67-71; C-in-c of St Mary Chap Castle Street Reading 71-77; Cogges Dio Ox from 77; Chap Luckley-Oakfield Sch Wokingham 73-75. *Cogges Priory, Witney, Oxon, OX8 6LA.* (Witney 2155)

LEBANON, *See* Jerusalem.

LEBENYA, Canon Gideon. **d** 31 **p** 34 St Jo Kaffr. C of Mt Fletcher 31-42; CF (S Afr) 42-45; P-in-c of Mt Fletcher 45-65; Can of St John's Cathl Umtata 58-65; Can (Emer) from 66; L to Offic Dio St John's from 65. *Fobane Mission, PO Kinira Drift, CP, S Africa.*

LEBOMBO, Lord Bishop of. *See* Sengulane, Right Rev Dinis Salomao.

LEBOMBO, Bishop Suffragan of. (Vacant)

LEBONA, Matthias. b 29. **d** 76 Les. d Dio Les. *St Paul's Rectory, PO Box LR 385, Leribe, Lesotho, S Africa.*

LEBOTSA, Mohomane Masimole. b 27. Fort Hare Univ Coll Alice BSc 50. Univ of Edin BSc 56. Univ of Lon MSc 62. **d** 75 **p** 76 Les. P Dio Les. *National University of Lesotho, PO Roma, via Maseru, Lesotho, S Africa.*

LE BRETON, Sydney Heywood. **d** 66 **p** 70 Wang. C of Seymour 66-67; Hon C of Wang Cathl 67-71; Benalla Dio Wang from 71. *1 Franklin Street, Wangaratta, Vic., Australia.*

LECHOANO, Paul Dennis Leepile. b 32. **d** and **p** 75 Les. P Dio Les. *PO Box MS 3, Maseru, Lesotho, S Africa.*

LECKEY, Canon Hamilton. b 29. TCD BA 51, MA 58. **d** 51 **p** 53 Down. C of St Martin Ballymacarrett Belf 51-55; Bangor 55-60; R of Drumgooland w Kilcoo 60-62; Comber 62-79; Priv Chap to Bp of Down 62-73; Dir of Ordinands Dio Down from 62; Can of Down Cathl from 74; I of Bangor Abbey Dio Down from 79. *34 Bryansburn Road, Bangor, Co Down, N Ireland.* (Bangor 5976)

LECKEY, Robert Hamilton. Univ of Tor BA 63. Wycl Coll Tor BTh 66. **d** 66 **p** 67 Tor. C of St John York Mills Tor 66-69; R of Bolton 71-76; St Richard of Chich Tor 76-80; Newmarket Dio Tor from 80. *Box 176, Newmarket, Ont., Canada.*

LE CRAS, Winter Charles. **d** 29 **p** 30 Montr. C of Quyon 29-32; R of Lachute 32-41; RD of St Andr 40-41; Bps' Miss in Ch Exten Work Dio Montr 41-48; R of St Paul Côte des Neiges Montr 48-60; P-in-c of St Andr E 60-66. *Fairhaven Home, Langton Avenue, Peterborough, Ont, Canada.*

LEDGARD, Canon Frank William Armitage. b 24. Wells Th Coll 49. **d** 52 **p** 53 St E. C of St Mary-le-Tower Ipswich 52-55; V of Tottington 55-62; Kirkby Malzeard w Dallagh Gill 62-66; R of Bedale Dio Ripon from 66; RD of Wensley from 78; Hon Can of Ripon Cathl from 80. *Rectory, Bedale, Yorks, DL8 1AF.* (Bedale 22103)

LEDGARD, Canon Thomas Callinan. b 16. Late Exhib of St Jo Coll Cam BA 38, MA 50. Westcott Ho Cam 38. **d** 39 **p** 40 Dur. C of Bp Wearmouth 39-42; Ryhope 42-44; V of St Mich AA Norton 44-46; Warcop w Musgrave R 46-50; R and V of Fulbourn 50-56; V of Kirkby Lonsdale w Mansergh 56-69; Cartmel 69-79; RD of Kirkby Lonsdale 64-69; Cartmel 69-70; Hon Can of Carl Cathl from 70; P-in-c of Warcop w Musgrave and Soulby w Crosby Garrett Dio Carl from 79. *Bridge End House, Warcop, Appleby, Cumb.* (Brough 217)

LEDGER, Charles Cecil. Univ of Manit BCom 54. Wycl Th Coll BTh 59. Union Th Sem NY MRE 60. Columbia Univ MA 65. **d** 59 **p** 60 Bran. C of St Matt Cathl Bran 59-61; Angl Ch of Canada Miss Dio Nam 61-68. *Unit 55, 547 Steeles Avenue W, Willowdale, Ont, Canada.*

LEDGER, James Henry. b 23. Oak Hill Th Coll 68. **d** 70 **p** 71 Stepney for Lon. C of Spitalfields Lon 70-74; V of St Cuthb Chitts Hill Wood Green Dio Lon from 75. *85 Wolves Lane, N22 5JD.* (01-888 6178)

LEDL, Milos. b 27. Canberra Coll of Min 74. **d** 74 **p** 75 C & Goulb. C of Junee 74-76; Cootamundra 76; P-in-c of Marulan 76-81; R of W Goulb Dio C & Goulb from 81. *128 Addison Street, Goulburn, NSW, Australia 2580.*

LEDWABA, Alfred. **d** 65 **p** 66 Pret. C of Mahwelereng Dio Pret from 65. *Box 55, Mahwelereng, N Transvaal, S Africa.*

LEDWABA, Samuel Malesela. b 42. St Pet Coll Alice 74. **d** 76 **p** 77 Pret. C of Atteridgeville 76-81; Mmakau Dio Pret from 81. *Box 28, De Wildt, Pretoria 0251, S Africa.*

LEDWARD, John Archibald. b 30. ALCD (2nd cl) 57, BD

58. Univ of Man MA 81. **d** 58 Warrington for Liv **p** 59 Liv. C of St Helens Lancs 58-62; V of Dearham 62-66; St Andr Mirehouse Whitehaven 66-71; St Geo Mart Daubhill Bolton 71-77; R of Newc L Dio Lich from 77. *Rectory, Seabridge Road, Newcastle-under-Lyme, ST5 2HS.* (Newc L 616397)

LEDWICH, William Delahoyde. b 46. TCD BA 68, MA 73. St Chad's Coll Dur BA (Th), Dipl Th 73. **d** 73 **p** 74 Man. C of Oldham 73-75; St Mary Blyth 75-78; M OGS from 75; V Cho Heref Cathl 78-79; Chap Cathl Sch Heref from 78. *Hereford Cathedral School, 29 Castle Street, Hereford, HR1 2NN.* (Heref 66679)

LEE, Alan Charles. b 49. SOC 77. **d** 79 Lon (APM). C of St Sav Acton Green 79-81; St Pet Acton Green Dio Lon from 81. *102 West Hill, Putney, SW15.*

LEE, Anthony Maurice. b 35. Bps' Coll Cheshunt 62. **d** 65 **p** 66 Lon. C of Pinner 65-71; Asst Youth Chap Glouc 71-72; V of Childs Wickham 72-73; R of Aston Somerville 72-73; V of Childswyckham w Aston Somerville Dio Glouc from 73. *Childs Wickham Vicarage, Broadway, Worcs.* (Broadway 2240)

LEE, Arnold John. b 17. St Edm Hall Ox 3rd cl Cl Mods 38, BA (2nd cl Lit Hum) 40, Dipl Th 41, MA 43. Wycl Hall Ox 40. **d** 42 **p** 43 Guildf. C of Claygate 42-45; CMS Miss Dio W Szech 45-51; S Perak 52-57; New Villages Selangor 57-59; St Paul Petaling Jaya 59-61; V 62-69; V of St Andr Ox 69-78; E Boldre w St Baddesley Dio Win from 78. *East Boldre Vicarage, Brockenhurst, Hants.* (East End 226)

LEE, Arthur. St Aid Coll 35. **d** 38 **p** 39 Man. C of St Phil Bradf Rd Man 38-40; Hanley w Hope 40-41; CF (EC) 41-46; C of St Luke Cannock (in C of St Thos Huntington) 46-47; V of Dawley Magna 47-50; R of Chilton Cantelo w Ashington 50-54; V of Stowey w Bp's Sutton 54-57; R of Kalamunda 57-64; St Mary W Perth 64-68; Nedlands 68-78; Perm to Offic Dio Perth from 78. *254 Geographe Bay Road, W Busselton, W Australia 6280.*

LEE, Arthur Donald. b 42. Bp's Univ Queb BA 69. Hur Coll Lon MDiv 72. **d** 72 **p** 73 Hur. C of St Jo Evang Kitchener 72-74; on leave 75-77 and from 79; R of Caledon E 77-79. *114 Lynden Circle, Georgetown, Ont, Canada.*

LEE, Arthur Gordon. b 32. Univ of Wales Swansea BA (2nd cl Hist) 52. St Mich Coll Llan 53. **d** 55 Swan B **p** 56 Mon for Swan B. C of Brynmawr 55-57; Llangyfelach w Morriston 57-60; V of Abbey-Cwmhir w Llanddewi Ystradenny 60-69; St Pet Cockett Swansea Dio Swan B from 69. *Cockett Vicarage, Swansea, W Glam.* (Swansea 581514)

LEE, Barry Joseph. Moore Coll Syd ACT ThL 74. **d** 76 Syd **p** 76 Bp Short for Syd. C of St John Camden 76-79; Perm to Offic Dio Syd from 79. *11 The Boulevard, Lewisham, NSW, Australia 2049.*

LEE, Brian. b 37. Linc Th Coll 78. **d** 80 **p** 81 Pet. C of Duston Dio Pet from 80. *St Francis House, Eastfield Road, Duston, Northampton.*

LEE, Brian John. b 51. AKC and BD 78. Coll of the Resurr Mirfield 78. **d** 79 **p** 80 S'wark. C of St Richard Ham Dio S'wark from 79. *188 Secrett House, Ham Close, Ham, Richmond, Surrey.* (01-940 8931)

LEE, Christopher Garfield. b 41. St Deiniol's Libr Hawarden 80. **d** 80 **p** 81 Swan B. C of St Pet Cocket Swansea 80-81; Oystermouth Dio Swan B from 81. *66 Queens Road, Mumbles, Swansea, W Glam.* (Swansea 60438)

LEE, Clive Warwick. b 34. St Pet Coll Ox BA (3rd cl Th) 58, MA 62. Coll of Resurr Mirfield 58. **d** 60 **p** 61 Win. C of W End Hants 60-65; St Jo Evang U Norwood 65-69; Chap and Asst Master Vinehall Sch from 69; Perm to Offic Dio Chich 69-75; L to Offic from 75. *Vinehall, Robertsbridge, E Sussex.* (Robertsbridge 880675)

LEE, Colin John Willmot. b 21. Wycl Hall Ox 57. **d** 59 Roch **p** 59 Bp Stannard for Roch. C of Gravesend 59-62; V of St Edm Dartford 62-67; C-in-c of St Bart Hallam Fields Ilkeston 67-69; Stanton-by-Dale w Dale Abbey 69-76; Adv to Bp on Industr Relations from 67; V of St Jo Evang Ilkeston Dio Derby from 76. *St John's Vicarage, Ilkeston, Derbys, DE7 5PA.* (Ilkeston 325446)

LEE, Cyril Herbert. b 16. St Jo Coll Dur BA 38, Dipl Th 39, MA 41. **d** 39 **p** 40 Ches. C of All SS Cheadle Hulme 39-42; Perm to Offic at Ch Ch Latchford 42-45; C of Tarvin (in c of St Phil Kelsall) 45-48; V of Milnthorpe and Chap Milnthorpe Hosp 48-55; Chelford 55-64; Chap Oakwood Hosp Maidstone 64-66; Perm to Offic Dio Cant from 74; Chap HM Pris Eastchurch from 81; Chap Keycol Hosp Newington from 81. *80 Church Lane, Newington, Sittingbourne, Kent.* (Newington 842704)

LEE, David B. d and **p** 76 Taejon. P Dio Taejon. *303 Dunpori, Dunpomyon, Asankun, Korea.*

LEE, David Hartley. d 63 **p** 64 Llan. C of Merthyr Dyfan 63-65; All SS Penarth 65-70; Chap Miss to Seamen Halifax Dio NS from 70. *Box 5147, Armdale, Halifax, NS, Canada.* (425-3643)

LEE, David John. b 49. Oak Hill Th Coll 76. **d** 79 Barking for Chelmsf **p** 80 Chelmsf. C of SS Pet & Paul Dagenham Dio Chelmsf from 79. *15 Felhurst Crescent, Dagenham, Essex, RM10 7XT.*

LEE, David John. b 46. Univ of Bris BSc 67. Univ of Lon Dipl Th (Extra-Mural) 73. Fitzwm Coll Cam BA 76. Ridley Hall Cam 74. **d** 77 **p** 78 S'wark. C of St Marg Putney 77-80; Tutor Bp Tucker Th Coll Mukono from 80. *Bishop Tucker College, Mukono, Uganda.*

LEE, David Stanley. b 30. Univ of Wales, BSc (2nd cl Civil Eng) 51. St Mich Coll Llan. **d** 57 Mon for Wales **p** 58 Llan. C of Caerau w Ely 57-60; Dioc Industr Chap and C of St Agnes Port Talbot 60-70; R of Merthyr Tydfil (w Cyfartha from 72) Dio Llan from 70. *Rectory, Merthyr Tydfil, Mid Glam.* (Merthyr 2992)

LEE, David Wight Dunsmore. b 39. Wells Th Coll 61. **d** 63 **p** 64 York. C of St Osw Middlesbrough 63-67; Northallerton w Kirby Sigston and Romanby 67-69; R of Limbe w Thyolo and Mulanje 69-71; S Highlands Malawi 71-75; V of Transfig N Newington 76-81; P-in-c of Sheriff Hutton Dio York from 81; Sec of Dioc Miss Coun from 81. *Vicarage, New Lane, Sheriff Hutton, York, YO6 1QU.* (Sheriff Hutton 336)

LEE, Donald Hugh Thomson. b 48. Bard Coll Annandale-on-Hudson NY BA 70. Keble Coll Ox BA 73, MA 78. St Steph Ho Ox 72. **d** 74 **p** 75 Bris. C of New Swindon (in c of St Sav) 74-79; St Jas W Hampstead Dio Lon from 79. *Flat 3, 8 Adamson Road, NW3 3HR.* (01-722 0253)

LEE, Canon Edwin Kenneth. b 06. St Chad's Coll Dur BA 30, Gabbett Pri 33 and 35, MA 35, MLitt 45. **d** 30 **p** 31 Newc T. C of Ponteland 30-33; Eston w Normandy 33-35; All SS Huntingdon 35-38; V of Poppleton 38-43; Org Dir ICF for NE Area 42-44; V of Ch Ch Lofthouse 43-51; Horsforth 51-75; Lect Leeds Univ 54-56; Exam Chap to Bp of Ripon from 58; RD of Headingley 70-72; Hon Can of Ripon 71-75; Can (Emer) from 75; Chap St Jo Bapt Hosp Ripon from 75. *The Flat, Minster House, Ripon, N Yorks.* (Ripon 3992)

LEE, Francis George. b 37. St Aid Coll 26. **d** 65 Warrington for Liv **p** 66 Liv. C of H Trin Wavertree 65-69; P-in-c of Mangrove Cay and S Andros Nass 69-72; V of Knowsley 72-77; Golden Square Dio Bend from 77. *St Mark's Vicarage, Maple Street, Golden Square, Vic, Australia 3555.*

LEE, Frederick Roydon. b 13. OBE 69. SOC 76. **d** 77 **p** 78 Roch (APM). C of Sundridge 77-81; L to Offic Dio Roch from 81. *Tranquil, Combe Bank, Sundridge, Sevenoaks, Kent TN14 6AD.*

LEE, Frederick William Maxwell. b 15. Univ of Dur LTh 40. St Pet Hall Ox BA (2nd cl Th) 47, MA 51. St Aid Coll 37. **d** 40 **p** 41 Man. C of Flixton 40-43; St Marg Whalley Range 43-44; Perm to Offic Dio Ox 44-47; C of H Trin Port of Spain 47-49; Exam Chap to Bp of Trinid 47-50; P-in-c of St Paul San Fernando 49-50; SPG Area Sec Co of York 50-53; V of Plumtree 53-58; Chap Plumtree Sch 53-58; L to Offic Dio Mashon 58; Asst Master Morgan High Sch 59-64; P-in-c of St Andr Arcadia 59-62; Exam Chap to Bp of Mashon 60-66; Commiss Mashon from 67; Perm to Offic Dio Ox 67-68; Dio Nor 68-70; Asst Master Thorpe Gr Sch Nor 68-70; Hitchin Girls' Gr Sch 70-80; Hon C of Hitchin 70-74; C of St Sav St Alb 74-80. *13 Sandpit Lane, St Albans, Herts.* (St Albans 57353)

LEE, Geoffrey Allen Billups. Fitzw Ho Cam BA 31, MA 37. Cudd Coll 32. **d** 33 **p** 34 Blackb. C of St Cath Burnley 33-37; Fleetwood (in c of St Nich) 37-38; Lytham 38-39; CF 39-62; V of Shrewton w Maddington and Rollestone 62-66; Winterbourne Stoke 62-66; C of All SS Nel 67-73; L to Offic Dio B & W 73-75; Perm to Offic Dio Sarum from 75. *Underhill Farm, East Knoyle, Salisbury, SP5 6BP.*

LEE, Harold. b 04. St Aid Coll 37. **d** 39 **p** 40 Sheff. C of Woodhouse 39-44; St Mich Macclesfield 44-49; V of St Mich AA Runcorn 49-58; Thelwall 58-61; Mortomley 61-65; Campsall 65-71; Surr 67-71; Hon C of Bakewell 71-75; Totley 75-80. *2 Cherry Tree Close, Sheffield, S11 9AF.*

LEE, Canon Hector. Kelham Th Coll 53. **d** 57 **p** 58 Southw. M SSM from 57; Tutor Kelham Th Coll 60-63; Asst P at Teyateyaneng 63-65; St Jas Mantsonyana 65-67; R of Teyateyaneng 67-69; Dir of SSM Miss Modderpoort Dio Bloemf from 69; Can of Bloemf from 80. *St Augustine's Priory, Modderpoort, OFS, S Africa.* (Modderpoort 1)

LEE, Henry. b 31. St Chad's Coll Dur BA 53, Dipl Th (w distinc) 55. **d** 55 **p** 56 Dur. C of St Ignatius Hendon Bp Wearmouth 55-60; St Marg (in c of St John Neville's Cross) Dur 60-65; PC of Medomsley Dio Dur 65-68; V 68-75; H Trin Darlington Dio Dur from 75; Chap Darlington Mem Hosp 75-79. *Holy Trinity Vicarage, 45 Milbank Road, Darlington, Co Durham.* (Darlington 65114)

LEE, Henry Welby. b 1896. Univ Coll Ox BA 21, MA 25. Cudd Coll 21. **d** 22 **p** 23 Wakef. C of Staincliffe 22-24; Penistone 24-28; St Mary Illingworth Halifax 28-30; V of Flockton w Denby Grange 30-35; R of Whitwood Mere 35-43; St Kessog Auchterarder 43-50; PC of Melbecks 50-59;

V of Muker 52-59; Escomb 59-64. *Ivy Cottage, Marske, Richmond, Yorks.*

LEE, Hock Beng. b 49. Univ of Leeds BA (Th) 73. Coll of Resurr Mirfield 72. **d** 75 W Mal. d Dio W Mal. *80-A Jalan Gereja, Seremban NS, Malaysia.*

LEE, Hugh Gordon Cassels. b 41. Univ of St Andr BSc 64. Edin Th Coll 64. **d** 67 **p** 68 Glas. C of St John Dumfries 67-70; St Andr Totteridge 70-73; R of St Jas Glas 73-80, Bishopbriggs Dio Glas from 80. *9 Meadowburn, Bishopbriggs, Glasgow.*

LEE, Hugo Moon Bum. b 26. **d** & **p** 69 Seoul. P Dio Seoul. *209-3 Hak Dong, Kangnam Ku, Seoul, Korea.*

LEE, Ivan Yin. b 56. Moore Th Coll Syd BD, ThL. **d** 81 Syd. C of St Matt Manly Dio Syd from 81. *1 Darley Road, Manly, NSW, Australia 2095.*

LEE, Jack. b 04. AKC 28. Linc Th Coll 28. **d** 28 Dover for Cant **p** 29 Cant. C of St Pet and St Paul Charlton-in-Dover 28-32; Battle 32-35; Perm to Offic at St Jo Bapt Beeston 35-36; C of H Trin Hastings 36-38; Chap RAF 38-46; V of St Pet Southwick 46-60; St Luke Brighton 60-68; R of Newtimber w Pyecombe 68-77. *212 Preston Road, Brighton, BN1 6RA.* (Brighton 508039)

LEE, James Gregory. Trin Coll Tor LTh 43. **d** 42 **p** 43 Ott. C of St John Ott 42-45; V of St Pet Ott 45-49; in Amer Ch 49-52; I of Epiph Scarborough 52-70; St Matthias Tor 70-80. *40 Homewood Avenue, Toronto, M4Y 2K2, Ont, Canada.*

LEE, Ven John Bang Hang. U Th Sem Foochow and Coll of H Cross Rang 35. Qu Coll Birm 47-48. **d** 36 **p** 37 Sing. P-in-c of H Trin Sing 37-65; All SS Kuala Lumpur 65-67; Hon Can of Sing 49-69; Archd of Centr Malaya 65-69; Can and Archd (Emer) and L to Offic Dio Sing from 70. *155 Taman, Permata, Singapore 20.*

LEE, John Chaejong. b 44. St Mich Sem Seoul 69. **d** and **p** 72 Seoul. P Dio Seoul. *250 Kwangch'ong Ni, Kanghwa, Kyonggi Do, 150-20, Korea.*

LEE, John Charles Hugh. b 44. Trin Hall Ox MA 66. Brunel Univ MTech 71. Ox Dioc Min Tr Scheme 78. **d** 81 Buckingham for Ox (NSM). C of St Mich AA Amersham-on-the-Hill Dio Ox from 81. *23 Whielden Street, Amersham, Bucks, HP7 0HU.*

LEE, John Foden. b 34. K Coll Lon and Warm AKC 61. **d** 61 Pet **p** 63 Lon. C of All SS Pet 61-63; St Andr Sudbury Middlx 63-65; Sherbourne (in c of St Paul) 65-67; R of Cheverell Magna 67; C-in-c of Erlestoke 67-68; V (w Cheverell Magna) 68-79; Seend w Bulkington Dio Sarum from 79. *Seend Vicarage, Melksham, Wilts, SN12 6NR.* (Seend 341)

LEE, John Ju Hoon. b 19. St Mich Sem Seoul 76. **d** 77 Taejon. d Dio Taejon. *483 Yongjungri, Chopyongmyon, Jonchonkun 330-35, Chungbuk, Korea.*

LEE, John Ross. **d** 56 **p** 57 Rupld. C of H Trin Winnipeg 56-58; R of Manitou 58-62; St Paul Winnipeg 62-69; Dir of Program Dio Montr 69-73; on leave. *1435 City Councillors Street, Montreal, Canada.* (514-288 5960)

LEE, John Royden. b 47. Univ of Wales (Swansea) BSc 70, MSc 73. Ripon Hall Ox. **d** 75 **p** 76 Swan B. C of St Pet Cockett Swansea 75-78. *St Botolph's Church, Aldgate, EC3N 1AB.* (01-283 1670)

LEE, John Samuel. b 47. Chich Th Coll 74. **d** 77 **p** 78 Ripon. C of Bramley Dio Ripon from 77. *18 Snowden Fold, Bramley, Leeds, LS13 2UH.* (Pudsey 568161)

LEE, Canon John William. b 27. Univ of Bris BA 47 (2nd cl Hist). Ely Th Coll 51. **d** 52 **p** 53 Glouc. C of St Steph Cheltm 52-56; C of St Mich AA Eccles Distr Blackpool 56-59; V of L Marsden Dio Blackb from 59; RD of Pendle from 78; Hon Can of Blackb from 81. *Vicarage, Bentley Street, Nelson, Lancs, BB9 0BS.* (Nelson 65888)

LEE, Joseph. **d** and **p** 77 Taejon. P Dio Taejon. *116 Daisori, Iryumyon, Chungbuk, Korea.*

LEE, Joseph Dae-Yong. b 42. Yonsei Univ Seoul BTh 64. **d** 77 **p** 78 Seoul. P Dio Seoul. *c/o 3 Chong dong, Chung Ku, Seoul 100, Korea.*

LEE, Canon Kenneth. b 13. St Jo Coll Dur BA 35, MA 38. **d** 36 **p** 37 Ches. C of St Mich Macclesfield 36-39; Hoylake 39-42; Heswall 42-44; V of St Barn Crewe 44-48; St Mary and St Paul Birkenhead 48-52; R of Heswall 52-79; Surr 53-79; Hon Can of Ches from 63; RD of Wirral N 75-79. *Greeba, Neston Road, Burton-in-Wirral, Chesh.*

LEE, Kenneth Peter. b 45. Em Coll Cam 2nd cl Th Trip pt i, 65, BA (2nd cl Th Trip pt ii) 67, MA 71. Cudd Coll 67. **d** 69 **p** 70 Ox. C of Stoke Poges 69-72; Witton 72-74; V of Frankby (w Greasby from 77) Dio Ches from 74. *14 Arrowe Road, Greasby, Mer, L49 1RA.* (051-678 6155)

LEE, Khi Liak. **d** 61 Borneo. L to Offic Dio Borneo 61-62; Dio Kuch from 62. *St John's Church, Jalan Tun Abang, Sibu, Sarawak, Malaysia.* (Sibu 22256)

LEE, Leslie John. b 19. St Aid Coll 44. Univ of Dur LTh 47. **d** and **p** 47 Nor. C of Wells-next-the-Sea 47-48; St John Lowestoft 48-49; Eyke w Bromeswell and Rendlesham 49-52; V of Metfield w Withersdale 52-55; R of Stiffkey w Morston 55-59; V of Watton 59-70; RD of Breckles from 65; R of Coltishall w Gt Hautbois Dio Nor from 70. *Coltishall Rectory, Norwich, NR12 7HL.* (Norwich 737255)

LEE, Ling Kwong. Trin Coll Sing 54. **d** 56 **p** 57 Sing. C of Selangor 56-63; P-in-c of St Mark Sungei-Buloh and Kepong Miss Distr 63-65. *c/o Bishopsgate, Singapore.*

LEE, Very Rev Lorne Francis. Trin Coll Tor STB 64. **d** and **p** 64 Bp Snell for Tor. C of Cobourg 64-65; St Paul Bloor Street Tor 65-66; on leave 66-68; I of Oyen 68-70; St Leo-on-the-Hilltop Red Deer 70-73; St Aug Lethbridge 73-80; Dean and R of St Alb Cathl Prince Albert Dio Sask from 80. *2641 6A Avenue West, Prince Albert, Sask, Canada.*

LEE, Luke Gun-hong. b 37. Univ of Yon Sei BTh 62. St Jo Coll Morpeth 66. **d** 67 **p** 68 Taejon. P Dio Taejon 68-71; Dio Seoul C of Bloxwich Dio Lich from 79. *6 Cresswell Crescent, Mossley Estate, Bloxwich, W Midl.* (Bloxwich 76647)

LEE, Maurice Charles. Moore Th Coll Syd ACT ThL 59. **d** 60 Syd **p** 61 Bp Kerle for Syd. C of St Steph Willoughby 61; Gladesville 62-64; Miss CMS Sabah 64-65; C of St Ives Provisional Distr 65-67; C-in-c of W Pymble Provisional Distr 67-75; Blakehurst 75-78; C in Miss Distr of St Jas and St John City and Dio Melb from 78. *8-12 Batman Street, West Melbourne, Vic, Australia 3003.* (329 0903)

LEE, Maurice Clifford. Univ of Bris BA (Th) 49. **d** & **p** 67 Perth. Asst Chap Ch Ch Gr Sch Claremont Dio Perth from 67. *15 Devon Road, Swanbourne, W Australia 6010.*

LEE, Moses Chong-sik. b 37. St Mich Sem Oryudong. **d** 68 **p** 69 Taejon. P Dio Taejon. *Box 22, Taejon 300, Korea.*

LEE, Very Rev Patrick Vaughan. Univ of Manit BA 53. St Jo Coll Winnipeg. **d** 56 **p** 57 Rupld. Miss at Eriksdale 56-58; R of St Bart Winnipeg 58-67; Portage la Prairie 67-75; Dean and R of St Paul's Cathl Ch Kamloops Dio Carib from 75; Exam Chap to Bp of Carib from 77. *443 Strathcona Terrace, Kamloops, BC, Canada.* (604-374 2779)

✠ **LEE, Right Rev Paul.** St Aug Coll Cant 57. **d** 52 **p** 53 Bp Chadwell for Korea. P Dio Korea 52-57 and 59-63; C of St Mary Wellingborough 57-59; Archd of Seoul and Warden Catechists' Sch Chong Chu 63-65; Cons Ld Bp of Seoul in St Mary and St Nich Cathl Seoul 27 May 65 by Bp in Korea; Bps of Hong; Sing; Kuch; Jess; Carib; Kobe; Taiwan (Amer Ch); and Philippines (Amer Ch); and Bps Chadwell; Longid (Amer Ch); Cabanban (Amer Ch); and Dayagbil (Philippines Ind Ch). *Anglican Church, 3 Chong Dong, Seoul, Korea.* (Seoul 75-6157)

LEE, Peter John. b 47. St Jo Coll Cam 2nd cl Hist Trip pt i 68, BA (2nd cl Hist Trip pt ii) 69, MA 73. St Jo Coll Nottm 72. **d** 73 Kens for Lon **p** 74 Lon. C of St Paul Onslow Sq Kens 73-76; R of Ch Ch Addington Durban 76-80; Orchards Dio Johann from 80. *18 High Road, Orchards, Johannesburg, S Africa.* (011-728 1561)

LEE, Peter Kenneth. b 44. Selw Coll Cam 2nd cl Cl Trip pt i, 64, BA (2nd cl Th Trip pt ii) 66, MA 69. Cudd Coll 67. **d** 69 **p** 70 Ripon. C of Manston 69-72; Bingley and Chap Bingley Coll of Educn 72-77; V of Cross Roads w Lees Dio Bradf from 77. *Vicarage, Cross Roads, Keighley, Yorks, BD22 9DL.* (Haworth 42210)

LEE, Raymond John. b 30. St Edm Hall, Ox BA (2nd cl Mod Lang) 53, MA 57. Tyndale Hall, Bris. **d** 56 **p** 57 S'wark. C of Tooting Graveney 56-59; St Jas Muswell Hill 59-62; V of St Mary-of-Bethany Woking 62-70; Gt Crosby Dio Liv from 70; Dioc Adv NSM from 79. *71 Liverpool Road, Liverpool, L23 5SE.* (051-924 1737)

LEE, Reginald Wilfred. b 09. Kelham Th Coll 27. **d** 32 **p** 33 Newc T. C of St Pet Wallsend 32-37; St Phil (in c of H Spirit) Newc T 37-39; Actg C of St Mich AA Maidstone 40-43; Min of Conv Distr of Hersden 43-49; Org Sec to Abp of Cant Thank-Offering Fund 46; Youth Chap Dio Cant 49-52; R of Gt Chart 50-57; C of St Marg U Norwood 58-71; St Martin Maidstone 71; Dep Chap Mayday and Queen's Hosps Croydon 71-75. *24b Blake Road, East Croydon, Surrey.*

LEE, Robert David. b 53. Qu Univ Belfast BD 75. Trin Coll Dub 77. **d** 77 **p** 78 Down. C of Comber Dio Down from 77. *32 Cherryvalley Crescent, Comber, Co Down, N Ireland.*

LEE, Robert William. b 31. Univ Coll of N Staff BA (2nd cl Hist and Phil) 54. St Cath S Ox BA (2nd cl Th) 58, MA 63. Ripon Hall, Ox 56. **d** 59 **p** 60 Lon. C of St Jerome Dawley 59-62; H Trin Bromley Common 62-65; R of Clayton Lancs 65-70; C-in-c of St Paul Bradford Lancs 65-70; Team V of Hemel Hempstead 70-72; St Pet and St Andr Corby w Gt and L Oakley 72-79; V of Weedon Lois w Plumpton and Moreton Pinkney and Wappenham Dio Pet from 80. *Vicarage, Weedon Lois, Towcester, Northants, NN12 8PN.* (Blakesley 278)

LEE, Ronald Ebsary. Qu Coll Newfld 60. **d** 61 **p** 63 Newfld. C of Hermitage 61-67; R of Bay D'Espoir 67-69; Buchans 67-71; Grand Bank Dio Newfld (Centr Newfld from 76) from

71. *Box 219, Grand Bank, Newfoundland, Canada.* (709-832-0404)

LEE, Shiu Ying. b 11. Lingnan Univ BSc 33. St Jo Coll Hong Kong. **d** 64 Hong **p** 65 Lon for Hong. C of St Martin-in-the-Fields Dio Lon from 64. *5 St Martin's Place, WC2N 4JJ.*

LEE, Steadworth Warren. Univ of W Indies BA 80. Codr Coll Barb 79. **d** 79 **p** 80 Antig. P Dio Antig 79-80; C of St Geo Cathl St Vincent Dio Windw Is from 80. *St George's House, Box 128, St Vincent, W Indies.*

LEE, Stephen George. b 57. Moore Th Coll Syd. **d** 81 Syd. C of St Paul Wahroonga Dio Syd from 81. *4 Ingram Road, Wahroonga, NSW, Australia 2076.*

LEE, Syn Hon. b 12. **d** 71 Kuch **p** 72 Sabah. P Dio Sabah. *Tg Aru, PO Box 25, Tanjong, Kota Kinabalu, Sabah, Malaysia.* (54774)

LEE, Thomas Richard. b 52. AKC 73. St Aug Coll Cant 74. **d** 75 **p** 76 Dur. C of St Andr Conv Distr Leam Lane Heworth Dio Dur from 75. *9 Lecondale Court, Leam Lane Estate, Gateshead, NE10 8QX.* (Gateshead 696691)

LEE, Tung Cheng. d 66 **p** 68 Hong. P Dio Hong 66-78. *13 Tai Hang Road, 8b Lai Sing Court, Hong Kong.* (5-772933)

LEE, Canon Walter Copeland. d 61 Bp Snell for Tor. C of Vespra 61-66; R of Innisfil 69-81; Can of Tor from 77. *317 Patterson Road, Barrie, Ont, Canada.*

LEE, William George. b 11. TCD BA 33, MA 48. **d** 34 Cork for Liv **p** 35 Liv. C of St Andr Southport 34-37; St Paul Cam 37-44; PC of Matlock Bath 44-49; V of St John Deptford 49-61; RD of Greenwich and Deptford 60; V of Ch Ch Chislehurst 61-76. *Dale Garth, Harmby, Leyburn, DL8 5PD.* (Wensleydale 22649)

LEE WARNER, Theodore John. b 22. Univ Coll Ox BA 49, MA 54. Wells Th Coll 50. **d** 51 **p** 52 Dur. C of St Mich AA Westoe S Shields 51-55; PC of Cassop w Quarrington 55-59; V of Peterlee 59-63; H Trin Darlington and Chap Darlington Mem Hosp 63-74; V of Norton 74-80; Gainford Dio Dur from 80; R of Winston Dio Dur from 80; RD of Barnard Castle from 80. *Gainford Vicarage, Darlington, Co Durham.* (darlington 730261)

LEECH, Christopher. b 16. Linc Th Coll 37. **d** 39 **p** 40 Wakef. C of Cudworth 39-41; Twerton-on-Avon (in c of St Pet) 41-43; R of H Trin Walcot Bath 43-47; C of St Patr Gwelo 47; Daramombe w Enkeldoorn and Umvuma 47-49; P-in-c of St Mary Hunyani S Rhod 49-52; PC of Easton Somt 53-54; P-in-c of St Bernard's Miss Marandellas S Rhod 54-57; V of St Geo Wigan 57-60; R of Combe Pyne w Rousdon Dio Ex 60-75; P-in-c 76-82; C of Axminster 77-79. *Kingdon Cottage, King Street, Colyton, Devon.*

LEECH, Canon Frank. b 14. St Aid Coll 44. **d** 46 **p** 47 Chelmsf. C of St Mich AA Gidea Pk 46-49; V of Becontree 49-55; Surr from 52; PC of St Jo Evang Mansfield 55-58; Chap of Mansfield Gen Hosp 55-58; V of Gidea Pk Dio Chelmsf from 58; C-in-c of St Alb Romford 63-68; RD of Havering 70-75; Hon Can of Chelmsf from 74. *St Michael's Vicarage, Gidea Park, Romford, Essex.* (Romford 41084)

LEECH, Kenneth. b 39. Univ of Lon BA (2nd cl Hist) and AKC 61. Trin Coll Ox BA (2nd cl Th) 63, MA 71. St Steph Ho Ox 62. **d** 64 **p** 65 Lon. C of H Trin w St Mary Hoxton 64-67; St Anne w St Thos Soho 67-71; Tutor St Aug Coll Cant 71-74; R of Bethnal Green 74-80; Field Officer for Race Relns from 80. *Church House, Dean's Yard, SW1P 3NZ.* (01-222 9011)

LEECH, Thomas Gill. b 04. AKC 35. Bps' Coll Cheshunt, 35. **d** 35 **p** 36 Lon. C of St John U Edmonton 35-37; St Sav Alexandra Pk 37-40; V of Gt Amwell 40-48; R of H Trin and C-in-C of St Paul Ramsgate 48-59; V of St Luke Woodside Croydon 59-68; R of Hertingfordbury 68-75; Perm to Offic Dio Cant from 75. *20 Manwood Road, Canterbury, Kent.*

LEEDS, Archdeacon of. *See* Comber, Ven Anthony James.

LEEFIELD, Michael John. b 37. Univ of Liv BA (2nd cl Geog) 60. K Coll Lon and Warm AKC and BD 65. **d** 66 **p** 67 Nor. C of Gt Yarmouth 66-70; V of Trowse 70-75; Arminghall 70-75; R of Caistor w Markshall 70-75; V of Lydney w Aylburton Dio Glouc from 75. *Vicarage, Lydney, Glos.* (Dean 42321)

LEEKS, Ronald Philip. b 16. Pemb Coll Ox BA (3rd cl Hist) 38, MA 42. Cudd Coll 38. **d** 39 **p** 40 Cant. C of St Andr Buckland-in-Dover 39-40; St Steph Norbury 40-42; St Alb S Norwood 42-49; St Mary Ashford (in c of Ch Ch S Ashford) 49-55; V of St Pet Whitstable 55-67; H Innoc S Norwood 67-81; Warden and Chap of Jesus Hosp Cant from 81. *The Warden's Lodge, Jesus Hospital, Sturry Road, Canterbury, CT1 1BS.* (Cant 63771)

LEEMAN, John Graham. b 41. NOC 78. **d** 80 **p** 81 York (NSM). C of St Mary Sculcoates Hull Dio York from 80. *St Mary's Vicarage, Eldon Grove, Beverley Road, Hull, HU5 2TJ.*

LEEMAN, Maurice Edward. b 27. TCD BA 49, Div Test (2nd cl) 50, MA 54. **d** 50 **p** 51 Connor. C of Carnmoney 50-53; St Pet Belf 53-59; R of Ahoghill (w Portglenone from 76) Dio Connor from 59; RD of Ballymena 66-74. *St Colmanell's Rectory, Ahoghill, Ballymena, Co Antrim, BT42 2PA, N Ireland.* (Ahoghill 871240)

LEEMING, Jack. b 34. Kelham Th Coll 56. **d** 61 **p** 62 S'wark. C of St Phil Sydenham 61-64; Chap RAF from 64. *c/o Ministry of Defence, Adastral House, WC1.*

LEEMING, John Maurice. b 24. MIMechE, MIProdE, CEng 59. N-W Ordin Course 72. **d** 75 Doncaster for Sheff **p** 76 Sheff. C of St Aug (APM) Brocco Bank Sheff 75-78; Norton 78-80; V of Bolsterstone Dio Sheff from 80. *Bolsterstone Vicarage, Sheffield, S30 5ZF.* (Sheff 882149)

LEEMING, Peter. b 23. Univ of Leeds, BA 50. Bps' Coll Cheshunt, 50. **d** 52 **p** 53 S'wark. C of St Jas Riddlesdown 52-56; Richmond 56-62; Sundon w Streatley 62-68; St Jo Bapt Moordown, Bournemouth 68-71; Hawarden 71-78; V in Rect Benef of Hawarden 78-81. *c/o 1 Church Cottages, Rectory Lane, Hawarden, Clwyd.*

LEES, Charles Alan. b 38. Qu Coll Birm 78. **d** 81 Birm (NSM). C of St Cypr Hay Mills Dio Birm from 81. *344 Barrows Lane, Yardley, Birmingham, B26 1QJ.*

LEES, Canon Jesse. b 1899. K Coll Lon 35. **d** 36 **p** 37 Lon. C of St Paul Finchley 36-39; PC of St Geo Gt Yarmouth 39-42; R of Fovant 42-51; Min of St Geo Conv Distr Oakdale 51-60; V 60-63; Surr from 53; RD of Poole 55-59; Can and Preb of Alton Australis in Sarum Cathl 61-67; Can (Emer) from 67; V of Market Lavington w Easterton 63-67. *47 Windsor Drive, Gloucester.*

LEES, Samuel Frederick. Univ of Syd BEcon 40. Moore Th Coll Syd ACT ThL (2nd cl) 59. **d** and **p** 60 Syd. C of St Andr Wahroonga 60-61; C-in-c of Narraweena w Ox Falls and Beacon Hill 61-65; R of S Canterbury 65-70; C-in-c of Abbotsford 70-74; R 74-75; Hosp Chap Concord Syd 75-78; C of St Steph Coorparoo Brisb 78-80; L to Offic Dio Syd from 80. *35 First Street, Blackheath, NSW, Australia 2785.*

LEES, William. b 08. Univ of Aber MA 32, BD 43. Edin Th Coll 31. **d** 49 Kens for Lon **p** 50 Lon. C of St Sav U Sunbury 49-50; Prin of St Thos Sch Kuch Borneo 50-54; R of Woodhead Dio Aber 54-55; Perm to Offic Dio St Alb 59-60; Dio B & W 62-69; Dio Aber 69-70. *Address temp unknown.*

LEES-SMITH, (Edward) Christopher John. b 21. CCC Ox BA 49, MA 65. Cudd Coll 49. **d** 50 **p** 51 Dur. C of St Luke Pallion Bp Wearmouth 50-54; M SSF from 54; LPr Dio Sarum 57-62; Dio Newc T from 62. *42 Balaam Street, Plaistow, E13 8AQ.*

LEESE, Arthur Selwyn Mountford. b 09. K Coll Lon AKC (1st cl) and BD 31. St Cath S Ox BA (2nd cl Th) 33, MA 44. Ripon Hall, Ox 31. **d** 33 **p** 34 Roch. C of Ch Ch Bexleyheath 33-37; Cockington w Chelston 37-39; PC of Langley Mill 39-51; V of Hawkhurst 51-74; Perm to Offic Dio Chich from 75; Dio Cant from 77. *84 Wickham Avenue, Bexhill-on-Sea, Sussex.*

LEESE, Frederick Henry Brooke. b 24. AKC 47. **d** 47 **p** 48 S'wark. C of St Mark Mitcham 47-50; St Thos-on-the-Bourne 50-54; V of St Martin Croydon 54-60; Pagham 60-70; Alderley Edge Chorley Dio Ches from 70. *Vicarage, Alderley Edge, Chesh, SK9 7UZ.* (Alderley Edge 583249)

LEESON, Martin Lister. b 25. ARCM 53, FRCO 76. Bps' Coll Cheshunt 57. **d** 59 **p** 60 Lon. C of Harringay 59-62; Hackney 62-64; Widford Essex 64-67; R of L Thurrock 67-76; V of St Luke Prittlewell Dio Chelmsf from 76. *St Luke's Vicarage, St Luke's Road, Southend-on-Sea, Essex, SS2 4AB.* (Southend 67620)

LEFA, David Sopoli. b 10. St Bede's Coll Umtata 70. **d** 70 Bp Sobukwe for St John's **p** 71 St John's. P Dio St John's. *P Bag 790, Matatiele, CP, S Africa.*

LE FEUVRE, Henry Mauger. b 21. Lich Th Coll. **d** 62 **p** 63 S'wark. C of Cheam 62-65; St Barn Dulwich 65-69; C-in-c of Dorrington 69-72; Stapleton 69-72; Cardington 69-71; R of St Lawr Jersey 72-80; R of Risby w Gt and L Saxham and Westley Dio St E from 80. *Risby Rectory, Bury St Edmunds, Suff, IP28 6RQ* (Bury St E 810416)

LE FEUVRE, Rollo Philip John. St Edm Hall Ox BA 57, MA 61. Univ of Capetn PhD 81. Clifton Th Coll 61. **d** 63 **p** 64 Capetn. C of St John Wynberg 63-65; Asst Chap Dioc Coll Rondebosch 65-70; R of Big Bend Swaz 71-73; Chap Univ of Capetn 73-77; St Paul's Th Coll Grahmstn from 77. *Box 77, Grahamstown, S Africa.*

LEFEVER, Henry Charles. b 06. Univ of Lon BA (2nd cl Phil) 30, BD 32. Univ of Tübingen PhD 34. **d** 65 **p** 66 S'wark. C of St Sav w All H S'wark 65-69; Hon C of Ascen Blackheath 69-75; Perm to Offic Dio Cant from 77. *8 Oaten Hill Place, Canterbury, Kent, CT1 3HJ.* (Canterbury 68304)

LE FEVRE, Ven Maurice Aubrey. Univ of NZ BCom 56. NZ Bd of Th Stud LTh 65. Coll Ho Ch Ch 54. **d** 57 Bp Rich for Wel **p** 57 Wel. C of All SS Palmerston N 57-59; Lower Hutt 59-63; V of Lyall Bay Wel 63-69; Carterton 69-76; Feilding Dio Wel from 76; Archd of Rangitikei from 79; Hon

Can of Wel from 79. *18 Camden Street, Feilding, NZ.* (37050)

LEFFLER, Christopher. b 33. Em Coll Cam BA 57, MA 61. Linc Th Coll. **d** 59 **p** 60 S'wark. C of Bermondsey 59-60; St Paul Herne Hill 60-63; C-in-c of St Steph Conv Distr Canley 63-67; R of L w Gt Glemham 67-72; C-in-c of Badwell Ash, Gt Ashfield, Hunston (and Langham and Stowlangtoft to 76) Dio St E 72; R from 72; Stowlangtoft w Langham from 76. *Badwell Ash Rectory, Bury St Edmunds, IP31 3DH.* (Walsham le Willows 575)

LEFROY, Christopher John Elton. b 25. Late Scho of Clare Coll Cam 2nd cl Math Trip pt ii 44, BA 46, MA 49. Ridley Hall Cam 47. **d** 49 **p** 50 Chelmsf. C of St Matt W Ham 49-51; Asst Chap Bradfield Coll 51-54; C of All S Langham Place 54-65; V of Highbury (w St Jo Evang Highbury Vale from 79 and St Sav Aberdeen Park from 82) Dio Lon from 65. *Christ Church Vicarage, Highbury Grove, N5 1SA.* (01-226 4544)

LEFROY, John Perceval. b 40. Trin Coll Cam BA 62. Cudd Coll 64. **d** 66 **p** 67 Cant. C of St Martin Maidstone 66-69; St Pet-in-Thanet 69-74; V of Barming Heath Maidstone Dio Cant from 74. *416 Tonbridge Road, Maidstone, Kent, ME16 9LW.* (Maidstone 26245)

LEGASSICK, Kenneth. Dioc Th Sch Fred 60. **d** 64 **p** 65 Fred. C of H Trin St John 64-70; R of Addington 70-73; Trin St John Dio Fred from 73. *50 Orange Street, St John, NB, Canada.*

LEGERTON, Ian Alfred Ford. b 50. Linc Th Coll 70. **d** 73 **p** 74 Ox. C of Chesham 73-75; H Cross Fenham 75-78; Bromborough Dio Ches from 78. *3 Croft Avenue, Bromborough.* (051-334 4181)

LEGG, John Andrew Douglas. b 32. Selw Coll Cam BA 55, MA 59. Wells Th Coll 57. **d** 59 Guildf for Cant for Col Bp **p** 59 Bunb. C of Albany 59-61; R of H Trin Northn 61-63; P-in-c of St Geo Carnarvon (all in N W Austr) 61-63; Chap at Rugby Sch 63-64; Commiss NW Austr 63-65; PC of Ashford w Sheldon 64-67; Chap Kuwait Oil Co and Episc P Kuwait 67-69; L to Offic Dio Melan 70-71; Chap and Ho Master St George's Sch Honiara 71-73; Asst Master L Ilford Comprehensive Sch from 73; P-in-c of Stapleford Tawney w Theydon Mount Dio Chelmsf from 78. *Rectory, Theydon Mount, Epping, Essex, CM16 7PW.* (Epping 75144)

LEGG, Reginald John. b 26. LRAM 50. Wells Th Coll 61. **d** 63 **p** 64 Glouc. C of Prestbury 63-66; V of Milnsbridge 66-67; Chap Miss to Seamen S Shields 67-70; Man 70-74; V of Methwold 74-80; RD of Feltwell 75-80; P-in-c of Dymock w Donnington and Kempley Dio Glouc from 80; Preston Dio Glouc from 80. *Rectory, Dymock, Glos.* (Dymock 270)

LEGG, Richard. b 37. Selw Coll Cam BA 62, MA 66. Brunel Univ MPhil 77. Coll of Resurr Mirfield, 63. **d** 65 **p** 66 Lon. C of St Pet Ealing 65-68; Chap Brunel Univ 68-78; C of Chipping Barnet w Arkley Dio St Alb from 81. *168 Mays Lane, Barnet, Herts.* (01-449 7758)

LEGG, Robert Anthony Christopher. Ch Coll Hobart ACT ThL 64. **d** 63 **p** 64 Tas. C of St Osw Launceston 63-64; St Jas New Town 64-65; P-in-c of Zeehan W Rosebery 65-66; R of Scottsdale 66-71; Kingston Dio Tas from 71. *Rectory, Kingston, Tasmania 7150.* (002-29 6150)

LEGG, Robert Richard. b 16. MBE (Mil) 45. Open Univ BA 78. St Aug Coll Cant 36. **d** 59 **p** 60 Win. C of Andover 59-62; R of E w W Tytherley 62-71; V of Kingsclere Dio Win from 71. *Kingsclere Vicarage, Newbury, Berks, RG15 8SL.* (Kingslere 298272)

LEGG, Roger Keith. b 35. Lich Th Coll 61. **d** 63 **p** 64 Portsm. C of Petersfield 63-66; Portsea (in c of St Faith) 66-70; R of Belvedere Mashon 70-75; V of Clayton Dio Lich from 75. *Vicarage, Clayton Lane, Clayton, Newcastle-under-Lyme, ST5 3DW.* (Newc-u-Lyme 614500)

LEGGE, Frederick John. b 10. Ridley Hall Cam 58. **d** 59 Croydon for Cant **p** 59 Cant. [f Free Ch Min]. C of St Mildred Addiscombe 59-60; V of St Jas Porchester Nottm 60-63; R of E Leake 63-76; C-in-c of Rempstone of Costock and of Stanford-on-Soar 70-76. *Parsonage House, 11 Chettle, Blandford Forum, Dorset, DT11 8DB.*

✠ **LEGGE, Right Rev William Gordon.** K Coll Halifax DD 73. Qu Coll Newfld. **d** 38 **p** 39 Newfld. C of Channel 38-41; I of Botwood 41-44; R of Bell Is 44-55; Archd of Avalon and Sec-Treas of Newfld Dioc Synod 55-68; Can of Newfld 55-68; Dioc Regr 57-68; Cons Ld Bp Suffr of Newfld in St Jo Bapt Cathl St John's 25 Jan 68 by Abp of Fred; Abp of Rupld (Primate); Bps of Newfld; NS; Queb; and Montr; Bps Suffr of Hur; NS; and Massachusetts (USA); Apptd Ld Bp of W Newfld 76; res 78. *Suite 311, Mill Brook Mall, Corner Brook, Newfoundland, Canada.*

LE GRICE, Very Rev Frederick Edwin. b 11. Qu Coll Cam 2nd cl Math Trip pt i 32, BA (2nd cl Th Trip pt i) 34, MA 45. Westcott Ho Cam 34. **d** 35 **p** 36 Ripon. C of St Aid Leeds 35-38; Paignton (in c of St Mich AA 40-46 and in c of St Andr 44-46;) 38-46; V of Totteridge 46-58; Can and Sub-Dean of St Alb Cathl 58-68; Exam Chap to Bp of St Alb 58-68; Dean of Ripon from 68; V of Ripon w Littlethorpe Dio Ripon from 68; M Gen Syn from 70; Ch Comm from 73. *The Minster House, Ripon, Yorks, HG4 1PE.* (Ripon 3615)

LE GRYS, Alan Arthur. b 51. AKC and BD 73. St Aug Coll Cant 73. **d** 74 **p** 75 St Alb. C of St Jo Bapt Harpenden 74-77; St John Hampstead 77-81; Chap Bedford and Westfield Colls from 81. *30 Lyndale Avenue, NW2 2QA.*

LEGUHONO, David. St Pet Coll Siota 63. **d** 65 **p** 67 Melan. P Dio Melan 65-75; Dio Ysabel from 75. *Hofi, Maringe, Santa Ysabel, Solomon Islands.*

LEGUVAKA, Ezekiel. **d** 57 **p** 60 Melan. P Dio Melan 57-75; Dio Ysabel from 75. *Nareabu, Maringe, Solomon Islands.*

LEHIBE, Jaona. b 48. **d** 76 **p** 77 Diego S. P Dio Diego S 77-79; Dio Antsir from 79. *BP 278, Antsiranana, Malagasy Republic.*

LE HURAY, James Rodwell. Moore Th Coll Syd ACT ThL 63. **d** 63 **p** 64 Syd. C of Killara 63-66; Neutral Bay 66-67; R of Denham Court w Rossmore 67-76; Kingsford Dio Syd from 76. *25 Sturt Street, Kingsford, NSW, Australia 2032.* (349-1424)

LE HURAY, Kenneth Rodwell. Univ of New Engl BA 61. Moore Th Coll Syd 47. ACT ThL 50. **d** and **p** 51 Syd. C of Kingsford 51-52; C-in-c of Sefton and Chester Hill 52-60; R of Leura 60-63; Kingsford 63-76; S Hurstville Dio Syd from 76. *31 The Mall, South Hurstville, NSW, Australia 2221.* (546-3236)

LEICESTER, Lord Bishop of. *See* Rutt, Right Rev Cecil Richard.

LEICESTER, Assistant Bishop of. *See* Mort, Right Rev John Ernest Llewelyn.

LEICESTER, Archdeacon of. *See* Silk, Ven Robert David.

LEICESTER, Provost of. *See* Warren, Very Rev Alan Christopher.

LEIEE, George William. **d** 33 **p** 34 Bp Haynes for Bloemf. Miss P Dio Bloemf 34-42; Dir of St Mary's Miss Brandfort 42-49; Miss St Aid Bethlehem 49-55; Ficksburg Miss 55-58; Dir 58-64. *PO Box 31, Teyateyaneng, Lesotho, S Africa.*

LEIGH, Arnold Robert. b 36. K Coll Lon and Warm AKC 60. **d** 61 **p** 62 S'wark. C of Lewisham 61-66; Stockwell Green 66-69; V 69-72; Team V in Withycombe Raleigh w Exmouth 72-74; R 74-79; P-in-c of St Bart Devonport Dio Ex 79-80; V from 80. *13 Outland Road, Milehouse, Plymouth, Devon.* (Plymouth 52623)

LEIGH, Preb Bernard Thomas. b 11. St Steph Ho Ox 30. **d** 34 **p** 35 Newc T. C of St Mary Blyth 34-36; St Andr and St Phil Notting Hill 36-39; Barrow Hill (in c of St Francis Hollingwood) 39-41; H Nativ Knowle Bris 41-49; Bathwick w Woolley 49-53; R of Wrington w Redhill 53-67; Preb of Wells Cathl from 65; V of St Jo Bapt Bathwick Bath 67-76; Chap Cheshire Home Axbridge 72-76. *The Cheshire Home, Axbridge, Somt.*

LEIGH, David. LTCL 56. **d** 61 **p** 63 Hong. V of St Mark Hunghom Kowloon Dio Hong 61-64; P-in-c from 67; Chap All SS Sch Homantin 64-67; P-in-c of St Mark Hung Hon Dio Hong 67-72; V from 73. *St Mark's Vicarage, Hunghom, Kowloon, Hong Kong.* (3-831007)

LEIGH, Dennis Herbert. b 34. Univ of Lon BSc (2nd cl Math) 56, Dipl Th 68. Chich Th Coll 58. **d** 60 **p** 61 S'wark. C of Roehampton 60-62; E Wickham 62-67; St Mark w St Marg Plumstead 67-73; C of Corby (in c of St Jo Bapt) 73-75. *14 Willowbrook Road, Corby, Northants.*

LEIGH, George Franklin. Wycl Coll Tor. **d** 25 **p** 26 Yukon. Miss at St Mary Mavo 25-30; Ch Extension Miss 30-32; I of Pointe Claire 32-33; R of Grace Ch Montr 33-40; and 45-54; Chap CASF 40-45; R of Chapleau 54-59; Chap Burwash Industr Farm Reform Dio Alg 59-64; I of Harriston 64-69. *c/o St George's Church, Harriston, Ont., Canada.*

LEIGH, Howard Vincent. b 46. Univ of Cant NZ BA 69. St Jo Coll Auckld 70. **d** 70 **p** 71 Waik. C of Stratford 70-74; V of Waihi 74-80; Huntly Dio Waik from 80. *Vicarage, Huntly, NZ.* (87-559)

LEIGH, James Ronald. b 32. SOC 63. **d** 67 **p** 68 S'wark. C of St Barn Purley 67-71; Prec St Ninian's Cathl Perth 71-73; R of Leven 73-78; Kirkcaldy Dio St Andr from 78. *Rectory, Townsend Place, Kirkcaldy, Fife.* (Kirkcaldy 263314)

LEIGH, Martin Francis. b 40. Univ of Sheff BSc 63. Cudd Coll 65. **d** 67 **p** 68 S'wark. C of Lambeth 67-70; Bakewell 70-74; V of Ockbrook w Borrowash Dio Derby from 74; RD of Ilkeston from 78; Surr from 79; M Gen Syn from 80. *Ockbrook Vicarage, Derby, DE7 3RL.* (0332 662352)

LEIGH, Philip Percival. b 16. AKC 43. Bp Collins Pri for Eccles Hist 43. **d** 43 **p** 44 Bris. C of St Luke Brislington 43-45; S Wraxall (in c of Atworth) 45-57; V of Enmore (Br Gui) 47-48; C of Bridport 48-49; V of Milborne St Andr w Dewlish 49-51; St Barn Oldham 51-55; PC of Treverbyn 55-62; C of Stapleton Glos 62-64; V of S Marston w Stanton Fitzwarren

65-73. *11 Banbury Close, Lawns Estate, Swindon, Wilts, SN3 1LQ.* (Swindon 31856)

LEIGH, Richard Kenyon. b 05. Univ of Liv BA 27. Westcott Ho Cam 44. **d** 44 **p** 45 Liv. C of St Jo Evang Walton-on-the-Hill 44-52; Asst Master Prescot Sch 45-52; V of St Cross Knutsford 52-72; Perm to Offic Dio Ches from 72. *Latrigg, Cuerdon Drive, Thelwall, Warrington, Ches WA4 3JV.* (Warrington 67426)

LEIGH-HUNT, Edward Christopher. Univ Coll Dur BA 47. Ely Th Coll 48. **d** 50 **p** 51 S'wark. C of St Anne Wandsworth 50-54; St Matt Bethnal Green 54-56; St Jo Bapt Southend Lewisham 56-57; St Barn Ealing 57-66; Asst Hosp St Bart Hosp and C of St Bart L 66-73; Chap Middx Hosp from 73. *c/o Middlesex Hospital, Mortimer Street, W1.* (01-636 8333)

LEIGH-WILLIAMS, Owen Charles. b 32. Late Exhib of BNC Ox BA (2nd cl Jurispr) 56, 2nd cl Th 58, MA 60. Wycl Hall, Ox 56. **d** 58 **p** 59 Chich. C of St Mary Southgate Crawley 58-64; Ch Ch Gt Warley 64-68; Dagenham 68-72; P-in-c of St Andr Basildon Dio Chelmsf from 72. *3 The Fremnells, Basildon, Essex, SS14 2QX.* (Basildon 20516)

LEIGH-WOOD, Kenneth James. Trin Coll Ox BA (2nd cl Th) 35, MA 39. Westcott Ho Cam 36. **d** 36 **p** 37 Lon. C of St Mary Abbots Kens 36-40; CF (EC) 40-45; V of Arnold 45-48; Chap of St Gabr Tr Coll Camberwell 48; R of St John-at-Hackney 48-51; C-in-c of All S Clapton Park 50-51; Warden ICF Tr Coll 51-52; CF 52-59; L to Offic Dio Ont from 59. *744 Alfred Crescent, Kingston, Ont., Canada.*

LEIGHLIN, Bishop of. *See* Cashel.

LEIGHLIN, Archdeacon of. *See* Patton, Ven Desmond Hilton.

LEIGHLIN, Dean of. *See* Bolton, Very Rev Frederick Rothwell.

LEIGHTON, Adrian Barry. b 44. Lon Coll of Div 65. **d** 69 **p** 70 Roch. C of St Paul Erith 69-72; St Marg Ipswich Dio St E from 72; C-in-c of St Helen Ipswich Dio St E from 75. *28 Grove Lane, Ipswich, Suffolk.* (Ipswich 217346)

LEIGHTON, Alan Granville. b 37. SOC 73. **d** 76 **p** 77 Chich. C of St Matt Silverhill, St Leonards-on-Sea 76-79; Eston w Normanby (in c of St George's Normanby) Dio York from 79. *465 Normanby Road, Normanby, Middlesbrough, Cleve, TS6 0EA.* (Eston Grange 460613)

LEIGHTON, Anthony Hindess. b 23. Univ of Lon BSc (2nd cl Physics) 44. Wells Th Coll 47. **d** 49 **p** 50 Leic. C of Melton Mowbray 49-54; V of Thorpe Acre w Dishley 54-61; R of Girton Dio Ely from 61; Proc Conv Ely 65-70; RD of N Stowe 68-76. *Rectory, 40 Church Lane, Girton, Cambridge.* (Cambridge 276183)

LEIGHTON, James Douglas. b 42. McMaster Univ W Ont BA 64, MA 65. Univ of W Ont DPhil 75. **d** 75 **p** 76 Hur. C of St Jo Evang Lon Ont 75-77; Lect Hur Coll Lon Ont from 77. *1349 Western Road, London, Ont., Canada.*

LEIGHTON, John Thomas. b 08. **d** 76 Warrington for Liv **p** 77 Liv. [f in CA] Hon C of Knowsley Dio Liv from 76. *22 Newlyn Avenue, Liverpool, L21 9LD.* (051-928 1957)

LEITCH, John Winston. Univ of Auckld, NZ Bd of Th Stud LTh (2nd cl) 65. St Jo Coll Auckld 62. **d** 64 **p** 65 Auckld. C of Kohimarama 64-68; Whangarei 68-70; V of Hauraki Plains 70-73; St Mary by the Sea Dio Auckld from 73. *753 East Coast Road, browns Bay, Auckland 10, NZ.* (47-86938)

LEITORO, Paul. **d** 77 **p** 78 Nak. P Dio Nak. *Box 42, Maralal, Kenya.*

LELA, Allan. **d** 78 **p** 79 Centr Melan. P Dio Centr Melan. *Maravovo Training Centre, Guadalcanal, Solomon Islands.*

✠ **LEMAIRE, Most Rev Ishmael Samuel Mills.** **d** and **p** 36 Accra. P Dio Accra 36-60; Can of Accra 60-63; Archd of Sekondi 61-63; Cons Asst Bp of Accra in H Trin Cathl Accra 5 May 63 by Abp of W Afr; Bp of Accra; and Bps Martinson and Dimieari; Apptd Ld Bp of Accra 68; Elected Abp and Metrop of W Afr 81. *Bishopscourt, PO Box 8, Accra, Ghana.* (Accra 62292)

LE MARCHAND, John Lewis Mansfield. b 43. BNC Ox BA 68. Sarum Th Coll 68. **d** 71 **p** 72 Roch. C of St William's Eccles Distr Roch 71-74; St Pet w St Marg Roch 74-76; R of Burham and Wouldham 76-81; V of Scopwick w Kirkby Green Dio Linc from 81; P-in-c of Martin w Martin Dales Dio Linc from 81; Timberland Dio Linc from 81. *Scopwick Vicarage, Lincoln, LN4 3NT.* (Metheringham 21047)

LEMMON, Ernest Albert. **d** 81 N Queensld (NSM). C of St Andr Gloncurry Dio N Queensld from 81. *c/o PO Box 54, Gloncurry, Qld, Australia 4824.*

LEMMON, George Colborne. Univ of NB BA 59, BD 65. Wycl Coll Tor LTh 62. **d** 62 **p** 63 Fred. I of Cant w Benton 62-65; R of Wilmot w Wicklow and Peel 65-69; Renforth 69-72; Sackville Dio Fred from 72; Dorchester Dio Fred from 72. *Rectory, Sackville, NB, Canada.*

LEMMON, John Richmond. b 40. Coll of Em & St Chad Sktn 78. **d** and **p** 80 Edmon. P-in-c of Battenburg Miss Dio Edmon from 80. *4811 - 53 Avenue, Bon Accord, Alberta, Canada. T0A 0K0.*

LEMMON, Canon Rowland. b 09. Keble Coll Ox BA (Hist) 31, MA 40. Wells Th Coll 31. **d** 32 **p** 33 Carl. C of St Jas Barrow-F 32-36; St Aid w Ch Ch Carl 36-40; V of St Bridget Beckermet 40-49; Ponsonby 41-49; H Trin Millom 49-62; RD of Gosforth 51-62; Hon Can of Carl 60-62; R of Hexham 62-75; Hon Can of Newc T 70-75; Can (Emer) from 75. *St Edward's, Barton Road, Bramley, Guildford, Surrey, GU5 0EB.* (Guildf 893711)

LEMON, Albert St John. b 22. St Chad's Coll Dur. **d** 56 **p** 57 Dur. C of Benfieldside 56-58; Perm to Offic Dio Momb 58-63; C of Stamford 64-66; V of Salter Street 66-77; R of Sheldon Dio Birm from 77. *165 Church Road, Birmingham, B26 3TT.* (021-743 2033)

LEMON, Clive William Henry. b 06. Univ of Dur LTh 32. St Aid Coll. **d** 32 **p** 33 Heref. C of Ludlow 32-36; Pr 34-36; C of H Trin Hull 36-37; V of Kirk Fenton 37-49; C of Sherburn-in-Elmet (in c of Barkston) 37-49; V of St Thos York 49-54; Anlaby 54-63; St Columb Scarborough 63-67; Barrowford 67-72. *40 Kingsmoor Road, Stockton-on-Forest, York.* (York 400339)

LEMON, Canon David Ernest. Univ of Tor BA 48. Wycl Coll Tor 48. **d** 50 **p** 51 Tor. C-in-c of Ch of Ap Miss Haviland Tor 50-51; I of Stayner 51-54; Cooksville S 54-62; Lindsay 62-72; Ch of Transfig City and Dio Tor from 73; Can of Tor from 72; Exam Chap to Bp of Calg from 74. *111 Manor Road, Toronto, Ont., Canada.* (416-489 7798)

LEMPRIERE, Norman Everard. b 28. Univ of Liv BEng 54. Ridley Hall Cam 55. **d** 57 **p** 58 St Alb. C of Ch Ch Ware 57-61; R of L Munden 61-64; R of Sacombe 61-64; Perm to Offic Dio Ex 64-66; C of Witheridge 66-69; R of Nymet Rowland w Coldridge 69-75; Wembworthy w Brushford 70-75; Denton w S Heighton and Tarring Neville 75-81; Sullington and Thakeham w Warminghurst Dio Chich from 81. *Thakeham Rectory, Pulborough, Sussex.* (W Chiltington 3121)

LENDON, Edward Charles. b 24. Peterho Cam BA (2nd cl Th Trip pt i) 48, MA 54. Ridley Hall Cam 48. **d** 50 **p** 51 Man. C of St Clem Higher Openshaw 50-52; Min of St Steph Conv Distr Cam 52-55; Org Sec CPAS for E Distr and Perm to Offic Dios Chelmsf, Ely, Linc and St Alb 55-59; V of Galleywood 59-68; Dagenham 68-81; RD of Barking 76-81; R of Peldon w Gt and L Wigborough Dio Chelmsf from 81. *Peldon Rectory, Colchester, Essex, CO5 7PT.* (Peldon 303)

LENDRUM, William Henry. b 24. Trin Coll Dub BA 50, Div Test (1st cl) 50, MA 62. **d** 50 **p** 51 Connor. C of St Mich Belf 50-53; Lisburn Cathl 53-61; C-in-c of Whiterock 61-69; R of St Mary Magd Belf Dio Connor from 69. *56 Windsor Avenue, Belfast, BT9 6EJ, N Ireland.* (Belfast 667516)

LENEMIRIA, Solomon. Weithaga Bible Sch 60. **d** 61 **p** 64 Nak. P Dio Nak 61-77. *PO Wamba, via Isiolo, Kenya.*

LENG, Bruce Edgar. b 38. St Aid Coll 68. **d** 69 Sheff **p** 70 Bp Gerard for Sheff. C of St Swith Sheff 69-74; Team V of All SS Speke 74-78; Yate New Town 78-81; R of Handsworth Dio Sheff from 82. *Handsworth Rectory, Sheffield, S13 9BZ.* (Woodhouse 2403)

LENGA, Johnson Nathan. **d** 76 **p** 77 Ysabel. P Dio Ysabel; VG from 77. *Tasia Training Centre, Santa Ysabel, Solomon Islands.*

LENKOE, Peter Lepoqo. b 52. St Pet Coll Pmbg 78. **d** 80 Bp Stanage for Johann. C of Evaton w Sebokeng Dio Johann from 80. *PO Box 5, Sebokeng, S Africa 1982.*

LENNARD, Edward Stuart Churchill. b 21. Ex Coll Ox MA 42. Cudd Coll 47. **d** 54 Buckingham for Cant **p** 55 Ox. L to Offic Dio Ox 54-57 and from 59; C of St Cuthb Tsolo 57-59. *228 Iffley Road, Oxford.*

LENNARD, Canon Guy Neville Beresford. St Jo Coll Morpeth. ACT ThL 36. **d** 37 **p** 38 Goulb. C of St Sav Cathl Goulb 37-38; P-in-c of Thuddungra 38-41; R of Narromine 41-53; Prec of St D Cathl Hobart 53-54; R of Deloraine 54-64; R of St Steph Sandy Bay Hobart Dio Tas from 64; Can of Tas from 81. *St Stephen's Rectory, Braddon Avenue, Sandy Bay, Tasmania 7005.* (002-25 1459)

LENNARD, Thomas Jay. b 21. MBE 54. **d** 76 **p** 77 Edin (APM). Hon C of St Andr Kelso Dio Edin from 76. *Kirkbank Station Cottage, Kelso, TD5 8LD.* (Crailing 248)

LENNERTON, David Bayne. K Coll NS BA 50, MSLitt 53, BD 60. **d** and **p** 53 NS. C of Ch Ch Dartmouth 53-57; R of H Spirit Dartmouth 57-64; Ch Ch Syd NS 64-68; Hon C of St Geo Hamilton 72-74; St Bart Hamilton Dio Niag from 74. *14 Chateau Court, Hamilton, Ont., Canada.* (416-388 5435)

LENNON, Alfred Dennis. b 32. Oak Hill Coll 72. **d** and **p** 74 Ely. C of Cam 74-77; P-in-c of St Barn Cam Dio Ely from 77. *St Barnabas's Vicarage, Cambridge, CB1 2BX.* (Cambridge 52924)

LENNON, George Bradley. b 50. Univ of Minn USA BA 74. Univ of Tor MA 76. Trin Coll Tor MDiv 80. **d** 80 Bp Read for Tor **p** 81 Bp Hunt for Tor. C of St Geo Mem Ch Oshawa

Dio Tor from 80. *51 Centre Street S, Oshawa, Ont, Canada, L1N 3Z9.*

LENNOX, Geoffrey Raymond. ACT ThDipl 70. **d** 64 **p** 66 Tas. C of St Steph Sandy Bay Hobart 64-66; P-in-c of Cooee 66-68; R of Franklin 68-73; New Norfolk 73-74; Perm to Offic Dio Tas 74-81. *1 Riverview Parade, Rosetta, Tasmania 7010.* (002-30 2622)

LENNOX, James. b 12. TCD BA 36. Div Test (2nd cl) 37, MA 40. **d** 38 **p** 39 Dur. C of Houghton-le-Spring 38-43; Darlington 43-47; V of Ch Ch Woodhouse 47-63; Surr from 50: V of Bingley 63-77; Perm to Offic Dio Bradf from 77. *30 Hazel Beck, Cottingley Bridge, Bingley, W Yorks, BD16 1LZ.* (Bradf 560189)

LENNOX, Robert McEwen. b 48. Univ of Winnipeg BA 70. Trin Coll Tor MDiv 73. **d** and **p** 73 Rupld. V of Fairford 73-74; C of St Luke Burlington 74-78; R of Ridgeway 78-81; Grace Ch Milton Dio Niag from 81. *317 Main Street, Milton, Ont, Canada.* (416-878 2411)

LENNOX, William Ernest Michael. b 28. Selw Coll Cam BA 52, MA 63. Univ of Leeds Certif Educn 55. St Bonif Coll Warm 62. **d** 63 **p** 64 Ripon. C of Bramley 63-66; Margate 66-71; R of Kingsnorth (w Shadoxhurst from 73) Dio Cant from 71; Shadoxhurst 71-73. *Kingsnorth Rectory, Ashford, Kent.* (Ashford 20433)

LENON, Philip John FitzMaurice. b 24. BD (Lon) 60. ARIBA 52. Wycl Hall, Ox 55. **d** 57 **p** 58 Lon. C of Ch Ch Crouch End Hornsey 57-60; Min of St Andr Conv Distr Sidcup 60-67; V of Crowborough Dio Chich from 67 *Vicarage, Crowborough, Sussex.* (Crowborough 2081)

LENOX-CONYNGHAM, Andrew George. b 44. Magd Coll Ox BA 65, MA 73. CCC Cam PhD 73. Westcott Ho 72. **d** 74 Stepney for Lon **p** 75 Lon. C of Poplar 74-77; Team V 77-80. *c/o Westerley, White Lane Close, Sturminster Newton, Dorset, DT10 1EJ.* (0258-72744)

LENS VAN RIJN, Robert Adriaan. St Jo Coll Nottm 78. **d** 80 Bradwell for Chelmsf **p** 81 Chelmsf. C of Gt Baddow Dio Chelmsf from 80. *10 Barrington Close, Great Baddow, Chelmsford, CM2 7AX.*

LENTHALL, Lionel Rossiter. St Barn Coll Adel ACT ThL 48. **d** 48 **p** 49 Adel. C of Ch Ch Mt Gambier 48-50; Miss Chap at Meadows 50-51; P-in-c 51-53; R of The Burra 53-58; P-in-c of Plympton 58-60; R 60-67; Mt Gambier 67-74; Sen Chap AMF 58-67; Hon Can of Adel 66-69; VG Dio Murray 70; Archd of the Murray 70-74; L to Offic Dio Adel 74-75; Perm to Offic Dio Brisb 75; L to Offic 76-78; M SSF Brookfield Queensld 75-77; L to Offic Dio Adel from 78. *56 High Street, Grange, S Australia 5022.*

LENTHALL, Raymond Arthur. b 48. ACT ThL 74. Ridley Coll Melb 72. **d** 77 **p** 78 Melb. C of St Mary Caulfield 77-79; P-in-c of Winchelsea Dio Melb from 79. *Vicarage, Winchelsea, Vic, Australia 3241.* (052-67 2042)

LENTON, Canon Leonard Gershom. Oak Hill Th Coll 60. **d** 61 Argent **p** 62 Central Brazil. Asst Chap of St Sav Belgrano Buenos Aires 61-67; V of H Trin Lomas de Zamora Buenos Aires Dio Argent from 67; Hon Can of St Jo Bapt Cathl Buenos Aires from 72. *Lavalle 188, Depto 6, Temperley, Buenos Aires, Argentina.*

LENTON, Robert Vincent. b 15. Clifton Th Coll 62. **d** 63 B & W for Maseno **p** 63 Maseno. Chap at Kericho 63-65; Thika 65-71; V of Lacock w Bowden Hill Dio Bris from 71. *Lacock Vicarage, Chippenham, Wilts.* (Lacock 272)

LEN VAI, d 61 Bp Ah Mya for Rang **p** 62 Rang. P Dio Rang 61-70; Dio Akyab from 70. *St Gabriel's Church, Myn Chy, Via Akyab, Burma.*

LENYGON, Canon Herbert Edward. b 11. Univ of Lon BD (2nd cl Th) 53. Kelham Th Coll 32. **d** 38 **p** 39 Newc T. C of St Pet Wallsend 38-41; St Gabr Heaton (in c of St Francis) 41-49; Chap United Hosps of Newc T 49-74; Hon Can of Newc T from 70. *48 Foxes Way, Warwick, CV34 6AY.* (Warwick 493954)

LENZ, Charles Allan. b 49. Trin Coll Tor BA 72. Vanc Sch of Th MDiv 79. **d** 79 **p** 80 Yukon. C of Carmacks Dio Yukon from 79. *c/o St George's Church, Carmacks, Yukon, Canada, Y0B 1C0.*

LEODI, Joseph Nteo. b 42. **d** and **p** 74 Les. P Dio Les. *St Michael's Mission, PO Mokhotlong, Lesotho, S Africa.*

LEOMY, Jonathan Emmanuel Akibo. b 12. **d** 74 **p** 78 Gambia. P Dio Gambia. *Eglise de la Toussaint, Mission Anglicane, Box 105, Conakry, Guinea, W Africa.*

LEONARD, Francis Joseph. b 09. Univ of Leeds BA 31. St Mich Th Coll Llan. **d** 33 **p** 34 Llan. C of St Tyfaelog Pontlottyn 33-36; Chap RN 36-64; Chap Miss to Seamen and I of St Thos-a-Becket Hamburg 64-68; V of Lemsford 68-78. *Rectory Cottage, Charlwood, Horley, Surrey, RH6 0EE.* (0293-862278)

✠ **LEONARD, Right Rev and Right Hon Graham Douglas.** b 21. PC 81. Ball Coll Ox BA 43, MA 47. Episc Th Sem Kentucky DD (hon causa) 74. Westcott Ho Cam 46. **d** 47 **p** 48 Ely. C of St Andr Chesterton 47-49; Perm to Offic at St Ives (Hunts) w Oldhurst and Woodhurst 49-50; C of Stansted Mountfitchet 50-52; V of Ardleigh 52-55; Dir of Relig Educn Dio St Alb 55-58; Publ Pr Dio St Alb 56-62; Hon Can of St Alb 55-57; Can Res 57-58; Can Emer 58-62; Gen Sec Nat S and Sec C of E Bd of Educn Schs Coun 58-62; Archd of Hampstead 62-64; Exam Chap to Bp of Lon 62-64; R of St Andr Undershaft 73; St Mary Axe Lon 62-64; Cons Ld Bp Suffr of Willesden in St Paul's Cathl 21 Sept 64 by Abp of Cant; Bps of Lon; St Alb; Pet; Chelmsf and Wakef; Bps Suffr of Stepney; and Kens; and Bps Wand, Reeves and Craske; Select Pr Univ of Ox 68; Trld to Truro 73; to Lon 81; Dean of Chapels R and Prelate of OBE from 81. *London House, 8 Barton Street, SW1P 3RX* (01-222 8661)

LEONARD, Jack Graham. ACT ThDip 61. **d** and **p** 77 C & Goulb. Chap RAAF from 77. *7 Trenwith Close, Spence, ACT, Australia 2617.*

LEONARD, John Francis. b 48. Lich Th Coll 69. **d** 72 **p** 73 Blackb. C of St Geo Chorley 72-75; H Trin (in c of St Nich) Blackpool 75-81; V of St Nich Marton Moss, Blackpool Dio Blackb from 81. *187 Common Edge Road, Marton Moss, Blackpool, FY4 5DL.* (Blackb 62658)

LEONARD, John James. b 41. Univ of Southn BSc (Maths) 62. Sarum Th Coll 63. **d** 65 **p** 66 Leics. C of Em Ch Loughborough 65-70; V of St Barn New Humberstone Leic 70-78; P-in-c of Conv Distr of Epiph Rushey Mead Dio Leic from 79. *St Theodore's House, 4 Sandfield Close, Rushey Mead, Leicester.* (Leicester 669956)

LEONARD, Pakake Heketoro. MBE 61, CBE 71. St Jo Coll Auckld. **d** 22 **p** 24 Wel. Miss to Maoris Rangitikei Distr Dio Well from 22; Asst Supt Maori Miss Dio Wel 33-44; Perm to Offic Dio Wel 44-46; Dio Wai 47-65. *106 Ranolf Street, Rotorua, NZ.*

LEONARD, Stanley Gwyn. b 15. St D Coll Lamp BA (2nd cl Engl) 36. Ripon Hall, Ox 36. **d** 41 Lich. C of Hengoed w Gobowen 41; L to Offic Dio Mon from 49. *St Ronan's, Old Penygarn, Pontypool, Gwent.*

LEONARD-JOHNSON, Philip Anthony. Selw Coll Cam BA 58, MA 62. Linc Th Coll 63. **d** 65 **p** 66 Nor. C of Wymondham 65-68; Bulawayo Cathl 69-72; R of Riverside Bulawayo Dio Matab from 74; P-in-c of Bembesi 72-74. *5 Bernafay Lane, Riverside, PO Hillside, Bulawayo, Zimbabwe.* (31309)

LEONARD-WILLIAMS, David Haigh. b 15. ARIBA 47. Coll of Resurr Mirfield 54. **d** 55 **p** 56 Ex. C of Tavistock 55-57; R of Yelden w Melchbourne 57-66; C-in-c of Dean w Shelton 57; V 58-66; RD of Riseley 64-66; R of Clifford Chambers w Marston Sicca 66-73; V of Northleach and Eastington w Hampnett (and Farmington from 74) 73-80. *The Corner House, Birlingham, Pershore, Worcs, WR10 5AD.*

LEONG, John. d and **p** 75 Kuch (APM). P Dio Kuch. *St Columba's Church, POB 233, Miri, Sarawak, Malaysia.*

LE PAGE, Dallas Arthur des Reux. b 17. Keble Coll Ox BA 49, MA 53. Cudd Coll 49. **d** 51 **p** 52 Lon. C of John Keble Ch Mill Hill 51-53; St Steph Hampstead 53-58; Asst Chap Michaelho Sch Dio Natal 58-63; Chap Dioc Coll Rondebosch 63-76; C of Fish Hoek 76-80; Sub-Dean and Prec of St Geo Cathl Capetn from 80. *7 Sir George Grey Street, Oranjezicht, Cape Town 8001, S Africa.*

LE PAGE, Eric Christopher. b 51. Mount Allison Univ NB BMus 73. Atlantic Sch of Th Halifax NS MDiv 78. **d** 78 Bp Hatfield for NS **p** 78 NS. C of Spryfield Dio NS from 78. *36 Kelly Street, Apt 310, Halifax, NS, Canada, B3N 1W2.*

LE PAGE, Herbert John. b 16. AKC 40. **d** 45 **p** 46 Win. C of St Helier Jersey 45-49; St Brelade (in c of St Aubin) 49-51; V of Aymestrey w Leinthall Earles 51-56; Alderney 56-65; V of St Pet Mile End w St Benet Stepney 65-70; Rosedale Dio York from 70. *Rosedale Abbey Vicarage, Pickering, Yorks. YO18 8SB.* (Lastingham 293)

LEPINE, (Timothy) Peter Gerald. b 27. St Francis Coll Brisb ACT ThL 56. **d** 57 **p** 58 N Queensld. C of Ayr 57-62; M SSF from 62; L to Offic Dio Brisb 66-67; Prin St Francis Coll Harurd Dio New Guinea 67-71; Dio Papua 71-80; P-in-c of H Redeemer Belf Dio Connor from 80. *The Friary, 75 Deerpark Road, Belfast 14, N Ireland.*

LE ROSSIGNOL, David Edward. b 45. Ridley Coll Melb ACT ThL 75. **d** 76 **p** 77 Tas. C of St John Launceston 76; St Jas New Town 76-79; P-in-c of Buckland Dio Tas from 79. *Rectory, Triabunna, Tasmania 7273.* (002-57 3321)

LE ROSSIGNOL, Edward Lawrence. b 10. **d** 76 **p** 78 Tas. Hon C of Sorell-Richmond 77-81; R of Hamilton Dio Tas from 81. *Rectory, Hamilton, Tasmania 7460.*

LE ROSSIGNOL, Richard Lewis. b 52. Univ of Aston in Birm BSc 75. Oak Hill Coll 76. **d** 79 Barking for Chelmsf **p** 80 Chelmsf. C of St Paul E Ham 79-81; Willesborough w Hinxhill Dio Cant from 81. *Christ Church House, 317 Hythe Road, Willesborough, Ashford, Kent.* (Ashford 38840)

LEROUX, André Georges. b 47. Wycl Coll Tor LTh 77. **d** 77 Bp Read for Tor **p** 79 Tor. C of St Marg West Hill Tor

77-78; Orillia S 78-80; I of Beeton, Tottenham and Palgrave Dio Tor from 80. *Box 39, Beeton, Ont, Canada.*

LERRY, Keith Doyle. b 49. Univ of Wales (Cardiff) Dipl Th 72. St Mich Coll Llan 69. **d** 72 **p** 73 Llan. C of Caerau w Ely 72-75; St Martin Roath Dio Llan from 75. *St Martin's Vicarage, Strathnairn Street, Roath, Cardiff, S Glam.* (Cardiff 482295)

LESHOELE, Matthew. St Bede's Th Coll Umtata 49. **d** 51 **p** 52 Basuto. P Dio Basuto 51-66; Dio Les from 66. *Box 145, Butha Buthe, Lesotho, S Africa.*

LESILWA, Yohana. St Phil Coll Kongwa 71. **d** and **p** 74 Centr Tang. P Dio Centr Tang. *Box 15, Dodoma, Tanzania.*

LESITER, Malcolm Leslie. b 37. Selw Coll Cam 2nd cl Th Trip pt i 59, BA (2nd cl Th Trip pt ii) 61, MA 65. Cudd Coll 61. **d** 63 **p** 64 Portsm. C of Eastney 63-66; Hemel Hempstead 66-71; Team V 71-73; V of Leavesden Dio St Alb from 73; RD of Watford from 81. *Leavesden Vicarage, Watford, Herts, WD2 7HJ.* (Garston 72375)

LESKE, Percy Eric. Ridley Coll Melb 79. **d** 79 **p** 80 N Terr. R of Numbulwar Dio N Terr from 79. *Rectory, Numbulwar, via Katherine, NT, Australia 5780.*

LESLIE, David Rodney. b 43. K Coll Lon and Warm AKC 67. **d** 68 Lon **p** 69 Willesden for Lon. C of St Anselm Belmont Lon 68-71; St Giles Cripplegate, Barbican w St Bart Moor Lane and St Alphage Lon Wall and St Luke Old Street w St Mary Charterhouse and St Paul Clerkenwell Lon 71-75; Team V of Kirkby Dio Liv from 76. *St Chad's Vicarage, Old Hall Lane, Kirkby, Liverpool, L32 5TH.* (051-546 5109)

✠ **LESLIE, Right Rev Ernest Kenneth.** OBE 72. Trin Coll Melb BA 31. ACT ThL 33. **d** 34 Melb **p** 35 Geelong for Melb. C of H Trin Coburg 34-37; R of Tennant Creek (w Alice Springs from 38) 37-40; Darwin 40-44; Chap AIF 42-45; R of Alice Springs w Tennant Creek 45-46; Vice-Warden St Jo Coll Morpeth 47-52; Chap C of E Gr Sch Timbertop 53-58; Cons Ld Bp of Bath in Syd Cathl 2 Feb 59 by Bp of Armid (Actg Metrop); Bps of River; Newc; and Bps Davies; Hilliard; Storrs; Kerle and Loane; res 80; Dean of Bath 59-71; Perm to Offic Dio Newc from 81. *51 Asca Drive, Green Point, NSW, Australia 2250.*

LESLIE, John Louis. b 13. Selw Coll Cam BA (3rd cl Cl Trip pt 1) 34, 3rd cl Th Trip pt i 35. Wells Th Coll 37. **d** 38 **p** 39 B & W. C of Yeovil w Preston Plucknett Kingston Pitney and Yeovil Marsh 38-40; Ilminster w Whitelackington 40-43; Chap RNVR 43-46; R of Curry Mallet w Curland 47-54; PC of Alcombe 54-66; Chap Commun St Mary Virg Wantage and L to Offic Dio Ox 66-75; R of Broughton Dio Pet from 75. *Rectory, Gate Lane, Broughton, Near Kettering, Northants, NN14 1ND.* (Kettering 790235)

LESLIE, Richard Charles Alan. b 46. AIB 71. **d** 79 St Alb. C of Redbourn Dio St Alb from 79. *12 Holts Meadow, Redbourn, Herts.*

LESOTHO, Lord Bishop of. *See* Mokuku, Right Rev Philip.

LESOTHO, Bishop Suffragan of. *See* Nestor, Right Rev Donald Patrick.

✠ **LESSER, Most Rev Norman Alfred.** CMG 71. Fitzw Hall Cam BA 23, MA 27. Ridley Hall Cam 23. ACT ThD 62. DD (Lambeth) 63. **d** 25 **p** 26 Liv. C of SS Simon and Jude Anfield 25-26; H Trin Formby 26-29; C-in-c of Ch Ch Conv Distr Norris Green W Derby 29-30; Chap of Cathl Liv and L to Offic Dio Liv 30-31; V of St Jo Evang Barrow-F 31-39; Hon Can R and Sub-Dean of All SS Cathl Ch Nairobi 39-47; Provost of Nairobi 42-47; Cons Ld Bp of Wai in Napier Cathl 11 June 47 by Abp of NZ; Bps of Waik; Dun; Auckld; Nel; and Wel; Bps Suffr of Aotearoa; and Bp Sedgwick; Elected Primate and Abp of NZ 61; res 71; L to Offic Dio Wai from 71. *4 Sealy Road, Napier, NZ.*

LESSO, Naboth Grugu. Univ of Ibad BA 66. **d** 69 Benin. d Dio Benin. *Uro Grammar School, PA Okpe-Isoko, via Kwale, Nigeria.*

LESTER, Preb Geoffrey. b 16. Trin Coll Cam BA 39, MA 43. Wycl Hall Ox 41. **d** 42 **p** 43 Lon. C of All S Langham Place w St Andr Wells Street 42-47; Chap of Westmr Abbey 43-44; C of Bywell w Riding Mill 47-48; Miss W Nile Distr 48-51; Chap All SS Cathl Nairobi 51; Chap Kampala 52-55; Provost and R of All SS Cathl Nairobi 55-60; R of Bath Abbey w St Jas Bath Dio B & W from 60; RD of Bath 61-71; Preb of Wells Cathl from 62; Proc Conv B & W 66-70. *1 George Street, Bathwick Hill, Bath, BA2 6BW.* (Bath 60361)

L'ESTRANGE, Canon Guy James Albert. b 24. Trin Coll Dub BA and Div Test 47, MA 50. **d** 47 Down **p** 48 Connor for Down. C of St Martin Ballymacarrett 47-51; Dean's V and Chapter Clk of St Patr Cathl Dub 51-63; Res Pr 52-63; News and Information Officer Ch of Ireland 61-63; Hd Master Cathl Choir Sch Cant 63-64; Min Can and Prec of Cant Cathl 63-68; Hon Can from 81; R of Saltwood Dio Cant from 68; RD of Elham 74-80. *Saltwood Rectory, Hythe, Kent, CT21 4QA.* (Hythe 66932)

L'ESTRANGE, Hilary Cecil Hurford. Trin Coll Dub. **d** 45 **p** 46 Down. C of St Mary Newry w Donaghmore 45-47; St Luke Belf 47-51; St Salvador Edin 51-54; C of H Cross E Pondoland 54-56; Matatiele 56-60; Beaufort W and of Vic W 60-62; R of Riversdale 62-70; Ladismith 62-70; Uniondale Dio Geo from 70; P-in-c of Jansenville 70-74; R of Beaufort W Dio Geo from 74. *21 Donkin Street, Beaufort West, CP, S Africa.* (2356)

LESUDAY, Bonface. St Phil Th Coll Kongwa, 65. **d** 67 Bp Madinda for Centr Tang **p** 67 Centr Tang. P Dio Centr Tang 67-70; L to Offic Centr Tang from 70. *Box 38, Babati, Tanzania.*

LE SUEUR, Canon Arthur Binet. Hatf Coll Dur LTh 22. St Paul's Miss Coll Burgh. **d** 24 Linc for Col **p** 25 S Rhod. C of St Mich Salisbury 24-28; St Alb Mazoe 28-31; P-in-c 31-34; C of St John Bulawayo 39-44; R of St Cuthb Gwelo 44-48; H Trin Belvidere 48-70; Can of Geo 56-70; Hon Can from 70. *Box 221, Knysna, CP, S Africa.* (Knysna 5231)

LE SUEUR, Arthur Gerald. Keble Coll Ox BA 34, MA 51. St Bonif Coll Warm 25. **d** 30 Bp Williams for Capetn **p** 32 Capetn. C of St Paul Faure 30-31; St Mary Woodstock 31-32; St Barn Ox 33-36; St Paul Capetn 32-33 and 36; Actg Warden of Zonnebloem Coll Capetn 36-37; R of St Matt Claremont 37-46; St Barn Capetn 46-54; L to Offic Dio Capetn 54-77; Perm to Offic from 77; Org Sec Bible S of S Africa from 64. *Box 139, Gordon's Bay 7150, CP, S Africa.*

Le SUEUR, Paul John. b 38. Univ of Lon BSc (2nd cl Geol) 59. Wycl Hall, Ox 60. **d** 62 **p** 63 S'wark. C of Mortlake w E Sheen 62-65; Witney 65-69; R of Sarsden w Churchill 69-74; P-in-c of Clifton Hampden w Burcot 74-77; H Trin Rotherfield Greys Dio Ox from 77. *Holy Trinity Vicarage, Henley-on-Thames, Oxon, RG9 1SE.* (Henley 4822)

Le Sueur, Richard Milo. b 54. Univ of Tor BA 76. Wycl Coll Tor MDiv 79. **d** 79 Bp Read for Calg **p** 80 Calg. C of St Aug Lethbridge Dio Calg from 79. *409-11th Street South, Lethbridge, Alberta, Canada T1J 2N9.*

LETCHER, Canon David John. b 34. Chich Th Coll 56. **d** 58 Truro **p** 59 Bp Wellington for Truro. C of St Austell 58-62; Southbroom 62-64; R of Odstock w Nunton and Bodenham 64-72; RD of Alderbury 68-73 and from 76; V of Downton Dio Sarum from 72; Can and Preb of Sarum Cathl from 79. *Downton Vicarage, Salisbury, Wilts, SP5 3QA.* (Downton 20326)

LETCHFORD, Roderick Ronald. b 56. Univ of Tas BSc 78. St Barn Coll Adel. **d** 80 Bal. Perm to Offic 80; C of St Pet w All SS Bal Dio Bal from 81. *All Saints Vicarage, Windermere Street, Ballarat, Australia 3350.*

LETCHFORD, Warwick Thomas. Univ of Syd BEcon 59. St Jo Coll Morpeth. ACT ThL 63. **d** 63 **p** 64 Bath. C of Wellington 63-65; H Trin Orange 65-66; Asst Chap All SS Coll Bath 66-67; C of Gilgandra 68-69; St Jas Syd 69-70; R of Brighton Tas 70-72; Mortlake 72-77; H Trin Launceston Dio Tas from 77. *35 Lawrence Street, Launceston, Tasmania 7250.* (003-314428)

LETEBELE, Abel Kgosiemang Jailor. St Bede's Coll Umtata 61. **d** 63 **p** 64 Kimb K. P Dio Kimb K from 63; Hon Chap to Bp of Kimb K 69-73; Can of St Cypr Cathl Kimb 73-80; R of Vaal Hartz Dio Kimb K from 74. *PO Box 4, Taung, CP, S Africa.* (Taung 147)

LETFORD, Peter Arthur. b 36. Oak Hill Th Coll 68. **d** 70 **p** 71 Cant. C of St Faith Maidstone 70-72; CF 72-75; C of St Luke Ramsgate 75-77; P-in-c of Eastling 77-79; Stalisfield w Otterden 78-79; St Elis Becontree Dio Chelmsf from 79. *St Elisabeth's Vicarage, Hewett Road, Dagenham, Essex, RM8 2XT.*

LETHBRIDGE, Courteney David. Bp's Univ Lennoxville BA. Univ of Ott MA. **d** 59 **p** 60 Ott. C of All SS Westboro Ott 59-63; I of Combermere 63-68; Navan 68-73; N Gower Dio Ott from 75; Exam Chap to Bp of Ott from 80. *Box 29, North Gower, Ont., Canada.* (1-613-489-3738)

LETHBRIDGE, John Graham. Univ of W Ont BA 46. Hur Coll BD 53, LTh 51. **d** 49 **p** 50 Hur. C of Thamesford 49-52; Chap to Westmr Hosp Lon 52-56; R of Old St Paul Woodstock 56-59; Exam Chap to Bp of Hur 57-61; Hon Can of Hur 61-70; R of All SS Windsor 64-70; Archd of Perth 70-74; R of St Jo Evang Kitchener 70-74; on leave. *480 Mayfair Drive, Oshawa, Ont., Canada.*

LETHEREN, William Neils. b 37. St Aid Coll 61. Dipl Th (Lon) 63. **d** 64 Warrington for Liv **p** 65 Liv. C of St Mich Liv 64-67; St Athanasius Kirkdale 67-69; Walsall Wood (in c of St Mark Shelfield) 69-71; V of St Mich Liv 71-75; St Jas W Derby Dio Liv from 75. *111 Mill Lane, West Derby, Liverpool, L12 7JA.* (051-228 3958)

LETIWA, Daniel. **d** 77 **p** 78 Nak. P Dio Nak. *Baragoi, PO Maralal, Kenya.*

LETLALA, Mpedi Paul. b 53. St Paul's Coll Grahmstn 78. **d** 80 Bp Ndwandwe for Johann. C of Evaton w Sebonkeng

Dio Johann from 80. *PO Box 5, Sebokeng, S Africa 1982.*

LETOYIA, David L. Ch Tr Centre, Kapsabet, 66. **d** 67 **p** 68 Nak. P Dio Nak. *AC Maralal, Thomson's Falls, Kenya.*

LETT, Leslie Alexander. Laurentian Univ Ont BA (Phil) 73. Codr Coll Barb 57. **d** 60 **p** 61 Antig. C of St Anthony Montserrat 60-62; St Anne Sandy Point St Kitts 62-64; P-in-c of St Geo Montserrat 64-66; R of St Martin Barb 67-71; St Geo and St Andr Barb 72-73; Sub-Dean of Kingstown Cathl St Vincent 73-74; Dean 74-77; Reg Co-Ordinator Caribbean Conf of Chs from 77; L to Offic Dio Antig from 77. *Box 911, St John's, Antigua, W Indies.*

LETTS, Charles Justice. LTh (S Afr) 57. **d** 58 Syd **p** 58 Bp Hilliard for Syd. C of St Phil Syd 58-59; R of Hartley 59-62; C-in-c of Granville S 62-70; C of Liverpool 70-72; L to Offic Dio Syd from 72. *8/35 Blaxcell Street, Granville, NSW, Australia.*

LETTS, Gerald Vincent. b 33. Univ of Wales BA (2nd cl Phil) 63. Univ of Birm Dipl Th 65. Qu Coll Birm 63. **d** 65 **p** 66 Leic. C of Birstall Leics 65-68; V of St Mich AA Belgrave 68-75; St Cuthb Firvale City and Dio Sheff from 75. *St Cuthbert's Vicarage, Horndean Road, Sheffield, S5 6UJ.*

LETTS, Kenneth John. b 42. Univ of Melb BA 65. Univ of Leeds Dipl Th 70. Coll of Resurr Mirfield 68. **d** 71 Melb **p** 72 Bp Dann for Melb. C of St Steph Mt Waverley 71-74; Chap Melb C of E Gr Sch from 74. *47 Kooyong Road, Caulfield, Vic, Australia 3162.* (03-509 0706)

LEUNG, Andrew. Union Th Coll Hong 63. **d** 66 **p** 67 Hong. V of Crown of Thorns Ch Hong 66-72; on leave 73-74; C of St Mary Hong 74-75; V of Kei Oi Dio Hong from 75. *17 Kwong Lee Road, Kowloon, Hong Kong.* (3-798165)

LEUNG, Canon Ching Wa James. Union Th Coll Canton. **d** 38 Canton for Vic **p** 39 Vic. P Dio Vic 38-46; P-in-c of Cantonese Congreations Kuala Lumpur and Malacca 47-48; P-in-c St Matt Neil Road Sing 48-73; Hon Can of Sing from 63; Exam Chap to Bp of Sing 69-73. *48 Blair Road, Singapore.*

LEUNG, Peter. Trin Th Coll Sing BTh 60, MTh 69. Univ of St Andr Scotld PhD 73. **d** 60 **p** 61 Sing. P Dio Sing 60-62 and 64-76; Dio Jess 62-64; Exam Chap to Bp of Sing 73-76. *6a Mount Sophia, Singapore 9.*

LEVER, Edmund Arthur. b 23. Sarum Th Coll 55. **d** 57 **p** 58 Man. C of St Werburgh Chorlton-cum-Hardy 57-59; St John Farnworth 59-60; Hon C of St Jas Leigh Essex 60-63; Asst Master Belfairs High Sch for Boys Leigh-on-Sea 60-63; V of St Geo Brentwood 64-73; Chap S Ockendon Hosp from 73. *42 Peartree Close, South Ockendon, Essex, RM15 6PU.* (0708 852933)

LEVER, Julian Lawrence Gerrard. b 36. Fitzw Ho Cam BA 60, MA 64. Sarum Th Coll 60. **d** 62 **p** 63 Sarum. C of Amesbury 62-66; R of Corfe Mullen 66-78; RD of Wimborne 73-75; P-in-c of Wilton w Netherhampton and Fugglestone Dio Sarum from 78. *Wilton Rectory, Salisbury, Wilts, SP2 0DL.* (Wilton 3159)

LEVERTON, Peter James Austin. b 33. Univ of Nottm BA 55. CEng, MIMechE 68. Ripon Coll Cudd 79. **d** 81 Worc. C of St John in Bedwardine City and Dio Worc from 81. *16 Heron Close, Worcester.* (Worc 426719)

LEVERTON, Peter Robert. b 25. Lich Th Coll 59. **d** 60 **p** 61 Leic. C of Shepshed 60-64; Chap Miss to Seamen N Queensld 64-69; V of Marsh Chapel 70-73; Grainthorpe w Conisholme 70-73; R of North Coates 70-73; Chap Miss to Seamen Immingham 73-77; P-in-c of Brislington Dio Bris from 77. *St Luke's Vicarage, Church Hill, Brislington, Bristol, BS4 4LT.* (Bristol 777633)

LEVESLEY, Canon Thomas Hogarth. b 12. **d** 54 **p** 55 Bradf. C of Heaton 54-57; V of Thornbury 57-65; St Marg Ilkley 65-80; RD of Otley 73-80; Hon Can of Bradf 77-80; Can (Emer) from 80. *12 Langford Road, Burley-in-Wharfedale, Ilkley, W Yorks, LS29 7NL*

LEVETT, Colin Andrew. b 13. **d** 69 Willesden for Lon **p** 71 Lon. C of Northwood 69-71; St Cuthb N Wembley 71-73; P-in-c of Oxgate 73-78. *19 Wilmington Court, Bath Road, Worthing, Sussex, DN11 3QN.* (0903-210744)

LEVETT, Howard. b 44. K Coll Lon and Warm AKC (1st cl) 67. **d** 68 **p** 69 S'wark. C of Rotherhithe 68-72; V of St Jo Evang Walworth 72-80; RD of S'wark and Newington 78-80; Chap of St Mark w All SS Alexandria Dio Egypt from 80. *Box 685, Alexandria, Egypt.*

LEVEY, Colin Russell. b 35. SOC 63. **d** 66 **p** 67 Roch. C of Rusthall 66-71; Youth Chap Dio Roch 71-75; Hon C of Riverhead 71-75; V of H Redeemer Lamorbey 75-81; Ch Ch Milton-next-Gravesend Dio Roch from 81. *48 Old Road East, Gravesend, Kent, DA12 1NR.* (Gravesend 54326)

LEVI, Samuel. **d** 62 **p** 63 Momb. P Dio Momb. *PO Box 440, Mombasa, Kenya.*

LEVICK, Brian William. b 30. Westcott Ho Cam 63. **d** 64 Linc **p** 65 Bp Otter for Linc. C of Bourne 64-69; Deeping St Jas 69-70; Hemel Hempstead 70-71; Team V 71-77; V of Firbank, Howgill and Killington Dio Bradf from 77; Hon C of Sedbergh, Cautley and Garsdale Dio Bradf from 77. *The Lune Vicarage, Highfield Road, Sedbergh, Cumb, LA10 5DH.* (Sedbergh 20670)

LEVICK, Canon Frank Hemsley. b 29. Kelham Th Coll 49. **d** 54 Warrington for Liv **p** 55 Liv. C of St Marg Anfield 54-58; V 58-67; Ribbleton Dio Blackb 67-80; R from 80; Hon Can of Blackb from 75; M Gen Syn Blackb from 75. *Ribbleton Rectory, Preston, Lancs, PR2 6QP.* (Preston 791747)

LEVINGSTON, Peter Owen Wingfield. b 31. Trin Coll Dub BA and Div Test 58. **d** 58 **p** 59 Cork. C of St Luke w St Ann Shandon Cork 58-60; Monkstown 60-62; Chap RAF from 62. *c/o Ministry of Defence, Adastral House, WC1.*

LEWERS, Very Rev Benjamin Hugh. b 32. Selw Coll Cam BA 60, MA 64. Linc Th Coll. **d** 62 **p** 63 Pet. C of St Mary Virg Northn 62-65; Hounslow Heath (in c of Good Shepherd) 65-68; Chap Heathrow Airport 68-75; V of Newark-on-Trent 75-80; P-in-c of Averham w Kelham 79-81; R of Newark w Hawton, Cotham and Shelton 80-81; Provost of Derby and V of All SS Cathl Ch Derby from 81. *Provost's House, 9 Highfield Road, Derby.* (Derby 42971)

LEWES, Lord Bishop Suffragan of. *See* Ball, Right Rev Peter John.

LEWES and HASTINGS, Archdeacon of. *See* Godden, Ven Max Leon.

LE WI, H Cross Coll Rang. **d** 59 **p** 60 Rang. P Dio Rang. *c/o Bishopscourt, 140 Pyidaungsu Yeiktha Road, Rangoon, Burma.*

LEWIN, William Donald. b 13. TCD BA 37, Div Test 39. **d** 39 **p** 40 Oss. C of Ferns 39-44; C-in-c Timahoe 44-47; I of Aghold w Mullinacuff 47-50; Chap Miss to Seamen Yorks and S Dur 50-54; Sen Chap Dub and Org Sec for Eire 54-60; Org Sec SW Engl 60-67; R of Hale w S Charford Dio Win from 67. *Hale Rectory, Fordingbridge, Hants.* (Breamore 307)

LEWIS, Alan Edgar. Ridley Coll Melb 69. **d** 72 **p** 73 Melb. C of St Columb Hawthorn 72-74; Frankston 74-75; St Jas Taunton 75-76; in Angl Inner City Min Dio Melb from 76. *55 Lucknow Street, Ascot Vale, Vic, Australia 3032.* (37-6502)

LEWIS, Albert Edward. b 02. K Coll Lon 46. **d** 48 **p** 48 Southw. C of St Jo Evang Mansfield 48-50; R of Colwick 50-52; Bestwood Pk 52-59; V of Kirkby Wharfe w Ulleskelf 59-66; Harby w Swinethorpe 66-70; V of Thorney w Wigsley and Broadholme 66-70; LPr Dio Southw from 70. *Fairview Road, Woodthorpe, Nottingham.*

LEWIS, Ven Albert John Francis. b 21. Univ Coll of S Wales BA (Econ) 46. St Mich Coll Llan. **d** 48 **p** 49 Llan. C of St Jo Bapt Cardiff 48-61; Dir of Relig Educn Dio Llan from 60; V of Pendoylan 61-81; RD of Llan 69-81; C-in-c of Welsh St Donats 71-73; V 73-81; Surr from 68; Can of Llan 76-81; Archd of Margam from 81. *Margam House, St Hilary, Cowbridge, S Glam, CF7 7DP.* (Cowbridge 2460)

LEWIS, Canon Alexander Thomas. b 20. Univ of Wales (Ban) BA 51. St Mich Coll Llan 50. **d** 52 **p** 53 Ban. C of Llanber w Barmouth 52-56; V of St Ann Llandygai (w Tregarth from 67) Dio Ban from 56; RD of Arllechwed from 73; Hon Can of Ban Cathl from 82. *St Ann's Vicarage, Bethesda, Gwyn.* (Bethesda 600357)

LEWIS, Allan Walter Morice. St Jo Coll Morpeth, ACT ThL 64. **d** 64 **p** 65 Adel. C of Burnside 64-66; P-in-c of Kingston w Robe 66-72; R of Port Elliot Dio Murray from 72. *Rectory, The Strand, Port Elliot, S Australia 5212.* (54 2022)

LEWIS, Canon Arthur Griffith. St D Coll Lamp BA 40. **d** 47 **p** 48 Swan B. C of Clydach 47-55; R of Aberyskir w Llanfihangel-Nantbran 55-63; V of Ystalyfera Dio Swan B from 63; RD of Cwmtawe from 79; Hon Can of Brecon Cathl 80-81; Can from 81. *Ystalfera Vicarage, W Glam.* (Glantawe 842257)

LEWIS, Arthur Jenkin Llewellyn. b 42. M Pharm Society 67. B Pharm. Coll of Resurr Mirfield 71. **d** 73 **p** 74 Llan. C of Cardiff 73-78; Christchurch w Mudeford 78-82; R of Lightbowne Dio Man from 82. *Lightbowne Rectory, Kenyon Lane, Manchester, M10 9HS.* (061-681 1308)

LEWIS, Arthur Roland. St Edm Hall, Ox BA (2nd cl Engl) 41, MA 45. St Steph Ho Ox 41. **d** 43 **p** 44 Southw. C of St Mich AA Sutton-in-Ashfield 43-45; Stirchley 45-47; UMCA Miss Msalabani 47-49; Kizara 49-50; P-in-c of Msalabani 50-53; Kihurio 53-55; C of Zanz Is 55-57; P-in-c of Milo 57-58; Rusape 58-60; Mandea 60-69; Archd of Inyanga 66-71; R of Makoni 69-77; L to Offic Dio Mashon 77-80; Dio Pret from 80. *Box 32640, Glenstantia 0010, S Africa.*

LEWIS, Ven Benjamin Alec. b 12. St D Coll Lamp BA (3rd cl Hist) 34. **d** 36 Swan B for St D **p** 37 St D. C of Cardigan 36-40; Ammanford 40-41; Bp's Messenger Dio St D 41-46; V of Ch Ch Llanelly 46-56; R of Hubberston from 56-70; Archd of St D from 70; Can of St D Cathl from 70; Dir of Relig Educn Dio St D from 70. *Archdeaconry, St Davids, Dyfed.* (St Davids 456)

LEWIS, Canon Bertie. b 31. Late Scho of St D Coll Lamp

BA (2nd cl Welsh) 54. Late Powis Exhib. St Cath Coll Ox BA (2nd cl Th) 57, Wycl Hall, Ox 54. **d** 57 **p** 58 St D. C of Cwmamman 57-60; St Mich Abth 60-62; V of Llanddewi-Brefi w Llanbadarn Odwyn 62-65; Henfynyw and Aberaeron w Llanddewi Aberarth 65-74; Lampeter 75-80; Can of St D from 78; R of Abth Dio St D from 80. *Rectory, Laura Place, Aberystwyth, Dyfed, SY23 2AU.* (Abth 617184)

LEWIS, Brian James. b 52. St Jo Coll Auckld 75. **d** 78 **p** 79 Ch Ch. C of Ashburton Dio Ch Ch from 78. *PO Box 400, Ashburton, NZ.*

LEWIS, Canon Brinley James. b 11. Univ of Wales BA 40. St D Coll Lamp 39. **d** and **p** 42 Swan B. C of Killay 42; St Thos Swansea 42-48; St Paul Stalybridge 48-51; V of St Jo Evang Dukinfield 51-60; Helsby 60-65; St Paul Stalybridge 65-79; RD of Mottram 76-79; Hon Can of Ches Cathl 78-79; Can (Emer) from 79. *77 Dewsnap Lane, Dukinfield, Chesh, SK16 5AW.* (330-0507)

LEWIS, Preb Charles Curwen Dickens. b 15. St D Coll Lamp BA 37. **d** 39 **p** 40 Mon. C of H Trin Christchurch Newport 39-42; CF (EC) 42-43; C of Cheddleton 43-47; V of St Mark Walsall 47-52; Burntwood 52-57; Hednesford 57-67; St Paul Walsall 67-80; Preb of Lich Cathl 79-80; Preb (Emer) from 80. *65 The Crescent, Walsall, W Midl.*

LEWIS, Charles William. b 04. Oak Hill Th Coll. **d** 60 **p** 61 Lon. C of St Andr Whitehall Pk 60-63; V of Knypersley 63-73. *Crestville, Summerfield Lane, Kidderminster, Worcs, DY11 7SA.* (Kidderminster 65561)

LEWIS, Christopher Andrew. b 44. Univ of Bris BA 69. CCC Cam PhD 74. Westcott Ho Cam 71. **d** 73 Dur **p** 74 Jarrow for Dur. C of Barnard Castle 73-76; Tutor (Sen Tutor from 79) of Ripon Coll Cudd 76-81; Vice-Prin from 81; P-in-c of Aston Rowant w Crowell 78-81. *The Old Red Lion, Great Milton, Oxford, OX9 7PB.* (Gt Milton 662)

LEWIS, Christopher Gouldson. b 42. K Coll Cam BA 64, MA 68. Cudd Coll 65. **d** 67 **p** 68 Newc T. C of All SS Gosforth 67-71; P-in-c of Bunuk Kuch 71-74; V of Round Green 74-80; Whitstable Dio Cant from 80; RD of Reculver from 80. *Vicarage, Whitstable, Kent.* (Whitstable 272308)

LEWIS, Canon Christopher Thomas Samuel. b 08. CCC Cam 3rd cl Cl Trip 28, BA (2nd cl Th Trip) 30, MA 39. Cudd Coll 30. **d** 32 **p** 33 Newc T. C of Ch Ch Tynemouth 32-36; SPG Miss Dio Rang 36-42 and 46-51; C of St Mary Hunslet Leeds 43-44; St Mich Newquay 44-46; Chap of Burma Oilfields 46; Chap Maymyo 46-49; Chap Rang Cathl 49-51; Hon Can of Rang 50-51; Can (Emer) from 51; V of St Gluvias 52-59; Illingworth Halifax 59-61; R of Cheriton Bp 61-74; RD of Kenn 72-74; Can Missr and P-in-c of Fajara Gambia 74-77; St Pet Dakar Gambia 74-77; Perm to Offic Dio Sarum from 77; Dio Antig 78. *7/8 Bearfield Buildings, Bradford-on-Avon, Wilts, BA15 1RP.*

LEWIS, Colbert Columbus. Codr Coll Barb 74. **d** 76 **p** 77 Windw Is. C of St George's Grenada 76-77; St Jas Layou 77-79; P-in-c of St Patr St Vincent Dio Windw Is from 79. *Rectory, Barrouallie, St Vincent, W Indies.* (809-45 87336)

LEWIS, Canon Cyril Vicar. d 69 **p** 70 Windw Is. C of St Patr Grenada 69-70; Calliaqua 70-73; P-in-c of Layou Dio Windw Is 73-77; Hon Can of St Geo Cathl Kingstown St Vinc from 76; Perm to Offic Dio Windw Is from 77. *Fountain, St Vincent, W Indies.* (84660)

LEWIS, Dan Roberts. b 17. St Francis Coll Brisb 77. **d** 78 **p** 79 Brisb. C of St Matt Grovely Dio Brisb from 78. *4 Chevalier Street, McDowall, Queensld, Australia 4053.*

LEWIS, David Austin. b 09. St D Coll Lamp BA 31. **d** 32 **p** 33 Ches. C of Tarvin 32-35; All SS Newport 35-42; V of St Illtyd Williamstown 42-49; Treherbert w Tynewydd and Ynsfeio 49-64; R of Llanwenarth Ultra 64-76; L to Offic Dio Mon from 77. *29 Fairfield, Penperlleni, Pontypool, Gwent.*

LEWIS, David Elliott Courthope. b 43. St Jo Coll Morpeth 70. **d** 72 **p** 73 Tas. C of St John Launceston 73-75; on leave 76; R of Deloraine Dio Tas from 77. *Rectory, Deloraine, Tasmania 7304.* (003-622010)

LEWIS, Canon David Gareth. b 31. Univ of Wales BA 52. Oriel Coll Ox BA (2nd cl Th) 59, MA 63. St Mich Coll Llan 56. **d** 60 **p** 61 Llan. C of Neath 60-63; Chap and Lect Sarum Th Coll 63-64; Vice-Prin 64-69; Perm to Offic Dio Llan 64-69; Publ Pr Dio Sarum 64-69; Dean and R of St Jo Bapt Cathl Bel 69-77; Exam Chap to Bp of Br Hond (Bel from 73) 70-77; V of St Mark Newport Dio Mon from 78; Dioc Missr and Can Res of Mon from 81. *St Mark's Vicarage, Newport, Gwent.* (Newport 63321)

LEWIS, David Glyn. Univ of Wales BA 36. Ripon Hall, Ox 36. **d** 39 **p** 40 Birm. C of St Mary the Virgin Acock's Green 39-45; Dioc Chap in c of St Laur Birm 45-49; V of Butler's Marston w Pillerton Hersey and Pillerton Priors 49-55; Long Itchington w Bascote 55-68; C-in-c of Ufton 67-68; V of Cubbington 68-79. *3 St James' Close, Kissing Tree Lane, Alveston, Stratford-on-Avon, Warws.*

LEWIS, David Gwynfor. b 12. Univ of Wales BA (3rd cl French) 34, 2nd cl Engl 35, MA 44. St Steph Ho Ox 37. **d** 39 **p** 40 St A. C of Colwyn 39-42; Welshpool 42-49; R of Llangynog w St Melangell 49-54; V of Gwernaffield 54-79; RD of Mold 68-79. *13 Lon Cae Del, Mold, Clwyd.* (Mold 55437)

LEWIS, David Howell Gwyn. b 05. St D Coll Lamp BA 48. **d** 49 **p** 50 Llan. C of Llantrisant 49-53; Pentyrch 53-54; Gelligaer 54-57; V of Abercanaid 57-67; Mathern w Mounton 67-74; Perm to Offic Dio Mon from 74. *4 St John's Court, Oakfield Road, Newport, Gwent, NPT4 LN.*

LEWIS, David Islwyn. b 15. St D Coll Lamp BA 37. St Mich Coll Llan 37. **d** 38 **p** 39 St D. C of Llanelly 38-47; V of Cwmparc 47-61; Baglan Dio Llan from 61; RD of Margam 71-81. *Baglan Vicarage, Port Talbot, W Glam, SA12 8ST.* (Briton Ferry 812199)

LEWIS, David Islwyn. b 06. **d** 69 **p** 70 Llan. Hon C of Tongwynlais Dio Llan from 69. *Sunningdale Bungalow, Cross Street, Tongwynlais, Cardiff, CF4 7NQ.* (Taff Wells 810897)

LEWIS, David Roy. b 18. Late Scho of St D Coll Lamp BA (2nd cl Hist) 39. St Mich Coll Llan 40. **d** 40 **p** 42 Llan. C of St Jo Bapt Cardiff 40-46; V of Port Mourant 46-54; Chap Pointe-à-Pierre (w Marabella 54-62) Trinid 54-66; V of Seven Sisters 66-77; Colwinston w Llandow & Llysworney Dio Llan from 77. *Rectory, Llandow, Cowbridge, S Glam.* (Wick 205)

LEWIS, David Sidney. St D Coll Lamp BA 28. **d** 28 St D for Swan B **p** 29 Swan B. C of Llandilo-Talybont 28-31; Cockett 31-33; C-in-c of Llanddewi-Ystradenny 33-35; V of Brawdy w Hayscastle 35-45; Llangennech 45-61; Llangain 61-64; Trelech-a'r-Bettws w Abernant 64-70. *Llwynrhyd, Meidrim, Dyfed.*

LEWIS, David Vaughan. b 36. Trin Coll Cam 2nd cl Hist Trip pt i 59, BA 60, 2nd cl Th Trip pt ii 61, MA 64. Ridley Hall Cam 60. **d** 62 Bp McKie for Cov **p** 63 Cov. C of St Matt Rugby 62-65; Asst Chap K Edw Sch Witley 65-71; Asst Master Abbs Cross Technical High Sch Hornchurch 71-76; Hon C of Rainham 71-76; V of St Pet Stoke Hill City and Dio Guildf from 76. *37 Hazel Avenue, Guildford, Surrey.* (Guildf 572078)

LEWIS, David Watkin. b 40. St D Coll Lamp BA 61. Wycl Hall, Ox 61. **d** 63 Llan **p** 64 Bp T M Hughes for Llan. C of Skewen 63-66; Field Tr Officer Prov Youth Counc Ch in Wales 66-68; C of Gabalfa 68-71; P-in-c of Marcross and Monkash w Wick Dio Llan 71-73; R from 73; Dioc Insp of Schs Dio Llan from 75; Asst Dioc Dir of Educn from 78; RD of Llantwit Major and Cowbridge from 81. *The Rectory, Wick, Cowbridge, S Glam, CF7 7QL.* (Wick 243)

LEWIS, Canon Donald Edward. b 30. St D Coll Lamp BA 53. Wycl Hall Ox 53. **d** 55 **p** 56 St A. C of Wrexham 55-59; R of Castle-Caereinion 59-62; CMS Area Sec Dios Ches, Ban, St A and S & M 62-65; V of Hale 65-77; Swansea Dio Swan B from 77; RD of Swan from 77; Hon Can of Brecon Cathl from 79. *Vicarage, Eden Avenue, Swansea, Glam.* (0792 298616)

LEWIS, Edward. b 13. Late Cho Scho of K Coll Cam 33, BA 36, MA 40. **d** 38 Ugan **p** 39 St D. CMS Miss Dio Ugan 36-39; C of Milford Haven 39-41; Min Can of St D Cathl 41-43; and 46-50; Chap RNVR 43-46; C-in-c of St Bride Liv 50-51; V 51-52; Bargoed 52-60; Llanrhian 60-63; Weedon Lois w Plumpton and Moreton Pinkney 63-73. *110 Lon-y-Gors, Pensarn, Abergele, Clwyd, LL22 7SA.* (0745-824255)

LEWIS, Edward John. b 15. Qu Coll Cam 3rd cl Nat Sc Trip pt i 35, BA 36, 3rd cl Th Trip pt i 37, MA 40. Ridley Hall, Cam 36. **d** 38 **p** 39 Liv. C of Litherland 38-41; Prescot 41-43; Chap RNVR 43-46; R of St Andrew Brechin 47-53; V of Copt Oak 53-56; PC of Swanwick w Pentrich (V of Pentrich) 56-74; P-in-c of Longstone 74-80. *5 Old Hall Gardens, Rainford, St Helens, Mer.* (Rainford 2242)

LEWIS, Elinor Glenys. b 11. **d** 49 **p** 78 Ch Ch. dss Dio Guildf 49-59; Chap Ch Ch NZ Hosp 60-63; Travel Comm Prov of NZ 63-65; Hd C Dio Auckld 66-69; Hostel of H Name 70-71; Perm to Offic Dio Ch Ch 73-78; Hon C of Sydenham-Beckenham Dio Ch Ch from 78. *10a Heybridge Lane, Christchurch 2, NZ.* (326-808)

LEWIS, Canon Elvet. b 23. Late Welsh Ch Scho of St D Coll Lamp BA (2nd cl Hist) 47. St Edm Hall Ox BA (2nd cl Th) 50; MA 54. St Mich Coll Llan 50. **d** 51 Swan B for St D **p** 52 St D. C of St Paul Llanelly 51-53; St Pet Carmarthen 53-58; V of Himbleton (w Huddington from 60) 58-65; V of Huddington 58-60; St Steph Worc 65-79; Kempsey and Severn Stoke w Croome D'Abitot 79-81; RD of Upton from 79; Hon Can Worc Cathl from 80. *25 Charles Way, Malvern, Worcs.* (Malvern 4983)

LEWIS, Eric. b 36. Sarum Wells Th Coll 74. **d** 77 Sarum **p** 78 Ramsbury for Sarum (APM). C of Oldbury Dio Sarum from 77. *St James House, Cherhill, Calne, Wilts.*

LEWIS, Eric Desmond. b 16. Worc Ordin Coll. **d** 57 **p** 58 Worc. [f Bapt Min] C of St Mary Kidderminster 57-60; Horsham (in c of St Mark) 60-64; V of Blackheath Birm

64-67; Old Windsor 67-73. *Mole End, Dockenfield, Farnham, Surrey.*

LEWIS, Ernest Henry. **d** and **p** 49 Calg. C of Taber Miss 49-52; R of Drumheller 52-59; Hon Can of Cal 55-59; I of Stoney Lake 59-64; Calvary Ch Tor 64-67; R of Bridgenorth Dio Tor 67-69. *PO Box 2335, Taber, Alta, Canada.* (223-3957)

LEWIS, Evan David Dyfrig. Univ of Wales BA 47. TD 67. St Mich Coll Llan. **d** 49 **p** 50 Llan. C of Llantwit Major 49-52; St Jo Bapt Cardiff 52-58; CF (TA) from 55; R of Llanmaes w Llanmihangel Dio Llan from 58; Dioc Insp of Schs Dio Llan from 58. *Llanmaes Rectory, Llantwit Major, CF6 9XR.* (Llantwit Major 2362)

LEWIS, Evan Edgar. b 07. St D Coll Lamp BA 28. Late Cho Scho of K Coll Cam 3rd cl Th Trip pt ii 30, BA 31, MA 35. **d** 31 **p** 32 St D. C of Henfynyw w Aberayron 31-32; Chap of St D Cathl 32-35; C of St Edm Roundhay 35-36; H Trin Worthing 36-40; V of Isleham 40-45; Kirknewton 45-50; Bettws-y-Crwyn w Newcastle 50-54; R of Taynton 54-57; Tibberton 54-57; V of Stoke St Milburgh w Heath 57-73; R of Abdon w Clee St Margaret 57-73; Cold Weston 57-73. *Yew Trees, Marston, Pembridge, Leominster, HR6 9JA.*

LEWIS, Evan Thomas Derwen. b 10. Univ of Wales BA (3rd cl Hist) 34. St D Coll Lamp 34. **d** 35 **p** 36 Swan B. C of Llansamlet 35-40; CF (EC) 40-46 (Men in Disp 45); V of St Pet Glasbury Dio Swan B from 46; Surr from 46; RD of Hay 60-62. *Glasbury Vicarage, Hereford.* (049-74229)

LEWIS, Francis Edward Walter. b 17. Univ of Wales BA (2nd cl Phil) 40. St Mich Coll Llan 41. **d** 42 **p** 43 Mon. C of St Jo Evang Newport Mon 42-46; Bracknell 46-51; V of Watlington 51-65; Linslade 65-73; St Luke Maidenhead 73-81; RD of Mursley 66-81. *26 Norfolk Road, Maidenhead, Berks, SL6 7AX.* (Maidenhead 22733)

LEWIS, Francis Norman. St Barn Th Coll Adel 66. **d** 68 **p** 69 Adel. C of Burnside 68-70; P-in-c of Maylands w Firle 70-74; R of Penola 74-76; C of Hawthorn 76-78; R of Payneham Dio Adel from 78. *6 Arthur Street, Payneham, S Australia 5070.* (337 1311)

LEWIS, Canon Frank Stanley. b 04. Late Scho of St Jo Coll Cam Bell Scho and 1st cl Math Trip pt i 24, Naden Stud and BA (Wrang) 26, 2nd cl Th Trip pt i 27, MA 30. Westcott Ho Cam 27. **d** 28 **p** 29 S'wark. C of St Anne S Lambeth 28-31; St Paul w St Mark Deptford 31-34; Missr Wel Coll Miss Walworth 34-37; V of St Mark Walworth 34-41; St Marg Putney 41-56; Ch Ch Sutton 56-74; Hon Can of S'wark 74; Can (Emer) from 74. *138 High Street, Pershore, Worcs.* (Pershore 553010)

LEWIS, Frederick. b 09. Univ of Wales BA 31. St Mich Coll Llan 30. FRAI 40. **d** 32 Llan for Ban **p** 33 St A for Ban. C of Holyhead 32-34; Llanaber w Barmouth 34-38; All SS U Norwood 38-41; V of Wymynswold and C-in-c of Aylesham Conv Distr 41-44; St Donat Abercynon 44-53; I of St Padarn's Welsh Ch Islington 53-55; Chap and Tutor of Whittington Coll 55-68. *45 Nelson Drive, Blairgowrie, Randburg, Transvaal, S Africa.*

LEWIS, Frederick Norman. b 23. Univ of Leeds BA (Engl) 47. Coll of Resurr Mirfield, 47. **d** 49 **p** 50 Liv. C of St Jas Haydock 49-51; Dresden 51-55; Stafford 55-56; V of Wednesfield 56-65; St Chad Shrewsbury 65-69; St Mary Kingswinford Dio Lich from 69; Surr from 69. *St Mary's Vicarage, Kingswinford, Brierley Hill, W Midl, DY6 7AA.* (Kingswinford 3716)

LEWIS, Canon George William. Nashota Th Sem. **d** 29 Bp Burstill for N Dakota **p** 33 Milwaukee. [f in Amer Ch] R of Biabou w Greggs and Stubbs 51-60; Grenadines N 60-64; Layou 64-68; Can of St Geo Cathl Kingstown St Vincent 63-69; Can (Emer) from 69. *400 Maine Street, Quincy, Illinois 62301, USA.*

LEWIS, Gruffudd Emyr. b 16. St D Coll Lamp BA (Math) 38. St Mich Coll Llan 38. **d** 39 **p** 40 St A. C of Rhosddu 39-44; Dwygyfylchi w Penmaenmawr 44-46; Llanfachraeth w Llanynghenedl and Llanfugael 46-49; R of Trefdraeth 49-79. *Neuadd Wen, Conway Road, Llandudno, Gwyn, LL30 1PR.*

LEWIS, Gwyn. b 10. St D Coll Lamp BA 31. Ridley Hall, Cam 32. BD 42. **d** 33 **p** 34 Swan B. C of Ystalyfera 33-36; St Mary Swansea 36-41; C-in-c St Mich Manselton 41-43; CF (EC) 43-47; V of Clydach 48-57; Surr 48-69; R of Methyr Tydfil 57-69; RD of Merthyr Tydfil 57-69; R of Litton Cheney 69-78; Puncknowle w Swyre 69-78. *37 East Road, Bridport, Dorset.* (Bridport 24057)

LEWIS, Harold Aneuryn. b 04. Univ of Wales BA 36. St Mich Coll Llan 36. **d** 37 **p** 38 St D. C of St Issell 37-39; St Ishmael w Llansaint and Ferryside 39-40; Min of St D (Welsh Ch) Paddington 40-55; V of St Thos Kensal Town Lon 55-74. *10 Kedleston Rise, Banbury, Oxon.*

LEWIS, Henry David. **d** 30 Malmesbury for Llan **p** 31 Llan. C of Eglwysilan 30-33; I of St Mary's Welsh Ch Camberwell 33-38; C of St Jo Evang Thornham w Gravel Hole 38-42; Chap HM Pris Birm 42-44; C of Festiniog w Maentwrog 44-50; C-in-c of Carno 50-55; V of Scouthead 55-68; Sarn 58-66. *40 Pengors Road, Llangyfelach, Swansea, W Glam.*

LEWIS, Hubert Godfrey. b 33. St D Coll Lamp BA 59, Dipl Th 60. **d** 60 **p** 61 Llan. C of Merthyr Tydfil 60-64; Caerphilly 64-66; Asst Master Ravensbourne Sch Bromley from 67. Perm to Offic Dio S'wark 66-76; Dio Cant from 76. *6 Hamlyn Gardens, Church Road, Upper Norwood, SE19 2NX.* (01-653 0193)

✠ **LEWIS, Right Rev Hurtle John.** St Mich Ho Crafers ACT ThL 51. **d** and **p** 51 Adel. M SSM from 51; Asst Tutor St Mich Ho Crafers and L to Offic Dio Adel 51-58; Chap Bro of St Barn Sch Ravenshoe 58-60; Sub-Prior of St Mich Ho Crafers 60-63; Prov of SSM in Austr 63-68; Commiss Melan 63-68; Prior SSM Japan 68-71; Cons Ld Bp of N Queensld in St Jo Cathl Brisb 2 Feb 71 by Abp of Melb; Bps of Newc; Rockptn; Carp; N Terr; and others. *Bishop's Lodge, Townsville, Queensland, Australia 4810.* (077-712297)

LEWIS, Ian. b 33. MB and BS (Lon) 57. MRCS and LRCP 57. Oak Hill Th Coll. **d** and **p** 64 Sarum. C of St Jo Evang Heatherlands Parkstone 63-66; Hd CMJ Ethiopia 66-73; Hon C of Walcot Bath 75-77; L to Offic Dio B & W from 78. *10 Northend, Batheaston, Bath, BA1 7EN.* (0225-859818)

LEWIS, Ivor. Univ of Wales BSc 21. St Mich Coll Llan 25. **d** 25 **p** 26 St A. C of Llangollen 25-29; Bracknell (in c of Chavey Down) 31-35; V of Evancoyd 35-44; C-in-c of Cascob 37-44; C of Ch Ch Westmr 44-47; Chap and Sub-Dean of St Geo Colleg Ch Jer 47-50; Chap Rio Tinto Mines Huelva 50-58; Palma 58-61. *147 Stoke Poges Lane, Slough, Berks.*

LEWIS, Jacob Brian. b 33. Univ of Wales BA 54. Fitzw Ho Cam BA 56, MA 60. Wells Th Coll 56. **d** 57 **p** 58 Llan. C of St Mary Virg Cardiff 57-61; St Francis Miss and Coll Sekhukuniland 61-63; Cowley St John Ox (in c of St Alban) 63-67; V of St Francis of Assisi Gladstone Pk Lon 67-75; R of Compton Parva and E Ilsley Dio Ox from 76. *Compton Rectory, Newbury, Berks, RG16 0RD.* (Compton 256)

LEWIS, James Edward. b 22. St D Coll Lamp BA 50. **d** 51 **p** 52 Swan B. C of Gorsienon 51-52; Defynock w Rhydbriw 52-56; R of Llangynllo w Troedyraur 56-61; V of Brynamman 61-72; Llangathen w Llanfihangel Dio St D from 72. *Vicarage, Llangathen, Dyfed.* (Dryslwyn 455)

LEWIS, Ven John. Worc Coll Ox BA 58, MA 62. Ridley Hall, Cam 58. **d** 60 **p** 61 Liv. C of Sutton 60-63; Asst Chap at Brussels 63-64; Chap St Jo Evang Montreux 64-69; The Hague Holland 69-81; RD of The Netherlands 69-75; Can of H Trin Cathl Brussels 81-82; Chan and Sen Can from 82; M Gen Syn from 81; Archd of N-W Eur from 81. *Ave Guillaume Gilbert 38, 1050 Brussels, Belgium.* (Brussels 6604649)

LEWIS, John Arthur. b 34. Jes Coll Ox BA (3rd cl Th) 56, MA 60. Cudd Coll 58. **d** 60 Glouc **p** 61 Tewkesbury for Glouc. C of St Mary Prestbury 60-63; Wimborne Minster 63-66; R of Eastington w Frocester 66-70; V of Nailsworth w Inchbrook and Shortwood 70-78; Cirencester w Watermoor Dio Glouc from 78. *Vicarage, 23 Chesterton Park, Cirencester, Glos.* (Cirencester 3142)

LEWIS, John Burrenston. b 14. Late Scho and Exhib of St D Coll Lamp BA (2nd cl Hist) 35. **d** 37 **p** 38 Swan B for St D. C of Llanstadwell 37-39; Steynton w Johnston 39-40; Pemb Dk 40-43; C-in-c of Treffgarne w Spital 43-46; C of Letterston w Llanfair Nant-y-Gof 46-47; v of Carew 47-64; St Paul Llanelly 64-72; R of Ludchurch w Templeton Dio St D from 73. *Ludchurch Rectory, Narberth, Dyfed.* (Llanteg 208)

LEWIS, John Herbert. b 42. Selw Coll Cam 2nd cl Th Trip pt i 62, BA (2nd cl Th Trip pt ii) 64, 2nd cl Th Trip pt iii 66. Westcott Ho Cam. **d** 66 **p** 67 Cov. C of Wyken 66-70; St Andr Bedford 70-73; Bp's Chap for Graduates and Libr Pusey Ho Ox 73-77; Team V of Woughton Dio Ox from 77. *1 Pencarron Place, Fishermead, Milton Keynes, Bucks, MK6.* (Milton Keynes 678281)

LEWIS, John Hubert Richard. b 43. K Coll Lon and Warm AKC 66. **d** 67 **p** 68 Newc T. C of Hexham 67-70; Ind Chap Dio Newc T 70-77; Communications Officer Dio Dur from 77. *Bishopton Vicarage, Stockton-on-Tees, Cleve, TS21 1HA.* (Sedgefield 30207)

LEWIS, Very Rev John Percival. b 19. Trin Coll Dub BA 44, Div Test 47. **d** 47 **p** 48 Tuam. C of Galway 47-51; I of Knappagh Tuam 51-74; RD of Tuam from 56; Can and Preb of Tuam Cathl from 70; Provost of Tuam from 73; I of Omey (or Clifden) Dio Tuam from 73. *Rectory, Clifden, Co Galway, Irish Republic.*

LEWIS, Canon John Rapley. b 02. Em Coll Cam BA 24, MA 28. **d** and **p** 37 Chelmsf. C of St Mary Virg Colchester 37-39; V of St Aug Thorpe Bay 39-47; Maldon 47-53; RD of Maldon 47-53; V of Gt Ilford 53-65; Chap K George V Hosp Ilford 53-65; St Mary's Hosp Ilford 59-65; Asst RD of Barking 58; RD 59-65; Hon Can of Chelmsf 60-71; Can (Emer) from 71; R of Downham 65-71; Publ Pr Dio Chelmsf from 71;

Perm to Offic Dios Sarum and Ox from 71. *Ravensbourne, Union Street, Ramsbury, Marlborough, Wilts SN8 2PR.* (Marlborough 20419)

LEWIS, John Thomas. b 02. Coll of Resurr Mirfield. **d** 40 **p** 41 Aber. C of St Olaf Kirkwall 40-41; C-in-c of St Mary's Miss Stromness 41-43; R of Ch of the H Rood Carnoustie 43-46; Wyberton 46-50; Belton Linc 50-55; PC of Manthorpe w Londonthorpe 51-55; R of Paulerspury 55-69; Chap Hickey's Almshouses Richmond from 69. *164 Sheen Road, Richmond, Surrey.* (01-940 6560)

LEWIS, John Thomas. b 47. Jes Coll Ox 1st cl Maths Mod (2nd cl Maths) BA 69, MA 73. St Jo Coll Cam 2nd Cl Th Trip pt ii BA 72. Westcott Ho Cam 71. **d** 73 **p** 74 Llan. C of Whitchurch 73-77; Llanishen w Lisvane 77-80; Asst Chap Univ Coll Cardiff from 80; Warden of Ordinands Dio Llan from 81. *St Andrew, High Street, Llandaff, Cardiff, CF5 2DX.* (0222-563089)

LEWIS, Ven John Wilfred. b 09. G and C Coll Cam 2nd cl Hist Trip pt i 32. Steel Stud Exhib and BA 33, MA 37. Westcott Ho Cam 33. **d** 35 **p** 36 Lon. C of St Marg Lothbury Lon 35-37; Hd and Chap of Ox Ho Bethnal Green 37-40; V of Kimbolton w Middleton-on-the-Hill and Hamnish 40-46; Dir of Educn Dio Heref 43-64; R of Cradley 46-60; Preb of Colwall in Heref Cathl from 48; Proc Conv Heref 50-55; RD of Stokesay 60-64; Archd of Ludlow 60-70; R of Wistanstow 60-70; Archd of Heref 70-76; Archd (Emer) from 76; Can Res of Heref 70-76. *9 Claremont Hill, Shrewsbury, Salop.* (Shrewsbury 65685)

LEWIS, Kenneth Lionel. b 22. Welsh Ch Exhib Univ of Wales 41. Keble Coll Ox (Th) 49, BA 50, MA 54. Ch Coll Cam Cert of Educn 52. Wycl Hall Ox 52. **d** 52 **p** 53 Roch. C of St John Bromley 52-55; St Marg Streatham 55-57; R of Tatsfield 57-72; L to Offic Dio S'wark 72-78; Perm to Offic Dio Cant 75-78. *Yew Tree Cottage, Ewell Minnis, Dover, Kent.*

LEWIS, Kenrick Ewart. Andover Newton Th Sem Mass STM 70. St Pet Coll Ja. **d** 59 Ja **p** 60 Kingston for Ja. C of Cross Roads 59-63; R of Snowdon w Providence and Prattville 63-68; on leave 68-70; C of Montego Bay 70-71; Actg Angl Warden UTCWI 71-72; Warden from 76; Tutor 71-75; Commiss Bel from 77; Exam Chap to Bp of Ja from 76. *UTCWI, Papine Road, Kingston 7, Jamaica, W Indies.* (093-79868)

LEWIS, Leslie. b 28. LRAM 56. St Aid Coll 61. **d** 63 **p** 64 Ches. C of Eastham 63-66; W Kirby 66-72; V of Rainow w Saltersford (and Forest from 73) Dio Ches from 72. *Rainow Vicarage, Macclesfield, Ches.* (Bollington 72013)

LEWIS, Malcolm John. b 50. St Steph Ho Ox 75. **d** 78 **p** 79 Cant. C of Sheerness 78-81; Burgess Hill Dio Chich from 81. *St Edward's House, 7 Dunstall Avenue, Burgess Hill, W Sussex, RH15 8PJ.* (Burgess Hill 41300)

LEWIS, Mathew Rice. b 1900. Lon Coll of Div. **d** 29 Llan **p** 30 Malmesbury for Llan. C of Gabalfa 29-32; Pembrey (in c of Burry Port) 32-36; R of Freystrop w Haroldstone 36-48; CF (EC) 40-45; V of Llechryd 48-56; R of St Mary Magd Colchester 56-66; Ravenstone 66-69. *8 Alder Way, West Cross, Swansea, W Glam, SA3 5PD.* (Swansea 403669)

LEWIS, Michael Augustine Owen. b 53. Mert Coll Ox BA 75, BA (Th) 77, MA 79. Cudd Coll 75. **d** 78 **p** 79 S'wark. C of Salfords 78-80; Chap Thames Poly from 80. *35 Elmdene Road, SE18 6TZ.* (01-855 6858)

LEWIS, Michael David Bennett. b 41. Univ of Wales Dipl Th 68. St Mich Coll Llan 65. **d** 68 Bp T M Hughes for Llan **p** 69 Llan. C of Penarth w Lavernock 68-72; Chap RAF 72-74; C of Llanishen w Lisvane 74-77; V of Penyfai w Tondu Dio Llan from 77. *Penyfai Vicarage, Bridgend, Mid-Glam.* (Bridgend 2849)

LEWIS, Michael Douglas. b 35. Late Exhib of Hertf Coll Ox 2nd cl Cl Mods 55, BA (2nd cl Th) 57, MA 60. Sarum Th Coll 58. **d** 59 Taunton for B & W **p** 60 B & W. C of Stogursey 59-65; V of N Curry Dio B & W from 65. *North Curry Vicarage, Taunton, Somt.* (N Curry 490255)

LEWIS, Michael John. b 37. St Aid Coll 64. **d** 66 Bp McKie for Cov **p** 67 Cov. C of Whitnash 66-69; Nuneaton 69-73; Team V of Basildon w Laindon (and Nevendon from 78) 73-79; V of St Jas W Bromwich Dio Lich from 79. *St James' Vicarage, Hill Top, West Bromwich, B70 0SB.* (021-556 0805)

LEWIS, Norman Eric. b 34. Open Univ BA 77. Lich Th Coll. **d** 63 **p** 64 Man. C of Hope 63-67; V of Hindsford 67-77; St Simon and St Jude Bolton-le-Moors Dio Man from 77. *46 Green Lane, Bolton, BL3 2EF.* (Bolton 23919)

LEWIS, Owen Alexander. b 06. Univ of Tor LTh 72. Wycl Coll Tor 71. **d** 72 **p** 73 Tor. C of St Phil City and Dio Tor from 72. *5 Lynn Haven Road, Toronto 392, Ont., Canada.* (416-783 5606)

LEWIS, Paul Wilfred. Late Exhib of Ch Ch Ox 2nd cl Cl Mods 58, BA (2nd cl Lit Hum) 60, Dipl Th 72. Chich Th Coll. **d** 64 Lon **p** 65 Willesden for Lon. C of H Cross w St Jude St Pancras 64-66; St Paul Park Lane and St Jo Div Vartry Road Tottenham 66-68; Tutor Codr Coll Barb 68-71; Lect Sarum and Wells Th Coll 72-74; Chap 73-74; Lon Sch of Econ 74-80; St Chris Hospice Sydenham from 80. *c/o 51-53 Lawrie Park Road, SE26* (01-778 9252)

LEWIS, Peter Anthony. b 25. Sarum Wells Th Coll 76. **d** 79 **p** 80 Portsm. C of St Simon Southsea Dio Portsm from 79. *2 Selsey Avenue, Southsea, Hants, PO4 9QL.*

LEWIS, Peter Goulstone. b 25. St D Coll Lamp BA 48. **d** 50 St D **p** 51 Bp R W Jones for St D. C of H Trin Aberystwyth 50-54; Caerphilly 54-60; V of Cwmbach 60-66; Tongwynlais 66-79; Llantrisant Dio Llan from 79. *Vicarage, Llantrisant, Mid-Glam.* (Llantrisant 223356)

LEWIS, Peter Graham. B 40. Linc Th Coll 70. **d** 81 Grimsby for Linc. C of L and Gt Coates w Bradley Dio Linc from 81. *16 Longfield Road, Grimsby, S Humb, DN34 5SB.*

LEWIS, Peter Richard. b 40. Univ of Dur BA (2nd cl Geog) 62. Univ of Birm Dipl Th 64. Qu Coll Birm. **d** 64 Aston for Birm **p** 65 Blackb for Birm. C of St Mary Moseley 64-67; Sherborne w Castleton and Lillington 67-71; P-in-c of Bishopstone w Stratford Tony 72-80; V of Amesbury Dio Sarum from 80. *Amesbury Vicarage, Salisbury, Wilts, SP4 7EU* (Amesbury 23145)

LEWIS, Philip Stacey. b 04. Univ of Liv BSc (1st cl Chem) 24, Campbell Brown Scho 24, PhD 26, FRIC 31. **d** 44 **p** 45 Lich. C of Cannock 44-47; V of Standish w Hardwicke 47-64; C-in-c of Haresfield 55-64; V of S Cerney w Cerney Wick 64-74. *6c The Avenue, Cirencester, Glos, GL7 1EH.* (Cirencester 2800)

LEWIS, Raymond John. b 26. **d** 77 **p** 78 Stepney fort Lon. C of Woodberry Down Dio Lon from 77; Chap at N Lon Ch and Centre for Deaf People from 77. *2D Grazebrook Road, Clissold Park, N16 0HS.*

LEWIS, Reginald William. Moore Th Coll Syd 60. **d** 61 **p** 62 Graft. C of Kempsey 60-62; Lismore 62-64; V of Dunoon 64-66; R of Nimbin 66-70; V of Mallanganee 70-72; S Graft 72-77; R of Kyogle Dio Graft from 77. *Rectory, Kyogle, NSW, Australia 2474.*

LEWIS, Richard. b 35. Fitzw Ho Cam BA 58, MA 63. Ripon Hall, Ox 58. **d** 60 **p** 61 Leic. C of Hinckley 60-63; Sanderstead 63-66; V of All SS S Merstham 67-72; H Trin (w St Pet from 74) S Wimbledon 72-79; C-in-c of St Pet S Wimbledon 72-74; V of St Barn Dulwich Dio S'wark from 79. *Vicarage, Calton Avenue, SE21 7DG.* (01-693 2936)

LEWIS, Richard Charles. b 44. Dipl Th (Lon) 68. ALCD 69. **d** 69 **p** 70 Carl. C of Kendal 69-72; Chipping Barnet 72-76; V of Ch Ch Watford Dio St Alb from 76. *Christ Church Vicarage, Leggatts Way, Watford, Herts.* (Garston 72240)

LEWIS, Richard Martin Lister. b 03. Bps' Coll Cheshunt 28. **d** 30 **p** 31 Chelmsf. C of Romford 30-32; Perm to Offic Ch Ch Swansea 32-33; C of St Jo Evang Holborn 33-35; St Columba Haggerston 35-37; Perm to Offic at St Andr Worthing 38-39; C 39-42; C-in-c of St Marg S Elmham w Flixton 42-44; R 44-53; C-in-c of St Pet S Elmham 44-53; V of Mendham 53-68; Weybread 53-68; R of Chillesford w Butley and Wantisden 68-74; Perm to Offic Dio St E from 75. *Dock Farmhouse, Boyton, Woodbridge, Suff.*

LEWIS, Richard Rice. b 03. Jes Coll Ox BA (2nd cl Mod Hist) 24, MA 28, Dipl Th 34. Ripon Hall Ox 33. **d** 34 **p** 35 Chelmsf. C of Brentwood 34-36; Asst Master Brentwood Sch 25-33 and 34-61; Asst Chap 36-47; Chap 47-61; serving w Army 40-41; CF (EC) 41-45; Men in Disp 45; CF (R of O) 50-58; Hon CF 46; PC of Claydon w Mollington 62-65; Perm to Offic Dio Glouc 65-73; Dio Ox 66-73; Dio St Alb from 73. *Lavender Barn, Lucas Lane, Hitchin, Herts, SG5 2JB.* (Hitchin 2047)

LEWIS, Robert. b 38. St Pet Coll Ox BA (2nd cl Th) 62, MA 66. Cudd Coll 62. **d** 64 Warrington for Liv **p** 65 Liv. C of Kirkby 64-67; Chap St Bonif Coll Warm 68-69; Tutor St Aug Coll Cant 69-70; C of Kirkby (in c of St Martin Southdene) 70-71; Team V 71-75; Dom Chap to Abp of York 76-79; R of Thirsk w S Kilvington, Carlton Miniott, Sand Hutton, Baldersby and Skipton-on-Swale Dio York from 79; M Gen Syn from 80. *Rectory, Thirsk, Yorks, YO7 1PR.* (Thirsk 23183)

LEWIS, Canon Robert Hugh Cecil. b 25. New Coll Ox BA and MA 50. Westcott Ho Cam 50. **d** 52 **p** 53 Man. C of Crumpsall 52-54; New Bury Farnworth 54-56; V of St Pet Bury 56-63; Poynton Dio Ches from 63; RD of Stockport from 72; Hon Can of Ches Cathl from 75; M Gen Syn from 75. *Poynton Vicarage, Stockport, Chesh.* (0625-872711)

LEWIS, Robert George. b 53. Univ of Lanc BEducn 76. **d** 78 **p** 79 Liv. C of Our Lady & St Nich Liv 78-81; Asst Dioc Dir of Educn (Youth) from 81. *9 Bellefield Avenue, West Derby, Liverpool, 12.* (051-228 3786)

LEWIS, Roger Edward. b 24. Qu Coll Cam BA 45, MA 49. Ridley Hall, Cam 47. **d** 49 **p** 50 Birm. C of Handsworth 49-52; R of Hadleigh Essex 52-58; V of Clacton-on-Sea 58-71; Chap Crossley Ho 58-71; V of St Matt Surbiton Dio S'wark from 71. *St Matthew's Vicarage, Kingsdowne Road, Surbiton, Surrey.* (01-399 4853)

LEWIS, Roger Gilbert. b 49. St Jo Coll Dur BA (Gen) 70. Ripon Hall Ox 70. **d** 72 **p** 73 Birm. C of Boldmere 72-76; St Pet Birm 76-77; Tettenhall Regis 77-80; Team V 80-81; V of Ward End Dio Birm from 81. *Ward End Vicarage, St Margaret's Avenue, Birmingham, B8 2BH.* (021-327 0555)

LEWIS, Preb Ronald Llewellyn. b 12. Univ of Leeds BSc 35. Coll of Resurr Mirfield, 35. **d** 37 **p** 38 Bris. C of St Cuthb Brislington 37-40; St Andr Montpelier Bris 41-46; SW Area Dir ICF 46-49; V of Kingston St Mary 49-63; V of Broomfield 53-63; H Trin Taunton 63-77; RD of Taunton N 60-63; Taunton S 65-71; Surr 71-77; Preb of Wells Cathl from 73. *23 Burton Place, Taunton, Somt, TA1 4HE.* (Taunton 74778)

LEWIS, Roy Dovery. d 37 Gambia **p** 38 St D for Gambia. Miss at Bathurst 37-41; C of Pontesbury (in c of Lea Cross) 41-44; CF (S Afr) 42-44; C of St John Walmer 44-46; R of Adelaide (S Afr) 46-49; Chap at Milan Genoa and Rapallo 49-50; R of St Geo Cathl Windhoek and Chap to Bp of Damar 50-54; LPr Dio Geo 54-59; P-in-c of Hout Bay 59-61; R of Worc 61-65; L to Offic Dio Capetn 65-80; Perm to Offic from 80. *Box 111, Grabouw 7160, CP, S Africa.* (Grabouw 0240)

LEWIS, Stanley Edward. b 43. Mem Univ Newfld BA 67, LTh 67. **d** 67 **p** 68 Newfld. I of Battle Harbour 68-71; Burgeo 72-76; Stephenville 76-81; St Pet City and Dio Edmon from 81. *11035-127 Street, Edmonton, Alta, T5M 0T3, Canada.*

LEWIS, Terence Arnold. b 15. Jes Coll Ox 2nd cl Cl Mods 35, BA (2nd cl Lit Hum) 37, 2nd cl Th 38, MA 41, BD 51. St Mich Coll Llan 38. **d** 39 Swan B for Llan **p** 40 Llan. C of St John Penydarren 39-41; Aberdare 41-44; Chap RNVR 44-47; Lect at St D Coll Lamp 47-55; Exam Chap to Bp of Swan B 47-55; R of Aston Clinton 55-64; C-in-c of Drayton Beauchamp 55-64; R of Aston Clinton, Buckland and Drayton Beauchamp Dio Ox from 64. *Aston Clinton Rectory, Aylesbury, Bucks, HP22 5JD.* (Aylesbury 630406)

LEWIS, Thomas Herbert. b 10. Univ of Wales BA (1st cl Phil) 31. St Mich Coll Llan 32, St Cath S Ox. **d** 33 **p** 34 Mon. C of Rhymney 33-37; Aberdare 37-39; Wolvercote 39-40; CF (EC) 40-47; Men in Disp 45; CF 49-50; SCF 50-60; R of Highclere (w Ashmansworth and Crux Easton from 68) 60-76. *16 Chesterfield Road, Newbury, Berks.*

LEWIS, Thomas James. b 17. Univ of Wales (Swansea) BA 49. St D Coll Lamp 49. **d** 51 **p** 52 Swan B. C of Llandrindod w Cefnllys 51-53; Llangyfelach w Morriston 53-57; V of Clyro w Bettws Clyro 57-73; Llowes and Glasbury 66-73; Penclawdd Dio Swan B from 73; RD of Hay 66-73. *Vicarage, Crofty, Swansea, W Glam.* (Penclawdd 285)

LEWIS, Thomas Peter. b 45. Selw Coll Cam BA 67. Ripon Hall Ox 68. **d** 70 **p** 71 St Alb. C of Bp's Hatfield 70-74; Borehamwood 74-79; Team V of Borehamwood Dio St Alb from 79. *Holy Cross Bungalow, Warren Grove, Borehamwood, Herts.* (01-953 2465)

LEWIS, Trevor Charlton Haselden. Qu Coll Birm 49. **d** 51 **p** 52 Glouc. C of St Aldate Glouc 51-54; Cirencester (in c of Watermoor) 54-55; C-in-c of St John Conv Distr Churchdown 55-64; V 64-65; R of Dursley w Woodmancote 65-70; Chap RN 70-71; in Amer Ch. *3333 West Second Street, Apt 206/54, Los Angeles, CA 90004, USA.*

LEWIS, Walter Alun. b 08. St D Coll Lamp BA 31. **d** 32 **p** 33 St A. C of Wrexham 32-44; V of Pontblyddyn 44-77. *29 Blaenwern, Gwernymynydd, Mold, Clwyd.*

LEWIS, Walter Arnold. b 45. Nat Univ of Ireland (Dub) BA 68, Div Test TCD 71. **d** 71 **p** 72 Connor. C of Whiterock 71-73; St Mark Ballysillan (in c of St Andr Glencairn) Belf Dio Connor from 73. *26 Lyndhurst Gardens, Belfast 13, N Ireland.* (Belf 743979)

LEWIS, Canon William Cooper. b 02. St D Coll Lamp BA 28. **d** 28 **p** 29 St D. C of Bettws w Ammanford 28-35; R of Lampeter Velfrey 35-48; Chap RAFVR 43-46; V of Rhymney 48-72; Surr from 48; RD of Bedwellty 56-72; Can of Mon from 58. *13 Norman Street, Caerleon, Newport, NP6 1BB.*

LEWIS, William Daniel. b 07. St Aid Coll 54. **d** and **p** 55 Wakef. C of Lightcliffe 55-57; V of St John Bradshaw Halifax 57-72. *121 Longfellow Crescent, Sholver, Oldham, Lancs.*

LEWIS, William Edwin Walker. d 62 Bp McKenzie for Wel **p** 63 Wel. C of Gonville 62-66; Wanganui Dio Wel from 66. *5a Rawhiti Place, St John's Hill, Wanganui, NZ.*

LEWIS, William George. b 14. Worc Ordin Coll 63. **d** and **p** 65 Ex. C of Egg Buckland 65-67; S Molton 67-70; R of Berrynarbor 70-80; Perm to Offic Dio Truro from 80. *16 Metha Road, St Newlyn East, Newquay, Cornw, TR8 5LP.* (Mitchell 636)

LEWIS, William George Melville. Open Univ BA. SOC. **d** 69 **p** 70 S'wark. C of Coulsdon 69-71; Perry Hill 71-74; V of St Barn Eltham 74-80; St Mark Reigate Dio S'wark from 80. *8 Alma Road, Reigate, Surrey, RH2 0DA.* (Reigate 44063)

LEWIS, William George Rees. b 35. Hertf Coll Ox BA (2nd cl Jurispr) 59, 2nd cl Th 61, MA 63. Tyndale Hall, Bris 61. **d** 63 **p** 64 St D. C of Tenby w Gumfreston 63-66; St Paul Llanelly 66-69; R of Letterston w Llanfair Nantygof (w Jordanston w Llanstinan 73-78; (w Puncheston w L Newcastle from 78) Dio St D from 69. *Rectory, Letterston, Haverfordwest, Dyfed.* (Letterston 336)

LEWIS, William Glyn. b 15. St D Coll Lamp BA 39. **d** 42 **p** 43 Llan. C of Garw Valley 42-45; Llantwit Major 45-48; Dinas and Penygraig 48-51; Llanishen w Lisvane 51-57; V of Miskin 57-63; St Jo Evang Brownswood Pk 63-80. *145 Heol-cae-Gurwen, Gwaun-cae-Gurwen, Ammanford, Dyfed.*

LEWIS, William Herbert. b 12. BNC Ox 2nd cl Cl Mods 33, BA (2nd cl Lit Hum) 35, 2nd cl Th 36, MA 40. Wycl Hall Ox 35. **d** 40 **p** 41 Ripon. C of Beeston 40-43; St Mich Farnley Leeds 43-44; CMS Miss Dio Momb 44-62; Asst Master Maseno Scho 44-47 and 50-51; Prin Embu Normal Sch 47-49; Supervisor of Schs Coast Prov Kenya 51-57; Miss Asst and Supervisor of Schs Taita RD 57-58; N Nyanza RD 58-61; Distr Manager of Schs Centr Nyanza 61; R of Llanddewi Skirrid w Llanvertherine 62-66; R of Llangattock Lingoed w Llanfair Chap 62-66; Bedwellty 66-80. *34 Albany Road, Blackwood, Gwent, NP2 1DZ.* (0495 228236)

LEWIS, William John. b 15. Univ of Wales, BA 36. Chich Th Coll 36. **d** 38 Leic **p** 39 Bp Willis for Leic. C of St Pet Leic 38-40; C-in-c of St Mich AA Woolwich 40-41; All SS Marg Street 41-43; Chap RNVR 43-46; Dom Chap to Bp of Ely 46-51; V of St Giles w St Pet Cam 51-68; St Anne Brookfield 68-76; Proc Conv Ely 55-64; Surr from 55; Perm to Offic Dio St Alb from 76; Dio Ely from 77. *75 High Street, Riseley, Bedford.* (Riseley 525)

LEWIS, William Meredith. b 15. Univ of Wales BA (2nd cl Phil) 37. St Mich Coll Llan 37. **d** 39 Mon for Llan **p** 40 Llan. C of Merthyr Tydfil 39-43; St Andr Major 43-47; St Jas Shirley Birm 47-50; Stratford-on-Avon 50-52; V of Priors Hardwick 52-56; Priors Marston 53-56; Ryton-on-Dunsmore 56-68; Chap to Police Coll 56-60; C-in-c of Bubbenhall 58-68; RD of Dunchurch 63-68; R of Shipston-on-Stour w Tidmington 68-80. *6 Margetts Close, Kenilworth, Warws.*

LEWIS, William Rhys. b 20. St Mich Coll Llan. **d** 55 **p** 56 Llan. C of Ystrad Mynach 55-58; Bassaleg 58-59; V of Cwmtillery 59-62; St Andr Lliswerry Newport 62-64; Ebbw Vale Mon 64-69; R 69-73; R of Llangattock w Llangynidr 73-78; V of St Luke Cwmbwrla Swansea Dio Swan B from 78. *St Luke's Vicarage, Cwmbwrla, Swansea, W Glam.* (Swansea 32300)

LEWIS, Wyndham Ronald. b 10. Late Exhib of Jes Coll Ox BA (2nd cl Mod Hist) 32, MA 36. **d** 34 Llan **p** 35 St A. C of Flint 34-38; St Mary Redcliffe 38-41; Wells Cathl 41-42; Chap RAFVR 42-46; C-in-c of Ryhill 47-48; V 48-53; Ardington w Lockinge 53-68; L to Offic Dio Ox 68-78; Perm to Offic Dio Ox from 78; Dio Mon from 80. *7 The Meadows, Usk, Gwent, NP5 1BT.*

LEWIS-NICHOLSON, Russell John. b 45. Oak Hill Coll 79. **d** 81 Bradf. C of St Jo Bapt Clayton Dio Bradf from 81. *103 Pasture Lane, Clayton, Bradford, BD14 6LR.*

LEWISHAM, Archdeacon of. *See* Davies, Ven Ivor Gordon.

LEWSEY, Ernest. b 1897. **d** 48 **p** 49 Ox. C of H Trin Headington Quarry Ox 48 and Warden Ball and New Coll Boys' Club 48-52; R of Bix 52-66; V of Pishill 54-66; C of Dinder 66-70. *11 Foster Close, Wells, Somt.* (Wells 73373)

LEWTHWAITE, David. b 39. K Coll Lon BD 75. St Aid Coll 63. **d** 65 Blackb **p** 66 Lancs for Blackb. C of Standish 65-68; St Andr and St Mich Cathl Bloemf 68-69; Team V of Welkom and P-in-c of H Cross Odendaalsrus 69-71; C-in-c of All SS Blackb 71-72; C of Kentish Tn 72-75; P-in-c of Wilden w Colmworth and Ravensden 75-79; V of Knottingley 79-81; R of Maulden Dio St Alb from 81. *Maulden Rectory, Bedford.* (Ampthill 403139)

LEY, John Andrew. b 16. St Deiniols Libr Hawarden 70. **d** 72 **p** 73 Heref. Hon C of Leintwardine w Adforton 72-76; Wigmore Abbey 76-80; L to Offic Dio Blackb 80-81. *Ocle Pychard Vicarage, Burley Gate, Hereford, HR1 3QR.* (Burley Gate 385)

LEY, John Rowland. Lich Th Coll 29. **d** 33 Bp Palmer for Glouc **p** 34 Glouc. C of Westbury-on-Severn 33-36; UMCA Miss Dio Masasi 36-65; P-in-c of Lukwika 42-46; Mindu 48-52; Lindi 54-58; Masasi 59-60; Lulindi 60-65; R of St Mary Virg Belize 65-70; P-in-c of Cat I Nass 70-72; Cayo 73-76. *Flat 11, Fairfield West, Huxtable Hill, Chelston, Torquay, TQ2 6RN.*

LEYD, Derrick. b 31. **d** 75 **p** 78 Bp Carter for Johann. C of Evaton w Sebokeng 75-80. *PO Box 2115, Johannesburg 2000, S Africa.*

LEYLAND, Derek James. b 34. Univ of Lon BSc (3rd cl Phys) 55. Univ of Birm Dipl Th 60. Qu Coll Birm 58. **d** 60 Burnley for York **p** 61 Blackb. C of Ashton-on-Ribble 60-63; Salesbury 63-65; V of St Osw Preston Lancs 65-67; Pendleton-in-Whalley 67-74; Dioc Youth Chap Blackb 67-69; Industr Youth Chap Blackb 70-74; R of Brindle 74-80; V of Ashton-on-Ribble Dio Blackb from 80. *St Andrew's Vicarage, Ashton-on-Ribble, Preston, Lancs, PR2 1EQ.* (preston 726848)

LEYSHON, Thomas Evan. b 04. Univ of Wales BSc 28. St Mich Coll Llan 28. **d** 29 **p** 30 Llan. C of Cymmer w Porth 29-33; Usk and Monkswood 33-35; C-in-c of Six Bells 33-38; V of Undy 38-73. *Tysta House, Undy, Magor, Newport, Gwent NP6 3SN.*

LEYTE, Edward. Qu Coll Newfld. **d** 48 **p** 49 Newfld. C of St John's Cathl 48-52; I of Flower's Cove 52-56; C of Corner Brook 56-60; R of Channel 60-69; Grand Falls 69-80; Assoc P of St Thos, St John's Dio E Newfld from 80. *36 Eastview Crescent, St John's Newfoundland, Canada.*

LI, Wing-Piu Michael. b 45. Lakehead Univ BA 70. Wycl Coll Tor MDiv 73. **d** 73 **p** 74 Tor. C of St Luke Tor 73-76; P-in-c of St Sav Tor 76-80; I of St Mark Oshawa Dio Tor from 80. *520 Beurling Street, Oshawa, Ont, Canada.*

LIBERTY, William Charles. Bp's Univ Lennox LST 68. **d** 68 Queb for Ott **p** 69 Ott. I of Combermere 68-71; Aylwin-River Desert 71-79. *Kazabazua, PQ, Canada.* (1-819-467-2163)

LICHFIELD, Lord Bishop of. *See* Skelton, Right Rev Kenneth John Fraser.

LICHFIELD, Dean of. *See* Lang, Very Rev John Harley.

LICHFIELD, Archdeacon of. *See* Ninis, Ven Richard Betts.

LICKESS, David Frederick. b 37. St Chad's Coll Dur BA 63, Dipl Th 65. **d** 65 **p** 66 York. C of Howden 65-70; V of Rudby-in-Cleveland w Middleton Dio York from 70. *Hutton Rudby Vicarage, Yarm, Cleve.* (Stokesley 700223)

LIDBETTER, Arthur Henry. ACT ThL (1st cl) 37. Moore Th Coll Syd 35. **d** 38 **p** 30 Syd. C of St Aug Neutral Bay 38-42; Actg R of St Alb Epping 42-45; Chap AIF 45-48; Miss Dio New Guinea 48-49; P-in-c of Wanigela 49-70; Chap Mart Mem Sch Agenhambo 71-74. *c/o 70 Bathurst Street, Sydney, NSW, Australia.*

LIDDELL, Peter Gregory. b 40. Univ of St Andr MA 63. Linacre Ho Ox BA (Th) 65, MA 70. Andover Newton Th Sch Mass DMin 76. Ripon Hall Ox 63. **d** 65 **p** 66 St Alb. C of Bp's Hatfield 65-71; in Amer Ch 71-76; P-in-c of Kimpton w Ayot St Lawr Dio St Alb from 77; Dir of Pastoral Counselling from 80. *Vicarage, Kimpton, Hitchin, Herts, SG4 8EF.* (Kimpton 832266)

LIDDLE, Alexander McDougal. Codr Coll Barb. **d** 66 Barb for Trinid **p** 67 Trinid. C of H Trin Cathl Port of Spain 66-68; All SS Port of Spain 68-71; St Mary and All SS Cathl Salisbury 70-76; Prec 71-76; R of Belvedere Dio Mashon from 77. *14 Clarendon Circle, Belvedere, Zimbabwe.*

LIDDLE, Harry. b 36. Late Exhib of Wadh Coll Ox BA 57, MA 61. Wycl Hall, Ox 62. **d** 64 Middleton for Man **p** 65 Man. C of St Paul Withington 64-68; R of St Jo Evang Broughton, Salford 68-73; V of Balby Dio Sheff from 73. *6 Greenfield Lane, Balby, Doncaster, Yorks, DN4 0PT.* (Doncaster 853278)

LIDDON, Albert Richard James. b 03. AKC 30. Cudd Coll 30. **d** 31 **p** 32 Ox. C of Cowley 31-33; Miss Dio Zulu 33-34; P-in-c Bremersdorp w Swaziland 34-46; Perm to Offic Dios Cant and S'wark 47; C of Northam w Westward Ho 48-49; V of Chalgrove w Berrick Salome 49-76; R of Newington 50-76. *3 St Mary's Green, Abingdon, OX14 1HJ.* (Abingdon 23062)

LIDDON, Alfred James. b 21. Univ of Lon BA 49. Oak Hill Th Coll 46. **d** 51 **p** 52 Southw. C of Stapleford 51-54; Lect of Watford 54-56; V of St Barn York 56-59; Org Sec CPAS in SE Distr 59-63; NE Distr 63-65; L Pr Dio York 63-65; R of St Pet Gunton 65-77; RD of Lothingland from 76; R of Bradwell Dio Nor from 77. *Bradwell Rectory, Great Yarmouth, Norf, NR31 8QQ.* (Gt Yarmouth 63219)

LIDSTONE, Ven Isaac Malcolm. McGill Univ Montr BA 16. Montr Dioc Th Coll Hon DD 63. **d** 27 Queb for Montr **p** 27 Montr. I of Greenfield Pk 27-31; R of Granby 31-68; Archd of Bedford 47-68; P-in-c of N Shefford and S Roxton 52-53. *1973 Le Clair, Apt 409, Waterloo, PQ, Canada J0E 2N0.*

LIEBENROOD, John Ernest Hancock. b 1900. Trin Coll Cam BA 22, MA 26. **d** 24 **p** 25 Lon. C of St Mark Tollington Pk Lon 24-25; Ch Ch Spitalfields 25-30; St Andr-the-Less Cam 31-35; I of Ch Ch Bromley Pk 36-44. *Braemar, Stonegate, Wadhurst, Sussex.*

LIETA, Jones Mpho. St Bede's Coll Umtata 66. **d** 68 **p** 69 Bloemf. C of Thaba 'Nchu 68-70; Welkom 70-72; Dir Witsieshoek Miss 73-78; R of St Clare Bothaville Dio Bloemf from 78. *Box 333, Bothaville, OFS, S Africa.*

LIETA, Ramokhutswane. d 77 Botswana. d Dio Botswana. *PO Box 456, Gaborone, Botswana.*

LIEW, That Lip. d 79 **p** 80 Sabah. P Dio Sabah. *PO Box 17, Sandakan, Sabah, Malaysia.*

LIFTON, Norman Reginald. b 22. Worc Ordin Coll 62. **d** 64 **p** 65 Glouc. C of Coleford w Staunton 64-66; Hersham 66-68; Milford 68-70; R of Spexhall w Wissett 70-77; V of Berkeley w Wick, Breadstone and Newport Dio Glouc from 77. *The Chantry, Berkeley, Glos, GL13 9BH.* (Dursley 810294)

LIGANGA, Martin. St Cypr Th Coll Tunduru 37. **d** 39 **p** 43 Masasi. P Dio Masasi 39-62. *USPG Tunduru, Lindi, Tanzania.*

LIGANGA, Petro. St Cypr Th Coll Namasakata. **d** 60 Masasi. d Dio Masasi. *USPG, Luatala, Tanzania.*

LIGHT, Ven Edwin Stanley. CD 56. Univ of Sask BA 47. Em Coll Sktn LTh 38, Hon DD 61. **d** 38 Sktn for Sask **p** 39 Sask. C of Spiritwood 38-41; RCAF 41-46; I of Turtleford Miss 46-48; Chap RCAF from 48; DCG and Dir of Relig Administration 60-66; Chap Gen 66-68; Archd RCAF 63-68; Gen Sec Angl Ch of Canada 68-79; Archd (Emer) Dio Sask from 69; Executive Officer Ont Prov Syn from 80. *c/o 600 Jarvis Street, Toronto, Ont, M4Y 2J6, Canada.*

LIGHT, Gordon Stanley. Carleton Univ BA 65. Trin Coll Tor STB 69. **d** 69 Tor for Carib **p** 69 Carib. C of St Paul's Cathl Kamloops 69-72; R of St Geo Edmon 72-77; I of St Luke Winnipeg Dio Rupld from 77; Exam Chap to Bp of Rupld from 81. *130 Nassau Street North, Winnipeg, Manit, Canada.*

LIGHT, Kenneth John. b 45. Univ of Otago BA 68. St Jo Coll Auckld LTh 70. **d** 70 **p** 71 Dun. C of Anderson's Bay 70-73; Invercargill 73-74; V of Wyndham 74-78; Waimea Plains Dio Dun from 78. *Vicarage, Meadow Street, Lumsden, NZ.*

LIGHTBOURN, Ven Gilbert Ord. OBE 46. Univ of Tor BA 22, MA 24. Wycl Coll Tor LTh 21, BD 26, DD 45. **d** 21 **p** 22 Tor. C of Swansea Ont 21-22; St Thos St John's Newfld 22-24; St Paul's Cathl Lon Ont 24-29; St Paul Tor 29-30; R of Trin Ch Aurora 30-40; RD of W York 39-40; Chap RCAF 40-45; C of Ch Ch Deer Park Tor 45-47; Sec CCCS 47-50; Hon Can of Sask 48-51; R of Shanty Bay 51-59; I of Craighurst and of Vespra 60-70; Archd of Simcoe 53-60; Archd (Emer) from 61. *119 Blake Street, Barrie, Ont, Canada.*

LIGHTBOURNE, Derek Hugh. Univ of Otago BA 63. St Jo Coll Auckld LTh 66. **d** 66 **p** 67 Auckld. C of Papatoetoe 66-69; E Coast Bays 60-71; Youth Dir Chr Educn Dio Auckld 71-74; V of Henderson 74-79; Heathcote- Mt Pleasant Dio Ch Ch from 79. *19 Martindales Road, Christchurch 2, NZ.*

LIGHTFOOT, Vernon Keith. b 34. Univ of Dur BA (2nd cl Phil) 58. Ripon Hall, Ox. **d** 60 **p** 61 Liv. C of Rainhill 60-62; Our Lady and St Nich Liv 62-65; V of St Anne Stanley Liv 65-75; St Luke Mt Albert City and Dio Auckld from 75. *704 New North Road, Mount Albert, Auckland, NZ.* (866-046)

LIGHTOWLER, Joseph Trevor. b 33. **d** 79 St Alb **p** 80 Hertf for St Alb. C of Leverstock Green Dio St Alb from 79. *19 Pancake Lane, Hemel Hempstead, Herts, HP2 4NB.*

LIGUNDA, Petro. St Cypr Th Coll 30. **d** 32 **p** 37 Masasi. P Dio Masasi 32-62. *USPG, Mkomaindo, Tanzania.*

LIGUNYA, Washington Aggrey. d 72 **p** 73 Momb. P Dio Momb 72-75; Dio Nai from 76. *Box 56682, Nairobi, Kenya.*

LIKEMAN, Martin Kaye. b 34. **d** 57 **p** 58 Ban. C of Llanwnog w Penstrowed 57-60; Llandudno 60-64; V of Llanrhian w Llanhowel and Carnhedryn 64-73; Llanstadwell Dio St D from 73; RD of Dewisland and Fishguard 71-73. *Llanstadwell Vicarage, Milford Haven, Dyfed.* (Neyland 600227)

LIKHANG, John. St Bede's Th Coll Umtata. **d** 50 **p** 52 Basuto. P Dio Basuto 50-66; Dio Les 66-77. *Box 239, Fiksburg, Lesotho, S Africa.*

LIKILIKI, Pauliasi Molevuka. b 41. St Jo Coll Auckld 70. **d** 71 Bp Halapua for Polyn **p** 72 Polyn. P Dio Polyn. *Box 25, Levuka, Fiji Islands.*

LIKOLECHE, Joseph. b 44. St Jo Sem Lusaka. **d** 72 **p** 73 Malawi. P Dio S Malawi. *c/o Diocesan Office, PO Kasupe, Malawi.*

LIKONDE, Canon Smithies Paul. St Cypr Coll Tunduru 55. **d** 57 **p** 60 SW Tang. P Dio SW Tang 57-71; Dio Ruv from 71; Can of Ruv from 72. *Box 7, Songea, Tanzania.*

LIKONDO, Dismas. St Cypr Th Coll Tunduru 50. **d** 52 **p** 55 Masasi. P Dio Masasi 52-75; Can of Masasi 69-75. *PO Box 92, Newala, Mtwara Region, Tanzania.*

LILES, Malcolm David. b 48. Univ of Nottm BA (2nd cl Th) 69. St Steph Ho Ox 69. **d** 71 **p** 72 Pet. C of Epiph Corby 71-74; St Aid New Cleethorpes 74-76; Team V of L Coates (and Gt Coates w Bradley from 78) Dio Linc from 76. *Church Centre, Wingate Road, Grimsby, Humb, DN37 9EL.*

LILEY, Christopher Frank. b 47. Univ of Nottm BEducn 70. Linc Th Coll 72. **d** 74 **p** 75 Lich. C of Kingswinford Wordsley 74-79; Team V of Ch Ch Stafford Dio Lich rom 79. *Marston Road Vicarage, Victoria Terrace, Stafford, ST16 3HA* (Stafford 52523)

LILLEY, Alan Charles. b 34. Univ of Nottm BA (2nd cl Hist) 55, MA 67. St Cath S Ox Dipl Th 59. Wycl Hall, Ox 57. **d** 59 Bp Maxwell for Leic **p** 60 Leic. C of H Ap Leic 59-63; St

Barn Leic 63-65; V of Copt Oak 65-78; Stud Counsellor Univ of Tech Loughborough and L to Offic Dio Leic from 78. *The Student Counselling Service, University of Technology, Ashby Road,* (Loughborough 63171 Ext 376)

LILLEY, Ivan Ray. Bps' Coll Cheshunt 58. **d** 61 **p** 62 Pet. C of Kettering 61-64; Gt Yarmouth 64-75; C-in-c of Tottenhill w Wormegay Dio Ely from 75; Watlington Dio Ely from 75; S Runcton w Holme and Wallington Dio Ely from 75. *Rectory, Watlington, King's Lynn, Norf, PE33 0HS.* (055-810305)

LILLEY, John. b 36. Univ of Liv Dipl Adv Educn Studs 70. **d** 81 Ban (NSM). C of Holyhead Dio Ban from 81. *12 Plas Hyfryd Crescent, Holyhead, Gwynedd, LL65 2AH.*

LILLIE, Henry Alexander. b 11. Trin Coll Dub BA and Div Test (1st cl) 36, MA 42. **d** 36 **p** 37 Arm. C of Portadown 36-41; I of Milltown 41-47; R of Kilmore and Diamond 47-52; Armagh 52-65; Preb of Tynan In Arm Cathl 52-60; Treas 60-61; Chan 61; Prec 61-65; Dean and Keeper of Publ Libr 65-79. *104 Drummanmore Road, Armagh, N Ireland, BT61 8RN.*

LILLIE, William Walter. b 07. Qu Coll Cam BA 29, MA 33. Wells Th Coll 30. **d** 31 Lincs **p** 32 Bp Hine for Linc. C of Louth w Welton 31-33; St Matt Ipswich 33-36; V of Oakington 36-38; R of Kingsdon 38-40; V of Cheddar 40-42; Kersey 42-46; R of Saxham 47-54; V of Swalcliffe w Shutford 54-59; R of Donhead St Mary w Charlton 56-69; Perm to Offic Dio Sarum from 76. *Grove Cottage, Mere, Warminster, Wilts.* (Mere 553)

LILLINGSTON, Peter John Edward. b 23. Pemb Coll Cam BA 47, MA 50. Cudd Coll 52. **d** 54 **p** 55 Southw. C of Bingham 54-56; Chap and Tutor St Jo Coll Diobu 56-59; Chap CMS Rural Tr Centre Asaba 59-67; Rural Development Co-ordinator Christian Coun Nig 67-69; Tutor Im Th Coll Ibadan 69; V of St Martin Ludgate City and Dio Lon from 70; Dep P-in-Ord to HM the Queen from 75; Dep Min Can of St Paul's Cathl Lon from 76. *St Martin's Vestry, Ludgate Hill, EC 4.* (01-248 6054)

LILLINGSTON-PRICE, Michael Christopher. b 31. Em Coll Cam BA 56, MA 60. Ripon Hall Ox 56. **d** 58 **p** 59 Roch. C of Belvedere 58-60; CF from 60. *c/o Ministry of Defence, Bagshot Park, Bagshot, Surrey.*

LILLISTONE, Brian David. b 38. SS Coll Cam 2nd cl Geog Trip pt i, 60, BA (2nd cl Th Trip pt 1a) 61, MA 65. St Steph Ho Ox 61. **d** 63 **p** 64 St E. C of All H Ipswich 63-66; Stokesay 66-71; C-in-c of Lyonshall w Titley 71-76; R of Martlesham w Brightwell Dio St E from 76. *Rectory, Lark Rise, Martlesham Heath, Ipswich, IP5 7SA.* (Ipswich 622424)

LIM, Cheng Ean. Trin Coll Sing. **d** 67 Sing. d Dio Sing 67-70; Dio W Mal from 70. *24 Jalan Cheras, Kuala Lumpur, Malaysia.*

LIM, Kok Heng. Trin Coll Sing. **d** 67 Sing. d Dio Sing. *2 Dundee Road, Singapore 3.*

LIM, Ven Michael Hong Chin. Sing Th Coll Cudd Coll 53. **d** 55 **p** 56 Borneo. P Dio Borneo 55-62; Dio Kuch 62-66; Dean 66-69; Can and Archd of Kuch (w Brunei and N Sarawak from 79) from 69; P-in-c of Sekama Dio Kuch from 69. *St Faith's Church, Kenyalang Park, Kuching, Sarawak.* (Kuching 24569)

LIM, Peng Soon. ACT ThL 55. **d** 56 **p** 57 Sing. C of St Hilda Sing 56-58; P-in-c 58-67; Exam Chap to Bp of Sing 65-67; C of Ch Ch N Adel 67-70; P-in-c of Kilburn 70-76; Croydon w Kilkenny Dio Adel from 76. *56 Elizabeth Street, Croydon, S Australia 5008.* (08-46 2036)

LIM, Poh Ham. b 46. Univ of Malaya BA 70. Ridley Coll Melb ACT ThL 74. BD (Lon) 76. **d** and **p** 77 Perth. C of Ch Ch Claremont 77-79; P-in-c of Forrestfield Dio Perth from 79. *6 Magnolia Way, Forrestfield, W Australia 6058.* (453 6786)

LIMBERT, Canon George William. b 1899. Univ of Leeds, BA 21. Coll of Resurr Mirfield. **d** 23 **p** 24 Lich. C of St Mary Tunstall 23-25; All SS Perry Street Northfleet 25-27; Milton-next-Gravesend (in c of St Faith) 27-30; R of Pemberton w Northcliffe W Austr 30-32; Harvey W Austr 33-35; C of Ch Ch Milton-next-Gravesend 36-37; R of Plaxtol 37-44; V of All SS Perry Street Northfleet 44-51; St Aug Gillingham 51-59; Proc Conv 51-55; RD of Gillingham 54-60; Hon Can of Roch 56-63; Can (Emer) from 63; R of Wrotham 59-63. *Manormead Nursing Home, Tilford Road, Hindhead, Surrey, GU26 6RA.*

LIMBERT, Kenneth Edward. b 25. MIMechE, CEng 69. SOC 72. **d** 75 Lon **p** 76 Willesden for Lon. C of St Edm Northwood Hills Pinner Dio Lon from 75. *55 York Road, Northwood Hills, Middx, HA6 1JJ.*

LIMBRICK, Warren Edmund. Univ of NZ BA 59, MA 60. NZ Bd of Th Stud LTh 64, Episc Th Sch Mass BD 66. Ch Ch Coll 55. **d** 60 Dun for Ch Ch **p** 62 Ch Ch. C of Merivale 60-63; Papanui 64-64; on leave 65-66; V of Banks Peninsula 66-69; Warden Selw Coll Dun 69-80; Exam Jt Bd of Th Stud 70-81; Exam Chap to Bp of Dun 71-80; Min Officer Dio Auckld from 80. *28 Corbett Scott Avenue, Epsom, Auckland 3, NZ.*

LIMENYA, Yusufu. **d** 37 **p** 42 Ugan. P Dio Ugan 37-60; Dio Ruw 60-72; Dio Boga-Z 72-74. *BP 154, Bunia, Zaire.*

EMLY, Lord Bishop of. *See* Empey, Right Rev Walton Newcombe Francis.

LIMERICK, Archdeacon of. *See* Snow, Ven Brian.

LIMERICK, Dean of. *See* Chambers, Very Rev George William.

LIN, Frank Yu-Shing. U Th Coll Hong Kong, 59. **d** 60 **p** 61 Hong. P Dio Hong. *St Mark's Church, Rua Pedro North da Silva, Macao, Hong Kong.* (Macao 5409)

LIN, Rinson Tang Kuen. b 29. Trin Th Coll Sing LTh 70. **d** 70 Sing. C of St Mich AA Sandakan 70-72; St Paul Dio Hong from 72. *St Paul's Church, Glenealy, Hong Kong.*

LIN YONE SIN, Paul. **d** 68 **p** 69 Rang. P Dio Rang 68-70; Dio Mand from 70. *Christ Church, Mong Shu, SSS, Burma.*

LINCOLN, Lord Bishop of. *See* Phipps, Right Rev Simon Wilton.

LINCOLN, Assistant Bishops of. *See* Otter, Right Rev Anthony; Healey, Right Rev Kenneth; Colin, Right Rev Gerald Fitzmaurice.

LINCOLN, Archdeacon of. *See* Adie, Ven Michael Edgar.

LINCOLN, Dean of. *See* Twistleton-Wykeham-Fiennes, Very Rev The Hon Oliver William.

LIND-JACKSON, Peter Wilfrid. b 35. Univ of Leeds, BA (2nd cl Th) 67. Linc Th Coll 67. **d** 68 **p** 69 Heref. C of St Martin 68-71; P-in-c of Burghill Dio Heref 71-78; V from 78. *Burghill Vicarage, Hereford.* (Hereford 760246)

LINDARS, Frank. b 23. Wycl Hall Ox 54. **d** 56 **p** 57 Ripon. C of St Luke Beeston Hill Leeds 56-59; St Wilfrid Harrogate 59-61; V of Shadwell 61-80; Masham and Healey Dio Ripon from 80; RD of Allerton 73-78. *Masham Vicarage, Ripon, N Yorks.* (Masham 255)

LINDARS, Canon (Barnabas) Frederick Chevallier. b 23. Late Scho of St Jo Coll Cam BA (1st cl Or Lang Trip pt i) 45. 1st cl Th Trip pt i 46, 2nd cl Th Trip pt ii 47, MA 48, BD 61, DD 73. Westcott Ho Cam 46. **d** 48 **p** 49 Dur. C of Pallion 48-52; L to Offic Dio Ely 52-78; M SSF from 54; Asst Lect in Div Univ of Cam 61-66; Lect 66-78; Exam Chap to Bp of Blackb 70-81; to Bp of Newc T 73-81; Dean and Fell Jes Coll Cam 76-78; Can Th of Leic from 77; Rylands Prof of Bibl Criticism Univ of Man and L to Offic Dio Man from 78; Perm to Offic Dio Ely from 79; M Gen Syn from 80. *Faculty of Theology, The University, Manchester, M13 9PL.* (061-273 3333 Ext 3541)

LINDBECK, Robert John. b 43. Canberra Coll of Min 71. **d** 71 **p** 72 C & Goulb. C of St Jo Bapt Canberra 71-74; S Wagga Wagga 74; P-in-c of Good Shepherd Canberra 74-75; R of Bribbaree 75-78; C of Albury 78-79; R of Berridale Dio C & Goulb from 79. *All Saints Rectory, Berridale, NSW, Australia 2628.*

LINDECK, Peter Stephen. b 31. Oak Hill Th Coll 57. **d** 59 **p** 60 Lon. C of St Luke Hackney 59-62; All SS Salterhebble Halifax 62-63; St Andr w St Matthias Islington 64-67; Perm to Offic Dios St Alb and Derby 67-68; Win and Lich 68; V of St Bede Toxt Pk Liv 68-74; St Geo Kano N Nig 74-76; C of Ollerton 77-80; Boughton 77-80; V of Whitgift w Adlingfleet and Eastoft Dio Sheff from 80; P-in-c of Swinefleet Dio Sheff from 81. *Whitgift Vicarage, Reedness, Goole, Humb, DN14 8HG.* (Reedness 256)

LINDEN, Gilbert John. Univ of Queensld BA 72. St Francis Coll Brisb 59. ACT ThL (2nd cl) 62. **d** 62 **p** 63 Rockptn. C of St Barn N Rockptn 62-67; R of Coolamon 67-69; Barcaldine 69-73; Blackwater 73; Winton 74-78; St Matt Pk Avenue City and Dio Rockptn from 78; Exam Chap to Bp of Rockptn from 78. *Rectory, Macalister Street, Park Avenue, Queensland, Australia 4701.* (079-272545)

LINDEN, Gregory. b 25. Roch Th Coll. **d** 65 **p** 66 Ripon. C of St Edm Roundhay 65-68; Highweek w Abbotsbury 68-72; V of Brampford Speke w Cowley Dio Ex from 72; R of Upton Pyne Dio Ex from 72. *Brampford Speke Vicarage, Exeter, Devon.* (Stoke Canon 268)

LINDHORST, Alan Max. b 49. Univ of Stellenbosch BA 71. Univ of Capetn BA 79. St Jo Coll Nottm Dipl Th 76. **d** 77 Swartz for Capetn **p** 78 Capetn. C of Milnerton 77-80; Bonteheuwel 80; R of Bot River Dio Capetn from 80. *Box 40, Bot River, Cape, S Africa.* (02824-772)

LINDISFARNE, Archdeacon of. *See* Smith, Ven David James.

LINDLEY, Geoffrey. b 22. St Jo Coll Ox BA 45, MA 47. Westcott Ho Cam 47. **d** 47 **p** 48 S'wark. C of St Mich E Wickham 47-51; St Mary Virg Welling 51-52; V of St Phil Lambeth and Chap of Lambeth Hosp 52-56; V of St Marg Ox 56-72; P-in-c of Pyrton w Shirburn 72-79; Lewknor 72-79; Shipton-under-Wychwood Dio Ox 79-80; V (w Milton-under-Wychwood, Fifield and Idbury) from 80; P-in-c of Milton-under-Wychwood 79-80. *Vicarage, Shipton-under-Wychwood, Oxon, OX7 6BP.* (S-u-W 830257)

LINDLEY, Harold Thomas. b 28. St Jo Coll Ox BA (3rd cl

Th) 51, MA 73. Wells Th Coll 51. **d** 53 **p** 54 Wakef. C of Normanton 53-57; C-in-c of St Jas Conv Distr Rawthorpe Huddersfield 57-63; PC of Longstone 63-67; V 68-74; C-in-c of Barrow-on-Trent w Twyford Dio Derby from 74; Swarkestone Dio Derby from 81. *Barrow-on-Trent Vicarage, Derby.* (Derby 701027)

LINDLEY, Milton. b 09. Univ of Leeds, BA (3rd cl Hist) 30. Coll of Resurr Mirfield, 27. **d** 32 **p** 33 Newc T. C of Ch Ch 32-36; St Matt (c of St Wilfred's Miss) Newc T 36-38; Chap Newc T Gen Hosp 38-42; V of H Trin North Shields 42-53; S Kirby 53-69; Horbury 69-74; Proc Conv Wakef 63-70; L to Offic Dio Ripon from 74. *37 Moseley Wood Green, Cookridge, Leeds, LS16 7HA.*

LINDLEY, Ven Ralph Adrian. CBE 75. St Jo Coll Dur BA (2nd cl div ii Pol and Econ) 51, Dipl Th 53. **d** 53 **p** 54 Blackb. C of St Steph Burnley 53-55; Chap RAF 55-70; Archd of the Gulf 70-78; Archd (Emer) from 78; Chap at Abu Dhabi w Qater 70-78; Gen Sec Jer and the Middle E Ch Assoc from 78; Commiss Cyprus from 78. *The Old Gatehouse, Castle Hill, Farnham, Surrey, GU9 0AE.*

LINDLEY, Richard Adrian. b 44. Univ of Hull, BA (2nd cl Th) 65. Univ of Man MA (Th) 79. Cudd Coll 66. **d** 68 **p** 69 Bradf. C of Ingrow 68-70; Perm to Offic Dio Birm 70-74; Team V of Ellesmere Port 74-79; V of St Francis Westborough City and Dio Guildf 79; Team R from 80. *Rectory, Beckingham Road, Guildford, Surrey, GU2 6BU.* (Guildf 504228)

LINDO, Astley. St Pet Coll Ja. **d** 66 **p** 67 Ja. P-in-c of Kew Pk 66-69; R of Grange Hill 69-74; Southfield Dio Ja from 74. *Rectory, Southfield, Jamaica.*

LINDO, Leithland Oscar. b 29. St Pet Coll Ja. **d** 56 **p** 57 Ja. C of Cross Roads 56-58; St Jo Evang w St Mary U Edmonton 58-62; Heston 62-66; V of Ch Ch Staines Dio Lon from 66. *Vicarage, Kenilworth Gardens, Staines, Surrey, TW18 1DR.* (Staines 55457)

LINDOP, Kenneth. b 45. Linc Th Coll 71. **d** 74 **p** 75 Leic. C of St Phil Leic 74-77; H Trin Cov 78-80; P-in-c of Cubbington Dio Cov 80-82; V from 82. *Cubbington Vicarage, Leamington, Warws.* (Leamington 23056)

LINDSAY, David Macintyre. b 46. Trin Hall Cam BA 68, MA 72. Univ of Ox Dipl Th 70. Cudd Coll 68. **d** 71 Bp Ramsbotham for Newc T **p** 72 Newc T. C of All SS Gosforth 71-74; Keele 74-76; C-in-c 76-77; Perm to Offic Dio St E 79-80; Dio St Alb from 80; Chap and Asst Master Haberdashers' Aske's Sch Elstree from 80. *72 Eastmoor Park, Harpenden, Herts.* (Harpenden 63738)

LINDSAY, Keith Malcolm. Univ of Adel BA 39. St Barn Coll Adel ACT ThL 41. **d** 41 **p** 42 Adel. C of Ch Ch N Adel 41-42; Miss Chap St Edw Kens Gdns Adel 42-44; M of Bro of St Jo Bapt Dio Adel 44-47; P-in-c of Tailem Bend Miss 47-50; C of Tue Brook Lancs 50-53; R of S Yorke Penin 53-57; St Mary Magd Adel 57-67; Chap of Adel Hosp 58-67; R of Ararat 67-71; Port Friary 71-74; P-in-c of Maylands-Firle 74-79; R of Toorak Gdns Dio Adel from 79. *42 Prescott Terrace, Toorak Gardens, S Australia 5065.* (30 4251)

✠ **LINDSAY, Right Rev Orland Ugham.** b 28. BD (Lon) 57. St Pet Coll Ja 53. Berkeley Div Sch Conn Hon DD 78. **d** 56 **p** 57 Ja. C of Vere 56-57; on leave 57-58; Asst Master Kingston Coll Ja 58-67; Chap 62-63; CF (Ja) 63-67; Sec of Synod Ja 62-70; Prin Ch Teachers' Coll Mandeville 67-70; Bps Exam Chap 69-70; Cons Ld Bp of Antigua in Cathl Ch of St Jago-de-la-Vega Spanish Town 24 Aug 70 by Abp of the WI and Bp of Guyana; Bps of Barb; Ja; Hond; Nass; Windw Is; Berm; and others. *Bishop's Lodge, PO Box 23, St John's, Antigua, W Indies.* (20151)

LINDSAY, Richard John. b 46. Sarum Wells Th Coll 74. **d** 78 **p** 79 Chich. C of Aldwick 78-81; Almondbury Dio Wakef from 81. *23 Wormald Street, Almondbury, Huddersfield, HD5 8NQ.* (Huddersfield 41446)

LINDSAY, Canon Richard John Alan. b 24. Late Scho of Trin Coll Dub BA (1st cl Mod) 46, Div Test 48, 1st cl Th Exhib 49. **d** 49 **p** 50 Carl. C of St Jas Carl 49-52; CMS Miss Ruanda 52-64; Chap and Tutor CMS Tr Coll Chislehurst 65-68; R of St Pancras (w St Jo Evang to 73) Chich 68-74; Chap at Maisons Laffitte Dio (Gibr in Eur from 80) Lon (N and C Eur) from 74; Can of H Trin Cathl Brussels from 81. *15 Avenue Carnot, Maisons Laffitte, France.* (962-3497)

LINDSAY, Canon Robert. b 16. St Jo Coll Dur BA 37, MA 40, Dipl Th 38. **d** 39 **p** 40 Dur. C of St Mary Gateshead 39-43; C-in-c of Sacriston 43-45; Benfieldside 45-46; V of Lanercost w Kirkcambeck 46-55; Hawkshead w Low Wray 55-70; R of Dean 70-74; RD of Derwent 70-81; Hon Can of Carl from 72; V of Loweswater w Buttermere 74-81. *58 Primley Road, Sidmouth, Devon, EX10 9LF.* (Sidmouth 77882)

LINDSAY, Robert Ashley Charles. b 43. Univ of Leeds BA 66. Univ of Ex BPhil 81. Coll of Resurr Mirfield, 66. **d** 68 Willesden for Lon **p** 69 Lon. C of John Keble Ch Mill Hill 68-72; Sherborne (in c of St Paul's) 73-78; Chap Coldharbour Hosp 73-78. *Diggory Venn, 32 Kings Road, Sherborne, Dorset.* (Sherborne 3146)

LINDSAY, Canon William Richard. Linc Th Coll 53. **d** 55 Linc **p** 57 Leic. C of Boultham 55-57; All S Leic 57-64; St Pet w St Hilda Leic 64-65; P-in-c of Bo'ness w Linlithgow 65-68; V of Jamestown 68-81; Archd and Can of St Hel 68-81; Can (Emer) from 81. *c/o USPG, 15 Tufton Street, SW1P 3QQ.*

LINDSAY-PARKINSON, Michael. b 28. Edin Th Coll 66. **d** 67 **p** 68 Edin. C of Ch Ch Morningside 67-70; St Mich AA Helensburgh 70-72; R of Lockerbie Dio Glas from 72; Annan Dio Glas from 72. *Rectory, Lockerbie, Dumfriesshire, Scotland.* (Lockerbie 2484)

LINDSEY, Archdeacon of. *See* Jarvis, Ven Alfred Clifford.

LINDSEY, Beverley Howard. Qu Univ Kingston Ont BA 62. Hur Coll BTh 65. **d** 65 **p** 66 Ont. I of Marysburg 65-68; R of N Hastings 68-73; Bath w Collins Bay 73-80; Gananoque Dio Ont from 80. *25 Princess Street, Gananoque, Ont, Canada.* (613-382 3557)

LINES, Victor William Nelson. St Aid Th Coll Bal ACT ThL 21. **d** 18 **p** 21 Bal. C of Ultima 18-20; Creswick 20-22; P-in-c of Tempy 22-23; C of Donald 23-24; P-in-c of Rokewood 24-26; V of Nhill 26-27; Linton 27-30; P-in-c of Harrow 30-35; Alvie w Beeac 35-40; V of Merino 40-48; R of Numurkah 48-52; Perm to Offic Dio Wang 52-53; Dio Bend 52-66; Dio Melb from 61. *17 Parkington Street, Kew, Vic, Australia 3101.*

LINFOOT, Edward. Angl Th Coll BC LTh 30. **d** 30 New Westmr for Koot **p** 30 Koot. I of Golden 30-33; High Prairie 33-37; V of Cumberland w Denman I 37-43; Chap CASF 43-46; R of Powell River 46-52; Edmonds 52-60; St Mark Vancouver 60-66. *PO Box 18, RR 1 Powell River, BC, Canada.*

LINFORD, John Kenneth. b 31. Univ of Liv BA 52. Chich Th Coll 54. **d** 56 **p** 57 Lich. C of Stoke-on-Trent 56-61; V of Tunstall 61-70; Sedgley 70-78; Surr from 72; R of Cannock Dio Lich from 78; V of Hatherton Dio Lich from 79. *11 Sherbrook Road, Cannock, Staffs.* (Cannock 2131)

LING, Charles Welchman. St Pet Coll Siota 64. **d** 68 **p** 69 Melan. P Dio Melan 68-75; Dio New Hebr 75-80; Dio Vanuatu from 80. *Box 122, Santo, Vanuatu.*

LING, William Robert. b 06. AIB 31. **d** 66 **p** 67 Portsm. C of St Jo Evang Sandown 66-70; C-in-c of Newchurch IW 70-74; Hon C of St Jo Evang Sandown Dio Portsm from 75. *Firdene, Broadway, Sandown, IW.*

LINGARD, Colin. b 36. Kelham Th Coll 58. **d** 63 **p** 64 York. C of St Martin Middlesbrough 63-66; Stainton-in-Cleveland 66-71; V of Sleights, Whitby 71-77; Team V of Redcar (in c of Kirkleatham) 77-78; V of Kirkleatham Dio York from 78. *130 Mersey Road, Redcar, Cleve, TS10 4DF.* (064-93 2073)

LINGARD, Keith Patrick. b 30. K Coll Lon and Warm AKC 53. **d** 54 **p** 55 Lon. C of St Mich AA Bedford Pk 54-56; Ruislip 56-58; Kempston 58-63; Metrop Area Sec UMCA 63-65; V of St Mark S Farnborough 65-75; R of Glaston w Bisbrooke 75-77; P-in-c of Morcott 75-77; R of Morcott w Glaston and Bisbrooke Dio Pet from 77. *Glaston Rectory, Uppingham, Leics, LE15 9BN.* (Uppingham 2373)

LINGORO, Bartholomew. d 77 **p** 78 New Hebr. P Dio New Hebr 77-80; Dio Vanuatu from 80. *Gaiogwo, Maewo, Vanuatu.*

LINGS, George William. b 49. Univ of Nottm BTh 74. St Jo Coll Nottm 70. **d** 75 Chelmsf **p** 76 Barking for Chelmsf. C of St Pet Harold Wood Hornchurch 75-78; Reigate 78-81; Dir of Training St Mary Reigate from 81. *63 Chart Lane, Reigate, Surrey, RH2 7EA.* (Reigate 43085)

LINGWOOD, David Peter. b 51. Univ of Lon BEducn 73. Univ of Southn BTh 80. Sarum Wells Th Coll 75. **d** 78 Lon **p** 79 Kens for Lon. C of St Hilda Ashford 78-81; Team V of the Ridge Redditch Dio Worc from 81. *3 St Peter's Close, Crabb's Cross, Redditch, Worcs.* (Redditch 45709)

LINI, Walter Hardie. St Jo Coll Auckld 66. **d** 69 **p** 70 Melan. P Dio Melan 69-75; L to Offic Dio New Hebr 75-80; Dio Vanuatu from 80. *PO Box 221, Vila, Vanuatu.*

LINKLATER, Paul Francis. Univ of Waterloo Ont BA 67. Huron Coll Ont MDiv 77. **d** 77 **p** 78 Hur. C of Trin Ch Cam 77-79; I of Port Rowan w Port Burwell Dio Hur from 79. *Box 115a, Port Rowan, Ont, Canada, N0E 1N0.*

LINKLATER, Robert William. McMaster Univ Ont BA 60. Wycl Coll Tor BTh 64. **d** and **p** 64 Niag. C of St Geo Guelph 64-68; R of Caledonia 68-70; on leave 70-74; Perm to Offic Dio Niag from 74. *45 Bunker Hill Drive, Hamilton, Ont., Canada.*

LINLEY, William Gerald. Trin Coll Tor BA 54, LTh and STB 57. **d** 56 **p** 57 Tor. C of St Mich AA Tor 56-59; P-in-c of St Pet Oshawa 59-63; R of St Laur Tor 63-78; Good Shepherd City and Dio Tor from 78; St Jas Just Downsview Tor 67-68. *1149 Weston Road, Toronto, Ont, M6N 3S3, Canada.*

LINN, Frederick Hugh. b 37. Em Coll Cam BA 61, MA 65. Ex Coll Ox BA (by incorp) 62. Ripon Hall Ox 61. **d** 63 **p** 64

Ches. C of Bramhall 63-68; V of St Mary Liscard 68-71; St Mary w St Columba Liscard 71-74; Wybunbury Dio Ches from 74. *Wybunbury Vicarage, Nantwich, Chesh.* (0270 841274)

LINN, John David Alan. b 29. MC 51. Ridley Hall Cam 73. **d** 75 Huntingdon for Ely **p** 76 Ely. C of H Trin & St Mary Ely 75-77; P-in-c of Fordham Dio Ely 77-81; V from 81; P-in-c of Kennett Dio Ely 77-81; V from 81. *Fordham Vicarage, Ely, Cambs.* (Fordham 266)

LINNEGAN, John McCaughan. TCD 55. ACCS (ACIS from 70) 48. **d** 57 **p** 58 Kilm. C of Billis 57-59; I of Cappagh Dio Derry from 59; Exam Chap to Bp of Derry from 79. *Erganagh Rectory, Omagh, Co Tyrone, N Ireland.* (Omagh 2572)

LINNEGAR, George. b 33. Kelham Th Coll 6LQ. **d** 62 **p** 63 Pet. C of St Mary Wellingborough 62-65; M CGA from 65; L to Offic Dio Lich 65-69; Dio B & W 69-80; C of All SS Lewes Dio Chich from 80. *18 Bradford Road, Lewes, BN7 1RB.*

LINNEY, Preb Gordon Charles Scott. b 39. **d** 69 **p** 70 Connor. C of Agherton 69-72; Dom Chap to Bp of Connor 70-72; Min Can of Down Cathl 72-75; St Patr Cathl Dub 75; V of St Cath w St Jas Dub 75-80; Preb of St Patr Cathl Dub from 77; R of Glenageary Dio Dub from 80. *St Paul's Vicarage, Silchester Road, Glenageary, Co Dublin, Irish Republic.* (Dub 801616)

LINNING, Alexander. b 19. Univ of Birm BA 40. BD (Lon) 42. **d** 61 **p** 62 Southw. Hon C of W Bridgford Dio Southw from 61; Asst Master W Bridgford Gr Sch 45-67; Asst Master W Bridgford Sch from 67. *7 Kingston Road, West Bridgford, Nottingham.* (Nottm 812959)

LINSKILL, Martin Paul Richard. b 50. Magd Coll Ox BA 72, BA (Th) 74, MA 75. St Steph Ho Ox 73. **d** 75 Willesden for Lon **p** 76 Lon. C of Pinner 75-80; Greenhill Dio Sheff from 80. *69 Westwick Crescent, Greenhill, Sheffield, S8 7DL.* (Sheff 351380)

LINSTER, James. Em Coll Sktn. **d** 66 **p** 67 Calg. I of Mirror 66-71; R of Olds Dio Calg from 71. *Box 102, Olds, Alta, Canada.* (226-3251)

LINTELL, Arthur Reginald. b 1892. Edin Th Coll 14. Univ of Dur LTh 16. **d** 16 **p** 17 Dur. C of St John Sunderland 16-17; St Mary w St Mary Magd Plymouth 17-19; Calstock 19-23; Camborne 23-24; St Winnow w St Nectan 24-27; V of Quethiock 27-75; RD of E Wivelshire 58-63. *23 Wyndham Square, Plymouth 1, 5EG.*

LINTON, Alan Ross. b 28. Dipl Th (Lon) 60. St Aid Coll 57. **d** 60 Liv **p** 61 Warrington for Liv. C of Blundellsands 60-62; St Phil Southport 62-63; Aigburth 63-66; V of Glazebury 66-68; C of Douglas 69-71; P-in-c of All SS Conv Distr Appley Bridge 71-76; Scorton Dio Blackb from 76; Admarsh in Bleasdale w Calder Vale Dio Blackb from 76. *Vicarage, Scorton, Preston, Lancs.* (Forton 791229)

LINTON, Alan Warren. Ridley Coll Melb ACT ThL 59. **d** 59 **p** 60 Gippsld. C of Moe 59-62; Warragul 62-63; V of Boolarra 63-66; R of Heyfield 66-70; Kensington 70-81; Commiss Centr Tang from 70; C of Magill and Chap Inter Ch Trade and Miss Dio Adel from 81. *1 Carunta Street, Wattle Park, S Australia 5066.*

LINTON, Ernest Lunn. **d** 59 **p** 60 Sask. I of Aborfield 59-61; Turtleford 61-65; R of Alberton 65-67; Stewiacke Dio NS from 68. *Stewiacke, NS, Canada.* (378-2470)

LINTON, John. b 10. St Francis Coll Brisb 75. **d** 76 **p** 78 Brisb. Hon C of St Andr Caloundra Dio Brisb from 76. *4 Bott Street, Dickey Beach, Vic., Australia 4551.*

LINTON, Joseph Edmund. b 19. Univ of St Andr MA 46. Sarum Th Coll 46. **d** 48 **p** 49 Newc T. C of St Mary Monkseaton 48-53; CF (TA) 50-54; C-in-c of St Aid Conv Distr Lynemouth 53-59; V of Beltingham w Henshaw Dio Newc T from 59. *Beltingham Vicarage, Bardon Hill, Hexham, Northumb.* (Bardon Mill 331)

LINTON, Sydney. b 07. Late Scho of Pemb Coll Ox 2nd cl Cl Mods 28, BA (3rd cl Lit Hum) 30, 2nd cl Th 31, MA 34. Westcott Ho Cam 31. **d** 32 **p** 33 Wakef. C of Morley 32-39; Hon Chap to Br Legation Helsinki 48-51; C of Limpsfield 51-57; V of H Trin Barnes 57-71; Commiss River from 69; R of Codford w Upton Lovell (and Stockton from 73) 71-77. *39 Lower Road, Bemerton, Salisbury, SP2 9NB.*

LINTOTT, William Ince. b 36. St Cath Coll Cam Math Trip pt i 56, BA (Th Trip pt ii) 58. Ely Th Coll 58. **d** 60 **p** 61 Chich. C of St Wilfrid Brighton 60-62; Chingford 62-66; Chap Fulbourn Hosp Cam 66-73; Lect at Cam Coll of Arts & Tech 73-74. *7 Haverhill Road, Stapleford, Cambridge.* (Cam 842008)

LINYEMBE, Jerome Gray. St Cypr Th Coll Tunduru 52. **d** 54 Zanz for Masasi **p** 63 Bp Soseleje for Masasi. P Dio Masasi. *Masasi, Tanzania.*

LINZEY, Andrew. b 52. AKC and BD 73. St Aug Coll Cant 75. **d** 75 **p** 76 Cant. C of SS Pet & Paul Charlton Dover 75-77; Chap and Lect N E Surrey Coll of Tech 77-81; Univ of Essex from 81. *Chaplaincy, University of Essex, Wivenhoe Park, Colchester, CO4 3SQ.* (Colchester 862286)

LIOMBA, John. b 37. **d** 69 **p** 70 S Malawi. P Dio S Malawi. *Box 53, Mangochi, Malawi.*

LIONG, Ern Sheh. **d** 66 **p** 67 Sing. P Dio Sing 66-70; Dio W Mal from 70. *29 Jalan Sikah China, Yong Peng, Johore, Malaya.*

LIOTSCOS, Barbara Jo-anne Ball. b 50. Qu Univ Kingston Ont BA 73. Vanc Sch of Th MDiv 79. **d** 80 Abp Somerville for New Westmr **p** 81 Abp Hambidge for New Westmr. C of St Faith Vanc Dio New Westmr from 80. *3214 W 4th Avenue, Vancouver, BC, Canada, V6K 1R9.*

LIPENDE, Canon William Steere. St Andr Coll Likoma, 32. **d** 36 **p** 38 Nyasa. P Dio Nyasa 36-61; Dio Lebom from 61; Archd of Kobwe 65-67; Massenjele 67-69; Can of Lebom from 69. *Caixa Postal 83, Vila Cabral, Moçambique.*

LIPOCHI, Benyamin Gerard. **d** 62 SW Tang. d Dio SW Tang 62-70; Dio Ruv from 71. *PO Luili, Tanzania.*

✠ **LIPP, Right Rev Richard Jacob.** b 08. [f in Lutheran Ch] Cons Bp in N Kerala on 21 April 54 by Bp of Madr and Trav (Ch in S India); Res 60; V of S Camberwell Melb 60-62. *7334 Susen, Gneisenaustr 5, W Germany.*

LIPPIATT, Michael Charles. b 39. BD (Lon) 71. Oak Hill Th Coll 67. **d** 71 **p** 72 Sheff. C of Ardsley 71-74; Lenton 74-78; V of H Trin Jesmond City and Dio Newc T from 78. *9 Collingwood Terrace, Jesmond, Newcastle-upon-Tyne, NE2 2JP.* (Newc T 811663)

LIPPINGWELL, Frank Henry Gilbert. **d** 65 **p** 66 New Westmr. I of Ladner 65-74; on leave. *3-3562 East 49th Avenue, Vancouver, BC, Canada.*

LIPSCOMB, Ian Craig. Wells Th Coll 61. ACT ThL 67. **d** 63 **p** 64 Lon. C of Feltham 63-65; H Trin Cathl Wang 66-68; Prec of St Sav Cathl Goulb 68-71; Perm to Offic Dio C & Goulb from 71. *10 Church Street, Goulburn, NSW, Australia.*

LIPSCOMBE, Brian. b 37. Univ of Bris BA (Th) 59. Tyndale Hall Bris. **d** 64 **p** 65 Warrington for Liv. C of Eccleston St Helens 64-66; St Pet Halliwell 66-69; H Trin Frogmore 69-72; V of Ch Ch Richmond 72-75; Team V of Ch Ch E Sheen Mortlake 76-80; V of H Redeemer Streatham Vale Dio S'wark from 80. *Vicarage, Churchmore Road, SW16.* (01-764 5808)

LIPSCOMBE, Walter Sidney. St Francis Coll Brisb. **d** 66 **p** 67 Brisb. C of Warwick 66-68; Miss at Kumbun 68-70; Kenainj 71-77; Mt Hagen w Kenainj 77-80; Perm to Offic Dio Brisb from 80. *7 Peter Parade, Miami, Queensld, Australia 4220.*

LIPSKEY, Edwin Ernst. b 06. Seager Hall Ont 62. CD 50. **d** 63 **p** 64 Sask. I of Medstead 63-65; C of St Alb Cathl Prince Albert 65-68; I of Hudson Bay 69-70; Macdowall 70-73; R of H Trin Prince Albert 71-73; L to Offic Dio Koot from 73. *PO Box 549, Sicamous, BC, Canada.*

LIPURA, Eldad. St Phil Coll Kongwa, 60. **d** 60 Bp Omari for Centr Tang **p** 60 Bp Wiggins for Centr Tang. P Dio Centr Tang 60-66; Dio W Tang from 66. *Bitale, Box 175, Kigoma, Tanzania.*

LISAUSYO, David Nicholas. b 40. **d** 75 **p** 76 S Malawi. P Dio S Malawi. *St Martin's School, Malindi, PO Mangachi, Malawi.*

LISEMORE, Canon Frederick John Henry. b 11. St Cath S Ox BA 37, MA 38. Ripon Hall, Ox 36. **d** 37 **p** 38 St E. C of St Jo Bapt Ipswich 37-39; CF (EC) 39-45; Men in Disp 40; Hon CF 45; C of St Andr Rugby (in c of St Pet) 46-48; V of St Nich Radford Cov 48-57; Ashbourne w Mapleton and Clifton 57-70; Surr 57-77; V of Repton 70-77; Foremark 70-77; Hon Can of Derby Cathl 75-77; Can (Emer) from 78. *36 Church Lane, Barton-under-Needwood, Burton-on-Trent, Staffs.* (Barton-under-Needwood 2554)

LISLE, Raymond James. b 15. Univ of Wales, BA 38. St D Coll Lamp 39. **d** 40 **p** 41 Mon. C of Risca 40-41; Aberystruth 41-44; New Tredegar 44-51; V of Nantyglo 51-57; R of Mamhilad w Llanfihangel Ponty-Moile 57-73; Tredunnoc w Llantrisant and Llanhenog Dio Mon from 73; RD of Usk from 72; Raglan from 77; Surr from 76. *Tredunnoc Rectory, Usk, NP5 1LY.* (Tredunnoc 231)

LISMORE, Bishop of. *See* Cashel.

LISMORE, Archdeacon of. *See* Armstrong, Ven Arthur Patrick.

LISMORE, Dean of. *See* Mayes, Very Rev Gilbert.

LISNEY, John Arthur Reginald. b 15. Clare Coll Cam 3rd cl Cl Trip pt i, 36, BA 37, 2nd cl Th Trip pt i, 38, MA 41. Ridley Hall, Cam 37. **d** 39 **p** 40 Birm. C of All SS Stechford 39-44; Temple Balsall 44-51; Perm to Offic Dio Cov 49-51; V of Shaw Hill 51-54; Witchford w Wentworth Dio Ely from 54. *Witchford Vicarage, Ely, Cambs, CB6 2HQ.* (0353 2341)

LISTER, David Ian. b 26. Roch Th Coll 61. **d** 62 **p** 64 York. C of Scarborough 62-66; St Aid Buttershaw 66-68; V of St

Geo Tufnell Pk Holloway Dio Lon from 68. *72 Crayford Road, N7 0ND.* (01-609 1645)

LISTER, Edmund. b 08. AKC 35. **d** 35 **p** 36 Ches. C of St Pet Birkenhead 35-36; Broadheath 36-40; RNVR 40-46; C of St Paul Stalybridge 47-48; R of Cotleigh w Monkton 48-50; V of W Bickleigh 50-60; Bp's Nympton 60-67; R of Rose Ash 60-67; C-in-c of Creacombe 65-67; RD of S Molton 65-67; R of Dunsfold 67-73; C of Bladon w Woodstock 73-75; Perm to Offic Dios Ex and Sarum from 73. *The Leys, Ware Lane, Lyme Regis, Dorset, DT7 3EL.* (Lyme Regis 3060)

LISTER, Frederick William. b 07. Wells Th Coll 71. **d** 71 Lon **p** 72 Bp of Fulham for Lon. Asst Chap St Jo and St Phil The Hague 71-75; Chap at Gothenburg 75-78; Hon C of St Pet Harrogate Dio Ripon from 78. *8 Tudor Court, Prince of Wales Mansions, Harrogate, N Yorks.* (0423-502162)

LISTER, John Field. b 16. Keble Coll Ox BA (2nd cl Th) 38, MA 42. Cudd Coll 38. **d** 39 **p** 41 Cov. C of St Nich Radford 39-44; St Jo Bapt Cov 44-45; V of St Jo Evang Huddersfield 45-54; Brighouse 54-71; Asst RD of Halifax 55-61; Proc Conv Wakef 59-72; Archd of Halifax 61-72; Hon Can of Wakef 61-72; Chap to HM the Queen 66-72; Exam Chap to Bp of Wakef 61-76; V and Provost of All SS Cathl Wakef 72-82; RD of Wakef 72-82. *5 Larkscliff Court, The Parade, Birchington, Kent, CT7 9NB.*

LISTER, Joseph Hugh. b 38. Tyndale Hall Bris. **d** 64 Warrington for Liv **p** 65 Liv. C of St Mark Newtown Pemberton 64-68; Warden Fellowship Afloat Charitable Trust and Hon C of Braintree 68-71; Darfield 71-73; P-in-c of St Swith Sheff 73-75; Team V of Sheff Manor 75-80; R of Winfarthing w Shelfanger 80-81; P-in-c of Gissing, Burston & Tivetshall 80-81; R of Winfarthing w Shelfanger w Burston, Gissing and Tivetshall Dio Nor from 81. *Winfarthing Rectory, Diss, Norf, IP22 2EA* (Diss 2543)

LISTER, Peter. b 42. Univ of Leeds, BA 64. Coll of Resurr Mirfield, 63. **d** 65 **p** 66 Newc T. C of St Pet Monkseaton 65-68; Cramlington 68-70; Asst Master Cramlington High Sch 71-74; Hon C of Cramlington 71-78; Walker Sch Newc T 75-78; C of Morpeth Dio Newc T from 79. *St Aidan's Parsonage, Grange Road, Stobhill, Morpeth, Northumb.*

LITANDA, Ven Edward. St Cypr Th Coll Tunduru 50. **d** 52 **p** 55 Masasi. P Dio Masasi; Archd of Luatala from 73; Can of Masasi from 73. *PO Masasi, Mtwara Region, Tanzania.*

LITHERLAND, Norman Richard. b 30. Univ of Lon BA (Latin) 51, BA (Greek) 52. Univ of Man MEducn 72. NOC 78. **d** 81 Man (NSM). C of St Mich Flixton Dio Man from 81. *151 Ullswater Road, Urmston, Manchester, M31 2SW.*

LITTLE, Andrew. b 27. K Coll Lon and Warm AKC 51. **d** 52 **p** 53 Lon. C of All SS Fulham 52-54; St Barn Epsom 54-61; V of Northwood 61-72; Stowe-by-Chartley Dio Lich from 72; C-in-c of Hixon Dio Lich from 72. *Vicarage, Stowe-by-Chartley, Staffs.* (Weston 270690)

LITTLE, Arthur Thomas. b 34. Univ of W Ont BA 56. Trin Coll Tor MDiv 72. **d** 72 **p** 73 Tor. C of St Pet Cobourg 72-74; I of St Geo Scarborough Tor 74-79; Port Credit Dio Tor from 79. *26 Stavebank Road, Mississauga, Ont, L5G 1L7, Canada.*

LITTLE, Denis Theodore. b 15. Late Scho of St Jo Coll Dur BA (2nd cl Engl) 36, MA 39. **d** 39 **p** 40 Dur. C of Bp Wearmouth 39-42; Tudhoe 42-46; Whitby 46-49; V of Kexby 49-54; Wilberfoss 49-54; Huntington York 54-61; Lythe 61-72; R of Dunnington 72-80; RD of Bulmer 78-80. *28 Kirklands, Strensall, York, YO3 5WX.*

LITTLE, Derek Peter. b 50. St Jo Coll Dur BA 72. Trin Coll Bris Dipl Th 75. **d** 75 **p** 76 Pontefract for Wakef. C of St Thos Bradley 75-78; St Geo Kidderminster 78-81; V of Lepton Dio Wakef from 81. *Lepton Vicarage, Huddersfield, W Yorks, HD8 0EJ.* (Huddersfield 602172)

LITTLE, George Nelson. b 39. Div Hostel Dub 70. **d** 72 **p** 73 Arm. C of Portadown 72-76; R of Newtownhamilton w Ballymoyer and Belleek 76-80; I of Aghaderg w Donaghmore (w Scarva from 81) Dio Down and Drom from 80. *Loughbrickland Rectory, Banbridge, Co Down, N Ireland.* (Banbridge 24073)

LITTLE, Harold Clifford. b 18. Univ of Lon BD 42. ALCD 42. **d** 42 **p** 43 Chelmsf. C of St Jo Evang Gt Ilford 42-44; St Mary Loughton (in c of St Mich AA) 44-48; V of Billesley Common 48-56; St Steph S Dulwich Dio S'wark from 56; Surr from 62. *St Stephen's Vicarage, College Road, SE21 7HN.* (01-693 3797)

LITTLE, Herbert Edwin Samuel. b 21. BA (Lon) 54, BD (Lon) 68. N-E Ordin Course 79. **d** 80 **p** 81 Dur (APM). C of St Cuthb City and Dio Dur from 80. *3 Whitesmocks Avenue, Durham, DH1 4HP.*

LITTLE, Ian Arthur Langley. b 24. ARICS 52. SOC 63. **d** 66 **p** 67 Roch. Hon C of Bickley 66-69; St Andr Bromley 69-77; Perm to Offic Dio Roch from 77. *23 Vale Road, Bickley, Kent, BR1 2AL.*

LITTLE, John Richardson. b 28. Magd Coll Ox BA (2nd cl Mod Hist) 49, MA 53, Dipl Th 50. Westcott Ho Cam 52. **d** 54 **p** 55 Man. C of Ch Ch Moss Side 54-57; St Aid Conv Distr Billingham 57-60; V of New Springs 60-65; H Cross Fenham 65-77; RD of Newc W 74-77; V of All SS Gosforth Dio Newc T from 77. *All Saints' Vicarage, Brackenfield Road, Gosforth, Newcastle, NE3 4DX.* (Gosforth 856345)

LITTLE, Malcolm Ross. Ch Coll Hobart ACT ThL 60. **d** and **p** 61 Tas. C of New Norf 61-62; R of Macquarie Plains w Maydena and Gretna 62-65; New Norfolk 65-70; Smithton 70-73; P-in-c of Pinnaroo 73-76; Perm to Offic Dio St Arn 74-76; R of Penola Dio Murray from 77. *Box 128, Penola, S Australia 5277.* (087-37 2457)

LITTLE, Richard Terence. b 17. BC Coll Bris 37. **d** 40 **p** 41 Lon. C of St Pet U Holloway 40-42; Chap RAFVR 42-47; V of St Ann Nottm 47-53; Skellingthorpe 53-70; R of Doddington 56-70; Chap at Düsseldorf 70-75; R of Meonstoke w Corhampton and Exton 75-78. *Address temp unknown.*

LITTLE, Sidney Charles. Montr Dioc Th Coll LTh 34. **d** 34 **p** 35 Montr. Asst in Ch Exten Work Dio Montr 34-36; C of St Jo Cathl Antig 36-38; I of Woodlands 38-39; C of Devonshire 39-42; Hamilton w Smiths 42-47; P-in-c of St Phil w St Steph Antig 49-51; L to Offic Dio Berm 51-56; V of St Luke Barb 56-57; P-in-c of St David's I Berm 57-60; R of Pebmarsh 60-63; V of White Colne 60-63; Foulness 63-65; Widdington Dio Chelmsf from 65. *28 Rylstone Way, Saffron Walden, Essex, CB11 3BS.*

LITTLE, Stephen Clifford. b 47. Univ of Man MEd 81. AKC 72. **d** 72 **p** 73 Ches. C of St Andr Runcorn 72-73; E Runcorn w Halton 73-75; C-in-c of St Pet Newbold Rochdale 75-77; Min for Social Responsibility Milton Keynes Chr Coun Dio Ox from 77; P-in-c of Broughton and Milton Keynes 77-81. *Broughton Rectory, Milton Keynes, MK10 9AA.* (Pineham 5298)

LITTLECHILD, William Bryant. b 02. St George's Windsor 52. **d** and **p** 53 Cov. C of Kenilworth 53-55; V of Sutton Courtenay w Appleford 55-67; RD of Abingdon 57-62; Surr 59-67; C-in-c of Chaffcombe 76-77; Knowle St Giles w Cricket Malherbie 76-77. *Kerris Vean, Chaffcombe, Chard, Somt.*

LITTLEFAIR, David. b 38. BD (Lon) 79. Trin Coll Bris 76. **d** 79 **p** 80 Win C of Bursledon Dio Win from 79. *15 Bursledon Heights, Long Lane, Bursledon, Southampton, SO3 8DB.*

LITTLER, Eric Raymond. b 36. Dipl Th (Lon) 67. Roch Th Coll 65. **d** 68 **p** 69 St Alb. C of Hatfield Hyde 68-73; Team V in Pemberton 73-74; V of Kitt Green 74-81; White Notley w Faulkbourne and Cressing Dio Chelmsf from 81. *White Notley Vicarage, Witham, Essex.* (Silver End 83194)

LITTLETON, Ambrose Francis. b 24. Qu Coll Birm. **d** 56 **p** 57 Lon. C of St Geo Headstone 56-59; CF 59-74; SCF 66-74. *c/o Lloyds Bank, 435 Pinner Road, Harrow, Middx, HA1 4HP.*

LITTLETON, Canon Thomas Arthur. b 12. St Edm Hall Ox BA (3rd cl Mod Hist) 35, MA 39. Univ of Leeds BD 48. Cudd Coll 36. **d** 37 **p** 38 Nor. C of Wymondham 37-39; Hexham 39-42; Barnsley (in c of St Paul) 42-45; St Mich AA Headingley 45-48; V of Dacre 48-53; Carlinghow 53-59; R of Croft 59-78; RD of Richmond E 65-70; Hon Can of Ripon 68-78; Can (Emer) from 78; RD of Richmond E, W and N 70-72; Richmond 72-75; P-in-c of Eryholme 70-78. *Stanwick Old Hall, Stanwick St John, Richmond, N Yorks, DL11 7RT.* (Piercebridge 565)

LITTLETON, Thomas John Harvard. b 41. Univ of Melb BA 63, BEd 67. Wm Temple Coll Rugby 67. **d** 69 **p** 71 Gippsld. Hon C of St Mary Morwell 69-73; Asst Master Morwell Sch 69-73; Educn Consultant Dio C & Goulb from 74; Team V of Weston Creek Canberra 74-77; P-in-c of All S Chapman Canberra Dio C & Goulb from 77. *1 Sideway Street, Chapman, ACT, Australia 2611.* (062-88 6153)

LITTLEWOOD, John Edward. b 50. Univ of E Anglia BSc 71. Ridley Hall Cam 72. **d** 75 Thetford for Nor **p** 76 Nor. C of Hellesden 75-78; Eaton Dio Nor from 78. *347 Unthank Road, Norwich, NR4 7QG.* (Norwich 53704)

LITTLEWOOD, John Richard. b 37. Ridley Hall Cam 69. **d** 72 Bp Graham-Campbell for Cant for Pet **p** 73 Pet. C of Rushden w Newton Bromswold 72-75; Chap Scargill Ho Skipton 75-77; V of Werrington Dio Pet from 77. *Werrington Vicarage, Peterborough.* (Peterborough 71649)

LITTLEWOOD, Walter. Coll of Resurr Mirfield 67. **d** 69 **p** 70 Cant. C of St Mich AA Maidstone 69-72; Romney Marsh Group 72-75; P-in-c of Brookland w Fairfield 75-78; P-in-c of Brenzett, Snargate, Snave and Old Romney w Midley (in Romney Marsh Group) 75-78; P-in-c of Ivychurch w Old Romney and Midley 76-78; V of Brookland w Fairfield and Ivychurch w Old Romney and Midley and Brenzett w Snargate and Snave 78-81; Hon C of N Holmwood Dio Guildf from 81. *17 Tollgate Road, Dorking, Surrey, RH4 2PP.*

LITTON, Alan. b 42. Ridley Hall Cam 66. **d** 69 Middleton for Man. C of St Bede Bolton 69-71; Ashton L 71-73; V of

Stonefold 73-77; Industr Chap Hull 77-81; Coppenhall Crewe Dio Ches from 81. *Vicarage, Stewart Street, Crewe, CW2 8LX.* (Crewe 60310)

LITTON, John Champernowne. b 24. Univ Coll Ox BA (2nd cl Mod Hist) 60, MA 63. Linc Th Coll 60. **d** 62 **p** 63 Lich. C of Cannock 62-66; R of Rockbourne (w Whitsbury 68-72) 66-72; Ch Oakley w Wootton Dio Win from 72; RD of Basingstoke from 78. *Church Oakley Rectory, Basingstoke, Hants.* (Basingstoke 780825)

✠ **LITUMBE, Right Rev Paulo Swithun.** St Bart Th Coll Msumba. **d** 60 **p** 61 Lebom. P Dio Lebom 60-76; Cons Bp Suffr of Lebom in St Cypr Ch Maputo 25 March 76 by Bp of Lebom; Bps of Pret and Swaz; and others; Trld to Niassa 79. *Missao Anglicana de Messumba, Metangula, Niassa, Moçambique.*

LIU, Alfred Yik Hin. **d** 62 **p** 65 Hong. P Dio Hong. *c/o Chu Oi School, Shek Lei Estate, Kwai Chung, Hong Kong.* (12-267424)

LIVERMORE, Canon Thomas Leslie. b 05. Late Exhib of G and C Coll Cam 2nd cl Nat Sc Trip pt i 26, BA (3rd cl Nat Sc Trip pt ii) 27, MA 31. Ridley Hall Cam 27. **d** 28 Dover for Cant **p** 29 Cant. C of Em S Croydon 28-32; Felixstowe 32-34; V of St Simon and St Jude Southport 34-36; Asst Sec BCMS 36-39; R of Fyfield 39-44; V of Berners Roding 39-44; St John Deptford (in c of St Nich from 45) 44-49; R of Morden 49-68; Proc Conv S'wark from 45; Surr 50-68; Hon Can of S'wark 56-68; Can (Emer) from 68; Exam Chap to Bp of S'wark 59-68; RD of Beddington 63-65; R of Poole 68-75; Perm to Offic Dio Nor 75-77; P-in-c of Sedgeford w Southmere Dio Nor from 77. *3 Church Farm Road, Heacham, King's Lynn, Norf.* (Heacham 70884)

LIVERPOOL, Lord Bishop of. *See* Sheppard, Right Rev David Stuart.

LIVERPOOL, Assistant Bishops of. *See* Baker, Right Rev William Scott; and Flagg, Right Rev John William Hawkins.

LIVERPOOL, Archdeacon of. *See* Spiers, Ven Graeme Hendry Gordon.

LIVERPOOL, Dean of. *See* Patey, Very Rev Edward Henry.

LIVERPOOL, Herman Oswald. b 25. Codr Coll Barb 74. **d** 77 Barb for Guy **p** 77 Bp George for Guy. C of St Phil Georgetn Dio Guy from 77. *Holy Redeemer Vicarage, West Ruimveldt, Greater Georgetown, Guyana.*

LIVESEY, Allan. b 09. Worc Ordin Coll. **d** 53 **p** 54 Liv. C of Huyton 53-56; V of St Mark Preston 56-64; Tockholes 64-74; L to Offic Dio Blackb from 79. *3 Rewe Close, Livesey, Blackburn, BB2 4PE.* (Blackb 670160)

LIVESEY, Kenneth. b 29. Codr Coll Barb 57. **d** 59 Barb for Gui **p** 60 Gui. C of St Phil Georgetn 59-62; R of Canje 62-73; V of Royton 73-81; P-in-c of H Trin Bury Dio Man from 81. *Holy Trinity Vicarage, Spring Street, Bury, Lancs, BL9 0RW.* (061-764 2006)

LIVESLEY, Alan Gardner. b 19. St Chad's Coll Dur BA (2nd cl Th) 43, MA 46. **d** 43 **p** 44 Liv. C of All SS Wigan 43-46; St Luke Bournemouth 46-48; H Trin Win 48-51; V of Ainstable (w Armathwaite from 54) 51-56; PC of Armathwaite 51-54; V of St Osw Millhouses Sheff 56-78; Beighton Dio Sheff from 78. *Beighton Vicarage, Sheffield, S Yorks, S19 6EE.* (Sheff 487635)

LIVINGSTON, Bertram. Trin Coll Dub BA 56. **d** 57 **p** 58 Oss. C of Enniscorthy 57-59; I of Carrickmacross (w Magheracloone from 61) 59-63; C-in-c of Derryvolgie 63-78; R 78-79; Monaghan Dio Clogh from 79. *Rectory, Monaghan, Irish Republic.* (Monaghan 136)

LIVINGSTONE, David George Lance. Moore Th Coll Syd ACT ThL 35, Th Scho 46. **d** 36 **p** 37 Syd. C of St Steph Kembla 36-38; P-in-c of Wilcannia 38-41; Streaky Bay 41-46; Asst Org Miss of BCAS 49-52; R of St Thos Auburn 52-54; Kingsford 54-63; St Anne Ryde 63-77; Hon Warden CA Tr Coll Croydon Syd 63-75; L to Offic Dio Syd from 77. *4 Glenview Road, Hunter's Hill, NSW, Australia 2110.* (89-1481)

LIVINGSTONE, Francis Kenneth. b 26. TCD BA (1st cl Mod Ment and Moral Sc). **d** 49 **p** 50 Dub. C of Santry U w Coolock 49-52; St Geo Dub 52-57; R of Castledermot U 57-62; C of Armagh 62-66; Hon V Cho of Arm Cathl from 63; I of St Sav Portadown Dio Arm from 66. *38 Vicarage Road, Portadown, Craigavon, N Ireland, BT62 4HF.* (Portadown 32664)

LIVINGSTONE, James Wayne. b 39. Calif State Univ Fullerton BA 69. Trin Coll Tor 73. **d** 75 **p** 76 NS. C of Lockeport & Barrington Dio NS 75-76; R from 76. *Rectory, Barrington, NS, Canada.*

LIVINGSTONE, Ven John Morris. b 28. Peterho Cam BA 53, MA 56. Cudd Coll 53. **d** 55 **p** 56 Ripon. C of Hunslet 55-60; Chap Liddon Ho Dio Lon 60-63; V of St Jo Evang Notting Hill Kens 63-74; C-in-c of St Mark Notting Hill 66-73; C-in-c of All SS Notting Hill 67-74; Proc Conv Lon 66-67; C-in-c of St Clem Notting Dale Kens 68-74; R of Notting Hill Lon 74-75; Chap St Geo Paris Dio (Gibr in Eur from 80) Lon (N and C Eur) from 75; Archd in N France from 80; M Gen Syn from 80; Hon Can of H Trin Cathl Brussels from 81. *Presbytère St Georges, 7 Rue Auguste-Vacquerie, 75116 Paris, France.* (1-720 22 51)

LIVINGSTONE, John Robert. Moore Th Coll Syd ACT ThL 64. **d** 64 **p** 65 Syd. C of Hunter's Hill 64-69; C-in-c of Rooty Hill 69-73; Res Min of New Housing Distr Green Valley 73-78; R of St Steph Normanhurst Dio Syd from 78. *2 Kenley Road, Normanhurst, NSW, Australia 2076.* (48-3122)

LIWA, Yoseke Dolo. Bp Gwynne Coll Mundri 61. **d** 62 **p** 63 Sudan. P Dio Sudan. *c/o Church Office, PO Box 110, Juba, Sudan.*

LIWEWE, Cyprian. St Andr Th Coll Mahulawe, 50. **d** 52 SW Tang **p** 55 Nyasa. P Dio Nyasa 62-65; Dio Malawi 65-71; Dio Lake Malawi from 71; Archd of Nkhotakota 70-72; Ntchisi 72-77. *PO Box 120, Mzuzu, Malawi.*

LLANCAVIL, Manoel. **d** 60 **p** 62 Argent. P Dio Argent 60-63; Dio Chile from 63. *Zanja, Chile.*

LLANDAFF, Lord Bishop of. *See* Poole-Hughes, Right Rev John Richard Worthington.

LLANDAFF, Assistant Bishop of. *See* Reece, Right Rev David.

LLANDAFF, Archdeacon of. *See* Clarke, Ven Herbert Lewis.

LLANDAFF, Dean of. *See* Davies, Very Rev Alun Radcliffe.

LLEWELLIN, Canon Harold Leslie. **d** and **p** 65 Niag. I of Glen Williams w Norval 65-68; R of St Mich Hamilton 68-76; Hon Can of Niag from 74; R of H Trin Welland Dio Niag from 76. *77 Division Street, Welland, Ont., Canada.* (416-734 3543)

LLEWELLIN, John Richard Allan. b 38. Fitzw Ho Cam BA 64, MA 78. Westcott Ho Cam 61. **d** 64 **p** 65 St Alb. C of Radlett 64-68; St Mary Virg Cathl Johann 68-71; V of Waltham Cross 71-79; R of Harpenden Dio St Alb from 79. *9 Rothamsted Avenue, Harpenden, Herts, AL5 2DD.* (Harpenden 2202)

LLEWELLYN, Brian Michael. b 47. Sarum Wells Th Coll 78. **d** 80 **p** 81 Guildf. C of Farncombe Dio Guildf from 80. *73 Binscombe Crescent, Farncombe, Nr Godalming, Surrey, GU7 3RA.*

LLEWELLYN, David John Patrick. b 16. AKC 40. Wells Th Coll. **d** 46 **p** 47 Guildf. C of St Martin Dorking 46-49; St Francis Dudley 49-50; Redditch 50-52; V of Bretforton 52-59; Wolverley 59-60; R of Uitenhage 60-64; St Mark and St Phil Port Eliz 64-65; P-in-c of Madinare 65-67; R of W Bulawayo 67-69; Sec USPG Ireland 70-73; R of Desertserges w Murragh and Killowen Dio Cork from 73; Kinneigh w Ballymoney Dio Cork from 76. *Rectory, Ballineen, Cork, Irish Republic.* (Bandon 023-47143)

LLEWELLYN, John Francis Morgan. b 21. MVO 82. Pemb Coll Cam BA 46, MA 48. Ely Th Coll 47. **d** 49 **p** 50 S'wark. C of Eltham 49-52; Chap and Asst Master K Coll Sch Wimbledon 52-58; Hd Master Cathl Choir Sch and Min Can of St Paul's Cathl Lon from 58-74; Jun Cardinal 65-68; Sacr and Warden Coll of Min Can 68-74; Dep P-in-Ord to HM the Queen 68-70 and from 75; P-in-Ord 70-75; Sub-Chap O of St John of Jer 70-74; Chap from 74; Chap of St Pet-ad-Vincula at HM Tower Lon from 74. *Chaplain's Residence, HM Tower of London, EC3N 4AB.* (01-709 0765)

LLEWELLYN, Ven Richard Vivian. St Paul's Coll Grahmstn. **d** 48 **p** 49 Johann. C of Brakpan 48-50; St Mary Rosettenville 50-51; Maitland 51-54; R of Roodebloem 54-57; Bellville 57-65; Caledon 65-72; Archd o Caledon from 71; R of Strand 73-76; Elgin Dio Capetn from 76. *Box 43, Elgin, CP, S Africa.* (Grabouw 395)

LLEWELLYN, William David. b 22. St D Coll Lamp BA 43. **d** 48 **p** 49 Llan. C of Llanishen w Lisvane 48-51; Whitchurch Glam 51-63; V of Treharris 63-70; Penmaen 70-77; St Mellons Dio Mon from 77. *St Mellons Vicarage, Cardiff, CF3 9UP.* (Cardiff 796560)

✠ **LLEWELLYN, Right Rev William Somers.** b 07. Ball Coll Ox BA 29, Dipl Th (w distinc) 34, MA 37. Wycl Hall Ox. **d** 35 **p** 36 Lon. C of Chiswick 35-37; V of Badminton w Acton Turville 37-49; CF (EC) 40-46; (TA) 48-51; (TA-R of O) 51-62; Hon CF from 62; V of Tetbury w Beverston 49-61; Surr from 50; RD of Tetbury 56-61; Archd of Lynn 61-72; C of Blakeney and of Stiffkey w Morston 62-63; Cons Ld Bp Suffr of Lynn in Westmr Abbey 18 Oct 63 by Abp of Cant; Bps of Lon; Win; St Alb; Nor; Roch; Sing; Bps Suffr of Tewkesbury; and Aston; and others; res 72; Hon Asst Bp of Glouc from 73; C-in-c of Boxwell w Leighterton 73-76; C of Tetbury w Beverston Dio Glouc from 77. *Scrubbetts, Kingscote, Tetbury, Glos, GL8 8YG.* (Leighterton 236)

LLEWELYN, John Dilwyn. b 18. St D Coll Lamp BA 40.

AKC 42. **d** 42 **p** 43 S'wark. C of St Mark Battersea Rise 42-45; Thame and Towersey w Aston Sandford 45-47; St Andr and St Mary Magd Maidenhead 47-51; C-in-c of St Aubyn Devonport 51-56; C of Merton 56-61; PC of St Simon Plymouth 61-68; V 68-82. *86 Edith Avenue, Plymouth, Devon, PL4 8TL.* (Plymouth 660654)

LLEWELYN, John Humphrey Norman. b 24. Down Coll Cam BA 49, MA 51. TD 70. Ridley Hall Cam 51. **d** 51 **p** 52 Leic. C of Oadby 51-54; V of Castle Donington 54-57; Hursley w Pitt 57-61; CF (TA) from 58; R of St Thos and St Clem w St Mich and St Swith Win 61-69; Surr from 62; V of Barton Stacey w Bullington 69-80; P-in-c of Longparish & Hurstbourne Priors 79-80; V of Barton Stacey and Bullington w Hurstbourne Priors and Longparish Dio Win from 80. *Longparish Rectory, Andover, SP11 6PB.* (Longparish 215)

LLEWELYN, Robert Charles. b 09. Pemb Coll Cam 2nd cl Math Trip pt i 30 BA 32, MA 36. **d** 36 **p** 38 Lon. Asst Master Westmr Sch 36-40; C of St Steph w St Mary Westmr 36-40; Hd Master Hallett War Sch Naini Tal 41-45; Chap Westmr Sch Lon 45-46; Hd Master St Jo Coll Nass 47-51; Prin of Sherwood Coll Naini Tal 51-66; Chap of St Mary Poona 67-71; P-in-c of Purundhar and of Panchgani 69-71; Archd of Poona 69-71; Warden Bede Ho Staplehurst 72-75. *80a King Street, Norwich, Norf.*

LLEWELYN, Robert John. b 32. Keble Coll Ox (3rd cl Mod Lang) 54, MA 58. Cudd Coll 65. **d** 66 **p** 67 St Alb. C of St Andr Bedford 66-69; St Luke w St John Cheltm 69-74; V of S Cerney w Cerney Wick 75-80; St Cath City and Dio Glouc from 80. *29 Denmark Road, Gloucester, GL1 3JQ.* (Glouc 24497)

LLOYD, Canon Alwyn Charles. St Paul's Coll CP, 46. **d** and **p** 46 Grahmstn. Chap St Paul's Coll Grahmstn 46; C of St Mary Port Elizabeth 46-47; R of Molteno w Steynsburg 47-51; St Paul Port Elizabeth 51-56; Swellendam 56-77; Archd of Riversdale 62-77; Hon Can of Geo from 77; R of Wellington 77-80; Perm to Offic Dio Capetn from 80. *77 Mitchell Street, Hermanus 7200, CP, S Africa.*

LLOYD, Arthur. Univ of Queensld BA 56. St Jo Coll Morpeth ACT ThL 49, Th Scho (2nd cl) 57. **d** 45 **p** 47 Armid. C of St Pet Cathl Armidale 45-46; St John Tamworth 46-49; V of Mary Valley 49-52; R of Oberon 52-54; Portland 54-58; H Trin Bend 58-62; Chap Camberwell Gr Sch 62-65; Perm to Offic Dio Melb 65-68 and from 74; C of Burwood 64-65. *3 King Street, Bayswater, Vic, Australia 3153.* (03-729 1736)

LLOYD, Bennett William. Montr Dioc Th Coll. **d** 54 **p** 55 Montr. C of St Luke Rosemount 54-55; C of St Paul's Pro-Cathl Regina 55-57; I of St Mich w St Luke Moose Jaw 57-61; R of St Marg Hamilton W 61-67; C of St Thos St Catharine's 67-69; St Luke Rosemount Montr 69. *540 Rosedale Avenue, Sarnia, Ont., Canada.*

LLOYD, Bernard James. b 29. K Coll Lon and Warm AKC 56. **d** 57 **p** 58 Chelmsf. C of Laindon w Basildon 57-65; V of St Geo E Ham Dio Chelmsf from 65; RD of Newham from 75. *St George's Vicarage, Buxton Road, E6.*

LLOYD, Bertram Trevor. b 38. Late Scho of Hertf Coll Ox BA (2nd cl Hist) 60, 2nd cl Th 62, MA 64. Clifton Th Coll 62. **d** 64 **p** 65 Lon. C of Ch Ch Mymms Barnet 64-70; V of Wealdstone Dio Lon from 70; RD of Harrow from 77; P-in-c of St Mich Harrow Weald Dio Lon from 80. *39 Rusland Park Road, Harrow, Middx, HA1 1UN.* (01-427 2616)

LLOYD, Preb Charles Henry. b 13. TCD BA (3rd cl Mods) 34, Abp King's Pri (2nd), Bp Foster's Pri (2nd) and Div Test (1st cl) 36. **d** 36 **p** 37 Dub. C of St Geo Dub 36-39; Rathfarnham 39-43; R of Moynalty w Moybologue 43-54; Gen Sec Hibernian CMS and L to Offic Dio Dub 54-70; I of New Ross Dio Ferns from 70; Preb of St Patr Cathl Dub from 73; Dioc Sec Dio Ferns 72-80. *Rectory, Ardross, New Ross, Co Wexford, Irish Republic.* (051-21391)

LLOYD, Clifford Arthur. Hur Coll Dipl Th 63. Seager Hall, Ont. **d** 63 **p** 64 Sask. I of Meadow Lake 63-65; Cumberland Ho 66-68. *Kamsack, Sask, Canada.*

LLOYD, Crewdson Howard. b 31. Ex Coll Ox BA (2nd cl Phil Pol and Econ) 54, MA 64. Wells Th Coll 64. **d** 66 **p** 67 Ex. C of St D Ex 66-69; Cirencester w Watermoor 69-72; Perm to Offic Dio Ox from 72. *12 Sandfield Road, Headington, Oxford, OX3 7RG.* (Ox 61755)

LLOYD, David John. b 52. St D Coll Lamp Dipl Th 76. Bp Burgess Hall Lamp 74. **d** 76 **p** 77 St D. C of Pembroke 76-77; Llanelly 77-80; V of Cilycwm w Ystradffin and Rhandirmwyn and Llanfair-ar-y-Bryn Dio St D from 80. *Vicarage, Cilycwm, Llandovery, Dyfed.* (Llandovery 20528)

LLOYD, David John Silk. St D Coll Lamp BA (Phil) 62. St Steph Ho Ox 71. **d** 73 **p** 74 Chelmsf. C of Brentwood 73-76; Hockley 76-80; Team V of Wickford and Runwell Dio Chelmsf from 80. *St Mary's Vicarage, Church End Lane, Runwell, Wickford, SS11 7JQ.*

LLOYD, David Jones. b 15. St D Coll Lamp BA 37. **d** 38 **p** 39 St D. C of Llannon 38-43; Llangathen w Llanfihangel Cilfargen 43-47; V of Yspyty Cynfyn 47-54; R of Cilgerran (w Bridell from 61) Dio St D from 54; RD of Kemes and Sub-Aeron 73-80; Can of St D Cathl 73-81. *c/o Rectory, Cilgerran, Dyfed.*

LLOYD, David Lewis. b 1891. St D Coll Lamp BA 16. **d** 17 Llan **p** 18 St A. C of Hope 17-19; Hawarden 19-21; St Paul Seacombe 21-27; St Luke Poolton 27-29; Llanrhos 31-37; V of Bwlchgwyn 37-57; Llantysilio 57-69. *21 Fern Avenue, Prestatyn, Clwyd.*

LLOYD, (Denys) David Richard. b 39. Late Exhib of Trin Hall Cam 2nd cl Mod Lang Trip pt i 59, BA (2nd cl Th Trip pt ia) 61, MA 65. Univ of Leeds MA (Th w Distinc) 69. Coll of Resurr Mirfield 61. **d** 63 **p** 64 Lich. C of St Martin Rough Hills Wolverhampton 63-67; M CR from 69; L to Offic Dio Wakef from 69; Tutor Coll of Resurr Mirfield 70-75; Vice-Prin from 75. *House of the Resurrection, Mirfield, Yorks.*

LLOYD, Preb George Arthur Lewis. b 04. MBE (Mil) 42. Univ of Lon BA (2nd cl Hist) 24, K Coll Lon Plumtre Engl Pri, Whichelow Reading Pri and AKC 26. **d** 27 **p** 28 Lon. C of St Jo Evang w St Sav Fitzroy Square 27-33; Succr and C of Cathl Derby 33-38; V of Bolsover 38-54; CF (R of O) 29-39 and from 45; CF 39-45; RD of Bolsover 46-54; Surr from 46; Hon Can of Derby 48-54; V of Chiswick 54-74; RD of Hammersmith 54-67; Preb of Sneating in St Paul's Cathl Lon 65-75; Preb (Emer) from 75; Commiss Bloemf 68-73; Hon C of K Chas Mart S Mymms 74-81. *4 St Mark's College, Audley End, Saffron Waldon, Essex.* (0799-25537)

LLOYD, George Stanley. b 16. Qu Coll Cam 2nd cl Hist Trip pt i 36, BA (2nd cl Hist Trip pt ii) 37, MA 41. Cudd Coll 38. **d** 39 **p** 40 Lich. C of Ch Ch Coseley 39-42; C-in-c of Oxley Conv Distr 42-46; V of Lapley w Wheaton Aston 46-48; Ellesmere 48-57; Sedgley 57-70; Atcham Dio Lich from 70. *Atcham Vicarage, Shrewsbury, Salop.* (Cross Houses 231)

LLOYD, Hamilton William John Marteine. b 19. Late Exhib of Jes Coll Ox BA (3rd cl Mod Hist) 41, MA 45. Ripon Hall Ox. **d** 43 **p** 44 Truro. C of K Chas Mart Falmouth 43-47; R of St Gerrans w St Anthony in Roseland 47-51; Min of H Epiph Conv Distr Bournemouth 51-53; V 53-60; Whitchurch w Tufton (w Litchfield from 68) 60-71; Lyndhurst (w Emery Down from 73) Dio Win from 71. *Vicarage, Lyndhurst, Hants.* (Lyndhurst 2154)

LLOYD, Harry James. St D Coll Lamp BA 50. **d** 51 **p** 52 Swan B. C of Hay w Llanigon 51-55; Hillingdon 55-56; Marlborough 56-60; PC of Kingston Dio Sarum 60-68; V from 68; V of Worth Matravers Dio Sarum from 60. *Kingston Vicarage, Wareham, Dorset.* (Corfe Castle 480254)

LLOYD, Henry Alexander. b 06. Univ of Wales BA 27, MA 37. St Mich Coll Llan 28. **d** 29 **p** 30 St A. C of Rhoysmedre 29-36; Llanrhos 36-38; R of Tregynon 38-76; CF (TA) from 50; RD of Cedewain 57-76; Cursal Can of Galfridi Ruthin in St A Cathl 60-66; Chan and Preb 66-76. *Riversdale, Newbridge, Wrexham, Clwyd.* (Ruabon 820105)

LLOYD, Very Rev Henry Morgan. b 11. DSO 41. OBE 59. Or Coll Ox BA 33, MA 37. Cudd Coll 33. **d** 35 **p** 36 Lon. C of St Mary Hendon 35-40; Chap RNVR 40-45; Prin of Old Rectory Coll Hawarden 46-48; Sec CACTM 48-50; Dean of Gibr 50-60; Dean of Truro and R of St Mary Truro 60-81; Dean (Emer) from 81. *3 Hill House, The Avenue, Sherborne, Dorset, DT9 3AJ.*

LLOYD, Canon Herbert James. b 31. St D Coll Lamp BA 57. **d** 58 **p** 59 St A. C of Wrexham 58-65; R of Llanferres (w Nercwys and Erryrys from 67) 65-71; V of Wrexham 71-74; Rhyl Dio St A from 75; Can of St A Cathl from 81. *Vicarage, Rhyl, Clwyd.* (Rhyl 53732)

LLOYD, James. b 04. St D Coll Lamp BA 27. **d** 28 **p** 29 St D. C of Yspitty-Ystwyth w Ystradmeurig 28-30; Ch Ch Llanelly 30-32; Llangollen (in c of Vron) 32-34; R of Jordanston 34-41; Heyope 41-44; V of Clyro w Bettws Clyro 44-56; Eglwsbrewis w St Athan 56-71. *48 Gwernyfed Avenue, Three Cocks, Brecon, Powys.*

LLOYD, John James. b 14. St D Coll Lamp BA 36. **d** 37 **p** 38 Llan. C of Ch Ch Ferndale 37-38; St Paul Grangetown Cardiff 38-41; Aberavon 41-50; V of Porth 50-63; Cadoxton-juxta-Neath 63-79. *16 Spoonbill Close, Rest Bay, Porthcawl, Mid Glam.*

LLOYD, John Philip. b 15. St Chad's Coll Dur BA 37, Dipl Th 38, MA 40. **d** 38 **p** 39 Liv. C of St Columba Anfield 38-41; Builth Wells w Alltmawr and Llanafan Fawr w Llanfihangel-Bryn-Pabuan 41-46; V of Llansantffraed-in-Elwel w Bettws Disserth 46-51; Eglwys Oen Duw and Llanfihangel Abergwessin w Llanddewi 51-64; Gatley 64-69; Bickerton 69-77; Perm to Offic Dio Ches from 77. *23 Alvaston Road, Monks Orchard, Nantwich, Chesh, CW5 5TT.* (Nantwich 626771)

LLOYD, Julian. b 21. Westcott Ho Cam 57. **d** 53 RC Bp of Lanc **p** 54 RC Abp of Liv. Rec into C of E by Bp of Derby 58. C of St Luke Derby 58-59; N Wingfield (in c of St John N Tupton) 59-60; V of Gorsley w Clifford's Mesne 60-64; R of Ruardean 64-69; E Allington 69-72; C of Dartmouth 73-77;

Team V of Oakmoor Dio Ex from 77. *Maycroft, 48 Clarence Hill, Dartmouth, Devon.*

LLOYD, Michael Broomfield. b 17. Rhodes Univ Grahmstn BA 37. **d** 77 Kimb K. C of Cathl Ch of St Cypr Kimberley 77-80; P-in-c of St Alb Kimberley Dio Kimb K from 80. *Box 369, Kimberley, CP, S Africa.*

LLOYD, Michael John. Univ of Leeds BCom 56. McGill Univ BD 63. Montr Dioc Th Coll LTh 63. **d** 63 **p** 64 Montr. C of St Paul Lachine Montr 63-65; Manager Dioc Book Room Montr 65-68; Angl Book Centre Tor from 68. *600 Jarvis Street, Toronto, Ont, M4Y 2J6, Canada.* (416-924 9192)

LLOYD, Nigel James Clifford. b 51. Univ of Nottm BTh 81. Linc. Th Coll 77. **d** 81 Sarum. C of Sherborne Dio Sarum from 81. *37 Ridgeway, Sherborne, Dorset, DT9 6DA.* (0935 814277)

LLOYD, Oscar Wynn. b 17. St D Coll Lamp BA 43. **d** 45 **p** 47 St A. C of Minera 45-48; Cerrig-y-Druidion UB 48-50; Witton 50-52; V of Pott-Shrigley 52-60; St Mark Birkenhead 60-66; Helsby 66-74; Ince 68-74; RD of Frodsham from 72; R of Dodleston w Higher Kinnerton Dio Ches from 74. *Dodleston Rectory, Kinnerton, Chester.* (Kinnerton 660257)

LLOYD, Paul Medley. b 23. St Jo Coll Cam BA (2nd cl Engl Trip pt i) 49, 2nd cl Engl Trip pt ii 50, MA 54. Cudd Coll 51. **d** 53 **p** 54 York. C of South Bank Middlesbrough 53-56; St Jas Piccadilly Westmr 56-58; St Steph w St John Westmr 58-59; V of St Martin Middlesbrough 59-60; Chap Shrewsbury Sch 61-63; C of Long Buckby w Brington 63-65; R of Barnack w Ufford and Bainton 65-74; V of Ramsgate 74-76; Ringmer Dio Chich from 76. *Ringmer Vicarage, Lewes, E Sussex, BN8 5LA.* (Ringmer 812243)

LLOYD, Peter John. b 32. TD 78. Wells Th Coll. **d** 61 **p** 62 Cant. C of Walmer 61-63; CF (TA) 62-67; C of Maidstone 63-66; V of Milton Regis-next-Sittingbourne 66-69; CF (TAVR) 67-73; R of Burrough Green w Brinkley and Carlton 69-73; CF 73-77; CF (TA) from 77; V of Chessington Dio Guildf from 77. *Vicarage, Garrison Lane, Chessington, Surrey.* (01-397 3016)

LLOYD, Peter Vernon James. b 36. St Jo Coll Cam BA 60. Ridley Hall Cam 60. **d** 62 **p** 63 B & W. C of Keynsham 62-65; Perm to Offic Dio Sarum from 65. *18 Cornelia Crescent, Branksome, Poole, Dorset.*

LLOYD, Raymond David. b 35. Univ of Wales (Cardiff) Dipl Th 61. Univ of Edin MPhil 74. Intern Th Sem Zurich BD 69. Edin Th Coll 71. **d** and **p** 72 Glas. C of Glas Cathl 72-76; Chap Angl Studs Glas 74-76; SSF from 78. *Friary, Hilfield, Dorchester, Dorset, DT2 7BE.* (030-03 345)

LLOYD, Rex Edward Ambrose. b 04. Worc Coll Ox BA 26, Dipl Th 27, MA 32. Wycl Hall Ox 29. **d** 29 **p** 30 Glouc. C of St Mary w St Matt Cheltenham 29-32; Ch Ch New Malden 32-35; PC of Kinson 35-43; V of St John Stourbridge 43-48; R of Fulmer 48-64; Hamsey w Offham 64-70; Dep Chap HM Pris Lewes 65-69; Perm to Offic Dio Chich from 70. *8 Church Street, Willingdon, Eastbourne, Sussex, BN20 9HP.* (Eastbourne 54663)

LLOYD, Richard Leslie Harris. b 09. Peterho Cam 2nd cl Hist Trip pt i 30, BA (2nd cl Hist Trip pt ii) 31, MA 35. Mert Coll Ox BA (by incorp) 32, MA and BLitt 36. St Steph Ho Ox 32. **d** 36 **p** 37 York. C of Middlesbrough 36-38; Northallerton 38-41; V of Dishforth and Marton-le-Moor 41-43; St Hilda York 43-50; Coxwold w Yearsley 50-56; Bishopthorpe 56-63; V of Acaster Malbis 56-63; RD of Ainsty 59-63; Chap and Lect Bede Coll Dur 63-74. *53 Tudhoe Village, Spennymoor, Co Durham, DL16 6LG.* (Spennymoor 815646)

LLOYD, Robert James Clifford. b 18. Selw Coll Cam BA 41, MA 49. Linc Th Coll 46. **d** 47 **p** 48 S'wark. C of Clapham 47-50; High Wycombe (in c of St Jo Evang) 50-53; CF (TA) 50-53; C of Hampstead 53-55; V of Wellington w W Buckland 55-66; C-in-c of Nynehead 56-57; V 57-66; Surr 57-66; RD of Wellington 59-66; R of Chartham 66-81; RD of W Bridge 75-81; Hon C of Elham Dio Cant from 81; Denton w Wootton Dio Cant from 81. *Cavendish House, 9 North Holmes Road, Canterbury, Kent, CT1 1QJ.* (Canterbury 57782)

LLOYD, Ronald Henry. b 32. St D Coll Lamp BA 52, LTh 54. **d** 54 **p** 56 Swan B. C of St Mich AA Swansea 54-56; Sketty 56-59; St Mary Swansea 59-63; CF (TA) 59-65; V of Elmley Castle w Netherton and Bricklehampton 63-69; Chap and Asst Master Dragon Sch Ox from 69; Chap Magd Coll Ox from 75; St Hugh Coll Ox 75-80; C-in-c of St Marg Ox 75-76; L to Offic Dio Ox from 76. *Dragon School, Oxford.*

LLOYD, Samuel. b 07. Univ of Wales (Cardiff) BA 48. St Deiniol's Libr Hawarden 69. **d** 69 **p** 70 Llan. C of Llangynwyd Dio Llan from 70. *9 Station Street, Maesteg, Mid Glam.* (Maesteg 2386)

LLOYD, Stephen Russell. b 47. Worc Coll Ox BA 69, MA 77. Oak Hill Coll Dipl Th 76. **d** 77 Stepney for Lon **p** 78 Lon. C of St Steph Canonbury Isl 77-81. *Address temp unknown.*

LLOYD, Stuart George Errington. b 49. TCD BA 72. **d** 75 **p** 76 Connor. C of Cloughfern 75-79; Cregagh Dio Down from 79. *21 Glensharragh Gardens, Belfast, BT6 9PE, N Ireland.* (Belfast 795985)

LLOYD, Thomas Colin. **d** 72 **p** 74 Bath. C of Coonamble Dio Bath from 72. *14 Aberford Street, Coonamble, NSW, Australia 2829.* (011-265)

LLOYD, Thomas Ernest. b 11. **d** 39 **p** 41 E Szech. CIM Miss at Pachung 39-42; Kwangyuen 42-44; furlough 44-45; R of Markfield w Stanton under Bardon 45-48; Midl Area Rep CIM 48-76; Trav Sec AIM 51-56; Home Sec 56-76. *26 Aldwick Crescent, Findon Valley, Worthing, Sussex.* (0903 65364)

LLOYD, Thomas Rees. b 03. Late Exhib of St D Coll Lamp BA 25, BD 34. **d** 26 Llan for St D **p** 27 Swan B for St D. C of St Issell 26-30; Llannon 30-32; Narberth w Robeston Wathen 32-35; V of Llanboidy 35-46; Newcastle Emlyn 46-68; Can of Clydey in St D Cathl 63-70. *Redcroft, Kilgetty, Dyfed.*

LLOYD, Timothy David Lewis. b 37. Clare Coll Cam BA 58, MA 62. Cudd Coll 58. **d** 60 Lon **p** 61 Kens for Lon. C of Stepney 60-64; St Alb Abbey St Alb 64-67; Prec 67-69; V of St Paul's Walden 69-78; R of Braughing (w L Hadham from 79) Albury, Furneux Pelham and Stocking Pelham Dio St Alb from 78; P-in-c of L Hadham 78-79; *Rectory, Furneux Pelham, Buntingford, Herts, SG9 0LD.* (Brent Pelham 287)

LLOYD, Canon William Eyton. Late Scho of Univ Coll of N Wales BA (2nd cl Gr) 20. Powis Exhib at Ch Ch Ox BA (2nd cl Th) 24, MA 30. **d** 23 Ban for St A **p** 24 St A. C of Flint 23-28; Gresford (in c of Llay) 28-32; V of Esclusham 32-44; CF (EC) 40-44; Hon CF 45; V of Alnwick 44-65; R of St John Lee 65-70; Exam Chap to Bp of Newc T 57-70; Hon Can of Newc T 64-70; Can (Emer) from 70; Dom Chap to Duke of Northumb from 44. *38 Wold Court, Hawarden, Clwyd, CH5 3LN.*

LLOYD, William Vincent Llewellyn. ACT ThL 35, Th Scho 46. Ridley Coll Melb. **d** 37 **p** 39 Melb. C of St Columb Hawthorn 37-40; Min of Broadmeadows 40-43; H Trin Hastings Melb 43-44; Chap AMF 44-46; Min of St Aug Mount Albert 46-50; V of E Kew 50-75; Perm to Offic Dio Melb from 75. *34 Roborough Avenue, Mount Eliza, Vic, Australia 3930.* (03-787 3744)

LLOYD, Winston. b 12. St D Coll Lamp BA 52. Dipl Th (Lon) 57. BD (Lon) 78. Lich Th Coll 52. **d** 53 Mon for Gui **p** 53 Gui. C of All SS New Amsterdam 53; P-in-c of Pt Mourant 54; V 55-57; R of Canje 57-63; Uggleshall w Sotherton Wangford and Henham 63-65; Risby 65-69; C of St Giles-in-the-Fields Holborn 69-71; V of St Paul Harringay 71-78; Gen Sec Guy Dioc Assoc from 75; Commiss to Abp of W Indies 77-80; Bp of Guy from 80; Perm to Offic Dio Ely 77-81; Dio Chelmsf from 81. *17 Leslie Road, Rayleigh, Essex, SS6 8PA.* (0268-776515)

LLOYD-JAMES, John Eifion. b 39. Clifton Th Coll 63. **d** 65 **p** 66 Chich. C of St Andr Burgess Hill 65-68; C-in-c of Good Shepherd Conv Distr Mile Oak Portslade 68-74; V of St Mich AA Lancing Dio Chich from 74. *Vicarage, Penhill Road, Lancing, Sussex.* (Lancing 3653)

LLOYD-JONES, William Richard. b 07. Jes Coll Ox BA (3rd cl Hist) 31, MA 35. St Mich Coll Llan 30. **d** 31 **p** 32 St D. C of Monkton 31-34; Eglwysnewydd 34-37; Seale 37-38; R of W Hallam 38-45; V of All SS w St John Isl Lon 45-49; PC of Ripley 49-57; Surr 49-57; C of St John's Cathl Napier 57-58; V of Newland w Redbrook 59-65; St Osw Croxley Green 65-75; Perm to Offic Dio St D from 76. *Pant-yr-Haf, Llangwyryfon, Aberystwyth, Dyfed, SY23 4HA.*

LO, James Shau Khi. **d** 80 **p** 81 Sabah. P Dio Sabah. *PO Box 88, Beaufort, Sabah, Malaysia.*

LOAKE, David Lorne. b 22. Ball Coll Ox BA 47, MA 48. ARCO 48. Qu Coll Birm 49. **d** 49 Kens for Lon **p** 50 Lon. C of St Steph Rochester Row Westmr 49-52; Sutton Coldfield 53-59; V of St Chad Sutton Coldfield 59-72; Sibsey w Frithville (and New Bolingbroke w Carrington from 80) Dio Linc from 72; P-in-c of New Bolingbroke and Carrington 76-80. *Vicarage, Sibsey, Boston, Lincs, PE22 0SJ.* (Boston 750305)

LOANE, Canon Kenneth Lawrence. Moore Th Coll Syd ACT ThL 42. **d** and **p** 43 Syd. C of Ch Ch Gladesville 43; Hon C 44-48; Chap AIF 44-48; I of Kiama 48-53; Castle Hill 53-56; R of Northbridge 56-60; Parramatta Dio Syd from 60; Can of St Jo Pro-Cathl Parramatta from 69. *9 Campbell Street, Parramatta, NSW, Australia 2150.* (635-9377)

✠ **LOANE, Most Rev Marcus Lawrence.** KBE 76. Univ of Syd BA 32, MA 37. Wycl Coll Tor Hon DD 58. Moore Th Coll Syd ACT ThL (1st cl) 33, Fell 55. Moorhouse Lect 76. **d** 35 **p** 36 Syd. C of Gladesville 35-37; Tutor Moore Th Coll Syd 35-38; Vice-Prin 39-53; Prin 54-58; Chap AIF 42-44; Can of Syd 49-58; Commiss in Austr for Centr Tang 51-66; Cons Bp Coadj of Syd in Syd Cathl 24 Feb 58 by Abp of Syd; Bp of Newc; and Bps Hilliard; Arthur; Kerle; and Davies; elected Abp of Syd (Metrop of Prov of NSW) 66; Primate of Austr

78; res 81. *18 Harrington Avenue, Warrawee, NSW, Australia 2074.*

LOASBY, Preb Edgar Harold. b 13. Late Exhib of BNC Ox BA (2nd cl Lit Hum) 35, MA 46. Cudd Coll 35. **d** 36 **p** 37 Dur. C of St Paul Gateshead 36-40; St Pet Mount Pk Ealing 40-45; V of St Alb Golders Green Lon 45-51; R of Gt Stanmore 51-61; St Luke Chelsea Dio Lon from 61; RD of Chelsea 61-73; Preb of St Paul's Cathl Lon from 71; Actg R of Strathfield 78; Select Pr Univ of Ox 80. *Rectory, Burnsall Street, SW3 3SR.* (01-352 6331)

LOBANOW-ROSTOVSKY RUSSELL, Andrew. b 17. Qu Coll Ox BA 38, MA 55. Cudd Coll 56. **d** 57 **p** 58 Glouc. C of All SS Cheltm 57-60; St Jas Milton (in c of St Patr) 60-64; Chap of St Bede's Ch for the Deaf Clapham 64-75; Chap to the Deaf Dio Guildf from 75. *1 Portland Terrace, 64 Harvey Road, Guildford, GU1 3LT.* (Guildford 70481)

LOBB, Edward Eric. b 51. Magd Coll Ox BA 74, MA 76. Wycl Hall Ox 73. **d** 76 **p** 77 Man. C of St Mary Virg Haughton 76-80; Rusholme Dio Man from 80. *166 Platt Lane, Rusholme, Manchester, M14 7PY.* (061-224 6776)

LOBO, Antonia Oscar. b 50. **d** and **p** 74 N Argent. P Dio N Argent. *Parsonage, Tucumán, N Argentina.*

LOCHRIDGE, Benjamin Sturges. b 38. Sarum Wells Th Coll 75. **d** 76 Gibr **p** 77 Centr Newfld. C of Grand Falls Dio Centr Newfld from 76. *13 Master's Lane, Windsor, Newfoundland, Canada.*

LOCK, David Stephen. b 28. **d** 63 **p** 64 S'wark. C of H Redeemer Streatham Vale 63-66; Hatcham 66-74; V of All SS Leyton Dio Chelmsf from 75. *All Saints Vicarage, Melbourne Road, Leyton E10.* (01-539 2170)

LOCK, Graham Robert. b 39. Hertf Coll Ox BA (3rd cl Th) 63. Ridley Hall Cam 62. **d** 64 **p** 65 Roch. C of St Pet Bexleyheath 64-66; St Justus Roch 66-71; St Mary w St Paulinus Cray 71-75; C-in-c of St Paul Chatham Dio Roch 75; V (w All SS) from 75. *Vicarage, Waghorn Street, Chatham, Kent, ME4 5LT.* (Medway 45419)

LOCK, Peter Harcourt D'Arcy. b 44. K Coll Lon and Warm AKC 67. **d** 68 **p** 69 Roch. C of Meopham 68-72; S Gillingham 72-77; R of Hartley Dio Roch from 77; M Gen Syn from 80. *Rectory, St John's Lane, Hartley, Dartford, Kent, DA3 8ET.* (Longfield 3819)

LOCK, Phyllis. b 44. Wycl Coll Tor LTh 72. **d** 72 **p** 77 Athab. I of Faust 72; McLennan 72-76; Beaverlodge Dio Athab from 76. *Box 390, Beaverlodge, Alta, Canada, T0H 0C0.* (403 354 3121)

LOCKE, Brian Henry. b 38. K Coll Lon and Warm AKC 61. **d** 62 Hulme for Man **p** 63 Man. C of St Pet Westleigh 62-65; St Mark Marske-in-Cleveland 65-68; V of Boosbeck w Moorsholm 68-72; Perm to Offic Dio Man from 78. *17 Cotswold Avenue, High Crompton, Shaw, Nr Oldham, Lancs.* (Shaw 46477)

LOCKE, Charles. Hur Coll Dipl Th 68. Seager Hall Ont. **d** 62 **p** 65 Moos. C of Kirkland Lake 62-64; I of Fort George 65-69; Matheson 69-75; Kirkland Lake Dio Moos from 75. *Box 692, Kirkland Lake, Ont, Canada.*

LOCKE, Roy Angus. **d** 58 **p** 59 Alg. I of Manitowaning 58-65; R of Englehart 65-70; Gravenhurst 70-75; Haileybury Dio Alg from 75. *PO Box 550, Haileybury, Ont., Canada.* (705-672 3428)

LOCKETT, Canon Arthur Stephen. b 18. Bps' Coll Cheshunt 61. **d** 63 **p** 64 Lon. C of Hillingdon 63-66; R of Barley 66-80; Hon Can of St Alb Cathl 77-80; Can (Emer) from 80. *50 Honeyway, Royston, Herts, SG8 7EU.* (Royston 43939)

LOCKETT, Paul. b 48. Sarum Wells Th Coll 73. **d** 76 **p** 77 Lich. C of Horninglow 76-78; Tewkesbury 78-80; P-in-c of St Pet W Bromwich Dio Lich from 80. *St Peter's Vicarage, Oldbury Road, Greets Green, W Bromwich.* (021-525 5147)

LOCKETT, Canon William Ernest Alfred. b 16. ARCA 39. Linc Th Coll 44. **d** 45 **p** 46 S'wark. C of Beddington 45-47; Lect City of Bath Tr Coll 47-50; Chap and Lect St Kath Tr Coll Liv 50-56; Lect in Fine Art Univ of Liv 56-69; Sen Lect from 69; Can Th Liv Cathl from 72. *The Croft, Ruff Lane, Ormskirk, Lancs.* (Ormskirk 72119)

LOCKHART, Antony William Castleton. b 25. Wells Th Coll 63. **d** 65 **p** 66 Guildf. C of Hale 65-69; Worplesdon 69-73; V of Weston, Surrey 73-79; Team V of St Francis Westborough City and Dio Guildf from 79. *St Luke's House, 32 Beckingham Road, Guildford, Surrey, GU2 6BT.*

LOCKHART, Preb Douglas Stuart Mullinger. b 06. Em Coll Cam BA 28, MA 32. Ridley Hall Cam 33. **d** 35 **p** 36 Liv. C of St Simon and St Jude Southport 35; All SS Southport 35-38; Clun 38-39; V of Clunbury (w St Mary Clunton) 39-48; Chap RAFVR 43-46; R of Bitterley w Middleton 48-78; PC of Hopton Cangeford 57-68; V 68-78; Preb of Nonnington in Heref Cathl from 61; P-in-c of Cold Weston 73-78; Stoke St Milborough 73-78; Clee St Margaret 73-78. *39 Charlton Rise, Ludlow, Salop, SY8 1ND.* (Ludlow 4351)

LOCKHART, Raymond William. b 37. Qu Coll Cam BA 58, LLB 60, MA 61. St Jo Coll Nottm 72. **d** 74 **p** 75 Southw. C of Aspley 74-76; R of Knebworth 76-81; V of Aspley Dio Southw from 81. *St Margaret's Vicarage, Aspley, Nottingham.* (Nottm 292920)

LOCKHART, Very Rev Robert Joseph Norman. b 24. TCD BA 46, MA 53. **d** 46 **p** 48 Connor. C of St Mary Magd Belf 46-49; Knockbreda 49-54; C-in-c of Carryduff w Killaney 54-60; R of Comber 60-62; St Donard Belf 62-70; Shankill Lurgan Dio Drom from 70; Prec of Drom 71-75; Dean from 75. *62 Banbridge Road, Lurgan, Craigavon, Co Armagh, BT66 7HG.* (Lurgan 3341)

LOCKLEY, Ven Harold. b 16. Univ of Lon BA 37, BD 43, MTh 49. Univ of Nottm PhD 55. Westcott Ho Cam 46. **d** 46 **p** 47 Leic. C of All SS Loughborough 46-48; Chap and Lect Loughborough Coll 46-51; V of S Wigston w Glen Parva 51-58; Dir of Post-Ordin Tr Dio Leic from 51; Exam Chap to Bp of Leic from 51; Can Res and Chan of Leic Cathl 58-63; Surr from 59; Proc Conv Leic 60-80; Archd of Loughborough from 63; V of All SS Leic 63-78. *c/o 1 Knighton Grange Road, Leicester.* (Leicester 707328)

LOCKWOOD, David. St D Coll Lamp BA 51. Qu Coll Birm 51. **d** 53 **p** 54 Worc. C of Halesowen 53-57; Ribbesford w Bewdley 57-60; R of Gt w L Witley and Hillhampton 60-64; V of Hanley Castle w Hanley Swan (and Welland from 79) 64-81. *Church Row, Llowes, Hereford.*

LOCKWOOD, Wilfred Eric. Univ of Leeds BA 49. Coll of Resurr Mirfield 49. **d** 51 **p** 52 Lich. C of Tettenhall 51-53; St Francis Bournemouth 53-57; V of St Mary Wardleworth Rochdale 57-62; Ch Ch Leeds w St John and St Barn Holbeck 62-71; R of Ducklington Dio Ox from 71. *Ducklington Rectory, Witney, Oxon.* (Witney 2484)

LOCKYER, David Ralph George. b 41. Wells Th Coll 65. **d** 67 **p** 68 Linc. C of Bottesford 67-69; Eling and Testwood Dio Win 69-73; Team V (w Marchwood) 73-77; Team R of Speke Dio Liv from 77. *Rectory, Parade Crescent, Liverpool, L24 2SH.* (051-486 1521)

LOCKYER, Desmond Edward Weston. b 18. K Coll Lon and Warm AKC 49. **d** 50 **p** 51 S'wark. C of W Norwood 50-52; St Matt Surbiton 52-54; Asst Chap United Sheff Hosps and C of St Phil w St Anne Sheff 54-56; C of Eastbourne 56-59; V of Hellingly 59-68; V of U Dicker 62-68; St Mich AA Eastbourne 68-75; St John w St Pet Preston Brighton Dio Chich from 75; Surr from 78. *35 Preston Drove, Brighton, BL1 6LA.* (B'ton 555033)

LOCKYER, Maurice David. b 19. AKC (1st cl) 43, Barry Pri and Knowling Pri 43. **d** 43 **p** 44 Sarum. C of St Mark Talbot Village 43-46; Laindon w Basildon 46-50; Horfield (in c of St Edm) 50-64; V of Huncote 64-76. *Pockford, Ellesborough Manor, Ellesborough, Aylesbury, Bucks, HP17 0XF.*

LOCKYER, Peter Eric. b 39. St Jo Coll Morpeth ACT ThL 63. **d** 63 **p** 64 Armid. C of Gunnedah 63-68; Glen Innes 68-69; P-in-c of Delungra 69-71; Team V of Tamworth 71-73; C of Lismore 73-75; R of Rosewood 75-78; V of Pine Rivers S Dio Brisb from 78. *33 Gertrude Street, Strathpine, Queensland, Australia 4500.* (205-3185)

LOCORO, Jephetha. **d** 79 **p** 80 Kara. P Dio Kara. *c/o Karamoja Diocesan Office, PO Box 44, Moroto, Uganda.*

LODER, Thomas Edgar. Qu Coll Newfld. **d** 12 **p** 13 Newfld. C-in-c of Grand Falls 12-13; TCF 17-19; Hon CF 19; R of Grand Falls 13-29; Corner Brook 29-54; Spaniard's Bay 54-59; Can of Newfld 54-60; R of Petty Harbour 59-60; Crapand 61-64. *Apt 710, Shore Line Towers, 2313 Lakeshore Boulevard, Toronto 14, Ont, Canada.*

LODGE, Anthony William Rayner. b 26. Wadham Coll Ox BA 51, MA 55. Cudd Coll 65. **d** 66 Barking for Chelmsf **p** 67 Chelmsf. C of St Pet Walthamstow 66-68; Chap Ripon Gr Sch and L to Offic Dio Ripon from 68. *Ripon Grammar School, Ripon, N Yorks, HG4 2DG.* (Ripon 2647)

LODGE, Guy Septimus. b 1899. St Bonif Coll Warm 32. **d** 33 **p** 34 Ex. C of Crediton 33-35; PC of Princetown 35-43; V of Egg Buckland 43-52; C of Sunninghill 52-55; R of Pt Antonio Jamaica 55-57; Perm to Offic Dio Linc 57; R of Tedburn St Mary 58-70; L to Offic Dio Ex 70-76; Dio Chich from 74. *Ramsay Hall, Byron Road, Worthing.* (Worthing 36880)

LODGE, John Alfred Ainley. b 29. Wells Th Coll 54. **d** 57 Wakef **p** 58 Pontefract for Wakef. C of St John Huddersfield 57-60; V of Shepley 60-64; St Jude Salterhebble Halifax 64-69; C-in-c of H Nativ Conv Distr Mixenden 69-75; V of Mixenden Halifax 75-76; Almondbury 76-79; Warmfield Dio Wakef from 79; RD of Almondbury 76-79; Chap to Bp of Wakef from 79. *Vicarage, Kirkthorpe Lane, Wakefield, W Yorks, WF1 5SZ.* (Wakef 893089)

LODGE, Roy Frederick. b 38. Tyndale Hall, Bris 63. **d** 66 **p** 67 Worc. C of Tardebigge w Webheath 66-67; Warden and Chap Probation Hostel Redditch 67-69; Chap RAF 69-75; C of Kinson 76; Asst Chap HM Pris Stafford 77-78; Chap HM Pris Ranby from 78. *Chaplain's Office, HM Prison, Ranby, Notts.*

LODWICK, Brian Martin. Univ of Leeds BA (2nd cl Hist)

61. Linacre Coll Ox Squire Scho 62, BA (4th cl Th) 63, MA 67, MPhil 76. St Steph Ho Ox 61. **d** 64 Bp T M Hughes for Llan **p** 65 Llan. C of Aberaman 64-66; Newton Nottage 66-73; R of Llansannor and Llanfrynach w Penllyn and Ystradowen Dio Llan from 73. *Llansannor Rectory, Cowbridge, S Glam.* (Cowbridge 2699)

LOEWENDAHL, David Jacob. b 50. SS Coll Cam BA 74, MA 77. **d** 77 **p** 78 S'wark. C of St Pet Walworth 77-80. *c/o Saltwood Grove, Walworth, SE17.*

LOEWENSTEIN, Philip Randolph. Univ of Witwatersrand BSc 33. **d** 74 **p** 75 Bloemf. C of Sasolburg 74-76; Asst Chap to Abp of Capetn from 76. *Bishopscourt, Claremont, CP, S Africa.* (71-2531)

LOFFHAGEN, Richard William. AKC 09. **d** 09 **p** 10 S'wark. C of St Mark Mitcham 09-12; P-in-c of Inhambane 12-19; C of Pret Cathl 19-21; V of H Name w St Sav Pret 20-21; P-in-c of Pietersburg Nat Miss Distr 21-24; V of Potgietersrust and P-in-c of Native Miss 24-27; Org Sec SPG Dio Man 27-28; P-in-c of Tsomo 28-33; LPr Dio Grahmstn 33-36; R of Clanwilliam 36-38; Durbanville 38-42; Malmesbury 42-63; L to Offic Dio Capetn 63-67. *Chaplain's Cottage, Bishopscourt, Claremont, CP, S Africa.*

LOFT, Edmund Martin Boswell. b 25. St Jo Coll Cam BA 49, MA 55. Ely Th Coll 49. **d** 51 **p** 52 Carl. C of H Trin Carl 51-54; Barrow-F 54-56; V of Allonby w Westnewton 56-62; Fillongley 62-76; St Barbara Earlsdon City and Dio Cov from 77. *24 Rochester Road, Earlsdon, Coventry, CV5 6AG.* (Coventry 74057)

LOFTHOUSE, Alexander Francis Joseph. b 30. Keble Coll Ox BA 54, MA 58. St Steph Ho Ox 54. **d** 56 **p** 57 Carl. C of St Jas Barrow 56-59; Castleford 59-60; V of Airedale w Fryston 60-70; Maryport 70-78; Surr from 73; V of Levens Dio Carl from 78; Underbarrow Dio Carl from 78; Helsington Dio Carl from 78. *Levens Vicarage, Kendal, Cumb.* (Sedgwick 60223)

LOFTS, Walter Henry. St Mich Coll Llan 49. **d** 52 **p** 53 Llan. C of St Luke Canton 52-54; All SS Llandaff 54-58; V of Colwinston 58-70. *3 Palace Road, Llandaff, Cardiff, CF5 2AF.* (Cardiff 566108)

LOGAN, Glen Vincent. St Paul's Coll Grahmstn Dipl Th 77. **d** 77 **p** 78 Grahmstn. C of St Mark E Lon Dio Grahmstn from 77-80; Cathl Ch of St Mich and St Geo and P-in-c of St Clem City and Dio Grahmstn from 80. *15 Trotter Street, Grahamstown, CP, S Africa.*

LOGAN, Kevin. b 43. Oak Hill Coll 73. **d** 75 Burnley for Blackb **p** 76 Blackb. C of Ch of The Sav Blackb 75-78; Leyland (in c of St John) Dio Blackb from 78. *St John's House, Leyland Lane, Leyland, Lancs.* (Leyland 23547)

LOGAN, Samuel Desmond. b 39. **d** 78 **p** 79 Down & Drom. C of Belvoir Dio Down from 78. *8 Casaeldona Crescent, Belfast, BT6 9RE.*

LOGUE, Edward Maurice. b 22. **d** 78 **p** 81 Glas. Hon C of Largs Dio Glas from 78. *31 Eastern Avenue, Largs, Ayrshire, KA30 9EG.*

LOMAS, Charles Linaker. St Andr Th Coll Whittlesford 36. **d** 39 **p** 40 Chelmsf. C of L Ilford 39-40; CF (EC) 40-47; I of Prince Rupert Coast Miss 47-51; Port Alice 51-67; L to Offic Dio BC from 67. *Twin Acres, Quatsino, BC, Canada.*

LOMAS, David. b 39. Cranmer Hall Dur 75. **d** 78 **p** 79 Dur. C of Chester-le-Street 78-81; P-in-c of All SS Newton Hall City and Dio Dur from 81. *c/o York Crescent, Newton Hall, Durham, DH1 5PT.*

LOMAS, Warwick John. St Jo Coll Morpeth, 64. **d** 64 **p** 65 Newc. C of Hamilton 64-66; Wyong 66-67; Maitland 67-72; R of Merriwa 72-74. *c/o 40 Gooch Street, Merriwa, NSW, Australia 2329.*

LOMAX, Barry Walter John. b 39. Lon Coll of Div 63. **d** 66 **p** 67 Roch. C of Sevenoaks 66-71; Ch Ch w St Andr Southport 71-73; V of St Matt Bootle 73-78; C-in-c of St Andr Litherland 76-78; V of St Jo Evang Wimborne Dio Sarum from 78. *Vicarage, St John's Hill, Wimborne, Dorset, BH21 1BX.* (Wimborne 883490)

LOMAX, Canon Frank. b 20. Univ of Leeds BA 42. Coll of Resurr Mirfield 42. **d** 44 **p** 45 Newc T. C of St Anthony Newc T 44-50; P-in-c of Sandakan 50-63; Can of Borneo 60-62; Jess 62-63; C of St Nich Newc T 63-64; V of Prudhoe 64-74; Hon Can and V of St Andr Cathl City and Dio Sing from 75. *St Andrew's Cathedral, Coleman Street, Singapore 6.*

LOMBARD, John Allan. Qu Univ Ont BA 64. Wycl Coll Tor LTh 66. **d** 66 Rupld for Ont **p** 67 Ont. C of St John Kingston 66-68; I of N Addington 68-71; I of N Frontenac 68-71; Marmora 71-76; Thamesville Dio Hur from 76. *Box 4, Thamesville, Ont., Canada.* (519-692 3837)

LOMIRI, Simasona Ladu. Juba Bible Inst. **d** 71 Sudan. d Dio Sudan. *Box 110, Juba, Equatoria Province, Sudan.*

LOMODONG, Charles. b 50. St Paul's Coll Limuru 75. **d** 77 Juba. d Dio Juba. *E.S.C., PO Box 110, Juba, Sudan.*

LOMONGIN, Ven Peter. b 44. Bp Tucker Coll Mukono 69. **d** 72 **p** 73 Soroti. P Dio Soroti 72-76; Dio Kara from 76; Archd from 78. *Box 44, Moroto, Uganda.*

LONARATA, Lionel. St Luke's Coll Siota 34. **d** 35 **p** 38 Melan. P Dio Melan 35-75; Dio Centr Melan from 75. *Maravovo Training Centre, Guadalcanal, British Solomon Islands.*

LONDON, Lord Bishop of. *See* Leonard, Right Rev and Right Hon Graham Douglas.

LONDON, Assistant Bishops in Diocese of. *See* Hodson, Right Rev Mark Allin; Knapp-Fisher, Right Rev Edward George; Woollcombe, Right Rev Kenneth John.

LONDON, Archdeacon of. *See* Harvey, Ven Francis William

LONDON, Dean of (St Paul's). *See* Webster, Very Rev Alan Brunskill.

LONG, Allan Elvey. b 14. AKC 41. **d** 41 **p** 42 Bris. C of St Jo Evang Clifton 41-44; All SS Friern Barnet 44-47; Chalfont St Peter 47-48; V of Kidmore End 48-53; St Francis Ewell 53-75; Perm to Offic Dio Bris from 79. *6 Jesmond Road, Clevedon, Avon, BS21 7SA.* (Clevedon 874941)

LONG, Anthony Auguste. b 45. Linc Th Coll 79. **d** 81 Lich. C of St Mary Kingswinford Dio Lich from 81. *4 The Village, Kingswinford, Brierley Hill, W Midl, DY6 8AY.*

LONG, Anthony Robert. b 48. Chich Th Coll 74. **d** 77 Lon **p** 78 Kens for Lon. C of St Nich w St Mary Magd Chiswick 77-80; Earley Dio Ox from 80. *3 The Knapp, Earley, Reading, RG6 2RT.* (Reading 67011)

LONG, Christopher William. b 48. Univ of Nottm BTh 78. Open Univ BA 80. Linc Th Coll 75. **d** 78 Doncaster for Sheff **p** 79 Sheff. C of St Chris Lower Shiregreen City and Dio Sheff 78-80; V from 81. *510 Bellhouse Road, Shiregreen, Sheffield, S5 0RG.* (Sheff 386526)

LONG, Canon Colin Angus. b 17. St D Coll Lamp BA 38. St Mich Th Coll Llan 39. **d** 40 Llan for Mon **p** 43 Mon. C of Beaufort 40; Panteg 42-47; St Paul Newport 47-51; V of Ynysddu 51-56; Pontypool 52-62; Maindee Dio Mon from 62; Can of Mon from 77. *Maindee Vicarage, Newport, NPT 8GR.* (Newport 277009)

LONG, Cuthbert Guy Desormeaux. b 11. Trin Coll Cam 3rd cl Th Trip pt i 32, BA (3rd cl Hist Trip pt ii) 34, MA 37. Westcott Ho Cam 36. **d** 37 **p** 38 Lon. C of St Mich Highgate 37-39; Chap RNVR 39-46; RN 46-60. *19 Hurst Farm Road, Weald, Sevenoaks, Kent, TN14 6PE.* (Weald 475)

LONG, David Harold. b 43. Hur Coll Ont BA 65, BTh 68. **d** 68 **p** 69 Tor. C of St Mich AA Tor 69-71; R of Elmvale 71-75; St Paul Rexdale City and Dio Tor from 76. *2182 Kipling Avenue North, Rexdale, Toronto, Ont, Canada.*

LONG, David William. b 47. K Coll Lon 67. St Aug Coll Cant 70. **d** 72 **p** 73 Warrington for Liv. C of St Anne Stanley Liv 72-73; St Luke W Derby 73-75; St Jude Cantril Farm Liv 75-79; V of St Barn Warrington Dio Liv from 79. *St Barnabas Vicarage, Warrington, Lancs.* (Warrington 33873)

LONG, Edward Percy Eades. b 14. Univ of Liv BA 36, MA 38. Linc Th Coll 73. **d** 73 **p** 74 Bradf. C of Sedbergh w Cautley and Garsdale Dio Bradf from 73. *4 Derry Cottages, Sedbergh, Cumbria.*

LONG, Edwin George. b 17. Univ of Leeds BA (2nd cl French) 49. Coll of Resurr Mirfield 49. **d** 51 **p** 52 Truro. C of St Mary Penzance 51-54; St Jo Div Romford 54-55; St Luke Woodside Croydon 55-59; Jarrow (in c of St Mark) 59-68; V of St Mark Jarrow 68-74; R of Easington Dio Dur from 74. *Easington Rectory, Peterlee, Co Durham, SR8 3BS.* (Easington 270287)

LONG, Eric Newton. b 12. **d** 77 **p** 78 Calg. Hon C of H Nativ Calg 77-80; P-in-c of St Aug Ogden City and Dio Calg from 80. *9815 Fairmont Drive SE, Calgary, Alta, Canada, T2J 0R9.* (255-6258)

LONG, Frank Rowland. b 01. Chich Th Coll 22. **d** 24 **p** 25 Sarum. C of Wareham 24-26; St Luke Hammersmith 26-30; Horsham (in c of St Mark) 30-35; Durrington 35-37; R of Ashington w Buncton 37-46; Seq of Ch of H Sepulchre Warminghurst 37-46; V of Peacehaven 46-59; St Andr Portslade 59-66; P-in-c of Hastings 66-69. *41 Steyning Avenue, Peacehaven, E Sussex, BN9 8HN.*

LONG, Frederick George Craigen. b 04. Worc Ordin Coll. **d** and **p** 64 Linc. C of Lenton 64-68; V of Thurlby 68-77; Perm to Offic Dio Linc from 77. *9 Leofric Avenue, Bourne, Lincs, PE10 9QT.*

LONG, George Alfred. Montr Dioc Th Coll. **d** 67 **p** 68 Montr. P-in-c of Grenville 67-71; R of Longueuil 71-76; Sutton Dio Montr from 76. *Box 531, Sutton, PQ, Canada.* (514-538 2736)

LONG, Henry. b 27. BEM 71. **d** 79 **p** 80 Down (APM). C of Carryduff & Killaney Dio Down from 79. *28 Cadger Road, Carryduff, Belfast, BT8 8AU.*

LONG, Canon John Henry. STh (St Jo Coll Winnipeg) 56. **d** 53 **p** 56 Moos. C of Moose Factory 53-56; R of Moos 56-60; Nakina Dio Moos 60-75; Hon C from 75; Hon Can of Moos 64-75; Can (Emer) from 75. *PO Box 133, Nakina, Ont., Canada.* (807-329 5330)

LONG, Ven John Sanderson. b 13. Qu Coll Cam 2nd cl Hist Trip pt i 34, BA (3rd cl Th Trip pt i) 35, MA 39. Cudd Coll 35. **d** 36 **p** 37 Cant. C of Folkestone 36-41; Chap RNVR 41-46; C of St Pet-in-Thanet 46; Dom Chap to Abp of Cant 46-53; V of Bearstead 53-59; Petersfield w Sheet 59-70; RD of Petersfield 62-70; Hon Can of Portsm 67-70; R of St Botolph Cam 70-81; Archd of Ely 70-81; Archd (Emer) from 81; Hon Can of Ely 70-81. *23 Thornton Road, Girton, Cambridge, CB3 0NP.* (Cam 276421)

LONG, Canon John Sydney. b 25. Univ of Lon BSc (Eng) 49. Wycl Hall Ox 50. **d** 51 **p** 52 Chelmsf. C of St Andr Plaistow 51-54; Keighley 54-57; C-in-c of Horton Bank Top Conv Distr 57-59; V of St Aid Buttershaw 59-64; Barnoldswick w Bracewell Dio Bradf from 64; Hon Can of Bradf from 77. *131 Gisburn Road, Barnoldswick, Colne, Lancs.* (Barnoldswick 812028)

LONG, Ven Leonard Wallace. Moore Coll Syd ThL 50. **d** and **p** 51 Syd. C of St Thos N Syd 51-53; Chap RAN 53-67; Sen Chap and Archd from 67; LPr Dio Melb 56-64; R of Killara Dio Syd from 74. *12 Springdale Road, Killara, NSW, Australia 2071.* (498-2137)

LONG, Michael David Barnby. b 32. K Coll Lon and Warm AKC 55. **d** 56 **p** 57 York. C of Whitby 56-59; Cottingham 59-61; V of Elloughton 61-66; C-in-c of Brantingham 61-66; V of St Cecilia Parson Cross Sheff 66-68; Flamborough 68-73; Surr 66-73; R of Litcham w Kempston and E w W Lexham 73-75; C-in-c of St Luke York 75-77; V 77-80; Hatton w Haseley and Rowington w Lowsonford Dio Cov from 80. *Hatton Vicarge, Warwick, CV35 7EX.* (Haseley Knob 332)

LONG, Peter Ronald. b 48. Univ of Nottm BA (Th) 69. Cudd Coll 71. **d** 73 Bp Lash for Truro **p** 74 Truro. In Amer Ch 72-73; C of Bodmin 73-75; Newquay 75-76; Asst Youth Chap Dio Truro 75-76; Chap 76-79; Publ Pr Dio Truro 77-79; P-in-c of St Mawgan-in-Meneage Dio Truro from 79; St Cury w Gunwalloe Dio Truro from 80. *Rectory, St Mawgan-in-Meneage, Helston, Cornwall, TR12 6AD.* (032 622293)

LONG, Robert Garth. b 09. K Coll Lon and Warm 51. **d** 53 **p** 54 Guildf. C of St Paul E Molesey 53-56; C-in-c of St Aug Conv Distr Aldershot 56-58; V 58-60; V of Hawley 60-75; Minley 60-75. *32 Coxheath Road, Church Crookham, Hants, GU13 0QG.* (Fleet 4473)

LONG, Robert George. Univ of Melb BA 39. St Barn Coll Adel ThL 41. **d** and **p** 41 Bal. C of Ch Ch Cathl Bal 41-42; St Luke and St Steph Bal 42-43; V of Koroit 43-45; Skipton and Lismore 45-46; R of Bright 47; Chap Ivanhoe Grammar Sch 48-49; Min of Eltham Par Distr 49-51; R of Donald 51-54; Bend N 54-61; I of W Brunswick 61-66; N Brighton 66-72; Altona 73-76; on leave 76-80; Perm to Offic Dio Melb from 81. *18 Luckins Road, Moorabbin, Vic, Australia 3189.* (97-2796)

LONG, Robert Milton. St Jo Coll Morpeth, 56. **d** and **p** 59 Perth. C of Wembley 59-60; Applecross 60-61; Asst Chap Miss to Seamen Melb 61-63; C of E St Kilda 63-64; P-in-c of Tocumwal 64-68; Asst Chap Miss to Seamen Port Melb and Perm to Offic Dio Melb from 68. *The Missions to Seamen, 1 Beach Road, Port Melbourne, Vic, Australia 3207.* (03-64 1527)

LONG, Robin Charles. b 48. ACT ThL 77. Canberra Coll of Min 76. **d** and **p** 78 C & Goulb. C of St John Canberra 78-80; H Cross Hackett 80-81; NW Belconnen Dio C & Goulb from 81. *8 Dodd Place, Spence, ACT, Australia 2615.*

LONG, Preb Samuel Ernest. b 18. ALCD 50 (LTh from 74). **d** 49 **p** 50 Down. C of St Clem Belf 49-52; Willowfield 52-56; I of Dromara and Garvaghy Dio Down from 56; RD of Dromore from 70; Preb of Down Cathl from 81. *Rectory, Dromara, Dromore, Co Down, BT25 2NE, N Ireland.* (Dromara 532234)

LONG, Simon Richard. Coll of Resurr Mirfield, 64. **d** 65 **p** 66 Win. C of St Francis Bournemouth 65-69. *3112 South Avenue A, Porteales, New Mexico 88130.*

LONG, William George. b 01. Wycl Coll Tor 50. **d** 68 Tor. C of St Mary Magd Dio Tor 68-74. *100 Gamble Avenue, Toronto 6, Canada.*

LONG, William Thomas. b 53. TCD Dipl Th 81. **d** 81 Down. C of St John Orangefield City and Dio Belf from 81. *412 Castlereagh Road, Belfast, N Ireland.*

LONGA, Yosia Kigwong. Bp Gwynne Coll Mundri, 61. **d** 65 Sudan. d Dio Sudan 65-69; Dio Soroti from 69. *Nakapiripirit Refugee Camp, Karamoja, Uganda.*

LONGARATA, Lionel. b 47. Bp Patteson Th Centre Kohimarama 71. **d** 74 Melan. d Dio Melan 74-75; Centr Melan from 75. *Marasa, Guadalcanal, Solomon Islands.*

LONGATABO, Beddeley. **d** 79 **p** 80 Centr Melan. P Dio Centr Melan. *Gaeta District, Gela Region, Solomon Islands.*

LONGBOTHAM, Richard Ashley. b 14. Sarum Th Coll 37. **d** 37 Lewes for Chich **p** 38 Chich. C of Ch Ch Eastbourne 37-40; Perm to Offic St D Scotstown 40-41; C of St Paul Durban 41-44; St Pet Maritzburg 44-46; R of Gatooma 47-52; St Martin Salisbury S Rhod 53-54; CF 54-57; V of Aldingbourne 57-59; R of Gwanda 59-60; Aston w Benington 60-62; Irene 62-72; Richmond Natal 72-74; Eersterust 75-78; Silverton and Cullinan w Bronkhorspruit 78-80. *St Marks House, Englefield, Nr Reading, Berks.*

LONGBOTTOM, Frank. b 41. Dipl Th (Lon) 68. Ripon Hall Ox 65. **d** 68 **p** 69 Guildf. C of Epsom 68-72; Chap Highcroft Hosp Erdington Dio Birm from 72. *46 Sunnybank Road, Wylde Green, Sutton Coldfield, W Midl.* (021-350 5823)

LONGBOTTOM, Gregory Keith. St Paul's Coll Grahmstn. **d** 74 **p** 75 Grahmstn. C of St Mark Cam 74-77; St Mich Queenstown Dio Grahmstn from 77; P-in-c of Sterkstroom 78-79; R of Molteno, Dordrecht and Indwe Dio Grahmstn from 79. *Box 88, Molteno 5580, CP, S Africa.*

LONGBOTTOM, Canon John Charles. b 1899. MBE 72. Univ of Man BA 20, MA 22. Cudd Coll 20. **d** 22 **p** 23 Liv. C of Warrington 22-28; V of Heckmondwike 28-38; R of Warrington 38-72; RD of Winwick 42-49; Warrington 49-57; Can of Liv 45-72; Can (Emer) from 72. *Down Court Cottage, Matching Road, Hatfield Heath, Bishops Stortford, Herts.* (Matching 490)

LONGBOTTOM, Paul Edward. b 44. K Coll Lon and Warm AKC 67. **d** 68 **p** 69 Roch. C of Rainham 68-71; Riverhead and of Dunton Green 71-75; V of H Trin Beckenham Dio Roch from 75. *64 Lennard Road, SE20 7LX.* (01-778 7258)

LONGFIELD, Claude Donald Hutton. **d** 61 Melb **p** 62 Bp Redding for Melb. C of St John Malvern E 61-62; St Paul Ringwood 62-64; V of Eltham w Panton Hill 64-69; Chadstone E 69-72; C in Dept of Industr Miss Dio Melb from 72. *47 Retreat Road, Newtown, Vic, Australia 3220.* (052-21 5935)

LONGFIELD, Thomas Edwin. b 29. St Jo Coll Nottm. **d** 71 **p** 72 Cov. C of St Mary Leamington Spa 71-74; V of Potters Green Dio Cov from 75. *Potters Green Vicarage, Coventry, CV2 2GF.* (Cov 613004)

LONGFOOT, Richard. b 46. Oak Hill Coll 76. **d** 78 Repton for Derby **p** 79 Derby. C of St Mary Chaddesden 78-81; St Martin Cam Dio Ely from 81. *171 Coleridge Road, Cambridge, CB1 3PN.* (Cam 247192)

LONGFORD, Canon Edward de Toësny Wingfield. b 25. Ch Ch Ox Squire Scho 43, BA (3rd cl Mod Hist) 48, MA 53. Wells Th Coll 49. **d** 51 **p** 52 St Alb. C of Stevenage 51-54; PC of Chettisham and Prec and Sacr of Ely Cathl 55-68; R of Gamlingay (w Hatley St Geo and E Hatley from 80) Dio Ely from 68; C-in-c of Everton w Tetworth 68-71; V 71-73; M Gen Syn Ely 74-80; P-in-c of Hatley St Geo 78-80; E Hatley 78-80; Hon Can of Ely Cathl from 79. *Gamlingay Rectory, Sandy, Beds, SG19 3EU.* (Gamlingay 50228)

LONGJOHN, Benjamin Jeremiah Dipamaokom. **d** 45 **p** 47 Niger. P Dio Niger 45-52; Dio Nig Delta from 52. *Kalabari, Nigeria.*

LONGLEY, Peter Albert. b 36. Univ of Keele BA (Engl & Pol) 61. K Coll Lon MA 75. Ripon Hall Ox 61. **d** 63 **p** 64 S'wark. C of Herne Hill 63-67; Lect Whitelands Coll of Educn Putney 67-72; Prin Lect Rachel McMillan Coll of Educn Deptford 72-77; Goldsmiths' Coll Univ of Lon from 77; L to Offic Dio S'wark from 68; Hon C of St Steph S Dulwich Dio S'wark from 77. *60 Chestnut Road, SE27 9LE.*

LONGMAN, Edward. b 37. Hatfield Coll Dur BSc 62. Fitz Ho Cam BA 66. Ridley Hall Cam 64. **d** 66 **p** 67 Lon. C of St Paul Lower Homerton 66-72; C of Parr Dio Liv 72-73; Team V from 73. *459 Fleet Lane, Parr, St Helens, Lancs.*

LONGMAN, Canon Edward George. b 35. St Pet Hall Ox BA (Th) 58, MA 62. Westcott Ho Cam 59. **d** 61 Sheff **p** 62 Bp Gerard for Sheff. C of St Mark Broomhall Sheff 61-65; V of St Thos Brightside Sheff 65-74; L to Offic Dio Brisb 72-73; V of Yardley Dio Birm from 74; RD of Yardley from 77; Hon Can of Birm Cathl from 81. *Yardley Vicarage, Birmingham, B33 8PH.* (021-783 2085)

LONGOLE, Isaac. b 43. Bp Tucker Coll Mukono 69. **d** 72 Soroti. d Dio Soroti. *Box 44, Moroto, Uganda.*

LONGRIDGE, Peter Nevile. b 12. St Edm Hall Ox BA 34, MA 59. Westcott Ho Cam 34. **d** 36 **p** 37 Lon. C of Ch Ch Southgate 36-39; Asst Chap Miss to Seamen Southampton 39-41; Newport 41-42; C of Barnstaple (in c of Sticklepath) 42-47; R of Coombe Pyne w Rousdon 48-59; Chap All H Sch Rousden 48-59; R of Highweek w Abbotsbury 59-77; Publ Pr Dio Ex from 77. *4 The Path, Irsha Street, Appledore, Devon, EX39 1RU.*

LONGRIDGE, Richard Nevile. b 15. Sarum Th Coll 46. **d** 48 Portsm **p** 49 Bp Kitching for Cant. C of St Mark Portsea 48-51; V of Bourton w Silton 51-63; R of Okeford Fitzpaine 63-67; Spetisbury w Charlton Marshall 67-77; Perm to Offic Dio Ex from 77. *41 Cross Street, Northam, Bideford, Devon.* (Bideford 3418)

LONGWELL, Canon Enid Marie. b 34. Angl Women's Tr Coll Tor STh 56. **d** 71 **p** 77 Athab. I of Colinton 71-72;

Grimshaw w Berwyn 72-80; Fort Vermilion Dio Athab from 80; Hon Can of Athab from 80. *Box 84, Fort Vermilion, Alta, T0H 1N0, Canada.* (927 3231)

LONGWORTH, Arthur Victor. b 24. Trin Coll Ox BA 48, MA 51. St Steph Ho Ox 48. **d** 49 **p** 50 Southw. C of Daybrook 49-51; LPr Dio Wakef 51-68; M CR from 54; Vice-Prin Coll of Resurr Mirfield 56-58; Tutor 58-64; Lect 64-68; Lect Bps Coll Cheshunt 68; C of All SS Clifton w St Mary Tyndall's Pk 68-69; Rubery 69-70; Vice-Prin Chich Th Coll 70-73; V of Walsgrave-on-Sowe 73-75; Bp's Tachbrook 75-80; Dioc Dir of Ordinands Cov 73-80; V of St Matt City and Dio Sheff from 80. *5 Broomgrove Crescent, Sheffield, S10 2LQ.* (Sheff 662299)

LONGWORTH-DAMES, Canon Francis Robert. b 12. Jes Coll Cam 3rd cl Engl Trip pt i, 33, BA (3rd cl Hist Trip pt ii) 34, MA 38. Westcott Ho Cam 36. **d** 37 **p** 38 S'wark. C of St Paul w St Mark Deptford 37-43; C-in-c of St Paul Bermondsey and Miss to Charterho in S'wark 43-48; V of St Jo Evang Middlesbrough 48-55; Surr from 49; V of Lewisham 55-65; Hon Can of S'wark from 60; RD of Lewisham 62-65; V of Warlingham w Chelsham and Farleigh 65-73; St Andr Catford 74-81. *Top Flat, 36 Evesham Road, Cheltenham, Glos, GL52 2AB.*

LONSDALE, Christopher Edwin. Angl Th Coll of BC STh 56. **d** 55 BC for Koot **p** 56 Koot. V of Armstrong 55-58; I of Comox 58-68; R of Strawberry Vale w View Royal 68-75; C of St John Vic 75-79. *308 Bessborough Road, Victoria, BC, Canada.* (604-479-6900)

LONSDALE, Canon Rupert Philip. Ridley Hall, Cam 47. **d** 48 **p** 49 Portsm. C of Rowner (in c of Bridgemary Miss Ch) 49-51; V of Morden w Almer and Charborough 51-53; Chap Uasin Gishu Dio Momb 53-58; R of Bentworth w Shalden 58-61; Chap Kisumu and L to Offic Dio Maseno 61-65; Can of Maseno 64-65; Can (Emer) from 65; V of Thornham w Titchwell 65-70; Chap Tenerife 70-73; Asst Chap at Madrid Dio Gibr from 73. *c/o British Embassy, Madrid.*

LOONG, John Shiu-Kee. Univ of Hong Kong, BSc 34, BA 36. **d** 40 Hong. Chinese Miss Calc 41-47; L to Offic Dio Calc 41-47; Sub Warden St John's Hall Hong Kong 47-50; Dioc Regr Dio Hong 49-71; Warden Ch Guest Ho Hong Kong 50-64; L to Offic Dio Hong from 72. *PO Box 837, 2 Upper Albert Road, Hong Kong.* (5-229205)

LOONG, Man Gon. Ling Nam Th Coll. **d** 55 **p** 56 Hong. V of H Carpenter Kowloon 56-58; Perm to Offic Dio Wel 59-63; V of Macao 63-65; P-in-c of Calvary Ch Kowloon 65-69; Missr Chinese Miss City & Dio Wel from 69. *3 Salisbury Terrace, Wellington, NZ.* (58-392)

LOPDELL-BRADSHAW, Humphrey Maitland. b 32. Edin Th Coll 58. **d** 61 Arg Is for Edin **p** 62 Edin. C of H Cross Davidson's Mains 61-65; St Barn Cathl Miss Edin 65-67; C-in-c of Oldbury Dio Birm 67-68; V 68-72; R of St Hilda Colinton Mains Edin 72-77; Hawick Dio Edin from 77. *St Cuthbert's Rectory, Hawick, Roxburgh.* (Hawick 2043)

LOPEZ, Francisco. **d** 75 Bp Leake for N Argent. d Dio N Argent. *Parsonage, Bagan, N Argentina.*

LOPEZ FERREIRO, Serafin Julio. Univ of Dur BA 74. St Jo Coll Dur Dipl Th 71. **d** 71 **p** 72 S'wark. C of St Steph S Lambeth 71-75; H Trin U Tooting Dio S'wark from 76; St Aug Tooting Dio S'wark from 76. *99 Broadwater Road, SW17 0DY.* (01-672 4712)

LOPUL, Niconor. **d** 79 Kara. d Dio Kara. *c/o Karamoja Diocesan Office, PO Box 44, Moroto, Uganda.*

LORAINE, Kenneth. b 34. Cranmer Hall Dur 63. **d** 66 Jarrow for Dur **p** 67 Dur. C of Stranton 66-69; Darlington (in c of St Columba) 69-72; V of Preston-on-Tees 72-79; Staindrop Dio Dur from 79. *Staindrop Vicarage, Darlington, Co Durham.* (Staindrop 60237)

LORD, Alexander. b 13. ALCD 43. **d** 43 **p** 44 Wakef. C of St Mary Wakef 43-45; C-in-c of St Jas Thornham 45-47; R of St Jas Clitheroe 47-55; V of Madeley 55-69; R of Illogan w Trevenson and Portreath 70-81; C of Weobley Dio Heref from 81. *Rectory, Staunton-on-Wye, Hereford, HR4 7LP.* (Moccas 302)

LORD, Charles James. b 12. Univ of Birm BSc 38. **d** 44 **p** 45 Birm. C of Yardley 44-49; Sutton Coldfield (in c of St Chad) 49-50; V of Eastern Green 50-53; Hatton w Haseley 53-71; Chap Rampton Hosp 71-81. *The Conifers, Back Street, Barnby-in-the-Willows, Newark, Notts.*

LORD, Edward. Codr Coll Barb Dipl Th 75, LTh 76. **d** 75 **p** 77 Trinid. Perm to Offic Dio Trinid 75-77; C of St Marg Port of Spain 77-81; R of St Paul San Fernando Dio Trinid from 81. *St Paul's Rectory, San Fernando, Trinidad.*

LORD, Hilton Nelson. b 46. Codr Coll Barb 65. **d** 69 Br Hond. C of St Mary Belize 69-71. *c/o Bishopthorpe, Southern Foreshore, Belize City, British Honduras.*

LORD, James Arthur. b 14. Trin Coll Tor STh 56. **d** 60 Niag. On leave; C of St Marg Hamilton Dio Niag from 76. *1109 King Street West, Hamilton, Ont, Canada, L8S 1L8.*

LORD, Canon John Fairbourne. b 19. Kelham Th Coll. **d** 43 **p** 44 Pet. C of St Mary Dallington 43-45; St Jas Gt Walthamstow 45-47; Langley-Marish 47-51; R of Thornage w Brinton (w Hunworth and Stody from 66) Dio Nor from 51; C-in-c of Hunworth w Stody 62-63; R 63-66; RD of Holt 64-79; Hon Can of Nor from 77. *Thornage Rectory, Holt, Norf, NR25 7AD.* (Melton Constable 860373)

LORD, Kenneth Frank. Clifton Th Coll 34. **d** 38 **p** 40 Sheff. C of St Cuthb Sheff 38-40; Actg C of Walkley 40-42; C of Ch Ch Moreton 42-44; V of Laithkirk 44-53; Skelton w Newby Dio Ripon from 53; Cundall w Norton-le-Clay 53-73. *Skelton Vicarage, Ripon, Yorks.*

LORD, Reginald Douglas. Keble Coll Ox BA 10, MA 16. Lich Th Coll 10. **d** 11 **p** 12 Liv. C of St Geo Wigan 11-13; St Thos Eccleston 13-16; All SS Wigan 16-17; SPG Miss Taian 17-18, 21-23 and 31-32; Yenchow 18-21 and 32-39; Pingyin 24-29; V of Waimate N NZ 40-42; New Lynn 42-47; R of Stratford Gippsld 47-49; V of Priddy 50-55; R of Bawdrip 55-61. *31 Jacka Crescent, Campbell, Canberra, ACT Australia.*

LORD, William Joseph. Trin Coll Tor. **d** 51 **p** 54 Ott. C-in-c of Eganville 51-52; Chap to Ashbury Coll Ott 52-54; Chap RCAF from 54. *c/o RCAFHQ Ottawa, Ont, Canada.*

LORING, John Henry. b 06. K Coll Cam BA 28, MA 32. Cudd Coll 29. **d** 31 **p** 32 St Alb. C of Knebworth 31-34; St Pet Southsea 34-45; V of Froxfield Hants 45-53; R of Haddiscoe w Toft Monks 53-58; V of Soulbury w Stoke Hammond 58-72. *8 Palmers, Wantage, Oxon.* (Wantage 4254)

LORMER, Arthur Robert. Moore Th Coll Syd ACT ThL 45. **d** 46 Syd **p** 46 Bp Pilcher for Syd. C of St Barn Syd 46-47; C-in-c of Berowra 46-53; R of S Kogarah Langlea 53-60; St Thos Auburn 60-74; Chap Prince Henry Hosp Dio Syd from 74. *22 Kain Avenue, Matraville, NSW, Australia 2036.* (661-1968)

LORU, James. **d** 79 **p** 80 Kara. P Dio Kara. *c/o Karamoja Diocesan Office, PO Box 44, Moroto, Uganda.*

LORUKUDE, Rufus. Buwalasi Th Coll 62. **d** 64 **p** 73 Soroti. P Dio Soroti 64-76; Dio Kara from 76. *c/o Karamoja Diocesan Office, PO Box 44, Moroto, Uganda.*

LOSACK, Marcus Charles. b 53. Ch Coll Cam BA (Th) 76, MA 78. Sarum Wells Th Coll 78. **d** 80 **p** 81 Ches. C of St Barn Hattersley Dio Ches from 80. *58 Callington Drive, Hattersley, Hyde, Cheshire.* (061-366 7036)

LOSEBY, Everitt James Carnall. b 22. **d** 66 Bp Horstead for Leic **p** 67 Leic. C of Thurmaston 66-70; R of Seagrave w Walton-le-Wolds 70-75; V of Ch Ch Thurnby Lodge City and Dio Leic from 75. *73 Nursery Road, Leicester, LE5 2HQ.* (Leic 413848)

LOTEN, Terrence Marshall. **d** 43 **p** 44 Aotearoa for Wai. C of Hastings 43-48; V of Takapau 48-50; Whakatane 50-58; Taradale 58-76; Woodville 76-80; Offg Min Dio Wai from 81. *c/o Waiapu House, Te Mata Road, Havelock North, NZ.*

LOTTER, Bryan Cecil. b 42. **d** 75 Bp Carter for Johann **p** 76 Johann. C of Benoni Dio Johann from 75. *4 Roseneath, Harrison Street, Benoni 1500, S Africa.*

LOUDEN, Terence Edmund. b 48. Ch Coll Cam Ba 70, MA 74. Sarum Wells Th Coll 72. **d** 75 **p** 76 Portsm. C of St Mark Portsea 75-78; P-in-c of St Clare Leigh Pk 78-81; R of Niton and of Chale Dio Portsm from 81. *Niton Rectory, Ventnor, IW.* (Niton 730595)

LOUGH, Arthur Geoffrey. b 12. K Coll Lon AKC (1st cl) and BD 34. PhD (Lon) 61. **d** 35 **p** 36 Glouc. C of St Paul Glouc 35-39; Dom Chap to Bp of Bom 39-42; P-in-c of St Paul Byculla Bom 40-42; C of Ch Ch St Geo-in-the-East Lon 42-44; Tuffley 44-48; Kingston-on-Thames 48-50; R of All SS Kingston Jamaica 50-54; V of Hennock Dio Ex from 54; RD of Moreton 66-69. *Hennock Vicarage, Newton Abbot, Devon.* (Bovey Tracey 833211)

LOUGHBOROUGH, Archdeacon of. *See* Lockley, Ven Harold.

LOUGHEED, Brian Frederick Britain. b 38. TCD BA 60, Div Test (2nd cl) 61. **d** 61 **p** 62 Dub. C of St Pet w St Audoen Dub 61-63; Glenageary 63-66; R of Rathmolyon U 66-80; Killarney U Dio Ardf from 80. *St Mary's Rectory, Killarney, Co Kerry, Irish Republic.* (064-31832)

LOUGHLIN, Canon Alfred. Clifton Th Coll 37. **d** 39 **p** 40 Blackb. C of St Mark Preston 39-44; Chap RAFVR 41-43; Org Sec SE Distr CPAS 44-48; V of St Chris Sneinton 48-54; Kinson 54-81; Can and Preb of Sarum Cathl 75-81; Can (Emer) from 81. *35 Southbourne Road, Southbourne, Bournemouth, BH6 5AE.*

LOUGHLIN, George Alfred Graham. b 43. Dipl Th (Lon) 68. Clifton Th Coll 65. **d** 69 Woolwich for S'wark **p** 70 S'wark. C of All SS Shooter's Hill 69-73; Ch Ch Bromley 73-76; P-in-c of Bothenhampton w Walditch 76-79; Team V of Bridport Dio Sarum 79. *Bothenhampton Vicarage, Bridport, Dorset.* (Bridport 23279)

LOUIS, Peter Anthony. b 41. St Cath Coll Ox BA 64. Wells Th Coll 66. **d** 68 **p** 70 Chich. C of St Mary Virg E Grinstead 68-75; Radcliffe-on-Trent 75-80; Hd Master Blue Coat

Comprehensive Sch Cov from 80. *c/o Blue Coat Comprehensive School, Coventry.*

LOURENS, William John Peter. b 49. St Pet Coll Alice Dipl Th 72. **d** 72 **p** 73 Capetn. C of Bonteheuwel 72-75; Bellville S 76-78; P-in-c of Grassy Pk Dio Capetn 78-80; R from 80. *Good Shepherd House, Victoria Road, Grassy Park 7800, CP, S Africa.* (72-2196)

LOUSADA, Horace Frank. St Aid Th Coll Bal ACT ThL 27. **d** 27 **p** 28 Bal. C of Marnoo 27-28; P-in-c 28-29; C of St Sav Gladstone 30-32; P-in-c of Paroch Distr of Miriam Vale 32-33; V of Wedderburn 36-38; P-in-c of Nyah W 38-40; L to Offic Dio Gippsld 62-74; Perm to Offic Dio Melb from 75. *3/41 Brighton Street, Frankston, Vic, Australia 3199.*

LOUSADA, John Matthews Hall. Moore Th Coll Syd ACT ThL 63. **d** 63 **p** 64 Syd. C of Neutral Bay 63-65; Miss CMS Dio Sing 66-70; Dio W Mal 70-77; R of H Trin Panania Dio Syd from 77. *201 Tower Street, Panania, NSW, Australia 2213.* (77-8097)

LOUTH, Andrew. b 44. St Cath Coll Cam BA 65, MA 69. Univ of Edin MTh 68. Edin Th Coll 66. **d** 68 **p** 69 Bris. C of Southmead 68-70; Fell and Chap Worc Coll Ox from 70; L to Offic Dio Ox from 70. *Worcester College, Oxford.*

LOUTTIT, Canon Redfern Ernest. Wycl Coll Tor 35. **d** 40 **p** 41 Moos. Miss at Factory R James Bay 40-53; U Albany Ojibway Miss 53-54; E Main 54-60; Paint Hills 60-63; Calstock 63-67; C of Moose Factory Dio Moos 67-71; R from 71; Hon Can of Moos from 71. *Box 30, Moose Factory, Ont., Canada.* (705-336 4800)

LOUW, Nicholas Tsoasane. **d** 68 **p** 69 Grahmstn. C of St Mich Herschel Dio Grahmstn from 68. *St Michael's Mission, All Angels, Hershel, via Zastron, OFS, S Africa.*

LOUW, Paul Leonard. Univ of Leeds BA 56. Coll of Resurr Mirfield 56. **d** 58 Aston for Birm **p** 59 Birm. C of Solihull 58-61; St Mich and St Geo Cathl Grahmstn 61-62; R of St Alb Cathcart 62-64; St Barn Port Eliz 64-68. *55 Main Road, Walmer, Port Elizabeth, CP, S Africa.*

LOVATT, Bernard James. Lich Th Coll 64. **d** 65 **p** 66 Heref. C of Burford (3rd Portion) w L Heref 65-67; Cleobury Mortimer w Hopton Wafers 67-68; Asst Master City of Cov Sch 65-68; C of Bradf-on-Avon 68-69; Wootton Bassett and of Broad Town 69-72; R of Bishopstrow and Boreham 72-79; V of St Anne Brighton Dio Chich from 79; P-in-c of St Geo Mart Brighton Dio Chich from 79. *33 Eaton Place, Brighton, Sussex, BN2 1EG.* (Brighton 699779)

LOVATT, Roy. b 45. Coll of Resurr 77. **d** 77 **p** 78 York (APM). C of Boston Spa 77-80; V of St Paul w Ch Ch & St Silas Sculcoates Dio York from 80. *Vicarage, St Paul Street, Hull, Yorks.* (Hull 29272)

LOVE, Ellsworth Frederick. b 12. Edin Th Coll 47. **d** 50 **p** 51 Edin. C of St Jas Leith 50-52; R of St Marg Easter Road Edin 52-69; W Linton 69-77. *3 Paisley Grove, Edinburgh, EH8 7LF.*

LOVE, Hector William. b 07. Trin Coll Dub BA and Div Test (2nd cl) 31, MA 34. **d** 31 **p** 32 Arm. C of Dundalk 31-35; P-in-c of Keady 35-41; I of Keady and Armaghbreague 41-61; Dep Dioc Regr Arm 40-42; Prov Regr Arm 43-79; Dir of Relig Educn Dio Arm 43-68; Preb of Mullabrack in Arm Cathl 55-65; Prec of Arm Cathl 65-73; Prec (Emer) from 73; Exam Chap to Abp of Arm 61-68; I of Heynestown U 61-66; Ballymascanlan w Carlingford and Omeath 66-73. *10 Vicars' Hill, Armagh, BT61 7ED, N Ireland.* (0861-522340)

LOVE, Richard Angus. b 45. K Coll Lon and Warm AKC 67. **d** 68 **p** 69 S'wark. C of Ascen Balham 68-71; Amersham w Coleshill 71-73; R of Scotter w E Ferry 73-79; P-in-c of Petham w Waltham and Lower Hardres w Nackington Dio Cant from 79. *Petham Vicarage, Canterbury, Kent, CT4 5RE.* (Petham 330)

LOVE, Robert. Univ of Bradf BSc 68, PhD 74. Trin Coll Bris Dipl Th 75. **d** 75 **p** 76 Bradf. C of Bowling 75-79; Team V of St Sav Forest Gate (in c of St Matt) Dio Chelmsf from 79. *c/o 12 Clova Road, Forest Gate, E7 9AH.*

✠ **LOVEDAY, Right Rev David Goodwin.** b 1896. Late Sizar of Magd Coll Cam 2nd cl Cl Trip pt i 21, BA (2nd cl Th Trip pt i) 22, MA 26. **d** 23 St Alb **p** 24 Ox for St Alb. Chap and Asst Master Aldenham Sch 22-25; Asst Master Clifton Coll 25-31; Asst Chap 25-30; Chap 30-31; Select Pr Univ of Cam 33 and 54; Trin Coll Dub 51; Univ of Ox 55 and 57; Hd Master Cranleigh Sch 31-54; Archd of Dorking and Exam Chap to Bp of Guildf 54-57; Cons Ld Bp Suffr of Dorchester in Cant Cathl 2 Feb 57 by Abp of Cant; Bps of Ox; Guildf; and Linc; Bps Suffr of Reading; and Whitby; and Bp Lenman; Proc Conv Ox from 59-64; res 71; Hon Asst Bp in Dio Ox from 71. *Wardington, Banbury, Oxon.*

LOVEDAY, Joseph Michael. b 54. AKC 75. St Aug Coll Cant 75. **d** 78 **p** 79 Pet. C of Kettering Dio Pet from 78. *13 Bowling Green Road, Kettering, Northants.*

LOVEGROVE, Walter John. b 19. St Aug Coll Cant 38. Univ of Dur LTh 44. **d** 42 **p** 43 Lich. C of Ogley Hay w Brownhills 42-43; St Giles Willenhall 43-45; Gt Yarmouth (in c of St James) 45-47; St Mary's Cathl Johann 47-49; R of Roodepoort 49-52; CF (S Afr) 52-54; R of N Suburbs Pret 54-64; Pietersburg 64-66; Fish Hoek 66-72; V of St Phil Chaddesden 72-75; C-in-c of Tintinhull 75; R (w Chilthorne Domer Yeovil Marsh and Thorne Coffin) 75-80; RD of Martock 78-80; P-in-c of St Phil Norbury Dio Cant 80-81; V from 81. *66 Pollards Hill North, SW16 4NY.* (01-764 1812)

LOVEJOY, Geoffrey William. b 08. St Chad's Coll Dur BA and LTh 31, MA 47. Dorch Miss Coll 28. **d** 32 **p** 33 B & W. C of H Trin Hendford Yeovil 32-34; M of Bro of Good Shepherd Dubbo 34-40; Cam Miss to Delhi 40-42; Chap of Kohat NWFP 42-44; C of All H Tottenham 45-46; R of Gatooma w Hartley S Rhod 46-47; Hartley 47-52; P-in-c of St Mark's Miss Mondoro 46-52; C of St Marychurch 52-54; C-in-c of Shiphay Collaton 54-57; PC 57-59; R of Cumberworth w Denby Dale 59-65; Gayhurst w Stoke Goldington 65-72; C-in-c of Ravenstone w Weston Underwood 67-72; Chap Sevenoaks Hosp 73-79; Hon C of St Jo Bapt Sevenoaks Dio Roch from 73; Dep Chap Orpington and Farnborough Hosps from 76. *73 Dartford Road, Sevenoaks, Kent, TN13 3TE.* (Sevenoaks 50595)

LOVEJOY, James Allan. b 06. Late Scho of Jes Coll Cam 1st cl Hist Trip pt i 27, BA (1st cl Hist Trip pt ii) 28, MA 35. Westcott Ho Cam 35. **d** 36 **p** 37 St Alb. C of All SS w St John Hertford 36-39; Miss (CUM) Dio Lah 39-49; Vice-Prin St Steph Coll Delhi 40-42; V of St Jas Delhi 42-47; V of Cathl Delhi and Exam Chap to Bp of Delhi 47-49; Shirehampton 49-58; Sec Conf of British Miss S 58-67; V of Westleton w Dunwich 67-74; Darsham 71-74. *28 Pembroke Road, Framlingham, Suff.* (Framlingham 723214)

LOVEJOY, John Geoffrey. K Coll Lon and Warm BD and AKC 60. **d** 61 **p** 62 Newc T. C of St Lawr Byker Newc T 61-64; Choppington 64-66; Usworth 66-70; L to Offic Dio Carl 73-78; R of Wyndham Dio NW Austr from 79. *Box 208, Wyndham, W Australia 6740.* (61 1386)

LOVELAND, John Michael. b 30. Roch Th Coll 65. **d** 67 **p** 68 Lon. C of St Hilda's Conv Distr Ashford Middx 67-71; Earley (in c of St Nicolas) 71-76; V of St Nicolas Earley 76-79; Kennington Dio Ox from 79. *Kennington Vicarage, Oxford, OX1 5PG.* (Ox 735135)

LOVELESS, Frederick William. St Jo Coll Morpeth. **d** 50 **p** 52 Bath. C of Cowra 50-51; Parkes 51-52; P-in-c of Stuart Town 53-54; C of Tamworth 54-56; V of Nundle 56-58; Tambar Springs 58-59; P-in-c of Trundle 62-67; Kandos 67; Woomelang w Tempy 69-72; Perm to Offic Dio Melb 72-76; Dio Wang from 77. *RMB 5105, Shelley, Vic, Australia 3700.*

LOVELESS, Kenneth Norman Joseph. b 11. VRD 61. Chich Th Coll 46. **d** 49 **p** 50 Lon. C of St Mark Dalston 49-51; St Pet w St John Lon Docks 51-54; Chap RNVR 53-58; RNR from 58; V of H Trin w St Mary Hoxton 54-68; Chap St Matt Hosp Shoreditch 55-68; RD of Shoreditch 64-67; Hackney 67-74; P-in-c of St Anne w St Sav and St Andr Hoxton 65-68; L to Offic Dio Lon from 76. *3 Clothworkers' Cottages, Bishop Street, N1 8PH.* (01-359 9179)

LOVELESS, Martin Frank. b 46. Wycl Hall Ox 72. **d** 73 Buckingham for Ox **p** 76 Reading for Ox. C of Caversham (in c of St Andr from 78) 75-81; V of Carterton Dio Ox from 81. *Carterton Vicarage, Oxford, OX8 3AA.* (Carterton 842429)

LOVELESS, Robert Alfred. Univ of Birm BA (2nd cl Hist) 66. Westcott Ho Cam 66. **d** 68 Cov **p** 69 Bp Daly for Cov. C of Kenilworth 68-72; Costessey 73-75; R of Colney 75-80; V of L Melton w Gt (w Marlingford to 80) and Bawburgh Dio Nor from 75. *Little Melton Vicarage, Norwich, NOR 45X.* (Norwich 810322)

LOVELESS, Canon William Harry. b 21. BSc (Econ) Lon 60. Ridley Hall Cam 61. **d** 63 **p** 64 Chelmsf. C of Danbury 63-65; St Mary Gt Cam 65-67; V of St Mark Cam Dio Ely from 67; Chairman Ely Dioc Bd for Social Responsibility 79-81; RD of Cam from 81; Hon Can of Ely from 81. *St Mark's Vicarage, Barton Road, Cambridge, CB3 9JZ.* (Cam 63339)

LOVELL, Alfred Frank. b 07. K Coll Lon BD, AKC and Jun Hebr Pri 34. St Steph Ho Ox 34. **d** 34 **p** 35 Chelmsf. C of St Jo Div Romford 34-37; Mkt Drayton 37-40; V of Loppington 40-46; Chap RNVR 43-46; Chap RN 46-50; HMS *Mauritius* 46-48; RN Sch of Music 48-50; V of St Gabr Pimlico Dio Lon from 50. *30 Warwick Square, SW1V 2AD.* (01-834 7520)

LOVELL, Charles Nelson. b 34. Or Coll Ox BA 57, MA 61. Wycl Hall, Ox. **d** 59 Stafford for Lich **p** 60 Lich. C of Walsall 59-63; St Giles-in-the-Fields Lon 63; H Trin Cam 64; Chap St Geo Coll Quilmes and All SS Quilmes Argent 64-67; V of Esh 67-75; V of Hamsteels 67-75; Chap Winterton Hosp Sedgefield Dio Dur from 75; Sec Dur Dioc Social Responsibility C'tee from 80. *Southdown, Winterton, Sedgefield, Stockton-on-Tees, Cleveland.* (Sedgefield 22066)

LOVELL, David John. b 38. Qu Coll Birm 60. **d** 61 Glouc **p** 62 Tewkesbury for Cant. C of St Steph Glouc 61-64; St Geo

Conv Distr Lower Tuffley Glouc 64-67; V of Lydbrook 67-73; R of Oatlands 73-75; Perm to Offic Dio Tas 76-81. *29 Lucas Street, Kingston, Tasmania 7150.* (002-29 5709)

LOVELL, Canon Ernest William O'Malley. b 22. Trin Coll Dub BA 44, Div Test 45, MA 59. **d** 45 **p** 46 Dub. C of Drumcondra w North Strand Dub 45-48; C-in-c of Mevagh 49-51; I of Badoney U 51-56; Camus-juxta-Mourne Dio Derry from 56; RD of Strabane from 71; Can of Derry from 75; Preb of St Patr Cathl Dub from 80. *Rectory, Newtown Street, Strabane, Co Tyrone, N Ireland.* (Strabane 882314)

LOVELL, Frederick Arthur. b 07. Chich Th Coll 31. **d** 34 **p** 35 Bris. C of St Mary Redcliffe (in c of St Mary Less 35-39) 34-41; Offg C-in-c of St Pet Bishopsworth 41-45; R of St Mary Cricklade 45-52; C-in-c of St Jo Bapt Latton 49-52; St Sampson Cricklade 50-52; Cricklade w Latton 52-53; R of Combe Martin from 53-73; RD of Shirwell 63-73; Perm to Offic Dios Ex and Truro from 74. *18 Trelawney Avenue, Poughill, Bude, Cornw.*

LOVELL, Canon Harold Guildford. b 1890. Ch Th Coll 13. **d** 14 Bp de Carteret for Abp of WI **p** 15 WI. C of All SS Kingston 14-17; TCF 17-19; R of St Jude and St Chris Stony Hill 19-21; Actg R of Halfway Tree 21-22; R 22-49; P-in-c of Mt James and Stony Hill 35-48; Hon Can of Cathl 39-50; Can (Emer) from 50; C of Bp's Hatfield (in c of St Mark Woodhill) 49-50; R of Wyddial 50-52; Anstey 50-52; Commiss 50-64; R of Essendon (w Woodhill from 59) 52-64; Perm to Offic Dio St Alb from 64. *1 Church Street, Hatfield, Herts.* (Hatfield 65275)

LOVELL, Keith Michael Beard. b 43. K Coll Lon and Warm 67. **d** 68 Colchester for Chelmsf **p** 69 Chelmsf. C of Romford (w Noak Hill from 69) 68-73; P-in-c of Elmstead 73-79; V of Tollesbury w Salcot Virley Dio Chelmsf from 79. *Tollesbury Vicarage, Maldon, Essex.* (Tollesbury 393)

LOVELL, Laurence John. St D Coll Lamp BA 54. Tyndale Hall Bris. **d** 56 **p** 57 Roch. C of Ch Ch w H Trin Penge 56-60; Illogan 60-63; V of St Keverne 63-68; C-in-c of St Paul Oatley Dio Syd 68-72; R from 72. *65 Rosa Street, Oatley, NSW, Australia 2223.* (57-5458)

LOVELOCK, John Herbert. b 03. St Jo Coll Dur BA 28, Dipl Th (w distinc) 29, MA 32. **d** 29 **p** 30 Dover for Cant. C of Milton Regis 29-32; St Luke Woodside Croydon 32-34; V of H Trin Selhurst 34-47; R of Denton w Wootton 47-52; Northbourne 52-59; Betteshanger w Ham 52-59; C of St Jude Thornton Heath 59-62; V of St Paul Thornton Heath 62-71; Perm to Offic Dio Cant from 71; Hon C of All SS Tooting 72-76; Perm to Offic Dio S'wark from 77. *3 St John's Hospital, Northgate, Canterbury, Kent, CT1 1BG.* (Cant 54108)

LOVELUCK, (Illtyd) Allan. St D Coll Lamp BA 53. Univ of Queensld BA 72. St Mich Coll Llan 53. **d** 55 **p** 56 Llan. C of Dowlais 55-58; M SSF from 58; Publ Pr Dio Chelmsf 62-64; Chap Univ of Queensld and L to Offic Dio Brisb 64-66; Perm to Offic Dio Brisb 66-79. *c/o 52 Ellerslie Crescent, Taringa, Queensland, Australia 4068.* (70 2804)

LOVELUCK, Arthur Howell. b 19. St Mich Coll Llan 46. **d** 49 **p** 50 Llan. C of Whitchurch 49-53; CF 53-56; V of St Osw Coney Hill Glouc 56-63; Williton Dio B & W from 63. *Williton Vicarage, Taunton, Somt.* (Williton 32560)

LOVELUCK, Graham David. b 34. Univ of Wales (Abth) BSc 55, PhD 58. St Deiniol's Libr Hawarden 76. **d** 78 **p** 79 Ban. Hon C of Llanfairmathafarneithaf Dio Ban from 78. *7 Garreg Lwyd, Benllech, Gwynedd, LL74 8RB.* (Tynygongl 2196)

LOVELY, Leslie Walter. Univ of Dur LTh 32. St Aug Coll Cant. **d** 32 **p** 33 Win. C of St Alb Southampton 32-35; Asst Chap at St Mark and All SS Alexandria 35-43; R of St Matt Riversdale 43-44; Victoria West 44-46; Graaff-Reinet 46-52; Benoni 52-56; Potchefstroom 56-61; Mayfair 61-66; Chap Johann Gen Hosp from 66. *5 Hagen Road, Greenside, Johannesburg, S Africa.* (011-724 1121)

LOVERIDGE, Barry Ernest. Coll Ho Ch Ch 56. **d** 56 **p** 7 Nel. C of Greymouth 56-58; Master Whakarewa Trust Sch 58-60; Hon C of Motueka 58-60; V of Ahaura-Brunnerton 60-67; Spring Creek 67-76; City Miss Dio Ch Ch 76-77; V of St John City and Dio Ch Ch from 77. *234 Hereford Street, Christchurch 1, NZ.* (67-744)

LOVETT, Ian James. b 49. SOC 73. **d** 76 Roch **p** 77 Cant. C of St Geo Gravesend 76-77; Willesborough w Hinxhill 77-82; Herne Dio Cant from 82. *c/o Herne Vicarage, Herne Bay, Kent, CT6 7HE.*

LOVEWELL, Robert Antony. b 34. Lich Th Coll. **d** 62 Bp Gerrard for York **p** 63 Sheff. C of St Aug Sheff 62-65; Chap Miss to Seamen and R of St Steph and St Lawr Lourenço Marques 65-73; Chap Miss to Seamen Port of the Tees 73-79; V of Wilton-in-Cleveland 73-79; Team V of Thornaby-on-Tees 79-81; Industr Chap HM Dkyard Devonport from 81. *Industrial Chaplain's Office, Devonport Dockyard, Devonport, Plymouth.*

LOVITT, Gerald Elliott. St Mich Coll Llan 59. **d** 61 Llan **p** 62 Bp Hughes for Llan. C of Aberdare 61-66; Whitchurch 66-71; V of St Paul Grangetown Canton 71-76; Rockfield w St Maughan Dio Mon from 76. *Rockfield Vicarage, Monmouth, NP5 3QB.* (Monmouth 2003)

LOVITT, Roy Cecil. Moore Th Coll Syd ACT ThL 56. **d** 49 **p** 50 Graft. C of Lismore 49-52; V of Burringbar w U Tweed 52-54; Dunoon 54-55; Healesville 55-59; Min of W Preston 59-61; Chap RAN 61-77; L to Offic Dio Syd 65-78; Asst Master Cranbrook Sch 77-78; R of St Jude Randwick Dio Syd from 79. *108 Avoca Street, Randwick, NSW, Australia 2031.* (399-3158)

LOW, Bernard Arthur. b 25. St Francis Coll Brisb 72. **d** 74 **p** 75 Brisb. C of St Pet Wynnum Brisb 74-77; V of Biggenden 77-80; St Geo Windsor City and Dio Brisb from 80. *18 Newmarket Road, Windsor, Qld, Australia 4030.* (57 4293)

LOW, David Anthony. b 42. K Coll Lon and Warm AKC 66. **d** 67 **p** 68 Roch. C of St Barn Gillingham 67-70; Wallingford 70-73; V of Spencer's Wood 73-82; Grazeley w Beech Hill 77-82; St Barn Gillingham Dio Roch from 82. *1 St Barnabas Close, Gillingham, Kent, ME7 4BU.* (Medway 51010)

LOW, David John. b 32. Univ of Bris BA 53. Wells Th Coll 55. **d** 57 **p** 58 Man. C of Ch Ch Bradf 57-59; Benchill 59-62; V of St Pet Newbold Rochdale 62-75; R of Moston Dio Man from 75. *47 Nuthurst Road, Moston, Manchester, M10 0EW.* (061-681 1201)

LOW, David Michael. b 39. Univ of Capetn BA 60. Cudd Coll 61. **d** 63 **p** 64 Portsm. C of St Cuthb Copnor 63-65; St Geo Cathl Capetn 65-67; Bredasdorp 67-69; St Faith Havant 69-72; V of St Helens IW Dio Portsm from 72; P-in-c- of St Pet Seaview Dio Portsm 80-81; V from 81. *St Helen's Vicarage, Ryde, IW.* (Bembridge 2630)

LOW, John Edmund. Univ of Lon BA (2nd cl Hist) 32. AKC 34. **d** 34 **p** 35 Lich. C of St Geo Newc L 34-37; Warrington (in c of St John) 37-43; St Mary Leigh 43-46; V of St Mary Magd Winton Man 46-51; St Thos Bedford Leigh 51-77; Perm to Offic Dios Ches and St A from 78. *9 Sunnyridge Avenue, Marford, Wrexham, Clwyd, LL12 8TE.* (Gresford 4614)

LOW, John Hallett. d 41 **p** 42 Edmon. C of Barrhead 41-45; R of St Nich Vanc 45-50; I of Quamichan w Cowichan 50-57; V of St Clem Lynn Valley Vanc 57-74. *Leek Road, RR2, Gibson's, BC, Canada.*

LOW, Terence John Gordon. b 37. Oakhill Th Coll 75. **d** 77 Willesden for Lon **p** 78 Lon. C of Kensal Rise 77-80; Longfleet Dio Sarum from 80. *55 Garland Road, Poole, Dorset, BH15 2LD.* (Poole 81907)

LOW, Canon William Laird. Bd of Th Stud NZ 39. **d** 40 **p** 41 Wel. C of Feilding 40-42; CF (NZ) 42-44; V of Hunterville 44-48; Waiwhetu 48-49; Ngaio Wel 49-62; Greytn 62-66; C of Lower Hutt (in c of Avalon) 66-71; Chap Wanganui Hosp Dio Wel from 69; Hon Can of Wel 73-78; Can (Emer) from 78; Offg Min Dio Wel from 78. *83 Duncan Street, Wanganui E, NZ.* (Wanganui 39-358)

LOW, William Roberson. b 50. Pemb Coll Cam BA 73, MA 77. Westcott Ho Cam 76. **d** 79 Stepney for Lon **p** 80 Lon. C of All SS Poplar Dio Lon from 79. *6 Mountague Place, Poplar, E14.* (01-515 5454)

LOWAL, Timothy. d 80 Kara. d Dio Kara. *c/o Karamoja Diocesan Office, PO Box 44, Moroto, Uganda.*

LOWCOCK, Brian Walter. b 23. Univ of Man LLB 43. Linc Th Coll 56. **d** 57 **p** 58 Linc. C of S Ormsby 57-62; PC of Drove End Gedney 62-67; C-in-c of Holbeach Hurn 62-65; V 65-67; C-in-c of St Nich Long Sutton 62-65; PC 65-67; Perm to Offic Dio Linc 68-73; L to Offic Dio Ely 70-74; C-in-c of St Mark w St Matt Holbeach Marsh 74-80; V of Edenham Dio Linc from 80. *Vicarage, Edenham, Bourne, Lincs, PE10 0LS.* (Edenham 272)

LOWE, Anthony Richard. b 45. Univ of York BA (2nd cl Pol) 66. Univ of Birm Dipl Th 68. Qu Coll Birm 66. **d** 69 Sheff **p** 70 Bp Gerard for Sheff. C of Greasborough 69-71; Thrybergh 71-74; P-in-c of St Mary w St Simon and St Matthias Sheff 75-77; V of St Hilda Shiregreen City and Dio Sheff from 77. *47 Firth Park Avenue, Sheffield, S5 6HF.* (Sheffield 386308)

LOWE, David Charles. b 43. Kelham Th Coll 62. **d** 67 **p** 68 Derby. C of Wingerworth 67-70; Greenhill Derbys 70-73; Team V of Eckington w Renishaw 73-78; V of St Geo Bury St Edms Dio St E from 78. *Vicarage, Acacia Avenue, Bury St Edmunds, Suff.*

LOWE, David Reginald. b 42. K Coll Lon and Warm BD and AKC 65. **d** 66 **p** 67 Heref. C of Tupsley 66-69; St Anne Lewes 69-73; H Trin Heref 73-77; P-in-c of Lyonshall w Titley Dio Heref from 77. *Lyonshall Vicarage, Kington, Herefs.* (Lyonshall 212)

LOWE, Derek Mayall. b 16. Univ of Man BA 51. ACII 39. Wells Th Coll 68. **d** 70 **p** 71 Ches. C of Wilmslow 70-75; V of Marthall w Over Peover Dio Ches from 75. *Marthall Vicarage, Knutsford, Ches, WA16 8SX.* (0625-861462)

LOWE, Derrick. b 34. Codr Coll Barb 58. **d** 60 Barb for Gui **p** 61 Gui. C of All SS New Amsterdam 60-62; P-in-c of Kwakwani w Berbice River 62-64; R of St Olaf Kirkwall w St Mary Stromness 65-69; St Bendict Ardwick City and Dio Man from 69. *St Benedict's Presbytery, Bennett Street, Manchester, M12 5BD.* (061-223 0154)

LOWE, Desmond Allen. b 38. Moore Coll Syd ACT ThL 68. **d** 70 **p** 71 Melb. C of Ch Ch S Yarra 70-71; All SS Geelong 71-73; P-in-c of Healesville 73-76; I 77-78; Berwick Dio Melb from 78. *Vicarage, Palmerston Street, Berwick, Vic, Australia 3806.* (707 1004)

LOWE, Donald. b 33. Lich Th Coll. **d** 60 **p** 61 Man. C of Horwich 60; St Martin's Conv Distr Wythenshawe 60-62; St Paul Bury 62-65; St Andr and St Mich Cathl Bloemf 65-67; St Marg Bloemf 67-69; V of Gannow Burnley 70-73; R of St Alb Virginia Bloemf 73-81; H Cross Odendaalsrus Bloemf 75-80; V of H Trin Colne Dio Blackb from 81. *49 Penrith Crescent, Colne, Lancs BB8 8JS.* (Colne 863431)

LOWE, Eric. b 29. Trin Coll Ox BA (3rd cl Th) 50, MA 54. St Steph Ho Ox 50. **d** 52 Bp Tubbs for Ches **p** 53 Ches. C of Ch Ch Ellesmere Port 52-55; Hucknall Torkard 55-56; Solihull 56-58; UMCA Area Sec for NW Engl 58-65; L Pr Dio Man 58-65; USPG Area Sec Dios Ches, Ban and St A from 65; Dio Liv from 73. *41 Church Lane, Upton, Chester, CH2 1DJ.* (Chester 382172)

LOWE, Eric. Em Coll Sktn BA 51, LTh 51. **d** 51 **p** 52 Sktn. R of Rosthern w Duck Lake 52-54; Loon Lake 54-56; P-in-c of St Andr Lah 56-60; Gojra 60-63; Mussorie 63-73; on leave 73-75; I of St Thos Vanc Dio New Westmr from 75. *5727 St Margaret's Street, Vancouver, BC, V5R 3H6, Canada.*

LOWE, Felix Benjamin. Codr Coll Barb 63. **d** 65 Barb for Guy **p** 66 Guy. C of St Jos Port Mourant 65-70; Bartica 70-75; V of Waramuri w Waini Dio Guy from 75. *Vicarage, Waramuri, Moruka River, Guyana.*

LOWE, Ven Frank McLean Rhodes. d 61 **p** 63 Gippsld. C of Sale Cathl 61-64; V of Bruthen 64-68; Newborough 68-71; Morwell Dio Gippsld from 71; Hon Can of Gippsld 73-81; Archd from 81; Exam Chap to Bp of Gippsld from 81. *Box 156, Morwell, Vic, Australia 3840.* (051-34 4674)

LOWE, Gilbert Albert. b 04. Late Jun and Sen Exhib of Trin Coll Dub BA (1st cl Mod) and Found Sch 26, BSc and Div Test 28, MA 76. **d** and **p** 29 Dub. C of St Kevin Dub 29-31; Ch Ch Leeson Pk Dub 31-39; Min Can St Patr Cathl Dub 30-36; Treas V 36-39; R of Stillorgan 39-41; CF (EC) 41-48; Min Can of St Patr Cathl Dub 48-51. *10 Camphill Court, West Byfleet, Weybridge, Surrey, KT14 6EQ.* (Byfleet 41476)

LOWE, James. b 21. Kelham Th Coll. **d** 44 **p** 45 Wakef. C of Royston 44-46; Brighouse 46-47; Dewsbury 47-51; CF 51-54; R of W Tanfield 54-57; Cranbrook W Austr 57-61; Hon Chap to Bp of Bunb 58-61; R of Bacton w Wyverstone 61-67; RD of S Hartismere 64-67; Samford 67-69; V of Bentley w Tattingstone 67-79. *Sunnibrae, The Heath, Tattingstone, Ipswich, Suff.* (Holbrook 377)

LOWE, Jerryl Mervyn Cresswell. Moore Coll Syd ThL 70. **d** and **p** 71 Syd. C of St Paul Wahroonga 71-72; Carlingford 73; Camden 73-75; R of St Leonard's Tas 75-79; Res Min of Doonside Blacktown Dio Syd from 79. *Rectory, Doonside, NSW, Australia 2767.* (621-8101)

LOWE, John Bethel. b 30. TCD BA 52, Th Exhib 55, BD 65. Ridley Hall, Cam 55. **d** 55 Connor **p** 56 Down and Dromore. C of St Mary Magd Belf 55-57; Tutor Bp Gwynne Coll Mundri 59-64; Bp Tucker Coll Mukono 64-74; Vice-Prin 68-74; Commiss Sudan from 65; Warden CMS Conf Centre Foxbury, Chislehurst 74-76; V of Kippington Dio Roch from 76. *Kippington Vicarage, Sevenoaks, Kent, TN13 2LL.* (Sevenoaks 52112)

LOWE, John Forrester. b 39. Univ of Nottm BA (3rd cl Th) 61. Lich Th Coll 61. **d** 64 **p** 65 Chelmsf. C of N Woolwich 64-69; V of Marks Gate, Chadwell Heath 69-74; Moulsham 74-79; N Woolwich w Silvertown Dio Chelmsf from 79. *St John's Vicarage, Manwood Street, North Woolwich, E16 2SX.* (01-476 2388)

LOWE, Joseph. b 14. Univ of Man BA 35, BD (w distinc) 38, MA 39. St Aid Coll 56. **d** 57 **p** 58 Ches. C of Lache w Saltney 57-59; V of Sutton 59-64; Bushbury 64-67; Shelton w Oxon 67-74; Surr 65-80; Hosp Chap Shrewsbury 74-80; Perm to Offic Dio B & W from 80. *16 Parkmead, Monkton Heathfield, Taunton, TA2 8PL.*

LOWE, Michael Arthur. b 46. BD (Lon) 67. Cranmer Hall Dur Dipl Th 75. **d** 76 **p** 77 Bradf. C of Thorpe Edge 76-79; N Ferriby Dio York from 79. *36 Dower Rise, Swanland, Humb, HU14 3QT.* (Hull 631271)

LOWE, Michael Sinclair. b 35. Open Univ BA 75. K Coll Lon and Warm AKC 61. **d** 62 Hulme for Man **p** 63 Man. C of Wm Temple Conv Distr Woodhouse Pk 62-66; V of Facit 66-70; St Barn Twerton Hill Bath (w Englishcombe from 77) 70-79; Bathford Dio B & W from 79. *Vicarage, Ostlings Lane, Bathford, Bath, BA1 7RW.* (Bath 858325)

LOWE, Raymond John. b 12. OBE (Mil) 67. St Edm Hall Ox BA (3rd cl Th) 34, MA 38. Sarum Th Coll 34. **d** 36 **p** 37 Lon. C of St Andr Hoxton 36-38; Chap RN 38-67; Hon Chap to HM the Queen from 65; C of St Mary Virg Ox 67-70; R of Padworth 70-77; V of Mortimer W End 70-77; Perm to Offic Dio Ox from 77. *Army and Navy Club, Pall Mall, SW1Y 5JN.*

LOWE, Canon Reginald Kenneth William. b 09. Trin Coll Dub BA 31, MA 34. **d** 32 **p** 33 Dub. C of Drumcondra w N Strand 32-42; I of Dunlavin 42-50; Rathdrum w Glenealy 50-65; Blessington w Kilbride 65-79; Can of Ch Ch Cathl Dub 58-79; Can (Emer) from 79; Treas 74-79; RD of Delgany 59-79. *Glenbride Cottage, Kilpedder, Co Wicklow, Irish Republic.*

LOWE, (Christopher) Richard. b 23. Univ of Birm BSc 44. Coll of Resurr Mirfield 46. M CR 67. **d** 48 **p** 49 Chelmsf. C of Ascen Victoria Docks 48-51; St Mark Swindon 51-56; R of Corringham 56-65; Proc Conv Chelmsf 65-66; L to Offic Dio Wakef 66-69; Dio Lon from 69; M Gen Syn from 80. *Royal Foundation of St Katharine, 2 Butcher Row, E14 8DS.* (01-790 3540)

LOWE, Canon Robert Arthur. Coll Ho Ch Ch LTh 52. **d** 52 **p** 53 Ch Ch. C of Highfield 52-54; Sydenham 54-56; V of Barrington Street 56-60; Geraldine 60-63; Adv Bd of Chr Educn Dio Ch Ch 63-66; V of Fendalton Dio Ch Ch from 66; Hon Can of Ch Ch from 74. *7 Makora Street, Christchurch 4, NZ.* (517-064)

LOWE, Sam. b 35. St D Coll Lamp 62. **d** 65 **p** 66 St D. C of Tenby w Gumfreston 65-67; Stourport 67-69; Halesowen w Hasbury and Lapal 69-72; V of St Andr and St Nich w St Pet Droitwich 72-73; Team V 73-77; V of St Geo (w St Mary Magd from 78) City and Dio Worc from 77. *Vicarage, St George's Square, Worcester, WR1 1HX.* (Worc 22698)

LOWE, Stephen Arthur. b 49. Univ of Nottm BSc 71. Cudd Coll 71. **d** 74 **p** 75 Southw. C of St Mark Mansfield 74-77; Chap of Martyrs' Sch Papua 77-78; P-in-c of Nambaiyufa 79; V of Kirkby Woodhouse Dio Southw from 80. *Vicarage, Skegby Road, Kirkby-in-Ashfield, Nottingham, NG17 9JE.* (Mansfield 759094)

LOWE, Stephen Richard. b 44. BSc (Econ) (Lon) 66. Ripon Hall Ox 66. **d** 68 Birm **p** 69 Aston for Birm. C of St Mich Gospel Lane Birm 68-72; P-in-c of Woodgate Valley Birm 72-75; V of E Ham w Upton Park Dio Chelmsf 75-76; Team R from 76. *Rectory, Navarre Road, E6.* (01-472 2073)

LOWE, William Ewing. Angl Th Coll of BC LTh 56. **d** 56 **p** 57 New Westmr. C of St John Shaughnessy 56-58; R of Ch K Brentwood Pk Burnaby 58-67; Hon C of St Bart City and Dio Tor from 68. *600 Jarvis Street, Toronto, Canada.*

LOWELL, Ian Russell. b 53. AKC 75. St Aug Coll Cant 75. **d** 76 **p** 77 Swan B. C of Llwynderw 76-79; Swansea Dio Swan B from 79. *Top Flat, 8 St James's Crescent, Uplands, Swansea, SA1 6DZ.* (Swansea 59227)

LOWEN, John Michael. b 47. Univ of Nottm BTh 77. Linc Th Coll 73. **d** 77 **p** 78 Southw. C of Beeston 77-80; Stratford-on-Avon Dio Cov from 80. *St James House, 61 Maidenhead Road, Stratford-upon-Avon.*

LOWERY, Ian Morton. b 30. Late Scho of Qu Coll Ox BA 53, MA 56. Cudd Coll 56. **d** 58 **p** 59 Portsm. C of H Spirit Southsea 58-61; V of St Jas Edgbaston 61-71; C-in-c 71-72; Perm to Offic Dio Birm from 73. *John Conolly Hospital, Bristol Road South, Birmingham 45.* (021-453 3771)

LOWETH, Ven Gerald Philip. Clark Univ Mass BA 50. Episc Th Sch Mass BD 53. Trin Coll Tor MTh 67. **d** 53 **p** 54 Conn. Im Amer Ch 53-65; Asst R of Grace Ch on-the-Hill Tor 65-69; Executive Sec Tor Urban Ch Bd 69-74; I of St Jo Div Scarborough Tor 74-79; St Mary Richmond Hill Dio Tor from 79; Archd of Scarborough 76-81; Archd (Emer) from 81. *10030 Yonge Street, Richmond Hill, Ont, L4C 1T8, Canada.*

LOWICK, Geoffrey William. Univ of Witwatersrand Johann BCom 57. Jes Coll Cam BA (3rd cl Th Trip pt ii) 61. Westcott Ho Cam 62. **d** 63 **p** 64 Johann. C of Orange Grove 63-68; R of H Trin Turfontein 70-72; L to Offic Dio Johann 72-79; C of Orchards Dio Johann from 79. *56 African Street, Orchards, Johannesburg, S Africa.*

LOWIN, Ernest William. Wycl Coll Tor LTh 67. **d** and **p** 67 Tor. C of Ch Ch Deer Pk Tor 67-69; R of St Andr Thistletown Tor 69-73; Lindsay 73-79; St Giles City and Dio Tor from 79. *37 Kecala Road, Scarborough, Ont, M1P 1K7, Canada.*

LOWLES, Martin John. b 48. Thames Poly Lon BSc 72. St Jo Coll Dur Dipl Th 78. **d** 78 Barking for Chelmsf **p** 79 Chelmsf. C of St Mary Leyton 78-81; Waltham Abbey Dio Chelmsf from 81. *St Laurence House, 46 Mallion Court, Ninefields, Waltham Abbey, Essex.*

LOWMAN, David Walter. b 48. AKC and BD 73. St Aug Coll Cant 73. **d** 75 Lon **p** 76 Kens for Lon. C of St Jo Notting Hill Kens 75-78; St Aug w St John Kilburn 78-81; Selection Sec and Vocations Adv ACCM and Chap to Ch Ho from 81.

Church House, Dean's Yard, SW1P 2NZ. (01-222 9011)

LOWNDS, Harold John. b 26. Bps' Coll Cheshunt 61. **d** 63 **p** 64 Derby. C of N Wingfield 63-67; C-in-c of Pilsley 67-70; R of Bonsall Dio Derby from 70; V of Cromford Dio Derby from 70. *Bonsall Rectory, Matlock, Derbys, DE4 2AE.* (Wirksworth 2124)

LOWNDS, Jon Richard. b 44. St Paul's Univ MTh 74. **d** 73 **p** 74 Fred. I of Ludlow & Blissfield Dio Fred from 74. *Box 205, Doaktown, NB, Canada.*

LOWRIE, Kenneth Johnson. St Aid Coll 39. **d** 40 **p** 41 York. C of H Trin Micklegate York 40-44; V of Newton-on-Ouse 44-55; R of St Aid Man 55-59; V of Ecchinswell w Sydmonton 59-72. *8 Little Lane, Haxby, York.* (York 760444)

LOWRIE, Robert Colledge. b 33. Univ of Leeds Dipl Th 57. Chich Th Coll 68. **d** 69 **p** 70 Ex. C of Sidmouth 69-74; V of W Hill 74-81; RD of Ottery from 77; Team R of Sidmouth, Woolbrook, Salcombe Regis & Branscombe Dio Ex from 81. *Rectory, Convent Fields, Sidmouth, Devon.* (Sidmouth 3431)

LOWRIE, Ronald Malcolm. b 48. Ripon Hall Ox 70. **d** 72 **p** 73 Birm. C of Knowle 72-75; Bourton-on-the-Water w Clapton 75-79; R of Broadwell 79-81; Evenlode 79-81; Oddington w Adlestrop 79-81; Team V of H Trin Trowbridge Dio Sarum from 81. *Vicarage, Chepstow Place, Trowbridge, Wilts.*

LOWRY, Canon Christopher Somerset. Trin Coll Dub BA 47, MA 65. **d** 47 **p** 48 Arm. C of Erriglе-Keerogue w Ballygawley and Killeshill 47-52; I of Grange Dio Arm from 52; Chap of St Luke's Mental Hosp Arm from 56; RD of Tynan from 71; Can of Arm from 79; R of Loughgall Dio Arm from 80. *Rectory, Main Street, Loughgall, Co Antrim, BT61 8HZ.* (Loughgall 587)

LOWRY, Robert Harold. b 19. Trin Coll Dub BA and Div Test 44, MA 49. **d** 44 Down **p** 45 Connor. C of St Mary Magd Belf 44-48; St Donard Belf 48-52; I of Drumgooland w Kilcoo 52-59; Aghalee 59-62; Willowfield 62-75; RD of Hillsborough 70-75; R of Lambeg Dio Connor from 75. *Lambeg Rectory, Lisburn, Co Antrim, N Ireland.* (Lisburn 3872)

LOWRY, William James. b 35. K Coll Lon BD abd AKC 69. **d** 71 **p** 72 Edmonton for Lon. C of All SS Edmonton 71-81; St Matt Ponders End Dio Lon from 81; Asst Master Bp Stopford's Sch Enfield (and Chap from 73) from 69. *8 Cromwell Court, Enfield, Middx, EN3 4LN.*

LOWRY-CORRY, Armar Douglas. b 29. Trin Coll Cam BA 52, MA 58. Cudd Coll 53. **d** 55 **p** 56 Lon. C of St Mary-of-Eton Hackney Wick 55-59; St Mary Virg Pimlico 59-64; Ch of Ch the Sav Ealing 64-68; V of Oakham (w Hambleton and Egleton from 72) 68-77; Perm to Offic Dio St E from 77. *Edwardstone Hall, Boxford, Colchester, CO6 5PH.* (Boxford 210233)

LOWSON, Christopher. b 53. AKC 75. Pacific Sch of Relig Berkeley Calif STM 78. St Aug Coll Cant 75. **d** 77 **p** 78 S'wark. C of Richmond 77-82; V of H Trin Eltham Dio S'wark from 82. *Vicarage, Southend Crescent, SE9 2SD.* (01-850 1246)

LOWSON, William Kenneth. b 12. Em Coll Cam 2nd cl Cl Trip pt i 32, BA (1st cl Cl Trip pt ii) 33, MA 37. Wells Th Coll 37. **d** 38 Roch **p** 39 Bp Linton Smith for Roch. C of Erith 38-40; Speldhurst 40-46; Deputation Sec CMS 46-60; Home Div Regr 60-77; Perm to Offic Dio Roch from 46. *9 King Harold's Way, Bexleyheath, Kent, DA7 5QU.* (01-310 3926)

LOWTHER, Leslie Cyril. b 20. St Jo Coll Dur BA (3rd cl Math) 41, Dipl Th 43, MA 44. **d** 43 **p** 44 Lich. C of St Paul Walsall 43-44; St Leon Bilston 44-47; Tideswell 47-52; R of Risley 52-57; Chap Risley Hall Approved Sch 52-57; V of St Jo evang Ilkeston 57-67; Dore Dio Derby (Dio Sheff from 74) from 67; Surr from 60. *Dore Vicarage, Sheffield, S17 3GX.* (Sheffield 363335)

LOWTHER, Thomas. b 14. St Jo Coll Dur BA and LTh 40. St Aid Coll 36. **d** 40 **p** 41 Dur. C of St Pet w St Cuthb Monkwearmouth 40-43; CMS Miss Dio Lagos 43-51; Tutor St Andr Coll Oyo 44-46; Melville Hall Ibad 47-51; V of St Jas and St Chris Lower Shiregreen Sheff 51-56; Commiss Ondo-B 52-57; V of Raughton Head w Gatesgill 56-61; Min of St Elisabeth's Eccles Distr Harraby 61-67; V 67-72; V of Borrowdale 72-79. *c/o Borrowdale Vicarage, Keswick, Cumb, CA12 5XQ.* (059684 238)

LOXHAM, Geoffrey Richard. b 40. Univ of Hull BA 62. Cranmer Hall Dur. **d** 65 Blackb **p** 66 Lanc for Blackb. C of St Barn Over Darwen 65-68; Leyland 68-72; V of St Mark Preston 72-79; Edgeside Dio Man from 79. *St Anne's Vicarage, Ashworth Road, Edgeside, Waterfoot, Rossendale, 25090)*

LOXLEY, Ronald Alan Keith. b 26. St John's Coll Ox BA (Eng) 51. MA 55. Cudd Coll 67. **d** 68 **p** 69 Bris. C of Swindon 68-71; Industr Chap (NE Lon) Dio Lon from 71. *12 The Orchard, N21 2DH.*

LOXTON, Albert Edward. Univ of Bris 29. Univ of Queensld BA (2nd cl Ment and Mor Phil) 57, MA 62. ACT Th Scho 46. Sarum Th Coll 30. **d** 33 **p** 34 Sherborne for Sarum. C of St Jas Southbroom 33-37; St Paul Ipswich 37-38; I of Nanango 38-43; R of St D Allora 43-48; St Thos Toowong Brisb 48-65; St Colomb Clayfield Brisb 65-75; Hon Can of Brisb 72-75. *48 Ryhill Road, Sunnybank Hills, Queensland, Australia 4109.* (345 4609)

LOXTON, John Sherwood. b 29. Univ of Birm BA (Th) 53. Univ of Bris BSc 50. **d** 80 Chich **p** 81 Horsham for Chich. [f Methodist Min]. C of Haywards Heath Dio Chich from 80. *85 Haywards Road, Haywards Heath, W Sussex, RH16 4HX.*

LOYIRA, Obadiya. Ngora Th Coll. **d** 54 **p** 56 U Nile. P Dio U Nile 54-61; Dio N Ugan from 61. *c/o PO Box 232, Gulu, Uganda.*

LOYNS, William John. St D Coll Lamp 51. St Mich Coll Llan 57. **d** 59 **p** 60 Llan. C of Llwynpia 59-65; Cadoxton-juxta-Barry 65-67; R of Marley 67-71; Southfield Ja 71-73; L to Offic Dio Lon from 73; USPG Area Sec Lon from 74. *15 Tufton Street, SW1P 3QQ.*

LUBEGA, George William. Bp Tucker Coll Mukono. **d** 65 **p** 67 Nam. P Dio Nam 65-72; Dio Mbale 72-74; Dio Nam from 74; Archd of Nam 75-77. *PO Box 14207, Kampala, Uganda.*

LUBEGA, Moses. b 41. **d** 77 Nam. d Dio Nam. *Namusaale Church of Uganda, PO Box 1030, Nakaseke, Uganda.*

LUBINA, Ven Ricardo. b 30. **d** 59 **p** 60 RC Bp of Venez. Rec into Angl Ch by Bp Suffr of Trinid 68. P Dio Trinid 68-72; Dio Venez from 73; Archd of E Venez from 73. *Calle Granada 5, Puerto Ordaz, Venezuela.*

LUBOGO, Samuel. b 42. Bp Tucker Coll Mukono 66. **d** 69 **p** 70 Nam. P Dio Nam 69-71; CF (Ugan) from 71. *Uganda Army, Box 406, Fort Portal, Uganda.*

LUBOWA, Isaka. d 45 Ugan. d Dio Ugan 45-61; Dio Nam 61-76. *PO Box 196, Mukono, Uganda.*

LUBWAMA, Danieri. d 39 **p** 41 Ugan. P Dio Ugan 39-60; Dio Nam from 60; Can of Ugan 50-60; Nam 60-72 and 74-76; Sub-Dean of St Paul's Cathl Kampala 52-58; Archd of Buganda 58-72. *PO Box 14297, Kampala, Uganda.*

LUBWAMA, Leubeni. Bp Tucker Coll Mukono. **d** 63 **p** 64 Nam. P Dio Nam. *PO Box 81, Lugazi, Uganda.*

LUCAS, Anthony Stanley. b 41. Univ of Man BA (2nd cl Hist) 62. Qu Coll Birm 63. **d** 65 Lon **p** 66 Kens for Lon. C of St Kath Westway Hammersmith 65-69; Ch Ch W Wimbledon 69-74; Caterham 74-78; V of Stockwell Dio S'wark from 78. *78 Stockwell Park Road, SW9 0DA.* (01-274 6357)

LUCAS, Arthur Edgar. b 24. Clifton Th Coll 60. **d** 62 **p** 63 Southw. C of St Paul Hyson Green Nottm 62-66; V of Willoughby-on-the-Wolds w Wysall 66-74; C-in-c of Widmerpool 71-74; R of The Saviour Collyhurst Man 75-80; Heapey Dio Blackb from 80. *Heapey Vicarage, Chorley, Lancs PR6 8EN.* (Chorley 3427)

LUCAS, Brian Humphrey. b 40. St D Coll Lamp BA 62. St Steph Ho Ox 62. **d** 64 Bp Hughes for Llan **p** 65 Llan. C of Cathl Ch Llan 64-67; Neath 67-70; Chap RAF 70-79; Sen Chap from 79. *c/o Ministry of Defence, Adastral House, Theobalds Road, WC1X 8PU.*

LUCAS, George Bromley. Trin Coll Melb BA 51. ACT ThL 52. **d** 53 **p** 54 St Arn. C of Mildura 53-55; R of Sea Lake 55-60; Dir of Youth and Relig Educn Dio St Arn 59-64; R of Charlton 60-64; Exam Chap to Bp of St Arn 61-64; V of Cheltm 64-70; Malvern Dio Melb from 70. *296 Glenferrie Road, Malvern, Vic, Australia 3144.* (03-20 3030)

LUCAS, Canon Harry McIntyre. Univ of Leeds BA 33. Coll of Resurr Mirfield. **d** 35 **p** 36 Ely. C of L Downham 35-38; St Thos w St John Scarborough 38-40; Langley Mill 40-42; Matlock 42-44; C-in-c of St Thos Scarborough 44-47; V of Burneston 47-48; R and Dir of Miss Gingindhlovu 49-52; Dir of Kambula Miss 52-59; Archd of W Zulu 52-59; VG of Zulu 53 and 57; Hon Can of Zulu from 58; Commiss Zulu 59-68; V of Brampford Speke w Cowley 59-64; R of Upton Pyne 59-64; V of Witton E 64-70. *28 Columbus Ravine, Scarborough, Yorks.* (Scarbro' 60545)

LUCAS, Henry Leonard Armstrong. b 18. Linc Th Coll 43. **d** 44 Carl **p** 45 Mon. C of H Trin Carl 44-45; St Mary Monmouth 45-48; C-in-c of Studham w Whipsnade 49; C of Hawkeshead 50-53; R of Gosforth 53-63; V of Netherton w Grasslot 63-65; V (C-in-c from 71) of Embleton w Wythop 65-76; P-in-c of Torpenhow 76-78; Perm to Offic Dio Carl from 80. *28 Langdale Close, Highfield, Cockermouth, Cumbria.*

LUCAS, Canon John Arthur. b 07. Keble Coll Ox BA (3rd cl Engl Lang and Lit) 29, MA 45. Cudd Coll 29. **d** 33 **p** 34 Ox. C of St Thos Mart Ox 33-35; St Wilfrid Brighton 35-37; St Pet Lon Dks (Radley Coll Missr) 37-39; V of St Mary Swanley 39-47; St Thos Mart Ox 47-74; P-in-c 74-78; Cler Sec Ox Dioc Conf 53-70; Hon Can of Ch Ch Ox from 70; C of St Mary Virg (in c of St Cross) City and Dio Ox from 78. *12 Lucas Place, Meadow Lane, Iffley, Oxford, OX4 4HA.* (Ox 774508)

LUCAS, John Maxwell. b 34. Cranmer Hall Dur 59. **d** 62 p 63 Blackb. C of Lancaster 62-65; St Cuthb Lytham 65-68; V of St Aid Blackb 68-72; Sparkhill 72-78; CF (TAVR) from 73; V of St Aug Edgbaston Dio Birm from 78. *9 Manor Road North, Edgbaston, Birmingham, B16 9JS.* (021-454 0127)

LUCAS, Ven John Michael. b 21. Lich Th Coll 40. **d** 44 Crediton for Ex **p** 45 Ex. C of St Mary Wolborough 44-50; Ashburton 50-52; R of Weare Giffard w Landcross and V of Monkleigh 52-62; Northam w Westward Ho 62-76; Chudleigh Knighton w Heathfield Dio Ex from 76; Archd of Totnes 76-81; Archd (Emer) from 81. *Chudleigh Knighton Vicarage, Newton Abbot, Devon, TQ13 0ET.* (Chudleigh 853230)

LUCAS, Kenneth Ashley. b 18. Wells Th Coll 68. **d** 69 Chich **p** 70 Lewes for Chich. C of Rye w Rye Harbour and Playden 69-73; R of W Chiltington Dio Chich from 74. *Rectory, East Street, West Chiltington, Pulborough, Sussex RH20 2JY.*

LUCAS, Mary Louise. b 48. York Univ Ont BA 70. Harvard Div Sch MDiv 75. **d** 75 **p** 76 Niag. C of Grace Ch St Catharines 75-78; St Jude Oakville 77-79; St Paul Jarvis 79-81; on leave. *132 Laurel Avenue, Islington, Ont, Canada, M9B 4T6.*

LUCAS, Paul de Neufville. b 33. Late Exhib of Ch Ch Ox 52, BA and MA 59. Cudd Coll 57. **d** 59 **p** 60 Lon. C of St Steph w St John Westmr 59-63; Chap Trin Hall Cam 63-69; V of Greenside 69-73; Chap Shrewsbury Sch 73-77; V of Batheaston Dio B & W from 78. *34 North End, Bath, Avon.* (Bath 858192)

LUCAS, Peter Stanley. Sarum Th Coll 48. **d** 50 **p** 51 Sarum. C of Gillingham 50-53; Min of Heald Green Conv Distr 53-58; V 58-62; Egremont 62-65; Surr 62-65; I of Mortlach 65-66; St Barn Moose Jaw 66-68; Kindersley 68-72; R of St Matt Regina 72-77; Archd of Assiniboia 74-77; Qu'App 77-81; Executive Sec of Syn Dio Qu'App 77-81. *c/o 1501 College Street, Regina, Sask, Canada.*

LUCAS, Raymond Charles Henry. b 15. ALCD 41. **d** 41 Bp Mann for Roch **p** 42 Roch. C of St Pet Southborough 41-43; H Trin St Philip's Bris 43-47; H Trin West Worthing (in c of St Matt) 47-50; V of St Jude Islington 50-54; St Matt Southborough 54-61; R of Branston 61-76; Parkham, Alwington and Buckland Brewer 76-79. *90 Cheverell Avenue, Salisbury, Wilts.*

LUCAS, Richard Charles. b 25. Trin Coll Cam BA 49, MA 57. Ridley Hall Cam. **d** 51 **p** 52 Roch. C of Sevenoaks 51-55; Cand Sec CPAS 55-61; Asst Sec 61-67; R of St Helen Bishopsgate (w St Andr Undershaft from 80) City and Dio Lon from 61; P-in-c of St Andr Undershaft Lon 77-80. *Rectory, Great St Helen's, EC3A 6AT.* (01-283 2231)

LUCAS, Robert Holdsworth Tindall. b 21. Tyndale Hall Bris 46. **d** 58 **p** 59 St Alb. [f Miss BCMS Ethiopia 49-58] C of Frogmore 58-60; R of Barnwell 60-69; Charmouth (w Catherston Leweston from 71) Dio Sarum from 69; R of Catherston Leweston 69-71. *Charmouth Rectory, Bridport, Dorset.* (Charmouth 60409)

LUCAS, Robert Keith. St Jo Coll Morpeth. ACT ThL 68. **d** 68 River. C of Deniliquin 68-78; Perm to Offic Dio Melb from 78. *c/o Vicarage, Robert Street, Parkdale, Vic, Australia 3195.*

LUCAS, Ronald Charles. b 26. St Mich Coll Llan 62. **d** 64 **p** 65 Mon. C of Rumney 64-66; L to Offic Dio Mon from 69; C of Llanishen w Lisvane Dio Llan from 72. *64 Fidlas Avenue, Llanishen, Cardiff.* (Cardiff 757119)

LUCAS, Ronald James. b 38. St Aid Coll 64. **d** 67 **p** 68 Bris. C of Swindon 67-71; St Martin Knowle 71-73; V of St Jo Bapt Park Swindon 73-77; R of St Jo Bapt and St Andr Swindon 77-80; V of Wroughton Dio Bris from 80. *Wroughton Vicarage, Swindon, Wilts.* (Wroughton 812301)

LUCAS, Simon Bruce Kechwenyamane. St Bede's Coll Umtata 63. **d** 66 **p** 67 Kimb K. C of St Matt Kimb 66-70; All SS Postmasburg 70-73; L to Offic Dio Kimb K 73-78. *PO Box 921, Kimberley, CP, S Africa.* (23870)

LUCAS, William Wallace. b 29. Sarum Th Coll 56. **d** 59 **p** 60 Dur. C of St Jo Bapt Stockton-on-Tees 59-63; V of St Mich AA Norton 63-81; R of Broseley w Benthall Dio Heref from 81; P-in-c of Jackfield Dio Heref from 81; Linley w Willey and Barrow Dio Heref from 81. *Rectory, Broseley, Salop.* (Telford 882647)

LUCHIGA, Bernard Kwiga. St Phil Th Coll Kongwa. **d** 66 Bp Madinda for Centr Tang **p** 67 Centr Tang. P Dio Centr Tang. *Box 1, Mpwapwa, Tanzania.*

LUCK, David William. Univ of Tor BA 49. McGill Univ Montr MA 60. Wycl Coll Tor LTh 52. **d** 51 **p** 52 Tor for Lah. Miss at Batala 52-63; Tutor St Jo Coll Agra 63-65; Serampore Coll 65-67; Nat Teachers' Coll Kyambogo 67-73; Lect Wycl Coll Tor 73-79; Exam Chap to Bp of Tor from 76; Assoc P of St Anne Tor 78-79; I of St Jo Div Scarborough City and Dio Tor from 79. *885 Scarborough Golf Club Road, Scarborough, Ont, Canada.*

LUCKCUCK, Anthony Michael. b 47. BA (Lon) 70. Wycl Hall Ox 70. **d** 77 **p** 78 Southw. C of Mansfield Woodhouse 77-79; Beeston Dio Southw from 79. *5 Ireton Street, Beeston, Nottingham.* (Nottm 226670)

LUCKETT, Canon Gerald Archer. b 13. Kelham Th Coll 31. **d** 39 **p** 40 Cant. C of Bearsted 39-41; Ashford 41-44; Lymington (in c of All SS) 44-50; R of Pluckley w Pevington 50-60; Lyminge w Paddlesworth 60-71; V of Cranbrook 71-81; Hon Can of Cant Cathl from 80. *Drokensford, Meonstoke, Hants.* (Droxford 307)

LUCKETT, Sidney. b 47. Univ of Stellenbosch BSc 69. Jes Coll Ox MPhil 72. Wycl Hall Ox 78. **d** and **p** 80 Capetn. C of St John Wynberg Dio Capetn from 80. *c/o St John's Vicarage, St John's Road, Wynberg 7800, Cape Town, S Africa.*

LUCKRAFT, Christopher John. b 50. AKC and BD 80. Ripon Coll Cudd 80. **d** 81 Sarum. C of Sherborne w Castleton & Lillington Dio Sarum from 81. *Craigness, Bristol Road, Sherborne, Dorset, DT9 4HS.*

LUCKRAFT, Ian Charles. b 47. Qu Coll Ox BA (Th) 70. CNAA BSc 81. Ripon Hall Ox 70. **d** 73 **p** 74 St Alb. C of Totteridge 73-76; Broxbourne w Wormley 76-78; Lect Harlow Tech Coll 78-81; Perm to Offic Dio St Alb 79-81; Graduate Demonstrator R Mil Coll of Sc Shrivenham from 82. *59 The Dormers, Highworth, Wilts.*

LUCKRAFT, Reginald Miller. Univ of Sask BA 15, MA 17. **d** 37 Sask **p** 38 Sktn for Sask. I of E Prince Albert 38-41; Miss at John Smith's Reserve 41-42; Chap Federal Penit Prince Albert 42-47. *13557 North Bluff, RR1, White Rock BC, Canada.*

LUDDINGTON, Tom Glenford. Ch Ch Ox BA 54, MA 58. AKC (2nd cl) and Plumptre Pri 38. **d** 38 Lon **p** 39 Willesden for Lon. C of St Andr Stoke Newington 38-40; St John-at-Hackney 40-41; St Pet Hereford 41-42; Ludlow 42-45; C-in-c of Diddlebury w Bouldon 45; V of Coalpit Heath 45-50; C of St Mich Ox 50-55; V of Seer Green 55-59; St Pet Kens Pk Road Kens 59-69; Perm to Offic Dios Lon and Chich from 69; S'wark from 80. *12 Woburn Court, Stanmore Road, Richmond-on-Thames, Surrey, TW9 2DD.* (01-940 8900)

LUDERS, Karl William. Moore Th Coll Syd ACT ThL 32. **d** 32 Syd **p** 33 Bp Kirkby for Syd. C of St Matt Manly 32-35; Kirton Point 35-40; V of Wyan w Rappville 40-42; Wilcannia 42-47; R of Culcairn w Henry 47-59; P-in-c of Crystal Brook (w Gladstone from 67) 59-71; Can of Willoch 63-70; Perm to Offic Dio C & Goulb from 72. *38 Birdwood Circle, Tuross Head, NSW, Australia 2537.*

LUDIDI, Gibson Sipambo. b 50. St Bede's Coll Umtata 74. **d** 75 Bp Sobukwe for St John's **p** 76 St John's. P Dio St John's. *Box 30, Tsolo, Republic of Transkei, S Africa.*

LUDLOW, Lord Bishop Suffragan of. *See* Wood, Right Rev Stanley Mark.

LUDLOW, Archdeacon of. *See* Woodhouse, Ven Andrew Henry.

LUDLOW, Arthur Percival. b 26. Chich Th Coll 48. **d** 51 **p** 52 Ripon. C of Manston Yorks 51-54; Seacroft 54-58; V of Stanground 58-72; R of Somersham w Pidley and Colne Dio Ely from 72. *Rectory, Rectory Lane, Somersham, Huntingdon, PE17 3EL.* (Ramsey 840676)

LUDLOW, Christopher George. b 18. AKC (2nd cl Th) 42. **d** 42 **p** 43 Lon. C of St Alb N Harrow 42-45; Gt Stanmore 45-49; Min Can (Sacr and Prec) of Cant Cathl 49-54; Asst Master K Sch Cant 50-54; R of Canewdon w Paglesham 54-57; Lect K Alfred's Coll Win 57-76; Chap 57-70. *Little Tolcarne, Burras, Helston, Cornwall, TR13 0HX.* (Praze 831631)

LUDLOW, Canon Leonard Arnot James. Qu Coll Newfld STh 43. **d** 45 **p** 46 Newfld. C of St Mary St John's 45-47; I of St Anthony 47-52; Greenspond 52-55; Harbour Grace 55-69; St Aug St John's Dio Newfld (E Newfld from 76) from 69; Can of E Newfld from 79. *1 Westerland Road, St John's, Newfoundland, Canada.* (709-753-1610)

LUDLOW, Noel. St Francis Coll Brisb 47. **d** and **p** 50 Brisb. C of Fortitude Valley Brisb 50-51; M of Bush Bro of St Paul 51-54; C of Warwick 54-55; V of Caboolture 55-57; R of Goondiwindi 57-64; Beaudesert 64-72; Ch Ch Yeronga City and Dio Brisb from 72. *21 Dublin Street, Yeronga, Queensland, Australia 4104.* (48 1638)

LUETCHFORD, Canon Albert Horace. b 1895. AKC (2nd cl) 22. Ely Th Coll 22. **d** 23 **p** 24 Lon. C of St Mark Notting Hill 23-25; St Aug Kilburn 25-35; V of St Pet Lon Docks 35-46; Chap St Geo-in-the-East Hosp 35-46; Radley Coll Miss 39-46; V of All SS Clifton (w St Mary Tyndall's Pk from 62) 46-68; Hon Can of Bris 59-80; Can (Emer) from 80; Cler Sec Bris Dioc Conf 59-65; Chap Conv of Sisters of Charity Knowle 68-80. *St John's Cottage, Tennis Road, Knowle, Bristol, BS4 2HG.* (Bristol 777738)

LUFF, Alan Harold Frank. b 28. Univ Coll Ox Dipl Th 52. MA 54. Westcott Ho Cam 54. **d** 56 **p** 57 Man. C of Stretford 56-59; Swinton 59-61; Prec of Man Cathl 61-68; V of Dwygyfylchi w Penmaenmawr 68-79; Prec and Sacr of

Westmr Abbey from 79. *7 Little Cloister, Westminster Abbey, SW1P 3PL.* (01-222 1386)

LUFF, Philip Garth. b 42. St Chad's Coll Dur BA (2nd cl Th) 63, Dipl Th 64. **d** 65 **p** 66 Ex. C of Sidmouth 65-69; Plymstock 69-71; Asst Chap Worksop Coll 71-74; V of St Jo Div Gainsborough 74-80; E Teignmouth Dio Ex from 80. *St Michael's Vicarage, Teignmouth, Devon.* (Teignmouth 4495)

LUFT, Canon Hyam Mark. b 13. Late Found Scho of St Jo Coll Dur BA (1st cl Cl) 34, Dipl TPT 35, MA 37, MLitt 53. FRHistS 72. **d** 37 **p** 38 Liv. C of St John Waterloo 37-40; Aintree (in c of St Giles) 40-41; Sefton 41-51; Asst Master at Merchant Taylors' Sch Crosby 41-56; C of Blundellsands 51-56; Hd Master of Blackpool Gr Sch 56-64; Merchant Taylors' Sch Crosby 64-79; Fell Em Coll Cam 69; Can Th of Liv Cathl from 79. *Highfurlong, St Michael's Road, Blundellsands, Liverpool 23.* (051-924 6034)

LUGENDO, Frank. b 24. **d** 72 Moro. d Dio Moro 72-75; Dio Zanz T from 75. *Box 5, Muheza, Tanzania.*

LUGG, Donald Arthur. b 31. St Aid Coll 56. **d** 59 Bp Rose for Cant **p** 60 Cant. C of H Trin w Ch Ch Folkestone 59-62; V of Seasalter 62-67; Chap at Masjed-e-Suleiman 67-73; V of Cliftonville Dio Cant from 74. *St Paul's Vicarage, Cliftonville, Margate, Kent.* (Thanet 20857)

LUGG, Stuart John. b 26. GOC 74. **d** 76 Glouc **p** 76 Tewkesbury for Glouc. C of Fairford 76-79; P-in-c of Kempsford w Whelford Dio Glouc from 79. *Parsonage, Kempsford, Fairford, Glos.* (Kempsford 241)

LUGOLOOBI, Henry Stades. Bp Tucker Coll Mukono, 59. **d** 65 **p** 67 Nam. P Dio Nam. *Mpigi, Box 67, Bombo, Uganda.*

LUI, Charles. St Pet Coll Siota 66. **d** 68 **p** 70 Bp Alufurai for Melan. P Dio Melan 68-75; Dio Malaita from 75. *Fooau, Malaita, Solomon Islands.*

LUJA, Cullwick. b 41. Bp Patteson Th Coll Kohimarama 71. **d** 73 Melan **p** 74 Bp Dudley for Melan. P Dio Melan 73-74; Dio Ysabel 75-76; Dio Centr Melan from 76. *Kirakira, Makira, Solomon Islands.*

LUJURON, Simona Nyoko. Bp Gwynne Coll Mundri, 61. **d** 66 Sudan. d Dio Sudan 66-76; Dio Omdurman from 76. *c/o Box 65, Omdurman, Sudan.*

LUKINDO, George. b 35. St Cypr Coll Ngala 75. **d** 77 Zanz T **p** 79 Bp Russell for Zanz T. P Dio Zanz T. *PO Kigongoi, Tanga, Tanzania.*

✠ **LUKINDO, Right Rev Yohana.** Kalole Th Coll 50. **d** 52 **p** 53 Zanz. P Dio Zanz 53-57; Asst Chap St Andr Coll Minaki 57-61; Archd of Korogwe 61-63; Magila 63-66; Cons Asst Bp in Zanz in H Cross Ch Magila 21 Mar 63 by Abp of E Afr; Bps of SW Tang; and Zanz; and Asst Bp in Centr Tang; VG of Zanz from 65; Archd of Korogwe w Zigualand 68-74. *PO Box 245, Korogwe, Tanzania.*

LUKWAGO, Fenekansi. b 23. **d** 74 **p** 75 Nam. P Dio Nam. *Kangulumira, PO Box 4889, Kangulumira, Uganda.*

LUKWAGO, Nathan. b 30. Bp Tucker Coll Mukono. **d** 70 Nam. d Dio Nam. *Box 20032, Kampala, Uganda.*

LUKWAGO, Paulo. **d** 77 Nam. d Dio Nam. *c/o St Paul's Cathedral, Kampala, Uganda.*

LUKWANG, Canon Nekemia. **d** 62 **p** 63 N Ugan. P Dio Ugan; Hon Can of N Ugan from 69. *Padibe, PO Box 23, Kitgum, Uganda.*

LUKYAMUZI, Yekosefati. Bp Tucker Coll Mukono. **d** 62 **p** 64 W Bugan. P Dio W Bugan. *COU, Kakabagyo, PO Buyamba-Kooki, Uganda.*

LULE, Andrea. **d** and **p** 75 Bunyoro. P Dio Bunyoro. *Box 159, Kiduma, Hoima, Uganda.*

LULE, Canon Robert. Bp Tucker Coll Mukono. **d** 48 **p** 49 Ugan. P Dio Ugan 48-60; Dio Nam from 60; Can of Nam from 78. *Anglican Church, Kira, PO Box 19011, Kasangati, Uganda.*

LULE, Yusufu. **d** 77 Nam. d Dio Nam. *Nateete Church of Uganda, PO Box 4497, Kampala, Uganda.*

LUMADE, Michael Oladipo. **d** 72 Ibad. d Dio Ibad. *St Paul's Church, Oyedeji, Nigeria.*

LUMAN, Arthur Cecil Rowe. b 11. St Paul's Coll Grahmstn LTh 37. St Aug Coll Cant 62. **d** 37 **p** 38 Capetn. C of St Mark Capetn 37-38; St Matt Claremont 38-41; CF (S Afr) 41-46; Asst C of St Geo Cathl Capetn 46-48; P-in-c of St Aid Lansdowne 49-53; R of Goodwood 53-59; Worc CP 59-61; Murston 62-80. *38 Headcorn Drive, Canterbury Kent.* (Cant 57831)

LUMB, David Leslie. b 28. Jes Coll Cam 3rd cl Cl Trip pt i 51, BA (3rd cl Th Trip pt i a) 52, MA 56. Oak Hill Th Coll 52. **d** 54 **p** 55 B & W. C of Walcot 54-58; Lenton 58-60; V of Handforth 60-71; St Jude Plymouth Dio Ex from 71. *St Jude's Vicarage, Knighton Road, Plymouth, PL4 9BU.* (Plymouth 61232)

LUMB, Dennis. b 36. Oak Hill Th Coll 77. **d** 79 **p** 80 Lich. C of Penn Fields Dio Lich from 79. *121 Church Road, Bradmore, Wolverhampton, WV3 7EN.* (Wolv 535607)

LUMBETA, Ven Cuthbert Mwansa. St Jo Sem Lusaka. **d** 63 N Rhod **p** 65 Zam. P Dio Zam 65-71; Dio N Zam from 71; Archd Dio N Zam from 78. *c/o Box 159, Mufulira, Zambia.*

LUMBWA, James. b 22. **d** 81 N Zam. d Dio N Zam. *St James Church, PO Box 25014, Buchi, Kitwe, Zambia.*

LUMBY, Jonathan Bertram. b 39. Em Coll Cam BA 62, MA 66. Ripon Hall Ox 62. **d** 64 **p** 65 Birm. C of St Mary Moseley 64-65; Asst Master Enfield Gr Sch 66-67; C of Hall Green 67-70; V of Melling 70-80; P-in-c of Milverton Dio B & W from 80; Fitzhead Dio B & W from 80. *Milverton Vicarage, Taunton, Somt, TA4 1LR.* (Milverton 400305)

LUMGAIR, Michael Hugh Crawford. b 43. BD (Lon) 71. Oak Hill Th Coll 66. **d** 71 **p** 72 St Alb. C of Chorley Wood 71-74; Prestonville 74-75; Attenborough w Toton 75-80; R of Tollerton Dio Southw from 80. *Rectory, Tollerton, Nottingham, NG12 4FW.* (Plumtree 2349)

LUMLEY, Arthur Peter. Univ of Leeds MA 46. Westcott Ho Cam. **d** 43 Bradf **p** 43 Bp Mounsey for Bradf. C of St Paul Shipley 43-45; V of Frizinghall 45-58; RD of Bradf 55-58; Proc Conv Bradf 56-58; V of Newport IW 58-64; Proc Conv Portsm 61-65; R of Sacr Trin Salford 64-65; Sen Chap to Bp of Man 64-65; R of Blandford St Mary 65-72; Bryanston 65-72; Durweston 67-72. *Becket's Corner, Priestlands Lane, Sherborne, Dorset.* (Sherborne 2395)

LUMLEY, Preb Ralph John Charles. b 05. Lich Th Coll 30. **d** 32 **p** 33 Lich. C of All SS Sedgley 32-35; St Mary Shrewsbury 35-40; C-in-c of St Andr Porthill 40-41; Offg Chap Worksop Coll 41-45; LPr Dio Southw 41-45; V of H Trin Oswestry 45-57; H Cross (The Abbey) Shrewsbury Dio Lich from 57; RD of Shrewsbury from 62; Surr from 64; Proc Conv Lich 64-70; Preb of Lich Cathl from 65. *Abbey Vicarage, Shrewsbury, Shropshire, SY2 6AP.* (Shrewsbury 56462)

LUMLEY, Robert. Trin Coll Dub BA 48, MA 54. **d** 49 Meath for Kilm **p** 50 Kilm. C of Drumgoon w Ashfield 49-54; I of Capreol 54-57; R of Elliot Lake 57-59; I of St Steph Port Arthur 59-67; Lake of Bays 67-73; St Jas Sudbury Dio Alg from 73. *207 Stewart Drive, Sudbury, Ont., Canada.* (705-522 3812)

LUMLEY, Theodore O'Driscoll. b 09. Keble Coll Ox BA 31, MA 36. St Steph Ho Ox 31. **d** 32 **p** 34 Worc. C of Headless Cross 32-34; Thames Ditton 34-36; CF 36-64; Lect NEET Coll Colchester from 64. *18 Inglis Road, Colchester, Essex.*

LUMLEY, William. b 22. TCD BA 44, MA 49, BD 49, QUB PhD 77. **d** 50 **p** 51 Dub, C of Drumcondra w N Strand 50-52; Cler V of Ch Ch Cathl Dub 52-54; C of All SS Clooney 54-59; R of Aghabog 59-63; V of Newhey 63-66; R of Ballybay 66-73; Derryvullan Dio Clogh from 73; Garvary Dio Clogh from 73. *Tamlaght, Enniskillen, Co Fermanagh, N Ireland.* (Lisbellow 236)

LUMMIS, Canon William Murrell. b 1886. MC 18. **d** 30 **p** 31 St E. C of St Matt Ipswich 30-33; V of Kesgrave 33-41; Chap K Edw VII Sanat Ipswich 34-41; V of H Trin (w St Mary from 46) Bungay 41-58; RD of S Elmham 42-58; Hon Can of St E 55-59; Can (Emer) from 59; L to Offic Dio St E from 59; Perm to Offic Dio Nor 59-73; RD of Higham 61-65; P-in-c Saham Toney 63-65; C-in-c of Tacolneston 67-70; Fundenhall 67-70. *32 Vimy Drive, Wymondham, Norfolk, NR18 0PB.* (Wymondham 3538)

LUMSDEN, Frank. b 20. Edin Th Coll 51. **d** 53 **p** 54 Dur. C of Usworth 53-56; V of Lynesack 56-76; R of Castle Eden w Monkhesleden Dio Dur from 76. *Rectory, Castle Eden, Co Durham.* (Wellfield 836230)

LUMSDON, Keith. b 45. Linc Th Coll 68. **d** 71 Dur. C of South Westoe 71-74; Jarrow Dio Dur 74-76; Team V from 76. *St John Baptist House, Nairn Road, Perth Green, Jarrow, T & W.* (Jarrow 892043)

LUND, George Radstone. St D Coll Lamp BA (2nd cl Hist) 38. Lich Th Coll 38. **d** 42 **p** 43 Ches. C of Bramhall 42-45. *Papworth Village Settlement, Cambridge.*

LUND, Ian Phillip. b 47. Rhodes Univ BA 68. St Paul's Coll Grahmstn Dipl Th 71. BD (Lon) 77. **d** 71 Natal **p** 74 Stepney for Lon. C of Ladysmith 71-72; St John Bethnal Green 74-76; Missr in Alford Group 76-78; Perm to Offic Dio Ely from 78. *1 Arbury Road, Cambridge, CB4 2JB.* (0223-61367)

LUND, John Edward. b 48. St Jo Coll Dur 78. **d** 80 **p** 81 Dur. C of Peterlee Dio Dur from 80. *14 Balliol Close, Peterlee, Co Durham, SR8 2NX.*

LUND, Peter. b 23. Late Scho of Or Coll Ox BA (2nd cl Mod Hist) and MA 49. Linc Th Coll 59. **d** 60 **p** 61 Dur. C of Barnard Castle 60-63; Staindrop w Cockfield (in C of Cockfield) 63-64; R of Cockfield 65-66; PC of Newton Aycliffe 66-69; C-in-c of Melsonby 69-71; R 71-72; C-in-c of Stanwick 69-71; V 71-72; C-in-c of Forcett 69-71; V 71-72; V of Startforth 72-75; Barnard Castle 76-79; P-in-c of Sark Dio Win

79-81; V from 81. *Vicarage, Sark, Via Guernsey, CI.* (Sark 2040)

LUND, Vernon Brian. Univ of Natal, BA 59. Wells Th Coll 63. **d** 65 B & W for Natal **p** 65 Natal. C of St Sav Cathl Pietermaritzburg 65-69; R of St Columba Durban 69-71; Chap Girls' Dioc Sch Grahmstn 71-75; R of Kirky Hilton Dio Natal from 75. *Box 282, Hilton, Natal, S Africa.* (Pmbg 31112)

LUNDA, James Ahibu. St Jo Sem Lusaka. **d** 65 **p** 67 Bp Mtekateka for Malawi. P Dio Malawi 65-71; Dio Lake Malawi 71-80; Archd of Nkhotakota 73-76. *Box 294, Lilongwe, Malawi.*

LUNDI, THE, Lord Bishop of. *See* Siyachitema, Right Rev Jonathan.

LUNDIMU, Kikuni. b 19. St Phil Coll Kongwa 75. **d** 77 Bukavu. d Dio Bukavu. *Kalima, II Parish, Bp 220, Kindu, Maniema, Zaire.*

LUNDU, Wilfred. b 18. **d** 71 **p** 72 S Malawi. P Dio S Malawi. *Ulande F.P. School, P/A Mkope, P.O. Mangochi, Malawi.*

LUNGLEY, John Sydney. b 41. St Pet Coll Ox BA (3rd cl Chem) 64, MA 70. St Steph Ho Ox 64. **d** 66 **p** 67 Lich. C of St Werburgh Burslem 66-70; Codsall 70-73; V of St Mark Evang Ocker Hill, Tipton Dio Lich from 73. *St Mark's Vicarage, Ocker Hill, Tipton, W Midl, DY4 0UT.* (021-556 0678)

LUNGU, Emmanuel Justin. b 50. **d** 77 **p** 79 Centr Zam. P Dio Centr Zam. *PO Box 70172, Ndola, Zambia.*

LUNGWA, Canon Denyeli. St Paul's Div Sch Limuru, 52. **d** and **p** 53 Centr Tang. P Dio Centr Tang 53-68 and from 69; Can of Centr Tang from 64; C of Middleton Lancs 68-69. *Box 15, Dodoma, Tanzania.*

LUNN, Christopher James Edward. b 34. K Coll Lon and Warm AKC 58. **d** 59 **p** 60 S'wark. C of Clapham 59-62; St Nich (in c of St Andr) Cranleigh 63-64; Ham Surrey (in c of St Richard) 64-66; V of St Richard Ham, Surrey 66-74; St Andr Coulsdon Dio S'wark from 75. *St Andrew's Vicarage, Julien Road, Coulsdon, Surrey.* (01-660 0398)

LUNN, David. b 47. Univ of Bris BSc 69. Univ of Dur BA 73, Dipl Th 74. St Jo Coll Dur 71. **d** 74 Warrington for Liv **p** 75 Liv. C of Aigburth 74-77; St Paul Slough 77-81; P-in-c of Haversham w L Linford Dio Ox from 81. *Haversham Rectory, Milton Keynes, Bucks, MK19 7DT.* (M Keynes 312136)

✠ **LUNN, Right Rev David Ramsay.** b 30. K Coll Cam BA 53, MA 57. Cudd Coll 53. **d** 55 **p** 56 Newc T. C of Sugley 55-59; N Gosforth (in c of St Aid) 59-63; Chap Linc Th Coll 63-66; Sub-Warden 66-70; V of St Geo Cullercoats 70-75; R 75-80; RD of Tynemouth 75-80; Cons Ld Bp of Sheff in York Minster 25 Jan 80 by Bp of Dur; Bps of Southw, Blackb, Bradf, Carl, Newc T, Liv, Wakef, Ripon and Man; Bps Suffr of Jarrow, Stockport, Burnley, Pontefract, Selby, Sherwood, Hulme, Whitby, Warrington, Doncaster, Hull, Knaresborough and Penrith; and others. *Bishopscroft, Snaithing Lane, Sheffield, S Yorks, S10 3LG.* (Sheffield 302170)

LUNN, Leonard Arthur. b 42. Trin Coll Bris 69. **d** 72 **p** 73 Barking for Chelmsf. C of Walthamstow 72-75; St Steph Walthamstow 72-75; V of St Jas Collier Row Romford Dio Chelmsf from 75. *St James's Vicarage, Lower Bedfords Road, Romford, RM1 4DG.* (Romford 49891)

LUNN, Canon William Bell. b 21. Edin Th Coll 47. **d** 50 **p** 51 Edin. C of H Trin Stirling 50-53; P-in-c of St Cath Bo'ness w St Mildred Linlithgow 53-57; R of St Mark Portobello 57-75; Can of Edin 68-75; R of Gordon Chap Fochabers Dio Moray from 75; Aberlour Dio Moray from 75; Can of St Andr Cathl Inverness from 79. *Gordon Chapel House, Fochabers, Morays, IV32 7DW.* (Fochabers 820337)

LUNNEY, Henry. b 31. AIB 57. Wycl Hall Ox 73. **d** 74 St E **p** 75 Dunwich for St E. C of St Aug of Hippo Ipswich 74-77; P-in-c of Westerfield w Tuddenham St Martin Dio St E from 77. *Westerfield Rectory, Ipswich, Suff, IP6 9AG.* (Ipswich 51073)

LUNNISS, Claude Marshall. G and C Coll Cam 3rd cl Hist Trip pt i 29, BA (3rd cl Th Trip pt i) 30. Coll of Resurr Mirfield 30. **d** 32 **p** 33 Chelmsf. C of The Ascen Vic Dks 32-36; LPr Dio Wakef 36-39; M CR from 38; Miss Sophiatown Johann 39-47; Ho of Resurr Mirfield 47-49; LPr Dio Lon 49-58; Dio Llan 59; Prior at St Teilo's Cardiff 58-59; Chap-Gen All SS Conv Holland Pk 59-61; Prior and Prov of St Pet Priory Rosettenville 61-67; P-in-c of H Cross Codrington Barb 67-69; V of St D Barb 69-76; L to Offic Dio Johann from 77. *Box 49027, Rosettenville, Johannesburg, S Africa.* (011-26 1933)

LUNNISS, David Oliver. b 51. St Barn Coll Adel 75. **d** 78 Adel. C of St Mich Mitcham 78-79; Alice Springs 80-81; Asst Chap Pulteney Gr Sch Adel 81; R of Naracoorte Dio Murray from 81. *Rectory, Jenkins Terrace, Naracoorte, S Australia 5271.*

LUNNON, Robert Reginald. b 31. K Coll Lon and Warm BD and AKC (2nd cl) 55. **d** 56 Dover for Cant **p** 57 Cant. C of St Mich AA Maidstone 56-58; Deal 58-62; V of Sturry 63-68; Norbury 68-77; Orpington Dio Roch from 77; Surr from 77; RD of Orpington from 79. *1a Keswick Road, Orpington, Kent, BR6 0EU.* (Orpington 24624)

LUNNY, William John. Univ of BC BA 52. Or Coll Ox BA 54, MA 59. Angl Th Coll BC LTh 60, BD 62. **d** 55 **p** 56 BC. I of Cowichan Lake 55-59; R of Sandwick 59-63; Courtenay 63-67; St Dunstan Vic Dio BC from 71; Cler Sec Dio BC from 81. *1793 Penshurst Street, Victoria, BC, Canada.* (604-477 1422)

LUNT, Derek. b 32. St Aid Coll 55. **d** 57 Liv **p** 58 Warrington for Liv. C of Toxt Pk 57-59; Prescot 59-61; V of Much Dewchurch w Llanwarne and Llandinabo 61-67; R of Pembridge w Moorcourt 67-74; Chap Lucton Sch 71-74. *c/o Pembridge Rectory, Leominster, Herefs.* (Pembridge 439)

✠ **LUNT, Right Rev Francis Evered.** b 1900. Univ Coll Dur LTh 34. Down Coll Cam MA 39, Hon Fell 66. Or Coll Ox MA 45. Lon Coll of Div 25. **d** 25 Ox **p** 27 Buckingham for Ox. C of St Andr and St Mary Maidenhead 25-31; St Barn Cam 31-34; L to Offic Dio Ely 33-43; Chap Down Coll Cam and Cam Past 34-43; Select Pr Univ of Cam 43; Sen Chap Ox Past 43-51; R of St Aldate Ox 43-51; Surr 43-51; Exam Chap to Bp of Ox 46-51; to Bp of Portsm 49-51; Dean of Bris 51-57; Cons Ld Bp Suffr of Stepney in St Paul's Cathl Lon 25 July 57 by Abp of Cant; Bps of Lon; Bris; Portsm; and Linc; Bps Suffr of Kens; Willesden; Malmesbury; Taunton; and Maidstone; and Bp T S Jones; Select Pr Univ of Cam 62; res 68. *Ridgeway House, Felpham, Bognor Regis, Sussex.*

LUNT, Canon Ronald Bryan. b 04. St Jo Coll Dur LTh 25, BA 28. St Edm Hall Ox BA and MA 48. **d** 27 **p** 28 Ches. C of St Mich Macclesfield 27-31; St Aldate Ox 31-37; V of St Andr w St Mary Magd Maidenhead 37-43; All SS Highfield 43-47; Great Malvern 47-74; RD of Powyke 59-74; Hon Can of Worc 59-74; Can (Emer) from 74. *1 Ranelagh Road, Malvern, Worcs.* (Malvern 61382)

LUNT, Canon Ronald Geoffrey. b 13. MC 43. Late Scho of Qu Coll Ox BA 35, MA 38, BD 67. Westcott Ho Cam 37. **d** 38 Ripon for Ox **p** 39 Dorch for Ox. Asst Master Radley Coll 38-40; CF (EC) 40-45; Hd Master of Liv Coll 45-52; Chief Master K Edw VI Sch Birm 52-74; Select Pr Univ of Cam 48 and 60; Univ of Ox 51-53; LPr Dio Birm 52-74; Hon Can of Birm 69-74; Can (Emer) from 74; C-in-c of Martley 74-78; Perm to Offic Dio Heref from 78. *The Station House, Ledbury, Hereford.* (Ledbury 3174)

LUNT, Ronald Sowden. b 30. Univ of Leeds BA (2nd cl Hist) 56. Ely Th Coll 56. **d** 58 **p** 59 Ches. C of St Thos Stockport 58-61; Ellesmere Port 61-65; V of Newton-in-Mottram 65-78; R of Ches Team Par Dio Ches from 78; RD of Ches from 79. *Rectory, Vicars Lane, Chester, CH1 1QX.* (0244-26357)

LUPTON, Brock William. b 48. Univ of BC BMus 70. Vanc Sch of Th MDiv 80. **d** 80 **p** 81 Yukon. I of Elsa Mayo Dio Yukon from 80. *Elsa, Yukon Territory, Canada, Y0B 1J0.*

LUPTON, George Arthur. St Francis Coll Brisb ACT ThL 41. **d** 41 **p** 43 Brisb. C of St Paul Ipswich Brisb 42-45; R of H Trin Goondiwindi 45-48; Coorparoo Brisb 48-57; Maryborough 57-61; Archd of Carp 61-63; The Downs 68-71; Moreton 71-75; Brisb 75-76; Hon Can of Brisb 63-68; Home Miss Sec Dio Brisb 63-66; R of St Luke Toowoomba 66-71; St Andr Lutwyche Brisb 71-76; C of Nambour Dio Brisb from 76. *1 Scrubb Road, Coolum, Queensland, Australia 4573.* (071-46 1168)

LUPTON, Lionel Cavendish. b 13. Edin Th Coll. **d** 55 Aber **p** 56 Arg Is for Aber. Asst Super Dio Aber 55-56; C of All SS Buckie 56-57; P-in-c of Portsoy 56-57; C of Gaywood w Mintlyn 58-59; V of Wiggenhall St German w St Mary Virg and Islington 59-64; PC of Sibford Gower w Sibford Ferris and Epwell 64-69; C-in-c of Broughton Pogis w Filkins 69-75; V 75-78. *The Cottage, Lower Bearwood, Pembridge, Nr Leominster, Herefs.* (Pembridge 513)

LUPTON, Canon Sidney Richard. Hur Coll 54. **d** 54 **p** 55 Hur. I of Pelee I 54-57; R of Kerwood 57-59; Kincardine 59-68; St Hilda w St Luke, St Thos 69-73; St Geo and H Trin Kitchener 73-79; Tillsonburg Dio Hur from 79; Dom Chap to Bp of Hur 75-78; Can of Hur from 80. *83 Bidwell Street, Tillsonburg, Ont, Canada.* (519-842 5124)

LURKINGS, Edward Henry. b 28. AKC 53. Univ of Lon BSc (2nd cl Econ) 68, MSc 70, PhD 81. **d** 54 **p** 55 Lon. C of St Mary Brookfield 54-59; Cricklewood (in c of L St Pet) 59-62; Industr Chap NW Lon 62-68; NE Lon 68-71; L to Offic Dio Lon 63-72; Perm to Offic from 72; Lect Middlesex Poly from 71; Hon C of St Mary Luton Dio St Alb from 72. *51 Elmwood Crescent, Luton, LU2 7HY.* (Luton 34380)

LURY, Anthony Patrick. b 49. AKC and BD 71. St Aug Coll Cant 71. **d** 72 **p** 73 S'wark. C of Richmond 72-76; P-in-c of St Marg Qu Streatham Hill 76-81; V of Ch K Salfords Dio

S'wark from 81. *Vicarage, Honeycrock Lane, Salfords, Redhill, Surrey.* (Redhill 62232)

LURY, Denys Patrick. b 15. Univ of Dur LTh 48. Bps' Coll Cheshunt 36. **d** 38 **p** 39 Lon. C of St Mich AA Bromley-by-Bow 38-40; All SS Carshalton 40-43; RN (Comb) 43-47; C of Ashford Kent 47-50; H Trin Reading 50-52; V of Charing 52-58; C-in-c of L Chart 52-58; V of Charing w L Chart 58-63; St Mich AA Maidstone 63-72; Chap St Monica's Home Westbury-on-Trym 72-80. *388 Wells Road, Knowle, Bristol, BS4 2QP.*

LUSAKA, Lord Bishop of. *See* Mumba, Right Rev Stephen Sebastian.

LUSCOMBE, John Nickels. b 45. K Coll Lon and Warm AKC 68. **d** 69 Lon **p** 70 Stepney for Lon. C of St Faith w Matthias and All SS Stoke Newington 69-74; V of St Phil Tottenham Dio Lon from 75. *St Philip's Vicarage, Philip Lane, N15.* (01-808 4235)

✠ **LUSCOMBE, Right Rev Lawrence Edward.** b 24. ACA 52. St Bonif Coll Warm. **d** 63 **p** 64 Glas. C of St Marg Newlands Glas 63-66; R of St Barn Paisley 66-71; Provost of St Paul's Cathl Dundee 71-75; Cons Ld Bp of Brech in St Paul's Cathl Dundee 21 June 75 by Bp of Arg Is (Primus); Bps of Edin, St Andr, Moray, Aber and Glas; and Bps Russell and Easson. *7 Shaftesbury Road, Dundee, DD2 1HF.* (0382-644215)

LUSCOMBE, Robert Keith. b 45. Moore Coll Syd ThL 69. **d** 70 **p** 71 Syd. C of Chatswood 70-74; R of Cabramatta W 74-79; St Paul S Coogee Dio Syd from 80. *21 Nymboida Street, South Coogee, NSW, Australia 2034.* (344-8270)

LUSEGA, Manase. **d** and **p** 78 Centr Tang. P Dio Centr Tang. *Box 270, Singida, Tanzania.*

LUSENGE, Sumaili. b 12. **d** 77 Bukavu. d Dio Bukavu. *Kailo Parish, BP 220, Kindu, Maniema, Zaire.*

LUSINDE, Joshua. b 35. St Phil Coll Kongwa 68. **d** 69 Bp Madinda for Centr Tang **p** 69 Moro. P Dio Moro 69-71; Dio Centr Tang from 71. *PO Kigwe Station, Tanzania.*

LUSINDE, Very Rev Naftali. St Phil Th Coll Kongwa 53. **d** 54 **p** 55 Centr Tang. P Dio Centr Tang; Archd of Buigiri 65-71; Dioc Sec 66-74; Can of Centr Tang from 71; Dir of Evang from 74; Dean of H Spirit Cathl Dodoma from 78. *Box 233, Dodoma, Tanzania.*

LUSINGO, Dunstan Esrom. b 35. St Phil Coll Kongwa. **d** and **p** 76 Centr Tang. P Dio Centr Tang. *Box 75, Zoissa, Kongwa, Tanzania.*

LUSWAZI, Canon Elliott Mvoweshumi. St Bede's Coll Umtata. **d** 38 **p** 43 St Jo Kaffr. C of Kokstad 39-41; Clydesdale 44-45; Holy Cross 45-54; Mount Frere 54-57; P-in-c of Ntsundwane 57-63; Ensikeni 63-72; Hon Can of St John's from 71. *Box 59, Umzimkulu 4660, S Africa.*

LUTALE, Yonasani. **d** 42 **p** 44 U Nile. P Dio U Nile 44-60; Dio Soroti from 60. *PO Otuboi, Teso, Uganda.*

✠ **LUTAYA, Right Rev Fesito.** Bp Tucker Mem Coll Mukono. **d** 31 **p** 32 Ugan. P Dio Ugan 31-39; PV of St Paul's Cathl Kampala 39-47; L to Offic Dio Ely 47-50; Can of Ugan and Sub-Dean of Kampala Cathl 50-52; Cons Asst Bp of Ugan in St Paul's Cathl Kampala 29 June 52 by Bp of Ugan; Bps of Momb; U Nile; Bps Carey; Tomusange; Beecher; Brazier; Balya; Trld to W Bugan 60; res 65. *Box 14067, Kampala, Uganda.*

LUTCHMAYA, Patrick Andrew. St Paul's Th Coll Maur LTh 64. **d** 64 Maur. d Dio Maur. *37 St James's Street, Port Louis, Mauritius.*

LUTEUTILWA, Isaaka Lutaligwa. **d** 56 Bp Omari for Centr Tang **p** 57 Centr Tang. P Dio Centr Tang 56-66; Dio W Tang 66-72; Dio Vic Nyan from 72. *Box 29, Geita, Tanzania.*

LUTHER, Richard Grenville Litton. b 42. BD (Lon) 64. Tyndale Hall, Bris 66. **d** 68 **p** 69 Blackb. C of St Mary Preston 68-70; Bishopsworth 70-71; Radipole Dio Sarum 72-77; Team V (w Melcombe Regis) from 77. *106 Spa Road, Weymouth, Dorset, DT3 5ER.* (Weymouth 71938)

LUTHER, Stuart Frank. b 26. BSc 57. MIEE 60, FIEE 77, CEng 66. Ripon Hall Ox 66. **d** 69 **p** 71 Chich. C of St Aug Bexhill 69-72; Romsey Dio Win from 72. *2 Church Road, Romsey, Hants, SO5 8EY.* (Romsey 515454)

LUTTON, Percy Theodore Bell Boyce. b 24. Univ of Dub BA 45, MA 48. **d** 46 **p** 48 Connor. C of Whitehouse 46-49; St Jo Evang Dudley 49-52; V of Stambermill 52-61; Wribbenhall 61-80; R of Castlemorton, Hollybush and Birtsmorton Dio Worc from 80. *Hollybush Vicarage, Ledbury, Herefs, HR8 1EX.* (Bromesberrow 218)

LUTWAMA, Yosiya. b 06. Mukono Th Coll 40. **d** 42 **p** 43 Ugan. P Dio Nam. *Kayindu School, Box 135, Bombo, Uganda.*

LUWAGA, Kezekia. Bp Tucker Coll Mukono. **d** 53 **p** 56 Ugan. P Dio Ugan 53-60; Dio W Bugan from 60. *COU Kabungo, Box 2801, Kalungu, Uganda.*

LUXMOORE, Canon Christopher Charles. b 26. Trin Coll Cam BA 50, MA 54. Chich Th Coll 50. **d** 52 **p** 53 Newc T. C of St Jo Bapt Newc T 52-55; C-in-c of St Bede's Eccles Distr Newsham Blyth 55-57; V 57-58; R of Sangre Grande Trinid 58-66; V of Headingley 67-81; Commiss Trinid from 68; M Gen Syn 75-81; Hon Can of Ripon Cathl 80-81; Can Res and Prec of Chich Cathl from 81. *The Residentiary, Canon Lane, Chichester, W Sussex, PO19 1PX.* (Chich 782961)

LUXMOORE-BALL, Cecil Michael. b 14. Keble Coll Ox BA (3rd cl Mod Hist) 36, MA 60. Cudd Coll 36. **d** 38 **p** 39 Lon. C of St Mary of Eton Hackney Wick 38-40; St Mich Golders Green 40-42; St Pet Parkstone 42-47; V of Chew Magna 47-70; Butleigh (w Baltonsborough from 78) 70-80. *Ladymead Cottage, Pound Lane, Bishop's Lydeard, Taunton, Somt.*

LUXTON, David William. Univ of W Ont BA 56. Cudd Coll 56. **d** 58 **p** 59 Hur for Tor. C of Grace Ch-on-the-Hill Tor 58-61; R of St Mich Hamilton 61-68; St Chris Burlington 68-74; Hon Can of Niag 72-73; R of St Geo-on-the-Hill City and Dio Tor from 73. *4600 Dundas Street West, Islington, Toronto, Ont., Canada.* (416-239 2341)

LUYT, Ven Norman. St Paul's Coll Grahmstn LTh 37. **d** 37 **p** 38 Johann. C of Brakpan 37-39; St Mary's Cathl Johann 39-47; R of Vereeniging 47-61; Orange Grove 61-70; Bryanston Dio Johann from 70; Archd of N Rand 65-70; Johann N from 70. *Rectory, Mount Street, Bryanston, Transvaal, S Africa.* (011-706 2828)

LUZINDA, Eriya Paulo. b 27. Bp Tucker Coll Mukono 73. **d** 74 **p** 75 Nam. P Dio Nam. *Box 14297, Kampala, Uganda.*

LWANDE, Jeremiah. Buwalasi Th Coll 59. **d** 60 U Nile. d Dio U Nile 60-61; Dio Mbale 61-72; Dio Bukedi from 72. *Lumino, Uganda.*

LWANGA, Canon Blasiyo. **d** 44 **p** 45 Ugan. P Dio Ugan 45-61; PV of St Paul's Cathl Kampala 52-58; Can 58-61; P Dio Nam from 61; Can of Nam from 75. *Box 837, Kampala, Uganda.*

LYAHI, Silvester. b 42. **d** 79 **p** 80 Centr Tang. P Dio Centr Tang. *PO Kilimatinde, via Manyoni, Tanzania.*

LYALL, Graham. b 37. St D Coll Lamp BA (2nd cl Hist) 61. Univ of Birm Dipl Th 63. Qu Coll Birm 61. **d** 63 **p** 64 York. C of Berwick Hills Middlesbrough 63-67; Kidderminster (in c of St Barn) 67-72; V of St Aug Dudley 72-79; P-in-c of St Steph Barbourne City and Dio Worc 79-81; V from 81. *1 Beech Avenue, Worcester.* (Worc 52169)

LYAWEYE, Jonas Abraham. **d** and **p** 78 Centr Tang. P Dio Centr Tang. *Box 52, Manyoni, Tanzania.*

LYNAS, Norman Noel. b 55. Univ of St Andr MTh 78. Div Hostel Dub 78. **d** 79 **p** 80 Down. C of Knockbreda 79-81; Holywood Dio Down from 81. *20 Princess Gardens, Holywood, Co Down, BT18 0PN.* (Holywood 2468)

LYNAS, Stephen Brian. b 52. St Jo Coll Nottm BTh 77. **d** 78 Lich **p** 79 Wolverhampton for Lich. C of Penn 78-81; Relig Programmes Org BBC Radio Stoke-on-Trent from 81. *Etruria Vicarage, Belmont Road, Etruria, Stoke-on-Trent, ST1 5NX.*

LYNCH, Alfred. b 1898. Univ of Dur LTh 23. St Bonif Coll Warm 21. **d** 23 Barking for Chelmsf **p** 24 Chelmsf. C of Barking 23-26; Perm to Offic at St Luke Ilford 26-27; V of Urswick 27-35; St Cath Horwich 35-39; R of Desford 39-44; Wootton Rivers 44-60; C-in-c of Savernake 56-60; R of Litton Cheney 60-69; R of Puncknowle w Swyre 60-69. *Highbank, Lockeridge, Marlborough, Wilts.* (Lockeridge 633)

LYNCH, Preb Donald MacLeod. b 11. CBE 72. Late Scho of Pemb Coll Cam 1st cl Cl Trip pt i 32, BA (2nd cl Th Trip pt i) 34, MA 37. Wycl Hall Ox 34. **d** 35 **p** 36 Lon. C of Ch Ch Chelsea 35-38; Tutor Oak Hill Th Coll Southgate and Publ Pr Dio St Alb 38-40; C of St Mich AA Stonebridge Pk 40-42; Min of All SS Queensbury Lon 42-50; V of St Luke Tunbridge Wells 50-53; Prin Ch Army Tr Coll Lon 53-61; LPr Dio Lon from 54; Chief Sec CA 60-76; Preb of Twyford in St Paul's Cathl Lon 64-76; Preb (Emer) from 76; Chap to HM the Queen 69-81; P-in-c of St Lawr Seal Dio Roch from 74; Underriver Dio Roch from 80; RD of Sevenoaks from 79. *St Lawrence Vicarage, Stone Street, Near Sevenoaks, Kent, TN15 0LQ.* (Sevenoaks 61766)

LYNCH, Frederick William. Univ of Manit BA 58. St Jo Coll Winnipeg LTh 62. **d** 58 **p** 59 Bran. C of Elgin 58-59; R 59-60; Boissevain 60-64; St Jas and St Pet Flin Flon 64-75; on leave. *69 Church Street, Flin Flon, Manit, Canada.*

LYNCH, Hollis Peter. b 34. Chich Th Coll 69. **d** 71 **p** 72 Ripon. C of Headingley 71-74; R of Balaclava and Siloah Dio Ja from 74; Exam Chap to Bp of Ja from 76. *Rectory, Balaclava PO, St Elizabeth, Jamaica, WI.* (096-32228)

LYNCH, James Kenrick. ACP 65. Ripon Hall, Ox. **d** 61 BurnleY for Blackb **p** 62 Blackb. C of Padiham w Higham 61-66; V of Chatburn 66-69; Chap Whittingham Hosp 69-72; V of St Lawr Barton 72-81. *11 St Lawrence Avenue, Barton, Preston, Lancs.*

LYNCH, Wayne Gary. b 48. Acadia Univ NS BA 72. Trin

Coll Tor MDiv 75. **d** 74 NS **p** 75 Bp Arnold for NS. C of Port Medway-Brooklyn Dio NS from 74. *The Rectory, Brooklyn, Queen's County, NS, Canada.* (354-3182)

LYNCH-WATSON, Graham Leslie. b 30. K Coll Lon and Warm AKC 55. **d** 56 **p** 57 S'wark. C of All SS New Eltham (in c of St Aid Edgebury from 58) 56-60; C of St Mary The Boltons Kens 60-62; V of St Bart Camberwell 62-66; St Barn Purley 66-77; C of Caversham (and Mapledurham from 81) Dio Ox from 77. *51 Galsworthy Drive, Caversham, Reading, Berks, RG4 0TR.* (0734 475152)

LYNDON, Philip John. b 09. St Bonif Coll Warm. **d** 36 Lon for Col **p** 37 Willoch. M of Bush Bro Quorn Willoch 36-42; Chap RAAF 42-46; C of St Jas Elmers End 47-48; V of St Marg of Antioch Leeds 48-53; St Aid Leeds and Surr 53-61; All SS Shrewsbury 61-74; Chap HM Pris Shrewsbury 64-70. *46 Underdale Road, Shrewsbury, Shropshire.*

LYNDS, Thomas George. b 34. ALCD 62 (LTh from 74). **d** 62 **p** 63 Chich. C of All S Eastbourne 62-65; Edgware (in c of St Andr) 65-72; V of St Luke Wimbledon Pk Dio S'wark from 72. *28 Farquhar Road, SW19 8DA.* (01-946 3396)

LYNE, Peter. b 27. Univ of Sheff BA 51. Qu Coll Birm 51. **d** 53 **p** 54 York. C of St Aug Newland 53-55; Harworth 55-56; Burbage w Harpur Hill 56-58; PC of Horsley Woodhouse 58-62; V of Rawcliffe 62-69; R of Shardlow w Gt Wilne, Elvaston, Thurlaston and Ambaston 69-74; Min of St Jo Bapt Ashbourne 74-80; P-in-c of Kniveton 75-80; Fenny Bentley 77-78; Osmaston w Edlaston 78-80; Holbrook and of L Eaton Dio Derby from 80; Surr from 78. *Vicarage, Moorside Lane, Holbrook, Derby, DE5 0TW.* (Derby 880254)

LYNE, Roger Howard. b 28. Mert Coll Ox BA 52, MA 56. Oak Hill Th Coll 52. **d** 54 **p** 55 Cov. C of St Matt Rugby 54-58; St Jo Evang Weymouth 58-61; V of Newchapel 61-65; C of Bucknall w Bagnall Dio Lich from 76. *14 Eaves Lane, Bucknall, Stoke-on-Trent, ST2 8JX.* (Stoke-on-T 267451)

LYNER, John Gregory. b 17. Sarum Th Coll 57. **d** 59 Leic **p** 60 Bp Maxwell for Leic. C of Knighton 59-62; V of Diseworth 62-69; Bringhurst w Gt Easton and Drayton 69-74; R of Stoney Stanton 74-80. *7 Croft Avenue, Aylestone, Leicester, LE2 8LF.*

LYNES, Brian Bell. St Francis Coll Brisb ACT ThL (2nd cl) 59. **d** 59 **p** 60 Brisb. C of St Luke Toowoomba 59-63; P-in-c of All SS Boianai 63-75; Chap ARA 75-76; R of St Luke Toowoomba Dio Brisb from 76. *152 Herries Street, Toowoomba, Queensland, Australia 4350.* (32 3440)

LYNETT, Anthony Martin. b 54. K Coll Lon BD 74, AKC 75. Sarum Wells Th Coll 75. **d** 78 **p** 79 Bris. C of Ch Ch Swindon 78-81; St Phil & St Jas Leckhampton w St Jas Cheltm Dio Glouc from 81. *c/o St Philip's Vicarage, Painswick Road, Cheltenham, Glos.*

LYNN, Lord Bishop Suffragan of. *See* Aitken, Right Rev William Aubrey.

LYNN, Archdeacon of. *See* Grobecker, Ven Geoffrey Frank.

LYNN, Dixon. b 09. Ely Th Coll 46. **d** 47 **p** 48 Newc T. C of St Gabr Heaton Newc T 47-52; V of Ulgham 52-55; PC of Whittonstall 55-57; R of Lerwick 57-62; Wark 62-75; V of Birtley 62-75. *Bridge House, Newbrough, Hexham, Northumb.*

LYNN, Edward Brown. Univ of Dur BA 35. Lich Th Coll 37. **d** 37 **p** 38 Dur. C of St Luke Pallion 37-40; Actg C of St Cuthb Benfieldside 40-41; Offg C-in-c of H Trin Gateshead 41-44; PC of Chopwell 44-51; Silksworth 51-55; Chap RAF 55-58; R of Brotton Parva 58-66; V of Mkt Weighton 66-77; R of Goodmanham 66-77; RD of Weighton 67-75; V of Trimdon Station (f Trimdon Grange) 77-79. *53 Alderside Crescent, Lanchester, Co Durham.*

LYNN, Frank Trevor. b 36. Keble Coll Ox BA 61, MA 64. St Steph Ho Ox 61. **d** 63 Warrington for Liv **p** 74 Liv. C of W Derby 63-65; Chorley 65-68; V of St Jo Evang Altrincham 68-72; Chap RN from 72. *c/o Ministry of Defence, Lacon House, Theobalds Road, WC1 8RY.*

LYNN, Geoffrey. St Aid Coll 55. **d** 57 **p** 58 Dur. C of Easington Colliery 57-60; R of Hetton-le-Hole Dio Dur from 60. *Rectory, Hetton-le-Hole, Co Durham.* (Hetton-le-Hole 3198)

LYNN, Gregory James. Laurentian Univ Ont BA 71. Trin Coll Tor MDiv 74. **d** 74 Alg. Chap Lakehead Miss to Seamen 74; R of Sundridge 74-76; on leave 77; I of Chibougamau Dio Moos from 78. *Box 272, Chibougamau, PQ, Canada.* (819-276 3451)

LYNN, Jeffrey. b 39. Moore Th Coll Syd 67. **d** 79 Repton for Derby **p** 80 Derby. C of Littleover 79-80; Allestree Dio Derby from 80. *4 Merridale Road, Littleover, Derby, DE3 7DJ.*

LYNN, John Cairns. b 40. Univ of Surrey BSc 63. Univ of Lon MSc 66. N-W Ordin Course 73. **d** 76 **p** 77 Liv (APM). C of Hunts Cross Dio Liv from 76; Hon Chap of Liv Cathl from 80. *2 Bancroft Close, Hunts Cross, Liverpool, L25 0LS.*

LYNN, Matthew James Frederick. b 26. TCD BA (2nd cl Hist Mod) 50, MA 57. **d** 62 **p** 63 Lim. C of St Mary and St Munchin Lim and Dean's V of Lim Cathl 63-65; R of Kinawley 65-71; I of Trin Ch 65-71; C of Weeke (in c of St Barn) 71-74; R of Headbourne Worthy Dio Win from 74. *King's Worthy Rectory, Winchester, Hants.* (Win 4281)

LYNN, Peter Anthony. b 38. Univ of Keele BA 62. St John's Coll Cam BA (2nd cl Th Trip pt ii) 64, MA 68, PhD 72. Westcott Ho Cam 67. **d** 68 Ely **p** 69 Huntingdon for Ely. C of Soham w Barway 68-72; Min Can St Paul's Cathl Lon 72-78; Hon Min Can from 78; L to Offic Dio Lon 73-78; Perm to Offic Dio St Alb from 78. *7 Heath Row, Bishop's Stortford, Herts.* (0279-58754)

LYON, Christopher David. b 55. Univ of Strathclyde LLB 75. Univ of Edin BD 81. Episc Th Coll Edin 78. **d** 81 Glas. C of Dumfries Dio Glas from 81. *28 Eastfield Road, Dumfries, Scotland.* (0387 68805)

LYON, Dennis. b 36. Dipl Th (lon) 66. Wycl Hall, Ox 64. **d** 67 **p** 68 Southw. C of St Mark Woodthorpe Nottm 67-70; Warden Walton Centre 70-72; V of Good Shepherd W Derby 72-81; Billinge Dio Liv from 81. *91 Newton Road, Billinge, Wigan, WN5 7LB.* (0744-892210)

LYON, Canon Donald Robert. b 20. Late Sch of Trin Coll Cam BA 41, PhD 44, MA 45. Linc Th Coll 46. **d** 47 **p** 48 Glouc. C of Dursley w Woodmancote 47-51; Brislington 51-52; V of St Mark City and Dio Glouc from 52; Hon Can of Glouc from 74; RD of Glouc City from 77. *19 Tewkesbury Road, Gloucester.* (Gloucester 24070)

LYON, Duncan Austin. b 39. St Chad's Coll Dur BA 60, Dipl Th 62. **d** 62 Warrington for Liv **p** 63 Liv. C of St Agnes Toxt Pk 62-65; Our Lady and St Nich Liv 65-68; R of Duxford 68-73; V of St Aug Wisbech 73-74; I of Sundridge Dio Alg from 76. *Box 157, Sundridge, Ont., Canada.*

LYON, Stephen Paul. b 49. Univ of Wales (Swansea) BSc 71. Trin Coll Bris 74. **d** 77 **p** 78 York. C of St John Newland Hull 77-81; Chap of Lee Abbey Fellowship Lynton from 81. *Lee Abbey Fellowship, Lynton, Devon.*

LYONS, Bruce Twyford. b 37. Dipl Th (Lon) 69. Tyndale Hall Bris 67. **d** 70 **p** 71 Dorking for Guildf. C of Virginia Water 70-73; Chap of St George's Knokke, St Mary's Bruges and the Engl Ch Ostend 73-78; V of St Paul E Ham Dio Chelmsf from 78. *227 Burges Road, E6 2EU.* (01-472 5531)

LYONS, Edward Charles. b 44. Univ of Nottm BTh 75. St Jo Coll Nottm 71. **d** 75 **p** 76 Ely. C of St Martin Cam 75-78; P-in-c of Bestwood Pk Dio Southw from 78. *36 Melksham Road, Bestwood Park Estate, Nottingham, NG5 5RX.*

LYONS, Frank. b 15. Codr Coll Barb. **d** and **p** 49 Trinid. C of H Trin Cathl Port of Spain 49-52; R of Princes Town and P-in-c of Gracechurch 52-63; Hon Can of Trinid 60-63; V of Annesley 63-80; Newstead 63-80. *Forest Lodge, Derby Road, Annesley, Notts.* (Mansfield 753304)

LYONS, James Robin. b 55. Univ of W Ont Lon BA 77. Hur Coll Lon Ont MDiv 80. **d** 80 **p** 81 Bp Townshend for Hur. C of St Geo Owen Sound Dio Hur from 80. *1560 6th Ave W, Apt 311, Owen Sound, Ont, Canada, N4K 5H8.*

LYONS, Kathleen May. **d** 64 **p** 78 Auckld. C of St Andr Epsom 64-76; R Oak 76-78; Mt Albert Dio Auckld from 78. *6 Coronation Road, Epsom, Auckland 3, NZ.* (688-679)

LYONS, Paul Benson. Qu Coll Birm 68. **d** 69 Bp J D McKie for Cov **p** 70 Cov. C of Rugby 68-70; St John Moston 70-72; PV of Llan Cathl 73-74; C of St Anne Highgate 74-75; Perm to Offic Dio Lon from 76. *181 Foundling Court, Brunswick Centre, WC1.* (01-278 2820)

LYONS, William. b 22. **d** 80 **p** 81 St Andr (NSM). C of Glenrothes Dio St Andr from 80. *13 Dovecot Park, Glenrothes, Fife.*

LYTH, Canon John. b 16. St Edm Hall Ox BA (2nd cl Geog) 38, MA 42. Linc Th Coll 38. **d** 40 **p** 41 Linc. C of Skegness 40-45; V of Wincobank 45-52; R of Sprotbrough w Cadeby 52-82; RD of Doncaster 59-82; Hon Can of Sheff from 64. *c/o Sprotbrough Rectory, Doncaster, Yorks.*

✠ **LYTH, Right Rev Richard Edward.** b 16. St Edm Hall Ox BA 38, MA 55. Oak Hill Th Coll. **d** 56 **p** 57 Carl. C of Arthuret 56-59; Hd Master Kigezi High Sch 60-64; Christian Rural Service Dio Ankole-K 64-67; Cons Ld Bp of Kigezi in Nam Cathl 8 Jan 67 by Abp of Ugan; Bps of Ankole-K; Mbale; Nam; N Ugan; Soroti; Nak; W Bugan; and Rwa; and Asst Bp in the Sudan; res 72; C of St Andr Chorleywood 74-81. *7 The Street, Warninglid, Haywards Heath, W Sussex, RH17 5TR.* (Warninglid 380)

LYTH, Canon Richard Francis. b 05. Univ of Dur LTh 25, BA 27. Edin Th Coll 22. **d** 28 **p** 29 Glas. C of St Marg Newlands Glas 28-32; Chap of St Ninian's Cathl Perth 32-39; R of St Andr Uddingston 39-75; C-in-c of St Marg Mossend 42-50; Hon Can of St Mary's Cathl Glas from 79. *26 Gardenside Street, Uddingston, Glasgow, G71 7BY.*

LYTLE, John Deaville. b 23. Wadh Coll Ox 3rd cl LitHum 49, BA 50, MA 52. Wycl Hall, Ox 50. **d** 51 **p** 52 Derby. C of Ilkeston 51-56; PC of Brassington 56-59; V of Bradbourne w

Brassington Dio Derby from 59; RD of Wirksworth from 78. *Brassington Vicarage, Derby.* (Carsington 281)

LYTTELTON, Edward Gascoigne. K Coll Cam BA 66. Ripon Hall Ox. **d** 69 S'wark. C of St Luke Camberwell 69-74. *41 Osborne Avenue, Toronto, Ont, Canada.*

M

MAABE, Henry. d 42 **p** 54 Melan. P Dio Melan 42-75; Dio Malaita from 75. *Ato, Malaita, British Solomon Islands.*

MAAGO, Festo. d 76 **p** 77 Ank. P Dio Ank 76-77; Dio W Ank from 77. *Box 2016, Kwashamaire, Uganda.*

MAANGI MATIU, Wiremu Petera. b 23. **d** 77 **p** 78 Aotearoa for Wai. C of Te Kaha Past Dio Wai from 77. *PO Box 73, Opotiki, NZ.*

MAANGI-MATIU, Waranga-Nui-o-Te Rangi. b 22. **d** 77 Aotearoa for Wai. C of Te Kaha Past Dio Wai from 77. *PO Waihau Bay, Bay of Plenty, NZ.*

MAARI, Eliphaz. Bp Tucker Coll Mukono 69. **d** 71 Ank. d Dio Ank 71-76; Dio Soroti from 76; Exam Chap to Bp of Soroti from 76. *Box 4, Mukono, Uganda.*

MABANDLA, Good Ngwendu. b 44. St Bede's Coll Umtata 76. **d** 78 **p** 79 St John's. P Dio St John's. *PO Box 76, Umzimkulu, Transkei.*

MABASO, Andreas Hamilton. St Pet Coll Rosettenville. **d** 53 **p** 54 Zulu. P Dio Zulu 53-63. *Chwezi BC School, PO Kwadladla, via Nkandhla, Zululand.*

MABASO, Paul Wilmot Mandlekosi. St Bede's Th Coll Umtata 58. **d** 59 **p** 61 Zulu. P Dio Zulu 59-74. *PB 117, Nkandla, Zululand.*

MABBE, Kiliona. d and **p** 75 Bunyoro. P Dio Bunyoro. *POB Bwijungu-Masindi, Uganda.*

MABENA, Petros. St Pet Coll Rosettenville 59. **d** 62 **p** 63 Pret. P Dio Pret 62-75; R of Sekhukhuniland 75-79; All SS Rethabile Dio Pret from 79. *1484 Mamelodi East, PO Rethabile, Pretoria 0122, S Africa.*

MABIJA, Arthur O'Brien Velile. St Pet Coll Alice. **d** 68 **p** 69 Kimb K for Grahmstn. P Dio Grahmstn 68-76; Dio Kimb K from 77. *30 Rotanang Street, Kimberley, CP, S Africa.*

MABIOR, Canon Kedhekia Barac. Bp Gwynne Coll 54. **d** 57 Bp Deng for Sudan **p** 58 Sudan. P Dio Sudan 58-76; Dio Juba from 76; Hon Can of Sudan 75-60; Juba from 76. *Box 110, Juba, Sudan.*

MABOE, Joseph Michael Johannes. b 37. St Pet Coll Alice 69. **d** 71 **p** 72 Johann. C of Kagiso 71-75; R of Jouberton Dio Johann from 75. *Box 4, Jouberton, Transvaal, S Africa.* (018-5704)

MABOEE, Austin Teboho. St Pet Coll Rosettenville LTh 45. **d** 44 **p** 45 Bloemf. C of Heilbron Miss 44-49; P-in-c of Thaba Nchu 49-50; Miss P St Aug Miss Modderpoort 50-56; Herzogville Miss 56-67; Harrismith Miss 67-69; Dir of St Mark Vrede 69-73; C of St Patr Miss Bloemf 73-74; H Cross Odendaalsrus 74-77; St Patr Maboee Dio Bloemf from 77. *Box 16023, PO Location, Bloemfontein, S Africa.*

MABONGA, Meshach. Buwalasi Th Coll 62. **d** 64 **p** 65 Mbale. P Dio Mbale 64-66; Dio Soroti 66-69; Mbale from 69. *PO Box 984, Mbale, Uganda.*

MABOVULA, Robert Deyi Ntamonde. St Bede's Coll Umtata 63. **d** 64 **p** 65 St John's. P Dio St John's. *P Bag 503, Cedarville 4720, S Africa.*

✠ **MABULA, Right Rev Joseph.** St Jo Sem Lusaka. **d** 65 Bp Mataka for Zam **p** 67 Zam. P Dio Zam 67-71; Cons Ld Bp of N Zam 7 Feb 71 in Lusaka Cathl by Abp of Centr Afr; Bps of Mashon; Lusaka; Matab; and Bp Mtekateka. *Box 159, Mufuliara, Zambia.* (024-4775)

MABUNO, Samusoni. Buwalasi Coll. **d** 48 **p** 50 U Nile. P Dio U Nile 48-61; Dio Mbale 61-72; Dio Bukedi 72-76. *Busolwe, Tororo, Uganda.*

MABURUKI, David. d 79 Kiga. d Dio Kiga. *BP 61, Kigali, Rwanda.*

MABUTO, Jacob Tokwe. St Pet Coll Rosettenville 37. **d** 38 St Jo Kaffr for Grahmstn **p** 40 Grahmstn. P Dio Grahmstn 40-70; Port Eliz 70-72. *PO Box 1079, Queenstown, CP, S Africa.*

MABUTO, Wellington. St Pet Coll Alice 62. **d** 64 **p** 65 Grahmstn. P Dio Grahmstn 64-70 and from 78; Dio Port Eliz 71-78. *Box 75, Mdantsane 5219, CP, S Africa.*

MABUZA, Meshack Boy. b 46. **d** 79 Swaz. d Dio Swaz. *Evelyn Baring High School, PO Box 21, Nhlangano, Swaziland.*

MABY, Harry Grant. b 09. Univ of Lon BSc 31. Westcott Ho Cam 35. **d** 35 **p** 36 S'wark. C of St Pet St Helier 35-40; Gt Bookham 40-43; Leatherhead (in c of All SS) 43-47; R of Fetcham 47-74. *21 Pewley Way, Guildford, Surrey.* (Guildford 66319)

McADAM, Alexander William. b 15. Univ of Wales, BA (1st cl Gr) 37. Jes Coll Ox 3rd cl Lit Hum 39, BA 40, MA 43. St Mich Coll Llan 39. **d** 41 **p** 42 Mon. C of Bedwas 41-44; Pontnewyndd 44-50; R of Grosmont w Skenfrith V Dio Mon from 50. *Rectory, Grosmont, Abergavenny, NP7 8LW.* (Pontrilas 421)

McADAM, Michael Anthony. b 30. Late Exhib K Coll Cam BA 52, MA 56. St Jo Coll Ox BA (by incorp) 52. Westcott Ho Cam 54. **d** 56 **p** 57 Pet. C of Towcester 56-59; Chap Hurstpierpoint Coll 60-68; Dom Chap to Bp of Lon 69-73; R of Much Hadham Dio St Alb from 73. *Rectory, Much Hadham, Herts.* (Much Hadham 2609)

McADAM, Robert Stephen Lett. Univ of Tor BA 36. Trin Coll Tor LTh 40. **d** 40 Tor **p** 41 Qu'App. C of St Geo Moose Jaw w Buffalo Lake 40-41; I 41-48; Milestone 48-51; Whitewood 51-56; Kindersley 56-68; Tisdale Dio Sask from 68; Star City 69-71; Hon Can of qu'App 63-68; I of Star City 73-74; R of St Geo Sktn 74-80; Delisle, Pk Lake 80. *72 Morris Drive, Saskatoon, Sask, Canada.*

McADAM, Stuart Lance Arthur. d 81 Fred (APM). Perm to Offic Dio Fred from 81. *232 University Avenue, Fredericton, NB, Canada, E3B 4H7.*

✠ **McADOO, Most Rev Henry Robert.** b 16. Late Scho of Trin Coll Dub, Bedell Scho, Kyle Pri and Downes Pri 37, BA (1st cl Mods) 38, Newport White Gr Pri and 2nd cl Div Test 39, PhD 40, BD 48, DD 49. Seabury-W Th Sem Hon STD 62. **d** 39 **p** 40 Cash. C of H Trin Cathl Waterf 39-43; I of Castleventry w Ardfield U (and Kilmeen from 47) 43-48; R of Kilmocomogue 48-52; RD of Glansalney West and Bere 48-52; Can of Kilbrittain in Cork Cathl and Can of Donoughmore in Cloyne Cathl 49-52; Dean and I of Cork Cathl 52-62; Can of St Patr 59-62; Hale Lect Seabury-W 62; Dean of Leigh 62-63; Cons Ld Bp of Oss Ferns and Leigh in Ch Ch Cathl Dub 11 Mar 62 by Abp of Dub; Bp of Meath; Bps of Cork; Killaloe; Cash; and Lim; Abp Barton; and Bps Harvey and Crozier; Trld to Dub (Abp of Dub and Bp of Glendal, Primate of Ireland and Metrop) 77. *See House, 17 Temple Road, Milltown, Dublin 6, Irish Republic.* (Dublin 977849)

McALDEN, Canon Joseph. d 16 **p** 17 NS. P-in-c at Westville NS 16-19; Miss at Greenwich 19-25; Min of Salisbury and Havelock 25-29; R of Andover 29-43; St Andr 43-61; Hon Can of Fred from 54. *St Andrew's, NB, Canada.*

McALEER, Michael. St Steph Ho Ox 31. **d** 20 **p** 21 RC Bp of Waterf and Lism. Received into Angl Commun by Bp of Glas 30. C of H Trin Paisley (in c of St Marg Renfrew) 31-33; R of St Jas Springburn Glas 33-41; St John Annan w Eastriggs 41-71. *Powfoot, Annan, Dumfriesshire.* (Annan 2169)

McALISTER, Ian James Walter. St Mich Ho Crafers. **d** 69 Bath **p** 71 N Queensld. C of H Trin Dubbo 69-71; St Jas Cathl Townsville 71-73; R of W Cairns 74-80; Ch Ch St Geo Dio Brisb from 80. *Rectory, Victoria Street, St George, Queensland, Australia 4393.*

McALISTER, Preb James Daniel Beaton. b 01. TCD BA 23, Toplady and Bp Forster Pri 23, Warren Pri and Div Test 24, MA 26. **d** 24 **p** 25 Arm. C of Portadown 24-26; Armagh 26-30; I of Kildress 30-39; R of Ballinderry w Tamlaght 39-50; I of Moy w Charlemont 50-62; RD of Tullyhogue 44-50; Dungannon 51-67; I of Eglish 62-72; Preb of Arm Cathl 66-72. *44 Coast Road, Cushendall, Co Antrim, BT44 0RX, N Ireland.* (Cushendall 436)

McALISTER, Kenneth Bloomer. b 25. TCD BA 51. **d** 51 **p** 53 Down. C of St Finnian Gregagh 51-54; St Patr Monaghan 54-57; St Mark Portadown 57-62; R of Ripley w Burnt Yates Dio Ripon from 62. *Ripley Rectory, Harrogate, Yorks.* (Harrogate 770147)

McALISTER, Randall George Leslie. b 41. TCD BA 63, MA 66. **d** 64 **p** 66 Arm. C of Portadown 64-67; R of Keady w Armaghbreague (and Derrynoose from 73) 67-74; Kirriemuir 74-81; St Jo Evang Greenock Dio Glas from 81. *24 Forsyth Street, Greenock, Renfrews, PA16 8DT.* (Greenock 20750)

McALISTER, Thomas George. b 20. Trin Coll Dub BA 42, MA 47. **d** 43 **p** 44 Down. C of Aghalee 43-45; St Pet Belfast 45-53; V of St Andr Southport 53-59; St Mary Spring Grove Osterley Isleworth 59-69; R of Haslemere 69-79; Chap of Wispers Sch 69-79; V of St Luke Slyne w Hest Dio Blackb from 79. *Hasty Brow Vicarage, Summerfield Drive, Slyne-with-Hest, Lancaster, LA2 6AQ.* (Hest Bank 822128)

McALLEN, James. b 38. BD (Lon) 71. Oak Hill Th Coll. **d** 66 **p** 67 S'wark. C of St Jo Evang Blackheath 66-69; St Thos Edin 69-73; V of St Jas Ap Selby 73-80; Wistow 73-80; Houghton Dio Carl from 80. *Houghton Vicarage, Carlisle, Cumb, CA6 4HZ.* (Carlisle 25808)

McALLEN, Robert. b 41. Bps' Coll Cheshunt 62. **d** 65 **p** 66 Down. C of Seagoe 65-68; Knockbreda 68-70; CF from 70.

c/o Ministry of Defence, Lansdowne House, Berkeley Square, W1X 6AA.

McALLISTER, Allan Bruce. b 48. Coll of Em & St Chad Sktn LTh 77. **d** 76 **p** 77 Sktn. I of Watson Sask 76-80; St Geo City and Dio Sktn from 80. *507 Avenue H South, Saskatoon, Sask, Canada.*

McALPIN, Craig Neal. Moore Th Coll Syd. **d** 52 Syd for Nel **p** 53 Nel. C-in-c of Suburban N 52-53; V 54-55; Motupiko 55-58; Cheviot 58-60; R of Mulgoa 60-62; C-in-c of Panania 62-70; L to Offic Dio Syd from 70; Staff Counsellor C of E Marriage Guidance Coun Syd 70-75. *2 Day Street, Chatswood, NSW, Australia 2067.* (41-8973)

McALPINE, Ian Douglas. b 47. Ont Bible Coll Tor BTh 70. Gordon-Conwell Th Sem USA MThStud 74. Hur Coll Ont 75. **d** 75 **p** 76 Hur. C of Trin Cam & Ch Ch Ayr 75-77; I of Florence 77-81; Walpole I Dio Hur from 81. *RR3, Wallaceburg, Ont, Canada N8A 4K9.*

MACAMO, Filipe. **d** 60 **p** 61 Lebom. P Dio Lebom from 60. *Caixa Postal 63, Jo£ao Belo, Mozambique.*

MACAN, Peter John Erdley. b 36. Bishop Gray Coll Capetn. **d** 60 **p** 61 Capetn. C of Matroosfontein 60-64; Good Shepherd Maitland 64-67; C of St Anne S Lambeth 68-71; V of St Silas Nunhead 72-81; P-in-c of H Spirit Clapham Dio S'wark from 81. *16 Elms Road, SW4 9EX.* (01-720 3677)

McANULTY, Alan Frederick. b 27. St Jo Coll Morpeth Dipl Th 69. **d** 63 **p** 69 Bath. C of St Barn Orange Dio Bath from 63. *9 Autumn Street, Orange, Australia 2800.* (62 1733)

McARDLE, Thomas. b 16. Edin Th Coll 47. **d** 48 Glas **p** 49 Arg Is for Glas. C of All SS Jordanhill (in c of St D Scotstoun) Glas 48-52; St Mary Hitchin 52-53; R of Sarratt 53-61; V of Lyndhurst 61-71; St Jas Pokesdown Bournemouth 71-77; P-in-c of Bentworth w Shaldon and Lasham Dio Win 77-79; R 79-81. *c/o Bentworth Rectory, Alton, Hants.* (Alton 63218)

McARTHUR, Peter Douglas. b 48. St Mich Ho Crafers Th Dipl 74. **d** and **p** 75 Perth. C of Kalamunda 76-78; R of Wanneroo-Yanchep Dio Perth from 78. *27 Leach Street, Wanneroo, W Australia 6065.* (405 1325)

MACARTNEY, William Horne. b 08. Qu Coll Cam 2nd cl Hist Trip pt i 29, BA (2nd cl Hist Trip pt ii) 30, MA 34. Ridley Hall Cam 31. 1 33 **p** 34 Newc. T. C of St Mich Byker 33-35; CMS Miss Buwalasi Tr Coll 35-41; CF (E Afr) 41-46; RD of Masaba 47-49; Asst Gen Sec C of E Coun on Foreign Relations 49-53; Chap to W Afr Studs Union 50-53; V of Upavon w Rushall 53-63; Area Sec CMS Dios Carl and Blackb 63-70; Chap Kako Gr Sch 70-73; Chap to Bp of W Buganda 70-73; L to Offic Dio Carl from 74. *Fishery Farm, Hutton Roof, Carnforth, Lancs.*

McATEER, Bruce James. ACA (Austr) 72. ACT ThDip 74. St Jo Coll Morpeth 72. **d** 73 **p** 75 Newc. C of Taree 73-78; Cessnock 78-79; P-in-c of Prov Distr Wyoming Dio Newc from 79. *30 Orange Parade, Wyoming, NSW, Australia 2251.* (043-25 3160)

McATEER, John Alexander. b 18. TCD BA and Div Test 44, MA 50. **d** 44 **p** 45 Lim. C of St Mary's Cathl 44-47; St Bart Dub 47-51; St Steph Kensington 51-52; All SS w St Columb Notting Hill Kens 52-59; V of H Innoc Hammersmith Dio Lon from 59. *35 Paddenswick Road, W6.* (01-748 5195)

McAUGHEY, Daniel Clinton. Univ of Idaho BSc 61. Ch Div Sch USA BD 65. **d** 65 Idaho for Athab **p** 65 Athab. C of Spirit River 65-67; St Pet Barb 67-69; P-in-c of St Sav I & Dio Barb from 69. *St Saviour's Vicarage, Barbados, W Indies.*

MACAULAY, John Roland. b 39. Univ of Man BSc 61. Wells Th Coll 61. **d** 63 Warrington for Liv **p** 64 Liv. C of Padgate 63-66; Up Holland (in c of Ch the Servant Digmoor from 70) 66-73; Team V 73-75; V of St Pet Hindley 75-81. *Address temp unknown.*

MACAULAY, Kenneth Lionel. b 55. Univ of Edin BD 78. Edin Th Coll 74. **d** 78 **p** 79 Glas. C of St Ninian Glas 78-80; P-in-c of St Matt Possilpark City and Dio Glas from 80. *200 Balmore Road, Glasgow, G22 6LJ.* (041-336 8147)

McAULEY, John Lalor. Univ of Syd BA 35. ACT ThL 37. **d** 37 **p** 38 Bath. C of Mudgee 37-39; M of Bro of Good Shepherd Dubbo 39-43; R of Geurie 43-47; Kandos 47-50; Prin of St Nich Boys' Home Glenroy 50-56; Min of Glenroy 56-61; Chap AMF 56-78; I of Sunshine 61-68; Mornington 68-78; Perm to Offic Dio Melb from 78. *20 Martin Street, Beaumaris, Vic, Australia 3193.* (99-3807)

McAULEY, Ross Leslie Stewart. b 44. M SSF 69-77; **d** 77 **p** 78 Wang. C of H Trin Cathl Wang 77-81; Chap Bro of St Laur Melb from 81. *67 Brunswick Street, Fitzroy, Vic, Australia 3065.*

McAULEY, Thomas Andrew. b 26. Bps' Coll Cheshunt. **d** 56 **p** 57 Connor. C of St Phil Belf 56-59; St Nich Belf 59-61; Maralin 61-64; I of Annahilt 64-70; Carrowdore and Millisle Dio Down from 70; Chap HM Borstal Millisle from 70. *40 Woburn Road, Millisle, Newtownards, Co Down, BT22 2HY, N Ireland.* (Millisle 861226)

McAULEY, Ven William Yaneh. St Aug Th Coll Accra, 49. **d** 52 **p** 54 Gambia. P Dio Gambia from 52; Can of St Mary's Cathl Bath Gambia 69-74; Archd of Guinea from 74. *Anglican Mission, Box 105, Conakry, Guinea.*

McAULIFFE, Geoffrey Raymond. b 44. ACT ThL 80. St Barn Coll Belair 77. **d** and **p** 80 River. C of Leeton Dio River from 80. *28 Main Avenue, Yanco, NSW, Australia 2703.* (069 557129)

McAUSLAND, William James. b 36. Edin Th Coll 56. **d** 59 **p** 60 Brech. C of St Mary Magd Dundee Dio Brech 59-64; R 71-79; H Cross Knightswood Glas 64-71; St Marg Lochee Dundee Dio Brech from 79. *19 Ancrum Road, Dundee, Angus, DD2 2JL.* (Dundee 67227)

McAVAN, Gordon William. OBE 62. AKC 41. **d** 41 **p** 42 Ox. C of W Wycombe 41-45; L to Offic Dio Ox 45-47; Chap at H Trin Rose Hill Maur 47-52; Warden of St Andr Sch Rose Hill Maur 47-63; L to Offic Dio Maur 52-63; Hon Can of Maur 60-63; Dom Chap to Bp of Maur 60-63; V of Cantley 63-79. *St Cecilia's Clergy House, Chaucer Close, Sheffield, S5 9QE.*

McAVOY, George Brian. b 41. MBE 78. Trin Coll Dub BA 61, MA 72. **d** 63 **p** 65 Cork. C of St Luke w St Ann Shandon Cork 63-66; I of Timoleague U 66-68; Chap RAF from 68. *c/o Ministry of Defence, Adastral House, Theobalds Road, WC1X 8RU.*

McBAY, Canon Walter Ernest. b 17. St Aid Coll 47. **d** 49 **p** 50 Worc. C of St Nich w St Pet Droitwich 49-51; Oleh 51-59; C-in-c of Shrawley 59-62; Miss Dio Ow 62-67; Can of Ow 66-67; Can (Emer) from 68; R of The Shelsleys 67-72; Thorpe-by-Newark 72-77; V of Farndon 72-77; Swinefleet 77-81. *c/o Swinefleet Vicarage, Goole, N Humb.* (Reedness 326)

MACBETH, Canon Colin Rowland. b 10. Late Exhib of Keble Coll Ox BA (2nd cl Mod Hist) 31, MA 35. Westcott Ho Cam 35. **d** 36 **p** 37 Win. C of Basingstoke 36-41; Chap RNVR 41-46; V of S Stoneham w Swaythling 46-53; Brockenhurst 53-69; RD of Lyndhurst 60-69; Hon Can of Win 67-75; Can (Emer) from 75; R of Weeke 69-75; RD of Win 71-73; Surr 73-75. *2 Brookside Cottages, Brighstone, IW.*

McBRIDE, Clive Sidney. **d** 58 **p** 59 Capetn. C of Good Shepherd Maitland 58-68; P-in-c of Factreton 68-80; Hosp Chap Dio Capetn from 80. *Mont Vue, Avenue Road, Mowbray 7700, CP, S Africa.*

McCABE, Alan. b 37. Univ of Lon BSc (Eng) 61. Ridley Hall Cam 61. **d** 63 **p** 64 Roch. C of Bromley 63-67; Succr and PV of Roch Cathl 67-70; V of H Trin Bromley Common 70-77; Westerham Dio Roch from 77; M Gen Syn 77-80. *Vicarage, Westerham, Kent, TN16 1TJ.* (Westerham 63127)

McCABE, Canon John Trevor. b 33. RD 78. Univ of Nottm BA (Econ & Soc Hist) 55. St Cath S Ox Dipl Th 59. Wycl Hall Ox 57. **d** 59 **p** 60 Ex. C of Em Plymouth 59-63; C-in-c of St Steph Ex 63-66; Chap RNR from 63; Chap Ex Sch 64-66; V of Capel 66-71; V of Scilly Is 71-74; Team R 74-81; Can Res of Bris Cathl from 81; Bp's Adv on Soc Responsibility from 81. *7 Mortimer Road, Clifton, Bristol, BS8 4EX.* (Bris 36312)

McCABE, Terence John. b 46. Sarum Wells Th Coll 71. **d** 74 Bp Daly for Cov **p** 75 Cov. C of St Nich Radford Cov 74-77; P-in-c of St Paul w St Barn Bris 77-80; Team V of St Aid E Bristol Dio Bris from 80. *St Aidan's Vicarage, Jockey Lane, St George, Bristol, BS5 8NZ.* (Bris 677812)

McCABE, William Alexander Beck. b 27. Qu Univ Belf BA 50, PhD 65. **d** and **p** 74 Sheff. Sec Sheff Coun of Chs from 71; Hon C of H Trin Millhouses Sheff 74-80; Team V of Sheff Manor Dio Sheff from 80. *45 Knowle Lane, Sheffield, S11 9SL.*

McCALL, Richmond James. Ridley Coll Melb ACT ThL 47. **d** 48 **p** 49 Melb. C of St Jas Ivanhoe 48-50; Min of Romsey w Lancefield 50-54; Greensborough w Diamond Creek 54-57; Oakleigh (Em w St Gabr) 57-63; Dir of C of E Boys' S and M Dept of Chr Educn Dio Melb 63-71; I of St John Bentleigh 71-81; St Steph Belmont Dio Melb from 81. *42 Regent Street, Belmont, Vic, Australia 3216.*

McCALL, William David Hair. St Mich Th Coll Crafers ACT ThL 64. **d** 63 **p** 64 Wang for River. C of Griffith 63-64; Broken Hill 64-67; P-in-c of Barellan 67-73; R of Corowa 73-78; Goodwood Dio Adel from 78. *34 Angus Street, Goodwood, S Australia 5034.* (272 9495)

McCALLA, Robert Ian. b 31. K Coll Lon and Warm AKC 55. **d** 56 **p** 57 Carl. C of St Jo Evang Barrow-F 56-58; Penrith 58-61; R of St Clem Greenheys Man 61-64; V of St Mark (w Ch Ch from 66) Glodwick Oldham 64-71; R of Distington 71-73; Howe Bridge Dio Man from 73. *Howe Bridge Vicarage, Atherton, Manchester, M29 0PH.* (Atherton 883359)

McCALLION, David John. b 16. McMaster Univ Hamilton Ont BA 42, MA 47. Brown Univ RI USA PhD 50. **d** 78 Bp Clarke for Niag **p** 79 Niag. C of Ch Ch Flamborough 78-79; Grace Ch Waterdown Dio Niag from 80. *722 Hiawatha Boulevard, Ancaster, Ont, Canada, L9G 3A7.* (416-648 1459)

McCALLUM, Edward Bruce. b 48. Carleton Univ BComm 69. Wycl Coll Tor 69. **d** and **p** 72 Tor. I of N Essa 72-77; Lakefield Dio Tor from 78. *Box 217, Lakefield, Ont, Canada.* (705-652 3196)

MacCALLUM, Howard Ross. b 48. Univ of Queensld BA 79. St Jo Coll Morpeth 76. **d** 77 **p** 78 Graft. C of Murwillumbah Dio Graft from 77. *11 Riverview Street, Murwillumbah, NSW, Australia 2484.*

McCALLUM, Canon Joseph Cyril. b 02. Keble Coll Ox BA 25, MA 30. Ripon Hall Ox. **d** 27 **p** 28 Birm. C of St Andr Bordesley 27-30; PC of St Hilda Warley Woods 30-59; Chap RNVR 43-46; V of Boldmere 59-74; Hon Can of Birm 65-74; Can (Emer) from 74. *93 Wylde Green Road, Sutton Coldfield, Warws.*

MacCALLUM, Norman Donald. b 47. Univ of Edin LTh 70. **d** 71 **p** 72 Edin. Team V of Livingston Dio Edin from 71. *St Columba's Manse, Sydney Street, Craigshill, Livingston, EH54 5HH.* (Livingston 32123)

McCALMAN, Peter Hugh. Univ of Birm BSc 53. Em Coll Sask LTh 64. **d** and **p** 64 Calg. R of Stettler 64-69; St Laur Calg 69-72; I of Salt Spring I 72-79; St Geo Mart Vic Dio BC from 79. *3909 St George's Lane, Victoria, BC, Canada.*

McCALMAN, Peter Hugh. Univ of Birm BSc 53. Em Coll Sask LTh 64. **d** and **p** 64 Calg. R of Stettler 64-69; St Laur Calg 69-72; I of Salt Spring I Dio BC from 72. *PO Box 214, Ganges, BC, Canada.*

McCAMLEY, Gregor Alexander. b 42. Trin Coll Dub BA 64, Div Test 65, MA 67. **d** 65 **p** 66 Down. C of Holywood 65-68; Bangor 68-72; I of St Gall Carnalea 72-80; St Columba Knock Belf Dio Down from 80. *Rectory, King's Road, Belfast, BT5 6JG.* (Belf 653214)

McCAMMON, John Taylor. b 42. QUB BSc 65. BD (Lon) 70. Clifton Th Coll Bris 67. **d** 71 **p** 72 down. C of Shankill, Lurgan 71-75; I of Kilkeel Dio Drom from 75. *Rectory, Manse Road, Kilkeel, Co Down, N Ireland.* (Kilkeel 62300)

McCANDLESS, Archibald Wylie. AKC 34. **d** 34 **p** 35 S'wark. C of St Thos Telford Pk 34-37; Melton Mowbray 37-39; R of Burrough-on-the-Hill 39-47; Chap RAF 43-46; V of Billesdon w Rolleston and Goadby 47-55; R of Glenfield 55-74; L to Offic Dio Leic from 74. *2 Windrush Drive, Oadby, Leicester.* (Leic 716658)

McCANDLESS, John Hamilton Moore. b 24. TCD 61. **d** 63 **p** 64 Connor. C of St Matt Shankill Belf 63-66; I of Termonmaguirke 66-69; C of Jordanstown 69-70; I of Ballinderry 70-74. *19 Steeple Green, Antrim, N Ireland.*

McCANN, David Terence. b 44. Univ of Dur BA 67, Dipl Th 69. St Chad's Coll Dur 63. **d** 69 Hulme for Man **p** 70 Man. C of Tonge Moor 69-73; Failsworth 73-76; C-in-c of St Alb Cheetwood City and Dio Man from 76. *21 Landfall Walk, Cheetham, Manchester, M8 8FB.* (061-792 2351)

✠ **McCANN, Most Rev James.** b 1897. QUB BA 19, DD (*jure dig*) 45, Hon LLD 66. TCD Eccles Hist Pri 18, Carson Pri 19, Div Test and President's Pri 20, BA (Resp) 26, MA and Elrington Th Pri (1st) 30, BD 35, PhD 44. **d** 20 **p** 21 Down. C of Ballymena 20-22; Ballyclare 22-24; Cavan Derryheen and Denn 24-28; Oldcastle U 28-30; I of Donaghpatrick w Kilshine 30-36; C-in-c of Colpe 36-40; R of St Mary Drogheda w Duleek 36-45; Surr 36-45; Exam Chap to Bp of Meath 43-45; Preb of Tipper in St Patr Cathl Dub 44-45; Cons Ld Bp of Meath in Arm Cathl 24 Aug 45 by Abp of Arm; Bps of Clogh; Derry; Down; and Connor; Select Pr 49 and 53; Trld to Arm 59; Res 69. *Belgravia Hotel, Belfast 9, N Ireland.*

McCANN, Roland Neil. b 39. Serampore Coll BD 73. Bp's Coll Calc Dipl Th 70. **d** 70 **p** 73 Calc. C of St Jas Calc 70-73; V of St Thos Calc 73-74; C of St Bart Earley 74-77; P-in-c of Ch Ch Miss Harlington Dio Lon from 77. *192 Waltham Avenue, Harlington, Middx.* (01-573 0112)

McCANN, Tom Saxon. b 22. St Aid Coll 57. **d** 59 **p** 60 Ches. C of Norbury Ches 59-62; V of Gee Cross 62-76; Surr from 67; R of Davenham Dio Ches from 76. *Davenham Rectory, Northwich, Chesh.* (Northwich 2450)

✠ **McCAPPIN, Right Rev William John.** b 19. Late Exhib of Trin Coll Dub BA (1st cl Or Lang Mod) 40, Hebr Pri 37, 38, and 39, Jellett Pri (2nd) 38, Wall Bibl Scho 39, Downes Pri Warren Pri and Div Test (1st cl) 41, Th Exhib 42, MA and BD 48. **d** 42 **p** 43 Arm. C of St Mark Arm 42-44; CF (EC) 44-47; C-in-c of Ardoyne 47-51; I of Jordanstown 51-59; Exam Chap to Bp of Connor 55-79; Chap Stranmillis Tr Coll Belf 56-68; R of St Bart Belf 59-71; Min Can of St Anne Cathl Belf 65-69; Archd of Connor 69-79; R of Carnmoney 76-81; Can of St Anne's Cathl Belf 79-81; Cons Ld Bp of Connor in St Anne's Cathl Belfast 30 Nov 81 by Abp of Arm; Bps of Meath, Tuam, Down, Cashel, Clogh, and Kilm; and Bps Butler, Heavener, Quin and West. *Bishop's House, 22 Deramore Park, Belfast 9, N Ireland.* (668442)

McCARRAHER, Seymour. b 26. Magd Coll Cam BA 48, MA 55. St Steph Ho Ox. **d** 55 Dur **p** 56 Jarrow for Dur. C of St Columba Southwick 55-59; Chap RN 59-75; C of Christchurch 75-81; V of Darton Dio Wakef from 81. *33 Roman Road, Darton, Barnsley, S Yorks, S75 5DE.* (Barnsley 384596)

McCARTER, Colin Heyes. b 13. Ch Coll Cam BA 34, MA 41. Lich Th Coll 37. **d** 39 **p** 40 Lich. C of Gnosall w Knightley 39-41; Chap RNVR 41-47; R of Hinstock 47-53; V of Baschurch 53-61; R of Woolstone w Oxenton and Gotherington 61-71; Broadwell w Evenlode 71-78; Oddington and Adlestrop 77-78; P-in-c of Sherborne, Windrush, The Barringtons & Aldsworth Dio Glouc from 80. *Vicarage, Windrush, Burford, Oxon.* (Windrush 276)

McCARTHY, Ernest Alfred. Em Th Coll Sktn 25. **d** 29 Athab **p** 30 Lon for Col Bp. C of Peace River 29-30; Miss at Terrace 30-31; R of Atlin 31-32; C of St Luke New Kentish Town 32-34; Chap HM Pris Wakef 34-37; H Trin Windsor 38-44; V of E Ruston 44-71; Perm to Offic Dio Nor from 71. *Anton House, St John's Road, Stalham, Norwich, NOR 34Z.*

McCARTHY, John Francis. b 38. Trin Coll Dub BA (2nd cl Mod) 61, MA 72. **d** 62 **p** 63 Down. C of Seapatrick 62-66; Seagoe 66-71; I of Moira 71-75; Heynestown Dio Arm from 75; R of Dundalk Dio Arm from 75. *Rectory, Haggardstown, Dundalk, Co Louth, Irish Republic.* (Dundalk 32402)

McCARTHY, Joseph William. Montr Dioc Th Coll. **d** and **p** 60 Montr. C of Cartierville and of Roxboro 61-63; Supt Old Brewery Miss Dio Montr from 63. *34 Davis Street, St Bruno, PQ, Canada.* (514-653 9183)

McCARTHY, Legh Beauchamp. b 08. Ch Ch Ox BA 29, MA 35. Wells Th Coll 32. **d** 33 **p** 34 Ex. C of Stoke Damerel 33-37; St Mary Banbury 37-39; CF (EC) 39-45; V of Tollesbury 45-50; L Clacton 50-61; Chap Clacton and Distr Hosp 50-61; V of Padbury w Adstock 61-65; R of Boxford 65-74. *12 Kennedy Close, Wash Common, Newbury, Berks.*

McCARTHY, Michael Scott. b 51. Univ of Guelph Ont BA 74. Wycl Coll Tor MDiv 78. **d** and **p** 78 Alg. C of St Paul Thunder Bay 78-81; I of Nipigon Dio Alg from 81. *Box 220, Nipigon, Ont, Canada.*

MacCARTHY, Robert Brian. b 40. TCD BA 63, MA 66. Univ Coll Cork MA 65. St Cross Coll Ox MA (by incorp) 81. Ripon Coll Cudd 77. **d** 79 Leigh **p** 80 Lism. C of Carlow Urglin & Staplestown 79-81; Libr Pusey Ho Ox from 81; Fell St Cross Coll Ox from 81; Publ Pr Dio Ox from 81; L to Offic Dios Cash, Waterf & Lism from 81. *Pusey House, Oxford, OX1 3LZ.*

McCARTHY, Terence Arthur. b 46. Kelham Th Coll 66. **d** 70 **p** 71 Chelmsf. C of Gt Burstead 70-74; Wickford 74-76; Team V of E Runcorn w Halton 76-80; V of H Trin Runcorn Dio Ches from 80. *Holy Trinity Vicarage, Grange Park Avenue, Runcorn, Chesh, WA7 5UT.* (Runcorn 72299)

McCARTNEY, Andrew. ACT ThL 42. **d** 42 **p** 43 Bath. Miss Bro of Good Shepherd 42-50; R of Kandos 50-54; Carcoar 54-58; Kandos 58-60; V of Inala 60-61; R of Peak Hill 61-67; V of Mitchell 67-71; St Mary Moorooka Brisb 71-73; R of Warren Dio Bath from 73. *Box 83, Warren, NSW, Australia 2824.* (068-4781 62)

McCARTNEY, Hugh Watt. St Mich Coll Crafers ThL 62. **d** 61 **p** 62 Melb. C of Ch Ch Brunswick 61-62; Sunshine 62-64; P-in-c of All SS w Sebastapol Bal 64; V 64-69; R of Koroit 69-71; P-in-c of Albert Pk 71-78; I of Mitcham Dio Melb from 78. *18 Edwards Street, Mitcham, Vic, Australia 3132.*

MacCARTY, Paul Andrew. b 34. Sarum Wells Th Coll 73. **d** 75 **p** 76 Southn for Win. C of St Andr Boscombe Bournemouth Dio Win from 75. *3 Douglas Avenue, Christchurch, Dorset, BH23 1JT.* (Christchurch 3807)

McCAUGHEY, Canon Robert Morley. Clifton Th Coll 33. **d** 35 **p** 36 Newc T. C of Walker 35-38; Ponteland 38-41; Benwell 41-43; V of St Luke Wallsend 43-52; Berwick-on-Tweed 52-61; RD of Norham 58-61; Proc Conv Newc T 60; V of Wisbech 61-74; Surr 61-47; RD of Wisbech 62-72; Hon Can of Ely 72-74; Can (Emer) from 74; L to Offic Dio Derry and Raphoe from 76. *Ballinahone House, Knockloughrim, Magherafelt, Co Londonderry, N Ireland.*

McCAULEY, Gary Francis. b 40. Hur Coll Lon Ont BA 63. Gen Th Sem NY STB 66. **d** 66 Moos **p** 67 NY for Moos. In Amer Ch 66-67; R of St Jas Moncton 71-79; Exam Chap to Bp of Fred 77-79; on leave. *600 Yale Avenue, Riverview, NB, Canada.*

McCAUSLAND, John George Alban Patrick. Bp's Univ Lennox BA 32, MA 37. **d** 31 **p** 32 Alg. C of St Bart Tor 33-34; I of White River 34-37; Capreol 37-40; M SSJE Bracebridge Dio Alg from 40; I of Gore Bay Dio Alg from 75. *Box 100, Gore Bay, Ont, Canada.*

McCAY, Alexander Wilson Michael. b 16. Keble Coll Ox BA 41, MA 45. Cudd Coll 41. **d** 43 **p** 44 Mon. C of St Mary Mon 43-48; Asst Warden of St John's Hostel Capetn 48-55; C of Somerset W 55-58; Chap Peterho Sch Rhod 58-61; Asst Chap 64-65; Chap Eagle Sch Umtali 61-63; Seaford Court Sch Malvern 66-67; L to Offic Dio Chich 67-69; Dio Worc

69-78; Chap St Mich Sch Barnstaple 78-81; P-in-c of St Pet Peebles Dio Edin from 81. *36 Wemyss Place, Peebles, EH45 8JT.* (0721 20571)

McCLATCHEY, Alfred Henry Bailey. b 20. Late Exhib of BNC Ox, Squire Scho 39, BA and MA 48. **d** 67 **p** 68 S'wark. C of St Mary Lambeth 67-69; Dom Chap to Bp of Dur 69-74; Bp of worc 74-79; V of Escomb 69-74; Witton Pk 69-74; R of Hartlebury w Bp's Wood Dio Worc from 74; Dir of Post Ordin Tr Dio Worc 74-79. *Rectory, Hartlebury, Kidderminster, Worcs, DY11 7TB.* (Hartlebury 250292)

McCLATCHIE, Prec Donald William. b 40. Trin Coll Dub BA 65, Div Test and Downes Pri for Liturgy and Comp 66. **d** 66 **p** 67 Dub. C of Clontarf 66-68; Cler V of Ch Ch Cathl Dub 68-71 and 75-80; Prec from 80; C-in-c of St Andr Dub 71-75. *Marine Lodge, Seafield Road, Killiney, Co Dublin, Irish Republic.*

McCLAUGHRY, Victor Thomas. b 13. Trin Coll Dub BA (2nd cl Ment and Mor Sc Mod) 34. MA 46. **d** 36 **p** 37 Cork. C Pr and Libr of St Fin Barre's Cathl Cork 36-41; C of Taney 41-45; S'wark Cathl and Res Chap of Guy's Hosp 45-48; Res Chap of Holloway Sanat Virginia Water 48-54; V of Gaydon w Chadshunt 54-56; Chap of Mickleover Hosp 56-60; PC of St Jo Evang Derby 60-63; Chap Dorothy Kerin Home of Healing Burrswood 63-66; V of Peasmarsh 66-70; E Preston w Kingston 70-79. *Collingwood, 2 West Avenue, Worthing, Sussex, BN11 5LY.* (Worthing 47001)

McCLELLAN, Bruce. b 44. Selw Coll Cam BA 66, MA 70. St Steph Ho Ox 66. **d** 68 Pet **p** 69 Bp Graham-Campbell for Pet. C of Uppingham 68-72; P-in-c of Gt w L Harrowden and Orlingbury 72-76; V of Hardingstone (w Horton and Piddington from 81) Dio Pet from 76; P-in-c of Horton w Piddington 79-81. *Hardingstone Vicarage, Northampton, NN4 0BY.* (Northampton 61811)

McCLELLAND, Canon William Hamilton Horace. Trin Coll Dub BA (2nd cl Ment and Mor Sc Mod 41) Div Test 42, MA 51. MBE (Mil) 61. **d** 43 **p** 44 Dub. C of Ch Ch Leeson Pk Dub 43-47; St Ann Dub 47-51; CF 51-67; Chap Shawnigan Lake Sch Dio BC from 67; Hon Can of BC from 78. *Shawnigan Lake School, Vancouver Island, BC, Canada.* (604-743 5516)

MACCLESFIELD, Archdeacon of. *See* Simpson, Ven Rennie.

McCLINTOCK, John DeWitt. Wycl Coll Tor. **d** 60 **p** 61 Calg. I of Vulcan 60-63; CF 63-67; Chap Kingston Hosp 67-70; R of St Paul Brockville 70-80; St Helen Vanc Dio New Westmr from 80. *4521 West 8th Avenue, Vancouver, BC, Canada.*

McCLINTOCK, Canon John (Jon) Herbert Tait. b 13. Late Exhib of Keble Coll Ox BA 35. Westcott Ho Cam 36. **d** 37 **p** 38 Carl. C of St Jas Barrow-F 37-43; Youth Org Dio Carl 43-46; LPr Dio Carl 43-46; V of St Barn Carl 46-52; P-in-c of St Andr and St Geo Rosyth 52-55; St Pet Inverkeithing 53-55; V of Fleetwood 55-67; Cross Canonby 67-78; Hon Can of Carl Cathl 73-78; Can (Emer) from 78. *144 Newtown Road, Carlisle, Cumb.*

McCLOGHRY, James. b 22. St Cath S Ox BA 49, MA 52. Qu Coll Birm 60. **d** 61 **p** 62 Pet. C of Marston w Warkworth 61-64; R of E Farndon 64-67; R of Marston Trussell 64-67; Oxenden w Marston Trussell and E Farndon Dio Pet from 67. *Oxenden Rectory, Market Harborough, Leics.* (Market Harborough 2052)

McCLOUGHLIN, Joshua. b 27. Div Hostel Dub 69. **d** 70 **p** 71 Clogh. C of Magheraculmoney 70-72; Cloughfern 73-77; R of Dunfanaghy 77-79; Drumkeeran, Muckross and Templecarne Dio Clogh from 79. *c/o Rectory, Kesh, Co Fermanagh, N Ireland.* (Kesh 31210)

McCLURE, David Joseph. b 07. Trin Coll Dub BA and Div Test 29, MA 41. **d** 30 **p** 31 Derry. C of Templemore (Par Ch Derry Cathl) 30-36; I of Castledawson 36-37; C of St Thos Telford Pk Streatham 38-41; R of Welbourn 41-49; Claypole 49-53; Perm of Offic Dio B & W 54-56; PC of Henton 56-60; PC of Theale 57-60; V of Braunston w Brooke 60-67; P-in-c of Gt w L Oakley 68-70; L to Offic Dio Pet from 70. *The Spinney, Stretton, Oakham, Leics.* (Castle Bytham 367)

McCLURE, Canon Hugh Norman. b 14. TCD BA (1st cl Mod and Gold Medal) and Ment and Mor Sc Research Pri 35, Div Test 37, MA 60. **d** 37 **p** 38 Down. C of St Anne's Cathl Belf 37-46; Dean's V 37-39; V Cho 39-46; I of Drummaul 46-56; Chap Windsor Sch Hamm BAOR 56-60 and 62-67; Chap Br Embassy Warsaw 59-60; Dir of Relig Stud Wymondham Coll 61-62; R of Wolverton w Ewhurst and Hannington 67-79; RD of Basingstoke 73-78; Hon Can of Win 77-79; Can (Emer) from 79. *Ardagh House, Baltimore, Co Cork, Irish Republic.* (Baltimore 33)

McCLURE, James. b 03. Edin Th Coll 46. **d** 47 **p** 48 Glas. C of St John Dumfries 47-53; R of Ch of Good Shepherd Hillington Glas 53-73. *32 Cresswell Avenue, Dumfries, DG1 2EZ.*

McCLURE, Roy. b 30. Div Hostel Dub 68. **d** 70 **p** 71 Clogh. C of Monaghan 70-72; St Matt Shankill Belf 72-76; Asst Chap HM Pris Liv 76-77; Chap HM Pris Preston from 77. *11 Chapman Road, Fulwood, Preston, PR2 4NX.* (Preston 774360)

McCLURE, Timothy Elston. b 46. St Jo Coll Dur BA 68. Ridley Hall Cam 68. **d** 70 **p** 71 Wakef. C of Kirkheaton 70-73; Chorlton-on-Medlock 74-79; Chap Man Poly Dio Man from 74; Team R of Whitworth City and Dio Man from 79. *27 Ladybarn Road, Fallowfield, Manchester, M14 6WN.* (061-224 4999)

McCOLL, Edmund Neil. McGill Univ. **d** 49 Montr for Athab **p** 50 Athab. C-in-c of North Star 49-52. I of Poltimore 52-56; Quyon 56-73; Vankleek Hill 73-81. *Box 542, Maxville, Ont, Canada.*

McCOLLIM, Keith Cameron. b 38. Canberra Coll of Min ACT ThL 76. **d** and **p** C & Goulb. P-in-c of Kameruka 77-80; R of Murrumburrah Dio C & Goulb from 80. *St Paul's Rectory, Albury Street, Murrumburrah, NSW, Australia 2587.*

McCOLLIN-MOORE, Eustace St Orban. b 45. St Jo Coll Winnipeg MDiv 79. **d** 79 **p** 80 Rupld. C of St Chad Winnipeg Dio Rupld from 79. *c/o 3390 Portage Avenue, Winnipeg, Manit, Canada, R3K 0Z3.*

McCOLLOUGH, John Keith. b 45. K Coll Lon and Warm AKC 66. **d** 68 Kens for Lon **p** 69 Lon. C of St Aug Kilburn 68-71; St Alb Mart w St Pet Holborn 71-74; St Mary Virg (in c of H Spirit) Kenton 74-80; V of St Hugh Eyres Monsell City and Dio Leic from 80. *St Hugh's Vicarage, Pasley Road, Eyres Monsell, Leicester, LE2 9BU.* (Leic 782954)

McCOLLUM, Graham Ronald. Trin Coll Dub BA (2nd cl Mod) 35, Div Test 36, MA 52. **d** 36 Warrington for Liv **p** 37 Liv. C of Maghull 36-39; Clontarf 39-41; Asst Chap Miss to Seamen Belf 41-43; Capetn 43-47; E Lon Grahmstn 47-72; R of Verulam 72-81. *4 Ocean View Road, Winklespruit, Natal, S Africa.*

McCOLLUM, Ven John Turquand. **d** 54 **p** 55 Arctic. Miss at Fort Smith 54-63; I of Beaver Lodge 63-70; Miss Hay River Episc Distr Mack 70-75; Dio Arctic from 75; Archd of Mack from 75. *Box 1023, Hay River, NWT, via Edmonton, Canada.*

McCOLLUM, Robert George. b 20. Trin Coll Dub BA 43, MA 60. **d** 44 **p** 45 Dub. C of Santry w Glasnevin 44-48; Taney 48-54; I of Donabate w Lusk 54-62; Clontarf Dio Dub from 62; RD of Finglas from 77. *Rectory, Seafield Road, Clontarf, Dublin, Irish Republic.* (Dublin 331181)

McCOMB, Samuel. b 33. Div Hostel Dub 70. **d** 71 **p** 72 Connor. C of St Mich Belf 71-74; Ch Ch Lisburn 74-79; I of Ballinderry Dio Connor from 79. *Rectory, Ballinderry, Co Antrim, N Ireland.* (Aghalee 651310)

McCOMBE, George Albert Stephen. Trin Coll Dub BA 50. **d** 51 **p** 52 Arm. C of Drumcree 51-54; St John Leytonstone 54-57; C-in-c of St Bride Liv 58-63; Chap R Masonic Sch Bushey 63-64; C of Prittlewell Essex 64-65; R of Maidstone-Paynton 66-70; Kingsclear Dio Fred from 70; New Maryland Dio Fred from 70. *St Peter's Rectory, RR6, Fredericton, NB, Canada.*

McCOMBE, Roger William. b 43. Univ of Tor BA 65. Wycl Coll Tor BTh 70. **d** 71 **p** 74 Alg. P Dio Alg 71-75; Dio Hur from 79. *6 Glenwood Road, Ingersoll, Ont, Canada.*

McCONCHIE, Stewart Donald. NZ Bd of Th Stud LTh (1st cl) 57. St Jo Coll Auckld 53. **d** 55 **p** 56 Auckld. C of Ellerslie 55-58; V of Paparoa 58-62; St Thos Wel 62-70; Wel S 70-72; Hon C of St Mark City and Dio Wel from 72. *17 Tamar Street, Island Bay, Wellington, NZ.*

McCONNELL, Brian Roy. b 46. St Paul's Coll Grahmstn Dipl Th 71. **d** 71 **p** 72 Capetn. C of Plumstead 71-74; St Geo Cathl Capetn 74-77; St Marg Prestwich 77-79; R of H Redeemer Sea Point Dio Capetn from 79. *82 Kloof Road, Sea Point 8001, CP, S Africa.* (44-1846)

McCONNELL, Dennis Malcolm. K Coll Lon and Warm BD and AKC 60. **d** 61 **p** 62 Cant. C of Maidstone 61-63; St Martin Rosebank Johann 63-64; Klerksdorp w Stilfontein 64-67; R of Roodepoort 67-72; Vanderbijl Pk 73-78; Nigel 78-80; L to Offic Dio Pret frm 81. *Box 258, Warmbaths, Transvaal, S Africa.*

McCONNELL, James Edward. ACT ThL 66. **d** 66 **p** 69 Brisb. Hon C of St Matt Holland Pk Brisb 66-78. *13 Avesnes Street, Holland Park, Queensland, Australia 4121.* (397 4512)

McCONNELL, James Frederick. St Paul's Coll Grahmstn. **d** 65 **p** 66 Bloemf. C of Kroonstad 65-66; Welkom 66-69; R of Stilfontein 70-75; Krugersdorp Dio Johann from 73. *Box 505, Krugersdorp, Transvaal, S Africa.* (011-660 3677)

McCONNELL, Philip. b 08. Keble Coll Ox BA 29, MA 33. Cudd Coll 30. **d** 31 **p** 32 Glouc. C of St Steph Glouc 31-34; C-in-c of St Osw Coney Hill 34-36; PC 36-45; V of Clearwell 45-52; PC of slad w Uplands 52-67; V of Maisemore 67-73; Perm to Offic Dio Ex from 74. *5 Avondale Road, Exmouth, Devon, EX8 2NQ.*

McCONNELL, Richard LeRoy. b 53. St Thos Univ Fred BA 75, MA 77. Trin Coll Tor MDiv 79. **d** 79 **p** 80 Fred. C of St Clem St John Dio Fred from 79. *50 Alward Street, Saint John, NB, Canada, E2K 2K2.*

McCORD, Robert Anthony Morgan. Laurentian Univ Ont BA 72. **d** 74 Alg. C of Sault Ste Marie Cathl Alg 75-77; I of Onaping 77-80; St Geo Guelph Dio Niag from 81. *99 Woolwich Street, Guelph, Ont, Canada.* (519-836 2254)

McCORMACK, Colin. b 47. Qu Univ Belf BSc 70. Univ of Nottm BA (Th) 77. St Jo Coll Nottm 75. **d** 78 Penrith for Carl **p** 79 Carl. C of St Jo Evang City and Dio Carl from 78. *68 Greystone Road, Carlisle, Cumbria, CA1 2DG.* (Carlisle 20893)

McCORMACK, David Eugene. b 34. Wells Th Coll 66. **d** 68 Bp McKie for Cov **p** 69 Cov. C of Lillington 68-71; The Lickey (in c of St Cath Blackwell) 71-75; V of Highter's Heath Dio Birm from 75. *Immanuel Vicarage, Pickenham Road, Hollywood, Birmingham.* (021-430 7578)

McCORMACK, Eustace Gilbert Geoffrey Modukpe. Fourah Bay Coll. **d** 65 **p** 67 Sier L. P Dio Sier L. *c/o Box 537, Freetown, Sierra Leone, W Africa.*

McCORMACK, Kevan Sean. b 50. Chich Th Coll 77. **d** 80 **p** 81 Heref. C of Ross-on-Wye Dio Heref from 80. *The Little House, Sussex Avenue, Ross-on-Wye, Herefs, HR9 5AJ.*

McCOULL, Denis Cecil. b 18. Angl Th Coll Vanc LTh 59. **d** 58 **p** 59 New Westmr. C of St Shaughnessy Vanc 58-61; Ceres Capetn 61-64; R of Elgin CP 64-71; Broughton-in-Airedale Bradf 72-77; Broughton w Marton & Thornton Dio Bradf from 77. *Broughton Rectory, Skipton, Yorks, BD23 3AN.* (Earby 2332)

McCOULOUGH, Thomas Alexander. b 32. K Coll Lon and Warm AKC 59. **d** 60 **p** 61 Dur. C of St Mich AA Norton Dur 60-63; USPG Miss Dio Chota N 63-67; C-in-c of St Jas Derby 67-72; Industr Chap Teesside Miss Dio York from 72. *109 Oxford Road, Middlesbrough, Cleve.* (0642 819499)

McCOY, Michael John. b 53. Rhodes Univ Grahmstn BA 74. Univ of Nottm BA 78. St Paul's Coll Grahmstn 79. **d** 79 **p** 80 Grahmstn. C of H Trin K Wm's Tn Dio Grahmstn from 79. *PO Box 256, King William's Town 5600, CP, S Africa.*

McCOY, Richard John. b 30. TCD BA (2nd cl Mod Ment and Mor Sc) 51, BD 56, MA 58, **d** 53 **p** 54 Connor. C of St Luke Belfast 53-56; Bangor Abbey 56-58; Chap of Ripon Hall Ox and L to Offic Dio Ox 58-60; PC of Hadfield 60-63; Exam Chap to Bp of Derby 60-63; I of Clonsast w Rathangan 63-67; Asst Master Portora R Sch Enniskillen 67-70; I of Dromore 70-72; Asst Master Bp's Sch Heref 72-77; Worc Girls Gr Sch from 77; L to Offic Dio Worc from 77. *20 Perry Mill Road, Peopleton, Pershore, Worcs.* (Worcester 840574)

McCRACKEN, Edward Paul. b 47. **d** 76 **p** 79 Fred. C of Riverview & Hillsborough 76-79; I of St Jas Moncton Dio Fred from 79. *101 Fairview Drive, Moncton, NB, Canada.*

McCREA, Basil Wolfe. b 21. QUB BA 49. Wycl Hall Ox 51. **d** 53 **p** 54 York. C of Hull 53-56; St Mark Dundela 56-59; H Trin w St Paul and St Pet Cork 59-61; R of Tullyaughnish 61-65; Rathkeale 65-68; H Trin Cork 68-72; Carrigaline U Dio Cork from 72. *Rectory, Carrigaline, Cork, Irish Republic.* (021-882224)

McCREADIE, Michael Cameron. b 51. Chich Th Coll 74. **d** 77 Knaresborough for Ripon **p** 78 Ripon. C of St Bart Armley 77-81. *Address temp unknown.*

McCREERY, William Robert Desmond. b 35. Oak Hill Th Coll 59. **d** 62 **p** 63 Down. C of Dundonald 62-66; St Donard Belf 66-69; I of Annalong 69-78; Dom Chap to Bp of Down 73-78; R of Knockbreda Dio Down from 78. *Knockbreda Rectory, Church Road, Belfast, N Ireland, BT8 4AN.* (Belfast 641493)

McCRORY, Peter. b 34. Chich Th Coll 63. **d** 67 Crediton for Ex **p** 68 Ex. C of St Marychurch 67-72; R of Kenn (w Mamhead to 75) 72-78; Publ Pr and Dom Chap to Bp of S'wark 78-81; V of Kew Dio S'wark from 81. *278 Kew Road, Richmond, Surrey.* (01-940 4616)

McCRORY, Walter Edward. b 38. Trin Coll Dub 66. **d** 69 **p** 70 Connor. C of Carrickfergus 69-73; Ballywillan (Portrush) 73-76; I of Armoy w Loughguile Dio Connor from 76. *Rectory, Armoy, Co Antrim, N Ireland.*

McCUAIG, Allan Kenneth. Angl Th Coll BC 66. **d** 67 Calg. I of S Alta 67-68; Blood Reserve 68-76; High River Dio Calg from 76. *Box 702, High River, Alta, Canada.* (652-2021)

McCUBBIN, David. b 29. K Coll Lon and Warm AKC 54. **d** 55 **p** 56 Taunton for B & W. C of Ch Ch Frome 55-57; Glastonbury 57-60; R of Dunoon 60-63; Kirkcaldy 63-70; Wallsend 70-79; St Jo Evang Aber 79-81; St Bride City and Dio Glas from 81; Surr 70-79. *St Bride's Rectory, 25 Queensborough Gardens, Glasgow, GL12 9QP.* (041-334 1401)

McCUE, James Bradley. b 55. Univ of Vanc BA 76. Trin Coll Tor MDiv 79. **d** 79 **p** 80 Bp Stiff for Tor. C of Cathl Ch of St Jas Dio Tor from 79. *65 Church Street, Toronto, Ont, Canada, M5C 2E9.*

McCULLAGH, Mervyn Alexander. b 44. Trin Coll Dub BA BEng 68. Div Hostel Dub 75; Div Test 79. **d** 79 **p** 80 Connor. C of Larne & Inver Dio Connor from 79. *7b Latharna House, Riverdale, Larne, Co Antrim, N Ireland.*

McCULLEY, Arthur. b 03. **d** 43 **p** 44 Chelmsf. C of West Ham 43-46; Org Sec CMJ and Perm to Offic Midl Distr 46-50; C of St Barn Leic 50-52; R of Gt w L Sheepy w Rathcliffe-Culey 52-75; L to Offic Dio Leic 76-81. *Address temp unknown.*

McCULLOCH, Derick William Brookes. b 50. Univ of Edin BD 74. Open Univ BA 80. Edin Th Coll 70. **d** 74 Arg is for Glas **p** 77 Ox. C of St Jo Evang Dumfries 74-75; Hon C of St Mary Boltons Kens 75-76; C of St Mich AA Amersham-on-the-Hill 76-78; Industr Chap Teesside Industr Miss 78-79; V of Leake w Over and Nether Silton and Kepwick Dio York from 79; P-in-c of Cowesby Dio York from 79. *Leake Vicarage, Knayton, Thirsk, N Yorks.*

McCULLOCH, Donald. b 25. Linc Th Coll 50. **d** 52 **p** 53 Ex. C of St Mark Ford Devonport 52-55; St Mary Virg Laira Plymouth 55-57; Wolborough (in C of St Leon) 57-59; C-in-c of Shiremoor Conv Distr 59-66; C of Cockington w Chelston 66-68; V of Whitleigh 68-74; Whipton Dio Ex from 74. *Vicarage, Whipton, Exeter, EX4 8ED.*

McCULLOCH, Geoffrey Kenneth. b 10. OBE (Mil) 57. Lon Coll of Div 62. **d** 64 **p** 65 York. [f Barrister-at-Law] C of Hull 64-67; C-in-c of St Matt Hull 68-71; St Barn Hull 70-71; V of St Matt w St Barn Hull 71-79; Perm to Offic Dio Lon from 79. *5 Roy Road, Northwood, Middx, HA6 1EQ.*

McCULLOCH, Joseph. b 08. Late Scho of Ex Coll Ox 3rd cl Cl Mods 29, BA (2nd cl Th) 31, MA 34. Ripon Hall Ox 31. **d** 31 Warrington for Liv **p** 33 S'wark. C of St Nich Blundellsands 31-32; Lee 32-34; Perm to Offic at St John Smith Sq Westmr 34-35; R of Turweston 35-38; Gt Warley 38-43; CF (EC) 39-43; R of Chatham 43-49; V of St Mary Warw 49-59; R of St Mary-le-Bow Lon 59-79. *c/o Rector's Lodgings, St Mary-le-Bow, Cheapside, EC2V 6AU.* (01-248 5139)

MacCULLOCH, Nigel John Howard. b 03. Edin Th Coll 29. TD 50. **d** 31 **p** 32 Glas. C of H Trin Ayr 31-33; P-in-c of St Fillan Kilmacolm w St Mary Bridge of Weir 33-41; CF (TA) 34-46; CF 46-56; R of Wetherden 56-58; C-in-c of Old Newton 56-58; R of Haughley w Wetherden 58-72. *3 Klondyke Cottages, Tollgate Lane, Bury St Edmunds, Suffolk, IP32 6DB.* (Bury St E 5859)

McCULLOCH, Ven Nigel Simeon. b 42. Selw Coll Cam BA 64, MA 69. Cudd Coll 64. **d** 66 **p** 67 Ches. C of Ellesmere Port 64-70; Chap Ch Ch Coll Cam 70-73; Perm to Offic Dio Liv 70-73; Dir of Th Stud Ch Coll Cam 70-75; Dioc Missr Dio Nor 73-78; R of St Thos w St Edm City and Dio Sarum from 78; Archd of Sarum from 79; Can and Preb of Sarum Cathl from 79. *Rectory, St Thomas' Square, Salisbury, Wilts.* (Salisbury 22537)

McCULLOCH, Robert David. St Jo Coll Morpeth ACT ThL 28. **d** 27 **p** 28 Newc. C of Lambton 27-28; Ch Ch Cathl Newc 28-31; Cessnock 31-32; P-in-c of Bellbird 32-34; S Maitland 34-37; C of St John Newc 37-38; R of Islington 38-42; Chap AIF 42-44; R of Cessnock 50-52; Taree 52-69; Hon Can of Newc 56-69; Perm to Offic Dio Newc from 69. *106 Stewart Avenue, Hamilton, NSW, Australia 2303.*

McCULLOCH, Robert Lewis. b 11. St Cath Coll Cam BA 35, MA 40. Linc Th Coll 35. **d** 37 Linc **p** 38 Grantham for Linc. C of Grantham 37-42 and 47-48; Chap RAF 42-46 and 48-61; Chap Univ of Liv 61-65; Hon Chap to Bp of Liv 61-65; R of Kingsdown w Mappiscombe 65-71; Chap at Tripoli 70-72; C of Worksop 72-74; P-in-c of All S w Ch Ch (and St Mich AA from 75) Radford 74-81. *Address temp unknown.*

McCULLOCH, Robert Lindo. Univ of Sask BA 69. St Pet Coll Ja 53. **d** 56 **p** 57 Ja. C of St Geo Kingston 56-58; R of Port Maria 58-61; Asst P to Bp Suffr of Mandeville 61-63; C of Ascen Montr 63-64; R of St Matt Sktn 64-73; Danville Dio Queb from 73. *Box 578, Danville, PQ, Canada.*

McCULLOUGH, Herbert Alexander. b 10. TCD BA (Resp) and Div Test (2nd cl) 32, MA 50. **d** 33 Malmesbury for Bris **p** 34 Bris. C of St Aldhelm Bedminster 33-35; Newington Surrey 35-37; Asst Chap Miss to Seamen Port of Lond and Publ Pr Dio Chelmsf 37-39; Perm to Offic Dio Roch 39; I of Aughrim w Clontuskert and Kiltormer 39-42; Creach 42-45; Surr 42-45; Chap Mental Hosp Ballinasloe 42-45; Chap Miss to Seamen for Tees Distr 45-51; L to Offic Dio York and Perm to Offic Dio Dur 45-51; Dios Derby and Ches 51-70; Chap Miss to Seamen Port of Man and L to Offic Dio Man 51-70; V of Kirk German 70-77; Surr 70-77. *26 Queens Drive, Peel, IM.*

McCULLOUGH, James. b 07. Wycl Hall Ox 41. **d** 42 **p** 43 Bris. C of St Mich Arch Bris 42-44; St Bart Penn (in C of St Osw) 44-48; V of St Gabr Fullbrook Walsall 48-54; R of Hinstock 54-59; Wrockwardine Wood 59-64; V of Sheriffhales w Woodcote 64-76; L to Offic Dio Lich from 76. *2 The Glebelands, High Ercall, Wellington, Telford, Salop.* (High Ercall 678)

McCULLOUGH, James Ronald. b 29. Acadia Univ NS BA 58, BTh 74. Univ of Winnipeg MDiv 75. **d** and **p** 76 Rupld. C of St Mich AA Winnipeg 76; I of St Geo Transcona 77-79; Fairford Area Dio Rupld from 79. *892 Consol Avenue, Winnipeg, Manit, R2K 1T5, Canada.*

McCULLOUGH, Robert Graham. Univ of NZ BA 57, MA 58. Berkeley Div Sch USA STB (*cum Laude*) 64. Ch Ch Coll. **d** 64 **p** 65 Ch Ch. C of Papanui 64-68; Chap Univ of Auckld and Perm to Offic Dio Auckld 68-75; Prin Ch Ch Coll Ch Ch from 74; Exam Chap to Bp of Ch Ch from 75. *100 Waimairi Road, Christchurch 4, NZ.* (41-891)

McCULLOUGH, Roy. b 46. Linc Th Coll 70. **d** 73 **p** 74 Blackb. C of Ashton-on-Ribble 73-77; Chap Highfield Priory Sch 73-77; V of Rishton Dio Blackb from 77. *Vicarage, Somerset Road, Rishton, Blackburn, BB1 4BP.*

McCULLUM, Canon James Alaxander. Qu Univ Ont BA 59. Wycl Coll Tor LTh 61. **d** 61 Yukon for Tor **p** 61 Tor. C of St Wilfrid Tor 61-62; R of St Paul's Cathl Dawson 62-64; Camp Takhini Whitehorse 64-66; C of Koot Boundary Reg Par 67-72; R of Kelowna 72-78; Hon Can of Koot 75-78; C of Ch Ch Cathl Vanc Dio New Westmr from 78; Can of New Westmr from 81. *690 Burrard Street, Vancouver, BC, Canada.*

McCURRY, James Gordon. Univ of Sask BTh. Coll of Em & St Chad Sktn. **d** 80 **p** 81 Bran. R of Minnedosa w Bethany and Clanwilliam Dio Bran from 80. *Minnedosa, Manit, Canada, R0J 1E0.*

McCURRY, Preb Norman Ernest. b 19. St Edm Hall Ox BA 40, MA 46. Chich Th Coll 40. **d** 46 **p** 47 Derby. C of St Jo Bapt Staveley 46-50; St Aid Leeds 50-52; W Wycombe 52-58; V of St Edw Holbeck 58-63; PC of Armley 63-67; C-in-c of Armley w New Wortley 67-72; V 72-73; R of Stepney Dio Lon from 73; RD of Tower Hamlets from 78; Preb of St Paul's Cathl Lon from 80. *Rectory, White Horse Lane, Stepney, E1 3NE.* (01-790 4120)

McCUTCHEON, William Steven. b 07. Univ of Wales BA 27. Late Scho of King's Coll Cam BA (3rd cl Th Trip pt i) 31, MA 35. St Mich Coll Llan 31. **d** 31 **p** 32 Llan. C of Llanblethian w Cowbridge 31-34; St Mellons w Llanedeyrn (in c of Cyncoed) 34-37; Prec of St Ninian's Cathl Perth 37-40; Min Can and Succr of Ripon Cathl 40-44; V of Kirkby Fleetham 44-59; R of Langton-on-Swale 47-59; Teversal 59-67; V of Kirklington w Hockerton 67-73; C-in-c of Winkburn 67-73; Perm to Offic Dio Southw from 73. *88 Blake Road, West Bridgford, Nottingham.* (Nottm 811886)

McDERMID, Canon Norman George Lloyd Roberts. b 27. St Edm Hall Ox BA 49, MA 52. Wells Th Coll 49. **d** 51 **p** 52 Ripon. C of Leeds (in c of Quarry Hill) 51-56; PC of Bramley 56-64; Surr 62-64; R of Kirkby Overblow 64-80; Chr Stewardship Adv Dio Ripon 64-76; Bradf and Wakef 73-76; M Gen Syn from 70; Hon Can of Ripon from 72; RD of Harrogate from 77; Ch Comm from 78; V of Knaresborough Dio Ripon from 80. *9 York Road, Knaresborough, N Yorks, HG5 0AF.* (0423 865273)

McDERMID, Richard Thomas Wright. b 29. St Jo Coll Dur BA (2nd cl Hist) 53, MA 81. Dipl Th 55. **d** 55 **p** 56 Ripon. C of Seacroft 55-61; V of St Mary Virg Hawksworth Wood Leeds 61-70; High Harrogate Dio Ripon from 70. *Christ Church Vicarage, St Hilda's Road, Harrogate, Yorks, HG2 8JX.* (Harrogate 883390)

McDermott, John Alexander James. b 52. Univ of Lon BSc 74, MSc, 78. K Coll Cam BA 80. Westcott Ho Cam 78. **d** 81 Stepney for Lon. C of St John w St Bart Bethnal Green Dio Lon from 81. *24 Mary MacArthur House, Warley Street, Bethnal Green, E2 0QD.* (01-981 0118)

McDERMOTT, John Michael. b 37. Open Univ BA 78. Chich Th Coll 68. **d** 71 Warrington for Liv **p** 72 Liv. C of Wigan 71-74; Fleetwood (in c of St Nich) 74-76; Leigh 76-79. *c/o 34 Grasmere Street, Leigh, Lancs, WN7 1XB.* (Leigh 606596)

McDERMOTT, Mark Charles. McMaster Univ BA 63, MA 64. Trin Coll Tor. **d** 67 Tor. C of St Simon Ap Tor 67-69; Hon C of St John Weston Tor 69-70; I of Dorchester 70-74; Shelburne 74-79; St Simon Oakville Dio Niag from 79. *1268 Redbank Crescent, Oakville, Ont, Canada.* (416-844 0877)

McDERMOTT, Marvin Gray. Univ of Tor MusBac 61. Trin Coll Tor STB 64. **d** and **p** 64 Carib. C of Prince Geo 64-65; I of Viking 65-69; C of St Jude Oakville 69-74; R of All SS Niag Falls 74-75; Norton and Springfield Dio Fred from 75. *RR2, Apophaqui, NB, Canada.*

McDERMOTT, Canon Robert Preston. b 11. Trin Coll Dub Scho and BA (2nd cl Mod Ment and Mor Sc) 32. Bp Forster Pri 33, Div Text (2nd cl) and Robert King Mem Pri 34, MA 49. **d** 35 **p** 36 Down. C of Ballymoney 35-38; St Pet Belf 38-40; C-in-c of Ardclinis 40-44; Sub-Warden St Deiniol's Libr Hawarden 44-45; I of Borrisoakane w Ardcroney and Aglishclohane 45-49; Killenaule 49; R of St Mary-le-Bow w St Mary-the-Less Dur 49-55; Chap to Univ of Dur 49-55; Exam Chap to Bp of Dur 52-67; Chap and Lect Bede Coll Dur 55-63; L to Offic Dio Dur 55-80; Lect in Th Univ of Dur 63-80; Hon Can of Dur Cathl from 75. *46 Westcott Drive, Durham, DH1 5AH.* (Dur 42646)

MACDONALD, Alastair Douglas. b 48. St Jo Coll Dur 71. **d** 74 **p** 75 S'wark. C of Mottingham 74-77; Woolich 77-81; V of St Andr Wimbledon Dio S'wark from 81. *47 Wilton Grove, SW19.* (01-542 1794)

MacDONALD, Derek. b 45. Univ of Lon Dipl Th 77. Oak Hill Coll 74. **d** 77 Bp Garrett for Leic **p** 78 Leic. C of St Pet Braunstone 77-80; R of Wongan Hills w Dalwallinu Dio Perth from 80. *Box 148, Wongan Hills, W Australia 6603.* (096-711152)

MACDONALD, Donald Courtenay. b 45. Univ of Nottm BTh 74. Kelham Th Coll 70. **d** 75 **p** 76 Bris. C of All SS Clifton Dio Bris from 75; Chap Derby Lonsdale Coll of Higher Educn from 79. *122 Uttoxeter New Road, Derby, DE3 3JE.*

McDONALD, Douglas Mark. b 28. Linc Coll Ox BA (2nd cl Th) 54. MA 59. Wells Th Coll 68. **d** 69 Chich **p** 70 Lewes for Chich. C of Horsham 69-76; Asst Master H Trin Sch Crawley 69-76; Team V of Kirkby Lonsdale 76-79; P-in-c of Tidmarsh w Sulham Dio Ox from 79. *Rectory, Tidmarsh, Reading.* (07357 2348)

MACDONALD, Duncan Fraser. Univ of Cant BA 69. St Jo Th Coll Auckld. **d** 70 **p** 71 Wel. C of Lower Hutt 70-73; Hon C of Waiwhetu 73-78; Taradale Dio Wai from 78. *3 Totara Street, Taradale, Napier, NZ.* (448-887)

MacDONALD, Eric Sutherland. b 41. Univ of Dalhousie NS MA 66, MA 71. Atlantic Sch of Th Halifax NS 77. **d** 79 **p** 80 NS. C of St Paul Rawdon 79-80; P-in-c of St D Conv Distr I and Dio Berm from 81. *Box 188, St David's, Bermuda.* (7-1231)

McDONALD, George Alexander. b 09. Trin Coll Dub BA (2nd cl Ment and Mor Sc Mod) 32, MA 43, BD 43. **d** 33 **p** 34 Down. C of St Andr Belf 33-37; Dioc C Dio Derry and Raph 37-45; C-in-c of Clondevaddock 45-80; Can of Raph 58-80; RD of Kilmacrenan E 62-80. *c/o Tamney Rectory, Letterkenny, Co Donegal, Irish Republic.*

MacDONALD, George Stewart. **d** 60 Graft **p** 73 Brisb. Hon C of Tweed Heads 60-62; Perm to Offic Dio Brisb 62-67; Hon C of St Francis Nundah City and Dio Brisb from 67. *48 Beams Road, Boondall, Queensland, Australia 4034.* (265 1840)

McDONALD, Gordon James Joseph. b 17. Wycl Hall Ox 50. **d** 52 **p** 53 Lon. C of Southall 52-55; CMS Tr Coll Chislehurst 55-56; Tutor/Bursar Buwalasi Th Coll 56-59; P-in-c of St Mark's Conv Distr Dallam Warrington 59-63; V of St Mark Newtown Pemberton 63-80; P-in-c of Easton w Letheringham Dio St E from 80. *Easton Rectory, Woodbridge, Suff, IP13 0ED.* (Wickham Market 746338)

MACDONALD, Canon Harold Gould. Trin Coll Tor BA 49, LTh 52, STB 53. **d** 51 **p** 52 Edmon. d Dio Edmon 51-52; R of Fort Saskatchewan 52-54; I of St D Edmon 54-56; R of St Faith Edmon 56-59; Assoc Sec Dept of Relig Educn 59-68; R of St Luke Winnipeg 68-77; Can of Rupld from 76; Chap Univ of Manit and St Jo Coll Winnipeg from 77. *116 Norquay Street, Winnipeg, Manit., Canada.*

McDONALD, Hector Egerton. St Pet Coll Ja LTh (Dur) 36. **d** 36 **p** 37 Ja. C of Claremont w Moneague 36-38; Lucea 38; Balaclava w Keynsham 38-40; R of Lucea 40-62; R of Green Is 42-62; All SS and St Alb Kingston 62-77; Can of Ja 69-77. *7 Breary Avenue, Trafalgar Park, Kingston, Jamaica, W Indies.* (093-66887)

MACDONALD, Henry George Warren. b 20. TCD BA 42, Div Test (1st cl) 43, MA 46, BD 46. **d** 43 **p** 44 Dub. C of St Thos and St Barn Dub 43-47; Chap RNVR 47-49; RN 49-75; Hon Chap to HM the Queen from 74; C of Fulford York 75-79; Perm to Offic Dio Ex from 79. *18 Abingdon Road, North Hill, Plymouth, PL4 6HZ.*

McDONALD, Ian Ferens. b 26. Kings Coll Lon LLB 58. St Jo Th Coll Auckld 71. **d** 72 Lon **p** 73 Auckld (APM). C of Paddington Lon 72-73; Hon C of Avondale 73-75; Mt Albert Dio Auckld from 75. *97 Alberton Avenue, Mt Albert 3, Auckland, NZ.* (867 250)

McDONALD, Ian Henry. b 40. St Aid Coll 65. **d** 68 **p** 69 York. C of Hull 68-70; Drumglass 70-73; R of Eglish 73-80; Killylea 73-80; Maghera Dio Derry from 80. *Rectory, Maghera, Londonderry, N Ireland.*

MACDONALD, Ian Huntley. Angl Th Coll BC 67. **d** 68 BC. C of Sooke 68-71. *2420 Meadowland Drive, Victoria, BC, Canada.*

McDONALD, Ivor Alfred Anthony. 1 45 Ripon for River **p** 46 River. C of St Mary Hunslet 45; St Pet Broken Hill 45-49; R of Moama 49-50; Chap BCOF Hiro Japan 50-51; R of Scottsdale 51-55; Prec of St D Cathl Hobart 55-57; Chap to Bp of Tas from 59; R of H Trin Launceston Dio Tas from 59. *35 Lawrence Street, Launceston, Tasmania.*

McDONALD, James Stewart. b 31. St Mich Coll Llan 59. **d** 62 **p** 63 Blackb. C of Haslingden 62-66; V of St Jude Preston 66-73; St Wilfrid Mereside, Blackpool Dio Blackb from 73.

Vicarage, Langdale Road, Mereside, Blackpool. (Blackpool 61532)

MACDONALD, James Younger. St Barn Coll Adel ACT ThL 48. **d** and **p** 48 Adel. C of Ch Ch N Adel 48-49; Miss P at Pinaroo 49; P-in-c 50-51; Mount Pleasant w Mannum Miss 51-54; R of Willunga 54-57; St Paul and Hosp and Gaol Chap Adel 57-62; R of Mitcham w Torrens Park 62-76; L to Offic Dio Adel from 76. *32 Jackson Avenue, Coromandel Valley, S Australia 5051.* (278 7535)

MACDONALD, John. b 16. St Cath S Ox BA (2nd cl Mod Hist) 38, 2nd cl Th 40, MA 42, BLitt 58. St Steph Ho Ox 39. **d** 41 **p** 42 Liv. C of St John Birkdale 41-44; Walton-on-the-Hill (in c of Miss of Good Shepherd) 44-49; Chap St Steph Ho Ox 49-54; L of Offic Dio Ox 49-60; Chap Ch Ch Cathl Ox 51-60; Chap New Coll Ox 52-60; Libr Pusey Ho Ox 54-60; Lect St D Coll Lamp and Chap Burgess Th Hall 60-76; Sub-Warden 62-76; L to Offic Dio St D 61-76; V of Edstaston Dio Lich from 76; Whixall Dio Lich from 76; Chap Chor Ches Cathl from 82. *Dean's Cottage, Abbey Street, Chester, CH1 2JF.*

MACDONALD, John Alexander. b 07. Tyndale Hall Bris 38. **d** 41 **p** 42 Man. C of St Marg Burnage 41-44; The Albert Mem Ch Man 44-46; V of St Mary Wakef 46-53; St Mark Byker Newc T 53-80. *135 Bosworth Gardens, North Heaton, NE6 5UP.* (657486)

McDONALD, John Cameron. Univ of Tor BA 56. Wycl Coll Tor LTh and BTh 56. **d** 55 Tor **p** 56 BC. C of Highland Creek 55-56; St John Vic 56-57; I of Metchosin Dio BC from 57. *Metchosin PO, BC, Canada.*

McDONALD, John Edward Walter. St Mich Ho Crafers 63. **d** 68 Bunb. C of Bosselton 68-70; Albany 70-72; R of Kondinin 72-75; Cranbrook 75-79; Collie Dio Bunb from 79. *Rectory, Collie, W Australia 6225.*

McDONALD, John Edwin. Moore Th Coll ACT ThL 58. **d** 59 Bp Hilliard for Syd **p** 59 Syd. C of St Luke Mosman 59-61; All SS N Parramatta 61-62; R of Stanmore 63-67; Artarmon Dio Syd from 67. *26 Broughton Road, Artarmon, NSW, Australia 2064.* (412-1315)

MACDONALD, John Hall. b 22. Trin Coll Dub BA (2nd cl Mod Hist and Pol Sc) 43, Div Test 44, MA 65. Westcott Ho Cam 44. **d** 45 **p** 46 Connor. C of St Luke Belf 45-48; All SS Grangegorman 48-51; Chap and Asst Master Rossall Sch 51-53; I of Kilscoran 53-55; Borris-in-Ossory w Aghavoe 55-58; R of St John Moston 58-62; C-in-c of St Mary's Eccles Distr Blackpool 62-65; V 65-78. *c/o 59 Stony Hill Avenue, South Shore, Blackpool, Lancs.* (Blackpool 42713)

McDONALD, John Richard Burleigh. b 17. Late Scho of Trin Coll Dub BA (1st cl Mods) 39, Downes Pri and Div Test (2nd cl) 40, BD 43. **d** 41 **p** 42 Down. C of St Pet Belf 41-45; Lect Bp Tucker Mem Coll Mukono 46-52; Prin Buwalasi Coll 52-61; Exam Chap to Bp of U Nile 53-61; Hon Can of U Nile 58-61; Educn Officer for Ch of Ireland 61-64; Prin Lect and Hd of Relig Stud Dept Stranmillis Coll Belf from 66. *76 Osborne Drive, Belfast, N Ireland, BT9 6LJ.* (Belfast 666737)

McDONALD, Joseph. d and **p** 21 Abp of Cardiff. Perm to Offic (Col Cl Act) 25; L to Offic Dio Ox 26-29; V of Shernborne (w Fring to 56) 29-78; R of Anmer 56-78. *c/o Shernborne Vicarage, King's Lynn, Norf.* (Snettisham 251)

McDONALD, Canon Keith. St Jo Coll Morpeth 52, ThL 56. **d** 54 Graft **p** 55 Bp Storrs for Graft. C of Lismore 54-59; V of Wyan w Rappville 59-61; R of Dorrigo 61-66; S Graft 66-72; Murwillumbah Dio Graft from 72; Hon Can of Graft from 79. *Rectory, Murwillumbah, NSW, Australia 2484.* (72 1070)

MACDONALD, Malcolm James. b 42. Sarum Th Coll 70. **d** 71 **p** 73 Kens for Lon. C of St Steph Hounslow 71-72; St Sav Shepherds Bush Lon 73-76; P-in-c of St Luke Shepherds Bush Dio Lon from 76. *St Luke's Vicarage, Uxbridge Road, W12.* (01-749 7523)

MacDONALD, Canon Murray Somerled. b 23. Late Exhib of Pemb Coll Cam BA 46, 2nd cl Th Trip pt i 47, MA 49. Ely Th Coll 47. **d** 48 **p** 49 Lon. C of Hendon 48-51; St Geo Hanover Sq Lon 51-53; R of Sawtry 53-54; C-in-c of Upton w Copmanford 53-54; R of Sawtry w Upton and Copmanford 54-57; V of Upwood w Gt and L Raveley 57-62; R of Wood Walton 57-62; V of Fenstanton 62-70; V of Hilton 62-70; RD of Huntingdon 69-76; R of Huntingdon Dio Ely from 70; V of St Mary w St Benedict Huntingdon Dio Ely from 70; Hon Can of Ely from 72; RD of Huntingdon from 81. *1 The Walks East, Huntingdon, PE18 6AP.* (Huntingdon 53105)

McDONALD, Canon Norman Womersley. Ridley Coll Melb ACT ThL 46. **d** 45 **p** 46 Gippsld. C-in-c of Neerim S w Noojee 45-46; V 46-48; Omeo 48-50; R of Drouin 50-55; Yallourn 55-60; Leongatha 60-69; Bairnsdale 69-76; Can of St Paul's Cathl Sale 68-69; Archd of Gippsld E 69-78; VG Dio Gippsld 76-78; Can of All SS Cathl Bend from 78; R of Mildura Dio Bend from 78. *St Margaret's Rectory, Eleventh Street, Mildura, Vic., Australia 3500.*

MacDONALD, Peter Stewart. K Coll Halifax NS BA 56, LTh 57. Trin Coll Tor STB 60. **d** 56 NS **p** 57 Tor for NS. R of Port Dufferin 57-61; Seaforth 61-63; I of Shelburne 63-70; R of St Paul Charlottetown 70-72; Ch Ch Dartmouth Dio NS from 72. *54 Wentworth Street, Dartmouth, NS, Canada.* (466-5644)

MACDONALD, Ranald Alexander. b 23. Fitzw Ho Cam BA 50, MA 55. Lon Coll Div. **d** and **p** 63 Lon. C of St Geo Headstone Hatch End 63-67; R of Parham and Wiggonholt w Greatham Dio Chich from 67. *Parham Rectory, Rackham, Pulborough, Sussex, RH20 2EU.* (Storrington 2209)

MACDONALD, Reginald Stephen. b 44. Richmond Coll Tor BA 75. Wycl Coll Tor LTh 74, MDiv 78. **d** and **p** 74 Bp Legge for Newfld. I of Cow Head 74-76; Hubbards Dio NS from 77. *Box 38, Hubbards, NS, Canada.* (857-9486)

McDONALD, Robert Wilkinson. Moore Th Coll Syd ACT ThL 63. **d** 62 Newc **p** 64 Syd. C of Woy Woy 62-64; Randwick 64-65; R of Corrimal 65-79; Heyfield Dio Gippsld from 79. *Rectory, Heyfield, Vic, Australia 3858.*

MacDONALD, Rodney Marshall. b 49. St Francis Coll Brisb. **d** 74 **p** 75 Brisb. C of St Aug Hamilton 74-75; Prec St John's Cathl Brisb 75-78; CF (Austr) from 79. *22 The Village, Balcombe, Vic, Australia 3935.* (059-74 2441)

McDONALD, Ronald Angus Fancourt. Ridley Coll Melb 79. **d** 81 NW Austr. Chap Wollaston Coll Perth from 81. *c/o Wollaston College, Mt Claremont, Perth, W Australia.*

McDONALD, Ross Francis. Moore Th Coll ACT ThL (2nd cl) 59. Melb Coll of Div Dipl Relig Educn 62. **d** 59 **p** 60 Armid. C of St Pet Cathl Armid 59-61; Moore 61-62; L to Offic Dio Syd 62-68 and from 70; Org Sec Syd Dioc Bd of Educn 64-68; R of Berrima w Moss Vale 68-70; Asst Master Syd Gr Sch 70-71; Abbotsleigh School Wahroonga 72-81; L to Offic Dio Syd from 70; Chap Abbotsleigh Sch from 81. *22 Woonona Avenue South, Wahroonga, NSW, Australia 2076.* (48-3020)

MACDONALD, Stephen Calliss. b 35. Selw Coll Cam 2nd cl Geog Trip pt i 57, BA (2nd cl Geog Trip pt ii) 58. Westcott Ho Cam 58. **d** 60 Croydon for Cant **p** 61 Cant. C of All SS Norwood 60-64; Chap Cov Cathl 64-68; Staff Chr Aid 68-70; Lect Coll of Further Educn Hitchin 70-74; Tutor from 74. *Crossways, Breachwood Green, Hitchin, Herts, SG4 8PL.*

✠ **MACDONALD, Right Rev Thomas Brian.** OBE 70. St Aid Col Bal ACT ThL 32. **d** 34 **p** 35 Bal. C of Ch Ch Warracknabeal 34; All SS Bal 34-35; P-in-c of Landsborough 35; R of Williams 35-39; Manjimup 39-40; Chap AIF 40-44; R of Claremont 44-50; Chap of St Pet Coll Sch Adel 50-59; Dean and R of St Geo Cathl Perth 59-61; Archd of Perth 61-67; Cons Bp Coadj of Perth in St Geo Cathl Perth 24 Feb 64 by Abp of Perth; Bps of NW Austr; Bunb; and Kalg; Bp Coadj of Melb; Asst Bp of Perth; and Bp Riley; res 79; Archd of Northam 70-72; Perth 73-77; Perm to Offic Dio Perth from 79. *33 Thomas Street, Nedlands, W Australia 6009.* (386 2049)

McDONALD, William Ivan Orr. b 19. Trin Coll Dub BA 48, MA 54, Div Test 49. Qu Coll Birm. **d** 50 **p** 51 Arm. C of St Mark Arm 50-57; Mullaglass 57-59; R 59-62; Dean's V of St Anne's Cathl Belf 62-70; V of Woolhope Dio Heref from 70; C-in-c of Mordiford w Dormington Dio Heref from 73. *Vicarage, Woolhope, Hereford.* (Fownhope 287)

MACDONALD-MILNE, Brian James. b 35. CCC Cam 2nd cl Th Trip pt i 56, BA (2nd cl Th Trip pt ii) 58, MA 62. MA (Oxon) 81. Cudd Coll 58. **d** 60 Lanc for York **p** 61 Blackb. C of Fleetwood 60-63; Sub-Warden St Pet Th Coll Siota 64-67; Actg Warden 68; Chap and Tutor Melan Bro Tabalia Solomon Is 69-72; Dioc Sec for Relig Educn Melan 65-72; Hd of Dept of Evang and Commun Educn Melan 73-75; VG and Dioc Sec Dio Centr Melan 75-77; M of Pacific Conf of Chs 78-80; L to Offic Dio New Hebr 78-80; Dio Ox from 81; Actg Chap Trin Coll Ox 81; St Pet Coll Ox 81-82; Relief Chap Grendon and Spring Hill Pris 81-82; Research Fell Qu Coll Birm from 82. *c/o Arden Lodge, Moat Lane, Prestwood, Great Missenden, Bucks.* (Gt Missenden 2167)

MacDONNELL, Charles Leonard. b 54. Univ of Bris BA 76. Ripon Coll Cudd 76. **d** 78 **p** 79 Bris. C of New Swindon 78-80; Westbury-on-Trym Dio Bris from 80. *16 Southfield Road, Westbury-on-Trym, Bristol, BS9 3BH.* (Bris 621336)

McDONNELL, Desmond Allen William. b 51. Austr Nat Univ Canberra BA 77. Trin Coll Melb 78. **d** 80 C & Goulb. C of St Sav Cathl Goulburn Dio C & Goulb from 80. *12e Church Street, Goulburn, NSW, Australia 2580.*

McDONNELL, Richard Patrick. b 45. Belknap Coll NH BD 71. CW Post Coll NY MA 74. U Th Coll NY BS 76, MDiv 77. **d** 79 **p** 80 Fred. C of Denmark Dio Fred from 79. *RR 2, New Denmark, NB, Canada, E0J 1T0.*

MACDONOGH, Jack Albert Middleton. b 14. Late Scho of TCD BA (1st cl Mod) 36, 1st cl Div Test 38, BLitt 39, MA 43, BD 50. **d** 39 **p** 40 Dub. C of St Steph Dub 39-42; Asst Master Rugby Sch 42-70; V of Orton-on-the-Hill w Twycross and Norton-by-Twycross 70-79. *9 Arden Street, Atherstone, Warws, CV9 1EB.*

McDOUGALL, David Alexander. Moore Th Coll Syd ACT ThL 64. **d** 65 **p** 66 Brisb. C of Kilkivan 65-69; R of Wyndham 69-74; Rushworth and Murchison 74-76; I of Cranbourne Dio Melb from 76. *Vicarage, Bakewell Street, Cranbourne, Vic, Australia 3977.* (059-96 1053)

McDOUGALL, Hugh John. Qu Univ Ont MSc 57. Wycl Coll Tor LTh 60. **d** 60 **p** 61 Tor. C of Trin E Tor 60-63; Chap Lakefield Prep Sch Ont 63-72; on leave. *St David's School, Squamish, BC, Canada.*

MacDOUGALL, Canon Ian William. TCD BA 43, MA 59, Div Test 43. **d** 43 **p** 44 Connor. C of St Steph Belf 43-45; Enniskillen and Trory 45-48; I of Drumlane 48-50; Ballinaclash U 51-54; R of Kilcleagh w Ballyloughloe and Ferbane 54-58; Mullingar U Dio Meath from 58; RD of Duleek and Slane from 58; Can of Meath from 81. *All Saints' Rectory, Mullingar, Co Westmeath, Irish Republic.* (Mullingar 8376)

McDOUGALL, Philip Ross. b 54. St Jo Coll Auckld LTh 80. **d** 80 Auckld. C of Manurewa Dio Auckld from 80. *33 Churchill Avenue, Manurewa, Auckland, NZ.*

McDOUGALL, Stuart Ronald. b 28. Roch Th Coll 64. **d** 66 **p** 67 Roch. C of St Aid Gravesend 66-69; St Thos Wells 69-70; Team V of Tong 70-73; V of Cononley w Bradley Dio Bradf from 73. *Vicarage, Meadow Close, Cononley, Keighley, Yorks, BD20 8LZ.* (Cross Hills 34369)

MacDOUGALL, William Duncan. b 47. Univ of Nottm BTh and LTh 74. St Jo Coll Nottm 69. **d** 74 Lon **p** 75 Stepney for Lon. C of St Aug Highbury 74-77; Chap at Salta Dio N Argent from 78. *Casilla 187, 4400 Salta, Provincia de Dalta, Argentina.*

McDOWALL, Alexander William. b 13. Univ of Nottm Dipl Educn 62. ACP 71. Qu Coll Birm 74. **d** 76 Repton for Derby **p** 77 Derby. C of St Luke Derby 76-78; Perm to Offic Dio Derby from 78; Dio Ex from 80. *12 Bristol Drive, Mickleover, Derby, DE3 5BT.*

MacDOWALL, Canon Garfield Harrison. b 44. Wycl Coll Tor 70. **d** and **p** 73 Caled. I of Port Edward 73-77; Kitwanga 77-80; Dawson Creek Dio Caled from 80; Hon Can of Caled from 81. *844-111th Avenue, Dawson Creek, BC, Canada.*

McDOWALL, Julian Thomas. b 39. CCC Cam BA 62, MA 67. Called to Bar, Gray's Inn 61. Linc Th Coll 62. **d** 64 Bp McKie for Cov **p** 65 Cov. C of Rugby 64-70; P-in-c of St Pet Conv Distr Stoke Hill 70-72; V of St Pet Stoke Hill Guildf 72-76; R of Elstead Dio Guildf from 76. *Elstead Rectory, Godalming, Surrey.* (Elstead 703251)

McDOWALL, Kenneth Stewart Patrick. b 08. Magd Coll Cam BA 30, MA 35. Westcott Ho Cam 46. **d** 48 Southn for Win **p** 49 Win. C of Milton 48-51; V of Ellingham (w Harbridge from 57) 51-65; R of Longparish w Hurstbourne Priors 65-71; Perm to Offic Dio Sarum from 71. *The Mill House, Wylye, Warminster, Wilts.*

McDOWALL, Robert Angus. b 39. K Coll Lon and Warm AKC 66. **d** 67 **p** 68 Dur. C of Bishopwearmouth 67-69; CF from 69; Sen Chap from 80. *c/o Lloyds Bank, Fawcett Street, Sunderland, Tyne & Wear, SR1 1SF.*

McDOWALL, Roger Ian. b 40. K Coll Lon and Warm AKC 64. **d** 65 **p** 66 Dur. C of Peterlee 65-68; St Luke w All SS Weaste Salford 68-70; St Aug Tonge Moor 70-73; V of Whitworth 73-80; Team V of Centr Torquay Dio Ex from 80. *All Saints Vicarage, Barton Road, Torquay, TQ1 4DT.* (Torquay 38865)

McDOWELL, Charles. b 16. BEM 65. Bps' Coll Cheshunt 64. **d** 66 **p** 67 Nor. C of Hilborough Group 66-70; R of Colkirk w Oxwick (w Whissonsett and Horningtoft from 74) 70-77; C-in-c of Whissonsett w Horningtoft 71-74; R of Gt Massingham 77-81; P-in-c of Harpley 77-79; R 79-81; Offg Chap RAF W Raynham from 76. *55 Queens Road, Fakenham, Norf. NR21 8BT.* (Fakenham 3646)

McDOWELL, Ian James. St Jo Coll Morpeth ACT ThL 58. **d** 61 **p** 62 Adel. C of St Paul Narracoorte 61-63; P-in-c of Elliston Miss 63-64; Elliston-Lock Miss 64-66; V of Ganton Yorks 67-71; C-in-c of Foxholmes w Butterwick Yorks 67-68; R 68-71; Angaston 71-76; Col Light Gardens Dio Adel from 76. *Bedford Square, Col Light Gardens, S Australia 5041.* (08-276 3993)

McDOWELL, Lindsay George. b 41. Canberra Coll of Min BTh 81. **d** 80 C & Goulb. C of St John Wagga Wagga Dio C & Goulb from 80. *63 Tarcutta Street, Wagga Wagga, NSW, Australia 2650.*

MACE, Alan Herbert. b 28. BA (2nd cl Engl) (Lon) 49. Wycl Hall Ox. **d** 60 **p** 61 Ches. C of Disley 60-63; H Trin Folkestone 63-67; L to Offic Dio Win from 67. *15 Bassett Heath Avenue, Southampton, SO1 7GP.* (Southampton 768161)

MACE, Arthur William Vernon. b 07. Univ of Lon BSc (1st cl Physics) 28. Wycl Hall Ox 35. **d** 36 **p** 37 Cant. C of St Luke Ramsgate 36-40; Asst Master Rugby Sch 40-61; Publ Pr Dio Cov 41-61; Lect in Physics Univ of Birm 61-65; Angl Chap Univ of Birm and Warden St Bart Ho 63-65; Perm to Offic Dio Birm 61-65; C of Beverley Minster 65-67; R of Rufforth w Moor Monkton 67-77; C-in-c of Long Marston 67-77; RD of Ainsty 69-77; C of Tadcaster Dio York from 78. *25 Stutton Road, Tadcaster, Yorks.* (Tadcaster 833655)

MACE, Francis Spencer. b 24. Univ of Birm Mus Bac (2nd cl) 49. Linc Th Coll 58. **d** 59 **p** 60 Sheff. C and Succr of St Pet and St Paul Cathl Sheff 59-61; C of St Jo Evang Ranmoor Sheff 61-65; R of Polebrook w Lutton (and Hemington from 78) Dio Pet from 65; P-in-c of Hemington 77-78. *Polebrook Rectory, Peterborough, PE8 5LN.* (Oundle 72500)

MACE, Frederick James. b 08. Ordin Test Sch Hawarden 30. Lich Th Coll 32. **d** 35 **p** 36 Shef. C of Owston 35-37; Wath-on-Dearne 37-43; V of Intake 43-58; Wadworth (w Loversall from 76) 58-77; Perm to Offic Dio Sheff from 78. *13 St Mary's Crescent, Tickhill, Doncaster, Yorks.*

MACE, Robert Alfred Beasley. b 16. Univ of Leeds BA 49. Coll of Resurr Mirfield. **d** 50 **p** 51 St Andr. C of St Andr Callander w St Mary Aberfoyle 50-53; St Mary Virg Newc T 53-54; St Silas Pentonville 54-56; Aylesbury 56-59; P-in-c of St Gabr Govan Glas 59-61; R of St Kiaran Campbeltown 61-65; V of St Pet (w St Jo Bapt from 72) Barnsley Dio Wakef from 65. *St Peter's Vicarage, Barnsley, Yorks.* (Barnsley 82220)

McEACHERN, Allan Hamilton. Hur Coll Dipl Th 63. **d** 63 Niag. C of H Trin Welland 63-67; R of St D and St Patr Guelph 67-73; Dunnville 73-81; St Pet Hamilton Dio Niag from 81. *705 Main Street East, Hamilton, Ont, Canada.* (416-545 1808)

McEACHRAN, Peter. b 20. **d** 75 **p** 76 Lah. P-in-c of Mardan Pakistan 75-76; Chap Lah Cathl 76-79; CMS Area Sec Dio Ox & St Alb from 79; Hon C of Haddenham w Cuddington & Kingsey Dio Ox from 79. *100 Churchway, Haddenham, Bucks, HP17 8DT.*

McELHINNEY, Samuel Herbert. b 08. Late Downes Exhib of Trin Coll Dub and Carson Bibl Pri 29 BA 30. MA 38. **d** 31 **p** 32 Down. C of Cath Ch Drom 31-36; St Patr Ballymacarrett 36-40; I of St Mich Belf 40-59; RD of Mid-Belf 55-59; R of Lambeg 59-74; Preb of Kilroot and Can of Connor Cathl 62-74. *5 Girona Avenue, Portrush, Co Antrim, N Ireland.*

McELVENEY, John William. Moore Th Coll ACT ThL 58. **d** 59 Bp Hilliard for Syd **p** 59 Syd. C of Bondi 59-61; Nowra 61-62; C-in-c of Villawood 62-65; CF (Austr) 65-73; R of Cremorne Point Dio Syd from 73. *42 Milson Road, Cremorne Point, NSW, Australia 2090.* (90-2110)

McENDOO, Neil. b 50. TCD BA 72, Div Test 75. Div Hostel Dub 72. **d** 75 **p** 76 Down. C of Cregagh 75-79; St Ann City and Dio Dub from 79. *33 Wellington Road, Ballsbridge, Dublin 4, Irish Republic.*

McENERY, Michael Joseph. b 35. Cant Sch of Min 77. **d** 80 **p** 81 Cant. C of Biddenden and of Smarden Dio Cant from 80. *Rectory, Biddenden, Ashford, Kent, TN27 8AH.*

McERLEAN, Lawrence Paul. b 50. Westmr Coll Penn USA BA 72. Wycl Coll Tor MDiv 77. **d** 77 Bp Read for Tor **p** 78 Tor. C of St John York Mills Tor 77-79; I of Fenelon Falls and Ch Ch Coboconk Dio Tor from 79. *Box 409, Fenelon Falls, Ont, Canada.*

MacEWAN, Alexander David. b 20. Launde Abbey Leic. **d** 69 **p** 70 Leic. C of Wigston Magna 69-75; V of Holmside 75-79; Blackfordby Dio Leic from 79. *Vicarage, Vicarage Close, Blackfordby, Burton-on-Trent, Staffs, DE11 8AZ.* (Burton/Trent 219445)

McEWIN, Robert Gavin Keith. Moore Coll Syd ThL 69. **d** 71 Syd **p** 72 Bp Begbie for Syd. C of Castle Hill 71-73; R of Leigh Creek 74-77; Missr at Mid-West and Transline Miss Dio Willoch from 77. *25 Cummins Street, Port Augusta, S Australia 5700.* (086-424784)

MACEY, Anthony Keith Frank. b 46. Univ Coll Cardiff Dipl Th 69. St Steph Ho Ox 69. **d** 71 **p** 72 Ex. C of St Thos Ex 71-76; V of Wembury Dio Ex from 76. *63 Church Road, Wembury, Plymouth, Devon.* (Wembury 862319)

MACEY, Ralph Arthur. b 14. Univ of Leeds BA 38. TD 63. Coll of Resurr Mirfield 38. **d** 40 **p** 41 Newc T. C of H Trin Tynemouth 40-42; St Andr Priory Hexham 42-45; Chollerton 45-47; Seghill w Seaton Delaval (in c of Seaton Delaval) 47-50; V of St Phil Newc T 50-60; CF (TA) 50-69; V of N Gosforth 60-67; Hon C of All SS Gosforth 67-76; St Geo Cullercoats Dio Newc T from 76; Asst Master Newc T Ch High Sch from 67. *22 Parkside, Tynemouth, North Shields, NE30 4JN.* (N Shields 70019)

McFADDEN, Ven Clement Francis Robert. Em Coll Sktn LTh 54. **d** 52 **p** 53 Sktn Sec-Treas and Trave Miss Dio Sktn 52-56; I of Bearskin Lake and Trout Lake 56-60; Atikokan 60-63; I of Humboldt 64-69; C of Trinian Sktn 69-76; Hon Can of Sktn 69-76; Archd of The Pas from 76; I of Flin Flon Dio Bran from 76; Exam Chap to Bp of Bran from 76. *72 Church Street, Flin Flon, Manit., Canada.*

McFADDEN, Canon Ronald Bayle. b 30. TCD BA 53,

Downes Oratory Pri (1st) 54, MA 55. **d** 54 **p** 55 Arm. C of Drumglass (Dungannon) 54-58; St Geo Cathl Capetn 58-62; Dundela 62-64; Dom Chap to Bp of Down 62-64; V of Pateley Bridge w Greenhow Hill 64-73; Knaresborough 73-79; P-in-c of H Trin Knaresborough 78-79; Can Res of Ripon Cathl from 79. *Canon's Lodge, Kangel Close, Dallamires Lane, Ripon, HG4 1DE.* (Ripon 700211)

McFADYEN, Phillip. b 44. K Coll Lon AKC and BD 69, MTh 70. St Aug Coll Cant 69. **d** 71 **p** 72 Sheff. C of St Mark Broomhall 71-74; Chap at Keswick Hall Nor 74-79; V of Swardeston Dio Nor from 79; P-in-c of Intwood w Keswick Dio Nor 79-81; R from 81; P-in-c of E Carleton Dio Nor 79-81; R from 81. *Swardeston Vicarage, Norwich, Norf.*

McFALL, Thomas Henry Crampton. b 13. TCD BA Ment and Mor Sc 35, Div Test 38, MA 40. **d** 37 **p** 38 Cash. C and Libr of Cathl Ch Waterf 37-39; R of Fiddown Castlane and Clonmore 39-49; Ferns w Kilbride and Tombe 49-79; Ed Oss Dioc Mag 40-49; Select Pr Univ of Dub 45; Dean of Ferns 49-79. *26 Nutley Avenue, Ballsbridge, Dublin 4, Irish Republic.* (01-692049)

McFARLAND, Allan Rowland. St Jo Coll Morpeth ACT ThL 45, Th Scho 52. BD(Lon) 58. **d** 46 **p** 47 Newc. C of Cessnock w Aberdare 46-48; Supt St Alb Home for Boys Murrurundi 48-50; R of Gundy 50-52; Jerry's Plains 52-56; Mossman 56-60; Atherton 60-67; Home Hill 67-71; Exam Chap to Bp of N Queensld 62-71; R of Chinchilla 71-75; Hervey Bay 75-80; C of St Matt Grovely City and Dio Brisb from 80. *67 Glenlee Street, Arana Hills, Queensland, Australia 4054.*

MacFARLANE, Cyril St Martin Bloomfield. b 13. Keble Coll Ox BA (3rd cl Th) 36, MA 46. Sarum Th Coll 37. **d** 38 **p** 39 Win. C of H Trin Southampton 38-40; St Aug Northam 40-42; St Mark Regent's Pk 42-44; St Aug Wembley Pk (to Offic in Annunc Miss Ch) 44-50; Hawarden (in c of St John Pentrobin and St Mary Broughton) 50-54; V of Lapley w Wheaton Aston 54-58; C of All SS Hobart 58-60; Lect in Th Ch Coll Hobart 58-63; R of Kempton Tas 60-63; PC of Burbage w Harpur Hill 63-68; V 68-74; R of Cranford w Grafton Underwood 74-81. *17 Bowhill, Kettering, Northants, NN16 8TT.* (0536-510199)

McFARLANE, Lloyd George. Wycl Coll Tor 46. **d** 49 Fred **p** 50 Tor. I of Kinmount 50-54; Mono Mills 54-62; R of Ft Frances 62-73; Hon Can of Keew 66-73; R of Addington Dio Fred from 74. *6 Aberdeen Street, Campbelltown, NB, Canada.*

McFARLANE, Percival Alan Rex. Columbia Univ NY BSc 61, MA 62. Dioc Coll Montr 50. **d** 51 Montr **p** 52 Qu'App. C of Assiniboia 51-52; St Paul's Pro-Cathl Regina 52-55; in Amer Ch 55-66; Chap to Bordeaux Gaol Montr 66-71; Leclere Inst Montr from 71; C of St Pet Mt Royal Montr 71-74; on leave. *12 Woburn Square, WC1.*

MACFARLANE, Richard Hosken. **d** 60 **p** 61 Graft. C of Murwillumbah 60-61; V of Coramba 61-64; R of Murwillumbah 64-72; Lismore 72-77; Maclean Dio Graft from 77. *Rectory, Maclean, NSW, Australia 2463.*

MACFARLANE, Robert Cephas. b 14. **d** 77 Birm. Hon C of St Martin City and Dio Birm from 77. *30 Inglewood Grove, Streetly, Sutton Coldfield, W Midl, B74 3LN.*

MACFARLANE, William Angus. b 17. Worc Coll Ox BA 39, MA 43. Wycl Hall Ox 39. **d** 40 **p** 41 Ex. C of Charles Plymouth (in c of St Aug 44-45) 40-45; St John Reading 45-47; CMS Men's Tr Coll Blackheath 47-48; C of H Trin Brompton 48-49; R of Bighton 49-52; V of Bp's Sutton 49-52; Southwold 52-59; Plaistow 59-71; Bexleyheath 71-79; Chap Sandhill Park Hosp Bp's Lydeard from 80. *Moorlands, Blue Anchor, Nr Minehead, Somerset.*

McFERRAN, Leonard Mack. Univ of Auckld BA 69. Em Coll Sktn 53, LTh 69. **d** 56 **p** 57 Sktn. I of Colonsay 56-58; C of St Jas Vancouver 58-59; Chap Centr City Miss Vancouver 59-60; Counsellor Alcoholism Found of BC Vancouver 60-65; and 69; Dir of Family Guidance Centre Dio Auckld 65-68; Hon C of Mt Roskill 69-72; Dir of Alcoholism and Drug Addiction Centre Auckld 69-71; V of St Luke Mt Albert Auckld 73-74; Hon C of Meadowbank 75-77; Chap John Howard S Vanc from 78. *834 West 62nd Avenue, Vancouver, BC, Canada.*

McFIE, James Ian. Lich Th Coll 59. **d** 61 **p** 62 Man. C of St Phil w St Steph Salford 61-65; V of Hey 65-75; All SS Elton, Bury Dio Man from 75. *All Saints' Vicarage, Tottington Road, Elton, Bury, Lancs, BL8 1LR.* (061-764 1431)

McGAVIN, Paul. b 43. Univ of New Engl NSW BA 70. Univ of Queensld MEcon 76. **d** 78 Graft. Actg Guardian Commun Servants of the Love of Ch Dio Graft 78-79; Perm to Offic Dio Melb from 79. *140 Graham Street, Broadmeadows, Vic, Australia 3047.*

McGECHIE, John Kenneth. St Jo Coll Auckld LTh 52. **d** 52 **p** 53 Wai. C of Tauranga 52-56; V of Edgecumbe 56-61; Porangahau 61-69; Puketapu Dio Wai from 69. *Vicarage, Puketapu, NZ.* (Napier 442-393)

McGEE, Peter John. b 36. Trin Coll Cam 2nd cl Hist Trip pt i 59, BA (Th Trip pt ia) 60. Chich Th Coll 60. **d** 62 **p** 63 Ex. C of St Thos N Keyham Devonport 62-63; St Mary Church 63-65; Dartmouth w Townstal 65-68; Cockington w Chelston 68-70; V of Exminster 70-77; P-in-c of Ottery St Mary Dio Ex 77-78; V from 78; P-in-c of Alfington Dio Ex 77-78; V from 78. *Vicar's House, Ottery St Mary, Devon, EX11 1DQ.* (040-481 2062)

McGEE, Stuart Irwin. b 30. TCD BA 53, Div Test 53, MA 68. **d** 53 **p** 54 Connor. C of St Simon Belfast 53-55; Chap Miss to Seamen Sing 55-58; I of Drumholm and Rossnowlach 58-65; CF from 65; DACG BAOR 77-80; SHAPE from 80. *c/o Ministry of Defence, Bagshot Park, Bagshot, Surrey, GU19 5PL.*

McGHEE, Henry Arthur. b 1896. Edin Th Coll 72. **d** and **p** 72 Glas. C of St Andr Wishaw (in c of St Cath Shotts) Dio Glas from 72. *4 Windsor Place, Shotts, Lanarks.*

McGILL, Donald Hugh. b 11. Cudd Th Coll 72. **d** and **p** 73 Ox (APM). C of Cudd 73; L to Offic Dio Ox from 73. *Cop Close, High Street, Long Crendon, Aylesbury, Bucks, HP18 9AN.*

McGILL, James. b 17. Univ of Edin MA 39. Edin Th Coll 39. **d** 41 **p** 42 Edin. C of St Pet Musselburgh 41-45; R 45-57; R of Troon Dio Glas from 57. *70 Bentinck Drive, Troon, Ayrshire.* (Troon 313731)

MacGILLIVRAY, Canon Alexander Buchan. b 33. Univ of Edin MA 55. Edin Th Coll 55. **d** 57 **p** 58 St Andr. Chap St Ninian's Cathl Perth 57-59; Aberlour Orphanage 60-62; C of St Marg Aberlour 60-62; R of Meldrum w Whiterashes Dio Aber from 62; Woodhead Dio Aber from 62; Insch Dio Aber from 74; Folla Rule Dio Aber from 74; Can of Aber from 78. *Rectory, Old Meldrum, Aberdeens.* (Old Meldrum 208)

McGINLEY, Jack Francis. b 36. ALCD 65. **d** 65 **p** 66 Roch. C of St Paul Erith 65-70; St Lawr Morden 70-74; V of Ch Ch New Catton Dio Nor from 74. *65 Elm Grove Lane, New Catton, Norwich, NR3 3LF.* (Nor 408332)

McGIRR, William Eric. b 43. Div Hostel Dub 68. **d** 71 **p** 72 Connor. C of St Nich Carrickfergus 71-74; Mt Merrion 74-77; R of Donacavey w Barr Dio Clogh from 77. *Doncavey Rectory, Co Tyrone, N Ireland.*

McGLASHAN, Alastair Robin. b 33. Late Scho of Ch Ch Ox 1st cl Cl Mods 53, BA (2nd cl Lit Hum) 57, MA 58. Late Scho of St Jo Coll Cam BA (1st cl Th Trip pt iii) 59, MA 63. Ridley Hall Cam 58. **d** 60 **p** 61 Liv. C of St Helens 60; Ormskirk 60-62; CMS India 62-74; in Amer Ch 74-75; C of H Redeemer Lamorbey 75-77; Chap W Pk Hosp Epsom from 77. *c/o West Park Hospital, Epsom, Surrey.*

MACGLASHAN, John Buchanan. b 48. Ridley Coll Melb 68. **d** 72 **p** 73 Melb. C of Ch Ch S Yarra 72-73; St John W Geelong 73-74; Sandringham 74; R of Avoca 75-76; I of Braybrook 76-80; Chap Brighton Jun Gr Sch Dio Melb from 80. *275 New Street, Brighton, Vic, Australia 3186.*

McGLAUGHLIN, Basil Gordon Young. b 10. Trin Coll Dub BA (Resp), Bp Forster Pri, Robert King Pri, Downes Div Pri and Div Test 35, BD 65. **d** 36 **p** 37 Oss. C of New Ross w Rosebercon Old Ross and Whitechurch 36-40; I of Cloughjordan w Modreeny 40-44; R of Stradbally (Castleconnell) 44-57; Chap to Bp of Killaloe 52-55; I of Bourney U 57-62; Drumcliffe and Kilnaboy 62-71; RD of U O'Mullod 62-73; Preb of Killaloe Cathl 63-67; Treas 67-72; I of Outeragh 71-81; RD of Edgeworthstown 78-81; Preb of Elphin Cathl 80. *31 Reubin Avenue, Dolphin's Barn, South Circular Road, Dublin 8, Irish Republic.*

McGONIGLE, Treas thoma. b 22. Trin Coll Dub BA (2nd cl Mod Lang) 45, MA 65. **d** 46 **p** 47 Arm. C of Drumglass 46-50; R of Clogherny 50-53; I of Magherafelt Dio Arm 53-61 and from 74; Portadown 61-74; Preb of Arm Cathl from 72; Treas from 79. *Rectory, Magherafelt, Co Londonderry, BT45 6AL, N Ireland.* (Magherafelt 32365)

McGORLICK, Canon Frank. Ridley Coll Melb 41. ACT ThL 43. **d** 42 Melb for Centr Tang **p** 43 Centre Tang. CMS Miss at Mpwapwa 43-45; Kibondo 45-48; 49-50 and 59-60; Miss at Murgwanza 50-59; and 60-63; Archd of W Lake 63-68; P-in-c of Katoke 63-66; Chap at Mwanza 67-73; Can of Vic Nyan 68-73; Can (Emer) from 73; Perm to Offic Dio Melb from 73; R of Foster 74-78; Perm to Offic Dio Melb from 78. *42 O'Shannessy Street, Nunawading, Vic., Australia 3131.*

McGOWAN, Ven Alan Brian. Ridley Coll Melb ACT ThL (1st cl) 59. **d** 59 **p** 60 Melb. C of H Trin Kew 59-60; Coburg 60-61; Melb Dioc Centre and P-in-c of St Luke Fitzroy 61-65; V of Moorabbin 65-70; R and Can Res of Darwin Cathl 70-73; R of Fremantle w Beaconsfield Dio Perth from 74; Archd of Fremantle from 79. *39 Fortescue Street, Fremantle, W Australia 6158.* (339 4696)

McGOWAN, James Rutherford. b 30. Late Scho and Exhib of Trin Hall Cam BA 53, MA 58. Ely Th Coll 53. **d** 55 **p** 56 Portsm. C of Copnor 55-58; Asst Chap St Edw Sch Ox 58-62; Chap Westmr Sch 62-68; Asst Master Waterford Sch

Mbabane 68-69; Chap K Sch ely 70-73; R of Duxford 73-79; Dep Dir of Educn Dio Ely 74-79; P-in-c of Ickleton 78-79; V of Buckland 79-80; Littleworth 79-80; R of Pusey 79-80. *Address temp unknown.*

MACGOWAN, John Boby. b 11. Univ of Dur Lth 39. Fitzw Ho Cam BA 49, MA 54. ARCO 36, FRCO 56. Oak Hill Th Coll 36. **d** 39 Worc for Col Bp 41 Syd. C of St Clem Marrickville 40-42; R of St Pet and St Paul Milton 42-43; All SS Sutton Forest 43-47; Chap RAAF 44-46; C of St Phil Cam 47-49; V of Donington 49-57; R of Nacton w Levington 57-63; V of Wethersfield 63-68; St Andr Leytonstone 68-71; V of Thorpe-le-Soken 71-76. *28 Hadleigh Road, Frinton-on-Sea, Essex.*

MacGOWAN, Kenneth French. Univ of Agra BA 30. Univ of Aligarh MA 35. **d** 57 **p** 58 Bom. Hd Master Ch Ch Sch Bom 57-63; L to Offic Dio Bom 59-63; C of All SS Cathl Allahabad 63-67; L to Offic Dio Syd from 67. *14 Dixon Street, Parramatta, NSW 2150, Australia.*

McGOWAN, Michael Hugh. St Cath Coll Cam BA 58, MA 62. Clifton Th Coll. **d** 60 **p** 61 Kens for Lon. C of Islington 60-63; Asst Chap Embassy Ch Paris 63-67; Chap at Lyons, Aix-les-Bains and Grenoble 63-67; Chantilly, Rouen, Caen and Le Havre 63-65; V of Maidenhead 68-81. *c/o St Mary's Vicarage, Maidenhead, Berks,* (Maidenhead 24908)

McGOWN, Robert Jackson. b 20. Keble Coll Ox BA 42, MA 46. Linc Th Coll 42. **d** 45 **p** 46 St E. C of St Mary-le-Tower Ipswich 45-47; Chap and Asst Master Brockhurst Sch 47-49; Perm to Offic Dio Ox 49-52; C of Astbury and Asst Dioc Insp of Schs Dio Ches 50-51; Min Can of Glouc Cathl and C of St Mary-de-Lode Glouc 51-54; C of W Kirby (in c of Caldy) Dio Ches 64-71. *16 Church Road, West Kirby, Wirral, Mer, L48 0RW.* (051-625 9481)

McGRATH, Alister Edgar. b 53. Wadh Coll Ox BA 75. Merton Coll Ox BA 78, MA 78, DPhil 78. Westcott Ho Cam 78. **d** 80 Southw **p** 81 Sherwood for Southw. C of Wollaton Dio Southw from 80. *4 Woodbank Drive, Wollaton, Nottingham, NG8 2QU.*

McGRATH, Dudley James. St Jo Coll Morpeth. **d** 56 **p** 57 Bath. Bro of Good Shepherd Dubbo 56-58; C of Dubbo 58-59; Bath Cathl 59-60; Cowra 60-62; P-in-c of Cudal 64-65; R 65-72; I of Deer Pk w St Alb 73-78; St Dunstan Camberwell Dio Melb from 78. *163 Wattle Valley Road, Camberwell, Vic, Australia 3124.* (299 4285)

McGRATH, Peter Henry. b 32. **d** 80 Port Eliz. C of St Nich Charlo Dio Port Eliz from 80. *PO Box 12075, Centrahil, Port Elizabeth 6006, S Africa.*

McGREEVY, Roy. b 34. Wycl Hall Ox 75. **d** 77 **p** 78 Ches. C of Poynton 77-80; V of St Berteline and St Chris Norton Dio Ches from 80. *Vicarage, Norton Hill, Runcorn, Cheshire, WA7 6QE.*

McGREGOR, Alistair Darrant. b 45. ALCD (2nd cl) 69. **d** 69 **p** 70 S'wark. C of Im w St Anselm Streatham 69-73; St Jas Somerset, Bermuda 73-76; Hatcham 76-80; Warden St Mich United Ch and Commun Centre New Cross 76-80; V of St Francis Heartsease City and Dio Nor from 80. *St Francis Vicarage, Rider Haggard Road, Heartsease, Norwich, NR7 9UQ.* (Nor 35399)

MACGREGOR, Alastair Gordon. St Paul's Th Coll Grahmstn. **d** 59 **p** 60 Capetn. C of Plumstead 59-63; St Aug Namaqualand 63-65; R of Bredasdorp 65-71; Robertson 71-76; P-in-c of All SS Lansdowne Dio Capetn from 76. *Rectory, O'okiep Road, Lansdowne, CP, S Africa.* (61-2015)

MACGREGOR, Colin Highmoor. b 19. Univ of Lon BSc (Econ) 45. Magd Coll Cam BA 47, MA 50. Wells Th Coll 54. **d** 56 **p** 57 S'wark. C of Camberwell 56-60; V of St Pet Clapham 60-73; Riddlesdown Dio S'wark from 73; Exam Chap to Bp of S'wark from 73. *Vicarage, St James's Road, Purley, Surrey, CR2 2DL.* (01-660 5436)

McGREGOR, Canon David Stuart. b 32. St Jo Coll Auckld 70. **d** 72 Bp McKenzie for Wel **p** 73 Wel. C of Ch Ch Wanganui 72-77; R of St Hugh City and Dio Port Eliz from 77; Can of Port Eliz from 79. *Box 7050, Newton Park, Port Elizabeth, CP, S Africa.* (041-335112)

McGREGOR, Francis Allan. Bp's Univ Lennox BA 57, LST 59. **d** 59 **p** 60 Ott. C of St Martin Ott 59-62; I of Russell 65-70; Carleton Place 71-75; St Steph City and Dio Ott from 75. *930 Watson Street, Ottawa, Ont, K2B 6B9, Canada.* (613-829 7824)

MacGREGOR, Gregor. b 33. Univ of St Andr MA 64, BD 67. **d** and **p** 77 St Andr (NSM). C of St Mich Elie 77-81; St John Pittenweem 77-81; R of Glenrothes Dio St Andr from 81. *1 Almond Way, Glenrothes, Fife.* (Glenrothes 752174)

McGREGOR, Canon Milton. Univ of New Engl BA 59. ACT ThL 50, Th Scho 54. **d** 50 **p** 51 Armid. C of Glen Innes 50-52; V of Boggabilla 52-60; Chap Univ of New Engl and New Engl Girls' Sch Armid 60-61; Exam Chap to Bp of Armid 60-62; C of St Anne Brondesbury w H Trin Kilburn 62-64; Warden Bro of St Barn Dio N Queensld 64-70; Hon Can of N Queensld 68-70 and from 81; Can 70-81; Warden St Mark's Coll in Univ of N Queensld from 70; Exam Chap to Bp of N Queensld from 71. *PO Box 199, Hermit Park, Townsville, Queensland 4810, Australia.* (077-795044)

MacGREGOR, Neil. b 35. Keble Coll Ox BA 60, MA 80. Wells Th Coll. **d** 65 **p** 66 B & W. C of St Mary Bathwick w Woolley 65-70; R of Oare w Culbone 70-74; C of Lynton w Brendon, Countisbury and Lynmouth 70-74; C-in-c of Kenn w Kingston Seymour 74-76; R 76-80; Lee Brockhurst Dio Lich from 80; R of Wem Dio Lich from 80. *Rectory, Wem, Shropshire, SY4 5TU.* (Wem 32550)

McGREGOR, Peter Louis. b 34. **d** 77 **p** 78 Johann. C of Modeor Dio Johann from 77. *175 Cadogan Avenue, Mondeor 2091, S Africa.*

McGREGOR, William. **d** 52 **p** 53 Sask. I of Leask 52-55; Meadow Lake 55-58; R of N Battleford 58-68; Hon Can of Sktn 67-68; I of St Cath St Cuthb and of St Sav Winnipeg 68-76; H Trin Winnipeg Dio Rupld from 76. *256 Smith Street, Winnipeg, Manit, Canada.*

McGRORY, Gregory Wayne. St Francis Coll Brisb. **d** 74 **p** 75 Brisb. C of Roma 74-75; Warwick 75-77; P-in-c of Mitchell Dio Brisb from 77. *30 Oxford Street, Mitchell, Queensland, Australia 4465.* (Mitchell 26)

MacGUFFIE, Alexander Henley. b 1888. MBE (Mil) 30. **d** 44 **p** 45 Egypt. Missr C of E Miss Aden 44-52; Chap St Mary Aden 45-50; C of Millom w Haverigg (in c of St Luke) 54-56; V of Mungrisdale 56-73, L to Offic Dio Carl from 74. *Mungrisdale Vicarage, Penrith, Cumb.* (Threlkeld 274)

McGUINESS, Hughie. St Jo Coll Morpeth ACT ThL 58. **d** and **p** 59 Perth. C of Northam 59-61; P-in-c of Northam W 61; C of Mosman Pk 62; R of Wongan Hills 62-67; Merredin 67-72; Toodyay 72-79; Kens Dio Perth from 79. *51 Brandon Street, South Perth, W Australia 6151.* (367 1918)

McGUIRE, Alec John. b 51. K Coll Cam BA 73, MA 76. Westcott Ho Cam 74. **d** 78 Buckingham for Ox **p** 79 Ox. C of Hungerford 78-81; St Pet Leeds Dio Ripon from 81. *4 St Peter's House, Kirkgate, Leeds, LS2 7DJ.* (452036)

McGUIRE, John. b 31. Oak Hill Th Coll 59. **d** 62 S'wark **p** 65 Derby. C of Tooting Graveney 62-64; Normanton-by-Derby 64-67; Chap RNR 67-81; Northern Area Sec ICM 67-71; R of Biddulph Moor Dio Lich from 71. *Biddulph Moor Rectory, Stoke-on-Trent, Staffs.* (Stoke-T 513323)

McHARDY, Iain William Thomson Duff. b 13. Univ of St Andr MA 36. Ely Th Coll 37. **d** 38 Pontefract for Wakef **p** 39 Wakef. C of S Kirkby 38-45; C-in-c of Dunblane 45; C of St Wilfrid Cantley 45-52; P-in-c of St Ninian Invergordon 52-74; Exam Chap to Bp of Moray from 60; Can of Inverness 64-77; Syn Clk Dio Moray 72-77; R of St Andr Fortrose w Cromarty 74-80; Dean of Moray, Ross and Caithness 77-80. *Beech Tree Cottage, Navity, Cromarty, Ross.*

MACHARIA, Lukas Wanjie. b 50. St Paul's Coll Limuru 74. **d** 75 **p** 76 Bp Ngaruiya for Mt Kenya S. On study leave. *c/o Box 40502, Nairobi, Kenya.*

MACHELL, Canon Bernard John. LTh (NZ) 45. ACT Th Scho 54. **d** 44 **p** 45 Nel. C of Blenheim 44-47; V of Reefton 47-53; Amuri 53-57; Richmond 57-71; Can of Nel from 62; V of Wakefield 71-78; Amuri Dio Nel from 78. *Vicarage, Culverden, NZ.*

MACHIHA, Canon Langton. **d** 43 **p** 44 S Rhod. P Dio S Rhod 43-52; Dio Mashon from 52; Hon Can of Mashon from 72. *St Oswald's Mission, PO Featherstone, Zimbabwe.*

MACHILI, Crispo. St Andr Dioc Coll Nkwazi 30. **d** 31 **p** 33 Nyasa. P Dio Nyasa 31-64; Dio Malawi 64-71; Can of St Pet Cathl Likoma 67-71; L to Offic Dio Lake Malawi from 72. *Chombo FP School, PO Nkhotakota, Malawi.*

MACHIN, Roy Anthony. b 38. Co for Nat Acad Awards BA 79. Oak Hill Coll 76. **d** 79 **p** 80 Man. C of St Pet Halliwell Dio Man from 79. *25 Redcar Road, Smithills, Bolton, BL1 6LL.* (Bolton 40255)

MACHIPWE, Akisoferi. **d** 64 Mbale. d Dio Mbale. *Bukabusi, PO Box 984, Mbale, Uganda.*

MACHITE, Harold. **d** 64 **p** 65 Centr Tang. P Dio Centr Tang 64-65; Dio Moro 65-80. *PO Berega, Tanzania.*

McHUGH, Brian. b 46. York Univ Ont BA 67. Gen Th Sem NY MDiv 73. **d** 72 NY for Tor **p** 73 Tor. Prior H Cross Priory Dio Tor from 73. *Holy Cross Priory, 3 Humewood Drive, Toronto, Canada.*

MACIE, Americo. **d** 66 **p** 68 Lebom. P Dio Lebom. *Caixa Postal 63, Jo£ao Belo, Mozambique.*

MACIE, Canon Josias. **d** 23 **p** 43 Lebom. P Dio Lebom; Hon Can from 71. *Missâo Anglicana de Maciene, CTT Chongoene, Joâo Belo, Mozambique.*

MACIE, Lucas Martins. **d** 66 **p** 68 Lebom. P Dio Lebom; Distr Supt of Maputo from 76. *Caixa Postal 57, Maputo, Mozambique.*

MACIE, Ven Silvestre. **d** 47 **p** 48 Lebom. P Dio Lebom; Archd of Maciene from 65. *Caixa Postal 63, Jo£ao Belo, Mozambique.*

McILLMURRAY, John Barron. Bps' Univ Lennox BA 65,

STB 68. **d** 66 **p** 68 Queb. C of St Pet Sherbrooke 66-68; Dioc Consultant Relig Educn and Youth Work Dio Queb 68-71; I of Seven Is 71-75; Dom Chap to Bp of Queb 71-77; R of Magog 75-77; St John Sarnia Dio Hur from 77. *144 Margaret Street, Sarnia, Ont., Canada.* (519-344 6522)

MacINNES, Canon David Rennie. b 32. Jes Coll Cam 2nd cl Engl Trip pt i 54, BA 55, 2nd cl Th Trip pt ii 56, MA 59. Ridley Hall Cam 55. **d** 57 **p** 58 Roch. C of St Mark Gillingham 57-61; C of St Helen Bishopsgate Lon 61-67; Prec of Birm Cathl 67-78; Dioc Missr and Hon Chap Birm Cathl from 79; Hon Can Birm Cathl from 81. *32 Salisbury Road, Moseley, Birmingham, B13 8JJ.* (021-449 1479)

McINNES, Raymond John. b 50. ACT ThL 76. St Jo Coll Morpeth 74. **d** 77 Melb **p** 78 Wang for Melb. C of H Trin Benalla 77-79; N Fitzroy and Clifton Hill Dio Melb from 79. *1 South Terrace, Clifton Hill, Vic, Australia 3068.* (48-4342)

MACINTOSH, Andrew Alexander. b 36. St Jo Coll Cam 1st cl Th Trip pt i 57, 2nd cl Th Trip pt ii 59, 2nd cl Th Trip pt iii 61, BA, 59, MA 63, BD 80. Ridley Hall Cam 60. **d** 62 **p** 63 Linc. C of S Ormsby 62-64; Lect St D Coll Lamp 64-67; L to Offic Dio St D 64-67; Dio Ely from 67; Chap St Jo Coll Cam 67-69; Fell, Tutor and Asst-Dean from 69; Dean from 79; Lect in Th from 70; Exam Chap to Bp of Carl from 69. *St John's College, Cambridge, CB2 1TP.* (Cambridge 61621)

McINTOSH, Andrew Malcolm Ashwell. b 43. Chich Th Coll 67. **d** 70 **p** 71 Bradwell for Chelmsf. C of Brentwood 71-74; Chingford 74-79; P-in-c of St Mary Maldon (w Mundon from 80) Dio Chelmsf from 79. *St Mary's Rectory, Park Drive, Maldon, Essex.* (Maldon 57191)

McINTOSH, David Henry. b 45. St Jo Coll Dur BSc 67, Dipl Th 69. Cranmer Hall Dur 67. **d** 70 Warrington for Liv **p** 71 Liv. C of Sutton Lancs 70-74; Team V 74-75; Chap Bethany Sch Goudhurst 75-80; V of St Thos Ap Douglas Dio S & M from 80; Dir of Relig Educn Dio S & M from 80. *St Thomas's Vicarage, Princes Road, Douglas, IM.* (Douglas 5609)

MACINTOSH, George Grant. b 41. St Jo Coll Dur BA 75, Dipl Th 76. **d** 76 **p** 77 Doncaster for Sheff. C of All SS Ecclesall Sheff 76-79; St Osw Millhouses Sheff 79-81; V of St Timothy Crookes City and Dio Sheff rom 81. *St Timothy's Vicarage, Slinn Street, Sheffield, S10 1NZ.* (Sheff 661745)

McINTOSH, Canon Hugh. b 14. Hatf Coll Dur LTh 41, BA 42, MA 45. Edin Th Coll 38. **d** and **p** 42 Brech. C of St Paul's Cathl Dundee 42-46; Chap St Mary's Cathl Edin 46-49; C of St Salvador Edin 49-51; R of St Adrian Gullane 51-54; St John Dumfries 54-66; Can of Glas 59-66 and from 70; Synod Clk 59-66; Provost of St Mary's Cathl Glas 66-70; R of Lanark Dio Glas from 70; Exam Chap to Bp of Glas and Gall from 75. *Christ Church Rectory, Lanark.* (Lanark 3065)

MACINTOSH, Ian Ross. Rhodes Univ BA 51. St Paul's Coll Grahamstn LTh 56. **d** 56 **p** 57 Pret. C of St Alb Cathl Pret 56-60; W Suburbs Pret 60; R 61-65; Worcester 65-68; Chap SAAF Pret 68-70; R of Orange Grove 71-80; Parkmore Dio Johann from 80. *Box 65366, Benmore, Johannesburg, S Africa.*

McINTOSH, John Alan. Univ of Syd BA 58. Westmr Th Sem USA BD 62. Moore Th Coll Syd ACT ThL O **d** 65 **p** 66 Syd. Lect Moore Th Coll Syd 65-67; C of Turramurra 67-69; CMS Miss Indonesia 70-80; Prin St Andr Hall Parkville from 80. *190 The Avenue, Parkville, Vic, Australia.*

MACINTOSH, Neil Keith. ACT ThL 61, Th Scho 66. Moore Th Coll Syd 61. BD (Lon) 63. **d** 61 Bp Kerle for Syd **p** 62 Syd. C of St Aug Neutral Bay 61-64; Kingsford 64-65; St Mark Darling Point Syd 65-68; C-in-c of Marsfield w Denistone E Provisional Distr 68-69; Asst Master N Syd Gr Sch 69-72; L to Offic Dio Syd 69-71 and 72-75; Libr Moore Th Coll 73-75; R of Sutton Forest 75-76; Chap KS Parramatta from 76. *The King's School, Parramatta, NSW, Australia 2150.* (630-0201)

McINTOSH, Patrick Ezekiel. b 47. Codr Coll Barb 74. **d** 76 **p** 77 Windw Is. C of H Trin St Lucia 76-77; S Patr Barrouallie 77-79; P-in-c of St Jas Layou Dio Windw Is from 79. *Rectory, Layou, St Vincent, W Indies.* (809-45 87424)

McINTOSH, St John. b 14. Cudd Coll 43. **d** 43 Chelmsf **p** 64 Portsm. C of St Sav Walthamstow 43; All SS Portsea 63-64. *Address temp unknown.*

MACINTYRE, Angus Greer. b 14. Late Scho of Linc Coll Ox BA (2nd cl Mod Hist) 36, Dipl in Th (w distinc) 39, MA 41. Men in Disp 46. Wycl Hall Ox 38. **d** 39 **p** 40 Ripon C of St Clem Leeds 39-40; Chap RAFVR 40-46; C of St Jo Evang Edin 46-48; R of St Jas Leith 48-52; Chap of Trin Coll Glenalmond 52-68; Can of St Ninian's Cathl Perth 66-68; V of Harborne 68-76; V of St Paul's Cathl St Hel 76-79; Hon C of Ch Ch Morningside City and Dio Edin from 79. *76 Polworth Gardens, Edinburgh 11.* (031-228 6182)

McINTYRE, Jack Simpson. b 18. **d** 62 **p** 63 St E. C of Wrentham w Benacre Covehithe and Henstead 62-64; St Jo Bapt Ipswich Dio St E from 70. *Flat 2, 27 Warrington Road, Ipswich, Suff.*

McINTYRE, James Whitelaw. b 37. BD (2nd cl) Lon 66. Edin Th Coll 59. **d** 62 **p** 63 Glas. C of St John Dumfries 62-66; C-in-c of H Name Cumbernauld 66-74; R of H Trin Stirling Dio Edin from 74. *18 Abercromby Place, Stirling.*

McINTYRE, John Charles. b 51. BD (Lon) 76. ACT ThL 75. Ridley Coll Melb 73. **d** 77 **p** 78 Melb. C of St Jas w St Luke Dandenong 77-79; P-in-c of Thomastown Dio Melb from 79. *Vicarage, Arundell Street, Thomastown, Vic, Australia 3074.* (465 4259)

McINTYRE, Kenneth. Univ of Syd BEcon 48. ACT ThL 58. Moore Th Coll. **d** 59 Bp Hilliard for Syd **p** 59 Syd. C of W Tyde 59-60; Org Sec Syd Dioc Bd of Educn 50-63; Adult Educn Officer 64; L to Offic Dio Syd 60-68; Dir of Chr Educn Dio Melb 68-72; Hd Master Selw Coll Guadalcanal 73-78; L to Offic Dio Centr Melan 75-78; R of Highgate 78-80; Leeming Dio Perth from 80. *Rectory, Ewing Avenue, Bull Creek, W Australia 6153.* (332-5344)

McINTYRE, Laurie. Wollaston Coll W Austr 63. ACT ThL 64. **d** and **p** 64 Perth. C of Wembley-Floreat Pk 65-66; R of Swan 66-67; L to Offic Dio Perth 67-72; Dio Syd 72-77; Asst Master Blue Mountains Gr Sch 72-77; Chap New Engl Girls' Sch Armid from 77. *St John's Lodge, NEGS, Armidale, NSW, Australia 2350.*

McINTYRE, Peter William. b 45. Univ of W Ont BA 66. Univ of Guelph MA 72. Trin Coll Tor MDiv 80. **d** 80 Niag **p** 81 Bp CM Mitchell for Niag. C of St Geo St Catharines Dio Niag from 80. *c/o St George's Church, Box 893, St Catharines, Ont, Canada L2R 6Z4.* (416-682 9232)

McINTYRE, Robert Marshall. b 08. Wells Th Coll. **d** 47 **p** 48 S'wark. C of St Phil Lambeth 47-49; St Pet St Helier 49-54; V of St Paul Newington 54-63; Wells 63-71; C-in-c of Chelwood 73-75; Compton Dando 73-75; V of Publow w Pensford (w Compton Dando and Chelwood from 75) 71-76. *1 Water Lane, Lopen, South Petherton, Somt, TA13 5JW.*

MACK, Charles Derrick. b 32. St D Coll Lamp BA 54. Qu Coll Birm 56. **d** 58 **p** 59 Ches. C of Sale 58-63; V of Bredbury Dio Ches 63-72; Asst Dioc Insp of Schs from 64; R of Christleton Dio Ches from 72. *Christleton Rectory, Plough Lane, Chester, CH3 7BA.* (Chester 35663)

McKAE, William John. b 42. Univ of Liv BSc 63. Univ of Bris Dipl Th 70. Wells Th Coll 68. **d** 71 **p** 72 Ches. C of St Paul w St Luke Tranmere 71-74; Midsomer Norton 74-75; Team V of Birkenhead Priory 75-80; R of Oughtrington Dio Ches from 80. *Oughtrington Rectory, Lymm, Chesh.* (Lymm 2388)

McKAVANAGH, Dermot James. b 51. AKC and BD 78. TCD BA 75. MA 78. **d** 78 **p** 79 Cant. C of St Sav Croydon Dio Cant from 78. *St Saviour's Lodge, 96a Lodge Road, Croydon, Surrey.*

McKAY, Brian Alexander. b 44. Univ of W Ont BA 67. Huron Coll Ont BTh 70. **d** 70 **p** 71 Bp Appleyard for Huron. C of Trin Ch Galt 71-73; I of St D Windsor 73-77; St Timothy Lon Dio Hur from 77; Dom Chap to Bp of Hur from 80. *181 Ellsworth Crescent, London, Ont., Canada.* (519-451 7780)

McKAY, Brian Andrew. b 39. Sarum Th Coll 69. **d** 71 **p** 72 Bp Ramsbotham for Newc T. C of Walker 71-74; Wooler w Doddington 74-77; Team V 77-81; V of St Mary Magd Long Benton Dio Newc T from 81. *St Mary's House, Blackfriars Way, Newcastle-upon-Tyne, NE12 8ST.* (Newcastle 662326)

MACKAY, Clive Vincent. ACT ThL 57. **d** 58 **p** 59 Melb. C of H Trin Coburg 58-60; N Geelong 60-61; Min of Whittlesea 61-67; C of Swan Hill 67-68; Perm to Offic Dio Melb from 68. *31 Church Street, Abbotsford, Vic, Australia 3067.* (03-42 5739)

McKAY, Ven David John. Univ of BC BA 63. Angl Th Coll BC. **d** 65 **p** 66 BC. C of Cedar Hill 65-67; P-in-c of Gold River 67-71; R of Campbell River 71-73; St Alb Port Alberni 73-81; Can of BC from 79; St Paul Nanaimo Dio BC from 81; Archd of Nanaimo from 81. *100 Chapel Street, Nanaimo, BC, Canada.*

MACKAY, Canon Douglas Brysson. b 27. Edin Th Coll 56. **d** 58 **p** 59 Moray. Prec of St Andr Cathl Inverness 58-61; R of Gordon Chap Fochabers 61-72; Can of St Andr Cathl Inverness 65-72; Hon Can from 72; Synod Clk Dio Moray 65-72; P-in-c of St Marg Aberlour 64-72; R of Carnoustie Dio Brechin 72; Can of St Paul's Cathl Dundee and Syn Clk Dio Brech from 81. *Rectory, Carnoustie, Angus, DD7 6AB.* (2202)

McKAY, Graham Bruce. b 50. Univ of NSW BEng 75. Univ of Lon BD 80. Moore Th Coll Syd ThL. **d** 81 Syd. C of St Phil Eastwood Dio Syd from 81. *8a Clanwilliam Street, Eastwood, NSW, Australia 2122.*

MACKAY, Hedley Neill. b 27. St Aid Coll 53. **d** 56 **p** 57 York. C of St Mary Beverley 56-59; Scarborough 59-60; CMS Miss Wusasa 61-70; V of St Andr Zaria 67-70; C of Wawne 70-71; Team V of Sutton-in-Holderness w Wawne 71-76; V of

Huntington City and Dio York 76-78; R from 78. *Huntington Rectory, York, YO3 9NU.* (York 768160)

MACKAY, Canon James. b 1895. **d** 31 **p** 32 Liv. C of St Geo Everton 31-32; St Alb Bevington 32-35; H Trin Wavertree 35-39; V of Hale 40-64; RD of Farnworth 50-64; Hon Can of Liv 60-64; Can (Emer) from 64. *The Old Vicarage, Swaffham Prior, Cambridge, CB5 0LE.* (Newmarket 741585)

MACKAY, James Alexander Nigel. b 11. TCD BA 38. Edin Th Coll 38. **d** 41 **p** 42 Edin. C of All SS Edin 41-45; R of St Mungo Alexandria 45-51; V of Kelstern w Calcethorpe 51-59; R of Ludford Magna w Ludford Parva 51-59; P-in-c of St Benet and All SS Kentish Town 60-62; V of Weasenham 62-67; V of Rougham 62-67. *29 Howbury Street, Bedford, MK40 3QU.*

McKAY, John Andrew. Chich Th Coll 72. **d** 74 Lon **p** 75 Edmon for Lon. C of St Mary Virg Primrose Hill Hampstead 74-77; V of Ch Ch w St Steph Battersea Dio S'wark from 77. *Christ Church Vicarage, Candahar Road, Battersea, SW11.* (01-228 1225)

McKAY, John William. b 41. Univ of Aber MA 62. Keble Coll Ox BA (Th) 64. Selw Coll Cam PhD 69. Ridley Hall Cam 66. **d** 70 **p** 71 York. Lect in Th Hull Univ from 69; Sen Lect from 78; C of Cottingham Dio York from 72. *77 Carr Lane, Willerby, Hull, HU10 6JS.* (Hull 658974)

McKAY, Leslie Jack. b 04. St Cath Coll Cam 2nd cl Hist Trip pt i 25, BA (2nd cl Hist Trip pt ii) 26, MA 30. Ridley Hall Cam 32. **d** 34 **p** 35 Sarum. C of Hamworthy 34-36; Perm to Offic at St Andr Nottm 36-37; C of Widcombe 37-38; Chap of Clifton Th Coll 38-42; C-in-c of Ch Ch Conv Distr Bedford 43-55; Min 55-58; V 58-73. *Manormead, Tilford Road, Hindhead, Surrey.*

McKAY, Canon Roy. b 1900. Magd Coll Ox (2nd cl Jurispr) 22, BA 23, MA 26. Ripon Hall Ox 24. **d** 26 **p** 27 S'wark. C of St Paul Kingston Hill 26-28; C-in-c of St Mark Londonderry Warws 28-31; V of Mountfield 31-36; Chap at Santa Cruz Teneriffe 36-37; Chap of Alleyn's Coll Dulwich 37-42; V of Goring 43-48; Chap of Canford Sch 48-55; Hd of Relig Broadcasting Dept BBC 55-63; Can and Preb of Hampstead in Chich Cathl 57-71; Can (Emer) from 71; Pr in Lincoln's Inn 58-59; R of St Jas Garlickhithe w St Mich Queenhithe and H Trin L Lon 64-70. *64 Thomas More House, Barbican, EC2.*

McKAY, Thomas Edison. St Pet Coll Ja 23. **d** 23 **p** 24 Ja. P Dio Ja 23-37; to Amer Ch 37-46; R of Moore Town w Fellowship 46-49; P-in-c of Gilnock 49-53; Lluidas Vale 53-56. *Labyrinth PO, Jamaica, W Indies.*

McKEACHIE, William Noble. b 43. Univ of the South, Sewanee BA (*summa cum laude*) 66. Trin Coll Tor STB 70. **d** 70 Tor **p** 70 Ox for Tor. Chap-Stud at St Jo Coll Ox 70-72; Dioc Th Consultant Tor 73-78; Chap Hart Ho and Hon C of St Jas Cathl Tor 74-78; Exam Chap to Bp of Tor 77-78; on leave. *University of the South, Sewanee, USA.*

McKEAN, Ven Robert Keith. Univ of Manit BA 61. St Jo Coll Winnipeg LTh 61. **d** 60 **p** 61 Rupld. C of St Aid Winnipeg 60-62; R of St Alb Winnipeg 62-65; All SS Peterborough Dio Tor from 65; Can of Tor 72-74; Archd of Pet from 74. *235 Rubidge Street, Peterborough, Ont., Canada.* (705-742 4311)

McKECHNIE, John Gregg. b 30. Em Coll Cam 3rd cl Hist Trip pt I 52, BA (2nd cl Th Trip pt ii) 54, MA 57. Ridley Hall Cam 54. **d** 55 **p** 56 S'wark. C of Morden 55-57; Tutor Clifton Th Coll Bris 57-62; Publ Pr Dio Bris 58-62; R of St Pancras w St Jo Chich 62-68; V of St Jo Evang and St Steph Reading Dio Ox from 68; Exam Chap to Bp of Ox from 79. *50 London Road, Reading, Berks, RG1 5AS.* (Reading 82366)

McKEE, David Carey. Univ of Manit BA 48. **d** 61 **p** 62 Niag. P-in-c of Winona 62-67. *26 Bernard Avenue, Toronto 5, Ont, Canada.*

McKEE, Douglas John Dunstan. b 34. Univ of W Austr BA 65. St Mich Th Coll Crafers 54. ACT ThL 58. M SSM 58. **d** 57 **p** 58 Adel. L to Offic Dio Adel from 57; Asst Chap St Barn Sch Ravenshoe 59-60; Tutor SSM Th Coll Crafers 60 and 65-68; Prior from 68; Tutor of Univ of W Austr and Perm to Offic Dio Perth 61-64; Prov of SSM in Austr 68-72; Dir SSM 72; 72-82; Pr Dio Southw from 73; L to Offic Dio Ox from 81. *SSM Priory, Willen, Milton Keynes, Bucks, MK15 9AA.* (Newport Pagnell 611749)

McKEE, Canon Harold Denis. b 30. Trin Coll Dub BA 53, MA 57. **d** 54 **p** 55 Dub. C of St Mary Donnybrook Dub 54-58; Treas V of St Patr Cathl Dub 56-61; C of St Bart Dub 58-61; Succr of Sheff Cathl 62-65; Prec from 65; Can Res from 65; M Gen Syn 70-75. *Flat 4, 46 Hill, Broomhill, Sheffield, S10 5BX.* (0742 685780)

McKEE, William Mulholland. b 05. **d** 49 **p** 50 Bradf. C of Pudsey 49-52; V of Silsden 52-58; R of Grenstead 58-74; P-in-c of Farnham 74-80. *Ivy Cottage, Burton End, Stansted, Essex, CM24 8UQ.* (Bp's Stortford 815888)

McKEE, William Thomas. b 18. Ch of Ireland Th Coll Dub 64. **d** 65 **p** 66 Connor. C of Ballymena 65-68; Willowfield 68-73; C-in-c of Magherally w Annaclone Dio Drom 73-77; R from 77. *46 Kilmacrew Road, Banbridge, Co Down, BT32 4EP, N Ireland.* (Banbridge 23655)

McKEEMAN, David Christopher. b 36. K Coll Lon and Warm AKC 58. **d** 60 **p** 61 S'wark. C of St Andr Catford 60-64; C-in-c of Em W Dulwich 64-69; LPr Dio Win from 70. *6 Montague Road, Bournemouth, BH5 2EP.* (Bournemouth 425641)

McKEGNEY, Herbert Austin. b 1898. St Aid Coll 26. **d** 27 **p** 28 Down. C of Coleraine 27-30; I of St Aug Derry 31-72; Can of Derry 48-72. *4 Sea View Drive, Portstewart, Londonderry, N Ireland.* (Portstewart 3178)

McKEGNEY, John Wade. b 47. TCD BA (Gen Stud) 70, MA 81. Div Hostel Dub 70. **d** 72 **p** 73 Down & Drom. C of Ballynafeigh 72-75; Bangor 75-80; R of Drumgath, Drumballyroney & Clonduff and of Drumgooland Dio Down from 80. *29 Cross Road, Hilltown, Rathfriland, Newry, BT34 5TF.* (Rathfriland 30304)

McKELLAR, John Lorne. b 19. Sarum Wells Th Coll 70. **d** 72 **p** 73 Sarum. C of Warminster and of Upton Scudamore 72-75; in Amer Ch 75-79; P-in-c of St Barn Colchester 79-81; in Amer Ch. *c/o St David's Rectory, Cottage Grove, W Oregon, USA.*

McKELLAR, John Walton. Univ of Syd BSc (2nd cl Biochemistry) 50. ACT ThL (2nd cl) 59. **d** 59 **p** 80 C & Goulb. C of St Paul Canberra 59-66; St Alb Canberra 66-80; Hon C of St Paul Manuka Dio C & Goulb from 80. *6 Ulverstone Street, Lyons, Canberra, Australia.*

McKELVEY, Robert Samuel James Houston. QUB BA (2nd cl Geog) 65. Trin Coll Dub Bp Forster Pri and Downes Oratory Pri (2nd cl) 67. **d** 67 **p** 68 Connor. C of Dunmurry 67-70; CF (TAVR) 70; C-in-c of Kilmakee Dio Connor from 70; R from 77; Ed Ch of Ireland Gazette from 75; N Ireland Educn Org for Ch Bd of Educn from 81. *60 Killeaton Park, Derriaghy, Dunmurry, Co Antrim, N Ireland.* (Dunmurry 610505)

McKELVIE, Alfred. b 10. TCD BA (Resp), Downes Oratory Pri (2nd), Ryan Pri, Past Th Pri and King Edw Pri 34, Div Test (2nd cl) 35, MA 43. **d** 35 **p** 36 Down. C of Ch Ch Lisburn 35-38; St Jude Ballynafeigh Belf 38-42; I of Templecorran and Islandmagee 42-46; St Donard Belf 46-56; St Jude Ballynafeigh Belf 56-80; RD of Hillsborough 63-66; Preb of Down Cathl 63-68; Treas 68-70; Chan 74-80; Archd of Down 70-74; L to Offic Dio Down from 80. *13 Dundela Gardens, belfast, BT4 3DH, N Ireland.* (Belfast 654902)

McKEMEY, Alfred Douglas. b 18. Tyndale Hall Bris 38. **d** 42 **p** 43 Lon. C of St Pet U Holloway 42-45; St John Heatherlands 45-48; Org Sec of CPAS and Perm to Offic in SE Distr 48-51; V of St Paul Plumstead 51-57; All S Eastbourne 57-68; St Andr Burgess Hill Dio Chich from 68; RD of Hurst from 80. *St Andrew's Vicarage, Burgess Hill, Sussex.* (Burgess Hill 2023)

McKEMEY, Robert. b 15. St Aid Coll 50. **d** 52 Burnley for Blackb **p** 53 Blackb. C of Ch Ch Blackb 52-53; PC of St Barn Blackb 53-57; L to Offic Dio Momb 57-59; Dio Nak 61-69; Exam Chap to Bp of Nak 62-69; BCMS Field Sec from 62; VG Dio Nak 63-69; Archd of Nak 64-69; I of Kilrea 69-73; R of Meysey Hampton w Marston Meysey 73-81; RD of Fairford 77-81; C-in-c of Clondevaddock Dio Raph from 81. *Rectory, Tamney, Letterkenny, Co Donegal, Irish Republic.*

MACKEN, Neil Robert. b 48. Macquarie Univ NSW BA 77. Moore Th Coll Syd 76. **d** 77 Bp Dain for Syd **p** 77 Syd. C of St Jas Turramurra 77-78; Lane Cove 79-81; Wentworthville Dio Syd from 81. *18 Pritchard Street, Wentworthville, NSW, Australia 2145.* (636 9737)

McKENNA, Dermot William. TCD BA 63, Div Test (2nd cl) 64, MA 66. **d** 64 **p** 65 Oss. C of Enniscorthy 64-66; I of Killeshin w Cloydagh, Killabban and Mayo Dio Leigh from 66. *Rectory, Ballickmoyler, Carlow, Irish Republic.*

MACKENNA, Richard William. b 49. Pemb Coll Cam BA 71, MA 75. Univ of Ox BA 77. Ripon Coll Cudd 75. **d** 78 Lon **p** 79 Kens for Lon. C of St Dionis Parsons Green Fulham 78-81; St Jas Paddington Dio Lon from 81. *45 Cleveland Square, W2.* (01-262 7841)

MACKENNA, Robert Christopher Douglass. b 44. Oriel Coll Ox BA 72, MA 75. Cudd Coll 71. **d** 73 Dorking for Guildf **p** 74 Guildf. C of Farncombe 73-77; Tattenham Corner & Burgh Heath 77-79; P-in-c of Hascombe Dio Guildf from 79. *Hascombe Rectory, Godalming, Surrey, GU8 4JA.* (Hascombe 362)

MACKENZIE, Canon Alan George Kett Fairbairn. b 11. OBE 81. Univ of Wales BSc 32. **d** 41 **p** 42 Ex. C of St Leon Ex 41-42; St Sidwell Ex 42-47; Chap Devon and Ex Miss to Adult Deaf and Dumb 41-47; Chap Coun for Deaf and Dumb Dio Ox 48-51; Asst Org Sec R Assc for Deaf and Dumb 51-52; Supt Chap 52-59; I of St Sav Old Oak Road Acton w All SS Norfolk Sq Paddington (for Deaf and Dumb) 52-59; Perm to Offic Dios S'wark Roch Guildf and Chelmsf 54-59; Cant 58-59; Chap-Sec Sarum Dioc Assoc for Deaf and

Hard of Hearing 59-74; Can of Sarum 72-77; Can (Emer) from 77; P-in-c of Corscombe 75-77; Halstock and E w W Chelborough 77; Perm to Offic Dio Chelmsf and Dio St Alb from 77. *23 Glebe End, Elsenham, Bishop's Stortford, Herts, CM22 6EL.*

McKENZIE, Very Rev Alexander George. Moore Th Coll Syd ACT ThL 59. **d** 54 **p** 55 Bend. C of All SS Cathl Bend 54-55; P-in-c of Kangaroo Flat 55; Kyabram 56; V of Tongala 56-62; R of H Trin Bend 62-67; Kyabram Bend 67-73; Dom Chap to Bp of Bend 64-72; Can of Bend 70-72; Dean from 72. *All Saints' Cathedral, MacKenzie Street, Bendigo, Vic, Australia 3550.* (054-43 4192)

MACKENZIE, Alfred Arthur. b 25. Bps' Coll Cheshunt, 61. **d** 61 Colchester for Chelmsf **p** 62 Chelmsf. C of Waltham Abbey 61-64; V of St Erkenwald Barking 64-72; Broomfield Dio Chelmsf from 72. *Vicarage, Butlers Close, Broomfield, CM1 5BE.* (Chelmsf 440318)

McKENZIE, Barrie. b 43. Qu Coll Birm 68. **d** 70 **p** 71 Dur. C of S Westoe 70-74; W Harton 74-77; St Mich AA Norton 77-79; R of Penshaw Dio Dur from 79. *Penshaw Rectory, Houghton-le-Spring, Co Durham, DH4 7ER.* (H-le-S 842631)

McKENZIE, David Robert. b 47. Wycl Coll Tor MDiv 74. **d** 74 **p** 75 Tor. C of Ch Ch Deer Pk Tor 74-76; Trail 76-78; I of St Steph Coquitlam Dio New Westmr from 79. *9887 Cameron Street, Burnaby, BC, Canada.*

MACKENZIE, David Stuart. b 45. Linc Th Coll 66. **d** 69 Dur **p** 70 Jarrow for Dur. C of St Mary Virg w St Pet Conv Distr Bp Wearmouth 69-72; St Giles Pontefract 72-74; Chap RAF from 74. *c/o Barclays Bank Ltd., 46-49 Broad Street, Stamford, Lincs.*

MacKENZIE, Canon Edward. St Pet Coll Rosettenville, 62. **d** 64 **p** 65 Johann. C of St Alb Johann 64-67; P-in-c of Westlea 67-75; R of Athlone 75-80; Crawford Dio Capetn from 80; Can of Capetn from 80. *Rectory, Belgravia Road, Athlone, CP, S Africa.* (67-7208)

MACKENZIE, George. b 09. Worc Coll Ox BA 31, MA 35. MBE (Mil) 46. TD and Bar 50, 2nd Bar 57. Wells Th Coll 32. **d** 33 **p** 34 Blackb. C of St Mary and All SS Whalley 33-36; Ashton-on-Ribble 36-44; CF (TA) 35-59; (TA-R of O) 59-64; V of Whaddon 45-47; R of Tattenhoe 45-47; W Grinstead w Partridge Green 47-52; Sullington 52-74; C-in-c of Storrington 52-53; R 53-74; RD of Storrington 63-70. *21 The Martlets, West Chiltington, Pulborough, Sussex.*

MACKENZIE, Iain MacGregor. b 37. Qu Coll Ox BA (Th) 59, MA 63. Univ of Edin MTh 69. Wycl Hall Ox. **d** 63 Win **p** 64 Southn for Win. C of Southn 63-66; Christchurch w Mudeford 66-69; R of H Trin Dunoon 69-74; V of All SS Southbourne 75-77; C of Woolston 78; St Giles-in-the-Fields Dio Lon from 79; Exam Chap to Bp of Lon from 81. *Higher Bosigran, Pendeen, Penzance, TR20 8YX.* (Penzance 796096)

McKENZIE, Jack Llewellyn. b 29. **d** 79 Lon **p** 80 Willesden for Lon. C of St Mich AA Stonebridge Willesden Dio Lon from 79. *2 Beckett Square, Chiltern Park, Berkhampsted, Herts.*

MACKENZIE, Ven John Andrews. Dalhousie Univ BA 57. Univ of K Coll Halifax LTh 59, BD 60. **d** 58 **p** 59 NS. R of Falmouth 58-63; C of St Aid Tor 64-68; on leave 68-73; I of Masset 74-78; Greenville Dio Caled from 78; Archd of Caled from 81. *Greenville, Naas River, BC, Canada.*

MACKENZIE, Lawrence Duncan. b 30. St Aid Coll 52. **d** 55 **p** 56 Blackb. C of St Gabr Blackb 55-58; Burnley 58-60; St Giles-in-the-Fields 60-63; V of Queensbury Dio Lon from 63. *Vicarage, Waltham Drive, Edgware, Middx, HA8 5PQ.* (01-952 4536)

McKENZIE, Malcolm. Univ of Melb BA 57. St Jo Coll Morpeth. **d** 57 **p** 58 Bal. C of Portland 57-58; P-in-c of Heywood 58-62; Prec St Geo Cathl Perth 63-64; Chap St Mark's Coll Adel 64-68; Master 68-77. *St Mark's University College, N Adelaide, S Australia 5006.* (08-267 2698)

MACKENZIE, Peter Thomas. b 44. Univ of Lon LLB 67. Univ of Nottm Dipl Th 68. Cudd Coll 68. **d** 70 **p** 71 Portsm. C of Leigh Pk 70-75; P-in-c of St Mary Milton Regis (St Mary Sittingbourne from 77) Dio Cant from 75. *88 Albany Road, Milton Regis, Sittingbourne, Kent, ME10 1EL.* (Sittingbourne 72535)

MACKENZIE, Ramsay Malcolm Bolton. b 1893. Trin Coll Ox BA 15, MA 19. Ely Th Coll 22. **d** 23 **p** 24 Lon. C of St Matthias Earl's Court 23-32; Sec ACS 32-34; Sec Centr Bd of Finance of C of E and Financial Sec of Ch Assembly 34-37; Proc Conv Lon 35-42; L to Offic Dio Lon 35-37; V of Shrewsbury 38-55; Surr from 38; Chap R Salop Infirm 38-48; RD of Shrewsbury 52-55; R of Edgmond 55-59; Perm to Offic Dio Chich from 59; Hon C of St Pet Eastbourne Dio Chich 59-71. *6 Pearl Court, Devonshire Place, Eastbourne, E Sussex, BN21 4AB.* (Eastbourne 23200)

MACKENZIE, Reginald James Sterling. b 11. Sarum Th Coll 55. **d** and **p** 57 Chich. C of Bognor 57-59; R of Tillington 59-67; V of St Kew 67-73; P-in-c of Perranuthnoe 73-78; St Hilary 73-78; St Hilary w Perranuthnoe 78-81; Perm to Offic Dio Truro from 81. *Higher Bosigran, Pendeen, Penzance, TR20 8YX.* (Penzance 796096)

MACKENZIE, Richard Graham. b 49. St Aug Coll Cant 72. **d** 73 **p** 74 Cant. C of Deal 73-78; Herne Dio Cant from 78. *Church View, Herne Street, Herne, Kent.* (Herne Bay 63113)

McKENZIE, Robert Leonard. ACT ThL 18. **d** 18 **p** 20 Bend. C of Koondrook 18-20; V 20-21; Mitiamo 21-24; LPr Dio River from 53. *Barham, NSW, Australia 2739.*

McKENZIE, Canon Thomas Allan. Coll Ho Ch Ch LTh 64. **d** 51 **p** 52 Ch Ch. C of Merivale 51-53; V of Banks Peninsula 54-58; Te Ngawi 58-60; Riccarton 60-66; P-in-c of Ascen Sing 66-69; V of Geraldine 69-74; L to Offic Dio Dun 74; Dio Ch Ch 74-76; V of St Alb Dio Ch Ch from 76; Hon Can of Ch Ch from 78. *138 Cranford Street, Christchurch 1, NZ.* (554-253)

MACKENZIE-LOWE, Cyril. Ripon Hall, Ox 64. **d** 66 **p** 67 S'wark. C of St Paul w St Mark Deptford 66-68; E Wickham 68-73; V of Newborough w Borough Fen Dio Pet from 73. *Newborough Vicarage, Peterborough.* (Newborough 682)

McKEON, James Ernest. b 22. TCD BA 45. **d** 46 **p** 47 Arm. C of Dundalk 46-48; St Geo Dub 48-52; I of Kilsaran 2 Dunleer 52-59; Drogheda 59-64; C-in-c of Termonfeckin and Beaulieu 62-64; Warden Wilson's Hosp Multyfarnham Dio Meath from 64. *Wilson's Hospital, Multyfarnham, Co Westmeath, Irish Republic.*

McKEON, Victor Edward Samuel. b 39. FCA (Ireland) 65. Div Hostel Dub. **d** 68 **p** 69 Clogh. C of Enniskillen 68-72; Accountant to Dios Connor, Down and Dromore from 72; R of Magherahamlet 77-79; Derryvullen N Dio Clogh from 79. *Rectory, Irvinestown, Co Fermanagh, N Ireland.* (Irvinestown 21225)

McKEOWN, Lydon Kenneth. Sir Geo Williams Univ Montr BA 57. McGill Univ BD 60. Montr Dioc Th Coll. **d** and **p** 60 Montr. C of Mt Royal 60-62; R of Hull 62-68; P-in-c of Chelsea 62-68; R of Stittsville 68-74; Hazeldean 74-78; St Aid City and Dio Ott from 78. *955 Wingate Drive, Ottawa, Ont, Canada.* (613-731 4309)

MACKERACHER, Alasdair John. b 22. Linc Th Coll 69. **d** 71 Sherborne for Sarum **p** 72 Sarum. C of Oakdale 71-73; Swanage w Herston 73-78; V of W Alvington 78-81; S Milton 78-81; Winkleigh Dio Ex from 81; Ashreigney Dio Ex from 81; Broadwoodkelly Dio Ex from 81; Brushford Dio Ex from 81. *Vicarage, Torrington Road, Winkleigh, Devon.* (Winkleigh 661)

McKEW, John Porter. b 09. TCD BA (Resp) 36, MA 61. **d** 39 **p** 40 Meath. C of Oldcastle 39-42; Ballymacelligott and Dioc C Dio Ardf 42-44; I of Kilflynn w Ratoo 44-49; Kilcornan w Ardcanny (w Kilkeedy from 53) 49-54; Cong 54-61; R of Dingle 61-72. *Tawlaght, Fenit, Co Kerry, Irish Republic.* (066-36192)

McKEW, Joseph Henry. b 1886. MC 17. CBE 44. Late Sen Exhib of Trin Coll Dub BA (Jun Mod) 10, MA 30. **d** 14 **p** 15 Clogh. C of Clones 14-15; CF 15-44; ACG E Command and Lon Distr 37-44; V of Bitterne 44-50; Hon Chap to HM the King 40-44; Chap Hosp of St Jo Bapt and Hosp of St Mary Magd Win 50-62; Asst Chap Win Coll 50-54. *The Friary, 19 St Cross Road, Winchester, SO23 9JA.*

MACKEY, John. b 34. Lich Th Coll. **d** 64 Penrith for Carl **p** 65 Carl. C of St Pet Kells Whitehaven 64-67; St Matt Barrow-F 67-70; R of Clayton 70-75; V of Low Marple Dio Ches from 75. *32 St Martin's Road, Marple, Chesh, SK6 7BY.* (061-427 2736)

MACKEY, William John Noel. b 07. TCD BA (3rd cl Mod, Ment and Mor Sc) 28, Ryan, Abp King and Bp Foster Pri 29, 1st cl Div Test and 3rd cl Mod Or Lang 30, 2nd cl Th Exhib 31, MA 51. **d** 31 **p** 32 Down. C of St Pet Belf 31-36; I of Billy 36-44; Warrenpoint w Clonallon 44-61; RD of Kilbroney 52-61; Newry and Mourne 58-61; Exam Chap to Bp of Down 57-71; Industr Officer Ch of Ireland 61-74. *86 North Road, Belfast 4, N Ireland.* (Belfast 658470)

McKIBBIN, Gordon. b 29. Dipl Th (Lon) 57. St Aid Coll 55. **d** 58 **p** 59 Down. C of Dundela 58-60; Knotty Ash 61-64; V of Gt Sankey Dio Liv from 64. *Parsonage, Parsonage Way, Great Sankey, Warrington, Lancs.* (Penketh 3235)

McKIBBON, James Thayer. Univ of W Ont BA 54. Hur Coll LTh 57. **d** 57 **p** 58 Hur. I of St Geo Kitchener 61-62; St Jo Evang Lon Ont 62-66; R of St Anselm Vancouver 66-68. *RR5, Concession 6, London, Ont, Canada.*

McKIE, Ian Alister. Ch Ch Coll LTh 64. **d** 59 Wel **p** 60 Bp Rich for Wel. C of St Pet Wel 59-60; Paraparaumu 60-61; Marton 61-62; V of Wainuiomata 62-66; Tawa 66-72; L to Offic Dio Wai from 72. *Box 897, Napier, NZ.*

MACKIE, Ian James. b 47. St Jo Coll Auckld 70. **d** 71 **p** 72 Ch Ch. C of Burwood 71-73; on leave 74-77; Dir of Marriage and Family Counselling Dio Perth from 77. *42 Ventnor Avenue, Perth, W Australia 6005.* (274 4422)

✠ **McKIE, Right Rev John David.** b 09. Trin Coll Melb BA 32. New Coll Ox BA (1st cl Th) 35, MA 44. Fell ACT 46.

Wells Th Coll 34. **d** 32 Melb **p** 34 Ox. Asst Chap C of E Gr Sch Melb 33; Chap and Lect Trin Coll Melb 36-40; Exam Chap to Abp of Melb 38-53; Chap AIF 39-44; I of Ch Ch S Yarra 44-46; Th Lect Trin Coll Melb 45-60; Cons Bp Coadj of Melb in St Paul's Cathl Melb 1 May 46 by Abp of Melb; Bps of Gippsld; Bend; Bal; St Arn; and Wang; and Bps Baker; Ashton; and Hart; res 60; Archd of Melb 46-60; Sen Chap AMF 47-60; VG Dio Melb 48; Actg Chap Gen 48; Chap and Sub-Prelate of O of St John of Jer from 50; Asst Bp of Cov 60; 60-81; of Berkswell 60-66; Commiss Melb 63-77; Adel from 66; Carp from 69; Exam Chap to Bp of Cov 65-81; V of Gt w L Packington 66-71. *Address temp unknown.*

MACKIE, Kenneth Johnston. Univ of NZ BA 45, MA 46. **d** 47 **p** 48 Auckld. C of Whangarie 47-51; P-in-c of S Hokianga 51-53; C of Gisborne 53-54; V of Opotiki 54-56; St Aug Napier 56-61; Gen Sec NZ Coun for Christian Educn 62-66; L to Offic Dios Ch Ch, Wai, Auckld and Dun 61-66; Gippsld 66-70; Chap Traralgon High Sch 66-70; Perm to Offic Dio Melb 70-72 and from 75; Miss Dio Papua 72-74. *20 Howard Street, Box Hill, Vic, Australia 3128.* (88-4333)

MACKIE, Robert. Bp's Univ Lennox. **d** 42 **p** 43 Queb. C of Frampton 42-43; I of Levis Miss 43-44; C of St Matthias Montr 44-45; R of St Paul Goodwin 45-48; I of Aylwin 48-50; River Desert 49-50; C of Ch Ch Deer Park Tor 50-52; I of St Timothy Agincourt 52-70; R of St Aid City and Dio Tor from 70. *71 Willow Avenue, Toronto, Ont., Canada.* (416-691 2222)

McKIM, Charles Ralph. Univ of Tor BA 53. Wycl Coll Tor. **d** 55 **p** 56 Niag. C-in-c of St Mich Hamilton 55-58; R 58-60; Dir of Christian Educn and LPr Dio Niag 60-64; Vice-Warden St Jo Coll Suva 64-69. *Box 321, King City, Ont, Canada.*

McKINLEY, Arthur Horace Nelson. b 46. Trin Coll Dub BA 69, Div Test 70, MA 79. **d** 70 **p** 71 Dub. C of Taney 71-76; V of Whitechurch Dub from 76. *Whitechurch Vicarage, Rathfarnham, Co Dublin, Irish Republic.*

McKINLEY, George Henry. b 23. Trin Coll Dub BA 44, MA 51. **d** 46 **p** 47 Cash. C of Waterf Cathl 46-49; R of Fiddown (w Kilmacow from 51) 49-54; C of St Paul S Harrow 54-58; V of St Mich Stonebridge Willesden 58-65; R of Hackney 65-77; V of Painswick w Sheepscombe Dio Glouc from 77. *Vicarage, Painswick, Stroud, Glos, GL6 6QB.* (Painswick 812334)

McKINLEY, John Gordon. Late Exhib of Trin Coll Dub BA 34, BD 51. **d** and **p** 35 Clogh. C of Drunkeeran and Magherculmoney 35-37; C-in-c of Donagh 38-43; R of Portarlington w Ballykean and Cloneyhurke 43-48; CF 49-51; V of Potton w Cockayne Hatley 51-57; Vice-Prin of Lich Th Coll 57-62; I of Donaghpatrick 62-70. *Tithe Cottage, Castleknock, Co Dublin, Irish Republic.* (Castleknock 212329)

McKINLEY, Reginald Michael. Trin Coll Dub BA 65, Div Test 66. **d** 66 **p** 67 Connor. C of St Simon Belf 66-68; St Pet Montr 68-70; St Geo St Cath 70-71; P-in-c of St Brendan Port Colborne 72-73; R of St Pet Hamilton 73-80; St Thos St Catharines Dio Niag from 80. *Box 1162, St Catharines, Ont, Canada.*

McKINNEL, Nicholas Howard Paul. b 54. Qu Coll Cam BA 75, MA 79. Wycl Hall Ox BA (Th) 79. **d** 80 **p** 81 Kens for Lon. C of St Mary Hammersmith Rd Fulham Dio Lon from 80. *72 Edith Road, W14.*

McKINNELL, Donald Stewart. Univ of BC BA 49, Angl Th Coll BC LTh 51. **d** 51 New Westmr **p** 52 Arctic. Miss at Fort Smith 51-53; V of Golden 53-59; Crescent Beach 59-63; R of Olds 63-65; V of All SS Calg 65-70; L to Offic Dio Calg 71-79; on leave. *469 Huntley Way, Calgary, Alta, Canada.* (274-1949)

MACKINNEY, James Alexander. b 52. Univ of Ex BA 74. Ripon Coll Cudd. **d** 78 **p** 79 Doncaster for Sheff. C of Wath-on-Dearne Dio Sheff from 78. *1 Church Street, Wath-upon-Dearne, Rotherham, S Yorks.*

McKINNEY, Mervyn Roy. b 48. St Jo Coll Nottm. **d** 81 Birm. C of St Pet Tile Cross Yardley Dio Birm from 81. *10 Kettlewell Way, Chelmsley Wood, Birmingham, B37 5JD.*

McKINNEY, Ronald Robert. Moore Th Coll Syd ACT ThL 65. **d** 67 **p** 68 Armid. C of Tamworth 67-68; Narrabri 68-69; V of Baradine 70-71; R of Littleton 71-74; Pitt Town 75-81; All S Leichhardt Dio Syd from 81. *126 Norton Street, Leichhardt, NSW, Australia 2040.* (569-2646)

McKINNEY, Ven Wilson. b 18. Trin Coll Dub BA 44, Div Test 44, MA 47. **d** 44 Down **p** 45 Connor. C of Ch Ch Lisburn 44-51; R of Ballyrashane w Kildollagh Dio Connor from 51; Dioc Sec from 71; RD of Coleraine 74-76; Archd of Dalriada from 76; Exam Chap to Bp of Connor from 76. *Ballyrashane Rectory, Coleraine, Co Derry, N Ireland.* (Coleraine 3061)

McKINNON, Archibald Vincent. b 07. **d** 77 **p** 78 Birkenhead for Ches. C of St Paul w St Luke Tranmere 77-79; St Bridget W Kirby Dio Ches from 79. *18 Newton Park Road, West Kirby, Wirral, Merseyside, L48 9XF.* (051-625 5998)

McKINNON, Neil Alexander. b 46. Wycl Hall Ox 72. **d** 74 **p** 75 S'wark. C of St Nich w Ch Ch Deptford 74-76; St Helier Morden 76-80; Min of Em Conv Distr W Dulwich Dio S'wark from 80. *94 Clive Road, SE21 8BN.* (01-670 2793)

MacKINNON, Reginald Beverley. b 51. St Thos Univ Fred BA, MDiv 80. Trin Coll Tor 79. **d** 80 Fred. C of Cant Dio Fred from 80. *PO Box 132, Canterbury, NB, Canada, E0H 1C0.*

MACKINTOSH, Canon Aeneas. b 27. Kelham Th Coll. **d** 52 **p** 53 Moray. Prec of St Andr Cathl Inverness 52-55; C of St Aug Wisbech 55-57; P-in-c of St Matt Possilpark Glas 57-60; R 60-61; H Trin Haddington 61-65; C of St Jo Evang City and Dio Edin 65-69; R 69-81; Dioc Insp of Ch Schs 63-69; Can of Edin Cathl from 75; R of N Berwick Dio Edin from 81; Gullane Dio Edin from 81. *Rectory, May Terrace, North Berwick, East Lothian.* (N Berwick 2154)

McKITTERICK, Canon John Henry Bernard. b 10. Selw Coll Cam 2nd cl Hist Trip 31, BA (2nd cl Th Trip) 32, MA 47. Cudd Coll 32. **d** 33 **p** 34 Guildf. C of Epsom 33-38; Min of St Jo Bapt Stoneleigh Conv Distr 38-43; V of St Paul The Hythe Egham 43-49; Oatlands 49-77; Surr from 48; RD of Emly 61-66; Can of Guildf 64-77; Can (Emer) from 77. *Little Croft, Luddington Avenue, Virginia Water, Surrey.* (Wentworth 4494)

McKITTRICK, Douglas Henry. b 53. St Steph Ho Ox 74. **d** 77 **p** 78 S'wark. C of St Paul Deptford 77-80; Tuebrook 80-82; V of Steph w St Cath City and Dio Liv from 82. *St Stephen's Vicarage, Grove Street, Liverpool, Mer.* (051-228 2316)

McKITTRICK, Noel Thomas Llewellyn. b 28. Trin Coll Dub BA 50, MA 57. BD 71. **d** 51 Derry **p** 53 Connor. C of Ch Ch Derry 51-52; St Aid Belf 52-54; Knockbreda 54-58; Keynsham 58-59; V of St Benedict Glastonbury 59-82; Surr from 70; V of St Paul Weston-super-Mare Dio B & W from 82. *St Paul's Vicarage, Clarence Road N, Weston-super-Mare, Avon.* (Weston-s-M 21888)

MACKLEY, Frederick Roy. b 05. Univ of Lon BA (1st cl Phil) 25. Coll of Resurr Mirfield 27. **d** 29 **p** 30 Cov. C of St Mary Nuneaton 29-48; V of Burton Dassett 48-56; Harbury Dio Cov from 56. *Harbury Vicarage, Leamington, Warws.*

MACKLIN, Reginald John. b 29. Univ of Bris BA (2nd cl Mod Hist) 52. Ely Th Coll 54. **d** 55 Kens for Lon **p** 56 Lon. C of St Barn W Hackney 55-58; St Mary Magd E Ham 58-61; Northolt (in c of St Richard) 61-64; Chap Bp's Sch Amman 64-68; Chap HBM Embassy Amman 64-68; Palma de Majorca 68-69; V of Stanwell Dio Lon from 69. *Vicarage, Stanwell, Staines, TW19 7JS.* (Ashford 52044)

MACKNEY, John Pearson. b 17. Univ of Wales (Cardiff) BA 39. MA (Lon) 81. St D Coll Lamp 39. **d** 41 **p** 42 Llan. C of Gellygaer 41-44; CF 44-47; C of Llangeinor 47-49; C-in-c of All SS Cardiff 49-58; Chap to HM Pris Cardiff 49-58; V of Mountain Ash 58-69. *Merlebank, Reading Road, Moulsford, S Oxon, OX10 9JG.*

McKNIGHT, John Andrew. b 49. **d** 78 **p** 79 Graft. C of Bangalow 78-80; Perm to Offic Dio Syd from 80. *Box A239, Sydney, NSW, Australia 2000.*

McKNIGHT, Richard Arthur. b 52. York Univ Ont BA 77. Trin Coll Tor MDiv 80. **d** 80 Bp Read for Tor **p** 81 Bp Hunt for Tor. C of St John Pet Dio Tor from 80. *99 Brock Street, Peterborough, Ont, Canada, K9H 2P2.*

McKNIGHT, Thomas Frederick. Univ of Syd MA 36. BEcon 40. ACT ThL 45, Th Scho 58. **d** and **p** 45 Syd. C-n-c of Blackheath Syd 45-48; CMS Miss Kongwa 48-50; Chap at Arusha 50-53; Morongoro 54-57; Iringa 57-58; R of St Aug Neutral Bay Dio Syd from 59; Commiss Nak from 70. *89 Wycombe Road, Neutral Bay, NSW, Australia 2089.* (90-1830)

McKNIGHT, Thomas George. **d** 65 **p** 66 Edmon. I of Mayerthorpe 65-72; St Mich City and Dio Edmon from 72. *13819-96th Street, Edmonton, Alta., Canada.* (403-476 5715)

McKNIGHT, Thomas Raymond. b 48. Qu Univ Belfast BEducn 71. Trin Coll Dub 74. **d** 77 **p** 78 Connor. C of Lisburn Cathl 77-80; St Nich Carrickfergus Dio Connor from 80. *7 Downshire Avenue, Carrickfergus, Co Antrim, BT38 7EL.*

MACKONOCHIE, Christopher. b 12. Pemb Coll Ox BA 34, MA 38. Cudd Coll 34. **d** 36 **p** 37 St Alb. C of Kempston 36-39; St Pet Dunstable 39-43; CF (EC) 43-47; V of Goldington 47-58; R of Dunstable 58-66; Surr 58-66; Hon Can of St Alb 60-66; C of Keynsham 66-67; V of Whitchurch 67-74; Weston Dio St Alb from 74. *Weston Vicarage, Hitchin, Herts.* (Weston 330)

MACKRELL, Arthur Thomas John. b 08. QUB BSc 30. St Aid Coll 31. **d** 32 **p** 33 Man. C of St Mark Worsley 32-34; Leyton 34-36; St Mark Dukinfield 36-38; V of Worsthorne 38-45; PC of St Geo Darwen 45-49; V of Ch Gresley 49-53; Dixon Green Farnworth 53-57; Surr 49-53; Asst Master Burnley Gr Sch 57-73; Perm to Offic Dio Blackb from 57. *2 Hall Park Avenue, Burnley, Lancs, BB10 4JJ.*

MacLACHLAN, Michael Ronald Frederic. b 39. Wycl Hall

Ox 75. **d** 77 **p** 78 Southw. C of SS Pet & Paul Mansfield 77-80; P-in-c of Ch Ch Newark 80; Team V of Newark w Hawton, Cotham and Shelton Dio Southw from 80. *Christ Church Vicarage, Boundary Road, Newark, Notts, NG24 4AJ.*

MACLAREN, Grant. b 12. St Cath Coll Cam 3rd cl Hist Trip pt i 36, BA (3rd cl Archaeol and Anthrop Trip) 37, MA 41. Wycl Hall Ox 37. **d** 39 **p** 40 S'wark. C of St Paul Greenwich 39-42; Ch Ch Gipsy Hill 42-45; Beccles 45-48; V of Oulton Broad 48-56; V of Ch Ch and C-in-c of H Trin Derby 56-57; V of Ch Ch w H Trin Derby 57-73; Stanley 73-80. *21 Tennessee Road, Chaddesden, Derby.*

McLAREN, Richard Francis. b 46. SOC 72. **d** 75 **p** 76 S'wark. C of Charlton 75-78; St Mary Abbots Kens Dio Lon from 79. *Flat 7 Argyll Court, 82/84 Lexham Gardens, Kensington, W8.* (01-373 0948)

McLAREN, Ronald. b 31. Kelham Th Coll. **d** 59 **p** 60 York. C of Redcar 59-62; Hornsea w Goxhill 62-65; V of St Thos Middlesbrough 65-70; Chap RN 70-73; R of Franklin 73-78; Lindisfarne Dio Tas from 78. *Rectory, Hume Street, Lindisfarne, Tasmania 7015.* (002-43 8134)

McLAREN, William Henry. b 27. Edin Th Coll 55. **d** 56 **p** 57 Bradf. C of Skipton 56-60; V of H Trin Bingley 60-65; Allerton Yorks 65-68; R of St Mary Aber 68-73; C-in-c of St Aug Newland Dio York 73-74; V 74-75; St Cuthb Hull 75-81; Hedon w Paull Dio York from 81. *44 New Road, Hedon, Hull, HU12 8BS.* (Hull 897693)

McLAUGHLIN, Arthur Melville. Moore Th Coll Syd 61. **d** 62 **p** 63 Syd. C of Waterloo 62; Balmain w Rozelle 63-64; R 64-67; R of Rozelle w Lilyfield Dio Syd from 67. *668 Darling Street, Rozelle, NSW, Australia 2039.* (82-1072)

McLAY, Robert James. b 49. Univ of Cant NZ BA 71. St Jo Coll Auckld LTh 73. **d** 73 **p** 74 Ch Ch. C of Fendalton 73-75; Yardley Birm 75-77; V of Banks Peninsula Dio Ch Ch from 77. *Vicarage, Okains Bay, Banks Peninsula, Canterbury, NZ.* (Okains 495)

MACLEAN, Alexander James. b 28. C Eng M IStructE 53. St Aid Coll 52. **d** 55 Warrington for Liv **p** 56 Liv. C of St Cath Wigan 55-57; Rainford 57-60; V of Em Chadderton 60-69; R of Largs 69-71; V of East Crompton 71-79; Turners Hill Dio Chich from 79. *Turners Hill Vicarage, Crawley, W Sussex.* (0342 715278)

MACLEAN, Allan Murray. b 50. Univ of Edin MA 72. Cudd Coll 72. **d** 76 **p** 77 Edin. Chap St Mary's Cathl Edin 76-81; R of H Trin Dunoon Dio Arg Is from 81. *Rectory, Dunoon, Argyll, PA23 7LN.* (0369-2444)

McLEAN, David John. b 40. SSM Th Coll Adel 76. **d** 79 **p** 80 Adel. C of St Jude Brighton Dio Adel from 79. *7 Dunluce Avenue, Brighton, S Australia 5048.*

McLEAN, Donald Stewart. b 48. TCD BA (Sem Lang) 70. Div Hostel Dub 70. **d** 72 **p** 73 Derry & Raph. C of Glendermott 72-75; I of Castledawson Dio Derry from 75; Dir of Ordinands Dio Derry from 79. *Castledawson Rectory, Magherafelt, Co Londonderry, N Ireland, BT45 8AZ.* (Castledawson 235)

McLEAN, Canon Douglas. b 12. Selw Coll Cam BA 34, MA 38. Cudd Coll 34. **d** 35 Bp Baynes for Birm **p** 36 Birm. C of St Mark Washwood Heath 35-41; Yardley (in c of St Mich) 41-48; C-in-c of Conv Distr St Mich AA S Yardley 48-51; V of Perry Barr 51-72; Exam Chap to Bp of Birm 57-78; Hon Can of Birm 61-72; Can Res from 72; RD of Handsworth 62-72; Dioc Dir of Ordinands Dio Birm 55-80; Exam Chap to Bp of Birm from 80. *83 Butlers Road, Handsworth Wood, Birmingham, B20 2NT.* (021-554 0567)

MacLEAN, Duncan Allan. Trin Coll Tor BA 48, BD 52. **d** 51 **p** 52 Tor. C of Oshawa 51-53; I of Walpole I 53-55; Dundalk 55-57; C of Ch Ch Tor 57-58; R of Lakefield 58-64; Chap RCAF 64-74; C of St Thos St Catharines 74-75; P-in-c of Resurr Thorold 74-75; Hornby 75-78; V of St Mark Hamilton Dio Niag from 78. *c/o 130 Bay Street South, Hamilton, Ont, Canada.* (416-529 7067)

McLEAN, Duncan William. b 41. Em & St Chad's Coll Sktn 70. **d** and **p** 73 Sask. I of Rosthern 73-74; St Geo Battleford 74-77. *Darquea 313, Aptdo 353-a, Quito, Ecuador.*

MACLEAN, Horace Yetman. KCNS. **d** 42 **p** 43 NS. I of Neil's Harbour 42-43; French Village 43-50; R of Digby 50-59; St Geo Sydney 59-67; Windsor 67-74. *PO Box 484, Bridgetown, NS, Canada.* (665-2428)

MACLEAN, Hugh Donald. Wycl Coll Tor STh 58. **d** 56 Tor for Calg **p** 57 Calg. I of Castor 57-60; R of McAdam 60-65; Niagara-on-the Lake 65-79; Ch of Ap Tor 79-81. *44 Reiner Road, Downsview, Toronto, Ont, Canada.*

MacLEAN, Ven James Aubrey. Montr Dioc Th Coll LTh 50. **d** 53 **p** 54 Montr. C of St Pet Montr 53-55; I of St Ignatius Montr 55-61; Cartierville Montr 61-70; R of Ste Anne de Bellevue Dio Montr from 70; Archd of St Andr 75; St Lawr from 75. *23 Perrault Avenue, Ste Anne de Bellevue 800, PQ, Canada.* (514-457 3999)

MacLEAN, John Lauchlin Langley. b 33. Acadia Univ NS BA 57. Trin Coll Tor BD 63. **d** and **p** 73 Keew. C of Kenora 73-74; R of Tangier 74-76; Canso w Queensport and Halfway Cove Dio NS from 76. *Box 59, Canso, NS, Canada.*

MACLEAN, John Raglan. MM 42. Univ of NZ BA 47. Cudd Coll 47. **d** 50 **p** 51 Bris. C of St Matt Moorfields Bris 50-53; Hastings NZ 53-58; V of Whakatane 58-64; Gisborne Dio Wai 64-70; Can of St John's Cathl Napier 66-70; P-in-c of Sunnynook Distr 70-71; C of Mt Albert 71-73; V of Grey Lynn Dio Auckld 73-80; P-in-c from 80. *Vicarage, Grey Lynn, Auckland, NZ.* (764-229)

MacLEAN, John Sandford Fleming. b 26. Hur Coll Lon BMin 72. **d** 72 **p** 73 Hur. I of Princeton Ayr & Drumbo 72-75; St Columba Waterloo Dio Hur from 75. *250 Lincoln Road, Waterloo, Ont., Canada.* (519-884 3681)

McLEAN, Michael Stuart. b 32. Univ of Dur BA 57. Cudd Coll 57. **d** 59 **p** 60 S'wark. C of Camberwell 59-61; L to Offic Dio Nor 61-68; R of Marsham 68-74; Burgh next Aylsham 68-74; RD of Ingworth 70-74; M Gen Syn from 73; C-in-c of St Pet Parmentergate w St Julian and St Etheldreda w St Pet Southgate Nor 74-75; Hon Min Can of Nor from 74; Team V of Parmentergate Team Min City and Dio Nor 75-77; R from 77. *10 Norman's Buildings, Rouen Road, Norwich, NR1 1QZ.* (0603-22509)

McLEAN, Canon Murdith Ronald. Univ of Alta BA 60. Univ of Birm MA 64. St Jo Coll Winnipeg LTh 63. **d** 63 **p** 64 Edmon. d Dio Edmon 63-64; Chap Univ of Alta 64-69; L to Offic Dio Edmon 64-69; Dio Athab 74-80; Warden and Vice-Chan of St John's Coll Winnipeg from 80; Can of Rupld from 80. *St John's College, University of Manitoba, Winnipeg 19, Canada.*

MacLEAN, Paul Thomas Allen Russell. b 45. Univ of Tor BA 67, MA 70. Episc Th Sch Mass BD 71. **d** 71 **p** 72 New Westmr. C of Horseshoe Bay 71; Oxton Ches 72-76; St Thos Tor 76-79; Consultants in Chr Educn Angl Ch of Canada from 79. *600 Jarvis Street, Toronto, Ont, Canada.*

McLEAN, Robert Hedley. b 47. St Jo Coll Dur BA 69. Ripon Hall Ox 69. **d** 71 **p** 72 S'wark. C of Redhill 71-74; St Mich AA S Beddington 74-77; Min of H Cross Conv Distr Motspur Pk, Raynes Pk Dio S'wark 77; V of H Cross Motspur Park from 77. *Vicarage, Douglas Avenue, New Malden, Surrey, KT3 6HT.* (01-942 3117)

McLEAN, William Duncan. Em & St Chad's Coll Sktn 70. **d** 73 Sktn. R of Rosthern, Wingard and Duck Lake Dio Sktn from 73. *Box 401, Rosthern, Sask, Canada.*

MACLEAY, Canon John Henry James. b 31. St Edm Hall Ox BA 54, MA 60. Coll of Resurr Mirfield 55. **d** 57 **p** 58 S'wark. C of St Jo Evang E Dulwich 57-60; St Mich Inverness 60-62; R 62-70; P-in-c of Grantown-on-Spey 70-78; Rothiemurchus 70-78; Can of St Andr Cathl Inverness 77-78; R of Ft William Dio Arg Is from 78; Can of St John's Cathl Oban from 80; Syn Clk Dio Arg Is from 80. *Rectory, Fort William, Inverness-shire.* (Fort William 2979)

McLEES, William Henry. b 27. Trin Coll Dub BA 53. St Aug Coll Cant. **d** 60 **p** 61 Down. C of Donaghadee 60-62; P-in-c of Good Shepherd Miss Pret 63-66; C of Dorking w Ranmore 66-68; R of Billis 68-71; C of St Jo Bapt W Byfleet 71-74; Gt Bookham 74-76; Ch Ch Epsom Dio Guildf from 77. *278 The Greenway, Epsom, Surrey.*

MACLEHOSE, Alexander. b 04. New Coll Ox 1st cl Cl Mods 25, BA (1st cl Lit Hum) 27. Stud Th (Lambeth) 65. Cranmer Hall Dur 65. **d** 65 **p** 66 Newc T. C of Sugley 65-67; St Jas Benwell Newc T 67-68; V of Lockerley and E Dean (w E and W Tytherley from 72) 68-76. *High Walls, Newton Toney, Wilts.*

McLELLAN, Canon Elmer Hugh. Univ of Tor BA 35. Trin Coll Tor. **d** 37 Bp Beverley for Tor **p** 38 Tor. C of St Bart Tor 37-38; I of H Trin Oshawa 40-52; R of Aurora 52-59; All H Tor 59-77; Can of Tor from 75; Hon C of St Patr Willowdale City and Dio Tor from 78. *412-50 Ruddington Drive, Willowdale, Toronto, Ont., Canada.*

McLELLAN, Eric Macpherson Thompson. b 16. St Jo Coll Dur BA 38, Dipl in Th 39, MA 41. **d** 39 **p** 40 Newc T. C of St Mark Byker Hill Newc T 39-44; Em Fazakerley 44-45; V of Em Ch Everton 45-54; R of Sevenoaks 54-70; Hon Can of Roch 68-70; Chap Br Embassy Ch Paris 70-80; St Mich Paris 75-79; RD of France 75-79; Archd in France 79-80; Perm to Offic Dio Roch from 80. *10 Stainer Road, Tonbridge, Kent, TN10 4DS.* (0732 356491)

McLELLAN, Canon Joseph Roderick. b 14. BD (Lon) 57. Edin Th Coll 52. **d** 54 **p** 55 Glas. C of St John Greenock 54-57; R of St John Baillieston 57-61; St John Johnstone 61-70; Lenzie 70-78; Can of Glas 74-80; Hon Can from 80; Dioc Chap Dio Glas 78-80. *2 Argyll Road, Kinross, KY13 7BB.*

McLELLAN, Kenneth Ian. b 40. St Jo Coll Auckld. **d** 78 **p** 79 Wel. C of Ch Ch Wanganui 78-80; V of Pongaroa Dio Wel from 80. *Box 42, Pongaroa, NZ.* (46-352)

MacLENNAN, Donald Hawkins. Wycl Coll Tor. **d** 26 **p** 27 Niag. C of Palermo and Omagh 26-29; Winoana 29-33; I of

Fergus Elora and Alma 33-41; St Geo Hamilton 41-66. *900 Easterbrook Avenue, Burlington, Ont, Canada.* (416-525 4756)

McLENNAN, Robert Eugene. Wycl Coll Tor. **d** 57 **p** 58 Tor. C of Oak Ridges 57-58; All SS Kingsway 58-62; I of St Gabr Richmond Hill 62-65; R of Cooksville S 65-79; on leave. *c/o Rectory, Cooksville South, Ont., Canada.* (416-279 2304)

McLEOD, Canon Alan Ralph. Angl Th Coll BC STB 67. **d** 67 New Westmr for Caled **p** 68 Caled. C of Burns Lake Miss 67-68; I 68-75; Vanderhoof Dio Caled from 76; Hon Can of Caled from 76. *Box 308, Vanderhoof, BC, Canada.*

MACLEOD, Alan Roderick Hugh. b 33. St Edm Hall Ox BA 56, MA 61. Wycl Hall, Ox 56. **d** 58 Chich **p** 59 Lewes for Chich. C of Bognor 58-61; Chap Wadh Coll Ox 62; Asst Master Picardy Boys' Sch Erith 63-69; C of Erith 63-69; L to Offic Dio Blackb from 70; Res Dean Lonsdale Coll Lanc 71-72; Asst Master Lanc R Gr Sch 72; K Edw Sch Totnes Devon 72-73; Perm to Offic Dio Ex from 72; L to Offic Dio Win from 73; Dir of Resources St Helier Boys' Sch from 73; Sec Jersey Coun of Chs 75-77. *Pippins Toft, Lashmars' Corner, East Preston, via Littlehampton, W Sussex*

McLEOD, Charles Joseph. **d** 23 **p** 25 Down. C of St Mich Belf 23-24; St Jude Ballynafeigh 25-31; I of Magheralin or Maralin 31-40; Ch Ch Lisburn 40-60; RD of Lisburn 50-56; Preb of Cairncastle in St Sav Cathl Connor 54-59; Chan 59-60. *21 Belvoir Crescent, Lisburn, Co Antrim, N Ireland.*

McLEOD, David Charles. b 35. Moore Th Coll Syd 75. **d** 76 Gippsld. C of Sale 76-77; Prec of St Paul's Cathl Sale 77-79; Chap RAAF from 79. *RAAF Base Butterworth, Penang, Malaysia.*

McLEOD, Donald James. St Paul's Coll Grahmstn 48. LTh (S Afr) 50. **d** 50 **p** 51 Grahmstn. C of St Sav E Lon 50-54; St Mich Queenstown 54-57 and 59-62; St Cuthb Port Eliz 57-59; Chap and Asst Master St Andr Coll Grahmstn 62-70 and 73-78; Dale Coll K Wm's Town 70-73; Chap St Jo Coll and L to Offic Dio Johann from 78. *St John's College, Houghton, Johannesburg, S Africa.*

MACLEOD, Canon Donald Norman. b 03. St Andr Coll Pampisford. **d** 47 **p** 48 Leic. C of St Barn Leic 47-50; Chap HM Prison Leic 48-53; C-in-c of St Aid New Parks Conv Distr Leic 50-52; Min 52-53; V of Ratby w Groby 53-60; Chap Markfield Sanat 55-69; RD of Sparkenhoe iii 59-64; V of Braunstone 60-64; Hon Can of Leic 60-80; Can (Emer) from 80; R of Nailstone w Carlton 64-69; Witherley w Atterton 69-80; RD of Sparkenhoe II from 74; L to Offic Dio Leic from 81. *56 The Meadows, Burbage, Hinckley, Leics.*

McLEOD, Graham. b 48. Univ of Newc NSW BA 69. ACT ThDip 73. St Jo Coll Morpeth 72. **d** 73 **p** 75 Newc. C of Toronto 73-79; P-in-c of Exper Pastoral Area of Gorokan Dio Newc from 79. *5 Galena Street, Gorokan, NSW, Australia 2263.*

McLEOD, Kenneth. b 22. St Chad's Coll Dur BA (2nd cl Phil) 50. Lightfoot Scho 50-52, Dipl Th 52. **d** 52 **p** 53 Ex. C of Holsworthy 52-55; Braunton (in c of Saunton) 55-58; R of Milton-Damerel and Newton St Petrock w Abbots Bickington and Bulkworthy 58-69; RD of Holsworthy 66-69; R of Langton-on-Swale Dio Ripon from 69; V of Kirkby-Fleetham w Fencote Dio Ripon from 69. *Kirkby-Fleetham Vicarage, Northallerton, Yorks.* (Kirkby-F 251)

McLEOD, Norman James. Bp's Univ Lennox BA 56. **d** 58 **p** 59 Ott. C of St Matthias Ott 58-60; R of Russell 60-64; Thedford 64-67; Perm to Offic Dio Ott from 70. *1977 Naples Avenue, Ottawa, Ont., Canada.*

McLEOD, Ronald. b 17. Univ of Lon BA 39, BD 71. Univ of Ex BA ([ad eund]) 56. Univ of Man MA 59. Bps' Coll Cheshunt 39. **d** 41 **p** 42 Ex. C of St Pet Plymouth 41-44; Chap RAF 44-73; Prin RAF Chap's Sch and Asst Chap-in-Chief 69-73; Hon Chap to HM the Queen from 72; R of Itchen-Abbas w Avington Dio Win from 73. *Itchen-Abbas Rectory, Winchester, Hants, SO21 1AX.* (096-278 244)

McLEOD, Wellington Alexander. Moore Th Coll Syd 31. ACT ThL 33. **d** 33 Bp Kirkby for Syd **p** 35 Syd. C of St Andr Lakemba 34-35; St Matt Manly 35-36; P-in-c of Minnipa 37-40; Croajingalong 40-42; Chap AIF 42-46; C of St Matt Manly 46-48; Chap Repatriation Hosp Concord and L to Offic Dio Syd from 48. *20 Argyle Avenue, Ryde, NSW, Australia 2112.* (80-3661)

McLOUGHLIN, Lindsay Thomas. b 51. St Jo Coll Morpeth ThDip 79. **d** and **p** 80 Newc. Cardiff Newc 80-81; Singleton Dio Newc from 81. *c/o The Rectory, High Street, Singleton 2330, NSW, Australia.*

MACLURE, Canon Andrew Seton. Late Tancred Stud of Ch Coll Cam BA 37, MA 41. Lon Coll of Div 37. **d** 39 **p** 40 Blackb. C of Leyland 39-41; Miss W Nile Distr 41-53; Goli 53-59; Arua Dio U Nile 59-61; Dio N Ugan 61-69; Dio M & W Nile from 69; Hon Can of U Nile 58-61; N Ugan 61-69; M & W Nile from 69; Dean of Em Cathl Mvara 69-72. *PO Box 37, Arua, Uganda.*

McMAHON, Alan Herbert. Moore Th Coll Syd 58. ACT ThL 60. **d** and **p** 61 Syd. C of Marrickville 61-63; P-in-c of Quorn 63-67; Chap Lidcombe Hosp and L to Offic Dio Syd 67-70; C of St Andr Cathl Sing 70-75; R of St Patr Tawau Dio Sabah from 80. *Box 279, Tawau, Sabah, Malaysia.*

McMAHON, Robert. St Jo Coll Morpeth. **d** 66 **p** 67 C & Goulb. C of Bega 66-69; Tumut 69-70; All SS Canberra 71-73. *10 Angus Street, Ainslie, Canberra, Australia.*

MACMANAWAY, Launcelot. b 12. TCD BA 36, MA 43. **d** 36 **p** 37 Down. C of Donaghcloney 36-39; Chap RN 39-67; Hon Chap to HM the Queen 65-67; Chan Malta Cathl 65-66; R of Youghal 67-74; C of Ardglass 74-79. *4 Heatherstone Road, Bayview, Bangor, Co Down, N Ireland.* (Bangor 58302)

McMANN, Duncan. b 34. Jes Coll Ox BA (2nd cl Mod Lang) 55, MA 60. Clifton Th Coll. **d** 58 **p** 59 Newc T. C of Newburn 58-60; St Gabr Bp Wearmouth 60-62; N Area Sec BCMS 62-66; Midlands Area Sec from 66; L to Offic Dio Man 63-66; Dio Cov from 66. *56 Cecily Road, Coventry, W Midl, CV3 5LA.* (Coventry 503691)

McMANNERS, Canon John. b 16. St Edm Hall Ox BA (1st cl Mod Hist) 39, Ma 45, DLitt 77. St Chad's Coll Dur Dipl Th 47. Officer of O of K Geo I (Greece) 48. FBA 78. **d** 47 **p** 48 Ripon. C of Leeds 47-48; Chap and Lect in Hist and Pol at St Edm Hall Ox 48-56; Fell 49-56; Dean 51-56; Exam Chap to Bp of Lich 54-56; Prof of Hist Univ of Tas 56-59; Univ of Syd 59-67; Univ of Leic 67-72; Regius Prof of Eccles Hist Univ of Ox from 72; Can of Ch Ch Ox from 72. *Christ Church, Oxford.*

McMANUS, Edward Joseph. **d** 77 Qu'App. C of Yorkton Dio Qu'App from 77. *213 Roslyn Avenue, Yorkton, Sask, Canada.*

McMANUS, James Robert. b 33. Wycl Hall Ox 56. **d** 58 **p** 59 Leic. C of H Trin Leic 58-60; Aylestone 60-63; CMS Miss in India 66-79; P-in-c of Ajni 67-71; in Ch of N India 70-79; V of St Barn Oldham Dio Man from 79. *1 Arundel Street, Oldham, Lancs, OL4 1NL.* (061-624 7708)

McMASTER, James Alexander. b 43. **d** 69 **p** 70 Down. C of Dundonald 69-73; Antrim 73-78; R of Tempo Dio Clogh from 78; Clabby Dio Clogh from 78. *Rectory, Clabby, Fivemiletown, Co Tyrone, N Ireland.* (Fivemiletown 697)

McMASTER, Richard Ian. Edin Th Coll 57. **d** 60 Penrith for Carl **p** 61 Carl. C of H Trin Carl 60-63; Chap St Andr Tr Coll Korogwe 63-66; V of Broughton Moor 66-69; St Steph Burnley 69-77; New Longton Dio Blackb from 77. *New Longton Vicarage, Preston, Lancs.* (Longton 613347)

McMILES, Anthony Ronald. ACT ThL 72. Moore Coll Syd 72. **d** and **p** 74 Syd. C of St Steph Willoughby 74-76; W Tamworth 76-78; C-in-c of Canley Heights Dio Syd from 78. *269 Canley Vale Road, Canley Heights, NSW, Australia.* (604-4428)

McMILLAN, Caldwell Allison Roe. Dalhousie Univ NS BA 65. **d** 66 NS. d Dio NS. *5 Whitman Court, Truro, NS, Canada.*

McMILLAN, Canon Hubert. **d** 71 **p** 76 Caled. C of St Pet New Aiyansh Dio Caled 71-80; I from 80; Hon Can of Caled from 81. *New Aiyansh, Naas River, Terrace, BC, Canada.*

MACMILLAN, John Nicholas. Ridley Coll Melb 58. **d** 61 **p** 62 Melb. C of Dandenong 61-63; Mount Waverley 63-64; V of Romsey w Sunbury and Lancefield 64-68; St Geo Reservoir 68-73; R of Naracoorte 73-76; I of Werribee Dio Melb from 76. *117 Synott Street, Werribee, Vic., Australia 3030.* (741-3396)

MACMILLAN, John Patrick. b 18. St Aid Coll. **d** 48 **p** 49 Ches. C of St Cath Higher Tranmere 48-49; Chap Thingwall Hosp 48-58; C of Ch Ch Latchford 49-51; V of St Ann Warrington 51-60; Em New Brighton Dio Ches from 60. *Emmanuel Vicarage, New Brighton, Chesh.* (051-639 2885)

✠ **McMILLAN, Right Rev Keith Alfonso.** St Pet Coll Ja. **d** 57 **p** 58. C of Cross Roads 57-59; P-in-c of Savanna la Mar 59-62; R 62-69; Christiana 69-72; Dioc Sec and Regr Dio Ja 72-80; Can of Ja 77-80; Cons Ld Bp of Belize in St Jo Bapt Cathl Belize City 24 Feb 80 by Bp of Windw Is; Bps of Antig, Trinid, Nass, Barb, Ja, Venez, Guy, Niag and Virgin Is (Amer Ch); Bp Suffr of Mandeville; and Bp H Edmonson. *Bishopthorpe, Box 535, Southern Foreshore, Belize City, Belize.* (02-3380)

McMILLAN, William George. b 12. **d** 69 Keew. I of Fort Alexander 71-72; Manning 72-74; St Paul River Labrador 74-76; Malbay Dio Queb from 76. *RR1, St George's de Malbaie, PQ, GOC 2XO, Canada.*

McMINN, Philip William. b 21. **d** 78 Bp Carter for Capetn **p** 78 Capetn. C of Wynberg (in-c of Kenwyn) 78-80; R of Manenberg Dio Capetn from 80. *Box 16, Manenberg, Athlone 7764, S Africa.*

McMONAGLE, William Archibald. b 36. TCD 65. **d** 68 **p** 69 Down. C of Magheralin 68-71; Bangor Abbey Dio Down from 71. *72 Abbey Park, Bangor, Co Down, N Ireland.* (Bangor 4401)

McMONIGLE, Donald William. b 49. Monash Univ Vic BA 72. Trin Coll Melb BD 79. **d** and **p** 79 Wang. R of St Luke Yea Dio Wang from 79. *St Luke's Rectory, PO Box 60, Yea, Victoria, Australia 3717.*

McMULKIN, Canon Francis Couldridge. Wycl Coll Tor. **d** 35 Hur for Tor **p** 36 Tor. C of St Barn Ches Tor 36-37; I of Apsley Miss 37-40; Mulmur 40-41; R of St Barn Tor 41-52; St Mark Tor 52-70; Can of Tor from 69. *33 Burnaby Boulevard, Toronto, Ont, Canada.*

McMULKIN, John Humphrey. Univ of Tor BA 49, STB and LTh 55. **d** 54 **p** 55 Niag. I of W Flamboro and C of Dundas' 54-58; R of St Patr Guelph 58-62; Georgetown 62-66; St Jo Evang Hamilton 66-71; Dean and R of St Alban's Cathl Prince Albert Sask 71-79; Exam Chap to Bp of Sask 75-79; Executive Sec Angl Found, Tor from 79; Hon C of St Geo Georgetown Dio Niag from 80. *600 Jarvis Street, Toronto, Ont, M4Y 2J6, Canada.*

✠ McMULLAN, Right Rev Gordon. b 34. QUB BSc (Econ) 61, PhD 71. ACIS 57. Ridley Hall Cam 61. **d** 62 **p** 63 Down. C of Ballymacarrett 62-67; Centr Adv on Chr Stewardship to Ch of Ireland 67-70; C of St Columba Knock Belf 70-71; I of St Brendan Belf 71-76; Dom Chap to Bp of Down 73-78; Exam Chap to Bp of Down 74-80; R of St Columba Knock Belf 76-80; Archd of Down 79-80; Cons Ld Bp of Clogh in St Patr Cathl Arm 7 Sept 80 by Abp of Arm; Bps of Connor, Kilm, Down, Cork, Cash, Tuam, Meath and Karamoja; and Bps Quin and Heavener. *The See House, Thornfield, Fivemiletown, Co Tyrone, N Ireland.*

McMULLAN, Paul Rex. Univ of Tor BA 61. Trin Coll Tor STB 64. **d** 64 Tor **p** 65 New Westmr. C of St Mary Vancouver 64-67; V of Agassiz Dio New Westmr from 67. *PO Box 7, Agassiz, BC, Canada.*

McMULLAN, Raymond Payne. St Chad's Coll Regina. **d** 62 **p** 63 Qu'App. I of Pense 62-64; R of St Mich Regina 64-66; L to Offic Dio Bran 66-78; P-in-c of Moose Lake 78-81; Russell Dio Bran from 81. *Russell, Manit., Canada.*

McMULLAN, Victor. TCD 65. **d** 68 **p** 69 Down. C of Donaghcloney w Waringstown 68-72; Magheraculmoney w Muckross and Templecarne 72-74; I of Mucknoe w Broomfield and Clontibret Dio Clogh from 74; Ballybay Dio Clogh from 74. *Rectory, Castleblayney, Co Monaghan, Irish Republic.* (Castleblayney 4)

McMULLEN, Alan John. b 14. Late Scho of K Coll Cam 1st cl Mod Lang Trip pt i 34, BA (2nd cl Mod Lang Trip pt ii) 36, MA 41. Cudd Coll 39. **d** 40 **p** 41 Lon. C of St Cypr St Marylebone Lon 40-49; Chap K Coll Cam 41-43; LPr Dio York from 49; V Cho Sub-Chanter and Sacr of York Minster 49-81; Chap HM Pris Askham Grange 65-69; Perm to Offic Dio York from 81. *Hilldrop Cottage, Low Way, Bramham, Wetherby, LS23 6QT.* (0937 842365)

McMULLEN, Canon Colin Archibald. Univ of BC BA 55. Angl Th Coll of BC LTh 57. **d** and **p** 57 Calg. C of St Steph Calg 57-58; I of Ch of Good Shepherd Calg 58-65; R of St Phil Elboya Calg 65-69; Stettler 69-75; Red Deer Dio Calg from 75; Hon Can of Calg from 75. *4767 56th Street, Red Deer, Alta, Canada.* (346 2263)

McMULLEN, Ronald Norman. b 36. TCD BA 61, MA 66. Ridley Hall Cam 61. **d** 63 **p** 64 Lon. C of St Mary Fulham 63-66; H Sepulchre Cam 66-70; St Ambrose (in c of St Timothy) Everton 70-73; Commun Work Course and Research Asst Univ of York 73-75; P-in-c of Heanor Dio Derby from 75; RD of Heanor from 76. *1a Mundy Street, Heanor, Derbys, DE7 7EB.* (Langley Mill 69800)

MacMULLIN, William Roland. b 45. Univ of NB BA 73. Wycl Coll Tor MDiv 76. **d** and **p** 75 Bp Read for Newfld. C of Port Saunders Dio Newfld (W Newfld from 76) 75; R from 75. *Box 99, Port Saunders, Newfoundland, Canada.* (709-861 3351)

McMURRAY, Brian Harold. b 44. **d** 67 **p** 68 Arm. C of St Mark Arm 67-68; St Bart Dub 68-71; St Mich AA Hull 71-72; New Eltham (in c of St Aidan) 72-75; P-in-c of Skelton 75-81; Prec of Gibr Cathl and Port Chap Gibr from 81; Hon Chap RN Gibr from 81. *Holy Trinity Cathedral, Cathedral Square, Gibraltar.* (72672)

McMURRAY, Raymond Carson. b 23. **d** and **p** 71 Rupld. C of St Sav Winnipeg Dio Rupld from 71. *640 Moncton Avenue, Winnipeg, Manitoba, R2K 1Y1, Canada.*

McMURRAY, Ritchie. Univ of Tor BA 50, MA 51, LTh 59, STB 59. **d** 58 **p** 59 Niag. C of St Jude Oakville 58-60; R of Beamsville 60-65; Smithville 62-65; Acton 65-68; Chap Univ of Guelph Ont from 68. *34 Dean Avenue, Guelph, Ont., Canada.* (519-821 6084)

MACNAB, Duncan Ivon. Univ of Tor BA 62. Trin Coll Tor STB 65. **d** 64 Bp Snell for Tor **p** 65 Tor. C of St Jo Bapt Norway Tor 64-66. *928 Bellvue Avenue, Halifax, NS, Canada.*

McNAB, John Ingram. BD (Lon) 58. STM (McGill) 63. McGill Univ PhD 72. St Pet Coll Ja 53. **d** 56 **p** 57 Ja. C of Half Way Tree Ja 56-57 and 59-62; Asst Master and Chap Ja Coll Kingston 62-64; Tutor and Chap St Pet Coll Ja 64-66; Warden United Th Coll of WI 66-74; P-in-c of Mona Heights Miss 64-69; Exam Chap to Bp of Ja 64-69 and 71-74; Bp of Br Hond 67-69; Prin Kingston Coll 74-78; Can of Ja 77-78; R of St Paul Cote-de-Neiges City and Dio Montr from 78. *3980 Cote-Ste-Catherine, Montreal, PQ, Canada H3T 1E3.* (514-739 0313)

McNAMARA, Victor James. Moore Coll Syd 72. **d** 72 **p** 73 Brisb. C of Dalby 72-75; V of Jandowae 75-79; R of Kilknan Dio Brisb from 79. *Rectory, Taylor Street, Murgeon, Queensland, Australia 4605.* (074-92 1450)

McNAMEE, William Graham. b 38. Univ of Birm BSocSc 59. St Jo Coll Dur BA (Th) 74. Dipl Th 75. Cranmer Hall Dur 73. **d** 75 Tonbridge for Roch **p** 76 Roch. C of St Steph Tonbridge 75-78; Drayton Bassett w Fazeley Dio Lich from 78; Canwell Dio Lich from 78; Hints Dio Lich from 78. *1 Rectory Close, Drayton Bassett, Tamworth, Staffs.* (Tamworth 60540)

McNAUGHT, James Gordon. b 1900. Sarum Th Coll 31. **d** 33 **p** 34 Worc. C of Cradley 33-36; Wimborne Minster 36-40; V of Allington 40-46; St Geo Claines Worc 46-51; Wilcot 51-62; R of Huish w Oare 51-62; RD of Pewsey 54-60; R of All SS Lockerbie 62-66. *Netheryett, Kirkpatrick Durham, Castle Douglas, Kirkcudbrightshire.* (Kirkpatrick Durham 306)

MACNAUGHTON, Alexander. b 15. Univ of Cam 1st cl Cl Trip pt i 36, (2nd cl Cl Trip pt ii) BA 37, MA 41. Linc Th Coll 40. **d** 41 **p** 42 Sarum. C of Melksham 41-44; St Bart Long Benton 44-47; Chap at St Paul's Cathl Ranchi 48-50; Exam Chap to Bp of Chota N 49-73; Prin Chota N Th Sch Murhu 51-62; P-in-c of Jamshedpur Chota N 63-73; L to Offic Dio Derby 74; Chap Derbys R Infirm 75-80. *Flat 12, St Mark's House, Radbourne Street, Derby, DE3 3BW.*

MACNAUGHTON, Canon Donald Allan. b 17. Or Coll Ox BA 40, MA 43. Westcott Ho Cam 40. **d** 41 **p** 42 Newc T. C of Ch Ch Tynemouth 41-45; Succr of Leeds Par Ch 45-49; V of St Barn Pendleton 49-53; St Luke Wallsend 53-58; Wooler 58-71; C-in-c of Branxton 60-67; RD of Glendale 58-71; C-in-c of Ingram 61-71; Ilderton 61-71; Kirknewton 68-71; Doddington 69-71; V of Berwick-upon-Tweed 71-82; St Mary Berwick-upon-Tweed 71-82; RD of Norham 71-82; Hon Can of Newc T 71-82; Chap of All SS Puerto de la Cruz Tenerife Canary Is Dio Gibr in Eur from 82. *All Saints, Apartado 28, Puerto de la Cruz, Tenerife, Canary Islands.*

MACNAUGHTON, James Alastair. b 54. St Jo Coll Ox BA 78. Fitzw Coll Cam BA (Th) 80. Ridley Hall Cam 78. **d** 81 Birm. C of St Jas Rounds Green Dio Birm from 81. *41 Harry Price House, Hartlebury Road, Oldbury, Warley, B69 1EQ.*

McNAUGHTON, John. b 29. St Chad's Coll Dur BA 53. **d** 54 **p** 55 Dur. C of St Pet Conv Distr Thorney Close 54-58; C-in-c of St Chad Conv Distr E Herrington 58-62; PC 62-66; CF from 66. *c/o Ministry of Defence, Bagshot Park, Bagshot, Surrey, GU19 5PL.*

MACNAUGHTON, William Malcolm. b 57. Qu Coll Cam BA 80. Ridley Hall Cam 79. **d** 81 Dur. C of Haughton-Le-Skerne Dio Dur from 81. *87 Hutton Avenue, Darlington, DL1 2AH.* (Darlington 58447)

MACNAUGHTON-JONES, Tilbury Cecil. b 02. Egerton Hall Man 32. **d** 34 **p** 35 Man. C of St Wilfrid Newton Heath 34-36; St Pet Stretford 36-38; V of Trowse 38-43; PC of Arminghall 38-43; CF (EC) 40-45; R of All SS w St Mich AA S Lynn and Seche Parva 45-51; Chap St Jas Hosp King's Lynn 46-51; R of Gt w L Ellingham 51-58; Tasburgh 58-70; V of Tharston 58-70; RD of Depwade 63-68; Perm to Offic Dio Nor from 70. *3 Chancel Close, Brundall, Norwich, NR13 5NA.* (Norwich 713657)

McNAUL, Robert Guthrie. b 42. Univ of Denver USA BA 65. Ch Div Sch of the Pacific BD 68. **d** 68 **p** 69 Colorado USA. C of Turramurra 70-72. *c/o Diocesan Office, Denver, CO 80218, USA.*

McNEAR, Ven John Terry. b 38. Wycl Coll Tor LTh 71. **d** 71 Tor **p** 71 Keew. C of Ch Ch Oshawa Tor 71-73; Fort Alexander Keew 73-74; Big Trout Lake 75-80; I of Thompson Dio Keew from 80; Archd of York from 80. *10 Caribou Road, Thompson, Manit, Canada.*

MACNEICE, Alan Donor. **d** 64 **p** 65 Connor. C of Ballymoney 64-67; R of Christiana Ja 67-69; C of Winchmore Hill 71-76; St Paul Harringay Lon 76-77; St Barn Kens 77-78; P-in-c 78-79. *c/o St Barnabas Vicarage, Addison Road, W14 8LH.*

McNEICE, Desmond Patrick. b 15. Univ of Lon BA 37. Ripon Hall Ox 37. **d** 38 **p** 39 Chelmsf. C of St Luke Leyton 38-42; Chap HM Pris Chelmsf (in c of Springfield) 42-45; V of St Jo Div Mawneys Romford 45-47; R of Wickham Bishops 47-55; V of Aveley 55-61; Melbourn 61-72; V of Meldreth 61-72; St Mary Magd Holmwood 72-81; RD of

Dorking 75-80. *Dormers, Leather Lane, Great Yeldham, Halstead, Essex.*

McNEIGHT, Herbert Frank. b 14. Chich Th Coll 79. **d** 79 **p** 80 Chich. Hon C of St Mich AA Southwick Dio Chich from 79. *12 Mile Oak Road, Southwick, Brighton, Sussex, BN4 4DP.*

McNEILE, Donald Hugh. b 30. Trin Coll Cam BA 53, MA 60. Coll of Resurr Mirfield 53. **d** 55 **p** 56 Liv. C of Wigan 55-57; Ch of Good Shepherd (in c of St Paul in Croxteth) W Derby 57-61. *Manor Farm, North Hinksey, Oxford.* (Oxford 45473)

McNEILL, George Edward. b 07. Wadh Coll Ox BA 28, MA 31. Clifton Th Coll 32. **d** 32 **p** 33 Cant. C of St Jo Bapt Folkestone 32-34; TCF Catterick 34-38; CF 38-54; V of Winterbourne Earls w Winterbourne Dauntsey and Winterbourne Gunner 54-57; Chap at Maisons Laffitte (N and C Eur) 57-63; Aiglon Coll Chesières-Villars Switzerland 63-65; C of Sidbury w Sidford 65-66; L to Offic Dio Ex 66-68; Dio Chich 68-69; Dio Guildf 69-79; Perm to Offic Dio Ex from 79. *8 Blueberry Downs, Budleigh Salterton, EX9 6NU.*

McNEISH, John. b 34. Edin Th Coll. **d** 61 **p** 62 St Andr. C of St Pet Kirkcaldy 61-64; Prec St Andr Cathl Aber 64-66; Chap RAF 66-72; C of Wootton Bassett 72-75; P-in-c of Stour Provost w Stour Row and Todber 75-79; Team R of Gillingham Dio Sarum from 79; RD of Blackmore Vale from 81. *Rectory, Gillingham, Dorset.* (Gillingham 2435)

McNICOL, Preb Malcolm. b 14. Oak Hill Th Coll 34. **d** 37 **p** 38 Lon. C of St Luke Hampstead 37-39; Ulverston 39-40; St Jas Alperton 40-41; CMS Miss 41-48; V of Madeley 48-54; St Mark Wolverhampton 54-75; P-in-c of Weston-on-Trent 75-81; RD of Stafford 77-81; Preb of Lich Cathl 79-81; Preb (Emer) from 81. *48 Glenridding Drive, Barrow-in-Furness, LA14 4PB.* (Barrow 26156)

McNUTT, Chan Albert Thompson. b 09. Trin Coll Dub BA 35; Newport White Greek Pri 38; MA 44; BD 50. **d** 38 **p** 39 Dub. C of Harold's Cross Dub 38-44; I of St Jude w St Laur Chapelizod Dub 44-80; RD of Monkstown 69-80; Preb of Dub Cathl 71-73; Treas 75-77; Chan 77-80. *c/o St Jude's Rectory, Kilmainham, Dublin, Irish Republic.* (Dublin 51880)

McNUTT, Preb John Alexander Miller. b 14. Edgehill Th Coll 37. **d** 47 **p** 48 Clogh. C-in-c of Currin (w Drummully from 51) 47-56; R of Trory 56-73; RD of Enniskillen 59-65; Chap to Bp of Clogh 65-73; RD of Kilskerry from 67; Ed Clogh Dioc Magazine 70-73; Preb of Clogh Cathl 73-80; Chan from 80; R of Magheracross Dio Clogh from 73. *Rectory, Ballinamallard, Co Fermanagh, N Ireland.* (Ballinamallard 238)

MACONACHIE, Alwyn. b 21. TCD Hebr Pri 42, BA (2nd cl Mod) 43 and Brooke Exhib 43, Div Test and Biblical Gr Pri (1st) 44, MA and BD 47. **d** 44 **p** 45 Derry. C of Ch Ch Londonderry 44-47; R of Killowen 47-64; RD of Limavady 60-65; N Sec CMS Ireland 64-70; Gen Sec 70-74; I of Glencraig Dio Down from 74; RD of Bangor from 78. *Glencraig Vicarage, 3 Seahill Road, Craigavad, Holywood, BT18 0DA.* (Holywood 2225)

MACONACHIE, Charles Leslie. b 27. TCD BA 71, MA 74. Angl Th Coll BC. **d** 50 **p** 51 Derry. C of All SS Clooney 50-54; C-in-c of Tamlaght O'Crilly Lower 54-61; Chap Newsham Gen Hosp 61-63; Chap RAF 63-67; C of Ch Ch (in c of St Pet) Derry 69-76; V of St Pet Belmont Derry 76-78; R of Culmore w Muff and Belmont Dio Derry from 78; Asst Warden for Ireland of the ChS Min of Healing from 78; Chap of O of St Luke 78-80; Warden for Ireland from 80; Exam Chap to Bp of Derry from 79. *Rectory, Heathfield, Londonderry, N Ireland.* (Derry 52396)

MACONCHY, Canon Richard Julian John Frederic. b 07. TCD Hebr Pri (1st) 28 and 29, BA and Weir Pri 30, Div Test (1st cl) Warren Pri and 2nd Downes Pri (Liturgy) 31, BD 56. **d** 31 **p** 32 Down. C of St Anne's Cathl Belf 31-34; Dean's V 32-34; C of St Ann Dub 34-40; I of Killanne w Templeudigan 40-45; C-in-c of Kilmeague w Feighcullen 45-56; C-in-c of Ballinafagh 45-56; V of All SS Blackrock 56-78; Preb of St Patrick's Cathl Dub from 75; Can of Ch Ch Cathl Dub 68-78; Can (Emer) from 78. *9 Oldcourt Grove, Bray, Co Wicklow, Irish Republic.* (Dublin 868725)

MACOURT, Ven William Albany. b 19. TCD BA 40, MA 46. **d** 42 **p** 43 Down. C of Ballymena 42-46; St Anne's Cathl (in c of Miss distr) Belf 46-48; I of Duneane w Ballyscullion 48-51; R of St Mark Ballysillan 51-64; Ch of Ireland Press Officer from 58-71; V of Ballymacarrett Dio Down from 64; Preb of Dub Cathl from 75; Archd of Down from 80. *155 Upper Newtownards Road, Belfast, BT4 3HX, N Ireland.* (Belfast 657180)

McPETRIE, Bruce Alexander. b 51. Univ of W Ont BA 74. Hur Coll Lon MDiv 77. **d** 77 **p** 78 Niag. C of St Jas Guelph 77-78; P-in-c of St Matthias Guelph 78-80; R of St Steph Niagara Falls Dio Niag from 80. *4500 Pettit Avenue, Niagara Falls, Ont, Canada.* (416-358 7775)

McPHAIL, Gordon Stuart. b 1898. Trin Coll Dub BA and Div Test 21, Downes Pri 20 and 21, MA 25, BD 35. **d** and **p** 22 Oss. C of New Ross and Hd Master John Ivory's Sch New Ross 22-30; C of St Werburgh Dub 30-36; Hon Cler V of Ch Ch Cathl 32-53; I of Santry w Glasnevin and Coolock 36-39; R of St Werburgh Dub 39-72; Can of Ch Ch Cathl Dub 53-68; Treas 68-72. *25 Charleville Road, Rathmines, Dublin, Irish Republic,*

McPHATE, Gordon Ferguson. b 50. Univ of Aber MB, ChB 74. Fitzw Coll Cam BA 77, MA 81. Westcott Ho Cam 75. **d** 78 **p** 79 S'wark. C of Sanderstead Dio S'wark from 78; Hon PV S'wark Cathl from 81. *Flat 12, Napier Court, 2 Outram Road, Croydon, CR0 6XG.*

McPHERSON, Albert Bayne. Univ of Melb BA (2nd cl Hist) 64. Trin Coll Melb ACT ThL (2nd cl) 66. **d** 66 **p** 67 Melb. C of St Geo Reservoir 66-67; St Jas Syd 67-69; St John N Frankston 69-70; W Heidelberg 70; on leave 70-71; C of St Paul's Cathl City and Dio Melb from 71. *82 Stevenson Street, Kew, Vic, Australia 3101.* (03-86 9679)

MACPHERSON, Anthony Stuart. b 56. Qu Coll Birm 77. **d** 80 **p** 81 Wakef. C of Morley w Churwell Dio Wakef from 80. *42 Manor Road, Churwell, Leeds, LS27 7RU.*

MACPHERSON, Archibald McQuarrie. b 27. Edin Th Coll 50. **d** 52 **p** 53 Aber. Jun Chap Aber Cathl 52-55; Prec 55-56; P-in-c of St Paul Airdrie 56-63; R of St Aug Dumbarton Dio Glas from 63. *St Augustine's Rectory, Dumbarton.* (Dumbarton 62852)

MacPHERSON, David Alan John. b 42. Univ of Lon Dipl Th (Extra-Mural Stud) 71, BD (Lon) 75. Trin Coll Bris 72. **d** 72 **p** 73 York. C of St Columba w St Andr & St Pet Drypool 72-76; C-in-c of Bessingby and Carnaby 76-78; Chap RAF from 78. *c/o Ministry of Defence, Adastral House, WC1.*

MacPHERSON, Ewan Alexander. b 43. Univ of Tor BA 74. Wycl Coll Tor MDiv 78. **d** 78 **p** 79 Tor. C of St Cuthb Leaside Tor 78-81; Ch of Ap City and Dio Tor from 81. *719 Sheppard Avenue West, Toronto, M3H 2L2, Ont, Canada.*

McPHERSON, James Murdoch. b 46. Univ of NSW BSc 67, PhD 70. ACT BTh 77. Coll of Min Canberra 75. **d** and **p** 78 C & Goulb. C of St Paul Canberra 78-80. *c/o Department of Theology, Abbey House, Palace Green, Durham, DH1 3RL.*

MacPHERSON, Leslie Ian. **d** 70 **p** 73 Ja (APM). P Dio Ja. *Box 602, Kingston 8, Jamaica, WI.* (092-92200)

MACPHERSON, Peter Sinclair. b 44. Lich Th Coll 68. **d** 71 Ex **p** 73 Plymouth for Ex. C of Honiton 71-72; Bideford 72-74; St Mark Ford, Devonport 74-75; V of Thorncombe 75-79; Team V of Dorchester Dio Sarum from 79. *St George's Vicarage, Dorchester, Dorset.* (Dorchester 2394)

MACPHERSON, Vernon John. Wycl Coll Tor STh 62. **d** 61 Bp Hunt for Ont **p** 62 Ont. I of Coe Hill 61-65; Maynooth 61-65; R of Elizabethtown 65-71; R of Rideau 71-80; St Luke Kingston Dio Ont from 80. *792 Old Colony Road, Kingston, Ont, Canada.* (613-384 3418)

McQUADE, William. b 09. **d** 49 Connor for Fred **p** 50 Fred. R of Hardwicke NB 50-51; C-in-c of Clongish and Clooncumber 51-52; Glencolumbkile 52-55; Preban w Moyne 55; I of Dingle U 55-57; Ballinaclough U 57-58; R of Bewcastle 58-66; V of Allhallows 66-76. *c/o Allhallows Vicarage, Mealsgate, Carlisle, Cumb.* (Low Ireby 355)

McQUAID, William Robert. Em Coll Sktn. **d** 68 **p** 69 Edmon. I of Kitscoty 68-70; Drayton Valley w Evansburg 70-78; C of All SS Cathl Edmon 78-81. *15035-86th Avenue, Edmonton, T5R 4B9, Alta., Canada.* (483-8792)

MacQUAIDE, Arthur John Allan. b 13. TCD BA 37, Div Test 38. **d** 38 **p** 39 Clogh. Dioc C Dio Clogh 38-39; C of Enniskillen 39-41; C-in-c of Lack (or Colaghty) 41-46; Derryvullan 46-58; C of Flint 58-60; R of Garrison w Slavin and Beleek U 60-80; Chap to Bp of Clogh 67-73; Preb of Clogh Cathl 73-80. *St Anne's Vicarage, Greenbank Road, Greenbank, Bristol, BS5 6HD.*

MACQUARRIE, Canon John. b 19. Univ of Glas MA (Ment Phil) 40, BD 43, PhD 54, DLitt 64, Hon DD 69. Univ of Ox MA 70; DD 81. **d** & **p** 65 NY USA. [f Lect Univ of Glas 53-62] In Amer Ch and Prof of Systematic Th U Th Sem NY 62-70; Lady Marg Prof of Div Univ of Ox from 70; Can of Ch Ch Ox from 70. *Christ Church, Oxford, OX1 1DP.* (Ox 43588)

McQUEEN, Duncan Robert. Muskingum Coll Ohio AB 50. Gen Th Sem NY LTh 54 STB 67. **d** and **p** 54 Long I USA. In Amer Ch 54-67 and from 75; Dean and V of Suva Cathl 67-74. *17 Exeter Drive, Auburn, Massachusetts, USA.*

McQUEEN, Elwood Duncan. **d** 27 **p** 28 Fred. Miss at Bright 27-30; Grand Falls 30; Bright 30-60; R of Stanley 60-63; I of Westmorland 63-67. *Zealand, NB, Canada.*

MacQUEEN, Kenneth Alexander. Moore Th Coll Syd ACT ThL 67. **d** 65 **p** 67 Brisb. C of St Bart Mt Gravatt Brisb 65-67; Booval 67-68; Dalby 68-72; P-in-c of Monto Dio Brisb 72-73; R from 73. *15 Bell Street, Monto, Queensland, Australia 4630.* (Monto 74)

MACQUEEN, Robert Lines. b 22. MRCS 51. LRCP 51. TD 71. **d** 71 **p** 72 Edmonton for Lon. C of St Geo Enfield

71-75; St Mary Magd Enfield 75-80; P-in-c of Barkway w Reed & Buckland Dio St Alb 80-81; R (w Barley) from 81. *Barkway Rectory, Royston, Herts, SG8 8EO.* (Barkway 260)

McQUEEN, Robert Roderick Grant. **d** 57 **p** 58 Perth. C of Mt Lawley 57-60; R of Moore 60-66; Pinjarra 66-68; Mt Barker 68-70; P-in-c of Pingelly 70-74; Perm to Offic Dio Perth from 74. *152 Victoria Street, Mosman Park, W Australia 6012.* (31 2757)

MACQUIBAN, Gordon Alexander. b 24. St D Coll Lamp BA 49. Ely Th Coll 49. **d** 51 **p** 52 Ches. C of Christleton 51-53; Disley 53-55; Heswall and Chap R Liv Children's Hosp Heswall 55-58; V of Norley 58-64; Ch Ch Ches 64-71; C of H Trin Without-the-Walls City and Dio Ches from 71; Sen Master Bps Middle Sch Blacon Ches from 71. *181 Saughall Road, Chester, CH1 5HG.* (Chester 372394)

McQUIE, Ronald Ernest. Univ of Melb Dipl in Educn (2nd cl) 22, BA 23. St Francis Coll Nundah. **d** 27 Brisb for N Queensld. C of H Trin Mackay 27-30; Chap Southport Sch 30-33; C of All SS Brisb 33-35; V of St Anne Nanango 35-36; Chap Prep Sch of Melb C of E Gr Sch 36-41; Chap AIF 41-44; V of Newport w Altona 44-49; I of Camberwell 49-64. *38 Summerhill Road, Glen Iris, Melbourne, Vic, Australia 3146.* (29-1508)

McQUILLEN, Brian Anthony. b 45. Ripon Hall Ox 73. **d** 75 **p** 76 Birm. C of Northfield 75-77; Sutton Coldfield 77-80; V of St Mary Virg Bearwood, Smethwick Dio Birm from 80. *27 Poplar Avenue, Birmingham, B17 8EG.* (021-429 2165)

McQUILLIN, Bernard Charles. Qu Coll Birm. **d** 54 **p** 55 Bris. C of St Steph Southmead 54-56; Cricklade w Latton 56-57; R of St Paul Kinross 57-60; Coates 66-71; Perm to Offic Dio Nor 60-66. *104 Giles Street, Sleaford, Lincs.*

McQUINN, Wallace Steward. b 03. Univ of Lon BD 36, BA 49, ALCD 36. **d** 36 **p** 37 Derby. C of St Chad Derby 36-39; Org Sec CPAS for NW Distr 39-41; V of H Trin Cloudesley Sq Islington Lon 41-50; C-in-c of St Thos Barnsbury Islington 44-50; V of St Jas W Ealing 50-60; St Antholin Lecturer in City of Lon 47-56; Surr 41-71; R of Ch Ch Brondesbury 60-71. *112 The Welkin, Lindfield, Haywards Heath, Sussex.*

MacQUIRE, Dominic Ronald. b 27. **d** 72 Carib. C of Westsyde 72-73; on leave. *201 Capitola Avenue, Santa Cruz, Calif, USA.*

McQUISTON, Thomas. b 30. Univ of Sask LTh. Coll of Em & St Chad Sktn. **d** and **p** 80 Bran. C of Glenboro Dio Bran from 80. *Box 491, Glenboro, Manit, Canada, R0K 0X0.*

MACRAE, Ernest Hugh. b 1893. CCC Ox 3rd cl Mods 14, BA 19. Edin Th Coll 34. **d** 36 **p** 37 Edin. C of St Pet Edin 36-40; R of St Marg Easter Road Edin 40-52; L to Offic Dio Edin 52-58. *82 Meadvale Road, Ealing, W5.*

McRAE, John Farquhar. Univ of Tor BA 49, MA 55, STB 58. Trin Coll Tor 55. **d** 57 Niag **p** 59 B'pore. Miss Dio B'pore 58-63; L to Offic Dio B'pore 63-64; R of Cranbrook 64-66; Dep Dir of Programme Dio Ott 66-70; Exam Chap to Bp of Ott 70-72; on leave. *202 Hickory Street, Ottawa 4, Ont, Canada.*

McRAE, Keith Alban. b 44. SOC 68. **d** 73 Chich **p** 74 Lewes for Cant for Chich. C of Crawley 73-78; Ifield Dio Chich from 78. *Plough Cottage, Ifield Street, Ifield, Crawley, RH10 0NN.* (Crawley 513629)

MacRAE, Peter Howard. Mt Allison Univ NB BA 61. McGill Univ BD 64. Univ of NB MA 69. Montr Dioc Th Coll LTh 64. **d** 64 **p** 65 Fred. C of Ch Ch Cathl Fred 65-68; Hon C of St Mary York 68-70. *264 George Street, Fredericton, NB, Canada.*

MacRAE, Canon Robert Daniel. Univ of BC BA 53, MSW 62. Em Coll Sktn LTh 58. **d** 58 Sask **p** 59 Carib. I of Ashcroft w Clinton 59-61; Westsyde 62-66; Asst Sec Coun for Chr Social Service 66-68; Nat World Program 68-69; Sec Primate's World Relief and Development Fund 70-77; R of St Jo Div Vic Dio BC from 77; Can of BC from 79. *1611 Quadra Street, Victoria, BC, Canada.*

McRITCHIE, Ven Frank Cuthbert. Univ of Tor BA 46. Wycl Coll Tor. **d** 30 **p** 31 Hur. C of St Jas Port Lambton Walpole I 30-31; I of Onondaga w Middleport 31-34; Bervie w Kingarf and Kinlough 34-40; R of St Thos Walkerton and RD of Bruce 40-42; Chap CASF 42-46; I of Aylmer 46-52; R of St Mary Walkerville 52-61; Can of Hur 58-61; R of Grace Ch Brantford 61-78; Archd of Brant 61-78; Archd (Emer) from 78. *Sombra, Ont, Canada.*

MACROBB, Graeme Lindsay. **d** and **p** 68 Gippsld. C of St Paul's Cathl Sale 68-70; V of Cann River 70-73; R of Mirboo N 73-75; Prin CA Coll of Evang and Perm to Offic Dio Syd from 76; Dio Newc from 77. *Box 107, French's Forest, NSW, Australia 2086.* (451-8395)

MACRORY, Robert Donald. b 13. Late Scho of Trin Coll Dub BA (1st cl Ment and Mor Sch Mod), Downes Pri (1st) 39, MA Downes Pri (1st) and Robert King Pri 40, BD 46. **d** 40 **p** 41 Cash. C of Clonmel w Innislonagh 40-42; St Steph Dub 42-49; Min Can of St Patr Cathl Dub 45-49; Vice-Prin Bps' Coll Cheshunt 49-57; Publ Pri Dio St Alb 50-57; C of St Geo Belf 59-60; Vice-Prin Ely Th Coll 60-64; L to Offic Dio Ely 60-64; Chap Bps' Coll Cheshunt 65-68; V of Stevington 68-76; Perm to Offic Dio Glouc from 77. *Flat 3, All Saints Court, All Saints Villas Road, Cheltenham, Glos, GL52 2HE.*

MACROW, David James. b 29. Bps' Coll Cheshunt. **d** 64 **p** 65 Lon. C of St Mich Wood Green 64-68; V of St Sav Alexandra Park 68-79; R of Cliffe-at-Hoo w Cooling City and Dio Roch from 79. *St Helen's Rectory, Church Street, Cliffe, Rochester, Kent.* (0634-220220)

McSHERRY, Harold Joseph. Em Coll Sktn BA and LTh 44, BD 47. **d** and **p** 44 Athab. R of Beaver Lodge 44-48; Chap and Exam Chap to Bp of Athab 46-48; Miss in Hiroshima Japan 49-57; R of St Alb Richmond 57-74; St Paul Vanc Dio New Westmr from 74. *1130 Jervis Street, Vancouver, BC, Canada.*

McSPARRON, Cecil. b 35. Trin Th Coll Sing MMin 77. **d** 68 Derry **p** 69 Clogh for Derry. C of Glendermott 68-70; St Andr Cathl and P-in-c of St Marg Sing 70-75; V of St John's and St Marg's 75-77; C of Portadown 78-80; Reg Sec Overseas Miss Fellowship from 80. *c/o Belmont, The Vine, Sevenoaks, Kent, TN13 3TZ.*

McSWEENEY, Irwin Vincent. Codr Coll Barb 57. **d** 60 Barb **p** 61 Nass. C-in-c of Exuma 60-61; Andros 61-68; P-in-c of Harbour I 71-72; Asst Master St Anne's Sch Nass 72-75; R of St Gregory Nass 75-78; L to Offic Dio Nass from 78. *PO Box N-4124, Nassau, Bahamas, W Indies.*

MACUA, Andrew. St Paul's Div Sch Limuru 46. **d** 48 **p** 49 Momb. P Dio Momb 48-61; Dio Ft Hall 61-65; Dio Mt Kenya 65-72. *Box 23029, Lower Kabete, Kenya.*

McVEIGH, Samuel. b 49. Div Hostel Dub 77. **d** 79 **p** 80 Derry. C of St Columb Drumragh Dio Derry from 79. *3 Anderson Gardens, Omagh, Co Tyrone, N Ireland.*

McVITTY, Brian Hugh. b 54. Univ of Tor BA 76. Wycl Coll Tor MDiv 79. **d** 79 Bp Read for Tor **p** 80 Tor. C of St Timothy Scarboro City and Dio Tor from 79. *4125 Sheppard Avenue East, Scarboro, Ont, Canada M1S 1T1.*

MacWILLIAM, Canon Alexander Gordon. b 23. Late Exhib of Univ of Wales BA 43. Univ of Lon BD (2nd cl Hons) 47, PhD (Th) 52. St Mich Coll Llan 43. **d** 46 **p** 47 Ban. C of Llanllyfni 46-49; Min Can of Ban Cathl 49-55; C of St Mary Ban 50-53; St Jas Ban 53-55; R of Llanfaethlu w Llanfwrog and Llanrhyddlad 55-58; R of Llanfairynghornwy w Llanrhwydrus 56-58; Lect Trin Coll Carmarthen from 58; L to Offic Dio St D from 60; Exam Chap to Bp of St D from 68; Can of St D from 78. *Pen Parc, Smyrna Road, Llangain, Dyfed.* (Llanstephan 333)

McWILLIAM, Charles Denis. b 24. Clare Coll Cam BA (1st cl Th) 49, MA 52. Cudd Coll 49. **d** 51 **p** 52 Ox. C of Cuddesdon and Tutor Cudd Coll Ox 51-54; C of St Geo Cathl Capetn 54-56; Prec 56-57; R of Roodebloem 57-61; R of Somt W 61-63; Exam Chap to Abp of Capetn 61-66; Chap Univ of Capetn 63-66; Perm to Offic Dio Sarum 67-73; Dio Fulham & Gibr 73-80; V of Heyhouses (or Sabden) Dio Blackb from 80. *St Nicholas Vicarage, Sabden, Blackburn, Lancs, BB6 9EH.* (padiham 71384)

MADABASI, Christopher Eiti. Bp Gwynne Coll Mundri, 61. **d** 64 Sudan. d Dio Sudan. *Clergy House, PO Box 135, Khartoum, Sudan.*

MADDEN, Canon Jack. St Francis Coll Brisb ACT ThL 50. **d** and **p** 51 Brisb. C of All SS Charleville 51-56; V of St Clem Stafford City and Dio Brisb 56-64; R from 64; Hon Can of Brisb from 68. *St Clement's Rectory, Stafford, Queensland, Australia 4053.* (56 4134)

MADDEN, John Harold. **d** 55 **p** 57 St Arn. C of Maryborough 55-57; V of Tresco 57-59; C of Port Adel 60-63; R of Hindmarsh 63-72; L to Offic Dio Adel from 72. *10 Turner Road, Elizabeth Park, S Australia 5113.* (252 0304)

MADDEN, Robert Willis. b 14. Late Scho of TCD BA (1st cl Mod Ment and Mor Sc) and Wray Pri (2nd) 36, Downes Pri (2nd) and Ryan Pri 37, Div Test (1st cl) 38, MA 40. **d** 39 Dorch for Ox **p** 40 Down. Tutor Wycl Hall Ox and L to Offic Dio Ox 39-40; C of Bangor 40-42; I of Ballyfin 42-49; C of St Jas Taunton 49-52; V of Mayfield 52-61; Thurnby w Stoughton 61-66; R of Misterton 66-79. *80 Duffield Road, Little Eaton, DE2 5DT.* (Derby 832388)

MADDEN, Sydney Richard William. b 11. TCD BA 38. **d** 40 Dub for Oss **p** 41 Oss. C of Ardamine w Glascarrig 40-44; C-in-c of Bannow w Duncormick 44-48; I of Kilrush w Ballycarney 48-52; Mothel w Bilbo 52-55; Ardamine U 55-80; Preb of Toome and Kilrush in Ferns Cathl 65-71; Treas 71-79; Chan 79-80. *Cranacrower Lodge, Ballycanew, Gorey, Co Wexford, Irish Republic.*

MADDEX, Patrick John. b 31. Univ of Edin BSc (Forestry) 54. Bps' Coll Cheshunt 55. **d** 57 **p** 58 St Alb. C of Baldock 57-61; All SS Oxhey 61-64; V of Codicote 64-82; R of Gt and L Wymondley w Graveley and Chivesfield Dio St Alb from 82. *Great Wymondley Rectory, Hitchin, Herts, SG4 7HA* (Stevenage 53305)

MADDICK, Albert Victor Stanley. Univ of NZ BA 42,

LTh 43. **d** 43 **p** 44 Ch Ch. C of Addington 43-45; R of Little River 45-47; Chap of St Pet Sch Cam Waik 47-51; L to Offic Dio Polyn 51-53; Hd Master Launceston Gr Sch and C of St John Launceston 53-57; Chap Mentone Gr Sch 58-63; Dir Coun Christian Educn in Schs and C of St Paul's Cathl Melb 63-68; I of Toorak 68-78; Chap Tintern C of E Gr Sch Dio Melb 78-79; I of S Camberwell 79-81; Perm to Offic Dio Melb from 81. *12 St James's Avenue, Kallista, Vic, Australia 3791.*

MADDISON, Norman. b 12. St Jo Coll Dur BA 34. **d** 35 Dur **p** 36 Jarrow for Dur. C of Dalton-le-Dale 35-37; Bp Wearmouth 37-43; V of St Jo Evang Barrow-F 43-48; Seaham w Seaham Harbour 48-60; R of Wolsingham (w Thornley from 64) 61-77; Perm to Offic Dio Dur from 77. *Whitfield Place, Wolsingham, Bishop Auckland, Co Durham.*

MADDOCK, David John Newcomb. b 36. Qu Coll Cam 2nd cl Th Trip pt i 58, BA (2nd cl Th Trip pt ii) 60, MA 64. Oak Hill Th Coll 60. **d** 62 **p** 63 Blackb. C of Bispham 62-65; Miss at Payne Bay 65-69; R of Frobisher Bay 70; Walsoken 70-77; Commiss Arctic from 70; V of Ch Ch Ore Dio Chich from 77. *Christ Church Vicarage, Canute Road, Ore, Hastings, E Sussex, TN35 5HT.* (0424-421439)

✠ **MADDOCK, Right Rev David Rokeby.** b 15. Univ of Bris BA 36. St Cath S Ox BA (3rd cl Th) 38, MA 42. Wycl Hall Ox 36. **d** 39 **p** 40 B & W. C of Chard 39-43; Sec B & W Dioc Youth Coun 43-45; V of Wilton 43-47; Chap Taunton Publ Asst Inst 45-47; R of Wareham w Arne 47-61; Surr from 47; Chap Wareham Publ Asst Inst 47-61; RD of Purbeck 48-61; C-in-c of Grange 50-61; Can and Preb of Warminster in Sarum Cathl 56-67; Archd of Sherborne 61-67; Sudbury 68-70; R of Bradford Peverell w Stratton 61-66; W Stafford w Frome Billet 66-67; Cons Ld Bp Suffr of Dunwich in St Paul's Cathl Lon 29 June 67 by Abp of Cant; Bps of Truro; Linc; St E; and Sarum; Bps Suffr of Stepney; Tonbridge; and Fulham; and Bps Wand; Harland; Hollis; and Cashmore; res 76; Provost and V of St Jas Cathl Ch Bury St Edms 76-80. *3 Norfolk Court, East Street, Bridport, Dorset, DT6 3LL.*

MADDOCK, Edward Watson. B 25. Univ of Manit BSc 48. **d** 75 Rupld. Hon C of Morden Area 75-78; St Thos Morden Dio Rupld from 78. *Box 411, Morden, Manit, R0G 1J0, Canada.*

MADDOCK, Eric John. b 1899. Oak Hill Th Coll 54. **d** 54 **p** 55 Roch. C of St John w Ch Ch Penge 54-56; V of Ponsbourne 56-59; Cler Sec ICM 59-62; Perm to Offic Dio S'wark 60-62; V of St Mary Preston 62-66; Dep Chap to HM Pris Preston 64-65; Perm to Offic Dio Ex from 66; Dio Truro from 73; Dio Chich from 79. *Christ Church Vicarage, Canute Road, Ore, Hastings, E Sussex, TN35 5HT.* (0424-421439)

MADDOCK, Eric Rokeby. St Pet Hall, Ox BA 33, MA 38. Wycl Hall, Ox 37. **d** 38 **p** 39 Heref. C of Ch Stretton 38-46; R of Chelvey w Brockley 46-60; Kelston 60-76; N Stoke 60-76. *3 Greyfield Road, High Littleton, Bristol.*

MADDOCK, Francis James Wilson. b 14. Univ of Bris BA 36. Wadh Coll Ox BA (3rd cl Hist) 38, MA 42. Cudd Coll 39. **d** 40 **p** 41 S'wark. C of St Barn Southfields 40-44; Horfield (in c of St Edm) 44-49; V of St Anne Brislington 49-56; St Pet Newlyn 56-60; Perm to Offic Dio Truro 60-64; R of Forrabury w Minster and Trevalga 64-74; C-in-c of Davidstow w Otterham 64-74; St Juliot w Lesnewth 64-74; RD of Trigg Minor 66-69; R of Boscastle w Davidstow 74-78; P-in-c of Port Isaac 78-79; Perm to Offic Dio Ex from 80. *8 Sylvan Close, Exmouth, Devon.*

MADDOCK, Henry Mervyn. ACT ThL 25. **d** 24 **p** 25 Tas. C of Glenorchy 24-26; R of King I 26-30; Kempton 30-35; Channel 35-38; Buckland 38-44; Hamilton 44-53; Richmond 53-60; L to Offic Dio Tas from 69. *26 Corinth Street, Howrah, Tasmania 7018.* (002-47 8414)

MADDOCK, Norman. b 15. St Jo Coll Dur BA 38, Capel Cure Pri 39, Dipl in Th 39. MA 41. **d** 39 **p** 40 Blackb. C of St Jas Chorley 39-42; All SS Marple Stockport (in c of St Paul Strines) 42-45; V of Tintwistle 45-49; R of H Trin Rusholme 49-55; Surr 50-79; V of St Thos Blackpool 55-69; Chatburn 69-79; Hon C of Warton Dio Blackb from 79. *The Parsonage, Priest Hutton, Nr Carnforth, Lancs.* (Burton 781264)

MADDOCK, Philip Arthur Louis. b 47. Oak Hill Th Coll 75. **d** 78 **p** 79 Ches. C of New Ferry Dio Ches from 78. *11 Cedar Avenue, Higher Bebington, Wirral, Cheshire.*

MADDOCK, Canon Philip Lawrence. b 20. Univ of Bris BA (2nd cl German and Phil) 42. Cudd Coll 42. **d** 43 **p** 44 Lon. C of St Aug Kilburn 43-48; All SS Weston-s-Mare 48-57; Chap Commun of Epiph Truro 57-60; Sub-Warden 60-63; Chap HM Pris Wandsworth 63-64; Birm 64-67; Ex 67-69; St Lawr Hosp Bodmin 69-76; Publ Pr Dio S'wark 64-65; Dio Truro 69-76; Can Res and Treas of Truro Cathl from 76. *Lemon Lodge, Lemon Street, Truro, TR1 2PE.* (Truro 2094)

MADDOCK, Sidney James. Wycl Coll Tor 66. **d** and **p** 69 Tor. C of St Hilda Fairbank, Tor 69-70; St Mary Westhill Tor 70-73; R of All SS Pentanguishene 73-77; St Jude Bramalea N Dio Tor from 77. *92 Massey Street, Brampton, Ont., Canada.*

MADDOCK-LYON, John Frederick. b 38. K Coll Lon and Warm AKC 62, BD 64. **d** 64 **p** 65 Ches. C of Woodchurch 64-67; Higher Bebington 67-70; V of Sandbach Heath 70-80; St John Egremont, Wallasey Dio Ches from 80. *7 Silver-Beech Road, Wallasey, Mer.* (051-638 4360)

MADDOCKS, Dennis Samuel. b 21. Univ of Sheff 39. Qu Coll Birm 47. **d** 50 **p** 51 Sheff. C of Attercliffe w Carbrook Sheff 50-53; Wombwell 53-55; R of Adwick-le-Street 55-60; V of Brixton Dio Ex from 60. *Brixton Vicarage, Plymouth, Devon, PL8 2AT.* (Plymouth 880292)

MADDOCKS, Ven Edward Henry. Em Coll Sktn LTh 18, BD 24, BA (Distinc) 36, Hon DD 56. **d** 18 **p** 19 Sask. C of Edgerton Alta 18-22; R of Humboldt 22-27; Ch Ch The Pas 27-29; Prof Em Coll Sktn 29-41; Montr Dioc Th Coll 41-44; P-in-c of Ch Ch Montr 43-44; R of St Steph Calg 44-60; Exam Chap to Bp of Calg 44-60; Hon Can of Calg 45-54; Archd of Bow Valley 54-60; Archd (Emer) from 60; Gen Sec of Gen Synod of Angl Ch of Canada 60-64; I of Brentwood Coll Mem Chap 64-73; Perm to Offic Dio BC from 73. *3493 Lovat Avenue, Victoria, BC, Canada.*

✠ **MADDOCKS, Right Rev Morris Henry St John.** b 28. Trin Coll Cam BA 52, MA 56. Chich Th Coll. **d** 54 **p** 55 Lon. C of St Pet Ealing 54-55; St Andr Uxbridge 55-58; V of Weaverthorpe w Helperthorpe 58-61; C in c of Luttons Ambo 61; V of St Martin Scarborough 61-71; Cons Ld Bp Suffr of Selby in Beverley Minster 25 Jan 72 by Abp of York; Bps of Dur; Ripon; Carl; Southw; Bris; Lich; Linc; Jarrow; Hull; Grimsby; Shrewsbury; and Bps Sansbury; Townley; Claxton; Sargent; Skelton; Bevan; and Cockin. *8 Bankside Close, Upper Poppleton, York, YO2 6LH.* (York 795342)

MADDOX, Bernard Thomas. b 31. St Steph Ho Ox 53. **d** 55 **p** 56 Lich. C of St Mary and St Chad Longton 55-60; V of St Werburgh Burslem 60-74; Chap Haywood and Stanfields Hosps 60-74; M Gen Syn from 70; P-in-c of St Mary Virg Shrewsbury 74-76; All SS Shrewsbury 74-76; St Mich Shrewsbury 74-76; V of Shrewsbury Dio Lich from 76. *37 Berwick Road, Shrewsbury, SY1 2LP.* (0743-3080)

MADDOX, David Pugh. b 16. St D Coll Lamp BA 39. **d** 49 **p** 50 St A. C of Rhosllanerchrugog 49-52; Mold 52-54; V of Llansantffraid-Glyn-Ceiriog 54-57; Tydweiliog w Llandudwen 57-59; Corris 59-62; R of Cerrigydrudion w Llangwm and Llanfihangel-Glyn-Myfyr (w Yspytty-Ifan and Petrefoelas from 66) 62-70; R of Bryneglwys w Llandegla 70-77; Llansantfraid-Glan-Conway w Eglwysbach 77-81. *Pemblemere, Arenig Street, Bala, Gwyn.*

MADDOX, Dewi David Morgan. b 22. St D Coll Lamp BA 42. Trin Coll Cam BA 61, MA 64. St Mich Coll Llan 42. **d** 45 **p** 46 Swan B. C of Llandilo-Talybont 45-49; Ewelme 49-51; R of Linton 51-56; V of Trumpington Dio Ely from 56; Surr from 61. *Trumpington Vicarage, Cambridge.* (Trumpington 3262)

MADDOX, Edwin Joseph Crusha. b 09. Dorch Miss Coll 38. **d** 41 **p** 42 Wakef. C of St John Wakef 41-43; St Cedd Canning Town 43-46; Gt Ilford (in c of St Alb) 46-50; V of H Trin Harrow Green 50-61; C-in-c of St Aug Miss Leytonstone 59-61; V of St Sav Walthamstow 61-71; St Jas Leigh 71-77. *43 Barnard Road, Leigh-on-Sea, Essex.*

MADDOX, Goronwy Owen. b 23. Univ of Wales BA 51. Sarum Th Coll 68. **d** 70 **p** 71 Sarum. C of Calne Dio Sarum from 70; Hd Master H Trin C of E Sch Calne from 58. *Holy Trinity School House, Calne, Wilts.* (Calne 813170)

MADDOX, Hugh Inglis Monteath. b 37. CCC Cam 2nd cl Hist Trip pt i 59, BA (2nd cl Th Trip pt ia) 60. Westcott Ho Cam 61. **d** 63 **p** 64 Sheff. C of Attercliffe w Carbrook Sheff 63-66; All SS w St Phil Maidstone 66-67; Folkestone 67-69; St Martin-in-the-Fields 69-73; R of Sandwich 73-81; V of St Peter in Thanet Dio Cant from 81. *Vicarage, St Peter in Thanet, Broadstairs, Kent.* (Thanet 69169)

MADELA, Philemon Mandlenkosi. **d** 69 **p** 71 Zulu. P Dio Zulu. *Private Bag 2045, Dundee, Natal, S Africa*

MADELEMU, Yohana. **d** and **p** 72 Centr Tang. P Dio Centr Tang. *Box 27, Kongwa, Tanzania.*

MADESI, Christopher Charles Tibahanana Muchenga. b 39. Bp Tucker Coll Mukono. **d** 69 **p** 70 Bp Rwakaikana for Ruw. P Dio Ruw. *COU Rwebisengo, Box 12, Fort Portal, Uganda.*

MADGE, Donald John. b 05. Worc Ordin Coll 64. **d** and **p** 65 Ex. C of St Mich AA Heavitree Ex 65-77; Publ Pr Dio Ex from 78. *3 Church Terrace, Heavitree, Exeter, EX2 5DU, Devon.*

MADGE, Douglas Grant. Hur Coll Dipl Th 63. **d** 63 Bp Appleyard for Hur **p** 64 Hur. C of Paisley 63-65; St Jo Evang Kitchener 65-67; I of St Columba Waterloo 67-74; H Trin Brantford Dio Hur from 74. *58 Cayuga Street, Brantford, Ont., Canada.* (519-756 5633)

MADGE, Francis Sidney. b 35. K Coll Lon and Warm

AKC 58. **d** 59 **p** 60 York. C of St Mary Bishophill Sen w St Clem York 59-62; St Mich AA Sutton-in-Holderness 62-64; St Jas Ex 64-69; R of Sutton-by-Dover w Waldershare 69-78; P-in-c of St Mary of Nazareth w Wickham Dio Cant 78-81; V from 81. *St Mary's Vicarage, The Avenue, West Wickham, Kent.* (01-777 3137)

MADI, Canon Samson. St Pet Coll Rosettenville 37. **d** 39 **p** 40 Zulu. C of Nkandhla 39-46; Utrecht 46-53; Dir of St John Blood River, Zulu 53-70; Hon Can of Zulu from 63. *Box 147, Eshowe, Zululand.*

MADI and WEST NILE, Bishop of. *See* Ringtho, Right Rev Remelia.

MADIDA, Milton Biozo. b 35. **d** 74 **p** 75 Matab. P Dio Matab. *89/7704 Mpopoma South, Bulawayo, Zimbabwe.*

MADIHI, John. b 46. St Phil Coll Kongwa. **d** 75 **p** 76 Centr Tang. P Dio Centr Tang. *PO Kibakwe, Tanzania.*

MADIKIDA, Canon John Baba. St Bede's Coll Umtata. **d** 52 **p** 54 St Jo Kaffr. P Dio St John's from 52; Can of St John's from 70. *St Mary's Mission, Qanqu, Transkei, S Africa.* (Qanqu 3)

MADILL, David George. Em Coll Sktn LTh 49. Univ of Sask BA 51. **d** 49 Qu'App **p** 50 Edmon. Chap RCAF 49-74; Westmr Hosp Lon Ont from 74. *c/o Westminster Hospital, London, Ont., Canada.*

✠ **MADINDA, Right Rev Yohana.** b 26. St Paul's Coll Limuru 56. **d** 57 Centr Tang **p** 58 Bp Omari for Centr Tang. V of H Spirit Cathl Dodoma 58-64 Cons Asst Bp in Centr Tang in H Trin Ch Moro 7 May 64 by Abp of E Afr; Bps of Centr Tang; Zanz; and Vic Nyan; Archd of Dodoma-Mvumi 65-71; Apptd Ld Bp of Centr Tang from 71. *Box 15, Dodoma, Tanzania.* (Dodoma 712)

MADLOPA, Philip. St Francis Th Coll Sekhukhuniland 62. **d** 64 **p** 65 Pret. C of Witbank 64-70; White River 71-78; R of Bushbuckridge Dio Pret from 78. *PO Box 173, Bushbuckridge, Transvaal 1280, S Africa.*

MADOKA, Allen. St Paul's Dioc Div Sch Limuru 44, Lon Coll of Div 48-49. **d** 45 **p** 49 Momb. P Dio Momb 49 58; CF (Kenya) 58-68; Can of Nai 67-70. *Chaplains' Dept, PO Box 30503, Nairobi, Kenya.*

MADONDOLA, Enoch Andrea. St Paul's Coll Limuru 58. **d** 59 **p** 60 Centr Tang. P Dio Centr Tang; Vice-Prin Msaloto Bible Sch Dodoma from 70. *Box 3103, Arusha, Tanzania.*

MADSSEN, John Andrew. St Francis Coll Brisb 53. **d** and **p** 56 Brisb. C of All SS Ipswich 56-58; Southport 58-60; Edenbridge (in c of St Paulinus Marlpit Hill) 61-62; V of Mt Gravatt Brisb 62-63; Caboolture 63-68; Perm to Offic Dio Brisb from 68. *16 Morcom Avenue, Corinda, Queensland, Australia 4075.* (379 8083)

MADUAKOLAM, Canon Godson Nwachukwu. Melville Hall Ibad 49. **d** 51 Bp Hall for Niger **p** 52 Nig Delta. P Dio Niger 51-52; Nig Delta 52-56; Niger 56-61; N Nig 61-68; Dio Ow from 68; Hon Can of Ow from 68. *Parsonage, PO Box 8, Akokwa, Ndizuogu, Nigeria.*

MADUMERE, Joseph Agomo. St Paul's Coll Anka 60. **d** 60 Nig Delta. d Dio Nig Delta. *St Matthew's Parsonage, c/o Box 49, Aba, Nigeria.*

MADZIRO, Ernest. **d** 79 **p** 80 Mashon. P Dio Mashon 70-81; Dio Lundi from 81. *Box 331, Fort Victoria, Zimbabwe.*

MADZIVANYIKA, Milton. St Jo Sem Lusaka 56. **d** 58 **p** 61 Mashon. P Dio Mashon. *c/o St Michael's Church, Harare, Zimbabwe.*

MADZIWA, Lovemore. **d** 76 Mashon. d Dio Mashon 76-81; Dio Mutare from 81. *St Luke's School, PB 8003, Rusape, Zimbabwe.*

MADZIYIRE, Peter. **d** 76 Mashon. d Dio Mashon. *St Augustine's School, PO Daramombe, via Enkeldoorn, Zimbabwe.*

MADZIYIRE, Salathiel. St Jo Sem Lusaka 66. **d** 68 **p** 69 Mashon. P Dio Mashon. *c/o All Saint's Rectory, Marandellas, Zimbabwe.*

MAE, Leonard. Maka Th Coll 36. **d** 37 Melan. d Dio Melan. *Reef Islands, British Solomon Islands.*

MAEKANE, Patrick Umzimkulu. **d** 31 **p** 32 Bloemf. Miss Dio Bloemf 32-40; P Dio Basuto 40-66; Dio Les 66-68; Can of Basuto 52-66; Les 66-68. *Marsite Mission, PO Maseru, Lesotho, S Africa.*

MAEMANE, Cecil. St Pet Coll Siota 54. **d** 56 **p** 59 Melan. P Dio Melan. *Melanesian Mission, British Solomon Islands.*

MAENDAENDA, Vincent. St Mark's Coll Dar-S 72. **d** 73 **p** 75 Ruv for Masasi. P Dio Masasi 73-75; Dio Ruv from 76. *PO Box 45, Tunduru, Tanzania.*

MAFABI, Abiasali. **d** 64 **p** 65 Mbale. P Dio Mbale 64-73. *Busano, PO Box 984, Mbale, Uganda.*

MAFABI, Christopher Levi. b 51. Bp Tucker Coll Mukono 77. **d** 80 Mbale. d Dio Mbale. *PO Box 1267, Mbale, Uganda.*

MAFABI, Mesusera. b 36. **d** and **p** 74 Mbale. P Dio Mbale. *Kalawa, PO Budadiri, Mbale, Uganda.*

MAFFEY, Canon Geoffrey Louis. NZ Bd of Th Stud LTh 38, Univ of NZ BA 36, MA (2nd cl) 37. St Jo Coll Auckld. **d** 38 **p** 39 Auckld C of Otahuhu 38-41; V of Hokianga 41-46; Kamo 46-48; New Lynn 48-51; Takapuna 51-63; One Tree Hill 63-70; Can of Auckld 68-80; Can Emer from 80; V of St Barn Mt Eden Auckld 70-80; Perm to Offic Dio Auckld from 80. *1027 Whangaparaoa Road, Hibiscus Coast, Auckland, NZ.*

MAFILIKA, Johnson. b 11. St Bede's Coll Umtata 71. **d** 71 **p** 72 St John's (APM). C of Cala Dio St John's from 71. *Box 34, Ugie 5470, Transkei, S Africa.* (Ugie 1840)

MAFUNE, Charles. Univ of E Afr Dipl Th 68. Bp Tucker Coll Mukono 65. **d** 67 Kig. d Dio Kig. *Box 255, Jinja, Uganda.*

MAFURA, Timothy. **d** 76 Mashon. d Dio Mashon 76-81; Dio Mutare from 81. *Holy Family School, PB 92, Inyazura, Zimbabwe.*

MAGADLA, Thamduxolo. b 41. St Bede's Coll Umtata 76. **d** 78 **p** 80 St John's. P Dio St John's. *St Andrew's Mission, Lusikisiki, Transkei.*

MAGADLELA, Elias Joshua Josiah. St Bede's Coll Umtata. **d** 53 **p** 54 Basuto. P Dio Basuto 53-65. *Box 87, Maseru, Lesotho, S Africa.*

MAGAHY, Canon Gerald Samuel. TCD BA (Mod) 45, MA 61, LLD 80. Univ Coll Galway, Higher Dipl Trin Coll Dub BA (Mod) 45, MA 61. Univ Coll Galway, Higher Dipl Educn 55. **d** 53 **p** 54 Lim. Dioc C Dio Lim and Hd Master Villiers Sch Lim 53-61; Chap and Hd Master K Hosp Sch Dub from 61; Can Treas of St Patr Cathl Dub from 80. *King's Hospital, Palmerstown, Dublin 20, Irish Republic.*

MAGAI, Ven Enok Riak. **d** 53 Bp Allison for Sudan **p** 55 Sudan. P Dio Sudan 53-76; Dio Rumbek from 76; Archd of Dinka from 71; Exam Chap to Bp of Sudan 71-76; Hon Can of All SS Cathl Khartoum 71-76. *Bishop's House, Rumbeck, Bahr-el-Ghazal, Sudan.*

MAGALA, Bethuel. b 33. St Phil Coll Kongwa 68. **d** and **p** 70 Centr Tang. P Dio Centr Tang. *Box 306, Moshi, Tanzania.*

MAGAMBO, William. b 41. Bp Tucker Coll Mukono 68. **d** 72 Ank. d Dio Ank. *Box 14, Mbarara, Uganda.*

MAGANGA, Canon Andreya. **d** 56 Bp Omari for Centr Tang **p** 57 Centr Tang. P Dio Centr Tang; Can of Centr Tang from 76. *Box 84, Mpwapwa, Tanzania.*

MAGARA, Matiya. Buwalasi Th Coll 56. **d** 59 U Nile **p** 61 N Ugan. d Dio U Nile 59-61; P Dio N Ugan 61-69; Dio M & W Nile from 69. *PO Box 212, Arua, Uganda.*

MAGAVA, Eli Bani. St Jo Coll Lusaka 51. **d** 53 **p** 54 Matab. P Dio Matab. *PO Box 2094, Bulawayo, Zimbabwe.* (64227)

MAGAWA, Simon. b 43. **d** 77 **p** 78 Moro. P Dio Moro. *PO Mkalama, Kilosa, Tanzania.*

MAGAWA, William Cidumuka. **d** 65 **p** 66 Centr Tang. P Dio Centr Tang. *Box 155, Iringa, Tanzania.*

MAGAYA, Andarea Manguboyo. **d** 47 **p** 50 Sudan. P Dio Sudan from 50. *CMS, Nzara, Yambio District, Southern Sudan.*

MAGEE, Frederick Hugh. b 33. Univ of Yale BA 56. Westcott Ho Cam 58. **d** 59 Man **p** 60 Hulme for Man. C of St Mark Bury 59-63; in Amer Ch 63-64; Chap St Paul's Cathl Dundee 74-79; R of St Andr St Andrews Dio St Andr from 79. *Rectory, St Andrews, Fife, KY16 9QF.* (St Andrews 73344)

MAGEE, Gregory Thomas David. ACT BTh 80. St Francis Coll Brisb. **d** 80 Brisb. C of H Spirit Kenmore Dio Brisb from 80. *Flat 5, 75 Cunningham Street, Taringa, Qld, Australia 4068.* (371 6602)

MAGEE, John Lawrence. b 19. BA (Lon) 52. **d** and **p** 78 Glouc. C of Westbury-on-Severn w Flaxley and Blaisdon Dio Glouc from 78. *Sharon, Blaisdon, Longhope, Glos, GL17 0AL.*

MAGEE, John Wallace. **d** and **p** 75 Syd. C of Epping 75-76; St Andr S Brisb 77-78; V of Rosewood Dio Brisb from 78. *76 John Street, Rosewood, Australia 4340.* (075-64 1430)

MAGEE, Malcolm Francis. b 24. Univ of Edin MA 49. **d** 54 **p** 55 RC Abp of Birm. In RC Ch 54-68; Rec into Angl Commun 71 by Bp of S'wark; L to Offic Dio S'wark 71-75; Hon C of St Mich AA Abbey Wood Plumstead 75-78; C of Mottingham (in-c of St Alb) Dio S'wark from 78. *132 William Barefoot Drive, Mottingham, SE9.* (01-857 7702)

MAGEE, Patrick Connor. b 15. Late Cho Scho King's Coll Cam 3rd cl Hist Trip pt i 36, BA (3rd cl Hist Trip pt ii) 37, MA 41. Westcott Ho Cam 38. **d** 39 **p** 40 Wakef. C of King Cross 39-43; Chap RNVR 43-46; Chap King's Coll Cam 46-52; Select Pr Univ of Cam 53; Commiss Jer from 47; V of Kingston T 52-60; Surr 53-60; Chap Bryanston Sch 60-70; V of Ryde 70-72; Surr 70-72; Chap Tiffin's Sch Kingston T 72-73; V of St Mich AA City and Dio Sarum 73-75; Team R of Bemerton Dio Sarum from 75. *Bemerton Rectory, Lower Road, Salisbury, Wilts.* (Salisbury 4632)

MAGGS, Roger James. Univ of Alta BSc (Eng) 52. Em Coll Sktn LTh 55. **d** 55 **p** 56 Edmon. C of Good Shepherd Edmon 55-56; R of St Phil Edmon 56-63; Langley 63-69; Port Coquitlam 69-72; on leave 73-80; Chap Oshawa Gen Hosp from 81. *Oshawa General Hospital, Oshawa, Ont., Canada.*

MAGILL, Peter George. b 49. McGill Univ Montr BTh 73. Montr Dioc Th Coll 74. **d** 75 **p** 76 Montr. C of Westmount 75-76; Ste Anne de Bellevue 76-78; St Ignatius City and Dio Montr from 78. *10439 Park George Boulevard, Montreal, PQ, Canada.* (514-321 3591)

MAGILL, Waller Brian Brendan. b 20. Found Scho TCD BA (1st cl Mod Ment and Mor Sc) 42, Div Test 43, Elrington Th Pri 45, BD 45. **d** 44 **p** 45 Down. C of St Columba Knock 44-47; Holywood 47-50; Vice Prin of Qu Th Coll Birm 50-55; Publ Pr Dio Birm 50-55; Lect in Th Univ of Birm 51-55; Chap Rugby Sch 55-62; Publ Pr Dio Cov 56-62; Lect in Div Nottm Coll of Educn 62-75; Trent Poly from 75; Perm to Offic Dio Southw 64-66; L to Offic from 66. *16 Parkcroft Road, West Bridgford, Nottingham.* (Nottingham 233293)

MAGIRA DOLLO, Abiaza. d 77 Rumbek. d Dio Rumbek. *ECS, Amadi, Sudan.*

MAGNESS, Anthony William John. b 37. New Coll Ox BA 62, MA 65. Coll of Resurr Mirfield 78. **d** 80 Liv **p** 81 Warrington for Liv. C of St Faith Gt Crosby Dio Liv from 80. *16 Alder Grove, Liverpool, L22 2AL.*

MAGODORO, Joy Munashe. b 47. Qu Coll Birm 73. **d** 75 Lich for Matab **p** 76 Matab. C of Sizinda Dio Matab 75-77; P-in-c 77-78; on leave. *7535/6 Tshabalala, Bulawayo, Rhodesia.*

MAGOFFIN, Richard David. d 78 N Queensld. Perm to Offic Dio N Queensld from 78. *73 Hodgkinson Street, Charters Towers, Qld, Australia 4820.*

MAGOKE, Ven Eliya. St Phil Coll Kongwa. **d** 65 **p** 66 Vic Nyan. P Dio Vic Nyan; Hon Can of Vic Nyan from 75; Archd of Usukuma from 80. *Box 144, Shinyanga, Tanzania.*

MAGOMBO, Tukani Lakulana. b 28. **d** and **p** 77 Boga-Z. P Dio Boga-Z. *BP 861, Kisangani, Zaire.*

MAGOR, Murray Churchill. McGill Univ Montr BA, BCL, BD and LTh 59. Dioc Th Coll Montr. **d** and **p** 59 Montr. C of Ch Ch Cathl Montr 59-62; R of Ste Agathe des Monts 62-64; Beaurepaire 64-70; Hon Can of Ch Ch Cathl Montr 70-73; Exam Chap to Bp of Montr 70-74; R of St Pet Mt Royal 70-74; Archd of St Andr 73-74; on leave; Prin St Geo Sch Montr from 81. *3282 Cedar Avenue, Westmount, PQ, Canada.* (514-933 6634)

MAGOWAN, Alistair James. b 55. Univ of Leeds BSc. 77. Trin Coll Bris 78. **d** 81 Sheff. C of Owlerton City and Dio Sheff from 81. *15 Morley Street, Hillsborough, Sheffield, S6 2PL.*

MAGOWAN, Harold Victor. b 34. QUB BA 55. Trin Coll Dub 55. **d** 57 **p** 58 Connor. C of Antrim 57-69. *Antrim House, Antrim, N Ireland.*

MAGSON, Thomas Symmons. b 09. St Jo Coll Cam BA 31, MA 35. Ripon Hall Ox 74. **d** 75 **p** 76 Bris (APM). C of Highworth Dio Bris from 75. *21 Cricklade Road, Highworth, Wilts, SN6 7BW.* (0793 762579)

MAGU, Canon Josiah Ngure. St Paul's Th Coll Limuru 44. Ridley Hall Cam 49. **d** 45 **p** 49 Momb. P Dio Momb 45-49 and 60-62; Tutor St Paul's Th Coll Limuru 49-51; Industr Missr 62-75; Can of Mt Kenya S from 75; V of Kirangari 75-77; Kiambu Dio Mt Kenya S from 77. *Box 116, Kiambu, Kenya.*

MAGU, Yusufu. St Paul's Dioc Div Sch Freetown 23. **d** 25 Ugan for Momb **p** 30 Momb. CMS P Dio Momb 25-51; Perm to Offic Dio Momb 51-61; Ft Hall 61-64; Dio Mt Kenya from 64. *PO Lower Kabete, Kenya.*

✠ **MAGUA, Right Rev Sospeter.** St Paul's Dioc Div Sch Limuru, 51. **d** 53 **p** 55 Momb. P Dio Momb 53-61; Ft Hall 61-64; Exam Chap to Bp of Ft Hall 61-63; Archd of Ft Hall 63-64; Mt Kenya 64-71; VG of Mt Kenya 71-73; Prov Sec Kenya 74-76; Cons Ld Bp of Mt Kenya S in Cathl Ch of St Jas and All Mart Murang'a 31 Oct 76 by Abp of Kenya; Bps of Nak, Maseno N, Mt Kenya E, Momb and Maseno S; and Bps Ngaruiya and Nzano. *PO Box 121, Murang'a, Kenya.* (Murang'a 53)

MAGUIRE, Brian William. b 33. Coll of Resurr Mirfield 70. **d** 72 Hull for York **p** 73 York. C of Guisborough 72-76; Team V of Haxby w Wigginton Dio York 76-77; R from 78. *Rectory, Westfield Close, Haxby, York, YO3 8JG.* (York 760455)

✠ **MAGUIRE, Right Rev Robert Kenneth.** Trin Coll Dub BA 45, Div Test 47, MA 50, DD 63. Montr Dioc Th Coll DD 63. Bp's Univ Lennox DCL 63. **d** 47 **p** 48 Arm. C of St Mark Arm 47-49; St Jas Ap Montr 49-52; Dean of Residence Trin Coll Dub and L to Offic Dios Dub Glendal and Kild 52-60; C-in-c of St Andr Dub 54-57; Min Can of St Patr Cathl Dub 55-58; Dean and R of Ch Ch Cathl Montr 61-63; Cons Ld Bp of Montr in Montr Cathl 8 Jan 63 by Bp of NS; Abps of Rupld; Alg; and Abp Dixon; Bps of Fred; Newfld; Queb; Ont; and Ott; Bp Coadj of NS (Davis); Asst Bp of Newfld (Seaborn); Bp of Vermont (USA); Abp Athenagoras; res 75. *4875 Dundas Street West, Islington, Ont, Canada.* (416-233 9561)

MAGUWO, Mikaeli. d 62 **p** 63 Centr Tang. P Dio Centr Tang. *Mnase, PO Kikombo, Tanzania.*

MAGUZI, Ahithopel. b 45. Bp Tucker Coll Mukono 70. **d** 72 Nam. d Dio Nam. *Box 829, Luweero, Uganda.*

MAGWAI, Filipo. d 54 **p** 55 Centr Tang. P Dio Centr Tang 54-65; Moro 65-70; L to Offic Dio Moro 70-74. *Box 169, Kilosa, Tanzania.*

MAGWAZA, Enoch. St Pet Coll Rosettenville. **d** 42 **p** 43 Pret. P Dio Pret 42-77. *Stand Q, 16 Mhluzi Location, Middleburg 1052, Transvaal, S Africa.*

MAHABIR, Eric. Codr Coll Barb 63. **d** and **p** 65 Trinid. Chap Pris and Hosps Dio Trinid. *30 Church Street, St James, Port of Spain, Trinidad, W Indies.*

MAHANZA, Yakoba. b 32. **d** 79 **p** 80 Centr Tang. P Dio Centr Tang. *c/o Box 993, Dodoma, Tanzania.*

MAHETANE, Fabiao. d 78 **p** 79 Lebom. P Dio Lebom. *CP 57, Maputo, Mozambique.*

MAHIAINI, Very Rev John. St Paul's Th Coll Limuru 56. **d** 57 **p** 59 Momb. P Dio Momb 57-61; Dio Ft Hall 61-64; Dio Mt Kenya 64-72; Exam Chap to Bp of Mt Kenya 66-72; to Bp of Nak 72-76; Provost of Nak Cathl from 72. *Box 244, Nakuru, Kenya.* (Nakuru 2569)

MAHITIRA, Ehasaph. d 74 **p** 75 Ank. P Dio Ank 74-76; Dio E Ank from 76. *PO Kiruhuura, Mbarara, Uganda.*

MAHLALELA, Efraim. St Aug Th Coll Maciene. **d** 64 Lebom **p** 67 Bp Pina-Cabral for Lebom; P Dio Lebom. *Missao Anglicana, Namaacha, Mozambique.*

MAHLALELA, Enock Mjabekwa. d and **p** 77 Swaz. P Dio Swaz. *St Michael's School, PO Box 15, Manzini, Swaziland.*

MAHLALELA, Ven Eric Josiah. St Bede's Coll Umtata 60. **d** 61 **p** 63 Zulu. P Dio Zulu 61-68; Dio Swaz from 68; Can of Swaz 76-79; Archd from 79. *PO Box 9, Luve, Swaziland.*

MAHLASELA, Daniel. St Bede's Coll Umtata, 46. **d** 47 **p** 49 St Jo Kaffr. C of Mount Fletcher 47-52; St Cuthb Tsolo 52-54 and 60-65; Kokstadt 54-56; P-in-c of Mt Fletcher 65-70; C of St Cuthb Tsolo 71-77; P-in-c of Xaxazana 77-81. *Umzimkulu Hospital, Transkei, S Africa.*

MAHN, Wilfried. d 71 Centr Tang. d Dio Centr Tang 71-80; Dio W Tang from 80. *c/o Box 15, Kasulu, Tanzania.*

MAHON, James Nicholas. b 12. Keble Coll Ox BA (3rd cl Hons Th) 33, MA 47. St Steph Ho Ox 33. **d** 35 **p** 36 Southw. C of St Mary Magd Hucknall Torkard 35-42; Wimborne Minster 42-50; R of Lytchett Matravers 50-77. *26 Keighley Avenue, Broadstone, Dorset, BH18 8HT.*

MAHOOD, Canon Brian Samuel. b 12. St Jo Coll Dur Barry Div Scho 38, BA (2nd cl Th) 39, MA 42. **d** 39 **p** 40 Chelmsf. C of St Laur Barkingside 39-41; CF (EC) 41-46; V of Hatfield Peverel 46-53; Squirrels Heath 53-79; Hon Can of Chelmsf 76-79; Can (Emer) from 79. *79 Tenterfield Road, Maldon, Essex, CM9 7EN.* (Maldon 55366)

MAHUIKA, Apirana Tuahae Kaukapakapa. St Jo Coll Auckld 57. Selw Coll Dun LTh 59. **d** 59 **p** 60 Auckld. C of Kawakawa 59-62; Chap St Steph Sch Bombay and L to Offic Dio Auckld 62-67; Dio Wel 67; V of Te Kaha Moari Past Wai 68-69; L to Offic Dio Wel from 72. *c/o Massey University, Palmerston North, NZ.*

MAHUMANE, Pedro. d 79 **p** 81 Lebom. P Dio Lebom. *CP 57, Maputo, Mozambique.*

MAHUNDO, Yonana. St Phil Th Coll Kongwa 62. **d** 65 Bp Madinda for Centr Tang **p** 65 Centr Tang. P Dio Centr Tang. *Ngaiti, PO Kintinku, Tanzania.*

MAHUPELA, Philemon. d 77 Botswana. d Dio Botswana. *c/o PO Box 769, Gaborone, Botswana.*

MAHYENGA, Mika Percival. St Paul's Coll Liuli. **d** 54 **p** 57 SW Tang. P Dio SW Tang 54-70; Dio Ruv 70-73; Can of Ruv 72-73; Dio Dar-S from 73. *PO Box 3321, Dar-es-Salaam, Tanzania.*

MAIDEN, William Edward. b 1899. Univ of Dur 31. Lich Th Coll 31. **d** 32 **p** 33 Lich. C of H Trin Oswestry 32-38; Tamworth (in c of Hopwas) 38-41; V of St Geo Dio Lich from 41. *St George Vicarage, Oakengates, Telford, Salop.* (Telford 613028)

MAIDMENT, Thomas John Louis. b 43. Univ of Lon BSc 65. St Steph Ho Ox. **d** 67 Lon **p** 68 Kens for Lon. C of St Steph Roch Row w St Jo Evang Westmr 67-73; P-in-c of H Trin Twickenham 73-77; V 77-80; Heston Dio Lon from 80. *147 Heston Road, Hounslow, Middx, TW5 0RD.* (01-570 2288)

MAIDSTONE, Lord Bishop Suffragan of. *See* Hardy, Right Rev Robert Maynard.

MAIDSTONE, Archdeacon of. *See* Smith, Ven Anthony Michael Percival.

MAIMANE, Julian. d 66 **p** 67 Pret. P Dio Pret. *P Bag X536, Mabopane, Pretoria, S Africa.*

MAIN, David Murray. b 28. Univ Coll Ox BA 52, MA 56. St Deiniol's Libr Hawarden 73. **d** 73 **p** 74 Glas. C of St Marg Newlands Glas 73-75; R of Challoch w Newton Stewart 75-79; H Trin Kilmarnock Dio Glas from 79; Commiss Ruv from 78. *1 Dundonald Road, Kilmarnock, Ayrshire.* (0563 23577)

MAIN, Ian Ross Macdonald. Wycl Hall, Ox. **d** 59 **p** 60 S'wark. C of Morden S'wark 59-62; R of Bloemhof 62-65; Ch Ch Addington Durban 65-73; Commiss Chile 72-77; L to Offic Dio Natal from 73. *Box 3865, Durban, Natal, S Africa.*

MAINA, Edward Kiragu. b 20. **d** 78 Mt Kenya S. d Dio Mt Kenya S. *Box 116, Kiambu, Kenya.*

MAINA, Edwin. b 25. **d** 78 Mt Kenya S. d Dio Mt Kenya S. *PO Box 22, Mukerenju via Thika, Kenya.*

MAINA, Elijah. d 76 **p** 77 Nak. P Dio Nak. *PO Box 9, Turbo, Kenya.*

MAINA, Manasse. b 42. **d** 71 **p** 72 Mt Kenya. P Dio Mt Kenya 71-75; Dio Mt Kenya S 75-76; Dio Mt Kenya E from 76. *Box 18, Kagio, Kenya.*

MAINA-WANJIGI, Hezron. Ch Tr Centre Kapsabet 66. **d** 67 **p** 68 Nak. P Dio Nak. *Nyandarua, Kenya.*

MAINDE, Canon Dunstan. St Cypr Th Coll Tunduru 54. **d** 55 **p** 58 Zanz. P Dio Zanz T; Can of Zanz T from 72. *Box 45, Tanga, Tanzania.*

MAINDONALD, Timothy Alexander. b 48. Waterloo Lutheran Univ BA 70. Trin Coll Tor MDiv 73. **d** 73 **p** 74 Tor. C of Ch Mem Ch Oshawa 73-75; CF (Canad) from 75. *CFB Bagotville, Alouette, PQ, Canada.*

MAINES, Trevor. b 40. Univ of Leeds BSc 63. Ripon Hall Ox 63. **d** 65 Warrington for Liv **p** 66 Liv. C of St Aid Speke 65-70; Stevenage 70-72; V of Dorridge 72-78; Cler Org Sec CECS Dio Ex 79-80; Hon C of Tiverton 79-80; Newton-Nottage w Porthcawl Dio Llan from 81; Org Sec CECS Wales from 80. *4 Queens Avenue, Porthcawl, Mid Glam, CF36 5HP.* (Porthcawl 771282)

MAINPRIZE, George Ronald. b 44. Univ of Newc BA 68, ThDip 79. St Jo Coll Morpeth 76. **d** and **p** 80 Newc. C of Raymond Terrace Dio Newc from 80. *9 Hunter Street, Raymond Terrace, NSW, Australia 2324.*

MAINSTONE, Sydney Alfred. Moore Th Coll Syd 26. **d** 30 **p** 31 Syd. C of Castle Hill w Baulkham Hills and Dural 30-33; St Matt Manly 33-35; Rockdale 35-36; C-in-c of Pennant Hills w Thornleigh 36-37; V 38-40; I of Kiama 40-48; R of Norwood 48-69; Commiss in S Austr for Centr Tang 55-67; L to Offic Dio Adel from 69. *33 Carlisle Road, Westbourne Park, S Australia 5041.* (71-3306)

MAINWARING, Islwyn Paul. b 52. Univ of Wales (Swansea) BD 75. St Mich AA Coll Llan 77. **d** 79 **p** 80 Llan. C of Llanilid w Pencoed Dio Llan from 79. *19 Dol Wen, Penprysg, Pencoed, Bridgend, Mid Glam.*

MAINWARING, William Douglas. b 26. Univ of Wales (Swansea) Dipl Th 73. St Mich AA Llandaff 72. **d** 74 **p** 75 Llan. C of St Fagan Aberdare 74-78; V of Seven Sisters 78-80. *3 Rhiw Nant, Abernant, Aberdare, Mid Glam.*

MAIR, James Fraser. b 24. St Pet Hall, Ox BA 49, MA 53. Wycl Hall, Ox 49. **d** 51 **p** 52 Ches. C of St Geo Stockport 51-55; V of Hollingworth 55-67; R of Bacton w Wyverstone 67-80; P-in-c of Cotton 76-80; V of Thurston Dio St E from 80. *Thurston Vicarage, Bury St Edmunds, Suff. IP31 3RU.* (Pakenham 30301)

MAIRS, Adrian Samuel. b 43. Oak Hill Coll 76. [f CA]. **d** 78 Bp McKie for Cov **p** 79 Cov. C of St Matt Rugby Dio Cov from 78. *5 Vicarage Road, Rugby, CV22 7AJ.*

MAITIN, Ito. b 36. Dipl Th (Lon) 67. Kelham Th Coll. **d** 68 **p** 69 Lich. C of St Jo bapt Longton 68-71; St Chad Lich 71-74; Tamworth 74-81; V of Penkhull Dio Lich from 81. *214 Queen's Road, Stoke-on-Trent, ST4 7LG.* (S-o-T 414092)

MAITLAND, Brodie Scott. b 29. Magd Coll Cam 2nd cl Engl Trip pt i, 51, BA (2nd cl Th Trip pt ia) 52, MA 56. Cudd Coll 59. **d** 59 **p** 60 Cov. Hon C of Sherbourne 59-64; Chap Warw Sch 60-64 and 65-68; Asst Chap Tonbridge Sch 64-65; L to Offic Dio Roch 64-65; Dio Cov 65-68; Hd Master Belmont Ho 68-72; Wells Ho Malvern Wells 72-75; Perm to Offic Dio Worc 72-75; Dio Win from 75; Dep Hd Ld Mayor Treloar Coll Froyle from 75; Hd of Lower Sch Ld Mayor Treloar Coll from 78. *Lord Mayor Treloar College, Froyle, Alton, Hants, GU34 4LA.*

MAITLAND, Henrison Emmanuel. Fourah Bay Coll 55. **d** 58 **p** 60 Sier L. P Dio Sier L. *Vicarage, Hastings, Sierra Leone.*

MAITLAND, Ven Ronald. Univ of Calif BA 51. Gen Th Sem NYSTB 58. **d** and **p** 58 NY. [f Amer Ch] Chap St Paul Palermo Buenos Aires 67-69; St Mich AA Martinez Buenos Aires 69-79; Cordoba Dio Argent from 79; Archd of Cordoba from 79. *St Paul's Church, Bahia Blanca 24, Cordoba, Argentina.*

MAITLAND, William Francis. Trin Coll Dub BA 46, Div Test 47, MA 52. **d** 47 **p** 48 Clogh. C-in-c of St Marg Clabby 47-51; Asst Chap Miss to Seamen Belfast 51-52; Chap Sunderland 52-55; Tyne and Blyth 55-60; Adel 60-80; Hon Chap from 81. *3 Manunda Street, Osborne, S Australia 5017.* (08-248 2308)

MAJA, Canon Lloyd. St Pet Coll Rosettenville. **d** 55 **p** 56 Bloemf. P Dio Bloemf; Can of Bloemf from 67. *Box 147, Witzieshoek 9870, OFS, S Africa.*

MAJEBE, John Silimela. St Pet Coll Alice. **d** 68 **p** 69 Kimb K. P Dio Kimb K; Exam Chap to Bp of Kimb K 75-76. *Box 100, Prieska, CP, S Africa.* (05942)

MAJEZI, Tamasanga. d 78 **p** 79 St John's (APM). P Dio St John's. *PO Box 142, Engcobo, Transkei.*

MAJIJA, Ashington Sizatu. St Bede's Coll Umtata, 65. **d** 66 **p** 67 St John's. P Dio St John's. *Box 308, Umtata 5100, Transkei, S Africa.* (Umtata 3527)

MAJKA, John Edwin. St Aid Coll 62. **d** 64 **p** 65 Ott. C of St Richard Ott 64-67; I of Pincourt Miss Ile-Perrot Dorion 64-68; R of St Cuthb City and Dio Montr from 68. *5355 Place d'Argenteuil, Montreal, PQ, Canada.* (514-332 1550)

MAJOLA, Vukile Mvelase. St Bede's Coll Umtata 64. **d** 65 **p** 67 St John's; C of Lusikisiki 65-70; H Cross 71-73; P-in-c of Butterworth Dio St John's from 73. *Ensikeni Mission, PO Hoha 4612, Transkei, S Africa.* (Hoha 3)

MAJOLA, Zilfred. b 43. **d** 76 **p** 78 Zulu. C of Vumanhlamvu Dio Zulu from 76. *PO Box 2, Nkandla 3855, Zululand.*

MAJOR, Charles Alan. b 24. Keble Coll Ox BA (2nd cl Mods 3rd cl LitHum) 47, MA 50. Edin Th Coll 51. **d** 53 **p** 54 Edin. C of St Salvador Stenhouse Edin 53-63; Perm to Offic Dio Guildf 63-65; C of Hythe Dio Cant from 65. *Flat D, Pine Hill, 29 Seabrook Road, Hythe, Kent.* (Hythe 65125)

MAJOR, John Austen. Angl Coll of BC Dipl Th 63. **d** 63 **p** 64 New Westmr. P-in-c of St Laur Coquitlam 63-70; R of St D, S Delta 70-80; Abbotsford Dio New Westmr from 80. *35382 Rockwell Drive, Abbotsford, BC, Canada.*

MAJOR, Richard James Edward. b 54. Trin Coll Bris 78. **d** 81 Warrington for Liv. C of Parr Dio Liv from 81. *12 Mather Avenue, Parr, St Helens, Merseyside, WA9 1SS.*

MAJORO, Filemon. b 27. **d** and **p** 75 Vic Nyan. P Dio Vic Nyan. *PO Box 182, Mwadui Mine, Tanzania.*

MAJUMBU, H Boas. d 77 **p** 78 W Tang. P Dio W Tang. *c/o St Stephen's Church, S.L.P. 161, Tabora, Tanzania.*

MAJWAKALA, Dani. Bp Tucker Coll Mukono. **d** 56 **p** 57 Ugan. P Dio Ugan. *NAC Kabarole, Box 37, Fort Portal, Toro, Uganda.*

MAJWAKARA, Dani. Bp Tucker Coll Mukono. **d** 56 Ugan **p** 58 Bp Balya for Ugan. P Dio Ugan 56-60; Dio Ruw 60-74. *Box 1201, Butiiti, Toro, Uganda.*

MAJWALA, Yokana. Bp Tucker Coll Mukono. **d** 56 Ugan **p** 58 Bp Balya for Ugan. P Dio Ugan 56-60; Dio Nam 60-72. *PO Box 43, Mukono, Uganda.*

MAK, Timothy Kwok Fai. Trin Coll Canton. **d** 50 **p** 56 Hong. Perm to Offic Dio Wel 50-56; Miss Chinese Miss 56-69; L to Offic Dio Wel from 68. *24 The Parade, Island Bay, Wellington, NZ.*

MAKA, Joel George. d 71 **p** 72 Carp. C-in-c of St Paul's Miss 71-73; C of Murray I 73-74; Badu I 74-76; P-in-c of Cowal Creek Dio Carp from 76. *PO Cowal Creek, Queensland, Australia 4875.*

MAKAHO, Elisha. d 61 **p** 62 Ft Hall. P Dio Ft Hall 62-64; Dio Mt Kenya 64-75; Dio Mt Kenya S from 75. *Kahumbu, Box 4, Saba Saba, Kenya.*

MAKAJA, Samuel. b 31. **d** 76 Les. d Dio Les. *St Saviour's Rectory, PO Box LR 38, Leribe, Lesotho, S Africa.*

MAKALIMA, Claudius. d 49 **p** 50 Pret. P Dio Pret 40-54; Dio Grahmstn 54-68; Dio St John's from 68. *Box 149, Matatiele, CP, S Africa.*

MAKALIMA, Philip Makhaya. St Bede's Coll Umtata 63. **d** 63 **p** 65 St John's. P Dio St John's. *Box 135, Butterworth, Transkei, S Africa.*

MAKALIMA, Robert. St Bede's Coll Umtata 55. **d** 56 **p** 58 St John's. P Dio St John's. *Box 3, Kentani, Transkei, S Africa.*

MAKAMBWE, Francis James. St Jo Sem Lusaka. **d** 65 Bp Mataka for Zam **p** 67 Zam. P Dio Zam 67-70; Dio Lusaka from 71; Can of Lusaka 71-75. *PO Box 154, Chipata, Zambia.*

MAKANDANJE, Stephen Anderson. d and **p** 59 Zulu. P Dio Zulu 59-71; Dio Swaz 71-77. *Box 23, Hlatikulu, Swaziland.*

MAKANYAGA, Stephen. b 43. **d** 79 Bp Mohamed for Centr Tang **p** 79 Centr Tang. P Dio Centr Tang. *c/o Box 2, Mpwapwa, Tanzania.*

MAKASI, Duncan Lifa Malizo. b 41. Univ of Fort Hare (SA) BA 69. St Pet Coll Alice 69. **d** 71 **p** 72 Port Eliz. P Dio Port Eliz 71-73; Grahmstn 73-80; Chap Fort Hare Univ 77-80. *Box 249, Alice, CP, S Africa.*

MAKATINI, Victor. b 25. **d** 77 **p** 78 Johann. C of St Aug

Orlando Dio Johann from 77. *1736 Dube South, Dube 1852, S Africa.*

MAKAU, Canon Fanuel. St Phil Th Coll Kongwa. **d** 57 Centr Tang **p** 58 Bp Omari for Centr Tang. P Dio Centr Tang 57-65; Dio Moro from 65; Hon Can of Moro from 77. *Box 124, Kilosa, Tanzania.*

MAKAYA, Frank. d 78 Matab. d Dio Matab. *c/o PO Box 2422, Bulawayo, Rhodesia.*

MAKEL, Arthur. b 39. K Coll Lon and Warm AKC 63. **d** 64 **p** 65 Dur. C of Beamish 64-68; Chap Teesside Industr Miss and L to Offic Dio York 68-72; Chap Scunthorpe Industr Miss and P-in-c of Scotton w Northorpe 72-81; R of Epworth Dio Linc from 81; Wroot Dio Linc from 81. *St Andrew's Rectory, Epworth, Doncaster, Yorks, DN9 1JL.* (Epworth 872471)

MAKEPEACE, James Dugard. b 40. Keble Coll Ox BA (2nd cl Th) 63, MA 67. Cudd Coll 63. **d** 65 **p** 66 Newc T. C of St Geo Cullercoats 65-68; Libr Pusey Ho and Chap Wadham Coll Ox 68-72; V of Romford 72-79; Tettenhall Regis Dio Lich 79-80; Team R from 80. *Rectory, Lloyd Road, Tettenhall, Wolverhampton.* (Wolverhampton 751622)

MAKHALANYANE, Canon Johannes Mohlauli. St Pet Coll Rosettenville. **d** 62 **p** 63 Bloemf. P Dio Bloemf from 62; Can of Bloemf from 75. *Box 12, Motsethabong, Welcom, OFS, S Africa.* (017-24152)

MAKHAYE, Matthew Mandlenkosi. St Bede's Coll Umtata, 58. LTh (S Afr) 60. **d** 60 **p** 61 Natal. P Dio Natal 60-64; Chap St Bede's Th Coll Umtata 64-68; L to Offic Dio Natal 68-70; R of Klip River Dio Natal from 71. *Box 228, Ladysmith, Natal, S Africa.*

✠ **MAKHETHA, Right Rev Fortescue.** St Pet Coll Rosettenville, LTh 48. **d** 48 **p** 49 Bloemf. C R Kroonstad 48-49; Leribe Miss 49-51; Dir of Thaba'nchu Miss 51-60; Can of Bloemf 54-60; P-in-c of Pro-Cathl of St Jas Maseru 60-78; Archd of N Basuto 60-72; S Les 72-77; Cons Ld Bp Suffr of Les in St Geo Cathl Capetn 23 April 67 by Abp of Capetn; Bps of Geo; St John's; Grahmstn; Kimb K; Damar; Les; Natal; Zulu; Johann; Pret; Les; and Mashon; and Bps Suffr of Capetn; and Lebom; res 78; Asst Bp of Bloemf from 78; R of St Patr City and Dio Bloemf from 78; Archd of Modderpoort from 81. *Box 16023, Batho Location, Bloemfontein, S Africa.*

MAKHOBA, Peter Cuthbert. St Bede's Coll Umtata LTh 55. **d** 54 **p** 55 Zulu. R of St Mary Nkonjeni 54-70; St Johns Blood River 70-78; Magogo Dio Zulu from 78. *Magogo, PO Nqutu, via Dundee, Natal, S Africa.*

MAKHONJWA, Harold Sizakele. St Bede's Coll Umtata, 65. **d** 66 **p** 67 St John's. P Dio St John's. *St Alban's Mission, PO Egoso, via Engcobo, CP, S Africa.*

MAKHUBU, Majawonkhe Gregory. St Bede's Coll Umtata 77. **d** 79 **p** 80 Swaz. P Dio Swaz. *Epiphany Church, PO Box 149, Mbabane, Swaziland.*

MAKHUBU, Victor Willie Tholinhlanhla. St Bede's Coll Umtata 66. **d** 68 **p** 69 Natal. P Dio Natal. *Box 8, Nqabeni, via Harding, Natal, S Africa.*

✠ **MAKHULU, Most Rev Walter Paul Khotso.** b 35. St Pet Coll Rosettenville, 55. **d** 57 **p** 58 Johann. P Dio Johann 57-61; Dio Matab 61-63; C of Poplar 64-66; St Silas Pentonville 66-67; St Clem Barnsbury 67-68; V of St Phil (w St Bart from 73) Battersea 68-75; Sec E Africa WCC Geneve 75-79; Cons Ld Bp of Botswana in H Cross Cathl Gaborone 10 June 79 by Abp of Centr Afr; and Bps of Matab and Johann; Elected Abp and Metrop of Prov of Centr Afr 80. *Bishop's House, PO Box 769, Gaborone, Botswana.*

MAKIN, Hubert. b 18. Open Univ BA 74. ACP 66. N-W Ordin Course. **d** 78 **p** 79 Wakef (NSM). C of Mount Pellon Dio Wakef from 78. *46 Upper Highfield, Gibb Lane, Mount Tabor, Halifax, Yorks, HX2 0UG.*

MAKIN, Walter Bradley. b 19. **d** 49 Free C of E **p** 75 Liv. [f in Free C of E]; Hon C of Clubmoor 75-77; Norris Green Dio Liv from 77. *14 Ogden Close, Liverpool, L13 0BB.* (051-226 9036)

MAKINDE, Samuel Bolaji. b 25. **d** 74 **p** 76 Ondo. P Dio Ondo. *St Michael's Vicarage, Ipe-Akoko, via Ikare, Nigeria.*

MAKIWA, Dunstan. b 42. **d** and **p** 76 Moro. P Dio Moro. *DM Idibo, PO Berega, Morogoro, Tanzania.*

MAKOBA, Yakobo. d 68 Centr Tang. d Dio Centr Tang. *Box 15, Dodoma, Tanzania.*

MAKOBWE, Andrea. b 39. St Phil Coll Kongwa 74. **d** and **p** 76 Vic Nyan. P Dio Vic Nyan. *PO Muleba, Bukoba, West Lake, Tanzania.*

MAKOI, Very Rev Ruben. Bp Gwynne Coll Mundri 57. **d** 60 **p** 61 Sudan. P Dio Sudan 60-76; Dio Rumbek from 76; Dean of Rumbek from 77. *ECS, Rumbek, Sudan.*

MAKOLO, Luke. St Paul's Coll Limuru 70. **d** 72 **p** 73 Nai. P Dio Nai. *Box 17056, Nairobi, Kenya.* (Nairobi 557409)

MAKONGIYO, Zakayo. St Paul's Dioc Div Sch Frere-town. **d** 29 **p** 33 Momb. CMS P Dio Momb 29-61. *Lubinu Parsonage, Private Bag, Mumiasi, Kenya.*

MAKONI, Basil Maurice. St Pet Coll Rosettenville 56. **d** 58 **p** 59 Mashon. P Dio Mashon. *St Mary's Mission, Hunyani, Private Bag 175H, Salisbury, Zimbabwe.*

MAKONI, Mark Malachi. St Jo Sem Lusaka. **d** 66 **p** 67 Mashon. P Dio Mashon. *St David's Mission, Bonda, Zimbabwe.*

MAKONI, Ven Nathanial Alban. d 59 **p** 60 Mashon. P Dio Mashon 59-81; Can of Mashon 75-81; Archd Dio Mashon 80-81; Dio Mutare from 81; P-in-c of Matsika Dio Mutare from 81. *c/o 115 Main Street, Umtali, Zimbabwe.* (62237)

MAKONYOLA, Charles Andrea. d 74 **p** 75 SW Tang. P Dio SW Tang. *PO Box 49, Chunya, Tanzania.*

MAKOROGO, Jonathan. b 44. St Phil Coll Kongwa 73. **d** 75 Vic Nyan. d Dio Vic Nyan 75-77. *Box 64, Geita, Tanzania.*

MAKOSHOLO, Vincent. St Bede's Coll Umtata 58. **d** 59 **p** 61 Basuto. P Dio Basuto 59-67; Dio Les from 67. *St Mark's Mission, Box 75, Maseru, Lesotho.*

MAKOWA, Frank. d 78 Matab. C of St Andr Wankie 78-81. *c/o Box 43, Wankie, Zimbabwe.*

MAKOWER, Malory. b 38. Trin Coll Dub BA 61, MA 68. St Jo Coll Ox MA 64, DPhil 64. Ridley Hall Cam 64. **d** 66 **p** 67 Lon. C of St Paul Onslow Square Kens 66-69; Tutor Ridley Hall Cam 69-71; Sen Tutor 71-76; L to Offic Dio Ely 69-76; C-in-c of Lode Dio Ely from 76; Dir of Tr for NSM Dio Ely from 76; Warden E Anglia Ministerial Tr Course 77-79; Prin from 79. *Lode Vicarage, Cambridge, CB5 9EW.* (Cam 811371)

MAKULILA, Emanuel Swinney. St Cypr Coll Lindi 76. **d** 77 **p** 78 Ruv. P Dio Ruv. *Chulu, PO Mbamba Bay, Tanzania.*

MAKULYE, Stephen. d 64 **p** 65 Mbale. P Dio Mbale; Dio Bulucheke from 71. *Church of Uganda, Bulucheke, Uganda.*

MAKUNDA, Petro. St Cypr Th Coll Tunduru 40. **d** 42 Masasi. d Dio Masasi 42-68. *USPG, Nantiela, Tanzania.*

MAKUNDI, Simon. St Phil Coll Kongwa 69. **d** and **p** 71 Centr Tang. P Dio Centr Tang 71-74 and from 76; on leave 74-76. *Box 15, Dodoma, Tanzania.*

MAKUNGU, Isaya. b 54. Catholic Faculty of Th Kinshasa Zaire LTh 77. **d** 77 Bukavu. d Dio Bukavu. *BP 2876, Bukavu, Zaire.*

MAKUWERERE, Simon. b 41. **d** 76 **p** 77 Matab. P Dio Matab 76-81; Dio Lundi from 81. *P Bag 9014, Gwelo, Zimbabwe.*

MAKWASI, Erisa. b 24. Bp Tucker Coll Mukono. **d** 67 **p** 69 Mbale. P Dio Mbale. *Box 1292, Mbale, Uganda.*

MAKWELA, Fanico Mzwendaba. b 34. **d** 76 Port Eliz. C of St Pet Zwide Dio Port Eliz from 76. *7407 Site & Service, Kwazakele, Port Elizabeth 6205, CP, S Africa.*

MAKWENDA, Joseph William. d 45 Masasi **p** 49 Nyasa. P Dio Nyasa 45-64; Dio Malawi 64-70; Dio Lebom from 71. *Augusto Cardoso, Vila Cabral, Messumba, Mozambique.*

MAKWENYA, Akland. b 21. St Cypr Coll Th Rondo 73. **d** 75 **p** 76 Masasi. P Dio Masasi. *KJT Mpindimbi, Private Bag PO Masasi, Mtwara Region, Tanzania.*

MALAITA, Lord Bishop of. *See* Pwaishiho, Right Rev Willie.

MALAN, Victor Christian de Roubaix. b 39. Univ of Capetn BA 60. Linacre Coll Ox BA 63, MA 68. St Jo Coll Cam MA (by Incorp) 69. Wycl Hall, Ox 61. **d** 63 **p** 64 Birm. C of St Chris Springfield 63-66; P-in-c 66-67; C of Windsor 67-69; Chap St Jo Coll Cam 69-74; L to Offic Dio Ely 70-74; V of All SS w St Kath Northn Dio Pet from 74. *2 The Drive, Northampton.* (Northn 32194 or 713468)

MALANGA, Elieza. d and **p** 77 Centr Tang. P Dio Centr Tang. *Box 34, Kongwa, Tanzania.*

MALANGO, Bernard. b 43. St Jo Sem Lusaka. **d** 71 **p** 72 S Malawi. P Dio S Malawi. *PO Chilema, Malawi.*

MALASA, Canon Martin Edward. St Andr Coll Lukomo 57. **d** 59 **p** 60 Nyasa. P Dio Nyasa 59-64; Dio Malawi 64-71; Dio S Malawi 71-76; Hon Can of S Malawi from 76. *c/o Agricultural Dept, PA Golomoti, Mtakataka, Malawi.*

MALATA, Ernest. b 10. **d** 74 Lake Malawi **p** 75 Bp Taylor for Lake Malawi. P Dio Lake Malawi 74-81. *Yofu Village, PO Likoma Island, Malawi.*

MALAU, Stephen. St Paul's Dioc Div Sch Limuru 50. **d** 53 **p** 54 Momb. P Dio Momb. *PO Box 23, Voi, Kenya.*

MALAVANOU, George Mishel. b 24. St Mark's Coll Dar-S. **d** 72 **p** 78 SW Tang. P Dio SW Tang. *c/o Luilo RC Mission, Manoa, Tanzania.*

MALAWI, SOUTHERN, Bishop of. *See* Ainani, Right Rev Dunstan.

MALAWI, SOUTHERN, Bishop Suffragan of. (Vacant)

MALAYSIA, WEST, Bishop of. *See* Savarimuthu, Right Rev John Gurubatham.

MALAZA, Canon Jeremiah. Coll of Resurr Rosettenville. **d** 56 **p** 57 Zulu. P Dio Zulu 56-69; Dio Swaz from 69; Can of

Swaz from 79. *PO Box 102, Siteki, Swaziland.* (Siteki 69)

MALBON, John Allin. b 36. Oak Hill Th Coll 62. **d** 65 **p** 66 Lich. C of St Jude Wolverhampton 65-68; All SS Hoole 68-71; C-in-c of Ch Ch Crewe 71-74; V 75-79; Plemstall w Guilden Sutton Dio Ches from 79. *Guilden Sutton Vicarage, Chester.* (Mickle Trafford 300306)

MALCOLM, Arthur Alistair. **d** and **p** 78 N Queensld. P-in-c of St Alb Yarrabah Dio N Queensld from 78. *St Alban's Rectory, Workshop Road, Yarrabah, Qld, Australia 4871.*

MALCOLM, Edward. b 34. BA (Lon) 60. Tyndale Hall, Bris 61. **d** and **p** 68 St E for Jer for Egypt. BCMS Miss Morocco 62-76; Asst Chap St John's Casablanca 69-76; V of St Silas Lozells 77-81; P-in-c of St Paul Lozells 77-81; V of St Luke Wolverhampton Dio Lich from 81. *122 Goldthorn Hill, Wolverhampton, Staffs.* (Wolverhampton 340261)

MALCOLM, George. b 03. Tyndale Hall, Bris 28. **d** 39 Buckingham for Ox **p** 40 Ox. C of Greyfriars Reading 39-45; R of Swepstone w Snarestone 45-56; V of Ch Ch Mountsorrel 56-64; R of Stoke Ash w Thwaite and Wetheringsett 64-76. *31 The Pines, Woodside, Hazelwood Road, Bristol, BS9 1QD.*

MALCOLM, John Douglas. Univ of NZ BSc 58, BA 60. Ch Ch Coll. **d** 60 Bp Rich for Wel **p** 61 Wel. C of Petone 60-62; Kelburn Wel 62-65; V of Eastbourne 65-71; Levin 71-78; Chap Porirua Hosp Dio Wel from 79. *25 St Edmund Crescent, Tawa, NZ.*

MALE, John. b 28. ACA 54. FCA 65. Linc Th Coll 59. **d** 61 **p** 62 Linc. Bursar Linc Th Coll 54-67; C of St Giles Linc 61-65; Dom Chap to Bp of Linc from 61; C of Boultham 65-68; St Pet-in-Eastgate w St Marg Linc 68-70; R of Riseholme w Grange-de-Lings 70-72; Warden of Dioc Ho Linc 68-72; C of Rosebank Dio Johann from 72. *Box 52139, Saxonwold, Transvaal, S Africa.* (011-47 3211)

MALEBETO, Peter Willison. St Phil Coll Kongwa 72. **d** 74 **p** 75 Centr Tang. P Dio Centr Tang. *Izazi, S.L.P. 343, Iringa, Tanzania.*

MALEBO, Ignatius Tobetsa. Coll of Resurr Rosettenville, 48. **d** 51 **p** 54 Basuto. C of St Jas Maseru 51-54; Mohales Hoek 54-56; Miss P Dio Basuto 56-66; Dio Les 66-74. *PO Box 127, Maseru, Lesotho, S Africa.*

MALECHELA, Petro Lusinde. **d** 39 **p** 40 Centr Tang. P at Dodoma 39-42 and 46-49; CF 42-46; P at Buigiri 49-61; Can of Centr Tang 54-61; L to Offic Dio Centr Tang from 61. *Kikuya, Box 47, Dodoma, Tanzania.*

MALECHELA, Canon Stefano. **d** 54 **p** 55 Centr Tang. P Dio Centr Tang; Can of Centr Tang from 73. *Box 15, Dodoma, Tanzania.*

MALEFODOLA, Augustine. St Pet Th Coll Siota 59. **d** 62 **p** 64 Melan. P Dio Melan 62-75; Dio Malaita from 75. *Saranigaula, N Malaita, Solomon Islands.*

MALEKA, Marcus Tau. Coll of Resurr Johann. **d** 05 **p** 13 Pret. C of Pret Native Miss 05-30. *Legkraal School, PO Makapanstad, Pretoria, Transvaal, S Africa.*

MALEKE, Jacob Raymond Hugh. St Pet Coll Rosettenville, 57. **d** 61 Bp Paget for Johann **p** 62 Johann. P Dio Johann from 61. *Box 31, Kwa-Xuma, Transvaal, S Africa.*

MALEKELA, Leonard. St Phil Th Coll Kongwa, 66. **d** 68 **p** 69 Moro. P Dio Moro. *PO Berega, Morogoro, Tanzania.*

MALEKELA, Yeremia. b 43. **d** 77 **p** 78 Moro. P Dio Moro. *Berega Hospital, PO Berega, Morogoro, Tanzania.*

MALEMA-MUKWELI, Absolom Michael. Bp Usher-Wilson Th Coll Buwalasi. **d** 64 **p** 65 Mbale. P Dio Mbale from 64; Dioc Sec from 80. *PO Box 473, Mbale, Uganda.*

MALENJE, Festo. Maseno Bible Sch 69. **d** 69 Maseno. d Dio Maseno N. *c/o PO Box 1, Maseno, Kenya.*

MALIBO, Canon Aaron Morikhihlane. St Bede's Coll Umtata, 46. **d** 47 **p** 49 Bloemf. P Dio Bloemf 47-51; Dio Basuto 51-66; Dio Les from 66; Can of Les from 66. *St Agnes's Mission, Teyateyaneng, Lesotho, S Africa.*

MALIMBIKA, Yustino Sewejo. **d** 38 **p** 39 Centr Tang. P Dio Centr Tang 38-65; Dio Moro from 65. *CMS, Berega, Tanzania.*

MALING, Charles Dudley. Ridley Coll Melb ACT ThL 44. **d** 40 Centr Tang **p** 44 Melb. CMS Miss HM Teachers' Tr Sch Katoke 40-42 and 44-47; Furlough 42-44; Supt Mvumi Miss Distr 47-50; Kilimatinde and Educn Sec for Dio Centr Tang 50-51; Miss at Dodoma 51-56; Can of H Spirit Cathl Dodoma 53-55; I of Northcote 56-64; V of Greensborough 64-77; Perm to Offic Dio Melb from 77. *Unit 13, 34 Fairlie Avenue, MacLeod, Vic, Australia 3085.*

MALING, Fred. Ridley Coll Melb BA (2nd cl hons) 50. ACT ThL 36. **d** 37 **p** 38 Melb. C of Moreland 38-39; Min of Melton 39-41; Chap AIF 41-44; R of Wongan Hills 44-46; Perm to Offic Dio Melb 46-50; V of Winchelsea 50-52; R of St Pet Sandy Bay 52-66; Swansea Tas 66-73. *43 Esplanade, Kingston Beach, Tasmania 7151.*

MALING'A, Canon Asanasiyo. **d** 37 **p** 38 U Nile. P Dio U Nile; Hon Can U Nile 54-61; Archd of Bukedi 61-74; Hon Can of Mbale 61-72; Bukedi from 81. *PO Box 170, Tororo, Uganda.*

MALINS, Donald Lockhart. Univ of BC STB 67. Angl Th Coll BC. **d** 67 **p** 68 Koot. C of Vernon 67-70; Koot Boundary Regional Par 70-73; I of Salmon Arm 73-81; H Trin Sidney Dio BC from 81. *11025 West Saanich Road, RR3, Sidney, BC, Canada.*

MALINS, Peter. b 18. Down Coll Cam BA 40, MA 47. Ridley Hall Cam 40. **d** 42 **p** 43 Cov. C of St Barbara Cov 42-44; CF (EC) 44-47; CF 47-73; ACG 67-73; Hon Chap to HM the Queen 72-73; V of Greenwich Dio S'wark from 73; P-in-c of H Trin and St Paul Greenwich Dio S'wark from 76. *Vicarage, Park Vista, SE10 9LZ.* (01-858 6828)

MALISA, Philip. **d** 76 **p** 77 Matab. C of Lower Gwelo Dio Matab (Dio Lundi from 81) from 77. *P Bag 9044, Gwelo, Zimbabwe.*

MALKINSON, Herbert Clifford James. b 11. Univ of Dur 36. Chich Th Coll 37. **d** 39 **p** 40 Lich. C of Ch Ch Tunstall (in c of St Sav Smallthorne 44-46) 39-46; V of Thorpe St Pet 46-80; Croft 48-80. *Northolme Cottage, Spilsby Road, Wainfleet, Skegness, Lincs.* (Skegness 880323)

MALKINSON, Michael Stephen. b 43. St Steph Ho Ox 65. **d** 68 **p** 69 Cant. C of New Addington 68-71; St Steph Blackpool 71-74; R of Wainfleet 74-81; V of St Mary Wainfleet 74-81; Lund Dio Blackb from 81; P-in-c of Croft 80-81. *Lund Vicarage, Clifton, Preston, Lancs, PR4 0ZE.* (Kirkham 683617)

MALLESON, Michael Lawson. b 42. Univ Coll of Swan BA 64. Linc Th Coll. **d** 70 Pontefract for Wakef **p** 71 Wakef. C of St Jo Bapt Wakef 70-73; C-in-c of St Andr Conv Distr Holmfield 73-75; V of Holmfield 75-80; St Alb Heworth Dio Dur from 80. *St Alban's Vicarage, Coldwell Park Drive, Gateshead, NE10 9BX.* (Felling 381720)

MALLETT, Michael William. b 18. **d** 69 **p** 70 Ches. C of Hyde 69-75; V of Broadheath Dio Ches from 75. *St Alban's Vicarage, Lindsell Road, Altrincham, Chesh, WA14 5NX.* (061-928 4820)

MALLETT, Ven Peter. b 25. CB 78. AKC 50. Men in Disp 57. St Bonif Coll Warm 50. **d** 51 Dover for Cant **p** 52 Cant. C of St Osw Norbury 51-54; CF 54-80; DACG 68-72; ACG 73-74; Chap-Gen 74-80; Hon Chap to HM the Queen from 73. *Everleigh Cottage, The Hollow, Shrewton, Wilts.* (Shrewton 620847)

MALLIN, Canon Stewart Adam Thomson. b 24. Edin Th Coll 58. **d** 61 **p** 62 Moray. Prec of St Andr Cathl Inverness 61-64; Itin P Dio Moray 64-68; R of Wick 68-77; P-in-c of Thurso 68-77; Can of Inverness Cathl from 74; R of Dingwall w Strathpeffer Dio Ross from 77; Syn Clk Dio Moray from 80. *Parsonage, Dingwall, Ross-shire.* (Dingwall 62204)

MALLINSON, Arnold. b 1896. Univ Coll Dur BA 22. St Steph Ho Ox 22. St Cath S Ox BLitt 24. **d** 24 **p** 25 Man. C of All SS Blackpool 24-26; St Thos Mart Ox 26-33; V of St Frideswide Ox 33-76; PC (V from 68) of Binsey 50-76. *Glenburn House, Mill Lane, Iffley, Oxford.*

MALLINSON, Ralph Edward. b 40. Or Coll Ox BA 63, MA 66. St Steph Ho Ox 63. **d** 66 **p** 67 Man. C of Bolton-le-Moors 66-68; All SS Elton Bury 68-72; V of St Thos (Ch the K from 76) Bury 72-81; P-in-c of Goodshaw Dio Man from 81. *Goodshaw Vicarage, Crawshawbooth, Rossendale, Lancs, BB4 8BW.* (Rossendale 213969)

✠ **MALLORY, Right Rev Charles Shannon.** b 36. Univ of California BA 58. Gen Th Sem NY STB 61. Rhodes Univ MA 71. **d** 61 Bp I I Curtis (USA) **p** 61 Damar. R of Tsumeb 61-62; Dir Ovamboland Miss 63-69; Archd of Ovamboland 64-69; Chap Dioc Girls Sch Grahmstn 70-71; Lect Makerere Univ Kampala 71-72; Cons Ld Bp of Botswana in RC Cathl Gaborone 31 Dec 72 by Bp of Mashon, Bps of Bloemf, Zulu, Matab, Swaz; and Bp Suffr of Capetn; res 78; Asst Bp of Long I (Amer Ch) 79-80; Apptd Bp of El Camino Real (Amer Ch) 80. *Box 1903, Monterey, California 93940, USA.*

MALLORY, George Henry. b 14. Univ of Lon BSc (Econ) 63. **d** 80 Bp Mort for Leic **p** 81 Bp Markham for Leic (NSM). C of Oaks in Charnwood and Copt Oak Dio Leic from 80. *2 Moscow Lane, Shepshed, Loughborough, Leics, LE12 9EX.*

MALMESBURY, Lord Bishop Suffragan of. *See* Temple, Right Rev Frederick Stephen.

MALONEY, William John. St Aug Coll Cant 38. St Francis Coll Brisb 40. ACT ThL 42. **d** 39 Lon for Col Bp **p** 43 Brisb. C of St Jas Cathl Townsville 40-41; Cairns 41-42; St Andr Brisb 42-43; M of Bush Bro of St Paul Brisb 43-46; C of St Francis Friar Park W Bromwich 46-47; Deptford (in c of St Mark) 47-49; St Edw Romford (in c of St Thos and St Geo) 49-50; V of West Vale Yorks 50-56; R of Norseman w Esperance 56-58; Lyndoch S Austr 58-61; V of Farcet 61-75. *45 Scarborough Road, Great Walsingham, Norf.*

MALONGA, Canon Yosiah. **d** 54 **p** 55 Centr Tang. P Dio Centr Tang; Can of H Spirit Cathl Dodoma from 67. *Mlali, PO Kongwa, Tanzania.*

MALOU ATER, John. b 35. Bp Tucker Coll Mukono 67. **d** 69 **p** 70 Sudan. P Dio Sudan from 71. *Rumbek Senior Secondary School, Omduram, PO Box 955, Sudan.*

MALPASS, Clive William. b 36. K Coll Lon and Warm AKC 60. **d** 61 **p** 62 S'wark. C of Malden 61-64; Horley (in c of St Francis) 64-69; Youth Chap Dio Dur 69-72; Adv in Lay Tr Dio Dur 72-76; V of Ven Bede Wyther Leeds Dio Ripon from 76. *Wyther Vicarage, Houghley Lane, Leeds LS13 2DT.* (Leeds 631361)

MALSBURY, Canon Reginald. b 17. Univ of Lon BA (2nd cl Hist) 40. Lich Th Coll 40. **d** 42 Burnley for Blackb **p** 43 Blackb. C of St Mary Penwortham 42-49; V of Scaptoft Dio Leic from 49; V of Hungarton Dio Leic from 49; Hon Can of Leic from 78. *Scraptoft Vicarage, Leicester.* (Leic 412318)

MALSOM, Laurence Michael. b 31. Selw Coll Cam 2nd cl Th Trip pt i, 53, BA (2nd cl Th Trip pt ii) 55, MA 59. Cudd Coll 55. **d** 57 **p** 58 Ex. C of Crediton 57-60; St Gabr Plymouth 60-62; Sidmouth (in c of St Francis) 62-64; V of Harberton 64-71; V of Harbertonford 64-71; RD of Totnes 70-75; V of S Brent 71-75; St Marychurch 75-79; P-in-c of Crownhill Plymouth Dio Ex 79-80; V from 80. *Crownhill Vicarage, Plymouth, Devon, PL5 3AF.* (Plymouth 773176)

MALTA, Dean of St Paul Valletta. *See* Satterthwaite, Right Rev John Richard.

MALTBY, Geoffrey. b 38. Univ of Leeds BA 62. Wells Th Coll 68. **d** 70 Sherwood for Southw **p** 71 Southw. C of St Mark Mansfield 70-73; V of Skegby 73-78; Carrington Dio Southw from 78. *6 Watcombe Circus, Nottingham, NG5 2DT.* (0602-621291)

MALTBY, Canon Keith Mason. b 19. Ch Coll Cam BA 47, MA 52. Univ of Man BD 52. Ridley Hall, Cam 47. **d** 49 **p** 50 Man. C of St Jas Birch-in-Rusholme 49-51; Min Can of Man Cathl 51-54; V of St Jo Bapt Bollington 54-57; Exam Chap to Bp of Ches from 57; V of Alderley Edge Chorley 57-69; Prin Lect in Div Coll of Educn Alsager 69-74; Can Res Libr and Treas of Ches Cathl from 74; Vice-Dean from 78. *13 Abbey Street, Chester, CH1 2JH.* (Ches 314408)

MALTIN, Basil St Clair Aston. b 24. Qu Coll Cam BA 49, MA 54. Westcott Ho Cam 50. **d** 51 **p** 52 Glouc. C of Dursley 51-53; Bathwick w Woolley 53-57; V of Ch Ch Frome 57-63; C-in-c of Marston Bigot 57-59; V of Bp's Lydeard 63-71; R of Pulborough w N Heath and Nutbourne Dio Chich from 71. *Rectory, Pulborough, Sussex.* (Pulborough 2673)

MALUGU, Canon Asani. **d** 54 **p** 55 Centr Tang; P Dio Centr Tang; Can of H Spirit Cathl Dodoma from 68. *Mvumi, PO Dodoma, Tanzania.*

MALULEKE, Willie. **d** 71 **p** 72 Pret. C of Sibasa Dio Pret from 71. *Private Bag 1183, New Union Mine, PO Malamulele, N Transvaal, S Africa.*

MAMA, Solomon Abu. **d** 45 **p** 47 Lagos. P Dio Lagos 45-55; Dio N Nig from 65. *St John's Vicarage, PO Box 14, Bida, Nigeria.*

MAMAH, Samuel Peter Odumbela. b 22. St Paul's Coll Awka. **d** 57 **p** 58 Nig Delta. P Dio Nig Delta. *St Michael's Parsonage, Oloibiri, via Nembe, Rivers State, Nigeria.*

MAMBETA, Alfred. St Mark's Coll Dar-S 70. **d** 70 Dar-S. d Dio Dar-S. *Box 25016, Ilala, Dar es Salaam, Tanzania.*

MAMBI, James. **d** 61 **p** 63 Centr Tang. P Dio Centr Tang. *Box 68 Kondoa, Tanzania.*

MAMBIRI, Yesaya Miraya. Bp Gwynne Coll Mundri, 59. **d** 63 **p** 64 Bp Dotiro for Sudan. P Dio Sudan 63-76; Dio Yambio from 76. *ECS, Nabanga, Equatoria, Sudan.*

MAME, Christopher Asu. Bp Gwynne Coll Mundri 57. **d** 59 Sudan. d Dio Sudan 59-64 and from 74; Vice-Prin Bp Gwynne Coll Mundri 64-74. *c/o Vicarage, Lainya, via Juba, Sudan.*

MAMENA, Philippe. St Paul Coll Ambatoharanana. **d** 50 **p** 52 Madag. P Dio Madag 50-69; Dio Tam from 69. *Ilaka, Madagascar.*

MAMVURA, Leonard. **d** 73 **p** 74 Mashon. P Dio Mashon. *Manyene Chapelry, Box 62, Enkeldoorn, Rhodesia.*

MAN, *See* Sodor and Man.

MAN, Archdeacon of. *See* Clague, Ven Arthur Ashford.

MANANA, Toswell. **d** 37 **p** 41 Melan. P Dio Melan. *San Cristoval, British Solomon Islands.*

MANAS, Inagie. St Paul's Th Coll Moa I 59. **d** 63 **p** 64 Carp. Miss at Badu I 65; C of Thursday I 66; Miss at Mabuiag I 67-70; Moa I 70-71; Bamaga 71-73; Yam I 73-75; P-in-c of Saibai I Dio Carp 76-77; Hon C from 77. *c/o Box 79, Thursday Island, Queensland, Australia 4875.*

MANASE, Abarayama Konyi. Bp Gwynne Coll Mundri, 57. **d** 59 **p** 61 Sudan. P Dio Sudan. *ECS, Kajo Kaji, Yei, Equatoria, Sudan.*

MANASWE, Johannes. **d** 66 **p** 67 Pret. P Dio Pret. *PO Box 63, Jane Furse Hospital, Transvaal, S Africa.*

MANCE, Herbert William. b 19. St Jo Coll Cam BA 40, MA 44. Oak Hill Th Coll 47. **d** 49 **p** 50 Ripon. C of St Geo and St Andr Leeds 49-53; CF 53-57; CMS Miss and Chap to Bp of Ibad 58-65; Chap of All SS Jericho Ibad 65-71; Hon Can of Ibad 70-71; C of Buckhurst Hill 71-75; P-in-c of Roydon Dio Chelmsf 75-79; V from 79. *153 High Street, Roydon, Harlow, Essex.* (Roydon 2103)

MANCHESTER, Lord Bishop of. *See* Booth-Clibborn, Right Rev Stanley Eric Francis.

MANCHESTER, Assistant Bishops of. *See* Hanson, Right Rev Richard Patrick Crosland; Ramsey, Right Rev Kenneth Venner; and Wickham, Right Rev Edward Ralph.

MANCHESTER, Archdeacon of. *See* Harris, Ven Reginald Brian.

MANCHESTER, Dean of. *See* Jowett, Very Rev Alfred.

MANCHESTER, Charles. b 28. Univ of Lon BD 54. Oak Hill Th Coll 50. **d** 55 **p** 56 Southw. C of St Nich Nottm 55-58; Kinson 58-61; R of Haworth 61-67; V of H Trin Aldershot Dio Guildf from 67; RD of Aldershot 73-78; M Gen Syn 74-75 and from 75. *2 Cranmore Lane, Aldershot, Hants.* (Aldershot 20618)

MANCHESTER, John Charles. b 45. BD (Lon) 69. ALCD 68. **d** 69 **p** 70 York. C of St Martin Scarborough 69-73; Abbey Ch of Our Lord St Mary and St Germain Selby 73-76; C-in-c of Old Malton Dio York 76-78; V from 79. *Gannock House, Old Malton Priory, N Yorks.* (Malton 2121)

MANCHESTER, Simon Lorimer. Univ of NSW BA. Moore Th Coll ThL 79. **d** 80 Syd **p** 80 Bp Short for Syd. C of St Mich Provisional Cathl Wollongong Dio Syd from 80. *Market Street, Wollongong, NSW, Australia 2500.* (29-1167)

MANCUELLO, Damasio. **d** and **p** 77 Parag. P Dio Parag. *Casilla 1124, Asuncion, Paraguay, S America.*

MANDALAY, Lord Bishop of. *See* Ba Maw, Right Rev Peter.

MANDALAY, Assistant Bishop of. *See* Kum Saung Tu, Right Rev James.

MANDALL, Arthur Wilfred. ALCD 32. **d** 32 **p** 33 Wakef. C of Rashcliffe 32-35; Asst Chap Missions to Seamen Port of Lon 35-37; Chap at Barry and Penarth 37-38; Chap RN 38-58; V of Sturminster Marshall 58-73. *28 Tynewydd Road, Barry, S Glam.*

MANDAMBWE, John. **d** 78 S Malawi. d Dio S Malawi. *Somola fps TA Chigalu, Lirangwe, Malawi.*

MANDER, Dennis Stanley. b 18. Bp's Coll Cheshunt, 60. **d** 62 **p** 63 Chelmsf. C of Moulsham 62-64; R of Didmarton w Oldbury-on-the-Hill and Sopworth 64-69; R of Middelburg 69-75; V of Hutts Gate 75-78; R of Lanteglos-by-Camelford w St Adwena Dio Truro from 78. *Rectory, Camelford, Cornw, PL32 9TP.* (Camelford 2286)

MANDER, Ronald Charles Ridge. b 13. Univ of Lon BD 50. Kelham Th Coll 32. **d** 38 **p** 39 S'wark. C of St John Walworth 38-42; St Mary Northolt 42-46; CF (EC) 43-47; C of Easton 47-48; St Thos Regent Street Lon 48-50; V of St Mich AA w All SS Paddington 50-55; Chap to Med Studs within Univ of Lon Chap 55-57; R of Nuthurst 57-61; Rumboldswyke Chich 61-67; Perm to Offic Dio Chich from 67; Asst Master Littlehampton Compr Sch 67-75. *90 Norfolk Gardens, Littlehampton, Sussex.* (Littlehampton 4154)

MANDER, Canon Thomas Leonard Frederick. b 33. Ely Th Coll 60. **d** 62 Bp McKie for Cov **p** 63 Cov. C of St Mary Magd Cov 62-66; V of Bp's Tachbrook 66-70; V of St Barbara Earlsdon Cov 70-76; R of Lighthorne w Chesterton and Newbold Pacey w Moreton Morrell Dio Cov from 76; Hon Can of Cov Cathl from 80. *Lighthorne Rectory, Warwick, CV35 0AR.* (Moreton Morrell 247)

MANDEVILLE, Lord Bishop Suffragan of. *See* Murray, Right Rev William Arthur.

MANDEVILLE, Maurice Valentine. b 03. CCC Cam 1st cl Cl Trip pt i 25, BA 26, (2nd cl Th Trip pt i), MA 33. Kelham Th Coll 31. **d** 33 Lewes for Chich **p** 34 Chich. C of St Andr Eastbourne 33-36; Vice-Prin Chich Th Coll 36-43; Asst Master Ardingly Coll 43-46; Chap 45-46; Chap King Edward VII Sanat Midhurst 47; Lect in Th and Sub-Warden Th Hostel K Coll Lon 48-57; L to Offic Dio Chich 47-48; Perm to Offic Dio Lon 48-58; Commiss Barb 52-58; V of St Patr Hove 58-64; Prec of Accra Cathl 64-66; P-in-c of Tema 66-69; Warden of Bps Coll 70-72; All SS Adabraka 72-76; Exam Chap to Bp of Accra 75-76; Hon Can of Accra 75-76. *Poulakerry House, Kilsheelan, Clonmel, Co Tipperary, Irish Republic.*

MANDIHLARE, Oliver. **d** 43 **p** 44 S Rhod. P Dio S Rhod 43-52; Dio Mashon from 52. *St Peter's Mission, Mandea, PB R7678, Umtali, Rhodesia.*

MANDLAZI, Davida. **d** 47 **p** 48 Lebom. C of Lourenço Marques Distr 47-48; Prin of St Chris Coll Maciene 48-62; P-in-c of Manjacaze Dio Lebom from 62. *Caixa Postal 63, Joao Belo, Mozambique.*

MANDOTA, Donald. b 26. **d** 74 **p** 75 S Malawi. P Dio S Malawi. *Masuku, P/A Mkumba, PO Namwera, Malawi.*

MANE, Ellison. St Pet Coll Maka. **d** 35 **p** 37 Melan. P Dio Melan. *Garafate, Santa Ysabel, British Solomon Islands.*

MANEARA, Gabriel. b 40. Bp Patteson Th Centre Kohimarama 71. **d** 74 Melan. d Dio Melan 74-75; Ysabel 75-76;

Dio Centr Melan 76-81; Dio Aipo from 81. *Anglican Church, Simbai, via Madang, Papua New Guinea.*

MANEBONA, John Patteson. St Pet Coll Siota. **d** 54 **p** 60 Melan. P Dio Melan 54-74. *Gaeta, Gela, Solomon Islands.*

MANELEE, Fredie. b 55. Patterson Th Centr Kohimarama Dipl Th 80. **d** 80 Centr Melan. d Dio Centr Melan. *c/o Church of Melanesia, PO Box 19, Honiara, Solomon Islands.*

MANENTSA, Rheuben Sipho. St Pet Coll Rosettenville. **d** 53 **p** 54 Johann. P Dio Johann. *Box 581, Benoni, Transvaal, S Africa.* (011-892 1704)

MANGA, Christopher. d and **p** 63 Zam. P Dio Zam 63-70; Dio Lusaka from 71. *St Peter's, Ncheka, Msoro, Fort Jameson, Zambia.*

MANGAN MORRIS, Christopher. b 47. Chich Th Coll 71. **d** 73 Wakef **p** 74 Pontefract for Wakef. C of Athersley 73-76; Kippax 76-78; Team V of Seacroft 78-81; V of Oulton w Woodlesford Dio Ripon from 81. *Woodlesford Vicarage, Leeds.* (823128)

MANGO, Justine. Buwalasi Th Coll 57. **d** 58 **p** 59 U Nile. P Dio U Nile 58-61; Dio Mbale 61-81. *PO Box 984, Mbale, Uganda.*

MANGOCHE, Patricio. d and **p** 75 Lebom. P Dio Lebom 75-79; Dio Niassa from 79. *Caboe, Lago, Niassa, Mozambique.*

MANGUBAYO, Anderia Magaya. b 14. Bp Gwynne Coll Mundri. **d** 47 **p** 51 Sudan. P Dio Sudan 47-76; Dio Yambio from 76. *ECS, Li Rangu, Yambio, Sudan.*

MANGWELA, Haruni Enoch. St Phil Th Coll Kongwa, 65. **d** 65 **p** 66 Centr Tang. P Dio Centr Tang. *PO Box 27, Kongwa, Tanzania.*

MANHIQUE, Juvencio. d 79 **p** 81 Lebom. P Dio Lebom. *CP 56, Maxixe, Mozambique.*

MANHIQUE, Paulino Tomas. d 66 **p** 68 Lebom. P Dio Lebom. *Caixa Postal 120, Maputo, Mozambique.*

MANHIRE, Ashley Lewin. b 31. K Coll Lon and Warm AKC 55. **d** 56 **p** 57 Ex. C of St Gabr Plymouth 56-59; Cockington 59-66; V of Barton Dio Ex from 66. *St Martin's Vicarage, Barton, Torquay, Devon.* (Torquay 37223)

MANICALAND, Diocese of. *See* Mutare, Diocese of.

MANIE, Gabriel. St Pet Coll Rosettenville, 46. **d** 48 **p** 49 Kimb K. C of St Matt Kimberley 48-52; St Mich Miss Batlharos 52-53; Dir 53-61; Good Shepherd Miss Mafeking 61-63; C of Kuruman Dio Kimb K 63-70; Exam Chap to Bp of Kimb K 61-67; Can of Kimb Cathl 64-73; R of Taung 70-73; C of Good Shepherd De Aar 73-80; Perm to Offic Dio Kimb K from 81. *c/o Box 48, Kuruman, CP, S Africa.*

MANIGILOGILO, Arthur. d 65 **p** 67 Melan. P Dio Melan 65-75; Dio Malaita from 75. *Gwaunaru, Malaita, Solomon Islands.*

MANIHAGI, Judah. St Pet Coll Siota. **d** 56 **p** 59 Melan. P Dio Melan. *Santa Ysabel, British Solomon Islands.*

MANIKAM, Butwan. St Pet Hall Sing BTh 61. **d** 61 **p** 62 Sing. P Dio Sing 61-70; Dio W Mal from 70. *3826 Jalan St Mark's, Butterworth, Province Wellesley, Malaysia.*

MANILLA, Canon Simeon Dappu Jungo. Univ of Ghana BA 64. St Paul's Coll Awka. **d** 55 **p** 56 Nig Delta. P Dio Nig Delta; Exam Chap to Bp of Nig Delta from 72; Can of Nig Delta from 72. *PMB 5053, Port Harcourt, Nigeria.*

MANJAWILA, David. b 30. **d** 72 **p** 73 Malawi. P Dio S Malawi. *Private Bag 4, Mangochi, Malawi.*

✠ **MANKTELOW, Right Rev Michael Richard John.** b 27. Late Scho of Ch Coll Cam BA 48, MA 52. Chich Th Coll 51. **d** 53 **p** 54 Linc. C of Boston 53-56; Lect 56-57; Chap Ch Coll Cam 57-61; Linc Th Coll 61-63; Sub-Warden 64-66; L to Offic Dio Linc 62-66; Commiss Nyasa 62-64; Malawi 64-78; V of Knaresborough 66-73; St Wilfrid Harrogate 73-77; RD of Harrogate 72-77; C-in-c of St Luke Harrogate 75-77; Hon Can of Ripon Cathl from 75; Cons Ld Bp Suffr of Basingstoke in Westmr Abbey 31 March 77 by Abp of Cant; Bps of Lon, Bradf, Ely, Glouc, Guildf, Lich, Portsm and Roch; Bps Suffr of Southn, Buckingham, Dorch, Edmon, Grimsby, Hertf, Horsham, Huntingdon, Jarrow, Kingston, Knaresborough, Malmesbury, Selby, Sherbourne, Shrewsbury, Stafford, Tonbridge, Willesden; and others; Res Can of Win Cathl from 77. *1 The Close, Winchester, Hants, SO23 9LS.* (Win 69374)

MANLEY, Gordon Noel. b 1900. Late Exhib of Magd Coll Cam BA 21, MA 25. Ripon Hall, Ox 57. **d** 58 **p** 59 Glouc. C of St Paul Cheltm 58-60; R of Frittenden 60-66; C of St Steph Cant 66-69. *12 Lovell Road, Rough Common, Canterbury, Kent, CT2 9DG.* (Canterbury 66627)

MANLEY, Gordon Russell Delpratt. b 33. Late Exhib and Tancred Stud of Ch Coll Cam 1st cl Th Trip pt i, 54, BA 56, 2nd cl Th Trip pt iii, 57, MA 60. Linc Th Coll 57. **d** 59 Glouc for Bris **p** 60 Bris. C of St Alb Westbury Pk Clifton 59-61; Chap Ch Coll Cam 61-66; Perm to Offic Dio Ely 62-66; V of Radlett 66-75; Faversham Dio Cant from 75. *Vicarage, Preston Street, Faversham, Kent, ME13 8PG.* (Faversham 2592)

MANLEY-HARRIS, Eric Francis. b 34. Sarum Th Coll 61. **d** 64 **p** 65 Ex. C of Plymstock 64-66; St Mary Arches Ex 67-68; Chap RN 68-74; C of St Jas Cathl Townsville 74-81; St Pet Townsville Dio N Queensld from 81. *Box 5471, Townsville, Qld, Australia.*

MANLIWOS, Ven Grergory. St Pet Coll Siota 63. **d** 65 **p** 67 Melan. P Dio Melan 65-75; Dio New Hebr 75-80; Dio Vanuatu from 80; Archd Dio Vanuatu from 80. *Vureas Bay, Vanualava, Vanuatu.*

MANN, David Peter. b 29. Ho of Sacred Miss 51. **d** 55 **p** 56 Newc T. C of St Matt Newc T 55-59; V of Ch Ch Shieldfield Newc T 59-75; St Andr Kingsbury Dio Lon from 75. *St Andrew's Vicarage, Church Lane, Kingsbury, NW9.* (01-205 7447)

MANN, Donald Leonard. Westcott Ho Cam. **d** 47 **p** 48 Southw. C of Southw Minster 47-49; Edwinstowe 49-51; St Paul St Alb 51-54; Baldock w Bygrave and Clothall 54-56; V of Guilden Morden 56-59; Rocester 59-63; Gnosall w Knightley 63-69; Sheen 69-76; C-in-c of Calton 72-76; Ellastone 76-77; Perm to Offic Dio Lich from 77. *Sheen Vicarage, Buxton, SK17 0ES.* (Hartington 486)

MANN, Eric. b 20. Edin Th Coll 55. **d** 57 **p** 58 Edin. C of Ch Ch Morningside Edin 57-59; C-in-c of St Barn Dep Miss Edin 59-62; PC of Natland 62-67; V 68-70; V of Netherton w Grasslot Dio Carl from 70; Surr from 79. *Netherton Vicarage, Maryport, Cumb., CA15 7PS.* (Maryport 2200)

MANN, Ivan John. b 52. Brunel Univ Middx BTech 74. Univ of Southn BTh 80. Sarum Wells Th Coll 78. **d** 78 **p** 79 St E. C of Hadleigh 78-81; Whitton w Thurleston and Akenham Dio St E from 81. *76 Congreve Road, Ipswich, IP1 6AL.* (Ipswich 461055)

MANN, John Owen. b 55. Qu Coll Belf BD 77. Div Hostel Dub 78. **d** 79 **p** 81 Connor. C of Cloughfern Dio Connor from 79. *40 Hillview Avenue, Newtownabbey, Co Antrim, N Ireland.* (Whiteabbey 63746)

✠ **MANN, Right Rev Michael Ashley.** b 24. RMC Sandhurst. Wells Th Coll 55. **d** 57 **p** 58 Ex. C of Wolborough 57-59; V of Sparkwell 59-62; V of Ch Ch Port Harcourt 62-67; Home Sec Miss to Seamen 67-69; Can Res of Nor Cathl 69-74; Industr Adv to Bp of Nor 69-74; Vice-Dean of Nor Cathl 73-74; Cons Ld Bp Suffr of Dudley in S'wark Cathl 29 March 74 by Abp of Cant; Bps of Win, Linc, Worc, Nor, St Alb and Chelmsf; Bps Suffr of Aston, Grantham and Thetford; and others; res 76; Archd of Dudley 75-76; Dean of Windsor and Dom Chap to HM the Queen from 76. *Deanery, Windsor Castle, Berks.* (Windsor 65561)

MANN, Peter Eric. b 51. St Jo Coll Dur BA (Th) 73. Westcott Ho Cam 73. **d** 75 **p** 76 Carl. C of St Jo Evang Barrow-F 75-78; Egremont 78-80; V of St Luke Morton City and Dio Carl from 80. *St Luke's Vicarage, Brownrigg Drive, Carlisle, Cumb, CA2 6PA.* (Carl 25695)

✠ **MANN, Right Rev Peter Woodley.** BD (Lon) 61. St Jo Coll Auckld LTh 53. **d** 53 **p** 54 Wai. C of St John's Cathl Napier 53-55; Rotorua 55-56; V of Porangahau 56-61; Dannevirke 61-66; Exam Chap to Bp of Wai 65-66; to Bp of Nel 66-71; V of Blenheim Nel 66-71; Archd of Marlborough 66-71; V of Timaru 71-75; Archd of Timaru 71-75; Exam Chap to Bp of Ch Ch 73-75; V of Lower Hutt 75-76; Cons Ld Bp of Dun in St Paul's Cathl Dun 24 Feb 76 by Abp of NZ; Bps of Auckld, Nel, Ch Ch, Wai and Wel; Bp Suff of Aotearoa; and Bp Spence. *Bishop's House, 10 Claremont Street, Roslyn, Dunedin, NZ.* (772-694)

MANN, (Christopher Stephen) Robert Francis. BD (2nd cl) Lon 56, PhD (Lon) 60. Kelham Th Coll 34. **d** 40 Linc for Southw **p** 41 Southw. C of St Geo Nottm 40-43; SSM Priory Liv 43-45; C of St Jo Evang Middlesbrough 45-47; St Cecilia Parson Cross Sheff 47-53; L to Offic Dio Southw 53-56; Dio Lon 54-56; Dio Ox 56-62; Asst Master Kilmorie Co Secondary Sch 62-65; L to Offic Dio S'wark 62-65; Hon C of St Chrys w St Jude Peckham 62-65; In Amer Ch from 65; Fell Johns Hopkins Univ Baltimore from 65; Prof of St Mary's Sem and Univ of Baltimore 67-69. *319 Homeland Southway, Baltimore, Md 21212, USA.*

MANN, Robin. b 45. Fitzwm Coll Can BA 76, MA 80. Ridley Hall Cam 73. **d** 77 Knaresborough for Ripon **p** 78 Ripon. C of Wetherby 77-80; V of Hipswell Dio Ripon from 80. *Vicarage, Piper Hill, Catterick Camp, Yorks, DL9 4PN.* (Richmond 833320)

MANN, Sydney. b 07. Ripon Hall Ox 63. **d** 64 Bp Mckie for Cov **p** 65 Cov. C of Beaudesert W Henley-in-Arden 64-66; Tamworth 66-69; V of Easington W Skeffling and Kilnsea 69-74; Hon C of All SS Leamington Priors Dio Cov from 75; Perm to Offic Dio Cov from 78. *10 Greville Smith Avenue, Whitnash, Leamington Spa, Warws, CV31 2HQ.* (0926 21837)

MANN, Victor James William. **d** 75 **p** 76 Rupld. Hon C of St Geo Transcona 75-77; Bp's C Dio Rupld 77-81; P-in-c of St Geo Transcona, Winnipeg Dio Rupld from 81. *111 St Claire Boulevard, Winnipeg, Manit, R2C 0V5, Canada.*

MANNALL, Michael John Frederick. b 37. St Mich Coll Llan 61. **d** 63 **p** 64 S'wark. C of H Spirit Clapham 63-66; St Bart Brighton 66-68; St Matt Willesden 68-69; Min of Little St Pet Conv Distr Cricklewood 69-73; R of Broughton 73-75; Perm to Offic Dio Lon from 75; Dio S'wark from 76; Hon C of St Luke w Good Shepherd Kingston-upon-Thames Dio S'wark from 76. *99 Elmbridge Avenue, Surbiton, Surrey.* (01-399 6345)

MANNING, Canon Arthur Lionel. b 16. Late Sizar of St Jo Coll Cam 2nd cl Cl Trip pt i 37, BA (3rd cl Th Trip pt i) 38, MA 44. Ridley Hall Cam 38. **d** 40 **p** 41 Ches. C of St Paul Portwood 40-41; Perm to Offic at St Mary and St Paul Birkenhead 42-49; V of Wrenbury w Baddiley 49-56; Gatley 56-64; Timperley 64-71; Hon Can of Ches 65-81; Can (Emer) from 81; V of Woodford 71-81. *2 Bro Helyg, Llandrillo, Corwen, Clwyd, LL21 0TR.*

MANNING, Brian Hawthorne. b 29. M IStructE 59. CEng. NW Ordin Course 70. **d** 73 Man **p** 74 Hulme for Man. C of Birch-in-Rusholme 73-75; St Gabr Prestwich Dio Man 75-80; St Mary Prestwich Dio Man from 80. *3 Willow Road, Prestwich, Manchester, M25 7DZ.*

MANNING, David Godfrey. b 47. Trin Coll Bris 73. **d** 76 S'wark. C of H Trin and Ch Ch Richmond 76-79; Anston Dio Sheff from 79. *18 Nursery Road, North Anston, Sheffield, S31 7BU.* (Dinnington 565191)

MANNING, David Tuini. NZ Bd of Th Stud LTh 67. **d** 67 Ch Ch **p** 68 Bp Warren for Ch Ch. C of Cashmere Hills 67-71; Ashburton 71-72; V of Kumara and of Chatham Is 72-75; Belfast-Redwood Dio Ch Ch from 75. *833 Main Road North, Christchurch 5, NZ.* (29-8942)

MANNING, Neville Alexander. b 41. BD (Lon) and ALCD 68. **d** 68 **p** 69 Roch. C of Belvedere 68-71; Hollington 71-73; Hersham 73-77; V of St Jerome Dawley Hillingdon Dio Lon from 77. *42 Corwell Lane, Dawley, Uxbridge, Middx.* (01-573 2084)

✠ **MANNING, Right Rev William James.** TCD BA 44, Div Test 44, MA 47. Oriel Coll Ox MA 50. **d** 44 **p** 45 Dub. C of St Mary Donnybrook 44-47; St Fin Barre's Cathl Cork 47-49; Chap Thomas Coram Sch Berkhamsted 49-51; C of St John Pembroke Berm 51-53; Can Res of Berm and Exam Chap to Bp of Berm 53-64; Chap at Zurich 64-66; Prec St Geo Cathl Capetn 67-72; Dean and R of St Mark's Cathl Geo 72-77; Cons Ld Bp of George in St Geo Cathl Capetn 5 Feb 78 by Abp of Capetn; Bps Suffr of Capetn; and Abp R S Taylor and Bp Barron. *Bishop's Lea, Box 227, George, CP, S Africa.* (George 2267)

MANNING, William Wybrants. Trin Coll Dub BA and Div Test 08, MA 20. **d** 09 **p** 10 Cork. C of Berehaven 09-14; Kilmocomogue 14-15; served in Wilts Regt 15-19; C of Bp's Hatfield 20-23; R of Lasham (w Herriard from 29) 23-39; Boyton w Sherrington 39-40. *Ardamine, Killrae Street, Bagenalstown, Co Carlow, Irish Republic.*

MANNOX, Canon Michael Edward Rathlin. b 08. Univ of Birm BA 34. Linc Th Coll 34. **d** 36 **p** 37 Pet. C of Irthlingborough 36-38; Shirehampton 38-46; CF (TA - R of O) 39-45; V of St Jo Div Fishponds 46-55; C-in-c of St Bede Bris 53-54; Hon Chap to Bp of Bris 50-62; V of St Steph Southmead 55-65; Hon Can of Bris 62-73; (Emer) from 73; R of Horfield 65-73; Surr 66-73; RD of Almondsbury 70-73; Perm to Offic Dio Ex from 73. *The Haven, Fry's Lane, Sidford, Sidmouth, Devon EX10 9SP.*

MANOLAS, Graeme Peter. b 52. St Mich Ho Crafers 69. **d** 74 **p** 75 Bunb. C of Albany 74-76; P-in-c of Williams 76-79; R of Cranbrook Dio Bunb from 79. *Rectory, Cranbrook, W Australia 6321.*

MANSBRIDGE, Michael Winstanley. b 32. Univ of Southn BA (2nd cl Hist) 54. Ridley Hall Cam 56. **d** 58 **p** 59 St Alb. C of Ware 58-60; Claverdon w Preston Bagot 60-62; Chap Univ Coll Nai 62-65; C of Nai 62-65; Hon Chap Nai Cathl 62-65; V of Chilvers Coton w Astley 65-75; RD of Nuneaton 67-74; Surr 74-75; V of H Trin Leamington Dio Cov from 75. *Clive House, Kenilworth Road, Leamington Spa, CV32 5TL.*

MANSEL, Canon James Seymour Denis. b 07. MVO 72. KCVO 79. Ex Coll Ox BA 32, MA 41. Westcott Ho Cam. **d** 41 **p** 42 Win. Asst Master Win Coll 39-65; Chap 41-65; Sub-Dean of HM Chapels R 65-79; Dep Clk of the Closet and Sub-Almoner 65-79; Dom Chap to HM the Queen 65-79; Chap from 79; Wiccamical Preb of Chich Cathl 71-81; Can (Emer) from 81; Chap O of St John of Jer from 71. *15 Sandringham Court, Maida Vale, W9.* (01-286 3052)

MANSELL, Henry Edward. St Francis Coll Brisb ACT ThL 51. **d** 51 **p** 52 N Queensld. C of Mackay 52-54; St Jas Cathl Townsville 54-56; R of Tully 56-61; L to Offic Dio Brisb 61-65; V of Jandowae 65-66; Chap RAAF from 66. *7 Hickeys Road, Wurruk, Australia 3851.*

MANSFIELD, David. Moore Th Coll Syd BTh 77. **d** and **p** 78 NW Austr. C of W Pilbara 78-80; St Luke Miranda Dio Syd from 80. *40 Malvern Road, Miranda, NSW, Australia 2228.* (525-9526)

MANSFIELD, Gordon Reginald. b 35. Clifton Th Coll 58. Dipl Th (Lon) 61. **d** 63 Penrith for Carl **p** 64 Carl. C of St Jo Evang Carl 63-65; Westcombe Pk 65-68; Hon C of Rashcliffe 68-70; V of Woodlands 70-80; Steeple Bumpstead w Helions Bumpstead Dio Chelmsf from 80. *Steeple Bumpstead Vicarage, Haverhill, Suff.* (Steeple Bumpstead 257)

MANSFIELD, Robert Stanley. St Chad's Coll Regina Div Test 52. **d** 52 **p** 53 Qu'App. C-in-c of Milden 52-53; P-in-c 53-56; R of Omemee 56-64. *436 Maple Wood Drive, Oshawa, Ont, Canada.*

MANSHIP, David. b 27. Keble Coll Ox BA (3rd cl Lit Hum) 52, MA 58. Qu Coll Birm 52. **d** 54 Kens for Lon **p** 55 Lon. C of St John-at-Hackney 54-58; Ascen Wembley 58-61; Asst Chap Lon Dioc Counc for Vol Relig Educn from 61; C (Chap and Youth Tr Officer from 62) of St Andr Holborn (Guild Ch) Lon 61-65; M Tr Officer C of E Youth Coun 65-68; Cl Tr Officer 68-70; Dir Relig Educn Dio Win 70-79; Hon Can of Win 74-79; R of Old Alresford 76-79; Exam Chap to Bp of Win 76-79; V of Abingdon Dio Ox from 79. *Vicarage, St Helen's Court, Abingdon, Oxon.* (Abingdon 20144)

MANSILLA, Gustavo Alberto. b 44. **d** 76 **p** 77 Parag. P Dio Parag. *a/c Casilla 1124, Asuncion, Paraguay.*

MANTHORP, Brian. b 34. Pemb Coll Ox BA (3rd cl Engl) 55, MA 59. Westcott Ho Cam. **d** 61 **p** 62 Guildf. C of Busbridge 61-62; Asst Master Charterhouse 62-65; L to Offic Dio S'wark 62-65; Asst Master Framlingham Coll 66-68; Aitchison Coll Lahore 68-70; Oakbank Sch Keighley 70-73; Hd Master H Trin C of E Aided Sch Halifax from 73; L to Offic Dio Wakef from 73. *Moor Bank, Ferncliffe Drive, Utley, Keighley, Yorks.*

MANTHORP, Canon Leslie Richard. b 05. Selw Coll Cam 2nd cl Engl Trip pt i 26, BA (2nd cl Geog Trip pt i) 27. MA 31. **d** 35 **p** 36 St E. C of H Trin Ipswich 35-40; R of Somersham w Flowton 40-47; LPr Dio Linc 48-50; Chap to de Aston School Market Rasen 47-50; V of Welland 50-53; Thorington w Wenhaston 53-60; RD of N Dunwich 57-60; Surr 58-75; R of Melton 60-75; Hon Can of St E 62-75; Can (Emer) from 75; RD of Woodbridge 72-75; Perm to Offic Dio St E from 76. *21 St George's Road, Felixstowe, Suff.*

MANTLE, John Ambrose Cyril. b 46. St Andr Univ MTh 74. Edin Th Coll 66. **d** 69 **p** 70 Brech. C of Broughty Ferry 69-71; Perm to Offic Dios Brech and St Andr 71-75; Dio Edin 75-77; Chap St Andr Univ 77-80; Fitzw Coll and New Hall Cam from 80; P-in-c of Elie and Pittenweem 78-80. *Fitzwilliam College, Cambridge, CB3 0DG.*

MANTLE, Canon Norman James. b 23. Selw Coll Cam BA 49, MA 54. Westcott Ho Cam. **d** 51 **p** 52 S'wark. C of St Jo Evang Redhill 51-55; Wimbledon 55-58; V of Rusthall Dio Roch from 58; RD of Tunbridge Wells 64-74; Hon Can of Roch from 73. *Rusthall Vicarage, Tunbridge Wells, Kent.* (Tunbridge Wells 21447)

MANTLE, Canon Rupert James. b 15. Univ of Edin MA 37. **d** 40 **p** 41 Glas. C of H Trin Paisley 40-42; St Cypr Lenzie 43; Chap Aber Cathl 44-46; R of St Machar Bucksburn 46-50; I of St Jo Evang Inverness 50-55; C-in-c of St Ninian Dundee 55-67; R of Torry w Cove 67-81; Can of St Paul's Cathl Dundee 70-76; St Cathl Aber 78-81; Hon Can from 81. *32 Craigiebuckler Terrace, Aberdeen, AB1 7SS.*

MANTON, Paul Arthur. b 45. Univ of Lon Dipl Th (Extra-mural) 75. BD (Lon) 77. Oak Hill Coll 73. **d** 77 Shrewsbury for Lich **p** 78 Lich. C of Penn Fields 77-80; Chap Ox Street Stores Lon from 80. *29 Finchley Way, N3 1AH.* (01-346 6735)

MANTON, Peter Geoffrey Kevitt. b 20. Wycl Hall, Ox. **d** 61 Southn for Win **p** 62 Win. C of St Mark Jersey 61-65; R of St John Jersey Dio Win from 65; Vice-Dean of Jersey from 75. *Rectory, St John, Jersey, CI.* (Central 0534-61677)

MANTSHONGO, Richard. St Bede's Coll Umtata, 32. **d** 33 **p** 38 St Jo Kaffr. C of Matatiele 33-38 and 46-63; St Barn Ntlaza 38-44; All SS 44-46; Nyanisos 63-71; L to Offic Dio St John's from 71. *PO Box 156, Matatiele, Transkei, S Africa.*

MANUEL, Canon Cyril Swamikan. Univ of Madras MA 49. Bp's Coll Calc 57. **d** 60 **p** 61 Calc. P Dio Calc 60-67; C of Cottesloe 67-68; Org Sec Angl Miss Coun of W Austr 68-72; R of Subiaco 72-78; Midland Dio Perth from 78; Can of Perth from 75. *Box 50, Midland, W Australia 6056.* (274 1464)

MANUEL, Raymond William. b 48. St Jo Coll Morpeth 73. **d** 76 **p** 77 Papua. P Dio Papua 76-77; Dio Port Moresby 77-80; Dio Newc from 81. *267 Excelsior Parade, Toronto, NSW, Australia 2283.*

MANWARING, John Lindsay. b 32. Linc Th Coll 69. **d** 71

Barking for Cant **p** 72 Barking for Chelmsf. C of Gt Ilford 71-73; Bexhill 73-75; Hon C of Eastbourne 76-78. *Address temp unknown.*

MANYAGA, Petro Nyamwaha. St Phil Th Coll Kongwa. **d** and **p** 62 Centr Tang. P Dio Centr Tang 62-66; Dio W Tang from 66. *Box 161, Tabora, Tanzania.*

MANYAMA, Yakobo. d 78 **p** 79 Vic Nyan. P Dio Vic Nyan. *Box 118, Mugumu, Tanzania.*

MANYAU, David. d 79 **p** 80 Mashon. P Dio Mashon 79-81; Dio Mutare from 81. *c/o Anglican Diocesan Offices, 115 Main Street, Umtali, Zimbabwe.*

MANYIKA, Musa. d 79 Bp Mohamed for Centr Tang **p** 79 Centr Tang. P Dio Centr Tang. *Box 1355, Dodoma, Tanzania.*

MANYWA, Hosea. b 24. **d** 77 **p** 78 Moro. P Dio Moro. *PO Ngiloli, Kilosa, Tanzania.*

MANZURU, Erikana Arama. Bp Gwynne Coll Mundri, 57. **d** 57 **p** 59 Sudan. P Dio Sudan 57-76; Dio Yambio from 76. *ECS, Ibba, Sudan.*

MAPER, Kedhekia Koot. b 54. **d** 81 Omdurman. d Dio Omdurman. *PO Box 65, Omdurman, Sudan.*

MAPLE, David Charles. b 34. Sarum Th Coll 64. **d** 66 Croydon for Cant **p** 66 Cant. C of Buckland-in-Dover 66-67; St Lawr-in-I of Thanet 67-71; Chap RAF 71-75; C-in-c of Newchurch and Burmarsh 75-78; C-in-c of Ivychurch and St Mary in the Marsh 75-76; R of Dymchurch (w Burmarsh and Newchurch from 78) 76-81; Hon Min Can of Cant Cathl from 79; Hon Chap to Abp of Cant from 81. *129 Ashford Road, Canterbury, Kent, CT1 3XR.* (Cant 53805)

MAPLE, Harold Walter James. b 04. **d** 60 **p** 61 Chich. C of Clayton w Keymer 60-64; R of Duncton 64-69; R of Burton w Coates 64-69; Seq of Up-Waltham 65-69; Perm to Offic Dio Cant from 73. *1 Moles Lane, Wyddial, Buntingford, Herts, SG9 0EX.*

MAPLE, John Philip. b 50. Chich Th Coll 71. **d** 74 Kens for Lon **p** 79 Stepney for Lon. C of St Mich AA w Ch Ch Notting Hill Kens 74-75; St D w St Clem Barnsbury 79-80; Cotham Dio Bris from 80. *182 St Michael's Hill, Bristol, BS2 8DE.* (Bristol 743198)

MAPLES, Canon Jeffrey Stanley. b 16. Down Coll Cam 2nd cl Engl Trip pt i, 37, BA 38, 2nd cl Th Trip pt i, 39, MA 46. Chich Th Coll 39. **d** 40 Portsm **p** 41 Bp Kitching for Portsm. C of St Jas Milton (in c of S Cross Miss Ch 41-46) 40-46; Watlington 46-48; V of Swinderby 48-50; St Mich-on-the-Mount Linc 50-56; Youth Chap and Asst Dir Educn 48-50; Dioc Dir of Educn 50-56; Can and Preb of Nassington in Linc Cathl 54-56; of Bishopstone in Sarum Cathl 57-60; of Bricklesworth and Chan 60-67; Can (Emer) from 67; Dioc Dir of Relig Educn and Publ Pr Dio Sarum 56-63; Proc Conv Sarum 58-69; Dir of Bible Reading Fellowship 63-67; V of Milton 67-73; RD of Portsm 68-73; Hon Can of Portsm 72-73; Bris from 74; Archd of Swindon 74-82. *c/o 25 Rowden Hill, Chippenham, SN15 2AQ.* (Chippenham 3599)

MAPOGO, Dunstan. d and **p** 78 Centr Tang. P Dio Centr Tang. *PO Chipogoro, Tanzania.*

MAPOMA, Charles Bantom Mcimbi. St Bede's Coll Umtata 59. **d** 60 **p** 63 St Jo Kaffr. P Dio St John's 63-73; Dio Grahmstn from 73. *PO Box 119, Stutterheim 4930, CP, S Africa.* (Mdantsane 113)

MAPPLEBECK, Anthony. b 16. SS Coll Cam BA 38, MA 42. Cudd Coll 39. **d** 40 **p** 41 Lon. C of H Cross Greenford 40-45; Bodmin 45-49; V of St Veryan 49-55; Mevagissey 55-81. *20 Polkirt Hill, Mevagissey, St Austell, Cornw,* (Mevagissey 842956)

MAPPLEBECKPALMER (formerly PALMER), Richard Warwick. b 32. CCC Cam BA 56, MA 60. Cudd Coll 56. **d** 58 **p** 59 York. C of Redcar 58-60; St John Drypool 61-63; V of St Ambrose Pendleton 63-77; P-in-c of Ambrosden w Merton and Piddington Dio Ox 77; V from 77. *Vicarage, Merton Bicester, Oxon, OX6 0NF.* (Charlton-on-Otmoor 212)

MAPSON, Albert. b 1896. Can Scho Linc 22. **d** 25 **p** 26 York. C of St Sav Scarborough 25-29; New Sleaford 29-30; St Andr Grimsby 30-33; Sub-Warden of St Mary's Home Stone 33-39; Perm to Offic Dios Cant and Lon 40; C of St Jo Bapt Margate 40-43; V of Challock w Molash 43-51; R of Staple 51-63; Perm to Offic Dio Cant from 64. *14 Oaten Hill Place, Canterbury, Kent, CT1 3HJ.* (Canterbury 66281)

MAPSON, John Victor. b 31. BA (Lon) 60. Oak Hill Th Coll 55. **d** 60 **p** 61 Derby. C of Littleover 60-62; St Mich Southfields 62-65; R of Willand 65-71; C-in-c of Axmouth 71-72; V (w Musbury from 75) 72-77; C-in-c of Musbury 73-75; RD of Honiton 76-77; V of Cullompton Dio Ex from 77; R of Kentisbeare w Blackborough Dio Ex from 77; RD of Cullompton from 81. *Vicarage, Cullompton, Devon, EX15 1DA.* (Cullompton 33249)

MAPUGA, Asher S. St Phil Th Coll Kongwa. **d** 57 Centr Tang **p** 58 Bp Omari for Centr Tang. P Dio Centr Tang. *Box 2, Mpwapwa, Tanzania.*

MAPUMA, Thomas. d 28 **p** 32 S Rhod. P Dio S Rhod 28-39; Asst P 39-42; P-in-c of St Patr Miss Gwelo 42-46; St Francis Miss Selukwe 46-50; St Matt Miss Gwelo 50-52; L to Offic Dio Matab 52-77. *Box 1047, Gwelo, Zimbabwe.*

MAPUNDA, Habil Oswald. b 42. St Mark's Coll Dar-S 77. **d** 79 **p** 80 Ruv. P Dio Ruv. *PO Box 7, Songea, Tanzania.*

MAPUNDA, Humphrey Patrick. St Cypr Coll Ngala 62. **d** 64 **p** 66 SW Tang. P Dio SW Tang 64-69; and from 72; Dio Dar-S 69-72. *Box 134, Kyela, Tanzania.*

MAPUTTA, Paul Alban. St Mark's Coll Dar-S 69. **d** 70 **p** 72 Dar-S. P Dio Dar-S 70-77; Dio S W Tang from 77. *c/o Box 32, Njombe, Tanzania.*

MAPUTWA, Maxwell. d 78 S Malawi for Lake Malawi. d Dio S Malawi for Lake Malawi. *Christian Council of Malawi, PO Box 805, Lilongwe, Malawi.*

MAQASHALALA, Canon Meshack. St Bede's Coll Umtata. **d** 38 **p** 41 St Jo Kaffr. P Dio St John's 38-42 and from 46; CF (S Afr) 42-46; Can of St John's from 67. *Box 216, Bizana, Transkei, S Africa.*

MAQUBELA, Caesar. St Bede's Coll Umtata. **d** 56 **p** 57 St John's. P Dio St John's 56-68; L to Offic Dio St John's from 68. *c/o PO Mjika, Transkei, S Africa.*

MARA, George. d 53 **p** 55 Carp. C of Torres Strait Miss 53-56; Miss at Saibai I 56-60; Mabuiag 60-62; Badu I 60-70; Cowal Creek 70-72; on leave 72-77; P-in-c of Umagico Dio Carp from 77. *Box 79, Thursday Island, Queensland, Australia 4875.*

MARAN ZAU YAW, d 60 Rang. d Dio Rang 60-70; Dio Mand from 71. *Emmanuel Church, Mohnyin, Burma.*

MARAU, Martin. b 45. Bp Patteson Th Centre Kohimarama 70. **d** 73 **p** 74 Melan. P Dio Melan 73-75; Centr Melan from 75. *Mwadoa, Ulawa Island, Solomon Islands.*

MARAU HELONGO, Joses. b 55. Patteson Th Centre Kohimarama Dipl Th 80. **d** 80 Centr Melan. d Dio Centr Melan. *c/o Church of Melanesia, PO Box 19, Honiara, Solomon Islands.*

MARC, Bira. St Paul's Coll Ambat. **d** 53 Madag. d Dio Madag 53-70. *Befandriana, Madagascar.*

MARCER, Graham John. b 52. Ripon Coll Cudd 75. **d** 78 **p** 79 Sarum. C of Sherborne 78-81; Christchurch Dio Win from 81. *31 Wickfield Avenue, Christchurch, Dorset, BH23 1JB.* (0202-483999)

MARCH, Charles Anthony Maclea. b 32. CCC Cam 2nd cl Econ Trip pt i 53, BA (2nd cl Hist Trip pt i) 55, MA 70. Oak Hill Th Coll 55. **d** 57 **p** 58 Cant. C of Em S Croydon 57-60; H Trin Eastbourne 60-63; V of St Andr Whitehall Pk U Holloway 63-67; H Trin w Ch Ch Tunbridge Wells Dio Roch from 67. *63 Claremont Road, Tunbridge Wells, Kent, TN1 1TE.* (Tunbridge Wells 26644)

MARCH, David Stanley. b 21. Linc Coll Ox BA (2nd cl Mod Lang) 51, MA 54. BD (Lon) 58, PhD (Lon) 67. Oak Hill Th Coll 53. **d** 55 **p** 56 Lon. C of St John U Holloway 55-58; V of St Paul Plumstead 58-65; St Paul W Ealing Dio Lon from 65. *102 Elers Road, W13.* (01-567 4628)

MARCH, John Vale. b 39. CCC Cam 2nd cl Econ Trip pt i 60, BA (3rd cl Law Trip pt ii) 62, MA 76. Linc Th Coll 62. **d** 64 Aston for Birm **p** 65 Birm. C of Sheldon 64-68; St Phil and St Jas Hodge Hill Dio Birm 68-72; Team V from 72. *1 Ayala Croft, Bromford Bridge, Birmingham, B36 8SN.* (021-747 9320)

MARCHAND, Rex Anthony Victor. b 47. AKC BD 69. St Aug Coll Cant 69. **d** 70 Bp Woolmer for Portsm **p** 71 Portsm. C of Leigh Pk Dio Portsm 70-73; Bp's Hatfield 73-80; R of Deal w Sholden Dio Cant from 80. *Rectory, Addelam Road, Deal, Kent, CT14 9BZ.* (Deal 4076)

MARCHANT, Frederick Percy. b 05. Univ of Leeds, BA (2nd cl Hist) 28. Coll of Resurr Mirfield, 28. **d** 30 Bp King for Roch **p** 31 Roch. C of St Botolph Northfleet 30-34; Crayford 34-36; Stone 36-38; Ascot Heath 38-45; V of Greenham 45-52; Winkfield (w Chavey Down from 53) 52-70. *Wyndhurst Villa, Water Lane, Somerton, Somt.*

MARCHANT, Ven George John Charles. b 16. St Jo Coll Dur LTh 38, BA 39, MA 42, BD 64. Tyndale Hall Bris 35. **d** 39 Willesden for Lon **p** 40 Lon. C of St Andr Whitehall Pk 39-41; L to Offic Dio Lon 41-44; C of St Andr L (in c of St Steph) Cam 44-48; PC of H Trin Skirbeck 48-54; V of St Nich Dur 54-74; RD of Dur 64-74; M Gen Syn Dur 70-80; Hon Can of Dur 72-74; Can Res from 74; Archd of Auckld from 74. *15 The College, Durham.* (Durham 47534)

MARCHANT, Iain William. b 26. Wells Th Coll 59. **d** 60 **p** 61 Carl. C of Dalston w Cumdivock 60-63; V of Hawkesbury 63-76; R of Newent Dio Glouc from 76. *Rectory, Newent, Glos.* (Newent 821641)

MARCHANT, Canon Ronald Albert. b 26. Late Scho and Stud Em Coll Cam BA 50, MA 52, PhD 57, BD 64. Ridley Hall Cam 50. **d** 54 York **p** 55 Whitby for York. C of St Steph Acomb York 54-57; Willian 57-59; V of Laxfield Dio St E from 59; RD of Hoxne 73-78; Hon Can of St E Cathl from 75. *Laxfield Vicarage, Woodbridge, Suff, IP13 8EB.* (Ubbeston 218)

MARCHINGTON, Graham William Kuranda. b 27. **d** and **p** 73 Zulu. C of Gingindhlovu Dio Zulu from 73. *Box 99, PO Mandini, Zululand.* (Mandini 42)

MARCON, John Neville. b 03. Or Coll Ox BA (3rd cl Th) 26, MA 30. Cudd Coll 29. **d** 29 **p** 30 Chelmsf. C of Chingford 29-34; W Tarring 34-37; V of Ch Ch Eastbourne 37-56; Loxwood 56-70. *Raydale, Fittleworth, Pulborough, Sussex.*

MARCON, Hubert John. b 39. Univ of Cant NZ LTh 80. St Jo Coll Auckld 77. **d** 79 **p** 80 Auckld. P-in-c of St Alb Balmoral Dio Auckld from 79. *37 Brixton Road, Balmoral, Auckland 3, NZ.*

MARCROFT, Harry Wycherley. b 08. St Jo Coll Dur BA 36. Egerton Hall Man 36. **d** 37 **p** 38 Man. C of St Paul Bury 37-44; V of St Paul Paddington 44-47; Edenfield 47-73. *Edenfield, Clatterbrune, Presteigne, Powys.* (Presteigne 516)

MARCUS, George Stephen. Bp Gray Coll Capetn. **d** 60 **p** 61 Capetn. C of St Aug O'Okiep 60-62; All SS Plumstead 62-71; P-in-c of St Helena Bay 71-76; R of Good Shepherd Maitland 76-80; St Phil City and Dio Capetn from 80. *Rectory, Roger Street, Cape Town 8001, S Africa.* (45-3580)

MARCUS, Justus Mauritius. Univ of Capetn BA 78. St Pet Coll Natal. **d** 78 **p** 79 Geo. C of St Barn Heidelberg Dio Geo from 78. *St Barnabas Rectory, Heidelberg, CP, S Africa.*

MARDEN, Peter Edgar. b 40. St D Coll Lamp BA (2nd cl Hist) 61. Linacre Ho Ox BA (3rd cl Th) 64, MA 68. St Steph Ho Ox 62. **d** 65 **p** 66 S'wark. C of Catford 65-70; Mortlake 70-73; V of St Phil Sydenham 73-75; Counsellor Mid-Kent Coll of Higher and Further Educn 76; Publ Pr Dio Cant from 77. *Mid-Kent College of Higher Educn, Maidstone Road, Horsted, Chatham, ME5 9UQ.* (Medway 41001)

MARDON, John Hedley. b 25. Lon Coll of Div 62. **d** 64 **p** 65 B & W. C of St Jas Taunton 64-66; V of Cullompton 66-77; Surr 68-77; RD of Cullompton 74-77; R of Kentisbeare w Blackborough 76-77; P-in-c of Locking Dio B & W 77-81; V from 81; Adv on Evang Dio B & W from 77. *Locking Vicarage, Weston-super-Mare, Avon.* (Banwell 823556)

MARGAM, Archdeacon of. *See* Lewis, Ven Albert John Francis.

MARI, Edward. **d** 77 Carp. C of Warraber I Dio Carp from 77. *Warraber Island, via Thursday Island, Queensland, Australia 4875.*

MARIERE, Canon Ruese Uvwieraerho Emekakao. Im Coll Ibad. **d** and **p** 66 Benin. P Dio Benin 66-77; Dio Warri from 77; Can of Warri from 80. *c/o PO Box 52, Warri, Nigeria.*

MARINGA, Johnson Nyaga. b 49. St Paul's Coll Limuru 74. **d** 76 **p** 78 Mt Kenya E. P Dio Mt Kenya E. *c/o Box 51, Marsabit, Kenya.*

✠ **MARINO, Right Rev Mario Lorenzo.** **d** 68 **p** 70 Argent. P Dio Argent 68-73; Dio N Argent 73-75; Cons Asst Bp of N Argent at Mision Chaquena 30 Sept 75 by Bps of N Argent, Parag and Argent and ES Amer; and Bp Leake. *Casilla 19, Ingeiero Juárez, Provincia de Formosa, Argentina.*

MARIPIL, Moises. **d** and **p** 76 Bp Bazley for Chile, P Dio Chile. *Casilla 26-D, Temuco, Chile.*

MARK, Robert James. b 36. K Coll Lon and Warm AKC 61. **d** 62 **p** 63 York. C of Guisborough 62-65; St Columba Middlesbrough 65-68; Thornaby-on-Tees (in c of St Mark from 70) 68-72; Team V 72-73; Team R of Staveley and Barrow Hill Dio Derby from 73. *Staveley Rectory, Chesterfield, Derbys, S43 3TN.* (Chesterfield 472270)

MARKBY, Archibald Campbell. b 15. Em Coll Cam BA 37, MA 41. Ridley Hall Cam 37. **d** and **p** 39 Bradf. C of St Clem Bradf 39-42; St Aldate Ox 42-46; V of St Mary Kilburn 46-53; Ch Ch Crouch End Hornsey 53-64; R of Ickenham 64-68; V of Crowfield w Stonham Aspal 68-71; Damerham w Martin 71-80. *Mead Cottage, Martin, Fordingbridge, Hants.* (Martin Cross 345)

MARKBY, Peter John Jenner. b 38. Em Coll Cam 3rd cl Math Trip pt i, 58, BA (2nd cl Th Trip pt ii) 60. Clifton Th Coll 62. **d** 64 **p** 65 Lon. C of St Geo Tufnell Pk 64-68; Crowborough 68-73; Polegate (in c of St Wilfrid) 73-77, R of St Jo Bapt Southover Lewes Dio Chich from 77. *Southover Rectory, Lewes, Sussex, BN7 1HT.* (Lewes 2018)

MARKER, John Howard. b 11. ALCD 34. **d** 34 **p** 35 Man. C of St Matt Bolton 34-37; St Paul Kersal 37-39; C-in-c of St Jo Bapt Little Hulton 39-40; R of St Jas Moss Side 40-48; V of St Andr Eccles 48-54; PC of Rowsley 54-68; R of Copford w Easthorpe 68-77. *7 Colne Springs, Ridgewell, Halstead, Essex, CO9 4RX.*

MARKEY, Michael John. b 42. Chich Th Coll 71. **d** 74 Willesden for Lon **p** 75 Lon. C of All SS Hillingdon 74-77; H Trin Reading 77-81; V of St Jos the Worker Northolt Dio Lon from 81. *430 Yeading Lane, Northolt, Middx, UB5 6JS.* (01-845 6161)

✠ **MARKHAM, Right Rev Bernard.** b 07. Univ of Leeds BA (2nd cl Hist) 28. Nashotah Ho Wisc Hon DD 79. Coll of Resurr Mirfield 28. **d** 30 Bradf **p** 31 S & M for Bradf. C of St Wilfrid Lidget Green 30-35; St Mich AA (in c of St Francis) N Kens 35-37; Stoke-on-Trent (in c of St Andr) 37-39; V of Bierley 39-46; R of St Benedict Ardwick 46-59; V of St Marg Toxt Pk 59-62; Cons Ld Bp of Nass in St Geo Cathl Georgetn 19 Aug 62 by Abp of W Indies; Bps of Antig; Barb; Trin; and Windw Is; Bps Mandeville and Shapley; and Bps of Puerto Rico; and Connecticut; res 72; Asst Bp of Southw 72-77; S'wark 77-80; R of E Bridgford 72-77; Commiss Nass from 72; P-in-c of Kneeton 73-77. *209 London Road, Balderton, Newark, Notts, NG24 3HB.* (Newark 703827)

MARKHAM, Canon Cecil Jeffries. KCWNS BA 19, MA 24, DCnL 58. **d** 21 **p** 22 Fred. C of Chatham 21-23; H Trin St John 23-26; R of Stanley 26-29; Sackville 29-32; Rothesay 32-64; CF (Canad) 40-44; RD of Kingston 47-48; Can of Fred from 59. *224 Gibbon Road, East Riverside, NB, Canada.*

MARKHAM, Cyril Guy. Qu Univ Kingston Ont BA 23. Hur Th Coll STh 55. **d** 55 **p** 56 Hur. I of St Timothy Lon 55-58; Regr Seager Hall 59-65. *478 Tecumseh Avenue, London, Ont, Canada.*

MARKHAM, David Christopher. b 17. Clifton Th Coll 67. **d** 69 **p** 70 Chich. C of H Trin Eastbourne 69-74; R of Elmswell 74-77; P-in-c of Danehill Dio Chich from 77. *Danehill Vicarage, Haywards Heath, W Sussex, RH17 7ER.* (Danehill 790269)

MARKHAM, Deryck O'Leary. b 28. Oak Hill Th Coll 66. **d** 68 **p** 69 S'wark. C of Purley 68-71; V of Bicton w E Budleigh Dio Ex from 71. *Vicarage, East Budleigh, Devon.* (Budleigh Salterton 3340)

MARKHAM, Canon Gervase William. b 1910. Trin Coll Cam BA 32, MA 36. Westcott Ho Cam 34. **d** 36 Jarrow for Dur **p** 37 Dur. C of Bp Wearmouth 36-39; Dom Chap to Bp of Dur and L to Offic Dio Dur 39-40; CF (EC) 40-46; V of St Steph Burnley 46-52; CF (TA) 50-52; CF (TA -R of O) from 52; V of Gt Grimsby 52-65; Surr 52-65; Preb and Can of Nassington in Linc Cathl 56-65; RD of Grimsby and Cleethorpes 62-64; Lowther 65-69; V of Morland w Thrimby and Gt Strickland Dio Carl from 65; Dioc Warden of Readers 69-74; Hon Can of Carl Cathl from 73; Bp's Officer for Stewardship 74-80. *Garden Flat, Morland House, Penrith, Cumb.* (Morland 654)

MARKHAM, John Gabriel. b 06. Linc Coll Ox BA 30, MA 70. Ely Th Coll 30. **d** 31 **p** 32 S'wark. C of St Jo Div Kennington Surrey 31-37; R of St Pet Walworth 37-44; Caister-on-Sea 44-60; Chap Reading and Distr Hosps 60-74. *22 Watlington Road, Benson, Oxon.* (Wallingford 35397)

MARKHAM, Canon John Vaughan. b 1900. Ex Coll Ox BA 22, MA 47. Westcott Ho Cam 39. **d** 40 **p** 41 Win. C of All SS Milford 40-42; C-in-c of All SS Margate 42-44; V 44-57; Chap R Sea Bathing Hosp 45-57; V of Elham 57-72; Hon Can of Cant 70-79; Can (Emer) from 79. *11c The Precincts, Canterbury, CT1 2EH.* (Cant 54693)

MARKHAM, John William. b 12. St Aid Coll 34. **d** 37 **p** 38 Man. C of St Mary Radcliffe 37-41; Hagley 41-44; Heswall Ches 45-51; Margate 51-52; R of Allington w St Nich Maidstone 52-60; V of Teynham 60-75. *16 Oaten Hill Place, Old Dover Road, Canterbury, Kent, CT1 3HJ.* (Canterbury 53988)

MARKLAND, Vincent Hilton. b 33. St D Coll Lamp BA 55. Ripon Hall Ox 67. **d** 68 **p** 69 Man. C of Worsley w Ellenbrook Dio Man from 68. *Brookfield House, Vicar's Hall Lane, Boothstown, Worsley, Manchester M28 4HT.* (061-790 5586)

MARKLE, Harvey. Wycl Coll Tor BA 39. **d** 41 **p** 42 Bran. C of Binscarth 41-42; I of Russell 42-46; Elgin 46-47; in Amer Ch 47-54; I of Stayner 54-60; R of Bolton Tor 60-71; Hon C of Penetanguishene Dio Tor from 78. *225 Russell Street, Midland, Ont., Canada.*

MARKS, Alfred Howard. b 02. Qu Coll Cam (3rd cl Hist Trip pt i) 24, BA 25, MA 29. Ridley Hall Cam 25. **d** 26 **p** 27 Birm. C of Aston-juxta-Birm 26-29; St Matt Surbiton 29-33; H Trin St Marylebone 33-35; V of St Asaph Birm 35-40; CF (EC) 40-45; Hon CF 45; V of Charles Plymouth and C-in-c of St Luke Plymouth 46-48; Surr 46-59; V of Shirley Hants 48-59; St Marg Ipswich 59-70; L to Offic Dio St E 70-80; Dio Lich from 81. *21 Hawthornden Gardens, Uttoxeter, Staffs, ST14 7PB.* (Uttoxeter 2018)

MARKS, Anthony Alfred. b 28. K Coll Lon and Warm AKC 53. **d** 54 **p** 55 Blackb. C of St Pet Fleetwood 54-58; V of St Cuthb Burnley 58-63; Chap RN from 63; Qu Hon Chap from 81. *c/o Ministry of Defence, Lacon House, Theobalds Road, WC1X 8RY.*

MARKS, Anthony Wendt. b 43. G and C Coll Cam 2nd cl Mod and Med Lang Trip pt i 61, BA (2nd cl Mod & Med Lang Trip pt ii) 63, MA 67, 1st cl Th Trip pt ia 64, PhD 70. BNC Ox MA, DPhil 72. St Steph Ho Ox 70. **d** 72 Man **p** 73 Middleton for Man. C of St Crispin Withington 72-75; Chap Univ of Lon 75-80; C of St Geo Hanover Square (in C of Grosvenor Chap) and Warden Liddon Ho Dio Lon from 80. *24 South Audley Street, W1Y 5DL.* (01-499 1684)

MARKS, David Frederick. b 14. Univ of Wales BA (2nd cl

Welsh) 37, 2nd cl Phil 38. Jesus Coll Ox BA (3rd cl Th) 40, MA 45. St Mich Coll Llan 40. **d** 41 **p** 42 St D. C of Llandilo Fawr 41-49; V of Llangathen w Llanfihangel Cilfargen 49-56; Exam Chap to Bp of St D from 50; Hd of Dept of Welsh at St D Coll Lamp from 56; C-in-c of Llancrwys 57-64; Sen Lect at St D Coll Lampeter from 74. *Wyngarth, Bryn Road, Lampeter, Dyfed.* (Lampeter 422474)

MARKS, John Alexander Rishworth. b 19. Trin Coll Dub BA (2nd cl Mod in Ment and Mor Phil) 41, Div Test 43, MA 61. **d** 43 **p** 44 Dub. C of Sandford Dub 43-45; Chap RNVR 45-46; RN 46-69; Perm to Offic Dio St Alb from 77. *1 Linten Close, Hitchin, Herts.*

MARKS, John Newman. KCNS BA 33. **d** 35 **p** 36 Fred. Miss at Westmorland 35-36; New Bandon 36-43; St Jo Bapt St John 43-52; on leave USA 52-56; P-in-c of St Jo Bapt St John Fred 56-72. *Apt 202, 55 Magazine Street, St John, NB, Canada.*

MARKS, Richard Frederick. Trin Coll Dub BA 53, MA 56. **d** 54 **p** 56 Derry. C of St Columb's Cathl Derry 54-57; Ch Ch Londonderry 57-60; Prec St Geo Cathl Capetn 60-67; R of St Cypr Retreat 67-72; Matroosfontein 72-80; St Mark Athlone Dio Capetn from 80. *Rectory, Church Street, Athlone, CP, S Africa.* (65-6550)

MARKS, Ronald Edward. Univ of Melb BA (1st cl Engl) 47, Dipl Educn 48. Worc Coll Ox BLitt 55. ACT ThL 50. **d** 53 Ox for Melb **p** 54 Buckingham for Cant for Melb. C of St Matt Ox 53-54; Min of Dingley 55-58; Gen Sec CMS Vic 58-65; Hon C of Melb Cathl 58-65; Asia Regional Sec CMS Austr 61-65; I of St Jas Glen Iris 65-67; Lect Univ of Queensld and Perm to Offic Dio Brisb from 67. *135 Ninth Avenue, St Lucia, Brisbane, Queensland, Australia 4067.* (370 1270)

MARKWELL, Donald Stanley. b 30. Vic Univ of Wel MA 53. **d** 79 **p** 80 S'wark. Hon C of Kingston Hill Dio S'wark from 79. *37 Queens Road, Kingston-upon-Thames, Surrey, KT2 7SL.* (01-546 0740)

MARLEY, Neville William Arthur. b 24. Em Coll Cam BA 46, MA 51. Ridley Hall Cam 48. **d** 50 **p** 51 Dur. C of Chester-le-Street 50-53; Darlington 53-54; St Mary Bury St E 54-56; V of St Thos Telford Pk Streatham Dio S'wark from 56; CF (TA) 59-64; CF (TA-R of O) 64-67. *39 Telford Avenue, SW2 4XL.* (01-674 4343)

MARLOR, Canon John Charles. Kansas Wesleyan Univ BA 60. St Chad's Coll Regina LTh 63. **d** 63 **p** 64 Calg. C of St Mich AA Calg 63-64; R of Strathmore 64-71; All SS City and Dio Sktn from 70; Dom Chap to Bp of Sktn from 71; Hon Can of Sktn from 80. *313 Taylor Street West, Saskatoon, Sask, Canada.*

MARLOW, Canon Howard Benjamin. b 19. Univ of Leeds BA 42. Coll of Resurr Mirfield 42. **d** 44 **p** 45 Lich. C of St Mary and St Chad Longton Staffs 44-48; St Anthony Montserrat 48-50; P-in-c of St Pet w St John and St Jas Montserrat Antig 50-52; C of St Steph Willenhall 52-53; PC of St Aid Small Heath 53-66; RD of Bordesley 57-66; Hon Can of Birm from 64; Surr from 64; V of Stirchley Dio Birm from 66; M of Gen Syn Birm from 70; Exam Chap to Bp of Birm from 78; Ch Comm from 78. *Stirchley Vicarage, 95 Cartland Road, Birmingham B30 2SD.* (021-458 3082)

MARLOW, Walter Geoffrey. b 29. K Coll Lon and Warm AKC (2nd cl) 57. **d** 57 **p** 58 Derby. C of Long Eaton 57-61; St Francis Mackworth 61-63; R of Stoke Albany w Wilbarston 63-68; V of Calow 68-73; R of Wingerworth 73-82; P-in-c of St Jas w St Phil and of St Pet Isl Dio Lon from 82. *1 Arlington Square, London, N1.* (01-226 4108)

MARLOWE, Keith Morris. b 47. Univ of Tor BA 68. Trin Coll Tor 70. **d** 72 Bp Bothwell for Niag; on leave. *c/o 260 Wilson Street, Ancaster, Ont., Canada.*

MARNHAM, Charles Christopher. b 51. Jes Coll Cam BA 73, MA 77. St Jo Coll Dur 75. **d** 77 Kens for Lon **p** 78 Lon. C of H Trin Brompton Kens and of St Paul's Onslow Sq Kens 77-80; St Barn Linthorpe Middlesbrough Dio York from 81. *23 Linden Grove, Linthorpe, Middlesbrough, Cleve.* (Middlesbrough 815961)

MAROLENG, David Josiah. b 28. **d** 75 **p** 76 Matab. P Dio Matab. *Box 43, Wankie, Zimbabwe-Rhodesia.*

MAROPONG, Canon Augustine Mocumi. St Bede's Coll Umtata 60. **d** 62 **p** 64 Kimb K. P Dio Kimb K from 62; Can of St Cypr Cathl Kimb from 80. *Box 9012, Galeshewe, CP, S Africa.* (41535)

MARPLES, Richard Bruce. b 48. Carleton Univ Ott BA 72. Trin Coll Tor MDiv 75. **d** and **p** 75 Ott. C of St Matthias Ott 75-77; I of Cumberland-Orleans Dio Ott from 77. *1093 Chateau Crescent, Orleans, Ont, Canada.*

MARQUET, John Michael. b 54. Univ of Otago BA 80. St Jo Coll Auckld 80. **d** 80 **p** 81 Dun. C of St John Div Invercargill Dio Dun from 80. *24 Jack Street, Invercargill, NZ.*

MARR, Donald Radley. b 37. St Aid Coll 61. **d** 64 **p** 65 Ches. C of Macclesfield 64-66; Sale 66-67; V of Marthall 67-72; C of West Kirby 72-75; V of Waverton Dio Ches from 76. *Waverton Vicarage, Chester.* (Chester 35581)

MARR, Keith Henderson. Moore Th Coll Syd. **d** and **p** 49 Syd. C of Campsie 49-50; St Mich Woollongong 50-51; CF (Austr) 51-56; R of Dural 56-58; I of Provisional Distr of Bexley N 58-62; Chap Long Bay State Penit from 62; L to Offic Dio Syd 64-77; Actg R of St Matt Botany Dio Syd from 77. *30 Clarence Road, Rockdale, NSW, Australia 2216.* (59-8569)

MARRAY, Santosh Kumar. b 57. Univ of WI Barb BA 81. Codr Coll Barb 77. **d** and **p** 81 Guy. C of All SS Berbice Dio Guy from 81. *11 Main & Trinity Streets, New Amsterdam, Berbice, Guyana.*

MARRETT, Charles Beauchamp. Univ of Syd BA 48, Dipl Educn 49. ACT ThL (1st cl) 61. **d** 60 **p** 61 Armid. C of Glen Innes 60-63; Narribri 63-64; V of Collarenebri 64-68; Bingara 68-72; Walcha Dio Armid from 72. *Vicarage, Walcha, NSW, Australia 2354.* (77-2543)

MARRETT, Hedley Charles Guille. b 09. St Bonif Coll Warm 29. **d** 34 **p** 35 S'wark. C of H Trin Woolwich 34-37; St Phil w St Mark Port Eliz 37-38; P-in-c of Barkly E 38-39; R of Colesberg 39-40; Swellendam 40-45; C of Benoni 45-47; V of St Luke Holbrooks Cov 47-50; St Simon Jersey 50-77; C-in-c of All SS Jersey 67-77. *11 Nicholas Meadow, Metherell, Callington, Cornw.*

MARRETT, Michael. St Pet Coll Ja, 61. **d** 61 **p** 62 Ja. C of Halfway Tree 61-64; R of Falmouth 64-71. *Rectory, Falmouth, Jamaica, W Indies.*

MARRIOTT, Canon David John. b 29. St Chad's Coll Dur BA 54, Dipl Th 56. **d** 56 **p** 57 Ripon. C of St Jas Manston 56-59; Asst Chap Cranleigh Sch 59-63; Hd Master Cathl Choir Sch Cant 64-67; Min Can of Cant Cathl 65-67; V of Wye w Brook Dio Cant from 67; Chap of Wye Coll Univ of Lon from 68; Warden of Readers Dio Cant from 75; Hon Can of Cant Cathl from 79; RD of W Bridge from 81. *Wye Vicarage, Ashford, Kent.* (Wye 450)

MARRIOTT, Frank Lewis. b 29. Lich Th Coll. **d** 60 **p** 61 Cov. C of St Barbara Cov 60-64; V of Tysoe w Compton-Wynyates and Oxhill 64-70; C-in-c of St Marg Cov 70-77; V of Long Itchington w Bascote Dio Cov from 77; R of Ufton Dio Cov from 77. *Long Itchington Vicarage, Rugby, Warws.* (Southam 2518)

MARRIOTT, James Henry. Kelham Th Coll 36. **d** 42 **p** 43 S'wark. C of St Dunstan Bellingham 42-45. St Pet St Helier 45-50; Perm to Offic Dio Ely 50-56; Cl Org Sec C of E Children's S Diocs Ely, Ox, Pet, and St Alb 55-56. *23 Kent Road, Peterborough.*

MARRIOTT, John Eric. b 31. Univ of Sask BA and B Educn 54. Wycl Coll Tor. **d** 58 **p** 59 Hur. C of St Jas Stratford 58-61; St Matt Winnipeg 61-64; V of Whytewold 63-65; St Cuthb Winnipeg 65-67; C of H Trin Winnipeg 67-69; R of St Matt Sktn 73-75; Perm to Offic Dio Edmon from 76. *601-8715 104th Street, Edmonton, Alta, Canada.*

MARRIOTT, Richard Ward. b 38. St Pet Hall Ox BA 62, MA 66. Linc Th Coll 62. **d** 64 **p** 65 Chelmsf. C of Wanstead 64-70; Grantham w Manthorpe 70-72; V of St Geo Barkingside Dio Chelmsf from 72; Hon Chap to Bp of Barking from 75. *St George's Vicarage, Woodford Avenue, Ilford, Essex.* (01-550 4149)

MARRIOTT, Stanley Richard. b 36. K Coll Lon and Warm AKC 60. **d** 61 **p** 62 Birm. C of Coleshill and of Maxstoke 61-64; V of Ansley 64-81. *c/o Ansley Vicarage, Church End, Nuneaton, Warwicks.* (Chapel End 392240)

MARRIOTT, Victor Gillespie. b 1897. Coll of the Resurr Mirfield 19. **d** 22 **p** 23 Mon. C of St Jo Bapt Newport Mon 22-28; C of St Chad Manningham 28-35; C-in-c of St Pet Toftshaw Conv Distr 35-39; V of Rawdon 39-62. *22 Warbeck Hill Road, Blackpool, Lancs, FY2 9SR.* (Blackpool 57429)

MARRIOTT, Wallace Falcon. Moore Th Coll Syd. ACT ThL 52. **d** 54 **p** 55 Nel. C-in-c of Hanmer 54; C of Ch Ch Cathl Nel 55-56; Reefton 56-58; Overseas Miss Fell S Perak 58-62 and 64-65; L to Offic Dio Ch Ch 63-64; C of Spreydon 64-66; Good Shepherd Ch Sing 67-71; V of St Matt Dun 71-80. *270 High Street, Dunedin, NZ.* (Dunedin 78-908)

MARRIOTT, William Ronald Thaw. b 16. Chich Th Coll 46. **d** 48 **p** 49 Derby. C of Long Eaton 48-53; St Kath Bournemouth 53-56; St Pet Acton Green 56-58; V of St Sav w St Gabr and St Steph Poplar 58-68; All SS Clevedon Dio B & W from 68; C-in-c Weston-in-Gordano Dio B & W from 71; Clapton-in-Gordano Dio B & W from 80; Walton-in-Gordano Dio B & W from 81. *All Saints Vicarage, Clevedon, Avon, BS21 6AX.* (Clevedon 873257)

MARRISON, Geoffrey Edward. b 23. Univ of Lon BA (2nd cl Malay) 48, PhD 67. Bps' Coll Cheshunt 49. Kirchliche Hochschule Th Coll Berlin 50. **d** 51 St Alb for Cant for Col Bp **p** 52 Sing. C of Wormley Dio St Alb 51-52; Selangor 52-55; C of St Andr Cathl Sing 55-56; Radlett 56-57; St Botolph Aldgate w H Trin Minories Lon 57-58; V of St Timothy Crookes Sheff 58-61; Linguistics Adviser BFBS 62-67; SPG

Miss Dio Assam 62-64; Perm to Offic Dio Cant 64-69; L to Offic from 69. *85 Warwick Road, Thornton Heath, Surrey, CR4 7NN.* (01-684 2806)

MARRO BAI, Samuel. d 66 **p** 67 Sier L. P Dio Sier L. *Box 2, Makeni, Sierra Leone,* (Makeni 437)

MARROW, David Edward Armfield. b 42. Univ of Nottm BA (2nd cl Th) 65. Tyndale Hall, Bris 65. **d** 67 **p** 68 Bris. C of Ch Ch w Em Clifton 67-70; BCMS Ethiopia 70-75; N Area Sec BCMS and Perm to Offic Dios Ches, Blackb, Bradf, Man, Liv, York, Carl and Newc T 75-77; Min of St Jas Ryde Dio Portsm from 77. *77 Argyle Street, Ryde, IW.*

MARROW, Canon Peter. b 13. Magd Coll Cam BA 34, MA 38. BC Coll Bris 37. **d** 37 **p** 38 Lon. C of St Paul Portman Sq 37-39; Chap RAFVR 39-46; V of Ch Ch Surbiton Hill 46-53; R of Broadwater 53-78; Can and Preb of Chich Cathl from 77. *Easter Cottage, Aldwick Street, Bognor Regis, W Sussex, PO21 3AW.* (Bognor Regis 821800)

MARRS, Robert Stuart Patrick. b 11. Univ of NZ BA 47. Univ of Lon LLB 53. St George's Windsor, 56. **d** 56 **p** 57 Roch. C of St John Bexley 56-59; V of Binsted Hants 59-65; R of Boyup Brook 65-68; P-in-c of Pinjarra 68-69; R 69-73; C of Headington 73-74; R of Bulmer w Welburn and Castle Howard Dio York from 74. *Bulmer Rectory, York, YO6 7BW.* (Whitwell-on-the-Hill 400)

MARSDEN, Andrew Robert. b 49. AKC 71. St Aug Coll Cant 71. **d** 72 **p** 73 Cant. C of New Addington 72-75; Prudhoe 75-77; Asst Chap HM Pris Wakef 77-78; Chap HM Borstal Portland 78-82; Onley from 82. *c/o Onley Prison, Rugby, Warws.*

MARSDEN, George Henry. b 28. Em Coll Sask LTh 51. Trin Coll Dub BA 57, MA 60. **d** 51 **p** 52 Sask. I of Fort Pitt 51-52; Arborfield w Carrot River 52-54; Rosthern w Duck Lake 54-55; C of Cavan U 55-58; Faversham 58-61; R of Willingale w Shellow and Berners Roding Dio Chelmsf from 61. *Willingale Rectory, Ongar, Essex.* (0277-86272)

MARSDEN, John Joseph. b 53. Univ of York BA 74. Univ of Nottm Dipl Th 78, MTh 81. St Jo Coll Nottm 77. **d** 80 **p** 81 Man. C of St Mary Leigh Dio Man from 80. *34 Grasmere Street, Leigh, S Lancs.*

MARSDEN, John Robert. b 22. Late Scho of Linc Coll Ox BA 48, MA 49. Ripon Hall Ox 57. **d** 58 **p** 59 Dur. C of St Cuthb Dur 58-61; Chap Dur Sch from 61; L to Offic Dio Dur from 64. *1 Pimlico, Durham.*

MARSDEN, Maori. NZ Bd of Th Stud LTh (2nd cl) 57. St Jo Coll Auckld. **d** 57 **p** 58 Waik. C of St Geo Frankton 57-59; Miss P Taranaki Maori Past 60-63; CF (NZ) 63-71; L to Offic Dio Auckld 63-70; Perm to Offic Dio Waik 63-70; Hon C of H Trin Devonport 71-74; Perm to Offic Dio Auckld 74-76; Hon C of H Trin Devonport Dio Auckld from 76. *Box 65, Te Kopuru, Northland, NZ.*

MARSDEN, Robert Edward. b 13. G and C Coll Cam BA 35, MA 53. Lon Coll of Div 35. **d** 37 **p** 38 Truro. C of Camborne 37-40; Falmouth 40-44; Org Sec CMS Dios Nor and Ely and LPr Nor 44-49; V of Pendeen 49-76; RD of Penwith 62-64; Perm to Offic Dio Truro from 76. *Ty-an-Radjel, North Carnmarth, Redruth, Cornw.* (Redruth 213871)

MARSDEN, Preb Robert William. b 24. Trin Coll Dub BA 49, MA 52, Div Test 50. **d** 50 **p** 51 Dub. C of St Jas Dub 50-54; Asst Chap Miss to Seamen Dub 54-58; R of Drum w Currin 58-66; I of Clones Dio Clogh from 66; I of Killeevan Dio Clogh from 66; Chap to Bp of Clogh 73-80; Preb of Clogh Cathl from 78. *Rectory, Killeevan, Co Monaghan, Irish Republic.* (Newbliss 52)

MARSDEN, Samuel Edward. b 44. Keble Coll Ox BA (2nd cl Th) 66. Linc Th Coll 66. **d** 68 **p** 69 Truro. C of Liskeard w St Keyne 68-72; R of St Gerrans w St Anthony-in-Roseland 72-77; V of Ch Ch Kowloon 77-81; P-in-c of Ingrave w Gt Warley and Childerditch Dio Chelmsf from 81. *Rectory, Great Warley, Essex.* (Brentwood 777)

MARSDEN, Canon Taki Wairua. b 26. St Jo Coll Auckld 70. **d** 71 Auckld **p** 72 Aotearoa for Auckld. Missr Maori Miss Dio Auckld 71-75; Dio Wel 75-81; Hon Can of Wel from 78; Team V of Mangere Dio Auckld from 81. *35 Cape Road, Mangere, NZ.*

MARSDEN, Thomas Arthur Stephen. b 1899. Chich Th Coll 27. **d** 30 **p** 31 Glouc. C of All SS Cheltm 30-32; Littlehampton 32-37; All SS Maidenhead (in c of St Paul) 37-44; V of E w W Challow 44-55; Thorpe St Mary 55-69; Chap Commun of H Name Malvern Link 69-73; L to Offic Dio Worc 70-73. *College of St Barnabas, Lingfield, Surrey, RH7 6NJ.*

MARSDEN-JONES, Watkin David. b 22. St D Coll Lamp BA 48. **d** 49 St A **p** 50 Ban for St A. C of Flint 49-54; Forest Row (in c of Ashurst Wood) 54-56; V of Copthorne 56-70; RD of E Grinstead 66-70; V of Bosham Dio Chich from 70. *Bosham Vicarage, Chichester, Sussex.* (Bosham 573228)

MARSH, Anthony David. b 29. Roch Th Coll 64. **d** 66 **p** 67 Truro. C of Liskeard 66-69; R of Wrentham w Benacre and Covehithe (w Frostenden and South Cove from 75) 69-80; P-in-c of Beyton w Hessett Dio St E from 80. *Beyton Rectory, Bury St Edmunds, Suff, IP30 9AL.* (Beyton 70318)

MARSH, Barry Graham. Moore Th Coll ACT ThL 57. **d** 58 Syd **p** 58 Bp Hilliard for Syd. C of W Manly 58-59; Chap at Norfolk I 59-61; C-in-c of Padstow w Revesby 61-65; R of Harris Pk and Rosehill 65-70; Narellan Dio Syd from 70. *Rectory, Cobbitty Road, Cobbitty, NSW, Australia 2570.* (046-51 2226)

MARSH, Ven Bazil Roland. b 21. Univ of Leeds, BA (2nd cl Hist) 42. Coll of Resurr Mirfield, 42. **d** 44 Bp Heywood for St Alb **p** 45 St Alb. C of Cheshunt 44-46; St Jo Bapt Cov 46-47; St Giles Reading 47-50; R of St Pet Townsville Queensld 51-56; V of St Mary Virg [f St Mary Far Cotton) Northn 56-64; R of St Pet Northn Dio Pet from 64; Archd of Northn from 64; Can of Pet from 64; Exam Chap to Bp of Pet from 64. *11 The Drive, Northampton, NN1 4RZ.* (Northampton 714015)

MARSH, David. b 32. St Jo Coll Dur BA (2nd cl Th) 54, Dipl Th 57. **d** 57 **p** 58 Lich. C of Bilston 57-62; L to Offic Dio Maseno 63-66; Chap Scargill Ho Kettlewell 67-69; Exam Chap to Bp of Maseno S 70-72; Archd of Maseno S 70-72; Commiss from 72; V of Meole Brace (w Sutton from 74) 72-77; St Andr Westlands Dio Lich from 77. *50 Kingsway West, Newcastle, Staffs, ST5 3PU.* (Newcastle 619594)

MARSH, Denis Wilton. b 08. AKC 31. M SSF 39. **d** 32 Ely **p** 33 Bp Price for Ely. C of All SS St Ives Hunts 32-36; LPr Dio Sarum 38-39; Chap St Francis Ho Cam 39-48; V of St Benedict Cam 46-48; Perm to Offic Dio Sarum from 48; Publ Pr 50-51; C-in-c of Compton Abbas West w Wynford Eagle and Toller Fratrum 51-56; Fr Guardian SSF 56-59; L to Offic Dio Newc T from 75. *The Friary of St Francis, Alnmouth, Alnwick, Northumb, NE66 3NJ.* (Alnmouth 213)

MARSH, Edward Frank. Dalhousie Univ NS BCom 56. Mem Univ Newfld BA 60. Qu Coll Newfld LTh 61, BD 69. **d** 59 **p** 60 Newfld. C of Corner Brook 59-63; I of Harbour Breton 63-69; C of Wickford 69-71; I of Indian Bay 71-73; C of St Jo Bapt Cathl, St John's 73-77; R of Cartwright Dio E Newfld from 77. *Cartwright, Labrador, Canada.* (709-224)

MARSH, Eric Arthur. St Aug Coll Cant. **d** 32 **p** 34 Lon. C of St Matt Willesden 32-34; All H Bromley-by-Bow 34-35; St Andr (in c of St Anne) Wigan 35-40; C-in-c of St Anne Conv Distr Wigan 40-44; CF (EC) 40-46; V of Over 46-53; C of St Phil Maidstone 54-56; V of Sheldwich Dio Cant from 56; R of Badlesmere W Leaveland Dio Cant from 56. *Sheldwich Vicarage, Faversham, Kent.* (Faversham 2782)

MARSH, Canon Ernest. b 1891. Keble Coll Ox BA (3rd cl Mod Hist) 13, MA 17. Leeds Cl Sch 13. **d** 14 **p** 15 Wakef. C of Wyke Bradford 14-17; Dewsbury 19-23; V of Ferry-Fryston 23-38; St Lawr w St Nich and New Fulford York 38-50; Mkt Weighton 50-61; Jt Sec York Dioc Conf 41-50; R of Goodmanham 51-61; Can and Preb of York Minster 47-76; Can (Emer) from 76; RD of City of York 48-50; Weighton 53-61; Surr 50-61. *62 Stockton Lane, York.* (York 54429)

MARSH, Ernest Henry. b 07. Lich Th Coll 56. **d** 57 **p** 58 Lich. C of Blurton 57-61; V of Gt Wyrley 61-70; P-in-c of Dilhorne 70-77. *40 Eccles Close, Hope, nr Sheffield, S30 2RG.*

MARSH, Francis John. b 47. Univ of York BA 69, DPhil 76. Oak Hill Coll 72. **d** 75 Huntingdon for Ely **p** 76 Ely. C of St Matt Cam 75-79; Pitsmoor w Wicker 79-81; St Thos Crookes City and Dio Sheff from 81. *79 Glebe Road, Sheffield, S10 1FB.* (0742-683463)

MARSH, Geoffrey John. b 38. K Coll Lon and Warm BD and AKC 60. **d** 61 **p** 62 Lon. C of St Pet and St Paul Teddington 61-63; Brierley Hill 63-66; Asst Master borough Green Sch 67-69; P-in-c of Bracknell 69-73; Speen 73-74; Stockcross 73-74; R of Boxford w Speen and Stockcross 74-80; PV of Truro Cathl and Chap Truro Cathl Sch from 80. *Cathedral School, Kenwyn, Truro, TR1 3DU.*

MARSH, Harry Carter. b 14. Chich Th Coll 48. **d** 49 **p** 50 Win. C of Ch Ch Portswood Southampton 49-51; St Thos w St Clem and St Mich w St Swith Win 51-52; V of St Columba Corby 52-60; Sholing 60-71; R of Michelmersh w Eldon and Timsbury (and Mottisfont from 74) 71-79. *Rose Croft, Manor Road, Hayling Island, Hants.* (H Island 3526)

✠ **MARSH, Right Rev Henry Hooper.** Wycl Coll Tor BA 21, MA 25. **d** 24 **p** 25 Tor. C of St Anne Tor 24-25; St Paul Tor 25-30; P-in-c of St Timothy Tor 30-36; R 36-62; Can of Tor 56-62; Cons Ld Bp of Yukon in Ch Ch Cathl Vic BC 25 March 62 by Abp of BC; Bps of New Westmr; Tor; Carib; Caled; and Koot; and Bp Sovereign; res 67. *Hedgerows, RR 3, Cobourg, Ont, Canada.*

MARSH, Ivor Frank. b 44. Chich Th Coll 74. **d** 76 **p** 77 Ex. C of Plymstock 76-79; P-in-c of St Aubyn Devonport Dio Ex 79-80; V from 80; Asst Chap HM Dkyard Devonport 79-80;

Team V of Sampford Peverell Dio Ex from 81. *Vicarage, Holcombe Regis, Wellington Somerset, Devon, TA21 0PA.* (Greenham 62243)

MARSH, Jack Edmund Bruce. b 08. Em Coll Cam 3rd cl Cl Trip pt i 29, BA (2nd cl Engl Trip pt i) 30, MA 34. **d** 73 **p** 74 Bris (APM). C of Yatton Keynell, Castle Combe and Biddestone w Slaughterford Dio Bris from 73. *Chaise House, Yatton Keynell, Chippenham, Wilts, SN14 7BA.* (Castle Combe 782365)

MARSH, Jeffrey Owen. b 53. Univ of Otago BTh 77. St Jo Coll Auckld 77. **d** 77 **p** 78 Dun. C of St Jo Invercargill 77-80; Wakatipu Dio Dun from 80. *1 Earl Street, Queenstown, NZ.* (330)

MARSH, John William. b 55. Univ of W Ont Lon BA 77. Hur Coll Lon Ont MDiv 80. **d** 80 Hur **p** 81 Bp Robinson for Hur. C of St Steph Lon Dio Hur from 80. *955 Wonderland Road, Apt 202, London, Ont, Canada, N6K 2H8.*

MARSH, Lawrence Allan. b 36. Sarum Th Coll 66. **d** 67 **p** 68 Portsm. C of Waterlooville 67-69; V of Shedfield 69-75; R of Fen Ditton Dio Ely from 76. *Rectory, High Street, Fen Ditton, Cambridge, CB5 8ST.* (Teversham 3257)

MARSH, Leonard Stuart Alexander. b 55. Univ of Hull BA 77. Linc Th Coll 74. **d** 79 S'wark. **d** 79 **p** 80 S'wark. C of St Barn Well Hall Eltham 79-81; Camberwell Dio S'wark from 81. *Flat C, St Giles Centre, Camberwell Church Street, SE5.* (01-708 1506)

MARSH, Margaret Anne. b 45. Univ of Auckld MA 66. Univ of Lon MPhil 70. **d** 78 **p** 79 Auckld. Hon C of St Aid Remuera 78-81; Asst in Dept of Chr Educn Dio Auckld from 81. *22 Sonia Avenue, Remuera, Auckland 5, NZ.*

MARSH, Peter Derek. b 29. Em Coll Sktn. **d** 59 **p** 60 Bran. I of Shoal Lake 59; R 60-62; C-in-c of St Frideswide's Didcot 62-64; L to Offic Dio Lon 64-71; V of St Mary Priory Road Hampstead 71-82. *St Paul's Church House, Cavendish Road, N4 1RT.* (01-340 9423)

MARSH, Robert John. b 20. Univ of Lon BA 49. Oak Hill Th Coll. **d** 50 **p** 51 Derby. C of St Chad Derby 50-53; Chap at Arusha Tang 53-57; V of St Geo Tufnell Pk 58-67; Newburn w Throckley 67-73; St Mark Siddal, Halifax 73-77; Rashcliffe Dio Wakef from 77. *37 Woodside Road, Beaumont Park, Huddersfield, W Yorks, HD4 5JJ.* (Huddersfield 653258)

MARSH, Roger Philip. b 44. AKC and BD 72. St Aug Coll Cant 73. **d** 73 St Alb **p** 74 Bedford for St Alb. C of St Luke Leagrave 73-76; Asst Youth Officer Dio St Alb 76-77; Resources Officer Dio St Alb 77-80; Chap Marlborough Coll from 80. *Marlborough Collrge, Marlborough, Wilts.*

MARSH, Ronald Clifford. Lich Th Coll. **d** 58 **p** 60 Bradf. C of Ch Ch Skipton 58-61. *Cunliffe House, Esholt, Shipley, Yorks.*

MARSH, Ronald James. St Francis Coll Brisb 74. **d** 76 **p** 77 Brisb. C of St Matt Sherwood Brisb 76-77; St Andr Lutwyche Brisb 77-79; V of St Martin Tara Dio Brisb from 79. *PO Box 27, Tara, Queensland, Australia 4421.* (Tara 233)

MARSH, William Gordon George. b 36. **d** 78 **p** 79 Waik. Hon C of St Andr Inglewood Dio Waik 78-81; V from 81. *Box 119, Inglewood, Taranaki, NZ.* (655)

MARSHALL, Canon Alexander Neil. St Francis Coll Brisb 59. **d** 61 Brisb for N Queensld **p** 62 N Queensld. C of Cairns 61-63; St Matt Townsville 63-65; Ayr N Queensld 65-69; R of Bowen 69-81; Edge Hill Dio N Queensld from 81; Hon Can of N Queensld from 76. *Box 1067, Cairns, Queensland, Australia.*

MARSHALL, Arthur. b 25. Oak Hill Th Coll 66. **d** 68 Southw **p** 69 Sherwood for Southw. C of St Jo Evang Worksop 68-71; R of Trowell 72-78; Abbas and Templecombe w Horsington 78-80; V of St Mark Newtown Pemberton Dio Liv from 80. *St Mark's Vicarage, Newtown, Wigan, Lancs, WN5 9BN.* (Wigan 43611)

MARSHALL, Arthur Gordon. Ridley Coll Melb ACT ThL 64. **d** 65 **p** 66 Melb. C of Niddrie 65-67; St Phil W Heidelberg 67-69; Dept of Evang & Ex Dio Melb 69-74; C-in-c of St Laur Doveton Dio Melb 69-74. *102 Power Road, Doveton, Vic 3177, Australia.*

MARSHALL, Basil Eustace Edwin. b 21. OBE 69. Westcott Ho Cam 71. **d** 73 **p** 74 Roch. C of Edenbridge 73-78; P-in-c of Lamberhurst Dio Roch from 78; Matfield Dio Roch from 78. *Lamberhurst Vicarage, Tunbridge Wells, Kent, TN3 8EL.* (Lamberhurst 890324)

MARSHALL, Bernard Godfrey Graham. b 35. Univ of Birm BA (2nd cl Th) 56, Dipl Th 59. Qu Coll Birm 58. **d** 60 Bp Stuart for Worc **p** 61 Worc. C of Gt and L Hampton 60-64; C-in-c of St Richard's Conv Distr Fairfield Evesham 64-65; Chap RN from 65. *c/o Ministry of Defence, Lacon House, Theobalds Road, WC1X 8RY.*

MARSHALL, Bryan John. b 40. Chich Th Coll 63. **d** 65 Burnley for Blackb **p** 66 Blackb. C of Poulton-le-Fylde 65-68; H Trin S Shore Blackpool 68-70; V of Wesham 70-74; PV of Chich Cathl 74-82; V of Boxgrove Dio Chich from 82; R of Tangmere Dio Chich from 82. *Vicarage, Church Lane, Boxgrove, Chichester, PO18 0ED.*

MARSHALL, Cecil Thomas. Univ of NZ BA 54. Coll Ho Ch Ch. **d** 54 **p** 55 Wel. C of Feilding 54-55; V of Par Distr of Wanganui 55-59; Kiwitea 59-64; Eltham 64-71; Chap Lower Hutt Hosp Dio Wel 69-75; Dir Chr Ministries and Hon C of Tawa-Linden 75-81; V of St Matt Palmerston N Dio Wel from 81. *109 College Street, Palmerston North, NZ.* (81-639)

MARSHALL, Christopher John Bickford. b 32. TD 78. K Coll Lon and Warm AKC 56. **d** 57 Guildf **p** 58 Kingston T for Guildf. C of Leatherhead 57-60; Crewkerne 60-63; V of Long Sutton (w Long Load from 72) 63-76; Wiveliscombe Dio B & W from 76; RD of Tone from 78. *Wiveliscombe Vicarage, Taunton, Somt.* (Wiveliscombe 23309)

MARSHALL, Christopher Robert. b 49. St Chad's Coll Dur BA 71. Sarum Wells Th Coll 72. **d** 74 **p** 75 Sheff. C of St Cecilia Parson Cross 74-77; St Gabr Fullbrook Walsall Dio Lich 77-78; U Gornal 78-80; V of St Andr Walsall Dio Lich from 80. *St Andrew's Vicarage, Birchills Street, Walsall, W Midl.* (Walsall 26844)

MARSHALL, David Charles. b 52. St Chad's Coll Dur BA 73. Trin Coll Bris 74. **d** 76 **p** 77 Lich. C of Meole-Brace 76-78; W Teignmouth w Kingway 78-80; Broadwater Dio Chich from 80. *St Stephens House, 80 Dominion Road, Worthing, BN14 8JJ.* (Worthing 30759)

MARSHALL, David Edward Francis. b 04. Lon Coll of Div 25. **d** 29 Guildf **p** 30 Lon for Guildf. C of St Sav Guildf 29-32; St Anne Tollington Pk 32-35; St Steph Clapham Pk 35-38; V of Loudwater 38-49; R of Farmborough 49-72. *Brunel, Woodview, Chilcompton, Bath, Somt.*

MARSHALL, Douglas Edwin. St Jo Coll Morpeth. **d** 58 Bp McKie for Bend **p** 59 Bend. C-in-c of Raywood 58-60; V of Birregurra 60-62; Perm to Offic Dio Melb 62-63; C of St Thos Ex 63-65; Headington Quarry Ox 65-66; CF 66-70; Min of Bellarine Par Distr 70-72; I of Burnley Dio Melb from 73. *290 Burnley Street, Burnley, Vic, Australia 3121.* (03-42 3284)

MARSHALL, Frank Bert Hamilton Harcourt. Codr Coll Barb 66. **d** 69 **p** 70 Barb. C of St Pet Barb 69-71; C of Ch Ch Barb 71-75; R of St Steph I and Dio Barb from 75. *St Stephen's Rectory, St Michael, Barbados, W Indies.*

MARSHALL, Frederick William. Dorch Miss Coll 27. **d** 30 **p** 31 Lon. C of St Cath Coleman Hammersmith 30-31; St Frideswide Poplar 31-36; St Mary Virg Tyndall's Pk Bris 36-38; St Alb Teddington 38-39; V of Goldthorpe 39-45; Poundstock 45-55; St Jas Southn 55-65; St Cury w St Gunwalloe 65-74; Perm to Offic Dio Truro from 74. *St Coventin Cottage, Borython Manor, Helston, Cornw.*

MARSHALL, Geoffrey Edward. b 31. Univ of Birm BA (2nd cl Gen) 52. Chich Th Coll 54. **d** 56 **p** 57 Pet. C of St Columba Corby 56-59; Abington 59-61; Min of St Steph Eccles Distr Rednal 61-70; C of Stevenage 70-71; V of Chells Stevenage 71-78; R of Walkern Dio St Alb from 78; RD of Stevenage from 78. *Rectory, Walkern, Stevenage, Herts.* (Walkern 322)

MARSHALL, Geoffrey Osborne. b 48. St Jo Coll Dur BA (Th) 71. Coll of Resurr Mirfield 71. **d** 73 **p** 74 St Alb. C of Waltham Cross 73-76; Digswell 76-78; P-in-c of Ch Ch Belper and Milford Dio Derby from 78. *Christ Church Vicarage, Belper, Derby.* (Belper 2193)

MARSHALL, George Sherwin. b 14. Univ of Leeds, BA 35. Qu Coll Birm 35. **d** 37 **p** 38 Southw. C of Warsop w Sookholm 37-41; St Mary Magd Newark-on-Trent 41-42; CF (EC) 42-45; CF 45-70; DACG BAOR 66-68; E Midl Distr 68-70; V of Norton Cuckney w Holbeck 70-79; Chap Welbeck Coll 70-79. *47 David's Drive, Wingerworth, Chesterfield, Derbys.*

MARSHALL, Godfrey Hibbert. b 05. CCC Cam BA 30, MA 37. Wells Th Coll 30. **d** 31 **p** 32 Newc T. C of St Geo Cullercoats 31-37; V of St Ignatius Hendon 37-58; Chap Radley Coll 58-65; V of Hayton w Talkin 65-73; L to Offic Dio Carl from 73. *Rookcroft, Johnby, Greystoke, Penrith, Cumb.*

MARSHALL, Graham George. b 38. Univ of Dur BA (2nd cl Mus) 60, Dipl Th 65. St Chad's Coll Dur 63. **d** 65 Blackb **p** 66 Lanc for Blackb. C of St Mich AA Ashton-on-Ribble 65-67; Lanc 67-71; R of Ch Eaton and C-in-c of Bradeley 71-75; Prec of Man Cathl 75-78; R of Reddish Dio Man from 78. *Rectory, St Elisabeth's Way, Reddish, Stockport, SK5 6BL.* (061-432 3033)

MARSHALL, Harold. ACT ThL 31, Th Scho 48. **d** 32 Newc **p** 33 Bath for Goulb. C of Canberra 32; Chap Canberra Gr Sch 33-34; C of Cardiff 34-35; Mayfield 35-37; Bellbird 37-40; Prec of Goulb Cathl 40-41; C and Prec of Ch Ch Cathl Newc 41-47; R of Mayfield 47-64; Can of Newc 58-78; R of E Maitland 64-78; Perm to Offic Dio Newc from 78. *199 Fishing Point Road, Rathmines, NSW, Australia 2283.*

MARSHALL, Harold Cecil. b 1894. TCD 16. **d** 18 **p** 19 Down. C of Derriaghy 18-25; Lambeg 25-29; I of Carrowdore

29-57; RD of Bangor 38-47; Preb of Down Cathl 53-55; Treas 55-59; Chan 59-64; I of Saul w Inch 57-64; P-in-c of Culfeightrin 64-69. *12 King's Road, Knock, Belfast, BT5 6JJ, N Ireland.* (Belfast 655587)

MARSHALL, Hugh Phillips. b 34. SS Coll Cam BA 57, MA 61. Linc Th Coll 57. **d** 59 **p** 60 Lon. C of St Steph w St John Westmr 59-65; V of Tupsley 65-74; Wimbledon Dio S'wark 74-78; R of Wimbledon Team Min from 78; Surr from 78; RD of Merton from 80. *Wimbledon Vicarage, Arthur Road, SW19 7DZ.* (01-946 2830)

MARSHALL, Ian James. b 51. St Mich Ho Crafers 72. **d** 78 **p** 79 Tas. C of Burnie 78-80; P-in-c of St Helens Dio Tas from 80. *Rectory, St Helens, Tasmania 7216.* (003 76 1144)

MARSHALL, Jack Edward. b 12. St Cath Coll Cam 2nd cl Th Trip pt 1, Sect A, 36, BA (2nd cl Th Trip pt i, Sect B) 37, MA 43. Wycl Hall Ox 37. **d** 38 **p** 39 Birm. C of St Mary Handsworth 38-40; Chapel-en-le-Frith (in c of Dove Holes) 40-43; St Jo Evang Penge 43-44; V of St Mary of Bethany Woking 45-53; R of St Pancras (w St John from 55) Chich 53-62; Chap St Richard's Hosp Chich 54-62; V of H Trin w St Matt Worthing 62-74; Stoke-sub-Hamdon 74-78; Perm to Offic Dio B & W from 79. *55 Linkhay, South Chard, Somt, TA20 2QS.*

MARSHALL, John. b 37. Kelham Th Coll. **d** 62 **p** 63 Derby. C of Winshill 62-64; S Chaddesden 64-65; V of Swinderby 65-77; Chap HM Borstal Morton Hall 65-77; R of Church Aston Dio Lich from 77. *Rectory, Wallshead Way, Church Aston, Newport, Salop TF10 9JG.* (Newport 810942)

MARSHALL, John Dixon. b 17. Edin Th Coll 40. Univ of Dur LTh 43. **d** 43 **p** 44 Edin. C of Old St Paul Edin 43-47; CF (EC) 47-52; Perm to Offic Dio Momb 47-53; Prec and Min Can of Ripon Cathl 53-54; R of St Olaf Kirkwall 54-59; St Pet Galashiels 59-65; St Andr Fortrose w St Regulus Cromarty 65-74; St Jo Evang Baillieston w St Serf Shettleston 74-82. *c/o Rectory, Swinton Road, Baillieston, Glasgow, G69 6DS.* (041-771 3000)

MARSHALL, John Douglas. b 23. Univ of Wales (Cardiff) BA 43. **d** 78 **p** 79 St Alb. C of Radlett Dio St Alb from 79. *12 Gills Hill, Radlett, Herts, WD7 8BZ.* (Radlett 7203)

MARSHALL, John Linton. b 42. Late Exhib of Worc Coll Ox BA 64, MA 68. Univ of Bris MLitt 75. Wells Th Coll 66. **d** 68 **p** 69 Bris. C of St Mary Virg Redcliffe w Temple and St Jo Bapt Bedminster 68-71; Tutor Sarum and Wells Th Coll 71-73; Asst Master Rutland Sixth Form Coll 74-76; Perm to Offic Dio Pet 74-77; Perm to Offic Dio Southw 76-77; Publ Pr 77-81; Asst Master Southw Minster Sch 77-81; Hon V Cho Southw Minster 79-81; R of Ordsall Dio Southw from 81. *Ordsall Rectory, Retford, Notts, DN22 7TP.* (Retford 702515)

MARSHALL, John William. b 24. St Andr Dioc Ordin Course 71. **d** 73 **p** 74 St Andr. C of Dunfermline Dio St Andr from 73. *16 Cromwell Road, Rosyth, Dunfermline, Fife.*

MARSHALL, Maurice Peter. b 23. Oak Hill Th Coll 59. **d** 61 **p** 62 Liv. C of St Mark Haydock 61-64; V of New Ferry 64-79; Hartford Dio Ches from 79. *Hartford Vicarage, Northwich, Chesh, CW8 1QQ.* (0606-74539)

✠ **MARSHALL, Right Rev Michael Eric.** b 36. Late Tancred Stud of Ch Coll Cam 2nd cl Hist Trip pt i 57, BA (2nd cl Th Trip pt ia) 58, MA 62. Cudd Coll 58. **d** 60 **p** 61 Birm. C of St Pet Birm 60-62; Tutor Ely Th Coll and Hon Min Can of Ely Cathl 62-64; Chap Univ of Lon 64-69; V of All SS Margaret Street St Marylebone 69-75; M Gen Syn Lon 70-75; Exam Chap to Bp of Lon 74-75; Commiss Johann from 75; Cons Ld Bp Suffr of Woolwich in Westmr Abbey 23 Sep 75 by Abp of Cant; Bps of Lon, S'wark, Derby, St Alb, Nor, Chich, Heref, Guildf, Ely and S & M; Bps Suffr of Willesden, Stepney, Kingston, Southn, Ramsbury, Aston, Basingstoke, Reading, Buckingham, Grantham and Tunbridge; and others. *4 College Gardens, SE21 7BE.* (01-693 2726)

MARSHALL, Peter. BD (Lon) 74. Moore Th Coll Syd ACT ThL 74. **d** and **p** 75 Syd. C of St Matt Manly 75-76; Perm to Offic Dio Syd 77-81. *c/o Church House, 417 Ann Street, Brisbane, Australia.*

MARSHALL, Peter Arthur. b 31. K Coll Lon and Warm AKC 58. **d** 59 **p** 60 Chelmsf. C of Hutton 59-61; Rickmansworth 61-66; R of Lexden Dio Chelmsf from 66. *1 Glen Avenue, Colchester, Essex, CO3 3RP.* (Colchester 78160)

MARSHALL, Peter James. b 48. Qu Coll Birm 78. **d** 80 Liv **p** 81 Warrington for Liv. C of Ormskirk Dio Liv from 80. *16 Jubilee Avenue, Ormskirk, Lancs, L39.*

MARSHALL, Canon Peter Jerome. b 40. McGill Univ Montr 58. Westcott Ho Cam 61. **d** 63 **p** 64 Chelmsf. C of E Ham 63-66; Woodford 66-70; V of St Pet Walthamstow 70-81; Commiss Venez 73-76; Dep Dir of Training Dio Chelmsf from 80; Can Res of Chelmsf Cathl from 81. *1 Harlings Grove, Waterloo Lane, Chelmsford, Essex.*

MARSHALL, Peter John. b 33. K Coll Lon 56. Codr Coll Barb 57. **d** 61 Barb for Trinid **p** 62 Trinid. C of H Trin Cathl Port of Spain 61-64; Chap Miss to Seamen Sing 64-67; CF from 67. *c/o Ministry of Defence, Lansdowne House, Berkeley Square, W1.*

MARSHALL, Peter John Charles. b 35. Univ of Bris BA 60. Ridley Hall, Cam 60. **d** 62 **p** 63 Chich. C of Lindfield 62-65; Trav Sec Script U from 65; Hon C of St Nich Nottm 65-67; St Andr Cheadle Hulme Dio Ches from 67. *1 Dennison Road, Cheadle Hulme, Chesh, SK8 6LW.* (061-485 1342)

MARSHALL, Robert Arthur. ACT ThL 34. **d** 36 **p** 37 Armid. C of Moree 36-39; P-in-c of Collarenebri 39-42 and 46-60; Chap AIF 41-46; Exam Chap to Bp of Armid 52-60; V of Narrabri 60-71; Can of Armid 66-71; Perm to Offic Dio Newc from 72. *43 Orange Parade, Wyoming, NSW, Australia 2251.*

MARSHALL, Rodney Henry. b 46. St Steph Ho Ox 72. **d** 75 **p** 76 Man. C of Our Lady of Mercy & St Thos of Cant Gorton 75-78; St Thos Bedford Leigh Dio Man from 78. *c/o Bedford Vicarage, Leigh, Lancs.*

MARSHALL, Timothy James. b 26. BNC Ox BA 48, BCL 49, MA 53. St Steph Ho Ox Dipl Th 51. **d** 52 **p** 53 Derby. [f Barrister] C of Staveley 52-60; PC of Shirebrook Dio Derby 60-68; V from 68. *Shirebrook Vicarage, Mansfield, Notts, NG20 8DN.* (0623-742395)

MARSHALL, Timothy John. b 53. GRSM 74. Oakhill Coll BA 79. **d** 79 Edmon for Lon **p** 80 Lon. C of St Jas Muswell Hill Dio Lon from 79. *67 St James's Lane, Muswell Hill, N10 3QY.* (01-883 7417)

MARSHALL, William Henry. b 06. St Chad's Coll Dur BA 30, MA 46. **d** 31 Ches for Liv **p** 32 Ches. C of St Jo Bapt Toxteth Pk 31; St Paul Crewe 31-33; Asst Missr All SS Miss White Lion Street Pentonville 33-34; Perm to Offic at St Thos Shepherd's Bush 34-39; C of St Mich AA Notting Hill 39-41; R of Bilborough w Strelley 41-47; V of Bole w Saundby 47-52; Chap of St Mary's Conv Rottingdean from 52. *St Mary's Convent, 30 Newlands Road, Rottingdean, Brighton, Sussex, BN2 7GD.*

MARSHALL, William John. b 35. TCD BA 57. Div Test 58. Th Exhib 59. BD 61, PhD 75. **d** 59 **p** 60 Down. C of Ballyholme 59-61; Miss of St Steph Hazaribagh Chota N 61-65; Lect in Hubback Th Coll Chota N 65-72; Asst Dean of Residence TCD 72-76; I of Rathmichael Dio Dub from 76. *Rathmichael Rectory, Shankill, Co Dublin, Irish Republic.*

MARSHALL, William Michael. b 30. Pemb Coll Ox BA 53, MA 57. Univ of Lon Dipl Th 67. Univ of Bris MLitt 72, PhD 79. Sarum Wells Th Coll 79. **d** 80 Taunton for B & W **p** 81 B & W (NSM). C of St Jo Bapt Glastonbury Dio B & W from 80; Asst Chap Millfield Sch from 80. *The Long House, Baltonsborough, Glastonbury, Somerset, BA6 8QP.*

MARSHALL-TAYLOR, Aubrey. b 11. Tyndale Hall Bris 32. Univ of Dur LTh 35. **d** 41 Rang **p** 42 Nagp. [f BCMS Lay Miss] BCMS Miss at Bina 41-43; Amarmow 43-45; Miss at Kyaukpyu Rang 47; C of Wel w Eyton 47-49; R of Pulverbatch 49-55; C-in-c of Smethcote w Woolstaston 53-55; R of Graveley w Chivesfield 55-78. *9 Charsley Close, Little Chalfont, Amersham, Bucks, HP6 6QQ.* (Little Chalfont 3749)

MARSHALL-WOOD, Leon. **d** 50 **p** 51 Bend. C of Raywood 50-52; V of Loddon 52-54; Mooroopna 54-59; I of Noble Pk 59-65; St Mark Fitzroy 65-69; Yarraville 69-73; St Mark Reservoir W Dio Melb from 73. *19 Beatty Street, Reservoir West, Vic, Australia 3073.* (47-1956)

MARSLAND, Duncan Reynolds William. Keble Coll Ox BA 05, MA 09, Leeds Cl Scho 05. **d** 06 **p** 07 Pet. C of St Barn New Humberstone Leic 06-10; Oswestry 10-22; V of St Martin 22-53. *Oaklands, Weston Lane, Oswestry, Salop.*

MARSON, Walter Jeffreys. OBE 56. ACT ThL (1st cl) 29. **d** 29 **p** 30 Brisb. C of St Jas Toowomba 29-34; V of Taringa Brisb 34-37; Chap RN 37-62; V of Palmwoods 62-73; Perm to Offic Dio Brisb from 73. *Whitecross Road, Bli Bli, Queensland, Australia 4560.* (Bli Bli 455 363)

MARSTON, David Howarth. b 48. St Jo Coll Dur BA 69. Episc Th Coll Edin 69. **d** 71 **p** 72 Carl. C of Kendal 71-75; Perm to Offic Dio Glas 75-78; Dio Carl from 78. *217 Rating Lane, Barrow-in-Furness, Cumb.* (Barrow 29023)

MARSTON, James Guy. Bp's Univ Lennox MA 49. **d** and **p** 40 Queb. C of Scotstown w Lake Megantic 40-41; St Pet Sherbrooke 41-42; I of Sandy Beach 42-46; Waterville 46-49; C of Ch Ch Cathl Montr 49-51; Dean of Residence Montr Dioc Th Coll 51-53; R of Danville 53-55; Sherbrooke 55-60; St Matt Queb 60-62; Archd of Queb 60-78; P-in-c of St Pet Limoilou Queb 62-72; R of St Matt Queb 67-72; Thetford Mines 72-78. *Box 29, Carleton Place, Ont, Canada.*

MARTEL, William Angus. b 37. Ch Ch Coll LTh 69. **d** 68 **p** 69 Wel. C of Porirua 68-72; V of H Trin Wainuiomata 72-76; Titahi Bay Dio Wel from 76. *45 Kapiti Crescent, Titahi Bay, NZ.* (8980)

MARTELL, Canon William Rigby. Trin Coll Tor. **d** and **p** 48 NS. R of New Germany 49-54; Wolfville 54-62; Truro NS 62-71; Archd of Northumb (NS) 69-71; Hon Can of NS from

71; Exam Chap to Bp of NS 70-75; R of Cornwallis Dio NS from 71. *RRI, Port Williams, NS, Canada.* (542-5041)

MARTIN, Canon Albert Harold Morris. b 10. Em Coll Cam 3rd cl Hist Trip pt i, 30, BA (3rd cl Th Trip pt i) 32, MA 35. Univ of Lon Dipl in Educn 39. Ridley Hal,l Cam 31. **d** 33 **p** 34 Chelmsf C of St Giles Colchester 33-36; Barking 36-37; CMS Miss at Salara (Sudan) 38-45; V of St Jo Evang Walthamstow 45-48; St Sav Westcliff-on-Sea 48-59; Surr from 51; RD of Canewdon and Southend 57-59; V of St Matt Surbiton 59-71; RD of Kingston 63-71; Hon Can of S'wark from 68; V of Betchworth 71-75. *Salara Cottage, Gill's Bridge, Outwell, Nr Wisbech, Cambs PE14 8TQ.*

MARTIN, Alexander Lewendon. b 26. Em Coll Cam BA (Nat Sc Trip pt i) 47, MA 51. Ridley Hall Cam 56. **d** 57 **p** 58 Guildf. C of Ashtead 57-59; Asst Chap Tonbridge Sch 59-64; LPr Dio roch 59-64; Chap Felsted Sch 64-74; Sedbergh Sch from 74; Publ Pr Dio Chelmsf 64-74; Perm to Offic Dio Bradf from 74. *Holmecroft, Station Road, Sedbergh, Cumb, LA10 5DW.* (Sedbergh 20443)

MARTIN, Anthony Bluett. b 29. St Jo Coll Cam BA 52, MA 56. Ridley Hall Cam 52. **d** 54 **p** 55 Pet. C of St Mary Rushden 54-57; St Geo Worthing 57-59; CSSM and L to Offic Dio Man 59-63; V of All SS Hoole Dio Ches from 63. *Hoole Vicarage, Chester.* (Chester 22056)

MARTIN, Anthony George. b 20. ALCD 42 (LTh from 74). **d** 43 **p** 45 Sarum. C of St Edm Sarum 43-46; H Trin Bradford-on-Avon 46-48; Sherborne w Castleton and Lillington 48-50; Keynsham 50-53; Qu Charlton 50-53; V of Puriton 53-58; Wookey 58-69; R of Ilchester w Northover 69-72; R of Limington 69-72; Axbridge (w Shipham and Rowberrow from 74) 72-80; Perm to Offic Dio B & W from 81. *4 The Rank, Upper Coxley, Wells, Somt, BA5 1QS.* (0749-75739)

MARTIN, Anthony Macdonald. St Francis Coll Brisb 60. **d** 63 Bp Hudson for N Queensld. C of St Jas Cathl Townsville 63-67; Chap All S Sch Charters Towers 67-73; CF (Austr) from 74. *Army Apprentice School, Balcombe, Vic, Australia.*

MARTIN, Canon Ashley Toll. b 09. St Pet Coll Rosettenville. **d** 43 Pret for Zulu **p** 44 Zulu. C of Mtunzini 43-44; R of Gingindhlovu 44-49; Nongoma and Dir of Nongoma Miss 49-54; Bremersdorp and Dir of Bremersdorp Miss 54-55; Mbabane and Dir of Mbabane Miss 55-64; Archd of Swaziland 55-64; Hon Can of Zulu from 63; Commiss Zulu 64-68; Swaz 68-76; R of Lezant 64-69; Lawhitton 64-69; Ladock 69-74; Team V of Probus, Ladock and Grampound w Creed 74-76; L to Offic Dio Truro from 76. *18 Lewman Road, Probus, Truro, TR2 4LL.* (St Austell 882062)

MARTIN, Barry Neil. b 34. Univ of Melb BA 64. La Trobe Univ BEducn 74. Ridley Coll Melb ACT ThL 57. **d** 60 **p** 61 Melb. C of All SS Niddrie 60-62; W Heidelberg 62; St John E Malvern 62-64; Melb Dioc Centre 64-70; P-in-c of St Mary N Melb 64-70; Exam Chap to Abp of Melb 70-74; Perm to Offic Dio Birm 75-76; Dir Inner City Min Melb 77-80; Asst Master Peninsula Sch Frankston from 80. *33 Liddesdale Avenue, Frankston, Vic, Australia 3199.*

MARTIN, David Geoffrey. b 34. K Coll Lon and Warm BD and AKC 60. **d** 61 **p** 62 Liv. C of Our Lady and St Nich Liv 61-63; Chap and Sub-Warden St Geo Coll Perth 63-65; R of Morawa 65-66; Chap and Lect K Coll Lon 66-70; V of St Jo Div Kennington 70-78; Chap of St Gabriel's Coll from 72; Exam Chap to Bp of Kens from 72; C of Ch Ch and St Jo Evang Clapham 78-81. *Address temp unknown.*

MARTIN, David Howard. b 47. AKC 70. Worc Coll Ox BEducn 79. St Aug Coll Cant 70. **d** 71 **p** 72 Lich. C of Sedgley 71-75; P-in-c of All SS Worc and Dioc Youth Chap 75-81; R of Newland, Guarlford and Madresfield Dio Worc from 81. *Madresfield Rectory, Malvern, Worcs, WR13 5AB.* (Malvern 4919)

MARTIN, Derrick Antonio. Univ Th Coll of WI. **d** 71 **p** 72 Ja. C of St Geo Kingston 71-73; Spanish Town Cathl 73-75; R of Black River Dio Ja from 75. *Rectory, Black River, Jamaica, WI.*

MARTIN, Donald Dales. b 30. Sarum Th Coll 53. **d** 55 **p** 56 Bradf. C of Guiseley 55-60; V of Manfield w Cleasby 60-73; Muker w Melbecks 73-78; Laithkirk Dio Ripon from 78; R of Romaldkirk Dio Ripon from 78. *Romaldkirk Rectory, Barnard Castle, Co Durham.* (Teesdale 50202)

MARTIN, Donald Phillip Ralph. b 30. Univ of Tor BA 52, MA 55. M SSM 60. **d** 54 Coadj Bp of Tor **p** 55 Tor. C of St Simon Tor 55-57; Tutor Kelham Th Coll 57-73; Prov of SSM in Engl 72-81; P-in-c of Willen 74-81; in Ch of Japan 81-82. *SSM Priory, Willen, Milton Keynes, Bucks, MK15 9AA.* (Newport Pagnell 611749)

MARTIN, Douglas Arthur. b 27. TD 72. Chich Th Coll 53. **d** 56 **p** 57 S'wark. C of St Steph Battersea 56-58; St Sampson Guernsey 58-59; St Jo Bapt Southend Lewisham 59-61; CF (TA) 60-67; CF (TAVR) 67-75; R of Syresham 61-64; R of Whitfield 61-64; Chap at St Sav (for Deaf and Dumb) Acton Middx 64-68; V of Laverstock 68-75; Acton w Worleston Dio Ches from 75. *St Mary's Vicarage, Chester Road, Acton, Nantwich, Chesh.* (Nantwich 626201)

MARTIN, Edward Eldred William. b 37. SOC 65. **d** 68 **p** 69 S'wark. C of Greenwich 68-71; Kidbrooke 71-75; V of St John (w St Andr from 78) Peckham 75-81; Chap Guy's Hosp from 81. *c/o Guy's Hospital, St Thomas Street SE1.*

MARTIN, Ven Ernest Vincent. KCNS BA 42, LTh w distinc 44. **d** 42 **p** 44 Fred. I of Musquash 44-49; Hampton 49-57; Woodstock 57-74; Archd of Fred 70-79; Exam Archd (Emer) from 79; Chap to Bp of Fred from 71; Dioc Treas from 74. *258 Inglewood Drive, Fredericton, NB, Canada.*

MARTIN, Frank. b 08. Men in Disp 43; AKC 32. **d** 32 **p** 33 S'wark. C of St Matt Brixton 32-39; CF (TA) 38-39; CF 39-48; R of Aston Rowant w Crowell 48-54; V of Mylor 54-75; RD of S Carnmarth 57-60 and 67-75. *New House, Mylor Creek, Falmouth, Cornw, TR11 5NL.* (Penryn 74343)

MARTIN, Frank Walter. b 13. Univ of Dur LTh 37. BC Coll Bris 34. **d** 37 **p** 38 Ox. C of St Paul Slough 37-40; Stapenhill 40-42; Publ Pr Dio Chelmsf 42-43; R of Bodiam 43-53; Chap Darvell Hall Sanat Robertsbridge 46-53; Ed 'The English Churchman' 45-64; R of Gt Horkesley 53-63; Chap Bexley Hosp 64-78; Perm to Offic Dio Roch from 79. *22a Hillside Avenue, Frindsbury, Rochester, Kent, ME2 3DB.* (Medway 77561)

MARTIN, Geoffrey Ernest. St Jo Coll Morpeth ACT ThL 28. **d** 28 Goulb **p** 29 Bp White for Goulb. C of Young 28-29; Wagga Wagga 29-31; Miss at Rabaul Melan 31-32; C of Albury 32-33; R of Barmedman 33-35; Adaminaby 35-38; C of St Mary Plaistow 38-40; C-in-c of St Andr Kyabram 41-42; V of Cohuna 42-46; Eaglehawk 46-52; Peterborough 52-56; R of South Road 56-70; L to Offic Dio Adel from 70. *10 Bonview Avenue, Panorama, S Australia 5041.* (276 3559)

MARTIN, Geoffrey Noel. b 1893. Westcott Ho Cam 45. **d** 45 Chich **p** 46 Roch for Chich. C of Uckfield 45-50; R of Sedlescombe w Whatlington 50-64. *Little Ven East, Milborne Port, Sherborne, Dorset.*

MARTIN, George. Univ of Dur BA 32, MA 62. Qu Coll Newfld. **d** 29 **p** 30 Newfld. I of Herring Neck 29-31; R of Burgeo 31-33; Pushthrough 33-36; Channel 36-60; Can of Newfld 54-71; Exam Chap to Bp of Newfld 54-70; R of Petty Harbour 60-67; Bp's Commiss from 60; I of Brigus w Salmon Cove 67-71. *35 Bell's Turn, St John's, Newfoundland, Canada.*

MARTIN, George. **d** 76 Mashon. d Dio Mashon. *Peterhouse, PB 741, Marandellas, Rhodesia.*

MARTIN, George. Ridley Coll Melb ACT ThL 58. **d** 60 **p** 61 Gippsld. C of Leongatha 60-62; Traralgon 62-64; V of Wonthaggi 64-68; Newport 68-70; Chap Prahram Tech Sch Dio Melb 71-78; Perm to Offic Dio Melb 70-72; C of Toorak 72-75; Armadale w Hawksburn 75-78; Chap Trin Gr Sch Kew from 78. *Trinity Grammar School, Wellington Road, Kew, Vic., Australia 3101.* (861 6713)

MARTIN, George Cobain. b 34. TCD BA and Div Test 57, MA 65. **d** 57 **p** 58 Down. C of Bangor 57-64; I of Kircubbin 64-74; R of Partney w Dalby (and Ashby-by-Partney, Skendleby and Candlesby w Scremby from 78) Dio Linc from 74; Ashby-by-Partney 74-78; Candlesby w Scremby 74-78; V of Skendleby 74-78. *Partney Rectory, Spilsby, Lincs.* (Spilsby 53570)

MARTIN, George Washington Leslie. b 05. Men in Disp 45 (twice); ALCD 40. **d** 40 **p** 41 Ripon. C of St Marg Horsforth 40-43; CF (EC) 43-48; Hon CF from 48; V of Pannal 48-57; Hd Master Rodbourne Ho Sch Malmesbury 57-58; Rodbourne Coll Gayhurst Bucks 58-69; Perm to Offic Dio Bris 57-69; Dio B & W 58-63; Dio Ox 63-69; R of St Jas Cupar 69-72; Perm to Offic Dio Ex from 72; Dio Ripon from 73. *3 Windsor Court, Holbeck Close, Scarborough, N Yorks, YO11 2XW,*

MARTIN, Gordon Albion John. b 30. K Coll Lon and Warm AKC and Bp Collins Pri 54. **d** 55 **p** 56 Lon. C of St Mary Magd Enfield 55-59; Palmers Green 59-61; V of St Martin Lower Edmonton 61-64; Culham 64-67; Asst Dioc Youth Officer Dio Ox 64-67; Bp's Youth Chap St Alb 67-73. C-in-c of Wareside 69-73; V of St Jo Bapt Harpenden Dio St Alb from 73; RD of Wheathampstead from 76. *St John's Vicarage, Harpenden, Herts, AL5 1DJ.* (Harpenden 2776)

MARTIN, Graham Rowland. b 39. Univ of Nottm BD 65. ACP 65. Univ of Bris BEducn 73. Wells Th Coll 71. **d** 71 **p** 72 Glouc. Hon C of St Cath Glouc 71-76; Asst Master Ribston Hall Sch Glouc from 68; P-in-c of Brookthorpe w Whaddon 76-78; Perm to Offic Dio Glouc 78-80; C of Hucclecote Dio Glouc from 80. *214b Stroud Road, Gloucester, GL1 5LJ.* (Gloucester 28721)

MARTIN, James. **d** 79 **p** 80 Mashon. P Dio Mashon 79-81; P-in-c of Chiredzi Dio Lundi from 81. *Box 174, Chiredsi, Zimbabwe.*

MARTIN, James Smiley. Trin Coll Dub 65. **d** 67 **p** 68 Connor. C of Glenavy 67-70; St Mary Belf 70-73; Carnmoney

73-74; I of Mallusk Dio Connor from 74. *Mallusk, Newtownabbey, Antrim, N Ireland.*

MARTIN, John. b 32. Roch Th Coll 61. **d** 64 Penrith for Carl **p** 65 Carl. C of St Matt Barrow-F 64-66; Netherton 66; Bp Wearmouth 66-67; Wigan 67-73; C-in-c of St Paul's Conv Distr Croxteth w Derby 73-79. *Address temp unknown.*

MARTIN, Canon John Bernard. b 27. Clare Coll Cam BA (3rd cl Nat Sc Trip) 51, MA 55. Ridley Hall, Cam 51. **d** 53 Liv for Leic **p** 54 Leic. C of H Ap Leic 53-56; Em Plymouth 56-59; V of Rounds Green 59-66; St Andr Ilford 66-76; Can Res (and Treas from 77) of Sheff Cathl 76-81; Can (Emer) from 81. *1 Silverdale Road, Sheffield, S11 9JJ.* (0742-368254)

MARTIN, John Frederick Theodore. b 07. St Andr Coll Whittlesford. **d** 37 **p** 38 Southw. C of Lowdham 37-47; R of W Leake w Ratcliffe-on-Soar and Kingston-on-Soar U 47-51; R of Newton w Haceby 51-54; V of Braceby w Sapperton 51-54; St Barn Pleasley Hill Mansfield 54-55; Chap St Aug Hosp Chartham 55-78. *Sherwood, Pilgrim's Lane, Chilham, Canterbury, Kent.*

MARTIN, John Henry. b 42. St Jo Coll Cam 2nd cl archaeol & Anthrop Trip pt i 61, (pt ii 63) BA, MA 67. Univ of Nottm BA (Th) 73. St Jo Coll Nottm 71. **d** 73 Doncaster for Sheff **p** 74 Sheff. C of Ecclesall 73-77; Hednesford (in C of St Mich Rawnsley from 80) Dio Lich from 77. *554 Littleworth Road, Rawnsley, Cannock, Staffs, WS12 5JD.* (Hednesford 76422)

MARTIN, John Hunter. b 42. K Coll Lon and Warm AKC 64. **d** 65 **p** 66 S'wark. C of Mortlake w E Sheen 65-69; Min of St Hugh's Conv Distr S'wark (Charterho Miss) 69-72; V of St Anne Bermondsey 72-78; P-in-c of Littleport w Little Ouse and St Matt Littleport Dio Ely from 78. *Littleport Vicarage, Ely, Cambs.* (Ely 860207)

MARTIN, John Keith. b 32. Sarum Wells Th Coll 76. **d** 79 **p** 80 B & W. C of St Mary Bathwick Bath Dio B & W from 79. *12 Abbey View, Bathwick, Bath, Avon, BA2 6DG.* (Bath 26192)

MARTIN, John McLean. b 35. Vanc Sch of Th 76. **d** 77 **p** 78 New Westmr. C of St Phil Vanc 77-79; I of Powell River Dio New Westmr from 79. *6984 Crofton Road, Powell River, BC, Canada.*

MARTIN, Canon John Pringle. b 24. Univ of Bris BA 50. Clifton Th Coll 50. **d** 52 **p** 53 Chelmsf. C of Braintree 52-56; St Paul (in c of St Luke) St Alb 56-59; V of Congleton 59-81; RD of Congleton from 74; Hon Can of Ches Cathl from 80; R of Brereton w Swettenham Dio Ches from 81. *Brereton Rectory, Sandbach, Cheshire.* (Holmes Chapel 33263)

MARTIN, John Stuart. b 11. St Jo Coll Dur BA 34. Wycl Hall Ox. **d** 35 **p** 36 Southw. C of St Pet Mansfield 35-37; Newhaven 37-39; Barcombe 39-43; V of H Trin Ox 43-46; Leafield w Wychwood 46-51; R of Rotherfield Greys 51-63; V of Highmore 55-63; R of Bow w Broad Nymet 63-65; V of Upottery 65-72; Team V of Farway w Northleigh and Southleigh 72-73; L to Offic Dios York and B & W from 75. *8 Church Road, Bawdrip, Bridgwater, Somt, TA7 8PU.* (Puriton 684092)

MARTIN, John Tidswell. b 24. Em Coll Cam BA 48, MA 52. Kelham Th Coll 48. **d** 53 Bp Linton for Cant **p** 54 Birm. C of Yardley Wood 53-55; Asst Gen Sec and Sec of Th Colls Dept of SCM 55-58; Gen Sec 58-62; R of St Chris Withington Lancs 62-68; V of Kingston-T Dio S'wark from 68. *15 Woodbines Avenue, Kingston-upon-Thames, Surrey, KT1 2AZ.* (01-546 2644)

MARTIN, John William. Clifton Th Coll 37. **d** 37 **p** 38 Roch. C of Ch Ch Tunbridge Wells 37-40; CF (EC) 40; C of Ch Ch Dartford 40-41; St Mary Eastbourne (In c of St Geo from 43) 41-47; Chap of St Mary's Hosp Eastbourne 42-47; C-in-c of Conv Distr of N Bersted 47-51 R of Itchingfield Dio Chich from 51. *Itchingfield Rectory, Horsham, Sussex.* (Slinfold 315)

MARTIN, Joseph Edward. Bp's Coll Cheshunt 58. **d** 60 Staff for Lich **p** 61 Shrewsbury for Lich. C of Short Heath 60-62; St Jo Evang Caterham 63-66; R of W Hallam (w Mapperley from 67) 66-70; C-in-c of Mapperley 66-67; V of Wykeham and Hutton Buscel 70-78; Askham Richard w Askham Bryan Dio York from 78; Chap HM Pris Askham Grange from 78. *Askham Bryan Vicarage, York, YO2 3QU.* (York 66581)

MARTIN, Kenneth. b 20. St D Coll Lamp 46, BA 47. **d** 48 **p** 49 Mon. C of Rumney 48-49; Griffithstown 49-51; Asst Master Monkton Ho Sch Cardiff 51-66; Bp of Llan High Sch from 66; Perm to Offic Dio Llan from 51; CF (TA) from 52. *21 Earls Court Road, Penylan, Cardiff, S Glam.* (Cardiff 493796)

MARTIN, Kenneth Cyril. b 31. SOC 71. **d** 73 Horsham for Chich **p** 74 Lewes for Cant for Chich. C of Hollington 73-76. Horsham (in c of H Trin) 76-79; P-in-c of St Osw Kidderminster 79-81; V 81; P-in-c of H Trin w St Matt Ronkswood City and Dio Worc from 81. *4 Silverdale Avenue, Worcester, WR5 1PY.* (Worc 353432)

MARTIN, Kenneth Granville. b 26. St Cath S Ox BA (2nd cl Th) 53, MA 58. Cudd Coll 53. **d** 54 **p** 55 St Alb. C of Sawbridgeworth 54-56; St Paul Bedford 56-60; Chap Miss to Seamen Antwerp 60-62; V of Kimpton 62-67; R of Baldock w Bygrave 67-79; V of King's Walden Dio St Alb from 79. *Vicarage, Church Road, King's Walden, Hitchin, Herts.* (Whitwell 278)

MARTIN, Canon Kenneth Roger. b 16. AKC (1st cl) 40. **d** 40 **p** 41 Ex. [f Solicitor] C of St Thos Ex 40-45; Perm to Offic Dio Cant 45-46; C of St Jo Evang U Norwood 46-47; Sidmouth (in c of St Francis Woolbrook) 47-51; Perm to Offic Dio Wakef 51-53; C of Ch Ch Reading (in c of St Agnes) 53-56; V of Summertown Ox 56-63; R of Rotherfield Greys 63-69; V of Highmore 63-69; R of Wokingham 69-81; RD of Sonning 77-80; Hon Can of Ch Ch Cathl Ox 80-81; Can (Emer) from 81; Perm to Offic Dio Ex from 81. *10 Kinsmans Dale, Moretonhampstead, Devon, TQ13 8LU.* (Moretonhampstead 774)

MARTIN, Canon Maurice Mitchell. b 01. St Edm Hall, Ox BA (2nd cl Th) 25, MA 29. Westcott Ho Cam 26. **d** 26 **p** 27 Chelmsf. C of Fryerning 26-27; Chelmsf (in c of All SS 27-31) 27-35; Prec of Chelmsf Cathl 31-35; R of St Jas Colchester (w All SS St Nich and St Runwald from 53) 35-69; Surr from 46; Chap Essex Co Hosp 48-69; Hon Can Chelmsf 54-75; Can (Emer) from 75; RD of Colchester 58-69; Chap to Bp of Colchester from 60; Dir of Ch Schs Dio Chelmsf 64-75; Publ Pr Dio Chelmsf from 69. *52 Creffield Road, Colchester, Essex, CO3 3HY.* (Colchester 66370)

MARTIN, Ven Michael Winnington. St Mich Th Coll Crafers ACT ThL 58. **d** 57 **p** 58 Wang. C of Corryong 58-60; Chap Mitchell River Miss 60-66; Edward River Miss Dio Carp 66; L to Offic Dio Wang 63-67; Archd of Cape York Peninsula 69-76; Admin Archd from 76; Dioc Commiss from 71; P-in-c of Weipa Miss Distr 75-76; Dioc Regr & Secr Dio Carp from 76; VG from 77. *PO Box 79, Thursday Island, Queensland, Australia 4875.* (117)

MARTIN, Nicholas Roger. b 53. St Jo Coll Dur BA 74. Ripon Coll Cudd 75. **d** 77 Ox **p** 78 Reading for Ox. C of Wolvercote w Summertown Ox 77-80; Kidlington Dio Ox from 80; Chap HM Detention Centre Kidlington from 80. *St John's Vicarage, The Broadway, Kidlington, Oxford, OX5 1EF.* (08675-5611)

MARTIN, Nicholas Worsley. b 52. Sarum Wells Th Coll 71. **d** 75 **p** 76 Llan. C of Llan Cathl 75-79; St Jo Bapt Cardiff 79; Caerphilly Dio Llan from 79. *71 Bartlett Street, Caerphilly, Mid Glam, CF8 1JT.*

MARTIN, Norman Duncan. Univ of Tor BA 48, MA 50. Univ of Illinois PhD 56. Wycl Coll Tor LTh 60. **d** 59 **p** 60 Tor. I of Perrytown Dio Tor from 59. *Gore's Landing, Ont., Canada.* (416-342 5680)

MARTIN, Norman George. b 22. Sarum Wells Th Coll 74. **d** 77 Taunton for B & W **p** 78 B & W (APM). C of Long Ashton 77-81; Walton-in-Gordano Dio B & W from 81. *7 Clynder Grove, Castle Road, Clevedon, Avon, BS21 7DF.* (Clevedon 873124)

MARTIN, Paul. b 50. Wabash Coll Indiana BA 72. Univ of the S Tenn 73. **d** 75 Ind USA **p** 76 Bp McKie for Cov. In Amer Ch 75; C of St Phil Norbury Dio Cant from 76. *45 Darcy Road, SW16.*

MARTIN, Paul Barri. b 58. St D Coll Lamp BA 79. St Steph Ho Ox 79. **d** 81 Llan for Mon **p** 82 Mon. C of St Mary Monmouth Dio Mon from 81. *9 Monkswell Road, Monmouth, Gwent, NP5 3PF.* (Mon 3828)

MARTIN, Philip John. b 06. Late Scho of St Jo Coll Ox 2nd cl Cl Mods 26, BA (2nd cl Lit Hum) 28, 2nd cl Th 29, MA 31. Wycl Hall, Ox 28. **d** 30 Glouc for Worc **p** 31 Worc. C of Halesowen 30-35; St John Dudley 35-39; C-in-c of St Geo Kidderminster 39-45; V 45-59; Longstock w Leckford 59-62; R of Hinton-on-the-Green 62-72; L to Offic Dio Worc from 72. *14 Swinford Road, Old Swinford, Stourbridge, W Mid, DY8 2LQ.* (Stourbridge 6204)

MARTIN, Raymond Sidney. b 43. St Jo Coll Morpeth ThDip 78. **d** and **p** 79 Newc. C of Singleton 79-80; R of Aberdeen/Gundy Dio Newc from 79. *16 Moray Street, Aberdeen, NSW, Australia 2336.*

MARTIN, Raymond William. b 32. BSc (Lon) 66. GOC 74. **d** and **p** 76 Glouc. C of St Mary-de-Lode w St Nich Glouc 76-77; Redmarley D'Abitot w Pauntley, Upleadon and Oxenhall Dio Glouc from 77. *Raysheil, Golden Valley, Upleadon, Newent, Glouc GL18 1HN.* (Tibberton 481)

MARTIN, Richard. Rhodes Univ Grahmstn BA 54. Em Coll Cam BA 57, MA 61. Wells Th Coll 57. **d** 59 Portsm **p** 60 Bloemf. C of St Mary Portsea 59-60; Bloemf Cathl 60-62; R of Wepener w Dewetsdorp 62-65; Odendaalsrus 65-69; R of St Hugh Port Eliz 69-76; Chap St Bede's Coll Umtata 77-79; R of Hillcrest Dio Natal from 81. *7 Elamgeni Road, Hillcrest 3600, Natal, S Africa.*

MARTIN, Richard Gibson. b 50. St Francis Coll Brisb 77. **d** 78 **p** 79 Brisb. C of St Barn Sunnybank 78-80; Southport

Dio Brisb from 80. *5/137 Nerang Street, Southport, Queensld, Australia 4215.*

MARTIN, Robin Hugh. b 35. Rhodes Univ Grahmstn BA 56. Univ of Birm Dipl Th 57, BD 61. Qu Coll Birm. **d** 58 **p** 59 Sheff. C of H Trin Darnall Sheff 58-62; C-in-c of St John's Conv Distr Kimberworth Park 62-65; L to Offic Dio Sheff 65-66; Dio Newc T 67-71; Perm to Offic Dio Man from 79. *696 Burnley Road, Lumb-in-Rossendale, Lancs.*

MARTIN, Canon Ronald William. b 12. MBE (Mil) 46. Late Exhib of Selw Coll Cam 3rd cl Hist Trip pt i, 33, BA 34, 3rd cl Th Trip pt i, 35, MA 38. Ridley Hall, Cam 34. **d** 36 Bedford for St Alb **p** 37 St Alb. C of Willian 36-40; C-in-c 40-42; Chap RAFVR 42-46; PC of Langleybury 46-68; V 68-77; RD of Watford 56-63; Hon Can of St Alb 61-77; Can (Emer) from 78; Surr 61-77; Chap Abbot's Hill Sch 66-80. *123 Hempstead Road, King's Langley, Herts, WD4 8AJ.* (King's Langley 68146)

MARTIN, Roy Ernest. b 29. Qu Coll Birm 74. **d** 77 Birm **p** 77 Bp Aston for Birm (APM). C of Marston Green Dio Birm from 77. *14 Walcot Green, Dorridge, Solihull, W Midl, B93 8BU.*

MARTIN, Russell Derek. b 47. St Jo Coll Dur 71. **d** 74 Jarrow for Dur **p** 75 Dur C of H Trin Hartlepool 74-77; St Jo Bapt Park Swindon 78-79; V of Penhill Dio Bris from 79. *Vicarage, Penhill, Swindon, Wilts.* (Swindon 721921)

MARTIN, Ven Stuart Morison. Montr Dioc Th Coll LTh 55. **d** 55 **p** 56 Montr. C of Ch Ch Cathl Montr 55-58; I of Lakeside Heights 58-65; R of St Matt City and Dio Montr from 68; Sec of Synod Montr 70-72; Archd of St Andr from 75. *4975 Dufferin Road, Montreal 254, PQ, Canada.* (514-484 9290)

MARTIN, Thomas Edward. Univ of Tor BA 60. Wycl Coll Tor LTh 63. **d** 63 Bp Snell for Tor **p** 64 Tor. C of St Jude Wexford Tor 63-65; I of Medonte (w Coldwater from 67) 65-67; Coldwater-Medonte 67-74; Beeton 74-79; on leave. *708 Burns Street West, Whitby, Ont., Canada.*

MARTIN, Thomas James. Trin Coll Dub BA 24, MA 29. Princeton Th Scm USA 23. **d** 36 **p** 37 Roch. [f Presbyterian Min] C of Gravesend 36-39; CF (TA) from 37; C of Chiddingfold 45-46; St Luke Redcliffe Sq S Kens 46-47; R of St Vincent Edin 47-53; V of Holy I 54-58; Barlestone 58-64 L to Office Dio Leic 64-67 R of Seagrave W Walton-le-Wolds 67-70. *Sophia St, Fairland, Johannesburg, S Africa.*

MARTIN, Thomas Robin. b 40. Bps' Coll Cheshunt 64. **d** 67 Repton for Derby **p** 68 Derby. C of Ripley 67-70; Ilkeston 70-74; V of Chinley w Buxworth Dio Derby from 74. *Buxworth Vicarage, Stockport, Chesh, SK12 7NH.* (Whaley Bridge 2243)

MARTIN, Canon Tom Davis. BEM 77. St Aid Th Coll Bal ACT ThL (2nd cl) 15. Univ of Dur LTh 16, BA 17. **d** 15 Bal **p** 16 Dur. LPr Dio Dur 15-16; C of Lumley Dur 16-18; Actg Chap RN 18; P-in-c of Ouyen 18-64; Chap to Bp of St Arn 26-64; Can of Ch Ch Cathl St Arn 42-64; Hon Can 64-76; Ch Ch Old Cathl St Arn from 77; Perm to Offic Dio St Arn 64-76; Dio Bend from 77. *Ramleh, Scott Street, Ouyen, Vic, Australia 3490.* (Ouyen 154)

MARTIN, Walter Gable. b 26. Nashotah Ho Wisconsin BD 56. **d** 56 S Florida **p** 57 Bp Moses. C of St Paul Long Island Nass 57-71; P-in-c of All SS Andros 71-76; in Amer Ch. *St James's Rectory, Griggsville, Illinois, 62340, USA.*

MARTIN, Walter Henry. Dorch Miss Coll 1898. Hatf Coll Dur BA 04, MA o8. **d** 1900 **p** 02 Grahmstn. C of Queenstn 1900-06; R of Tarkastad 06-09; Cam 09-12; P-in-c of New Hanover Natal 12-14; V of Newcastle Natal 14-24; Prin of St Chad's Coll and P-in-c of Native Miss Ladysmith 24-27; V of Greytown 27-31; St Thos Durban 31-46; Can of St Sav Cathl Maritzburg 37-50; Hon Can of Maritz 50-55; Archd of Durban 42-50; L to Offic Dio Natal 50-54; Dio Johann 54-65. *41 Commissioner Street, Kempton Park, Transvaal, S Africa.*

MARTIN, William Benjamin. d 61 Niag. On leave; C of St D Welland Dio Niag from 76. *234 Willson Street, Welland, Ont, Canada, L3C 2T8.*

MARTIN, William Henry Blyth. b 10. Late Scho of Keble Coll Ox 1st cl Cl Mods 31, BA (1st cl Lit Hum) and Liddon Stud 33, MA 36. Cudd Coll 35. **d** 36 **p** 37 Dur. C of St Mary Tyne Dk 36-39; Chap of Bps' Coll Cheshunt 39-45; Vice-Prin 45-48; CF (EC) 41-45; PC of St Aug Chesterfield 49-62; V of Long Eaton 62-80. *69 Deerings Road, Hillmorton, Rugby, Warws.* (Rugby 70949)

MARTIN, William John. b 16. OBE 55. United Th Coll of WI 70. **d** 72 **p** 73 Bp Clark for Ja. C of Kingston Ja 72-74; Chap at Marbella, Algeciras and Estapona 74-75; C of Par Ch Kingston 75-79; St John's Cathl Antig 79-80; St Anthony Plymouth, Montserrat Dio Antig from 80. *c/o St Anthony Rectory, Plymouth, Montserrat, W Indies.*

MARTIN, William Matthew. b 28. Ch Coll Cam BA 52, MA 56. Ridley Hall, Cam 52. **d** 54 **p** 55 Man. C of St Luke w All SS Weaste 54-56; V 56-61; CF (TA) 58-61; CF from 61; DACG from 73. *40 Jepps Avenue, Barton, Preston, PR3 5AS.* (0772-862166)

MARTIN-HARVEY, Martin. b 11. DSC 45. Worc Coll Ox BA 34, MA 38. Ridley Hall, Cam 34. **d** 36 **p** 37 Worc. C of Ch Ch Malvern 36-38; Asst Chap Embassy Ch Paris and St Mark Versailles 38-40; Chap RNVR 40-46; Asst Chap and Ho Master St Lawr Coll Ramsgate 47-72. *Admiralty Cottage, Harbour Street, Broadstairs, Kent.* (0843-67907)

MARTINDALE, Joseph William. b 1895. Univ of Dur BSc 16. **d** 58 **p** 59 Carl. C of Kirkby Stephen 58-60; V of Isel 60-61; PC of Setmurthy 60-61; V of Isel w Setmurthy 61-67; L to Offic Dio Carl from 67. *13 Oak Road, High Carleton, Penrith, Cumb.* (Penrith 67067)

MARTINEAU, Canon Christopher Lee. b 16. Trin Hall Cam 2nd cl Hist Trip BA 38. MA 70. Linc Th Coll 39. **d** 41 **p** 42 Leic. C of Hinckley 41-43; Chap RNVR 43-46; C of St Albans Abbey 46-48; V of St Paul Balsall Heath 48-54; Publ Pr Dio Birm 54-58; V of Shard End 58-65; R of Skipton-in-Craven Dio Bradf from 65; Exam Chap to Bp of Bradf from 66; Hon Can of Bradf from 72. *Rectory, Skipton-in-Craven, N Yorks, BD23 1ER.* (Skipton 3622)

MARTINEAU, David Richards Durani. b 36. K Coll Lon and Warm AKC 59. **d** 60 **p** 61 Ches. C of St Jo Bapt Ches 60-64; St Mark's Cathl Geo 64; Riversdale 64-66; R of Beaufort W 66-69; R of Vic W 66-69; C of St Paul Jarrow Dio Dur 69-72; Team V 72-75; R from 76. *St Peter's House, York Avenue, Jarrow, T & W, NE32 5LP.* (Jarrow 891925)

MARTINEAU, Jeremy Fletcher. b 40. K Coll Lon and Warm BD (3rd cl) and AKC 65. **d** 66 **p** 67 Dur. C of St Paul Jarrow 66-73; Industr Adv to Bp of Dur 69-73; Chap to Agr and P-in-c of Raughton Head 73-80; Chap to Agr and Industry Dio Bris from 80. *The Cathedral, Bristol, BS1 5TJ.* (Bristol 23944)

✠ **MARTINEAU, Right Rev Robert Arnold Schurhoff.** b 13. Late Scho of Trin Hall Cam 1st cl Math Trip pt i 33, 2nd cl Math Trip pt ii 34, BA (Math Trip pt iii w distinc) 35, Tyson Med 35, MA 39. Westcott Ho Cam 36. **d** 38 **p** 39 Sarum. C of Melksham 38-41; Chap RAFVR 41-46; V of St Geo Ovenden Halifax 46-52; Asst RD of Halifax 51-52; Chap R Aux AF 47-52; V of Allerton 52-66; Hon Can of Liv 61-66; RD of Childwall 64-66; Proc Conv Liv 64-66; Cons Ld Bp Suffr of Huntingdon in S'wark Cathl 6 Jan 66 by Abp of Cant; Bps of Linc; Ely; S'wark; and Portsm; Bps Suffr of Maidstone; Buckingham; Grantham; and Warrington; Bps Walsh; Dunlop; Martin; Chase; and Healey; and Bp of Calif; Trld to Blackb 72; res 81. *Gwenallt, Park Street, Denbigh, Clwyd, LL16 3DB.* (Denbigh 4089)

MARTINSON, John Cecil. St Jo Coll Winnipeg, 48. **d** 50 **p** 51 Keew. C of St Paul Churchill 51-52; Miss at Fort George 52-60; V of Peguis Ind Reserve 60-61; R of Stonewall 61-71; Can of Rupld 66-67; Archd of Selkirk 67-71; I of Kitkatla Dio Caled from 71. *Kitkatla, BC, Canada.*

MARTINSON, Peter Stephen Douglas. b 15. Univ of Lon BA 42. AKC 48. Teacher's Dipl 50. **d** 49 **p** 50 S'wark for Cant for Col Bp. C of Kennington 49-53; Asst Chap and Lect at St Monica's Tr Coll Mampong 53-55; Perm to Offic Dio Cant 55-63; Chap Univ Coll of Cape Coast 63-66; Area Sec USPG Dio Guildf 66-80; Commiss Kum from 73. *17 Yeomans Lane, Liphook, Hants, GU30 7PN.*

MARTLEW, Andrew Charles. b 50. Univ of Nottm BTh 76. Univ of Lanc MA 80. Linc Th Coll 72. **d** 76 Burnley for Blackb **p** 77 Blackb. C of Poulton-le-Fylde 76-79; Hon C of Ch Ch Lanc 79-80; V of Ch Ch Melaka Dio W Mal from 81. *c/o National Westminister Bank, Bailrigg, Lancaster, LA1 4XZ.*

MARTYN, George Robert. Univ of Sask BA 51. Trin Coll Tor LTh 54, STB 55. **d** 54 **p** 56 Sktn. Miss at Meota 54-56; R of Perdue 56; in Amer Ch 56-63; Hon C of Epiph Scarborough Tor 63-66; St Jo Div Scarborough City and Dio Tor from 67. *348 Rouge Highland Drive, West Hill, Ont, Canada.*

MARTYR, James Graham de Garlieb. b 1883. Cudd Coll 18. O of Sacred Treas cl v (Japan) 38. **d** 19 **p** 20 Lon. C of H Trin Stroud Green 19-21; Org Sec Korean Miss 21-27; Actg C of St Mary Graham Street and St Anne Lambeth 22-27; in service of Japanese Govt 28-37; Perm to Offic at St Paul Kandy and Actg Chap to Bp of Colom 45-47; P-in-c of St Mark Badulla and St Paul Kandy 47-50; H Trin Nuwara Eliya 55-59; L to Offic Dio Colom 46-61 P-in-c of St Matt Dematagoda 59-61. *Address temp unknown.*

MARUFU, Thomas Moyo. d 78 **p** 79 Matab. C of Que Que Dio Matab 78-80; P-in-c of Torwood Dio Matab 80-81; Dio Lundi from 81. *L 121 Torwood, Redcliff, Zimbabwe.*

MARUPEN, David Martin. b 31. **d** 76 **p** 77 Pret. C of Eersterus Dio Pret from 76. *345 Furst Avenue, Eersterus 0022, S Africa.*

MARURU, Reuben. St Pet Coll Siota. **d** 52 Melan. d Dio Melan. *San Cristoval, British Solomon Islands.*

MARVELL, John. b 32. Univ of Lon BD 63. Univ of Leic MEducn 73. Oak Hill Coll 79. **d** 80 Chelmsf **p** 81 Colchester for Chelmsf (NSM). C of Ch Ch Colchester Dio Chelmsf from 80. *13 Mossfield Close, Colchester, Essex, CO3 3RG.*

MARWA, James. St Phil Th Coll Kongwa, 64. **d** 66 Vic Nyan **p** 67 Bp Madinda for Vic Nyan. P Dio Vic Nyan. *PO Box 26, Tarime, Tanzania.*

MASA, Johnson. d 63 Centr Tang **p** 64 Bp Madinda for Centr Tang. P Dio Centr Tang 64-65; L to Offic Dio Moro from 64. *Berega, PO Kilosa, Tanzania.*

✠ **MASABA, Right Rev Erisa Kabiri.** MBE 55. **d** 33 **p** 34 U Nile. P Dio U Nile 33-40; Tutor Buwalasi Th Coll 40-43; CF (E Afr) 43-48; P Buwalasi 48; Buhugu 49-52; Mbale 52-61; Archd of Mbale 53-61; Bugisa 61; Hon Can of Mbale 61-64; Cons Ld Bp of Mbale in St Andr Cathl Mbale 23 Aug 64 by Abp of Ugan; Bps of Soroti; W Bugan; N Ugan; and Ankole-K; and Asst Bps of N Ugan; and Nam; res 75; Dean of St Andr Cathl Mbale 70-75. *Box 473, Mbale, Uganda.*

MASAKALE, Andrew. St Bede's Coll Umtata 61. **d** 62 **p** 64 St John's. P Dio St John's from 64. *Box 33, Matateile, S Africa.*

MASALAKUFENI, Albert. b 16. **d** 76 **p** 77 Matab. P Dio Matab. *P Bag 5285 Q, Bulawayo, Zimbabwe.*

MASANCHE, Alfred. b 15. **d** and **p** 72 S Malawi. P Dio S Malawi. *Mpilisi, Box 184, Balaka, Malawi.*

MASANGO, Archibald Wele. St Pet Coll Rosettenville. **d** 61 **p** 62 Grahmstn. P Dio Grahmstn 61-65; P-in-c of St Marg of Scotld Jansenville 65-78; St John Oudtshoorn Dio Geo from 78. *Box 594, Oudtshoorn, CP, S Africa.*

MASANIKA, Yona. St Phil Th Coll Kongwa, 65. **d** 67 Bp Madinda for Centr Tang **p** 67 Centr Tang. P Dio Centr Tang. *Box 15, Dodoma, Tanzania.*

MASANJA, Abednego. b 47. St Phil Coll Kongwa 75. **d** and **p** 77 Vic Nyan. P Dio Vic Nyan. *St Peter's Church, Choma cha Nkola, PO Nzega, Tanzania.*

MASANJA, Joseph. b 47. St Phil Th Coll Kongwa 68. **d** 70 **p** 71 Vic Nyan. P Dio Vic Nyan 71-77; *PO Box 3015, Malya, Tanzania.*

MASANO, Ven John Walter. St Jo Sem Lusaka 64. **d** 65 Bp Mtekateka for Malawi **p** 67 Malawi. P Dio Malawi 65-71; Dio S Malawi from 71; Archd of Shire from 78. *P Bag 514, Limbe, Malawi.*

MASASI, Lord Bishop of. *See* Chisonga, Right Rev Gayo Hillary.

MASASI, Assistant Bishop of. (Vacant).

MASAULWA, Dani. b 50. St Phil Coll Kongwa 78. **d** 80 **p** 81 Centr Tang. P Dio Centr Tang. *c/o Box 68, Kondoa, Tanzania.*

MASAULWA, Lister. d and **p** 78 Centr Tang. P Dio Centr Tang. *Box 15, Mpwapwa, Tanzania.*

MASCALL, Canon Eric Lionel. b 05. Late Math Scho of Pemb Coll Cam 24, 2nd cl Math Trip pt i, 25, BA (Math Trip pt ii, Wrang w distinc and Foundress Scho) 27, MA 31, BD 43, DD 58. Univ of Lon BSc (1st cl) 26. Univ of Ox MA and BD (by incorp) 45, DD 48. Univ of St Andr Hon DD 67. FBA 74. Ely Th Coll 31. **d** 32 **p** 33 S'wark. C of St Andr Stockwell Green 32-35; St Matt Westmr 35-37; M OGS from 37; Sub-Warden Linc Th Coll and L to Offic Dio Linc 37-45; Select Pr Univ of Cam 43 and 59; Lect in Th at Ch Ch Ox 45; Student and Tutor 46-62; Student (Emer) from 62; Lect in Phil of Relig Univ of Ox 47-62; L to Offic Dio Ox 46-63; Bampton Lect Univ of Ox 56; Columb Univ NY 58; Prof of Hist Th Univ of Lon 62-73; Prof (Emer) from 73; Dean of Th 68-72; L to Offic Dio Lon from 62; Commiss Capetn 64-73; Boyle Lect 65-66; Fell of K Coll Lon from 68; Gifford Lect Edin 70-71; Exam Chap to Bp of Willesden 70-73; to Bp of Truro from 73; to Bp of Lon from 81; Hon Can of Truro from 74. *30 Bourne Street, SW1.* (01-730 2423)

MASCALL, Sydney Charles. b 16. ALCD 40. **d** 40 Roch **p** 43 Lon. C of H Trin Penge 40-41; w YMCA HM Forces 41-43; C of Bow 43-47; V of Sedgeford w Southmere R 47-51; Ch Ch New Catton 51-55; Chap Roundway Hosp Devizes 55-71; Supply Chap Miss to Seamen 72-81; Residential Care Officer Waverley Ho Melksham 72-81. *50 Long Street, Devizes, Wilts, SN10 1NP.* (Devizes 4232)

MASDING, John William. b 39. Late Demy of Magd Coll Ox BA (2nd cl Hist) 61, MA 65. Ridley Hall, Cam 63. **d** 65 **p** 66 Birm. C of Boldmere 65-71; V of St Paul Hamstead Dio Birm from 71. *Hamstead Vicarage, Walsall Road, Birmingham, B42 1ES.* (021-357 1259)

MASEMOLA, Malachi. Coll of Resurr Rosettenville. **d** 43 **p** 44 Pret. P Dio Pret 43-69. *Sekhukhuniland, PO Soetveld, via Middelberg, Transvaal, S Africa.*

MASEMOLA, Ven Richard Mlokothwa. St Pet Coll Rosettenville 58. **d** 60 **p** 61 Natal. P Dio Natal. Archd of Pmbg from 75. *Box 41, Edendale, Pietermaritzburg, Natal, S Africa.*

MASEMOLA, Sipho. St Pet Coll Rosettenville, 57. **d** 59 Johann **p** 60 Bp Paget for Johann. P Dio Johann. *Box 5017, Bathobotlhe 1766, Transvaal, S Africa.*

MASENO NORTH, Lord Bishop of. *See* Mundia, Right Rev James Israel.

MASENO SOUTH, Lord Bishop of. *See* Okullu, Right Rev Henry

MASEREKA, Yahoo. d 65 **p** 66 Ruw. P Dio Ruw. *Lake Kative, Busongora, Uganda.*

MASEREKAI, Yonasani. d and **p** 75 Bunyoro. P Dio Bunyoro. *Box 20, Hoima, Uganda.*

MASH, Neil Beresford. b 30. Em Coll Sktn Div Test 54. **d** 54 **p** 55 Sask. I of Fort Pitt 54-57; Chap and Asst Master Seaford College Sussex 57-58; C of Buckhurst Hill (in c of St Elis) 58-61; R of Wilby w Brundish 61-67; V of Swaffham 67-76; Old Catton Dio Nor from 76; Surr from 68. *St Margaret's Vicarage, 4 Colkett Drive, Old Catton, Norwich, Norf.*

MASHEDER, Peter Timothy Charles. b 49. AKC 71. St Aug Coll Cant 71. **d** 72 **p** 73 Barking for Chelmsf. C of St Francis of Assisi Barkingside 72-75; Chingford Dio Chelmsf from 75. *Old Church House, Priory Avenue, Chingford, E4 8AA.* (01-529 0110)

MASHEDER, Richard. b 36. K Coll Lon and Warm AKC 59. **d** 60 Lanc for York **p** 61 Blackb. C of St Matt Preston 60-62; Padiham w Higham (in c of St John Higham) 62-65; P-in-c of Worsthorne 65; V 65-73; CF (TA) 65-67; P-in-c of St Jude Blackb 74-78; V of St Thos (w St Jude from 78) Borough and Dio Blackb from 76. *197 Burnley Road, Blackburn, Lancs, BB1 3HW.* (Blackburn 52958)

MASHEDER, Richard Oswald. b 06. Keble Coll Ox BA 31. Ely Th Coll 29. **d** 33 **p** 34 Cant. C of St Paul Ramsgate 33-35; St Mich AA Croydon 35-38; St Bart Charlton-in-Dover 38-41; All SS E Finchley 41-47; V of Gt Bardfield (w L Bardfield from 69) 47-74; RD of Dunmow 63-70. *65 Rock Road, Cambridge, CB1 4UG.* (Cambridge 40420)

MASHICILA, Leonard Silumko. b 18. **d** and **p** 77 Capetn (APM). C of Guguletu 77-79; St Chad Butterworth Dio St John's from 79. *Box 201, Butterworth, Transkei.*

MASHIKINYA, Ven Jonah Matobe. d 47 **p** 48 Pret. P Dio Pret; Can of Pret 71-77; Archd of Pret Distr from 77. *Boithutong Centre, Soshanguve, Transvaal, S Africa.*

MASHIMBA, Elikana. b 38. St Phil Coll Kongwa 70. **d** 71 **p** 72 Vic Nyan. P Dio Vic Nyan. *Box 44, Chato, Biharamulo, Tanzania.*

MASHINGAIDZE, Gabriel. St Jo Sem Lusaka, 66. **d** 68 Mashon. d Dio Mashon. *St Peter's Mission, Maudea, PB R3678, Umtali, Rhodesia.*

MASHIYI, Douglas Herben Ndafika. St Bede's Coll Umtata. **d** 48 **p** 50 St Jo Kaffr. P Dio St John's 48-81. *PO St Cuthberts, Transkei, S Africa.*

MASHONALAND, Lord Bishop of. *See* Hatendi, Right Rev Ralph Peter.

MASHONALAND, Lord Bishop Suffragan of. (Vacant)

MASIH, Samuel Ghulam. b 40. **d** 81 Cyprus. d Dio Cyprus. *PO Box 8884, Salalah, Oman.*

MASIH-DAS, James Nathaniel. b 27. Wilfred Laurier Univ Ont BA 60. **d** 80 Barb **p** 80 Guy. C of All SS New Amsterdam Berbice Dio Guy from 80. *11 Trinity Street, New Amsterdam, Berbice, Guyana.*

MASINDUKA, Kosiya. d 75 **p** 77 Ruw. P Dio Ruw. *Box 37, Fort Portal, Uganda.*

MASIRA, Daniel. b 26. **d** 76 Maseno S. d Dio Maseno S. *PO Box 121, Kisii, Kenya.*

MASLEN, Stephen Henry. b 37. CCC Ox BA 62, MA 65. Ridley Hall, Cam. **d** 64 **p** 65 B & W. C of Keynsham w Qu Charlton 64-67; Cheltnm 67-71; C-in-c of St Mary Lambeth 72-74; Team V of North Lambeth 74-79; V of Horley Dio S'wark from 79. *Vicarage, Massetts Road, Horley, Surrey.* (Horley 2218)

MASLEN, Trevor. b 51. Chich Th Coll 77. **d** 80 Chelmsf **p** 81 Barking for Chelmsf. C of St Mary Magd Harlow Dio Chelmsf from 80. *280 Carters Mead, Harlow Common, Harlow, Essex.*

MASOGO, David. d 65 **p** 66 Pret. P Dio Pret. *Magoshi School, Private Bag XO3, PO Neanderlal 0714, S Africa.*

MASON, Adrian Stanley. b 54. Hatfield Poly BSc 77. Ripon Coll Cudd 77. **d** 80 **p** 81 St Alb. C of St Pet Mill End Rickmansworth Dio St Alb from 80. *98 Tudor Way, Mill End, Rickmansworth, Herts, WD3 2HT.*

MASON, Alan Hambleton. b 27. BD (Lon) 59. Wycl Hall Ox 56. **d** 59 **p** 60 S'wark. C of St Pet Norbiton 59-63; V of Thornton 63-73; St Pet Norbiton Dio S'wark from 73. *21 Wolsey Close, Kingston-on-Thames, Surrey, KT2 7ER.* (01-942 8330)

MASON, Albert Christian. b 37. Univ of Syd BAgr 59. Ridley Coll Melb 61. **d** 63 **p** 64 Armid. C of Tamworth 63-65; Quirindi 65-69; Perm to Offic Dio Bend from 69. *2 Davies Court, Bendigo, Vic., Australia 3550.*

MASON, Charles Oliver. b 51. Jes Coll Cam BA 73. St Jo

Coll Dur BA 79. **d** 80 **p** 81 Glouc. C of Cheltenham Dio Glouc from 80. *1 Crescent Terrace, Cheltenham, Glos, GL50 3PE.*

MASON, Canon Charles Patrick Vaughan. b 12. Qu Coll Birm 32. Univ of Dur LTh 42. **d** 36 **p** 37 Glouc. C of St Mark Glouc 36-39; Asst P Korogwe 39; Zanz 39-43; P-in-c of St D Miss Bonda 43-59; Can of Mashon 58-67; Hon Can from 67; St Pet Miss Mandea 59-60; Archd of Umtali 60-65; P-in-c of Rusape 60-61; R of Makoni 61-65; Borrowdale Rhod 65-67; Oddington w Adlestrop 68-77; Perm to Offic Dio Glouc from 79. *55 Park Avenue, Longlevens, Gloucester.* (Glouc 20149)

MASON, Clive Ray. b 34. Univ of Dur BA (2nd cl Th) 57. Qu Coll Birm 57. **d** 59 **p** 60 Dur. C of Gateshead 59-62; Ch Ch Bp Wearmouth 62-64; V of St Jo Evang Darlington 64-74; C-in-c of Southwick Dio Dur from 75. *Southwick Rectory, Sunderland, SR5 2DU.* (Sunderland 491349)

MASON, David John. b 42. Sarum Wells Th Coll 72. **d** 74 Bp Vockler for Sarum **p** 75 Lon. C of St John of Jer w Ch Ch S Hackney 75-78; All SS Haggerston 78-80; V of St Cedd Canning Town Dio Chelmsf from 80. *301 Newham Way, E16 4ED.* (01-476 2021)

MASON, Ernest Walter. b 20. SOC 74. **d** 77 **p** 78 S'wark. C of H Spirit Clapham Dio S'wark from 77. *35 Klea Avenue, Clapham, SW4 9HG.*

MASON, Frederic. b 13. SS Coll Cam MA 38. Univ of Malaya Hon LLD 60. St Aug Coll Cant 60. **d** 61 **p** 62 Cant. Prin Ch Ch Coll Cant 61-75; Hon C of St Steph Mackington Cant 61-67; L to Offic Dio Cant 67-75; Perm to Offic Dio Ex from 75. *The Old School House, Lustleigh, Newton Abbot, Devon, TQ13 9TD.* (Lustleigh 251)

MASON, Frederick Michael Stewart. b 15. Kelham Th Coll 32. **d** 39 **p** 40 Bris. C of St Mark Swindon (in c of St Luke from 44) 39-49; St Paul Ox 49-51; All SS (in c of St Barn) Heref 51-56; Min of St Francis's Eccles Distr Radford Dio Cov 56-59; V from 59. *Vicarage, Treherne Road, Coventry, Warws.* (Coventry 595178)

MASON, Geoffrey Charles. b 48. AKC and BD 74. St Aug Coll Cant 74. **d** 75 **p** 76 S'wark. C of Hatcham Park 75-78; V of Bellingham Dio S'wark from 78. *St Dunstan's Vicarage, Bellingham Green, SE6 3JB.* (01-698 3291)

MASON, John Evans. b 32. Linc Th Coll 57. **d** 59 **p** 60 S'wark. C of Putney 59-62; Berry Pomeroy w Bridgetown 62-64; Chap RN 64-68; V of Hopton 68-72; R of Diss 72-80; P-in-c of St Remigius Roydon 72-76; Dir of YMCA Cam from 80. *c/o Bishop Woodford House, Barton Road, Ely, Cambs, CB7 4DX.*

MASON, John Frederic Wears. Univ of Syd BA 41. Moore Th Coll 41. ACT ThL 42. **d** 42 **p** 43 Syd. C of St John Parramatta 42-46; R of Berrima w Moss Vale 47-51; V of St John Bal 51; Asst Master C of E Gr Sch N Syd 52-53; Chap 53-60; R of Northbridge 61-64; L to Offic Dio Syd 64-66; Chap Cathl Sch Syd 67-70; Prec and Min Can of Syd Cathl 71-73; C-in-c of Mowbray 73; R 73-77; Actg Chap Blue Mountains Gr Sch and C of Ch Ch Springwood Dio Syd from 78. *5 Meers Crescent, Faulconbridge, NSW, Australia 2776.* (047-51 1096)

MASON, John Graham. Univ of Syd BA 67. BD (Lon) 69. Moore Th Coll Syd ACT ThL 67. **d** 69 **p** 70 Syd. C of Yagoona 69-73; St Mich Wollongong 73-74; Chester-le-Street Dur 74-76; Perm to Offic Dio C & Goulb 76-77; P-in-c of St Matt Wanniassa Dio C & Goulb from 77. *28 McBryde Crescent, ACT, Australia 2903.*

MASON, John Henry. b 04. St D Coll Lamp BA 35. **d** 35 **p** 36 Llan. C of Pontlottyn 35-38; Llangynwyd 38-42; V of Gilfach Goch 42-46; Chap RAF 46-61; R of Bratton Clovelly w Germansweek 61-72; Perm to Offic Dio St D from 72. *40 West Haven, Cosheston, Pembroke Dock, Dyfed, SA72 4UL.* (Pembroke 3775)

MASON, John Joseph Edward. **d** 33 **p** 35 Tor. C of St Jo Evang Tor 33-35; Cardiff w Monmouth 35-37; I of Wyebridge w Tay 37-39; Manvers 40-47; Craighurst w Crown Hill 47-53; C of St D Tor 54-57; I of Kinmount 57-69. *Apt 310, 1728 Lawrence Avenue, Toronto 15, Ont.*

MASON, John Leslie. St Jo Coll Morpeth. **d** 62 **p** 63 Bath. C of Orange 62-65; Dubbo 65-68; R of Warren 69-73; Peak Hill Dio Bath from 74. *Rectory, Peak Hill, NSW, Australia 2869.* (068-6922 36)

✠ **MASON, Right Rev Kenneth Bruce.** Univ of Queensld BA 66, Dipl Div 64. St Jo Coll Morpeth ACT ThL (1st cl) 53. **d** 53 **p** 54 Bath. Bro of Good Shepherd 53-64; P-in-c of Gilgandra 53-58; P-in-c of Darwin 59-61; R of Alice Springs 62; L to Offic Dio Brisb 63-64; Dio Melb 64-68; Asst Chap Trin Coll Univ of Melb 65; Dean 66-67; Cons Ld Bp of N Terr in St Jo Evang Cathl Brisb 24 Feb 68 by Abp of Brisb; Abp of Melb; Bps of Bath; Rockptn; New Guinea; Newc; and Carp; Coadj Bps of Brisb (Hudson); and Syd (Dain); Asst Bp of New Guinea (Ambo); Abp Moline and Bp Muschamp. *PO Box 2267, Darwin, N Territory, Australia 5794.* (089-81 6888)

MASON, Kenneth Staveley. b 31. Univ of Lon BSc (Chem) 53, BD (1st cl) 64. ARCS 53. Wells Th Coll 56. **d** 58 **p** 59 York. C of St Martin Hull 58-61; Pocklington and Millington w Gt Givendale 61-63; V of Thornton w Allerthorpe and Melbourne 63-69; Sub-Warden K Coll Lon at St Aug Coll Cant 69-76; Abp's Adv in Pastoral Min Dio Cant 76-81; Dir Cant Sch of Min 77-81; Prin from 81; Sec Cant Dioc Bd of Min from 78; Six Pr in Cant Cathl from 79; Exam Chap to Abp of Cant from 80. *1 Lady Wootton's Green, Canterbury, Kent, CT1 1TL.* (Canterbury 59401)

MASON, Canon Lancelot. b 05. Trin Coll Cam BA 26, MA 30. Westcott Ho Cam 27. **d** 28 **p** 29 Ely. C of Soham 28-32; Res Chap to Bp of Chich 32-38; R of Plumpton w E Chiltington 38-46; Hon Chap to Bp of Chich 39-46; Chap RNVR 39-46; Men in Disp 46; Archd of Chich 46-73; Exam Chap to Bp of Chich 48-73; Can Res of Chich Cathl 49-73; Can (Emer) from 73; Select Pr Univ of Cam 50; Perm to Offic Dio Southw from 73. *The Stables, Morton Hall, Retford, Notts.* (Retford 705477)

MASON, Peter Charles. b 45. AKC and BD 72. St Aug Coll Cant 72. **d** 73 Repton for Derby **p** 74 Derby. C of Ilkeston 73-76; St Mary Magd Bridgnorth 76-78; Team V of Bridgnorth Dio Heref from 78. *41 Innage Lane, Bridgnorth, Salop, WV16 4HS.* (Bridgnorth 2235)

MASON, Peter Joseph. b 34. Univ of Lon BA (2nd cl Russian) 58. Coll of Resurr Mirfield, 58. **d** 60 **p** 61 Chelmsf. C of Belhus Pk Eccles Distr 60-63; L to Offic Dio Gibr 63-64; Asst Chap Univ of Lon 64-70; Chap City Univ Lon 66-70; R of St Mary Stoke Newington 70-78; V of Writtle (w Highwood from 81) Dio Chelmsf from 78; P-in-c of Highwood 78-81. *Vicarage, Lodge Road, Writtle, Chelmsford, CM1 3HY.* (Chemsford 421282)

MASON, Peter Ralph. McGill Univ BA 64, BD 67. Montr Dioc Th Coll LTh 67. **d** 67 **p** 68 Montr. C of St Matt Hampstead Montr 67-69; I of Hemmingford 69-71; R of St Clem Verdun 71-75; St Pet Mt Royal 75-80; St Paul Halifax Dio NS from 80. *129 Glenforest Drive, Clayton Park, Halifax, NS, Canada B3M 1J2.*

MASON, Richard Frank. b 51. Laurentian Univ of Sudbury Ont BA 74. Trin Coll Tor MDiv 79. **d** and **p** 79 Alg. R of St Paul Wawa Dio Alg from 79. *PO Box 79, Wawa, Ont, Canada, P0S 1K0.*

MASON, Ven Richard John. b 29. Linc Th Coll 55. **d** 58 **p** 59 St Alb. C of Bp's Hatfield 58-64; Dom Chap to Bp of Lon 64-69; V of Riverhead 69-73; Edenbridge Dio Roch from 73; C-in-c of Dunton Green 69-73; Archd of Tonbridge from 77; P-in-c of Crockham Hill Dio Roch from 81. *Vicarage, Crockham Hill, Edenbridge, Kent, TN8 6RL.* (Edenbridge 866515)

MASON, Roger Arthur. b 41. BSc (Lon) 65. K Coll Lon and Warm BD and AKC 68. **d** 69 Willesden for Lon. **p** 70 Lon. C of Enfield 69-72; P-in-c of Westbury 72-78; R 78; P-in-c of Yockleton 72-78; R 78; P-in-c of Gt Wollaston 77-78; V 78; V of Willesden Dio Lon from 78. *Willesden Vicarage, Neasden Lane, NW 10 2TT.* (01-459 2167)

MASON, Ronald William. b 06. ALCD 38. **d** 38 Tewkesbury for Glouc **p** 39 Glouc. C of St Paul Cheltm 38-41; St Luke Weaste 41-42; St Mary Virg Colchester 42-46; V of St Jo Evang Colchester 46-54; St Pet Bocking 54-65; Chap St Mich Hosp Braintree 54-65; Surr 54-71; R of Gt Warley 65-71; Perm to Offic Dio Ely 72-80. *Address temp unknown.*

MASON, Walter Cecil. b 15. Bp's Coll Cheshunt 41. **d** 43 **p** 44 Mon. C of Bedwellty 43-45; Llanfrechfa 45-46; Filton 46-48; Henbury w Hallen (in c of Aust and Northwick) 48-52; Littleham w Exmouth (in c of St Andr Exmouth) 52-56; V of Kilmington 56-57 C of Sidmouth (in C of St Francis Woolbrook) 57-59; PC of Eastville w Midville 59-61; R of Marksbury 61-80; R of Stanton Prior 61-80. *19 Westfield Park South, Bath, Avon, BA1 3HT.* (Bath 24056)

MASON, William Frederick. b 48. Linc Th Coll 75. **d** 78 **p** 79 St E. C of St Aug of Hippo Ipswich 78-81; Team V of Dronfield Dio Derby from 81. *Holmesdale Vicarage, Green Lane, Dronfield, Sheffield.*

MASON, William Hugh Owen. b 28. Qu Coll Ox BA (3rd cl Hons Engl) 52, MA 57. Cudd Coll 52. **d** 54 **p** 55 S'wark. C of All SS W Dulwich 54-57; S Barn Northolt 57-60; St Mary Magd Munster Square St Pancras 60-62; V of St Clem Notting Dale Kens 62-68; Commiss Wang 63-68; L to Offic Dio Nor from 69; R of Kedington Dio St E from 72. *Kedington Rectory, Haverhill, Suff.* (Haverhill 702725)

MASON, William Peter. b 1899. Univ of Sask BA 30. Em Coll Sktn LTh 30, BD (1st cl) 34. **d** 30 **p** 31 Bran. C of Reston 30; R of Miniota 30-31; Miss at Grand Rapids 31-33; Perm to Offic (Col Cl Act) at St Mich AA Bishopston 34; Ch Ch Clifton 34-36; C 36; Org Sec CCCS for E Distr and L to Offic Dio Ely 37-42; V of St Jas Ap Selby 42-56; C-in-c of Wistow 52-56; V of Stillington w Marton Moxby and Farlington 56-63; Skidby 63-67. *98 Finkle Street, Cottingham, N Humb.* (Hull 849983)

MASSA, Erisa. **d** 64 **p** 65 Mbale. P Dio Mbale from 64. *Bukonde, PO Box 297, Mbale, Uganda.*

MASSEY, Denton. MIT BSc 26. OBE 46. **d** 60 Huron **p** 61 Bp Luxton for Hur. I of Point Edward 60-62; R of Ch of H Sav Waterloo 62-70. *5135N Wilkinson Road, Paradise Valley, Arizona 85253, USA.*

MASSEY, Frederick. b 02. Univ of Wales BA (2nd cl Econ and Mod Hist) 30. **d** 30 **p** 31 St A. C of Newtown 30-33; St Jas w St Pet Nottm 33-35; Clun w Chapel Lawn 35-38; PC of Hentland w Hoarwithy 38-44; V of Dixton w Wyesham 44-52; Clehonger 52-55; R of Eaton Bp 52-55; Tedstone Delamere w Edvin Loach and Tedstone Wafer 56-60; C of Rottingdean (in c of St Nich Saltdean) 60-66; Perm to Offic Dio Chich 66-76; Dio Derby from 77. *2a St Mary's Close, Alvaston, Derby, DE2 0GF.* (0332-752442)

MASSEY, Frederick. b 14. Edin Th Coll 43. **d** 44 **p** 45 Glas. C of Ch of Good Shepherd Hillington (in c of Ascen Mosspark from 45) 44-46; St Paul Preston 46-47; PC of Edale 47-48; V of Brownhill 48-52; The Sav Ch Bolton 52-54; R of Margaret River and of Albany W Austr 54-59; St Geo Wigan 59-64; Commiss Bunb from 59; Chap St John's Hosp Linc 64-69; V of Long Sutton 69-74; R of Denton 74-80. *88 Station Road, Burgh-le-Marsh, Skegness, Lincs.*

MASSEY, Frederick Michael. b 17. AKC 47. **d** 47 **p** 48 S'wark. C of Clapham 47-49; Eccleshall-Bierlow Sheff 49-53; R of Walesby Dio Linc from 53; V of Usselby 53-74; Kingerby w Osgodby and Kirkby 55-74; C-in-c of Stainton-le-Vale w Kirmond-le-Mire 74-80; Claxby w Normanby-le-Wold 74-80; Tealby 74-80; N Willingham 74-80. *Walesby Rectory, Market Rasen, Lincs.*

MASSEY, Keith John. b 46. Oak Hill Th Coll 69. **d** 72 **p** 73 S'wark. C of St Jas w Ch Ch Bermondsey 72-76; Benchill Dio Man from 76. *St Luke's House, Brownley Road, Wythenshawe, Manchester, M22 4PT.* (061-998 2071)

MASSEY, William Cyril. b 32. Lich Th Coll 58. **d** 61 **p** 62 Heref. C of St Martin Heref 61-66; V of Kimbolton w Middleton-on-the-Hill and Hamnish 66-74; Alveley Dio Heref from 75; P-in-c of Quatt Malvern Dio Heref from 81. *Alveley Vicarage, Bridgnorth, Salop, WV15 6ND* (Quatt 780326)

MASSHEDAR, John Frederick. b 50. Univ of Dur BEducn 74. Linc Th Coll 76. **d** 78 **p** 79 York. C of Pocklington 78-81; Ascen Middlesbrough Dio York from 81. *2 Melsonby Avenue, Park End, Middlesbrough, Cleve.* (0642-319627)

MASSIAH, Hubert Arden Christopher. Sir Geo Williams Univ Montr BA 57. McGill Univ BD 59. Montr Dioc Th Coll LTh 59. **d** 58 **p** 59 Ont. C of Ch Ch Belleville 59-61; R of Camden E 61-64; on leave. *692 Burrard Street, Vancouver, BC, Canada.*

MASSINGBERD-MUNDY, John. b 07. Pemb Coll Cam BA 30, MA 46. Cudd Coll 31. **d** 32 **p** 33 Chelmsf. C of St Martin Dagenham 32-34; St Cuthb Sheff 34-37; St Barn Linthorpe (in c of St Jas) 37-40; V of Sewerby w Marton Grindall and Ergham 40-43; Mkt Weighton 43-50; R of Goodmanham 46-50; C-in-c of Bedale 50-59; R 59-65; Surr 50-65; V of Brocklesby w Limber Magna 65-72; V of Kirmington 65-72. *Quaker's Garth, Carlton, Leyburn, Yorks, DL8 4BA.*

MASSINGBERD-MUNDY, Roger William Burrell. b 36. St D Coll Lamp BA 59. Ridley Hall Cam 59. **d** 61 **p** 62 Newc T. C of St Jas Benwell Newc T 61-64; CF (TA) 63-68; (TAVR) from 71; C of Whorlton (in c of St Wilfrid Newbiggin Hall) Dio Newc T 64-72; Team V 73; C-in-c of Healey Dio Newc T from 73; Dioc Stewardship Adv Dio Newc T from 73. *Healey Vicarage, Riding Mill, Northumb.* (Riding Mill 316)

MASSON, Philip Roy. b 52. Hertf Coll Ox BA 75. Univ of Leeds BA 77. Coll of the Resurr 75. **d** 78 Bp Reece for Llan **p** 79 Llan. C of Port Talbot Dio Llan from 78. *89 Talbot Road, Port Talbot, W Glam.* (Port Talbot 897017)

MASTERMAN, Malcolm. b 49. Chich Th Coll 76. **d** 77 **p** 78 Dur. C of Peterlee 77-80; Chap Basingstoke Distr Hosp from 80. *The Lodge, Park Prewett, Basingstoke District Hospital, Hants.* (Basingstoke 3202)

✠ **MASTERS, Right Rev Brian John.** b 32. Qu Coll Cam BA 55, MA 59. Cudd Coll 62. **d** 64 **p** 65 Lon. C of Stepney 64-69; V of H Trin w St Mary Hoxton 69-82; P-in-c of St Anne w St Sav and St Andr Hoxton 69-75; St Anne w St Columba Hoxton 75-80; M Gen Syn from 73; Cons Ld Bp Suffr of Fulham 25 March 82 in St Paul's Cathl Lon by Abp of Cant; Bps of Lon and Nor; Bps Suffr of Aston, Dorchester, Edmon, Kens, Stepney, Plymouth and Willesden; and Bps Capper, Hodson, Woollcombe, Weekes, Arden, Ellison, Goodchild and Reindorp. *c/o 19 Brunswick Gardens, W8 4AS.*

MASTERS, Charles Frederick. b 51. Univ of Guelph BSc 73. St Jo Coll Nottm Dipl Th 76. **d** 78 Bp Clarke for Niag **p** 79 Niag. C of St Luke Burlington 78-80; R of Lowville Dio Niag from 80. *379 McNabb Crescent, Milton, Ont, Canada, L9T 3G3.* (416-878 4384)

MASTERS, Kenneth Leslie. b 44. Univ of Leeds BA (2nd cl Phil and Th) 68. Cudd Coll 68. **d** 70 **p** 71 Lich. C of St Paul Wednesbury 70-71; Tettenhall Regis 71-75; Team V of Chelmsley Wood 75-79; R of Harting Dio Chich from 79. *Rectory, Harting, Petersfield, Hants, GU31 5QB.* (Harting 234)

MASTERS, Leslie. b 31. Ripon Hall Ox 73. **d** 75 **p** 76 Bris. C of Hanham 75-78; Team V of St Agnes and St Simon w St Werburgh City and Dio Bris from 78. *St Werburgh Vicarage, St Werburgh's Park, Bristol 2.* (0272-558863)

MASTERS, (Austin) Raymond. b 26. Kelham Th Coll 45. M SSM 51. **d** 52 Llan for Bloemf **p** 53 Bloemf. C of Kroonstad Miss 52-56; Miss P St Patr Miss Bloemf 56-57; St Aug Miss Modderpoort 58-59; Dir 59-64; Warden 64-65; Can of Bloemf 58-65; Perm to Offic Dio Blackb 65-68; Chap St Martin's Coll Lanc 68-70; Asst Sec Bd of Miss and Unity Gen Syn 71-77; Hon C of St Pet Harrow 72-77; Commiss Taejon from 73; Team V of Ex Centr Dio Ex from 77; Dioc Missr and Ecumen Officer from 77; Warden of Commun of St Jo Bapt Clewer from 79. *c/o Diocesan Office, Palace Gate, Exeter, EX1 1HY.* (0392-72686)

MASTERTON, Paul Robert. b 35. Clifton Th Coll 63. **d** 66 **p** 67 Birm. C of Selly Hill 66-68; Sutton Coldfield 68-72; Aldridge 72-74; Gt Crosby 74-76; P-in-c of Manuden w Berden Dio Chelmsf from 76. *Manuden Vicarage, Bishop's Stortford, Herts, CM23 1DG.* (Bp's Stortford 812228)

MASTIN, Brian Arthur. b 38. Late Scho of Peterho Cam BA 60, MA 63, BD 80. Mert Coll Ox MA (*ad eund*) 63. **d** 63 Ban **p** 64 Chelmsf for Ban. Chap Ban Cathl 63-65; Asst Lect Univ Coll N Wales 63-65; Lect from 65; Perm to Offic Dio Chelmsf from 64; Dio Lich 66-70; L to Offic Dio Ban from 65. *University College of N Wales, Bangor, Gwynedd, LL57 2DG.*

MASUBA, Erifazi. b 20. Bp Tucker Coll Mukono 73. **d** and **p** 74 Mbale. P Dio Mbale. *Bumasifa, Box 769, Mbale, Uganda.*

✠ **MASUKO, Right Rev Elijah Musekiwa.** St Jo Sem Lusaka 66. **d** 68 **p** 70 Matab. P Dio Matab 68-81; Can of Matab 79-81; Cons Ld Bp of Mutare 4 Oct 81. *115 Main Street, Umtali, Zimbabwe.*

MASURAA, Canon William Atkin. **d** 41 **p** 46 Melan. P Dio Melan 41-74; Can of Melan 56-74; Hon Can from 74. *Palasu'u, S Malaita, Solomon Islands.*

MASUSELA, Edward Gusha. b 26. **d** 76 **p** 77 Matab. P Dio Matab 76-81; Dio Lundi from 81. *PO Box 974, Gwelo, Zimbabwe.*

MASYA, David Masila. b 39. St Paul's Coll Limuru 69. **d** 74 Nai. d Dio Nai. *Box 100, Kitui, Kenya.*

MATABELELAND, Lord Bishop of. *See* Mercer, Right Rev Robert William Stanley.

MATABELELAND, Dean of. *See* Ewbank, Very Rev Robert Arthur Benson.

MATAGARAKIKAI, Adam. b 20. St Aid Coll Dogura. **d** 64 New Guinea **p** 72 Papua. d Dio New Guinea 64-71; P Dio Papua from 72. *Gwede, via Rabaraba, MBD, Papua, New Guinea.*

MATANA, Jonathan Mlandeli. St Pet Coll Rossettenville, 51. **d** 54 **p** 56 Grahmstn. Miss (O of Ethiopia) Dio Grahmstn 54-59; Dio St John's 59-70; Dio Port Eliz from 70. *St Mark's Mission, Box 201, Kirkwood, CP, S Africa.*

MATANDA, Amos. **d** 73 **p** 74 Mashon. P Dio Mashon. *Mondoro Mission District, PB 812, Hartley, Zimbabwe.*

MATAVATA, Albano Pedro. **d** 76 Lebom (APM). d Dio Lebom. *CP 1420, Beira, Mozambique.*

MATAYO, Yona. b 56. St Phil Coll Kongwa 79. **d** 81 Centr Tang. d Dio Centr Tang. *PO Saranda Station, Tanzania.*

MATCHETT, Edward James Boyd. b 19. TCD BA 43, MA 60. **d** 43 **p** 44 Down. C of St Mary Belfast 43-45; Asst Chap Miss to Seamen Belf 45-46; Port Chap Miss to Seamen Basra Iraq 47-50; Chap Miss to Seamen Sunderland 50-52; Sen Chap at Belf and Org Sec for N Ireland 52-64; Chap Miss to Seamen Wel 64-69; Reg Dir E Reg 69-74; Perm to Offic Dios Ely, Linc, St E and Pet 69-74; Dio Southw 70-74; L to Offic Dio Nor 70-74; Dio Hong from 74; Sen Port Chap Hong from 74. *c/o Missions to Seamen, Hong Kong.* (3-688261)

✠ **MATE, Right Rev Martin.** Bp's Univ Lennox BA (1st Cl Th and Phil) 66, MA 67. Qu Th Coll Newfld LTh 49. **d** 52 **p** 53 Newfld. C of St Jo Bapt Cathl Newfld 52-53; R of Pushthrough 53-58; I of St Anthony 58-64; R of Cookshire 64-67; Catalina 67-72; Pouch Cove 72-76; Dioc Treas Dio E Newfld 76-80; Cons Ld Bp of E Newfld and Labrador in St John's Cathl Newfld 25 May 80 by Bp of Fred (Actg Metrop) and Abp Seaborn; Bps of Montr, W Newfld, Centr Newfld, NS and Queb; and Bps Legge, Brown and Matthews. *31 Dundas Street, St John's, Nfld, Canada.* (709-722 6788)

MATEBESE, David Thamsanga. d 59 **p** 60 Johann. P Dio Johann from 59. *PO Box 50, Katlehong, Germiston, Transvaal, S Africa.*

MATEEKA, Stanley. Buwalasi Th Coll 64. **d** 65 Ank. d Dio Ank 65-71; Dio Kig from 71. *PO Box 13, Kabale, Kigezi, Uganda.*

MATEMA, Horace Bakari. St Phil Th Coll Kongwa, 66. **d** 68 **p** 69 Moro. P Dio Moro. *Iyogwe, Berega Kilosa, Tanzania.*

MATESO, Alfej Daudi. St Cypr Th Coll Tunduru. **d** 47 **p** 50 Masasi. P Dio Masasi 47-72; Archd of Newala 64-72. *PO Box 92, Newala, Tanzania.*

MATHE, Alfred Legau. b 55. St Bede's Coll Umtata 76. **d** 78 **p** 79 Bloemf. L to Offic Dio Bloemf 78-79; C of St Aug Thaba Nchu Dio Bloemf from 79. *Box 9, Thaba Nchu, OFS, S Africa.*

MATHEKGA, Abbey Danny. b 36. Univ of S Afr BSc 63. **d** 76 **p** 77 Pret. C of Letaba & Namakgale Dio Pret from 76. *PO Box 313, Phalaborwa 1390, S Africa.*

MATHER, Bernard Edelston. b 13. BCM and Th Coll Clifton, 36. **d** 39 **p** 40 Ches. C of St Mark Evang New Ferry 39-42; St Geo Millom 42-45; R of Burlingham St Andr w St Pet 45-53; V of St Sav Bacup 53-56; R of Haversham (w L Linford from 73) 56-80; C-in-c of L Linford 56-73. *Glendale, Tresmere, Launceston, Cornw, PL15 8QY.* (Canworthy Water 219)

MATHER, Cuthbert. b 15. Tyndale Hall Bris 36. **d** 40 **p** 41 Ches. C of Bebington 40-42; Stapenhill 43-51; St Andr L Cam 51-52; Dagenham 53-57; V of Needham w Rushall 57-80. *2 Church Close, Hunstanton, Norfolk, PE36 6BE.* (Hunstanton 33084)

MATHER, Geoffrey Crewe. b 10. St Paul's Coll Burgh 32. **d** 35 **p** 36 Man. C of St Clem Ordsall 35-37; H Trin Bury 37-40; Tong w Tong Street 40; C-in-c of Horton Bank Top Conv Distr 40-41; C of Eye w Braiseworth 41-43; Chap RNVR 43-46; C of Wells 46-47; PV 47-48; Min Can of Carl 48-49; R of St Matt Ardwick Man 49-52; Stock Gaylard w Lydlinch 52-56; Perm to Offic Dio Lon 57-58; V of Lapley w Wheaton Aston 58-61; Chap Magd Coll Ox 60-61; R of Shalstone w Biddlesden 61-62; V of Beer 62-66; R of Barrowden w Wakerley 66-69; Perm to Offic Dio Cant 69-73; Dios St E and Chelmsf 73-81; Dio Ox from 81. *Crewe House, 18 Gloucester Street, Faringdon, Oxon, SN7 7HY.* (Faringdon 20336)

MATHER, James Malcolm. b 31. Trin Coll Cam BA 54, MA 59. Cudd Coll 54. **d** 56 **p** 57 York. C of S Bank 56-60; St Mich Sutton in Holderness 60-61; St Thos Hanwell 61-63; PC of H Trin Ilkeston 63-72; P-in-c of U Langwith 72-77; R (w Whaley Thorns from 80) 77-80; P-in-c of Whaley Thorns 77-80; Watlington w Pyrton and Shirburn Dio Ox 80-81; V from 81. *Watlington Vicarage, Oxford, OX9 5AD.* (Watlington 2494)

MATHER, John. d 58 **p** 59 Moos. I of Hearst 58-60; Schumacher 60-64; R of Bourlamaque 64-69; C of H Trin Winnipeg 73-74; R of Buckingham 74-78; C of Trin Ch Cornw 78-81. *209-323 Second Street East, Cornwall, Ont, Canada.*

MATHER, Robin William. b 48. Univ of Manit BA 69. Hur Coll Ont MDiv 72. **d** and **p** 72 Rupld. C of H Trin Winnipeg 72-74; I of St Thos Winnipeg 75-77; Hon C of St Mary Winnipeg Dio Rupld from 77. *67 Portland Avenue, Winnipeg, Manit, Canada.*

MATHER, William Bernard George. b 45. St Jo Coll Nottm 45. **d** 79 Chich **p** 80 Lewes for Chich. C of St Leon St Leonards-on-Sea Dio Chich from 79. *7 Boscobel Road, St Leonards-on-Sea, E Sussex, TN38 0LU.*

MATHERS, Alan Edward. b 36. Oak Hill Th Coll 61. **d** 64 **p** 65 Ox. C of St Matt Grandpont w St Luke Ox 64-66; St Leon Bootle 66-68; Hampreston 68-70; C-in-c of Damerham 70-71; V of Queniborough 71-76; in Amer Ch 76-77; V of St Matt Tipton Dio Lich from 77; P-in-c of St Paul Tipton Dio Lich from 77. *107 Dudley Road, Tipton, W Midl.* (021-557 1929)

MATHERS, David Michael Brownlow. b 43. Em Coll Cam 2nd cl Th Trip pt i, 63, BA (2nd cl Th Trip pt ii) 65, MA 69. Clifton Th Coll 65. **d** 67 Sarum **p** 68 Sherborne for Sarum. C of St Clem Parkstone 67-70; Ch Ch Bromley Park 70-73; V of Bures 73-80; in Episc Ch of Brazil 80-82. *c/o 38 Fairfield Avenue, Felixstowe, Suff.*

MATHESON, Alan. b 02. Univ of Melb BA 29, ACT ThL (1st cl) 29. Ridley Coll Melb 23. **d** 30 Bp White for Goulb **p** 31 Goulb. M of Commun of the Ascen and L to Offic Dio Goulb 30-33; C of H Trin Launceston Tas 33-34; Perm to Offic (Col Cl Act) 34; C of Grantham 35-36; R of Nevendon 36-40; Ashingdon w S Fambridge 40-49; Clifton Camville w Chilcote (w Statfold from 67) 49-72; C-in-c of Thorpe Constantine 70-72; Perm to Offic Dio Glouc from 72. *14 Naunton Park Close, Cheltenham, Glos, GL53 7DL.* (Cheltenham 32512)

MATHESON, David Melville. b 23. McGill Univ Montr BA 55, BD 61. Linc Th Coll 77. **d** 77 Buckingham for Ox **p** 78 Reading for Cant for Ox (APM). Chap of Blue Coat Sch Reading Dio Ox from 77; Hon C of St Pet Earley Dio Ox from 78. *Reading Blue Coat School, Sonning, Berks, RG4 0SU.*

MATHESON, John Alexander. b 55. K Coll Halifax NS BA. Harvard Div Coll MDiv 80. **d** 80 Fred. C of Derby & Blackville Dio Fred from 80. *PO Box 82, Renous, NB, Canada, E0C 1K0.*

MATHESON, John Edward. Univ of Manit BSC 52. Trin Coll Tor LTh 57. **d** 56 Tor for NS **p** 57 Rupld for NS. C of Pugwash 56-58; R 58-61; R of River John 58-61; I of Liscomb 63-70; R of St Jo Moose Jaw 70-80; Yorkton Dio Qu'App from 80. *166 Second Avenue North, Yorkton, Sask, Canada.*

MATHESON, Neil Robin. Moore Th Coll Syd ACT ThL 65. **d** 65 **p** 66 Syd. C of Kangaroo Valley 66-67; Dural 67-69; R of Littleton 69-71; Perm to Offic Dio Syd from 78. *124 Kenthurst Road, Kenthurst, NSW, Australia 2154.* (654-1070)

MATHESON, Ronald Stuart. b 29. BA (2nd cl Hist) Lon 50. Ely Th Coll 52. **d** 54 **p** 55 Newc T. C of St Anthony Newc T 54-57; Hedworth 57-59; V of St Mary S Hylton Bp Wearmouth 59-65; P-in-c of Leslie Miss (w Glenrothes) 65-72; P-in-c of Glenrothes 65-69; R 69-73; St Marg Lochee 73-79; USPG Miss Dio Bel Centr Amer from 79. *PO Box 66, Anglican Rectory, 7th Ave S, Corozal Town, Belize.*

MATHESON, Roy Keith. St Jo Coll Auckld 61. ACT ThL 65. NZ Bd of Th Stud LTh 65. **d** 62 **p** 63 Waik. C of Morrinsville 62-63; Te Aroha 63-65; V of Mangakino 65-67; Hon P-in-c of Kawhia Miss Distr 68-70; Perm to Offic Dio Waik 70-72 and from 74; Hon C of St Pet Cathl Hamilton 72-74. *10 Vine Street, Hamilton, NZ.* (63-697)

MATHEW, Barry Charles. St Jo Coll Morpeth 46. **d** 50 **p** 52 River. C of Broken Hill 50-52; R of Moama 52-56; Lockhart 59-62; C of Melb Dioc Centre 62-66; Chap Sunbury Ment Hosp 62-66; Bal Ment Hosp 66-73; Perm to Offic Dio Melb from 73. *5 Crocker Street, Ballarat, Vic, Australia 3350.* (34-1018)

MATHEW, Madazil Pathen. d 39 **p** 40 Trav. In CSI 39-57; P Dio Momb from 57. *PO Box 72, Mombasa, Kenya.*

MATHEWS, Arthur Kenneth. b 06. OBE (Mil) 42. DSC 44. Late Exhib of Ball Coll Ox 3rd cl Mod Hist 28, BA 32, MA 36. Cudd Coll 31. **d** 32 **p** 33 Wakef. C of Penistone 32-34; L to Offic Dio Wakef 34-38; V of Forest Row 38-44; Chap RNVR 39-44; L to Offic Dio Chich 44-46; V of Rogate 46-54; Seq of Terwick 46-54; Commiss Sing 49-64; Wel 60-72; RD of Midhurst 49-54; Hon Chap to Bp of Portsm 50-59; Centr Coll of Angl Communion 54-55; Dean of St Alb 55-63; R of Abbey Ch St Alb 55-63; St Pet Peebles 63-68; V of Thursley 68-76; RD of Godalming 69-74; Hon Chap to Bp of Nor 69-71; Perm to Offic Dio Ox from 77. *The Tallat, Westwell, Burford, Oxon.*

MATHEWS, Laurence William. b 08. TD 50. OBE (Mil) 56. Qu Coll Cam BA 30, MA 34. Ridley Hall Cam 30. **d** 32 **p** 33 Liv. C of All H Allerton 32-36; C-in-c of St Matt St Helens Lancs 36-39; CF 39-66; Men in Disp 44; DACG 53-60; ACG 61-66; Hon Chap to HM the Queen 64-66; Dom Chap to Bp of Chelmsf 67-71; Chap SW France 71-76; C-in-c of Oare w Culbone Dio B & W from 76. *Oare Rectory, Brendon, Devon.* (Brendon 270)

MATHEWS, Richard Twitchell. b 27. Bp's Coll Cheshunt, 57. **d** 59 **p** 60 Leic. C of St Phil Leic 59-63; Chap of Qatar and the Trucial States 63-67; V of Riddlesden 67-74; Dom Chap to Bp of Bunb 74-76; R of Narrogin 76-78; R of Medbourne w Holt and Stockerston w Blaston Dio Leic from 78. *Medbourne Rectory, Market Harborough, Leics.* (Medbourne Green 228)

MATHEWS, Ronald Peel Beresford. b 24. Trin Coll Dub. **d** 64 **p** 65 Cash. C of Blessed Trin Cathl Waterf 64-65; Dean's V 65-66; I of Clonbroney w Killoe 66-71; Drumgoon w Ashfield 71-74; Deputn Sec of Leprosy Miss from 74. *Leprosy Mission, 20 Lincoln Place, Dublin 2, Irish Republic.* (Dublin 61066)

MATHEWS, William Henry Robert. b 11. Bps Coll Cheshunt 49. **d** 52 **p** 53 Lon. C of St Pet Harrow 52-55; St Luke Enfield 55-56; Area Sec UMCA 56-62; V of All SS Hanley 62-66; Asst Sec New Guinea Miss 66-68; R of Eastwell 69-79; Goadby Marwood 69-76; P-in-c of Eaton 75-79; Stathern 75-76; Perm to Offic Dio Pet from 80. *56 Neale Avenue, Kettering, Northants, NN16 9HE.* (Kettering 81941)

MATHIAS, John Maelgwyn. b 15. Late Scho of St D Coll Lamp, Eldon Scho 37, BA (2nd cl Hist) 38. St Mich Coll Llan 40. **d** 40 **p** 41 Ban. C of St Mary Ban 40-44; St Pet Cockett 44-49; V of Dihewyd w Mydroilyn Felinfach 49-54; R of Cellan w Llanfair Clydogau Dio St D from 54; Asst Master

St Jo Coll Ystrad Meurig from 58. *Cellan Rectory, Lampeter, Dyfed.*

MATHIAS, William James. Late Scho and Exhib of St D Coll Lamp BA 41, Univ of Lille, B ès Lettres, 48. Univ of Brussels L en Phil 50. St Ephrem's Inst Solna Sweden DD 79. **d** 42 **p** 43 Llan. C of Treherbert 42-43; Coity w Nolton 43-47; Hampton 47-48; V of Penn St w Holmer Green 48-51; St Mark Victoria Park 51-55; St Andr Stoke Newington 55-63; Can Res of Cathl of H Cross Geraldton 63-65; Exam Chap to Bp of NW Austr 64-65; V of Abertillery 65-77. *95 Gladstone Street, Abertillery, Gwent, NP3 1NG.* (Abertillery 3968)

MATHIESON, Eric. b 25. Down Coll Cam BA 47, MA 52. St Steph Ho Ox. **d** 50 **p** 51 Man. C of St Aug Tonge Moor 50-54; V of St Cath Burnley 54-59; St Alphege S'wark Dio S'wark from 59. *St Alphege Clergy House, Pocock Street, SE1.* (01-928-6158)

MATHODE, Alfred Mbofheni. b 32. St Francis Coll Sekhukhuniland 66. **d** 70 **p** 71 Pret. C of Sibasa Dio Pret from 70. *c/o St Mary's Church, PO Shayandima, via Louis Trichardt, S Africa.*

MATHONSI, Thomas Bhekinkosi. St Bede's Coll Umtata 60. **d** 61 **p** 63 Zulu. P Dio Zulu. *Box 6, Ingwavuma, Zululand, S Africa.*

MATIMA, Canon Bernard. St Bede's Coll Umtata. **d** 56 **p** 58 St Jo Kaffr. P Dio St John's; Hon Can of St John's from 78. *Fobane Mission, PO Kinira Drift, Mount Fletcher, Transkei, S Africa.*

MATIMBA, Elfric. **d** 26 **p** 29 S Rhod. C Dio S Rhod 26-52; Dio Mashon 52-56 *c/o St Faith's Mission, Rusape, Rhodesia.*

MATLALA, Ven Magodi Paul. St Pet Coll Rosettenville, 61. **d** 63 **p** 64 Pret. P Dio Pret; Archd of Centr Transvaal from 78. *PO Box 4, Seshego, Transvaal, S Africa.*

MATLATSA, Canon Marcellianus Setsoho. St Bede's Coll Umtata 46. **d** 48 **p** 49 Bloemf. P Dio Basuto 48-66; Dio Les from 66; Can of Les from 71. *St Bartholomew's Mission, Sekameng, PB Mafeteng, Lesotho.*

MATLEY, Robert Dudley. Melb Coll of Div LTh 65. **d** 70 **p** 71 Syd. C of Cronulla 70-72; Jamberoo 72-74; R of Smithfield Dio Syd from 74. *Lot 1, Justin Street, Smithfield, NSW, Australia 2134.* (604-5414)

MATLHOLA, James Hamilton. b 33. St Bede's Coll Umtata 69. **d** 73 **p** 74 Kimb K. P Dio Kimb K. *Box 150, Vryburg, CP, S Africa.*

✠ **MATOLENGWE, Right Rev Patrick Monwabisi.** St Pet Coll Alice 63. **d** 65 Capetn for Grahmstn **p** 66 Grahmstn. P Dio Grahmstn 65-68; P-in-c of Nyanga Dio Capetn 69-76; Can of Capetn 75-76; Cons Ld Bp Suffr of Capetn in Cathl Ch of St Mich and Geo Grahmstn 21 Nov 76 by Abp of Capetn; Bps of Natal, Geo, St John's, Bloemf, Johann, Grahmstn, Port Eliz, Swaz, Zulu, Pret, Les and Lebom; and others. *Bishop's House, 79 Kildare Road, Newlands, CP. S Africa.* (64-2444)

MATOLWENI, Ven Warrant Xel'tole. St Pet Coll Rosettenville, 50. **d** 52 **p** 53 Johann. P Dio Johann 52-61; Dio St John's from 61; Hon Can of St John's 77-81; Archd of E Griqualand from 81; P-in-c of Clydesdale Dio St John's from 81. *Box 76, Umzimkulu 4660, Transkei, S Africa.*

MATOMELA, Shadrack Tembile. b 33. St Bede's Coll Umtata 73. **d** 74 **p** 75 St John's. P Dio St John's. *Box 217, Cala, Republic of Transkei, S Africa.*

MATON, Oswald. b 24. St Aug Coll Cant 75. **d** 77 **p** 78 Roch. C of St Steph Chatham Dio Roch from 77. *304 Maidstone Road, Chatham, Kent.*

MATONYA, David. b 54. St Phil Coll Kongwa 77. **d** 79 Bp Mohamed for Centr Tang **p** 79 Centr Tang. P Dio Centr Tang. *Box 34, Kongwa, Tanzania.*

MATONYA, Samuel Enock. **d** 56 **p** 57 Centr Tang. P Dio Centr Tang. *Iringa-Mvumi, Tanzania.*

MATONYA, Canon Yeremiya. **d** and **p** 48 Centr Tang. P Dio Centr Tang 48-67; Can of Dodoma from 67. *Ikowa, Tanzania.*

MATSHAI, Solomon Modise. St Pet Coll Rosettenville LTh 40. **d** 40 **p** 42 Bloemf. C of Tala Miss 40-43; Thaba'nchu Miss 43-49; P-in-c of Goldfields Miss 49-52; Miss P at St Mary's Miss Odendaalsrus 52-54; Dir of Winburg Miss Distr and of St Clem Miss Winburg 54-60; Kroonstad Miss Distr 60-64; C of Rustenberg 64-68; P-in-c of Rustenberg W Dio Pret 68-70; R 70-75; Saulsville Dio Pret from 75. *PO Box 1, Atteridgeville 0008, S Africa.*

MATSHISI, Ernest. St Bede's Coll Umtata 73. **d** 73 **p** 74 Port Eliz. C of St Patr Humansdorp Dio Port Eliz from 73. *Box 66, Humansdorp, CP, S Africa.*

MATSINHE, Carlos Simao. St Mark's Coll Dar-S 75. **d** 79 **p** 80 Lebom. P Dio Lebom. *CP 82, Maputo, Mozambique.*

MATSON, Howard Kenneth. Wycl Coll Tor BA 48. Wycl Coll Tor LTh 51. **d** 50 **p** 51 Tor. C of St Paul Halifax 50-52; I of Elmvale 53-55; R of St Phil Etobicoke Tor 55-64; Dalhousie 64-68. *138 Citation Drive, Willowdale, Ont, Canada.*

MATTEN, Derek Norman William. Wycl Hall, Ox 54. **d** 56 **p** 57 Liv. C of Farnworth 56-59; H Trin Walton (in c of Good Shepherd) Aylesbury 59-62; Chap Kampala and Entebbe 62-69; Chap Univ of Karlsruhe 69-73; L to Offic Dio Lon (N & C Eur) from 69. *Adlerweg 13, D-7824 Hinterzarten, W Germany.* (07652/234)

MATTHEW, Andrew Foster. b 45. Oak Hill Th Coll 68. **d** 70 **p** 71 St Alb. C of St Paul St Alb 70-74; Harwell (w Chilton from 76) 74-77; Chilton 74-76; V of St Keverne Dio Truro from 77; RD of Kerrier from 80. *St Keverne Vicarage, Helston, Cornw, TR12 6NE.* (St Keverne 280277)

MATTHEW, George Kenneth. b 18. Worc Ordin Coll 62. **d** 64 **p** 65 S'wark. C of Putney (in c of St John from 65) 64-67; R of Beyton w Hessett 67-73; Medstead w Wield Dio Win from 74. *Medstead Rectory, Alton, Hants.* (Alton 62050)

MATTHEW, Ven John Michael. MBE (Mil) 46. St Jo Coll Rangoon 39-40. Ridley Hall Cam 47-48. **d** 39 **p** 40 Rang. Asst Master St John's Coll Rang 39-40; C of H Trin Cathl Rang 40-42; St Thos Calc 42-43; CF (India) 43-47; Hon CF 46; C of Liv 47; L to Offic Dios Liv and Ely 47-48; Asst Chap H Trin Cathl Rang 48-52; P-in-c of H Cross Kokine 52-66; V of H Trin Cathl Rang 66-78; Hon Can of Rang from 70; Archd from 78. *64 Shwe Dagon Pagoda Road, Rangoon, Burma.*

MATTHEWMAN, Canon Ronald. **d** 53 Lon for Col **p** 54 Hur. C of St Jo Evang Kitchener 53-56; I of St Mark Brantford 56-58; R of Aylmer 58-69; Ascen Windsor Dio Hur from 69; Can of Hur from 70. *1385 University Ave West, Windsor 11, Ont., Canada.* (519-256 4341)

MATTHEWS, Allen. b 06. Univ of Bris BSc 26. **d** and **p** 67 Glouc. C of Newent 67-75; Perm to Offic Dio Glouc from 76. *Wilton Cottage, Culver Street, Newent, Glos.*

MATTHEWS, Ven Anthony Francis Hall. St Francis Coll Brisb 60, ACT ThL 62. **d** 63 **p** 64 Carp. C of Darwin 63-66; Chap Aerial Miss and R of Normanton w Croydon 66-76; Hon Can of Carp 70-76; Archd of Cape York Peninsula from 76; P-in-c of Cooktown Dio Carp from 76. *Box 21, Cooktown, Queensland, Australia 4871.*

MATTHEWS, Arthur. Coll of Resurr Mirfield, 57. **d** 57 **p** 58 Zulu. C of Eshowe 57-58; R of Empangeni 58-61; V of Dundee 61-65; R of St Alphege Pietermaritzburg 65-70; Chap Univ of Natal 65-70; R of Karkloof 70-80; Perm to Offic Dio Natal from 80. *8 Archbell Crescent, Howick, Natal, S Africa.*

MATTHEWS, Barry Alan. b 46. K Coll Lon and Warm AKC 68. **d** 69 **p** 70 Kimb K. C of De Aar 70-71; St Aug Kimb 71-73; St Aid Leeds 74-77; R of St Steph Vryburg 77-81; Exam Chap Dio Kimb K from 81. *c/o PO Box 150, Vryburg 8600, S Africa.* (01451)

MATTHEWS, Basil Wilfrid Barrow. b 1887. Coll of Resurr Mirfield 05. Univ of Leeds BA 09. **d** 11 **p** 12 Lon. C of St Jas Moore Pk Fulham 11-14; St Jas Hampstead Rd 14-18; TCRN 18-19; C of Kingston T 19-23; Hosp of St Thos Hosp 23; V of H Trin Lambeth 23-39; St Laur Catford 39-51; C-in-c of New Bentley 51-57; V of Eastoft 57-60; Perm to Offic Dio S'wark 60-71. *107 Swan Court, Chelsea Manor Street, SW3 5RY.* (01-352 4641)

MATTHEWS, Bertram. b 06. Univ of Lon BA 50. Lich Th Coll 30. **d** 32 **p** 33 Lich. C of Bloxwich 32-36; Cannock (in c of Heath Hayes) 36-39; V of Chasetown 39-56; Colwich 56-71. *80 Gaia Lane, Lichfield, Staffs.*

MATTHEWS, Brian. b 32. ARIC 55. Cranmer Hall Dur 59. **d** 62 **p** 63 Leic. C of Belgrave 62-65; Whitwick 65-69; L to Offic Dio Leic 69-71; P-in-c of Bardon Hill 71-78; V of Whitwick St Andr w Thringstone Dio Leic from 78. *St Andrew's Vicarage, Loughborough Road, Thringstone, Leicester, LE6 4LQ.* (Coalville 222380)

MATTHEWS, Ven Brian Benjamin. OBE 73. Hertf Coll Ox 3rd cl Mod Hist 35, BA 36 MA 40. Chich Th Coll 35. **d** 37 Guildf **p** 38 Bp Golding-Bird for Guildf. C of St Mich Aldershot 37-41; Chap RNVR 41-46; C of Tewkesbury Abbey 46-48; Chap Denstone Coll 48-58; Monte Carlo Dio Gibr (Gibr in Eur from 80) from 58; Can of St Paul's Angl Cathl Malta from 73; Archd of The Riviera from 76. *St Paul's House, Avenue de Grand Bretagne, Monte Carlo.* (307106)

MATTHEWS, Campbell Thurlow. b 33. Univ of Lon BA (2nd cl Geog) 56. St Jo Coll Nottm 70. **d** 71 Dur **p** 72 Bp Skelton for Dur. C of Ryton 71-74; Lect Sunderland Coll of Educn 64-74; V of Greenside Dio Dur from 74. *Greenside Vicarage, Ryton, T & W.* (Ryton 2422)

MATTHEWS, Charles. b 17. MIMechE 51. Wells Th Coll 64. **d** 66 **p** 67 Ches. C of Neston 66-73; V of St Thos Liscard, Wallasey 73-79; Over Tabley w High Legh Dio Ches from 79. *Over Tabley Vicarage, Knutsford, Chesh, WA16 0PL.* (Knutsford 52221)

MATTHEWS, Canon Charles Edwin. b 10. Keble Coll Ox BA (4th cl Th) 31, MA 35. Sarum Th Coll 32. **d** 33 **p** 34 S'wark. C of St Chrys Peckham 33-37; St Clem E Dulwich 37-39; Mortlake (in c of All SS E Sheen) 39-41; V of St Nich

Plumstead 41-48; St Mich AA S Beddington 48-63; Hon Can of S'wark from 58; RD of Beddington 60-63; V of Lingfield 64-77; Perm to Offic Dios Chich and S'wark from 77. *28 Halsford Park Road, East Grinstead, Sussex, RH19 1PS.*

MATTHEWS, Preb Clarence Sydney. b 11. Univ of Lon BA (2nd cl French) 30, BD 38, K Coll Lon Kitchener Scho 30, AKC (1st cl) 32. **d** 34 **p** 35 Lon. C of St Ann Stamford Hill 34-38; Barnes 38-40; V of St Osw Fulham 40-54; Lect in Th at Nat S Tr Coll Hampstead 47-54; V of St Steph Ealing 54-81; Surr from 64; RD of Ealing E 68-79; Preb of St Paul's Cathl Lon 75-81; Preb (Emer) from 81; Hon C of St Dunstan City and Dio Cant from 81. *5 Linden Grove, Canterbury, Kent, CT2 8AB.* (0227-66078)

MATTHEWS, Clifford James. K Coll NS. **d** 53 **p** 54 NS. C of Glace Bay 53-55; I of Musquodoboit Harbour 55-57; Louisbourg Dio NS from 62. *Louisbourg, NS, Canada.* (733-2030)

MATTHEWS, Colin John. b 44. Jes Coll Ox BA 67, MA 71. Fitzw Coll Cam BA 70, MA 74. Ridley Hall Cam 68. **d** 71 **p** 72 Kens for Lon. C of St Paul Kens 71-74; H Ap Leic 74-78; Bible Use Sec Script U from 78. *52 Agraria Road, Guildford, GU2 5LF.* (0483-33412)

MATTHEWS, Daniel Fairbairn. b 40. Bp Patteson Th Centre Kohimarama 71. **d** 73 **p** 74 Melan. d Dio Melan 74-75; Centr Melan from 75. *Patteson House, Honiara, Solomon Islands.*

MATTHEWS, Canon Donald Francis. b 12 Sarum Th Coll 39. **d and p** 41 Glouc. C of St Barn Tuffley 41-47; Berkeley w Sharpness 47-50; PC of St Aldate Glouc 50-68; V 68-75; RD of Glouc City 61-76; Hon Can of Glouc from 64; R of Hempsted Dio Glouc from 75. *Hempsted Rectory, Gloucester.* (Gloucester 24550)

MATTHEWS, Frank. AKC 22. **d** 23 **p** 24 Lon. C of St Mary Ealing 23-29; C-in-c of Ramsbury w Axford 29-30. *77 Gresham Road, Staines, Middx.*

MATTHEWS, Preb Frederick Albert John. b 13. Ex Coll Ox BA (2nd cl Mod Lang) 33, MA 38. Wycl Hall Ox 34. **d** 36 Crediton for Ex **p** 37 Ex. C of Stoke Damerel 36-44; V of Pinhoe 44-61; RD of Aylesbeare 57-61; V of Plympton Dio Ex from 61; Archd of Plymouth 62-78; Preb of Ex from 78. *St Mary's Vicarage, Plympton, Devon, PL7 4LD.* (Plymouth 336157)

MATTHEWS, Frederick Peter. b 45. Grey Coll Dur BA (2nd cl Th) 66, MA 68. Sarum Wells Th Coll 70. **d** 72 **p** 73 Cant. C of W Wickham 72-75; Sholing 75-78; Publ Pr Dio Win from 78; Asst Master Bellemoor Sch Southn 78-79; V of Woolston Dio Win from 79. *117 Swift Road, Woolston, Southampton.* (Southn 448542)

MATTHEWS, George Charles Wallace. b 27. Sarum Th Coll 58. **d** 60 **p** 61 Ches. C of St Paul Coppenhall 60-63; St Anne Lewes 63-67; V of Wheelock 67-76; Mossley Dio Ches from 76. *Mossley Vicarage, Congleton, Chesh.* (Congleton 3182)

MATTHEWS, Gerald Charles. b 1899. **d** 41 **p** 42 Ox. [f Bapt Min] C of Cowley 41-44; St Mary Reading 44-47; V of Headington Quarry Ox 47-55; R of Newbury 55-69; Surr 59-69; L to Offic Dio Sheff from 70. *36 Rupert Road, Sheffield 7.*

MATTHEWS, Gerald Lancelot. b 31. Ripon Hall Ox 55. **d** 57 Birm **p** 58 Aston for Birm. C of The Quinton 57-60; Olton 60-63; V of Brent Tor w N Brentor Chap 63-72; P-in-c (R from 72) of Lydford w Bridestowe and Sourton (w Brent Tor and N Brentor Chap from 72) 70-78; P-in-c of Black Torrington, Bradford and Thornbury Dio Ex from 78. *Rectory, Black Torrington, Beaworthy, Devon, EX21 5PU.* (Black Torrington 279)

MATTHEWS, Gerrit. d 68 **p** 69 Pret. C of St Sav W Suburbs Dio Pret from 69. *Box 19028, Pretoria West, S Africa.* (79-5528)

MATTHEWS, Gilbert Brian Reeves. b 19. Keble Coll Ox BA 42, MA 48. St Steph Ho Ox 41. **d** 44 Ox for Chich **p** 45 Chich. C of St Wilfrid Brighton 44-49; Ch Ch St Leonards-on-Sea 49-55; Finedon 55-58; R of Rushton (w Pipewell from 78) w Glendon (and Thorpe Malsor from 79) 58-81; Dioc Chap for Youth 58-64; P-in-c of Thorpe Malsor 76-80. *c/o Rushton Rectory, Kettering, Northants.* (Kettering 710415)

MATTHEWS, Harold James. b 46. Univ of Leeds BSc 68. Fitzw Coll Cam BA 70, MA 74. Westcott Ho Cam 68. **d** 71 Warrington for Liv **p** 72 Liv. C of Mossley Hill 71-74; St Anne Stanley Liv 74-76; Team V of St Jas Clapton in Hackney Team Min 76-78; Chap of Forest Sch Snaresbrook from 78. *11 Isabella Road, Hackney, E9.* (01-986 8584)

MATTHEWS, Canon Hubert Samuel. MBE 66. Ripon Hall Ox 29. **d** 34 **p** 35 York. C of St Aug Newland Hull 34-36; Chap of Valparaiso 36-39; V of Rudston 39-46; Lowthorpe w Ruston Parva 46-54; CF 47-49; CF (TA) 50-54; Chap at Limassol Cyprus 54-74; Hon Can of St Geo Colleg Ch Jer 73-75; Can (Emer) from 76; L to Offic Dio Cyprus from 78. *Kato Polemidhia, Limassol, Cyprus.*

MATTHEWS, John. b 22. TD 66. Trin Coll Cam BA 48, MA 51. Bps' Coll Cheshunt, 49. **d** 51 **p** 52 Sheff. C of Woodlands 51-54; St Andr Sharrow Sheff 54-57; CF (TA) from 53; V of St Barn Sheff 57-62; Gt Dunmow Dio Chelmsf from 62; C-in-c of L Canfield 62-70; Gt Easton Dio Chelmsf from 70; M Gen Syn 70-80; RD of Dunmow from 75. *Vicarage, Great Dunmow, Essex, CM6 2AE.* (Gt Dunmow 2504)

MATTHEWS, John David. K Coll Lon and Warm AKC 55. **d** 56 **p** 57 Sarum. C of E w W Harnham 56-59; St Mary's Colleg Ch of Port Eliz 59-63; R of Primrose 64-67; Linden Dio Johann from 67. *75 Eighth Street, Linden, Johannesburg, Transvaal, S Africa.* (011-46 1392)

MATTHEWS, John Gilbert. St Jo Coll Winnipeg. **d** 54 **p** 55 Rupld. C of St Luke Winnipeg 54-56; R of Manitou 56-59; I of Chemainus 59-65; R of Ch Ch 65-71; I of Fort McMurray 71-75; Nipawin Dio Sask from 76. *Box 701, Nipawin, Sask, Canada.*

MATTHEWS, Lewis William. b 29. St Jo Coll Dur BA (2nd cl Gen) 53, MSc 76, Dipl Th 55. **d** 55 Selby for York **d** 56 York. C of Eston 55-57; H Trin Wicker Sheff 57; Industr Miss Dio Sheff 57-61; V of Copt Oak 61-64; Braunstone 64-70; Team R of Thornaby-on-Tees 70-78; Dir Lon Dioc Bd for Social Responsibility from 80. *c/o 30 Causton Street, SW1P 4AU.*

MATTHEWS, Melvyn William. b 40. St Edm Hall, Ox BA (2nd cl Mod Lang) 63, MA 67. K Coll Lon and Warm BD (2nd cl) and AKC (2nd cl) 67. **d** 67 **p** 68 Lon. C of Enfield 67-70; Asst Chap Univ of Southn and L to Offic Dio Win 70-72; Lect Univ of Nai and L to Offic Dio Nai 73-76; V of All SS Highgate Lon 76-79; P-in-c of St Paul Ap Clifton Dio Bris from 79; Sen Chap Univ of Bris from 79. *9 Leigh Road, Bristol, BS8 2DA.* (Bristol 37427)

MATTHEWS, Oswald John. St Edm Hall, Ox BA 37, MA 40. Ripon Hall, Ox 35. **d** 37 **p** 38 York. C of Beverley Minster 37-41; V of St Pet Drypool 41-48; Fridaythorpe w Fimber and Thixendale 48-53; Chap Mission to Seamen Buenos Aires 53-54; Wel 55-64; V of Taita 64-69; Wanganui E 69-77; Perm to Offic Dio Wel from 78. *55a Jellicoe Street, Wellington, NZ.* (39-540)

MATTHEWS, Canon Percival Charles Halls. b 15. Em Coll Cam 2nd cl Hist Trip pt i, 36, BA (3rd cl Th Trip pt ii) 37, MA 41. Wycl Hall, Ox 37. **d** 38 **p** 39 Birm. C of St Steph Selly Hill 38-41; Org Sec CPAS for Midls 41-45; Publ Pr Dio Birm 42-44; V of St Chrys Birm 44-49; H Trin N Harborne Smethwick 49-53; St Geo Douglas 53-57; St Geo and St Barn w All SS Douglas 57-80; Proc Conv S & M 64-80; RD of Douglas 71-80; Can of St German Cathl Peel 75-80; Can (Emer) from 80. *Edelweiss, Glen Loch Circle, Glen Vine, IM.*

MATTHEWS, Peter Henry. b 22. Sarum Th Coll 62. **d** 64 **p** 65 Sarum. C of Wareham w Arne 64-67; P-in-c of Houghton 67; Sholing (in c of St Francis) 67-69; R of Hilperton w Whaddon 69-78; P-in-c of St Paul Staverton 71-72; V 72-78; P-in-c of Milborne St Andrew w Dewlish Dio Sarum from 78. *Milborne St Andrew Vicarage, Blandford, Dorset, DT11 0JP.* (025-887227)

✠ **MATTHEWS, Right Rev Ralph Vernon.** St Jo Coll Auckld NZ Bd of Th Stud LTh (1st cl) 58. **d** 55 **p** 56 Wai. C of Hastings 55-60; V of Waipukurau 60-70; Hon Can of St John's Cathl Wai 69-70; Can 70-76; V of Taupo 70-76; Gisborne 76-79; Archd of Wai 76-79; Cons Ld Bp of Wai in Cathl Ch of St Jo Evang Napier 31 Aug 79 By Abp of NZ; Bps of Nel, Ch Ch, Auckld, Wel, Polyn and Newc T; and others. *8 Cameron Terrace, Napier, NZ.*

MATTHEWS, Robert Gregory. St Chad's Coll Regina. **d** 54 **p** 55 Qu'App. C of Medicine Hat 54-56; St Geo Willowdale Tor 56-59; I of Beeton 56-60; C of Kelowna 60-65; I of Cowichan Lake 65-67; R of Arrow Lakes 68-71; Summerland Dio Koot from 71. *Box 697, Summerland, BC, Canada.* (494-3466)

MATTHEWS, Rodney Charles. b 36. Sarum Th Coll 62. **d** 64 **p** 65 Chelmsf. C of Gt Clacton w L Holland 64-68; St Mary Virg (in-c of St Mich AA) Loughton Dio Chelmsf 68-74; Team V 74-76; V of All SS Goodmayes Dio Chelmsf from 76. *All Saints' Vicarage, Broomhill Road, Goodmayes, Essex, IG3 9SJ.* (01-590 1476)

MATTHEWS, Canon Roy Ian John. b 27. TD 71. St Cath S Ox BA (Th) 52, MA 56. St Steph Ho Ox 52. **d** 54 **p** 55 Wakef. C of St Mary Barnsley 54-58; V of Staincliffe 58-65; CF (TA) 58-67; (TAVR) from 67; V of Penistone w Midhope 65-72; Brighouse Dio Wakef from 72; Surr from 65; Hon Can of Wakef Cathl from 76. *Vicarage, Brighouse, Yorks, HD6 1AU.* (Brighouse 714032)

MATTHEWS, Royston Peter. b 39. St D Coll Lamp BA 61. Univ of Wales, Dipl Th 64. St Mich Coll Llan. **d** 64 Bp T M Hughes for Llan **p** 65 Llan. C of Fairwater Conv Distr Cardiff 64-67; Cadoxton-Juxta-Barry 67-71; R of Henllys w

Bettws 71-80; V of Bettws Dio Mon from 80. *St David's Rectory, Bettws, Newport, Gwent.* (Newport 855193)

MATTHEWS, Ruth Helenor. b 16. **d** 64 **p** 77 Queb. I of St Francis of Assisi Dio Queb from 77. *276 Heriot Street, Drummondville, Quebec, J2C 1K1, Canada.*

MATTHEWS, Stuart James. b 37. St Jo Coll Dur BA 60. Bps' Coll Cheshunt. **d** 62 **p** 63 Chich. C of Horsham 62-65; Rednal Birm 65-67; Min of St Bede's Eccles Distr Brandwood 67-68; C of Northfield 68-72; V of Thurcroft Dio Sheff from 72; RD of Laughton from 79. *122 Green Arbour Road, Thurcroft, Rotherham, Yorks, S66 9ED.* (Wickersley 542261)

MATTHEWS, Terence Leslie. Handsworth Coll 55. **d** 61 **p** 62 York. C of W Acklam 61-64; V of Horden 64-72; R of Witton Gilbert 72-77; P-in-c of Grangetown Dio Dur 77-81; V from 81. *St Aidan's Vicarage, Grangetown, Sunderland, SR2 9RS.* (Sunderland 43485)

MATTHEWS, Thomas Ernest. b 04. **d** 52 **p** 53 Bradf. C of Keighley (in c of All SS) 52-56; R of Creeton w Counthorpe and Swinstead 56-77; Swayfield 60-77; Perm to Offic Dio Linc from 77. *22 Station Road, Little Bytham, Grantham, NG33 4RA.*

✠ **MATTHEWS, Right Rev Timothy John.** b 07. Bp's Univ Lennox LST 32, STh 42, BA 44. CD 63. **d** 32 **p** 33 Edmon. C of Viking 33-37; I of Edson 37-40; R of Coaticook 40-44; Kenogami 44-52; R and Archd of Gaspé 52-57; R of Lennoxville 57-71; Archd of St Francis 57-71; Cons Ld Bp of Quebec on 28 Sept 71 by Bp of NS; Bps of Newfld; Montr; Bps Suffr of NS; Newfld; and Bp Waterman; res 77. *23 High Street, Lennoxville, PQ, Canada.*

MATTHEWS, Victor Bruce Thorne. Acadia Univ NS BA 63. Mansfield Coll Ox BA 65, MA 69. Trin Coll Tor STB 66. **d** and **p** 66 Tor. C of St Jas Cathl Tor 66-69; Lect McMaster Univ Hamilton Ont 69-72; Laurentian Univ of Ont 72-76; Univ of tor from 76. *University of Toronto, Toronto, Ont, Canada.*

MATTHEWS, Victoria. b 54. Univ of Tor BA 76. Yale Div Sch MDiv 77. **d** 79 Bp Read for Tor **p** 80 Tor. C of St Andr Scarboro City and Dio Tor from 79. *2333 Victoria Park Avenue, Scarborough, Ont, Canada, M1R 1W6.*

MATTHEWS, William Andrew. b 44. Univ of Reading BA (2nd cl Engl) 65. St Steph Ho Ox 65. **d** 67 **p** 68 Bris. C of St Alb Westbury Pk Clifton 67-70; Marlborough 70-73; C-in-c of Winsley 73-75; V 75-81; Bradford-on-Avon Dio Sarum from 81. *Holy Trinity Vicarage, Bradford-on-Avon, Wilts.* (B-on-A 4444)

MATTHEWS-PAYNE, James. St D Coll Lamp BA 41. Lich Th Coll 41. St Mich Coll Llan 46. **d** 46 **p** 47 Llan. C of Merthyr Dyfan 46-51; St Cath Canton Cardiff 51-53; Aberavon 53-55; R of Southn Berm 55-60; V of Woolston 60-65; R of Bridgetown Bunb 65-68; Narrogin 68-71; Morley w Hampton Park 71-79; Morley-Noranda 79-80; Perm to Offic Dio Perth from 80. *Unit 11, 22 Freedman Road, Mount Lawley, W Australia 6050.*

MATTHEWSON, James Scott. b 15. Wycl Hall, Ox 54. **d** 56 **p** 57 Newc T. C of Walker 56-58; H Trin Jesmond Newc T 58-62; V of Widdrington Dio Newc T from 62; Ulgham Dio Newc T from 62. *Vicarage, Widdrington Station, Morpeth, Northumb, NE16 5PU.* (Morpeth 790389)

MATTHIAE, David. b 40. Fitzw Ho Cam BA 63, MA 69. Linc Th Coll 63. **d** 65 Cant **p** 66 Dover for Cant. C of New Addington 65-70; SS Pet and Paul Charlton Dover 70-75; V of St Greg Gt (All SS from 76) City and Dio Cant from 75. *All Saints Vicarage, Military Road, Canterbury, Kent, CT1 1PH.* (Cant 63505)

MATTHIAS, Edwin. b 23. AKC (2nd cl) 50. St Bonif Coll Warm 50. **d** 51 **p** 52 Leic. C of St Mary Hinckley 51-54; Putney (in c of All SS) 54-58; V of Bolney 58-65; R of Chailey Dio Chich from 65. *Chailey Rectory, Lewes, Sussex.* (Newick 2286)

MATTHIAS, George Ronald. b 30. St Deiniol's Libr Hawarden 76. **d** 78 **p** 79 St A. C of Broughton Dio St A from 78. *Sandown, Westminster Road, Moss, Wrexham, Clwyd.*

MATTINGLEY, Brian John. b 14. Univ of Tas BA. **d** 80 Bp Jerrim for Tas **p** 81 Tas. Hon C of Scottsdale Dio Tas from 80. *Westwood Street, Bridport, Tasmania 7254.*

MATTOCK, Donald Walter. b 26. Univ of Tor BComm 49. Ex/Truro Min Tr Scheme. **d** 81 Ex (NSM). C of St Greg Dawlish Dio Ex from 81. *White House, Ideford, Newton Abbot, Devon.*

MATTY, Horace Anthony. b 36. Ely Th Coll 61. **d** 63 **p** 64 Glouc. C of Minchinhampton w Box 63-66; Hunslet w Stourton 66-69; Team V in Shingay Group 69-71; V of Parson-Drove 71-74; Southea w Murrow 71-74; Coven Dio Lich from 74. *Coven Vicarage, Wolverhampton, Staffs.* (Standeford 230)

MATUMBO, Luxford. St Phil Th Coll Kongwa. **d** 58 Bp Omari for Centr Tang **p** 58 Centr Tang. P Dio Centr Tang 58-77; w Bible S of Tanzania from 80. *Box 175, Dodoma, Tanzania.*

MATUMBO, Stephen. **d** 69 **p** 70 Moro. P Dio Moro 69-79. *Primary School, PO Magole, Tanzania.*

MATUTA, Julius. **d** 74 **p** 75 S Malawi. P Dio S Malawi. *Central High School, Box 5023, Limbe, Malawi.*

MAUBE, Canon Filemon. St Phil Th Coll Kongwa. **d** 57 Centr Tang **p** 58 Bp Omari for Centr Tang. P Dio Centr Tang 57-65; Dio Moro from 65; Hon Can of Moro from 77. *Iwogwe, PO Berega, Morogoro, Tanzania.*

MAUDE, Alan. b 41. BD (Lon) 69. STh (Lambeth) 74. Oak Hill Th Coll. **d** 69 Hulme for Man **p** 70 Man. C of Balderstone Rochdale 69-73; St Matt Crumpsall 73-75; Chap R Vic Infirm Newc T from 75. *Royal Victoria Infirmary, Newcastle-on-Tyne.*

MAUDE, Ralph Henry Evelyn. b 09. St Pet Hall, Ox BA 33, MA 37. St Steph Ho Ox 32. **d** 33 **p** 34 Bris. C of St Geo Brandon Hill Bris 33-36; St Steph Bournemouth 36-45; R of St Jas Shaftesbury 45-57; V of St Paul Weymouth 57-66; St Pet Devizes 66-74. *6 Titan Barrow, Bathford, Bath, Somt.*

MAUDSLEY, George Lambert. b 27. St Jo Coll Nottm 74. **d** 75 Bp Parker for Cov **p** 76 Bp McKie for Cov. C of Binley 75-77; Chap Barn Fellowship Winterborne Whitechurch from 77. *Whatcombe House, Winterborne Whitechurch, Blandford Forum, Dorset, DT11 0PB.* (Milton Abbas 880280)

MAUDSLEY, Keith. b 51. Univ of York BA 72. Ripon Hall ox 72. **d** 75 Bp Parker for Cov **p** 76 Bp McKie for Cov. C of Rugby 75-78; St Mary Gt Cam Dio Ely from 79. *30 Eachard Road, Cambridge, CB3 0HX.* (Cam 354349)

MAUDSLEY, Michael Peter. b 38. Univ of St Andr BSc (2nd cl Chem) 61. Oak Hill Th Coll 65. **d** 67 **p** 68 Blackb. C of St Mark Layton Blackpool 67-70; Hartford Chesh 70-72; R of Balerno 72-82; V of Stapenhill w Caldwell Dio Derby from 82. *Vicarage, Stapenhill Road, Stapenhill, Burton-on-Trent, Staffs.* (0283-64589)

MAUGER, Canon Lennard Gaudin. St Barn Coll Adel. **d** 50 **p** 51 Bunb. C of Manjimup 50-53; R of Lake Grace 53-59; Manjimup 59-68; Cranbrook 68-75; Can of Bunb 67-75; Can (Emer) from 75; Perm to Offic Dio Perth from 75; Dio Bunb from 76. *115 Currie Street, Warnbro, W Australia 6169.* (095-27 3189)

MAUGHAM, James Reavley. Men in Disp 44. Roch Th Coll. **d** 60 **p** 61 Chelmsf. C of St Mary Virg Loughton 60-62; Chap Versailles 62-68; Chap Maisons Laffitte 62-68; V of St Jo Evang Seven Kings 68-73; P-in-c of Panfield 73-79. *c/o 23 Mildmay Road, Burnham on Crouch, Essex.*

MAUGHAN, Bruce Edward. St Francis Coll Brisb. **d** 79 Brisb. Perm to Offic Dio Brisb from 79. *c/o Southport School, Surch Avenue, Southport, Queensland, Australia 4215.*

MAUGHAN, Geoffrey Nigel. b 48. CCC BA 69, MA 73. Oak Hill Coll 75. **d** 77 **p** 78 S'wark. C of New Malden w Coombe 77-81; Abingdon (in-c of Ch Ch) Dio Ox from 81. *69 Northcourt Road, Abingdon, Oxon.* (Abingdon 20115)

MAUGHAN, John. Keble Coll Ox BA 51, MA 55. Linc Th Coll. **d** 53 **p** 54 Dur. C of Heworth 53-56; Winlaton (in c of St Barn Rowlands Gill) 56-59; R of Penshaw 59-72; V of Cleadon Park Dio Dur from 72. *218 Sunderland Road, South Shields, Co Durham.* (South Shields 60091)

MAUGHAN, Canon Joseph. b 02. St Jo Coll Durham BA 30, Dipl in Th 31, MA 33. **d** 31 **p** 32 Dur. C of St Aid W Hartlepool 31-33; Wolsingham 33-35; V of St Cuthb Dur 35-44; R of Jarrow 44-55; PC of Seaton Carew 55-61; Hon Can Dur 55-78; Can (Emer) from 78; V of Kelloe 61-74. *1 Foxton Way, High Shincliffe, Durham.*

MAULIDI, Sifaeli. St Phil Th Coll Kongwa, 63. **d** 65 Bp Madinda for Centr Tang **p** 65 Centr Tang. P Dio Moro. *Box 320, Morogoro, Tanzania.*

MAULTSAID, John Wesley. Univ of Manit BA 61. St Chad's Coll Regina 59. **d** 61 Qu'App. C of St Paul's Pro Cathl Regina 61-63; I of Nokomis 63-66; R of St Timothy Sktn 66-70; C of St John Cathl Bel 70-71; L to Offic Dio Br Hond (Bel from 73) from 71. *111 Albert Street, Belize City, British Honduras.*

✠ **MAUND, Right Rev John Arthur Arrowsmith.** b 09. CBE 75. MC 46. Univ of Leeds BA 31. Coll of Resurr Mirfield 31. **d** 33 **p** 34 Worc. C of Evesham 33-36; All SS Blackheath 36-38; Asst P Pret Native Miss Dio Pret 39-40 and 46-50; CF (S Afr) 40-46; Men in Disp 42; Cons Ld Bp of Basuto (Les from 66) in St Geo Cathl Capetn 19 Nov 50 by Abp of Capetn; Bps of Natal; S Rhod; St Jo Kaffr; Grahmstn; Pret; Bloemf; Geo; St Helena; Kimb K; Zulu; Lebom; Johann; Damar; and Bps Lavis; Peacey; and Stainton; res 76; Perm to Offic Dio St E from 77. *Hengrave Community, Bury St Edmunds, Suff.* (Culford 338)

MAUNDRELL, Canon Wolseley David. b 20. Late Exhib of New Coll Ox BA (2nd Cl Phil Pol and Econ) 41, Dipl Th 42, MA 45. **d** 43 **p** 44 Guildf. C of Haslemere 43-49; Dom Chap to Bp of Chich 49-50; V of Sparsholt w Lainston 50-56;

R of Weeke (or Wyke) 56-61; Can Res of Win 61-70; Treas 61-70; Vice-Dean 66-70; Exam Chap to Bp of Win 62-70; Asst Chap H Trin Brussels 70-71; V of Icklesham 72-81; RD of Rye from 78; Can and Preb of Chich Cathl from 81; Team R of Rye Dio Chich from 82. *Rectory, Gun Garden, Rye, E Sussex, TN31 7HH.* (Rye 2430)

MAUNG KWAI, Luke. **d** 36 **p** 37 Rang. P Dio Rang 36-70; Archd of Moulmein 67-70; P Dio Pa-an 70-80. *Nat Shin Naung Road, Toungoo, Burma.*

MAUNG MAUNGH, Joseph. H Cross Coll Rang. **d** 59 **p** 60 Rang. P Dio Rang. *St Michael's Church, Kemmendine Road, Rangoon, Burma.*

MAUNG SEIN, **d** 77 **p** 78 Akyab. P Dio Akyab. *Emmanuel Church, Tui Kan Vum, Burma.*

MAUNSELL, Colin Wray Dymock. b 33. Pemb Coll Cam BA (3rd Cl Mech Sc Trip pt i) 56. Dipl Th (Lon) 58. Tyndale Hall Bris. **d** 58 Kingston T for Guildf **p** 59 Guildf. C of Virginia Water 58-60; w BCMS from 60. *c/o 251 Lewisham Way, SE4 1XF.*

MAUNSELL, John Harcourt. **d** 48 **p** 50 Br Colum. I of Cowichan 49-55; Chap Shawnigan Lake Sch 55-57; V of Keremeos 57-60; Waihi 60-61; Frankton 61-65; R of Glandore 65-67; C of St Barn Vic Dio BC from 71. *5-1005 St Charles Street, Victoria, BC, Canada.*

MAURICE, Canon David Powys. b 31. K Coll Lon and Warm 51. **d** 55 **p** 56 CheLmsf. C of Prittlewell 55-59; H Trin Fareham 59-63; V of Costessey 63-70; N Walsham w Antingham 70-78; Hon Can of Nor from 77; R of Cley-next-the-Sea w Wiveton Dio Nor from 78; Blakeney Dio Nor from 78; Letheringsett w Bayfield w Glandford Dio Nor from 78. *Blakeney Rectory, Holt, Norf, NR25 7NJ.* (Cley 740686)

MAURICE, Canon Lionel Selwyn. b 1899. St Jo Coll Ox BA (3rd cl Th) 22, MA 45. Bps' Coll Cheshunt, 22. **d** 23 **p** 24 S'wark. C of St Marg Lee 23-29; R of Offord d'Arcy w Offord Cluny 29-38; Cottenham 38-64; RD of N Stowe 56-64; Hon Can of Ely 61-69; Can (Emer) from 69. *15a Perry Road, Buckden, Huntingdon, Cambs, PE18 9XG.* (Huntingdon 810314)

MAURICE, Peter David. b 51. St Chad's Coll Dur BA 72. Coll of Resurr Mirfield 73. **d** 75 **p** 76 S'wark. C of St Paul Wimbledon Pk 75-79; Team V of Mortlake w E Sheen Dio S'wark from 79. *86 East Sheen Avenue, SW14 8AU.* (01-876 4201)

MAURICK, Bernardus Johannes Catharina. b 25. **d** 74 **p** 75 Johann. C of Roodepoort Dio Johann from 74. *8 Eider Road, Florida Lake, Florida Tvl 1710, S Africa.* (011-672 3051)

MAURITIUS, Lord Bishop of. *See* Huddleston, Most Rev Ernest Urban Trevor.

MAURITIUS, Dean of. *See* Cathan, Very Rev Paul Ambrose.

MAW, Dwai. **d** 36 **p** 37 Rang. P Dio Rang. *Anglican Mission, Pa-an, Karen State, Burma.*

MAWA, William. St Pet Coll Rosettenville 58. **d** 60 **p** 61 Kimb K. P Dio Kimb K 60-70; Dio Port Eliz 71-78; Dio Grahmstn from 78. *PO Box 159, Port Alfred, CP, S Africa.*

MAWER, David Ronald. Late Exhib of Keble Coll Ox BA 55, MA 58. Univ of Dur BA 57. Wells Th Coll 58. **d** 59 **p** 60 Newc T. C of St Geo Cullercoats 59-61; Chap Qu Coll St John's 61-64; Vice Prin 64-65; Research Stud Faculty of Div McGill Univ 65-73; Lect Em Coll Sktn and L to Offic Dio Sktn 74-81; Exam Chap to Bp of Sktn 76-78. *c/o 71 Bronson Avenue, Ottawa, Ont, Canada.*

MAWHINNEY, Stanley Allen. b 32. **d** 79 **p** 80 Dun. Hon C of St John Div Invercargill Dio Dun from 79. *20 Frome Street, Invercargill, NZ.*

MAWSON, Canon Arthur Cyril. b 35. St Pet Coll Ox BA (2nd cl Nat Sc) 56, MA 61. Wycl Hall Ox 61. **d** 62 **p** 63 Lich. C of Walsall 62-66; V of H Trin Millhouses Sheff 66-73; Selection Sec ACCM 73-79; L to Offic Dio Lon 73-79; Can Res and Treas of Ex Cathl from 79; Dioc Dir of Ordinands Dio Ex from 81. *9 The Close, Exeter, Devon, EX1 1EZ.* (Ex 79367)

MAWSON, David Frank. b 44. Selw Coll Cam BA 65, MA 69. Linc Th Coll 79. **d** 80 Stafford for Lich **p** 81 Lich. C of Ch Ch Tunstall Dio Lich from 80. *7 Park Terrace, Tunstall, Stoke-on-Trent, Staffs, ST6 6BP.* (Stoke/Trent 819175)

MAWSON, Frank. b 18. ACIS 70. N-W Ordin Course 74. **d** 77 Ches **p** 78 Stockport for Ches. C of St Mary Stockport 77-79; P-in-c of Harthill w Burwardsley Dio Ches from 79. *Vicarage, Harthill Road, Tattenhall, Chester, CH3 9NU.* (Tattenhall 70067)

MAWSON, Robert. St Jo Coll Morpeth ThL 37. **d** 38 **p** 39 Newc. C of Waratah 38-39; St Jas Morpeth 39-40; Miss Chap Dio Brisb 40; C of Ch Ch Cathl Newcastle 40-43; Chap RAN 43-46; Chap Miss to Seaman Dio Newc 46-48; R of Raymond Terrace 48-49; Woolloongabba 49-55; Gympie 55-60; Glouc 60-66; Morpeth 66-79; Can of Newc 76-79; Perm to Offic Dio Newc from 79. *58 New England Highway, Lochinvar, NSW, Australia 2321.* (30 7351)

MAWSON, Robin Charles. b 40. St Jo Coll Auckld LTh 77. **d** 76 **p** 77 Wai. C of St Aug Napier 76-78; V of Mahora Dio Wai from 78. *821 Ngaio Street, Hastings, NZ.* (82-665)

MAX, Alexander Llewhellin. St D Coll Lamp BA 34. St Mich Coll Llan 35. **d** 35 **p** 36 Mon. C of H Trin Newport 35-37; St Andr Newport 37-39; St Jas Sutton 39-41; Conv Distr of Carlin How w Skinningrove 41-44; St Annes-on-the-Sea 44-47; R of Thurlton w Thorpe-next-Haddiscoe 47-50; Earsham 50-77; C-in-c of Denton 50-56. *7 Mill Gardens, Woodton, Bungay, Suff.*

MAXFIELD, Stephen John Farquhar. b 50. Chich Th Coll 77. **d** 80 **p** 81 Heref. C of Cleobury Mortimer w Hopton Wafers Dio Heref from 80. *Glebe House, New Road Gardens, Cleobury Mortimer, Nr Kidderminster, 59)*

MAXTED, Canon Kenneth Edward. Hur Coll LTh 64. **d** 63 Bp Snell for Tor **p** 64 Tor. C of St Anne Tor 64-65; St John York Mills Tor 65-68; R of Ch of Comforter Tor 68-72; St Luke Tor 72-77; V of H Trin City and Dio Tor from 77; Can of Tor from 78. *10 Trinity Square, Toronto, Ont., Canada.* (416-362 4521)

MAXWELL, Barry Colin Clarke. Moore Th Coll ACT ThL 64. **d** 64 **p** 65 Syd. C of Miranda 64-67; Wahroonga 67-68; C-in-c of Mascot 68-74; Asst Master Shore C of E Gr Sch N Syd 74-80; L to Offic Dio Syd from 74; Asst Master St Andr Cathl Sch Syd from 80. *130 Boundary Road, Pennant Hills, NSW, Australia 2120.* (84-2242)

MAXWELL, Bill. **d** 75 B & W. C of Ch Ch Clevedon 75. Missr Dio Chile from 76. *Casilla 26-D, Temuco, Chile.*

MAXWELL, Bunty Te Wiremate. b 20. **d** 77 **p** 78 Aotearoa for Wai. Hon C of Te Kaha Past Dio Wai from 77. *Torere PO, Opotiki, Bay of Plenty, NZ.*

MAXWELL, Christopher John Moore. b 31. Qu Coll Cam MA 75. MRCS 59. LRCP 59. Trin Coll Bris 74. **d** 75 B & W **p** 76 Chile. C of Ch Ch Clevedon 75; SAMS Miss Dio Chile from 75. *Mision Anglicana, Casilla 26D, Temuco, Chile.*

MAXWELL, Eric Linton. Univ of Dur LTh 30, BA 33. St Pet Coll Ja. **d** 30 **p** 31 Ja. C of St Matt Kingston 30-32; Asst Master Kingston Coll 31-32; R of St Matt Allman Town Kingston 33-35; Buff Bay w Birnamwood 35-36; Port Maria 36-39; Spanish Town 39-44; Can of Ja Cathl 39-44 and 51-57; CF (WI) 44-46; R of St Anne's Bay 46-48; St Luke Cross Rds 48-74; Archd of Surrey 57-73; Kingston 74-78; Chap Up Park Camp 52-57 and 62-63; Commiss Antig from 71. *5 Gloucester Avenue, Kingston 6, Jamaica, W Indies.* (093-76578)

MAXWELL, Ian Charles. b 17. Ch Coll Cam BA 40, MA 44. Ridley Hall Cam 40. **d** 42 **p** 43 Roch. C of Ch Ch Dartford 42-45; CF (EC) 45-47; V of St Jas Aston 47-51; CMS Area Sec and L to Offic Dios Newc T and Dur 51-53; CMS Area Sec Dios Ox Sarum and Win 53-55; V of All SS Belvedere 55-61; R of Stanhope 61-74; Gt w L Somerford and Seagry Dio Bris from 74. *Great Somerford Rectory, Chippenham, Wilts.* (Seagry 720220)

MAXWELL, James Edmund. Univ of Tor BA 39. Trin Coll Tor LTh 41. **d** and **p** 41 Niag. C of Grand Valley w Colbeck 41-42; Jarvis and Cheapside 42-44; C of St Thos St Catharines 46-47; I of Hornby 47-75; Hon Can of Niag 65-75. *RR5, Georgetown, Ont., Canada.*

MAXWELL, Canon Malcolm Aubrey. Codr Coll Barb. **d** 51 Barb for Windw Is **p** 52 Windw Is. C of Castries St Lucia 52-54; V of St Sav 54-61; St Aug Barb 61-67; St Paul Barb 67-76; Chap of Gen Hosp Barb 68-76; R of Ch Ch I and Dio Barb from 76; Can of Barb from 76. *Rectory, Christ Church, Barbados, W Indies.*

MAXWELL, Malcolm Garth. b 44. Univ of K Coll Halifax BA 66, MSLitt 72. **d** 72 **p** 73 Fred. C of Ch Ch St Anne's Fred 72-76; I of Tobique Dio Fred from 76. *Box 284, Plaster Rock, NB, Canada.*

MAXWELL, Marcus Howard. b 54. Univ of Liv BSc 76. Univ of Nottm BA 79. St Jo Coll Nottm 77. **d** 80 **p** 81 Man. C of St Matt Chadderton Dio Man from 80. *35 Clevedon Road, Chadderton, Oldham, Manchester, OL9 0AH.*

MAXWELL, Richard Renwick. b 23. Mert Coll Ox BA (3rd cl Hist) 49, MA 49. Westcott Ho Cam 49. **d** 51 **p** 52 Win. C St Jo Bapt Moordown Bournemouth 51-55; UMCA Miss Mapanza 55-62; R of Livingstone 62-65; C of N Holmwood 65-67; R of Harrietsham 67-73; Blean Dio Cant from 73. *24 Tyler Hill Road, Blean, Canterbury, Kent.* (Blean 261)

MAXWELL, Robert Ian. Ch Coll 64. **d** 65 **p** 66 Tas. C of St Osw Launceston 65-67; P-in-c of Richmond w Risdon 67-69; L to Offic Dio Tas 70-81. *11 Pirie Street, New Town, Tasmania 7008.* (002-28 4323)

MAXWELL, Canon Thomas Winston. Univ of Alta BA 58. St Chad's Coll Regina LTh 57. Trin Coll Tor STB 63. **d** 56 Qu'App for Edmon **p** 57 Edmon. V of Good Shepherd Edmon 57-62; C of Grace Ch Tor 64-65; R of Transcona 65-70; Roxboro Pierrefonds Dio Montr from 70; Hon Can of

Montr from 79. *7 Raimbault Street, Dollard Des Ormeaux 970, PQ, Canada.* (514-684 0348)

MAY, Anthony John. b 30. Sarum Th Coll. **d** 63 **p** 64 Sarum. C of Bridport 63-67; Kirkby (in c of Tower Hill) 67-69; C-in-c of St Thos Old Charlton Woolwich 69-74; Chap Warlingham Pk Hosp from 74. *Chaplain's House, Warlingham Park Hospital, Warlingham, Surrey, CR3 9YR.* (Upper Warlingham 2101)

MAY, Arthur Harry. b 10. Univ of Lon BA (2nd cl French) 32. St Cath S Ox BA (3rd cl Th) 47, MA 63. Wycl Hall, Ox. **d** 47 **p** 48 Lon. C of H Trin Southall 47-50; Prec and Chap Sheff Cathl 50-52; CMS Miss Dio Lagos 52-62 Prov Chap to Abp of W Afr 52-55; Chap St Sav Lagos 55-62; C of H Trin Kens 62-63; R of St Mary Wavertree 63-68; Sub-Warden St Deiniol's Libr Hawarden 68-73; V of Middleton w Cropton 73-80; RD of Pickering 75-80. *Old School House, Fletching, Uckfield, E Sussex, TN22 3SP.* (Newick 2533)

MAY, Arthur John. b 16. Linc Th Coll 40. **d** 42 **p** 43 Lon. C of St Matt Stepney 42-46; St Andr Plaistow 46-48; V of St Barn Silvertown 48-53; C-in-c of St Jo Evang N Woolwich 48-53; V of Upton Park 53-63; Min of All SS Eccles Distr Belhus Pk Dio Chelmsf 63-68; V from 68. *All Saints' Vicarage, Foyle Drive, South Ockendon, Essex.* (South Ockendon 3246)

MAY, Barry John. ACT ThDip 69. St Barn Coll Adel 66. **d** 69 **p** 70 Adel. C of Mt Gambier 69-70; P-in-c of St Martin Boroko 71-72; R of Waikerie 72-75; Burra 76-79; Dongara Greenough w Walkaway and Mingenew Dio NW Austr from 80. *Church Street, Dongara, W Australia 6525.* (099-27 1164)

MAY, Charles Henry. b 29. ALCD 58 (LTh from 74). **d** 58 **p** 59 Lon. C of St Jas L Bethnal Green 58-62; Woking 62-64; Org Sec CPAS W Midl Distr 64-67; V of St Luke Hackney 67-80; Home Sec SAMS from 80. *c/o Allen Gardiner House, Pembury Road, Tunbridge Wells, Kent, TN2 3QU.*

MAY, Denis Harry. b 31. ARICS 56. **d** 63 **p** 64 S'wark. C of Eltham 63-65; Hon C of Charing w L Chart 66-70; L to Offic Dio Cant from 70. *19 Malvern Road, Ashford, Kent, TN24 8JA.* (Ashford 38816)

MAY, Donald Charles Leonard. b 25. Chich Th Coll 72. **d** 73 Barking for Chelmsf **p** 74 Chelmsf. C of Barkingside 73-77; V of Aldersbrook Dio Chelmsf from 77. *St Gabriel's Vicarage, Aldersbrook Road, E12 5HH.* (01-989 0315)

MAY, Ernest Herdman Langton. b 13. Trin Coll Dub BA 35, Div Test 36. **d** 37 **p** 38 Oss. C of Enniscorthy w Clone and Clonmore 37-40; CF (EC) 40-47; I of Ballingarry w Lockeen 47-51; Rathgraffe (Castlepollard) w Mayne and Foyran 51-58; Athlone 58-81; RD of Ardnurcher and Clonmacnoise 64-81; C-in-c of Forgney 68-81; Can of Meath 69-81. *The Lodge, Barrettstown House, Newbridge, Co Kildare, Irish Republic.*

MAY, Ernest William Lees. b 08. Keble Coll Ox BA 32, MA 36. St Steph Ho Ox 32. **d** 34 **p** 35 Dur. C of Houghton-le-Spring 34-37; V of Grindon and Dom Chap to 7th Marq of Londonderry 37-45; Chap RAFVR 39-46; Chap RAF 46-62; V of Effingham w L Bookham 63-70; R of Ewelme 70-75; Britwell Salome w Britwell Prior 70-75. *Swallows' Rest, Bridge, Winsham, Chard, Somt.* (Winsham 488)

MAY, George Louis. b 27. Selw Coll Cam BA 52, MA 56, Ridley Hall Cam 52. **d** 54 **p** 55 Roch. C of St Mary Cray w St Paul's Cray 54-56; St Barn Conv Distr Cray 56-57; C-in-c of Elburton Conv Distr Plymstock 57-66; Asst Master Guthlaxton Sch Wigston Magna 67-70; Ixworth Sch Suff 70-72; Thurston Upper Sch Suff 73-74; Curriculum Co-ordinator Perias Sch New Alresford from 75; Hon C of Ropley w W Tisted Dio Win from 78. *High View, Gundleton, Alresford, Hants.*

MAY, John Alexander Cyril. b 52. K Coll Lon BD 77. Linc Th Coll 79. **d** 80 Newc T **p** 81 Bp Gill for Newc T. C of Ch Ch Tynemouth Dio Newc T from 80. *35 Blanchland Terrace, North Shields, T & W, NE30 2BB.* (N Shields 583701)

MAY, Canon John Lovett. MBE (Mil) 46. Univ of Tas BA 36. Ch Coll Hobart ACT ThL 37. Worc Coll Ox BA 48 MA 57. **d** 38 **p** 39 Tas. C of All SS Hobart 38; Staff Hutchins Sch Hobart 38-39; H Trin Launceston Tas 40; Chap AIF 41-46; Min Can and Prec of St David's Cathl Hobart 46; R of Scottsdale 49-51; RD of NE Deanery 49-51; Chap R Mil Coll Duntroon 51-55; C of All SS Hobart 55-57; Warden Ch Coll Hobart and Can Chan of Hobart Cathl 58-63; Can of Newc 63-74; Warden St Jo Coll Morpeth 63-74; R of Sandy Bay Dio Tas 74-79; Can of Tas 77-80; Can (Emer) from 80. *Coningham, Snug, Tasmania 7154.*

MAY, Canon Malcolm Ivor. LTh (S Afr) 59, St Paul's Th Coll Grahmstn. **d** 58 **p** 59 Natal. C of St Jas Durban 58-60; V of Drakensberg 60-61; St Barn Durban 62-64; Oxford-Cust 64-68; Kens-Otipua 68-71; St Pet U Riccarton Dio Ch Ch from 71; Chap of Commun of the Sacred Name Dio Ch Ch from 75; Hon Can of Ch Ch from 78. *24 Main South Road, Christchurch 4, NZ.* (45-653)

MAY, Norman Gowen. b 20. AKC 48. St Bonif Coll Warm 48. **d** 49 **p** 50 Chich. C of St Matthias Brighton 49-51; Horsham 51-54; St John Blackpool 54-56; V of H Trin Blackb 56-61; C of St Pet Earley (in c of St Nich) 61-68; R of Balcombe 68-78; P-in-c of Lurgashall 78-81; Lodsworth 78-81; Selham 78-81; V of Lurgashall w Lodsworth and Selham Dio Chich from 81. *Vicarage, Lodsworth, Petworth, W Sussex, GU28 9DE.* (Lodsworth 274)

MAY, Oscar Henry Edward. **d** 14 **p** 15 Rupld. C of Plumas 14-16; I of Reston Manit 16-21; Perm to Offic at Neasden 22-24; C of Ashford Middx 24-28; Ash next Sandwich w Westmarsh 28-34; V of Bredgar 34-59. *Old Rectory, Norton, Faversham, Kent.*

MAY, Canon Peter de Denne. b 13. Late Scho of CCC Cam 2nd cl Cl Trip pt i 33, BA (1st cl Th Trip pt i) 35, MA 40. Cudd Coll 35. **d** 36 **p** 37 Win. C of Basingstoke 36-40; Vice Prin Westcott Ho Cam 40-44; Select Pr Univ of Cam 44; Prin Bp's Coll Calc 45-48 and 50-58; Vice-Prin 48-50; Exam Chap to Bp of Calc 49-58; Hon Can of Calc 57-58; Portsm 63-69; Can (Emer) from 69; V of St Mark N End Portsea 59-69; Surr 61-68; R of Newmarket w St Agnes Exning 69-78; Exam Chap to Bp of St E 70-78; Surr 70-78; RD of Mildenhall 72-78; Perm to Offic Dio Ely from 79; Dio St E from 78. *21 Moulton Avenue, Kentford, Newmarket, Suff, CB8 8QX.*

MAY, Peter Dudfield. b 12. Late Scho and Stud of St Jo Coll Cam BA 34, LLB 35. Ripon Hall Ox 38. **d** 39 **p** 40 Birm. C of All SS Gravelly Hill 39-43; St Jas Trowbridge 43-46; V of Preshute and Chap Marlborough Children's Convalesc Hosp 46-53; R of Stoke Abbott 53-82; V of Netherbury w Solway Ash 54-82. *c/o Lloyds Bank, Beaminster, Dorset.*

MAY, Peter Richard. b 43. St Jo Coll Cam BA 64, MA 68. Trin Coll Bris 77. **d** 79 **p** 80 Blackb. C of St Thos Lanc Dio Blackb from 79. *80 Aldcliffe Road, Lancaster, Lancs, LA1 5BB.*

MAY, Richard Grainger. b 19. St Cath Coll Cam BA 40. Linc Th Coll 41. **d** 42 St Alb **p** 69 Sarum. C of Cheshunt 42-43; M SSF 44; Hon C of St Andr Plaistow from 70; Chap of Plaistow Maternity and Balaam Street Hosps 72-75; L to Offic Dio Chelmsf 73-75. *The Friary, Hilfield, Dorchester, Dorset.*

MAY, Canon Robert John Montague. b 09. Kelham Th Coll 26. **d** 32 Bp Lander for St Alb **p** 33 St Alb. C of Gt Berkhamsted 32-36; Hitchin (in c of St Mark) 36-40; V of St Jo Evang Cleckheaton 40-47; Lanteglos-by-Fowey 47-52; Par 52-61; V of St Sampson 59-61; King's Heath 61-74; RD of Moseley 64-71; Hon Can of Birm 71-74; Can (Emer) from 74; C of Par Dio Truro from 74. *Hendra, Kilhallon, Par, Cornw.*

MAY, Canon Samuel. b 01. Late Scho of St D Coll Lamp BA 24, BD 38. **d** 24 **p** 25 Ches. C of Ch Ch Macclesfield 24-30; V of Godley w Newton Green 30-74; Hon Can of Ches 60-74; Can (Emer) from 74; C-in-c of Newton-in-Mottram 64-65. *32 St Paul's Hill Road, Hyde, Chesh, SK14 2SW.*

MAYAKA, Justus. St Cypr Coll Lindi 76. **d** 77 **p** 78 Ruv. P Dio Ruv. *PO Perahimo, Songea, Tanzania.*

MAYAKA, Mikael. Hegongo Th Coll 36. **d** 38 **p** 40 Zanz. P Dio Zanz 38-69; L to Offic Dio Zanz T from 70. *Box 35, Muheza Tanga Region, Tanzania.*

MAYANJA, Canon Christopher Mukibi. **d** 48 **p** 49 Ugan. P Dio Ugan 48-61; Dio Nam from 61; Can of Nam from 75. *Box 14297, Kampala, Uganda.*

MAYBURY, David Kaines. b 32. G and C Coll Cam BA 55, MA 59. Ridley Hall Cam 55. **d** 57 **p** 58 S'wark. C of H Trin Sydenham 57-60; Rainham 60-63; R of St Jas L Leith 63-75; St Jo Evang Jedburgh Dio Edin from 75. *Rectory, Jedburgh, Roxburghs, TD8 6BN.* (Jedburgh 2493)

MAYBURY, Canon Henry Kilworth. b 21. Pemb Coll Ox MA 46. Chich Th Coll. **d** 46 Ox **p** 47 Roch. C of W Wycombe 46-47; All SS Perry Street Roch 47-48; in Amer Ch 48-74; Hon Can of Milwaukee (USA) from 60; P-in-c of St Mary Buxted 75-79; Hadlow Down 75-79; C of Selsey Dio Chich from 80. *18 Glen Crescent, Selsey, Chichester, PO20 0QT.* (Selsey 5236)

MAYBURY, Canon John Montague. b 30. G and C Coll Cam BA 53, MA 57. Ridley Hall Cam 53. **d** 55 **p** 56 Liv. C of All H Allerton 55-59; Rowner 59-62; V of Wroxall 62-67; St Simon Southsea 67-78; Crofton Dio Portsm from 78; Hon Can of Portsm Cathl from 81. *Crofton Vicarage, Vicarage Lane, Stubbington, Fareham, Hants PO14 2JX.* (Stubbington 2007)

MAYCOCK, Herbert Guy. Ex Coll Ox 3rd cl Hist 23, BA 24, Ripon Hall Ox 32. **d** 33 **p** 34 Ex. C of Okehampton 33-37; R of Coates 37-42. *Neopardy Fold, Neopardy, Crediton, Devon.*

MAYEKISO, Shadrach Zwelibanzi. b 55. St Bede's Coll Umtata 78. **d** 80 Bloemf. **d** Dio Bloemf 80-81; Dio Johann from 81. *PO Box 6200, Johannesburg, S Africa.*

MAYER, Alan John. b 46. K Coll Lon AKC 70. St Aug Coll Cant 70. **d** 71 **p** 72 Ripon. C of Stanningley 71-74; St Helier Morden 74-79; Team V of Wimbledon Dio S'wark from 79. *55 Alwyne Road, Wimbledon, SW19 7AE.*

MAYER, Graham Keith. b 46. St Cath Coll Ox BA 68. Linc Th Coll 78. **d** 80 **p** 81 Ex. C of Paignton Dio Ex from 80. *St Boniface House, Belfield Road, Paignton, TQ3 3UZ.*

MAYES, Andrew Dennis. b 56. AKC and BD 79. St Steph Ho Ox 80. **d** 81 Edmon for Lon. C of St Alphage Hendon Dio Lon from 81. *18 Montrose Avenue, Burnt Oak, Edgware, HA8 0DW.* (01-952 1635)

MAYES, Very Rev Gilbert. b 15. Trin Coll Dub BA (2nd cl Ment and Mor Sc Mod) 43, Div Test (1st Cl) 44, MA 61. **d** 44 **p** 45 Arm. C of St Mark Arm 44-47; Hd Master Cathl Sch Arm and Dioc C Dio Arm 47-48; I of Donaghmore Upper w Pomeroy 48-52; Ed of Arm Dioc Mag 48-57; R of Dundalk 52-61; RD of Dundalk 57-61; Commiss Gambia 58-66; Dean of Lism from 61; I of Lism and Cappoquin w Clashmore Dio Lism from 61; Ardmore and Templemichael 61-71; Tallow w Kilwatermoy Dio Lism from 71; Dungarvan from 80. *Deanery, Lismore, Co Waterford, Irish Republic.*

MAYES, John. b 44. Bps' Coll Cheshunt 63. **d** 67 Arm. C of Portadown Arm 67-74; I of Kilrea Dio Derry from 74; Aghadowey Dio Derry from 76. *Kilrea Rectory, Coleraine, Co Derry, N Ireland.*

MAYES, Leonard Harry. b 25. Ely Th Coll. **d** 61 **p** 62 St Alb. C of Norton 61-65; Biscot 65-69; V of St Mich AA Watford 69-78; Liscard Dio Ches from 78. *107 Manor Road, Wallasey, Merseyside, L45 7LU.* (051-639 1553)

MAYES, Michael Hugh Gunton. b 41. TCD BA (2nd cl Hebr and Or Lang Mod) 62. **d** 64 **p** 65 Arm. C of Portadown 64-67; St Columba Portadown 67-68; USPG Kobe Japan 68-69; Tokyo 69-70; Yokkaichi Japan 70-74; Area Sec for Cashel, Cork, Lim and Tuam from 75; I of St Mich Blackrock w St Nich Dio Cork from 75. *St Michael's Rectory, Blackrock, Cork, Irish Republic.*

MAYES, Stephen Thomas. b 47. St Jo Coll Nottm 67. **d** 71 **p** 72 Ex. C of Cullompton 71-75; St Mark Cheltm (in c of St Barn) Dio Glouc from 75. *21 Brooklyn Road, Cheltenham, Glos.* (0242-22568)

MAYES, Thomas David Dougan. b 08. TCD BA 30. **d** 31 **p** 32 Arm. C of Armagh 31-33; CMS Miss Owo 36-38; Ado-Ekiti 33-36 and 38-39; R of Woods Chap 39-46; I of Clonfeacle 46-64; Dioc Sec 50-63; Preb of Tynan in Arm Cathl 60-61; Chan 61-65; R of Ballymore 64-73; Archd of Arm 65-73. *42 Castle Gardens, Richhill, Co Armagh, N Ireland.*

MAYFIELD, Ven Christopher John. b 35. G and C Coll Cam BA 57, MA 61. Linacre Ho Ox Dipl Th 63. Wycl Hall Ox 61. **d** 63 Bp Warner for Birm **p** 64 Birm. C of St Martin Birm 63-67; Lect 67-71; V of Luton (w E Hyde to 76) 71-80; RD of Luton 74-79; Archd of Bedford from 79. *Archdeacon's House, The Ride, Totternhoe, Dunstable, Beds, LU6 1RH.* (Dunstable 68100)

MAYGER, Francis John. St Mich Ho Crafers 48. **d** 52 **p** 53 Adel. Perm to Offic Dio Adel 52-53; C of Rose Park 53-54; Glenelg 54-55; Miss at Tailem Bend 55-57; P-in-c of Morialta 57-61; R of Lyndoch 61-67; Enfield 67-79; Belair Dio Adel from 79. *Box 156, Belair, S Australia 5052.* (278 3114)

MAYHEW, Charles. b 40. K Coll Lon and Warm BD (2nd cl) and AKC 64. **d** 65 **p** 66 Southw. C of St Mary Virg Nottm 65-69; V in Cawston Group (R of Cawston and C-in-c of Felthorpe w Haveringland) 69-74; R of Barnack w Ufford and Bainton Dio Pet from 74; RD of Barnack from 77. *Barnack Rectory, Stamford, Lincs.* (Stamford 740234)

MAYHEW, Peter. b 10. MBE 46. Univ of Lon BSc (Econ) 31. Univ of Ox MLitt 79. Ely Th Coll. 34. **d** 35 **p** 36 Man. C of St Alb Cheetwood 35-38; OMC Miss Calc 38; C of St Mary Shrewsbury 38-39; CF (TA - R of O) 39-46; Men in Disp 45; V of St Aid Leeds Yorks 46-53; Surr 50-53; M Bush Bro of St Paul Charleville 53-59; Hd Master Slade Sch Warwick 53-58; R of Mt Isa Dio N Queensld 59-62; Archd of the W 59-62; V of St Jo Div Kennington 62-69; Warden Bro of St Barn Dio N Queensld 70-74; Hd Master St Barn Sch Ravenshoe 72-74; Chap All SS Sisters of the Poor Ox from 74; Commiss River from 78. *14a Magdalen Road, Oxford.*

MAYLAND, Canon Ralph. b 27. VRD 63 and Bar 73. Ripon Hall, Ox 57. **d** 59 **p** 60 S'wark. C of Lambeth 59-62; Chap RNR from 61; C-in-c of St Paul's Conv Distr Manton 61-68; V of St Marg Brightside 68-72; Chap Industr Miss Dio Sheff 68-81; V of Ecclesfield 72-81; Can Res, Preb and Treas of York Minster from 82. *3 Minster Court, York, YO1 2JD.*

MAYNARD, John William. b 37. BSc (1st cl Eng) Lon 58. Ripon Hall, Ox 60. **d** 62 **p** 63 Cant. C of St Laur-in-Thanet 62-67; Ch Ch Ashford 67-70; V of Pagham Dio Chich from 70. *Pagham Vicarage, Bognor Regis, Sussex, PO21 4NX.* (Pagham 2713)

MAYNARD, Raymond. b 30. **d** 77 Ox **p** 78 Buckingham for Ox (NSM). C of Hedsor w Bourne End 77-80; Newport Pagnell w Lathbury Dio Ox from 80. *108 Wolverton Road, Newport Pagnell, MK16 8JG.*

MAYNARD, Richard Edward Buller. b 42. K Coll Lon and Warm AKC 66. **d** 67 **p** 68 Truro. C of St Ives 67-71; K Chas Mart Falmouth 71-74; V of St Germans Dio Truro from 74; Tideford Dio Truro from 74; RD of E Wivelshire from 81. *Vicarage, St Germans, Saltash, Cornw, PL12 5LH.* (0503-30305)

MAYNE, Charles Richard Thomas. b 10. Univ of Wales, BA 35. St D Coll Lamp 36. **d** 37 **p** 38 Lon. C of St Anne Tollington Pk 37-40; Wormhill 40-42; Beddington 42-44; CF (EC) 44-47; C of St Pet St Alb 47-54. *58 Hook Road, Surbiton, Surrey.*

MAYNE, George Shearer. b 1900. Univ of Lon BSc 24. **d** 43 **p** 44 Chelmsf. C of St Jo Bapt Tilbury Docks 43-45; Perm to Offic Dio Worc 45-47; C of Ch Ch w St Andr Gt Malvern 47-50; V of U Arley 50-53; R of Grendon 53-58; V of Budbrooke w Hampton-on-the-Hill 58-64. *6 Knapp Ridge, Ledbury, Herefs, HE8 1BJ.*

MAYNE, Isaac. b 1899. Trin Coll Dub BA 22, MA 53. **d** 30 **p** 32 Kilm. Publ Pr Dio Kilm 30-34; I of Kiltullagh 34-39; Killinagh w Kiltyclogher 39-40; Elph U 40-45; Hd Master Bp Hodson's Gr Sch Elph and Preb of Kilcooley in Elph Cathl 40-45; Warden of Wilson's Hosp Multyfarnham 45-64; Preb of St Patr Cathl Trim 55-64; Preb of Tipper in St Patr Cathl Dub 58-64. *Robinstown, Kilskyre, Kells, Co Meath, Irish Republic.*

MAYNE, Very Rev John Andrew Brian. b 34. QUB BA (2nd cl Hist) 55. BD (2nd cl) Lon 62. Trin Coll Dub Div Test (1st cl) 57. **d** 57 **p** 58 Connor. C of Ballymoney 57-60; St Columba Knock 60-62; C-in-c of Knocknagoney 62-68; Belvoir 68-71; R 71-80; Warden of Readers Dio Down 69-80; Dio Cashel from 80; Exam Chap to Bp of Down 73-80; Dean of Waterf from 80. *Deanery, Grange Park Road, Waterford, Irish Republic,* (Waterford 74119)

MAYNE, Canon Michael Clement Otway. b 29. CCC Cam 2nd cl Engl Trip pt i 53, BA 54, 3rd cl Th Trip pt ii 55, MA 58. Cudd Coll 55. **d** 57 **p** 58 St Alb. C of St Jo Bapt Harpenden 57-59; Dom Chap to Bp of S'wark 59-65; V of Norton 65-72; Hd of Relig Programmes BBC Radio 72-79; Hon Can of S'wark from 75; V of St Mary Gt w St Mich AA Cam Dio Ely from 79. *39 Madingley Road, Cambridge.* (Cam 355285)

MAYNIER, Anne Jaqueline. **d** 77 **p** 78 Bran. C of St John Reston & Ch Ch Melita Dio Bran from 77. *Box 134, Reston, Manit, Canada, R0M 1X0.*

MAYO, Gordon Edwin. b 18. St Jo Coll Dur LTh 42, BA 45, MA 61. Oak Hill Th Coll. **d** 42 **p** 43 Ches. C of Cheadle 42-44; St Nich Dur 44-45; Chap RAFVR 45-48; C of All S Langham Place and L to Offic at St Pet Vere Street Lon 48-50; Chap at Nakuru and Distr 50-57; Dioc Can of Momb, Can Missr and Chap R Tech Coll Nairobi 57-59; Asst Warden Lee Abbey 60-64; Warden Lee Abbey Internat Stud Club 64-71; R of Coulsdon 71-78; Dir of Chr Stewardship and Publ Pr Dio S'wark from 78. *56 Schubert Road, SW15 2QZ.*

MAYO, Inglis John. b 46. ACA 69. Ripon Coll Cudd 75. **d** 77 **p** 78 Win. C of Bitterne Park Dio Win from 77. *24 Lacon Close, Bitterne Park, Southampton, Hants.* (Southampton 553132)

MAYOH, John Harrison. b 23. Univ Coll of Southn BA (Lon) 50. Wycl Hall Ox 52. **d** 53 Liv **p** 54 Warrington for Liv. C of St John and St James Litherland 53-55; CMS Miss at Lusadia and at Ahmedabad 57-60; C of St Mary Upton 61-62; V of Em Ch Everton 62-69; Ch Ch Bridlington 69-80; R of Aythorpe Roding w Leaden Roding and High Roding Dio Chelmsf from 80. *Rectory, Stortford Road, Leaden Roding, Dunmow, Essex.* (White Roding 387)

MAYOR, Henry William. b 39. Or Coll Ox BA 62. Westcott Ho Cam 62. **d** 64 Aston for Birm **p** 65 Birm. C of The Quinton 64-66; Dudley 67-71; R of St Agnes Birch-in-Rusholme Dio Man from 71. *St Agnes Rectory, Slade Lane, Manchester, M13 0GN.* (061-224 2596)

MAYOR, Santiago. **d** 76 Parag. d Dio Parag. *a/c Casilla, 1124 Asuncion, Paraguay.*

MAYOSS, (Aidan) Anthony. b 31. Univ of Leeds BA 55. Coll of Resurr Mirfield 55. **d** 57 **p** 58 Lich. C of Meir 57-62; L to Offic Dio Wakef 62-72 and from 78; M CR from 64; C of Stellenbosch 73-75; Chap to Stellenbosch Univ 74-75; Asst Chap Univ of Lon 76-78; L to Offic Dio Lon 76-78. *House of The Resurrection, Mirfield, W Yorks, WF14 0BN.* (0924-494318)

MAYS, George Alonzo. b 12. St Aid Coll. **d** 54 Stockport for Ches **p** 55 Ches. C of St Geo Stockport 54-57; V of St Matt Chadderton 57-61; Blawith w Lowick 61-72. *29 Templand Park, Allithwaite, Grange-over-Sands, Lancs, LA11 7QS.*

MAZENGO, James. **d** 59 Bp Omari for Centr Tang **p** 60 Centr Tang. P Dio Centr Tang. *Box 15, Dodoma, Tanzania.*

MAZIBUKO, Cleopas Posselt Zwelibanzi. b 19. **d** 76 **p** 78 Zulu. C of St Aug Nqutu Dio Zulu from 76. *PO St Augustine's 3006, Zululand.*

MAZIBUKO, Oliver Bonus Knowles. St Pet Coll Rossettenville. **d** 54 **p** 55 Johann. P Dio Johann. *St Paul's Rectory, Mohlakeng, Transvaal, S Africa.* (011-669 4616)

MAZO, Dennis Mbulelo. b 28. St Bede's Coll Umtata 60.

d 62 **p** 64 St John's. P Dio St John's. *PO Box 65, Umtata, Transkei.*

MAZOMBO, Munyatwa. b 32. **d** 76 Boga-Z **p** 77 Bukavu. P Dio Bukavu. *Gongomeka Parish, BP 220, Kindu, Maniema, Zaire.*

MAZUA, Weston Wordsworth. b 14. **d** and **p** 73 Lake Malawi. d Dio Lake Malawi. *c/o Diocesan Registrar, Box 5133, Limbe, Malawi.*

MAZUNGULA, Isaac Mpumelelo. St Bede Th Coll Umtata 67. **d** 69 **p** 71 Grahmstn. P Dio Grahmstn 69-77. *Box 155, Lady Frere, CP, S Africa.*

MBAALU, Christopher. Buwulasi Th Coll 65. **d** 66 **p** 69 Nam. P Dio Nam. *Nabiswera, PO Nakasongola, Uganda.*

MBABAZI, John. d 78 **p** 79 Ruw. P Dio Ruw. *c/o Box 37, Fort Portal, Uganda.*

MBACHU, Canon Clement Arinze. Trin Coll Umuahia 60. **d** 62 Niger. d Dio Niger 62-70; Dio Enugu from 70; Hon Can of Enugu from 81. *All Saints Parsonage, Gra, Enugu, Nigeria.*

MBAEKWE, Simon Umeanwe. d 43 Bp Patterson for Niger **p** 44 Niger. P Dio Niger 43-52; Dio Nig Delta 52-56; Dio Niger 56-59; Dio Ow 59-73. *St Paul's Parsonage, Urualla, Orlu, Nigeria.*

MBAGO, Benyamini. d 57 Centr Tang **p** 59 Uka U for Centr Tang. P Dio Centr Tang. *Box 52, Manyoni, Tanzania.*

MBAJUNWA, Canon Nelson Sunday Akushiobike. Im Coll Ibad 56. **d** 58 Bp Nkemena for Niger **p** 59 Niger. P Dio Niger 58-70; Dio Ow from 70; Exam Chap to Bp of Niger 70; Hon Can of Ow from 73. *St Augustine's College, Nkwerre, Nigeria.*

MBAKA, Arthur. Weithaga Bible Sch. **d** & **p** 61 Ft Hall. P Dio Ft Hall 62-64; Dio Mt Kenya 64-75; Mt Kenya S from 75. *Box 116, Kiambu, Kenya.*

MBALE, Lord Bishop of. *See* Wesonga, Right Rev Akisoferi.

MBALI, Escourt Zolile. b 40. Univ of Fort Hare (SA) BA 68. Univ of Ox BA 71. St Bede's Coll Umtata 62. **d** 71 Natal **p** 72 Bp Hallowes for Natal. P Dio Natal 71-73; Dio Grahmstn 73-74; Dio Botswana 74-81; Exam Chap to Bp of Botswana 77-81; V of Preston-on-Tees Dio Dur from 81. *Eaglecliffe, Stockton, Cleve, TS16 9BD.*

MBALULA, Arthur. b 18. **d** 72 **p** 73 Johann. C of Orlando H Cross Dio Johann from 72. *Box 15, Dube, Transvaal 1800, S Africa.* (011-981 344)

MBANE, Howard Tembekile. b 29. **d** 77 **p** 80 Grahmstn. C of Mdantsane Dio Grahmstn from 77. *PO Box 74, Mdantsane 5219, East London, S Africa.*

MBARA, Samuel. St Paul Th Coll Ambat. **d** 63 **p** 68 Madag. P Dio Madag 63-69; Dio Diego S 69-70; Dio Tam from 70. *Ampahomanitra, Madagascar.*

MBARAZI, Nehemia Naftali. St Phil Th Coll Kongwa 65. **d** 65 Centr Tang. d Dio Moro. *c/o Box 320, Morogoro, Tanzania.*

MBARUKU, George Kimweri. St Mark's Coll Dar-S 73. **d** 73 **p** 75 Dar-S. P Dio Dar-S. *Box 9030, Dar-es-Salaam, Tanzania.*

MBATHA, Emmanuel Nkosinathi. b 49. St Pet Coll Alice 70. **d** 73 **p** 74 Zulu. P Dio Zulu. *Box 4, Nqutu, Natal, S Africa.*

MBATHA, Ezra. Isandhlwana Coll 24. **d** 24 **p** 28 Zulu. P Dio Zulu 24-57; Dir of Mvunyane Miss Dio Zulu 57-59. *PO Box 14, Blood River, via Dundee, Natal, S Africa.*

MBATHA, Hamilton. St Bede's Coll Umtata 67. **d** 68 **p** 70 Zulu. C of St Matthias Utrecht 68-70; St Luke Paulpietersburg 71-73; P-in-c of Vumanhlamvu 74-77; R of Kwa Magwaza Dio Zulu from 77. *P Bag 802, Melmouth, Zululand.*

MBATHA, Canon Philip James. McKenzie Mem Coll Isandhlwana. **d** 33 **p** 35 Zulu. P Dio Zulu 33-76; CF (S Afr) 42-44; Dir of Inlwati Miss 52-62; Can of Zulu 54-63; Dir of Eshowe Miss 62-63; Archd of W Zulu 63-67; N Zulu 67-76; Hon Can of Zulu 77-79; Can (Emer) from 79. *Box 67, Nongoma, Zululand.*

MBATHA, Canon Vincent McClagan. St Pet Coll Rosettenville. **d** 57 **p** 58 Zulu. P Dio Zulu; Can of Zulu from 77. *P Bag 513, Eshowe, Zululand, S Africa.*

MBEBE, Slingsby Mwezi. b 35. **d** 80 St John's (APM). d Dio St John's. *Private Bag 5005, Umtata, Transkei.*

MBEKELU, Reuben Esau. d 62 **p** 66 Momb. P Dio Momb from 62. *PO Box 63, Taveta, Kenya.*

MBELEDOGU, Francis Ifenwobi. d 45 **p** 47 Niger. P Dio Niger 45-72. *c/o St Philip's Church, Ogidi, Nigeria.*

MBELESIA, Ezekiel. b 37. Bp Tucker Coll Mukono 66. **d** 70 Nam. d Dio Nam 70-72; Dio Kamp 72-74; Dio Nai from 75. *Box 13084, Nairobi, Kenya.*

MBELWA, Stephen. b 37. St Cypr Coll Rondo 69. **d** 72 **p** 73 Zanz T. P Dio Zanz T. *Box 3, Handeni, Tanzania.*

MBENANGA, Elisha. b 43. St Phil Coll Kongwa 68. **d** & **p** 70 Centr Tang. P Dio Centr Tang. *Idifu, PO Mvumi, Tanzania.*

MBENSE, Joseph Siyethemba Abednego. b 31. St Bede's Coll Umtata 68. **d** 69 Natal **p** 70 Swaz. P Dio Swaz 70-73; Dio Natal from 73. *PO Box 41, Edenvale, Natal, S Africa.* (Greytown 3903)

MBEWANA, Simon Sabelo. b 31. St Bede's Coll Umtata 71. **d** 72 **p** 74 St John's. C of Mandileni 72-81; Ntsundwane Dio St John's from 81. *P Bag Mission Halt, Nggeleni, Transkei, S Africa.*

MBEZI, Andrea. d 77 Zanz T **p** 80 Bp Russell for Zanz T. P Dio Zanz T. *PO Box 35, Korogwe, Tanzania.*

MBEZI, Marko. b 25. St Cypr Coll Ngala 62. **d** 64 Bp Lukindo **p** 66 Bp R N Russell. P Dio Zanz T. *PO Handeni, Tanzania.*

MBEZI, Samwil. St Cypr Th Coll Tunduru 58. **d** 60 Zanz. d Dio Zanz T. *PO Kwankono, Sindeni, Tanzania.*

MBIJILI, Daudi. d and **p** 72 Centr Tang. P Dio Centr Tang. *Bahi, PO Bahi Station, Tanzania.*

MBINDA, Robert. b 50. St Phil Coll Kongwa 73. **d** 75 **p** 76 Centr Tang. P Dio Centr Tang. *Box 15 PO, Dodoma, Tanzania.*

MBINHE, Elisha. St Phil Coll Kongwa 71. **d** and **p** 74 Centr Tang. P Dio Centr Tang. *Dosidosi, Box 57, Kongwa, Tanzania.*

MBITI, John Samuel. BA (Lon) 53. Barrington Coll USA BA 56, BTh 57. Fitzw Ho Cam PhD 63. Westcott Ho Cam 60. **d** 63 **p** 64 St Alb for Cant for Col Bp. C of St Mich w Childwick St Alb 63-64; Lect Makerere Univ Kampala from 64. *Makerere University, Kampala, Uganda.*

MBIU, Peter. b 36. St Phil Coll Maseno. **d** 69 Maseno **p** 71 Nak. P Dio Nak from 69. *Box 96, Njoro, Kenya.*

MBIZA, Benaiah Sheldon. St Andr Nkwazi, 26. **d** 27 **p** 31 Nyasa. P Dio Nyasa 27-29; Hd Master St Mich Coll Lik 20-30; P Dio Nyasa 31-64; Dio Malawi 64-66; Can of Lik Cathl from 44. *Malango Village, Box 22, Ntchisi, Malawi.*

MBOGO, Danyeli. d 32 **p** 33 Centr Tang. C of Buigiri 32-35; Dodoma 35-41; Kongwa 41-59; Hon Can of Centr Tang 47-59. *Box 2, Mpwahwa, Tanzania.*

MBOGO, Elias. b 13. **d** 79 **p** 80 Centr Tang. P Dio Centr Tang. *Box 134, PO Arusha, Tanzania.*

MBOGO, Canon Manuel Roger. d 60 Momb. d Dio Momb 60-66 and from 68; Dio Nai 66-68; Chap to Bp of Momb from 74; Can of Momb from 76. *PO Rabai, Mombasa, Kenya.*

MBOGO, Renson. b 45. **d** 71 **p** 72 Mt Kenya. P Dio Mt Kenya 71-75; Dio Mt Kenya S 75-77; Mt Kenya E from 77. *Box 1046, Kianyaga, Kenya.*

MBOGONI, Canon Dan. d 54 **p** 55 Centr Tang. P Dio Centr Tang; Can of Centr Tang from 66. *Box 27, Kongwa, Tanzania.*

MBOGU, Mathias Igboanugoudu. Trin Coll Umuahia. **d** 61 **p** 62 Niger. P Dio Niger. *St Simon's Church, Nnobi, via Nnewi, Nigeria.*

MBOIZI, Erisa. d 52 Bp Tomusange for U Nile **p** 54 U Nile. P Dio U Nile 52-61; Dio Mbale 61-72; Dio Bukedi 72-76. *PO Bulangira, Mbale, Uganda.*

MBOJE, Nimirodi Junias. d and **p** 69 Momb. P Dio Momb. *PO Shimba Hills, Mombasa, Kenya.*

MBOMBO, George Loyiso Luvuyo. b 53. St Bede's Coll Umtata 74. **d** 75 Bp Sobukwe for St John's. d Dio St John's 75-81; Dio Natal from 81. *Box 464, Umkomaas 4170, Natal, S Africa.*

✠ **MBONA, Right Rev Kolin.** b 45. Bp Tucker Coll Mukono. **d** 69 **p** 71 Ruw. P Dio Ruw 69-76; Dio Bukavu 76-80; Cons Asst Bp of Bukavu 7 Sept 80 at Boga by Abp of Uganda; Bps of M & W Nile, Butare and Boga-Z. *BP 3296 Lubumaashi, Shaba Region, Zaire.*

MBONU, Ven Christopher Agonsi. Trin Coll Umuahai. **d** 54 Niger **p** 56 Bp Hall for Niger. P Dio Niger 54-68; C of Goole 68-69; Upton 69-70; P Dio Niger from 70; Hon Can of Niger 70-76; Archd of Onitsha from 76. *Christ Church, Onitsha, Nigeria.*

MBONU, Wilfred Obiebezie Nwafo. d 50 **p** 51 Niger. P Dio Niger 50-59; Dio Ow from 59. *St Michael's Parsonage, Ife-Ezinihitte, PA Mbawsi, Nigeria.*

MBONYANA, Duncan Phathwa. b 54. St Bede's Coll Umtata 74. **d** 76 **p** 77 Kimb K. C of St Jas Galeshewe Dio Kimb K 76-79; R from 79. *POB 8016, Galeshewe 8330, CP, S Africa.* (23870)

MBUGUA, Joseph. d 77 **p** 78 Nak. P Dio Nak. *Box 56, Nakuru, Kenya.*

MBUGUA, Canon Leonard. St Paul's Th Coll Limuru 58. **d** 59 Momb **p** 61 Ft Hall. P Dio Ft Hall 61-64; Dio Nai from 64; Hon Can of Nai and Exam Chap to Bp of Nai from 72. *PO Box 13084, Nairobi, Kenya.* (Nairobi 22233)

MBUGUA, Samuel. b 35. **d** 71 **p** 72 Mt Kenya. P Dio Mt Kenya 71-75; Mt Kenya S from 75. *PO Ithanga, Thika, Kenya.*

MBUGWA, Nelson. d 60 Momb **p** 61 Nak. P Dio Nak

60-69. *Anglican Church, Nasokol, Private Bag, Kitale, Kenya.*

MBUI, Richard. Weithaga Bible School 60. **d** 61 **p** 62 Ft Hall. P Dio Ft Hall 61-64; Dio Mt Kenya 64-75; Dio Mt Kenya E from 75; Exam Chap to Bp of Mt Kenya E 75-78 and from 80. *Box 97, Kianyaga, Kenya.*

MBUJI, Petro F. d and **p** 74 Centr Tang. P Dio Centr Tang 74-77; Dio Zanz T from 77. *PO Handeni, Tanzania.*

MBUKURE, Job. d 75 Kamp. d Dio Kamp. *c/o Box 335, Kampala, Uganda.*

MBULI, Francis Themba. b 45. St Pet Coll Alice 68. **d** 71 **p** 72 Zulu. P Dio Zulu. *PO Umvunyane, Vryheid, Natal, S Africa.*

MBULINYINGI, Canon Mattiya. St Cypr Coll Ngala 58. Edin Th Coll 61. **d** 59 **p** 62 Zanz. P Dio Zanz 59-65; Synod Sec Dio Dar-S 65-69; P Dio Zanz T 69-78; Can of Zanz T from 76; Lect St Mark's Th Coll Dar-S from 78; L to Offic Dio Dar-S from 78. *Box 2537, Dar-es-Salaam, Tanzania.*

MBUNGANABWO, Canon Asanasio. Bp Tucker Coll Mukono. **d** 51 **p** 53 Ugan. P Dio Ugan 51-61; Dio Ruw from 61; Can of Ruw from 72. *Box 248, Fort Portal, Uganda.*

MBUWAYESANGO, Lawrence. d 70 **p** 71 Mashon. P Dio Mashon 70-78; Dio Matab 78-81; Dio Lundi from 81. *Box 99, Que Que, Zimbabwe.* (Que Que 2512)

MBWANA, Erasto. St Cypr Th Coll Namasakata 52. **d** and **p** 63 Zanz. P Dio Zanz T from 63. *PO Box 33, Mnyuzi, Tanzania.*

MBWANA, Canon Martin. Univ of E Afr BA 66. Gen Th Sem NY STB 68. **d** 66 Bp Russell for Zanz T **p** 68 Zanz T. P Dio Zanz T 68-71; Warden Angl Th Coll Dar-S 71-78; Prov Sec Tanzania from 78; Can of Zanz T from 80. *Box 899, Dodoma, Tanzania.*

MBWILA, Frederick. d 75 **p** 76 W Tang. P Dio W Tang. *PO Box 15, Kibondo, Tanzania.*

MCHAKAMA, Ven George Alexander Godfrey. St Jo Sem Lusaka 62. **d** 63 **p** 65 Malawi. P Dio Malawi 65-71; S Malawi from 71; Archd of Mangochi E from 78. *PO Malindi, Mangochi, Malawi.*

MCHUNU, Christopher Celakuye. b 49. **d** 77 **p** 78 Zulu. C of St Mary Nkonjeni Dio Zulu from 77. *St Mary's Parish, Private Bag 39, Mahlabathini 3865, Zululand, S Africa.*

MCILONGO, Joseph McIntynne Mvuleni. b 36. St Pet Coll Alice 73. **d** 75 **p** 76 Grahmstn. C of H Name Stutterheim 75-81; Khutsong Dio Johann from 81. *PO Box 6088, Oberholzer, 2502, S Africa.*

MDAKA, Sydwell Themba. b 09. **d** 78 **p** 79 St John's (APM). P Dio St John's. *PO All Saints, Transkei.*

MDHLADHLA, Ewert Ivine. St Pet Coll Rosettenville. **d** 57 **p** 58 Natal. P Dio Natal 57-80; Perm to Offic from 80. *c/o PO Box 36239, Ntokozweni, Natal, S Africa.*

MDHLADHLA, Canon Garland Clement. LTh (S Africa) 40. **d** 40 **p** 42 Natal. C of Umlazi 40-53; P-in-c 53-74; Hon Can of St Sav Cathl Pmbg 57-61 and from 74; Capitular Can 61-74. *2 Old Hospital Road, Umlazi, Natal, S Africa.*

MDHLULI, Matthews Tshidisho. b 49. St Bede's Coll Umtata 68. **d** and **p** 78 Bloemf. C of St Pet Rocklands Dio Bloemf from 78. *PO Box 18007, Ga-Sehunelo, Bloemfontein 9315, S Africa.*

MDIMU, Herbert. d 22 **p** 25 Zanz. d Dio Zanz 22-25; P-in-c 25-37; Chap Kiwanda Sch 37-40; P-in-c from 40. *USPG, Msalabane, Muheza, Tanga, Tanzania.*

MDLETSHE, Ephraim. b 19. **d** 78 Zulu. d Dio Zulu. *Private Bag 526, Nongoma 3950, Zululand.*

MDLETSHE, Sipho Daniel. St Bede's Coll Umtata 67. **d** 68 **p** 70 Natal. C of Springvale 68-70; Klip River 70-76; R of Indududu 76-79; Hammarsdale Dio Natal from 79. *Box 606, Hammarsdale, Natal, S Africa.*

MDLULWA, Joshua Jonald Ndafika. St Bede's Coll Umtata. **d** 61 **p** 62 Gramhstn. P Dio Grahmstn 61-66. *PO Idutywa, Transkei, S Africa.*

MDUMULLA, Jonas Habel. b 50. St Phil Coll Kongwa 70. **d** 74 **p** 75 Centr Tang. P Dio Centr Tang. *Box 15, Dodoma, Tanzania.*

MDUNA, Jasper Amm. St Bede's Coll Umtata 42. **d** 44 **p** 46 St Jo Kaffr. C of H Cross Miss Dio St Jo Kaffr 44-47; L to Offic Dio Johann 48; Dios Cant and York 48-51; C of St Aug Miss Penhalonga 51-60; P-in-c of Standerton 60-62; C of St Cuthbert's 62-68. *c/o Box 36, Umtata, Transkei, S Africa.*

MEACHAM, John David. b 24. K Coll Lon and Warm AKC 51. Lambeth STh (2nd cl) 77. **d** 52 **p** 53 Ox. C of St Luke Maidenhead 52-55; Croydon 55-58; V of Sittingbourne 58-74; Brenchley Dio Roch from 74; Surr 58-74. *Vicarage, Brenchley, Kent.* (Brenchley 2140)

MEAD, Arthur Hugh. b 39. K Coll Cam BA 60, MA 64. New Coll Ox BA (by incorp) 61, BLitt 66. St Steph Ho Ox 61. **d** and **p** 80 Kens for Lon (APM). C of St Jo Evang Hammersmith Dio Lon from 80. *22 Spencer Road, Chiswick, W4.* (01-994 4112)

MEAD, Arthur William Rushton. Univ of Auckld BA 63, MA 69. St Jo Coll Auckld LTh 64. **d** 64 **p** 65 Auckld. C of Henderson 64-67; L to Offic Dio Auckld 67-68; C of Thames 68-70; V of Bay of Is 70-80; Titirangi Dio Auckld from 80. *541 South Titirangi Road, Titirangi, NZ.* (817-7300)

MEAD, George Thomas. b 26. Nor Ordin Course 74. **d** 76 **p** 77 Nor. C of Thorpe-Episcopi Dio Nor from 76. *28 Telegraph Lane East, Norwich, NR1 4AL.*

MEAD, John Harold. b 37. Wells Th Coll 69. **d** 71 **p** 72 Glouc. C of Charlton Kings 71-75; R of Stratton w Baunton Dio Glouc from 75. *Stratton Rectory, Gloucester Road, Cirencester, Glos, GL7 2LJ.* (Cirencester 3359)

MEAD, Nigel Gerrish. b 31. Tyndale Hall, Bris 62. **d** 64 **p** 65 Win. C of Shirley Southn 64-67; C of Alverdiscott w Huntshaw and Newton Tracey 67-71; Beaford w Roborough 67-71; St Giles-in-the-Wood 67-71; Yarnscombe 67-71; V of Shebbear w Buckland Filleigh and Highampton w Sheepwash Dio Ex from 71. *Shebbear Vicarage, Beaworthy, Devon, EX21 5RU.* (Shebbear 424)

MEAD, William John. b 19. Lich Th Coll 65. **d** 66 Buckingham for Ox **p** 67 Ox. C of St Mary Upton cum Chalvey, Slough 66-73; P-in-c of Ivinghoe w Pitstone (and Slapton from 76) Dio Ox 73-76; R from 76; P-in-c of H Cross Slapton 73-76. *Ivinghoe Vicarage, Leighton Buzzard, LU7 9EB.* (Cheddington 668260)

✠ **MEADEN, Right Rev John Alfred.** Qu Coll Newfld. Univ Coll Dur LTh 16, BA 17, MA 35. Bp's Univ Lennox Hon DCL 57. Trin Coll Tor Hon DD 59. Mem Univ Newfld Hon LLD 61. **d** 17 NS for Newfld **p** 18 Newfld. I of White Bay 17-21; R of Burin 21-29; Pouch Cove 29-34; Sec Treas of Exec C'tte of Newfld Dioc Synod 34-47; Exam Chap to Bp of Newfld 43-47; Can of St D in Newfld Cathl 38-57; Prin of Qu Coll St John's 47-57; Cons Ld Bp of Newfld in St John's Cathl 28 Oct 56 by Abp of Queb; Bps of NS; Montr; and Maine USA; res 65; Dean of St John's Cathl 56-65. *Sungdast Manor, 6909 9th Street South, Petersburg, Fla 33705, USA.*

MEADEN, Philip George William. b 40. Open Univ BA 75. Lich Th Coll 64. **d** 66 **p** 67 Birm. C of Aston-juxta-Birm 66-70; V of St Paul Lozells 70-76; Asst Chap HM Pris Brixton 76-77; Chap HM Pris Lewes from 77. *1 The Drive, Brighton Road, Lewes, BN7 1EF.*

MEADER, Philip John. b 44. Oak Hill Coll 73. **d** 75 **p** 76 Chelmsf. C of St Paul E Ham 75-78; CMJ from 78. *136 Beechwood Avenue, St Albans, Herts.*

MEADES, George Edward Everart. d 56 **p** 57 Tor. C-in-c of Manvers 56-60; R of Bobcaygeon and Dunsford 60-71; Hon C of Haliburton 72-79. *41 Kawartha Drive, Lindsay, Ont, Canada.*

MEADOWCROFT, John Grey. b 28. Univ of NZ BA 49, LTh 52. Princeton Th Sem MTh 66. **d** 51 **p** 52 Nel. C of Greymouth 51-53; V of Awatere 53-55; on leave 55-56; Miss at Sukkur 57-58; H Trin Karachi 58-60; Lect United Th Sem Gujranwala 61-65; Princeton Th Sem USA 65-66; Exam Chap to Bp of Lah 69-75; L to Offic Dio Ch Ch 75; C of Cashmere Hills 76; V of Papanui 76-80; St Matt City and Dio Dun from 80. *270 High Street, Dunedin, NZ.* (Dun 775743)

MEADOWS, Donald Ian. BD (Lon) 67. Moore Th Coll Syd ACT ThL 66. **d** 66 **p** 67 Syd. C of Eastwood 66-70; C-in-c of Prov Distr Pendle Hill (w Girraween 73-75) 71-78; R of Newtown Dio Syd from 78. *189 Church Street, Newtown, NSW, Australia 2042.* (51-2043)

MEADOWS, John Michael. b 27. St Jo Coll Cam BA 50, MA 55. Ridley Hall, Cam 51. **d** 53 **p** 54 Man. C of St Geo Mart Daubhill Bolton-le-Moors 53-55; CIM Miss in Perak State 57-61; Saigon-Cholon 62-75; L to Offic Dio Cant from 75; Dio Glouc from 78; Dios Worc and Win from 79. *1 Canute Drive, Bransgore, Christchurch, Dorset.*

MEADOWS, Canon Roy Sidney. b 15. Univ of Lon BA (2nd cl Hist) 52. **d** 38 **p** 39 S'wark. C of St John Deptford 38-41; Gen Deputn Work; BCMS 41-42; Org Sec Northern Area 42-43; LPr Dio Blackb 43; Chap RAF 43-67; V of Kimbolton 67-82; Stow Longa 67-82; Ed Ely Dioc Gazette 70-81; RD of Leightonstone 74-82; Hon Can of Ely from 75. *48 Newtown, Kimbolton, Huntingdon.*

MEADOWS, Canon Stanley Percival. b 14. St D Coll Lamp BA 46, TD 61. **d** 47 **p** 48 Man. C of St Mark Worsley 47-49; CF (TA) 48-64; Littleborough 49-51; V of St Geo Charlestown 51-61; R of St Geo w St Barn Oldham Road Man 61-72; Chap Ancoats Hosp from 64; Hon Can of Man Cathl from 71; R of St Cuthb Miles Platting City and Dio Man from 72; RD of Ardwick from 77. *Rectory, Shetland Road, Miles Platting, Manchester, M10 7JB.* (061-205 8774)

MEADS, William Ivan. b 35. Univ of Lon BA 56. ACIS 67. Linc Th Coll 75. **d** 77 **p** 78 Glouc. C of St Luke Cheltenham 77-81; Chap HM Pris Pentonville from 81. *42 Grenoble Gardens, N13 6JG.*

MEADUS, Wilfred Glosson. Qu Coll Newfld. **d** 29 **p** 30 Newfld. C-in-c of Griquet 29-30; I 30-34; Miss of Cartwright

34-36; R of Ecum Secum 37-41; Musquodoboit 41-43; Chap RCN 43-46; R of Port Hill PEI 46-49; Conquerall 49-50; Hubbards 50-53; St John Halifax 53-63; I of Indian Harbour 63-66; R of St Pet Halifax 66-70. *O'Hara Apt 110, Bedford Highway, Halifax, NS, Canada.* (443-4261)

MEAGER, Frederick William. b 18. St Mich Coll Llan 46. **d** 48 **p** 49 Llan. C of St Fagan Aberdare 48-51; Hawarden 51-54; Willian 54-56; PC of Wildmore w Langrick and Thornton-le-Fen 56-59; V of Old Warden 59-64; Min of St Pet Conv Distr Watford Dio St Alb 64-67; V from 67; RD of Watford 70-75. *St Peter's Vicarage, Westfield Avenue, Watford, Herts.* (Watford 26717)

MEAKER, Maxwell Ralph. d 64 **p** 72 Rockptn. Supt St Geo Homes for Children Parkhurst 64-74; R of Killarney 74-78; V of St John Enoggera City and Dio Brisb from 78. *42 Harding Street, Enoggera, Brisbane, Australia 4051.* (356 7889)

MEAKES, Daniel Edward. b 49. Univ of BC BA 75. Vanc Sch of Th MDiv 78. **d** 78 Yukon, C of Dawson 78-81; Co-ordinator of Tr Min Dio Carib from 81. *RR2, Heffley Creek, BC, V0E 1Z0, Canada.*

MEAKIN, Albert Richard. b 1895. Ripon Hall Ox 55. **d** and **p** 56 Sheff. C of Worsborough Dale 56-58; St Jas Benwell (in c of Ven Bede) Newc T 58-62; R of Allendale 62-69. *Ravensmere Nursing Home, Avenue Victoria, Scarborough, Yorks.*

MEAKIN, Alfred Reginald. b 03. Lich Th Coll 29. **d** 30 **p** 31 Pet. C of Finedon 30-33; Knighton 33-38; V of Long Clawson 38-47; Barlestone 47-51; R of Appleby Magna 51-61; RD of Akeley W 53-61; Surr from 59; R of Em Ch Loughborough 61-69. *Wynsford, Blandford Road North, Beacon Hill, Poole, BH16 6AD.*

MEAKIN, Anthony John. b 28. Down Coll Cam BA 52, MA 56. Westcott Ho Cam. **d** 54 **p** 55 Newc T. C of All SS Gosforth 54-60; V of St Paul Alnwick 60-71; St Jo Bapt Edlingham w Bolton Chapel Newc T 62-71; R of Whickham Dio Dur from 71; RD of Gateshead W from 78. *Rectory, Whickham, Newcastle-on-Tyne.* (Whickham 887397)

MEAKIN, Canon James William Robinson. Bp's Univ Lennox LST 26. **d** 27 **p** 28 Ott. Miss-in-c of Montague and Franktown 27-30; C of St Matt Ott 30-32; R of Clayton 32-40; Richmond 40-51; Hawkesbury 51-56; Can of Ott 52-64; Hon Can from 64; R of Almonte 56-64. *931 Pinecrest Road, Ottawa 14, Ont, Canada.*

MEAKIN, John Allan Douglas. Bp's Univ Lennox BA 52. Trin Coll Tor LTh 55. **d** 55 **p** 56 Ott. C of Trin Ch Ott 55-58; I of Colinton 58-63; St Aug Grand Prairie 63-65; Wembley 65-66; St Paul Ott 66-69; R of Arnprior 69-77; St John Nepean City and Dio Ott from 77. *105 Slack Road, ottawa, Ont, Canada.*

MEAKIN, Ven John Ernest. Kelham Th Coll 30. **d** 36 **p** 37 Lon. C of St Matt Stepney 36-39; St Steph Cheltm 39-41; Knottingley 41-43; C-in-c of St Phil Stepney 43-46; Chap Miss to Seamen at Santos 46-51; Singapore 51-55; Port Adel and Outer Harbour Adel 55-60; Chap RANR 56-63; R of Port Linc 60-68; Port Pirie 68-74; Jt and Assoc R 74-76; Archd of Eyre Peninsula 68-70; Willoch 70-80; Willoch (Outer) from 80; R of Whyalla 76-80; VG Dio Willoch from 80. *Staddlestones, Elder Street, Moonta Mines, S Australia 5558.* (088-25 2816)

MEALLY, Robert Ferguson. b 08. Hur Coll STh 61. **d** 58 **p** 59 Hur. I of Blyth 58-65; R of Killoughter U 65-73; L to Offic Dio Kilm 74-76; Dio Dub from 76. *11 Claremont Villas, Glenageary, Co Dublin, Irish Republic.*

MEANLEY, Hubert Edward Sylvester. b 10. Trin Coll Cam BA 32. **d** 34 **p** 35 Wakef. C of Sandal Magna 34-38; Penistone 38-40; Huddersfield 40-44; V of Cawthorne 44-53; St Geo Barnsley 53-62; Askham Bryan 62-68; V of Askham Richard 62-68; R of Settrington 68-76; C-in-c of Thorpe Bassett 72-76. *11 Hillshaw Park Way, Ripon, N Yorks.*

MEAR, Robert William. b 11. Clifton Th Coll 38. **d** 40 **p** 41 Liv. C of St Mary Bootle 40-41; Maghull 41-42; Ch of the Marts Leic 42-45; Heworth York 45-48; V of St Jude Newc T 48-52; St Barn York 52-56; CMS Area Sec Dios Blackb Bradf and Carl 56-62; R and V of Silloth 62-77. *Tetley Cottage, Cartmel, Grange-over-Sands, Cumbria.*

MEARA, David Gwynne. b 47. Oriel Coll Ox BA (Lit Hum) 70, BA (Th) 72, MA 73. STh (Lambeth) 76. Cudd Coll 71. **d** 73 **p** 74 Ox. C of Reading 73-77; Chap Univ of Reading from 77. *University Chaplaincy Centre, Whiteknights, Reading, Berks.*

MEARDON, Brian Henry. b 44. Univ of Reading BSc 66, PhD 71. Oakhill Coll 77. **d** 79 Reading for Ox **p** 80 Ox. C of SS John & Steph Reading Dio Ox from 79. *2 Church House, Orts Road, Reading, Berks.*

MEARNS, Christopher Lee. b 30. Worc Coll Ox BA (2nd cl Mod Hist) 54, 2nd cl Th 56, MA 58. Ripon Hall, Ox. **d** 57 **p** 58 Lon. C of Greenhill Harrow 57-60; Vice-Prin Qu Coll St John's Newfld 60-62; Lect Ripon Tr Coll from 63; C-in-c of Marton-le-Moor 67-75; Sen Lect Coll Ripon and York St John from 74. *14 Primrose Drive, Ripon, HG4 1EY.* (Ripon 2695)

MEARS, Ian Roland. Univ of Syd BSc 63. BD (Lon) 74. Moore Coll Syd ThL 70. **d** 71 **p** 72 Syd. C of Univ of Syd BSc 63. Moore Coll Syd ThL 70. **d** 71 **p** 72 Syd. C of Seaforth 71-74; Lect Moore Th Coll Syd 74-79; Editor Bd of Educn Syd from 79. *155 Charles Street, Ryde, NSW, Australia 2122.* (807-6098)

MEARS, Canon John Cledan. b 22. Univ of Wales, BA (2nd cl Phil) 43, MA 48. Wycl Hall, Ox 43. **d** 47 **p** 48 St A. C of Mostyn 47-49; Rhosllannerchrugog 49-56; V of Cwm 56-59; Chap St Mich Coll Llan 59-67; Sub-Warden 67-73; Lect in Th Univ of S Wales Cardiff 59-73; L to Offic Dio Llan 59-73; Exam Chap to Bp of Llan from 60; V of Gabalfa Dio Llan from 73; Hon Can of Llan from 81. *St Mark's Vicarage, Gabalfa, Cardiff, S Glam.* (Cardiff 23611)

MEARS, Phillip David. b 40. Univ of Dur BA (3rd cl Th) 62, Dipl Th 63. **d** 65 Blackb **p** 66 Lanc for Blackb. C of St John Sandylands Heysham 65-68; St Geo Chorley 68-71; V of St Ambrose Leyland 71-81; Chap Warrington Distr Gen Hosp from 81. *Warrington General Hospital, Warrington, Chesh.*

MEASEY, George. b 08. Roch Th Coll 67. **d** 68 **p** 69 Portsm. C of Rowner 68-72; St Geo Worthing 72-78. *21 Woodlea Road, Worthing, Sussex.*

MEASURES, Canon Douglas Brian. b 33. Sarum Th Coll. **d** 57 **p** 58 Leic. C of Braunstone 57-60; Hucknall Torkard (in c of St John) 60-63; Dioc Insp Schs Dio Southw 60-63; Dio Truro 63-68; V of St Cubert 63-68; Dir of Relig Educn St E 68-73; Hon Can of St E from 70; V of Leiston w Sizewell 73-75; Perm to Offic Dio Portsm 75-81; Dio Guildf from 81. *23 Green Leys, Church Crookham, Aldershot, Hants, GU13 0PN.* (Fleet 24358)

MEATH AND KILDARE, Lord Bishop of. *See* Caird, Most Rev Donald Arthur Richard.

MEATH, Archdeacon of. *See* Corrigan, Ven Thomas George.

MEATS, Alan John. b 41. Univ of Wales (Cardiff) BA (2nd cl Welsh) 62. Univ of Lon BD 70. St Mich Coll Llan 68. **d** 70 **p** 71 Bp Hughes for Llan. C of Pontypridd 70-73; V in R Benef of Ystradyfodwg 73-75; V of Llandilo Talybont Dio Swan B from 75; RD of Llwchwr from 81. *Vicarage, Pontardulais, W Glam.* (Pontardulais 882468)

MECHANIC, Rodney Ian. b 48. Trin Coll Bris 76. **d** 78 Bp Carter for Capetn **p** 78 Capetn. R of St Andr Ceres Dio Capetn from 78. *St Andrew's Rectory, Munnik Lane, Ceres 6835, Cape, S Africa.*

MECHI, Richard. b 32. **d** 76 **p** 78 Centr Zam. P Dio Centr Zam. *PO Box 70172, Ndola, Zambia.*

MEDA, Canon Meshaki. d 54 **p** 55 Centr Tang. P Dio Centr Tang 54-66; Archd of Kilimatinde 66-69; Arusha Moshi 70-71; Dean of Dodoma Cathl 71-74; Can from 71; V of Vinghawi 74-75; Chap Wilson Carlile Sch Chamwino from 75. *PO Chamwino, Buigiri, Tanzania.*

MEDCALF, John Edward. b 19. Oak Hill Th Coll. **d** 50 **p** 51 Cov. C of St Matt Rugby 50-53; PC of Chell 53-61; V of Heath Town Dio Lich from 61; Surr from 65. *Heath Town Vicarage, Wolverhampton, W Midl.* (Wolverhampton 731213)

MEDCALF, William Henry. b 15. TCD Downes Div Premium (1st cl) 45, BA 45, Div Test (1st cl) 46, MA 49. **d** 46 **p** 47 Connor. C of St Mich Belf 46-48; St Pet Bedford 48-50; Org Sec CMJ SE Distr 50-63; Exhib Dir 63-80; Publ Pr Dio St Alb 67-80. *185 Dibdin House, Maida Vale, W9 1QQ.* (01-328 3133)

MEDCOF, Mary Alice. b 35. Univ of Tor BA 58. Trin Coll Tor MDiv 79. **d** 79 Bp Read for Tor **p** 80 Tor. C of St Paul Lorne Park Dio Tor from 79. *1190 Lorne Park, Mississauga, Ont, Canada, L5H 3A4.*

MEDFORTH, Allan Hargreaves. b 27. Qu Coll Cam BA 48, MA 52. Westcott Ho Cam 50. **d** 51 **p** 52 Newc T. C of Hexham 51-55; PV of Southw Minster 55-59; V of Farnsfield 59-72; RD of Southw 66-72; V of St Pet City & Dio St Alb from 72; RD of St Alb from 74. *23 Hall Place Gardens, St Albans, Herts, AL1 3SB.* (St Albans 51464)

MEDHURST, Phillip. b 48. Wadham Coll Ox BA (Engl) 70, BA (Th) 72. Ripon Hall Ox 72. **d** 73 **p** 74 S'wark. C of St Mich AA Abbey Wood 73-76; Asst Master John Cleveland Coll Hinckley 76-78; Earl Shilton Commun Coll Leic from 78; Perm to Offic Dio Leic from 78. *42a Hobson Road, Leicester, LE4 2AQ.*

MEDLEY, Arnold Theodore. d 73 Ja (APM). d Dio Ja. *St Paul's PA, Manchester, Jamaica, WI.*

MEDWAY, Kerry Edward. b 46. Moore Th Coll Syd 70. **d** 73 Syd **p** 73 Armid. C of Moree 73-74; Tingha 74-76; P-in-c of Coober Pedy w NW Miss 76-81. *Box 266, Coober Pedy, S Australia 5723.* (73 5038)

MEE, Alan George. Ridley Coll Melb ACT ThL 33. **d** 34

Melb **p** 35 Geelong for Melb. C of St John Footscray 34-35; St Mary Caulfield 35-38; Min of Broadmeadows 38-40; W Preston 40-45; Chap AIF 40-43; Min of Hampton 45-52; Chap RAAF 52-58; I of S Caulfield 58-64; Chap and Vic Sec Miss to Seamen Dio Melb 65-70; Chap Dunkirk and N France 71-74. *8 St Clements Street, Highett, Vic, Australia 3190.*

MEE, James Alexander. Trin Coll Dub BA 30, Div Test (2nd cl) 31, MA 39. **d** 31 **p** 32 Derry. C of Omagh 31-35; Chap (Eccles Est) Dio Lah 36; Murree 37; Asst Chap Peshawar 36-37; Chap 38-40; Kohat 40-42; Jullundur 42-43; Quetta ii 43-44; Peshawar 43-47; Murree 47; Hon CF 47; P-in-c of St Mary's Cathl Auckld 48-49; V of Papatoetoe 49-51; St Helier's Bay (f Tamaki W) 51-70; Exam Chap to Bp of Auckld 51-64; Chap Commun of H Name Auckld 59-61; L to Offic Dio Auckld from 70. *123 St Johns Road, Meadowbank, Auckland 5, NZ.*

MEED, Henry Robert. b 15. Ripon Hall, Ox 50. **d** 51 **p** 52 Man. C of Ch Ch W Didsbury 51-55; V of Falinge 55-62; R of Nash w Thornton and Beachampton 62-75; RD of Wolverton 67-70; C-in-c of Thornborough 69-75; V of Wingrave w Rowsham, Aston Abbotts and Cublington 75-81. *Blyth Cottage, Church Road, Felsham, Bury St Edmunds, Suff.*

MEEHAN, Cyril Frederick. b 52. Univ of Nottm BTh 80. St Jo Coll Nottm 77. **d** 80 **p** 81 Cov. C of Keresley w Coundon Dio Cov from 80. *39 Bennetts Road South, Keresley, Coventry, CV6 2FN.*

MEEK, George Edward. b 08. Univ of Leeds BA 30. Coll of Resurr Mirfield 26. **d** 32 Bp E J Palmer for Glouc **p** 33 Glouc. C of St Mark Glouc 32-35; Stroud 35-37; Cirencester 37-39; V of Ixworth 39-48; CF (R of o) from 39; C-in-c of Ixworth Thorpe 46-48; R of W Monkton 48-53; Byfleet 53-58; V of Wombourn 58-68; C-in-c of Whaddon w Tattenhoe 68-75; Newton Longville (R w Stoke Hammond, Whaddon and Tattenhoe from 75) 68-77; Stoke Hammond 72-75; RD of Mursley 73-77. *28 Titian Road, Hove, BN3 5QS.* (0273-773065)

MEEK, Canon John Conway. b 33. Univ of Lon BSc (2nd cl Math) 55, AKC 56. St Cath S Ox BA (3rd cl Th) 59, MA 63. Wycl Hall Ox 57. **d** 59 **p** 60 S'wark. C of Im w St Anselm Streatham 59-62; Bilston 63-65; V of St Mary Bredin City and Dio Cant from 65; Chap Kent and Cant Hosp 65-73; M Gen Syn from 70; RD of Cant 76-82; Hon Can of Cant Cathl from 79. *57 Nunnery Fields, Canterbury, Kent, CT1 3JN.* (Canterbury 62479)

MEERES, John Reginald. b 14. Univ of Liv BA (2nd cl Med and Mod Hist) 36. Univ of Leeds BD 50, PhD 59. BSc (2nd cl Econ) (Lon) 55. Sarum Th Coll 36. **d** 44 **p** 45 Ches. C of Grappenhall 44-46; Carlton 46-50; Stoke-on-Trent 50-52; CF 52-55; Asst Master Longton High Sch Stoke-on-Trent 55-63; Lect Kingston-upon-Hull Coll of Educn and Perm to Offic 63-78; V of Langtoft w Foxholes, Butterwick and Cottam Dio York from 79. *Langtoft Vicarage, Driffield, N Humb.* (Langtoft 226)

MEERING, Laurence Piers Ralph. b 48. Univ of Man Inst of Sc & Tech BSc. 70. Trin Coll Bris 79. **d** 81 Bris. C of Ch Ch Downend Dio Bris from 81. *73 Westbourne Road, Blackhorse, Downend, Bristol.* (0272 561413)

MEERS, John Cyril. b 04. Univ of Lon BSc (1st cl Eng) 25. Lon Coll of Div 32. **d** 32 **p** 33 Ox. C of St Paul Slough 32-35; Iver 35-36; V of St Silas Toxt Pk 36-44; St Paul Hyson Green Nottm 44-53; Thurnby w Stoughton 53-61; Chudleigh 61-70; LPr Dio Ex 71-78; Dio Ox from 78. *Ellesborough Manor, Butler's Cross, Nr Aylesbury, Bucks, HP17 0XF.* (Wendover 622336)

MEGAHEY, Alan John. b 44. Selw Coll Cam BA 65, MA 69. QUB PhD 69. Westcott Ho Cam 69. **d** 70 **p** 71 Lich. Asst Master Wrekin Coll 67-72; Asst Chap 70-72; Asst Master Cranleigh Sch from 72. *Cranleigh School, Surrey.* (Cranleigh 4486)

MEGGS, Peter Antony Harsant. Trin Coll Tor BA 48. Bp's Univ Lennox LST 63. **d** 63 **p** 64 Ott. C of St Matt Ott 63-65; Hon C of All S City and Dio Tor from 69. *27 Ambrose Street, Willowdale, Ont, Canada.*

MEGICKS, Wentworth. St D Coll Lamp BA 15. Jes Coll Ox BA and MA 25. **d** 25 **p** 26 Llan. C of Whitchurch 25-30; Chap of Llan Cathl 30-31; Min Can of Man Cathl 31-61; Prec 38-61. *26 Portarlington Road, Bournemouth, Hants.*

✠ **MEHAFFEY, Right Rev James.** b 31. Trin Coll Dub BA 2nd cl Ment and Mor Sc (Mod) 52, Th Exhib 54, MA and BD 56. QUB PhD 75. **d** 54 **p** 55 Down. C of Ballymacarrett 54-56; St John Deptford 56-58; Down Cathl 58-60; C-in-c of St Chris Ballymacarrett 60-62; I of Kilkeel 62-66; Cregagh 66-80; Priv Chap to Bp of Down 72-80; Can Missr Dio Down 76-80; Cons Ld Bp of Derry and Raphoe in St Patr Cathl Arm 7 Sept 80 By Abp of Arm; Bps of Meath, Connor, Kilm, Cork, Down, Cash, and Tuam; and Bps Quin and Heavener. *The See House, 112 Culmore Road, Londonderry, BT48 8JF, N Ireland.* (Londonderry 51206)

MEHARRY, Robert Cyrus. St Jo Coll Auckld 53. **d** 54 **p** 55 Waik. C of Te Awamutu 54-57; V of Katikati 57-61; C of St Andr Cam 61-64; V of Taumarunui 64-68; Te Kauwhata 68-76; Perm to Offic Dio Waik 76-80; Dio Auckld from 80. *24 Rawhiti Road, Manly, Whangaparaoa, NZ.*

MEIER, David Vernon. b 36. Univ of W Austr BA 61, B Educn 66. BD (Lon) 73. Moore Coll Syd 70. **d** and **p** 74 Perth. C of Midl 74-76; R of Narembeen-Bruce Rock 76-79; on leave 79-80; Perm to Offic Dio Perth from 80. *34/537 William Street, Mount Lawley, W Australia 6050.*

MEIER, Niklaus Rudolf. b 26. Univ of W Ont BA 65. Hur Coll Lon LTh 63. **d** 73 **p** 74 Hur. I of Markdale 73-76; on leave. *1385 Commissioner's Road, London, Ont., Canada.*

MEIGH, Simon John. b 52. Univ York BA 74. St Mich AA Coll Llan 78. **d** 80 Bp Woollcombe for Lon **p** 82 Lon. C of St Aug w St John Kilburn Paddington Dio Lon from 80. *151 Dibdin House, Maida Vale, W9 1QG.*

MEIKLE, David Skene. b 39. St Cath Coll Cam 3rd cl Th Trip pt i, 58, BA (3rd cl Th Trip pt ii) 60. **d** 63 **p** 64 Edin. C of St Cuthb Hawick 63-67; C-in-c of St Phil Edin 67-72; C of Banbury 72-73; Team V 74-78; R of St Matt Ipswich Dio St E from 78. *St Matthew's Rectory, Ipswich, Suff.* (Ipswich 51630)

MEIKLEJOHN, Canon Kenneth Walter. b 07. Late Scho of Ch Coll Cam 1st cl Cl Trip pt i, 27, BA (2nd cl Cl Trip pt ii) 28, MA 34. Univ of Lon BD (2nd cl) 48. **d** 36 Bp Golding-Bird for Guildf **p** 37 Guildf. Chap St John's Sch Leatherhead and L to Offic Dio Guildf 36-60; CF (R of O) 39-45; Hon CF 45; R of St Pet and All SS Dorch 60-73; RD of Dorch 67-75; Can and Preb of Sarum Cathl 71-75; Can (Emer) from 75. *31 Broadmead, Broadmayne, Dorchester, Dorset.*

MEIMANE, Cecil. St Pet Coll Siota. **d** 56 **p** 59 Melan. P Dio Melan 56-75; Dio Ysabel from 75. *Koge, Hograno, Santa Ysabel, Solomon Islands.*

MEIN, James Adlington. b 38. Univ of Nottm BA (2nd cl Th) 60. Westcott Ho Cam 63. **d** 63 **p** 64 Edin. C of St Columba Edin 63-67; Sec Chr Commun Chs and L to Offic Dio Malawi (S Malawi from 71) 67-72; R of Grangemouth Dio Edin from 72; P-in-c of Bo'ness Dio Edin from 77. *7 Ronaldshay Crescent, Grangemouth, Stirlingshire, FK3 9JH.* (Grangemouth 482438)

MEIN, Peter Simon. b 27. Univ of Nottm BA (1st cl Th) 55, MA 59. Kelham Th Coll 48. MSSM 54-70. **d** 55 **p** 56 Southw. Tutor and Chap Kelham Th Coll 55-61; Warden 62-64; Prior and Warden 64-70; Chap and Asst Master St Andrew's Sch Delaware from 71. *St Andrew's School, Middletown, Delaware 19709, USA.*

MEIRION-JONES, Huw Geraint. b 39. R Agr Coll Cirencester NDA and MRAC 61. K Coll Lon AKC 69, BD 71. St Aug Coll Cant 69. **d** 70 **p** 71 Lich. C of Harlescott 70-73; Worplesdon 73-77; V of Ash Vale Dio Guildf from 77. *203 Vale Road, Ash Vale, Aldershot, Hants.* (Aldershot 25295)

MEISSNER, Charles Ludwig Birkbeck Hill. b 26. Trin Coll Dub 60. **d** 62 **p** 63 Clogh. C of Monaghan 62-64; Kildallon Dio Kilm 64-65; R 65-71; R of Kinawley Dio Kilm from 71; I of Trin Ch Dio Kilm from 71; Surr from 71. *Kinawley Rectory, Derrylin, Co Fermanagh, N Ireland.* (Derrylin 284)

MEJA, Samuel. **d** 57 Centr Tang **p** 60 Johann. d Dio Centr Tang 57-60; P Dio Johann 60-63; Dio Vic Nyanza 63-73; Hon Can of Vic Nyan 68-73. *Box 26, Tarime, Tanzania.*

MEJE, Simon Sims. St Pet Coll Rosettenville 56. **d** 59 Johann **p** 60 Bp Paget for Johann. P Dio Johann from 59. *PO Box 3, Kagiso, Krugersdorp, Transvaal, S Africa.* (01-664 2700)

MEKA, Bernard Nwabueze. b 36. Im Coll Ibad 77. **d** 78 **p** 79 Asaba. P Dio Asaba. *St John's Parsonage, Abbi, Bendel State, Nigeria.*

MEKE, Canon Samisoni. **d** 68 Bp Halapua for Polyn **p** 71 Polyn. Hon C of Levuka Dio Polyn from 68; Can of Suva Cathl from 75. *PO Box 25, Levuka, Fiji.*

MEKOA, Archie Amos. St Pet Coll Rosettenville 52. **d** 54 **p** 55 Johann. P Dio Johann. *c/o 634 Fourth Avenue, Payneville, Transvaal, S Africa.*

MELANESIA, Metropolitan of Province of. *See* Palmer, Most Rev Norman Kitchener.

MELANESIA, CENTRAL, Lord Bishop of. *See* Palmer, Most Rev Norman Kitchener.

MELANESIA, CENTRAL, Assistant Bishop of. (Vacant)

MELANO, Cecil. St Pet Coll Siota. **d** 68 **p** 70 Melan. P Dio Melan 68-75; Dio Malaita 75-76; Dio Centr Melan from 76. *Vanikoro Island, Temotu Region, Solomon Islands.*

MELBOURNE, Lord Archbishop of, and Metropolitan of Province of Victoria. *See* Dann, Most Rev Robert William.

MELBOURNE, Bishops Coadjutor of. *See* Grant, Right Rev James Alexander; and Shand, Right Rev David Hubert Warner.

MELBOURNE, Dean of. *See* Thomas, Very Rev Tom William.

MELBOURNE, Te Waaka. St Jo Coll Auckld 65. **d** 66 **p** 67 Waik. C of Tokoroa 66-67; Taumarunui 67-68; P-in-c of Waitomo Maori Past 68-71; V of Mangakino 71-76; Chap Te Wai Pounamu Coll Ch Ch 76-78; P-in-c of Rangiatea Maori Past Dio Wel from 78. *59 The Ruaparaha Street, Otaki, NZ.* (8030)

MELHUISH, Douglas. b 12. St Pet Hall Ox BA (3rd cl Mod Hist) 34, MA 38. Wycl Hall Ox 39. **d** 39 Lon **p** 40 Guildf. Asst Master Haberdashers' Aske's Sch Hampstead 37-40; St John's Sch Leatherhead and L to Offic Dio Guildf 40-42; Asst Master Bedford Sch (Chap from 43) and LPr Dio St Alb 42-46; Lect and Tutor Trin Coll Carmarthen 46-48; Prin CMS Tr Coll Buwalasi 48-53; Asst Master Kagumo Coll 53-58; Hd Master Kagumo Sch 58-67; L to Offic Dio Momb 53-61; Dio Ft Hall 61-64; Dio Mt Kenya 64-67; Perm to Offic Dio Nak 68; Dio Sarum from 69; Dio Win 70-74; P-in-c of St Lawr IW 74-79. *27 Sturford Lane, Corsley, Warminster, Wilts.* (Chapmanslade 396)

MELINSKY, Canon Michael Arthur Hugh. b 24. Ch Coll Cam BA 47, MA 49. Ripon Hall Ox 57. **d** 57 **p** 59 Sherborne for Sarum. C of Wimborne Minster 57-59; Wareham w Arne 59-61; V of St Steph Nor 61-68; Chap Norf and Nor Hosp 61-68; Hon Can and Can Missr of Nor 68-73; Can (Emer) from 73; Chief Sec ACCM Westmr 73-77; Perm to Offic Dio S'wark 73-77; Prin N Ordin Course from 77; Publ Pr Dio Man from 77; Perm to Offic Dios Blackb, Bradf, Ches, Derby, Liv, Ripon, Sheff, Wakef and York from 77. *75 Framingham Road, Brooklands, Sale, Chesh, M33 3RH.* (061-962 7513)

MELLA, William. **d** 61 **p** 62 Mbale. P Dio Mbale. *PO Kapchorwa, Mbale, Uganda.*

MELLING, John Cooper. b 44. ALCD 73. St Jo Coll Nottm 68. **d** 72 **p** 73 Edmon for Lon. C of Enfield 72-76; St Jas and of Em Didsbury 76-79; R of St Mich w St Bart Gt Lever Dio Man from 79. *355 Green Lane, Great Lever, Bolton, Lancs, BL3 2LU.* (Bolton 26510)

MELLING, Leonard Richard. b 13. St Aid Coll 38. **d** 41 York **p** 42 Hull for York. C of W Acklam 41-45; Scarborough 45-48; Min of St Mark Newby Eccles Distr Scarborough 48-54; P-in-c of Seria Dio Borneo 54-59; Area Sec USPG Dios Cov and Ox 59-64; Dio York 64-67; L to Offic Dio York 64-67; V of Osbaldwick w Murton 67-78; RD of Bulmer 72-78; V of St Columba Miri 78; Dean of St Thos Cathl Kuch 78-81. *Clergy Flat, St Thomas's Cathedral, Kuching, Sarawak.*

MELLIS, John Charles. b 46. Princeton Th Sem 67. **d** 71 **p** 72 BC. Chap of Columb Coast Miss City and Dio BC from 71; Archd of Quatsino 79-80; on leave. *c/o Box 759, Port McNeill, BC, Canada.* (604-956 4210)

MELLISH, John. b 26. Cranmer Hall Dur 67. **d** 69 Penrith for Carl **p** 70 Carl. C of Ulverston 69-72; V of Bromfield (w Waverton from 73) 72-79; P-in-c of Westnewton 76-79; V of Shap Dio Carl from 79. *Shap Vicarage, Penrith, Cumb.* (Shap 232)

MELLISH, Peter Robert. b 21. **d** 81 Pret. C of St Wilfrid Hillcrest Dio Pret from 81. *140 Banket Road, Waterkloof 0181, S Africa.*

MELLISS, Laurence John Albert. b 21. DSM 45. RD 69. K Coll Lon and Warm AKC 52. **d** 53 Dover for Cant **p** 54 Cant. C of Norbury 53-56; Folkestone 56-60; Chap RNR from 56; R of St John U St Leonards 60-64; V of Littlehampton 64-76; RD of Arundel 75-76; V of Findon 76-81; R of Catsfield and Crowhurst Dio Chich from 81. *Rectory, Church Lane, Catsfield, Battle, TN33 9DR.* (Ninfield 892319)

MELLOR, Canon Alexander. Lich Th Coll 32. **d** 35 **p** 36 Trinid. C of All SS Port of Spain 35-37; St John Longsight Man 37-38; St Paul San Fernando 38-40; V of Toco 40-44; C of St Matthias w St Laur (in c 44-46) Barb 44-47; V of St Mark w St Cath Barb 47-48; St Marg Barb 48-52; C of Advent Ch Montr 52-53; R 53-66; Valois 66-77; Sec Montr Dioc Synod 66-69; Hon Can of Montr 74-77; Can (Emer) from 78; P Assoc of St Geo St Catharines 77. *Apt 412, 363 Geneva Street, St Catharines, Ont., Canada.* (416-684 6488)

MELLOR, David John. b 49. Univ of Nottm BTh 72. Kelham Th Coll 68. **d** 72 **p** 73 Lich. C of Horninglow 72-74; St Mich Tividale, Tipton (in c of H Cross) 74-77; Team V of St Bertelin Stafford Dio Lich from 77. *St Bertelin's House, Holmcroft Road, Stafford, ST16 1VG.* (Stafford 52874)

MELLOR, Kenneth Paul. b 49. Univ of Southn BA (Th) 71. Univ of Leeds MA 72. Cudd Coll 72. **d** 73 **p** 74 York. C of Cottingham 73-76; Ascot Heath 76-80; V of St Mary Magd Tilehurst Dio Ox from 80. *270 Kentwood Hill, Tilehurst, Reading, Berks, RG3 6DR.* (Reading 27234)

MELLOR, Robert Frederick. b 14. ACIS 37. Tyndale Hall Bris 38. Univ of Dur LTh 42. **d** 41 **p** 42 Liv. C of St Chrys Everton 41-43; St Cath Tranmere 43-46; Org Sec NW Area BCMS and Perm to Offic Dios Liv Blackb Man and Ches 46-50; R of Albert Mem Ch Man 50-56; V of St Mark Haydock 56-65; St Cath Tranmere 65-79. *5 Fleet Croft Road, Arrowe Park, Wirral, Mer, L49 5LY.* (051-678 7717)

MELLORS, James. b 32. Kelham Th Coll 52. **d** 56 **p** 57 Wakef. C of Horbury 56-61; V of Scholes 61-72; Mirfield Dio Wakef from 72. *Vicarage, Mirfield, Yorks.* (Mirfield 492188)

MELLOWS, Alan Frank. b 23. Qu Coll Cam BA 45, MA 49. Tyndale Hall Bris 47. **d** 49 S'wark for Cant **p** 50 S'wark. C of Morden 49-54; V of Brimscombe 54-62; R of Mileham 62-74; C-in-c of Stanfield 62-74; Beeston-next-Mileham 62-66; R 66-74; P-in-c of Gt w L Dunham 70-73; R of Ashill (w Saham Toney from 79) Dio Nor from 74; P-in-c of Saham-Toney 78-79. *Rectory, Ashill, Thetford, Norf.* (Holme Hale 440247)

MELLSOP, Denis Heywood. Univ of NZ BA 57. St Jo Coll Auckld LTh 61. **d** 60 **p** 61 Auckld. C of New Lynn 60-62; St Mark Remuera Auckld 62-65; Asst Dir of Christian Educn 65-66; V of Kamo-Hikurangi 66-71; Taiere 71-74; Assoc P of Invercargill 74-76; Chap St Pet Sch Cam Dio Waik from 76. *St Peter's School, PB Cambridge, NZ.* (6933)

MELLY, Aleck Emerson. b 24. Oak Hill Th Coll 50. **d** 53 **p** 54 Man. C of Chadderton 53-56; St Mark Cheltm 56-59; PC of St Paul Tipton 59-68; R of Kemberton w Sutton Maddock (w Stockton from 81) Dio Lich from 68; C-in-c of Stockton 74-81. *Kemberton Rectory, Shifnal, Salop, TF11 9LH.* (Telford 583971)

MELOCHE, William Joseph Bertram. St Chad's Coll Regina 38. **d** and **p** 38 Qu'App. C of Limerick 38; I of Eston 39-42; Cupar 42-44; Baie Comean 44-48; R of St Matt Aldershot 48-50; St Jas Guelph 50-56; St Mary Virg 56-68; Hon C of St Barn Danforth Ave Tor 68-76; Perm to Offic Dio BC from 76. *302-505 Trutch Street, Victoria, BC, Canada.*

MELROSE, Kenneth Mark Cecil. b 15. Ex Coll Ox BA (2nd cl Mod Hist) 37, Dipl in Th 38, 2nd cl Th 39, MA 41. Ripon Hall Ox 37. **d** 39 **p** 40 Bris. C of St Jo Evang Clifton 39-41; Asst Master Dean Close School Cheltm and L to Offic Dio Glouc 41-42; Chap RNVR 42-46; RNV(S)R 46; Asst Master Cheltm Coll 46-47; Bedford Sch and L to Offic Dio St Alb 47-49; V of St Aldhelm Bedminster 49-55; Hurstbourne Tarrant 55-63; St Denys Southn 63-71; V of Bovey Tracey Dio Ex from 71. *Vicarage, Coombe Lane, Bovey Tracey, Devon.* (Bovey Tracey 833213)

MELROSE, Michael James Gervase. b 47. St Chad Coll Dur BA (2nd cl Th) 69. Dipl Th 70. **d** 71 Bradwell for Cant **p** 72 Chelmsf. C of All SS Chelmsf 71-74; St Pet Eaton Square 74-80; R of St Chrys Vic Park Dio Man from 80. *Rectory, Daisy Bank Road, Victoria Park, Manchster, M14 5QH.* (061-224 4152)

MELVILLE, Malcolm Charles Crompton. b 13. Univ of Birm BSc 36. Lich Th Coll 37. **d** 39 **p** 40 Bris. C of St Paul Swindon 39-42; Treas V and Sacr Lich Cathl 42-43; Chan V 43-46; C of St Mich Lich 42-43; Chap RNVR 46-48; Chap St Paul's Sch São Paulo 48-52; C of All SS Margaret Street 52-63; Hd Master All SS Choir Sch 52-63; C-in-c of Clifton w Glapton 63-65; C of Heacham 65-67; Perm to Offic Dio St Alb from 67. *45 Beverley Crescent, Bedford.*

MEMBERY, Donald Percy. b 20. K Coll Lon BSc 50 and AKC 51. **d** 79 Ox **p** 80 Buckingham for Ox (NSM). C of Aston Rowant w Crowell 79-81; P-in-c of Swyncombe Dio Ox from 81. *Rectory, Swyncombe, Henley on Thames, Oxon, RG9 6EA.* (Nettlebed 641249)

MEME, Caleb Oyiana. **d** 28 **p** 29 Niger P Dio Niger. *Agbor, Nigeria.*

MENA, Ven Alberto. **d** 66 **p** 67 Chile. P Dio Chile; Archd of Temuco from 72; Hon Can of Chile from 77. *Casilla 26-D, Temuco, Chile, S America.*

MENCHIONS, Clayton. **d** 66 **p** 67 Newfld. I of Brooklyn 66-69; Botwood 72-76; Hon C of Bell I Dio E Newfld from 77. *c/o St Boniface School, Bell Island, Newfoundland, Canada.*

MENDEL, Thomas Oliver. b 57. Down Coll Cam BA. Cranmer Hall Dur 79. **d** 81 Ely. Chap Down Coll Cam from 81. *Downing College, Cambridge, CB2 1DQ.*

MENDEZ, Ernesto. b 09. **d** and **p** 66 Argent. P Dio Argent 66-73; N Argent from 73. *Parsonage, Vertientes, N Argentina.*

MENDS, Edward Thomas. St Aug Th Coll Accra 56. **d** 58 **p** 59 Accra. P Dio Accra 58-73; Dio Kum from 73. *St Cyprian's Cathedral, Box 144, Kumasi, Ghana.*

MENE, Ibegan. b 31. **d** 80 Carp. C of Badu I Dio Carp from 81. *Badu Island, Queensland, Australia.*

MENEAR, John Lawrence. Moore Th Coll Syd BTh 79. **d** 80 Syd **p** 80 Bp Short for Syd. C of St Phil Caringbah Dio Syd from 80. *17 Combara Avenue, Caringbah, NSW, Australia 22229.* (524-5174)

MENEGBE, Patrick Nda. **d** 81 Kano. d Dio Kano. *Holy Trinity Church, PO Box 170, Maiduguri, Nigeria.*

MENEY, Brian James. b 42. Univ of Glas MA 63. Edin Th Coll 63. **d** 65 **p** 66 Brech. C of St Paul's Cathl Dundee 65-69; L to Offic Dio Edin 69-71; H Cross Davidson's Mains 71-73; Asst Sec Rep Ch Coun 73-81; P-in-c of St Barn Edin 73-81; Chap Bede House Staplehurst from 81. *Bede House, Staplehurst, Kent.*

MENIN, Malcolm James. b 32. Univ Coll Ox BA 55, MA 59. Cudd Coll 55. **d** 57 **p** 58 Portsm. C of H Spirit Southsea Portsea 57-59; Fareham 59-62; V of St Jas w Pockthorpe 62-73; C-in-c of St Martin-at-Palace Nor 62-74; St Mary Magd City and Dio Nor 68-72; V (w St Jas from 73) from 72; RD of Nor E from 81. *St Mary Magdalene Vicarage, Crome Road, Norwich, NR3 4RQ.* (Norwich 25699)

MENKENS, Arthur Eric. b 18. St Francis Th Coll Brisb 68. **d** 69 N Queensld. C of All SS, Gordonvale 69-73; P-in-c of Prosperine 73-79; Home Hill Dio N Queensld from 79. *Box 343, Home Hill, Queensland, Australia.*

MENNELL, John Alfred Atkinson. Hur Th Coll. **d** 52 **p** 58 Hur. C of Ch of Ascen Windsor 52- 56; I of Wheatley 56-60; C of Leamington 60-62; I of Wheatley 62-65. *2121 Chilver Road, Windsor, Essex, Ont, Canada.*

MENNIGKE, Stuart Michael. b 53. St Paul's Th Coll Grahmstn 78. **d** 80 Bp Stanage for Johann. C of Florida Dio Johann from 80. *PO Box 65, Florida, S Africa 1710.*

MENON, Nicholas Anthony Thotekat. b 39. Mert Coll Ox BA (2nd cl Engl) 61, MA 65, Dipl Th 62. St Steph Ho Ox 61. **d** 63 **p** 64 Lon. C of Ch Ch Lanc Gate Dio Lon 63-66; Hon C 66-70; V of Thorpe St Mary 70-76; SS Phil and Jas w St Marg Ox 76-79; Chap Univ of Surrey and Bp of Guildf Chap for Higher Educn from 79. *6 Cathedral Close, Guildford, Surrey, GU2 5TL.* (Guildford 76380)

MENSAH, Albert Wellington Yamoak. Kelham Th Coll 59. **d** 62 **p** 63 Accra. P Dio Accra 62-74; Dio Kum from 75. *Box 5, Bekwai, Ashanti, Ghana.*

MENTERN, Richard John. b 19. ALCD (2nd cl) 48. **d** 48 **p** 49 Chelmsf. C of Barking 48-53; R of St Anne Newton Heath 53-57; V of Broadheath 57-74; C-in-c of Bradford Abbas w Clifton Maybank Dio Sarum from 74. *St Mary's House, Bradford Abbas, Sherborne, Dorset.* (Yeovil 4969)

MENYATSO, Josiah Dikgobelo Hosea. b 29. **d** 78 **p** 80 Bp Ndwandwe for Johann (NSM). C of Ikageng Dio Johann from 78. *1270 Ikageng, Potchefstroom, S Africa 2520.*

MENZIES, Alastair Charles Vass. b 16. AKC 38. Univ of Lon BA (2nd c l Hist). TD 66. Lich Th Coll 39. **d** 39 **p** 40 Lich. C of Ch Ch Stafford and Asst Chap HM Pris 39-41; CF (EC) 41-45; Chap and Asst Master Epsom Coll and L to Offic Dio Guildf 45-77; CF (TA) 53-67. *Clare Cottage, Neacroft, Bransgore, Christchurch, Dorset, BH23 8JS.* (Bransgore 72380)

MENZIES, Donald William. Univ of Glas MB ChB 46. Univ of Melb PHD 62. Ridley Coll Melb. **d** 57 **p** 58 Melb. C of St Mark Camberwell Melb 57-58; Hon C of Melb Cathl 58-63; Perm to Offic Dio Melb 64-66. *c/o Provincial Laboratory, Regina, Sask, Canada.*

MENZIES, George Keith. Univ of Tor BA 51. Wycl Coll Tor. **d** 54 **p** 55 Alg. I of Port Carling 55-59; R of Petrolia Dio Hur from 59. *Box 565, Petrolia, Ont., Canada.* (519-882 1430)

MENZIES, Ian Hamilton. b 06. **d** and **p** 73 Ch Ch. Hon C of Parklands 73-76; Ch Ch Cathl 76-77; P-in-c of Avonside Dio Ch Ch from 77. *Rehutai, Menzies Bay, Little Akaloa, Banks Peninsula, NZ.*

MEOBA, Emmanuel Ekwughelie. b 42. Univ of Lon Dipl Th (Extra-Mural) 73. Trin Coll Umuahia 71. **d** 73 **p** 74 Niger. P Dio Niger. *St Mary's Church, Ukpo, Nigeria.*

MEPSTED, Leonard Charles. b 34. Univ of Leeds BA (2nd cl Gen) 61. Coll of Resurr Mirfield 61. **d** 63 Sheff **p** Jarrow for Dur. C of Goldthorpe 63-65; S Shields 65-69; Woodston 69-71; V of Fridaybridge w Coldham 71-72; C of Moss Side 72-74; C-in-c of All SS Farnworth 75-76; C of Lawton Moor 76-78; C-in-c of Falinge Dio Man from 78. *Falinge Vicarage, Rochdale, Lancs, OL12 6PL.* (Rochdale 46272)

MERA, James. St Pet Coll Siota 63. **d** 66 **p** 67 Melan. P Dio Melan 66-75; Dio New Hebr 75-80; Dio Vanuatu from 80. *Mota Lava, Banks Islands, Vanuatu.*

MERANATADU, Mark. Patteson Th Centre Kohimarama. **d** 72 Melan. d Dio Melan 72-75; Dio New Hebr from 75. *Lobaha, Aoba, New Hebrides.*

MERCER, David Emery. b 45. St Mary's Univ Halifax BA 69. Dalhousie Univ BEd 70. **d** 71 **p** 72 Fred. C of Ch Ch Cathl Fred 71-74; I of Derby w Blackville Dio Fred from 74. *Box 73, Blackville, NB, Canada.*

✠ **MERCER, Right Rev Eric Arthur John.** b 17. Kelham Th Coll. **d** 47 **p** 48 Ches. C of Coppenhall 47-51; C-in-c of St Cath Conv Distr Heald Green 51-53; R of St Thos Stockport 53-59; St Bridget w St Martin Ches 59-65; Ches Dioc Missr 59-65; Hon Can of Ches 64-65; Cons Ld Bp Suffr of Birkenhead in Ches Cathl 7 Nov 65 by Abp of York; Bps of Dur; Liv; Ches; Blackb; Southw; and others; Trld to Ex 73; Chairman CEMS 74-77. *The Palace, Exeter, Devon, EX1 1HY.* (Ex 72362)

MERCER, Gordon Gladstone. Univ of Tor BA 42. **d** 40 **p** 41 Arctic for Newfld. C of St Alb Tor 41-44; Trin Mem Ch Montr 44-47; Chap Kingston Coll Jamaica 47-51; CF (Canad) from 51. *6 Donaldson Avenue, Birch Cove, Halifax, NS, Canada.*

MERCER, John David. Montr Dioc Th Coll LTh 67. **d** 67 Montr. C of Vaudreuil 67-69; R of Waterloo 69-74; St Paul Cote des Neiges Montr 74-75; I of Arundel 75-78; on leave. *1350 Windingtrail, Mississauga, Ont, Canada L4Y 2T8.*

MERCER, Canon John James Glendinning. b 20. Trin Coll Dub BA 49, MA 55. **d** 50 **p** 51 Down. C of St Mark Newtownards 50-53; Bangor 53-55; I of Ballyholme Dio Down from 55; RD of Bangor 71-78; Can of Belf Cathl from 76. *Ballyholme Rectory, Bangor, Co Down, N Ireland.*

✠ **MERCER, Right Rev Robert William Stanley.** St Paul's Th Coll Grahmstn LTh 59. M CR 65. **d** 59 **p** 60 Matab. C of Ascen Bulawayo 59-63; L to Offic Dio Wakef 64-66; Perm to Offic Dio Llan 66-68; R of St Mary Stellenbosch 68-70; Sch Chap St Aug Penhalonga 70-71; R of Borrowdale 72-77; Cons Ld Bp of Matab in City Hall Bulawayo 1 May 77 by Abp of Centr Afr; Bps of Mashon and Botswana; Bps Suffr of Capetn (Bp Swartz) and Mashon; Chap O of St John of Jer from 80; Sub-Prelate from 81. *PO Box 2422, Bulawayo, Zimbabwe.* (19-65059)

MERCER, Ronald Tucker. Qu Univ Kingston Ont BA 50. **d** and **p** 49 Newfld. C of Corner Brook 49-53; St Mary St John's 53-56; I of Twillingate 56-59; R of Bay L'Argent 59-62; C of St Mary Virg St John's 62-64; R of Mt Pearl 64-80. *Box 250, Mount Pearl, St John's, Newfoundland, Canada.* (709-368-5693)

MERCER, Timothy James. b 54. Fitzw Coll Cam BA 76, MA 80. Westcott Ho Cam 78. **d** 81 Roch. C of SS Pet & Paul Bromley Dio Roch from 81. *13 Rochester Avenue, Bromley, Kent, BR1 3DB.*

MERCER, William Douglas. Qu Coll Newfld LTh 50. **d** 40 **p** 41 Newfld. Asst Master Bp Feild Coll St John's 40-41; C of Channel 41-43; Vice-Prin Qu Coll Newfld 43-49; R of Fogo 51-55; Bonavista 55-59; Upper I Cove 59-62; Watford 62-68; Ch of Resurr Lon Dio Hur from 68. *800 Fleet Street, London 25, Ont., Canada.* (519-451 4984)

MERCER, William Herbert John. b 12. Trin Coll Cam BA 34. Ely Th Coll 36. **d** 38 **p** 39 Dur. C of Ryhope 38-40; Stratford-on-Avon 40-44; S Kirkby 44-48; V of Carleton 48-66; Hackness w Harwood Dale 66-77. *40 Garth End Road, West Ayton, Scarborough, N Yorks, YO13 0JH.*

MERCHANT, Alan Naylor. b 11. Univ of Man Dalton Math Scho 30 and 31, BSc (1st cl Math) 32. Bps' Coll Cheshunt 32. **d** 34 **p** 35 Man. C of St Wilfrid Northenden 34-38; St Marg Hollinwood 38-43; R of Ascen Lower Broughton 43-50; V of Tottington 50-55; Chap RAF 55-58; Asst Master and Chap Dioc Coll Rondebosch 59-60; V of Pinetown 61-66; C-in-c of Stand Lane 66-67; C of K William's Town 67-68; R of St Paul Pmbg 69-71; Margate Natal 72; C of St Barn Dulwich 73-78. *72 Dulwich Village, SE21 7AJ.*

MERCHANT, David Clifford. b 17. Univ of Wales BA (2nd cl French) 37, 2nd cl Engl 38. Univ of Birm MA 70. St Mich Coll Llan 45. **d** 46 **p** 47 Mon. C of St Julian Newport 46-48; Hawarden 48-50; V Cho of St A Cathl 50-53; Area Sec for SPG in Midls 53-57; Publ Pr Dio Birm 54-57 and from 65; Dio Lich 54-57; V of St Jas W Bromwich 57-65; Sen Lect and Chap of Westhill Coll of Educn Birm from 65; Hon C of Northfield Dio Birm from 74. *28 Weoley Park Road, Selly Oak, Birmingham 29.*

MERCHANT, Canon William Moelwyn. b 13. Late Exhib of Univ of Wales (Cardiff) BA (1st cl Engl) 33, 2nd cl Hist 34, MA 50, DLitt 60. **d** 40 **p** 41 Mon. C of Llangattock-juxta-Caerleon 40-42 and 46-55; Lect Univ Coll Cardiff 39-50; Sen Lect 50-61; Reader 61; Prof of Engl Univ of Ex 61-73; Exam Chap to Bp of Sarum from 64; Can and Preb of Sarum Cathl 67-73; Can (Emer) from 73; Chan 67-70; V of Llanddewi-Brefi w Llanbadarn Odwyn 74-78. *16 St Mary's Road, Leamington Spa, Warws.* (Leamington 314253)

MERCIER, David Cuthbert. St Pet Hall, Ox BA 32, MA 36. Wycl Hall, Ox 35. **d** 37 **p** 38 Liv. C of St Mary Edge Hill 37-41; St Mary Gt Sankey Warrington (in c of St Mary's Miss Penketh) 41-44; St Pet Parr 44-49; V of Langford Budville w Runnington 49-54; R of St Phillack w St Gwithian 55-59; V of Marton and Chap Dioc Girls' Sch Marton 59-64; V of Par Distr of Kiwitea 64-76; Perm to Offic Dio Wel from 76. *Scott's Ferry, RD2, Bulls, NZ.*

✠ **MEREDITH, Right Rev Bevan Stanley.** St Francis Coll Brisb. **d** 61 **p** 62 Brisb. C of Toowong 61-62; Miss at Koeno 62-66; Archd of N New Guinea 66-67; New Guinea Is 67-77;

Cons Asst Bp of New Guinea in St Jo Evang Cathl Brisb 26 Feb 67 by Abp of Brisb; Bps of New Guinea; N Queensld; Carp; and Rockptn; Bp Coadj of Brisb; and Asst Bps of New Guinea (Ambo and Chisholm); Apptd Bp of New Guinea Is 77. *PO Box 159, Rabaul, Papua New Guinea.*

MEREDITH, Claison Charles Evans. b 26. St D Coll Lamp BA 51. **d** 54 Bp Sara for Heref **p** 55 Heref. C of Bromyard 54-56; St Paul Weston-s-Mare 56-59; R of Norton-sub-Hamdon 59-68; C-in-c of Chiselborough 59-68; V of Westonzoyland 69-80; Puriton w Pawlett Dio B & W from 80. *Puriton Vicarage, Bridgwater, Somt.* (Puriton 683500)

MEREDITH, James Noel Michael Creed. b 17. Keble Coll Ox 3rd cl Mod Hist 39, BA 40, MA 43. Westcott Ho Cam 39. **d** 40 S'wark **p** 42 Woolwich for S'wark. C of Woolwich 40-44; CF 44-47; Chap St John's Sch Leatherhead 47-48; Hd of Oxford Ho Bethnal Green 48; R of Ch Ch Moss Side Man 48-56; Savannah la Mar 56-57; Hd Master de Carteret Coll Mandeville Ja 57-61; R of Stoke Cov 61-71; RD of Cov E 69-71; V of Hessle 71-78; R of Milton Abbas, Hilton w Cheselbourne and Melcombe Horsey 78-80; V in R Benef of Llandudno Dio Ban from 80. *Vicarage, Morfa Road, West Shore, Llandudno, Gwyn.* (Llandudno 75781)

MEREDITH, Nial. b 32. Univ of Dur BA (2nd cl Social Stud) 56, Van Mildert Exhib 57-58, Dipl Th 58. Cranmer Hall Dur 58. **d** 58 Warrington for Liv **p** 59 Liv. C of St Matt Bootle 58-61; C-in-c of St Mich Liv 61-63; V 63-71; Chap Liv Cathl 62-71, C-in-c of St Jas w St Matt and H Trin Toxt Pk 66-68; V of St Pet Newton-in-Makerfield Dio Liv from 71; Chap Red Bank Sch from 75. *St Peter's Vicarage, Newton-le-Willows, Mer.* (Newton-le-Willows 4815)

MEREDITH, Robert. b 21. Bps' Coll Cheshunt. **d** 58 **p** 59 St Alb. C of St Andr Bedford 58-61; V of All SS Luton 61-67; Kimpton (w Ayot St Lawr from 75) 67-76; RD of Wheathampstead 72-76; R of Hunsdon (w Widford and Wareside from 80) Dio St Alb from 76; Widford 76-80. *Rectory, Acorn Street, Hunsdon, Ware, Herts.* (Ware 870171)

MEREDITH, Roland Evan. b 32. Trin Coll Cam 3rd cl Hist Trip pt i 54, BA (2nd cl Th Trip pt i) 55, MA 59. Cudd Coll. **d** 57 **p** 58 Dur. C of Bp Wearmouth 57-59; Dioc Chap Dio Birm 59-60; C of Kirkby (in c of St Mark Northwood) 60-63; V of Hitchin 63-72; Surr 65-72, 73-79 and from 80; V of Preston 72-76; R 76-79; RD of Preston 73-79; Hon Can of Blackb 78-79; R of Witney Dio Ox from 79; P-in-c of Hailey w Crawley Dio Ox from 79. *Rectory, Church Green, Witney, Oxon.* (Witney 2517)

MEREDITH, Ronald Duncan d'Esterre. b 09. K Coll Lon BD and AKC (1st cl) 32. **d** 32 **p** 33 Cant. C of Milton Regis 32-35; St Sav Croydon 35-39; St Pet-in-Thanet (in c of St Andr Broadstairs) 30-42; C-in-c 42-44; Chap RNVR 44-45; V of Chislet 45-50; H Trin Sittingbourne 50-62; R of Dymchurch w Eastbridge Orgarswick Blackmanstone (and Burmarsh to 63) 62-68; V of Seasalter 68-76; Ed Cant Dioc Notes 66-80; Six Pr Cant Cathl from 73; Perm to Offic Dio Cant 76-78; SB O St J from 76; Hon C of St Pet-in-Thanet Dio Cant from 80. *64 Beacon Road, St Peter in Thanet, Broadstairs, Kent.* (Thanet 69883)

MEREDITH-JONES, Richard. b 26. K Coll Lon. **d** 54 **p** 55 S'wark. C of St Geo Perry Hill Catford 54-56; C-in-c of H Trin New Charlton 56-58; V of Cinderford 58-62; Chap Dilke Mem Hosp Cinderford 58-62; V of St Jo Div Richmond 62-66; Industr Chap Dio Wakef 66-70; Chap of Frenchay and Glenside Hosps Dio Bris from 70. *Gordano, Blackberry Hill, Stapleton, Bristol, BS16 1DB.*

MERENJE, James Paolo. **d** 59 **p** 62 Masasi. P Dio Masasi. *Chivinja, Tanzania.*

MERINO, Herminio. **d** 61 **p** 62 Argent. Chap at Quepe Dio Argent from 62. *c/o Mission Anglicana, Casilla 26d, Temuco, Chile.*

MERIONETH, Archdeacon of. *See* Hughes, Ven Thomas Bayley.

MERIVALE, Charles Christian Robert. b 44. St Jo Coll Dur 76. **d** 78 Lon **p** 79 Stepney for Lon. C of Ch Ch Highbury 78-81; V of Hawes Dio Ripon from 81; Hardraw w Lunds Dio Ripon from 81. *Vicarage, Hawes, N Yorks, DL8 3NP.* (Hawes 553)

MERRETT, James Douglas. b 47. Univ of Tor BA 69. Trin Coll Tor MDiv 73. **d** 73 **p** 74 Tor. C of St Simon Ap Tor 73-77; I of St Pet Oshawa 77-81; Our Sav City and Dio Tor from 81. *1 Laurentide Drive, Don Mills, Toronto, Ont, Canada.*

MERRETT, Jonathan Charles. b 55. Univ of Wales (Bangor) BMus 77, MMus 78. Ripon Coll Cudd 78. **d** 81 Cov. C of Kenilworth Dio Cov from 81. *145 Albion Street, Kenilworth, Warwicks, CV8 2FY.*

MERRIMENT, John Robert. Moore Th Coll Syd ACT ThL (2nd cl) 64, Th Scho NT 66. **d** 64 **p** 65 Syd. C of Seven Hills w Lalor Pk 64-69; Chap of Nor I 69-71; Res Min New Housing Distr Tregear Dio Syd from 72. *105 Ellsworth Drive, Tregear, NSW, Australia 2770.* (628-6028)

MERRY, David Thomas. b 48. St Chad's Coll Dur BA 70, AKC 73. St Aug Coll Cant 73. **d** 74 **p** 75 Tewkesbury for Glouc. C of Cirencester 74-78; team V of Bridgnorth Dio Heref from 78; P-in-c of Quatford Dio Heref from 81. *32 Goodwood Avenue, Bridgnorth, Shropshire.*

MERRY, James Thomas Arthur. Univ of Tor BA 58. Wycl Coll Tor BTh 62. **d** 61 Bp Wilkinson for Moos **p** 62 Moos. R of St Paul Fort Albany 61-67; I of Gillam 67-69; I of Pikwitonei 67-69; Fort Geo Moos 69-72; L to Offic Dio Sktn 72-74 and from 78; R of Souris 74-76; on leave 76-78. *112-105th Street, Saskatoon, Sask, Canada.*

MERRY, Rex Edwin. b 38. K Coll Lon and Warm AKC 67. **d** 68 **p** 69 Linc. C of St Jo Bapt Spalding 68-73; Boxmoor Dio St Alb from 73. *23 Beechfield Road, Boxmoor, Herts.* (Hemel Hempstead 53102)

MERWOOD, Raymond George. b 27. K Coll Lon and Warm. **d** 54 Sarum **p** 56 Sheff. C of Wareham 54-55; Rawmarsh 55-58; Thrybergh 58-62; Brixham 62-67; V of Newton Poppleford w Harpford Dio Ex from 67. *Newton Poppleford Vicarage, Sidmouth, Devon.* (0395-68390)

MESSENGER, Paul. b 38. St D Coll Lamp BA 63. Coll of Resurr Mirfield 63. **d** 65 **p** 66 S'wark. C of St Luke Battersea 65-69; Ainsdale 69-71; V of St Steph Wigan 71-74; Asst Chap St Marg Conv E Grinstead and Chap Kingsley St Mich Sch 74-76; C-in-c of Southwater Dio Chich 77-81; V from 81. *Southwater Vicarage, Horsham, W Sussex.* (0403-730229)

MESSER, Ralph Edwin. b 32. N-W Ordin Course 76. **d** 79 **p** 80 York (APM). Hon C of Escrick 79-81; Area Sec USPG 79-81; P-in-c of Cawood Dio York from 81; Ryther Dio York from 81. *Cawood Vicarage, Selby, Yorks.* (Cawood 273)

MESSOM, Alan George. St Chad's Coll Dur BA 63, Dipl Th 65. **d** 65 **p** 66 Newc T. C of St Gabr Heaton 65-68; Tongnae 69-72; P-in-c of N Pusan 74-77; V of St Bart Borough and Dio Derby from 78. *49 Addison Road, Derby.* (Derby 47709)

META, Stephen. **d** 65 **p** 66 Maseno. P Dio Maseno 65-70; Dio N Maseno from 70. *Anglican Church, Sigalame, Kenya.*

METCALF, Michael Ralph. b 37. Clare Coll Cam BA (2nd cl Math Trip pt ii) 61, 2nd cl Th Trip pt ii 62, 2nd cl Th Trip pt iii 63, MA 65. Univ of Birm MA 80. Ridley Hall Cam 63. **d** 64 **p** 65 Bris. C of Downend 64-67; Perm to Offic Dio Birm 68-78; Dio Lich 72-81; Lect W Midl Coll of Educn Walsall 72-77; Sen Lect 77-81. *67 Park Hall Road, Walsall, W Midl, WS5 3HL.* (Walsall 33546)

METCALF, Robert Laurence. b 35. Univ of Dur BA 60, Dipl Th 62. Cranmer Hall Dur 60. **d** 62 Warrington for Liv **p** 63 Liv. C of Ch Ch Bootle 62-65; Farnworth (in c of St John) 65-67; V of St Cath Wigan 67-75; R of Wavertree Dio Liv from 75. *Holy Trinity Rectory, Hunters Lane, Liverpool, L15 8HL.* (051-733 2172)

METCALFE, Alan. b 22. St aid Coll 49. **d** 52 **p** 53 Wakef. C of St John Cleckheaton 52-55; Todmorden 55-56; Thornhill Lees (in c of Savile Town) 56-58; V of Middlestown w Netherton 58-60; S Crosland 60-64; Upwood w Gt and L Ravely 64-69; St Matt W Town w St Jo Bapt Dewsbury 69-71; Warden Bridgehead Hostel Cardiff 71-73; Field View Hostel Stoke Prior 73-75; McIntyre Ho Nuneaton 75-79; Perm to Offic Dio Cov 75-79; C of Southam Dio Cov from 79. *66 Linley Road, Southam, Leamington Spa, CV33 0JY.* (Southam 4437)

METCALFE, Charles Gordon. Trin Coll Dub BA 11. **d** 13 **p** 14 Kilm. C of Mohill w Termonbarry 13-16; C-in-c of Annaduff 28-31; I of Kilmore (wAnnaduff E 32-57) 16-57; Can of Kilmacallan in Elph Cathl 49-57. *Kilmore Rectory, Carnick-on-Shannon, Co Leitrim, Irish Republic.*

METCALFE, Canon Eric Albert. b 10. Univ of Leeds BA 32. Coll of Resurr Mirfield 32. **d** 34 **p** 35 S'wark. C of St Luke w St Paul Charlton 34-40; L to Offic in Ch Ch Salfords 40-45; V of Ascen Ch Plumstead Common 45-57; Chap St Nich Hosp Plumstead 51- 57; V of St Geo Perry Hill 57-66; St Marg Qu Streatham Hill 66-76; Hon Can of S'wark Cathl 72-76; Can (Emer) from 76; L to Offic Dio Roch from 77. *14 Burnhill Road, Beckenham, Kent, BR3 3LA.*

METCALFE, James. b 17. St Pet Hall Ox BA 39, MA 44. Wycl Hall Ox 39. **d** 41 Bp Mann for Roch **p** 42 Roch. C of Ch Ch Dartford 41-43; CF (EC) 43-47; C of Goole 47-49; V of St Thos Batley 49-55; Mexborough 55-71; R of Wickersley Dio Sheff from 71. *Wickersley Rectory, Rotherham, Yorks, S66 0ES.* (Wickersley 3111)

METCALFE, John Burgess. b 21. Magd Coll Cam MB, BChir 46, MA 48. Qu Coll Birm 72. **d** 75 **p** 76 Heref (NSM). C of Wistanstow Dio Heref from 75; Centr Telford Dio Lich from 75. *The Villa, Madeley, Telford, Shropshire, TF7 5AE.*

METCALFE, Neville Sidney. b 14. DSO 42. St Pet Hall Ox BA (2nd cl Mod Hist) 36, MA 63. Wycl Hall Ox 36. **d** 38 **p** 39 Southw. C of St Pet Old Radford 38-39; CF (R of O) 39-47 (Men in Disp 40 and 42); CF 47-72; ACG 65-72; Hon Chap to HM the Queen 69-72; Chap Co Hosp York and C of St

Steph Acomb York 72-74. *56 Ouse Lea, Shipton Road, Clifton, York, YO3 6SA.*

METCALFE, Percy. Egerton Hall, Man 23. **d** 24 **p** 25 Man. C of All S Ancoats 24-28; Ripley 28-31; V of S Wingfield 31-36; R of Brotton Parva (w Carlin How 36-41) 36-52; V of Ruswarp w Sneaton 52-59. *8 Oxford Street, Saltburn-by-the-Sea, Yorks.*

METCALFE, Reginald. b 38. **d** 79 St Alb. C of Apsley End Dio St Alb from 79. *30 Manorville Road, Apsley, Hemel Hempstead, Herts.*

METCALFE, Ronald. b 41. Edin Th Coll 67. **d** 69 **p** 70 York. C of Saltburn-by-the-Sea 69-72; P-in-c of Crathorne and Dioc Youth Officer Dio York 73-77; Adult Tr Officer from 78. *Rectory, Barton-le-Street, Malton, N Yorks.*

METCALFE, Thomas William. b 16. Selw Coll Cam BA 38, MA 42. Ripon Hall Ox 39. **d** 39 Knaresborough for Ripon **p** 40 Ripon. C of St Chad Far Headingley 39-42; Barwick-in-Elmet 42-46; CF 46-71; V of Wragby 71-77. *14 Ellam Avenue, Neville's Cross, Durham, DH1 4PG.* (Durham 44184)

METCALFE, William Bernard. b 47. St Jo Coll Cam BA (Architecture) 69, MA 73. Ball Coll Ox BA (Th) 71. Ripon Hall Ox 70. **d** 72 Ox **p** 73 Buckingham for Ox. C of Caversham 72-75; Aylesbury and Industr Chap Ox 75-79; Team V of Thamesmead Dio S'wark from 79. *21 Northwood Place, Thamesmead, Erith, Kent, DA18 4HN.* (01-311 7967)

METCALFE, Canon William Nelson. b 15. St Jo Coll Dur BA 39, MA 54. St Aid Coll LTh 35. **d** 39 **p** 40 Southw. C of St Leodegarius Old Basford 39-42; Chap RAFVR 42-47; C of Melton Mowbray 47; V of Bunny w Bradmore 47-59; R of Bottesford (w Muston from 62) Dio Leic from 59; RD of Framland I 61-80; Surr from 69; Hon Can of Leic from 75. *Bottesford Rectory, Nottingham.* (Bottesford 42335)

METE, Hohepa Matiu. b 44. **d** 81 Auckld. C of Parengarenga Ahipara Peria Dio Auckld from 81. *36 Bonnetts Road, Kaitaia, NZ.*

METE, Maaka Matiu. St Jo Coll Auckld LTh 50. **d** 51 **p** 52 Auckld. C of Otahuhy w Panmure 51-55; V of Bombay NZ 55-60; Kamo 60-66; Maori Missr Dio Ch Ch 66-69; V of Phillipstown 69-74; P-in-c of Kawakawa Miss Distr 74-75; Ruawai 75; on leave 76; V of Birkenhead Dio Auckld from 77. *187 Hinemoa Street, Birkenhead, Auckland, NZ.* (487-260)

METHUEN, Alan Robert. b 11. Dorch Miss Coll 37. **d** 41 **p** 42 Linc. C of St Hugh Old Brumby 41-42; Letchworth 43-46; Clewer (in c of All SS Dedworth) 50-57; P-in-c of Conv Distr of All SS Dedworth 57-75; Gt Haseley w Albury, Tiddington and Waterstock Dio Ox from 75. *Great Haseley Rectory, Oxford, OX9 7JG.* (Great Milton 303)

METHUEN, John Alan Robert. b 47. BNC Ox BA (2nd cl Th) 69, MA 74. Cudd Coll 69. **d** 71 Buckingham for Ox **p** 72 Reading for Ox. C of Fenny Stratford 71-74; P-in-c of Dorney and Warden Eton Coll Project 74-77; V of St Mark Reading Dio Ox from 77. *88 Connaught Road, Reading, RG3 2UF.* (Reading 587400)

METIVIER, Robert John. b 31. STh (Lambeth) 61. Ch Div Sch of the Pacific BD 66. Univ of Lon BA 68. Codr Coll Barb. **d** 60 Barb **p** 61 Trinid. C of St Crisp Port of Spain 61-64; w USPG 66-67; R of Tacarigua 68-77; St Andrew 77-78; C of Gt Berkhamsted Dio St Alb from 78. *All Saints House, Shrublands Road, Berkhamsted, Herts.*

METTERS, Anthony John Francis. b 43. K Coll Lon and Warm AKC (2nd cl) 65. **d** 68 **p** 69 Ex. C of Heavitree Ex 68-73; V of Crownhill 74-79; RD of Plymouth 77-79; Chap RN from 79. *c/o Ministry of Defence, Lacon House, Theobald's Road, London, WC1X 8RY.*

METTHAM, Maurice Desmond. b 20. Sarum Wells Th Coll 73. **d** 74 Basingstoke for Win **p** 75 Win. C of St Sav Guernsey 74-81; Perm to Offic Dio Win from 81. *Merryhill, La Rue D'Albecq, Albecq, Castel, Guernsey, CI.*

METZGER-COKER, Johannes Bankole Clement. Fourah Bay Coll 61. **d** 62 **p** 63 Sier L. P Dio Sier L. *Vicarage, Regent, Sierra Leone.*

MEUX, Kenneth John. b 07. Selw Coll Cam 2nd cl Hist Trip pt i 28, BA 29, 2nd cl Th Trip pt i 30, MA 36. Westcott Ho Cam 30. **d** 31 **p** 32 S'wark. C of St John Southend Lewisham 31-34; St Geo Camberwell 34-36; St John (in c of St Kentigern) Edin 36-40; R of Winlaton 40-49; Chap Gibside 40-49; V of St Osw Dur 49-64; Proc Conv Dur 55-64; RD of Dur 58-64; Buxton 66-71; Hon Can of Dur 58-64; V of Buxton 64-71; Surr 66-74; R of Thorpe Morieux w Preston and Brettenham 71-74. *38 Paradise Row, Melcombe Bingham, Dorchester, Dorset, DT2 7PQ.* (Milton Abbas 880532)

✠ **MEYER, Right Rev Conrad John Eustace.** b 22. Pemb Coll Cam BA 46, MA 48. Westcott Ho Cam. **d** 48 **p** 49 Bris. C of St Francis Ashton Gate Bedminster 48-51; Chap RNVR 50-54; C of Kenwyn 51-53; Falmouth 54-55; V of Devoran 54-64; Chap Falmouth Hosp 55; Dioc Youth Chap Dio Truro 55-60; Asst Dir of Relig Educn 59-60; Relig Insp for Schs 60-69; Dioc Sec for Educn 60-69; P-in-c of St Wenn 64-68; Hon Can of Truro from 66; Archd of Bodmin 69-79; Provost of W Div Woodard Corp from 69; Exam Chap to Bp of Truro 73-79; Cons Ld Bp Suffr of Dorchester in Westmr Abbey 25 Jan 79 by Abp of Cant; Bps of Lon, Ox, Truro, B & W, Heref, Nor, Portsm, Roch, Linc, Lich and St E; Bps Suffr of Jarrow Buckingham, Grantham, Hertford, Shrewsbury, Tonbridge and St Germans; and others. *151 Wroslyn Road, Freeland, Oxford, OX7 2HR.*

MEYER, Frederick Herbert. Moore Th Coll ACT ThL 27. **d** 26 **p** 27 Syd. C of All S Leichardt 27-29; Perm to Offic Dio Syd and Asst Sec Bush Ch Aid S for Austr and Tas 29-31; C of St Nich Coogee 31-34; C-in-c of St John Maroubra 34-37; St Aug Stanmore 37-41; R of St Luke Liv 41-50; L to Offic Dio Syd 51-54; Chap Ld Howe Is 54-57; C of Dapto 57-58; Chap St Geo Hosp Kogarah 58-61. *68 Farrar Brown Court, Nuffield Village, Castle Hill, NSW, Australia.*

MEYER, Rex Sydney Rudolf. Univ of Queensld BA 52, BEducn 57. Moore Th Coll ACT ThL 41. **d** 42 **p** 43 Syd. C of St Mich Wollongong 42-43; C-in-c of Prov Distr of Abbotsford w Russell Lea 43-45; V of Wyan w Rappville 45-49; R of Rozelle 49-58; C-in-c of Ultimo 54-57; Dir of Dept of Promotion Dio Syd 58-59; L to Offic Dio Syd 58-59; C of Leichhardt 59-60; Roseville 60-63; Lane Cove 63-65; Chap Callan Pk and Broughton Hall Psychiatric Hosps Dio Syd from 65. *1 Belgium Avenue, Roseville, NSW, Australia 2069.* (82-0266)

MEYER, Richard Ernest. b 44. St Jo Coll Dur BA 66. Coll of Resurr Mirfield 71. **d** 73 Tewkesbury for Glouc **p** 73 Glouc. C of Up Hatherley 73-74; Wotton St Mary Without (or Longlevens) 74-77; V of Gt and L Hampton Dio Worc from 77. *Hampton Vicarage, Evesham, Worcs.* (Evesham 6381)

MEYER, Stuart Thomas. b 45. GLCM 69. Trin Coll Bris 76. **d** 78 **p** 79 Heref. C of St Jas and of St Pet w St Owen Heref 78-80; Chap K Coll Cam from 80. *King's College, Cambridge.*

MEYER, Vernon Francis. St Barn Coll Adel. ACT ThL 33. **d** 33 **p** 34 Adel. C of Glenelg 33-36; Miss Chap Loxton 36-38; P-in-c of S Yorke's Peninsula 38-42; Chap AIF 40-45; R of Ch Ch Yankalilla 45-54; V of W Dereham w Wereham 54-57; LPr Dio Adel 57-58; R of Balaklava 58-62; Broadview 62-67; Lyndoch 68-74; L to Offic Dio Adel from 74. *Rectory, Lyndoch, S Australia 5351.*

MEYERS, John William. b 47. St Pet Coll Imbali Dipl Th 80. **d** 80 Kimb K. d Dio Kimb K. *Box 514, Udington, S Africa.*

MEYNELL, Andrew Francis. b 43. Westcott Ho Cam 70. **d** 73 **p** 74 Ox. C of Cowley (in c of St Jas from 75) 73-79; Team V 79-80; V of Wendover Dio Ox from 81; P-in-c of Halton Dio Ox from 81. *Vicarage, Dobbins Lane, Wendover, Aylesbury, Bucks.* (Wendover 622230)

MEYNELL, Canon Mark. b 14. Ch Ch Ox BA 37, MA 44. Cudd Coll. **d** 40 **p** 41 St Alb. C of Abbey Ch St Alb 40-46; R of Folkington 46-49; Marlesford 49-56; R of Campsea Ashe 51-56; Cogenhoe 56-63; V of Leamington Hastings 65-79; Exam Chap to Bp of Cov from 65; Can Th of Cov 73-78; Can Th (Emer) from 78; C-in-c of Birdingbury 73-74; R 74-79; Perm to Offic Dio St E from 80. *2 Double Street, Framlingham, Woodbridge, Suffolk.* (Framlingham 723898)

MEYRICK, Cyril Jonathan. b 52. St Jo Coll Ox BA (Th) 73. Sarum Wells Th Coll 74. **d** 76 **p** 77 Dorchester for Ox. C of Bicester 76-78; Dom Chap to Bp of Ox 78-81; Tutor Codrington Coll Barb from 81. *Codrington College, Barbados, W Indies.*

MFEKA, Edmund Lammetjie. St Pet Coll Alice 62. **d** 64 **p** 65 Zulu. P Dio Zulu 64-77; Dio Natal from 77. *Box 45, Tongaat, Natal, S Africa.*

MFENYANA, Mlami Mafu. b 41. St Pet Coll Alice 66. **d** 69 **p** 71 Grahmstn. C of Mdantsane 69-71; St Mich Miss Grahmstn 71-73; R of H Trin Ft Beaufort 73-77; St Andr Queenstown 77-78; P-in-c of Nyanga Dio Capetn from 78. *c/o Box 1932, Cape Town, S Africa.* (62-1702)

MFENYANA, Naphtali Mtutuzeli. St Pet Coll Rosettenville. **d** 44 **p** 46 Grahmstn. Asst Miss St Phil E Lon 44-48; St Phil Grahmstn 48-50; Miss at St Agnes Noupoort 50-62; R of St Andr Queenstown 62-76; Can of Grahmstn Cathl 71-74 and 77-80; Archd of Queenstown 74-76. *Box 123, Whittlesea, CP, S Africa.*

MFOCWA, Newton Pennington Mbele. St Bede's Coll Umtata. **d** 55 **p** 56 St John's. P Dio St John's. *PO Cofimvaba, Transkei, S Africa.*

MGANGA, Herbert. Hegongo Th Coll 43. **d** 44 **p** 48 Zanz. Asst P Dio Zanz 60-74; Chap of Kiwanda Tr Coll Dio Zanz T 61-68; Chap St Andr Coll Dio Dar-S 71-78. *PO Box 35, Korogwe, Tanzania.*

MGANGA, Samwil. St Cypr Th Coll Tunduru 58. **d** 60 Zanz. d Dio Zanz T 60-74; and from 79. *Box 35, Korogwe, Tanzania.*

MGAYA, Petro. d 80 Bp Russell for Zanz T (NSM). d Dio

Zanz T. *PO Mkuzi, Muheza, Tanga Region, Tanzania.*

MGAYA, Philip. Kalole Th Coll 53. **d** 54 **p** 57 Zanz. P Dio Zanz T. *Magoma, PO Kwata, Korogwe, Tanzania.*

MGAZA, Archie. b 32. St Cypr Coll Rondo 69. **d** 72 **p** 73 Zanz T. P Dio Zanz T. *Box 140, Handeni, Tanzania.*

MGBEMENA, Canon Louis Chukujindu. Trin Coll Umuahia, 55. **d** 57 **p** 58 Niger. P Dio Ow 57-62; Dio Niger from 62; Hon Can of Niger from 76. *Diocesan Lay Training Centre, Nnewi, Nigeria.*

MGBEMENE, Canon Amos Egwuekwe Daniel. b 23. BSc (Lon) 49. Im Coll Ibad 71. **d** 71 **p** 72 Niger. P Dio Niger; Can of Niger from 74. *All Saints' Cathedral, Box 361, Onitsha, Nigeria.*

MGINA, Staffano Yahana. St Cypr Th Coll Ngala, 59. **d** 60 **p** 63 S W Tang. P Dio SW Tang; Can of SW Tang from 80. *Mlangali, PO Itundu, Tanzania.*

MGOMBA, Hadad. b 28. **d** 73 Moro. d Dio Moro. *P.O. Turiani, Morogoro, Tanzania.*

MGOMBE, Charles. b 12. **d** 74 Lake Malawi **p** 75 Bp Taylor for Lake Malawi. P Dio Lake Malawi 74-79. *Mgombe Village, P/A Chia, Nkhotakota, Malawi.*

MGONGO, Yohana. St Cypr Th Coll Ngala, 60. **d** 62 Zanz. d Dio Zanz T from 62. *St Cyprian's Theological College, Ngala, PO Box 212, Lindi, Tanzania.*

MHANDO, Tito. St Cypr Coll Ngala. **d** 66 Bp Russell for Zanz T **p** 68 Zanz T. P Dio Zanz T. *Box 140, Handeni, Tanzania.*

MHANDO, Canon Yonah Chadibwa. **d** 56 Bp Omari **p** 57 Centr Tang. P Dio Centr Tang 56-65; Dio Moro from 65; Hon Can of Moro from 77. *Tunguli, PO Berega, Morogoro, Tanzania.*

MHINA, Denis Kibaja. **d** 73 **p** 75 Dar-S. P Dio Dar-S. *Box 25016, Dar-es-Salaam, Tanzania.*

MHLABI, John. St Jo Coll Lusaka. **d** 58 **p** 60 Matab. P Dio Matab. *4313 Tshaka, PO Luveve, Bulawayo, Zimbabwe.*

MHLAULI, Mteteli. **d** 74 **p** 76 Grahmstn. C of St Matt's Miss Grahmstn 74-77. *PO St Matthew's, Grahamstown, S Africa.*

MHLAULI, Sydwell Sithilanga Mkhuphanyathi. b 40. St Bede's Coll Umtata 69. **d** 71 **p** 72 St John's. C of All SS St John's 71-77; P-in-c of Xugxwala Dio St John's from 77. *PO Viedgesville, Transkei, S Africa.* (Viedgesville 16)

MHLOPE, Canon Andrew. **d** 23 **p** 33 Lebom. P Dio Lebom; Can of Maciene Cathl from 52. *Caixa Postal 57, Lourenco Marques, Portuguese East Africa.*

MHOGOLO, Godfrey Mdimi. St Phil Coll Kongwa 70. **d** 74 **p** 75 Centr Tang. P Dio Centr Tang 74-75; Dio Melb 75-80; Prin St Phil Th Coll Kongwa from 80. *Box 26, Kongwa, Tanzania.*

MIAKO, Solomon Manumingi. Bp Gwynne Coll Mundri. **d** 62 **p** 63 Sudan. P Dio Sudan 62-76; Archd of Moru 75-75. *ECS, Lui, Sudan.*

MICHAEL, Anthony David. St Jo Coll Morpeth 63. **d** 66 **p** 67 Graft. C of Casino 66-70; Guildford 70-71; CF (Austr) 71-74; Perm to Offic Dio Wang 72-74; C-in-c of Provisional Par Mascot 74-80; Actg R of Botany 76-77; w CMS from 80. *93 Bathurst Street, Sydney, NSW, Australia 2000.*

MICHAEL, David Henry Vincent. b 12. Univ of Wales (Swansea) BA 35. St D Coll Lamp. **d** 39 **p** 40 Waik. C of St Geo Frankton 39-41; C-in-c of H Trin Ngaruawahia 41-43; CF (NZ) 43-45; C of Northwich 46-48; R of St Jo Evang Wick 48-54; P-in-c of St Pet and H Rood Thurso 54-61; Perm to Offic Dio Birm from 61. *29 Mayall Drive, Four Oaks, Sutton Coldfield, Warwicks.*

MICHAEL, Ernest Stanley Rees Mackay. b 11. Late Exhib of St D Coll Lamp BA (3rd cl Hist) 32. St Mich Coll Llan. **d** 34 **p** 35 St D. C of St Paul Llanelly 34-37; Llanedy 37-39; Tenby 39-41; R of Bosherton w St Twynnells 41-48; V of Monkton 48-53; CF (EC) 41-46; CF 53-65; Chap to HM the Queen at HM Tower Lon 65-68; V of Magor w Redwick (and Undy from 74) 68-81; RD of Netherwent 80-81. *4 Sycamore Terrace, Magor, Newport, Gwent, NP6 3ET.* (Magor 880659)

MICHAEL, Ian MacRae. b 40. Univ of Aber MA 62. Hertf Coll Ox DPhil 66. Westcott Ho Cam 77. **d** 79 **p** 80 Birm. C of King's Heath Dio Birm from 79. *6c Cambridge Road, King's Heath, Birmingham, B13 9UD.* (021-444 2311)

MICHANGULA, Enosse. St Chris Th Coll Maciene 49. **d** 50 **p** 51 Lebom. P Dio Lebom from 50. *Caixa Postal 57, Lourenço Marques, Mozambique.*

MICHELL, Canon Douglas Reginald. b 19. St Jo Coll Dur BA 41, MA 44. Westcott Ho Cam 41. **d** 43 **p** 44 Chelmsf. C of H Trin Hermon Hill 43-45; Chap St Jo Coll Dur and L to Offic Dio Dur 45-48; R of St Jas Moss Side 48-53; V of Horwich 53-61; Surr from 53; V of Evington 61-80; Hon Can of Leic from 67; RD of Christianity N 74-79; Gartree I from 81; V of Billesdon (and Skeffington from 82) w Rolleston and Goadby Dio Leic from 80. *Billesdon Vicarage, Leicester, LE7 9AE.* (Billesdon 284)

MICHELL, Francis Richard Noel. b 42. St Cath Coll Cam 2nd cl Geog Trip pt i 63, BA (3rd cl Geog Trip pt ii) 64, MA 68. Tyndale Hall Bris 64. **d** 66 **p** 67 Pet. C of St Giles Northn 66-69; Gateacre 69-72; V of St Paul, Hatton Hill Litherland 72-79; Rainhill Dio Liv from 79. *Vicarage, View Road, Rainhill, Prescot, Lancs.* (051-426 4666)

MICHELL, Jocelyn Ralph Stamerham. b 21. Trin Coll Cam BA 43, MA 55. Ridley Hall, Cam 45-46 and 50. **d** 51 Liv **p** 55 Chich. C of Sutton St Helens 51-55; St John Meads Eastbourne 55-56; V of St Geo Huyton 56-61; St Andr Kowloon 61-68; Longstock w Leckford 69-79; Dioc Missr Dio Asaba from 80. *c/o Bishopscourt, Box 216, Asaba, Bendel State, Nigeria.*

MICHELO, Vincent. **d** 72 **p** 73 Lusaka. P Dio Lusaka. *PO Mapanza, via Choma, Zambia.*

MICHIE, John. Oak Hill Th Coll. **d** 46 **p** 47 Man. C of H Trin Rusholme 46-48; Lenton (in c of Priory Ch of St Anthony) 49-50; V of Rufforth 50-55; C-in-c of Askham Bryan 51-54; R of H Trin Rusholme 55-64; V of H Trin w St Luke Warrington 64-68; Miss Rhod Rly Miss 71-76. *Box 835, Bulawayo, Rhodesia.* (19-60663)

MICHIE, William John Riach. St Columb's Hall Wang 64. **d** 67 **p** 68 Gippsld. C of Morwell 67-69; Bairnsdale 69-71; V of Newborough 71-74; on leave 75-76; Perm to Offic Dio Melb from 76. *2-38 Westbury Street, Balaclava, Vic, Australia 3183.* (527-6844)

MIDDLEDITCH, Terry Gordon. b 30. St D Coll Lamp BA 62. **d** 63 Lanc for Blackb **p** 64 Blackb. C of Poulton-le-Fylde 63-67; C-in-c of St Jas Heysham 65-67; C of St Pet Cheltm Dio Glouc from 75. *44 Long Mynd Avenue, Cheltenham, Glos.*

MIDDLEMOST, Sidney Harold Arthur. St Paul Coll Grahmstn 64. **d** 66 **p** 68 Capetn. C of Wynberg 66-71; CF (S Afr) from 71. *Box 1, Monte Vist, CP, S Africa.* (98-3911)

MIDDLESEX, Archdeacon of. *See* Perry, Ven John Neville.

MIDDLETON, Lord Bishop Suffragan of. *See* Tytler, Right Rev Donald Alexander.

MIDDLETON, Alan Derek. b 46. St Jo Coll Dur BA (2nd cl Gen) 68. Univ of Birm Dipl Th 71. Qu Coll Birm 70. **d** 72 **p** 73 Lich. C of Cannock 72-75; Warden of St Helen's Millbank Youth and Commun Centre Bp Auckland 76-79; V of St Jo Evang Darlington Dio Dur from 79. *343 Yarm Road, Darlington, Co Durham, DL1 1BD.* (Darlington 57748)

MIDDLETON, Barry Glen. b 41. Lich Th Coll 68. **d** 70 **p** 71 Man. C of Westhoughton 70-73; St Marg Prestwich 73-74; Team V of Buxton 75-77; Chap Worc R Infirmary Hosp and L to Offic Dio Worc from 77. *Chaplain's Office, Worcester Royal Infirmary, Worcester.* (Worc 27122)

MIDDLETON, Edmund Rawstone. St Paul's Hostel Grahmstn 13. **d** 14 **p** 16 Bp Balfour for Bloemf. C of Mafeteng 14-19; Dir of Miss at Sekubu 19-23; Mafeteng 23-29; Leribe 29-41; Sekubu 41-47; Fouriesburg and Brindisi Miss 47-63. *Brindisi, Fouriesburg, OFS, S Africa.*

MIDDLETON, Hugh Charles. Univ of Nottm BTh 77. Linc Th Coll 73. **d** 77 **p** 78 Linc. C of New Sleaford Dio Linc from 77. *29 St Denys Avenue, Sleaford, Lincs.*

MIDDLETON, Canon Kenneth Frank. b 28. Keble Coll Ox BA (3rd cl Hons Mod Hist) 52, 3rd cl Hons Th 54, MA 64. St Steph Ho Ox 52. **d** 55 **p** 56 Leic. C of St Matt Leic 55-58; St Barn W Hackney 58-60; V of St Matt (w St Geo from 61) City and Dio Leic from 60; RD of Christianity N from 79; P-in-c of St Alb City and Dio Leic from 80; St Mich Belgrave City and Dio Leic from 81; Hon Can of Leic Cathl from 80. *St Matthew's Vicarage, Taylor Road, Leicester, LE1 2JN.* (Leicester 23038)

MIDDLETON, Leonard James. b 33. Bps' Coll Cheshunt 55. **d** 58 **p** 59 Roch. C of Beckenham 58-60; Wallingford 60-64; V of Codnor 64-71; E Tilbury 71-77; P-in-c of W Tilbury 71-77; R of Copford w Easthorpe Dio Chelmsf from 77. *Rectory, Copford Green, Colchester, Essex, CO6 1DB.* (Colchester 210253)

MIDDLETON, Michael John. Univ of Dur BSc 62. Fitzw Ho Cam BA (2nd cl Th Trip pt ii) 66. Westcott Ho Cam 63. **d** 66 **p** 67 Newc T. C of St Geo Jesmond Newc T 66-69; Chap St Geo Gr Sch Capetn 69-72; K S Tynemouth 72-77; V of St Geo Jesmond City and Dio Newc T from 77; M Gen Syn from 80. *St George's Vicarage, Jesmond, Newcastle-upon-Tyne, NE2 2TF.* (Newc T 811628)

MIDDLETON, Thomas Arthur. b 36. K Coll Lon and Warm AKC 61. **d** 62 **p** 63 Dur. C of Sunderland 62-63; St Helen Bp Auckland 63-67; Winlaton (in c of St Barn Rowlands Gill) 67-70; P-in-c St Thos Conv Distr Pennywell Bp Wearmouth 70-79; R of Boldon Dio Dur from 79. *Rectory, West Boldon, Co Durham.* (Boldon 7370)

MIDDLETON, Trevor. Moore Th Coll Syd 62. ACT ThL 67. **d** and **p** 65 C and Goulb. C of Berridale 65-67; N Goulb 67-69; Engadine 69-72; C-in-c of Provisional Distr Oak Flats Dio Syd 72-75; R from 75. *40 Fisher Street, Oak Flats, NSW, Australia 2527.* (56-1024)

MIDDLETON-DANSKY, Serge Wladimir. b 45. Ripon Coll Cudd 75. **d** 77 Huntingdon for Ely **p** 78 Ely. C of Wisbech 77-79. *c/o Hillview Farm, Northaw Road West, Northaw, Herts.*

MIDDLEWICK, Robert James. b 44. BD (Lon) 76. Ripon Coll Cudd 75. **d** 77 **p** 78 Roch. C of Bromley 77-81; Belvedere (in c of St Andr Bostall Heath) Dio Roch from 81. *276 Brampton Road, Bexley Heath, Kent, DA7 5SF.* (01-303 9332)

MIDGLEY, Edward Graham. b 23. St Edm Hall Ox BA (1st cl Engl Lang and Lit) 47, MA 48, BLitt 50. Cudd Coll 56. **d** 56 **p** 57 Ox. Fell and Tutor St Edm Hall Ox from 56; Dean 56-78; Vice-Prin 70-78; Chap from 78; L to Offic Dio Ox from 56; M Liturgical Comm of Gen Syn from 81. *St Edmund Hall, Oxford.*

MIDLANE, Colin John. b 50. Univ of Lon BA 72. Sarum Wells Th Coll 77. **d** 78 Lon **p** 79 Stepney for Lon. C of St Pet w St Thos Bethnal Green Dio Lon from 78. *3 Queen Margaret Flats, St Jude's Road, Bethnal Green, E2.* (01-729 2225)

MIDLIGE, Canon Benjamin Angus. Bp's Univ Lennox LST 47. **d** 47 **p** 48 Montr. C of St Jo Div Verdun Montr 47-51; I of St Marg Montr 51 and 58-63; St Chad Montr 51-58; R of St Paul Lachine City and Dio Montr from 63; Hon Can of Montr from 74. *379 44th Avenue, Lachine 610, PQ, Canada.* (514-634 2758)

MIGHALL, Robert. b 33. St Pet Hall Ox BA (3rd cl Th) 57, MA 61. Wycl Hall Ox 57. **d** 58 **p** 59 Cov. C of St Mich Stoke Cov 58-62; Rugby (in c of St Pet) 62-64; V of Newbold-on-Avon w Long Lawford 64-75; Kineton Dio Cov from 76; Combroke w Compton Verney Dio Cov from 76. *Kineton Vicarage, Warwick, CV35 0LL.* (Kineton 640248)

MIHILL, Dennis George. b 31. St Alb Dioc Min Tr Scheme. **d** 81 St Alb. C of St Nich Harpenden Dio St Alb from 81. *5 Dalkeith Road, Harpenden, Herts.*

MIKAYA, Ven Henry. b 40. St Cypr Coll Rondo 69. **d** 71 **p** 72 Lake Malawi. P Dio Lake Malawi from 71; Archd of Lilongwe from 75. *Box 294, Lilongwe, Malawi.*

MIKEKEMO, Zephaniah. Warner Mem Th Coll 56. **d** 58 **p** 59 Bp Brazier for Ugan. P Dio Ugan 58-60; Dio Rwanda B 60-65; Dio Ankole-K 65-67; Dio Kig from 67. *Iryaruvumba, Box 1017, Kisoro, Uganda.*

MILBURN, John. b 15. Univ of Lon BA (2nd cl Engl) 38. AKC 40. **d** 40 **p** 41 Lon. C of St Sav Hoxton 40-43; Perm to Offic at St Pet Limehouse 43-46; St Swith Worc 46-49; Chap Hostel of God Clapham 49-53; V of St Steph w St Cath Liv 53-64; St Paul Brighton Dio Chich from 64. *St Paul's Vicarage, Brighton, Sussex, BN1 2RG.* (Brighton 25297)

MILBURN, John Kenneth. b 13. St Jo Coll Dur BA 39, MA 42. **d** 40 **p** 41 Dur. C of St Aid Blackhill 40-43; Asst Chap Miss to Seamen Tyne Station and L to Offic Dio Dur 43-44; C of Princetown and Asst Chap HM Pris Dartmoor 44-46; C-in-c of St Aug Plymouth 46-47; V 47-56; Churchstow w Kingsbridge 56-81; RD of Woodleigh 58-65 and 76-80; P-in-c of Charleton w Buckland-tout-Saints 80-81. *3 Willows Close, Frogmore, Kingsbridge, Devon.* (Frogmore 374)

MILBURN, Very Rev Robert Leslie Pollington. b 07. Late Scho of SS Coll Cam 1st cl Cl Trip pt i 28, BA (Aegr Cl Trip pt ii) 30, Jeremie Hellenistic Pri 31, Geo Williams Pri 32, MA 34. New Coll Ox Hall-Houghton LXX Pri (Jun) 33. **d** 34 **p** 35 Ox. Fell and Chap Worc Coll Ox 34-57; Tutor 45-57; Jun Bursar 36-46; Estates Bursar 46-57; Select Pr Univ of Ox 42-44; Univ Lect in Ch Hist 47-59; Exam Chap to Bp of S'wark 51-57; Ox 52-57; Bampton Lect 52; Dean of Worc 57-68; Dean (Emer) from 68; Exam Chap to Bp of Worc 60-68; Select Pr Univ of Cam 63; Master of the Temple, Lon 68-80; Hon Fell Worc Coll Ox from 78. *Wallcroft, Winslow, Bromyard, Herefs.* (Bromyard 83469)

MILDENHALL, Pamela Ann. b 32. St Jo Coll Auckld 75. LTh (extra-mural) 67. **d** 75 **p** 78 Wel. C of St Matt Masterton 75-81; V of Manaia Dio Wel from 81. *Vicarage, 35 Ngatai Street, Manaia, NZ.*

MILES, Alfred Charles. ACT ThL 20. Ridley Coll Melb. **d** 20 **p** 21 Gippsld. C of Wonthaggi 20-22; V of Blackwood Forest w Bass 22-26; C of St Matt Prahran 26; Min of Hastings 26-30; Mt Dandenong 30-36; Blackburn 36-47; I of H Trin Thornbury 47-56; Gardenvale 56-64. *3/507 Middleborough Road, Box Hill North, Vic, Australia 3129.* (03-89 9223)

MILES, Archibald Geoffrey. b 22. New Coll Ox BA 47, 2nd cl Th and MA 48. Chich Th Coll 49. **d** 50 **p** 51 Pet. C of St Mich AA Northampton 50-53; St John's Pro-Cathl Bulawayo 53-54; Ascen Hillside Bulawayo 54-59; Headley Hants 59-60; R of Bentley Surrey 60-63; Riverside Bulawayo 63-73; St John's Cathl Bulawayo 73-74; V of Shrewton and Rollestone 75-80; New Marston City and Dio Ox from 80; P-in-c of Winterbourne Stoke 75-80. *8 Jack Straw's Lane, Headington, Oxford, OX3 0DL.* (Oxford 42803)

MILES, Charles Francis. b 09. Univ of Dur LTh 33. Lon Coll of Div 32. **d** 32 **p** 33 Lon. C of St Sav Tollington Pk 32-34; Coleford w Staunton 34-38; Trent Vale 39-40; R of Eastington 40-47; Hilperton w Whaddon 47-50; C of Tiverton 52-55; C-in-c of Chevithorne and Cove 55-58; V 58-74; Perm to Offic Dio Ex 74-78; Dio Glouc from 78. *5 Latymer Croft, Churchdown, Glos.*

MILES, Charles Reginald. ACT ThL 28. Ridley Coll Melb 26. **d** 28 **p** 29 Bend. C of St Paul Bend 28-31; All SS Tatura 31; V of Sebastian 31-35; R of Milloo 35-37; Woodend (in c of Trentham from 42) 37-44; St Luke N Fitzroy 44-47; St Matt E Geelong 47-49; Richmond 50-60; Min of Springvale 60; Glen Waverley 60-64; V of Mt Eliza 65-69; Perm to Offic Dio Wang from 80. *Lease Street, Katunga, Vic, Australia 3640.* (82-2858)

MILES, Canon Charles Reginald. Tyndale Hall Bris 36. **d** 39 **p** 40 Lich. C of St Luke Wolverhampton 39-43; Bucknall w Bagnall 43-46; R of Dibden Dio Win from 46; Hon Can of Win Cathl from 75. *Rectory, Beaulieu Road, Dibden Purlieu, Southampton, SO4 5PT.* (Hythe 843204)

MILES, Edward Harford. Univ of W Ont BA 64. Hur Coll BTh 67. **d** 66 Hur. C of St Jo Evang Lon Ont 66-67. *21 Nelson Street, Simcoe, Ont., Canada.*

MILES, Edward Rowland. **d** 77 **p** 79 Geo. C of Knysna 77-80; P-in-c of Ugie Dio St John's from 80. *Box 17, Ugie, S Africa.*

MILES, Eric Victor. b 28. St Mich Coll Llan 55. **d** 57 Mon for Wales **p** 58 Llan. C of Grangetown Canton 57-60; Roath 60-62; UMCA Area Sec Wales, Glouc and Heref 62-64; USPG Area Sec Bris and Glouc from 65; Commiss SW Tang from 75. *65 Windmill Road, Minchinhampton, Stroud, GL6 9EB.* (Brimscombe 883145)

MILES, Frank Norman. b 07. Univ of Wales BA 28, MA 33. Univ of Lon BD 46. St Mich Coll Llan. **d** 41 **p** 42 Llan. C of Llanwonno 41-47; L to Offic Dio Llan from 47; Asst Master Pontypridd Boys' Gr Sch 31-72. *Marcross, The Avenue, The Common, Pontypridd, Mid Glam CF37 4DF.* (Pontypridd 402706)

MILES, Gerald Christopher Morgan. b 36. Peterho Cam Ba 57, MA 72. Cranfield Inst of Tech Bedford MSc 72. Wycl Hall Ox 74. **d** 76 **p** 77 Roch. C of St Jas Tunbridge Wells 76-80; V of Leigh Dio Roch from 80. *Leigh Vicarage, Tonbridge, Kent.* (Hildenborough 833022)

MILES, Gilbert Henry. b 1899. **d** 57 **p** 58 Southw. C of All S w Ch Ch Radford 57-60; V of Whatton-in-the-Vale w Aslockton 60-65; C-in-c of Awsworth w Cossall 65-69; Perm to Offic Dio Southw 69-80; Dio Chich from 80. *Flat 7, Glyne Hall, De La Warr Parade, Bexhill-on-Sea, TN40 1LY.* (Bexhill 217689)

MILES, Harold Leslie. b 14. **d** 45 Ripon for River **p** 46 River. [f in CA] C of Belmont 45-46; St Thos Narrendera 46-47; Broken Hill 47-49; Wensley (in c of Leyburn) Yorks 49-51; R of Saxby w Stapleford V 51-54; Wyfordby 51-54; Saxby w Stapleford Garthorpe and Wyfordby 54-64; Finningham w Westhorpe Dio St E from 64. *Finningham Rectory, Stowmarket, Suffolk.* (Bacton 781207)

MILES, Hubert Richard. **d** 59 **p** 60 Auckld. C of St Luke Mt Albert 60-62; Thames 62-64; V of Waimate N 64-67; Warkworth 67-75; Offg Min Dio Auckld from 76. *39 Bertram Street, Warkworth, Auckland, NZ.* (8260)

MILES, James. St Francis Coll Brisb. **d** 59 **p** 60 Kalg. C of Boulder 59-61; Geraldton 61-63; R of Pingelly 63-65; Donnybrook 65-66; C of Albany 66-68; P-in-c of Ringarooma w Derby 68-70; Perm to Offic Dio Melb from 70. *190 The Avenue, Parkville, Vic 3052, Australia.*

MILES, Lawrence. b 24. St D Coll Lamp BA 48. **d** 50 **p** 51 Llan. C of Ton Pentre 50-54; St Jo Bapt Cardiff 54-61; V of Cwmparc Dio Llan from 61. *Vicarage, Cwmparc, Treorchy, Mid Glam CF42 6NA.* (Treorchy 773303)

MILES, Malcolm Robert. b 36. K Coll Lon and Warm AKC 60. **d** 61 **p** 62 Pet. C of St Mary Virg Northn 61-63; E Haddon 63-67; R of Broughton 67-73; Asst Chap Univ of Nottm 73-74; V of H Trin Northn Dio Pet from 75. *24 Edinburgh Road, Northampton, NN2 6PH.* (Northn 711468)

MILES, Richard Henry. St Jo Coll Morpeth. **d** 46 **p** 47 Bath. Bro of Good Shepherd 46-47 and 48-54; Chap All SS Coll Bath 47-48; C-in-c of Cobar 48-51; Warden of Hostels Dubbo 51-54; Prin St Paul's Tr Sch for Boys Newhaven Philip I 54-56; Supt of St Laur Home Grange 56-57; P-in-c of Kilburn 57; All SS Cathl Bath 58-59; Warden St John's Hostel Forbes 60; St Francis's Ho Dubbo 61; All SS Hostel Charleville 62; V of Ascen Morningside Brisb 62-79; Perm to Offic Dio Brisb from 79. *15 Barton Road, Hawthorne, Queensland, Australia 4171.* (399 3317)

MILES, Canon Robert George. b 01. Clifton Th Coll 35. **d** 36 **p** 37 Lon. C of Em Maida Hill 36-38; St Jo Bapt Isl 38-41; V 41-49; Highley 49-61; St Nich w Ch Ch Deptford 61-73; Hon Can of S'wark from 72. *Mabledon, London Road, Southborough, Tunbridge Wells, Kent TN4 0UZ.* (0732-35 8645)

MILES, Canon Robert William. b 27. Magd Coll Camb BA

50, MA 55. Westcott Ho Cam 50. **d** 52 **p** 53 Man. C of Bury 52-55; Dom Chap to Bp of Chich and L to Offic Dio Chich 55-58; Provost of Momb Cathl 58-63; R of St Mary Dalmahoy 65-70; Batsford w Moreton-in-Marsh 70-77; Perm to Offic Dio Glouc from 79; Can of Momb Cathl from 80. *Boilingwell, Sudeley, Winchcombe, Cheltenham, Glos.* (Winchcombe 603337)

MILEY, Reginald John Austin. St Jo Coll Morpeth. **d** and **p** 36 Perth. C of S Perth 36-38; St John Northam 38-40; St Geo Cathl Perth 40-43; Chap AIF 43-46; R of Meckering-Cunderin 46-52; Canning Dio Perth from 52. *147 Treasure Road, Queen's Park, W Australia 6107.* (68 2633)

MILFORD, Canon Theodore Richard. b 1895. Magd Coll Ox BA (1st cl Lit Hum) 21, MA 33. Westcott Ho Cam 30. **d** 31 **p** 34 Luckn. Lect St Jo Coll Agra 31-35; Exam Chap to Bp of Luckn 33-35; Sec SCM and C of All H Lombard Street Lon 35-37; Study Sec SCM 37-38; V of St Mary Virg (Univ Ch) Ox 38-47; Can and Preb of Norton Episcopi in Linc Cathl 47-68; Can (Emer) from 68; Chan 47-58; Master of the Temple 58-68; Select Pr Univ of Ox 59-60. *1 Kingsman Lane, Shaftesbury, Dorset, SP7 8HD.* (Shaftesbury 2843)

MILL, John Joseph. **d** 59 Melb for Tas **p** 60 Tas. C of St Geo Launceston 59-60; Moonah 60-62; P-in-c of Richmond Tas 62-66; C of Corowa 66-67; Perm to Offic Dio Melb 67-70; C of St Pet Box Hill 70-72; P-in-c of St Paul Kingsville 72-76; I 76-81; St Steph Highett Dio Melb from 81. *25 Donald Street, Highett, Vic, Australia 3190.*

MILLAM, Peter John. b 36. St D Coll Lamp BA 58. Ridley Hall, Cam 58. **d** 63 **p** 64 Glouc. C of Ch Ch Cheltenham 63-66; Sen Chap Ch Ch Cathl Port Stanley Falkld Is 66-70; V of Pulloxhill w Flitton 70-79; St Paul Luton Dio St Alb from 79. *105 London Road, Luton, Beds, LU1 3RG.* (Luton 31591)

MILLANIR, Guillermo. **d** 66 **p** 68 Chile. P Dio Chile. *Casilla 26d, Temuco, Chile, S America.*

MILLAR, Alan Askwith. b 26. Qu Coll Birm 59. **d** 60 **p** 61 York. C of Redcar and of Kirkleatham 60-64; V V of St Aid Middlesbrough 64-72; Cayton w Eastfield Dio York from 72. *Eastfield Vicarage, Scarborough, N Yorks, YO11 3EE.* (Scarborough 582428)

MILLAR, Andrew Charles. b 48. Univ of Hull BSc 69. Cudd Coll 71. **d** 73 **p** 74 St E. C of Rushmere 73-76; Ipswich 76-79; Dioc Youth Chap Dio Sheff from 79. *91 Tenter Balk Lane, Adwick-le-Street, Doncaster, S Yorks.* (Doncaster 722243)

MILLAR, Ven Douglas Stewart. Univ of NZ BA 30, MA (1st cl Lat and Fr) 31. Auckld Th Coll 32. **d** 32 **p** 33 Auckld. Asst Chap K Coll Otahulu 32-36; R of Moora 36-40; V of Wakatipu 40-42; St Thos Auckld 42-46; St Columba Grey Lynn 46-49; Takapuna 49-51; Exam Chap to Bp of Auckld 49-51; to Bp of Dun 69-73; V of Invercargill 51-55; Hon Can of Dun 55-74; Warden Selw Coll Dun 55-69; Archd and VG of Dun 65-75; Archd (Emer) from 75; V of Warrington 69-75; Hosps Chap Dun 70-73; Hon C of St Paul's Cathl Dun 75-80; L to Offic Dio Dun from 80. *112 Glenpark Avenue, Maryhill, Dunedin, NZ.* (Dunedin 35-163)

MILLAR, Edward John Michael. Univ of Melb BA (2nd cl Phil) 58. Trin Coll Melb ACT ThL (2nd cl) 59. **d** 60 **p** 61 Melb. C of Dandenong 60-61; Ringwood 61-62; Coburg 62-63; R of Boort 63-68; Exam Chap to Bp of St Arn 65-68; V of W Preston w NE Coburg 68-72; I of Chadstone E 72-77; Perm to Offic Dio Melb from 77. *794 Burke Road, Camberwell, Vic, Australia 3124.* (82-5956)

MILLAR, Frank. b 38. Sarum Th Coll 67. **d** 69 **p** 70 S'wark. C of H Trin S'wark 69-72; Saltdean 72-76; Cler Org Sec CECS for Dios Guildf, S'wark and Chich 75-76; P-in-c of Tendring Dio Chelmsf 76-80; R (w L Bentley, Beaumont and Moze) from 80; C of Gt Oakley 76; P-in-c of Beaumont w Moze 76-80. *Tendring Rectory, Clacton-on-Sea, Essex, CO16 0BW.* (Weeley 830406)

MILLAR, John Alexander Kirkpatrick. b 39. Trin Coll Cam BA 62, MA 66. St Jo Coll Dur 74. **d** 76 Lon **p** 77 Kens for Lon. C of H Trin Brompton Road w St Paul Onslow Sq Kens Dio Lon from 76. *St Paul's Church House, Onslow Square, SW7.* (01-589 3933)

MILLAR, Lynn Hartley. Fitzw Hall Cam 2nd cl Engl Trip pt i 23, BA (3rd cl Th Trip pt ii) 24, MA 28. Trin Coll Dub MA 42, BD 43, PhD 44. **d** 24 Ely **p** 26 Natal. C of St Mary L Cam 24-26; C of St Luke Miss Maritzburg 26-29; Chap of All SS Home and Asst Master St Geo Gr Sch Capetn and Ed S Afr Ch Directory 30-31; P-in-c of Fish Hoek 32-33; Perm to Offic Dio Lon 33; Dio Roch 34-37; Chap and Tutor Coll of St Columba Rathfarnham 37-42; Dir of Educn for Episc Ch in Scotld 43-46; Dom Chap to Bp of Edin 43-46; Perm to Offic Dio Edin 46-48; R of St Andr Strathtay w St Marg Miss Aberfeldy 48-49; Chap Woolmer's Sch Kingston 49-50; St Cath Conv Parmoor 51-52; Area Sec UMCA Metrop Area 52-53; Hd Master St Chad's Coll Caldecote 53-56; St Mich Coll Belize Br Hond 56-60; Chap Crookham Court Sch Newbury 61-62; St Monica Mampong 63-64; Sen Lect in Educn Malaga 65-67; C of Howden 67-68; Perm to Offic Dio Roch from 68. *48 High Street, Chislehurst, Kent.* (01-467 8850)

MILLAR, Stanley. b 21. **d** 73 **p** 75 Rupld. Hon C of St John's Cathl Ch Winnipeg 73-78; Hon Asst to Bp of Rupld from 78. *60 Mortimer Place, Winnipeg, Manit, Canada.*

MILLARD, Albert George. b 17. Chich Th Coll. **d** 64 **p** 65 Ox. C of Wokingham 64-71; V of Kintbury w Avington Dio Ox from 71; C-in-c of Enborne w Hamstead Marshall 74-78. *Kintbury Vicarage, Newbury, Berks.* (Kintbury 243)

MILLARD, Malcolm Edoric. b 38. Univ of Lon BA 60. AKC 60. **d** 77 Gambia. d Dio Gambia. *PO Box 428, Banjul, The Gambia, W Africa.*

MILLARD, Murray Clinton. b 29. Ex Coll Ox BA 50, Dipl Th 52, MA 58. St Steph Ho Ox 51. **d** 53 **p** 54 Bris. C of St Greg Horfield 53-55; St Steph Guernsey 55-61; R of St Mary Jersey 61-71; St Sampson Guernsey 71-81; V of St Steph Guernsey Dio Win from 81. *St Stephen's Vicarage, Guernsey, CI.* (Guernsey 20268)

MILLEN, Canon Peter Elton. Univ of W Ont BA 57. **d** 57 Hur for Calg **p** 57 Calg. C of Red Deer 57-60; R of Crow's Nest 60-63; R of Bowness w Montgomery 63-67; Banff 67-71; Ch Ch City & Dio Sktn from 71; Hon Can of Sktn from 80. *505 Rusholme Road, Saskatoon, Canada.*

MILLER, Alexander Barrett. Wadh Coll Ox BA 30, MA 41. Called to Bar Middle Temple 32. St Andr Coll Pampisford 40. **d** 41 **p** 42 Newc T. C of Howdon Panns 41-42; Chollerton w Thockrington 42-45; Fleetwood (in c of St Marg) 45-47; P-in-c of Naaruawahia 47-51; V of Ohura 51-52; CF (NZ) 52-56. *c/o Department of Justice, Wellington, NZ.*

MILLER, Alfred Ernest. St Francis Coll Brisb 60. ACT ThL (2nd cl) 63. **d** 62 Bp Hand for Melb **p** 62 Bp Redding for Melb. C of St John Camberwell 62-64; Miss Dio New Guinea 64-69; Dioc Archd New Guinea 68-69; Chief Exec Officer Miss to Streets and Lanes and L to Offic Dio Melb from 70. *64 Williams Road, Blackburn, Vic, Australia 3130.* (03-878 8593)

MILLER, Anthony Talbot. b 37. St D Coll Lamp BA 59. Coll of Resurr Mirfield. **d** 61 **p** 62 Mon. C of Panteg w Llanddewi Fach and Llandegveth 61-63; Monmouth 63-65; V of Holm Cultram 65-76; Dir Ellesmere Coll Arts Centre and L to Offic Dio Lich 76-78; P-in-c of Wrockwardine Wood Dio Lich from 78. *Rectory, Wrockwardine Wood, Telford, Salop, TF2 7AH.* (Telford 613865)

MILLER, Augustus Powell. b 1888. St Aid Coll 13. **d** 13 **p** 14 Liv. Org Sec Sunday Sch Inst Dio Liv 13-15; C of Sefton (in c of Hightown) 13-19; V of St Mark Newtown Pemberton 19-23; St Lawr Kirkdale and Chap Kirkdale Homes 23-27; Surr from 22; CF (TA) from 26; TD 43; V of St Luke Liv 27-32; Gt Crosby 32-43; R of St Olave Hart Street and All H Staining w St Cath Coleman Lon 43-59; Commiss U Nile 48-59; Chap O of St John of Jer from 54; Perm to Offic Dio Dur 59-60; Dio S'wark 61-67; Dio Liv from 69. *Sharston House, Manor Park South, Knutsford, Chesh.*

MILLER, Barry. b 42. Open Univ BA 78. Linc Th Coll 63. **d** 65 **p** 66 Jarrow for Dur. C of Greenside 65-68; Bp Auckland 68-71; L to Offic Dio Leic 71-77 and from 80; Asst Chap Univ of Leic 77-80; C of St Nich Leic 77-80; Adv C of E Bd of Educn from 80. *Church House, Dean's Yard, SW1P 3NZ.*

MILLER, Cecil. St Jo Coll Morpeth. **d** 46 **p** 47 Bath. R of Eugowra 48-75; Can of Bath 64-75. *Rosedurnate Centre, Orange Street, Parkes, NSW, Australia 2870.*

MILLER, Charles Ernest. Worc Ordin Coll 67. **d** 68 **p** 69 York. C of Filey 68-70; V of Bilton-in-Holderness 70-75; C-in-c of Osmotherley Dio York 75-78; V (w E Harsley and Ingleby Arncliffe) from 78. *Osmotherley Vicarage, Northallerton, N Yorks.* (Osmotherley 282)

MILLER, Charles Irvine. b 35. Univ of Nottm BEd 76. Bps' Coll Cheshunt 61. **d** 63 **p** 64 York. C of St Mark Anlaby 63-66; Whitby 66-68; R of Ingoldmells w Addlethorpe 68-72; C-in-c of Bp's Norton w Atterby 72-76; V of Scunthorpe Dio Linc from 76. *St John's Vicarage, Normanby Road, Scunthorpe, Humb, DN15 6AR.* (Scunthorpe 842691)

MILLER, Cyril Stephen Harry. **d** 34 **p** 35 Graft. C of Liston 34-35; P-in-c 35-36; P-in-c of Grevillea 36-37; V of Copmanhurst 37-40; R of Eureka w Clunes 40-48; Coramba 48-52; H Trin Lower Macleay 52-55; L Pr Dio Newc 55-58; L to Offic Dio Graft from 59. *228 Ballina Road, Goonellabah, Lismore, NSW, Australia.*

MILLER, David George. b 54. Ripon Coll Cudd BA (Th) 80. Or Coll Ox BA (Hist) 76, MA 80. **d** 81 Chich. C of Henfield, Shermanbury & Woodmancote Dio Chich from 81. *41 Furners Mead, Henfield, BN5 9JA.* (Henfield 3011)

MILLER, David James Tringham. b 45. AKC 70. Sarum Wells Th Coll 76. **d** 77 **p** 78 Pet. C of SS Pet & Paul Abington 77-80; Team V of St Pet and St Andr Corby w Gt and L

Oakley Dio Pet from 80. *Vicarage, Beanfield Avenue, Corby, NN18 0EH.* (Corby 67620)

MILLER, David John. Chich Th Coll 60. **d** 62 **p** 63 Portsm. C of H Spirit Southsea 62-65; Roehampton 67-68; Chap at Luxembourg 68-72; Lausanne Dio (Gibr in Eur from 80) Lon (N and C Eur) from 72. *1 bis Avenue de l'Eglise Anglaise, Lausanne, Switzerland.*

MILLER, David Reginald. b 29. K Coll Lon and Warm AKC 54. **d** 55 **p** 56 St Alb. C of Hockerill 55-58; Combe Down 58-61; V of Pill 61-70; Wedmore (w Theale from 74 and Blackford from 78) Dio B & W from 70; Surr from 71; RD of Axbridge from 77; C-in-c of Blackford 77-78. *Vicarage, Wedmore, Somt, BS28 4EJ.* (Wedmore 712254)

MILLER, David Samuel. b 31. Lich Th Coll 62. **d** 63 **p** 64 Lich. C of Leek 63-66; Blurton 66; St Kath Southbourne Bournemouth 66-71; V of E Worldham w W Worldham and Hartley Mauditt w Kingsley and Oakhanger 71-76; Team V of Buckhurst Hill 76-80; V of St Nich Elm Pk Hornchurch Dio Chelmsf from 80. *Vicarage, St Nicholas Avenue, Elm Park, Hornchurch, Essex RM12 4PT.* (Hornchurch 51451)

MILLER, David Samuel Clifford. b 11. AACCA 46. ACIS 49. **d** 69 **p** 70 B & W. C of N Petherton 69-80; Perm to Offic Dio B & W from 80. *27 Bridgwater Road, North Petherton, Bridgwater, Somt.*

MILLER, Derek Charles. b 47. Ridley Coll Melb 68. **d** 71 Melb **p** 72 Bp Grant for Melb. C of Warrnambool 71-74; St Pet Hammersmith 74-76; Asst Chap St Mark Florence 76-77; C of Portsea 77-80; V of Bodenham w Hope-under-Dinmore, Felton and Preston Wynne Dio Heref from 80. *Bodenham vicarage, Hereford.* (Bodenham 370)

MILLER, Donald James. Ridley Coll Melb ThL 71. **d** 72 **p** 73 Melb. C of St John Bentleigh 72-74; St Andr Brighton 74-76; P-in-c of Newport w Altona N Dio Melb from 76. *61 Mason Street, Newport, Vic., Australia 3015.* (391-1206)

MILLER, Canon Donald Sydney. St Jo Coll Morpeth 55. **d** 57 **p** 60 Adel. C of Henley Beach 57-58; St Pet Glenelg 58-61; P-in-c of Koolunga 61-64; Hillcrest 64-66; R of Waikerie 66-72; Millicent 72-76; Hon Can of The Murray from 75; C of O'Halloran Hill Dio Murray 77; P-in-c 77-79; R from 79. *Rectory, Main South Road, O'Halloran Hill, S Australia 5158.* (08-3813039)

MILLER, Edward Jeffery. b 24. St Jo Coll Cam BA 48, MA 50. Wells Th Coll 48. **d** 50 **p** 51 B and W. C of S Lyncombe 50-53; Ch of S India 54-67; C-in-c of Wootton Courtenay Dio B & W 68-74; R from 74; C-in-c of Timberscombe Dio B & W 68-74; V from 74; P-in-c of Selworthy Dio B & W from 79. *Selworthy Rectory, Minehead, Somt.* (Porlock 862445)

MILLER, Edward Sidney. b 08. Hatf Coll Dur BA 31, Dipl in Th and Hatf Exhib 32, MA 34. Bps' Coll Cheshunt 32. **d** 32 **p** 33 Win. C of Sholing 32-36; Benoni 36-41; R of Ermelo 41-46; Potchefstroom 46-49; P-in-c of Elgin 49-58; R of Kalk Bay 58-61; W Coker 61-62; Fish Hoek 62-66; C of Welwyn (in c of St Mich Woolmer Green) 66-68; R of Barton-Mills 68-76; C-in-c of Herringswell 71-76; Perm to Offic Dio St E from 76. *54 The Street, Barton Mills, Bury St Edmunds, Suff.*

MILLER, Frederick Ernest. Tor Dioc Tr Sch 65. **d** 65 Bp Snell for Tor **p** 65 Tor. C of All SS Kingsway Tor 65-67; R of Unionville 67-74; C of H Trin Tor 74-77; on leave. *72 Kenilworth Avenue, Toronto, Ont., Canada.*

MILLER, Geoffrey Edward. Univ of Leeds BA 56. Coll of Resurr Mirfield 53. **d** 57 **p** 58 Birm. C of St Aid Small Heath 57-59; St Paul Grove Pk Chiswick 59-61; St Pet Barnsley 61-63; R of N w S Claypole 63-76; C-in-c of Westborough w Dry Doddington and Stubton 63-65; R 65-76; P-in-c of Bierley Dio Bradf 76-78; V from 78. *St John's Vicarage, Bierley Lane, Bradford, BD4 6AA.* (Bradford 681397)

MILLER, Canon George Charles Alexander. b 20. Trin Coll Dub BA 45, Div Test 46. **d** 46 **p** 47 Oss. C of Wexford w Rathaspeck 46-49; Asst Chap Miss to Seamen Belf 49; Immingham Dk 49-51; Chap at Pernis Rotterdam 51-55; I of Billis w Ballyjamesduff 55-57; Knockbride U 57-65; Urney U Dio Kilm from 65; Can of Kilm Cathl from 77. *Rectory, Cavan, Irish Republic.* (049-31975)

MILLER, Hanson Orlo. **d** 63 **p** 64 Hur. C of St Paul's Cathl Lon Ont 63-65; R of Mitchell w Sebringville 65-70; Pt Edw 70-77. *183 Gammage Street, London, Ont., Canada.*

MILLER, Harold Creeth. b 50. TCD BA 73. Univ of Nottm BA (Th) 75. St Jo Coll Nottm 73. **d** 76 **p** 77 Connor. C of Carrickfergus 76-79; Dir of Ex Stud St John's Coll Nottm from 79. *St John's College, Bramcote, Nottingham, NG9 3QS.* (Nottm 251114)

MILLER, Harold John. b 04. AKC 34. **d** 34 **p** 35 Lon. C of St Geo Brentford 34-36; All SS (in c of St Aug) S Lambeth 36-39; V of Roydon 39-44; Gt Wakering 44-48; St Edm S Chingford 48-56; R of Rochford 56-72; Chap Rochford Gen Hosp 56-72; Tone Vale Hosp Somt from 72. *St Christopher's Cottage, Old Cleeve, Minehead, Somt.* (Washford 624)

MILLER, Harry Baxter. **d** 50 **p** 52 Sask. C of Hudson Bay 50-55; Miss at Peigan 55-56; Blackfoot Miss 56-60; I of St Geo Moose Jaw 60-65; on leave 65-79; I of Canora Dio Qu'App from 79. *Box 1255, Canora, Sask, Canada.*

MILLER, Henry Arthur. **d** 73 **p** 75 Ja (APM). P Dio Ja. *PO Nairn, Jamaica, WI.*

MILLER, Henry Galtir Darrin. St Andr Coll Lagos. **d** 23 Bp Oluwole for Lagos **p** 24 Lagos. CMS P Dio Lagos 23-43; C of Ch Ch Cathl Lagos 43-45; Bassa Country Dio Lagos 45-52; Dio N Nigeria 52-65. *St Bartholomew's, Zaria, Nigeria.*

MILLER, Ian Norman. b 13. St Pet Hall, Ox BA 38, MA 47. Wycl Hall, Ox 38. **d** 40 **p** 41 Roch. C of Strood 40-44; St Pet Battersea 44-47; V of All SS Hatcham Pk 47-53; Foleshill 53-63; Dunchurch w Thurlaston 63-77; RD of Dunchurch 68-75; L to Offic Dio Linc from 78. *36 St Nicholas Close, Barkston, Grantham, NG32 2ND.*

MILLER, James. b 36. Trin Coll Dub BA 63, Div Test (1st cl) 64, MA 66. **d** 64 **p** 65 Derry. C of Ch Ch Londonderry (in c of St Pet from 66) 64-69; R of Tamlaght O'Crilly U and Lower Dio Derry from 69; RD of Kilrea from 76. *Hervey Hill Rectory, Kilrea, Londonderry, BT51 5TT, N Ireland.* (Kilrea 40296)

MILLER, James. b 43. **d** and **p** 73 Newfld (APM). C of H Trin w Trin E Dio Newfld (Centr Newfld from 76) from 73. *New Bonaventure, Newfoundland, Canada.* (709-464 3729)

MILLER, James Edward. b 12. Men in Disp 43 and 46. Kelham Th Coll 28. **d** 35 **p** 36 Lich. C of St Andr W Bromwich 35-37; Marske-in-cleveland (in c of St Thos New Marske) 37-39; St Paul Wood Green (in c of St Luke) Wednesbury 39-41; Chap RAFVR 41-47 V of St Jas West Bromwich 47-56; St Germain Edgbaston 56-71; The Lickey w Blackwell 71-76. *23 Leadbetter Drive, Bromsgrove, Worcs.* (0527-33181)

MILLER, James Ivimey. b 33. Late Exhib of Trin Hall Cam BA and Research Stud 55, MA 59. Ridley Hall Cam 56. **d** 61 **p** 62 St E. C of Beccles 61-63; Blackpool 63-67; Kirk Ella 67-73; R of Cockfield, Suff 73-78; Perm to Offic Dio St E from 78. *3 Grosvenor Gardens, Bury St Edmunds, Suff, IP33 2JS.* (Bury St E 62839)

MILLER, John David. b 50. Univ of Nottm BTh 73. Kelham Th Coll 68. **d** 74 Jarrow for Dur **p** 75 Dur. C of Horden 74-79; Team V of St Aid Billingham Dio Dur from 79. *22 Tintern Avenue, Billingham, Cleve, TS23 2DF.* (Stockton 533487)

MILLER, John Douglas. b 24. FCA 60. N-W Ordin Course 74. **d** 77 **p** 78 Ches. C of Prestbury 77-80; V of Ashton Hayes Dio Ches from 80. *Ashton Hayes Vicarage, Chester.*

MILLER, John Gareth. b 57. St Jo Coll Dur BA (Th) 78. Ridley Hall Cam 79. **d** 81 Cant. C of Addiscombe Dio Cant from 81. *68 Elgin Road, Addiscombe, Surrey, CR0 6XA.* (01-654 6925)

MILLER, John Selborne. b 32. Univ of Lon Dipl Bibl Stud 68. SOC 64. **d** 71 **p** 72 Willesden for Lon. C of Kenton 71-74; St Etheldreda w St Clem Fulham 74-79; Hon Chap RAFVR 75-79; Perm to Offic Dio Truro 79-80; Dio Lon from 81. *6 Croydon House, Wootton Street, SE1 8TS.* (01-928 1157)

MILLER, John Stephen Corfield. b 16. Selw Coll Cam BA 38, 1st cl Th Trip pt i 39, MA 41. Westcott Ho Cam 39. **d** 40 **p** 41 Ripon. C of Leeds 40-43; Asst Chap Marlborough Coll 43-44; Chap 44-53; Gen Sec SCM in Schs 53-61; R of St Helen Bishopsgate Lon 53-61; Hd Master St Pet Colleg Sch Adel 61-78; Asst Master Bp Reindorp Sch Guildf 78-81; Perm to Offic Dio Guildf from 78. *8 St Omer Road, Guildford, Surrey.* (Guildford 60359)

MILLER, Kenneth Huitson. b 30. Univ of Dur BA 55, Lich Th Coll 58. **d** 60 **p** 61 Newc T. C of St Geo Jesmond Newc T 60-63; N Gosforth 63-67; Subchanter and Sacr of Lich Cathl and Asst Master (Chap 70-75) Cathl Sch 67-75; V of Wolstanton Dio Lich 75-79; Team R from 79; RD of Newc L from 77; Surr from 77. *Wolstanton Rectory, Knutton Road, Wolstanton, Newcastle, Staffs, ST5 0HU.* (0782-627708)

MILLER, Kenneth Leslie. b 50. Univ of Lanc BEducn 74. N Ordin Course 78. **d** 80 **p** 81 Liv. C of St Pet Formby Dio Liv from 80. *14 Wrigleys Lane, Formby, Merseyside.*

MILLER, Norman Alfred Leslie. b 06. Qu Coll Cam 3rd cl Engl Trip 27, BA (3rd cl Anthrop Trip) 28, MA 32. Ridley Hall Cam 28. **d** 29 **p** 30 Lon. C of St Luke S Kens 29-32; Chap at Momb Cathl 32-35; Perm to Offic at St Mary-le-Park Battersea 35-37; St Jas Piccadilly 37-38; Publ Pr Dio Win 40-42; Dio S'wark 42-44; V of H Trin Woolwich 44-47; Titchfield 47-73; C-in-c of Locks Heath 54-55; RD of Alverstoke 57-62. *The Bakehouse, Easterton, Devizes, Wilts.*

MILLER, Patrick Figgis. b 33. Ch Coll Cam 1st cl Th Trip pt i 54, BA (2nd cl Th Trip pt ii) 56, MA 60. Cudd Coll. **d** 58 **p** 59 Portsm. C of St Cuthb Copnor 58-61; St Mary Gt w St Mich AA Cam 61-63; SCM Sec Univ of Cam 61-63; Asst Master Man Gr Sch 63-69; Can Res and Libr of S'wark Cathl 69-72; Lect Qu Mary's Coll Basingstoke 72-79; Prin Sunbury

Coll 79-80; Esher Coll from 81. *31 Hare Lane, Claygate, Esher, Surrey.* (0372-67563)

MILLER, Paul. b 49. Oak Hill Th Coll 71. **d** 74 **p** 75 Ex. C of St Mary Magd Upton Torquay 74-77; Farnborough Hants 77-78; P-in-c of St Luke Torquay Dio Ex 78-81; V from 81. *St Luke's Vicarage, Torquay, Devon.* (Torquay 27974)

MILLER, Paul Richard. b 37. K Coll Lon AKC BSc 60. Linc Th Coll 60. **d** 62 Bp Gerard for Sheff **p** 63 Sheff. C of St Geo w St Steph Sheff 62-65; Bottesford w Ashby (in c of Riddings Estate) 65-67; Bp of Linc Youth Chap and C of Corringham 67-69; Dioc Youth Adv Dio Ripon 69-74; Hd of Youth Dept Nat Coun of Social Service and Sec Nat Coun for Vol Youth Services 74-79; Publ Pr Dio St Alb 74-79; P-in-c of Woburn Dio St Alb 79-80; V (w Eversholt, Milton Bryan, Battlesden and Pottesgrove) from 80; P-in-c of Battlesden and Pottesgrove 79-80; Eversholt w Milton Bryan 79-80. *Vicarage, Park Street, Woburn, Milton Keynes, MK17 9PG.*

MILLER, Canon Paul William. b 18. Qu Coll Birm Dipl Th 50. **d** 50 Derby **p** 51 Bp O'Ferrall for Derby. C of Staveley 50-53; Matlock 53-55; V of Codnor 55-61; C of All SS Cathl Derby 64-66; Can Res and Prec from 66; Chap to HM the Queen from 81. *22 Kedleston Road, Derby.* (Derby 44773)

MILLER, Peter Laird. ACT ThL 65. St Mich Ho Crafers 61. **d** 66 **p** 67 Adel. C of Eliz Downs Adel 66-73; P-in-c of Kingston-Robe 73-77; R of Berri-Barmera Dio Murray from 77. *3 Strawbridge Street, Berri, S Australia 5343.* (085-82 1175)

MILLER, Peter Tennant. b 21. Keble Coll Ox BA 47, MA 63. Ripon Hall Ox 62. **d** 63 **p** 64 Roch. C of Wigmore w Hempstead 63-68; V of St Paul Manton Worksop 68-73; C-in-c of St Cath w St Luke Nottm 74-75; C of St Mary Nottm 75-77; R of Edith Weston w Normanton, N Luffenham and Lyndon w Manton Dio Pet from 77. *Rectory, Church Lane, Edith Weston, Leics, LE15 8EY.* (Stamford 720931)

MILLER, Philip David Bevington. b 1899. St Steph Ho Ox 23. **d** 23 Southn for Win **p** 24 Win. C of St Luke Bournemouth 23-26 and 27-30; St Paul New Southgate 26-27; St D (in c of St Mich AA) Ex 30-36; V of W Wycombe 36-44; R of St Jo Bapt Cov 44-47; R and V of St Giles Reading 47-66; RD of Reading 62-65; Hon Can of Ch Ch Ox 64-66; L to Offic Dio Chich from 67. *20 Roman Road, Hove, BN3 4LA, Sussex.* (Brighton 416132)

MILLER, Philip Howard. b 40. Tyndale Hall Bris 67. **d** 72 Parag **p** 73 N Argent. P Dio N Argent 72-73; C of H Trin Rusholme Man 73-74; SAMS Miss Dio Parag 74-77; C of St Cypr w Ch Ch Toxteth 78-80; V of Burscough Bridge Dio Liv from 80. *Vicarage, Burscough, Ormskirk, Lancs.* (Burscough 893205)

MILLER, Raymond Kenneth. b 15. Qu Coll Cam 2nd cl Hist Trip 36, BA 37, 2nd cl Th Trip 38, MA 41. Ridley Hall Cam 37. **d** 39 **p** 40 St Alb. C of Luton 39-43; Gravesend 43-47; V of St Mary Pype Hayes Erdington 47-53; St Barn Woodside Park Finchley 53-81; Preb of St Paul's Cathl Lon 79-81. *Paradise House, Paradise Row, Sandwich, Kent, CT13 9AS.*

MILLER, Richard Bracebridge. b 45. Wycl Hall Ox 68. **d** 70 **p** 71 S'wark. C of Good Shepherd Lee 70-74; Roehampton 74-77; Earley 77-80; V of Aldermaston w Wasing and Brimpton Dio Ox from 80. *Aldermaston Vicarage, Reading, Berks, RG7 4LX.* (Woolhampton 2281)

MILLER, Robert George. b 15. Univ of Bris BA (3rd cl Hist) 37. BC Coll Bris 37. **d** 39 **p** 40 S'wark. C of St Jas W Streatham 39-41; St John Weymouth 41-42; H Trin Brompton 42-43; V of St Jas Holloway 43-47; St Jas U Edmon 47-79; Chap N Middx Hosp from 48. *81 The Chine, Grange Park, N18 2EE.* (01-360 5269)

MILLER, Robert William Harry. b 46. K Coll Lon AKC 69. St Aug Coll Cant 70. **d** 70 **p** 71 Lon. C of Hayes 70-73; St Mary Bryanston Square, St Marylebone Lon 73-75; M CGA 75-76; Asst Master Sir William Romney Sch Tetbury 76-78; Perm to Offic Dio Glouc 76-81; V of Elkesley w Bothamsall Dio Southw from 81. *Elkesley Vicarage, Maple Drive, Retford, Notts.* (Gamston 293)

MILLER, Ronald Anthony. b 41. City Univ Lon BSc (C Eng) 63. SOC 69. **d** 72 Dorking for Guildf **p** 80 (NSM). C of Crookham 72-73; and from 80. *6 Velmead Close, Fleet, Hants, GU13 9LR.*

MILLER, Samuel Wardell. **d** 52 **p** 53 NS. I of Newport and Walton 52-55; Hubbards 55-60; R of New Glasgow 60-72; Trenton 67-72; St Phil Halifax Dio NS from 72. *George Dauphinee Avenue, Halifax, NS, Canada.* (455-9543)

MILLER, Stephen Murray. Univ of Syd BSc 72. Moore Coll Syd ACT ThL 75. BD (Lon) 75. **d** 76 Syd **p** 77 Bp Short for Syd. C of St Luke Dapto 76-78; Chatswood 79; Res Min of St Steph Cabramatta W Dio Syd from 80. *391 Cabramatta Road, Cabramatta West, NSW, Australia 2166.* (602-2986)

MILLER, Wilfred Howard. b 10. Qu Coll Cam BA 32, MA 36. Wycl Hall Ox 34. **d** 35 Chelmsf for St E **p** 36 St E. C of Beccles 35-38; Maidenhead 38-39; Eling 39-40; CF (EC) 40-46; V of St Martin Barnehurst 46-50; R of N Cray 50-57; Severn Stoke 57-63; CF (TA) 51-56; CF (TA-R of O) from 56; V of Wellow 63-71; C-in-c of Foxcote w Shoscombe 63-71. R of Wellow with Foxcote and Shoscombe 71-75. *11 Lenborough Road, Buckingham, Bucks.*

MILLER, William David. b 45. Univ of Man BA 66. Linc Th Coll 69. **d** 71 **p** 72 Newc T. C of St Geo Jesmond 71-74; Corbridge 74-77; N Gosforth (in c of St Aid) 77-81; Team V of Whorlton Dio Newc T from 81. *Whorlton Rectory, Westerhope, Newcastle-upon-Tyne, NE5 1NN.*

MILLER-KEELEY, Diane Marie. b 47. St Jo Coll Auckld. **d** 77 **p** 78 Wai. Offg Min Dio Wai 77; Hon C of Hastings 78-80; Gisborne Dio Wai from 80. *237 Crawford Road, Gisborne, NZ.* (89535)

MILLETT, Canon Francis Henry Walter. b 19. AKC 48. St Bonif Coll Warm. **d** 49 **p** 50 S'wark. C of St Nich Plumstead 49-54; Wimbledon (in c of St Matt) 54-61; V of St Jo Bapt Timberhill w All SS and St Mich Thorn Nor 61-75; St Jo Bapt de Sepulchre Nor 61-75; R (w St Pet Parmentergate) 75-77; Hon Min Can of Nor Cathl 63-77; RD of Nor E 70-81; V of St Giles w St Benedict City and Dio Nor from 77; Hon Can of Nor from 77. *St Giles Vicarage, Heigham Road, Norwich, NR2 3AU.* (Nor 23724)

MILLETT, William Hugh. b 21. AKC 49. St Bonif Coll Warm 49. **d** 50 **p** 51 Worc. C of St Steph Barbourne Worc 50-53; V of Catshill 53-58; R of Richard's Castle 58-78; P-in-c of Stoke Lacy w Much Cowarne and Moreton Jeffries Dio Heref from 78. *Stoke Lacy Rectory, Bromyard, Herefs.* (Munderfield 257)

MILLICAN, Anthony Gordon. b 28. Ridley Hall Cam 58. **d** 60 **p** 61 S'wark. C of St Jas Hatcham 60-63; Woodmansterne 63-65; St Giles-in-the-Fields Lon 65-68; V of St Chris Brislington Dio Bris from 68. *29 Runswick Road, Bristol, BS4 3HY.* (Bristol 776819)

MILLIER, Gordon. St Aid Coll 63. **d** 65 **p** 66 B & W. C of Congresbury 65-69; C-in-c of Badgworth w Biddisham 69-76; R of Weare w Badgworth w Biddisham Dio B & W from 76; C-in-c of Compton Bishop Dio B & W from 81. *Weare Rectory, Axbridge, Somt.* (Axbridge 732378)

MILLIGAN, Dennis Edward. b 18. **d** 65 **p** 66 Portsm. C of Elson 65-69; Hayling (in c of St Pet) 69-71; C-in-c of St Pet Conv Distr Hayling N 71-73; R of Gatcombe w Chillerton Dio Portsm from 73. *Gatcombe Rectory, Newport, IW, PO30 3EF.* (Chillerton 246)

MILLIGAN, William Edward. b 03. TCD BA 25, Div Test 28, MA 29. **d** 28 **p** 29 Down. C of St Mary Belf 28-32; C-in-c of Drumgath w Drumballyroney (w Clonduff from 36) 32-36; R 36-41; C-in-c of Scarva 41-53; I of Ballee w Bright (w Killough from 68) 53-73; RD of Lecale E 61-70. *24 Seymour Road, Bangor, Co Down, BT19 1BL, N Ireland.* (Bangor 65165)

MILLIGAN, Canon William John. b 28. Em Coll Cam BA 49. Cudd Coll 53. **d** 55 **p** 56 Portsm. C of St Mark Portsea 55-62; V of All SS New Eltham 62-71; Roehampton 71-79; Can Res of St Alb Cathl from 79. *2 Sumpter Yard, St Albans, Herts.* (St Albans 61744)

MILLIKEN, Michael Sturge. b 20. Pemb Coll Cam BA 48, MA 63. Wells Th Coll 63. **d** 65 **p** 66 Win. C of St Alb Bournemouth 65-69; R of Fawley 69-79; V of Chilworth and N Baddesley Dio Win from 79. *Vicarage, Crescent Road, North Baddesley, Southampton, SO5 9HU.* (0703-732393)

MILLINER, Llewelyn Douglas. b 14. Univ of Wales BSc (1st cl Chem) 35. **d** 38 Llan **p** 39 Swan B for Llan. C of St Fagan Aberdare 38-41; St Mary Wellingborough 41-43; CF 43-63; Asst Master K Cathl Sch Worc 63-66; P-in-c of St Luke's Conv Distr Chelmsf 66-69; Dep Hd Master Widford Lodge Prep Sch Chelmsf 69-80; Perm to Offic Dio Chelmsf 69-80; Dio Ex from 80. *Fordings, Weare Giffard, Bideford, Devon.* (Bideford 3729)

MILLING, David Horace. b 29. Or Coll Ox BA (2nd cl Lit Hum) 51, 2nd cl Th 52, MA 54. Magd Coll Cam PhD 74. Cudd Coll 54. **d** 56 **p** 57 Bris. C of St Mary Redcliffe Bedminster 56-59; St John Fishponds 59-62; Lect United Th Coll Bangalore 62-69; Burgess Hall St D Univ Coll Lamp 73-75; C of Caversham (and Mapledurham from 81) Dio Ox from 77. *St Andrew's House, Harrogate Road, Caversham, Reading, RG4 7PW.* (0734-472788)

MILLINGTON, Kenneth Cecil. b 03. St Chad's Coll Dur BA 25, Dipl Th 26, MA 28. **d** 26 **p** 27 Lich. C of St Andr Walsall 26-32; Coseley 32-34; SSC Dio Lich 34-38; V of St Mary and All SS Palfrey Walsall 38-56; R of W Felton 56-73. *83 Oakhurst Road, Oswestry, Salop.*

MILLINGTON, Robert William Ernest. b 51. Univ of Sheff BA 73. St Jo Coll Dur Dipl Th 75. **d** 76 **p** 77 Liv. C of Ormskirk 76-79; St Paul Hatton Hill 79-81; V of Ch Ch Bootle Dio Liv from 81. *1 Breeze Hill, Bootle, Mer, L20 9EY.* (051-525 2565)

MILLINGTON, Stuart. b 45. Lich Th Coll 67. **d** 70 **p** 71 Repton for Derby. C of Boulton 71-73; Moseley 73-75; Team V of Staveley w Barrow Hill from 76. *Vicarage, Cedar Street, Hollingwood, Nr Chesterfield, S43 2LE.* (Chesterfield 472486)

MILLINS, Leslie Albert. b 20. St Paul's Th Coll Grahmstn. **d** 53 **p** 54 Mashon. C of Avondale 53-56; R of Mabelreign 56-59; C of St Jo Evang Kensal Green 60-61; St Jude on the Hill Hampstead 61-62; Old St Pancras w St Matt Oakley Square Lon 62-69; V 69-75; St Alphege Edmonton Dio Lon from 76. *St Alphege's Vicarage, Rossdale Drive, N9 7LG.* (01-804 2255)

MILLMAN, Geoffrey. b 11. Pemb Coll Ox BA (3rd cl Mod Hist) 37, MA 41. Wycl Hall Ox 37. **d** and **p** 39 Birm. C of Aston-juxta-Birm 39-44; Gerrard's Cross 44-46; V of St Jas Plumstead (w St Jo Bapt from 53) 46-64; Greetham w Stretton and Clipsham 64-65; Lect Salford Coll of Technology from 65; Perm to Offic Dio Man from 65; Dio Ches from 72. *71 The Avenue, Sale, Chesh, M33 4GA.* (061-973 4524)

MILLMAN, Canon Thomas Reagh. Univ of Tor BA 31, MA 33. Wycl Coll Tor LTh 33, BD 38. McGill Univ Montr PhD 43. Univ of W Ont DD 53. Univ of K Coll Halifax NS Hon LLD 74. **d** 33 **p** 34 Tor. C of Grafton and Centreton 33-35; Tutor and Dean Montr Dioc Coll 36-41; R of Dunham w St Armand E 41-49; I of Alvinston w Inwood 49-51; Dean and Prof of Ch Hist Hur Coll 51-54; Prof of Ch Hist Wycl Coll Tor 54-74; Gen Synod Archivist 55-74; Hon C of St Timothy Tor 57-74; Exam Chap to Bp of Tor 64-74; Can of Tor from 69. *27 Brookdale Avenue, Toronto, Ont., Canada.*

MILLMAN, William John. Univ of W Ont BA 52. Hur Coll LTh 57, BD 62. **d** 57 **p** 58 Hur. R of Thedford 57-62; Burford 62-67; All SS Woodstock 67-70; St Matt Windsor Dio Hur from 70; Exam Chap to Bp of Hur 68-70. *3190 Massey Court, Windsor 21, Ont., Canada.* (519-969 1510)

MILLS, Alan Francis. b 29. Late Exhib of Ch Coll Cam BA 52. Linc Th Coll 52. **d** 54 **p** 55 Southw. C of Hucknall Torkard 54-58; St Jo Bapt Bathwick 58-70; V of Drayton 70-76; Muchelney 70-76; Alcombe Dio B & W from 76. *Vicarage, Alcombe, Minehead, Somt.* (Minehead 3205)

MILLS, Alexander Lake. ACT ThL 57. **d** 45 Bal **p** 46 Bend for Bal. C of Swan Marsh 45-46 ; P-in-c 46-47; Cobden 47-48; Natimuk 48-50; V of Beaufort 50-57; Inverleigh 57-60; Lara 60-66; Mornington 66-68; Chelsea 69-73; Perm to Offic Dio Melb from 73. *6 Clarke's Town Avenue, Mount Eliza, Vic, Australia 3930.* (787-4839)

MILLS, Arthur Maurice Broughton. b 04. TCD BA 26, MA 29, Div Test 31. **d** 31 **p** 32 Down. C of Bangor 31-36; I of Ballingarry w Lockeen 36-43; Dom Chap to Bp of Killaloe 36-43; Offerlane w Borris in Ossory 43-46; Templemichael 46-59; Exam Chap to Bp of Kilm from 51; RD of Newtownforbes 53-60; I of New Ross 60-70; Donagh w Tyholland 70-78; Errigal-Trough w Errigal-Shanco 70-78. *18 Sherwood Road, Bangor, Co Down, N Ireland.* (Bangor 55727)

MILLS, Canon Clifford James Holden. b 13. AKC (2nd cl) 39. **d** 39 Ely **p** 40 Bp Eyre Price for Ely. C of Sutton-in-the-Isle 39-41; Hitcham 41-45; R of St Mary Troston (w Gt Livermere from 46) 45-55; C-in-c of Ampton w L Livermere 45-55; RD of Blackburne 50-70; R of Stanton 55-70; Reydon 70-78; Surr 62-70; Hon Can of St E 63-81; Can (Emer) from 81; RD of Halesworth 73-81; Perm to Offic Dio St E from 81. *16 St Peter's Path, Holton, Halesworth, Suff, IP19 8NB.* (Halesworth 2884)

MILLS, David Francis. b 51. Oak Hill Coll Dipl of Higher Educn 78. **d** 79 **p** 80 Bris. C of Rodbourne Cheney Dio Bris from 79. *2 Cherhill Court, Moredon, Swindon, Wilts, SN2 3HB.*

MILLS, Canon Donald. b 16. K Coll Lon BD and AKC 40. **d** 40 **p** 41 S'wark. C of St Geo Mart S'wark 40-42; Rusthall 42-45; St Barn Gillingham 45-48; V of Slade Green 48-56; St Barn Gillingham 56-81; Hon Can of Roch 73-81; Can (Emer) from 81; RD of Gillingham 75-81; Surr 75-81. *St Barnabas House, Bramley Avenue, Faversham, Kent.* (Faversham 6403)

MILLS, Edgar Parker. b 1896. Trin Coll Dub BA 19, MA 36. **d** 19 **p** 21 Kilm. C of Annagh w Quivvy 19-23; St Luke's Cork 23-27; Min Can and C of St Fin Barre's Cathl Cork from 27; Can and Preb of Brigown in Cloyne Cathl 59-65; Treas of Cloyne and Can of Cahirlag in Cork Cathl 65-67; Prec of Cloyne and Can of Killaspugmullane in Cork Cathl 67-73; Prec of Cork 69-73. *5 Hanover Place, Washington Street, Cork, Irish Republic.* (Cork 24461)

MILLS, Eric Charles. Trin Coll Tor STB 64. **d** and **p** 64 Niag. I of Palermo 64-66; R of Georgetown 66-71; St Jo Evang Hamilton 71-78; St Barn St Catharines Dio Niag from 78. *31 Queenston Street, St Catharines, Ont, Canada.* (416-682 5319)

MILLS, Francis Peter. Perry Hall, Melb. **d** 66 **p** 67 Melb. C of Ascot Vale 66-69; Melb Dioc Centre 69-72; R of Lynwood w Langford and Ferndale 73-76; Chap Miss to Seamen Fremantle 76-77; R of Exmouth w Ashburton 77-79; Derby Dio NW Austr from 80. *Box 90, Derby, W Australia 6728.*

MILLS, Geoffrey Charles Malcolm. b 33. Wycl Hall, Ox 59. **d** 61 Colchester for Chelmsf **p** 62 Chelmsf. C of Buckhurst Hill 61-65; All SS Ecclesall Sheff 65-69; V of St Aug Sheff 69-78; R of Whiston Dio Sheff from 78. *Whiston Rectory, Rotherham, S Yorks.* (Rotherham 64430)

MILLS, Gordon Derek. b 35. Lich Th Coll 60. **d** 63 Warrington for Liv **p** 64 Liv. C of W Derby 63-65; Clifton w Glapton 65-67; V of St Faith N Wilford 67-72; Farnsfield Dio Southw from 72; P-in-c of Kirklington w Hockerton Dio Southw from 77. *Farnsfield Vicarage, Newark, Notts, NG22 8ER.* (Mansfield 882247)

MILLS, Harold James. St Jo Coll Armid ACT ThL 22. **d** 22 **p** 23 Goulb. C of Junee 22-23; P-in-c of Michelago 23-24; C of Quirindi 25-26; P-in-c of Delungra 26-33; V of Emmaville 33-37; on leave 37-40; Boggabri 40-44; RD of Tamworth 42-47; C of Tamworth 44-47; R of St Barn Rockptn 47-53; L to Offic Dio Brisb 50; V of Narrabri 53-57; LPr Dio Armid from 57. *139 Upper Street, Tamworth, NSW, Australia.*

MILLS, Hubert Cecil. b 44. TCD BA 66, Div Test 67, MA 71. **d** 67 **p** 68 Dub. C of Rathfarnham 67-72; St Ann and of St Steph Dub 72-77; Min Can of St Patr Cathl Dub from 69; Succr from 77; R of Holmpatrick w Kenure and Balbriggan Dio Dub from 77. *Holmpatrick Rectory, Northcliffe Heights, Skerries, Co Dublin, Irish Republic.* (01-491321)

MILLS, Jack Herbert. b 14. Selw Coll Cam 3rd cl Econ Trip pt i 36, BA (3rd cl Th Trip pt i) 38, MA 42. Cudd Coll 39. **d** 40 S'wark **p** 41 Roch for S'wark. C of St Geo Camberwell 40-42; St Barn Southfields 42- 46; Jt Metrop Sec SPG for Dios Lon S'wark and Chelsmf and LPr Dio S'wark 46-47; Chap Hurstpierpoint Coll 47-52; L to Offic Dio Chich 47-52; Chap K Coll Otahuhu and Perm to Offic Dio Auckld 52-56; Asst Chap St Pet Colleg Sch Adel 57-59; Chap and Tutor St Paul's College Sch Hamilton NZ 59-61; Asst Chap Guildf Gr Sch Perth 62-63; Chap 63-66; Hd Master Carp Coll Darwin 66-74; L to Offic Dio Carp 66-68; Dio N Terr 68-74; Hd Master of St Wilfrid's Sch Ex and Chap of Commun of St Wilfrid 74-79; Hon C of Bodiam and Ewhurst Dio Chich from 79; Perm to Offic Dio Ex from 81. *Tysons, Market Place, Colyton, Devon, EX13 6JS.* (0297-52361)

MILLS, Jeffray. Moore Th Coll Syd ACT ThL 38. **d** 40 **p** 41 Syd. C of St Andr Summer Hill 40-41; C-in-c of Harris Pk 41; R of St Mary w Rooty Hill 42-44; Earlwood 44-49; Lithgow 49-54; St Paul Chatswood 54-58; Campsie 59-76; L to Offic Dio Syd from 76. *1/89 Oaks Avenue, Dee Why, NSW, Australia 2099.* (981-3351)

MILLS, Canon John. Late Exhib of Keble Coll Ox BA (3rd cl Mod Hist) 45, MA 47, Dipl Th 48. BD (Lon) 57. Wycl Hall, Ox 47. **d** 49 **p** 50 Carl. C of Cleator Moor 49-51; St Paul Barrow-F 51-53; V of St Jo Evang Barrow-F 53-57; R of St Mary Wavertree Dio Liv 57-63; Ed Liv Dioc Leaflet 60-77; V of Prescot Dio Liv from 63; RD of Prescot from 72; Hon Can of Liv from 74. *Vicarage, Prescot, Lancs.* (Prescot 6719)

MILLS, John Arthur. K Coll NS BA 68, BST 69. **d** 69 Fred. C of St Anne Fred 69-72; R of Renforth 72-76; Newcastle and Nel Dio Fred from 76. *216 Pleasant Street, Newcastle, NB, Canada.*

MILLS, Leslie. b 17. Wycl Hall, Ox 68. **d** 68 Bp Cornwall for Win **p** 69 Southn for Win. C of Basingstoke 68-77; Old Basing 77-80; Camberley w Yorktown Dio Guildf from 80. *St Martin's House, 229 Upper College Ride, Old Dean, Camberley, 58)*

MILLS, Mary Alice Maud. b 14. Qu Univ Kingston Ont BA 55. Wycl Coll tor LTh 50. **d** 69 **p** 76 Hur. C of Kirkton 75-76; R 76-80. *Box 252, Glencoe, Ont, Canada, N0L 1M0.*

MILLS, Michael Henry. AKC 73. St Aug Coll Cant 73. **d** 74 **p** 75 Dur. C of Newton Aycliffe 74-78; Padgate Dio Liv 78-79; Team V from 79. *Vicarage, Briers Close, Fearnhead, Warrington, Chesh, WA2 0DN.*

MILLS, Murray John. Univ of NZ MA 58. St Jo Coll Auckld LTh (1st cl) 60. **d** 60 **p** 61 Auckld. C of Papakura 60-63; Whangarei 63-65; V of Bay of Is 65-70; Matamata 70-75; Exam Chap to Bp of Waik 74-79; and from 80; Adv in Chr Educn Dio Waik 76-81; Archd of Waik 76-80; VG from 78; V of Tokoroa Dio Waik from 81. *Box 164, Tokoroa, NZ.* (67-565)

MILLS, Philip. b 43. Univ of Wales BSc (2nd cl Geog) 65. Linacre Coll Ox BA 68, MA 72. Wycl Hall Ox 65. **d** 68 **p** 69 Man. C of Droylsden 68-70; St Thos Bedford-Leigh 70-73; V of Calderbrook 73-78; Southowram Dio Wakef from 78. *Vicarage, Church Lane, Southowram, Halifax, Yorks HX3 9TD.* (Halifax 65229)

MILLS, Reginald Edward. St Jo Coll Morpeth ACT ThL (2nd cl) 56. **d** 55 **p** 56 Bath. Bush Bro of Good Shepherd 55-60; C of Gilgandra 55-56; V of Cobar 56-60; C of All H N Greenford 60; Bundaberg 61; V of Palmwoods 61-62; Caloundra Dio Brisb 62-65; R from 65; Commiss Carp from 69.

46 Upper Gay Terrace, Caloundra, Queensland, Australia 4551. (91 1632)

MILLS, Canon Robert Archibald Clarke. Hur Coll 54. **d** 54 **p** 55 Hur. I of Kirkton 54-56; Watford 56-62; R of St Ann Lon 62-68; Aylmer Dio Hur from 68; Can of Hur from 75. *74 Centre Street, Aylmer, Ont., Canada.* (519-773 8031)

MILLS, Very Rev Robert Scott. Univ of NZ LLB 57. NZ Bd of Th Stud LTh (1st cl) 59. Union Th Sem NY STM 66. St Jo Coll Auckld 57. **d** 59 **p** 60 Auckld. C of Whangarei 59-63; St Mary's Cathl Auckld 63-65; Ch Ch Cathl Nel 66-69; Exam Chap to Bp of Nel 66-69; V of Blockhouse Bay 69-73; Exam Chap to Bp of Auckld 70-72; to Bp of Dun 73-80; Dean and V of St Paul's Cathl City and Dio Dun from 73; P-in-c of Warrington from 78. *Deanery, 268 Stuart Street, Dunedin, NZ.* (Dunedin 770-276)

MILLS, Stanley. b 18. Linc Th Coll 78. **d** 78 **p** 79 Sheff (APM). C of Stannington Dio Sheff from 78. *187 Oldfield Road, Stannington, Sheffield, S6 6DX.* (Sheff 340250)

MILLS, Walter George. Montr Dioc Th Coll LTh 66. **d** 66 Bp Appleyard for Hur **p** 67 Hur. C of Old St Paul Woodstock 66-69; I of Ox Centre 69-72; Thedford 72-75; St Jas Cam Dio Hur from 75. *22 Harvey Street, Cambridge, Ont., Canada.* (519-658 4547)

MILLS, William. St D Coll Lamp BA 33. **d** 33 **p** 34 Man. C of H Trin Coldhurst 33-36; St Marg Hollinwood 36-37; P-in-c of St Phil Bloemf 37-41; CF (S Afr) 41-46; C of Blakenall Heath 46-48; R of Grindon 48-52; V of Butterton 48-52; R of Forton 52-56; Belvedere 56-63; Hardwicke 63-68; Chap HM Pris Aylesbury 65-68; L to Offic Dio Capetn 69-77; Perm to Offic from 77. *603 Monreith, Hall Road, Sea Point, CP, S Africa.* (442939)

MILLS, William Keith. Seager Hall, Ont STh 61. **d** 61 Hur **p** 62 Bp Townshend for Hur. I of Ox Centre 61-64; St Phil Windsor 64-71; Harrow 70-75; St Jas Brantford Dio Hur from 75. *132 Grand Street, Brantford, Ont., Canada.* (519-753 1709)

MILLYARD, Alexander John. b 29. St Jo Coll Dur BA (2nd cl Gen) 53. Qu Coll Birm 53. **d** 54 York **p** 55 Whitby for York. C of St Aid Middlesbrough 54-56; Pocklington and of Millington 56-58; Rickmansworth 58-61; R of Wormley 61-65; Asst Chap HM Pris Pentonville 65-67; Chap HM Pris Leeds 67-69; Ex 69-71; Wandsworth 72-73; V of Snibston 73-75; All S Leic 75-79; Blakesley w Adstone Dio Pet from 79. *Vicarage, Blakesley, Towcester, Northants, NN12 8RB.* (Blakesley 507)

✠ **MILMINE, Right Rev Douglas.** St Pet Hall, Ox BA and MA 46. Clifton Th Coll. **d** 47 **p** 48 Ex. C of St Phil w St Jas Ilfracombe 47-50; St Paul Slough 50-53; Miss at Mquehue-Pelal 54; Temuco 55-60; Santiago Dio Argent 61-63; Dio Chile 63-73; Archd of N Chile 64-69; Hon Can of Chile 69-77; Cons Ld Bp of Parag in Ch of the Good Shepherd Lima 18 March 73 by Bp Flagg, Bps of Argent, Chile and Venez, Abp Kratz (Primate of Brazil), and Bps of Ecuador, Columbia and Puerto Rico and Bp Howe. *Iglesia Anglicana, Casilla 1124, Asuncion, Paraguay.*

MILN, Peter. b 43. Univ of Wales (Swansea) BA 65. Univ of Nottm MTh 81. E Midl Jt Ordin Tr Scheme 76. **d** 79 **p** 80 Lich. Hon C of Uttoxeter Dio Lich from 79; Lect Burton Tech Coll from 79. *41 Balance Street, Uttoxeter, Staffs, ST14 8JQ.*

MILNE, Charles Alexander. **d** 58 **p** 59 Moos. I of St Cuthb Cochrane (Ch on Wheels) 58-60; R of Moosonee 60-64; Hornepayne 64-70; Calstock w Hearst 69-70; Geraldton Dio Moos from 70. *Box 233, Geraldton, Ont., Canada.* (807-854 1465)

MILNE, Frederic James. b 08. **d** 60 **p** 61 Ripon. C of Bramley 60-64; V of St John Drypool 64-69; C of St Mary Virg Middleton 69-73; Hon C 73-74. *8 Hillcourt Avenue, Leeds 13.*

MILNE, Robert Luther. Moore Th Coll ACT ThL 54. **d** and **p** 54 Syd. Asst Chap Miss to Seamen Syd 54-55; C-in-c of Canley Vale 55-59; R of Castle Hill 59-78; Dir New Areas C'tte Dio Syd from 78. *39b Pennant Parade, Epping, NSW, Australia 2121.* (871-1758)

MILNE, Canon William. b 04. St Paul's Coll Burgh, 24. **d** 29 **p** 30 Wakef. C of Ossett 29-32; P-in-c of Grantown-on-Spey w Rothiemurchus and Kingussie 32-37; C of St Marg Newlands (in c of St Aid Clarkston) Glas 37-38; P-in-c of St Aid Clarkston Glas 38-42; R of St Mary Aber 42-65; Can of St Andr Cathl Aber 62-65; Hon Can from 78; R of Kirriemuir 65-73; Chap to Glamis Chap from 73. *Elmslea, Elm Road, Kirriemuir, Angus, DD8 4DG.* (Kirriemuir 2742)

MILNE, William Young. b 10. Late Th Exhib Univ of Dur LTh 34, Hatf Exhib 35, BA (3rd cl Th) 36. Edin Th Coll 31. ATCL 29. **d** 36 **p** 37 Edin. C of Old St Paul Edin 36-39; P-in-c of Armadale w Bathgate 39-45; C of Cradley Heath 45-48; Hagley 48-50; V of Malvern Wells 50-81. *Vicarage, Wilden, Stourport-on-Severn, Worcs, DY13 9LP.*

MILNER, Darryl Vickers. St Chad's Coll Dur Dipl Th 66. **d** 66 **p** 67 Lich. C of H Trin Oswestry 66-69; C of Mobini 69-72; St Martin Durban N 72-73; R of Umhlanga 73-76; V of Mangere E 76-81; Northcote Dio Auckld from 81. *47 Church Street, Northcote, NZ.*

MILNER, David. b 11. St Jo Coll Ox BA (3rd cl Mod Lang) 33, MA 47. Ripon Hall, Ox 33. **d** 35 **p** 36 Roch. C of St Mary Shortlands 35-38; Cathl Ch Birm 38-41; V of St Paul Swanley 41-56; Asst Master New Beacon Sch Sevenoaks 56-59; Vicar's Hill Sch Boldre Lymington 62-63; Chap Dunchurch-Winton Hall Sch 63-66; L to Offic Dio Cov 63-68. *39 Queensway, Mildenhall, Suff.*

MILNER, David. b 38. St Aid Coll 63. **d** 66 Penrith for Carl **p** 67 Carl. C of H Trin Ulverston 66-68; All SS Mickleover 68-71; St John Mickleover Dio Derby 68-71; V from 71. *7 Onslow Road, Mickleover, Derby, DE3 5JJ.* (Derby 514862)

MILNER, Eric. b 10. Mert Coll Ox BA (1st cl Mod Hist) 33, Liddon Stud 34, 2nd cl Th 35, MA 37. Linc Th Coll 35. **d** 36 **p** 37 Wakef. C of Hemsworth 36-39; Dewsbury 39-40; St Jas Elmers End 40-42; All SS Chatham 42-44; Chap RNVR 44-46; RN 46-65; V of Bentley 67-80. *Borrowdale, Hillcrest Avenue, Ossett, W Yorks, WF5 9PL.* (Ossett 271740)

MILNER, Leslie. b 35. Univ of Birm BSc (2nd cl Chem) 57. St Jo Coll Cam BA 59. Wells Th Coll 61. **d** 63 **p** 64 Birm. C of Yardley 63-66; Seacroft 66-71; Dir St Basil's Centre Deritend from 71; P-in-c of Deritend 73-78. *St Basil's Centre, Heath Mill Lane, Deritend, Birmingham 9.* (021 772 2483)

MILNER, Raymond John. b 50. Univ of Cant NZ BEng 74. St Jo Coll Auckld 77. **d** 77 **p** 78 Dun. C of All SS Dun 77-79; V of Milton-Tuapeka Dio Dun from 79. *165 Union Street, Milton, NZ.* (8244)

MILNER, Robert Reginald. Univ of Dur BA 1896. **d** 01 **p** 02 Dur. C of Rainton Co Dur 01-07; Boldon 07-08; Offley 08-13; St Pet Birm 13-16; St Bart Gt Lon 17-18; w CA 18-19; Perm to Offic Dio Lon 19-21; C of St Leon Shoreditch 21-23; V of St Jas Curtain Rd Shoreditch 23-27; St Mary Woodlands Sevenoaks 27-56. *The Grafton Hotel, Beltonge Road, Herne Bay, Kent.*

MILNER, Canon Ronald James. b 27. Pemb Coll Cam 2nd cl Engl Trip pt i, 47, BA (2nd cl Th Trip pt i) 49, MA 52. Wycl Hall Ox 51. **d** 53 **p** 54 Sheff. C and Succr of St Pet and St Paul Cathl Sheff 53-58; V of Westwood 58-64; St Jas Fletchamstead 64-70; R of St Mary w H Trin Southn 70-72; C-in-c of St Matt Southn 70-72; L to Offic Dio Win 72-73; R of Southn (City Centre) Team Min Dio Win from 73; Hon Can of Win Cathl from 75. *The Deanery, Chapel Road, Southampton, SO1 1NH.* (Southn 333754)

MILNES, David Ian. b 45. Chich Th Coll 74. **d** 76 Chelmsf **p** 77 Barking for Chelmsf. C of St Sav Walthamstow 76-80; Chingford Dio Chelmsf from 80. *49 Hawkwood Crescent, Chingford, E4.* (01-529 3929)

MILNES, Canon Lewis Percival. b 01. Late Found Scho of K Coll Cam 2nd cl Cl Trip pt i, 21, BA (1st cl Cl Trip pt ii) 22, MA 26. Cudd Coll 24. **d** 25 **p** 26 Ripon . C of St Bart Armley 25-28; Guisborough 28-31; PC of Oulton Yorks 31-38; V of Wetherby 38-46; Middleton Tyas (w Barton from 56) 46-62; RD of Richmond E 52-60; Surr 38-46 and 53-71; C-in-c of Barton 53-56; Hon Can Ripon 55-71; Can (Emer) from 71; R of Kirklington 62-71; Proc Conv Ripon 64-71; Perm to Offic Dio Ripon from 71. *16 Whitcliffe Grove, Ripon, Yorks, HG4 2JW.* (Ripon 2036)

MILROY, Arthur Rundle. b 26. Late Exhib of SS Coll Cam 2nd cl Hist Trip pt 1, 49, BA (2nd cl Hist Trip pt ii) 50, MA 52. Ridley Hall, Cam 50. **d** 52 **p** 53 Nor. C of H Trin Heigham 52-54; Tutor St Aid Coll Birkenhead 54-56; Chap 56-59; Vice-Prin 59-62; L to Offic Dio Ches 56-62; V of Downend 62-72; P-in-c of Rowsley 72-79; Dir of Chr Stewardship Dio Derby 72-78; Dioc Dir of Ordinands Dio Derby from 78; V of Quarndon Dio Derby from 79. *Quarndon Vicarage, Derby, DE6 4JA.* (Derby 559333)

MILTON, Claudius James Barton. b 29. K Coll Lon and Warm BD 52, AKC (2nd cl) 52. **d** 53 **p** 54 Lon. C of St Andr Sudbury 53-57; Asst Chap and Asst Master Bedford Sch 57-65; Chap and Asst Master Cranbrook Sch 65-74; Clayesmore Sch, Iwerne Minster from 74. *28 Oakwood Drive, Iwerne Minster, Dorset.* (Fontmell Magna 811792)

MILTON, Jeffrey Roderick. b 52. Worc Coll Ox BA 75, MA 78. St Mich AA Coll Llan 74. **d** 76 **p** 77 Llan. C of Llanfabon 76-77; Hon C of St Luke Cardiff 78; R of Bulawayo W Dio Matab from 78. *Rectory, Kinmont Avenue, Barham Green, Bulawayo, Zimbabwe.* (66409)

MILTON, Thomas Charles. Moore Th Coll Syd ACT ThL 64, Th Sch 66. BD (Lon) 68. **d** 66 **p** 67 Tas. C of Burnie 66-68; R of King Is 69; Perm to Offic Dio Brisb 70-71; P-in-c of Biggenden 71-72; C of Liv 72-73; C-in-c of Prov Distr Greenacre 73-75; C of St Mary Magd St Marys 76; Green Valley Dio Syd 76-78; Res Min from 78. *1 Spica Street, Sadleir, Australia 2168.* (607-0536)

MILTON-SMITH, Charles Henry. Wycl Hall Ox. **d** 63 **p**

64 Worc. C of Kidderminster 63-66; V of Foxdale 66-71; R of St Paul's Cathl St Hel 71-76; V of Maker w Rame 76-81. *c/o Maker Vicarage, Fore Street, Kingsand, Cornw, PL10 1NB.* (Plymouth 822302)

MILTON-THOMPSON, David Gerald. OBE 76. Em Coll Cam BA 39, MA, MB, BChir 49. MRCS (Engl) and LRCP (Lon) 42. **d** 64 **p** 65 Momb. L to Offic Dio Momb from 64. *St Luke's Hospital, PO Kaloleni, Mombasa, Kenya.*

MILVERTON, The Lord Fraser Arthur Richard Richards. b 30. Bp's Coll Cheshunt. **d** 57 **p** 58 Roch. C of Beckenham 57-59; St Jo Bapt Sevenoaks 59-60; Gt Bookham 60-63; V of Okewood w Forest Green 63-67; R of Chr Malford w Sutton Benger and Tytherton Kellaways Dio Bris from 67. *Rectory, Christian Malford, Chippenham, Wilts, SN15 4BY.* (Seagry 466)

MILVERTON, Frederic Jack. b 15. Univ of Lon BSc 37. Univ of Leeds MEd 40. Ripon Hall Ox. **d** 57 **p** 58 Sheff. C of Ecclesall 57-60; V of Thurcroft 60-61; Lect Nottm Coll of Educn 61-67; Weymouth Coll of Educn 67-76; Dorset Inst of Higher Educn 76-79; Publ Pr Dio Southw 62-67; Dio Sarum 67-79; Team V of Oakdale Dio Sarum from 79. *16 Rowbarrow Close, Canford Heath, Poole, Dorset, BH17 9EA.* (Broadstone 699807)

MILWARD, Terence George. b 23. Ripon Hall, Ox 66. **d** 68 Bp Sinker for Birm **p** 69 Birm. C of Selly Oak 68-70; St Bart Edgbaston 70-75; Team V of St Swithun Bournemouth 75-80; R of Smannell w Enham Alamein Dio Win from 80. *Rectory, Enham Alamein, Andover, Hants* (Andover 52877)

MIMPRISS, Timothy John. b 40. Jes Coll Cam BA 61, BChir 64, MB 65, MA 65. FFA (RCS) 68. St Jo Coll Nottm 69. **d** 71 Southw for Centr Tang **p** 72 Centr Tang. Miss Dio Centr Tang 71-74; L to Offic Dio Ely from 76. *c/o Nat West Bank, High Street, Bangor, Gwyn.*

MINALL, Peter. b 26. Univ of Lon BSc 47. Bps' Coll Cheshunt 51. **d** 53 **p** 54 St Alb. C of Bp's Stortford 53-57; Luton 57-63; St Barn Tuffley Glouc 63-65; Asst Youth Chap Dio Glouc 65-69; V of Stroud Dio Glouc from 69; RD of Bisley from 78. *Vicarage, Church Street, Stroud, Glos, GL5 1JL.* (Stroud 4555)

MINANI, Anthony Utu. b 48. St Paul's Coll Limuru 73. **d** 76 **p** 77 Boga-Z. P Dio Boga-Z 76-77; Dio W Tang 77-78; Dio Bukavu from 78. *BP 145, Beni, Zaire.*

MINAY, Francis Arthur Rodney. b 44. Westcott Ho Cam 66. **d** 68 **p** 69 Roch. C of Edenbridge 68-73; St Mark Bromley 73-75; V of Tudeley w Capel 75-79; Team V of Littleham-cum-Exmouth Dio Ex from 79. *Glebe House, Littleham Road, Exmouth, Devon,* (Exmouth 72312)

MINCHER, John Derek Bernard. b 31. M OSB 54. **d** 60 **p** 61 Ox. L to Offic Dio Ox from 60. *Nashdom Abbey, Burnham, Bucks.*

MINCHEW, Donald Patrick. b 48. Univ of Wales (Cardiff) BD 76. St Mich AA Llan 72. **d** 76 **p** 77 Glouc. C of St Aldate Glouc 76-80; P-in-c of Sharpness w Purton & Brookend Dio Glouc 80-81; V from 81. *The Venns, Sanigar Lane, Sharpness, Glos, GL13 9NF.* (Dursley 811360)

MINCHIN, Anthony John. b 35. St Cath Coll Cam 1st cl Mod Lang Trip pt i, 58, BA (2nd cl Th Trip pt ia) 59. Wells Th Coll 59. **d** 61 Glouc **p** 62 Tewkesbury for Glouc. C of St Pet Cheltm 61-64; St Jas Bushey 64-67; V of St Mich Cheltm 67-74; Lower Cam Dio Glouc from 74. *St Bartholomew's Vicarage, Lower Cam, Dursley, Glos.* (Dursley 2679)

MINCHIN, Basil George Francis. b 10. Univ of Bris BSc 31. Coll of Resurr Mirfield, 31. **d** 34 **p** 35 Bris. C of St Francis Ashton Gate 34-36; St Mich Two Mile Hill Bris 36-39; St Barn Swindon 39-46; V of Bedminster 46-60; Sec Fellowship of St Alb and St Sergius 60-68; C of St John Notting Hill 63-69; V of Lynsted w Kingsdown 69-75; R of Norton 70-75; Six Pr in Cant Cathl from 74. *5 The Precincts, Canterbury, Kent, CT1 2EE.* (Cant 53895)

MINCHIN, Charles Scott. b 51. Trin Coll Cam BA 72, MA 75. Linc Th Coll 73. **d** 75 **p** 76 Lich. C of Gt Wyrley 75-78; Team V of Wilnecote 78-81; Tamworth Dio Lich from 81. *14 Cowley, Glascote, Tamworth, B77 2RD.* (Tamworth 61853)

MINCHIN, George Reginald. b 05. Trin Coll Dub BA 31, MA 43. **d** 31 **p** 32 Derry. C of Ch Ch Derry 31-35; C-in-c of Mevagh 35-46; Camus-juxta-Bann Dio Derry 46-65; R 65-75; RD of Limavady 65-75; Can of Derry 70-75. *4 Fortview, Portballintrae, Bushmills, Co Antrim, N Ireland.*

MINCHIN, Horace William. Trin Coll Dub BA 32, MA 46. **d** 33 **p** 34 Down. C of St Nich Belf 33-37; Drumglass 37-38; C-in-c of Drumnakilly Dio Arm 40-43; R from 43. *Drumnakilly, Omagh, Co Tyrone, N Ireland.*

MINCHIN, Canon James Blundell. Univ of Melb BA (2nd cl Cl) 65. Trin Coll Melb ACT ThL (1st cl) 65. **d** 66 **p** 67 Melb. C of St Geo Malvern 66-67; St Andr Cathl Sing 68-71; P-in-c of Our Sav Sing 68-71; Asst Chap Trin Coll Melb 71-73; Perm to Offic Dio Ox 74-75; C in Angl Inner City Min Melb 76-77; R and Can Res of Ch Ch Old Cathl St Arn Dio Bend from 77. *Rectory, Queen's Avenue, St Arnaud, Vic, Australia 3478.*

MINCHIN, Kells Arthur. Univ of Tor BA 50. Wycl Coll Tor Lth 52. **d** 52 Edmon. C Dio Edmon 51-52; I of Westlock 52-54; C of H Trin Edmon 54-55; V of Vermillion 55-59; I of Minnow Lake 59-60; CF (Canad) from 60. *Chaplaincy Service, Department of National Defence, Ottawa 4, Ont, Canada.*

MINCHIN, Canon Sidney Frederick. b 14. Univ of Lon BA 36. Lich Th Coll 36. **d** 38 Stafford for Lich **p** 39 Lich. C of St Andr W Bromwich 38-42; Tatenhill 42-46; Tamworth (in c of Glascote) 46-49; V of Stowe-by-Chartley 49-54; R of Flixton w S Elmham 54-65; V of Brandeston w Kettleburgh 65-79; RD of S Elmham 59-65; Loes 70-78; Hon Can of St E Cathl 74-79; Can (Emer) from 79. *24 Fore Street, Weston Zoyland, Bridgwater, Somt.* (W Zoyland 606)

MINGI, John Barge. b 54. **d** 80 New Guinea Is for Aipo. d Dio Aipo. *Anglican Church, Aiome, via Madang, Papua New Guinea.*

MINHINNICK, Leslie. Jes Coll Ox, Hall Houghton Jun Gr Test Pri 39, BA (1st cl Th) 39, Liddon Stud 40, MA 43. Wycl Hall, Ox 40. **d** 41 **p** 42 Llan. C of St Clem Briton Ferry 41-43; St John Canton Çardiff 43-45; Tutor St Aid Coll Birkenhead 45-50; Vice-Prin 50-51; V of St Jo Evang Over 51-54; St Mark Birkenhead 54-60; Exam Chap to Bp of Ches 53-60; to Bp of Blackb 62-81; V of Preston 60-61; Chipping 61-66; St Jo Div Lytham 66-81. *Old School House, Cemaes, Anglesey, Gwyn, LL67 0NG.*

MINIMAH, F[illegible] St Paul's Coll Awka. **d** 73 **p** 74 Nig Delta. P Dio Nig Delta. *St James Parsonage, Ogoloma Town, Box 19, Okrika, Nigeria.*

MINJA, Jason. **d** 61 Ft Hall **p** 62 Mt Kenya. P Dio Mt Kenya 62-75; Dio Mt Kenya E from 75. *Box 40, Karaba, Kenya.*

MINNS, John Alfred. b 38. Oak Hill Th Coll 63. **d** 68 **p** 69 Ches. C of St Andr Cheadle Hulme 68-72; Hartford 72-74; V of Wharton Dio Ches from 74. *Vicarage, Wharton, Winsford Chesh.* (Winsford 3215)

MINNS, John Arthur. **d** 75 **p** 76 Wai. C of Gisborne 75; P-in-c of Waikohu 76-81; V of Woodville Dio Wai from 81. *Vicarage, Woodville, NZ.* (8777)

MINORS, Graham Glyndwr Cavil. b 44. **d** and **p** 79 Glouc. C of St Bart Lower Cam Dio Glouc from 79. *37 Orchard Leaze, The Quarry, Cam, Dursley, Glos GL11 6HY.*

MINSHALL, Douglas Arthur. E Midl Min Tr Course. **d** 81 Sherwood for Southw. C of Worksop Priory Dio Southw from 81. *49 Kilton Glade, Worksop, Notts, S81 0PX.*

MINSHALL, Neville David. b 37. K Coll Lon and Warm AKC 64. **d** 65 Lich **p** 66 Stafford for Lich. C of St Paul Wolverhampton 65-66; C of Stafford 66-68; Rugeley 68-69; H Cross Shrewsbury 69-73; P-in-c of Wrockwardine Wood 73-77; R of Brierley Hill 77-81; Worthen Dio Heref from 81; Hope w Shelve Dio Heref from 81; Middleton-in-Chirbury Dio Heref from 81. *New Rectory, Worthen, Shrewsbury, SY5 9HW.* (Worthen 476)

MINSHULL, William Howell. b 15. BEM (Mil) 43. Men in Disp 44 and 45. Worc Ordin Coll 59. **d** 61 **p** 62 Chesh. C of St Jas Birkenhead 61-64; R of Kilve w Stringston Kilton and Lilstock 64-78; C-in-c of E Quantoxhead 75-78; W Quantoxhead 77-78; Holford w Dodington 78; RD of Quantockshead 68-73; Quantock 73-78; R of Quantoxhead Dio B & W from 78. *Kilve Rectory, Bridgwater, Somt.* (Holford 310)

MINSON, Roger Graham. b 41. Univ of Leeds BA 64. Coll of Resurr Mirfield 64. **d** 66 **p** 67 Bris. C of St Greg Horfield 66-70; Southmead 70-73; V of Lawrence Weston 73-81; Team V of Knowle Dio Bris from 81. *Vicarage, St Martin's Road, Knowle, Bristol, BS4 2NH.*

MINSULA, Godwin. **d** 73 **p** 74 Centr Zam. P Dio Centr Zam. *Box 80042, Kabwe, Zambia.*

MINTER, Richard Arthur. Worc Coll Ox BA (2nd cl Mod Hist) 29, 3rd cl Th 31, MA 33, BD 55. St Steph Ho Ox 29. **d** 32 **p** 33 Man. C of St Chrys Vic Pk and Tutor Egerton Hall Man 32-34; Vice-Prin St Paul's Miss Coll Burgh 34-36; C of All SS Stoneycroft 36-37; St Geo Kingston 37-38; P-in-c of Claremont 38-40; Asst Master Munro Coll Jamaica 40-42; Manchester Sch Jamaica 42-45; V of Stow w Quy Dio Ely from 46. *Quy Vicarage, Cambridge.* (Cambridge 811277)

MINTON, David Samuel Haynes. **d** 50 **p** 51 Bran. C of Melita 50-52; I of Souris 52-56; Lockeport 56-58; R of Crapand 58-60. *Breadalbane, PEI, NS, Canada.*

MINTON, Richard Reginald. b 09. BC Coll Bris 32. **d** 35 Bp Crick for Derby **p** 36 Derby. C of Ch Ch Derby 35-39; Perm to Offic Dio Lon 39-42; V of Chiddingstone Causeway 42-48; L to Offic as Chap to Wallingford Farm Tr Sch 48-50; C of H Trin Worthing (in c of St Matt) 50-54; V of Westhampnett and Chap Graylingwell Hosp 54-61; St Alb Streatham Pk 61-65; R of Corley 65-77; Perm to Offic Dio Ex from 77; Chap All H Sch Rousdon 78-81. *c/o Flat B, Old Vicarage, Fore Street, Seaton, Devon.*

MINTY, Kenneth Desmond. b 25. Ch Ch Ox BA (Lit Hum)

48, MA 51. Qu Coll Birm 72. **d** 73 Lich **p** 74 Shrewsbury for Lich. Asst Chap Wrekin Coll Dio Lich from 73; Asst Master from 75; C of Lawley (Telford Central from 76) 74-81; Wrockwardine Dio Lich from 81. *Wrekin College, Wellington, Telford, Shropshire.*

MINTY, Norman Basil. Moore Th Coll Syd ACT ThL 36. **d** 37 **p** 38 Syd. C of Picton w The Oaks and Yerranderie 37-39; Mortlake w Penshurst 39-42; Chap AIF 42-46; St Jude Randwick 46-47; R of St Steph Hurlstone Pk 47-62; Granville 62-73; L to Offic Dio Syd from 73. *474 Victoria Road, Rydalmere, NSW, Australia 2116.*

MINTY, Selwyn Francis. b 34. St D Coll Lamp. **d** 61 Llan **p** 62 Bp T M Hughes for Llan. C of Tonyrefail 61-66; Pontypridd 66-69; V of Cilfynydd Dio Llan from 69. *Vicarage, Cilfynydd, Pontypridd, Mid Glam, CF34 4EH.* (Pontypridd 402933)

MIRARO, Herbert. St Phil Th Coll Kongwa. **d** 66 Bp Madinda for Centr Tang **p** 67 Centr Tang. P Dio Centr Tang 66-74. *Itigi Station, PO Itigi, Tanzania.*

MIRRINGTON, Robert Norman. Univ of Syd MSc 62, PhD 65. Univ of Lon BD 77. Moore Th Coll Syd ThL 76. **d** 78 Syd **p** 78 Bp Robinson for Syd. C of Glenbrook 78-81; R of Pitt Town Dio Syd from 81. *St James's Rectory, Pitt Town, NSW, Australia 2756.* (045-72 3014)

MISHITA, Mikaeli. **d** 54 **p** 55 Centr Tang. P Dio Centr Tang 54-66; Dio W Tang 66-80; Archd of W Tang 66-80. *Box 15, Kibondo, Tanzania.*

MISI, Alden. St Jo Sem Lusaka 66. **d** 69 Bp Mtekataka for Malawi **p** 70 Malawi. d Dio Zam 66-70; P Dio Lake Malawi from 71. *PO Koronga, Malawi.*

MISIGARO, Samuel. **d** 69 **p** 70 Bur. P Dio Bur 69-75; Dio Buye from 75. *EPEB, Buhiga, Bujumbura, Burundi.*

MISITANA, Samuel. Patteson Th Centre Kohimarama. **d** 72 Melan. d Dio Melan 72-75; Dio Malaita from 75. *Bio Training Centre, N Malaita, Solomon Islands.*

MISSO, Christopher Carrol. Div Sch Colom 61. **d** 64 **p** 65 Colom. C of Ch Ch Cathl Colom 64-68; Dehiwala 68-70; Dioc Adv in Relig Educn Colom 70-72; C of Grovely 72-74; V of Caboolture 74-80; All SS Chermside City and Dio Brisb from 80. *501 Hamilton Road, Chermside, Queensland, Australia 4032.* (59 2062)

MISSO, Edward Geoffrey. **d** 52 **p** 53 Colom. C of Moratuwa 52-57; I of Panadura 57-59; H Em Moratuwa 59-64; C of Redcliffe Queensld 64-65; St Mich AA Polwatte Colom 65-69; I of Nugegoda 69-72; R of Boulder 72-73; Malacca 73-76; L to Offic Dio Perth 76-77; R of Kalamunda Dio Perth from 77. *Rectory, Railway Road, Kalamunda, W Australia 6076.* (93 1160)

MITANDE, Ambrosio. St Athan Th Coll Hegongo 24. **d** 25 **p** 26 Zanz. Asst Miss Dio Masasi 26-29; P-in-c of Machombe 29-45; Chilimba 45-49; Tunduru 49-55. *USPG, Mumbaka, Masasi, SP, Tanzania.*

MITCHELL, Allan. b 52. Kelham Th Coll 71. **d** 78 Penrith for Carl **p** 79 Carl. C of St Pet Kells Whitehaven 78-81; St John Bapt Upperby City and Dio Carl from 81. *382 London Road, Carlisle, Cumb.* (Carlisle 24619)

MITCHELL, Andrew Robert. b 52. St Jo Coll Auckld. **d** 78 Ch Ch. C of Kaiapoi Dio Ch Ch from 78. *35 Blackwell Crescent, Kaiapoi, NZ.*

MITCHELL, Brooke Elizabeth. b 55. McMaster Univ Ont BA 76. **d** 80 Abp Somerville for New Westmr **p** 81 Abp Hambidge for New Westmr. C of Four Saints Langley Dio New Westmr from 80. *20955 Old Yale Road, Langley, BC, Canada V3A 7P8.*

MITCHELL, Cecil Robert. b 32. QUB BSc 54. TCD 63. **d** 65 **p** 66 Connor. C of St Mary Magd Belf 65-68; St Mark Ballysillan Belf 68-70; Sec Dio Connor 70-74; I of Ballywalter Dio Down from 74. *2 Whitechurch Road, Ballywalter, Newtownards, Co Down, N Ireland.* (Ballywater 252)

MITCHELL, Charles Albert. Bp's Univ Lennox BA 61. Univ of Niag NY MSc (Educn) 76. St Chad's Coll Regina LTh 61. **d** 56 Qu'App for Tor **p** 57 Tor. C of St Clem N Tor 56-59; on leave 59-61; St Jas Cathl Tor 61-63; R of St Barn St Catherines 63-70; Hon C of Thorold 73-78; St Geo St Catharines Dio Niag from 78. *37 Spruce Street, St Catherines, Ont, Canada.*

MITCHELL, Ven Charles Edward Solly. **d** 34 **p** 36 Tas. C of Ringarooma 34-38; R of Pontville 38-40; Chap AIF 40-43; R of Smithton 44-45; St Helens Tas 45-50; Sorell 50-56; Kempton and Archd of Hobart 56-59; Archd (Emer) from 59. *Glenview, Main Road, Glenorchy, Tasmania.*

✠ **MITCHELL, Right Rev Clarence Malcolm.** Univ of W Ont BA 53. Hur Coll LTh 54. **d** and **p** 54 Niag. C of Welland 54-56; R of Port Dalhousie 56-58; Burlington 58-68; Ascen Hamilton 68-70; St Geo Guelph 70-80; Hon Can of Niag 60-70; Archd of Trafalgar 70-74; Wellington 74-80; Cons Bp Suffr of Niag in Ch Ch Cathl Hamilton 8 June 80 by Abp of Ont; Bps of Niag, Hur, Ott, Alg, Qu'App, Edmon and Ja; Bps Suffr of Hur (Robinson and Parke-Taylor) and Tor; and others. *67 Victoria Avenue South, Hamilton, Ont, L8N 2S8, Canada.*

MITCHELL, Clarence Searle. **d** 67 Mashon **p** 68 Matab for Mashon. C of Avondale 67-80; Archd of N Mashon 72-74; Perm to Offic Dio River from 81. *16 Evatt Street, Griffith, NSW, Australia.*

MITCHELL, Claude. St Paul's Th Coll Grahmstn 62. **d** and **p** 64 Pret. C of St Wilfrid Hillcrest Pret 64-66; R of Witbank 66-71; Middelburg 66-71; Elgin 71-76; Hermanus Dio Capetn from 76. *Box 87, Hermanus, CP, S Africa.* (hermanus 02831)

MITCHELL, David George. b 35. QUB BA 56. Sarum Th Coll 59. **d** 61 **p** 62 Bris. C of Westbury-on-Trym 61-64; Cricklade w Latton and Eisey 64-68; V of St Jo Div Fishponds 68-77; RD of Stapleton 76-77; Team R of E Bristol Dio Bris from 77. *St Ambrose Vicarage, Stretford Avenue, Bristol, BS5 7AN.* (Bristol 517299)

MITCHELL, David Leslie. b 45. Univ of Keele BA 68, St Jo Coll Nottm 68. **d** 71 **p** 72 Southw. C of Bramcote 71-73; C-in-c of Meerbrook 73-75; Asst in Relig Broadcasting BBC Man from 75; Publ Pr Dio Derby from 75; Perm to Offic Dio Man from 77. *13 Sundown Close, New Mills, Stockport, Cheshire.* (New Mills 44122)

MITCHELL, Canon David Nelson. Trin Coll Tor STh 52. **d** 44 **p** 45 Moos. Miss at Rupert's House 44-49; R of St Paul St Porcupine and Dioc Sec and Asst Treas Regr Dio Moos 49-54; Can of Moos and Dom Chap to Bp of Moos 52-54; R of St Luke Fort William 54-59; Bracebridge Dio Alg from 59; Hon Can of Alg from 73. *Box 273, Bracebridge, Ont., Canada.* (705-645 2164)

MITCHELL, David Norman. b 35. Tyndale Hall, Bris. **d** 67 **p** 68 Ches. C of Marple 67-70; St Helen's Liv 70-72; V of St Steph S Lambeth 72-78; P-in-c of Ch Ch Brixton 73-75; SE Area Sec CPAS 78-81; Perm to Offic Dio Cant 79-81; R of Uphill Dio B & W from 81. *Uphill Rectory, Weston-super-Mare, Avon.* (W-s-M 20156)

MITCHELL, Edwin. b 44. Univ of Nottm BTh 74. St Jo Coll Nottm 70. **d** 74 **p** 75 Southw. C of St Jo Evang Worksop 74-77; Waltham Abbey 77-80; V of Whiston Dio Liv from 80. *90 Windy Arbor Road, Whiston, Mer, L35 3SG.*

MITCHELL, Eric Sidney. b 24. Sarum Wells Th Coll 79. **d** 80 **p** 81 Sarum (NSM). C of Portland Dio Sarum from 80. *10 Underhedge Gardens, Southwell, Portland, Dorset.*

MITCHELL, Frank. b 06. Late Scho of St Jo Coll Dur BA (3rd cl Math) and Lightfoot Scho 29, Capel Cure Pri 30, Dipl in Th 31, MA 32. **d** 30 **p** 31 Dur. C of St Edm Gateshead 30-33; Bp Wearmouth 33-35; PC of Dipton 35-38; V of Clay Cross 38-55; Farington 55-68; Yealand Conyers 68-74. *Tanglin, Norton, Presteigne, Powys, LD8 2EN.*

MITCHELL, Frank. b 21. Ely Th Coll 49. **d** 51 **p** 52 Ripon. C of St Aid Leeds 51-54; V of Bramham 54-62; St Sav (w All SS from 73) Scarborough Dio York from 62. *1 Manor Road, Scarborough, Yorks.* (Scarborough 60648)

MITCHELL, Canon Frank Leonard. St Cath S Ox BA 39, MA 47. Wycl Hall, Ox 46. **d** 48 **p** 49 Roch. C of Rainham 48-50; V of St Matt Borstal 50-56; Meopham 56-65; RD of Cobham 58-65; R of Hayes 65-76; Hon Can of Roch from 76; C of Speldhurst w Groombridge and Ashurst 76-79; Perm to Offic Dio Chich from 80. *10 Beechwood Close, Burwash, Etchingham, TN19 7BS.* (Burwash 822601)

MITCHELL, Frederick Rudolph. b 13. Trin Coll Dub BA 38, MA 50. **d** 38 **p** 39 Oss. C of Kilnamanagh U 38-40; Mariners' Ch Kingstown 40-42; I of Achill and Dugort 42-45; Monasterevan 45-51; Derralosary U 51-57; Asby w Ormside 57-59; Drumlease U 59-62; V of St Cuthb Carl 62-66; R of Kirkbride w Newton Arlosh 66-78. *91 Moorehouse Road, Belle Vue, Carlisle, Cumb, CA2 7QH.* (0228-27909)

MITCHELL, Geoffrey Peter. b 30. Univ of Liv BEng 57. Univ of Man MSc 68. Wells Th Coll 57. **d** 59 **p** 60 Man. C of Ch Ch Bradf 59-61; R of St Pet w St Jas L Man 61-64; L to Offic Dio Man from 64; Hon C of St Geo Unsworth Dio Man from 68. *7 Chadderton Drive, Unsworth, Bury, BL9 8NL.* (061-766 8572)

MITCHELL, Canon George Alfred. b 23. Trin Coll Dub BA (2nd cl Mod Hist and Pol Sc) 45, MA 56. **d** 46 **p** 47 Connor. C of St Matt Belf 46-48; Ballymoney 48-51; C-in-c of St Anne's Miss Distr Belf 51-52; R of St Matt Lisburn 52-58; Carrickfergus 59-70; Bangor Dio Down from 70; Can of St Anne's Cathl Belf from 78. *2 Raglan Road, Bangor, Co Down, N Ireland.* (Bangor 65230)

MITCHELL, Glen. St Mich Ho Crafers 64. **d** 68 Perth. C of Nedlands 68-69; Narembeen 69-70. *c/o Church Office, Box W 2067, Perth 6001, W Australia.*

MITCHELL, Gordon Frank Henry. b 26. Sarum Wells Th Coll 74. **d** 77 **p** 78 Sarum (NSM). C of St Mary Alderbury and of St John W Grimstead Dio Sarum from 77. *Seefeld, Southampton Road, Whaddon, Salisbury, Wilts.*

MITCHELL, Graham Bell. b 40. Univ of Otago BA 64,

MA 65. Worc Coll Ox BA 73. St Chad's Coll Dur 66. **d** 68 **p** 69 Bris. C of St Agnes w St Simon Bris 68-71; St Mich AA Bris 73-76; V of St Pet Bp Auckland 76-78; Vice-Prin Chich Th Coll from 78. *5 North Pallant, Chichester, W Sussex.*

MITCHELL, Canon Henry Gordon. b 20. St Chad's Coll Dur BA (2nd cl Th) 44, Dipl Th 45, MA 47. **d** 45 **p** 46 Liv. C of St Mary Walton-on-the-Hill 45-52; R of Fulbeck Dio Linc 52-72; RD of Loveden 64-72; Can and Preb of S Scarle in Linc Cathl from 67; C-in-c of Carlton Scroop w Normanton 69-72; V of New Sleaford Dio Linc from 72. *Vicarage, Sleaford, Lincs, NG34 7SH.* (Sleaford 302177)

MITCHELL, James William. St John's Episc Th Sch Cam Mass 28. **d** and **p** 28 Washington. In Amer Ch 28-71; R of Fellowship Ja 71-76; C of Pedro Plains Dio Ja from 77. *Watchwell P.A., Jamaica, W Indies.*

MITCHELL, John Harry. b 33. Dipl Th (Lon) 58, BD (Lon) 63, MTh (Lon) 69. Wycl Hall Ox. **d** 62 Penrith for Carl **p** 63 Carl. C of Ambleside w Rydal 62-65; Wolborough 65-71; V of Tor Mohun 72-74; Team V of Centr Torquay Dio Ex from 74-80; V of St Marychurch Dio Ex from 80. *Vicarage, St Marychurch, Torquay, Devon.* (Torquay 37661)

MITCHELL, John Irvin. MBE 56. Sarum Th Coll 35. **d** and **p** 39 Ja. C of St Luke Cross Roads Ja 39-41; R of Falmouth 41-44; Chapelton Ja 44-49; C of Perranzabuloe w Perranporth Cornwall 49; St Luke Eltham 49-51; St Andr Plaistow (in c of St Martin) 51-53; V of St Martin Barb 54-57; I of New Ross 57-62. *c/o Church House, Cross Roads, Jamaica.*

MITCHELL, Keith Adrian. b 47. Kelham Th Coll 66. **d** 70 **p** 71 Dur. C of St Jas Conv Distr Owton Manor, Hartlepool 70-73; St Thos Middlesbrough 73-76; M SSF 76-81; P-in-c of St D Pilton 79-81; C of Horden Dio Dur from 81. *St Mary's Vicarage, Horden, Peterlee, Co Durham.* (0783-864423)

MITCHELL, Lawrence William. Univ of Calg BA 64. Em Coll Sktn LTh 67. **d** 66 **p** 67 Sask. C of Sturgeon Valley 66-67; I of Fort Pitt 67-68; C of Ch Ch Edmon 68-71; R of Wainwright 71-76; St Steph City and Dio Sktn from 76. *1219 Cairns Avenue, Saskatoon, Sask, Canada.*

MITCHELL, Leonard David. ACA 56, FCA 67. Wells Th Coll 60. **d** 61 **p** 62 Nor. C of Hilborough w Bodney of Oxburgh w Foulden of Cockley Cley w Gooderstone of Gt Cressingham and of L Cressingham w Threxton 61-64; V of St Aid Ernesettle Plymouth 64-67; Hon C of Highland Creek 67-68; West Hill Tor 68-69; Tillsonburg 69-71; Woodstock 75-76. *98 Sunset Drive, St Thomas, Ont., Canada.*

MITCHELL, Norman Emmanuel. b 18. Qu Coll Cam BA 39, MA 47. Bp's Coll Cheshunt 46. **d** 48 **p** 49 Guildf. C of All SS Weston Thames Ditton 48-51; Weybridge (in c of St Mich AA) 51-54; Chap Nat Nautical Sch Portishead 55-57; R of Radstock 57-64; C-in-c of Writhlington 61-64; Warden Hollywood Manor Probation Home 65-71; Lect Chiswick Poly 71-73; Hon C of Ightam 71-76; R of Neatishead w Irstead Dio Nor from 76; P-in-c of Barton Turf Dio Nor 76-77; V from 77; Adv to Dioc Bd for Social Responsibility Dio Nor from 76; RD of Tunstead from 79. *Neatishead Rectory, Norwich, NR12 8BT.* (Horning 375)

MITCHELL, Very Rev Patrick Reynolds. b 30. Mert Coll Ox BA (2nd cl Th) 52, MA 56. Wells Th Coll 52. **d** 54 **p** 55 Southw. C of St Mark Mansfield 54-57; Chap Wells Th Coll and PV of Wells Cathl 57-61; L to Offic Dio B & W 59-61; V of St Jas Milton 61-67; Frome Selwood 67-73; C-in-c of Woodlands 67-73; Bp's Chap for Ordin Tr 70-74; Dean of Wells from 73; M Advisory Bd for Redundant Chs from 78; M of Cathls Advisory Comm for Engl from 81. *Dean's Lodging, 25 The Liberty, Wells, Somt, BA5 2SZ.* (Wells 72192)

MITCHELL, Peter Cyril. b 29. St Jo Coll Auckld LTh 72. **d** 69 **p** 70 Waik. C of St Mary New Plymouth 70-73; V of Ngaruawahia 73-77; Tokoroa 77-81; Fitzroy Dio Waik from 81. *8 Henui Street, New Plymouth, NZ.* (83-611)

MITCHELL, Peter Derek. b 30. Roch Th Coll 67. **d** 69 **p** 70 Ox. C of Wargrave 69-72; V of Lund 72-80; Badsey Dio Worc from 80; Wickhamford Dio Worc from 80. *Vicarage, Badsey, Evesham, Worcs, WR11 5EW.* (Evesham 830343)

MITCHELL, Richard. b 06. Univ of Dur LTh 29. Bp Wilson Th Coll IM 26. **d** 29 **p** 30 Liv. C of St Paul Widnes 29-33; St Matt and St Jas Mossley Hill 33-38; V of St Anne Warrington 38-42; Chap RAF 40-58; V of St Paul's Walden 58-68. *25 Sandiways, Wallasey Village, Merseyside, L45 3HJ.*

MITCHELL, Robert McFarlane. b 50. Univ of Man BA (Th) 72. Wycl Hall Ox 73. **d** 75 **p** 76 Roch. C of Tonbridge 75-80; CF from 80. *Ministry of Defence, Bagshot Park, Bagshot, Surrey, GU19 5PL.*

MITCHELL, Roger Sulway. b 36. Chich Th Coll 70. **d** and **p** 71 Roch. C of Sidcup 71-74; Pembury 74-76; Chap St Lawr Hosp Bodmin from 76. *10 Queen's Crescent, Bodmin, Cornw, PL31 1QW.* (Bodmin 3281)

MITCHELL, Ronald Bruce. Ridley Coll Melb ACT ThL 65. **d** 64 **p** 65 Adel. C of Ch Ch Adel 64-67; P-in-c of Port Broughton 67-69; R of Balmoral 69-73; Deniliquin Dio River from 73. *PO Box 279, Deniliquin, NSW, Australia 2710.* (058-81 2092)

MITCHELL, Canon Stanley. b 04. Egerton Hall, Man 33. **d** 35 **p** 36 Man. C of St Mary Virg Davyhulme 35-38; All SS Elton 38-40; V of Crawshawbooth 40-48; St Luke Benchill 48-62; Hon Can of Man 57-71; Can (Emer) from 71; R of Heaton Moor 62-71; RD of Heaton 65-71; L to Offic Dio Blackb from 79. *26 The Strand, Rossall, Fleetwood, Lancs, FY7 8NR.* (Fleetwood 4497)

MITCHELL, Stephen John. b 51. Univ of Ex BA 73. Fitzw Coll Cam BA 78. Ridley Hall Cam 76. **d** 79 **p** 80 Worc. C of Gt Malvern 79-81; Prec of St Martin's Cathl City and Dio Leic from 82. *17 Cooden Avenue, Leicester, LE3 0JS.*

MITCHELL, Tom Good. K Coll NS STh 62. **d** 63 **p** 64 NS. I of Barrington 63-68; R of Dominion and of New Waterford 68-73; Alberton 73-81; V of Misterton w W Stockwith Dio Southw from 81. *25 Gringley Road, Misterton, Doncaster, S Yorks, DN10 4AP.*

MITCHELL, Victor Sidney William. b 03. Moore Th Coll Syd 25. ACT ThL 28. **d** 27 **p** 28 Syd. C of H Trin Dulwich Hill 27-29; Missr Bush Ch Aid S for Austr and Tas 29; Vic Sec 30-32; Org Sec CCCS NW Area and L to Offic Dio Liv 32-36; V of Constable Lee 36-39; St Sav Nottm 39-55; Surr from 40; R of Costock 55-69; Rempstone 55-69; Perm to Offic Dio Chich from 70. *2 The Hop Gardens, South Harting, Petersfield, Hants, GU31 5QL.* (Harting 439)

MITCHELL, Wilfred Christopher. b 15. Lich Th Coll 51. **d** 53 **p** 54 Southw. C of Bilborough w Strelley 53; V of St Mich AA Radford 59-68; V of All SS Linc 68-81. *46 Fairleas, Branston, Lincoln, LN4 1NW.* (Linc 792710)

MITCHELL, William Blanchard. b 26. St Aid Coll 53. Dipl Th (Lon) 54. **d** 55 **p** 56 Carl. C of Kendal 55-59; Dalton-in-Furness 59-60; V of Nicholforest 60-61; CF 61-77; V of Nicholforest w Kirkandrews-on-Esk Dio Carl from 77. *Nicholforest Vicarage, Penton, Carlisle, Cumb.* (Nicholforest 221)

MITCHELL, William James. Ridley Coll Melb ACT ThL 49. **d** 50 River **p** 50 Bp James for River. C of Menindee 50; P-in-c 51-55; V of Balmoral 55-60; C of Franston 60-62; I of Clayton 62-72; C in Dept of Evang and Ex Dio Melb from 72. *44 South Parade, Blackburn, Vic, Australia 3130.* (03-877 3881)

MITCHELL, William John. **d** 27 **p** 28 Kilm. C of Annagh (Belturbet) w Quivvy 27-30; C-in-c of Derrylane 30-42; I of Killinkere w Mullagh 42-73; Lurgan w Loughan 61-73; Can of Drumlease in Kilm Cathl 65-73; *c/o Killinkere, Virginia, Co Cavan, Irish Republic.*

MITCHELL-INNES, James Alexander. b 39. Ch Ch Ox BA 64, MA 66. Lon Coll of Div 65. **d** 67 Crediton for Ex **p** 68 Ex. C of Cullompton 67-71; N Nig 71-75; P-in-c of Puddletown w Athelhampton and Burleston Dio Sarum 75-78; V (w Tolpuddle) from 78. *Puddletown Vicarage, Dorchester, Dorset, DT2 8SL.* (Puddletown 216)

MITCHELL-JONES, Leslie James. b 11. St Aug Coll Cant 61. **d** 62 **p** 63 B & W. C of Weston-s-Mare 62-64; V of Witham Friary 64-70; C-in-c of Marston Bigot 64-70; R of Cheddon Fitzpaine 70-81. *c/o Cheddon Fitzpaine Rectory, Taunton, Somt.*

MITCHINSON, Frank. b 37. K Coll Lon and Warm AKC 60. **d** 61 **p** 62 Lich. C of Cross Heath 61-64; Forrabury w Minster and Trevalga 64-68; Harpenden 68-70; R of Southwick Dio Chich from 70. *Southwick Rectory, Brighton, BN4 4GB.* (Brighton 592389)

MITCHINSON, Ronald. b 35. Linc Th Coll 66. **d** 68 **p** 69 Dur. C of Heworth 68-72; Banbury 72-73; Team V 73-76; St Luke Rotorua 76-79; Hon C of Glen Innes Dio Auckld from 79; Co-Dir Industr Miss Dio Auckld from 79. *35 Strong Street, Auckland 6, NZ.* (583-885)

MITFORD, Bertram William Jeremy. b 27. Wells Th Coll 62. **d** 64 **p** 65 Man. C of Hollinwood 64-67; Atherton 67-68; Frome Selwood 68-71; V of Cleeve-in-Yatton 72-74; Cleeve w Chelvey and Brockley 74-79; Chap HM Pris Shepton Mallet from 79. *2 Charlton Road, Shepton Mallet, Somt, BA4 5NY.* (S Mallet 2825)

MITTON, Michael Simon. b 53. Univ of Ex BA (Th) 75. St Jo Coll Nottm 76. **d** 78 Reading for Cant for Ox **p** 79 Buckingham for Ox. C of St Andr Hatters Lane High Wycombe Dio Ox from 78. *7 Kendalls Close, High Wycombe, Bucks, HP13 7NN.*

MITYANA, Bishop of. *See* Mukasa, Right Rev Yokana Balikuddembe.

MIZEN, Johannes Robert. **d** 71 **p** 72 St John's. C of Umtata Cathl Dio St John's from 71. *80 King Edward Road, Umtata, Transkei, S Africa.*

MJWAUZI, Eustace. b 34. **d** and **p** 75 Vic Nyan. P Dio Vic Nyan. *PO Box 1033, Bukoba, Tanzania.*

MKANDLA, Frank. b 16. **d** 76 **p** 77 Matab. P Dio Matab.

St Francis Mission, PO Tjolotjo, Zimbabwe.

MKANDLA, Sidney Kuza. **d** 75 **p** 76 Matab. P Dio Matab 75-81; Dio Lundi from 81. *Box 974, Gwelo, Zimbabwe.*

MKATA, Ven Frank Barnabas. **d** 57 **p** 58 Nyasa. P Dio Nyasa 57-64; Dio Malawi 64-71; Dio Lake Malawi from 71; Dean 74-78; Archd of Likoma from 74. *Box 133, Nkhotakota, Malawi.*

MKATE, Andrew Daniel. St Mark's Coll Dar-S 69. **d** 72 **p** 73 SW Tang. P Dio SW Tang 72-76; Dio Ruv from 77. *PO Mbamba Bay, Tanzania.*

MKAYERUZA, Methuen. St Andr Th Coll Lik 38. **d** 39 Nyasa. d Dio Nyasa 39-64; Dio Malawi from 64. *USPG, Mpondas, Fort Johnston, Malawi.*

✠ **MKHABELA, Right Rev Bernard Lazarus.** St Pet Coll Rosettenville 56. **d** 58 **p** 59 Zulu. P Dio Zulu 59-68; Dio Swaz 68-75; Can of Swaz 68-75; Archd of E Swaz 73-75; Cons Ld Bp of Swaz in St Aug Ch Nqutu 11 Sep 75 by Abp of Capetn; Bps of St John's and Natal; Bps Suffr of Natal and St John's; and Bp Zulu. *Bishop's House, Box 118, Mbabane, Swaziland, S Africa.* (2333)

✠ **MKHIZE, Right Rev Alfred.** St Bede's Coll Umtata 53. **d** 55 **p** 56 Natal. P Dio Natal 55-80; Can of St Sav Cathl Pmbg from 73-80; Cons Ld Bp Suffr of Natal at Jan Smuts Stadium Pmbg 13 April 80 by Abp of Capetn; Bps of Grahmstn, Port Eliz, Pret, Kimb K, Les, St John's, Natal and Zulu; and Bps Hallowes and Zulu. *Box 899, Pietermaritzburg, Natal, S Africa.*

MKHIZE, Bonginkosi Andreas. b 51. St Bede's Coll Umtata. **d** 77 **p** 78 Natal. C of Ekuvukeni Kwa Mashu 77-80; St Chad Klip River Dio Natal from 80. *PO Box 228, Ladysmith, Natal, S Africa.*

MKHIZE, Elliot Lawrence Danane. St Pet Coll Alice, 64. **d** 66 **p** 68 Natal. C of Kwa Mashu 66-70; St Faith Durban 70-72; R of St John Tongaat 72-77; Lect Federal Th Sem Pmbg and L to Offic Dio Natal from 78. *P Bag X505, Plessislaer 4500, Natal, S Africa.*

MKHIZE, Simon Peter Ndoda. St Bede's Coll Umtata 65. **d** 67 **p** 68 Natal. C of St Aug Umlazi 67-69; R of St John Tongaat 69-72; Umzimkulwana 72-77; Clermont Dio Natal from 77. *Box 24, Clernaville, Natal, S Africa.* (Clernaville 12)

MKHIZE, Victor Patrick Sipho. Univ of S Afr BA 66. Selw Coll Cam 2nd cl Th Trip pt i 67, BA (3rd cl Th Trip pt ii) 69. St Bede's Coll Umtata 60. **d** 69 **p** 70 Natal. C of St Faith Durban 69-70; Kwa Mashu 70-73; Chap St Chris Sch Luyengo 73-76; Vice-Prin St Bede's Coll Umtata 76-79; I of Umlazi Dio Natal from 80. *Box 36224, Ntokozweni, Natal, S Africa.*

MKHULISE, Meshak. St Bede's Coll Umtata 64. **d** 65 St John's. d Dio St John's. *Ensikeni Mission, PO Hoha, Transkei, S Africa.*

MKIZE, Alfred. Coll of Resurr Rosettenville, LTh 42. **d** 42 **p** 43 Zulu. Asst P Nkandhla 42-48; Vryheid Native Miss Distr 48-54; St Aug Miss Hlazakazi 54-68; R of Inhlwathi 69-77; Can of Zulu 70-77. *PB 523, Inhlwathi, Nongoma, Zululand.*

MKIZE, Ven Calvin Sidlosenkosi Bekwakhe. St Bede's Coll Umtata. **d** 56 **p** 58 St Jo Kaffr. P Dio St Jo Kaffr 58-60; Dio St John's from 60; Archd of St Barn from 80. *PO Ntlaza 5114, Transkei, S Africa.* (Ntlaza 3)

MKIZE, Selby Bonkinkosi. St Bede's Coll Umtata 52. **d** 54 **p** 55 Zulu. P Dio Zulu 54-71. *PO Box 171, Piet Retief, Zululand.*

MKOLE, Yohana. **d** 68 **p** 69 W Tang. P Dio W Tang. *Kalinzi, PB Kigoma, Tanzania.*

MKOMAWANTHU, Frank Ananias Philip. b 35. Univ of Cape Coast Ghana BA 66. **d** 77 **p** 78 S Malawi. P Dio S Malawi. *Box 600, Blantyre, Malawi.*

MKONGOSO, Francis Nathan. St Andr Th Coll Lik 57. **d** 59 Nyasa. d Dio Nyasa 59-64; Dio Malawi from 64. *St Andrew's College, Likoma, Malawi.*

MKOSA, Titus Samson. b 39. St Phil Coll Kongwa 75. **d** and **p** 77 Vic Nyan. P Dio Vic Nyan. *PO Box 64, Ngudu, Tanzania.*

MKOSANA, Ozias Martin. b 30. **d** 75 **p** 76 Matab. P Dio Matab; Dioc Youth Chap from 81. *20 Cleeve Road, Montrose, Bulawayo, Zimbabwe.*

MKOWEKA, Arthur. St Jo Sem Lusaka, 64. **d** 65 **p** 67 Bp Mtekateka for Malawi. P Dio Malawi 65-71; Dio S Malawi 71-73; Dio Lake Malawi from 73. *Box 2, Nkhotakota, Malawi.*

MKUCHU, Amos. b 38. St Phil Coll Kongwa 71. **d** 72 Moro. d Dio Moro 72-80. *Ibuti, Gairo, PO Kilosa, Tanzania.*

MKUCHU, Canon Filemoni Chimosa Gamalieli. **d** 55 **p** 56 Centr Tang. P Dio Tang 55-65; Dio Moro 65-80; Hon Can of Moro from 77. *Box 124, Kilosa, Tanzania.*

MKUCHU, Frederick Clement. b 39. St Phil Th Coll Kongwa 68. **d** 70 **p** 71 Moro. P Dio Moro. *Box 71, Kidatu, Tanzania.*

MKUNDA, Daudi. **d** 66 **p** 67 Moro. P Dio Moro. *Box 26, Gairo, Kilosa, Tanzania.*

MKWIJI, Chad. **d** 73 **p** 74 Zanz T. P Dio Zanz T. *Magila, Box 35, Korogwe, Tanzania.*

MLANDU, John. b 49, **d** 76 **p** 77 St John's. P Dio St John's. *PO Holy Cross, Republic of Transkei, S Africa.*

MLANGWA, Christopher. St Cypr Th Coll Ngala. **d** 62 Zanz. d Dio Zanz T 62-72; Dio Dar-S 72-76; Dio Lebom from 76. *CP 82, Maputo, Mozambique.*

✠ **MLELE, Right Rev Joseph Williard.** **d** 52 **p** 55 SW Tang. P Dio SW Tang from 55; Can of SW Tang from 64; Archd of Njombe from 65; Cons Asst Bp of SW Tang in H Cross Pro-Cathl Luili 24 Aug 65 by Abp of E Afr; Bp of SW Tang; Asst Bp of Masasi; and Bp Thorne; Apptd Bp of SW Tang 74. *Box 32, Njombe, Tanzania, E Africa.*

MLELWA, Michael. **d** 74 **p** 75 SW Tang. P Dio SW Tang. *PO Box 146, Njombe, Tanzania.*

MLEMETA, Hezron. b 23. **d** 71 **p** 72 Vic Nyan. P Dio Vic Nyan 71-77; Dio Moro from 77. *Box 320, Morogoro, Tanzania.*

MLOMBI, Ammonias Mhlambiso. St Bede's Coll Umtata, 58. **d** 59 **p** 61 St John's. P Dio St John's. *Box 165, Mount Frere, Transkei, S Africa.*

MLOMBILE, Canon Michael Mkhanyisi. St Bede's Coll Umtata. **d** 55 **p** 57 St Jo Kaffr. P Dio St Jo Kaffr 57-60; Dio St John's from 60; Hon Can of St John's from 78. *Box 64, Engcobo 5050, Transkei, S Africa.*

MLOSA, Ephraim. **d** and **p** 67 Moro. P Dio Moro 67-74. *Gairo, PO Kilosa, Tanzania.*

MLOWEZI, Ernesti. b 45. St Phil Coll Kongwa 77. **d** 79 Bp Mohamed for Centr Tang **p** 79 Tang. P Dio Centr Tang. *Box 15 PO, Dodoma, Tanzania.*

MLUNGUSYE, Rafael. St Cypr Coll Ngala, 64. **d** 66 Masasi. d Dio Masasi. *Box 16, Masasi, Tanzania.*

MMANYWA, Edward. **d** 68 **p** 69 Centr Tang. P Dio Centr Tang. *PO Box 904, Dodoma, Tanzania.*

MNCWANGO, Cyprian Thandeka. b 38. **d** 76 **p** 78 Zulu. C of Melmoth 76-77; KwaMagwaza Dio Zulu from 77. *Private Bag 802, Melmoth 3835, Zululand.*

MNDALA, Dennis. b 27. **d** 71 **p** 72 Lake Malawi. P Dio Lake Malawi. *Box 39, Nkhata Bay, Malawi.*

MNDOLI, Habeli. **d** 70 **p** 70 Centr Tang. P Dio Centr Tang. *DCT Chiwondo, Box 941, Dodoma, Tanzania.*

MNGOMEZULU, Percy Sipho. b 38. **d** and **p** 78 Swaz. P Dio Swaz. *PO Box 781, Mbabane, Swaziland.*

MNGOMEZULU, Posselt. b 28. **d** 77 **p** 78 Zulu. C of Ubombo Dio Zulu 77-78; P-in-c from 78. *PO Box 26, Ubombo 3970, Zululand, S Africa.*

MNIPALIKA, Boniface. St Cypr Th Coll Namasakata, 50. **d** 52 **p** 55 Masasi. P Dio Masasi from 52. *Nambunga, Masasi, Tanzania.*

MNKANDLA, Sydney. b 45. **d** 74 Matab. d Dio Matab. *1605 Old Makoba, Gwelo, Rhodesia.*

MNONGONE, Canon Mikael Sila. St Cypr Th Coll Tunduru 32. **d** 34 **p** 37 Masasi. Asst Miss Dio Masasi 34-35; P-in-c of Mumbaka 45-50; Mindu 50-52; Nanyindwa 53-59; Can of Masasi from 53; P-in-c of Nanguruwe 59-64; Asst P of Mkomaindo 64-70; Dio Masasi 70-72. *PO Box 16, Masasi, Tanzania.*

MNQATHU, John Norton Natal. St Bede's Coll Umtata, 66. **d** 67 **p** 68 St John's. P Dio St John's. *Rectory, Mqanduli, Transkei, S Africa.* (Mqanduli 21)

MNUONA, Eliya. St Cypr Th Coll Namasakata 50. **d** 52 **p** 55 Masasi. P Dio Masasi. *Minjale, Lindi, Masasi, Tanzania.*

MNYANDU, William Alfred. b 29. St Pet Coll Alice 68. **d** 71 **p** 72 Zulu. P Dio Zulu. *St Augustine's Church, PO St Augustine's, Natal, S Africa.*

MNYANDU, Ziphozonke. b 46. St Pet Coll Alice 72. **d** 74 **p** 75 Zulu. C of Maphophoma 74-78; P-in-c of Esikhawini Dio Zulu from 78. *Box 88, Esikhawini, Zululand.*

MNYANDWA, Hosea Sekwao. **d** 39 **p** 41 Centr Tang. Asst P Kimamba 39-42; Kigoma 42-43; Berega 43-44; Kilosa 44-50; Berega 50-57. *CMS, Berega, Kilosa, Tanzania.*

MNYANGWILA, Alexander. **d** and **p** 77 Centr Tang. P Dio Centr Tang. *DCT, Ikasi, Tanzania.*

MNYANJOKA, Stephen. **d** and **p** 77 Centr Tang. P Dio Centr Tang. *PO Mlali, Tanzania.*

MNYORORO, Joshua. **d** 56 **p** 57 Centr Tang. P Dio Centr Tang. *Manhyali, Tanzania.*

MOATT, Richard Albert. b 54. AKC and BD 76. Linc Th Coll 80. **d** 81 Carl. C of Egremont w Haile Dio Carl from 81. *9 St John's Terrace, Bigrigg, Nr Egremont, Cumbria, CA22 2TU.* (Cleator Moor 811155)

MOBBS, Bernard Frederick. b 26. SOC 71. **d** 72 **p** 73 S'wark. C of St Barn Purley 72-74; Vice-Prin SOC 74-80;

P-in-c of St Bart Sydenham Dio S'wark from 80. *4 Westwood Hill, SE26.* (01-778 5290)

MOBERLY, Richard Hamilton. b 30. Trin Hall Cam BA 53, MA 57. Cudd Coll 53. **d** 55 **p** 56 Liv. C of Walton-on-the-Hill 55-59; St Mary Abbots Kens 59-63; R of Chingola Zam 63-66; V of St Anselm Kennington Cross 67-73; Team V of North Lambeth 74-80; Chap S Lon Industr Miss from 80. *South London Industrial Mission, 27 Blackfriars Road, SE1.*

MOBERLY, Robert Walter Lambert. b 52. New Coll Ox MA 77. Selw Coll Cam MA 80. Trin Coll Cam PHd 81. Ridley Hall Cam 74. **d** 81 Birm. C of Knowle Dio Birm from 81. *1713 High Street, Knowle, Solihull, W Midl, B93 0LN.*

MOBLEY, Ronald John. Worc Ordin Coll. **d** 62 Bp Stuart for Worc **p** 63 Worc. C of Cropthorne w Charlton 62-65; Kingswood Surrey 65-68; R of Eastleach Martin w Eastleach Turville and Southrop 68-73; V of Newland w Redbrook 73-80. *c/o Newland Vicarage, Coleford, Glos.* (Coleford 3220)

MOCKFORD, Preb John Frederick. b 28. Em Coll Cam BA (2nd cl Geog Trip pts i and ii) 52, MA 56. Ridley Hall, Cam 52. **d** 54 **p** 55 Man. C of St Silas Ardwick 54; Ch Ch Harpurhey 54-57; V of St Leon Bootle 57-64; CMS Miss Nam 66-72; Dioc Sec Kamp 72-73; Can Miss Kamp 72-73; V (R from 77) of Bushbury Dio Lich from 73; Surr from 73; Preb of Lich Cathl from 81. *Rectory, Bushbury Lane, Wolverhampton, Staffs, WV10 8JP.* (Wolverhampton 782226)

MODISAESI, Jacob Molupe. b 39. **d** 75 Bp Carter for Johann **p** 76 Johann. C of Natalspruit Dio Johann from 75. *Box 12050, Katlehong 1832, S Africa.* (011-917)

MODUDULA, Lawrence. d 57 **p** 63 New Guinea. P Dio New Guinea 57-71; Dio Papua from 71; Dom Chap to Bp of New Guinea 59-71. *Menapi, PO Dogura, via Boroko, Papua New Guinea.*

MOEKETSI, Gasebame Petrus. b 34. **d** 70 Bp Carter for Johann. C of Emdeni Dio Johann from 70. *470a Naledi, PO Kwa-Uma, Tvl, S Africa.*

MOEKETSI, Seth. d 72 **p** 73 Mashon. P Dio Mashon 72-81; Dio Mutare from 81. *Holy Name Parish, Sakubva, Umtali, Zimbabwe.*

MOELLER, Preb Edward Jack. b 09. St Chad's Coll Dur BA 36, Dipl Th 37, MA 39. **d** 37 **p** 38 Bris. C of St Jo Evang Clifton 37-39; St Sav w St Pet S'wark and PV of S'wark Cathl 39-41; Paignton 41-43; Chap RAFVR 43-47; V of Whipton 47-74; RD of Christianity 51-57; Preb of Ex Cathl from 62. *26 Kennerley Avenue, Whipton, Exeter, Devon.* (Ex 66447)

MOFFAT, Donald Keith. St Jo Coll Morpeth ACT ThL (2nd cl) 62. **d** 63 Bp Sambell for Melb for Bal **p** 64 Melb for Bal. C of Horsham 63-64; P-in-c of St Aug Betong 66-69; C of Ch Ch St Laur Syd 69-76; R of Enmore w Stanmore Dio Syd from 76. *61a Albany Road, Stanmore, NSW, Australia 2048.* (569 4332)

MOFFAT, George. b 46. Univ of Edin BD 77. Edin Th Coll 67. **d** 72 Papua **p** 73 Edin. C of Falkirk 73-76; St Pet Lutton Place Edin 76-81; Angl Chap to Univ of Edin 77-81; C of Heston Dio Lon from 81. *24 Hogarth Gardens, Heston, Middx, TW5 0QS.* (01-579 9388)

MOFFATT, Canon Gerald Early. b 1896. Bp's Univ Lennox MA 46. Trin Coll Tor BD 44. **d** 42 **p** 43 Tor. C of St Jas Cathl Tor 42-47; I of Fenelon Falls 47-48; Lorne Park 48-52; R and Can of St Pet Cathl Charlottetown 52-58; R of St Mark Port Hope 58-70; Epiph Scarborough Tor 70-75; Can of Tor from 72; I of Campbellford Dio Tor from 75. *Box 557, Campbellford, Ont, Canada.* (705-653 1663)

MOFFATT, James Ronald. Kelham Th Coll 1899. **d** 12 **p** 13 N Rhod. UMCA Miss P Dio N Rhod 12-19; C of St Mary Johann 19-20; St Sav St Alb 20-21; R of Barberton 21-25; P-in-c of Sekukuniland and Supt of Jane Furse Mem Hosp 25-29; R of St Aug Kimb 29-32; P-in-c of Endhlozana Miss and R of Piet Retief 32-35; Broken Hill 38-44; Fort Jameson 44-47; C of St Cypr Cathl Kimberley (in c of Barkly W w Windsorton and Holpen) 47-50; St Alb Copnor Portsm 50-51; Itin P S Africa 51-54; R of Barkly W 54-56. *Gardens Hotel, Queenstown, CP, S Africa.*

MOFFATT, Neil Thomas. b 46. Fitzw Coll Cam BA 68, MA 72. Qu Coll Birm 69. **d** 71 **p** 72 S'wark. C of Old Charlton 71-74; C of St Pet Walworth 74-77; V of Dormansland Dio S'wark from 77. *Dormansland Vicarage, Lingfield, Surrey, RH7 3RA.* (0342 832391)

MOFFATT, Canon Percy Elliott. b 15. St Aug Coll Cant 38. **d** 40 **p** 41 York. C of St Jo Evang Middlesbrough 40-43; Selby Abbey 43-45; Skelton-in-Cleveland 45-49; CF 49-65; V of Bulkington 65-71; RD of Bedworth 68-71; R of Stoke Cov 71-76; C-in-c of Wyken 74-76; R of Caludon Team Min Cov 76-78; Hon Can of Cov Cathl from 76; V of Dunchurch w Thurlaston Dio Cov from 78. *Dunchurch Vicarage, Rugby, Warws, CV22 6PJ.* (Rugby 810274)

MOFFET, William Brown. b 05. Tyndale Hall Bris 27. **d** 30 **p** 31 St Alb. C of Ch Ch Ware 30-33; BCMS Miss at Akyab 33-42; CF (Ind) 43-46; V of Bovingdon 46-54; St Martin Dover 54-69; C-in-c of Hougham-by-Dover 54-69; C of All SS Eastbourne 69-72; Perm to Offic Dio Chich from 71. *55 Freeman Avenue, Hampden Park, Eastbourne.* (Eastbourne 54188)

MOGAPI, Peter. St Bede's Coll Umtata 58. **d** 60 **p** 61 Kimb K. P Dio Kimb K 60-76. *Box 60, Kuruman, CP, S Africa.*

MOGFORD, Canon Stanley Howard. b 13. St Pet Hall Ox BA (2nd cl Mod Lang) 35, Dipl Th 36, MA 39. Westcott Ho Cam 36. **d** 37 **p** 38 Llan. C of Aberdare 37-41; Cathl Ch Llan 41-48; V of Cyfarthfa 48-54; Pontypridd 54-63; Llanblethian w Cowbridge (w Llandough and St Mary Church from 66) 63-80; RD of Llantwit Major and Cowbridge from 69; Can of Llan from 71. *c/o Llanblethian Vicarage, Cowbridge, S Glam.* (Cowbridge 2302)

MOGGA, Yoasa Wurbe. Bp Gwynne Coll Mundri. **d** 61 **p** 63 Sudan. P Dio Sudan 61-76; Dio Juba from 76; Dioc Sec from 77. *Box 170, Juba, Sudan.*

MOGOILLE, Harun Chiwaye. St Phil Coll Kongwa. **d** 74 **p** 75 Centr Tang. P Dio Centr Tang. *Box 15, Dodoma, Tanzania.*

MOGOKONYANE, Benjamin. St Bede's Coll Umtata. **d** 57 **p** 59 Kimb K. P Dio Kimb K. *Box 87, Mafeking, CP, S Africa.*

MOGOROSI, Shadrach. St Pet Coll Rosettenville, 45. **d** 47 **p** 49 Bloemf. C of Thaba 'Nchu Miss 48-49; NE Free State Miss 49-53; Miss P at Vredefort 53-61; Sasolburg Miss 61-64; Winburg 64-71; Brandfort 69-71; Virginia 71-73; P-in-c of Bultfontein Dio Bloemf from 73. *Box 152, Bultfontein, OFS, S Africa.* (480)

✠ **MOHAMED, Right Rev Alpha Francis.** Ridley Coll Melb ThL 72. St Phil Th Coll Kongwa, 65. **d** 67 Bp Madinda for Centr Tang **p** 67 Centr Tang. P Dio Centr Tang 67-71; on leave 72; Prin Msalato Sch Dodoma 73-76; Cons Asst Bp of Centr Tang in Dodoma Cathl 15 Aug 76 by Abp of Tanzania; Bps of Centr Tang and Vic Nyan; and Bp Stanway. *c/o Box 15, Dodoma, Tanzania.*

MOHAMMED, Samuel Buddah. Im Coll Ibadan, 60. **d** 63 **p** 64 N Nig. P Dio N Nig. *PO Box 16, Kaduna, Nigeria.*

MOHAN, Bernard Patrick. St Edm Hall, Ox BA (3rd cl Engl) 25, Dipl Th 26, MA 38. Wycl Hall, Ox 26. **d** 27 **p** 28 Guildf. C of H Trin Aldershot 27-31; H Trin Heigham 31-33; V of Ludham 33-36; St Jo Evang Penge 36-46; C-in-c of Ch Ch Penge 43-46; Reg Sec BFBS 46-55; Perm to Offic Dios Ox and St Alb 48-55; Lon and Chelmsf 52-55; Distr Sec Canad Bible S Cape Breton and Newfld 55-67; Asst Master Edgehill Sch Windsor NS 67-69. *RR3, Sydney, NS, Canada.*

MOHASOA, Petrus Bushy. b 35. St Pet Coll Alice 72. **d** 74 **p** 75 Johann. C of Kagiso 74-77; R of Marico Dio Johann from 77. *Box 194, Zeerust, Transvaal, S Africa.* (014-282 Ext 669)

MOHOTO, Abrham Fikile. b 30. **d** 78 Bp Stanage for Johann **p** 79 Johann (NSM). C of Wattville Dio Johann from 78. *1196 Poto Street, Wattville, S Africa 1500.*

MOHUTSIOA, Zachariah Austin Tuêlo. St Pet Coll Alice. **d** 67 **p** 68 Johann. C of St Paul Jabavu 67-70; R of St Aug Marico and Zeerust 71-77; Natalspruit Dio Johann from 77. *Box 12050, Katlehong, Transvaal, S Africa.* (011-917)

MOI, Ven Stephen Gill. b 32. **d** 68 Bp Ambo for New Guinea **p** 70 New Guinea. P Dio New Guinea 68-71; Dio Papua 71-77; Dio New Guinea Is from 77; Archd of New Guinea Is from 78. *Anglican Church, Menpa, PMB Gasmata, Via Kimbe, Papua New Guinea.*

MOILOA, Gilbert Kgosinkwe. b 30. **d** 74 **p** 77 Johann. C of Tladi 74-75; Senaoane Dio Johann 75-81; L to Offic Dio Johann from 81. *2078a Naledi, Kwa-Xuma, Johannesburg, S Africa.*

MOIR, David William. b 38. St Aid Coll 64. **d** 67 Barking for Chelmsf **p** 68 Chelmsf. C of Danbury 67-70; St Jo Bapt Bollington 70-72; V of St Jas Sutton Chesh 72-81; Prestbury Dio Ches from 81. *Vicarage, Prestbury, Chesh.* (Prestbury 829288)

MOISOVEN, Judah. Patteson Th Centre Kohimarama. **d** 72 Melan. d Dio Melan 72-75; Dio New Hebr from 75. *Loh, Torres Islands, New Hebrides.*

MOKINYO, Harun David. St Paul's Dioc Div Sch Limuru, 50. **d** 52 **p** 54 Momb. P Dio Momb 52-64; Dio Nai from 64. *PO Kajiado, Kenya.*

MOKIWA, Canon Leonard. St Cypr Coll Namasakata. **d** 54 **p** 57 Zanz. P Dio Zanz 54-65; Dio Dar-S from 65; Can of Dar-S from 71. *PO Box 28004, Kisarawe, Dar-es-Salaam, Tanzania.*

MOKOENA, Samuel Laolao. d 74 **p** 75 Bloemf. St Pet Coll Alice 72. C of Thaba 'Nchu 74-78; R of Springfontein 78-81; P-in-c of St Aug Thaba Nchu Dio Bloemf from 81. *Box 9, Thaba Nchu, OFS, S Africa.*

MOKOSAN, Alison Madragyi. Bp Gwynne Coll Mundri, 60. **d** 64 **p** 65 Bp Ngalamu for Sudan. P Dio Sudan. *Malakal United Church, PO Box 40, Malakal, Upper Nile Province, Sudan.*

MOKOTSO, Ishmael Tseliso. b 41. **d** 76 Les. d Dio Les. *St Agnes Mission, PO Box TY 22, Teyateyaneng, Lesotho, S Africa.*

✠ **MOKUKU, Right Rev Philip.** St Pet Coll Rosettenville, 57. **d** 59 **p** 61 Basuto. P Dio Basuto 59-67; Dio Les 67-77; Dean and R of St Mary and St Jas Cathl Maseru 77-78; Cons Ld Bp of Les in St Mary and St Jas Cathl Maseru 11 June 78 by Bp of Bloemf; Bps of Zulu, Swaz and Kimb K; and Bp D Tutu. *Bishop's House, Box MS 87, Maseru, Lesotho.*

MOLALE, Michael. St Pet Coll Rosettenville. **d** 61 **p** 62 Johann. P Dio Johann 61-75; Dio Botswana from 75; Dean of Botswana 76-81. *c/o Box 573, Gaborone, Botswana.*

MOLD, Peter John. Univ of W Austr BA 62. Linc Th Coll. **d** 63 **p** 64 Linc. C of Boston 63-67; Scarborough 67-68; Prec of St Geo Cathl Perth 68-79; R of York Dio Perth from 79. *Rectory, Suburban Road, York, W Australia 6302.* (096-41 1081)

MOLD, Philip Geoffrey. b 18. AKC 40. Univ of Lon BD 40. Westcott Ho Cam 40. **d** 41 **p** 42 Leic. C of Birstall 41-44; Whitwick (in c of St D Broom Leys) 44-50; V of Fleckney w Saddington 50-57; Thornley Dio Dur from 57. *Vicarage, Thornley, Durham, DH6 3EN.* (Wellfield 820363)

MOLE, Arthur Penton. b 10. Univ of Witwatersrand BA 30. Bps' Coll Cheshunt 33. **d** 35 **p** 36 Win. C of All SS W Southbourne 35-37; Wolborough 37-44; R of Goldsborough 44-49; Dir of Relig Educn and Publ Pr Dio St Alb 49-51; PC of St Mark Barnet Vale 51-59; RD of Barnet 55-59; V of St Kath Southbourne 59-71; R of Old Alresford (w Brown Candover, Chilton Candover, Swarraton and Northington from 74) 71-76; C-in-c of Swarraton w Northington and Brown Candover and Chilton Candover 72-76; L to Offic Dio Worc from 76. *15 Garden Stiles, Pershore, Worcs, WR10 1JW.* (Pershore 554167)

MOLE, David Eric Harton. b 33. Em Coll Cam BA 54, Lightfoot Sch 57, MA 58, PhD 62. Ridley Hall, Cam 55. **d** 59 Birm **p** 59 Aston for Birm. C of St Steph Selly Hill 59-62; Tutor St Aid Coll 62-63; Chap and Fell of Peterho Cam 63-69; Lect Univ of Ghana 69-72; Chap and Fell Legon Hall 70-72; Lect Qu Coll Birm 72-76; Tutor USPG Coll of The Ascen Selly Oak from 76. *College of the Ascension, Weoley Park Road, Selly Oak, Birmingham B29 6RD.* (021-472 1667)

MOLE, Eric Edward. b 1900. OBE 61. **d** and **p** 74 Birm. Hon C of Hall Green Dio Birm from 74. *67 Lovelace Avenue, Solihull, W Midl, B91 3JR.* (705 5291)

MOLEFE, Abel Mampa. b 31. **d** 76 Bp Carter for Johann **p** 77 Johann. C of Moroka Dio Johann from 76. *1246 Rockville, Moroka 1860, S Africa.*

MOLEFE, Christian Paul. St Pet Coll Rosettenville, 39. **d** 41 **p** 42 Johann. C of Orlando Native Miss Johann 41-45; P-in-c of Vereeniging Miss Distr 45-49; Brakpan Miss Distr 49-56; Pimville Johann 56-64; Klerksdorp 64-66; R of Mamelodi 66-69; C of St John Orlando 69-76. *Box 119, Orlando East, Transvaal, S Africa.*

MOLESWORTH, Canon Anthony Edward Nassau. b 23. Pemb Coll Cam BA 45, MA 48. Coll of Resurr Mirfield 45. **d** 46 **p** 47 Newc T. C of St Mary Blyth 46-51; St Phil Newc T 51-52; Usuthu 52-59; P-in-c of Piggs Peak 59-62; R and Dir 62-71; Can of Zulu 63-68; Swaz 68-71; Can (Emer) from 71; R of Huish Episcopi w Pitney 71-78; Commiss Swaz from 73; C-in-c of High Ham 76-78; Low Ham 76-78; Team R of Langport w Huish Episcopi Dio B & W from 78. *Rectory, Huish Episcopi, Langport, Somt.* (Langport 250480)

MOLESWORTH, Bruce Robert. Moore Th Coll Syd ACT ThL 55. **d** 56 **p** 57 Syd. C of W Manly 56-58; Southborough 58-59; C-in-c of Marsfield w Denistone E Provisional Distr 60-67; Westmead 68-71; R 71-77; Hosp Chap Dio Armid from 77. *Upper Street, Tamworth, NSW, Australia.*

MOLETSANE, Felix Tsepho. b 51. St Bede's Coll 78. **d** 78 St John's. d Dio St John's. *St Bede's College, Umtata, Transkei.*

MOLETSANE, Moses Thamsanqa Lehlohonono. b 44. St Pet Coll Alice 70. **d** 72 **p** 73 Grahmstn. C of St Mich AA Queenstown 72-74; Zwelitsha 74-76; P-in-c of St Cypr Langa Dio Capetn from 76. *St Cyprian's Church, Langa, CP, S Africa.* (53-3287)

MOLETSHE, Anthony Thembinkosi. b 40. St Pet Coll Alice. **d** 71 **p** 72 Swaz. C of Manzini Dio Swaz from 71. *Box 68, Manzini, Swaziland.*

MOLIFE, Walker Pickford Nathaniel. **d** 56 **p** 59 Natal. P Dio Natal from 56. *581 Smith Drive, Sobantu Village, Pietermaritzburg, Natal, S Africa.*

MOLL, Randell Tabrum. b 41. BD (Lon) 65. Wycl Hall Ox. **d** 66 **p** 67 York. C of Drypool 66-70; Netherton and of Sefton 70-72; Industr Chap in Netherton Liv and SW Lancs 70-75; Ostende 75-76; P-in-c of Brockmoor 76-81. *c/o Brockmoor Vicarage, Brierley Hill, Staffs, DY5 3UR.* (Brierley Hill 78375)

MOLLAN, Very Rev Robert Augustine. b 1895. Trin Coll Dub BA 19, Div Test 21, MA 22. **d** 21 **p** 22 Down. C of St Donard Belf 21-23; Dioc C of Clogh 23-27; C of Ch Ch Lisburn 27-32; I of Glenavy 32-35; R of Kilwaughter w Cairncastle and Raloo 36-42; Cathl Ch Clogh 42-51; Can of Clogh and Preb of Tullycorbet 44-51; Prec of Clogh Cathl 51-60; R of Ballybay Aughnamullen and Crossduff 51-66; RD of Ballybay 51-66; Can and Preb of Donaghmore in St Patr Cathl Dub 60-62; Dean of Clogh 62-66. *95 Leinster Road, Rathmines, Dublin 6, Irish Republic.* (Dublin 973142)

MOLLER, Cyril Crawford. **d** 61 **p** 62 Rockptn. C of St Luke Wandal Rockptn 61-62; P-in-c of Barlaba 62-63; Pialba 63-67; R of Gayndah 67-70; Perm to Offic Dio Brisb from 70. *102 Churchill Street, Childers, Queensland 4660, Australia.*

MOLLER, George Brian. b 35. TCD BA 60, MA 64. **d** 61 **p** 62 Connor. C of St Pet Belf 61-64; Larne 64-68; C-in-c of Rathcoole Dio Connor 68-69; I from 69. *3 Strathmore Park North, Belfast, N Ireland, BT15 5HQ.* (Belfast 776085)

MOLLOY, Neale Gordon. OBE 75. Trin Coll Melb BA 34. ACT ThL 36. **d** 37 **p** 38 Melb. C of St Andr Brighton 37-40; Dir St John's Boys' Home Cant Dio Melb 40-76; Can of Melb 70-80; Perm to Offic Dio Melb from 80. *37 Mount View Road, North Balwyn, Vic, Australia 3104.* (85-8169)

MOLLOY, Terrence Harold. b 36. St Jo Coll Auckld LTh 76. **d** 71 **p** 72 Auckld. C of St Paul Auckld 71-76; V of Mt Roskill Dio Auckld from 76. *1352 Dominion Road, Mount Roskill, Auckland 4, NZ.* (699-574)

MOLOI, Aaron Mphani. St Pet Coll Rosettenville. **d** 59 Johann **p** 60 Bp Paget for Johann. P Dio Johann from 59. *Box 6, Tembisa, Transvaal, S Africa.*

MOLOI, Canon Bertram Joseph Lehlohonolo. St Pet Coll Rosettenville. **d** and **p** 50 Johann. P Dio Johann 50-63 and from 65; Dio Bloemf 63-65; Dir Dept of Miss and Can of Johann from 77. *Box 49027, Rosettenville, 2130, S Africa.*

MOLOI, Cyprian Daniel. St Pet Coll Rosettenville 61. **d** 63 **p** 64 Johann. P Dio Johann. *Box 163, Standerton, Transvaal, S Africa.* (014-81 3478)

MOLOI, Canon Sima Kok. Coll of Resurr Rosettenville. **d** 40 **p** 41 Johann. C of Ermelo 40-42; Wakkerstroom Native Miss Dio Johann 42-45; P-in-c from 45; Hon Can of Johann from 80. *St Mary's Mission, Daggakraal, PO Vlakpoort, E Transvaal, S Africa.*

MOLOINYANE, Gustave Tholo. St Bede's Coll Umtata, 60. **d** 61 **p** 63 Bloemf. P Dio Bloemf 61-63; Dio Basuto 63-66; Dio Les From 66. *St Mary's Mission, Khukhune, PO Buthe Buthe, Lesotho.*

MOLOLO, Gidion. **d** and **p** 78 Centr Tang. P Dio Centr Tang. *Box 15, Dodoma, Tanzania.*

MOLOMO, William Hilary. St Pet Coll Alice, 61. **d** 64 **p** 65 Pret. P Dio Pret 64-73. *PO Jane Furse Hospital, Middelburg, Transvaal, S Africa.*

MOLONY, Nicholas John. b 43. Univ of Dur BA 67. Univ of Birm Dipl Th 70, MA 78. Qu Coll Birm 67. **d** 70 **p** 71 Ox. C of Beaconsfield 70-75; P-in-c of Ch Ch Chesham 75-80; Team V of Gt Chesham 80-81; P-in-c of Weston Turville Dio Ox from 81. *Weston Turville Rectory, Aylesbury, Bucks.* (Stoke Mandeville 3212)

MOLSON, Walter Kingsbury. McGill Univ Montr BA 38. Trin Coll Tor STB 67. **d** 67 Ott. I of Eganville 67-71; St Martin Ott 71-73; on leave. *RR3, Killaloe, Ont., Canada.*

MOLYNEAUX, George. b 12. Tyndale Hall Bris 35. Kaiser-i-Hind Medal 43. **d** 38 S'wark for Col Bp **p** 39 Rang. C of St Phil E Rang 38-39; BCMS Miss at Akyab 39; Minbya 39-42; Eccles Est CF (Ind) 42-44; Hon CF 46; Org Sec BCMS N Area and LPr Dio Man 44-46; BCMS Miss Burma 46-50; Org Sec for NW Engl and LPr Dio Man 50-51; C of Kinson 51-54; V of Bovingdon 54-78. *Address temp unknown.*

MOLYNEUX, Arthur Robert Joseph. Chich Th Coll 41. **d** 45 St Andr for Edin **p** 46 Brech for Edin. C of All SS Edin 45-49; P-in-c of St Ninian Comely Bank Edin 49-55; St D of Scotld Pilton Edin 55-59; C of All SS Cathl Edmon 59-61; R of St Mark Edmon 61-68; Hon C of St Mich Edmon 68-72; St Steph City and Dio Edmon 72-76; P-in-c 76-77; I from 77. *6219 144a Avenue, Edmonton, T5A 1S3, Alta, Canada.*

MOLYNEUX, Fred. Univ of Man BA 22. Ridley Hall Cam 22. **d** 24 **p** 25 Ex. C of St Mary Magd Upton Torquay 24-28; Chap Toc H (E and N Yorks and Lincs) 28-29; Miss to Seamen Newport Mon 29-32; Hamburg 32-33; Dunkirk France 33-36; Chap of Yenangyaong Oilfields 36-38; Moulmein 38-40; R of Moora 40-46; Rosalie 46-56; Asst Chap Miss to Seamen Port of Lon 56; Org Sec Miss to Seamen Dio Ex 56-58; P-in-c of St Aid Bentley W Austr 58-60; R of Spearwood w Hilton Pk 60-64; L to Offic Dio Perth from 64. *51 Jameson Street, Mosman Park, W Australia 6012.* (31 4173)

MOLYNEUX, Horace William Hubert. b 1889. Sarum Th

Coll 23. **d** 24 **p** 25 Win. C of St Jas Southampton 24-30; All SS Alton 30-35; V of Hythe 35-66; L to Offic Dio Win from 66. *1 Morley Close, Winkton, Christchurch, Hants.*

MOLYNEUX, Raymond Jurgen Frederic. Wollaston Coll W Austr 63. **d** and **p** 66 Perth. C of Wembley-Floreat Pk 66-68; P-in-c of Wyalkatchem 68-69; R 69-72; Lockridge w Eden Hill 72-73; Min of Applecross 73-74; Assoc P of Gosnells-Maddington 74-78; R of Gingin Dio Perth from 78. *Rectory, Gingin, W Australia 6503.* (095-752 285)

MOLYNEUX, William. b 01. Bp Wilson Th Coll IM 30. **d** 32 **p** 33 Liv. C of St Mary Bootle 32-35; St Cath Wigan 35-37; V of St Matt Blackb 37-52; St Mary Kirkdale 52-71. *88 Grange Road, Southport, Lancs, PR9 9AD.*

MOLYNEUX, William Arthur. Tyndale Hall Bris 29. **d** 33 **p** 34 Vic. Miss at Momeng 33-39; R of Downe St Mary 40-45; Clannaborough 43-45; V of St Jo Bapt Harborne 45-48; w 'C of E in S Africa' 48-55; R of Ch Ch Addington Durban 55-57; Mowbray 57-80. *1 Roughmoor Road, Mowbray 7700, CP, S Africa.*

MOMADI, Petro. b 36. St Mark's Coll Dar-S 79. **d** 80 Dar-S. M SSF; on study leave. *PO Box 250017, Dar-es-Salaam, Tanzania.*

MOMBASA, Lord Bishop of. *See* Mwang'ombe, Right Rev Peter.

MOMBASA, Dean of. *See* Mwadime, Very Rev Jefferson Willie.

MONAGHAN, Leslie Frank. Moore Th Coll Syd ACT ThL 63. **d** 63 **p** 64 Syd. C of Albion Pk 63-65; C-in-c of Villawood 65-70; R of Lawson 70-73; Panania 74-77; Dongara-Greenough 77-80; Field Rep Angl Home Miss S Dio Syd from 80. *25 Springdale Road, Wentworthville, NSW, Australia 2145.* (631-9767)

MONALA, Canon Peter. St Pet Coll Rosettenville. **d** 32 **p** 35 Johann. C Dio Johann 32-36; P-in-c of Lichtenburg Miss Distr 36-42; Krugersdorp Miss 42-59; Can of Johann 53-65; Hon Can from 65; P-in-c of Crown Mines 59-69; R of St John Orlando Johann 66-69; C of St Pet in Chains Natalspruit 69-74; L to Offic Dio Johann from 74. *Box 60, Boksburg, Transvaal, S Africa.*

✠ **MONCREIFF, Right Rev Francis Hamilton.** b 06. St Jo Coll Cam BA 27, MA 31. Univ of Glas Hon DD 67. Cudd Coll 28. **d** 30 **p** 31 Ely. C of St Giles Cam 30-35; St Aug Kilburn 35-41; C-in-c of St Salvador Edin 41-47; R 47-51 (w St Steph from 49); Chap HM Pris Edin 42-51; Can of St Mary's Cathl Edin 50-52; Dioc Missr Edin 51-52; Cons Ld Bp of Glas and Gall in St Mary's Cathl Glas 15 July 52 by Bp of Arg Is (Primus); Bps of Moray; Aber; Brech; Edin; St Andr; Derry; and Bp Jackson; Elected Primus of Episc Ch in Scotld 62; res 74. *19 Eglinton Crescent, Edinburgh, EH12 5BY.* (031-337 1523)

MONCUR, Henry Alexander. b 11. AKC 43. **d** 43 Cant **p** 44 Dover for Cant. C of St Osw Norbury 43-46; Ashford 46-52; V of Bardon Hill 52-56; Stoke Golding w Dadlington 56-79. *56 Beaufort Drive, Barton Seagrove, Kettering, Northants.*

MONDS, Edward Henry. Tyndale Hall, Bris 38. **d** 41 **p** 42 Lich. C of Ch Ch Burton-on-Trent 41-43; Org Sec ICM for S of Engl and LPr Dio S'wark 43-48; R of Hampreston 48-78. *4 Dewwentwater Road, Merley, Wimbourne, Dorset, BH21 1PS.*

MONEY, Jack Humphrey. b 25. Sarum Th Coll 58. **d** 59 **p** 60 Chich. C of St Anne Lewes 59-63; V of Stanmer w Falmer and Moulsecoomb 63-75; R of Heene Worthing Dio Chich from 75. *4 Lansdowne Road, Worthing, W Sussex, BN11 4LY.* (Worthing 202312)

MONK, Joseph Albert. b 06. ACP 33. Launde Abbey Leic 74. **d** 75 **p** 76 Leic. C of Ch Langton 75-77; L to Offic Dio Leic from 77. *19 Thornborough Close, Little Bowden, Market Harborough, Leics.*

MONK, Nicholas John. b 32. Westcott Ho Cam 61. **d** 63 **p** 64 Bris. C of H Cross Inns Court Bris 63-67; Stoke Bp 67-69; V of All SS Swindon 69-75; Ashton Keynes w Leigh Dio Bris from 75. *Ashton Keynes Vicarage, Swindon, Wilts, SN6 6PP.* (Cirencester 861566)

MONK, Ronald Henry. b 35. SOC 72. **d** 75 **p** 76 S'wark. C of Ch of Good Shepherd Lee (in c of St Pet from 78) 75-81; V of Earlsfield Dio S'wark from 81. *Vicarage, Waynflete Street, SW18 3QE.* (01-946 4214)

MONKS, John Stanley. St D Coll Lamp 38. AKC 42. **d** 42 **p** 43 Liv. C of St Elph Warrington (in c of St John's Miss Ch) 42-45; H Sav Priory Ch Tynemouth 45-49; V of Spittal 49-54; St Marg Scotswood 54-66; St Cuthb Blyth Dio Newc T from 66. *29 Ridley Avenue, Blyth, Northumb, NE24 3BA.* (Blyth 2410)

MONKS, Kenneth Bevan. McGill Univ Montr BSc (Agr) 37. **d** 53 **p** 56 Tor. I of Stoney Lake 53-55; N Essa 55-58; Chap Ashbury Coll Ott 58-65. *Montebello, Quebec, Canada.*

MONKS, Roger James. b 39. G and C Coll Cam BA 61. Coll of Resurr Mirfield, 61. **d** 63 **p** 64 Pet. C of Higham Ferrers 63-66; Cheshunt 68-70; Chap Dartington Hall Sch 70-71; Warden of Cranstoun Project 72. *Address temp unknown.*

MONMOUTH, Lord Bishop of. *See* Childs, Right Rev Derrick Greenslade.

MONMOUTH, Archdeacon of. *See* Evans, Ven John Barrie.

MONMOUTH, Dean of. *See* Jenkins, Very Rev Frank Graham.

MONROE, James Allen. b 35. St Aid Coll 63. **d** 64 **p** 65 Connor. C of St Mich Belf 64-68; Coleraine 68-71; I of Ballynure w Ballyeaston 71-77; Coleraine Dio Connor from 77. *St Patrick's Rectory, Mountsandel Road, Coleraine, Co Derry, N Ireland.* (Coleraine 3429)

MONTAGUE, Canon William John. b 18. Late Found Scho of K Coll Cam 1st cl Mod and Med Lang Trip pt i, 38, BA (2nd cl Hist Trip pt ii) 40, MA 44. Linc Th Coll 40. **d** 42 **p** 43 Worc. C of St Geo Redditch 42-44; St Nich Liv 44-47; Marlborough 47-50; Min of Conv Distr of St Edm of Cant Weymouth 50-54; C of St Pancras 55-57; Vice-Prin Bps' Coll Cheshunt 57-61; Can Missr Dio Wakef 62-74; Proc Conv Wakef 64-74; Vice Provost of Wakef 73-74; R of Buckland Dio S'wark from 74; Adv in-Service Tr to Bp of S'wark from 74. *Buckland Rectory, Betchworth, Surrey.* (Betchworth 3360)

MONTAGUE-YOUENS, Canon Hubert Edward. b 30. Ripon Hall, Ox 55. **d** 58 **p** 59 Worc. C of Redditch 58-59; Halesowen 59-62; V of Kempsey 62-68; St Geo Kidderminster 68-72; R of Ribbesford w Bewdley and Dowles 72-81; RD of Kidderminster 76-81; Hon Can of Worc 78-81; Can (Emer) from 81; R of Bridport (Allington, Bothenhampton w Walditch and Bradpole) Dio Sarum from 81. *Bridport Rectory, Dorset.* (Bridport 22138)

✠ **MONTEFIORE, Right Rev Hugh William.** b 20. St Jo Coll Ox BA (1st cl Th) 46, MA 47, Liddon Stud 48. SS Coll Cam MA (by incorp) 47, BD 63. Univ of Aber Hon DD 77. Westcott Ho Cam 48. **d** 49 **p** 50 Newc T. C of St Geo Jesmond Newc T 49-51; Chap and Tutor Westcott Ho Cam 51-53; Vice-Prin 53-54; Exam Chap to Bp of Newc T 53-70; to Bp of Worc 57-60; to Bp of Cov 57-70; to Bp of Blackb 66-70; Fell and Dean of G and C Coll Cam 54-63; Select Pr Univ of Cam 54 and 63; Asst Lect Univ of Cam 56-59; Lect 59-63; Can Th of Cov 59-69; V of St Mary Gt w St Mich AA Cam 63-70; Proc Conv Ely 66-70; Hon Can of Ely 69-70; Cons Ld Bp Suffr of Kingston-upon-Thames 29 Sept 70 in S'wark Cathl by Abp of Cant; Bps of Lon, Ely, Man, Leic, Newc T, Bris, Guildf, Pet, Sarum, Derby, Birm and St Alb; and others; M Gen Syn S'wark 75-78; Trld to Birm 78. *Bishop's Croft, Harborne, Birmingham, B17 0BG.* (021-427 2062)

MONTEGO BAY, Bishop Suffragan of. *See* Reid, Right Rev Alfred Charles.

✠ **MONTEITH, Right Rev George Rae.** Univ of NZ BA 28. St Jo Coll Auckld **d** 28 Auckld **p** 29 NZ for Auckld. C of St Matt Auckld 28-29; Actg V of Hauraki Plains NZ 30; Perm to Offic (Col Cl Act) at Stoke-on-Trent (in c of St Paul Mt Pleasant) 31-33; C 33; V of Dargaville 34-37; St 2BI*R5 Mt Eden Auckld 37-49; Dean of St Mary's Cathl Auckld 49-69; VG 63-76; Cons Asst Bp of Auckld in St Mary's Cathl Auckld 24 Feb 65 by Abp of NZ; Bps of Auckld, Aotearoa, Ch Ch, Dun, Waik and Wel; and Bp McKenzie; res 76; L to Offic Dio Auckld from 76. *7 Cathedral Place, Auckland 1, NZ.* (374-449)

MONTGOMERIE, William Arthur. b 31. Oak Hill Th Coll 56. **d** 59 **p** 60 Man. C of Ch Ch Chadderton 59-62; V of Tunstead 62-69; H Trin w St Luke Warrington Dio Liv from 69. *6 Palmyra Square North, Warrington, Chesh, WA1 1JQ.* (Warrington 30057)

MONTGOMERY, Archdeacon of. *See* Thomas, Ven Owen.

MONTGOMERY, Canon Anthony Allan. b 33. Trin Hall Cam BA 56. Edin Th Coll 56. **d** 58 **p** 59 Glas. C of Dumfries 58-63; P-in-c of St Paul Airdrie 63-67; R 67-68; Chap Gordonstoun Sch from 68; Can of St Andr Cathl Inverness from 81. *Gordonstoun School, Moray.* (Alves 282)

MONTGOMERY, Charles George Greathead. b 08. AKC 33. **d** 33 **p** 34 Roch. C of All SS Perry Street Northfleet 33-40; Actg C-in-c of St Gennys 42-44; V of Poundstock 44-45. *Jasmine Cottage, Ash Cross, Bradworthy, Holsworthy, Devon.*

MONTGOMERY, Harry Reid. Univ of W Ont BA 49, LTh 49. **d** 49 **p** 50 Hur. I of Oakwood Corners and St Steph Sarnia 49-51; R of Watford 51-56; Wallaceburg 56-61; St Martin-in-the-Fields Lon 61-69; St Aid Windsor 69-76; Exam Chap to Bp of Hur 64-70; I of Ch of Transfig Lon Dio Hur from 76. *480 Castlegrove Boulevard, London, Ont., Canada.*

MONTGOMERY, Ian David. b 44. Univ of St Andr LLB 66. ACA 69. Wycl Hall Ox 71. **d** 75 **p** 76 Lon. C of St Dionis

Parsons Green Fulham 75-78; in Amer Ch from 78. *758 North Pleasant Street, Amherst, Mass 01002, USA.* (413-549 5929)

MONTGOMERY, James Ivan. b 31. **d** 75 Bp Carter for Johann **p** 76 Johann. C of Westlea Dio Johann from 75. *18 Soutpansberg Avenue, Bosmont 2093, S Africa.*

MONTGOMERY, Canon John Alexander. b 11. Trin Coll Dub BA (Resp) 34. **d** 35 **p** 36 Clogh. Dioc C Dio Clogh 35-37; C of St Simon Belf 37-40; Dioc C Dios Kilm, Elph and Ard 40-45; C-in-c of Drumshambo 45-50; R of Taunagh w Kilmactranny 50-54; I of Garvary 54-59; Kilkeevin 59-67; Ardagh (w Kilcommick from 71) 67-80; RD of S Elphin 66-67; Newtownforbes 67-80; Can and Preb of Elph and Ard Cathl 78-80. *Grange Courtyard, Linlithgow, W Lothian, EH49 7RH.*

MONTGOMERY, John Alford. b 36. Episc Th Sem Ky USA 72. **d** 74 Lexington for NS **p** 74 NS. C of Port Hill 74-77; L to Offic Dio Calg from 77. *24 Moreuil Wood Drive SW, Calgary, Alta, Canada.*

MONTGOMERY, Pembroke John Charles. b 24. Codr Coll Barb. **d** 53 Nass **p** 55 Windw Is. C of St Geo Cathl St Vincent 55-56; R of Biabou 56-65; Calliaqua 65-73; Can of Kingstown Cathl 63-73; C-in-c of St Jas City and Dio Derby 73-74; V from 74. *Vicarage, Malcolm Street, Derby, DE3 8LS.* (Derby 43911)

MONTIZAMBERT, Charles Kenneth. Wycl Coll Tor 58. **d** 62 Keew **p** 63 Ont for Keew. R of Keew 63-69; Ignace 69-70; L to Offic Dio Rupld from 70. *490 Telfer Street S, Winnipeg 10, Canada.*

MONTJANE, Norman Kuduudu. St Pet Coll Rosettenville 56. **d** 58 **p** 60 Pret. P Dio Pret 58-71; Dio Johann from 72. *Box 119, Orlando 1804, Johannesburg, S Africa.*

MONTJANE, Stephen Masikane Letlape. b 33. Univ of Leeds BA 57. **d** 76 Bp Carter for Johann **p** 78 Johann. C of St Mary's Cathl Johann 76-81; R of Pimville Dio Johann from 81. *2498 Zone 2, Pimville 1808, Johannesburg, S Africa.*

MONTOYA, Julio. **d** and **p** Peru. P Dio Peru. *Apartado 5152, Lima 18, Peru.*

MONTREAL, Lord Bishop of. *See* Hollis, Right Rev Reginald.

MONTREAL, Assistant Bishops of. *See* Brown, Right Rev Russel Featherstone; and Hill, Right Rev Henry Gordon.

MONTREAL, Archdeacon of. *See* Doidge, Ven John Nicholls.

MONTREAL, Dean of. *See* Shepherd, Very Rev Ronald Francis.

MONYANE, Nathaniel. St Bede's Coll Umtata. **d** 66 **p** 68 Les. p Dio Les. *St Joseph's Mission, Mohloka, PO Lebian Falls, Lesotho.*

MOODY, Aubrey Rowland. Coll of Resurr Mirfield 53. **d** 55 **p** 56 Chelmsf. C of Wanstead 55-57; V of Feering Dio Chelmsf from 57. *Feering Vicarage, Colchester, Essex, C05 9NL.* (Kelvedon 70226)

MOODY, Cecil John Kingston. Univ of Sask BA 63. Em Coll Sktn LTh 63. **d** 63 Dub for Keew. C of Emo 63-64; I 64-66. *311 First Street East, Fort Frances, Ont, Canada.*

MOODY, Christopher John Everard. b 51. New Coll Ox BA 72. Cudd Coll BA (Th) 74. **d** 75 Lon **p** 76 Kens for Lon. C of All SS Fulham 75-79; C-in-c of St Andr Surbiton Dio S'wark from 79. *33 Cheyne Hill, Surbiton, Surrey.* (01-399 7948)

MOODY, Derek Frank. b 41. Univ of Wales BA (3rd cl Hist) 62. Chich Th Coll 63. **d** 65 **p** 66 Ches. C of Ellesmere Port 65-69; St John Southend Lewisham (in c of St Mark Downham) 69-73; Team V of Catford (Southend) and Downham 73-74; V of St Richard Ham Surrey Dio S'wark from 75. *Vicarage, Ashburnham Road, Ham, Surrey.* (01-948 3758)

MOODY, Ernest. b 1900. **d** 45 **p** 46 Dur. C of St Nich (in c of St Mary) Bp Wearmouth 45-48; St Luke Ferryhill 48-50; Cockfield w Staindrop (in c of Staindrop) 50-52; PC of Dipton 52-60; Waterhouses 60-70. *Sherburn Hospital, Durham.*

MOODY, Geoffrey Sidney. b 13. St Cath S Ox BA 35, MA 39. **d** 54 **p** 55 Bp Stuart for Worc. C of Belbroughton w Fairfield 54-56; R of Abberley 56-61; V of Norton w Whittington 61-67; Holly Bush w Birtsmorton 67-78; P-in-c of Castle Morton 72-78; L to Offic Dio Lich from 78. *30 Meadow Lane, Derrington, Stafford, Staffs, ST18 9NA.*

MOODY, George Henry. b 27. Cranmer Hall 69. **d** 71 York **p** 72 Hull for York. C of Marske-in-Cleveland 71-74; Dioc Chap to the Deaf Dio Lich from 74. *86 Charlotte Street, Walsall, WS1 2BA.*

MOODY, John Kelvin. St Francis Coll Brisb ACT ThL 55. **d** 56 **p** 57 Brisb. C of Warwick 56-57; Southport 57-58; Dalby 58-61; St Cuthb Kens 61-64; Chap at Ankara 64-69; Istanbul 64-66; Palma 69-75; Tangier 75-79; Can of Gibr 74-79. *c/o 8 Rue Cujas, Tangier, Morocco.*

MOODY, Sydney George. b 08. **d** 66 Bp Horstead for Leic **p** 67 Leic. C of Braunstone 66-69; R of Frolesworth w Leire and Ashby Parva 69-79; Perm to Offic Dio Chelmsf from 80. *The Dower House Cottage, Castle Hedingham, Halstead, CO9 3DG.*

MOON, Arthur Thomas. b 22. ACP 53, LCP 56. Dipl Th (Lon) 66. Sarum Th Coll 65. **d** 66 Lanc for Blackb **p** 67 Blackb. C of Fulwood 66-71; All H Bispham Dio Blackb from 71. *Church Villa, All Hallows Road, Bispham, Blackpool.*

MOON, Aubrey Douglas. b 1893. Qu Coll Ox BA 17, MA 53. **d** 17 **p** 19 Birm. C of St Pet Maney 17-20; Bp Ryder Ch Birm 20-21; Chap of Enham Village Centre 21-22; Lille 22-27; R of St Phillipe de Torteval Guernsey 27-31; V of Helston 31-65; Perm to Offic Dio Ex from 66. *Cedar Cottage, Buckerell, Honiton, Devon.*

MOON, John Charles. b 23. Sarum Th Coll 49. **d** 51 **p** 52 Linc. C of Bottesford w St Paul Ashby 51-54; Habrough w Immingham 54-55; V of Immingham 55-61; St Luke w All SS Weaste Salford 61-67; St Jo Bapt Spalding Dio Linc from 67. *Vicarage, Hawthorn Bank, Spalding, Lincs.* (Spalding 2816)

MOON, Leslie Richard John. b 07. Dorch Miss Coll 28. **d** 31 **p** 32 Lon. C of All SS S Acton 31-32; St John Cinderford 33-35; St Jas Gt Walthamstow 35-36; Lymington 36-44; R of Hale w S Charford and Woodgreen 44-56; V of St John Guernsey 56-66; R of Millbrook 66-73. *44 Riverside Gardens, Romsey, Hants, SO5 8HN.*

MOON, Canon Ronald Earl. St Jo Coll Morpeth. **d** and **p** 56 C & Goulb. C of Tumut 56-57; R of Tarcutta 57-63; Binda 63-66; Field Officer Dept Chr Educn Dio C & Goulb 66-71; R of Cootamundra 71-80; Ainslie Dio C & Goulb from 80; Can of C & Goulb from 80. *1 Bonney Street, Ainslie, ACT, Australia 2602.*

MOON, Thomas Arnold. b 24. Univ of Lon BA 51. Oak Hill Th Coll 49. **d** 52 **p** 53 Liv. C of Fazakerly 52-56; V of St Benedict Everton 56-70; St Luke Formby Dio Liv from 70. *St Luke's Vicarage, Formby, Liverpool, L37 2DE.* (Formby 77655)

MOOR, David Drury. b 18. St Edm Hall Ox BA 39, MA 44. Wells Th Coll 46. **d** 48 **p** 49 Glouc. C of St Barn Tuffley 48-52; C-in-c of Symondsbury w Eype and Broadoak 52-53; R 53-61; V of St Andr Bournemouth 61-69; St Mich AA Bournemouth Dio Win from 69. *6a Portarlington Road, Bournemouth, Hants.* (B'mth 763514)

MOOR, Maurice Albert Charles. St Paul's Coll Burgh 30. **d** 34 **p** 35 Wakef. C of St Geo Ovenden Halifax 34-36; Slaithwaite 36-40; Calne 40-44; V of Chute w Chute Forest 44-62; L to Offic Dio Ban from 63. *Edensor Lodge, Llwyngwril, Gwyn.* (0341-250495)

MOORE, Adrian Roberts. b 40. Ridley Coll Melb ThL 72. **d** 72 **p** 73 Melb. C of St Jas Ivanhoe 72-74; St John Croydon 74-75; P-in-c of Pakenham 75-80; S Pilbara Dio NW Austr from 80. *30 Joffre Avenue, Paraburdoo, W Australia.*

MOORE, Alan Keith. Moore Th Coll Syd ThL 80. **d** 80 Brisb. C of St John Dalby Dio Brisb from 80. *6 Connelly Street, Dalby, Qld, Australia 4405.* (074 62 2071)

MOORE, Anthony Richmond. b 36. Clare Coll Cam BA 59, MA 63. Linc Th Coll 59. **d** 61 **p** 62 S'wark. C of Roehampton 61-66; All SS New Eltham (in c of St Aid Edgebury) 66-70; Missr of Blackbird Leys Conv Distr Ox 70-81; Team V of Dorchester (in C of Marsh and Toot Baldon and Nuneham) Dio Ox from 81. *Marsh Baldon Rectory, Oxford.*

MOORE, Arthur Lewis. b 33. Univ of Dur BA 58, Dipl Th 59, PhD 64. Cranmer Hall Dur 58. **d** 62 **p** 63 Roch. C of Stone 62-66; Clevedon 66-68; Chap and Tutor Wycl Hall Ox 68-70; Vice-Prin from 70. *3 Norham Gardens, Oxford.* (Oxford 55796)

MOORE, Arthur Robert. b 15. Sarum Th Coll 62. **d** 63 **p** 64 Sarum. C of Calne 63-67; V of Steeple Ashton w Semington 67-79; C-in-c of Keevil 71-72; V 72-79; P-in-c of Southwick w Boarhunt Dio Portsm from 79. *1 High Street, Southwick, Fareham, Hants.* (Cosham 382113)

MOORE, Bernard Geoffrey. b 27. New Coll Ox BA (2nd cl Jurispr) 47, MA 52. Ely Th Coll 49. **d** 51 **p** 52 Blackb. C of St Pet Chorley 51-54; Dom Chap to Bp of Blackb 54-55; C-in-c of St Mich AA Eccles Distr Blackpool 55-67; Chap Vic Hosp Blackpool 58-67; V of St Barn Morecambe 67-81; R of Standish Dio Blackb from 81. *Standish Rectory, Wigan, Lancs.* (Standish 421396)

MOORE, Bernard George. Qu Coll Birm 57. **d** 60 **p** 61 York. C of St Columba Middlesbrough 60-62; St Cypr Cathl Kimberley 62-64; R of St Matt Kimberley 64-69 Chap RN 70-74; C of Milton 74-76; V of Glenfield 76-80; Kaitaia Dio Auckld from 80. *47 Church Road, Kaitaia, NZ.*

MOORE, Preb Brian Birkett. b 24. Oak Hill Th Coll 51. **d** 53 **p** 54 York. C of H Trin Heworth York 53-55; Cheadle 55-57; R of Corley 57-64; Chap High View Hosp 61-64; Chap at Barcelona 64-67; V of St John Southall 67-74; Surr from 69; RD of Ealing W 72-74; V of Wembley Dio Lon from 74; Chap Wembley Hosp from 74; RD of Brent from 77; Preb of

St Paul's Cathl Lon from 80. *St John's Vicarage, Crawford Avenue, Wembley, Middx, HA0 2HX.* (01-902 0273)

MOORE, Brian Philip. b 51. AKC 72. St Aug Coll Cant 72. **d** 74 **p** 75 St Alb. C of Bp's Hatfield 74-78; Radlett 78-81; V of Eaton Bray w Edlesborough Dio St Alb from 81. *Eaton Bray Vicarage, Dunstable, Beds, LU6 2DN.* (0525 220261)

MOORE, Ven Bruce Macgregor. Univ of NZ BA 55. Coll of Resurr Mirfield. **d** 57 **p** 58 Blackb. C of St Steph Blackpool 57-61; Manurewa 61-63; V of Panmure 63-73; All SS Ponsonby Auckld 73-79; Exam Chap to Bp of Auckld from 77; Can of H Trin Cathl Auckld from 78; V of Howick Dio Auckld from 79; Archd of Manukau from 81. *13 The Glebe, Howick, Auckland, NZ.* (46-864)

MOORE, Clive Granville. b 31. Late Exhib of St Pet Hall Ox BA (3rd cl Th) 54, MA 58. Wycl Hall Ox 54. **d** 55 **p** 56 Carl. C of St Paul Barrow-F 55-57; CF 57-61; R of Stone 61-69; Chap Joyce Green Hosp Dartford 61-69; R of Radstock (w Writhlington from 71) Dio B & W from 69; C-in-c of Writhlington 69-71; Surr from 72; RD of Midsomer Norton from 81. *Radstock Rectory, Bath, Somt.* (Radstock 33182)

MOORE, Colin Frederick. b 49. Div Hostel Dub 69. **d** 72 **p** 73 Arm. C of Drumglass 72-80; R of Newtownhamilton w Ballymoyer Dio Arm from 80. *71 Ballymoyer Road, Whitecross, Co Armagh, N Ireland, BT60 2LA.* (Glenanne 256)

MOORE, David. b 36. St D Coll Lamp BA 61. Magd Coll Cam BA (3rd cl Th Trip pt ii) 63, MA 68. Linc Th Coll 63. **d** 65 **p** 66 York. C of Saltburn-by-the-Sea 65-69; Northallerton w Kirby Sigston and Romanby 69-72; V of Kirk Levington Dio York from 72; V of High and Low Worsall Dio York from 72. *Vicarage, Kirk Levington, Yarm, Cleve, TS15 9LQ.* (Eaglescliffe 782439)

MOORE, David Leonard. **d** 80 S'wark. Hon C of St Matt Brixton Dio S'wark from 80. *230 Links Road, Mitcham, SW16.* (01-769 7319)

MOORE, David Metcalfe. b 41. Univ of Hull BA 64, PhD 69. Trin Coll Bris 76. **d** 78 **p** 79 Ches. C of All SS Marple Dio Ches from 78. *125 Church Lane, Marple Stockport, Cheshire, SK6 7LD.* (061-427 1467)

MOORE, David Roy. b 39. Clare Coll Cam BA 61. Ripon Hall, Ox 61. **d** 63 **p** 64 Leic. C of Melton Mowbray 63-66; St Steph Walbrook Lon and Dep Dir The Samaritans 66-73; C of Daybrook Dio Southw 77-80; V from 80. *Vicarage, Oxclose Lane, Daybrook, Nottingham, NG5 6FB.* (Nottingham 262686)

MOORE, Canon Dennis Charles. b 19. Univ of Lon BD 46. Tyndale Hall Bris 39. **d** 43 S'wark for Chich **p** 44 Chich. C of Broadwater 43-47; Org Sec CPAS E Distr and Perm to Offic Dios Nor; Chelmsf; St E; Pet; St Alb; and Linc 47-51; L to Offic Dio Ely 48-51; V of St Luke Eccleston 51-55; St Luke New Catton 55-62; Wellington w Eyton 62-70; Surr 65-70; RD of Wrockwardine 66-70; V of Watford (w St Jas from 73) Dio St Alb from 70; C-in-c of St Jas Watford 70-73; RD of Watford 75-81; Surr from 78; Hon Can of St Alb from 80. *Vicarage, Watford, Herts.* (Watford 25189)

MOORE, Donald Frederick. Em Coll Sktn LTh 50. **d** 50 **p** 51 Edmon. C of H Trin Edmon 50-52; All SS Cathl Edmon 52; V of Jasper 52-55; Sedgewick 55-60; R of Fort Sask 60-65; V of St Ambrose Barb 65-68; Hon C of All SS Cathl City and Dio Edmon from 70. *Apt 1010, 13910 Stony Plain Road, Edmonton, Alta, Canada.*

MOORE, Ven Edward Alexander. b 28. TCD BA 50, Div Test 51, MA 65. **d** 51 **p** 52 Derry. C of Drumragh and Mountfield 51-57; I of Inver w Mountcharles (and Killaghtee from 61) 57-72; RD of Boylagh from 61; Can of Raph 68-76; R of Taughboyne Dio Raph from 72; Dean of Raph 76-80; Exam Chap to Bp of Derry from 76; Archd of Raph from 80. *Taughboyne Rectory, Carrigans, Lifford, Co Donegal, Irish Republic.* (074-40135)

✠ **MOORE, Right Rev Edward Francis Butler.** b 06. Late Exhib and Scho of Trin Coll Dub 1st cl Ment and Mor Phil 27, BA (1st cl Mod) 28, Toplady Pri 29, Downes Pri for Comp and for Oratory and Warren Pri 30, MA 40, PhD 44, Hon DD 59. **d** 30 **p** 31 Dub. C of Bray 30-32; Hon Cler V of Ch Ch Cathl Dub 31-35; C of Clontarf 32-34; I of Castledermot w Kinneagh 34-40; Greystones 40-58; Chap to Duke of Leinster 34-40; RD of Delgany 50-58; Can of Ch Ch Cathl Dub 51-58; Archd of Glendal 57-58; Cons Ld Bp of Kilm and Elph and Ard in St Patr Cathl Arm 6 Jan 59 by Abp of Arm; Bps of Down; Connor; Meath; Tuam; Clogh; and Cashel; res 81. *Drumlona, Sea Road, Kilcoole, Co Wicklow, Irish Republic.*

MOORE, Edward James. b 32. Trin Coll Dub BA 56, MA 59. **d** 56 **p** 57 Connor. C of St Luke Belf 56-59; CF 59-62; C of Dunmurry (in c of St Hilda) 62-64; C-in-c of Kilmakee 64-70; R of H Trin Belf 70-80; Jordanstown Dio Connor from 80. *122 Circular Road, Jordanstown, Newtownabbey, Co Antrim, BT37 0RH. N Ireland.* (Whiteabbey 62119)

MOORE, Ernest Roy. b 21. Univ of Man MA (Th) 76. N-W Ordin Course. **d** 73 Stockport for Ches **p** 74 Ches. C of Cheadle 73-78; Bramhall Dio Ches from 78. *3 Thorn Road, Bramhall, Stockport, Chesh.* (061-439 8173)

MOORE, Chan Evelyn Garth. b 06. Trin Coll Cam BA 27, MA 31. Cudd Coll 62. **d** and **p** 62 Ely. [Called to Bar Gray's Inn 28]; Lect in Law CCC Cam 47-73 and Fell from 47; Chan and VG Dio S'wark from 48; Dur from 54; Glouc from 57; High Bailiff Ely Cathl from 61; L to Offic Dio Ely from 62; Ch Comm 64-77; Mere's Select Pr Univ of Cam 65; V of St Mary Abchurch City and Dio Lon from 72. *St Mary Abchurch, EC4N 7BA.* (01-626 0306); *and Corpus Christi College, Cambridge, CB2 1RH.*

MOORE, Canon Fred. b 11. St Jo Coll Dur LTh BA 44. St Aid Coll. **d** 43 **p** 44 Man. C of St Barn Openshaw 43-45; St Bart Westhoughton 45-47; Thornham w Gravel Hole 47-49; V of Tunstead 49-54; Camerton w Seaton 54-72; RD of Maryport 67-70; Hon Can of Carl Cathl 70-77; Can (Emer) from 77; RD of Solway 70-77; V of Gt Broughton 72-77. *30 Braeside, Seaton, Workington, Cumb.*

MOORE, Frederick George. KCNS. **d** and **p** 35 NS. C of River John 35-38; Port Morien 38-41; R of Woodside 41-67. *4 Tupper Street, Dartmouth, NS, Canada.* (466-4064)

MOORE, George Guy. Selw Coll Cam BA 10, MA 19. Wells Th Coll. **d** 21 **p** 22 Win. C of Albury w Chilworth 21-28; V of Send 28-35. *c/o Lloyds Bank, Lymington, Hants.*

MOORE, Henry James William. b 33. TCD BA 55. **d** 56 **p** 57 Arm. C of Mullabrack 56-61; Drumglass 61-63; I of Clogherny 63-81; Ballinderry w Tamlaght and Arboe Dio Arm from 81. *Rectory, Ballinderry, Cookstown, Co Tyrone, N Ireland.*

MOORE, Henry Wylie. b 23. Univ of Liv BCom 50, Univ of Leeds MA 72. Wycl Hall Ox 50. **d** 52 **p** 53 Liv. C of Farnworth 52-54; St Leon Middleton 54-56; CMS Miss at Khuzistan Oil Fields 57-59; R of Burnage 60-63; Middleton 63-74; Home Sec CMS 74-80; Dep Gen Sec from 80. *CMS, 157 Waterloo Road, SE1 8UU.*

MOORE, Herbert Alexander. b 15. Univ of Wales, BA (Latin and French) 36. BD (Lon) 54. Tyndale Hall, Bris 36. **d** 38 **p** 39 Chich. C of Broadwater 38-40; Actg C of Ramsgate 40-41; I of St Luke's Chap Leamington Priors 41-42; CF (EC) 42-47; V of Woodmancote w Popham and E Stratton 47-51; Org Sec E Distr CPAS 52-55; PC of Ch Ch St Alb 55-60; Metrop Sec CCCS SE Distr 60-64; V of Widcombe 64-66; Chap and Asst Master Cloverley Hall Sch Salop 66-67; Kingsmead Sch Hoylake 67-71; Hillstone Sch Malvern 71-80. *28 Blackmore Road, Malvern, Worcs, WR14 1QT.* (Malvern 5661)

MOORE, Preb Herbert Alfred Harold. b 17. Late Squire Scho of Ex Coll Ox 3rd cl Cl Mods 38, BA (3rd cl Th) 40, MA 43. Cudd Coll 40. **d** 41 **p** 42 Lon. C of St Mary of Eton Hackney Wick 41-44; Thornhill Lees (in c of St Mary Savile Town) 44-46; Min Can and Sacr of Ely Cathl 46-47; PC of Chettisham 46-47; V of Fenstanton 47-61; V of Hilton 47-61; Asst Insp of Schs Dio Ely 59-61; Trav Sec Ch U 61-64; C of St Mich Bedford Pk 61-64; V of St Pet Acton Green 64-71; St Steph Glouc Rd Kens Dio Lon from 71; RD of Kens from 76; P-in-c of H Trin Kens Gore w All SS S Kens Dio Lon from 78; Preb of St Paul's Cathl Lon from 80. *9 Eldon Road, W8 5PU.* (01-937 5083)

MOORE, Hugh Desmond. b 37. St Cath Coll Ox BA (2nd cl Engl) 58, 2nd cl Th 60, MA 64. St Steph Ho Ox 58. **d** 61 **p** 62 S'wark. C of St Luke Kingston T 61-68; Asst Chap Univ of Lon 68-70; V of St Alphage Hendon Dio Lon from 70; Chap Edgware Gen Hosp from 70. *St Alphage Vicarage, Montrose Avenue, Burnt Oak, Edgware, Middx HA8 0DN.* (01-952 4611)

MOORE, James Brooksbank. Late Scho of St D Coll Lamp BA (3rd cl Hist) 31. St Mich Coll Llan 31. **d** 32 **p** 33 Mon. C of St Jo Evang Maindee 32-35; H Ap Charlton Kings 36-38; Perm to Offic at Walton-on-Thames 38-39; Lydney w Aylburton 39-42; PC of Stanley St Leon 42-44; C of St Mary Cheltenham 44-46; Chap and Asst Master Abbey Sch Malvern Wells 46-49; Chap Heron's Ghyll Sch and L to Offic Dio Chich 49-54; R of Bearwood 54-80. *c/o Rectory, King Street Lane, Winnersh, Wokingham, Berks.* (West Forest 5460)

MOORE, James Edward. b 33. Trin Coll Dub BA (2nd cl Ment and Mor Sc) 54, MA 64. **d** 56 **p** 57 Down. C of St Columba Knock 56-60; Bangor 60-62; C-in-c of Belvoir 62-68; R of Groomsport 68-75; R of St Mark Dundela Belf Dio Down from 75; RD of Holywood from 76. *St Mark's Rectory, Sydenham Avenue, Belfast, BT4 2DR.*

MOORE, James Frederick. b 12. Univ of Sheff BSc 35, MSc 36. **d** 38 **p** 40 Br Hond. Hd Master Tela Ch Sch 38-43; St Mich Coll Belize 43-54; L to Offic Dio Bradf from 55; Asst Master Keighley Gr Sch 55-77. *215 Bradford Road, Riddlesden, Keighley, W Yorks, BD20 5JR.*

MOORE, James Kenneth. b 37. K Coll Lon and Warm AKC 62. **d** 63 **p** 64 Dur. C of St Osw W Hartlepool 63-66;

C-in-c of Manor Pk Conv Distr Sheff 66-75; Team V of Manor Park Sheff 75-78; Team R of Frecheville w Hackenthorpe Dio Sheff from 78. *Frecheville Rectory, Sheffield, S12 4XS.* (Sheff 399555)

MOORE, James Richard Finkle. Univ of Tor BA 48, BD 54, MTh 60. **d** 60 Bp Snell for Tor **p** 61 Tor. C of Richmond Hill 60-63; R of Lakefield 64-66; Ch of the Annunc Tor 66-78; N Hastings Dio Ont from 78. *Bancroft, Ont, Canada.* (613-332 2622)

MOORE, John. b 26. St D Coll Lamp BA 51. Oak Hill Th Coll 51. **d** 53 **p** 54 Truro. C of Illogan 53-57; H Trin Margate 57-58; Abingdon 58-67; V of St Sav Retford 67-73; R of Aspenden w Layston and Buntingford Dio St Alb from 73. *Vicarage, Vicarage Road, Buntingford, Herts.* (Royston 71552)

MOORE, John. St Aid Coll. **d** 57 **p** 58 Connor. C of Glenavy 57-59; St Mich Belf 59-60; R of Kingscourt U 60-63; C of Carmoney (in c of St Brigid) 63-65; C-in-c of Templepatrick w Donegore Dio Connor 65-68; R from 68. *Vicarage, Templepatrick, Co Antrim, N Ireland.* (Templepatrick 32213)

MOORE, John Arthur. b 33. Cudd Coll 70. **d** 71 **p** 72 Chelmsf. Hon C of Gt Burstead 71-74; Asst Master K Edw Sch Chelmsf 71-74; Chap Barnard Castle Sch from 74. *Littlemoor, Mount Eff Lane, Barnard Castle, Co Durham, DL12 8UW.* (Teesdale 38601)

MOORE, John Cecil. b 37. TCD BA 61, Div Test 62, MA 67, BD 69. **d** 62 **p** 63 Connor. C of St Matt Shankill Belf 62-65; Holywood 65-70; R of Ballyphilip w Ardquin 70-77; Mt Merrion 77-79; Donaghcloney Dio Drom from 79. *Rectory, Waringstown, Co Down, N Ireland.* (Waringstown 218)

MOORE, John David. b 30. St Chad's Coll Dur BA (3rd cl Th) 54, Dipl Th 55. **d** 56 **p** 57 Newc T. C of St Pet Wallsend 56-60; Leamington Priors (in c of St Alb Mart) 60-62; V of Longford 62-75; P-in-c of St Mary Nuneaton Dio Cov 75-77; V from 77. *St Mary's Abbey Vicarage, Nuneaton, Warws, CV11 6HU.* (Nuneaton 382936)

MOORE, John Keith. b 26. Sarum Wells Th Coll 78. **d** 81 Guildf (NSM). Hon C of All SS Onslow Village City And Dio Guildf from 81. *30 London Road, Guildford, Surrey, GU1 2AF.*

MOORE, John Lawrence. b 46. Univ of Manit BA 71. Em Th Coll Sask MDiv 72. **d** and **p** 72 Rupld. C of St John's Cathl Winnipeg 72-75; I of Emerson 75-78; St Thos Morden Dio Rupld from 78. *Box 233, Morden, Manit, Canada.*

MOORE, John Michael. b 48. Em Coll Cam BA 70, MA 73. Cudd Coll 72. **d** 74 **p** 75 Wakef. C of Almondbury 74-77; Team V of Basingstoke Dio Win from 77. *219 Paddock Road, Basingstoke, Hants, RG22 6QP.* (Basingstoke 64393)

MOORE, John Richard. b 35. ALCD 59 (LTh from 74). **d** 59 **p** 50 Lon. C of Em Northwood 59-63; V of Burton Dassett 63-66; Youth Chap Dio Cov 63-71; Dir Lindley Lodge Educl Trust Nuneaton 71-82; Team R of Kinson Dio Sarum from 82. *Rectory, Millhams Road, Kinson, Bournemouth, Dorset.* (Northbourne 3650)

MOORE, Leonard Richard. b 22. Univ of Leeds BA 47 (2nd cl Latin). Coll of Resurr Mirfield 47. **d** 49 Kens for Lon **p** 50 Lon. C of St Mary Hendon 49-54; Stevenage (in c of St Pet Broadwater) 54-60; V of All SS Bedford 60-68; Asst Master Hendon Gr Sch 68-72; Hastingsbury Sch Kempston from 72; Publ Pr Dio St Alb from 68; C-in-c of H Trin Bedford 70-74. *22 Dart Road, Bedford.* (Bedford 57536)

MOORE, Lewis. Trin Coll Dub Div Test 34, MA 47. **d** 34 **p** 35 Oss. C of Rathdowney 34-36; Thurles 36; I of Mothel 36-39; R of Fenagh w Myshall 39-42; Chap RAFVR 42-57; RAf 47-61; Chap St Mich and St Geo Sch Iringa Centr Tang 61-63; R of Coates Northants 63-66; Umzinto 66-70 and 73-79; Richmond 70-73. *Box 237, Winklespruit, Natal, S Africa.*

MOORE, Marilyn June. b 47. St Mary's Univ Halifax NS BA 75. Wycl Coll Tor MDiv 78. **d** and **p** 80 Queb. C of All SS Seven Is Dio Queb from 80. *45 Ungava Street, Seven Islands, Que, Canada, G4R 4E4.*

MOORE, Matthew Edward George. b 38. Oak Hill **d** 77 **p** 78 Connor. C of Larne w Inver 77-80; R of Desertmartin Dio Derry from 80. *Rectory, Desertmartin, Co Derry, N Ireland.* (Magherafelt 32455)

MOORE, Mervyn. Univ of Leeds, BA (2nd cl Hist) 40. Coll of Resurr Mirfield 40. **d** 42 Hull for York **p** 43 York. C of St Martin Middlesbrough 42-45; Helmsley 45-49; V of Osbaldwick w Murton 49-54; R of Uitenhage 54-60; St Sav E Lon 60-65; St Geo Parktown 65-76; Rosebank Dio Johann from 76. *Box 52139, Saxonwold, Johannesburg, S Africa.* (011-47 3211)

MOORE, Mervyn Edward. St Paul's Coll Grahmstn LTh 65. **d** 65 **p** 66 Natal. C of St Paul Durban 67-73; CF (S Afr) from 73. *PO Box 113, Simonstown, S Africa.* (021-869)

MOORE, Canon Michael Mervlyn Hamond. b 35. Pemb Coll Ox BA 60, MA 63. Wells Th Coll 60. **d** 62 **p** 63 Lon. C of St Matt Bethnal Green 62-66; Angl Chap in Rumania, Yugoslavia and Bulgaria 66-67; Asst Gen Sec C of E Coun on Foreign Relns 67-70; Gen Sec 70-72; C of St Dunstan-in-the-W 67-73; Hon C of St Pet Walworth 73-80; Abp of Cant Chap for Foreign Relns 72-82; Can of Cant Cathl from 74. *c/o 222 Lambeth Road, SE1 7LB.*

MOORE, Norman Aubrey. AKC 35. **d** 35 **p** 36 Wakef. C of Mt Pellon 35-38; Thornhill Lees (in c of St Mary Savile Town) 38-44; V of Denby Dio Wakef from 44. *St John's Vicarage, Denby, Huddersfield, Yorks.* (Huddersfield 861270)

MOORE, Norman Butler. b 25. St Jo Coll Dur BA 50, Dipl Th 52. **d** 52 Birm **p** 53 Bp Linton for Cant. C of Aston 52-55; Gravesend 55-57; V of St Jas Aston 57-59; PC of Warley Woods 59-64; Bp's Chap for Youth and Asst Dir of Educn Dio Worc 65-66; L to Offic Dio Worc 65-66; V of Lucton w Eyton 66-69; Hazelwell 69-75; St Andr Watford Dio St Alb from 75. *64 The Avenue, Watford, Herts.* (Watford 24858)

MOORE, Paul Austin. Trin Coll Tor BA 50, BD 53. **d** 52 Bp Wells for Tor **p** 53 Niag. C of St Jo Bapt Norway Tor 52-53; Miss at St Columba St Catherine's 53-57; C of Ch Ch Cathl Hamilton 57-59; R of St Aug Hamilton 59-61; C of Ch Ch Cathl Vanc 61-63; I of St Monica Vanc W 63-66; R of St Mark Vanc 66-70; Tutor Patteson Th Centre Kohimarama 71-74; I of Lowville w Nassagaweya 74-76; R of Wainfleet w Welland Junction 76-79; Ch Ch Wainfleet 79-80; Assoc R of St Jas Port Colborne 79-80; P Assoc of St Luke Burlington Dio Niag from 80. *1382 Ontario Street, Burlington, Ont, Canada.* (416-634 5887)

MOORE, Percival Spencer. Moore Th Coll Syd. Abbott Scho 10, Barker Scho 11. Univ of Dur LTh 11. St Jo Coll Dur BA 19, MA 23. **d** 11 **p** 12 Syd. C of St John Bishopsthorpe NSW 12-13; St Jas Syd 14-16; TCF 16-19; on leave 19-20; C of All SS Petersham NSW 20-21; R of Grenfell NSW 21-24; V of Ch Ch Cathl Bal 24-34; RD of Bal 32-34; Org Sec CCCS for S Distr 34-36; Chap at Geneva 37-40; Actg R of Gosford 41-43. *Wagstaffe, NSW, Australia.*

MOORE, Canon Percy Byron. d 60 C & Goulb **p** 74 Melb. C of St Luke Canberra 60-66; C-in-c of Bungarimbil Boys' Home Tumbarumba 66-68; Perm to Offic Dio Melb 68-76; R of Maffra Dio Gippsld from 76; Can of Gippsld from 81. *Rectory, Maffra, Vic, Australia 3860.* (051-47 1056)

MOORE, Peter. b 21. Univ of Leeds BA 47. Coll of Resurr Mirfield 46. **d** 48 Southn for Win **p** 49 Win. C of N Stoneham 48-51; St Alb Copnor 51-53; V of H Trin N Shields 53-58; PC of St Mary Thetford 58-65; R of Mundford w Lynford 65-75; C-in-c of Ickburgh w Langford 65-75; C-in-c of Cranwich w Colveston 65-75; RD of Thetford 69; V of Whitley St Helen Dio Newc T from 76. *Whitley Vicarage, Hexham, Northumb.* (Slaley 379)

MOORE, Peter Albert. b 44. Univ of Queensld BEng 69, BD 76. St Francis Coll Brisb 74. **d** 75 **p** 76 Queensld. C of St John Cairns 75-78; R of Charters Towers Dio N Queensld from 78. *73 Hodgkinson Street, Charters Towers, Qld, Australia 4820.*

MOORE, Ven Peter Bonnell. Univ of W Ont BA 57. Hur Coll BTh 59. **d** 58 **p** 59 Hur. I of St Clair Beach 58-61; C of St Paul's Cathl Lon 61-67; R of St Hilda Oakville 67-70; St Thos St Catharine's 70-80; Hon Can of Niag 74-80; Archd of Wellington from 80; R of St Geo Geulph Dio Niag from 80. *99 Woolwich Street, Guelph, Ont, Canada N1H 3V1.* (519-836 2254)

MOORE, Peter Callan. b 25. Clare Coll Cam BA 49, MA 59. ACIS 56. **d** 61 **p** 62 Ox. C of All SS Highfield Ox 61-64; C-in-c of St Richard of Chich Conv Distr Hanworth Dio Lon 64-65; Min 65-71; V of St Richard of Chich Hanworth 72-78; Stowmarket Dio St E from 78; RD of Stowmarket from 81. *Vicarage, Ipswich Road, Stowmarket, Suff, IP14 1BD.* (Stowmarket 3576)

MOORE, Very Rev Peter Clement. b 24. Ch Ch Ox BA 45, MA 48, DPhil 54. Cudd Coll 45. **d** 47 Cant **p** 48 Guildf for Cant. Min Can of Cant Cathl and Asst Master Cathl Choir Sch 47-49; C of Bladon w Woodstock 49-51; Chap New Coll Ox 49-51; V of Alfrick w Lulsley 52-59; Hurd Libr to Bp of Worc 53-62; V of Pershore w Pinvin and Wick 59-67; Surr from 59-67; RD of Pershore 65-67; Can Res of Ely Cathl 67-73; Treas 69; Vice-Dean 71; Dean and R of Cathl and Abbey Ch St Alb from 73. *Deanery, St Albans, Herts.* (St Albans 52120)

MOORE, Peter Norman. b 43. Trin Coll Cam BA 65, MA 68. Westcott Ho Cam 68. **d** 73 Woolwich for S'wark. C of St Andr Catford 73-74. *60 Wellington Road, Hampton, Middx.*

MOORE, Richard Noel. b 34. Trin Coll Dub BA (Or Lang Mod) 56, MA 60. **d** 57 **p** 58 Derry. C of St Columb's Cathl Derry 57-60; I of Clondehorky 60-66; Stranorlar w Kilteevogue and Meenglas 66-76; Glendermott Dio Derry from 76. *Glendermott Rectory, Londonderry, N Ireland.* (Londonderry 3001)

MOORE, Richard Norman Theobald. b 39. Univ of St

Andr BSc 62. BD (Lon) 66. Clifton Th Coll. **d** 66 **p** 67 St E. C of Stowmarket 66-69; St Barn New Humberstone 69-72; C-in-c of the Martyrs City and Dio Leic 73; V from 73. *Martyrs' Vicarage, Westcotes Drive, Leicester, LE3 0QT.* (Leic 57769)

MOORE, Robert Allen. b 32. Univ of the Pacific BA 54. Univ of Boston STB 58, STM 59. Methodist Min 59-62. **d** and **p** 63 Minn (USA). In Amer Ch 63-80; V of Farington Dio Blackb from 80. *150 Croston Road, Farington, Preston, Lancs, PR5 3PR.* (Preston 38999)

MOORE, Canon Robert Denholm. b 23. Trin Coll Dub BA 45. **d** 46 **p** 47 Derry. C of Ch Ch Derry 46-49; Clontarf 49-53; I of Clondehorky 53-60; RD of Kilmacrenan 59-60; R of Clonleigh w Donaghmore 60-65; I of Tamlaghtfinlagan Dio Derry from 65; Can of Derry from 80. *77 Ballykelly Road, Limavady, Co Londonderry, N Ireland, BT49 9DS.* (Limavady 2743)

MOORE, Canon Robert George Chaffey. b 11. Kelham Th Coll 28. **d** 39 Linc **p** 40 Grimsby for Linc. C of St Giles Linc 39-42; Chap RAF 42-47; R of Compton Abbas 49-73; RD of Shaftesbury 58-63 and 68-73; Can and Preb of Sarum Cathl from 72; Team V of Shaston 73-77; Hon C of St Thos City and Dio Sarum from 77. *48 Rectory Road, Salisbury, SP2 7SD.*

MOORE, Ronald Spencer. b 09. Univ of Leeds BA 33. Coll of Resurr Mirfield 33. **d** 35 **p** 37 Ches. C of Ellesmere Port 35-37; L to Offic Dio Ches 37-40; C of Odd Rode (in c of Rode Heath) 40-44; V of Eaton 44-47; R of Ashton-upon-Mersey 47-59; V of Buglawton 59-63; R of Warburton 63-74. *2 Russell Avenue, Sale, Cheshire, M33 2ET.* (061-973 2157)

MOORE, Canon Ronald William Trevor. b 12. AKC 35. Sarum Th Coll 35. **d** 36 **p** 37 Derby. C of Brimington 36-40; Buxton (in c of St Jas w St Anne) 40-48; R of Newbold w Dunston 48-72; Sec Derby Dio Youth Council 42-50; Surr 59-81; M Gen Syn Derby 64-80; Hon Can of Derby 67-81; Can (Emer) from 81; RD of Chesterfield 67-72; V of Melbourne 72-81; RD of Melb 78-81. *Upper Hillside Farm, Taylor's Lane, Ashleyhay, Wirksworth, Derby.* (Wirksworth 3576)

MOORE, Stanley. St Jo Coll Dur BA 35. St Aid Coll 30. **d** 35 **p** 36 Southw. C of St Mary Bulwell 35-38; CMS Miss Dio U NIle 38-58; Hd Master High Sch Gulu 40-53; Miss At Boroboro 53-56; Gulu U Nile 56-58; Perm to Offic Dio Melb 58-62; CMS Miss Groote Eylandt 62-64; Umbacumba Miss 64-70; Chap Roper River Miss N Terr 70-73; Perm to Offic Dio Melb from 73. *9 Paddington Road, Oakleigh, Vic, Australia 3166.*

MOORE, Preb Stanley Ernest. b 10. Late Exhib of Fitzw Ho Cam 3rd cl Hist Trip pt i 32, BA (3rd cl Hist Trip pt ii) 33, MA 38. Wells Th Coll 33. **d** 34 **p** 35 Ches. C of Witton 34-36; Gt Budworth 37-38; V of Worfield 38-56; CF (R of O) from 39; R and RD of Cheadle 56-71; Preb of Lich Cathl 70-79; Preb (Emer) from 79; R of Standon 71-79; C-in-c of Croxton w Broughton 74-79; Perm to Offic Dio St E from 79. *65 Horsecroft Road, Bury St Edmunds, Suff.* (Bury St E 5005)

MOORE, Terry Chappel. b 47. BD (Lon). Trin Coll Bris 65. **d** 80 **p** 81 BC. C of St Barn Vic Dio BC from 80. *1522 Coldharbour Road, Victoria, BC, Canada, V8R 1H5.*

MOORE, Canon Thomas Frank. **d** 56 **p** 70 Alg. C of Nipigon (in c of Red Rock) 56-57; I of St Steph Thunder Bay Dio Alg from 59; Hon Can of Alg from 76. *120 Autumn Wood Road, Postal Station F, Thunder Bay, Ont., Canada.* (807-344 4865)

MOORE, Thomas Robert. b 38. TCD 65. STh (Lambeth) 79. **d** 68 **p** 69 Dub. C of Drumcondra w N Strand 68-70; St Columba Portadown 70-72; R of Kilskeery w Trillick Dio Clough from 72. *Rectory, Kilskeery, Co Tyrone, N Ireland.* (Trillick 228)

MOORE, Thomas Sydney. b 50. St Paul's Coll Grahmstn. **d** 79 **p** 80 Capetn. C of St Thos Rondebosch Dio Capetn from 79. *St Thomas Church, Campground Road, Rondebosch 7700, CP, S Africa.*

MOORE, William Ernest. Wycl Coll Tor 56. **d** and **p** 61 Tor. C of St Jas Cathl Tor 61-64; I of St Gabr Richmond Hill 65-68; R of Ch Mem Ch Oshawa 69-74; St John Pet Dio Tor from 74. *99 Brock Street, Peterborough, Ont., Canada.* (705-745 7624)

MOORE, William Henry. b 14. St Bonif Coll Warm 34. **d** 38 39 St Alb. C of St Pet Mill End 38-41; Tring 41-44; Gt Yarmouth (in c of St John) 44-46; I of Waihi 46-50; V of Prebbleton NZ 50-52; R of Houghton Conquest w Houghton Gildaple 52-56; Dundalk Ont 56-59; Filby w Thrigby 60-62; C-in-c of Mautby 60-62; Perm to Offic Dio Nor 62-71; Asst Master Mildenhall Secondary Sch 68-73; Heartsease Sch Nor 73-75; C of Mildenhall 71-73. *c/o 12 Fishley View, Acle, Norwich, NR13 3EL.*

MOORE, William James Foster. b 26. TCD BA 50. **d** 50 **p** 51 Connor. C of Glenavy 50-53; Coleraine 53-57; R of Rasharkin w Finvoy 57-66; I of St Matt Broomhedge Lisburn Dio Connor from 66. *Broomhedge Rectory, Lisburn, Co Antrim, N Ireland.* (Maze 229)

MOORE, William John. Dalhousie Univ 47. K Coll Halifax NS LTh 59. **d** and **p** 53 NS. I of Liscomb 53-58; R of Eastern Passage 58-68; St Marg of Scotld Halifax Dio NS from 68. *3761 Robie Street, Halifax, NS, Canada.* (455-2451)

MOORE, William Morris. b 33. QUB BSc 55. Trin Coll Dub. **d** 61 **p** 62 Connor. C of St Mich Belf 61-64; All SS Belf 64-70; R of St Mich Belf 70-80; St Jude Ballynafeigh Belf Dio Down from 80; RD of Mid-Belfast 79-80. *11 Bladon Avenue, Belfast, BT9 5JL, N Ireland.* (Belfast 667500)

MOORES, George. b 1885. Univ of Lon BSc 08. **d** and **p** 45 Man. C of St Mary Prestwich 45-48; V of Ch Ch Glodwick 48-51; PC of Edale 52-55; C of St Keverne 57-58; St Mich Stanwix 59-60. *69 Penrhyn Avenue, Rhos-on-Sea, Clwyd, LL28 4RD.*

MOORGAS, Geoffrey Gordon. b 30. Sarum Wells Th Coll 80. **d** 81 S'wark. C of St Matt Brixton Dio S'wark from 81. *1 St Matthew's Road, Brixton, SW2.*

MOORHEAD, Henry Robert Leishman. b 14. G and C Coll Cam BA 36, MA 54. Sarum Th Coll 66. **d** 67 **p** 68 Sarum. C of Gillingham 67-71; Perm to Offic Dio Sarum from 72. *The Old Forge, Frome St Quintin, Dorchester, Dorset, DT2 0HG.* (Evershot 548)

MOORHEAD, John Francis. K Coll Halifax NS LTh 50. **d** and **p** 50 Fred. C of St Marg Fred 50-51; CF (Canad) 51-55; C of Trin Ch St John 55-57; R of Burton 57-60; St Jude w St John 60-63; Dauphin 63-72; Exam Chap to Bp of Bran 65-72; I of Gordon w Lorne 72-76; Chatham Fred 76-79; Waterford and St Mark Dio Fred from 79. *Rectory, Sussex Corner, NB, Canada.*

MOORHOUSE, Asheleigh Edward. b 24. Univ of Manit BArch 49. SW Th Sem LTh 54. **d** and **p** 54 Milwaukee. in Amer Ch 54-69; I of St Mich AA Lon Ont 69-70. *94 Allard Street, Apt 414, Sault Ste Marie, Ont., Canada.* (705-254 7976)

MOORHOUSE, Franklin Glyndwr. b 12. Ely Th Coll 60. **d** 61 Bp Graham for Carl **p** 62 Carl. C of St Geo Barrow-F 61-66; R of Whicham w Whitbeck 66-72; V of Ravenstonedale w Newbiggin-on-Lune 72-80. *c/o Ravenstonedale Vicarage, Kirkby Stephen, Cumb, CA17 4NG.*

MOORHOUSE, Geoffrey Edgar. **d** 56 **p** 57 Melb. C of Dandenong 56-58; C-in-c of Croydon 58; Min of Diamond Creek 58-61; Lorne 61-66; C-in-c of Bayswater 66-68; I 68-79; E Kew Dio Melb from 79. *17 Hale Street, East Kew, Vic, Australia 3102.* (859-1352)

MOORHOUSE, Humphrey John. b 18. Oak Hill Th Coll 37. **d** 41 Lon **p** 42 Chelmsf. C of St Mark Dalston 41-42; St Chad Chadwell Heath 42-45; R of Vange Dio Chelmsf from 45. *782 Clay Hill Road, Basildon, Essex, SS16 4NG.* (Basildon 553248)

MOORHOUSE, Canon John Baldwin. Trin Coll Tor BA 49, LTh 52, STB 53. **d** 51 **p** 52 Edmon. C Dio Edmon 51-52; R of Wainwright 52-55; Portage la Prairie 55-59; on leave 59-60; Assoc Sec Dept of Relig Educn Angl Ch of Canada 60-65; R of St Sav Penticton 65-69; I of H Trin Winnipeg 70-74; St Aid Winnipeg Dio Rupld from 75; Can of Rupld from 76. *274 Campbell Street, Winnipeg, Manit., Canada.*

MOORHOUSE, Llewellyn Owen. b 14. Ely Th Coll 63. **d** 64 Penrith for Carl **p** 65 Carl. C of Kirkby Stephen w Mallerstang 64-66; St Geo Barrow-F Carl 66-68; V of Grayrigg 68-75; P-in-c of Sawrey 75-80. *17 Church Street, Beaumaris, Gwyn.*

MOORHOUSE, Norman. b 12. **d** 48 **p** 49 Nor. C of Tittleshall w Godwick and Wellingham 48-49; Lowestoft (in c of St Pet) 49-53; St Aug Queen's Gate Kens 53-55; Min of St Pet Distr Ch Becontree 55-59; V 59-64; St Geo Everton 64-68; Chap John Bagot Hosp 64-67; R of Rock w Heightington 68-75; Perm to Offic Dio Nor from 75. *34 Primrose Road, Thorpe Hamlet, Norwich, Norf.*

MOORHOUSE, Peter. b 42. Univ of Liv BSc 64. Linc Th Coll 79. **d** 81 Knaresborough for Ripon. C of Horsforth Dio Ripon from 81. *7 Featherbank Walk, Horsforth, Leeds, LS18 4QN.*

✠ **MOORMAN, Right Rev John Richard Humpidge.** b 05. Em Coll Cam BA 27, 2nd cl Th Trip pt i 28, MA 31, BD 41, DD 45, Hon Fell 59. Univ of Leeds Hon LittD 64. Univ of St Bonaventure USA Hon LittD 66. Westcott Ho Cam 28. **d** 29 **p** 30 Ripon. C of St Matt Holbeck 29-33; Leighton Buzzard 33-35; R of Fallowfield 35-42; Hon Chap to Bp of Man 40-44; Exam Chap 40-44; Select Pr Univ of Cam 44; Univ of Ox 63; Birkbeck Lect Trin Coll Cam 48-49; V of Lanercost w Kirkcambeck 45-46; Exam Chap to Bp of Carl 45-59; Prin of Chich Th Coll and Chan of Chich Cathl 46-56; LPr Dio Carl 47-59; Preb of Heathfield in Chich Cathl 56-59; External Exam K Coll Lon 56-58; Cons Ld Bp of Ripon in York Minster 11 June 59 by Abp of York; Bps of Dur; Sheff; Carl;

Man; Ches; Bradf; and Wakef; and others; res 75; Hale Mem Lect Evanston USA 66; Chairman Angl-RC Preparatory Comm 67-68; Pres Henry Bradshaw S from 77. *22 Springwell Road, Durham.* (Durham 63503)

MOORSE, Frank Robert. b 08. Clifton Th Coll. **d** 59 **p** 60 Ex. C of Em Plymouth 59-62; R of Dolton 63-78; C-in-c of Iddesleigh w Dowland 64-68; R 68-78; C-in-c of Monk Okehampton 65-68; R 68-78; Publ Pr Dio Ex from 78. *25 Seymour Road, Newton Abbot, Devon, TQ12 2PT.* (N Abbot 2953)

MOORSOM, Robert Coverdale. b 23. ARCM 48. Cudd Coll 49. **d** 50 **p** 51 Bradf. C of Sedbergh 50-54; Grahmstn Cathl 54-59; P-in-c of St Mark Port Eliz 59-64; V of Bierley 65-71; C of Wareham 71-79; Team V of Gillingham Dio Sarum from 79. *Vicarage, Stour Provost, Gillingham, Dorset, SP8 5RU.* (East Stour 216)

MOOSONEE, Lord Bishop of. *See* Lawrence, Right Rev Caleb James.

MOOSONEE, Lord Bishop Suffragan of. (Vacant)

MOOSONEE, Dean of. *See* Fowler, Very Rev John Richard Hart.

MOOTE, Ven Clayton Thomas Gilbert. **d** 61 **p** 62 Niag. C of Queenston 61-63; St Geo St Catherines 63-66; Kinistino 66-73; Dom Chap to bp of Sask from 71; Miss at Lac La Ronge Dio Sask from 70; Archd of Sask from 75. *Box 96, Lac La Ronge, Sask., Canada.*

MOOTI, Andereya. **d** 63 **p** 66 Ruw. P Dio Ruw. *c/o Box 37, Fort Portal, Uganda.*

MORAES, Basil Tyson. b 21. Lingnan Univ Canton BA 45. Columb Univ MA 47. Jes Coll Cam BA 56, MA 60. Wycl Hall Ox 50. **d** 52 **p** 53 Ox. C of St John Reading 52-54; St Phil Cam 54-56; Chap St Mark's Sch Hong Kong 56-63 and 72-75; Prin 63-72; P-in-c of H Nativ Ch Hong Kong 63-72; C 72-75; L to Offic Dio Hong 56-75; Chap Scargill Ho Skipton and Perm to Offic Dio Bradf 75; C of St Cath Wigan 75-77; H Trin St Helens 77-78; Hemel Hempstead (in c of St Steph) 78-81; Perm to Offic Dio St Alb from 81. *10 St Mary's Court, Hemel Hempstead, Herts, HP2 5HZ.* (Hemel Hempstead 48838)

MORAKA, Olson Mokhoane. St Pet Coll Rosettenville 54. **d** 56 **p** 57 Bloemf. P Dio Bloemf 56-75; Can of Bloemf 70-75; R of Rustenburg W 75. *Box 2, Tihabane, Pretoria, S Africa.*

MORAKINYO, Emanuel Akinkunmi. Melville Hall Oyo 34. **d** 35 **p** 36 Lagos. P Dio Lagos 35-42. *Ijebu Ode, Lagos, Nigeria.*

MORAKINYO, Erastus Aderinwale Akinboade. **d** 61 **p** 63 Ibad. P Dio Ibad 61-76. *PO Box 62, Ile-Ife, Nigeria.* (Ile-Ife 2146)

MORALES, Rafael. **d** 76 Bp Bazley for Chile. d Dio Chile. *Casilla 4, Chol-Chol, Chile.*

MORAY, ROSS and CAITHNESS, Lord Bishop of. *See* Sessford, Right Rev George Minshull.

MORAY, ROSS and CAITHNESS, Dean of. *See* Barnes, Very Rev Cyril Arthur.

MORCOM, Canon Anthony John. b 16. Clare Coll Cam 2nd cl Hist Trip pt i 37, BA (3rd cl Th Trip pt i) 38, MA 42. Cudd Coll 38. **d** 39 **p** 40 Lon. C of St Mary Magd Paddington 39-42; St Mary Bourne Street Pimlico 42-47; Dom Chap to Bp of Lon 47-55; Archd of Middx 53-66; V of St Cypr Clarence Gate St Marylebone 55-66; St Mary L Cam 66-73; RD of Cam 71-73; Can Res of Ely Cathl from 73; Treas from 76. *Powchers Hall, Ely, Cambs, CB7 4DL.* (Ely 2336)

MORCOM-HARNEIS, Canon Theophilus William. b 03. AKC and Jelf Pri 34. **d** 34 **p** 35 Lon. C of St Leon Shoreditch 34-37; Missr of St Hilda Tottenham 37-39; PC of St Jo Bapt Gt Cambridge Rd Tottenham 39-41; R of Shellingford 41-47; Actg C of Longcot w Fernham 45-47; V of St Luke Maidenhead 47-60; Surr 47-69; RD of Maidenhead 57-74; PC of Littlewick 60-69; V 69-74; Hon Can of Ch Ch Ox from 66. *9 Suzan Crescent, Wantage, Oxon, OX12 7DD.*

MORDEN, Donald Richard. b 53. Univ of Sask BA 76. Coll of Em & St Chad BTh 79. **d** 79 **p** 80 Edmon. I of Mayerthorpe Dio Edmon from 79. *PO Box 487, Mayerthorpe, Alberta, Canada, T0E 1N0.*

MORDEN, Ven John Walter Henshaw Grant. Univ of Tor BA 49. Wycl Coll Tor LTh 52, BD 53, DD (*hon causa*) 63. U Th Sem NY STM 54. Gen Th Sem NY DTh 61. **d** 51 **p** 52 Tor. C of All S Lansing Tor 51-53; on leave in USA 53-56; R of Eatonville 56-58; Asst Prof of Th Hur Coll 58-61; Prof of Th and Vice-Prin 61-62; Dean of Th 62-66; Prin from 62; Archd of Hur 69-73; Archd (Emer) from 74. *1349 Western Road, London, Ont., Canada.*

MORDI, Samuel Chiweta. b 23. **d** 73 **p** 74 Benin. P Dio Benin. *Iyi-Agor Grammar School, Box 6, Ubulu-uku, Nigeria.*

MORE, Richard David Antrobus. b 48. St Jo Coll Dur BA (Th) 70, Dipl Th 71. Cranmer Hall Dur 70. **d** 72 **p** 73 Ches. C of Macclesfield 72-77; Chap of Lee Abbey Lynton Dio Ex from 77. *Lee Abbey, Lynton, Devon.* (Lynton 2621)

MORELAND, John Ralph Hardwicke. ALCD 34. St Jo Coll Dur LTh 34, BA 36, MA 41. **d** 36 Bedford for St Alb **p** 37 St Alb. C of Watford 36-39; Beverley Minster 39-42; V of Eye 42-47; E Budleigh w Bicton 47-71. *51 Brackendale Road, Queen's Park, Bournemouth, BH8 9HY.*

MORENO, Miguel Silvano. b 08. **d** 74 N Argent. d Dio N Argent. *Parsonage, Tucumán, N Argentina.*

MORESBY, Tracy Anstruther. Univ of NZ MusB 34. **d** and **p** 35 Wai. C of Gisborne 35-38; V of Te Puke 39-40. *Pohunga Crescent, Parnall, Auckland, NZ.*

MORETON, Eric Wilson. b 03. Hatf Coll Dur LTh 27, Exhib and BA 28. St Bonif Coll Warm. **d** 29 **p** 30 S'wark. C of H Trin S Wimbledon 29-31; SPG Chap of Dhanbad Chota N 31-36; R of Cubley w Marston Montgomery 37-46; PC of Darley Abbey 46-51; UMCA Area Sec and L to Offic Dio Worc 51-57; V of N Stoke w Ipsden and Mongewell 57-69. *The Crest, Alby, Norwich, NR11 7PJ.*

MORETON, Mark. b 39. Jes Coll Cam BA 64, MA 68. Westcott Ho Cam. **d** 65 **p** 66 Portsm. C of All SS Landport Portsea 65-70; St Martin-in-the-Fields Westmr 70-72; Chap Jes Coll Cam 72-77; R of Stafford Dio Lich from 77; P-in-c of Ch Ch Stafford 77-79. *32 Rowley Avenue, Stafford, ST17 9AG.* (Stafford 58511)

MORETON, Michael Bernard. b 44. St Jo Coll Cam BA 66, MA 70. Ch Ch Ox BA 66, MA and DPhil 69. St Steph Ho Ox 66. **d** 68 Dorking for Guildf **p** 69 Bp Stannard for Guildf. C of Banstead 68-74; R of Alburgh 74-75; Denton 74-75; Middleton Cheney w Chacombe Dio Pet from 75. *Middleton Cheney Rectory, Banbury, Oxon., OX17 2NZ.* (Middleton Cheney 710254)

MORETON, Michael Joseph. b 17. Univ Coll Lon BA (2nd cl Hist) 40. Ch Ch Ox BA (2nd cl Th) 47, MA 53. Wells Th Coll 47. **d** 48 **p** 49 B & W. C of St Andr Taunton 48-52; Ilfracombe 52-59; Lect in Th Univ of Ex from 57; R of St Mary Steps City and Dio Ex from 59; Exam Chap to Bp of Ex from 61. *St Mary Steps Rectory, Matford Road, Exeter, EX2 4PE.* (Ex 77685)

MORETON, Philip Norman Harley. b 28. Linc Th Coll. **d** 57 **p** 58 York. C of Howden 57-60; Bottesford w Ashby 60-65; PC of St Giles Linc 65-70; V of Bracebridge Heath 70-77; Seasalter Dio Cant from 77. *Seasalter Vicarage, Whitstable, Kent.* (Whitstable 2798)

MORETON-JACKSON, Alfred Moreton. b 08. Univ of Bris MA 78. Qu Coll Birm 32. **d** 41 **p** 42 Lich. C of Penn Staffs 41-43; St Pet w St Nich Droitwich 43-46; R of Leigh w Bransford 46-75; Chap to High Sheriff of Worc 69-70; Dom Chap to Bp of Worc 72-75. *Falconchase, Golden Valley, Birtsmorton, Worcs, WR13 6AA.* (Birtsmorton 372)

MOREY, Preb Desmond James. b 16. Em Coll Cam 2nd cl Law Trip BA 37, MA 41. Wycl Hall, Ox 39. **d** 40 **p** 41 Roch. [Called to Bar Innr Temple 38] C of Erith 40-43; St Andr Plymouth 43-45; St Pet Norbiton 45-48; V of St John Southall 48-61; Taunton 61-81; Preb of Wells Cathl from 74. *64 Anglesey Avenue, Loose, Maidstone, Kent, ME15 9SY.* (Maidstone 46294)

MORGAN, Alan Wyndham. b 40. St D Coll Lamp BA 62. St Mich Coll Llan 62. **d** 64 **p** 65 Swan B. C of Llangyfelach w Morriston 64-69; Cockett 69-72; St Mark w St Barn Cov 72-73; Team V of Cov E Dio Cov from 73; Bp's Officer for Social Responsibility Dio Cov from 78; M Gen Syn from 80. *Corley Rectory, Tamworth Road, Corley, Coventry, CV7 8AA.* (Fillongley 40314)

MORGAN, Allen Bruce. b 42. St Mich Coll Llan 64. **d** 67 Bp T M Hughes for Llan **p** 68 Llan. C of St Jo Bapt Cardiff 67-70; Bassaleg 70-72; C-in-c of St Hilary's Conv Distr Greenway 72-75. *Address temp unknown.*

MORGAN, Arthur Boyd. b 49. Mem Univ of Newfld BA 71. Qu Coll St Jo Newfld LTh 73. **d** and **p** 73 Newfld. R of Battle Harbour 73-76; Belleoram Dio Centr Newfld from 76. *Box 9, Belleoram, Newfoundland, Canada.* (709 2311)

MORGAN, Barry Cennydd. b 47. Univ of Lon BA (Hist) 69. Selw Coll Cam BA (2nd cl Th Trip pt ii) 71, MA 75. Westcott Ho Cam 70. **d** 72 **p** 73 Llan. C of St Andr w Dinas Powis and Michaelston-le-Pit 72-75; Lect at St Mich Coll Llan and Univ of Wales 75-77; Ed Welsh Churchman from 75; Warden of Ch Hostel Ban from 77; Chap and Lect Univ Coll Ban from 77; Exam Chap to Abp of Wales from 78; L to Offic Dio Ban from 77. *Anglican Chaplaincy, Prince's Road, Bangor, Gwyn.* (Bangor 53566)

MORGAN, Basil Henry Trevor. *See* Trevor-Morgan, Basil Henry Trevor.

MORGAN, Basil Ivor. b 1887. Late Math Exhib of Jes Coll Ox BA 10, MA 13. Wycl Hall Ox and Egerton Hall Man 10. **d** 11 **p** 12 Man. C of Ch Ch Bradford 11-12; St Jas Higher Broughton 12-14; Chertsey 15-16; Chap (CCCS) of Cochin and Munaar 16-20; (ACIS) Jhelum 20-22; (Eccles Est) Nowshera 22-24; Lah Cathl 24-26; Hyderabad 27-30; furlough 26-27; 30-31; 34 and 38; Sialkot 31-34; Risalpur 34-35; Dagshai 36; Jullundur 35 and 36-39; Hazara 39-40; Karachi 41;

Ambala 41-42; Can of Lah 42-43; Perm to Offic Dio Natal from 47; Dio St D from 68. *c/o National and Grindlay's Bank, 23 Fenchurch Street, EC3P 3ED.*

MORGAN, Bernard Spencer Trevor. b 32. K Coll Lon and Warm AKC 55. **d** 56 **p** 57 Portsm. C of Havant 56-62; Yatton Keynell 62-65; R of Kessingland Dio Nor from 65; C-in-c of Mutford w Rushmere 65-67; P-in-c of Gisleham 65-67; RD of Lothingland 71-76; P-in-c of Gisleham Dio Nor from 81. *Kessingland Rectory, Lowestoft, Suff.* (Lowestoft 740256)

MORGAN, Bevil Victor. Bp Cray Th Coll Capetn 61. **d** 63 **p** 64 Capetn. C of St Phil Capetn 63-67; Bellville 67-69; R of Good Shepherd Maitland 69-76; Woodstock 76; Salt River Dio Capetn from 76. *Cecil Road, Salt River, CP, S Africa.* (55-1233)

MORGAN, Brian. b 35. Univ of Lon BA (3rd cl Cl) 58. Wells Th Coll 59. **d** 61 **p** 62 Man. C of W Withington 61-63; Rochdale 63-65; P-in-c of Mayaro w Rio Claro 65; La Brea 66-69; V of St Jas Heywood 69-74; Chap Miss to Seamen Momb 74-77; Pernis 77-78; Antwerp 78-80; V of St Chad Skerton Dio Blackb from 80. *St Chad's Vicarage, St Chad's Drive, Lancaster, LA1 2SE.* (Lanc 63816)

MORGAN, Chandos Clifford Hastings Mansel. b 20. CB 73. Jes Coll Cam BA 42, MA 46. Ridley Hall Cam 42. **d** 44 **p** 45 Roch. C of H Trin Tunbridge Wells 44-51; Staff of CSSM 47-51; Chap RN 51-75; Chap of the Fleet and Archd of the RN 72-75; Chap Dean Close Sch Cheltm from 76. *Dean Close School, Shelburne Road, Cheltenham, Glos, GL51 6HE.* (Cheltm 519275)

MORGAN, Chesney Lawrence. Univ of Manit LTh 50, BA 56. St Jo Coll Winnipeg. **d** 50 **p** 51 Bran. C of Em Ch Holland 50-51; R 51-52; The Pas 52-56; St Cuthb Winnipeg 56-60; L to Offic Dio Rupld from 60; Chap Deer Lodge Hosp Winnipeg from 70. *222 Overdale Street, St James 12, Manit., Canada.*

MORGAN, Christopher Basil. b 22. Hertf Coll Ox BA 50, MA 54. Chich Th Coll 48. **d** 51 **p** 52 Nor. C of Diss 51-52; Lowestoft 52-56; R of Hevingham Dio Nor from 56; R of Brampton Dio Nor from 56. *Hevingham Rectory, Norwich, Norf.* (Buxton 238)

MORGAN, Christopher Heudebourck. b 47. Univ of Lon Dipl Th (Extra-Mural) 70. Univ of Lanc BA 73. Kelham Th Coll 66. **d** 73 **p** 74 Leic. C of Birstall 73-76; Asst Chap H Trin Brussels 76-80; P-in-c of St Geo Redditch 80-81; Team V of The Ridge, Redditch Dio Worc from 81. *Vicarage, St George's Road, Redditch, Worcs, B98 8EE.* (Redditch 63017)

MORGAN, Christopher John. b 46. Linc Th Coll 70. **d** 72 Ox **p** 73 Buckingham for Ox. C of Earley 72-76; Epsom (in c of St Steph) 76-79; V of Stoneleigh Dio Guildf from 79. *59 Stoneleigh Park Road, Stoneleigh, Surrey, KT19 0QU.* (01-393 3738)

MORGAN, Daniel M. b 54. **d** and **p** 80 Gambia. P Dio Gambia. *Mission Anglicane, PO Box 105, Conakry, Guinea.*

MORGAN, David Farnon Charles. b 43. Univ of Leeds BA (2nd cl Phil and Th) 68. Coll of Resurr Mirfield 68. **d** 70 **p** 71 Man. C of Swinton 70-73; All SS and Martyrs Langley Man 73-75; R of St Clem Ordsall Salford Dio Man from 75. *Rectory, St Clement's Drive, Ordsall, Salford, M5 3WQ.* (061-872 0948)

MORGAN, David Joseph. b 47. Bp Burgess Hall Lamp 66. **d** 74 **p** 75 St D. C of Pembroke Dock 74-77; Burry Port w Pwll 77-80; Asst Chap Miss to Seamen Tilbury 80; Port Chap Miss to Seamen Port of Lon from 81; Publ Pr Dio Chelmsf from 81. *Missions to Seamen, Flying Angel Club, Tilbury Docks, Essex.* (Tilbury 2080)

MORGAN, David Maldwyn Lewis. b 15. M OSB. **d** 47 **p** 49 Ox. L to Offic Dio Ox from 47; C of Burnham 74-77; P-in-c of Bierton w Hulcott Dio Ox from 77. *Bierton, The Vicarage, Aylesbury, Bucks.* (Aylesbury 23920)

MORGAN, David Reginald. St D Coll Lamp. **d** 42 **p** 47 St A. C of Brymbo 42-50; Eglwys-Rhos (in c of Deganwy) 50-54; R of Brynford 54-64; V of Brymbo Bwlchgwyn 64-71; R of Llanelian (and Bettws-yn-Rhos from 74) 71-80. *c/o Llanelian Rectory, Colwyn Bay, Clwyd.* (Colwyn 55305)

MORGAN, David Watcyn. b 14. St D Coll Lamp. **d** 64 **p** 65 St D. C of Cardigan 64-69; R of Herbrandston (w St Ishmael and Hasguard from 70) Dio St D from 69. *Herbrandston Rectory, Milford Haven, Dyfed.* (Milford Haven 3263)

MORGAN, Denis. b 36. Cudd Coll 67. **d** 69 Willesden for Lon **p** 70 Lon. C of St Steph Bush Hill Pk 69-72; St Nich Stevenage 72-75; Chap Lister DG Hosp 72-75; V of St Osw Croxley Green Dio St Alb from 75. *159 Baldwins Lane, Croxley Green, Rickmansworth, Herts, WD3 3LL.* (Watford 32387)

MORGAN, Preb Dewi (David) Lewis. b 16. Univ of Wales BA 37. St Mich Coll Llan 38. **d** 39 Swan B for Llan **p** 40 Llan. C of St Andr Cardiff 39-43; Aberdare 43-46; Aberavon 46-50; Press Officer SPG from 50; Edit and Press Sec from 54; Perm to Offic Dios S'wark and Lon 51-62; Ed *St Martin's Review* 53-55; Hon Chap St Bride Fleet Street Lon 55-62; R of St Bride Fleet Street w Bridewell and H Trin Gough Square City and Dio Lon from 62; Preb of St Paul's Cathl Lon from 76; P-in-c of St Dunstan-in-the-West 78-79. *St Bride's Rectory, Fleet Street, EC 4.* (01-353 1301)

MORGAN, Donald Sinclair. Qu Coll Newfld 54. **d** 60 **p** 61 Newfld. C of Gander 60-61; St Mich AA St John's 61-64; I of Smith's Sound 64-66; C of St Mary Virg St John 66-70; R of Bell I 70-73; Rose Blanche Dio Newfld (W Newfld from 76) from 73. *PO Box 190, Rose Blanche, Newfoundland, Canada.* (709-27)

MORGAN, Canon Edgar Francis Andrew. b 07. St Jo Coll Dur BA 34, MA 38. **d** 34 **p** 35 Birm. C of St Jas Ashted 34-37; Ch Ch Weston-s-Mare 37-41; V of H Trin Bordesley 41-50; St Martin Barnehurst 50-58; Coleshill 58-75; V of Maxstoke 61-75; RD of Coleshill 67-75; Hon Can of Birm 69-75; Can (Emer) from 75. *34 Severn Avenue, Weston-super-Mare, Somt.*

MORGAN, Edward Jacob Earle. Univ of NB BA 63. Trin Coll Tor STB 68. **d** 68 **p** 69 Koot. C of Nelson 68-74; R of Londonderry-Bible Hill Dio NS from 74. *345 Pictun Road, Truro, NS, Canada.* (895-5025)

MORGAN, Evan Griffith. b 07. St D Coll Lamp. **d** 32 **p** 33 St D. C of Fishguard 32-34; Landore 34-42; R of Llanbadarn Fawr 42-50; V of St Nicholas-on-the-Hill Swansea 50-67; Surr from 51; R of Reynoldston (w Llandewi and Knelston 67-72; w Penrice from 72) 67-77. *634 Gower Road, Upper Killay, Swansea, W Glam, SA2 1EX.* (Swansea 203146)

MORGAN, Evan Tom Parry. b 10. St D Coll Lamp, BA 31. St Mich Coll Llan 32. **d** 34 **p** 35 St D. C of Llanelly 34-40; C-in-c of Walton W w Talbenny 40-41; V of Eglwyswrw w Meline 41-56; Ch Ch Llanelly 56-60; R of Llangoedmor w Llechryd 60-78. *c/o Llangoedmor Rectory, Dyfed, SA43 2LH.* (Cardigan 2414)

MORGAN, Frank Charles. b 14. Bps' Coll Cheshunt 53. **d** 54 **p** 55 Blackb. C of St John Preston 54-57; V of St Aid Bamber Bridge 57-65; St Andr Cleveleys 65-81. *27 Parkside Road, St Annes on Sea, Lancs, FY8 3SZ.*

MORGAN, Gareth Morison Kilby. b 33. Univ of Bris BA (2nd cl Hist) 56. Cudd Coll 57. U Th Sem Bangalore 59. **d** 61 **p** 62 S'wark. C of St Pet St Helier 61-65; Chap Scargill Conf Ho Kettlewell 65-70; Asst Dir of Educn Dio Linc 71-74; Dir of Educn and L to Offic Dio St E 74-81; Team R of Hanley Dio Lich from 81. *Rectory, Harding Road, Hanley, Stoke-on-Trent, ST1 3BQ.* (0782-266031)

MORGAN, Geoffrey. b 51. AKC 72. St Aug Coll Cant 73. **d** 74 **p** 75 Man. C of The Ascen Hulme Man 74-77; Nantwich 77-79; Bp's Hatfield Dio St Alb from 79. *31 Homestead Road, Hatfield, Herts.* (Hatfield 62897)

MORGAN, Gerald. b 16. St Mich Coll Llan 46. **d** 47 **p** 48 Llan. C of Glyntaff 47-52; Townstal w St Sav Dartmouth 52-54; Org Sec Miss to Seamen E Distr 54-57; Chap Miss to Seamen Newport and Cardiff and Org Sec for Wales 57-64; Chap Shoreham Harbour and SE Area Sec 64-70; V of Marystowe w Coryton (and Stowford, Lew-Trenchard and Thrushelton from 79) 70-81; P-in-c of Lew Trenchard w Thrushelton 78-79; Stowford 78-79; Hon C of Braunton w Saunton Dio Ex from 82. *St Anne's Parsonage, Saunton, Braunton, Devon.* (Braunton 812412)

MORGAN, Gerallt. b 12. St Cath S Ox BA 47. MA 51. Wycl Hall Ox. **d** 47 **p** 48 Pet. C of St Giles Northtn 47-51; C-in-c of St Hilda's Conv Distr Hunts Cross 51-57; V 57-59; St Andr Southport 59-65; R of Whiston 65-78. *7 Heathwood Avenue, Barton-on-Sea, New Milton, Hants, BH25 7LW.*

MORGAN, Glyn. b 33. Univ of Wales BA 55, MA 69. Coll of Resurr Mirfield. **d** 57 **p** 58 Ban. C of Dolgellau 57-60; Conway 60-63; V of Corris 63-68; Asst Master Friars Sch Ban 69-70; Oswestry Boys' Sch 70-74; Oswestry High Sch for Girls 74-79; Fitzalan Sch Oswestry from 79; C of H Trin Oswestry 71-79; L to Offic Dio Ban from 70. *Hawthorns, Weston Lane, Oswestry, Salop.* (Oswestry 5817)

MORGAN, Glyn. b 21. Oakhill Coll 73. **d** 76 **p** 77 Pet. C of Barton Seagrave w Warkton Dio Pet from 76. *St Edmund's House, Warkton, Kettering, Northants.*

MORGAN, Grenville. b 15. Univ of Leeds BA (2nd cl Latin) 40. Coll of Resurr Mirfield 40. **d** 42 **p** 43 Southw. C of St Mary Magd Newark 42-45; PV of Southw Minster 45-46; Dioc Dir of Youth Dio Southw 46-47; V of Dallington 47-60; Market Drayton 60-72; R of Adderley 60-72; RD of Hodnet 60-72; Surr 60-72; V of Finchingfield w Cornish Hall End 72-80. *12 Ramsey Close, Canterbury, Kent.* (Cant 57904)

MORGAN, Gwilym Howell Rowland. Univ of Wales (Cardiff) BA 39. Clifton Th Coll 40. **d** 41 **p** 42 Llan. C of St Cath Canton 41-44; TCF 44-48; C of St Mary Haverfordwest 48-51; Chap HM Pris Maidstone 51-53; HM Pris Leyhill 53-58; V of Tidenham w Beachley and Lancaut 58-75; R of Tibberton w Taynton 75-80. *1 Elm Court, Woolaston, Lydney, Glos.*

MORGAN, Canon Gwilym Owen. b 17. Univ of Lon BSc (2nd cl Econ) 47. Westcott Ho Cam 46. **d** 48 **p** 49 Man. C of

Bury 48-51; Chap Salford R Hosp 51-71; R of St Phil Salford (w St Steph from 59) 51-71; St Steph Salford 54-59; Proc Conv Man 57-80; ACCM from 58; RD of Salford 57-71; Hon Can of Man 62-71; Can Res of Man Cathl from 71; Sub-Dean from 72; Bp's Adv on Hosp Chaps from 72. *20 Lyndhurst Road, Manchester, M20 0AA.* (061-434 2732)

MORGAN, Harold Evan. b 17. Late Scho and Exhib of St D Coll Lamp BA (2nd cl Engl) 38. **d** 40 **p** 41 Birm. C of Oldbury 40-42; Northleach 42-43; CF(EC) 43-47; V of Milford 47-50; R of Yerbeston w Loveston 50-51; C-in-c of Uzmaston w Boulston 51-53; R of Llanilid w Pencoed 53-68; V of Newc Dio Llan from 68. *Vicarage, St Leonard's Road, Bridgend, Mid Glam.* (Bridgend 3553)

MORGAN, Harold Vincent. Univ of Wales (Swansea) BA 45, BD 49. St Mich Coll Llan 51. **d** 53 **p** 54 Ban. C of Llangefni w Tregaian 53-55; Rhymney 55-57; Aberdare 57-59; V of Nantymoel 59-61. *20 Scott Avenue, Weddington, Nuneaton, Warws.*

MORGAN, Hector. b 03. Bp's Coll Calc 29. **d** 30 Rang **p** 32 Cant for Col Bp. Perm to Offic at H Trin Sheerness 32; Asst Chap Cathl Ch Rang 30-31 and 33; Chap at Insein 33-36; R of Pickwell w Leesthorpe 36-43; V of Owston w Withcote R 38-43; CF (TA) - R of O) from 39; V of Goodmayes 43-47; Surr 47; V of Shapwick w Ashcott 47-55; St Luke New Kentish Town (w St Paul Camden Square from 56) 55-61; H Trin S Wimbledon 61-65; R of Barton-Mills 65-68. *Abbots Loft, The Manor, Dod Lane, Glastonbury, Somt.*

MORGAN, Henry. b 45. Hertf Ox BA (2nd cl Th) 68. Westcott Ho Cam 68. **d** 70 **p** 71 S'wark. C of St Marg Lee 70-73; St Paul Lorrimore Sq Newington 73-75; St Mich AA w All S and Em Camberwell Dio S'wark from 75. *St Michael's Vicarage, Bethwin Road, SE5.* (01-701 2456)

MORGAN, Preb Hubert Charles Trevor. b 05. St D Coll Lamp BA 31. **d** 31 Bp De Salis for B & W **p** 32 B & W. C of St Luke S Lyncombe 31-36; V of Wedmore 36-70; RD of Axbridge 45-67; Preb of Wells Cathl from 56. *5 Abbey Close, Wookey, Wells, Somt.* (Wells 72526)

MORGAN, James Edward. Qu Coll Newfld. **d** 32 **p** 33 Newfld. I of Tack's Beach 32-34; Heart's Delight 34-42; Chap RCN 42-45; I of Exploits 45-48; Miss at St Martin and Black River 48-52; R of Derby w Blackville 52-74. *RR2, Chatham, NB, Canada.*

MORGAN, John Aeron. St D Coll Lamp. **d** 40 **p** 41 St D. C of Pembrey 40-52; Ch Stretton 52-62; R of Harley w Kenley 62-73; C-in-c of Hughley 65-73; V of Pencarreg w Llanycrwys Dio St D from 73. *Pencarreg Vicarage, Lampeter, Dyfed.* (Lampeter 221)

MORGAN, John Geoffrey Basil. b 21. Wells Th Coll 59. **d** 60 **p** 61 Sarum. C of Oakdale 60-64; St Mark Talbot Village (in c of St Thos Ensbury Pk) 64-67; Min of St Thos Eccles Distr Ensbury 67-69; V of St Thos Ensbury Dio Sarum from 69. *42 Coombe Avenue, Bournemouth, Dorset.* (Bournemouth 514286)

MORGAN, John Laurence. b 41. Univ of Melb BA (2nd cl Hist) 62. Or Coll Ox BA (2nd cl Th) 69, MA 73. **d** 68 Gippsld **p** 69 Ox for Gippsld. Actg Chap Or Coll Ox 69; Chap 70-78. *University of Melbourne, Parkville, Vic, Australia 3052.*

MORGAN, John Roland. b 31. Univ of Birm BA (2nd cl Th) 54. Bps' Coll Cheshunt 54. **d** 55 **p** 56 Birm. C of Selly Oak 55-57; Yardley Wood 57-58; Hamstead 58-61; V of St Chad Smethwick 61-68; Balsall Common Dio Birm from 68. *St Peter's House, Balsall Common, Coventry, CV7 7EA.* (Berkswell 32721)

MORGAN, John William Miller. b 34. Univ of Lon BSc 56. Wycl Hall Ox 61. **d** 63 **p** 64 St Alb. C of Ch Ch St Alb 63-68; V of St Matt Luton 68-79; Mangotsfield Dio Bris from 79. *Mangotsfield Vicarage, Bristol, BS17 3JA.* (Bris 560510)

MORGAN, Kenneth James. b 14. Selw Coll Cam BA 36. MA 43. Wells Th Coll 36. **d** 38 Lewes for Chich **p** 39 Chich. C of Moulsecoomb 38-40; Preston 40-41; Chap RAFVR 41-47; Chap Miss to Seamen Tyne Station and L to Offic Dio Dur 47; Chap at Oslo Norway 47-51; V of Ch Ch Blacklands Hastings 51-58; V of St Jo Evang Weston Bath 58-66; Shalford Dio Guildf from 66. *Shalford Vicarage, East Shalford Lane, Guildford, Surrey, GU4 8AE.* (Guildford 62396)

MORGAN, Martin Paul. b 46. St Steph Ho Ox 71. **d** 73 **p** 74 Pet. C of St Mary Virg Kettering 73-76; Fareham 76-79; V of Ch of Ascen Portsea Dio Portsm from 80. *Vicarage, Kirby Road, Portsmouth, Hants, PO2 0PW.* (Portsm 660123)

MORGAN, Mervyn Thomas. b 24. Ch Coll Cam BA 48, MA 71. Chich Th Coll 79. **d** 80 Chich **p** 81 Lewes for Chich (APM). C of Lewes 80-81; Glynde w W Firle & Beddingham Dio Chich 81-82; P-in-c from 82. *The Parsonage, Firle, Lewes, BN8 6NP.* (Glynde 227)

MORGAN, Michael. b 32. Univ of Lon BSc 57, MSc 67, PhD 63. FRIC 68. **d** 74 **p** 75 Portsm (APM). C of Portsdown Dio Portsm from 74. *33 Mansvid Avenue, Cosham, Portsmouth, PO6 2LX.*

MORGAN, Morley Roland. b 47. St D Coll Lamp BA 76. St Steph Ho Ox 76. **d** 77 Llan **p** 78 Bp Reece for Llan. C of Merthyr Dyfan 77-78; Llantrisant 78-80; Team V of Caludon Dio Cov from 80. *14 St Austell Road, Wyken, Coventry, W Midl, CV2 5AE.* (Cov 445029)

MORGAN, Murray Charles. b 46. St Jo Coll Auckld 68. **d** 71 **p** 72 Auckld. C of Whangarei 73-74; Mangere 74-77; Picton Dio Nel from 77. *Vicarage, Picton, NZ.*

MORGAN, Nicholas John. b 50. AKC and BD 71. St Aug Coll Cant 72. **d** 73 Man **p** 74 Hulme for Man. C of Woodhouse Pk 73-76; Southam w Stockton 76-79; V of Brailes w Winderton Dio Cov from 79; R of Sutton-under-Brailes Dio Cov from 79. *Brailes Vicarage, Banbury, Oxon, OX15 5HT.* (Brailes 230)

MORGAN, Canon Oliver Constant McDowall. St D Coll Lamp LDiv 23. **d** 23 **p** 24 Chelmsf. C of St Sav Westcliff-on-Sea 23-25; St Mich Cricklewood 25-27; Reigate 27-32; V of Billesdon w Rolleston and Goadby 32-37; St Andr Watford 37-46; St Marg w Ch Ch Ward End 46-59; RD of E Birm 48-58; Yardley 58-59; Hon Can of Birm 54-59; Cov 65-70; Can (Emer) from 70; V of St Mary Warw 59-70; C-in-c of Sherbourne 69-70; Surr 61-70; Perm to Offic Dio Heref 70-73; Dio Mon 71-73; Dio Birm 73; Dio Cov from 74; Hon Chap Birm Cathl from 76. *96 Knightsbridge Road, Olton, Solihull, W Midl, B92 8RB.* (021-743 3385)

MORGAN, Owen. b 06. St Mich Coll Llan 51. **d** 53 **p** 54 Ban. C of Llanidan w Llanddaniel-fab 53-55; Festiniog w Maentwrog 55-57; R of Llanbrynmair w Dylife 57-63; V of Penisarwaen w Llanddeiniolen 63-74. *6 Goronwy Street, Gerlan, Bethesda, Gwynedd.*

MORGAN, Peter Birkett. b 30. Ch Ch Ox BA (2nd cl Hist) 52, MA and BLitt 61. Ripon Hall Ox 52. **d** 56 **p** 57 Lon. C of St Marylebone 56-60; V of Wealdstone 60-69; Enfield Dio Lon from 69; RD of Enfield from 82. *Vicarage, Silver Street, Enfield, EN1 3EG.* (01-363 8676)

MORGAN, Philip. b 51. Univ Coll Cardiff BD 78. BSc (Lon) 75. St Mich AA Llan 75. **d** 78 **p** 79 Swan B. C of St Nich-on-the-Hill Swansea 78-81; Morriston Dio Swan B from 81. *8 Heol Rhosyn, Clasemont Park, Morriston, Swansea, W Glam.* (Swan 71866)

MORGAN, Canon Philip Brendan. b 35. G and C Coll Cam BA 59, MA 63. Wells Th Coll 59. **d** 61 **p** 62 Lon. C of Ch Ch Lanc Gate 61-66; V in Trunch Group 66-68; P-in-c of St Steph Nor 68-72; Sacr of Nor Cathl 72-74; Can and Sub-Dean of St Alb 74-81; R of Bushey Dio St Alb from 81; Hon Can of St Alb Cathl from 81. *Rectory, High Street, Bushey, Watford, WD2 1BD.* (01-950 1546)

MORGAN, Philip Reginald Strange. b 27. St D Coll Lamp BA (2nd cl Hist) 51. Keble Coll Ox BA (3rd cl Th) 53, MA 57. Wells Th Coll 57. **d** 57 **p** 58 Mon. C of Fleur-de-Lys 57-59; Bassaleg 59-62; V of Dingestow (w Wonastow to 65; w Penrhos from 65) 62-66; R of Machen (w Rudry to 75) 66-76; V of Llangattock-juxta-Caerleon Dio Mon from 76. *Caerleon Vicarage, Newport, Gwent.* (Caerleon 420248)

MORGAN, Philip Richard Llewelyn. b 27. Wadh Coll Ox BA (3rd cl Mod Hist) 50, MA 52. St Steph Ho Ox 53. **d** 55 **p** 56 S'wark. C of Warlingham 55-58; Chap Haileybury and Imperial Service Coll 58-73; Hd Master Haileybury Jun Sch Dio Oxon from 74. *Clewer Manor, Windsor, Berks, SL4 3RS.* (Windsor 66330)

MORGAN, Reginald Graham. b 25. St D Coll Lamp BA 46, LTh 48. **d** 48 St D for St A **p** 49 St A. C of Chirk 48-50; Llangollen w Trevor 50-55; R of Llanwyddelan w Manafon 55-66; V of Rhuddlan Dio St A from 66; RD of St A from 78. *Vicarage, Rhuddlan, Clwyd.* (Rhuddlan 590402)

MORGAN, Reginald Graham Tharle. b 46. St Jo Coll Nottm LTh 75. **d** 75 Leic **p** 76 Bp Mort for Leic. C of Oadby 75-79; St Agnes Kloof Dio Natal from 79. *Box 33, Kloof, Natal 3640, S Africa.*

MORGAN, Richard Dennis. Univ of BC BA 63. Angl Th Coll BC STB 66. **d** 66 **p** 68 New Westmr. C of St John Vancouver 66-68; I of Gibsons 69-71; V of St Mary Virg Vancouver Dio New Westmr from 71. *6414 Chester Street, Vancouver 15, BC, Canada.*

MORGAN, Robert Chowen. b 40. Late Scho of St Cath Coll Cam 1st cl Th Trip pt i 61, BA (2nd cl Th Trip pt ii) 63, 1st Cl Th Trip pt iii 64. St Chad's Coll Dur 64. **d** 66 Lanc for Blackb **p** 67 Blackb. C of Lancaster 66-76; Lect Univ of Lanc 67-75; Sen Lect 76; Lect Univ of Ox and Fell of Linacre Coll from 76. *37 Hugh Allen Crescent, Marston, Oxford, OX3 0HL.* (Oxford 721566)

MORGAN, Robert Harman. b 28. Univ of Wales BA 55. Coll of Resurr Mirfield 55. **d** 57 Mon for Wales **p** 58 Llan. C of Penarth w Lavernock 57-61; Caeru w Ely 61-67; V of Glan Ely Dio Llan from 67. *Vicarage, Grand Avenue, Ely, Cardiff, S Glam.* (Cardiff 591633)

MORGAN, Robert Oscar Thomas. b 05. Univ of Wales, BA 27. St Mich Coll Llan 30. **d** 30 **p** 31 Ban. C of Amlwch 30-34; Eglwys-rhos 34-36; Rhosddu 36-39; R of Pont Robert 39-44; V of Glascombe w Rhulen 44-48; Org Sec Miss to

Seamen E Distr 48-54; NW Distr (Dios Blackb; Carl and Man) 54-57; Miss to Seamen Dio Momb 57-61; Area Sec NW Distr 61-64; Chap Dunkirk and N France 64-71; L to Offic Dio Blackb from 78. *84 Palatine Avenue, Lancaster.* (Lanc 66777)

MORGAN, Roger. b 32. Univ of Bris BA 59. Tyndale Hall Bris 56. **d** 61 **p** 62 Lon. C of St Cuthb Chitts Hill Wood Green 61-64; R of Kingham (and Daylesford from 69) 64-78; C-in-c of Sarsden w Churchill 74-78; V of St Cuthb W Hampstead Dio Lon from 78. *13 Kingscroft Road, NW2 3QE.* (01-452 1913)

MORGAN, Roger William. b 40. Merton Coll Ox BA 62. Univ of Cam MA 67. Ridley Hall Cam 80. **d** 81 Ely (APM). Fell of CCC Cam from 67; C of St Paul Cam Dio Ely from 81. *11 Emmanuel Road, Cambridge.*

MORGAN, Samuel. b 07. St D Coll Lamp BA 32. **d** 32 **p** 33 St D. C of Llandyssul 32-35; Chap (S Amer MS) of Chubut Welsh Coll 35-42; V of Llanwenog w Llanwnen 42-64; RD of Lampeter 54-64; V of Felinfoel 64-77; RD of Kidwelly 72-77; Can of St D 72-79. *10 Ty'rfran Avenue, Llanelli, Dyfed.* (Llanelli 2977)

MORGAN, Samuel. b 32. **d** 74 **p** 78 Gambia. P Dio Gambia. *Eglise de la Toussaint, Mission Anglicane, Box 105, Conakry, Guinea, W Africa.*

MORGAN, Steve Shelley. b 48. Univ of Wales Dipl Th 70. St Mich Coll Llan 67. **d** 71 **p** 72 Llan. C of Llan Cathl 71-74; Llanharan w Peterstone 71-74; Neath w Llantwit 74-77; S Wales Area Sec Div Healing Miss from 74; V in R Benef of Merthyr Tydfil and Cyfarthfa Dio Llan from 77. *Christchurch Vicarage, Georgetown, Cyfarthfa, Merthyr Tydfil, Mid Glam.* (0685-71995)

MORGAN, Thomas Curtis. b 12. Univ of Wales BA 41. St D Coll Lamp 41. **d** 43 **p** 44 Llan. C of Cadoxton-juxta-Neath 43-47; Oakwood 47-52; Penhow and St Bride Netherwent 52-54; R of Panteg w Llanddewi-Fach and Llandegveth Dio Mon from 54. *Panteg Rectory, Pontypool, NP4 5TS.* (Pontypool 3724)

MORGAN, Thomas Frederick. Ridley Coll Melb ACT ThL 53. **d** 53 Bunb for Melb **p** 54 Melb. C of Coburg 53-55; V of Beech Forest w Apollo Bay 55-61; I of St Aug Moreland 61-68; V of Doncaster Dio Melb from 68. *106 Church Road, Doncaster, Vic, Australia 3108.* (03-848 1139)

MORGAN, Thomas John Walford. b 16. Univ of Wales BA (French) 37. St D Coll Lamp 37. **d** 39 Ban for Llan **p** 40 Llan. C of Roath 39-42; Heavitree 42-45; Merton 45-5o; CF 50-71; V of Swallowfield 71-81. *7 Mateo Drive, Tiburon, California 94920, USA.*

MORGAN, Canon Thomas Meurig. St D Coll Lamp BA 32. **d** 32 **p** 33 St A. C of Llanrhaiadr yn Mochnant 32-37; Llangystenyn 37-39; R of Garthbeibio 39-49; V of Meifod (w Llangynyw from 61) 49-76; RD of Caereinior from 56; Cursal Can of St A Cathl 69-76; Can (Emer) from 76. *Vicarage, Dolanog, Welshpool, Powys.*

MORGAN, Thomas Oliver. Univ of Sask BA 62. BD (Lon) 65. Tyndale Hall, Bris 62. **d** 66 Lanc for Blackb **p** 67 Blackb. C of Ch of the Sav Blackb 66-69; I of Porcupine Plain 69-73; Kinistino and Fort La Corne 73-77; Shellbrook Dio Sask from 77; Exam Chap to Bp of Sask from 79. *Box 352 Shellbrook, Sask., Canada.*

MORGAN, Thomas Scott. b 20. ACP 67. R Mil Coll Sandhurst. Oak Hill Th Coll. **d** 51 **p** 52 S'wark. C of St Jo Evang Blackheath 51-54; Perm to Offic Dio St Alb from 80. *Old Stocks, Chenies Road, Chorley Wood, Herts, WD3 5LY.* (Chorley Wood 3232)

MORGAN, Trevor. b 12. Univ of Wales (Swansea) BA 37. St Mich Coll Llan 44. **d** 44 **p** 45 St A. [f Min in Presb Ch of Wales] C of Llanrhaiadr-ym-Mochnant w Llanarmon 44-46; Caerphilly 46-48; Walsall 48-52; V of Gt Wyrley 52-60; Almeley 60-66; R of Moreton-on-Lugg w Pipe and Lyde 66-77. *Address temp unknown.*

MORGAN, William Badham. b 40. Univ of Wales (Cardiff) BSc (Econ) 65. Ripon Hall Ox 70. **d** 72 **p** 73 Llan. C of Merthyr Tydfil 72-76; P-in-c of Penydarren Dio Llan from 76. *Vicarage, Penydarren, Merthyr Tydfil, Mid Glam.* (Merthyr Tydfil 5559)

MORGAN, William Charles Gerwyn. St D Coll Lamp BA 52. St Mich Coll Llan 52. **d** 56 **p** 57 St D. C of Hubberston 56-62; V of Ambleston w St Dogwells 62-68; Fishguard w Llanychaer Dio St D from 68. *Vicarage, Fishguard, Dyfed.* (Fishguard 2895)

MORGAN, William John. b 11. St D Coll Lamp BA 42. **d** 43 **p** 44 Llan. C of St John Miskin 43-47; Coity w Nolton 47-56; V of Cilfynydd 56-68; R of Llanilid w Pencoed 68-78. *6 St Paul's Court, Heol Fair, Llandaff, Cardiff, CF5 2ES.*

MORGAN, William John. b 38. Selw Coll Cam BA 62, MA 66. Cudd Coll 62. **d** 65 **p** 66 Llan. C of St Jo Bapt Cardiff 65-68; Asst Chap Univ Coll Cardiff 68-70; Perm to Offic Dio Lon 70-73; C of Ch Ch Albany Street St Pancras 73-78; P-in-c of St Dunstan E Acton Dio Lon 78-80; V (w St Thos) from 80. *Vicarage, Perryn Road, W3 7NA.* (01-743 4117)

MORGAN, William Stanley Timothy. b 41. St D Coll Lamp BA 63. Wycl Hall Ox 63. **d** 66 Llan for St D **p** 67 St D. C of St Mich AA Aberystwyth 66-69; V of Ambleston w St Dogwell 69-74; R of E Walton w Llysyfran 70-74; V of Llannon 74-80; Lampeter Dio St D from 80. *Vicarage, Lampeter, Dyfed.* (Lampeter 422460)

MORGAN, Winston Kenneth. St Francis Coll Brisb. **d** and **p** 57 Graft. C of Lismore 57-62; V of Caboolture 62-63; Pine Rivers 63-65; C of Ch of Annunc Camp Hill Brisb 65-66. *210 Pacific Highway, South Murwillumbah, NSW, Australia.*

MORGAN-JONES, Christopher John. b 43. Univ of Bris BA 66. Univ of Chicago MBA 68. McMaster Univ Ont MA 69. Cudd Coll 70. **d** 73 **p** 74 Cant. C of St Sav Folkestone 73-76; P-in-c of Swalecliffe 76-81; V of Addington Dio Cant from 82. *Addington Vicarage, Spout Hill, Croydon, CR0 5AN.* (Lodge Hill 42167)

MORGAN-JONES, Richard James. b 46. Em Coll Cam BA 68. Ripon Hall Ox 73. **d** 75 Tonbridge for Roch **p** 76 Roch. C of St Mark Bromley 75-77; Perm to Offic Dio Roch 77-81. *15 Wendover Road, Bromley, Kent.*

MORGANS, Thomas. St D Coll Lamp BA 12. St Mich Coll Llan 12. **d** 12 **p** 14 St D. C of Llansadwrn w Llanwrda 12-15; served in RAMC 15-19; C of Llangathen (in c of Court Henry) 19-23; V of Taliaris 23-33; R of Jeffreyston w Reynalton 33-46; V of Penally 46-52. *Address temp unknown.*

MORIARTY, William Warren. Univ of Syd MSc 51. Univ of Melb BA 60. ACT ThL (2nd cl) 58. **d** 60 **p** 61 Melb. C of Brunswick 60-61; Glenroy 61-62; Footscray 62; Min of Altona 62-66; C of Melb Dioc Centre 66-70; Perm to Offic Dio Melb from 70. *30 Rowen Street, Burwood, Vic, Australia 3125.* (20-4587)

MORISON, Ernest Harvey. St Aug Coll Cant 05. **d** 09 **p** 10 St Alb. C of L Ilford 09-11; Asst Miss of St Mich Miss Hershel 11-15; Miss-in-c 17-26; St Matt Miss Keiskama Hoek 15-17; Miss at St Chad King William's Town 25-29; V of Nigel 29-32; R of Modderfontein 32-35; P-in-c of St Cypr Native Miss Johann 35; R of L Burstead 35-52; C of St Mary-in-the-Marsh (in c of All SS St Mary's Bay) 52-54. *c/o Barclays Bank, 73 Oxford Street, East London, CP, S Africa.*

MORISON, Canon John Donald. b 34. ALCD (2nd cl) 60. **d** 61 **p** 62 Chelmsf. C of Rayleigh 61-64; St Austell 64-67; V of Meltham Mills 67-71; Youth Chap Dio Cov 71-76; Dir of Relig Educn and Miss Dio Port Eliz from 76; Chap Univ of Port Eliz from 77; Can of Port Eliz from 80. *2 Brebner Street, Parson's Hill, Port Elizabeth, CP, S Africa.*

MORLEY, Athelstan John. b 29. Linc Coll Ox BA 52, MA 56. Ridley Hall Cam. **d** 54 **p** 55 S'wark. C of St Matt Surbiton 54-57; Succr of Chelmsf Cathl Ch 57-60; Prec 60; R of Mistley w Manningtree and Chap Royal E Cos Hosp 60-69; Hadleigh Dio Chelmsf from 69; Ed 'Essex Churchman' 68-75; Hon Sec Essex Chs Support Trust from 78. *50 Rectory Road, Hadleigh, Benfleet, Essex, SS7 2ND.* (Southend 558992)

MORLEY, Edward Paul. Wycl Coll Tor 42. Bp Snell's Dioc Tr Sch 59. **d** 62 **p** 63 Tor. C of Ch Ch Brampton 62-64; I of St Matt Ap Oriole City and Dio Tor from 64. *70 George Henry Boulevard, Willowdale, Ont., Canada.* (416-447 4194)

MORLEY, Frank. b 15. Worc Ordin Coll 63. **d** 65 **p** 66 Sarum. C of Melksham 65-68; V of Overton w Fyfield and E Kennett 68-73; Urchfont w Stert 74-81; C of Much Birch w L Birch, Much Dewchurch, Llanwarne and Llandinabo Dio Heref from 81. *St David's House, Copper Beeches Close, Much Dewchurch, Hereford, HR2 8DX.* (0981-540734)

MORLEY, George Ashley. Wycl Coll Tor. **d** 58 **p** 59 Tor. I of St Andr Tor 58-59; C of St Timothy Tor 59-63; I of St Barn Tor 63-65; Otonabee Dio Tor from 65; St Alb Pet 65-73; Stony Lake 73-74; Dixie 74-81; on leave. *1805-1300 Bloor Street West, Mississauga, Ont, Canada.* (416-277 0462)

MORLEY, Henry Brian Standen. b 27. Selw Coll Cam BA 51, MA 55. Ridley Hall Cam 51. **d** 53 **p** 54 Pet. C of St Pet Rushden 53-56; Edgware 56-59; Min of St Luke Eccles Distr Watford 59-65; PC of St Jo Evang Wimborne 65-68; V 68-78; H Trin Skirbeck 78-80; Lindfield Dio Chich from 80. *Vicarage, Lindfield, Haywards Heath, W Sussex, RH16 2HR.* (Lindfield 2386)

MORLEY, John. b 43. St Deiniol's Libr Hawarden. **d** 68 Bp J D McKie for Cov **p** 69 Bp Daly for Cov. C of Newbold-on-Avon 68-73; Solihull (in c of St Francis Elmdon Heath) 73-77; Chap RAF from 77. *c/o Ministry of Defence, Adastral House, WC1.*

MORLEY, Ven John Sydney. St Jo Coll Morpeth, 58. **d** 61 **p** 62 Adel. C of Ch Ch Adel 61-62; Chap AMF 62-72 and from 77; P-in-c of Parkside and Chap Mental Hosp Parkside 63-68; R of Kadina 68-74; Burra 74-75; Mt Barker 75-79; Murray Bridge Dio Murray from 79; Archd of The Murray from 79; Exam Chap to Bp of The Murray from 79. *8 Mannum Road, Murray Bridge, S Australia 5253.* (085-32 2275)

MORLEY, Keith. b 44. St Chad's Coll Dur BA (2nd cl Th)

66, Dipl Th 67. **d** 67 Birm **p** 68 Aston for Birm. C of St Mich AA S Yardley 67-70; Solihull (in c of St Francis Elmdon Heath) 70-73; V of St Mary and St John Shaw Hill, Saltley Birm 73-77; Lavington (or Lenton) w Osgodby, Keisby, Hanby and Ingoldsby 77-79; P-in-c of Bassingthorpe w Westby and Bitchfield 77-79; Burton-le-Coggles 77-79; R of Boothby Pagnell 77-79; Ingoldsby w Lavington (or Lenton), Osgodby, Keisby, Hanby, Bassingthorpe, Westby, Bitchfield, Burton-le-Coggles and Boothby Pagnell Dio Linc from 79. *Ingoldsby Rectory, Grantham, Lincs, NG33 4EW.* (047-685 699)

MORLEY, Keith Dudley. Moore Th Coll Syd ACT ThL 61. **d** 62 **p** 63 Tas. C of Glenorchy 62-65; Guildford 65-67; R of Smithfield 67-74; Maroubra Dio Syd from 74. *341 Maroubra Road, Maroubra, NSW, Australia 2035.* (349-2160)

MORLEY, Canon Leonard. b 04. Egerton Hall, Man 35. **d** 37 **p** 38 Man. C of All S Bolton-le-Moors 37-40; Padiham (in c of Higham) 40-43; C-in-c of All SS Blackpool 43-46; V of Timperley 46-56; PC of Kingsley Ches 56-68; V 68-72; RD of Frodsham 61-72; Hon Can of Ches 69-72; Can (Emer) from 72; Perm to Offic Dio Cant from 79. *12 Ghyllside Road, Northiam, Rye, Sussex.* (Northiam 2324)

MORLEY, Canon Leslie James. b 45. K Coll Lon and Warm AKC and BD 67, MTh 68. **d** 69 **p** 70 Birm. C of St Pet Birm 69-72; St Mary Boltons Kens 72-74; Chap Univ of Nottm 74-80; Can Res of Southw Minster from 80; Dir of Post-Ordin Tr from 80. *5 Vicar's Court, Southwell, Notts, NG25 0HP.* (Southwell 815056)

MORLEY, Philip Charles. b 51. Trin Coll Tor MDiv 78. **d** 78 Tor. C of Ch Ch Scarborough Tor 78-79; Richvale 79-80; I of Coldwater-Medonte Dio Tor from 80. *Box 132, Coldwater, Ont, Canada.*

MORLEY, Terence Martin Simon. b 49. St Steph Ho Ox 71. **d** 74 **p** 75 York. C of St Alb Hull 74-76; Middlesbrough 76-77; Perm to Offic Dio Dur 77-78; Hon C of St Andr Worthing 78-80; C of St Patr Hove Dio Chich from 80. *The Flat, St Patrick's Vicarage, Cambridge Road, Hove, E Sussex.* (0273-735430)

MORLEY, Trevor. b 39. Univ of Man BSc 62. MPS 62. Ripon Hall, Ox 65. **d** 67 Crediton for Ex **p** 68 Ex. C of Em Plymouth 67-70; Chap Hammersmith Hosp from 70. *63 Primula Street, W12.* (01-749 2333)

MORLEY, Very Rev William Fenton. b 12. CBE 80. Late Scho of St D Coll Lamp BA (2nd cl Engl) and Engl Pri 32. Or Coll Ox BA (3rd cl Th) 34, MA 38. Univ of Lon BD (1st cl) 45. Wycl Hall, Ox 35. **d** 35 **p** 36 Llan. C of Caerau w Ely 35-38; Newton Nottage 38-43; V of Penrhiwceiber 43-46; Gt Haseley 46-50; Lect in Hebr and Gr and Dir of Mus Cudd Coll 46-50; Exam in NT Gr and Hebr Univ of Lon and Ext Lect in Biblical and Relig Studies from 47; Educn Sec Overseas Coun of Ch Assembly 50-56; Publ Pr Dio Roch 51-56; Ed E and W Review 53-64; Can Res and Prec of S'wark Cathl 56-61; Chap and Lect St Gabriel's Coll Lon 56-61; V of Leeds 61-71; Hon Can of Ripon 61-71; RD of Leeds 61-71; Warburton Lect Linc Inn 63-65; Proc Conv Ripon 64-71; Sarum 72-77; Chap to HM the Queen 65-71; Ch Comm 68-77; Dean of Sarum 71-77; (Dean Emer) from 77; Exam Chap to Bp of Sarum 72-77; Chairman C of E Pensions Bd 74-80. *5 Cavendish Place, Bath, Avon.* (Bath 312598)

MORLEY-BUNKER, John Arthur. b 27. ACIS 64. Wells Th Coll 67. **d** 68 **p** 69 Bris. C of Horfield 68-71; C-in-c of All H Easton Bris 71-75; V 75-82; RD of Bris City 74-79; V of St Greg Horfield Dio Bris from 82. *St Gregory's Vicarage, Bristol, BS7 0PD.* (Bristol 692839)

MOROA, Pilane Abraham. b 48. **d** 80 Bp Ndwandwe for Johann (NSM). C of St Aug Orlando Dio Johann from 80. *10382b Orlando West, Phirima, S Africa 1848.*

MOROGORO, Lord Bishop of. *See* Chitemo, Right Rev Gresford.

MORONEY, Ven John Burbury. Fitzw Ho Cam BA 56, MA 60. Ridley Coll Melb ACT ThL 49 **d** 49 **p** 50 Melb. C of Melb Dioc Centre 49; Chap R Melb Hosp 50-53; Fitzw Ho Cam 54-56; I of Williamstown 56-65; Exam Chap to Abp of Melb from 62; V of St Columb Hawthorn Dio Melb from 65; Can of Melb from 69; Archd of Kew 70; Malvern 71-78; Melb from 78. *448 Burnwood Road, Hawthorn, Vic, Australia 3122.* (03-81 1805)

MORONY, Ross Allan. b 45. St Barn Coll Adel Dipl Th 79. **d** 80 **p** 81 Adel. C of St Columba Hawthorn Dio Adel from 80. *99 Cross Road, Hawthorn, S Australia 5062.*

MORPHET, George Thexton. ACT ThL 47. **d** 38 **p** 39 Bend. C of Bridgewater 38-39; V of White Hills 39-40; Chap AIF 40-44; R of St Mary Woodend 44-48; Ch Ch Echuca 48-53; Chap Miss to Seamen Townsville 53-59; Wakehurst Inst Wickham and of Newc 59-62; Vic Dks Lon 62-68; Brisb 68-77; Perm to Offic Dio Brisb from 77. *68 Spowers Street, Bribie Island, Queensland, Australia 4507.* (48 1635)

MORPHET, Mark Stephen. b 53. AKC 76. Chich Th Coll 76. **d** 77 Chich **p** 78 Lewes for Chich. C of St Mary Eastbourne 77-80. *c/o 6 Bay Pond Road, Eastbourne, Sussex.*

MORRALEE, Arnold Melvin. b 06. St Bonif Coll Warm 35. **d** 36 **p** 37 Willoch. M of Bush Bro Quorn 36-39; Hon Can of Willoch 40; R of St Geo Goodwood 40-47; Chap AIF 43-45; R of Elton 48-58; Chesterton w Haddon 48-59; V of St Aug Barb 58-59; St Matthias Barb 59-62; Hon CF Barb 60; V of Finchingfield 62-71; Perm to Offic Dio Syd from 77. *8 Derby Street, Vaucluse, NSW, Australia 2030.* (337-2686)

MORRELL, (Dunstan) Athol Henry. b 09. Kelham Th Coll 29. **d** 34 **p** 35 Bris. M SSM 34-53; C of Bedminster 34-37; St Bernard Distr Ch Parson Cross 37-39; St Cecilia Parson Cross Sheff 39-42; St Geo Nottm 42-45; L to Offic Dio Southw 46-53; Dio Ox from 54; M OSB from 53. *Nashdom Abbey, Burnham, Bucks.*

MORRELL, Geoffrey Bernard. b 45. K Coll Lon and Warm AKC 68. **d** 69 **p** 71 Portsm. C of St Alb W Leigh Conv Distr Havant 69-76; V of Shedfield Dio Portsm from 76. *Shedfield Vicarage, Southampton, SO3 2HY.* (Wickham 2162)

✠ **MORRELL, Right Rev James Herbert Lloyd.** b 07. AKC 30, FKC 60. Ely Th Coll 30. **d** 31 **p** 32 Lon. C of St Alphage Hendon 31-36; St Mich AA Brighton 36-40; Chap for Work among Men and Boys Dio Chich and Chap Supt Brighton Boys' Hostel 40-41; Lect for C of E Moral Welfare Coun and L to Offic Dio Chich 41-44; V of Roffey 44-46; Archd of Lewes 46-59; Cons Ld Bp Suffr of Lewes in Westmr Abbey 30 Nov 59 by Abp of Cant; Bps of Ely; Sarum; Lich; and Chich; Bp Suffr of Dover; and Bps Mackenzie; Warde and Gwyer; Res 77; Asst Bp of Chich from 78; Preb of Chich Cathl from 59; Provost of S Div Woodard Corpn from 61. *83 Davigdor Road, Hove, Sussex, BN3 1RA.* (Brighton 733971)

MORRELL, Nigel Paul. b 38. SOC. **d** 76 **p** 77 St Alb. C of St Paul Letchworth Dio St Alb from 76; St Mich Letchworth Dio St Alb from 81. *38 Townley, Letchworth, Herts.*

MORRELL, Robin Mark George. b 29. Cudd Coll 58. **d** 60 **p** 61 Portsm. C of Petersfield 60-63; C-in-c of Stockwood Conv Distr 63-71; Publ Pr Dio Bris 71-72; R of Honiton w Gittisham and Combe Raleigh 72-78; Surr 74-78; Lay Tr Officer Dio S'wark from 78. *27 Dartmouth Row, SE10 8AW.* (01-692 9448)

MORREY, Frederick Albert. St Jo Coll Morpeth **d** 57 **p** 59 Gippsld. C of Morwell 57-61; V of Bruthen 61-63; R of Myrtleford 63-66; Alexandra 66-70; P-in-c of Mossman 70-73; V of Frenchville Rockptn 73-77; Blackall Dio Rockptn from 77; Hon Can of Rockptn 77-78. *c/o 23 Raymond Street, Sale, Vic, Australia 3850.*

MORRIS, Alan Ralph Oakden. b 29. Roch Th Coll 59. **d** 61 **p** 62 Roch. C of Riverhead 61-62; St Pet w St Marg Roch 62-66; C of Wrotham (in c of Good Shepherd Borough Green) 66-74; V of Biggin Hill Dio Roch from 74. *St Mark's Vicarage, 10 Church Road, Biggin Hill, Kent, TN16 3JU.* (Biggin Hill 72312)

MORRIS, Albert Edgar Njoro. b 06. **d** 68 Bp Horsted for Leic **p** 69 Leic. C of Houghton-on-the-Hill 68-70; St Aid New Parks Leic 70-74. *32 Fairfield Crescent, Glenfield, Leicester, LE3 8EH.* (Leic 871803)

MORRIS, Albert George. b 15. Tyndale Hall, Bris. **d** 48 **p** 49 Chelmsf. C of Dagenham 48-51; St Paul Clacton-on-Sea 51-53; V of All SS Clapham Pk 53-58; R of Beeston-next-Mileham 58-61; C-in-c of Brisley 59-61; V of W Aberdares 61-64; Asst Master Kapsabet Secondary Sch 64-65; St Andr Sch Turi 65-67; C of Rowner 67-68; C-in-c of St Matt Conv Distr Bridgemary, Gosport 68-80. *128 Skipper Way, Lee-on-Solent, Hants, PO13 8HD.*

MORRIS, Alexander Dorner. b 23. Late Exhib of Jes Coll Cam 2nd cl Cl Trip pt i 47, BA 48, 2nd cl Th Trip pt i 49, MA 53. Linc Th Coll 49. **d** 51 **p** 52 Sheff. C of St Thos Wincobank 51-53; Rotherham 53-54; C-in-c of Manor Pk Conv Distr Sheff 54-59; Relig Instruction Org Dio Bom 59-63; Chap St Paul Poona 59-61; Thana Bom 61-63; V of Bexley 63-71; Leatherhead Dio Guildf from 71; RD of Leatherhead 72-77. *Vicarage, St Mary's Road, Leatherhead, Surrey.* (Leatherhead 72313)

MORRIS, Alexander James Pitman. McGill Univ Montr BA and LTh 59. **d** and **p** 59 Montr. P-in-c of St Hilda w St Chad Montr 59-61; C of St Lambert 61-63; I of Valleyfield 63-66; R of Lakeside Heights 66-75; Chap Veterans' Hosp Ste Anne De Bellevue Dio Montr from 75. *Veterans' Hospital, St Anne de Bellevue, PQ, Canada.* (514-457 3440)

MORRIS, Alfred Ronald. Univ of Syd. **d** and **p** 53 C & Goulb. C of St Jo Bapt Canberra 53-54; Asst Master Canberra Gr Sch 54-58; Chap 58-64; Asst Master Mart Mem Sch Agenehambo 65-71; Hd Master 71-79; Insp of Schs Dio Aipo from 79. *PO Box 240, Goroka, Papua New Guinea.* (72-2618)

MORRIS, Alfred Thomas. b 01. St Aid Coll 28. **d** 31 **p** 32 Blackb. C of St Jas Darwen 31-35; Clayton-le-Moors 35-37; V of St Cuthb Preston 37-70; L to Offic Dio Blackb from 79.

11 Fairways, Broughton, Preston, Lancs. (Gt Eccleston 70248)

MORRIS, Arthur Ronald. Jes Coll Ox BA (2nd cl Mod Lang) 38, MA 42. St Steph Ho Ox 38. **d** 40 **p** 41 St A. C of Rhosddu 40-42; Buckley 42-45; Miss P Dio Masasi 46-51; Asst Master Chidya Sch Dio Masasi 50-51; P-in-c of Fiwila 51-53; Livingstone 53-55; V of St Alb Sneinton 55-59; V of St Steph Sneinton 55-59; R of Livingstone 59-62; C of St Martin Barton 63-66; V of St Mich Edmon 66-71; Inglewood 71-73; R of St Alb Auchenflower City and Dio Brisb from 73. *395 Milton Road, Auchenflower, Brisbane, Queensland, Australia 4066.* (370 2566)

MORRIS, Bernard Lyn. b 28. St Aid Coll 55. **d** 58 **p** 59 Bris. C of Hartcliffe Conv Distr 58-61; Bishopston 61-63; R of St Thos Ardwick 63-69; Surr 64-69; R of Aylton w Pixley Munsley and Putley 69-79; P-in-c of Tarrington w Stoke Edith 72-77; R 77-79; P-in-c of Qu Camel w W Camel, Marston Magna w Rimpton and Corton Denham Dio B & W 79-80; R from 80. *Rectory, Englands Lane, Queen Camel, Yeovil, Somt, BA22 7NN* (0935-850326)

MORRIS, Cecil Hubert Musgrave. b 25. **d** 79 Bp Stanage for Johann **p** 80 Johann (NSM). C of Bedfordview Dio Johann from 79. *7 Lancaster Road, Parkdene, Boksburg, S Africa 1460.*

MORRIS, Christopher John. b 45. K Coll Lon and Warm AKC 67, BD 68. **d** 68 **p** 69 Lich. C of W Bromwich 68-72; Porthill 72-74; Ecumen Liaison Officer BBC Radio Carl and Min Can of Carl Cathl 74-77; V of Thursby Dio Carl from 77; Dioc Communications Officer Dio Carl from 77. *Thursby Vicarage, Carlisle, CA5 6PF.* (Dalston 710303)

MORRIS, Colin. b 28. Qu Coll Ox BA (1st cl Mod Hist) 48, 1st cl Th 51, MA 53. Linc Th Coll 51. **d** 53 Ox **p** 54 Reading for Cant. Fell, Chap and Lect in Mod Hist and Th Pemb Coll Ox 53-69; Lect in Mod Hist Univ of Ox 53-59; Prof of Medieval Hist Univ of Southn from 69. *Department of History, University, Southampton.*

MORRIS, Colman Montenac. b 19. **d** 73 **p** 75 Bp J T Clark for Ja (APM). C of Kingston Dio Ja from 73. *4 Silver Road, Hughendon Park, St Andrew, Jamaica, WI.*

MORRIS, David Edmond. b 27. Univ of Wales BA 56. St D Coll Lamp. **d** 57 **p** 58 St D. C of Llanfihangel-ar-Arth 57-59; Asst Master St Jo Coll Ystrad Meurig 59-61; C of Yspytty Ystwyth w Ystrad Meurig 59-61; CF 61-81; ACG SW Distr 78-81; Hon Chap to HM the Queen from 78; V of Penllergaer Dio Swan B from 81. *Penllergaer Vicarage, Swansea, W Glam.* (Gorseinon 892603)

MORRIS, (Augustine) David Freestone. b 05. Univ of Lon 22. M OSB 24. **d** 36 **p** 37 Ox. C of Taplow 36-39; Beaconsfield (in C of St Mich) 41-43; Prior Nashdom Abbey 45-48; Abbot 48-74; L to Offic Dio Ox from 54. *Nashdom Abbey, Burnham, Bucks, SL1 8NL.* (Burnham 3176)

MORRIS, David Meeson. b 35. Late Scho of Trin Coll Ox BA (2nd cl Chem) 56, MA 60. Chich Th Coll 57. **d** 60 **p** 61 Lon. C of St Steph w St John Westmr 60-65; Libr of Pusey Ho Ox 65-68; L to Offic Dio Ox 66-68; Chap Wadh Coll Ox 67-68; Chap Industr Miss Sheff 68-72; C of St Leon Norwood Sheff 68-69; Brightside 69-72; V of Market Drayton Dio Lich from 72; R of Adderley Dio Lich from 72. *Vicarage, Market Drayton, Shropshire, TF9 1AQ.* (Market Drayton 2527)

MORRIS, David Pryce. b 39. Univ of Wales Dipl Th 62. St Mich Coll Llan 62. **d** 63 **p** 64 St A. C of Colwyn Bay 63-70; R of St Geo or Kegidog 70-79; V of Bodelwyddan 76-79; Connah's Quay Dio St A from 79. *Connah's Quay Vicarage, Deeside, Clwyd.*

MORRIS, David William. McMaster Univ Ont BA 54. Trin Coll Tor LTh 58. **d** and **p** 58 Niag. C of Ch Ch Niagara Falls 58-60; I of Mayo 60-65; P-in-c of Governor's Harbour Eleuthera 65-68; Asst Master St Jo Coll Nass 68-75; I of Ch Ch Lon Ont 75-80; All SS Waterloo Dio Hur from 80. *682 Glen Forest Boulevard, Waterloo, Ont, Canada.*

MORRIS, Dennis Gordon. ALCM 58. St D Coll Lamp Dipl Th 67. **d** 67 Bp TM Hughes for Llan **p** 68 Llan. C of Neath w Llantwit Dio Llan from 67. *18 Woodland Road, Neath, W Glam, SA11 3AL.* (Neath 55738)

MORRIS, Edwin Alfred. b 32. Wells Th Coll 62. **d** 64 Bp McKie for Cov **p** 65 Cov. C of St Chad Cov 64-66; L to Offic Dio Cov 66-74; Industr Chap Dio Cov from 68; P-in-c of Churchover w Willey Dio Cov from 74; RD of Rugby from 78. *Churchover Rectory, Rugby, Warws.* (Rugby 832420)

MORRIS, Eustin John. Montr Dioc Th Coll. **d** 67 **p** 68 Montr. C of St Paul Lachine Montr 67-69; I of St Ignatius Montr 69-74; St Lawr La Salle Dio Montr from 74. *596 Terrace Beauce, La Salle, PQ, Canada.* (514-363 9923)

MORRIS, Frank Leo. b 20. St Steph Ho Ox 50. **d** 53 **p** 54 Roch. C of Bickley 53-55; Letchworth 55-61; V of Wareside 61-65; Gt w L Hormead (and Anstey w Brent Pelham and Meesden from 79) Dio St Alb from 65; R of Wyddial Dio St Alb from 65; RD of Buntingford 68-75; P-in-c of Anstey 79; Brent Pelham w Meesden 79. *Great Hormead Vicarage, Buntingford, Herts.* (Great Hormead 258)

MORRIS, George Edis. St Jo Coll Armid. **d** 08 **p** 12 Graft A. C of Glen Innes NSW 08-10; Urala 10; Inverell 10-13; C-in-c of Wauchope 13-19; R of Cobargo 19-24; Marulan 24-32; Gundagai 32-54; L to Offic Dio Syd from 61. *147 Harbord Road, Harbord, NSW, Australia.*

MORRIS, George Erskine. Codr Coll Barb. **d** 62 Bp Stuart for Worc **p** 63 Worc. C of St Jo Bapt Kidderminster 62-66; R of Digby 66-70; R of Weymouth 69-70; P-in-c of Port Morien 70-72; on leave. *PO Box 957, Sydney, NS, Canada.* (539 6684)

MORRIS, Gwilym Alun. b 09. CBE 64. Qu Coll Birm 38. **d** 39 **p** 40 York. C of St Barn Linthorpe Middlesbrough 39-42; CF (EC) 42-46; Men in Disp 45; Chap Palestine Police Force 46-48; Min of St Mich AA Legal Distr N Hull 48-54; Chap at Bahrain 54-65; Hon Can of St Geo Colleg Ch Jer 60-67; Archd of E Arabia and The Gulf 62-65; Abp's Sec for Pilgrimages to H Land 65-67; Dir NE Reg Miss to Seamen and L to Offic Dio York 68-70; V of Coxwold 70-75; Perm to Offic Dio York from 75. *Captain Cook's House, Grape Lane, Whitby, N Yorks, YO22 4BA.* (Whitby 602434)

MORRIS, Henry James. b 47. Univ of Lon BSc 69. Wycl Hall Ox BA (Th) 78. **d** 79 Chelmsf **p** 80 Barking for Chelmsf. C of Woodford Wells Dio Chelmsf from 79. *8 Firs Walk, Woodford Green, Essex.*

MORRIS, Ian Henry. b 42. Sarum Wells Th Coll 73. **d** 75 **p** 76 Bris. C of Lawrence Weston 75-78; St Buryan, St Levan & Sennen 78-81; P-in-c of Lanteglos-by-Fowey Dio Truro from 81. *Lanteglos-by-Fowey Vicarage, Polruan, Fowey, PL23 1PR.* (Polruan 213)

MORRIS, Ian James Patrick. b 43. Univ of Dur BA 65. Westcott Ho Cam 67. **d** 69 **p** 70 Ely. C of Wisbech 69-72; Gaywood 72-76; Asst Chap Basingstoke Hosp 76-78; Chap Seacroft, Killingbeck, Newton Green and Meanwood Park Hosps Leeds from 78. *Seacroft Hospital, York Road, Leeds, LS14 6UQ.* (Leeds 648164)

MORRIS, John. b 01. Em Coll Sktn LTh 28. **d** 28 Yukon **p** 29 M'Kenz R. Miss at Teslin 28-29; Fort MacPherson 29-32; Coppermine River 32-34; C of Belgrave 35-38; R of Nether Broughton 38-46; V of St Pet Mountsorrel 46-53; H Trin Ashby de la Zouch 53-59; R of Newbold de Verdun 59-62; All SS Birm 62-68; V of Shuttington w Amington 68-71; C of Tamworth 72-82. *17 Strawberry Lane, Blackfordby, Burton-on-Trent, DE11 8AH.*

MORRIS, John. b 25. Westcott Ho Cam. **d** 65 **p** 66 St Alb. C of St Mich St Alb 65-68; V of Leverstock Green 68-80; Team R of Chambersbury, Hemel Hempstead Dio St Alb from 80. *Leverstock Green Vicarage, Hemel Hempstead, Herts.* (Hemel Hempstead 64860)

MORRIS, John Derrick. b 18. MRCS LRCP 43. Lon Coll Div 62. **d** 64 **p** 65 Nor. C of Cromer 64-67; V of Broadway 67-71; Hon C of St Leonards-on-Sea Dio Chich from 71. *Dene Cottage, Maple Avenue, Bexhill-on-Sea, E Sussex, TN39 4ST.*

MORRIS, John Dudley. b 33. Ball Coll Ox BA 57, 2nd cl Chem 58, Dipl Th 59, MA 61. Wycl Hall, Ox 58. **d** 60 **p** 61 Roch. C of Tonbridge 60-65; Cockfosters (in c of St Paul Hadley Wood) 65-69; Chap and Asst Master Elstree Sch Woolhampton 70-74; L to Offic Dio Ox 73-74; Hd Master Handcross Park Sch from 74. *Handcross Park School, Haywards Heath, W Sussex, RH17 6HF.* (Handcross 400526)

MORRIS, John Edgar. b 20. Keble Coll Ox BA 42, MA 50. Wycl Hall Ox 42. **d** 44 Warrington for Liv **p** 45 Liv. C of St Thos Eccleston 44-48; H Trin Warrington (in c of St Luke) 48-50; V of All SS Newton-le-Willows 50-57; R of Wavertree 57-66; PC of Ainsdale Dio Liv 66-68; V from 68. *708 Liverpool Road, Ainsdale, Southport, Mer, PR8 3QE.* (Southport 77760)

MORRIS, John Edward. b 1896. **d** 44 **p** 45 Lah. Asst Chap Lah Canton 44-45; CF (Ind) 45-46; Hon CF 46; C of St Aid Leeds 46-48; R of St Colman Is of Yell Shetland 48-49; C of St Aid Leeds 49-51; PC of Barrington 51-55; V of Rennington w Rock 55-61. *22 Buckstone Crescent, Edinburgh 10.* (031-445 3234)

MORRIS, John Howes. b 06. Univ of Lon BSc (2nd cl Botany) 29. ARCS 29. Westcott Ho Cam 29. **d** 31 **p** 32 Lon. C of S Hackney 31-34; Friern Barnet 34-40; St Mary Hendon (in c of Holders Hill) 40-45; V of St Mary Virg Tottenham 45-51; St Mich Harrow Weald 51-59; Ch Ch Turnham Green 59-72; Perm to Offic Dio Cant from 73. *Flat 3, 176 Sandgate Road, Folkestone, Kent, CT20 2LQ.* (Folkestone 58998)

MORRIS, John Marcus Harston. b 15. BNC Ox Colquitt Exhib 34, BA (2nd cl Lit Hum) 37, 2nd cl Th 39, MA 47. Wycl Hall, Ox 37. **d** 39 **p** 40 Liv. C of St Bart Roby 39-40; Gt Yarmouth 40-41; Chap RAFVR 1941-43; R of Weeley 43-45; L to Offic in Weeley Village Hall 44-45; V of St Jas Birkdale 45-50; Ed *The Anvil* 46-50; *Eagle* 50-59; Perm to Offic Dio Lon from 50; Hon Chap of St Bride Fleet Street City and Dio

Lon from 52. *Mill House, Midford, Nr Bath, Avon, BA2 7DE.* (0225-833939)

MORRIS, John Rhys Oakley. b 16. Univ of Wales, BA (2nd cl Lat) 38. St Mich Coll Llan **d** 48 Swan B. C of Oystermouth 48; Perm to Offic Dio St A from 49. *55 Cysgod-y-Coleg, Bala, Gwyn.*

MORRIS, Canon John Richard. b 23. Or Coll Ox BA (2nd cl Th) 48, MA 52. Westcott Ho Cam **d** 50 **p** 51 Birm. C of St Geo Birm 50-52; King's Norton 52-57; PC of Longbridge 57-64; R of Sanderstead 64-70; Exam Chap to Bp of S'wark from 68; V of Battersea Dio S'wark from 70; RD of Battersea 76-80; Hon Can of S'wark Cathl from 76; P-in-c of St Mary-le-Park Battersea 76-79. *32 Vicarage Crescent, SW11 3LD.* (01-228 9648)

MORRIS, Kenneth Richard. Clifton Th Coll 59. **d** 62 **p** 63 Ex. C of St Jude Plymouth 62-65; Chap RAF from 65. *c/o Ministry of Defence, Adastral House, WC1.*

MORRIS, Canon Leon Lamb. Univ of Syd BSc 34. Univ of Lon BD (1st cl) 43, MTh 46. Fitzw Ho Cam PhD 52. Univ of Melb MSc 66. Moore Th Coll Syd ACT ThL (1st cl) 37. **d** 38 **p** 39 Syd. C of Campsie 38-40; P-in-c of Minnipa 40-45; Perm to Offic Dio Melb 45-48; Vice-Prin Ridley Coll Melb 45-60; Prin 64-79; C of H Trin Coburg 48-50 and 53-55; IVF Travelling Fell 50-51; Chap Deaconess Tr Ho Fairfield Melb 53-60; Warden of Tyndale Ho Cam 60-63; Can of Melb 64-79; Can (Emer) from 79; Perm to Offic Dio Melb from 80. *17 Queens Avenue, Doncaster, Vic, Australia 3108.*

MORRIS, Leslie Nathaniel. **d** 54 **p** 55 Ch Ch. C of Fendalton 54-57; V of Bryndwr 57-60; Woolston 61-66; Belfast-Styx 66-67; L to Offic Dio Ch Ch 74-76 and from 77; P-in-c of Kumara 76; Highfield 77. *141a Rockinghorse Road, Christchurch 7, NZ.*

MORRIS, Martin Geoffrey Roger. b 41. Trin Coll Cam BA 63, MA 67. St D Coll Lamp 63. **d** 66 **p** 67 Mon. C of St Paul Newport 66-72; R of Lampeter Velfrey (and Llanddewi Velfrey from 74) Dio St D from 72. *Lampeter Velfrey Rectory, Narberth, Dyfed, SA67 8UH.* (Llanteg 241)

MORRIS, Michael Alan. b 46. Jes Coll Cam BA 70, MA 74. Coll of the Resurr Mirfield 79. **d** 81 Cov. C of All SS Leamington Priors Dio Cov from 81. *35 Portland Street, Leamington Spa, CV32 5EY.*

MORRIS, Norman. Hur Coll LTh 55. **d** 49 **p** 50 Hur. C of Kitchener 49-50; R of Florence 50-56; Forest 56-61; C of St Paul Charlottetown 61-62; R of Loughborough 62-76; Can of Ont 74-77. *RR3, Iona Station, Ont, Canada.*

MORRIS, Norman Foster Maxwell. b 46. Univ of Ex BA 68, MA 72. SOC 75. **d** 78 **p** 79 S'wark. C of All SS N Beddington 78-81; Chap Tonbridge Sch from 81. *Tonbridge School, Tonbridge, Kent, TN9 1JP.*

MORRIS, Paul David. b 56. St Jo Coll Nottm BTh 79. **d** 80 Chelmsf **p** 81 Bradwell for Chelmsf. C of Billericay Dio Chelmsf from 80. *72 Tylands, Billericay, Essex, CM12 9PB.*

MORRIS, Peter. b 45. Tyndale Hall Bris 68. **d** 71 Warrington for Liv **p** 72 Liv. C of St Simon & St Jude, Southport 71-74; Min of Netherley 74-76; V of Bryn Dio Liv from 76. *12 Bryn Road, Ashton-in-Makerfield, WN4 0AA.* (Ashton-in-Makerfield 727114)

MORRIS, Canon Peter Arthur William. b 23. Bps' Coll Cheshunt, 57. **d** 58 **p** 59 St Alb. C of Croxley Green 58-62; V of Sawbridgeworth 62-74; S Gillingham 74-79; P-in-c of Pleshey Dio Chelmsf from 79; Chap Pleshey Retreat Ho from 79; Warden from 80; Can of Chelmsf Cathl from 81. *Pleshey Vicarage, Chelmsford, Essex.* (Pleshey 236)

MORRIS, Peter Michael Keighley. b 27. Late Mansell Exhib and Pusey and Ellerton Hebr Scho of St Jo Coll Ox BA (2nd cl Th) 50, 2nd cl Or Lang 52, Liddon Stud and Jun Kennicott Sch 51, MA 56. Westcott Ho Cam 51. **d** 54 **p** 55 Mon. C of Bedwellty 54-55; Lect St D Coll Lamp 55-69; Sen Lect from 69; Exam Chap to Bp of Mon 55-68; and from 73; LPr Dios Mon and St D from 55. *St David's College, Lampeter, Dyfed.*

MORRIS, Philip Gregory. b 50. Univ of Leeds BA 71, M Phil 74. Coll of Resurr Mirfield 71. **d** 73 **p** 74 Llan. Research in Th Univ of Leeds 73-74; C of Aberdare 74-77; Neath w Llantwit 77-80; V of Cymmer and Porth Dio Llan from 80. *Vicarage, Maesgwyn, Porth, Mid Glam, CF39 9HW.* (Porth 2219)

MORRIS, Raymond John Walton. b 08. OBE 69. Em Coll Cam BA 33, MA 37. Lon Coll of Div 33. **d** 34 **p** 35 Lon. C of St Steph E Twickenham 34-37; Cathl Ch Bradf 37-40; Succr 38-40; V of Em Plymouth 40-45; St Steph E Twickenham 45-56; Chap Embassy Ch Paris 56-69; RD of France 56-69; V of H Trin Brompton 69-75. *Culver Cottage, Laundry Lane, Shaftesbury, Dorset.* (0747-3422)

MORRIS, Reginald Brian. b 31. St Mich Coll Llan 56. **d** 59 **p** 60 Worc. C of St Jo Bapt-in-Bedwardine Worc 59-61; P-in-c of Ch Ch Tolladine 61-62; CF 62-78; V of Cheswardine Dio Lich from 78; Hales Dio Lich from 78. *Cheswardine Vicarage, Market Drayton, Salop.* (Cheswardine 204)

MORRIS, Richard Samuel. b 10. TCD BA 35, MA 39. Edgehill Th Coll Belf 31. **d** 58 **p** 59 Down. C of St Donard Belf 58-60; Dundela 60-62; I of Aghalee 62-64; R of Magheradroll 64-69; I of Kilsaran w Dunleer and Drumcar w Dunany 69-75. *26 Kingsway Park, Belfast, N Ireland.* (Dundonald 3175)

MORRIS, Richard William. **d** and **p** 58 St Arn. C of Swan Hill 58; V of Quambatook 58-60; R of Sea Lake 60-66; Skipton 66-69; V of Moe w Newborough 69-78; R of Port Augusta 78-81; Burra Dio Willoch from 81. *Box 47, Burra, S Australia 5417.*

MORRIS, Robert. b 07. Lich Th Coll 32. **d** 34 **p** 36 Lich. C of St Mary Kingswinford 34-35; All SS W Bromwich 35-37; Wensley (in c of Leyburn) 37-39; CF (EC) 39-45; V of St Simon Leeds 46-55; All H w St Simon Leeds 55-58; Killinghall 58-75. *52 Clotherholme Road, Ripon, N Yorks, HG4 2DL.* (Ripon 4393)

MORRIS, Robert John. b 45. Univ of Leeds BA 67. Coll of Resurr Mirfield 74. **d** 76 **p** 77 Ripon. C of Holbeck 76-78; Moseley Dio Birm from 78. *4 Woodrough Drive, Moseley, Birmingham, B13 9EP.* (021-449 2564)

MORRIS, Robin Edward. b 32. St Jo Coll Ox BA 55, MA 60. **d** 57 **p** 58 Man. C of St Thos Halliwell 57-61; V of Castleton Moor 61-71; St Geo Stalybridge 71-80; R of Heswall Dio Ches from 80. *Heswall Rectory, Wirral, Chesh.* (051-342 3471)

MORRIS, Samuel Harry. b 03. Univ of Dur BA 25. St Paul's Coll Burgh 25. **d** 26 **p** 27 Zanz. Miss at Mkuzi 26-27; Korogwe 27-29; Asst P at Mkuzi 29-32; Tongwe 32-35; C of St Andr W Bromwich 35-39; V of St Steph Willenhall 39-50; All SS Bromsgrove Dio Worc 50-52; UMCA Miss at Mapanza 52-53; P-in-c of Tanga 54-57; V of Snibston 58-63; St Jas Aylestone Pk 63-71; L to Offic Dio Leic from 71. *609 Welford Road, Leicester, LE2 6FP.* (Leic 886613)

MORRIS, Stanley Cottrill. Univ of W Ont BA 46. **d** 63 Alg. Hon C of Ascen Sudbury 63-69; St Phil Etobicoke City and Dio Tor from 69. *1514 Bridge Road, Oakville, Ont, Canada.*

MORRIS, Stanley James. b 35. Keble Coll Ox BA 58, MA 63. Chich Th Coll 59. **d** 61 **p** 62 Lich. C of Tunstall 61-64; W Bromwich 64-67; V of Wilnecote Dio Lich from 67. *Wilnecote Vicarage, Tamworth, Staffs, B77 2PH.* (Tamworth 280806)

MORRIS, Stephen Francis. b 52. Univ of Nottm BTh 79. St Jo Coll Nottm 74. **d** 79 Reading for Ox **p** 80 Ox. C of N Hinksey Dio Ox from 79. *142 North Hinksey Lane, Oxford, OX2 0LZ.*

MORRIS, Stuart Collard. b 43. K Coll Lon and Warm AKC 66. **d** 67 **p** 68 Bris. C of Hanham w Hanham Abbots 67-71; Whitchurch 71-74; P-in-c of Dodington w Wapley and Codrington 74-77; Westerleigh 74-77; R of Munslow w Bouldon and Diddlebury Dio Heref from 77; P-in-c of Holdgate w Tugford Dio Heref from 77; Abdon Dio Heref from 77; The Heath Dio Heref from 77. *Munslow Rectory, Craven Arms, Salop.*

MORRIS, Thomas Ernest Gilbert. b 06. Men in Disp 40. Late Scho of St D Coll Lamp BA (Hist) 28. Ex Coll Ox 28. **d** 30 **p** 31 Swan B. C of St Mary Swansea 30-36; CF (TA) 32-36; TCF Chatham 36-39; CF 39-58; Can of Accra 55-56; R of Roggiett w Llanfihangel Roggiett 58-69; RD of Netherwent 61-69; Surr from 61; V of Rockfield and Llangattock-Vibon-Avel w Llanfaenor and St Maughan 69-77. *c/o Rockfield Vicarage, Monmouth, NP5 3QB.* (Monmouth 2003)

MORRIS, Timothy David. b 48. Univ of Lon BSc 69. Trin Coll Bris 72. **d** 75 **p** 76 Edin. C of St Thos Edin 75-77; R of St Jas L Leith Dio Edin from 77. *29 Dudley Gardens, Edinburgh, EH6 4PU.* (031-554 3520)

MORRIS, Wilfred. b 1896. **d** 29 **p** 30 Graft. M of Bro of Our Sav Liston 29-31; V of Upper Macleay 31-35; N Grafton 35-37; Llanllugan 37-48; R of Nantglyn 48-57; Bodfari 57-69; L to Offic Dio St A from 70. *Waen View, Tal-y-Cafn, Colwyn Bay, Clwyd.*

MORRIS, William Humphrey. b 29. Univ of Wales BA (Phil) 54, MA 72. Univ of Birm Dipl Th 58. Univ of Man MEducn (Phil) 76, PhD 80. Qu Coll Birm 56. **d** 58 **p** 59 Ches. C of Prestbury 58-60; Neston 60-65; V of Sandbach Heath 65-68; Asst Master Wilmslow Gr Sch 68-76; L to Offic Dio Ches from 69; Research Fell Univ of Man 76-81. *Chantry Cottage, Smallwood, Sandbach, Chesh, CW11 0XF.* (Smallwood 306)

MORRIS, William James. b 23. St Deiniol's Libr Hawarden 72. **d** 73 **p** 74 Swan B (APM). C of Brecon Dio Swan B from 73. *School House, Cwmdu, Crickhowell, Powys.* (Bwlch 355)

MORRIS, William Sparkes. Late Scho of Univ of Bris BA (1st cl Phil and Engl Lit) 39. Univ of Chicago, DPhil 55. Hur Coll Lon Hon DD 69. Wycl Hall Ox 41. **d** 43 **p** 44 Bris. C of Kingswood 43-45; Inter Coll Sec SCM for Newc T and Dur 45-48; L to Offic Dio Dur 46-48; Fell in Div Sch of Univ of

Chicago 48-51; L to Offic Dio Chicago 48-55; Dio Hur from 55; Prof Hur Coll 55-68; Dean of Th 61-62; Assoc Prof of Phil Lakehead Univ 68; Prof from 69; L to Offic Dio Hur 68; Perm to Offic Dio Alg 68-70. *281 Worseley Street, Thunder Bay, Ont., Canada.* (807-577 2990)

MORRIS, William Thomas Edmund. b 07. St D Coll Lamp BA 31. **d** 31 **p** 32 Swan B. C of Clydach 31-35; St Mark Lyncombe 35-41; PC of Theale 41-50; R of Bawdrip 50-55; V of Mark 55-72; Surr 65-72; RD of Burnham 68-71. *White-croft, Grants Lane, Wedmore, Somt, BS28 4EA.*

MORRISBY, Alexander Rupert Babington. Moore Th Coll Syd 38. ACT ThL 39. **d** 40 **p** 41 Syd. C of St Steph Willoughby 40-41; St Matt Botany 41-42; Actg C of St John Wallerawang 42-44; Chap AIF 44-46; Org Sec CMS Dio Brisb 46-54; L to Offic Dio Syd 51-54; R of Ashbury 54-59; Milton 60-67; L to Offic Dio Syd 67-69 and from 73; R of Cook's River 69-73; Rep Bible S for NSW 73-76; Field Sec 76-80; Vic Sec SAMS from 80. *12/18 Larnes Street, Forest Hill, Vic, Australia 3131.*

MORRISON, Alexander Grant. **d** 66 Syd for Carp **p** 67 Carp. C of All S Cathl Thursday I 66-69; P-in-c of Moa I 69-73; Kowanyama 73-74; R of Mossman Dio Carp from 74. *St David's Rectory, Mossman, Queensland, Australia 4873.*

MORRISON, Andrew Leslie. b 11. TD 53. Pemb Coll Ox BA (3rd cl Mod Hist) 33, MA 37. Westcott Ho Cam 33. **d** 35 Dur **p** 36 Jarrow for Dur. C of S Westoe 35-38; PC of Castleside 38-42; CF (TA) from 39; R of Branston 46-49; V of Ch Ch Gateshead 49-55; Chap Bensham Gen Hosp 50-55; R of Fenny Compton w Wormleighton 55-64; RD of Dassett Magna 59-64; V of Bury w Houghton 64-76; Perm to Offic Dio Chich from 76. *14 Guildford Place, Chichester.* (Chichester 784310)

MORRISON, Barry John. b 44. Pemb Coll Cam 2nd cl Anthrop Trip pt i 64, BA (2nd cl Anthrop Trip pt ii) 66, MA 70. ALCD 69. **d** 69 **p** 70 Bris. C of Stoke Bishop 69-72; Edgware 72-76; Chap Poly of Centr Lon from 76. *Flat A, 37-49 Riding House Street, W1P 7PT.* (01-580 4204)

MORRISON, Cecil. b 10. Men in Disp 45. St Chad's Coll Dur BA 32. Dipl Th 33, MA 35. Cudd Coll 33. **d** 34 York **p** 35 Whitby for York. C of St Olave w St Mich-le-Belfry York 34-37; Drypool (in c of St Bart) 37-39; CF (TA - R of O) 39-45; V of Osbaldwick w Murton 45-49; St Aid w St Alb Mart Middlesbrough 49-56; R of Guisborough w St Pet-in-Commondale 56-64; V of Greenwich 64-73; Publ Pr Dio S'wark from 73. *1 Alexander Court, Kidbrooke Grove, SE3 0LH.* (01-858 9905)

MORRISON, David Noel. Univ of Melb BA 49, ACT ThL 52. **d** and **p** 53 Brisb. C of Clayfield 53-54; M of Bush Bro of St Paul 54-55; Perm to Offic Dio Melb 55-59; Chap Ivanhoe Gr Sch Melb 55-59; I of Middle Pk 59-70; St Geo W Footscray 70-78; Aberfeldie Dio Melb from 78. *27 St Kinnord Street, Essendon, Vic, Australia 3040.* (337 8059)

MORRISON, Frederick George. b 37. Lich Th Coll 61. **d** 63 **p** 65 Chich. C of All SS Sidley Bexhill 63-66; Chap RAF from 66. *c/o Ministry of Defence, Adastral House, WC 1.*

MORRISON, Gladstone Ashbourne. St Pet Coll Ja 65. **d** 65 Kingston for Ja **p** 66 Ja. P-in-c of Manchioneal w Rural Hill and Boston 65-67; R of Montpelier 67-71; Harewood 72-74; Chapelton Dio Ja from 74. *Rectory, PO Chapelton, Jamaica, W Indies.* (098-72268)

MORRISON, Gordon Robert. Univ of Melb BA 48, MA 52. St Jo Coll Morpeth ACT ThL 52. **d** and **p** 53 Adel. C of Mt Gambier 53-54; Walkerville 54-57; Broken Hill 57-63; Exam Chap to Bp of River 60-75; R of Wentworth 63-65; Broken Hill 65-75; Hon Can of River 64-75; R of Dubbo Dio Bath from 75. *Box 158, Dubbo, NSW, Australia 2830.* (068-82 4050)

MORRISON, Herbert Andrew. b 09. Dallas Th Sem Texas BD 36. K Coll Lon 37. **d** and **p** 38 Chich. C of Lindfield 38-39; Chap RAFVR 39-46; RAF 46-50; R of Elvetham 50-52; Windlesham 52-56; Chap at Amsterdam 56-58; Hon Chap Cant Cathl 58-61; V of Thurnham w Detling 58-61; Gilling 61-66; R of Freshwater 66-77. *5 Millers Field, Great Shefford, Berks.* (Gt Shefford 553)

MORRISON, Iaian Edward. b 36. St Steph Ho Ox 76. **d** 78 **p** 79 Chich. C of St Aug Preston 78-80; Felpham w Middleton Dio Chich from 81. *54 Springfield Road, Brighton, Sussex, BN1 6DE.*

✠ **MORRISON, Right Rev Ian Archibald.** **d** 61 **p** 62 Argent. Chap at Araucanian Miss Temuco Chile 62-77; Cons Asst Bp in Chile (Bp of Cautin and Malleco) in H Trin Ch Temuco 12 June 77 by Bps of Chile and Parag; and Bp Flagg. *Casilla 26d, Temuco, Chile.*

MORRISON, Ian David. K Coll Halifax NS BA 64, LTh 65. **d** 64 **p** 65 NS. C of St Paul Halifax 64-65; St Jas Montr 65-67; on leave. *University of P.E.I., Charlottetown, P.E.I., Canada.* (892-1388)

MORRISON, James Wilson Rennie. b 42. Univ of Aber MA 65. Linc Th Coll 76. **d** 78 Buckingham for Ox **p** 79 Ox. C of Ch Ch Reading 78-81; R of Burghfield Dio Ox from 81. *Rectory, Burghfield Common, Reading, Berks, RG7 3BH.* (Burghfield Common 3243)

MORRISON, John. b 18. **d** 76 Brech (APM). Perm to Offic Dio Brech 76-77; C of Ch Ch Reading Dio Ox from 77. *32 Bourne Avenue, Reading, RG2 0DU.* (Reading 862203)

MORRISON, John Anthony. b 38. Jes Coll Cam BA 60, MA 64. Linc Coll Ox MA 68. Chich Th Coll 61. **d** 64 **p** 65 Birm. C of St Pet Birm 64-68; St Mich Ox 68-74; Chap Linc Coll Ox 68-74; Exam Chap to Bp of Ox from 73; V of Basildon Berks Dio Ox from 74; RD of Bradfield from 78; M Gen Syn from 80. *Upper Basildon Vicarage, Reading, Berks, RG8 8LS.* (Upper Basildon 223)

MORRISON, Leonard Haslett. b 16. CCC Cam BA 38, MA 48. Cudd Coll 47. **d** 49 **p** 50 Glouc. [Called to Bar 47] C of Leckhampton 49-51; Chap Cheltm Coll 51-55; Asst Master 55-62; Chap Rugby Sch 62-69; Charterho 69-78; Team V of Lynton Dio Ex from 78. *Laurel Cottage, Parracombe, Barnstaple, Devon.* (Parracombe 435)

MORRISON, The Hon Nial Ranald. b 32. Jes Coll Ox BA 54, MA 57, Dipl Th 55. Ripon Hall, Ox 54. **d** 56 **p** 57 Glouc. C of St Cath Glouc 56-58; Stroud 59-62; V of Randwick Dio Glouc from 62; Min Can of Glouc from 80. *Randwick Vicarage, Stroud, Glos.* (Stroud 4727)

MORRISON, Robin Victor Adair. b 45. Univ of Nottm BA (2nd cl Th) 67. Ripon Hall Ox 68. **d** 70 **p** 71 Stepney for Lon. C of St John-at-Hackney 70-73; Asst Chap Univ of Newc T 73-76; C-in-c of Teversal 76-78; Asst Master Deans Commun High Sch Livingston 78-79; R of St Columba Edin 80-81; Chap of Guild of Students Univ of Birm from 81. *c/o University of Birmingham, PO Box 363, Birmingham, B15 2TT.*

MORRISON, Walter Edward. b 15. ALCD 41. **d** 41 **p** 42 S'wark. C of Morden 41-44; Reigate 44-49; V of H Trin Richmond 49-55; H Trin Anerley 55-56; Ch Ch w H Trin Penge 56-66; St Luke Bath 66-81. *15 Ashley Road, Clevedon, Avon, BS21 7UX.* (Clevedon 876088)

MORRISON, Preb Walter John Raymond. b 30. Jes Coll Cam BA 55, MA 58. Westcott Ho Cam 55. **d** 57 **p** 58 Lon. C of St Mark Dalston 57-60; Totteridge 60-63; V of St Paul Letchworth 63-71; RD of Hitchin 70-71; Research Fell Qu Coll Birm 71-72; R of Ludlow Dio Heref from 72; RD of Ludlow from 78; Preb of Heref Cathl from 78; Pastoral Care of Ashford Carbonell w Ashford Bowdler, Caynham, Ludford and Richards Castle 80-81. *4 College Street, Ludlow, Salop, Sy8 1AN.* (Ludlow 2073)

MORRISON, William Elwyn. b 44. Univ of Waterloo BA 66. Univ of Tor MA 67. Trin Coll Tor MDiv 76. **d** 76 **p** 77 Yukon. I of Carcross w Atlin 76-79; Cassiar Dio Yukon from 79; Exam Chap to Bp of Yukon from 79. *Box 306, Cassiar, BC, Canada V0C 1E0.*

MORRISON, William Kingsburgh. Trin Coll Tor BA 26. **d** 28 **p** 29 NS. C of Arichat 28-29; P-in-c 29-30; R of Coxheath 30-42; RD of Syd 38-42; R of Fort McMurray w Waterways 42-46; Durham w Egremont and Allan Park 46-49; Dutton Tyrconnell and Burwell Park 49-50; Dutton w W Lorne 50-51; I of Roseland 51-60; R of Port Stanley 60-67. *35028 Millwood Drive, Woodlake, Calif 93286, USA.*

MORRISON-WELLS, John Frederick Pritchard. b 42. St D Coll Lamp BA 65. Coll of Resurr Mirfield, 65. **d** 67 Birm **p** 68 Aston for Birm. C of St Mich AA Bartley Green 67-70; St Andr Handsworth 70-73; V of Perry Barr 73-80; St Aid Small Heath Dio Birm from 80; Exam Chap to Bp of Birm from 78; RD of Bordesley Dio Birm from 80. *St Aidan's Clergy House, Herbert Road, Birmingham, B10 0PR.* (021-772 0318)

MORROW, Derek James. b 15. Trin Coll Dub BA 42, MA 47. Div Test 46. **d** 46 **p** 47 Down. C of Donaghadee 46-49; R of Rathmolyon and Laracor 49-51; Tullamore Lynally and Rahan 51-64; Drogheda w Duleek and Slane 64-81; RD of U and Lower Kells and Fore 64-77; Can of Meath 69-81; Dioc Regr Dio Meath 77-81; Archd of Meath 79-81. *4 Cyprus Avenue, Belfast 5, N Ireland.* (Belf 653984)

MORROW, Edward Sydney. b 34. Qu Coll Birm 73. **d** 74 Bp Wood for Damar **p** 75 Damar. On study leave 74-75; VG Dio Damar (Namibia from 80) from 75. *Box 57, Windhoek, SW Africa.* (2-7122)

MORROW, George Frederick. b 07. TCD BA 45. **d** 46 **p** 47 Meath. C of Oldcastle w Lougherew and Mountnugent 46-47; C-in-c of Kilbixy and Leney U 47-51; I 51-52; Easkey U 52-60; Fenagh U 60-64; Rathaspeck U 64-69; Kiltegan (w Hacketstown, Clonmore and Moyne from 76) 69-79; Preb of Kilkenny and of Leigh 76-79. *135 Balrothery Estate, Tallaght, Co Dublin.*

MORROW, Grant. b 47. St Barn Coll Adel 74. **d** 77 **p** 78 Melb. C of St Steph Belmont 77-79; P-in-c of Fawkner Dio Melb from 79. *6 Seacombe Street, Fawkner, Vic, Australia 3060.* (359 2186)

MORROW, Harry Hugh. Trin Coll Dub BA 49. **d** 49 **p** 50 Dub. C of St Thos Dub 49-52; Rathmolyon 52-56; R 56-58; I of Killoughter U 58-62; C of Portadown 62-65; R of Ballinderry w Tamlaght 65-70; Bordertown 70-73; P-in-c of Findon w Seaton 73-76; Dir Social Welfare Dept Dio Adel from 76. *c/o 18 King William Road, N Adelaide, S Australia.* (267 1411)

MORROW, Henry. Montr Dioc Th Coll LTh 55. **d** 54 **p** 55 Alg. C of Epiph Sudbury 55-57; I of Ascen Sudbury 57-61; St Matt Sault Ste Marie 61-69; R of New Liskeard 69-73; St John Thunder Bay Dio Alg from 73. *226 Pearl Street, Thunder Bay, Ont., Canada.* (807-345 6898)

MORROW, Joseph John. b 54. Univ of Edin BD 79. Edin Th Coll 76. **d** 79 **p** 80 Brech. Chap to St Paul's Cathl Dio Brech from 79. *25 Blackness Avenue, Dundee, DD2 1EW.*

MORSE, Victor Sidney Edward. **d** 66 **p** 67 Tor. C of St Andr Scarborough 66-68; I of Cookstown 68-72; St Geo Pet Tor 72-77; on leave. *2050 Sperling Avenue, Burnaby, BC, Canada.*

MORSHEAD, Ivo Francis Trelawny. b 27. ACA 52, FCA 63. Cudd Coll 61. **d** 63 **p** 64 Bris. C of St Mary Redcliffe w Temple Bedminster 63-68; Wimbledon (in c of St Jo Bapt) 68-73; V of Elham 73-78; V of Whitchurch Dio Ex from 78. *Whitchurch Vicarage, Whitchurch Road, Tavistock, Devon, PL19 9DQ.* (Tavistock 2185)

MORSON, Preb John Basil. b 10. MC 43. TD 53. OBE 56. Linc Th Coll 30. **d** 33 Ches for Wakef **p** 34 Wakef. C of Liversedge 33-35; Tarporley 35-37; Pontesbury (1st and 2nd portions) (in c of Lea Cross) 37-43; V of Minsterley 45-54; R of Habberley 45-54; CF (TA - R of O) 39-59; Dioc Missr Dio Lich and V of Sambrook 54-62; Hon Chap to HM the Queen 57-59; Preb of Lich 61-79; Preb (Emer) from 79; R of Wem 62-79; V of Lee Brockhurst 62-79; RD of Wem and Whitchurch 63-79. *St Chads Cottage, Claremont Bank, Shrewsbury, Salop, SY1 1RW.*

MORT, Jacob. b 1890. **d** 28 **p** 29 Man. C of St Mark Heyside 28-29; Castleton Moor 29-31; St Paul Kersal 31-33; C-in-c of Lumb-in-Rossendale 33-34; V 34-48; Bardsley 48-52; Prestolee 52-56; PC of Birtles 56-64; Perm to Offic Dio Chelmsf 64-74. *53 Blenheim Road, Clacton-on-Sea, Essex.*

✠ **MORT, Right Rev John Ernest Llewelyn.** b 15. CBE 65. St Cath Coll Cam 3rd cl Hist Trip pt i 37, BA (3rd cl Hist Trip pt ii) 38, MA 42. Ahmadu Bello Univ Zaria Hon LLD 70. Westcott Ho Cam 38. **d** 40 **p** 41 Worc. C of Dudley 40-44; Priv Chap to Bp of Worc 44-52; L to Offic Dio Worc 44-48; V of St Jo Bapt-in-Bewardine Worc 48-52; Cons Ld Bp of N Nigeria in Worc Cathl 24 June 52 by Abp of Cant; Abp of Wales; Bps of Worc; Birm; and Lich; and Bps Fyffe; Lasbrey; A W Smith; Curtis and Sara; res 69; Can Res and Treas of Leic Cathl from 70; Asst Bp in Dio Leic from 72. *7 St Martin's East, Leicester, LE1 5FX.* (Leicester 530580)

MORTENSEN, Carl August Albert. b 1900. St Andr Coll Pampisford 48. **d** 49 **p** 50 Dur. C of Dawdon 49-51; V of Pelton 51-59; St Matt Darlington 59-61; Ushaw Moor 61-62; PC of Trimdon Grange 65-68; V 68-71. *Address temp unknown.*

MORTER, Ian Charles. b 54. AKC 77. Coll of the Resurr Mirfield 77. **d** 78 Chelmsf **p** 79 Colchester for Chelmsf. C of St Jas Colchester Dio Chelmsf from 78. *13 Roman Road, Colchester, Essex, CO1 1UR.* (Colchester 73038)

MORTIBOYS, John William. AKC and BD 69. Sarum Th Coll 71. **d** 71 **p** 72 Ox. C of All SS Reading Dio Ox from 71. *14 Downshire Square, Reading, Berks, RG1 6NH.* (Reading 52000)

MORTIMER, Anthony John. b 42. Sarum Wells Th Coll 68. **d** 71 **p** 72 Heref. C of St Martin Heref 71-79; V of Kingstone Dio Heref from 79; P-in-c of Clehonger Dio Heref from 80; Eaton Bp Dio Heref from 80. *Kingstone Vicarage, Hereford.* (Golden Valley 250350)

MORTIMER, Arthur James. b 12. Fitzw Ho Cam BA 33, MA 37. Coll of Resurr Mirfield 33. **d** 35 **p** 36 Chelmsf. C of Stanford-le-Hope 35-38; Barking 38-39; Hornchurch (in c of St Geo) 39-45; V of Canvey I 45-53; St Aug Thorpe Bay 53-56; St John L Thurrock 56-77; Chap Thurrock Hosp 56-73. *2 Gateley Gardens, Norwich, NR3 3TU.*

MORTIMER, Charles Edward. Em Coll Sktn 63. **d** & **p** 67 Calg. I of Carbon 67-70; Big Country 70-75; Brooks Dio Calg from 75. *Box 514, Brooks, Alta, Canada.* (882-3300)

MORTIMER, Charles Philip. b 38. Linc Th Coll 68. **d** 70 Pontefract for Wakef **p** 71 Wakef. C of Penistone 70-74; P-in-c of Luddenfoot 74-77; V of Luddenden 74-77; Chap RAF from 77. *c/o Ministry of Defence, Adastral House, Theobalds Road, WC1.*

MORTIMER, Douglas Hayman. b 10. Lich Th Coll 32. **d** 35 **p** 36 Southw. C of St Mich AA Sutton-in-Ashfield 35-42; Min of Forest Town 42-47; R of Bilborough w Strelley 47-53; C-in-c of Lytchett Minster 53-54; V 54-78. *5 Haven Road, Corfe Mullen, Wimborne, Dorset, BH21 3SY.* (Broadstone 699565)

MORTIMER, Canon Hugh Augustine. Bp's Univ Lennox. **d** 40 Montr **p** 42 Fred for Montr. C of St Matthias Westmount 40-42; Trin Mem Ch Montr 42-45; I of Fort St John 45-49; R of St Steph Buckingham 49-52; Chap RCN 52-72; Hosp Chap Dio BC from 72; Hon Can of BC from 78. *1723 Green Oaks Terrace, Victoria, BC, Canada.* (604-598 8272)

MORTIMER, Prec Hugh Sterling. b 23. Trin Coll Dub BA 44, MA 53. **d** 46 **p** 47 Connor. C of St Polycarp Finaghy 46-49; Dean's V of St Anne's Cathl Belf 49-53; V Cho 53-55; I of Tartaraghan 55-61; Hon V Cho of Arm Cathl from 57; R of Magherafelt 61-66; Armagh Dio Arm from 66; Preb of Arm Cathl 67-72; Treas of Arm Cathl 72-73; Chan 73-75; Prec from 75. *Rectory, Armagh, N Ireland.* (Armagh 522970)

MORTIMER, John Lionel. b 15. St Edm Hall Ox 34. Univ of Dur LTh 39. Dorch Miss Coll 36. **d** 39 Bp Golding-Bird for Guildf **p** 40 Guildf. C of St Martin Dorking 39-43; St Mark S Farnborough 43-47; St Sav w St Pet S'wark 47-48; SPCK Films Officer 48-50; Chap of Elmhurst Sch Camberley and L to Offic Dio Guildf 50-76. *Foxlease, High Street, Maiden Bradley, Warminster, Wilts.* (Maiden Bradley 345)

MORTIMER, Lawrence George. b 45. St Edm Hall Ox BA (2nd cl Th) 67, MA 71. St Chad Coll Dur Dipl Th 68. **d** 70 **p** 71 Cov. C of Rugby 70-75; V of Styvechale Dio Cov from 75. *16 Armorial Road, Coventry, CV3 6GJ.* (Cov 414524)

MORTIMER, Tom. b 1896. Keble Coll Ox BA (*sc* Th w distinc) 21, MA 24. Wells Th Coll 21. **d** 22 **p** 23 Ex. C of Gt Torrington 22-24; M of Bush Bro of St Barn N Queensld 24-29; C of St Mary Redcliffe 29-32; R of Horwood w Newton Tracey 32-37; V of Burrington 37-41; Salcombe 41-46; Westleigh 46-60; Hon Chap to Bp of Ex from 50; R of Cotleigh w Monkton 60-62. *Rectory, Feniton, Honiton, EX14 0ED.* (Honiton 850253)

MORTIMER, William Raymond. b 31. St Deiniol's Libr Hawarden 68. **d** 69 **p** 70 St A. C of Flint 69-71; L to Offic Dio St A 72-73; V of Llanwddyn w Llanfihangel-yng-Ngwynfa w Llwydiarth Dio St A from 73. *Llanwddyn Vicarage, Oswestry, Salop., SY10 0LX.* (Llanwddyn 663)

MORTIMER-TANNER, Richard Sutherland. St Jo Coll Morpeth ThL 40. **d** 41 **p** 42 Graft. C of Casino 41-44; P-in-c of Liston 44-45; V of All SS Monto 47-49; H Trin Fortitude Valley Brisb 49-52; Chap Launceston Gr Sch 53-54; C-in-c of Cullenswood 54-55; Lect Univ of Queensland from 55. *25 Latrobe Street, East Brisbane, Queensland, Australia.*

MORTIMORE, Robert Edward. b 39. Wells Th Coll. **d** 69 Dorking for Guildf **p** 70 Guildf. C of Byfleet 69-72; Fitzroy 72-75; St Aid Remuera 76; Fitzroy 77-79; V of Te Kuiti Dio Waik from 79. *Box 313, Te Kuiti, NZ.*

MORTLEY, Eric George. Univ of Syd BA 62. BD (Lon) 67. Moore Th Coll Syd ACT ThL 43. **d** and **p** 43 Syd. C of St Steph Newtown 43-44; Harris Pk 44-48; Home Sec NSW Branch of CMS 48-50; Actg Gen Sec from 50; R of W Ryde w Ermington 50-53; Prin of Bible Tr Inst Strathfield 53-56; R of Eastwood 56-64; Chap to Abp of Syd 57-64; R of All SS Woollahra 64-75; L to Offic Dio Syd from 75. *33 Wheeler Parade, Dee Why, NSW, Australia 2099.* (98-5824)

MORTON, Alan McNeile. b 28. Univ of Lon BD 49. K Coll Lon and Warm AKC 51. MTh (Lon) 68. BA (Lon) 78. **d** 52 **p** 53 Guildf. C of St Paul Egham Hythe 52-55; Dom Chap to Bp of St E 55-58; Youth Chap Dio St E 56-58; C of St Mary Stoke Ipswich 58-59; V of St Francis Ipswich 59-64; Hon Chap to Bp of St E 60-64; Exam Chap to Bp of St E 63-64; Perm to Offic Dio Ely 68-69; Chap and Asst Master Reading Sch 69-78; Perm to Offic Dio Ox from 69; Hdmaster St Sebastian Sch Nine Mile Ride Wokingham from 78. *16 Erleigh Road, Reading, Berks.*

MORTON, Albert George. b 34. Univ of Sask BA 61. McGill Univ Montr MA 73. Em & St Chad's Coll Sktn LTh 61. **d** 61 Edmon for Arctic **p** 61 Arctic. Miss at Inuvik 61-65; C of Stanford-le-Hope 66-69; V of Swallowbeck 69-82; R of L Munden and Sacombe Dio St Alb from 82. *Little Munden Rectory, Dane End, Ware, Herts.* (092-084 255)

MORTON, Alexander Francis. Late Scho of St D Coll Lamp BA 30, BD 36. Coll of Resurr Mirfield 30. **d** 32 **p** 33 S'wark. C of St Anne Wandsworth 32-35; St Mark Noel Pk 35; St Andr Stockwell Green 35-40; Chap at All SS Maymo 40-42; CF (Ind) 42-46; Hon CF 46; Asst Chap Rang Cathl and Chap Ch Ch Canton Rang 46-48; Chap HM Pris Wakef 48-52; V of Sutton w Lound 52-73; Perm to Offic Dio Southw from 74. *5 Chequers Close, Ranby, Retford, Notts.*

MORTON, Alfred Bruce. b 21. TCD BA (2nd cl Mod Ment and Mor Sc) 42, MA 47. Linc Th Coll. **d** 44 **p** 45 Newc T. C of Hexham 44-47; R of St Ninian Alyth w St Marg Meigle 47-51; St Pet Kirkcaldy 51-57; Northfield 57-73; RD of King's Norton 62-73; Chap and Sec Partis Coll Bath from 73. *1 Partis College, Bath, Somt, BA1 3QD.*

MORTON, Andrew Edward. b 51. Univ of Lon BA 72. AKC and BD 74. St Aug Coll Cant 75. **d** 76 Lon **p** 77 Kens for Lon. C of Feltham 76-79; Pontlottyn w Fochriw 79-81; V of Ferndale w Maerdy Dio Llan from 81. *Vicarage, North Terrace, Maerdy, Rhondda, Mid Glam.* (Maerdy 651)

MORTON, Arthur. b 15. CVO 79. OBE 61. Jes Coll Cam BA 36, MA 40. Wycl Hall Ox 36. **d** 38 **p** 39 Willesden for Lon. C of Neasden 38-41; Chap Miss to Seamen at Man 41-51; Asst Dir NSPCC 51-54; Dir 54-79; M of Home Office Advisory Coun on Child Care and Centr Tr Coun in Child Care 56-68. *25 Cottes Way, Hill Head, Fareham, Hants, PO14 3NF.*

MORTON, Clive Frederick. b 47. BA (Lon) 70. St Jo Coll Dur 78. **d** 80 **p** 81 Leic. C of Countesthorpe w Foston Dio Leic from 80. *4 Central Street, Countesthorpe, Leicester, LE8 3QJ.*

MORTON, Francis Henry. **d** 34 **p** 36 St Arn. C of Manangatang 34-36; V 36-38; Dunolly 38-41; Donald 41-50; Whittlesea 50-51; I of Lillydale 51-54; W Coburg 54-60; Essendon 60-67; Mentone 67-72; Perm to Offic Dio Melb from 73. *6 Downward Street, Mornington, Vic, Australia 3931.* (059-75 4819)

MORTON, Harold Christopherson. **d** 59 **p** 60 Edmon. I of Vegreville 59-67; Sedgewick 67-72; Vegreville 72-79. *114 Parkview Manor, Vegreville, Alta, Canada.*

MORTON, Howard Knyvett. b 30. St Jo Coll Cam BA 51, MA 67. Linc Th Coll 55. **d** 57 **p** 58 St Alb. C of Hatfield Hyde 57-60; Asst Master Heaton Gr Sch Newc T 60-66; Sec Adult Educn C'tte Dio Newc T 63-66; CMS 66-72; Asst Master Heaton Comp Sch Newc T 72-75; Heworth Comp Sch Gateshead from 75. *1 Ashleigh Grove, Newcastle-upon-Tyne, NE2 3DJ.*

MORTON, John Francis Eric. b 17. Univ of Leeds BA (2nd cl Lat) 38. Coll of Resurr Mirfield 38. **d** 40 **p** 41 Ripon. C of St Wilfrid Leeds 40-43; C-in-c of Hough End Conv Distr 43-46; CF (EC) 46-47; CF 47-55; V of Hudswell w Downholme 55-60; C-in-c of Marske 58-60; V of H Spirit Beeston Hill 60-78. *St Barnabas House, Windmill Approach, Leeds, LS10 3DT.*

MORTON, John Ivan. b 32. Linc Coll Ox BA (2nd cl Mod Hist) 55, MA 59. Wells Th Coll. **d** 57 **p** 58 Lich. C of St Chad Shrewsbury 57-60; Dunham Massey 60-62; Sen Div Master Altrincham Gr Sch 60-62; PC of St Luke Derby 62-70; St Andr w Kirby 70-75; St Matt Northn Dio Pet from 75; RD of Northn from 79. *Vicarage, St Matthew's Parade, Northampton, NN2 7HF.* (Northampton 713615)

MORTON, Canon John Peter Sargeson. b 12. Late Exhib of Keble Coll Ox 3rd cl Cl Mods 33, BA (3rd cl Th) 35, MA 39. Lich Th Coll 35. **d** 36 **p** 37 Carl. C of St Jo Evang Barrow-F 36-38; St Aid w Ch Ch Carl 38-43; V of St Jas Barrow-F 43-54; H Trin Carl 54-67; Ambleside W Rydal and Brathay 67-78; Hon Can of Carl 62-78; Can (Emer) from 78. *35 Gretton Road, Winchcombe, Cheltenham, GL54 5EG.* (Winchcombe 603384)

MORTON, Murray James. St Jo Coll Morpeth, ACT Thl (2nd cl) 67. **d** 68 **p** 69 Melb. C of Balwyn 68-70; Ringwood 70-71; I of St Mark Spotswood 71-74; Ocean Grove Dio Melb from 74. *90 Asbury Street, Ocean Grove, Vic, Australia 3226.* (052-55 1996)

MORTON, Rupert Neville. b 25. St Steph Ho Ox 51. **d** 54 **p** 55 Guildf. C of St Mich Aldershot 54-57; Prec of Guildf Cathl 57-58; Chap Carter Bequest Hosp 58-62; V of St Chad Middlesbrough 58-62; Bramley 62-79; Grafham 62-79; Hon Chap to Bp of Kimb K 68-71; RD of Cranleigh 71-76; M Gen Syn Guildf from 73; R of Haslemere Dio Guildf from 79. *Rectory, Derby Road, Haslemere, Surrey.* (Haslemere 4578)

MORTON, William Derek. b 28. Wells Th Coll 67. **d** 69 Bp Horstead for Leic **p** 70 Leic. C of Kibworth Beauchamp w Kibworth Harcourt 69-72; Industr Chap K Lynn Dio Nor from 72. *12 Coniston Close, Sandy Lane, South Wootton, PE30 3NL.* (King's Lynn 674158)

MORVEN, Herbert Baldwin. b 43. **d** 76 Caled. C of New Aiyansh Dio Caled from 76. *New Aiyansh, Naas River, via Terrace, BC, Canada.*

MOSBY, Canon Eddie Jaban. St Paul's Th Coll Moa I 55. **d** 60 **p** 62 Carp. C of All S Cathl Thursday I 60-64; Chap Bamaga Govt Settlement Dio Carp 64-80; Hon Can of Carp from 70; P-in-c of Yorke I Dio Carp from 80. *Yorke Island, Queensland, Australia.*

MOSBY, Morrison Ted. b 49. St Jo Coll Morpeth 78. **d** 81 Carp. C of Weipa S Dio Carp from 81. *Weipa South, Queensland, Australia.*

MOSEA, Ven Albert Edwin. St Pet Coll Rosettenville. **d** 62 **p** 63 Bloemf. P Dio Bloemf from 62; Archd of N Free State and Can of Bloemf from 77. *Box 5009, Lengau, Kroonstad, OFS, S Africa.* (01411-7623)

MOSEDALE, Hugh Alfred. b 14. AKC 48. St Bonif Coll Warm. **d** 49 **p** 50 Liv. C of W Derby 49-52; Lewisham 52-55; St Mary Walton 55-57; V of Middleton Junction 57-61; R of Elsworth w Knapwell Dio Ely from 61; Boxworth Dio Ely from 61; RD of Bourn 72-81. *Boxworth Rectory, Cambridge, CB3 8LZ.* (Elsworth 226)

MOSEKI, Itumeleng Baldwin. b 40. **d** 76 Bp Carter for Johann **p** 77 Johann C of Dobsonville Dio Johann from 76. *1076 Dobsonville, Roodepoort 1715, S Africa.*

MOSELANE, Tebogo Geoffrey. St Pet Coll Alice. **d** 71 **p** 72 Johann. P Dio Johann. *Box 17, Sharpeville, Johannesburg, S Africa.*

MOSELEY, Arthur William. b 27. Lich Th Coll. **d** 60 **p** 61 Lich. C of Castlechurch 60-64; Bloxwich 64-66; V of Bradley, Staffs 66-72; C of Stoke-upon-Trent 73-74; V of Brown Edge Dio Lich from 74. *Brown Edge Vicarage, Stoke-on-Trent, Staffs.* (S-o-T 502134)

MOSELEY, Colin Francis. **d** 79 **p** 80 Bris (APM). Hon C of St Mary Fishponds Dio Bris from 79. *7 Prospect Close, Winterbourne Down, Bristol, BS17 1BD.*

MOSELEY, David John Reading. b 30. Univ Coll Ox BA 54, MA 58. Wells Th Coll 54. **d** 56 **p** 57 Man. C of St Jo Evang Farnworth 56-59; V of Laventille w Morvant and Barataria Trinid 59-63; St Paul Bedminster 63-75; Team V of Bedminster 75-78; V of Kilmington w Shute Dio Ex from 78. *Kilmington Vicarage, Axminster, Devon, EX13 7RG.* (Axminster 33156)

MOSELEY, Eric Hugh. St D Coll Lamp 23. Lon Coll of Div 27. **d** 28 **p** 29 Llan. C of Gilfach Goch 28-31; Stourport 31-36; St Pet Gt Worc 36-40; L to Offic Dio Worc 40-60; Cler Org Sec C of E Children's S Dios Birm; Cov; Heref; Leic; Lich and Worc 43-60; Perm to Offic Dio Heref 43-60; V of Sellack w K Capel and Foy 60-81. *The Rowans, Grove Common, Sellack, Ross-on-Wye, Herefs.*

MOSELEY, Hugh Martin. b 47. St Jo Coll Dur BA 70. Westcott Ho Cam 71. **d** 73 Cant **p** 74 Dover for Cant. C of Hythe 73-77; P-in-c of Eythorne (w Waldershare from 80) Dio Cant from 77; Waldershare 78-80. *Eythorne Rectory, Barfreystone Road, Dover, Kent.* (Shepherdswell 830241)

MOSELEY, Roger Henry. b 38. Edin Th Coll 60. **d** 63 **p** 64 Lon. C of All SS Friern Barnet 63-66; Grantham 66-69; C-in-c of Swaton w Spanby 69-73; Horbling 69-73; V of Soberton w Newtown 73-79; Sarisbury w Swanwick Dio Portsm from 79. *Sarisbury Vicarage, Bridge Road, Sarisbury Green, SO3 7EN.* (Locksheath 2207)

MOSES, H Cross Rang **d** 59 **p** 60 Rang. P Dio Rang. *Ko-ohn Circle, c/o St Luke's Compound, Toungoo, Burma.*

MOSES, Canon Haydn. b 28. St D Coll Lamp BA 51. St Mich Coll Llan 51. **d** 53 **p** 54 Llan. C of Aberdare 53-56; Neath w Llantwit and Tonna 56-60; CF (TA) from 59; R of Cilybebyll 60-71; V of Llangyfelach w St Teilo-Clase 71-77; Llanelli Dio St D from 77; Can of St D Cathl from 80. *Vicarage, Old Road, Llanelli, Dyfed.* (Llanelli 2072)

MOSES, John Anthony. Univ of Queensld MA 63. Univ of Erlangen PhD 65. **d** 77 **p** 78 Brisb. Hon C of H Spirit Kenmore City and Dio Brisb from 77. *11 Wexford Street, Kenmore, Queensland, Australia 4069.*

MOSES, Very Rev John Henry. b 38. Univ of Nottm BA 59, PhD 65. Linc Th Coll 62. **d** 64 **p** 65 St Alb. C of St Andr Bedford 64-70; P-in-c of St Pet Cov 70-73; St Mark w St Barn Cov 71-73; Exam Chap to Bp of Cov 72-77; RD of Coventry E 73-77; R of Cov E Team Min 73-77; Surr 73-77; Archd of Southend 77-82; Bp of Chelmsf Officer for Industry and Commerce 78-82; R and Provost of Chelmsf and Dir of Cathl Centre for Research and Tr from 82. *Provost's House, Harlings Grove, Waterloo Lane, Chelmsford, CM1 1YQ.* (Chelmsford 354318)

MOSES, Leslie Alan. b 49. Univ of Hull BA 71. Univ of Edin BD 76. Edin Th Coll 73. **d** 76 **p** 77 Edin. C of Old St Paul Edin 76-79; R of Leven Dio St Andr from 79. *Rectory, Victoria Road, Leven, Fife, KY8 4EX.* (Leven 26488)

MOSES, Norman. b 22. AKC (2nd cl) 37. **d** 37 **p** 38 Dur. C of St Mary Heworth 37-40; C-in-c of Grindon 40-44; V of St Jude S Shields 44-58; Grangetown 58-77. *1 Wayside, Sunderland, T & W, SR2 7QJ.*

MOSES, Ponniah Elisha. b 41. Bp's Coll Calc. **d** and **p** 74 W Mal. P Dio W Mal. *Emmanuel Church, Tapah, Perak, Malaysia.*

MOSFORD, Denzil Huw Erasmus. b 56. St D Coll Lamp Dipl Th 77. Sarum Wells Th Coll 77. **d** 79 **p** 80 Swan B. C of Clydach Dio Swan B from 79. *6 Twyn-y-Bedw Road, Clydach, Swansea, SA6 5EN.*

MOSHER, Ven Leonard Weldon. **d** 29 **p** 30 NS. C of St Geo Halifax 29-31; R of Weymouth 31-34; St Alb Woodside 34-41; Bridgetown 41-46; Asst Sec Dio NS 47-49; R of Hantsport 49-52; Kentville 52-77; Hon Can of NS 59-77; Archd of Annapolis 60-77; Archd (Emer) from 77. *192 Pleasant Street, Dartmouth, NS, Canada.*

MOSHESH, Godfrey Kopano. b 09. St Bede's Coll Umtata 74. **d** 74 St John's. d Dio St John's. *St Bede's College, Umtata 5100, S Africa.*

MOSHOEU, Reuben. **d** 57 **p** 58 Kimb K. P Dio Kimb K.

Box 63, Taung Station, Kimberley, CP, S Africa.

MOSIMA, Esau. **d** 77 Botswana. d Dio Botswana. *PO Box 159, Nahalapye, Botswana.*

MOSLEY, Edward Peter. b 38. Clifton Th Coll 62. **d** 67 **p** 68 Carl. C of St Andr Mirehouse Whitehaven 67-69; St Paul Newbarns w Hawcoat Barrow-F 69-72; R of Aikton 72-77; C-in-c of Gt Orton 72; R 72-77; V of Silloth 77-78; CF from 78. *c/o Ministry of Defence, Bagshot Park, Bagshot, Surrey, GU19 5PL.*

MOSLEY, William. McGill Univ Montr MD and CM 28. Univ of Tor DPH 37. **d** 63 Bp Snell for Tor. C of Ch of the Comforter City and Dio Tor from 63. *20 Lankin Boulevard, Toronto, 359, Ont., Canada.*

MOSOLA, Paul Nathanial. **d** 81 Geo. d Dio Geo. *St John's Rectory, Bongulethu, Oudtshoorn, S Africa.*

MOSOTHOANE, Canon Ephraim Khotso. St Bede's Th Coll Umtata, LTh 63. Qu Coll Birm Dipl Th, MA. **d** 65 **p** 66 Bloemf. Miss P of St Patr Miss Bloemf 65-68; Tutor St Bede's Coll Umtata Dio St John's 68-76; Prin 77-81; Can of St John's from 77; Lect Univ of Transkei from 81. *P Bag X5092, Umtata, Transkei, S Africa.* (Umtata 2151)

MOSS, Arthur Robinson. b 15. St D Coll Lamp BA 40. **d** 40 **p** 41 Liv. C of Ch Ch Bootle 40-42; St Mich Garston 42-43; Ormskirk 43-46; R of Hopesay w Edgton 46-52; V of Beckwithshaw and Chap Qu Ethelburga Sch Harrogate 52-58; V of Cannington 58-80; C-in-c of Aisholt Dio B & W from 69. *1 Withiel Drive, Cannington, Somt, TA5 2LY.*

MOSS, Barrie. b 42. BD (Lon) 65. ALCD (1st cl) 64. **d** 65 **p** 66 Lon. C of St Matt Willesden 65-67; St Andr Kingsbury 67-70; Harrow Weald (in c of St Barn) 70-74; P-in-c of Radwinter 74-78; R (w Hempstead) 78-80; P-in-c of Hempstead 74-78; V of Beamish Dio Dur from 80. *St Andrew's Vicarage, Stanley, Co Durham, DH9 0DU.* (Stanley 32252)

MOSS, Very Rev Basil Stanley. b 18. Qu Coll Ox BA (2nd cl Lit Hum) 41, 2nd cl Th 42, Quested Exhib 42, MA 45. Linc Th Coll 42. **d** 43 **p** 44 Man. C of Leigh 43-45; Tutor Linc Th Coll 45-46; Sub Warden 46-51; LPr Dio Linc 45-51; Sen Tutor St Cath Cumberland Lodge 51-53; V of St Nath Cotham 53-54; C-in-c of St Kath Bishopston 53-54; V of St Nath w St Kath Bris 54-60; Exam Chap to Bp of Bris 56-73; to Bp of Blackb 62-66; Dir of Ordin Tr Dio Bris 56-66; Hon Can of Bris 59-60 and 66-73; Can Res 60-66; Chief Sec ACCM 66-73; Provost of Birm from 73. *10 Carisbrooke Road, Birmingham, B17 8NW.* (021-429 3398)

MOSS, Bernard Stanley. **d** 60 Bp Paget for Johann **p** 61 Johann. C of Germiston 60-62; R of Belgravia Johann 62-68; Nigel w Heidelberg 68-78; P-in-c of Regent Hill Dio Johann from 81. *32 South Road, The Hill, Johannesburg, S Africa.*

MOSS, Denis. b 32. **d** 74 **p** 75 Auckld (APM). Hon C of St Geo Epsom 74-77. *107 Campbell Road, One Tree Hill, Auckland, NZ.* (662-720)

MOSS, Francis Duncan. b 23. AKC (2nd cl) 43. Wells Th Coll 53. **d** 54 **p** 55 Guildf. C of St Paul Nork 54-56; Tewkesbury 56-57; V of Gt w L Barrington and Taynton 57-60; C-in-c of St Geo Conv Distr Lower Tuffley Glouc 60-64; R of Kemerton 64-80; Mobberley Dio Ches from 80. *Rectory, Mobberley, Chesh.* (Mobberley 3218)

MOSS, Guy Ernest James. b 18. chich Th Coll 41. **d** 42 S'wark **p** 43 Kingston T for S'wark. K Coll Lon 39. Chich Th Coll 41. **d** 42 S'wark **p** 43 Kingston T for S'wark. C of St Chrys Peckham 42-44; St Nich Guildf 44-48; L to Offic Dio Leic 48-49; Burnham 49-50; R of Shimplingthorne w Alpheton 50-55; V of Hoxne w Denham 55-59; L to Offic Dio Nor 60-65; Chap All H Conv Ditchingham 60-63; Sub Warden 63-65; R of Chedgrave w Hardley and Langley Dio Nor from 65. *Chedgrave Rectory, Norwich, NOR 20W.* (Loddon 535)

MOSS, Harold George Edward. b 20. Glouc Sch for Min 79. **d** 80 Tewkesbury for Glouc **p** 81 Glouc. C of Cirencester Dio Glouc from 80. *57 Queen Elizabeth Road, Cirencester, Glos, GL7 1DH.*

MOSS, Howard George. b 1891. St Mich Coll Llan. **d** 24 **p** 25 Llan. C of Merthyr Tydfil 24-26; Kingswood Glos 26-31. *Address temp unknown.*

MOSS, Ivan Douglas Francis. **d** 76 Chich **p** 77 Horsham for Chich. C of Crawley Dio Chich from 76. *Turks Croft, Rusper Road, Ifield, Crawley, W Sussex.*

MOSS, James Wilfred. b 15. Oak Hill Coll 75. **d** 76 St Alb **p** 77 Hertford for St Alb. C of H Trin Frogmore St Alb 76-78; St Luke Watford 78-81. *139 Parkside Drive, Watford, Herts, WD1 3BA.* (Watford 23518)

MOSS, Kenneth Charles. b 37. Univ of Lon BSc 59, DIC and PhD 62. ARCS 59. **d** 66 **p** 68 BC. Hon C of St Barn Vic BC 67-73; Lazenby Chap Univ of Ex from 73. *c/o Chemistry Department, Exeter University, Exeter, EX4 4QJ.*

MOSS, Preb Leonard Godfrey. b 32. K Coll Lon and Warm BD and AKC 59. **d** 60 **p** 61 S'wark. C of St Marg Putney 60-63; Cheam 63-67; V of Much Dewchurch w Llanwarne and Llandinabo 67-72; Dioc Ecumen Officer Dio Heref from 69; V of Marden w Amberley (and Wisteston from 78) Dio Heref from 72; M Gen Syn from 70; Preb of Heref Cathl from 79. *Marden Vicarage, Hereford.* (Sutton St Nich 256)

MOSS, Peter Hextall. b 34. Clare Coll Cam 2nd cl Hist Trip pt i 57, BA (2nd cl Th Trip pt ii) 59, MA 62. Linc Th Coll 59. **d** 61 **p** 62 Dur. C of Easington Colliery 61-63; Whickham 63-65; C-in-c of St Bede Town End Farm Conv Distr Sunderland 65-72; V in Dereham Group (in c of Mattishall; Mattishall Burgh; Welborne and Yaxham) Dio Nor from 72. *Mattishall Vicarage, East Dereham, Norf.* (Dereham 850243)

MOSS, Peter Lindsay. b 42. Ridley Th Coll ACT ThL 70. **d** 71 **p** 72 Melb. C of Camberwell Melb 71-72; St Matt Kens 72-74; Greensborough 74-80; I of Wattle Pk Dio Melb from 80. *109 Broughton Road, Surry Hills, Vic, Australia 3127.*

MOSS, Ralph Naboth Gilmore. Qu Coll Newfld LTh 65. **d** 63 **p** 64 Newfld. C of Fogo 63-66; R of Rose Blanche 66-69; Badger's Quay 70-77. *c/o Box 119, Badger's Quay, Bonavista Bay, Newfoundland, Canada.*

MOSS, Ven Stanley Charles. Trin Coll Melb BA (1st cl Hist) 48. Worc Coll Ox BA (3rd cl Th) 64. ACT ThL (1st cl) 50. **d** 50 **p** 52 Melb. C of Melb Dioc Centre 50-52; Min of Kallista 52-56; Mentone 56-61; I of St Geo Malvern 61-70; Exam Chap to Abp of Melb 61-62; Archd of Kew 69-70; Melb 70-78; Malvern from 78; Dir Angl Inner-City Min Dio Melb 72-76; I of Toorak Dio Melb from 78. *86 Clendon Road, Toorak, Vic, Australia 3142.* (24 4981)

MOSS, Victor Charles. b 25. Oak Hill Th Coll BD (Lon) 65. **d** 66 **p** 67 Ches. C of Macclesfield 66-68; Belper 69-71; V of Ch Ch Chesterfield Dio Derby from 71. *Christ Church Vicarage, Chesterfield, Derbys.* (Chesterfield 73508)

MOSS, Wilfrid Maurice. b 10. St Jo Coll Dur LTh 34, BA 35, MA 41. Tyndale Hall Bris 31. **d** 35 **p** 36 Blackb. C of All SS Preston 35-38; Min of Trin Episc Chap Buxton 38-42; R of Albert Mem Ch Man 42-50; V of Ch Ch Sidcup 50-75; RD of Sidcup 70-75; Perm to Offic Dio Ex from 75. *Highfield, Rock Hill, Georgeham, Devon.* (Croyde 890653)

MOSS, Preb William Henry Osmund. b 11. St Bonif Coll Warm 31. **d** 36 Sherborne for Sarum for Bris **p** 37 Bris. C of St Mich AA Windmill Hill 36-39; Chap RN 39-48; V of Marshfield (w Cold Ashton from 54) 48-54; R of W Kington 54-55; V of St Luke Brislington 55-66; Uttoxeter w Bramshall Dio Lich from 66; C-in-c of Stramshall Dio Lich from 67; Surr from 67; RD of Uttoxeter from 76; Preb of Lich Cathl from 79. *Vicarage, Uttoxeter, Staffs, ST14 8AA.* (Uttoxeter 2668)

MOSS, William Stanley. b 07. MBE 43. Univ of Liv BA (2nd cl Geog) 28, MA 31. Ripon Hall, Ox 32. **d** 33 **p** 34 Man. C of H Trin Littleborough 33-38; Chap and Tutor Coll of St Mark and St John Chelsea 38-39; CF (TA) 39-45; Hon SCF 45; Chap and Lect Trin Coll Carmarthen 45-73; LPr Dio St D from 46. *20 Limegrove Avenue, Carmarthen, Dyfed.*

MOSSMAN, Preb Donald Wyndham Cremer. b 13. OBE 65. ALCD 39, (LTh from 74). **d** 39 Willesden for Lon **p** 40 Lon. C of St Jas L Bethnal Green 39-42; Offg C-in-c of St Simon Zelotes U Chelsea Lon 42-44; V 44-49; Chap Leysin and Montana Switzerland 49-51; Ch Ch Amsterdam w Haarlem and Den Helder 51-55; Zürich 55-64; RD of Switzerland 55-64; Austria 55-63; Preb of St Paul's Cathl Lon from 60; PC of Ch Ch Crouch End Hornsey 64-69; C of St Mich Highgate 69-71; Commiss N and C Eur 64-80; and Gibr 71-80; RD of W Haringey 67-71; R of St Jas Garlickhythe w St Mich Queenhythe and H Trin L City and Dio Lon from 71; Hon Embassy Chap Warsaw from 77; Hon Can of H Trin Pro-Cathl Brussels from 80. *1 Bishop Street, Prebend Street, N1 8PH.* (01-359 6688)

MOSSOP, Henry Watson. b 08. Lich Th Coll 52. **d** 54 **p** 55 Pet. L to Offic in the Culworth Deanery 54-55; C of Eydon and of Moreton Pinkney and of Culworth 55-57; V of Mears Ashby and R of Hardwycke 57-59; Colby w Banningham and Tuttington 59-66; Twyford w Guist 66-73. *Gatehouse, Antingham, North Walsham, Norf, NR28 0NH.* (N Walsham 403561)

MOSSOP, Canon Robert Owen. b 09. Peterho Cam BA 30, MA 35. Westcott Ho Cam 32. **d** 33 **p** 34 Ox. C of Earley 33-40; Chap RAFVR 40-46; R of Ruan Laniharne w Philleigh 46-50; V of Constantine 50-73; RD of Kerrier 59-73; Hon Can of Truro from 69. *Westwood, Carnmenellis, Redruth, Cornw.*

MOSTYN, Francis William. Moore Coll Syd ACT ThL 73. **d** 75 Syd **p** 76 Bp Robinson for Syd. C of St Paul Lithgow 75-79; R of St Barn Littleton Dio Syd from 79. *86 Rabaul Street, Lithgow, NSW, Australia 2790.* (51-4047)

MOTAUNG, Archibald Ezra Tau. b 42. St Bede's Coll Umtata 65. **d** 69 **p** 71 Natal. C of Springvale 69-70; L to Offic Dio Natal 71-73; R of Springvale 73-81; Meadowlands Dio Johann from 81. *450 Maseru Street, Zone 7, Meadowlands, Johannesburg, S Africa.*

MOTAUNG, Cyril. **d** 46 **p** 48 Natal. P Dio Natal 46-79.

PO Box 464, Umkomaas, Natal, S Africa.

MOTAUNG, Daniel. St Bede's Coll Umtata. **d** 60 **p** 62 Basuto. P Dio Basuto 60-66; Dio Les from 66. *St Hilda's Mission, PO Schonghong, via Qacha's Nek, Lesotho, S Africa.*

MOTEBE, Abraham Hans. St Pet Coll Rosettenville. **d** 53 **p** 54 Johann. P Dio Johann 53-62; Dio Pret 62-67. *10877 Matlale Street, Daveyton, East Rand, Transvaal, S Africa.*

MOTHIBA, Nehemiah. b 40. **d** 69 **p** 70 Pret. C of Mahwelereng 69-76; R of Turfloop w Matoks Dio Pret from 76. *P Bag 506, Dwarsriver, N Transvaal, S Africa.*

MOTHIBI, Canon Ariel Clayton Nako. St Pet Coll Rosettenville. **d** 56 **p** 57 Bloemf. P Dio Bloemf 57-65; Dio Natal from 65; Can of Natal from 76. *PO Box 14225, Madadani, Natal, S Africa.*

MOTHIBI, Freddy Mogomotsi. b 39. St Bede's Coll Umtata 69. **d** 70 **p** 71 Bloemf. C of St Patrick Bloemf 71-74; P-in-c of St Pet Rocklands 74-76. *Box 317, Odendaalsrus, OFS, S Africa.*

MOTION, Alexander William. b 08. Pemb Coll Cam BA 31, LLB 32, MA 36. St Bonif Coll Warm. **d** 51 **p** 52 Newc T. C of St Geo Jesmond 51-53; V of St Andr Newc T 53-77. *34 Alwinton Terrace, Newcastle upon Tyne 3.*

MOTLEY, Edward William John. b 01. Bps' Coll Cheshunt 35. **d** 36 **p** 37 Lon. C of St Martin-in-the-Fields 36-41; V of John Keble Ch Mill Hill 41-57; Redbourn 57-67. *The Lodge, Standen, East Grinstead, W Sussex.*

MOTLOI, William James. b 16. St Francis Coll Sekhukhuniland 68. **d** 70 **p** 72 Pret. C of Mamelodi W 70-73; Rethabile Dio Pret from 73. *Box 54, Mamelodi, Pretoria, S Africa.*

MOTSA, Canon Gilbert Dlebankomo. St Pet Coll Rosettenville, 61. **d** 63 **p** 64 Zulu. P Dio Zulu 63-68; Dio Swaz from 68; Can of Swaz from 80. *PO Box 137, Nhlangano, Swaziland.*

MOTSA, Stephen. b 24. **d** 70 Bp Carter for Johann **p** 71 Johann. C of Emdeni Dio Johann from 70. *Bonegang HP School, 847 Moletsane, PO Kwa Xuma, Transvaal, S Africa.*

MOTSEPE, Kenneth Mmutle. St Francis Coll Sekhukuniland. **d** 66 **p** 67 Pret. C of St Andr Rustenburg 66-70; R of St Andr Mmakau 70-81; St John Temba Dio Pret from 81. *Box 36, Temba, Pretoria 0401, S Africa.*

MOTT, Julian Ward. b 52. Loughborough Univ of Tech BSc 77. Ripon Coll Cudd 78. **d** 81 Leic. C of St Andr Aylestone City and Dio Leic from 81. *58 Belvoir Drive, Aylestone, Leicester, LE2 8PA.*

MOTT, Peter John. b 49. Ch Coll Cam BA 70, MA 75. Univ of Dundee PhD 73. Univ of Nottm BA 79. St Jo Coll Nottm 77. **d** 80 **p** 81 York. C of St John Newland Hull Dio York from 80. *75 Desmond Avenue, Beverley High Road, Hull HU6 7JX.*

MOTTAHEDEH, Iraj. U Th Sem Bangalore. **d** 59 **p** 60 Iran. P Dio Iran. *St Paul's Church, Nik Street, Avenue Roosevelt, Teheran, Iran.*

MOTTERSHEAD, Derek. b 39. Open Univ BA 74. Co for Nat Acad Awards BEducn. Chich Th Coll 65. **d** 69 Barking for Chelmsf **p** 70 Chelmsf. C of St Barn w St Jas Gtr Walthamstow 69-72; All SS Chelmsf 72-77; Asst Master Gt Baddow Sch 74-80; P-in-c of Cold Norton w Stow Maries 77-80; V of St Andr Leytonstone Dio Chelmsf from 80. *St Andrew's Vicarage, Forest Glade, E11 1LU.* (01-989 0942)

MOTTRAM, Andrew Peter. b 53. AKC 77. Ripon Coll Cudd 77. **d** 78 Lon **p** 79 Kens for Lon. C of Bedfont 78-81; Bp's Hatfield Dio St Alb from 81. *Church Cottage, Church Street, Hatfield, Herts.* (Hatfield 72119)

MOTYER, John Alexander. b 24. Trin Coll Dub Cl Sizarship 42, BA (2nd cl Ment and Mor Phil Mod) 46, MA 51, BD 51, Carson Bibl Pri Bp Forster Pri and Abp King Pri 46, Div Test Downes Pri Hebr Pri (1st cl) Eccles Hist Pri 47. **d** 47 **p** 48 Lich. C of Penn Fields 47-50; H Trin Bris 50-54; Tutor Clifton Th Coll Bris 50-54; Vice-Prin 54-65; V of St Luke W Hampstead 65-70; Dep Prin Tyndale Hall Bris 70-71; L to Offic Dio Bris 70-81; Prin Trin Coll Bris 71-81; Min of Ch Ch Westbourne, Bournemouth Dio Win from 81. *43 Branksome Dene Road, Bournemouth, Dorset, BH4 8JW* (0202-762164)

MOTYER, Stephen. b 50. Pemb Coll Cam BA 73, MA 77. Univ of Bris MLitt 79. Trin Coll Bris 73. **d** 76 **p** 77 St Alb. Lect Oak Hill Coll from 76. *2 Farm Lane, Chase Side, Southgate, N14 4PP.*

MOUGHTIN, Ross. b 48. St Cath Coll Cam BA 70. St Jo Coll Dur Ba (Th) 75. **d** 76 **p** 77 Liv. C of St Paul Hatton Hill Litherland 76-79; Heswall Dio Ches from 79. *15 Castle Drive, Heswall, Wirral, Mersyside.* (051-342 5946)

MOULD, William Douglas Gordon. b 10. ALCD 38. **d** 38 Lon **p** 39 Willesden for Lon. C of St Paul Ealing 38-41; Hampreston 41-43; St Clem Ox 43-44; R of St Pet Thetford 44-48; V of Ch Ch High Wycombe 48-54; Chudleigh 54-61; R of All Cannings w Etchilhampton 61-63; Combe Hay 63-70. *4 Shakespeare Avenue, Bath, Somerset.*

MOULDEN, Ven Donovan Edward Faulkner. Vanc Sch of Th Dipl Th 71. **d** 71 New Westmr for Calg **p** 72 Calg. C of St Barn Calg 71-73; Chap Alta Inst of Tech 71-73; C Of Oak Bay 73-77; R of St Luke Vic Dio BC from 77; Dom Chap to Bp of BC from 80; Archd Dio BC from 81. *3821 Cedar Hill Cross Roads, Victoria, BC, Canada.*

MOULDER, James Edward. b 37. Rhodes Univ Grahmstn BA 61. PhD 77. **d** 77 Grahmstn (APM). C of Cathl Ch of St Mich & St Geo Grahmstn 77-80. *c/o Rhodes University, Grahamstown 6140, S Africa.*

MOULDER, Kenneth. b 53. Univ of Lon BEducn 75. Ridley Hall Cam 78. **d** 81 Chelmsf. C of St Pet Harold Wood Hornchurch Dio Chelmsf from 81. *22 Gubbins Lane, Harold Wood, Essex, RM3 0QA.*

MOULE, Charles Francis Digby. b 08. Late Scho of Em Coll Cam 1st cl Cl Trip pt i 29, BA (1st cl Cl Trip pt ii) and Evans Pri 31, Jeremie Septuagint Pri 32, Crosse Scho 33, MA 34, Hon Fell Em Coll Cam 72. Hon DD Univ of St Andr 58. FBA 66. Ridley Hall Cam 31. **d** 33 Ely **p** 34 Bp Price for Ely. C of St Mark Cam and Tutor Ridley Hall Cam 33-34; St Andr Rugby 34-36; St Mary Gt Cam 36-40; Vice-Prin Ridley Hall Cam 36-44; L to Offic Dio Ely from 41; Dean of Clare Coll Cam 44-51; Fell from 44; Select Pr Univ of Cam 42, 48 and 53; Ox 54 and 73; Lect in Div Univ of Cam 47-51; Lady Marg Prof of Div in Univ of Cam 51-76; Can Th of Leic Cathl 55-76; Commiss St John's from 80; Perm to Offic Dio Chich from 81. *1 King's Houses, Pevensey, E Sussex, BN24 5JR.*

MOULE, George William Henry. b 04. Em Coll Cam (2nd cl Cl Trip pt i) 25, BA (2nd cl Cl Trip pt ii) 26, MA 30. **d** 36 **p** 37 Glouc. Asst Master and Chap of Dean Close Sch Cheltm 26-39; Berkhamsted Sch 39-45; Asst Master and Asst Chap Repton Sch 45-49; Asst Master and Chap Kelly Coll Tavistock 49-51; R of Oborne w Poyntington 52-53; Asst Master and Chap Rose Hill Sch Alderley 53-55; St Bees Sch Cumb 55-59; V of Damerham 59-70. *Herne Cottage, St Bees, Cumb, CA27 0ED.*

MOULE, Kevin David. b 54. Coll of Resurr Mirfield 77. **d** 80 **p** 81 Edmonton for Lon. C of All SS Finchley Dio Lon from 80. *61 Park Hall Road, East Finchley, N2.* (01-883 9344)

MOULTON, Paul Oliver. b 43. N Ordin Course 77. **d** 80 Ches **p** 81 Stockport for Ches. C of Wilmslow Dio Ches from 80. *25 Stanneylands Road, Wilmslow, Cheshire.*

MOULTON, Thomas Wilson. Qu Coll Newfld 59. **d** 61 **p** 62 Newfld. C of Channel 61-64; I of St Anthony 64-70; R of Deer Lake Dio Newfld (W Newfld from 76) from 70. *Box 148, Deer Lake, Newfoundland, Canada.* (709-635-2326)

MOULTON, William Arthur. b 11. Univ of Leic MEducn 64. FCP 57. Wells Th Coll 47. **d** 48 Kens for Lon **p** 49 Lon. Asst Chap and Sen Lect Coll of St Mark and St John Chelsea 48-62; Prin Lect Bp Grosseteste Coll Linc from 62; L to Offic Dio Linc from 62; Hon PV of Linc Cathl from 76. *49 Main Street, Anwick, Sleaford, NG34 9SJ.* (Ruskington 833384)

MOULTON, William Ernest Ross. b 54. Univ of Tor BA 76. Wycl Coll Tor MDiv 79. **d** 79 **p** 80 Ont. C of Land O'Lakes Dio Ont from 79. *Plevna, Ontario, Canada, K0H 2M0.* (613-479 2432)

MOUMAKOE, Kantoro David. b 54. St Bede's Coll Umtata Dipl Th 81. **d** 78 Pret. C of Moletjie & Matlala Dio Pret from 78. *PO Box 4, Seshego 0742, S Africa.*

MOUNSEY, William Lawrence Fraser. b 51. Univ of St Andr BD 75. Edin Th Coll 76. **d** 78 **p** 79 Edin. C of Portobello Dio Edin from 78. *5 Brighton Place, Portobello, Edinburgh.*

MOUNTAIN, Geoffrey. b 27. Ch Coll Cam 2nd cl Cl Trip pt i 47, BA (3rd cl Engl Trip pt i) 48, Dipl Th 50, MA 53. Wycl Hall Ox. **d** 51 **p** 52 Sheff. C of Darfield 51-53; Fulwood 53-58; R of St Paul York 58-70; Asst Lect York Technical Coll 70-72; Asst Master The Mount Sch York from 72; C of Dringhouses City and Dio York from 70. *4 Beckfield Lane, Acomb, York, Y02 5RL.* (York 791172)

MOUNTFORD, Brian Wakling. b 45. Univ of Newc T BA 66. Univ of Cam MA 73. Westcott Ho Cam 66. **d** 68 **p** 69 Lon. C of St Steph w St Jo Evang Roch Row Westmr 68-69; C of Lanc Gate Paddington 69-73; Fell and Chap Sidney Sussex Coll Cam 73-78; V of Southgate Dio Lon from 78. *1 The Green, Southgate, N14 7EG.* (01-886 0384)

MOUNTFORD, John. b 55. Univ of Nottm BEducn 77. Univ of Birm MA (Th) 80. Linc Th Coll 73. **d** 78 **p** 79 Lich. C of Wombourne 78-80; U Gornal Dio Lich from 80. *8 Eve Lane, Upper Gornal, Dudley, DY1 3TY.* (Sedgley 73900)

MOUNTFORD, Reginald Arthur. b 04. Bp's Coll Cheshunt 36. **d** 37 Lich **p** 38 Stafford for Lich. C of Cannock 37-39; Dresden (in c of St Luke Florence) 39-42 and 46-47; Chap RAF 42-46; V of St Mary Sedgley 47-62; Kinnerley w Melverley 62; C of Cricklewood 62-69. *5 Verlands Close, Niton, Ventnor, IW.*

MOUNTFORT, Canon Gerald Woolfield. Univ of NZ BA 54. NZ Bd of Th Stud LTh 64. Coll Ho Ch Ch. **d** 54 **p** 55 Ch

Ch. C of Avonside 54-56; Ashburton 56-59; Hokitika 59; V of Kumara 59-60; Rakaia 60-63; Maniototo 63-66; Oamaru 66-71; Mornington 71-75; Flagstaff-Brockville 75-76; Taieri Dio Dun from 76; Hon Can of Dun from 77. *48 Ayr Street, Mosgiel, NZ.* (6250)

MOUNT KENYA EAST, Lord Bishop of. *See* Gitari, Right Rev David Mukuba.

MOUNT KENYA SOUTH, Lord Bishop of. *See* Magua, Right Rev Sosipeter.

MOUNT KENYA SOUTH, Assistant Bishop of. *See* Ngaruiya, Right Rev Ezbon.

MOUNTNEY, Frederick Hugh. St Chad's Coll Dur BA (3rd cl Th) 36, MA 39. Lich Th Coll 36. **d** 37 **p** 38 Derby. C of Beighton 37-39; Spondon 39-40; St Lawr Newc T 40-44; C-in-c of St John Backworth 44-48; V of N Gosforth Newc T 48-51; R of Lillingstone Dayrell w Lillingstone Lovell 51-56; V of All SS Heref 56-75; Chap Vic Eye Hosp Heref 56-75; Dioc Ecumen Officer 63-69; Chap at Bonn and Cologne 75-79. *Wayside, New Radnor, Presteigne, Powys.*

MOUNTNEY, John Michael. b 47. St Chad Coll Dur BA 69. Cudd Coll 69. **d** 71 Bp Ramsbotham for Newc T **p** 72 Newc T. C of Morpeth 71-75; Long Benton 75-77; Sub-Warden Commun of All H Ditchingham Dio Nor from 77. *St Edmunds, Ditchingham, Bungay, Suff.* (Bungay 2139)

MOUNTNEY, Robert Griffith. ACT ThL 45. **d** 46 **p** 47 Melb. C of St Mary Warburton 46-48; Min of Berwick 48-51; on leave 51-52; I of Vermont 52-65; S Caulfield 65-77; Perm to Offic Dio Melb from 77. *Flat 1, 2 Berwick Street, Camberwell, Vic, Australia 3124.* (82-1891)

MOVE, Karabutega. b 43. **d** 80 Boga-Z. d Dio Boga-Z. *EAZ Bukiringi, BP 154, Bunia, Haut-Zaire.*

MOVIN, William. **d** 41 **p** 47 Rang. P Dio Rang 41-70; Dio Pa-an from 70. *St Matthew's Church, Moulmein, Burma.*

MOWAT, Geoffrey Scott. b 17. CCC Ox BA (2nd cl Mod Hist) 39, MA 49. Ripon Hall Ox 58. **d** 59 **p** 60 Bris. C of Ch Ch Clifton 59-61; Lect and Chap St Mary's Coll Cheltm 61-64; R of Quenington w Coln St Aldwyn and Hatherop 64-76; RD of Fairford 74-76; V of St Paul Penang 77-79; St Mary Kuala Lumpur Dio W Mal from 79. *St Mary's Vicarage, Jalan Raja, Kuala Lumpur, Malaysia.*

MOWATE, Arthur Jack. b 12. M IMechE 47, CEng. Qu Coll Birm 71. **d** and **p** 74 Worc (APM). Hon C of St Geo Kidderminster Dio Worc from 74. *16 Linden Avenue, Kidderminster, Worcs, DY10 3AB* (Kidderminster 3296)

MOWBRAY, David. b 38. Fitzw Ho Cam 2nd cl Engl Trip pt i 59, BA (2nd cl Engl Trip pt ii) 60, MA 64. BD (Lon) 62. Clifton Th Coll **d** 63 **p** 64 Pet. C of St Giles Northn 63-66; Lect of Watford 66-70; V of Broxbourne (w Wormley from 77) Dio St Alb from 70; Surr from 73. *Vicarage, Broxbourne, Herts.* (Hoddesdon 62382)

MOWBRAY, Derek David Whitfield. Univ of Lon BD 42. Univ of Dur MLitt 52. PhD (Sheff) 58. PhD (Leeds) 59. ALCD 42. **d** 42 S'wark **p** 43 Kingston T for S'wark. C of Morden 42-45; Asst Master Parmiter's Found Sch Lon 48-50; Res Tutor All Nations Bible Coll Ox 50-52; C of Doncaster 54-55; V of Kettlewell w Conistone 55-60; Wrangthorn 60-70; R of St Jo Bapt w St Mary-le-Port Bris 71-74; Perm to Offic Dio Bris from 75. *16 Russell Road, Bristol, BS6 7UB.* (Bristol 624862)

MOWLL, Basil Christopher. b 1890. Em Coll Cam BA 12, MA 21. Ridley Hall Cam 12. **d** 13 **p** 14 Roch. C of St Pet Southborough 13-16; Ch Ch Brixton 16-18; V of Ch Ch N Brixton 18-27; R of Broadwater 27-53; V of Hemingford Grey 53-55. *1 Courtlands, Ravens Way, Milford-on-Sea, Hants.* (Milford-on-Sea 2671)

MOWLL, John Edward. b 12. St Edm Hall Ox BA 34, MA 39. Westcott Ho Cam 35. **d** 36 **p** 37 Wakef. C of Normanton 36-41; Slaithwaite 41-43; Armley 43-46; V of St Wilfrid Leeds 46-60; Golcar 60-77. *Jersey House, The Bishop's Avenue, Finchley, N2 0BE.*

MOWLL, John Kingsford. b 33. Em Coll Cam 3rd cl Hist Trip pt i 56, BA (2nd cl Th Trip pt ia) 57, MA 61. BD (Lon) 60. Clifton Th Coll. **d** 59 **p** 60 Man. C of Halliwell 59-62; Cheadle 62-66; Miss at La Paz 66-69; Formosa Argent 70-80; V of Buglawton Dio Ches from 80. *Buglawton Vicarage, Congleton, Chesh.* (Congleton 3294)

MOWLL, John William Rutley. b 42. Sarum Th Coll 63. **d** 66 **p** 67 Sheff. C of Oughtibridge 66-69; Hill Birm 69-72; V of U Arley and Industr Chap in Kidderminster and Distr 73-78; R of Upton Snodsbury w Broughton Hackett (and the Flyfords and N Piddle from 79) Dio Worc from 78; Grafton Flyford w N Piddle and Flyford Flavell 78-79. *Rectory, Grafton Flyford, Worcs, WR7 4PG.* (Upton Snodsbury 247)

MOXLEY, Cyril Edward. b 09. Ch Coll Cam 2nd cl Hist Trip pt i 31, BA (2nd cl Hist Trip pt ii) 32, MA 37. Ely Th Coll 33. **d** 35 Madr **p** 37 Lon for Col. M of St Pet Bro Dio Madr 35-37; C of H Redeemer Clerkenwell 37-41; Perm to Offic Dio Cant 41-42; C of St John U Norwood 42-44; Chap RAFVR 44-50; R of Charlton Mackrell w Charlton Adam 50-52; Chap RAF 52-65; Prin RAF Chaps' Sch 60-64; Asst Chap-in-Chief RAF Germany 64-65; V of S Stoneham w Swaythling Win 65-74; Hon Chap of Win Cathl from 79. *2 Sutton Gardens, St Peter Street, Winchester, Hants, SO23 8HP.*

MOXON, Canon Charles. b 16. Late Cho Scho of K Coll Cam 3rd cl Hist Trip pt i 37, BA (3rd cl Hist Trip pt ii) 38, MA 42. Cudd Coll 38. **d** 39 **p** 40 Pet. C of Towcester w Easton Neston 39-41; Newport Pagnell (in c of St Luke from 43) 41-46; Min Can of St Paul's Cathl Lon 46-52; Hon Min Can from 52; Jun Cardinal and Sacr and L to Offic Dio Lon 47-52; Chap to R Cancer Hosp 48-52; V of St Anselm Hatch End 52-62; Sub-Chap O of St Jo of Jer from 52; R of Weybridge 62-67; V of St Matt Northn 67-75; Hon Min Can of Pet Cathl 68-75; Can Res and Prec of Sarum Cathl from 75. *54 The Close, Salisbury, Wilts, SP1 2EL.* (Salisbury 22996)

MOXON, David John. b 51. Univ of Cant BA 74. Massey Univ NZ MA 76. Univ of Ox BA 78 **d** 78 Wai. C of Havelock N Dio Wai from 78. *8 Lipscombe Crescent, Havelock North, NZ.* (775-609)

MOXON, Donald. b 05. MC 45. Linc Th Coll 30. **d** 30 **p** 31 Newc T. C of Seaton Hirst 30-34; St Bart Armley 34-36; Cathl Chap Rang 36-39 and 47-48; Mingaladon 39-41; CF (Ind) 41-46; Hon CF 46; Archd of Rang 46-48; V of Felkirk w Brierley 48-51; Brighouse 51-53; C of Brandon w Wangford 56-57; Gateshead (in c of St Aid) 57-59; V of Leadgate 59-68; Boadnell 68-73. *Long Row, Howick, Alnwick, Northumberland.*

MOXON, Harold. b 1900. **d** 34 **p** 35 Bradf. C of H Trin Bradf 34-35; Perm to Offic Dio Nor 36-43; R of Burnham Deepdale 43-50; V of E Halton 50-53; Killingholme 50-53; PC of All SS Linc 53-60; V of Cowbit 60-76. *1 Thames Road, Spalding, Lincs.* (Moulton Chapel 66489)

MOXON, Michael Anthony. b 42. Univ of Lon BD 78. Sarum Th Coll 67. **d** 70 **p** 71 Nor. C in Lowestoft Group 70-74; Min Can of St Paul's Cathl Lon 74-81; Sacr 77-81; Warden of Coll of Min Can 79-81; V of Tewkesbury w Walton Cardiff Dio Glouc from 81. *Abbey House, Tewkesbury, Glos.* (Tewkesbury 293333)

MOXON, William James. b 25. Qu Coll Birm 68. **d** 69 **p** 70 St Alb. C of St Paul Letchworth 69-72; P-in-c of Ecumen Exper N Bedford Area 72-76; Chap at Puerto de la Cruz, Tenerife 76-78; Chap Miss to Seamen Port Said 78-79; Chap of St Mark w All SS Alexandria 79-80; V of St Jo Evang Altrincham Dio Ches from 81. *52 Ashley Road, Altrincham, WA14 2LY.* (061-928 3236)

MOXON, William John. b 18. Keble Coll Ox BA (Geog) 39, MA 42. Westcott Ho Cam 40. **d** 41 **p** 42 Ox. C of Earley 41-44; Windsor 44-45; Chap at St Luke Haifa 45-49; Deputn Sec Jer and the East Miss 49-50; V of Walsgrave-on-Sowe 50-57; Bidford-on-Avon 57-68; Bengeworth 68-77; R of Redmarley D'Abitot (w Bromsberrow from 81) w Upleadon, Pauntley and Oxenhall Dio Glouc from 77; P-in-c of Bromsberrow 79-81. *Redmarley Rectory, Gloucester, GL19 3HS.* (Bromsberrow 245)

MOYER, David Lloyd. b 51. Whittier Coll Calif BA 73. Seabury-Western Th Sem Chicago MDiv 76. **d** and **p** 76 E Newfld. C of St Thos St John's Dio E Newfld from 76. *33 MacDonald Drive, St John's, Newfoundland.*

MOYI, Henry Okeno. b 43. St Phil Sch Maseno 73. **d** 75 **p** 76 Maseno S. P Dio Maseno S. *AC Kisumu, PO Box 43, Kisumu, Kenya.*

MOYLE, Edward Philip. b 38. Wycl Coll Tor LTh 70. **d** 70 Bp Clarke for Moos **p** 71 Moos. C of Kashechewan 70-72; Burgeo 72-75; I of Foleyet 73-76; Hornepayne 76-78; St Luke Thunder Bay Dio Alg from 78. *205 Cameron Street, Thunder Bay, Ont, Canada.*

MOYLE, Francis Charles Blake. univ of Melb BA 41. St Jo Coll Morpeth 41. **d** 41 **p** 42 Goulb. C of Cootamundra 41-43; Shepparton 44-45; R of Yackandanah w Kiewa 45-49; Benalla 49-58; Priv Chap to Bp of Wang 55-58; Can of Wang 57-58; V and Sub-Dean of Ch Ch Cathl Bal 58-67; Hon Can of Bal 58-62; Can Res 62-67; V of Ch Ch Essendon Dio Melb from 67. *1 Marco Polo Street, Essendon, Vic, Australia 3040.* (03-379 2770)

MOYLE, Frank William. Kelham Th Coll **d** 22 **p** 23 Southn for Win. C of St Jas Southampton 22-24; St Alb Mart Birmingham 25-28; Perm to Offic at All H Gospel Oak 29-30; C of St Andr Plaistow 30-32; Eye and Braisworth Suff 32-34; R of Saxmundham 34-66; Surr 41-66. *25 Morley Avenue, Woodbridge, Suff.* (Woodbridge 2262)

MOYNAN, William John. b 20. Trin Coll Dub BA 44. **d** 44 **p** 45 Dub. C of St Jude Dub 44-49; Drumcondra w N Strand 49-56; Cler V of Ch Ch Cathl Dub 52-56; R of Portarlington U 56-63; I of Donabate w Lusk Dio Dub from 63; I of Swords w Kilsallaghan and Clonmethan Dio Dub from 68. *Rectory, Swords, Co Dublin, Irish Republic.* (Dublin 402308)

MOYO, Elliot Reginald. St Jo Th Sem Lusaka, 64. **d** 67 **p** 68 Matab. C of Bulawayo Cathl 68-70; P-in-c of H Cross

Miss Luvere 70-72; Pris Chap Dio Matab from 72. *Connemara Prison, Hunter's Road, Zimbabwe-Rhodesia.* (Hunter's Road 3)

MOYO, Laymond. **d** 76 Mashon. d Dio Mashon. *Holy Trinity School, PB 710, Enkeldoorn, Rhodesia.*

MOYO, Obert Joseph. **d** 77 **p** 78 Matab. P Dio Matab. *Box 43, Wankie, Zimbabwe.*

MOYO, Simon. **d** 76 Mashon. d Dio Mashon. *St Nicholas Church, PO Box 81, Odzi, Rhodesia.*

MPAGALALE, Ezekiel. b 37. St Phil Coll Kongwa 72. **d** and **p** 74 Vic Nyan. P Dio Vic Nyan. *Box 722, Mwanza, Tanzania.*

MPAGI, Amunoni. Bp Tucker Coll Mukono. **d** 56 Ugan **p** 58 Bp Balya for Ugan. P Dio Ugan 56-61; Dio Nam from 61. *Church of Uganda, Vukula, Box 36, Kalire, Uganda.*

MPALANYI, Ven Livingstone. Bp Tucker Coll Mukono. **d** 69 **p** 70 Nam. P Dio Nam. Archd of Nam from 77. *c/o Box 14297, Kampala, Uganda.*

MPAMBICHILE, Laurence. St Cypr Th Coll Tunduru **d** 42 **p** 45 Masasi. P Dio Masasi 42-76. *PO Chuingutwa, Tanzania.*

MPANDANYAMA, Geoffrey. **d** 55 **p** 56 Mashon. P Dio Mashon; L to Offic Dio Mashon from 70. *PB 8083, Rusape, Rhodesia.*

MPANGA, Nasani Kibanga. Bp Tucker Coll Mukono. **d** 69 **p** 70 W Bugan. d Dio W Bugan. *Church of Uganda, Kiwoomya, PO Box 380, Masaka, Uganda.*

MPANGAZA, Ven Festus. **d** 54 Bp Brazier for Ugan **p** 55 Ugan. P Dio Ugan 54-64; Archd of N Rwanda Dio Rwanda B 64-66; Dio Rwa from 66. *Anglican Church, Gahini, Kigali, Rwanda.*

MPANYANE, Annet Tumelo. b 43. St Pet Coll Alice 67. **d** 69 **p** 70 Bloemf. C of Bultfontein Miss 69-70; Thaba 'Nchu Miss 70-74; St Patr Miss Bloemf 74-76; R of St John Wepener Dio Bloemf from 76. *Box 132, Wepener, OFS, S Africa.*

MPELUMBE, Dunford. St Cypr Th Coll Tunduru **d** 57 Masasi. d Dio Masasi 57-79; Dio Dar-S from 79. *Box 16, Bagamoyo, Tanzania.*

MPERA E, **d** 42 **p** 44 Ugan. P Dio Ugan. *PO Kakeri, Busiro, Uganda.*

MPHAKI, Cornelius. b 30. St Pet Th Coll Rossettenville 67. **d** 69 Bp Carter for Johann **p** 70 Johann. P Dio Johann from 70. *PO Box 54, Dube, Johannesburg, S Africa.*

MPHENYEKE, Gabriel Alfred Puseletso. St Pet Coll Rosettenville, 56. **d** 58 **p** 59 Johann. P Dio Johann 58-77. *2686 Zone 2, Pimville, Johannesburg, S Africa.*

MPHUNYANE, Job Malefetsane. St Bede's Coll Umtata. **d** 57 **p** 60 Basuto. P Dio Basuto 57-66; Dio Les from 66. *St John's Mission, Hantja, PO Lebihan Falls, Maseru, Lesotho.*

MPIKWANE, Adonis. St Bede's Coll Umtata. **d** 55 **p** 56 Kimb K. P Dio Kimb K. *PO Box 8016, Kimberley, CP, S Africa.* (0571-3704)

MPINGANJIRA, Jonathan. b 33. **d** 75 **p** 76 S Malawi. P Dio S Malawi. *PO Chinseu, Masaula, Malawi.*

MPOFU, Joseph William. b 30. **d** 76 **p** 77 Matab. C of Gweletshena Dio Matab from 76. *P Bag 5403 T, Bulawayo, Zimbabwe.*

MPOYOLA, Festo Francis. St Phil Coll Kongwa 67. **d** and **p** 71 Centr Tang. P Dio Centr Tang. *Box 340, Dodoma, Tanzania.*

MPUNZI, Ananias Nduna. b 46. St Pet Sem Alice 69. **d** 71 **p** 72 Kimb K. C of St Jas Galeshewe Kimb 71-74; Taung 74-75; Vaal Hartz 75-77; R of St Phil Vryburg Dio Kimb K 77-79. *c/o Box 517, Vryburg, CP, S Africa.*

MQUQO, Davidson Njengele. b 29. St Bede's Coll Umtata. **d** 69 **p** 70 Grahmstn. O of Ethiopia. C of St Pet Uitenhage 70-71; P-in-c of H Cross Miss Katlehong 71-76; R of St Steph Langa Dio Capetn 77-79; P-in-c from 79. *31 Moshesh Avenue, Langa 7455, S Africa.* (53-5115)

MRUKA, Walter. b 41. St Phil Sch Maseno 73. **d** 75 **p** 76 Maseno S. P Dio Maseno S. *Box 31, Bondo, Kenya.*

MSAKAFU, John Abdallah. b 36. **d** and **p** 77 Vic Nyan. P Dio Vic Nyan. *PO Box 69, Musoma, Tanzania.*

MSAKWIZA, Ven Matthew George. St Jo Th Sem Lusaka. **d** 64 Nyasa **p** 65 Bp Mtekateka for Malawi. P Dio Malawi 65-71; Dio S Malawi 71-72; Dio Lake Malawi from 72; Archd Dio Lake Malawi from 80. *Box 11, Ntchisi, Malawi.*

MSALA, George. St Cypr Th Coll Namasakata, 50. **d** 52 **p** 55 Masasi. P Dio Masasi. *Box 16, Masasi, Mtwara Region, Tanzania.*

MSAMATI, Basil. St Cypr Th Coll Ngala, 63. **d** 64 **p** 66 Masasi. P Dio Masasi. *PO Kilwa, Masoko, Tanzania.*

MSAMATI, Benjamin Evans. St Cypr Coll Tunduru 57. **d** 59 Masasi **p** 63 Bp Soseleje for Masasi. P Dio Masasi. *PO Mtwara, Tanzania.* (Mtwara 2357)

MSAMWERA, Aidan Anderson Cyril. **d** 62 SW Tang. d Dio SW Tang 62-70; Dio Ruv from 71. *Linda, PO Mbamba Bay, Tanzania.*

MSANE, Midian Thembumusawenkosi. **d** 56 **p** 57 Zulu. P Dio Zulu 56-65; Can of Zulu 65-72; L to Offic Dio Zulu 73-77; R of Polela 77-78; Tongaat Dio Natal from 78. *Box 45, Tongaat, Natal, S Africa.*

MSEGU, Isaka Meshak. St Phil Th Coll Kongwa 65. **d** 67 **p** 68 Moro. P Dio Moro 67-75; Dio Vic Nyan 75-79; Dio Moro from 79. *PO Berega, Tanzania.*

MSEI, Canon Anthony Michael. **d** 74 **p** 75 Zanz T. P Dio Zanz T; Can of Zanz T from 80. *PO Box 45, Tanga, Tanzania.*

MSEKAWANTHU, Canon Matthias Alexander. St Andr Th Coll Likoma, 35. **d** 39 **p** 45 Nyasa. P Dio Nyasa 39-64; Dio Malawi 64-71; Dio Lake Malawi from 71; Can of Malawi 64-71; Dean 68-74; Archd of Likoma 71-74; Can of Lake Malawi from 74. *Mbamba, PO Likoma Island, Malawi.*

MSELE, Arnold Yeremia. b 22. **d** 70 **p** 71 Moro. P Dio Moro 70-80. *Kibedya Primary School, Gairo, Kilosa, Tanzania.*

MSELE, Stephano Chinyami. **d** 39 **p** 41 Centr Tang. P Dio Centr Tang 39-65; Dio Moro 65-74. *Gairo, PO Kilosa, Tanzania.*

MSENGANA, Sobantu Silberbauer. b 10. **d** 75 **p** 76 Capetn (APM). C of Langa Dio Capetn from 75. *Box 50, Langa 7455, CP, S Africa.*

MSHAMA, Wilson. b 53. St Phil Coll Kongwa 73. **d** 75 **p** 76 Centr Tang. P Dio Centr Tang. *PO Mvumi, Tanzania.*

MSHAMU, Andrea. St Cypr Coll Lindi 71. **d** 74 **p** 75 Masasi. P Dio Masasi. *Box 19, Nachingwea, Lindi, Tanzania.*

MSHOKA, Sylvester. **d** 72 **p** 73 Lusaka. P Dio Lusaka. *Box 19, Petauke, Zambia.*

MSHOMI, William. b 40. **d** 77 **p** 78 Moro. P Dio Moro. *DM Ngiloli, c/o Gairo Rural Deanery, PO Gairo-Kilosa, Tanzania.*

MSIMANG, Henry Ludger. St Pet Coll Rosettenville 50. **d** 52 **p** 53 Zulu. P Dio Zulu 52-58; Dio Natal 58-64; Dio Pret 64-71; Dio Bloemf from 71. *Box 4, Heilbron, OFS, S Africa.*

MSOKOSELA, Canon Francis Lester. St Jo Sem Lusaka. **d** 55 **p** 56 N Rhod. P Dio N Rhod 55-64; Dio Zam from 64-70; Dio Lusaka from 71; Hon Can of Lusaka 75-76; Can from 76. *PO Box 3457, Lusaka, Zambia.*

MSOMI, Abel Le Roy. **d** and **p** 43 Centr Tang. P Dio Centr Tang 43; in c of St Mary Pietermaritzburg (C of E in S Africa) from 43. *c/o Christ Church Rectory, Durban, Natal, S Africa.*

MSONTHI, Canon Bartolomayo Caleb. **d** 45 **p** 49 Nyasa. P Dio Nyasa 45-64; Dio Malawi 64-71; Dio Lake Malawi from 71; Archd of Ntchisi 70-72; Hon Can of Lake Malawi from 73. *Church of St Andrew, Chalundu, Ntchisi, Malawi.*

MSUNZA, Jonas. St Phil Th Coll Kongwa 64. **d** 66 **p** 67 Centr Tang. P Dio Centr Tang. *PO Box 68, Kondoa, Tanzania.*

MSUSA, Valentino. St Cypr Coll Tunduru. **d** 54 Zanz for Masasi **p** 57 Masasi. P Dio Masasi 57-68. *USPG, Nanyindwa, Masasi, Lindi, Tanzania.*

MTAMBO, Michael. b 20. **d** 74 **p** 75 S Malawi. P Dio S Malawi. *Matope, P/Bag 514, Limbe, Malawi.*

MTANGO, Elisha Lazaro. St Phil Th Coll Kongwa 65. **d** 65 **p** 66 Centr Tang. P Dio Centr Tang. *PO Mvumi, Tanzania.*

MTEBENE, Stephen. St Cypr Th Coll Ngala. **d** 62 Zanz T. d Dio Zanz T. *PO Box 23, Mnyuzi, Tanzania.*

✠ **MTEKATEKA, Right Rev Josia.** St Andr Th Coll Likoma 36. **d** 39 **p** 43 Nyasa. P Dio Nyasa 43-52; P-in-c Dio SW Tang 52-65; Can of SW Tang 59-65; Archd of Njombe 62-65 Cons Ld Bp Suffr of Malawi in Likoma Cathl 27 May 65 by Abp of Centr Afr; Bps of Malawi; and Mashon; and Bps Mataka and Thorne; Apptd Bp of Lake Malawi 71; res 77. *Box 27, Ntchisi, Malawi.*

MTEMI, Amos. St Phil Coll Kongwa 69. **d** and **p** 71 Centr Tang. P Dio Centr Tang. *Ilangali, PO Dodoma, Tanzania.*

MTETEMELA, Donald Leo Weston. St Phil Coll Kongwa 69. **d** and **p** 71 Centr Tang. P Dio Centr Tang 71-74 and from 76; Dioc Sec from 78; on leave 75-76. *Box 15, Dodoma, Tanzania.*

MTHETHWA, Arthur Magama. St Pet Coll Rosettenville, 51. **d** 53 **p** 54 Johann. P Dio Johann from 54. *PO Box 74, Heidelberg, Transvaal, S Africa.* (015-1 3591)

MTHETHWA, Oliver Eric Mkumbuzi. b 17. **d** 71 **p** 72 Johann. C of Natalspruit Dio Johann from 71. *Box 12050, Katlehong, Germiston, Transvaal 1832, S Africa.* (Katlehong 44)

MTHETHWA, Zebulon Cleopas. St Pet Coll Rosettenville 60. **d** 62 **p** 63 Zulu. P Dio Zulu 62-72; Dir Dept of Educn CPAS 72-73; Prov Dir of Chr Educn S Africa 73-77; L to Offic Dio Zulu from 77. *P Bag 802, Melmoth, Zululand, S Africa.*

MTHSWENI, Elijah Alijatgelwa. St Pet Coll Rosettenville

d 62 **p** 63 Pret. P Dio Pret from 62. *Stand Q 16 Mhlunzi Location, Middleburg 1052, S Africa.*

MTIBUA, Ernest. St Cypr Coll Lindi 71. **d** 73 **p** 75 Zanz T. P Dio Zanz T. *Box 35, Korogwe, Tanzania.*

MTIZI, Athanasio. d and **p** 77 Centr Tang. P Dio Centr Tang. *Chipanga, PO Kigwe, Tanzania.*

MTOWE, Nelson Paul. d 61. Centr Tang **p** 62 Bp Omari for Centr Tang. P Dio Centr Tang. *Holy Trinity Church, Moshi, Tanzania.*

MTUBATWA, Timotheo R. b 38. **d** 75 **p** 76 Centr Tang. P Dio Centr Tang. *PO Chenene, Tanzania.*

MTUNGUJA, Dunstan. St Cypr Th Coll Ngala. **d** 62 Zanz T. d Dio Zanz T from 62-69; P-in-c of Mombo 69-70; Pemba 70-74; Kiwanda 74-77; Magila Dio Zanz T from 77. *Box 123, Tanga, Tanzania.*

MTUPILA, Very Rev Manuel Noel. d 66 **p** 68 Lebom. P Dio Lebom 66-79; Dio Niassa from 79; Dean of Niassa from 81. *Missae Anglicana de Messuma, Lago, Niassa, Mozambique.*

MTWESI, Julius Pasika. St Bede's Coll Umtata. **d** 32 **p** 36 St Jo Kaffr. P Dio St John's. *St Alphege, Mandileni, CP, S Africa.*

MTWEVE, Lunyilike Adriano. St Paul's Coll Liuli. **d** 54 **p** 57 SW Tang. P Dio SW Tang. *Box 32, Njombe, Tanzania.*

MUANGE, John. d 66 **p** 69 Nai. C of Kithangathini 69-70; C-in-c of Syongila 71; C of All SS Cathl Nai 72-76; V of Ukia Dio Nai from 77. *St Andrew's Church, Ukia, Kenya.*

MUBBALA, Erezefani. Buwalasi Th Coll 62. **d** 64 **p** 65 Mbale. P Dio Mbale 64-72; Dio Bukedi from 72; Dioc Sec from 81. *Box 170, Tororo, Uganda.*

MUBEHO, Yohana Eliya. St Phil Coll Kongwa 74. **d** and **p** 76 Centr Tang. P Dio Centr Tang. *PO Box 35, Babati, Tanzania.*

MUBIRU, Titus Kasozi. d 73 Nam **p** 76 Melb for Nam. P Dio Nam 73-75; C of St Jas Ivanhoe 76-77; St Mark Camberwell 78-79; Perm to Offic Dio Melb from 79. *4/2 Georgina Parade, Camberwell, Vic, Australia 3124.*

MUCHIIRI, Francis Kabanya. b 32. **d** 78 Mt Kenya S. d Dio Mt Kenya S. *PO Box 271, Limuru, Kenya.*

MUCKPAH, Jimmy. b 36. Arthur Turner Tr Sch Pangnirtung 70. **d** 72 Arctic **p** 73 Qu'App for Arctic. Miss at Eskimo Point Dio Arctic from 72. *St Francis Mission, Askimo Point, NWT, Canada.*

MUCOKORI, Yosamu. Bp Tucker Coll Mukono. **d** 59 Ugan. d Dio Ugan 59-60; Dio Ankole-K 60-67; Dio Ank from 67. *PO Ibanda, Mbarara, Ankole, Uganda.*

MUDALA, Gideon. d 64 **p** 65 Centr Tang. P Dio Centr Tang 64-66; Dio W Tang from 66. *Mwese, PO Mpanda, Tanzania.*

MUDAMBI, Samusoni. Bp Tucker Coll Mukono. **d** 63 **p** 64 Nam. P Dio Nam 63-70. *Kiyunga, PO Box 4533, Bulopa Busoga, Uganda.*

MUDDIMAN, John Bernard. b 47. Keble Coll Ox BA (2nd cl Cl) 67, 1st cl Th 69, MA 72, DPhil 76. Selw Coll Cam BA (1st cl Th Trip pt iii) 71, MA 75. Westcott Ho Cam 69. **d** 72 Dorchester for Ox **p** 73 Win for Ox. Hon C of St Giles City and Dio Ox from 72; Chap New Coll Ox 72-76; Tutor St Steph Ho Ox from 76; Vice-Prin from 80. *St Stephen's House, Oxford.*

MUDFORD, Canon Walter Cyril. K Coll Cam BA 21. MA 34. Cl Tr Sch Cam 21. **d** 22 Ox for St Alb **p** 23 St Alb. LPr Dio St Alb and Asst Chap Bedford Sch 22-25; C of St Mary Magd Sunderland 25-29; I of St Aug Chesterfield 29-34; Chap St Jo Coll Johann 34-38; R of Boksburg 38-41; Miss P Dio Gambia 42-48; Archd of The Gambia 42-48; P-in-c of Msoro 48-66; Mazabuka 66-69; Livingstone 69-70; Archd of Msoro 60-66; Hon Can of Zam 60-70; Can (Emer) from 70; Chap at Costa Blanca 71-77. *c/o Casita del Camino, Jesus Pobre, Por Gata de Gorgos, Alicante, Costa Blanca, Spain.*

MUDGE, Frederick Alfred George. b 31. Univ of Leeds BSc (1st cl Gen) 58. Univ of Wales BD 67. St Mich Coll Llan 58. **d** 61 **p** 62 Llan. C of Cwmavon 61-64; PV of Llan Cathl 64-70; R of Llandough w Leckwith Dio Llan from 70; Exam Chap to Bp of Llan from 73. *103 Penlan Road, Llandough, Penarth, S Glam.* (Penarth 703349)

MUDHOO, Canon James. d 35 **p** 36 Maur. C of H Trin Rose Hill 35-37; V of Brisee Verdiere w Poudre and Beau-Champ 37-44; Souillac 45-62; Can of Maur from 62; P-in-c of St Paul Vacoas 63; R of Beau-Bassin 64-73; Pamplemousses w Montagne Longwe and Beau-Champ Dio Maur from 73. *Rectory, Pamplemousses, Mauritius.* (33-549)

MUDONYI, Jonathan Peter. Buwalasi Th Coll. **d** 57 U Nile. d Dio U Nile 57-61; Dio Mbale from 61. *PO Box 614, Mbale, Uganda.*

MUDZINGANYAMA, Cyril. d 73 **p** 74 Mashon. P Dio Mashon. *Tsonzo Church District, PB 8075, Rusape, Rhodesia.*

MUERS, Robin Peter. Univ of Cant NZ BEng 65. ACT ThL 72. BD (Lon) 73. Moore Coll Syd 72. **d** and **p** 74 Syd. C of Hornsby 74-75; Castle Hill 76-78; C-in-c of Blakehurst Dio Syd from 79. *9 Centre Street, Blakehurst, NSW, Australia 2221.* (546-6523)

MUGAI, Abed. b 44. St Paul's Coll Limuru 73. **d** 75 **p** 78 Mt Kenya E. d Dio Mt Kenya E 75-78; P Dio Mt Kenya E from 78. *Box 6086, Embu, Kenya.*

MUGALULA, Canon Kapuliam. Bp Tucker Mem Coll Mukono. **d** 51 **p** 52 Ugan. P Dio Ugan 51-61; Dio Nam from 61; Can of Nam from 75. *PO Box 16312, Kampala, Uganda.*

MUGARURA-MUTANA, Benoni Jack. b 41. Univ of W Ont BMin 77. Bp Tucker Coll Mukono 70. **d** 72 **p** 73 Kig. P Dio Kig 72-74; C of St Geo St Catharines Dio Niag from 77. *Unit 603, Carriage Road, St Catharines, Ont, Canada, L2P 2K2.* (416-684-6706)

MUGASA, Manasse. b 45. Butare Th Coll 71. **d** 74 Rwa. d Dio Rwa. *E.A.R. Gehini, B.P. 22 Kigali, Rwanda.*

MUGE, Solomon. b 38. **d** 78 Lango. d Dio Lango. *PO Lira, Uganda.*

MUGENGA, Canon Fred. b 30. Bp Tucker Coll Mukono 70. **d** 72 **p** 73 Kig. P Dio Kig; Archd of Kig from 77. *PO Karuhinda, Kinkizi, Kigezi, Uganda.*

✠ **MUGERA, Right Rev Tibafa Sylivestre.** b 30. Bp Tucker Coll Mukono. **d** 69 **p** 70 Bp Rwakaikara for Ruw. P Dio Ruw 69-72; Dio Boga-Z 72-80; Cons Ld Bp of Kisangani at Boga 7 Sept 80 by Abp of Rwanda B and Boga-Z and Abp of Uganda; Bps of Boga-Z, Butare and M & W Nile; and others. *BP 861, Kisangani, Zaire, Africa.*

MUGERWA, Blasius. Bp Tucker Mem Coll Mukono. **d** 55 Ugan **p** 61 Nam. P Dio Ugan 55-61; Dio Nam from 61. *Box 50, Kapeeka, Uganda.*

MUGGLETON, Major George. b 25. Chich Th Coll 55. **d** 57 **p** 58 Man. C of Oldham 57-59; Ashton L 59-61; V of H Trin Selhurst Croydon 61-68; R of Stisted (w Bradwell-juxta-Coggleshall and Pattiswick from 69) Dio Chelmsf from 68; C-in-c of Pattiswick 68-69; C-in-c of Bradwell-juxta-Coggleshall 68-69. *Stisted Rectory, Braintree, Essex, CM7 8AP.* (Braintree 25367)

MUGOYA, Adoniya. Buwalasi Th Coll 58. **d** 59 **p** 60 U Nile. P Dio U Nile 59-61; Dio Mbale 61-72; Dio Bukedi from 72. *Buwesa, PO Busolwe-Tororo, Uganda.*

MUGRIDGE, Alan John. b 52. Univ of Syd BA. Moore Th Coll Syd BD, ThL. **d** 81 Syd. C of St Jas Turramurra Dio Syd from 81. *The Curate's Cottage, St James' Lane, Turramurra, NSW, Australia 2074.*

MUGWIMI, James Godfrey. b 40. St Paul's Coll Limuru 73. **d** and **p** 76 Mt Kenya S. P Dio Mt Kenya S. *Box 229, Nyeri, Kenya.*

MUHALYA, Benjamin. d 77 **p** 78 Nak. P Dio Nak. *Box 244, Nakuru, Kenya.*

MUHAYA, Yuel Ruhigira. d 48 **p** 51 Ugan. P Dio Ugan 48-60; Ruw 60-67; Dio W Bugan from 67. *Nakyenyi, PO Box 298, Masaka, Uganda.*

MUHEMBANO, Athanasio. Hur Coll Lon Ont. **d** and **p** 48 Centr Tang. P Dio Centr Tang 48-81. *Kilimatinde, PO Manyoni, Tanzania.*

MUHEMBANO, Canon Eliya. St Phil Th Coll Kongwa. **d** 57 Centr Tang **p** 58 Bp Omari for Centr Tang. P Dio Centr Tang from 57; Can of H Spirit Cathl Dodoma from 78. *Box 26, Kongwa, Tanzania.*

MUHERYA, Kezekiya. d 39 **p** 41 Ugan. P Dio Ugan 39-61; Dio Ruw 61-66. *c/o PO Box 20, Hoima, Uganda.*

MUHIA, James Dan. b 22. **d** 74 Mt Kenya **p** 76 Bp Ngaruiya for Mt Kenya S. P Dio Mt Kenya 74-75; Mt Kenya S from 75. *Kanjuka, Box 679, Thika, Kenya.*

MUHOLOVE, Elias. d and **p** 75 Lebom. P Dio Lebom. *CP 120, Maputo, Mozambique.*

MUHORO, Canon Samuel. St Paul's Dioc Div Sch Limuru. **d** 48 **p** 49 Momb. P Dio Momb 48-53 and 55-61; Tutor St Paul's Dioc Div Sch 53-55; P Dio Ft Hall 61-65; Dio Mt Kenya 65-75; Dio Mt Kenya S from 75; Can of St Jas and All Marts Cathl Ch Ft Hall from 69. *Kiruri, PO Kangema, Murang'a, Kenya.*

MUHOZI, Ven Erifazi. Bp Tucker Mem Coll Mukono, 57. **d** & **p** 58 Ugan. P Dio Ugan 58-69; Dio Ank 70-77; Archd of Ank 70-77; Bweranyangi from 77; Can of Ank 72-77; Bp's Commiss Dio W Ank 77-78. *Po Kabwohe, Mbarara, Uganda.*

MUIANGA, Very Rev Gabriel. St Aug Th Coll Maciene. **d** 60 **p** 61 Lebom. P Dio Lebom; Dean of Lebom from 76; Distr Supt of Maciene from 76. *CTT Changoene, Xai Xai, Mozambique.*

MUIR, Anthony Wright. b 13. TCD BA & Div Test 36, MA 39. **d** 36 **p** 37 Wakef. C of St Pet Huddersfield 36-43; Chap RNVR 43-46; C of Epsom (in c of St John) 47-50; Min of Conv Distr of Good Shepherd Tadworth 50-55; V 55-77; Perm to Offic Dio St E from 77. *25 Greys Close, Cavendish, Sudbury, Suff, CO10 8AB.*

MUIR, David Murray. b 49. Univ of Glas MA 70. Univ of

Nottm BA (Th) 72. St Jo Coll Nottm 76. **d** 76 Kens for Lon **p** 77 Lon. C of St Mary W Kens 76-79; St Marg Aspley 80; in Ch of N India from 81. *Box 3568, New Delhi 110024, India.*

MUIR, Ian Gordon. b 17. St Paul's Coll Grahmstn LTh 46. **d** 46 **p** 47 Johann. C of Boksburg 46-48; Rosebank Johann 48-52; Bloemf Cathl and Douglas Missr 52; R of Ladybrand 52-54; C-in-c of Milnerton 54-56; C of St Paul Knightsbridge and Chap St Geo Hosp Lon 56-58; at USPG Lon 63-64; Chap HM Publ Insts Dio Trinid 64-66; R of Point Fortin 66-68; I of Elkhorn w Shoal River 69-70; C of St Mary Willesden 70-72; C-in-c of St Mich Cricklewood Dio Lon from 72. *160 Anson Road, NW2 6BH.* (01-452 8160)

MUIR, John William. b 38. Univ of Dur BA 59. Mansfield Coll Ox MA 65. Chich Th Coll 78. **d** 78 **p** 79 Wakef. [f Congregational Min]. C of Brighouse 78-80; V of Northowram Dio Wakef from 80. *Northowram Vicarage, Halifax, HX3 7HH.* (Halifax 202551)

MUJETSI, Erukana. d 54 **p** 56 U Nile. P Dio U Nile 54-61; Dio Mbale 61-73. *Mulatsi, Box 480, Mbale, Uganda.*

MUKANDLA, Sydney. b 45. **d** 74 **p** 75 Matab. P Dio Matab. *1605 Old Mkoba, Gwelo, Rhodesia.*

MUKASA, Abusolomu. Bp Tucker Mem Coll Mukono, 42. **d** 42 **p** 44 Ugan. P Dio Ugan. *Anglican Church, Timmina, PO Bombo, Uganda.*

MUKASA, Amos. Bp Tucker Mem Coll Mukono, 56. **d** 57 Ugan. d Dio Ugan 57-61; Dio Nam from 61. *Box 67, Brombo, Uganda.*

MUKASA, Canon Disani. d 33 **p** 34 Ugan. P Dio Ugan 33-60; Dio Nam 60-62; Can of St Paul's Cathl Kampala from 62. *Box 14106, Kampala, Uganda.*

MUKASA, Ephraim. d 68 **p** 69 Ruw. P Dio Ruw; Dioc Treas from 76. *Box 37, Fort Portal, Uganda.*

MUKASA, Frederick James. d 77 Nam. d Dio Nam. *Kkungu Church of Uganda, PO Box 30366, Kampala, Uganda.*

MUKASA, Ven Nasaneri. Bp Tucker Mem Coll Mukono. **d** 62 **p** 63 Ruw. P Dio Ruw 62-72; Dio Boga-Z 72-76; Dio Bukavu from 76; Hon Can of Boga-Z 72-76; Bukavu from 76; Archd of Goma from 76. *BP 363, Goma, Nord Kivu, Zaire.*

MUKASA, Samuel. b 50. **d** 77 Nam. d Dio Nam. *Nsangi Church of Uganda, PO Box 1, Kitemu, Uganda.*

✠ **MUKASA, Right Rev Yokana Balikuddembe.** Bp Tucker Mem Coll Mukono. Ridley Hall, Cam 56. **d** 54 **p** 57 Ugan. P Dio Ugan 57-60; Dio Nam from 61; Exam Chap to Bp of Soroti 66-77; Dean of St Paul's Cathl Kampala 67-74; Can 67-77; Cons Ld Bp of Mityana in St Andr Cathl Mityana 29 May 77 by Abp of Ugan; Bps of Nam, Bunyoro, Ruw, W Bugan, Busogo and Mbale; and others. *PO Box 102, Mityana, Uganda.*

MUKIRANE, Ven Stephen. Bp Tucker Mem Coll Mukono. **d** 65 **p** 66 Ruw. P Dio Ruw from 65; Archd of Kasese from 73. *Box 142, Kasese, Uganda.*

MUKISA, Fredrick. d and **p** 75 Bunyoro. P Dio Bunyoro. *Box 132, Bulindi, Hoima, Uganda.*

MUKOMBOLA, Daniel Paulo. St Phil Th Coll Kongwa, 60. **d** 60 Bp Wiggins for Centr Tang **p** 61 Centr Tang. P Dio Centr Tang 60-65; and from 69; Dio Moro 65-68. *Chinyika, PO Chipogoro, Tanzania.*

MUKULA, Ven Yovani. Buwalasi Th Coll 51. **d** 52 Bp Tomusange for U Nile **p** 54 U Nile P Dio U Nile 54-60; Dio Soroti from 60; Hon Can of Soroti from 72; Archd of Soroti from 75; Exam Chap to Bp of Soroti from 75. *c/o Box 107, Soroti, Uganda.*

MUKULU, Erukana. Buwalasi Th Coll. **d** 55 **p** 56 U Nile. P Dio U Nile 55-61; Dio Mbale 61-73; Dio Bukedi 73-74; Dio Nam from 75. *Box 22016, Nakifuma, Uganda.*

MUKUNDI, Zabron Paul Wacira. b 34. **d** 78 Mt Kenya S. d Dio Mt Kenya S. *Box 23068, Lower Kabate, Kenya.*

MULCOCK, Edward John. b 16. Univ of Leeds BA 37. Coll of Resurr Mirfield 37. **d** 39 **p** 40 Derby. C of Long Eaton 39-48; V of St Hilda Leeds 48-55; St German Roath 55-60; Min of S Kenton Conv Distr Wembley 61-66; V of St John (w St Jas from 76) Walham Green Dio Lon from 66; C-in-c of St Jas Fulham 68-69; V 69-76. *Vicarage, Maxwell Road, SW6 2JW.* (01-736 4574)

MULENGA, Canon George. d 41 **p** 43 N Rhod. P Dio N Rhod 41-56; Can of N Rhod 56-64; Zam 64-65; Archd of N Zam 65-70; P-in-c of Luanshya Dio Centr Zam from 71; Hon Can of Centr Zam from 71; VG from 75. *PO Box 90506, Luanshya, Zambia.*

MULHOLLAND, John David. York Univ Ont BA 70. Montr Dioc Th Coll LTh 66, Trin Coll Tor MDiv 73.**d** 73 **p** 74 Bp Read for Tor. C of St John York Mills Tor 73-75; I of St Andr-by-the-Lake (P-in-c from 80) and Chap Miss to Seamen City and Dio Tor from 75; P-in-c of St Crisp Tor 77-80. *Unit 3, 10 Buller Avenue, Toronto, Ont, Canada.*

MULHOLLAND, Nicholas Christopher John. b 44. Chich Th Coll 77. **d** 79 **p** 80 Glouc. C of Thornbury Dio Glouc from 79. *26 Gloucester Road, Thornbury, Nr Bristol.*

MULHONDI, Yosamu. b 48. Tucker Coll Mukono 79. **d** 80 Ruw. d Dio Ruw. *PO Box 13, Kasese, Uganda.*

MULINDA, Andrea. d 32 N Rhod. d Dio N Rhod 32-35. *USPG, Chipili, Kasama, Zambia.*

MULLANE, Ven John Murdoch. Univ of Auckld BA 56, MA 57. St Jo Coll Auckld 53. NZ Bd of Th Stud LTh (1st cl) 60. **d** 58 **p** 59 Auckld. C of New Lynn 58-62; Tutor St Jo Coll Auckld 62-64; L to Offic Dio Auckld 62-64; V of Clevedon 64-67; Dir Chr Educn Dio Ch Ch 67-72; Dio Auckld from 72; Exam Chap to Bp of Auckld from 72; Hon Can of Auckld from 78; P-in-c of St Matt City and Dio Auckld 79-81; V from 81; Archd of Auckld from 81. *21 Hepburn Street, Auckland 1, NZ.*

MULLARD, George Edward. b 14. St D Coll Lamp BA 38. Sarum Th Coll 38. **d** 39 **p** 40 Ex. C of Hartland 39-42; St Gabr Plymouth 42-45; Northam w Westward Ho (in c of H Trin Westward Ho) 45-48; V of E Coker (w Sutton Bingham from 69) 48-79; C-in-c of Sutton Bingham 58-69. *Alvington Cottage, Nr Yeovil, Somt, BA22 8TH.* (Yeovil 71752)

MULLEN, Lester Royce. Qu Univ Kingston, Ont BA 64. Wycl Coll Tor LTh 65. **d** 62 **p** 64 Ont. C of St John Kingston 62-64; R of Camden E 64-69; I Dio of Lantz 69-73; on leave. *RR4, Digby, NS, Canada.*

MULLEN, Peter John. b 42. Univ of Liv BA 70. **d** 70 **p** 71 Ripon. C of Manston 70-72; All SS Stretford 72-73; Oldham 73-74; L to Offic Dio Man from 74; Asst Master Whitecroft High Sch Bolton 74-77; V of Tockwith (and Bilton w Bickerton from 78) Dio York from 77; Bilton-in-Ainsty 77-78. *Vicarage, Tockwith, N Yorks.* (Tockwith 338)

MULLENGER, Alan Edward. BD (Lon) 64. Kelham Th Coll M SSM 39. **d** 40 **p** 41 Sheff. C of St Cecilia Parson Cross Sheff 40-48; St Patr Bloemf 48-52; Vice-Prin Modderpoort Sch 52-54; Miss P at St Patr Miss Bloemf 54-56; R of Mantsonyane 56-61; Perm to Offic Dio Ox 63-64; Dio Nor 64-65; P-in-c of Mampong 65-73; Hon Can of Kum 73-74; R of St John Maseru Dio Les from 73. *PO Box 270, Maseru, Lesotho.* (Maseru 2154)

MULLENGER, William. b 44. Linc Th Coll 68. **d** 69 Stepney for S'wark **p** 70 S'wark. C of St Jo Evang Clapham 69-73; Hook Dio S'wark from 73. *276 Hook Road, Hook, Chessington, Surrey.* (01-397 0063)

MULLENS, John Langford. b 06. Selw Coll Cam BA 28, MA 52. Westcott Ho Cam 29. **d** 29 **p** 30 Newc T. C of Benwell 29-36; Hexham 36-39; V of Delaval w Seaton Sluice and New Hartley 39-54; R of Farthinghoe w Thenford 54-71; Perm to Offic Dio Roch from 72; Dio Cant from 74. *29d Frant Road, Tunbridge Wells, Kent, TN2 5JT.* (Tunbridge Wells 27770)

MULLER, Brian Edwin. b 41. St Jo Coll Morpeth. **d** 70 **p** 72 Newc. C of Cessnock 70-74; Mayfield 75-77; Chap Mitchell Coll of Advanced Educn Bath from 77. *c/o Mitchell College Education, Bathurst, NSW, Australia 2795.* (31-1722)

MÜLLER, Cyril. b 47. St Pet Coll Alice 70. **d** 72 **p** 73 Port Eliz. C of St Kath Uitenhage 72-81; R of St Mary Magd Salt Lake Dio Port Eliz from 81. *Box 17048, Saltville, Port Elizabeth, CP, S Africa.*

MULLER, Hugo. Seager Hall, Ont STh 61. **d** 60 Hur for Moos **p** 61 Moos. C of Swastika 60-63; I of Rouyn 63-65; Chapais and Chibougamau 65-70; R of Noranda 70-75; Fort Frances Dio Keew from 75. *358 Church Street, Fort Frances, Ont., Canada.* (807-274 9777)

MULLER, Raymond John. Ch Ch Coll NZ Bd of Th Stud LTh 64. **d** 62 Bp McKenzie for Wel **p** 63 Wel. C of All SS Palmerston N 62-68; V of Patea 68-71; L to Offic Dio Wel 72-74; V of Tawa-Linden Dio Wel from 74. *Vicarage, Ngatitoa Street, Tawa, NZ.* (Tawa 6415)

MULLER, Wolfgang Wilhelm Bernard Heinrich Paul. b 28. ALCD 54. **d** 55 **p** 56 Roch. C of Tonbridge 55-56; St Steph Chatham 56-59; Min of Wigmore w Hempstead Eccles Distr 59-65; V of St Matt Wigmore Gillingham 65-72; S Gillingham 72-73. *5 Koln 51, Lindenallee 61, Germany.*

MULLETT, Alfred James. b 14. Qu Coll Birm 33. St Aid Coll 34. **d** 37 **p** 38 Man. C of Middleton 37-42; R of St Paul Bradf 42-49; V of All SS Northmoor Oldham Dio Man from 49; Chap Westhulme Hosp from 49. *All Saints' Vicarage, Barton Street, Oldham, Lancs, OL1 2NR.* (061-624 4768)

MULLETT, John St Hilary. b 25. St Cath Coll Cam BA 47, MA 49. Linc Th Coll. **d** 50 **p** 51 Lon. C of All H Tottenham 50-52; R of Que Que Rhod 52-61; V of St Jo Bapt Bollington 61-69; Oxton 69-73; Proc Conv Ches 66-77; M Gen Syn 71-77; R of Ashwell Dio St Alb from 77. *Ashwell Rectory, Baldock, Herts.* (Ashwell 277) (046-274 2277)

MULLIN, George Orchard. Univ of Syd BA 40. St Jo Coll Morpeth ACT ThL 41. **d** 42 **p** 43 Newc. C of Singleton 42-44; Waratah 44-45; Chap AIF 45-46; C of Waratah 47-48; P-in-c of Camden Haven 48-52; R of Dungog 52-58; Wyong 58-62; Hamilton 62-70; St Mary W Maitland Dio Newc from 70. *68 Church Street, Maitland, NSW, Australia 2320.* (33-5302)

MULLINEAUX, John. b 16. Univ of Man BA (Engl) 38. Kelham Th Coll 38. **d** 41 **p** 42 Bris. C of St John Bedminster

41-44; CF (EC) 44-47; C and Sacr of Blackb Cathl 47-50; V of Brierfield 50-60; Ch Ch Lanc 60-67; Caton w Littledale 67-81; Hon Chap to Bp of Blackb 70. *10 Ashfield Avenue, Lancaster, LA1 5DZ.* (0524-36769)

MULLINER, Denis Ratliffe. b 40. BNC Ox BA (2nd cl Mod Lang) 62, MA 66. Linc Th Coll 70. **d** 72 Ox **p** 73 Buckingham for Ox. C of Sandhurst 72-76; Chap Bradfield Coll Dio Ox from 76. *Bradfield College, Reading.*

MULLINGS, Peter. St Pet Coll Ja. **d** 63 **p** 64 Ja. P-in-c of Old Harbour 63-68; R 68-71; P-in-c of Bartons 68-71; Actg Dir of Youth Work 71-74; R of Mona Heights Dio Ja from 74. *1 Palmetto Avenue, Kingston 6, Jamaica.* (092-76436)

MULLINS, George Austin. Univ of Melb BA 64, MA 67, PhD 73. St Jo Coll Morpeth ThL 59. **d** 57 C & Goulb **p** 59 Melb. C of Bega 57; Braybrook 58-59; Box Hill 60-62; V of H Trin E Ringwood 63-69; C of Ascot Vale Dio Melb 69-71; I from 71. *9 Roxburg Street, Ascot Vale, Vic, Australia 3032.* (03-37 6979)

MULLINS, Joe. MC 45. Trin Coll Ox BA 49. Ridley Hall Cam. **d** 50 **p** 51 Lon. C of St Paul Portman Square Lon 50-52; in Ch of S India 52-56; P-in-c of St Pet Canberra Dio C & Goulb from 77. *24 Bunny Street, Weston, ACT, Australia 2611.*

MULOBA, Bukanga. b 20. **d** 76 Boga-Z **p** 77 Bukavu. P Dio Bukavu. *Kihembwe Parish, BP 220, Kindu, Maniema, Zaire.*

MULOCHO, Obadiya. **d** 46 **p** 48 U Nile. P Dio U Nile 46-48; Asst P Kisoko 48; Tororo 49-61; Dio Mbale 61-72; Dio Bukedi 72-76; Hon Can of Mbale 69-72; Can of Bukedi 72-76. *Box 856, Mbale, Uganda.*

MULOLO, Gilbert. **d** 75 **p** 76 Centr Zam (APM). P Dio Centr Zam. *PO Box 70172, Ndola, Zambia.*

MULONGO, Isaac. **d** 76 d Dio Lusaka. *PO Mapanza, via Choma, Zambia.*

MULREADY, David Gray. b 47. Moore Coll Syd ACT ThL 70. **d** 71 Syd **p** 71 Bp Delbridge for Syd. C of Camden 71-75; P-in-c of Tambar Springs 75-77; V of Walgett 77-81; Manilla Dio Armid from 81. *Vicarage, Hill Street, Manilla, NSW, Australia 2346.*

MULRENAN, Richard John. b 12. Tyndale Hall Bris 37 and 45. ACA 36, FCA 60. **d** 46 **p** 48 E Szech [f Lay Miss] C of St Phil and St Jacob Bris 46; Bucknall w Bagnall (in c of St John Abbey Hulton) 51-53; V of Bayston Hill 53-57; PC of St Clem Parkstone 57-66; V of Braintree 66-77; Chap Wm Julien Courtauld Hosp 66-77; P-in-c of Glympton Dio Ox from 80. *Church Bungalow, Glympton, Woodstock, Oxon, OX7 1AT.* (Woodstock 812188)

MULULA, Yoel. St Phil Coll Kongwa 69. **d** and **p** 71 Centr Tang. P Dio Centr Tang. *Mhayungu, Box 913, Dodoma, Tanzania.*

MULUMBA, Eros. **d** 42 **p** 44 Ugan. P Dio Ugan. *CMS, Bale, Bulemezi, Uganda.*

MULUYA, George. Buwalasi Th Coll 64. **d** 65 **p** 67 Nam. P Dio Nam 65-69; Dio Bugembe from 69. *c/o PO Box 4013, Bugembe, Uganda.*

MULVANEY, Francis James. Hur Coll Dipl Th 67. **d** 67 Bp Queen for Hur **p** 68 Hur. R of Florence 67-72; St Thos Owen Sound 72-78; on leave. *1390 8th Avenue West, Owen Sound, Ont., Canada.* (519-376 4986)

MULWANYI, Patrick Saul. Buwalasi Th Coll 61. **d** 64 Nam. d Dio Nam. *Anglican Church, Masulita, PO Kakine-Kampala, Uganda.*

✠ **MUMBA, Right Rev Stephen Sebastian.** St Jo Bapt Th Sem Lusaka. **d** 65 Bp Mataka for Zam **p** 67 Zam. P Dio Zam 67-70; Dio Centr Zam 71-75; Dioc Sec Dio N Zam 75-81; Can of N Zam 76-81; P-in-c of St Barn Chingola 76-81; Cons Ld Bp of Lusaka in Cathl of The H Cross Lusaka 8 Feb 81 by Abp of Centr Afr; Bps of N Zam; Centr Zam and Lake Malawi. *Bishops's House, Box 30183, Lusaka, Zambia.*

MUMFORD, David Bardwell. b 49. St Cath Coll Cam BA 71, MA 75. Cudd Coll 73. **d** 75 Bris. C of St Mary Redcliffe Bedminster 75-79; Perm to Offic Dio Bris from 79. *3 Redland Terrace, Bristol, BS6 6TD.*

MUMFORD, Edward Corey. Em Coll Sktn LTh 60. **d** 60 **p** 61 Edmon. C of Sedgewick 60-61; I of Hardisty 61-62; Bon Accord 62-65; Miss at Inuvik 65-68; R of Kimberley 69-74; on leave 75-78; I of Keremeos Dio Koot from 78. *Box 211, Keremeos, BC, Canada.*

MUMFORD, Grenville Alan. b 34. **d** and **p** 78 Colchester for Chelmsf. [F Methodist Min] C of Witham 78-81; Min of St Marg Conv Distr Ilford Dio Chelmsf from 81. *58 Brisbane Road, Ilford, Essex.* (01-554 7542)

MUMFORD, Canon Hugh Raymond. b 24. Oak Hill Th Coll 50. **d** 53 Kens for Lon **p** 54 Stepney for Lon. C of St Jas L Bethnal Green 53-57; Lect and C of Watford 57-59; R of St Pet Thetford 59-69; RD of Thetford 68-69; V of Cerne Abbas w Upcerne 69-72; Nether Cerne 69-72; R of Godmanstone 69-72; Minterne Magna 69-72; V of Cerne Abbas w Godmanstone and Minterne Magna Dio Sarum from 72; RD of Dorch 74-79; Can of Sarum Cathl from 77. *Vicarage, Back Lane, Cerne Abbas, Dorchester, Dorset, DT2 7JW.* (Cerne Abbas 251)

MUMFORD, John Alexander. b 52. Univ of St Andr MTh 75. Ridley Hall Cam 75. **d** 77 Sarum **p** 78 Sherborne for Sarum. C of Canford Magna Dio Sarum from 77. *2 Chichester Walk, Wimborne, Dorset, BH21 1SN.* (Wimborne 886674)

MUMFORD, Michael David. b 29. **d** 79 St Alb **p** 80 Bedford for St Alb. Chap Lister Hosp Dio St Alb from 79. *Lucas's Farmhouse, Rustling End, Codicote, Hitchin, Herts.* (Stevenage 820168)

✠ **MUMFORD, Right Rev Peter.** b 22. Univ Coll Ox BA 50, MA 54. Cudd Coll 50. **d** 51 **p** 52 Sarum. C of St Mark Sarum 51-55; Abbey Ch St Alb 55-57; V of St Luke Leagrave Luton 57-63; St Andr Bedford 63-69; Proc Conv St Alb 64-70; R of Crawley 69-73; Can and Preb of Chich Cathl 72-73; Archd of St Alb 73-74; Cons Ld Bp Suffr of Hertf in S'wark Cathl 29 March 74 by Abp of Cant; Bps of Win, Linc, St Alb, Nor, Roch and Chelmsf; Bps Suffr of Aston, Grantham, Bedford and Thetford; and others; Trld to Truro 81. *Lis Escop, Truro, Cornw, TR3 6QQ.* (Devoran 862657)

MUMFORD, Peter Lindsay. b 40. St Jo Coll Morpeth ACT ThL 76. **d** 76 Newc **p** 77 Bp Parker for Newc. Hon C of Muswellbrook 76-78; C of Taree 78-80; R of Murrurundi Dio Newc from 80. *Rectory, Mount Street, Murrundi, NSW, Australia 2338.* (065-466157)

MUMFORD, William Thomas. Univ of Dur LTh 17. **d** 14 Bp de Carteret for Abp of WI **p** 15 WI. C of Halfway Tree 14-16; R of Mavis Bank w Clifton 16-24; Darliston 24-28; R of Southfield and Mayfield 28-36; Balaclava w Keynsham 36; Mile Gully 36-55; P-in-c of Pedro Plains 62-70. *Munro College, PO Jamaica, W Indies.*

MUMMELELE, Matthayo. St Cypr Th Coll Ngala 63. **d** 64 **p** 66 Masasi. P Dio Masasi. *Box 92, Newala, Tanzania.*

MUN, Zachariah. b 34. St Mich Sem Oryudong 61. **d** 63 **p** 64 Korea. P Dio Korea 63-65; Dio Seoul 65-70; Dio Taejon 70-74; Dio Pusan from 74; VG Dio Taejon 70-73. *On-Chongdong 183-38; Dong Rae Ku, Pusan 601-02, Korea.* (Pusan 52-1930)

MUNA, Justin. Weithaga Bible Sch 59. **d** 59 Momb **p** 61 Ft Hall. P Dio Ft Hall 59-64; Dio Mt Kenya 64-75; Dio Mt Kenya S from 75. *Gitugi, Box 253, Murang'a, Kenya.*

MUNBY, Philip James. b 52. Pemb Coll Ox BA 75, MA 80. St Jo Coll Nottm 76. **d** 78 **p** 79 S'wark. C of Gipsy Hill Dio S'wark from 78. *9 Gatestone Road, Upper Norwood, SE19.* (01-653 3084)

MUNCEY, William. b 49. Oak Hill Coll BA 80. **d** 80 **p** 81 S'wark. C of St Mich AA Southfields Dio S'wark from 80. *3 Hambledon Road, Southfields, SW18.*

MUNDA, Eluzai Gyima. Bp Gwynne Coll Mundri, 60. **d** 63 **p** 68 Sudan. d Dio Sudan; P Dio Sudan from 70: Prin Bp Gwynne Coll Mundri from 73. *c/o Bishop Gwynne College, Mundri, Sudan.*

MUNDEN, Alan Frederick. b 43. St Jo Coll Nottm BTh 74. Univ of Birm MLitt 80. **d** 74 **p** 75 Tewkesbury for Glouc. C of Cheltenham 74-76; Clayton Mem Ch Jesmond Dio Newc T from 76. *21 Windsor Terrace, Jesmond, Newcastle upon Tyne, NE2 4HE.* (Newc T 811490)

✠ **MUNDIA, Right Rev James Israel.** St Paul's Th Coll Limuru, 59. **d** 60 Momb **p** 62 Maseno. P Dio Maseno 60-65; Dioc Youth Adviser Dio Maseno 65-70; Cons Ld Bp of Maseno N in H Trin Ch Enyaita 2 Oct 70 by Abp of Kenya; Bps of Mt Kenya; Momb; Maseno S; and Asst Bp of Nak. *PO Box 416, Kakamega, Kenya.*

MUNDO, Adonikam. St Phil Th Coll Kongwa, 60. **d** 60 Bp Wiggins for Centr Tang **p** 61 Centr Tang. P Dio Centr Tang 60-65; Dio Moro from 65. *Rubeho, Tanzania.*

MUNDY, William Basil. Trin Coll Tor BA (Hons) 51, LTh 54. **d** 53 **p** 54 Niag. C of St Aid Oakville 53-54; R 54-55; Eganville 55-59; I of Evansburgh 59-60; Sherwood Pk 60-61; R of Creston 61-62; R of St Francis Caulfield W Vanc 66-70; I of Lake Hill 74-78. *71 Bronson Avenue, Ottawa, Ont., Canada.*

MUNGAI, Benson. **d** 77 **p** 78 Nak. P Dio Nak. *PO Tambach, Kenya.*

MUNGANGA, Marangbalu. b 43. **d** and **p** 77 Boga-Z. P Dio Boga-Z. *BP 154, Bunia, Zaire.*

MUNGAVIN, Gerald Clarence. b 27. Edin Th Coll 51. **d** 54 St Andr **p** 55 Glas. C of H Trin Dunfermline 54-55; Good Shepherd Hillington Glas 55-57; CF 57-60; C of Stanwix 60-62; Chap RAf 62-75; R of St Congan Turriff 75-81; Cuminestown 75-81; Bannf 75-81; Banchory Dio Aber from 81; Kincardine O'Neil Dio Aber from 81. *Rectory, Banchory, Kincardineshire.* (Banchory 2783)

MUNGUNO, Lourenco. **d** 77 **p** 78 Lebom. P Dio Lebom.

CP 57, Maputo, Mozambique.

MUNGWA, Isaac. d 32 **p** 33 N Rhod. Miss P Dio N Rhod 33-64; L to Offic Dio Lusaka from 71. *Msoro Mission, Fort Jameson, Zambia.*

MUNIGE, Ven Yusufu Kabarole. b 39. Bp Tucker Coll Mukono 72. **d** 74 **p** 75 Boga-Z. P Dio Boga-Z 74-79; Archd from 79. *EAZ Bunia, BP 154, Bunia, Zaire.*

MUNIOKANO, John Yeseri Kantebuka. Buwalasi Th Coll. **d** 56 Ugan **p** 58 Bp Balya for Ugan. P Dio Ugan 56-61; Dio Nam from 61. *Training College, Bukote, Uganda.*

MUNN, Harold Thomas. b 46. Univ of Vic BC BA 67. Trin Coll Tor MDiv 73. **d** 73 **p** 74 Yukon. C of Elba, Mayo and Pelly 73-76; P Assoc of Ch Ch Cathl Whitehorse 77-80; R of Ch Ch City and Dio Edmon from 80. *10210-121 Street, Edmonton, Alta, Canada.*

MUNN, Quentin Lindsay Carlyle. b 1938. Univ of Wales BA 60. St Steph Ho Ox 60. **d** 62 **p** 63 Llan. C of St Mary Virg Cardiff 62-64; Aberaman 64-65; L to Offic Dio Lon from 69; Asst Master Dormers Wells High Sch from 74. *29 Mostyn Avenue, Wembley, Middx.* (01-902 3679)

MUNN, Richard Probyn. b 45. Selw Coll Cam 2nd cl Th Trip pt i 65, BA (2nd cl Div i Th Trip pt ii) 67. Cudd Coll 67. **d** 69 **p** 70 Glouc. C of Cirencester w Watermoor 69-72; Chap to St Mark's Sch Mapanze 72-74; R of Livingstone 75-80; Archd of S Prov Zam 80; P-in-c of King's Stanley Dio Glouc from 80. *King's Stanley Rectory, Stonehouse, Glos.* (Stonehouse 2419)

MUNNS, Canon Kenneth Barry. Univ of Newc BA 67. St Jo Coll Morpeth ACT ThL (2nd cl) 63. **d** 65 **p** 66 Newc. C of Cessnock 65-69; Asst Sec ABM for NSW 70-72; Perm to Offic Dios C & Goulb and Syd 70-72; R of Enmore w Stanmore 72-76; Waratah Dio Newc from 76; Dioc Can Miss Dio Newc from 80. *Rectory, Bridge Street, Waratah, NSW, Australia 2289.* (68 1077)

MUNNS, Stuart Millington. b 36. OBE 77. St Cath Coll Cam 3rd cl Th Trip pt i 56, BA (3rd cl Th Trip pt ii) 58, MA 62. Cudd Coll 58. **d** 60 **p** 61 Derby. C of Allenton w Shelton Lock 60-63; St Thos Brampton 63-65; C-in-c of Ch of the Ascen Conv Distr Loundsley Green 65-66; Bp's Chap for Youth Dio Derby 66-72; Dir of Commun Industry 72-77; Perm to Offic Dio Lon 72-77; Hon C of Ch Ch Crouch End Hornsey 72-77; V of Knowsley Dio Liv from 77; Dio Missr Dio Liv from 77. *Vicarage, Tithebarn Road, Knowsley Village, Mer, L34 0JA.* (051-546 4266)

MUNRO, Basil Henry. b 40. Ripon Hall Ox 73. **d** 75 **p** 76 St Alb. C of N Mymms 75-78; St Steph City and Dio St Alb 78-80; V from 80. *14 Watling Street, St Albans, Herts.* (St Alb 62598)

MUNRO, Donald Alexander. b 08. Clifton Th Coll. **d** 46 **p** 47 Raph. C of Rossnowlagh w Drumholm 46-48; Chilvers Coton 48-51; V of Ansley 51-57; Shapwick w Ashcott 57-69; R of Kilmington Wilts Dio B & W from 69. *Kilmington Rectory, Butts Lane, Warminster, Wilts, B12 6RB.* (Maiden Bradley 293)

MUNRO, Duncan John Studd. b 50. Magd Coll Ox BA 72, BA (Th) 75, Can Hall Gr NT Pri 75, MA 76. Wycl Hall Ox 73. **d** 76 **p** 77 Doncaster for Sheff. C of All SS Ecclesall Sheff 76-78; St Barn and St Mary Sheff 78-80; L to Offic Dio Sheff from 80. *36 Thompson Road, Sheffield, S11 8RB.* (Sheff 682063)

MUNRO, John Alexander. Univ of Melb BA (1st cl Phil and Hist) 43. ACT ThL 39. Univ of Lon MTh 48, PhD 51. **d** and **p** 43 Bal. C of Warrnambool 43-46; St Martin-in-the-Fields Trafalgar Square Lon 46; Bp's Chap to Univ of Lon 48-50; Dean and V of Ch Ch Cathl Bal 51-53; Austr Broadcasting Comm and Perm to Offic Dio Melb 53-56; Dio Syd 57-63; Federal Supervisor Relig Broadcasts 56-61; Federal Dir of Gen Programmes 61-63; R of Dee Why w Brookvale 63-66; St Paul Canberra 66-72; Albury and Archd of Albury 72-73; Chairman ABM and L to Offic Dio Syd 73-76. *109 Cambridge Street, Stanmore, NSW, Australia 2048.*

MUNRO, John Alexander. Trin Coll Tor **d** and **p** 51 Niag. C of Oakville 51-53; CF (Canad) 53-59; R of St Matt Lon 59-63; I of St Mark Brantford 63-80; Can of Hur 75-80. *Box 220, St George, Ont, Canada.*

MUNRO, Canon Louis Cecil Garth. b 16. Univ of Leeds BA 40. Coll of Resurr Mirfield, 40. **d** 42 **p** 43 Man. C of St Sav Ringley 42-44; St Mark North End Portsea (in C of St Nich from 45) 44-55; V of Forton 55-81; RD of Alverstoke 66-72; Hon Can of Portsm Cathl 71-81; Can (Emer) from 81; Perm to Offic Dio Portsm from 81. *7 St Helen's Road, Alverstoke, Gosport, Hants, PO12 2RL.* (Gosport 85494)

MUNRO, Robert Angus. Brisb Th Coll ACT ThL 27. **d** 26 **p** 27 Brisb. C of St Paul Ipswich 26-28; St Paul Maryborough 28-31; V of Chinchilla 31-33; Brisb Valley 33-38; R of Stanthorpe 38-40; Bellbird 40-44; Coopernook 44-49; Tor 48-61; Williamtn 61-66; Perm to Offic Dio Newc from 66; Dio Syd from 79. *2 Sylvania Avenue, Springwood, NSW, Australia 2777.* (047-51 3920)

MUNRO, Terence George. b 34. Jes Coll Cam BA 56, MA 60. Linc Th Coll 59. **d** 61 **p** 62 Ripon. C of Far Headingley 61-64; P-in-c of Vaughansfield 64-70; R of Methley w Mickletown 70-79; V of St Pet w St Cuthb Hunslet Moor Dio Ripon from 79. *139 Dewsbury Road, Hunslett Moor, Leeds 11.* (Leeds 716321)

MUNROE, Very Rev John Austin. Univ of K Coll Halifax, BA 52, BS Litt 55, BD 64. **d** 54 **p** 55 NS. I of Rawdon 54-59; R of Aylesford 59-63; Horton 63-68; Lunenburg 68-79; Exam Chap to Bp of NS from 71; Dean and R of All SS Cathl Halifax Dio NS from 79. *Deanery, 1350 Tower Road, Halifax, NS, Canada.* (423-3222)

MUNSON, Arthur George. b 1898. Univ of Bris BA 23. Ripon Hall Ox 23. **d** 24 **p** 25 Chelmsf. C of Barking 24-27; St Luke Gt Ilford 27-28; All SS w St Pet Maldon 28-32; R of Wickford 32-55; Perm to Offic Dio Chelmsf 55-64; LPr from 64. *St Mark's College, Audley End, Nr Saffron Walden, Essex.*

MUNT, Cyril. b 28. K Coll Lon and Warm AKC 52. **d** 53 Dover for Cant **p** 54 Cant. C of Ashford 53-56; Dorking 56-60; R of Cheriton w Newington 60-68; Harbledown Dio Cant from 68. *Harbledown Rectory, Canterbury, Kent, CT2 8NW.* (Canterbury 64117)

MUNT, Donald James. b 20. ALCD 53 (LTh from 74). **d** 53 **p** 54 S'wark. C of Ch Ch Purley 53-56; St Jas Hatcham (in c of St Mich) 56-61; V of Oulton Broad 61-69; St Pet Brockley 69-75; R of Litcham w Kempston and E and W Lexham Dio Nor from 76; P-in-c of Mileham and of Beeston-next-Mileham and of Stanfield Dio Nor from 81. *Litcham Rectory, King's Lynn, Norf, PE32 2NZ.* (Litcham 223)

MUNT, Canon Neil. b 20. AKC 43. Linc Th Coll **d** 44 **p** 45 S'wark. C of St Pet St Helier 44-46; Redhill 46-51; Uckfield Isfield and L Horsted 51-53; V of St Jas Malden 53-62; Surr from 71; Godmanchester 62-74; H Trin w St Mary City and Dio Ely from 74; Chettisham Dio Ely from 76; Prickwillow Dio Ely from 76; Hon Can of Ely from 74. *Vicarage, St Mary's Street, Ely, Cambs, CB7 4ER.* (Ely 2308)

MUNTON, Canon Peter John. Coll Ho Ch Ch NZ Bd of Th Stud LTh 51. **d** 51 **p** 52 Wel. C of Palmerston N 51-55; V of Pauatahanui 55-56; Paeroa 56-61; Tokoroa 61-64; Morrinsville 64-68; Can of St Pet Cathl Hamilton 67-68; V of Hastings 68-76; Te Hapara Dio Wai from 76; Can of Wai from 73. *776 Childers Road, Gisborne, NZ.* (4928)

MUNTU, Boaz. Bp Tucker Coll Mukono 70. **d** 72 Ank. d Dio Ank. *Ryakasinga, PO Kemikyera, Mbarara, Uganda.*

MUNYAMALE, Emanuel. St Phil Th Coll Kongwa, 66. **d** 68 Bp Madinda for Centr Tang. **p** 68 Centr Tang. P Dio Centr Tang. *PO Mwitikira, Tanzania.*

MUNYAMPARA, Canon Yosefi. d 65 Rwanda B **p** 66 Rwa. P Dio Rwa 65-75; Dio Kiga from 75; Can of Rwa 72-75; Kiga from 75. *Shyogwe, BP 27, Gitarama, Rwanda.*

MUNYANGABE, Yosia. d 65 Rwanda B **p** 66 Rwa. P Dio Rwa 65-75; Dio Kiga from 75; Archd of S Rwa 75. *PO Box 43, Gikongero, Rwanda.*

MUNYANGAJU, Jerome. b 53. St Phil Coll Kongwa 73. **d** and **p** 75 Vic Nyan. P Dio Vic Nyan. *PO Box 278, Mwanza, Tanzania.*

MUNYANGERI, Wycliffe. d 54 **p** 56 Bp Brazier for Ugan. P Dio Ugan 54-60; Dio Ankole-K 60-67; Dio Kig from 67. *PO Box 1212, Mparo, Kigezi, Uganda.*

MUNYANGWILA, Canon Yona Munyambwa. d 41 **p** 43 Centr Tang. P Dio Centr Tang 41-65; Can from 65. *c/o PO Box 15, Dodoma, Tanzania.*

MUNZENDA, Musubaho. b 42. Bp Tucker Coll Mukono 72. **d** 74 **p** 75 Boga-Z. P Dio Boga-Z 74-76; Bukavu from 76. *BP 2876, Bukavu, Zaire.*

MUOGHERE, Vincent Omasheho. Im Coll Ibad. **d** and **p** 66 Benin. P Dio Benin 66-72; Dio Warri from 80; C of Sparkhill 72-78; Exam Chap to Bp of Warri from 80. *c/o Box 396, Warri, Bendel State, Nigeria.*

MURAGURI, Ben Nyahu. Weithaga Bible Sch 59. **d** 60 Momb **p** 61 Ft Hall. P Dio Ft Hall 60-65; Mt Kenya from 65. *Anglican Church, Muguru, PO Kangema, Kenya.*

MURCH, Derrick Gabriel Newbery. b 19. Sarum Th Coll 66. **d** 68 **p** 69 Sarum. C of Wimborne Minster 68-71; P-in-c of Buckland Newton 71-72; Wootton-Glanville w Holnest 71-72; V of Dilton Marsh (w Brokerswood from 73) 72-77; P-in-c of Halstock 77-79; Corscombe 77-79; E w W Chelborough 77-79; Team V of Melbury Dio Sarum from 79. *Corscombe Vicarage, Dorchester, Dorset, DT2 0NU.* (093-589247)

MURCH, Robin Norman. b 37. Wells Th Coll. **d** 67 Ely **p** 68 Huntingdon for Ely. C of St Aug Wisbech 67-70; C of Basingstoke (in c of St Gabr) 70-73; Whitstable 73-76; V of Queenborough Dio Cant from 76. *Vicarage, High Street, Queenborough, Kent.* (Sheerness 2648)

MURCHISON, Canon Laurence Maxwell. Univ of Syd BA 40. ACT ThL 45. ARCO 51. ARCM 51. **d** 43 **p** 44 Goulb. C of Young 43-46; St John Canberra 46-47; Ch Ch S Yarra

47-48; L to Offic Dio Melb 48-49; C of All SS Geelong 49-51; Prec and Organist of St Sav Cathl Goulb 51-59; R of St Paul Canberra 60-66; Exam Chap to Bp of C & Goulb from 60; Can of St Sav Cathl Goulb from 60; Tutor St Mark's Libr Canberra Dio C & Goulb from 66. *237 Antill Street, Watson, ACT, Australia.* (062-48 0875)

MURCHISON, Morris Duncan. Univ of W Ont BA 61. Hur Coll BTh 63. **d** 62 **p** 63 Hur. P Dio Hur 62-64; C of All SS Ott 64-67; Ingleside 67-73; R of St Matt Lon Ont 73-77; St Jas Sarnia Dio Hur from 77. *957 Bond Street, Sarnia, Ont., Canada.* (509-542 3232)

MURCOTT, Hugh Gordon. St Cath Coll Ox BA (3rd cl Th) 35, MA 42. Univ of Pret MA 32. Univ of Stellenbosch MEducn 38. **d** 62 **p** 63 Johann. C of Benoni 62-67; R of Ermelo 67-72; Randfontein 72-76; Auckld Pk 76-80. *c/o Box 1032, Pretoria 0001, S Africa.*

MURDIN, Frank Laurence. b 11. Univ of Leeds BA (2nd cl Hist) 34. Coll of Resurr Mirfield 34. **d** 36 **p** 37 Pet. C of St Paul Pet 36-41; R and V of Culworth 41-58; RD of Culworth (formerley Brackley i) 50-58; Weldon 64-65; V of Moreton Pinkney 55-58; R of Brampton Ash w Dingley 58-65; V of Greetham w Stretton and Clipsham 65-76. *48 Pinewood Close, Bourne, Lincs, PE10 9RL.* (Bourne 3696)

MURDOCH, Alexander Edward Duncan. b 37. Oak Hill 68. **d** 71 **p** 73 Kens for Lon. C of St Helen w H Trin Kens 71-72; St Barn Kens 73-74; CF 74-77; C of St Bridget W Kirby (in c of the Resurr and All SS) Dio Ches from 78. *13 Caldy Road, W Kirby, Wirral, Merseyside, L48 2HE.* (051-625 7611)

MURDOCH, Genevieve Theresa. b 28. **d** 76 **p** 78 Rupld. Hon C of Selkirk 76-81; R of W Beaches Dio Rupld from 81. *c/o 212 Eveline Street, Selkirk, Manit, Canada.*

MUREWA, Bamidele Olusesan. b 54. Im Coll Ibadan 75. **d** 78 **p** 79 Ijebu. P Dio Ijebu. *Holy Trinity Church, Ibefun, Ijebu-Ode, Nigeria.*

MURFET, Edward David. Qu Coll Cam BA 59, MA 63. Chich Th Coll 59. **d** 61 **p** 62 Cant. C of St Mich AA Croydon 61-64; Hunslet w Stourton 64-65; St Mary of Eton Hackney Wick 65-69; Asst Chap St Ursula Bern 69-71; Chap of Naples 71-74; All SS Rome 74-77; Publ Pr Dio Bris 78-81; Gen Sec C of E Men's Society from 81. *18 Hertford Street, Coventry, CV1 1LF.* (Cov 22053)

MURFET, Gwyn. b 44. Linc Th Coll 71. **d** 74 **p** 75 York. C of Scalby w Ravenscar 74-77; P-in-c of S Milford Dio York from 77. *South Milford Rectory, Leeds, LS25 5AP.* (S Milford 683349)

MURGATROYD, Canon Eric. b 17. Open Univ BA 76. Lich Th Coll. **d** and **p** 46 Bradf. C of All SS Otley 46-49; Skipton 49-51; V of Grindleton 51-56; St Andr Yeadon 56-66; Cottingley 66-77; Woodhall Dio Bradf from 77; Hon Can of Bradf Cathl from 77. *Vicarage, Galloway Lane, Pudsey, W Yorks, LS28 8JR.* (Bradford 662735)

MURIITHI, Jacob. St Paul's Coll Limuru 68. **d** and **p** 71 Mt Kenya. P Dio Mt Kenya 71-75; Dio Mt Kenya E 75-78. *Nyangwa, Box 158, Embu, Kenya.*

MURIITHI, Stephen Kamici. St Paul's Th Coll Limuru. **d** 80 Mt Kenya E. d Dio Mt Kenya E. *PO Box 97, Kianyaga, Kenya.*

MURPHY, David. b 14. Univ of Lon BA 50, BD 52. **d** 49 **p** 50 Drom. C of Drom Cathl 49-51; I of Drumlane 51-55; C of Seapatrick 55-61; Derriaghy 61-63; Seghill 63-66; V of Haverton Hill 67-73; West Pelton Dio Dur from 73. *West Pelton Vicarage, Stanley, Co Durham, DH9 6RT.* (Beamish 700275)

MURPHY, John Gervase Maurice Walker. b 26. TCD BA 52, MA 55. **d** 52 **p** 53 Down. C of Lurgan 52-55; CF 55-77; DACG Rhine 69-71; Sen Chap RMA Sandhurst 71-73; ACG BAOR 73-75; ACG S East 75-77; V of Ranworth W Panxworth 77-79; Bp's Chap Norf Broads 77-79; RD of Blofield 79; R of Sandringham Group Dio Nor from 79; Dom Chap to HM the Queen from 79. *Sandringham Rectory, King's Lynn, Norf.* (Dersingham 40587)

MURPHY, Peter Frederick. b 40. K Coll Lon and Warm AKC 65. **d** 67 Lon **p** 68 Kens for Lon. C of St Jo Evang w St Mich AA Paddington 67-72; Team V of All SS Basingstoke 72-81; V of Hythe Dio Win from 81. *14 Atheling Road, Hythe, Southampton, SO4 6BR.* (Hythe 842461)

MURPHY, Ven Raymond Herbert. K Coll NS. **d** 41 **p** 42 Fred. C of Musquash 41-42; R 42-43; Kingston 43-45; Newcastle 45-59; Bathurst Dio Fred from 59; Archd of Chatham from 68; Exam Chap to Bp of Fred from 71. *426 King Avenue, Bathurst, NB, Canada.*

MURPHY, Rodney Morris. St Jo Coll Auckld 52. **d** 54 **p** 55 Wai. C of Napier Cathl 54-56; Rotorua 56-60; P-in-c of Murupara 60-61; V of Waipawa 61-63; R of Blackall 63-68; Archd of The West 65-69; V of Keppel 68-69; R of Young 69-72; C of Gisborne 72-74; V of Masterton 74-80; Avalon Dio Wel from 80. *966 High Street, Lower Hutt, NZ.* (677-710)

MURPHY, Thomas. b 20. TCD BA (2nd cl Or Lang Mod) 56, Div Test (1st cl) and Abp King Pr (2nd) 57, MA 64. **d** 57 **p** 58 Connor. C of Carrickfergus 57-60; Ch Ch Belf 60-63; R of Newtownhamilton and Ballymoyer 63-76; Hon V Chor of Arm Cathl from 69; R of Sixmilecross w Termonmaguirke Dio Arm from 76. *Sixmilecross Rectory, Omagh, Co Tyrone, N Ireland.* (Beragh 218)

MURPHY, William Albert. b 43. BD (Lon) 73. Qu Univ Belf MTh 78. Trin Coll Bris 69. **d** 73 **p** 74 Connor. C of Ch Ch Cathl Lisburn 73-79; Supt and Chap Ulster Inst for the Deaf from 79. *5/6 College Square North, Belfast, BT1 6AR. N Ireland.* (Belfast 21733)

MURRAY, Alan. b 37. Sarum Th Coll 62. **d** 64 **p** 65 Newc T. C of St Phil Newc T 64-68; Seaton Hirst (in c of St Andr) 68-73; V of Seghill Dio Newc T from 74. *Seghill Vicarage, Cramlington, Northumb, NE23 7EA.* (Seaton Delaval 371601)

MURRAY, Alexander John Mackie. Kelham Th Coll 58. **d** 63 Newc T **p** 66 Stafford for Lich. C of Ch Ch Shieldfield Newc T 63-64; Fenton 66-69; Rugeley 69-71; St Paul w St Luke Tranmere 71-77; V of Barnton 77-80. *c/o Barnton Vicarage, Northwich, Chesh, CW8 4JH.* (Northwich 74358)

MURRAY, Carl Cyrus. Codr Coll Barb 51. **d** 55 Barb for Antig **p** 56 Antig. C of St Jo Cathl Antig 55-60; R of St Mary Antig 61-64; V of St Clem Barb 64-65; C of St Matthias Barb 65-66; R of St Mary St Kitts 66-68; C of Kingston 68-73; R of St Ambrose I and Dio Barb from 76. *Rectory, Lady Meade Gardens, Bridgetown, Barbados, WI.*

MURRAY, Christopher James. b 49. Open Univ BA 78. St Jo Coll Nottm 79. **d** 81 Sarum. C of St Jo Evang Parkstone Dio Sarum from 81. *91 Churchill Road, Parkstone, Poole, Dorset, BH12 2LR.*

MURRAY, David McIlveen. b 36. ALCD 61. **d** 61 **p** 62 S'wark. C of Mortlake w E Sheen 61-64; Lyncombe Bath 64-67; Horsham 67-73; V of St Bart Devonport 73-79; Chalfont St Pet Dio Ox from 79. *Vicarage, Austen Way, Chalfont St Peter, Gerrard's Cross, Bucks.* (Gerrard's Cross 82389)

MURRAY, David Owen. St Mich Th Coll Crafers ACT ThL 68. **d** 68 **p** 69 Bunb. C of St Bonif Cathl Bunb 68-70; R of Lake Grace 70-74; Jerramungup 74-79; Mt Barker Dio Bunb from 79; Chap to Bp of Bunb from 78. *Rectory, Mount Barker, W Australia 6324.* (098-51 1060)

MURRAY, Desmond Theodore. b 30. **d** 80 Trin. C of St Mark Point Fortin Dio Trin from 80. *18 Canaan Road, Point Fortin, Trinidad, WI.*

MURRAY, Frederick Gordon. St Barn Coll N Adel ACT ThL 38. **d** 38 Bunb for Perth **p** 39 Perth. C of St Mary Perth 38-41 and 42-43; R of Toodyay 41-43; St Mary W Perth 43-44; Chap AIF 44-46; R of Dongarra w Mingenew 46-49. *Dongarra, W Australia.*

MURRAY, Gordon John. b 33. St Cath Coll Cam BA (2nd cl Engl Trip pt i) 56, 2nd cl Th Trip pt ia 57, MA 61. Clifton Th Coll 57. **d** 59 **p** 60 Heref. C of St Jas Heref 59-62; Uphill 62-65; PC of St Mary Chap Castle Street Reading 65-68; Ed *Engl Churchman* 65-71; Prin Kensit Coll Finchley 68-75; Asst Master Sandown High Sch 76-78. *8 Mill Lane, Felixstowe, Suff.*

MURRAY, Gordon Stewart. b 33. Univ of Lon BSc 72. Ripon Coll Cudd 76. **d** 78 Bp McKie for Cov **p** 79 Cov. C of Kenilworth 78-81; V of Potterspury w Furtho and Yardley Gobion Dio Pet from 81. *Potterspury Vicarage, Towcester, Northants, NN12 7PX.* (Yardley Gobion 542428)

MURRAY, Harold Frederick. Qu Coll Ont. **d** 64 **p** 66 Ont. I of Wolfe I 64-69; Tamworth 69-80; St Paul Brockville Dio Ont from 80. *37 Victoria Avenue, Brockville, Ont, Canada.* (613-342 8541)

MURRAY, Hugh Peter William. b 13. New Coll Ox BA 36, MA 47. **d** and **p** 75 Tewkesbury for Cant for Glouc (APM). C of Coln St Aldwyn 75-81; Perm to Offic Dio Glouc from 81. *Hinton House, Ablington, Cirencester, Glos., GL7 5NY.*

MURRAY, Ian Hargraves. b 48. Univ of Man BSc 71. St Jo Coll Nottm 79. **d** 81 Roch. C of St Paul Northumberland Heath Erith Dio Roch from 81. *113 Belmont Road, Erith, Kent, DA8 1LF.*

MURRAY, Ivan Cameron. **d** 63 **p** 65 Fred. C of St Geo St John 63-67; Hon C of Lancaster Dio Fred from 67. *480 De Monts Street, Lancaster, NB, Canada.*

MURRAY, James Henry. St Pet Th Coll Jamaica, 49. **d** 52 **p** 53 Jamaica. C of St Luke Cross Roads 52-53 and 55-56; P-in-c of Porus 53-55; R of Golden Grove 56-58; Port Antonio 58-66; Highgate-St Mary 66-67; Snowdon w Providence and Pratville Dio Ja from 68. *Rectory, Newport PO, Jamaica, W Indies.*

MURRAY, James Stirling. St Mich Th Coll Crafers 58. ACT ThL (2nd cl) 60. **d** 61 **p** 62 Melb. C of Dioc Task Force Broadmeadows Area 61-63; Chaps' Dept Dio Melb 63-65; C of St Jas City and Dio Syd from 65. *c/o St James's Church, King Street, Sydney, NSW, Australia.*

MURRAY, Canon John Desmond. b 16. TCD BA 38, Div Test (2nd cl) 39, MA 46. **d** 39 **p** 40 Dub. C of St Werburgh

Dub 39-41; Ch Ch Leeson Pk 41-43; H Trin Rathmines Dub 43-49; Min Can of St Patr Cathl Dub 43-53; R of Powerscourt 49-53; Chap RN 53-55; R of Dalkey 55-70; St Phil Milltown City and Dio Dub from 70; Hon Chap to Abp of Dub 73; Can of Ch Ch Cathl Dub from 79. *2 Dartry Park, Dublin 6, Irish Republic.* (Dub 975854)

MURRAY, John Douglas. b 16. Late Exhib of Keble Coll Ox BA (2nd cl Mod Hist) 38, MA 46. Bps' Coll Cheshunt, 38. **d** 40 **p** 41 Carl. C of Lowther w Askham 40-41; St Geo Barrow-F 41-43; CF (EC) 43-47; V of Brigham 47-50; Asst Master Workington Gr Sch 48-50; Lect St Pet Coll of Educn Saltley and Publ Pr Dio Birm 50-79; P-in-c of Streat w Westmeston Dio Chich from 79. *Streat Rectory, Hassocks, Sussex, BN6 8RX.* (Plumpton 890607)

MURRAY, John Grainger. b 45. Div Hostel Dub 67. **d** 70 Oss **p** 71 Leigh. C of Carlow 70-72; Lim Cathl 72-77; I of Rathdowney U Dio Oss from 77. *Rectory, Rathdowney, Leix, Irish Republic.* (Rathdowney 42)

MURRAY, John Robert. b 40. Univ of BC LTh 74. Vanc Sch of Th 71. **d** 73 **p** 74 BC. I of H Trin Sooke 73-79; Quamichan Dio BC from 79. *RR5, Duncan, BC, Canada.*

MURRAY, John Thomas. Edin Th Coll 63. **d** 66 Wakef **p** 67 Pontefract for Wakef. C of Golcar 66-70; R of Suddie w Queenstown 70-72; Ft Wel Guy 72-74. *Flat L, 163 Gloucester Terrace, W2 6DX.*

MURRAY, Kimberley David. b 52. Univ of Alta BA 73. Trin Coll Tor MDiv 76. **d** 76 **p** 77 Edmon. C of St Jo Evang Edmon 76-80; I of St Marg Miss City and Dio Edmon from 80. *11612-44a Avenue, Edmonton, Alta, Canada.*

MURRAY, Puti Hopaea. b 22. **d** 75 **p** 78 Auckld. C of Ponsonby 75-78; Maori Missr Dio Auckld from 78. *15 Fulton Crescent, Otara, NZ.*

MURRAY, Reginald James. d 59 **p** 60 Hur. C of St Paul Windsor 59-60; I of St Luke Windsor 60-67. *254 Josephine Avenue, Windsor 11, Ont, Canada.*

MURRAY, Robert Desmond. b 16. TCD BA 39. **d** 39 **p** 40 Down. C of Cathl Ch Drom 39-43; Rathkeale w Nantenan 43-44; I of Cloughjordan w Modreeny 44-55; Asst Chap Miss to Seamen Belf 55-58; V of E Crompton 58-70; Old w New Hutton Dio Carl from 70; P-in-c of Grayrigg Dio Carl from 76. *New Hutton Vicarage, Kendal, Cumb, LA8 0AS.* (Kendal 22149)

MURRAY, Ronald Thomas. b 09. St Pet Hall Ox BA (3rd cl Th) 33, MA 37. Clifton Th Coll 32. **d** 33 **p** 34 Bris. C of St Mich Arch Bris 33-36; Lect Clifton Th Coll 34-36; C of St Mich Bishopston (in c of Ch of Good Shepherd) 36-40; V of St Mich AA Windmill Hill Bris 40-43; Chilvers Coton 43-49; R of Southam 49-74; Surr 50-78; Proc Conv Cov 51-55; RD of Southam 57-66; C-in-c of Ufton 58-64; Perm to Offic Dio Cov from 80. *4 Barrowfield Court, Barrowfield Lane, Kenilworth, CV8 1EQ.* (Leamington Spa 59480)

MURRAY, Stewart Welsley. b 54. Carleton Univ Ott BA 76. Huron Coll Lon Ont MDiv 79. **d** and **p** 79 Ott. C of St Richard Ott 79-81; I of Vankleek Hill Dio Ott from 81. *Vankleek Hill, Ont, Canada, K0B 2P0.*

MURRAY, Thomas. Em Coll Sask STh 41. **d** 26 **p** 27 Sask. C-in-c of Prairie River 26-28; I of Perdue 28-30; Miss in c of Aklavick 30-35; C of Ripley (in c of St John) 36-40; V of St Chad Tonge Fold 40-42; H Trin Horwich 42-53; Surr 42-53; V of Ashton Keynes w Leigh 53-62; C of St Thos and St Clem w St Mich and St Swith Win 62-66. *1539 Foster Street, White Rock, BC, Canada.*

MURRAY, Thomas Barry. Hur Coll LTh 57. **d** 55 **p** 57 Hur. I of Muncey 55-57; Hyde Pk 57; C of All SS Windsor 57-59; R of Markdale 59-61; St Paul and St John Chatham Ont 61-66; St Marg Lon 66-71; All SS Woodstock Dio Hur from 71. *Rectory, Woodstock, Ont., Canada.* (519-537 3650)

MURRAY, Thomas Brian. b 29. Wycl Hall Ox 69. **d** 70 Warrington for Liv **p** 71 Liv. C of St Helen's 71-73; Chap to the Deaf Bris 73-74; Org Sec C of E Coun for Deaf from 75; Hon C of Enfield Dio Lon from 76. *Church House, Dean's Yard, SW1P 3NZ.* (01-222 9011)

✠ **MURRAY, Right Rev William Arthur.** Univ of Dur LTh 48. AKC 54. Columbia Univ NY MA 67. U Th Sem NY BD 62. **d** 50 **p** 51 Ja. C of St Mich Kingston 51-52; Asst Master and Chap Kingston Coll Ja 52-54; L to Offic Dio Lon 52-54; Chap Univ Coll of W Indies 54-62; R of Lluidas Vale 62-66; on leave USA 66-67; P-in-c Linstead and St Thos-Ye-Vale 67-69; Lluidas Vale 70-71; Prin Ch Coll Mandeville from 71; Exam Chap to Bp of Ja 71-76; Cons Ld Bp Suffr of Mandeville in St Mark Ch Mandeville 29 June 76 by Bp of Windw Is; Bps of Antig, Ja and Barb; Bps Suffr of Kingston and Montego Bay; and others. *PO Box 159, Mandeville, Jamaica, W Indies.* (096-22662)

MURRAY, William George. b 04. Late Scho of St D Coll Lamp BA (2nd cl Hist) 26, BD 71. Keble Coll Ox 3rd cl Th 29, BA and MA 52. St Mich Th Coll 29. **d** 30 **p** 31 Mon. C of St Mary Mon 30-32; Perm to Offic at Timperley 33-37; Chap of Leavesden Hosp 37-44; V of E Tilbury 44-53; R of W Tilbury 44-53; V of St Andr Westcliff-on-Sea 53-60; Bradfield 60-65; Exam Chap to Bp of Chelmsf 63-72; R of St Botolph w H Trin and St Giles Colchester 65-74. *7 Beverley Road, Colchester, Essex, CO3 3NG.* (Colchester 72949)

MURRAY, William Robert Craufurd. b 44. St Chad's Coll Dur BA (Social Stud) 66, Dipl Th 68. **d** 68 **p** 69 Carl. C of Workington 68-71; St Wilfrid Harrogate 71-74; V of Winksley-cum-Grantley w Aldfield and Studley 74; C-in-c of Sawley 74; R of Fountains 75-81; V of U Hutt Dio Wel from 81. *Vicarage, Logan Street, Upper Hutt, NZ.* (85-533)

MURRAY, THE, Lord Bishop of. *See* Porter, Right Rev Robert George.

MURRAY-LESLIE, Adrian John Gervase. b 46. Lich Th Coll 67. **d** 69 Sheff **p** 70 Ripon for Sheff. C of St Cuthb Firvale 69-73; Mosborough 73-80; P-in-c of Edale Dio Derby from 80; Warden Champion Ho Youth Centre Edale from 80. *Edale Vicarage, Sheffield, S30 2ZA.* (Hope Valley 70254)

MURRAY-STONE, Albert Edmund Angus. b 18. Im Coll Ibad 58. **d** and **p** 68 Accra. Hon C of Takoradi Accra 69-70; Port Chap Supt British Sailors S Takoradi Accra 68-74; Asst P Kumasi 73-74; Sen Chap BSS & State Sec Miss to Seamen Fremantle 74-76; Warden BSS Falmouth 76-78; Hon C of All SS Falmouth 76-77; St Gwennap 77-78; P-in-c of Boscastle w Davidstow 78-81; V of All SS Falmouth Dio Truro from 81. *2 Wodehouse Terrace, Falmouth, Cornw, TR11 4QX.* (Falmouth 314654)

MURRELL, John Edmund. b 28. Westcott Ho Cam. **d** 66 **p** 67 Cant. C of Ivychurch w Old Romney and Midley 66-70; R of Bardwell 70-75; Perm to Offic Dio Ely 75-77; V of Thorington w Wenhaston, Bramfield and Walpole Dio St E from 77. *Wenhaston Vicarage, Halesworth, Suff.* (Blythburgh 239)

MURRIE, Clive Robert. b 44. Ripon Coll Cudd. **d** 79 **p** 80 Newc T. C of Kenton 79-80; Prudhoe Dio Newc T from 80. *12 Leaway, Prudhoe, Northumb, NE42 6QE.*

MURRIN, Raymond. d 65 **p** 66 Qu'App. I of Last Mountain 65-68; R of Sumner 68-70; V of Sapperton 70-79; St Jo Evang N Vanc Dio New Westmr from 79. *220 West 8th Avenue, North Vancouver, BC, Canada.*

MURSELL, Alfred Gordon. b 49. Brasenose Coll Ox BA (Mod Hist) 70, BA (Th) 72. Cudd Coll 71. **d** 73 Warrington for Liv **p** 74 Liv. C of Walton-on-the-Hill Liv 73-77; V of St Jo Evang E Dulwich Dio S'wark from 77. *62 East Dulwich Road, SE22 9AU.* (01-639 3807)

MURY, Claude. Univ of Alta BEducn 78. Newmann Coll Edmon BTh 80. **d** 81 Athab. On leave. *Box 3191, St Paul, Alta, Canada, T0A 3A0.*

MUSA, Titus Adebola. b 36. Im Coll Ibad 75. **d** 78 Ondo. d Dio Ondo. *St Luke's Vicarage, Akure, Ondo State, Nigeria.*

✠ **MUSAAD, Right Rev Ishaq.** St Aid Coll 50. **d** 52 Bp Allen for Egypt **p** 53 Egypt. C of Old Cairo 52; C-in-c of Giza 52-60; Chap at Heliopolis 60-71; Hon Can of All SS Cathl Cairo 65-71; Commiss in Egypt for Abp in Jer 71-74; Archd in Egypt 71-74; Cons Ld Bp in Egypt in All SS Cathl Cairo 1 Nov 74 by Bp Stopford (VG in Jer), Bps in Jordan and Iran; and Bps L Ashton and G Allen; Episc Can of St Geo Jer from 76. *c/o PO Box 87, Distribution Zamalek, Cairo, Egypt.* (62315)

MUSAFIRI, Ndela Salumu. b 45. Ridley Hall Cam 77. **d** 78 St Alb for Boga-Z. d Dio Boga-Z. *Eglise Anglicane, BP 861 Kisangani, Zaire.*

MUSAJAKAWA, Y. d 42 **p** 44 Ugan. P Dio Ugan 42-61; Dio Nam from 61; Archd of Ndejje 67-73. *PO Box 95, Bombo, Uganda.*

MUSANA, Onesifolo Susane Tolofini. b 29. Bp Tucker Coll Mukono 74. **d** 76 Bp Kauma for Nam **p** 77 Nam. P Dio Nam. *PO Banunaanika, Uganda.*

✠ **MUSCHAMP, Right Rev Cecil Emerson Barron.** b 02. Univ of Tas BA 24. ACT ThL (2nd cl) 25. St Cath S Ox BA (3rd cl Th) 27, MA 34. St Steph Ho Ox 26. **d** 27 Bris for Win **p** 28 Win C of St Luke Bournemouth 27-30; Aldershot (in c of St Alb and St Aid) 30-32; Withycombe Raleigh (in c of All SS Exmouth) 32-37; Chap Ex City Ment Hosp 36-37; V of St Mich Ch Ch 37-50; Chap RNZAF 42-45; Cons Ld Bp of Kalgoorlie in Perth Cathl 21 Dec 50 By Abp of Perth; Abp of Brisb; Bp of NW Austr; and Bp Elsey; res 67; Archd of Northam 53-55; Asst Bp of Perth 50-55; Dean of Brisb 67-72; Perm to Offic Dio Perth from 72; Dio Bunb from 73. *9 Samson Street, Mosman Park, W Australia 6012.* (384-5185)

MUSENGEZI, Martin. St Pet Coll Rosettenville 50. **d** 53 **p** 54 Mashon. P Dio Mashon. *St Albans Mission, PO Glendale, Rhodesia.*

MUSGRAVE, James Robert. b 20. Trin Coll Dub BA 43. MA 51. **d** 44 Down **p** 45 Connor. C of St Andr Belf 44-46; Derriaghy 46-51; I of Duneane w Ballyscullion 51-54; R of St

MWANZA, Nathan Thomas. St Jo Sem Lusaka. **d** 67 Bp Mataka for Zam **p** 67 Zam. P Dio Zam 67-70; Dio Lusaka from 71. *St Bartholomew's Church, P Bag 49, Chipata, Zambia.*

MWARABU, Simon. b 49. St Phil Coll Kongwa 77. **d** 81 Centr Tang. d Dio Centr Tang. *PO Mvumi, Tanzania.*

MWASHIGADI, Canon Edward. **d** 62 **p** 65 Momb. P Dio Momb from 62; Can of Momb from 76. *Anglican Church, PO Box 80, Mariakani, Kenya.*

MWASSI, John Matthew. St Jo Sem Lusaka. **d** 54 **p** 56 Nyasa. P Dio Nyasa 55-64; Dio Malawi 64-71; Dio S Malawi 71; Dio Lake Malawi from 71; Can of Lake Malawi 74-78; Archd 78-80. *Box 133, Nkhotakota, Malawi.*

MWASUMBI, Andaluisye. b 28. **d** 76 **p** 77 Moro. P Dio Moro 76-80. *PO Box 691, Morogoro, Tanzania.*

MWASYA, Timotheo. St Paul's Th Coll Limuru. **d** 64 **p** 66 Mt Kenya. P Dio Mt Kenya 64-75; Dio Mt Kenya E from 75. *Karaba, Box 448, Embu, Kenya.*

MWATULEVILE, Bernard Lugano. St Cypr Coll Ngala 73. **d** 72 **p** 74 SW Tang. P Dio SW Tang. *Box 54, Njombe, Tanzania.*

MWAURA, Leonard Mbogo. St Paul's Th Coll Limuru, 58. **d** 59 Momb **p** 61 Ft Hall. d Dio Momb 59-61; P Dio Ft Hall 61-64; Dio Mt Kenya 64-75; Dio Mt Kenya S from 75; Exam Chap to Bp of Mt Kenya 73-75; Mt Kenya S from 75. *Box 121, Murang'a, Kenya.*

MWAZO, Herbert Peter. St Paul's Dioc Div Sch Limuru 51. **d** 53 **p** 55 Momb. P Dio Momb 53-69; Dio Nai from 69. *c/o PO 30333, Nairobi, Kenya.*

MWEBESA, Yosia. b 50. St Phil Coll Kongwa 73. **d** and **p** 75 Vic Nyan. P Dio Vic Nyan. *Kanyinya, PO Box 14, Rulenge, West Lake, Tanzania.*

MWELA, Yakobo. **d** 28 **p** 32 S Rhod. P Dio S Rhod 28-52; Dio Mashon 52-67; Hon Can of Mashon 62-74; L to Offic Dio Mashon from 67. *Post Bag 175H, Salisbury, Rhodesia.*

MWELE, Edgell. **d** and **p** 77 New Hebr. P Dio New Hebr 77-80; Dio Vanuatu from 80. *Abwatuntora, Pentecost, Vanuatu.*

MWENDA, Canon Jameson. St Andr Dioc Coll Nkwazi, 30. **d** 31 **p** 33 Nyasa. P Dio Nyasa 31-64; Dio Malawi 64-71; Dio Lake Malawi 71-74; Can of Likoma Cathl from 52. *c/o Box 83, Nkhotakota, Malawi.*

MWENDI, Yonah Hosea. St Phil Th Coll Kongwa 60. **d** 60 Bp Wiggins for Centr Tang **p** 61 Centr Tang. P Dio Centr Tang. *Box 35, Mpwapwa, Tanzania.*

MWENGWE, Julius. St Jo Sem Lusaka **d** 63 N Rhod **p** 65 Zam. d Dio N Rhod 63-64; P Dio Zam 64-70; Dio Centr Zam from 71. *c/o Diocesan Registrar, Box 45, Ndola, Zambia.*

MWENGWE, Canon William. **d** 41 **p** 43 N Rhod. Miss P Dio N Rhod 41-64; L to Offic Dio Centr Zam 71-75; Hon Can of Centr Zam from 71. *Box 7, Mkushi, Zambia.*

MWERI, Ven Nathaniel. St Paul's Dioc Div Sch Limuru **d** 48 **p** 49 Momb. P Dio Momb from 48; Can of Momb 66-76; Archd Dio Momb from 77. *PO Box 263, Malindi, Kenya.*

MWESIGYE, Yoramu. **d** 76 **p** 77 Ank. P Dio Ank 76-77; Dio W Ank from 77. *Box 2022, Rwashamaire, Uganda.*

MWIGOWE, Suleman Malekela. **d** 39 **p** 41 Centr Tang. P Dio Centr Tang; Mlali 39-49; Uponela 49-51. *Uponela, c/o CMS, Berega, Kilosa, Tanzania.*

MWIHAMBI, Petro. **d** 61 **p** 62 Centr Tang. P Dio Centr Tang. *Meia Meia, Tanzania.*

MWIJUMBE, Phinehas. b 36. **d** 74 **p** 75 Centr Tang. P Dio Centr Tang. *Box 30, Itigi, Tanzania.*

MWIMA, Canon Erikz. **d** 46 **p** 48 U Nile. P Dio U Nile 46-61; Dio Mbale 61-63; Hon Can of Mbale 63-72; Can of Bukedi from 72. *Box 170, Tororo, Uganda.*

MWINUKA, Reuben Japhet. **d** 74 **p** 75 SW Tang. P Dio SW Tang. *PO Box 32, Njombe, Tanzania.*

MYA HAN, Andrew. H Cross Coll Rang. **d** 66 **p** 67 Rang. P Dio Rang 66-70 and from 72; Dio Mand 70-72; Archd of Rang 72-78; Prov Sec and Treas Burma from 72; V of H Trin Cathl City and Dio Rang from 78. *446 Bogyoke Aung San Road, Rangoon, Burma.*

MYA SHWE, b 43. **d** 74 **p** 75 Pa-an. P Dio Pa-an. *St George's Church Parsonage, Old Thandaung, Thandaung Township, Karen State, Burma.*

MYA THAN, John. **d** 68 **p** 69 Rang. P Dio Rang 69-70; Dio Mand from 70. *All Saints' Church, Shwebo, Burma.*

MYA WA, Timothy. **d** 61 **p** 62 Rang. P Dio Rang 61-70; Dio Mand from 70. *St Luke's Church, Langkho, Burma.*

MYAT SOE, **d** 74 **p** 75 Rang (APM). P Dio Rang. *Ywathitgon Village, Hmawbi Township, Burma.*

MYATT, James. b 14. **d** 73 Stockport for Ches **p** 74 Ches. C of Mobberley 73-77; Perm to Offic Dio Ches from 77; Ches Dioc Schs Adv 74-81. *Nethway, Town Lane, Mobberley, Cheshire.*

MYATT, Philip Bryan. b 29. Wycl Hall Ox 54. **d** 57 **p** 58 Portsm. C of St Jo Evang Fareham 57-61; Westgate 61-64; R of Woodchester 64-70; Walcot Bath Dio B & W from 70. *6 Rivers Street, Bath, Avon.* (Bath 25570)

MYBURGH, Edwin Arthur. b 35. **d** 77 Johann. C of Westlea Dio Johann from 77. *1007 Bernard Flats, Steytler Street, Newclare 2093, S Africa.*

MYCOCK, Geoffrey John Arthur. b 22. Open Univ BA 76. St Deiniol's Libr Hawarden 76. **d** 77 **p** 78 Ches. C of H Trin Ches 77-79; P-in-c of Hargrave 79-80; Chap to Bp of Ches 79-80; V of Sandbach Heath Dio Ches from 80. *Sandbach Heath Vicarage, Sandbach, Chesh.* (Sandbach 3673)

MYEGETA, Yeremia William. St Cypr Coll Ngala 66. **d** 68 Bp Mlele for SW Tang. d Dio SW Tang. *Mlangali, Box 32, Njombe, Tanzania.*

MYERS, Canon Arnold George. b 23. Keble Coll Ox BA 44, MA 48, Dipl Th 46. St Steph Ho Ox. **d** 47 **p** 48 Carl. C of Harrington 47-50; Our Lady and St Nich Liv 50-53; V of St Dunstan Edge Hill 53-62; R of W Derby Dio Liv 62; RD of W Derby 71-78; Hon Can of Liv from 74. *West Derby Rectory, Liverpool, L12 5EA.* (051-226 3878)

MYERS, Harry. b 20. Cudd Coll 60. **d** 62 **p** 63 Newc T. C of St Pet Monkseaton 62-66; St Pet Bywell 66-68; Stafford 68-77; St Mary Kingswinford 77-80; P-in-c of Fulford-in-Stone Dio Lich from 80; Hilderstone Dio Lich from 80. *20 Tudor Hollow, Fulford, Stone, Staffs.* (Blythe Bridge 7073)

MYERS, John Bulmer. b 19. Worc Ordin Coll 64. **d** 66 **p** 67 York. C of St Barn Linthorpe Middlesbrough 66-68; St Jo Evang Huddersfield 76-79; V of Cornholme Dio Wakef from 79. *Cornholme Vicarage, Todmorden, Lancs.* (Todmorden 3604)

MYERS, Lorne Arthur. b 28. McMaster Univ Ont BA 49. Bp's Univ Queb LST 52, BD 57. **d** 51 **p** 52 Niag. C of St Jas Hamilton 51-53; R of St Mark Hamilton 53-58; Thorold 58-62; Exam Chap to Bp of Niag 61-62; I of Point Edward Dio Hur from 77. *565 Errol Road West, Sarnia, Ont, Canada, N7V 2B9.*

MYERS, Milton. Moore Th Coll Syd ACT ThL 66. **d** 66 **p** 67 Syd. C of Kingsgrove 67-69; R of Cabramatta 69-74; Summer Hill 74-78; Robertson Dio Syd from 78. *Rectory, Robertson, NSW, Australia 2577.* (048-851210)

MYERS, Paul Henry. b 49. Qu Coll Birm 74. **d** 77 **p** 78 Bradf. C of Baildon 77-80; W Bromwich Dio Lich from 80. *50 Wilford Road, W Bromwich, B71 1QN.* (021-588 3440)

MYERS, Ralph George. b 12. ACP 36. **d** 77 Liv. Hon C of Sutton Dio Liv from 77. *109 Oxford Street, St Helen's, Merseyside.* (St Helen's 25809)

MYERSCOUGH, Robin Nigel. b 44. K Coll Lon BD 69. Coll of the Resurr Mirfield 81. **d** 81 Nor. Hon C of Diss Dio Nor from 81. *The Old Palace, The Close, Norwich, NR1 4DD.*

MYHILL, Christopher John. b 47. Oak Hill Th Coll Dipl Higher Educn 79. **d** 79 Bradwell for Chelmsf **p** 80 Chelmsf. C of Stanford-le-Hope Dio Chelmsf from 79. *4 Hall Close, Stanford-le-Hope, Essex, SS17 8HJ.*

MYHILL, Frederick Robert. b 13. Univ of Lon BA 33, BD 36. ALCD 36. **d** 36 **p** 37 Southw. C of St Pet Old Radford 36-38; Chap St Paul's Coll Hong Kong 38-46; St Steph Coll Stanley Hong Kong 46-55; V of Cofton Hackett 55-78. *135 Victoria Avenue, Hull, N Humb, HU5 3DP.* (Hull 493098)

MYHILL-TAYLOR, Frederic Harry. St Jo Coll Morpeth, 52. **d** 53 **p** 54 Graft. C of Port Macquarie 53-56; P-in-c of Tamber Springs 56-59; C of Inverell 59-61; St Jo Kalg 61-62; R of The Rock 62-73; Ganmain 73-77; Coolamon Dio River from 77. *Box 51, Coolamon, NSW, Australia 2701.*

MYITTA, **d** 67 **p** 68 Rang. P Dio Rang 68-70; Dio Mand from 70. *St Luke's Church, Bilumyo, Burma.*

MYLCHREEST, Horace. b 1886. St Aid Coll 11. Univ of Dur LTh 13. **d** 11 **p** 12 Newc T. C of St Silas Byker 11-13; St Steph Elswick 13-15; All S Eastbourne 16-19; TCF 16-19; Hon CF 19; C of Cheam 19-20; R of Chedington 21-22; Thornbury 22-29; V of Buckfastleigh 29-42; R of Berrynarbor 42-51. *Bowcombe Cottage, Kingsbridge, Devon.*

MYLES, David Sterling. K Coll Halifax, NS BA 61, LTh 65. **d** 65 **p** 66 NS. I of Rawdon 65-69; New Lon 69-70; C of Dartmouth 71-75; R of Amherst Dio NS from 75. *53 Havelock Street, Amherst, NS, Canada.* (667-8790)

MYLES, Peter Rodney. b 42. St Aug Coll Cant 70. **d** 71 **p** 72 Derby. C of Tideswell 71-74; St Mary The Boltons Kens 74-79; P-in-c of St Pet Kens Pk Rd Notting Hill Dio Lon from 79. *48 Ladbroke Road, W11 3NW.* (01-229 7275)

MYLES, William Arthur. Univ of Tor BA 54, BSW 55. Trin Coll Tor STB 63. **d** 62 **p** 63 Tor. C of St Leon Tor 62-64; R of St Dunstan Tor 64-66; Uxbridge 66-71; P-in-c of St Alb Pet 71-75; Hon C of Our Sav Don Mills City and Dio Tor from 75. *647 Broadview Avenue, Toronto, Ont, Canada.*

MYLNE, Canon Angus Fletcher. CCC Ox BA 22, MA 30. Westcott Ho Cam 25. **d** 27 Win for Portsm **p** 28 Portsm. C of Petersfield 27-30; Bulawayo 30-36; V of Alfred County 36-44; P-in-c of Springvale Miss 44-49; V of St Pet Maritz 49-64; Can of St Sav Cathl Pietermaritzburg 52-66; Hon Can from

66; R of St D Pietermaritzburg 64-69; Chap St Jo Sch Pmbg 69-72; C of Scottsville Dio Natal from 72. *18 Taylor Road, Scottsville, Pietermaritzburg, Natal, S Africa.* (2-1708)

MYNETT, Colin. b 25. Roch Th Coll 61. **d** 63 **p** 64 Truro. C of Liskeard w St Keyne 63-66; R of Lifton 66-71; R of Kelly w Bradstone 66-71; Team V of St Aubyn Devonport 71-75; V of Cinderford Dio Glouc from 75. *St John's Vicarage, Cinderford, Glos.* (Cinderford 23123)

MYNORS, James Baskerville. b 49. Peterho Cam BA 70, MA 74. St Jo Coll Nottm 77. **d** 78 Bp Mort for Leic **p** 80 Guildf. Hon C of H Ap Leic 78-79; C of Virginia Water Dio Guildf from 79. *c/o Christ Church Vicarage, Virginia Water, Surrey.*

MZAMANE, Joshua Bernard Mbizo. St Pet Coll Rosettenville 56. **d** 58 **p** 59 Johann. P Dio Johann. *Kwa Thema, Transvaal, S Africa.* (011-886 82)

MZAMANE, Mhlauli Mothoo. b 17. **d** 79 **p** 80 Bloemf. C of St Mark Vrede Dio Bloemf from 79. *PO Box 227, Vrede 2455, S Africa.*

MZAMANE, Sithembele Tobela. b 52. St Bede's Coll Umtata 74. **d** 75 **p** 77 Bp Sobukwe for St John's. P Dio St John's. *Box 187, Engcobo, Republic of Transkei, S Africa.*

MZENGA, David. b 45. St Phil Coll Kongwa 77. **d** 79 Bp Mohamed for Centr Tang **p** 79 Tang. P Dio Centr Tang. *Box 38, Babati, Tanzania.*

MZIKILA, Elliott Alexander. St Cypr Th Coll Ngala. **d** 62 **p** 64 SW Tang. P Dio SW Tang 62-70; Dio Ruv from 71. *PO Litumba, Peramiho, Tanzania.*

MZIZI, Ephraim. St Alb Coll Natal. **d** 30 **p** 46 Natal. P Dio Natal; L to Offic Dio Natal from 58. *Umtwalumi, Natal, S Africa.*

MZUGA, Canon Simeon Judah. St Paul's Dioc Div Sch Limuru. **d** 48 **p** 49 Momb. P Dio Momb from 48; Can of Momb from 66. *PO Kigombo, Kenya.*

MZUNGU, Canon David. St Paul's Dioc Div Sch Limuru. **d** 48 **p** 49 Momb. P Dio Momb; Can of Momb from 76. *c/o Box 80072, Mombasa, Kenya.*

N

NABETA, Tucker Tamusoni Thomas. Trin Hall Cam BA 58. Westcott Ho Cam 56. **d** 58 **p** 60 Ugan. P Dio Ugan 58-60; Dio W Bugan 60-67; Dio Nam 67-72; Exam Chap to Bp of W Bugan 63-67; P Dio Kamp from 72. *Box 7062, Kampala, Uganda.*

NABUGOMU, Canon Gideon. d 64 **p** 65 Mbale. P Dio Mbale; Can of Mbale from 78. *Box 1117, Mbale, Uganda.*

NABUGUZI, Erika Jemera. d 48 **p** 50 Ugan. P Dio Ugan 48-61; Dio Nam from 61. *Anglican Church, Kibaale, PO Box 53, Busembatia, Uganda.*

NACHICHA, Beda. b 28. St Cypr Coll Rondo. **d** 72 **p** 73 Abp Sepeku for Masasi. P Dio Masasi. *PB Masasi, Mtwara Region, Tanzania.*

NADEN, Anthony Joshua. b 38. Jes Coll Ox 1st cl Th 60, BA (2nd cl Or Stud) 62, MA 64. Wycl Hall Ox 60. **d** 62 **p** 63 Portsm. C of Rowner 62-66; Fisherton Anger 70-72. *PO Box 378, Tamale, Ghana.*

NADERER, Gordon Kenneth Charles Maximilian. b 14. Wycl Hall Ox. **d** 44 **p** 45 Roch, C of St Paul Chatham 44-46; Bp's Chap to German Prisoners of War Dio Roch 46-48; to Foreign Workers Dio Roch and Min of Conv Distr of St Jas Walderslade and St Phil Wayfield 49-55; Seq and C-in-c of Penhurst w Ashburnham 55-58; R of Rodmell w Southease 58-74; V of Westham Dio Chich from 74. *Westham Vicarage, Pevensey, E Sussex, BN24 5DE.* (Eastbourne 762294)

NADIN, Dennis Lloyd. b 37. St D Coll Lamp BA (2nd cl Hist) 60. Univ of Man MEducn 81. Ridley Hall Cam 63. **d** 64 Warrington for Liv **p** 65 Liv. C of Childwall 64-67; Seacroft 67-69; Project Officer Grubb Inst Behavioural Stud Lon 67-70; Lect CA Tr Coll Blackheath Lon 70-72; Publ Pr Dio Chelmsf 73. *9 Bishopsfield, Harlow, CM19 6UK.*

NADKARNI, Edward Wasant. b 41. Trin Coll Cam 2nd Cl pt i 62, BA (3rd cl Th pt ii) 64, MA 67. Cudd Coll 68. **d** 69 Colchester for Chelmsf **p** 70 Chelmsf. C of E Ham 69-71; St Andr Hertford 71-74; Chap for Educn Deanery of Bedford 74-78; Chap Univ of Lanc from 78. *Chaplaincy Centre, Bailrigg, Lancaster.* (Lancaster 67128)

NAESMYTH of POSSO (formerly WEBB), George Cresswell Naesmyth. b 1895. Wells Th Coll. **d** 25 **p** 26 Birm. C of St Pet Harborne 25-30; V of St Nich Birm 30-31; Publ Pr Dio Birm 31-32; Dir ICF for SW Area and Publ Pr Dio Bris 33-35; R of Oare w Culbone 35-44; Seq of Southwick w Boarhunt 44-75. *The White House, Southwick, Hants.*

NAFUYE, Firimoni. d 64 **p** 65 Mbale. P Dio Mbale. *Church of Uganda, Butandiga, PO Box 297, Mbale, Uganda.*

NAGLE, Charles Edgar. St Jo Coll Morpeth 31. ThL 51. **d** 33 Bath for Goulb **p** 35 Goulb. C of Cootamundra 33-35; P-in-c of Cobargo 35-38; R of Adaminaby 38-43; Tumbarumba 43-48; C of St Sav Cathl Goulb 48-49; R of W Goulb w Lake Bathurst 49-57; Woodburn 57-60; S Graft 60-66; C of All SS N Parramatta 66-68; P-in-c of Lake Bath 68-71; Perm to Offic Dio C & Goulb 71-74; Dio Wang from 74. *Box 282, Albury, ACT, Australia 2640.*

NAHABEDIAN, Harold Joseph. b 39. Univ of Tor BA 63, MA 66, STB 70. Trin Coll Tor 69. **d** 73 Tor **p** 74 New Westmr. C of St Jas Vanc 74-76; Chap Trin Coll Tor 76-81. *c/o Trinity College, Hoskin Avenue, Toronto, Ont., Canada.*

NAIDOO, Henry Leonard Gonasulan. b 50. St Paul's Coll Grahmstn. **d** 77 **p** 78 Natal. C of Ch Ch Overport 77-80; Wentworth Dio Natal from 80. *37 Lakhimpur Road, Merebank, Natal, S Africa.*

NAILENGE, Olavi Ijaloo. b 29. **d** 71 Damar. **p** 72 Bp Wade for Capetn for Damar. P Dio Damar 71-80; Dio Namibia from 80. *PO Box 57, Windhoek, SW Africa.* (061-22345)

NAINBY, Canon Winston Manby. Em Coll Sktn BA and LTh 31. **d** 30 **p** 31 Edmon. C of Hardisty 30-32; I of Sedgewick 32-37; Ponoka 37-40; RD of Wetaskiwin 37-40; R of St Faith Edmon 40-42; H Trin Edmon 42-58; Can of Edmon 44-56; Exam Chap to Bp of Edmon 53-58; Archd of Edmon S 56-58; I of St Jo Evang Port Hope 58-70; Can of Tor from 64; Hon C of Trin Ch Barrie Dio Tor from 70. *271 Wellington Court, E Barrie, Ont., Canada.*

NAIRN, Frederick William. b 43. Trin Coll Dub 64. **d** 67 **p** 68 Connor. C of Larne (Inver) 67-70; Chap RAF 70-74; C-in-c of Harmston Dio Linc from 75; Coleby Dio Linc from 75. *Vicarage, Harmston, Lincoln.* (Lincoln 720282)

NAIRN, Ian Charles. St Jo Coll Auckld LTh 67. **d** 67 Auckld **p** 68 Bp Monteith for Auckld. C of St Phil St Heliers Bay Auckld 67-70; E Coast Bays 70-72; P-in-c 72-73; V of Hauraki Plains 73-75; P-in-c of S Hokianga Miss Distr 75-79; V of Point Chevalier Dio Auckld from 79. *13 Dignan Street, Point Chevalier, Auckland 2, NZ.* (865-102)

NAIRN, Leonard Hilton. St Francis Th Coll Brisb. **d** 65 **p** 66 Brisb. C of St Luke Toowoomba 65-68; St Paul Ipswich 68-69; Asst Chap C of E Gr Sch Brisb 69-70; Chap Canberra Gr Sch 70-78; Perm to Offic Dio C & Goulb from 79. *10 Hacking Crescent, Narrabundah, ACT, Australia 2604.*

NAIRN, Stuart Robert. b 51. AKC and BD 75. St Aug Coll Cant 75. **d** 76 Lynn for Nor **p** 77 Thetford for Nor. C of E Dereham 76-80; Team V of Hempnall Dio Nor from 80. *24 Triple Plea Road, Woodton, Nr Bungay, Suffolk.* (Woodton 397)

NAIRN-BRIGGS, George Peter. b 45. AKC 69. St Aug Coll Cant 69. **d** 70 **p** 71 S'wark. C of Catford 70-73; Raynes Park 73-75; V of Ch K Salfords 75-81; St Pet, St Helier Morden Dio S'wark from 81; M Gen Syn from 80. *St Peter's Vicarage, Bishopsford Road, Surrey.* (01-648 6050)

NAIROBI, Lord Archbishop of, and Metropolitan of Province of Kenya. *See* Kuria, Most Rev Manasses.

NAIROBI, Assistant Bishop of. *See* Nzano, Right Rev Crispus.

NAIROBI, Provost of. (Vacant)

NAISH, Raymond William. Univ of NZ BSc 61. St Jo Coll Auckld LTh (1st cl) 64. **d** 64 **p** 65 Dun. C of Invercargill 64-68; V of Bluff w Stewart Island 68-70; Hon C of Fitzroy Dio Waik from 71. *146b Seaview Road, New Plymouth, NZ.* (35-265)

NAISUKWA, Paul. d 77 **p** 78 Nak. P Dio Nak. *Box 745, Eldoret, Kenya.*

NAIWERO, Emanueri. b 28. **d** and **p** 74 Mbale. P Dio Mbale. *Bukiga, Box 984, Mbale, Uganda.*

NAKABALI, Bokomo Kwale. d 42 **p** 44 Ugan. P Dio Ugan 44-60; Dio W Bugan from 60. *Church of Uganda, Lubaale, PO Kanoni-Mpigi, Uganda.*

NAKAJUMO, Mikael. St Cypr Th Coll Tunduru 37. **d** 39 **p** 43 Masasi. P Dio Masasi. *USPG, Kanyimbi, Masasi, Tanzania.*

NAKAYAMA, Canon Gordon Goichi. Angl Th Coll BC. **d** 32 **p** 34 New Westmr. Miss Ch of Ascen Vancouver 32-42; Miss to Japanese Slocan Dio Koot 42-45; Dio Calg 45-71; Can of Calg 66-71; Can (Emer) from 72; Perm to Offic Dio New Westmr from 79. *845 Semlin Drive, Vancouver, BC, Canada.*

NAKHOSI, Ven Robert. d 61 **p** 62 Mbale. P Dio Mbale; Archd and Can of Mbale from 78. *PO Box 851, Mbale, Uganda.*

NAKOOLAK, Bobby. b 36. Arthur Turner Tr Sch Pangnirtung 76. **d** 79 **p** 80 Arctic. C of Lake Harbour Dio Arctic from 79. *St Paul's Anglican Mission, Lake Harbour, NWT X0A 0N0, Canada.*

NAKURU, Lord Bishop of. (Vacant)

NAKURU, Assistant Bishop of. (Vacant)

NALEDI, Ven Theophilus. St Bede's Th Coll Umtata. **d** 59 **p** 60 Kimb K. P Dio Kimb K 59-70; Dio Matab 71-72; Dio Botswana from 72; Dioc Archd from 76. *Box 359, Lobatse, Botswana.*

NALUMPA, Emilius. St Jo Sem Lusaka 57. **d** 58 **p** 60 N Rhod. P Dio N Rhod 58-64; Dio Zam 64-70; Dio Lusaka from 71. *St Bartholomew, Mapanza, Choma, Zambia.*

NALUWUNGU, Kezeroni. Bp Tucker Coll Mukono. **d** 50 **p** 51 Ugan. P Dio Ugan 50-60; Dio W Bugan from 60. *Kawungeera, PO Box 167, Mityana, Uganda.*

NAMANGO, Isaac. d 71 **p** 72 Maseno N (APM). P Dio Maseno N. *Box 46, Bungoma, Kenya.*

NAMASIME, Dasani. d 64 **p** 65 Mbale. P Dio Mbale. *Church of Uganda, Buluganya, Uganda.*

NAMBINA, Benjamin. St Paul's Coll Ambat. **d** 52 **p** 54 Madag. P Dio Madag 52-63. *Marolambo, Madagascar.*

NAMBUTA, Bartolomayo Stefano. St Cypr Th Coll Tunduru 57. **d** 59 **p** 62 Masasi. P Dio Masasi. *Kigongoi, Tanga, Tanzania.*

NAMIBIA, Lord Bishop of. *See* Kauluma, Right Rev James Hamupanda.

NAMIBIA, Bishop Suffragan of. (Vacant)

NAMIREMBE, Lord Bishop of. *See* Nsubuga, Right Rev Dunstan Kasi.

NAMIREMBE, Assistant Bishop of. *See* Kauma, Right Rev Misaeri.

NAMIREMBE, Dean of. *See* Sengenda-Zake, Very Rev Justin Gustavus.

NAMO, Jacob Ranthite. St Pet Coll Rosettenville 55. **d** 57 **p** 58 Johann. C of St Mich AA Alexandra Township Johann 58-62; R 62-74; Emdeni Dio Johann from 74. *Box 33, Kwa-Xuma, Transvaal, S Africa.* (011-934 Ext 454)

NAMOK, William. St Paul's Th Coll Moa I 63. **d** 63 Carp. C of Lockhart River 63-67; Bamaga 67-71. *Lockhart River, Queensland, Australia.*

NAMPESYA, Gayo. St Cypr Th Coll Tunduru. **d** 42 **p** 45 Masasi. P Dio Masasi. *USPG, Chilimba, Tanzania.*

NAMUYENGA, Asanasio. Bp Tucker Mem Coll Mukono. **d** 15 **p** 17 Ugan. P Dio Ugan 15-52. *Kimwanyi, PO Box 446, Masaka, Uganda.*

NAMUYENGA, Saulo. Bp Tucker Mem Coll Mukono. **d** 15 **p** 17 Ugan. P Dio U Nile 15-30; Dio Ugan 30-37. *Bamusuta, Singo, Uganda.*

NAMUYENGA, Yoasi. Buwalasi Th Coll. **d** 69 W Bugan. d Dio W Bugan. *Church of Uganda, Ssinde, PO Katera, Kampala, Uganda.*

NANCARROW, Keith Carl. Ridley Coll Melb. ACT ThL 50. **d** 51 **p** 52 Gippsld. C of Bairnsdale 51-52; V of Moe 52-55; Asst Sec CMS for Victoria and Perm to Offic Dio Melb 55-58; R of St Aid Launceston 58-80; Sec CMS for Tas from 59; R of St Pet Sandy Bay Dio Tas from 80. *St Peter's Rectory, Grosvenor Street, Sandy Bay, Tasmania 7005.* (002 23 6281)

NANDI, Petrus. d 64 Damar. d Dio Damar. *c/o St mary's Mission, Odibo, PO Oshikango, Ovamboland, SW Africa.* (Oshikango 5)

NANGOLI, Zimulani. Buwalasi Th Coll. **d** 61 **p** 62 Mbale. P Dio Mbale. *PO Box 473, Mbale, Uganda.*

NANJUBU, Cyprian Joel. Bp Tucker Coll Mukono 62. **d** 63 Nam. d Dio Nam. *Buwanya, Uganda.*

NAN KENG, d 69 Rang **p** 71 Akyab. P Dio Akyab. *St James's Church, Tlen Thang Vum, Burma.*

NANKIVELL, Christopher Robert Trevelyan. b 33. Late Exhib of Jes Coll Ox BA (2nd cl Geog) 55, MA 63. Linc Th Coll 56. **d** 58 **p** 59 Lich. C of Bloxwich 58-60; St Mary Stafford 60-64; C-in-c of Malins Lee 64-72; Social Welfare Sector Min to Milton Keynes Chr Coun 73-76; Lect in Non-Res Tr Qu Coll Edgbaston Birm from 76. *Queen's College, Somerset Road, Birmingham, B15 2QH.*

NANSEERA, Charles Edmund. Bp Tucker Coll Mukono. **d** 51 **p** 53 Ugan. P Dio Ugan 51-60; Dio W Bugan from 60. *Anglican Church, Kinunka, Kabula, PO Lyantonde, Uganda.*

NANTAGYA, Canon Amosi. d 43 **p** 45 Ugan. CMS P Dio Ugan 43-60; Dio W Bugan from 60; Can of W Bugan from 70. *Church of Uganda, Mpenja, PO Mpenja Mpigi, Uganda.*

NAPARTUK, Abelie. b 40. Arthur Turner Tr Sch Pangnirtung 70. **d** 72 Arctic **p** 73 Qu'App for Arctic. Miss at Sugluk 72-74; Povungnituk 75-77; on leave 77-81; P-in-c of St Steph Fort Chimo Dio Arctic from 81. *Box 143, Fort Chimo, Queb, J0M 1C0, Canada.*

NAPE, Masekwa David. St Pet Coll Rosettenville 59. **d** 62 **p** 64 Johann. P Dio Johann. *Box 248, Ventersdorp, Transvaal, S Africa.* (014-832 Ext 291)

NAPETE, Sosipateri. d 64 **p** 65 Mbale. P Dio Mbale 64-72; Dio Bukedi from 72. *Church of Uganda, Kibuku, PO Budaka, Uganda.*

NAPIER, Charles John Lenox. b 29. Univ Coll Ox BA 52, MA 57. **d** and **p** 60 RC Bp of Cilicium. Rec into C of E by Bp of Ely 63. C of Illogan 63-66; Tutor Lon Coll of Div (St Jo Coll Nottm from 70) 66-73; Team V of S Molton 73-80; R of Drewsteignton Dio Ex from 80; Hittisleigh Dio Ex from 80; Spreyton Dio Ex from 80. *Rectory, Drewsteignton, Exeter, EX6 6QW.* (Drewsteignton 227)

NAPLEY, David John. b 13. SOC 65. **d** 68 **p** 69 S'wark. C of Hurst Green 68-71; Ham 71-74; Team V of Quidenham 74-77; P-in-c of Earsham Dio Nor 77-79; R (w Alburgh and Denton) from 79; P-in-c of Alburgh 77-79; Denton 77-79. *Earsham Rectory, Bungay, Suff.* (Bungay 2147)

NAPPER, Harold Stuart. b 01. Univ of Dur LTh 37. St Aug Coll Cant 33. **d** 35 **p** 36 Lon. C of St Matthias Poplar 35-38; Chap at Jamalpur India 38-48; R of Bencubbin 48-50; C of St Patr Perth 50-52; Perm to Offic Dio Lon 52-53; C of Harpenden 52-54; V of St Jas Bermondsey (w Ch Ch from 56) 54-66; L to Offic Dio S'wark from 67. *20 Millstream House, Jamaica Road, SE16.* (01-237 1000)

NARAIN, Errol Lloyd. St Pet Coll Natal 77. **d** 80 Natal. C of St Agnes Kloof Dio Natal from 80. *PO Box 33, Kloof 3640, S Africa.*

NARANSAMY, Anthony Eric Lancelot. b 33. **d** 75 Bp Carter for Johann **p** 76 Johann. C of Benoni Dio Johann from 75. *155 Wynberg Street, Actonville 1500, S Africa*

NARBEY, Dudley Cyril. b 26. Ch Ch Coll 68. **d** 69 **p** 70 Nel. C of Motueka 70-71; All SS Nel 71-73; V of Amuri 73-76; Havelock 76-78; Dom Chap to Bp of Nel from 78. *64 Brooklands Road, Nelson, NZ.*

NARRAWAY, Donald Quinton. b 46. St Paul's Coll Grahmstn 70. **d** 72 **p** 73 Pret. C of St Alb Cathl Pret 72-75; Ch Ch Pietersburg 75 and 78-81; R of Zoutpansberg 75-78; Chap Pret Hosp from 81. *92 Duxbury Road, Hillcrest, Pretoria 0083, S Africa.*

NARUSAWA, Masaki Alec. b 53. AKC and BD 77. Linc Th Coll 77. **d** 78 Lon **p** 79 Edmon for Lon. C of St Alphage Hendon 78-81; St Lawr Eastcote Dio Lon from 81. *33 Sunningdale Avenue, Eastcote, Ruislip, HA4 9SS.* (01-868 9994)

NASH, Alan Frederick. b 46. Sarum Wells Th Coll 72. **d** 75 **p** 76 Worc. C of H Innoc Kidderminster 75-79; P-in-c of Mildenhall 79-82; Team V of N Wingfield Dio Derby from 82. *Tupton Vicarage, The Gables, Ankerbold Road, Tupton, Chesterfield, Derbys.* (Chesterfield 864543)

NASH, Arthur John. Em Coll Sktn LTh 68. **d** 68 **p** 69 Sask. C of Montreal Lake 68-69; I of Sturgeon Lake and of Sturgeon Valley 69-72; V of Aldergrove 73-79; St D Delta Dio New Westmr from 79. *1115-51a Street, Delta, BC, Canada.*

NASH, Arthur Lloyd. b 40. Em Coll Sktn. **d** 70 **p** 71 Bran. R of Glenboro 71-72; I of Lockeport 72-76; Sydney Mines and Baddeck Dio NS from 76. *11 Queen Street, Sydney Mines, NS, Canada.*

NASH, Brian John. b 54. St Jo Coll Dur BSc 75. St Jo Coll Nottm 77. **d** 80 **p** 81 Birm. C of St Luke City and Dio Birm from 80. *63 Princess Road, Edgbaston, Birmingham, B5 7PZ.*

NASH, Bryon William. Bps' Univ Lennox BA 67. **d** and **p** 69 Tor. C of Thornhill 69-70; St Matt Islington Tor 70-73; R of St Jas Brampton Dio Tor from 73. *133 Cornwall Heights, Brampton, Ont., Canada.* (416-451 7711)

NASH, David. b 25. K Coll Lon and Warm BD and AKC 51. **d** 52 **p** 53 Chelmsf. C of St John Buckhurst Hill 52-58; Min of St Cedd's Conv Distr Westcliff 58-63; Eccles Distr 63-66; R of Rivenhall Dio Chelmsf from 66. *Rectory, Church Road, Rivenhall, Witham, Essex CM8 3PQ.* (0376-511161)

NASH, David John. b 41. Pemb Coll Ox BA (Th) 64, MA 70. Wells Th Coll 65. **d** 67 **p** 68 Lon. C of Ch of Ascen Wembley 67-70; Team V of Hackney 70-75; H Trin Clifton Notts 76-82; V of Winchmore Hill Dio Lon from 82. *St Paul's Vicarage, Church Hill, N21.*

NASH, Eric John Hewitson. b 1898. Trin Coll Cam BA 25, MA 29. Ridley Hall Cam 25. **d** 27 **p** 28 Lon. C of St John W Ealing 27-28; Perm to Offic at Em Wimbledon 28-29; Chap Wrekin Coll Wel 29-31; Missr CSSM and Trav Sec Script U 32-69. *10 Craufurd Rise, Maidenhead, Berks.* (Maidenhead 21034)

NASH, Canon Harry Neville. b 1899. Univ of Lon BSc 21. St Steph Ho Ox. **d** 29 **p** 30 Ox. C of St Mary and St John Ox 29-36; Hd Master UMCA Kiungani High Sch 36-38; Kiwanda Centr Sch 38-43; P-in-c of Korogwe 43-50; Can of St Cypr in Ch Ch Cathl Zanz 48-60; Hon Can from 68; Prin of St Andr Tr Coll Minaki 50-58; P-in-c of Kideleko Dio Zanz 58-60; V of St Barn Ox 60-67; Chap Commun of H Family Baldslow 67-74. *17 Old Park Close, Broad Street, Cuckfield, Sussex.* (Hayward's Heath 55791)

NASH, Paul Alexander. b 20. GOC 73. **d** 76 Glouc **p** 76 Tewkesbury for Glouc. C of St John Coleford Dio Glouc from 76. *16 Orchard Road, Coombs Park, Coleford, Glos, GL16 8AU.*

NASH, Reginald Frank. b 15. **d** 66 **p** 67 Glouc. C of St Jas

Glouc 66-69; C-in-c of Sharpness w Purton and Brookend 69-75; R of Dymock w Donnington (and Kempley from 77) 75-80. *31 Woodview Road, Norman Hill, Dursley, Glos, GL11 5RJ.*

NASH, Reginald Trevor. b 09. **d** 48 **p** 49 Mon. C of St Jas Pontypool 48-50; Ch Ch Ellacombe Torquay 50-52; V of Plaistow 52-58; R of St Bride Stretford 58-63; Panfield 63-73; C of Newchurch 73-76; Winwick 76-81. *24 Bradwell Road, Lowton, Warrington, Lancs, WA3 2PB.* (Leigh 67448)

NASH, Richard Edward. b 10. Westcott Ho Cam 54. **d** 56 Sherborne for Sarum **p** 57 Sarum. C of H Trin Weymouth 56-59; R of Graffham w Woolavington 59-65; C-in-c of St Thos w All SS Lewes 65-68; V of Eridge Green 68-72; C-in-c of Stinsford 73-75; Winterbourne Came w Whitcombe 73-75. *Corner Cottage, Neighbourne, Oakhill, Bath, Somt, BA3 5BQ.*

NASH, Ronald. Montr Dioc Th Coll LTh 65. **d & p** 65 Ont. I of Ameliasburg 65-69; Chap Collins Bay Penit Dio Ont from 69. *RR1, Kingston, Ont, Canada.* (613-544 3321)

NASH, Canon Trevor Gifford. b 30. Clare Coll Cam BA 53, MA 57. Cudd Coll 53. **d** 55 **p** 56 St Alb. C of Cheshunt 55-57; CF (TA) 56-67; C of Kingston T 57-61; C of Stevenage (in C of St Andr Bedwell) 61-63; V of St Luke Leagrave 63-67; Sen Chap St Geo Hosp Lon 67-73; R of St Maurice w St Laur and St Swith City and Dio Win from 73; P-in-c of H Trin City and Dio Win from 77; RD of Win from 78; Hon Can of Win Cathl from 80. *Rectory, Colebrook Street, Winchester, Hants.* (Win 68056)

NASH, William Henry. Oak Hill Th Coll 58. **d** 61 Bp McKie for Cov **p** 62 Cov. C of New Milverton 61-64; St Philemon (in c of St John) Toxt Pk 64-67; V of Bryn 67-76; NW Area Sec CPAS from 76; LPr Dio Man from 76; V of Penn Fields Dio Lich from 82. *St Philip's Vicarage, Church Road, Bradmore, Wolverhampton, WV3 7EN.* (0902-36943)

NASH, William Warren. b 09. Trin Coll Dub BA 35, Div Test 36, MA 58. **d** 36 Ches **p** 38 Kilm for Arm. C of St Paul Birkenhead 36; L to Offic Dio Kilm 37-38; C of Portadown 38-40; C-in-c of Cooneen w Mullaghfad 40-44; Drummully 44-51; I of Aghadrumsee 51-74; RD of Clones 67-72. *27 Langley, Bretton, Peterborough.* (Pet 266024)

NASH-WILLIAMS, Piers le Sor Victor. b 35. Trin Hall Cam BA 57, MA 61. Cudd Coll 59. **d** 61 **p** 62 Win. C of Milton 61-64; Asst Chap Eton Coll 64-66; Perm to Offic Dio Ox 65-66; Asst Master Hurst Court Sch Hastings 66-68; Perm to Offic Dio Chich 66-68; C of St Pet Maidenhead 69-72; V of St Geo Wash Common Newbury 72-73; Team V of Newbury Dio Ox from 73. *206 Andover Road, Newbury, Berks, RG14 6NU.* (Newbury 41249)

NASHAK, James Isaiah. b 46. Arthur Turner Tr Sch Pangnirtung 76. **d** 79 **p** 80 Arctic. C of Payne Bay Dio Arctic from 79. *Holy Trinity Anglican Mission, Payne Bay, Queb J0M 1A0, Canada.*

NASOOK, Canon Noah. d 61 **p** 64 Arctic. Miss at Igloolik Dio Arctic from 61; Hon Can of Arctic from 72. *Igloolik, NWT, via Montreal AMF, Canada.*

NASSAU AND THE BAHAMAS, Lord Bishop of. *See* Eldon, Right Rev Michael Hartley.

NASSAU AND THE BAHAMAS, Assistant Bishop of. (Vacant)

NASSAU, Dean of. *See* Granger, Very Rev William James.

NATAL, Lord Bishop of. *See* Nuttall, Right Rev Michael.

NATAL, Suffragan Bishop of. *See* Mkhize, Right Rev Alfred.

NATAL, Assistant Bishop of. *See* Stainton, Right Rev Thomas William.

NATAL, Dean of. *See* Forbes, Very Rev John Franey.

NATANA, Very Rev Ephraim Adulluru. Bp Gwynne Coll Mundri 61. **d** 64 **p** 66 Sudan. P Dio Sudan 64-76; Dio Omdurman from 76; Provost of All SS Cathl Khartoum from 73; Dioc Sec Dio Omdurman from 76. *Clergy House, PO Box 135, Khartoum, Sudan.*

NATEI, Bartholomew. St Pet Coll Siota 59. **d** 62 **p** 64 Melan. P Dio Melan 62-75; Dio Centr Melan from 75. *Reef Islands, Santa Cruz, Solomon Islands.*

NATERS, Charles James Reginald. b 20. Selw Coll Cam BA 45, MA 47. Coll of Resurr Mirfield. **d** 47 **p** 48 Man. C of St Benedict Ardwick 47-52; M SSJE from 54; C of St Cypr Miss Langa Capetn 59-60; St Cuthb Miss Tsolo Transkei 60-68; L to Offic Dio Ox 69-76; Dio Lon from 76. *22 Great College Street, SW1P 3QA.*

NATHAN, Ngati-Pare. b 27. St Jo Coll Auckld 69. **d** 72 **p** 73 Auckld. C of Otahumu 72-76; V of Warkworth Dio Auckld from 76. *1 Bambro Street, Warkworth, NZ.* (8054)

NATHANAEL, Martin Moses. b 43. Univ of Lon BEducn 73. K Coll Lon MTh 77. Ripon Coll Cudd 77. **d** 79 Kens for Lon **p** 80 Lon. C of All SS Hampton Dio Lon from 79. *44 The Avenue, Hampton, TW12 3RS.* (01-979 8916)

NATHANIEL, Ivan Wasim. Punjab Univ MA 65. Bp's Coll Calc 59. **d** 62 **p** 64 Amrit. P Dio Amrit 62-68; C of St Aug Newland 68-70; Hon C of Crawley and Asst Master Thos Bennett Sch Crawley 70-76; Hd Relig Stud H Trin C of E Sch Crawley from 76. *8 Lincoln Close, Tilgate, Crawley, Sussex, RH10 5ET.* (Crawley 22401)

NATTRASS, Michael Stuart. b 41. Univ of Man BA 62. Cudd Coll 62. **d** 64 **p** 65 Dur. C of Easington Colliery 64-65; Silksworth 65-68; Perm to Offic Dio Southw 68-72; L to Offic Dio Dur 72-76; Perm to Offic Dio Lon 76-78; Hon C of Pinner Dio Lon from 78. *81 Cecil Park, Pinner, Middx, HA5 5HL.* (01-866 0217)

NAUMANN, Canon David Sydney. b 26. Ripon Hall Ox 54. **d** 55 Croydon for Cant **p** 56 Cant. C of Herne Bay 55-58; Asst Chap United Sheff Hosps 58-60; V of Reculver 60-64; Chap Qu Mary's Hosp Carshalton 64-65; R of Eastwell w Boughton Aluph 65-67; V of Westwell 65-67; Youth Chap Dio Cant 63-70; Warden St Gabr Retreat Ho Westgate 68-70; V of Littlebourne 70-82; Secr Cant Dioc Adv C'tte from 70; RD of E Bridge from 78; Hon Can of Cant Cathl from 81; R of Sandwich Dio Cant from 82. *Rectory, Knightrider Street, Sandwich, Kent, CT13 9ER.* (Sandwich 613138)

NAUMANN, John Frederick. St Francis Coll Brisb ACT ThL (2nd cl) 66. **d** 66 **p** 67 Brisb. C of St Matt Holland Pk Brisb 66-70; V of Pine Rivers 70-74; Sunnybank City and Dio Brisb 74-77; R from 77. *189 Lister Street, Sunnybank, Queensland, Australia 4109.* (345 1535)

NAUNTON, Hugh Raymond. b 38. Open Univ BA 75. Chich Th Coll 60. **d** 63 **p** 64 Ely. C of Stanground 63-66; Perm to Offic Dio S'wark 66-78; Dio Guildf from 75; Hd Relig Educn Ch (Ecumen) Sch Richmond from 78; Hon C of St Phil Cheam Common Dio S'wark from 79. *34 Windsor Road, Worcester Park, Surrey, KT4 8EW.* (01-330 6303)

NAVARETTE, David. b 37. **d** 69 Argent. d Dio Argent 69-73; N Argent from 73. *Parsonage, Saucelito, N Argentina.*

NAW MAI, d 65 **p** 66 Rang. P Dio Rang 65-70; Dio Mand from 70. *Emmanuel Divinity School, Mohnyin, Myitkyina District, Burma.*

NAY LYNN, Noel. b 45. **d** 70 Bp Aung Hla for Rang **p** 71 Rang. P Dio Rang 70-71; Dio Pa-an from 71. *c/o Bishopkone, Pa-an, Karen State, Burma.*

NAYLOR, Bruce Allan. Univ of Melb Dipl Mus 56. ARCM 60. ARSCM 65. Univ of Adel BMus 68, MMus 73. **d** 65 Perth **p** 79 Adel. Hon C of St Geo Cathl Perth 65-67; Perm to Offic Dio Adel 75-76; C of Hawthorn Dio Adel from 79. *97 Cross Road, Hawthorn, S Australia 5062.* (71-9228)

NAYLOR, Canon Charles Basil. b 11. Keble Coll Ox BA (2nd cl Lit Hum) 34, MA 39. **d** 39 **p** 40 Liv. L to Offic Dio Liv 39-45; Chap to Liv Coll 41-44; Chap RNVR 44-46; L to Offic Dio Bom 44-46; Chap and Dean of St Pet Coll Ox 46-56; Fell 50-56; Tutor in Th 50-56; C of St Pet-le-Bailey Ox and L to Offic Dio Ox 46-56; Exam Chap to Bp of Blackb from 51; Sen Proc Ox Univ 52-53; Exam Chap to Bp of Liv from 55; Can Res and Chan of Liv Cathl from 56; Dioc Dir of Ordin 56-72; Clergy Tr from 72. *Cathedral, Liverpool, L1 7AZ.* (051-709 6271)

NAYLOR, Frank. b 36. Univ of Lon BA 58. Univ of Liv MA 63. N-W Ordin Course 75. **d** 75 Warrington for Liv **p** 76 Liv (APM). Dep Hdmaster Prescot Sch Knowsley from 75. *27 Daresbury Road, Eccleston, St Helens, Merseyside, WA10 5DR.* (St Helens 57034)

NAYLOR, Frederick. b 11. St Aug Coll Cant 34. **d** 38 Pontefract for Wakef **p** 39 Wakef for Col Bp. C of Dewsbury Moor 38-41; Chap S Afr Ch Rly Miss 41-51; V of Cross Stone 51-53; Paddock 53-60; Bossall w Buttercrambe 60-66; Bp Burton 66-77. *North End Farm Cottage, Bishop Burton, Beverley, N Humb.*

NAYLOR, Henry Harrison. b 12. Univ of Dur LTh 37. Qu Coll Birm 37. **d** 37 **p** 38 Sheff. C of All SS Sheff 37-41; Hillsborough w Wadsley Bridge 41-45; Stocksbridge 45-47; Attercliffe Parishes 47-48; C-in-c of St Mich AA Neepsend Sheff 48-53; Asst Chap to Sheff United Hosps 50-53; V of Arksey and Chap to Doncaster Royal Infirm 53-61; Eastoft 61-72; Bramley 72-78; Perm to Offic Dio Sheff from 78. *32 West Park Drive, Swallownest, Sheffield.*

NAYLOR, (Gregory) Ian Frederick. b 47. K Coll Lon AKC 70. St Aug Coll Cant 70. **d** 71 **p** 72 S'wark. C of St Giles Camberwell 71-74; M OSB from 74. *Nashdom Abbey, Burnham, Slough, SL1 8NL.* (Burnham 3176)

NAYLOR, James Barry. b 50. Univ of Lon BSc 71, St Benet's Hall Ox BA 75. Wycl Hall Ox 72. **d** and **p** 76 S'wark. C of Catford (Southend) and Downham Dio S'wark 76-78; Team V from 78. *St Luke's House, Northover, Bromley, Kent, BR1 5JR.* (01-698 1354)

NAYLOR, John Herbert. St Jo Coll Manit LTh 33. **d** 34 **p** 35 Calg. C of Hanna 34-36; I of Brooks w Bassano 36-41; Drumheller 41-45; RD of Drumheller 44-45; R of Port Coquitlam and Port Moody 45-49; St Agnes N Vanc 49-72. *1234 Grand Boulevard, North Vancouver, BC, Canada.*

NAYLOR, John Watson. b 26. Trin Hall Cam 3rd cl Hist

Trip pt i 51, BA (3rd cl Th Trip pt ia) 52, MA 56. Ripon Hall Ox 64. **d** 66 **p** 67 Newc T. C of St Andr Newc T 66-69; Otterburn (in c of Corsenside) 69-72; V of Husborne Crawley w Ridgmont 72-76; Chap of Caldicott Sch 76-80; P-in-c of Chollerton Dio Newc T from 80. *Chollerton Vicarage, Hexham, Northumb, NE46 4TF.*

NAYLOR, Canon Peter Aubrey. b 33. Ely Th Coll 57. **d** 58 **p** 59 Lon. C of St Steph Shepherd's Bush 58-62; St Mark Portsea 62-66; Chap HM Borstal Portsm 64-66; V of H Innoc Kidderminster 66-74; Maidstone (w Tovil from 81) Dio Cant from 74; P-in-c of Tovil 79-81; Hon Can of Cant Cathl from 79; RD of Sutton from 80. *Vicarage, Priory Road, Maidstone, Kent.* (Maidstone 56002)

NAYLOR, Peter Edward. b 30. Linc Th Coll 58. **d** 61 **p** 62 S'wark. C of St Mich AA S Beddington 61-64; V of St Anne S Lambeth 64-77; Nork Park Dio Guildf from 77. *Nork Vicarage, Banstead, Surrey.* (Burgh Heath 53849)

NAYLOR, Peter Henry. b 41. Chich Th Coll 64. **d** 67 **p** 68 Bris. C of Filton 67-70; Brixham 70-72; Leckhampton 72-76; V of Brockworth Dio Glouc from 76. *Vicarage, Court Road, Brockworth, Gloucester.* (Witcombe 2725)

NAYLOR, Robert James. b 42. N-W Ordin Course 74. **d** 77 **p** 78 Liv. C of Aigburth 77-80; Social Responsibility Adv Dio Glouc from 80. *Rectory, Over Old Road, Hartpury, GL19 3BJ.* (Hartpury 556)

NAYLOR, Ross John. b 48. Univ of Dur BA 76. St Jo Coll Morpeth ACT ThL 70. **d** 70 **p** 71 Newc. C of Merewether 70-71; Wallsend 72-73; St Helen Bp Auckland 73-75; Waratah 78-79; Tutor St Jo Coll Morpeth from 79; Perm to Offic Dio Brisb 79-80; Dio Newc from 80. *54 Alton Road, Raymond Terrace, NSW, Australia 2324.*

NAYLOR, Russell Stephen. b 45. Univ of Leeds BA (2nd cl Engl & Th) 70. St Chad's Coll Dur Dipl Th 72. Ho of Resurr Mirfield 64. **d** 72 Knaresborough for Ripon **p** 73 Ripon. C of Chapel Allerton 72-75; Industr Chap in Netherton Liv Industr Miss 75-81; P-in-c of Burtonwood Dio Liv from 81. *Vicarage, Chapel Lane, Burtonwood, Warrington, Chesh.* (Newton-le-Willows 5371)

NAYLOR, Stanley. b 29. N-W Ordin Course 76. **d** 79 **p** 80 Bradf. Hon C of Girlington 79-80; C of Tong w Holme Wood Dio Bradf from 80. *c/o St Christopher's Vicarage, Broadstone Way, Holme Wood, Bradford, W Yorks.*

NAYLOR-SMITH, Alan. b 39. Trin Coll Cam 2nd cl Econ Trip pt i 60, BA (2nd cl Th Trip pt ii) 62, MA 72. Linc Th Coll 62. **d** 64 **p** 65 Sheff. C of Stocksbridge 64-68; Team V of Hemel Hempstead Dio St Alb from 68. *33 Craigavon Road, Grovehill, Hemel Hempstead, Herts, HP2 6BA.* (Hemel Hempstead 54229)

NAZER, George. b 48. St Chad's Coll Dur BA (2nd cl Geog) 69. Sarum Wells Th Coll 70. **d** 71 Dorking for Guildf. C of Leatherhead Dio Guildf from 72. *8 Clinton Road, Leatherhead, Surrey.*

NAZER, Raymond. b 20. St Chad's Coll Dur LTh 42, BA 43. Edin Th Coll 39. **d** 43 **p** 44 Lon. C of St Benet Fink Tottenham 43-46; Beckenham 46-50; St Mary Virgin Kettering 50-55; R of Stoke Albany w Wilbarston 55-62; V of All H Ipswich 62-71; V of Castle Acre w Newton Dio Nor from 71; R of Southacre Dio Nor from 71. *Castle Acre Vicarage, Kings Lynn, Norfolk.* (Castle Acre 256)

NCACA, Ven John Patrick. St Pet Coll Alice. **d** 66 **p** 67 Grahmstn. P Dio Grahmstn; Archd Dio Grahmstn from 80. *PO Box 35, Zwelitsha, CP, S Africa.* (Peddie 73)

NCAME, Adonijah Mzimkhulu. b 25. **d** 79 Port Eliz (APM). C of B Mizeki Miss Kwazakele Dio Port Eliz from 79. *79 Gqamlana Street, New Brighton, Port Elizabeth 6200, S Africa.*

NCUBE, Stanley. b 27. **d** 74 **p** 75 Matab. C of St Chad Selukwe Dio Matab (Dio Lundi from 81) 74-78; P-in-c from 78. *Box 93, Selukwe, Zimbabwe-Rhodesia.*

NDABA, Johannes Harrison Themba. St Pet Coll Rosettenville 59. **d** 62 **p** 63 Johann. P Dio Johann 62-73; Dio Swaz from 73. *PO Box 762, Manzini, Swaziland.*

NDABA, Walter. St Bede's Coll Umtata 42. **d** 43 **p** 45 Natal. Asst P Umlazi Miss 45-48; Ladysmith Miss 48-50; P-in-c of Umzimkulwana 50-64; R 64-72; St Laur Ngcwayi 72-77; Perm to Offic Dio Natal from 77. *PO Box 583, Port Shepstone, Natal, S Africa.*

NDABABONYE, Emmanuel. b 45. Butare Th Coll 71. **d** 74 Rwa. d Dio Rwa 74-75; Dio Kiga from 75. *E.A.R. Maranyundo, BP 61, Kigali, Rwanda.*

NDABARORA, Andrew. **d** 60 **p** 61 Rwanda B. P Dio Rwanda B 60-66; Dio Rwa 66-75; Dio Kiga from 75. *Anglican Church, PO Box 22, Nyabisindu, Rwanda.*

NDAGI, Paul Brahima. **d** and **p** 55 N Nig. P Dio N Nig 55-65. *c/o PO Box 72, Kaduna, Nigeria.*

NDAHAGALIKIYE, Canon Daniel. St Paul's Coll Limuru 56. **d** 57 **p** 58 Centr Tang. P Dio Centr Tang 57-63; Dio Vic Nyan 63-78; Hon Can of Vic Nyan from 77. *Box 25, Ngara, Tanzania.*

NDAHANI, John David. St Phil Coll Kongwa. **d** 65 **p** 66 Centr Tang. P Dio Centr Tang. *Luwaka, Dodoma, Tanzania.*

NDAHANI, Noel David. St Phil Coll Kongwa. **d** 66 Bp Malinda for Centr Tang **p** 67 Centr Tang. P Dio Centr Tang 66-78; Dioc Sec 74-78; V of Minaki 78-80; C of Upanga Dio Dar-S from 80. *Box 2184, Dar es Salaam, Tanzania.*

NDAHANI, Sospeter. b 50. St Phil Coll Kongwa 79. **d** 81 Centr Tang. d Dio Centr Tang. *Box 931, Dodoma, Tanzania.*

NDAHURA, Canon Tomasi. **d** 46 Ugan. d Dio Ugan 46-60; Dio Ruw 60-72; Dio Boga-Z 72-77; Hon Can of Boga-Z from 72. *BP 154, Bunia, Zaire.*

NDAKISA, Michael Tembekile. St Bede's Coll Umtata 58. **d** 59 **p** 61 St John's. P Dio St John's. *PO All Saints, Transkei, S Africa.*

NDALE, Hannington. Maseno Bible Sch 69. **d** 69 Maseno. d Dio Maseno N. *Box 1, Maseno, Kenya.*

✠ **NDANDALI, Right Rev Justin.** Clifton Th Coll 65. **d** 67 S'wark for Lon for Col **p** 68 Rwa. Dioc Sec Rwa 67-75; Cons Ld Bp of Butare in Cathl Ch of Butare Rwa 19 Oct 75 by Abp of Ugan; Bps of Kigali, Busoga, Mbale, Ank and Buye; and others. *BP 225, Butare, Rwanda.*

NDANGA, Denys Donald. b 28. **d** 71 **p** 72 Matab. P Dio Matab 71-81; P-in-c of St Patr Gwelo Dio Lundi from 81; VG Dio Lundi from 81. *Box 1017, Gwelo, Zimbabwe.*

NDARASHERE, George. **d** 63 Centr Tang. d Dio Centr Tang. *St Philip's College, Kongwa, Tanzania.*

NDARUSEHELE, George. **d** 63 Vic Nyan. d Dio Vic Nyan. *PO Box 70, Ngara, Tanzania.*

NDATILA, Lukas. St Phil Coll Kongwa 72. **d** 74 **p** 75 Centr Tang. P Dio Centr Tang. *PO Kibakwe, Tanzania.*

NDAYANSE, Johnasani. b 39. **d** 79 **p** 80 W Tang. P Dio W Tang. *c/o PO Box 175, Kigoma, Tanzania, E Africa.*

NDAYISABA, Canon Sezi. **d** 66 **p** 67 Bur. P Dio Bur 66-75; Dio Buye from 75; Can of Buye from 77. *Buye, PO Box 58, Ngozi, Burundi.*

NDEBELE, Alphaeus Manzini. St Bede's Coll Umtata 62. **d** 63 **p** 65 Zulu. P Dio Zulu. *PB 6027, Hluhluwe, Zululand.*

NDEBELE, Nimrod Ntonga. Matab Ordin Course. **d** 80 Matab. d Dio Matab. *Tjolotjo, Zimbabwe.*

NDEKE, Mbelo. b 14. Trin Coll Nai 74. **d** 75 **p** 76 Boga-Z. P Dio Boga-Z. *BP 861, Kisangani, Zaire.*

NDERITU, Samuel. **d** 78 Nak. d Dio Nak. *c/o Box 244, Nakuru, Kenya.*

NDHLOVU, Napoleon Kayser. St Bede's Coll Umtata 52. **d** 53 **p** 55 Natal. P Dio Natal. *St Barnabas's Mission, Durban, S Africa.*

NDIA, Meshack. b 36. **d** 74 Mt Kenya. d Dio Mt Kenya 74-75; Mt Kenya E from 75. *Box 1069, Kianyaga, Ngiriambu, Kenya.*

NDIETSHE, Anthony Thembinkosi Bonga. St Pet Coll Alice 71. **d** 71 **p** 72 Swaz. C of St Geo Manzini 71-75; R of St Matthias Barberton Dio Pret from 75. *Box 151, Barberton 1300, Pretoria, S Africa.* (267)

NDIFWA, Canon Nelson Luka. St Paul's Coll Liuli. **d** 55 **p** 58 SW Tang. P Dio SW Tang; Can of SW Tang from 72. *Box 32, Njombe, Tanzania.*

NDIHO, Peter. b 46. **d** 71 **p** 72 Mt Kenya. P Dio Mt Kenya 71-75; Dio Mt Kenya S from 75. *Karura, Box 23029, Lower Kabete, Kenya.*

NDIJENYENE, Wilson. **d** 67 **p** 68 W Tang. P Dio W Tang. *Shunga, PB Kasulu, Tanzania.*

NDIKUMWAMI, Simon. Warner Mem Th Coll Ibuye 61. **d** 63 Rwanda B. d Dio Rwanda B 63-66; Dio Bur from 66. *Buhiga, Bujumbura, Burundi, Centr Africa.*

NDIMATAMU, Paul. b 38. Bp Tucker Coll Mukono 74. **d** 78 M & W Nile. d Dio M & W Nile. *PO Box 370, Arua, Uganda.*

NDIMBIRWE, Canon Shem. Bp Tucker Coll Mukono. **d** 41 **p** 43 Ugan. P Dio Ugan 41-60; Dio Ankole-K 60-67; Can of Ankole-K 64-67; Kig from 67; Archd 67-75. *PO Box 3, Kabale, Uganda.*

NDIZANA, Horace. St Bede's Coll Umtata 54. **d** 55 **p** 57 St J Kaffr. P Dio St Jo Kaffr 55-60; Dio St John's from 60. *Box 96, Idutywa, Transkei, S Africa.*

NDLAMLENZE, Edward Wellington Musawayo. St Bede's Coll Umtata. **d** 55 **p** 57 Zulu. P Dio Zulu. *St Luke's Church, Location, Paulpietersburg, S Africa.*

NDLAZULWANA, Arthur. **d** 77 **p** 78 Matab. P Dio Matab. *P Bag Q5294, Bulawayo, Zimbabwe.*

NDLOVU, Erastus Vusi. b 40. **d** 76 Natal, C of Enwabi 76-79; Tongaat Dio Natal from 79. *PO Box 45, Tongaat, Natal, S Africa.*

NDLWANA, Bernard Mandlonke. **d** 73 **p** 74 Grahmstn. C of Bolotwa 73-75; Zwelitsha 75-77; R of St Barn Port Alfred 77-80; St John Bolotwa Dio Grahmstn from 80. *Mission House, PO Bolotwa 5325, CP, S Africa.*

NDOMONDO, George. d 74 p 75 S Malawi. P Dio S Malawi. *PO Chilipa, Malawi.*

NDONDE, Samuel George. St Paul's Th Coll Limuru. **d** 67 **p** 68 Nak. P Dio Nak 67-73; Dio Dar-S from 73. *Box 2537, Dar-es-Salaam, Tanzania.*

NDORI, Evans. St Paul's Dioc Div Sch Limuru 54. **d** 55 **p** 57 Momb. P Dio Momb 55-61; Dio Maseno 61-69; Dio N Maseno from 70. *Anglican Church, Namasoli, Kenya.*

NDU, Canon Lawson Nbachi. b 16. Trin Coll Umuahia 54. **d** 56 **p** 57 Nig Delta. P Dio Nig Delta; Can of Nig Delta from 77. *St Martin's Parsonage, Ogu, Port Harcourt, Nigeria.*

NDUA, Luka Mandu. d 57 Bp Deng for Sudan **p** 58 Sudan. P Dio Sudan. *ECS, Angobi, Yei, Equatoria, Sudan.*

NDUIGA, Herbert. St Paul's Dioc Div Sch Limuru 43. **d** 43 **p** 45 Momb. P Dio Momb 43-61; Dio Ft Hall 61. *Karungu, PO Runyenjes, Embu, Kenya.*

NDUKA, Jeremiah Ehosiem. Trin Coll Umuahia 58. **d** 60 **p** 61 Ow. P Dio Ow. *Parsonage, Inyishi, Owerri, Nigeria.*

NDULUMANI, Daudi. d and **p** 77 Centr Tang. P Dio Centr Tang. *DCT, Msanga, Tanzania.*

NDUMO, Shadrack Moeketsi. b 43. St Bede's Coll Umtata 68. **d** 69 Les **p** 70 Bp Makhetha for Les. C of St Sav Leribe Dio Les from 69. *Box 38, Leribe, Lesotho.*

NDUMULLA, Stanley Yusufu. b 45. St Phil Coll Kongwa 72. **d** 74 **p** 75 Centr Tang. P Dio Centr Tang. *Box 15, Dodoma, Tanzania.*

NDUNGANE, Foster Flintoft Tuniswa. St Bede's Coll Umtata 35. **d** 37 **p** 40 St Jo Kaffr. C of Qumbu 37-41; Kokstad 51-59; St Cypr Miss Langa 59-65; P-in-c of Guguletu 65-76. *PO Mqanduli, Republic of Trenskei, S Africa.* (Umtata 2869)

NDUNGANE, Canon Joseph Ephraim Bede. St Bede's Coll Umtata. **d** 42 **p** 45 St Jo Kaffr. C of Qumbu 42-50; H Cross Miss E Pondoland 50-58; P-in-c of Mzizi 60-66; Xugswala 66-72; Hon Can of St John's 69-73; Can 73-76; Can (Emer) from 77; Archd of Kokstad (Pondoland from 75) 73-76; P-in-c of H Cross Miss 72-76. *Box 5, Mqanduli, CP, S Africa.*

NDUNGANE, Reginald Solomzi. d 53 **p** 54 St John's. P Dio St John's. *Box 347, Idutywa, Transkei, S Africa.*

NDUNGANE, Winston Hugh Njongonkulu. b 41. AKC and BD 78. St Pet Coll Alice 71. **d** 73 Capetn. C of Athlone Capetn 73-75; St Mark Mitcham 75-76; St Pet Hammersmith 76-77; St Mary Virg w St Paul Hampstead 77-79; Chap & Tutor St Pet Coll Plessislaer from 80. *c/o St Peter's College, POB 505, Plessislaer, Natal, S Africa.*

NDUNG'U, James William. b 41. **d** 74 Mt Kenya. d Dio Mt Kenya 74-75; Mt Kenya E 75-76; Dio Mt Kenya S from 77. *Box 47, Murang'a, Kenya.*

NDUNGU, Javanson Kiumbe. b 33. **d** 78 Mt Kenya S. d Dio Mt Kenya S. *PO Box 89, Banana Hill, Limuru Read, Kenya.*

NDUWAYO, John Wesley. b 50. Bp Tucker Coll Mukono 73. **d** 75 **p** 76 Buye. P Dio Buye. *BP 58 Ngozi, Burundi, E Africa.*

✠ **NDWANDWE, Right Rev Mfaniseni Sigisbert.** b 28. Pontifical Urbaniana Univ Rome DCnL 62. **d** and **p** 55 RC Bp of Eshowe. Rec into Angl Ch by Bp of Johann 68; C of St Mary's Cathl Johann 70-72; R of Jouberton 72-75; Sharpeville 75-78; Archd of Klerksdorp from 78; Cons Ld Bp Suffr of Johann in St Mary Virg Cathl Johann 19 May 78 by Abp of Capetn; Bps of Johann, Kimb K, Natal, Bloemf, Port Eliz, Swaz and Pret; and Bp Nye. *Box 17, 1933 Sharpeville, Transvaal, S Africa.*

NDYABAGYERUKA, Erisa. d and **p** 79 W Ank. P Dio W Ank. *Box 2018, Rwashamaire, Uganda.*

NDYABAHIKA, Barirarahe David. b 33. Bp Tucker Coll Mukono 65. **d** 67 **p** 68 Kig. P Dio Kig. *PO Kambuga, Kigezi, Uganda.*

NDYABAHIKA, James. b 40. Bp Tucker Coll Mukono 65. **d** 68 **p** 69 Kig. P Dio Kig; Dioc Sec Dio Kig 70-73. *Box 3, Kabale, Uganda.*

NDYANABO, Amos. b 27. **d** 77 E Ank. d Dio E Ank. *PO Box 14, Mbarara, Uganda.*

NDYANABO, Eriya. d 45 Ugan. d Dio Ugan 45-60; Dio Ankole-K 60-67; Dio Kig from 67. *Muko, PO Murole, Uganda.*

NEAL, Anthony Terrence. b 42. Chich Th Coll 65. **d** 68 Ripon **p** 69 Knaresborough for Ripon. C of St Sav w St Hilda Leeds 68-73; Hawksworth Wood 73-78; Asst Chap and Asst Master Abbey Grange High Sch 73-81; C of Farnley 78-81; P-in-c of St Erth Dio Truro from 81; Dioc Adv in Relig Educn Dio Truro from 81. *Vicarage, School Lane, St Erth, Hayle, Cornw, TR27 6HN.* (Hayle 753194)

NEAL, Christopher Charles. b 47. St Pet Coll Ox BA (Th) 69. Ridley Hall Cam 69. **d** 72 **p** 73 Cant. C of Addiscombe 72-76; St Paul Camberley (in c of St Mary) Dio Guildf from 76. *37 Park Road, Camberley, Surrey.* (Camberley 22085)

NEAL, Geoffrey Martin. b 40. K Coll Lon and Warm AKC 63. **d** 64 **p** 65 S'wark. C of St Paul Wimbledon Pk 64-66; in Amer Ch 66-68; St Mark Reigate 68-70; C-in-c of St Faith Wandsworth 70-72; V 72-75; C-in-c of Houghton Regis Dio St Alb 50-75; V from 75. *Vicarage, Houghton Regis, Beds, LU5 5DJ.* (Dunstable 65741)

NEAL, John Edward. b 44. Univ of Nottm BTh 74. Linc Th Coll 70. **d** 74 **p** 75 S'wark. C of Lee 74-77; Ch Ch & St John Clapham 77-81; P-in-c of St Barn Eltham Dio S'wark from 81. *449 Rochester Way, SE9.* (01-856 8294)

NEAL, John Raymond. Univ of Melb BA 52, MA 53. BD 56. ACT ThL 54. Harvard Univ Mass ThD 72. **d** 55 **p** 56 Melb. C of Hampton 55-57; P-in-c of E Essendon 57-61; Sub-Warden St Geo Coll Perth 61-63; Executive Sec Austrn Coun of Chs 63-67; L to Offic Dio Syd 63-67; on leave 67-72; R of Floreat Pk 72-75; Exam Chap to Abp of Perth 73; Chap St Geo Coll and Univ of W Austr 75-80; Perm to Offic Dio Perth from 81. *64 John Street, Inglewood, W Australia 6052.* (271-6575)

NEAL, Canon John Richard. McMaster Univ Ont BA 55. Trin Coll Tor LTh 58, BD 66. **d** and **p** 58 Niag. C of St Jas Hamilton 58-60; R of Tapleytown and Woodburn 58-60; C of St Geo Cathl Kingston 60-64; R of Bath 64-68; Deseronto and Kingsford 69-71; St Thos Kingston 71-79; Picton Dio Ont from 79; Can of Ont from 78. *Box 222, Picton, Ont, Canada.* (613-476 3303)

NEAL, John Vernon. St Jo Coll Auckld LTh 68. **d** 68 **p** 69 Nel. C of Stoke 68-70; I of St Clem Miss Harrington Harbour 71-75; V of Westport Dio Nel from 75. *Vicarage, Westport, NZ.* (8348)

NEALE, Alan James Robert. b 52. Univ of Ox BA 76, MA 81. Univ of Lon BSc 73. Wycl Hall Ox 74. **d** 77 **p** 78 Ex. C of St Andr Plymouth 77-80. *84 Highfield Lane, Southampton.* (550372)

NEALE, Geoffrey Arthur. b 41. St Aid Coll 63. **d** 65 Bp McKie for Cov **p** 66 Cov. C of St Mich Stoke Cov 65-68; H Trin Fareham 68-71; Team V 71-72; R of Binstead 72-77; Bottesford w Ashby 77-80; V of Horncastle w Low Toynton Dio Linc from 80. *Vicarage, Horncastle, Lincs, LN9 6HA.* (Horncastle 3537)

NEALE, James Edward McKenzie. b 38. Selw Coll Cam 3rd cl Th Trip pt i 59, BA (3rd cl Th Trip pt ii) 61. Clifton Th Coll 61. **d** 63 **p** 64 Liv. C of St Ambrose w St Timothy Everton (in C of St Ambrose from 67) 63-72; Relig Adv to Radio Merseyside 72-76; V of St Matt Bestwood Dio Southw from 76. *Vicarage, Padstow Road, Bestwood Estate, Nottingham.* (Nottm 276107)

✠ **NEALE, Right Rev John Robert Geoffrey.** b 26. K Coll Lon and Warm AKC (Jelf Pri) 54. **d** 55 **p** 56 S'wark. C of St Pet St Helier Morden 55-58; Chap at Ardingly Coll 58-62; Recruitment Sec CACTM 63-66; ACCM 66-68; R of Hascombe 68-74; Hon Can and Can Missr of Guildf and Dir Post Ordin Tr 68-74; Archd of Wilts 74-80; Cons Ld Bp Suffr of Ramsbury in Westmr Abbey 24 Jan 74 by Abp of Cant; Bps of Sarum, Ox, Glouc, Ely, Worc, Pet, Birm, Bradf, Guildf and Derby; Bps Suffr of Edmon, Kens, Tonbridge, Dorking, Basingstoke and Sherborne; and others; Area Bp Wilts Pars Sarum from 81. *Chittoe Vicarage, Bromham, Chippenham, Wilts, SN15 2EL.* (Bromham 850651)

NEAT, Harry Lewis. b 10. St Chad's Coll Dur BA (2nd cl Hist) 32, MA 35. **d** 33 **p** 34 Dur. C of St Steph Ayres Quay 33-36; St Cuthb Dur 36-44; V of Haverton Hill 44-49; PC of Bearpark 49-70; Chap Dur Hosp 64-70; V of Sherburn 70-81. *7 Elvet Moor, Durham, DH1 3PR.*

NEATE, Charles Edward Burnell. b 08. Chich Th Coll 33. **d** 34 **p** 35 Chich. C of Storrington 34-36; St Andr Eastbourne 36-38; Chap to Preb Sch Chich 38-41; Chap of Chich Cathl 38-40; PV 38-41; Sub-Dean 39-41; Chap of Eastbourne Coll 41-45; Chap of St Geo Paris 45-48; Radley Coll Berks 49-58; V of St Steph Bournemouth 58-62; Sub-Warden of Radley Coll Berks 62-68; Chap St Mary's Sch Wantage 68-70; Actg Chap K Coll Taunton 70-71; R of Crowcombe 71-75; Hon C of St Jo Evang Taunton Dio B & W from 75. *Carrick, Shepton Beauchamp, Ilminster, Somt, TA19 0LY.* (S Petherton 40948)

NEAUM, Andrew David Irwin. Univ of Rhodesia BA 68. St Paul's Coll Grahmstn 72. **d** 74 **p** 75 Mashon. C of St Mary and All SS Cathl Salisbury Dio Mashon from 74. *Cathedral of St Mary & All Saints, Box 981, Salisbury, Zimbabwe.*

NEAUM, Canon David. Lich Th Coll 34. **d** 37 **p** 38 Lich. C of All SS Burton-on-Trent 37-39; Cannock (in c of Heath Hayes) 39-43; V of Kingston w Gratwich 43-46; R of Leigh Staffs 46-52; Chap of Tristan da Cunha 52-55; P-in-c of St Bernard's Miss Marandellas 56-60; St Jo Bapt Miss Chikwaka 60-64; R of Highlands Salisbury Dio Mashon from 64; Archd of E Mashon 66-68; W Mashon 68-71; Hon Can of Mashon from 72. *89 Enterprise Road, Highlands, Salisbury, Zimbabwe.*

NECHIRONGA, Webster Wulfstan Hwiridzai. St Pet Coll Rosettenville LTh 52. **d** 51 **p** 52 S Rhod. C at St Aug Miss Penhalonga 51-52; St Mich Miss Salisbury 52-54; St Mary Portsea 54-56; Lomagundi 56-60; P-in-c of Mabruku 60-63; Chikwake 64-67; Rusape 67-74; C of Matsika 75-77; Chap Mpilo Hosp 77-80; Warden St Barn Centre Salisbury from 80. *191 Westwood, Southerton, Salisbury, Zimbabwe.*

NEECH, Canon Alan Summons. b 15. Univ of Dur LTh 37. Tyndale Hall Bris 34. **d** 39 **p** 40 Luckn. BCMS Miss Dio Luckn 37-64; Dioc Missr Dio Luckn 60-64; Can of Luckn 64-66; Can (Emer) from 66; Overseas Sec BCMS 64-66; Gen Sec 66-81; Hon Can of Centr Tang from 72; Hon C of St Paul Slough 75-81. *Address temp unknown.*

NEED, Philip Alan. b 54. AKC 75. Chich Th Coll 76. **d** 77 **p** 78 S'wark. C of Ch Ch and St John Clapham 77-80; All SS w St Pet Luton Dio St Alb from 80. *48 Harefield Road, Luton, Beds.* (Luton 31901)

NEEDHAM, Canon Geoffrey. b 14. Keble Coll Ox BA 37, MA 43. Lich Th Coll 37. **d** and **p** 39 Bradf. C of Otley 39-44; V of Riddlesden 44-49; Kimberworth Sheff 49-60; Ranmoor 60-79; RD of Hallam 69-75; Hon Can of Sheff Cathl 71-79; Can (Emer) from 80. *33 Park Street, Worksop, Notts.*

NEEDHAM, Canon George. b 01. Univ of Sheff BA 23. Late Exhib of Trin Coll Cam 2nd cl Mor Sc Trip pt i 25, BA (1st cl Th Trip pt ii) 26, MA 35. Bps' Coll Cheshunt 26. **d** 27 **p** 28 Sheff. C of St Geo Doncaster 27-32; Chap at Doncaster Infirm 28-32; R of Braithwell w Bramley 32-36; V of St Phil Sheff 36-40; Chap Sheff R Infirm 36-40; St Phil w St Anne Sheff 40-42; V of Conisborough 42-45; R of Wombwell 45-52; V of Kendal 52-70; RD of Kendal 53-70; Surr from 53; Proc Conv Carl 55-64; Hon Can of Carl from 59. *5 Thornleigh Road, Kendal, Cumb.* (Kendal 20395)

NEEDHAM, George Oswald. b 18. Univ of Man BA 49. Wycl Hall Ox 49. **d** 51 **p** 52 Ches. C of Macclesfield 51-53; W Kirby 53-56; V of Wrenbury w Baddiley 56-64; R of Thurstaston 64-79. *14 Gills Lane, Barnston, Wirral, Mer, L61 1AD.*

NEEDHAM, Gregory. Univ of Syd BA 33. Lucas-Tooth Scho Univ of Lon MA (Educn w distinc) 50. ACT ThL 36. **d** 37 **p** 38 Newc. C of Singleton 37-40; Young 40; Wagga Wagga 40; Chap of Armid Sch 41-42; Chap RAAF 43-46; Commiss Armid 46-49; Perm to Offic Dio Lon 46-48; Dio Roch 48-49; Chap to Hutchin's School Hobart 50; Lect in Educn Univ of Queensld 51-75; Perm to Offic Dio Brisb 51-69; Hon C of St Matt Sherwood 69-71; Miss Chap Dio Brisb 76. *5 Dunkeld Street, Toowoomba, Queensland, Australia 4350.*

NEEDHAM, John. b 09. St Jo Coll Dur BA (2nd cl Hist) 30, MA and Dipl Th 33. **d** 32 **p** 33 Dur. C of St Gabr Bp Wearmouth 32-35; St Cuthb Darlington 35-37; V of St Sepulchre Cam 37-47; CF (EC) 40-45; V of St John Cherry Hinton Cam 47-55; Surr 52-55; V of Walney I 55-63; Aspatria 63-72; C-in-c of St Jas Hayton 67-72; V of Torpenhow 72-75; L to Offic Dio Carl from 75. *Priory Close, St Bees, Cumb, CA27 0DR.* (St Bees 572)

NEEDHAM, Thomas Paul Richard. b 42. **d** and **p** 78 Keew. I of Gillam 78-80. *Box 640, Gillam, Manit, Canada, R0B 0L0.*

NEEDLE, Paul Robert. b 45. Dipl Th (Lon) 70. Oak Hill Coll 67. **d** 70 **p** 71 Bradf. C of St Jo Evang Gt Horton Bradf 70-74; Pudsey 74-77; Chap St Luke's Hosp Bradf and Hon C of All SS Bradf 78-80. *c/o 17 Glebe Street, Pudsey, W Yorks.* (Pudsey 574533)

NEELANDS, William David. b 43. Univ of Tor BA 65, MA 66. Trin Coll Tor MDiv 78. **d** 77 **p** 79 Tor. Regr Trin Coll Tor from 77; C of St Mary Magd City and Dio Tor from 79. *Trinity College, Toronto, M5S 1H8, Canada.*

NEELS, Raymond James. St Jo Coll Auckld LTh 61. **d** 61 **p** 62 Waik. C of Te Awamutu 61-63; New Plymouth 63-64; V of Pio Pio w Aria 64-67; Tokoroa 67-72; Chap Waik Publ Hosp 72-78; New Plymouth Hosp from 78. *153 Seaview Road, New Plymouth, NZ.* (34-689)

NEELY, George Edward. b 20. **d** 60 **p** 62 S'wark. C of Ascen Balham Hill 60-61; St Luke Camberwell 61-62; Rotherhithe (in c of Epiph) 62-67; V of St Bart Camberwell (S Bermondsey from 78) Dio S'wark from 67. *Vicarage, Barkworth Road, SE16 3BY.* (01-237 1238)

NEELY, William George. b 32. BD (Lon) 62. **d** 56 **p** 57 Down. C of Cregagh 56-62; C-in-c of Mt Merrion 62-68; R 68-76; Dioc Missr Down 70-76; Preb of Down Cathl 74-76; R of Kilcooley w Littleton, Crohane and Killenaule Dio Cash from 76; C-in-c of Fertagh Dio Oss from 79. *Rectory, Grange Barna, Thurles, Tipperary, Irish Republic.* (Kilkenny 34147)

NEEP, Edwin Phipps. b 18. St Cath S Ox BA (Th) 50, MA 54. Ripon Hall, Ox 46. **d** 51 **p** 52 Guildf. C of St Mich Aldershot 51-54; Walton-on-Thames 54-57; R of Bladgdon w Charterhouse Dio B & W from 57; C-in-c of Butcombe 71-72. *Blagdon Rectory, Bristol.* (Blagdon 62495)

NEEVE, Eric John. St Francis Th Coll Brisb 52. **d** and **p** 56 Brisb. C of Sherwood Brisb 56-57; Bundaberg 57-59; Toowoomba 59-60; V of Mary Valley 60; R of Noosa 61-67; N Ipswich Dio Brisb from 67. *17 Lawrence Street, North Ipswich, Queensland, Australia 4305.* (81 3271)

NEIGHBOUR, William. Oak Hill Th Coll 48. **d** 50 **p** 51 Lon. C of St Pet U Holloway 50-52; St Jo Evang (in c of St Steph) Reading 52-54; R of St Sav Chorlton-on-Medlock 54-57; V of St Jo Bapt Islington 57-62; Tytherington Dio Glouc from 62. *Tytherington Vicarage, Wotton-under-Edge, Glos.* (Thornbury 2289)

NEIL, Alan George. b 47. Univ of Cant BA 71. St Jo Coll Auckld 71. **d** 73 **p** 74 Ch Ch. C of Papanui 73-75; Shirley 75-77; Rangiora Dio Ch Ch from 77. *134 White Street, Rangiora, NZ.* (7467)

NEIL, Richard Wilfred. b 16. Dipl Th (Lon) 57. Lon Coll Div 51. **d** 53 **p** 54 S'wark. C of Ch Ch E Greenwich 53-55; St Jas Hatcham 55-56; V of Cowling 56-60; St Mich Devonport Dio Ex 60-81; L to Offic Dio Ex from 81. *22 Park Street, Plymouth, PL3 4BL.* (Plymouth 558974)

NEIL-SMITH, John Christopher. b 20. Pemb Coll Cam BA 43, MA 46. Westcott Ho 43. **d** 44 **p** 45 Dur. C of Bishopwearmouth 44-46; Actg C of St Steph Rochester Row Westmr 46-47; C of Christ the Sav Ealing 47-53; V of Ponders End 53-59; St Sav Hampstead Dio Lon from 59. *30 Eton Villas, NW3 4SQ.* (01-722 4621)

NEILL, Charles Christopher Stanley. b 33. G and C Coll Cam BA 57, MA 60. Cudd Coll. **d** 66 **p** 67 Heref. C of St Jo Bapt Heref 66-67; V Cho of Heref Cathl and Chap Cathl Sch Heref 67-78; Sen Chap Abingdon Sch 78-80; Team V of Wolvercote w Summertown City and Dio Ox from 80. *34 Oakthorpe Road, Oxford, OX2 1BE.* (Ox 58835)

NEILL, Canon Erberto Mahon. b 16. TCD BA 40, MA 43. **d** 39 **p** 40 Dub. C of Portarlington 39-42; Irish Staff Worker Scripture U 42-70; I of St Jas Bray 47-61; Castleknock w Mulhuddart and Clonsilla 61-75; RD of Dub St Mary 71-77; Can of Ch Ch Cathl Dub from 72; Chap to Pres of Irish Republic 73-74; C-in-c of St Andr Dub 75-77; V of Harold's Cross City and Dio Dub from 77. *2 Avondale Road, Killiney, Co Dublin, Irish Republic.* (855393)

NEILL, Gerald Monro. b 02. G and C Coll Cam BA 25, MA 29. **d** 26 **p** 28 Dur. C of St Aid Grangetown 26-29; Warden of Caius Coll Miss Battersea 29; Chap Aysgarth Sch 29-34; Hd Master of Bannel Head Sch Kendal and L to Offic Dio Carl 34-35; R of St Steph S Shields 35-38; V of St Mary Heworth 38-46; Ryhope 46-48; Chap Sunderland Borough Mental Hosp 46-48; R of Swanton Morley w Worthing 48-58; V of Bedwyn Magna 58-64; Savernake Forest 58-64; RD of Pewsey 60-66; V of Chute w Chute Forest 64-73; C-in-c of Chettle 73-80. *32 Campbell Road, Salisbury, Wilts.*

NEILL, Very Rev Ivan Delacherois. b 12. Men in Disp 45. Knight Officer O of Orange Nassau (with swords) 46. OBE 58. CB 63. Jes Coll Cam BA 35, MA 38. Lon Coll of Div 35. **d** 36 **p** 37 Lon. C of St Mary Fulham 36-38; Perm to Offic at Ch Ch Crouch End 38-39; CF 39-66; Chap Gen to the Forces 60-66; Hon Chap to HM the Queen 60-62; Chap 62-66; V and Provost of Cathl Ch (w St Paul and St Jude Moorfields) Sheff 66-74; Provost (Emer) from 74; Perm to Offic Dio Glouc from 74. *Rodborough Crest, Rodborough Common, via Stroud, Glos, GL5 5BT.* (045-387 3224)

NEILL, James Purdon. b 41. Oak Hill Th Coll 60. Dipl Th (Lon) 63. **d** 64 Penrith for Carl **p** 65 Carl. C of St Thos Kendal 64-68; Chap Pk Hill Flats Sheff 68-71; P-in-c of St Jo Evang Mansfield 71-77; V of St Ann w Em Nottm Dio Southw from 77. *17 Robin Hood Chase, Nottingham.* (Nottm 55471)

NEILL, John Robert Winder. b 45. Late Scho of TCD BA 1st cl Hebr and Or Lang Mod 66, MA 69, Jes Coll Cam BA (2nd cl Th Trip pt ii) 68, MA 72. Ridley Hall Cam 67. **d** 69 **p** 70 Dub. C of Glenageary 69-71; Lect Div Hostel Dub 70-71; Bp's V, Libr and Chapter Regr of St Canice's Cathl Kilkenny 71-74; Regr Dio Oss Ferns and Leighlin 71-74; I of Abbeystrewry 74-78; V of St Bart w Ch Ch Leeson Pk City and Dio Dub from 78. *12 Merlyn Road, Dublin 4, Irish Republic.* (Dub 694813)

NEILL, Robert Chapman. b 51. TCD Div Test 77. **d** 77 **p** 78 Down. C of Shankill Lurgan Dio Drom from 77. *35 Gilford Road, Lurgan, Craigavon, Co Armagh, N Ireland.*

NEILL, Canon Robert Purdon. b 10. Fitzw Ho Cam BA 33, MA 37. Wycl Hall, Ox 34. **d** 35 **p** 36 Carl. C of St Jas Carl 35-38; Ch Ch Barnet 38-39; R of Burslem 39-41; V of Fremington 41-45; R of March 45-50; V of St Andr L Cam 50-57; Surr from 55; V of Lenton Notts 57-62; St Jo Evang Worksop 62-73; RD of Worksop 65-72; Hon Can of Southw 68-75; Can (Emer) from 75; C-in-c of Caunton 73-75; Maplebeck 73-75. *27 Alvey Road, Balderton, Newark, Notts.*

✠ **NEILL, Right Rev Stephen Charles.** b 1900. Late Scho of Trin Coll Cam Jun Carus Gr Test Pri 19; Davies Scho and 1st cl Cl Trip pt i 20; Craven Scho, Jeremie LXX Pri, Evans Pri and Members' Latin Essay Pri 21; BA (1st cl Cl Trip pt ii) 22;

1st cl Th Trip pt ii, Scholefield Pri, Sen Carus Gr Test Pri, Stud Crosse Scho, and Chan Cl Med 23; 2nd Win Reading Pri 24; MA 26. DD 80. Trin Coll Tor Hon DD 50. Univ of Hamburg Hon ThD 57. St Univ Tokyo LittD 60. Univ of Glas Hon DD 61. Univ of Uppsala Hon ThD 65. FBA 69. **d** 26 Tinn **p** 28 Ely for Tinn. Itin Miss Dio Tinn 26-27; Fell Trin Coll Cam 24-28; Lect U Ch Coll Alwaye and Miss Dio Tinn 28-30; Warden Bp's Th Coll Nazareth 30-39; Exam Chap to Bp of Tinn 29-39; Cons Ld Bp of Tinn in Dorn Cathl 8 Jan 39 by Bp of Calc; Bps of Dorn; Madr; Guildf; Nagp; Iran; and Tranquebar; Bp Suffr of Aotearoa; and Bps Elliott; Tarafdar and Johnson; res 45; Chap Trin Coll Cam and Lect Univ of Cam 45-47; Select Pr Univ of Ox 45 and 77; Cam 48 and 73; Hulsean Lect Cam 46-47; Asst Bp to Abp of Cant 46-49; Co-Dir Study Dept World Coun of Chs 47-48; Assoc Gen Sec 48-51; Gen Ed World Chr Books 52-62; Dir 62-68; Prof of Miss and Ecumen Th Univ of Hamburg 62-68; Bampton Lect Ox 64; Prof of Philos and Relig Studs Univ of Nairobi 69-73; Commiss Dios Egypt and Iran from 76; Jer and Cyprus and the Gulf from 77; Hon Asst Bp of Ox from 79. *c/o Wycliffe Hall, Oxford, OX2 6PW.*

NEILL, William Barnett. b 30. Trin Coll Dub BA (1st cl Heb and Or Lang Mod) 61. **d** 63 Down **p** 64 Tuam for Down. C of St Clem Belf 63-66; Dundonald 66-72; R of Drumgath 72-80; Drumgooland 76-80; Mt Merrion Dio Down from 80. *122 Mount Merrion Avenue, Belfast, BT6 0FS.* (Belf 644308)

NEILL, William Benjamin Alan. b 46. Open Univ BA 76. Div Hostel Dub 68. **d** 71 **p** 72 Connor. C of St Colman Dunmurry 71-74; Coleraine 75-77; St Anne w St Steph Dub 77-78; r of Convoy and Donaghmore w Monellan 78-81; Faughanvale Dio Derry from 81. *21 Main Street, Eglinton, Co Derry, N Ireland.* (Eglinton 810217)

NEILSON, John William. b 12. AKC 35. **d** 35 **p** 37 S'wark. C of St Paul Plumstead 35-39; St Jas (in c of St Mich) Hatcham 39-41; Offg C-in-c of Newington and Hartlip 41-45; V of Lympne w W Hythe Dio Cant from 45; RD of N Lympne 64-75. *Lympne Vicarage, Hythe, Kent.* (Hythe 66526)

NEILSON, Robert Geoffrey. Univ of NZ BA 55. St Jo Coll Auckld LTh (2nd cl) 57. **d** 57 **p** 58 Wai. C of Gisborne 57-60; P-in-c 60; V of Murupara-Roporoa 61-65; Otane 65-70; Wakatipu 70-77; Wel S City and Dio Wel from 77. *17 Gordon Place, Wellington 2, NZ.* (894-932)

NEILSON, Terrence Gary. b 38. Vanc Sch of Th Dipl Th 74. **d** 74 Koot **p** 74 Carib. I of Lytton Indian Miss and Shulus Dio Carib from 74. *Box 1345, Merritt, BC, Canada.*

NEISH, Donald Arthur. Univ of K Coll Halifax BA 51, BSLitt 54, BD 68. **d** and **p** 54 NS. R of Antigonish and C-in-c of Country Harbour 54-61; Elora and Drayton 61-64; Ch Ch St Catherines 64-71; Spryfield 70-76; R of H Spirit Dartmouth Dio NS from 76. *21 Lynn Drive, Dartmouth, NS, Canada.* (466-6116)

NEISH, Gordon Charles. K Coll NS BA 63. **d** 65 **p** 66 NS. d Dio NS 65-66; R of Port Dufferin 66-73; on leave. *Herring Cove PO, NS, Canada.* (477-1481)

NEISH, Robert Arthur. Dalhousie Coll Halifax BA 11. **d** 22 **p** 23 NS. C of Neill's Harbour 22; R of Arichat 23-24; Granville 24-30; Seaforth 31-45; New Ross 45-49; Petite Rivière 49-51; Melford 51-58; Rosette 59-64. *Granville Ferry, NS, Canada.*

NEISON, Robert Wayne. b 31. St Jo Coll Auckld. **d** 78 Bp Spence for Auckld **p** 79 Auckld. Hon C of Devonport Dio Auckld from 78. *25 Hastings Parade, Devonport, Auckland, NZ.* (453-575)

NELL, George Alfred Montague. St Jo Coll Armid ACT ThL 22, Th Scho (2nd cl) 39. **d** 23 **p** 24 Armid. C of Glen Innes 23-24; P-in-c of Bukkulla 24-26; C of Quirindi 26-29; Canberra 29-30; R of Moruya 30-36; Binda 36-44; Can of Goulb Cathl 43-78; R of Crookwell 44-50; Junee 50-68; L to Offic Dio C & Goulb 68-78. *12 Prince Street, Goulburn, NSW, Australia.*

NELLOR, William Charles Frank. Ridley Coll Melb ACT ThL 44. **d** 42 **p** 44 Bend. C of St Paul Bend 42-44; Actg C-in-c of Par distr of Tongala 44-45; C of All SS Cathl Bend 45-46; R of Milloo w Mitiamo 46-52; Tatura 52-57; C of St Mary Caulfield 57-60; Melb Dio Centre 60-64; Chap Prince Henry's Hosp Melb 60-64; V of Gardenvale 64-77; I of Black Rock Dio Melb from 77. *35 Arkaringa Crescent, Black Rock, Vic., Australia 3193.* (598-8348)

NELSON, Lord Bishop of. *See* Sutton, Right Rev Peter Eves.

NELSON, Dean of. *See* Hurd, Very Rev Michael John.

NELSON, Allen James. b 29. Trin Coll Dub 53. **d** 55 **p** 56 Dub. C of Glenageary 55-57; Clontarf 57-60; I of Bailieborough w Mullagh 60-75; C-in-c of Knockbride (w Shercock from 72) 66-75; I of Julianstown w Colpe Dio Meath from 75; Drogheda Dio Meath from 81. *Julianstown Rectory, Eastham Road, Bettystown, Drogheda, Co Louth, Irish Republic.* (Drogheda 27345)

NELSON, Arthur Basil. b 20. Wells Th Coll 63. **d** 64 **p** 65 Ex. C of Littleham w Exmouth 64-67; R of Sampford Peverell (w Uplowman, Holcombe Rogus w Hockworthy and Burlescombe from 76) Dio Ex from 67; R of Uplowman 67-76; C-in-c of Holcombe Rogus w Hockworthy 76. *Sampford Peverell Rectory, Tiverton, Devon.* (Sampford Peverell 206)

✠ **NELSON, Right Rev Aruna Kodjo.** St Aug Coll Kumasi. **d** and **p** 32 Accra. P Dio Accra 32-63; Hon Can of Accra 59-63; Provost of Accra Cathl 63-77; Cons Asst Bp of Accra in Accra Cathl 11 Dec 66 by Abp of W Afr; Bps of Accra; and Ibadan. *Holy Trinity Cathedral, PO Box 8, Accra, Ghana.* (Accra 66103)

NELSON, Colin Gordon. ACT ThL 74. Moore Coll Syd 74. **d** 74 Syd. C of Green Valley 74-76; Res Min of Tregear 76-79; Glenquarie Dio Syd from 79. *32 Edgar Street, Macquarie Fields, NSW, Australia 2564.* (605-5463)

NELSON, Frank. b 12. Jes Coll Ox BA 35, MA 40. BSc (Lon) 44. **d** 78 Reading for Cant for Ox **p** 78 Ox (NSM). Hon C of Sutton Courtenay w Appleford Dio Ox from 78. *6 Tullis Close, Sutton Courtenay, Abingdon, OX14 4BD.*

NELSON, Frank Derek. b 55. Univ of Capetn BA 76. St Paul's Coll Grahmstn 77. **d** 78 **p** 79 Bloemf. C of St Matthias Welkom 78-81; St Andr and St Mich Cathl City and Dio Bloemf from 81. *PO Box 1523, Bloemfontein, S Africa.*

NELSON, Ian Walter. Coll Ho Ch Ch NZ Bd of Th Stud LTh 65. **d** 56 **p** 57 Nel. C of Ahaura w Brunnerton 56-58; V of Motupiko 58-60; Cheviot 60-66; Granity w Waimangaroa 66-71; Ellerslie 71-81; E Otago Dio Dun from 81. *78 Beach Street, Waikouaiti, NZ.* (309)

NELSON, Kenneth Edmund. b 10. St Jo Coll Cam BA (2nd cl Cl pts i and ii) 33, MA 36. Qu Coll Birm 46. **d** 47 Wakef **p** 48 Pontefract for York. C of Huddersfield 47-50; Pocklington 50-52; V of Brotton Parva 52-58; Sheriff Hutton 58-65; V of L Aden and Chap BP Oil Refinery 65-67; C-in-c of Crayke w Brandsby and Yearsley 67-68; R 68-78; Perm to Offic Dio York from 78; Dio Ripon from 81. *Flat 1, Holly Mount, 23b Ripon Road, Harrogate, N Yorks.* (Harrogate 68460)

NELSON, Matthew. b 13. St Aid Coll 45. **d** 47 **p** 48 Man. C of St Thos Radcliffe 47-49; Deane 49-50; R of St Cypr Ordsall Salford 50-55; V of St Andr Radcliffe 55-63; St Jas Heywood 63-68; R of St Paul Blackley 68-78; Hon C of St Leon Middleton Dio Man from 80. *32 Moss Lane, Middleton, Manchester, M24 1WX.* (643-4472)

NELSON, Melbourne William. NZ Bd of Th Stud LTh (2nd cl) 68. **d** 67 **p** 68 Bath. C of Wellington 68-69; P-in-c of Cakaudrove 69-70; V 70-72; Exam Chap to Bp of Polyn 73-76; Dioc Educn Officer Dio Polyn 73-76; R of Bulahdelah Dio Newc from 76. *Rectory, Stroud Street, Bulahdelah, NSW, Australia 2423.*

NELSON, Michael. b 44. Univ of Lon BD (2nd cl) 66. Coll of Resurr Mirfield 66. **d** 68 Repton for Derby **p** 69 Repton for Cant. C of Newbold w Dunston 68-72; N Gosforth (in c of St Aid) 72-77; V of Seaton Hirst Dio Newc T from 77. *Seaton Hirst Vicarage, Ashington, Northumb.* (Ashington 813218)

NELSON, Michael. b 44. Univ of Newc (Aus) BSc 68, BA 72. St Jo Coll Cam BA 74. Westcott Ho Cam 74. **d** 75 Newc T for Newc (Aus). Perm to Offic Dio Newc T 75; C of Egglescliffe 75-76; Cessnock 76-77; Industr Chap and Perm to Offic Dio Newc from 77. *9 Day Street, East Maitland, NSW, Australia 2323.*

NELSON, Nelson John. b 21. Ripon Hall Ox 64. **d** 65 **p** 66 Birm. C of The Quinton 65-68; V of St Paul W Smethwick Dio Birm from 68; RD of Warley from 79. *Vicarage, West Park Road, W Smethwick, Warley, W Midl B67 7JH.* (021-558 0470)

NELSON, Owen Ignatius. **d** 75 Ja (APM). C of All SS Kingston Dio Ja from 75. *30 Highland Drive, Kingston 8, Jamaica, W Indies* (092-44157)

NELSON, Ralph Archbold. b 27. St Cuthb S Dur BA 50. Bps' Coll Cheshunt 50. **d** 52 **p** 53 Blackb. C of St Mary Penwortham 52-57; C of Eglingham 57-58; V of Featherstone 58-80; Kirkham Dio Blackb from 80. *Kirkham Vicarage, Preston, Lancs, PR4 2SL.* (Kirkham 683644)

NELSON, Raymond George. St Jo Coll Morpeth 60. **d** 61 **p** 62 Graft. C of Coffs Harbour 61-62; Port Macquarie 62-64; Casino 64-65; V of SW Rocks 65-66; Asst Sec ABM for NSW 67-69; C of Gosford 69-72; P-in-c of Islington-Carrington Dio Newc from 72. *3 Norfolk Avenue, Islington, NSW, Australia 2296.* (61-2180)

NELSON, Robert Gibson. b 34. ALCD 61. **d** 61 Kens for Lon **p** 62 Lon. C of St Mary Osterley Isleworth 61-64; C-in-c of St Barn Conv Distr Reading 64-69; R of Margaret River 69-72; V of St Jo Evang Guernsey 72-78; R of Ste Marie du Castel Guernsey Dio Win from 78. *Castel Rectory, Guernsey, CI.* (Guernsey 56793)

NELSON, Robert Towers. b 43. Liv Coll of Tech BSc 65. N-W Ordin Course 76. **d** 79 **p** 80 Liv (APM). Hon C of Our

Lady & St Nich City and Dio Liv from 79. *5 Sedbergh Road, Wallasey, Merseyside.*

NELSON, Warren David. b 38. TCD BA 67. **d** 68 **p** 69 Connor. C of St Mich Belf 68-70; I of Kilcooley 70-76; Hon Chap Coalbrook Fellowship Hosp Ho Thurles from 76. *Coalbrook Fellowship, Halfhandkerchief Wood, Coalbrook, Thurles, Tipperary, Irish Republic.*

NELSON, William. b 38. Oak Hill Coll 74. **d** 76 Penrith for Carl **p** 77 Carl. C of Hensingham 76-81; V of St Paul Widnes Dio Liv from 81. *28 Fairfield Road, Widnes, WA8 6SG.* (051-424 2221)

NEMAKHUVHANI, Matthew Ramboho. St Francis Th Coll Sekhukhuniland 62. **d** 64 **p** 65 Pret. P Dio Pret. *St Mary's Church, PO Shayandina, via Louis Trichardt, N Transvaal, S Africa.*

NEMBHARD, Justin Albert. Univ of WI BA (Th) 73. United Th Coll of WI 71. **d** 71 **p** 72 Ja. C of St Andr Half-Way Tree 71-72; on leave 73-74; R of Highgate Dio Ja from 75. *Rectory, Highgate, Jamaica, W Indies.*

NEMEYINKIKO, Ernest. Warner Mem Th Coll Ibuye 61. **d** 63 Rwanda B. d Dio Rwanda B 63-66; Dio Rwa 66-75; Dio Kiga from 75. *Kigeme, Butare, Rwanda.*

NENER, Thomas Paul Edgar. b 42. Univ of Liv MB, ChB 66. FRCS Edin 71, FRCS 71. Coll of Resurr Mirfield 78. **d** 80 Liv **p** 81 Warrington for Liv. C of Warrington Dio Liv from 80. *133 Church Street, Warrington, Cheshire, WA1 2TL.*

NESBITT, Charles Howard. b 13. St Jo Coll Dur LTh 34, BA 35. Bp Wilson Th Coll IM 31. **d** 35 **p** 36 Liv. C of St Chris Norris Green 35-37; St Matt Blackb 37-41; St John Gt Harwood 41-46; V of St Jas Wrightington 46-58; Baxenden Accrington 58-68; Stalmine 68-74. *40 Stanley Road, Sandilands, Morecambe, Lancs.*

NESBITT, Charles Maurice Grillet. b 09. Univ Coll Lon BA (2nd cl Engl) 31, Teacher's Dipl 32. St George's Windsor **d** 50 **p** 51 St E. C of St Greg w St Pet Sudbury 50-52; V of Friston w Snape 52-55; R of Farnley Leeds 55-63; V of All S Harlesden 63-74; Hon C of St Paul City and Dio Bris from 81. *5 Ryland Place, St Werburgh's, Bristol, BS2 9YZ.* (Bris 555921)

NESBITT, Thomas Edward. b 46. Montr Dioc Th Coll LTh 70. **d** 70 Rupld. C of St Aid Winnipeg 70-72; on leave 73-75; C of Gtr Coaticook 76-78. *33-4804 Cote des Neiges, Montreal, PQ, Canada.*

NESBITT, William Ralph. b 17. Sarum Th Coll 70. **d** 70 **p** 71 Win. C of Iford 70-76; All SS, St Chris and St Kath Southbourne Bournemouth Dio Win from 76. *6 Foxholes Road, Southbourne, Bournemouth, BH6 3AS.*

NESHAM, George Dove. b 20. ALCD 50. **d** 50 **p** 51 Carl. C of Harrington 50-52; Ferryhill 52-55; V of Stanley 55-62; Woodkirk 62-76; Ripponden w Rishworth 76-80; Satley Dio Dur from 80; RD of Stanhope from 81. *St Cuthbert's Vicarage, Saltley, Bishop Auckland, DL13 4HU.* (Tow Law 730091)

NESHAM, Robert Harold. b 15. Men in Disp 47. **d** 68 **p** 69 Glouc. C of Upton St Leon 68-72; V of Poulton (w Down Ampney from 73) Dio Glouc from 72; C-in-c of Down Ampney 72-73. *Poulton Vicarage, Cirencester, Glos, GL7 5HU.* (Poulton 383)

NESLING, Horace William. St Aid Coll 37. TD 51. **d** 38 **p** 39 St E. C of Ipswich 38-39; CF (TA - R of O) 39-46; CF 46-62; CF (R of O) 62-64; Perm to Offic Dio St E 62-64; R of Abbess w Beauchamp Roding 64-69; R of White Roding 64-69; V of Boxted (w Langham from 76) 69-78; C-in-c of Langham 75-76; Hon C of Horseheath Dio Ely from 79; W Wickham Dio Ely from 79. *Horseheath Rectory, Cambridge, CB1 6QA.*

NESS, Michael Ross. St Chad's Coll Regina 44. **d** 47 **p** 48 Qu'App. C of Eston 47-48; I of Alsask 48-50; Rosetown 50-54; R of Port Medway 54-59; Alberton 59-64; Crapaud 65-76. *131 North River Road, Charlottetown, PEI, Canada.*

✠ **NESTOR, Right Rev Donald Patrick.** b 38. Ex Coll Ox BA (4th cl Th) 63, MA 66. Qu Coll Birm 63. **d** 65 **p** 66 Wakef. C of Woodkirk 65-68; Forton 68-72; Asst Chap Univ of botswana, Lesotho and Swaz 72-74; Chap 74-79; Cons Ld Bp Suffr of Les in St Geo Cathl Capetn 14 Oct 79 by Abp of Capetn; Bps of Grahmstn, Les, Natal, Johann, Port Eliz and Geo; Bps Suffr of Capetn (Swartz and Matolengwe); and others. *c/o Box LR 43, Leribe, Lesotho.*

NETHERCOTE, Richard Arthur. Ridley Coll Melb ACT ThL 65. **d** 65 **p** 66 Bend. C of All SS Cathl Bend 65-68; Kyabram 68-69; V of Loddon w Raywood 69-73; I of St Steph Richmond 73-77; Perm to Offic Dio Melb from 77; Dio Bend from 78. *97 Clarendon Street, Maryborough, Vic, Australia 3465.*

NETTLESHIP, Charles. b 08. OBE (Mil) 45. St Aug Coll Cant. **d** 62 **p** 63 Cov. C of Bilton 62-65; V of Leek Wooton Dio Cov from 65. *Leek Wootton Vicarage, Warwick.*

NEUBECKER, Francis Stanley. d 54 **p** 55 Bath. C of Gilgandra 54-55; P-in-c of Brewarrina 56-57; M of Bro of Good Shepherd N Territory 58; Chap at Tennant Creek 57-62; P-in-c of Bourke 62-64; R of Barcaldine 64-69; Bothwell 69-71; Keppel 71-74; Bright 74-78; P-in-c of Edward River Dio Carp from 78. *Edward River, via Normanton, Qld, Australia.*

NEUDEGG, Leslie. b 35. SOC 77. **d** 80 **p** 81 Roch (NSM). C of Chalk Dio Roch from 80. *40 Dennis Road, Gravesend, Kent, DA11 7NW.*

NEUHAUS, Theodore Frederick Charles. b 19. Univ of Syd BA (2nd cl Engl) 40. BD (Lon) 58. **d** 70 **p** 71 Centr Tang. P Dio Centr Tang 70-74; C-in-c of Provisonal Distr of Berala Dio Syd from 74. *17 Crawford Street, Berala, NSW, Australia 2141.* (649-6100)

NEVE, Keith Edward. Ridley Coll Melb ACT ThL 58. **d** 60 **p** 61 Melb. C of St Geo Bentleigh 60-62; Moreland 62-64; V of Warburton 64-71; I of St Paul Fairfield 71-80; St Geo Bentley Dio Melb from 80. *12 Mavho Street, Bentleigh, Vic, Australia 3204.*

NEVE, Raymond David. Ridley Coll Melb ACT ThL 58. **d** 59 **p** 60 Adel. C of Ceduna 59-61; P-in-c of Wilcannia 61-65; Menindee 65-69; Kambalda 69-71; R of Norseman 71-75; N Midlands 75-80; Mundaring Dio Perth from 80. *Rectory, Mann Street, Mundaring, W Australia 6073.* (295 1029)

NEVELL, Frederick George. b 24. Univ of Lon BA 51. Oak Hill Th Coll. **d** 51 **p** 52 Lon. C of Ch Ch Spitalfields 51-54; St Mary Becontree 54-56; V of St Matt W Ham 56-64; St Luke w St Simon and St Jude W Kilburn 64-73; St Barn Clapham Common Dio S'wark from 73. *12 Lavender Gardens, SW11 1DL.* (01-223 5953)

NEVETT, David Richard. b 42. Univ of Sask BA 72. Em & St Chad's Coll Sktn. **d** 72 **p** 73 Qu'App. C of Balcarres Dio Qu'App from 72. *Box 683, Balcarres, Sask., Canada.* (334-2532)

NEVILLE, Graham. b 22. Late Scho and Stud of CCC Cam 1st cl Cl Trip pt i 42, BA 47, 1st cl Th Trip pt i 48, MA 49. Chich Th Coll 48. **d** 50 **p** 51 Southw. C of Sutton-in-Ashfield 50-53; Chap Univ of Sheff 53-58; R of Culworth 58-63; Eydon 58-63; RD of Culworth 62-63; Exam Chap to Bp of Pet 62-69; Chap and Lect Ch Ch Coll Cant 63-68; L to Offic Dio Cant from 63; Dio Chich from 73; Chap Sutton Valence Sch Maidstone 68-73; Six Pr Cant Cathl 69-78; Exam Chap to Abp of Cant 70-75; Lect Eastbourne Coll of Educn 73-76; E Sussex Coll of Higher Educn 76-79; Brighton Poly 79-80; Dioc Dir of Educn Dio Linc from 80. *23 Stonefield Avenue, Lincoln, NL2 1QL.* (0522 32922)

NEVIN, Ronald. Linc Th Coll 63. **d** 64 **p** 65 Dur. C of Norton 64-66; R of Cockfield 66-70. *Box 92, Quantico, Maryland 21856, USA.*

NEW, David John. b 37. Univ of Lon BSc (2nd cl Eng) 58. Chich Th Coll 65. **d** 67 **p** 68 Cant. C of Folkestone 67-72; All SS K Heath 72-74; V of St Mich AA S Yardley Dio Birm from 74. *60 Yew Tree Lane, South Yardley, Birmingham, B26 1AP.* (021-706 2563)

NEW, John Bingley. b 29. BD (Lon) 70. Chich Th Coll 77. **d** 77 Win **p** 78 Basingstoke for Win. C of Sholing 77-79; V of Micheldever & E Stratton and Woodmancote w Popham Dio Win from 79. *Vicarage, Micheldever, Winchester, SO21 3DA.* (Micheldever 233)

NEW, Philip Harper. b 08. St Jo Coll Dur LTh 32, BA 33. St Aid Coll 29. **d** 33 **p** 34 Leic. C of Melton Mowbray 33-37; St Aug Leic 37-38; R of W Leake w Ratcliffe-on-Soar and Kingston-on-Soar 38-47; CF (EC) 43-46; V of Pleasley Hill 47-53; R of Kimberley 53-59; V of Thurgarton w Hoveringham 59-69; Beckingham 69-73; C-in-c of Walkeringham 69-73; Perm to Offic Dio Southn from 74. *Overdale, Old Melton Road, Normanton-on-the-Wolds, Nottingham, NG12 5NL.*

NEW, Canon Thomas. b 30. K Coll Cam BA 52, MA 56. Cudd Coll 52. **d** 54 **p** 55 Lon. C of H Cross Greenford 54-55; Old St Pancras and St Matt Oakley Square 55-58; Woodham 58-64; V of All SS Guildf 64-72; Banstead Dio Guildf from 72; Exam Chap to Bp of Guildf from 75; RD of Epsom 76-80; Hon Can of Guildf from 79. *Vicarage, Banstead, Surrey, SM7 2NQ.* (Burgh Heath 51134)

NEW GUINEA, *See* Papua New Guinea.

NEW HEBRIDES, Diocese of. *See* Vanuatu.

NEW WESTMINSTER, Lord Bishop of. *See* Hambidge, Most Rev Douglas Walter.

NEW WESTMINSTER, Dean of. *See* Burke, Very Rev Northcote Richard.

NEW ZEALAND, Metropolitan of. *See* Reeves, Most Rev Paul Alfred.

NEWALL, Arthur William. b 24. St D Coll Lamp BA 49. Chich Th Coll 49. **d** 51 **p** 52 Man. C of St Phil Hulme Man 51-53; Fallowfield 53-55; V of St Barn Oldham 55-60; Aspull 60-68; R of Foots Cray 68-78; V of Henlow Dio St Alb from 78. *Vicarage, Henlow, Beds, SG16 6AN.* (Hitchin 812257)

NEWALL, Peter Frederick. Univ of Syd BA 56. Moore Th

Coll ACT ThL (2nd cl) 50. **d** and **p** 50 Syd. C of St Andr Cathl Syd 50-53; H Trin Miller's Point Syd 50-52; Chap of Cranbrook Gr Sch Edgecliffe and C of St Andr Cathl Syd 53-56; R of Leura 56-60; Clovelly 60-64; P-in-c of Glenunga Dio Adel 64-69; R 69-70; Dean and V of St Pet Cathl Armid 70-77; Commiss Centr Tang from 69. *c/o Deanery, Armidale, NSW, Australia 2350.* (72-2269)

NEWALL, Richard Lucas. b 43. K Coll Lon and Warm AKC 66. **d** 66 Warrington for Liv **p** 67 Liv. C of Roby 66-69; St Geo Douglas IM 69-71; L to Offic Dio Man 72-75; C of St Mary Bangor 75-77; R of Newborough w Llangeinwen, Llangaffo and Llanfair yn y Cwmwd Dio Ban from 77. *Rectory, Dwyran, Anglesey, Gwyn.* (Newborough 285)

NEWARK, Archdeacon of. *See* Leaning, Ven David.

NEWBOLD, Hugh Edward Stonehewer. b 13. St Steph Ho Ox 32. **d** 36 **p** 37 Ox. C of High Wycombe 36-38; All SS E Clevedon 38-40; CF (EC) 40-45; C of High Wycombe 45-50; Wooburn 50-51; V of Soulbury 51-57; R of Stoke Hammond 53-57; V of E and W Wellow 57-70; St Jo Evang Bournemouth 70-79; P-in-c of Cold Waltham Dio Chich from 80. *Cold Waltham Vicarage, Nr Pulborough, Sussex.*

NEWBON, Eric. b 23. Fitzw Ho Cam BA 51, MA 55. Ridley Hall Cam 51. **d** 53 **p** 54 Liv. C of Garston 53-57; V of Bickershaw 57-65; All S Southport Dio Liv from 65. *19 Norwood Avenue, Southport, Mer, PR9 7EG.*

NEWBON, Kenneth. b 29. Wells Th Coll 67. **d** 69 **p** 70 Heref. C of Ch Stretton 69-72; C-in-c of Cressage w Sheinton 72-75; V of St Pet Braunstone City and Dio Leic 75-81; Team R from 81. *Braunstone Vicarage, Leicester, LE3 3AL.* (Leic 824102)

NEWBURY, John Allan. b 02. Ripon Hall Ox 55. **d** 56 **p** 57 Chelmsf. C of Leyton 56-58; V of Wethersfield 58-63; R of Sandon 63-67; V of St Andr Leytonstone 67-68; Perm to Offic Dios Cant and Chelmsf from 71. *38 Church Road, Rivenhall, Witham, Essex.*

NEWBURY, Robert. b 22. St D Coll Lamp BA 46. **d** 48 **p** 49 Swan B. C of Killay 48-55; V of Glascwm w Rhulen and Cregrina 55-63; Manselton Swansea Dio Swan B from 63. *Manselton Vicarage, Swansea, W Glam.* (Swansea 54848)

NEWBY, Geoffrey Peter. b 43. Ridley Coll Melb Th Dipl 74. **d** 75 **p** 77 Perth. d Dio Perth 75-77; C of Spearwood-Willagee Dio Perth from 77. *85 Phoenix Road, Spearwood, W Australia 6163.* (418 1005)

NEWBY, Lindsay Raymond John. b 40. Oak Hill Coll Lon 79. **d** and **p** 80 Armid. C of Quirindi Dio Armid from 80. *Henrey Street, Quirindi, NSW, Australia 2343.*

NEWBY, Matthew Truran. Univ of Tor BA 26, MA 27. Wycl Coll Tor Dipl Th 29; Hon DD 68. **d** 29 **p** 30 Tor. C of Advent Tor 29-31; St Matt Tor 31-38; I of Scarboro' Junction and Sandown Pk 38-39; R of Islington 39-47; Chap of Trin Coll Tor 47-73; Exam Chap to Bp of Tor 53-73; Can of Tor 55-79. *61 Lynwood Avenue, Toronto, Ont., Canada.*

NEWBY, Peter Gordon. b 23. **d** 64 **p** 65 Leic. C of St Phil Leic 64-69; R of L Bowden 69-72; V of Gouray Jersey 72-77; Chap Jersey Group of Hosps 78-80; R of Much Birch w L Birch, Much Dewchurch, Llanwarne and Llandinabo Dio Heref from 80. *Much Birch Rectory, Hereford.* (Golden Valley 540558)

NEWBY, Tom Berrington. b 08. FCA 60. Wycl Hall Ox 50. **d** 52 **p** 53 Southw. C of St Chrs Sneinton 52-54; Bp Hannington Mem Ch Hove (in c of H Cross) 54-57; V of St Andr L Cam 57-65; Surr 61-65; V of Packington w Normanton-le-Heath 65-68; C of St Alb Streatham Pk 71-72; Perm to Offic Dio Portsm 73-74; C-in-c of St Jas Ryde 74-77; Perm to Offic Dio Nor from 80. *2 Balmoral Crescent, Heacham, Norf, PE31 7EL.* (Heacham 71549)

NEWCASTLE, Lord Bishop of (Province of York). *See* Graham, Right Rev Andrew Alexander Kenny.

NEWCASTLE, Assistant Bishop of (Province of York). *See* Gill, Right Rev Kenneth Edward.

NEWCASTLE, Provost of (Province of York). *See* Spafford, Very Rev Christopher Garnett Howsin.

NEWCASTLE, Lord Bishop of (Province of NSW). *See* Holland, Right Rev Alfred Charles

NEWCASTLE, Assistant Bishops of (Province of NSW). *See* Stibbard, Right Rev Leslie; and Parker, Right Rev Geoffrey Frank.

NEWCASTLE, Dean of (Province of NSW). *See* Beal, Very Rev Robert George.

NEWCOMBE, Kenneth Harry. b 27. Ridley Hall Cam 70. **d** 72 **p** 73 Leic. C of St Mary Melton Mowbray 72-78; W Bridgford (in c of St Paul) Dio Southw from 78. *St Paul's Parsonage, Boundary Road, West Bridgford, Nottingham, NG2 7DB.* (Nottm 233492)

NEWCOMBE, Timothy James Grahame. b 47. AKC 75. St Aug Coll Cant 75. **d** 76 **p** 77 Heref. C of St Martin Heref 76-79; Hitchin Dio St Alb from 79. *67 Whitehill Road, Hitchin, SG4 9HP.* (Hitchin 57402)

NEWCOME, James William Scobie. b 53. Trin Coll Ox BA 74, MA 78, Selw Coll Cam BA 77, MA 81. Ridley Hall Cam 75. **d** 78 **p** 79 St Alb. C of Leavesden Dio St Alb from 78. *41 Horseshoe Lane, Garston, Watford, Herts, WD2 7HJ.* (Garston 70318)

NEWELL, Aubrey Francis Thomas. b 20. St D Coll Lamp BA 43. **d** 45 **p** 46 St A. C of Rhosddu 45-49; Llanwnog 49-50; Gabalfa 50-53; Gt Marlow 53-57; R of Lavendon w Cold Brayfield 57-62; V of Gawcott w Hillesden 62-77; P-in-c of Radclive w Chackmore 69-72; RD of Buckingham 70-76; P-in-c of Padbury w Adstock 72-77; V of Lenborough Dio Ox from 77. *Gawcott Vicarage, Buckingham.* (Buckingham 3162)

NEWELL, Cameron Percy. b 1895. Univ of Dur LTh 17. Lon Coll of Div 14. **d** 19 **p** 21 Chelmsf. C of Leyton 19-22; Chepstow 22-23; Ch Ch Ware 23-27; Ch Ch Ramsgate 27-29; V of St Thos Crookes 29-34; R of Ruckinge 34-35; V of St Pet Ipswich (w St Mary at Quay from 42) 35-64; L to Offic Dio St E from 64. *1 Colchester Road, Ipswich, Suff.* (Ipswich 56924)

NEWELL, Charles John Cuthbert. b 09. Or Coll Ox BA 31, MA 46. St Aug Coll Cant 31. **d** 32 **p** 33 Ripon. C of St Mich Headingley 32-35; SPG Miss at Ahmadnagar 35-37; Kolhar 37-43; Chap (Eccles Est) Belgaum Bom 43-46; on furlough 46; Chap of Ahmadnagar 47; Poona 47-49; SPG Miss Kolhapur 49-55; Exam Chap to Bp of Bom 50-55; V of Wetherby 55-67; Pakenham (w Norton and Tostock from 79) 67-80; P-in-c of Gt Livermere 71-74; Norton w Tostock 76-79; Perm to Offic Dio St E 80-81; Dio Ripon from 81. *23 Greengate Lane, Knaresborough, N Yorks, HG5 9EL.*

NEWELL OF STAFFA, Gerald Frederic Watson. b 34. Sarum Th Coll. **d** 59 **p** 60 Win. C of St Pet Southn 59-61; Overton w Laverstoke and Freefolk 61-63; CF (TA) 61-63; CF 63-67; R of Spennithorne 67-69; Finghall 67-69; Hauxwell 67-69; Hon C of Durrington 70-75; Steyning 75-78. *Freswick Castle, Caithness.*

NEWELL, Kenneth Ernest. b 22. Sarum Wells Th Coll 77. **d** 79 **p** 80 Ex (APM). C of Lynton Dio Ex from 79. *Mole End, Lydiate Lane, Lynton, N Devon.*

NEWELL, Ven Phillip Keith. Univ of Melb BSc 53, BEducn 60, MEducn 69. Trin Coll Melb ACT ThL (2nd cl) 59. **d** 60 **p** 61 Melb. C of All SS St Kilda 60-62; St Andr Brighton 62-63; St Jas Syd 63-67; Chap Syd Hosp 63-67; R of Ch Ch St Lucia City and Dio Brisb from 67; Can Res of Brisb from 73; Archd of Lilley from 76. *3 Baty Street, St Lucia, Brisbane, Queensland, Australia 4067.* (370 8887)

NEWELL, Richard Barry. St Jo Coll Morpeth ACT ThL 59. **d** 59 **p** 60 Newc. C of New Lambton 59-63; R of Kendall 63-69; N Lake Macquarie 69-75; Coopernook Dio Newc from 75. *Rectory, Lansdowne Road, Coopernook, NSW, Australia 2426.* (065-56 3132)

NEWELL, Samuel James. b 28. TCD BA (2nd cl Or Lang Mod) and Wall Bibl Scho 53, Downes Div Pri (2nd) and Div Test (1st cl) 54, MA 63. **d** 54 **p** 55 Connor. C of St Mary Belf 54-57; Derriaghy 57-60; Reading 60-63; V of Ch Ch Chesham w St Geo Tylers Hill 63-74; C-in-c of Wraysbury 74-78; Team V of Riverside Dio Ox from 78. *57 Welley Road, Wraysbury, Staines, TW19 5ER.* (Wraysbury 2740)

NEWETT, Neville David. b 36. ACT Dipl Th 71. Ridley Coll Melb 71. **d** 72 **p** 73 Tas. C of Smithon-Stanley 72-73; P-in-c of Stanley 73-76; R of Queenstown 76-79; St John New Tn Dio Tas from 79. *St John's Rectory, New Town, Tasmania 7008.* (002 28 1131)

NEWFOUNDLAND, CENTRAL, Lord Bishop of. *See* Genge, Right Rev Mark.

NEWFOUNDLAND, EASTERN and LABRADOR, Lord Bishop of. *See* Mate, Right Rev Martin.

NEWFOUNDLAND, EASTERN and LABRADOR, Dean of. *See* Rusted, Very Rev Edward Charles William.

NEWFOUNDLAND, WESTERN, Lord Bishop of. *See* Payne, Right Rev Sidney Stewart.

NEW GUINEA ISLANDS, Lord Bishop of. *See* Meredith, Right Rev Bevan Stanley.

NEWHAM, Canon Raymond George. b 14. K Coll Lon and Warm AKC 49. **d** 49 **p** 50 Guildf. C of Haslemere 49-53; V of St John Drypool Hull 53-58; C-in-c of Lowfield Heath 58; Industr Chap of Crawley 58-62; L to Offic Dio Chich 58-62; Industr Adv Dio Chich from 62; V of St Anne Brighton 62-76; Can and Preb of Chich Cathl from 74; C-in-c of Hamsey Dio Chich from 76. *Hamsey Rectory, Offham, Lewes, E Sussex, BN7 3PX.* (Lewes 4356)

NEWHOUSE, Ven Robert John Darrell. b 11. Late Scho of Worc Coll Ox 1st cl Cl Mods 33, BA (2nd cl Lit Hum) 35, MA 38. Cudd Coll 35. **d** 36 **p** 37 Pet. C of St Jo Bapt Pet 36-40; St Giles Cam 40-46; Chap RNVR 41-46; R of Ashwater 46-56; RD of Holsworthy 54-56; Aylesbeare 65-66; V of Littleham w Exmouth 56-66; Surr 62-66; Archd of Totnes and Can Res of Ex Cathl 66-76; Treas of Ex Cathl 70-76; Archd (Emer) and Can (Emer) from 76. *Pound Cottage, Northlew, Okehampton, Devon.* (Beaworthy 532)

NEWING, Canon Brian Charles. Wollaston Th Coll W Austr ACT ThL 65. **d** 65 **p** 66 Bunb. C of St Bonif Cathl Bunb 65-67; R of Ravensthorpe w Jerramungup 67-74; Pinjarra Dio Bunb from 74; Can of Bunb from 74. *Rectory, Pinjarra, W Australia 6208.* (095-31 1248)

NEWING, Edward George. ACT ThL 58. BD (Lon) 59. MTh (Lon) 61. Moore Th Coll Syd 57. **d** 59 Bp Hilliard for Syd **p** 59 Syd. C of Toongabbie 59-60; R of H Trin Miller's Point Syd 60-62; P-in-c of Moro 62-64; Lect St Phil Coll Kongwa 64-66; St Paul's Coll Limuru 66-70; on leave 70-72; L to Offic Dio Syd 73-76; R of Hornsby 76-80; Warden St Pet Hall, Sing from 80. *6a Mount Sophia, Singapore 0922.*

✠ **NEWING, Right Rev Kenneth Albert.** b 23. Selw Coll Cam BA 53, MA 57. Coll of Resurr Mirfield 53. **d** 55 **p** 56 Ex. C of Plymstock 55-63; R of Plympton St Maurice 63-82; RD of Plympton 71-76; M Gen Syn from 73; Preb of Ex from 75; Archd of Plymouth 78-82; Cons Ld Bp Suffr of Plymouth 2 Feb 82 in Westmr Abbey by Abp of Cant; Bps of Lon, Win, Ex, Birm, Bris, Derby, Ely, Glouc, Lich, Ox, Southw and Truro; Bps Suffr of Crediton, Barking, Basingstoke, Bedford, Bradwell, Croydon, Colchester, Edmon, Grantham, Hull, Maidstone, Ramsbury, Sherborne, Sherwood, Shrewsbury, Southn, Stockport and Willesden; and Bps Coggan, Hodson, Patterson, Woollcombe, Claxton and others. *9 Fore Street, Plympton St Maurice, Plymouth, Devon, PL7 3LZ.* (Plymouth 336274)

NEWING, Peter. b 38. Univ of Dur BA (3rd cl Soc Stud) 63. ACP 67. Univ of Bris BEducn 76. **d** 65 **p** 66 Glouc. C of Blockley w Aston Magna 65-69; C-in-c of Taynton 69-75; Tibberton 69-75; Asst Master Selw Sch Glouc 70-73; R of Brimpsfield w Elkstone and Syde Dio Glouc from 75. *Rectory, Brimpsfield, Gloucester, Glos, GL4 8LD.* (Witcombe 3621)

NEWLYN, Edwin. b 39. K Coll Lon and Warm AKC 64. **d** 65 **p** 66 Leic. C of St Mich AA Belgrave 65-68; Chap Miss to Seamen Santos 68-69; Asst Chap Glas and C of St Gabr Govan Glas 69-73; Chap Miss to Seamen E Lon Grahmstn 73-76; R of St Pet W Bank E Lon 75-76; Chap Miss to Seamen Immingham Dock 77-81; V of Fylingdales and Hawsker w Stainsacre Dio York from 81; P-in-c of Hawsker 81. *Fylingdales Vicarage, Robin Hood's Bay, N Yorks, YO22 4RN.* (Whitby 880386)

NEWMAN, Alan George. b 18. Lich Th Coll 41. **d** 44 Lich for B & W **p** 45 Taunton for Cant. C of St Mich Twerton-on-Avon 44-52; CF (TA) 50-56; V of Clandown 52-56; PC (V from 69) of Ch Ch Bradf-on-Avon 56-76; R of Monkton Farleigh w S Wraxall Dio Sarum from 76. *Monkton Farleigh Rectory, Bradford-on-Avon, Wilts, BA15 2QD.*

NEWMAN, Alfred John Gordon. b 19. Qu Coll Birm 71. **d** and **p** 74 Birm. C of St Pet Hall Green Dio Birm from 74. *15 Ashleigh Road, Solihull, W Midl, B91 1AE.* (021-705 2068)

NEWMAN, Arthur Maurice. b 18. St Jo Coll Ox BA (3rd cl Hist) 40, Dipl Th 41. **d** 42 **p** 43 Dur. C of St Paul Jarrow 42-48; St Columba Southwick Dur 48-52; V of Gorefield 52-59; Southea w Murrow 59-67; V of Parson Drove 59-67; C-in-c of Gt w L Stukeley Dio Ely 67-68; R 68-82. *6 Fairfield Crescent, St Ives, Cambs, PE17 4QH.*

NEWMAN, Brian Edward. **d** 68 Adel for Willoch **p** 69 Willoch. C of Melrose 68-70; R of Quorn 70-74; Kadina Dio Willoch from 74. *Box 176, Kadina, S Australia 5554.* (088-21 1219)

NEWMAN, Cecil Ernest. Roch Th Coll 61. Western Th Coll USA BA 58, Dipl Th 58. **d** 62 **p** 63 Ex. C of Tiverton 62-64; Wolborough 64-67; Chap Darenth Pk Hosp Dartford from 67. *6 Birtrick Drive, Meopham, Kent.* (Meopham 813678)

NEWMAN, David Maurice Frederick. b 54. Hertf Coll Ox BA 75, MA 79. St Jo Coll Nottm. **d** 79 **p** 80 Roch. C of Ch Ch Orpington Dio Roch from 79. *43 Haileybury Road, Orpington, Kent.*

NEWMAN, Dennis Gerard. b 30. Univ of Nottm Dipl Th 55, BA 55. Univ of Wisconsin MTh 69. Roch Th Coll 60. **d** and **p** 61 Chich. C of Hampden Pk 61-63; Wadhurst and of Tidebrook 63-65; V of Ch Ch Eastbourne 65-71; St Pet St John Preston Brighton 71-74; Hampden Park Dio Chich from 74. *St Mary's Vicarage, Brassey Avenue, Hampden Park, Eastbourne, Sussex.* (Eastbourne 53166)

NEWMAN, Douglas Graff. Wollaston Th Coll W Austr 58. **d** 59 **p** 60 Perth. C of Northam 59-62; R of Merredin 62-67; Bassendean 67-71; Wongan Hills 72-76. *c/o Rectory, Wongan Hills, W Australia 6603.* (Wongan Hills 93)

NEWMAN, Edmund Hannibal. Univ of NZ BA 35. NZ Bd of Th Stud LTh (1st cl) 37. Univ of Melb BD 39. **d** 37 **p** 38 Nel. C of Blenheim 37-38; Ch Ch Cathl Nel 38-40; V of Ahaura w Brunnerton 40-41; Actg V of Cheviot 41-46; V of Woodend 46-52; Hinds 52-58; Leeston 58-63; Otaio w Blue Cliffs 63-68; Oxford-Cust 68-71; Perm to Offic Dio Ch Ch from 75. *15 Hayes Avenue, Christchurch, NZ.* (41-691)

NEWMAN, Eric William. b 26. Angl Th Coll BC STh 65. **d** 56 **p** 57 New Westmr. C of H Trin New Westmr 56-57; Chap Miss to Seamen New Westmr 56-64; Vic Dks Lon 67-68; Newport 69-78; S Shields from 78; V of St Timothy Vanc 65-67. *Missions to Seamen, South Shields, T & W.*

NEWMAN, Geoffrey Maurice. b 22. Ox NSM Course 77. **d** 80 **p** 81 Ox. C of Binfield Dio Ox from 80. *8 Yarnold Close, Wokingham, Berks, RG11 1SD.*

NEWMAN, Graham Anthony. b 44. Ripon Coll Cudd 79. **d** 81 Bp Gill for Newc T. C of Walker Dio Newc T from 81. *610 Welbeck Road, Walker, Newcastle-on-Tyne, NE6 3AB.* (Wallsend 634095)

NEWMAN, Harrison. b 15. Bps' Coll Cheshunt, 54. **d** 56 **p** 57 Lon. C of Old St Pancras and of St Matt Oakley Square Lon 56-59; Jes Ch (in c of St Giles) Forty Hill Enfield 59-63; V of St Pet de Beauvoir Town 63-72; Chap Hackney Hosp Group from 72. *Chaplain's Office, Hackney Hospital, E9.* (01-985 5555)

NEWMAN, Harry Folinsbee. Univ of Tor BA 37. Wycl Coll Tor LTh 40. **d** 40 **p** 41 NS. C of St Paul Halifax 40-42; Kensington NS 42-44; MSCC Miss Palumpur 44-49. *Apt 4, 560 Park Crescent, Fairport Beach, Ajax, Ont, Canada.*

NEWMAN, John Humphrey. b 17. ALCD 49. **d** 49 Lewes for Chich **p** 50 Chich. C of Bp Hannington Mem Ch Hove 49-52; V of Welling 52-64; St Jo Evang Penge 64-74; R of Knockholt Dio Roch from 74. *Knockholt Rectory, Sevenoaks, Kent, TN14 7PP.* (Knockholt 33132)

NEWMAN, Laurence Victor. b 23. Wells Th Coll. **d** 66 **p** 67 Cant. C of Hythe 66-69; Milton Hants 69-71; Asst Chap Wandsworth Pris 71-72; Chap Ashford Remand Centre 72-77; HM Pris Win from 77. *c/o HM Prison, Winchester, Hants.*

NEWMAN, Michael Alan. b 40. Chich Th Coll 67. **d** 70 **p** 71 Lon. C of St Aug Kilburn 70-73; St Mary Cable Street Stepney 75-77. *April Cottage, Georges Lane, Storrington, Pulborough, W Sussex.*

NEWMAN, Michael John. b 50. Univ of Leic BA 72, MA 75. Ex Coll Ox Dipl Th 74. Cudd Coll Ox 73. **d** 75 Stafford for Lich **p** 76 Lich. C of Tettenhall Regis 75-79; Uttoxeter 79-82; R of Norton Canes Dio Lich from 82. *81 Church Road, Norton Canes, Cannock, Staffs, WS11 3PQ.* (Heath Hayes 79982)

NEWMAN, Michael Reginald. b 16. Merton Coll Ox Squire Scholar 35, BA (2nd cl Th) 39, MA 46. Cudd Coll 46. **d** 47 **p** 48 Leic. C of Glen Parva w S Wigston 47-49; Horsell 49-52; Haslemere (in c of St Chris) 52-54; R of Wetherden 54-56; C-in-c of Old Newton 54-56; V of Combe Bissett w Homington 56-61; Chap Sarum Tr Coll 56-61; V of Warnham 61-74; RD of Horsham 68-74; V of Willingdon 74-81. *22 Rother View, Burwash, Etchingham, E Sussex, TN19 7BN.* (Burwash 882456)

NEWMAN, Canon Michael Robert. K Coll Lon BD 61. St Jo Coll Auckld LTh 53. **d** 54 **p** 55 Auckld. C of Whangarei 54-58; St Steph Hampstead 58-61; V of Bay of Is 61-65; Thames 65-71; Team V of Mangere Miss Distr 71-73; V of Otara Miss Distr Dio Auckld from 73; Hon Can of Auckld from 80. *15 Fulton Crescent, Otara, NZ.* (27-49778)

NEWMAN, Paul Anthony. b 48. BSc (Lon) 70. Univ of Leeds Dipl Th 75. Coll of Resurr Mirfield 73. **d** 76 **p** 77 S'wark. C of St Laur Catford 76-82; Team V of Grays Dio Chelmsf from 82. *St Mary's House, Rectory Road, Grays Thurrock, Essex.* (0375 73685)

NEWMAN, Philip John. K Coll Lon and Warm BD and AKC 66. **d** 67 Bp Arnott for Melb **p** 68 Melb. C of All SS E St Kilda 67-69; Box Hill 69-70; P-in-c of Ch of Ascen Burwood E Dio Melb 70-72; I 72-74; Dioc and Exam Chap to Abp of Melb 74-77; I of Templestowe Dio Melb from 77. *6 Dellfield Drive, Templestowe Lower, Vic, Australia 3107.* (850-2160)

NEWMAN, Richard David. b 38. Late Exhib of BNC Ox 2nd cl Cl Mods 58, BA (3rd cl Lit Hum) 60, MA 63. Lich Th Coll 60. **d** 62 **p** 63 Chich. C of E Grinstead 62-66; Gt Grimsby (in C of St Martin) 66-73; Team V 73-74; V of St Nich-at-Wade w Sarre (and Chislet w Hoath from 75) 74-81; H Innoc S Norwood Dio Cant from 81; C-in-c of Chislet w Hoath 74-75. *192a Selhurst Road, SE25 6XX.* (01-653 2063)

NEWMAN, Richard Frank. b 37. Lich Th Coll. **d** 62 **p** 63 Pet. C of Kettering 62-65; Foleshill 65-69; R of Kislingbury w Rothersthorpe 69-79; V of Stannington Dio Sheff from 79. *Stannington Vicarage, Sheffield, S6 6DB.* (Sheffield 345586)

NEWMAN, Robert Stevenson. Univ of Tor BA 39. Wycl Coll Tor LTh 42. **d** 42 **p** 45 Sktn. I of Sutherland 42-47; Perdue 47-50; High Prairie w McLennan 50-56; Berwyn 56-58; Can of Athab 52-58; Warden of Montr Dioc Th Coll and Prof of Pastoral Th 58-61; I of Bordeaux 61-66; Chomedey 64-66; Valleyfield 66-71. *PO Box 487, Beaverton, Ont., Canada.*

NEWMAN, Robert Vivian. Em & St Chad's Coll Sktn 70. **d** 73 Sktn. C of H Trin Sktn 73-75; I of Lintlaw 75-76; on leave 76-77; I of Parkland Dio Sktn from 78. *Box 217, Lashburn, Sask, Canada.*

NEWMAN, Ronald William. b 26. **d** and **p** 71 Wel. Hon C of Feilding Dio Wel from 71. *29 Norfolk Crescent, Feilding, NZ.*

NEWMAN, Preb Thomas Percival. b 20. Lich Th Coll 55. **d** 57 **p** 58 Lich. C of St Paul Wednesbury 57-61; V of St Mark Ocker Hill Tipton 61-65; Willenhall Dio Lich from 65; Preb of Lich Cathl from 81. *St Giles Vicarage, Willenhall, W Midl.* (Willenhall 65722)

NEWMARCH, Ven Walter Henry. Univ of Syd BA 58. Moore Th Coll Syd ACT ThL (2nd cl) 49. **d** and **p** 50 Syd. C of Ch Ch Gladesville 50; Asst Chap KS Parramatta 51-53; Asst Master 69-76; CMS Miss at Tawau 54-68; Hon Can of Jess 62-68; L to Offic Dio Syd from 70; Archd of Parramatta w Camden from 77. *348 Marsden Road, Carlingford, NSW, Australia 2118.* (872-2690)

NEWNHAM, Eric Robert. b 43. Sarum Wells Th Coll 70. **d** 75 **p** 76 S'wark. C of Ch of Ascen Blackheath Dio S'wark from 75. *27 Morden Hill, SE13 7NN.* (01-692 6507)

NEWNHAM, Osmond James. b 31. Univ of Leeds, BA 55. Coll of Resurr Mirfield, 55. **d** 57 Sherborne for Sarum **p** 58 Sarum. C of St Mark Sarum 57-60; Pewsey 60-62; CF (R of O) from 59 (TAVR) from 71; R of Chickerell w Fleet Dio Sarum from 62. *Chickerell Rectory, Weymouth, Dorset.* (Weymouth 784915)

NEWNS, Donald Frederick. b 07. St Aid Coll 34. **d** 37 **p** 38 Man. C of St Steph Elton Bury 37-39; St Andr Nottm 39-40; St Jo Evang Mansfield 40-43; Actg C of Stoke-on-Trent and Offg Chap Stoke-on-Trent Hosp and Inst 43-44; Chap Sheff Royal Infirm and Hosp 45-49; V of Eastwood 49-51; Deputy Chap to HM Pris Wandsworth 52-53; Chap to HM Pris Parkhurst 53-59; C-in-c of E w W Lexham 59-61; R of Litcham w Kempston and P-in-c of E & W Lexham 59-61; R of Lilcham w Kempston w E w W Lexham 61-72. *Crow Hall, West Lexham, King's Lynn, Norf, PE32 2SA.* (Weasenham St Peter 255)

NEWPORT, Archdeacon of. *See* Wright, Ven Royston Clifford.

NEWPORT, Derek James. b 39. Sarum Wells Th Coll 74. **d** 76 **p** 77 Ex. C of Tavistock 76-78; R of Gambo Dio Centr Newfld from 78. *Anglican Rectory, Gambo, Newfoundland, Canada.*

NEWSAM, Bernard Hugh. b 01. Selw Coll Cam 3rd cl Hist Trip pt i 25, BA (2nd cl Anthrop Trip) 26, MA 31. Cudd Coll 27. **d** 28 Hull for York **p** 29 York. C of Saltburn-by-the-Sea 28-34; C-in-c of St Osw Conv Distr Middlesbrough 34-36; V 36-50; Baldersby 50-69; Skipton-on-Swale 50-69. *4 Herisson Close, Pickering, N Yorks, YO18 7HB.*

NEWSAM, Rowland. b 1894. Selw Coll Cam BA (3rd cl Th Trip pt i) 22, MA 26. Cudd Coll 22. **d** 23 **p** 24 Man. C of Bolton 23-26; Lect Bolton Chy Estates 25-26; V of St Aug Tonge Moor 26-33; Ch Ch E Coatham 33-43; R of Beeford w Lissett and Dunnington 43-52; RD of N Holderness 49-52; PC of Martindale 52-59. *14 Main Street, Beeford, Driffield, N Humb, YO25 8As.*

NEWSHAM, Richard John. CD 62. Univ of Tor BA 51. Wycl Coll Tor. **d** 51 **p** 52 Tor. C of St Paul Bloor Street Tor 51-54; I of St Andr-by-the-lake Tor 54-55; Hon C of St Thos City and Dio Tor from 55. *115 Torbarrie Road, Downsview, Ont, Canada.*

NEWSOME, John Keith. b 49. Merton Coll Ox BA 73, MA 76. Ripon Coll Cudd 73. **d** 76 **p** 77 Newc T. C of St Pet Bywell 76-78; H Trin Berwick-on-Tweed Dio Newc T from 78. *9 Lovaine Terrace, Berwick-on-Tweed, TD15 1LA.* (Berwick 7317)

NEWSON, John David. b 32. Univ of Southn BSc 53, PhD 57. Cudd Coll 64. **d** 65 Cant **p** 66 Dover for Cant. C of St Greg Gt (All SS from 76) Cant 65-77; Lect Ch Ch Coll Cant 65-80. *124 Queen's Road, Buckhurst Hill, Essex, IG9 5BJ.* (01-505 7748)

NEWSUM, Alfred Turner Paul. b 28. Coll of Resurr Mirfield 52. **d** 53 **p** 54 Llan. C of St German Roath 53-59; St Matt Westmr 59-60; St Mark Washwood Heath Saltley 60-68; C-in-c of St Greg Small Heath 68-78; V of St Aid Small Heath 72-80; Stockland Green Dio Birm from 80. *Vicarage, Bleak Hill Road, Birmingham, B23 7EL.* (021-373 0130)

NEWTH, Barry Wilfred. b 33. Univ of Bris BA 56. ALCD (2nd cl) 58. **d** 58 **p** 59 Ches. C of Upton 58-62; Kimberworth 62-63; V of Clifton 63-72; St Thos (and St John from 74) Radcliffe 72-81; R of Heaton Mersey Dio Man from 81. *15 Priestnall Road, Heaton Mersey, Stockport, SK4 3HR.* (061-432 2165)

NEWTH, Canon Frederick John. Keble Coll Ox BA (2nd cl Th) 28, MA 35. Cudd Coll 28. **d** 30 **p** 31 York. C of St Mary Bishophill Sen York 30-33; Leckhampton 33-38; PC of Wotton St Mary Without 38-48; C-in-c of St Catharine Glouc 42-46; Asst RD of Glouc 46-51; V of St Barn Tuffley Glouc 48-50; R of Springs 50-61; Archd of Heidelberg 57-61; Johann 61-67; Prov Executive Officer in S Afr 67; R of Rosebank 68-74; Hon Can of Johann from 68; L to Offic Dio Johann from 76. *11a-12th Avenue, Parktown North, Johannesburg, Transvaal, S Africa.*

NEWTH, Melville Cooper. Univ of Syd BA 38. Moore Coll Syd ThL 42. **d** 41 **p** 42 Syd. Hd Master of Cathl Choir Sch from 41; C of St Andr Cathl City and Dio Syd 41-47; Prec 47-54; Min Can from 54; L to Offic Dio Syd from 79. *5-7 Hinemoa Avenue, Normanhurst, NSW, Australia 2076.* (48-3094)

NEWTON, Barrie Arthur. b 38. Univ of Dur BA 61. Wells Th Coll 61. **d** 63 Warrington for Liv **p** 64 Liv. C of Walton-on-the-Hill 63-67; King's Lynn 67-69; Asst Chap The Lon Hosp 69-71; Chap K Coll Hosp Lon 72-77; C-in-c of Stowey w Bp's Sutton 77-81; Compton Martin w Ubley 79-81; St Jo Bapt Bridgwater w Chedzoy B & W from 81. *St John's Rectory, Monmouth Street, Bridgwater, Somt.* (Bridgwater 422540)

NEWTON, Brian Karl. b 30. Keble Coll Ox BA (3rd cl Mod Hist) 55, MA 59. Wells Th Coll 56. **d** 58 **p** 59 Carl. C of St Geo Barrow-F 58-61; H Trin Cathl Port of Spain 61-62; R of H Cross Marabella 62-69; Gen Ed USPG 69-71; R of St Sav Curepe and St Jo San Juan Trinid 71-77; Team V of Gt Coates Dio Linc from 77. *St Nicolas Vicarage, Great Coates, Grimsby, Humb.*

NEWTON, Cecil. b 19. St Aid Coll 55. **d** 57 **p** 58 Dur. C of St Andr Monk Wearmouth 57-60; V of St Pet Preston 60-63; Holme Eden 63-73; R of Distington 73-78; L to Offic Dio Win from 78. *5 Marlborough Mansions, Christchurch Road, Bournemouth, BH7 6DR.* (0202 427938)

NEWTON, Canon Christopher Wynne. b 25. Trin Hall Cam 2nd cl Geog Trip pt i 45, BA (2nd cl Th Trip pt i) 46. Westcott Ho Cam 48. **d** 50 **p** 51 Dur. C of Ch Ch Gateshead Dio Dur 50-52; C-in-c of St Clem Miss Labrador 52-55; C of All SS Harrow Weald (in c of St Barn) 55-58; V of Radlett 58-66; RD of St Alb 63-66; V of Hemel Hempstead 66-71; R 71-72; RD of Milton Keynes 72-77; Claydon from 78; Team V in Swan Dio Ox from 78; Hon Can of Ch Ch Cathl Ox from 80; Dioc Ecumen Officer from 79. *Marsh Gibbon Rectory, Bicester, OX6 0AP.* (086 97297)

NEWTON, David Ernest. b 42. Sarum Wells Th Coll 72. **d** 74 Warrington for Liv **p** 75 Liv. C of Wigan 74-80; V Cho of York Minster from 80; Sub-Chanter from 81. *36 High Petergate, York, YO1 2EH.* (York 24159)

NEWTON, Derek Lewis. b 14. K Coll Lon BA 36. Wycl Hall, Ox 54. **d** 55 **p** 56 Chelmsf. C of St John Southend-on-Sea 55-58; Chap of St Paul's Coll Abeokuta Lagos 58-59; Prin of St Pet Coll Kaduna N Nig 60-70; St Paul Coll Zaria 71-72; Kufena Coll Zaria 72-78; C of Woodford Dio Chelmsf from 78. *49b Buckingham Road, Woodford, E18.* (01-505 8157)

NEWTON, Edgar James. b 12. Wells Th Coll 67. **d** 68 **p** 69 Bris. C of Hengrove 68-71; Ch Ch Swindon 71-78; L to Offic Dio B & W from 78. *16 Mullins Way, Ansford, Castle Cary, Somt.* (0963 50058)

NEWTON, Gerald Blamire. b 30. Lich Th Coll. **d** 69 **p** 70 Ripon. C of St Wilfrid Halton 69-73; Gt Yarmouth (in c of St Jas) 73-74; P-in-c of Cattistock w Chilfrome and Rampisham and Wraxall 74-77; V of St Osw Coney Hill Glouc 77-79; Bryneglwys and Llandegla Dio St A from 79; Llanarmon-yn-Ial Dio St A from 80. *Rectory, Llandegla, Wrexham, Clwyd.* (Llandegla 362)

NEWTON, Graham Hayden. b 47. AKC 69. St Aug Coll Cant 70. **d** 70 **p** 71 S'wark. C of St Mary-at-Lambeth 70-73; Team V of Catford (Southend) and Downham 73-78; P-in-c of Porthill 78-79; Team V of Wolstanton Dio Lich from 79. *14 Dorrington Grove, Porthill, Newcastle, ST5 0HY.* (0782 561709)

NEWTON, Canon Harold Leech. Em Coll Sktn BA and LTh 40. **d** 40 **p** 41 Bran. C of Ch Ch Hamiota 40-41; R 41-42; R of Killarney 42-47; RD of Tiger Hills 44-47; R of St Mary Virg Bran 47-52; Can of Bran 49-52; C of H Trin Winnipeg 52-54; I of St Patr Tor 54-60; R of St Jude Winnipeg 60-67; P-in-c of Grace Ch Winnipeg 60-67; R of St Bart Winnipeg 67-74; P Supervisor River N Pars 74-75; Can of Rupld 74-75; Hon Can from 75; P Assoc of St John's Cathl Winnipeg 76-79. *230 Roslyn Road, Winnipeg, Manit, R2L 0H1, Canada.*

NEWTON, Herbert. b 11. St Aid Coll 38. **d** 40 **p** 41 Southw. C of St Chris Sneinton 40-41; Selston 41-46; V of Shireoaks 46-78. *99 Garside Street, Worksop, Notts.*

NEWTON, James William Logan. b 04. ACIS 32, FCIS 35. **d** 61 **p** 62 Derby. C of Bolsover 61-68; C-in-c of St Andr Conv Distr Malvern 68-75. *5 Georgina Avenue, Worcester.* (Worc 425291)

NEWTON, John. b 39. K Coll Lon and Warm AKC 65. **d** 66 **p** 67 Ex. C of Whipton 66-68; Plympton 68-74; R of Lifton 74-81; Kelly w Bradstone 74-81; V of Broadwoodwidger 74-81; Chap All H Sch Ropusdon from 81. *Woodlands, Rousdon, Lyme Regis, Dorset.* (Lyme Regis 5265)

NEWTON, John David. b 48. Montr Dioc Th Coll 73. **d** and **p** 74 Montr. C of St Jas Montr 74-77; R of Good Shepherd Cartierville Montr 7-80; St Jo Bapt Pointe Claire Dio Montr from 80. *233 St Claire Avenue, Pointe Claire, PQ, Canada H9S 4E3.* (514-697 1714)

NEWTON, John Richard. b 25. St Jo Coll Dur 76. **d** 78 **p** 79 York. C of Cottingham 78-80; R of Beeford w Lissett and Dunnington Dio York from 80; Foston-on-the-Wolds Dio York from 80; N Frodingham Dio York from 80. *Beeford Rectory, Driffield, N Humb, YO25 8BA.* (Beeford 320)

NEWTON, Keith. b 52. AKC and BD 73. St Aug Coll Cant 74. **d** 75 **p** 76 Chelmsf. C of St Mary Gt Ilford 75-78; Team V of Wimbledon Dio S'wark from 78. *St Matthew's House, Melbury Gardens, SW20 0DF.* (01-946 0092)

NEWTON, Kenneth. b 24. Open Univ BA 74. STh (Lambeth) 75. St Aid Coll 49. **d** 52 Jarrow for Dur **p** 53 Dur. C of Ch Ch Felling 52-54; PC of St Geo Gateshead 54-56; V of Llanveynoe w Crasswall 56-59; Clodock and Longtown w Crasswall and Llanveynoe 59-61; All S Bolton 61-63; All SS Belize 63-64; R of Failsworth 64-70; V of Frizington 70-76; P-in-c of St Geo Dio Berm 76-77; V from 77. *Parsonage, Chapel of Ease Road, St David's, Bermuda.*

NEWTON, Lloyd Frank. Moore Th Coll Syd 31. **d** 33 Bp Kirkby for Syd **p** 37 Syd. C of St John Bishopthorpe Syd 33-35; Castle Hill w Baulkham Hills and Dural 35-37; R of Emu w Castlereagh 37-40; St Luke Berry 40-47; Denham Court and Rossmore 47-59, Enmore 59-61; Kurrajong 61-71; L to Offic Dio Syd from 71. *73 Shirlow Avenue, Faulconbridge, NSW, Australia 2776.*

NEWTON, Maurice Gray. b 01. Pemb Coll Ox BA 27, MA 29. Ridley Hall, Cam 27. **d** 28 **p** 29 Lon. C of St John W Ealing 28-33; Iver 33-34; St Ebbe Ox 35-36; St Steph Wandsworth 36-39; V of Charsfield 39-44; R of Oldbury 44-48; I of St Jo Evang Chich 49-54; V of Childerditch w L Warley 54-64; R of Gt Easton Essex 64-70. *Chapel Cottage, Bromeswell, Woodbridge, Suff.* (Eyke 354)

NEWTON, Peter. b 35. Sarum Wells Th Coll 74. **d** 77 **p** 78 Reading for Ox. Hon C of St Barn Reading 77-79; C of Bracknell Dio Ox from 79. *St Andrew's House, Priestwood Court Road, Bracknell, Berks, RG2 1TU.* (Bracknell 25229)

NEWTON, Peter. b 39. St Jo Coll Nottm 73. **d** 75 Southw **p** 76 Sherwood for Southw. C of St Jas Porchester Nottm 75-79; R of Wilford Dio Southw from 79. *Wilford Rectory, Nottingham, NG11 7AJ.* (Nottm 815661)

NEWTON, Raymond David. b 43. K Coll Lon BSc 65. Linc Th Coll 65. **d** 67 Dunwich for St E **p** 68 St E. C of St Matt Ipswich 67-71; E w W Barkwith 71-74; R of Chelmondiston w Harkstead (and Shotley w Erwarton from 78) Dio St E from 74; C-in-c of Shotley w Erwarton 75-78. *Chelmondiston Rectory, Ipswich, Suffolk.* (Woolverstone 214)

NEWTON, Richard. b 47. Univ of Lon Dipl Th (Extra-Mural Stud) 72. Trin Coll Bris 72. **d** 73 **p** 74 Portsm. C of St Jo Evang Fareham 73-76; St Mark Cheltm Dio Glouc from 76. *30 Russet Road, Arle, Cheltenham, Glos, GL51 7LW.* (Cheltenham 580496)

NEWTON, Richard Edward. b 1899. Wadh Coll Ox BA (Nat Sc) 22. Wycl Hall Ox 22. **d** 24 Lon for Col **p** 25 Trav. CMS Miss at Kottayam 24-27; Asst Master St Geo Sch Harpenden 27-32; Hd Master Kingsfield Sch Oxhey 32-40; Davenies Sch Beaconsfield 40-68. *Ditton Meads, Pinkneys Green, Maidenhead, Berks.* (Maidenhead 25922)

NEWTON, William Barrett. Moore Th Coll Syd ACT ThL 66. **d** 67 **p** 68 Syd. C of Newtown 67-68; Nowra 68-70; C-in-c of Lurnea 70-73; R of Cleve Cowell and Kimba 74-76; Riverstone Dio Syd from 76. *53 Elizabeth Street, Riverstone, NSW, Australia 2765.* (627-1015)

NEWTON, Canon William Ronald. b 12. Univ of Birm BA (2nd cl Hist) 43. Westcott Ho Cam 41. **d** 43 Birm for Truro **p** 44 Truro. C of St Paul Truro 43-48; PV of Truro Cathl 45-46; PC of Treslothan 48-52; V of Moulsecoomb (w Stanmer and Falmer from 56) 52-63; St Paul Truro 63-73; St Mary w St Paul Penzance Dio Truro from 73; Surr from 66; Hon Can of Truro Cathl from 71. *Vicarage, Chapel Street, Penzance, Cornw, TR18 4AP.* (Penzance 3079)

NEWTON, William Shakespeare. b 1898. St Andr Coll Pampisford, 46. **d** 47 **p** 48 Cov. C of St Geo Cov 47-51; R of Lighthorne 51-59; V of Chesterton 51-59; Butlers Marston w Pillerton Hersey and Pillerton Priors 59-70; RD of Stratford-on-Avon 64-69; Perm to Offic Dio Cov from 70. *4 St James Close, Kissing Tree Lane, Alveston, Stratford-on-Avon.* (Stratford-on-Avon 4609)

NEWTON-SMITH, Jack William. Univ of Tor BA 37. Wycl Coll Tor. **d** 39 **p** 40 Tor. C of St Anne Tor 39-41; I of Medonte 41-45; St Geo Allandale (w St Paul Innisfil and St Pet churchill 45-52) 45-57; St Gabr Richmond Hill 58-61. *106 Durham Street West, Lindsay, Ont, Canada.*

NEY, Ven Reginald Basil. OBE 78. ARCM 55. Lich Th Coll 41. **d** 45 **p** 46 Lich. C of Gnosall w Knightley 45-47; Chap at Gibr and Prec of Gibr Cathl 47-54; Chap and Asst Hosp of St Bart's Hosp Lon 54-59; Chap HBM Embassy Madrid Dio Gibr (Gibr in Eur from 80) from 56; Can of Gibr from 62; Archd from 63; Chap at Algeciras and Bilbao Dio Gibr (Gibr in Eur from 80) from 70. *c/o British Embassy, Madrid, Spain.* (2 745155)

NG, Ho Le. d 24 **p** 27 Sing. P Dio Sing. *14 Brighton Avenue, Singapore 19.*

NG, Peter Danson Kim Yiu. b 46. Trin Coll Sing 67. **d** 71 Kuch. d Dio Kuch. *Box 79, Kuala Belait, Brunei, Malaysia.*

NG, Seng Chuan. Trin Th Coll Sing 73. **d** 77 **p** 78 Sing. P Dio Sing. *St Paul's Church, Upper Serangoon Road, Singapore 1953.*

NGAAGA, Onesifolo. Buwalasi Th Coll. **d** 64 **p** 66 W Bugan. P Dio W Bugan. *PO Box 323, Masaka, Uganda.*

NGACHENGO, Titus Fillipo. b 34. St Phil Coll Kongwa 71. **d** 71 **p** 72 Vic Nyan. P Dio Vic Nyan. *Box 875, Mwanza, Tanzania.*

✠ **NGAHYOMA, Right Rev Maurice Dastan Lazaro.** St Paul's Coll Liuli. St Aug Coll Cant 64. **d** 55 **p** 58 SW Tang. P Dio SW Tang 55-71; Cons Bp of Ruvuma in Pro-Cathl Ch of H Cross Liuli 2 July 71 by Bp of Sw Tang; Bp of Lake Malawi; Asst Bp of Sw Tang; and Bp Thorne; Dean of Ruvuma from 74. *Box 7, Songea, Tanzania.*

✠ **NGALAMU, Most Rev Elinana Jabi. d** 53 **p** 55 Sudan. P Dio Sudan 53-61; Archd of Dinka Moru 61-71; Moru 71-74; Cons Asst Bp in the Sudan in Juba Par Ch 25 Jan 63 by Abp in Jer; Bp in Sudan; and Bp of W Bugan; Apptd Ld Bp in the Sudan 74; Bp of Juba 76; Elected Abp and Metrop of Prov of The Sudan 76. *Box 110, Juba, S Region, Sudan.* (Juba 64)

NGALYA, Gabriel. St Phil Coll Kongwa 71. **d** and **p** 74 Centr Tang. P Dio Centr Tang. *PO Mvumi, Tanzania.*

NGAMA, Ven Amosa Rakpi. b 12. Div Sch Yei. **d** 46 **p** 48 Sudan. P Dio Sudan 47-55; Hon Can of Sudan 55-76; Archd of S Sudan 61-63; Provost of All SS Cathl Juba 63-71; Exam Chap to Bp of Sudan 67-76; R of Nzara Dio Yambio from 76; Archd of Zande-Moru 71; Zande 72-76; Yambio from 77; Can from 77. *ECS, Nzara, Sudan.*

NGANGA, John Patteson. St Pet Coll Siota. **d** 57 **p** 60 Melan. P Dio Melan 57-75; Dio Centr Melan from 75. *Marasa, Guadalcanal, Solomon Islands.*

N'GAN GAM, Yawhan. d 55 **p** 56 Rang. P Dio Rang 55-70; Dio Mand from 70. *Christ Church, Myitkyina, Burma.*

NGANZIYO, Petero Mambere. d 70 Sudan. d Dio Sudan 70-76; Dio Yambio from 76. *ECS, Maridi, Equatoria Province, Sudan.*

NGARACU, Joseph. CMS Div Sch Limuru. **d** 34 U Nile for Momb **p** 39 Momb. P Dio Momb 34-65; Dio Ft Hall 61-62. *Muthiria, PO Box 141, Fort Hall, Kenya.*

NGARAMBE, Zachary Prudence. d 79 Mt Kenya E. d Dio Mt Kenya E. *PO Box 338, Kerugoya, Kenya.*

NGARI, Lazaro. b 27. **d** 78 **p** 79 Mt Kenya E. P Dio Mt Kenya E. *Box 6093, Runyenje's, Kenya.*

NGARINDA, William. Bp Tucker Coll Mukono 62. **d** 63 **p** 65 Ankole-K. P Dio Ankole-K 63-67; Dio Ank from 67. *PO Rwashamaire, Mbarara, Uganda.*

✠ **NGARUIYA, Right Rev Ezbon.** St Paul's Dioc Div Sch Limuru. **d** 43 **p** 45 Momb. P Dio Momb 43-45; and 50-61; Tutor St Paul's Dioc Div Sch Limuru 49-50; P Dio Ft Hall 61-64; Dio Mt Kenya from 64; Can of Cathl Ch of St Jas and Marts Ft Hall 69-72; Cons Asst Bp of Mt Kenya (Mt Kenya S from 75) in Cathl Ch of St Jas Ft Hall 24 June 72 by Abp of Kenya; Bps of Maseno N, Maseno S and Mt Kenya. *PO Box 121, Murang'a, Kenya.*

NGATAI, Mita-Kiwara. b 28. **d** 77 **p** 79 Aotearoa for Wai. C of Nuhaka Past Dio Wai from 77. *PO Box 118, Nuhaka, NZ.*

NGBAGA, Yakobo Sirigi. Bp Gwynne Coll Mundri, 59. **d** 63 **p** 64 Bp Dotiro for Sudan. P Dio Sudan 63-76; Dio Yambio from 76. *ECS, Yambio, Sudan.*

NGBANDIA, Martin Khamis. d 70 **p** 72 Sudan. P Dio Sudan 70-76; Dio Yambio from 76. *ECS, Ibba, Equatoria Province, Sudan.*

NGCAMA, Ashton Nombula. b 17. St Bede's Coll Umtata 79. **d** 79 St John's. d Dio St John's. *St Bede's College, Umtata, Transkei.*

NGCANGCA, Jesse David. St Pet Coll Rosettenville, 56. **d** 58 **p** 59 Grahmstn. P Dio Grahmstn 58-70; Dio Port Eliz from 70. *Box 66, Humansdorp, CP, S Africa.* (04232 379)

NGCOBO, Francis. St Bede's Coll Umtata, 67. **d** 68 **p** 69 Zulu. P Dio Zulu. *PB 523, Nongoma, Zululand.*

NGCONGO, Philip Zebulon. St Pet Coll Rosettenville 46. **d** 48 **p** 50 Natal. P Dio Natal 48-60 and from 64; Dio Zulu 60-64. *c/o Stoffelton School, Impendhle, Natal, S Africa.*

NGELEOKA, Emmanuel Onyeabo. b 40. Trin Coll Umuahia 73. **d** 75 **p** 76 Aba. P Dio Aba 75-80. *c/o St Luke's Parsonage, Olokoro, Umuahia, Nigeria.*

NGEMA, Isaac. St Pet Coll Alice. **d** 69 **p** 70 Zulu. P-in-c of Ch K Ngutu 70-72; Perm to Offic Dio Zulu from 72. *Box 4, Nquthu, via Dundee, Natal, S Africa.*

NGENDANZI, Timoteo. Warner Th Coll Buye 64. **d** 66 **p** 67 Bur. P Bur 66-75. *Nyabigina, DS 12, Bujumbura, Burundi.*

NGERE, Amuzai Paris. Bp Gwynne Coll Mundri 61. **d** 62 **p** 63 Sudan. P Dio Sudan 62-76; Dio Rumbek from 76. *ECS, Lui, Sudan.*

NGEWU, Alban Bansil Vuyisile. St Bede's Coll Umtata, 63. **d** 64 **p** 65 St John's. P Dio St John's. *Box 299, Mount Frere, Transkei, S Africa.*

NGEWU, Canon Cameron Kenati. St Bede's Coll Umtata 23. **d** 24 **p** 28 St Jo Kaffr. P Dio St Jo Kaffr 24-60; Dio St John's 60-66; L to Offic Dio St John's from 66; Can of St John's Cathl Umtata 55-66; Can (Emer) from 66; Archd of Centr Transkei 57-66. *St Mary's Mission, Qanqu, Qumbu, Transkei, S Africa.* (Qanqu 3)

NGEWU, Livingstone Lubabalo. b 50. St Bede's Coll Umtata 73. **d** 74 **p** 76 St John's. P Dio St John's 74-80; on leave. *Fort Hare University, Fort Hare, Transkei, S Africa.*

NGEWU, Zulu Zachariah Brownlee. St Bede's Coll Umtata 47. **d** 48 **p** 50 St Jo Kaffr. P Dio St Jo Kaffr 50-60; Dio St John's from 60. *Box 82, Bizana 4800, Transkei, S Africa.* (Redoubt 5)

NGHAMBI, Obadia. b 58. St Phil Coll Kongwa 79. **d** 81 Centr Tang. d Dio Centr Tang. *PO Kikomba, Tanzania.*

NGIKA, Musa. b 39. **d** 75 **p** 77 Vic Nyan. P Dio Vic Nyan. *PO Box 44, Chato, Tanzania.*

NGIMAH, Andrew. **d** 75 **p** 77 Ruw. P Dio Ruw. *Box 37, Fort Portal, Uganda.*

NGIRIRIMANA, Joseph. b 42. St Paul's Coll Limuru 71. **d** 75 Boga-Z **p** 77 Bukavu. P Dio Bukavu. *BP 2876, Bukavu, Zaire.*

NGOBESE, Wilmot Ronala. St Pet Coll Alice. **d** 67 **p** 70 Zulu. C of Maphophoma 67-70; Natalspruit 70-74; Senaoane 74-76; R of Wesselton 76-80; Vosloorus Dio Johann from 80. *Box 12140, Rusloo 1468, Transvaal, S Africa.*

NGODWANE, Canon Elijah Ngqele. St Pet Coll Alice, 63. **d** 65 **p** 66 Grahmstn. P Dio Grahmstn; Can of Grahmstn from 79. *PO Box 161, Ezibeleni, Transkei, S Africa.*

NGOLIGA, Elieza. **d** 64 **p** 65 Centr Tang. P Dio Centr Tang. *Chamkoloma, Dodoma, Tanzania.*

NGOMBANE, Arthur John. **d** 77 **p** 79 St John's (APM). P Dio St John's. *PO Box 44, Ugie 5470, S africa.*

NGOMBANE, Gladwyn. **d** 77 **p** 79 St John's (APM). P Dio St John's. *Private Bag X5009, Umtata, Transkei.*

NG'ONJA, Gilead. **d** 69 **p** 70 Centr Tang. P Dio Centr Tang. *DCT Lamaiti, PO Mundemu, Tanzania.*

NGOOBI, Livingstone. b 42. **d** 77 Nam. d Dio Nam. *c/o Namirembe Cathedral, PO Box 14297, Kampala, Uganda.*

NGOTA, Simeon Obululu. b 39. **d** 74 **p** 76 Maseno N. P Dio Maseno N. *PO Box 4, Nambale, Kenya.*

NGOYI, Philemon Perry. **d** 65 St John's. d Dio St John's. *Readsdale School, Cooper Store, PO Glencarry, Transkei, S Africa.*

NGQUMEYA, Daniel Matthew Molifi. b 43. St Pet Coll Alice 68. **d** 70 Bp Carter for Johann **p** 71 Johann. C of Daveyton 70-73; R of Wattville 74-77; Lichtenburg Dio Johann from 77. *Box 745, Lichtenburg, Transvaal, S Africa.*

NGRIRIMANA, Joseph Mohr. b 47. St Paul's Coll Limuru 74. **d** 74 Boga-Z. d Dio Boga-Z. *BP 154, Bunia, Zaire.*

NGUBANE, Emmanuel Victor. St Bede's Coll Umtata, 57. **d** 58 **p** 60 Natal. P Dio Natal 58-80; Archd Dio Natal 79-80. *c/o Box 224, Ntokozweni, Natal, S Africa.*

NGUBANE, Jotham. Coll of Resurr Rosettenville, 39. **d** 42 **p** 43 Zulu. C of St Aug Nqutu 42-44; St Alb Mvunyane 44-47; St Paul Nkwenkwe 47-48; Lansdowne Miss 48-52; Empangeni 52-55. *Heatonville, Zululand.*

NGUBANE, Mdaluyazi Nkosingiphile Theophilus. St Pet Coll Alice LTh 66. **d** 65 Grahmstn for Zulu **p** 67 Zulu. P Dio Zulu. *PO Box 14, Blood River, via Dundee, S Africa.*

NGUGHU, Naftali. St Phil Coll Kongwa 81. **d** 79 **p** 80 Centr Tang. P Dio Centr Tang. *PO Mundemu, Tanzania.*

NGUMA, Timothy. **d** 66 **p** 67 Momb. P Dio Momb. *Box 72, Mombasa, Kenya.*

NGUNDA, Barnaba. b 34. St Cypr Coll Rondo 69. **d** 72 **p** 73 Abp Sepeku for Masasi. P Dio Masasi. *PB Masasi, Mtwara Region, Tanzania.*

NGUNDU, Ehasaph. **d** 74 **p** 75 Ank. P Dio Ank 74-76; Dio E Ank from 76. *PO Kikagate, Mbarara, Uganda.*

NGUNI, James. **d** 78 Nak. d Dio Nak. *c/o Box 244, Nakuru, Kenya.*

NG'URWEGI, Fesoto. Bp Tucker Coll Mukono. **d** 56 Ugan **p** 58 Bp Balya for Ugan. P Dio Ugan 56-60; Dio Nam from 60. *Anglican Church, Kakira, Uganda.*

NG'WANZANOGU, Samson. b 14. **d** 76 **p** 77 Vic Nyan. P Dio Vic Nyan. *PO Box 2246, Mwanza, Tanzania.*

NGWATI, Arthur Mbaka. Weithaga Bible Sch 60. **d** 61 Ft Hall. d Dio Ft Hall 61-64; Dio Mt Kenya from 64. *All Saints' Church, Limuru, Kenya.*

NGWENYA, Jabula Jimmy. St Bede's Coll Umtata. **d** 62 **p** 64 Natal. P Dio Natal 62-68; Dio Swaz from 68. *c/o PO Box 741, Manzini, Swaziland,*

NGWESO, Emmanuel Malili. b 45. St Phil Coll Kongwa 70. **d** 72 **p** 73 Vic Nyan. P Dio Vic Nyan. *Box 40, Sengerema, Geita, Tanzania.*

NHAGUIOMBE, Canon Roberto. **d** 50 **p** 51 Lebom. P Dio Lebom from 50; Hon Can of Lebom from 65. *Caixa Postal 56, Inhambane, via Lourenço Marques, Mozambique.*

NHAGUMBE, Jose Chamuce. St Mark's Coll Dar-S 75. **d** 79 **p** 80 Lebom. P Dio Lobom. *CP 57, Maputo, Mozambique.*

NHAQUILE, Pedro Roberto. **d** 79 **p** 81 Lebom. P Dio Lebom. *CP 56, Maxixe, Mozambique.*

NHEMA, Daniel. St Jo Coll Lusaka, 56. **d** 58 **p** 60 Mashon. P Dio Mashon. *St Werburgh's Mission, Post Box 43, Umtali, Rhodesia.*

NHONYA, Yusto Asheri. St Phil Coll Kongwa, 62. **d** and **p** 65 Bp Madinda for Centr Tang. P Dio Moro 65-80. *Berega, PO Kilosa, Tanzania.*

NHUKUWALA, Eliya Tadayo. St Phil Coll Kongwa. **d** 65 **p** 66 Centr Tang. P Dio Centr Tang. *Box 233, Dodoma, Tanzania.*

NIA NIA, Huatahi. b 38. **d** 77 **p** 78 Aotearoa for Wai. C of Turanga Past Dio Wai from 77. *PO Te Hapara, Gisborne, NZ.*

NIAGARA, Lord Bishop of. *See* Bothwell, Right Rev John Charles.

NIAGARA, Suffragan Bishop of. *See* Mitchell, Right Rev Clarence Malcolm.

NIAGARA, Dean of. *See* Fricker, Very Rev Joachim Carl.

NIAS, John Charles Somerset. b 18. Worc Coll Ox BA (2nd cl Th) 40, MA 45, BD 46. Wells Th Coll 40. **d** 41 Bp Kitching for Portsm **p** 42 Portsm. C of St Mary Portsea 41-44; L to Offic Dio St A 44-46; Chap of Heswall Nautical Sch 44-46; C of St Barn Northolt Park 46-47; R of Blandford St Mary 47-54; Sec Gen of Oratory of the Good Shepherd 50-52; R of Bryanston 52-54; V of Uttoxeter w Bramshall 54-56; PC (V from 68) of Ramsden Dio Ox from 56; V of Finstock Dio Ox from 56; C-in-c of Wilcote Dio Ox from 56; Dir of Stud C of E Bd of Educn Study Centre (Centr Readers Bd from 63) from 61. *Ramsden Vicarage, Oxford.* (Ramsden 394)

NIASSA, Bishop of. *See* Litumbe, Right Rev Paulo Swithun.

NIBLETT, David John Morton. b 24. Wells Th Coll 51. **d** 54 **p** 55 Lon. C of St Dunstan w All SS Stepney 54-59; V of Syston 59-65; St Pet w H Trin Barnstaple 65-75; S Brent Dio Ex from 75. *Church House, South Brent, Devon.* (S Brent 3247)

NIBLOCK, David Hale Alt. St Jo Coll Auckld. **d** 41 **p** 42 Auckld. C of Takapuna 41-45; P-in-c of Hauraki Plains 45; Actg C of Pukekohe 46; V of Kaitaia 46-49; Waitara 49-52; Woodville 52-57; C of Cam 57-60; Thames 60-62; V of Pukekohe 62-64; L to Offic Dio Wai from 64. *9 Kowhai Street, Tauranga, NZ.*

NIBLOCK, Peter Armour. Univ of Tor BA 51. Wycl Coll Tor LTh and BTh 58, BD 61. **d** 58 Tor for Rupld **p** 58 Rupld. C of St Geo Winnipeg 58-61; R of Transcona 61-65; St Mark Calg 65-72; on leave 72-73; C of St Mary Kerrisdale Vanc Dio New Westmr from 74. *2490 West 37th Avenue, Vancouver, BC, Canada.*

NICE, John Edmund. b 51. Univ Coll of N Wales (Bangor) BA 73. Coll of Resurr Mirfield 74. **d** 76 **p** 77 Ches. C of St Sav Oxton 76-79; St Mary Liscard Dio Ches from 79. *28 Denton Drive, Wallasey, Wirral, Mer.* (051-639 9913)

NICHOLAS, Brian Arthur. b 19. St Edm Hall Ox BA 47, MA 53. Wycl Hall Ox 62. **d** 64 **p** 65 Ox. C of Gerrard's Cross 64-66; Ch Ch Reading 66-69; V of Chudleigh Knighton w Heathfield 69-76; St Mark City and Dio Ex from 76. *36 Polsloe Road, Exeter, EX1 2DN.* (Ex 56478)

NICHOLAS, Gwynfryn Lloyd. Univ of Wales, BA (2nd cl Lat) 39. St D Coll Lamp 39. **d** 40 **p** 41 Llan. C of Dowlais 40-44; Llantrisant 44-49; Eglwysilan 49-54; Cadoxton-juxta-Neath 54-56; V of Llandyfodwg 56-66; C of Roath 66-68. *8 Llanina Grove, Trowbridge Estate, Rumney, Cardiff, S Glam.*

NICHOLAS, Herbert Llewellyn. b 19. St D Coll Lamp 51. **d** 53 **p** 54 Llan. C of Merthyr Tydfil 53-65; V of St Matt Pontypridd Dio Llan from 65. *Vicarage, Hospital Road, Pontypridd, Mid Glam.* (Pontypridd 402671)

NICHOLAS, Maurice Lloyd. b 30. Kelham Th Coll 54. **d** 58 **p** 59 Lon. C of Stepney 58-60; St Jo Bapt Sevenoaks 60-65; Chap RADD 65-75; C of Northolt (in c of St Hugh) Dio Lon from 75. *12 Crawford Gardens, Northolt, Middx.* (01-578 0663)

NICHOLAS, Patrick. b 37. Selw Coll Cam 3rd cl Econ Trip pt i 58, BA (2nd cl Th Trip pt ii) 60, MA 65. Wells Th

Coll 60. **d** 62 **p** 63 S'wark. C of Camberwell 62-63; Warlingham w Chelsham and Farleigh 63-65; Oxted 65-68; Chap St John's Cathl Hong 68-74; C of St Mary Portsea 75. *Address temp unknown.*

NICHOLAS, Paul James. b 51. St D Coll Lamp Dipl Th 73. Coll of Resurr Mirfield 73. **d** 74 **p** 75 St D. C of St Paul Llanelly 74-78; Roath Dio Llan from 78. *St Philip's House, Cairnmuir Road, Tremorfa, Cardiff, S Glam.* (0222-24600)

NICHOLAS, Samuel Richard Stephen. MBE 57. Fourah Bay Coll BA 21, Dipl Th 22, MA 24. **d** 45 Lagos **p** 45 Bp Akinyele for Lagos. Prin of Ijebu Ode Gr Sch 46-58; L to Offic Dio Accra from 58. *c/o Christ Church House, Cape Coast, Ghana.*

NICHOLAS, Trevor Graeme. b 53. Univ of Otago BSc 74. St Jo Coll Auckld 77. **d** 77 **p** 78 Dun. C of H Trin Gore 77-79; V of Wyndham Dio Dun from 79. *Vicarage, Redan Street, Wyndham, NZ.* (345)

NICHOLAS, William Ronald. b 06. St D Coll Lamp BA 28. Wells Th Coll 28. **d** 29 **p** 31 St D. C of H Trin Aberystwyth 29-31; Tenby w Gumfreston 31-36; R of St Lawr w Ford 36-42; V of Lamphey w Hodgeston 42-53; Johnston w Steynton 53-74. *Address temp unknown.*

NICHOLL, John Hawdon. b 41. GRSM 63. Ex Coll Ox BA 66, MA 71. Cudd Coll 74. **d** 75 **p** 76 Ripon. C of Headingley 75-78; V of Hawksworth Wood w Moor Grange Dio Ripon from 78. *St Mary's Vicarage, Cragside Walk, Leeds, LS5 3QE.* (Horsforth 582923)

NICHOLL, Joseph Edward Chancellor. b 20. MC 45. Qu Coll Cam BA 46, MA 48. Ridley Hall Cam. **d** 48 **p** 49 Roch. C of St Jo and Ch Ch Penge 48-50; Chap Sutton Valence Sch 50-59; Asst Chap Stowe Sch 59-60; Chap 60-62; Asst Chap and Ho Master 62-72; Chap 72-75; C-in-c of Stowe 75-81; R of Angmering w Ham & Bargham Dio Chich from 82. *Rectory, Angmering, W Sussex, BN16 4JU.* (Rustington 4979)

NICHOLL, Samuel Amos. **d** 40 **p** 41 Ch Ch. C of St Albans 40-42; Lyttelton 42-44; Offg Min Ch Ch 48-52; V of Chatham Is 52-60; L to Offic Dio Ch Ch from 60. *396 Port Hills Road, Hillsborough, Christchurch 2, NZ.*

NICHOLLS, Alan Fryer. Univ Coll Ex BA (3rd cl Cl) 50. Sarum Th Coll 50. **d** 52 **p** 53 Sarum. C of Wootton Bassett 52-55; Chesterfield 55-56; V of Ringley 56-60; PV of Chich Cathl and Chap and Asst Master of Prebendal Sch 60-63; V of Selmeston w Alciston 63-65; Chap Woodbridge Sch 65-66; Ho Master and Asst Chap from 66; L to Offic Dio St E from 80. *School House, Woodbridge School, Woodbridge, Suff.* (Woodbridge 3118)

NICHOLLS, Charles Geoffrey William. Late Scho of St Jo Coll Cam BA 47, MA 49. Norrisian Pri 50. Wells Th Coll 51. **d** 52 **p** 53 Ox. C of Wendover 52-55; Chap Angl Studs in Edin 55-60; Assoc Prof St Jo Coll Winnipeg 60-61; Prof of Relig Stud Univ of BC from 61; L to Offic Dio New Westmr from 61. *3670 West 34 Avenue, Vancouver 13, BC, Canada.*

NICHOLLS, David Gwyn. Univ of Lon BSc (1st cl Econ) 57. K Coll Cam PhD 62. Yale Univ STM 62. Univ of Ox MA (Special Decree) 73. Chich Th Coll 61. **d** 62 **p** 63 Lon. C of Bloomsbury 62-66; Lect Univ of the W Indies 66-73; L to Offic Dio Trinid 70-73; Chap, Lect and Fell of Ex Coll Ox 73-78; P-in-c of Littlemore Dio Ox from 78. *Vicarage, St Nicholas Road, Littlemore, Oxford, OX4 4PP.* (Ox 773738)

NICHOLLS, Derek Frederick. Em Coll Sktn 65. **d** 65 Edmon **p** 66 Chelmsf. C of All SS Cathl Edmon 65-66; Saffron Walden 66-67; Aveley 67-68; Basingstoke (in c of St Pet) 68-71; R of Elsa 71-73; Carmacks 73-75; St D Powell River 75-80; Westlock Dio Edmon from 80. *Box 935, Westlock, Alta, Canada.*

NICHOLLS, John. b 43. K Coll Lon and Warm AKC 66. **d** 67 **p** 68 Man. C of St Clem w St Cypr Salford 67-69; All SS and Marts Langley 69-72; V 72-78; Dir of Past Studs Coll of the Resurr Mirfield from 78. *College of the Resurrection, Mirfield, W Yorks.*

NICHOLLS, John Gervase. b 15. Qu Coll Cam BA 38, MA 42. Lon Coll of Div 38. **d** 39 **p** 40 Lon. C of St Steph E Twickenham 39-43; Youth Org Dio S'wark 43-45; V of St Mary Summerstown 45-50; PC of St Francis Sarum 50-57; Lect St Paul Durban 57-59; Can Res and V of All SS Cathl Nairobi 59-63; Archd of Nairobi 61-63; V of Herne Bay 63-67; Archd in Cyprus 67-75; Chap at Nicosia 67-75; R of St Clem w H Trin Ipswich 75-81; Commiss Cyprus from 76; P-in-c of Wilby w Brundish Dio St E from 81. *Wilby Rectory, Diss, Norfolk.* (Stradbroke 333)

NICHOLLS, John Glasson. b 18. Edin Th Coll 50. **d** 52 St Andr **p** 53 Edin for St Andr. C of St Pet Kirkcaldy 52-54; CF (TA) from 53; C of Newark 54-55; C-in-c of Conv Distr of St Jo Bapt Carlton Colwick 55-58; V 58-60; Camberwell 60-68; R of St Mary Woolnoth Lon 68-74; Chap to HM the Queen at HM Tower Lon from 68; to Ld Mayor of Lon 72-73; R of Chiddingfold Dio Guildf from 74. *Rectory, Chiddingfold, Surrey, GU8 4QA.* (Wormley 2008)

NICHOLLS, Leonard Samuel. b 07. Ex Coll Ox BA (2nd cl Mod Hist) 29, MA 34. Bps' Coll Cheshunt 30. **d** 32 **p** 33 Guildf. C of All SS Headley Hants 32-34; St Gabr Warwick Square 34-41; C of Haslemere (in c of St Chris) 41-49; R of Monken Hadley 49-54; C of Bletchingley 54-60; Uckfield of Horsted Parva and of Isfield 60-61; Waldron 61-65; Durrington 67-68; Etwall w Egginton 68-71. *Old Post House, Framfield, Uckfield, Sussex.*

NICHOLLS, Michael Stanley. K Coll Lon and Warm AKC 59. **d** 60 **p** 61 Ex. C of St Martin's Conv Distr Barton 60-63; St Mary Virg E Grinstead 63-66; Min of Ch K Eccles Distr Salfords 66-68; V 68-75; V of St Barn Tunbridge Wells Dio Roch from 75. *31 Lansdowne Road, Tunbridge Wells, Kent.* (Tunbridge Wells 23609)

NICHOLLS, Prestonia Delisle. Codr Coll Barb 66. **d** 69 **p** 70 Barb. C of St Leon Barb 69-70; St Geo Barb 70-72; All S I and Dio Barb from 72. *Husbands, St Michael, Barbados, W Indies.*

NICHOLLS, Raymond Arthur Bertram. St Columb's Hall Wang ACT ThL 41. **d** 40 **p** 41 Wang. C of Holy Trin Cathl Wang 40-42; P-in-c of St Steph Rutherglen 42-43; Miss Dio New Guinea 43-50; P-in-c of Mukawa 44-49; Eroro 49-50; Cobram 50-51; Prin of St Paul's Home for Boys Newhaven Philip Is 51-52; I of Inverleigh w Meredith 52-54; R of Proserpine 54-56; Marceba 56-58; Yea 58-60; L to Offic Dio Brisb 60-63; CF (Austr) 60-62; I of St Luke Frankston E 62-68; Perm to Offic Dio Melb from 70. *10 Discon Street, Mentone, Vic, Australia 3194.* (90-7438)

NICHOLLS, Richard. b 09. Keble Coll Ox BA 30, MA 35. Ely Th Coll 31. **d** 32 **p** 34 Lich. C of All SS Leek 32-37; Blakenall Heath 37-41; C-in-c of Marchington w Marchington Woodlands 41-46; V of Foxt w Whiston 46-51; R of Marston Montgomery w Cubley 51-58; C of Middleton-by-Wirksworth 59-65. *Address temp unknown.*

NICHOLLS, Robert William. b 10. Univ of Lon BA 31. AKC 33. St Steph Ho Ox 33. **d** 33 **p** 34 Lon. C of St Etheldreda Fulham 33-37; All SS Sidley 37-39; Horsham 39-49; C-in-c & Seq of St Patr Hove 49-58; V of St Matthias Preston 58-69; Barnham 69-71. *Old Rectory Cottage, Worth, Crawley, W Sussex, RH10 4RT.* (Crawley 883193)

NICHOLLS, Stanley Charles. b 28. St Chad's Coll Dur BA (2nd cl Th) 53. Bp's Coll Cheshunt 53. **d** 54 York **p** 55 Selby for York. C of St Thos Middlesbrough 54-59; Hornsea 59-60; V of Newington 60-62; Liverton 62-68; Ruswarp w Sneaton 68-78; Kirkby-in-Cleveland Dio York from 78. *Vicarage, Kirkby-in-Cleveland, Middlesbrough, TS9 7AQ.* (0642 712394)

NICHOLLS, Stephen Frank Sergius. Univ of Tas BA 68. Ch Coll Hobart 64. **d** 68 **p** 69 Tas. P-in-c of Risdon Vale Miss Distr 69-75; R of St Mary Magd City and Dio Adel from 75. *144 Wright Street, Adelaide, S Australia 5000.* (08-223 2521)

NICHOLLS, Trevor. b 42. Univ of Leic BA (2nd cl Hist) 64. Tyndale Hall Bris 65. **d** 67 **p** 68 Southw. C of Lenton 67-68; Attenborough w Chilwell 68-70; St Mary Ealing 70-72; R of Parkham w Alwington 72-75; C-in-c of Buckland Brewer 73-75; Asst Master Oaklands Sch Waterlooville 75-81; St Greg Comprehensive Sch Tunbridge Wells from 81. *c/o St Gregory's Comprehensive School, Tunbridge Wells, Kent.*

✠ **NICHOLLS, Right Rev Vernon Sampson.** b 17. Clifton Th Coll 38. **d** and **p** 41 Bris. C of St Osw Bedminster Down 41-42; St Martin Liskeard w St Keyne 42-44; CF (EC) 44-46; Hon CF 46; V of Meopham 46-56; RD of Cobham 54-56; V of Walsall RD of Walsall 56-67; Surr 56-67; Chap Walsall Gen Hosp 56-67; Preb of Curborough in Lich Cathl 64-67; Archd of Birm 67-74; Proc Conv Birm 67-74; Cons Ld Bd of S & M in York Minster 11 June 74 by Abp of York; Bps of Ripon, Wakef, Southw, Sheff, Carl, Birm, Lich and Derby; Bps Suffr of Jarrow, Stockport, Burnley, Penrith, Pontefract, Selby, Doncaster, Birkenhead and Aston; and others; Dean of St German's Cathl Peel from 74. *Bishop's House, Quarterbridge Road, Douglas, IM.* (Douglas 0624 22108)

NICHOLS, Alan Charles. Moore Th Coll ACT ThL (2nd cl) 61. **d** 61 Bp Kerle for Syd **p** 62 Syd. C of Kingsgrove 61-64; Padstow w Revesby 64-65; C-in-c of St D w St John Greenacre 65-67; R of Wentworthville 68-70; Ch Information Officer Syd 70-73; Dir 73-77; R of St Steph Newtown 74-77; I of St Jas Old Cathl and Missr St Jas and St John Miss City and Dio Melb from 78. *8/12 Batman Street, Melbourne West, Australia 3003.* (329 6133)

NICHOLS, Albert Percival. b 18. Tyndale Hall Bris. **d** and **p** 57 Moos. C of Kirkland Lake 57; P-in-c of Bourlamaque 57-59; C of Attenborough w Bramcote and Chilwell (in c of St Pet Toton) 59-60; R of E Chinnock 60-77; Middle Chinnock (w W Chinnock from 70) 60-78; C-in-c of W Chinnock 60-70; RD of Martock 75-78; R of Norton-sub-Hamdon w Chiselborough, W Chinnock and Middle Chinnock Dio B &

W from 78. *Middle Chinnock Rectory, Crewkerne, Somt, TA18 7PN.* (Chiselborough 202)

NICHOLS, Anthony Howard. Univ of Syd BA 59. Moore Th Coll Syd ACT ThL 66. BD (2nd cl) Lon 67. **d** 66 **p** 67 Syd. C of Chatswood 67; Tutor Moore Th Coll Syd 68-72; CMS Miss Indonesia from 72. *Fakultas Theologia, Universitas IKIP, Kristen-satya, Jateng, Indonesia.*

NICHOLS, Barry Edward. b 40. SOC. **d** 69 **p** 70 S'wark. Hon C of Surbiton Dio S'wark from 69. *32 Corkran Road, Surbiton, Surrey, KT6 6PN.* (01-390 3032)

NICHOLS, Charles Philip. b 37. K Coll Lon and Warm 60. **d** 65 **p** 66 Portsm. C of Leigh Pk 65-68; M SSF 68-69; Betong 69-71; Boianai 71-72; Kingston-T 73-77; Ch Ch S Ashford (in c of St Francis) 77-81; Team V of Quidenham Dio Nor from 81. *Banham Rectory, Norwich, Norf, NR16 2HN.* (Quidenham 562)

NICHOLS, David Stanley. b 38. St Barn Coll Adel 70. **d** 72 **p** 73 Wang. C of Shepparton 72-74; R of Myrtleford 74-77; Numurkah Dio Wang from 77. *Rectory, Numurkah, Vic, Australia 3636.* (058 621048)

NICHOLS, Dennis Harry. b 25. Kelham Th Coll 47. **d** 52 **p** 53 Pet. C of Oakham 52-55; St Mary Virg Kettering 55-57; PC of St Paul Spalding 57-61; V of H Trin Bury 61-81; St Gluvias Dio Truro from 81. *St Gluvias Vicarage, Penryn, Cornw.* (Penryn 73356)

NICHOLS, Frank Bernard. b 43. Kelham Th Coll 64. **d** 68 St Alb **p** 69 Hertf for Cant. C of St Andr Luton 68-72; Cheshunt 72-76; Min of H Cross Conv Distr Marsh Farm Luton Dio St Alb from 76. *40 Purway Close, Marsh Farm, Luton, LU3 3RT.* (Luton 55757)

NICHOLS, Ian David. Univ of Tor BA 61. Wycl Coll Tor LTh and BTh 64. **d** 64 **p** 65 Fred. C of Ch Ch St Anne's and of St Marg Fred 64-67; R of Stanley 67-72; C of St Wilfrid Islington Tor 72-74; R of St Nich Birch Cliff Tor 74-78. *1512 Kingston Road, Scarborough, Ont., Canada.*

NICHOLS, Matthew William Hardwicke. b 04. St D Coll Lamp BA 26. Wells Th Coll 28. **d** 28 **p** 29 Swan B. C of Ch Ch Swansea 28-32; Chap HM Pris Swansea 30-32; C of St Andr Worthing 32-37; PV of Truro Cathl and Chap Truro Cathl Sch 37-38; Perm to Offic at St Jude-on-the-Hill Hampstead Garden Suburb 38-39; R of Clapham w Patching 39-46; St Paul San Fernando 46-49; PC of Ambergate 50-53; Chap Hostel of God Clapham Common 53-54; V of St Aug w St Steph Haggerston 54-59; P-in-c of Aruba Antig 59-62; V of St Thos Huddersfield 64-75; Chap St Marg Conv Aber 75-78. *22 The Quadrangle, Newland, Malvern, WR13 5AX.*

NICHOLS, Canon Paul Randolph Shalders. b 1891. Ball Coll Ox BA 13, MA 17. Cudd Coll 14. **d** 16 **p** 17 Ox. C of All SS Wokingham 16-18; St Jas (w c of St Phil Miss) Edin 18-19; St Pet Eaton Sq 19-21; St Mich Chester Sq Lon 21-25; V of St Mich AA w All SS Paddington 25-31; St Jo Evang Paddington 31-41; R of Chatham 41-43; V of Gt Crosby 43-59; RD of Bootle 48-59; Can Dioc of Liv 55-59; Can (Emer) from 66; V of Sancreed 59-61; R of Sennen 61-63. *2 Raven Meols Lane, Formby, Mer.*

NICHOLS, Raymond Maurice. b 22. ALCD 53. **d** 53 **p** 54 Liv. C of Childwall 53-56; Chap at Mt Kenya 56-60; Dir of Relig Educn Prov of E Afr 60-64; C of St Mark Nairobi 60-64; Home Sec SPCK 64-71; Overseas Sec 67-73; Publisher 73-74; L to Offic Dio Lon 64-74; P-in-c of Dorchester-on-Thames w Berinsfield 74-78; Newington 77-78; R of Dorchester Dio Ox from 78; V of Warborough Dio Ox from 78. *Rectory, Dorchester-on-Thames, Oxon, OX9 8HZ.* (Oxford 340007)

NICHOLS, Robert Oswald. St Barn Coll Adel 47. ACT ThL 49. **d** 50 **p** 51 Adel. C of Hindmarsh 50-52; Miss Chap Plympton 52-53; C of Mt Gambier 53; P-in-c of Kangaroo I 53-57; R of Clare 57-61; Yankalilla 61-74; Lyndoch Dio Adel from 74. *Rectory, Lyndoch, S Australia 5351.* (08-524 4022)

NICHOLSON, Brian Warburton. b 44. ALCD 73 (LTh from 74). St Jo Coll Nottm 70. **d** 73 **p** 74 Sarum. C of Canford Magna 73-77; St Steph E Twickenham 77-80; V of St John Colchester Dio Chelmsf from 80. *St John's Vicarage, Evergreen Drive, Colchester, Essex.* (Colchester 843232)

NICHOLSON, Cyril William. b 09. ALCD 35. **d** 35 **p** 36 Chelmsf. C of St Chad Chadwell Heath 35-37; H Trin Bris 37-39; Becontree 39-40; Waltham Abbey (in c of St Thos Upshire) 40-46; C of Battle 46-49; V of St Paul Sheerness 49-62; Chap of HM Pris Eastchurch 50-62; V of H Trin Sittingbourne 62-75. *29 Ashley Close, Minster, Sheppey, Kent, ME12 3ED.*

NICHOLSON, Cyrus Elephint. d 75 **p** 77 Ja (APM). C of Port Maria Dio Ja from 75. *Box 43, Port Maria, Jamaica, WI.*

NICHOLSON, Canon Donald. b 10. St Chad's Coll Dur BA (2nd cl Hist) and De Bury Scho 32, Jenkyns Scho 33, Dipl Th (w distinc) 34, MA 35. **d** 33 **p** 34 Dur. C of H Trin Darlington 33-36; St Steph S Kens 36-39; St Martin Ruislip 39-43; Beaconsfield (in c of St Mich) 43-46; Missr of Conv Distr of St Mich Beaconsfield 46-47; V of St Barn Ox 47-55; Proc Conv Ox 55-56; Vice-Prin Edin Th Coll 56-64; Commiss New Guinea 56-71; V of St Mary Virg Pimlico 64-71; Hon Chap St Mary's Cathl Edin 56-64; Hon Can from 64; Chap Stacklands Retreat Ho 71-75; Hon Chap 75-80; Perm to Offic Dios Edin from 75; Aber & Moray from 80; Chap St Marg Conv Aber from 80. *St Margaret's Convent, 17 Spital, Aberdeen, AB2 3HT.* (0224 638407)

NICHOLSON, Ernest Wilson. b 38. TCD BA (1st cl Mod) 60, MA 64. Wolfson Coll Cam MA (by incorp) 67, BD 71. Pemb Coll Cam DD 78. Univ of Glas PhD 64. Westcott Ho Cam 69. **d** 69 Huntingdon for Ely **p** 70 Ely. [f Lect in Or Lang TCD 62-67] Lect in Div Univ of Cam 67-79; Fell, Chap and Dir of Th Stud Pemb Coll Cam from 69; Dean 73-78; Or Prof of the Interpretation of H Script Ox from 79. *Oriel College, Oxford.*

NICHOLSON, Gary Roy. b 51. Univ of Syd BA. Moore Th Coll Syd BD, ThL. **d** 81 Syd. C of H Trin Panania Dio Syd from 81. *37 Fromelles Avenue, Milperra, NSW, Australia 2214.*

NICHOLSON, George Edward. b 32. St D Coll Lamp BA 54, LTh 56. **d** 56 **p** 57 Mon. C of Llanhilleth 56-58; C-in-c of Nantyglo 58-60; V 60-66; CMS Area Sec Dios Nor and St E 66-77; P-in-c of Potter Heigham Dio Nor from 77; Repps w Bastwick Dio Nor from 77. *Potter Heigham Vicarage, Great Yarmouth, Norf.* (Potter Heigham 779)

NICHOLSON, George Henry. b 1895. Lon Coll of Div 28. **d** 30 **p** 31 Chelmsf. C of Ch Ch Leyton 30-32; CF 32-35; Chap RAF 35-38; R of Burghfield 38-71. *24 Brading Way, Purley, Reading, RG8 8BS.*

NICHOLSON, Godfrey Carruthers. b 48. Univ of Cant NZ BSc 67. St Jo Coll Auckld BD 72. **d** 71 **p** 72 Ch Ch. C of Fendalton 71-74; on leave. *129 Fendalton Road, Christchurch 4, NZ.*

NICHOLSON, Guy Colville. Univ of NZ BE 45. Oak Hill Th Coll 51. **d** 53 **p** 54 Roch. C of Ch Ch Beckenham 53-56; V of Hemswell w Harpswell 56-63; V of Lentworth 56-63; RD of Aslackhoe 60-63; V of Ellerslie 63-71; L to Offic Dio Auckld from 71. *49 Landscape Road, Papatoetoe, NZ.* (27-85 985)

NICHOLSON, John Malcolm. b 08. Late Exhib of K Coll Cam BA 31, MA 36. Cudd Coll 31. **d** 32 **p** 33 Newc T. C of St Jo Bapt Newc T 32-36; V of St Mary Monkseaton 36-38; Sugley 38-46; St Geo Cullercoats 46-55; Exam Chap to Bp of Newc T 45-53; to Bp of Sheff 55-59; V of Melton-on-the-Hill 55-59; C-in-c of Marr 55-59; Archd of Doncaster 55-59; Hd Master of K Sch Tynemouth 59-70; Select Pr Univ of Cam 58-59; R of Brightwalton w Catmore (and Leckhampstead, Chaddlesworth and Fawley from 74) 70-74; V of Leckhampstead 70-74; C-in-c of Chaddleworth 72-74; Fawley Berks 72-74. *12 Carrsfield, Corbridge, Northumberland.* (Corbridge 2483)

NICHOLSON, Joseph. b 14. Late Organ Scho of St Jo Coll Dur BA 35, Dipl Th 37, MA 38. LRAM 45. **d** 37 **p** 38 Dur. C of St Pet Auckland 37-39; St Paul W Pelton 39-42; Gainsborough 42-45; Asst Master Tettenhall Coll 45-50; Chap Romsey Coll 50-53; Perm to Offic Dio Win 50-53; V of St Thos York 55-58; Healaugh w Wighill and Bilbrough 58-60; R of Moresby 60-63; V of Eppleton 63-69; Asst Master Penhill Secondary Sch Swindon 69-75; Perm to Offic Dio Bris 69-75; Dio Mon 75-77; P-in-c of Blaenavon w Capel Newydd 77-79. *52 Seacroft Road, Mablethorpe, LN12 2DJ.* (Mablethorpe 7574)

NICHOLSON, Joseph Smith. b 16. St Jo Coll Dur BA 40, Dipl Th 41, MA 43. **d** 41 **p** 42 Dur. C of St Paul Darlington 41-43; Chap Miss to Seamen Port of London 43-44; Mersey 44-45; C of Alnwick 45-47; Chap RNVR 47-49; RNR from 56; C-in-c of Holywell 49-52; V of Howdon Panns 52-57; Chap HM Pris Man 57-60; Dur 60-63; Walton 63-66; Wandsworth 66-70; Leyhill 70-73; Styal Chesh 73-76; Dur 76-82; L to Offic Dio Ches 73-76. *43 Broom Hill Drive, Broompark, Ushaw Moor, Durham, DH7 7NX.*

NICHOLSON, Kinross. Univ of NZ BA 37. AKC 38. St Jo Coll Auckld. **d** 38 Wel **p** 39 Bp Sprott for Wel. C of Ch Ch Wanganui 39-42; V of Opunake 42-47; C of St Andr Cathl Sing and Dioc Regr 47-48; V of Negri Sembilan 48-50; St Andr Cathl Sing and Dioc Regr of Sing 50-51; PC of St Jo Evang Mansfield (Col Cl Act) 51-54; V of Te Kuiti 54-61; L to Offic Dio Auckld 61-64; Perm to Offic Dio Melb from 64. *2 Munro Street, Middle Brighton, Vic 3186, Australia.*

NICHOLSON, Leonard William Eugene. d and **p** 69 Pret. Hon C of Hercules Pret 69-71; L to Offic Dio Port Eliz from 79. *23 Louise Michael Drive, Lovemore Heights, Port Elizabeth, S Africa.*

NICHOLSON, Nigel Patrick. b 46. Sarum Wells Th Coll 72. **d** 75 **p** 76 Guildf. C of Farnham 75-78; Worplesdon 78-81; P-in-c of Compton Dio Guildf from 81. *Compton Rectory, Guildford, Surrey, GU3 1ED.* (Guildf 810328)

NICHOLSON, Peter Charles. b 25. Chich Th Coll. **d** 59 St

Alb **p** 60 Bedford for St Alb. C of Sawbridgeworth 59-62; Min Can, Prec and Sacr of Pet Cathl 62-67; V of Wroxham w Hoveton 67-74; Hon Min Can of Nor from 67; V of Lyme Regis 74-80; Gen Sec St Luke's Hosp for the Clergy from 80; Hon C of SS Pet & Paul Harlington Dio Lon from 81. *29 St Paul's Close, Harlington, Hayes, UB3 5AA.*

NICHOLSON, Peter Charles. b 44. Oak Hill Coll 74. **d** 76 **p** 77 Cant. C of Ch Ch Broad Green Croydon 76-80; Gt Baddow Dio Chelmsf from 80. *164 Meadgate Avenue, Chelmsford, Essex.* (Chelmsf 71516)

NICHOLSON, Ven Reginald John. LTh 64. St Jo Coll Auckld. **d** 59 **p** 60 Waik. C of St Pet Cathl Hamilton 60-61; V of Ohura 61-63; Ngaruawahia 63-68; W New Plymouth 68-72; Te Aroha Dio Waik from 72-81; Archd of Piako 80-81; Waik from 81; V of Claudelands Dio Waik from 81. *25 Thames Street, Hamilton, NZ.*

NICHOLSON, Robert Carruthers. Univ of NZ BA 36. NZ Bd of Th Stud LTh 36. **d** and **p** 38 Nel. C of All SS Nel 38-40; V of Collingwood 40-44; Awatere w Seddon and Ward 44-53; Spring Creek 53-59; Can of Nel 57-77; V of Westport 59-67; Takaka 67-70; Wairau Valley 70-77; Perm to Offic Dio Nel from 77. *125a Weld Street, Blenheim, NZ.*

NICHOLSON, Rodney. b 45. Merton Coll Ox BA 68, MA 71. Ridley Hall Cam 69. **d** 72 **p** 73 Blackb. C of Colne 72-75; Blackpool 75-78; V of St Bart Ewood Blackb Dio Blackb from 78. *Ewood Vicarage, Bolton Road, Blackburn, Lancs.* (Blackb 51206)

NICHOLSON, Roland. b 40. Sarum Wells Th Coll 72. **d** 74 Lanc for Blackb **p** 75 Blackb. C of St Barn Morecambe 74-78; V of Feniscliffe Dio Blackb from 78. *Vicarage, St Francis Road, Feniscliffe, Blackburn, BB2 2TZ.* (Blackb 21757)

NICHOLSON, Trevor Parry. b 35. St Edm Hall Ox BA (4th cl Th) 58. Wycl Hall Ox 58. **d** 60 **p** 61 Chich. C of Ch Ch Eastbourne 60-63; Ifield (in c of Langley Green) 63-67; Asst Youth Chap Win 67-73; Chap Shoreham Gr Sch 73-78; P-in-c of Capel Dio Guildf from 78. *Capel Vicarage, Dorking, Surrey.* (Dorking 711260)

NICHOLSON, William George. Ridley Coll Melb 57. **d** 59 **p** 61 Melb. C of Ch Ch Essendon 59-61; Cheltm 61-63; Chap Vic Miss to Seamen Melb 63-65; R of Milloo w Lockington 65-68; St Francis Nundah 68-71; Pittsworth 71-79; Cardiff 79-81; All SS Preston Dio Melb from 81. *239a Murray Road, Preston, Vic, Australia 3072.*

NICHOLSON, William Surtees. b 15. Coll of Resurr Mirfield 39. **d** 41 **p** 42 Ches. C of Wilmslow 41-44; St Pet Wallsend 44-48; C-in-c of St Pet Conv Distr Balkwell 49-61; V of Ashington 61-74; Bamburgh (and Lucker from 74) 74-81. *Pepperclose Cottage, The Wynding, Bamburgh, Northumberland, NE69 7DB.*

NICKALLS, Frederick William. b 13. Oak Hill Th Coll 49. **d** 51 **p** 52 Roch. C of St Jo Evang Penge 51-53; Lenton (in c of St Mary Wollaton Pk) 53-55; V of Em Everton 55-58; Barnehurst 58-67; R of Nailsea 67-78; Perm to Offic Dios Bris & Sarum from 79. *41 Church Street, Wootton Bassett, Wilts, SN4 7BQ.*

NICKALLS, Vivian James. b 14. St Pet Hall Ox BA 37, MA 41. Wells Th Coll 38. **d** 38 **p** 39 Liv. C of Walton-on-the-Hill (in c of Good Shepherd from 40) Liv 38-44; V of St Geo Everton 44-51; Ascott-under-Wychwood 51-59; C-in-c of Leafield 55; V 56-59; R of Norbury w Snelston 59-65; V of Haddenham 65-74; V of Kingsey 65-74; C-in-c of Cuddington 72-74; Minster Lovell 74-77; Perm to Offic Dio Ox from 77. *1 The Maples, Wendover, Aylesbury, Bucks.*

NICKELS, John Alfred. Bps' Coll Cheshunt 37. **d** 40 **p** 41 Lon. C of St Mich Wood Green 40-41; Chap RNVR 41-46; Org Sec C of E Children's S 47-49; C-in-c of St Mary The Boltons Kens 49-52; Chap HM Pris Maidstone 52-55; Chap R Canad Navy 59-62; Nat Cathl Sch and Assoc Can Washington DC 62-63; Kingston Penit Ont 63-68; Chief of Chap Services Canad Penit Service ottawa 68-79; Perm to Offic Dio Ott 70-79; on leave. *Address temp unknown.*

NICKISSON, Theodore Philip. b 07. ALCD 32. **d** 32 **p** 33 Lich. C of St Luke Leek 32-33; Quarry Bank 33-34; Beaminster 34-38; Newport Pagnell 38-40; R of Gt Linford 40-45; V of Blewbury 45-51; C of All SS Notting Hill 51-53; H Sav Hitchin 53-58; V of Gt Waxham w Palling 58-60; C-in-c of Horsey 58-60; C of Clewer 60-67; Headington Quarry Ox 67-73. *Woodlands View, Bell Lane, Cassington, Oxford.*

NICKLES, Albert Arthur. Late Scho of Ch Coll Cam BA 38. Cudd Coll 38. **d** 39 **p** 40 Bradf. C of All SS Horton Bradf 39-43; St John Bierley (in c of St Pet Toftshaw) Bradf 43-46; Miss Dio Madag 46-52; Archd of Imerina Dean of Madag and Exam Chap to Bp 52-53; SPG Miss Dio Accra 53-73; Synod Sec Dio Accra 55-58; L to Offic Dio Accra 59-73; Master Achimota Sch Ghana 59-61; Cler Rep of Synod of Prov of W Afr 61-67; P-in-c of Tema 62-66; Chap Univ of Ghana and Tutor Trin Coll Legon 67-73; Dioc Sec Dio Diego S 73-79; Dio antsir 79; Tutor St Paul's Th Coll Ambatoharanana from 79. *St Paul's College, Ambatoharanana, Malagasy Republic.*

NICKLESS, Christopher John. b 58. St D Coll Lamp BA (Th) 79. Coll of the Resurr Mirfield 79. **d** 81 Mon. C of Bassaleg Dio Mon from 81. *2 Highcross Drive, Rogerstone, Newport, Gwent, NP1 9AB.*

NICKLESS, Canon Victor George. b 08. Univ of Dur BA and LTh 34. Lon Coll of Div 30. **d** 34 **p** 35 Roch. C of H Trin Beckenham 34-37; St Jo Evang Bexley 37-41; CF (EC) 41-45; V of St Jo Evang Bexley 45-50; Strood 50-63; Surr 50-77; R of Wrotham 63-77; Hon Can of Roch 70-77; Can (Emer) from 78; RD of Shoreham 75-77. *Ford Place, Wrotham Heath, Sevenoaks, Kent.*

NICKLIN, John Marcus. b 31. Univ of Birm MA 73. ALCD 54. **d** 55 **p** 56 Nor. C of St Cath Mile Cross 55-58; St Paul Newbarns w Hawcoat 58-59; St Mary Becontree 59-61; Min of St Paul's Eccles Distr Harold Hill Hornchurch 61-65; Chap Rubery Hill Hosp Birm 65-74; St Aug's Coll Cant 74-76; Cler Org Sec CECS Dios Cant and Roch from 76. *7 Stanmore Court, New Dover Road, Canterbury, Kent.*

NICKOLAS, Merryn George Scott. St Jo Coll Morpeth. **d** 35 **p** 36 Newc. C of Morpeth 35-36; Gosford 36-37; Mayfield 37-39; Singleton 39-41; P-in-c of Woy Woy 41-45; R 45-47; New Lambton 47-79; Perm to Offic Dio Newc from 79. *83 Queens Road, New Lambton, NSW, Australia 2305.*

NICKOLS-RAWLE, Peter John. b 44. Sarum Wells Th Coll 76. **d** 78 **p** 79 Ex. C of St Thos Ex 78-80; Old and New Shoreham Dio Chich from 80. *Church House, Adur Avenue, Shoreham-by-Sea, BN4 5NN.* (Shoreham 4648)

NICOL, Ajayi Eleborra. b 44. Fourah Bay Coll. **d** 70 Sier L. C of St Patr Kissy Dio Sier L from 70. *3a Upper Easton Street, Freetown.*

NICOL, Ernest. b 25. SOC 71. **d** 74 Edmon for Lon **p** 75 Lon. C of Ch Ch Crouch End Hornsey 74-75; St Geo Hornsey Dio Lon from 76. *75 Nightingale Lane, N8.* (01-340 7650)

NICOLAS, Patricia Frances. **d** 77 Bp Spence for Wai **p** 78 Auckld. d Dio Wai 77-78; Hon C of St Matt City and Dio Auckld from 78. *16 Wallace Street, Herne Bay, Auckland 2, NZ.*

NICOLL, Alexander Charles Fiennes. b 34. Dipl Th (Lon) 66. Lon Coll of Div 66. **d** 68 **p** 69 Lich. C of Trentham 68-71; Hednesford 72-74; V of Longnor Dio Lich from 74; P-in-c of Quarnford Dio Lich from 74; Sheen Dio Lich from 80. *Longnor Vicarage, Buxton, Derbys.* (Longnor 316)

NICOLL, George Lorimer. b 23. **d** 75 Glas. C of Clydebank Dio Glas from 75. *19 McKenzie Avenue, Clydebank, Dunbartonshire, G81 2AT.*

NICOLLE, Russell Fredrick Allister. b 38. **d** 77 **p** 78 Alg. C of Manitouwadge and Marathon 77-80; I of Elliot Lake Dio Alg from 80. *120 Hillside Drive South, Elliot Lake, Ont, Canada.*

NICOLSON, Paul Roderick. b 32. Cudd Coll 65. **d** 67 Dorch for Ox **p** 68 Ox. C of Farnham Royal 67-70; LPr Dio St Alb from 70. *Tallents, Kimpton, Hitchin, Herts.* (Kimpton 832364)

NICOLSON, Canon Ronald Brian. Univ of Natal BA (Engl) 60, (Th) 64, PhD 70. Chich Th Coll 60. **d** and **p** 62 Natal. C of St Sav Cathl Pmbg 62-65; R of Karkloof 65-70; Pinetown 70-81; Can of Natal 77-80; Hon Can from 81; Archd Dio Natal 80; Perm to Offic Dio Natal from 81. *35 King Edward Avenue, Pietermaritzburg 3201, S Africa.*

NIDUHA, Edson. b 54. St Phil Coll Kongwa 73. **d** and **p** 75 Vic Nyan. P Dio Vic Nyan. *PO Box 93, Ngara, West Lake, Tanzania.*

NIEHUS, Robert John. b 43. ACT ThL 68. Univ of Tas BA 74. Univ of Adel BA 75. St Mich Th Coll Crafers 64. **d** 69 **p** 70 Adel. C of Gawler 69-71; Asst Chap Ch Coll Hobart 71-74; C of Crafers 74-75; R of Maitland 75-77; Port Pirie 77-81; Semaphore Dio Adel from 81. *243 Military Road, Semaphore, S Australia 5019.*

NIELD, Colin. b 35. Sarum Th Coll 58. **d** 60 **p** 61 Wakef. C of Mirfield 60-62; Blandford Forum and Langton Long 62-64; V of Beighton 64-68; Laxton 68-70; C-in-c (V from 69) of Egmanton 68-70; R of W Retford Dio Southw from 70. *Rectory, North Road, Retford, Notts.* (Retford 3116)

NIELSEN, Ronald Marius Boniface. b 09. M OSB. **d** 51 **p** 52 Ox. L to Offic Dio Ox from 51. *Nashdom Abbey, Burnham, Bucks.*

NIGER, Lord Bishop on the. *See* Onyemelukwe, Right Rev Jonathan Arinzechuku.

NIGER DELTA, Lord Bishop on the. *See* Fubara, Right Rev Yibo Alalibo.

NIGER DELTA, Assistant Bishop on the. (Vacant).

NIGERIA, Metropolitan of Province of. *See* Olufosoye, Most Rev Timothy Omotayo.

NIGHTINGALE, George Crispin Charsley. St Jo Coll Morpeth. **d** 27 **p** 28 Bath. M of Bro of Good Shepherd Dio Bath 27-33; C of St Mich AA Stoke Newington 33; Asst P

Kuching 33-35; Perm to Offic (Col Cl Act) Dio Cant 35-37; P-in-c of St Thos St Kitts Antig 37-42; P-in-c of Moana 46-49; C of Broken Hill 49-50; Perm to Offic Dio Melb from 60. *19 Mascoma Street, Strathmore, Vic, Australia.*

NIGHTINGALE, John Brodie. b 42. Late Scho of Pemb Coll Ox BA (2nd cl Phil Pol and Econ) 64. Univ of Bris Dipl Social Stud 65. Qu Coll Cam BA (2nd cl Th Trip pt ii) 67. Westcott Ho Cam 65. **d** 67 **p** 68 Man. C of St Martin Wythenshawe 67-70; w Inst of Ch & Society Ibadan 70-76; Adult Educn Adv and P-in-c of Amberley w N Stoke 76-79; Asst Home Sec Bd of Miss and Unity Gen Syn from 80. *Church House, Dean's Yard, SW1P 3NZ.* (01-222 9011)

NIGHTINGALE, William. b 11. ACCS 52. St Aug Coll Cant. **d** 61 **p** 63 S'wark. C of Ch Ch S'wark 61-65; Industr Chap Dio S'wark from 75; Hon C St Mary Wimbledon Dio S'wark from 75. *14 Melbury Gardens, SW20 0DJ.* (01-946 8361)

NIKANI, Mason Sipho Wele. St Bede's Coll Umtata 70. **d** 71 **p** 72 St John's. Miss O of Ethiopia Dio St John's 71-75 and from 80; Dio Grahmstn 75-78. *PO Kentani, Transkei, S Africa.*

NIKORA, Kahutiaiterangi. b 36. **d** 78 **p** 79 Wai. Hon C of Whangara Past Dio Wai from 78. *5 Halley Street, Gisborne, NZ.*

NIKORA, Tamaro Charles Tiniwai. b 02. **d** 77 **p** 78 Aotearoa for Wai. C of Ruatoki-Whakatane Past Dio Wai from 77. *Flat 4, 66 Hinemoa Street, Whakatane, NZ.*

NIL, Elias. St Jo Coll Rangoon. **d** 49 Rang. Sec and Treas Dio Rang from 49. *Saya Elias, 104a Inya Road, Kokine, University PO, Rangoon, Burma.*

NI LONE, John. d 70 **p** 71 Rang. d Dio Rang. *St Mark's Church, Prome, Burma.*

NIMIK, Edward Joseph. b 31. St Jo Coll Winnipeg BMin 78. **d** 78 Rupld for Caled **p** 79 Caled. I of St Paul New Masset Dio Caled from 78. *Box 677, Masset, BC, Canada.*

NIMMO, Alexander Emsley. b 53. Univ of Aber BD 76. Edin Th Coll 76. **d** 78 **p** 79 Moray. Prec St Andr Cathl Inverness 78-81; P-in-c of St Pet Stornoway Dio Arg Is from 81. *10 Springfield Road, Stornoway, Isle of Lewis, PA87 2PT.* (Stornoway 3609)

NIN, Alan. b 24. Wells Th Coll 63. **d** 65 Ox **p** 66 Reading for Ox. C of Sandhurst Berks 65-67; Youth Chap and L to Offic Dio Birm 67-70; Ed Birm Dioc Directory 70-71; Chap to Br Embassy Bonn and All SS Cologne 70-72; V of Four Oaks 72-77; Dir of Educn Dio Guildf from 77. *St Mark's House, Franklyn Road, Godalming, Surrey, GU7 2LD.* (Godalming 29275)

NIND, Ven Anthony Lindsay. Ball Coll Ox BA and MA 50. Cudd Coll 50. **d** 52 **p** 53 Sarum. C of St Jas Southbroom 52-54; Wareham 54-56; Chap Miss to Seamen for Hong Kong 56-61; R of Langton Matravers 61-70; St Paul's S£ao Paulo Argent 70-75; Chap Ch Ch Vienna 75-80; St Andr Zurich Dio Gibr in Eur from 80; Archd in Switzerland from 80; Hon Can of H Trin Cathl Brussels from 81. *Promenadegasse 9, Zurich 8001, Switzerland.* (01-472241)

NIND, Robert William Hampden. b 31. Ball Coll Ox BA (3rd cl Engl) 54, MA 60. Cudd Coll 54. **d** 56 **p** 57 Linc. C of Spalding 56-60; Vere Ja 60-63; R 63-67; C-in-c of St Bart Battersea 67-70; Commiss Br Hond (Bel from 73) from 67; Ja 70-77; V of St Matt Brixton Dio S'wark from 70. *5 St Matthew's Road, SW2.* (01-274 3553)

NINDI, Charles Frederick. d 57 Centr Tang **p** 58 Bp Omari for Centr Tang. P Dio Centr Tang 57-67; L to Offic Dio Centr Tang from 67. *Box 87, Iringa, Jary, Tanzania.*

NINEHAM, Canon Dennis Eric. b 21. Late Scho of Qu Coll Ox 1st cl Cl Mods 41, BA (1st cl Lit Hum) 43, Squire Scho 40, Liddon Stud 43, 1st cl Th 45, MA 46, BD 64, DD 78. Cam BD (by incorp) 64. Berkeley Div Sch USA Hon DD 65. Univ of Birm Hon DD 72. Linc Th Coll 44. **d** 44 **p** 45 York. Asst Chap Qu Coll Ox 44-46; Chap and Fell 46-54; Exam Chap to Bp of Ripon from 47; to Abp of York from 48; to Bp of Sheff 47-54; to Bp of Nor 60-71; Prof of Bibl and Hist Th at K Coll Lon 54-58; Select Pr Univ of Ox 54-55; Univ of Cam 59; Proc Conv Univ of Lon 55-64; Prof of Div Univ of Lon 58-64; Fell K Coll Lon from 63; Commiss N Ugan from 61; Regius Prof of Div Univ of Cam and Fell of Em Coll Cam 64-69; Warden of Keble Coll Ox 69-79; Hon Fell from 80; Proc Conv Univ of Cam 64-69; Univ of Ox 69-75; Prof of Th and Hd of Th Dept Univ of Bris from 80; Hon Can of Bris Cathl from 80; Exam Chap to Bp of Bris from 81. *Department of Theology, Royal Fort House, Tyndell Avenue, Bristol, BS8 1UJ.* (Bristol 24161)

NINGENZA, Justin. d 75 **p** 76 Buye. P Dio Buye. *c/o Kirundo BP, 18 Kirundo, Burundi.*

NINHAM, Canon Cecil Ronald. b 08. AKC (1st cl) 31. Univ of Lon Collins Pri and Trench Gr Pr 30, BD and McCaul Hebr Pri (Jun) 31, 1st cl Gr NT and Apoc 35. **d** 31 **p** 32 Dur. C of Esh 31-35; Perm to Offic at W Harton 35-36; PC 36-41; V of St Andr Nor 41-52; R of St Mich at Plea w St Pet Hungate Nor 47-52; V of Loddon w Sisland 52-73; RD of Loddon 53-60; Surr from 53; Hon Can of Nor 59-79; Can (Emer) from 79. *21 St Mary's Road, Poringland, Norwich, NOR 4ZW.* (Framingham Earl 2346)

NINIS, Ven Richard Betts. b 31. Linc Coll Ox BA 53, MA 62. Linc Th Coll 53. **d** 55 **p** 56 Lon. C of Poplar 55-62; V of St Martin Heref 62-71; V of Bullinghope w Grafton 68-71; R of Dewsall w Callow 68-71; Dioc Missr Dio Heref 69-74; Preb of Heref Cathl 70-74; Archd of Stafford 74-80; Lich from 80; Can Res and Treas of Lich Cathl from 74. *24 The Close, Lichfield, Staffs, WS13 7LD.* (Lichfield 23535)

NISBETT, Joshua Mastine Samuel. b 46. Univ of WI Ja BA 75. U Th Coll of WI 71. **d** 74 **p** 75 Antig. P-in-c of St Geo I and Dio Antig 75-76; R from 77. *St George's Rectory, Box 177, St John's, Antigua, WI.*

NISBETT, Thomas Norman. Codr Coll Barb 59. **d** 62 **p** 63 Barb. C of St Phil Barb 63-65; St Jas Sandys 65-66; P-in-c of St David's I 66-71; C of Pembroke Berm 71-74; Chap to Bp of Berm from 73; V of Devonshire Dio Berm from 74. *PO Box 401, Devonshire, Hamilton, Bermuda.*

NISHI, Daudi. St Phil Th Coll Kongwa 68. **d** and **p** 69 Vic Nyan. P Dio Vic Nyan. *PO Box 64, Geita, Tanzania.*

NISSEN, Peter Boy. b 46. Univ of BC BA 69. Vanc Sch of Th MDiv 73. **d** 73 **p** 75 Yukon. C of Cassiar 73-76; I of Old Crow 76-79. *c/o Rectory, Old Crow, Yukon Territory, Canada.*

NIXEY, Richard Edward. Moore Th Coll Syd ACT ThL 77. **d** and **p** 78 Syd. C of Eastwood 78-81; St Clem Mossman Dio Syd from 81. *69 Shadforth Street, Mossman, NSW, Australia 2088.* (969-2449)

NIXON, Canon Bernard Lawrence. b 26. St Jo Coll Dur BA 55, Dipl Th 56. **d** 56 **p** 57 Sheff. C of Goole 56-60; Chap of Wm Baker Tech Coll (Dr Barnardo's Homes) and L to Offic Dio St Alb 60-67; V of Silsoe Dio St Alb from 67; Surr from 69; RD of Ampthill from 75; Hon Can of St Alb from 79. *Vicarage, Silsoe, Beds, MK45 4ED.* (0525 60458)

NIXON, Canon Charles Hunter. b 07. Men in Disp 45. Late Scho of Keble Coll Ox 2nd cl Cl Mods 28, BA (3rd cl Lit Hum) and Liddon Stud 30, 2nd cl Th 31, MA 47. Dorch Miss Coll 31. **d** 33 **p** 34 Lon. C of St Pet Lon Dks 33-35; Perm to Offic at All SS Miss White Lion Street Pentonville 35-36; Perm to Offic Dio Ox 36-38; L to Offic 38-39; Chap Dorch Miss Coll 36-38; Vice-Prin 38-39; C of St Pet Lon Dks 39-47; CF (EC) 43-46 (Men in Disp 45); V of St Mary Swanley 47-64; R of Woodston 64-73; Coveney 73-77; RD of Yaxley 64-71; Surr 64-77; Hon Can of Ely 70-78; Can (Emer) from 78. *2 Bramley Drive, Colkirk, Fakenham, Norf.*

NIXON, Charles Richard Harris. b 39. Dalhousie Univ BComm 61, BEducn 64. Atlantic Sch of Th Halifax NS MDiv 78. **d** 77 NS **p** 78 Bp Hatfield for NS. C of Rawdon 77-78; R of Annapolis and Granville 78-81; C of Pembroke Dio Berm from 81. *c/o Rectory, Pembroke, Bermuda.*

NIXON, John David. b 38. Univ of Leeds BSc 60. CEng, MICE 70. Linc Th Coll 76. **d** 78 Bp McKie for Cov **p** 79 Cov. C of Rugby Dio Cov from 78. *19 Elsee Road, Rugby, Warwicks, CV21 3BA.*

NIXON, Michael Willoughby. St Jo Coll Morpeth. **d** and **p** 70 Bath. C of Bourke 70-75; P-in-c of Sag Sag 75-77; Sec Angl Centre Dio Aipo from 78. *Box 340, Madang, Papua New Guinea.*

NIXON, Neville Douglas. St Mich Ho Crafers ACT ThL 69. **d** 69 **p** 70 Brisb. C of St Pet Wynnum 69-74; V of St Mary Gin Gin 74-79; Ch of Ascen Morningside City and Dio Brisb from 79. *706 Wynnum Road, Morningside, Queensland, Australia 4170.* (399 4129)

NIXON, Phillip Edward. b 48. Ch Ch & Wolfson Coll Ox MA 73, DPhil 73. Trin Coll Cam BA (Th) 80. Westcott Ho Cam 78. **d** 81 Knaresborough for Ripon. C of Halton Dio Ripon from 81. *67 Morritt Drive, Leeds, LS15 7HZ.*

NIXON, Roy Herbert. St Chad's Coll Regina Dipl Th 54. **d** 54 Qu'App **p** 55 Alg. C of Sudbury 54-55; I of Lake of Bays 55-59; R of Haileybury 59-62; P-in-c of Temiskaming 63-65; C of St Pet Brockville 65-66; Chap Brockville Psychiatric Hosp from 66. *Box 113, Maitland, Ont, Canada.* (613-348 3659)

NIXSON, Peter. b 27. Ball Coll Ox BA 51, MA 59. Coll of Resurr Mirfield. **d** 53 Ex **p** 54 B & W for Ex. C of Babbacombe 53-56; St Mark Swindon 56-57; All SS Boyne Hill 57-60; Min of St Mary's Conv Distr Bayswater Headington Ox 60-66; Perm to Offic Dio Ex 66-67 and from 70; Dio Lich 67-69; Asst Master Oswestry High Sch for Boys 67-70; Tiverton Gr Sch 70-75; Knowles Hill Sch Newton Abbot from 75; L to Offic at H Trin Oswestry 69-70. *34 Osney Crescent, Paignton, Devon, TQ4 5EY.*

NJAKARE, Bernard. b 27. **d** 74 **p** 75 S Malawi. P Dio S Malawi. *Box 5564, Limbe, Malawi.*

NJAMU, James. St Jo Sem Lusaka 56. **d** 57 **p** 59 N Rhod. P Dio N Rhod 57-60; Dio Ruw 60-64; Dio Zam 64-70; Dio N

Zam 71-75; Dio Centr Zam from 75. *Box 70172, Ndola, Zambia.*

NJAMU, Joseph Kombe. St Jo Sem Lusaka. **d** 68 Zam **p** 69 Bp Mataka for Zam. P Dio Zam 68-71; Dio N Zam from 71. *PO Box 159, Mufulira, Zambia.*

NJAU, Daniel Karobia. b 36. **d** 76 **p** 77 Nak. P Dio Nak. *PO Wanjohi, via Ol'Kalou, Kenya.*

NJAWA, Jairus Andrea. b 22. **d** 76 **p** 77 Vic Nyan. P Dio Vic Nyan. *PO Box 144, Shinyanga, Tanzania.*

NJEGOVAN, James Dusan. b 54. Univ of Man BA 75. St Jo Coll Winnipeg MDiv 78. **d** 78 **p** 79 Rupld. C of Portage Plains 78-81; St Paul Winnipeg Dio Rupld from 81. *830 North Drive, Winnipeg, Manit, Canada.*

NJENGA, Cephas. b 45. **d** 71 **p** 72 Mt Kenya. P Dio Mt Kenya 71-75; Dio Mt Kenya S from 75. *Weithaga, Box 107, Murang'a, Kenya.*

NJERU, Elijah. b 39. **d** 71 **p** 72 Mt Kenya. P Dio Mt Kenya 71-75; Dio Mt Kenya E from 75. *Box 712, Embu, Kenya.*

NJERU, Sospeter. **d** 67 **p** 69 Mt Kenya. P Dio Mt Kenya 67-75; Dio Mt Kenya E 75-77 and from 80. *Box 6084, Runyenje's, Kenya.*

NJIRI, John Elphas. b 41. **d** 78 **p** 79 Mt Kenya E. P Dio Mt Kenya E. *Box 132, Kianyanga, Kenya.*

NJIRU, Elias. **d** 61 Ft Hall **p** 62 Mt Kenya. P Dio Mt Kenya 61-74. *Nyangwa, Box 158, Embu, Nigeria.*

NJIRU, Ezekiel. St Paul's Dioc Div Sch Limuru 51. **d** 53 **p** 55 Momb. P Dio Momb 53-61; Dio Ft Hall 61-64; Dio Mt Kenya from 64. *Nyangwa, PO Embu, Kenya.*

NJIRU, Canon Musa. St Paul's Dioc Div Sch Lumuru. **d** 34 U Nile for Momb **p** 39 Momb. P Dio Momb 34-61; Dio Ft Hall 61-64; Dio Mt Kenya 64-65; Hon Can of Ft Hall 62-64; Mt Kenya 64-75; Can (Emer) from 75. *Kigari, PO Box 119, Embu, Kenya.*

NJOGI, George William. Bp Tucker Coll Mukono, 67. **d** 68 **p** 70 W Bugan. P Dio W Bugan. *Church of Uganda, Lugala, PO Box 164, Mpigi, Uganda.*

NJOGU, Jeremiah. b 44. St Paul's Coll Limuru 73. **d** 75 **p** 76 Mt Kenya E. P Dio Mt Kenya E. *Box 189, Embu, Kenya.*

NJOGU, Nehemiah Milton. b 48. **d** 78 **p** 79 Mt Kenya E. P Dio Mt Kenya E. *Box 841, Embu, Kenya.*

✠ **NJOJO, Right Rev Patrice Byankya.** b 38. Montr Th Coll 79. **d** 79 Boga-Z **p** 80 Montr for Boga-Z. P Dio Boga-Z 79-80; Cons Ld Bp of Boga-Z at Boga 7 Sept 80 by Abps of Rwanda and Uganda; Bps of Butare, M & W Nile; and Bp Ridsdale. *BP 154, Bunia, Zaire.*

NJOKU, Samuel Onyekachi. b 45. Trin Coll Umuahia 77. **d** 80 Aba. d Dio Aba. *St Michael's Cathedral, PO Box 818, Aba, Nigeria.*

NJOKWENI, Canon Lennox Oscar Maziza. St Pet Coll Rosettenville. **d** 44 **p** 46 Grahmstn. Asst Miss St Mich Herschel 44-46; St Steph Port Eliz 46-51; C of Graaff-Reinet 51-54; Miss at St Anne Uitenhage 54-56; St Phil E Lon 56-65; St Phil Grahmstn 65-68; Archd of Albany 64-68; R of St Anne Uitenhage 68-69; C of St Matt Miss Grahmstn 69-75; R of Bolotwa 75-79; Hon Can of Grahmstn from 75; P-in-c of St Thos Fort White Dio Grahmstn from 79. *Box 5011, Kwa-Dimbaza, CP, S Africa.*

NJOLIBA, John. **d** 59 Bp Omari for Centr Tang **p** 66 Centr Tang. P Dio Centr Tang. *Chinyika, PO Box 2, Mpwapwa, Tanzania.*

NJOLOKO, Kyabutwabubi. b 11. **d** 75 **p** 76 Boga-Z. P Dio Boga-Z 75-76; Dio Bukavu from 76. *Lukalakala Parish, BP 220, Kindu, Maniema, Zaire.*

NJOROGE, David. St Paul's Th Coll Limuru 68. **d** and **p** 71 Mt Kenya. P Dio Mt Kenya 71-75; Dio Mt Kenya S from 75. *CPK Nanyuki, Box 271, Limuru, Kenya.*

NJOROGE, Gad Karanja. **d** 76 **p** 77 Nak. P Dio Nak. *Box 1253, Nakuru, Kenya.*

NJOROGE, John Stephen Gitunda. b 34. **d** 78 Mt Kenya S. d Dio Mt Kenya S. *PO Box 48, Kahuhia, Murang'a, Kenya.*

NJUE, Joseph. **d** 78 **p** 79 Mt Kenya E. P Dio Mt Kenya E. *Box 189, Embu, Kenya.*

NJUGUNA, George Muiru Manasseh. St Paul's Th Coll Lumuru. **d** and **p** 68 Nak. P Dio Nak. *Naivasha, Kenya.*

NJUGUNA, Henry. Weithaga Bible Sch 60. **d** 61 **p** 62 Ft Hall. P Dio Ft Hall 62-64; Dio Mt Kenya from 64. *Box 23021, Lower Kabete, Kenya.*

NJUGUNA, James Frederick. St Phil Coll Maseno 69. **d** 69 Maseno **p** 71 Nak. P Dio Nak. *PO Marigat, via Nakuru, Kenya.*

NJUGUNA, Samson. **d** 67 **p** 69 Mt Kenya. P Dio Mt Kenya 67-75; Dio Mt Kenya S from 75. *Box 121, Murang'a, Kenya.* (Murang'a 53)

NJUGUNA, Solomon Kamau. b 38. **d** 76 Nak. d Dio Nak. *Nabkoi Full Primary School, PO Ainabkoi, Kenya.*

NJUKI, Linus. **d** 67 **p** 69 Mt Kenya. P Dio Mt Kenya 67-75; Dio Mt Kenya E from 75; Exam Chap to Bp of Mt Kenya E from 78. *Box 113, Embu, Kenya.*

NJUMBE, Johana. St Paul's Dioc Div Sch Limuru. **d** 34 U Nile for Momb **p** 39 Momb. P Dio Momb. *CMS, Mutira, PO Kerugoya, Kenya.*

NJUMBUXA, Adolphus Bikitsha. b 42. St Pet Coll Alice Dipl Th 74. **d** 74 **p** 75 Johann. C of Natalspruit 74-77; R of Thokoza Dio Johann from 77. *Box 7, Thokoza, Johannesburg, S Africa.*

NJUNWOHA, Lazaro. Bp Tucker Coll Mukono. **d** 56 Ugan **p** 58 Bp Balya for Ugan. P Dio Ugan 56-60; Dio Ankole-K 60-67; Dio Ank from 67. *Church of Uganda, Bujaga, Ankole, Uganda.*

NKADIMENG, Ntobeng Clement Hendrik. b 35. St Pet Coll Alice 68. **d** 70 **p** 71 Pret. C of Sekhukhuniland 70-75; R of Turfloop Dio Pret from 75. *PO Box 26, Sovengo 0727, S Africa.*

NKALUBO, Samuwiri Nkangaali. b 24. Bp Tucker Coll Mukono 71. **d** 72 W Bugan. d Dio W Bugan. *Lwemiyaga, PO Sembabule, Mawogola, Uganda.*

NKAYAMBA, Amos. b 26. **d** 80 **p** 81 W Tang. P Dio W Tang. *PO Box 33, Kaliua, Kigoma, Tanzania.*

NKAZAMUREGO, Erasto. **d** 60 **p** 61 Rwanda B. P Dio Rwanda B 60-66; Dio Rwa 66-75; Dio Kiga from 75. *Anglican Church, Post Box 43, Gikongero, Rwanda.*

NKIDUMWAMI, Simon. Warner Mem Th Coll Ibuye 61. **d** 63 Rwanda B. d Dio Rwanda B 63-66; Dio Dur from 66. *Buhiga, Bujumbura, Burundi.*

NKOANE, Very Rev (Simeon) Joseph. St Pet Coll Rosettenville 52. **d** 54 **p** 55 Pret. P Dio Pret 54-56; L to Offic Dio Wakef 58-61; M CR from 59; Dio Llan 61-63; Lect St Pet Coll Alice and L to Offic Dio Grahmstn 65-66; P Dio Johann from 66; Archd of E Rand 72-77; Johann Centr 77-78; Johann E from 78; Dean and R of St Mary Virg Cathl City and Dio Johann from 77. *Box 2029, Johannesburg, Transvaal, S Africa.* (011-22 1506)

NKONGA, Henry. **d** and **p** 63 Zam. P Dio Zam 63-70; Dio N Zambia 71-80. *c/o Chungupengu Govt School, Mansa, Zambia.*

NKOPO, Wilberforce Maxasa. b 31. St Pet Coll Alice 67. **d** 69 Grahmstn **p** 70 Port Eliz. C of H Spirit Kwazakele 70-72; Alexandria Dio Port Eliz from 72. *PO Box 99, Alexandria, Port Elizabeth, S Africa.* (04652-214)

N'KOWANE, Wiseman Briton Bonakele. St Bede's Coll Umtata, 46. **d** 48 **p** 53 Grahmstn. C of St Steph Port Eliz 48-50; St Andr Queenstown 50-52; St Mich Sterkspruit 52-53; Humansdorp 53-56; Miss of H Trin Beaufort 56-58; Asst Miss St Steph Port Eliz 58-62; C of St Jas Miss Cradock 62-64; P-in-c of Langa Dio Capetn from 65. *Langa, CP, S Africa.* (533287)

NKUMANDA, Nqabisile Stanford. b 38. St Bede's Coll Umtata 77. **d** 78 **p** 79 Grahmstn. C of St John Debe Marelas Dio Grahmstn from 78. *PO Debe Nek 5604, CP, S Africa.*

NKUMBUYE, James. **d** 78 **p** 79 Ruw. P Dio Ruw. *c/o Box 1401, Kamwenge, Uganda.*

NKUMIRA, Johnstone. b 47. St Phil Coll Kongwa 78. **d** 80 **p** 81 W Tang. P Dio W Tang. *PO Box 149, Kasulu, Kogoma, Tanzania.*

NKUSSI, Wilson. Buwalasi Coll 63. **d** 64 Nam. d Dio Nam. *Nawaikoke, PO Box 80, Kaliro, Uganda.*

NKWARE, Anania. b 44. St Phil Th Coll 68. **d** and **p** 70 Vic Nyan. P Dio Vic Nyan. *Box 2, Ngara, Tanzania.*

NKWARE, Andrea Bukuru. b 22. **d** and **p** 77 Vic Nyan. P Dio Vic Nyan. *PO Box 93, Ngara, West Lake, Tanzania.*

NKWE, Ven David Cecil Tapi. St Pet Coll Rosettenville, 59. **d** 62 **p** 63 Johann. P Dio Johann Archd of Johann W from 78. *PO Box 197, Kwa Xuma, Transvaal, S Africa.*

NLADZULUANIA, Arthur. **d** 77 Matab. d Dio Matab. *c/o Box 2422, Bulawayo, Rhodesia.*

NMEZI-IGBOKWE, Theophilus Onyema. **d** 65 **p** 66 Accra. P Dio Accra. *PO Box 364, Accra, Ghana.*

NNAMA, Bedford Chukwukadibie Chukwudumogu. b 39. Trin Coll Umuahia 66. **d** 68 **p** 70 Niger. P Dio Niger. *66 Mount Hod Road, SW16.*

NNAMANI, Ernest Chinwese Uwadiegwu. b 39. Trin Coll Umuahia 72. **d** 74 Enugu. d Dio Enugu. *Emmanuel Church, Nenwe PA, Awgu Division, ECS, Nigeria.*

✠ **NOAKES, Right Rev George.** b 24. Univ of Wales (Abth) BA (2nd cl Phil) 48. Wycl Hall Ox 49. **d** 50 Sarum for St D **p** 52 St D. C of Lampeter 50-56; V of Eglwyswrw w Meline 56-59; Tregaron 59-67; Eglwys Dewi Sant Cardiff 67-76; R of Abth 76-80; Can of St D Cathl 77-79; Archd of Cardigan 79-82; V of Llanychaiarn 80-82; Cons Ld Bp of St D in Ban Cathl 2 Feb 82 by Abp of Wales; Bps of St A, Mon, Llan, Swan B, Man and Down. *Llys Esgob, Abergwili, Dyfed, SA31 2JG.*

NOAKES, Harold Isaac. b 05. St Jo Coll Cam BA 28, MA 31. Bps' Coll Cheshunt. **d** 31 **p** 32 Chelmsf. C of Waltham Abbey (or H Cross) 31-37; Perm to Offic at Cathl Ch Chelmsf 38-42; Prec 38-42; CF (TA) 33-37; V of St Andr Leytonstone

42-45; Chap HM Pris Chelmsf 45-46; R of St Mary-at-the-Walls Colchester 46-65; Hon Chap to Bp of Chelmsf 48-51; R of Ampton w L Livermere and Ingham 65-68. *Rutlands, Willows Green, Chelmsford, Essex.* (Great Leighs 243)

NOAKES, Kenneth William. b 43. Late Scho of Trin Coll Ox BA 65, MA 68, DPhil 71. Cudd Coll 66. **d** 68 **p** 69 Glouc. C of Prestbury 68-71; Libr Pusey Ho Ox 71-76; L to Offic Dio Ox 71-76; P-in-c of Marhamchurch (w Launcells from 77) Dio Truro 76-78; R from 78; M Gen Syn from 80. *Marhamchurch Rectory, Bude, Cornw, EX23 0AR.* (Widemouth Bay 203)

NOAKES, Ronald Alfred. b 14. Open Univ BA 76. **d** and **p** 37 Waik. C of Ch Ch Taumarunui 37-38; P-in-c of Whangamomona 38-39; Chap RN (NZ) 39-42; Asst Master St Pet Sch and Offg Min Cam 42-47; C of Hayling I 47-48; Chap at Marseilles and to Med Miss to Seamen 48-52; Chap RAF 52-62; V of Whixley w Green Hammerton Dio Ripon from 62. *Whixley Vicarage, York.* (Green Hammerton 30269)

NOBBS, John. b 1900. AKC (1st cl) 26. Ely Th Coll 26. **d** 26 **p** 27 Man. C of St Mary Virg Prestwich 26-31; PC of Barrow Hill 31-40; V of St Aug Tonge Moor 40-46; Winterbourne Down 46-57; St Jo Bapt Sevenoaks 57-62; R of Belstone w Sticklepath Chap 62-67; L to Offic Dio Ex from 68. *Carey Castle Lodge, 34 Church Road, Torquay, Devon, TQ1 4QY.* (Torquay 34500)

NOBBS, John Ernest. b 35. Tyndale Hall Bris 60. **d** 63 **p** 64 Chelmsf. C of Walthamstow 63-66; Braintree 66-69; St Andr w St Mary Wakef 69-71; Tooting Graveney 71-74; Woking 74-78; St Geo Worthing Dio Chich from 78. *177 Lyndhurst Road, Worthing, Sussex.* (Worthing 200387)

NOBES, Edward Arthur. b 36. Ch Ch Ox BA 58, MA 65. St Steph Ho Ox 58. **d** 60 **p** 61 Lich. C of Rushall 60-63; Asst Chap King's Sch Ely and Perm to Offic Dio Ely 63-66; Hon Min Can of Ely Cathl 64-69; C of St Mary w H Trin Ely 66-69; V of Cople 69-76; C-in-c of St Lawr Willington 71-76; V of Thornbury Dio Glouc from 76. *Vicarage, Castle Street, Thornbury, Avon, BS12 1HQ.* (Thornbury 413209)

NOBLE, Alexander Eric Lionel Edward. b 17. Wycl Hall Ox. **d** and **p** 58 Roch. C of St Thos Southborough 58-60; Sec S'wark Dioc Dilapidations Bd 60-63; Asst Sec S'wark Pastoral Reorg C'tte 60-61; Sec 61-65; Asst Sec S Lon Ch Fund and S'wark Dioc Bd of Finance 60-61; Sec 61-65; V of Bedfont 66-75; Chap St Jas Oporto 75-77; Alassio 77-78; Las Palmas Dio Gibr in Eur from 81. *Holy Trinity, Rafael Ramirez, Las Palmas, Canary Islands.*

NOBLE, Alexander Frederick Innes. b 30. Selw Coll Cam BA 53, MA 57. Lon Coll Div 53. **d** 55 **p** 56 Bris. C of Stratton St Marg 55-57; Brislington 57-59; Chap and Asst Master Pierrepont Ho Sch Frensham 59-61; Asst Chap and Asst Master Repton Sch 61-63; Chap 63-66; Blundell's Sch Tiverton 66-72; Asst Master St John C of E U Sch Cowley 73-76; Chap Cranbrook Sch 76-81; St Geo Sch Harpenden from 81. *St George's School, Harpenden, Herts.*

NOBLE, Anthony Norman. b 47. St Barn Th Coll Adel 76. **d** 79 **p** 80 Adel. C of Woodville w Woodville Gdns 79-80; St Martin Campbelltown Dio Adel from 80. *2 Marea Court, Campbelltown, S Australia 5074.*

NOBLE, Arthur. b 12. TCD BA 35, Div Comp Pri Downes Pri (1st) for Reading Liturgy and Div Test 36, MA 38. **d** 36 **p** 37 Down. C of Newtownards 36-39; St Mark Ballysillan (in c of St Bride) 39-41; Shankill Lurgan 41-44; R of Finvoy w Rasharkin 44-49; St Aid Belf 49-61; Ch Ch Lisburn 61-82; RD of Lisburn 67-72; Preb of Connor Cathl 74-79; Prec 79-82. *38 King's Road, Knock, Belfast, N Ireland.*

NOBLE, Arthur. b 03. ALCD 31. **d** 31 **p** 32 Newc T. C of St Marg Scotswood 31-34; Carlton-in-the-Willows 34-37; R of St Barn Openshaw 37-44; St Thos Heaton Norris 44-52; V of Davyhulme 52-60; Chap to Pk Hosp 59-60; V of Gisburn 60-66; Oxenhope 66-70; Perm to Offic Dio York from 76. *9 Prospect Bank, Bramham, Wetherby, W Yorks, LS23 6QR.*

NOBLE, Charles Brain. Univ of Tor BA 39. Trin Coll Tor LTh 41. **d** 42 **p** 43 Alg. C of Mindemoya 42-47; I of Korah 47-80; Hon Can of Alg 60-65; Archd of Alg 65-76; Dom Chap to Bp of Alg 76-80. *365 Fourth Avenue, Sault Ste Marie, Ont, Canada.*

NOBLE, David Harvey. Univ of Queensld BA 61. St Francis Coll Brisb ACT ThL (2nd cl) 63. **d** 63 Bp Hudson for Brisb **p** 63 Brisb. C of St Clem Stafford Brisb 63-65; M of Bush Bro of St Paul Cunnamulla 65-68; Chap Ch Coll Hobart 68-69. *c/o General Theological Seminary, New York, N Y, 10011, USA.*

NOBLE, Douglas. b 24. Wycl Hall Ox 61. **d** 62 **p** 63 Derby. C of St Werburgh Derby 62-65; V of H Trin S Wimbledon 65-72; Ch Ch Newark 72-74; Dioc Insp of Schs Southw 73-74; V of St Jo Evang Bexley 74-80; Frindsbury w Upnor Dio Roch from 80; Surr from 75; RD of Strood from 80. *4 Parsonage Lane, Frindsbury, Rochester, Kent, ME2 4UR.* (Medway 77580)

NOBLE, Canon Douglas Oswald. b 12. Univ of Aber MA 39. Edin Th Coll 39. **d** 40 **p** 41 Aber. C of St Jas Aber 40-42; R of St Jas Cruden 42-45; St Andr Alford 45-51; St Jo Evang Forfar 51-59; CF (TA) 52-57; SCF (TA) 57-60; Can of St Ninian's Cathl Perth 57-59; R of St Mich AA Helensburgh 59-71; R of St Columba Largs 71-78; Can of St Mary's Cathl Glas 71-78; Hon Can from 78. *18 Market Street, St Andrews, Fife, KY16 9NS.* (St Andr 77419)

NOBLE, Francis Alick. Late Exhib of Trin Coll Cam 2nd cl Math Trip pt i, 31, BA (Sen Opt pt ii) 33, MA 37. Linc Th Coll 33. **d** 36 Wakef **p** 37 Pontefract for Wakef. C of St Edw Barnsley 36-38; St Mich Castleford 38-40; Shelton 41-43; V of Edensor 43-50; Min of Eccles Distr of St Paul Crofton Orpington 50-59; V 59-67; R of Guiseley 67-78. *16 Parc Aberconwy, Prestatyn, Clwyd, LL19.* (Prestatyn 6820)

NOBLE, John Ashley. St Francis Coll Brisb ACT ThL 65. **d** 65 **p** 68 Brisb. C of St Steph Coorparoo Brisb 65-69; Booval 69-70; Perm to Offic Dio Bris 70-76; Hon C of N Mackay 77-79; Asst Chap Colleg Sch of St Pet Adel from 79. *22a Trinity Street, College Park, S Australia 5069.*

NOBLE, John Leroy. St Jo Coll Morpeth ACT ThL 35. **d** 36 **p** 37 Armid. C of St John Tamworth 36-37; St Cypr Narrabri 37-38; P-in-c of Collareneberi 38-39; Tambar Springs 39-42; C of Tamworth 42-43; Chap AIF 43-58; BCOF Japan 45-51; Ingleburn 51-58; State Sec ABM 57; R of N Rockptn 58-61; L to Offic Dio Brisb 61-64; and from 68; R of Gayndah 64-67; V of Pialba 67-68. *2 Hornibrook Esplanade, Contarf Beach, Australia 4019.* (84-7132)

NOBLE, Peter Hirst. b 37. BD (Lon) 68. Univ of Leeds MPh 72. Cranmer Hall Dur 65. **d** 68 **p** 69 Wakef. C of Honley w Brockholes 68-72; V of Askern Dio Sheff from 72; C-in-c of Moss 72-81. *Askern Vicarage, Doncaster, S Yorks.* (Doncaster 700404)

NOBLE, Philip David. b 46. Univ of Glas BSc 67. Univ of Edin BD 70. Edin Th Coll 67. **d** 70 **p** 71 Edin. C of Ch Ch Morningside 70-72; Port Moresby 72-73; P-in-c of Sakarina 73-75; R of Cambuslang Dio Glas from 76; Uddington Dio Glas from 76. *58 Elm Drive, Cambuslang, Glasgow.* (041-641 9541)

NOBLE, Robert. b 18. TCD Dipl Bibl Stud 56. **d** 57 **p** 58 Down. C of Ballymacarrett 57-62; C-in-c of St Chris Belf 62-65; R 65-72; Kilwarlin 72-81; RD of Hillsborough 75-80; Chap RAF from 81. *2 Newport Road, Albrighton, Wolverhampton.*

NOBLE, Robert. b 43. TCD BA (2nd cl Mod) 66, Div Test (1st cl) 68, BD 73. **d** 68 **p** 69 Down. C of Holywood 68-71; Chap RAF from 71. *c/o Ministry of Defence, Adastral House, WC 1.*

NOBLE, William Samuel. Em Coll Sktn BA and LTh 34. **d** 34 Sktn **p** 35 Sask. C of Unity 34-35; Miss at Kinistino 35-36; I of Melfort 36-38; Can of St Alb Cathl Prince Albert Sask 39-52; R 39-52; Waterdown 52-75; Dom Chap to Bp of Niag 56-61; P-in-c of Palermo Dio Niag from 75. *Apt 922, 690 Regency Court, Burlington, Ont, Canada.* (416-681 1066)

NOBLETT, William Alexander. b 53. Univ of Southn BTh 78. Sarum Wells Th Coll 74. **d** 78 Dub **p** 79 Win. C of Sholing 78-80; R of Ardamine U Dio Ferns from 80. *Ardamine Rectory, Gorey, Co Wexford, Irish Republic.*

✠ **NOCK, Right Rev Frank Foley.** Univ of Tor BA 38. Trin Coll Tor BD 46, Hon DD 57. **d** 40 **p** 41 Tor. C of St Matt Tor 40-42; P-in-c of Korah 42-45; R of Bracebridge 45-48; Sudbury 48-57; Exam Chap to Bp of Alg 47-74; Dean and R of Sault Ste Marie Cathl 57-74; P-in-c of St Steph Miss Sault Ste Marie 57-74; Cons Ld Bp of Alg in Sault Ste Marie Cathl 10 Jan 75 by Abp of Moos and Abp W L Wright; Bps of Tor, Ont, Ott, Niag and Hur; Bps Suffr of Moos, Hur and Tor. *Box 1168, Sault Ste Marie, Ont., Canada.* (705-256 7379)

NOCK, Peter Arthur. b 15. Keble Coll Ox BA 36, MA 42. Bps' Coll Cheshunt 37. **d** 39 **p** 40 Blackb. C of Gt Harwood 39-40; Lancaster Priory Ch Lanc 40-45; V of Ch Ch Wyresdale 45-50; St Cuthb Darwen 50-64; Sparkhill 64-71; RD of Bordesley 67-71; V of St Pet Maney 71-81. *West View, Dufton, Appleby, Cumb, CA16 6DB.* (Appleby 51413)

NOCKELS, Donald Reginald. b 09. Univ of Leeds BA (2nd cl Cl) 32. Coll of Resurr Mirfield 32. **d** 34 **p** 35 Cant. C of St Sav Westgate-on-Sea 34-38; Perm to Offic at St Andr Croydon 38-39; C of St Anne Derby 39-40; H Trin Bingley 40-44; Min of St Cuthb Wrose Bradf 44-54; V of Cottingley 54-63; Cononley w Bradley 63-73. *1 Highfield Court, Oakworth, Keighley, W Yorks. BD22 7JA.* (Haworth 43912)

NOCKELS, John Martin. b 46. Qu Coll Birm 72. **d** 73 **p** 74 Bradf. C of Eccleshill 73-76; Fawley 76-78; V of Shirley Warren Dio Win from 78. *94/98 Chestnut Road, Shirley Warren, Southampton, SO1 6BU.* (Southn 774603)

NODDER, Jonathan James Colmore. b 37. Dipl Th (Lon) 64. Tyndale Hall Bris 63. **d** 65 **p** 66 Chesh. C of Bebington 65-71; V of St Mark Edgeley Stockport Dio Ches from 71. *St Mark's Vicarage, Edgeley, Stockport, Chesh.* (061-480 5896)

NODDER, (Arnold) Thomas Arthur. b 20. K Coll Lon 58. **d** 60 **p** 61 S'wark. C of Rotherhithe 60-63; M SSF from 63; L Pr Dio Chelmsf 63-66; C-in-c of St Phil and St Jas Plaistow 66-68; LPr Dio Birm from 70. *Friary, Hilfield, Dorchester, Dorset, DT5 7BE.*

NODDINGS, John Henry. b 39. Chich Th Coll 80. **d** 81 Roch. C of Southborough Dio Roch from 81. *Fairview, London Road, Southborough, Tunbridge Wells, Kent.*

NOEL, Douglas Earle. Wycl Coll Tor. **d** 42 Tor **p** 43 NS. C of St Paul Halifax 43-45; R of New London NS 45-48; C of St Thos St John's Newfld 48-54; Grace Ch-on-the-Hill Tor 54-56; R of Southn Ont 56-60; Waterford Ont 60-63; Hosp Chap Hamilton 63-72; C of Ch Ch Cathl Hamilton 72-77; Chap Hamilton Gen Hosp from 77. *Apt 702, 90 Duke Street, Hamilton, Ont., Canada.* (416-522 8741)

NOEL, Dugald Clifford. Mem Tr Sch Tennessee. **d** and **p** 28 Tennessee. I of Battle Harbour 30-38; Herring Neck 39-42; Neil's Harbour 42-50; on sick leave 50-54; R of Kings Cove 55-65. *St Luke's Homes, St John's, Newfoundland, Canada.*

NOEL, Frank Arthur. b 20. Trin Coll Dub BA 44, Div Test 45, MA 49. **d** 45 **p** 46 Down. C of Aghalee 45-48; Portadown 48-51; R of Ballinderry w Tamlaght 51-59; I of Tullaniskin w Clonoe 59-63; R of Mullabrack w Kilcluney 63-75; Acton and Drumbanagher Dio Arm from 75; RD of Mullabrack from 75. *Drumbanagher Vicarage, Jerrettspass, Newry, Co Down, BT35 6LW, N Ireland.*

NOEL, Samuel Maurice. b 16. Oak Hill Th Coll 40. **d** 41 Pontefract for Wakef **p** 42 Wakef. C of St Andr Wakef 41-44; Newtownards 45-47; Portadown 47-50; R of Creggan and Forkill (w Jonesborough from 60; Killeavy from 65; Ballymascanlon, Carlingford and Omeath from 73) Dio Arm from 50; RD of Creggan 67-75. *Jonesborough Rectory, Newry, Co Down, N Ireland.* (Killeavy 227)

NOEL, William Donald Keven. Qu Coll Newfld 58. **d** 63 **p** 64 Newfld. C of Grand Falls 63-64; P-in-c of Bay St Geo 64-69; I of Harbour Breton 69-73; Indian Bay Dio Newfld (Centr Newfld from 76) from 73. *PO Box 17, Trinity, Bonavista Bay, Newfoundland, Canada.* (709-678-2507)

NOEL-COX, Edward Lovis. b 1899. Bps' Coll Cheshunt 22. **d** 23 **p** 25 Chelmsf. C of St Martin's Conv Distr Plaistow 23-24; Latchingdon 24-25; All SS Southend-on-Sea 25-27; Sandhurst 27-29; Minehead 29-35; V of Langport 35-42; C of St Mary Virg (in c of St Sav) Reading 42-51; Chap Qu Mary's Hosp for Children Carshalton 51-64; Perm to Offic Dio Cant 52-58; Dio Chich from 65. *7 Willow Court, Grand Avenue, Worthing, Sussex.*

NOGEA, Isaac. **d** 75 **p** 76 Zanz T. P Dio Zanz T. *Box 45, Tanga, Tanzania.*

NOISE, Robin Allan. b 31. K Coll Lon and Warm. **d** 57 **p** 58 Cov. C of Wyken 57-60; R of Churchover w Willey 60-66; C-in-c of Harborough Magna 62-66; Chap St Mary's Hosp Harborough Magna 62-66; V of St Jo Bapt Leamington 66-81; Alveston Dio Cov from 81. *Alveston Vicarage, Stratford-on-Avon, Warws.* (Stratford-on-Avon 292777)

NOKES, Peter Warwick. b 48. Univ of Leic BA 71. Westcott Ho Cam 79. **d** 81 Birm. C of Northfield Dio Birm from 81. *Flat 1, 34 Woodland Road, Northfield, Birmingham, B31 2HS.* (021-477 9719)

NOKES, Robert Harvey. b 39. Keble Coll Ox BA (2nd cl Mod Hist) 61, MA 65. Univ of Birm Dipl Th 63. Qu Coll Birm 61. **d** 63 **p** 64 St Alb. C of Totteridge 63-67; Dunstable 67-73; V of Langford Dio St Alb from 73. *Langford Vicarage, Biggleswade, Beds.* (Hitchin 700248)

NOLAN, James Charles William. b 44. Chich Th Coll 75. **d** 77 **p** 78 Ches. C of St Andr Crewe 77-79; Sale (in c of St Francis) Dio Ches from 79. *193 Northenden Road, Sale Moor, Sale, Cheshire, M33 2JG.* (061-969 7061)

NOLAN, James Joseph. b 16. Cranmer Hall Dur. **d** 61 **p** 62 Southw. C of St Jo Evang Worksop 61-63; V of St Cath Edge Hill 63-66; H Trin Heworth w St Cuthb Peaseholme 66-72; Dep Sec CPAS 72-74; R of Bridlington Dio York from 74. *Rectory, Church Green, Bridlington, Yorks, YO16 5JX.* (Bridlington 2221)

NOLAN, John. b 25. TCD BA and Div Test 51, MA 55. **d** 51 **p** 52 Connor. C of Carrickfergus 51-53; Dean's V of St Anne's Cathl Belf 53-55; V Cho 55-79; Min Can from 60; Bp's C of St Jo Bapt U Falls Dio Connor from 79. *28 Upper Green, Dunmurry, Belfast, BT17 0EL.*

NOLAN, Robert William. b 47. St Francis Coll Brisb 68. **d** 70 **p** 71 Brisb. C of St Paul Ipswich 70-74; R of Childers 74-76; P-in-c of Jindalee-Middle Pk Brisb 77-80; V of St Cath Centenary Suburbs City and Dio Brisb from 80. *McFarlane Street, Middle Park, Queensland, Australia 4074.* (376 4052)

NOLLAND, John Leslie. Univ of New Engl BSc 70. BD (Lon) 71. Moore Coll Syd ThL 70. **d** 71 **p** 72 Syd. C of W Cabramatta 71-72; Res Min St Steph W Cabramatta 73-74; on leave. *37 Kingarth Street, Busby, NSW, Australia 2168.*

NOLLY, Joseph Harold. b 46. St Pet Coll Alice 73. **d** 75 **p** 76 Capetn. C of St Cypr Retreat 75-78; Athlone 78-80; Wesfleur Dio Capetn from 80. *26 Anna Avenue, Atlantis 7349, CP, S Africa.*

NOLO, Yona. **d** 69 Centr Tang **p** 69 Moro. P Dio Centr Tang. *Ndebwe, PO Mvumi, Tanzania.*

NOMA, Dick Shepherd. Newton Coll Dogura 68. **d** 71 Bp Ambo for Papua **p** 72 Bp Meredith for Papua. C of Mt Waverley 72-73; Perm to Offic Dio Melb 73-74; P-in-c of Asai 74-76; Hon C of Madang 77-80; V of Apugi Dio New Guinea Is from 80; Exam Chap to Bp of New Guinea Is from 80. *Apugi, via Kandrian, Papua New Guinea.*

NOMBEKELA, Wycliffe Delford Bkizitha. b 46. St Bede's Coll Umtata 69. **d** 70 Bp Sobukwe for St John's **p** 72 St John's. C of St Andrew Umtata 70-72; Ntlaza 72-75; H Cross Miss Dio St John's 75-79; Dioc Youth Org from 79. *Box 65, Umtata, Transkei, S Africa.*

NOMLALA, Nelson Ncoba. St Pet Coll Rosettenville, 49. **d** 51 **p** 53 St Jo Kaffr. P Dio St Jo Kaffr 51-60; Dio St John's from 60. *Box 155, Engcobo, Transkei, S Africa.*

NOMPUKU, Alfred Vuyisile Pomomo. b 47. St Bede's Coll Umtata 75. **d** 77 **p** 78 St John's. P Dio St John's. *PO Holy Cross, Transkei.*

NOON, Canon Edward Arthur. b 16. Selw Coll Cam 2nd cl Mod and Med Lang Trip pt i 36, BA (3rd cl Th Trip pt i) 38, MA 42. Bps' Coll Cheshunt 38. **d** 40 **p** 41 S'wark. C of St Jo Evang Kingston T 40-43; St Barn Dulwich 43-48; C-in-c of St Pet S Wimbledon 48-50; V 50-55; St Mark Mitcham 55-65; Horley Surrey 65-77; RD of Reigate 72-76; Hon Can of S'wark from 72; C-in-c of St Barn Purley Dio S'wark from 77. *84 Higher Drive, Purley, Surrey, CR2 2HJ.* (01-660 3251)

NOONAN, Daniel Edward. Trin Coll Tor BA 48, BD 51. **d** 50 Calg for Bran **p** 51 Bran. R of Pilot Mound 50-54; St Geo Bran 54-59; Portage la Prairie 59-67; Can of Rupld 62-66; Archd of Selkirk 66-67; Winnipeg 67-71; Dir of Program Dio Rupld 67-71; Hon C of St Jude Winnipeg 71-72; St Bede Winnipeg 73-76; R of Souris 76-79; St Jo Div Vic Dio BC from 79. *1611 Quadra Street, Victoria, BC, Canada.*

NOONE, Ronald Martin. b 49. Trin Coll Melb BTh 76. **d** 77 **p** 78 Melb. C of St D Moorabbin 77-78; Asst Chap Geelong Gr Sch 78-81; on leave. *Geelong Grammar School, Corio, Vic, Australia 3214.* (052-75 1142)

NOOTT, Arthur Jenner. Wells Th Coll. **d** 53 **p** 54 Win. C of St Alb Southn 53-54; Christchurch w Mudeford (in c of All SS Mudeford) Dio Win 54-58; R of St Mary Pembroke Tobago 58-60; Couva Dio Trinid 60-62; V of Westbury-on-Severn 62-76. *10 Marine Parade, Shaldon, S Devon, TQ14 0DP.*

NOOTT, Canon Eric Hervey Jenner. b 1899. St Jo Coll Cam BA 20, MA 24. **d** 22 **p** 23 Worc. C of Ch Ch Malvern 22-27; Asst Master KS Glouc 27-36; Min Can of Glouc Cathl 27-36; Sacr 32-36; Hon Min Can 36-42; Prec 42-51; V of Barnwood 36-47; Chap of Barnwood Ho Glouc 37-51; Asst RD of Glouc 40-46; Hd Master KS Glouc 42-51; Hon Can of Glouc from 48; R of Withington (w Compton Abdale from 62) 51-69. *2 St Mary's Street, Gloucester.*

NOPECE, Bethlehem Nceba. b 50. Univ of S Africa BTh. St Bede's Coll Umtata 77. **d** 78 **p** 80 St John's. P Dio St John's. *PO Box 135, Butterworth, Transkei.*

NORBERT, Henri Narson. St Paul's Coll Ambat 53. **d** 63 Bp Seth for Madag **p** 65 Madag. P Dio 63-69; Dio Tam 69-74; Dio Antan from 75. *Ambohipiainana, Fihaonana, Ankazobe, Malagasy Republic.*

NORBURN, Very Rev Richard Evelyn Walter. b 21. Univ of Witwatersrand BA 44. St Paul's Coll Grahmstn 49. **d** 51 **p** 53 Pret. Vice-Prin Dioc Tr Coll Dio Pret 51-56; Dir of Relig Educn Dio Pret 56-62; R of Potgietersrus 56-62; C of St Sav Croydon 63-64; V of St Phil Norbury 65-75; Addington 75-81; Surr 75-81; Hon Can of Cant Cathl 79-81; Can (Emer) from 81; RD of Croydon Addington 81; Dean of Botswana from 81. *Box 769, Gaborone, Botswana.* (Gaborone 53280)

NORBURN, Canon Richard Henry. b 32. St Edm Hall Ox BA (2nd cl Mod Hist) 57, Dipl Th 58. Wycl Hall Ox. **d** and **p** 59 St E. C of St Greg w St Pet Sudbury 59-65; Youth Chap Dio St E 65-74; R of Ampton w L Livermere and Ingham 74-81; C-in-c of Gt Livermere 74-81; RD of Thingoe from 78; R of Ingham w Ampton and Gt and L Livermere Dio St E from 81; Hon Can of St E from 81. *Ingham Rectory, Bury St Edmunds, Suff.* (Culford 430)

NORCOTT, James William. QUB BA 22. **d** 48 **p** 49 Connor. C of Derriaghy 48-52; I of Macroom U 52-58; Berehaven w Glengarriff 58-72. *Rectory, Glengarriff, Co Cork, Irish Republic.*

NORCROSS, Norman Jon. Univ of BC BA 60. Angl Th Coll of BC LTh 63. **d** 63 **p** 64 Calg. C of Ch Ch Calg 63-65; V of Rimbey 65-67; Chap RCN from 67. *82 Pinecrest Drive, Dartmouth, NS, Canada.*

NORFOLK, Archdeacon of. *See* Dawson, Ven Peter.

NORFOLK, Ven Edward Matheson. b 21. Univ of Leeds BA (2nd cl Hist) 44. Coll of Resurr Mirfield 41. **d** 46 Kens for Lon **p** 47 Lon. C of H Cross Greenford 46-47; K Chas Mart

South Mymms 47-50; Bushey 50-53; PC of Waltham Cross 53-59; V of Welwyn Garden City 59-69; R of Gt Berkhamsted 69-81; Hon Can of St Alb Cathl from 72; V of King's Langley 81-82; Archd of St Alb from 82. *6 Sopwell Lane, St Albans, Herts, AL1 1RR.* (St Alb 57973)

NORGATE, Canon Cecil Richard. St Chad's Coll Dur BA 47, Dipl Th 49. **d** 49 **p** 50 Newc T. C of St Pet Wallsend 49-54; Miss P at Newala 54-56; Masasi 56-58; P-in-c of Mkomaindo Dio Masasi from 58; Can of Masasi Cathl from 73. *USPG, Mkomaindo, PO Box 16, Masasi, Tanzania.*

NORGATE, Norman George. b 32. Qu Coll Cam BA 55, MA 58. Ridley Hall Cam. **d** 57 **p** 58 Roch. C of Northumb Heath Erith 57-60; St Steph E Twickenham 60-63; V of St Pet Bexleyheath 63-70; St Mary-of-Bethany Woking Dio Guildf from 71. *St Mary's Vicarage, West Hill Road, Woking, Surrey.* (Woking 61269)

NORMAN, Andrew Herbert. b 54. AKC and BD 77. St Steph Ho Ox 77. **d** 78 **p** 79 Cant. C of Deal w Sholden 78-81; Maidstone Dio Cant from 81. *25 Wayfair Avenue, Maidstone, Kent.* (Maidstone 677682)

NORMAN, Arthur Leslie Frayne. b 08. Sarum Th Coll 29. **d** 31 **p** 33 Swan B. C of St Jude Swansea 31-37; St Gabr Swansea (in c of St Aug Brynmill) 37-46; Surr from 47; V of St John Swansea 46-58; Ch Ch Swansea 58-75; Chap HM Pris Swansea 58-75. *4 Malvern Terrace, Brynmill, Swansea, W Glam.* (Swansea 59310)

✠ **NORMAN, Right Rev Edward Kinsella.** b 16. MC 43. DSO 45. Univ of NZ BA 39. Westcott Ho Cam 46. **d** 47 **p** 48 Newc T. C of Berwick-on-Tweed 47-49; V of Waiwhetu 49-52; Levin 52-59; Tauranga 59-65; Karori Wel 65-73; Archd of Wel 69-73; Cons Ld Bp of Wel in St Paul's Cathl Wel 31 May 73 by Abp of NZ; Bps of Nel, Auckld, Dun, Wai and Ch Ch; and others. *Bishopscourt, 28 Eccleston Hill, Wellington 1, NZ.* (723-183)

NORMAN, Edward Leslie. b 11. Univ of Wales BA (2nd cl Phil) 33. Lich Th Coll 33. **d** 35 **p** 36 Sheff. C of Doncaster 35-37; St Mich Wood Green Lon 37-42; L to Offic Dio Dur 43 and Asst Chap Miss to Seamen 42-43; Dio Chelmsf 43-44 and Asst Chap Miss to Seamen Port of Lon 43-44; C of Bexleyheath 44-45; Min of St Pet Conv Distr Bexleyheath 45-51; V of Hoo St Werburgh 51-61; Borstal 61-77; C-in-c of Wouldham 73-75; *11 Roebuck Road, Rochester, Kent, ME1 1UE.* (Medway 44069)

NORMAN, Edward Robert. b 38. Selw Coll Cam BA 61, PhD 64, MA 65, BD 67, FRHistS 72. DD 78. **d** 65 **p** 71 Ely. Fell of Selw Coll Cam 62-64; Jes Coll Cam 64-71; Lect in Hist Univ of Cam from 64; Fell and Dean of Peterho Cam from 71. *Peterhouse, Cambridge.*

NORMAN, Garth. b 38. St Chad's Coll Dur BA (2nd cl Th) 62, Dipl Th (w distinc) 63, MA 68. **d** 63 **p** 64 S'wark. C of St Anne Wandsworth 63-66; Trunch w Swafield 66-71; Team R of Trunch Group Dio Nor from 71; RD of Repps from 75. *Mundesley Rectory, Norwich, NR11 8DG.* (Mundesley 720520)

NORMAN, John Alan. b 28. Keble Coll Ox BA (2nd cl Th) 51, MA 55. Westcott Ho Cam 51. **d** 53 **p** 54 Derby. C of Ilkeston 53-57; PC of Ashford w Sheldon 57-64; R of Breadsall 64-71; V of Ticehurst 71-74; R of Sullington 74-77; Storrington Dio Chich from 74; Surr from 75; RD of Storrington 76-81. *Storrington Rectory, Pulborough, W Sussex, RH20 4EF.* (Storrington 2888)

NORMAN, Canon John Ronald. b 15. Univ of Lon BA (2nd cl Hist) 40. Linc Th Coll 40. **d** 42 Hull for York **p** 43 York. C of Yarm 42-43; Stokesley 43-46; R of St Ternan Muchalls 46-50; V of Kirkby Ireleth 50-55; R of Greystoke w Penruddock 55-60; C-in-c of Matterdale 56-60; Warden of St Andr Coll Greystoke 56-60; Chap Commun of H Paraclete and St Hilda's Sch Whitby 60-61; R of Dunnington 61-72; RD of Bulmer 65-72; R of Bolton Percy w Colton Dio York from 72; Worship Adv Dio York from 72; Sec Dioc Advisory C'tte Dio York 75-80; Can and Preb of York Minster from 77. *Rectory, Bolton Percy, York.* (Appleton Roebuck 213)

NORMAN, John William Leneve. b 15. Clifton Th Coll 40. **d** 42 **p** 43 Chelmsf. C of Chingford 42-44; LPr Dio Nor and C-in-c of Bodham 44-47; C-in-c of Hempstead-by-Holt 45-47; C of Brentwood 47-51; St Botolph Colchester (in c of St Steph) 51-53; V of St Steph Colchester 53-62; Paulton (in c of Farrington Gurney 73-77) 62-81; Farrington Gurney 77-81. *c/o Vicarage, Paulton, Bristol, Avon, BS18 5LG.* (Midsomer Norton 412234)

NORMAN, Malcolm. Qu Coll Newfld. **d** 34 **p** 35 Newfld. C-in-c of Tack's Beach 34-35; I 35-41; R of Simonds 43-47; Miss of Gordon and Lorne 47-52; R of McAdam 52-60; Good Shepherd Ont 60-75. *322 Brock Street, Kingston, Ont, Canada.* (613-546 7517)

NORMAN, Michael Heugh. Qu Coll Cam BA 48. Westcott Ho Cam 48. **d** 50 Dover for Cant **p** 51 Cant. C of St Pet-in-I of Thanet 50-52; Retreat 52-62; P-in-c of Bergvliet 62; R of St Steph Pinelands Dio Capetn from 62. *St Stephen's Rectory, Central Square, Pinelands, CP, S Africa.* (533350)

NORMAN, Paul Gordon. b 22. ALCD 55. **d** 55 **p** 56 Lon. C of St Anne Limehouse 55-58; Erdington (in c of St Marg) 58-62; R of Ashover Dio Derby from 62. *Ashover Rectory, Chesterfield, Derbys, S45 0AU.* (Ashover 246)

NORMAN, Roy Albert. b 23. **d** 65 **p** 66 Glouc. C of Brockworth 65-67; Thornbury Glos 67-70; P-in-c of Woolaston w Alvington Dio Glouc 70-80; R from 80. *Rectory, Main Road, Alvington, Lydney, Glos, GL15 6AT.*

NORMAN, Canon William Beadon. b 26. Late Scho of Trin Coll Cam BA 49, MA 55. Ridley Hall Cam 52. **d** 52 **p** 53 Roch. C of St Jo Bapt Beckenham 52-54; CMS Miss and Tutor Buwalasi Th Coll Uganda 55-65; Exam Chap to Bp of Soroti 61-65; Hon Can of Mbale 63-65; V of Alne w Aldwark 65-74; Blackheath 74-79; RD of Warley 74-79; Hon Can of Birm Cathl from 78; Team R of King's Norton Dio Birm from 79. *King's Norton Rectory, Birmingham, B30 3EX.* (021-458 3289)

NORMAN, William John. St Andr Coll Whittlesford. **d** 44 Bp Golding-Bird for Guildf **p** 45 Guildf. C of Stoke-next-Guildf 44-47; Org Sec BFBS 47-50; R of Ruan Lanihorne w Philleigh 50-52; PC of St Edm Gateshead 52-54; CMS Area Sec Dios Lon and S'wark 54-66; Dios Chich, Guildf and Portsm 54-74; SE Reg Sec 56-74; R of Buriton 74-79. *22 Middlehill Road, Colehill, Wimborne, Dorset.*

NORMAND, John Stanley. Moore Th Coll. BD (Lon) 74. **d** and **p** 75 Syd. C of Seaforth 75-76; CMS Miss 77-80; C-in-c of Manly Vale w Allambie Heights Dio Syd from 80. *1 King Street, Manly Vale, NSW, Australia 2093.* (949-1451)

NORMINGTON, Eric. b 16. SOC. **d** 63 **p** 64 S'wark. C of Coulsdon 63-66; Bath Abbey 66-70; R of All SS Weston Bath (w N Stoke from 78) 70-81; RD of Keynsham 75-76; C of Sidbury w Sidford Dio Ex from 81. *St Peter's Vicarage, Newlands Close, Sidmouth, Devon.* (Sidmouth 2016)

NORNABELL, Canon Edward Raymond. Bp's Univ Lennox LST 32. **d** 31 **p** 32 Alg. C of St Thos Tor 32-34; R of Huntsville 34-48; St Barn St Catharines 48-56; I of Burk's Falls 56-60; Espanola 60-71; Hon Can of Alg from 66; I of Port Syd Alg 71-79. *Box 2736, Fairy Avenue, Huntsille, Ont, Canada.*

NORRIS, Allan Edward. b 43. St Jo Coll Dur BA 72, Dipl Th 73. Cranmer Hall Dur 69. **d** 73 **p** 74 S'wark. C of St John w St Jas and St Paul Plumstead 73-78; St Geo w St Andr Battersea 78-82; St Sav Battersea Pk 78-82; V of Isle of Grain w Stoke Dio Roch from 82. *Parsonage, Isle of Grain, Rochester, Kent, ME3 0BS.* (Medway 270263)

NORRIS, Arthur Henry. b 1900. St Chad's Coll Dur BA (2nd cl Th) 21, MA 24. **d** 24 **p** 25 Dur. C of St Osw Dur 24-28; St John Darlington 28-30; Min of St Mark Darlington 30-39; V of St Osw W Hartlepool 39-56; Chap W Hartlepool Gen Hosp 45-56; R of Foston w Flaxton 56-65; RD of Bulmer 60-65; C-in-c of St Mich-le-Belfrey w H Trin Goodramgate York 66-68. *6 The Coppice, Bishopthorpe, York.* (York 706806)

NORRIS, Barry John. b 46. Open Univ BA 80. **d** 70 **p** 71 RC Archbp of S'wark. In RC Ch 71-72; Rec into Angl Commun by Bp of Ely 76; C of St Pet Wisbech (in c of St Mary) 76-78; Team V of E Ham 78-81; Chap RAF from 81. *c/o Ministry of Defence, Adastral House, Theobalds Road, WC1.*

NORRIS, Canon Basil Charles. K Coll Cam BA 37, MA 41. Cudd Coll 38. **d** 39 Chelmsf **p** 40 Lon. C of St Jas Clacton 39-40; St Mary Virg Kenton 40-43; Rickmansworth 43-47; Chap Cho of Ches Cathl 47-49; Hd Master of Choir Sch Newc T and Prec of Newc T Cathl 49-59; Dir of Educn Dio York from 59; R of St Mary Castlegate w St Mich Spurriergate City and Dio York from 59; Sec York Educn C'ttee from 59; Can and Preb of York Minster from 66. *9 Lawnway, York, YO3 0JD.* (York 59281)

NORRIS, Clifford Joseph. b 29. Codr Coll Barb. **d** 61 Antig **p** 68 Lon. C of St John's Cathl Antig 61-62; C of St Silas Pentonville Islington 68-70; St Dunstan and All SS Stepney 70-73; P-in-c of St Jas w St Jude Bethnal Green Dio Lon from 73; Commiss Antig from 73. *331 Bethnal Green Road, E2 6LG.* (01-739 0010)

NORRIS, Canon Edward Colston. b 06. St Cath S Ox BA 37, MA 41. Ridley Hall Cam 37. **d** 38 **p** 39 Bris. C of St Aug Swindon 38-40; Offg C-in-c 40-42; CF (EC) 42-46 (Men in Disp 44); Chap Napsbury Ment Hosp 47-81; Hon Can of St Alb 69-81; Can (Emer) from 81. *c/o 8 Westwick Close, Leverstock Green, Hemel Hempstead, Herts.* (Hemel Hempstead 53018)

NORRIS, Eric Richard. b 43. Ripon Hall Ox 66. **d** 69 Warrington for Liv **p** 70 Liv. C of Huyton 69-72; Mexborough 72-74; V of Dalton 74-78; Cler Org Sec CECS Dio Carl from 78. *Hazel Rigg, Abbeytown, Carlisle, CA5 4RL.* (Abbeytown 674)

NORRIS, Gerald Leigh. **d** 53 **p** 54 Queb. I of Peninsula

53-55; Bury 55-59; R of Waterloo 59-63; in Amer Ch 63-68; R of Conquerall Dio NS from 68; New Dublin Dio NS from 68. *St Augustine's Church, Conquerall, NS, Canada.* (688-2630)

NORRIS, Harold Alexander. b 05. Univ of Leeds BA (2nd cl Hist) 28. Coll of Resurr Mirfield 28. **d** 30 Liv **p** 31 Cov. C of St Dunstan Earle Rd Edge Hill 30-31; St Jo Bapt Cov 31-35; All H N St Pancras 35-39; R of St Joseph Port Mourant 39-45; Commiss Guy 46-66 and from 67; SW Area Sec SPG 46-55; PC of St Aldhelm Branksome 55-60; Chap St Bernard's Hosp Southall and L to Offic Dio Lon 60-73. *255 Pope's Lane, W5 4NH.* (01-567 6209)

NORRIS, John Henry. b 03. St Jo Coll Cam BA 25, MA 29. Ridley Hall Cam 26. **d** 27 **p** 29 Blackb. C of All SS Clayton-le-Moors 27-33; H Trin Darwen 33-35; V of St Jas Darwen 35-56; Lund 56-72. *17 Windermere Road, Kendal, Cumb. LA9 4QJ.*

NORRIS, William Basil. b 06. Late Exhib of St Jo Coll Ox BA (2nd cl Hist) 26, MA 30. Trin Coll Dub MA (*ad eund*) 34. Cudd Coll 28. **d** 29 **p** 30 Ox. C of Gt Marlow 29-33; Chap of St Andr Cathl Aber 33-36; C of Hessle 36-37; R of St Paul Kinross 37-44; V of Carlinghow 44-48; Exmoor 48-61; R of Challacombe 57-61; N Waltham w Steventon (and Dummer to 68; Ashe w Deane from 72) 61-76; C-in-c of Ashe w Deane 68-72. *2 Wonston Manor Cottages, Sutton Scotney, Winchester, Hants, SO21 3PD.*

NORRISS, Victor William. Univ of Lon BA (2nd cl Cl) 32. Cudd Coll 38. **d** 39 **p** 40 Win. C of St Mark Woolston 39-42; Chap RNVR 42-46; RN 46-66; Chap N Foreland Lodge 67-68; C of Ringwood (in c of St Paul Bisterne and St Jo Bapt Poulner) 68-71; R of Wonston w Sutton Scotney Dio Win 71-81; R of Wonston from 81. *Wonston Rectory, Winchester, Hants.* (Sutton Scotney 240)

NORTH, Albert. b 13. Univ of Lon BA (2nd cl French) 35. Sarum Th Coll 64. **d** 65 Barking for Chelmsf **p** 66 Chelmsf. C of Squirrel's Heath 65-70; V of Gt w L Saling 70-72; St Osyth 72-81. *9 Woburn Avenue, Kirby Cross, Frinton-on-Sea, Essex, CO13 OPX.*

NORTH, David Roland. b 45. Qu Coll Birm 72. **d** 73 **p** 74 Blackb. C of Salesbury 73-76; Marton 76-79; V of St Leon Penwortham Dio Blackb from 79. *Vicarage, Marshall's Brow, Penwortham, Preston, Lancs PR1 9HY.* (Preston 742367)

NORTH, George Lewis. b 16. AKC 41. **d** 41 **p** 42 Pet. C of St Mary Virg Far Cotton Northampton 41-46; Whitchurch w Doddington 46-49; V of Ch Ch Northampton 49-52; Chap to LCC Residential Sch Hutton 52-57; R of Brington w Molesworth and Old Weston Dio Ely from 57; V of Leighton Bromswold Dio Ely from 68. *Brington Rectory, Huntingdon, Cambs, PE18 0PU.* (Bythorn 305)

NORTH, Michael Anthony. Moore Th Coll Syd ACT ThL 67. **d** 67 **p** 68 Syd. C of E Roseville 67-68; Summer Hill 68-69; Seaforth Dio Syd from 70. *22 Frenchs Forest Road, Seaforth, NSW 2092, Australia.*

NORTH, Robert. b 54. Univ of Lon BSc 77. Ripon Coll Cudd 78. **d** 81 Heref. C of SS Pet & Paul Leominster Dio Heref from 81. *10 The Meadows, Leominster, Herefs.* (Leom 5417)

NORTH, Vernon Leslie. b 26. Bps' Coll Cheshunt 61. **d** 63 **p** 64 Guildf. C of N Holmwood 63-65; Dunstable 65-68; V of Stotfold Dio St Alb from 68; P-in-c of Radwell Dio St Alb from 76; RD of Shefford from 79. *Vicarage, Church Road, Stotfold, Hitchin, Herts.* (Hitchin 730218)

NORTHALL, Malcolm Walter. b 26. Ely Th Coll 63. **d** 64 **p** 65 Worc. C of Bromsgrove 64-67; V of Blockley w Aston Magna Dio Glouc from 67. *Blockley Vicarage, Moreton-in-Marsh, Glos, GL56 9ES.* (Blockley 700283)

NORTHAM, Cavell Herbert James Cavell. b 32. St Steph Ho Ox 53. **d** 56 **p** 57 Ox. C of W Wycombe (in c of Downley from 58) 56-61; CF (TA) 60-63; V of Lane End 61-68; Stony Stratford Dio Ox from 68; Surr from 68; C-in-c of Calverton 69-72; R from 72. *Stony Stratford Vicarage, Milton Keynes, MK11 1JA.* (Milton Keynes 562148)

NORTHAMPTON, Archdeacon of. *See* Marsh, Ven Bazil Roland.

NORTHCOTE, John George. **d** 52 Jarrow for Dur **p** 53 Dur. C of St Cuthb Dur 52-53; Princetown and Asst Chap HM Pris Dartmoor 53-55; Chap HM Pris and LPr Dio Man 55-56; HM Pris Walton Liv 56-63; L Pr Dio Liv 56-63; R of Kingswood 63-65; Perm to Offic Dio Leic from 66. *23 Pytchley Drive, Loughborough, Leics, LE11 2RH.* (Loughborough 31546)

NORTHCOTT, Canon Geoffrey Stephen. b 21. Univ of Leeds BA 42. Coll of Resurr Mirfield 40. **d** 47 **p** 48 S'wark. C of St Andr Stockwell Green 47-54; St Sav St Alb 54-57; PC of St Sav Luton Dio St Alb 57-68; V from 68; Hon Can of St Alb Cathl from 72. *Vicarage, St Saviour's Crescent, Luton, Beds.* (Luton 30445)

NORTHCOTT, Michael Stafford. b 55. St Chad's Coll Dur BA (Th) 76, MA 77. St Jo Coll Dur 80. **d** 81 Man. C of St Clem Chorlton-cum-Hardy Dio Man from 81. *94 Hardy Lane, Chorlton-cum-Hardy, Manchester, M21.*

NORTHCOTT, William Mark. b 36. Clifton Th Coll 61. **d** 64 **p** 65 Chelmsf. C of St Luke Walthamstow 64-68; H Trin Idle 68-70; N Sec CMJ 70-79; L to Offic Dio Man 71-79; Perm to Offic Dios Southw, Lich and Dios of N Prov 71-79; V of Withnell Dio Blackb from 79. *Withnell Vicarage, Chorley, Lancs, PR6 8SN.* (0254 830256)

NORTHCROFT, Henry William. Te Aute Th Coll. **d** 39 **p** 40 Wai. C of Wairoa 39-40; Waiapu Pastorate 40-41; on active service 41-46; V of Te Ngae Pastorate 46-50; Waipawa Maori Pastorate 50-53; Wairoa Maori Distr 53-56. *c/o 43 Hunter Brown Street, Wairoa, NZ.*

NORTHERN ARGENTINA, Lord Bishop of. *See* Leake, Right Rev David.

NORTHERN ARGENTINA, Assistant Bishop of. *See* Marino, Right Rev Mario Lorenzo.

NORTHERN FRANCE, Archdeacon of. *See* Livingstone, Ven John Morris.

NORTHERN TERRITORY, Lord Bishop of the. *See* Mason, Right Rev Kenneth Bruce.

NORTHERN UGANDA, Lord Bishop of. *See* Ogwal-Abwang, Right Rev Benoni Yovani.

NORTHFIELD, John Frederick. b 40. Ridley Coll Melb ThL 71. **d** 72 **p** 73 Melb. C of St Mark Camberwell 72-74; P-in-c of Thomastown 74-78; I of Niddrie Dio Melb from 78. *138 Hoffman's Road, Niddrie, Vic, Australia 3042.* (379 6363)

NORTHMORE, Solomon Roy. b 12. Wycl Hall Ox 58. **d** 59 **p** 60 Leic. C of Melton Mowbray 59-61; R of Osgathorpe 61-64; C-in-c of Woolfardisworthy w Buck Mills 64-67; V 67-69; R and Arch-P of Haccombe w Coffinswell 69-77; Perm to Offic Dio Ex from 78. *34 Charles Road, Kingskerwell, Newton Abbot, Devon, TQ12 5JW.*

NORTHOLT, Archdeacon of. *See* Butler, Ven Thomas Frederick.

NORTHRIDGE, Herbert Aubrey Hamilton. b 16. Trin Coll Dub BA 40, MA 43. **d** 41 **p** 42 Derry. C of Ch Ch Derry 41-45; C-in-c of Convoy 45-47; I 47-50; Derg (w Termonamongan from 71) 50-81; Can of Derry 72-81. *Goblusk, Ballinamallard, Co Fermanagh, N Ireland.*

NORTHRUP, Albert Aubrey Taylor. K Coll NS BA 49. **d** 49 **p** 50 Fred. R of Aberdeen and Brighton 49-51; Grand Manan 51-54; Summerland 54-61; Revelstoke 61-62; Port Moody 62-69; St Simon Deep Cove Vanc 69-72; C of St Paul Vanc 72-76; R of H Trin Vanc 76-79. *1710-143b Street, White Rock, BC, Canada.*

NORTHUMBERLAND, Archdeacon of. *See* Unwin, Ven Christopher Philip.

NORTHWOOD, Michael Alan. b 36. BSc (Phys) Lon 60. Wells Th Coll 62. **d** 64 **p** 65 Chich. C of Eastbourne 64-66; All SS Sanderstead 66-68; Marlborough Deanery Chap Dio Sarum from 68; C-in-c of Alton Barnes w Alton Priors and Stanton St Bernard 69-75; Publ Pr Dio Sarum from 75. *Danecourt, East Grimstead, Salisbury, Wilts.*

NORTON, Anthony Bernard. b 40. Univ of Man BA (2nd cl Hist) 62. Linc Th Coll 63. **d** 65 **p** 66 Bris. C of Westbury-on-Trym 65-68; St Agnes w St Simon Bris 68-70; C-in-c of St Werburgh Bris 70-73; Team V of St Agnes and St Simon w St Werburgh Bris 73-77; V of St Alb Lakenham Dio Nor from 77. *St Alban's Vicarage, Eleanor Road, Norwich, NR1 2RE.* (Norwich 21843)

NORTON, David Jeffrey. b 45. Univ of W Ont BA 67. Hur Coll Lon BTh 70, BD 75. **d** 76 **p** 77 Hur. P-in-c of Chippewa w Oneida 76-81; on leave. *570 William Street, Apt 605, London, Ont, Canada, N7B 3E9.*

NORTON, Eric Charles. b 14. ACP 66. Oakhill Th Coll 77. **d** 80 **p** 81 Barking for Chelmsf. Hon C of St Anne Chingford Dio Chelmsf from 80. *24 Larkshall Crescent, Chingford, E4 6NS.*

NORTON, Eric Hugh Pepler. b 1899. G and C Coll Cam BA 20, MA 25. FCA 29. Cudd Coll 33. **d** 34 **p** 35 Wakef. C of Brighouse 34-38; V of Carlton 38-43; CF (EC) 39-41; V of Birkenshaw w Hunsworth 43-53; Almeley 53-59; Hon C of St Pet Bournemouth Dio Win from 60. *Flat 71, Bath Hillcourt, Parsonage Road, Bournemouth, BH1 2HW.*

NORTON, Harold Mercer. b 06. Linc Th Coll 28. **d** 31 **p** 32 York. C of St Chad York 31-33; St Cuthb Middlesbrough 33-36; Willington 36-41; V of Deaf Hill w Langdale 41-44; Carlton-in-Cleveland 44-49; V of Faceby 44-49; CF 49-60; V of Brill w Boarstall 60-72; Perm to Offic Dio York from 72. *Carr Hall Bungalow, Briggswath, Whitby, N Yorks.* (Whitby 810764)

NORTON, Canon Horace Ewart. Kelham Th Coll 17. **d** 23 **p** 24 Cov. C of St Mary Virg Nuneaton 23-26; All SS Engcobo 26-28; P-in-c of Indawana 28-40; H Cross E Pondoland 40-54; Archd of Pondoland 46-58; Can of St John's Cathl Umtata 46-66; Canon (Emer) from 66; R of Umzimkulu and

P-in-c of Clydesdale Miss 54-65; Archd of Kokstad 58-65; L to Offic Dio St John's 65-69; Dio Grahmstn 69-71. *Plough Hotel, Ixopo, Natal, S Africa.*

NORTON, Howard John. b 41. Fitzw Coll Cam BA 64, MA 72. St Jo Coll Nottm 79. **d** 80 **p** 81 S'wark. C of Ch Ch S'wark Dio S'wark from 80. *14a Christchurch Park, Sutton, Surrey, SM2 5TN.*

NORTON, James Herbert Kitchener. b 37. Qu Coll Birm 78. **d** 81 Lich (APM). C of Donnington Wood Dio Lich from 81. *17 Queen's Road, Donnington, Telford, Shropshire, TF2 8DB.* (Telford 605737)

NORTON, John Colin. b 25. Magd Coll Ox BA (2nd cl Phil Pol and Econ) 50, MA 54. Cudd Coll 50. **d** 52 Malmesbury for Bris **p** 53 Bris. C of St Mary Redcliffe Bedminster 52-57; Bitterne Pk 57-61; C-in-c of St Mary Virg w St Pet Conv Distr Bp Wearmouth 63-68; V of All SS Clifton (w St Mary Tyndall's Pk to 76 and St Jo Evang from 78) 68-80; Commiss Papua from 71; Hon Can of Bris Cathl 77-80; V of Penistone Dio Wakef from 80. *Penistone Vicarage, Sheffield, S Yorks, S30 6DY.* (Barnsley 763241)

NORTON, Leslie Miles. b 10. Sarum Th Coll 46. **d** 48 **p** 49 S'wark. C of St Barn Dulwich 48-52; Cheam (in c of St Alb) 52-55; V of St Pet Dulwich Common Dio S'wark from 55. *St Peter's Vicarage, Lordship Lane, SE22.* (01-693 6885)

NORTON, Michael George Charles. b 34. Kelham Th Coll 55. **d** 59 Shrewsbury for Lich **p** 60 Staff for Lich. C of Sedgley 59-63; Wombourn 63-65; Stafford 65-67; V of St Pet W Bromwich 68-76; Wigginton Staffs Dio Lich from 76. *Wigginton Vicarage, Tamworth, Staffs.* (Tamworth 4537)

NORTON, Michael James Murfin. b 42. Lich Th Coll 66. **d** 67 **p** 68 Lich. C of St Francis Friar Pk W Bromwich 67-70; C of Ch Ch Wellington 70-72; All SS (in c of St Marg) Upper Norwood 72-76; V of Elstow Dio St Alb from 76. *Elstow Abbey Vicarage, Bedford, MK42 9XT.* (Bedford 61477)

NORTON, Peter Eric Pepler. b 38. TCD BA 61. G and C Coll Cam PhD 64. St Jo Coll Dur 78. **d** 80 **p** 81 Penrith for Carl. C of Ulverston Dio Carl from 80. *18 Church Walk, Ulverston, Cumbria, LA12 7EN.* (0229 56133)

NORTON, William Fullerton. b 23. Selw Coll Cam BA 46, MA 52. Wycl Hall Ox 46. **d** 48 **p** 49 Leic. C of H Ap Leic 48-52; C of St Matt Sing 52-54; Miss At New Village Selangor 54-56; Kampong Tawas New Village 56-60; V of St Pet Ipoh 60-63; R of St Steph Manila 63-66; C of St Luke's Hackney 67; Tooting Graveney 68-71; V of St Sav w St Paul Holloway Dio Lon from 71. *St Saviour's Vicarage, Hanley Road, N4 3DQ.* (01-272 1246)

NORWICH, Lord Bishop of. *See* Wood, Right Rev Maurice Arthur Ponsonby.

NORWICH, Archdeacon of. *See* Handley, Ven Anthony Michael.

NORWICH, Dean of. *See* Edwards, Very Rev David Lawrence.

NORWOOD, Christopher Leslie. b 46. St Chad's Coll Dur BA (Th) 68. Coll of Resurr Mirfield 68. **d** 70 **p** 71 Ripon. C of Armley 70-74; Chap St John's Sch Tiffield 74-75; C-in-c of Ch Ch Conv Distr Dunscroft 75-78; V of Dunscroft 78-81; Team V of Frecheville w Hackenthorpe Dio Sheff from 81. *61 Sheffield Road, Hackenthorpe, Sheffield, S12 4LR.*

NORWOOD, Canon Clarence William. b 1900. AKC (1st cl) 22. Univ of Lon BD 23. **d** 23 **p** 24 S'wark. C of H Trin Barnes 23-27; Miss SPG at Bangkok 27-39; Chap of Ch Ch Bangkok 35-39; P-in-c of St Andr Subiaco 40-43; R of St Luke Cottesloe 43-53; Can of Perth 49-53; Hon Can 53-67; Can (Emer) from 67; Commiss Perth from 54; Willoch from 72; V of Sutton Valence w E Sutton 54-63; Chap HM Borstal Inst E Sutton Pk 54-63; R of Southchurch 63-80. *34 High Street, Ramsgate, Kent.*

NORWOOD, David John. b 40. Linc Th Coll 65. **d** 68 **p** 69 St Alb. C of Hitchin 68-72; P-in-c of Luanshya 72-76; C of St Mary Littlehampton 76-77; Chap R Cornw Hosp Treliske and P-in-c of Chacewater 77-79. *91 Chosen Drive, Churchdown, Glos, GL3 2QS.* (0452 855680)

NORWOOD, Philip Geoffrey Frank. b 39. Em Coll Cam 2nd cl Th Trip pt i 60, BA (3rd cl Th Trip pt ii) 62, MA 66. Cudd Coll 63. **d** 65 **p** 66 Cant. C of St Edw K and Confessor New Addington 65-69; Chap to Abp of Cant 69-72; V of Hollingbourne 72-78; P-in-c of Wormshill 74-78; Huckinge 74-78; St Laur-in-Thanet w Manston Dio Cant from 78. *St Laurence-in-Thanet Vicarage, Ramsgate, Kent.* (Thanet 52478)

NOSEWORTHY, Ven Donald Wilbur. b 21. McGill Univ Montr BA 42. Montr Dioc Th Coll LTh 47. **d** 46 **p** 47 Montr. C of Aylwin River Desert 46-47; I 47-48; R of Shawville 48-50; in Amer Ch 50-71; R of St Paul St John Dio Fred from 71; Can of Fred 74-80; Dioc Archd from 80. *162 Mt Pleasant Avenue, St John, NB, Canada, E2K 3V2.*

NOSEWORTHY, Ian. b 54. Memorial Univ Newfld BA 75. Trin Coll Tor 75. **d** 78 Centr Newfld. C of Hermitage 78-81. *c/o Anglican Rectory, Hermitage, Hermitage Bay, Newfoundland.*

NOTMAN, Canon Eric. b 34. K Coll Lon and Warm AKC 58. **d** 59 **p** 60 Carl. C of St Jas Gt Barrow-F 59-63; Penrith 63-66; V of St Jo Evang Barrow-F Dio Carl from 66; Hon Can of Carl Cathl from 75; RD of Furness from 81. *St John's Vicarage, Barrow-in-Furness, Cumb. LA14 2TS.* (Barrow-in-Furness 21101)

NOTT, Albert James Loriot. St Francis Coll Brisb ACT ThL (2nd cl) 53. **d** and **p** 54 Brisb. C of St Columb Clayfield 54-55; St Matt Groveley Brisb 55-56; M of Bush Bro of St Paul 56-61; L to Offic Dio Syd 61-63; V of Mary Valley 61-72; Jandowae 72-74; R of Oakey Dio Brisb from 74. *St Augustine's Rectory, Oakey, Queensland, Australia 4401.* (91 1193)

NOTT, George Thomas Michael. b 34. Late Hasker Scho of Ex Coll Ox BA (2nd cl Th) 58, MA 62. Coll of Resurr Mirfield. **d** 60 Birm **p** 61 Aston for Birm. C of Solihull (in c of St Francis from 63) 60-69; Min Can of Worc 69-77; Chap K Sch Worc 69-77; P-in-c of St Nich City and Dio Worc from 77. *11 St George's Square, Worcester, WR1 1HX.* (Worc 24855)

NOTT, Michael John. b 16. K Coll Lon Wordsworth Pri 36, Whichelow Pri and AKC 38. BD (2nd cl) 39, Fell 72. Linc Th Coll 39. **d** 39 **p** 40 Pet. c of Abington 39-45; St Mary Reading 45-46; V of St Andr Kettering 46-54; RD of Weldon ii 52-54; Chap Kettering Hosp 52-54; Surr 53-54; Chap and Warden of Heritage Craft Sch and Hosp Chailey 54-57; L to Offic Dio Chich 55-57; V of Seaford w Sutton 57-64; Surr 57-64; RD of Seaford 61-64; Sen Chap to Abp of Cant 64-65; Can Res of Cant 65-72; Archd of Maidstone 65-67; Cant 67-72; Provost and V of Cathl Ch Portsm 72-82; Hon Chap RN from 79. *c/o Provost's House, 13 Pembroke Road, Old Portsmouth, PO1 2NJ.* (Portsm 82440)

✠ **NOTT, Right Rev Peter John.** b 33. Fitzw Ho Cam BA 61, MA 65. Westcott Ho Cam 58. **d** 61 **p** 62 St Alb. C of Harpenden 61-64; Chap Fitzw Ho (Fitzw Coll from 66) Cam 64-69; Fell 67-69; L to Offic Dio Ely 66-69; R of Beaconsfield 69-77; Surr 70-77; M Gen Syn 75-77; Preb of Wells Cathl from 77; Cons Bp Suffr of Taunton in St Paul's Cathl Lon 18 Oct 77 by Abp of Cant; Bps of Lon, B & W, Ox, Linc, Lich and Nor; Bps Suffr of Fulham & Gibr, Stepney, Buckingham, Horsham, Pontefract, Sherborne and Tonbridge; and Bps M Hodson and M Hollis and others. *Sherford Farm House, Sherford, Taunton, Somt.* (Taunton 88759)

NOTTAGE, Terence John. b 36. Oak Hill Th Coll 62. **d** 65 **p** 66 Lon. C of St Paul Finchley 65-68; Edgware 68-72; V of St Mark Harlesden Dio Lon from 72. *99 Furness Road, NW10 5UJ.* (01-965 6349)

NOTTINGHAM, Archdeacon of. *See* Williamson, Ven Robert Kerr.

NOTTINGHAM, Birman. b 29. St Chad's Coll Dur BA 53, MA 56. MEducn 64. Univ of Lanc PhD 75. Ely Th Coll 53. **d** 55 Dur **p** 56 Jarrow for Dur. C of Ven Bede Monk Wearmouth 55-58; L to Offic Dio Dur 58-70. *The Senior Common Room, St Martin's College, Lancaster.*

NOURSE, John. b 22. Late Cho Scho of St Jo Coll Cam BA 43, MA 47. Wells Th Coll 48. **d** 49 Win **p** 51 Southn for Win. C of St Aug Bournemouth 49-51; Asst Master Hurstpierpoint Coll 51-52; C of Shere w Peaslake (in C of Peaslake) 52-57; Eton (in c of Eton Wick) 57-62; Min Can of St Geo Windsor and Asst Master St Geo Choir Sch 57-67; Succr 61-67; V of Amesbury and Offg Chap RAF 67-69; Min Can and Prec of Cant Cathl 69-73; V of Charing w L Chart from 73. *Charing Vicarage, Ashford, Kent, TN27 0LP.* (Charing 2598)

NOURSE, Peter. b 10. RD 43. Fitzw Ho Cam BA 36, MA 39. Wells Th Coll 37. **d** 37 Guildf **p** 38 Bp Golding-Bird for Guildf. C of Gt Bookham 37-39; Chap RNVR 39-45; V Cho of Sarum 45-52; Succr 47-52; V of Bromfield 52-60; Succr, Sacr and Sub-Treas of Ex Cathl and Custos of Coll of Vs Cho 60-62; V of Eardisland 62-76; C-in-c of Shobdon 65-76; Perm to Offic Dio Heref from 76. *Priory End, Church Street, Leominster, Herefs.* (Leominster 3936)

NOVA SCOTIA, Lord Bishop of. *See* Hatfield, Right Rev Leonard Fraser.

NOVA SCOTIA, Bishop Suffragan of. (Vacant)

NOWE, Canon Joseph William Beamish. KCNS BA 41, Div Test and LTh 43, BSLitt 51. **d** 42 **p** 43 NS. C of Alberton 42-43; R 43-49; Coxheath 49-55; Glace Bay 55-58; R of Merritton 58-64; R of Grace Ch Hamilton 64-74; Fonthill Dio Niag from 74; Hon Can of Niag from 76. *Box 536, Fonthill, Ont., Canada.* (416-892 2155)

NOWELL, John David. b 44. K Coll Lon and Warm AKC 67. **d** 68 Wakef **p** 69 Pontefract for Wakef. C of Lindley 68-70; Lightcliffe 70-72; V of Wyke 72-80; Silsden Dio Bradf from 80. *Silsden Vicarage, Keighley, Yorks.* (Steeton 52670)

NOY, Frederick William Vernon. b 47. Sarum Th Coll 67. **d** 71 **p** 72 Bris. C of St Jo Bapt Swindon 71-75; V of Stinsford,

Winterbourne Came w Whitcombe and Winterbourne Monkton 75-80; Chap Sarum Dioc Assoc for Deaf and Hard of Hearing from 75-80. *54 Casterbridge Road, Dorchester, Dorset.* (Dorchester 64269)

NOYCE, Colin Martley. b 45. Ridley Hall Cam 74. **d** 76 Ely **p** 77 Huntingdon for Ely. C of St Jas Cam 76-78; Chap RN 78-82; R of Mistley w Manningtree Dio Chelmsf from 82. *Rectory, 47 High Street, Manningtree, Essex.* (Manningtree 2200)

NOYES, Robert Charles. **d** 63 **p** 64 New Westmr. C of St Mary Kerrisdale Vancouver 63-64; I of St Simon Deep Cove N Vancouver 64-69. *6146 Kathleen Street, South Burnaby, BC, Canada.*

NOYES, Roger. b 39. Linc Th Coll 65. **d** 67 **p** 68 Ripon. C of Adel 67-70; Chap Aldenham Sch 70-74; Aldborough and Dunsforth w Boroughbridge and Roecliffe Dio Ripon from 74. *Vicarage, Church Lane, Boroughbridge, Yorks, YO5 9BA.* (Boroughbridge 2433)

NQINI, Stanley Sipo. St Bede's Coll Umtata 51. **d** 53 **p** 56 Grahmstn. Asst Miss (O of Ethiopia) Grahmstn 53-56 and 62-66; Umtata 56-62; Uitenhage 66-68; P-in-c of St Steph Langa 68-77; St Cypr Miss Port Alfred Dio Grahmstn from 77. *St Cyprian's Mission, Port Alfred, CP, S Africa.*

NQODI, Ranton Diliza. St Bede's Coll Umtata 62. **d** 63 **p** 64 St John's. P Dio St John's. *Box 174, Maclear, CP, S Africa.*

NSALE, A. **d** 43 **p** 44 Ugan. P Dio Ugan 43-60; Dio W Bugan 60-66; Dio Nam from 66. *PO Box 4828, Jinja, Uganda.*

NSENGIYUMVA, Emmanuel. b 53. St Phil Coll Kongwa 76. **d** 79 **p** 80 W Tang. P Dio W Tang. *c/o PO Box 74, Kasulu, Tanzania.*

NSERA, Cranmer. **d** 46 Ugan. d Dio Ugan 46-61; Dio Nam from 61. *Church of Uganda, Luwero PO, Uganda.*

NSEREKO, Yekoyada. b 21. Bp Tucker Coll Mukono 70. **d** 72 Nam. d Dio Nam. *Buzzibwera, PO Kikyusa, Bombo, Uganda.*

NSHAKIRA, Ernest. Div Sch Kabale 63. **d** 64 **p** 66 Ankole-K. P Dio Ankole-K 64-67; Dio Kig from 67. *Nyakinoni, PO Karuhinda, Uganda.*

NSHAMIHIGO, Augustin. b 50. Butare Th Coll 71. **d** 74 Rwa. d Dio Rwa 74-75; Dio Kiga from 75. *BP 61, Kigali, Rwanda.*

NSHIMBA, Nicholas. b 19. **d** 73 N Zam (APM). d Dio N Zam. *PO Box 46, Mansa, Zambia.*

NSIAH, Emmanuel. b 43. **d** and **p** 74 Kum. P Dio Kum. *Box 1, Fumesua, Ashanti, Ghana.*

NSONGORA, Augustin. **d** 75 **p** 77 Ruw. P Dio Ruw. *Box 37, Fort Portal, Uganda.*

✠ **NSUBUGA, Right Rev Dunstan Kasi.** St Paul's Univ Tokyo Hon DD 58. Bp Tucker Coll Mukono. **d** 44 **p** 45 Ugan. P Dio Ugan; Can and Sub-Dean of St Paul's Cathl Kampala 58-61; Dean of Nam 61-65; Cons Asst Bp of Nam in St Paul's Cathl Kampala 7 June 64 by Abp of Ugan; Bps of Mbale; Soroti; W Bugan; N Bugan; Ankole-K; and Ruw; Asst Bp on Nig Delta; Bp Balya; and Bp of Bukoba (Swedish Ch); Apptd Bp of Nam 65. *PO Box 14297, Mmengo, Kampala, Uganda.* (Kampala 46208)

NSUBUGA, Erika. **d** 39 **p** 41 Ugan. P Dio Ugan 39-61; Dio Nam from 61. *Anglican Church, Kavumba, Uganda.*

NSUBUGA, Livingstone. b 49. Bp Tucker Coll Mukono 74. **d** 76 **p** 77 Nam. P Dio Nam. *PO Box 30737, Kampala, Uganda.*

NTAATE, George. b 31. Bp Tucker Coll Mukono 73. **d** 74 **p** 75 Nam. P Dio Nam. *Ssempa, Box 15, Wobulenzi, Uganda.*

NTABUSANZWE, Timoteo. **d** 80 Kiga. d Dio Kiga. *BP 17, Byumba, Rwanda.*

NTAGAZWA, Denis. Warner Th Coll Buye 67. **d** 69 Bur. d Dio Bur. *c/o PO Box 58, Ngozi, Burundi.*

NTAHINDWA, Timotheo. b 37. St Phil Coll Kongwa 77. **d** 79 **p** 80 W Tang. P Dio W Tang. *PO Box 15, Kibondo, Tanzania, E Africa.*

NTAHOMBAYE, Pierre. **d** 74 Bur **p** 75 Buye. P Dio Buye. *c/o BP 58 Ngozi, Burundi..*

NTAKULA, Wilkie. b 22. **d** and **p** 75 Vic Nyan. P Dio Vic Nyan 75-77; Dio Masasi from 78. *c/o Mtandi, Private Bag PO, Masasi, Mtwara Region, Tanzania.*

NTAMWISHIMIRO, Gregoire. **d** 75 **p** 76 Buye. P Dio Buye. *BP 58 Ngozi, Burundi.*

NTANCHUTI, William John. b 44. St Phil Coll Kongwa 75. **d** and **p** 77 Vic Nyan. P Dio Vic Nyan. *PO Box 15, Biharamulo, Tanzania.*

NTANDU, Musa. **d** 61 **p** 62 Centr Tang. P Dio Centr Tang. *Box 82, Manyoni, Tanzania.*

NTARANKE, Mikeairi. Bp Tucker Coll Mukono 61. **d** 62 **p** 63 Ruw. P Dio Ruw. *Anglican Church, Bukuku, Uganda.*

NTATE, Adoniya. Bp Tucker Coll Mukono. **d** 35 **p** 37 Ugan. P Dio Ugan 35-60; Dio W Bugan 60-69; Hon Can of W Bugan 64-69. *Bukomero, PO Katera, Kampala, Uganda.*

NTAWIMENYA, Andre. **d** 74 Bur **p** 75 Buye. P Dio Buye. *Murama BP 66 Muyinga, Burundi.*

NTE, Jacob Owubosigha Jetegwu. St Paul's Coll Awka. **d** 55 **p** 57 Nig Delta. P Nig Delta. *St Silas's Parsonage, Umuahia, Nigeria.*

NTHIGA, Albert Kithua. St Paul's Coll Limuru 74. **d** 76 **p** 78 Mt Kenya E. P Dio Mt Kenya E. *Box 748, Embu, Kenya.*

NTHIGA, Epaphras. Weithaga Bible Sch 60. **d** 60 **p** 62 Ft Hall. P Dio Ft Hall 62-64; Dio Mt Kenya 64-75; Dio Mt Kenya E from 75; Exam Chap to Bp of Mt Kenya E from 75. *Box 338, Kerugoya, Kenya.*

NTIBAZONKIZA, Stephen. Warner Mem Th Coll Ibuye 61. **d** 63 Rwanda B. d Dio Rwanda B 63-66; Dio Bur from 66. *Matana, Burundi.*

NTIGACIKA, Yofesi. Warner Th Coll Buye 64. **d** 66 **p** 67 Bur. P Dio Bur. *Ruyenzi, DS 127, Bujumbura, Burundi.*

NTIGEZA, Joseph. **d** 69 Bur. d Dio Bur. *c/o PO Box 58, Ngozi, Burundi.*

NTINTILI, Linford Sipho. St Bede's Coll Umtata 59. **d** 60 **p** 67 St John's. P Dio St John's. *Box 28, Mount Ayliff 4850, Transkei, S Africa.*

NTIRUKA, Francis Nzaganya. Moore Th Coll Syd ACT ThL 62. **d** 62 **p** 63 Centr Tang. P Dio Centr Tang 62-66; Dio W Tang 66-77; Perm to Offic Dio Syd 77-80. *Box 13, Kasulu, Tanzania.*

NTLALI, Ebenezer St Mark. b 54. St Bede's Coll Umtata 79. **d** 80 St John's. d Dio St John's. *St Bede's College, Umtata, Transkei.*

NTLOLA, Wilson Lulamile Tozana. b 46. St Bede's Coll Umtata 69. **d** 70 Bp Sobukwe for St John's **p** 72 St John's. C of St Ignatius Tsomo 70-73; Idutywa 73-76; Zwelitsha 77-78; R of H Trin Dimbaza Dio Grahmstn from 78. *Box 5032, Kwa-Dimbaza, CP, S Africa.*

NTOGOTA, Adonia. Bp Tucker Coll Mukono. **d** 59 Ugan. d Dio Ugan 59-61; Dio Ruw from 61. *Box 37, Fort Portal, Uganda.*

NTOMBELA, Philip Gabriel. b 47. St Pet Coll Alice 68. **d** 71 **p** 72 Zulu. P Dio Zulu; Chap Univ of Zulu from 74. *Box 73, Kwa Dlangezwa, Zululand.*

NTOW, Ebenezer Ayesuh. b 39. **d** and **p** 75 Accra. P Dio Accra. *Box 2, Nkoranza, Ghana.*

NTOW, Martin Kofi. **d** 63 **p** 64 Accra. P Dio Accra 63-75. *PO Box 80, Aburi, Ghana.*

NTSANGANE, Meshack. b 34. **d** 74 **p** 75 Johann. C of Khuma Stilfontein Dio Johann from 74. *318506, Khuma, Stilfontein, Tvl 2550, S Africa.*

NTSEARE, Canon Benjamin Theko. Coll of Resurr Rosettenville 44. **d** 46 **p** 47 Johann. P Dio Johann; Can of Johann 72-79; Hon Can from 80. *Box 1017, Brencania, Brakpan, Transvaal, S Africa.*

NTSHANGASE, Nimrod. St Bede's Coll Umtata 67. **d** 68 **p** 70 Zulu. C of H Name Empangeni 68-74; R of St Alb Umvunyane 74-77; H Name Empangeni Dio Zulu from 77. *Box 392, Empangeni, Zululand.*

NTSHANGASE, Philip. St Bede's Coll Umtata 67. **d** 68 **p** 70 Zulu. C of St Marg Nongoma 68-73; P-in-c of Ingwavuma Dio Zulu from 73. *PO Box 6, Ingwavuma, Zululand, S Africa.* (Ingwavuma 19)

NTSHIDI, Israel Sandile. b 30. St Bede's Coll Umtata 68. **d** 69 **p** 71 St John's. C of St Barn Ntlaza 69-70; St Ignatius Tsomo 71-73; Idutywa Dio St John's from 73. *Box 233, Umtata, Transkei, S Africa.*

NTSHUCA, Stephen Gwebityala. b 26. St Bede's Coll Umtata 75. **d** 75 Bp Sobukwe for St John's **p** 76 St John's. P Dio St John's. *P Bag Lower Gwadu, Willowvale, Republic of Transkei,*

NTULI, Clement Edgar. St Pet Coll Rosettenville. **d** 55 **p** 56 Zulu. P Dio Zulu. *Box 544, Vryheid, Natal, S Africa.*

NTULI, Hendrick. b 42. St Pet Coll Alice 74. **d** 76 **p** 77 Pret. C of St Matthias Barberton 76-78; Nsikazi Dio Pret from 78. *PO Box 27, Kabokweni 1245, S Africa.*

NTULI, Michael. St Bede's Coll Umtata. **d** 43 **p** 44 Zulu. P Dio Zulu. *Indulindi, PO Inyoni, Rail, Zululand.*

NTUNYE, Hendrik Mbeji. b 13. St Bede's Coll Umtata 70. **d** 70 Bp Sobukwe for St John's **p** 71 St John's. C of St Barn Miss Ntlaza Dio St John's from 70. *St Barnabas' Mission, PO Ntlaza, Via Umtata, Transkei, S Africa.*

NTUZA, Amos. b 39. St Phil Coll Kongwa 75. **d** 76 **p** 77 Vic Nyan. P Dio Vic Nyan. *PO Box 16, Musoma, Tanzania.*

NUDDS, Douglas John. b 24. St Aid Coll 48. **d** 51 **p** 52 Nor. C of E Dereham w Hoe 51-55; St Jas Birstall 55-58; V of Bardon Hill 58-62; St Mich AA Belgrave 62-68; St Marg Leic and Chap Leic R Infirm 68-72; Chap High Royds Hosp Menston 72-79; V of Lidget Green Dio Bradf from 79. *Lidget Green Vicarage, Bradford, BD7 2LU.* (Bradford 72504)

NUGA, Majekodunmi Adeoye. b 45. Im Coll Ibad 73. **d** 76

Lagos. d Dio Lagos 76; Dio Ijebu from 76. *St Saviour's Church, Igbile, Box 187, Ijebu-Ode, Nigeria.*

NUGENT, Alan Hubert. b 42. Univ of Dur BA (2nd cl Th) 65, MA 78. Wycl Hall Ox 65. **d** 67 Warrington for Liv **p** 68 Liv. C of St Matt and St Jas Mossley Hill 67-71; St Mary Magd Bridgnorth 71-72; Chap Univ and Hatfield Colls Dur 72-78; P-in-c of Ch Ch Bp Wearmouth Dio Dur from 78. *Christ Church Vicarage, St Bede's Park, Sunderland, T & W, SR2 7DZ.* (Sunderland 58077)

NUGENT, Eric William. b 26. Bps' Coll Cheshunt 56. **d** 58 **p** 59 Chelmsf. C of Rochford 58-61; Eastwood 61-62; Min of St D Eccles Distr Eastwood 62-66; V 66-79; P-in-c of Weeley Dio Chelmsf 79-81; V (w L Clacton) from 81; V of L Clacton 80-81. *Vicarage, Holland Road, Little Clacton, Clacton-on-Sea, CO16 9RD.* (Clacton 860241)

NUGENT, Percy. b 1897. Edin Th Coll 28. **d** 33 **p** 34 St Andr. C of Burntisland w Aberdour and Kinghorn Miss 33-37; St Ninian's Cathl Perth (in c of St Finnian Lochgelly) 37-39; P-in-c of St Colman Burravoe 39-44; R of St Marnan Aberchirder 44-49; Monymusk w Kemnay 49-55; St Jo Evang New Pitsligo 55-62. *16 South Street, Aberchirder, Huntly, Aberdeenshire, AB5 5TR.*

NUNAN, Robert James. St Francis Coll Brisb ACT ThL 57. **d** 58 **p** 59 N Queensld. C of Charters Towers 58-59; Mundingburra 59-60; MacKay 61-63; Twickenham 64-65; Chap RN 65-69; R of Broadford 69-73; Alexandra Dio Wang from 73. *St John's Rectory, Alexandra, Vic, Australia 3714.* (057-72 1053)

NUNN, Adrian Peter. b 40. Melb Coll of Div LTh 80. St Jo Coll Auckld 79. **d** 80 Auckld. C of Kaitaia Dio Auckld from 80. *53 Church Road, Kaitaia, NZ.*

NUNN, Geoffrey William John. b 24. St Jo Coll Dur BA 51. **d** 52 **p** 53 Chelmsf. C of Upminster 52-58; V of St Martin Dagenham Dio Chelmsf from 58. *St Martin's Vicarage, Goresbrook Road, Dagenham, Essex.* (01-592-0967)

NUNN, Peter. b 32. Kelham Th Coll 53. **d** 57 Warrington for Liv **p** 58 Liv. C of St Geo Wigan 57-60; Warrington 60-62; V of St Pet Warrington 62-65; Chap Winwick Hosp Warrington from 65; Offg Chap RAF from 80. *Chaplain's Residence, Winwick Hospital, Warrington, Lancs.* (Warrington 55221 Ext 8)

NUNN, Peter Michael. b 38. Sarum Th Coll 64. **d** 66 **p** 67 Lon. C of St Geo Hornsey 66-71; Cleator Moor w Cleator 71-72; V of St Luke's Carl 72-79; Wotton St Mary Without (or Longlevens) Dio Glouc from 79. *Holy Trinity Vicarage, Church Road, Longlevens, Gloucester.* (Glouc 24129)

NUNNELEY, James Edward. St Bonif Coll Warm 34. **d** 37 **p** 38 York. C of Easington w Skeffling and Kilnsea 37-39; St Botolph Linc 39-43; PC of H Trin Gainsborough 43-50; V of Bottesford w Ashby 50-59; Surr 48-78; R of Raithby w Hallington 59-78; Withcall 59-78; V of Tathwell w Haugham 59-78. *28 Grosvenor Road, Louth, LN11 0BB.*

NUNNERLEY, William John Arthur. b 27. St D Coll Lamp BA 54. St Chad's Coll Dur Dipl Th 56. **d** 56 **p** 57 Mon. C of St Geo Tredegar 56-60; Chap RN 60-81; R of Barnoldy-le-Beck Dio Linc from 81; Waltham Dio Linc from 81. *Waltham Rectory, Grimsby, S Humb, DN37 0PN.* (Grimsby 822172)

NUNNS, Ven Arthur Ernest de Lisle. Trin Coll Dub Div Test 08, BA 09, MA 25. **d** 09 **p** 10 Derry. C of Ch Ch Londonderry 09-13; V of Metchosin 13-16; R of St Steph S Saanich BC 16-19; Killaghtee 19-24; St Mary Oak Bay 24-57; Hon Can of Ch Ch Cathl Vic 29-37; Archd of Vic 37-68; LPr Dio BC 57-68. *12-1006 St. Charles Street, Victoria, BC, Canada.*

NUNTULOA, Henry. St Pet Coll Siota 62. **d** 64 **p** 65 Melan. P Dio Melan 64-75; Dio Malaita from 75. *Kwaiabu, Malaita, Solomon Islands.*

NURSE, Donald William Charles. b 03. **d** 56 **p** 57 Nor. C of Attleborough 56-63; R of Erpingham w Calthorpe 63-79; Perm to Offic Dio Nor from 79. *4 Skeyton Road, North Walsham, Norf, NR28 0SB.*

NURSE, Edward Michael. Univ of Tor BA 63. Trin Coll Tor STB 66. **d** 66 **p** 67 Tor. C of St John Pet 66-70; R of Sioux Lookout 70-73; on leave 73-74; R of Indian Harbour Dio NS from 74. *RR1, Tantallon, Box 1, Site 20, Hfx Co., NS, Canada.* (823-2624)

NURSE, Ralph McCulloch. b 18. **d** and **p** 68 Lon. [f Bapt Min] C of St Alb Golders Green 68-71; R of Ch Ch w St Laur Brondesbury 71-75; V of Southea w Murrow and Parson Drove Dio Ely from 75; P-in-c of Guyhirn w Ring's End Dio Ely from 79. *Southea Vicarage, Parson Drove, Wisbech, Cambs.* (Wisbech 700426)

NURSE, Selwyn. St Andr Th Coll Trinid Dipl Th. **d** 80 Trinid. C of St Agnes St James Port of Spain Dio Trinid from *c/o St Agnes Rectory, Clarence Street, St James, Trini- WI.*

URSER, Canon John Shelley. b 29. Peterho Cam 1st cl Trip pt i 49, BA (1st cl Hist Trip pt ii) 50, MA 54, PhD 58. Wells Th Coll 58. **d** 58 **p** 59 Sheff. C of Tankersley 58-61; Dean and Fell of Trin Hall Cam 61-68; Warden of St Mark's Libr Canberra 68-74; R of Freckenham w Worlington 74-76; Can and Chan of Linc Cathl from 76; Exam Chap to Bp of Linc from 76. *The Chancery, 11 Minster Yard, Lincoln, LN2 1PJ.* (Lincoln 25610)

NURTON, Robert. b 44. Univ of Wales (Lamp) BA 67. Ridley Hall Cam 67. **d** 69 **p** 70 Bris. C of Hartcliffe 69-73; St Mary Stoke Ipswich 73-77; Chap RN from 77. *c/o Ministry of Defence, Lacon House, Theobalds Road, WC1X 8RY.*

NUTTALL, George Herman. b 31. St Jo Coll Dur BA 59, Dipl Th 61. Cranmer Hall Dur 59. **d** 61 York for Bradf **p** 62 Bradf. C of Eccleshill 61-65; V of St Barn Oldham 65-70; Area Sec CMS Lich and Derby 70-81; Reg Sec CMS Midl from 78; V of St Aug City and Dio Derby from 81. *155 Almond Street, Derby, DE3 6LY.* (Derby 766603)

✠ **NUTTALL, Right Rev Michael.** Univ of Natal BA 55. Rhodes Univ BA 56. G and C Coll Cam BA 57, MA 62. BD (Lon) 65. St Paul's Coll Grahmstn 63. **d** 64 **p** 65 Grahmstn. C of St Mich and St Geo Cathl Grahmstn 64-69; P-in-c of Sidbury 66-69; L to Offic Dio Grahmstn 69-75; Dean and Archd of Grahmstn 75; Cons Ld Bp of Pret in Cathl of St Mich and St Geo Grahmstn 16 Nov 75 by Abp of Capetn; Bps of St John's, Natal, Johann, Bloemf, Kimb K, Lebom, St Hel, Grahmstn, Swaz, Zulu and Port Eliz; and Others; Trld to Natal 81. *Bishops House, 5 Chaceley Place, Morningside, Durban 4001, S Africa.* (338069)

NUTTALL, Michael John Berkeley. b 36. K Coll Lon and Warm AKC 60. **d** 61 **p** 62 Ripon. C of Chap Allerton 61-64; Stanningley 64-68; V of Epiph Gipton Leeds 68-76; R of N Witham Dio Linc from 76; S Witham Dio Linc from 76; P-in-c of Stainby w Gunby Dio Linc from 76. *South Witham Rectory, Grantham, Lincs, NG33 5QB.* (Thistleton 612)

NUTTALL, Robert. b 10. Westcott Ho Cam 73. **d** 74 **p** 75 Chelmsf (APM). C of Gt Wakering 74-76; Chap Southend Gen Hosp and Publ Pr Dio Chelmsf 76-82; Perm to Offic Dio Ches from 82. *69 The Avenue, Sale, Chesh, M33 4GA.* (061-962 8790)

NUTTALL, William Neville Edge. b 03. Univ of Natal MA 25. **d** and **p** 73 Natal. C of Drakensberg Dio Natal from 73. *Box 67, Underberg, Natal, S Africa.* (Underberg 2804)

✠ **NUTTER, Most Rev harold Lee.** Mt Allison Univ NB BA 44; Hon LLD 72 Dalhousie Univ NS MA 47. K Coll NS BSLitt 47, DD 60. **d** 46 NS for Fred **p** 47 Fred. Miss of Simonds and Upham 47-51; R of Woodstock 51-57; St Mark St John 57-60; Exam Chap to Bp of Fred 58-71; Dean of Fred 60-71; Commiss Fred 63-71; Cons Ld Bp of Fred in St Dunstan's Ch Fred 2 Nov 71 by Bp of NS; Bps of Newfld; Montr; Queb; Ott; Berm; Maine; and others; Elected Abp and Metrop of Prov of Canada 80. *808 Brunswick Street, Fredericton, NB, Canada E3B 1H8* (506-455 8667)

NVIRI, Yoeri. Bp Tucker Mem Coll 37. **d** 39 Ugan for U Nile. d Dio U Nile 39-61; Dio Nam 61-67. *Box 30366, Kampala, Uganda.*

NWABUFO, Ebenezer Chukwukelu. b 34. Trin Coll Umuahia 65. **d** 68 **p** 69 Niger. P Dio Niger. *St Mark's Nibo, Nr Awka, ECS, Nigeria.*

NWABUOKU, Stephen Ibebukwu. Awka Coll. **d** 29 **p** 31 Niger. P Dio Niger 29-60. *Anglican Church, Okpanam, via Asaba, Nigeria.*

NWABUOKU, Stephen Oseloka. b 30. **d** 73 **p** 74 Benin. P Dio Benin 73-77; Dio Asaba 77-81; CF (Nigeria) from 81. *Chaplaincy HQ, Lagos, Nigeria.*

NWACHUKU, Frank Kanu. b 27. Trin Coll Umuahia 72. **d** 74 **p** 75 Aba. P Dio Aba. *St Matthew's Parsonage, Aba, Nigeria.*

NWACHUKU, Harry Chukunedum Agomo. Trin Th Coll Umuahia. **d** 50 **p** 51 Niger. P Dio Niger 50-52; Dio Nig Delta 52-71. *c/o St Michael's Parsonage, Okaiuga, Nigeria.*

NWACHUKU, Canon Israel Chiawulamoke. b 28. Trin Coll Umuahia 61. **d** 63 **p** 64 Nig Delta. P Dio Nig Delta 64-72; Dio Aba from 72; Hon Can of Aba from 80. *Christchurch Parsonage, Umunteke, Asa, Nigeria.*

NWACHUKWUGURU, Godfrey Chukwuemeka Sunday. b 33. **d** 77 Aba. d Dio Aba. *Government College, Umuahia, Nigeria.*

NWAFOR, Lazarus Nwalozie. b 36. Trin Coll Umuahia 76. **d** 76 Nig Delta. d Dio Nig Delta *St George's Parsonage, PO Box 15, Egwanga, Opobo, Rivers State, Nigeria.*

NWAGWU, Erasmus Nduka-Uba. d 72 **p** 73 Owerri. P Dio Owerri. *St Barnabas' Church, Umudim, Atta, Via Owerri, Nigeria.*

NWAGWU, Gabriel Madugba. b 30. Trin Coll Legon 69. **d** and **p** 73 Aba. P Dio Aba. *St Michael's Cathedral, Box 818, Aba, Nigeria.*

NWAGWU, Samual Chikwudinma Isaiah. b 36. St Paul's

Coll Awka 76. **d** 77 Aba. d Dio Aba. *Holy Innocents Parsonage, c/o PO Box 818, Aba, Nigeria.*

NWAIGWE, Abraham Chukwunyere. b 35. Trin Coll Legon 69. **d** and **p** 73 Aba. P Dio Aba. *St Barnabas Parsonage, Ihie, via Nbawsi, Nigeria.*

NWAKA, Lawrence Chuku. b 19. **d** 70 **p** 71 Lagos. d Dio Lagos. *7 Sheteolu Street, Lagos, Nigeria.*

NWAMA, Joshua O. Trin Coll Umuahia 80. **d** 81 Ow. d Dio Ow. *St Peter's Church, PO Box 8, Akokwa, via Orlu, Nigeria.*

NWAMBIRE, Samuel. St Paul's Coll Limuru. **d** 64 **p** 65 Momb. P Dio Momb. *Box 72, Mombasa, Kenya.*

NWANGWU, Geoffrey Aforka Chukwujekwu. b 39. Trin Coll Umuahia 65. **d** 68 Bp Uzodike for Niger **p** 68 Niger. P Dio Niger. *St Andrew's Church, Amichi, ECS, Nigeria.*

✠ **NWANKITI, Right Rev Benjamin Chukuemeka.** Univ of Dur BA (2nd cl Phil) 58. Dipl Th (Lon) 51. Melville Hall Ibad 49. **d** Bp Hall for Niger **p** 52 Niger. P Dio Niger 52-60; C of St Gabr Sunderland 58; w Nigerian Broadcasting Service 62-68; Archd of Ow 68-69; Cons Asst Bp of Ow 28 April 68 by Abp of W Afr; Bps of Ow; Nig Delta; Apptd Bp of Ow 69. *Box 31, Owerri, Nigeria.* (Owerri 117)

NWANKWO, James Chukwunweike. Awka Tr Coll. **d** 45 **p** 47 Niger. P Dio Niger 45-73; Hon Can of Niger 64-69; Synod Sec Dio Niger 64-70. *St Andrew's Obosi, Onitsha, Nigeria.*

NWEZE, David Ogwu. b 29. **d** 76 **p** 77 Enugu. P Dio Enugu. *Holy Trinity Church Obinagu, PO Box 16, Udi, Nigeria.*

NWIGWE, Hezekiah Okafo. Awka Tr Coll. **d** 45 **p** 47 Niger. P Dio Niger. *Nrewi, Uruagwie, S Nigeria.*

NWIGWE, Obed C.. Trin Coll Umuahia 80. **d** 81 Ow. d Dio Ow. *c/o Christ Church, PO Box 73, Owerri, Nigeria.*

NWOBA, Canon Jacob Eboh. b 23. Trin Coll Umuahia 58. **d** 60 **p** 61 Nig Delta. P Dio Nig Delta; Can of Nig Delta from 77. *Box 336, Port Harcourt, Nigeria.*

NWOGBE, Benson Enyinnaya. b 32. Trin Coll Umuahia 66. **d** 68 **p** 69 Nig Delta. P Dio Nig Delta 69-72; Dio Aba from 72. *St Barnabas Parsonage, Omoba, Box 5, Nigeria.*

NWOGU, Friday Onwukanjo. b 50. Trin Coll Umuahia 76. **d** and **p** 79 Aba. P Dio Aba. *St Peter's Parsonage, Obegu via Aba, Nigeria.*

NWOGWUGWU, Canon Jumbo Onyeubani. Trin Coll Umuahia 60. **d** 62 **p** 63 Nig Delta. P Dio Nig Delta 62-72; Dio Aba from 72; Can of Aba from 75. *St Stephen's Parsonage, Umuahia, Nigeria.*

NWOKENNA, Vincent Osueke. Trin Coll Umuahia 59. **d** 61 **p** 62 Ow. P Dio Ow. *Parsonage, Amauzari, via Owerri, Nigeria.*

NWOKO, Benjamin Ukauzo. b 23. St Paul's Coll Awka. **d** 74 **p** 75 Aba (APM). P Dio Aba. *St Stephen's Church, Umuahia, Nigeria.*

NWOKOLO, Felix Chukunenye. **d** 63 **p** 64 Ow. P Dio Ow. *PO Box 33, Orlu, Nigeria.* (Orlu 70)

NWORIE, Felix Ubochi. Awra Tr Coll 47. **d** 48 Bp Onyeabo for Niger. d Dio Niger 48-59; Dio Ow from 59. *St Paul's Parsonage, Ezeoke, Nsu PA, Umuahia, Nigeria.*

NWOSE, Isreal Idechukwu. b 42. Trin Coll umuahia 72. **d** 74 Niger. d Dio Niger. *Federal Radio, Enugu, Nigeria.*

NWOSU, Benjamin Chukukadibia Ejefoberi. **d** 36 Bp Gelsthorpe for Niger **p** 38 Niger. P Dio Niger 36-52; and from 70; Archd of Owerri 52-55; Onitsha 55-70. *Ozubulu, Nigeria.*

NWOSU, David Onwumelu. Trin Coll Umuahia 48. **d** 50 **p** 51 Niger. P Dio Niger 50-52 and 63-72; Dio Nig Delta 52-63. *Parsonage, Uga, Nigeria.*

NWOSU, Canon Felix. b 32. Trin Coll Umuahia 63. **d** 65 **p** 66 Niger. P Dio Niger 66-70; Dio Enugu from 70; Hon Can of Enugu from 81. *St Peter's Parsonage, Ogbete, Enugu, Nigeria.*

NWOSU, Godwin Enyidedeya. b 27. Trin Coll Umuahia 66. **d** 69 **p** 70 Nig Delta 70-72; Dio Aba from 72. *St Barnabas Parsonage, Box 2, Imo River, Nigeria.*

NWOSU, Ikechi Nwachukwu. b 49. Trin Coll Umuahia 75. **d** 78 Aba. d Dio Aba. *St Michael's Cathedral, PO Box 818, Aba, Nigeria.*

NWOSU, Canon Isaac. **d** 53 **p** 54 Nig Delta. P Dio Nig Delta 53-72; Dio Aba from 72; Can of Aba from 72. *Christ Church Parsonage, Akwete, Nigeria.*

✠ **NWOSU, Right Rev Rowland Nwafo Chukwunweike.** Trin Coll Umuahia 55. Dipl Th (Lon) 57. **d** 57 **p** 58 Niger. P Dio Niger 57-69; Dio Enugu 69-77; Can of Enugu 71-74; Hon Can 74-77; Cons Ld Bp of Asaba in St Matt Cathl Benin City 6 Aug 77 By Abp of W Afr; Bps of Lagos, Niger, Gambia, Nig Delta, Ibad, Ondo, N Nig, Ow, Ekiti, Enugu, Aba, Kum, Kwara, Ilesha, Egba-Egbado, Accra and Ijebu. *Bishopscourt, PO Box 216, Asaba, Bendel State, Nigeria.*

NXUMALO, Andreas Benyoni. **d** 78 **p** 79 Swaz. P Dio Swaz. *PO Box 1211, Mbabane, Swaziland.*

NXUMALO, Joshua. b 24. **d** 72 **p** 73 Johann. C of Meadowlands Dio Johann from 72. *Box 30, Iketlo, Johannesburg 1852, S Africa.* (011-989 193)

NYABAGABO, Erenesiti. **d** 41 **p** 49 Ugan. P Dio Ugan 41-61; Dio Nam 61-67; Dio Kig from 67. *PO Box 14, Mbarata, Uganda.*

NYABWERE, Nekemiya. **d** 76 **p** 77 Ank. P Dio Ank 76-77; Dio W Ank from 77. *PO Kabwohe, Mbarara, Uganda.*

NYACHIKO, Jairus. St Phil Coll Kongwa 69. **d** and **p** 71 Centr Tang. P Dio Centr Tang. *Box 15, Dodoma, Tanzania.*

NYACHIKO, Canon Petro. **d** 59 Bp Omari for Centr Tang **p** 60 Centr Tang. P Dio Centr Tang; Can of H Spirit Cathl Dodoma from 78. *DCT, Nara, Tanzania.*

NYAGA, Alfred Johnson. b 48. **d** 75 **p** 76 Mt Kenya E. P Dio Mt Kenya E. *PO Kutus, Via Kerugoya, Kenya.*

NYAGA, Bernard. b 38. **d** 78 **p** 79 Mt Kenya E. P Dio Mt Kenya E. *Anglican Church, Kanyuambora, Embu, Kenya.*

NYAGA, Julius. b 48. **d** 78 **p** 80 Mt Kenya E. P Dio Mt Kenya E. *Anglican Church, PO Box 133, Embu, Kenya.*

NYAGA, Phinehas Isaiah. St Paul's Coll Limuru 61. **d** 63 Ft Hall **p** 64 Mt Kenya. P Dio Mt Kenya 63-72; CF (Kenya) from 72. *Box 48702, Nairobi, Kenya.*

NYAHWA, Edward. St Pet Coll Rosettenville. **d** 47 **p** 48 S Rhod. P Dio S Rhod 47-52; Dio Mashon from 52; L to Offic Dio Matab 68-70. *c/o PO Box 7, Salisbury, Rhodesia.*

NYAHWA, Stanley Musa. Edin Th Coll 62. **d** 65 **p** 66 Ripon. C of Chapel-Allerton 65-67; Exec Officer for Radio and Television Christian Coun Zam from 67; L to Offic Dio Zam 67-71; Dio Lusaka from 71. *Box 183, Lusaka, Zambia.*

NYAKADO, Peter. St Phil Th Coll Kongwa. **d** 65 **p** 66 Vic Nyan. P Dio Vic Nyan. *Box 12, Tarime, Tanzania.*

NYAKUBIHA, Paulo Balihuta. **d** 65 **p** 66 Bp Kahurananga for W Tang. P Dio W Tang. *Box 15, Kibondo, Tanzania.*

NYAKURA, Philip. **d** 77 **p** 79 Matab. P Dio Matab. *c/o Box 99, Que Que, Zimbabwe.*

NYAMANE, Isaiah. St Pet Coll Rosettenville. **d** 58 **p** 59 Bloemf. P Dio Bloemf. *Box 85, Jagersfontein, OFS, S Africa.*

NYAMBELE, Jackson Munyanga. b 44. **d** and **p** 77 W Tang. P Dio W Tang. *DWT Matiazo, Kalinzi Private Bag, Kigoma, Tanzania.*

NYAMBU, Andarea. CMS Div Sch Momb 28. **d** 29 Momb. d Dio Momb. *PO Box 72, Mombasa, Kenya.*

NYAMUSESA, Erisa. Mukono Th Coll 49. **d** 51 **p** 52 Ugan. P Dio Ugan 51-60. *Bamadu, Uganda.*

NYAMWATA, Frederick. St Paul's Coll Limuru 75. **d** 76 Maseno N. d Dio Maseno N. *PO Box 384, Kakamega, Kenya.*

NYANDA, Victor Felix Mwelase. **d** 61 **p** 62 Grahmstn. P Dio Grahmstn 61-74; Perm to Offic Dio St John's 74-77; P-in-c of Manzana 77-81; *P O All Saints, Transkei, S Africa.*

NYANDURA, Yona. b 48. St Phil Coll Kongwa 78. **d** 80 **p** W Tang P Dio W Tang. *PO Box 49, Nyumbigwa, Kasulu, Tamzania.*

NYANG, Haggai. Ch Tr Centre, Kapsabet, 66. **d** 67 **p** 68 Nak. P Dio Nak. *Box 79, Nandi Hills, Kenya.*

NYANGASA, Patriki. St Cypr Th Coll Tunduru 58. **d** 60 Zanz. d Dio Zanz T. *Box 33, Mnyuzi, Tanzania.*

✠ **NYANJA, Right Rev Peter Nathaniel.** b 40. St Cypr Coll Rondo 69. **d** 71 **p** 72 Lake Malawi. P Dio Lake Malawi 71-78; Archd of Nkhotakota 76-78; Cons Ld Bp of Lake Malawi in All SS Ch Nkhotakota 25 June 78 by Abp of Centr Afr; Bps of Lusaka and N Zambia; and Bp Mtekateka. *Bishop's House, Box 133, Nkhotakota, Malawi.*

NYANZI, Eria. b 42. Bp Tucker Coll Nukono 68. **d** 70 **p** 72 Nam. P Dio Nam. *Box 14297, Kampala, Uganda.*

NYANZI, Semei. **d** 27 **p** 29 U Nile. P Dio U Nile 27-40; Dio Ugan 40-44; Dio W Bugan 60-63; Can of Ugan 52-60; Can and Sub-Dean of W Bugan 63-64; Archd 64-69. *PO Box 120, Bbombo, Uganda.*

NYAPERA, Timotheo. Ch Tr Centre Kapsabet 62. **d** 63 **p** 65 Nak. P Dio Nak 63-75; Dio Maseno N from 76. *Box 51, Butere, Kenya.*

NYARONGA, Ven Gershom. St Paul's Coll Limuru. **d** 56 **p** 57 Centr Tang. P Dio Centr Tang 56-63; Dio Vic Nyan from 63; Archd of E Lake from 63; Dioc Sec Dio Vic Nyan 63-66; Dioc Regr from 66. *Box 69, Musoma, Tanzania.*

NYARUBONA, Swithini. Bp Tucker Coll Mukono. **d** 53 **p** 56 Ugan. P Dio Ugan 53-60; Dio Ruw 60-72; Archd of Bunyoro 67-72. *Box 132, Hoima, Bunyoro, Uganda, E Africa.*

NYE, Charles Stanley. b 11. St Pet Hall Ox BA (2nd cl Th) 31, Liddon Stud 32, MA and BD 35. **d** 34 **p** 35 Win. Chap Lect and Tutor in Engl Lit and Div K Alfred's Coll Win 34-36; L to Offic Dio Win 34-37; Dio Swan B 35-37; Dir of Relig Educn 36-41; L to Offic Dio Dur 36-37; R of Rainton 37-41;

V of St Mary Virg Nelson 41-44; Blundellsands 44-61; Lect St Aid Coll 53-61; R of Tiverton 61-75; RD of Tiverton 65-67. *62 Mill Hill Road, Cowes, IW.*

NYE, David Charles. b 39. BD (Lon) 65. St Bonif Coll Warm 62. **d** 63 **p** 64 Glouc. C of Charlton Kings 63-67; Yeovil (in c of Preston Plucknett) 67-70; V of Lower Cam 70-74; St Mary-de-Lode w St Nich 74-76; Dir of Ordin Tr and Min Can of Glouc 74-79; V of Maisemore 76-79; Chap Grenville Coll Bideford 79-81; V of St Phil and St Jas Leckhampton w St Jas Cheltm Dio Glouc from 81. *St Phillip's Vicarage, Painswick Road, Cheltenham, Glos, GL50 2EX.* (Cheltm 25460)

NYE, John Arthur Keith. b 04. Mert Coll Ox BA (2nd cl Engl) 25, MA 29. Univ of Man BD 27. Egerton Hall Man 25. **d** 27 **p** 28 Man. C of St Jas Gorton 27-30; Lancaster 30-34; V of Clayton-le-Moors 34-42; Admarsh in Bleasdale w Calder Vale 42-52; Chipping 52-61; Ribby w Wrea 61-69; L to Offic Dio Blackb from 71. *Fosbrooke House, Clifton Drive, Lytham, Lancs.* (Lytham 736411)

✠ **NYE, Right Rev Mark.** Late Scho of St Jo Coll Ox BA (3rd cl Hist) 31, MA 36. Cudd Coll 32. **d** 33 **p** 34 S'wark. C of St Luke Richmond Surrey 33-36; R of Prieska w Upington 36-42; Douglas and Dir of Miss in Griqualand W 42-45; Makefing 45-50; P-in-c of Native Miss Pret 50-60; P-in-c of Good Shepherd Miss 54-58; R of St Wilfrid Hillcrest Pret 60-65; Dean and R of St Alb Cathl Pret 65-73; Archd of Pret 65-66; N Transv 73-77; Cons Ld Bp Suffr of Pret in St Alb Cathl Ch Pret 19 June 73 by Abp of Capetn; Bps of Bloemf, Pret, Kimb K, Johann, Lebom, Natal and Swaz; and Bp Suffr of Johann; res 77; Can (Emer) of Pret from 78; R of St Barn City and Dio Capetn from 78. *34 Camp Street, Tamboerskloof, Cape Town, S Africa.* (41-2057)

NYE, Canon Nathaniel Kemp. b 14. AKC 36. Cudd Coll 36. **d** 37 **p** 38 S'wark. C of St Pet St Helier 37-40; Chap RAFVR 40-46; R of H Trin Clapham 46-54; V of St Pet St Helier 54-61; All SS (w St Phil from 62) Maidstone 61-66; Hon Can of Cant 61-79; Can (Emer) from 79; RD of Sutton 65-66; Tait Missr Dio Cant 66-72; Warden Dioc Retreat Ho Westgate 70-72; Archd of Maidstone 72-79; Dioc Clergy Widows Officer from 79. *Lees Cottage, Boughton Lees, Nr Ashford, Kent.* (Ashford 26175)

NYENWE, Sunday Amesi. b 24. Trin Coll Umuahia 65. **d** 65 **p** 66 Nig Delta. P Dio Nig Delta. *All Saints Parsonage, Rumuokwrusi, Obio, via Port Harcourt, Nigeria.*

NYESI, John. Fitzwm Coll Cam BA 73, MA 77. Ridley Hall Cam. **d** 67 **p** 68 Nai. C of All SS Cathl Nai 67-70; on leave 70-73; V of St Steph Kisumu 73-74; Tutor St Paul's Coll Limuru 74-75; Prin 76-78; on leave. *1325 North College Avenue, Claremont, CA 91711, USA.*

NYILIKA, Wilson. b 37. **d** 75 **p** 76 Matab. P Dio Matab. *P Bag Q5294, Zimbabwe.*

NYINDO, Festo. d 74 **p** 75 Ank. P Dio Ank 74-77; Dio W Ank from 77. *PO Mutooma, Bushenyi, Uganda.*

NYIRIMANZI, Andre. d 80 Kiga. d Dio Kiga. *BP 489, Kigali, Rwanda.*

NYMAN, Canon Lewis. St Jo Coll Morpeth. **d** 61 **p** 62 Newc. C of E Maitland 62-63; Gosford 64-65; CF (Austr) 66-73; R of Swan Hill Dio St Arn (Dio Bend from 77) from 73; Can of St Arn 74-76; Ch Ch Old Cathl St Arn from 77. *79 McCallum Street, Swan Hill, Vic., Australia 3585.* (050-32 1246)

NYOKANA, Albert Madlubutshana. b 26. **d** 79 **p** 80 St John's (APM). P Dio St John's. *Gqwesa Store, Qumba, Transkei.*

NYOMA, Noel Lotio. Juba Bible Inst. **d** 71 Sudan. d Dio Sudan. *Box 110, Juba, Equatoria Province, Sudan.*

NYOMBI, Misaeri. Bp Tucker Coll Mukono. **d** 60 **p** 62 W Bugan. P Dio W Bugan 60-65; Dio Ruw 65-72; Dio Bunyoro from 72. *Munsa, PO Box 251, Kahumiro, Bunyoro, Uganda.*

NYONG'O, Ven Hesbon. St Paul's Dioc Div Sch Limuru, 44. **d** 45 **p** 49 Momb. P Dio Momb 45-53; CF (Afr) 53-57; P Dio Momb 57-61; Dio Maseno 61-62 and 63-70; C of St Mary Doncaster 62-63; P Dio Maseno S from 70; Hon Can of Maseno 68-70; Maseno S from 70; Exam Chap to Bp of Maseno S 70-75; Archd of Ng'iya from 72. *Box 71, Maseno, Kenya.*

NYONI, Daniel. St Jo Th Sem Lusaka. **d** 58 **p** 60 Matab. P Dio Matab 58-80. *Box 9044, Gwelo, Zimbabwe.*

NYORO, Felix. St Paul's Dioc Div Sch Limuru. **d** 43 **p** 45 Momb. P Dio Momb 43-61; Dio Ft Hall 61-64; Dio Mt Kenya 64-75; Dio Mt Kenya S from 75. *Box 221, Murang'a, Kenya.*

NYOROZI, Alfred. Bp Tucker Coll Mukono, 60. **d** 62 **p** 64 Ankole-K. P Dio Ankole-K 62-67; Dio Ank from 67. *Box 103, Mbarara, Uganda.*

NZABAMWITA, Francis. d 78 **p** 79 Ruw. P Dio Ruw. *c/o Box 351, Fort Portal, Uganda.*

NZAKARA, Levi Hassan. Bp Gwynne Coll Mundri, 61. **d** 64 **p** 66 Sudan. P Dio Sudan. *ECS, Maridi, Equatoria Province, Sudan.*

✠ **NZANO, Right Rev Crispus.** St Paul's Th Coll Limuru. **d** and **p** 67 Momb. P Dio Momb 67-68; Prin CA Tr Coll Nai 68-69; Asst Gen Sec CA in E Africa 69-70; Gen Sec from 71; Cons Asst Bp of Nai in All SS Cathl Nai 23 Feb 75 by Abp of Kenya; Bps of Momb, Maseno N, Mt Kenya and Maseno S; and others. *PO Box 72584, Nairobi, Kenya.* (Nairobi 23233)

NZIKO, Gresford Kata Malandi. St Phil Th Coll Kongwa 69. **d** 71 **p** 72 Moro. P Dio Moro. *Songe, Via Handeni, Tanzania.*

NZISEHERE, Sebastian. b 29. **d** 76 **p** 77 Vic Nyan. P Dio Vic Nyan. *Murgwanza, Ngara, West Lake, Tanzania.*

NZOTTA, Titus Nwanguma. Trin Coll Umuahia 56. **d** 58 **p** 59 Nig Delta. P Dio Nig Delta 58-72; Dio Aba 72-79. *St Barnabas's Church, Nbawsi, Nigeria.*

NZUKUMA, Arthur Benjamin Cuthbert. St Paul's Coll Grahmstn 61. **d** 62 **p** 63 Grahmstn. P Dio Grahmstn 62-71. *Linge Bantu Township, Malibini, CP, S Africa.*

O

O, Basil Sang-ok. b 15. **d** 66 **p** 68 Taejon. P Dio Taejon. *498 Kwanghyewon, Chingchon, Ch'ungbuk 330-33, Korea.*

O, David Yongsam. b 33. St Mich Sem Seoul 64. **d** 67 **p** 68 Taejon. P Dio Taejon 67-72. *3533 N Albany Avenue, Chicago 60618, USA.*

OADE, John Leonard. b 09. ALCD 37. **d** 36 **p** 37 Wakef. C of Rashcliffe 36-38; Bingley 38-40; CF (EC) 40-46; Hon CF from 46; R of Oswaldkirk 46-53; C-in-c of Yearsley 46-53; V of Riddlesden 53-56; R of Rylstone 56-63; Severn Stoke 63-72; Perm to Offic Dio Glouc from 76. *Dean Bungalow, Lynwood Road, Primrose Hill, Lydney, GL15 5SG.* (0594 422331)

OADES, Michael Anthony John. b 45. Sarum Wells Th Coll 71. **d** 73 **p** 74 S'wark. C of St Luke Eltham 73-77; St Andr (in c of St Francis) Coulsdon 77-81; V of St Jas Merton Dio S'wark from 81. *St James Vicarage, Beaford Grove, SW20.* (01-540 3122)

OADES, Peter Robert. b 24. Fitzw Ho Cam BA 47, MA 53. **d** and **p** 67 Portsm. C of Warblington w Emsworth 67-68; V Cho Sarum Cathl 68-74; Chap and Asst Master Sarum Cathl Sch 68-74; V of Sturminster Newton w Hinton St Mary 74-81; R of Stock w Lydlinch 75-81; RD of Blackmore Vale 78-81; V of Woodford Valley Dio Sarum from 81. *Middle Woodford Vicarage, Salisbury, SP4 6NR.* (072 273 310)

OAKE, Ven Frederick Raymond. Bp's Univ Lennox BA 55. Qu Coll Newfld BD 65. **d** 48 **p** 49 Newfld. I of Exploits 48-52; White Bay 52-53; R of Belleoram 54-60; Bay St Geo 60-64; Bonavista 64-74; Dir of Programme Dio Newfld (E Newfld from 76) from 74; Can and Archd of E Newfld from 76; Dioc Regr and Sec from 76; Treas from 81. *19 King's Bridge Road, St John's, Newfoundland, Canada.*

OAKES, Graham. b 42. Univ of Leeds Dipl Th 68. Chich Th Coll 68. **d** 70 **p** 71 Man. C of Ascen Hulme Man 70-74; All SS Clifton w St Mary Tyndall's Park 74-76; P-in-c of St Mark Chadderton Dio Man 76-78; V from 78. *Vicarage, Milne Street, Chadderton, Oldham, OL9 0HR.* (061-624 2005)

OAKES, Hugh Roy Gilbert. Univ of Syd BA 54. Austrn Nat Univ MA 66. Moore Th Coll Syd ACT ThL 54. **d** and **p** 54 C & Goulb. C of Cooma 54-55; P-in-c of Adelong 55-56; R of Tumbarumba 56-60; Lake Bath 60-63; Berridale 63-68; Dioc Regr Dio Gippsld 68-70; Hon Can of St Paul's Cathl Sale 70-73; Educn Dir Dio Gippsld 70-73; Hon C of St Paul's Cathl Sale 73-77; Perm to Offic Dio Wang from 77. *35 Acacia Street, Sheppartan, Vic, Australia 3630.*

OAKES, Canon Hugh Toft. b 16. Bp Wilson Th Coll IM 39. **d** 41 Bp Duppuy for Worc **p** 42 Worc. C of St John Dudley 41-44; St Andr Pershore 44-46; R of All SS Wainfleet 46-54; V of Humberston Dio Linc from 54; Can and Preb of Linc Cathl from 79. *Vicarage, Tetney Road, Humberston, Grimsby, S Humb, DN36 4JF.* (Grimsby 813158)

OAKES, Jeremy Charles. b 51. ACA 75, FCA 81. Westcott Ho Cam 75. **d** 78 Bp Garrett for Leic **p** 79 Leic. C of St Denys Evington Leic 78-81; SS Pet & Paul Ringwood Dio Win from 81. *Tumble Barn, Linford Road, Poulner, Ringwood, Hants, BH24 1TY.* (Ringwood 79389)

OAKES, John Cyril. b 49. AKC 71. St Aug Coll Cant 71. **d** 72 **p** 73 Heref. C of Broseley w Benthall 72-76; Cannock (in c of St John Heath Hayes) Dio Lich 76-79; Team V from 79.

226 Hednesford Road, Heath Hayes, Cannock, WS12 5DZ. (Heath Hayes 78478)

OAKES, Leslie John. b 28. K Coll Lon and Warm AKC 53. **d** 54 **p** 55 Man. C of St Thos Bedford Leigh 54-58; C of Walsall 58-60; Chap Selly Oak Hosp Birm 60-64; PC of Longbridge Dio Birm 64-68; V from 68. *220 Longbridge Lane, Birmingham 31.* (021-475 3484)

OAKES, Melvin. b 36. Linc Th Coll 77. **d** 79 Barking for Chelmsf **p** 80 Chelmsf. C of St Mich AA L Ilford Dio Chelmsf from 79. *56 Second Avenue, Manor Park, E12 6JE.* (01-478 1595)

OAKHAM, Archdeacon of. *See* Fernyhough, Ven Bernard.

OAKLEY, Barry Wyndham. b 32. TD 72. SS Coll Cam BA (3rd cl Mech Sc Trip pt i) 53, MA 57. Ridley Hall Cam 56. **d** 58 **p** 59 Portsm. C of St Mary Alverstoke 58-61; CF (TA) from 59; C of Bermondsey 61-63; V of Crofton 63-78; M Gen Syn Portsm 74-78; V of Edmon Dio Lon from 78; P-in-c of St Mich Edmon Dio Lon from 80. *All Saints' Vicarage, All Saints' Close, Edmonton, N9 9PB.* (01-803 9199)

OAKLEY, Frederick Charles. **d** 59 **p** 60 Gippsld. C of Bairnsdale 59-62; Moe 62-63; V 63-65; R of Kilmore 65-71; Perm to Offic Dio Gippsld from 72. *62 Narracan Drive, Newborough, Vic., Australia 3828.* (051-27 3585)

OAKLEY, Hilary Robert Mark. b 53. Univ of Wales (Bangor) BSc 75. Univ of Ox BA (Th) 78. Ripon Coll Cudd 76. **d** 79 **p** 80 Birm. C of St Pet City and Dio Birm from 79. *51 Kelsall Croft, Birmingham, B1 2PS.*

OAKLEY, Raymond. b 09. Ripon Hall Ox 58. **d** and **p** 60 Birm. C of St Nich Kings Norton (in c of St Anne W Heath) 60-66; V of St Mary Virg Bearwood Smethwick 66-79; Perm to Offic Dio Birm from 80. *21 Poplar Avenue, Birmingham, B17 8EG.*

OAKLEY, Richard John. b 46. K Coll Lon AKC 69. St Aug Coll Cant 69. **d** 70 **p** 71 Hulme for York. C of Wm Temple Ch Woodhouse Pk 70-75; V of H Trin Ashton L 75-80. *House of the Resurrection, Mirfield, W Yorks, WF14 0BN.*

OAKLEY, Robin Ian. b 37. Ripon Hall Ox 68. **d** 70 **p** 71 St Alb. C of Leighton Buzzard 70-73; St Mich AA Watford 73-76; R of Ickleford (w Holwell from 80) Dio St Alb from 76. *Rectory, Turnpike Lane, Ickleford, Hitchin, Herts SG5 3XB.* (Hitchin 2925)

OAKLEY, Timothy Crispin. b 45. Qu Coll Cam BA 66, MA 70. St Jo Coll Nottm 73. **d** 76 **p** 77 Roch. C of St Aug Bromley Common 76-79; St Jo Div Fairfield Liv 79-82. *c/o 28 Edge Grove, Liverpool, L7 0HW.* (051-228 6632)

OAKLEY, Trevor John William. b 51. Moore Th Coll Syd BTh. **d** 81 Syd. C of St Jo Bapt Sutherland Dio Syd from 81. *Ninth Avenue, Loftus, NSW, Australia 2232.*

OAKLEY, William Ernest Bernard. b 49. Univ of Manit BA 70. Montr Dioc Th Coll BTh 74. **d** 74 **p** 75 Rupld. C of St Matt Winnipeg 74-76; I of St Paul Middlechurch and of St Mart River N Angl Pars Dio Rupld from 76. *162 Smithfield Avenue, Winnipeg, Manit, R2V 0C2, Canada.*

OAKLEY, William John Terence. b 08. MM 41. **d** 32 **p** 33 Wakef. C of Drighlington 32-34; Ch Ch Woodhouse (in c of Good Shepherd) 34-36; R of S Cross 36-38; Norseman 38-39; TCF (AIF) 39-41; TCF 41-45; Chap 115 AGH Heidelburgh Melbourne 46; C of Atherton 47-48; V of Cloughfold 48-52; E Kirkby w Miningsby 52-56; PC of Hagnaby 52-56; R of Tansor w Cotterstock and Fotheringhay 56-73. *3 The Glebe, Flore, Northants, NN7 4LX.* (Weedon 40831)

OAKS, Ernest James. b 26. Univ of NZ BCom 62. St Jo Coll Auckld 75 **d** 76 **p** 77 Wai. C of Taupo Dio Wai from 76. *134 Taharepa Street, Taupo, NZ.* (89-466)

OATES, Alan. b 32. SOC 79. **d** 80 Bradwell for Chelmsf **p** 81 Chelmsf (NSM). C of Rayleigh Dio Chelmsf from 80. *7 Glebe Drive, Rayleigh, Essex, SS6 9HJ.*

OATES, Austin Edwin. Worc Ordin Coll. **d** 63 **p** 64 Ches. C of Prestbury 63-67; V of Plemstall w Guilden Sutton 67-74; Crowton Dio Ches from 74. *Crowton Vicarage, Northwich, Chesh.* (Kingsley 88310)

OATES, Donald Allan. b 21. Oak Hill Coll 78. **d** and **p** 81 Barking for Chelmsf (NSM). C of Gt Parndon Dio Chelmsf from 81. *37 Copse Hill, Great Parndon, Harlow, Essex, CM19 4PN.*

OATES, Canon John. b 30. Kelham Th Coll 53. **d** 57 **p** 58 Lon. C of St Mary Virg of Eton Hackney Wick 57-60; Development Officer C of E Youth Coun 60-64; Development Sec C of E Coun Commonwealth Settlement 64-65; Gen Sec from 65; Sec C of E C'tte on Migration and Internat Affairs from 68; Commiss Perth and NW Austr from 68; Jer 69-75; Bunb from 69; Hon Can of Bunb from 69; V of Richmond Dio S'wark from 70; P-in-c of St Jo Div Richmond 75-79; RD of Richmond & Barnes from 79. *Vicarage, Ormond Road, Richmond, Surrey.* (01-940 0362)

OATES, John Francis Titus. Worc Coll Ox BA 50, MA 54. Qu Coll Birm 50. **d** 52 **p** 53 Ripon. C of Hunslet 52-56; Chap RN 56-67; in Amer Ch from 67. *St Thomas Parish Church, Chestnut Street, Camden, Maine 04843, USA.*

OATEY, Michael John. b 31. Chich Th Coll 57. **d** 60 Lon **p** 61 Kens for Lon. C of W Drayton 60-66; V of St Mich Sutton Court Chiswick 66-74; Tywardreath Dio Truro from 74; R of St Sampson Dio Truro from 74. *Vicarage, Tywardreath, Par, Cornw, PL24 2PL.* (Par 2998)

OATEY, Canon Richard Oliver. b 02. AKC 37. **d** 37 **p** 38 Truro. C of Liskeard 37-42; V of St Teath w Delabole and Michaelstow 42-48; RD of Trigg Minor 47-48; Powder 58-61; R of St Erme 48-64; Hon Can of Truro 56-78 Can (Emer) from 78; C-in-c of St Allen 59-64; V of Devoran 64-71. *9 The Green, East Leake, Loughborough, Leics.* (East Leake 3836)

OATWAY, Hugh Malcolm. Moore Th Coll Syd ACT ThL 60. **d** 58 **p** 59 Nel. C of Ch Ch Cathl Nel 58-60; V of Wairu Valley 60; Chap RNZAF 60-66; V of Cheviot 66-70; Highfield 70-79; Ngaio Dio Wel from 79. *11 Abbott Street, Wellington 4, NZ.* (796-936)

OBADOFIN, Canon Michael Obafemi. Melville Hall, Ibad. **d** 48 **p** 49 Lagos. P Dio Lagos 48-52; Dio Ondo-B 52-62; Dio Ondo from 62; Hon Can of Ondo from 75. *Box 15, Ifon, Nigeria.* (Ifon 5)

OBAN, Provost of. *See* Abbott, Very Rev Nigel Douglas Blayney.

OBASORO, Aoron Akanbi. **d** 40 **p** 44 Lagos. P Dio Lagos 40-52; Dio Ondo-B 52-62; Dio Ondo from 62. *c/o CMS, Ifira, Okene, Nigeria.*

OBAWEYA, Canon Joseph Clement. Melville Hall, Ibad. **d** 50 **p** 51 Lagos. P Dio Lagos 50-52; Dio Ondo-B 52-62; Dio Ondo 62-66; Dio Ekiti from 66; Can of Ekiti from 66. *St John's Vicarage, Igbemo, Ekiti, Nigeria.*

OBAYA, Fesito. **d** 56 Ugan **p** 58 Bp Balya for Ugan. P Dio Ugan 56-60; Dio Ruw from 60. *Kigaya, Uganda.*

OBAYOMI, Canon Joseph Olanipekun. Im Coll Ibad 62. **d** 64 **p** 65 Lagos. P Dio Lagos 64-77; Dio Ijebu from 77; Can from 79. *St Paul's Church, Odogbolu, Nigeria.*

OBEE, Douglas Walter. b 18. Roch Th Coll 65. **d** 67 **p** 68 Roch. C of Beckenham 67-71; V of Oldridge 71-75; R of Whitestone 71-75; V of Ivybridge Dio Ex from 76; C-in-c of Harford Dio Ex from 75. *Vicarage, Ivybridge, Devon, PL21 0AD.* (Ivybridge 2592)

O'BEIRNE, Peter Donald Moray. b 20. Kelham Th Coll 39. **d** 43 Lewes for Chich **p** 44 Chich. C of Portslade w Hangleton 43-46; All SS Fulham 46-50; Dorking 50-54; V of Latton 54-63. *5 Burley Close, Loxwood, Billingshurst, Sussex.*

OBELI, Lamech. Buwalasi Th Coll 58. **d** 59 **p** 60 U Nile. P Dio U Nile 59-61; Dio Mbale 61-65; Dio N Ugan 65-74; Dio Bukedi from 74. *PO Box 170, Tororo, Uganda.*

O'BENEY, Robin Mervyn. b 35. Ely Th Coll 61. **d** 64 **p** 65 Portsm. C of Liss 64-65; St Cuthb Copnor 65-68; L to Offic Dio Portsm 68-71; Dio Nor 72-74; Hon C of Wymondham 74-76; R of Newton Flotman w Swainsthorpe 76-80. *c/o Swainsthorpe Rectory, Norwich, NR14 8PH.* (Swainsthorpe 399)

OBENG, Clement Ani. **d** and **p** 58 Accra. P Dio Accra. *Box 47, Obo-Kwahu, Ghana.*

OBERLIN-HARRIS, Osric. Late Cl Scho of Univ of Tas BA 03, 2nd cl Ment and Mor Sc 04, MA 11. Late Scho and Sen Col Stud of St Jo Coll Ox BA (2nd cl Th) 07. Cudd Coll 07. **d** 08 **p** 09 St Alb. C of The Ascen Vic Dks 08-11; St Anne Nanango 11-15; V 15-19; Chap of Yarrabah Miss N Queensld 19-20; R of Cairns N Queensld 21-22; C of St Cypr Durban 22-24; St Jas Isipinge 24-26; P-in-c of Par Distr of Clairwood and Bluff (w St Raphael's Miss from 28) Durban 26-33; V of St Jas Stamford Hill Natal 33-46; Th Tutor Dio Natal 37-46; Can of St Sav Cathl Maritzburg 44-46; V of Gt Staughton 46-52; Commiss Natal 47-55; R of Broughton 52-55; R of King's Ripton 52-55. *32 Church Street, New Norfolk, Tasmania.*

OBIA, Hilkiah. **d** 66 **p** 67 N Ugan. P Dio N Ugan 66-69; Dio M & W Nile from 69. *Church of Uganda, Box 272, Arua, West Nile, Uganda.*

OBIANABA, frederick Mbanugo. b 48. Trin Coll Umuahia 79. **d** 81 Asaba. d Dio Asaba. *All Saint's Church, Iselle Uku, Bendel State, Nigeria.*

OBIANWU, Ernest Nwabueze. Im Coll Ibad 62. **d** 64 **p** 65 N Nig. P Dio N Nig 64-67; Dio Niger 68-75. *c/o PO Box 72, Kaduna, Nigeria.*

OBIAYI, Ezekiel. b 11. Dioc Tr Centre Arua. **d** 69 **p** 70 Madi. P Dio Soroti. *Box 44, Moroto, Uganda.*

OBIDIKE, Elijah Egbuna. Awka Tr Coll. **d** 45 **p** 47 Niger. P Dio Niger 45-52 and 55-67; Dio Nig Delta 52-55. *Nibo, Nigeria.*

OBIEFUNA, Samuel Obiegbu. Trin Th Coll Umuahia 58. **d** 59 **p** 60 Ow. P Dio Ow 59-72; Dio Niger from 72. *Parsonage, Umudim, Box 15, Nnewi, Nigeria.*

OBIERO, Ainea Paulo. b 22. St Paul's Coll Limuru 51. **d** 54 **p** 55 Momb. P Dio Momb 54-59; Dio Maseno S from 77.

PO Box 353, Luanda, Kenya.

OBIERO, Charles. Maseno Bible Sch 69. **d** 69 Maseno. d Dio Maseno 69-70; Dio Maseno N from 70. *Box 1, Maseno, Kenya.*

OBIJIAKU, Lazarus Okafor Akunekwe. St Paul's Coll Awka. **d** 55 **p** 57 Niger. P Dio Niger 55-59; Dio Ow 59-70; Can of All SS Cathl Egbu 70-74. *Parsonage, Akokwa, Via Orlu, Nigeria.*

OBINYA, Canon Uju Otuokwesiri Wachukwu. b 34. Trin Coll Umuahia 62. **d** 64 **p** 65 Nig Delta. P Dio Nig Delta 65-72; Dio Aba from 72; Can of Aba from 75. *PO Box 818, Aba, Nigeria.*

OBIRI, Joisrael Esimajotayomi. Melville Hall Ibad 48. **d** 52 **p** 53 Odutola for Ondo-B. P Dio Ondo-B 53-60; Dio Ibad from 60. *St Andrew's Vicarage, Edidi-Oja, via Offa, Nigeria.*

OBISESAN, Thomas Oyelami. b 21. **d** 76 **p** 78 Ibad. P Dio Ibad. *St Peter's Vicarage, Orile-Owu, via Ibadan, Nigeria.*

OBODAI, Canon Alfred Codjoe. **d** 52 **p** 53 Accra. P Dio Accra; Hon Can of Accra 68-75; Can from 75. *Box 4, Tema, Accra, Ghana.*

OBODAI, Samiel Nii Torgbor. b 45. Trin Coll Legon 71. **d** and **p** 75 Accra. P Dio Accra; CF (Ghana) from 79. *Ministry of Defence, Burma Camp, Accra, Ghana.*

OBONIYE, Jeremiah. Im Coll Ibad 78. **d** 81 Benin. d Dio Benin. *c/o Registrar, PO Box 82, Benin City, Nigeria.*

OBOTE, Isaiah. b 43. Bp Tucker Coll Mukono 64. **d** 71 **p** 72 Soroti. P Dio Soroti. *Box 107, Soroti, Uganda.*

O'BRIEN, Donogh Smith. b 34. St Pet Hall Ox BA 56, MA 60. Ripon Hall Ox 56. **d** 57 Warrington for Liv **p** 58 Liv. C of Gt Sankey 57-63; Farnworth 63-66; Asst Master Wade Deacon Gr Sch Widnes and L to Offic Dio Liv from 66. *178 Lunt's Heath Road, Widnes, Lancs.* (051-424-0147)

O'BRIEN, George Edward. b 32. Clifton Th Coll 61. **d** 64 Penrith for Carl **p** 65 Carl. C of St Jas Denton Holme 64-68; V of St Thos Stafford Dio Lich from 68; Chap HM Pris Stafford 77-80. *Vicarage, Doxey, Stafford, ST16 1EQ.*

O'BRIEN, Canon James Henry. b 10. Bps' Coll Cheshunt, 42. **d** 44 **p** 45 Blackb. C of St Jo Evang Blackb 44-47; V of St Aid Blackb 47-67; M Gen Syn Blackb 59-75; St Cuthb Darwen 67-75; Surr from 49; Proc Conv Blackb from 59; RD of Darwen 64-75; Hon Can of Blackb 73-75; Can (Emer) from 75; C of Adlington 75-79; L to Offic Dio Blackb from 79. *10 Crompton Place, Blackburn, Lancs, BB2 6LW.* (Blackb 64799)

O'BRIEN, John. b 41. St Jo Coll Cam BA 63, MA 67. Ridley Hall Cam. **d** 65 **p** 66 Glouc. C of Wotton (or Longlevens) 65-69; Youth Chap Glouc 67-69; Lect St Mary's Coll of Educn Cheltm 69-74; Sen Lect 74-79; Coll of St Paul & St Mary Cheltm from 79; Hon C of St Jo Evang Churchdown Dio Glouc from 69. *10 Keriston Avenue, Churchdown, Gloucester, GL3 2BU.* (0452 713169)

O'BRIEN, Neville Ernest Bruce. St Jo Coll Morpeth ACT ThL (2nd cl) 59. **d** 59 **p** 60 Newc. C of E Maitland 59-61; Ch Ch St Laur Syd 62; Cessnock 62-63; R of Coopernook 63-71; Dungog 71-77; L to Offic Dio Newc from 77. *18 Celebes Street, Ashtonfield, E Maitland, NSW, Australia 2323.*

O'BRIEN, Peter Thomas. Univ of Man PhD 71. Moore Th Coll Syd ACT ThL 60. BD (Lon) 61. **d** 61 Bp Kerle for Syd **p** 62 Syd. C of Provisional Distr of Padstow w Revesby 61-63; CMS India 64-68 and 71-73; C of Cheadle 68-71; Lect Moore Th Coll Syd from 74. *Moore Theological College, Carillon Avenue, Newton, NSW, Australia 2042.* (51-3072)

O'BRIEN, Robert Stephen. b 36. SOC 67. **d** 71 Guildf. C of Ch Ch Esher 71-73; St Lawr Jewry City and Dio Lon from 73. *c/o St Lawrence Jewry Vicarage, Guildhall, EC2.*

O'BRIEN, Ronald Arthur. MBE 72. Moore Th Coll Syd. **d** 31 **p** 32 Syd. C of St John Balman N 31-33; St John Camden NSW 33-36; Toowoomba 36; St Pet Hornsby 37; C-in-c of Dural 37-42; Chap AIF 42-46; R of Dural 47-49; Canterbury 49-57; Burwood 57-77; L to Offic Dio Syd from 77. *69 Springdale Road, Killara, NSW, Australia 2071.* (498-4006)

O'BRIEN, Thomas Joseph. St Jo Coll Morpeth ACT ThL 47. **d** 46 **p** 47 Goulb. C of Cathl Goulb 46-47; Wagga Wagga 47-49; R of Cobargo 49-50; Barmedman 50-52; Chap RAAF and LPr Dio C & Goulb 52-56; R of Gunning 56-61; Regr Dio St Arn 61-67; Can of St Arn 64-67; V of Mortlake 67-71. *War Veterans Home, Legacy Park, Narrabeen, NSW, Australia.*

OBULI, Charles. Bp Tucker Coll Mukono 63. **d** 64 **p** 65 Mbale. P Dio Mbale 64-72; Dio Bukedi from 72. *Church of Uganda, Buhehe, PO Box 1034, Busia, Uganda.*

OBURA, Canon Samusoni. **d** 52 Bp Tomusange for U Nile **p** 54 U Nile. P Dio U Nile 52-67; Dio N Ugan 67-76; Archd of Lango 67-72; Aduku 73-76; Can of Lango from 76; Prin Dioc Th Coll Mukono from 76. *PO Box 4, Mukono, Uganda.*

OBURU, Allen Nweyilobu. b 27. **d** 76 Nig Delta. d Dio Nig Delta. *Holy Trinity Parsonage, Nonwa, Tai-Eleme, Port Harcourt, Rivers State, Nigeria.*

OBUWA, Yokonani. **d** 58 **p** 59 U Nile. P Dio U Nile 58-61; Dio N Ugan 61-74. *Lira Town, Uganda.*

OBWONG, Dixon John. b 41. **d** 74 **p** 76 Maseno N. P Dio Maseno N. *Box 5067, Funyula, Kenya.*

O'BYRNE, Francis Michael. b 12. Tyndale Hall Bris 41. **d** 44 Warrington for Liv **p** 45 Liv. C of St Luke Eccleston 44-46; St Kevin Dub 46-49; C-in-c of Rynagh w Clonmacnoise U 49-54; Athboy U Dio Meath 54-56; R 56-81; Can of Meath 76-81. *Birch Lea, Old Connaught Avenue, Bray, Co Wicklow, Irish Republic.*

O'BYRNE, Canon James. b 21. TCD BA (2nd cl Ment and Mor Sc Mod). Abp King and Bp Forster Pri 48. Downes Div Pri (1st cl), Div Test (1st cl) and Th Exhib (1st cl) 49. BD (1st cl) 50. MA 55. **d** 50 **p** 51 Dub. Chap and Tutor of ICM 50-51; C of Ch Ch Belfast 51-52; Tutor and Libr Lon Coll Div 53; C of Burnage 53-55; V of Tunstead 55-62; Sen Tutor Clifton Th Coll 62-65; Vice-Prin 65-69; Prin 69-72; C-in-c of St Steph City and Dio Nor from 72; Exam Chap to Bp of Nor from 73; Hon Can of Nor Cathl from 75; Asst Dioc Dir of Ordinands from 76. *12 The Crescent, Norwich, NR2 1SA.* (Norwich 23045)

OCAMA, Yonasani. Buwalasi Th Coll 51. **d** 53 **p** 54 U Nile. P Dio U Nile 53-61; Dio N Ugan 61-72. *PO Apach, Akokoro, Uganda.*

OCAYA, Kileopa. **d** 65 **p** 66 Bp Wani for Soroti. P Dio Soroti 66-69; P Dio M & W Nile from 69. *PO Agwoko, Uganda.*

OCCOMORE, Albert Ernest. b 06. Ridley Hall Cam. **d** 64 **p** 65 Chelmsf. Hon C of Gidea Pk Dio Chelmsf 64-67; C 67-76; Perm to Offic Dio Chelmsf from 77. *446 Upper Brentwood Road, Gidea Park, Romford, Essex, RM2 6JB.* (Romford 49597)

OCEATRE, Justus. **d** 62 **p** 63 N Ugan. P Dio N Ugan 62-69; Dio M & W Nile from 69. *PO Moyo, Uganda.*

OCEN, Canon Erinaye. **d** 61 **p** 62 N Ugan. P Dio N Ugan 61-76; Lango from 76; Hon Can of Lango from 76. *PO Alemere, Lira, Uganda.*

OCEN, John William. Bp Usher-Wilson Coll Buwalasi. **d** 64 **p** 65 N Ugan. P Dio N Ugan. *Alito, Uganda.*

OCEN, Ven Yekoakazi. Buwalasi Th Coll 59. **d** 61 **p** 62 N Ugan. P Dio N Ugan 61-76; Dio Lango from 76; Archd of Lango from 76. *PO Aduku, Lira, Uganda.*

OCHAMA, Yonasani. **d** 52 Bp Tomusange for U Nile **p** 54 U Nile. P Dio U Nile 52-61; Dio Mbale from 61. *PO Nagongera, Uganda.*

OCHANA, Geoffrey. St Paul's Th Coll Limuru 73. **d** 73 **p** 74 Nak. P Dio Nak. *PO Box 381, Nakuru, Kenya.*

OCHE, Peter. **d** 56 Momb **p** 61 Nak. P Dio Momb 56-61; Dio Nak 61-70; Dio Mt Kenya from 70. *BCMS PO Marsabit, Kenya.*

OCHIENG, Ignatius. **d** 62 **p** 65 Maseno. P Dio Maseno 65-69; Dio Nak from 70. *PO Box 651, Nakuru, Kenya.*

OCHOLA, Macleord Baker. b 36. Bp Tucker Coll Mukono 69. **d** 72 N Ugan. d Dio N Ugan 72-77; Dio Boga-Z from 77. *BP 154, Bunia, Zaire.*

OCHUNG'A, Joash Anaminyi. St Paul's Dioc Sch Limuru. **d** 52 **p** 55 Momb. P Dio Momb. *PO Box 30175, Nairobi, Kenya.*

OCKFORD, Paul Philip. b 46. St Chad's Coll Dur BA 67. St Steph Ho Ox 68. **d** 70 **p** 71 S'wark. C of St Pet Streatham 70-74; Cheam (in c of St Osw) 74-77; P-in-c of Eastrington 77-79; Team V of Howden Dio York from 79. *Eastrington Vicarage, Goole Humb, DN14 7QE.* (Eastrington 282)

OCKIYA, Daniel Nana. **d** 65 **p** 66 Accra. P Dio Accra 65-70; Dio Benin from 71; Can of Benin 74-77. *Parsonage, Edherie, via Oleh, Nigeria.*

OCKIYA, Isaac Ayebainaemi Abraham. Trin Coll Umuahia 59. **d** 61 **p** 62 Nig Delta. P Dio Nig Delta. *St Cyprian's Church, PO Box 15, Port Harcourt, Nigeria.*

OCKIYA, Jonathan Fanyo Obiriango. Awka Coll Nigeria. **d** 42 Bp Onyeabo for Niger **p** 44 Niger. P Dio Niger 42-52; Dio Nig Delta 52-72. *c/o St Luke's Church, Nembe, Nigeria.*

OCKWELL, Canon Herbert Grant. b 12. Kelham Th Coll 30. **d** 36 **p** 37 S'wark. C of St Matt Newington 36-40; CF (EC) 40-46; V of St Phil Lambeth 46-52; St Andr Surbiton 52-62; Proc Conv S'wark 55-62; Commiss Bloemf 58-69; V of Ascen Balham 62-70; Hon Can of S'wark 64-70; Can (Emer) from 70; R of Blendworth w Chalton and Idsworth 70-81. *72 Bowes Hill, Rowlands Castle, Hants, PO9 6BS.* (Rowlands Castle 2301)

OCOM, Robert. b 54. **d** 78 Lango. d Dio Lango. *PO Minakulo, Lira, Uganda.*

O'CONNOR, Alfred Stanley. b 20. Trin Coll Dub BA 43, MA 60. **d** 43 **p** 44 Down. C of St Mich Belf 43-45; Cavan U 45-49; R of Killesher 49-54; Roscrea U 54-62; RD of Ely O'Carroll 60-62; R of Camlough w Killeavy 62-65; Drumglass Dio Arm from 65. *Rectory, Dungannon, Co Tyrone, N Ireland.* (Dungannon 2614)

O'CONNOR, Brian Michael McDougal. b 42. St Cath Coll

Cam 3rd cl Th Trip pt i, 65, BA (2nd cl Th Trip pt ii), 67, MA 69. Cudd Coll 67. **d** 69 **p** 70 Ox. C of St Andr Headington 69-71; P-in-c of Merton 72-76; M Gen Syn Ox 75-80; Roch from 80; Sec Ox Pastoral C'tte and Redundant Chs Uses C'tte 72-79; V of Rainham Dio Roch from 79; RD of Gillingham from 81. *80 Broadview Avenue, Rainham, Kent, ME8 9DE.* (Medway 31538)

O'CONNOR, Daniel. b 33. Univ of Dur BA (2nd cl Engl) 54, MA (Th) 67. Univ of St Andr PhD (Th) 81. Cudd Coll 56. **d** 58 **p** 59 Dur. C of St Pet Stockton-on-Tees 58-62; St Aid W Hartlepool 62-63; Chap and Lect St Steph Coll Delhi 63-72; Chap Univ of St Andr 72-77; R of Good Shepherd Edin 77-82; Prin Coll of Ascen Selly Oak Birm from 82. *College of Ascension, Weoley Park Road, Birmingham, B29 6RD.*

O'CONNOR, John Goodrich. b 34. Keble Coll Ox BA (1st cl Hist) 58, (3rd cl Th) 60. Lich Th Coll. **d** 61 Lanc for Blackb **p** 62 Blackb. C of St Steph Blackpool 61-66; Holbeck 66-68; Hendon 68-73; Team V of Thornaby-on-Tees Dio York 73-79; Team R from 79. *St Mark's Rectory, Trenchard Avenue, Thornaby, Cleve, TS17 0EF.* (Stockton 761655)

O'CONNOR, Larry Charles. Univ of Tor BA 62. Wycl Coll Tor BTh 65. **d** 65 Bp Hunt for Tor **p** 66 Tor. C of Ch of Transfig Tor 65-73; R of St Timothy-by-the-Humber Tor 73-81; Dixie S Dio Tor from 81. *1506 Larchview Trail, Mississauga, Ont., Canada.*

O'CONNOR, Nigel George. b 23. TD 66. Linc Th Coll 53. **d** 55 **p** 56 Linc. C of S Ormsby 55-58; R of Partney w Dalby 58-65; R of Ashby-by-Partney 59-65; V of Skendleby 59-65; CF (TA) 62-67; CF (TAVR) 67-71; CF (R of O) from 71; R of Romney Marsh Group 65-74; V of S w N Hayling Dio Portsm from 74. *Vicarage, Havant Road, Hayling Island, Hants, PO11 0PR.* (Hayling I 2914)

O'CONNOR, Preb Ronald Charles Clifford. b 12. Late Exhib of Trin Coll Dub BA (Resp), King Edw Pri and Weir Pri 35, Div Test (2nd cl) 36, MA 62. **d** 36 Lim for Arm **p** 37 Derry for Arm. V Cho of St Patr Cathl Arm and C of Arm 36-39; I of Kildress 39-43; R of Desertlyn w Ballyeglish Dio Arm from 43; RD of Tullyhogue from 51; Hon V Cho of Arm Cathl from 57; Can and Preb of Yagoe St Patr Cathl Dub from 65. *Desertlyn, Moneymore, Co Derry, N Ireland.* (Moneymore 200)

O'CONNOR, Samuel John. b 18. Linc Th Coll. **d** 69 **p** 70 Cant. C of Walmer 69-72; Faversham 72-75; C-in-c of Teynham 75; V of Ringwood Dio Win from 75. *Vicarage, Ringwood, Hants, BH24 1AS.* (Ringwood 3219)

O'CONNOR, William Goodrich. b 04. Bps' Coll Cheshunt 36. **d** 36 **p** 38 Lich. C of Trent Vale 36-38; Fenton 38-40; St Jo Bapt Ches 40-43; St Pet ad Vincula Stoke-on-Trent 43-48; V of St Chad West Coseley 48-50; St Paul Coppenhall Crewe 50-56; St Laur Morecambe 56-66; Holbeck (w St Edw Holbeck from 68) 66-75; C-in-c of St Edw Holbeck 66-68; Hon C of Mottram-in-Longdendale 75-78; Perm to Offic Dio Ches from 78. *33 Eaton Mews, Handbridge, Chester.*

O'CONNOR-FENTON, Kenneth de ffenton. St Aug Coll Cant 26. **d** 31 **p** 32 Southw. C of Hucknall Torkard 31-33; St Paul Capetn 33-34; Calvinia 34-35; P-in-c 35-36; R of Namaqualand 36-37; Saldanha Bay 37-42; P-in-c of Camps Bay 42-53; Sec Capetn Dioc Bd of Miss 46-54; P-in-c of Landsowne 53-59; St Paul Capetn 59-73. *c/o Diocesan Registry, Cartwright's Corner House, Adderley Street, Cape Town, S Africa.*

ODALA, Canon Ernesto. St Bart Th Coll Msumba. **d** 60 **p** 61 Lebom. P Dio Lebom 61-69; Dio Malawi 69-71; Dio S Malawi from 71; Hon Can of S Malawi from 73. *Malindi, PO Mangochi, Malawi.*

ODDIE, Samuel. b 02. Bp Wilson Th Coll IM 27. **d** 28 **p** 29 S & M. C of Malew IM 28-31; Old Radford 31-34; LPr Dio Southw (in c of Ch Ch Chilwell) 34-38; Offg CF Chilwell 37-38; V of St Jo Bapt Plumstead 38-45; St Thos Launceston 45-53; R of St Mewan 53-61; V of Bourton 61-70. *30 Lyons Road, St Austell, Cornwall.* (St Ausell 3950)

ODDIE, William John Muir. b 39. Trin Coll Dub BA 64, MA 80. Univ of Leic PhD 70. Univ of Ox MA 81. St Steph Ho Ox 75. **d** 77 **p** 78 Bris. C of Westbury-on-Trym 77-80; Libr Pusey Ho Ox from 80; Fell St Cross Coll Ox from 81. *Pusey House, Oxford, OX1 3LZ.*

ODDY, Andrew Dick. b 49. Univ of Syd LLB 73. Trin Coll Melb BD 77. **d** 77 **p** 78 Melb. C of St Steph Mt Waverley 77-79; Glenroy 79-81; I of St John Frankston Dio Melb from 81. *4 Monterey Boulevard, North Frankston, Vic, Australia 3200*

ODDY, Frederick Brian. b 29. St D Coll Lamp BA 50. Linc Th Coll 50. **d** 52 **p** 53 Blackb. C of Em Preston 52-55; St Anne's-on-Sea (in c of St Marg) 55-57; V of St Jas Chorley 57-64; Warton (w Yealand Conyers from 76) Dio Blackb from 64; C-in-c of Yealand Conyers 74-76. *Warton Vicarage, Carnforth, Lancs.* (Carnforth 2946)

ODDY, John Scotthorn. b 35. St Cath Coll Ox BA (3rd cl Th) 60, MA 64. Clifton Th Coll 60. **d** 62 **p** 63 Lon. C of St Jas Muswell Hill 62-67; V of Ardsley 67-77; RD of Wath 75-77; Chap at Bordeaux 77-80; Selection Sec ACCM from 80. *Church House, Dean's Yard, SW1P 3NZ.* (01-222 9011)

ODEBA, Yotham. **d** 66 **p** 67 N Ugan. P Dio N Ugan 66-69; Dio M & W Nile from 69. *Church of Uganda, PO Paidha, West Nile, Uganda.*

ODEDEJI, David Ademola. b 25. **d** 75 **p** 76 Ibad. P Dio Ibad. *c/o Ikereku PA, via Ibadan, Nigeria.*

ODEDELE, Samuel Morolayo. Im Coll Ibad 59. **d** 62 **p** 63 Ibad. P Dio Ibad. *St Matthew's Vicarage, Akufo, Ibadan, Nigeria.*

ODEFADEHAN, Timothy Opayemi. Im Coll Ibad Dipl Th 70. **d** 71 **p** 72 Ondo. P Dio Ondo. *Vicarage, Araromi-Obu, Ondo, Nigeria.*

ODEKE, Amulam. **d** 63 **p** 64 Soroti. P Dio Soroti. *Ngariam, Uganda.*

ODEKE, Seperiya. **d** 54 **p** 56 U Nile. P Dio U Nile 56-60; Dio Soroti from 60. *Malera, PO Bukedea, Uganda.*

ODENDAHL, Robert Thomas Frederic. **d** 53 **p** 54 Hur. C of Muncey 53-54; I of Cayugas 54-58; Ohsweken 58-65; W Par Six Nations Reserve 65-69; R of Lucknow 69-72; L to Offic Dio Koot from 72. *954 Vernon Avenue, Penticton, BC, Canada.*

ODENEYE, Samuel Ajayi. **d** 50 **p** 51 Lagos. P Dio Lagos 50-52 and from 55; Dio N Nig 52-55. *Adeola Odutola College, Ijebu Ode, Nigeria.*

ODERA, Eliud Okiring'. St Paul's Coll Limuru 75. **d** 76 Maseno N. d Dio Maseno N. *PO Box 100, Butere, Kenya.*

ODERE, Ven Yakobo. Buwalasi Th Coll. **d** 58 **p** 59 Soroti. P Dio Soroti; Hon Can of Soroti from 72; Actg Archd of Ngora 77; Archd from 78. *Box 3001, Ngora, Uganda.*

ODETUNDE, Benjamin Adegoke. Melville Hall Ibad 51. **d** 52 **p** 53 Ondo-B. P Dio Ondo-B 52-62; Dio Ibad from 62. *Eripa, Ibadan, Nigeria.*

ODHIAMBO, Andarea. St Paul's Dioc Div Sch Limuru. **d** 39 **p** 43 Momb. P Dio Momb 39-61; Dio Maseno 61-68. *PO Funyula, Kenya.*

ODIDA, Balunaba. **d** 52 Bp Tomusange for U Nile **p** 54 U Nile. P Dio U Nile 52-61; Dio N Ugan 61-67. *c/o PO Box 232, Gulu, Uganda.*

ODIIT, Enosi. CMS Coll Buwalasi, 38. **d** 39 **p** 41 U Nile. P Dio U Nile 39-61; Dio Soroti from 61; CF (E Afr) 44-47; Hon Can of U Nile 54-61; Soroti 61-77; Archd of Teso 66-72; Ngora 72-76; Karamoja 66-70; Exam Chap to Bp of Soroti 66-77; Prin Dioc Tr Coll Ngora from 76. *Box 3001, Ngora, Uganda.*

ODILORA, Abel Orizu. b 34. Trin Coll Umuahia 65. **d** 68 Bp Uzodike for Niger **p** 68 Niger. P Dio Niger. *St Thomas's Parsonage, Umuchu, Via Aguata, East Central State, Nigeria.*

ODINAH, Emmanuel. Trin Coll Umuahia 62. **d** 64 **p** 65 Niger. P Dio Niger. *St Jude's Church, Adazi-Ani, Nigeria.*

ODLING-SMEE, Charles William. b 04. Univ of Lon BSc 25. AMICE 31. Westcott Ho Camb 39. **d** 40 **p** 41 Ripon. C of Headingley 40-45; V of Manfield w Cleasby 45-60; Nidd w Brearton 60-81; P-in-c of Brearton Dio Ripon from 81. *Greenwich Cottage, Brearton, Harrogate, N Yorks, HG3 3DD.*

ODLING-SMEE, George William. b 35. K Coll Dur MB BS 59. FRCS 68. **d** 77 **p** 78 Connor (APM). Hon C of St Thos Belf Dio Connor from 77. *10 Deramore Park South, Belfast, BT9 5JY.*

ODLUM, Michael Julian. b 24. DFC 45. **d** 56 **p** 57 Mon. C of Risca 56-59; St Vincent 60-65; R of Calliaqua w Mesopotamia and Evesham Windw Is 60-65; C-in-c of Spaxton w Charlynch 65-67; V of Sampford Arundel 67-74; Asst Chap HM Pris Wandsworth 74-75; Chap HM Pris Standford Hill from 75. *c/o HM Prison, Church Road, Eastchurch, Sheerness, ME12 4DU.* (Eastchurch 441)

ODO, Eze Ernest. b 43. Trin Coll Umuahia 72. **d** 74 Enugu. d Dio Enugu. *Holy Trinity Church, Akwu-Achi, Box 12, Oji River, ECS, Nigeria.*

ODO, Joshua Babalola. Melville Hall, Ibad. 56. **d** 57 **p** 59 Lagos. P Dio Lagos. *PO Box 13, Epe, Ijebu-Waterside, Nigeria.*

ODOMO, Julius Folorunso. b 44. Im Coll Ibad 67. **d** 70 **p** 71 Ondo. P Dio Ondo. *Holy Trinity Church, Yaba, Ondo, Nigeria.*

ODONGO, Canon Erifasi. **d** 64 **p** 66 N Ugan. P Dio N Ugan 64-76; Dio Lango from 76; Hon Can of Lango from 78. *Omoro, PO Aloi, Lira, Uganda.*

ODONGO, Gideon. **d** 64 **p** 66 N Ugan. P Dio N Ugan 64-76; Dio Lango 76-77. *Box 19, Apach, Uganda.*

ODONGO, Jacob. b 38. **d** 78 Lango. d Dio Lango. *PO Alito, Lira, Uganda.*

ODONGO, Jotham Elisha. b 45. **d** and **p** 77 Vic Nyan. P Dio Vic Nyan. *PO Box 160, Musoma, Tanzania.*

O'DONOHUE, Kevin Paul. b 22. Qu Coll Birm. **d** 56 **p** 57 Newc T. C of Alston w Garrigil 56-59; C-in-c 59-60; Berwick-on-Tweed 60-61; Otterburn and of Horsley w Byrness 61; V of Choppington 61-80; R of Castle Carrock w Cumrew and Croglin Dio Cumb from 80. *Castle Carrock Rectory, Carlisle, Cumb, CA4 9LZ.* (Hayton 231)

O'DONOVAN, Ven Bartholomew John. St Jo Coll Morpeth 62. **d** 63 **p** 64 River. C of Leeton 63-68; Broken Hill 68-69; P-in-c of Lockhart 70-73; R 73-76; Broken Hill Dio River from 76; Archd of Darling from 78. *PO Box 185, Broken Hill, NSW, Australia 2880.* (Broken Hill 3221)

O'DONOVAN, Martin William. b 49. Univ of Melb BA 78. Trin Coll Melb 78. **d** 79 **p** 80 Melb. C of St John Bentleigh 79-81; St Martin Deepdene Dio Melb from 81. *31 Ropley Avenue, Balwyne, Vic, Australia 3103.*

O'DONOVAN, Canon Oliver Michael Timothy. b 45. Ball Coll Ox BA 68, MA 71, DPhil 75. Wycl Hall 68. **d** 72 Dorchester for Ox **p** 73 Reading for Ox. Tutor Wycl Hall Ox 72-77; Asst Prof Wycl Coll Tor 77-80; Assoc Prof 80-82; Exam Chap to Bp of Tor 79-81; Can of Ch Ch Ox from 82; Regius Prof of Ox Univ from 82. *Christ Church, Oxford, OX1 1DP.*

O'DRISCOLL, Very Rev Percival Richard. Bp's Univ Lennox BA 64, STB 65. **d** 64 Ott. C of St Matthias Ott 64-67; St Jo Evang Kitchener 67-70; I of St Mich AA Lon Hur 70-75; St Bart Sarnia 75-80; Dean and R of St Paul's Cathl Lon Dio Hur from 80. *472 Richmond Street, London, Ont, Canada, N6A 3E6.* (519-434 3225)

O'DRISCOLL, Very Rev Thomas Herbert. Trin Coll Dub BA 51. **d** 52 **p** 53 Dub. C of Monkstown 52-54; Ch Ch Cathl Ott 54-56; R of Carp 56-62; St John Ott 62-68; Can of Ott 67-68; Dean and R of Ch Ch Cathl Vancouver Dio New Westmr from 68. *690 Burrard Street, Vancouver, BC, V6C 2L1, Canada.*

ODUBOGUN, Emanuel Adesanya. d 41 **p** 43 Lagos. P Dio Lagos 41-70. *Box 23, Ijebu-Ode, Nigeria.*

ODUCHE, Canon Kenneth Igwealo. Trin Coll Umuahia 62. **d** 64 **p** 65 Niger. P Dio Niger 64-69; Dio Enugu from 69; Hon Can of Enugu from 81. *St Mary's Parsonage, Ngwo, Enugu, Nigeria.* (Enugu 2397)

ODUKOYA, Emmanuel Ayodele. b 28. Im Coll Ibad. **d** 73 **p** 74 Lagos. P Dio Lagos; Prov Treas Nigeria from 79; Commiss Kano from 80. *Box 78, Lagos, Nigeria.*

ODULI, Walter Amolo. St Paul's Coll Limuru 69. **d** 71 Nak **p** 72 Bp Kuria for Nak. P Dio Nak. *Box 391, Eldoret, Kenya.*

ODUMA, Canon Boaz. St Paul's Div Sch Limuru 51. **d** 54 **p** 55 Momb. P Dio Momb 54-61; Dio Maseno 61-70; Dio Nai 70-74; Dio Maseno S from 74; Hon Can of Maseno S from 75; Exam chap to Bp of Maseno S from 75. *PO Ramugi, Kenya.*

ODUNUGA, Samuel Adedoyin Folajunmi. d 44 **p** 45 Niger for Lagos. P Dio Lagos 44-52 and 62-67; Dio Ondo-B 52-62; Hon Can of Ondo-B 55-62; Ondo 62-67; Archd of Offa Ilorin 67-72. *c/o St Saviour's Church, Ijebu Ode, Nigeria.*

ODUOR, James Apollo. b 33. Bp Tucker Coll Mukono 71. **d** 71 **p** 72 Nam. P Dio Nam 71-76; Maseno S from 77. *PO Box 25, Songhor, Kenya.*

ODUOR, Timothy Oluoch. Ch Tr Centre Kapsabet 62. **d** 63 **p** 65 Nak. P Dio Nak. *Kitale, Kenya.*

ODUR, Azaliya. Buwalasi Th Coll 56. **d** 58 **p** 59 U Nile. P Dio U Nile 58-61; Dio N Ugan from 61. *c/o PO Box 14, Gulu, Uganda.*

ODURO, Paul. b 24. **d** and **p** 74 Kum. P Dio Kum. *c/o St Justin's Church, Nkawie, Ashanti, Ghana.*

ODUSANYA, Canon Emmanuel Oyerinade. Im Coll Ibad 57. **d** 58 **p** 60 Ondo-B. P Dio Ondo-B 58-62; Dio Ondo from 62; Hon Can of Ondo from 75. *St Peter's Vicarage, Ile-Oluji, Ondo, Nigeria.*

ODUSEUN, Julius Titus. b 05. **d** 72 **p** 73 Ekiti. P Dio Ekiti. *St David's Church, Iludun, Ileje, Ekiti, Nigeria.*

ODUSUSI, David Sodeinde. Melville Hall, Ibad. **d** 52 Bp Phillips for Lagos **p** 53 W Afr. P Dio Lagos 52-67. *c/o St Paul's Vicarage, PO Box 7, Shagamu, Nigeria.*

ODUTAYO, Canon Daniel Adesanya. Univ of Dur BA 50. **d** 66 Bp Jadesimi for Lagos **p** 67 Lagos. P Dio Lagos 66-76; Dio Egba from 76; Can of Egba from 76. *St John's Vicarage, Igbein, Abeokuta, Nigeria.* (Igbein 100)

✠ **ODUTOLA, Right Rev Solomon Odunaiya.** OBE 61. O Federal Republic of Nigeria 64. Fourah Bay Coll Univ of Dur BA 28, Dipl Th 30, MA 37. Univ of Nigeria Hon DD 62. Hur Coll Hon DD 63. **d** 29 **p** 30 Bp A W Smith for Lagos. P Dio Lagos 29-40; Tutor 38-40; Hon Can of Lagos 43-52; Exam Chap to Bp of Lagos 44-53; Archd in N Provs Nigeria 45-50; Ondo 50-52; Cons Ld Bp of Ondo-B in Lagos Cathl 24 Feb 52 by Abp of W Afr; Bps Akinyele; S C Phillips; Martinson; and D B Hall; Trld to Ibad 60; res 71. *Bishopscourt, PO Box 3075, Ibadan, Nigeria.*

ODWUSI, Theodocius Oladipo Folorunso. b 34. **d** 79 **p** 81 Egba. P Dio Egba. *St Peter's Church, Agoro, PO Box 4, Ijoko, Nigeria.*

O'DWYER, Charles Sidney Firmin O'Rourke. b 04. SS Coll Cam 3rd cl Med and Mod Lang Trip 26, BA 30, MA 33. Ridley Hall, Cam 30. **d** 31 **p** 32 Chelmsf. C of Leyton 31-34; Chap RN 34-38; Perm to Offic Dio Chich 38-39; C of St Paul Furzedown Streatham 39-40; Asst Master R Gr Sch Guildf 40-70; Perm to Offic Dio Guildf from 40. *27 Daryngton Drive, Merrow, Guildford, Surrey.* (Guildford 73520)

OELSNER, Willy. b 1897. Univ of Berlin DD 29. **d** 39 **p** 40 Chich. C of Preston 39-40; Hon Chap to Bp of Chich 41; C of Moulsecoomb 41-44; Org Sec CMJ 44-50; C-in-c of H Trin Conv Distr Hove 50-71. *16 Wilbury Avenue, Hove, Sussex.*

OEPPEN, John Gerard David. b 44. St D Coll Lamp Dipl Th 67. **d** 67 Bp T M Hughes for Llan **p** 68 Llan. C of Cymmer w Abercregan 67-70; Team V in Rectorial Benef of Glyncorrwg w Afan Vale and Cymmer Afan 70-71; C of Whitchurch 71-74; V of H Trin Aberavon 74-78; Bargoed and Deri w Brithdir Dio Llan from 78. *Vicarage, Moorland Road, Bargoed, Mid-Glam.* (Bargoed 831069)

OESTREICHER, Canon Paul. b 31. Univ of NZ BA 53, MA 56. Humboldt Research Scho Univ of Bonn 55. Linc Th Coll 56. **d** 59 **p** 60 Lon. C of H Trin Dalston 59-61; Asst Relig Broadcasting BBC 61-64; C of K Chas Mart S Mymms 61-68; Assoc Sec Internat Dept Br Coun of Chs 64-69; V of Ch of Ascen Blackheath 68-81; Dir of Tr Dio S'wark 69-72; M Gen Syn from 70; Hon Chap to Bp of S'wark 75-80; Hon Can of S'wark Cathl from 78; Publ Pr Dio S'wark from 81; Asst Gen Secr & Secr of the Div of Intern Affairs of the BCC from 81. *50 Handen Road, SE12.* (01-852 5766)

OFEI-KWATIA, Canon Albert. d 52 Accra. d Dio Accra; Hon Can of Accra from 68. *PO Box 12, Accra, Ghana.* (Accra 76628)

O'FERRALL, Basil Arthur. b 24. CB 79. TCD BA 48, MA 65. **d** 48 **p** 49 Connor. C of Coleraine 48-51; Chap RN 51-75; Chap of the Fleet and Archd for the RN 75-80; Hon Chap to HM the Queen 75-80; Chap from 80; Hon Can of Gibr 77-80; V of Ranworth w Panxworth and Woodbastwick Dio Nor from 80; Bp's Chap Norf Broads from 80. *Ranworth Vicarage, Norwich, NR13 6HT.* (South Walsham 263)

OFFER, Clifford Jocelyn. b 43. Univ of Ex BA 67. Westcott Ho Cam 67. **d** 69 **p** 70 Roch. C of Bromley 69-74; Team V of Southn (City Centre) Dio Win from 74. *13 The Avenue, Southampton, SO1 2SQ.* (Southampton 29132)

O'FLYNN, Canon Norman Peter. Trin Coll Tor BA 57. **d** 59 Tor for Koot **p** 60 Bp Rhea (USA) for Koot. C of Summerland 59-62; R of St Patr Guelph 62-66; Chippawa 66-70; Fonthill w Port Robinson 70-74; I of Penticton Dio Koot from 74; Can of Koot from 79. *150 Orchard Avenue, Penticton, BC, Canada.* (493-1326)

OFOMA, Jude Egbunize. Trin Coll Umuahia 61. **d** 63 **p** 64 Niger. P Dio Niger 63-71; Dio Enugu from 72. *Emmanuel Parsonage, Umuabi, Nigeria.*

OFWONO, Astaluko Apollo. Buwalasi Th Coll 64. **d** 66 **p** 67 Mbale. P Dio Mbale 66-69; CF Ugan from 69. *c/o PO Box 473, Mbale, Uganda.*

OGABA, Pulcinate. d 61 **p** 62 N Ugan. P Dio N Ugan. *Awere, Uganda.*

OGBEHA, James Cekula. d 65 **p** 68 Ondo. d Dio Ondo. *Ecewu, via Lokoja, Nigeria.*

OGBO, Geoffrey E. O.. b 24. **d** 74 **p** 77 Lagos. P Dio Lagos. *Bishop Tugwell Memorial Church, Sheteolu Street, Lagos, Nigeria.*

OGBONNA, Abel Onyenweaku. b 34. St Paul's Coll Awka 78. **d** and **p** 79 Aba. P Dio Aba. *Holy Innocents Parsonage, c/o PO Box 397, Aba, Nigeria.*

OGBONNA, David Obasi Onukwube. b 38. Trin Coll Umuahia 71. **d** 73 **p** 74 Enugu. P Dio Enugu. *St Stephen's Parsonage, Box 14, Udi, ECS, Nigeria.*

OGBONNEWO, Martin Okoro. Im Coll Ibad. **d** 74 **p** 75 Ibad. P Dio Ibad. *St Paul's Church, Oyan, Oshogbo, Nigeria.*

✠ **OGBONYOMI, Right Rev Titus Eyiolorunsefunmi.** Melville Hall Ibad. **d** 55 **p** 56 N Nig. P Dio N Nig 55-59; CF (Nigeria) 59-75; Can of N Nig 69-75; Cons Ld Bp of N Nig in Ch Ch Cathl Lagos 29 June 75 by Abp of W Afr; Bps of Aba, Ibad, Lagos, Ondo, Niger, Eketi, Enugu and Ilesha; and Bp Adeniyi; Apptd Bp of Kaduna 80. *Bishopscourt, PO Box 72, Kaduna, Nigeria.* (23220)

OGBUJI, Princewill Enyinna. b 25. **d** 75 **p** 76 Aba. P Dio Aba. *St Peter's Parsonage, Itungwa, via Aba, Nigeria.*

OGDEN, Cyril Newton. AKC 39. **d** 39 **p** 40 S'wark. C of St Andr Coulsdon 39-40; Old Charlton 40-42; Chap RAFVR 42-46; L to Offic Dio S'wark 48-60; V of Whaplode 60-77; PC (V from 69) of Holbeach Fen 60-77; Perm to Offic Dio Linc from 77. *6 Woodside East, Thurlby, Bourne, Lincs, PE10 0HT.* (Bourne 224398)

OGDEN, Canon David Edgar Foster. b 21. St Chad's Coll Dur BA 48. Bps' Coll Cheshunt 48. **d** 50 **p** 51 Blackb. C of Ribbleton 50-52; Skerton 52-55; V of Cockerham 55-60;

Barrowford 60-66; Bp's Insp of Schs 60-65; Hon Chap to Bp of Blackb 65-66; Can Res of Newc T 66-78; Dir of Relig Educn Dio Newc T 66-78; Asst Sec to Dioc Syn 70-78; Master of Greatham Hosp Dio Dur from 78; V of Greatham Dio Dur from 78; RD of Hartlepool from 78; Can (Emer) of Newc T from 78. *Master's House, Greatham Hospital, Hartlepool, Cleve, TS25 2HS.* (Hartlepool 871148)

OGDEN, Eric. N-W Ordin Course 73. **d** 76 **p** 77 Man. Hon C of Lydgate Dio Man from 76. *40 Burnedge Lane, Grasscroft, via Oldham, OL4 4EA.* (Saddleworth 3661)

OGDEN, Canon Eric Grayson. b 06. AKC 32. St Steph Ho Ox 32. **d** 32 **p** 33 Lon. C of St Sav Ealing 32-37; Chap of Chich Th Coll 37-40; Commiss Colom 38-46; CF (EC) 40-45; C of St Mary Walton-on-Thames 45-48; V of Fairwarp 48-51; All S Clive Vale Hastings 51-54; St Mich AA (w All SS from 56) Brighton 54-65; Seq of All SS Brighton 54-56; R of St Jo Evang U St Leonards 65-72; Asst Chap at E Costa del Sol 72-76; Chap at Malaga 76-78; Can of Gibr 78-79; Hon Can from 79; Hon C of St Andr Worthing Dio Chich from 79. *Ramsay Hall, Byron Road, Worthing, Sussex.* (Worthing 36880)

OGDEN, Graham Sydney. Univ of Syd BA 58. BD (Lon) 62. Moore Th Coll Syd ACT ThL (1st cl) 62. Univ of Dur MLitt 65. Princeton Th Sem NJ PhD 75. **d** 62 **p** 64 Dur. Asst Tutor St Jo Coll Dur and L to Offic Dio Dur 62-64; CMS Miss Melb and L to Offic Dio Melb 64-66; Tokyo 66-68; Lect St Pet Hall Mt Sophia Sing 68-74; Exam Chap to Bp of Sing 70-72; Perm to Offic Dio Syd from 75; Lect United Th Coll Enfield 76-80. *20 lane 2, Sec 2, Yang Teh Highway, Shihlin, Taiwan.*

OGDEN, Harry. K Coll Lon and Warm AKC 57. **d** 58 **p** 59 Man. C of Hollinwood 58-60; St Aid Conv Distr Langley 60-61; R of Lightbowne 61-69; V of Farnworth 69-72; St Steph and All Marts Lower Moor Oldham 72-79; R of Ch Ch Moss Side Dio Man from 79. *Rectory, Monton Street, Moss Side, Manchester 14.* (061-226 2476)

OGDEN, Ralph. Univ of Syd BA 51. Moore Th Coll Syd 36. ACT ThL 38. **d** 39 **p** 40 Syd. C of St Matt Manly 39-40; C-in-c of Glen Davis 40; R of Wallerawang 40-46; Milson's Pt 46-55; Oatley W 55-58; Exam Chap to Abp of Syd 56-58; Chap Repatriation Gen Hosp Concord 58-68; L to Offic Dio Syd from 63. *Unit 25, Blue's Point Tower, North Sydney, NSW, Australia 2060.* (92-6785)

OGDEN, Stephen Gower. b 14. Univ of Lon BD 54. St Aid Coll 45. **d** 46 **p** 47 Liv. C of Em Ch Fazakerley 46-48; C-in-c of St Matt Conv Distr Eccleston 48-51; V 51-55; CF 55-59; Chap St Jas Hosp Leeds 59-66; Fairfield Hosp Stotfold from 66; CF (TAVR) from 68. *223 High Street, Arlesey, Beds, SG15 6SZ.* (Hitchin 731206)

OGDEN-SWIFT, Geoffrey William. b 21. Pemb Coll Cam BA 46, MA 48. Cudd Coll 47. **d** 49 **p** 50 Ripon. C of All S Leeds 49-52; Dom Chap to Bp of Ely 52-55; R of Fincham 55-62; R of Boughton 55-62; RD of Fincham 59-62; V of Ramsey 62-66; Soham w Barway 66-80; RD of Fordham 70-78; P-in-c of Over Dio Ely from 80. *Over Vicarage, Cambridge, CB4 5NH.* (Swavesey 30329)

OGE, Sergius. Newton Coll Dogura 70. **d** 73 Papua. d Dio Papua. *Box 26, Popondota, Papua, New guinea.*

OGEDEGBE, Canon Peter Irabor. Im Coll Ibad 58. Dipl Th (Lon) 58. **d** 58 Ibad **p** 60 Ondo-B. P Dio Ondo-B 58-62; Dio Benin from 62; Can of Benin from 76. *University of Ibadan, Nigeria.*

OGEDENGBE, Abraham T'Olorunjube. Melville Hall, Ibad. **d** 52 Bp Phillips for Lagos **p** 53 W Afr. P Dio Lagos Dio Ondo-B 56-62; Dio Ondo 62-65. *c/o PO Box 31, Akure, Nigeria.*

OGENDO, John. d 62 Maseno. d Dio Maseno 62-69; Dio N Maseno from 70. *Khwisero, Kenya.*

OGHENEKARO, Joseph Abi. b 27. **d** 73 **p** 74 Benin. P Dio Benin. *St John's Parsonage, Box 18, Ughelli, Nigeria.*

OGHOLI, Raphael Oghenerobo. Trin Coll Umuahia 61. **d** 63 **p** 64 Benin. P Dio Benin. *St Augustine's Parsonage, Aviara, Ughelli, Nigeria.*

OGIDI, William Onwubiko. Trin Coll Umuahia 57. **d** 59 **p** 60 Niger. P Dio Niger. *Parsonage, Uga, via Awka, Nigeria.*

OGILVIE, Gordon. b 42. Univ of Glas MA (2nd cl Cl) 64. BD (2nd cl) Lon 67. ALCD (1st cl) 66. **d** 67 **p** 68 Guildf. C of St Giles Ashtead 67-72; V of New Barnet 72-80; Dir of Pastoral Stud Wycl Hall Ox from 80. *3a Norham Gardens, Oxford, OX2 6PS.* (0865 52397)

OGILVIE, Ian Douglas. b 37. Em Coll Cam 3rd cl Cl Trip pt i, 58, BA (2nd cl Engl Trip pt i) 59, MA 63. Linc Th Coll 59. **d** 61 **p** 62 S'wark. C of Clapham 61-63; St Mary Gt Cam 63-66; Chap Sevenoaks Sch 66-77; Malvern Coll from 77; Hon Chap to Bp of Roch 74-77; Exam Chap from 77. *Chaplain's House, The College, Malvern, Worcs, WR14 3HT.* (Malvern 63548)

OGILVIE, Joseph John. Bp Gray Coll Capetn 60. **d** 62 **p** 63 Capetn. C of Athlone 62-68; Lower Paarl 68-72; Elgin 72-74; P-in-c of Bp Lavis Matroosfontein 74-80; R of St Mary Woodstock Dio Capetn from 80. *Rectory, Station Street, Woodstock, CP, S Africa.* (55-2864)

OGINGO, John Edward. b 39. **d** 78 Lango. d Dio Lango. *PO Nambieco, Lira, Uganda.*

OGIRA, Matthew. St Phil Bible Sch Maseno 69. **d** 69 **p** 70 Maseno. P Dio Maseno S. *Box 82, Sidindi, Kenya.*

OGLE, Albert Joy. b 54. Univ of Wales (Bangor) BD 75. TCD 75. **d** 77 **p** 78 Connor. C of Derriaghy 77-81. *c/o 9 Ballycolin Road, Dunmurry, Belfast, BT17 0NN.*

OGLE, Walter John. St Jo Coll Morpeth ACT ThL 68. **d** 68 **p** 69 Newc. C of New Lambton 68-69; Cardiff 69-71; Cessnock 71-75; L to Offic Dio Graft 75-76; P-in-c of Normanton 76; Exam Chap to Bp of Carp 77-78; Asst Chap Ch Ch Gr Sch Perth 78-79; Perm to Offic Dio Adel from 79. *St Michael's House, Crafers, S Australia 5152.*

OGLE, Winton Archibald. b 11. Dioc Ordin Tr Scheme. Codr Coll Barb 71. **d** 71 Stabroek for Guy **p** 72 Guy. C of Kitty 71-75; V of Bartica Dio Guy from 75. *Vicarage, Bartica, Essequibo River, Guyana.*

OGLESBY, Leslie Ellis. b 46. Univ Coll Ox BA 69, MA 73. City Univ Lon MPhil 73. Fitzw Coll Cam BA 73, MA 77. Ripon Coll Cudd 77. **d** 78 **p** 79 St Alb. C of St Mary Shephall Stevenage 78-80; V of Markyate Dio St Alb from 80; Dir St Alb Min Tr Scheme from 80. *Vicarage, Markyate, St Albans, Herts, AL3 8PD.* (Luton 841701)

OGLEY, John. b 40. Oak Hill Th Coll 62. **d** 65 **p** 66 Sheff. C of Ardsley 65-68; Carlton-in-the-Willows 68-71; P-in-c of Tollerton 71-79; V of Skegby Dio Southw from 79. *Skegby Vicarage, Sutton-in-Ashfield, Notts, NG17 3ED.* (Mansfield 558800)

OGOIGBE, Canon Christopher Abiodun. Im Coll Ibad 62. **d** and **p** 64 Benin. P Dio Benin; Can of Benin from 78. *c/o St Matthew's Cathedral, Benin, Nigeria.*

OGOMBE, Thoma. d 59 Momb **p** 62 Maseno. P Dio Momb 59-61; Dio Maseno from 61. *Lugare, PO Ukwala, Kenya.*

OGONIBA, Morris Okpara. d 60 **p** 61 Nig Delta. P Dio Nig Delta. *Box 14, Bori-Ogoni, Nigeria.*

OGONY, Jeremiah. Buwalasi Th Coll 58. **d** 59 **p** 60 U Nile. P Dio U Nile 59-61; Dio N Ugan from 61. *PO Box 14, Gulu, Uganda.*

O'GORMAN, Paul Anthony. b 46. Portsmouth Poly BSc (Soc) 79. Oakhill Coll 79. **d** 81 Barking for Chelmsf. C of Leyton Dio Chelmsf from 81. *27 Crawley Road, Leyton, E10 6RJ.*

O'GRADY, Brian John. Ridley Coll Melb ACT ThL 59. **d** 59 Bal **p** 61 Adel. C of Beech Forest w Apollo Bay 59-61; Ceduna 61-63; Chap Hydro Camps Tas 63-65; P-in-c of Wilcannia 65-69; L to Offic Dio Gippsld 69-70; Hon C of St Paul's Cathl Sale Dio Gippsld 69-70. *Diocesan Registry, 23 Raymond Street, Sale 3850, Vic., Australia.*

OGUCHI, Alexander Onwuegbu. b 33. Trin Coll Umuahia 72. **d** 74 Niger. d Dio Niger. *Immanuel Church, Adazi-Enu, Nigeria.*

OGUGU, Stephen. d 76 **p** 77 Soroti. P Dio Soroti. *Kacerede, Kumi County, South Teso, Soroti, Uganda.*

OGUJIOFOR, Frank Ottah. b 20. Trin Coll Umuahia 62. **d** 64 **p** 65 Nig Delta. P Dio Nig Delta 65-72; Dio Aba from 72. *Holy Trinity Parsonage, Apumiri Ubakala, Umuahia, Nigeria.*

OGUMA, Dishon. St Paul's Dioc Div Sch Limuru 50. **d** 52 **p** 54 Momb. P Dio Momb 52-61; Dio Maseno 61-70; Dio Maseno S 70-74. *c/o PO Box 68, Pap-Onditi, Kisumu, Kenya.*

OGUNBAJO, Solomon Adegboyega. b 37. Im Coll Ibad 69. **d** 72 **p** 73 Lagos. d Dio Lagos. *Christ Church Vicarage, Odosenbora, via Ijebu-Ode, Nigeria.*

OGUNBANJO, Canon Festus Olajide Olufeyisan. Melville Hall Ibad. **d** 46 **p** 48 Lagos. O Dio Lagos 46-62 and from 70; Dio Ibad 62-66; L to Offic 66-69; Hon Can of Ibad 69-71; Succr Dio Lagos from 70; Can of Lagos from 71; Exam Chap to Bp of Lagos from 77. *Box 161, Agege, Lagos, Nigeria.*

OGUNDANA, Ven Elijah Oluremi Ige. Univ of Lon Dipl Th (Extra-Mural) 61. BD (Lon) 68. Im Coll Ibad 56. **d** 59 **p** 60 Ibad. P Dio Ibad 59-62; C of St Ambrose Bris 62-64; St Sav Walthamstow 64-66; P Dio Ibad from 69; Can of Ibad 75-80; Archd and Exam Chap to Bp of Ibad from 80. *PO Box 23, Oyo, Ibadan, Nigeria.*

OGUNDELE, Ven Joseph Moses. Im Coll Ibad 55. **d** 57 **p** 59 Ibad. P Dio Ibad; Archd of Oyo 74-76; Oshogbo from 76. *Box 26, Oshogba, Nigeria.*

OGUNDIMITE, John Olayoriju. Univ of Ibad BA 77. Im Coll Ibad Dipl Th 74. **d** 77 **p** 78 Ondo. P Dio Ondo. *Box 132, Ondo, Nigeria.*

OGUNDIPE, Ephraim Ayodele. Im Coll Ibad 64. **d** 66 **p** 67 Ondo. P Dio Ekiti. *c/o PO Box 12, Ado-Ekiti, Nigeria.*

OGUNFUYE, Timothy Obafemi. b 36. BA (Lon) 60. NY Univ MA 69. Im Coll Ibad. **d** 72 **p** 73 Lagos. P Dio Lagos.

Methodist Teacher Training College, Box 23, Sagamu, Nigeria.

OGUNHIBE, Ilemobayo Olusola. **d** 78 **p** 79 Ilesha. P Dio Ilesha. *St Phillip's Church, Iwara, Ilesha, Nigeria.*

OGUNLADE, Joseph Oluwasegun. Im Coll Ibad. **d** 66 Bp Jadesimi for Ibad **p** 67 Ibad. P Dio Ibad 66-72; C of Rugby 72-73. *St Paul's Vicarage, PO Box 56, Ikirun, Nigeria.*

OGUNLEYE, Lucas Babasanmi. Im Coll Ibad 69. **d** 72 **p** 73 Ibad. P Dio Ibad; Dom Chap to Bp of Ibad from 75. *Bishopscourt, Bodija Estate, Ibadan, Nigeria.*

OGUNLEYE, Michael Olajide. Im Coll Ibad 58. **d** 60 **p** 61 Ibad. P Dio Ibad. *Vicarage, Oba, Nigeria.*

OGUNLOWO, Ven Joseph Akin. Melville Hall, Ibad 56. **d** 57 **p** 58 Lagos. P Dio Lagos 57-76; Dio Egba from 76; Archd of Egba from 76; Exam Chap to Bp of Egba from 76. *Box 8, Ilaro, Nigeria.*

OGUNMILADE, Canon Joel Johnson. Im Coll Ibad 59. **d** 61 Ibad **p** 62 Lagos. P Dio Lagos; Can of Lagos from 77. *4a Police Lane, Apapa, Lagos, Nigeria.*

OGUNOIKI, Alfred Oguyale Tanimowo. b 15. **d** 72 **p** 74 Lagos. P Dio Lagos. *St Peter's Church, Igan-Alade, via Ilaro, Nigeria.*

OGUNRINDE, Joseph Adewale. b 13. **d** 72 **p** 73 Ekiti. P Dio Ekiti. *St Peter's Anglican Church, Box 40, Ikole, Ekiti, Nigeria.*

OGUNRO, Moses Akinola. Im Coll Ibad 62. **d** 64 **p** 65 Ondo. P Dio Ondo 64-67; Dio Ekiti from 67. *St Paul's Vicarage, Odo-Owa, Nigeria.*

OGUNROTIMI, Isaac Adegite. Melville Hall, Ibad. **d** 56 **p** 57 Ondo-B. P Ondo-B 56-62; Dio Ondo 62-67; Dio Ekiti from 67. *Vicarage, Ogotun, Ekiti, Nigeria.*

OGUNSAKIN, David Oladipo. b 41. Im Coll Ibad Dipl Th 72. **d** 72 **p** 73 Ondo. P Dio Ondo. *University of Ibadan, Ibadan, Nigeria.*

OGUNSAKIN, Elijah Taiwo. Im Coll Ibad. **d** 71 **p** 72 Ondo. P Dio Ondo. *Box 4, Ondo, Nigeria.*

OGUNSANYA, Samuel Omosanya. Im Coll Ibad 61. **d** 63 **p** 64 Lagos. P Dio Lagos. *Oke-Jaga, Box 47, Ijebu-Igbo, Lagos, Nigeria.*

OGUNSEEIJU, Ven Emmanuel Olatubosun. Im Coll Ibad 58. **d** 60 **p** 61 Ibad. P Dio Ibad 60-75; Dio Kwara 75-76; Dio Ilesha from 77; Hon Can of Kwara 75-76; Archd Dio Ilesha from 77. *St Matthew's Church, Ijebu-Ijesha, Nigeria.*

OGUNSEYE, Titus Olodotun. **d** 58 **p** 59 Lagos. P Dio Lagos. *St James's Church, Orile-Ilugun, Ibadan Road, Abeokuta, Nigeria.*

OGUNSUSI, Canon Ezekiel Adewolu. Im Coll Ibad 58. **d** 60 **p** 61 Ondo-B. P Dio Ondo-B 60-62; Dio Ondo from 62; C of Hyde Chesh 70-72; Hon Can of Ondo from 77. *PO Box 14, Ilara-Akure, Nigeria.*

OGUNTIMILEHIN, David Adewumi. b 28. **d** 72 **p** 74 Ibad. P Dio Ibad. *PO Box 27, Ipetu-Modu, Ife, Nigeria.*

OGUNTUGA, Michael Olayide. b 42. Im Coll Ibad 73. **d** 76 Lagos. d Dio Lagos 76; Dio Ijebu from 76. *St John's Church, Odosimadegun, via Ijebu-Ide, Nigeria.*

OGUNYEMI, Christopher Olanrewaju. b 37. **d** 74 Lagos **p** 76 Ijebu. d Dio Lagos 74-76; P Dio Ijebu from 76. *St Andrew's Church, Imuwen, Box 250, Ijebu-Ode, Nigeria.*

OGUNYEYE, Richardson Abimbola. **d** 64 **p** 68 Lagos. P Dio Lagos 64-76; Dio Ijebu 76-81. *c/o Emmanuel Church, Isonyin, Ijebu-Ode, Nigeria.*

OGUNYIMIKA, Gabriel Adedeji. Im Coll Ibad 58. **d** 60 **p** 61 Ibad. P Dio Ibad. *St Mark's Vicarage, Offa, Ilorin, Nigeria.*

OGUZIE, Robert Stevenson Amajuoyi. Trin Coll Legon 69. **d** 72 **p** 73 Ow. P Dio Ow. *St Andrew's Parsonage, Amala, Okpala, Via Aba, Nigeria.*

OGWAL, David. b 42. **d** 78 Lango. d Dio Lango. *PO Bala, Lira, Uganda.*

OGWAL, Lewis. b 47. Bp Tucker Coll Mukono 73. **d** 75 N Ugan **p** 77 M & W Nile. P Dio Lango from 77. *Diocese of Lango, PO Box 6, Lira, Uganda.*

OGWAL, Michael. **d** 61 **p** 62 N Ugan. P Dio N Ugan 61-76; Dio Lango from 76. *PO Aboke, Lira, Uganda.*

OGWAL, Canon Ruebeni. **d** 46 **p** 50 U Nile. P Dio U Nile 46-61; Dio N Ugan 61-76; Hon Can of N Ugan from 66. *Box 6, Lira, Uganda.*

OGWAL, Temoceo. **d** 62 **p** 63 N Ugan. P Dio N Ugan 62-76; Dio Lango from 76. *Box 167, Lira, Uganda.*

✠ **OGWAL-ABWANG, Right Rev Benoni Yovani.** b 42. Univ of W Ont BMin 74. Bp Tucker Coll Mukono 66. **d** and **p** 69 N Ugan. C of Ch Ch Gulu 69; Asst Prov Sec Ugan 70-72; on leave 72-74; Cons Ld Bp of N Ugan in St Phil Pro-Cathl Gulu 29 Sept 74 by Abp of Uganda, Rwanda, Burundi and Boga-Z; and others; C of St Mich AA City and Dio Tor from 78. *PO Box 232, Gulu, Uganda; and c/o 611 St Clair West, Toronto, Ont, Canada.*

OGWAL-OMARA, Lewis. **d** 76 Lango. d Dio Lango. *PO Box 6, Lira, Uganda.*

OGWANG, Yesero. Buwalasi Th Coll. **d** 57 **p** 58 U Nile. P Dio U Nile 57-61; Dio N Ugan 61-76; Dio Lango from 76. *Box 20, Aboke, Uganda.*

OGWO, Edmund Chike. b 42. Trin Coll Umuahia 71. **d** 73 **p** 74 Nig Delta. P Dio Nig Delta. *St John's Parsonage, Bishop Johnson Street, PO Box 627, Port Harcourt, W Africa.*

OGWO, Moses Wamadi. St Paul's Coll Awka. **d** 63 **p** 74 Nig Delta. P Dio Nig Delta. *c/o St Paul's Parsonage, Ogbakiri, via Port Harcourt, Nigeria.*

OHAERI, Elijah Nlewedim. b 32. St Paul's Coll Awka 61. **d** 73 **p** 74 Aba. P Dio Aba. *St Thomas Anglican Parsonage, Azumini-Ndoki, via Aba, Nigeria.*

OHAGA, John Mark. b 39. **d** 71 **p** 73 Maseno S. P Dio Maseno S. *Ng'iya Girls' High School, PO Ng'iya, via Kisumu, Kenya.*

OHAME, Paul Onwuharameze. b 37. St Paul's Coll Awka 78. **d** and **p** 79 Aba. P Dio Aba. *St John's Parsonage, c/o PO Box 818, Aba, Nigeria.*

O'HANLON, Canon William Douglas. b 11. Peterho Cam BA 32, MA 37. BCM and Th Coll Clifton 32. **d** 37 **p** 38 Sarum. C of St John Heatherlands 37-39; Chap RAFVR 39-46; R of Langton Matravers 46-51; V of Calne (w Blackland from 63) 51-69; C-in-c of Heddington 53-63; Surr from 51; Non-Res Can and Preb of Sarum Cathl from 61; V of [illegible] Hemington 69-72; R of Studland Dio Sarum from 72. *Studland Rectory, Swanage, Dorset.* (Studland 200)

O'HARA, Reginald Herbert Edward. St Jo Coll Morpeth ACT ThL 30. **d** 31 **p** 32 Armid. C of Narrabri 31-33; Gunnedah 33-35; P-in-c of Collarenebri 35-38; Delungra 38-40; Manly 40-41; R of Kameruka 41-42; Perm to Offic Dio Goulb 42-45. *9 Short Street, Granville, NSW, Australia.*

OHIDA, Samuel Ogbadayin. Im Coll Ibad 59. **d** 61 **p** 62 Ondo-B. P Dio Ondo. *Okeagbe, North Akoko, Nigeria.*

OHITO, Canon Shem. St Paul's Dioc Div Sch Limuru. **d** 52 **p** 54 Momb. P Dio Momb 52-61; Dio Maseno 61-70; Dio S Maseno from 70; Hon Can from 70; Exam Chap to Bp of S Maseno from 71. *Box 221, Ukwala, Kenya.*

OHS, Douglas Fredrick. b 49. Univ of Sask BA 74. Em & St Chad's Coll Sktn LTh 75. **d** 74 BC for Sask **p** 75 B & W for Sask. C of Bridgwater 75-77; R of Macdowall Dio Sask from 77. *Box 34, Macdowall, Sask, Canada.*

OHUONU, Daniel Ogbonna. b 30. **d** 72 **p** 73 Aba. P Dio Aba. *St Peter's Parsonage, Owerrinta, Nigeria.*

OJANGO, Isack. Ch Tr Centre, Kapsabet, 66. **d** 67 **p** 68 Nak. P Dio Nak. *Box 245, Kitale, Kenya.*

OJARA, Apolo. **d** 62 **p** 63 N Ugan. P Dio N Ugan. *Keyo, Uganda.*

OJI, Erasmus Oluchukwu. b 43. BSc (Lon) 66. LRCP 70. FRCS 76. Oak Hill Th Coll 75. **d** 78 Lon for Niger. C of St Jo W Ealing 78-81. *c/o 3 Regency Close, Ealing, W5 2LP.*

OJIAMBO, Alistaliko. St Paul's Th Coll Limuru. **d** 59 Bp Wiggins for Centr Tang **p** 60 Centr Tang. P Dio Centr Tang 59-63; Dio Vic Nyan 63-64; Dio Nam from 64. *Church of Uganda, Walukuba, PO Jinja, Uganda.*

OJO, Ven James Adefemi. b 26. Melville Hall, Ibad. **d** 52 **p** 53 W Afr. P Dio Lagos 52-76; Dio Kwara from 76; Archd of Lokoja from 77; Exam Chap to Bp of Kwara from 77. *Box 11, Lokoja, Nigeria.*

OJO, John Olaniyi. b 26. Univ of Lon BA 60. Im Coll Ibad 73. **d** 75 **p** 76 Ondo. P Dio Ondo 75-76; Dio Ibad from 77. *Obagun Church, Ikirun, Nigeria.*

OJO, Jonathan Kayode. Im Coll Ibad 56. **d** 57 **p** 58 Ondo-B. P Dio Ondo-B 57-62; Dio Ondo 62-66; Dio Ekiti from 66. *Holy Trinity Vicarage, Aisegba, Nigeria.*

OJO, Samson Ademola. Im Coll Ibad 63. **d** 65 **p** 66 Ibad. P Dio Ibad 65-72; Dio Ekiti from 72. *St Peter's Vicarage, Ikere, Nigeria.*

OJOK, Canon Yokana. Buwalasi Th Coll 51. **d** 52 Bp Tomusange for U Nile **p** 54 U Nile. P Dio U Nile 54-61; Dio N Ugan from 61; Hon Can of N Ugan from 67. *Koich, Uganda.*

OJOM, Henry. b 40. **d** 78 Lango. d Dio Lango. *PO Adwari, Lira, Uganda.*

OJOMO, Canon Joseph Adebowale. Im Coll Ibad 58. **d** 60 **p** 61 Lagos. P Dio Lagos 60-76; Dio Ijebu from 76; Hon Can from 79. *St Paul's Church, Omu, Via Ijebu-Ode, Nigeria.*

OJULE, David. b 54. Bp Tucker Coll Mukono 78. **d** 80 Bukedi. d Dio Bukedi. *PO Box 170, Tororo, Uganda.*

OJURONGBE, Samuel Oyodele. Im Coll Ibad 56. **d** 58 **p** 59 Ondo-B. P Dio Ondo-B 58-62; Dio Ondo from 62. *St Peter's Vicarage, Ijare, Akure, Nigeria.*

OJURUKA, Charles Ibeabuchi. b 32. St Paul's Coll Awka 75. **d** 76 **p** 77 Aba. P Dio Aba. *St Luke's Parsonage, Amakama, Umuahia, Nigeria.*

OKADA, Canon Amnon. b 30. Bp Tucker Coll Mukono 63. **d** 65 **p** 66 Bp Wani for N Ugan. P Dio N Ugan 65-76; Dio

Lango from 76; Hon Can of Lango from 76. *PO Box 6, Lira, Uganda.*

OKADAPAU, Yesse. St Paul's Dioc Div Sch Limuru 50. **d** 52 **p** 54 Momb. P Dio Momb 52-61; Dio Maseno from 61. *Katakwa, PO Myanga, Kenya.*

OKAFO, Christian Baldwin Akubudike. Trin Th Coll Umuahia 58. **d** 59 **p** 60 Ow. P Dio Ow. *Parsonage, Uvuru, via Owerri, Nigeria.*

OKAFOR, Canon Isaac Chinweubs. Trin Th Coll Umuahia 49. **d** 51 **p** 52 Niger. P Dio Niger 51-59 and from 64; Dio Ow 59-64; Dio Niger from 64; Hon Can from 72. *Igbo-Ukwe, Awka, Nigeria.*

OKAFOR, Shadrach Okechuku. b 43. Univ of Lon Dipl Th (Extra-Mural) 73. Trin Coll Umuahia 71. **d** 73 **p** 74 Niger. P Dio Niger. *St Peter's Church, Onitsha, ECS, Nigeria.*

OKAFOR, Vincent Odiuke. St Paul's Coll Awka. **d** 55 **p** 57 Niger. P Dio Niger 55-58; Dio N Niger 58-68; Dio Ow 69-80. *St Paul's Church, Ezeoke, via Umuahia, Nigeria.*

OKAI, Winfred Ayitey-Adjin. Univ of Ghana 62. **d** 64 **p** 65 Accra. P Dio Accra. *PO Box 8, Accra, Ghana.* (Accra 27817)

OKAKA, Ven Wilson. **d** 64 **p** 66 N Ugan. P Dio N Ugan 64-76; Dio Lango from 76; Archd of Lira from 73; Hon Can of Lango from 78. *Box 71, Lira, Uganda.*

OKALEBO, Othniel. b 33. **d** 79 **p** 80 Soroti. P Dio Soroti. *PO Box 1, Ngora, Uganda*

OKARE, Yesero. **d** 76 **p** 77 Soroti. P Dio Soroti. *c/o Amuria County, North Teso, Soroti, Uganda.*

OKAUCHEMBI, Sengi. b 41. **d** 80 Boga-Z. d Dio Boga-Z. *EAZ Mambasa, BP 154, Bunia, Haut-Zaire.*

OKE, Isaiah Oloromo. **d** 49 **p** 50 Bp Akinyele for Lagos. P Dio Lagos 49-52; Dio Ondo-B 52-60; Dio Ibad 60-65. *c/o PO Box 3075, Ibadan, Nigeria.*

OKECH, Apolo. Buwalasi Th Coll 49. **d** 50 U Nile **p** 53 Bp Tomusange for U Nile. P Dio U Nile 50-61; Dio N Ugan 61-69; Dio M & W Nile from 69. *PO Box 42, Pakwach, Uganda.*

OKECHUKU, Henry Lewis Olisaemeka. **d** 43 Bp Patterson for Niger **p** 44 Niger. P Dio Niger 43-46; 48-52; and 59-64; Dio Lagos 46-48; Dio Nig Delta 52-59; Archd of Enugu 64-76. *St Mary's Church, Obosi, Nigeria,*

OKECHUKWU, Erastus Ikedionu. b 36. Trin Coll Umuahia 69. **d** 73 **p** 74 Niger. P Dio Niger. *Immanuel Church, Nawfija, Aguata, ECS, Nigeria.*

OKEDI, Samuel. Buwalasi Th Coll 61. **d** 62 **p** 63 Soroti. P Dio Soroti. *PO Box 4, Ngora, Uganda.*

OKEKE, Gideon O.C.. Trin Coll Umuahia 80. **d** 81 Ow. d Dio Ow. *Christ Church, PO Box 73, Owerri, Nigeria.*

OKEKE, Benson Nnama. Im Coll Ibad. **d** 59 **p** 60 Niger. P Dio Niger. *Parsonage, Nawfia, Awka, Nigeria.*

OKEKE, David. b 41. Trin Coll Umuahia 66. **d** 68 Niger **p** 70 Sier L. P Dio Niger. *St Paul's Parsonage, Oba, Via Onitsha, Nigeria.*

OKEKE, George Ezeanurumbu. Trin Coll Umuahia 61. **d** 63 **p** 64 Ow. P Dio Ow. *All Saints' Parsonage, Egbu, PO Box 31, Owerri, Nigeria.*

OKEKE, Joseph Prince Chikwendu. Trin Coll Umuahia. **d** 61 **p** 62 Niger. P Dio Niger; Exam Chap to Bp of Niger from 80. *Bishop Crowther Seminary, Awka, Nigeria.*

OKEKE, Very Rev Lazarus Chike. **d** 55 **p** 56 Liberia. P Dio N Nig 63-70; Dio Enugu from 71; Can of Enugu 75-76; Provost from 76. *St Bartholomew's Cathedral, Box 444. Asata, Enugu, Nigeria.*

OKEKE, Nicholas Chukwuzubelu. b 42. Trin Th Coll Umuahia 78. **d** 81 The Niger. d Dio The Niger. *PO Box 361, Onitsha, Anambra State, Nigeria.*

OKEKE, Robinson Ejiofor. b 42. Trin Coll Umuahia 66. **d** 68 **p** 70 Niger. P Dio Niger 68-72. *St Stephen's Parsonage, Mgbakwu, Via Awka, East Central State, Nigeria.*

OKEKE, Rufus. **d** 75 **p** 76 Niger. P Dio Niger. *c/o Box 361, Onitsha, Nigeria.*

OKELLO, Mackay. **d** 63 **p** 64 Soroti. P Dio Soroti. *Box 107, Soroti, Uganda.*

OKELLO, Samuel Baker. **d** 62 **p** 63 N Ugan. P Dio N Ugan 62-76; Dio Lira from 76. *PO Anyeke, Lira, Uganda.*

OKELLO, Zadok. Buwalasi Th Coll 57. **d** 59 **p** 60 U Nile. P Dio U Nile 59-61; Dio N Ugan 61-76; Dio Lango from 76. *Box 506, Dokolo, Uganda.*

OKELO, Hesbon. **d** 62 **p** 65 Maseno. P Dio Maseno 62-70; Dio Maseno S from 70. *Box 136, Siaya, Kenya.*

OKELO, Pesito. **d** 63 **p** 64 Soroti. P Dio Soroti. *Box 139, Soroti, Uganda.*

OKERE, Robinson Obasi. Dipl Th (Lon) 59. Im Coll Ibad 57. **d** 59 Ow **p** 60 Bp Nkemena for Ow. P Dio Ow; Can of Ow from 75. *Parsonage, Obizi, Owerri, Nigeria.*

OKERE, William Akarahu. b 24. St Paul's Coll Awka 60. **d** 73 **p** 74 Aba. P Dio Aba. *St Luke's Parsonage, Amakama, Box 104, Umuahia, Nigeria.*

OKEREMI, Rufus Morakinyo. b 40. Univ of Lagos BSc. **d** 80 Ibad. d Dio Ibad. *St Paul's Church, Odo-Ona, PMB 5603, Ibadan, Nigeria.*

OKERO, Joseph. **d** 77 **p** 78 Kara. P Dio Kara. *c/o Karamoja Diocesan Office, PO Box 44, Moroto, Uganda.*

OKERRI, Moses Makumum. St Paul's Coll Awka 57. **d** 57 **p** 58 Niger. P Dio Niger 57-62; Dio Benin from 62; Can 69-77. *St Andrew's Parsonage, Umuoru, Nigeria.*

OKETI, Abel. b 35. **d** 78 Lango. d Dio Lango. *PO Onyakedi, Lira, Uganda.*

OKEYO, Walter Philip. St Paul's Coll Limuru 75. **d** 77 Maseno S. d Dio Maseno S. *PO Box 43, Kisumu, Kenya.*

OKIA, Yason. Buwalasi Th Coll 65. **d** 66 Soroti. d Dio Soroti 66-72. *Malera, Bukedea, Uganda.*

OKIDI, Salathiel. **d** 64 **p** 65 N Ugan. P Dio N Ugan. *Church of Uganda, Lira Palwo, PA Patango, Gulu, Uganda.*

OKILLE, Nicodemus Eng'walas. Bp Tucker Coll 70. **d** 73 **p** 74 Bukedi. P Dio Bukedi. *St Peter's Church, Box 170, Tororo, Uganda.*

OKINDA, James. **d** 65 **p** 66 Maseno. P Dio Maseno 65-69; Dio N Maseno from 70. *Esiandumba, PO Box 124, Maseno, Kenya.*

OKINDA, Peter. **d** 77 **p** 78 Nak. P Dio Nak. *Box 272, Kitale, Kenya.*

✠ **OKINE, Right Rev Robert Garshong Allotey.** Kelham Th Coll 58. **d** 64 **p** 65 Accra. P Dio Accra 64-81; Archd of Koforidua 81; Cons Ld Bp of Koforidua 18 Oct 81. *Box 166, Koforidua, Ghana.*

OKIROR, Richard. b 48. **d** 79 **p** 80 Soroti. P Dio Soroti. *PO Box 107, Soroti, Uganda.*

✠ **OKODI, Right Rev William.** **d** 63 **p** 64 N Ugan. P Dio N Ugan 63-76; Sec and Treas Dio N Ugan 71-76; Dio Lango 76-80; Cons Asst Bp of Lango 80. *PO Box 6, Lira, Uganda.*

OKOH, Nicholas Dikeriehi. b 52. Im Coll Ibad 78. **d** 79 **p** 80 Asaba. P Dio Asaba. *Sultan Bello Hall, University of Ibadan, Ibadan, Nigeria.*

OKOLE, Simeon Bokeno Polly. b 34. St Paul's Coll Awka 56. **d** 73 **p** 74 Benin. P Dio Benin. *St Matthew's Vicarage, Box 4, Ekoabetu, via Benin City, Nigeria.*

OKOLI, Abel. **d** 75 **p** 76 Niger. P Dio Niger. *c/o Box 361, Onitsha, Nigeria.*

OKOLI, Jeremiah Robins Nwankwo. Trin Coll Umuahia 57. **d** 59 **p** 60 Niger. P Dio Niger 59-69; Dio Enugu from 69. *St Mark's Parsonage, Awgu, Nigeria.*

OKOLI, Musa. Buwalasi Th Coll 63. **d** 64 Soroti. d Dio Soroti 64-69. *Bishop Kilching Teacher's Training College, Ngora, Uganda.*

OKOLI, Theodore Madueke. b 32. Trin Coll Umuahia 65. **d** and **p** 68 Niger. P Dio Niger. *St Mark's Church, Ogbunike, ECS, Nigeria.*

OKOLO, Edward Onuzulike Chinwe. b 39. Trin Coll Umuahia 64. **d** 66 Niger **p** 68 Bp Uzodike for Niger. P Dio Niger. *St Stephen's Parsonage, Umudin Nnewi, Nigeria.*

OKOLO, Samuel Chukinuekezie. b 30. Trin Coll Legon. **d** 72 **p** 74 Enugu. P Dio Enugu. *Box 11, Amokwe, Udi, ECS, Nigeria.*

OKOLO, Simeon Chibuzo. St Paul's Coll Awka 62. **d** 62 **p** 63 Niger. P Dio Niger. *St Paul's Church, Alor, Nigeria.*

OKOLO, Simon. **d** 75 **p** 76 Niger. P Dio Niger. *c/o Box 361, Onitsha, Nigeria.*

OKOLO, Stephen Onwuanwa. St Paul's Coll Awka 57. **d** 57 **p** 58 Niger. P Dio Niger 57-71; Dio Enugu 71-79. *c/o Christ Church, Achi, Nigeria.*

OKOLUGBO, Emmanuel. Univ of Ibad. **d** 66 **p** 68 Benin. P Dio Benin 66-68 and from 73; Dio Ibad 69-72; Can of Benin 74-77. *Institute of Education, Benin City, Nigeria.*

OKO MINIMAH, Emmanuel Ibifila. b 26. **d** 73 Nig Delta. d Dio Nig Delta. *St Cyprian's Parsonage, Box 15, Port Harcourt, W Africa.*

OKONGO, Nafutali. **d** 62 **p** 65 Mbale. P Dio Mbale 2-72; Dio Bukedi from 72. *Apokori, PO Tororo, Uganda.*

OKONKWO, Edwin Obi. b 43. Trin Coll Legon ThL 72. **d** 72 Niger. d Dio Niger. *St Andrew's Church, Obosi, Nigeria.*

OKOR, Frank Agala. Trin Coll Umuahia 61. **d** 63 **p** 64 Nig Delta. P Dio Nig Delta. *81 Calabar Road, Box 74, Calabar, Cross River State, Nigeria.*

OKORI, Wilson. **d** 75 N Ugan **p** 76 Lango. P Dio Lango. *Lango College, PO Box 86, Lira, Uganda.*

OKORO, John Onovuhe. b 23. **d** 74 **p** 75 Benin. P Dio Benin. *Okpolo Primary School, Enhwe, via Ughelli, Nigeria.*

OKORO, Richard Joseph Nwokeleme. b 40. Trin Coll Umuahia 71. **d** 73 **p** 74 Aba. P Dio Aba. *St John's Parsonage, c/o Asa-Umunka PA, via Aba, Nigeria.*

OKOROUDO, Godson Chibuzo. b 42. Trin Coll Umuahia 78. **d** 81 The Niger. d Dio The Niger. *St John's Church Fegge Onitsha, PO Box 828, Onitsha, Anambra State, Nigeria.*

OKOSA, Yosam. b 16. Bp Tucker Coll Mukono 70. **d** 71 **p**

73 Soroti. P Dio Soroti. *Katinge, Kaberamaido, Teso, Uganda.*

OKOTH, John William. St Phil Th Coll Kongwa. **d** 60 Bp Omari for Centr Tang **p** 60 Bp Wiggins for Centr Tang. P Dio Centr Tang 60-63; Dio Vic Nyan 63-64; Dio Maseno S from 70. *PO Ahero, Kenya.*

✠ **OKOTH, Right Rev Yona.** Buwalasi Th Coll. **d** 54 **p** 56 U Nile. P Dio U Nile 54-61; Dioc Treas Dio Mbale 61-64; Prov Sec Ch of Ugan 65-72; Cons Ld Bp of Bukedi in St Paul's Cathl Kampala 6 Aug 72 by Abp of Ugan; Bps of W Bugan, Nam, Ank, Kig, M & W Nile, Mbale, Soroti, Ruw, N Ugan, Boga-Z, and others. *Box 170, Tororo, Uganda.* (Tororo 326)

OKOTO, Pinekasi. **d** 63 **p** 64 Soroti. P Dio Soroti. *Kacumbala, Uganda.*

OKOYE, Eugene Ikwunne. b 46. Trin Coll Umuahia 74. **d** 76 Niger. d Dio Niger. *St Mark's Church, Nnewi, Nigeria.*

OKOYE, Gabriel. **d** 75 **p** 76 Niger. P Dio Niger. *c/o Box 361, Onitsha, Nigeria.*

OKOYE, James Igboamalu Eugene. Trin Coll Umuahia, 62. **d** 63 **p** 64 Niger. P Dio Niger. *St Philip's Church, Ogidi, Onitsha, Nigeria.*

OKPALA, Ven Clifford Uzoechi. Trin Coll Umuahia. **d** 56 **p** 57 Niger. P Dio Niger; Hon Can of Niger 76-80; Archd of Awka from 80. *St Faith's Church, Awka, Nigeria.*

OKPALA, Gius Ifejika Chukuma. **d** 65 N Nig. d Dio N Nig. *PO Box 1, Makurdi, Nigeria.*

OKPALA, Godwin Izundu Nmezinwa. b 44. Trin Coll Umuahia 74. **d** 76 Niger. d Dio Niger. *St Faith's Church, Awka, Nigeria.*

OKPALEKE, Godwin. b 44. Trin Coll Umuahia 72. **d** 74 Niger. d Dio Niger; CF (Nigeria) from 80. *Nigerian Army, Yaba, Lagos, Nigeria.*

OKPAROCHA, John Ghibuzo Ikpo. Trin Coll Umuahia 56. **d** 58 **p** 59 Niger. P Dio Niger 58-61; Dio Enugu 69-76; Hon Can of Enugu 73-76. *Christ Church, Owerri, Nigeria,*

OKPIDAMA, Julius Doka. b 29. **d** 73 **p** 74 Benin. P Dio Benin. *Udu Primary School, Uwheru, c/o PO Ughelli, Nigeria.*

OKPORI, Shadrach Cyrus. b 32. Trin Coll Umuahia 68. **d** 73 **p** 74 Nig Delta. P Dio Nig Delta. *St Paul's Parsonage, Diobu, Box 53, Diobu, Port Harcourt, Nigeria.*

OKUBANJO, Josiah Ademola. Im Coll Ibad 64. **d** 66 **p** 67 Lagos. P Dio Lagos. *St John's Vicarage, Odosimadegun, Ijebu-Ode, Nigeria.*

✠ **OKULLU, Right Rev Henry.** Virginia Th Sem BD 65, Hon DD 73. Bp Tucker Coll Mukono, 57. **d** 58 **p** 60 Ugan. P Dio Ugan 58-60; Dio Nam 60-63; L to Offic Dio Nam 63-67; Dio Nai 68-71; Provost of All SS Cathl Nairobi 71-74; Exam Chap to Bp of Nai 73-74; Cons Ld Bp of Maseno S in Pro-Cathl Ch of St Steph Kisumu 24 Feb 74 by Abps of Kenya and Ugan; Bps of Momb, Maseno N, Bukedi and N Ugan; and others. *PO Box 114, Kisumu, Kenya.*

OKULO-AWANY, Tom. **d** 75 N Ugan **p** 76 Lango. P Dio Lango. *Town College, PO Box 125, Lira, Uganda.*

OKUMU, Ven Isaka. Bp Tucker Coll Mukono. **d** 56 **p** 58 U Nile. P Dio U Nile 56-61; Dio N Ugan from 61; Hon Can of N Ugan 67-69; Archd of Acholi 69-72; Gulu from 73. *c/o Box 232, Gulu, Uganda.*

OKUNFULURE, David Ibikunle. Melville Hall, Ibad. **d** 46 Asst Bp for Lagos **p** 47 Lagos. P Dio Lagos 46-52; Dio Ondo-B 52-62; Dio Ondo 62-77; Hon Can of Ondo-B 56-62; Ondo 62-64; Archd of Akure 64-77; Exam Chap to Bp of Ondo 64-77. *c/o Box 20, Ile-Oluji, Ondo, Nigeria.*

OKUNMUYIDE, Ven David Okunlola. Melville Hall Ibad. **d** 49 **p** 50 Lagos. P Dio Lagos 50-55; Ibad 55-74; Ilesha from 74; Hon Can of Ibad 69-73; Archd of Offa-Ilorin 73-74; Ilesha from 74. *PO Box 2, Ipetu-Ijesha, Nigeria.*

OKUNNUGA, Bandele Oladejo. b 44. Im coll Ibad 67. **d** 70 **p** 71 Lagos. P Dio Lagos. *c/o University of Lagos, Lagos, Nigeria.*

OKUNSANYA, Babafunmilayo Joseph. b 11. **d** 74 Lagos. d Dio Lagos. *28 Jebba Street, Box 45, Ebbute Metta, Nigeria.*

✠ **OKUNSANYA, Right Rev Isaac Oyelaja Sonola.** Univ of Dur (Fourah Bay Coll) LTh 31, BA 33. St Andr Coll Oyo. **d** 32 Lagos **p** 33 Bp Howells for Lagos. C Dio Lagos 32-43; ETC Owo 43-47; Prin ETC Owo 47-56; Hon Can of Lagos 47-52; Exam Chap to Bp of Ondo-B 52-63; Sec Dioc Synod Ondo-B 52-58; Archd of Owo 52-59; Akure 59-64; Supt Akure Distr 56-59; Sec Prov Synod of W Afr 57-63; Cons Ld Bp of Ondo in St Steph Cathl Ondo 24 Feb 64 by Abp of W Afr; Bps of Ibad; Ow; Nig Delta; Benin; and Lagos; and Bps Afonya; Uzodike; and Awosika; res 71. *PMB 5390, Ibadan, Nigeria.*

OKURUT, Lazaro. **d** 76 **p** 77 Soroti. P Dio Soroti. *Malera, Bukedea County, South Teso, Soroti, Uganda.*

OKURUT, Canon Thomas. Buwalasi Th Coll 58. **d** 59 Bp Tomusange for U Nile **p** 60 U Nile. P Dio U Nile 58-63; Dio Soroti 63-69; and from 72; Hon Can of Soroti from 77. *Box 2016, Serere, Uganda.*

OKWENGE, Misalom. b 37. **d** 78 Lango. d Dio Lango. *PO Kungu, Lira, Uganda.*

OKWEZUZU, Elisha Boe. Trin Coll Umuahia, 62. **d** and **p** 64 Benin. P Dio Benin. *St Stephen's Parsonage, Ilue-Ologbo, PA Otibio, Ughelli, Nigeria.*

OKWUADI, Francis Eze. St Paul's Coll Awka. **d** 47 Niger. d Dio Niger 47-62; Dio Benin from 62; Can of Benin 66-73. *Igbodo, via Agbor, Nigeria.*

OLADAPO, Samuel Akamji. b 25 **d** 74 **p** 76 Ondo. P Dio Ondo. *St Paul's Vicarage, Ifon, Owo, Nigeria.*

OLADAPO, William Ejide. b 41. Im Coll Ibad 73. **d** 76 Lagos **p** 77 Egba. P Dio Egba. *St Peter's Church, Ilogbo-Oldfin, Box 90, Abeokuta Nigeria.*

OLADETOUN, Canon Gabriel Adebolu. Melville Hall, Ibad. **d** 56 **p** 57 Ondo-B. P Dio Ondo-B 56-62; Dio Ondo 62-65; Dio Lagos 65-72; Dio Ibad from 73; Can of Ibad from 75. *Box 3395, Ibadan, Nigeria.*

OLADUGBA, Daniel Ifedayo Bamidele. Melville Hall Ibad. **d** 57 **p** 58 Ondo-B. P Dio Ondo-B 57-62; Dio Ondo 62-68. *NBC, Ibadan, Nigeria.*

OLAFIMIHAN, James Bukoye. Melville Hall, Ibad 54. St Aug Coll Cant 63. **d** and **p** 55 N Nig. P Dio N Nig 55-60 and 65-77; Provost of N Nig 65-77; P Dio Soroti 60-65; Exam Chap to Bp of N Nig 65-77. *PO Box 48, Offa, Nigeria.*

OLAGBUJI, Joseph Adetula. b 36. Im Coll Ibad 67. **d** 70 **p** 71 Ondo. P Dio Ondo; Bp's Chap Dio Ondo from 77. *Box 25, Ondo, Nigeria.*

OLAGUNDOYE, Moses Olafioye. Im Coll Ibad 62. **d** 64 **p** 65 Lagos. P Dio Lagos. *c/o PO Box 13, Lagos, Nigeria.*

OLAGWA, Benjamin. **d** 64 **p** 65 Mbale. P Dio Mbale 64-72; Dio Bukedi from 72. *Church of Uganda, Kidoko, PO Box 422, Tororo, Uganda.*

OLAITAN, Daniel Ademola. St Andr Coll Oyo, 29. **d** 30 Bp Oluwole for Lagos **p** 31 Lagos. P Dio Lagos 30-52; Dio Ibad 52-66; Hon Can of Lagos 52-57; Can of Ibad 54-60; Archd of Offa Ilorin 60-66. *St Mark's Vicarage, Offa Ilorin, Nigeria.*

✠ **OLAJIDE, Right Rev gideon Isaac Oladipo.** Melville Hall, Ibad 51. Dipl Th (Lon) 54. **d** and **p** 54 Ondo-B. P Dio Ondo-B 54-61; Perm to Offic Dio Ely 61-62; P Dio Ibad 62-81; Exam Chap to Bp of Ondo 64-77; Ekiti 67-81; Can of Ekiti from 71; Provost of St Jas Cathl Ibad 79-81; Cons Ld Bp of Ilesha in St Jas Cathl Ibad 1 March 81 by Abp of Prov of Nigeria; Bps of Aba, Enugu, Lagos, Ekiti, Kaduna, Ijebu, Benin, Asaba, Egba-Egbado, Kano, Jos and Warri; and others. *Box 237, Ilesha, Nigeria.*

OLAJUBE, Isaac Oladele. b 48. Im Coll Ibad 74. **d** 77 Ilesha. d Dio Ilesha. *All Saints Anglican Church, Esa-Odo, Via Ilesha Oyo State, Nigeria.*

OLAL, Andrew. **d** 66 **p** 67 N Ugan. P Dio N Ugan 66-69; Dio M & W Nile from 69. *PO Box 22, Moyo, uganda.*

✠ **OLANG', Most Rev Festo Habakkuk.** Univ of the S Tenn Hon DD 77. St Paul's Div Sch Limuru 44. **d** 45 **p** 50 Momb. RD of Centr Nyanza 51-55; Cons Asst Bp to Bp of Momb in St Paul's Cathl Namirembe Kampala 15 May 55 by Abp of Cant; Bps of Sudan; Momb; Centr Tang; Ugan; U Nile; Nig Delta; and Zanz; Asst Bps of Ugan; and U Nile; and Bp C E Stuart; Apptd Bp Suffr of Maseno 58; Bp of Maseno 61; Trld to Nai 70; Elected Abp and Metrop of Prov of Kenya 70; res 79. *PO Box 1 Maseno, Kenya.*

OLANIPEKUN, Gabriel Ayilara. b 38. Im Coll Ibad Dipl Th 72. **d** 72 **p** 73 Ekiti. P Dio Ekiti. *St Paul's Anglican Church, Ishan, Ekiti, Nigeria.*

OLAOYE, Samuel Ayotunde. Im Coll Ibad 58. **d** 61 **p** 63 Ibad. P Dio Ibad. *St Paul's Vicarage, Omu-Aran, via Ilorin, Nigeria.*

OLASODE, Emmanuel Oba. b 27. Im Coll Ibad 80. **d** 79 **p** 81 Egba. P Dio Egba. *PO Box 267, Ibara, Abeokuta, Nigeria.*

OLASODE, Canon Michael. Melville Hall Ibad 56. **d** 57 **p** 58 Ondo-B. P Dio Ondo-B 57-63; C of Earl Shilton w Elmesthorp Leic 63-64; P Dio Ondo from 64; Hon Can of Ondo from 72. *Box 8, Igbara-Oke, Ondo, Nigeria.*

OLASUYAN, Solomon Osekorede. b 36. **d** 74 **p** 76 Ondo. P Dio Ondo. *St Christopher's Vicarage, Odeaye, via Okitipupa, Nigeria.*

OLATUNJI, Cornelius Obafemi. Im Coll Ibad. **d** 71 Ibad. d Dio Ibad 71-74; Dio Ilesha from 74. *Vicarage, Erin Oke, Nigeria.*

OLAWUMI, Joshua Oni. Im Coll Ibad. **d** 67 **p** 68 Ondo. P Dio Ondo. *Vicarage, Ipele, Ondo, Nigeria.*

OLAYANJU, Samuel Sunday. b 39. Univ of Ibad BA 77.

Im Coll Ibad Dipl Th 73. **d** 73 **p** 74 Ondo. P Dio Ondo. *PMB 17, Owo, Ondo, Nigeria.*

OLAYEMI, Joseph Bamgboye. Melville Hall, Ibad. **d** 38 **p** 39 Lagos. P Dio Lagos 38-52; Dio Ondo-B 52-57 and 58-61; Hon Can of Ondo-B 55-62; C of St Cypr Edge Hill 57-58; Archd of Oshogbo 62-72. *All Saints', Oshogbo, Nigeria.*

OLAYEMI, Kuyebi Michael. b 32. **d** 74 Lagos. d Dio Lagos. *St Paul's Vicarage, Box 7, Shagamu, Nigeria.*

OLAYINKA, David Oladiji. BA Lon 56. **d** 69 **p** 70 Ibad. Prin Oduduwa Coll Ile-Ife 69-73; Bapt High Sch Iree 74-80; Atakumosa Gr Sch from 80. *Atakumosa Grammar School, Oshu, Nigeria.*

OLD, Arthur Anthony George. b 36. Clifton Th Coll 69. **d** 71 **p** 72 Blackb. C of St Jas Clitheroe 71-73; Bispham 73-77; V of Stonefold 77-81; Team V of Lowestoft Group Dio Nor from 81. *c/o 16 Corton Road, Lowestoft, Suff.* (Lowestoft 3046)

OLDAKER, Dennis McLean. AKC (1st cl) Trench Pri and Jun McCaul Pri 33. OT Scho 34. Univ of Lon BD 33. **d** 33 **p** 34 Lon. C of St Mich Cricklewood 33-34; St Ann Stamford Hill 34-36; Harrow 36-40; St Botolph Bishopsgate Lon 40-45; V of St Luke Hackney 45-47; R of St Luke Old Street 47-52; C-in-c of St Mary Charterho w St Thos and St Paul Finsbury 50-52; R of St Jo Div Chatham 52-54; C-in-c of Chatham 52; RD of Roch 53-64; Surr from 54; R of St Mary w St John Chatham 51-64; Hon Can of Roch 59-70; V of Sidcup 64-70; RD of Sidcup 64-70; R of Seale 70-81. *1 Park Road, Farnham, Surrey.* (Farnham 724208)

OLDALE, Harry. b 17. Bps' Coll Cheshunt, 51. **d** 53 **p** 54 Sheff. C of St Pet Warmsworth 53-56; Woodlands 56-58; V of Moor Ends 58-60; R of Edgefield 60-71; Chap Kelling Hosps from 64; P-in-c of Weybourne Dio Nor 71-76; V (w U Sheringham) from 76; P-in-c of Kelling w Salthouse Dio Norf from 71; R from 76. *Vicarage, Weybourne, Norf.* (Weybourne 268)

OLDEN, Canon Aidan Ronald Cuming. b 17. Trin Coll Dub BA 38, MA 41. Div Test 39. **d** 40 **p** 41 Down. C of St Mary Newry 40-41; Dean's V Belf Cathl 41-42; Succr of St Patr Cathl Dub 42-47; I of Enniskeen 47-60; Can of Meath from 58; Ed Meath Dioc Magazine 57-65; I of Kells Dio Meath from 60; Preb of St Patr Cathl Dub from 64; RD of Clonard and Trim from 67. *Rectory, Kells, Co Meath, Irish Republic.* (Ceanannus Mor 40151)

OLDFIELD, Henry John Herbert. Univ of BC BA (2nd cl Phil) 41. Angl Th Coll Vancouver LTh 43. **d** 43 Br Columb for Bran **p** 44 Bran. C of Pilot Mound 43-46; R of Hamiota 46-49; Sardis w Rosedale 49-55; I of Princeton BC 55-59; C of St Edm Roundhay Yorks 59-63; I of Burquitlam 63-79. *8530 West Saanich Road, RR2 Saanichton, BC, Canada.*

OLDFIELD, Roger Fielden. b 45. Qu Coll BA 67, MA 71. Trin Coll Bris BD 75. **d** 75 **p** 76 Man. C of St Pet Halliwell Dio Man 75-80; V from 80. *Vicarage, Harper's Lane, Smithills, Bolton, Lancs.* (Bolton 42820)

OLDHAM, Canon Arthur Charles Godolphin. b 05. AKC (2nd cl) 33. **d** 33 **p** 34 Guildf. C of Witley 33-36; V of Brockham Green 36-43; R of Merrow 43-50; RD of Guildford 49-50; V of Godalming 50-62; RD of Godalming 57-62; Exam Chap to Bp of Guildf 58-71; Hon Can of Guildf 59-61; Can Res 61-71; Can (Emer) from 72; Dir of Ordin Tr 58-71; Asst Dir 71-73. *Dora Cottage, Beech Hill, Hambledon, Surrey.* (Wormley 2087)

OLDHAM, Charles Harry. b 14. St D Coll Lamp BA 47. **d** 48 **p** 49 Man. C of Atherton 48-53; V of St Alb Rochdale 53-59; PC (V from 68) of Goff's Oak 59-79. *94 Prestbury Drive, Warminster, Wilts.* (Warminster 213678)

OLDHAM, Dale Raymond. Ridley Hall Cam 64. **d** 67 **p** 68 Guildf. C of St Mary-of-Bethany Woking 67-70; Papanui 71-74; CMS Miss Dio Centr Tang 74-81. *c/o PO Box 164, Dodoma, Tanzania.*

OLDHAM, Canon John. b 19. Kelham Th Coll 38. **d** 44 **p** 45 Derby. C of Staveley 44-49; Chap S Afr Rly Miss Beira Sect 49-52; C-in-c of Melfort S Rhod 52-54; C of Staveley 54-57; PC of Somercotes 57-64; St Bart Derby 64-72; Proc Conv Derby from 65; Surr from 68; V of Buxton 72-74; R (w Burbage and King Sterndale) Dio Derby from 74; Ch Comm from 78; Hon Can of Derby Cathl from 79. *17 Lismore Road, Buxton, Derbys, SK17 9AN.* (Buxton 2151)

OLDLAND, John Leyshon. b 06. Chich Th Coll 29. **d** 33 **p** 34 Lon. C of St Sav Poplar 33-37; H Trin Hoxton 37-38; Fulwell 39-40; St Thos Acton Vale 40-41; L to Offic as C-in-c at St Sav Pimlico 41-43; C of Carshalton (in c of Ch of Good Shepherd) 43-48; V of St Jo Div Balham 48-61; Perm to Offic Dio Lon 62-63; C of S Elmsall 63-65; C-in-c of Athersley and New Lodge 65-71; Chap of Commun of St Pet Horbury 71-73. *5 St James Close, Bishop Street, Islington, N1 8PH.*

OLDMAN, Reginald William. NZ Bd of Th Stud LTh 64. St Jo Coll Auckld 62. **d** 64 **p** 65 Waik. C of New Plymouth 64-67. *13 Carlton Terrace, Gonville, Wanganui, NZ.*

OLDMEADOW, Russell Henry. Univ of Melb BA 47, BD 60. **d** and **p** 59 C & Goulb. C of Queanbeyan 59; Wagga Wagga 59-63; R of Gundagai 63-66; Albury 66-71; Archd of Albury 66-71; L to Offic C & Goulb from 71. *Box 682, Albury, NSW, 2640, Australia.*

OLDNALL, Frederick Herbert. b 16. Ripon Hall Ox. **d** 57 **p** 58 Cov. C of St Nich Cov 57-59; Stratford-on-Avon 59-62; V of Rosliston w Coton-in-the-Elms Dio Derby from 62. *Rosliston Vicarage, Burton-on-Trent, Staffs.* (Burton 761438)

OLDRIDGE, Gary Douglas. b 50. New Coll of Univ of S Fla BA 73. Hur Coll Lon MDiv 76. **d** and **p** 77 Bp Robinson for Hur. I of Ridgetown Dio Hur from 77. *Box 613, Ridgetown, Ont, Canada, N0P 2C0.*

OLDROYD, Colin Mitchell. b 30. Down Coll Cam BA 54, MA 60. Wells Th Coll 60. **d** 61 **p** 62 Man. C of All SS Elton Bury 61-63; St D Ex 63-66; V of Cleobury Mortimer w Hopton Wafers 66-78; C-in-c of Neen Sollars w Milson 66-78; Doddington 66-78; RD of Ludlow 75-78; R of Ledbury (w Eastnor from 81) Dio Heref from 78; P-in-c of Eastnor 78-81; RD of Ledbury 78-81; Surr from 78. *Ledbury Rectory, Herefs, HR8 1PL.* (Ledbury 2571)

OLDROYD, James Healey. Worc Ordin Coll **d** 55 **p** 56 Worc. C of Kidderminster 55-57; Tardebigge 57-61; V of St Mark-in-the-Cherry Orchard Worc 61-75. *135 Bath Road, Worcester.*

OLDROYD, Trevor. b 33. Univ of Dur BA 55. BD (2nd cl) Lon 60. Wycl Hall Ox 60. **d** 61 **p** 62 S'wark. C of Barnes 61-66; Wimbledon (in c of St Mark) 66-68; Chap K Sch Gutersloh 68-73; Asst Master Dudley Gr Sch from 73. *7 Gigmill Way, Norton, Stourbridge, Worcs.* (Stourbridge 6420)

OLHAUSEN, William John. b 37. Trin Coll Dub BA 60, MA 63. Ridley Hall Cam 60. **d** 62 Warrington for Liv **p** 63 Liv. C of Grassendale 62-66; Asst Chap Bede Coll Dur from 66-70; Lect 66-68; Sen Lect 68-70; V of Hazlemere Dio Ox from 70; RD of Wycombe from 78. *Hazlemere Vicarage, High Wycombe, Bucks, HP15 7PZ.* (High Wycombe 23191)

OLI, Luke. b 22. **d** 76 **p** 77 Polyn. P Dio Polyn. *PO Box 3744, Samabula, Fiji.*

OLIBA, Solomon. **d** 76 **p** 77 Soroti. P Dio Soroti. *Otuboi, Kaberamaido County, Central Teso, Soroti, Uganda.*

OLIELO, Justin. St Phil Th Coll Kongwa 60. **d** 61 Bp Wiggins for Centr Tang. d Dio Centr Tang 61-63; Dio Vic Nyan from 63. *Box 26, Tarime, Tanzania.*

OLIIT, Yosamu. Buwalasi Th Coll. **d** 56 **p** 59 U Nile. P Dio U Nile 56-61; Dio N Ugan from 61. *Box 232, Gulu, Uganda.*

OLING, Leuben. **d** 64 **p** 67 N Ugan. P Dio N Ugan. *Awach, Gulu, Uganda.*

OLIPHANT, David Glen. b 42. Univ of Syd BArchit 67. Melb Coll of Div BD 76. **d** and **p** 76 C & Goulb. C of St John Canberra 76-78; Perm to Offic Dio Birm 79-80; P-in-c of Aranda Dio C & Goulb from 80. *13 Bindel Street, Aranda, ACT, Australia 2614.*

OLIVER, Anthony Grant. b 09. OBE (Mil) 42. Wells Th Coll 59. **d** 60 **p** 61 Chich. C of Haywards Heath 60-68; V of Jarvis Brook 68-75; L to Offic Dio Bunb from 75. *PO Box 239, Denmark, W Australia 6330.*

OLIVER, Arthur Edmund. St Chad's Coll Dur BA 26, MA 29. Cudd Coll 28. **d** 29 **p** 30 York. C of St Olave w St Giles York 29-32; Scarborough (in c of St Paul) 32-38; V of St Jude (w St Steph from 57) Hull 38-61; Cloughton 61-78. *15 Grosvenor Road, Scarborough, Yorks.*

OLIVER, Arthur Norman. b 16. Worc Ordin Coll. **d** 65 **p** 66 Chich. C of Willingdon 65-69; St Jo Div W Worthing 69-71; R of Etchingham Dio Chich from 71; V of Hurst Green Dio Chich from 72. *Rectory, High Street, Etchingham, Sussex.* (Etchingham 235)

OLIVER, Bernard John. b 31. M IMechE, CEng 65. SOC 75. **d** 78 Barking for Chelmsf **p** 79 Chelmsf. C of Chipping Ongar Dio Chelmsf from 78. *72 Longfields, Ongar, Essex, CM5 9DE.*

OLIVER, Ven Beverley Stephen. Lich Th Coll 58. **d** 60 Lich for Capetn **p** 61 Bp Cowdry for Capetn. C of Goodwood 61; R of H Trin Paarl 61-69; Camps Bay 69-78; St Paul Capetn 74-78; Milnerton 78-80; Newlands Dio Capetn from 80; Archd of Capetn from 80. *77 Kildare Road, Newlands 7700, CP, S Africa.* (64-3851)

OLIVER, David Nelson. b 51. Montr Dioc Th Coll 74. **d** 75 **p** 76 Montr. C of St Phil Montr 75-77; R of Iberville Dio Montr from 77. *148 Jacques Cartier Street North, St Jean, Quebec, Canada.* (514-346 6505)

OLIVER, David Ryland. b 34. Late Scho and Pri of St D Coll Lamp BA (Welsh) 56. Powis Exhib to St Cath S Ox BA (Th) 58, MA 62. Wycl Hall Ox 56. **d** 58 **p** 59 St D. C of St Pet Carmarthen 58-61; Llangyfelach w Morriston 61-63; R of Aberedw w Llandeilo-Graban and Llanbadarn-y-Garreg 63-66; Llanbadarn Fawr w Llandegley and Llanfihangel Rhydithon 66-68; L to Offic Dio Llan 68-70; Asst Master Porth Boys' Gr Sch Rhondda 68-70; Llanidloes High Sch 70-73; L to Offic Dio Ban 70-73; V of Nefyn w Carngiwch and Pistyll and Tudweiliog w Llandudwen and Edern and

Ceidio 73-74; Abercraf w Callwen 74-77; Llangyfelach 77-79; R of Llanllwchaearn Dio St D from 79. *Rectory, New Quay, Dyfed, SA45 9RE.* (New Quay 273)

OLIVER, Eric Edwin. Bp Wilson Th Coll IM 37. **d** 38 **p** 39 Man. C of St Geo Bolton 38-41; Kendal 41-43; V of Staveley (w Kentmere from 52) 43-76; L to Offic Dio Blackb from 76. *96 Park Avenue, Euxton, Chorley, Lancs.* (Chorley 71881)

OLIVER, Erwin Henry. b 38. Hur Coll Ont BMin 74. **d** 74 **p** 75 Hur. C of All SS Windsor 74-75; Six Nations Reserve E Parish Dio Hur from 75. *Caledonia, Ont., Canada.*

OLIVER, Frank Leslie. MBE 56. Trin Coll Melb BA and MA 23. ACT ThL 23. AKC 23. **d** 23 **p** 24 Melb. C of St John E Malvern Melb 23-24; Chap RAN 24-28; RAN (Emy List) 28-58; Chap Miss to Seamen at Stockton NSW 28-30; Melb 30-39; Sen Chap 30-60; Chap RAN 39-43; I of Mt Dandenong 60-68; Perm to Offic Dio Melb from 68. *2 Rubens Grove, Canterbury, Vic, Australia 3126.* (82-6796)

OLIVER, Frederick Charles. Lon Coll of Div. **d** 28 **p** 29 Roch. C of St Paul Chatham 28-30; St Dunstan-in-the-E Lon 30-32; Org Sec C of E Children's S Dios Chich; Guildf; Portsm and Sarum 32-33; Min of St Hilda's Conv Distr Tottenham 33-36; Camp Chap Dio Argent 36-38; R of Cricket Malherbie and PC of Knowle St Giles 38-40; C of St Clem Parkstone 45-48; Perm to Offic Dio Sarum 48-49; R of Ludgershall 49-65. *Fairwinds, The Douard, Whitchurch, Ross-on-Wye, Herefs.*

OLIVER, George. b 1895. Lon Coll of Div 30. **d** 32 **p** 33 Lon. C of St Pet U Holloway 32-35; R of Kencot 35-38; Mursley 38-55; RD of Mursley 51-55; Surr 53-65; Seq of Swanbourne w L Horwood 53-54; R of Eastrop 55-65. *2 Morley Close, Winkton, Christchurch, Dorset.*

OLIVER, Graham. St Barn Th Coll Adel. **d** 68 **p** 69 N Terr. C of Alice Springs Dio 68-70; Morwell 70-72; Prec of St D Cathl Hobart 72-77; R of Brighton Dio Tas from 77. *St Mark's Rectory, Pontville, Brighton, Tasmania 7403.* (002-68 1221)

OLIVER, John. St Jo Coll Dur LTh 41. BA and Long Reading Pri 42. BCM and Th Coll 38-41. **d** 42 **p** 43 S'wark. C of New Malden and Coombe 42-44; Gorleston 44-47; C of E in S Africa 47-58; L to Offic Dio Johann 54-58. *170 Corlett Drive, Bramley, Johannesburg, S Africa.*

OLIVER, John Andrew George. b 28. St Jo Coll Dur. BA 53, Dipl Th 55. **d** 55 **p** 56 S'wark. C of Bermondsey 55-58; St Barn Dulwich 58-61; Chap RN from 61; Hon Chap to HM Queen from 79. *c/o Ministry of Defence, Lacon House, Theobalds Road, WC1 8RY.*

OLIVER, John Graham Wyand. b 47. Ridley Hall Cam 76. **d** 78 **p** 79 Roch. C of Shortlands 78-81; St Paul Hammersmith Dio Lon from 81. *22 Colet Gardens, Hammersmith, W14 9DH.* (01-741 2492)

OLIVER, John Keith. b 35. G and C Coll Cam BA 59, MA 63, MLitt 65. Westcott Ho Cam. **d** 64 **p** 65 Nor. C of Hilborough w Bodney 64-68; Chap and Asst Master Eton Coll 68-72; V of S Molton w Nymet St Geo 73-75; Team R of S Molton (w Kingsnympton, Romansleigh, N Molton and Twitchen from 79) Dio Ex from 75; C-in-c of Warkleigh w Satterleigh and Chittlehamholt 73-75; High Bray w Charles 73-75; Filleigh w E Buckland 73-75; Surr from 74; RD of S Molton 74-80; P-in-c of N Molton w Twitchen 77-79; M Gen Syn from 80; Team R of Ex Cent Dio Ex from 82. *3 Spicer Road, Exeter, Devon.*

OLIVER, John Michael. b 39. St D Coll Lamp BA 62. Ripon Hall, Ox 62. **d** 64 **p** 65 Ripon. C of St Pet Harrogate 64-67; Bramley 67-72; V of St Mary Low Harrogate w Harlow Hill 72-78; St Mary Beeston Dio Ripon from 78; Ecumen Officer for Leeds Metrop Coun of Chs from 81. *16 Town Street, Beeston, Leeds, LS11 8PN.* (Leeds 705529)

OLIVER, John Rodney. Trin Coll Melb BA 53. ACT Th Scho 68. Univ of Lon MTh 73. Bps' Coll Cheshunt 54. **d** 56 St Alb **p** 57 Melb for Bal. C of Much Hadham 56-57; Chap Bal Gr Sch 58-69; C of Thorley 70-73; V of Aberfeldie 74-77; Exam Chap to Abp of Melb from 75; Chap Trin Coll Melb from 77. *Trinity College, University of Melbourne, Parkville, Vic., Australia 3052.* (347-1044)

OLIVER, Canon Keith Llewellyn. b 12. Late Exhib of St D Coll Lamp BA and Harford Scho 36. **d** 36 **p** 37 Swan B. C of St Paul Landore 36-40; St Julian Newport 40-46; V of Ynysddu 46-50; St Jo Bapt Newport 50-79; Can of Mon Cathl from 71. *5a Hazeldene Road, Weston-super-Mare, BS23 2XL.* (0934 416027)

OLIVER, Kenneth Cyril. b 08. OBE 49. CBE 60. St Edm Hall Ox BA 30, MA 34. Westcott Ho Cam 31. **d** 32 **p** 33 Ripon. C of St Edm Roundhay 32-34; St Cypr Hay Mill 34-36; Chap Toc H for S Lon Area 36-39; CF 39-60; Hon Chap to HM the Queen 59-60; Chap Milton Abbey Sch 60-62; L to Offic Dio Sarum 60-62; Chap HM Pris Ford 69-74; P-in-c of Clymping 74-77; V 77-80. *c/o St Mary's Vicarage, Clymping, Littlehampton, Sussex.* (Littlehampton 5882)

OLIVER, Paul Robert. b 41. Dipl Th (Lon) 65. Tyndale Hall, Bris 63. **d** 66 **p** 67 Guildf. C of Virginia Water 66-70; w Script U (E Region) 70-74; L to Offic Dio Nor 70-75; Team V of Thetford Dio Nor from 75. *44 Nunsgate, Thetford, Norf.*

OLIVER, Philip Maule. b 38. Univ of Birm LLB (3rd cl) 59. Wells Th Coll 62. **d** 64 **p** 65 Lich. C of Chesterton 64-67; Tettenhall Wood 67-71; V of Milton 71-78; Ixworth w Ixworth Thorpe and Bardwell Dio St E from 78; P-in-c of Honington w Sapiston & Troston Dio St E from 81. *Ixworth Vicarage, Bury St Edmunds, Suff, IP3 2HE.* (Pakenham 30311)

OLIVER, Ven Philip Newton. Moore Th Coll Syd ACT ThL 62. **d** 62 **p** 63 Syd. C of Mittagong 62-64; Gladesville 64; C-in-c of Yagoona 64-68; R of Lane Cove 68-73; Gen Sec CMS Vic and L to Offic Dio Melb 74-78; Dir of Ch Information 78-80; Archd of Syd and Cumberland from 80. *St Andrew's House, Sydney Square, Sydney, Australia 2000* (269-0642)

OLIVER, Roland John. b 29. Lich Th Coll. **d** 59 Stafford for Lich **p** 60 Lich. C of Sedgley 59-62; V of The Lodge (Weston Rhyn) 62-77; L Aston Dio Lich from 77. *Little Aston Vicarage, Walsall Road, Little Aston, Sutton Coldfield, W Midl.* (021-353 0356)

OLIVER, Stephen John. b 48. K Coll Lon AKC 70. St Aug Coll Cant 70. **d** 71 **p** 72 Southw. C of Clifton 71-75; P-in-c of Ch Ch Newark 75-79; R of Plumtree Dio Southw from 79. *Plumtree Rectory, Nottingham.* (Plumtree 4245)

OLIVER, Stephen Melbourne. Wycl Coll Tor. **d** 57 **p** 58 Tor. C of St Anne Tor 57-58; St Cuthb 58-60; R of St D Hardington 61-71; St Marg City and Dio Tor from 71. *33 Burnaby Boulevard, Toronto, Ont., Canada.* (416-483 9749)

OLIVER, Terence Maule. b 07. Univ Coll Dur BA 32. Linc Th Coll 31. **d** 36 **p** 37 Southw. C of St Mark Mansfield 36-37; C-in-c of St Aid Conv Distr Mansfield 37-47; CF 47-51; V of St Mark Seremban and Miss Negri Sembilan 51-56; USPG Miss Dio Sing 56-66; V of Shilbotel 66-76. *Restharrow, Longhorsley, Morpeth, Northumb.* (Longhorsley 253)

OLIVER, Thomas Gordon. b 48. Univ of Nottm BTh 72, ALCD 72 (LTh from 74). St Jo Coll Nottm 68. **d** 72 **p** 73 Bradf. C of Thorpe Edge 72-76; St Mark Woodthorpe, Nottm 76-80; V of Huthwaite Dio Southw from 80. *Huthwaite Vicarage, Sutton-in-Ashfield, Notts, NG17 2QT.* (Mansfield 555053)

OLIVEY, Hugh Charles Tony. b 35. St Mich AA Coll Llan 77. **d** 79 **p** 80 Truro. C of St Winnow & of St Veep 79-81; C of Lostwithiel and of Lanhydrock and of Lanivet Dio Truro from 81. *6 Barn Park, Lostwithiel, Cornwall, PL22 0EY.*

OLLIER, Cecil Rupert. b 13. St Edm Hall Ox BA (3rd cl Th) 34. MA 42. Ely Th Coll 34. **d** 36 Man for Ches **p** 37 Ches. C of St Mary-without-the-Walls Ches 36-38; St Jo Bapt Bollington 38-40; Stoke-on-Trent 40-46; V of Normacot 46-52; Fauls Salop 52-54; R of Naracoorte Dio Adel 54-57; Chap Qu Eliz Hosp Birm 57-58; V of Fenton 58-73; R of Moreton Saye 73-78; Hon C of Kettering 78-80; Chap Berkeley's Hosp Worc from 80. *c/o Chaplain's House, Berkeley's Hospital, The Foregate, Worcester, WR1 3QG.*

OLLIER, Timothy John Douglas. b 44. Trin Hall Cam 2nd cl Hist Trip pt i, 64, BA (2nd cl Th Trip pt ii) 66, MA 69. Cudd Coll 66. **d** 68 **p** 69 Dur. C of Silksworth 68-71; St Marylebone w H Trin Lon 71-74; Winlaton (in c of Rowlands Gill) 74-77; R of Redmarshall Dio Dur from 77; V of Bishopton w Gt Stainton Dio Dur from 77. *Rectory, Redmarshall, Stockton-on-Tees, TS21 1EP.* (Sedgefield 30810)

OLLIFFE, Gregory Brian. Moore Th Coll Syd ThL 71. **d** and **p** 72 Syd. C of Darling Point 72-73; St Swith Pymble 73-75; Fairfield 75-80; V of All SS Jakarta Dio Sing from 80. *All Saints' Church, Jalan Hakim 5, Jakarta Pusat, indonesia.*

OLNEY, Desmond Ronald. b 29. **d** 73 Bp Monteith for Auckld **p** 74 Auckld (APM). Hon C of Marsden-Waipu Miss Dio Auckld from 73. *Marsden Point Road, RD 1, Ruakaka, NZ.* (Ruakaka 479)

OLOFIN, Samuel Ajayi. b 36. Im Coll Ibad Dipl Th 70. **d** 70 **p** 71 Ondo. P Dio Ondo. *Box 32, Akure, Nigeria.*

OLOGUN, Joseph Omobamidele. b 51. Im Coll Ibad 76. **d** 79 **p** Ijebu. P Dio Ijebu. *St Andrew's Church, Imuwen, PO Box 106, Ijebu-Imusin, Nigeria.*

OLOGUNTOYE, Amos Oluranti. b 36. **d** 77 Ilesha. d Dio Ilesha. *St Mark's Vicarage, Iperindo, Nigeria.*

OLOJO, Canon James Oladosu. b 31. Im Coll Ibad 58. **d** 60 **p** 61 Lagos. P Dio Lagos 60-76; Dio Ijebu from 76; Can of Ijebu from 77. *Emmanuel Vicarage, Italupe, via Ijebu-Ode, Nigeria.*

OLOKUNBOLA, Ven Joshua Monday. Melville Hall Ibad. **d** 57 **p** 58 Ibad. P Dio Ibad 57-74; Dio Ilesha 74-76; Dio Ondo from 77; Hon Can of Ilesha 74-76; Archd of Owo from 78. *Box 4, Owo, Ondo, Nigeria.*

OLOLO, Cornelius Onywero. St Paul's Th Coll Limuru 63. **d** 66 **p** 67 Maseno. P Dio Maseno 67-71; Dio Maseno S from

71. *PO Ng'iya, Via Kisumu, Kenya.*

OLOMODOSI, Very Rev Adeneye Olufemi. Melville Hall Ibad. **d** 57 **p** 58 Lagos. P Dio Lagos 57-76; Dio Egba from 76; Hon Can of Lagos 68-76; Provost of St Pet Cathl Ch Ake from 76. *St Peter's Cathedral, Box 182, Ake, Abeokuta, Nigeria.* (Abeokuta 151)

OLOMU, Daniel Osanyin Atitebe. Im Coll Ibad 58. **d** 60 **p** 61 Ondo-B. P Dio Ondo-B 60-62; Dio Ondo 62-67; Dio Ekiti from 67. *St Luke's Vicarage, Iro, Ikere-Ekiti, Nigeria.*

OLONIYO, Canon Gabriel Babalola. Im Coll Ibad 60. **d** 62 **p** 63 Lagos. P Dio Lagos 62-76; Dio Egba from 76; Can of Egba from 76; Exam Chap to Bp of Egba from 76. *Egba-Owoke Grammar School, PMB 2055, Abeokuta, Nigeria.*

OLONIYO, Canon Joshua Sapaye. Melville Hall, Ibad. **d** 49 **p** 50 Lagos. P Dio Lagos 49-52; Dio Ondo-B 52-62; Dio Ondo 62-67; Dio Ekiti from 67; Can of Ekiti from 68. *St Philip's Vicarage, Aramoko-Ekiti, Nigeria.*

OLOO, Joash. **d** 59 Momb **p** 62 Maseno. d Dio Momb 59-62; P Dio Maseno 62-70; Dio Maseno S from 70. *Box 1710, Kisumu, Kenya.*

OLORUNTOBA, Peter. **d** 81 Benin. d Dio Benin. *St Luke's Church, Afuze Emai, Nigeria.*

O'LOUGHLIN, Canon Gordon Raymond. b 32. Late Scho of Linc Coll Ox BA 56, MA 60. Wells Th Coll 56. **d** 58 **p** 59 Win. C of St Francis Bournemouth 58-62; St Barn Tunbridge Wells 62-65; Chap Roch Th Coll 65-67; Sub-Warden 67-69; V of St Alb Hull 69-78; Can and Preb of York Minster from 78; Dioc Dir of Post Ordin Tr Dio York from 77; Team V of All SS (in c of St Martin w St Helen) Pavement 78-82; V of St Andr Bromley Dio Roch from 82. *St Andrew's Vicarage, Burnt Ash Lane, Bromley, Kent.* (01-460 0481)

O'LOUGHLIN, Michael Wilfrid Bryan. b 23. Ch Coll Cam BA 47, MA 58, PhD 64. **d** 81 Ely (APM). C of Linton Dio Ely from 81; Lect Cam Coll of Arts & Tech from 81. *Ditches Close, Linton, Cambridge.*

OLOWO, Besweri Christopher. **d** 76 **p** 77 Nam. P Dio Nam. *PO Box 196, Mukono, Uganda.*

OLOWO, Yesero. Buwalasi Th Coll 57. **d** 58 **p** 59 Mbale. P Dio Mbale 58-72; Dio Bukedi from 72. *PO Box 126, Tororo, Uganda.*

OLOWOFOYEKU, Moses Ayodele. b 12. Melville Hall, Ibad 48. **d** 53 **p** 55 Ondo-B. P Dio Ondo-B 53-62; Dio Ondo 62-70; Dio Lagos from 71. *Vicarage, Iworo, Box 7, Badagry, Nigeria.*

OLOWOKURE, Ven Jacob Olabode Kehinde. Univ of Ibad BA 65, MA 70. **d** 61 **p** 62 Ondo-B. P Dio Ondo; Hon Can of Ondo 73-76; Exam Chap to Bp of Ilesha from 74; to Bp of Ondo from 76; Archd of Ondo from 76. *Box 55, Ondo, Nigeria.* (Ondo 2031)

OLOWOYO, Canon Abraham Sunday Oluwole. Univ of Lon Dipl Th (Extra-Mural) 69. Univ of Ibad BA 70. Im Coll Ibad 65. **d** 68 Bp Jadesimi for Ibad **p** 69 Ibad. P Dio Ibad. Hon Can of Ilesha from 77; Exam Chap to Bp of Ilesha from 81. *PO Box 515, Ibadan, Nigeria.*

OLOWU, Isaac Ojo. **d** 75 Ibad. d Dio Ibad 75-77. *Christ Anglican Church, Shaki, via Iseyin, Nigeria.*

OLSEN, Arthur Barry. Univ of NZ BA 61. Ridley Coll Melb ACT ThL 63. **d** and **p** 64 Nel. C of All SS Nel 64-67; V of Ahuara 67-69; Motupiko 69-70; Amuri 70-73; Maori Miss and C of St Matt Dun 73-76; V of Brooklyn Wel 77-81; on leave. *13 Garfield Street, Brooklyn, Wellington, NZ.*

OLSEN, Bruce Roger. b 29. **d** 74 **p** 75 Ott. C of Ch of Ascen City and Dio Ott 74-75; I from 75. *251 Echo Drive, Ottawa, Ont., Canada.* (613-235 6112)

OLSON, Albert Carl. **d** 80 **p** 81 (NSM). C of St John Cairns Dio N Queensld from 80. *c/o PO Box 52, Cairns, Qld Australia 4870.*

✠ **OLUFOSOYE, Most Rev Timothy Omotayo.** St Paul's Univ Tokyo Hon DD 58. Univ of BC STh 59, Melville Hall Ibad. **d** 46 Asst Bp for Lagos **p** 47 Lagos. P Dio Lagos 46-52; Dio Ondo 52-65; Regr Dio Ondo 53-65; Can of Ondo Cathl 54-65; Provost 60-65; Exam Chap to Bp of Ondo 57-65; Cons Ld Bp of Gambia and the Rio Pongas in St Steph Cathl Ondo 10 Oct 65 by Abp of W Afr; Bps of Ibad; N Nig; Ow; Sier L; Lagos; Ondo; Accra; Benin; and Nig Delta; trld to Ibad 71; Elected Abp and Metrop of Prov of Nigeria 79. *Bishopscourt, Box 3075, Mapo, Ibadan, Nigeria.*

OLUGASA, Justus Olorunfemi. b 38. Univ of Ibad BA 64. Im Coll Ibad 70. **d** 70 **p** 72 Ondo. P Dio Ondo; Prin Ilogbo High Sch from 75. *Ilogbo High School, Ilogbo-Ekiti, Nigeria.*

OLUGUA, Thomas Freeman Okovunuye. b 24. **d** 73 **p** 74 P Dio Benin. *St Barnabas Church, Ivrogbo, via Ughelli, Nigeria.*

OLUKOJU, Zaccheus Subero. Melville Hall, Ibad. **d** 50 **p** 51 Lagos P Dio Lagos 50-52; Dio Ondo-B 52-62; Dio Ondo 62-74; Hon Can of Ondo 69-74. *St Andrew's Vicarage, Kabb, Nigeria.*

OLUMA, Canon Enosi. **d** 64 **p** 65 N Ugan. P Dio N Ugan 64-76; Dio Lango from 76; Hon Can of Lango from 78. *Box 6, Lira, Uganda.*

OLUMAKAIVE, Ven Theophilus Akin. Im Coll Ibad 56. **d** 58 Ondo-B. d Dio Ondo-B; Dio Ondo 62-75; Dio Kwara from 75; Archd of Kwara from 75. *St Michael's Church, Esie, Kwara State, Nigeria.*

OLUMIDE, Canon Adeyinka. Univ of Dur BA 48. St Cath S Ox Dipl Th 49. Wycl Hall, Ox 48. **d** 50 **p** 51 Sheff. C of Heeley 50-52; Chap of Lagos Cathl 52-57; L to Offic Dio Lagos from 57; Hon Can of Lagos from 57; L to Offic Dio Nai from 71. *c/o Nigerian Broadcasting Corporation, Ikoyi, Lagos, Nigeria.*

OLUMIDE, Oluseye Abiola. b 42. Clifton Th Coll 68. **d** 71 Man **p** 72 Hulme for Man. C of St Osw w St Cath Collyhurst 71; St Pet Halliwell 71-72; St Phil w St Steph Salford 72; Perm to Offic Dio Lon 72-73; C of St Mich-at-Bowes Bowes Pk 73; C-in-c 73; C of Stanmer w Falmer (in c of St Mary Magd Coldean) (and Moulescomb to 76) 73-76; St Jas w St Clem Moss Side 76; The Ascen Hulme Man 76-77; C-in-c of St Mary Hulme Man 76-77, Asst Chap N Man Gen Hosp 77-80; Chap St Bernard's Hosp Southall from 80. *St Bernard's Hospital, Southall, Middx.* (01-574 8141 ext 315)

OLUMOYA, Ven Josiah Olufemi. **d** 53 **p** 54 W Afr. P Dio Lagos; Archd of Ijebu Remo from 77. *Box 7, Sagamu, Lagos, Nigeria.*

OLUMOYA, Canon Justus Bayode. Melville Hall, Ibad. **d** 54 **p** 55 Lagos. P Dio Lagos 54-55; Dio Ibad 55-74; Dio Ilesha from 74; Dom Chap to Bp of Ibad 66-69; Hon Can of Ilesha from 77. *St Peter's Church, Ikeji-Arakeji, Nigeria.*

OLUMUYIWA, Gabriel Olubayode. b 34. **d** 77 **p** 79 Ijebu. P Dio Ijebu. *St Michael's Church, Owu, Via Ijebu-Ode, Nigeria*

OLUNWA, Raymond Obudein. b 24. Im Coll Ibad 71. **d** 72 **p** 73 Nig Delta. P Dio Nig Delta. *St Peter's Parsonage, Hospital Road, Port Harcourt, Nigeria.*

OLUPITAN, Isaac Albert Oladenusi. Im Coll Ibad 61. **d** 63 **p** 65 Lagos. P Dio Lagos. *St John's Church, Ode-Lemo, Shagamu, Nigeria.*

OLUPONA, Ven michael Alatake. Im Coll Ibad 56. **d** 57 **p** 58 Ondo-B. P Dio Ondo-B 57-62; Dio Ondo 64-71; Dio Ibad from 71; C of Kingswood Bris 62-64; Hon Can of Ondo 69-71; Can of Ibad 71-74; Archd of Oke-Osun 74-76; Ife from 76. *Box 30, Ile-Ife, Nigeria.*

OLURUNTOLA, Samuel Olufemi. b 28. **d** 80 **p** 81 Ijebu. P Dio Ijebu. *St Michael's Vicarage, Ododeyo c/o Odosimadegun, PA Ijebu-Ode, Nigeria.*

OLUSANYA, Isaac Olumoyebo. b 25. **d** 72 **p** 74 Lagos. P Dio Lagos 72-76; Dio Ijebu from 76. *St Thomas's Vicarage, Abigi, Ijebu Waterside, via Ijebu-Ode, Nigeria.*

OLUWASANMI, Matthew Oluwadare. b 46. Im Coll Ibad 70. **d** 73 **p** 74 Ibad. P Dio Ibad. *St Paul's Church, Oyedeji, c/o Apatere PA, via Ibadan, Nigeria.*

OLUWATOBA, Samuel Oladugba. **d** 63 **p** 65 Ondo. P Dio Ondo. *Vicarage, Idogun, via Owo, Nigeria.*

OLUWATOPE, William. b 41. Univ of Ibad Dipl Educn 69. **d** 79 **p** 81 Egba. P Dio Egba. *St Paul's Church, Igbore, Abeokuta, Nigeria.*

OLUWATUSIN, Samuel Oladipo. Im Coll Ibad 65. **d** 68 Bp Jadesimi for Ibad **p** 69 Ibad. P Dio Ibad. *Vicarage, Ilobu, Oshogbo, Nigeria.*

OLUWOLE, Alao Raphael Sunday. Im Coll Ibad 58. **d** 60 **p** 61 Ondo-B. P Dio Ondo-B 60-62; Dio Ondo from 62. *c/o PO Box 25, Ondo, Nigeria.*

OLUWOLE, Samuel Sunday. Im Coll Ibad 58. **d** 60 Ondo-B **p** 61 Ibad. d Dio Ondo-B 60-61; P Dio Ibad from 61. *St Paul's, Esa Oke, Ilesha, Nigeria.*

OLYOTT, Ven Leonard Eric. b 26. Univ of Lon BA 50. Westcott Ho Cam 50. **d** 52 **p** 53 S'wark. C of St Geo Camberwell 52-55; Bp's Hatfield (in c of St Mich AA Birchwood) 55-60; V of Chipperfield 60-68; Crewkerne 68-71; R of Crewkerne w Wayford 71-77; RD of Crewkerne 72-77; Preb of Wells Cathl from 76; Archd of Taunton from 77. *Summerhayes, Higher Street, Curry Mallet, Taunton, Somt, TA3 6SY.* (Hatch Beauchamp 480758)

OMADANG, Yekoyasi. **d** 58 **p** 59 U Nile. P Dio U Nile 58-61; Dio Mbale from 61. *Apokori, PO Tororo, Uganda.*

OMALA, Mika. Bp Tucker Coll Mukono 63. **d** 64 **p** 65 Mbale. P Dio Mbale 64-72; Dio Bukedi from 72. *Church of Uganda, Pajwenda, PO Box 242, Tororo, Uganda.*

OMAN, Brian Malcolm. b 14. Qu Coll Cam 2nd cl Hist Trip pt i 35, BA (2nd cl Th Trip pt i) 36, MA 46. Chich Th Coll 36. **d** 37 **p** 38 Man. C of Our Lady of Mercy and St Thos Gorton 37-40; Perm to Offic Dio Ox 40-42; Chap St Mary's Abbey West Malling 42-46; Perm to Offic Dio Heref 44; C of St Barn Tunbridge Wells 46-55; V of St Mary Cardiff 55-62; R of Gt Greenford 62-74; V of King's Sutton Dio Pet from 74. *King's Sutton Vicarage, Banbury, Oxon.* (Banbury 811364)

OMAND, William Donald. b 03. **d** 54 Reading for Cant **p** 55 Ox. [f Free Church Min] C of Thatcham 54-55; Bracknell (in c of Easthampstead) 55-56; R of Winterbourne Abbas w Steepleton 56-59; PC of Chideock 59-69; V 69-71; Perm to Offic Dio Ex from 72; Dio Sarum from 75; Dio Truro 76-78. *29 Higher Street, Cullompton, Devon, EX15 1AJ.* (Cullompton 3459)

OMDURMAN, Lord Bishop of. *See* Shukai, Right Rev Butrus Tia.

O'MEALLY, Ven Walter Samuel. St Pet Th Coll Ja. **d** 39 **p** 40 Ja. C of St Mich Kingston 39-41; R of Porus 41-47; Chantilly w Cumberland 47-52; Pratville 51-52; Balaclava and Siloah 52-60; H Trin Montego Bay 60-64; Mandeville Dio Ja from 64; Can of Ja 70-78; Archd of Mandeville from 78. *Mandeville, Jamaica, W Indies.* (096-22360)

OMENUWOMA, Jeremiah. Trin Coll Umuahia 64. **d** 66 Benin. d Dio Benin. *St Andrew's Parsonage, Box 52, Warri, Nigeria.*

OMIGBODUN, Canon Julius Ladunjoye. Univ of Dur (Fourah Bay Coll) BA 50. Im Coll Ibad 59. **d** 59 **p** 61 Ibad. Prin Oshogbo Gr Sch Dio Ibad from 61; Can of Ibad from 73. *PO Box 98, Oshogbo, Nigeria.* (Oshogbo 2119)

OMINDO, Helikia. b 50. St Phil Coll Kongwa 75. **d** and **p** 77 Vic Nyan. P Dio Vic Nyan; Dioc Treas from 80. *PO Box 278, Mwanza, Tanzania.*

OMING, James. Buwalasi Th Coll 58. **d** 60 **p** 61 N Ugan. P Dio N Ugan 60-69. *PO Lira, Uganda.*

OMING, Nikanori. Gulu Th Coll 61. **d** 62 **p** 63 N Ugan. P Dio N Ugan 62-76; Dio Lango from 76. *PO Anyeke, Lira, Uganda.*

OMIYINKA, Isaiah Olayeni. b 24. **d** 75 **p** 76 Ibad. P Dio Ibad. *c/o Idiayunre PA, via Ibadan, Nigeria.*

OMODARA, Adeboye. b 43. **d** 74 **p** 75 Ondo. P Dio Ondo. *St Paul's Vicarage, Iju-Odo, via Okitipupa, Nigeria.*

OMODIN, Yekolam. **d** 63 **p** 64 Soroti. P Dio Soroti. *Latome, PO Kaangole, Karamoja, Uganda.*

OMOERA, Sunday Isikhuenmen. b 39. Univ of Lon Dipl Th 69. Yale Div Sch Conn STM 78. Univ of Lanc MA 79. Im Coll of Th Ibad 66. **d** 69 **p** 70 Benin. P Dio Benin; Exam Chap to Bp of Benin from 79; Dioc Sec from 80. *St James Anglican Church, PO Box 111, Benin City, Nigeria.*

OMOITI, Tolofemo. **d** 64 **p** 65 Mbale. P Dio Mbale 64-72; Dio Bukedi from 72. *Church of Uganda, Kalaiti, PO Tororo, Uganda.*

OMOJOLA, David Ayodele. **d** 58 Lagos. d Dio Lagos 58-62; Dio Ondo 62-67; Dio Ibad from 67. *PO Box 3075, Ibadan, Nigeria.*

OMOKOGBO, James Oriloye. Im Coll Ibad 58. **d** 61 **p** 63 Ibad. P Dio Ibad. *PO Box 102, Ile-Ife, Nigeria.*

OMOLE, Nathaniel Oakhena. b 07. **d** 74 **p** 75 Benin. P Dio Benin. *St John's Church, c/o Box 9, Sabongidda Ora, Nigeria.*

OMOLERE, Samuel Adejoro. Univ of Ife Nigeria BA 71. **d** 77 Ondo. d Dio Ondo. *PMB 256, Epinmi-Akoko, via Ikare-Akoko, Ondo, Nigeria.*

OMOLO, Very Rev Jonathan Daniel. St Paul's Th Coll Limuru 56. **d** 57 **p** 59 Momb. P Dio Momb 57-61; Maseno 61-68; L to Offic Dio Nai 68-71; P Dio Maseno S from 72; Archd of Kisumu 72-76; Exam Chap to Bp of Maseno S from 72; Provost of St Steph Cathl Kisumu from 76. *PO Box 43, Kisumu, Kenya.*

OMONGIN, Samuson. **d** 63 **p** 64 Soroti. P Dio Soroti. *Ngariam, Uganda.*

OMONIJE, Joseph Ayelade Babalola. b 32. ACP 67. Im Coll Ibad 62. **d** and **p** 64 Ibad. P Dio Ibad; Exam Chap to Bp of Ibad from 77. *St Paul's Vicarage, Odo-Ona, Moor Plantation, Ibadan, Nigeria.*

OMONIJO, Gamaliel Omotayo. Im Coll ibad. **d** 63 **p** 65 Ibad. P Dio Ibad. *St Stephen's, Ora, Nigeria.*

OMONIYI, Daniel Akingbode. **d** 24 **p** 26 Bp Oluwole for Lagos. P Dio Lagos 24-52; Dio Ondo-B 52-62. *c/o Bishopscourt, Box 12, Ado-Ekiti, Nigeria.*

OMOSEIBI, Joshua Omoyele Omosola. Im Coll Ibad. **d** 62 Ondo-B **p** 63 Ondo. P Dio Ondo 62-67 and from 77; Dio Ekiti 67-71; C of H Trin Chesterfield 72-73. *St Stephen's Vicarage, Iju, Akure, Nigeria.*

OMOSOLA, Thomas Oyewole. b 34. Im Coll Ibad 62. **d** 65 **p** 66 Lagos. P Dio Lagos 65-76; Dio Egba from 76. *St John's Vicarage. Ajilete, Egbado, Nigeria.*

OMOSUYI, Rufus Oluwadare. b 36. **d** 73 **p** 75 Ondo. P Dio Ondo. *St Silas's Vicarage, Omuo-Ekiti, via Ikole, Nigeria.*

OMOTARA, Canon Peter Olatunji. Melville Hall Ibad. **d** 56 **p** 57 Ibad. P Dio Ibad; Can of Ibad from 76. *St Peter's Vicarage, Ikeji-Titun, Nigeria.*

OMOTUYI, Samuel Adegboye. b 07. **d** 72 **p** 73 Ekiti. P Dio Ekiti. *All Saints Church, Okebola, Box 57, Ikole, Ekiti, Nigeria.*

OMOWARE, James Kolawole. b 38. **d** 74 **p** 76 Ondo. P Dio Ondo. *Box 20, Ile-Oluji, Nigeria.*

OMOYAJOWO, Canon Joseph Akinyele. Dipl Th (Lon) 63. Univ of Ibad BA 66, PhD 71. Im Coll Ibad 61. **d** 63 **p** 65 Ondo. P Dio Ondo; Exam Chap to Bp of Ekiti from 71; to Bp of Ondo from 77; Hon Can of Ondo from 76. *Public Service Commission's Office, Akure, Nigeria.*

OMUJONG, Absolom. Buwalasi Th Coll. **d** 62 **p** 63 Mbale. P Dio Mbale. *Church of Uganda, Buyobo, PO Box 297, Mbale, Uganda.*

OMULO, Reuben. **d** 24 **p** 28 Momb. P Dio Momb 24-37 and 47-61; Perm to Offic Dio Momb 37-47; Dio Maseno 61-62. *Marenyo, PO Yala, Kenya.*

OMUSALA, Canon Nelson. St Paul's Dioc Div Sch Limuru. **d** 52 **p** 54 Momb. P Dio Momb 52-61; Dio Maseno 61-69; Dio Maseno N from 70; Hon Can of Maseno 68-69; Maseno N from 70; Exam Chap to Bp of Maseno N from 70. *PO Nambale, Kenya.*

OMWIRIKHA, Aggrey. b 42. **d** 74 **p** 76 Maseno N. P Dio Maseno N. *Box 167, Mumias, Kenya.*

ONAIKA, David. b 41. **d** 75 **p** 76 S Malawi. P Dio S Malawi. *Likwenu, PO Kasupe, Malawi.*

ONDO, Lord Bishop of. *See* Idowu, Right Rev Emanuel Olawale.

ONDOA, Elikana. **d** 58 **p** 59 U Nile. P Dio U Nile 58-61; Dio N Ugan 61-69; Dio M & W Nile from 69. *PO Box 216, Arua, Uganda.*

✠ **O'NEIL, Most Rev Alexander Henry.** Hur Th Coll LTh 29. **d** 29 **p** 30 Hur. C of Atwood w Henfryn and Elma 29-35; R of Gorrie Fordwich and Wroxeter 35-39; St Paul Clinton 39-41; Actg Prin of Hur Coll 41-43; Prin 43-52; Gen Sec of BFBS In Canada and C of St Clem Eglinton Tor 52-57; Cons Ld Bp of Fred In Ch Ch Cathl Fred 25 Jan 57 By Abp of Queb; Abp of Alg; Bps of Montr; NS; Tor; Newfld; and Maine; Bps Suffr of Hur; and Tor; and Bp Moorhead; Elected Metrop of Prov of Canada 63; res 71. *1 Grosvenor Street, London, Ont., Canada.*

O'NEIL, Canon James Francis. Univ of Tor BA 49. Wycl Coll Tor LTh 51. **d** 51 Tor **p** 52 Br Columb for Tor. C of St Jo Bapt Norway Tor 51-53; R of Haliburton 54-57; Richmond Hill 57-69; St John York Mills City and Dio Tor from 69; Can of Tor from 72. *174 Old Yonge Street, York Mills, Willowdale, Ont., Canada.* (416-225 6611)

O'NEIL, John Fitzgerald. ED 49. Univ of Manit BA 37. St Jo Coll Manit LTh 37. **d** 37 **p** 38 Calg. Miss of Rocky Mountain House 37-39; I of Pincher Creek w Cowley Livingstone Lundbreck and Waterton Lakes 39; Armed Services CASF 39-44; Chap 44-45; V of St Mich Canmore w Exshaw and Cochran; 46-49; R of Port Coquitlam and Port Moody 49-53; Chap Essondale Hosp 53-70; L to Offic Dio Carib from 75. *271 West St Paul Street, Kamloops, BC, Canada.* (374-4703)

O'NEIL, Thomas Arthur. b 11. St Chad's Coll Dur Found Scho 29, Cl Scho 31, BA (1st cl Cl), Lightfoot Scho and Maltby Pri 32, Jenkyns Scho 33, 3rd cl Th 34, MA 50. **d** 34 Warrington for Liv **p** 35 Liv. C of Walton-on-the-Hill 34-36; C-in-c of Bannow w Duncormick 36-39; Kilscoran 39-44; Asst Chap Miss to Seamen Belf 44; Port of Lon 44-46; C of St Steph Paddington 46-49; Ch Ch Ealing 50-51; Perm to Offic Dio Lon 51-63; Dio Cant from 67; Chap St Steph Coll Broadstairs 63-67; Asst Master Gillingham Gr Sch (Howard Sch from 75) 67-76. *144 Minnis Road, Birchington, Kent.*

O'NEILL, Christopher John. b 53. Worc Coll Ox BA 75, MA 80. Ripon Coll Cudd 77. **d** 78 Bp McKie for Cov **p** 79 Cov. Asst Chap Rugby Sch 78-80; Asst Master Charterho Godalming from 81. *Charterhouse, Godalming, Surrey.* (Godalming 4437)

O'NEILL, Gary. b 57. AKC and BD 79. Westcott Ho Cam 80. **d** 81 Man. C of St Mary Oldham Dio Man from 81. *44 Godson Street, Oldham, OL1 2DB.* (061-678 7617)

O'NEILL, Preb Nevil. b 23. Trin Coll Dub BA 45, MA 55. **d** 46 Meath for Down **p** 47 Down. C of Drom Cathl 46-48; Enniskillen and Trory 48-51; R of Galloon (w Drummully from 66) 51-81; Preb of Clogh Cathl from 80; R of Clogher w Errigal-Portclare Dio Clogh from 81. *Cathedral Rectory, Clogher, Co Tyrone, N Ireland.* (Clogher 235)

O'NEILL, Wilfrid Stephen. b 1886. Univ of Leeds BA (3rd cl Hist) 10, MA 23. Coll of Resurr Mirfield. **d** 12 Wakef **p** 13 Dover for Cant. C of Whitstable 12-14; Frome Selwood 14-16; SPG Miss Dio Madag 16-17; Civil Chap of Seychelles 17-19; C of Hagley 20-21; Chap of St Andr Lah 21-22; Prin Bp Cotton Sch Simla 22-27; Chap at Kohat 27-32; Gulmarg 32; Risalpur 32-33; Rawalpindi 33-34, 37 and 41-42; Sialkot 34-37; Peshawar 38-39; Dalhousie 39-41; Murree and Chaklala 42-46; V of Wootton St Laur 46-49; Hon CF 47; V of Emery Down 49-58; Perm to Offic Dio Truro 58-68. *Trewood Cottage, St Ives, Cornw.*

O'NEILL, William Lloyd. b 11. Trin Coll Dub BA 32, MA 38. **d** 34 **p** 35 Down. C of Derriaghy 34-35; Drumragh 35-38;

Chap RAF 38-66; C-in-c and Seq of Portfield 67-79. *1 Fishbourne Road, Chichester, Sussex, PO19 3HS.* (Chichester 782603)

O'NEILL-FITZSIMONS, Terence Michael. TCD 76. **d** and **p** 78 Matab. C of Que Que Dio Matab 78-79; P-in-c 79-80. *c/o 18 Renin Road, Redcliff, Que Que, Zimbabwe.* (68482)

ONEN, Ven Kezeroni. d 62 **p** 63 N Ugan. P Dio N Ugan; Archd of Kitgum from 73. *PO Box 10, Kitgum, Uganda.*

ONG, Ming King. Trin Coll Sing BTh 72. **d** 72 **p** 73 Sing. P Dio Sing. *1 Leedon Road, Singapore 10.*

ONGANY, Yason. d 62 **p** 63 N Ugan. P Dio N Ugan. *Anaka, Uganda.*

ONGLEY, Albert Edwin Alexander. Trin Coll Tor BA 40. LTh 42. **d** 42 Tor **p** 43 Niag. C of St Clem N Tor 42-43; St Geo St Catherines 43-46; Youth Chap Dio Niag 46-48; I of Winona 48-51; Canon Davis Mem Ch Sarnia 51-55; Ch of Redeemer Lon 55-63; Exam Chap to Bp of Hur 60-63. *179 Appleby Line, Burlington, Ont, Canada.*

ONGLEY, Ven Frederick George. Trin Coll Tor BA 36, MA 38. **d** 38 **p** 39 Tor. C of St Clem Tor 38-41; Actg C of Collingwood 40-42; Chap RCAF 42-47; R of St Matt Pro-Cathl Bran 47-54; Can of Bran 52-54; R of St John Pet 54-63; Archd of Pet 56-63; R of St Geo Oshawa 63-77; Can of Tor 64-69; P-in-c of St Pet Oshawa 66-73; Archd of Scarborough 69-74; Dur 74-77; Archd (Emer) from 78; P-in-c of Apsley 78-79. *Buckhorn, Ont, Canada.*

ONGORA-ATWAI, Yekoyakim. b 39. Bp Tucker Coll Mukono 71. **d** 74 **p** 75 N Ugan. P Dio N Ugan 74-76; Dio Lango from 77. *Lango Dept of Religious Education, PO Box 6, Lira, Uganda.*

ONI, Amos Omoniyi. Im Coll Ibad 62. **d** 64 **p** 65 Ibad. P Dio Ibad. *St John's, Akinmorin, Oye, Nigeria.*

ONI, David Omotayo. Im Coll Ibad 62. **d** 64 **p** 65 Lagos. P Dio Lagos. *St Saviour's Church, Ikenne, Shagamu-Remo, Nigeria.*

ONI, Joseph Adejumo. Melville Hall Ibad. **d** 60 Bp Awosika for Ondo-B **p** 61 Ondo-B. P Dio Ondo-B 60-62; Dio Ondo from 62; Prec of St John's Cathl Ilesha from 76. *Box 45, Ilesha, Nigeria.*

ONI, Olumide Olawanle. b 32. Fourah Bay Coll Sier L BA 58. Univ of Birm MEducn 64. **d** 74 **p** 75 Ondo. P Dio Ondo; Prin Ondo Gr Sch from 76. *Ondo Grammar School, Ondo, Nigeria.*

ONI, Samuel Adeluse. d 75 **p** 76 Ondo. P Dio Ondo. *c/o Box 25, Ondo, Nigeria.*

ONI, Samuel Olorunda. b 34. **d** 73 **p** 75 Ondo. P Dio Ondo. *Vicarage, Igbatako, via Okitipua, Nigeria.*

ONI, Samuel Owolabi. Melville Hall, Ibad. **d** and **p** 38 Lagos. P Dio Lagos 38-52 and 55-63; Dio Ondo-B 52-55; Dio Ibad from 63. *c/o Grammar School, Oyan, Nigeria.*

ONI, Theophilus Ajaja. Im Coll Ibad 64. **d** 67 **p** 68 Ondo. P Dio Ondo. *Box 74, Owo, Nigeria.*

ONIBERE, Simon Godknows Azuinov. b 43. Im Coll Ibadan BA 69, MA 73. Dipl Th 74. **d** 80 Warri. d Dio Warri. *Dept of Religous Studies, University of Ife, Ile-Ife, Nigeria.*

ONIONS, John Vincent. St Jo Coll Morpeth ACT ThL 57. **d** 57 **p** 58 Newc. C of Waratah 58, Taree 57-61, Singleton 61-63; Belmont (in c of Swansea) 63-65; R of Wingham Dio Newc from 65. *Rectory, Bent Street, Wingham, NSW, Australia 2429.* (065-53 4043)

ONIYA, Emmanuel Gbolahan. b 41. Univ of Ibad BA 77. Im Coll Ibad 71. **d** 74 Ibad. d Dio Ibad. *University of Ibadan, Ibadan, Nigeria.*

ONIYIDE, Michael. b 33. **d** 79 Egba. d Dio Egba. *St Peter's Church, Ikanna Balogun, PO Box 1750, Abeokuta, Nigeria.*

ONIYINDE, Cornelius Adebowale. b 32. Im Coll Ibad 80. **d** 79 **p** 81 Egba. P Dio Egba. *PO Box 1233, Abeokuta, Nigeria.*

ONO, Benjamin Nwafo. b 36. St Paul's Coll Awka 75. **d** 76 **p** 77 Enugu. P Dio Enugu. *Anglican Diocese of Enugu, PO Box 418, Enugu, Nigeria.*

ONONOGBO, Canon Jonathan. St Paul's Coll Awka 46. Umuahia Th Coll 52. **d** 54 **p** 55 Nig Delta. P Dio Nig Delta 54-70; Dio Ow from 70; Hon Can of Ow from 73. *Ezeoke, Owerri, Nigeria.*

ONSLOW, Charles Norman. St Jo Coll Morpeth. **d** 53 **p** 54 Newc. C of Muswellbrook 53-56; Singleton 56-57; Cessnock 57-58; P-in-c of Dora Creek 58-64; R of Bulahdelah 64-75; C of Cessnock Dio Newc from 75. *Rectory, Wollombi Road, Millfield, NSW, Australia 2325.* (98 1396)

ONTARIO, Metropolitan of Province of. *See* Garnsworthy, Most Rev Lewis Samuel.

ONTARIO, Lord Bishop of. *See* Read, Right Rev Allan Alexander.

ONTARIO, Dean of. *See* Baker, Very Rev Grahame Brinkworth.

ONUAGULUCHI, Canon Albert Maduabueke. b 37. Univ of Nig Nsukka BA 66. St Jo Coll Nottm 71. **d** 72 **p** 73 Enugu. P Dio Enugu; Dioc Sec from 76; Hon Can of Enugu from 81. *41 Colliery Avenue, Enugu, Nigeria.*

ONUCHUKU, Frederick Oke. b 29. St Paul's Coll Awka. **d** 73 **p** 74 Nig Delta. P Dio Nig Delta. *St Michael's Church, Box 14, Omuku, Port Harcourt, Nigeria.*

ONUNWA, Rufus Udobata. b 47. Trin Coll Umuahia 71. **d** 74 **p** 75 Ow. P Dio Ow. *University of Nigeria, Nsukka, Nigeria.*

ONUOHA, Hart Onyebuchi. b 36. St Paul's Coll Awka 76. **d** 77 Aba. d Dio Aba. *Bishop Johnson Memorial Church, c/o St Stephen's Church, Umuahia, Nigeria.*

ONWUAMA, Ebenezer Chukunyem. St Paul's Coll Awka. **d** 61 W Afr for Benin **p** 62 Benin. P Dio Benin 61-72. *St Matthew's Church, Idumuje-Ugboko, Isseli-Uku, Nigeria.*

ONWUBIKO, John Nwankoro. b 12. **d** 75 **p** 76 Aba. P Dio Aba. *St John's Parsonage, Osusu, via Aba, Nigeria.*

ONWUDIWE, Alphonso Chukwuemeka. b 35. Trin Coll Umuahia 66. **d** 68 **p** 70 Niger. P Dio Niger. *St Jude's Church, Oraifite, Nigeria.*

ONWUJEKWE, Felix Batrick Okoye. Trin Coll Umuahia. **d** 63 **p** 64 Niger. P Dio Niger. *St James' Church, Nanka, Nigeria.*

ONWUKA, Ven Benson Ihechituru. Trin Coll Umuahia. **d** 56 **p** 57 Nig Delta. P Dio Nig Delta 56-73; Dio Aba from 72; Can of Aba from 72; Archd Dio Aba from 80. *St Matthew's Parsonage, Aba, Nigeria.*

ONWUKA, Samuel Chiemeka. Trin Coll Umuahia, 49. **d** 51 **p** 53 Niger. P Dio Niger 51-59; Dio Ow 59-74; Can of Ow 64-74. *Parsonage, Obollo, Owerri, Nigeria.*

ONWURA, Isaiah Nnaoum. Trin Coll Umuahia. **d** 63 **p** 64 Niger. P Dio Niger. *St James Church, Enugwuabo, Awka, Nigeria.*

ONWURAH, Polycarp Emeka. b 46. Trin Coll Umuahia Dipl Th 73. **d** 73 **p** 74 Niger. P Dio Niger. *c/o St James' Church, Enuguabo, Ajalli PA, ECS, Nigeria.*

ONWUZULU, Phanuel Dike. St Paul's Coll Awka. **d** 62 **p** 63 Niger. P Dio Niger. *St Silas Church, Ihiala, Nigeria.*

ONYAIT, Christopher. d 76 **p** 77 Soroti. P Dio Soroti. *c/o Katakwi, Usuk County, North Teso, Soroti, Uganda.*

ONYANGA, Peter. d 77 Lango. d Dio Lango. *PO Box 91, Lira, Uganda.*

ONYANGO, James. b 37. St Phil Sch Maseno 73. **d** 75 **p** 76 Maseno S. P Dio Maseno S. *PO Sawagongo, Kenya.*

ONYANGO, Wilfred John. Buwalasi Th Coll 59. **d** 61 **p** 62 N Ugan. P Dio N Ugan 61-76; Dio Lango from 76. *PO Arocha, Lira, Uganda.*

ONYEANUSI, Frederick. b 47. Trin Coll Legon 69. **d** 72 **p** 73 Enugu. P Dio enugu. *Box 14, Udi, ECS, Nigeria.*

ONYEBUENYI, Chibundu Anameje. d 72 **p** 73 Ow. P Dio Ow. *St John's Church, Isu, via Orlu, Imo State, Nigeria.*

ONYECHI, Jacob Aniemeka. Trin Coll Umuahia 49. **d** 51 **p** 52 Nig Delta. P Dio Nig Delta 51-65; Dio Niger from 65. *Holy Trinity Church, Abatete, Onitsha, Nigeria.*

ONYEIBOR, Benson Chukwukelue Bemegbunem. b 46. Dipl Th (Lon) 74. Trin Coll Umuahia 72. **d** 74 Enugu. d Dio Enugu. *c/o St Mary's Parsonage, Box 394, Enugu, ECS, Nigeria.*

ONYEJEKWE, Onwurah Isaac Paul. Trin Coll Umuahia 58. **d** 59 **p** 60 Ow. P Dio Ow 59-74; Can 71-74. *Box 197, Sabon, Kano, Nigeria.*

✠ **ONYEMELUKWE, Right Rev Jonathan Arinzechuku.** b 29. BD (Lon) 63. Univ of Birm MA 68. **d** 55 **p** 57 Niger. P Dio Niger 55-59 and from 62; C of Walton Breck Liv 61-62; Can of Niger 69-75; Archd of Awka 70; Prin Trin Coll Umuahia 71-75; Cons Ld Bp on the Niger in All SS Cathl Egbu 23 Feb 75 by Abp of W Afr; Bps of Aba, Accra, Ibad, Kum, Ow, Enugu, Ondo and Nig Delta; and others. *Bishopscourt, PO Box 42, Ozala, Onitsha, Nigeria.*

ONYEMUZE, Godwin Chukwueloka. Im Coll Ibad 64. **d** 67 **p** 68 Ibad. P Dio Ibad 67-72; Dio Niger from 72. *St John's Parsonage, Ukpor, via Nnewi, Nigeria.*

ONYEWUCHI, Rufus. b 40. **d** 74 **p** 75 Queb. R of Baie Common 74-76; I of Magd Is Miss 77-78; on leave. *Leslie PO, Grosse Isle, Magdalene Island, PQ, Canada.*

ONYIAGHA, Christopher Anabuike. d 64 N Nig. d Dio N Nig 64-66; Dio Niger from 67. *St Mary's Church, Isseke, via Ihiala, Nigeria*

ONYINGE, Yusufu Lucepo. b 07. **d** 65 M & W Nile **p** 67 N Ugan. P Dio N Ugan. *Ngeyo Ma-kome, Pagen Labongo, Box 47, Kitgum, Uganda.*

OOI, Clement Kok Leong. d 58 Sing **p** 58 Bp Koh for Sing. P Dio Sing. *c/o Diocesan Office, St Andrew's Cathedral, Singapore 6.*

OOI, Luke Lah Kar. Ridley Coll Melb ACT ThL 56. **d** 56 Sing. C of Johore Bahru 56-58; St Mary Kuala Lumpur 58-60; P-in-c of St Pet Sing 60-63; V of Malacca 63-68; Sandakan 70-73; Hon Can and Archd of Sabah 70-73; V of

Petaling Jaya Dio W Mal from 74; Exam Chap to Bp of W Mal from 75. *St Paul's Church, Jalan Utara, Petaling, Jaya, Malaysia.*

OOMMEN, Ampatu Cheriyan. Univ of Trav Serampore Coll BD 51. **d** 59 **p** 60 Ugan. Lect at Bp Tucker Mem Coll Mukono Dio Nam from 59. *PO Box 4, Mukono, Uganda.*

OO THA, Gregory. **d** 34 **p** 36 Rang. P Dio Rang 36-70; Dio Pa-an from 70. *Tantabin, Toungoo, Burma.*

OPADINA, Canon John Oyeniran. Melville Hall, Ibad 53. **d** 54 **p** 55 Ondo-B. P Dio Ondo-B 54-62; Dio Ondo 62-67; Dio Ekiti from 67; Can of Ekiti from 69. *St Peter's Vicarage, Aiyede-Ekiti, Nigeria.*

OPARA, Canon Moses Ukachukwu. St Paul's Coll Awka. **d** 62 **p** 63 Ow. P Dio Ow; Hon Can of Ow from 75. *Parsonage, Atta, Nigeria.*

OPARAH, Godson Ekeamadi. Im Coll Ibad 62. **d** 64 **p** 65 N Nig. P Dio N Nig 64-67; Dio Niger from 68. *BCM Church, Onitsha, Nigeria.*

OPELAMI, Joel Odukoya. **d** 59 Ibad **p** 61 Ondo-B for Ibad. Prin St Pet Teachers' Tr Coll Ilesha 59-65; St Luke's Tr Coll Ibad 65-67; P Dio Ibad 59-80; Archd of Ife 73-76; Ibad N 76-80. *c/o Box 4843, Ibadan, Nigeria.*

OPETO, Canon Erenesiti. **d** 52 Bp Tomusange for U Nile **p** 54 U Nile. P Dio U Nile 52-61; Dio N Ugan 61-70; Hon Can of N Ugan from 67. *PO Ibuje, Lira, Uganda.*

OPIE, Edward Charles. St Wilfrid's Coll Tas 26. ACT ThL 27. **d** 26 **p** 27 Tas. C of Burnie Tas 26-28; St Paul Harringay 28-30; St Geo Hanover Sq 30-33; Cler Sec Dr Barnardo's Homes for Dios B & W Bris and Glouc 33-35; Metrop Sec Ch Dept 35-41; V of St Martin Kensal Rise 41-42; Perm to Offic Dio Lon 42-45 and from 57; in c of Chelsea Old Ch 43; in c of St Andr Undershaft 43-45; Chap S Lon Crematorium from 45; C of St Jude Courtfield Gdns 46-48; C of St Andr Undershaft Lon 49-55; Chap Streatham Pk Cem 55-56; C-in-c of Ch Ch Woburn Square 56-61. *1 St George's Buildings, Bourdon Street, W1.*

OPIE, Roderick Preston. Qu Coll Birm 54. **d** 55 **p** 56 Newc T. C of St Jas Benwell Newc T 55-58; L to Offic Dio Adel 58-60; C of Mt Gambier 60-61; Coromandel Valley 61-62; P-in-c of Tumby Bay 62-64; Perm to Offic Dio Adel 64-65 and 69-72; C of Eliz 65-68; H Cross Cathl Geraldton 68; Ch Ch N Adel 72-73; P-in-c of Eliz N 73-79; R of Yankalilla Dio Murray from 79. *Rectory, Main Road, Yankalilla, S Australia 5203.* (085-582019)

OPII, Henry. Ngora Th Coll. **d** 54 **p** 56 U Nile. P Dio U Nile 54-61; Dio N Ugan 61-67. *PO Kaberamaido, Teso, Uganda.*

OPIO, Canon Becweri. Buwalasi Th Coll 58. **d** 59 **p** 60 U Nile. P Dio U Nile 59-61; Dio N Ugan 61-76; Dio Lango from 76; Hon Can of Lango from 76. *Box 150, Lira, Uganda.*

OPIO, Canon Hosea Wacibira. Buwalasi Th Coll. **d** 51 **p** 53 U Nile. P Dio U Nile 51-61; Dio N Ugan 61-69; Hon Can of N Ugan 67-69; M & W Nile from 69. *PO Box 370, Arua, Uganda.*

OPIO, John Wilson. b 42. Bp Tucker Coll Mukono 70. **d** 72 N Ugan. d Dio N Ugan. *Box 10, Kitgum, Uganda.*

OPIO, Sezi. **d** 77 Lango. d Dio Lango. *Box 6, Lira, Uganda.*

OPOKU, Albert George. St Aug Th Coll Accra 56. **d** and **p** 58 Accra. P Dio Accra 58-73; Dio Kum from 73. *PO Box 144, Kumasi, Ghana.*

OPOLOT, Gideoni. **d** 63 **p** 64 Soroti. P Dio Soroti. *Atiira, PO Serere, Uganda.*

OPOLOT, John Peter. **d** 63 **p** 64 Soroti. P Dio Soroti 63-69. *Box 5, Ngora, Uganda.*

OPOLOT, Wilson. Bp Tucker Coll Mukono, 67. **d** 69 Soroti. d Dio Soroti; Dioc Treas from 74. *Box 107, Soroti, Uganda.*

OPOLOT, Canon Yusufu. Buwalasi Th Coll. **d** 50 U Nile **p** 53 Bp Tomusange for U Nile. P Dio U Nile 50-60; Dio Soroti from 60; Hon Can of Soroti from 66. *Mukongoro, Uganda.*

OPORI, Canon Barakirya. Bp Tucker Coll Mukono. **d** 56 **p** 57 U Nile. P Dio U Nile 56-61; Dio N Ugan 61-76; Dio Lango from 76; Hon Can of N Ugan 69-76; Lango from 76. *PO Aduku, Lira, Uganda.*

OPOTI, Shadrack Waswa Aphrodite. St Paul's Th Coll Limuru 56. **d** 57 **p** 59 Momb. P Dio Momb 57-75; Dio Nak from 75. *Box 24, Soy, Kenya.*

OPPENHEIM, Raymond Leonard Leander. b 42. **d** 69 Alaska for Calif **p** 70 Alaska. In Amer Ch 69-75; V of Timaru 75-79; Avonside Dio Ch Ch from 79. *1 Trinity Lane, Christchurch 1, NZ.* (896-948)

OPUDU, Silvanus Igoni. St Paul's Coll Awka. **d** 55 **p** 57 Nig Delta. P Dio Nig Delta. *PO Box 11, Okrika, Nigeria.*

OPUKOK, Simon Toonee. b 50. Arthur Turner Tr Sch Pangnirtung 72. **d** 75 **p** 76 Arctic. C of Spence Bay 75-77; on leave. *Spence Bay, NWT, Canada.*

ORAM, Canon Geoffrey William James. b 14. Late Thorpe Exhib and Scho of Em Coll Cam 1st cl Cl Trip pt i 35, BA (1st cl Th Trip pt i) 37. MA 40. Ridley Hall Cam 36. **d** 38 **p** 39 S'wark. C of Tooting Graveney 38-40; Rugby 40-41; PC of St Thos Ipswich 41-49; R of E Bergholt 49-64; Hon Chap to Bp of St E 54-67; Exam Chap from 57; Hon Can of St E from 59; RD of Samford 59-64; V of Aldeburgh w Hazlewood 64-80; P-in-c of St Mich Ipswich Dio St E from 81. *12 Cheltenham Avenue, Ipswich, Suff, IP1 4LN.* (Ipswich 211371)

ORAM, John Ernest Donald. b 34. Tyndale Hall Bris 58. Open Univ BA 74. **d** 61 **p** 62 Man. C of St Luke Cheetham Man 61-64; Gt Baddow 64-67; V of St Barn Blackb 67-72; Chap to Bp of Sheff for Soc Responsibility 72-79; Chap-Psychotherapist Dio Sheff from 79. *12 Montgomery Road, Sheffield, S7 1LQ.* (Sheffield 582332)

✠ **ORAM, Right Rev Kenneth Cyril.** Univ of Lon BA 39. AKC (1st cl) 41. Linc Th Coll 42. **d** 42 **p** 43 Cant. C of Cranbrook 42-45; H Trin Upington w Prieska and Kenhardt 46-50; R of Prieska and Dir of Miss 50-52; Mafeking and Dir of Miss 52-60; Archd of Bechuanaland 53-60; Dean of Kimberley 60-64; Grahmstn 64-74; Archd of Grahmstn 64-74; Exam Chap to Bp of Kimb K 69-74; Cons Ld Bp of Grahmstn in St Thos Ch Durban 8 Nov 74 by Abp of Capetn; Bps of Zulu, Les, Kimb K, St John's, Pret, Geo, Port Eliz, Bloemf, Lebom and Swaz; and others. *Bishopsbourne, PO Box 162, Grahamstown, CP, S Africa.* (Grahamstown 2500)

ORAM, Roland Martin David. b 45. Trin Coll Cam BA 68. Cranmer Hall Dur Dipl Th 78. **d** 78 **p** 79 Southw. C of Aspley 78-81; Chap of Alleyn's Sch Dulwich from 81. *c/o Alleyn's School, Dulwich, SE22.*

ORANGE, David Copley. Univ of Melb BA 46. Univ of Syd BD 50. St Paul's Coll Syd 48. **d** 48 **p** 49 C & Goulb. C of St Sav Cathl Goulb 48-50; R of Cobargo 50-54; Koorawatha 54-57; C of Cooma 57-60; R of Lakes Entrance 60-66; Perm to Offic Dio Melb from 67. *69 Severn Street, Box Hill, Vic, Australia 3128.* (88-5458)

ORBELL, John Heddle Ray. b 16. Late Scho of CCC Ox BA 38, MA 41. Dipl Th 39. Wycl Hall, Ox 38. **d** 40 **p** 41 Bris. C of St Andr Clifton 40-43; St Giles Ashstead 43-44; St Mich AA (in c of Ch of Good Shepherd) Bishopston 44-50; Chap HM Pris Horfield 47-50; V of St Chris Brislington 50-61; R of Compton Greenfield Dio Bris from 61; P-in-c of Pilning w Severn Beach and Northwick Dio Bris from 80. *Compton Greenfield Rectory, Easter Compton, Bristol, BS12 3RU.* (Pilning 2440)

ORCHARD, George Richard. b 41. Ex Coll Ox BA (2nd cl Hist) 62, 2nd cl Th 64, MA 66. Ripon Hall Ox 62. **d** 65 **p** 66 Derby. C of Greenhill 65-70; M Ecumen Team Min Sinfin Moor 70-78; V of Sinfin Moor 76-78; Team R of Dronfield w Unstone Dio Derby from 78. *Rectory, Church Street, Dronfield, Sheffield, S18 6QB.* (Dronfield 412328)

ORCHARD, Harry Frank. b 23. Roch Th Coll. **d** 63 **p** 64 Sarum. C of Sturminster Newton 63-65; Miss to Seamen Argent 65-67; V of Preston w Sutton Poyntz 67-71; R of Teffont Ewyas w Teffont Magna 71-73; V of Dinton 71-73; Chap in Nadder Valley Group from 75; RD of Chalke from 80. *Downstream, Bulcombe, Salisbury, Wilts, SP2 0EJ.* (Wilton 2322)

ORCHARD, Ven John David. **d** 49 **p** 50 Wel. C of St Thos Wel 49-51; V of Wanganui E 52-59; Pohangina 59-64; Paraparaumu 64-73; Johnsonville 73-81; Levin Dio Wel from 81; Archd of Kapiti from 77. *120 Cambridge Street, Levin, NZ.* (85-955)

OREBANJO, Philip Ayayi. St Andr Coll Oyo. **d** 42 **p** 43 Lagos. P Dio Lagos 42-62; Dio N Nig 62-69; Archd of Kano 60-69. *11 Raboyijo Street, Ojowo, Ijebu-Igbo, Nigeria.*

ORECH, William. b 33. **d** 78 Lango. d Dio Lango. *PO Aroma, Lira, Uganda.*

OREDUGBA, Ven Thomas Laitan. **d** 41 **p** 43 Lagos. P Dio Lagos 41-52 and 60-75; Dio N Nig 52-60; Archd of Kano 55-60; Exam Chap to Bp of N Nig 56-60; to Bp of Lagos 67-75; Hon Can of Lagos 62-67; Archd of Lagos 67-74; Archd (Emer) from 74. *50 Olatilewa Street, Ikate, Lagos, Nigeria.*

O'REILLY, Charles Temple Meyrick Mandeville. b 1893. Trin Coll Dub BA 14, MA 17. **d** 15 Dub for Waterf **p** 17 Cash. C of Drumcannon w Dunhill 15-17; St Jo Div Fairfield Liv 18; TCF 18-19; Hon CF 21; C of St Jas Dover 22-23; Assoc Sec Dr Barnardo's Homes Dios Cant Roch and Chich 23-25; Asst Metrop Sec 26-29; Perm to Offic Dio St Alb 29-31; Dio Lon 29-33; St John w St Paul Battersea 33-34; C of St Mary Spring Grove Isleworth 34-35; V of Ch Ch High Wycombe 35-38; H Trin w St Paul Kilburn 38-42; St Mich AA Stoke Newington Common 42-50; St Jo Bapt Islington 50-57; R of Ludgershall 57-62; Perm to Offic Dio St Alb 62-67; Dio Ox from 67. *12 Ambrose Rise, Wheatley, Oxon.* (Wheatley 3304)

OREKOYA, Gabriel Adebiyi. b 15. Fourah Bay Coll. BA

(Dur) 50. **d** 70 **p** 71 Lagos. P Dio Lagos. *48 Shipeolu Street, Ijebutedo, Shomolu, Nigeria.*

ORFORD, Barry Antony. b 49. Univ of Wales BA 71. St Steph Ho Ox 71. **d** 73 **p** 74 Mon. C of Monmouth 73-77; C and V Cho of St A Cathl from 73. *Groesffordd, Mount Road, St Asaph, Clwyd.* (St Asaph 582650)

ORFORD, Keith John. b 40. E Midl Jt Ordin Tr Scheme 76. **d** 79 Repton for Derby **p** 80 Derby. Hon C of Matlock Bank Dio Derby from 79. *27 Lums Hill Rise, Matlock, DE4 3FX.* (0629 55349)

ORHEWERE, Canon Alfred Babatope. **d** 51 W Afr **p** 52 Ondo-B. P Dio Ondo-B 52-62; Dio Ondo 62-66; Dio Lagos 66-76; Dio Egba from 76; Can of Lagos 75-76; Hon Can of Egba from 76. *Box 169, Abeokuta, Nigeria.*

ORIAKU, Harold Erisonwengibia. **d** 36 Bp Glesthorpe for Niger **p** 39 Niger. P Dio Niger 36-52; Dio Nig Delta 52-67; Can of Nig Delta 53-67. *St Peter's Church, Box 11, Okrika, Nigeria.*

ORIMOLOYE, Ezekiel Adewole. Im Coll Ibad 55. **d** 57 **p** 58 Ibad. P Dio Ibad 57-62; Dio Ondo from 62. *Box 16, Idanre, via Akure, Nigeria.*

ORINGO, Alukipo. **d** 64 **p** 65 Mbale. P Dio Mbale 64-72; Dio Bukedi from 72. *Church of Uganda, PO Nagongera-Tororo, Uganda.*

ORIOMA, Joseph Aziakdono Edmund. b 35. Trin Coll Umuahia 72. **d** and **p** 73 Benin. P Dio Benin *St Peter's Parsonage, Okpe-Isoko, PA Okpe-Isoko, via Ughelli, Nigeria.*

ORKNEY, Bishop of. *See* Aberdeen.

ORKNEY, Archdeacon of. (Vacant).

ORLAND, Canon Ernest George. b 28. Lich Th Coll 61. **d** 62 **p** 63 Pet. C of St Mich AA Northn 62-65; R of Gayton w Tiffield 65-69; V of St Pet and St Andr Corby Dio Pet 69-72; R of Team Min w Gt and L Oakley 72-81; RD of Corby 79-81; Can of Pet from 79; V of All SS City and Dio Pet from 81. *208 Park Road, Peterborough.* (Peterborough 54130)

ORME, John. Sarum Th Coll 58. **d** 60 **p** 61 Ches. C of Heald Green 60-64; Ellesmere Port 64-67; Chap Harperbury Hosp St Alb 67-73; C-in-c of All SS (w St Pet from 76) Luton Dio St Alb 73-79; V from 79. *Vicarage, Shaftesbury Road, Luton, Beds.* (Luton 20129)

ORME, Martin Kitchener. b 27. Univ of Lon BD 50. AKC 50. Open Univ BA 75. St Bonif Coll Warm 50. **d** 51 **p** 52 Blackb. C of St Pet Blackb 51-54; St Cath Burnley 54-57; Chap RN 57-78; R Hosp Sch Holbrook from 78; L to Offic Dio St E from 78. *48 Royal Hospital School, Ipswich, Suffolk.* (Ipswich 328847)

ORME, Peter John. b 45. Univ of Cam BA 65, MA 69. Trin Coll Tor MDiv 76. **d** 76 Bp Clarke for Niag **p** 77 Niag. C of St Geo Guelph 76-81; R of Ch Ch St Catharines Dio Niag from 81. *4 Lisgar Street, St Catharines, Ont, Canada.* (416-684 4049)

ORME, Stewart. b 22. Univ of Leeds BA 49. Open Univ BA 75. St Steph Ho Ox 50. **d** 52 **p** 55 Guildf. C of Leatherhead 52-57; C-in-c of Lightwater Conv Distr 57-59; R of Albury w St Martha Dio Guildf from 59. *Albury Rectory, Guildford, Surrey.* (Shere 2533)

ORME, Sydney. b 27. Oak Hill Th Coll 54. **d** 58 **p** 59 Man. C of St Pet Halliwell 58-61; V of Friar Mere 61-73; Knypersley Dio Lich from 73. *Knypersley Vicarage, Stoke-on-Trent, Staffs.* (S-on-T 512240)

ORMEROD, Edward Thomas. St Jo Coll Morpeth. **d** 31 Graft for Newc **p** 31 Graft. C of St Mary W Maitland 31; P-in-c of Liston 31-33; V of N Grafton 33-34; C of Casino 34-35; R of Bowraville 35-36; C of Ch Ch Gunnedah 36-37; P-in-c of Boggabilla 37-41; Chap RAAF 41-46; V of Uralla 46-50; Moree 50-59; Can of Armid 51-60; V of Werris Creek 59-60; Bingara 60-61. *Bingara, NSW, Australia.*

ORMEROD, Henry Lawrence. b 35. Pemb Coll Cam 3rd cl Cl Trip pt i, 57, BA (2nd cl Th Trip pt 1a) 58, MA 63. Univ of Birm Dipl Th 59. Qu Coll Birm 58. **d** 60 **p** 61 Chelmsf. C of Chigwell 60-64; Thundersley 64-68; Canvey I 68-72; V of Stanground Ely 72-77; R (w Farcet) 77-81; St Jo & St Andr Swindon Dio Bris from 81. *Rectory, Verwood Close, Park North, Swindon, Wilts, SN3 2LE.* (Swindon 611473)

ORMISTON, Albert Edward. b 26. Oak Hill Th Coll 53. **d** 56 **p** 57 Southw. C of St Jo Evang Worksop 56-58; St Chrys (in c of St Polycarp) Everton 58-59; V of St Polycarp Everton 59-63; Org Sec SAMS Dios Carl, Ches, Blackb, Bradf, Liv and Man 63-67; V of Gateacre 67-73; St Steph Tonbridge Dio Roch from 73. *St Stephen's Vicarage, Brook Street, Tonbridge, Kent.* (Tonbridge 353079)

ORMOS, Claude Patrick. b 51. Univ of Indiana MA 75. Montr Dioc Th Coll. **d** 78 **p** 79 Montr. C of St Phil Montr W 78-80; Roxboro-Pierrefonds Dio Montr from 80. *4525 Sources Boulevard, Roxboro, PQ, Canada, H8Y 3C2.* (514-684 8259)

ORMSBY, Robert Daly. b 22. CCC Ox BA 42, MA 48. Sarum Wells Th Coll 77. **d** 78 **p** 79 Ex. C of Lydford w Bridestowe, Sourton & Brent Tor Dio Ex from 78. *Lipscliffe, Coryton, Okehampton, Devon.* (Chillaton 344)

ORMSTON, Derek. b 43. St D Coll Lamp Dipl Th 67. **d** 67 **p** 68 Lich. C of Ogley Hay w Brownhills 67-70; Tettenhall Regis 70-74; P-in-c of All SS Leek Dio Lich 74-79; Team V from 79. *All Saints Vicarage, Compton Leek, Staffs, ST13 5PT.* (Leek 382588)

ORMSTON, Joseph. b 24. Oak Hill Th Coll 47. **d** 51 Dur **p** 53 S'wark. C of Ven Bede Gateshead 51-52; St Steph Wandsworth 52-54; St John Reading 54-56; V of Shenstone 56-65; St Luke Wimbledon Pk 65-71; R of St Geo w St Paul Stamford Dio Linc from 71; Surr from 79. *St George's Rectory, Stamford, Lincs.* (Stamford 3351)

ORODHO, Ezekiel. St Paul's Dioc Div Sch Limuru, 46. **d** 49 **p** 51 Momb. P Dio Momb 49-61; Dio Nak 61-64; Dio Maseno 64-70; Dio Maseno N from 70. *PO Box 167, Mumias, Kenya.*

OROGE, Ven Michael Ajayi. Melville Hall Ibad. **d** 49 **p** 50 Lagos. P Dio Lagos 49-52; Dio Ibad from 52; Can of Ibad 69-76; Archd of Oke-Osun from 76. *Box 6, Gbongan, Ibadan, Nigeria.*

ORORI, Randolph. Newtown Coll Dogura 70. **d** and **p** 73 Papua. P Dio Papua. *Agaun PMB, via Alotau, Papua New Guinea.*

ORPWOOD, Canon William Warren Coverdale Lipscomb. b 01. Pemb Coll Ox BA and MA 30. Ridley Hall, Cam 24. **d** 26 **p** 27 Lon. C of St Paul Ealing 26-29; St Clem Ox 29-30; CMS Miss at Kabale 31-35; Buhiga 36-37; Kabale 37-39; Chap RAFVR 39-45; C of Em Weston-s-Mare 46-47; V of St Matt Kingsdown 47-53; St Paul w St Clem (and St Barn from 55) Bris 53-61; Alveston 61-70; RD of Almondsbury 65-70; Hon Can of Bris 67-70; Can (Emer) from 70. *12 Southdown Road, Westbury-on-Trym, Bristol, BS9 3NN.* (Bris 500589)

ORR, David Cecil. b 33. Trin Coll Dub BA 56, MA 68. **d** 57 Derry **p** 58 Dub. C of Drumragh 57-60; I of Convoy 60-70; RD of Raphoe 66-70; I of Maghera 70-80; Drumragh w Mountfield Dio Derry from 80. *Rectory, Omagh, Co Tyrone, N Ireland.*

ORR, Nathaniel Blair. Wycl Hall Ox 63. **d** 64 **p** 65 Liv. C of Ainsdale 64-66; R of Offord D'Arcy w Offord Cluny 66-75; C-in-c of Gt Paxton 67-75; V of St Aug Tynemouth 75-81. *c/o St Augustine's Vicarage, Jackson Street, North Shields, NE30 2HY.* (0632 579179)

ORR, Owen Robinson. Univ of Tor BA 46. Univ of Harvard, MA 50. Gen Th Sem NY 50. **d** 51 **p** 52 Hur. C of St Jo evang Lon 51-55; R of St Mark Parkdale Tor 57-60; Hon C of Ch of Redeemer Tor 60-63; I of Port Perry 63-64; Hon C of St Martin City and Dio Tor from 65; P-in-c of St Crisp City and Dio Tor from 80. *110 Pacific Avenue, Toronto 9, Ont, Canada.*

ORR, Reginald Henry Pache. b 11. Qu Coll Cam BA 36, MA 40. Bps' Coll Cheshunt 36. **d** 38 **p** 40 York. C of Hessle 38-42; Huntington 42-43; Banstead 43-47; V of All SS Guildf 47-63; Frimley Green 63-74; R of Shackleford 74-79; Peper Harow 74-79. *163 Stoke Road, Guildford, Surrey, GU1 1EY.* (Guildf 61471)

ORRELL, Joseph Albert. b 30. BD (Lon) 56. Lich Th Coll 60. **d** 61 **p** 62 Liv. C of Orford 61-63; V of Hollinfare 63-71; New Springs Wigan 71-77; Asst Master Aspull High Sch Wigan 77-81; Wigan Deanery High Sch from 81. *24 Kenyon Road, Wigan, Lancs, WN1 2DQ.* (Wigan 35285)

ORRITT, Crofton Paul. Trin Coll Tor 73. **d** 74 Calg for Newfld **p** 75 Bp Legge for Newfld. C of Burgeo w Ramea 74-75; I of Ramea 76-79; L to Offic Dio E Newfld from 79. *Queen's College, St John's, Newfoundland, Canada.*

ORTIZ, Eliseo. b 51. **d** 77 Chile. d Dio Chile. *Casilla 675, Santiago, Chile.*

ORTIZ, José. b 49. **d** 77 Chile. d Dio Chile. *Casilla 675, Santiago, Chile.*

✠ **ORTIZ, Right Rev Omar.** **d** 61 **p** 62 Argent. Chap at Temuco 61-62; Angl Centre Santiago 62-72; Valparaiso 72-81; Asuncion 81-82; Cons Asst Bp of Parag 82. *Casilla 1124, Ascuncion, Paraguay.*

ORTIZ, Roberto. b 24. **d** 68 **p** 69 Argent. P Dio Argent 68-73; N Argent from 73. *Parsonage, Yegua Alta, N Argentina.*

ORTON, Richard. b 33. Keble Coll Ox BA 56, MA 60. Lich Th Coll 60. **d** 61 **p** 64 Wakef. C of Penistone 61-62; Hon C of Meltham 62-69; Horsforth 69-72; C of Far Headingley 72-75; V of Hellifield 75-80; R of Hutton Dio Chelmsf from 80; RD of Bowland 78-79. *Hutton Rectory, Brentwood, Essex, CM13 1RX.* (Brentwood 210495)

ORUAMA, Canon Jason Esau. b 15. Trin Coll Umuahia 51. **d** 53 **p** 55 Nig Delta. P Dio Nig Delta; Can of Nig Delta from 72. *PO Box 8, Nembe, Nigeria.*

ORUFA, Maxwell Amineterima. b 27. **d** 76 Nig Delta. d Dio Nig Delta. *St Peter's Parsonage, Yenagoa, via Ahoada, Rivers State, Nigeria.*

O'RYAN, John Whiteford. b 26. Trin Coll Dub BA 47, MA 59. **d** 49 **p** 50 Arm. C of St Mark Portadown 49-52; St Bart Belf 52-53; St Andr Croydon 53-55; St Phil Norbury 55-56; Coulsdon 56-62; V of St Mary Edge Hill 62-72; St D Childwall Dio Liv from 72. *Vicarage, Rockey Lane, Liverpool, L16 1JA.* (051-722 4549)

OSANYINTOLU, Amos Ilesanmi. b 41. Im Coll Ibad 69. **d** 72 Ibad. d Dio Ibad. *St Paul's Vicarage, Agbamu, via Offa, Nigeria.*

OSBALDESTON, Michael. b 53. Univ of Dur BA 74. Westcott Ho Cam 74. **d** 76 **p** 77 Barking for Chelmsf. C of Woodford 76-80; Bp's Hatfield (in c of St John) Dio St Alb from 80. *St John's House, Bishop's Rise, Hatfield, Herts.* (07072 62689)

OSBORN, David Ronald. b 42. Clifton Th Coll 62. **d** 66 **p** 67 Southw. C of Fardon 66-69; W Bridgford 69-72; P-in-c of Kirkandrews-on-Eden w Beaumont and Grinsdale 72-77; Asst Dir of Educn Dio Carl 72-77; Asst Master and Chap Dauntsey's Sch W Lavington from 77. *Dauntsey's School, West Lavington, Devizes, Wilts, SN10 4HE.* (Lavington 2223)

OSBORN, Frederick Oriel. b 13. **d** 43 **p** 44 Waik. C of St Geo Frankton 43-45; P-in-c of Whangamomona 46-48; C of Onehunga Auckld NZ 48-49; H Trin Lamorbey (Col Cl Act) 49-52; Caterham (in c of St Paul) 52-55; St Mary Magd Wandsworth Common 55-59; V of St Bart Battersea 59-66; R of Gt w L Addington 66-71; C of St Paul S Harrow 71-72; Keyworth 72-75; V of Scrooby w Ranskill 75-78. *40 Highland Avenue, Bognor Regis, W Sussex, PO21 2BJ.*

OSBORN, Frederick William. Univ of Birm BA (2nd cl Cl) 44. **d** 45 **p** 46 Lich. C of St John The Pleck Walsall 45-48; Stoke on Trent 48-52; V of Horninglow 52-57; R of Longsight 57-65; V of Meir 65-77; C of St Paul Burton-on-Trent Dio Lich from 77. *11 Needwood Street, Burton-on-Trent, Staffs.*

OSBORN, John Geoffrey Rowland. b 33. Jes Coll Cam 2nd cl Math Trip pt i, 53, BA (3rd cl Math Trip pt ii) 55, MA 59. Wells Th Coll 63. **d** 65 **p** 66 Ox. C of Easthampstead 65-68; Asst Master R Gr Sch Lanc and L to Offic Dio Blackb 68-70; Prin St Marg Sch Seria 70-75; V of Tockholes and Asst Dir of Relig Educn Dio Blackb 75-77; Dir of Relig Educn Dio B & W from 77. *c/o The Old Deanery, Wells, Somt.*

OSBORN, Maurice. b 25. Univ of Wales BA 50. Wycl Hall Ox 55. **d** 55 **p** 56 S'wark. C of E Wickham 55-57; Chap Dauntsey's Sch W Lavington 57-72; Asst Master 58-78; P-in-c of Bp's Lavington Dio Sarum from 79. *Greensand Cottage, West Lavington, Wilts.* (Lavington 3244)

OSBORN, Peter George. b 14. Univ of Syd BA (1st cl Hist) 35. Cudd Coll 61. **d** 63 **p** 64 Portsm. C of forton 63-66; Chap Geelong Gr Sch 66-68; Abingdon Sch 68-75; C-in-c of Hawkley 74; P-in-c of St Cypr City and Dio Adel from 75; C of St Pet Cathl City and Dio Adel from 75; Asst Chap Colleg Sch of St Pet Adel 77-78. *Flat 9, 58 High Street, Grange, S Australia 5022.* (08-356 3806)

OSBORN, Reginald Richardson. Worc Coll Ox BA (1st cl Mod Hist) 32, MA 38, BLitt 38. Ridley Hall Cam 46. **d** and **p** 47 Lich. C of St Laur Darlaston 47-49; V of Hanbury 49-53; Chap HM Pris Stafford (Draycott-in-the-Clay) 49-53; V of All SS Goodmayes 53-63; Exam Chap to Bp of Chelmsf 58-63; to Bp of Roch 63-77; V of St Luke Bromley Common 63-77; Tutor SOC 70-73; P-in-c of Syresham w Whitfield Dio Pet from 77. *Syresham Rectory, Brackley, Northants.* (Syresham 638)

OSBORN-JONES, Arthur. b 09. Wycl Hall Ox 39. ACP 22. **d** 41 **p** 42 Leic. C of St Phil Leic 41-43; Chap RAFVR 43-46; V of Hoddesdon 46-54; Broadway 54-67; St Paul Cliftonville 67-73; L to Offic Dio Ban 74-77; C of St Mich Highgate 77-79. *24 Ainsworth Avenue, Ovingdean, Brighton, BN2 7BG.* (0273 309067)

OSBORNE, Alexander Deas. b 34. Univ of Liv BSc 54, PhD 57. Oak Hill Coll 78. **d** 81 St Alb (NSM). C of Redbourn Dio St Alb from 81. *19 Rickyard Meadow, Redbourn, St Albans, AL3 7HT.* (Redbourn 3749)

OSBORNE, Anthony Russell. b 47. Sarum Wells Th Coll 77. **d** 79 **p** 80 Heref. C of Holme Lacy Dio Heref from 79. *St Cuthbert's House, Holme Lacy, Hereford.*

OSBORNE, Arthur Frederick. b 09. K Coll Lon 28. BD (2nd cl) and AKC 44. **d** 33 **p** 34 Ox. C of Beaconsfield 33-35; St Benet Fink Tottenham 35-36; E Barnet 36-38; V of Lindsell 38-44; PC of St Mark Barnet Vale 44-51; RD of Barnet 48-51; Sen Lect in Div and Chap Salisbury Dioc Tr Coll 51-56; V of Bradf-on-Avon 56-65; Chap and Prin Lect Kirkby Fields Coll of Educn Liv 65-72; Northn Coll of Educn 72-75; Perm to Offic Dio Linc from 72. *37 King Street, West Deeping, Peterborough, PE6 9HP.* (Market Deeping 342397)

OSBORNE, Bernard Francis. Em Coll Sktn 66. **d** 69 **p** 70 Athab. I of Fort Chipewyan 70-72; Sedgewick 72-74; Camrose Dio Edmon from 74. *Box 1955, Camrose, Alta., Canada.* (403-672 2640)

OSBORNE, Brian Charles. b 38. Univ of St Andr MA 61. Clifton Th Coll 61. **d** 63 Grantham for Linc **p** 64 Linc. C of H Trin Skirbeck 63-68; C-in-c of New Clee 68-71; V 71-75; St Aug Derby 75-80; H Trin Skirbeck Dio Linc from 80. *Holy Trinity Vicarage, Spilsby Road, Boston, Lincs.* (Boston 63657)

OSBORNE, Brian Murray. b 31. St Jo Coll Morpeth Dipl Th 72. **d** 71 **p** 72 Graft. Hon C of Eureka-Clunes w Dunoon 71-73; R of Dorrigo 73-78; S Graft 78-81; Mullumbimby Dio Graft from 81. *Box 52, Mullumbimby, NSW, Australia 2482.*

OSBORNE, Cecil Alfred. Univ of Bris BA 36. Ridley Hall Cam 36. **d** 38 Bris **p** 39 Malmesbury for Bris. C of St Thos Ap Eastville Bris 38-41; St Paul Brixton 41-43; St Martin-in-the-Fields 43-45; V of St Osw Bedminster 45-53; PC of St Thos Ap Hanwell 53-57; Min Can of Graft Cathl 57-59; C of Ch Ch Cathl Graft 57-59; R of Port Macquarie 59-65; Good Shepherd Canberra 65-74; Bega Dio C & Goulb from 74; Archd of Monaro S Coast and Exam Chap to Bp of C & Goulb 74-79; Perm to Offic Dio C & Goulb from 79. *6 Embley Street, Holder, ACT, Australia 2611.*

OSBORNE, Coles Alexander. CIE 45. **d** and **p** 47 Syd. Hon C of St Andr Cathl Syd 47-53; Darling Point Syd 53-66; Hon Chap to Abp of Syd 59-66; L to Offic Dio Syd from 66. *126 Hopetown Avenue, Vaucluse, NSW, Australia 2030.* (337-2959)

OSBORNE, David Robert. b 50. Univ of Birm BSc 71. Univ of Nottm Dipl Th 72. St Jo Coll Dur 78. **d** 80 **p** 81 Lich. C of Penkridge Dio Lich from 80. *Wayside, Top Road, Acton Trussell, Stafford.* (Penkridge 2408)

OSBORNE, David Victor. b 36. Univ of Dur BA 59, Dipl Th 62. Cranmer Hall Dur 59. **d** 62 **p** 63 S'wark. C of St Anselm w St Jas Kennington Cross 62-66; Sandal Magna w Newmillerdam 66-67; R of All S Ancoats Man 67-73; V of H Angels Claremont Pendleton, Salford 73-80; Breedon-on-the-Hill w Isley Walton and Worthington Dio Leic from 80. *Breedon-on-the-Hill Vicarage, Derby, DE7 1AJ.* (Melbourne 2154)

OSBORNE, Canon Derek James. b 32. Tyndale Hall Bris 53. **d** 57 **p** 58 Sarum. C of Weymouth 57-60; St Mary Southgate Crawley 60-63; V of Ch Ch Croydon 63-71; Cromer Dio Nor from 71; C-in-c of Gresham Dio Nor from 71; Hon Can of Nor from 77. *Vicarage, Cromwell Road, Cromer, Norfolk.* (Cromer 512000)

OSBORNE, Hayward John. b 48. New Coll Ox BA (Th) 70, MA 73. Westcott Ho Cam 71. **d** 73 **p** 74 Roch. C of Bromley 73-77; Halesowen w Hasbury and Lapal Dio Worc 77-79; Team V from 79. *55 Quarry Lane, Halesowen, W Midl.* (021-550 8744)

OSBORNE, John David. d 63 Bp Snell for Tor **p** 64 Tor. C of Ch Ch Oshawa 63-67; I of Fort McPherson 69-75; Wolfe I 77-78; Marysburgh Dio Ont from 78. *Milford, Ont, Canada.* (613-476 2324)

OSBORNE, Kenneth Arnold. St Barn Th Coll Adel ThL 48. **d** 49 **p** 50 Adel. C of St Marg Woodville 49-51; Miss Chap Balaklava w Owen and Hamley Bridge 50-51; P-in-c 51-53; R of Minlaton 53-57; Gawler 57-62; P-in-c of Mallala 57-62; R of Wagga Wagga 62-81; Archd of Wagga Wagga 62-81; Consultant in Ch Development Dio C & Goulb from 81. *Jamieson House, Constitution Avenue, Reid, ACT, Australia 2601.*

OSBORNE, Malcolm. b 19. AKC 50. St Bonif Coll Warm 50. **d** 50 **p** 51 Portsm. C of St Mary Portsea 50-58; Chap St James's Hosp Balham 58-60; V of Whitehawk 60-65; R of St Mawnan w St Michael's 65-69; Chap at Ankara 69-70; Radcliffe Infirm Ox 71; P-in-c of Marsworth and Cheddington w Mentmore Dio Ox from 72; R of Cheddington w Mentmore and Marsworth 76-79; P-in-c of Seer Green Dio Ox from 79. *Vicarage, Long Grove, Seer Green, Beaconsfield, Bucks, HP9 2YN.* (Beaconsfield 5013)

OSBORNE, Ralph. b 38. Univ of Kent Dipl Th 80. Clifton Th Coll 63. **d** 66 Hulme for Man **p** 67 Man. C of Harpurhey 66-68; St Sav Chorlton-on-Medlock 68-71; Wilmington 71-73; V of Cray St Mary w St Paulinus (St Paulinus to 77) Dio Roch from 74. *Vicarage, Main Road, St Paul's Cray, Orpington, Kent, BR5 3EN.* (Orpington 27697)

OSBORNE, Reginald Eric. Bp's Univ Lennox BA 34. **d** 33 **p** 34 Ott. L to Offic Dio Ott 33-34; C of St John Smith's Falls 34-37; I of Cobden 37-41; R of N Gower 41-43; C of St Matt Ott 43-47; R of St Martin Tor 47-51; St Matt Ott 51-73; Hon Can of Ott 58-61; Archd of Ott 62-73. *Apt 707, 2050 De Maisonneuve West, Montreal, PQ, Canada.*

OSBORNE, Canon Robert John. b 45. Univ of Sask BA 72. Em & St Chad's Coll Sktn LTh 71. **d** and **p** 72 Carib. C of St Paul's Cathl Kamloops Dio Carib from 72; Dom Chap to Bp of Carib 75-80; Can of Carib from 80. *3041 Westsyde Road, Kamloops, BC, V2B 7G1, Canada.*

OSBORNE, Canon Robin Orbell. b 29. Univ of Leeds BA (Th) 54. Coll of Resurr Mirfield 52. **d** 54 **p** 55 Pet. C of All H Wellingborough 54-58; Oxhey (in c of All SS) 60-61; V of Woburn 61-65; R of Battlesden w Pottesgrove 61-65; V of

Cheshunt Dio St Alb from 65; RD of Cheshunt 70-81; Hon Can of St Alb from 76. *Vicarage, Church Gate, Cheshunt, Herts.* (Waltham Cross 23121)

OSBORNE-BROWN, William St Andrew. Moore Th Coll Syd 34. **d** and **p** 38 Nel. C of Cobden w Runanga 38; P-in-c 38-39; V 39-44; Chap NZEF 41-44; C of St Silas Waterloo 45; R of St Alb Corrimal 45-50; Narrabeen Dio Syd from 50. *St Faith's Rectory, McTier Street, Narrabeen, NSW, Australia 2101.* (98-8146)

OSBOURNE, David John. b 56. Linc Th Coll 78. **d** 79 **p** 80 Dur. C of Houghton-le-Spring 79-82; St Jo Bapt Spalding Dio Linc from 82. *44 West Parade, Spalding, Lincs.* (0775 61486)

OSCROFT, Robert James. St Francis Th Coll Brisb 41. **d** 46 **p** 47 Brisb. C of St Luke Toowoomba 46-47; St Paul's Cathl Rockptn 48; M St Andr Bush Bro from 49; P-in-c of Dawson Valley Distr 49-50; P-in-c of Gracemere Distr Rockptn 59-60; R of Blackall 60-63; V of Buninyong 64-67; R 67-69; Merbein 69-75; Perm to Offic Dio St Arn 75-76. *Box 319, Yenda, NSW, Australia 2681.*

OSEI, Robert. **d** 76 **p** 77 Kum. P Dio Kum. *Box 144, Kumasi, Ghana.*

OSEMBO, Carson. Newton Coll Dogura 71. **d** 70 **p** 73 Bp Kendall for Papua. P Dio Papua. *Anglican Church, Manau, via Popondota, Papua New Guinea.*

OSEMBO, Kenneth. **d** 72 **p** 73 Bp Kendall for Papua. P Dio Papua. *Maramathana, via Dogura, Papua New Guinea.*

OSEMEIKHIAN, Elijah Aikhairaiyi Masterwell. b 13. **d** 73 **p** 74 Benin. P Dio Benin. *St John's Church, Box 13, Idumebo, Ebpoma, Nigeria.*

OSGATHORP, Canon Herbert James. b 1897. Univ of Man BA 22. Linc Th Coll 22. **d** 24 **p** 25 Newc T. C of Morpeth 24-29; V of Ulgham 29-36; Walker 36-44; Bedlington 44-69; Surr 37-69; RD of Bedlington 56-69; Hon Can of Newc T 60-69; Can (Emer) from 69. *9 Towers Avenue, Jesmond, Newcastle-upon-Tyne, NE2 3QE.* (Newc T 812115)

OSGERBY, John Martin. b 34. Univ of Sheff BSc 56, PhD 59. Linc Th Coll 75. **d** 77 Doncaster for Sheff **p** 78 Sheff. C of Rotherham 77-80; P-in-c of W Bessacarr Conv Distr Doncaster Dio Sheff from 80. *39 Sturton Close, W Bessacarr, Doncaster, S Yorks.* (Doncaster 58487)

OSGOOD, Graham Dean. b 39. BSc (Lon) 62. St Jo Coll Bramcote ALCD 71. **d** 71 **p** 72 Ches. C of Bebington 71-76; V of Gee Cross Dio Ches from 76. *Gee Cross Vicarage, Hyde, Chesh.* (061-368 2337)

OSHO-WILLIAMS, George Nathaniel. **d** 43 **p** 45 Sier L. P Dio Sier L. *Parsonage, Wilberforce, Sierra Leone.*

OSINOWO, Emanuel Osiyemi. **d** 44 **p** 45 Lagos. P Dio Lagos. *Box 2, Ijebu-Igbo, Nigeria.*

OSIRU, Elkana Matthew. St Paul's Th Coll Limuru. **d** 56 **p** 58 Momb. P Dio Momb 56-61; Dio Nak from 61. *Box 272, Kitale, Kenya.*

OSISANYA, Canon Noah Ebun-Olorun Adenuga. BA (2nd cl Hist) Lon 53. **d** 64 **p** 65 Lagos. P Dio Lagos 64-74; Dio Ondo 74-76; Dio Ijebu from 76; Can of Ijebu from 77; Exam Chap to Bp of Ijebu from 81. *St Matthew's Church, Ojowo, Ijebu-Igbo, Nigeria.*

OSMAN, David Thomas. b 49. Univ of Bradf BTech 72. Trin Coll Bris 75. **d** 78 **p** 79 Dir. C of Stranton 78-81; St Jas Denton-Holme City and Dio Carl from 81. *118 Dalston Road, Carlisle, Cumb.* (Carl 22938)

OSMAN, Ernest. b 35. St Aid Coll 61. **d** 64 Middleton for Man **p** 65 Man. C of Ch Ch Heaton 64-68; V of St Pet Farnworth 68-77; St Martin Dio Lich from 77. *Vicarage, St Martin's, Oswestry, Salop, SY11 3AP.* (Chirk 2295)

OSMERS, John Robert. Univ of NZ BA 57, MA (2nd cl) 58. Coll of Resurrection Mirfield 59. **d** 61 Sheff **p** 62 Bp Gerard for Sheff. C of Rawmarsh 61-65; Asst P of Mohales Hoek 65-66; R of Quthing 66-72; Masite Dio Les from 72. *Masite Mission, PO Maseru, Lesotho.* (Morija 217)

OSMOND, Alec Edward. b 15. AKC 38. **d** 39 **p** 40 Ex. C of Plympton St Mary 39-45; Berry Pomeroy w Bridgetown (in c of Bridgetown) 45-49; V of Woodbury w Exton Dio Ex from 49. *Woodbury Vicarage, Exeter, Devon.* (Woodbury 32315)

OSMOND, David Methuen. b 38. Qu Coll Birm 75. **d** 77 **p** 78 Birm. C of Yardley 77-80; V of Wythall Dio Birm from 80. *27 Lea Green Lane, Wythall, Birmingham, B47 6HE.* (Wythall 823381)

OSMOND, Oliver Robert. b 44. Ch Coll Cam BA 66, MA 70. Trin Coll Tor STB 69. Cudd Coll 66. **d** 69 **p** 70 Tor. C of St John York Mills 69-71; R of N Essa Ont 71-74; Westmorland and Assoc P of St Paul Sackville NB 74-77; P-in-c of St Francis Lower Sackville NS 77-81; V of John Keble Ch Mill Hill Dio Lon from 81. *Vicarage, Deans Lane, Edgware, Middx, HA8 9NT.* (01-959 1312)

OSMOND, Thomas Lindbergh. b 37. **d** 74 Mack. C of Aklavik 74-77; I of Fort McPherson Dio Arctic from 77. *Box 65, Fort McPherson, NWT, Canada.*

OSO, Michael. b 18. **d** 80 **p** 81 Egba. P Dio Egba. *24 Iporo Ake Street, Abeokuta, Nigeria.*

OSODO, John. St Phil Bible Sch Maseno 69. **d** 69 Maseno. d Dio Maseno 69-71; Dio Maseno S 71-77. *Box 33, Ndhiwa, Kenya.*

OSSAI, Mbanugo. b 35. **d** 73 **p** 74 Benin. P Dio Benin. *BCM Parsonage, c/o PA Aboh-Kwale, Nigeria.*

OSSELTON, Richard Scupham. b 20. Univ of Lon BA (2nd cl Engl) 51. Qu Coll Birm 52. **d** 53 **p** 54 Ripon. C of Bramley 53-59; V of Wortley 59-66; Gt w L Ouseburn (and Marton w Grafton from 71) 66-79; C-in-c of Marton w Grafton 66-71; R of Wickmere w Itteringham and L Barningham Dio Nor from 79. *Rectory, Itteringham, Norf, NR11 7AX.* (Saxthorpe 360)

OSSORY, FERNS AND LEIGHLIN, Lord Bishop of. *See* Cashel.

OSSORY, Archdeacon of. *See* Willis, Ven Frederick Andrew Graves.

OSSORY, Dean of. (Vacant).

OST, Audley Desmond. AKC 38. **d** 38 **p** 39 Chelmsf. C of E Hanningfield 38-39; Euston w Barnham and Fakenham 39-41; LPr Dio St E 41-44; R of E Hanningfield Dio Chelmsf from 44. *East Hanningfield Rectory, Chelmsford, Essex, CM3 5AF.* (Chelmsf 400217)

OSTLE, Arthur John. McGill Univ Montr 32. St Aid Coll 38. **d** 38 **p** 39 Liv. C of St Luke Gt Crosby 38-40; CF (EC) 40-46; C of Sephton 46-47; V of St Mary Bootle 47-51; I of Chesley w Tara 52-56; C of St Paul's Cathl Lon Ont 56-60; R of St Andr Lon Ont 60-76. *Apt 311, 400 Sandringham Crescent, London, Ont., Canada.*

OSTLER, Kenneth George. b 48. Univ of K Coll BA 72. Trin Coll Tor 74. **d** 75 Fred **p** 76 Alg. On leave 75-76; I of Manitowaning 76-78; C of H Trin Sault Ste Marie Dio Alg from 78. *1561 Queen Street East, Sault Ste Marie, Ont, Canada.*

OSTLING, William Harold. Moore Th Coll Syd ACT ThL 57. **d** and **p** 57 Syd. C of Miranda 57; C-in-c of Gymea Provisional Distr 58-62; R of Roseville E 62-69; Chap RN Shore Hosp and L to Offic Dio Syd 69-72; R of Marrickville Dio Syd from 72. *90 Petersham Road, Marrickville, NSW, Australia 2204.* (55-0315)

OSUIGWE, Cornelius Ogechukwu Nneka. b 39. Trin Coll Legon 69. **d** 73 **p** 74 Niger. P Dio Niger. *Iyi Enu Hospital, Box 67, Ogidi, ECS, Nigeria.*

OSUNLUSI, Canon Ezekiel Bankole. b 21. Im Coll Ibad 61. **d** 63 **p** 64 Lagos. P Dio Lagos 63-76; Dio Egba from 76; Hon Can of Egba from 79. *Vicarage, Oke Odan, Egbado, Nigeria.*

OSUNTUSA, Samuel Makinde. b 34. **d** 76 **p** 80 Ibad. P Dio Ibad. *St John's Church, Eruwa, via Ibadan, Nigeria.*

OSWALD, John Edward Guy. b 39. Late Exhib of Qu Coll Cam 1st Cl Th Trip pt i 61, BA (2nd cl Or Stud Trip pt i) 63, MA 67. Ridley Hall Cam. **d** 68 **p** 69 Bris. C of St Paul Chippenham w Langley Burrell 68-72; Hengrove 72-75; C-in-c of Hardenhuish 75-79; St Mich Kington 75-79; Team V of St Paul Chippenham w Hardenhuish and Langley Burrell and Kington St Mich Dio Bris from 79. *Hardenhuish Vicarage, Malmesbury Road, Chippenham, Wilts.* (Chippenham 50787)

OSWALD, Ronald William. b 17. Trin Coll Dub BA (Resp) 38, MA 53, Div Test 55, BD 57, 1st cl Or Lang Mod 59. **d** 55 **p** 56 Dub. C of St Geo Dub 55-58; St Jas Taunton 58-60; Hon Chap Br Embassy Ch and Hd of CMJ Tunis 60-67; V of Castle Hedingham 67-80; R of Panfield Dio Chelmsf from 80. *Panfield Rectory, Braintree, Essex.* (Braintree 24615)

OSWALD, William Harrison. b 01. Qu Coll Cam 2nd cl Hist Trip pt i 21, BA (3rd cl Hist Trip pt ii) 22, 2nd cl Th Trip pt ii 24, MA 26. Ridley Hall Cam 22. **d** 24 **p** 25 S'wark. C of Ch Ch Gipsy Hill 24-26; CMS Miss Panyam 26-30; Exam Chap to Bp of Lagos 32 and 35; Warden Melville Hall St Andr Coll Oyo 30-36; V of St Mark Oulton Broad 36-41; R of H Trin Heigham 41-50; Proc Conv Nor 45-50; R of Angmering 50-69; Perm to Offic Dio Bris from 69. *Glebe Cottage, Latton, Swindon, Wilts.* (Swindon 750384)

OSWIN, Frank Anthony. b 43. Chich Th Coll 69. **d** 71 Bp McKie for Cov **p** 72 Cov. C of St Nich Radford Cov 71-74; Shrub End 74-76; V of Layer-de-la-Haye 76-80; St D Eastwood Dio Chelmsf from 80. *400 Rayleigh Road, Eastwood, Leigh-on-Sea, Essex.* (Southend 523126)

OTAALA, Washington. **d** 62 **p** 63 Soroti. P Dio Soroti. *Box 9, Kumi, Uganda.*

OTAMIRI, Jonathan Irondi. b 28. Im Coll Ibad 72. **d** 72 **p** 73 Nig Delta. P Dio Nig Delta. *St John's Parsonage, c/o Ndele PA, via Ahoada, Nigeria.*

OTARI, Lancelot. **d** 71 Bp Ambo for Papua **p** 71 Papua. P Dio Papua. *Box 26, Popondota, Papua, New Guinea.*

OTEDO, Androniko. **d** 62 Maseno. d Dio Maseno. *Akoko, PO Sare, S Nyanza, Kenya.*

OTHIENO-OLUOCH, Simeon. b 25. **d** 70 **p** 72 Momb. P Dio Momb 70-76; Maseno S from 77. *Ramula, PO Box 353, Luanda, Kenya.*

OTI, John Chukuneyeremaka. Trin Coll Umuahia. **d** 56 **p** 57 Niger. P Dio Niger 56-59 and 63-73; Nig Delta 59-61; Dio Ow from 74; Hon Can of Niger 73-74. *Parsonage, Orogwe, Nigeria.*

OTIANG, Hebron Amos. St Phil Bible Sch Maseno 69. **d** 69 **p** 70 Maseno. P Dio Maseno 69-71; Dio Maseno S from 71. *Box 25, Ndori, Kenya.*

OTIENO, John. St Phil Coll Kongwa 64. **d** 65 **p** 66 Vic Nyan. P Dio Vic Nyan 68-69; Dio Maseno S from 70. *Box 136, Siaya, Kenya.*

OTIENO, Noah Reuben. St Paul's Dioc Div Sch Limuru. **d** 53 **p** 55 Momb. P Dio Momb 53-61; Dio Maseno from 61. *Rengea, PO Yala, Kenya.*

OTIENO-ANGELA, Johannes. b 52. St Paul's Coll Limuru 74. **d** 76 Maseno S. d Dio Maseno S. *PO Box 11, Maseno, Kenya.*

OTIKOR, Owen Adango. b 27. St Paul's Coll Awka. **d** 60 **p** 61 Nig Delta. P Dio Nig Delta. *PO Box 10, Elele, Nigeria.*

✠ **OTIM, Right Rev Melkizedek.** b 35. Bp Tucker Th Coll Mukono 67. **d** 69 **p** 70 N Ugan. P Dio N Ugan 69-75; Cons Ld Bp of Lango in St Paul's Cathl Nam 11 Jan 76 by Abp of Ugan; Bps of Bukedi, Ank, Bunyoro, Busoga, Mbale, Nam, N Ugan, Ruw, W Bugan, Buj and Buye. *PO Box 6, Lira, Lango, Uganda.*

OTOHA, Franklin. **d** 71 Bp Ambo for Papua **p** 71 Papua. P Dio Papua. *Box 26, Popondota, Papua, New Guinea.*

OTT, Gavin Melville. St Francis Coll Brisb ACT ThL (2nd cl) 65. **d** 65 **p** 66 Brisb. C of All SS Chermside Brisb 65-68; Bundaberg 68-71; R of Dimboola 70-74; L to Offic Dio Rockptn 74-81; R of Bowen Dio N Queensld from 81. *Box 32, Bowen, Queensland, Australia.*

OTTAWA, Lord Bishop of. *See* Lackey, Right Rev Edwin Keith.

OTTAWA, Dean of. *See* Downey, Very Rev Thomas Edward.

OTTAWAY, Bernard Wyndham. b 15. Keble Coll Ox BA 38, MA 43. Cudd Coll 38. **d** 39 **p** 40 Chelmsf. C of St Luke Vic Dks 39-40; St Alb Mart Westcliff-on-Sea 40-43; Upminster 43-47; V of St Pet Becontree 47-55; R of Loughton 55-71; Birdbrook w Sturmer (w Ridgewell and Ashen from 76) 71-81; C-in-c of Ashen w Ridgewell 74-76; P-in-c of Farnham Dio Chelmsf from 81. *Farnham Rectory, Bishops Stortford, Herts, CM23 1HR.* (Farnham 318)

OTTAWAY, Michael John. b 17. Merton Coll Ox 3rd cl Mod Hist 39, BA 40, MA 44. Cudd Coll 40. **d** 41 **p** 42 Chelmsf. C of St Marg Leytonstone 41-45; Kettering 45-48; Kibworth 48-49; V of Wolvercote City and Dio Ox 49-76; Team V (w Summertown) from 76. *Wolvercote Vicarage, Oxford.* (Oxford 55640)

✠ **OTTER, Right Rev Anthony.** b 1896. Trin Coll Cam BA 20, MA 25. Westcott Ho Cam 24. **d** 25 Lon **p** 26 Willesden for Lon. C of H Trin St Marylebone 25-31; Lon Sec SCM 26-31; V of Lowdham w Gunthorpe 31-49; Chap of Lowdham Grange Borstal Inst 31-45; Ed Southw Dioc Magazine 41-46; Hon Can of Oxton Secunda Pars in Southw Cathl 42-49; RD of Gedling 46-49; Cons Ld Bp Suffr of Grantham in S'wark Cathl 18 Oct 49 by Abp of Cant; Bps of Nor; S'wark; Linc; Southw; and Wakef; Bps Suffr of Woolwich; Grimsby; Willesden; and Jarrow; and Bp Western; res 65; R of N and S Stoke w Easton 49-65; Dean of Stamford 49-71; Preb of Brampton in Linc Cathl 50-65; Can (Emer) from 65; Asst Bp in Dio Linc from 65. *The Old Rectory, Belton, Grantham, Lincs.* (Grantham 2061)

OTTER, Anthony Frank. b 32. Kelham Th Coll 54. **d** 59 **p** 60 Lon. C of St Jo Evang Bethnal Green 59-63; Aylesbury (in C of St Pet) 63-68; V of Hanslope w Castlethorpe 68-77; P-in-c of S w N Moreton Dio Ox 77-79; R (w Aston Tirrold) from 79; Aston Tirrold 77-79. *South Moreton Rectory, Didcot, OX11 9AF.* (Didcot 812042)

OTTER, William Rodney. NZ Bd of Th Stud LTh 67. Coll Ho Ch Ch. **d** 57 Bp Rich for Wel **p** 57 Wel. C of Ch Ch Wanganui 57-61; V of Raetihi 61-64; CF (NZ) 64-70; L to Offic Dio Ch Ch 64-70; V of Cheviot 70-76; Greytown 76-80; Silverstream Dio Wel from 80. *13 Terminus Street, Silverstream, NZ.* (282-203)

OTTEWELL, Lewis. b 12. St Aid Coll 33. **d** 37 **p** 39 Ripon. C of Ch Ch U Armley 37-40; Hunslet 40; CF (EC) 40-46; Chap Miss to Seamen 47-54; R of Rochford (w Eastham from 59) 54-64; RD of Lindridge 57-64; V of St Francis Dudley 64-74. *65 Aldersley Avenue, Tettenhall, Wolverhampton, Staffs.*

OTTEY, John Leonard. b 34. Univ of Nott BA (1st cl Th) 70. K Coll Lon and Warm AKC (1st cl) 60. **d** 61 **p** 62 Linc. C of Grantham 61-64; R of Keyworth Dio Southw from 70; C-in-c of Stanton-on-the-Wolds Dio Southw from 71. *Keyworth Rectory, Nottingham.* (Plumtree 2017)

OTTLEY, David Ronald. Univ of Lanc BA 78. Sarum Wells Th Coll. **d** 81 Man. C of St Clem Urmston Dio Man from 81. *157 Stretford Road, Urmston, Manchester, M31 1IW.* (061-748 8411)

OTTLEY, Ernest Sydney. Univ of Tor BA 32. Wycl Coll Tor LTh 32. **d** and **p** 32 Niag. C of Ascen Hamilton 32-35; St Paul Tor 35-37; R of Streetsville 37-42; Ch Ch Edmon 42-60; Exam Chap to Bp of Edmon 43-60; Can of Edmon 49-60; I of Our Sav Don Mills Tor 60-65; R 65-71. *6 Marmion Avenue, Toronto 12, Ont., Canada.*

OTTO, Francis James Reeve. Late Exhib of New Coll Ox BA (2nd cl Engl) 64, 2nd cl Th and MA 68. Wells Th Coll 68. **d** 69 **p** 70 Truro. C of St Steph-by-Saltash 69-72; Newquay 72-73; V of Lanteglos-by-Fowey 73-79; St Goran w Caerhays Dio Truro from 79. *Vicarage, Goran, St Austell, Cornw.* (Mevagissey 842437)

OTTOSSON, Krister Alexander. b 39. Univ of Lon BSc (2nd cl Econ) 61. Ch Div Sch Calif MDiv 65. Wycl Hall, Ox 62. **d** 65 Dur **p** 66 Jarrow for Dur. C of Chester-le-Street 65-68; NW Area Sec Chr Educn Movement 68-71; Sec Educn Dept BCC 71-76; Lay Tr Adv Dio Dur 76-81; Adult Educn Officer C of E Bd of Educn from 81. *Church House, Dean's Yard, SW1P 3NZ.* (01.222 9011)

OTTREY, Raymond Ivor. Univ of Sask BA 67. Em Coll Sktn LTh 67. **d** 67 **p** 68 Sktn. I of Battleford Dio Sktn from 67; I of Meota 67-71; Swift Current 71-77; St Barn Medicine Hat Dio Calg from 77. *635-4th Street SE, Medicine Hat, Alta, Canada.*

OTUBELU, Christopher Otubelu. b 26. Trin Coll Umuahia 71. **d** 73 **p** 74 Niger. P Dio Niger. *Emmanuel Church, Adazienu, Njikoka Division, ECS, Nigeria.*

✠ **OTUBELU, Right Rev Gideon Nweke.** Univ Coll Ibad BA (Lon) 52, BD (Lon) 55. Ridley Hall Cam 57. **d** 58 Chelmsf for Cant for Col Bp **p** 59 Niger. P Dio Niger 58-69; Can of Niger 67-69; Cons Ld Bp of Enugu in St Geo Cathl Freetown Sier L 29 June 69 by Abp of W Afr; Bps of Sier L, Gambia and Guildf; Asst Bps of Sier L and Accra. *Bishop's House, Uwani, Box 418, Enugu, Nigeria.* (Enugu 3088)

OTUBUE, Thomas Chenekohwiroro. b 33. Im Coll Ibad 66. **d** 69 **p** 70 Benin. P Dio Benin. *Anglican Parsonage, PA Agbarha-Otor, via Ughelli, Mid-West State, Nigeria.*

OTUKOL-EKITELA, John. b 52. Bp Tucker Coll Mukono 77. **d** 80 Bukedi. d Dio Bukedi. *PO Box 170, Tororo, Uganda.*

OTUOGBAI, Samuel Iseemi. Melville Hall Ibad 45. **d** 47 **p** 48 Lagos. P Dio Lagos 47-52; Dio Ondo-B 52-65; Dio Benin from 65. *PO Box 82, Benin City, Nigeria.*

OUDU, Saradu. b 53. St Phil Coll Kongwa 77. **d** 80 Boga-Z. d Dio Boga-Z. *E.A.Z. Bunia, BP 154, Bunia, Haut-Zaire.*

OUKO, George Jacob. b 33. **d** 76 **p** 77 Maseno S. P Dio Maseno S. *PO Box 35, Ahero, Kenya.*

OULDS, Terence James Gregory. b 49. St Paul's Coll Grahmstn. **d** 75 **p** 76 Natal. C of St Paul Durban 75-77; V of Eltham 78-81; Johnsonville Dio Wel from 81. *22 Bassett Road, Johnsonville, NZ.* (788-384)

OULESS, John Michael. b 22. AKC 49. Ridley Hall Cam 49. **d** 50 **p** 51 Pet. C of St Mary Dallington Northampton 50-55; Evesham 55-56; R of Halewood 56-62; V of Southwick w Glapthorn 62-71; Chap Glapthorn Road Hosp Oundle 63-71; R of Cogenhoe Dio Pet from 71; Whiston Dio Pet from 71. *Cogenhoe Rectory, Northampton, NN7 ILS.* (Northampton 890338)

OURUMU, Fenekasi. Buwalasi Th Coll. **d** 61 **p** 62 Mbale. P Dio Mbale 61-73; Dio Bukedi from 73. *PO Box 4010, Pallisa, Uganda.*

OUSKUN, Johnson Caleb Matthias. b 43. St Jo Coll Winnipeg 78. **d** 79 **p** 80 Keew. C of St Jas Thompson Dio Keew from 79. *72 Lynx Crescent, Thompson, Man, R8N 0L8, Canada.*

OUTHWAITE, Stephen Anthony. b 35. Wells Th Coll 62. **d** 64 **p** 65 Win. C of Ascen Bitterne Pk 64-67; Min of Tadley St Mary Conv Distr 67-71; R of Milton Dio Win from 71. *Rectory, New Milton, Hants., BH25 6QN.* (New Milton 615150)

OUTRAM, David Michael. b 42. Univ Coll of N Wales Ban BA 77, BD 79. Coll of the Resurr Mirfield 79. **d** 80 **p** 81 Ban. C of Llandegfan w Beaumaris and Llanfaes w Penmon and Llangoed w Llanfihangel Dinsylwy Dio Ban from 80. *22 Mill Lodge, Llandegfan, Menai Bridge, Anglesey, Gwyn.*

OUTRAM, Edmund Paul Augustus Charles. b 03. Chich Th Coll 26. **d** 29 Bp King for Roch **p** 30 Roch. C of Stone 29-32; Swaffham 33-37; Perm to Offic at N Mundham w Hunston 37-39; V 39-68; CF (EC) 43-46; Perm to Offic Dio Portsm from 68. *49 Oxford Road, Southsea, Hants, PO5 1NP.* (Portsmouth 811348)

OUTTA, Julius Jacob. St Phil Coll Kongwa 63. **d** 64 Centr Tang **p** 64 Vic Nyan. P Dio Vic Nyan 64-72. *Biharamulo, Tanzania.*

OVENDEN, Edward Clifford Lewis. b 10. Chich Th Coll 31. **d** 33 **p** 34 Lon. C of St Mary Virg Kenton 33-40; Epping 40-47; V of Aveley 47-55; Epping 55-75. *1 Highlands Drive, St Leonards-on-Sea, Sussex.* (Hastings 425194)

OVENDEN, John Anthony. b 45. Open Univ BA 80. Sarum Wells Th Coll 71. **d** 74 Doncaster for Sheff Sheff **p** 75 Sheff. C of Handsworth 74-77; Uckfield 77-80; Prec and Sacr of Ely Cathl from 80; P-in-c of Stuntney Dio Ely from 80. *Precentor's House, The College, Ely, Cambs, CB7 4JU.* (Ely 2526)

OVENDEN, Nigel John. b 23. Ripon Hall Ox 58. **d** 60 **p** 61 St Alb. C of St Paul Bedford 60-64; V of N Baddesley 64-73; R of Compton w Shawford Dio Win from 73. *Compton Rectory, Winchester, Hants, SO21 2AS.* (Twyford 713189)

OVENDEN, Richard Reginald. b 1900. Sarum Th Coll 24. **d** 27 Bris for Sarum **p** 28 Sarum. C of Mere 27-30; Milford-on-Sea 30-36; V of Stourpaine 36-54; R of Steepelton Iwerne 36-53; Durweston 53-54; V of W Alvington 54-69. *12 Rodney Road, Backwell, Bristol, BS19 3HW.*

OVERELL, Alan Herbert. b 25. St Edm Hall Ox 2nd cl Engl 48, BA 49, Dipl Th 50, MA 53. St Steph Ho Ox 49. **d** 51 **p** 52 Lich. C of St Mary and St Chad Longton 51-56; St Pet Plymouth (in c of St Matt Stonehouse) 56-60; R of St Alb Cheetwood Man 60-65; Sacred Trin Salford 65-70; Exam Chap to Bp of Man 65-77; Sen Chap Univ and Poly of Leeds from 71; C-in-c of Em Leeds Dio Ripon from 71. *7 North Grange Mount, Leeds, LS6 2BY.* (Leeds 785830)

OVEREND, Barry Malcolm. b 49. AKC and BD 71. St Aug Coll Cant 71. **d** 72 **p** 73 Glouc. C of Nailsworth w Inchbrook and Shortwood 72-74; Asst Master Henry Gotch Sec Sch Kettering 74-75; C of Ch Ch High Harrogate 75-78; V of Collingham w Harewood Dio Ripon from 78. *Collingham Vicarage, Wetherby, W Yorks, LS22 5AU.* (Collingham Bridge 73975)

OVERINGTON, David Vernon. b 34. ALCD 60. **d** 60 Tonbridge for Cant **p** 61 Roch. C of Ch Ch w H Trin Penge 60-62; Lenton 62-65; PC of Brackenfield w Wessington 65-71; C-in-c of Cubley w Marston Montgomery 71-76; R of Bridgetown 76-79; Denmark Dio Bunb from 79. *Rectory, Denmark, W Australia 6333.*

OVERTHROW, Terence Reginald Charles. b 36. Bris & Glouc Th Course 76. **d** and **p** 79 Glouc (APM). C of St Geo Lower Tuffley City and Dio Glouc from 79. *33 Courtfield Road, Quedgeley, Gloucester, GL2 6UQ.*

OVERTON, Charles Henry. b 51. CCC Ox BA 74, MA 77. Fitzw Coll Cam BA 79. Ridley Hall Cam 77. **d** 80 **p** 81 Roch. C of Tonbridge Dio Roch from 80. *14 Salisbury Road, Tonbridge, Kent.* (Tonbridge 355200)

OVERTON, John Eric. b 15. Worc Coll Ox BA 39, MA 44. St Steph Ho Ox 39. **d** 41 Ripon **p** 42 Ox. C of H Spirit Beeston Hill Leeds 41-42; Wantage 42-48; St Jo Evang Newbury (in c of St Geo Wash Common) 48-55; V of Downton 55-59; Shiplake 59-67; St Barn w St Paul Ox 67-80. *43 Court Road, Malvern, Worcs.*

OVERTON, Keith Charles. b 28. E Anglian Min Tr Course 78. **d** 81 Ely (apm). C of Duxford Dio Ely from 81. *12 Greenacres, Duxford, Cambridge, CB2 4RB.*

OVERTON, Thomas Vincent Edersheim. b 34. New Coll Ox 2nd cl Cl Mods 56, BA (3rd cl Lit Hum) 58, Dipl Th 59, MA 61. Wycl Hall Ox 58. **d** 60 Lon **p** 61 Kens for Lon. C of H Trin Hampstead 60-63; St Geo Leeds 63-67; Perm to Offic Dio Lon 68; Miss in Thailand 71-78; R of Knossington w Cold Overton 78-81; V of Owston w Withcote 78-81; R of St Jo Bapt and St Leon Bedford Dio St Alb from 81. *St John's Rectory, St John's Street, Bedford.* (Bedf 54818)

OVERY, Arthur William. b 19. Nor Ordin Course 73. **d** 76 Lynn for Nor **p** 77 Nor (APM). Hon C of St Marg Lowestoft Dio Nor from 76. *The Hollies, Warren Road, Lowestoft, Suffolk, NR32 4QD.*

OWADARA, Josiah Olorummoroti. b 32. **d** 74 **p** 76 Ondo. P Dio Ondo. *St John's Vicarage, Aiyeteju Ikeram, via Ikare Akoko, Nigeria.*

OWADASA, Isaac. Im Coll Ibad 67. **d** 71 **p** 72 Ondo. d Dio Ondo. *Box 4, Owo, Ondo State, Nigeria.*

OWADAYO, Matthew Oluremilekun. Univ of Ibad BA 71. Im Coll Ibad Dipl Th 64. **d** 64 **p** 65 Ondo. P Dio Ondo. *University of Jos, Plateau State, Nigeria.*

OWADE, Ven Charles. **d** 62 **p** 65 Maseno. P Dio Maseno 62-71; Dio Maseno S from 71; Archd Dio Maseno S from 78. *Box 121, Kisii, Kenya.*

OWALA-KOLA, David. b 48. Bp Tucker Coll Mukono 70. **d** 72 **p** 73 Nam. P Dio Nam 72-75; Dio Maseno S from 75. *PO Box 380, Kisumu, Kenya.*

OWEN, Chan Cledwyn. b 15. Univ of Wales, BA 36. Dorch Miss Coll 36. **d** 38 Mon for Ban **p** 39 Bp Wentworth-Shields for Ban. C of Llanwnog 38-40; Llandudno 40-47; R of Henllan 47-57; V of Llanfair Caereinion w Llanllugan 57-67; Surr from 57; R of Newtown w Llanllwchaiarn and Aberhafesp 67-74; Cursal Can of Radulphi Birkenhead in St A Cathl 69-76; V of Llangollen w Trevor Traian and Llantysilio Dio St A from 74; Chan and Preb from 76. *Vicarage, Abbey Road, Llangollen, Clwyd.* (Llangollen 860231)

OWEN, David Thomas. b 03. St D Coll Lamp BA 25. St Mich Coll Llan 25. **d** 26 Llan for St D **p** 27 St D. C of Laugharne 26-35; V of Llanddewi Velfrey w Crinow R 35-73. *Milton Bank, Laugharne, Dyfed.* (Laugharne 214)

OWEN, David William. b 31. Down Coll Cam 2nd cl Cl Trip pt i 54, BA (2nd cl Th Trip pt ia) 55, MA 58. Linc Th Coll 55. **d** 57 Hulme for Man **p** 58 Man. C of St Phil w St Steph Salford 57-61; Grantham (in c of Ascen Harrowby) 61-65; V of Messingham w E Butterwick 65-70; V of Spilsby w Hundleby 70-77; R of Aswardby w Sausthorpe 70-77; Langton-by-Partney w Sutterby 70-77; C-in-c of Halton Holgate 71-77; Gt Steeping and Firsby 75-77; L Steeping 75-77; R of Louth Dio Linc from 77. *Rectory, Louth, Lincs.* (Louth 603213)

OWEN, Derek Malden. b 29. Oak Hill Coll 74. **d** 76 Chich **p** 77 Lewes for Chich. C of H Trin Eastbourne 76-78; Walthamstow (in c of St Steph) 78-79; Team V desig 79-81; R of Ditcheat & E Pennard w Pylle Dio B & W from 81. *Rectory, Ditcheat, Shepton Mallet, Somt.* (Ditcheat 429)

OWEN, Canon Derwyn Randulph Grier. Trin Coll Tor BA 36, MA 37, LTh 40, PhD 41. CCC Ox BA 38, MA 42. St Jo Coll Winnipeg Hon DD 58. Wycl Coll Tor Hon DD 59. K Coll Halifax, NS Hon DD 59. Em Coll Sktn Hon DD 64. Bp's Coll Lennox Hon DCL 65. **d** 41 **p** 42 Tor. C of St Cuthb Tor 41-57; Lect Trin Coll Tor 41-57; Provost from 57; Chap CASF 41-46; Can of Tor from 69. *Trinity College, Toronto, Ont, Canada.*

OWEN, Edward Goronwy. b 01. Univ of Wales, BA 21, 3rd cl Phil 22. Jes Coll Ox BA (2nd cl Th) 28, MA 35. **d** 28 **p** 29 St A. C of Colwyn Bay 28-31; Colwyn 31-36; V of Cwm 36-39; Llansantffraid-Glyn-Ceiriog 39-54; RD of Llangollen 51-54; Edeirnion 58-63; Llanrwst 66-71; R of Corwen w Rhug 54-64; Cursal Can of David Ap Howell in St A Cathl 61-69; Can (Emer) from 69; Preb of Meifod and Sacr 69-71; V of Llanrhos 64-71. *44 Dinerth Road, Colwyn Bay, Clwyd.*

OWEN, Edward Joseph. b 1892. St D Coll Lamp LDiv 29. **d** 29 St D for Llan **p** 30 Mon for Llan. C of Pontlottyn 29-31; Netherton Dudley 31-41; R of Romsley 41-56; V of Crowle 56-63. *166 Bromyard Road, Worcester, WR2 5EE.* (Worcester 422628)

✠ **OWEN, Right Rev Edwin.** b 10. TCD Cluff Mem Pri 31, Hebr Pri 32, BA (Mod Hist and Polit Sc Mod) 32, MA 41. **d** 34 **p** 35 Dub. C of Glenageary 34-36; Ch Ch Leeson Pk Dub 36-38; Min Can of St Patr Cathl Dub 35-36; Chan V 36-38; Succr 38-42; I of Birr w Eglish 42-57; RD of Ely O'Carroll 46-57; Can of Rath in Killaloe Cathl 54-57; R of Killaloe and Dean of Killaloe 57-72; Dioc Sec of Killaloe and Kilfenora 57-72; RD of U O'Mullod and of Traderry 57-60; Kilfenora and of Corkovasker 60-72; Cons Ld Bp of Killaloe in St Flannan's Cathl Killaloe 25 Jan 72 by Abp of Dub; Bps of Cash; Cork; Oss; and Lim; Bp of United Dios of Limerick w Killaloe 76; res 81. *5 Frankfort Avenue, Rathgar, Dublin 6, Irish Republic.*

OWEN, Ekpenyong. **d** 76 Nig Delta. d Dio Nig Delta. *3 Infantry Division Headquaters, Nigerian Army, Jos, Nigeria.*

OWEN, Eric Alexander. b 06. Late Scho and Exhib of St D Coll Lamp BA (1st cl Hist) 26, BD 35. St Mich Th Coll Llan 28. **d** 29 **p** 30 Ban. C of Criccieth 29-32; Conway w Gyffin 32-37; Harlech w Llanfair-juxta-Harlech 37-39; Llandegfan w Beaumaris 39-42; R of Bryncoedifor 42-51; CMS Area Sec to Dios S & M, Ban, St A and Archds of Ches and Cardigan 51-61; V of Birkenhead 61-69; Middlewich 69-71. *Portland, Cae Mair, Beaumaris, Anglesey.* (Beaumaris 565)

OWEN, Ethelston John Charles. b 20. St D Coll Lamp BA 42. **d** 48 St D for St A **p** 49 St A. C of Gresford 48-50; Abergele 50-55; R of Llanfynydd 55-58; Chap Mersey Miss to Seamen 58-60; V of Clehonger 60-80; R of Eaton Bp 60-80. *3 Yew Tree Close, Kingstone, Hereford, HR2 9HG.* (Golden Valley 250785)

OWEN, George Charles. b 14. Linc Th Coll. **d** 52 **p** 53 Linc. C of St Swith Linc 52-55; PC of Sutton St Edm 55-59; V of Lavington (or Lenton) w Osgodby Keisby Hanby and Ingoldsby 59-75; C-in-c of Bassingthorpe w Westby and Bitchfield 59-60; V 60-75; C-in-c of Boothby Pagnell 59-60; V 60-75; C-in-c of Burton-le-Coggles 59-60; V 60-75; R of Bassingham 75-79; Aubourn w Haddington 75-79; Carlton-le-Moorland w Stapleford 75-79; Skinnand 75-79; Thurlby w Norton Disney 75-79; Chap HM Pris Beckingham from 81. *6 Hilldales, Metheringham, Lincoln.*

OWEN, Gerald. St D Coll Lamp BA 49. **d** 50 **p** 51 St A. C of Minera 50-54; V of Foxt w Whiston 54-57; St Mich Shrewsbury 57-63; Wednesbury Dio Lich from 63; Surr from

67. *Vicarage, Wednesbury, Staffs.* (Wednesbury 0378)

OWEN, Gordon Campbell. b 41. Univ of Wales (Bangor) BD 76. **d** 81 Ban. C of Ban Cathl from 81. *6 Belmont Avenue, Bangor, Gwyn, LL57 2HT.*

OWEN, Gordon Percival. b 07. Univ of Wales 24. Clifton Th Coll 32. **d** 34 **p** 35 Lich. C of St Matt Wolverhampton 34-37; Cannock (in c of Chadsmoor) 37-42; C-in-c of Shawbury 42-43; C of St Luke Eltham 44-49; Harpenden (in c of All SS) 49-51; V of Stopsley 51-55; C of All SS Bedford 55-57; V of Humbleton w Elsternwick 57-58; V of Burton Pidsea 57-58; C of St Jas Enfield Highway 59-60; Chap St Mich Home Axbridge 60-61; Commun of St Anne Emsworth 61-62; C of Bladon w Woodstock 62-64; V of Wootton 64-76; Perm to Offic Dio Ox from 76. *16 Hill View Lane, Wootton, Boars Hill, Oxford, OX1 5JT.* (Oxford 730742)

OWEN, Griffith Oliver. b 1892. Jes Coll Ox 14. **d** 17 **p** 19 St A. C of Llanycil w Bala 17-19; Abergele 19-25; C-in-c of Llanfihangel-Glyn-Myfyr 25-28; Abp's Messenger 28-33; V of Brynymaen (w Trofarth from 49) 33-53. *Penrhyn, West Parade, West Shore, Llandudno, Gwyn.*

OWEN, Harry Dennis. b 47. Oak Hill Coll 73. **d** 76 Kens for Lon **p** 77 Lon. C of Ch Ch Fulham 76-81; V of St Mark Byker City and Dio Newc T from 81. *37 Lesbury Road, Heaton, Newcastle-on-Tyne 6.* (Newc T 656912)

OWEN, James. b 31. Trin Hall Cam 2nd cl Hist Trip pt i 52, BA (2nd cl Hist Trip pt ii) 53, MA 58. Ely Th Coll. **d** 56 **p** 57 Lon. C of St Mary The Boltons Kens 56-60; All SS Clifton 60-62; Chap Jes Coll Cam 62-66; Repton Sch 66-67; Asst Chap Univ of Nottm 67-69; Chap and Southw Dioc Lect 69-74; V of St Mary L Cam Dio Ely from 74; Asst Chap O St John from 76. *Little St Mary's Vicarage, Cambridge, CB3 9EX.* (0223-350733)

OWEN, James Thomas. b 48. Linc Th Coll 77. **d** 80 **p** 81 Edmonton for Lon. C of Palmers Green Dio Lon from 80. *509 Green Lanes, Palmers Green, N13 4BS.* (01-886 8174)

OWEN, Ven John Bradley. b 14. McGill Univ BA 38. Montr Dioc Th Coll LTh 41, BD 43. **d** and **p** 41 Montr. C of Ch of Advent Westmount Montr 41-42; Exam Chap to Bp of Athab 42-44; I of Goodwin 42-45; Quyon 45-50; R Grande Prairie 50-57; Hon Can of Athab 52-57; I of Watrous 57-62; R of Carp Ott 62-71; Dioc Missr and Sec-Treas Dio Athab 71-77; Dioc Regr 77-79; Archd of Athab 71-79; Archd (Emer) from 79. *RR1, Weir, Quebec, Canada, J0T 2V0.*

OWEN, John Glyndwr. b 20. St D Coll Lamp BA 48. **d** 49 **p** 50 Llan. C of Merthyr Tydfil 49-52; CF 52-58; C of St Sav St Alb 58; C of Sundon w Streatley 58-60; V of St Barn Pendleton 60-61; Walford w Bishopswood 61-71; R of Honington w Sapiston (and Troston from 73) 71-81. *93 Mill Lane, Sawston, Cambridge.*

OWEN, John Peregrine. b 19. Univ of Wales BA (2nd cl Hist) 41. St Mich Coll Llan 41. **d** 43 **p** 44 St D. C of Llandilo Fawr 43-46; Skewen 46-56; V of Nantymoel 56-59; R of Dowlais 59-76; Surr from 61; RD of Merthyr Tydfil 69-76; R of Wenvoe w St Lythans Dio Llan from 76. *Rectory, Wenvoe, S Glam.* (0222-593392)

OWEN, John Edward. b 52. Middx Poly BA 75. Sarum Wells Th Coll BTh 81. **d** 81 Cant. C of S Ashford Dio Cant from 81. *37 Clockhouse, Ashford, Kent, TN23 2HD.* (Ashford 31644)

OWEN, Canon Lawrence William. Univ of W Ont BA 40. **d** 41 Hur **p** 41 Chich for Col Bp. On Mil Service 41-46; I of Bervie Kingarf and Kinlough 46-48; Port Elgin Southampton 48-51; Simcoe 51-70; Can of Hur 69-79; Can (Emer) from 79; R of New St Paul Woodstock 70-76; Dover 76-79. *Apt 502, 770 Wonderland Road, London, Ont, Canada.*

OWEN, Lionel Edward Joseph. b 19. SOC 66. **d** 69 Dover for Cant **p** 70 Cant. C of Hythe 69-73; Deal 73-75; V of Teynham Dio Cant from 75; RD of Ospringe from 80. *Teynham Vicarage, Sittingbourne, Kent.* (Teynham 521238)

OWEN, Preb Noah. b 10. St D Coll Lamp BA 34. **d** 34 Taunton for B & W **p** 35 Bp de Salis for B & W. C of Winford 34-40; Wellow 40-44; CF (EC) 44-47; V of Dulverton 47-64; RD of Wiveliscombe 52-64; Surr 53-77; R of Chew Stoke (w Nempnett Thrubwell from 73) 64-77; C-in-c of Norton Malreward 67-77; V 77; C-in-c of Nempnett Thrubwell 71-73; RD of Chew Magna 71-77; Preb of Wells Cathl 76-77; and from 80; Perm to Offic Dio B & W from 79. *West Grove, Popleswell, Crewkerne, Somt, TA18 7ES.* (Crewkerne 74023)

OWEN, Owen Hugh. Univ of Wales, BA 47. St Steph Ho Ox 47. **d** 49 **p** 50 Ban. C of Llanfairisgaer 49-53; Chap RAF 53-77; Hon Chap to HM the Queen 76-77; V of L Houghton w Brafield-on-the-Green Dio Pet from 77. *Brafield Parsonage, Northampton, NN7 1BA.* (Northamptom 890885)

OWEN, Owen Thomas. b 19. Univ of Liv 37. St Chad's Coll Dur Dipl Th 45. Univ of Lanc MA 77. **d** 45 **p** 46 Dur. C of Easington Colliery 45-48; Chap and Tutor St Jo Coll York and L to Offic Dio York 48-51; V of Hedgefield 51-56; R of St Mary-le-Bow w St Mary L Dur 56-60; Chap to Univ of Dur 56-60; R of Clifton w Glapton 60-62; Chap and Sen Lect Nottm Tr Coll 60-62; Sen (Prin from 65) Lect City of Liv Coll of Higher Educn Liv and L to Offic Dio Liv from 62. *1 Oakwood Road, Halewood, Liverpool 26.* (051-486 8672)

OWEN, Peter Russell. b 35. Univ of Wales Dipl Th 63. St Mich Coll Llan. **d** 63 **p** 64 St A. C of Wrexham 63-64; Connah's Quay 64-65; Asst Chap Mersey Miss to Seamen 66-69; C of All SS U Norwood (in c of St Marg) 69-72; Hawarden (in c of St Mary Broughton) 72-75; R of Nannerch w Ciclain (and Rhydymwyn from 79) Dio St A from 75. *Nannerch Rectory, Mold, Clwyd, CH7 5RD.* (Hendre 207)

OWEN, Phillip Clifford. b 42. G and C Coll Cam BA 65, MA 69. Ridley Hall Cam 71. **d** 73 **p** 74 St E. C of Stowmarket 73-76; Headley Hants (in c of St Mark Bordon) Dio Guildf 76-81; Team V from 81. *29 Hollybrook Park, Bordon, Hants, GU35 0OL.* (Bordon 4200)

OWEN, Raymond Philip. b 37. Univ of Man BSc (3rd cl Chem Eng) 60. Chich Th Coll 65. **d** 67 Pontefract for Wakef **p** 68 Wakef. C of Elland 67-70; Lindley w Quarmby 70-73; V of St John Bradshaw, Halifax 73-80; Industr Chap Teesside Industr Miss from 80. *6 Albert Road, Eaglescliffe, Stockton, Cleve, TS16 0DD.* (Eaglescliffe 782073)

OWEN, Richard Ellis. b 12. Clifton Th Coll 48. **d** 50 Derby **p** 51 Bp O'Ferrall for Derby. C of Littleover 50-53; Whitchurch Salop 53-55; R of Elkstone w Syde and Winstone 55-61; V of Gt and L Badminton w Acton Turville 61-71; Kemble w Poole Keynes 71-73; V of Pebworth w Dorsington Dio Glouc from 73. *Pebworth Vicarage, Stratford-on-Avon, Warws, CV37 8XG.* (Stratford/Avon 270245)

OWEN, Canon Richard Llewelyn. b 27. St D Coll Lamp BA (2nd cl Welsh) 51. St Mich Coll Llan. **d** 53 **p** 54 Ban. C of Holyhead 53-57; Portmadoc 57-59; R of Llanfechell w Bodewryd Rhosbeirio and Llanfflewin 59-67; V of Penrhyndeudraeth w Llanfrothen 67-77; R of Llangefni w Tregaean W Llangristiolus w Cerrig Ceinwen Dio Ban from 77; Dioc Sec for World Miss from 77; Can of Ban from 82. *Rectory, Llangefni, Gwynedd, LL7 7EA.* (Llangefni 723104)

OWEN, Robert David Glyn. b 06. Bps' Coll Cheshunt, 37. **d** 39 **p** 40 St A. C of Cerrig-y-Druidion w Llangwm and Llanfihangel-glyn-myfyr 39; C-in-c of Llannefydd 46-50; V of Capel Garmon 50-54; C of Norton 54-58; R of Grindon 58-63; V of Butterton 58-63; St Paul Burslem 63-67. *55 Grove Road, Fenton, Stoke-on-Trent, Staffs, ST4 3AY.* (Stoke/Trent 322312)

OWEN, Robert Glynne. b 33. Univ of Wales 53. St Mich Coll Llan 56. **d** 58 Ban **p** 59 St A for Ban. C of Machynlleth w Llanwrin 58-62; Llanbeblig w Caernarvon 62-65; V of Carno w Trefeglwys 65-69; Hon C of Dorking 69-75. *77 Ffordd Pentre, Mold, Clwyd, CH7 1UY.* (Mold 2038)

OWEN, Robert Lee. b 56. Univ of Wales (Cardiff) BD 79. Qu Coll Birm 79. **d** 81 St A. C of Holywell Dio St A from 81. *The Close, Well Street, Holywell, Clwyd, CH8 7PL.*

OWEN, Ronald Alfred. b 44. Sarum Wells Th Coll 80. **d** 81 Tewkesbury for Glouc. C of Wotton St Mary Without (or Longlevens) Dio Glouc from 81. *68 Windermere Road, Longlevens, Gloucester, GL2 0LZ.* (Glouc 22069)

OWEN, Ronald Roy. b 25. Bp's Univ Lennoxville BA 47. **d** 77 Queb. Hon C of All SS Heref Dio Queb from 77. *Bishop's College School, Lennoxville, PQ, Canada.*

OWEN, Stanley Alfred George. b 17. Worc Ordin Coll 57. **d** 59 **p** 60 Birm. C of Bickenhill w Elmdon Dio Birm 59-60; R of Elmdon and V of Bickenhill from 60. *Elmdon Rectory, Tanhouse Farm Road, Elmdon, Solihull, W Midl, B92 9EY.* (021-743 6336)

OWEN, Canon Thomas John. b 1893. Western Coll Cotham Bris 14. **d** 31 **p** 32 Mon. [f Congregational Min] C of Risca 31-35; C of Cathl Ch Newport 35; Chap 35-39; V of Llantilio-Pertholey 39-67; Ed Mon Dioc Year Book 40-66; RD of Abergavenny 62-67; Hon Can of Mon from 64; L to Offic Dio Mon from 67. *7 Grosvenor Road, Abergavenny, NP7 6AH.* (Abergavenny 3126)

OWEN, Preb Thomas Robert. b 07. Trin Coll Cam 2nd cl Hist Trip pt i 30, BA (2nd cl Hist Trip pt ii) 31, MA 40. Bps' Coll Cheshunt 31. **d** 33 **p** 34 York. C of South Bank 33-37; Heavitree 37-40; Chap RAFVR 40-46; V of H Trin Barnstaple 46-52; Chap N Devon Infirm Barnstaple 48-52; V of Braunton w Saunton and Knowle 52-67; Yelverton 67-74; RD of Barnstaple 58-67; Preb of Ex from 59. *Tresco, Oakland Avenue, Barnstaple, N Devon.* (Barnstaple 3014)

OWEN, Tuddyd. Welsh Ch Scho Univ of Wales, BA 35. St Mich Coll Llan 36. **d** 36 **p** 37 Ban. C of Llanbeblig 36-40; CF (EC) 40-48; R of Llechylched w Ceirchiog (and Llanfihangel-yn-Nhowyn from 52) 48-57; V of Towyn 57-77. *Box 1424, Valley Woods, Stellarton, NS, Canada.*

OWEN, William. OBE 71. Univ of Lon BD 55. Tyndale Hall Bris 27. **d** 30 Bris for Col Bp **p** 31 U Nile. BCMS Miss Lake Rudolf Distr 30-34; Taposa 34-36; Nasokol 36-37; Chap Nyanza 37; CMS Miss Butere 38-39; Maseno 39-44; furlough 45-46; Actg Prin St Paul's Dioc Div Sch Limuru 46-48; RD of Southern Highlands 47-48; Prin Embu Normal

Sch 49-53; Chap Kangaru Sch 54-58; Hd Master 58-60; Njiri's High Sch 61-70; Starehe Boys Centre Nai 74-81; L to Offic Dio Ft Hall 61-64; Dio Mt Kenya 64-70; Exam Chap to Bp of Maseno 61-70; L to Offic Dio Nai 70-81. *51 Bridge Down, Bridge, Nr Canterbury, Kent, CT4 5BA.*

OWEN, William David. b 17. Univ of Wales BA (2nd cl Phil) 39. Wycl Hall Ox 40. **d** 41 **p** 42 St D. C of Fishguard 41-45; Old Swinford 45-49; Min of Astwood Bank w Crabbs Cross Conv Distr 49-50; V 50-63; St Jo Bapt Claines Dio Worc from 63. *Claines Vicarage, Worcester.* (Worcester 51251)

OWENS, Ashby. b 43. Univ of Man BA 65. Fitzw Coll Cam BA (3rd cl Th Trip pt ii) 67, MA 71. Ridley Hall Cam 65. **d** 68 **p** 69 Ches. C of St Phil Alderley Edge Chorley 68-71; Ch Ch Barnston Ches 71-74; V of Alsager Dio Ches from 74. *37 Eaton Road, Alsager, Stoke-on-Trent, ST7 2BQ.*

OWENS, Christopher Lee. b 42. Linc Th Coll 66. **d** 69 Lon **p** 70 Stepney for Lon. C of H Trin Dalston 69-72; St Mark (in c of St Francis) N End Portsea 72-81; Team V of E Ham Dio Chelmsf from 81. *70 William Morley Close, Priory Road, East Ham, E6 1QZ.* (01-472 1067)

OWENS, Ernest Amman. St D Coll Lamp BA 42. Ridley Hall, Cam. **d** 44 **p** 45 St A. C of St Giles Wrexham 44-47; Ulverston 47-50; V of Drigg (w Irton from 55) 50-57; Tonge w Alkrington 57-59. *15 The Mall, Sandown, IW.*

OWENS, Philip Roger. b 47. Univ of Wales (Ban) Dipl Th 70. Wells Th Coll 71. **d** 71 **p** 72 St A. C of Colwyn Bay 71-74; Wrexham 74-77; Team V 77-80; P-in-c of Yoxford Dio St E from 80. *Yoxford Vicarage, Saxmundham, Suff.* (Yoxford 247)

OWENS, Canon Rodney Stones. b 19. Univ of Lon BA 53. Bps' Coll Cheshunt. **d** 50 **p** 51 Roch. C of Darenth 50-51; Wokingham 51-55; R of Gt Livermere w Troston 55-59; C-in-c of Ampton w L Livermere 55-59; V of St Aug of Hippo Ipswich 59-65; Asst Master Ipswich Sch 65-74; L to Offic Dio St E 65-74; R of Coddenham (w Gosbeck and Hemingstone w Henley from 75) Dio St E from 74; Gosbeck 74-75; C-in-c of Hemingstone w Henley 74-75; RD of Bosmere from 78; Hon Can of St E from 81. *Rectory, School Road, Coddenham, Ipswich, IP6 9PS.* (Coddenham 419)

OWENS, Stephen Graham Frank. b 49. Ch Coll Cam BA 71, MA 75. Qu Coll Birm 73. **d** 75 **p** 76 Worc. C of St Mich AA Norton 75-81. *Address temp unknown.*

OWERRI, Lord Bishop of. *See* Nwankiti, Right Rev Benjamin Chukuemeka.

OWERS, Donald William. b 50. Ridley Coll Melb 79. **d** 80 Armid. C of W Tamworth Dio Armid from 80. *18 Church Street, West Tamworth, NSW, Australia 2340.*

OWERS, Ian Humphrey. b 46. Em Coll Cam 3rd cl Th Trip pt i 66, BA (2nd cl th Trip pt ii) 68, MA 72. Westcott Ho Cam 71. **d** 73 **p** 74 S'wark. C of St Sav Denmark Pk Peckham 73-77; V 77-82; Ch Ch w St Andr & St Mich E Greenwich Dio S'wark from 82. *52 Earlswood Street, SE10.*

OWINO, Oswald Samuel. b 38. Trin Coll Nai 72. **d** 71 **p** 72 Nai. P Dio Nai. *Box 41584, Nairobi, Kenya.*

OWITI, Peter. St Paul's Dioc Div Sch Limuru, 48. **d** 49 **p** 51 Momb. P Dio Momb 49-61; Dio Maseno from 61. *PO Ng'iya, Kenya.*

OWOLABI, Joseph Oladunjoye. Im Coll Ibad 58. **d** 61 **p** 63 Ibad. P Dio Ibad. *Igangan, Nigeria.*

OWOLABI, Canon Theophilus Adeleke. b 18. Melville Hall, Ibad. **d** 52 **p** 53 W Afr. P Dio Lagos 52-76; Dio Egba from 76; Hon Can of Egba from 76. *Holy Trinity Church, Okenla Ifo, Nigeria.*

OWOPETU, Nathaniel Olusanya. b 21. **d** 81 Ilesha. d Dio Ilesha. *St Stephen's Anglican Church, Ere-Ijesha, via Ilesha, Nigeria.*

OWORI, Ezekiel Matthew. **d** 44 **p** 46 U Nile. P Dio U Nile 44-61; Dio Mbale 61-72; Dio Bukedi 72-74. *Box 225, Tororo, Uganda.*

OWST, Clifford Samuel. b 09. FCII 34. Linc Th Coll 77. **d** 77 Grimsby for Linc **p** 78 Linc. Hon C of St Mary Mablethorpe (w Trusthorpe from 78) Dio Linc from 77. *Tennyson's Cottage, Quebec Road, Mablethorpe, Lincs, LN12 1LU.* (Mablethorpe 2369)

OWSTON, Ronald Howard Thomas. Univ of Tor BA 55. Trin Coll Tor LTh 58, STB 59. **d** 57 **p** 58 Tor. C of St Jo Bapt Norway, Tor 57-60; R 65-68; R of St Chris-on-the-Heights Tor 61-65. *51 Bond Street, Toronto 5, Canada.*

OWU, Simeon Olusegun. b 47. **d** 76 Ijebu. d Dio Ijebu. *St Andrew's Church, PO Box 155, Imobu, Ijebu-Ode, Nigeria.*

OXBROW, Mark. b 51. Univ of Reading BSc 72. Fitzw Coll Cam BA 75; MA 79. Ridley Hall Cam 73. **d** 76 **p** 77 Roch. C of Ch Ch Luton 76-80; Team V of the Epiph (in c of St Hugh) City and Dio Newc T from 80. *14 Thropton Crescent, Gosforth, Newcastle upon Tyne, NE3 3HT.* (0632 858792)

OXENFORTH, Colin Bryan. b 45. St Chad's Coll Dur BA 67, Dipl Th 69. **d** 69 **p** 70 Roch. C of St Andr Bromley 69-72; Nunhead 72-76; V of St Marg Toxt Dio Liv from 76. *St Margaret's Vicarage, Princes Road, Liverpool, L8 1TG.* (051-709 1526)

OXFORD, Lord Bishop of. *See* Rodger, Right Rev Patrick Campbell.

OXFORD, Archdeacon of. *See* Weston, Ven Frank Valentine.

OXFORD, CHRIST CHURCH, Dean of. *See* Heaton, Very Rev Eric William.

OXFORD, Leonard. b 47. Univ of WI Barb LTh 81. Codr Coll Barb 78. **d** and **p** 81 Guy. C of St Marg Berbice Dio Guy from 81. *St Margaret's Vicarage, 78 Village, Corriverton, Corentyne, Skeldon, Berbice, Guyana.*

OXFORD, Victor Thomas. b 41. Chich Th Coll 65. **d** 68 **p** 69 Lich. C of Norton-le-Moors 68-73; Norton Canes 73-75; Cannock (in c of St Aidan W Chadsmoor) 75-76; Team V 77-81; V of Chesterton Dio Lich from 81. *Chesterton Vicarage, Newcastle-under-Lyme, Staffs, ST5 7HJ.* (Newc-u-Lyme 562479)

OXLEY, Christopher Robert. b 51. Univ of Sheff BA 73. Univ of Ox BA (Th) 78. Wycl Hall Ox 76. **d** 79 **p** 80 Sheff. C of Greasborough Dio Sheff from 79. *35 Acorn Croft, Munsbrough, Rotherham, S Yorks.*

OXLEY, Herbert. b 02. Univ of Lon BSc 31. Bps' Coll Cheshunt. **d** 54 Reading for Cant **p** 55 Ox. C of Crowthorne 54-57; V of Clanfield (w Kelmscot from 60) 57-62; R of Lerwick 62-67; P-in-c of Burravoe 62-67. *Nant Logyn, Trecastle, Brecon, Powys.*

OXLEY, John Rice. Ridley Coll Melb 58. ACT ThL (2nd cl) 60. **d** 61 **p** 62 Melb. C of Kingsville w Spotswood 61-63; St Silas Geelong 63-65; Dept of Chaps Dio Melb 65-67; and from 70; V of Carrum w Seaford 67-70. *48 Suffolk Road, Surrey Hills, Vic 3127, Australia.*

OYAKO, Erick. **d** and **p** 75 Bunyoro. P Dio Bunyoro. *Box 17, Kigorobya, Waaki, Hoima, Uganda.*

OYAMO, Wilson. St Phil Coll Maseno 69. **d** 69 Maseno **p** 71 Nak. P Dio Nak. *St Andrew's Church, Kapenguria, Kitale, Kenya.*

OYAT, Festo. Buwalasi Th Coll 52. **d** 54 **p** 56 U Nile. P Dio U Nile 54-61; Dio N Ugan from 61. *St Philip's, Gulu, Uganda.*

OYATOYE, John Adeyemi Igbayiloye. Im Coll Ibad 62. **d** 64 **p** 65 Lagos. P Dio Lagos. *Ibefun, PO Box 22, Ijebu-Ode, Nigeria.*

OYEBADE, Jacob. b 33. **d** 73 **p** 74 Ibad. P Dio ibad. *St Matthew's Vicarage, Kutayi, c/o Apatere PA, Ibadan, Nigeria.*

OYEBAJO, Emmanuel Olajide. b 15. Melville Hall Ibad. **d** 51 **p** 52 W Africa. P Dio Lagos 51-62 and from 72; Dio Ondo 62-67; Dio Ekiti 67-68; Dio Ibad 68-72. *PO Box 72, Oshodi, Nigeria.*

OYEBODE, Gabriel Oluwasola. b 38. Howard Univ Washington DC MDiv 76, DMin 78. Im Coll Ibad Dipl Th 70. **d** 69 **p** 70 Ondo. P Dio Ondo 69-73; on leave. *c/o Howard University, Washington DC, WA 20001, USA.*

OYEDEJI, Canon Claudius Oyewo. Melville Hall, Ibad 37. **d** and **p** 38 Lagos. P Dio Lagos 38-52; Dio Ibad 52-62; Hon Can of Ibad from 62. *St Andrew's Vicarage, Bamgbola, Igbo-Elerin, Apatere PO, Ibadan, Nigeria.*

OYEDIRAN, Christopher Bamgboye. Melville Hall, Ibad 54. **d** 56 **p** 58 Ibad. P Dio Ibad. *Inisha, Ibadan, Nigeria.*

OYEDOKUN, Theophilus Oyebanji. b 42. Im Coll Ibad 73. **d** 76 Ibad. d Dio Ibad. *St Barnabas Anglican Church, Apomu, via Ibadan, Nigeria.*

OYEJOLA, James Oladejo. b 24. **d** 75 **p** 76 Ilesha. P Dio Ilesha. *St Bartholomew's Church, Odo, Nigeria.*

OYEKANMI, Joshua Ojo. b 27. **d** 72 **p** 74 Ibad. P Dio Ibad. *Box 102, Ile-Ife, Nigeria.*

OYEKANMI, Samuel Adegboye. b 22. **d** 75 **p** 76 Ibad. P Dio Ibad. *St Matthew's Church, Kutayi, c/o Apatere P.A., Ibadan, Nigeria.*

OYELADE, Amos Adebayo. Im Coll Ibad 56. **d** 58 **p** 60 Ibad. P Dio Ibad. *St Paul's Vicarage, Iseyin, Oyo, Nigeria.*

OYELADE, Solomon Olaife. Univ of Ife BA 68. Dipl Th (Lon) 62. Im Coll Ibad. **d** 61 **p** 63 Ibad. P Dio Ibad; Exam Chap to Bp of Ibad 72-76. *c/o PO Box 125, Ibadan, Nigeria.*

OYELEYE, Amos Oyewo. Im Coll Ibad 56. **d** 57 **p** 58 Ibad. P Dio Ibad. *PO Box 63, Ogbomoshe, Nigeria.*

OYELEYE, Stephen Olamilekan. b 46. Im Coll Ibad 73. **d** 76 **p** 77 Ibad. P Dio Ibad. *University of Ife, Nigeria.*

OYET, Julius Isotuk. b 39. Im Coll Ibad Dipl Th 70. **d** 70 **p** 72 Nig Delta. P Dio Nig Delta. *Box 3, Bonny, Nigeria.*

OYET, Paulo. Buwalasi Th Coll. **d** 64 **p** 65 N Ugan. P Dio N Ugan. *PO Aboke, Lira, Uganda.*

OYETADE, Ven Ezekiel Adigun. Melville Hall, Ibad. **d** 49 **p** 50 Lagos. P Dio Lagos 49-52; Dio Ibad 52-61; Dio N Nig 61-80; Archd of Jos from 72; Exam Chap to Bp of N Nig 72-80. *PO Box 12, Jos, Nigeria.*

OYINLADE, David Kehinde. b 43. Im Coll Ibad 78. **d** 81 Egba. d Dio Egba. *Christ Church, Ilaro, Nigeria.*

OYINLADE, Ven Moses David Oluwafemi. Melville Hall Ibad. **d** 51 Lagos **p** 52 Ibad. P Dio Ibad 51-69; Dio Ondo from 69; Hon Can of Ibad 65-69; Archd of Akoko 69-76; Akure from 77; Exam Chap to Bp of Ondo from 74. *Box 34, Akure, Nigeria.* (Akure 2204)

OYINLOLA, Festus Aderibigbe Sunday. b 40. **d** 75 Ibad. d Dio Ibad. *St John's Church, Oba, via Oshogbo, Nigeria.*

OYINLOLA, Joshua Sunday. b 55. Im Coll Ibadan 75. **d** 78 **p** 79 Ijebu. P Dio Ijebu. *St Michael's Church, Owu, via Ijebu-Ode, Ogun State, Nigeria.*

OYOO, Barnaba. **d** 54 Centr Tang **p** 57 Bp Omari for Centr Tang. P Dio Centr Tang 54-63; Dio Vic Nyan from 63. *Box 5, Tarime, Tanzania.*

OYUKO, Michael. **d** 77 Lango. d Dio Lango. *PO Iceme, Lira, Uganda.*

OYWAYA, Canon Esau. St Paul's Dioc Div Sch Freretown 28. **d** 29 **p** 33 Momb. P Dio Momb 33-59; TCF 40-46; RD of Southern Highlands 48-50; N Nyanza 50-59; Hon Can of Momb 49-59; Nak from 64; Archd of Eldoret 59-61; Nak 61-64; Exam Chap to Bp of Nak 61-76; Miss W Pokot 62-64. *PO Box 16, Maseno, Kenya.*

OZANNE, John Bowstead Sausmarez. St Francis Coll Brisb ACT ThL 64. **d** 65 **p** 66 Carp. C of Darwin 64-68; Mudgee 68-72; R of Moama 73-74. *PO Box 96, Moama, NSW, Australia 2739.*

OZIGBO, Emmanuel Chukwudike Benito. b 33. St Paul's Coll Awka 62. **d** 76 **p** 77 Enugu. P Dio Enugu. *St Andrew's Church Adani, Box 16, Nsukka, Enugu, Nigeria.*

OZIMATI, Stanley. **d** 65 **p** 67 N Ugan. P Dio N Ugan 65-69; Dio M & W Nile from 69. *Box 37, Arua, Uganda.*

OZOKO, Chrstopher Ngwu. b 30. Trin Coll Legon 69. **d** 72 **p** 73 Enugu. P Dio Enugu. *St Paul's Parsonage, Oji River, via Enugu, ECS, Nigeria.*

P

PAAN, Peter. **d** 38 **p** 43 Hong. BCMS Miss Dio Hong from 38. *Diocesan Office, Hong Kong.*

PA-AN, Lord Bishop of. *See* Kyaw Mya, Right Rev George.

PACE, Lindsay Young. Univ of Melb BA 59. ACT ThL 46. **d** 47 **p** 48 Melb. C of Ch of Epiph Northcote 47-48; St John Heidelberg 48-49; Min of Lara 49-54; St Silas N Geelong 54-58; Ferntree Gully 58-63; I of Balaclava 63-69; Hampton 69-79; Heathmont Dio Melb from 79. *207 Canterbury Road, Heathmont, Vic, Australia 3135.* (870 7119)

PACEY, Edgar Prentice. b 29. Univ of Edin MA 50. Edin Th Coll 52. **d** 54 **p** 55 Glas. C of H Trin Motherwell 54-56; St Mary's Cathl Glas 56-61; R of Coatbridge 61-70; Perm to Offic Dio Glas 70-77; C of St Martin City and Dio Glas from 77. *25 Midlothian Drive, Glasgow, G41 3QX.* (041-632 7451)

PACEY, Ronald Grant. b 43. St Jo Coll Morpeth 76. **d** 76 **p** 77 Graft. C of Lismore 76-79; R of Bonalbo Dio Graft from 79. *Box 58, Bonalbo, NSW, Australia 2470.*

PACK, Wilfred George. b 02. Chich Th Coll 26. **d** 28 **p** 29 Win. C of Weeke 28-35; St Clem Bournemouth 35-37; St Luke Bournemouth 37-39; V of Vernham Dean w Linkenholt R 39-45; Ringwood w Bisterne (and Harbridge to 57) 45-61; St Mary Bourne (w Litchfield to 68; w Woodcott 68-70) 61-70; C-in-c of Woodcott 66-68. *Otway, North Street, Rogate, Petersfield, Hants, GU31 5BH.* (Rogate 473)

PACKER, James. b 21. St Mich Coll Llan 63. **d** 65 Burnley for Blackb **p** 66 Blackb. C of St Geo Chorley 65-68; P-in-c of St Marg Conv Distr Ingol 68-70; Chap HM Pris Preston 70-73; Gartree 73-77; Wymott, Leyland from 77; L to Offic Dio Leic 73-77. *c/o HM Prison, Wymott, Ulnes Walton, Leyland, Lancs.*

PACKER, James Innell. b 26. CCC Ox BA 48, MA 52, D Phil 55. Wycl Hall, Ox 49. **d** 52 Bp Linton for Birm **p** 53 Birm. C of St Jo Bapt Harborne 52-54; Lect Tyndale Hall Bris and LPr Dio Bris 55-61; Libr Latimer Ho Ox 61-62; Warden 62-69; L to Offic Dio Ox 66-69; Prin Tyndale Hall Clifton Bris 70-72; L to Offic Dio Bris 70-78; Assoc Prin Trin Coll Bris 72-78; Prof of Hist Th Regent Coll Vanc from 78. *2130 Wesbrook Mall, Vancouver, BC, Canada.*

PACKER, John Richard. b 46. Keble Coll Ox BA (2nd cl Mod Hist) 67, 2nd cl Th 69. Ripon Hall Ox 67. **d** 70 **p** 71 S'wark. C of St Pet St Helier 70-73; Chap St Nich Abingdon 73-77; Tutor Ripon Hall Ox 73-75; Ripon Coll Cudd 75-77; V of Wath-upon-Dearne w Adwick-upon-Dearne Dio Sheff from 77. *Vicarage, Barnsley Road, Wath-upon-Dearne, Rotherham, S63 6PY.* (Rotherham 872299)

PACKER, Canon John William. b 18. Late Exhib of Univ of Lon BA (2nd cl Hist) 40, BD (2nd cl) 41. AKC (1st cl Th) 41, MTh (Ch Hist) 48. **d** 41 **p** 42 Southw. C of Attenborough w Bramcote 41-44; Asst Master Lanc Royal Gr Sch 44-46; and 47-49; Warden of Whalley Abbey and Asst Dir of Relig Educn Dio Blackb 46-47; Lect in Relig Educn Univ of Leeds 50-53; Hd Master Canon Slade Gr Sch Bolton and L to Offic Dio Man 53-77; Hon Can of Man 75-78; Can (Emer) from 78; Perm to Offic Dio Cant from 78. *Netherbury, Meadow Close, Bridge, Canterbury, Kent, CT4 5AT.* (0227 830364)

PACKER, Roger Ernest John. b 37. Pemb Coll Cam 2nd cl Hist Trip pt i 59, BA (3rd cl Th Trip pt ia) 60, MA 64. ARCO 59. Cudd Coll 60. **d** 62 **p** 63 Bris. C of Chippenham 62-65; Caversham 65-70; R of Sandhurst Dio Ox from 70. *155 High Street, Sandhurst, Camberley, Surrey, GU17 8HR.* (Yateley 872168)

PACKER, Thomas Leonard Graham. b 15. AKC 42. **d** 42 **p** 43 Chelmsf. C of H Trin Barkingside 42-49; Camberley w Yorktown 49-54; Mayfield 54-67; P-in-c of St Andr Portslade 67-76; R of Eastergate 78-79; Barnham and Eastergate Dio Chich from 79. *Eastergate Rectory, Barnham Road, Barnham, PO22 0EQ.* (Yapton 552077)

PACKHAM, Herbert John Victor. b 16. Trin Coll Dub BA and Div Test 39, MA 46. **d** and **p** 40 Lim. C of Ballymacelligott and Dioc C of Ardf and Agh 40-42; I of Kilnaughton w Ballylongford and Kilfergus 42-43; C of Ch Ch Leeson Pk Dub 43-52; V of Rathcoole w Newcastle Lyons 52-63; Chap Peamount Sanat 52-63; I of Harold's Cross 63-73; C-in-c of Castledermot Dio Glendal from 73. *Castledermot, Athy, Co Kildare, Irish Republic.* (0503 44121)

PACKWOOD, John William. b 35. Kelham Th Coll 55. **d** 59 Warrington for Liv **p** 60 Liv. C of St Marg Anfield 59-63; Ribbleton 63-65; V of St Pet Accrington 65-73; Asst Chap HM Pris Man 73; Chap HM Pris Preston 73-77; HM Pris Gartree 77-79; L to offic Dio Leic 77-79; V of Kilby 79-81; Wistow w Newton Harcourt 79-81; P-in-c of Glen Magna w Stretton Magna 81. *Address temp unknown.*

PADDISON, Michael David William. b 41. Oak Hill Coll 75. **d** 77 Bradwell for Chelmsf **p** 78 Chelmsf. C of Ch Ch Gt Warley 77-80; Rayleigh Dio Chelmsf from 80. *13 Sir Walter Raleigh Drive, Rayleigh, SS6 9JB.*

PADDOCK, Canon Gerald Alfred. b 39. Oak Hill Th Coll 66. **d** 69 Lon **p** 70 Stepney for Lon. C of St Andr Whitehall Pk U Holloway 69-73; Edgware (in c of St Pet) 73-76; P-in-c of Ab-Kettleby w Wartnaby and Holwell 76-81; Can Missr and Hon Can of Leic Cathl from 80; V of Oaks-in-Charnwood w Copt Oak Dio Leic from 81. *Oaks-in-Charnwood Vicarage, Loughborough, Leics.* (Shepshed 3246)

PADDOCK, John Allan Barnes. b 51. Univ of Liv BA 74. St Steph Ho Ox 75. **d** 80 **p** 81 Glouc. C of Matson Dio Glouc from 80. *8 Barleycroft Close, St Leonard's Park, Gloucester.*

PADDOCK, William Frank. b 02. St Jo Coll Dur ThL 26, BA 27. Lon Coll of Div 23. **d** 27 Win for Guildf **p** 28 Guildf. C of Stoke-next-Guildf 27-30; V of St Jas Holloway 31-36; St Luke W Kilburn 36-47; All SS Burton-on-Trent 47-50; Ch Ch Fulham 50-59; St John Ealing Dean 59-66; R of Broadwell w Evenlode 66-71; Perm to Offic Dio Glouc from 71. *96 Orchard Avenue, Cheltenham, GL51 7LE.* (Cheltnm 23164)

PADGET, William Thomas. b 19. **d** 77 **p** 78 Bris (APM). C of Rodbourne-Cheney Dio Bris from 77. *59 Avonmead, Greenmeadow, Swindon, Wilts, SN2 3NY.*

PADOA, Cecil Rhodes. b 20. **d** 74 **p** 75 Johann. C of Benoni Dio Johann from 74. *104 Cranbourne Avenue, Benoni Tvl 1500, S Africa.* (011-54 1726)

✠ **PAE, Right Rev Mark.** b 26. Nashotah Ho Wisc DTh 75. St Mich Coll Ch'ongju. **d** 54 **p** 56 Korea. P Dio Korea 54-65; Dio Taejon from 65; Archd of Ch'ung-Ch'ong 65-71; Cons Ld Bp of Taejon in St Nich Cathl Seoul 1 June 74 by Bp of Seoul; Bps of Kuch, Sing, Sabah, Vic Hong Kong and W Malaysia; and others. *Anglican Church, PO Box 22, Taejon 300, Korea.* (3-5261)

PA E, Stephen. **d** 69 Rang **p** 71 Mand. d Dio Rang 69-70; P Dio Mand from 71. *St Paul's Church, Pang Long, Burma.*

PAENGA, Ven Te Keepa. St Jo Coll Auckld. **d** 49 **p** 50 Wai. C of Rotorua 49-52; V of Te Ngae 52-58; Wai Maori Past 58-63; Waipatu-Moteo Maori Past 63-68; Whangara Maori Past Dio Wai from 68; Archd of Wai from 79. *Vicarage, Wainui Road, Whangara, Gisborne, NZ.* (84-965)

PAETKAU, John. b 44. Em & St Chad's Coll Sktn 70. **d** 73 **p** 74 Rupld. C of St Geo Winnipeg 73-74; St John Vanc 74-78; I of Sechelt Dio New Westmr from 78. *1 Coopers Road, Halfmoon Bay, BC, Canada.*

PAFFORD, Basil Ruby. Qu Coll St John's 53. **d** 58 **p** 59 Newfld. I of Cow Head 58-64; R of Fogo 64-68; P-in-c of Bay St Geo 69-70; R of Arnold's Cove 70-77; Portugal Cove Dio E Newfld from 77. *Box 100, Portugal Cove, Newfoundland, Canada.* (709-895 6677)

PAGAN, Keith Vivian. b 37. Univ of Dur BA 60, MA 66.

Chich Th Coll 60. **d** 62 **p** 63 Chelmsf. C of St Jas Clacton-on-Sea 62-64; Wymondham 64-70; V of Hindolveston 70-80; C-in-c of Guestwick 70-80; Kettlestone 70-79; R of Campbeltown Dio Arg Is from 80. *Rectory, Campbeltown, Argyll.*

PAGE, Canon Alan George. b 24. Em Coll Cam BA 48, MA 52. Wycl Hall, Ox 49. **d** 51 **p** 52 Lon. C of St Andr Thornhill Square Islington 51-53; CMS Miss at Weithaga Momb 53-56; Miss Asst Embu Distr Momb 57-58; Tutor at St Paul's United Th Coll Limuru 59-60; Chap to Bp of Ft Hall 61-64; Mt Kenya 64-65; Exam Chap to Bp of Ft Hall 61-64; Mt Kenya 64-71; V of Ft Hall 61-65; Tutor MacGregor Bible Sch Weithaga 66-70; Tutor at St Paul's United Th Coll Limuru 70-71; Hon Can of Mt Kenya 71-75; Mt Kenya S from 75; C of St Luke S Lyncombe, Bath 71-72; R of Freshford w Limpley Stoke (and Hinton Charterhouse from 76) Dio B & W from 72; Commiss Mt Kenya S from 75. *Freshford Rectory, Bath, BA3 6EB.* (Limpley Stoke 3135)

PAGE, Alan Richard Benjamin. b 38. St D Coll Lamp BA 60. St Mich Coll Llan 60. **d** 62 **p** 63 Llan. C of St Andr Cardiff 62-64; St Julian Newport 64-67; H Trin Hoxton 67-69; H Trin Winchmore Hill 69-71; V of St Mich w All SS and St Thos Camden Town Dio Lon from 71. *St Michael's Vicarage, Bartholomew Road, NW 5.* (01-485 1256)

PAGE, Alfred Charles. b 12. CCC Cam BA 34, MA 38. Wycl Hall Ox. **d** 36 **p** 37 Ripon. C of Wortley-de-Leeds 36-40; Leeds (in c of St Mary and Good Shepherd) 40-44; V of St Mark Woodhouse 44-55; Rothwell 55-69; RD of Whitkirk 61-69; Proc Conv Ripon 64-69; Hon Can of Ripon 66-69; V of Arthington 69-72; Archd of Leeds 69-81. *602 King Lane, Alwoodley Park, Leeds, LS17 7AN.*

PAGE, Brian Tindall. Linc Coll Ox BA (2nd cl Engl Lang and Lit) 33, MA 37. Wells Th Coll 33. **d** 35 **p** 36 Cant. C of St Mark S Norwood 35-38; St Geo Cathl Capetn 38-40; C-in-c of St Cypr Retreat 40-43; R of Worc 43-46; C of St Jas Vancouver 46-49; Min of St Geo Conv Distr New Addington 49-52; R of Duncan 52-62; Hon Can of Ch Ch Cathl Vic BC 59-77; R of St Barn Vic 62-76. *912 Vancouver Street, Victoria, BC, Canada.*

PAGE, Christopher Charles Edward. b 54. Univ of Vic BC BA 77. Wycl Coll Tor MDiv 80. **d** 80 Tor for Rupld **p** 80 Rupld. C of St Geo Winnipeg Dio Rupld from 80. *168 Wilton Street, Winnipeg, Manit, Canada, R3M 3C3.*

PAGE, Canon Clifford Kemp. **d** 60 **p** 61 Bend. C of Heathcote 60-63; R of Tatura 63-72; V of Daylesford 72-77; Can of Bend 73-77; Can (Emer) from 77; Perm to Offic Dio Wang from 80. *48 Hastie Street, Tatura, Vic, Australia 3616.*

PAGE, David George. b 42. St Jo Coll Winnipeg 78. **d** and **p** 79 Qu'App. Hosp Chap Dio Qu'App from 79. *1501 College Avenue, Regina, Sask, S4P 1B8.*

✠ **PAGE, Right Rev Dennis Fountain.** b 19. G and C Coll Cam 3rd cl Cl Trip 40, BA (3rd cl Th Trip) 41, MA 45. Linc Th Coll 41. **d** 43 **p** 44 Cov. C of St Andr Rugby (in c of St Geo Hillmorton) 43-49; R of Hockwold w Wilton 49-65; Weeting 49-65; RD of Feltwell from 53; Hon Can of Ely 63-65 and from 68; V of Yaxley 65-75; Archd of Huntingdon 65-75; Cons Ld Bp Suffr of Lanc in Blackb Cathl 1 March 75 by Abp of York; Bps of Blackb, Wakef, Sheff, Bradf, Carl, Ches and Ely; Bps Suffr of Stockport, Burnley, Penrith, Pontefract, Birkenhead and Huntingdon; and others. *Vicarage, Church Lane, Winmarleigh, Preston, Lancs PR3 0LA.* (Garstang 2577)

PAGE, John Fountain. CCC Cam 2nd cl Hist Trip pt i, 37, BA 38, 3rd cl Th Trip pt i, 39, MA 42. Linc Th Coll 40. **d** 41 **p** 43 Chich. C of Petworth 41-42; S Bersted 42-43; Lowestoft 47-52; R of Kessingland 52-56; C of St Steph Calg 56-57; I of Colwood w Langford 57-59; Chap Univ Sch Vic BC 59-60; Asst Chap Vevey 61-63; Chap 63-68. *Chaucey, Blonay, Vaud, Switzerland.*

PAGE, John Knott. b 12. Men in Disp 45; MBE 46. Oak Hill Th Coll 32. **d** 35 **p** 36 Southw. C of St Paul Hyson Green 35-39; Felixstowe 39-40; St Paul Slough 40-42; Chap RAFVR 42-47; V of Greyfriars Reading 47-68; St Jo Evang Weymouth 68-77; Hosp Chap 68-78. *96 Oakbury Drive, Preston, Weymouth, Dorset.* (Preston 3664)

PAGE, John Laurance Howard. b 40. Lon Coll of Div 62. **d** 65 Stepney for Lon **p** 66 Lon. C of Spitalfields 65-69; Winchester 69-72; C of Ringwood 72-76; V of Lockerley and E Dean w E and W Tytherley Dio Win from 76. *Lockerley Vicarage, Romsey, Hants.* (Lockerley 40635)

PAGE, John Thomas. b 11. **d** 72 **p** 74 Stepney for Lon (APM). C of St Mark Vic Pk Dio Lon from 72. *12 McKenna House, Wrights Road, Bow, E.3.* (01-980 8268)

PAGE, Leonard Arthur. Em Coll Sktn STh 46. **d** 43 **p** 46 Sask. C of St Geo E Prince Albert 43-50; R of Roslin 50-51; Shannonville 51-56; St Marg Belleville 51-62; All SS Niagara Falls 62-69; Orangeville 69-75; Hon Can of Niag 70-75. *412 Highland Road, Peterborough, Ont., Canada.*

PAGE, Michael Bruce Richard. b 36. St Edm Hall Ox BA 57, MA 64. Chich Th Coll 78. **d** 79 **p** 80 Willesden for Lon. C of S Ruislip 79-81; Perm to Offic Dios Lon and Chich from 81. *9 Wood Street, Bognor Regis, W Sussex, PO21 2PT.*

PAGE, Michael John. b 42. K Coll Lon and Warm BD and AKC 66. **d** 67 **p** 68 Sheff. C of Rawmarsh w Parkgate 67-72; C-in-c of Gleadless Valley Conv Distr 72-74; R of Gleadless Valley Team Min 74-77; V of Lechlade Dio Glouc from 77; RD of Fairford from 81. *Vicarage, Sherbourne Street, Lechlade, Glos, GL7 3AH.* (Lechlade 52262)

PAGE, Richard Dennis. b 23. G and C Coll Cam BA 48, MA 50. Ridley Hall, Cam 48. **d** 50 **p** 51 Sheff. C of Ecclesfield 50-52; Chap St Lawr Coll Ramsgate 52-58; Dean Close Sch Cheltm 58-60; and 62-64; Netherton Tr Sch 60-62; V of Ecclesfield 64-71; RD of Ecclesfield 66-71; R of Wells-next-the-Sea 71-78; C-in-c of Hockham 71-78; RD of Burnham and Walsingham 72-78; V of Hemsby Dio Nor from 78. *Hemsby Vicarage, Great Yarmouth, Norf.* (Gt Yarmouth 730308)

PAGE, Trevor Melvyn. b 41. Univ of Dur BA 63. Fitzw Coll Cam BA (2nd cl Th Trip pt iii) 67, MA 72. Westcott Ho Cam 64. **d** 67 **p** 68 Sheff. C of H Trin Millhouses Sheff 67-69; Chap Univ of Sheff 69-74; V of Intake Dio Sheff from 74. *Vicarage, Kingston Road, Intake, Doncaster, Yorks, DN2 6LS.* (Doncaster 23167)

PAGE, William Wilson. b 14. Wycl Hall, Ox. **d** 59 **p** 60 Birm. C of Erdington (in c of St Chad) 59-63; V of Kingsbury w Hurley 65-68; C of Coleshill 68-71; Lavington w Osgodby, Keisby, Hanby and Ingoldsby 71-74; Bassingthorpe w Westby and Bitchfield 71-74; Boothby Pagnell 71-74; Burton-le-Coggles 71-74; R of Gt Casterton, Pickworth, Tickencote and L Casterton Dio Pet from 74. *Great Casterton Rectory, Stamford, Lincs.* (Stamford 4036)

PAGE-TURNER, Edward Gregory Ambrose Wilford. b 31. Qu Coll Birm 57. **d** 60 **p** 61 York. C of Helmsley 60-64; St Phil Earl's Court 64-67; Walton-on-Thames 67-70; V of Seend (w Bulkington from 71) 70-79; R of Woodstock w Bladon Dio Ox from 79; P-in-c of Begbroke and of Shipton-on-Cherwell and of Hampton Gay Dio Ox from 80. *Woodstock Rectory, Oxford, OX7 1UQ.* (Woodstock 811415)

PAGE-WOOD, Ivan Thomas. b 05. Univ of Bris BA 25. Sarum Th Coll 26. **d** 28 **p** 29 Bris. C of St Mary Fishponds Bris 28-32; Kingswood (in c of Ascen) 32-35; V of St Leon Redfield Bris 35-42; St Barn Swindon 42-50; St Cuthb Brislington 50-57; Staverton w Boddington 57-64; PC of Lower Cam 64-70; Perm to Offic Dios Glouc and Bris from 70. *34 Hollis Gardens, Hatherley, Cheltenham, Glos., GL51 6JQ.* (Cheltenham 512122)

PAGET, Alfred Ivor. b 24. St Aid Coll 56. **d** 59 **p** 60 Ches. C of Hoylake 59-62; Chap Miss to Seamen Hong Kong 62-63; Melb 63-64; C of St Geo Hyde 64-66; R of Gt Henny (w L Henny and Middleton from 68) 66-74; L Henny 66-68; Middleton Chelmsf 66-68; C of Gt Holland (in c of Holland) 74-79; V of Holland-on-Sea Dio Chelmsf from 79. *297 Frinton Road, Holland-on-Sea, Essex, CO15 5SP.*

PAGET, Canon Arthur Gordon Westwood. b 1893. St Chad's Coll Dur BA 19, MA 25. Ely Th Coll 19. **d** 20 **p** 22 Ely. C of St Mary Whittlesey 20-23; St Pet Mancroft Nor 23; Thorpe Hamlet 23-25; St James w Pockthorpe 25-27; Asst Min Can of Nor 23-31; V of St Mich-at-Thorn Nor and Asst Master Winton Sch Nor 27-31; Asst Master K S Pet 32; Min Can and Prec and Sacr of Pet Cathl 31-33; Hon Min Can of Nor from 42; Chap All H Hosp Ditchingham 33-39; R of Hedenham 33-59; St Clem w St Edm and St Geo Colegate Nor 59-60; C of St Teath w Michaelstow (in c of Delabole) 60-62; R of Letheringsett w Bayfield and Glandford 62-67; Perm to Offic Dio St E from 67; Hon Can (Emer) St E Cathl from 74. *8 The College of St Mark, Audley End, Saffron Walden, Essex, CB11 4JD.*

PAGET, David Rolf. b 54. Worc Coll Ox BA 78. St Steph Ho Ox BA (Th) 80. **d** 81 Cant. C of Sheerness Dio Cant from 81. *29 Wheatsheaf Gardens, Sheerness, Kent, ME12 1YH.*

PAGET, Harold Leslie. b 09. Univ of Birm 30. St Aug Coll Cant 53. **d** 54 Bp Sara for Heref **p** 55 Heref. [F Methodist Miss] C of Holmer w Huntington 54-56; R of Ickham 56-64; Swalecliffe 64-76; Perm to Offic Dio Cant from 76. *70 Marine Parade, Whitstable, Kent.*

PAGET, John Rodborough. b 05. AKC 35. **d** 35 **p** 36 St Alb. C of Leighton Buzzard 35-39; St Mary Bedford 39-40; C-in-c of St Francis Conv Distr Broadfield 40-44; V of Deeping St Jas 44-47; Horley 47-49; Surr 48-49; Chap to Moor Park Coll for Adult Christian Educn Farnham and L to Offic Dio Guildf 49-52; R of Duloe w Herodsfoot 52-61; R of St Pinnock 52-61; V of St Kew 61-67; R of Tillington 67-70; Perm to Offic Dio Chich 71-73; C-in-c of Trotton w Chithurst 73-76; Perm to Offic Dio Chich from 76. *8 Heathfield Park, Midhurst, GU29 9HL.*

PAGET, Robert Edward. St Francis Coll Brisb 79. **d** 79 **p** 80 Brisb. Hon C of St Jas Kelvin Grove Dio Brisb from 79. *44 Settlement, The Gap, Queensld, Austrlaia 4061.* (30 2568)

PAGET, Robert James Innes. b 35. K Coll Lon and Warm AKC 59. **d** 60 **p** 61 Southw. C of Attenborough w Bramcote and Chilwell 60-63; St Mark Cheltm 63-72; C-in-c of Pilsley 72-73; Team V of N Wingfield Dio Derby from 73. *Pilsley Vicarage, Chesterfield, Derbys., S45 8EF.* (Tibshelf 2348)

PAGET, Robert John. St Francis Coll Brisb. **d** 80 Brisb. C of Ch Ch Bundaberg Dio Brisb from 80. *2 Wynter Street, Bundaberg, Qld, Australia 4670.* (071 722 139)

PAGET-WILKES, Michael Jocelyn James. b 41. ALCD 69. **d** 69 Kingston T for S'wark **p** 70 S'wark. C of Wandsworth 69-74; V of Hatcham Dio S'wark from 74. *St James Vicarage, Hatcham, SE14.* (01-692 1921)

PAIA, Matthew. **d** 78 **p** 79 Centr Melan. P Dio Centr Melan. *Siota Provincial Secondary School, Gela, Solomon Islands.*

PAICE, Alan. b 26. K Coll Lon and Warm AKC 53. **d** 55 **p** 56 Lich. C of Leek 55-59; Haslemere 59-63; Eton (in c of St Jo Bapt Eton Wick) 63-74; P-in-c of The Lee Dio Ox from 74; Hawridge w Cholesbury Dio Ox from 74; St Leonards Dio Ox from 79. *The Lee Vicarage, Great Missenden, Bucks, HP16 9LZ.* (The Lee 315)

PAICE, James. Selw Coll Cam 3rd cl Th Trip pt i, 28, BA (3rd cl Th Trip pt ii) 29, MA 33. St Bonif Coll Warm 24. **d** 29 **p** 30 Newc T. C of All SS Gosforth 29-32; P-in-c of Koorda 32-37; R of Midl Junction 37-44; Chap to Abp of Perth 40-51; R of Victoria Pk 42-46; St Patr Mt Lawley City and Dio Perth from 46; RD of Perth 46-65; Exam Chap to Abp of Perth 49-74; Can of Perth 50-74; Archd of Swan 67-74. *1 Derril Avenue, Dianella, W Australia 6062.* (49 8104)

PAICE, Michael Antony. b 35. Kelham Th Coll. **d** 60 **p** 61 Southw. C of Skegby 60-62; St Jo Bapt Carlton 62-66; V of Misterton w W Stockwith 66-81; P-in-c of Olveston w Aust Dio Bris from 81; Littleton-on-Severn w Elberton Dio Bris from 81. *Olveston Vicarage, Bristol, BS12 3DA.* (Almondsbury 612296)

PAICE, William Henry. b 08. Worc Ordin Coll. **d** 57 **p** 58 Worc. C of Holly Hall 57-59; Redditch 59-62; Hayling I 62-68; C-in-c of All SS Conv Distr Gurnard 68-73. *1 Morley Close, Burton, Christchurch, Dorset, BH23 7LA.* (Christchurch 476255)

PAIN, Canon David Clinton. b 36. K Coll Lon 56. **d** and **p** 64 Benin. P Dio Benin 64-67; L to Offic Dio Accra from 67; Hon Can of Accra from 80. *Box 4683, Accra, Ghana.*

PAIN, John Alcuin Odell. b 1895. Lich Th Coll 51. **d** 52 **p** 53 Carl. C of Appleby 52-55; Murton w Hilton 52-55; V of Gilsland w Over and Nether Denton 55-60; Witham Friary 60-64; C-in-c of Marston Bigot 60-64; L to Offic Dio Carl 64-69; and from 74; Perm to Offic Dio Capetn 69-70 and 72-73; L to Offic Dio Ex 71-72. *84 Skinburness Road, Silloth, Carlisle, Cumb, CA5 4QH.* (Silloth 31746)

PAIN, Lawrence Percy Bernard. b 11. Univ of Lon BA 32. Wells Th Coll 48. **d** 49 **p** 50 Guildf. C of St Nich Cranleigh 49-52; V of Frimley Green 52-63; Cove w S Hawley 63-70; RD of Aldershot 65-69; V of Rowledge 70-81. *49 Parkhouse Road, Minehead, Somt, TA24 8AD.*

PAIN, Michael Broughton George. b 37. Univ of Dur BA 61. Wycl Hall, Ox 61. **d** 63 **p** 64 Bris. C of Downend 63-67; Swindon 67-70; V of Alveston 70-78; Ch Ch City and Dio Guildf from 78. *25 Waterden Road, Guildford, Surrey, GU1 2AZ.* (Guildford 68886)

PAINE, Andrew Liddell. b 40. Jes Coll Cam 2nd cl Hist Trip pt i 62, BA (2nd cl Th Trip pt ii) 64, MA 67. Ridley Hall, Cam 63. **d** 65 **p** 66 St Alb. C of Luton w E Hyde 65-69; V of Essington 69-75; R of St Mich on Greenhill Lich 75-79; P-in-c of St Mary Lich 78-79; R (w St Mich) 79-80. *Birch Heys, Cromwell Range, Manchester, M14 6HU.* (061-225 1000)

PAINE, David Stevens. b 24. St Jo Coll Cam MB and BChir 47, MA 52. Ridley Hall Cam 52. **d** 54 **p** 55 Portsm. C of Rowner 54-56; Freshwater 56-59; V of S Cerney w Cerney Wick 59-64. *42 Newton Road, Cambridge.* (Cambridge 53300)

PAINE, Douglas Leonard. b 24. AKC 50. St Bonif Coll Warm 51. **d** 51 **p** 52 Win. C of St Andr Boscombe 51-53; Chap St John Calc 53-55; C of Eastleigh 55-58; V of Bursledon 58-73; Sway Dio Win from 73. *Sway Vicarage, Lymington, Hants, SO4 0BA.* (Sway 2358)

PAINE, Canon Ernest Liddell. b 11. Trin Coll Bris 34. **d** 37 **p** 38 Blackb. C of All H Bispham 37-40; Org Sec BCMS for Midls and Publ Pr Dio Derby 40-44; Chap Russell-Coates Nautical Sch 44-48; Castle Court Sch Parkstone 48-53; V of St John Heatherlands 44-53; Proc Conv Sarum 51-55; Cov 55-64; V of St Matt Rugby 53-63; RD of Rugby 56-63; Cler Sec Cov Dioc Conf 56-63; Surr 59-63; Hon Can of Cov 61-63; R of Bradfield w Buckhold and Southend 63-71; C-in-c of Stanford-Dingley 66-71; Chesterton 71-76; Lighthorne 71-76; Moreton Morell w Newbold Pacey 76; RD of Dassett Magna 75-76. Hon Can of Cov Cathl 75-76; Can (Emer) from 76; Perm to Offic Dio Sarum from 76. *1 Abbey Court, Cerne Abbas, Dorchester, Dorset, DT2 7JH.* (Cerne Abbas 358)

PAINE, Harold William. Wycl Hall, Ox. **d** and **p** 57 Roch. C of Farningham 57-59; R of Colton 59-66; V of Easton 59-66. *Address temp unknown.*

PAINE, Humphrey John. b 06. Trin Coll Cam BA 28, MA 37. Cudd Coll 29. **d** 30 **p** 31 Newc T. C of Ch Ch Tynemouth 30-33; St Aug Tonge Moor 33-37; Chap of Penang 37-41; Chap RNVR 42-44; R of Gt Melton 45-69; C-in-c of Marlingford 55-69; RD of Humbleyard 62-69; V of Fressingfield 69-74; V of Weybread 69-74. *38 Arlington Lane, Norwich, NR2 2DB.*

PAINE, John Henry Fairman. b 08. Ely Th Coll 59. **d** 60 **p** 61 Linc. C of Grimsby 60-62; V of Hogsthorpe 62-70; V of Mumby 63-70; Tetney 71-81. *15 Remillo Avenue, Grimsby, Lincs.* (Grimsby 55208)

PAINE, Kevin Adrian Martin. b 56. Univ of Wales (Cardiff) Dipl Th 81. St Mich AA Llan. **d** 81 Mon. Chap to St Woolos Cathl Newport Dio Mon from 81. *9 Clifton Road, Newport, Gwent.*

PAINE, Peter Cecil. St Francis Th Coll Brisb 57. ACT ThL 59. **d** 59 **p** 60 Bath. M Bro of Good Shepherd. C of Darwin 60-61; R of Katherine 62-65; Childers w Howard 66-69; Ch of Annunc Camp Hill Brisb 69-79; Perm to Offic Dio Brisb from 79. *127 Lunga Street, Camp Hill, Queensland, Australia 4152.*

PAINE, Peter Stanley. b 46. K Coll Lon BD 69. Cudd Coll 69. **d** 71 Ripon **p** 72 Knaresborough for Ripon. C of St Aidan Leeds 71-74; St Wilfrid Harrogate 74-78; V of H Spirit Beeston Hill Dio Ripon from 78. *114 Stratford Street, Leeds, LS11 7EQ.* (Leeds 701446)

PAINEL, Huenchu. **d** 74 **p** 75 Bp Bazley for Chile. P Dio Chile. *Casilla 4, Chol-Chol, Chile.*

PAINTER, David Scott. b 44. LTCL 65. Worc Coll Ox BA (2nd cl Th) 68, MA 72. Cudd Coll 68. **d** 70 **p** 71 Ex. C of St Andr Plymouth 70-73; Chap Plymouth Poly 71-73; C of All SS Margaret Street St Marylebone and Tutor in Inst of Chr Stud 73-76; Dom Chap to Abp of Cant 76-80; Dir of Ordinands Dio Cant 76-80; Perm to Offic Dios Ex and S'wark 76-80; V of Roehampton Dio S'wark from 80. *31 Roehampton Close, SW15 5LU.* (01-876 6461)

PAINTER, Jack. BD (Lon) 63. ACT ThL (2nd cl) 61, Th Scho 64. Melb Coll of Div Dipl Relig Educn 63. Moore Th Coll Syd. **d** 61 Bp Kerle for Syd **p** 62 Syd. C of Turramurra 61-63; St John Darlinghurst Syd 63-65; Tutor St Jo Coll Dur 65-68; Perm to Offic Dio Dur 65-68; Prec of St Andr Cathl Syd 68-71; L to Offic Dio Capetn 71-76; Exam Chap to Abp of Capetn 71-76; Lect La Trobe Univ Bundoore from 76; Perm to Offic Dio Melb from 77. *La Trobe University, Bundoora, Australia 3083.*

PAINTER, John. b 25. Selw Coll Cam BA (3rd cl Th Trip pt i) 48, MA 53. Ripon Hall, Ox 48. **d** 50 **p** 51 Lon. C of St Mary Stoke Newington 50-55; St Barn Woodside Pk 55-56; Llanguicke (Pontardawe) 56-59; C-in-c of St Jo Bapt Hafod Swansea 59-60; R of Chipstable w Raddington 61-64; V of Audenshaw 64-66; Sandown 66-72; R of Keinton Mandeville (w Lydford-on-Fosse from 77) Dio B & W from 72; C-in-c of Lydford-on-fosse 76-77; RD of Castle Cary from 81. *Keinton Mandeville Rectory, Domerton, Somt, TA11 6EP.* (Charlton Mackrell 3216)

PAINTER, Michael Roderick. Univ of W Austr BA 60. Wollaston Th Coll W Austr ACT ThL 61. **d** 63 **p** 64 Perth. C of Nedlands 63-66; P-in-c of Morawa 66-67; R 67-70; R of E Claremont 70-74; Gosnells-Maddington 74-79; Mt Hawthorn w Osborne Pk Dio Perth from 79. *98 Flinders Terrace, Mount Hawthorn, W Australia 6016.* (444 1447)

PAINTER, Canon Wilfred George Patrick Douglas. AKC 30. Univ of Lon BD 30. Sarum Th Coll 30. **d** 30 **p** 31 Glouc. C of The Slad w All SS Uplands 30-33; R of Dalwallinu 33-34; C of St Geo Perth 34-37; R of Wembley 37-43; Parkerville 43-44; Midl Junction 44-51; E Fremantle (w Palmyra from 55) 51-71; N Fremantle 60-65; Hon Can of St Geo Cathl Perth 64-67; Can 67-77; Can (Emer) from 77; R of St Mary W Perth 71-77; Perm to Offic Dio Perth from 77. *20 Excelsior Street, Shenton Park, Australia 6008.* (381 6584)

PAISLEY, James. b 05. Edin Th Coll 27. **d** 29 **p** 30 Carl. C of Dalton-in-Furness 29-31; Jesselton N Borneo 32-33; Hd Master St Mich Sch Sandakan 33-34; St Thos Sch Kuching 35-36; P-in-c of St Jas Kudat 36-40; St Thos Cathl Kuching 40-42; Beverley w Brookton 42-43; R of Harvey 43-45; serving w Borneo Civil Affairs Unit 45-47; V of Compton Parva 47-70; V of Hampstead Norreys 47-70; Perm to Offic Dio Ex from 70. *15 Wilton Way, Abbotskerswell, Newton Abbot, Devon.* (Newton Abbot 3728)

PAISLEY, John Joseph. b 17. Oak Hill Th Coll 46. **d** 49 **p** 50 Lon. C of St Paul Canonbury 49-51; Newburn (in c of Throckley) 51-53; V of Ch Ch Blackb 53-65; St Mark Layton Blackpool Dio Blackb from 65. *163 Kingscote Drive, Layton, Blackpool, Lancs.* (Blackpool 32895)

PAISLEY, Ronald Gordon. b 15. Clifton Th Coll 50. **d** 52 **p** 53 Lon. C of St Pet Upper Holloway 52-55; V of Newchapel

55-60; St Alb Becontree 60-73; St Clem Toxt Pk 73-80. *Restalrig, Hall Road, Ecclefechan, Lockerbie, Dumfries.*

PAISLEY, William Clifford. Wayne State Univ BA 61. Hur Coll BTh 64. **d** 64 Hur for Moos **p** 65 Moos. I of Pickle Crow 64-66; Upham 66-70; Gordon w Lorne 70-72; Campobello 72-76; Stanley Dio Fred from 76. *Rectory, Stanley, NB, Canada.*

PAK, Francis Kyongjo. b 44. St Mich Sem Seoul 71. **d** 74 **p** 75 Seoul. P Dio Seoul. *1-1 1 Ka Tongsong dong, Songbuk Ku, Seoul 132, Korea.* (Seoul 93-2290)

PAK, John. St Mich Sem Oryudong, 61. **d** and **p** 64 Korea. P Dio Korea 64-65; Dio Taejon 65-69; Dio Seoul 69-76. *236 Libby Street, Honolulu, Hawaii.*

PAK, Laurence. St Mich Sem Oryudong, 61. **d** and **p** 64 Korea. P Dio Korea 64-65; Dio Seoul from 65; Arch P of Seoul 73-77. *11 Kyo Dong, Suwon 170, Korea.*

PAK, Ven Mark Sung-si. St Mich Sem Oryudong. **d** 67 **p** 68 Taejon. P Dio Taejon; Can of Taejon 75; Archd of Centr Taejon from 76. *Anglican Church, Yesaneup, Yesankun 340, Korea.*

PAK, Stephen. St Mich Sem Oryudong 61. **d** 63 **p** 64 Korea. P Dio Korea 63-65; Dio Taejon 65-70 and 71-73; Dio Seoul from 73; C of Warrnambool 70-71; Arch P of Seoul 73-77. *234-55 Yondu Dong, Seoul 131, Korea.*

PAKENHAM, Charles Wilfrid. Trin Coll Ox BA (3rd cl Th) 40, MA 52. Wycl Hall Ox 40. **d** 41 **p** 42 Liv. C of Sutton 41-44; CMS Miss Dio Lagos 44-49; C of Cheltenham 49-52; V of Waterloo Dio Liv from 52; CF (TA) 63-67. *17 Alexander Road, Liverpool 22.* (051-928 2796)

PAKENHAM, Stephen Walter. b 29. Qu Coll Cam 2nd cl Econ Trip pt i, 55, BA (3rd cl Th Trip pt ii) 57, MA 61. Linc Th Coll 57. **d** 59 **p** 60 Birm. C of St Jas Handsworth 59-61; St Andr (in c of St Francis) Handsworth 61-64; V of Donnington 64-75; Apuldram 64-75; Durrington 75-81; St Mary Bourne w Woodcott Dio Win from 81. *St Mary Bourne Vicarage, Andover, Hants.* (St Mary Bourne 308)

PALACIOUS, James Edwin. b 52. Univ of WI BA (Th) 75. Codr Coll Barb 71. **d** 75 Nass. C of St Barn Nass 75; Dom Chap to Bp of Nass 75-81; Dioc Sec Dio Nass 77-81; on leave. *c/o Box N 656, Nassau, Bahamas.*

PALAVECINO, Hector Mario. b 43. **d** 76 N Argent. d Dio N Argent. *Casilla 19, Ing Juarez, Pcia de Formosa, Argentina.*

PALENG, Edmund. Ho of Epiph Kuching 52. **d** 55 **p** 56 Borneo. P Dio Borneo 55-62; Dio Kuch from 62. *c/o Box 120, Bintulu, Sarawak, Malaysia.*

PALFREY, Canon Claude Hugh. b 13. Linc Th Coll 44. **d** 46 **p** 47 Nor. C of Wymondham 46-49; Thorpe-Episcopi 49-55; Dep Master of Choristers at Nor Cathl 49-58; Hon Min Can of Nor 55-58; Prec and Min Can from 58; V of Bawburgh 56-58; V of L Melton 56-58; R of St Jo Bapt Maddermarket Nor 58-81; Hon Can of Nor from 75. *60 The Close, Norwich, NR1 4EH.* (Norwich 28084)

PALFREY, James Edgar Martin. Wycl Coll Tor. **d** 56 Suffr Bp for Tor **p** 57 Tor. C-in-c of Medonte 56-58; R of Cavan 58-62; Hosp Chap Dio Tor from 62; Hon C of Ch of Ascen Tor 63-76. *c/o Ste 1, 5 Cheviot Place, Islington, Ont, Canada.*

PALIN, John Edward. b 47. Univ of Wales (Cardiff) Dipl Th 70, St Mich Coll Llan 67. **d** 71 **p** 72 Derby. C of St Jo Bapt Staveley 71-74; Nottm 74-76; V of Greetham (and Thisleton from 79) w Stretton and Clipsham Dio Pet from 77; P-in-c of Thistleton 77-79. *Greetham Vicarage, Oakham, Leics, LE15 7NF.* (Oakham 812015)

PALIN, Canon Reginald Culliford. b 03. St Jo Coll Dur BA 25, MA 28. **d** 27 Liv for Ches **p** 29 Ches. C of St Paul Birkenhead 27-30; All SS Hoole 30-34; CMS Miss at Mboga 34-39; Archd of W Prov Ugan 45-50; Ugan 50-60; Prov Sec Ugan 61-64; Can of Nam 61-64; Hon Can from 64; V of Wichenford 64-72; Commiss Boga-Z from 72; C-in-c of Tibberton w Bredicot and Warndon 73-75. *14 Broom Meadow Road, Fernhill Heath, Worcester, WR3 7TJ.* (Worcester 53190)

PALIN, Roy. b 34. Univ of Man BA (2nd cl Engl) 56. Ripon Hall, Ox 65. **d** 67 Repton for Derby **p** 68 Derby. C of Ilkeston 67-70; Wollaton 70-71; V of Thorney w Wigsley and Broadholme 71-79; Harby w Swinethorpe (and Thorney w Wigsley, Broadholme and N and S Clifton from 79) 71-80; P-in-c of N and S Clifton 75-79; V of Tuxford w Weston and Markham Clinton Dio Southw from 81; P-in-c of Markham Clinton 80; Weston 80; Laxton Dio Southw from 80. *Tuxford Vicarage, Newark, Notts.* (Tuxford 870497)

PALINGO, Jackson. b 31. **d** 79 **p** 80 Centr Tang. P Dio Centr Tang. *PO Kwa Mtoro, Kondoa, Tanzania.*

PALLANT, Roger Frank. b 35. Trin Coll Cam 2nd cl Hist Trip pt i 56, BA (2nd cl Th Trip pt ia) 57, MA 61. Wells Th Coll 57. **d** 59 Stafford for Lich **p** 60 Lich. C of Stafford 59-62; St Mary-le-Tower Ipswich and Dioc Youth Chap Dio St E 62-65; Development Officer C of E Youth Coun from 65; C of Putney 66-71; R of Hintlesham w Chattisham 71-80; Sec St E Dioc Syn from 76; V of All H Ipswich Dio St E from 80. *All Hallows' Vicarage, Reynolds Road, Ipswich, Suff, IP3 0JH.* (Ipswich 77467)

PALMER, Alfred Kingsmill. b 1899. TCD BA and BAI 23, MA 28. Clifton Th Coll 35. **d** 36 **p** 37 Oss. C of Wexford 36-38; C-in-c of Cleenish 38; I of Shillelagh 38-41; Thurles 41-49; Killiskey 49-53; Kilcullen w Carnalway 53-60; Geashill and Killeigh 60-71; C-in-c of Ballycommon 60-71; Preb of Kild Cathl 80-81; Treas 64-71; RD of Clonbullogue 63-71. *2 Silchester Park, Glenageary, Co Dublin, Irish Republic.*

PALMER, Alister Gordon. **d** 80 **p** 81 Bris. C of Patchway Dio Bris from 80. *1a Police Houses, Southsea Road, Patchway, Bristol, BS12 5DP.*

PALMER, Angus Douglas. b 40. St Chad's Coll Dur BA (2nd cl Th) 62, Dipl Th (w distinc) 63. **d** 63 **p** 64 Newc T. C of Wallsend 63-66; H Cross Fenham 66-69; Bottesford w Ashby 69-70; R of Penicuik Dio Edin from 70; W Linton Dio Edin from 77. *Rectory, Broomhill Road, Penicuik, Midlothian, EH26 9EE.* (Penicuik 72862)

PALMER, Angus Elor. St Jo Th Coll Morpeth 29. ACT ThL 31. **d** 31 Melb for Wang **p** 32 Wang. C of Longwood 31-33; St Mich Camden Town Lon 33-36; All SS Brisb 36-37; All SS St Kilda 37-39; C-in-c of St Bart Burnley 38; C of Broken Hill 39-40; P-in-c of Allansford w Panmure 40-41; All SS Bal and Wendouree 41-44; Chap AIF 44-46; P-in-c of Skipton 46-48; Chap Miss to Seamen Hobart 48-53; R of Launceston 53-57; Chap to Bp of Tas 54-57; I of Hawksburn 57-70; St Jas E St Kilda 70-72; Perm to Offic Dio Melb from 73. *Flat 2, 30 Denby Road, Armadale, Vic., Australia 3143.*

PALMER, Basil Charles Donaldson. b 06. St Jo Coll Auckld. Univ of NZ BA 33. **d** 30 **p** 31 Auckld. C of Ellerslie 30-31; Otahuhu 31-34; Windlesham 34-36; Bridport 36-38; PC of Derry Hill 38-45; V of Whiteparish 45-51; R of E Knoyle 51-75; PC of Sedgehill 51-67; V 68-75; RD of Tisbury 59-69; Perm to Offic Dios Ex, Sarum and B & W from 75. *Watersmeade, Underway, Combe St Nicholas, Chard, Somt TA20 3NS.*

PALMER, Bernard Joseph. b 20. St Cath Ox BA (3rd cl Mod Hist) 49, MA 64. Worc Ordin Coll 64. **d** 66 **p** 67 Truro. C of St Stephen-by-Saltash 66-69; R of Harvington 69-78; V of Stoulton w Drakes Broughton and Pirton Dio Worc from 78. *Broughton Vicarage, Drakes Broughton, Pershore, Worcs, WR10 2AQ.* (Worc 840528)

PALMER, Very Rev Clifford George. Univ of NZ BA 33. St Jo Coll Auckld 29. **d** 32 **p** 33 Auckld. C of St Andr Epsom NZ 32-35; St Jas Croydon 36-37; Perm to Offic at St Aug Pendlebury 37-38; V of Bay of Is 38-40; CF (NZ) 40-46; Men in Disp 43; Perm to Offic Dio Ox 46; V of St Thos Cov 47-53; Commiss Auckld 48-53; V of Whangarei 53-57; Archd of Waimate 53-57; Dean and V of St Pet Cathl Hamilton 57-74; Dean (Emer) from 74; Perm to Offic Dio Waik 74-75; Hon C of Forest Lake Dio Waik from 75. *10 Defoe Avenue, Hillcrest, Hamilton, NZ.* (69-842)

PALMER, Canon David Henry. b 33. Univ of Bris BA 54. Linc Th Coll 56. **d** 58 **p** 59 S'wark. C of St Jo Evang E Dulwich 58-62; All SS (in c of Dogsthorpe from 63) Pet 62-68; V of H Trin Northn 68-74; Chap to Br Embassy Ankara 74-77; Br Embassy and All SS Rome Dio Gibr (Gibr in Eur from 80) from 77; Can of Malta Cathl from 79. *Via del Babuino 153b, 00187 Rome, Italy.* (679 4357)

PALMER, David Roderick. b 34. St Jo Coll Dur BA 56. Univ of Birm Dipl Th 58. Qu Coll Birm. **d** 60 **p** 61 Chelmsf. C of Loughton 60-63; St Gabr Westmr 63-64; Chap Miss to Seamen 64-67; CF 67-74; Chap Luxembourg 74-80; P-in-c of Exton and Winsford and Cutcombe w Luxborough Dio B & W from 80. *Winsford Vicarage, Minehead, Somt.* (Winsford 301)

PALMER, Ven Derek George. b 28. Selw Coll Cam BA 51, MA 55. Wells Th Coll 51. **d** 52 **p** 53 Bris. C of Stapleton 52-54; Bishopston 54-58; Min of Hartcliffe Conv Distr 58-62; V 62-68; Swindon 68-76; Gen Syn 70-81; Hon Can of Bris 74-76; Can of Roch Cathl from 76; Archd of Roch from 76. *Archdeaconry, Rochester, Kent, ME1 1SX.* (Medway 42527)

PALMER, Derek James. b 54. Univ of Man BA (Th) 77. Qu Coll Birm 77. **d** 79 **p** 80 Lich. C of St Edw Leek Dio Lich from 79. *6a Wallbridge Precinct, Leek, Staffs.*

PALMER, Donald Cameron. b 48. Ridley Coll Melb 72. **d** 75 Melb for St Arn **p** 76 Melb. C of Mildura 75; St Barn Balwyn 75-78; on leave 78-80; I of St Pet and St Andr Braybrook Dio Melb from 80. *67 Darnley Street, Braybrook, Vic, Australia 3019.*

PALMER, Francis Harvey. b 30. Late Exhib of Jes Coll Cam 2nd cl Cl Trip pt i, 51, BA 52, 2nd cl Th Trip pt ii, 53, MA 56. Wycl Hall, Ox 53. **d** 55 **p** 56 Liv. C of Knotty Ash 55-57; St Mary Southgate Crawley 58-60; Chap Fitzw Ho Cam 60-64; L to Offic Dio Ely 61-64; V of H Trin Cam 64-71; Surr 66-72; Prin of Ridley Hall Cam 71-72; R of Worplesdon 72-80; Ecumen Officer to Bp of Guildf 74-80; Dios Missr and

P-in-c of Blymhill w Weston-under-Lizard Dio Lich from 80. *Blymhill Rectory, Shifnal, Salop, TF11 8LL.* (Weston-under-Lizard 273)

PALMER, Francis Noel. b 1897. Wadh Coll Ox BA 21, MA 43. Drew Th Sem NJ BD 25. **d** 31 Montr for Tor **p** 32 Niag for Tor. C of St Anne Tor 32-33; R 33-38; V of St Sav Everton 38-41; St Luke Prestonville 41-45; Prin CA Mem Tr Coll 45-47; Dioc Missr Dio Ex 47; R of Shillingstone 47-52; Hanover w Allan Park 52-54; V of St Jo Evang Bromley 54-68; Perm to Offic Dio Cant from 68. *44 Princess Margaret Avenue, Cliftonville, Margate, Kent CT9 3DZ.* (Thanet 25853)

PALMER, Frank Reginald Charles. b 07. AKC 30. **d** 30 **p** 31 Lon. C of St Mich AA Stoke Newington 30-32; St Mary-le-Strand Lon 32-44; C-in-c 44; R of St Adamnan Duror 44-46; Actg C of All SS Ennismore Gdns Lon 46-47; C 47-50; V of St Martin Lower Edmonton 50-54; C of St Geo Hanover Square Lon 54-56; R of Easton-in-Gordano 56; C of Lon Dks 56-60; Perm to Offic Dio Lon 60-62 and from 71; Dio York 63; Dio Ox 65-67. *11 Hampstead Hill Gardens, NW3 2PH.*

PALMER, Frederick Thomas Montgomery. Brisb Th Coll ACT ThL 13. **d** 13 **p** 15 Brisb. C of H Trin Fortitude Valley 13-14; St Paul Roma 14-15; St Andr Pittsworth 15-18; St Paul Ipswich 18-19; St John Dalby 20-22; V of Noosa 22-24 (all in Queensld) furlough 24-25; C of St Mark Warwick 25-27; V of Biggenden 27-29; Coolangatta 29-31; Wyan w Rappville 31-32; Nimbin 32-42; P-in-c of Gundy 42-45; R of Nabiac 45-52; P-in-c of Clarence Town 52-61. *13 Averley Street, Kahibah, NSW 2290, Australia.*

PALMER, Canon George Henry. b 14. AKC 37. **d** 37 **p** 38 Roch. C of St Jas Gravesend 37-40; St Steph Norbury 40-42; Ch Ch Reading (in c of St Agnes Reading) 42-48; V of Benson 48-63; Deddington w Clifton and Hempton 63-78; RD of Deddington 65-78; Hon Can of Ch Ch Cathl Ox from 77. *Preston House, Preston Crowmarsh, Benson, Oxford, OX9 6SL.* (Wallingford 38296)

PALMER, Very Rev George Llewellyn Otolorin. Fourah Bay Coll BA 40, MA 45. **d** 42 **p** 43 Sier L. C of Ch Ch Freetown 42-44; CF (W Afr) 44-46; P-in-c of Gloucester Sier L 46-48; C of Drypool Hull Yorks 48-49; V of Hastings Sier L 49-52; LPr Dio Accra 56-62; Dio Sier L from 62; Prin Secondary Sch Kazeima 62-64; CMS Gr Sch Freetown Sier L 64-70; Exam Chap to Bp of Sier L from 67; Dean of St Geo Cathl Freetown from 70. *Box 1174, Freetown, Sierra Leone.* (Freetown 30141)

PALMER, Graham. b 31. Em Coll Cam BA 53, MA 57. Qu Coll Birm 56. **d** 58 **p** 59 S'wark. C of Camberwell 58-61; St Aug Kilburn 61-67; C-in-c of St Alb Fulham Dio Lon 67-73; V from 73. *St Alban's Vicarage, Margravine Road, W6 8HJ.* (01-385 0724)

PALMER, Canon Harold Ernest. Univ of Melb BA 39. Gen Th Sem NY STB 56. Ridley Coll Melb. **d** 39 **p** 40 Goulb. C of St Sav Cathl Goulb 39-41; Wagga Wagga 41-43; Chap AIF 43-46; R of Port Moresby 47-50; P-in-c of Dogura 50-54; Sub-Dean and Can of Dogura Cathl and Dioc Chap to Bp of New Guinea 50-54; Can Dioc 54-62; on leave 54-56; P-in-c of Mukawa 56-57; I of Agenehambo 57-62; R of St Luke Canberra 62-67; Can, Vice-Dean and R of St Sav Cathl Goulb Dio C & Goulb from 67. *134 Cowper Street, Goulburn, NSW, Australia.* (048-21 2206)

PALMER, Harvey. **d** 77 **p** 78 N Queensld. C of All SS Gordonvale Dio N Queensld from 77. *PO Box 181, Gordonvale, Qld, Australia 4865.*

PALMER, Herbert Harrison. Late Scho of New Coll Ox BA (1st cl Math) 1900, MA 07. **d** 01 **p** 02 Liv. C of Em Ch Everton 01; St John Waterloo Liv 01-03; Chap RN 03-16; R of Greystead 16-17; C of Bp's Hatfield 19-20; Asst Master Liv Coll 20-26; L to Offic Dio Liv 21-26; P-in-c of Bulwer w Himeville and Underberg 27-30; V of Mid Illovo 30-58; Camperdown 40-58; L to Offic Dio Natal from 58. *Chapter Close, Taunton Road, Pietermaritzburg, Natal, S Africa.*

PALMER, Hugh. b 50. Pemb Coll Cam BA 72, MA 76. Ridley Hall Cam 73. **d** 76 **p** 77 Nor. C of H Trin Heigham 76-80; Bp's Chap for Tr and Miss Dio Nor from 80. *59 Bury Street, Norwich, Norf.* (Nor 22343)

PALMER, Hugh Maurice Webber. Magd Coll Cam BA 3rd cl Th Trip 51, MA 55. Cudd Coll 51. **d** 53 **p** 54 Win. C of Bitterne Pk 53-57; Chap Rhod and Nyasa Rly Miss Dios Mashon and Matab 57-60; Asst P Umtali Dio Mashon 60-62; V of Owslebury w Morestead 62-65; R of St Luke Que Que 65-68; C of St Mary and All SS Cathl Salisbury 68-70; Headbourne Worthy 70-71; R of Haynford (w Stratton Strawless from 77) Dio Nor from 72; C-in-c of Stratton Strawless 72-77. *Haynford Rectory, Norwich, Norf. NOR 85X.* (Norwich 898330)

PALMER, Ian Stanley. b 50. K Coll Lon BD 71. Cranmer Hall Dur 73. **d** 75 Warrington for Liv **p** 76 Liv. C of Huyton 75-78; Chap Univ of Dur from 78. *Trevelyan College, Durham, DH1 3LN.* (Durham 61133)

PALMER, James Asa. Hur Coll Ont. **d** 56 **p** 58 Hur. I of Bervie 56-59; St Steph Stratford 59-62; R of St Mark Windsor 62-65; St James Winnipeg 65-70; P-in-c of Forest Ont 71-75. *Wiarton, Ont., Canada.*

PALMER, John Charles. b 52. Univ of Otago BTh 78. St Jo Coll Auckld. **d** 77 **p** 79 Dun. C of Caversham 78-80; St John Invercargill 80-81; on leave. *30 Norfolk Street, St Clair, Dunedin, NZ.* (878-802)

PALMER, John Michael Joseph. b 18. VRD 62. Qu Coll Cam BA 40, MA 48. **d** 61 **p** 62 Pet. C of Oakham 61-64; Chap RNR from 62; R of Parham w Wiggonholt and Greatham 64-67; V of Fernhurst 67-72; Dom Chap to Bp of Willesden 73; to Bp of Truro 73-74; L to Offic Dio Lon 73; Dio Truro 73-75. *York Hill Cottage, Alderney, CI.*

PALMER, John Richard Henry. b 29. K Coll Lon and Warm AKC 52. **d** 53 **p** 54 Guildf. C of Englefield Green 53-57; Bro of the Good Shepherd and P-in-c of Brewarrina Dio Bath 57-62; C of Wareham 62-63; PC of St Jo Evang Derby 63-66; Chap Holloway Sanat Virginia Water 66-70; Brookwood Hosp from 70. *Red Gables, Brookwood Hospital Estate, Knap Hill, Woking, Surrey GU21 2RG.* (Brookwood 4545)

PALMER, John Russell. b 25. Univ of Birm BSc 46. Cudd Coll 70. **d** 71 Southn for Win **p** 72 Win. C of Weeke Dio Win 71-76; V of Four Marks Dio Win from 76. *Four Marks Vicarage, Alton, Hants.* (Alton 63344)

PALMER, Keith. b 33. Wycl Hall, Ox 64. **d** 66 Hulme for Man **p** 67 Man. C of St Paul Halliwell 66-67; Bispham 67-70; H Trin Darwen 70-74; Team V of St Pet Darwen w St Paul Hoddlesden 74; V of Foulridge Dio Blackb from 74. *Foulridge Vicarage, Colne, Lancs.* (Colne 865491)

PALMER, Michael Christopher. b 43. K Coll Lon and Warm AKC 67. **d** 68 **p** 69 Ox. C of Easthampstead 68-71; Chap Miss to Seamen Lon 71-72; Hong Kong 73; on leave 74-76; L to Offic Dio Ox 76-79; Dio Truro from 79. *Sophies Cottage, Treworthal, Ruan Highlanes, Truro, Cornwall, TR2 5LR.* (Veryan 667)

PALMER, Canon Neville William Jarvis. Univ of Witwatersrand, BSc 31. St Paul's Coll Grahmstn LTh (S Afr) 35. **d** 35 **p** 36 Johann. C of St Dunstan Benoni 35-41; CF (S Afr) 41-46; Chap of St Jo Coll Johann 46-66; L to Offic Dio Johann 46-66; C of St Mary Cathl Johann 67-74; Can of Johann 72-79; Hon Can from 80. *1 Seymour Avenue, Parktown, Johannesburg, S Africa.* (31-3302)

PALMER, Norman Ernest. b 28. BD (Lon) 59. Dipl Th (Lon) 56. Roch Th Coll 66. **d** and **p** 67 Ox. C of Chipping Norton 67-69; V of Bozeat w Easton Maudit Dio Pet from 69. *Bozeat Vicarage, Wellingborough, Northants, NN9 7LZ.* (Wellingborough 663216)

✠ **PALMER, Most Rev Norman Kitchener.** MBE 75. St Jo Coll Auckld NZ Bd of Th Stud LTh 65. **d** 64 Auckld for Melan **p** 66 Melan. C of Glen Innes 64-65; Asst Master All H Sch Pawa 65-67; Hd Master St Barn Sch Alangaula 67-69; St Nich Sch Honiara 69-72; Res Can of St Barn Cathl Honiara 69-72; Dean 73-75; Cons Ld Bp of Centr Melan in St Barn Cathl Honiara 1 Nov 75 by Bp of Ysabel, Bps of Malaita, New Hebr, Papua, Graft and Polyn; and others; Apptd Abp and Metrop of Prov of Melan 75. *Archbishop's House, Box 19, Honiara, Solomon Islands.* (Honiara 893)

PALMER, Peter Malcolm. b 31. Chich Th Coll 56. **d** 59 **p** 60 St Alb. C of Leighton Buzzard 59-63; Apsley End 63-65; H Sav Hitchin 65-69; R of Ickleford 69-76; V of St Matt Oxhey Dio St Alb from 76. *Vicarage, St Matthew's Close, Eastbury Road, Oxhey, Herts, WD1 4PT.* (Watford 41420)

PALMER, Peter Parsons. **d** 59 **p** 61 Alg. SSJE Miss At Bracebridge Alg 59-79; Perm to Offic Dio Leic from 80. *St John's House, 2 Woodland Avenue, Leicester, LE2 3HG.*

PALMER, Robert William. b 28. Wells Th Coll 63. **d** 65 Bp McKie for Cov **p** 66 Cov. C of St Barbara Earlsdon Cov 65-69; P-in-c of St Mark Cov 69-71; Hon C of Binley 72-75; V of St Paul Ecclesfield Dio Sheff from 76. *St Paul's Vicarage, Wheata Road, Sheffield, S5 9FP.* (Sheff 468137)

PALMER, Roland Ford. Trin Coll Tor LTh 15, BA 16, Hon DD 43. MSSJE 22. **d** 16 **p** 17 Alg. C of North Bay 16; Englehart 16; I of St Geo w St Mich Port Arthur Ont 17-19; in Amer Ch 19-27; P-in-c of Emsdale 27-28; Superior SSJE in Canada 27-48; and 63-66; Miss at Bracebridge Dio Alg from 69; I of Sorrento 47-48; on leave 48-52; Dioc Miss Dio Alg 52-66; Hon Can of Alg 56-79; P-in-c of Ch Ch Lon 66-69. *St Anne's Tower, Apt 1105, 661 Dufferin Street, Toronto 145, Ont., Canada.* (416-537 9827)

PALMER, Ronald Harrison. Univ of Syd BEcon 49. Moore Th Coll Syd ACt ThL 46. **d** and **p** 47 Syd. C of St Andr Summer Hill 47-48; Erskineville 48; R of Wingecarribee 49-51; Austinmer w Clifton and Thirroul 51-54; Earlwood 54-67; Forestville 67-69; Chap Concorn Hosp Dio Syd from 69. *9 Rushall Street, Pymble, NSW, Australia 2073.* (44-3688)

PALMER, Stephen Charles. b 47. Oak Hill Th Coll 71. **d** 74 **p** 75 Portsm. C of Crofton 74-77; Dom Chap to Bp of Portsm 77-80; Hon Chap from 81; Chap RNR from 78; R of Brighstone w Brooke and Mottistone Dio Portsm from 80. *Brighstone Rectory, Newport, IW, PO30 4AQ.* (Brighstone 740267)

PALMER, Stephen Roundell. b 23. Ch Ch Ox BA 50, MA 54. Cudd Coll 51. **d** 53 **p** 54 Portsm. C of H Spirit Southsea 53-58; R of Weston under Penyard 58-72; R of Hope Mansel 58-72; L to Offic Dio Carl from 73. *The Croft, Croft Avenue, Penrith, Cumberland.*

PALMER, Terence Henry James. b 34. Late Scho Stud and Pri St D Coll Lamp BA (2nd cl Hist) 55, LTh 57. St Edm Hall Ox BA (2nd cl Th) 65, MA 69. **d** 57 **p** 58 Mon. C of Griffithstown 57-60; Min Can and C of St D Cathl 60-63; Perm to Offic Dios B & W and Ox 63-65; C of Monmouth 65-69; C-in-c of St Hilary's Conv Distr Greenway 69-72; R of Roggiett w Llanvihangel Roggiett (and Portskewett from 80) Dio Mon from 72. *19 Main Road, Portskewett, Newport, Gwent, NP6 4SG.* (Caldicot 420313)

PALMER, William Frederick. b 15. Kelham Th Coll 33. **d** 40 **p** 41 S'wark. C of St Pet St Helier 40-41; St Jo Div Earlsfield 41-44; Burnham (in c of St Andr Cippenham) 44-49; V of Langley Marish 49-68; R of Chalfont St Giles 68-73; V of St Mich AA Mill Hill 73-81; Perm to Offic Dio St Alb from 81. *22 The Sycamores, Baldock, Herts, SG7 5BJ.* (Baldock 892456)

PALMER, William John. St D Coll Lamp BA 33. **d** 34 **p** 35 St D. C of Milford Haven 34-35; Northbourne 35-38; Deal 38-40; St Paul w St Geo (in c of St Barn) Edin 40-41; Alnwick 41-45; V of Amble 45-53; Slaley 53-68; Dinnington 68-74. *Cheviot View, Brunswick Village, Newcastle-upon-Tyne.*

PALOMINOS, Luis. d 76 Bp Bazley for Chile. d Dio Chile. *Casilla 561, Vina del Mar, Chile.*

PAMFLETT, Thomas Macdonald. St Jo Coll Morpeth 59. ACT ThL 60. **d** 60 Bp Redding for Bal **p** 61 Bal. C of Warrnambool 60-63; P-in-c of Nhill Dio Bal 63-64; R 64-70; R of Beaufort 70-76; V of Ballan w Bungaree Dio Bal from 76. *Vicarage, Ballan, Vic, Australia 3343.* (053-681342)

PAMMENT, Gordon Charles. b 31. TCD BA 54. Linc Th Coll 56. **d** 58 **p** 60 St Alb. C of Hemel Hempstead 58-63; Gedney Drove End 63-65; I of Macroom U 65-72; Rathcormac Dio Cloyne from 72; Castlelyons (Aghern) Dio Cloyne from 72; Fermoy U Dio Cloyne from 78. *Rectory, Glenville, Co Cork, Irish Republic.* (Cork 880140)

PAMPLIN, Richard Lawrence. b 46. Univ of Lon BSc (Eng) 68. Univ of Dur BA 75. Wycl Hall Ox 75. **d** 77 **p** 78 Dur. C of Greenside 77-80; St Barn & St Mary City and Dio Sheff from 80. *St Mary's Vicarage, Charlotte Road, Sheffield, S1 4TL.* (Sheff 24987)

PANG, Canon Andrew Wing Cheung. b 25. Chinese Univ Hong Chung Chi Coll Dipl 57. **d** 51 S China **p** 54 Hong. V of St Mary Dio Hong from 70; Hon Can of Hong from 73. *2a Tai Hang Road, Causeway Bay, Hong Kong.* (5-265355)

PANKHURST, Donald Araunah. b 28. Univ of Birm Dipl Th 64. Qu Coll Birm 62. **d** 64 Warrington for Liv **p** 65 Liv. C of St John Pemberton 64-68; V of Aspull 68-76; R of Newchurch Dio Liv from 76. *Newchurch Rectory, Culcheth, Warrington, Chesh.* (Culcheth 6300)

PANNELL, Roy Charles. b 45. K Coll Lon AKC 69. St Aug Coll Cant 69. **d** 70 Bp Gerard for Sheff **p** 71 Sheff. C of St Cecilia Parson Cross Sheff 70-75; V of New Bentley 75-82; St Pet Greenhill Dio Sheff from 82. *St Peter's Clergy House, Reney Avenue, Sheffield, S8 7FN.* (Sheff 377522)

PANNETT, Philip Anthony. b 36. MPS 59. K Coll Lon and Warm AKC 63. **d** 64 **p** 65 Chich. C of Moulsecoomb w Stanmer and Falmer 64-68; Hangleton 68-72; L to Offic Dio Cant from 72; Dio Chich from 76. *35 Dudley Road, Brighton, BN1 7GN.*

PAN SHWE, d 70 Pa-an. d Dio Pa-an. *Western Hills, Toungoo Area, Burma.*

PANTER, Canon Noel. b 09. Ex Coll Ox BA (3rd cl Engl Lang and Lit) 31, Dipl Th 32, MA 35. Wycl Hall, Ox 31. **d** 33 **p** 34 Worc. C of St Geo Kidderminster 33-36; St Francis Dudley 36-41; R of Churchill in Halfshire w Blakedown 41-68; RD of Kidderminster 63-68; Hon Can of Worc from 66; V of Ch Ch Malvern 68-77. *2 Park View, Oatleys Road, Ledbury, Herefs, HR8 2BN.* (Ledbury 2789)

PANTER, Richard James Graham. b 48. Oak Hill Th Coll 73. **d** 76 **p** 77 Man. C of H Trin Rusholme 76-80; St Cypr w Ch Ch Toxteth Dio Liv from 80. *6 Carstairs Road, Nesham Park, Liverpool.* (051-220 8822)

PANTING, John. b 36. K Coll Cam BA 60, MA 64. Ridley Hall, Cam 60. **d** 62 **p** 63 Guildf. C of Woking 62-65; Chap Dean Close Sch Cheltm 65-68; L to Offic Dio York 68-70; C of Stratford-on-Avon Dio Cov 70-75; Team V of Shottery 75-79; V of Keresley w Coundon Dio Cov from 79. *34 Tamworth Road, Coventry, CV6 2EL.* (Keresley 2717)

PANTON, Alan Edward. b 45. K Coll Lon and Warm BD and AKC 67. **d** 68 **p** 69 S'wark. C of Eltham 68-73; Horley 73-78; V of St Mary Dallington Northn Dio Pet from 78. *Vicarage, The Barton's Close, Dallington, Northants.* (Northampton 51478)

PAO, Benjamin. Union Th Coll Hong LTh 65. **d** 65 Hong. d Dio Hong; Exam Chap to Bp of Hong 71-73; on leave 74-77; and from 78; Hosp Chap Dio Hong 77-78. *c/o 1 Lower Albert Road, Hong Kong.*

PAPANE, Shadrach Kgosimang. St Bede's Coll Umtata 70. **d** and **p** 74 Bloemf. C of Thaba'Nchu 74-76; P-in-c of Clocolan Dio Bloemf from 76. *Box 255, Clocolan, OFS, S Africa.*

PAPE, Nicholas. d 78 **p** 79 Centr Melan. P Dio Centr Melan. *Bola District, Gela Region, Solomon Islands.*

PAPE, Timothy Vernon Francis. b 39. BSc (2nd cl) Lon 63. Wells Th Coll 63. **d** 65 **p** 66 Worc. C of Pershore 65-69; Perm to Offic Dio Bris 69-73; Publ Pr Dio Sarum from 75; Dep Hd Master Southbroom C of E Sch 75-81; Hd Master Chirton Primary Sch from 81. *Old Brewery House, Shaw, Melksham, Wilts.* (Melksham 702259)

PAPPAS, Anastassius Haralabus. Ridley Coll Melb 59. ACT ThL 63. **d** 63 Bp Sambell for Melb **p** 64 Melb. C of W Footscray 63-65; V of W Heidelberg 65-70; R of Mansfield 70-77; Chap C of E Gr Sch Geelong from 77. *Geelong Grammar School, Corio, Vic., Australia 3214.* (052-75 1142)

PAPPRILL, Leonard Arthur. St Francis Coll Brisb ACT ThL 51. **d** 48 **p** 49 Graft. C of Graft Cathl 48-52; R of Bowraville 52-55; Centr Macleay 55-76; Perm to Offic Dio Graft from 76. *Cnr Lord and Gabrielle Avenue, East Kempsey, NSW, Australia 2440.*

PAPROTH, Darrell Neil. b 44. BD (Lon) 72. Ridley Coll Melb ThL 73. **d** 73 **p** 74 Bp Dann for Melb. C of Rosanna 73-75; Caulfield 75-76; P-in-c of Northcote 76-80; Lakes Entrance Dio Gippsld from 80. *Box 151, Lakes Entrance, Vic, Australia 3909.*

PAPUA NEW GUINEA, Metropolitan of Province of. *See* Hand, Most Rev Geoffrey David.

PAPWORTH, John. b 21. BSc (Lon) 52. **d** 75 **p** 76 Lusaka (APM). P Dio Lusaka. *Box RW 549, Lusaka, Zambia.*

PARACHINI, David Charles. Univ of Penn BA 65. Hur Coll BTh 68. **d** 68 Hur **p** 69 Bp D J Campbell for Hur. L to Offic Dio Hur 68-69. *140 Sargent Street, Newton, Mass 02158, USA.*

PARAGUAY, Lord Bishop of. *See* Milmine, Right Rev Douglas.

PARAGUAY, Assistant Bishop of. *See* Ortiz, Right Rev Omar.

PARDOS, Marcus Leon. b 39. **d** 76 N Argent. d Dio N Argent. *Casilla 19, Ing Juarez, Pcia de Formosa, Argentina.*

PARE, Philip Norris. b 10. K Coll Cam 2nd cl Cl Trip pt i, 31, BA (2nd cl Th Trip pt i) 33, MA 37. Cudd Coll 33. **d** 34 **p** 35 S'wark. C of All SS W Dulwich 34-37; Asst Chap Bps' Coll Cheshunt 37-39; Vice-Prin 39-40; C of St Mary L Cam 40; Chap RNVR 40-46; V of Cheshunt 46-57; RD of Ware 49-56; Exam Chap to Bp of St Alb 51-56; Can Missr Stipendiary Dio Wakef 57-62; Dir of Ordinands Dio Wakef 59-68; Stewardship Adviser Dio Wakef 60-68; V and Provost of All SS Cathl Wakef 62-71; Ch Comm 68-71; V of Cholsey 73-82; Provost of N Div Woodard Corp 77-82. *c/o Cholsey Vicarage, Wallingford, Oxon, OX10 9PP.* (0491 651216)

PARE, Stephen Charles. b 53. Univ of Sussex BEducn 75. Univ of Wales (Cardiff) Dipl Th 80. St Mich AA Coll Llan 78. **d** 80 **p** 81 Llan. C of St Jo Bapt Cardiff Dio Llan from 80. *17 Brithdir Street, Cathays, Cardiff, CF2 4LE.*

PARFITT, Brian John. b 49. Ex Coll Ox BA 71, MA 76. Wycl Hall Ox 71. **d** 74 **p** 75 Mon. C of St Mark Newport Gwent 74-78; R of Aberystruth (Blaina) Dio Mon from 78. *Rectory, Brynteg Road, Blaina, Gwent, NP3 3HN.* (Blaina 290079)

PARFITT, Graeme Stanley. b 36. Qu Coll Birm 77. **d** 79 **p** 80 Bris. C of St Jo Div Fishponds Dio Bris from 79. *306 Lodge Causeway, Fishponds, Bristol, BS16 3RD.*

PARFITT, John Arthur. b 49. Univ of Nottm BTh 81. St Jo Coll Nottm 77. **d** 81 Southw. C of Radcliffe-on-Trent Dio Southw from 81. *44 Clumber Drive, Radcliffe-on-Trent, Nottingham, NG12 1DB.*

PARFITT, John Hubert. b 29. Univ of Birm Dipl Th 66. Univ of Southn MA 72. Qu Coll Birm 78. **d** 80 Worc **p** 81 (APM). C of Fladbury, Moor & Wyre Piddle Dio Worc from 80. *1 The Green, Fladbury, Pershore, Worcs, WR10 2QA.*

PARFITT, Keith John. b 44. K Coll Lon AKC and BD 68. St Aug Coll Cant 69. **d** 70 Bp Graham-Campbell for Pet **p** 71 Pet. C of St Andr Kettering 70-74; Asst Social and Industr Adv Dio Portsm 74-81; RD of Alverstoke from 79; P-in-c of St Matt Conv Distr Bridgemary, Gosport Dio Portsm from 81. *Church House, Wych Lane, Bridgemary, Gosport, Hants PO13 0NL.* (Fareham 280419)

✠ **PARFITT, Right Rev Thomas Richards.** b 11. St Jo Coll

Ox 3rd cl Cl Mods 31, BA (2nd cl LitHum) 33, 2nd cl Th 34, MA 36. Cudd Coll 34. **d** 35 Bp Crick for Derby **p** 36 Derby. C of New Mills 35-39; Rugby (in c of H Trin) 39-43; Chap RNVR 43-46; V of St Andr Derby 46-52; RD of Derby 51-52 Cons Ld Bp in Madag in S'wark Cathl 25 Jan 52 by Abp of Cant; Bps of S'wark; Derby; St E; Bps Suffr of Kingston T; Woolwich; and Kens; and Bps O'Ferrall and Vernon; res 61; Dean of Cathl Ch of St Laur Antan 52-61; Asst Bp of Derby from 61; R of Matlock w Tansley 62-80; Hon Can of Derby from 62; RD of Wirksworth 73-78. *St Paul's Vicarage, Old Chester Road, Derby, DE1 3SA.* (Derby 381093)

PARHAM, (Barnabas) Earl Leander. St Mark's Coll Dar-S 73. **d** 73 **p** 74 Dar-S. M SSF 74. P Dio Dar-S. *Box 2227, Dar-es-Salaam, Tanzania.*

PARISH, John Raymond. d and **p** 59 Graft. C-in-c of U Macleay 59-60; V of Copmanhurst 60-64; R of Alstonville Dio Graft from 64. *Rectory, Alstonville, NSW, Australia.* (28 0231)

PARISH, Stephen Richard. b 49. Univ of Lon Dipl Th (Extra-Mural Stud) 77. Oak Hill Coll 74. **d** 77 Man **p** 78 Bp Hulme for Man. C of Ch Ch Chadderton 77-81; Team V of Chell Dio Lich from 81. *c/o St Michael's Rectory, Stoke-on-Trent, Staffs, ST6 6JT.*

PARK, Allan. b 38. Lich Th Coll 61. **d** 64 Penrith for Carl **p** 65 Carl. C of St Mary Westfield Workington 64-67; Lawton Moor 67-69; R of Lightbowne 69-81; M Gen Syn from 80; V of Peel Green w Barton Dio Man from 81. *St Michael's Vicarage, Peel Green, Manchester, M30 7LP.* (061-789 3751)

PARK, Canon John Raymond. b 11. Keble Coll Ox BA (3rd cl Hist) 33, MA 37. Linc Th Coll 34. **d** 35 **p** 36 Newc T. C of St Gabr Newc T 35-39; C-in-c of St John's Conv Distr Wallsend 39-44; V of Lindley 44-51; H Trin Southport 51-56; R of Lee St John 56-64; Wigan 64-74; RD of Wigan 65-74; Hon Can of Liv from 66; R of W Tanfield and Well w Snape 74-76; Perm to Offic Dio York from 76. *52 Longridge Lane, Upper Poppleton, York.* (York 794658)

PARK, Robert William. b 12. Univ of Man BA 38. Bps' Coll Cheshunt, 35. **d** 39 **p** 40 Birm. C of St Gabr Weoley Castle w St Mich Bartley Green 39-43; St Jas Handsworth 43-49; V of Shuttington w Amington 49-56; Dioc Chap (in c of World's End) Dio Birm 56-59; V of St Bonif Birm 59-62; R of Shackerstone w Congerstone 62-77. *Greenhill, Clarence Road, Craig-y-Don, Llandudno, Gwyn LL30 1TW.*

PARK, Trevor. b 38. BA (1st cl) Lon 64. STh (Lambeth) 81. Linc Th Coll 64. **d** 66 **p** 67 Carl. C of Crosthwaite 66-68; Asst Chap Solihull Sch 69-71; V of St Bees 71-77; Chap St Bees Sch 71-77; M Gen Syn Carl from 75; V of Dalton-in-Furness Dio Carl from 77. *Vicarage, Dalton-in-Furness, Cumb.* (D-in-F 62526)

PARKE, Edmund George. b 14. Trin Coll Dub BA 37. MA 47. **d** 38 **p** 39 Lich. C of St Giles Newc T 38-42; Chap RAFVR 42-48; RAF 48-69; Chap and Welfare Officer Social Work Dept of Dundee Corp 69-75; Tayside Reg Coun Dundee Div 75-79. *8 Westwood Terrace, West Newport-on-Tay, Fife, DD6 8JF.*

PARKE, Canon George Reginald. b 09. Linc Th Coll 40. **d** 42 **p** 43 Newc T. C of Horton 42-46; St Geo Cullercoats 46-48; PC of H Cross Fenham Newc T 48-64; Proc Conv Newc T 62-64; V of St Gabr Heaton 64-73; Beadnell 73-80; RD of Newc T W 64; Newc T E 72-73; Hon Can of Newc T from 70. *West House, Dunstan, Alnwick, Northumb, NE66 3TB.*

✠ **PARKE-TAYLOR, Right Rev Geoffrey Howard.** Univ of Tor BA (1st cl Or Lang) 42, MA 44. Wycl Coll Tor LTh 44, BD 61, DD 67. **d** 44 **p** 45 Tor. Lect Wycl Coll Tor 44-46; Prof 47-51; I of Fenelon Falls and Coboconk 51-53; Thistletown 53-55; Queensway 55-59; Prof of NT Angl Th Coll Vancouver 59-64; OT Hur Coll 64-76; Dean of Th 66-76; Can of Hur 73-76; Cons Bp Suffr of Hur in St Paul's Cathl Lon Ont 14 Sept 76 by Abp of Moos; Bps of Hur, Tor, Ont, Niag and Alg; Bps Suffr of Hur, Niag and Tor; and others; Elected Bp Suffr of Tor 81. *135 Adelaide Street East, Toronto, Ont, Canada, M5C 1L8.*

PARKER, Alan Ronald. Univ of NSW BSc 66. Moore Th Coll Syd 79. **d** 80 Syd **p** 80 Bp Robinson for Syd. C of SS Jas & John Mt Druitt Dio Syd from 80. *12 Falkirk Place, Dharruk, NSW, Australia 2770.* (625-7301)

PARKER, Alfred. b 20. Univ of Man BA (2nd cl Hist) 47. Wycl Hall, Ox 47. **d** 49 **p** 50 Man. C of Droylsden 49-53; St Jas Farnworth (in c of St Geo New Bury) 53-54; C-in-c of St Bart Bolton 54-56; V 56-61; C-in-c St Mich Gt Lever 59-61; R of St Mich w St Bart Gt Lever 61-65; V of Belmont Dio Man from 65. *Vicarage, Belmont, Bolton, BL7 8AA.* (Belmont Village 221)

PARKER, Arthur Townley. b 14. Worc Ordin Coll 59. **d** 61 **p** 62 Worc. C of St Steph Barbourne Worc 61-63; St Cypr Cathl Kimberley 63-64; R of Rock w Heightington 64-68; C of W Wycombe (in c of St Mary and St Geo) 68-70; St Jo Watford 70-71; Thornton w Martin 73-75; Chap Hostel of God Dio S'wark 71-73; Asst Chap Wandsworth Pris 71-73. *6 Coronation Road, Bridgwater, Somt, TA6 7DS.* (0278-425889)

PARKER, Brian. b 40. Coll of Em and St Chad Sktn 62. **d** 65 **p** 66 Qu'App. I of Eston Dio Qu'App 65-69; Balcarres 69-72; Valleyview Dio Athab from 72. *Box 506, Valleyview, Alta, TOH 3NO, Canada.* (403-524 3798)

PARKER, Cecil William. b 11. Bps' Coll Cheshunt, 46. St Andr Th Coll Pampisford, 48. **d** 48 **p** 49 Chelmsf. C of St Barn Little Ilford 48-51; St Jas Colchester 51-53; Min of St Anne's Distr Colchester 53-59; V of St Andr Walthamstow 59-80. *Robins Croft, The Crescent, Tenbury Wells, Worcs, WR15 8DJ.*

PARKER, Charles Julian. b 06. Univ of Lon BA 28, BD 31. Lon Coll of Div 30. **d** 31 **p** 32 S'wark. C of St Sav Herne Hill Road 31-34; H Trin Wallington 34-38; V of Ch Ch Richmond 38-49; St Jas W Streatham 49-57; R of Burgh Castle 58-70; R of Belton 58-70; C of Royston 70-72; L to Offic Dio Guildf from 73. *26 Grindstone Crescent, Knaphill, Woking, Surrey, GU21 2RY.* (Brookwood 3706)

PARKER, David Anthony. b 38. St Chad's Coll Dur BA 62, Dipl Th 64. **d** 64 **p** 65 Lon. C of St Jo Evang Palmers Green 64-65; St Mary Virg Kenton 65-71; W Hyde Rickmansworth 71-75; P-in-c of St Aug Brinksway Stockport Dio Ches 75-80; V from 80. *8 Tillard Avenue, Cheadle Heath, Stockport, Gtr Man.* (061-477 3541)

PARKER, David Arthur. b 48. Kelham Th Coll Dipl Th 71. **d** 71 **p** 72 Ramsbotham for Newc T. C of Shieldfield 71-74; St Ignatius Mart Hendon Bp Wearmouth 74-79; P-in-c of St Cuthb Conv Distr Southwick Dio Dur from 79. *St Cuthbert's Vicarage, Rotherham Road, Red House, Sunderland, T & W.* (Sunderland 491261)

PARKER, David Charles. b 53. Univ of St Andr MTh 75. Emm Coll Cam Dipl Th 76. Ridley Hall Cam 75. **d** 77 Edmon for Lon **p** 78 Lon. C of St Paul Mill Hill 77-80; Woodstock w Bladon Dio Ox from 80; C of Begbroke and of Shipton-on-Cherwell and of Hampton Gay Dio Ox from 81. *2 Crecy Walk, Woodstock, Oxon.* (Woodstock 811499)

PARKER, David John. b 33. St Chad's Coll Dur BA 55. Linc Th Coll 57. **d** 59 **p** 60 Newc T. C of Tynemouth 59-60; Ponteland 60-63; St Mich Byker 63-64; C-in-c of St Martin's Conv Distr Byker Newc T 64-69; V of Whorlton 69-72; R 73-80; Industr Chap Dio Linc from 80. *46 Yarborough Crescent, Lincoln, LN1 3LU.* (Linc 20057)

PARKER, David Louis. b 47. Univ of Lon LLB 70. Wycl Hall Ox BA (Th) 79. **d** 80 **p** 81 Chich. C of St Mary Broadwater Dio Chich from 80. *28 Loxwood Avenue, Worthing, BN14 7QY.*

PARKER, David William. b 21. GOC 77. **d** and **p** 81 Glouc. Hon C of Cromhall & Tortworth Dio Glouc from 81. *22 Durham Road, Charfield, Wotton-under-Edge, Glos, GL12 8TH.*

PARKER, Dennis. b 22. Tyndale Hall, Bris 63. **d** 64 **p** 65 Chich. C of Polegate 64-68; C-in-c of St Mary Chap Castle Street Reading 68-70; R of Newdigate Dio Guildf from 70. *Newdigate Rectory, Dorking, Surrey, RH5 5DL.* (Newdigate 469)

PARKER, Douglas Llewellyn. Seager Hall Ont Dipl Th 64. **d** 63 **p** 64 Hur. I of Thorndale 63-65; Lion's Head 65-69; C of Grace Ch Brantford 69-70; R of Burford Dio Hur from 70. *Box 55, Burford, Ont., Canada.* (519-449 2279)

PARKER, Douglas Stephen. b 30. Moore Th Coll Syd ACT ThL 58. **d** 58 **p** 59 Armid. C of W Tamworth 58-60; Inverell (in c of Tingha) 60-66; V of Tenterfield 66-74; P-in-c of Blakehurst Syd 74-75; C of Bickenhill w Elmdon 75-76; Nowra 77-78; C-in-c of Pendle Hill 78; R of Toongabbie Dio Syd from 79. *Box 68, Pendle Hill, NSW, Australia 2145.* (631-8761)

PARKER, Eric. b 16. St Chad's Coll Dur BA 43, MA 49, Dipl Th 44. **d** 44 **p** 45 Liv. C of St Mich AA Wigan 44-48; St Faith Gt Crosby 48-49; Selby Abbey 49-50; St Mich AA Wigan 50-53; V of St Hilda Audenshaw 53-56; Foxton 56-60; R of Eynesbury 60-61; Chap Cho of Ches Cathl and Asst Master at Cathl Choir Sch 61-66; V of Mackworth 66-70; R of Kirk Langley 66-70; C of Allestree 70-73. *20 Rossall Crescent, Sleaford, Lincs, NG34 7JF.*

PARKER, Eric Clince. b 09. Hatf Coll Dur BA 33. Lich Th Coll 33. **d** 35 **p** 36 Blackb. C of St Osw Knuzden 35-37; Ch Kirk 37-38; Polesworth 38-40; Em Loughborough 40-43; St Nich Leic 43-45; R of Bruntingthorpe 45-50; V of Oaks-in-Charnwood 50-55; Foxton w Gumley 55-62; R of Stathern 62-75; C of Bakewell 75-77; P-in-c of Innerleithen Dio Edin from 77. *St Andrew's Parsonage, Innerleithen, Peeblesshire, EH44 6HR.* (Innerleithen 830447)

PARKER, Frank Maxwell Lewis. b 12. **d** 67 Lon **p** 68 Willesden for Lon. C of Winchmore Hill 67-69; Edmonton 69-71; V of St Barn Temple Fortune Lon 71-76; Long Buckby w Watford Dio Pet from 76. *Long Buckby Vicarage, Northampton, NN6 7QU.* (Long Buckby 842318)

PARKER, Gary Mervyn. St Jo Coll Morpeth ACT ThL 63. **d** 63 **p** 64 Newc. C of Wallsend 63-65; Miss P Dio New Guinea 65-70; P-in-c of Southlakes 70-75; R of Mt Vincent 75-79; Hamiltom Dio Newc from 79. *148 Denison Street, Hamilton, NSW, Australia 2303.* (61 1980)

✠ **PARKER, Right Rev Geoffrey Frank.** Univ of Syd BA 38. Worc Coll Ox BA 51, MA 55. Moore Th Coll Syd ACT ThL 39. **d** 40 **p** 41 Syd. Master Cathl Choir Sch Syd 40-41; Chap Tr Gr Sch Summer Hill 41-44; R of St Steph Hurlstone Park 44-47; Chap RAAF 47-49; L to Offic Dio Syd 49-51; C of Oddington w Adlestrop 51; Chap Ch Gr Sch Launceston Tas 52-53; R of Aberdeen NSW 53-55; Singleton 55-64; Vice-Warden St Jo Coll Morpeth 64-70; Commiss Polyn 65-70; R of Muswellbrook 70-74; Cons Asst Bp of Newc in St Andr Cathl Syd 24 June 74 by Abp of Syd; Bps of Newc; Armid, Bath, C & Goulb, Graft and River; and others; Exam Chap to Bp of Newc from 79. *250 Darby Street, Newcastle, Australia 2300.*

PARKER, George Alexander. St Jo Coll Morpeth ACT ThL (2nd cl) 64. **d** and **p** 64 Newc. C of Singleton 64-68; Wallsend 69-70; P-in-c of W Wallsend 70-75; Exper Pastoral Distr of Gateshead 75-80; R of N Lake Macquarie Dio Newc from 80. *80 Main Road, Boolaroo, NSW, Australia.*

PARKER, George Arthur. b 17. St Pet Hall, Ox BA (Th) 39, MA 43. Wycl Ox 39. **d** 40 **p** 41 Blackb. C of St Bart Gt Harwood 40-41; C-in-c of 41-45; Sacr of Blackb Cathl 45; V of St Paul Blackb 45-55; Succr of Blackb Cathl 46-48; Prec 52-56; Asst Master Qu Eliz Gr Sch Blackb 53-56; Ch Sch Bury 65-73 and 77-79; V of Mytton 56-68; C of Bury 72-73; Whalley Dio Blackb from 73. *8 Limefield Avenue, Whalley, Blackburn, Lancs.*

PARKER, George Jeffrey. b 24. LCP 69. Cudd Coll 70. **d** 70 **p** 71 Lich. Hdmaster St Nich Sch Codsall from 68; C of Codsall 70-76; Lapley w Wheaton Aston 76-80; L to Offic Dio Lich from 80. *Cranham, Pinfold Lane, Wheaton Aston, Staffs, ST19 9PD.* (Wheaton Aston 840862)

PARKER, George William. b 29. Univ of K Coll Halifax NS BS Litt 53, BD 59. **d** 53 **p** 54 Calg. C of Cath Ch of Redeemer Calg 53-55; I of Cardston 55-59; C of St Barn W Hackney 59-61; V of Haggerston Lon 61-68; C of St Mark North End Portsea 73-75; V of St Jo Evang Darlington 75-78; R of Ste Agathe Des Monts 78-81; Digby Dio NS from 81. *Box 1307, Digby, NS, Canada B0V 1A0.*

PARKER, Canon Harvey Lloyd. Hur Coll LTh 47. Univ of W Ont BA 47. **d** 47 **p** 48 Hur. I of Ailsa Craig w Brinsley 47-49; Chesley w Tara 49-52; R of Wingham 52-56; Owen Sound 56-62; New St Paul Woodstock 62-70; Simcoe Dio Hur from 70; Can of Hur from 75. *73 Colborne Street South, Simcoe, Ont., Canada.* (519-426 0501)

PARKER, Hugh James. b 30. ACP 55. TCD MA 57. **d** 63 **p** 64 Connor. L to Offic Dio Connor from 63; Dioc C of Connor from 70; Hd Master Larne High Sch from 81. *29 Ransevyn Drive, Whitehead, Co Antrim, BT38 9NW, N Ireland.*

PARKER, Hugh White. b 12. AKC (2nd cl) 39. **d** 39 Willesden for Lon **p** 40 Lon. C of H Trin Wealdstone 39-41; Burnham (in c of St Andr Cippenham) 41-44; Taplow 44-51; R of Wexham 51-64; Waddesdon w Westcott Over Winchendon and Fleet Marston 64-79; Perm to Offic Dio Ox from 79. *4 St Mary's Close, Bicester, Oxon, OX6 8BW.* (Bicester 42421)

PARKER, Ian Saunders. b 44. Dipl Th (Lon) 67. Kelham Th Coll 63. **d** 68 **p** 69 Ches. C of H Trin Ches 68-71; Chap RN 71-75; Min of St Marg Conv Distr Ilford 75-80; R of Doddinghurst Dio Chelmsf from 80; V of Mountnessing Dio Chelmsf from 81. *Rectory, Church Lane, Doddinghurst, Brentwood, Essex, CM15 0NJ.* (Blackmore 821366)

PARKER, James Rollin. Univ of Oregon USA BA 59. Angl Th Coll BC LTh 62. **d** 62 **p** 63 BC. C of St Mary Oak Bay 62-63; St Paul Vancouver 63-66; I of St Luke Vancouver 66-70; St Andr w St Matt Vanc Dio New Westmr from 71. *2016 West 47th Avenue, Vancouver 13, BC, Canada.*

PARKER, John Bristo. b 26. Edin Th Coll 61. **d** 64 Penrith for Carl **p** 65 Carl. C of St Jo Evang Barrow-F 64-68; V of Sledmere (and Wetwang w Cowlam from 73) 68-79; R of Cowlam 68; C-in-c of Wetwang 69; V of Kirkby Ireleth Dio Carl from 79. *Vicarage, Kirkby-in-Furness, Lancs.* (Kirkby-in-Furness 256)

PARKER, John William. b 39. St Steph Ho Ox 66. **d** 78 **p** 79 Truro (APM). Hon C of St Mary Penzance 78-82; Hdmaster St Mary's Sch Penzance 78-82; Ch Ch Sch Albany St Lon from 82; Hon C of St Mary Magd Munster Sq Dio Lon from 82. *5 Swinley House, Redhill Street, NW1.*

PARKER, Canon John William. AKC 34. Sarum Th Coll 34. **d** 35 **p** 36 Linc. C of St Aid New Cleethorpes 35-37; St Martin Linc 37-41; V of Gosberton Clough 41-46; R of St Jo Bapt w St Clem Stamford 46-62; Dom Chap to Marq of Ex 46-59; Chap S Geo Residential Est Stamford 48-58; Confrater Browne's Hosp Stamford 58-62; V of Coates 62-75; R of Willingham-by-Stow 62-75; R of Stow w Sturton 62-75; C-in-c of Scampton Brattleby and Aisthorpe 62-63; Can and Preb of Linc Cathl from 74. *6 Minster Yard, Lincoln, LN2 1PJ.*

PARKER, Joseph Donaldson. b 28. TCD 60. **d** 62 **p** 63 Down. C of St Donard Belf 62-64; Chap and Org Sec Miss to Seamen Belf 64-74; Chap Miss to Seamen Vanc from 75. *50 North Dunlevy Avenue, Vancouver, BC, Canada.*

PARKER, Preb Joseph French. b 09. St Chad's Coll Dur BA 37, Dipl Th 38, MA 40. **d** 38 **p** 39 Liv. C of Warrington 38-40; St Mary Shrewsbury 40-42; St Pet Wolverhampton 42-46; V of St Mary Kingswinford 46-51; St Agnes Toxt Pk 51-60; Proc Conv Liv 59-61; V of W Bromwich 61-76; RD of W Bromwich 61-76; Surr 62-76; Preb of Lich Cathl 67-76; Preb (Emer) from 76. *Tea Rose Cottage, Edenhall, Penrith, Cumb.* (076-881 543)

PARKER, Kenneth Gilbert. St Paul's Coll Grahmstn 64. **d** and **p** 65 St John's. C of Matatiele 65-75; P-in-c of Swartberg 75-80; Perm to Offic Dio Natal from 81. *278 Bulwer Street, Pietermaritzburg, Natal, S Africa.*

PARKER, Kenneth William. St Jo Coll Morpeth ThL 66. **d** 69 Bp Sambell for Melb **p** 70 Melb. C of Beamaris 69-71; H Trin Cathl Wang 71-73; Angl Inner-City Min (in c of St Phil Collingwood and N Richmond) 73-78; I of St Paul Gisborne Dio Melb from 78. *St Paul's Vicarage, Fisher Street, Gisborne, Vic, Australia 3437.* (054-28 2280)

PARKER, Lorenzo Hillary. **d** 75 **p** 77 Ja (APM). C of Bog Walk Dio Ja from 75. *Box 43, Linstead, Jamaica, WI.*

PARKER, Maurice Edwin. b 44. Dipl Th (Lon) 73. Oak Hill Coll 70. **d** 73 **p** 74 Roch. C of Bexley Dio Roch from 73. *6 Tile Kiln Lane, Bexley, Kent, DA5 2BD.* (Crayford 528923)

PARKER, Peter Edward. b 32. Univ of Edin MA 55. Sarum Wells Th Coll 73. **d** 74 Penrith for Carl **p** 75 Carl. C of Kirkby Lonsdale 74-76; All SS w St Jo Evang Kingston T 76-80; Chap to Poly of the S Bank from 80. *110 St George's Road, SE1 6EU.*

PARKER, Peter John. b 47. Univ of Vic BA 69, MDiv 74. Vanc Sch of Th 71. **d** 73 **p** 74 BC. C of N Saanich 73-77; I of Gold River 77-81; Parksville Dio BC from 81. *Box 457, Parksvile, BC, Canada.*

PARKER, (Raphael) Ramon Lewis. b 36. Kelham Th Coll 56. **d** 61 **p** 62 Man. C of Tonge Moor 61-64; H Redeemer Clerkenwell 64-65; V of St Hilda Prestwich 65-71; M SSF from 71; Chap St D Coll Lamp from 81. *Friary, Vicarage Road, Llandudno, LL30 1PT, Gwyn.* (0570-422330)

PARKER, Reginald Boden. b 01. Univ of Lon BSc 23, Dipl Educn 24. St Cath S Ox 3rd cl Math Mods 33, BA (2nd cl Th) 35, MA 39. MRST 36. Ripon Hall, Ox 32. **d** 35 **p** 36 Liv. C of Childwall 35-37; C of St Marg Westmr and Trav Sec AEGM 37-39; Asst Master and Asst Chap Oundle Sch 39-48; Prin of Igbobi Coll Lagos 48-58; Can (Res) of Liv 58-61; Bp's Chap in Univ of Liv 58-61; Select Pr Univ of Ox 60; Asst Master of Wel Coll Berks 61-64; R of Bentham 64-72. *3 Yew Tree Cottages, Sheepscombe, Stroud, Glos., GL6 7RB.* (Painswick 812650)

PARKER, Richard Frederick. b 36. Oak Hill Coll 72. **d** 74 Bedford for St Alb **p** 75 St Alb. C of Wootton 74-76; Bp Hannington Mem Ch Hove 76-81; R of Northwood IW Dio Portsm from 81; V of H Trin Cowes Dio Portsm from 81. *Northwood Rectory, Cowes, IW.* (Cowes 293938)

PARKER, Robert. b 43. BSc (3rd cl Math) Lon 65. Cudd Coll. **d** 67 **p** 68 Sheff. C of St Cuthb Firvale 67-70; Asst Chap Cheltm Coll 70-74; R of Yate 74-77; Yate New Town 77-80; C of E Development Officer from 80. *Church House, Dean's Yard, SW1P 3NZ.* (01-222 9011)

PARKER, Robert Lawrence. b 34. ALCD (1st cl) 59. **d** 59 **p** 60 Bris. C of St Paul Chippenham 59-61; Ch Ch Swindon 61-63; St Andr Epsom Auckld 63-64; V of Glen Eden 64-71; Nether Stowey (w over-Stowey from 73) Dio B & W from 71; C-in-c of Over Stowey 71-73. *Nether Stowey Vicarage, Bridgwater, Somt.* (Nether Stowey 732247)

PARKER, Robert Vlieland. b 09. Trin Hall Cam 3rd cl Cl Trip pt i 29, 2nd cl Th Trip pt i BA 30, MA 35. Wycl Hall, Ox 31. **d** 33 **p** 34 Win. C of H Trin Bournemouth 33-35; St Jas Milton and Org Sec Portsm Dioc Coun for Youth 35-38; C of Ch Ch Woking 38-39; V of King's Teignton 39-46; Chesham 46-56; St Paul Cliftonville 56-67; Surr 46-56; V of St Jo Evang Weston Bath 67-74. *Little Croft, Green Lane, Chesham Bois, Amersham, Bucks.*

PARKER, Robert William. b 18. Linc Th Coll 81. **d** 81 Linc. C of Mablethorpe Dio Linc from 81. *9 Marine Avenue, Sutton-on-Sea, Lincs.*

PARKER, Roland John Graham. b 48. AKC 72. St Aug Coll Cant 71. **d** 74 Grantham for Linc **p** 75 Linc. C of St Faith w St Martin Linc 74-78; V of Appleby and Chap Scunthorpe Industr Miss Dio Linc from 78. *Vicarage, Appleby, Scunthorpe, S Humb, DN15 0AR.* (0724 732157)

PARKER, Ronald. b 25. E Anglian Min Tr Course 78. **d** 81 Ely (NSM). C of Bassingbourn Dio Ely from 81. *44 Walnut Tree Close, Bassingbourn, Royston, Herts, SG8 5PB.* (0763 42803)

PARKER, Russell Edward. b 48. Dipl Th (Lon) 77. Univ of Man BA 80. St Jo Coll Nottm 80. **d** 81 Man. C of Walmsley Dio Man from 81. *38 Queen's Avenue, Bromley Cross, Bolton, Gtr Man.*

PARKER, Theodore William Lake. b 21. Univ of Lon BSc (Eng) 44. Kelham Th Coll 51. **d** 55 Man **p** 57 Carl. C of Ascen Ch Lower Broughton 55; Keswick 56-60; Skerton 60-63; C-in-c of St Alb w St Paul Conv Distr Burnley 63-64; Min 64-66; C of St Wilfrid Mereside Blackpool 66-71; Padiham 71-77. *c/o The Vicarage, Whalley Road, Padiham, Burnley, BB12 8JS.*

PARKER, Thomas Henry Louis. b 16. Em Coll Cam BA 38, MA 42, BD 50, DD 61. Lon Coll of Div 38. **d** 39 **p** 40 Ox. C of Chesham 39-42; St Phil Cam 42-43; St Andr L Cam 43-45; Luddesdown 45-48; PC of Brothertoft w Kirton Holme 48-55; R of L Ponton (w Stroxton to 59) 55-61; R of Gt Ponton 58-61; V of Oakington 61-71; Lect in Th Univ of Dur 71-75; Reader 75-81. *Address temp unknown.*

PARKER, Thomas Maynard. b 06. Late Scho of Ex Coll Ox BA (1st cl Mod Hist) 27, Liddon Stud 28, 1st cl Th 29, MA 31, BD and DD 56. FRHistS 56. St Steph Ho Ox 27. **d** 30 **p** 31 Chich. C of St Bart Chich 30-31; Libr and Tutor Chich Th Coll 30-32; L to Offic Dio Chich 31-32; C of St Mary Virg Somers Town 32-35; Libr Pusey Ho Ox 35-52; L to Offic Dio Ox from 35; Exam Chap to Bp of Bradford 43-55; Asst Chap Ex Coll Ox 46-52; L to Offic Dio Bradf 45-55; Bampton Lect Univ of Ox 50; Lect in Th Univ of Ox 50-73; Lect in Th Pemb Coll Ox 52-60; Fell, and Praelector in Th and Mod Hist Univ Coll Ox 52-73; Fell (Emer) from 73; Chap Univ Coll Ox 52-70; Regr 66-73; Exam in Hons Sch of Mod Hist Univ of Ox 53-55; in Th 63-65; in Mod Hist QUB 64-66; Commiss St Jo Kaffr 53-55; Select Pr Univ of Cam 55; Univ of Ox 60-61; Birkbeck Lect Trin Coll Cam 56-57. *36 Chalfont Road, Oxford, OX2 6TH.* (Ox 58494)

PARKER, Preb Thomas Reginald. St Jo Coll Dur LTh 38, BA 39. St Aid Coll 35. **d** 39 **p** 40 Lich. C of St John Hanley 39-41; St Chad Shrewsbury 41-43; Penkridge w Stretton 43-46; V of Gt Wyrley 46-52; St Martin Rough Hills Wolverhampton 52-60; Kingswinford 60-73; Preb of Lich Cathl from 69. *c/o Rectory, Wordsley, Stourbridge, Worcs.* (Kingswinford 3101 and 3221)

PARKER, Timothy Maxwell Bailey. Univ of W Ont BA 29, BD 35. Hur Th Coll LTh 29, Hon DD 60. **d** 29 **p** 30 Hur. C of Hensall and Staffa 29-34; R of Morpeth Clearville and Howard 34-39; St Luke Broughdale 40-46; Regr Bursar and Lect Hur Coll 46-53; Dir Dept Lit and Supplies 54-67; R of Burford 67-70. *897 Richmond Street, London 11, Ont, Canada.*

PARKER, William Albert Stuart. b 26. Wells Th Coll 68. **d** 70 **p** 71 Birm. C of Bartley Green 70-72; Sutton Coldfield 72-75; V of Allen's Cross Dio Birm from 75. *148 Frankley Beeches Road, Northfield, Birmingham, B31 5LW.* (021-475 8329)

✠ **PARKER, Right Rev William Alonzo.** b 1897. Univ of Man BCom 25, MA (Com) 39. Kelham Th Coll 27. **d** 28 **p** 29 Sheff. C of Cathl Ch Sheff 28-30; Chap St Geo Colleg Sch and Br Commun Jer and Br Chap to Bp in Jer 31-37; V of St Matt Gosport 37-42; St Chad Shrewsbury 42-45; R of Stafford 45-55; Archd of Stafford 45-59; Preb of Tachbrook in Lich Cathl 55-59; Can Res and Treas 55-59; Chap O of St John of Jer 55-60; Sub-Prelate from 60; Cons Ld Bp Suffr of Shrewsbury in Westmr Abbey 30 Nov 59 by Abp of Cant; Bps of Ely; Sarum; B & W; Chich; and Lich; Bps Suffr of Dover; and Stafford; and Bps O'Ferrall; Mackenzie; Gwyer; Hamilton; Stewart; and Ward; res 69; Preb of Freeford in Lich Cathl 60-67; Provost of Denstone Coll 60-67. *104 Stretton Farm Road, Church Stretton, Salop, SY6 6DX.*

PARKER, William Burdick. b 23. Albany Law Sch NY LLB 44. Hur Coll Ont MDiv 74. **d** 74 Hur **p** 75 Bp Robinson for Hur. C of Gorrie w Fordich 74-75; I 75-76; P-in-c of Pelee I Dio Hur from 76. *Pelee Island, Ont., Canada.*

PARKER, William Joseph. b 10. Univ of Man BA 37. Ridley Hall, Cam 35. **d** 37 **p** 38 Man. C of Albert Mem Ch Man 37-40; CF (EC) 40-46; V of H Trin Burton-on-Trent 46-54; St Jo Evang Park Sheff 54-66; R of Barnburgh 66-77; Perm to Offic Dio Ban & St A from 78. *23 Victoria Park, Colwyn Bay, Clwyd.* (Colwyn Bay 2057)

PARKER, Ven William Samuel. b 11. TCD Hebr Pri 32, BA 33, MA 39. **d** 34 **p** 35 Dub. C of Portarlington 34-39; R of Baltinglass w Ballynure 39-47; I of Gorey (w Kilnahue from 55) Dio Ferns from 47; RD of New Ross and Wexford 56-57; Carnew 60-65; Ferns from 65; Can of Ferns 59-65; Treas 65-69; Chan 69-71; Archd of Ferns from 71. *Rectory, Gorey, Co Wexford, Irish Republic.* (055-21383)

PARKES, Alfred David. b 37. Ex Coll Ox BA (2nd cl Music) 62, MA 66. Cudd Coll 62. **d** 64 **p** 65 Dur. C of St Luke Pallion Bp Wearmouth 64-66; Gateshead 66-70; V of Ch Ch Gateshead 70-77; L to Offic Dio Dur 77-81; P-in-c of Bearpark Dio Dur from 81. *Vicarage, Bearpark, Co Durham.*

PARKES, Geoffrey Johnson. b 06. **d** and **p** 38 Berm. C of St Geo Berm 38-45; Minehead 45-46; Clayton-le-Moors 46-50; Chapel-en-le-Frith (in c of St Paul Dove Holes) 50-57; Wilmslow 57-59; V of Lostock Gralam 59-67; C of St John Egremont Wallasey 67-71; Hon C from 72. *54 Canterbury Road, Wallasey, Ches.*

PARKES, James William. b 1896. Late Cl Scho of Hertf Coll Ox BA 22, MA 26, DPhil 34. Univ of Southn DLitt (*hon causa*) 69. Ripon Hall, Ox 22. Cudd Coll 25. **d** 25 **p** 26 Lon. C of St Steph Hampstead 25-28; Warden Stud Movement Ho 26-28; Sec Internat Stud Service 28-34; Publ Pr Dios St Alb and Roch 35-64; Dio Sarum from 64. *Netherton, Iwerne Minster, Blandford, Dorset.* (Fontmell Magna 367)

PARKES, Norman John. b 34. Edin Th Coll 78. **d** and **p** 76 Glas. [f Bapt Min]. Hon C of St Mark E Kilbridge 76-78; C of St Marg Newlands Glas 78-80; R of Challoch w Newton Stewart Dio Glas from 80. *All Saints Rectory, Challoch, Newton Stewart, Wigtownshire, DG8 6RB.* (Newton Stewart 2101)

PARKES, Robert Stephen. b 12. Selw Coll Cam BA 35, MA 40. Linc Th Coll 37. **d** 38 **p** 39 Win. C of Eastleigh 38-48; Bp of St Alb's Chap for Youth 49-54; LPr Dio St Alb 49-50; R of Lilley 50-54; PC of St Geo Tilehurst 54-65; R of Pangbourne 65-77; RD of Bradfield 69-75. *22 Arle Close, Alresford, Hants.*

PARKES, Victor Daniel. St D Coll Lamp BA (Hist) 26. St Mich Coll Llan 26. **d** 27 **p** 28 Llan. C of St Luke Canton 27-29; Llandough w Leckwith and Cogan 29-30; All SS Fishponds 30-31; Perm to Offic at Wimblington 33-34; St Thos Brampton 34-37; C of Ogley Hay w Brownhills 37-38; Hebden Bridge (in c of St John) 38-41; C-in-c of Llanddewi-Ystradenny 41-53; V of Llanafan Fawr w Llanganten 53-68. *Address temp unknown.*

PARKHILL, Alan John. b 43. TCD BA 66, Div Test 68. **d** 67 **p** 68 Down. C of Knockbreda 67-70; Asst Warden Elswick Lodge Newc T 71-72; C of Bangor 73-78; Bp's C of Ch Ch Kilmore Dio Down from 78. *Rectory, Church Road, Crossgar, Co Down, N Ireland.* (Crossgar 830371)

PARKIN, Alan Morley. b 28. Ripon Coll Cudd 75. **d** 77 **p** 78 Waik. C of St Andr Cam 77-80; V of Morrinsville Dio Waik from 80. *Vicarage, Thames Street, Morrinsville, NZ.* (Morrinsville 5260)

PARKIN, George David. b 37. Univ of Dur BA 60, Dipl Th 62. Cranmer Hall, Dur 60. **d** 62 **p** 63 Man. C of Balderstone Rochdale 62-65; H Trin Tunstead 65-67; Gateshead Fell 69-73; CMS Miss in Nigeria 74-76; V of Walton Breck Dio Liv from 80. *Holy Trinity Vicarage, Richmond Park, Liverpool, L6 5AD.* (051-263 1538)

PARKIN, John Francis. b 40. Linc Th Coll 65. **d** 68 **p** 69 Newc T. C of St Geo Cullercoats 68-72; Stony Stratford 72-73; Team V of L Coates 73-76. *16 Longfield Road, Grimsby, Lincs, DN34 5SB.* (Grimsby 78612)

PARKIN, Trevor Kinross. b 37. Cranmer Hall, Dur 63. **d** 66 **p** 67 York. C of St Martin Hull 66-69; St Jo Evang w St Steph Reading 69-73; Industr Chap Dio Lon & L to Offic Dio Lon 73-80; Industr Chap Dio Ely from 80. *31 Thornton Close, Girton, Cambridge, CB3 0NF.* (Cam 276657)

PARKINS, Barry Harold. Moore Coll Syd 79. **d** and **p** 80 Syd. C of St Faith Narrabeen Dio Syd from 80. *97 Claudare Street, Collaroy Plateau, NSW, Australia 2098.* (98-0347)

PARKINS, Frederick Harrison. b 43. **d** 81 Pret. C of St Steph Lyttelton Dio Pret from 81. *241 Pretorious Avenue, Lyttelton, Verwoerdburg 0140, S Africa.*

PARKINSON, Andrew. b 56. Keble Coll Ox BA 77, MA 80. Westcott Ho Cam 78. **d** 80 Burnley for Blackb **p** 81 Blackb. C of H Trin S Shore Blackpool Dio Blackb from 80. *427 Lytham Road, South Shore, Blackpool, Lancs.*

PARKINSON, Arthur Norman. b 09. QUB 27. Trin Coll Dub BA and Brooke Exhib 32, Div Test 33. **d** 33 **p** 34 Arm. C of Armagh 33-36; Portadown 36-38; C-in-c of Mullavilly 38-40; I 40-46; Grange 46-52; Kilmore w Diamond 52-63; RD of Creggan 63-65; R of Acton w Drumbanagher 63-75; Treas of Arm Cathl 65-72; Chan 72-73; Prec 73-75. *34 Old Rectory Park, Portadown, Craigavon, Co Armagh, BT62 3QH., N Ireland.*

PARKINSON, David Thomas. b 42. Linc Th Coll 77. **d** 79 **p** 80 Bris. C of St Mary Yate Dio Bris from 79. *18 Melrose Avenue, Yate, Bristol, BS17 5AL.* (0454 314235)

PARKINSON, Derek Leslie. b 29. Ripon Hall Ox 64. **d** 66 **p** 67 Guildf. C of Ch Ch Guildf 66-69; P-in-c of St Sav w St Jas Ap Preston 69-74; Fontmell Magna 74-81; Ashmore 74-81; Kingswood and Alderley w Hillesley Dio Glouc from 81. *Kingswood Rectory, Wotton-under-Edge, Glos, GL12 8RS.* (W-under-E 3361)

PARKINSON, Edward James. TCD BA 50, Div Test 51, MA 54. **d** 51 **p** 52 Kilm for Connor. C of St Mary Belf 51-53; Lanc 53-55; CF (TA) from 54; R of St Anne Limehouse 55-60; V of Hampton 60-69; L to Offic Dio Newc T 74-80; Master of The Charterhouse Kingston-upon-Hull from 80. *Master's House, The Charterhouse, Charterhouse Lane, Kingston-upon-Hull, HU2 8AF.*

PARKINSON, Edwin. Bp's Univ Lennox BA 28, LST 30. **d** 30 **p** 31 Fred. Miss in Drummond 30-42; I of Malbay Miss 42-44; Grand Manan 44-49; R of H Trin St Stephen 49-70. *RR1, Canterbury, NB, Canada.*

PARKINSON, Francis Wilson. b 37. Open Univ BA 80. Dipl Th (Lon) 63. St Aid Coll 59. **d** 62 **p** 63 Dur. C of St Andr Monkwearmouth 62-64; Speke 64-67; CF from 67; Publ Pr Dio York from 73. *c/o Ministry of Defence, Lansdowne House, Berkeley Square, W1.*

PARKINSON, George Rodney. b 11. Late Pemberton Scho of Univ Coll Dur BSc (2nd cl Physics) 33. Sarum Th Coll 35. **d** 35 **p** 36 Wakef. C of St Geo Lupset 35-40; Thornhill 40-41; Halifax (in c of St Mary) 41-43; V of St Mary Halifax 43-48; Asst Chap K William's Coll IM 48-57; and from 71; Chap 57-71; Ho Master from 54. *8 Scarlett Close, Castletown, IM.*

PARKINSON, George Stanley. Late Scho and Exhib of St Jo Coll Dur BA (Th) 47, Dipl Th (w distinc) 48. **d** 48 **p** 49 Liv. C of St Paul Widnes 48-51; Bradf Cathl (in c of St Jo Bowling) 51-55; V of Greengates 55-58; Pennington 58-71; Eccles 71-80; Churt Dio Guildf from 80. *Churt Vicarage, Farnham, Surrey.* (Headley Down 3368)

PARKINSON, James Henry. b 20. **d** and **p** 74 Wai. Hon C of Opotiki Dio Wai from 74. *1 Mary Henry Place, Whakatane, NZ.*

PARKINSON, Preb John Fearnley. b 30. ALCD 54. **d** 55 **p** 56 Ex. C of St Andr Plymouth 55-59; Metrop Sec United S for Christian Lit 59-62; V of St Budeaux Devonport 62-66; Relig Adv Westward TV 62-81; SW TV from 82; CF (TA) 63-77; Co Chap Devon ACF from 77; V of Kenton (w Mamhead from 75 and R of Powderham from 79) Dio Ex from 66; Preb of Ex from 75. *Kenton Vicarage, Exeter, Devon.* (Starcross 890214)

PARKINSON, John Reginald. b 32. Qu Coll Birm 79. **d** 81 Worc (NSM). Hon C of Catshill Dio Worc from 81. *15 Ferndale Close, Catshill, Bromsgrove, Worcs, B61 0PR.*

PARKINSON, Joseph Greenwood. Tyndale Hall, Bris 30. **d** 34 **p** 36 Lich. C of St Martin (in c of St Luke Gt Bridge) Tipton 34-36; St Sav (in c of St Marg) Nottm 36-37; St Paul St Alb and Asst Chap Hill End Mental Hosp 37-38; R of Elton 38-46; V of Thornton w Bagworth 49-51; R of Burslem 51-56; Surr 53-56; CF 55-58; V of Onecote w Bradnop 58-75. *Causeway Head, The Ford, Oncote, Leek, Staffs, ST13 7RW.* (Oncote 394)

PARKINSON, Canon Keith Edgar Hollyer. b 17. AKC (1st cl) Trench Gr Pri and Knowling Pri 41, Collins Eccles Hist Pri 40. Univ of Lon BD (1st cl) 41, MTh 46. **d** 41 **p** 42 Ox. C of Banbury 41-43; Weeke 43-46; St Pet Bournemouth (in c of St Swith) 46-51; V of St Aug Bournemouth 52-82; Visiting Lect in Th Univ of Southn 57-76; Exam Chap to Bp of Win 62-75; Hon Can of Win from 77. *39 Bell Street, Swanage, Dorset, BH19 2RY.* (Swanage 2542)

PARKINSON, Kenneth Frank Armstrong. b 32. Pemb Coll Ox BA (3rd cl Mod Hist) 56, MA 60. Linc Th Coll. **d** 58 **p** 59 York. C of Selby Abbey 58-61; St Mary Portsea 61-63 and 66-68; Botley 63-66; Cowplain 68-71; R of Shanklin Dio Portsm from 71. *Rectory, Shanklin, IOW.* (Shanklin 2407)

PARKINSON, Peter. b 23. Roch Th Coll 61. **d** 63 **p** 64 Linc. C of St Mary le Wigford w St Martin Linc 63-65; Skegness (in c of St Clem) 65-68; V of Newton-on-Trent 68-73; R of Kettlethorpe w Laughterton 68-73; R of N Coates Dio Linc from 73; V of Marsh Chapel Dio Linc from 73; Grainthorpe w Conisholme Dio Linc from 73. *Marshchapel Vicarage, Grimsby, Lincs, DN36 5SX.* (Marshchapel 393)

PARKINSON, Raymond Neville. b 21. Univ of Bris BA (2nd Th) 53. Tyndale Hall, Bris 50. **d** 54 **p** 55 Chich. C of Bp Hannington Mem Ch Hove 54-57; St Jo Evang Reading 57-59; R of Folke w Long Burton N Wootton and Haydon 59-69; V of H Trin Ashby-de-la-Zouch 69-79; Whitwick St Geo w Swannington and Coleorton Dio Leic from 79. *17 & 19 Loughborough Road, Coleorton, Leicester, LE6 4HJ.* (Coalville 222686)

PARKINSON, Ronald Curnow. b 06. Em Coll Cam BA 28, MA 32. Cudd Coll 28. **d** 29 **p** 30 York. C of St John Middlesbrough 29-34; Marske-in-Cleveland (in c of St Thos New Marske) 34-36; SPG Miss at Hiratsuka 36-39; Tsuruni 39-40; Shidzuoka 40; Chap RNVR 40-46; C of Folkestone 46-47; Chap The Quintin Sch 47-62; Sir R Manwood's Sch Sandwich 62-71; L to Offic at Palermo 73-75; Chap at St Jean de Luz 75-76; Perm to Offic Dio Ox from 77. *133 Banbury Road, Oxford.* (Ox 54449)

PARKINSON, Simon George Denis. b 39. St D Coll Lamp BA 66. Westcott Ho Cam 65. **d** 67 **p** 68 Ripon. C of Rothwell 67-70; Chap RAF 70-73; C of Leeds 74-75; V of Horbury Junction Dio Wakef from 76. *Horbury Junction Vicarage, Wakefield, W Yorks, WF4 5DU.* (0924 275274)

PARKINSON, Thomas Alan. b 40. N-W Ordin Course 75. **d** 78 Doncaster for Sheff **p** 79 Sheff. C of St Cecilia Parson Cross Sheff 78-82; Goldthorpe Dio Sheff from 82. *The Clergy House, Goldthorpe, Rotherham, S Yorks.* (0709 892184)

PARKS, Canon Geoffrey Harper. b 14. MC 45. Kelham Th Coll 30. **d** 37 **p** 38 Lon. C of All SS Friern Barnet 37-39; CF (EC) 39-45; Hon CF 46; V of Flitcham w Anmer 45-48; Stoneleigh (W Ashow R) 48-75; Hon Can of Cov 63-75; Can (Emer) from 75; Sub Treas Chich Cathl from 78. *3 Newtown, Chichester, PO19 1UG.* (0243 781848)

PARKS, John Mordaunt Crofton. b 08. Keble Coll Ox BA 30, MA 45. Ripon Hall. **d** 57 **p** 58 Roch. Hon C of St Nich Sevenoaks and Chap Sevenoaks Sch 57-64; V of St Lawr Seal 64-74; Hon C of St Luke Sevenoaks Dio Roch from 74. *5 Nursery Close, Wickenden Road, Sevenoaks, Kent.* (Sevenoaks 55177)

PARKYN, Michael Sean. b 51. Wadh Coll Ox MA 74. Univ of Nottm Dipl Th 77. St Jo Coll Nottm 76. **d** 79 Southw **p** 80 Derby. C of St Paul Hyson Green Nottm 79-80; Stanton-by-Dale Dio Derby from 80. *92 Wharncliffe Road, Ilkeston, Derbys, DE7 5HF.* (0602 324683)

PARLETT, Gordon Alec. Oak Hill Th Coll 46. **d** 49 **p** 50 Roch. C of St Marg Roch 49-51; St Mark S Norwood 51-56; R of Buckland-in-Dover 56-72; Hon Chap Miss to Seamen from 58; Chap Buckland Hosp 59-72; V of Loose Dio Cant from 72. *Loose Vicarage, Maidstone, Kent, ME15 0AG.* (Maidstone 43513)

PARMENTIER, Martinus Franciscus Georgius. b 47. Univ of Utrecht DTh 71, Pemb Coll Ox DPhil 74. Old Catholic Sem Amersfoort 65. **d** and **p** 71 Abp Kok (Old Catholic Ch of Netherlands). On study leave 71-73; C of St Pet Wolvercote 74-76; on study leave 76-78; R of Old Cathl Ch Haarlem Dio (Gibr in Eur from 80) Lon (N & C Eur) from 78. *Kinderhuissingel 78, 2013 Av Haarlem, Netherlands.* (023-326878)

PARNELL, Bryan Donald. b 38. Chich Th Coll 66. **d** 69 **p** 70 S'wark. C of St Jo Bapt Southend Lewisham 69-72; Asst Chap St Pet Colleg Sch Adel 72-76; R of Angaston 76-78; Chap RAN from 78. *c/o 12 Schilling Street, Angaston, s Australia 5353.*

PARNELL-HOPKINSON, Clive. b 46. Sarum Wells Th Coll 75. **d** 78 Bradwell for Chelmsf **p** 79 Chelmsf. C of Maldon 78-81; Chandler's Ford Dio Win from 81. *St Martin's House, Randall Road, Chandler's Ford, Eastleigh, Hants, 4469)*

PARR, George. MC 45. St Jo Coll Dur BA 37. **d** 38 **p** 39 Liv. C of H Trin Walton Breck 38-40; CF (EC) 40-46; Men in Disp 45; Hon CF 46; Org Sec CMS for Dios Liv, Man and S & M 46-49; V of St Paul Southport 49-54; St Thos Ap Douglas 54-59; H Trin Ripon 59-78. *22 South Grange Road, Ripon, N Yorks, HG4 2NH.* (Ripon 4163)

PARR, Canon James Edwin Cecil. b 20. Trin Coll Dub BA 42, Div Test (1st cl) 43. MA 47. **d** 43 **p** 44 Connor. C of Ch Ch Lisburn 43-48; CF 48-50; C of Whitehouse (in c of Cloughfern) 50-52; C-in-c of Ascen Cloughfern Dio Connor 52-59; R from 59; Can of Connor Cathl from 80. *Cloughfern Rectory, Newtownabbey, Co Antrim, N Ireland.* (Whiteabbey 2437)

PARR, John. b 53. St Edm Hall Ox BA 74. BD (Lon) 79. Trin Coll Bris 75. **d** 79 **p** 80 Liv. C of St Luke Great Crosby Dio Liv from 79. *53 Cranfield Road, Great Crosby, Liverpool, L23 9TY.*

PARR, Patrick William Denis. Univ of NZ BA 46. **d** 48 **p** 49 NZ. C of St Pet Riccarton 48-50; CF 50-52; C of St Mary Bryanston Square Lon 52-54; Chap Ch Coll Ch Ch 54-62; St Paul Colleg Sch Hamilton 62-78; Offg Min Dio Wai 79-81; Dio Auckld from 81. *40 Toroa Street, Torbay, Auckland, NZ.*

PARR, William George Hossack Redmond. b 08. Kelham Th Coll 24. **d** 31 **p** 32 Cov. C of St Thos Cov 31-35; St Jo Evang Bethnal Green 35-40; C-in-c of St Aug of Cant Whitton 40-45; V of St Barn Bethnal Green 45-49; St Andr Stoke Newington 49-54; Cowfold 54-62; R of Frenchay 62-73. *8 Queens Gardens, Herne Bay, Kent, CT6 5BS.*

PARRETT, Stanley Frederick Donald. **d** 78 **p** 79 Heref. C of Whitchurch w Ganarew Dio Heref from 78. *The Stores, Whitchurch, Nr Ross-on-Wye, Herefords.*

PARRISH, Arthur Geoffrey. b 13. St Cath S Ox BA 35, MA 41. Ripon Hall Ox. **d** 41 **p** 42 Birm. C of St Laur Birm 41-43; All SS Gravelly Hill 43-44; St Geo Leeds 44-46; Chap Ripon Hall Ox 46-47; V of St Pet Preston 47-51; Slyne w Hest 51-78; RD of Tunstall 71-74. *Reed How, Wansfell Road, Ambleside, Cumb, LA22 0EG.*

PARROTT, Geoffrey. Univ of Sask BA 48, Em Coll Sktn LTh 38. **d** 38 Sktn for Caled **p** 39 Calg. Miss at Rolla 38-39;

C of St Steph Calg 39-41; V of Merritt BC 41-43; R of St Geo Stettler w Castor Coronation 43-44; L to Offic Dio New Westmr 44-74; Chap St Geo Sch Vanc 44-67. *Terry's Cross, Brighton Road, Henfield, W Sussex, BN5 9SX.*

PARROTT, George. b 37. Univ of Leeds, BA (2nd cl Cl) 61. Bps' Coll Cheshunt 61. **d** 63 **p** 64 Worc. C of Stourport 63-65; C-in-c of St Richard's Conv Distr Fairfield Evesham 65-68; P-in-c of Mufulira Zam 68-70; C of St Pet Cleethorpes (in c of St Francis) 70-75; R of Withern 75-80; Withern Group of Pars Dio Linc from 80; P-in-c of Authorpe w Tothill, Gayton-le-Marsh, N w S Reston & Castle Carlton, Belleau w Claythorpe Aby & Greenfield, Swaby w S Thoresby, Strubby w Woodthorpe 76-80; R of Reston Dio Linc from 80. *Withern Rectory, Alford, Lincs.* (Withern 363)

PARROTT, Canon Gerald Arthur. b 32. St Cath Coll Cam BA 56, MA 60. Chich Th Coll **d** 58 **p** 59 Newc T. C of Ashington 58-61; St Pet Brighton 61-63; V of St Wilfrid Leeds 63-68; St Jo Bapt Southend Lewisham 68-73; R of Catford (Southend) and Downham 73-77; RD of E Lewisham 75-77; Can Res and Prec of S'wark Cathl from 77. *7 Temple West Mews, West Square, SE11 4SN.* (01-735 5924)

PARRY, Albert. b 09. Univ of Wales BA 32. St Mich Coll Llan 32. **d** 33 **p** 34 Ban. C of Llandudno 33-36; Llandrillo-yn-Rhos 36-39; V Cho of St A Cathl 39-42; V of Briton Ferry 42-76; RD of Neath 69-76; Hon C of Llantwit Major Dio Llan from 76. *Ashgrove Bungalow, Ashgrove, Llantwit Major, S Glam, CF6 9SS.* (L Major 2644)

PARRY, Ven Alfred Charles Ascough. Univ of Natal BA 58. Westcott Ho Cam 59. **d** 61 **p** 62 Chelmsf for Lon for Natal. C of E Ham 61-63; St Martin Durban N 63-64; R of H Trin Newcastle Natal 64-70; C of Kloof 70-76; Dir of Chr Educn Dio Natal 70-80; C of H Nativ Cathl Pmbg 76-80; R of Estcourt Dio Natal from 80; Archd of Ladysmith from 80. *Box 123, Estcourt, Natal, S Africa.*

PARRY, Alfred Morgan. St D Coll Lamp 25. Lich Th Coll 29. **d** 33 St D for Llan **p** 34 Llan. C of Tonyrefail 33-36; St Mary Magd S'wark 36-38; Chap Dr Barnardo's Boys' Garden City Woodford Bridge 38-40; R of Barnston Dio Chelmsf from 40; V of L Dunmow Dio Chelmsf from 47. *Little Dunmow Vicarage, Dunmow, Essex.*

PARRY, Arfon. b 19. Univ of Wales BA 50. St Mich Coll Llan. **d** 48 St A for Wales **p** 49 Ban. C of Penmaenmawr w Dwygyfylchi 48-51; Festiniog w Maentwrog 51-54 V Cho of St A Cathl 54-55; V of Capel Garman 55-59; Scissett Dio Wakef from 59. *Scissett Vicarage, Huddersfield, Yorks.* (Huddersfield 863321)

PARRY, Bryan Horace. b 33. St Mich Coll Llan 65. **d** 67 **p** 68 Ban. C of Holyhead 67-71; Team V 71-73; C of St Aid Small Heath (in c of St Greg Gt) 73-78; V of St Greg Gt Small Heath 78-80; Perry Barr Dio Birm from 80. *Perry Barr Vicarage, Church Road, Birmingham, B42 2LB.* (021-356 7998)

PARRY, Brychan Vaughan. b 13. Univ of Wales, Dipl Th 37. St Andr Coll Pampisford 41. **d** and **p** 42 Bris. C of St Paul Bedminster 42-44; CF (EC) 44-46; V of St Anne Greenbank Bris 46-53; CF 53-69; V of Gt Barton 69-78. *c/o National Westminster Bank, Queensway, Bletchley, Milton Keynes, Bucks.*

PARRY, Christopher Loton. Bps' Coll Cheshunt 30. **d** 33 **p** 34 Lon. C of St Paul Hammersmith 33-36; Ramsey St Mary w Pondsbridge 36-37; V 37-40; R of Orton Longueville w St Botolph Bridge 40-41; Chap RAFVR 41-45; V of Alderton 45-46; Perm to Offic Dio Chich 49-52; Toc H Padre NW and Man Area 52-54. *2 Copeland Road, Rondebosch, CP, S Africa.*

PARRY, David Owen Raymond. b 17. St D Coll Lamp BA 40. **d** 41 **p** 42 Chelmsf. C of L Ilford 41-43; CF (EC) 43-45; C of St Andr (in c of St Francis of Assisi) Coulsdon 46-50; R of Pitsea 50-54; V of Bentley Common and Chap Lon Hosp Annexe Brentwood 54-67; R of L Waltham Dio Chelmsf from 67. *Little Waltham Rectory, Chelmsford, Essex.* (Chelmsford 360241)

PARRY, David Thomas Newton. b 45. Selw Coll Cam 1st cl Th Trip pt i 65, BA (2nd cl Th Trip pt ii) 67, MA 71. STh (Lambeth) 76. Cudd Coll 67. **d** 69 Hulme for Man **p** 70 Man. C of Oldham 69-73; Brooklands 73-74; Tutor Sarum Wells Th Coll 74-78; V of St Pet Westleigh Dio Man from 78. *Vicarage, Firs Lane, Leigh, Lancs.* (Leigh 673626)

PARRY, Dennis John. b 38. St D Coll Lamp BA 60. St Mich Coll Llan 60. **d** 62 **p** 63 Llan. C of Caerphilly 62-64; St Fagan Aberdare 64-67; Miss at Povungnituk 67-69; R of Gelligaer 69-75; V of Llanwnog and Caersws w Carno Dio Ban from 75. *Llanwnog Vicarage, Caersws, Powys, SY17 5JG.* (Caersws 318)

PARRY, Derek Nugent Goulding. b 32. Ely Th Coll 60. **d** 63 **p** 64 Portsm. C of Fareham 63-67; St Mark North End Portsea 67-74; C-in-c of Piddletrenthide Plush Alton Pancras and Piddlehinton Dio Sarum from 74. *Piddletrenthide Vicarage, Dorchester, Dorset.* (Piddletrenthide 300)

PARRY, Eric Gordon. b 1900. Late Exhib of Univ Coll Ox BA (2nd cl Th) 22, MA 26. Ridley Hall Cam 22. **d** 23 **p** 24 Wakef. C of All SS Almondbury 23-25; Tutor St Aid Coll Birkenhead 25-26; CMS Miss Egypt 27-49; Dio Sudan 49-56; Exam Chap to Bp in Egypt 37-56; to Bp in the Sudan 52-56; Hon Can Khartoum Cath 52-56; C of Richmond 57-58; V of Sharow w Copt Hewick 58-70; RD of Ripon 62-70; L to Offic Dio Ripon from 70. *65a Clotherholme Road, Ripon, HG4 2DN.* (Ripon 4323)

PARRY, Frederick Rocke Pryce. b 07. Magd Coll Cam BA 35, MA 39. Westcott Ho Cam 35. **d** 36 **p** 37 Ripon. C of St Steph Kirkstall 36-39; LPr Dio Man and SCM Intercolleg Sec Man Univ 39-42; Univ of Liv 40-42; V of Selly Oak 42-56; R of Washington 56-64; V of St Matt and St Jas Mossley Hill 64-75. *Bridge House, Rowton Bridge Road, Christleton, Chester, CH3 7BD.* (Chester 32066)

PARRY, Ian Austin. St Francis Coll Brisb ACT ThL 66. **d** 66 **p** 67 Brisb. C of St Luke Toowoomba 66-70; Palmwoods Dio Brisb from 70. *Vicarage, Palmwoods, Queensland, Australia.*

PARRY, Irvon Meredydd. b 38. Univ of Wales BSc 59, BD 62. St Mich Coll Llan 59. **d** 62 **p** 63 Ban. V of Penbryn w Blaenporth 68-70; Ystradmeurig 70-74; Hd Master St Jo Coll Ystradmeurig 70-81. *Address temp unknown.*

PARRY, John Idris. b 16. St D Coll Lamp BA (Th) 37. **d** 52 Sudan **p** 53 Liv for York for Sudan. CMS Miss Dio Sudan 41-61; Exam Chap to Bp of Sudan 59-61; CMS Area Sec Dios Dur and Newc T 61-66; V of Kirkwhelpington 66-68; Warden CMS Fellowship Ho Foxbury 68-74; V of Langton Green 74-81. *48 South Drive, Rhyl, Clwyd.*

PARRY, John Iorwerth. b 04. Univ of Wales BA (2nd cl Latin) 27. St Steph Ho Ox 32. **d** 33 **p** 34 Ban. C of Llanwnda w Llanfaglan 33-35; Llanbedr-y-Cennin 35-38; Perm to Offic at Rhoscolyn 39-42; R of Newborough 42-75; RD of Menai and Mallraeth 62-75. *Ty Newydd Cytir, Brynsiencyn, Anglesey, Gwyn, LL61 6TJ.* (Brynsiencyn 360)

PARRY, John Seth. b 22. Tyndale Hall Bris 40 and 47. **d** 48 **p** 49 Liv. C of St Mark St Helens 48-52; Bilton 52-55; R of Clitheroe 55-60; PC of Chaddesden 60-69; V 69-76; Ravenhead Dio Liv from 76. *Vicarage, Regent's Road, St Helens, Mer.* (St Helens 23601)

PARRY, Canon Kenneth Charles. b 34. Ripon Hall, Ox 56. **d** 58 **p** 59 Cov. C of Stoke 58-61; Chap RN 61-65; V of Cradley 65-70; H Trin Malvern Dio Worc from 70; RD of Malvern from 74; Surr from 78; Hon Can of Worc Cathl from 80. *Holy Trinity Vicarage, Malvern, Worcs.* (Malvern 4380)

PARRY, Maldwyn Tegid. b 10. Univ of Wales BA 36. St Mich Coll Llan 37. **d** 38 **p** 39 Ban. C of Llandinorwic 38-41; Llanfaethlu w Llanfwrog 41-43; CF (EC) 43-47; C of Dwygyfylchi 47-50; V of Penmon w Llangoed w Llanfihangel Dinsylwy 50-71; Glanadda w Penrhosgarnedd 71-79. *8 Belmont Avenue, Bangor, Gwyn, LL57 2HT.*

PARRY, Merfyn. b 19. St Steph Ho Ox 46. St D Coll Lamp BA 46. **d** 48 **p** 49 Ban. C of Glanadda 48-51; Chap RAF 51-57; V of Penley 57-61; Eglwysbach 61-72; R of Trefnant Dio St A from 72; RD of Denbigh from 80. *Rectory, Trefnant, Denbigh, Clwyd, LL16 5UF.* (Trefnant 377)

PARRY, William. b 10. St D Coll Lamp BA 35. **d** 40 **p** 41 Ely. C of St Matt Cam 40-41; Ramsey 41-44; R of Syresham 44-48; Chap Devon Ment Hosp Exminster 48-63; Exe Vale Hosp Group 63-75; L to Offic Dio Ex 48-75; Dio Ban from 76. *24 Tyddyn Isaf, Menai Bridge, Gwynedd.*

PARRY, William Bruce. Hur Th Coll. **d** 54 **p** 55 Tor. C of St Mary Magd Tor 54-56; R of Wainfleet 56-60; Kimberley 62-64. *SSJE, Bracebridge, Ont, Canada.*

PARRY, William Daniel. b 09. St Chad's Coll Dur BA 31, Dipl Th 32, MA 34. **d** 32 **p** 33 Ban. C of Towyn 32-36; Dwygyfylchi w Penmaenmawr 36-38; Llanaber w Barmouth 38-45; V of Arthog 45-48; Llandinam (w Trefeglwys w Penstrowed from 72) 48-78; RD of Arwystli 53-73; Surr 53-78; Can Res of Ban Cathl 60-70; Chan of Ban Cathl 70-78. *Vicarage, Llannerch-y-Medd, Anglesey, LL71 8EH.* (Llannerch-y-Medd 525)

PARRY OKEDEN, John Patrick Edmund. b 30. Keble Coll Ox BA (2nd cl Lit Hum) 53, MA 56. Cudd Coll 53. **d** 55 **p** 56 Ox. C of Woodstock 55-58; Wakef Cathl 58-61; P-in-c of Potgietersrus Miss Distr 61-64; R of St Paul Potgietersrus 64-66; V of Cowley Dio Ox 66-79; Team R 79-80. *Turnworth, Little Blenheim, Yarnton, Oxford.*

PARRY-CHIVERS, Stanley. b 06. St Paul's Hostel 25. **d** 29 St Arn **p** 32 Willoch. C of Wycheproof 29-31; Robinvale 31; P-in-c of St Matt Quorn 32-33; Perm to Offic (Col Cl Act) at Teddington 33-34; C of St Bart Battersea 34-35; St Andr Yeadon 35-36; R of Fiddington 36-42; V of Compton Bp 42-47; CF (EC) 40-46; Hon CF 46; V of St Laur Brondesbury Pk 47-70; Perm to Offic Dio Ex 70-73; C-in-c of St Mary Magd Barnstaple 73-74. *4 Chestnut Close, Acland Park, Braunton, Devon.*

PARRY-JENNINGS, Christopher William. Lon Coll of Div 57. **d** 60 **p** 62 Ches. C of Claughton w Grant 60-63; H Trin Folkestone 63-67; Shirley 67; V of Linc Ch Ch 67-72; Riccarton Dio Ch Ch from 72. *69 Riccarton Road, Christchurch 4, NZ.* (44-368)

PARSK, William. b 09. **d** 77 **p** 78 Calg. Hon C of Cathl Ch of the Redeemer Calg 77-80; on leave. *302, 602 1st Street S.E, Calgary, Alta, Canada, T2G 4W4.*

PARSLOW, Ven John Henry. MBE 74. Qu Coll Birm 47. **d** 50 **p** 51 Worc. C of Ribbesford w Bewdley 50-53; C-in-c of Conv Distr of Ronkswood 53-60; V of H Trin Worc 58-60; Chap at Blantyre 60-64; P-in-c of St Pet Cathl Likoma 64-67; R of Blantyre Dio Malawi 67-71; Dio S Malawi from 71; Archd of Shire Highlands from 69. *PO Box 326, Blantyre, Malawi.* (34749)

PARSON, George Percivale. Univ of W Ont BA 38. Hur Th Coll. **d** 30 **p** 31 Hur. C of Walter's Falls 30-32; I of Kirkton w Saintsbury 32-38; R of Shelburne w Primrose 38-41; St Paul Windsor 41-44; St Mary's (w Ch Ch Lakeside from 48) 44-50; St Geo Tor 50-55; Distr Sec U Canada Bible S 55-58; R of Port Credit 58-68. *724 Rathbourne Avenue, Woodstock, Ont, Canada.*

PARSONAGE, Robert Leslie. b 20. St Aid Coll 43. **d** 46 **p** 47 Liv. C of St Luke Farnworth 46-48; Bowdon 48-51; CF (TA) 49-52; V of St Geo Everton 51-52; Chap City Hosp N Liv 51-52; CF 52-74; V of St Matt Bayswater Dio Lon from 74. *27 St Petersburgh Place, W2 4LA.* (01-229 2192)

PARSONS, Andrew David. b 53. Univ of E Anglia BA 74, MA 81. Fitzw Coll Cam BA 77. Westcott Ho Cam 75. **d** 78 **p** 79 Nor. C of Hellesdon Dio Nor from 78. *51 Marlpit Lane, Norwich, NR5 8XR.*

PARSONS, Arthur. b 45. St Jo Coll Nottm 70. **d** 75 **p** 76 Guildf. C of Cuddington 75-78; Liskeard w St Keyne and St Pinnock 78-81; P-in-c of St Ludgvan Dio Truro from 81. *Rectory, Churchtown, Ludgvan, Penzance, Cornwall.* (Cockwells 740784)

PARSONS, Arthur Gordon Boyd. b 20. TD 50. Ripon Hall Ox 54. **d** 56 **p** 57 Sheff. C of St Mary Doncaster 56-58; V of N Wilford 58-60; R of W w E Allington and Sedgebrook 60-66; C-in-c of Woolsthorpe 60-64; R 64-66; PC of St Anne Grantham 66-69; V of Friskney 69-73; R of Tansor w Cotterstock and Fotheringhay 73-76; V of Forest Town 76-78; Sutton w Lound Dio Southw from 78. *Sutton Vicarage, Retford, Notts.*

PARSONS, Bernard. b 26. Ely Th Coll 60. **d** 62 **p** 63 Linc. C of Bourne 62-64; PC of W Pinchbeck 64-68; V 68-71; V of Sutton Bridge Dio Linc from 71. *St Matthew's Vicarage, Sutton Bridge, Spalding, Lincs.* (Sutton Bridge 350288)

PARSONS, Christopher James Hutton. b 54. Univ of Wales (Bangor) BA 75. Univ of Birm Dipl Th 78. Qu Coll Birm 76. **d** 79 Reading for Ox **p** 80 Ox. C of Crowthorne Dio Ox from 79. *44 Greenwood Road, Crowthorne, Berks.*

PARSONS, David. b 37. Qu Coll Cam Cl Trip pt i (Th Trip pt ii) BA 61. Ridley Hall Cam. **d** 62 Warrington for Liv **p** 63 Liv. C of Ormskirk 62-65; Beccles 65-68; V of St Jo Evang Woodbridge 68-73; Asst Master and Chap Edgarley Hall School Glastonbury 73-78; Hd of Cl Bruton Sch for Girls from 78. *13 Ivythorn Road, Street, Somt.*

PARSONS, Derek Adrian. b 27. Clare Coll Cam BA 49, MA 52. Ridley Hall, Cam 51. **d** 53 Ox **p** 54 Reading for Cant. C of Maidenhead 53-55; CF (TA) 55-67; CF (TAVR) 67-81; Asst Chap K Edw Sch Witley 55-62; Chap 62-75; Ho Master 59-74; P-in-c of Alfold 75-78; Asst Master Howard of Effingham Sch from 75. *3 Rodney Way, Guildford, Surrey, GU1 2NY.* (Guildf 61874)

PARSONS, Desmond John. Coll of Resurr Mirfield, 65. **d** 66 **p** 67 S'wark. C of St Mark Woodcote Purley 66-70; V of All SS (w Em from 78) W Dulwich Dio S'wark from 71. *165 Rosendale Road, SE 21.* (01-670 0826)

PARSONS, Douglas Cyril. b 05. Oak Hill Th Coll 60. **d** 61 **p** 62 Man. C of St Clem Higher Openshaw 61-64; R of Knossington w Cold Overton 64-73; V of Owston w Withcote 64-73; P-in-c of All S Eastbourne 73-79. *Glebelands Cottage, Gilberts Drive, East Dean, Eastbourne, BN20 0DJ.*

PARSONS, Edgar Llewellyn. **d** 38 **p** 39 Newfld. C of Heart's Content 38-39; Grand Falls 39-41; R of Ecum Secum 41-48; Newport 48-50; Mahone Bay 50-58; Liv NS 58-68; Ch Ch Syd 68-73; I of Lantz Dio NS from 73. *PO Box 63, Lantz, NS, Canada.* (883-2280)

PARSONS, Ernest Francis. Wells Th Coll. **d** 66 **p** 67 Bris. C of Bishopsworth 66-67; Highworth 67-70; V of Em Sparkbrook Dio Birm from 71. *301 Golden Hillock Road, Sparkbrook, Birmingham 11.* (021-772 1553)

PARSONS, Geoffrey Fairbanks. b 35. Trin Coll Cam 2nd cl Cl Trip pt i 57, BA (2nd cl Cl Trip pt ii) 58, Th Trip pt ia 60, MA 68. Ridley Hall Cam 59. **d** 61 **p** 62 Ches. C of Over 61-64; Heswall 64-69; V of St Steph Congleton 69-75; Weaverham Dio Ches from 75. *Weaverham Vicarage, Northwich, Chesh, CW8 3NJ.* (Weaverham 852110)

PARSONS, George Edward. b 35. St D Coll Lamp BA 60. Ripon Hall Ox 60. **d** 62 **p** 63 Heref. C of Leominster 62-66; Bromfield, of Culmington w Onibury and of Stanton Lacy 67-70; Perm to Offic Dio Heref 71-73; L to Offic 73-77; Asst Master Ludlow Sch 66-79; Pastoral Charge of St Mary Caynham Dio Heref 77-79; Perm to Offic Dio Glouc from 79; Asst Master Oakley Secondary Sch Cheltm from 79. *116 Linden Avenue, Prestbury, Cheltenham, Glos, GL52 3DR.* (Cheltm 42464)

PARSONS, George Horace Norman. b 19. SOC 65. **d** 68 **p** 69 S'wark. C of St Cath Hatcham 68-72; Horley (in c of St Wilfrid) 72-76; V of All SS Wimbledon 76-79; C of St Mary Caterham 80-82; Chap St Lawr Hosp Caterham from 82. *Elmwood, St Lawrence's Hospital, Caterham, Surrey.* (Caterham 46411)

PARSONS, Gilbert Harvey. b 20. St Pet Hall Ox BA and MA 46, 2nd cl Th 48. Cudd Coll 48. **d** 50 **p** 51 S'wark. C of St Pet Clapham 50-51; St Luke w St Paul Old Charlton 51-56; V of Stokenchurch (w Cadmore End from 61) 56-72; PC of Cadmore End 56-61; C-in-c of Radnage 65-68; Ibstone 65-72; RD of Aston 66-72; V of Burford w Fullbrook (and Taynton from 75) Dio Ox from 72. *Vicarage, Burford, Oxford, OX8 4SE.*

PARSONS, Very Rev Jeffrey Michael Langdon. b 41. Univ of Wales BA 72. St Jo Coll Morpeth ACT ThL 62. **d** 66 **p** 68 Adel. C of Nara Coorte 66-69; Chap Bancroft's Sch Woodford Green 72-75; R of Lambourne w Abridge and Stapleford Abbots 75-78; Chap St Pet Colleg Sch Stonyfell Adel 78-80; Dean and R of St D Cathl Hobart Dio Tas from 80. *Deanery, 9 Pillinger Street, St Dynnyrne, Tasmania.*

PARSONS, John Banham. b 43. Selw Coll Cam 2nd cl Th Trip pt i 63, BA (2nd cl Th Trip pt ii) 65, 2nd cl Th Trip pt iii 67. Ridley Hall Cam 65. **d** 67 **p** 68 Bris. C of Downend 67-71; P-in-c of Area Ecumen Exper Withywood 71-77; Hengrove Dio Bris from 77. *Christ Church Vicarage, Hengrove, Bristol, BS14 9BP.* (Whitchurch 832346)

PARSONS, John Christopher. b 27. Keble Coll Ox BA (4th cl Jurispr) 52, MA 56. St Steph Ho Ox 52. **d** 54 **p** 55 Chelmsf. C of Chingford 54-57; Chap RN 57-59; R of Ingham w Sutton 59-65; C of Lowestoft (in c of St Pet) 66-69; Chap RADD Essex Area and Publ Pr Dio Chelmsf 69-71; L to Offic Dio Truro 71-74; Social Worker for the Deaf Cornw from 71; Perm to Offic Dio Ex 73-74; P-in-c of Godolphin 74-80; St Enoder Dio Truro from 80. *St Enoder Rectory, Summercourt, Newquay, Cornw, TR8 5DF.* (0726 860724)

PARSONS, Laurie. b 19. Keble Coll Ox BA 41. Wells Th Coll 41. **d** 43 **p** 44 Cov. C of Westwood 43-49; C-in-c of Galley Common Conv Distr Stockingford 49-57; V of Priors Marston 57-69; V of Priors Hardwick 57-69; Radford Semele Dio Cov from 69. *Radford Semele Vicarage, Leamington Spa, Warws, CV31 1TA.* (Leamington Spa 27374)

PARSONS, Martin. b 07. Qu Coll Cam 3rd cl Hist Trip pt i 27, BA (2nd cl Hist Trip pt ii) 28, MA 32. Lon Coll of Div 29. **d** 30 **p** 31 Lon. Tutor Lon Coll of Div 30-34; CMJ Miss Warsaw 34; Hd of Miss and Br Chap 35-39; R of St Kevin Dub 39-44; Gen Sec Hibernian CMS 44-48; V of St Jo Evang Blackheath 48-56; Proc Conv S'wark 55-59; V of Em Northwood 56-64; PC of St Andr Ox 64-69; Commiss Chile 65-72; Extension Sec CMJ 69-72; Perm to Offic Dio B & W from 72. *61 Elm Tree Road, Locking, Weston-super-Mare, BS24 8EL.* (Banwell 822090)

PARSONS, Michael William Semper. b 47. St Cath Coll Ox BA 69, MA 74, DPhil 74. Selw Coll Cam BA 77. Ridley Hall Cam 75. **d** 78 Edmon for Lon **p** 79 Lon. C of All SS Edmon 78-81; Research Fell (Th) Univ of Dur from 81. *Dept of Theology, Abbey House, Palace Green, Durham, DH1 3RS.* (0385 64466)

PARSONS, Montague Richard. St Jo Coll Dur BA 32, MA 38. K Coll Lon BD 36, MTh 39, PhD 66. **d** 31 **p** 32 Lon. C of Ch Ch Highbury 31-37; Lect Lon Coll of Div 36-37; R of S Hackney 37-55; Acton Dio Lon from 55. *Rectory, Acton, W3 9NR.* (01-992 8876)

PARSONS, Richard Edgar. b 46. AKC BD 69, MTh 70. St Aug Coll Cant 69. **d** 71 **p** 72 Sheff. C of Intake 71-73; Lect Ch Army Tr Coll Blackheath 73-79; Hon C of Blackheath Dio S'wark from 73; Selection Sec ACCM from 79. *44 Heathlee Road, SE3.*

PARSONS, Robert Arthur Frederick. b 15. **d** 57 Llan for Wales **p** 58 Swan B. C of Clydach 57-60; R of Whitton w Pilleth (w Norton to 64) Dio Swan B from 60; Cascob and of Llangynllo & Bleddfa Dio Swan B from 79. *Whitton Rectory, Knighton, Powys.*

PARSONS, Robert Martin. b 43. Qu Coll Cam 3rd cl Music Trip pt i 64, BA (3rd cl Th Trip pt ia) 65, MA 69. ALCD 68. **d** 68 **p** 69 Sheff. C of Chapeltown 68-71; St Jo Evang Park Sheff 71-75; V of Swadlincote Dio Derby from 75; RD of Repton from 81. *Swadlincote Vicarage, Burton-on-Trent, DE11 8LF.* (B-o-T 217756)

PARSONS, Roger John. b 37. Sarum Th Coll 62. **d** 65 **p** 66

Win. C of Bitterne Pk 65-69; H Redeemer w St Phil Clerkenwell 69-72; St Andr Willesden 72-76; St Laur-in-I-of-Thanet (in c of St Chris Newington) 76-81; Warden St Benedict's Sch Aldershot 77-81; Hosp Chap Luton & Dunstable Hosp w St Mary's Hosp Luton from 81; C of All SS Luton Dio St Alb from 81. *Luton & Dunstable Hospital, Luton, Beds.*

PARSONS, Ronald Francis. d and **p** 55 Athab. I of Chipewyan 55-61; New Lon 61-63; R of Tangier 63-67; Sackville 67-70; Canso w Queensport 70-73; on leave. *5877 Columbus Street, Halifax, NS, Canada.* (454-5488)

PARSONS, Ronald Vincent. St Aid Coll 63. **d** 65 **p** 66 Ches. C of St Geo Altrincham 65-68; Big Country 68-70; R of Sumner 70-80. *8 McDonald Crescent, Swift Current, Sask, Canada.*

PARSONS, Stephen Christopher. b 45. Keble Coll Ox BA (2nd cl Th) 67, MA 72, BLitt 78. Cudd Coll Ox 68. **d** 70 **p** 71 Cant. C of Whitstable 70-71; St Sav Croydon 71-74; Perm to Offic Dio Ox 74-76; C of St Laur-in-Thanet 76-79; V of Lugwardine w Bartestree (and Weston-Beggard from 81) Dio Heref from 79. *Lugwardine Vicarage, Hereford.* (Bartestree Cross 244)

PARSONS, Canon Thomas Roy. b 04. MBE 50. Chich Th Coll 28. **d** 31 **p** 32 Lon. C of St Mary Magd Munster Square St Pancras 31-34; Actg R of St Geo Cathl Kingstown St Vincent 34-35; P-in-c of St Paul Grenada 35-36; Actg R of Gouyave 36; V of Woodford Halse 37-45; Chap RAF Castle Archdale 41-43; No 7 Radio Sch Lon 43-44; Upper Heyford 44-45; Staff Chap 85 Wing BAFO 46-48; Yatesbury 48-50; Command HQ MEAF 50-52; Halton 52-56; Warden and Prin RAF Moral Leadership Centre Cologne 56-59; Industr Chap in Croydon 60-62; V of St Martin Ludgate Lon 62-70; Actg Missr Lon Healing Miss and Perm to Offic Dio Lon 77-79; Hon Can of St Geo Cathl Kingstown St Vincent from 77. *Abbotscliffe House, Capel Le Ferne, Folkestone, Kent, CT18 7HZ.*

PARSONS, Wilfrid Herbert. b 09. ALCD 36. **d** 36 **p** 37 Roch. C of Sevenoaks 36-38; Tonbridge (in c of St Sav) 38-39; CF (EC) 39-45; Men in Disp 46; PC of Bothenhampton w Walditch 46-49; V of St Luke Wimbledon 49-53; R of Puncknowle w Swyre 53-59; R of Litton Cheney 53-59; C-in-c of Long Bredy w L Bredy 53-57; RD of Abbotsbury 55-59; V of St Pet Colchester 59-70; Surr 69-76; V of Bothenhampton w Walitch 70-76; Perm to Offic Dio Sarum from 76. *Westerly, Bowhayes, Bothenhampton, Bridport, Dorset.* (Bridport 23225)

PARSONS, William George. b 20. Em Coll Cam BA 47, MA 50. Wells Th Coll. **d** 51 **p** 52 Bris. C of St Osw Bedminster 51-54; St Mich AA Bishopston 54-58; C-in-c of Lawrence Weston Conv Distr Bris 58-63; V 63; Prin Bro of the Good Shepherd Dio Bath 63-68; V of Warmley 68-71; C-in-c of Syston 68-71; Commiss Bath from 69; Publ Pr Dio Bris from 71. *Parsonage, Luckington, Chippenham, Wilts, SN14 6PG.* (Sherston 249)

PARTINGTON, Peter John. b 57. Peterho Cam BA (Th) 79. St Jo Coll Nottm 79. **d** 81 Cov. C of H Trin City and Dio Cov from 81. *10 Newby Close, Cheylesmore, Coventry.*

PARTINGTON, Brian Harold. b 36. St Aid Coll. **d** 63 Middleton for Man **p** 64 Man. C of Em Didsbury 63-66; Deane 66-68; V of Kirk Patrick Dio S & M from 68; RD of Peel from 76; P-in-c of St Jo Bapt German Dio S & M 77-78; V from 78; P-in-c of Foxdale Dio S & M 77-78; V from 78. *Kirk Patrick Vicarage, Peel, IM.* (Peel 2637)

PARTINGTON, Fred. b 31. Univ of Lon BSc (2nd cl Econ) 53. Ridley Hall, Cam 59. **d** 61 **p** 62 Liv. C of St Matt Bootle 61-63; Cove w S Hawley 63-67; Lect Watford Coll of Technology 67-70; Hendon Coll of Technology from 70. *8 Cecil Road, NW9.*

PARTINGTON, Kenneth. b 41. Ripon Hall Ox. **d** 70 Hulme for York **p** 71 Man. C of Atherton 70-72; Kippax 72-75; V of St Mary Crosthwaite Dio Carl from 75; Cartmel Fell Dio Carl from 75; Witherslack Dio Carl from 75; Winster Dio Carl from 77. *Crosthwaite Vicarage, Kendal, Cumbria, LA8 8HT.* (Crosthwaite 276)

PARTON, John Denoon. St Francis Coll Brisb. **d** 62 **p** 63 Bath. C of Brewarrina 62-66; Moorabbin 67-68; on leave 69-76; P-in-c of Mt Isa 77-78; V of Moorooka City and Dio Brisb from 78. *10 Edgehill Street, Nathan, Queensland, Australia 4111.* (277 7110)

PARTRIDGE, Canon Alfred Joseph. b 08. Late Scho of Univ of Sheff BA (1st cl Hist) 30, MA 39. TD 54. Linc Th Coll 30. **d** 32 **p** 33 Cov. C of Stockingford 32-34; Kenilworth 34-39; V of All SS Cov 39-50; CF (TA) from 38; R of Farnborough w Avon Dassett 50-59; RD of Dassett Magna 57-59; R of Bilton 59-73; RD of Rugby 63-73; Hon Can of Cov 65-73; Can (Emer) from 73; Perm to Offic Dio Linc from 73. *15 Church Street, Heckington, Sleaford, NR34 9RF.* (Sleaford 60211)

PARTRIDGE, Anthony John. b 38. St D Coll Lamp BA (2nd cl Engl) 61. Linacre Ho Ox BA (Th) 63. K Coll Lon PhD 77. St Steph Ho Ox 61. **d** 64 **p** 65 S'wark. C of All SS Sydenham Dio S'wark 64-67; Hon C 67-74; Publ Pr Dio S'wark from 74; Sen Lect Thames Poly Dio S'wark 73-75; Prin Lect from 75. *c/o Thames Polytechnic, Wellington Street, SE18.*

PARTRIDGE, David John Fabian. b 36. Ball Coll Ox BA (2nd cl Mod Hist) 60. Westcott Ho Cam 60. **d** 62 **p** 63 Man. C of St Thos Halliwell 62-65; St Martin-in-the-Fields Westmr 65-69; R of Warblington w Emsworth Dio Portsm from 69. *Rectory, Church Path, Emsworth, Hants.* (Emsworth 2428)

PARTRIDGE, Nathanael Fred. b 1899. Selw Coll Cam 19. Ely Th Coll 22. **d** 23 **p** 25 Sheff. C of St Osw Abbeydale Sheff 23-27; Cathl Ch Sheff 27-29; PC of Ridgeway 29-44; V of Tresmere w Treneglos and Tremaine 44-48; Burrington 48-50; R of Shobrooke 50-54; Offwell w Widworthy 54-68; Perm to Offic Dio Truro 68-69; L to Offic from 69. *East Portholland, St Austell, Cornwall, PL26 6NA.*

PARTRIDGE, Ronald Malcolm. b 49. Dipl Th (Lon) 73. Cudd Coll 74. **d** 75 **p** 76 Bris. C of Hartcliffe 75-78; St Geo E Bris Dio Bris from 78. *St George's House, Lambley Road, St George, Bristol 5, BS5 8JQ.* (Bris 556200)

PARTRIDGE, Timothy Reeve. b 39. Univ of Lon BSc and AKC 60. Wells Th Coll 60. **d** 62 Tewkesbury for Glouc **p** 63 Glouc. C of St Cath Glouc 62-65; Lutton 65-74; R of Bugbrooke Dio Pet from 74. *Bugbrooke Rectory, Northampton, NN7 3PD.* (Northampton 830373)

✠ **PARTRIDGE, Right Rev William Arthur.** b 12. Univ of Birm BA (2nd cl Hist) 33. Linc Th Coll 33. **d** 35 **p** 36 Worc. C of The Lye 35-38; SPG Miss Dio Madr 39-51; Chap RAFVR 43-46; Lect Meston Tr Coll Madr 47-51; Metrop's Commiss and VG in Nandyal 51-63; Cons Asst Bp of Calc (Bp in Nandyal) in St Thos Cathl Bom 4 Jan 53 by Bp of Calc (Metrop); Bps of Rang; Chota N; Bhag; Nasik; Kurun; Bom; Luckn; Colom; Nagp; Assam; Lah; and Delhi; and Bps Aung Hla; Ah Mya; Richardson and Wilkinson; res 63; V of Ludford 63-69; Asst Bp of Heref 63-75; Preb of Heref Cathl 63-77; Preb (Emer) from 77; Commiss Nand from 63. *50 The Crescent, Colwall, Malvern, Worcs, WR13 6QN.* (Colwall 40050)

PASCOE, Harold John. b 42. St D Coll Lamp BA 65, Dipl Th 67. **d** 67 **p** 68 Lich. C of U Gornal 67-70; St Gabr Fullbrook Walsall 70-73; V of St Andr Walsall 73-80; Donnington Wood Dio Lich from 80. *St Matthew's Vicarage, Donnington Wood, Telford, Shropshire, TF2 8NN.* (Telford 604239)

PASH, Stephen James. b 51. Univ of Adel BA 73. St Barn Coll Adel ACT ThL 75. **d** 76 **p** 77 Adel. C of Edwardstown w Ascot Park 76-78; P-in-c of Kilburn 78-79; Chap St Mark's Coll and C of St Pet Cathl City and Dio Adel from 80. *St Mark's College, Pennington Terrace, N Adelaide, S Australia 5006.* (267 2211)

PASIPANODYA, Fabian. d 47 **p** 47 S Rhod. P Dio S Rhod 47-52; Dio Mashon 52-81; Dio Mutare from 81. *PB 7094, Umtali, Zimbabwe.*

PASK, David James. b 51. St Jo Coll Auckld 78. **d** 79 **p** 80 Wai. C of Edgecumbe-Kawerau Dio Wai from 79. *Vicarage, Edgecumbe, NZ.*

PASKINS, David James. b 52. St D Coll Lamp BA 73. Trin Hall Cam BA (Th) 76. Westcott Ho Cam 74. **d** 77 **p** 78 Cant. C of St Pet-in-Thanet 77-80; Swanage Dio Sarum from 80. *9 Cecil Road, Swanage, Dorset.* (Swanage 2953)

PASLEY, Canon Charles Victor. b 19. **d** 58 **p** 59 Dub. C of St Jude Dub 58-61; I of Skreen U Dio Killala from 61; RD of Straid from 66; Dom Chap to Bp of Tuam from 69; Can of Achon Cathl from 75. *Skreen Rectory, Co Sligo, Irish Republic.* (Sligo 72117)

PASLEY, James. Trin Coll Dub. **d** 61 **p** 62 Dub. C of St Cath Dub 61-62; St Jude Dub 62-63; Deputn Sec Hibernian Bible S for Ireland from 63; I of Athy Dio Glendal from 70. *Athy, Co Kildare, Dublin, Irish Republic.*

PASSI, Very Rev Dave. St Paul's Th Coll Moa I 56. **d** 62 **p** 63 Carp. C of All S Cathl Thursday I 62-66; Mabuiag I 66-69; Archd of Torres Strait 71-76; Res Can of Carp 74-76; C of St Paul's Cathl Rockptn 76-80; Dean of Carp from 81. *Deanery, Thursday Island, Queensland, Australia 4875.*

PASSI, Sam. d 73 Carp. C of Murray Island Dio Carp from 73. *c/o Box 79, Thursday Island, Queensland, Australia 4875.*

PASSINGHAM, Eric Albert. b 27. Wells Th Coll 69. **d** 70 **p** 71 Roch. C of St Steph Chatham 70-74; Crawley (in c of Three Bridges) Dio Chich 74-79; Team V from 79. *St Richard's House, Cross Ways, Three Bridges, Crawley, W Sussex, RH10 1QF.* (Crawley 21978)

PASTERFIELD, Canon Dunstan Patrick. Clare Coll Cam BA 49, MA 53. Cudd Coll 49. **d** and **p** 51 St E. C of Badingham and of Dennington Dio St E 51-53; I of Shaunavon 53-57; Estevan 57-63; St Mary Regina 64-74; R of St Mich AA City and Dio Calg from 74; Exam Chap to Bp of Calg from 74; Hon Can of Calg from 78. *Box 3221, Station B, Calgary, Alta, Canada.* (289-5960)

✠ **PASTERFIELD, Right Rev Philip John.** b 20. Trin Hall Cam 2nd cl Hist Trip pt i 48, BA 49, MA 53. Cudd Coll 49. **d** 51 **p** 52 S'wark. C of Streatham 51-54; V of W Lavington 54-60; R of Woolbeding 55-60; Chap K Edw VII Hosp Midhurst 54-60; V of Oxton 60-68; RD of Birkenhead 66-68; Can and Sub-Dean of St Alb 68-74; Commiss New Guinea 69-71; Papua from 71; RD of St Alb 71-74; Cons Ld Bp Suffr of Crediton in Westmr Abbey 18 Oct 74 by Abp of Cant; Bps of Nor, Southw, Cov, Portsm, St Alb and Ex; Bps Suffr of Basingstoke, Bedford, Dover, Hertf, Kingston T, Maidstone, Plymouth, Dorch, Reading, Tonbridge and Willesden; and others. *10 The Close, Exeter, Devon, EX1 1EZ.* (Exeter 73509)

PASWANI, Geoffrey. d 78 **p** 79 Matab. C of St Francis Selukwe Dio Matab (Dio Lundi from 81) from 78. *Box 50, Mashaba, Zimbabwe.*

PATCHING, William Albert. d 79 **p** 80 N Queensland (NSM). C of St Mary Atherton Dio N Queensld from 79. *c/o PO Box 218, Atherton, Qld, Australia 4883.*

PATE, David James. St Jo Coll Manit BA and BTh 65, M Div 76. **d** 64 Bp Anderson for Rupld **p** 65 Rupld. C of St Matt Winnipeg 65-66; V of Woodlands 66-69; Emerson 69-71; I of St Mark Winnipeg 71-80; St Paul Winnipeg Dio Rupld from 80. *830 North Drive, Winnipeg, Manit, Canada.*

PATEMAN, Donald Herbert. b 15. ALCD 48. **d** 48 Lon **p** 49 Stepney for Lon. C of St Jas-the-Less Bethnal Green 48-51; All H Bromley-by-Bow 54-56; Hon Sec S for Relief of Distress 52-66; V of St Mark w St Bart Dalston Dio Lon from 56. *St Mark's Vicarage, Sandringham Road, E8 2LL.* (01-254 4741)

PATEMAN, Edward Brian. b 29. Univ of Leeds BA 51. Qu Coll Birm 51. **d** 53 **p** 54 Dur. C of St Pet Stockton-on-Tees 53-57; Lect of Bolton 57-58; PC of Coxhoe 58-65; V of Dalton-le-Dale Dio Dur from 65; Surr from 65; RD of Houghton-le-Spring 72-75. *Dalton-le-Dale Vicarage, Church Lane, Murton, Co Durham, SR7 9RD.* (Hetton-le-Hole 262410)

PATEMAN, Norman Carter. b 10. AIB 31. Univ of Lon BA (1st cl Chinese) 50. **d** 39 **p** 40 E Szech. [f Lay Miss] CIM Miss Dio E Szech 39-44; Sec CIM Lon 44-66; OMF 66-74; Perm to Offic Dio Nor from 75. *26a Morley Road, Sheringham, Norf, NR26 8JE.* (Sheringham 2313)

PATEN, Richard Alfred. b 32. Ch Coll Cam BA (3rd cl Mech Sc Trip pt i) 56, MA 60. C Eng MICE 61. Ripon Hall Ox 61. **d** 63 **p** 64 Leic. C of Oadby 63-67; St Mark Pet 67-71; Chap for Commun Relns Pet 71-73; Hon Chap from 73; Dioc Chap Dio Pet from 73. *198 Lincoln Road, Peterborough, PE1 2NQ.*

PATERNOSTER, Canon Michael Cosgrove. b 35. Late Scho of Pemb Coll Cam BA 59, MA 63. Cudd Coll 59. **d** 61 **p** 62 S'wark. C of St Andr Surbiton 61-63; Dioc Super and Chap Qu Coll Dundee 63-68; Chap Dundee Univ 67-68; Sec Fellowship of St Alb and St Sergius 68-71; R of St Jas Dollar 71-75; Stonehaven Dio Brech from 75; Hon Can St Paul's Cathl Dundee from 81. *St James's Rectory, Gurney Street, Stonehaven, AB3 2EB.* (Stonehaven 62694)

PATERSON, Albert Ernest. b 06. Sarum Th Coll **d** 57 **p** 58 Ox. C of Buckingham 57-60; PC of Penn Street w Holmer Green 60-67; C of St Marg Leic 69-73; V of Arnesby w Shearsby 73-78; Industr Chap Dio Leic from 78; L to Offic Dio Leic from 78. *88 Ruskington Drive, Wigston Fields, Leicester.* (Leic 888006)

PATERSON, David. b 33. Late Scho of Ch Ch Ox BA 55, MA 58. Linc Th Coll 56. **d** 58 **p** 59 Worc. C of Kidderminster 58-60; St Geo Wolverhampton 60-63; V of St Pet Loughborough Dio Leic from 63. *129 Ashby Road, Loughborough, Leics, LE11 3AB.* (Loughborough 63047)

PATERSON, David Alexander. St Paul's Coll Grahmstn 60. **d** 62 Capetn **p** 72 Geo. C of St Mark's Cathl Dio Geo 71-73; R of Balmoral 74-77; Millicent Dio Murray from 77. *Rectory, George Street, Millicent, S Australia 5280.* (087-332090)

PATERSON, Donald Alexander. b 33. Univ of Leeds, BA (3rd cl Psychol) 57. Wycliffe Hall, Ox. **d** 68 Warrington for Liv **p** 69 Liv. C of Speke 68-70; Ch Ch U Armley 70-74; Warden St Geo Crypt Leeds Dio Ripon from 75. *49 Sutherland Avenue, Leeds, LS8 1BY.* (Leeds 663634)

PATERSON, Douglas Monro. b 30. Em Coll Cam 2nd cl Hist Trip pt i 52, BA (2nd cl Th Trip pt ii) 54, MA 57. Tyndale Hall Bris. **d** 57 **p** 58 B & W. C of Walcot 57-60; St Paul Portman Square St Marylebone 60-62; Min of St John Downshire Hill Hampstead 62-65; L to Offic Dio Rwa and Lect Stanley-Smith Th Coll 67-73; C of St Thos Edin 73-75; Lect Lebanon Miss Bible Coll Berwick-upon-Tweed from 75; L to Offic Dio Newc T from 75; Perm to Offic Dio Edin from 75. *Lebanon Missionary Bible College, Berwick-upon-Tweed, TD15 1PA.*

PATERSON, Eric Beaumont. Univ of Tor BA 57. Trin Coll Tor LTh 59. **d** 58 **p** 59 Alg. I of W Thunder Bay 59-62; R of Haileybury 62-69; I of St Matt Sault Ste Marie 69-74; Ch of Epiph Sudbury Dio Alg from 74; Sec Dioc Syn Alg from 77. *85 Larch Street, Sudbury, Ontario, Canada.* (705-675 2279)

PATERSON, Geoffrey Gordon. b 45. Ch Ch Coll NZ LTh 69. **d** 69 **p** 70 Ch Ch. C of Belfast-Redwood 70-74; V of Mayfield Mt Somers P-in-c of Astwood Bank w Crabbs Cross 79-80. *Address temp unknown.*

PATERSON, Gordon Ronald. b 16. MBE (Mil) 57. Ripon Hall Ox 58. **d** 59 **p** 60 Portsm. C of Warblington w Emsworth 59-62; V of Swanmore Dio Portsm from 62; RD of Bp's Waltham from 79. *Swanmore Vicarage, Southampton, SO3 2QT.* (Bishop's Waltham 2105)

PATERSON, Hugh Edward James Trevor. b 1891. AKC 24. Univ of Lon BD 24. **d** 24 **p** 25 Win. C of H Trin w St Mary Guildf 24-30; Jt Ed Guildf Dioc Gazette 29-32; V of Addlestone 30-45; Chap Princess Mary Village Homes 30-45; Asst RD of Emly 43-45; V of Camberley w Yorktown 45-61; Surr 45-61; R of Holford w Dodington 61-69. *Dogdole, Church Street, Merriott, Somt.*

PATERSON, Hugh Stanley. Univ of NZ BSc 59. NZ Bd of Th Stud LTh 65. Ch Ch Th Coll 57. **d** 60 Dun for Ch Ch **p** 62 Ch Ch. C of Highfield 60-63; Hokitika 63-66; V of Kumara 63-66; Malvern Dio Ch Ch from 66. *St Ambrose's Vicarage, Sheffield, NZ.* (Sheff 14)

PATERSON, Ivor David John. b 20. McGill Univ Montr BTh 72. Montr Dioc Th Coll 70. **d** and **p** 73 Montr. C of Greenfield Park 73-75; R of Mascouche 75-78; Dunham Dio Montr from 78. *Box 148, Dunham, PQ, Canada J0E 1M0.* (514-295 2201)

PATERSON, Canon James Beresford. b 21. DSC 42. Westcott Ho Cam 59. **d** 61 **p** 62 St E. C of Woodbridge 61-64; R of Broughty Ferry 64-72; L to Offic Dio Brech 72-75; Sec Scot Chs Action for World Development 72-79; P-in-c of Glencarse Dio Brech from 76; Hon Can of St Paul's Cathl and Dioc Sec Dundee from 79. *Rectory, Glencarse, Perth, Scotland.* (Glencarse 386)

PATERSON, James Douglas Jun. Wycl Coll Tor BA 37, LTh 39, BD 44. **d** 39 **p** 40 Tor. C of Mono E 39-42; I of Ch Ch Oshawa 42-45; Chap RCAF 45-46; C of St Timothy Tor 46-47; I of Woodbridge and Castle 47-54; R of Mimico 54-59; Epiph Tor 59-79. *820 Burnhamthorpe Road, Etobicoke, Ont, Canada.*

PATERSON, John Alexander. Hur Coll STh 59. **d** and **p** 59 Niag. C of Port Colborne 59-62; R of St Brendan Port Colborne 62-64; Palmerston 64-69; on leave 70-75; Chap Mid-W Reg Centre Palmerston and Hon C of Arthur w Grand Valley Dio Niag from 75. *Box 68, Harriston, Ont, Canada.* (519-338 3214)

PATERSON, John Campbell. b 45. Univ of Auckld BA 66. LTh 69. **d** 69 **p** 70 Auckld. C of Whangarei 69-71; P-in-c of Waimate N Maori Past 71-76; Hon C of Maori Miss Dio Auckld from 76; Chap Qu Vic Sch Auckld from 76. *11 Glanville Terrace, Parnell, Auckland 1, NZ.* (373-162)

PATERSON, John Charles. b 47. Moore Coll Syd ThL 71. **d** and **p** 73 Syd. C of Gladesville 73-75; H Trin Adel 75-78. *c/o Box 198, Armidale, NSW, Australia.*

PATERSON, Very Rev John Thomas Farquhar. b 38. TCD BA (Or Lang) 61, Div Test 63, MA 64, BD 71. **d** 63 **p** 64 Arm. C of Drumglass 63-65; St Bart Dub 66-68; C-in-c of St Mark Dub 68-71; Min Can of St Patr Cathl Dub from 67; Asst Dean of Residence TCD 68-72; I of St Bart w Leeson Pk Dub 72-78; Kildare w Lackagh, Kilmeague and Feighcullen Dio Kild from 78; Dean of Kild from 78. *Dean's House, Curragh Camp, Co Kildare, Irish Republic.* (045-41654)

PATERSON, Noel Bruce. Sir Geo Williams Univ Montr BA 62. Hur Coll BTh 65. **d** 65 **p** 66 Edmon. P-in-c of St Mich AA Edmon 65-70; I of Hinton 70-72; C of Grace Ch Brantford 72-73; I of St D Sarnia 73-76; St Barn Lon Dio Hur from 76. *1774 Seeley Drive, London, Ont., Canada.* (519-451 6854)

PATERSON, Rex Douglas Trevor. b 27. K Coll Lon and Warm AKC 54. **d** 55 **p** 56 Ox. C of St Luke Maidenhead 55-58; Littlehampton 58-62; V of Woodingdean 62-73; Ferring Dio Chich from 73. *19 Grange Park, Ferring, Worthing, Sussex, BN12 5LS.* (Worthing 41645)

PATERSON, Very Rev Robert Gary. Univ of W Ont BA 60. Hur Coll BTh 63. **d** 63 **p** 64 Hur. C of Ascen Windsor 63-65; I of Churchill 65-70; Can of St Alb Pro-Cathl Kenora 68-70; Archd of York 68-70; Dean and R of St Andr Cathl Prince Rupert Dio Caled from 70. *200 Fourth Avenue West, Prince Rupert, BC, Canada.* (604-624 4766)

PATERSON, Robert Mar Erskine. b 49. Late Scho of St Jo Coll Dur BA 71, Dipl Th 72. **d** 72 Man **p** 73 Swan B. C of Harpurhey 72-73; Sketty 73-78; R of Llangattock and

Llangynidr Dio Swan B from 78. *Llangattock Rectory, Crickhowell, Powys.* (Crickhowell 810270)

PATERSON, Torquil John MacLeod. b 52. Rhodes Univ Grahmstn BSc 73, BD 76, MA 77. St Paul's Th Coll Grahmstn 77. **d** 78 Bp Ndwandwe for Johann **p** 79 Johann. Lect Rhodes Univ from 78. *Rhodes University, Grahamstown, S Africa 6140.*

PATERSON, Canon William John McCallum. b 19. Univ of Leeds, BA 41. Coll of Resurr Mirfield, 41. **d** 43 Knaresborough for Ripon **p** 44 Ripon. C of St Wilfrid Harehills Leeds 43-46; Knaresborough 46-52; R of St Luke Miles Platting Man 52-56; V of Bardsey 56-69; R of Spennithorne 69-79; Finghall 69-79; Hauxwell 69-79; RD of Wensley 70-79; Hon Can of Ripon Cathl from 75; R of Kirk Hammerton w Nun Monkton and Hunsingore Dio Ripon from 79. *Kirk Hammerton Rectory, York, YO5 8BX.* (Green Hammerton 30766)

PATERSON, William Lawrence. b 07. **d** 33 **p** 34 Roch. C of St Alb Dartford 33-38; R of Gt Hanwood 38-49; CF 40-45; V of Madley w Tyberton Dio Heref from 49; C-in-c of Preston-on-Wye w Blakemere Dio Heref from 71. *Madley Vicarage, Hereford.* (Golden Valley 250245)

PATERSON-SMYTH, Canon John. Trin Coll Tor BA 47, BD 51, LTh 51. **d** 51 **p** 52 Tor. C of Ch Ch Deer Park Tor 51-53; I of Belmont 53-57; R of St Cypr Tor 57-66; R of St Alb Tor 63; St Chad Tor 66-77; Exam Chap to Bp of Tor from 73; Can of Tor from 75; R of St Cuthb Leaside City and Dio Tor from 77. *1399 Bayview Avenue, Toronto, Ont., Canada.* (416-485 0329)

PATEY, Colin Frank. b 49. SS Coll Cam BA 71, MA 75. St Steph Ho Ox 72. **d** 74 Hertf Coll Ox BA 37, MA 45. Univ of Liv LLD 80. Westcott Ho Cam 38. **d** 39 40 Chelmsf. C of Hedworth 74-78; St Paul Weymouth 78-81; V of Grimethorpe Dio Wakef from 81. *Grimethorpe Vicarage, Barnsley, S Yorks, S72 7JB.* (0226 711331)

PATEY, Donald Weare. b 08. Univ of Wales, BA 35. Coll of Resurr Mirfield, 35. MCR 48. **d** 37 **p** 38 Derby. C of Long Eaton 37-41; Burbage (in c of St Jas Harpur Hill) 41-45; L to Offic Dio Wakef 47-51; and from 55; Dio Llan 49-55; Dio Mashon 65-66. *House of the Resurrection, Mirfield, Yorks.*

PATEY, Very Rev Edward Henry. b 15. Hertf Coll Ox BA 37, MA 45. Univ of Liv LLD 80. Westcott Ho Cam 38. **d** 39 **p** 40 Chelmsf. C of St Mary Virg Colchester 39-42; Bishopswearmouth 42-50; Chap for Youth to Bp of Dur 46-50; V of Oldland w All SS Longwell Green 50-52; Sec Youth Dept Br Coun of Churches 52-56; Asst Gen Sec 56-58; Can (Res) of Cov 58-64; Select Pr Univ of Ox 61; Dean of Liv from 64. *Cathedral, Liverpool, L1 7AZ.* (051-709 6271); *and 197 Queens Drive, 2)*

PATFIELD, Ven Kenneth Allan. St Jo Coll Armid ACT ThL 50. **d** 50 **p** 51 Armid. C of Narrabri 50-53; W Tamworth 53-54; V of Mungindi 54-56; Bundarra 56-63; Walcha 63-68; Tamworth 68-79; Can of Armid 74-79; Perm to Offic Dio Wang 79; Archd of Albury from 79; R of St Matt Albury Dio C & Goulb from 79. *Box 682, Albury, ACT, Australia 2640.*

PATFIELD, Ronald. Moore Coll Syd ThL 48. **d** and **p** 49 Syd. C of Eastwood 49; St Paul Wahroonga 50-51; Min of St Steph Normanhurst 52; R of Annandale 53-58; Wentworthville 58-68; Seaforth Dio Syd from 68. *1 French's Forest Road, Seaforth, NSW, Australia 2092.* (94-1997)

PATIENT, Peter Leslie. b 39. Chich Th Coll 63. **d** 66 **p** 67 Ox. C of St Andr Headington Ox 66-69; St Lawr Stroud 69-72; St Mary Virg Welwyn 72-75. *28 Young's Rise, Welwyn Garden City, Herts, AL8 6RU.*

PATO, Luke Luscombe Lungile. b 49. Fort Hare Univ BA. Univ of Manit MA. St Bede's Coll Umtata 71. **d** 73 St John's **p** 75 Bp Sobukwe for St John's. C of Tsomo 73-76; Mahlubini 76-78; on leave 78-81; Vice Prin St Bede's Th Coll Umtata from 81. *Box 328, Umtata, Transkei.*

PATON, Canon David Macdonald. b 13. BNC Ox BA 36, MA 39. **d** 39 Ches for Col **p** 41 Hong. C of St Steph Hong Kong 39-41; L to Offic Dio E Szech 41-44; Chap and Libr Westcott Ho Cam 45-46; L to Offic Dio Ely 45-46; C of St Alb Abbey 45-46; L to Offic Dio Fukien 47-50; Chap and Exam Chap to Bp of Fukien 47-50; Perm to Offic Dio St Alb 51-52; V of Yardley Wood 52-56; Managing Dir and Ed of SCM Press 56-59; L to Offic Dio S'wark 56-69; Sec Ch Assembly Coun for Ecumen Co-operation 59-63; Assembly Miss and Ecumen Coun 64-69; Regional Officer Br Is 65-68; Hon Can of Cant from 66-81 Can (Emer) from 81; R of St Mary de Crypt w St Jo Bapt Glouc 69-81; V of Ch Ch Glouc 79-81; Chap to HM the Queen from 72. *37a Cromwell Street, Gloucester, GL1 1RE.* (0452-422051)

PATON, George Hemsell. b 23. Wadh Coll Ox MA 49. Oak Hill Th Coll 50. **d** 52 **p** 53 Nor. C of St Anne Earlham 52-54; Darfield 54-56; CMS Area Sec Ely 56-62; Dios St E and Nor 56-66; Publ Pr Dio Nor 60-66; PC of St Mark Kemp Town Brighton 66-67; V of St Mark w St Matt Kemp Town Brighton 67-71; R of Ripe w Chalvington 71-77; Laughton w Ripe and Chalvington 77-78; V of Iford w Kingston and Rodmell Dio Chich from 78. *Vicarage, Kingston, Lewes, E Sussex, BN7 3NS.* (Lewes 2384)

PATON, Ian Fisher. Univ of Leeds BA 36. Coll of Resurr Mirfield 36. **d** 38 **p** 39 Sarum. C of Blandford Forum 38-41; St Geo Hanover Square Westmr 41-44; Chap RNVR 44-47; RN 47-57; Perm to Offic Dio Bris 58-62; C of St Teath 62-67; R of Margaret River 67-68; C of Geraldton 68-72. *c/o Box 271, Geraldton, W Australia 6530.*

PATON, Ven Michael John Macdonald. b 22. Magd Coll Ox BA 49, MA 54. Linc Th Coll 52. **d** 54 **p** 55 Newc T. C of All SS Gosforth 54-57; V of Norton Woodseats Sheff 57-67; Chap United Sheff Hosps 67-70; V of St Mark Broomhall Sheff 70-78; Archd of Sheff and Res Can of Sheff Cathl from 78. *62 Kingfield Road, Sheffield, S11 9AU.* (Sheffield 57782)

PATON, Waller. b 1888. Univ of St Andr MA 10. Edin Th Coll 12. **d** 14 **p** 15 Glas. C of St Andr Ardrossan 14-16; Yatton 16-19; TCF 18-19; Hon CF 19; C and Prec St Andr Cathl Inverness 20-21; C of St Nich w St Leon Bris 21-25; Streatham 25-27; St Mary Balham 27-29; H Trin Westmr 29-30; Ch Ch Turnham Green 30-33; V of New Brentford 33-45; R of Exbury 45-59; C of Windlesham (in c of St Alb) 63-69. *24 Croft Road, Selsey, Sussex.*

PATON, William Robin. St Mich Th Coll Crafers ACT ThL 51. **d** 53 **p** 54 Graft. C of Ch Ch Cathl Grafton 53-54; Min Can 54-55; C of Casino 55-57; Youth Dir Dio Tas 57-59; R of Queenstown 59-67; Wynyard 67-73; All SS Hobart Dio Tas from 73. *4 Adelaide Street, South Hobart, Tasmania 7000.* (002-23 1795)

PATRICK, Canon Alan Reginald. Univ of New Engl BA 74. Moore Th Coll Syd ACT ThL 65. **d** 65 **p** 66 Syd. C of Forestville 66; C-in-c of French's Forest 67-71; R 71-75; Camden Dio Syd from 76; Can of St Mich Prov Cathl Wollongong from 78. *Rectory, Menangle Road, Camden, NSW, Australia 2570.* (046-668012)

PATRICK, George. d 49 **p** 50 Perth. C of St Pet Vic Pk Perth 49-50; St Hilda Perth 50-51; R of N Midlands 51-55; C of Chesterfield 55-57; Chap of Commun of St Pet Walkerburn 57-58; C of St Sav Folkestone 58-59; Chap St Mary's Home Hastings and L to Offic Dio Chich 59-71. *4 Morden College, Blackheath, SE3 0PW.*

PATRICK, Hugh Joseph. TCD BA 62, MA 66. **d** 63 Down **p** 64 Tuam for Down. C of Drom Cathl 63-66; Shankill 66-70; Rothwell, Leeds 70-73; V of St Hilda Thurnscoe E 73-78; Wales Dio Sheff from 78; P-in-c of Thorpe Salvin 78-82. *Wales Vicarage, Sheffield, S31 8PD.* (Worksop 771111)

PATRICK, Canon James Barry. Univ of Lon BSc (2nd cl Sociology) 54. Wycl Coll Tor BTh 58. **d** 57 **p** 58 Tor. C of St Paul Bloor Street Tor 57-61; R of Nipawin 61-64; R of St Leon-on-the-Hill Red Deer 64-70; R of St Gabr City and Dio Calg from 70; Can of Calg from 81. *14 Cornell Place NW, Calgary 43, Alta, Canada.* (282-8192)

PATRICK, James Scott King. b 06. Univ of Glas MA 29. Ripon Hall, Ox 35. **d** and **p** 35 Birm. C of Hall Green 35-36; St Luke Glas 36-37; Perm to Offic at King's Norton 37-39; C of Sutton Coldfield 39-48; Chap HM Pris Leeds 48-49; L to Offic Dio Ripon 48-49; C of Wortley de Leeds 49-50. *6b Bainbrigge Road, Leeds, LS6 3AD.*

PATRICK, John. St Jo Coll Winnipeg. **d** 47 **p** 48 Keew for Bran. C of Somerset 47-49; R 49-51; P-in-c of Sherridon and Waboroden 51-54; P-in-c of Gladstone and of Neepawa 54-55; I of MacGregor 55-56; Steveston Dio New Westmr from 57. *Box 432, Steveston, BC, Canada.*

PATRICK, John Peter. b 23. K Coll Lon. **d** 52 Jarrow for Dur **p** 53 Dur. C of Westoe S Shields 52-55; Woodhouse Dio Wakef 55-58; Batley 58-59; V of Upperthong 59-75; Slaithwaite w E Scammonden 75-80; Donington Dio Linc from 80. *Donington Vicarage, Spalding, Lincs.*

PATRICK, Peter John. d 75 **p** 76 Trinid. R of St Andr Tobago Dio Trinid from 78. *St Andrew's Rectory, Scarborough, Tobago, W Indies.*

PATSTON, Raymond Sidney Richard. b 26. Kelham Th Coll 47. **d** 51 **p** 52 Lon. C of H Innoc Hammersmith 51-53; St Pet Acton Green 53-56; UMCA Area Sec for E Cos 56-62; C of St Luke Chesterton 56-59; R of Downham Mkt w Bexwell 61-71; V of Old Clee Dio Linc from 71. *202 Clee Road, Grimsby, S Humb.* (Cleethorpes 61800)

PATSTONE, Arthur Job. Queen's Coll Birm. **d** 08 **p** 10 Calg. Miss at Rimby w Bentley Alta 08-10; I of St Bypr Lacombe 10-16; Doaktown 16-20; Miss of Grand Falls 20-24; R of Westfield 24-29; St Paul Newmarket 29-41; I of Stayner 41-51; P-in-c of Hastings w Roseneath 51-61; Hon C of All SS Pet Dio Tor from 61. *636 Lundy's Lane, Peterborough, Ont, Canada.*

PATSTONE, John Douglas. b 46. Wycl Coll Tor LTh 76. **d** 76 **p** 77 Fred. C of Ch Ch Fred 76-81; I of St Alb Port Alberni Dio BC from 81. *FBox 115, Port Alberni, BC, Canada.*

PATTEN, John. b 27. Qu Coll Birm 74. **d** 76 Lich **p** 77

Stafford for Lich (APM). C of Armitage 76-79; St Mich City and Dio Lich from 79. *31 Trent Valley Road, Lichfield, WS13 6EZ.* (Lich 28245)

PATTENDEN, Henry Albert. b 11. Lich Th Coll 53. **d** 54 **p** 55 Lich. C of Rugeley 54-57; C-in-c of Rickerscote Conv Distr Stafford 57-62; V of 62-66; Leighton-under-the-Wrekin w Eaton Constantine 66-67; Etruria 67-72; C of Wymering 72-73. *22 George Hill Court, Stafford.*

PATTERSON, Brian Raymond. **d** 80 Armid. C-in-c of Tingha Dio Armid from 80. *Vicarage, Sapphire Street, Tingha, NSW, Australia 2369.*

✠ **PATTERSON, Right Rev Cecil John.** b 08. CBE 54, CMG 58. Late Exhib of St Cath Coll Cam 3rd cl Cl Trip pt i 29, BA (2nd cl Hist Div 1 Trip pt ii) 30, MA 34, Hon Fell from 62. Hon DD (Lambeth) 63. Univ of Nigeria Hon DD 64; Bps' Coll Cheshunt 30. **d** 31 **p** 32 Lon. C of H Innoc Kingsbury 31-34; CMS Miss Dio Niger 34-42; Cons Asst Bp on the Niger in St Paul's Cathl 2 Feb 42 by Abp of Cant; Bps of Lon; Leic; Ox; Worc; and Korea; Bps Suffr of Buckingham and Stepney; Apptd Ld Bp on the Niger 45; Abp and Metrop of W Afr 61; res 69; Hon Can of Guildf 66-69; Can (Emer) from 69; Hon Asst Bp in Dio Lon 70-76; Abps' of Cant and York Rep for Commun Relns 70-72. *6 High Park Road, Kew, Richmond, Surrey.* (01-876 1697)

PATTERSON, Charles David Gilliat. b 40. Univ of Lon (Extra-Mural) Dipl Th 74. Oak Hill Coll 71. **d** 74 Lon **p** 75 Kens for Lon. C of H Trin Brompton Lon 74-77; St Mary Isleworth 77-80; V of Bures Dio St E from 80. *Vicarage, Bures, Suff, CO8 5AA.* (Bures 227315)

PATTERSON, Conrad Brenton. Univ of Adel BA 61. ACT ThDip 76. **d** 61 **p** 62 Willoch. C of Port Pirie 61-63; Pet 63-65; R of Bordertown 65-70; Loxton 70-75; P-in-c of O'Halloran 75-77; R of Morphett Vale Dio Murray from 77. *Box 118, Morphett Vale Central, S Australia 5162.* (08-382 2182)

PATTERSON, Curtis. b 45. **d** 77 **p** 79 Queb. C of Harrington Harbour 77-79; I of St Clem W, Harrington Harbour Dio Queb from 79. *Harrington Harbour, Duplessis Co, PQ, Canada, G0G 1N0.*

PATTERSON, Forde. **d** 32 **p** 33 Arm. C of Portadown 32-36; C-in-c of Aghavilly 36-45; R 45-56; RD of Aghaloo 55-64; Tynan from 64; R of Killylea 56-73. *Rectory, Killylea, Co Armagh, N Ireland.*

PATTERSON, Francis Jennings. Trin Coll Dub BA, Div Test (2nd cl) 25. **d** 25 **p** 26 Kilm. C of Killeshandra w Killegar 25-29; C-in-c of Killasnett w Ballaghmeehan 29-42; I of Laragh w Lavey 42-67. *Larah Rectory, Poles, Cavan, Irish Republic.*

PATTERSON, Canon Frederick George de Joncourt. b 1900. Hertf Coll Ox BA 22, MA 26, Cudd Coll 22. **d** 23 **p** 24 Ripon. C of St Bart Armley 23-27; P-in-c of Selukwe and Chap of Shabani 27-31; C of Dewsbury (in c of St Jas) 31-34; Dom Chap to Bp of Wakef and Dioc Chap Wakef 34-38; Hon Chap to Bp of Wakef from 38; Commiss Geo 37-56; V of St Matt W Town Dewsbury 38-49; Birstall 49-59; RD of Birstall 50-59; Surr from 51; Hon Can Wakef 52-62; Can (Emer) from 62; R of Emley 59-62; Clifford Chambers (w Marston Sicca from 64) 62-66. *Address temp unknown.*

PATTERSON, Hugh John. b 38. K Coll Lon and Warm AKC 63. Univ of Southn MPhil 76. **d** 64 **p** 65 Guildf. C of Epsom 64-65; Chap and Lect Ewell Coll 65-68; Asst Chap and Lect Bp Otter Coll Chich 68-71; Lect Dudley Coll of Educn from 71; Sen Lect Wolverhampton Poly from 77. *10 Severnvale, Eardington, Bridgnorth, Salop, WV16 5JW.* (Bridgnorth 5298)

PATTERSON, Ian Francis Riddell. Trin Coll Dub BA 55. **d** 55 **p** 56 Connor. C of St Mary Belf 55-59; Finaghy 59-63; I of Craigs w Dunaghy and Killogan 63-66; Trin Coll Miss Belf 66-68; H Redeemer Belf 68-80; Kilroot Dio Connor from 80. *Kilroot Rectory, Carrickfergus, Co Antrim, N Ireland.*

PATTERSON, James Rowan Colebrooke. **d** 56 **p** 57 Moos. R of Swastika 56-61; I of Sturgeon Falls 61-66. *Box 22, Grayling, Michigan, USA.*

PATTERSON, John. b 27. Bps' Coll Cheshunt 60. **d** 61 **p** 62 Ox. C of St Luke Maidenhead 61-65; Chap RAF 65-72; V of St Jas Ashton L 72-78; in Amer Ch. *c/o Diocesan Office, 1055 Taylor Street, San Francisco, CA 94108, USA.*

PATTERSON, John Norton. b 39. TCD BA 64, MA 68. **d** 65 **p** 66 Connor. C of St Paul Belf 65-68; Larne and Inver 68-72; R of Ballintoy 72-78; R of Rathlin 72-78; Dunseverick Dio Connor from 78. *Ballintoy Rectory, Ballycastle, Co Antrim, N Ireland.* (Ballycastle 62411)

PATTERSON, Kenneth William. St Chad's Coll Regina, LTh 64. **d** and **p** 64 Niag. C of St Andr Grimsby Ont 64-67; I of Palermo 67-72; I of St Simon Oakville 67-72; St Jas St Catharines 72-79; St Eliz Burlington Dio Niag from 79. *5324 Bromley Road, Burlington, Ont, Canada.* (416-639 2987)

PATTERSON, Ven Lester James. Univ of W Ont BA 38, BD 50. Hur Coll Ont LTh 39, Hon DD 74. **d** 39 **p** 40 Hur. C of Lucknow Ripley Port Albert and Dungannon 39-40; R of Huntingford w Zorra 40-41; I of Canon Davis Mem Ch Sarnia 41-47; All SS Lon 47-53; R of H Trin Chatham 53-56; Exam Chap to Bp and R of New St Paul Woodstock 56-62; Archd of Saugeen 62-66; Essex from 66; R of St Geo Owen Sound 62-66; St Barn Windsor Dio Hur from 66. *2041 Verdun Avenue, Windsor 20, Ont., Canada.* (519-254 3584)

PATTERSON, Lewis David Malcolm. b 06. Lon Coll Div 51. **d** 53 **p** 54 Chich. C of Crowborough 53-56; St Paul St Marylebone 56-58; V of Rye Harbour w Camber 58-65; Min of St Paul Eccles Distr Camelsdale 65-69; V of Camelsdale 69-75. *4 Stone Court, Petersfield Road, Midhurst, GU29 9LP.*

PATTERSON, Marwood Francis. Wycl Coll Tor. **d** 55 **p** 56 Tor. I of Stoney Lake Miss 55-59; P-in-c of St Jas Just Downsview Tor 59-67. *36 Shady Lane Crescent, Thornhill, Ont, Canada.*

PATTERSON, Norman John. b 47. Peterho Coll Cam BA 69. St Jo Coll Nottm 70. **d** 73 Warrington for Liv **p** 74 Liv. C of St Ambrose w St Timothy Everton 73-74; St Pet Everton Dio Liv 74-79; Team V from 79. *115 Shaw Street, Everton, Liverpool, L6 1HW.* (051-207 2994)

PATTERSON, Patrick Douglas MacRae. b 51. Univ of Vic BC BA 73. Wycl Hall Ox 73. **d** 76 Ches **p** 77 BC. C of Bebington Ches 76-79; St John Vanc Dio New Westmr from 79. *2641 West 41st Avenue, Vancouver, BC, Canada.*

PATTERSON, Canon Peter William. St Mich Th Coll Crafers ACT ThL (2nd cl) 51. **d** 51 **p** 52 Adel. L to Offic Dio Adel 51; C of St Paul Port Adel 51-53; Miss Chap at Meadows-Mylor 53-56; P-in-c of Mt Pleasant 56-58; R 58-62; Gawler 62-67; P-in-c of Mallala 62-67; Two Wells 64-67; R of Plympton 67-73; Fullarton Dio Adel from 73; Hon Can of Adel from 81. *9 Staunton Avenue, Fullarton, S Australia 5063.* (08-71 4223)

PATTERSON, William Alfred. Wycl Hall Ox 77. **d** 79 **p** 80 Ches. C of Partington w Carrington Dio Ches from 79. *Beechfield, Chapel Lane, Partington, Urmston, Manchester.* (061-775 7666)

PATTERSON, Ven William James. b 30. Ball Coll Ox BA 53. Ely Th Coll 53. **d** 55 **p** 56 Newc T. C of St Jo Bapt Newc T 55-58; P-in-c of Mayaro w Rio Claro Trinid 58-65; R of Esher 65-72; Downham L w Pymoor 72-79; RD of Emly 68-72; Chap to Bp of Ely 73-74; P-in-c of Coveney 78-80; Archd of Wisbech from 79; V of St Mary Wisbech Dio Ely from 80. *St Mary Vicarage, Wisbech, Cambs, PE13 4RN.* (Wisbech St Mary 596)

PATTINSON, Canon Charles Kenneth. b 04. St Jo Coll Dur BA 25, Dipl Th 26, MA 28. **d** 27 **p** 28 Dur. C of St Andr Monk Wearmouth 27-29; L to Offic Dio Dur 30-36; R of Edmundbyers 36-44; V of Escomb 44-48; Dom Chap to Bp of Dur 29-36; Chap 36-52; Prec and Sacr of Dur Cathl 48-72; L to Offic Dio Dur from 50; Hon Can of Dur 62-74; Can (Emer) from 74. *55 South Street, Durham.*

PATTINSON, George Henry. b 14. Dorch Miss Coll 39. **d** and **p** 42 York. C of St Paul Middlesbrough 42-48; Hessle 48-49; Selby Abbey 49-53; V of Elloughton 53-61; C-in-c of Brantingham 56-61; V of Barney w Thursford Dio Nor from 61; C-in-c of Fulmodeston w Croxton Dio Nor from 70. *Barney Vicarage, Fakenham, Norf, NR21 0AD.* (Thursford 309)

PATTISON, Alan Frank. Ridley Coll Melb ACT ThL 55. **d** 56 **p** 57 Melb. C of Cheltm 56-57; Min of Hastings 57-59; Chap AMF 59-60; C of St Paul Ringwood 60-61; V of H Trin Ringwood 61-63; Heathmont 63-66; St John Bentleigh 66-71; R of Scarborough 71-80; Wodonga Dio Wang from 80. *225 Beechworth Road, Wodonga, Vic, Australia 3690.*

PATTISON, Alan Thomas. Univ of Syd BA 38. **d** 38 **p** 39 Syd. C of All SS Petersham 38-39; St John Ashfield 39; St Mark Darling Pt Syd 39-43; R of St Faith Narrabeen w Pittwater 43-46; Denham Court w Rosemore 46-47; Mittagong 47-53; Longueville 53-67; Maroubra 67; L to Offic Dio Syd from 67. *4 Harriman Court, Nuffield Village, Castle Hill, NSW, Aistralia 2154.* (634-7702)

PATTISON, Edwin Gibson. b 25. Oak Hill Th Coll 66. **d** 67 **p** 68 Ex. C of Ashton w Trusham 67-71; V of Dunsford w Doddiscombsleigh Dio Ex from 72; Sec Dioc Advisory C'tte Ex from 75; RD of Kenn 76-80. *Dunsford Vicarage, Exeter, Devon, EX6 7AA.* (Christow 52490)

PATTISON, George Linsley. b 50. Univ of Edin MA 72, BD 77. **d** 77 **p** 78 Newc T. C of St Jas Benwell 77-80; P-in-c of Kimblesworth Dio Dur from 80. *210 Gilesgate, Durham.* (Dur 62246)

PATTISON, Graham Bentley. b 39. Open Univ BA 75. Kelham Th Coll 59. **d** 64 **p** 65 Dur. C of Beamish 64-66; Benfieldside 66-67; Barnsley 67-70; Team V of Tong w Holme Wood 70-74; R 74-77; Master of Sherburn Hosp and Social Responsibility Officer Dio Dur from 77. *The Master's House, Sherburn Hospital, Durham, DH1 2SE.* (Durham 720332)

PATTISON, Ronald Wells. b 43. Carleton Univ Ott BA 72. Episc Th Coll Cam USA MDiv 67. **d** and **p** 72 Ott. I of Petawawa 72-80; Metcalfe Dio Ott from 80. *Box 84, Metcalfe, Ont, Canada.* (613-821 1922)

PATTISON, Stephen Bewley. b 53. Selw Coll Cam BA 76. Edin Th Coll 76. **d** 78 **p** 80 Newc T. C of All SS Gosforth 78-79; Hon Chap St Nich Hosp Gosforth from 78; Hon C of St Thos Mart City and Dio Newc T from 80. *1 Greenfield Place, Newcastle-upon-Tyne, NE4 6AX.* (Newc T 329104)

PATTON, Ven Desmond Hilton. b 12. TCD BA and Div Test 35. **d** 36 **p** 37 Oss. C of Killermogh 36-38; Wexford 38-40; R of Mothel 40-41; Adhade W Ardoyne 41-51; I of Clonenagh W Roskelton (and Ballyfin from 58) 51-59; RD of Aghade 57-60; Dunleckney 60-62; I of Carlow U 59-77; Preb of Tecolme in Leigh Cathl 60-71; Preb of Blackrath in Oss Cathl 60-62; Archd of Oss and Leigh 62-76; Archd (Emer) from 76; Exam Chap to Bp of Oss 62-77. *Lyttleholme, Delgany, Co Wicklow, Irish Republic.* (875207)

PATUAWA, George Wiki Nathan. b 39. St Jo Coll Auckld 71. **d** 73 Bp Monteith for Auckld **p** 74 Auckld. C of Whagarei 73-75; Maori Miss Dio Auckld 75-78; Chap Waiouru Mil Camp and Hon C of Taihape Dio Wel from 78. *Chaplain's Office, Waiouru MC, NZ.*

PAU, Peter. Union Th Coll Hong Kong LTh 65. **d** 65 Hong. C of St Thos Kowloon 65-72; V of Crown of Thorns Ch Kowloon Dio Hong from 72. *Vicarage, Texaco Road, Kowloon, Hong Kong.* (12-201082)

PAUL, David Brown. b 47. Univ of Keele BEduc 70. St Steph Ho Ox 72. **d** 74 **p** 75 Dur. C of St Mary Magd Millfield 74-79; P-in-c of St Andr Romford Dio Chelmsf 79-80; R from 80. *St Andrew's Rectory, London Road, Romford, Essex, RM7 9QD.* (Romford 64192)

PAUL, Francis Lincoln. Univ of Cant BA 65. NZ Bd of Th Stud LTh 65. **d** 65 Bp McKenzie for Wel **p** 66 Wel. C of Johnsonville 65-71; V of Pahiatua 71-77; Wanganui E 77-79 Chap Wanganui Hosp and Perm to Offic Dio Wel from 79. *99 Ikitara Road, Wanganui, NZ.* (38-717)

PAUL, Francis. **d** 75 Sudan **p** 77 Rumbek. P Dio Rumbek. *ECS, Lui, Sudan.*

✠ **PAUL, Right Rev Geoffrey John.** b 21. Qu Coll Cam MA 46. K Coll Lon MTh AKC 48. **d** 48 **p** 49 Chelmsf. C of Little Ilford 48-50; Ch of S India 50-65; Can Res of Bris 66-71; Hon Can from 71; Exam Chap to Bp of Bris 66-77; Dir of Ordin Tr Bris 66-71; Warden of Lee Abbey Devon 71-77; RD of Hull 77-81; Cons Ld Bp Suffr of Hull in York Minster 25 March 77 by Abp of York; Bps of Dur, Southw, Man, Newc T, Wakef, and Derby; Bps Suffr of Jarrow, Stockport, Burnley, Penrith, Pontefract, Selby, Knaresborough, Sherwood, Hulme, Whitby, Doncaster and Plymouth; and Bps Tomkins, Cockin, Sargent and Treacy; Trld to Bradf 81. *Bishopscroft, Ashwell Road, Heaton, Bradford, W Yorks, BD9 4AU.* (Bradford 45414)

PAUL, John Douglas. b 28. Univ of Edin MA 52. Ely Th Coll 52. **d** 54 **p** 55 Portsm. C of Ascen Portsm 54-56; Asst P Msumba Dio Nyasa 56-60; Dio Lebom 60-70; Archd o Metangula 65-70; R of Castle Douglas 70-75; St Mark Portobello 75-80; Elgin w Lossiemouth Dio Moray from 80. *Rectory, Gordon Street, Elgin, Morays, IV30 1JG.* (Elgin 7505)

PAUL, John Graham. b 32. **d** 75 **p** 77 Tas. C of St D Cathl Hobart 75-77; Hon C of Lindisfarne 77-79; Ch Ch Cathl Darwin Dio N Terr from 79. *Christ Church Cathedral, Darwin, NT, Australia.*

PAUL, John Wilfred. b 30. St Jo Coll Morpeth, ACT ThL 52. **d** 51 **p** 54 Newc. C of Hamilton 51-57; Ascen Mitcham 57-59; V of St Jo Evang Clapham 59-65; CF (TA) 60-67; V of St Mary Balham Dio S'wark from 65. *220 Balham High Road, SW12 9BS.* (01-675 3968)

PAUL, Lionel John. b 18. Codr Coll Barb 47. **d** 49 Barb **p** 50 Windw I. C Dio Barb 49-50; St Geo Cathl Kingstown 50-52; R and P-in-c of Stann Creek and Valley Br Hond 52-58; C of St Barn Walthamstow 58-60; R of Walkern 60-69; C of St Jo Bapt Harpenden 69-73; Min of St Benedict Conv Distr Apsley End 73-79; R of Cockfield Dio Dur from 79. *Cockfield Rectory, Bishop Auckland, Co Durham, DL13 5AA.* (Bp Auckld 718447)

PAUL, Naunihal Chand. b 40. **d** 69 **p** 70 Simla. C of Ch Ch Simla 69-70; V of St Jas Kangra w Dharamsala 70-74; C of St Clem Urmston 75-77; C-in-c of St Pet Farnworth 77-80; Team V of E Farnworth and Kearsley Dio Man from 80. *St Peter's Vicarage, Braiford Street, Farnworth, Lancs, BL4 9JY.*

PAUL, Roger Philip. b 53. Clare Coll Cam BA 74. Westcott Ho Cam 78. **d** 81 Cov. C of Caludon Team Min Dio Cov from 81. *111 Mones Boulevard, Binley Road, Coventry, CV2 5NB.*

PAULEY, Denniss Franklyn. b 19. Chich Th Coll. **d** 57 **p** 58 Lon. C of St Mich AA Bromley 57-59; Gt Greenford 59-62; Tonge Moor 62-69; St Silas Pentonville Dio Lon from 69. *87a Richmond Avenue, Islington, N1 0LX.*

PAULIN, Canon James Marmaduke. b 06. Open Univ BA 73. St Andr Th Coll Whittlesford 35. **d** 37 **p** 38 Newc T. C of Morpeth (in c from 39) 37-41; C-in-c of St Mary St Barn and St Simon Sheff 41-43; V of St Mary Bramall Lane (w St Simon from 46) Sheff 43-48; RD of Ecclesall 47-48; Corbridge 66-71; V of Longhirst w Hebburn 48-57; Bywell St Pet 57-71; Dioc Insp of Schs 50-71; Hon Can of Newc T from 64; Proc Conv Newc T 64-71. *11 Trinity Terrace, Corbridge, Northumberland.* (Corbridge 2414)

PAULL, Canon Francis Harold. Trin Coll Tor LTh 20. **d** 21 **p** 22 Tor. C of Grace Ch Tor 21-22; I of Atwood w Henfryn 22-25; R of Bayfield w Varna and Middleton 25-33; I of St Aid Windsor 33-45; Listowel and Atwood 45-64; Hon Can of Hur 61-65; Can (Emer) from 66. *353 Dalhousie Street, Bayfield, Ont, Canada.*

PAULO, Charles. **d** 80 Bp Russell for Zanz T. d Dio Zanz T. *PO Box 208, Wete, Pemba, Tanzania.*

PAULSE, John Albert. b 36. Federal Th Coll Alice 68. **d** 70 **p** 71 Capetn. C of St Aid Lansdowne 70-74; R of Namaqualand 74-77; St Phil City and Dio Capetn from 77. *101 Roger Street, Cape Town 8001, S Africa.* (41-2863)

PAVADAY, Joseph Lhorgeedassen. **d** 65 **p** 66 Maur. C of Curepipe 65-70; R 70-73; Reduit Dio Maur from 73. *La Caverne, Vacoas, Mauritius.* (Vacoas 221)

PAVEY, Gordon Sidney Alfred. b 19. Univ of Lon BD 47. Univ of Leeds MEd 56. Chich Th Coll [illegible] C of K Chas Mart S Mymms 42-44; St Mich AA Bedford Park Lon 44-48; H Trin Taunton 48-50; UMCA Org Sec for N Midl 50-54; V of St Thos Huddersfield 54-64; Dioc Chap for Youth 54-57; Sen Div Master Qu Eliz Gr Sch Wakef 57-64; Prin Lect in Th St Martin's Coll Lanc 64-68; L to Offic Dio Blackb 64-68; Dio Bris from 68; Prin Lect Coll of St Matthias Fishponds Bris from 68; Bris Poly from 77. *2 Carey's Close, Clevedon, Avon, BS21 6BA.* (Clevedon 872623)

PAVEY, Michael Trevor. b 32. ALCD 59. **d** 59 Thetford for Nor **p** 60 Nor. C of St Pet Mancroft Nor 59-61; N Walsham w Antingham 61-63; Chap RAF 63-80; Perm to Offic Dios Ex, Truro; B & W, Glouc, Heref, Bris & Sarum from 80. *28 Birchwood Avenue, Weston-s-Mare, BS23 3JE.* (0934 26821)

PAVEY, Peter John. b 29. Univ of Lon BD (2nd cl) and ALCD 54. Univ of Edin 54. **d** 55 **p** 56 Roch. C of Bexleyheath 55-58; Tutor St Aid Coll 58-63; Chap 62-63; L to Offic Dio Ches 59-63; Chap St Luke Haifa 63-66; Exam Chap to Abp in Jer 65-66; Vice Prin Ridley Hall Cam 66-70; Actg Prin 70-71; L to Offic Dio Ely 67-71; V of St Paul Letchworth (w Willian from 77) Dio St Alb from 71; RD of Hitchin from 73. *177 Pixmore Way, Letchworth, Herts, SG6 1QT.* (Letchworth 3083)

PAWLEY, Clive. b 35. K Coll Lon and Warm AKC 59. **d** 60 **p** 61 Chelmsf. C of St Barn L Ilford 60-63; St Thos-on-the-Bourne 63-67; V of Tongham Dio Guildf from 67. *Tongham Vicarage, Farnham, Surrey.* (Runfold 2224)

PAWLEY, Duncan Medway. b 45. Univ of Syd BSc 66. BD (Lon) 73. Moore Coll Syd ThL 71. **d** 73 Syd **p** 73 Bp Robinson for Syd. C of Guildford 73; Punchbowl 73-75; Port Kembla 75-76; Kiama 76-78; R of Merrylands Dio Syd from 78. *4 Denmark Street, Merrylands, NSW, Australia 2160.* (637 2522)

PAWSEY, Jack Edward. b 35. Trin Coll Ox BA (3rd cl Jurispr) 59, MA 65. Westcott Ho Cam 64. **d** 66 **p** 67 S'wark. Sec Dioc Coun for Social Aid S'wark 66-75; Race Relns Worker Dio S'wark 75-78. *Cambridge House, 131 Camberwell Road, SE5.*

PAWSON, Geoffrey Philip Henry. b 04. Late Rustat Scho of Jes Coll Cam 2nd cl Cl Trip pt i 25, BA (2nd cl Th Trip pt ii) 26, Hulsean Pri 27, MA 31. Wells Th Coll 26. M CR 46. **d** 27 **p** 28 Worc. C of St Steph Redditch 27-29 SPG Miss Dio Chota N 30-31; C of King Cross Halifax 31-32; Tutor Lich Th Coll 32-33; Lect 32-36; Chap 33-36; C of Cathl Ch Wakef 37-38; V of St Mary L Cam 38-44; Perm to Offic Dio Ripon 48-52; Vice-Prin of Coll of Resurr Mirfield 52-56; Prin of Coll of Resurr Rosettenville Johann 56-60; L to Offic Dio Wakef 61-66 and from 69; Vice-Prin Coll of Resurr Mirfield 62-65; Proc Conv Wakef 62-65; Prior and Prin of Codr Coll Barb 66-69; *House of the Resurrection, Mirfield, Yorks, WF14 0BN.*

PAWSON, John Walker. b 38. Kelham Th Coll 58. **d** 63 **p** 64 York. C of St Mich AA N Hull 63-67; L Gornal 67-70; V of St Jo Evang Tipton 70-78; Meir Heath Dio Lich from 78. *Vicarage, Meir Heath, Stoke-on-Trent, Staffs, ST3 7LH.* (Blythe Bridge 3189)

PAWUN, Thomas Taban. **d** 76 Sudan. d Dio Sudan 76; Dio Omdurman from 76. *Box 65, Omdurman, Sudan.*

PAXMAN, Denis James. St Edm Hall Ox BA (2nd cl Mod Hist) 50, Dipl Th 51, MA 54. Ely Th Coll 52. **d** 53 Dover for Cant **p** 54 Cant. C of Bearsted 53-56; Chap Solihull Sch 56-65;

Warden and Hd Master St Mich Coll Tenbury 65-77; PC (V from 69) of St Mich AA Tenbury Wells 65-77; Chap of Howell's Sch Denbigh from 77. *58 Park Street, Denbigh, Clwyd, LL16 3DE.* (Denbigh 2193)

PAXON, Robin Michael Cuninghame. b 46. St Jo Coll Dur BA 69. Westcott Ho Cam 69. **d** 71 **p** 72 Cant. C of St Pet Croydon 71-77; Saffron Walden w Wendens Ambo and Littlebury 77-80; P-in-c of Plaistow Dio Chelmsf from 80. *24 Richmond Street, Plaistow, E13 9AA.* (01-471 8775)

PAXTON, Cyril. b 14. SOC 64. **d** 67 **p** 68 S'wark. C of Riddlesdown 67-74; Isfield 74-76; Horsted Parva 74-76; Uckfield 74-76; Hon C of S Petherton Dio B & W from 77. *Cobblers, Hinton St George, Crewkerne, Somt, TA17 8SA.* (Crewkerne 72741)

PAXTON, Geoffrey Joseph. Moore Th Coll Syd ACT ThL 66. **d** 66 **p** 67 Brisb. C of St Barn Ithaca Brisb 66-69; Perm to Offic Dio Brisb 69-79. *c/o 76 West Avenue, Wynnum, Queensland, Australia 4178.*

PAXTON, John Ernest. b 49. Univ of Ex BA 71. Westcott Ho Cam 74. **d** 74 **p** 75 Worc. C of Redditch 74-77; Chap at Dubai 77-81; Industr Missr Dio Man from 81. *113 Tudor Avenue, Bolton, BL1 4NB.*

PAXTON-HALL (formerly HALL), Canon Michael Arthur. St Francis Coll Brisb ACT ThL 44. **d** 44 **p** 45 Brisb. C of St Paul Ipswich 44-48; M of Bush Bro of St Paul from 48; V of Caboolture 53-55; R of Childers 55-59; Indooroopilly 59-68; Warwick Brisb 68-73; Bundaberg Dio Brisb from 73; Hon Can of Brisb from 70. *233 Bourbong Street, Bundaberg, Queensland, Australia 4670.* (71 2467)

PAY, Maurice Clement. Univ of Melb BA 27, MA 29. Univ of Lon BD 31. **d** 31 Melb **p** 32 Gippsld. Asst Chap Melb Gr Sch 31-32; V of Neerim 32-34; Asst Chap C of E Gr Sch Brisb 35-38; R of Coorparoo Brisb 39-48; Miss Chap Dio Brisb 48-50; R of Gatton 50-59; St Matt Groveley Brisb 59-61; Boonah Brisb 61-71; Perm to Offic Dio Brisb from 71. *Noojee, Kangaroo Avenue, Bribie Island, Queensland, Australia 4507.* (Bribie Island 48 1312)

PAY, Norman John. b 50. St Jo Coll Dur BA 72. Cranmer Hall Dur Dipl Th 73. **d** 74 **p** 75 Dur. C of South Moor 74-78; Rawmarsh (in c of St Nicolas Ryecroft) 78-80; C-in-c of New Cantley Conv Distr Doncaster Dio Sheff from 80. *St Hugh's House, Levet Road, Cantley, Doncaster, DN4 6JQ.* (Doncaster 55739)

PAYN, Peter Richard. b 33. Moore Th Coll Syd ACT ThL (2nd cl) 59. **d** and **p** 60 Syd. C of Pittwater 60-61; St Matt Kensington S Austr 61-63; St Jas w St John Melb 63-65; V of St Matt E Geelong 65-79; C of Ch Ch Blackb 79-80; V of Ch Ch Lowestoft Dio Nor from 80. *Vicarage, 1 Beeching Drive, Lowestoft, Suff, NR32 4TB.* (Lowestoft 2444)

PAYNE, Alan Frank. b 19. Bps' Coll Cheshunt 63. **d** 65 **p** 66 Ripon. C of Horsforth 65-69; V of Woodlesford (w Oulton from 75) 69-80; Thurgoland Dio Wakef from 80. *Vicarage, Halifax Road, Thurgoland, Sheffield, S Yorks, S30 4AL.*

PAYNE, Anthony Charles Prideaux. b 08. Pemb Coll Ox 2nd cl Cl Mods 28, 3rd cl Lit Hum 30, BA 36, MA 64. Ely Th Coll 35. **d** 36 **p** 37 Linc. C of Bourne 36-39; Sleaford 39; C-in-c of Swineshead 39-41; Chap RAFVR 41-46; C of Isham 47-49; R of Syresham 49-61; C-in-c of Wappenham 49-52; R 52-58; C-in-c of Whitfield 60-61; R of St Mich Lich 61-74. *29 Chapel Lane, Rode Heath, Stoke on Trent, ST7 3SD.* (Alsagar 2705)

PAYNE, Canon Charles Thomas Leonard. b 11. Kelham Th Coll 29. **d** 34 **p** 35 S'wark. C of St John Southend Lewisham 34-39; Old Malden 39-42; V of Ch Ch Streatham Hill 42-79; Chap to CA Hostel Streatham 48-79; RD of Streatham 73-79; Hon Can of S'wark from 75; Perm to Offic Dio St E from 79. *6 Cedar Walk, Acton Sudbury, Suff.*

PAYNE, Colin. K Coll Lon and Warm AKC 66. **d** 67 Bp McKie for Cov **p** 68 Cov. C of St Pet Cov 67-68; St Mary Virg Nuneaton 68-70; L to Offic Dio Southw from 71. *207 Windmill Lane, Nottingham.*

PAYNE, Cyril Douglas. b 16. Sarum Th Coll 46. **d** 49 **p** 50 Pet. C of St Columba Corby 49-51; Wellingborough 51-54; V of Stourpaine and R of Durweston 54-59; Edith Weston w Normanton 59-63; V of All SS Wellingborough 63-82. *32 London Road, Canterbury, Kent.*

PAYNE, Cyril Gordon. b 26. Univ of Bris BA 53. Linc Th Coll 53. **d** 55 **p** 56 Lon. C of H Trin Southall 55-58; Christchurch (in c of St Mary Somerford) 58-63; V of Otterbourne Win 63-75; Milford Dio Win from 75. *Vicarage, Lymington Road, Milford-on-Sea, Hants, SO4 0QN.* (Milford-on-Sea 3289)

PAYNE, David James. b 31. Clare Coll Cam BA 54, MA 61. Wycl Hall, Ox 60. **d** 62 Ox **p** 63 Guildf. C of Faringdon w L Coxwell 62-63; Ch Ch Guildf 63-66; R of Shackleford 66-73; R of Peper Harow 66-73; R of Odell 73-78; V of Pavenham 73-78; Warden Old R Crowhurst and Dir of Div Healing Miss for UK Dio Chich from 78. *The Old Rectory, Crowhurst, Nr Battle, Sussex.*

PAYNE, Canon Denis Alfred. b 22. Or Coll Ox BA (2nd cl Mod Hist) 50, MA 53. Wells Th Coll 50. **d** 51 **p** 52 Sheff. C of St Geo w St Steph Sheff 51-55; Chap and Lect Makerere Coll Univ of E Afr 55-67; Ministry Sec ACCM 67; Sen Selection Sec 69-73; Exam Chap to Bp of St E from 67 and Dioc Dir of Ordins and Clergy Tr from 73; Can Res of St E from 73; M Gen Syn 75-80; *2 Abbey Precincts, Bury St Edmunds, Suff.* (Bury St Edm 3396)

PAYNE, Eric Llewellyn. Codr Coll Barb 48. **d** 51 Barb for Antig **p** 52 Puerto Rico for WI. C of St Jo Cathl Antig 51-59; V of St D Barb 59-68; R of St John I and Dio Barb from 68. *St John's Rectory, Barbados, W Indies.*

PAYNE, Francis Michael Ambrose. b 18. Keble Coll Ox BA 39, MA 43. Ely Th Coll 39. **d** 41 **p** 42 Leic. C of St Pet Leic 41-45; Upton w Chalvey 45-48; V of Long Clawson 48-53; Shepshed 53-58; Ashby-de-la-Zouch 58-62; Surr from 59; RD of Akeley W 61-62; R of Henley-on-Thames 62-78; RD of Henly 73-78; P-in-c Remenham 75-78; R of Ecton Dio Pet from 78. *Ecton Rectory, Northampton, NN6 0QE.* (Northampton 406442)

PAYNE, Frederick. **d** 41 **p** 42 Ont. I of Loughboro Miss Ont 41-47; R of Elizabethtown 47-50; Prescott 50-78; Can of St Geo Cathl Kingston 62-70; Archd of St Lawrence 70-78. *Box 483, Prescott, Ont, Canada.*

PAYNE, Frederick Gates. b 19. Jes Coll Cam BA 40, MA 43. Lon Coll of Div 40. **d** 42 **p** 43 Taunton for B & W. C of St Jas Bath 42; Walcot 42-45; CF (EC) 45-48; Hd of CMJ Miss Ethiopia 48-67; SW Org Sec CMJ from 68. *83 Penn Lea Road, Weston, Bath, Somt, BA1 3RQ.* (Bath 23092)

PAYNE, Geoffrey. b 47. Em Coll Cam BA 69, MA 73. Trin Coll Ox BA 73, MA 78. Cudd Coll 71. **d** 74 **p** 75 Birm. C of Perry Barr 74-78; Chap RAF from 78. *Ministry of Defence, Adastral House, Theobalds Road, WC1X 8RU.*

PAYNE, Harold Womack. b 41. Pfeiffer Coll N Carolina BA 63. Virginia Th Sem USA 63. **d** 66 **p** 67 Bp Fraser for N Carolina. In Amer Ch 66-76; R of Our Lady & St Steph Bimini 77-78. *Address temp unknown.*

PAYNE, Canon James John Henry. MBE 69. St Pet Hall Ox BA (2nd cl Th) 53, MA 59. Linc Th Coll 53. **d** 53 **p** 54 Liv. Asst Chap Mersey Miss to Seamen Liv 53-55; C of Stoneycroft Dio Liv 55-57; Chap and Asst Master Igbobi Coll Lagos 57-62; Chap St Sav Lagos Dio Lagos from 62; Hon Can of Lagos from 71; Exam Chap to Bp of Lagos from 77. *St Saviour's Chaplaincy, PO Box 836, Lagos, Nigeria.* (Lagos 23078)

PAYNE, James Richmond. MBE 82. Moore Th Coll Syd 45. ACT ThL 49. **d** 47 **p** 48 Graft. C of Lismore 47-50; R of Nimbin 50-52; Chap RAAF 52-57; R of St Steph Coorparoo Brisb 57-62; Dean and R of St Geo Cathl Perth 62-68; BFBS Commonwealth Sec for Austr and Perm to Offic Dio C and Goulb from 68; L to Offic Dio Syd from 68; Commiss Centr Tang from 70. *Bible House, Garema Place, Canberra City, ACT 2601, Australia.*

PAYNE, John Charles. b 04. St Aid Coll 50. **d** 51 **p** 52 Carl. C of Stanwix 51-53; Dalton-in-Furness w Newton 53-55; V of Ch Ch Glodwick Oldham 55-62; St Sav Preston 62-69. *59 Castle Syke View, Pontefract, Yorks.*

PAYNE, John Michael. St Francis Coll Brisb 59. **d** 63 N Queensld **p** 64 Brisb for N Queensld. C of Mundingburra Townsville 63-66; Dir Dept of Miss Dio N Queensld 66-67; C of Gulliver Townsville 67-69; P-in-c of Prosperine 69-73; R of Ayr 74-77; Mt Isa 77-81; Archd of the West 78-81; R of W Mackay Dio N Queensld from 81. *Box 559, Mackay, Qld, Australia.*

PAYNE, John Percival. b 49. Univ of Nottm BA (2nd cl Th) 70. Cudd Coll 70. **d** 72 **p** 73 Ox. C of Tilehurst 72-76; St Sav w St Hilda Cross Green Leeds (in c of St Hilda) 76-79; Chap St Hilda's Priory Sneaton Castle Dio York from 79. *St Hilda's Priory, Sneaton Castle, Whitby, Yorks.*

PAYNE, Canon John Vernon. b 17. Univ of Wales, BA (3rd cl Gr) 39. St Mich Coll Llan 39. **d** 40 **p** 41 Llan. C of Llantrisant 40-49; Aberdare (in c of Cwmbach) 49-52; V of Llanharan w Peterston-super-Montem 52-64; V of St Cath Pontypridd Dio Llan from 64; RD of Pontypridd from 67; Can Llan Cathl from 71. *St Catherine's Vicarage, Pontypridd, Mid Glam, CF37 2BS.* (Pontypridd 402021)

PAYNE, Canon Joseph Marshall. b 17. Trin Coll Dub BA 38, MA 52. **d** 40 **p** 41 Down. C of St Aid Belf 40-43; Ballynafeigh 43-44; Chap RAF 44-72; Asst Chap-in-Chief 65-72; Hon Chap to HM the Queen 70-72; V of Malew Dio S & M from 72; RD of Castletown from 77; Can of S & M from 78; Treas from 80. *Malew Vicarage, Ballasalla, IM.* (Castletown 2469)

PAYNE, Kenneth Alan. b 45. Pemb Coll Ox BA 68, MA 71. Qu Coll Birm 71. **d** and **p** 74 Birm. C of Perry Barr 74-78; St Paul Ruislip Manor 78-79; Hawksworth Wood (in c of Moor Grange) Dio Ripon from 79. *St Andrew's House, Butcher Hill, Leeds, LS16 5BG.* (Leeds 755195)

PAYNE, Leonard Vivian. b 20. St D Coll Lamp BA 42. Lich Th Coll 42. **d** 44 **p** 46 Llan. C of Whitchurch 44-50; St

Paul Weston-s-Mare 50-55; V of St Paul Bedminster 55-62; St Paul Weston-s-Mare 62-81; Surr 63-81. *c/o St Paul's Vicarage, Weston-super-Mare, Avon.*

PAYNE, Ralfe Dudley. b 22. Univ of Lon BA 50. Qu Coll Birm. **d** 52 Lich **p** 53 Stafford for Cant. C of Tettenhall Wood 52-57; Tamworth 57-60; V of Gayton w Fradswell 60-63; Brockmoor 63-75; C of Kinver 75-79; V of Swindon Dio Lich from 79; R of Himley Dio Lich from 79. *Swindon Vicarage, Dudley, W Midl, DY3 4PG.* (Kingswinford 278532)

PAYNE, Richard Derek. b 29. K Coll Lon and Warm 51. **d** 55 **p** 56 St Alb. C of Stevenage 55-58; Clayton w Keymer 58-60; C-in-c of Coldean Conv Distr 60-63; R of Telscombe w Piddinghoe (and Southease from 75) 63-76; Chap and Asst Master Holmswood Ho Sch Tunbridge Wells 76-78; Cler Org Sec CECS Dios Cant, Roch, Chich, Guildf and S'wark from 78; Perm to Offic Dio Cant from 79. *Greystones, Duddleswell, Uckfield, Sussex.* (Nutley 2314)

PAYNE, Robert Christian. b 42. Univ of Wales, Dipl Th 65. St Mich Coll Llan 62. **d** 65 **p** 66 Glouc. C of Charlton Kings 65-69; Waltham Cross 69-71; V of Falfield (w Rockptn from 72) 71-76; C-in-c of Rockptn 71-72; Chap HM Detention Centre Eastwood Pk 71-76; HM Borstal Everthorpe 76-79; HM Borstal Glen Parva from 79. *c/o 5 Eden Close, Oadby, Leics.*

PAYNE, Robert Harold Vincent. b 44. St Jo Coll Nottm 77. **d** 79 **p** 80 Man. C of St Jas Didsbury Dio Man from 79. *6 Barlow Moor Road, Didsbury, Manchester 20 0TR.*

PAYNE, Robert Sandon. b 48. Univ of Reading BSc 69. ARICS 72. Ripon Coll Cudd 77. **d** 80 **p** 81 Heref. C of Bridgnorth Dio Heref from 80. *15 Stourbridge Road, Bridgnorth, Salop.* (Bridgnorth 61900)

✠ **PAYNE, Right Rev Sidney Stewart.** Qu Coll St John's BA 58, LTh 59, BD 67. **d** 57 **p** 58 Newfld. I of Happy Valley Miss 57-65; Bay Roberts 65-70; R of St Anthony Newfld 70-78; Exam Chap to Bp of Newfld 70-73; Cons Ld Bp Coadj of W Newfld in Cathl of H Redeemer Corner Brook 23 June 78 by Abp of E Newfld; Bps of NS, Montr, Fred, Queb, W Newfld and Centr Newfld; and others; Apptd Bp of W Newfld July 78. *Bishop's Lodge, 13 Cobb Lane, Newfoundland, Canada.* (709-634 9987)

PAYNE, Victor John. b 45. Univ of Wales Dipl Th 69. St Mich Coll Llan 66. **d** 70 Bp Hughes for Llan **p** 71 Llan. C of Ystrad-Mynach 70-72; Whitchurch 72-75; CF (TAVR) 74-75; CF from 75. *c/o Ministry of Defence, Bagshot Park, Bagshot, Surrey.*

PAYNE, Walter Richard Stanley. b 29. BSc (Lon) 54. FRIC 64. CChem 76. SOC 75. **d** 78 **p** 79 Roch. C of H Trin Lamorbey Dio Roch from 78. *120 Hurst Road, Sidcup, Kent, DA15 9AF.*

PAYNE, Warwick Martin. K Coll Lon and Warm AKC 51. **d** 52 Bp Weller for Southw **p** 53 Southw. C of St Pet Mansfield 52-56; P-in-c of Kristi Kunda Dio Gambia 56-58; C of Winlaton (in c of Rowlands Gill) Dio Dur 59-62; R of Qacha's Nek 63-77; P-in-c of Butterworth 77-80; St John and St Martin Swartberg Dio St John's from 80. *Rectory, Swartberg, Transkei, S Africa.*

PAYNE, William George. b 1896. **d** 49 **p** 50 Dur. C of St Paul Darlington 49-50; Winlaton (in c of St Patr High Spen) 50-54; V of Esh w Langley Park 54-55; PC of Shiney Row 55-61; St Barn Hendon Bp Wearmouth 61-66. *8 The Oaks West, Mowbray Road, Sunderland, T & W, SR2 8HZ.* (Sunderland 71139)

PAYNE, William Vines. Moore Th Coll Syd. **d** and **p** 56 C and Goulb. C of Queanbeyan 56-57; P-in-c of Batlow 57-59; on leave 59; C of Westcombe Pk Kent 59-60; C-in-c of Provisional Distr of All SS Albion Pk 61-64; R of Clovelly 64-66; Dir Counselling Service Home Miss S Dio Syd 67-76; Welfare C of E Homes from 77; L to Offic Dio Syd from 67. *43 Carroll Street, Kogarah Bay, NSW, Australia 2217.* (529-7628)

PAYNE COOK, John Andrew Somerset. b 43. St Pet Coll Ox BA 65. Coll of Resurr Mirfield 65. **d** 68 Bradwell for Chelmsf **p** 69 Chelmsf. C of Latton 68-71; Gt Berkhamsted 71-76; Min of Goldington (N Brickhill) Bedford Conv Distr Dio St Alb from 76. *Vicarage, Calder Rise, North Brickhill, Bedford.*

PAYNE-CROSTON, Canon Eric Tuson. St Barn Th Coll Adel 37. ACT ThL 39. **d** 39 Adel **p** 40 Bp Thomas for Adel. C of St Pet Glenelg 39-41; Miss Chap Tailem Bend Miss 41-44; Mid-Yorke's Peninsula Miss Minlaton 44-45; R of Minlaton 45-48; Lyndoch 48-58; Benalla Dio Wang from 58; Hon Can of Wang from 76. *Rectory, Benalla, Vic, Australia 3672.* (061-62 2061)

PAYNTER, Norman Catchlove. Univ of Adel BA (1st cl Hist) 37. St Barn Th Coll Adel 38. ACT ThL 39. **d** 39 Adel **p** 40 Bp Thomas for Adel. C of Ch Ch N Adel 39-41; Miss Chap Kangaroo Is Miss 41-42; P-in-c of Murray Bridge Miss Distr 42-43; L to Offic Dio Adel and Chap RAN 44-46; P-in-c of Berri Miss 46-47; R of St Thos Balhannah (in c of St Jas Blakiston) 47-52; Chap RAN 52-54; Chap St Mark's Univ Coll Adel 54-60; Dom Chap to Bp of Adel and Prec of Adel Cathl 59-60; Perm to Offic Dio Cant 60-62; R of St Paul Adel 62-68; Broadview 68-70; Archd of Adel 70-79; Exam Chap to Bp of Adel 70-79; Org Chap Bp's Home Miss S Dio Adel 70-79; L to Offic Dio Adel from 79. *253 Stanley Street, North Adelaide, S Australia 5006.* (08-267 1074)

PAYNTER, Richard Ambrose Leslie. b 50. Univ of WI BA 77. Codr Coll Barb 74. **d** 76 **p** 77 Windw Is. C of St Geo Cathl St Vincent 76-77; St Geo Grenada 77-80; P-in-c of St Paul St Vincent Dio Windw Is from 80. *PO Box 483, St Vincent, W Indies.* (809-45 84332)

PAYNTON, Paul Alexander. b 42. Linc Th Coll 72. **d** 74 **p** 75 Pet. C of Uppingham w Ayston 74-77; R of Teigh w Whissendine (and Market Overton from 79) Dio Pet from 77; P-in-c of Market Overton 77-79. *Whissendine Vicarage, Paddock Close, Leics, LE15 7HW.* (Whissendine 333)

PAYTON, Canon Arthur Edward. b 16. MA (Lambeth) 81. **d** 39 **p** 40 Antig. C of St Geo St Kitts 39-42; St Osw Bris 42-44; Org Sec British Empire Leprosy Relief Assoc 44-49; C-in-c of St Jo Bapt Toxt Pk 49-50; V 50-56; R of Salcott Virley w Salcott Wigborough 56-64; V of Highwood 64-66; Hon C of Feering 66-69; Kelvedon Dio Chelmsf from 69; Hon Can of Gibr from 73. *Runton Grange, West Runton, Cromer, Norf.* (026 375 400)

PAYTON, John Vear. b 36. Bps' Coll Cheshunt, 60. **d** 63 **p** 64 St Alb. C of Hatfield Hyde 63-72; V of Farley Hill Luton Dio St Alb from 72. *Vicarage, Rotherham Avenue, Farley Hill, Luton, Beds, LU1 5PP.* (Luton 29466)

PAYTON, Robert James. Univ of Sask BA 65. Trin Coll Tor STB 68. **d** 68 **p** 69 Sask. C of Brampton 68-70; Miss Lac La Ronge 70-72; I of Birch Hills 72-79; St Mich Archangel City and Dio Tor from 80. *66 Haven Hill Square, Scarborough, Ont, Canada M1V 1M5.*

PAYTON, Ven Walter Frederick. Univ of Tor BA 32. St Jo Coll Winnipeg Hon DD 60. Wycl Coll Tor. **d** 32 Niag for Tor **p** 32 Tor. C of St Geo Graft 32; R of Perrytown 32-37; Humber Bay 37-42; Can Missr Dio Sask 42-56; Sec 42-66; Treas 42-62; Archd of Prince Albert 56-66; Archd (Emer) from 66; Exam Chap to Bp of Sask 60-66; Chap Dominion Penit Prince Albert 66-76. *633 21st Street West, Prince Albert, Sask, Canada.*

PAYTON, Wilfred Ernest Granville. b 13. Em Coll Cam BA 36, MA 40. CB 65. Ridley Hall Cam 36. **d** 38 **p** 39 Derby. C of Heanor 38-41; Chap RAF 41-69; Asst Chap-in-Chief Bomber Commd 59-61; FEAF 61-63; Prin RAF Chaps' Sch 64-65; Chap-in-Chief and Archd 65-69; Can and Preb of St Botolph in Linc Cathl 65-69; Hon Chap to HM the Queen 65-69; V of Abingdon w Shippon 69-79; RD of Abingdon 76-79. *Westwood, Ladder Hill, Nailsworth, Glos, GL6 0AW.* (Nailsworth 4340)

PEABODY, Gordon Shepard. Bp's Univ Lennox 61. **d** and **p** 65 Queb. I of Malbay 65-68; R of Drummondville 68-73; Maberly-Lanark 73-78; Renfrew Dio Ott from 78; Sec of Syn Dio Ott from 76. *140 Hall Avenue East, Renfrew, Ont, Canada.*

PEACE, Geoffrey. b 23. SOC. **d** 68 Kens for Lon. C of St Hilda's Conv Distr (St Hilda from 73) Ashford Middx 68-80; Spilsby w Hundleby Dio Linc from 80. *4 Station Road, Halton Holgate, Spilsbury, PE23 5PB.* (Spilsby 52121)

PEACH, Canon Harold Edwin Arthur. Hur Coll LTh 46. Univ of W Ont BA 46. **d** 46 Hur for Calg **p** 47 Calg. C of St Steph Calg 46-48; V of Stettler w Outstations 48-53; St Martin Calg 53-64; R of St John Windsor 64-74; Can of Hur from 73; I of St Luke Lon Dio Hur from 74. *1068 The Parkway, London, Ont., Canada.* (519-432 1270)

PEACH, Malcolm Thompson. b 31. St Chad's Coll Dur BA 56. Sarum Th Coll 56. **d** 58 **p** 59 Dur. C of Beamish 58-61; L to Offic Dio Dur 61-65; Chap Grey Coll Dur Univ and SCM Intercolleg Sec NE Engl 61-65; Chap St Aid Coll Dur 64-65; C-in-c of St Mark's Conv Distr Stockton-on-Tees 65-72; P-in-c of St Nich Bp Wearmouth Dio Dur 72-81; V from 81. *17 Humbledon Park, Sunderland, T & W, SR3 4AA.* (Sunderland 226444)

PEACH, Sidney John Elias. b 11. St Bonif Coll Warm 34. **d** 37 **p** 38 Swan B. C of Llandilo-Talybont 37-39; Uitenhage S Afr 40-41; CF (S Afr) 41-45; C of St Pet St Helier 46-47; St Laur Upminster Essex 47-49; SPG Miss Borneo 49-53; V of Kuching Cathl Borneo 51-53; Sec Borneo New Cathl Fund 53-54; Miss P Dio Borneo 54-56; V of St John Bury St Edms 56-68; C-in-c of St Mary-at-Elms Ipswich 68-75. *2 Woodbury Avenue, Wells, Somt, BA5 2XN.*

PEACOCK, Clifford Alan. St Jo Coll Morpeth. **d** 68 **p** 69 River. L to Offic Dio River 68-69; P-in-c of Urana River 69-72; R 72-74; Hay 74-76; C of St Luke Wandal City and Dio Rockptn from 76. *1 Bapaume Street, Wandal, Rockhampton, Queensland, Australia 4700.*

PEACOCK, Frederick Harold. b 04. Lon Coll of Div 39. **d**

40 **p** 41 Sarum. C of St John Heatherlands 40-43; V of Hennock 43-53; PC of St Mary Castle Street Reading 53-61. *119 Gladys Avenue, North End, Portsmouth, PO2 9BD.*

PEACOCK, Hubert Henry Ernest. b 14. St Edm Hall Ox BA (2nd cl Hist) 35, MA 44. Linc Th Coll 39. **d** 39 Linc for Johann **p** 40 Johann. Asst Chap of St Jo Coll Johann 39-44; C of Springs 44-45; R 45-49; Kensington Johann 49-51; Chap Bedford Sch 51-56; Hd Master St Geo Gr Sch Capetn 56-64; Hon Can of Capetn 58-64; C of Fish Hoek 73-78; Lect Hewat Tr Coll Capetn 74-77; L to Offic Dio Cash, Waterf and Lism from 78; R of Kilrossanty & Stradbally Dio Lism from 80. *Rectory, Stradbally, Co Waterford, Irish Republic.* (051-93129)

PEACOCK, John. ALCD 60. **d** 60 Croydon for Cant **p** 61 Cant. C of Addiscombe 60-62; Felixstowe 62-65; Chap RAF 65-70; C-in-c of Panania 71-74; R of Strathfield 74-81; Chap Gladesville Hosp from 81. *75 Fullers Road, Chatswood, NSW, Australia 2067.*

PEACOCK, John Oswald. Montr Dioc Th Coll LTh 37, Hon DD 74. **d** 37 **p** 38 Montr. C of St Matt Montr 37-39; C-in-c of Cowansville 39-45; R 45-79; Hon Can of Montr 73-74; Archd of Bedford 74-79; Hon C of Knowlton Dio Montr from 79. *107 Bruce Boulevard, Cowansville, PQ, Canada J2K 3A5.* (514-263 7226)

PEACOCK, Leslie John Frederick. b 11. MBE 58. Sarum Th Coll 50. **d** 51 **p** 52 Win. C of St Pet Maybush Peel Shirley 51-53; CF 53-59; V of Pateley Bridge 59-63; V of Greenhow Hill 59-63; R of Bonnington w Bilsington 63-73; C-in-c of Fawkenhurst 63-73; Newington and Bobbing w Iwade 73-77; Perm to Offic Dio Ex from 77. *11 Chettle, Blandford, Dorset.*

PEACOCK, Mansel Reginald. b 1888. TD 25. Trin Coll Cam BA 09, MA 13. Sarum Th Coll 09. **d** and **p** 13 Roch. C of St Mary Shortlands 13-14; Served in Army 14-19; Asst Master and Chap Kelly Coll Tavistock 19-27; V of Monks Kirby w Withybrook and Copston 27-48; R of Dickleburgh 48-66; C-in-c of Thelveton w Frenze 60-66. *The Firs, Pulham St Mary, Diss, Norf.* (Pulham Market 376)

PEACOCK, Thomas Edward. Univ of Dur BSc 55, PhD 58. **d** 64 **p** 65 S'wark. C of St Sav S'wark 64-67; Lect Univ of Queensld and Perm to Offic Dio Brisb 67-68 and from 69; C of Jarrow 68-69; Dir of External Stud St Francis Coll Brisb 72-76; Miss Chap Dio Brisb from 76; Exam Chap to Abp of Brisb from 76. *9 Bergamot Street, Bald Hills, Queensland, Australia 4036.* (261 1711)

PEACOCK, William John. b 15. Worc Ordin Coll 65. **d** 67 **p** 68 Worc. C of St Francis Dudley 67-69; St Andr Netherton Dudley 69-74; V in R Benef of Ebbw Vale 74-78; V of Caerwent w Dunham and Llanfair Discoed Dio Mon from 78. *Caerwent Vicarage, Newport, Gwent, NP6 4AW.* (Caldicot 421871)

PEACOCKE, Arthur Robert. b 24. Ex Coll Ox BA 46, BSc 47, MA and DPhil 48, DSc 62. Univ of Birm Dipl Th 60, BD 71. **d** and **p** 71 Ox. Lect in Biochemistry Univ of Ox from 63; Fell and Tutor St Pet Coll Ox 65-73; M Abp's Commiss on Chr Doctrine 69-76; Dean of Clare Coll Cam from 73; Select Pr Univ of Ox 73; Hulsean Pr Univ of Cam 76; Bampton Lect Univ of Ox 78; Bp Wm's Mem Lect Japan 81. *Clare College, Cambridge, CB2 1TL.* (0223 358681)

✠ **PEACOCKE, Right Rev Cuthbert Irvine.** b 03. TD 51. Trin Coll Dub BA (3rd cl Mod Hist and Pol Sc) 25, Div Test 26, MA 28. **d** 26 Derry for Down **p** 27 Down. C of Seapatrick 26-30; Hd of Ch of I Miss Belf 30-33; R of Derriaghy 33-35; St Mark Dundela 35-56; CF (TA R of O) from 38; Priv Chap to Bp of Down and Drom 45-56; RD of Holywood 48-50; Archd of Down and Can of Belf 50-56; Dean of St Anne's Cathl Belf and V of Belf 56-70; Cons Ld Bp of Derry and Raphoe 6 Jan 70 in St Anne's Cathl Belf by Abp of Arm; Bps of Connor and Kilm; Bps Elliott and Mitchell; res 75. *Culmore House, Culmore, Londonderry, N Ireland.*

PEAKE, Charles Clifford. b 17. St Jo Coll Ox BA (2nd cl Mod Hist) 38. Qu Coll Birm 38. **d** 40 **p** 41 Bradf. C of St Paul Shipley 40-42; Ilkley 43; CF(EC) 43-47; C of Pudsey St Lawr 47-49; V of Wyke 49-56; V of Bellerby 56-68; V of Leyburn 56-68; Surr from 67; PC of Starbeck 68-78; R of Farnham w Scotton and Staveley w Copgrove Dio Ripon from 78. *Staveley Rectory, Knaresborough, N Yorks.* (Copgrove 275)

PEAKE, David George. b 49. Ridley Coll Melb ThDip 72. **d** 73 Melb **p** 74 Bp Grant for Melb. C of Ch Ch S Yarra 73-74; Glenroy 74-76; Frankston E 76-80; I of St Mark Fitzroy Dio Melb from 80. *268 George Street, Fitzroy, Vic, Australia 3065.*

PEAKE, Frank Alexander. Em Coll Sktn LTh 43. Univ of Sask BA 47. Ch Div Sch Berkeley, California, BD 49. Univ of Alberta, MA 52. Hur Coll DD 65. Thorneloe Univ Ont DLittS 74. **d** 41 **p** 42 Edmon. C of Clandonald 41-43; V of Onoway 43-46; Ponoka 46-48; RD of Wetaskiwin 47-48; West Field Sec of Gen Bd of Relig Educn in Canada 48-53; Regr and Prof of Ch Hist Angl Th Coll of BC Vancouver 53-54; Prof of Pastoral Th 54-59; Dir of Educn Dio Hur 59-66; R of Glanworth 59-66; Exam Chap to Bp of Koot 55-60; Asst Prof of Hist Laurentian Univ of Ont 66-69; Prof from 69; Hon C of Epiph Sudbury 66-78; Pres and Vice-Chan Thorneloe Univ Sudbury 70-74. *234 Wilson Street, Sudbury, Ont., Canada.* (705-522 4125)

PEAKE, Herbert Edward. Em Coll Sktn 57. **d** 62 **p** 63 Yukon. C of Watson Lake 62-65; Fort St John 65-68; I of Chetwynd 68-73; Fort St John 73-78; Hon Can of Caled 76-78; on leave. *9311-107 Avenue, Fort St John, BC, Canada.* (604-785 4708)

PEAKE, Simon Jeremy Brinsley. Worc Coll Ox BA 54, MA 56. St Steph Ho Ox 53-55 and 57. **d** 57 **p** 58 Chich. C of St Andr Eastbourne 57-60; Ch the K Claremont 60-61; R of Rondebloem 61-65; Good Shepherd Maitland 65-69; C of St Mich AA Kitwe 69-70; R of Kitwe 71-77; Chap St Paul Athens Dio Gibr (Gibr in Eur from 80) from 77. *6 Karneadou Street, Athens, Greece.* (714906)

PEAL, John Arthur. b 46. AKC BD 70. St Aug Coll Cant 70. **d** 71 **p** 72 Portsm. C of All SS Portsea and of St John Bapt Rudmore 71-74; Westbury w Westbury Leigh and Dilton 74-77; V of Borstal Dio Roch from 77; Chap to HM Pris Cookham Wood Roch from 78. *Borstal Vicarage, Rochester, Kent.* (Medway 45948)

PEAL, William John. b 26. K Coll Lon BSc 47, PhD 52. St Jo Coll Nottm 79. **d** 80 **p** 81 Leic. C of Coalville Dio Leic from 80. *4 Maplewell, Coalville, Leics, LE6 3RE.*

PEARCE, Alfred Edward. b 16. AKC 48. **d** 48 Dover for Cant **p** 49 Cant. C of Croydon 48-55; V of Wye (w Brook from 62) 55-66; Chap Wye Coll Cant 55-66; C-in-c of Brook 59-62; R 62-66; R of St Steph Hackington City and Dio Cant from 67. *St Stephen's Rectory, Canterbury, Kent.* (Canterbury 65391)

PEARCE, Arthur Cyril Reginald. d 68 **p** 69 Portsm. Hon C of Havant 68-70; Hon C of Kapiti 70-79; Offg Min Dio Wel from 79. *5 Arthur Street, Paraparaumu Beach, NZ.* (P Beach 5603)

PEARCE, Brian Edward. b 39. Kelham Th Coll 59. **d** 64 **p** 65 Birm. C of St Matt Smethwick 64-68; King's Norton 68-72; Team V 72-80; R of Dorcan Swindon Dio Bris from 80. *Vicarage, St Paul's Drive, Covingham, Swindon, Wilts, SN3 5BY.* (Swindon 25130)

PEARCE, Bryan William. McGill Univ Montr BA 61, BD 64. Montr Dioc Th Coll. **d** 64 **p** 65 Montr. C of St Geo Montr 64-66; Chap Montr Gen Hosp from 68. *Box 977, Hudson, PQ, Canada.* (514-458 5910)

PEARCE, Clive. b 40. Late Exhib of St D Coll Lamp BA 63. St Steph Ho Ox 63. **d** 65 Lon **p** 66 Kens for Lon. C of St Pet Acton Green 65-67; Eastcote 67-73; V of St Anselm Hatch End Dio Lon from 73. *Vicarage, 50 Cedar Drive, Hatch End, Pinner, HA5 4DE.* (01-428 4111)

PEARCE, David Langley John. St Mich Th Coll Crafers ACT ThL 52. **d** 53 **p** 54 Tas. C of Burnie 53-56; R of Zeehan 56-60; Avoca w Fingal 60-63; Prec of St D Cathl Hobart 63-72; R of Bellerive 72-79; Wynyard Dio Tas from 79. *Rectory, Wynyard, Tasmania 7325.* (004 42 2116)

PEARCE, David Murray Anderson. Qu Coll St Johns, 53. **d** 57 **p** 58 Newfld. C of Channel 57-60; R of Harbour Buffett 60-63; Badger's Quay 63-69; Harbour Grace 69-76; Burin 76-78; U Is Cove Dio E Newfld from 78. *Upper Island Cove, Newfoundland, Canada.*

PEARCE, Dennis William Wilfrid. b 25. Bps Coll Cheshunt. **d** 58 **p** 59 Chelmsf. C of L Ilford 58-62; Leytonstone 62-65; V of Harrow Green 65-81; C-in-c of St Aug Conv Distr Leytonstone 65-74; P-in-c of St Luke Leyton 78-81; R of Capel St Mary w L Wenham Dio St E from 81. *Capel St Mary Rectory, Ipswich, Suff, IP9 2LA.* (Gt Wenham 310236)

PEARCE, Canon Douglas Albert. b 22. K Coll Lon BD and AKC 47, MTh 50. **d** 47 **p** 48 Ox. C of St Mary Thatcham 47-51; Buckhurst Hill 51-56; R of Farnborough w W Ilsey 56-68; RD of Wantage 67-77; V of W w E Hanney Dio Ox from 68; Hon Can of Ch Ch Ox from 73; Asst Dir of Educn Dio Ox from 77. *Hanney Vicarage, Wantage, Berks.* (West Hanney 249)

PEARCE, (Justin) Edmund James. b 03. SS Coll Cam BA 24, MA 28. Cudd Coll 25. M CR 37. **d** 27 Bris **p** 28 Malmesbury for Bris. C of St Mark Swindon 27-34; Chap RAFVR 39-45; Warden of St Teilo's Hall 52-55; Prior 52-58; Prior Codr Coll Barb 58-61; L to Offic Dio Barb 58-67; Exam Chap to Bp of Barb 60-67. *House of the Resurrection, Mirfield, Yorks.*

PEARCE, Preb Eustace Kenneth Victor. b 13. BSc Lon 65. ALCD 37. **d** 37 **p** 38 Liv. C of St Clem Toxt Pk 37-40; Sutton 40-42; Fordington 42-44; V of All SS Camberwell 44-50; R of Bucknall w Bagnall 50-71; Surr 51-81; CF (TA) 66-67; CF (TAVR) 67-81; Preb of Lich Cathl 67-81; Preb (Emer) from 81; V of Audley 71-81. *15 Kinnersley Avenue, Kidsgrove, Stoke-on-Trent, ST7 1AP.* (07816 73325)

PEARCE, Francis Charles. **d** 55 **p** 56 Wel. C of Karori Wel 55-57; V of Pauatahanui 57-66; Shannon 66-72; P-in-c of Titahi Bay 72; Hon C 73-76; P-in-c of Tawa-Linden 73-74; Perm to Offic Dio Wel from 76. *15 Haunui Road, Pukerua Bay, NZ.* (Pukerua Bay 427)

PEARCE, Canon Frank. b 31. St Aid Coll. **d** 57 **p** 58 Southw. C of Worksop Priory 57-61; C-in-c of W Retford Dio Southw 61-62; R 62-70; R of Kettering Dio Pet from 70; Surr from 73; Hon Can of Pet from 78. *Rectory, Kettering, Northants.* (Kettering 3385)

PEARCE, Ven George Carman. Hur Coll 46. **d** 46 **p** 47 Hur. C of Thorndale w Grace Ch Nissouri 46-49; Brantford 49-50; I of Burford 50-56; St D Lon 56-59; R of Old St Paul Woodstock 59-71; St Geo Sarnia Dio Hur from 71; Can of Hur 69-72; Archd of Lambton from 72. *138 Charlotte Street, Sarnia, Ont., Canada.* (519-344-5167)

PEARCE, George Roland. McGill Univ Montr BA 57, BD 60. Montr Dioc Th Coll. **d** and **p** 60 Montr. P-in-c of Aylwin and of River Desert 60-64; R of Ste Agathe des Monts 64-68. *PO Box 147, Sharbot Lake, Ont, Canada.*

PEARCE, Canon Gerald Nettleton. b 25. St Jo Coll Dur BA 49, Dipl Th 51. **d** 51 **p** 52 St E. C of St Mary Bury St Edmunds 51-54; Attenborough w Bramcote and Chilwell 54-56; V of Selston w Westwood 56-61; R of Wilford 61-73; V of Radcliffe-on-Trent Dio Southw from 73; Shelford Dio Southw from 73; C-in-c of Holme-Pierrepont w Adbolton Dio Southw from 73; RD of Bingham from 73; Surr from 75; Hon Can of Southw Minster from 77. [illegible] *Radcliffe-on-Trent, Nottingham, NG12 2FB.* (R-on-T 2203)

PEARCE, Herbert Malcolm. AKC 40. ARCM 33. **d** 40 **p** 41 Ox. C of St Mich Ox 40-42; Kirkley 42-45; St Hilda Crofton Pk 45-46; R of Foxearth 46-54; C-in-c of Sturmer 52-54; V of Mendlesham 54; V and Sin R of Gestingthorpe 54-56; R 56-62; C-in-c of Ashen 59-62; V of St Chad Manningham 62-69; Salt 69-77; P-in-c of Keyston w Bythorn Dio Ely from 78. *Keyston Rectory, Huntingdon, Cambs, PE18 0RE.* (Bythorn 259)

PEARCE, Jack Edwin. b 33. Trin Coll for LTh 80. **d** 80 Niag **p** 81 Bp CM Mitchell for Niag. C of Ch of the Ascen Hamilton Dio Niag from 80. *c/o Church of the Ascension, Forest Avenue at John Street South, 1.* (416-527 3505)

PEARCE, John. b 13. MBE 63. **d** 68 **p** 69 Truro. Bp of Truro's Chap for Social Concern from 68; C-in-c (V from 73) of St Sithney 72-76; Hon Chap to Bp of Truro from 76. *Lanner Court, Helston, Cornw.* (Helston 4000)

PEARCE, Preb John Frederick Dilke. b 32. Ex Coll Ox BA (3rd cl Th) 55, MA 59. Westcott Ho Cam. **d** 57 **p** 58 Lon. C of St Mark Dalston 57-60; Ch Ch Chelsea 60-63; R of St Paul L Homerton 63-81; Preb of St Paul's Cathl from 70; C-in-c of All S Clapton Pk Dio Lon from 72; V from 77; RD of Hackney 74-79; V of St Barn w St Paul L Homerton Dio Lon from 81. *111 Homerton High Street, E9 6DL.* (01-985 2764)

PEARCE, John Gilbert. Bp's Univ Lennox BA 50, LST 52. **d** 52 **p** 53 Montr. Miss Dio Montr 52-55; C of St Columba Montr 55-64; R of Clarendon Shawville 64-72; St Pet City and Dio Ott from 72. *1334 Laperriere Avenue, Ottawa, Ont., Canada.* (1-613-729-2889)

PEARCE, Kenneth Jack. b 25. Linc Th Coll 62. **d** 63 **p** 64 Sarum. C of Wootton Bassett and of Broad Town 63-66; P-in-c of St Andr Derby 66-68; V of St Mark City and Dio Derby from 68. *119 Francis Street, Derby, DE2 6DE.* (Derby 40183)

PEARCE, Michael Hawkins. b 29. Sarum Th Coll 61. **d** 62 **p** 63 Bris. C of St Aldhelm Bedminster 62-65; Bishopston (in c of Good Shepherd) 65-68; R of Jacobstow w Warbstow 68-74; V of Treneglos 68-74; St Teath w Delabole Dio Truro from 74. *St Teath Vicarage, Bodmin, Cornwall, PL30 3JF.* (Bodmin 850292)

PEARCE, Reginald Frederic George. b 15. St Aug Coll Cant. **d** 40 **p** 41 Man. C of St Mark Bury 40-42; St Luke Salt River 42-44; R of Touws River 44-46; Clanwilliam and Calvinia 46-48; Durbanville 48-53; St Matt Claremont 53-57; Chap at Recife Brazil 57-58; C of St John Wynberg 58-61; R of Namaqualand 61-64; St Anne Maitland 64-67; Hosp Chap Port Eliz 67-68; V of Laneast w St Clether (w Tresmere from 76) 68-78; C-in-c (V from 70) of Tresmere 68-76; P-in-c of St Erth 78-80; Perm to Offic Dio Truro from 80. *Sunshine Cottage, Churchtown, St Agnes, Cornw.* (St Agnes 3252)

PEARCE, Ronald Albert. Wollaston Coll Perth 58. **d** 59 **p** 60 Perth. C of Wembley 59-63; R of Dalwallinu 63-68; Riverton 68-74; Wembley Downs Dio Perth from 74. *57 Brompton Road, City Beach, W Australia 6015.* (41 2655)

PEARCE, Ronald Edgar John. St D Coll Lamp BA 42. Lich Th Coll 42. **d** 44 **p** 45 St D. C of Tenby 44-46; St Matt Stepney 46-47; Swansea 47-50; Chap Cho of Ches Cathl and Asst Master of Choir Sch 50-53; V of Ch Ch Ches 53-56; Prec and Sacr of Bris Cathl 56-61; V of Warmley 61-68; R of Siston 62-68; Chap R Wolverhampton Sch from 68. *c/o Royal Wolverhampton School, Wolverhampton, Staffs.*

PEARCE, Stephen Wilson. b 34. K Coll Lon and Warm. **d** 62 **p** 63 Blackb. C of St Jas Chorley 62-64; St Steph w St Phil and St Ann Sheff 64-66; Warton 66-69; V of St Chad Skerton 69-77; and 78-80; P-in-c of Ch Ch Sktn 77-78; C of St Pet Fleetwood (in c of St Nich) 80-81; Team V of Raveningham Dio Nor from 81. *Vicarage, School Lane, Heckingham, Norf.* (Raveningham 289)

PEARCE, Trevor John. b 27. Roch Th Coll 65. **d** 67 **p** 68 Cant. C of Cheriton Street 67-69; Willesborough w Hinxhill 69-73; V of St Barn Devonport 73-79. *c/o Flat 1, Cummings House, N Devon District Hospital, Barnstaple, Devon.* (Barnstaple 72577 ext 450)

PEARCE-HIGGINS, Canon John Denis. b 05. Late Scho of G and C Coll Cam 1st cl Cl Trip pt i 25, BA (1st cl Cl Trip pt ii, w distinc in Phil) Warr Scho and Research Stud 27, MA 30. Ripon Hall, Ox 34. **d** 37 **p** 38 Birm. C of St Agnes Cotteridge 37-40; CF (EC) 40-45; V of Hanley Castle 45-53; Lect Worc Tr Coll 46-53; V of Putney 53-63; Chairman Modern Churchmen's U 58-68; Vice-Chairman Churches' Fellowship for Psychical Study from 60; Exam Chap to Bp of S'wark from 61; Can and Vice-Provost of S'wark Cathl 63-71; Can (Emer) from 71. *Address temp unknown.*

PEARCEY, Paul Alan Cyril. b 37. Univ of Dur BA 59, Dipl Th 61. Cranmer Hall, Dur. **d** 61 **p** 62 Man. C of Deane 61-65; Chap Redbank Approved Sch 65-66; C-in-c of St Mark's Conv Distr Blackley 66-73; R of Llanelwedd w Llanfaredd and Cwmbach-Llechryd Dio Swan B from 73; [illegible] in Elwell w Bettws Disserth and Cregina Dio Swan B from 79. *Llanelwedd Rectory, Builth Wells, Powys, LD2 3TY.* (Builth Wells 553701)

PEARCY, Vernon Charles. b 23. K Coll Lon and Warm BD 56, AKC (2nd cl) 56. **d** 56 **p** 57 S'wark. C of St Pet St Helier Surrey 56-59; St Jas Piccadilly Westmr 59-61; Chap St Geo Sch Harpenden 61-62; C of St Nich Sutton Surrey 62-63; St Pet Croydon 63-67; Belmont 68-70; Wimbledon 70-76; Hayling 77; R of Warbleton and Bodle Street Green Dio Chich from 78. *Warbleton Rectory, Rushlake Green, Nr Heathfield, E Sussex, TN21 9QJ.* (Rushlake Green 830421)

PEARCY, Victor Joseph. b 14. C Chem MRSC 48. **d** and 72 Portsm. C of St Sav Portsea 72-75; St Mark N End Portsea Dio Portsm from 75. *34 Madeira Road, Portsmouth, Hants, PO2 0SZ.*

PEARE, Canon Oliver Arthur Patrick. b 17. TCD BA 43, Div Test 46, MA 55. **d** 46 **p** 47 Cash. C of Clonmel 46-52; I of Tallow w Kilwatermoy 52-55; Youghal (w Killeagh from 59) 55-63; R of Abbeystrewry 63-66; I of Kinsale U Dio Cork from 66; Can of Cork and Cloyne from 80. *St Multose Rectory, Kinsale, Co Cork, Irish Republic.* (021-72220)

PEARMAIN, Andrew Neil. b 55. AKC and BD 79. Ridley Hall Cam 79. **d** 81 Guildf. C of Cranleigh Dio Guildf from 81. *22 Orchard Gardens, Cranleigh, Surrey, GU6 7LG.*

PEARMAIN, Brian Albert John. b 34. BD (Lon) 68. Roch Th Coll 63. **d** 66 Dover for Cant **p** 67 Cant. C of Shirley 66-69; Selsdon 69-73; C-in-c of H Trin Louth 73-75; Team V of Louth 75-79; R of Scartho Dio Linc from 79. *Rectory, Woodrow Park, Scartho, Humb, DN33 2EF.*

PEARMAN, Geoffrey William. b 09. ALCD 50. BD (1st cl) (Lon) 51. **d** 46 Lon for Niger **p** 47 Niger. CMS Miss Dio Niger 46-48; LCD 48-51; Exam Chap to Bp on the Niger 51-57; to Bp of Nig Delta 52-57; Tutor Trin Coll Umuahia 52-55; Prin 56-57; C of Buckhurst Hill 57-59; V of Greenstead Green 59-65; Exam Chap to Bp of Chelmsf 64-70; R of Goldhanger w L Totham 65-71; Widdington 71-74. *11 Bramley Close, Lexden, Colchester, CO3 3RU.*

PEARS, John Barbour. b 10. Sarum Th Coll 46. **d** 48 **p** 49 Newc T. C of St Phil Newc T 48-51; Horton 51-56; Asst Chap Sheff United Hosps 56-58; Chap City Gen Hosp and Firvale Infirm Sheff 58-67; N Gen Hosp Sheff 67-73; Dioc Chap Dio Sheff 73-78; Hon C of St Cuthb Firvale City and Dio Sheff from 79. *5 Devon Road, Sheffield, S4 7AJ.* (Sheffield 386703)

PEARS, William Steuart. b 19. Ex Coll Ox BA and MA 45. Wells Th Coll 48. **d** 49 **p** 50 Lon. C of St Martin-in-the-Fields Trafalgar Square 49-52; St Mary Hampton 52-53; V of All SS Perry Street Northfleet 53-56; R of Penshurst 56-61; V of Ch Ch Crewe 61-66; C-in-c (R from 67) of Ashton w Trusham 66-72; C-in-c (R from 67) of Bridford 66-72; C-in-c (R from 67) of Dunsford w Doddiscombsleigh 66-72; C-in-c of Christow 68-72; R of Christow w Bridford and Ashton w Trusham Dio Ex from 72; RD of Kenn 74-76. *Christow Rectory, Exeter.* (Christow 52658)

PEARSE, Andrew George. b 46. Wycl Hall Ox 71. **d** 74 Stepney for Lon **p** 75 Lon. C of St Luke Hackney 74-77; Em Chadderton 77-81; R of The Saviour Collyhurst City and Dio Man from 81. *Rectory, Eggington Street, Manchester, M10 7RN.* (061-205 2808)

PEARSE, Nicholas James Donald. b 1898. St Mich Coll Llan 23. **d** 25 **p** 26 Glas. C of St Marg Newlands Glas 25-28; All SS Heref 28-29; Perm to Offic at H Trin Marylebone

34-37; Witney 37-43; C of High Wycombe (in c of St Anne Wycombe Marsh) 43-50; R of Lavendon w Cold Brayfield 50-56; C-in-c of Asthall w Asthalleigh 63-67; Perm to Offic Dio Ox from 67. *Mignonette, The Square, Bampton, Oxford.*

PEARSE, Percy George Hedley. b 13. Univ Coll Dur LTh 35, BA 36, MA 39. ALCD 35. **d** 36 **p** 37 S'wark. C of St Jas Kidbrooke 36-38; St Paul Kingston Hill 38-40; Actg Chap Kingston Hosp 40-41; St Geo Leeds 41-44; Gt Ilford 44-48; R of Stanford-le-Hope 48-59; Surr 55-78; R of Doddinghurst 59-72; R of Stondon Massey 59-72; Debden 72-78; RD of Saffron Waldon 74-78. *3 Chalfont Avenue, Christchurch, Dorset.*

PEARSE, Ronald Thomas Hennessy. b 26. K Coll Lon and Warm AKC 52. **d** 53 **p** 54 Leic. C of St Pet w St Hilda Leic 53-55; St Thos Ap Hanwell 55-58; R of Asfordby Dio Leic from 58; C-in-c of Scalford w Wycombe and Chadwell 75-76. *Rectory, Church Lane, Asfordby, Melton Mowbray, Leics, LE14 3RU.* (Melton Mowbray 812327)

PEARSON, Andrew George Campbell. b 41. Qu Coll Ox BA (Mod Hist) 63, BA (Th) 66. Wycl Hall 63. **d** 71 **p** 72 Roch. C of St Mark Gillingham 71-72; Billingshurst 72-77; St Mich w St Phil Ches Sq Dio Lon from 77. *c/o 4 Chester Square, SW1.*

PEARSON, Brian. b 29. Sarum Wells Th Coll 71. **d** 73 **p** 74 Roch. C of Rainham 73-77; Pembury 77-80; V of St Aid Gravesend Dio Roch from 80. *Vicarage, St Gregory's Crescent, Gravesend, Kent.* (Gravesend 52500)

PEARSON, Brian Edward. b 53. York Univ Ont BA 75. Trin Coll Tor MDiv 80. **d** 81 Tor. C-in-c of Cookstown Dio Tor from 81. *29 Church Street E, Cookstown, Ont, Canada, L0L 1L0.*

PEARSON, Brian Robert. b 35. Univ of Leeds, BA (2nd cl Hist) 59. Coll of Resurr Mirfield. **d** 61 **p** 62 Derby. C of Chesterfield 61-66; P-in-c of St Jo Evang Derby 66-72; St Anne Derby 66-72; R of Thorpe Episcopi Dio Nor from 72. *Thorpe Rectory, Norwich, NR7 0PZ.* (Norwich 33578)

PEARSON, Brian William. b 49. Brighton Poly BSc 71. City Univ Lon MSc 80,. **d** 79 **p** 80 S'wark. Hon C of All SS Shooters Hill Plumstead 79-80; Perm to Offic Dio Chich from 81. *Tilings, Goring Road, Steyning, Sussex.*

PEARSON, Christian David John. Open Univ BA 76. CCC Cam 1st cl Th Trip pt i, BA (2nd cl Th Trip PT ii) 79. K Coll Lon and Warm AKC 65. **d** 66 **p** 67 Dur. C of Pallion 66-68; Peterlee 68-71; M SSF from 71; L to Offic Dio Sarum 71-73; Dio Dar-es-Salaam 74-75; Ely from 75. *15 Botolph Lane, Cambridge, CB2 3RD.* (Cam 353903)

PEARSON, Edgar. b 13. Tyndale Hall Bris 37. **d** 41 Bp Tubbs for Ches **p** 42 Lah. C of St Chad Handforth 41; Miss U Burma 42; Chap Peshawar 42-43; Multan 43; Nowshera 44; Gharial 45; Razmak 45-46; New Delhi Canton 46-47; C of Lahore Cathl and Kashmir and Chap Waziristan 47; Hon CF 47; Chap Valparaiso and Vina del Mar Chile 50-55; C of St Paul's Cathl Melb 55-56; R of Eureka 56-59; P-in-c of Dunoon 60-61; Adaminaby NSW 61-65; R of Dallinghoo w Pettistree Dio St E from 65; C-in-c of Bredfield w Boulge Dio St E from 74. *Dallinghoo Rectory, Woodbridge, Suff.* (Charsfield 247)

PEARSON, Geoffrey Seagrave. b 51. St Jo Coll Dur BA 72, Dipl Th 73. Cranmer Hall Dur 72. **d** 74 **p** 75 Wakef. C of Kirkheaton 74-77; Ch Ch (in c of Ch of Redeemer) City and Dio Blackb from 77. *255 Rothesay Road, Shadsworth, Blackburn, BB1 2HZ.*

PEARSON, Canon George Arthur. Univ of Melb BA 38, ACT ThL 39. **d** 40 **p** 41 Melb. C of St Aug Moreland 40-43; Hd Master Dodoma Secondary Sch Tang 43-47; Kongwa 48; Home Sec CMS Melb 49; Supervisor Village Schs Mvumi 49-50 and 58-59; Berega 50-55; Miss at Mpwapwa 55-57; Dioc Sec Centr Tang 57-61; Exam Chap to Bp of Centr Tang 57-61; Archd of Mpwapwa 57-59; W Tang and P-in-c of Kigoma 60-61; Can of Centr Tang 56-61; Hon Can from 61; L to Offic Dio Syd 61-63 and from 75; V of Richmond 63-72; I of St Jas Dandenong 72-75; Dep Prin Ridley Coll and L to Offic Dio Melb 75-80; Perm to Offic from 80. *c/o Ridley College, Walker Street, Parkville, Vic, Australia 3052.*

PEARSON, Harold Geoffrey. b 21. Ch Coll Cam BA (2nd cl Hist Trip pt ii) 43, MA 47. Chich Th Coll 43. **d** 45 **p** 46 Sherborne for Sarum. C of H Trin Weymouth 45-48; M SSF from 48; L to Offic at St Benedict Cam 50-54; at St Phil and St Jas Plaistow 54-59; P Koki Miss Port Moresby 59-60; St Francis Friary Jegarata 60-67; Prov Min Pacific Prov SSF 67-70; Min Gen SSF from 70. *Friary, Hilfield, Dorchester, Dorset.* (Cerne Abbas 345)

PEARSON, Harry MacGregor. b 02. Univ of Lon BSc (Eng) 24. Ely Th Coll 63. **d** 64 **p** 65 Chelmsf. C of Canvey I 64-67; Hutton 67; Abertillery 68-69; Overbury 69-71. *Tan-y-Graig, Sunbank, Llangollen, Clwyd, LL20 8EG.* (0978 860414)

PEARSON, Henry Gervis. b 47. Mansfield Coll Ox BA 72, MA 76. St Jo Coll Nottm 72. **d** 74 Lewes for Chich **p** 75 Horsham for Chich. C of St Mary Southgate, Crawley (in c of H Trin Tilgate from 76) Dio Chich 74-79; Team V from 79. *Holy Trinity House, Titmus Drive, Tilgate, Crawley, Sussex.* (Crawley 25809)

PEARSON, James David. b 51. Univ of Capetn BSocSc 74. St Paul's Coll Grahmstn 76. **d** 78 **p** 79 Capetn. C of St Geo Cathl Capetn 78-80; R of Caledon Dio Capetn from 80. *Rectory, PO Box 25, Caledon, CP, S Africa 7230.*

PEARSON, James Stuart. b 28. St Jo Coll Dur BA 57. Cranmer Hall Dur 57. **d** 58 **p** 59 Wakef. C of Halifax 58-63; V of Alverthorpe 63-70; Knottingley 70-78; Woolley Dio Wakef from 78; Bp's Adv for Social Responsibility Dio Wakef from 78. *Woolley Vicarage, Wakefield, W Yorks, WF4 2JU.* (Barnsley 382550)

PEARSON, James William. b 20. FCA 59. Qu Coll Birm 75. **d** 78 **p** 79 Worc. C of Beoley Dio Worc from 78. *Ringwood, Rowney Green, Alvechurch, Birmingham, B48 7QE.*

PEARSON, John Alfred Fowler. b 12. AKC 33. Ely Th Coll 34. **d** 35 **p** 36 Lon. C of St Luke Enfield 35-40; St Mark Bush Hill Pk 40-43; V of St Matt Willesden 43-53; St Mary Brookfield 53-61; St Mich Golders Green 61-76; L to Offic Dio Chich from 76. *30 Gerald Road, Worthing, W Sussex.*

PEARSON, John Edwin. b 26. Westcott Ho Cam. **d** 61 **p** 62 Chich. Educn Sec UMCA 55-62; Home Sec 62-65; C of Clayton w Keymer 61-65; V of U Beeding 65-69; R of Bramber w Botolphs 65-69, C-in-c and Seq of St Patr Hove 69-74; R of St Jo Bapt-sub-Castro Lewes 74-76; L to Offic Dio Chich from 76. *Tile Cottage, Balcombe, Nr Haywards Heath, Sussex.* (Balcombe 411)

PEARSON, John Graham. Selw Coll Cam BA (3rd cl Th) 67, MA 71. Sarum Th Coll 68. **d** 69 **p** 70 Win. C of St Francis Bournemouth 69-73; C-in-c of St Jas Shaftesbury 73; Team V of Shaston 73-79; V of St Luke Winton Bournemouth Dio Win from 79. *31 Lonsdale Road, Bournemouth, Dorset, BH3 7LY.* (Bournemouth 516653)

PEARSON, John Nigel. b 45. E Midl Min Tr Course 78. **d** 81 Derby. [f in CA]. C of Stapenhill Dio Derby from 81. *150 Hawthorn Crescent, Stapenhill, Burton-on-Trent, Staffs, DE15 9QW.*

PEARSON, John Thomas. b 26. St Francis Coll Brisb 77. **d** 78 **p** 79 Brisb. C of H Trin Goondiwindi 78-80; St Nich Sandgate City and Dio Brisb from 80. *24 Yaraan Street, Bracken Ridge, Queensld, Australia 4017.* (269 6921)

PEARSON, Kevin. b 54. Univ of Leeds BA 75. Univ of Edin BD 79. Edin Th Coll 76. **d** 79 **p** 80 Dur. C of Horden 79-81. *Address temp unknown.*

PEARSON, Michael John. b 53. Univ of Southn BTh 78. Sarum Wells Th Coll 74. **d** 78 **p** 79 Ex. C of Paignton Dio Ex from 78. *St Andrew's Parsonage, St Andrew's Road, Paignton, S Devon.* (Paignton 559602)

PEARSON, Peter. b 09. Tyndale Hall Bris 32. **d** 35 **p** 36 Lich. C of St Matt Tipton 35-37; Cobridge (in c of St Andr Sneyd Green) 37-40; V of Buildwas 40-45; Fremington 45-74; Proc Conv Ex 63-70; Publ Pr Dio Ex 75; C-in-c of Coldridge (or Coleridge) 75-77; P-in-c of Chawleigh w Cheldon 77-78; L to Offic Dio Ex from 79. *25 Grange Avenue, Barnstaple, Devon, EX31 2DS.*

PEARSON, Raymond. b 06. AKC 31. St Steph Ho Ox. **d** 31 **p** 32 S'wark. C of St Laur Catford 31-33; St Luke W Norwood 33-36; Godstone 36-40; Chap RAFVR 40-46; R of Horne 46-49; Chap Kuwait Oil Co Kuwait 49-55; PC of Fen Drayton w Conington 56-72. *2 St Lawrence House, Chobham, Woking, Surrey, GU24 8BT.* (Chobham 8100)

PEARSON, Raymond Joseph. b 44. AKC 71. St Aug Coll Cant 71. **d** 72 **p** 73 Ripon. C of Wetherby 72-75; Goring 75-77; C of Bramley (in c of St Marg) Dio Ripon from 77. *St Margaret's House, Newlay Lane, Bramley, Leeds, LS13 2AJ.* (Pudsey 574811)

PEARSON, Robert Forster. b 22. St Barn Coll Adel 67. **d** 70 **p** 71 Adel. C of Croydon 71-72; R of Elliston 72-74; Jt and Assoc R of Port Augusta 74-77; C of St John Salisbury 77-81; Chap Flinders Med Centre Dio Adel from 81. *9 Howard Street, Beulah Park, S Australia 5067.*

PEARSON, Roderick Percy. b 21. Linc Th Coll 74. **d** 75 **p** 76 Dur. C of St Cuthb Darlington 75-80; V of Bp Middleham Dio Dur from 80. *Vicarage, Bishop Middleham, Ferryhill, Co Durham, DL79 9AE.* (Ferryhill 51360)

PEARSON, Roy Barthram. b 35. K Coll Lon and Warm 56. **d** 60 **p** 61 Lon. C of St Mary Brookfield Lon 60-64; St Cypr Clarence Gate St Marylebone 64-70; V of Tottenham Dio Lon from 70. *The Priory, Church Lane, N17.* (01-808 2470)

PEARSON, Stephen. d 43 Lon for Alg **p** 44 Blackb. C of Ribchester 43; I of White River 43-47; C of Rayleigh 47-49; Newburn (in c of Throckley) 49-51; V of Chilcompton 51-54; St Matt Bolton 54-57; Goodshaw 57-61; R of Brome w Oakley 61-69; Luddington w Hemington and Thurning 69-77; C-in-c of Clopton 69-77. *Address temp unknown.*

PEARSON, Thomas Henry Edward. b 10. Univ of Edin BSc 33. Worc Ordin Coll 62. **d** 64 **p** 65 Edin. C of H Trin Stirling 64-65; St Mark Portobello 65-68; St Fagan Aberdare 68-69; R of St Geo Maryhill Glas 69-75; Hon P-in-c of Girvan 76-80. *Ivybank, Main Street, Inverkip, Greenock, PA16 0AT.* (Wemyss Bay 521693)

PEARSON, Tom Vivian. Selw Coll Dun LTh 40. **d** 37 **p** 38 Wel. C of Masterton 37-43; CF (NZ) 41-43; V of Mangatainoka-Pongaroa 43-46; Eltham 46-50; Otaki 50-54; St Mark Wel 54-60; V of Gisborne 60-64; Trentham 64-78; Archd of Belmont 70-78; C of Roturua 78-79; Ohinemutu Dio Wai from 79. *217 Pukehangi Road, Rotorua, NZ.* (88-106)

PEARSON, William Robert. St Francis Coll Brisb. **d** 59 **p** 60 N Queensld. C of St John Townsville 59-62; R 62-66; Chap Miss to Seamen Townsville 59-62; R of W Cairns 67-71; Chap RANVR from 68; R of St Francis Nundah City and Dio Bris from 71. *68 Cavendish Street, Nundah, Queensland, Australia 4012.* (266 2174)

PEARSON-MILES, David. b 37. St Jo Coll Nottm 74. **d** 76 **p** 77 Reading for Ox. C of Hazlemere 76-79; R of Waddesdon w Westcott Over Winchenden and Fleet Marston Dio Ox from 79. *Waddesdon Rectory, Aylesbury, Bucks, HP18 0JQ.* (Aylesbury 651312)

PEART, John Graham. b 36. Bps' Coll Cheshunt 65. **d** 68 **p** 69 St Alb. C of Cheshunt 68-70; St Pet St Alb 70-73; R of Hunsdon 73-76; Widford 73-76; Industr Chap Dio St Alb from 76. *7 Ch[illegible] Luton, Beds.* (Luton 391869)

PEART, Urban Humphrey. b 06. Wells Th Coll. **d** 62 **p** 63 Ex. C of St Sidwell Ex 62-64; Hd Master St Sidwell's Sch Ex 53-64; V of Holcombe Rogus w Hockworthy 64-74; RD of Cullompton 71-74; Hon C of Paignton 74-76; Shaston 77-80; Hon C of St Alkmund City and Dio Derby from 80. *48 Brayfield Road, Littleover, Derby, DE3 6GT.* (Derby 760877)

PEASE, John Alfred. b 29. St Aid Coll 58. **d** 60 **p** 61 Sheff. C of Swinton 60-63; St Cecilia Parson Cross Sheff 63-65; V of Bolton-upon-Dearne 65-70; V of S Kirkby 70-81; St Jo Evang Bovey Tracey Dio Ex from 81. *St John's Vicarage, Bovey Tracey, Newton Abbot, Devon.* (Bovey Tracey 833451)

PEASGOOD, David Herbert Edward. Univ of Tor BA 61, MA 67. Wycl Coll Tor BTh 64. **d** 64 Bp Snell for Tor **p** 65 Tor. C of St Timothy Tor 64-68; I of Markham 68-77; St Geo Oshawa Dio Tor from 77. *963 Mohawk Street, Oshawa, Ont, Canada.*

PEASTON, Canon Monroe. Late Exhib of BNC Ox BA (2nd cl LitHum) 36, Dipl Th 37, MA 43, Univ of Lon BD 48. Union Th Sem NY ThD 64. Wycl Hall, Ox 36. **d** 38 **p** 39 Liv. C of St Helens 38-40; Claughton w Grange 40-43; Org Sec CMS for Dios Bradf Blackb and Carl and Perm to Offic Dios Blackb and Bradf 43-45; Asst Chap Wrekin Coll Wellington and Perm to Offic Dio Lich 45-48; V of Wadestown Wel 48-51; Master of Coll Ho Ch Ch 51-59; Exam Chap to Bp of Ch Ch 53-64; Vice-Prin of Ch Ch Coll 59-64; Hon Can of Ch Ch 61-64; Montr 66-80; Can (Emer) from 80; Prin Montr Dioc Th Coll 65-74; Assoc Prof Pastoral Psychol McGill Univ 64-80. *3481 University Street, Montreal, PQ, Canada H3A 2A8.*

PEAT, David William. b 37. Clare Coll Cam BA 59, PhD 63. Westcott Ho Cam 73. **d** 75 Huntingdon for Ely **p** 76 Ely. C of St Andr Chesterton 75-77; Chap of Coll of Ripon and York St John York from 77. *College of Ripon and York St John, Lord Mayor's Walk, York, YO3 7EX.*

PEAT, Lawrence Joseph. b 28. Linc Th Coll 55. **d** 58 **p** 59 Ripon. C of Bramley 58-61; R of All SS Heaton Norris 61-65; PC (V from 68) of Bramley 65-73; C-in-c of All SS and St Erkenwald Southend 73-74; R of Southend-on-Sea 74-79; V of Skelsmergh w Selside and Longsleddale Dio Carl from 79. *Skelsmergh Vicarage, Kendal, Cumbria, LA9 6NU.* (Kendal 24498)

PEATFIELD, Canon Alfred Charles Henry. b 22. New Coll Ox BA (2nd cl Hist) and MA 48, 2nd cl Th 50. Ripon Hall Ox 48. **d** 51 **p** 52 Lon. C of St Jo Bapt Hackney 51-54; V of St Paul Battersea 54-56; Wellesley and Kedah 56-64; St Geo Penang 64-70; Archd of N Malaya 64-70; Hon Can of Sing 65-70; Chap and V Temporal of Hornchurch Dio Chelmsf from 70; Commiss W Mal from 70; Sing from 73; RD of Havering 75-80; Hon Can of Chelmsf from 80. *222 High Street, Hornchurch, Essex, RM12 6QP.* (Hornchurch 41571)

PEATTIE, Colin Hulme Reid. Univ of Natal, BSc 59. Ripon Hall Ox 61. **d** 63 **p** 64 Lon. C of St Anselm Belmont Middx 63-65; St Columba Durban 65-69; R of St Jas Dundee 69-72; Chap St Andr Sch Bloemf 72-76; R of St Alphege Pmbg Dio Natal from 77. *70 New England Road, Pietermaritzburg, Natal, S Africa.* (Pmbg 24195)

PECK, David George. b 11. Late Exhib of Jes Coll Cam BA 32, MA 48. Linc Coll Ox MA 51. St Steph Ho Ox 32. **d** 34 **p** 35 S'wark. C of St Jo Div Richmond Surrey 34-37; Wimbledon 37-39; Perm to Offic at Wanstead 39-40; Org Sec ICF for SW Area 40-43; V of Bedwyn Parva 43-51; Perm to Offic Dio Ox 51-53; R of Godington w Stratton Audley 53-59; Chap and Asst Master Cokethorpe Pk Sch 59-63; R of Shellingford Dio Ox from 63; Seq of Longcot w Fernham 63-65; Ed Ox Dioc Mag 65-72; Hon Chap to Bp of Ox from 72. *Shellingford Rectory, Faringdon, Oxon, SN7 7QA.* (Stanford-in-the-Vale 277)

PECK, Douglas Cyrus. b 26. Univ of BC BComm 48, BA 49. Vanc Sch of Th 71. **d** and **p** 73 Sask. R of Spiritwood and of Pelican Lake 73-76. *15 Esterbrooke Avenue, Willowdale, Ont., Canada.*

PECK, Canon Jack Percy. Hur Coll BA 55, LTh 58, BD 63. McMaster Univ MA 67. **d** 56 **p** 58 Hur. C-in-c of Princeton Centre 56-61; R of Southn Ont 61-64; I of Trin Sarnia 64-70; R of Ch of H Sav Waterloo 70-76; Can of Hur from 73; I of All SS Windsor Dio Hur from 76. *1539 Victoria Avenue, Windsor, Ont., Canada.*

PECK, Robert Logan. Univ of Miami, BA 55. Episc Th Sem Kentucky BD 59. **d** 58 **p** 59 Lexington. [f in Amer Ch] V of Manaia 64-68; Hon C of Wadestown 68-75; V of Ruapehu Dio Wel from 75; P-in-c of Wainuiarus Maori District Dio Wel from 75. *124 Seddon Street, Raetihi, NZ.* (154)

PECK, Trevor Paul Owen. b 47. Lich Th Coll 69. **d** 72 Doncaster for Sheff **p** 73 Sheff. C of Hatfield 72-74; St Marg Swinton 74-77; Team V of Gt Grimsby 77-81; V of Glentworth Dio Linc from 81; Hemswell w Harpswell Dio Linc from 81. *Vicarage, Stoney Lane, Glentworth, Gainsborough, DN21 5DF.* (Hemswell 402)

PECK, William Gerard. b 18. AKC (2nd cl) 40. Lich Th Coll 40. **d** 41 **p** 42 Southw. C of Bulwell 41-45; CF (EC) 45-46; CF 46-49; Hon CF 49; R of Wetheringsett w Brockford 49-56; Chap HM Pris Strangeways Man 56-57; Hollesley Borstal Inst 57-59; HM Pris Stafford 59-63; R of Fornham All SS Dio St E from 63. *Fornham All Saints' Rectory, Bury St Edmunds, Suff.* (Bury St Edmunds 66971)

PECKETT, Desmonde Claude Brown. b 19. **d** 77 St Germans for Truro **p** 78 Truro. C of Charlestown Dio Truro from 77. *The Smugglers, Porthpean, St Austell, Cornwall.*

PECKETT, John Freeman. b 20. Clifton Coll Bris. **d** 74 **p** 76 Nai. Hon C of St Steph Nai 74-77; C of Harringay 77-79; Palmers Green Dio Lon from 80. *135 Palmerston Road, N22 4QX.*

PECKOVER, Cecil Raymond. b 16. Ridley Hall, Cam 62. **d** 63 Bp Gelsthorpe for Southw **p** 64 Southw. C of Selston w Westwood 63-64; Newark-on-Trent (in c of Cotham Hawton Shelton and of Sibthorpe from 65) 64-66; V of Emneth 66-78; R of Clenchwarton 78-80. *Address temp unknown.*

PEDDLE, Gerald Eugene. b 46. Mem Univ Newfld BA, LTh. **d** 69 **p** 70 Newfld. C of Burgeo w Ramea 70-71; I of Random 72-75; CF (Canad) from 75. *c/o Chaplain's Department, War Office, Ottawa, Ont., Canada.*

PEDLAR, John Glanville. b 43. Univ of Ex BA (3rd cl Th) 68. St Steph Ho Ox 68. **d** 70 **p** 71 Ex. C of Tavistock 70-73; Prec of Portsm Cathl 73-77; St Alb Cathl 77-81; V of Redbourn Dio St Alb from 81. *Redbourn Vicarage, St Albans, Herts.* (Redbourn 3122)

PEDLEY, Geoffrey Stephen. b 40. Qu Coll Cam 2nd cl Hist Trip pt i 62, BA (2nd cl Th Trip pt ii) 64, MA 67. Cudd Coll 64. **d** 66 Warrington for Liv **p** 67 Liv. C of Our Lady and St Nich Liv 66-69; H Trin Cov 69-71; P-in-c of Kitwe Zambia 71-77; H Trin Stockton Dio Dur from 77; V of St Pet Stockton Dio Dur from 77. *77 Yarm Road, Stockton-on-Tees, TS18 3PJ.* (Stockton-on-Tees 66625)

PEDLOW, Henry Noel. b 37. QUB BA 59. Trin Coll Dub 59. **d** 61 **p** 62 Connor. C of St Phil Belf 61-66; St Nich Belf 66-70; I of Eglantine Dio Connor from 70. *All Saints Vicarage, Eglantine, Hillsborough, Co Down.*

PEEBLES, Canon Alexander Paterson. b 21. Westcott Ho Cam 62. **d** 63 **p** 64 St Alb. C of Bp's Hatfield 63-65; C of Swan Group (Barton Hartshorne w Chetwode, Grendon Underwood w Edgcott, Marsh Gibbon, Preston Bissett, and Twyford) Dio Ox 65-68; C-in-c 68-73; RD of Claydon 71-73; R of Glenrothes 73-81; Can of St Ninian's Cathl Perth from 78; Dioc Super Dio St Andr from 81. *5 Hillside Place, Newport-on-Tay, Fife, DD6 8DH.* (0382-543095)

PEEK, John Richard. b 51. Univ of Bris BSc 72. Univ of Nottm BA (Th) 75, St Jo Coll Nottm 73. **d** 76 **p** 77 Dur. C of St Jo Evang Hebburn 76-78; Dunston 78-81; R of Armthorpe Dio Sheff from 81. *Rectory, Armthorpe, Doncaster, S Yorks, DN3 3AD.* (Doncaster 831231)

PEEK, Roland Denys. b 17. Sarum Th Coll 69. **d** 70 **p** 71 Ex. C of St Matt Ex 70-74; R of Moretonhampstead (w Manaton and N Bovey from 78) Dio Ex from 74; P-in-c of Manaton 78; N Bovey 78. *Rectory, Moretonhampstead, Devon.* (Moretonhampstead 332)

PEEL, Basil Headley. Trin Coll Dub BA (2nd cl Mod Hist) 52, MA 55. Wells Th Coll 52. **d** 54 **p** 55 Lich. C of Oswestry 54-59; Leek 59-62; V of Chesterton 62-68; Short Heath 68-79; Longsdon Dio Lich from 79. *Longsdon Vicarage, Stoke-on-Trent, Staffs. ST9 9QF.* (Leek 385318)

PEEL, David Charles. b 41. AKC 75. St Aug Coll Cant 75. **d** 76 **p** 77 Newc T. C of St Paul Whitley Bay Cullercoats 76-79; St John Percy, Tynemouth Dio Newc T from 79. *96 Murray Close, North Shields, Tyne & Wear, NE29 6HB.*

PEEL, Derek. b 46. Chich Th Coll 69. **d** 72 **p** 73 Willesden for Lon. C of St Pet Ealing 72-74; St Matt Gt Pet Str Westmr 74-78; V of St Francis Bournemouth Dio Win from 78. *Clergy House, Charminster Road, Bournemouth, Dorset, BH8 9SH.* (Bournemouth 59336)

PEEL, Derrick. b 50. Linc Th Coll 75. **d** 78 **p** 79 Bradf. C of Otley Dio Bradf from 78. *73 St Clair Road, Otley, W Yorks, LS21 1DE.* (Otley 463756)

PEEL, Donald Naylor. Wycl Coll Tor BA 46, LTh 49, MA, BD. Univ of Indiana PhD. **d** 48 **p** 49 Tor for Sktn. Miss at Macklin 48-53; Tarn Taran 53-58; Kotgarh 58-63; St Paul's Cathl Ambala 63-69; C of Erindale 69-70; C of St Jo Evang Huron 70-73; Hosp Chap Dio Tor 74-79; Asst Chap Wycl Coll Tor from 80. *Wycliffe College, Hoskin Avenue, Toronto, Ont, Canada.*

PEEL, Edward Beechey. b 13. Late Demy of Magd Coll Ox 2nd cl Cl Mods 34, 2nd cl Lit Hum 36, BA 37, MA 41. Westcott Ho Cam 38. **d** 38 **p** 39 Blackb. L to Offic Dio Blackb 38-65; Dio Glouc from 65; Asst Master Rossall Sch 36-65; Chap 51-65; Chap Cheltm Coll 65-70; L to Offic Dio Chich from 70. *Foxcombe House, South Harting, Petersfield, Hants.* (Harting 357)

PEEL, Canon Jack. Linc Th Coll 31. **d** 33 **p** 34 Wakef. C of St Paul Morley 33-37; C-in-c of Lundwood Conv Distr 37-41; V of Kinsley 41-45; Dioc Youth Chap Wakef 45-49; C of Wakef Cathl and Org Sec Wakef Dioc Appeal 45-49; Gen Sec York Prov Coun for Relig Educn 48-55; Sec W Yorks Youth C'tte of the Chs 46-55; Surr 49-55; V of Pontefract 49-55; Proc Conv Wakef 50-51; R of Kingston Ja 55-61; Sec Ja Synod 58-61; R of Sandys 61-65; Pembroke Berm 65-72; Hon Can of Berm 65-72; Can (Emer) from 73; Chap at Marseilles 72-73; Santa Cruz 73-74; Bonn and Cologne 74-75; Las Palmas Dio Gibr (Gibr in Eur from 80) from 75. *Albeniz 1, Las Palmas, Canary Islands.*

PEEL, John Bruce. b 30. TCD BA (2nd cl Hist and Pol Sc) 54, MA 68. Wells Th Coll 69. **d** 70 **p** 71 Stockport for Ches. C of Wilmslow 70-75; V of Weston (w St Mark Shavington) Dio Ches from 75. *Weston Vicarage, Crewe, Chesh.* (Crewe 582585)

PEEL, Michael Jerome. b 31. Univ of Bris BA (2nd cl French) 55, MLitt 73. St Cath S Ox Dipl Th 59. Univ of Man BD 65. Wycl Hall Ox 57. **d** 59 **p** 60 Man. C of Stretford 59-61; St Ambrose Chorlton-on-Medlock and Chap Univ of Man 61-62; C of Chorlton-cum-Hardy 62-65; V of Chirbury 65-68; C-in-c of Marton-in-Chirbury 65-68; R of Iver Heath Dio Ox from 68. *Iver Heath Rectory, Iver, Bucks, SL0 0ND.* (Iver 654470)

PEELING, William Henry. Qu Univ Ont BA 48. Trin Coll Tor BD and LTh 51. **d** 51 **p** 52 Alg. I of Vickers Heights 51-53; R of Marathon 53-55; Lloydminster 55-60; St Jas Winnipeg 60-65; Fort Nelson 65-68. *c/o Synod Office, 837 West Hastings Street, Vancouver, 1 BC, Canada.*

PEERS, Francis Pittaway. Lon Coll of Div 31. **d** 32 **p** 33 Liv. C of St Jo Evang Everton 32-34; R of Hopton Wafers w Doddington V 34-50; C of St Giles-in-the-Fields Lon 50-51; St Cath Coleman Hammersmith 54-55; St Mary Pet 57-58. *c/o Barclays Bank, Four Ways, Cradley Heath, Staffs.*

PEERS, John Caldwell. b 10. Tyndale Hall Bris 33. **d** 36 Liv **p** 37 Ches. C of St Mark Haydock 36-37; Cheadle 37-40; R of St Cath Collyhurst 40-44; V of St Geo Mart Daubhill 44-50; St Phil Penn Fields 50-67; Standon 67-76; Proc Conv Lich 65-71. *5 High Street, Findon, Worthing.* (Findon 3209)

PEERS, John Edward. b 39. Bps' Coll Cheshunt 60. **d** 63 **p** 64 Roch. C of Crayford 63-67; St Jas Elmers End Beckenham 67-69; Winlaton (in c of St Patr) 69-72; P-in-c of Silkworth 72-81; R of L Bowden Dio Leic from 81. *Little Bowden Rectory, Market Harborough, Leics, LE16 8AS.* (Market Harborough 62926)

✠ **PEERS, Right Rev Michael Geoffrey.** Univ of BC Vanc BA 56. Trin Coll Tor LTh 59, Hon DD 78. **d** 59 **p** 60 Ott. C of St Thos Ott 59-61; Trin Ott 61-63; Chap Carleton Univ Ott 63-66; R of St Bede Winnipeg 66-72; Archd of Winnipeg 71-74; P Supervisor River N Pars 72-74; Dean and R of St Paul's Pro-Cathl Regina 74-77; Exam Chap to Bp of Qu'App 74-77; Cons Ld Bp of Qu'App in St Paul's Cathl Regina 6 Oct 77 by Abps E W Scott (Primate) and G F Jackson; Bps of Calg, Rupld, Sask, Sktn, Arctic, Keew, Athab, Bran, Edmon and N Ugan; Bp Suffr of Niag; and Bp H V Stiff. *1501 College Avenue, Regina, Sask, Canada.* (306-527 8606)

PEET, Derek Edwin. b 26. Univ of Sheff BA 51, Univ of Lon Dipl Th 57. Qu Coll Birm 66. **d** 67 Pontefract for Wakef **p** 68 Wakef. C of Hebden Bridge 67-70; V of Darton 70-79; Team R of Gleadless Valley Dio Sheff from 79. *St John's Vicarage, Blackstock Close, Sheffield, S14 1AE.* (Sheff 398632)

PEET, John Michael. b 44. K Coll Lon and Warm AKC (2nd cl) 67. **d** 68 **p** 72 S'wark. c of St Pet Battersea 68-69; St Nich Sutton Surrey 69-74; Perry Hill 74-78; Team V of Stepney 78-81; P-in-c of St Bart Stamford Hill Dio Lon from 81. *St Bartholomew's Vicarage, Craven Park Road, Stamford Hill, N15 6AA.* (01-800 1554)

PEET, Norman William. b 07. St Jo Coll Dur BA 37, MA 40. **d** 38 **p** 39 Blackb. C of St Mich AA Blackb 38-42; Chap Miss to Seamen Port of Suez 42-44; Org Sec for W Centr Distr and LPr Dios Heref Lich Cov Birm and Worc 44-48; C of Thornton-le-Fylde (in c of St Jo Little Thornton) Dio Blackb 48-52; Chap Miss to Seamen Port Sudan 52-55; Capetn 55-56; Org Sec Miss to Seamen Dios Sheff and Wakef 56-59; V of Rivington 59-67; Weeton 67-73. *41 Meadows Avenue, Thornton, Blackpool, FY5 2TN.*

PEEVER, Canon Johnston Bain. Sir Geo Williams Univ BA 61. McGill Univ BD 63. Montr Dioc Th Coll LTh 63. **d** 62 **p** 63 Alg. I of Mindemoya 64-66; C of St Luke's Cathl Sault Ste Marie 66-69; Dir of Leadership Tr Newfld 69-72; Sec Information and Stewardship Comm Ont 72-77; Can of Ont 77; Ott from 80; R of Trin Ch Cornw Dio Ott from 77. *105 Second Street West, Cornwall, Ont, Canada.* (613-932 3622)

PEGG, Charles William. b 06. St Aid Th Coll Bal ACT ThL 31. **d** 31 **p** 33 Bal. C of H Trin Jeparit 32-33; Miss Chap of Waikerie Miss 33-35; Koolunga Miss 35-37; R of H Trin Riverton 37-40; Ch Ch Balaklava 40-46; P-in-c of St Thos Hamley Bridge w St Luke Owen 43-46; Chap RAAF 45-46; C of St Pet Kirkley 46-47; V of Betley 47-58; Oakengates 58-74; C-in-c of Gt Bircham w Bircham Newton and Bircham Tofts 74-78. *31 Church Lanes, Fakenham, Norf, NR21 9DG.* (Fakenham 3392)

PEGG, John Mayall. b 39. St Jo Coll Dur 59. Sarum Th Coll 62. **d** 64 B & W **p** 65 Taunton for B & W. C of Bridgwater w Chilton Trinity 64-68; H Trin Hendford Yeovil 68-70; Bathwick 70-72; Ross-on-Wye 72-74; R of Thrybergh 74-81; Lympstone Dio Ex from 81. *Lympstone Rectory, Exmouth, Devon.* (Exmouth 3525)

PEGLAR, Bruce Adolphe. Univ of Tor BA 37. Wycl Coll Tor. **d** and **p** 36 Niag. C of Ch of Ascen Hamilton 36-38; I of Mt Forest Riverstown and Farewell 38-41; Chap CASF 41-64; R of Fergus Dio Niag from 64. *320 Union Street East, Fergus, Ont, Canada.* (519-843 2024)

PEGLER, Albert Dahl. b 22. St D Coll Lamp BA 48. **d** 49 **p** 50 Llan. C of Garw Valley 49-51; Cilybebyll w Alltwen Dio Llan 51-56; Aberavon 56-60; V of Bedlinog 60-69; R of Bettws Dio Llan from 69. *Bettws Rectory, Bridgend, Mid Glam.* (Aberkenfig 646)

PEGLER, Frederic Arthur. Selw Coll Cam BA 46, MA 48. Qu Coll Birm 46. **d** 47 Chich **p** 49 St Alb. C of St Jo Bapt Crawley w St Pet West Crawley 47-49; Rickmansworth 49-50; V of Sark 50-52; PV of Southw Minster 52-55; R of Southn w Port Elgin 55-56; R of Swastika 63-74; on leave. *1004-65 Southport Street, Toronto, Ont, Canada.*

PEIRCE, Ven Frederick Warwick. McMaster Univ Ont BA 46. Wycl Coll Tor LTh 50. **d** 50 Niag **p** 51 Rupld. C of St Geo Winnipeg 50-52; R of Manitou 52-53; C of Ch Ch Cathl Hamilton 53-56; R of St Jas Guelph 56-61; St Steph Calg 61-68; Ch Ch Edmon 68-79; Can of Edmon 72-78; Archd of Strathcona 78-80; Edmon from 80; Exam Chap to Bp of Edmon from 78; Dioc Sec and Treas from 80. *13813 Summit Drive, Edmonton, Alta, T5N 3S8, Canada.*

PEIRCE, John. b 35. Worc Coll Ox BA (3rd cl Th) 59, MA 64. Wycl Hall Ox 59. **d** 61 **p** 62 Lon. C of H Trin Brompton 61-64; Wareham 64-68; V of Sturminster Newton w Hinton St Mary 68-74; Kingswood 74-79; Publ Pr Dio Ex from 79. *Council for Christian Care, 96 Old Tiverton Road, Exeter, Devon.*

PEIRCE, John Martin. b 36. Jes Coll Cam BA 59, MA 65. Westcott Ho Cam 65. **d** 66 **p** 67 Cant. C of Croydon 66-70; C of H Trin Fareham 70-71; Team V 71-76; R of Langley Marish Dio Ox from 76; RD of Burnham from 77. *St Mary's Rectory, Langley, Slough, Berks.* (Slough 42068)

PEIRCE, Roy Willis. Bp's Univ Queb. **d** 44 **p** 46 Queb. C of St Maurice 44-45; Fitch Bay 45; Cape Cove 45-46; St Matt Queb 46-49; P-in-c of Saguenay Miss 49-53; CF (Canad) 53-62; R of Stanstead 62-72; I in Team Ministry of Gtr Coaticook Dio Queb from 73. *Stanstead, PQ, Canada.*

PEIRSON, Peter Kenneth. b 16. Worc Coll Ox BA 37, MA 46. Lich Th Coll 53. **d** 54 **p** 55 Lich. C of Coseley 54-55; Cannock (in c of St Paul and Mosswood) 55-57; Friern Barnet 57-59; Kenton (in c of H Spirit) 59-61; PC of St Jo Div Vartry Road Tottenham 61-64; V of St Martin Lower Edmon 64-77; C-in-c of St Pet Lower Edmon 65-66; R of Preston w Ridlington and Wing w Pilton Dio Pet from 77. *Preston Rectory, Uppingham, Leics, LE15 9NN.* (Manton 287)

PELHAM, John. b 36. New Coll Ox BA 61, MA 65. **d** 79 **p** 80 Edin. Hon C of Balerno Dio Edin from 79. *2 Horsburgh Bank, Balerno, Midlothian, EH14 7DA.*

PELINI, Sibanja. b 42. **d** 77 Bukavu. d Dio Bukavu. *Beni Parish, BP 145, Nord-Kivu, Zaire.*

PELL, Archibald James. b 42. Univ of Tor BA 64, MSocial Work 69. Univ of Windsor Ont MA 71. Trin Coll Tor STB 67. **d** 67 **p** 68 Hur. Hon C of L Trin Tor 67-69; C of All SS Windsor Hur 69-71; Hon C of Stoney Creek 71-74; P-in-c of Good Shepherd Hamilton 74-75; R of St Phil Burlington Dio Niag from 75. *1525 Mountain Grove Avenue, Burlington, Ont., Canada.* (416-637 2212)

PELL, George Russell. b 49. Carleton Univ Ott BA 72. Hur Coll Ont MDiv 75. **d** 75 **p** 76 Hur. C of Princeton & Drumbo 75; I of Ox Centre 75-78; Chap Bp's Univ Lennoxville 78-81; St Clement's Centre St Aug Dio Queb from 81. *St Augustine, Duplessie, PQ, Canada.*

PELLANT, Walter Reginald Guy. OBE 79. AKC 42. Cudd Coll 42. **d** 43 **p** 44 S'wark. C of St Paul Lorrimore Square Newington 43-45; St Jo Div Kennington 45-48; Chap RAF 48-69; Res Chap St Clem Danes Westmr 69-71; Chap at Geneva 71-80. *c/o 59 rue de Lyon, Geneva, Switzerland.* (45 53 32)

PELLEGRIN, Victor Bruce Holker. b 37. Univ of BC BA 65. Univ of Wisc (Stout) MSc 66. Univ of Kansas PhD 70. Vanc Sch of Th LTh 61. **d** 61 **p** 62 Koot. R of Arrow Lakes 61-64; in Amer Ch 64-68; Lect Univ of Manit 68-71; Consulting Psychologist Rupld Found 71-75; C of Ch of Good Shepherd Winnipeg 68-72; St Mich AA Winnipeg 72-77; Exam Chap to Bp of Rupld 75-80; to Bp of Keew 77-80; Dean of Div St Jo Coll Winnipeg 77-80; Dir of Ex Programme 78-80; Co-ordinator of Special Min Dio Ott from 80. *21 Woodhill Crescent, Ottawa, K1B 3B7, Canada.*

PELLEY, John Lawless. b 34. Oak Hill Th Coll 67. **d** 69 **p** 70 Portsm. C of St Jo Evang Fareham 69-72; H Trin Frogmore St Alb 72-76; V of Standon Dio St Alb from 76. *Vicarage, Kents Lane, Standon, Ware, Herts, SG11 1PJ.* (Ware 821390)

PELLING, John Arthur. b 30. ARCA 54. Chich Th Coll 55. **d** 58 **p** 59 Lewes for Chich. C of Hangleton 58-61; St Mary Abbots (in c of Ch Ch) Kens 61-75; V of St Sav Hammersmith 75-79; Chap of H Trin Nice Dio Gibr (Gibr in Eur from 80) from 79. *11 rue de la Buffa, Nice, France.* (87 1983)

PELLOE, Canon John Parker. b 05. Qu Coll Ox BA and Dipl Econ 35, MA 42. Cudd Coll 35. **d** 36 **p** 38 Dur. C of St Columba Southwick 36-39; St Cuthb Kens 39-42; C-in-c of Chettisham 42-43; Dom Chap to Bp of Ely 42-46 and 65-66; V of Wisbech 46-60; Surr 46-67; RD of Wisbech 46-53; Hon Can of Ely 52-53; Archd of Wisbech 53-64; V of Stuntney 60-68; Hon Can of Ely from 65; Chap to HM the Queen 64-75. *14 Lynn Road, Ely, Cambs.* (Ely 2232)

PELLY, Canon Raymond Blake. b 38. Worc Coll Ox BA (2nd cl Th) 61, MA 69. **d** 63 **p** 64 Newc T. C of All SS Gosforth 63-65; Kings Lynn 69-70; Vice Prin Westcott Ho Cam 71-76; L to Offic Dio Ely 72-76; Perm to Offic Dio St E 74-76; Warden St Jo Coll Auckld from 77; Hon Can of Auckld from 78; Hon C of Cathl Ch of St Mary Dio Auckld from 78. *St John's College, St John's Road, Auckland 5, NZ.* (587-086)

PELTON, Ian Simpson. b 30. Keble Coll Ox 50. Sarum Th Coll 55. **d** 57 **p** 58 Dur. C of Crook 57-61; Harton 61-65; PC (V from 69) of Coxhoe Dio Dur from 65. *Vicarage, The Avenue, Coxhoe, Durham.* (Durham 770222)

PELTOR, Lawrence Frank. b 08. Keble Coll Ox BA (3rd cl Th) 33, MA 37. Linc Th Coll 33. **d** 34 **p** 35 Linc. C of St Nich w St John Newport Linc 34-37; St Paul (in c of H Cross) Middlesbrough 37-39; Whitby (in c of St Mich AA) 39-40; CF (EC) 40-45; Hon CF 45; PC of St John Spitalgate and Chap Hill View Hosp Grantham 46-55; V of Kilburn 55-57; V of Thirkleby w Kilburn and Bagby 57-60; R of Willey w Barrow 60-72; C-in-c of Linley 61-72; C of Wybunbury (in c of St Mark Shavington) 72-73. *37 Conduit Lane, Bridgnorth, Shropshire.* (Bridgnorth 3173)

PELZ, Werner. Univ of Lon BA 49. Linc Th Coll 50. **d** 51 **p** 52 Man. C of St Jas Birch-in-Rusholme 51-54; C-in-c of Lostock Conv Distr Bolton 54-63. *c/o 14 Henrietta Street, WC2.*

PEMBERTON, Arthur. b 48. Trin Coll Bris 76. **d** 79 **p** 80 Birm. C of St John Harborne Dio Birm from 79. *58 Station Road, Harborne, Birmingham, B17 9LX.*

PEMBERTON, David Charles. b 35. K Coll Lon and Warm 57. **d** 61 **p** 62 Win. C of Pokesdown 61-65; St Mary W Derby 65-67; C-in-c of St Jude's Conv Distr Cantril Farm Liv 67-71; V 71-74; St Bonif Devonport Dio Ex from 74. *1 Normandy Way, Plymouth, Devon, PL5 1SW.* (Plymouth 31137)

PEMBERTON, Jeremy Charles Baring. b 56. Mert Coll Ox BA, MA 81. Fitzw Coll Cam BA 80. Ridley Hall Cam 79. **d** 81 Jarrow for Dur. C of Stranton w Hartlepool Dio Dur from 81. *76 Colwyn Road, Hartlepool, Cleve, TS26 9AZ.* (Hartlepool 65471)

PEMBERTON, Michael Burman Wolfe. b 38. St D Coll Lamp BA 61. Cranmer Hall, Dur 61. **d** 65 **p** 66 Ches. C of Over 65-68; St Geo Stockport 68-69; Bromborough 69-71; CA Lon 71-73; C of St Jo Bapt Bollington 73-78; Davenham (in c of Good Shepherd) Dio Ches from 78. *8 Standford Drive, Leftwich, Northwich, Chesh.* (Northwich 45727)

PEMBERTON, Thomas Warwick Winstanley. b 26. St Jo Coll Cam BA 50, MA 55. Cudd Coll 62. **d** 63 Shrewsbury for Lich **p** 64 Lich. C of St Chad Shrewsbury 63-66; V of St Pet Rickerscote Stafford 66-73; Titchfield Dio Portsm from 73. *Titchfield Vicarage, Fareham, Hants, PO14 4AG.* (Titchfield 42324)

PEMBERTON, Canon Wilfred Austin. b 16. Univ Coll Nottm 36. Univ of Nottm PhD 52. Univ of Lon BA (2nd cl Hist) 39, BD 42. AKC 41. **d** 41 **p** 42 Chelmsf. C of St Giles Colchester 41-43; C-in-c 43-46; PC of Stonebroom 46-51; Chap Morton Hosp 49-51; R of Breaston (w Wilne and Draycott from 61) Dio Derby from 51; Chap Draycott Hosp from 62; Hon Can of Derby Cathl from 80. *Breaston Rectory, Derby.* (Draycott 2242)

PENA, Juan Elias. **d** 69 RC Bp of Peru **p** 74 Venez. P Dio Venez. *Calle Granada 5, Urb Los Olivos, Puerto Ordaz, Edo Bolivar, Venezuela.*

PENDER-SMITH, John. b 28. **d** and **p** 73 Natal. P-in-c of Merebank Dio Natal from 73. *16 Park Drive, Westville, Natal, S Africa.* (Durban 859671)

PENDLETON, David Julian. b 24. K Coll Lon and Warm BD and AKC 54. **d** 54 **p** 55 Birm. C of Shard End 54-59; Northfield (in c of Shenley Green) 59-65; Min of Shenley Green Eccles Disr 65-70; V of St D Shenley Green Dio Birm from 70. *49 Shenley Green, Birmingham, B29 4HH.* (021-475 4874)

PENDLETON, George. b 39. St Deiniol's Libr Hawarden 76. **d** 78 **p** 79 St D. C of Pembroke Dock 78-80; R of Llangwm Dio St D from 80; Freystrop Dio St D from 80. *Rectory, Llangwm, Haverfordwest, Dyfed.*

PENDLETON, John Thomas. b 12. Dorch Miss Coll 39. **d** 41 **p** 42 Blackb. C of Padiham w Higham 41-44; PC of Cornholme 44-49; V of Slaithwaite w E Scammonden 49-61; C-in-c of St Luke Cleckheaton 61-62; V 62-77. *25 Meadow Close, Robertown, Liversedge, W Yorks.*

PENDLETON, Mervyn Boulton. b 13. SS Coll Cam 2nd cl Cl Trip pt i 34, BA (2nd cl Th Trip pt i) 35, MA 42. Chich Th Coll 35. **d** 37 **p** 38 Chich. C of All S Hastings 37-39; U Beeding and Bramber w Botolphs 39-42; W Tarring 42-44; Actg C of Rusthall 44-45; R of Brington 45-52; V of Wollaston w Strixton 52-60; Chap St Steph Coll Broadstairs 60-62; Chap and Asst Master Ringwood Gr Sch Bournemouth 65-68; Warden and Chap of Whittington Coll Almshouses Felbridge 68-69; C of Yateley 69-71; R of Kimpton w Thruxton and Fyfield 71-78. *20 Owers Way, West Wittering, Sussex.*

PENDORF, James Gordon. b 45. Drew Univ NJ BA 67. Episc Div Sch Mass BD 71. **d** 71 Newark (USA) **p** 71 Bp Rath for Newark (USA). In Amer Ch 71-76; V of H Trin Colne 76-80; Sen Stewardship Adv Dio Chelmsf from 80. *Guy Harlings, 53 New Street, Chelmsford, CM1 1NG.*

PENFOLD, Gilbert Murray. b 17. Univ of Dur LTh 40. Oak Hill Th Coll 36. **d** 40 **p** 42 Kens for Lon. C of St Mary Fulham 40-43; St Paul Slough 43-45; St John Worksop 45-47; Ecclesfield 47-51; V of All SS Sheff 51-59; R of Longhope Dio Glouc from 59. *Rectory, Longhope, Glos.* (Longhope 830298)

PENFOLD, Kenneth Duncan. b 32. Univ of Leeds BA 56. Coll of Resurr Mirfield 57. **d** 59 Roch **p** 60 Tonbridge for Cant. M CGA. C of All SS Belvedere 59-61; L to Offic Dio Glouc 63-67; Dio Pet 67-74; Dio Bradf 75-78; Prior CGA from 77; Perm to Offic Dio Glouc 78-80; Dio Ex from 78; P-in-c of St Mary Magd w St Mich AA Manningham Dio Bradf from 79. *28 White's View, Bradford, W Yorks, BD8 8NN.* (Bradf 42886)

PENG, Andrew Yung-Cheong. **d** 51 **p** 54 Hong. Asst Supt Tai Po Orph and L to Offic Dio Hong 51-52; C of H Trin Kowloon 52-55; All SS Kowloon 55-57; St Paul Hong Kong 57-59; St Matt Hong Kong 59-63; V of St Pet N Point Hong Kong 63-69. *St Peter's Vicarage, North Point, Hong Kong.*

PENG, Peter Yun-Cheong. Lingnan Univ BA 50. Union Th Coll Canton 50. **d** 50 Hong **p** 53 Bp Moyung for Hong. C of All SS Yaumati Kowloon 50-62; V of H Trin Kowloon 62-67; P-in-c of Good Shepherd Miss Vancouver Dio New Westmr from 67. *2649 West 23rd Avenue, Vancouver 8, BC, Canada.*

PENGELLEY, Laurence Maxwell. Moore Th Coll Syd. **d** 52 **p** 53 Gippsld. C of Neerim S 52; V 53-54; R of Toora 54-60; V of Omeo 60-66; V of Boolarra 66-71; Missr Aboriginal Miss Roelands 71-75; Perm to Offic Dio Bunb from 75. *4 Woonar Street, Carey Park, W Australia 6320.*

PENGELLEY, Peter John. b 22. Sarum Wells Th Coll 72.

d 74 **p** 75 B & W. C of Midsomer Norton 74-78; R of Stogursey w Fiddington Dio B & W from 78. *Stogursey Rectory, Bridgwater, Somt, TA5 1PN.* (Nether Stowey 732884)

PENGELLY, Paul Jeremy Charles. CCC Ox BA (3rd cl Hist) 60. Pemb Coll Cam BA (3rd cl Th) 62. Ridley Hall, Cam 61. **d** 63 **p** 64 Man. C of St Phil w St Mark Man 63-65. *Address temp unknown.*

PENHALLURICK, Harold. b 08. Univ of Wales BA 34. St Mich Coll Llan 34. **d** 35 **p** 36 Llan. C of St Gwladys Bargoed 35-37; St Jo Bapt Cardiff 38-41; CF (EC) 41-47; CF 47-59. *24 Glanrhyd Road, Ystradgynlais, Swansea, W Glam.*

PENMAN, Canon David John. Univ of NZ BA 62. Univ of Karachi MA 69, PhD 77. Ch Ch Th Coll LTh 64. **d** 61 **p** 62 Wel. C of Wanganui 61-65; CMS Miss Kar 66-72; Hon C of Ch Ch Kar 67-69; Presbyter United Ch of Pakistan 71-72; CMS Miss Dio Jordan 72-75; Hon C of All SS Beirut 72-75; Prin St Andr Hall Melb and L to Offic Dio Melb 76-79; Commiss Jer 77-79; Hon Can of Wel from 79; V of Palmerston N Dio Wel from 79; Exam Chap to Bp of Wel from 81. *Box 549, Palmerston North, NZ.* (82-400)

PENMAN, Robert George. b 42. St Jo Coll Auckld 63. NZ Bd of Th Stud LTh 66. **d** 65 **p** 66 Auckld. C of Mt Roskill 65-68; C of Henderson 69-70; V of Glen Innes 71-72; C of Alverstoke 73-74; CF 74-77; C of St Mary Bridgwater 77-80; P-in-c of Haselbury Plucknett w N Perrott and Misterton Dio B & W 80-81; R from 81. *Haselbury Plucknett Vicarage, Crewkerne, Somt, TA18 7PB.* (Crewkerne 72063)

PENN, Canon Arthur William. b 22. Univ of Man BA 49. Wycl Hall Ox 49. **d** 51 **p** 52 Ches. C of Bowdon 51-53; Alston w Garrigill 53-56; V of Kirkdale w Nawton 56-67; Brampton Dio Carl from 67; RD of Brampton from 74; P-in-c Gilsland w Over Denton (and Nether Denton to 77) Dio Carl from 75; Hon Can of Carl from 78. *Vicarage, Brampton, Cumb, CA8 1BU.* (Brampton 2486)

PENN, Barry. b 46. Univ of Wales (Swansea) BA 72. St Jo Coll Nottm 77. **d** 79 **p** 80 St Alb. C of New Barnet Dio St Alb from 79. *159 Victoria Road, New Barnet, Herts, EN4 9PB.* (01-449 2306)

PENN, Christopher Francis. b 34. ACII 63. Wells Th Coll 68. **d** 70 **p** 71 Win. C of Andover 70-72; Odiham 72-75; Keynsham 75-76; Team V 76-81; R of Chilcompton w Downside & Stratton-on-the-Fosse Dio B & W from 81. *Chilcompton Vicarage, Bath, Somt.* (Stratton/Fosse 232219)

PENN, Clive Llewellyn. b 12. Oak Hill Th Coll 47. **d** 48 **p** 49 S'wark. C of St Luke Deptford 48-50; St Sampson Guernsey 50-54; P-in-c of Cummins S Austr 55-56; Miss Chap of Somerton Pk and Warradale 56-59; R of Port Elliot w Goolwa Adel 59-65; V of Gouray Jersey 66-71; L to Offic Guernsey & Jersey Dio Win from 71. *30 Upper Mansell Street, St Peter Port, Guernsey, CI.*

PENNAL, David Bernard. b 37. Ripon Hall Ox 64. **d** 67 Birm **p** 68 Aston for Birm. C of St Mary Moseley 67-71; Bridgwater 71-73; C-in-c of Hilton w Cheselbourne and Melcombe Horsey 73-76; V (w Milton Abbas) 76-78; P-in-c of Spetisbury w Charlton Marshall Dio Sarum from 78. *Spetisbury Rectory, Blandford Forum, Dorset.* (Blandford 53153)

PENNANT, Philip Vivian Rogers. b 14. TD 69. Trin Coll Cam BA 47, MA 48. St Mich Coll Llan 48. **d** 49 **p** 50 Ely. C of St Jo Evang Cherry Hinton 49-52; I of Strathmore Dio Calg 52-56; V of Blyth w Barnby Moor (and Ranskill to 59) 56-65; C-in-c of Scofton w Osberton 56-61; V 61-65; R of Sutton Bonington 65-79; P-in-c of Normanton-on-Soar 65-79; Goodnestone w Chillenden and Knowlton Dio Cant from 79; Adisham Dio Cant from 79. *Parsonage House, Goodnestone, Canterbury, Kent, CT3 1PJ.* (Nonington 840282)

PENNELL, Charles Walter Ernest. b 18. St Aid Coll. **d** 49 **p** 50 Lanc for Blackb. C of St Andr Ashton-on-Ribble 49-52; R of HEsketh w Becconsall 52-60; V of St Mary Virg Waterloo Dio Liv from 60. *St Mary's Vicarage, Waterloo, Liverpool 22.* (Waterloo Liv 3587)

PENNELL, Canon James Henry Leslie. b 06. Univ of Edin BL 27. TD and clasp 50. Edin Th Coll 29. **d** 29 **p** 30 Moray. C and Prec of St Andr Cathl Ch Inverness 29-32; Dioc Chap 30-32; R of St Mary Dunblane 32-49; Offg Chap Qu Vic Sch Dunblane 32-49; CF (TA) 34-50; DACG 45; Provost of St Andr Cathl Inverness 49-65; Hon Can from 66; R of Foxearth w Pentlow 65-72; C-in-c of Liston w Borley 67-72; Perm to Offic Dio St E from 73. *The Croft, Hundon, Sudbury, Suffolk.*

PENNEY, David Richard John. b 39. Univ of Dur BA (3rd cl Th) 63, Dipl Th 65. Cranmer Hall Dur 66. **d** 67 Bp McKie for Cov **p** 68 Cov. C of Chilvers Coton 67-70; Styvechale 70-72; P-in-c of Ansty w Shilton 72-77; Withybrook 73-77; R of Easington w Liverton Dio York from 77. *Easington Rectory, Saltburn-by-Sea, Cleve.* (Guisborough 41348)

PENNEY, Herbert Richard. b 07. Trin Coll Dub BA 33, MA 45. **d** 34 **p** 35 Killaloe. C of Birr 34-36; I of Kilcornan w Ardcanny 36-45; Chap Miss to Seamen Bris 45-51; Port of Lon 51-54; Org Sec Miss to Seamen SE Distr 54-58; V of Parkfield 58-62; Plumpton Wall 62-73. *22 Lingmoor Rise, Kendal, LA9 7NR.* (Kendal 25722)

PENNEY, John Edward. b 12. St Jo Coll Dur LTh 33, BA 34, MA 37. Clifton Th Coll 30. **d** 35 Lon **p** 36 Willesden for Lon. C of St Paul Roxeth 35-36; St Mich AA Northn 36-38; Shere (in c of Peaslake) 38-43; V of St Paul S Harrow 43-51; Wisborough Green 51-77; Perm to Offic Dio Ex from 77. *28 Oakleigh Road, Exmouth, EX8 2LN.* (Exmouth 4863)

PENNEY, Robert Affleck. b 13. K Coll Lon and Warm 53. **d** 54 Dover for Cant **p** 55 Cant. C of St Jo Evang Shirley 54-58; V of Patrixbourne w Bridge 58-63; V of Bekesbourne 58-63; St Sav Croydon 63-68; Petham w Waltham 68-70; Perm to Offic Dio Cant from 79. *116 North Road, Hythe, Kent, CT21 5DY.* (Hythe 66118)

PENNEY, William Affleck. b 41. K Coll Lon and Warm BD and AKC 63. **d** 66 **p** 67 Roch. C of St Steph Chatham 66-70; Industr Chap and C-in-c of Bredhurst 70-72; Industr Chap and Hon C of S Gillingham 72-74; Industr Chap and Hon C of Eynsford w Farningham and Lullingstone 74-77; Chap to Bp of Roch from 74. *82 Hayes Road, Bromley, Kent, BR2 9AB.*

PENNICEARD, Clifford Ashley. Monash Univ Austr BA (2nd cl Phil) 65. Linacre Coll Ox BA (3rd cl Th) 67. St Steph Ho Ox 65. **d** 68 Bp McKie for Cov **p** 69 Cov. C of St Jo Bapt Leamington 68-71; Perm to Offic Dio Melb from 71. *5-27 Hill Street, Hawthorn, Vic, Australia 3122.*

PENNICOOK, Ian Donald. b 46. Univ of S Austr BTh 77. Moore Coll Syd ThL 71. **d** 73 Syd **p** 73 Bp Delbridge for Syd. C of St Luke Dapto 73-75; Dural 76-77; C-in-c of Kenthurst Dio Syd from 77. *Pitt Town Road, Kenthurst, NSW, Australia 2154.* (654-1445)

PENNIE, Canon Gibb Niven. b 09. Univ of Aber MA (2nd cl Cl) 30. BD 44. Edin Th Coll 34. **d** 36 **p** 37 Edin. C of Good Shepherd Murrayfield Edin 36-37; Ch Ch Morningside Edin 37-41; Lect Edin Th Coll 38-41; Chap 42-45; P-in-c of Ch Ch Dalbeattie 45-49; R 49-51; Exam Chap to Bp of Glas and Gall 49-69; R of St Mary Hamilton 51-57; St Jo Evang Greenock 57-77; Can of Glas 61-77; Hon Can from 77. *111 Earlbank Avenue, Glasgow.*

PENNING, Frank Philip. **d** 56 **p** 57 Madr. In Ch of S India 56-68; R of Leederville 69-77; P-in-c of St Mary W Perth Dio Perth from 77. *8-11 Outram Street, W Perth, W Australia 6005.* (325 5243)

PENNINGTON, Frederick William. b 11. K Coll Lon and Warm. **d** 55 **p** 56 Ex. C of St Pet Tiverton 55-58; R of Bradford Devon 58-66; R of Thornbury 58-66; V of N Molton w Twitchen 66-77; C-in-c of Molland 68-77; Publ Pr Dio Ex from 77. *Vicarage, Woolsery, Bideford, Devon.*

PENNINGTON, John Kenneth. b 27. Univ of Man LLB (2nd cl) 48. Linc Th Coll 51. **d** 52 Warrington for Liv **p** 53 Liv. C of Wavertree 52-56; Rotherham 56-59; P-in-c of All S Kanpur 59-63; V of St Phil Nelson 64-66; USPG Area Sec for Dios Derby Leic and Southw 66-71; Derby and Sheff 71-75; Lect at St Mary Virg Nottm and Deanery Chap from 75. *St Catharine's Vicarage, St Ann's Well Road, Nottingham, NG3 1EJ.* (Nottm 52497)

PENNINGTON, John Michael. b 32. Em Coll Cam BA 54, MA 58. Wells Th Coll 58. **d** 60 **p** 61 Ches. C of St Geo Stockport 60-64; V of St Steph Congleton 64-68; Chap Nor Sch 68-70; V of Hattersley 70-72; C-in-c of Ch of Resurr Conv Distr of Upton Priory Macclesfield 72-75; V of Upton Priory 75-79. *c/o 152 Prestbury Road, Macclesfield, Chesh.* (Macclesfield 26257)

PENNINGTON, Michael John. Univ of Adel BA 67. St Jo Coll Morpeth ACT ThL 60. **d** 61 **p** 62 Adel. C of S Elizabeth 61-66; R of Port Hedland 66-72; Spearwood-Willagee 72-77; Applecross Dio Perth from 77. *2 Mitchell Street, Ardross, W Australia 6153.* (64 2015)

PENNISTON, Canon Joe Cyril. b 12. Ely Th Coll 35. **d** 35 **p** 36 Wakef. C of Ravensthorpe 35-37; Perm to Offic at Hebden Bridge 37-38; St Thos York 38-39; C of St Aid w St Alb Mart Middlesbrough 39-40; Whitby (in c of St Mich) 40-47; Chap RAFVR 44-47; V of St Luke Thornaby-on-Tees 47-65; Surr from 57; Proc Conv York 59-80; R of Whitby Dio York from 65; RD of Whitby from 65; Can and Preb of York Minster from 72. *Rectory, Whitby, N Yorks, YO21 1JP.* (Whitby 2590)

PENNOCK, John Harding Lovell. b 16. Ripon Hall Ox 63. **d** 65 **p** 66 Birm. C of St Geo Edgbaston 65-68; V of Hill 68-78; P-in-c of Sculthorpe w Dunton Dio Nor from 78. *Rectory, Sculthorpe, Fakenham, Norf.* (Fakenham 3315)

PENNY, Edwin Arthur. b 10. Univ of Lon BA 45. LRAM 34. Univ of Birm Dipl Th 60. Ripon Hall Ox 60. **d** 60 **p** 61 Birm. Hd Master St Laur Sch Northfield 53-70; Hon C of Northfield 60-64; Frankley 64-66; L to Offic Dio Birm 66-70; C of Shenley Green 70-73; Northfield 74-75; Perm to Offic

Dio Heref from 76; Dio Swan B from 78. *Rylands, Walton Green, Presteigne, Powys, LD8 2PU.*

PENNY, Edwin John. b 43. Univ of Leeds BA (2nd cl Engl) 64. Coll of Resurr Mirfield 64. **d** 66 **p** 67 Birm. C of Acock's Green 66-69; Wombourne 69-71; St Paul Wednesbury 71-74; V of Kingshurst 74-79; Chap All H Conv Ditchingham from 79. *St Fursey, Ditchingham, Bungay, Suffolk, NR35 2DZ.* (0986-2482)

PENNY, Michael John. b 36. Linc Th Coll 78. **d** 80 **p** 81 Leic. C of St Mary Magd w St Guthlac Knighton City and Dio Leic from 80. *47 Aberdale Road, Knighton, Leicester, LE2 6GD.*

PENNY, Wilfred Joseph. b 05. St Bonif Coll Warm 29. **d** 32 **p** 33 Lon. C of St John-at-Hackney 32-38; LDHM of Ch Ch Staines Dio Lon 38-51; Min 51-57; V of Compton Dundon 57-62; R of Winford 62-73. *3 Overvale Mansions, 17 Montpelier, Weston-super-Mare, Avon.* (W-s-M 32145)

PENRICE, James Allen. Univ of BC BA 60. Angl Th Coll BC LTh 60. **d** 60 **p** 61 New Westmr. I of St Pet Vanc 60-76; St Luke Vanc 71-76; St D Vanc Dio New Westmr from 76. *2475 Franklin Street, Vancouver, BC, Canada.*

PENRITH, Lord Bishop Suffragan of. *See* Hacker, Right Rev George Lanyon.

PENTREATH, Canon Arthur Godolphin Guy Carleton. b 02. Late Scho of Magd Coll Cam 2nd cl Cl Trip pt i 23, BA (1st cl Cl Trip pt ii) 25, MA 28. Westcott Ho Cam 25. **d** 28 **p** 29 Natal. Chap Michaelhouse Coll Natal 28-30; Master Westmr Sch 30-34; Hd Master Colleg Sch of St Pet Adel 34-44; Wrekin Coll 44-51; Cheltm Coll 52-58; Select Pr Univ of Ox 54-55; Univ of Cam 55; Can Res of Roch 59-65; Can (Emer) from 65. *Wooden Walls, Dock Lane, Beaulieu, Hants.* (0590 612348)

PENTREATH, Canon Harvey. b 29. Wells Th Coll 54. **d** 57 Bris **p** 58 Malmesbury for Bris. C of St Ambrose Bris 57-60; Leatherhead 60-63; Haslemere 63-65; R of Elstead 65-72; V of Cuddington 72-80; Helston Dio Truro from 80; Hon Can of Guildf from 80. *Vicarage, Church Lane, Helston, Cornw, TR13 8NQ.* (Helston 2516)

PENWARDEN, Canon Peter Herbert. b 21. Keble Coll Ox BA (2nd cl Th) 42, MA 46. Linc Th Coll 42. **d** 44 **p** 45 S'wark. C of All SS New Eltham 44-49; V of All SS S Wimbledon 49-61; Benhilton 61-71; Vice-Provost and Can Res of S'wark Cathl from 71. *122 Kennington Road, SE11 6RE.* (01-735 8322)

PEPELA, John. Bp Patteson Th Centre Kohimarama 68. **d** 70 **p** 74 Melan. P Dio Melan 70-75; Dio Ysabel 75-76; Dio Centr Melan from 76. *c/o Box 19, Honiara, Solomon Islands.*

PEPPER, Leonard Edwin. b 44. Ex Univ BA (Th) 71. Ripon Hall Ox 71. **d** 73 **p** 74 York. C of Cottingham 73-76; Kingshurst 76-80; Dir of Pastoral Stud St Steph Ho Ox from 80. *c/o St Stephen's House, Marston Street, Oxford, OX4 1JX.*

PEPPERDENE, Liddon Max Muller. Wycl Coll Tor. **d** 26 **p** 27 Tor. C of All SS Tor 26-30; R of Trin Queb 31-38; La Tuque 38-42; St Luke St John 42-45; L to Offic Dio Fred 45-50; R of Sussex 50-57; Chatham 57-69. *Box 28, Petitcodiac, NB, Canada.*

PEPPIATT, Martin Guy. b 33. Trin Coll Ox 2nd cl Cl Mods 55, BA (2nd cl Lit Hum) 57, 2nd cl Th 59, MA 60. Wycl Hall Ox 57. **d** 59 **p** 60 Lon. C of All S Langham Place Lon 59-63; V of Nakuru 65-69; V of St Steph E Twickenham Dio Lon from 69. *21 Cambridge Park, Twickenham, Middx, TW1 2JE.* (01-892 5258)

PEPPIN, Philip Hamilton. b 07. K Coll Lon AKC 33. **d** 55 **p** 56 Carl. C of St Aid w Ch Ch Carl 55-57; St Sav w St Mark Hull 57-62; Howden and of Barmby Marsh and Wressle 62-66; St Hilda w St Pet Middlesbrough 66-67; L to Offic Dio Mon from 68. *The Chantry, Monmouth, Gwent, NP5 3PA.*

PEPPLE, Jezreel Godwin. b 25. **d** 76 Nig Delta. d Dio Nig Delta. *St Simon's Parsonage, Ikuru Town, Andoni, Obolo, Agafor PA, via Opobo, Nigeria.*

PERALTA, Noe. d 75 Bp Leake for N Argent. d Dio N Argent. *Parsonage, Yuto, N Argentina.*

PERCEY, William Kenneth. Ridley Coll Melb ACT ThL 63. **d** 64 **p** 65 Tas. C of Burnie 64-66; R of King I 66-68; Cressy 68-72; Latrobe 72-75; Rep BFBS Tas 75-79; Perm to Offic Dio Tas 75-79; R of Oatlands 79-80; Chap Inter-Ch Trade & Industr Miss N Region Dio Tas from 80. *Inter-Church Trade & Industry Mission, 25 Veulalee Ave, Trevallyn, Tasmania 7250.* (003 31 8723)

PERCIVAL, Alson Bastin. b 46. Codr Coll Barb 77. **d** 77 **p** 78 Antig. C of St John's Cathl Antig 78-79; R of St Pet Montserrat Dio Antig from 79. *St Peter's Rectory, Montserrat, W Indies.*

PERCIVAL, Douglas Hodson. Moore Th Coll Syd ACT ThL 54. **d** and **p** 54 Syd. C of Pymble 54-55; C-in-c of Berala 55-58; Org BFBS 58-60; CF (Austr) from 60; L to Offic Dio Syd from 60; Dio C & Goulb 64-67; Perm to Offic from 81. *Department of Defence, Canberra, Australia 2600.*

PERCIVAL, Geoffrey. b 46. Ridley Hall Cam 73. **d** 76 **p** 77 Bradf. C of Eccleshill 76-79; Otley Dio Bradf from 79. *170 Weston Drive, Otley LS21 2DT.* (Otley 463632)

PERCIVAL, Keith Thompson. Moore Th Coll Syd ACT ThL 58. **d** 59 Bp Hilliard for Syd **p** 59 Syd. C of Coogee 59-60; Carlingford 60-62; C-in-c of Old Guildf and E Fairfield 62-65; Girraween w Toongabbie Provisional Distr 65-73; Chap Lidcombe Hosp Dio Syd from 73. *Lidcombe Hospital, Joseph Street, Lidcombe, NSW, Australia 2141.* (646-8216)

PERCIVAL, Martin Eric. b 45. BSc (Eng) (Lon) 66. Linacre Coll Ox BA (Th) 70. MA 74. Wycl Hall Ox 67. **d** 70 **p** 71 Warrington for Liv. C of St Marg Anfield 70-73; Witney 73-74; Team V of Bottesford w Ashby 74-76; Grantham 76-80; R of Coningsby w Tattershall Dio Linc from 80. *Coningsby Rectory, Lincoln.* (Coningsby 42223)

PERCIVAL, Robert Standring. Univ of Sheff BA 55. Qu Coll Birm. **d** 59 **p** 60 Man. C of Lightbowne 59-62; St Marg Prestwich 62-63; V of St Aug Pendlebury 63-68; Lect Glouc Technical Coll and Perm to Offic Dio Glouc from 68. *5 Firwood Drive, Tuffley, Gloucester, GL4 0AB.* (Glouc 22739)

PERCY, Donald. b 45. Kelham Th Coll 66. **d** 71 Dur **p** 72 Bp Skelton for Dur. C of St Ignatius Hendon Bp Wearmouth 71-75; Our Lady of Mercy & St Thos Gorton 75-77; St Thos Middlesbrough Dio York from 77. *St Thomas Clergy House, Longlands Road, Middlesbrough, TS3 9DH.*

PERCY, George Thomas. d 60 Newc. C of Belmont 60-73. *49 Walter Street, Belmont, NSW, Australia.*

PERCY, Gordon Reid. b 46. St Jo Coll Dur BA (2nd cl Th and Phil) 68, Dipl Th 70. Cranmer Hall 69. **d** 71 **p** 72 Man. C of St Jo Flixton 71-76; Charlesworth Dio Derby 76-77; P-in-c from 77; Dinting Vale Dio Derby from 80. *Church House, Winster Mews, Gamesley, Glossop, Derbys, SK13 0LU.*

PERCY, Harold John. b 42. York Univ Ont BA 69. Wycl Coll Tor 73. **d** 75 Bp Read for Tor **p** 76 Tor. C of Mississauga 75-77; on leave 77-80; Assoc P Trin E City and Dio Tor from 80. *115 Marion Street, Toronto, Ont, M6R 1E6, Canada.*

PERDUE, Ernest Cope Todd. b 30. TCD BA (Cl Mod) 52, BD 56, MEducn 73, MPsychSc. **d** 54 **p** 55 Dub. C of Drumcondra and N Strand 54-58; Booterstown w Carysfort 58-60; Dean of Residence Trin Coll Dub 60-68; C-in-c of St Mark Dub 66-68; St Steph Dub 68-69; I of Rathmichael 69-76; Asst Chap Kings' Hosp Sch Dub 77-80; C of Taney Dio Dub from 80. *44 Seaview Park, Shankhill, Co Dublin, Irish Republic.* (01-856370)

✠ **PERDUE, Right Rev Richard Gordon.** Trin Coll Dub BA (Resp) 31, Div Test (1st cl) 33, MA and BD 38. **d** 33 **p** 34 Dub. C of Drumcondra w N Strand 33-36; Rathmines 36-40; I of Castledermot w Kinneagh 40-43; Roscrea 43-54; Archd of Killaloe and Kilfenora and Exam Chap to Bp of Killaloe 51-54; Cons Ld Bp of Killaloe; Kilfen; Clonf; and Kilmac in Ch Ch Cathl Dub 2 Feb 54 by Abp of Dub; Bps of Meath; Lim; Cash; Cork; and Oss; Trld to Cork 57; res 78. *Clonleigh, Kinsale, Co Cork, Irish Republic.*

PERDUE, Canon Richard Keith. Trin Coll Tor BA 31. **d** 33 **p** 34 Tor. C of St Geo Tor 33-36; P-in-c of Lakeview Miss 36-40; I of Aurora 40-48; Chap CASF 42-46; R of St Matt Tor 48-63; Can of Tor from 59; Dom Chap to Bp of Tor 63-74; R of St Matt Islington 64-73. *52 Arnold Avenue, Thornhill, Ont., Canada.*

PERERA, George Anthony. b 51. Univ of Edin BD 74. Linc Th Coll 74. **d** 76 **p** 77 Liv. C of H Trin Wavertree and Chap Mabel Fletcher Tech Coll 76-79; Team V of Maghull (in c of St Jas) Dio Liv from 79. *St James Vicarage, Green Link, Green Park, Maghull, Liverpool L31 8DW.*

PEREZ, Marciano. b 13. **d** and **p** 66 Argent. P Dio Argent 66-73; N Argent from 73. *Parsonage, Maria Cristina, N Argentina.*

PEREZ, Mariano. b 13. **d** and **p** 66 Argent. P Dio Argent 66-73; N Argent from 73. *Parsonage, Santa Teresa, N Argentina.*

PEREZ, Santiago. b 44. **d** 74 N Argent. d Dio N Argent. *Parsonage, Crevaux, N Argentina.*

PERFECT, Leslie Charles. b 12. Keble Coll Ox BA (2nd cl Mod Hist) 35, MA 39. Wells Th Coll 35. **d** 36 **p** 37 Swan B. C of Llanelly 36-40; Lect and C of Henbury (in c of Northwick and Aust) 40-43; Chap RAFVR 43-46; V of Deeping St Nich (in c of St Mich Tongue End from 48) 46-51; Cleobury Mortimer (w Hopton Wafers from 54) 51-60; Surr from 52; R of Wootton 60-70; R of Kiddington 60-70; V of Effingham and R of L Bookham 70-80. *Radford House, 109 Camelot Drive, Bedford, NH03102, USA.*

PERHAM, Michael Francis. b 47. Keble Coll Ox BA 74, MA 78. Cudd Coll 74. **d** 76 **p** 77 Cant. C of St Mary BV Addington 76-81; Dom Chap to Bp of Win from 81; Sec C of E Doctrine Comm from 79; Consultant C of E Liturgical Comm from 81. *Wolvesey, Winchester, Hants, SO23 9ND.* (Win 3720)

PERINI, Paul Frederick. b 51. Univ of Syd BA 73. BD (Lon) 76. Moore Th Coll Syd ACT ThL 76. **d** 77 Bp Dain for Syd **p** 77 Bp Robinson for Syd. C of St Jas & St John Mt Druitt 77-80; St Clem Mosman 80; Chap Barker Coll Hornsby from 81. *Barker College, Hornsby, NSW, Australia 2077.* (477-3556)

PERKIN, David Arthur. b 30. Pemb Coll Ox BA 54, MA 58. Linc Th Coll 54. **d** 56 **p** 57 Lon. C of St John's Wood 56-61; Chap and Lect Univ of Technology Loughborough and L to Offic Dio Leic from 61. *University of Technology, Loughborough, Leics.* (Loughborough 63171)

PERKIN, Paul John Stanley. b 50. Ch Ch Ox BA 71, MA 75. Wycl Hall Ox 78. **d** 80 **p** 81 Roch. C of St Mark Gillingham Dio Roch from 80. *The Garden House, Vicarage Road, Gillingham, Kent, ME7 5JA.* (Medway 53687)

PERKINS, Alban Leslie Tate. b 08. Kelham Th Coll 28. M SSM 33. **d** 34 **p** 35 Southw. C of St Geo Nottm 34-37; St Patr Miss Bloemf 37-44; Dir 44-58; Chap St Andr Dioc Sch 38-47; Can of Bloemf 52-67; R of Welkom and Dir of Welkom Miss 58-63; Prov of SSM in S Afr 63-67; C of St Geo w St Jo Bapt Nottm 68-72; Prior St Agnes Priory Les 72-76; R of All SS Modderpoort 76-80; L Pr Dio Man from 81. *S.S.M. Priory, 11 Upper Lloyd Street, Moss Side, Manchester M14 4HY.*

PERKINS, Claude Ambrose. b 07. Lich Th Coll 27. **d** 31 **p** 32 Derby. C of H Trin Chesterfield 31-33; St Mary Wirksworth 33-35; Eckington 35-37; PC of Clifton 37-53; Charlesworth 53-63; V of Weston 63-74; Perm to Offic Dio Ches 74. *Dulverton Hall, St Martins Square, Scarborough, YO11 2DQ.*

PERKINS, Colin Blackmore. b 35. FCII 65. Lon Coll Div 68. **d** 70 Sherwood for Southw **p** 71 Southw. C of Hyson Green 70-73; V of Clarborough w Hayton 73-79; Tythby w Cropwell Butler Dio Southw from 79; P-in-c of Cropwell Bp Dio Southw from 79; Colston Bassett Dio Southw from 79; Granby w Elton Dio Southw from 79; Langar w Barnstone Dio Southw from 79. *Cropwell Butler Vicarage, Nottingham, NG12 3AJ.*

PERKINS, David John Elmslie. b 45. Univ of Dur BA 66, Dipl Th 68. Cranmer Hall Dur. **d** 69 Sheff **p** 70 Bp Gerard for Sheff. C of Wadsley 69-71; Shortlands 71-73; Perm to Offic Dio Lon 76-78; Dio B & W from 78. *Rainbows End, Montacute Road, Stoke-sub-Hamdon, Somt, TA14 6UQ.* (Martock 3314)

PERKINS, Douglas Brian. b 32. Or Coll Ox BA 56, MA 63. St Steph Ho Ox 56. **d** 58 Blackb **p** 60 Lon. C of St Cath Burnley 58-59; St Alb Teddington 59-60; Hon C St Barn Ox 63-64; Chap and Asst Master Beechwood Pk Sch 64-66; LPr Dio St Alb 64-66; Dio Lon 66-68; C of St Alb Mart Holborn 69-79; P-in-c of Ch Ch Streatham Dio S'wark from 79. *Christ Church Vicarage, Streatham Hill, SW2 3ET.* (01-674 5723)

PERKINS, Canon Eric William. b 08. Univ of Leeds BA (3rd cl Hist) 29. Coll of Resurr Mirfield 26. **d** 31 **p** 32 S'wark. C of St Paul Lorrimore Square Newington Lon 31-33; St Mark Washwood Heath Birm 34-35; Fenny Stratford (in c of St Marg) 35-38; St Mary Virg (in c of St Mark) Reading 38-44; V of Boyne Hill Maidenhead 44-56; Surr 52-76; R of Upton w Chalvey Slough 56-76; Hon Can of Ch Ch Ox 62-79; Can (Emer) from 79; Proc Conv Ox 65-73; RD of Burnham 69-74; Sub-Warden of Commun of St Jo Bapt Clewer Windsor from 70. *School House, Church Road, Farnham Royal, Slough, SL2 3AW.* (Farnham Common 5801)

PERKINS, Frederick William Benjamin. Univ of Leeds, BA (2nd cl Hist) 34. BD (Lon) 56. Coll of Resurr Mirfield, 34. **d** 36 **p** 37 S'wark. C of St Pet Vauxhall 36-39; Potters Bar 39-43; St Jas Enfield (in c of St Pet and St Paul Miss Ch Enfield) 43-47; Min of St Pet and St Paul Conv Distr Enfield 47-50; M OGS from 48; Prior 60-74; Warden of Selw Coll Univ of Otago NZ 50-55; Lect Univ of Otago 51-55; V of St Francis Gladstone Pk 55-67; Chap and Lect Berridge Ho Tr Coll Hampstead 56-64; Lect in Div Inst of Educn Univ of Lon 56-78; Coll of All SS Tottenham 64-78; Hon C of Potters Bar Dio Lon from 68; Exam Chap to Bp of Edmon from 72; Lect in Educn Stud Univ of Lon 74-78. *16 Oakmere Avenue, Potters Bar, Herts, EN6 5ED.* (P Bar 54224)

PERKINS, Graeme Stanley. b 53. Ridley Coll Melb 76. **d** 78 **p** 79 Gippsld. Perm to Offic Dio Gippsld 78-81; C of St Jas Dandenong Dio Melb from 81. *c/o 7 Wilson Street, Dandenong, Vic, Australia 3175.*

PERKINS, Harry. St Jo Coll Morpeth. **d** 39 **p** 40 Graft. C of Lismore 39-40; V of Bowraville 40-45; C of St Paul Ipswich 45-47; Pialba 47-54; R of Nanango 54-74; Perm to Offic Dio Brisb from 74. *14 Falkinder Avenue, Paradise Point, Queensland, Australia 4216.* (Gold Coast 30 9443)

PERKINS, Canon John Stanley Heathcote. Univ of NZ BA 39. LTh 40. **d** 39 **p** 40 Ch Ch. C of St Mary Timaru 39-44; CF (NZ) 42-44; V of Amberley NZ 44-49; Kensington-Otipua 49-52; Te Ngawai 52-58; Hokitika 58-62; Rangiora 62-68; Sumner-Heathcote 68-77; Sumner Redcliffs 71-77; Hon Can of Ch Ch 75-77; Can (Emer) from 77. *55 Celia Street, Christchurch 8, NZ.*

PERKINS, Malcolm Bryan. b 20. SS Coll Cam BA 41, MA 45. Wycl Hall Ox 41. **d** 43 **p** 44 Roch. C of Rainham 43-47; St Jo Evang Bexley 47-50; C-in-c of Chalk 50-51; V 51-56; Borstal 56-61; Chap of St Bart Hosp Roch 59-74; Medway Hosp Gillingham 65-67; C-in-c of St Mary Virg Strood 61-65; R of Wouldham 65-73; Toc H Staff Padre from 73; C of Roch Dio Roch from 74. *20 Gordon Terrace, Rochester, Kent, ME1 1SB.* (Medway 402414)

PERMAN, George Hayward. b 01. Tyndale Hall, Bris 31. **d** 34 **p** 35 Man. C of St Marg Burnage 34-37; St Pet Southborough 37-38; St Andr Holborn 38-39; V of St Pet Clerkenwell 39-53; RD of Finsbury and Holborn 47-53; Proc Conv Lon 51-55; V of Ealing 53-67; RD of Ealing 54-60. *2 Wakehurst Court, St George's Road, Worthing, BN11 3DJ.* (Worthing 38540)

PERRENS, Eric George. Univ of Sheff BA 38. Lich Th Coll 38. **d** 40 **p** 41 Ches. C of St Matt Stockport 40-44; Ecclesfield 45-47; C-in-c of New Edlington Conv Distr 47-51; V of Mortomley 51-60; Thorpe Salvin 60-69; Rawcliffe 69-77; R of Bradfield Dio Sheff from 77. *Bradfield Rectory, Sheffield, S6 6LG.* (Sheff 81225)

PERRENS, Everard George. b 15. Scho of St Cath Coll Cam BA (1st cl Nat Sc Trip pt i) 36, 2nd cl pt ii, 37, MA 42. Linc Th Coll 40. **d** 42 **p** 43 Cov. C of St Andr Rugby 42-44; CF (EC) 44-47; Master and Chap Nabumali High Sch Ugan 47-59; Hd Master Nyakasura Sch Ugan 59-65; Chap St Marg Sch Bushey 65-74; King Henry VIII Sch Cov 74-79; C of St Chris Allesley Pk 79-80; Hon C of St Barbara Earlsdon City and Dio Cov from 80. *68 Warwick Avenue, Coventry, W Midl, CV5 6DG.* (Cov 74841)

PERRETT-JONES, Reginald James Archibald. b 04. Univ of Wales BA 34. Dorch Miss Coll 34. **d** 37 **p** 38 Mon. C of Mon 37-39; Glyntaff 39-50; V of Forthampton w Chaceley 50-54; R of Matson 54-61; Cliddesden (w Winslade to 76) Dio Win from 61; Commiss Venez 76-81. *Rectory, Wood's Lane, Cliddesden, Basingstoke, Hants RG25 2JG.* (Basingstoke 22876)

PERRIN, Donald Barton Edward. b 05. TCD BA 33, MA 36. **d** 33 **p** 34 Down. C of St Mark Dundela 33-40; C-in-c of Craigs 40-45; R 45-46; I of Ballywillan (Portrush) 46-69; C-in-c of Culfeightrin (Actg C-in-c from 76) Dio Connor from 69; Can of Belf Cathl 61-65; Archd of Dalriada 65-76. *17 Drumavoley Park, Ballycastle, Co Antrim, N Ireland.* (Ballycastle 62552)

PERRINS, Harold. b 21. Kelham Th Coll 38. **d** 44 **p** 45 Lich. C of Fenton 44-49; Talke 49-53; R of Armitage 53-61; V of Lapley w Wheaton Aston 61-65; Priors Lee 65-69; R of Harlaston 69-77; V of Edingale 69-77; St Aid Shobnall Burton-on-Trent Dio Lich from 77. *St Aidan's Vicarage, Shobnall Road, Burton-on-Trent, Staffs, DE14 2BB.* (B-on-T 68392)

PERRIS, Anthony. b 48. Univ of Wales (Abth) BSc 69. Selw Coll Cam BA 76, MA 79. Ridley Hall Cam 74. **d** 77 Wakef. C of Sandal Magna 77-80; St Andr Plymouth Dio Ex from 80. *39 Lambhay Hill, The Hoe, Plymouth, PL1 2NW.* (Plymouth 667574)

PERRIS, John Martin. b 44. Univ of Liv BSc 66. Trin Coll Bris Dipl Th 70. **d** 72 **p** 73 Roch. C of Sevenoaks 72-76; Bebington 76-79; V of Redland Dio Bris from 79. *151 Redland Road, Bristol 6.* (Bristol 37423)

PERROTT, John Alastair Croome. Univ of NZ LLB 60. Clifton Th Coll 62. **d** 64 **p** 65 Roch. C of St Pet Tunbridge Wells 64-67; Stanford-le-Hope 67-78; R of Elmswell Dio St E from 78. *Elmswell Rectory, Bury St Edmunds, Suff.* (Elmswell 512)

PERROTT, Joseph John. b 19. St Aid Coll 63. **d** 64 **p** 65 Dub. C of St Geo Dub 64-71; Drumcondra 71-72; R of Drimoleague 72-75; Mallow U 75-78; I of Ballydehob Dio Cork from 78; Aghadown w Kilcoe Dio Cork from 78; RD of Cork and Ross 74-80. *Rectory, Ballydehob, Co Cork, Irish Republic.* (Ballydehob 9)

PERROTT, Michael John Lankester. b 51. Univ of Syd BA 72. Keble Coll Ox BA (Th) 75. St Steph Ho Ox 75. **d** 77 **p** 78 S'wark. C of St Paul Deptford 77-80; Higham Ferrers w Chelveston Dio Pet from 80. *Higham Ferrers Vicarage, Wellingborough, NN9 8DL.* (Rushden 2433)

PERROTTET, Henry Holbrook. b 1897. Trin Coll Melb BA 24. ACT ThL 22. **d** 21 Gippsld for Melb **p** 22 Melb. C of St Pet Melb 21-23; Min of Meredith Vic 23-25; C of Corowa NSW 25-26; St Jas Syd 26-28; Perm to Offic All SS Miss Pentonville 28-29; C of St Mich AA Bromley-by-Bow 29-31; P-in-c of Bimini w Berry I 31-32; L to Offic Dio River 36-39; P-in-c of Wentworth 39-43; Chap AIF 43-46; C of H Trin Bingley 46-47; CF 47-55; Perm to Offic Dio Cant 55-77. *Terry's Cross, Woodmancote, Henfield, Sussex, BN5 9SX.*

PERRY, Anthony Robert. Kelham Th Coll 48. **d** 52 **p** 53 Sheff. C of St Cecilia Parson Cross Sheff 52-56; Welkom

56-58; St Jas Mantsonyane 59-60; Teyateyaneng 60-66; Chap Morija Tr Coll 66-68; R of Teyateyaneng 69-70; Chap Univ of Natal and St John's Conv 71-77; L to Offic Dio Natal from 78; Hosp Chap from 79. *61 Ogwini Street, Durban 4001, Natal, S Africa.*

PERRY, Canon Arthur Sidney. b 11. AKC (2nd cl) 38. Univ of Lon BD (2nd cl) 47, MTh 51. **d** 38 **p** 39 S'wark. C of St Pet Norbiton 38-42; Caterham 42-48; V of St Bart Sydenham 48-57; Surr from 53; V of St Barn Dulwich 57-79; Chap Alleyn's Coll of God's Gift 57-79; RD of Dulwich 67-78; Hon Can of S'wark 68-79; Can (Emer) from 79; Perm to Offic Dios Nor and Chelmsf from 79. *Baverstock House, Bridewell Street, Walsingham, Norf, NR22 6BJ.* (032 872319)

PERRY, Christopher Hugh. b 14. NW Ordin Course 73. **d** 74 Repton for Derby **p** 75 Derby. C of Wingerworth Dio Derby from 74. *2 Wheatcroft Close, Wingerworth, Chesterfield, Debys, S42 6PE.* (Chesterfield 73856)

PERRY, Canon Colin Charles. b 16. Late Chor Scho of K Coll Cam 3rd cl Cl Trip pt i 37, BA 38 2nd cl Th Trip pt ii 39, MA 42. Westcott Ho Cam 39. **d** 40 **p** 41 S'wark. C of St Sav Denmark Pk 40-42; St Jo Evang Redhill 42-44; Chap Achimota Sch Ghana 45-56; V of Aldbourne 56-64; V of Baydon 57-64; PC of St Francis Sarum 64-71; V of Preston w Sutton Poyntz 71-81; RD of Weymouth 74-79; Can and Preb of Sarum Cathl from 77; Team R of Preston w Sutton Poyntz and Osmington w Poxwell Dio Sarum from 81. *Vicarage, Preston, Weymouth, Dorset, DT3 6BX.* (Preston 833142)

PERRY, Canon Colin Edward Herschel. Univ of Leeds, BSc 32. Coll of Resurr Mirfield 32. **d** 34 **p** 35 Llan. C of St Sav Cardiff 34-38; Chap HM Pris Cardiff 37-38 HM Borstal Roch 39-40; Asst Chap Wormword Scrubs 38; Chap HM Pris Maidstone 38-40; Chap RAF 40-46; Chap HM Prison Win 46-50; Hants Co Coun Remand Homes and Purbrook Approved Sch 48-50; R of St Martin w St Paul Cant 50-63; Chap HM Pris Cant 50-63; and 66-68; V of Patrixbourne w Bridge and Bekesbourne 63-79; RD of E Bridge 63-79; Hon Can of Cant from 67; Proc Conv Cant 68-70; Chap HM Borstal Dover from 79. *132 New Dover Road, Canterbury, Kent, CT1 3EJ.* (Cant 58668)

PERRY, David William. b 42. St Chad's Coll Dur BA (2nd cl Cl) and Lightfoot Scho 64, Dipl Th 66. **d** 66 **p** 67 Ripon. C of St Mary Virg Middleton 66-69; Bedale 69-71; Marton-in-Cleveland 71-75; V of Skirlaugh w Long Riston Dio York from 75. *Skirlaugh Vicarage, Hull, Humb, HU11 5HE.* (0401-62259)

PERRY, Edna Lenora. b 23. Univ of Manit BPed 71, BA 75, BEducn 75. St Jo Coll Winnipeg. **d** 80 **p** 81 Rupld. Hon C of River N Angl Pars Winnipeg Dio Rupld from 80. *130 Elliot Avenue, Bird's Hill, Manit, Canada, F0E 0H0.*

PERRY, Edward John. K Coll Lon and Warm AKC 62. **d** 63 **p** 64 Ex. C of St Francis Honicknowle Devonport 63-65; Ashburton w Buckland-in-the-Moor 65-70; V of Cornwood Dio Ex from 70; Asst Dir of Relig Educn Dio Ex from 71. *Cornwood Vicarage, Ivybridge, Devon.* (Cornwood 237)

PERRY, Eric Akers. ACIS 70. Qu Coll Birm 56. **d** 58 **p** 59 Glouc. C of Lydney w Aylburton 58-64; R of Wickwar (w Rangeworthy from 76) Dio gloucfrom 64; CF (TAVR) from 64; RD of Hawkesbury from 77. *Wickwar Rectory, Glos.* (Wickwar 267)

PERRY, Geoffrey. b 33. K Coll Lon and Warm BD and AKC 57. **d** 58 **p** 59 Truro. C of Falmouth 58-63; St Jo Div Fishponds 63-66; R of St Ive (w Quethiock from 75) Dio Truro from 66; RD of W Wivelshire 73-76. *St Ive Rectory, Liskeard, Cornw, PL14 3LX.* (Callington 2327)

PERRY, George Lysle. Ridley Hall, Melb 31. ACT ThL 33. **d** 33 **p** 36 Gippsld. C-in-c of Yarragon 33-36; C of St Paul's Cathl Sale 36-37; Footscray 38-40; Min of Lara 40-44; Chap AMF 41-44; I of Rutherglen 44-47; R of Yea 47-52; Numurka 52-65; C of Sandringham 65-67; Chap Miss to Seamen Melb 67-69; Perm to Offic Dio Gippsld from 70. *c/o L Deane, Shady Creek, Yarragon, Vic, Australia 3823.* (056-86 220)

PERRY, Graham Henry. b 36. St Francis Th Coll Bris 68. **d** 70 **p** 72 Rockptn. Hon C of St Paul's Cathl Rockptn 70-71; St Luke Wandal Rockptn 71-73; St Sav Gladstone 73-74; P-in-c of Brisb Valley Dio Brisb 74-75; R from 75. *Rectory, Toogoolawah, Queensland, Australia 4313.* (83 1128)

PERRY, Harold George. St Aid Coll 58. **d** 60 Blackb **p** 61 Lanc for Blackb. C of Chorley 60-62; Ashton L 62-64; V of Earby 64-68. *17 Sussex Drive, Helmshare, Rossendale, Lancs.*

PERRY, John. b 09. TD 60. Univ of Edin MA 28, BD 34, PhD 50. Edin Th Coll 30. **d** 32 **p** 33 Edin. C of Ch Ch Edin 32-35; St Jas Inverleith-row (in c of St Phil) Edin 35-38; P-in-c of Armadale and Bathgate Miss 38-39; CF (R of O) 39-48; CF (TA) 48-59; R of Monymusk w Kemnay 46-49; St Congan Turriff 49-53; Exam Chap to Bp of Aber 49-53; to Bp of St Andr 55-77; R of Newport w Tayport 53-65; Can of St Ninian's Cathl Perth 61-77; R of Comrie 65-77; Ed Scottish Episc Ch Yr Bk 70-75. *29 Balhousie Street, Perth, PH1 5HJ.* (Perth 26594)

PERRY, John Freeman. b 35. ALCD 59 (LTh from 74). **d** 59 **p** 60 Guildf. C of Ch Ch Woking 59-62; Chorleywood (in c of St Andr) 62; Min of St Andr Eccles Distr Chorleywood 63-66; V 66-77; RD of Rickmansworth 72-77; Warden of Lee Abbey Lynton Dio Ex from 77; RD of Shirwell from 80. *Lee Abbey, Lynton, Devon, EX35 6JJ.* (Lynton 2621)

PERRY, Ven John Neville. b 20. Univ of Leeds BA 41. Coll of Resurr Mirfield 41. **d** 43 **p** 44 Lon. C of All SS Poplar 43-50; V of St Pet De Beauvoir Square W Hackney 50-63; Feltham 63-75; RD of Hounslow 67-75; Archd of Middx from 75. *63 Alexandra Road, Hounslow, Middx, TW3 4HP.*

PERRY, Kenneth James. Univ of Melb BA 49. Ridley Coll Melb 51. **d** 52 **p** 53 Melb. Chap Melb Dioc Centre 52-53; P-in-c of Sunbury 53-54; Asst Sec CMS Vic 54-55; Miss at Tawau 55-60; L to Offic Dio Sing 60-63; V of Klang 63-65; Gen Sec CMS Vic 65-72; C of St Paul's Cathl Melb 65-73; I of St John Cranbourne 73-76; H Trin Oakleigh 76-79; Perm to Offic Dio Melb 79. *190 The Avenue, Parkville, Vic, Australia 3052.* (380 4954)

PERRY, Martin Herbert. b 43. Cranmer Hall Dur 66. **d** 70 **p** 71 Dur. C of St Mark Millfield Bp Wearmouth 70-74; Haughton-le-Skerne 74-77; V of St Matt (and St Luke from 79) Darlington Dio Dur from 77. *63a Brinkburn Road, Darlington, Co Durham.* (Darlington 63412)

PERRY, Michael Arnold. b 42. BD (Lon) 64. MPhil (Southn) 74. Ridley Hall Cam 63. **d** 65 Warrington for Liv **p** 66 Liv. C of St Helens 65-68; Bitterne 68-72; V 72-81; R of Eversley Dio Win from 81. *Eversley Rectory, Basingstoke, Hants, RG27 0LX.* (Eversley 733237)

PERRY, Ven Michael Charles. b 33. Trin Coll Cam 1st cl Nat Sc Trip pt i 54, BA (1st cl Nat Sc Trip pt ii) 55, 1st cl Th Trip pt ii 57, MA 59. Westcott Ho Cam 56. **d** 58 Lich **p** 59 Stafford for Lich. C of Berkswich 58-60; Chap Ripon Hall Ox 61-63; L to Offic Dio Ox 62-64; St Alb 65-70; Perm to Offic Dio Lon 63-70; Chief Asst Home Publishing SPCK 63-70; Exam Chap to Bp of Lich 65-74; Archd of Dur and Can Res of Dur Cathl from 70. *7 The College, Durham, DH1 3EQ.* (Durham 61891)

PERRY, Richard Douglas. Univ of Tor St Chad's Coll Regina LTh 56. **d** 55 **p** 56 Qu'App. R of Wawota 56-59; Grenfell 59-67; Pipestone 67-69; C of Cleethorpes 69-72; R of Jarvis 72-75; St Aid Oakville Dio Niag from 75. *7 Washington Avenue, Oakville, Ont., Canada.* (416-844 6643)

PERRY, Robert Anthony. b 21. Univ of Leeds, BA 47. Coll of Resurr Mirfield 47. **d** 49 Whitby for York **p** 50 York. C of St John Middlesbrough 49-54; Prin of St Aug Sch Betong 54-59; P-in-c of Betong 56-59; Provost of St Thos Cathl Kuch 59-66; R of Hasfield w Tirley 66-69; Asst Chap HM Pris Man 69; L to Offic Dio Leic 70-73; Chap HM Pris Gartree 70-73; C-in-c of St Edw Mottingham 73-75; V of St Columba Miri 76-78; Warden Ho of Epiph Kuching 78-80; P-in-c of Presteigne w Discoyd Dio Heref 80; R from 80; P-in-c of Lingen Dio Heref from 81; Kinsham Dio Heref from 81. *Rectory, St David's Street, Presteigne, Powys, LD8 2BF.* (Presteigne 7777)

PERRY, Roy John. b 28. Chich Th Coll 71. **d** 72 Taunton for B & W **p** 73 B & W C (APM to 76) of H Trin Hendford, Yeovil 72-77; Team V in Withycombe Raleigh w Exmouth Dio Ex from 77. *All Saints Vicarage, Church Road, Exmouth, Devon, EX8 1RZ.* (Exmouth 3572)

PERRY, Thomas Victor. b 08. TCD BA 32. **d** 32 **p** 33 Oss. C of Carlow 32-35; Chap (Eccles Est) of Bolarum 35-37; Calicut 37; St Geo Cathl Madr 37-38; St Thos Mt w Pallavaram and Vellore 38; furlough 38-39; H Trin Bangalore 39-41; Chap of St Mary Fort St Geo and St Thos Mount Madr 41-42; St Jo Secunderabad 42-43; CF (Ind) 43-47; (Men in Disp 45) Hon CF 46; I of Kilmallock w Athlacca and Bruree 49-54; R of Kilmessan w Galtrim 54-57; I of Trim 57-79; Can of Meath 57-79; Dean of Clonmacnoise 61-79. *Seaview Cottage, Whitehill Road, Carnlough, Co Antrim.*

PERRY, Victor Harry. b 16. AKC 48. **d** 49 Dover for Cant **p** 50 Cant. C of Faversham 49-52; Ashford 52-60; V of St Mich AA Tenterden 60-70; St Jude Thornton Heath 70-81; Hon C of St Steph Norbury Dio Cant from 81. *23 Beechwood Avenue, Thornton Heath, Croydon, Surrey.* (01-684 2605)

PERRY-GORE, Noel Arthur. b 07. St Edm Hall Ox BA 32, MA 34. Westcott Ho Cam 32. **d** 32 **p** 33 S'wark. C of St Paul w St Mark Deptford 32-37; C-in-c of St Paul Distr Arbourthorne Sheff 37-38; V 38-47; V of St John's Wood Ch 47-72; Surr 48-72; RD of St Marylebone 51-59 and 62-63. *67 Military Road, Rye, Sussex.* (Rye 2441)

PERRY-GORE, Raymond George Ralph. St Jo Coll Morpeth 24. **d** 28 Bath **p** 31 Truro. C of Gilgandra NSW 28-29; St Steph-in-Brannel 30-34; Westbury 34-35; R of St Geo Tortola 35-41; V of St Clem Ste Madeleine 41-44; To Amer Ch 44-46; R of St Dominic 46-59; V of St Gluvias w Ponsanooth and Penryn Borough 56-69; C-in-c of St Anne's St Kitts 71-73. *Box 205, Roadtown, Tortola, British Virgin Islands, W Indies.*

PERRY-GORE, Walter Keith. St D Coll Lamp BA 59. Westcott Ho Cam 60. **d** 61 **p** 62 Truro. C of St Austell 61-64; V of H Innoc I and Dio Barb 64-70; R of New Carl 70-75; N Hatley Dio Queb from 75. *Rectory, North Hatley, PQ, Canada.*

PERRYMAN, David Francis. b 42. Brunel Univ Middx BTech 64. Oak Hill Coll 74. **d** 76 **p** 77 Cant. C of H Trin Margate 76-80; R of Ardingly Dio Chich from 80. *Ardingly Rectory, Haywards Heath, Sussex, RH17 6UR.* (Ardingly 892332)

PERRYMAN, John Frederick Charles. b 49. Merton Coll Ox BA 71, MA 74. Ridley Hall Cam 72. **d** 74 **p** 75 Roch. C of Shortlands 74-78; Asst Chap St George's Hosp Tooting from 78. *109 Kenlor Road, SW17.*

PERSAUD, Isaac Anthony. b 56. Univ of the WI (Barb) BA 79. Codr Coll Barb 75. **d** 79 Stabroek for Guy. C of St Jos Port Mourant 79-80; H Redeemer Georgetn Dio Guy from 80. *Holy Redeemer Vicarage, West Ruimveldt, Georgtown, Guyana.*

PERSIA, *See* Iran.

PERSSON, William Michael Dermot. b 27. Or Coll Ox BA 51, MA 55. Wycl Hall Ox 51. **d** 53 Dover for Cant **p** 54 Cant. C of Em S Croydon 53-55; St John Tunbridge Wells 55-58; V of Ch Ch Mymms Barnet 58-67; R of Bebington 67-79; M Gen Syn Ches from 75; Commiss Chile from 77; V of Knutsford w Toft Dio Ches from 79; Exam Chap to Bp of Lon from 81. *Vicarage, Knutsford, Chesh, WA16 8QL.* (Knutsford 2834)

PERTH, Lord Archbishop of, and Metropolitan of Province of Western Australia. *See* Carnley, Most Rev Peter Frederick.

PERTH, Assistant Bishop of. *See* Challen, Right Rev Michael Boyd.

PERTH, Dean of (W Australia). *See* Robarts, Very Rev David Oswald.

PERTH, Provost of (Dio St Andrews). *See* Watt, Very Rev Alfred Ian.

PERU, Lord Bishop of. *See* Evans, Right Rev David Richard John.

PESCOD, John Gordon. b 44. Univ of Leeds BSc (3rd cl Chem Eng) 70. Univ of Birm Dipl Th 71. Qu Coll Birm 68. **d** 72 **p** 73 S'wark. C of St Geo Camberwell 72-75; Chap R Philanthropic S Sch Redhill 75-80; P-in-c of Nunney w Wanstrow and Cloford Dio B & W from 80. *Nunney Rectory, Frome, Somt.*

PESKETT, Osmond Fletcher. b 12. Univ of Dur LTh 44. Tyndale Hall Bris. **d** 37 **p** 38 Hong. C of Nanning 38-39; V 39-43; C of St Pet and St Paul Felixstowe 45; BCMS Miss at Nanning Kwangsi 45-50; V of Ch Ch Chadderton 51-55; St Steph Tonbridge 55-65; R of Em Moro 65-67; Chan of Moro 65-68; Hon Can of Moro from 68; V of St Keverne 68-77; Perm to Offic Dio Truro from 77; Commiss Moro from 81. *Smelters Rest, Quay Road, Devoran, Truro, Cornwall.*

PESKETT, Richard Howard. Selw Coll Cam BA 64, MA 68. Ridley Hall Cam 64. **d** 68 Bp Ramsbotham for Newc T **p** 69 Newc T. C of Jesmond Newc T 68-71; Lect Discipleship Tr Centre and Asian Centre for Th Stud Sing from 71. *33a Chancery Lane, Singapore 11.*

PESTAINA, Foster Bancroft. Univ of Dur (Codr Coll Barb) BA 53. **d** 51 **p** 52 Nass. C of St Agnes Nass 51-53; P-in-c of Exuma 53-55; C of St Sav w St Gabr and St Steph Poplar 55-56; P-in-c of St Patr Governor's Harbour Eleuthera 56-63; Long I 63-66; H Cross New Providence 66-71; Archd of Grand Bahama 71-80; R of Ch K Grand Bahama I and Dio Nass from 71. *PO Box F-87, Freeport, Grand Bahama, W Indies.* (3525402)

PETA, David Scholtz. St Bede's Coll Umtata, 43. **d** 47 Bp Etheridge for Grahamstn **p** 51 Grahmstn. Asst Miss O of Ethiopia at New Brighton 47-51; Port Alfred 51-55; P-in-c O of Ethiopia 55-60; Miss of St Barn Alicedale 60-64. *St Paul's Mission, Alicedale, Grahamstown, CP, S Africa.*

PETA, Pere Frederick. b 29. **d** 78 **p** 79 Wai. Hon C of Wairoa-Mohaka Past 78-80; Waipatu-Moteo Past Dio Wai from 80. *48 Napier Terrace, Napier, NZ.* (55153)

PETA, Yusuf. **d** 73 **p** 75 Zanz T. P Dio Zanz T. *Box 45, Tanga, Tanzania.*

PETER, John. **d** 73 **p** 77 Carp. C of Bamaga 73-77; P-in-c of Boigu I Dio Carp from 77. *c/o Box 79, Thursday Island, Queensland, Australia 4875.*

PETERA, Harold Wilfred. b 36. **d** 81 Auckld. C of Parengarenga Ahipara Peria Dio Auckld from 81. *78 North Road, Kaitaia, NZ.*

PETERBOROUGH, Lord Bishop of. *See* Feaver, Right Rev Douglas Russell.

PETERBOROUGH, Assistant Bishops of. *See* Rogers, Right Rev Alan Francis Bright; Franklin, Right Rev Alfred; and Burrough, Right Rev John Paul.

PETERBOROUGH, Dean of. *See* Wise, Very Rev Randolph George.

PETERKEN, Peter Donald. b 28. K Coll Lon and Warm BD and AKC 51. **d** 52 **p** 53 Roch. C of St Mary Swanley 52-55; and 62-65; Ch Ch Isle of Dogs Poplar 55-57; R of S Perrott w Mosterton and Chedington 57-59; V of Skeldon w Leeds and Chap of Paramaribo Gui 59-62; R of Killamarsh 65-70; V of St Luke City and Dio Derby from 70; M Gen Syn Dio Derby from 78; RD of Derby N from 79. *Vicarage, Peet Street, Derby, DE3 3RF.* (Derby 45720)

PETERO, Daudi. St Paul's Dioc Div Sch Limuru. **d** 47 **p** 49 Momb. P Dio Momb 47-52; and 57-61; Dio Ft Hall 61-64; Dio Mt Kenya 64-75; Dio Mt Kenya E from 75; Exam Chap to Bp of Mt Kenya E from 78. *Box 6051, Runyenjes, Kenya.*

PETERS, Andrew Emmanuel. b 50. ACT ThL 78. Trin Coll Melb BTh 80. **d** 80 Bal. C of Colac Dio Bal from 80. *7 Marks Street, Colac, Vic, Australia 3250.*

PETERS, Arthur Gordon. K Coll NS BA 60, STB 63. **d** 62 **p** 63 NS. d Dio NS 62-63; R of Weymouth 64-68; Annapolis 68-73; R of Granville 68-73; Ch Ch Syd Dio NS from 73. *793 George Street, Sydney, NS, Canada.* (564-5315)

PETERS, Canon Cyril John. b 19. Fitzw Ho Cam BA 42, MA 45. Chich Th Coll 40. **d** 42 Chich **p** 43 Lewes for Chich. C of St Mich AA Brighton 42-45; CF (EC) 45-47; C of St Mich AA Brighton 47-50; Chap Brighton Coll and L to Offic Dio Chich 50-69; R of Uckfield Dio Chich from 69; Isfield Dio Chich from 69; Horsted Parva Dio Chich from 69; RD of Uckfield from 73; Surr from 75; Can & Preb of Chich Cathl from 81. *Rectory, Uckfield, Sussex.* (Uckfield 2251)

PETERS, Ven Daniel Stephen George. St Pet Coll Alice 66. **d** 68 **p** 69 Kimb K. C of St Barn Kimberley 68-72; Douglas Dio Kimb K from 72; Archd of De Aar from 81. *PO Box 108, Douglas, CP, S Africa.* (Douglas 310)

PETERS, David Lewis. b 38. Ch Ch Ox BA 62, MA 66. Westcott Ho Cam 63. **d** 65 **p** 66 Man. C of St Mary w St Pet Oldham 65-70; C of Stand (in c of St Andr Hillock) 70-74; V of Hillock Dio Man from 74. *St Andrew's House, Mersey Drive, Whitefield, Manchester, M25 6LA.* (061-766 5561)

PETERS, Douglas John. Univ of Syd BA 47, Dipl Educn 48. **d** and **p** 55 Bath. Warden St Francis Hostel Dubbo 55-59; R of Portland 59-63; Gilgandra 63-72; Forbes Dio Bath from 72. *Rectory, Forbes, NSW, Australia 2871.* (068-52 2223)

PETERS, Kenneth. b 54. Univ of Wales (Cardiff) Dipl Th 77. St Mich AA Coll Llan 74. **d** 77 Llan **p** 78 Bp Reece for Llan. C of Mountain Ash 77-80; Chap Miss to Seamen from 80. *Kingston House, James Street, Liverpool, L2 7PG.* (051-236 2432)

PETERS, Kenneth Maxwell. b 40. ACT ThDip 76. Ridley Coll Melb 74. **d** 77 Melb **p** 77 Bp Grant for Melb. C of St Mary Magd Dallas 77-80; I of St Pet Bundoora Dio Melb from 80. *12 Alma Road, Bundoora, Vic, Australia 3083.*

PETERS, Lionel Victor. b 1900. St Jo Coll Dur BA (2nd cl Th) 25, MA 28. Wells Th Coll 26. **d** 26 **p** 27 Glouc. C of St Phil and St Jas Leckhampton 26-28; Welwyn 28-32; R of Beeston St Lawr w Ashmanhaugh V (w Hoveton St Pet from 35) 32-50; V of Tunstead w Ruston Sco 47-50; LPr Dio Chich 50-78; Bursar and Tutor St Jo Coll Dur 50-53; Perm to Offic Dio Portsm 61-75. *High Bank, North Lane, South Harting, Petersfield, GU31 5NN.*

PETERS, Michael. b 41. Chich Th Coll 75. **d** 77 **p** 78 Truro. C of Redruth Dio Truro 77-79; Team V (w Lanner from 80) from 79. *Vicarage, Pencoys, Four Lanes, Redruth, TR16 6LR.* (Redruth 215035)

PETERS, Peter William. Univ of New Engl Armid BA 67. Moore Th Coll Syd 60. **d** 62 Armid. C of St Pet Cathl City and Dio Armid from 62. *St John's Hostel, Armidale NSW, Australia.*

PETERS, Ralph Strafford. b 25. Trin Coll Dub BA 48, MA 57. **d** 48 **p** 50 Connor. C of All SS Belfast 48-51; Miss (DUM) at Hazaribagh Dio Chota N 51-57; C of Donaghadee 57-60; C-in-c of Loughinisland 60-62; R 62-65; V of Newry 65-81; Preb of Drom Cathl 75-77; Treas 77-81; R of Down w Holly Mount Dio Down from 81. *Rectory, Downpatrick, Co Down, N Ireland.* (Downpatrick 2286)

PETERS, Richard Henry Lawrence. **d** 76 Melb **p** 77 Bp Muston for Melb. C of St Paul Frankston 76-78; P-in-c of St Silas N Geelong Dio Melb from 78. *112 Spark's Road, Norlane, Vic, Australia 3214.* (052-78 1257)

PETERS, Richard Paul. b 13. Univ Coll Ox BA 35, MA 39. Cudd Coll 37. **d** 38 **p** 39 Portsm. C of Portsea 38-44; V of Easebourne 44-55; Henfield 55-69; RD of Hurst 65-69; Warden of Crowhurst Ch's Ministry of Healing Battle 69-78. *Jason's Keep, Blackstone, Henfield, Sussex.*

PETERS, Robert David. b 54. Coun for Nat Acad Awards BA (Th) 76. Oak Hill Coll 78. **d** 79 **p** 80 Ches. C of St Geo Hyde Dio Ches from 79. *120 Great Norbury Street, Hyde, Cheshire, SK14 1HX.* (061-366 6955)

PETERS, Robert Warren. b 47. St Jo Coll Auckld LTh 74. **d** 73 **p** 74 Wel. C of Lower Hutt 73-75; Johnsonville 75-77; V of Newlands-paparangi 77-81; Adv in Chr Educn Dio Waik from 81. *11 Tudor Crescent, Hamilton, NZ.* (57-066)

PETERS, Stephen Eric. b 45. Westcott Ho Cam 74. **d** 77 Barking for Chelmsf **p** 78 Chelmsf. C of Wanstead 77-79; St Marg Leigh 79-81; P-in-c of Purleigh Dio Chelmsf from 81; Cold Norton w Stow Maries Dio Chelmsf from 81. *Purleigh Rectory, Chelmsford, Essex.* (Purleigh 743)

PETERS, Canon William John. d 66 **p** 68 Kimb K. C of Ritchie 66-72; R 72-74; Homevale 74-75; All SS Kimberley Dio Kimb K from 75; Can of St Cypr Cathl Kimb from 73. *127 Barkly Road, Kimberley, CP, S Africa.* (Kimb 26001)

PETERSEN, George Archibald. St Pet Coll Alice. **d** 68 **p** 69 Capetn. C of Hopefield 68-78; Perm to Offic Dio Capetn from 78. *79 Glenhaven Avenue, Glenhaven, Belville 7530, Cape, S Africa.* (95-1839)

PETERSEN, Gordon James. b 47. St Francis Coll Brisb ACT Dipl Th 71. **d** 70 **p** 71 Brisb. C of Toowoomba 70-73; V of Surat 73-77; Inala City and Dio Brisb from 77. *Vicarage, Poinsettia Street, Inala, Queensland, Australia 4077.* (372 1216)

PETERSEN, Reginald Henry. St Paul's Coll Grahmstn 36, LTh (S Afr) 38. **d** 38 **p** 39 Capetn. C of St Mark Capetn 38-40; Hopefield 40-42; R of Calvinia 42-46; St Matt Claremont 46-53; St Mark Capetn 53-59; C of St Mary's Cathl Johann 59-62; R of St Andr Standerton 62-70; C of Linden Dio Johann from 70. *75 Eighth Street, Linden, Johannesburg, S Africa.* (011-46 1392)

PETERSON, David Gilbert. BD (Lon) 68. Univ of Man PhD 78. Moore Th Coll Syd ACT ThL 68. **d** 68 **p** 69 Syd. C of St Matt Manly 68-70; Lect Moore Th Coll and L to Offic Dio Syd 71-75; C of Cheadle 75-78; R and Can of St Mich Cathl Wollongong Dio Syd from 80. *Rectory, Church Hill, Wollongong, NSW, Australia 2500.* (042-289132)

PETERSON, Dennis. Oak Hill Th Coll 51. **d** 54 **p** 55 Chelmsf. C of All SS Leyton 54-56; St Geo Leeds 56-58; V of St Jude E Brixton 58-79. *c/o St Jude's Vicarage, Dulwich Road, SE24.* (01-274 3183)

PETERSON, Leslie Ernest. Univ of W Ont BA 52. Huron Th Coll LTh 54. **d** 54 **p** 55 Alg. I of Coniston 54-59; Elliot Lake 59-63; Ch Ch N Bay 63-78; Parry Sound Dio Alg from 78. *10 McMurray Street, Parry Sound, Ont, Canada.*

PETERSON, Canon Norman Edwin. McGill Univ BA 20. Montr Th Coll LTh 23. **d** 22 **p** 23 Montr. C of St Alb (Bp Carmichael Mem) Montr 22-26; R of Waterloo 26-29; C of St Columba Montr 29-35; R 35-64; Hon Can of Montr 59-64; Can (Emer) from 64. *Box 370, Rawdon, PQ, Canada J0K 1S0.*

PETFIELD, Bruce Le Gay. b 34. N-E Ordin Course 76. **d** 79 **p** 80 Newc T (NSM). C of Morpeth Dio Newc T from 79. *42 Grange Road, Stobhill Grange, Morpeth, Northumberland, NE61 2UF.*

PETHER, Christopher James. Univ of NZ BA 61. Univ of Cant MA 65. St Jo Coll Auckld NZ Bd of Th Stud LTh (1st cl) 65. **d** 65 Bp McKenzie for Wel **p** 66 Wel. C of Karori 65-71; V of Wanganui Par Distr 71-75; Chap Univ of Vic Wel 75-77; V of Miramar Dio Wel from 77. *89 Miramer Avenue, Wellington, NZ,* (888-640)

PETHER, Richard John. Wollaston Coll W Austr ACT ThL 65. **d** and **p** 65 Perth. C of Mt Hawthorn 65-66; P-in-c of Osborne Pk 66-68; Mt Newman 68-70; Perm to Offic Dio Perth 70-74; Chap Miss to Seamen Portland 76-77; Perm to Offic Dio Perth from 80. *3 Christie Court, Wanneroo, W Australia 6065.* (405-1346)

PETHYBRIDGE, Richard Hamlin. Ridley Coll Melb ACT ThL 30. **d** 30 **p** 32 Bend. C of All SS Pro-Cathl Bend 31-32; V of Long Gully 32-33; Home Sec CMS Melb 33-34; R of Cullenswood 34-40; Scottsdale 40-42; V of Yallourn 42-43; R 43-45; Northcote 45-56; Min of Springvale 56-59; I of Port Melb 59-61; Angl Prov Immigration Chap 61-69. *5 Chadree Court, Dingley, Vic, Australia 3172.* (551 2189)

PETITE, Robert. b 46. Univ of Tor BA 69. Trin Coll Ont MDiv 72. **d** 71 Bp Arnold for NS **p** 72 NS. C of All SS Cathl Halifax 72-75; Chap Delhousie Univ Halifax from 75. *1663 Oxford Street, Halifax, NS, Canada.* (423-2811)

PETITPIERRE, (Robert) Max Charles. b 03. Late Postmaster of Mert Coll Ox BA 24, 3rd cl Nat Sc 25, MA 32. St Paul's Coll Burgh 25. **d** 27 Buckingham for Ox for St D **p** 28 St D. Chap and Tutor of S Wales and Mon Tr Coll Carmarthen 27-30; Chap and Lect Bede Coll Dur and L to Offic Dio Dur 30-35; V of St Giles Nor 35-40; Chap St Aug Lodge Lady Lane Nor 39-40; Chap Toc H Lon 40-44; LPr Dio Lon 42-47; Warden of St Anne's Ho Soho 44-47; M OSB from 48; L to Offic Dio Ox from 54. *Nashdom Abbey, Slough, SL1 8NL.* (Burnham 3176)

PETO, Ven Cyril Henry Gilbert. d 37 **p** 38 Alg. C-in-c of Murillo 37-41; R of Parry Sound Dio Alg 41-43 and 46-67; CF (Canad) 43-46; Archd of Muskoka 57-66; Archd (Emer) from 67. *Apt 506, 22a Belvedere Avenue, Parry Sound, Ont, Canada.*

PETRIE, Albert Leslie. Hur Coll Dipl Th 69. **d** 69 Hur for Fred. C of Restigouche 69-70; I 70-72; R of Stanley 72-76; Simonds Dio Fred from 76. *Upper Loch Lomond, RR5, NB, Canada*

PETRIE, Alistair Philip. b 50. Univ of Lon Dipl Th (Extra-Mural Stud) 76. Oak Hill Th Coll 73. **d** 76 **p** 77 York. C of Eston w Normanby 76-79; C-in-c of Prestwick 79-81; R 81-82; I of Brentwood Mem Chap Dio BC from 82. *Brentwood Memorial Chapel, 792 Sea Drive, Brentwood Bay, Victoria, BC, Canada.*

PETT, Douglas Ellory. b 24. Univ of Lon BA 46, BD 48, AKC 48, PhD 74. St Bonif Coll Warm 48. **d** 49 **p** 50 Chelmsf. C of Prittlewell 49-54; C of St Mary de Lode Min Can Glouc Cathl and Publ Pr Dio Glouc 54-58; Sacr 55-58; St Mich Ches Square 58-61; V of St Gulval 61-66; Chap St Mary's Hosp Paddington from 66. *28 Warrington Crescent, W9 1EL.* (01-289 1195)

PETTENGELL, Ernest Terence. b 43. K Coll Lon and Warm. **d** 69 **p** 70 Ox. C of Chesham 69-72; Farnborough Hants 72-75; Asst Master K Alfred Sch Burnham-on-Sea 75-78; C of Bp's Cleeve 78-80; P-in-c of Shipton Moyne and Westonbirt w Lasborough and Chap and Asst Master Westonbirt Sch Dio Glouc from 80. *Rectory, Shipton Moyne, Tetbury, Glos, GL8 8PW.* (Westonbirt 244)

PETTERSEN, Alvyn Lorang. b 51. TCD BA 73. Univ of Dur BA 75, PhD 81. Sarum Wells Th Coll 78. **d** 81 Ely. Chap Clare Coll Cam from 81. *Etheldreda, Chesterton Lane, Cambridge, CB4 3AA.* (0223-311737)

PETTET, Reginald Stanley Thomas. St Barn Coll Adel 41. ACT ThL 43. **d** and **p** 43 Adel. C of St Columba Hawthorn 43-44; P-in-c of Millicent 44-48; R of The Burra 48-53; P-in-c of Angaston 53-54; R 54-56 (all in Dio Adel) V of Edlington w Wispington and R of Thimbleby Dio Linc 56-59; P-in-c of Woodville Gardens 59-63; Dioc Sec SPCK from 60; R of Mt Barker 63-68; Henley Beach 68-72; L to Offic Dio Adel from 72. *11 Cambridge Avenue, West Beach, S Australia 5024.* (356 1220)

PETTETT, David Bramwell. d 78 Syd. C of Leichhardt Dio Syd from 78. *11/35 Lilyfield Road, Leichhardt, NSW, Australia 2040.*

PETTIFER, Bryan George Ernest. b 32. Qu Coll Cam BA 55, MA 59. Ridley Hall Cam 57. **d** 59 **p** 60 Sheff. C of Attercliffe w Carbrook Sheff 59-61; Ecclesall Sheff 61-65; Chap and Lect Bath Tech Coll 65-74; Dioc Adult Educn Officer Dio Bris 75-80; Perm to Offic Dio B & W from 80; Dir of Pastoral Th Sarum Wells Th Coll from 80. *19a The Close, Salisbury, Wilts, SP1 2EE.* (Sarum 332235)

PETTIFER, John Barrie. b 38. Linc Th Coll 63. **d** 65 **p** 66 Man. C of St Matt Stretford 65-67; Stand 67-71; V of H Trin Littleborough Dio Man from 71. *Littleborough Vicarage, Manchester.* (Littleborough 78334)

PETTIFER, Leslie Stuart. b 15. Ridley Hall Cam 65. **d** 67 Win **p** 68 Southn for Win. C of Ringwood 67-70; R of Knights Enham w Smannell 70-74; Smannell w Enham Alamein 74-80. *Holmesley, Hillside, Colyton, E Devon.*

PETTIFOR, David Thomas. b 42. Ripon Coll Cudd 78. **d** 81 Cov. C of Binley Dio Cov from 81. *3 Tysoe Croft, Binley, Coventry, CV3 2FF.*

PETTIGREW, James Askey. Moore Th Coll Syd ACT ThL 65. **d** 65 **p** 66 Syd. C of Ryde 66-67; Liverpool 67-70; Randwick 70-72; C-in-c of Provisional Par The Oaks 72-74; R 74-77; Condoblin 77-80; Concord and Burwood Dio Syd from 80. *17 Burton Street, Concord, NSW, Australia 2137.* (747-4483)

PETTIGREW, Stanley. b 27. Trin Coll Dub BA 49, MA 62. **d** 50 **p** 51 Down. C of Newc 50-53; Clontarf 53-57; I of Derralossary 57-62; R of Wicklow w Killiskey Dio Glendal from 62. *Rectory, Wicklow, Irish Republic.* (Wicklow 2132)

PETTIT, Archibald Benjamin. b 06. Worc Ordin Coll 63. **d** 65 **p** 66 Leic. C of Lutterworth 65-68; Oadby 68-69; V of Whitwick w Thringstone 69-77. *18 Rockville Drive, Embsay, Skipton, N Yorks.*

PETTIT, Arthur George Lifton. St D Coll Lamp BA 29. Jes Coll Ox BA (Th) 31, MA 35. St Steph Ho Ox 32. **d** 32 **p** 33 St D. C of Llanelly 32-38; V of Rhosmarket 28-48; R of Bosherston w St Twynnells 48-50; Remenham 50-75; Exam Chap to Bp of St D 49-50. *13 Merlin Close, Tenby, Dyfed.*

PETTIT, Dennis Sidney Jack. b 1897. Linc Th Coll 41. **d** 43 **p** 44 Pet. C of Duston 43-47; V of Spratton 47-68; Hon C of Duston 68-76; Perm to Offic Dio Nor from 80. *Address temp unknown.*

PETTITT, Donald. b 09. Bps' Coll Cheshunt, 57. **d** 57 **p** 58 Nor. R of Ickburgh 57-62; C-in-c of Cranwich w Didlington and Colveston 57-62; R of Ashby w Thurton Claxton and Carleton 62-69; V of Worstead w Westwick and Sloley 69-78. *Arbor Road, Cromer, Norf.* (Cromer 512539)

PETTITT, Maurice. b 13. Clare Coll Cam BA 35, MA 57. Mus Bac 37. Lich Th Coll. **d** 57 **p** 58 Pet. Asst Chap Wellingborough Sch 57-62; C-in-c of Welbury 62-63; R of W and

E Rounton (w Welbury from 63) 62-69; V of Riccall 69-78; RD of Escrick 73-78. *Holbeck House, Lastingham, York.* (Lastingham 517)

PETTITT, Mervyn Francis. b 39. Qu Coll Birm Dipl Th 66. **d** 66 Barking for Chelmsf **p** 67 Chelmsf. C of St Jas w All SS St Nich and St Runwald Colchester 66-69; Loughton 69-72; R of Downham (w S Hanningfield from 78) Dio Chelmsf from 72; P-in-c of S Hanningfield 77-78. *Downham Rectory, Billericay, Essex.* (Basildon 710370)

PETTITT, Simon. b 50. Univ of Nottm BTh 74. Kelham Th Coll 70. **d** 75 **p** 76 Pontefract for Wakef. C of Penistone (w Midhope to 76) 75-78; Youth Officer Dio Wakef 77-80; Dioc Schs Officer and P-in-c of Hintlesham w Chattisham Dio St E from 80. *Hintlesham Rectory, Ipswich, Suff.* (Hintlesham 258)

PETTY, Brian. b 34. St Aid Coll 59. **d** 62 **p** 63 Lich. C of Meole Brace 62-65; Chap RAF 65-69; C of St Paul Ipswich Brisb 69-70; R of Heyfield Gippsld 70-75; P-in-c of Kimbolton w Middleton-on-the-Hill and Hamnish 75-79; Pudleston-cum-Whyle w Hatfield Docklow, Stoke Prior and Humber 76-79; P-in-c of Haddenham Dio Ely 79-80; V from 80. *Haddenham Vicarage, Ely, Cambs.* (Ely 740309)

PETTY, John Fitzmaurice. b 35. Trin Hall Cam BA (Mech Sc) 59, MA 65. Cudd Coll 64. **d** 66 **p** 67 Sheff. C of St Cuthb Firvale Sheff 66-69; St Helier S'wark 69-75; V of Hurst Dio Man from 76. *Hurst Vicarage, Ashton-under-Lyne, Gtr Man, OL6 8EZ.* (061-330 1935)

PEUBA, Robin Kora. Newton Coll Dogura 69. **d** 71 **p** 72 Bp Ambo for Papua. P Dio Papua 71-77; Dio New Guinea Is from 78. *Anglican Church, PB Sag Sag, Kimbe, Papua New Guinea.*

PEVERLEY, William Robinson. b 09. AKC 47. **d** 47 **p** 48 S'wark. C of St Cath Hatcham 47-50; Abbots Langley 50-54; C-in-c of Bolnhurst of Colmworth of Ravensden and of Wilden 54-57; R of Wilden w Colmworth and Ravensden 57-62; V of St Matt Oxhey 62-76. *41 Priory Gardens, Usk, Gwent.* (Usk 2159)

PEYTON, Nigel. b 51. Univ of Edin MA 73. Edin Th Coll BD 76. U Th Sem NY STM 77. **d** 76. **p** 77 Brech. Chap St Paul's Cathl Dundee 76-82; Dioc Youth Chap Dio Brech from 76; Chap of Invergowrie Dio Brech 79-82; P-in-c from 82. *All Souls Church, Main Street, Invergowrie, Dundee, DD2 5AG.* (Invergowrie 525)

PEYTON, Noel Christopher. Univ of Sask BA 59, B Educn 65. Em Coll Sktn LTh 59. **d** 59 **p** 60 Sask. I of Macdowall 59-63; Asst Chap Ashbury Coll Ott 65-66; Perm to Offic Dio Ott from 72. *11 Wallford Way, Ottawa, Ont., Canada.*

PEYTON JONES, Donald Lewis. b 14. DSC 42. St Bonif Coll Warm 59. **d** 61 **p** 62 Ex. C of Withycombe Raleigh w Exmouth 61-63; V of Salcombe Regis 63-73; Appledore 73-78; C-in-c of Lundy I 73-78; Hon Chap Miss to Seamen Plymouth from 78. *Fort Cottage, Cawsand, Cornw.*

PEZZACK, Margery Marie. b 19. **d** 71 **p** 77 Tor. C of St John York Mills Dio Tor from 71. *224 - 24 The Links Road, Willowdale, Ont., Canada, M2P 1P9.*

PFANKUCH, Canon Lester Edward. Univ of NZ BA 50. NZ Bd of Th Stud LTh 64. **d** 51 **p** 52 Ch Ch. C of Sumner 51-55; Pudsey Dio Bradf 55; Chap CSSM and Scripture U Dio Sing 56-59; Miss at Prov Wellesley and Kedah 59-63; V of Belfast-Styx 63-66; Woolston 66-74; Chap at Twizel 74-76; V of Richmond Dio Nel from 76; Hon Can of Nel from 79. *27 Dorset Street, Richmond, NZ.* (4-8844)

PFITZNER, Errold Prosper. St Barn Coll Adel 38. ACT ThL 40. **d** 40 Bp Thomas for Adel **p** 41 Adel. C of Ch Ch N Adel 40-41; P-in-c of Penola Miss 41-44; M of Bro of St Jo Bapt 44-46; R of St Mark Maylands 46-69; L to Offic Dio Adel from 69. *40 First Avenue, Sefton Park, Adelaide, S Australia 5083.* (44 6145)

PFUKURI, Andrew. **d** 60 **p** 61 Rwanda B. P Dio Rwanda B 60-66; Dio Rwa 66-75; Dio Kiga from 75; Can of Kiga from 74; Dioc Archd of Rwa 74-75; Kiga 75-79; Dir Stanley Smith Bible Coll Gahini from 79. *BP 22, Kigali, Rwanda.*

PHAGO, Edward Methi Joseph. b 02. Univ Coll of Fort Hare BA 53. St Francis Coll Sekhukhuniland 70. **d** 70 **p** 74 Pret. C of St Pet Ga-Rankuwa 70-78; P-in-c of St Pet Witbank Dio Pret from 78. *PO Box 1385, Witbank 1035, S Africa.*

PHAIR, Edgar Nevill. b 15. Trin Coll Dub Downes Pri 37, BA 39, MA 46. **d** 40 **p** 41 Oss. C of Carlow 40-43; Chap RAFVR 43-47; RAF 47-53; I of Clogher 53-60; Preb of Clogh Cathl 55-60; Chap O of St John of Jer from 57; V of St Mildred Addiscombe 60-72; Benenden 72-81; Chap Beneden Hosp from 81. *1 Marling House, Durgates, Wadhurst, E Sussex.* (Wadhurst 3824)

PHAIR, Henry Lloyd. b 17. Trin Coll Dub BA 42. **d** 42 **p** 43 Down. C of St Jas Belf 42-45; C-in-c of Drumlane 45-47; Chap Miss to Seamen Belf 47-48; C-in-c of Mullaghdun 48-51; R of Lissan 51-55; Chap RAF 55-72; V of High Ercall Dio Lich from 76; Rowton Dio Lich from 76. *High Ercall Vicarage, Telford, Salop.* (High Ercall 206)

PHALANE, William Malesela. b 24. **d** 79 Pret. C of St Cypr Pietersburg Dio Pret from 79. *Private Bag 7895, Pietersburg 0700, S Africa.*

PHALO, Arthur. b 25. St Bede's Coll Umtata. **d** 52 **p** 54 St Jo Kaffr. M SSJE. C of Tsolo 53-55; Mt Fletcher 55-59; St Cuthb Dio St John's 59-76. *c/o St Edward's House, 20 Great College Street, SW1P 3QA.*

PHA MU, H Cross Coll Rang. **d** 60 Rang. d Dio Rang 60-70; Dio Pa-an from 70. *St Andrew's Church, Kwambi, Burma.*

PHANG, Andrew See Yin. b 48. **d** 79 **p** 81 W Mal. P Dio W Mal. *c/o 1-A Fair Park, Ipoh, Perak, Malaysia.*

PHARAOH, Douglas William. b 18. Worc Ordin Coll 68. **d** 69 **p** 70 Worc. C of Ch Ch Malvern 69-71; Area Sec to Leprosy Miss 65-68 and 71-72; C-in-c of St Cuthb Bensham, Gateshead 72-73; V of New Seaham 73-76; Wymeswold (and Prestwood w Hoton from 78) 76-80; P-in-c of Grandborough w Willoughby and Flecknoe Dio Cov 80-81; V from 81. *Willoughby Vicarage, Rugby, Warws, CV22 8BX.* (Rugby 890327)

PHAROAH, Donald James. b 05. AKC (2nd cl) 27. **d** 28 Roch **p** 29 Bp King for Roch. C of St Jo Bapt Sevenoaks 28-32; H Trin Lamorbey (in c of Day's Lane Miss) 32-33; St Andr Deal 33-39; V of St Greg Gt Cant 39-57; Chap St Jo Hosp Cant 39-57; RD of Cant 51-57; V of Headcorn 57-71. *5 Springshaw Close, Bessels Green, Sevenoaks.* (Sevenoaks 56542)

PHATLANE, Levi Phadima. St Pet Coll Rosettenville, 35. **d** 38 **p** 39 Pret. P Dio Pret 38-48; L to Offic Dio Johann 67-74; Dio Pret from 74. *PO Box 1, Atteridgeville 0008, S Africa.*

PHEELY, William Rattray. Edin Th Coll 57. **d** 60 **p** 61 Glas. C of St Mary's Cathl Glas 60-63; St Martin Sarum 63-66; St Phil Georgetown Guy 66-67; R of Suddie w Queenstown 67-70; V of Enmore 70-72; Port Mourant 72-73; St Phil Georgetn Dio Guy from 73. *St Philip's Vicarage, Georgetown, Guyana.* (02-65638)

PHEIFFER, John Leslie. b 18. Wells Th Coll. **d** 67 Lon **p** 68 Willesden for Lon. C of Northwood Hills Pinner 67-69; Chap Twickenham Prep Sch 69-71; C of Chobham w Valley End 71-76; Highcliffe 76-79; V of St Denys's Southn Dio Win from 79. *St Denys Vicarage, Abbotts Way, Highfield, Southampton.* (Southampton 557786)

PHELAN, Frederick James Lawrence. b 44. Edin Dioc tr for Min 77. **d** 81 **p** 82 Edin. C of St John Jedburgh Dio Edin from 81. *Ancrum Craig Cottage, Jedburgh, Roxburghshire.*

PHELANE, Howard Neo. b 55. St Bede's Coll Umtata 79. **d** 80 St John's. d Dio St John's. *St Bede's College, Umtata, Transkei.*

PHELPS, Arthur Charles. b 26. St Cath Coll Cam BA 50, MA 55. Ridley Hall Cam 51. **d** 53 **p** 54 Liv. C of St Lawr Kirkdale 53-56; Rainham Essex 56-60; Min of St Jas Eccles Distr Collier Row Romford 60-66; V 66-75; R of Thorpe Morieux w Preston and Brettenham Dio St E from 75. *The New Rectory, Thorpe Morieux, Bury St Edmunds, Suff, IP30 0NW.* (Cockfield Green 828355)

PHELPS, Ian James. b 29. Oak Hill Th Coll 53. **d** 56 **p** 57 S'wark. C of St Mary Magd Peckham 56-59; V of S Croxton w Gaddesby 59-67; R of Beeby 59-67; CF (TA) 60-67; CF (R of O) from 67; Dioc Youth Officer and L to Offic Dio Leic from 67. *1 Weir Lane, Houghton-on-the-Hill, Leics.* (Leicester 416599)

PHELPS, Ian Ronald. b 28. BSc (Zool) (Lon) 53. Univ of Lon PhD 57. FLS 60. Chich Th Coll 57. **d** 59 **p** 60 Chich. C of Good Shepherd Preston 59-61; Sullington and of Storrington 62-64; R of Newtimber w Pyecombe 64-68; V of St Luke Brighton 68-74; Team V of The Resurr Brighton 74-76; V of Peacehaven Dio Chich from 76. *41 Bramber Avenue, Peacehaven, E Sussex, Bn9 8HR.* (Peacehaven 3149)

PHENNA, Peter. b 31. ALCD 63. **d** 63 **p** 64 Lon. C of All S Langham Place St Marylebone 63-69; V of St Martin Cam Dio Ely from 69. *Vicarage, Suez Road, Cambridge, CB1 3QD.* (Cambridge 248648)

PHILIP, Peter Wells. b 35. Ridley Hall Cam 64. **d** 67 Stepney for Lon **p** 68 Lon. C of St Mark w St Anne Tollington Pk Holloway 67-70; St Pet Battersea 70-72; Hon C of St Paul Auckld 74; V of Titirangi 74-80; C of Blockhouse Bay Dio Auckld from 80. *14 Hepburn Road, Glen Eden, Auckland 7, NZ.*

PHILIPSON, John Wharton. b 05. **d** 66 **p** 67 Newc T. C of Gosforth 66-79. *1 Otterburn Terrace, Newcastle upon Tyne, NE2 3AP.*

PHILLIP, Rubin. b 47. St Pet Coll Alice CP Dipl Th 71. **d** 71 **p** 72 Natal. C of St Gabr Wentworth 71-77; R of Overport Dio Natal from 77. *Box 37008, Overport, Natal, S Africa.* (88-5090)

PHILLIPS, Anthony Charles Julian. b 36. Univ of Lon BD (1st cl) and AKC (1st cl) 63. G and C Coll Cam PhD 67. St Jo

Coll Ox MA 75, DPhil 80. Coll of the Resurr Mirfield. **d** 66 Huntingdon for Ely **p** 67 Ely. C of Good Shepherd Conv Distr Chesterton Cambs 66-69; Fell, Dean, Chap and Dir of Th Stud Trin Hall Cam 69-74; Hon Chap to Bp of Nor 69-71; Fell and Chap St Jo Coll Ox from 75; Lect Jes Coll Ox from 75; Exam Chap to Bp of Ox from 79; to Bp of Man from 80. *St John's College, Oxford.*

PHILLIPS, Brian Edward Dorian William. b 36. Univ of Bris BA 58. Ripon Hall Ox 58. **d** 60 **p** 61 Heref. C of Ross-on-Wye 60-64; Chap RAF 64-68; C of Fringford 68-73; Chap and Asst Master Howell's Sch Denbigh 73-76; Team V of Cleobury Mortimer w Hopton Wafers 76-80; V of Dixton w Wyesham Dio Heref from 80. *Dixton Vicarage, Gwent.*

PHILLIPS, Brian Robert. b 31. Clare Coll Cam BA 53, MA 57. Linc Th Coll 54. **d** 56 **p** 57 Glouc. C of St Barn Tuffley 56-59; Southgate 59-62; R of Luckington w Alderton 62-69; V of Highworth w Sevenhampton, Hannington, and Inglesham Dio Bris from 69. *Highworth Vicarage, Swindon, Wilts.* (Highworth 762206)

PHILLIPS, Charles. **d** 61 **p** 62 Gippsld. Hon C of Bairnsdale 61-66; R of Lakes Entrance 66-76; Perm to Offic Dio Gippsld from 76. *Box 565, Bairnsdale, Vic, Australia 3875.*

PHILLIPS, Christopher George. b 49. Barrington Coll RI, USA BA 73. Sarum Wells Th Coll 73. **d** 75 Bris. C of Southmead Dio Bris from 75. *182a Ullswater Road, Southmead, Bristol.*

PHILLIPS, David Elwyn. **d** 64 Bp Hughes for Llan **p** 65 Llan. C of Ferndale 64-68; Port Talbot 68-70; V of Abercanaid Dio Llan from 70. *St Peter's Vicarage, Abercanaid, Merthyr Tydfil, Mid Glam.* (Ynysowen 247)

PHILLIPS, Donald David. b 54. Univ of W Ont BSc 76, MSc 78. Hur Th Coll Lon Ont MDiv 81. **d** 81 Athab. Perm to Offic Dio Athab from 81. *c/o Diocese of Athabasca, Synod Office, Box 279, Peace River, Alta, Canada, T0H 2X0.*

PHILLIPS, Duncan Laybourne. b 08. Wycl Hall Ox 45. **d** 47 **p** 48 Bradf. C of Keighley 47-49; C-in-c of St Pet Keighley 49-51; V of Morval 51-57; Chap HM Pris Wandsworth 57-66; Camp Hill 66-67; Albany IW 67-69; V of Eye (w Croft w Yarpole and Lucton from 73) 69-81; C-in-c of Croft w Yarpole and Lucton 69-73; L to Offic Dio Heref from 81. *82 Westcroft, Leominster, Herefs.* (0568-3564)

PHILLIPS, Edward Leigh. b 12. St Edm Hall Ox BA 34, MA 47. Wycl Hall Ox 33. **d** 35 **p** 36 Glouc. Asst Chap Dean Close School Cheltm 35-37; C of Highfield 37-38; C-in-c of Ch K Conv Distr Patcham 39-41; CF (EC) 41-46; V of Ide Hill 46-49; Moulsecoomb 49-52; Kingston w Iford (and Rodmell from 75) 52-78; RD of Lewes 65-77. *35 Woodland Green, Upton St Leonards, Gloucester, GL4 8BD.*

PHILLIPS, Eric Lionel. **d** 51 **p** 52 Tas. P-in-c of Sheffield 51-55; R of Buckland 55-58; Channel 58-61; Cygnet 61-64 and 66-69; New Norf 64-65; L to Offic Dio Tas 65-66; and from 70. *1 Danina Street, Chigwell, Tasmania 7011.*

PHILLIPS, Frank Austin. b 43. Canberra Coll of Min ThDip 79. **d** and **p** 79 C & Goulb. C of Kambah 79-80; R of Koorawatha Dio C & Goulb from 81. *St James' Rectory, Greenethorpe, NSW, Australia 2809.*

PHILLIPS, Canon Frederick Wallace. b 12. Univ of Wales BA 34, MC 43. St Mich Coll Llan 34. **d** 36 Llan **p** 37 Swan B for Llan. C of Fochriw and Deri 36-38; Roath 38-40; CF (EC) 40-46; C of Ch Ch Epsom 46-47; R of Harrietsham 47-56; V of Faversham 56-64; RD of Ospringe 56-64; Thanet 64-74; V of Margate 64-74; Hon Can of Cant from 66; R of Smarden Dio Cant from 74; Biddenden Dio Cant from 80. *Rectory, Smarden, Kent, TN27 8ND.* (Smarden 313)

PHILLIPS, Canon Geoffrey John. b 23. BNC Ox BA 47, MA 56. Ridley Hall Cam 54. **d** 56 **p** 57 Pet. C of St Andr Kettering 56-59; Tideswell 59-62; Chap Miss to Seamen Colom 62-65; R of Gillingham w Geldeston and Stockton 65-70; V of Eaton 70-81; RD of Nor S 71-81; Hon Can of Nor Cathl from 78; Chap Ch Ch Vienna w Prague and Budapest Dio Gibr in Eur from 81. *Jauresgasse 17, 1030 Vienna, Austria.*

PHILLIPS, Ven George Edward. St Jo Coll Manit LTh 32, Hon DD 67. **d** 32 **p** 33 Bran. C of Roblin 32-34; R of Shoal Lake 34-37; St Patr Winnipeg 37-61; Chap RCAF 42-45; Archd of Selkirk 58-66; Winnipeg 66-67; Archd (Emer) from 67; R of Charleswood (St Mary Charleswood Winnipeg from 67) 61-71; Headingley 67-71; P-in-c of Woodlands 71-72. *201 Robindale Road, Winnipeg 20, Manit., Canada.*

PHILLIPS, George William. Ridley Coll Melb ACT ThL 49. **d** 50 **p** 51 Melb. C of St Mark Camberwell 50; Ivanhoe 50-52; I of Bacchus Marsh 52-57; Min of Melton 54-57; I of Yarraville 57-65; Min of Mulgrave 65-72; Glen Waverley 65-72; I 72-78; St Mary Caulfield Dio Melb from 78. *4 Hood Crescent, Caulfield, Vic, Australia 3161.* (528 5541)

PHILLIPS, Gordon Joshua. b 14. St D Coll Lamp BA 36. Ely Th Coll 36. **d** 38 Llan **p** 39 Ban for Llan. C of Glyntaff 38-46; St Mich AA N Kens 46-56; PC of St Mary Virg Isleworth Dio Lon 56-68; V from 68. *St Mary The Virgin Vicarage, Bridge Road, Isleworth, Middx.* (01-560 6166)

PHILLIPS, Gordon Lewis. b 11. Late Scho and Exhib of BNC Ox BA (1st cl Lit Hum) 33, 3rd cl Th 35, MA 37. Kelham Th Coll 35. **d** 37 **p** 38 Mon. C of St Julian Newport 37-40; R of Northolt 40-55; Chap Univ of Lon 55-68; R of Bloomsbury 56-68; Exam Chap to Bp of St Alb 57-68; Preb of St Paul's Cathl Lon 60-68; Proc Conv Lon 60-65; Commiss SW Tang 62-68; Select Pr Univ of Cam 63; Univ of Ox 64-65; Dean and V of Llan 68-71; Chap Luxembourg 72-74. *Ty Cornel, Cilycwm, Llanymddyfri, Dyfed.*

PHILLIPS, Gwilym Caswallon Howell. b 07. Bro of St Paul Bardfield 30. **d** 32 **p** 33 Waik. C of St Pet Cathl Hamilton 32-35; V of All SS Uruti 35-37; C of Gore 37-38; Chap Buckingham Coll Harrow 38-39; Perm to Offic at Roos Yorks 39-40; C of H Ap Charlton Kings 41-44; All SS Bromsgrove 44-45; St Sav Luton 45-48; V of Stotfold 48-61; Evenley 61-72. *1 The Glebe, Flore, Northampton, NN7 4LX.* (Weedon 40423)

PHILLIPS, Harvey Royden. b 18. Clifton Th Coll 40. **d** 42 **p** 43 Portsm. C of H Trin Fareham 42-45; Newbury 45-46; Actg C of Newquay 46-47; CF 47-51; V of Clawton 51-54; V of Tetcott w Luffincott 51-54; SPCK Port Chap Southn 54-58; V of St Jo Bapt w Winnall Win 58-62; Dioc Insp of Schs 59-62; Chap Kuwait 62-66; V of Townstal w St Sav Dartmouth Dio 66-78; St Petrox (w St Barn to 75) Dartmouth 66-78; P-in-c of Shaldon Dio Ex from 78. *Vicarage, Shaldon, Teignmouth, Devon.* (Shaldon 2396)

PHILLIPS, Henry Gordon. **d** 60 **p** 61 Ont. I of Leeds Rear 60-62; Columb Coast Miss BC 62-63; Atikokan 63-67. *413 Amethyst Crescent, Thunder Bay, Ont., Canada.* (807-577 2990)

PHILLIPS, Horace George. b 38. Univ of Man BA (2nd cl French) 60. Univ of Birm Dipl Th 62. Qu Coll Birm 60. **d** 62 Tewkesbury for Cant **p** 63 Glouc. C of Wotton-St Mary-Without 62-65; Standish w Hardwicke and Haresfield 65-68; Cirencester (in c of Watermoor) Glouc 68-74; V of St Jo Evang Churchdown 74-79; P-in-c of Beckford w Ashton-under-Hill Dio Glouc from 79. *Vicarage, Beckford, Tewkesbury, Glos, GL20 7AD.* (Evesham 881380)

PHILLIPS, Canon Ivor. St D Coll Lamp BA 39. St Mich Coll Llan 40. **d** 41 **p** 42 St A. C of Denbigh 41-51; V of Llanarmon-yn-Ial (w Erryrys Mold from 55) 51-64; R of Corwen (w Llangar from 66) Dio St A from 64; Can of St A Cathl from 81; RD of Edeynnion from 81. *Rectory, Corwen, Clwyd.* (Corwen 2322)

PHILLIPS, Ivor Lloyd. b 04. Univ of Wales BSc 25. MC 45. St Mich coll Llan 30. 1 31 Mon **p** 32 Llan for Mon. C of Machen 31-34; St Jo Evang Maindee 34-39; CF (R of O) 39-46; Men in Disp 45; Hon CF 46; V of Pontnewynydd 46-49; St Paul Newport 49-65; CF (TA) 49-55; Hon Can of Mon 56-62; Can 62-73; Warden of Ordinands 62-73; Archd of Newport 64-73; R of Tredunnoc w Kemeys Inferior and Llantrisant 65-73. *2 Pier House, Crackwell Street, Tenby, Dyfed.*

PHILLIPS, Ivor Lynn. b 44. Univ of Leeds BA 70. Cudd Coll Ox 69. **d** 71 **p** 72 Llan. C of Bedlinog and Trelewis 71-73; Roath 73-77; Team V of Wolverhampton 77-81. *Address temp unknown.*

PHILLIPS, Jack Leslie Lawton. b 46. St Mich Ho Crafers 73. **d** 75 Brisb for Perth **p** 76 Bp Holland for Perth. C of Girrawheen 75-77; Broken Hill 77-79; P-in-c of Coleambally and Darlington Point Dio River from 79. *Rectory, Coleambally, NSW, Australia 2707.* (544164)

PHILLIPS, Canon John Bertram. b 06. Em Coll Cam 3rd cl Cl Trip pt i 26, BA (2nd cl Engl Trip pt i) 27, MA 33. DD (Lambeth) 66. Hon DLitt (Ex) 70. Ridley Hall Cam 28. **d** 30 Barking for Roch **p** 30 Roch. C of St Jo Evang Penge 30-33; St Marg Lee 36-40; V of Good Shepherd Lee 40-44; St Jo Evang Redhill 45-55; Perm to Offic Dio Sarum 55-64; Wiccamical Preb of Exceit in Chich Cathl 57-60; Can and Preb of Torleton in Sarum Cathl 64-70; Can (Emer) from 70. *17 Gannett's Park, Swanage, Dorset.* (Swanage 3122)

PHILLIPS, John Freeman. b 14. K Coll Lon BSc 38. Bps' Coll Cheshunt 58. **d** 60 **p** 61 Heref. Hon C of Welsh Newton w Llanrothal 60-73; Perm to Offic Dio Mon 61-75; Dio S'wark 75-80; Dio St D from 80. *20 Merlins Hill, Haverfordwest, Dyfed, SA61 1PQ.* (0437-2071)

✠ **PHILLIPS, Right Rev John Henry Lawrence.** b 10. Trin Hall Cam BA 32, MA 37. DD (Lambeth) 60. Ridley Hall Cam 32. **d** 34 **p** 35 Ripon. C of Ch Ch Harrogate 34-35; Methley 35-38; R of Farnley 38-45; Surr 39-45; Chap RNVR 42-45; Dir of Service Ordin Cands 45-48; Gen Sec CACTM 48-49; Archd of Nottm 49-60; V of Radcliffe-on-Trent 49-57; V of Shelford 49-57; C-in-c of Clifton w Glapton 58-60; Chap to HM the Queen 59-60; Cons Ld Bp of Portsm in Westmr Abbey 25 Mar 60 by Abp of Cant; Bps of Lon; Win; Ely; Heref; B & W; Chich; Nor; St E; Chelmsf; Leic; Pet; and Wakef; Bps Suffr of Kens; Fulham; Tonbridge; Barking; and Whitby; and Bps Cowdry; Carpenter-Garnier; Kitching;

Simpson; Wand; Robin; Cockin; Chase; Bayne; and Craske; Abp of Utrecht; and Bp of Deventer; res 75; C-in-c of W and E Lulworth 75-79; Perm to Offic Dio St E from 79. *Highlands, Harkstead, Ipswich, Suffolk.* (Holbrook 328261)

PHILLIPS, John William. b 47. Univ of Tor BA 73. Wycl Coll Tor MDiv 78. **d** 80 Bp Read for Tor **p** 81 Bp Tonks for Tor. C of All SS Kingsway Dio Tor from 80. *2850 Bloor Street W, Toronto, Ont, Canada, M8X 2N1.*

PHILLIPS, John William Burbidge. b 39. Univ of Dur BSc 60. BD (2nd cl) Lon 68. Tyndale Hall, Bris 65. **d** 68 Pet **p** 69 Bp Graham-Campbell for Pet. C of Barton Seagrave 68-71; C of All SS Northn 71-75; R of Irthlingborough Dio Pet from 75. *Irthlingborough Rectory, Wellingborough, Northants, NN9 5TY.* (Wellingboro' 650278)

PHILLIPS, Joseph Benedict. b 11. **d** 37 **p** 38 RC Bp of Nottm. Rec into Angl Commun 43 by Bp of Linc. C of Lambeth 47-50; St Jo Bapt Woking (in c of H Trin Knaphill) 50-53; V of St Jas Burton 53-59; St Andr Listerhills Bradf 59-66. *100 Ruskin Avenue, Lincoln, LN2 4BT.*

PHILLIPS, Kenneth John. b 37. Coll of Resurr Mirfield 67. **d** 67 **p** 68 Blackb. C of St Jas Blackb 67-69; P-in-c of St Chris Conv Distr Lea Dio Blackb 70-80; V from 80. *848 Blackpool Road, Lea, Preston, PR2 1XL.* (Preston 729716)

PHILLIPS, Lamont Wellington Sanderson. b 33. SOC 73. **d** 76 **p** 78 Edmon for Lon. C of St Paul tottenham Dio Lon from 76. *63 Bruce Castle Road, N17 8NL.*

PHILLIPS, Laurence George. Wycl Coll Tor. **d** 43 Bp Beverley for Niag **p** 44 Niag. C of Ch of Ascen Hamilton 43-44; Chap CASF 44-46; I of Harriston w Farewell 46-47; P-in-c of St Andr Thistletown Tor 59-67; R 67-69; P-in-c of Bridgenorth 69-73; on leave 73-76; Hon C of Shelburne Dio Niag from 80. *Box 967, Shelburne, Ont., Canada.* (519-925 3503)

PHILLIPS, Martin Nicolas. b 32. Em Coll Cam 3rd cl Th Trip pt i 55, BA (3rd cl Th Trip pt ii) 57, MA 61. Linc Th Coll 57. **d** 59 Leic **p** 60 Bp Maxwell for Leic. C of St Luke Conv Distr Stocking Farm Leic 59-63; V of St Silas Sheff 63-71; Birstall Dio Leic from 72; Wanlip Dio Leic from 72. *Birstall Vicarage, Birstall Road, Birstall, Leicester.* (Leicester 674517)

PHILLIPS, Michael. St Pet Coll Alice 71. **d** 73 **p** 74 Port Eliz. C of Ch the King Port Eliz 73-76; Namaqualand 76-78; R of Ch K Port Eliz 78-80; Namaqualand Dio Capetn from 80. *Box 12, O'okiep 8270, CP, S Africa.*

PHILLIPS, Michael John. b 54. Council for Nat Acad Awards BA (Law) 77. Sarum Wells Th Coll 78. **d** 81 Swan B. C of Killay Dio Swan B from 81. *79 Ashgrove, Killay, Swansea, W Glam.* (0792-206631)

PHILLIPS, Owen Henry. ACT 53. **d** 53 **p** 54 Centr Tang. Miss Dio Centr Tang 53-55; LPr Dio Natal 55-56; C of St Paul Durban 56-59; P-in-c of The Bluff 59-61; St Paul Durban 62-64; R of St Pet Pmbg 64-76; Commiss Centr Tang from 70; R of Drakensberg Dio Natal from 76. *Box 21, Himeville, Natal, S Africa.* (Himeville 13)

PHILLIPS, Patrick Noble Stowell. b 22. Univ of Edin MA (Geog) 50. ALCD 52. **d** 52 Roch for Cant **p** 53 Niger. Tutor St Mark's Coll Awka 52-54; St Paul's Coll Awka 54-55; C of Mossley Hill Dio Liv 55-56; R of Milverton Dio Hur 56-60; Prin Angl Gr Sch Benin 60-63; R of Moresby 63-66; Mapleton Rupld 66-71; Arthuret Dio Carl from 71. *Arthuret Rectory, Netherby Road, Longtown, Carlisle, CA6 5NT.* (Longtown 791338)

PHILLIPS, Percy Graham. b 26. St Aid Coll 46. **d** 51 **p** 52 Ches. C of Wallasey 51-54; Thrybergh 54-58; St Mich du Valle Guernsey 58-60; V of Heytesbury w Tytherinton and Knook 60-65; St Mich Stonebridge Willesden 65-70; Vernham Dean w Linkenholt R 70-78; C of Farnham Dio Guildf from 78. *6 High Park Road, Farnham, Surrey, GU9 7JL.* (Farnham 722514)

PHILLIPS, Peter. b 26. Oak Hill Th Coll 63. **d** 65 **p** 66 Chich. C of All S Eastbourne 65-69; St Paul St Alb 69-73; V of Riseley (w Bletsoe from 79) Dio St Alb from 73. *Riseley Vicarage, Church Lane, Riseley, Bedford.* (Riseley 234)

PHILLIPS, Raymond Arthur. b 29. K Coll Lon and Warm 49. **d** 53 **p** 54 Lon. C of St Aug w St Phil Stepney 53-56; Asst P at Kitwe 56-61; P-in-c of Chipili 61-65; R of Broken Hill Zam 65-68; V of St Faith w St Matthias and All SS Stoke Newington 68-73; R of Sangre Grande 73-80; V of All SS Hillingdon Dio Lon from 80. *Vicarage, Ryefield Avenue, Hillingdon, Uxbridge, Middx.* (Uxbridge 33991)

PHILLIPS, Canon Rees William Hippesley. b 12. Late Exhib of Jes Coll Ox 3rd cl Cl Mods 33, BA (2nd cl Lit Hum) 35, 2nd cl Th 36, MA 38. Cudd Coll 36. **d** 37 **p** 38 Ely. C of St Giles w St Pet Cam 37-39; Clee w Cleethorpes 39-41; Chap of Rugby Sch 41-42; LPr Dio Cov 41-42; C of St Mary Swanley 42-47; Exam Chap to Bp of Mon 44-45; Proc Conv Roch 45-50; Libr Pusey Ho Ox 46-52; L to Offic Dio Ox 47-52; Warden St Jo Sem Lusaka 52-64; R of Outwell 64-73; Can (Emer) of Zam from 65; Exam Chap to Bp of Ely 68-73; Chap to Commun of Epiph 73-77; Subwarden 74-77; Perm to Offic Dio Ox from 77. *107 Bloxham Road, Banbury, Oxon, OX16 9JT.* (Banbury 51765)

PHILLIPS, Richard. b 08. Em Coll Sktn LTh 37. **d** 37 **p** 38 Sktn. C-in-c of Unity 37-39; Asst Chap Mwanza 39-40; Asst Master Arusha European Sch 40-44; CF (E Afr) 44-50; C of Old Radford 50-52; R of Bilsthorpe 52-61; V of St Geo Charlestown 61-70; Prestolee 70-75. *35 Holcombe Crescent, Kearsley, Lancs, BL4 8JX.*

PHILLIPS, Canon Richard William. b 06. Kelham Th Coll 23. **d** 29 **p** 30 Chelmsf. C of Brentwood 29-35; Acomb and St Sampson York 35-36; R of Dunton Waylett 36-38; C-in-c of Wrangbrook Conv Distr 38-43; V of St Pet Barnsley 43-65; Proc Conv Wakef 55-80; V of Womersley 65-81; C-in-c of Kirk Smeaton 65-81; Dep Prolocutor Lower Ho of Conv York from 65-81; Can of Wakef from 68. *Marsh End Cottage, Howden, Goole, N Humb, DN14 7DF.*

PHILLIPS, Robin Michael. b 33. K Coll Lon and Warm AKC 58. **d** 59 **p** 60 Lon. C of St Mellitus Hanwell 59-61; St Marg-on-Thames 61-64; Hangleton 64-68; PC (V from 69) of Mellor Dio Derby from 68. *Mellor Vicarage, Stockport, Chesh, SK6 5LX.* (Marple 1203)

PHILLIPS, Roy. KCNS. **d** and **p** 35 NS. C of Ch Ch Dartmouth 35-39; R of Mahone Bay 39-41; CF (Canad) 41-46; R of Seaforth 46-49; Windsor 49-53; Prin of Shingwauk Hall 54-64; I of Petite Rivière 64-72. *2733 Connolly Street, Halifax, NS, Canada.* (454 1165)

PHILLIPS, Stephen. b 38. QUB BA 60. Linc Th Coll 60. **d** 62 **p** 63 Linc. C of Waddington 62-65; Gt Grimsby 65-72; V of Limber Magna w Brocklesby Dio Linc from 72; Kirmington Dio Linc from 72. *Great Limber Vicarage, Grimsby, Lincs.* (Roxton 641)

PHILLIPS, Thomas Wynford. b 15. Univ of Wales BA 37, BD 40. St Mich Coll Llan. **d** 43 **p** 44 St A. C of Shotton 43-46; Rhyl (in c of St John) 46-50; Hall Green 50-52; V of Shustoke w Bentley and C-in-c of Maxstoke 52-55; PC of Clay Cross 55-68; R of Upton Magna 68-73; V of Withington 68-73; R of Roche 73-80; Withiel 73-80; RD of St Austell 76-80. *Brynawelon, Wheal Quoit Avenue, St Agnes, Cornw.*

PHILLIPS, William Jepson. b 13. Late Scho of St D Coll Lamp BA (2nd cl Hist) 37. St Mich Coll Llan 37. **d** 39 Swan B for Llan **p** 40 Llan. C of Treherbert 39-42; All SS Penarth 42-43; CF (EC) 43-47; C of Ton Pentre 47-49; V of St Steph Hampstead 49-63; Asst Master Woodside Secondary Boys Sec Sch Tottenham 63-68; Somerset Boys' Compr Sch Tottenham from 68; Hon C of Ch Ch W Green Tottenham 68-76; Southgate, Dio Lon from 76. *3 Arundel Gardens, Winchmore Hill, N21 3AG.* (01-886 9294)

PHILLIPS, William Thomas. St Mich Coll Llan 50. **d** 51 **p** 52 Llan. C of Merthy-Dyfan w E Barry 51-58; Penarth w Lavernock 58-59; R of Oxwich w Penrice 59-69. *Address temp unknown.*

PHILLIPS, William Ufelgwyn Maundy. b 11. St D Coll Lamp BA 3. **d** 34 **p** 35 Mon. C of St Geo Tredegar 34-37; Aberavon 37-46; C-in-c of St Samson Cardiff 46-53; V of St Sav Roath 51-73; Margam 73-80; Surr 73-80; P-in-c of Llanharry Dio Llan from 81. *1 St Paul's Court, Llandaff, Cardiff.*

PHILLIPS-SMITH, Edward Charles. b 50. AKC 71. St Aug Coll Cant 72. **d** 73 **p** 74 Lich. C of Wolverhampton 73-77; Chap St Pet Colleg Sch Wolverhampton from 77. *32a Lonsdale Road, Penn, Wolverhampton, Staffs.*

PHILLIPSON, Christopher Quintin. b 14. Late Exhib of Ch Coll Cam BA 36, 3rd cl Th Trip pt i 37, MA 40. Ridley Hall Cam 36. **d** 38 Lon **p** 39 Willesden for Lon. C of Ch Ch Turnham Green 38-40; St Ann Stamford Hill 40-44; CMS Miss Dio Luckn 44-54; Chap of St John Sikandra Agra and of Ch Ch Mathura 50-54; V of Southbourne 54-62; R of W Thorney 56-62; Ardingly 62-70; Aldingbourne 70-81. *91 Little Breach, Chichester, Sussex, PO19 4TZ.*

PHILLPOT, Donald John. b 27. St Jo Coll Dur BA (2nd cl Social Stud) 53, Dipl Th 55. **d** 55 **p** 56 Bris. C of Southmead 55-60; Brislington 60-63; V of Dorrington 63-68; R of Stapleton and Asst Dir Dioc Youth Work 63-68; Bridgnorth w Tasley 68-78; C-in-c of Astley Abbotts 68-78; Surr 70-78; V of Lillington Dio Cov from 78; Surr from 81. *Lillington Vicarage, Leamington Spa, Warws, CV32 7RH.* (Leamington Spa 24674)

PHILLPOT, Greig. b 54. ACT ThL 77. St Jo Coll Morpeth 75. **d** 78 **p** 79 Tas. C of Devonport 78-79; Cathl Ch of Tas 79-80; on study leave. *c/o 125 Macquarie Street, Hobart, Tasmania 7000.*

PHILLPOTTS, Joshua Eden. b 29. St Pet Coll Ja 52. **d** 58 **p** 60 Kingston for Ja. C of St Mich Kingston Ja 58-59; Harewood 59-62; R of Manchioneal 62-65; I of Watson Lake 65-70; C of Whitehorse (in c of St Chris Haines Junct) 70-74; I of High Prairie Dio Athab from 75. *Box 1022, High Prairie, Alta, TOG 1EO, Canada.*

PHILP, Very Rev David Edgar Haldon. St Francis Coll Brisb 60. **d** 62 N Queensld. C of Cairns 62-65; Ingham 65-67;

St Matt Mundingburra Townsville 67-69; R of Mirani 69-71; Home Hill 71-74; Mt Isa 74-76; Archd of the West 74-77; Dean and R of St Jas Cathl Townsville Dio N Queensld from 78; Exam Chap to Bp of N Queensld from 78. *Deanery, Cleveland Terrace, Townsville, Queensland, Australia 4810.* (077-712247)

PHILP, Canon Robert Henry Haldon. St Francis Coll Brisb. **d** 59 **p** 60 N Queensld. C of Mt Isa 59-62; R of Hughenden 62-65; C in Dept of Chaps Melb 65-67; R of St Luke Wandal City and Dio Rockptn from 67; Exam Chap to Bp of Rockptn from 69; Hon Can of Rockptn from 71. *Rectory, Wandal, N Queensland, Australia 4700.* (079-2 1971)

PHILPOT, William Thomas Archibald. b 05. Wadh Coll Ox BA 28, MA 34. Ripon Hall Ox 35. **d** 37 Birm **p** 46 Truro. C of Erdington 37; Libr Ripon Hall Ox 39-46; C of St Jo Bapt Penzance 46-48; R of Tregony w St Cuby (and Cornelly from 73) 48-74; Perm to Offic Dio Ox from 74. *21 Chapel Lane, Chalgrove, Oxon, OX9 7RF.*

PHILPOTT, Eric William. St Barn Coll Adel 27. ACT ThL 30. **d** 30 **p** 31 Adel. C of Ch Ch Mt Gambier 30-32; Miss Chap Tailem Bend Miss 32-34; Tatiara Miss 34-36; P-in-c of St John Mt Pleasant 36-44; St Edw Kens Gardens 44-46; R of Ch Ch Balaklava and P-in-c of Owen Miss 46-50; L to Offic Dio Adel 51-56 and from 71; P-in-c of Meadows Miss 58-71; Perm to Offic Dio Murray 71-77. *PO Box 1, Aldgate, S Australia 5154.* (08-339 1851)

PHILPOTT, John David. b 43. Univ of Leic BA (Hist) 64. Trin Coll Bris 69. **d** 72 **p** 73 Ches. C of Knutsford 72-75; Toft 72-75; Bickenhill w Elmdon 75-79; V of St Luke w St Thos City and Dio Birm from 79. *St Luke's Vicarage, Bristol Street, Birmingham, B5 7AY.* (021-622 2435)

PHILPOTT, John Wilfred. b 44. K Coll Lon and Warm BD and AKC 67. **d** 68 **p** 69 Cant. C of St Steph Norbury 68-71; St Mildred Addiscombe 71-75; V of Whitfield w Guston Dio Cant from 75. *Whitfield Vicarage, Dover, Kent, CT16 3EZ.* (Dover 820314)

PHILPOTT, Samuel. b 41. Kelham Th Coll 60. **d** 65 Malmesbury for Bris **p** 66 Bris. C of St Mark Swindon 65-70; Barton 70-73; C-in-c of All SS Exmouth 73-74; V of All SS Exmouth in Withycombe Raleigh Team Min 74-76; V of Shaldon 76-78; P-in-c of St Pet w All SS Plymouth Dio Ex 78-80; V from 80. *23 Wyndham Square, Plymouth, Devon, PL1 5EG.* (Plymouth 62110)

PHILPOTT, Theodore Guy. b 31. Univ of Melb BComm 59. **d** 70 **p** 72 Gippsld. C of St Paul Cathl Sale Gippsld 70-72; Bairnsdale 72-73; R of Omeo 73-76; Heyfield 76-79; Dom Chap to Bp of Gippsld 76-79. *Christ Church, Coonabarabran, NSW, Australia 2857.*

PHILPS, Mark Seymour. b 51. Worc Coll Ox BA 73, MA 78. St Jo Coll Nottm 77. **d** 80 Barking for Chelmsf. C of Chadwell Heath Dio Chelmsf from 80. *3 St Chad's Road, Chadwell Heath, Romford, Essex.*

PHILSON, James Alexander Summers. Edin Th Coll 48. **d** 51 **p** 52 Edin. C of Ch Ch Falkirk 51-53; R of St Mary Dunblane 53-62; Beverley 62-64; Victoria Pk 64-75; Cottesloe Dio Perth from 75. *240 Marmion Street, Cottesloe, W Australia 6011.* (384 8530)

PHIPPS, David John. b 46. Univ of Bris BSc 68. Trin Coll Bris 75. **d** 78 St Germans for Truro. C of St Madron w Morvah 78-80; St Jo Evang Kenilworth Dio Cov from 80. *21 Caesar Road, Kenilworth, Warws, CV8 1DL.*

PHIPPS, Ernest. Em Coll Sktn. **d** 52 **p** 53 Calg. C of Cathl Ch of Redeemer Calg 52-53; I of St Cypr Calg 53-57; Montague Dio Ott from 57. *PO Box 2000, Smith's Falls, Ont., Canada.* (1-613-283-1629)

PHIPPS, Frederick George. Kelham Th Coll 50. **d** 54 **p** 55 Derby. C of Staveley 54-59; St Mary and St Nich Cathl Seoul 59-61; P-in-c of St Andr Onsuri 61-63; St Mich Inchon Korea 63-65; Dom Chap to Bp of Korea 64-65; C of Warrnambool 65-69; V of St Luke w St Steph and St Mark Bal 69-72; R of Natimuk 72-74; Port Fairy Dio Bal from 74. *St John's Rectory, Port Fairy, Vic., Australia 3284.* (055-68 2211)

PHIPPS, John Maclean. b 14. Em Coll Cam 3rd cl Engl Trip pt i 37, BA (3rd cl Th Trip pt i) 38, MA 50. Cudd Coll 38. **d** 39 Ox **p** 40 Dorchester for Ox. C of Banbury 39-41; C-in-c of St Andr Cambois 41-46; C of Newport Pagnell 47-53; V of St Mary Speenhamland Newbury 53-71; Buckland Oxon 71-79; Littleworth 71-79; R of Pusey 71-79. *15 Meadow Close, Farmoor, Oxford.* (Cumnor 2955)

✠ **PHIPPS, Right Rev Simon Wilton.** b 21. MC 45. Trin Coll Cam BA 48, MA 53. Westcott Ho Cam 48. **d** 50 **p** 51 Wakef. C of Huddersfield 50-53; Chap of Trin Coll Cam 53-58; Industr Chap Dio Cov 58-68; C of St Mich Cathl Cov 58-68; Hon Can of Cov 65-68; Cons Ld Bp Suffr of Horsham in S'wark Cathl 25 Apr 68 by Abp of Cant; Bps of Chich; Edin; Cov; Birm; and Leic; Bps Suffr of Lewes; and Tewkesbury; and Bps Hunter and Graham-Campbell; Trld to Linc 75. *Bishops House, Eastgate, Lincoln, LN2 1QQ.* (Linc 34701)

PHIZACKERLEY, Ven Gerald Robert. b 29. Late Exhib of Univ Coll Ox BA (2nd cl Engl) 52, MA 56. Wells Th Coll 52. **d** 54 Penrith for Carl **p** 55 Carl. C of St Barn Carl 54-57; Chap Abingdon Sch 57-64; R of Gaywood w Bawsey and Mintlyn 64-78; RD of Lynn 68-78; Surr 74-78; Hon Can of Nor Cathl 75-78; Archd of Chesterfield from 78; P-in-c of Ashford w Sheldon Dio Derby from 78; Hon Can of Derby Cathl from 78. *Vicarage, Ashford-in-the-Water, Bakewell, Derbys, DE4 1QN.* (Bakewell 2298)

PHOENIX, Harold. b 11. Kelham Th Coll 28. **d** 34 **p** 36 Lich. C of St Jo Evang W Bromwich 34-36; N Ormesby 36-40; Hitchin 40-46; CF (EC) 46-47; V of Willington 47-70; V of Moggerhanger 47-70. *18 West Way, Moggerhanger, Bedford.* (Biggleswade 40250)

PHOOFOLO, Canon Vincent Khobotlo. MBE 64. St Pet Th Coll Rosettenville LTh 55. **d** 55 **p** 56 Basuto. P Dio Basuto 55-66; Dio Les from 66; Can of Les from 66. *Box 11, Mafeteng, Lesotho.* (Mafeteng 288)

PHOTOLO, Benjamin. St Pet Th Coll Rosettenville 59. **d** 61 **p** 62 Johann. P Dio Johann. *Box 192, Orlando, Transvaal, S Africa.*

PHUTSISI, Ephraim. St Pet Th Coll Rosettenville. **d** 51 **p** 52 Bloemf. P Dio Bloemf. *c/o PO Box 9, Thaba 'Nchu, OFS, Africa.*

PHYALL, Albert Thomas. b 02. AKC 31. **d** 31 **p** 32 Lon. C of St Alphage Hendon 31-34; Chap H Cross Retreat Ho Limpsfield 34-36; C of St Andr Willesden Green 36-40; C-in-c of St Paul Paddington 40-44; V of St Anselm Hayes 44-75; Hon C of Ch of the Annunc St Marylebone 75-80; Hon P-in-c of St Jo Bapt Holland Road Kens 79-81; Perm to Offic Dio Lon from 81. *93 Delaware Mansions, Maida Vale, W9.* (01-289 0023)

PHYPERS, David John. b 39. Univ of Leic BA 60. BD (Lon) 65. Linc Th Coll 76. **d** 78 Repton for Derby (APM) **p** 79 Derby. C of Normanton-by-Derby 78-80; St Steph Sinfin Dio Derby from 80. *1 Chesterton Avenue, Sunnyhill, Derby, DE3 7GS.*

PHYSICK, Gregory William Arthur. b 47. York Univ Ont BA 70. Trin Coll Tor MDiv 75. **d** 75 Bp Read for Tor **p** 76 Tor. C of St Clem Eglinton Tor 75-78; R of Dunbarton Dio Tor from 78. *882 Kingston Road, Pickering, Ont, Canada.* (416-839 7907)

PHYTHIAN, Kenneth. d and **p** 59 Moos. I of Malartic 59-60; C of St Matt Cathl Timmins 60-61; R of Landsowne Rear 61-72; on leave. *1350 Windsor Drive, Brockville, Ont, Canada.*

PIACHAUD, Preb François Allen. b 12. Univ of Lon BA (Hons Hist) 32, BD 35. Selw Coll Cam Jun Patteson Stud 35, BA (Th Trip pt ii) 37, MA 41. Westcott Ho Cam 37. **d** 37 **p** 38 Newc T. C of St Osw Walkergate Newc T 37-40; St John Edin 40-44; V of Wrangthorn 44-51; Ch Ch Chelsea Dio Lon from 51; Robt Boyle Lect 53-55; Exam Chap to Bp of Lon 56-73; Dir of Cler Stud Dio Lon 57-64; Preb of St Paul's Cathl Lon from 61; Proc Conv Lon 65-75 and 76-80; Commiss Colom 65-77; RD of Chelsea 74-77. *27 Tite Street, SW 3.* (01-352 5106)

PIASO, Andrew. St Pet Coll Siota 63. **d** 66 **p** 70 Melan. P Dio Melan 66-75; Dio Ysabel 75-76; Dio Centr Melan from 76. *Olevuga, Gela, Solomon Islands.*

PIBWORTH, John David. b 23. OBE 79. Ripon Hall Ox. **d** 61 **p** 62 Win. C of N Stoneham w Bassett 61-66; V of Pennington Dio Win from 66. *Pennington Vicarage, Lymington, Hants.* (Lym 2646)

PICK, William Harry. b 23. Open Univ BA 77. St Aid Coll 51. **d** 54 Warrington for Liv **p** 55 Liv. C of St Geo Wigan 54-57; V of All SS Newton-in-Makerfield 57-67; Stoneycroft 67-79; R of N Meols Dio Liv from 79. *North Meols Rectory, Bankfield Lane, Southport, Mer, PR9 7NJ.* (Southport 28325)

PICKARD, Donald Henry. b 1888. MC 18. K Coll Lon 48. **d** 48 Dover for Cant **p** 49 Cant. C of St Pet Croydon 48-53; V of Leysdown w Harty 53-55; Woodnesborough 55-59; L to Offic Dio Cant from 59. *8 Sheppey Road, Maidstone, Kent.* (Maidstone 43547)

PICKARD, Francis William James. b 21. Worc Ordin Coll 64. **d** 66 **p** 67 Win. C of Shirley 66-68; V of Old Warden 68-73; P-in-c of All SS Caldecote 72-73; Hinxworth w Newnham (and Radwell 73-76) Dio St Alb from 73. *Rectory, Hinxworth, Baldock, Herts.* (Ashwell 2144)

PICKARD, Frank Eustace. b 31. Univ of Lon BSc (Econ) 52. St Cath S Ox BA 56, MA 63. St Steph Ho Ox. **d** 57 **p** 58 Liv. C of Haydock 57-59; Davenham 59-60; Asst Master St Dunstan's Sch Lon 60-63; KS Pet and Hon Min Can of Pet Cathl 63-72; C-in-c (V from 68) of Newborough 67-72; R of Isham w Pytchley 72-76; Abington Dio Pet from 76. *5 Abington Park Crescent, Northampton, NN3 3AD.* (Northampton 31041)

PICKARD, Hedley Arthur Mitchell. b 27. Linc Th Coll 61.

d 63 **p** 64 York. C of H Trin Bridlington 63-66; V of Bempton 66-71; L Hulton 71-75; Chap at Palma Dio Gibr (Gibr in Eur from 80) from 75. *Calle José Villalonga 82, El Terreno, Palma de Mallorca, Spain.* (237279)

✠ **PICKARD, Right Rev Stanley Chapman.** CBE 68. Dorch Miss Coll 33. **d** 37 **p** 38 S'wark. C of St Cath Hatcham 37-39; Kota Kota 39-40; Likoma 40-49; P-in-c of Msumba 49-58; Archd of Msumba 50-58; Exam Chap to Bp of Nyasa 54-58; Cons Ld Bp of Lebom in Cathl Ch of St Michael and St George Grahmstn 23 Nov 58 by Abp of Capetn; Abp of Matab; Bps of Grahmstn; Nyasa; Pret; Geo; Kimb K; Basuto; Natal; Damar; St Jo Kaffr; Bloemf; and Zulu; Asst Bp of Capetn; and Bps Fisher; Paget; and Stainton; res 68; Dean of St Aug Cathl Maciene 58-68; Asst Bp of Johann from 68; Prov Exec Officer 68-72; R of Belgravia Dio Johann from 72. *170 Park Street, Belgravia, Johannesburg, Transvaal, S Africa.* (011-24 1219)

PICKARD, Stephen Kim. b 52. Univ of Newc BComm, BD. St Jo Coll Morpeth 77. **d** and **p** 80 Newc. C of Singleton Dio Newc from 80. *13 Gibson Close, Singleton Heights 2330, NSW, Australia.*

PICKARD, William Priestley. Clifton Th Coll 56. **d** 59 **p** 60 S'wark. C of St Matthias U Tulse Hill 59-63; Asst Warden Shaftesbury Crusade Bris from 63. *21 Rylestone Grove, Stoke Bishop, Bristol 9.* (Bristol 620372)

PICKBURN, Prosper de Mestre. St Jo Coll Morpeth, ACT ThL 29. **d** 32 Goulb **p** 33 Bath for Goulb. C of Cobargo 32; Junee 32-34; Albury 34-37; Binalong 37-40; Canberra 40; C-in-c of Bungendore 40-42; R 46-51; Commiss C and Goulb 51-54; Chap RAAF 42-46; R of Moruya 54-56; Morwell 56-60; Trafalgar 60-61; L to Offic Dio Gippsld from 61. *Morwell, Vic, Australia.*

PICKBURN, Thomas Henry. St Aid Coll Bal 32. St Columb's Hall, Wang 33. ACT ThL 34. **d** 34 **p** 36 Bal. C of Ch Ch Cathl Bal 35-36; P-in-c of Apollo Bay 36-39; Beech Forest 39-50; R of Binda 50-57; C of Young 57-60; R of Yea 60-73; Perm to Offic Dio C & Goulb from 73. *Bimbimbie, Meribula, NSW, Australia 2548.*

PICKEN, James Hugh. b 51. Univ of Vic BMus 75. Ripon Coll Cudd BA (Th) 79. **d** 80 **p** 81 Dur. C of Jarrow Dio Dur from 80. *112 Wansbeck Road, Jarrow, T & W, NE32 5SR.*

PICKEN, William Middlewood Martin. b 06. SS Coll Cam BA 28, MA 32. Westcott Ho Cam 29. **d** 30 **p** 31 Wakef. C of Elland 30-34; St Mary Truro and PV of Truro Cathl 34-37; Hon PV from 37; R of St Martin-by-Looe 37-71. *2 Stratton Terrace, Falmouth, Cornwall*

PICKERILL, Jack Hill. b 09. Kelham Th Coll 32. **d** 38 **p** 39 Lon. C of St Mary Willesden 38-43; LDHM at St Mary Virg E Hounslow 43-49; R of Boulder 49-53; Bruce Rock (and Narembeen to 56) 53-59; Subiaco 60-72; Hosp Chap Dio Perth 72-79; Perm to Offic Dio Perth from 80. *13 Blencowe Street, West Leederville, W Australia 6007.* (381 3659)

PICKERING, David Colville. b 41. Kelham Th Coll 61. **d** 66 **p** 67 Derby. C of St Phil Chaddesden 66-70; New Mills 70-72; Buxton (in c of St Mary) 72-74; V of SS Aug Chesterfield Dio Derby from 74. *Saint Augustine's Vicarage, Chesterfield, S40 3HJ.* (Chesterfield 73942)

PICKERING, Canon David William. Univ of NZ BEng (2nd cl) 59. ACT ThL (1st cl) 60. BD (Lon) 66. **d** 60 **p** 61 Nel. C of Ch Ch Cathl Nel 60-65; V of Murchison 65-66; Chap and Tutor Ch Ch Coll 66-70; V of Spreydon 70-77; Addington 73-77; Blenheim Dio Nel from 77; Hon Can of Ch Ch Cathl 75-77; Exam Chap to Bp of Ch Ch 74-77; Bp of Nel from 77; Hon Can of Nel from 78. *Vicarage, Andrew Street, Blenheim, NZ.* (3909)

PICKERING, Ven Fred. b 19. St Pet Hall Ox BA (3rd cl Phil Pol and Econ) 41, MA 45. St Aid Coll 41. **d** 43 **p** 44 Blackb. C of St Andr Leyland 43-46; Islington 46-48; Sec CPAS (NE Distr) 48-51; V of All SS Burton-on-Trent 51-56; St Jo Evang Carl 56-63; PC of St Cuthb Chitts Hill, Wood Green 63-68; V 68-74; RD of E Haringey 68-73; Exam Chap to Bp of Edmonton from 73; Archd of Hampstead from 74. *177 Winchmore Hill Road, N21 1QN.* (01-886 2680)

PICKERING, James. Div Hostel Dub 68. **d** 71 **p** 72 Sheff. C of St Nath Sheff 71-73; Conwall w Gartan 73-80; I of Ardagh Group Dio Ard from 80. *Tashinny Rectory, Colehill, Co Longford, Irish Republic.* (Colehill 5434)

PICKERING, John Alexander. b 41. TCD BA 63, Div Test 65, MA 66. **d** 65 **p** 66 Down. C of Magheralin 65-67; C-in-c (V from 68) of Oughteragh 67-71; Deputn Sec Hibernian Bible S 71-74; I of Drumgoon w Ashfield 74-80; R of Keady w Armaghbreague and Derrynoose Dio Arm from 80. *31 Crossmore Road, Keady, Co Armagh, N Ireland.*

PICKERING, John Michael Staunton. b 34. Sarum & Wells Th Coll 71. **d** 72 Lynn for Nor **p** 73 Nor. C of Gaywood w Bawsey and Mintlyn 72-77; P-in-c of Foulsham Dio Nor from 77; Hindolveston and of Guestwick Dio Nor from 80. *Foulsham Rectory, E Dereham, Norf.* (Foulsham 275)

PICKERING, John Roger. b 28. Fitzw Ho Cam BA 52, MA 56. Linc Th Coll 62. **d** 63 York **p** 66 Chelmsf. [f Congregational Min] C of Haxby w Wigginton 63-64; CF 66-69; C of H Trin Folkestone 71-73; P-in-c of Buckland Newton 73-77; Wootton-Glanville w Holnest 73-77; Osmington w Poxwell 77-79. *c/o Osmington Vicarage, Weymouth, Dorset.* (Preston 832202)

PICKERING, Malcolm. b 37. Sarum Th Coll 65. **d** 68 **p** 69 Portsm. C of Milton Hants 68-70; Stanmer w Falmer and Moulsecoombe 70-75; R of Ninfield 75-80; V of Hooe 75-80; Ventnor Dio Portsm from 80; H Trin Ventnor Dio Portsm from 80. *Ventnor Vicarage, Park Avenue, Ventnor, IW.* (Ventnor 852130)

PICKERING, Mark Penrhyn. b 36. Univ of Liv BA (1st cl Lat) 59. St Cath Coll Ox BA (3rd cl Th) 62, MA 67. Wycl Hall Ox 60. **d** 63 **p** 64 Ches. C of Claughton w Grange 63-67; Newland 67-72; Team V (in c of St Hilda Gt Field) of Marfleet 72-76; V of St Nich Hull Dio York from 76. *898 Hessle High Road, Hull, HU4 6SA.* (Hull 507944)

PICKERING, Robert Henry. Univ of Man BA (Econ & Soc Stud) 72. Oak Hill Th Coll 54. **d** 56 **p** 57 Carl. C of Ulverston 56-58; V of Birtle (or Bircle) and Chap of Fairfield Gen Hosp Bury 58-62; V of Ch Ch Chadderton 62-72; St Paul Slough Dio Ox from 72. *196 Stoke Road, Slough, Berks.* (Slough 21497)

PICKERING, Stephen Philip. b 52. Coll of the Resurr 78. **d** 79 **p** 80 Newc T. C of St Luke Wallsend Dio Newc T from 79. *Church House, Hugh Street, Wallsend, Tyne & Wear.*

PICKERING, Thomas. b 07. Late Scho of Ch Coll Cam 1st cl Math Trip pt i 26, BA (2nd cl Math Trip pt ii) 28, MA 32. Ely Th Coll 30. **d** 30 **p** 31 Leic. Asst Master Alderman Newton's Sch Leic 28-72; C of St Mary de Castro Leic 30-35; St Geo Mart Leic 35-46; L to Offic Dio Leic from 46. *10 Park Hill Drive, Aylestone, Leicester.* (Leicester 831242)

PICKERING, William Stuart Frederick. b 22. K Coll Lon AKC and BD 49, Cleave-Cockerill Stud 53, PhD 58. Univ of Manit Hon DCL 81. **d** 50 **p** 51 Linc. C of Frodingham 50-53; L to Offic Dios Guildf and Linc 55-56; Dio Newc T from 66; Tutor K Coll Lon 55-56; Asst Prof of Sociology St Jo Coll Univ of Manit 56-62; Assoc Prof 62-66; Lect Univ of Newc T 66-74; Sen Lect from 74; Perm to Offic Dio Ely from 77. *Department of Social Studies, University of Newcastle upon Tyne, NE1 7RU.*

PICKERSGILL, Ernest. b 21. Worc Ordin Coll 64. **d** 66 Ripon **p** 67 Knaresborough for Ripon. C of Rothwell 66-70; V of Elsecar 70-75; Burton Pidsea w Humbleton and Elsternwick 75-81; Shadwell Dio Ripon from 81; RD of S Holderness 78-81. *2 Church Farm Garth, Shadwell, Leeds, LS17 8HD.* (Leeds 661521)

PICKETT, Charles Edward. Univ of K Coll NS 66. **d** 68 **p** 69 Fred. C of Musquash 68-71; R of Salisbury w Havelock 71-74; on leave. *Box 218, Salisbury, NB, Canada.*

PICKETT, Leslie Anniss. b 09. Univ of Leeds BA 31. Coll of Resurr Mirfield 30. **d** 32 **p** 33 Liv. C of St Andr Wigan 32-35; St Marg Ilkley 35-46; CF (EC) 40-46; CF (TA) 51-59; HCF (TARO) from 59; V of Bierley 46-53; H Trin Bury 53-60; Chap Hostel of God Clapham 60-66; V of Froyle 66-75; Hon C of St Mary Swanley 78-80; Perm to Offic Dio Chich from 80. *10 Old Coach House, Belsize Close, Belsize Road, W Worthing, Sussex BN11 4RT.* (0903-38036)

PICKFORD, Canon Edward Henry. ACT ThL 23. **d** 23 **p** 24 Wang. Tutor St Columb's Hall and C of Milawa 23-24; R of Dookie 24-27; Violet Town 27-29; Kilmore 29-36; St Paul Bend 36-57; Chap to Bp of Bend 38-57; Can of Bend 42-57; Can (Emer) from 57; Perm to Offic Dio Bend 57-66; Dio Melb 57-76; *Parlington Street, Canterbury, Vic, Australia 3126.* (03-82 6571)

PICKFORD, Walter Edgar. Seager Hall, Ont. **d** 62 **p** 63 Hur. I of Alvinston 62-64; St D Windsor 64-66; Tilbury 66-70. *5 gladstone Avenue, Tilbury, Ont., Canada.*

PICKLES, Harold. b 13. Sarum Th Coll 34. **d** 36 **p** 37 Derby. C of Wirksworth w Carsington 36-39; Chesterfield 39-42; C-in-c of Bolsover 42-45; Burbage 45-46; V of Beighton 46-57; Edwinstowe w Carburton 57-78. *24 Afton Road, Bishop's Stortford, Herts.* (Bp's Stortford 54414)

PICKLES, Hugh John. b 18. Univ Coll Ox BA 46, MA 46. Cudd Coll 40. **d** 42 **p** 43 Ox. C of St Mary and St John Cowley Ox 42-43; Wantage 43-53; Chap of Worksop Coll and L to Offic Dio Southw 53-63; V of Blewbury Dio Ox from 63; C-in-c of Upton Dio Ox 68-74; R from 74. *Blewbury Vicarage, Didcot, Oxon.* (Blewbury 850267)

PICKLES, Sydney George. b 09. Dorch Miss Coll 30. **d** 33 **p** 34 Dur. C of St Pet Jarrow 33-36; Benfieldside 36-37; C-in-c of St Cuthb Conv Distr Monk Wearmouth 37-39; PC of St Steph Ayres Quay Bp Wearmouth 39-42; V of Hedgefield 42-48; C of Almondbury 48-50; LPr Dio York and Area Padre E Yorks Toc H 49-53; V of Newport 53-59; Nafferton w Wansford 59-74. *8 Baker Fold, Raglan Gardens, Halifax, Yorks, HX1 5TX.*

PICKSTONE, Charles Faulkner. b 55. BNC Ox MA 77. Univ of Leeds BA (Th) 80. Coll of the Resurr Mirfield 78. **d** 81 Ches. C of Birkenhead Priory Dio Ches from 81. *St Anne's Vicarage, Ashville Road, Birkenhead, Merseyside, L41 8AU.*

PICKTHORN, Canon Charles Howard. b 25. Linc Coll Ox BA 48, MA 52. Sarum Th Coll 48. **d** 50 **p** 51 Ripon. C of Ch Ch High Harrogate 50-54; Cheam (in c of St Osw) 54-60; R of Bourton-on-the-Water w Clapton Dio Glouc from 60; Surr from 61; RD of Stow from 67; P-in-c of Gt Rissington 68-81; Hon Can of Glouc Cathl from 77. *Bourton-on-the-Water Rectory, Cheltenham, Glos.* (Bourton 20386)

PICKUP, Harold. St Pet Hall Ox BA 39, MA 46. Ridley Hall, Cam 46. **d** 47 **p** 48 Man. C of Middleton 47-50; Publ Pr (in c of St Mary Gravesend) Dio Roch 50-51; V of St Mary Gravesend 51-57; R of Stanley Tas 57-62; Chap to Bp of Tas 58-62; Asst Chap Ch Gr Sch Launceston 62-63; Chap 63-73; Perm to Offic Dio Tas 73-75; Hon C of St Geo Launceston Dio Tas from 75. *69 Haig Street, Launceston, Tasmania 7250.* (003-262820)

PICTON, Arthur David. b 39. Ch Ch Ox BA (2nd cl Pol Phil and Econ) 62, MA 67. Chich Th Coll. **d** 65 Hulme for Man **p** 66 Man. C of St Phil Hulme Man 65-67; Swinton (in C of All SS Wardley) 67-71; R of St Pet Stretford 71-79; P-in-c of Knight's Enham Dio Win from 79. *1 Ryon Close, Caerlon Drive, Knight's Enham, Andover, Hants.*

PICTON, Clive William. **d** 66 Newc. C of Cessnock Dio Newc from 66. *View Street, Cessnock, NSW, Australia 2325.*

PICTON, Canon David Hugh Thomas. St D Coll Lamp BA 39. St Mich Coll Llan 44. **d** 44 St D **p** 45 Llan for St D. C of Manorbier 44-45; Fishguard w Llanychaer 45-46; CF 46-48; C of Goole 48-50; V of Cotmanhay and Shipley 50-60; Chap of Ilkeston Gen Hosp 50-60; Surr 57-60; Chap of Darrang Distr Dio Assam 60-62; Oslo 62-67; Copenhagen 67-81; Hon Can of H Trin Cathl Brussels from 81; R of Gt w L Bromley Dio Chelmsf from 81. *Great Bromley Rectory, Colchester, Essex, CO7 7TS.* (Colchester 230344)

PICTON, William James. b 13. Oak Hill Th Coll 46. **d** 48 E Szech **p** 52 Chich. [f Lay Miss CIM] Miss Dio E Szech 49-51; C of Bp Hannington Mem Ch Hove 52-54; CF 54-65; SCF 65-69; Perm to Offic Dio Momb 56-62; V of St Luke w Holloway 69-78; Perm to Offic Dio S'wark from 78. *49a Manor Avenue, SE4 1TD.*

PIDD, Arthur Tom. Univ of Melb BA (Sociology) 25, MA 27. ACT ThL 25. **d** 25 **p** 27 Melb. C of St Andr Brighton 25-28; Asst Master Brighton Gr Sch Melb 28-30; Actg Hd Master 30-31; Dir Relig Educn Dio Melb 34-41; Chap AMF 41-45; Lect Trin Coll Melb 36-38 and 48-50; I of St Cath Caulfield 45-50; R of Claremont 50-66; L to Offic Dio Perth 66-72; Perm to Offic Dio Melb from 73. *22 The Pass, South Croydon, Vic, Australia 3136.* (03-870 7259)

PIDDINGTON, Michael Christopher Wren. Wycl Coll Tor LTh 55. **d** 55 Br Columb for Keew **p** 56 Keew. C-in-c of Split Lake 55-60; R of Sioux Lookout 60-62; I of Black River 62-67; Shulus Indian Miss 67-74; C of Prince Geo 75-79; I of Sooke Dio BC from 79. *Box 519, Sooke, BC, Canada.*

PIDGEON, Richard Hain. Ridley Coll Melb BA 48, ThL 49. **d** 49 **p** 50 Melb. C of All SS St Kilda 49-50; Min of Drysdale and Portarlington 50-54; Mount Dandenong 54-57; I of Werribee 57-62; V of Portland 62-67; R 67-69; St John Bal 69-74; Can of Bal 71-74; I of Balwyn 74-79; Mornington Dio Melb from 79. *Vicarage, Mornington, Vic, Australia 3931.* (059-75 2214)

PIDSLEY, Christopher Thomas. b 36. ALCD 61. **d** 61 Kens for Lon **p** 62 Lon. C of Cockfosters 61-66; Rainham (in c of St John and St Matt S Hornchurch) 66-70; V of Chudleigh Dio Ex from 70. *Chudleigh Vicarage, Newton Abbot, Devon.* (Chudleigh 853241)

PIDSLEY, Garnett Clifford. **d** 77 **p** 78 N Queensld. C of St Marg W Cairns Dio N Queensld from 77. *c/o PO Box 118, Manunda, Qld, Australia 4870.*

PIERARD, Canon Beaumont Harold. MBE 72. St Jo Coll Auckld. **d** 46 Wel **p** 51 Waik. C of St Pet Wel 46-47; Cambridge 50-51; Chap St Pet Sch Cambridge NZ 51-53; Hurstpierpoint Coll Sussex 53-54; Worksop Coll 54-57; V of Waitara 57-59; Chap Dioc Sch Hamilton Dio Waik from 59; Can of Waik from 64; JP from 68. *287 Peachgrove Road, Hamilton, NZ.* (57-000)

PIERCE, Anthony Edward. b 41. Univ of Wales BA (Hist) 63. Linacre Coll BA (Th) 65, MA 71. Ripon Hall Ox 63. **d** 65 **p** 66 Swan B. C of St Pet Cockett Swansea 65-67; St Mary Swansea 67-74; Bp's Chap at Univ Coll Swansea 71-74; V of Llwynderw Dio Swan B from 74. *Llwynderw Vicarage, Fairwood Road, West Cross, Swansea, SA3 5TP.* (Swansea 68913)

PIERCE, Canon Claude Anthony. OBE (Mil) 46. Late Exhib of Magd Coll Cam BA (2nd cl Th Trip pt i) 47, MA 49, BD 53. Kaye Pri 55. Ely Th Coll 47. **d** 48 **p** 49 Derby. C of Chesterfield 48-51; Chap Magd Coll Cam 51-56; Lect in Th 54-56; CF (TA) 50-56; Select Pr Univ of Cam 54; Warden of Wollaston Coll 56-71; LPr Dio Perth from 56; Hon Can of Perth 64-66; Can from 66. *61 Hawkestone Street, Cottesloe, W Australia 6011.* (384 5559)

PIERCE, Duncan Dennis. Moore Th Coll. **d** 58 Syd **p** 58 Bp Hilliard for Syd. Asst Chap Miss to Seamen Syd 58-66; C of Wembley Floreat Pk 66-70; R of N Midlands 70-75; Riverton Dio Perth from 75. *39 Beatrice Avenue, Shelley, W Australia 6155.* (457 2406)

PIERCE, Neil David. b 42. Univ of Cant NZ BA 63, MA 64. Univ of Leeds Dipl Th 70. Coll of Resurr Mirfield. **d** 70 **p** 71 Pontefract for Wakef. C of Huddersfield 70-74; Prec of St John's Cathl Bulawayo Dio Matab from 75. *28 Gifford Avenue, North End, Bulawayo, Zimbabwe.*

PIERCE, Oliver George. b 30. Trin Coll Dub BA 55, MA 58. **d** 56 **p** 57 Connor. C of Ch Ch Belf 56-58; St Pet Parr 58-60; St Mark Portadown 60-62; R of Mullaglass 62-64; Clogh w Drumsnatt 64-73; Trory (w Killadeas from 80) Dio Clogh from 73. *Rectory, Rossfad, Ballinamallard, Co Fermanagh, N Ireland.*

PIERCE, Thomas. b 25. St Mich Coll Llan 57. **d** 59 **p** 60 St A. C of Minera 59-65; R of Brynford w Ysceifiog 65-76; V of Minera w Coedpoeth Dio St A from 76. *Minera Vicarage, Coedpoeth, Wrexham, Clwyd, LL11 3TN.* (Wrexham 755679)

PIERCEY, Canon Albert. Wycl Coll Tor. **d** 45 Tor for Sktn **p** 46 Sktn. I of All SS Sktn 45-48; R of Milton and Rustico PEI Dio NS from 48; P-in-c of Cherry Valley Dio NS from 62; Can of St Pet Cathl PEI from 68. *Milton, PEI, Canada.* (894-5080)

PIERCY, Henry Graham. b 05. Armstrong Coll Dur BSc 27. Ridley Hall Cam 27. **d** 29 **p** 30 Bradf. C of St Steph Bowling Bradf 29-31; CMS Miss Dio Hok 31-35; Chap Obuse Sanat 35-36; C of Portchester 37-39; Hawarden (in c of St Jo Bapt Pentrobin) 39-42; R of Charlton Mackrell w Charlton Adam 42-50; V of St Geo Jesmond Newc T 50-68; Hon Chap Hunters Moor Hosp Newc T 69-79. *65 Glamis Avenue, Melton Park, Newcastle-upon-Tyne, NE3 5SY.* (0632-362738)

PIERPOINT, Wilfred. **d** 63 Qu'App. C of St Jas Regina 63-69. *1013 Fort Street, Regina, Sask, Canada.*

PIERRE, Phillip Gunn Lawrence. b 06. **d** 72 Bp Read for Tor **p** 73 Tor. P Dio Tor 72-74. *30 Carabob Court, Apt 1008, Agincourt, Ont., Canada.*

PIERRE, William Antonin. Univ of NZ BA 23, MA 24. **d** 62 **p** 63 Ch Ch. C of Fendalton 62-74; Hon C from 75. *28 Alpha Avenue, Christchurch 5, NZ.* (558-580)

PIERSSENE, (Jeremy) Anthony Rupert. b 31. CCC Cam 2nd cl Engl Trip pt i 54, BA (2nd cl Engl Trip pt ii) 55, 3rd cl Th Trip pt ii 57. Ridley Hall Cam 56. **d** 58 **p** 59 Lon. C of Cockfosters 58-61; Trav Sec Scripture U 61-69; Chap Rugby Sch 69-76; R of Windlesham Dio Guildf from 76. *Rectory, Windlesham, Surrey.* (Bagshot 72363)

PIETERMARITZBURG, Dean of. *See* Forbes, Very Rev John Franey.

PIGGOTT, Raymond George. Univ of Leeds BA 38. Coll of Resurr Mirfield 38. **d** 40 Bp Willis for Leic **p** 41 Leic. C of St Mark Leic 40-42; St Mary Magd Munster Square 42-47; Chap RN 47-53; C of St Jo Bapt Felixstowe 53-54; V of Barney w Thursford 54-56; St Marg Ilkley 56-65; Roffey 65-80; P-in-c of Lynch w Iping Marsh Dio Chich from 80. *Lynch Rectory, Milland, Liphook, Hants, GU30 7LU.* (Milland 285)

PIGOTT, Graham John. b 44. BD (Lon) 73. Dipl Th (Lon) 71. St Jo Coll Nottm 79. **d** 81 Southw. C of St Jo Bapt Beeston Dio Southw from 81. *1 Burton Drive, Chilwell, Nottingham, NG9 5NS.*

PIGOTT, Canon John Drummond. b 26. TCD BA 50, MA 56. **d** 51 Connor **p** 52 Kilm for Connor. C of St Phil Belf 51-54; Jordanstown 54-56; Chap RAF 56-59; V of U Clatford w Goodworth Clatford 59-65; Warley Woods 65-74; Boldmere Dio Birm from 74; RD of Warley 72-74; Surr from 74-75; Hon Can of Birm Cathl from 81. *Vicarage, Church Road, Boldmere, Sutton Coldfield, B73 5RX.* (021-373 0207)

PIGOTT, Nicholas John Capel. b 48. Qu Coll Birm 75. **d** 78 Dur **p** 79 Cant. C of Belmont 78-79; St Sav Folkestone Dio Cant from 79. *42 Dolphins Road, Folkestone, Kent.* (Folkestone 50307)

PIGREM, Terence John. b 39. Oak Hill Th Coll 66. **d** 69 Lon **p** 70 Stepney for Lon. C of St Andr Isl 69-73; Barking 73-75; Team V 75-77; C (in c of St Francis) of St Luke W Holloway Dio Lon 77-79; V from 79. *St Francis' Church Centre, North Road, N7 9EY.* (01-609 3708)

PIHAVAKA, John. b 49. Bp Patteson Th Coll Kohimarama 73. **d** 76 **p** 77 Ysabel. P Dio Ysabel. *Church of Melanesia, Gizo, Solomon Islands.*

PIKE, Andrew Patrick. TCD BA 65, Div Test 66. **d** 66 **p** 67 Down. C of Bangor 66-71; St Jo Vanc 71-74; Powell River

74-79; I of St Faith Vanc Dio New Westmr from 79. *2170 West 49th Avenue, Vancouver, BC, Canada.*

PIKE, Ven Eric. St Paul's Coll Grahmstn Dipl Th 68. **d** 68 **p** 69 Grahmstn. C of St John E Lon 68-71; Komga 71-73; R of Cam E Lon 73-79; Can of Grahmstn from 76; Dir of Lay Tr and Archd Dio Grahmstn from 79. *5 Botha Road, Selborne, East London, CP, S Africa.*

PIKE, Eric Sydney. b 13. BSc (Lon) 52. SOC 78. **d** 79 **p** 80 S'wark (APM). Hon C of Em Ch Wimbledon Dio S'wark from 79. *67 Durham Road, SW20 0DE.*

PIKE, Horace Douglas. b 13. AKC 48. **d** 48 **p** 49 Pontefract for Wakef. C of Todmordon 48-52; C-in-c of Lundwood 52-55; V of Gawber 55-59; Baildon 59-71; R of Burnsall 71-78; Perm to Offic Dio York 78-81; P-in-c of Langton w Birdsall Dio York from 81. *Langton Rectory, Malton, N Yorks, YO17 9QP.* (Burythorpe 234)

PIKE, James. Qu Coll Newfld. **d** 37 **p** 38 Newfld. C of St Mary St John's 37-39; I of Random 39-43; Heart's Delight 43-44; Botwood 44-53; R of Rosette 53-58; Digby 58-66; Cornwallis 66-70; Hubbards 70-77. *Ingrahamport, Halifax Co, NS, Canada.*

PIKE, James. b 22. Trin Coll Dub 66. **d** 68 Derry **p** 69 Clogh for Derry. C of All SS Clooney 68-72; R of Ardstraw (w Baronscourt from 76) Dio Derry from 72. *Rectory, Bunderg Road, Newtownstewart, Co Tyrone, N Ireland.* (Newtownstewart 342)

PIKE, Robert James. b 47. Kelham Th Coll 66. **d** 70 Bp McKie for Cov **p** 71 Cov. C of St Pet Cov 70-74; Bilton 74-76; P-in-c of St Geo Southall 76-81; V of St Paul S Harrow Dio Lon from 81. *St Paul's Vicarage, Corbins Lane, South Harrow, Middx.* (01-422 2991)

PIKE, Roger Walter. b 31. Roch Th Coll 65. **d** 67 Dorch for Ox **p** 68 Ox. C of St Paul Wokingham 67-70; Ch Ch Whitley Reading 70-76; P Missr of St Jo Conv Distr California Finchampstead 76-80; V of St Faith W Cowes Dio Portsm from 80. *St Faith's Vicarage, W Cowes, IW.*

✠ **PIKE, Right Rev St John Surridge.** Trin Coll Dub BA 32, MA 35, DD *(jure dig.)* 58. **d** 32 **p** 34 Dub. C of Taney 32-37; Hd of S Ch Miss Ballymacarrett Belf 37-47; SPG Miss Dio Gambia 47-52; R of St Geo Belf 52-57; Commiss (in N Ireland) for Gambia 54-57; Cons Ld Bp of Gambia and the Rio Pongas in St Geo Cathl Sier L 16 Feb 58 by Abp of W Afr; Bp of Ondo-B; and Bp P J Jones; res 63; Asst Bp of Guildf from 63; V of Ewshott 63-71; Botleys and Lyne Dio Guildf from 71; Long Cross Dio Guildf from 71. *Vicarage, Lyne and Long Cross, Chertsey, Surrey.* (Ottershaw 3551)

✠ **PIKE, Right Rev Victor Joseph.** b 07. OBE 44. Men in Disp 46. CBE (Mil) 50. CB 53. Trin Coll Dub BA 29, Div Test 30, MA 37, DD *(jure dig)* 55. **d** 30 **p** 31 Dub. C of Taney 30-32; TCF Aldershot 32-36; CF 36-60; Hon Chap to HM the King 48-52; to HM the Queen 52-53; Chap to HM the Queen 53-60; Chap-Gen to the Forces 51-60; Hon Can of Cant 51-60; Preb of Sarum Cathl from 60; Cons Ld Bp Suffr of Sherborne in S'wark Cathl 24 Jun 60 by Abp of Cant; Bps of Sarum, Leic, Ches, Gambia and the Rio Pongas and Meath; Bps Suffr of Willesden, Fulham and Maidstone; Bps Jones and Johnston; res 76; Chap to Retired Clergy in Rural Deanery of Sarum from 78. *53 The Close, Salisbury, Wilts, SP1 2EN.* (0722-5766)

PIKE, William Aubrey Monsell. b 05. Magd Coll Cam BA 26. Cudd Coll 27. **d** 28 **p** 29 Dur. C of H Trin Sunderland 28-30; Airedale w Fryston 30-33; C-in-c of Wrangbrook Conv Dist 34-37; C of St John Bulawayo 38-39; Chap RNVR 40-45; R of Hawnby w Old Byland 45-48; Min Can of St Geo Chap Windsor 48-54; L to Offic Dio Ox 49-54; V of St Mich Wakef 54-56; R of Burnham-Deepdale 56-70; R of Brancaster 56-70. *18 St John's Road, Cambridge, CB5 8AN.* (Cam 355751)

PILBROW, Rory Charles Gerald. b 51. Univ of Cant Ch Ch BA 75. St Jo Coll Auckld LTh 79. **d** 80 **p** 81 Dun. C of N Invercargill Dio Dun from 80. *126 Catherine Street, Invercargill, NZ.*

PILCHER, Noel James. Moore Th Coll Syd 58. ACT ThL 60. **d** 61 Syd **p** 61 Bp Kerle for Syd. C of Bondi 61-64; C-in-c of Oaks w Burragorang 64-68; Asquith w Mt Colah 69-74; R 74-76; Richmond Dio Syd from 76. *Rectory, Windsor Street, Richmond, NSW, Australia 2753.* (78-1205)

PILCHER, Canon Norman Donald. Univ of Tor BA 36. Bp's Univ Lennox MA 57. **d** 38 **p** 39 Queb. C of Kenogami 38-39; Cathl Ch Queb 39-41; St Jo Bapt St John NB 41-43; R of St Geo Drummondvile 43-49; Prin of Ind Res Sch Prince Albert 49-52; Gordon's Ind Res Sch Punnichy 52-55; Warden St Chad's Coll Regina 55-63; Exam Chap to Bp of Qu'App 57-63; to Bp of Queb 63-67; Hon Can of Qu'App 59-63; R of St Matt Queb 63-67; Asst Distr Sec Canad Bible S 67-69; I of St Marg Montr 70-74; R of Trin Ch St Bruno Montr 74-80; Hon Can of Montr 77-80; Can (Emer) from 80; P Assoc of St Jude Oakville Dio Niag from 80. *Apt 202, 150 Allan Street, Oakville, Ont, Canada L6J 3N8.* (416-842 3784)

PILGRIM, Graeme Edward. b 51. Massey Univ Palmerston N NZ BSc 73. St Jo Coll Auckld LTh 76. **d** 76 Bp McKenzie for Wel **p** 77 Wel. C of Levin 76-79; V of Hunterville Dio Wel from 79. *Vicarage, Hunterville, NZ.*

PILGRIM, Richard Colin Laurence. b 26. Pemb Coll Cam BA (2nd cl Hist Trip) 50, MA 55. Ridley Hall Cam 50. **d** 52 **p** 53 Guildf. C of Esher 52-55; Min of New Cathl Conv Distr Guildf 55-57; R of Puttenham w Wanborough 57-65; Industr Chap Dio Roch 65-74; Hon C of Chislehurst 65-74; R of Gravesend Dio Roch from 74. *St George's Rectory, Gravesend, Kent.* (Gravesend 534965)

PILKINGTON, Charles George Willink. b 21. Trin Coll Cam BA 42, MA 64. Westcott Ho Cam. **d** 63 Hulme for Man **p** 64 Man. C of Pendleton and of Brindle Heath 63-65; Chorlton-cum-Hardy 65-68; R of St Chris Withington Dio Man from 68. *Rectory, Moorgate Avenue, Withington, Manchester, M20 8HE.* (061-445 2008)

PILKINGTON, Canon Christopher Frost. b 23. Trin Coll Cam BA 50, MA 60. Ridley Hall Cam 50. **d** 52 **p** 53 Worc. C of St Jo Bapt-in-Bedwardine Worc 52-55; V of St Mark-in-the-Cherry-Orchard Worc 55-60; Bromsgrove 60-68; Surr 60-68; R of St Steph w St Nich and St Leon (w All SS 68-73) City and Dio Bris from 68; Hon Can of Bris Cathl from 79. *Rector's Room, St Stephen's Street, Bristol, BS1 1EQ.* (Bristol 277977)

PILKINGTON, Edward Russell. b 39. ALCD 65. **d** 65 **p** 66 Bradf. C of Eccleshill 65-68; Billericay 68-72; V of St Geo Thundersley 72-78; R of Theydon Garnon Dio Chelmsf from 78. *Theydon Garnon Rectory, Fiddlers Hamlet, Epping, Essex.* (Epping 72608)

PILKINGTON, Canon Evan Matthias. b 16. Keble Coll Ox BA (3rd cl Th) 39, MA 46. Cudd Coll 39. **d** 40 Grimsby for Linc **p** 41 Linc. C of Bottesford w Ashby 40-42; H Trin Southall 42-44; St Jo Div Kennington 44-46; V of E Kirkby w Miningsby 46-52; H Trin U Tooting 52-61; Kingston-T 61-67; Can Res of Bris 68-76; St Paul's Cathl Lon from 76; Chap to HM the Queen from 69. *3 Amen Court, EC4M 7BU.* (01-248 4554)

PILKINGTON, John Rowan. b 32. Magd Coll Cam 2nd cl Econ Trip pt i 53, BA (2nd cl Econ Trip pt ii) 55, MA 59. Ridley Hall Cam 57. **d** 59 **p** 60 Guildf. C of Ashtead 59-61; Wimbledon (in c of St Mark) 62-65; R of Newhaven 65-75; Farlington Dio Portsm from 75. *27 Farlington Avenue, Cosham, Portsmouth, PO6 1DF.* (Cosham 375145)

PILKINGTON, Canon Peter. b 33. Jes Coll Cam BA 55, MA 59. Westcott Ho Cam 58. **d** 59 **p** 60 Derby. C of Bakewell 59-62; Asst Master and Chap Eton Coll 62-75; Perm to Offic Dio Ox 66-75; Hd Master K Sch Cant from 75; Hon Can of Cant Cathl from 75. *14 The Precincts, Canterbury, Kent.* (Cant 62963)

PILLANS, Canon Daile. St Paul's Coll Grahmstn LTh. **d** 45 Bp Etheridge for Grahmstn **p** 46 Grahmstn. C of St Sav E Lon 45-48; R of Barkly East w Dordrecht and Indwe 48-51; Stutterheim 51-57; St Paul Port Eliz 57-67; Alexandria Grahmstn 67-71; St Francis Port Eliz 71-75; All SS Ficksburg 75-78; N Suburbs Pret 78-80; Sundays River Valley Dio Port Eliz from 80; Hon Can of Port Eliz from 81. *Box 60, Sunlands 6115, CP, S Africa.*

✠ **PILLAR, Right Rev Kenneth Harold.** b 24. Qu Coll Cam BA 48, MA 53. Ridley Hall Cam 48. **d** 50 **p** 51 Liv. C of Childwall 50-53; Chap Lee Abbey and L to Offic Dio Ex 53-57; V of St Paul Beckenham 57-62; St Mary Bredin Cant 62-65; Commiss Arctic 63-70; Warden Lee Abbey and L to Offic Dio Ex 65-70; V of Waltham Abbey 70-82; RD of Chigwell (Epping Forest from 78) 76-82; Cons LD Bp Suffr of Hertf in Westmr Abbey 2 Feb 82 By Abp of Cant; Bps of Lon, Win, St Alb, Chelmsf, Birm, Bris, Derby, Ely, Glouc, Lich, Ox, Southw and Truro; Bps Suffr of Barking, Basingstoke, Bedford, Bradwell, Croydon, Colchester, Edmon, Grantham, Hull, Maidstone, Ramsbury, Sherborne, Sherwood, Shrewsbury, Southn, Stockport and Willesden; and Bps Coggan of Cant, Hodson, Patterson, Woollcombe, Claxton and others. *Hertford House, Abbey Mill Lane, St Albans, Herts.* (St Alb 66420)

PILLAR, Kenneth James. b 50. St Jo Coll Nottm 70. **d** 74 **p** 75 Roch. C of St Mich AA Wilmington 74-79. *Address temp unknown*

PILLING, James Arthur. b 1889. Univ of Leeds BA (2nd cl Cl) 10. Coll of Resurr Mirfield. **d** 12 **p** 13 Linc. C of St Swith Linc 12-21; V of Gosberton Clough 21-32; Cowbit 32-59; Chap Pinchbeck Road Hosp Spalding 46-59; Perm to Offic Dio Linc from 59. *14 Buckthorn Avenue, Skegness, Lincs.*

PILLING, John Turton. St Jo Coll Winnipeg LTh 61. **d** 61 **p** 62 Bran. R of Virden 61-69; R of Miniota 61-69; St Matt Regina 69-71; Exec Sec of Synod Dio Qu'App 71-77; Dioc Archd Dio Qu'App 74-77; R of Swift Current 77-80; St Andr

City and Dio Calg from 80. *5011 46th Avenue SW, Calgary, Alta, Canada, T3E 6L2.* (250-2469)

PILLING, William Edward. b 03. Kelham Coll 25.Lon Coll of Div 29. **d** 30 **p** 31 Man. C of St John Farnworth 30-33; St Marg Leic 33-34; C-in-c of St Chris Park Estate Leic 34-37; R of Long Whatton 37-40; V of Quorn 40-54; R of Market Bosworth w Shenton 54-60; RD of Sparkenhoe i 54-60; Surr from 54; Hon Can of Leic 58-60; R of Alderley 60-69. *25 Redesmere Drive, Alderley Edge, Chesh, SK9 7UR.* (Alderley Edge 4570)

PILMER, James David. b 38. Perry Hall Melb 69. **d** 69 **p** 70 Melb. C of All SS East St Kilda 69-72; P-in-c of St Luke N Fitzroy and St Andr Clifton Hill 72-77; I of Surrey Hills Dio Melb from 77. *177 Union Road, Surrey Hills, Vic, Australia 3127.* (89 2605)

PIMLOTT, Stephen John. b 45. SS Coll Cam BA 67, MA 71. Trin Coll Ox BA 73. Cudd Coll 71. **d** 74 **p** 75 Derby. C of Newbold 74-78; St Jo Evang Walworth 78-82; V of St Benedict Bordesley Dio Birm from 82. *Vicarage, Hobmoor Road, Birmingham, B10 9AY.* (021-772 2726)

PIMPERTON, Raymond Swindale. b 12. Linc Th Coll 77. **d** 77 Grantham for Linc **p** 78 Linc. C of Holbeach Dio Linc from 77. *6 Chestnut Avenue, Holbeach, Lincs.*

PINCHES, Donald Antony. b 32. Pemb Coll Cam 2nd cl Engl Trip pt i, 54, BA (2nd cl Engl Trip pt ii) 55, MA 60. Linacre Ho Ox BA (2nd cl Th) 67. Wycl Hall, Ox. **d** 67 Dorch for Ox **p** 68 Ox. C of H Trin aylesbury 67-71; Em Plymouth 71-74; Team V of Lydford 74-77; V of Shiphay Collaton Dio Ex from 77. *83 Cadewell Lane, Shiphay, Torquay, Devon.* (Torquay 63361)

PINCHIN, Antony Peter. b 57. St Jo Coll Cam BA 79. Coll of the Resurr Mirfield 79. **d** 81 Guildf. C of Hawley Dio Guildf from 81. *295 Fernhill Road, Farnborough, Hants, GU14 9EW.*

PINDER, Canon Charles. b 21. K Coll Lon and Warm AKC 49. **d** 50 **p** 51 S'wark. C of Raynes Pk 50-53; V of All SS Hatcham Pk 53-60; C-in-c of CCC Miss Camberwell 58-60; V of Catford 60-73; Hon Chap to Bp of S'wark 63-80; Sub-Dean of S Lewisham 68-73; Borough Dean of Lambeth from 73; Can (Emer) of S'wark Cathl from 73; P-in-c of Ch Ch Brixton 75-80; St Jas Camberwell 76-77. *97 Kingsmead Road, Tulse Hill, SW2 3HZ.* (01-674 6091)

PINDER, Derrick Bibby. Bps' Coll Cheshunt. **d** 57 **p** 58 B & W. C of H Trin Taunton 57-59; Stepney 59-61; V of St Jas Fulham 62-68. *Address temp unknown.*

PINDER, John Ridout. b 43. Peterho Cam 2nd cl Hist Trip pt i 63, BA (2nd cl Th Trip pt ii) 65, MA 69. Cudd Coll 65. **d** 73 **p** 74 St Alb. C of Leavesden 73-77; Gen Sec Melan Miss from 77. *c/o 15 Denewood Close, Watford, Herts, WD1 3SZ.* (Watford 26351)

PINE, David Michael. b 41. Lich Th Coll 68. **d** 71 **p** 72 Ex. C of Northam 71-74; R of Toft w Caldecote and Childerley 74-80; Hardwick 74-80; V of St Andr Ipswich Dio St E from 80. *229 Britannia Road, Ipswich, Suff.* (Ipswich 78204)

PINK, Canon David. b 34. Qu Coll Cam 2nd cl Hist Trip pt i 57, BA (3rd cl Th Trip pt ia) 58, MA 62. Linc Th Coll 58. **d** 60 **p** 61 Chelmsf. C of L Ilford 60-63; Lect of Boston Lincs 63-65; V of Kirton-in-Holland 65-71; St Jo Evang Spitalgate Grantham 71-77; Ecumen Officer Lincs and S Humb and P-in-c of Canwick Dio Linc from 77; Can and Preb of Linc Cathl from 77. *Canwick Vicarage, Lincoln, LN4 2RN.* (Lincoln 22170)

PINK, James William. b 20. Dipl Th (Lon) 55. Codr Coll Barb 53. **d** 55 Guy **p** 56 WI. C of Enmore 55-57; P-in-c Berbice River Miss 57-60; V of Mackenzie 60-65; St Phil Georgetn 65-68; Ruimveldt 69-73; Asst Chap HM Pris Pentonville 73; Chap HM Pris Haverigg 73-76; Holloway from 76; L to Offic Dio Carl 73-76; Dio Lon from 76. *HM Prison, Holloway, N7.* (01-607 6747)

PINKER, Colin Stuart. b 43. Vic Univ of Wel BA 70. St Jo Coll Auckld LTh 71. **d** 71 **p** 72 Bp McKenzie for Wel. C of Johnsonville 72-81; V of Brooklyn Dio Wel from 81. *13 Garfield Street, Brooklyn, Wellington, NZ.* (899-687)

PINKHAM, Charles Ernest. LTh S Afr 40. **d** 40 **p** 41 Capetn. C of St Mark Capetn 40-43; R of Hopefield 43-47; Touws River 47-53; Bredasdorp 53-58; Durbanville 58-65; C of Ceres 65-67; Somerset W 67-73; L to Offic Dio Capetn 73-80; Perm to Offic from 80. *Box 331, Somerset West, S Africa.* (22456)

PINKNEY, Canon Morley Edward. Sir Geo Williams Coll BA 50. McGill Univ Montr BD 54. Montr Dioc Th Coll LTh 54. Gen Th Sem NY STM 59. **d** 54 **p** 55 Hur. C of Thedford and Grand Bend 54-57; on leave 57-59; I of St Timothy Lon 59-62; Chap Renison Coll Waterloo 62-63; I of Paris 63-69; R of St Ann Lon Dio Hur from 69; Can of Hur from 77; Exam Chap to Bp of Hur from 78. *1357 Commissioner's Road West, London 61, Ont., Canada.* (519-471 0800)

PINNER, John Philip. b 37. K Coll Lon BA (2nd cl Hist) 59. Westcott Ho 69. **d** 71 **p** 72 Cant. C of Dover 71-74; Chap Felsted Sch from 74. *Garnetts, Felsted, Essex.* (0371-820598)

PINNER, Terence Malcolm William. b 35. K Coll Lon and Warm AKC 59. **d** 60 **p** 61 S'wark. C of St Barn Eltham 60-64; St Mich and St Geo Cathl Grahmstn (in c of St Clem from 66) 64-67; On staff USPG 67-69; R of K Wm's Town 69-72; St Nich Beacon Bay E Lon Grahmstn 72-74; Sec for Home Affairs Conf of Miss Societies 74-76; Adult Educn Officer Dio Lich from 76; P-in-c of Hinstock 76-80. *Rectory, Standon, Stafford.* (Standon Rock 265)

PINNIGER, Jonathan. ACT ThL 73. Ridley Coll Melb 71. **d** 74 **p** 75 Melb. C of St Mark Camberwell 74-76; St John Blackburn 76-77; in Angl Inner-City Min Melb 77; Chap at San Pedro 78-80; C of All SS Greensborough Dio Melb from 80. *80 Watsonia Road, Watsonia, Vic, Australia 3087.*

PINNIGER, Timothy. b 41. **d** 71 **p** 72 Gippsld. C of Bairnsdale 71-75; P-in-c of Bunyip 75-77; R 77-79; I of Moreland Dio Melb from 79. *10 Davies Street, Brunswick, Vic, Australia 3056.* (386 6810)

PINNOCK, Geoffrey Gilbert. b 16. K Coll Lon and Warm 47. **d** 50 **p** 51 Lon. C of St Mich AA Paddington 50-52; R of Parys Bloemf 52-54; Hosp Chap Dio Johann 54-57; P-in-c of Jeppestn 57; Perm to Offic Dio Lon 57-66; Actg Chap Nat Hosp Qu Sq Lon 60; St Steph Hosp Chelsea 61-62; Asst Chap Univ Coll Hosp Lon 62-66; in Amer Ch 66-72; Perm to Offic Dio Lon 72-73; S'wark 73-74; C of St Phil w St Bart Battersea 74-75; P-in-c of Bradoc (w Boconnoc 75-78) 75-81; Perm to Offic Dio Ox from 81; Dio Lon from 82. *11 Drove Acre Road, Oxford, OX4 3DF.* (Oxford 47355)

PINSENT, Ewen Macpherson. b 30. Edin Th Coll 67. **d** 69 Nor **p** 70 Lynn for Nor. C of Holt 69-72; R of St Andr Kelso Dio Edin from 72. *Rectory, Forestfield, Kelso, Roxburghshire.* (Kelso 24163)

PINSON, Wilfrid John. b 41. Univ of S Pacific Suva BD 70. Pacific Th Coll Suva. **d** and **p** 71 Newc. C of Maitland 71-72; Tutor Bp Patteson Th Centre Kohimarama 73-75; Hon Chap to Bp of Bal from 76. *Box 423, Warnambool, Vic, Australia 3280.* (055-651413)

PIPER, Gary Quentin David. b 42. Nottm Coll of Educn Dipl Educn 71. Oak Hill Th Coll 75. **d** 78 Lon **p** 79 Kens for Lon. Hon C of St Matt Fulham Dio Lon from 78. *28 Ashcombe Street, Fulham, SW6 3AN.*

PIPER, John Howard. b 09. St Chad's Coll Dur BA 31. **d** 32 **p** 34 Lich. Asst Chap Denstone Coll 32-34; C of H Nativ Knowle 34-41; Sidmouth (in c of St Francis Woolbrook) 41-44; Chap RAFVR 44-46; Actg C of St Mark Cov 46-49; C-in-c of St Andr Paignton 49-55; C of St Budeaux (in c of Whitleigh) 55-57; V of St Chad Whitleigh Plymouth 57-68; R of Ratcliffe-on-the-Wreake w Rearsby (and Thrussington from 78) 68-82; P-in-c of Thrussington 77-78. *52 Avenue Road, Queniborough, Leics.* (Leicester 606603)

PIPER, Canon Leonard Arthur. b 08. Clifton Th Coll 32. **d** 35 **p** 36 Lon. C of Ch Ch w St Mary and St Steph Spitalfields 35-37; St Cuthb Darlington (in c of Blackwell) 37-39; R of Hurworth-on-Tees 39-74; CF 40-46 & 64; Hon CF 50-82; Surr from 46; Dinsdale w Sockburn 61-74; Hon Can of Dur 70-74; Can (Emer) from 74. *Bridge Cottage, Over Dinsdale, Darlington, Co Durham, DL2 1PW.* (Dinsdale 2864)

PIPER, Reginald John. Univ of Syd BSc 63. Moore Th Coll Syd ACT ThL 66. **d** 66 **p** 67 Syd. C of Willoughby 66-69; Lalor Pk 69-72; C-in-c of Provisional Par Hurstville Grove 72-74; R of Kiama 75-80; H Trin City and Dio Adel from 80. *87 North Terrace, Adelaide, S Australia 5000.* (51 3862)

PIPPEN, Brian Roy. b 50. Bp Burgess Hall Lamp 71. **d** 73 **p** 74 Mon. C of Maindee 74-77; V in R Benef of Cwmbran Dio Mon from 77. *St Mary's Vicarage, Croesyceiliog, Cwmbran, NP4 2LF.*

PIRIE, John Henry. b 07. Univ of Leeds BA 29. Coll of Resurr Mirfield 26. **d** 32 **p** 33 Bradf. C of Tong w St John Tong Street 32-38; Haigh w Aspull (in c of New Springs) 38-40; Missr of Clare Coll Miss Rotherhithe 40-56; C-in-c of All SS Rotherhithe 41-52; V of St Jo Evang Walworth 56-71; C-in-c of St Mark Walworth 56-57; Publ Pr Dio S'wark from 72. *31 Walter's Close, Brandon Street, SE17 1NE.*

PIRIE, William Trevor Mark. Edin Th Coll 61. **d** 64 **p** 65 Glas. C of St Jo Evang Greenock 64-68; Dumfries 68-73; Annan (in c of Eastriggs) Dio Glas from 73. *Winston Hotel, Rae Street, Dumfries.*

PITCAIRN, Andrew. KCNS. **d** 40 **p** 41 NS. C of H Trin Liv 40-43; Port Medway 43-46; P-in-c of Blandford 46-50; R of Port Greville 50-54; U Falmouth 54-58; I of Musquodoboit Harbour 58-63; Stewiacke 63-68; R of Bridgetown 68-70; Em Dartmouth Dio NS from 70. *Dartmouth, NS, Canada.* (469-2365)

PITCHER, Abraham. KCNS 31. **d** 34 **p** 35 NS. C of Neil's Harbour 34-38; Liscomb 38-45; R of Rossette 45-53; Lockeport 53-54; New Dublin 54-66. *RR 1 Pleasantville, Lunenburgh Co, NS, Canada.*

PITCHER, David John. b 33. Ely Th Coll 55. **d** 58 **p** 59

Stafford for Lich. C of St Mary Kingswinford 58-61; Kirkby Lancs (in c of St Mark from 63) 61-66; R of Ingham w Sutton 66-72; V of Lakenham 72-76; R of Framlingham w Saxtead Dio St E from 76; Surr from 76. *Rectory, Framlingham, Nr Woodbridge, Suff.* (Framlingham 723653)

PITCHER, Canon Edwin Harold Victor. Univ of Syd BA 39, MA 62. St Jo Coll Morpeth ACT ThL 41. Th Scho 57. 42 **p** 43 Newc. C of Waratah 42-44; Singleton 44-45; R of Bulahdelah 45-49; C of Singleton 49; R of Aberdeen 49-53; St Paul W Maitland 53-55; Scone 55-60; L to Offic Dio Newc 60-69; Chap St Jo Coll Morpeth 61-69; Lect from 61; Can of Newc from 63; R of Merewether Dio Newc from 69; Exam Chap to Bp of Newc from 79. *Rectory, Winsor Street, Merewether, NSW, Australia 2291.* (63-1388)

PITCHER, Ronald Charles Frederick. b 21. AKC 50. St Bonif Coll Warm 47. **d** 51 **p** 52 Man. C of St Marg Burnage 51-53; St Jas Heywood 53-55; C-in-c of St Francis Conv Distr Newall Green Dio Man 55-61; V 61-73; Chap Baguley and Wythenshawe Hosps 64-73; C-in-c of Danesholme Conv Distr Corby 73-81; V of Estover Dio Ex from 80. *14 Dover Road, Estover, Plymouth, PL6 8ST.*

PITCHES, Reginald Morgan. b 09. Keble Coll Ox BA 30, MA 34. Cudd Coll 30. **d** 31 **p** 32 S'wark. C of St Anselm Kennington Cross 31-36; St Laur Catford 36-41; All SS Lewisham 41-43; Heckmondwike 44-49; Prec of St Paul's Cathl Dundee 49-50; R of St Martin Dundee 50-60; R of Wetheral w Warw 60-69; V of Bridekirk 69-76; Perm to Offic Dio Carl from 77. *Fife Lodge, Lorton, Cockermouth, Cumb.* (Cockermouth 297)

PITCHFORD, Herbert John. b 34. Univ of Dur BA 60. Ridley Hall Cam 60. **d** 62 **p** 63 Heref. C of St Martin Heref 62-68; R of Much Birch w L Birch (and Much Dewchurch, Llanwarne and Llandinabo from 78) 68-80; P-in-c of Much Dewchurch w Llanwarne and Llandinabo 73-78; M Gen Syn Heref 75-80; V of Grange Pk Dio Lon from 80. *St Peter's Vicarage, Langham Gardens, Grange Park, N21 1DN.* (01-360 2294)

PITCHFORD, Hubert Dunn. b 1890. **d** 49 **p** 50 Bradf. C of Keighley 49-51; V of Windhill 51-53; R of Wilby 53-61; Clipston 61-65. *Ellesborough Manor, Butler's Cross, Aylesbury, Bucks.*

PITHERS, Brian Hoyle. b 34. Chich Th Coll 63. **d** 66 Huntingdon for Ely **p** 67 Ely. C of Wisbech 66-70; V of Fenstanton 70-75; St Mary Magd Hilton 70-75; St Matt Habergham Eaves Burnley Dio Blackb from 75; P-in-c of H Trin Habergham Eaves Burnley Dio Blackb from 78. *Vicarage, Fern Road, Burnley, Lancs.* (Burnley 24849)

PITIKOE, Joseph Tsiliso. St Pet Coll Rosettenville 50. **d** 52 **p** 53 Pret. P Dio Pret 52-72; Dio Johann from 73. *Box 281, Westonaria 1780, Transvaal, S Africa.*

PITMAN, Clifford George. b 19. St D Coll Lamp BA 48. **d** 49 **p** 50 Llan. C of Llangynwyd w Maesteg 49-52; Caerphilly 52-54; Llanharan w Brynna 54-59; Neath 59-60; V of Tonna Dio Llan from 60. *8 Park Street, Tonna, Neath, W Glam, SA11 3JS.* (Neath 2779)

PITMAN, Cyrus Clement James. b 44. Mem Univ of Newfld BA 67, LTh 67. **d** 67 **p** 68 Newfld. C of Channel 67-70; I of Flower's Cove 70-76; Meadows Dio W Newfld from 76. *Meadows, RR2 Corner Brook, Newfoundland, Canada.*

PITMAN, Ernest Charles. b 07. St Chad's Coll Regina 27. **d** 30 **p** 31 Qu'App. C of Milden 30-31; I 31-32; R of H Trin Canora 34-35; Perm to Offic (Col Cl Act) at St Mark S Norwood 33-34; and 35-36; C of H Trin Milton Regis 36-39; Eaton 39-40; CF (EC) 40-46; Hon CF from 46; R of Kingsnorth 46-51; Shadoxhurst 46-51; CF 51-56; R of Orlestone w Ruckinge 56-58; V of Em W Dulwich 58-63; Commiss Qu'App 58-74; Hon Can of Qu'App 61-74; V of Caistor w Holton-le-Moor and Clixby 63-67; R of Withern 67-71; N w S Reston and Castle Carlton 67-71; V of Strubby w Woodthorpe 67-71; R of Denton 71-73. *4 Warley Dale Crescent, Grantham, Lincs.* (Grantham 61023)

PITOUT, Frederick Geoffrey Arthur. b 48. St Paul's Coll Grahmstn Dipl Th 79. **d** 79 **p** 80 Pret. C of Letaba 79-80; Trin Lynnwood Dio Pret from 80. *459 Lovers Walk, Lynnwood 0081, S Africa.*

PITSO, Cottrell James Teboho. St Pet Th Coll Rosettenville 59. **d** 61 **p** 62 Bloemf. P Dio Bloemf. *Box 232, Winburg, OFS, S Africa.*

PITT, George. Qu Univ Belf BD 79. Ch of Ireland Th Coll Dub 79. **d** 81 Connor. C of St Mary Belf Dio Connor from 81. *17 Cardigan Drive, Belfast, BT14 6LX.*

PITT, John Alfred. **d** and **p** 53 Athab. C of Fort Vermilion 53-55; Miss at Sexsmith 55-59; R of St Barn New Westmr 59-69. *828A 3 Road, Richmond, BC, Canada.*

PITT, John Matcham. b 50. Macquarie Univ NSW BA 73. ACT ThL 76. BD (Lon) 77. Moore Coll Syd 74. **d** and **p** 78 C & Goulb. C of Cootamundra 78-80; Cooma Dio C & Goulb from 80. *10 Boundary Street, Cooma, NSW, Australia 2630.*

PITT, John Victor Cavill. b 23. Univ of K Coll NS BTh 74. **d** 73 **p** 74 NS. Chap of Cole Harbour Hosp Dio NS from 73. *Cole Harbour Hospital, 15 Windmill Road, Dartmouth, NS B3A 1C6, Canada.* (466-6888)

PITT, Louis Wetherbee. b 23. Univ of Columb BA 44. Episc Th Sch BD 47. **d** and **p** 47 Bp Lawrence. In Amer Ch 47-73. Dean and R of H Cross Cathl Lusaka 73-77. *c/o Deanery, PO Box 477, Lusaka, Zambia.*

PITT, Mervyn George Mottram. b 10. Qu Coll Cam 3rd cl Hist Trip pt i, 31, BA (2nd cl Hist Trip pt ii) 32, MA 36. Wells Th Coll 32. **d** 34 **p** 35 S'wark. C of Putney (in c of All SS) 34-39; C-in-c of H Trin Crownhill Conv Distr 39-46; Chap RAFVR 41-46; V of King's Teignton 46-48; Chap Haileybury Coll 49-51; V of St Denys Southn 51-62; R of Over Wallop w Nether Wallop 62-78. *Ellers, Hayes Close, King's Somborne, Stockbridge, Hants.* (K Somborne 5667)

PITT, Robert Edgar. b 37. Chich Th Coll 70. **d** 73 **p** 74 Bris. C of Knowle 73-77; St Cuthb Wells w Ch Ch Coxley and Wookey Hole 77-81; Team V of Wellington & Distr Dio B & W from 81. *Vicarage, Rockwell Green, Wellington, Somt, TA21 9DH.* (Wellington 2742)

PITT, Trevor. b 45. Univ of Hull BA (1st cl Th) 66, MA 69. U Th Sem NY STM 70. Linc Th Coll 68. **d** 70 Bp Gerard for Sheff **p** 71 Sheff. C of St Geo Sheff 70-74; Team V of Hemsworth in Gleadless Valley 74-77; R 77-79; P-in-c of Elham Dio Cant from 79; Vice-Prin Cant Sch of Min from 81. *Elham Vicarage, Canterbury, Kent, CT4 6TT.* (Elham 219)

PITT, Canon William Edward. b 24. Keble Coll Ox BA (2nd cl Th) and MA 49. St Steph Ho Ox 48. **d** 50 **p** 51 Lon. C of H Cross Greenford 50-54; Sub-Warden St Jo Bapt Sem Lusaka 54-61; Vice-Prin St Bede's Coll Umtata 61-68; R of Stoke Albany w Wilbarston 68-73; Burton Latimer Dio Pet from 73; Can of Pet Cathl from 80. *Burton Latimer Rectory, Kettering, Northants.* (Burton Latimer 2098)

PITT-OWEN, Albert Thomas. Univ of Syd BA 35. Moore Th Coll Syd 33. ACT ThL 35. **d** 36 **p** 37 Syd. C of St Luke Liv w Holsworthy 36; Asst Chap Miss to Seamen Syd 37-41; C of St Phil Syd 37-47; Chap AIF 41-46; Cranbrook Sch 46-48; R of Dural 49-53; Hd Master C of E Gr Sch Wentworth Falls and L to Offic Dio Syd 53-67; R of Haberfield 67-78; L to Offic Dio Syd from 78. *Highfields, Hume Highway, Picton, NSW, Australia 2571.* (046-771754)

PITTIS, Stephen Charles. b 52. Univ of Lon Dipl Th (extra-mural stud) 75. Oak Hill Coll 73. **d** 76 **p** 77 Southn for Win. C of Ch Ch Win 76-79; Chap Colls of Further and Higher Educn Bournemouth and Poole from 79. *14 Crescent Road, Branksome, Poole, Dorset.*

PITTOCK, John Leslie. b 10. St Aug Coll Cant. **d** 61 **p** 62 Cant. C of Hythe 61-64; R of Pluckley 64-78; Perm to Offic Dio Cant from 78. *112 Sandyhurst Lane, Ashford, Kent, TN25 4NT.* (Ashford 23700)

PITTS, Frederick John Hewlett. Hur Coll LTh 46. **d** 45 **p** 46 Tor. I of Belmont, Havelock, Norwood and Westwood 45-48; Cannington w Sunderland Tor 48-49; R of Delhi 50-54; St Jas Brantford 54-59; Kitchener 59-76; Port Burwell 76-78. *81 Waddell Street, Stratford, Ont, Canada.*

PITTS, Michael James. b 44. Worc Coll Ox BA 67. Qu Coll Birm 67. **d** 69 Dur **p** 70 Jarrow for Dur. C of St Thos Conv Distr Pennywell Bp Wearmouth 69-72; H Trin Darlington 72-74; Chap and Miss to Seamen Dunkirk 74-79; V of Tudhoe 79-81; Chap of Helsinki w Moscow Dio Gibr in Eur from 81. *Aarnivalkeontie, 10E Espoo, Helsinki 00330, Finland.*

PITUVAKA, John Rufus. St Pet Coll Siota 62. **d** 64 **p** 66 Melan. P Dio Melan 64-75; Dio Centr Melan from 75. *Maravovo, Guadalcanal, Solomon Islands.*

PIVA, Alan. St Francis Coll Brisb 42. **d** 46 Brisb for Melan **p** 53 Melan. P Dio Melan 46-75; Dio Malaita from 75. *Sikaiana, Solomon Islands.*

PIVA, Leslie. St Jo Coll Auckld 64. **d** 67 **p** 68 Melan. P Dio Melan 67-74; L to Offic Dio Centr Melan 75-80; Dio Melb from 80. *18 Neill Court, East Bentleigh, Vic, Australia 3165.*

PIX, Stephen James. b 42. Late Scho of Ex Coll Ox BA 64, Dipl Th 65, MA 68. Clifton Th Coll 66. **d** 68 Warrington for Liv **p** 69 Liv. C of St Helens 68-71; L to Offic Dio S'wark 71-76; Hon C of H Trin Wallington Dio S'wark from 76. *31 Heathdene Road, Wallington, SM6 0TB.* (01-647 2439)

PIZZEY, Lawrence Roger. b 42. Univ of Dur BA (2nd cl Th) 64. Westcott Ho Cam 65. **d** 67 Dunwich for St E **p** 68 St E. C of Bramford 67-71; Tutor Woodbridge Abbey and Asst Chap Woodbridge Sch 71-77; R of Culford w W Stow and Wordwell Dio St E from 77; P-in-c of Flempton w Hengrave (and Lackford from 79) Dio St E from 77. *West Stow Rectory, Bury St Edmunds, Suff, IP28 6ET.* (Culford 220)

PJEAUNG, Li. **d** 71 Akyab. d Dio Akyab. *Pi Chaung, Paletwa, Burma.*

PLACE, Canon Ralph Harrison. b 03. St Chad's Coll Dur BA 28, MA and Dipl Th 31. **d** 29 **p** 30 Bradf. C of St Barn Heaton 29-35; Min of St Cuthb Wrose 35-38; V of H Trin Bingley 38-44; Ch Ch Skipton 44-53; Sec Bradf Dioc Conf

51-53; V of Penistone w Midhope 53-56; Menston-in-Wharfedale w Woodhead 56-65; Proc Conv Bradf 56-70; Hon Can of Bradf 57-77; Can (Emer) from 77; R of Burnsall 65-71. *3 Abbeyfield, Woodlands Drive, Gargrave Road, Skipton, N Yorks.* (Skipton 3219)

PLACE, Rodger Goodson. b 37. St Chad's Coll Dur BA 60, Dipl Th 62. **d** 62 **p** 63 Heref. C of Pontesbury 62-65; St Martin Heref 65-68; V of Ditton Priors 68-75; R of Neenton 68-75; C-in-c of Aston Botterell w Wheathill and Loughton 69-75; Burwarton w Cleobury 69-75; Dacre w Hartwith Dio Ripon 75-76; V from 76. *Vicarage, Dacre Banks, Harrogate, HG3 4ED.* (Harrogate 780262)

PLAISTER, Keith Robin. b 43. K Coll Lon and Warm BD (2nd cl) and AKC 65. **d** 66 Colchester for Chelmsf **p** 67 Chelmsf. C of Laindon w Basildon 66-71; V of Gt Wakering (w Foulness from 78) Dio Chelmsf from 71. *2 New Road, Great Wakering, Essex, SS3 0AH.* (Southend 219226)

PLAISTOWE, Ven Ronald Percy Frank. b 11. St Jo Coll Dur LTh 34, BA 35. Clifton Th Coll. **d** 35 **p** 36 Bris. C of St Ambrose Bris 35-39; St Alb Westbury Pk Clifton 39-42; PC of Cleeve 42-48; V of St Pet Palmerston N 48-53; Timaru 53-63; Archd of Timaru 53-63; V of Sumner-Heathcote 63-68; Archd of Sumner 63-68; Ch Ch 68-71; Archd (Emer) from 71; Dep VG of Ch Ch 68-71; VG 71-76; V of Merivale 68-75; Exam Chap to Bp of Ch Ch 73-75; Chap of St Geo Hosp Ch Ch from 75. *165 Main Road, Christchurch 8, NZ.* (849-632)

PLAMBECK, James Allan. Univ of Ill MSc 62, PhD 65. **d** 72 **p** 73 Edmon. C of St Geo City and Dio Edmon 72-73; Hon C from 74. *11736 - 83 Avenue, Edmonton, Alta., Canada.* (403-433 1313)

PLANT, James Francis. Bp's Univ Lennox BA 52. **d** 52 **p** 53 Ott. I of Mattawa 52-54; S March 54-56; C of St Luke Ott 56-61; R of St Mich AA City and Dio Ott from 61. *1124 Field Street, Ottawa 4, Canada.*

PLANT, Richard George Nicholas. b 45. Univ of Man BA 67. Coll of Resurr Mirfield 68. **d** 71 **p** 72 Wakef. C of St Jo Cleckheaton 71-74; Adel w Ireland Wood 74-78; V of Ireland Wood 78-82; Armley w New Wortley Dio Ripon from 82. *Armley Vicarage, Wesley Road, Leeds, LS12 1SR.* (Leeds 638620)

PLANT, Robert David. b 28. Univ of Birm BSc 49. St Deiniol's Libr Hawarden 74. **d** 76 St A **p** 80 Cant (APM). C of Llandrillo-yn-Rhos 76-79; C of St Nich-at-Wade w Sarre & Chislet w Hoath Dio Cant from 79. *4 Sandalwood Drive, St Nicholas-at-Wade, Birchington, Kent, CT7 0PE.*

PLASTOW, Graham Henry George. b 40. St Jo Coll Nottm 68. **d** 71 **p** 72 Lon. C of St Marylebone w H Trin 71-74; Marlborough 74-77; P-in-c of N Shoebury Dio Chelmsf from 77. *North Shoebury Vicarage, Weare Gifford, Shoeburyness, Essex, SS3 8AB.* (0702 584053)

PLATT, Andrew Martin Robert. b 41. Oak Hill Coll 74. **d** 76 **p** 77 St Alb. C of St Paul St Alb 76-79; V of Gazeley w Dalham and Moulton Dio St E from 79. *Gazeley Vicarage, Newmarket, Suff.* (Newmarket 750719)

PLATT, Canon Ernest Wilfrid. b 10. Univ of Sheff BA 32. Lich Th Coll 32. **d** 34 **p** 35 Sheff. C of Eastwood 34-36; Succr of Leic Cathl 36-45; Chap RAFVR 41-46; V of St Anne Leic 46-56; Hinckley Dio Leic from 56; Surr from 56; RD of Sparkenhoe ii 60-71; Hon Can of Leic Cathl from 74. *Hinckley Vicarage, Leicester.* (Hinckley 637691)

PLATT, George Herbert. b 06. Linc Th Coll 30. **d** 33 **p** 34 Sheff. C of Tinsley 33-36; St Chad Norton Woodseats 36-38; V of Hook 38-45; Offg C-in-c of Airmyn 40-45; V of Oughtibridge 45-51; Chap Middlewood and Wharncliffe Hosps 47-50; V of Barkston w Syston 51-56; Chap St John's Hosp Linc and LPr Dio Linc 56-64; R of Willoughby w Sloothby 64-71; C-in-c of Ulceby w Fordington 64-68; R 68-71; C-in-c of Claxby and Dexthorpe 64-70; R 70-71. *1 Croft Drive, Tranby Lane, Anlaby, Hull, Yorks, HU10 7DZ.* (Hull 653053)

PLATT, Harold Geoffrey. b 27. Down Coll Cam BA 50, MA 52. Ridley Hall Cam. **d** 53 **p** 54 Ely. C of St Paul Cam 53-56; Min of St Martin's Conv Distr Cam 56-57; R of St Clem Broughton Salford 57-66; C-in-c of St Matthias w St Simon Salford 62-66; L to Offic Dio Man 66-76; Dio Worc from 76. *Island House, Belbroughton, Nr Stourbridge, W Midl, DY9 0DX.*

PLATT, James Henry. b 1898. Bp Wilson Th Coll IM 34. **d** 36 **p** 37 Derby. C of St Alkmund Derby 36-39; Ripponden (in c of Rishworth) 39-41; V 41-46; St Jo Div Sowerby 44-46; Skelmanthorpe 46-49; Wragby 49-55; R of Cumberworth 55-59; Saxby 59-60; V of Bonby 59-60; R of Ballaugh 60-66; V of Kirk German 66-69. *3 Ballakneale Avenue, Port Erin, IM.* (Port Erin 832569)

PLATT, John Dendy. b 24. Magd Coll Cam BA 49, MA 55. Wells Th Coll 50. **d** 52 **p** 53 Guildf. C of Headley 52-56; Haslemere 56-58; R of Skelton w Hutton-in-the-Forest 59-71. *c/o Lloyds Bank, 6 Pall Mall, SW1.*

PLATT, John Emerson. b 36. Pemb Coll Ox BA (2nd cl Th) 59, MA 65, DPhil 77. Univ of Hull MTh 72. Cudd Coll 59. **d** 61 **p** 62 Blackb. C of Adlington 61-64; St Mich AA Sutton-in-Holderness 64-68; St Giles Ox 68-71; Asst Chap Pemb Coll Ox 68-69; Chap from 69. *57 Great Clarendon Street, Oxford, OX2 6AX.* (Oxford 57660)

PLATT, Michael Robert. b 39. SS Coll Cam BA 61. Cudd Coll 62. **d** 64 Ripon. C of Far Headingley 64-65; Asst Master Belmont Coll Barnstaple 65-68; Qu Coll Taunton from 68; Ho Master from 72. *Howard Vivian House, Wild Oak Lane, Taunton, Somt.*

PLATT, Reginald Thomas. BD (Lon) 62. Moore Th Coll Syd ACT ThL 61. **d** 62 Bp Hudson for Syd **p** 63 Syd. C of Pagewood 62-64; C-in-c of Matraville 64-67; Gen Sec CMS Queensld and L to Offic Dio Brisb 67-74; R of Longueville Dio Syd from 74. *37 Arabella Street, Longueville, NSW, Australia 2066.* (42-2581)

PLATT, William David. b 31. St Chad's Coll Dur BA 54. Coll of Resurr Mirfield 54. **d** 56 **p** 57 Lon. C of St John-on-Bethnal-Green 56-60; Pinner 60-65; V of St Kath N Hammersmith 65-72; Woodham Dio Guildf from 72. *Woodham Vicarage, Woking, Surrey, GU21 5SH.* (Woking 62857)

PLATTEN, Stephen George. b 47. Univ of Lon BEd 72. Trin Coll Ox Dipl Th 74. Cudd Coll 72. **d** 75 Reading for Ox **p** 76 Buckingham for Ox. C of St Andr Headington 75-78; Chap and Tutor Linc Th Coll from 78. *Lincoln Theological College, Lincoln, LN1 3BP.* (0522-38885)

PLATTEN, Canon Thomas George. b 1899. Late Exhib and Scho of St Jo Coll Cam 1st cl Nat Sc Trip pt i 21, BA (1st cl Anthrop Trip) 22, MA 26. Westcott Ho Cam 22. **d** 23 **p** 24 Man. C of St Chrys Vic Pk Man 23-27; Dom and Dioc Chap to Bp of Wakef and L to Offic Dio Wakef 27-28; Miss at Trin Coll Kandy 28-32; Chap Coll of St Mark and St John Chelsea 32-35; Warden of Bp Heber Hall and Prof in Madr Coll 36-46; Exam Chap to Bp of Madr 38-46; Prin of Saltley Tr Coll Birm 47-68; Hon Can Birm 52-68; Can (Emer) from 68; Perm to Offic Dio Cov 68-74; P-in-c of Honington w Idlicote 71-81. *Fexhole Cottage, Lower Brailes, Banbury, Oxon.* (Brailes 319)

PLAWA, Stephen. H Cross Coll Rang. **d** 66 **p** 67 Rang. P Dio Rang 66-70; Dio Pa-an from 70. *St Mark's Church, Kundaw, Kawthoolei, Burma.*

PLAXTON, Ven Cecil Andrew. b 02. St Edm Hall Ox BA 24, MA 28. Cudd Coll 25. **d** 26 **p** 27 B & W. C of Chard 26-28; St Martin Sarum 28-32; V of Southbroom 32-37; H Trin Weymouth 37-51; R of Pewsey 51-65; Surr from 35; RD of Weymouth 44-51; Can and Preb of Sarum Cathl from 48; Archd of Wilts 51-74; Archd (Emer) from 74. *St Edmund's Way, Potterne Road, Devizes, Wilts.* (Devizes 3391)

PLAXTON, Edmund John Swithun. b 36. K Coll Lon and Warm AKC 60. **d** 61 **p** 62 S'wark. C of Crofton Pk 61-65; Coulsdon (in c of St Francis) 65-69; V of St Paul Forest Hill 69-80; Belmont Dio S'wark from 80. *Vicarage, Belmont Rise, Sutton, Surrey, SM2 6EA.* (01-642 2363)

PLAYFAIR, Ven Ross Patrick Lyon Ferris. Bp's Univ Lennox BA (Th) 54. **d** 54 Queb **p** 55 Ott. Miss at Mattawa 54-59; C of All SS Ott 61; R of St Geo City and Dio Ott from 61; Archd of Ott E from 73. *8 Cobalt Avenue, Ottawa, Ontario, Canada.* (1-613-235-1636)

PLESTER, Geoffrey Eversden. d 58 St Arn **p** 64 NW Austr. Hon C of Maryborough 58-60; Geraldton 60-62; C of Greenough 62-63; Hon Chap Miss to Seamen Geraldton from 63; Hon C of Geraldton Cathl 63-64; C 64-65; R of Dongara w Greenough-Walkaway 65-69; Prec St Jo Bapt Cathl Kalg 69; R of Boulder 69-70; C of H Cross Cathl Geraldton Dio NW Austr from 70. *18 Carson Terrace, Geraldton, W Australia 6530.* (099-213639)

PLIMLEY, Canon William. b 17. St Aid Coll 50. **d** 52 **p** 53 Ches. C of Norbury Stockport 52-55; V of Laisterdyke Dio Bradf from 55; RD of Calverley 65-78; Hon Can of Bradf from 67. *Laisterdyke Vicarage, Parsonage Road, Bradford, BD4 8PY, Yorks.* (Bradford 664565)

PLOWMAN, Richard Robert Bindon. b 38. [f Solicitor]. Ridley Hall Cam 76. **d** 78 Taunton for B & W **p** 79 B & W. C of Combe Down w Monkton Combe (and S Stoke from 81) Dio B & W from 78. *77b Bradford Road, Combe Down, Bath, Avon, BA2 5BP.* (Combe Down 832191)

PLOWRIGHT, Ernest William. b 1900. Univ of Bris BA 29. Sarum Th Coll 28. **d** 30 **p** 31 Bris. C of Shirehampton 30-32; St Mich AA (in c of the Good Shepherd) Bishopston 32-36; V of Hanham w Hanham Abbots 36-58; Chap Hanham Hall 50-58; RD of Bitton 51-58; Hon Can Bris 55-58; PC of Drayton 58-70; Muchelney 58-70; Perm to Offic Dio B & W from 70. *8 Davis Terrace, Tucker Street, Wells, Somt, BA5 2DX.* (Wells 73486)

PLOWRIGHT, Joseph Arnold. b 22. Univ of Leeds BA 43. Coll of Resurr Mirfield 40. **d** 45 Stepney for Lon **p** 46 Kens for Lon. C of Great Greenford 45-47; St Martin Knowle Bris 47-50; St Mark Mansfield 50-53; Chap RN 53-75; C of Ch Ch w St Paul St Marylebone 75-78; Hon C of St Jo Bapt Portland 78-80. *Address temp unknown.*

PLUMB, Bernard Outing. **d** and **p** 31 Nel. V of Murchison 31-33; C of Ch Ch Cathl Nel 33-35; Blenheim 35-36; St Luke Oamaru 36-39; V of Waimea Plains 39-41; CF (NZ) 42-46; V of Banks Peninsula 46-49; Opawa 49-55; L River 55-63; L to Offic Dio Ch Ch from 63. *298 Keyes Road, Christchurch 7, NZ.*

PLUMBRIDGE, Canon William Edward. b 1891. St Cath Coll Ox BA (3rd cl Mod Hist) 12, MA 27. **d** 21 **p** 22 Wakef. C of All SS Cathl Wakef 21-45; Asst Master Gr Sch Wakef 13-51; Chap St Pet Conv Horbury 45-71; Hon Chap to Bp of Wakef 56-71; Hon Can of Wakef 60-71; Can (Emer) from 71. *College of St Barnabas, Blackberry Lane, Lingfield, Surrey, RH7 6NJ.*

PLUMLEY, Jack Martin. b 10. Univ of Dur Th Exhib 30, Hebr Scho 31. St Jo Coll Dur BA (3rd cl Th) 32, MLitt 39. K Coll Cam MA (*ad eundem*) 50. **d** 33 **p** 34 Lon. C of St Luke Hackney 33-35; Enfield 35-37; H Trin Kingsway 37-40; Actg C of St Geo Mart w H Trin Holborn 40-41; V of Ch Ch Hoxton 41-45; St Paul Tottenham 45-47; R of Milton 47-57; Select Pr Univ of Cam 55 and 59; Prof of Egyptology Univ of Cam and Fell of Selw Coll Cam from 57; P-in-c of Longstone Dio Ely from 80; Actg Dean of Pemb Coll Cam 81-82. *Selwyn College, Cambridge.*

PLUMLEY, Paul Jonathan. b 42. St Jo Coll Nottm 71. **d** 74 **p** 75 Nor. C of St Cath Mile Cross Nor 74-77; P-in-c of Stoke Ash w Thwaite and Wetheringsett 77-79; Wickham Skeith 77-79, Assoc Min of St Jo Evang Woodbridge Dio St E from 74. *5 Bury Hill, Melton, Woodbridge, Suff, IP12 1LF.*

PLUMMER, Arthur Jasper. b 09. Keble Coll Ox BA (3rd cl Hist) 31, MA 36. Ely Th Coll 31. **d** 32 **p** 33 S'wark. C of Lady Marg Walworth 32-34; Actg C of Credition 40-45; R of High Bickington (w Atherington from 57) 45-74; Perm to Offic Dio Ex 74-77; Dio B & W from 80; Actg Chap Ch of the Ascen Cadenabbia 77. *Ferndale, Rockford, Brendon, N Devon.* (Brendon 207)

PLUMMER, Canon Charles Henry. b 06. St Aid Coll 40. **d** 40 Bp Tubbs for Ches **p** 41 Ches. C of St John Bollington 40-43; Bp of Ches Chap for Youth and L to Offic Dio Ches 43-48; C-in-c of St Marg Lothbury Lon 48-51; Chap and Sec of Lon Dioc Coun for Children Youth and for Further Educn 48-51; V of Ch Ch Southgate 51-58; Chap Halliwick Cripples' Sch 54-58; CF (TA) from 54; Surr from 57; V of Hemel Hempstead 58-66; Chap W Herts and St Paul's Hosps 59-66; C-in-c of St Paul Hemel Hempstead 60-62; Hon Can of St Alb 61-66; Can (Emer) from 66; R of Dereham Group (V of E Dereham w Hoe 66-73; C-in-c of Mattishall 70-73; Mattishall Burgh 70-73; Hockering 70-73; N Tuddenham 70-73; Welborne 70-73; Yaxham 70-73; RD of Mitford from 66; Chairman of Youth Comm Dio Nor 71-81; Chap to Dereham Hosp from 66; Hon Chap to Bp of Nor from 81. *27 Quebec Road, Dereham, Norfolk.* (Dereham 3971)

PLUMPTON, Paul. b 50. Keble Coll Ox BA 72. St Steph Ho Ox 72. **d** 74 **p** 75 Man. C of Tonge Moor 74-76; Atherton 76-79; V of St Jas Oldham Dio Man from 79. *8 Rosedale Close, Oldham, Lancs, OL1 4BU.* (061-633 4441)

PLUMPTRE, John Basil. b 25. Pemb Coll Cam BA 49, MA 54. Launde Abbey Leic 75. **d** 75 **p** 76 Leic. C of St Pet Leic 75-80; E Leake Group Dio Southw from 81. *Rectory, Stanford on Soar, East Leake, Loughborough, Leics.*

PLUMRIDGE, George William. Em Coll Sktn. **d** 28 Sask for Keew **p** 29 Keew. C of Redditt 28-30; I of Ignace 30-34; Dryden w Eagle River and Minnitaki 34-39; Exam Chap to Bp of Keew 39-48; Hon Can of Keew 44-48; Archd of Kenora and Rainy River 48-62; Keew 62-71. *Box 301, Dryden, Ont., Canada.*

PLUNKETT, Michael Edward. b 38. Univ of Leeds BSc (2nd cl) 61. Ely Th Coll 61. **d** 63 Warrington for Liv **p** 64 Liv. C of Kirkby 63-68; Lect of Stockton-on-Tees 68-72; L to Offic Dio Dur 72-73; Team V of Stockton-on-Tees Centr 73-75; V of St Jude Cantril Farm 75-81; Melling Dio Liv from 81; Sec Dioc Bd of Miss and Social Responsibility Dio Liv from 81. *Melling Vicarage, Liverpool, L31 1EE.* (051-526 6013)

PLUNKETT, Pelham Stanley. b 12. Trin Coll Dub BA 36, MA 39. **d** 59 Roch **p** 59 Bp Stannard for Roch. C of Tonbridge 59-62; Hildenborough 62-63; V 63-68; Lect Poole 68-69; V of St Cath Nor 69-81; Commiss Dio Kigezi from 75; Hon C of Hordle (in c of St Andr Tiptoe) Dio Win from 81. *c/o Church Cottage, Sway Road, Tiptoe, Lymington, Hants.* (New Milton 616670)

PLUNKETT, Peter William. b 30. Oak Hill Th Coll. **d** 61 **p** 62 Liv. C of Em Fazakerley 61-64; St Mark St Helens Lancs 64-68; V of St Paul N Shore Kirkdale 68-79; P-in-c of SS Mary w John Bootle 77-79; V of SS Mary w Paul Bootle 79-81; St Paul Goose Green Dio Liv from 81. *St Paul's Vicarage, Warrington Road, Goose Green, Wigan, WN3 6QB.* (0942-42984)

PLYMOUTH, Lord Bishop Suffragan of. *See* Newing, Right Rev Kenneth Albert.

PLYMOUTH, Archdeacon of. *See* Ellis, Ven Robin Gareth.

POARCH, John Chilton. b 30. Univ of Bris BA (2nd cl Hist) 54. Ridley Hall Cam 54. **d** 56 **p** 57 Bris. C of Ch Ch Swindon 56-59; Corsham 59-61; R of Praslin Seychelles 61-63; V of St Cuthb Brislington 63-69; Archd of Seychelles and R of St Paul's Cathl Mahé 69-72; V of Warmley Dio Bris from 72; R of Syston Dio Bris from 72; Commiss Sey from 73; RD of Bitton from 79; P-in-c of Bitton Dio Bris from 80. *Vicarage, Warmley, Bristol, BS15 5JJ.* (Bris 673965)

PO CHO, Jonathan. H Cross Coll Rang 60. **d** 64 **p** 65 Rang. P Dio Rang 64-70; Dio Pa-an from 70; Sec and Treas Dio Pa-an from 80. *Dioceson Office, Nat Shin Naung Road, Toungoo, Burma.*

POCKLINGTON, Canon Eric Charles. b 12. Kelham Th Coll 28. **d** 35 Dur **p** 36 Jarrow for Dur. C of St Columba Southwick 35-41; St Geo Cullercoats 41-43; Miss at Msumba 43-49; P-in-c of Likwenu 49-55; Chap at Blantyre 55; R 56-62; V of St Phil Georgetown Br Gui 62-65; Tonge Moor 65-70; St Oswald-in-Lee w Bingfield and Wall 70-78; RD of Hexham 71-78; Hon Can of Newc T from 74; P-in-c of Eyemouth Dio Edin from 78. *Parsonage, Eyemouth, Berwicks.* (0390-50000)

POCOCK, Frank Lovell. b 08. OBE 59. Em Coll Cam BA 32, MA 36. Ridley Hall Cam 33. **d** 33 **p** 34 Ex. Chap of Newton Coll Newton Abbot 34-36; Chap RN 36-63; V of Martin 63-67; R of Ringwould w Oxney 67-77; P-in-c of St Jo Evang Kingsdown 74-77; Perm to Offic Dio Cant from 79. *55 Balfour Road, Walmer, Deal, Kent.* (Deal 2314)

POCOCK, George Shiel. St Pet Th Coll Ja. **d** and **p** 39 Ja. C of Buff Bay w Birnamwood 39; R 39-44; R of Swanswick (w Falmouth from 45) 44-49; C of H Cross Cant 49; V of Elsenham 50-55; R of L Thurrock 55-56; Falmouth Ja 56-58; Golden Grove 58-63; Buff Bay w Birnamwood 63-70. *The Muschette Home, Duncans PO, Jamaica, W Indies.*

POCOCK, Lawrence Bruce. b 38. Hur Coll Lon Ont MDiv 78. **d** 78 Bp Robinson for Hur **p** 79 Hur. C of Bp Cronyn Mem Ch Lon 78-80; I of Lucan Dio Hur from 80. *Box 539, Lucan, Ont, Canada, N0M 2J0.*

POCOCK, Lawrence Victor. Wycl Coll Tor. **d** 28 **p** 29 Tor. C of St Matt Tor 29; R of Blyth w Auburn and Belgrave 30-35; Florence w Aughrim 35-39; I of Hespeler 39-51; St D Lon Ont 51; Chap Publ Inst 51-52; I of Ingersoll 56-63; Riverside 63-66; R of St Aid Windsor 66-68; Cayuga 68-73. *59 Norton Crescent, Georgetown, Ont., Canada.*

POCOCK, Leonard Richard. CD 58. Univ of BC BA 50. Wycl Coll Tor LTh 54, BD 67. **d** 52 **p** 53 Tor. C of Birch Cliff 52-53; I of Cavan 53-55; CF (Canad) 55-74. *3811 Quesnell Drive, Vancouver, BC, Canada.*

POCOCK, Nigel John. b 47. Univ of Lon BSc 68. Lambeth STh 78. Oak Hill Th Coll 69. **d** 72 **p** 73 Roch. C of St Jas Tunbridge Wells 72-75; Heatherlands 75-78; V of St Chris City and Dio Leic from 78. *St Christopher's Vicarage, Marriott Road, Leicester, LE2 6NU.* (Leic 832679)

POCOCK, Raymond Ernest. St Jo Coll Morpeth 60. ACT ThL (2nd cl) 63. **d** 63 **p** 64 Adel. C of Unley 63-65; P-in-c of Penola 65-71; Meadows 71-74; Norton Summit (w Montacute from 76) 74-79; Dir Inter-Ch trade & Industr Miss Tas from 79. *Inter-Ch Trade & Industry Mission, 58 Forest Road, W Hobart, Tasmania 7000.* (002 23 6285)

PO DAN, Dunstan. H Cross Coll Rang. **d** 63 Rang. d Dio Rang 63-70; Dio Pa-an from 70. *St Mary's Church, Kappali, Myitkyina District, Burma.*

PODGER, Richard Philip Champeney. b 38. K Coll Cam BA 61, Th Trip pt ii 62, MA 66. Cudd Coll 62. **d** 64 **p** 65 Sheff. C of Doncaster 64-68; Orpington (in c of Ch of Unity Ramsden) 68-74. *2 Pound Cottages, Risby, Bury St Edmunds, IP28 6QJ.* (Bury St Ed 810057)

POER, Raymond Beresford. b 1894. Trin Coll Dub Downes Pri (1st) and Div Test (2nd cl) 16, BA 17, MA 24. **d** 17 **p** 18 Cash. C of Portlaw 17-22; Dioc C of Cork Cloyne and Ross 22-27; I of Kinsale U 27-46; Dean of Ross Cathl, Preb of H Trin in Cork Cathl and R of Ross w Rathbarry (w Kilmacabea U from 59) 46-68; RD of Timoleague 50-68. *6 Sydenham Terrace, Monkstown, Co Cork, Irish Republic.* (Cork 841132)

POGGO, Benaia Duku. Bp Gwynne Coll Mundri, 61. **d** 64 Bp Dotiro for Sudan **p** 66 Sudan. P Dio Sudan. *c/o Church Office, PO Box 110, Juba, Equatoria Province, Sudan.*

POGMORE, Edward Clement. b 52. Sarum Wells Th Coll 76. **d** 79 **p** 80 Sarum. C of Calne w Blackland Dio Sarum from 79. *30 Warren Crescent, Calne, Wilts, SN11 9BL.*

✠ **POGO, Right Rev Ellison Leslie.** b 47. St Jo Coll Auckld LTh 79. **d** 79 **p** 80 Dun. C of Andersons Bay 79-80; Cons Ld Bp of Ysabel 1 Nov 81 by Abps of Melan and Papua; Bps of Vanuatu, Temotu, Malaita and Dun; and Bps Alufurai and Tuti. *Bishop's House, Jejevo, Ysabel, Solomon Islands.*

POGO, Harry. **d** 57 Melan. d Dio Melan 57-74. *Vatupura, Gela, Solomon Islands.*

POGSON, Ruth Elena. b 24. Univ of Tor BA 47. Univ of Columbia NY MA 53. Wycl Coll Tor LTh 54. **d** 77 **p** 78 Rupld. Dir of Field Educn (Div) St Jo Coll Winnipeg from 77; Hon C of St Aid Winnipeg Dio Rupld from 78. *1750 Pembina Hy, Apt 118W, Winnipeg, Manit, Canada, R3T 4J5.*

POHL, Wilfred Ernest. Univ of Natal BA 49. Coll of Resurr Mirfield. **d** 56 **p** 57 Zulu. P Dio Zulu 56-58; Dio Johann from 58. *Box 59052, Kengray, Johannesburg, S Africa.*

PO HLA, Luke. H Cross Coll Rang. **d** 59 **p** 60 Rang. P Dio Rang 59-70; Dio Pa-an from 70. *St Peter's Mission, Toungoo, Burma.*

POIL, Ronald Wickens. b 30. AKC 56. **d** 57 **p** 58 Cant. C of Willesborough 57-60; Chap RAF 60-76; C-in-c of Edith Weston w Normanton 65-67; V of Southbourne (w W Thorney from 80) Dio Chich from 76; P-in-c of W Thorney 76-80; RD of Westbourne from 78. *Southbourne Vicarage, Emsworth, Hants, PO10 8JE.* (Emsworth 2436)

POINTS, John David. b 43. Qu Coll Birm 78. **d** 80 **p** 81 Lich. C of Wood Green Dio Lich from 80. *315 Crankhall Lane, Wednesbury, W Midl, WS10 9QQ.*

PO KHAI, d 39 **p** 40 Rang. P Dio Rang. *St Luke's School, Toungoo, Burma.*

POKU, Canon Daniel Kofi. St Aug Coll Kumasi. **d** and **p** 32 Accra. P Dio Accra 32-71; Dio Kum 73; Hon Can of Kum from 73. *PO Box 4117, Kumasi, Ghana.*

PO KUN, Canon Luke. St Jo Coll Rang. **d** 27 **p** 28 Rang. P Dio Rang; Archd of the Delta 45-70; Hon Can of Rang Cathl from 45. *Bishop's Home, 44 Prome Road, Rangoon, Burma.*

POLE, Francis John Michael. b 42. **d** 67 RC Bp of Arundel & Brighton **p** 68 RC Abp of S'wark. In RC Ch 68-75; Rec into Angl Commun by Bp of Chelmsf (APM). C of St Pet Walthamstow 75; H Trin Beckenham 76-77; St John Shirley 77-79; Perm to Offic Dio Cant 79; Asst Chap of St Phil and St John The Hague Dio Lon (N & C Eur) from 79. *Riouwstr 2, The Hague, Netherlands.*

POLGEN, Norman. **d** 69 Perth **p** 74 Rockptn. L to Offic Dio Perth 69-70; C of H Cross Cathl Geraldton 70-72; Asst St Geo Homes Parkhurst 72-80; P-in-c of St Geo Miss Palm I Dio N Queensld from 80. *St George's Mission, Palm Island, Queensland, Australia 4816.*

POLHILL, Arthur John Henry. b 20. Sarum Th Coll 65. **d** 67 **p** 68 Ex. C of Tor Mohun 67-71; V of Tipton St John w Venn Ottery Dio Ex from 71. *Tipton St John Vicarage, Sidmouth, Devon, EX10 0AQ.* (Ottery St Mary 2760)

POLITT, Robert William. b 47. Oak Hill Coll 73. **d** 76 **p** 77 Roch. C of St Pet Bexleyheath Dio Roch from 76. *46 Berkeley Avenue, Bexleyheath, Kent, DA7 4UA.* (01-304 6726)

POLKINGHORNE, John Charlton. b 30. Trin Coll Cam MA 56, PhD 55, ScD 74. Westcott Ho Cam 79. **d** 81 Ely (NSM). Fell of Trin Coll Cam from 54. C of St Andr Chesterton Dio Ely from 81. *22 Belvoir Road, Cambridge, CB4 1JJ.*

POLLAK, Peter Henry. b 18. Worc Ordin Coll 67. **d** 69 **p** 70 Worc. C of Claines 69-73; V of Grimley w Holt Dio Worc from 73. *Grimley Vicarage, Worcester, WR2 6LT.* (Worc 640242)

POLLARD, Canon Clifford Francis. b 20. AKC 49. St Bonif Coll Warm 49. **d** 50 **p** 51 Heref. C of Leominster 50-53; Luton 53-56; V of Stopsley 56-60; Toc H Chap in Kent and Sussex 60-64; R of Mersham 64-68; Asst Dir Educn Dio Cant 68-69; Dir from 69; Hon Can of Cant from 72. *6 Lady Wootton's Green, Canterbury, Kent, CT1 1NQ.* (Canterbury 61674)

POLLARD, (David-Matthew) David Stanley. b 49. AKC and BD 80. **d** 80 **p** 81 Bradf. M CGA. C of St Mary Magd Manningham Dio Bradf from 80. *28 White's View, Bradford, BD8 8NN.*

POLLARD, David. b 55. Univ of Lon BSc 77. Trin Coll Bris 78. **d** 80 **p** 81 Arctic. P-in-c of Coppermine Dio Arctic from 80. *St Andrew's Anglican Mission, Coppermine, NWT X0E 0E0, Canada.*

POLLARD, Geoffrey. Ely Th Coll. **d** 65 **p** 66 Lon. C of St Mary Brookfield 65-68; St Mary Magd Munster Square St Pancras 68-71; V of St Sav w St Jas L Westmr Dio Lon from 71. *75 St George's Square, SW1 3QW.* (01-821 9526)

POLLARD, James Adrian Hunter. b 48. Univ of Nottm BTh 78. St Jo Coll Nottm 74. **d** 78 **p** 79 Liv. C of Much Woolton 78-81. *Haygrass House, Taunton, Somt, TA3 7BS.*

POLLARD, John Edward Ralph. b 40. ALCD 68. **d** 67 **p** 68 Southw. C of Ollerton 67-71; H Trin Walton 71-74; V of Haddenham (w Cuddington and Kingsey from 77) Dio Ox from 74; Kingsey 74-77; P-in-c of Cuddington 74-77. *Haddenham Vicarage, Aylesbury, Bucks, HP17 8AF.* (Haddenham 291244)

POLLARD, Noel Stewart. Univ of Syd BA (3rd cl Hist) 51, BD 56. Ch Ch Ox BA (2nd cl Th) 58, MA 63. Moore Th Coll Syd. **d** and **p** 53 Syd. C of Rose Bay w Vaucluse 53; Prec of St Andr Cathl Syd 53-56; C of Ch Ch Cathl Ox 57-58; H Sepulchre Cam Dio Ely 58-61; Lect and Libr Moore Th Coll Syd 62-68; L to Offic Dio Syd 67-72; Master New Coll Univ of NSW 68-72; Lect St John's Coll Nottm and Univ of Nottm from 72; Publ Pr Dio Southw from 73. *c/o St John's College, Nottingham.*

POLLARD, Roger Frederick. b 32. Univ of Sheff BSc 52. Univ of Lanc MA 78. Bp's Hostel Linc 56. **d** 58 **p** 59 S'wark. C of Catford 58-63; V of Takoradi 63-66; C of St Osw Fulford York 66-67; St Geo Camberwell 67; Asst Master Roch Valley Sch Milnrow 68-69; S Craven Sch Cross Hills from 69; Perm to Offic Dio Bradf from 70. *High Close Barn, New House Lane, Long Preston, Skipton, Yorks.*

POLLARD, Samuel Lister. McGill Univ BA (1st cl Hist and Med) 29, MA 30. Montr Dioc Th Coll LTh 32. **d** 34 **p** 35 Montr. C of Poltimore 34-37; I of Bordeaux w Cartierville and Ahuntsic Montr 37-57; Ahuntsic from 57; Chap of St Vinc de Paul 57-68. *422 St Louis Avenue, Pointe Claire, PQ, Canada, H9R 2A2.*

POLLARD, William Gilbert. b 12. Late Scho of CCC Cam 2nd cl Cl Trip pt i 32, BA (3rd cl Th Trip pt i) 34. Linc Th Coll 34. **d** 36 **p** 37 Win. C of Ch Ch Freemantle 36-39; Welwyn Garden City 39-41; Schs Sec SCM 41-42; Chap RNVR 42-46; YMCA w BAOR 47-49; Tutor St Paul's Coll Awka 49-51; Dennis Mem Gr Sch Onitsha 51-54; Prin of Ngwa High Sch Aba 54-60; St Aug Gr Sch Nkwerre 62-65; Chap Schlenker Secondary Sch Port Loko 66-69; Lect Ecole Normale Bangui 71-75; Chap Miss to Seamen Port Harcourt 76-77; Perm to Offic Dios Roch and Chich from 80. *2 Regency Terrace, Cambridge Gardens, Tunbridge Wells, Kent, TN2 4SD.*

POLLESEL, Michele Frank. b 49. Laurentian Univ Sudbury Ont BA 72. Trin Coll Tor MDiv 79. Bp Read for Tor **p** 80 Tor. C of St Simon-Ap City and Dio Tor from 79. *525 Bloor Street E, Toronto, Ont, Canada, M4W 1J1.*

POLLIT, Preb Michael. b 30. Worc Coll Ox BA 54, MA 58. Wells Th Coll 54. **d** 56 **p** 57 Lich. C of Cannock 56-59; Codsall (in c of H Cross Bilbrook) 59-62; V of St Pet W Bromwich 62-67; Proc Conv Lich from 64; R of Norton-le-Moors 67-76; RD of Leek 72-76; Surr from 73; V of St Chad Shrewsbury Dio Lich from 76; Preb of Lich Cathl from 81. *St Chad's Vicarage, Shrewsbury, Salop.* (Shrewsbury 3761)

POLLITT, Graham Anthony. b 48. Coun for Nat Acad Awards BA 79. Oak Hill Coll 76. **d** 79 **p** 80 Man. C of Rusholme Dio Man from 79. *102 Platt Lane, Manchester, M14 5WJ.* (061-224 1061)

POLLOCK, Daniel Harvey. St Francis Coll Brisb. **d** 74 **p** 75 Brisb. C of Bundaberg 74-75; St Nich Sandgate Brisb 75-77; V of Texas Dio Brisb from 77. *Vicarage, Broadway Street, Texas, Queensland, Australia 4385.* (Texas 30)

POLLOCK, Hugh Gillespie. Oak Hill Th Coll 61. **d** 64 **p** 65 Cant. C of St Luke Maidstone 64-68; Washfield 68-73; Chap Lee Abbey Lynton 73-76; V of Dersingham (w Anmer and Shernborne from 80) Dio Nor from 76; P-in-c of Anmer and of Shernborne 79-80. *Dersingham Vicarage, King's Lynn, Norf.* (Dersingham 214)

POLLOCK, James Colin Graeme. b 53. St Chad's Coll Dur BA 76. Ripon Coll Cudd 77. **d** 78 **p** 79 Dur. C of St Osw W Hartlepool Dio Dur from 78. *56 Wiltshire Way, Throston Grange, Hartlepool, Cleve, TS26 0TB.* (0429 79575)

POLLOCK, John Charles. b 23. Late Scho of Trin Coll Cam BA 46, MA 48. Ridley Hall Cam 49. **d** 51 **p** 52 Lon. C of St Paul Portman Sq St Marylebone 51-53; R of Horsington 53-58; Ed *The Churchman* 53-58; Perm to Offic Dio Ex from 61. *Rose Ash House, South Molton, Devon, EX36 4RB.* (Bishop's Nympton 403)

POLLOCK, John Gordon. b 26. Sarum Wells Th Coll 71. **d** 73 Ches. C of Lache w Saltney 73-75; Wilton 75-78; V of St Matthias Preston Dio Chich from 78. *45 Hollingbury Park Avenue, Brighton, Sussex, BN1 7JQ.* (Brighton 508178)

POLLOCK, Neil Thomas. b 38. Dipl Th (Lon) 68. Lich Th Coll. **d** 67 Lon **p** 68 Willesden for Lon. C of L Stanmore 67-72; C-in-c of St Marg Uxbridge 72-81; R of Norwood Dio Lon from 81. *Norwood Rectory, Norwood Green, Middx, UB2 4LE.* (01-574 1362)

POLLOCK, Norman Harvey. **d** 75 Brisb. Hon C of All SS Brisb 75-77; St Andr City and Dio Brisb from 77. *158 Wynnum Road, Norman Park, Brisbane, Queensland, Australia.* (399 3078)

POLLOCK, Norman Stuart. b 09. Dorch Miss Coll 33. **d** 35 **p** 36 Lon. C of St Aug Haggerston 35-36; St Jude Hampstead Garden Suburb 36-37; St Gabr Cricklewood 37-39; Perm to Offic at Ch Ch Ealing 39-41; Offg C-in-c of Dunblane 41-45; C of Ch Ch Esher 45-49; Chiswick 49-50; PC of St Francis Isleworth 50-65; R of Lichborough w Maidford 65-72; Commiss Lebom from 62; C in Hambleden Valley Group 72-79; Chap St Kath Conv Parmoor Dio Ox from 72; Warden from 80; Chap HM Borstal Finnamopre Wood

73-76. *Cedar Cottage, St Katharine's Convent, Parmoor, Bucks.* (High Wycombe 881446)

POLYNESIA, Lord Bishop in. *See* Bryce, Right Rev Jabez Leslie.

POLYNESIA, Assistant Bishop in. (Vacant)

POMEROY, Michael James. b 26. Sarum Th Coll 64. **d** 66 **p** 67 Sarum. C of Broadstone 66-69; C-in-c of Ibberton w Belchalwell and Woolland Dio Sarum 69-72; R (with Okeford Fitzpaine from 73) from 72. *Ibberton Rectory, Blandford, Dorset.* (Hazelbury Bryan 260)

POMERY, David John. b 45. Chich Th Coll 75. **d** 77 **p** 78 Lich. C of Ch Ch Coseley Dio 77-79; Stocksbridge (in c of Deepcar) 79-81; V of Bentley Dio Sheff from 81. *St Peter's Vicarage, High Street, Bentley, S Yorks, DN5 0AA.* (0302-874224)

POMFRET, Albert. Univ of Wales (Cardiff) BSc 57. Univ of Lon MA 69. Oak Hill Coll 72. **d** 75 Tonbridge for Roch **p** 76 Roch (APM). Hon C of Ch Ch Dartford 75-80; Lect Dartford Coll 61-79; Perm to Offic Dio Roch from 80. *70 Wentworth Drive, Dartford, Kent, DA1 3NG.*

POND, Nigel Peter Hamilton. b 40. K Coll Lon and Warm AKC 65. **d** 66 **p** 67 Nor. C of E Dereham 66-69; Chap RN from 69. *c/o Ministry of Defence, Lacon House, Theobalds Road, WC1X 8RY.*

POND, Wilfred Oscar. b 12. **d** 74 **p** 77 Antig. C of St Geo Dominica Dio Antig from 74. *Loubiere, Dominica, WI.*

PONT, Gordon John Harper. b 35. Univ of Glas BSc 56, BD 65. Edin Th Coll 56. **d** 59 **p** 60 St Andr. C of H Trin Dunfermline 59-62; Motherwell 62-65; R of Largs 65-68; Dioc Super Brech 68-71; Chap Univ of Dundee 68-73; R of St Luke Downfield Dundee 71-74; Hon Chap Dundee Cathl from 74. *5 Westpark Road, Dundee, DD2 1NU.* (Dundee 69883)

PONT, Philip Roy. b 03. Edin Th Coll 56. **d** and **p** 56 Glas. C of H Cross Knightswood Glas 56-58; R of Wishaw w Shotts 58-64; St Jo Evang Moffat Dio Glas from 64. *Rectory, Moffat, Dumfriesshire, DG10 9DS.* (Moffat 20176)

PONTEFRACT, Lord Bishop Suffragan of. *See* Hare, Right Rev Thomas Richard.

PONTEFRACT, Archdeacon of. *See* Unwin, Ven Kenneth.

PONTER, John Arthur. b 37. Univ of Wales BA (2nd cl Engl and Phil) 61. Linacre Ho Ox BA (2nd cl Th) 63, MA 68. Univ of E Anglia PhD 81. Wycl Hall Ox 61. **d** 63 **p** 64 Chelmsf. C of Gidea Pk 63-67; Min (V from 69) of St Anne's Eccles Distr Colchester 67-72; Chap Univ of E Anglia 72-77; Chelmsf Cathl from 78; V of St John Moulsham Dio Chelmsf from 79. *St John's Vicarage, Vicarage Road, Chelmsford, CM2 9PH.* (Chelmsf 352344)

PONTON, William Clifford. b 08. St D Coll Lamp BA (2nd cl Hist) 30. St Mich Th Coll Llan 31. **d** 32 Mon **p** 33 Llan for Mon. C of Mynyddisllwyn 32-35; St Paul Newport 35-40; V of Cwmtillery 40-46; Malpas 46-77; RD of Newport 67-77; Can of Mon Cathl 71-77. *1 Montgomery Road, Malpas, Newport, NP7 6QE.* (Newport 855929)

POODHUN, Lambert David. b 30. Univ of Natal BA 53. Edin Th Coll 54. **d** 56 Edin for Natal **p** 57 Natal. C of St Aid Durban 56-60; P-in-c of St Paul Pmbg 60-64; R 64-67; Ch Ch Overport Durban 67-76; Archd of Durban 75-76; C of Upton-cum-Chalvey (in c of St Pet) Slough 77-80; Chap Kingston Hosp 80-81; Tooting Bec Hosp from 81. *55A Fassett Road, Kingston upon Thames, Surrey, KT1 2TE.* (01-546 0190)

POOE, Motheo William. b 55. St Pet Coll Pmbg 78. **d** 80 Bp Stanage for Johann. C of St Mary Orlando Dio Johann from 80. *PO Box 19, Orlando, S Africa 1804.*

POOH, Tin Chee. Trin Coll Sing 60. **d** 63 **p** 64 Sing. C of Ch Ch Malacca 64-65; P-in-c of St Pet Ipoh 66-71; V of St Phil and St Jas Sungei Patani 72-73; Johore 73-74; St Matt City and Dio Sing from 74. *184 Neil Road, Singapore 2.*

POOLE, Aquilla James. McGill Univ BA 35, STM 55. Montr Dioc Th Coll LTh 37, BD 44. **d** 37 **p** 38 Montr. L to Offic Dio Montr 37-38; C of St Alb (Bp Carmichael Mem Ch) Montr 38; I of Arundel 38-39; Aylwin 39-42; R of Streetsville 42-43; Chap Ashbury Coll Ott 43-46; I of Vanleek Hill 46-55; R of Richmond 55-72. *1574 Birchwood Drive, Mississauga, Ont., Canada.*

POOLE, Arthur James. b 09. Qu Coll Birm 36. **d** 38 Pontefract for Wakef **p** 39 Wakef. C of Kirkburton 38-41; St Barn Crosland Moor 41-43; Chap Toc H Southampton and Perm to Offic Dio Win 43-44; V of All SS Pontefract 44-50; Crosland Moor 50-56; Childs Ercall 56-65; C-in-c of Stoke-on-Tern 56-57; R 57-65; V of Gt Haywood 65-78; R of Ingestre w Tixall 65-78; Perm to Offic Dio Lich from 78. *18 Balmoral Road, Baswich, Stafford, ST17 0AN.* (0785-40245)

POOLE, Denis Tom. b 19. St Jo Coll Dur 39. St Aid Coll 41. **d** 43 Liv **p** 44 Warrington for Liv. C of St Silas Toxt Pk 43-45; St Lawr Kirkdale 45-48; Chap Mariners' Ch Glouc and Glouc R Infirm 48-51; V of St Andr Lambeth 51-54; C-in-c of St Thos Lambeth 51-54; V of New Ferry 54-63; Biddulph Dio Lich from 63; Chap Biddulph Hosp from 63; Surr from 64. *Vicarage, Congleton Road, Biddulph, Stoke-on-Trent, ST8 7RG.* (Stoke-T 513247)

POOLE, John. b 19. Peterho Cam MA 44. St Alb Ministerial Tr Scheme 77. **d** 80 St Alb **p** 81 Hertf for St Alb. C of St Andr Bedford Dio St Alb from 80. *35 Falcon Avenue, Bedford.*

POOLE, John Denys Barlow. b 33. Qu Coll Cam 2nd cl Cl Trip pt i, 56, (2nd cl Th Trip pt ia) BA 57, MA 61. Cudd Coll 57. **d** 59 **p** 60 St Alb. C of St Luke Leagrave Luton 59-62; Raynes Pk 62-65; Apsley (in c of St Benedict) 65-72; R of W Wickham Dio Cant from 73. *22 Gates Green Road, West Wickham, Kent, BR4 9JW.* (01-462 4001)

POOLE, John Robert. b 46. Univ of Lon BSc 69. Univ of Bris Dipl Th 71. Clifton Coll Bris 69. **d** 72 **p** 73 Bradf. C of All SS Little Horton Bradf 72-75; Otley 75-79; V of Bankfoot Dio Bradf from 79. *Vicarage, Carrbottom Road, Bankfoot, Bradford, W Yorks.* (Bradf 726529)

POOLE, Canon Joseph Weston. b 09. Late Scho and Exhib of Jes Coll Cam 2nd cl Cl Trip pt i 30, BA 31, 3rd cl Th Trip pt i 32, MA 39. Westcott Ho Cam 32. **d** 33 **p** 34 Chelmsf. C of St Mary Virg Colchester 33-35; L to Offic Dio Lon 35-36; Min Can of Cant Cathl 36-49; Prec and Sacr 37-49; R of Merstham (w Gatton from 56) 49-58; C-in-c of Gatton 50-56; Hon Can of Cov 58-63; Prec 58-77; Can (Res) 63-77; Can (Emer) from 77. *21a Beauchamp Avenue, Royal Leamington Spa, Warws.* (Leamington 24614)

POOLE, Canon Maurice Philip. St Jo Coll Manit BA 42, LTh 44. **d** 44 **p** 45 Rupld. C of St Luke Winnipeg 44-46; I of St Mary Charleswood and H Trin Headingley 46-49; C of St Clem N Tor 49-50; R of All SS Peterborough 51-64; St John W Tor City and Dio Tor from 64; Dom Chap to Bp of Tor from 63; Can of Tor from 75; I of Stouffville Dio Tor from 80. *288 Humberside Avenue, Toronto, Ont, Canada.*

POOLE, Maurice Philip. Wilfrid Laurier Univ Ont BA 74. Trin Coll Tor MDiv 77. **d** 77 Tor Read for Tor. **p** 78 Tor. C of H Trin Thornhill Dio Tor from 77. *Box 185, Thornhill, Ont., Canada, L3T 3N3.*

POOLE, Peter William. b 35. St Pet Hall Ox BA 59, MA 63. Wells Th Coll 59. **d** 61 **p** 62 Cant. C of Cheriton Street 61-64; Birchington w Acol 64-67; V of Newington 67-73; Bearsted 73-76; C-in-c of Lower Halstow 72-73. *4 Albion Road, Booker, High Wycombe, Bucks.* (H Wycombe 29675)

POOLE, Richard Roderick. b 11. St Pet Hall Ox BA (3rd cl Engl Lang and Lit) 34. Ripon Hall Ox 34. **d** 36 **p** 37 Lon. C of H Trin St Marylebone 36-38; St Geo Bloomsbury 38-39; Waldron (in c of St Bart) 39-42; St Barn Hove 42-45; Slaugham 45-48; Stoke Bishop 48. *The Lodge, Botton Hall, Danby, Whitby, Yorks.*

POOLE, Ronald John Ajax. b 10. Selw Coll Cam BA 32, MA 36. Wells Th Coll 32. **d** 33 **p** 35 Lich. C of St Chad Wolverhampton 33-37; Asst Master St Mich Sch Tenbury 37; Min Can of Llan Cathl and Asst Master Cathl Sch 37-46; L to Offic Dio Llan 38-46; V of Penyfai 46-51; Sec Dioc Coun for Educn 51-64; R of Llandow w Llysworney 51-60; V of Tondu 60-73; Perm to Offic Dio Llan from 73. *20 Park Place, Brycethin, Bridgend, Mid Glam.*

POOLE, Roy John. b 26. Univ of Lon BD 54. ALCD 54 (LTh from 74). **d** 54 **p** 55 Newc T. C of St Aid Newc T 54-57; M of Bush Bro St Paul Charleville 57-59; C of Warw Queensld 59-61; R of Ch Ch Bradf 61-66; Area Sec Chr Aid Dept BCC 66-68; Regional Supervisor S & E Engl 68-74; Actg Dir of Home Missions Dio Perth 74-75; Executive Officer Angl Health and Welfare Services Dio Perth 75-77; Gen Sec W Austr Coun of Chs from 77. *199 Northstead Street, Scarborough, W Australia 6019.* (41 3679)

POOLE, Stanley Burke-Roche. b 09. K Coll Lon BA (1st cl Hist), Inglis Stud and Gladstone Pri 31, MA 34. Qu Coll Birm 36. **d** 38 **p** 39 Birm. C of St Germain Edgbaston and Lect Qu Coll Birm 38-39; Asst Master KS Cant 39-55; Asst Chap 39-48 and 55-64; Lect St Aug Coll Cant 49-50 and 52-53; V of Littlebourne 48-70. *13 Chaucer Court, New Dover Road, Canterbury, Kent, CT1 3AU.* (Cant 51586)

POOLE, William Harry Hardwicke. St Jo Coll Auckld 63. **d** 65 **p** 66 Wai. C of Rotorua 65-68; V of Waipiro Bay 68-74; Edgecumbe-Kawerau 74-76; C of St Paul Auckld 76-78; V of Manurewa Dio Auckld from 78. *Vicarage, Lupton Road, Manurewa, NZ.* (266-5266)

POOLE, Wynton Hardwicke. b 08. **d** and **p** 74 Wai. Hon C of Tauranga Dio Wai 74-80 and from 81; V of Waipaoa Par Distr 80-81. *Wairoa Road, RD1, Tauranga, NZ.* (25-737)

✠ **POOLE-HUGHES, Right Rev John Richard Worthington.** b 16. Hertf Coll Ox BA 39, MA 45. Wells Th Coll 45. **d** 47 **p** 48 St D. C of St Mich AA Aberystwyth 47-50; Miss at Korogwe 50-53; Sub-Warden St Cypr Th Coll Tunduru Dio Masasi 53-57; Chap St Mich Th Coll Llan 57-59; Home Sec UMCA 59-62; Cons Ld Bp of SW Tang in the Ch of St Matt

Idunda Njombe 31 May 62 by Abp of E Afr; Bps of Masasi; Mauritius; and Nyasa; and Asst Bp of Centr Tang; res 74; Asst Bp of Llan 75; Elected Bp of Llan 75; Enthroned 76; C of Llantwit Major w St Donat 75. SW Tang from 75. *Llys Esgob, The Green, Llandaff, Cardiff, CF5 2YE.* (Cardiff 562400)

POOLEY, Christopher Young. b 13. St Bonif Coll Warm. **d** 38 **p** 40 Br Hond. Miss at Castilla 38-39; La Ceiba Hond Repub 40-47; furlough 47; C of H Trin Brompton 47-48; Rugby 48-52; R of Salwarpe 52-56; V of Rowde 56-63; Alderbury Dio Sarum from 63; R of W Grimstead Dio Sarum from 64. *Alderbury Vicarage, Salisbury, Wilts.* (Salisbury 710229)

POOLEY, Francis William. Univ of Tor BA 31; Wycl Coll Tor LTh 34. **d** 34 **p** 35 Tor. C of Albion 34-35; I 35-39; Sunderland 39-42; Omemee w Emily 42-51; Ch of Atonement Alderwood 51-64; R of St Matt First Avenue Tor 64-77; Hon C of Erindale Dio Tor from 78. *1183 Garden Road, Mississauga, Ont, Canada.*

POOLEY, Peter Owen. b 32. Kelham Th Coll 54. **d** 58 **p** 59 Lon. C of St Mary Magd Paddington 58-62; R of Rockland St Mary w Hellington 62-67; Asst Master Thomas Lethaby Sch 67-70; St Phil Gr Sch Edgbaston 70-74; Lordswood Gr Sch Edgbaston 74-80; Hon C of St Geo Edgbaston 77-80; R of Elton Dio Ely from 80; P-in-c of Stibbington Dio Ely from 80; Water Newton Dio Ely from 80. *Elton Rectory, Peterborough, PE8 6SA.* (Elton 222)

POOLMAN, Alfred John. b 46. K Coll Lon BD and AKC 69. St Aug Coll Cant 69. **d** 70 **p** 71 Ripon. C of Headingley 70-74; Moor Allerton 74-78; Monk Bretton 78-80; V of Copley Dio Wakef from 80. *1 Riverwood Drive, Halifax, W Yorks, HX3 0TH.* (Halifax 52964)

POORE, Leonard Arthur. b 07. Univ of Lon BA (2nd cl Engl) 27, BD 43. Edin Th Coll 41. **d** 42 Hull for York **p** 43 York. C of St Maurice York 42-43; Asst Chap and Lect St Jo Coll York and LPr Dio York 43-67. *20 Bridge Close, Bursledon, Southampton, SO3 8AN.*

POPE, Charles Guy. b 48. AKC 70. St Aug Coll Cant 70. **d** 71 **p** 72 Edmonton for Lon. C of Southgate 71-74; St Steph Hampstead 74-77; All H Gospel Oak 74-77; V of St Paul New Southgate Dio Lon from 77. *11 Woodland Road, N11.* (01-361 1946)

POPE, Colin. b 51. Linc Th Coll 75. **d** 78 **p** 79 Liv. C of Ch of Good Shepherd W Derby 78-81; V desig of St Phil Westbrook. *89 Lander Close, Old Hall, Great Sankey, Warrington, Chesh.* (Warrington 574932)

POPE, Daniel Legh. b 23. Cudd Coll 67. **d** 68 **p** 69 St D. C of Llanelly 68-71; V of Radley Dio Ox from 71. *Radley Vicarage, Abingdon, Oxon.* (Abingdon 24309)

POPE, David Allan. b 20. Or Coll Ox BA 45, MA 72. Ely Th Coll 45. **d** 47 **p** 48 Cant. C of St Mary and St Eanswythe Folkestone 47-51; V of Tovil 51-54; R of E Horsley 54-63; Ivychurch w Old Romney and Midley 63-65; C-in-c of Brenzett w Snargate and Snave 64-65; Newchurch 64-65; St Mary in the Marsh 64-65; Burmarsh 64-65; R of Broadstairs 65-73; P-in-c of Berwick 73-76; Arlington 73-75; Selmeston w Alciston 74-76; Rusper 76-79; R of Colsterworth 79-81; P-in-c of Erpingham w Calthorpe Dio Nor from 81; Alby w Thwaite Dio Nor from 81. *Erpingham Rectory, Norwich, NR11 7QX.* (Hanworth 8073)

POPE, David John. Ridley Coll Melb. **d** 59 **p** 61 St Arn. C of Maryborough 59-62; Cheltm 63-65; V of St Matthias N Richmond 65-69; Perm to Offic Dio Melb 69; and from 71; R of Wentworth 69-70; C of St Luke N Altona 70-71; Perm to Offic Dio Melb 71-72 and 76-77; I of St Pet Brighton Beach 77-79. *1 Moffat Brighton Beach, Vic, Australia 3186.* (92-2397)

POPE, Donald Keith. b 35. **d** 76 **p** 77 Mon. C of Llangattock-juxta-Caerleon Dio Mon from 76. *Yew Tree Cottage, Candwr Lane, Ponthir, Caerleon, Gwent. NP6 1HU.*

POPE, Michael John. b 37. Sarum Th Coll 62. **d** 65 **p** 66 Heref C of Broseley w Benthall 65-68; St Giles Shrewsbury 68-71; P-in-c of St Geo Shrewsbury 71-75; V 75-79; Gnosall Dio Lich from 79. *Gnosall Vicarage, Stafford, Staffs, ST20 0ER.* (Stafford 822213)

POPE, Michael Ronald. b 41. Bps' Coll Cheshunt 65. **d** 68 **p** 69 St Alb. C of H Trin Lyonsdown 68-72; Seaford 72-76; R of Hurstpierpoint 76-81; *c/o Rectory, Hurstpierpoint, Hassocks, Sussex.* (Hurstpierpoint 832203)

POPE, Robert William. b 16. OBE 70. Univ of Dur LTh 40. St Aug Coll Cant 35. **d** 39 **p** 40 Roch. C of H Trin Milton-next-Gravesend 39-41; St Nich Guildf 42-43; Shere (in c of Peaslake) 43-44; Chap RN 44-71; Fleet Chap Malta 63-65; Actg Chan of St Paul's Cathl Valletta 63-65; V of Whitchurch w Tufton and Litchfield 71-77; Dean of Gibr 77-82. *c/o The Deanery, Gibraltar.*

POPE, Rodney John. b 22. St D Coll Lamp BA 48, BD 67, MA 71. **d** 49 **p** 50 Ches. C of Bredbury 49-52; W Kirby 52-53; V of Egremont 53-62; Eastham Ches 62-72; Commiss Qu'App from 62; Surr 62-72; Dioc Insp of Schs Ches 68-72; Dep Dir Coll of Prs 72-73; V of Gt w L Saling Dio Chelmsf from 72. *Great Saling Vicarage, Braintree, Essex, CM7 5DT.* (Gt Dunmow 850296)

POPE, William Davis. Univ of Tor BA 49. Wycl Coll Tor. **d** 52 **p** 53 Alg. C of Port Arthur 52-53; St John Shaughnessy Vancouver 53-55; I of Hope 55-63; Foothills Miss 64-70; Raymore 70-80; New Sumner Dio Qu'App from 80. *Box 269, Esterhazy, Sask, Canada.*

POPONDOTA, Lord Bishop of. *See* Ambo, Right Rev George.

POPOOLA, James Afolabi. b 49. Im Coll Ibad 72. **d** 75 **p** 76 Ibad. P Dio Ibad 75-79; Dio Egba from 79. *Box 208, Abeoka, Nigeria.*

POPPLE, Dennis. St Aid Coll 59. **d** 52 Hulme for Man **p** 63 Man. C of Walkden 62-65; Chap Miss to Seamen 65-71; I of St Hilda Sechelt 71-73; R of St Laur Coquitlam Dio New Westmr from 73. *805 St Laurence Street, Coquitlam, BC, Canada.*

POPPLEWELL, Andrew Frederick. b 53. St Jo Coll Dur BA 75. Wycl Hall Ox 76. **d** 78 **p** 79 York. C of St Phil and St Jas Clifton York 78-81; St Chad City and Dio Lich from 82. *38 St Chad's Road, Lichfield, Staffs.* (Lich 51009)

POROWAI, Elijah. d 72 **p** 74 Melan. P Dio Melan 72-74; L to Offic Dio Centr Melan from 75. *King George VI School, Honiara, Solomon Islands.*

PORRIOR, Canon Eric Vernon. K Coll Halifax. **d** 52 **p** 53 NS. R of Lakeside and Timberlea 53-54; Lantz 54-56; CF (Canad) from 56; Can of Ott from 80. *Dept of Defence, Ottawa, Ont, Canada.*

PORRIT, Ralph Eugene. Wycl Coll Tor. **d** 50 **p** 51 Niag. C of Lowville 50-51; R (w Milton Heights from 53) 51-55; Arthur 55-67; Hon C of St John Ancaster Dio Niag from 80. *4 Millbank Place, Hamilton, Ont., Canada.*

PORT ELIZABETH, Lord Bishop of. *See* Evans, Right Rev Bruce Read.

PORT ELIZABETH, Assistant Bishop of. *See* Cowdry, Right Rev Roy Walter Frederick.

PORT STANLEY, Dean of. *See* Tucker, Right Rev Cyril James.

PORTEOUS, Eric John. b 34. K Coll Lon and Warm AKC 58. **d** 59 **p** 60 S'wark. C of St Paul Wimbledon Pk 59-62; Leeds 62-66; V of Wortley Ripon 66-72; RD of Armley 70-72; R of Woolwich 72-79; Sub Dean of Woolwich 74-77; C-in-c of St Mich AA Woolwich 75-77; Chap Whipps Cross Hosp Leytonstone from 79. *64 Elmhurst Drive, South Woodford, E18.*

PORTEOUS, Canon Lawrence William. Coll Ho Ch Ch 51. **d** 51 **p** 52 Wel. C of Ch Ch Wanganui 51-53; V of Waverley-Waitotara 53-58; Johnsonville Wel 58-73; Waikanae 73-80; Hon Can of Wel 78-80; Can (Emer) from 80; Perm to Offic Dio Wel from 80. *2 Kaitawa Street, Waikanae, NZ.*

PORTEOUS, Michael Stanley. b 35. SOC 70. **d** 73 **p** 74 S'wark. C of St Mich AA Barnes 73-76; Perm to Offic Dio Lon 76-78; C of The Annunc Brighton Dio Chich from 78. *51 Stanley Road, Brighton, BN1 4NH.*

PORTER, Anthony. b 52. Hertf Coll Ox BA (Engl) 74, MA 78. Fitzw Coll Cam BA (Th) 76, MA 80. Ridley Hall Cam 74. **d** 77 Edmon for Lon **p** 78 Lon. C of Edgware 77-80; St Mary Haughton Dio Man from 80. *6 Bacon Avenue, Haughton Green, Denton, Manchester, M34 1LT.* (061-320 5968)

PORTER, Arnold Murray. Univ of Tor BA 58. Trin Coll Tor 58. **d** 61 **p** 62 Alg. C of Sault Ste Marie Cathl 61-64; I of Manitouwadge 64-69; R of St Jas w French River Sudbury 70-71; on leave. *676 King Street, Apt 211, Midland, Ont, Canada.*

PORTER, Arthur William. b 29. St Deiniol's Libr Hawarden 70. **d** 70 **p** 71 Willesden for Lon. C of St Martin Ruislip 70-80; V of Kingsbury Dio Lon from 80. *54 Roe Green, NW9.* (01-204 7531)

PORTER, Brian John Henry. b 33. Ex/Truro Jt Tr Scheme 78. **d** 81 Ex. (NSM). C of St Andr Plymouth Dio Ex from 81. *4 Delgany Villas, Derriford, Plymouth, Devon, PL6 8AG.* (0752 771653)

PORTER, Brian Meredith. b 39. Monash Univ Vic BA 66. Trin Hall Cam BA (2nd cl Th Trip pt ii) 75, MA 79. Univ of New Engl NSW BLitt 79. Cudd Coll 66. **d** 68 **p** 71 Melb. C of H Trin Kew 68-69; Asst Master Trin Gr Sch Kew 68-69; Perm to Offic Dio Melb 69-71; Asst Master The King's Sch Parramatta 70-73; C of St Jas Syd 71-73; Perm to Offic Dio Ely 73-75; C of St Paul Canberra 75-78; Asst Master Canberra Gr Sch from 75; Chap from 79; Lect Canberra Coll of Min from 79; Editor St Mark's Review from 81. *Canberra Grammar School, Monaro Crescent, Redhill, ACT, Australia 2603.* (956747)

PORTER, Charles Victor. b 13. G and C Coll Cam BA 34, MA 38. ALCD 36. **d** 36 **p** 37 Cov. C of St Mark New Milverton 36-39; Ch Ch Paignton (in c of St Paul Preston) 39-44; V of Ch of Good Shepherd Romford 44-60; St Andr

Ilford 60-66; Perm to Offic Dio Nor from 67. *21 The Rise, Sheringham, Norf.* (Sheringham 822245)

PORTER, David Anthony. b 34. Wycl Hall Ox 73. **d** 75 **p** 76 St Alb. C of St Luke Watford 75-78; Worting 78-81; V of Snettisham Dio Nor from 81; P-in-c of Fring and of Ingoldisthorpe Dio Nor from 81. *Vicarage, Station Road, Snettisham, King's Lynn, Norf.* (Dersingham 41301)

✠ **PORTER, Right Rev David Brownfield.** b 06. Hertf Coll Ox BA 27, Dipl Th 29, MA 31. Wycl Hall Ox. **d** 29 **p** 30 Ripon. C of St Aug Wrangthorn 29-31; Tutor of Wycl Hall Ox 31-35; L to Offic Dio Ox and Chap of Wycl Hall Ox 33-35; Chap of Wadh Coll Ox 34-35; V of All SS Highfield 35-43; Darlington 43-47; R of St Jo Evang Edin 47-61; Commiss St Jo Kaffr 49-56; Dean of Edin 54-61; Hon Can of Birm from 62; Cons Ld Bp Suffr of Aston in Westmr Abbey 2 Feb 62 by Abp of Cant; Bps of Birm; Glas; Lon; Chich; St E; Leic; Worc; Ox; Bradf; and others; res 72. *Silver Leys, Brockhampton, Cheltenham.*

PORTER, David Michael. b 37. Ely Th Coll 61. **d** 64 **p** 65 Heref. C of Clun w Chapel Lawn 64-67; Scarborough 67-69; St Osw Fulford 69-71; V of Strensall 71-78; Easingwold w Raskelfe Dio York from 78. *Easingwold Vicarage, York, YO6 3JT.* (Easingwold 21394)

PORTER, Dennis Percy. b 26. AKC 49, BSc 47. Univ of Birm Dipl Th 58. **d** 72 Sheff **p** 73 Doncaster for Sheff (APM). C of Ecclesall Sheff 72-79; Chap Dioc Conf Centre Whirlow Grange from 78; L to Offic Dio Sheff from 79. *75 Marsh House Road, Bents Green, Sheffield, S11 9SQ.* (0742 362058)

PORTER, Frederick. Ridley Coll Melb ACT ThL 29. **d** 28 Melb **p** 29 Bp Stephen for Melb. C of Belgrave w Emerald 28-32; Lorne 32-39; V of H Trin Bacchus Marsh 39-49; I of St Osw Glen Iris 49-60; Chap AIF 40-46; I of Brighton Beach 60-72; Perm to Offic Dio Melb from 72. *25 Beddoe Street, East Brighton, Vic, Australia 3187.* (92-9462)

PORTER, Geoffrey Ernest. b 14. AKC 48. **d** 48 **p** 49 Chelmsf. C of St Andr Ilford 48-53; R of W Horndon w Ingrave 53-61; Ingrave 61-78. *25 Station Road, Mursley, Milton Keynes, Bucks.*

PORTER, John Dudley Dowell. b 33. St Edm Hall Ox BA 60, MA 61. Qu Coll Birm 57. **d** 59 **p** 60 Birm. C of Londonderry 59-62; Tettenhall Regis 62-65; Chap RAF 65-69; V of Wombourne 69-75; St Pet Rickerscote 75-81; P-in-c of Whitmore Dio Lich from 81; Maer Dio Lich from 81; Chap Chorlton Dio Lich from 81. *Whitmore Rectory, Snape Hall Lane, Whitmore Heath, Newcastle, Staffs,*

PORTER, Preb John Robert Hugh. b 17. Trin Coll Dub BA 40, BD 58. **d** 40 **p** 41 Oss. C of Enniscorthy 40-43; CF 43-47; I of Ballysodare U 47-55; Gen Sec SAMS for Ireland 55-61; I of Drumcannon w Dunhill Dio Waterf from 61; Dom Chap to Bp of Cash from 65; RD of Dungarvan and Waterford 67-81; Preb and Treas of Waterf Cathl from 74. *Rectory, Tramore, Co Waterford, Irish Republic.* (Waterford 81301)

PORTER, Canon Joshua Roy. b 21. Late Exhib of Mert Coll Ox BA (1st cl Mod Hist) and Liddon Stud 42, 1st Cl Th 44, MA 47, Kennicott Hebr Fell 55, Sen Denyer and Johnson Scho 58. St Steph Ho Ox 42. **d** 45 **p** 46 Portsm. C of St Mary Portsea 45-47; Res Chap to Bp of Chich 47-49; Hon Chap 49-50; Exam Chap from 50; Fell, Chap and Lect Or Coll Ox 49-62; Tutor 50-62; Lect in Th Univ of Ox 50-62; Select Pr Univ of Ox 53-55; Univ of Cam 57; TCD 58; Prof of Th Univ of Ex from 62; L to Offic Dio Ex from 62; Proc Conv Ex 64-75; Other Univs (Cant) from 75; Can and Preb of Wightring and Th Lect in Chich Cathl from 65; Exam Chap to Bps of Pet and Truro from 73; to Bp of Lon from 81. *Jasin, Taddyforde, Exeter.* (Ex 70413)*; and Queen's Building, University of Exeter.* (Ex 77911)

PORTER, Kenneth Wilfred. St Aid Coll 58. **d** 61 **p** 62 Bradf. C of Queensbury 61-63; St Paul Oldham 63-65; V of Wardle Dio Man from 65. *59 Alpine Drive, Wardle, Rochdale, OL12 9NY.* (Rochdale 78148)

PORTER, Leopold Victor. b 1897. **d** 40 **p** 41 Sarum. C of W Lavington w L Cheverell 40-43; V of Keevil 43-46; V of Bulkington 44-46; Swallowcliffe w Ansty 46-51; R of Chilmark 51-58; Gt w L Cheverell 58-63; L to Offic Dio Sarum from 63. *28 St George's Road, West Harnham, Salisbury, Wilts.*

PORTER, Michael Edward. b 44. Trin Coll Bris 75. **d** 77 **p** 78 Pet. C of St Columba Corby 77-81; S Hornchurch Dio Chelmsf from 81. *Parsonage, South End Road, Rainham, Essex, RM13 7XT.* (Rainham 55260)

PORTER, Canon Nigel Oram. b 11. Late Exhib of Hatf Coll Dur BA and LTh 37, MA 46. St Bonif Coll Warm 33. **d** 37 **p** 38 Lon. C of St John w St Sav Fitzroy Square 37-39; L Ilford 39-43; Barking (in c of St Paul) 43-45; V of St Barn L Ilford 45-76; Proc Conv Chelmsf 64-70; Hon Can of Chelmsf 68-76; Can (Emer) from 76; Bp of Chelmsf Advisor for Commun Relns 76-81. *36 Church Road, Rivenhall, Witham, Essex.* (Witham 511876)

✠ **PORTER, Right Rev Robert George.** OBE 52. St Jo Coll Morpeth and Moore Coll Sydney ACT ThL (2nd cl) 48. **d** 47 **p** 48 Bath. C of Ch Ch Cathl Bal 47-49; P-in-c of Isivita 49-51; Agenehambo New Guinea 51-57; VG and Archd of Bal 57-70; Exam Chap to Bp of Bal 58-70; Cons Asst Bp of Bal in St Paul's Cathl Melb 21 Sept 67 by Abp of Melb; Bps of St Arn; Bend; and Bal; and Bps Sambell and Arnott; Apptd Bp of The Murray 70. *48 Eleanor Terrace, Murray Bridge, S Australia 5253.* (085-32 2240)

PORTER, William Albert. b 28. Univ of NZ (Otago) BA 51, MA 52. Coll of Resurr Mirfield, 53. **d** 55 **p** 56 Birm. C of Perry Bar 55-58; V of Port Chalmers 59-61; Warrington 61-62; Tutor St John's Coll Suva 62-63; Asst Supt Melanesian Miss 62-64; Supt 64-67; Can and Prec of H Trin Cathl Suva 65-67; C of Wimbledon (in c of St Mark) 68; Asst Chap HM Pris Walton Liv 69-70; Chap HM Pris Brixton 70-74; HM Pris Long Lartin 74-79; HM Pris Liv from 79. *c/o HM Prison, Hornby Road, Walton, Liverpool.*

PORTER, William George Ernest. b 17. Ripon Hall Ox 60. **d** 60 **p** 61 Southw. C of Brinsley w Underwood 60-62; C-in-c of Conv Distr of St Martha Broxtowe 62-63; PC 63-67; V of Brinsley w Underwood 67-82; Dioc Insp of Schs 63-82. *6 Ringwood Avenue, Mansfield, Notts, NG18 4DA.* (Mansfield 21656)

PORTER, William Newington. Univ of Tor BA 33. Trin Coll Tor LTh 34. **d** 34 **p** 35 Niag. C of Moorefield W Rothsay and Drayton Ont 34-35; I 35-36; Perm to Offic (Col Cl Act) at St Martin Brighton 36-37; C of St Thos Brampton 37-39; C-in-c of Morpeth W Howard and Clearville 39-41; I of Stafford 41-44; R of Grand Turk w Salt Cay and E Caicos 44-46; I of Maberly 46-51; Eganville 51-55; New Carlisle 55-63; Fitch Bay 63-69; Portneuf 69-72; I in Team Ministry of Eaton-Dudswell 73-74. *RR4, North Augusta, Ont, Canada.*

PORTEUS, Canon Alan Cruddas. b 12. St Chad's Coll Dur BA (3rd cl Mod Hist) 32, Dipl Th 34. **d** 35 Whitby for York **p** 36 York. C of Haxby w Wigginton 35-37; H Trin Tynemouth 37-40; Seghill (in C of St Steph Seaton Delaval) 40-47; PC of Ridgeway 47-52; V of St Osw-in-Lee w Bingfield (Wall) 52-60; Ponteland 60-77; RD of Newc W 64-74; Hon Can of Newc T from 72; P-in-c of Blanchland w Hunstanworth 77-79. *14 Wembley Avenue, Monkseaton, Whitley Bay, T & W.*

PORTEUS, James Michael. b 31. Late Scho of Worc Coll Ox BA (3rd cl Th) 55, MA 58. Cudd Coll. **d** 57 **p** 58 Blackb. C of Fleetwood 57-60; St Mary Virg Ox 60-62; in Amer Ch 62-69; Chap Univ Lon 69-74; V of St Jude-on-the-Hill Hampstead Garden Suburb Dio Lon from 74. *Vicarage, Central Square, NW11 7AH.* (01-455 7206)

PORTEUS, Matthew Thomas. b 10. Trin Coll Dub BA 32, Div Test (2nd cl) 33. **d** 33 **p** 34 Dub. C of St Steph Dub 33-34; Clontarf 34-38; C-in-c of Drumlane 38-41; I of Drumgoon (Cootehill) w Ashfield 41-56; C-in-c of Killeshesdony 50-56; Exam Chap to Bp of Kilm 51-56; V of W Haddon w Winwick 56-73. *12 North Hill Way, Bridport, Dorset, DT6 4JX.*

PORTEUS, Robert John Norman. b 50. TCD BA 72, Div Test 75. **d** 75 Armagh. C of Portadown 75-79; R of Ardtrea w Desertcreat Dio Arm from 79. *50 Lower Grange Road, Cookstown, Co Tyrone, N Ireland.* (Cookstown 63206)

PORTEUS, Wilfrid Beilby. b 10. Univ of Dur LTh 34. St Aid Coll 31. **d** 34 **p** 35 Blackb. C of St Pet Chorley 34-36; Morecambe 36-37; Burnley 37-40; Offg C-in-c of St Jude Preston 40-46; V of Feniscowles 46-59; St Thos Ap Garstang 59-75. *30 Manor Road, Slyne with Hest, Lancaster, LA2 6LB.* (Hest Bank 823008)

PORTHOUSE, John Clive. b 32. BD (2nd cl) Lon 58. Oak Hill Th Coll 58. **d** 60 **p** 61 Chelmsf. C of All SS Leyton 60-62; St Thos Kendal 62-64; V of Flimby 64-68; St Andr Sidcup 68-74; St Jo Bapt Beckenham Dio Roch from 74; RD of Beckenham from 80. *Vicarage, Eden Park Avenue, Beckenham, Kent, BR3 3JN.* (01-650 3515)

PORTHOUSE, Roger Gordon Hargreaves. b 39. Tyndale Hall Bris 66. **d** 69 **p** 70 Lich. C of All SS Wellington 69-71; St Mary Cheadle (in c of St Cuthb) 71-75; R of Spixworth w Crostwick 75-81; Frettenham w Stanninghall 75-81; V of Hailsham Dio Chich from 81. *Vicarage, Hailsham, E Sussex, BN27 1BL.*

PORTMAN, William Gordon. St Chad's Coll Regina. **d** 55 **p** 56 Qu'App. I of Hazenmore 55-58; Milden 58-60; C of Cannock Staffs 60-61; Mortlach 61-65; Lumsden 65-66; P-in-c of Balgonie 66-70; I of Avonlea and Ogema 70-74; Weyburn Dio Qu'App from 74. *206 Bison Avenue, Weyburn, Sask., Canada.* (842-2470)

PORT MORESBY, Lord Bishop of. *See* Hand, Most Rev Geoffrey David.

PORTSMOUTH, Lord Bishop of. *See* Gordon, Right Rev Archibald Ronald McDonald.

PORTSMOUTH, Assistant Bishops of. *See* Curtis, Right Rev Ernest Edwin; Eastaugh, Right Rev Cyril; Hunt, Right Rev William Warren; Roberts, Right Rev Edward James Keymer.

PORTSMOUTH, Provost of. (Vacant).

PORTSMOUTH, Archdeacon of. *See* Scruby, Ven Ronald Victor.

PORTSMOUTH, Canon William. b 10. Late Newby, Hebr and De Bury Scho of St Jo Coll Dur BA (2nd cl Th) 34, MA 37. **d** 35 Dur **p** 36 Jarrow for Dur. C of St Pet Auckland 35-37; St Marg (in c of St John Neville's Cross) Dur 37-46; CF (TA-R of O) 39-46; V of Leadgate 46-59; Stannington 59-62; Birtley 62-79; RD of Chester-le-Street 74-79; Hon Can of Dur from 74. *26 Seatonville Road, West Monkseaton, Whitley Bay, T & W.*

POSHOLI, Philip Tefelo. b 41. **d** and **p** 74 Les. P Dio Les. *St Stephen's Mission, PO Box MH 22, Mohales Hoek, Lesotho, S Africa.*

POST, David Charles William. b 39. Jes Coll Cam BA 61, MA 65. Oak Hill Th Coll 61. **d** 63 **p** 64 Roch. C of Ch Ch Orpington 63-66; Fulwood Sheff 66-68; V of Lathom 68-75; Poughill 75-78; Braddan 78-79; P-in-c of Santan 78; V 78-79; Dioc Missr Dio S & M 78-79; V of Sherburn-in-Elmet w Barkston Dio York from 79. *Vicarage, Sherburn-in-Elmet, Leeds, LS25 6BJ.* (S Milford 682122)

POSTILL, John Edward. b 35. Oak Hill Th Coll 64. **d** 67 **p** 68 Chich. C of St Mary Crawley 67-70; Bowling 70-74; V in Winfarthing Group 74-79; R of Slaugham Dio Chich from 79. *Rectory, Handcross, Haywards Heath, RH17 6BU.* (Handcross 400221)

POSTILL, Richard Halliday. b 37. Univ of Hull BSc 59. Westcott Ho Cam 66. **d** 68 Bp Sinker for Birm **p** 69 Birm. C of Wylde Green 68-72; St Mary Kingswinford (in c of Ascen Wall Heath) 72-75; V of Yardley Wood Dio Birm from 76. *Vicarage, School Road, Birmingham, B14 4EP.* (021-474 2012)

POSTLES, Donald. b 29. MPS 51. Univ of Birm Dipl Th 59, MA 65. Qu Coll Birm 56. **d** 59 **p** 60 Liv. C of H Trin Southport 59-62; Prescot (in c of St Paul Bryer Estate) 62-63; V of St Steph Whelley Wigan 63-71; St Luke Farnworth Dio Liv from 71. *Vicarage, Coroner's Lane, Widnes, Chesh, WA8 9HY.* (051-424 2735)

POSTLETHWAITE, Alan James. b 38. Univ of Dur BA (2nd cl Pol and Econ) 60. Linc Th Coll 60. **d** 62 **p** 63 York. C of Cottingham 62-65; Cockermouth 65-68; V of Seascale 68-77; P-in-c of Drigg 75-77; V of Whitehaven Dio Carl from 77. *Vicarage, Oak Bank, Whitehaven, Cumb, CA28 6HY.*

POSTON, Ralph. b 08. K Coll Cam 2nd cl Mod Lang Trip pt i 28, BA (3rd cl Hist Trip pt ii) 30, MA 57. Cudd Coll 57. **d** 58 **p** 59 Bris. C of Cricklade w Latton 58-60; V of Bp's Lavington 60-65; R of Portland 65-69; Chap HM Pris Verne 65-76. *Rufus Gate, Church Ope Road, Wakeham, Portland, Dorset DT5 1HY.* (Portland 820223)

POSTON, Robert Charles. b 12. St Edm Hall Ox BA (2nd cl Th) 36, MA 59. Bps' Coll Cheshunt 35. **d** 37 **p** 38 Chelmsf. C of Mistley w Bradfield 37-39; Halstead 39-42; CF (EC) 42-46; Hon CF 46; Perm to Offic Dio Chelmsf 47; V of St Luke Leyton 48-61; St Andr Westcliff-on-Sea 61-73; Perm to Offic Dios Chelmsf and St E from 73. *Clement's House, Gt Horkesley, Colchester, Essex, CO6 4HA.* (Colchester 271344)

POTAKA-DEWES, Eru. Univ of Cant BA 62. St Jo Coll Auckld. **d** 67 Bp McKenzie for Wel **p** 69 Wel. C of Wel Maori Past Dio Wel from 67. *c/o 26 Nottingham Street, Wellington, NZ.*

POTHEN, John. b 25. Univ of Madras MA 49. K Coll Lon and Warm AKC 52, BD 53. **d** 52 **p** 53 Roch for Lon. C of Erith 52-54; Asst Chap St Thos Cathl Bomb and Colaba 55; Chap St John Calc 55-60; Dom Chap to Bp of Calc 55-60; Chap St Paul's Cathl Calc 60-61; V 61-69; C of St Jas Enfield 69-71; V of St Alphege Edmon 71-75; Exam Chap to Bp of Edmon from 73; Oakwood Dio Lon from 75. *2 Sheringham Avenue, N14 4UE.* (01-360 1749)

PO THET, Moses. d 33 **p** 34 Rang. P Dio Rang 33-70. *c/o St Michael's Church, Shwelaung, PO Wakema, Burma.*

POTT, Canon Roger Percivall. b 09. St Steph Ho Ox. **d** 33 **p** 34 Lon. C of Ch Ch Chelsea 33-35; SPG Sec and Treas L to Offic Dio S Tokyo and Hd Master Yokohama Internat Sch 35-40; Offg C-in-c of H Trin Paddington 40-42; Chap RNVR 42-44; C of Brentwood 44-45; V of Heacham Dio Nor from 45; Hd Master St Mich Sch Ingoldisthorpe 46-70; R of Ingoldisthorpe 46-81; Hon Can of Nor Cathl from 81. *Vicarage, Heacham, King's Lynn, Norf.* (Heacham 70268)

POTTER, Andrew Eldon. Univ of Alta BSc (Eng) 48. Trin Coll Tor LTh 55. **d** 54 **p** 55 Edmon. I of Kitscoty 55-60. *8 Windsor Crescent SE, Calgary, Alta, Canada.* (252-0642)

POTTER, Charles Elmer. b 42. Georgetn Univ Washington BS 65. Wycl Coll Tor MDiv 81. **d** 81 Warrington for Liv. C of Ch Ch Southport Dio Liv from 81. *20 Talbot Street, Southport, Merseyside, PR8 1HP.*

POTTER, George Koszelski St John. b 22. Em Coll Cam BA 43, MA 47. ARCM 45. St Cath S Ox Dipl Th 53. Wycl Hall Ox 51. **d** 53 Lon **p** 54 Kens for Lon. C of St Luke Chelsea 53-56; V of St Aid Sudden Rochdale 56-62; Riverhead 62-68; C-in-c of Dunton Green 67-68; Asst Master Harris High Sch Rugby and Perm to Offic Dio Cov 68-77; V of Langcliffe w Stainforth Dio Bradf from 77; P-in-c of Horton-in-Ribblesdale Dio Bradf from 80. *Stainforth Vicarage, Settle, N Yorks, BD24 9PQ.* (Settle 3564)

POTTER, Graham Frederick. b 34. Qu Coll Birm 62. **d** 65 **p** 66 Bris. C of Ashton Gate 65-68; St Jo Bapt Park Swindon 68-70; M (Social and Industr) E Swindon Group 70-74; Bp's Social and Industr Adv Swindon from 74. *12 Canterbury Close, Swindon, SN3 1HU.* (Swindon 20178)

POTTER, Guy Anthony. b 18. St Jo Coll Cam BA 40, MA 44. Cudd Coll Ox 40. **d** 41 **p** 42 Win. C of St Jo Bapt Moordown Bournemouth 41-46; V of Marton w Grafton 46-55; C-in-c of Aldborough w Dunsforth 50-52; V 52-55; V of All SS Alton 55-65; Chap Henry Gauvain Hosp Alton 55-61; St Mary's Home Alton 57-65; R of Heene Worthing 65-75; RD of Worthing 71-75; M Gen Syn 73-75; R of Black Notley Dio Chelmsf from 75. *Black Notley Rectory, Braintree, Essex.* (0376-26935)

POTTER, Harry Drummond. b 54. Em Coll Cam MA 79, MPhil 81. Westcott Ho Cam 79. **d** 81 S'wark. C of St Paul Deptford Dio S'wark from 81. *6 Walnut House, Clyde Street, Deptford, SE8.*

POTTER, James David. b 35. K Coll Lon and Warm AKC 66. **d** 67 Birm **p** 68 Aston for Birm. C of Longbridge 67-70; Publ Pr Dio Birm 71-73; Asst Master Handsworth New Road Boys' Sch Birm 71-73; V of H Trin Smethwick (w St Alb from 78) Dio Birm from 73; C-in-c of St Alb Smethwick 76-78. *69 South Road, Smethwick, W Midl, B67 7BP.* (021-558 0373)

POTTER, Canon John Buchanan. b 38. New Coll Ox BA (2nd cl Phil, Pol and Econ) 61. Wells Th Coll 62. **d** 63 Bp McKie for Cov **p** 65 Cov. C of Wyken 63-66; Warden Hall of Residence Lanchester Coll Cov 66-70; V of Writtle 70-78; Res Can of Derby Cathl from 78. *24 Kedleston Road, Derby, DE3 1GU.* (0332-363425)

POTTER, John Daniel. Univ of Syd BA 50. ACT ThL 51. **d** 51 **p** 53 Armid. C of Gunnedah 52-54; St Pet Cathl Armid 54-55; Glen Innes 55-57; V of Wee Waa 57-59; Chap Geelong C of E Gr Sch Timbertop 59-65; C of Harrogate Yorks 65-66; Chap St Mary's Sch Wantage 66-68; St John's Sch Sing 68-71; I of St Paul Cant Dio Melb from 71. *2 Margaret Street, Canterbury, Vic, Australia 3216.* (03-83 7431)

POTTER, John Henry. b 26. Univ of Lon BA 50. Oak Hill Th Coll 50. **d** 52 Lon **p** 53 Kens for Lon. C of Islington 52-55; Kinson 55-58; V of St John U Holloway 58-65; R of St Illogan w Trevenson and Portreath 65-69; P-in-c of St Phil and St Jas Ilfracombe 69-72; V 72-76; R of Poole Dio Sarum from 76; RD of Poole from 80. *Rectory, Poole, Dorset.* (Poole 2694)

POTTER, John Michael. b 28. ALCD 56. **d** 56 **p** 57 Cant. C of St Mary Magd Addiscombe 56-60; V of Kettlewell w Conistone (and Hubberholme from 80) 60-82; P-in-c of Arncliffe w Halton Gill 75-78; Hubberholme 78-80; R of Somersham w Flowton and Offton w Willisham Dio St E from 82. *Rectory, Somersham, Ipswich, Suff.*

POTTER, Keith Clement. b 39. Chich Th Coll 62. **d** 64 **p** 65 Sheff. C of Ch Ch Doncaster 64-68; Tong 68-70; V of St Columba Horton w St Andr Listerhills Bradf 70-79; St Andr Yeadon Dio Bradf from 79. *St Andrew's Vicarage, Yeadon, Nr Leeds, LS19 7XO.* (Rawdon 503989)

POTTER, Malcolm Emmerson. b 48. Univ of Lon BSc 70. St Jo Coll Nottm. **d** 75 **p** 76 Ches. C of St Mary Upton 75-78; on staff CPAS 78-80. *Address temp unknown.*

POTTER, Martin. b 33. Fitzw Ho Cam 2nd cl Hist Trip pt i 58, BA (2nd cl Hist Trip pt ii) 59, MA 63. Linc Th Coll 63. **d** 65 **p** 66 Man. C of Rochdale 65-67; L to Offic Dio Zam 68-72; Hon C of St Matt Hastings 72-74; Perm to Offic Dio Waik from 74. *Kahu Street, Ohura, NZ.*

POTTER, Michael William. b 48. La Trobe Univ Vic BA 69. Univ of Melb BD 77. Trin Coll Melb 74. **d** 77 **p** 78 Melb. C of St John E Bentleigh 77-79; Lara 79-80; H Nativ Corio Dio Melb from 80. *8 Rodbrough Crescent, Corio, Vic, Australia 3214.* (052-75 4597)

POTTER, Richard Antony. b 36. K Coll Cam BA 60, MA 64. Ridley Hall Cam 60. **d** 62 **p** 63 St Alb. C of Luton 62-72; V of H Trin Lyonsdown Dio St Alb from 72. *18 Lyonsdown Road, New Barnet, Barnet, Herts, EN5 1JE.* (01-449 0382)

POTTER, Canon Rupert Marshall. d 57 **p** 58 Tas. C of Clarence 57-59; Cressy 59-60; R of Penguin 60-63; Moonah 63-79; Bellerive Dio Tas from 79; Can of Tas from 80. *St Mark's Rectory, Clarence Street, Bellerive, Tasmania 7018.* (002 44 1296)

POTTER, Timothy John. b 49. Univ of Bris BSc 71. Oak Hill Coll 73. **d** 76 **p** 77 S'wark. C of Wallington 76-79; Hampreston 79-81; Team V of Stratton St Margaret w South

Marston and Stanton Fitzwarren Dio Bris from 81. *South Marston Vicarage, Swindon, SN3 4SR.* (Swindon 827021)

POTTER, William Robert. Late Pri of Univ of Melb BA 43. ACT ThL 43. **d** 44 **p** 45 Melb. C of S Yarra 44-47; Cranbourne 47-51; V of Glenroy 51-56; Balaclava 56-63; Mont Albert N 63-72; I of Ringwood Dio Melb from 72. *40 Warrandyte Road, Ringwood, Vic, Australia 3134.* (03-870 6074)

POTTIER, Ronald William. b 36. SOC 73. **d** 76 **p** 77 S'wark. C of St Mich AA Lower Sydenham Dio S'wark from 76. *12 Neiderwald Road, Sydenham, SE26.* (01-699 4375)

POTTON, Frederick Hedley. **d** and **p** 57 Cov. C of Barford 57-58; Claverdon 58-60; Lillington 60-68. *11 Hadrian Close, New Cubbington, Leamington Spa, Warws.* (Leamington Spa 23348)

POTTS, Canon George Chapman. b 1898. Keble Coll Ox BA (2nd cl Mod Hist) 23, MA 43. Cudd Coll 22. **d** 23 **p** 24 Carl. C of St Jas Barrow-F 23-28; Dioc Org Sec CETS from 28; LPr Dio Carl 29; R of Distington 29-35; Wetheral w Warwick 35-45; CF (EC) 40-46; Men in Disp 45; Hon CF 46; V of Casterton 46-52; Lect of St Martin Birm 52-67; Chap of St Basil and St John Birm 54-59; Hon Can of Birm 65-67; Can (Emer) from 67. *13 The Paddock, Upton, Wirral, Mer, L49 6NP.*

POTTS, Henry Arthur. b 16. Trin Coll Cam BA 48. St Steph Ho Ox 48. **d** and **p** 50 Roch. C of the Annunc Chislehurst 50-52; St Mich Cathl Barb 52-53; V of St Luke Barb 53-56; Publ Pr Dio Roch 56-57; V of St Luke Gillingham 57-69; chap D Kerin Trust Burrswood 69-74; P-in-c of St Jas w St Pet Bris 74-77; R of Balsham Dio Ely from 77. *Balsham Rectory, Cambridge, CB1 6DX.* (West Wratting 204)

POTTS, Canon Hugh Cuthbert Miller. b 07. Linc Coll Ox BA 29, MA 41. St Steph Ho Ox 37. **d** 37 **p** 38 Glouc. C of Cirencester w H Trin Watermoor 37-44; V of St Arvan's w Penterry 44-49; R of Eastington 49-52; Stow-on-the-Wold w Broadwell 52-61; C-in-c of Evenlode 52-61; RD of Stow 59-61; V of St Cath Glouc 61-80; Hon Can of Glouc from 69; Sub-Chap Order of St Jo from 72. *5 Hilton Close, Hempsted, Gloucester, GL2 6LQ.*

POTTS, James. b 30. AKC and BD 56. **d** 57 Wakf **p** 58 Pontefract for Wakef. C of Brighouse 57-59; P Dio Zanz 59-61; Sub-Warden St Cypr Th Coll Ngala 61-66; Warden 66-69; Warden Angl Th Coll Dar-S 69-71; C-in-c of St Helen's Conv Distr Athersley and New Lodge 71-73; V of Athersley 73-77; Madeley Dio Lich from 77. *Madeley Vicarage, Crewe, Chesh, CW3 9PX.* (Stoke-on-Trent 750205)

POTTS, Wilfrid Mark Allinson. b 11. Ch Ch Ox BA 33, MA 37. Cudd Coll 34. **d** 36 **p** 37 Sarum. C of Gillingham Dorset 36-39; Perm to Offic at St Pet w St Paul Huddersfield 39-40; C of Bp's Hatfield 40-43; V of St Jo Bapt Harpenden 43-64; RD of St Alb 57-63; Proc Conv St Alb 59-60; V of Carisbrooke 64-81; V of St Nich-in-Castro Carisbrooke 64-81. *10 Sparkford Close, Winchester, Hants.* (Win 66056)

POTTS, William Gilbert. b 17. Bps' Coll Cheshunt, 46. **d** 49 **p** 50 Lich. C of Fenton 49-52; St Andr w St Mich W Bromwich 52-53; Ashbourne w Mapleton and Clifton 53-57; V of Beighton 57-64; PC (V from 68) of Winshill Dio Derby from 64; Surr from 68. *Winshill Vicarage, Mill Hill Lane, Burton-on-Trent, Staffs.* (Burton 63779)

POULTER, Alan John. b 39. St Aid Coll 64. **d** 67 **p** 68 Ches. C of Heswall 67-72; V of Bredbury 72-78; Oxton Dio Ches from 78. *Oxton Vicarage, Birkenhead, L43 2JZ.* (051-652 1194)

POULTER, Joseph William. b 40. Univ of Dur BA 61, 2nd cl Th 66, Dipl Th (w distinc) 67. Cranmer Hall Dur 66. **d** 67 Barking for Chelmsf **p** 68 Chelmsf. C of Harlow New Town 67-71; H Trin Washington 71-76; C-in-c of St Bede Town End Farm Conv Distr Sunderland Dio Dur from 76. *Town End Farm House, Bootle Street, Town End Farm Estate, 3)*

POULTNEY, Wilfred Howard. b 25. Qu Coll Birm 71. **d** 73 Bp McKie for Cov **p** 74 Cov (APM) C of St Jo Bapt Leamington Dio Cov from 73. *22 St Catherine's Crescent, Whitnash, Leamington Spa, Warws, CV31 2LA.*

POULTON, Arthur Leslie. K Coll Lon BA (2nd cl Engl) and AKC 53. BD (2nd cl) (Lon) 60. Tyndale Hall Bris 53. **d** 55 **p** 56 Nor. C of New Catton 55-56; St Anne Earlham 56-58; Chorley Wood 58-61; R of E Barnet 61-64; Chap and Sen Lect Ches Coll of Educn from 64; L to Offic Dio Ches from 66. *Chester College, Cheyney Road, Chester.* (Chester 375444)

POULTON, Christopher John. b 03. Univ of Lon BA (3rd cl Cl) 27. Wells Th Coll 27. **d** 28 **p** 29 Ex. C of Plympton St Mary 28-33; Dawlish 33-43; V of Holcombe Burnell 43-49; St Mark Ex 49-62; Chap Ex Sch 49-62; RD of Christianity 59-62; Aylesbeare 66-69; V of Budleigh Salterton 62-71; Publ Pr Dio Ex from 71. *34 East Budleigh Road, Budleigh Salterton, Devon.* (Budleigh Salterton 2383)

POULTON, Canon John Frederick. b 25. K Coll Lon BA (2nd cl) 50. Ridley Hall Cam 50. **d** 52 **p** 53 Chich. C of Bp Hannington Mem Ch Hove 52-54; CMS Miss Bp Tucker Mem Coll Mukono 55-60; Actg Prin Bp Tucker Coll Mukono 61-62; Dir of Ch of Ugan Lit and Radio Centre Mukono 63-66; Research Sec World Assoc for Chr Broadcasting 66-68; Research and Development Officer Abps' Coun on Evang 69-72; Executive Sec 73-78; Can Res of Nor Cathl from 78. *27 The Close, Norwich, NR1 4DZ.* (Norwich 28506)

POUNCE, Alan Gerald. Univ of Lon BSc 55. Wycl Hall Ox 57. **d** 59 **p** 60 Lich. C of Heath Town 59-61; St Pet w St Owen Heref 61-63; R of Gt w L Dunham 63-69; Asst Master Windsor Gr Sch from 69. *38 Longdown Road, Sandhurst, Camberley, Surrey.* (Crowthorne 2870)

POUNCEY, Canon Cosmo Gabriel Rivers. b 11. Qu Coll Cam BA 32, 2nd cl Th Trip pt i 33, MA 36. Cudd Coll 33. **d** 34 **p** 35 S'wark. C of St Jo Div Kennington 34-44; Sec Ch Educn League 43-46; V of Woodham 46-63; Surr 57-63; RD of Woking 57-63; Proc Conv Guildf 58-64; Glouc 64-70; Hon Can of Guildf 62-63; V of Tewkesbury w Walton Cardiff 63-81; P-in-c of Tredington w Stoke Orchard 63-81; Deerhurst w Apperley 74-80; RD of Tewkesbury 68-81; Hon Can of Glouc Cathl 72-81; Can (Emer) from 81; Perm to Offic Dio Worc from 81. *Gannicox, Birlingham, Pershore, Worcs, WR10 3AB.* (Evesham 750720)

POUNCY, Anthony Grenville. Qu Coll Cam BA 37, MA 41. Tyndale Hall, Bris 37. **d** 38 **p** 39 Sarum. C of St John Weymouth 38-41; V of Ch Ch Cov 41-46; Ed Sec BCMS and Perm to Offic Dio Roch 46-54; R of Bebington 54-67; V of Woking 67-79. *47 Brook Gardens, Emsworth, Hants.*

POUND, Arthur Gilbert. b 02. Univ of Birm BA (2nd cl Hist) 23, MA 27. St Cath S Ox MA 46. Ripon Hall, Ox 38. **d** 38 **p** 39 Birm. C of St Paul Bordesley Green 38-46; PC 46-68; V 68-74; CF (EC) 40-46. *185 Long Lane, Halesowen, W Midl, B62 9EP.* (Halesowen 2280)

POUND, Keith Salisbury. b 33. St Cath Coll Cam 3rd cl Engl Trip pt i 53, BA (2nd cl Hist Trip pt ii) 54, MA 58. Cudd Coll. **d** 57 **p** 58 S'wark. C of St Pet St Helier 57-61; Tr Officer of Hollowford Tr and Conf Centre Sheff 61-64; Warden 64-67; R of H Trin (w St Matt from 74) S'wark 68-78; C-in-c of St Matt Newington 68-74; RD of S'wark and Newington 73-78; R of Thamesmead Dio S'wark from 78. *1 Glendale Way, Thamesmead, SE28 8HA.* (01-310 7573)

POUNDE, Nigel. b 46. Univ of Edin MA (2nd cl Econ) 69. Cranmer Hall Dur Dipl Th 71. **d** 72 **p** 73 Portsm. C of St Simon Southsea 72-75; Clayton w Keymer 75-79; P-in-c of St Paul Pulau Pinang Dio W Mal from 80. *56 Jalan Macalister, Pulau Pinang, Malaysia.*

POUNTAIN, Eric Gordon. b 24. Sarum Th Coll 65. **d** 66 Blackb for Man **p** 67 Man. C of St Jas New Bury Farnworth 66-76; Perm to Offic Dio Man from 77; Dio Blackb 78-79; Chap Preston Poly and P-in-c of St Mark Preston 79-81; V of Salesbury Dio Blackb from 81. *Salesbury Vicarage, Blackburn, Lancs, BB1 9HX.* (Blackburn 48072)

POVALL, Charles Herbert. b 18. Univ of Man MEducn 71. St Deiniol's Libr Hawarden 75. **d** 76 **p** 77 Ches. C of St Thos Norbury Dio Ches from 76. *3 Magda Road, Great Moor, Stockport, SK2 7LX.* (061-483 6713)

POVALL, Graham Arthur William. Univ of Leeds BA 60. Coll of Resurr Mirfield 60. **d** 62 Lon for Natal **p** 62 Natal. C of St Alphege Pmbg 52-65; St John Pinetown 70-77; St Paul Durban Dio Natal from 77. *400 Currie Road, Durban, Natal, S Africa.*

POVEY, Kenneth Vincent. b 40. K Coll Lon and Warm AKC 62. **d** 63 **p** 64 Ches. C of Ch Ch Crewe 63-66; Neston 66-69; St Mary Abbots Kens 69-72; R of H Trin without-the-Walls 72-81; Chap of St Alb Copenhagen Dio Gibr in Eur from 81. *Rosenvaengets Havedvej 21a, 2100 Copenhagen, Denmark.*

POVEY, William Charles Alfred. b 10. St Andr Coll Whittlesford 38. **d** 40 Bp Willis for Leic **p** 41 Leic. C of Glen Parva w S Wigston 40-41; St Steph Leic 41-42; All SS Leek 42-46; St Paul S Harrow (in c of St Mark) 46-47; V of St Jo Evang Edmonton 47-54; All SS Child's Hill 54-73; C of St Mary Finchley 73-75; Perm to Offic Dio Heref from 75. *35 St Mary's Street, Bridgnorth, Shropshire, WV16 4DR.* (Bridgnorth 5937)

POW, Lionel George. b 28. **d** 80 Trinid. C of H Sav Curepe Dio Trinid from 80. *41 Eleventh Street, Mt Lambert, San Juan, Trinidad, WI.*

POWDRILL, Wilfred Roy. b 23. St Aid Coll 54. **d** 56 **p** 57 Leic. C of The Martyrs Leic 56-59; C-in-c of Ch Ch Eccles Distr Thurnby Lodge 59-61; Min 61-69; CF (R of O) 59-78; R of Anstey Leics 69-75; V of Glen Parva w S Wigston 75-81. *Flat 4, Arnold Smith House, Bridge Street, Shepshed, Leics.* (Shepshed 4862)

POWE, Eric James. b 23. Late Scho and Pri of St D Coll Lamp BA (2nd cl Phil) 50, BD 61. St Steph Ho Ox 50. **d** 52 Croydon for Cant **p** 53 Cant. C of H Trin Ramsgate 52-54; Buckland-in-Dover 54-57; CF 57-72; DACG 72-73; R of

Broadstairs Dio Cant from 73. *Rectory, Broadstairs, Kent.* (Thanet 62921)

POWE, Roger Wayne. b 46. Univ of Lon BEducn 70, MA 78. SOC 73. **d** 76 **p** 77 S'wark. Hon C of St Andr Surbiton 76-79; Asst Chap Giggleswick Sch 79-80; Hurstpierpoint Coll from 81; C of All SS Marg Street 80-81. *Hurstpierpoint College, Hassocks, W Sussex.*

POWELL, Abner Leslie. Univ of WI BA (Th) 73. United Th Coll of WI 73. **d** 73 **p** 74 Ja. C of St Geo Kingston 73-74; R of Frankfield Dio Ja from 74. *c/o Frankfield PO, Jamaica.*

POWELL, Albert George Clifton. b 1893. Selw Coll Cam BA 18, MA 21. Cudd Coll 19. **d** 20 **p** 21 Ches. C of St Mary Disley 20-23; St Cath Hatcham 24-29; Cathl Ch Bury St E 29-35; V of St Mich AA Knighton 35-54; Dunton Bassett 54-61; L to Offic Dio Leic 61-77. *Leaholm Nursing Home, St Michaels Road, W Worthing.*

POWELL, Anthony James. b 51. Sarum Wells Th Coll 78. **d** 79 **p** 80 Roch. C of Larkfield and of Leybourne Dio Roch from 79. *73 Rectory Lane, Leybourne, W Malling, Kent.*

POWELL, Canon Arthur George. Ridley Coll Melb ACT ThL 17, Th Scho 27. **d** 17 **p** 18 Gippsld. C of Loch 17-19; Bairnsdale 19-20; Warden and Tutor of Bro of St Jo Evang Gippsld 20-23; V of Drouin 23-25; R of Orange E 25-38; Mudgee 38-59; Exam Chap to Bp of Bath 37-59; Can of Bath 44-59; Can (Emer) from 59; L to Offic Dio Syd from 59. *33 Warrina Village, Castle Hill, NSW, Australia 2154.*

POWELL, Baden Clarence. **d** 65 **p** 66 Melb. C of St John Camberwell 65-67. *7 Nardoo Street, O'Connor, Canberra, ACT 2601, Australia.*

POWELL, Colin Arthur. b 32. Univ of Dur BA (2nd cl Mod Hist) 53. Oak Hill Th Coll 56. **d** 58 **p** 59 Blackb. C of Leyland 58-61; St Thos Lanc 61-64; St Cath Higher Tranmere 64-65; R of St Luke Cheetham Man 65-81; Team V of Oldham Dio Man from 81. *Holy Trinity Vicarage, 46 Godson Street, Oldham, OL1 2DB.* (061-665 2502)

POWELL, Dennis John. Tyndale Hall, Bris. **d** 62 Calg **p** 63 Tor for Calg. C of St Cuthb Tor 62-63; I of Crow's Nest 63-65; Amherst I 65-67; R of Lansdowne Front 67-73. *PO Box 119, Lansdowne, Ont, Canada.*

POWELL, Donald Miles. McMaster Univ BA 62. Trin Coll Tor STB 65. **d** and **p** 65 Niag. C of Ch Ch Cathl Hamilton 64-67; on leave 67-69; R of St Aid Oakville 69-74; Ch of the Transfig St Catharines 74-79; Dom Chap to Bp of Niag from 79; Chap St Pet Centre and Dir of Miss to Seamen Hamilton from 79. *431 East 14th Street, Hamilton, Ont, Canada.*

POWELL (formerly POPPLEWELL), Douglas Louis. b 16. Hertf Coll Ox BA (1st cl Hist) 38, 2nd cl Th 40, MA 56. St Steph Ho Ox 39. **d** 41 **p** 42 Roch. C of The Annunc Chislehurst 41-50; Asst Hosp to St Thos's Hosp 50-53; Vice-Prin St Chad's Coll Dur 53-63; L to Offic Dio Dur 54-63; Lect in Th Univ of Ex 63-67; Sen Lect from 67; L to Offic Dio Ex from 64. *Queen's Building, University, Exeter, Devon.* (Exeter 77911)

POWELL, Dudley John. Tyndale Hall Bris 65. **d** 69 Blackb **p** 70 Lanc for Blackb. C of Sav Blackb 69-71; Rodbourne Cheney 71-74; P-in-c of St Matt Kingsdown Bris 74-79; V from 79-80; Stoke Gifford Dio Bris from 80. *Stoke Gifford Vicarage, Bristol.* (Bristol 692486)

POWELL, Canon Edward. **d** 30 **p** 31 Lon for Col Bp. Perm to Offic at Monk's Kirby w Withybrook and Copston 30-31; C of Hungerford 31-32; R of Southwood w Limpenhoe V 32-33; C of Newport Pagnell 33-36; Charlbury w Chadlington and Shorthampton (in c of Chadlington) 36-37; V of Ambrosden w Arncot and Blackthorn 37-42; CF 39-42; V of Belchamp St Paul Dio Chelmsf from 42; C-in-c of Ovington w Tilbury-juxta-Clare Dio Chelmsf 42-43; R from 43; RD of Belchamp 48-74; Surr from 52; Hon Can of Chelmsf from 80. *Vicarage, Belchamp St Paul, Sudbury, Suff.* (Clare 277210)

POWELL, Eric Douglas. Univ of BC BA 58. M Social Work 71. Angl Th Coll Vancouver LTh 59. **d** 58 **p** 59 New Westmr. P-in-c of St Geo Ind Miss Kingcome 58-60; R of St D Powell River 61-63; on leave 63-64; C of St John Shaughnessy Heights Vancouver 64-66; R of Prince Geo 66-69; on leave 69-71; Dir of Programme Dio New Westmr from 71. *692 Burrard Street, Vancouver, BC, Canada.*

POWELL, Francis David Claude. b 09. Univ of Leeds BA 31. Coll of Resurr Mirfield 31. **d** 33 **p** 34 Roch. C of St Barn Tunbridge Wells 33-36; St Mary Pimlico 36-45; Chap RNVR 42-45; Miss Dio Masasi 45-65; Dean and R of St Jo Bapt Cathl Belize 65-69; V of St Matt w Kens Hammersmith 70-75; Perm to Offic Dios St Alb and Ox from 75. *St Martha's Lodge, Park Road, Tring, Herts, HP23 6BP.*

POWELL, Frank. b 29. K Coll Lon and Warm AKC 52. **d** 53 **p** 54 Cov. C of Stockingford 53-56; St Andr Netherton (in c of St Pet Darby End) Dudley 56-60; Ch of Good Shepherd W Bromwich 60-66; C-in-c of St John W Bromwich 60-66; V of Good Shepherd w St John W Bromwich 66-69; Bilston (St Leon w St Luke from 72) 69-76; C-in-c of Hanbury Dio Lich from 76. *Hanbury Vicarage, Burton-on-Trent, Staffs.* (Burton-on-T 813357)

POWELL, Frederick James. b 1894. Univ of Dur BMus 23. St Aid Coll 27. **d** 29 **p** 30 Down. C of Bangor 29-32; C-in-c of Ashfield 32-36; I of Kilkeevin U (Castlerea) 36-40; Rathaspick w Streete Coolamber 40-49; Teampol-na-mbocht (or Altar) 49-55; Castlemartyr 55-59; Chap Kingston Coll Mitchelstown and C-in-c of Brigown and Farahy 59-65. *11 Kingston College, Mitchelstown, Co Cork, N Ireland.*

POWELL, Geoffrey Peter. b 25. Chich Th Coll 54. **d** 56 Bris **p** 57 Malmesbury for Bris. C of St Agnes Bris 56-58; Sherston Magna w Pinkney and Easton Grey 58-62; V of Wanborough 62-75; R of Lyddington w Wanborough 75-80; Preb of Lyddington 75-80; V of St Cleer Dio Truro from 80. *St Cleer Vicarage, Liskeard, Cornw, PL14 5DJ.* (Liskeard 43240)

POWELL, Canon Henry James. b 1892. **d** 30 **p** 31 Roch. C of H Trin Penge 30-33; R of Milton-next-Gravesend 33-50; V of Aylesford 50-64; RD of Cobham 50-54; Malling 54-64; Surr 50-64; Hon Can of Roch 56-64; Can (Emer) from 64. *Dulverton, Barnfield, Marlborough, Wilts.* (Marlborough 2015)

POWELL, James. b 51. Sarum Wells Th Coll 78. **d** 79 Roch. C of Larkfield and of Leybourne Dio Roch from 79. *73 Rectory Lane, Leybourne, W Malling, Kent.*

POWELL, James Alexander. b 41. McMaster Univ Ont BA 72. Trin Coll Tor 71. **d** 73 **p** 74 Niag. Perm to Offic Dio Niag 73-74; R of St Phil Grimsby Beach 74-76; Perm to Offic Dio Edmon 76-79; R of St James St Catharines Dio Niag from 79. *405 Merritt Street, St Catharines, Ont, Canada.* (416-682 8853)

POWELL, John Arthur. b 34. St Jo Coll Auckld 56. **d** 59 **p** 60 Auckld. C of Remuera 59-62; Avondale 62-64; V of Islands 64-67; Helensville 67-70; Otara Miss Distr 70-73; St John Campbell's 73-76; Hon C of Henderson Dio Auckld from 76. *50 Jaemont Avenue, Te Atatu South, Auckland, NZ.*

POWELL, John Edward Henry. b 14. Late Scho of St D Coll Lamp BA 52. **d** 54 **p** 55 St A. C of Hope 54-57; Llandrillo-yn-Rhos 57-59; R of Shelton 59-63; V of Gayton w Fradswell Dio Lich from 63. *Gayton Vicarage, Stafford, ST18 0HQ.* (Weston 270278)

POWELL, John Hughes. b 28. Univ of Wales (Cardiff) BSc 48. **d** 80 **p** 81 Llan (NSM). Hon C of Llanfabon Dio Llan from 80. *64 High Street, Nelson, Mid-Glam, CF46 6HA.*

POWELL, John Reginald. b 36. Univ of Nottm BA (2nd cl Th) 59. St Cath S Ox Dipl Publ and Social Admin 60. Ripon Hall Ox 59. **d** 61 **p** 62 Wakef. C of Hebden Bridge 61; Thornhill 61-64; C-in-c of St Aug Halifax 64-67; Asst Master R Gr Sch Lanc 67-68; Hon C of Ch Ch Lanc 67-69; V of Holland Fen w Amber Hill and Chap Hill 69-73; Asst Master Norton Sch 73-76; Perm to Offic Dio York from 73; L to Offic Dio Ely from 76; Chap K Sch Ely from 77. *6 The Gallery, Ely, Cambs, CB7 4DH.*

POWELL, Kelvin. b 49. Wycl Hall Ox 71. **d** 74 Warrington for Liv. **p** 75 Liv. C of Prescot 74-77; Ainsdale 77-79; V of Bickershaw Dio Liv from 79. *Vicarage, Bickershaw, Wigan, Lancs, WN2 4AE.* (Wigan 866139)

POWELL, Kenneth John. b 14. Univ of Lon MB BS 38. **d** 62 **p** 63 Ex. C of St Paul's Conv Distr Burnt House Lane Ex 62-65; Crediton 65-75; Heavitree Ex 76-80; Hon C of Broadhembury w Payhembury Dio Ex from 80. *The Old Vicarage, Payhembury, Honiton, Devon, EX14 0HA.* (Broadhembury 362)

POWELL, Llewellyn. b 28. Glouc Th Course 67. **d** 70 **p** 71 Glouc. C of Quinton 70-73; C-in-c 73-76; V of Ch Honeybourne w Cow Honeybourne Dio Glouc from 76. *Vicarage, Honeybourne, Worcs, WR11 5PP.* (Evesham 830302)

POWELL, Llewellyn Montague Saxon. St D Coll Lamp BA 29. **d** 29 **p** 30 Malmesbury for Llan. C of St Mary Virg Cardiff 29-35; Chap (Eccles Est) at Chakrata 36 and 37-38; Luckn 36-37; Surr 36; Benares 37; Naini Tal 39; Allahabad 38 and 39; Jhansi 40; Chaubattia 40-42; Jhansi 42-45; Allahabad Canton 45-46; Dehra Dun 46-49; Hon CF 47; Perm to Offic Dio Lon 49; Chap at Lausanne 49-59; St John Ghent 59-73; Chap at St Geo Mem Ch Ypres 61-73. *33 Turnaware Road, Falmouth, Cornw.*

POWELL, Ralph Dover. b 49. Chich Th Coll 71. **d** 74 **p** 75 Ches. C of St Mich Coppenhall Crewe 74-77; H Trin Heref 77-80; V of St Barn Crewe Dio Ches from 80. *Vicarage, West Street, Crewe, Cheshire.* (0270 2418)

POWELL, Randall Ingram. St Pet Coll Ja. **d** 56 **p** 57 Ja. C of Montego Bay 56-57; P-in-c of Marley 57-60; Balaclava Keynsham and Siloah 60-63; R of Christiana 64-67; On leave. *Box 23, Mandeville, Jamaica, W Indies*

POWELL, Raymond Leslie. b 35. K Coll Lon and Warm AKC 61. **d** 62 **p** 63 Lon. C of Hendon 62-67; Huntingdon (in c of St Barn Oxmoor from 69) 67-75; V of St Barn Huntingdon 75-79; P-in-c of Sawston Dio Ely from 79. *Vicarage, Church Lane, Sawston, Cambridge, CB2 4JR.* (Cambridge 832248)

POWELL, Richard Michael Wheler. b 19. St Edm Hall Ox BA 45. Wells Th Coll 47. **d** 49 **p** 50 Ches. C of St Pet Hale 49-52; V of Crowle Worcs 52-56; Chap Suez Contractors' Services Co Egypt 56-57; V of Kempsey 57-62; R of Tarporley 62-72; C-in-c of L Budworth 69-70; R of Overton w Laverstoke and Freefolk 73-81; P-in-c of Damerham w Martin Dio Sarum from 81. *Vicarage, Martin, Fordingbridge, Hants.* (Martin Cross 215)

POWELL, Richard Penry. Univ of Dur LTh 38. St Aid Coll 34. **d** 38 Stafford for Lich **p** 39 Lich. C of Brierley Hill 38-42; St Chad Derby 42-45; Uttoxeter w Bramshall 45-47; V of Alton 47-60; Bradley-le-Moor 48-60; R of Drayton Bassett 60-64; C-in-c of St Mary's Conv Distr Canwell 60-64; V of Wrockwardine 64-80; Uppington w Aston 64-80. *34 Herbert Avenue, Wellington, Telford, Salop.*

POWELL, Richmond Roscow ffolliott. b 09. **d** 45 **p** 46 Lagos. Dom Chap to Bp of Lagos 46-52; Actg Supt Niger Ch Group Lagos 49-52; Warden St Andr Bro Okene 52-53; R of Evershot w Frome St Quintin and melbury Bubb 53-59; C of Milford 59-74. *The Coach House, Woodland Way, Milford-on-Sea, Lymington, Hants SO4*

POWELL, Ronald Mercer. b 18. **d** 75 **p** 77 Kimb K. C of St Cypr Kimb Dio Kimb K from 75. *85 Central Road, Kimberley 8301, CP, S Africa.* (22171)

POWELL, Canon Samuel Frederick William. St Aug Coll Cant 35. **d** 35 **p** 37 Pet. C of All SS Pet 35-38; Yeoville Johann 38-40; Actg C of Daventry 40-41; C-in-c of St Columba Conv Distr Corby 41-44; V of Bozeat 44-49; R of Daventry 49-57; Surr from 51; RD of Daventry 55-68; R of Barby 57-72; V of Kilsby 57-72; Hon Can of Pet 67-78; Can (Emer) from 78; R of Clipston 72-78. *34 St Augustin Way, Daventry, Northants.* (Daventry 3189)

POWELL, Samuel John. Qu Coll Ox BA (2nd cl Th) 53, MA 57. **d** 47 **p** 48 Ox. L to Offic Dio Ox 47-53; C of Pontnewynydd 53-55; Ashchurch 55-56; L to Offic Dio Ox 56-58; Asst Master Escola Britânica de S£ao Paulo 58-64; Prof of Engl Faculdades of Taubaté and Mogi das Cruzes, S£ao Paulo from 64. *Vila Estremadura, Caixa Postal 161, Campos do Jord£ao, SP, Brazil.*

POWELL, Sydney Roswell. St Pet Coll Kingston. **d** 59 Ja **p** 60 Kingston for Ja. C of St Mich Kew Pk 59-62; P-in-c of Gilnock 62-63; Frankfield 63-67; P-in-c of Mile Gully 63-67; L to Offic Dio Antig from 80. *St Anthony's Rectory, Plymouth, Montserrat, W Indies.*

POWELL, William Michael. b 33. Bps' Coll Cheshunt 58. **d** 61 Kens for Lon **p** 62 Lon. C of St Mich Golders Green 61-64; St Cath Hatcham 64-67; Woodham 67-72; V of All SS Onslow City and Dio Guildf from 72; RD of Guildf from 78. *Vicarage, Abbots Close, Onslow Village, Guildford, Surrey, GU2 5RW.* (Guildford 72006)

POWELL-DAVIES, Noel Winston. b 14. Oriel Coll Ox MA 50. **d** 75 **p** 77 Tas. Hon C of St D Cathl Hobart Dio Tas from 75. *28 Rosny Esplanade, Rosny, Tasmania 7018.* (002-44 4821)

POWER, Alan Edward. Worc Coll Ox BA 50, MA 53. Lich Th Coll. **d** 57 **p** 58 Birm. C of Ch Ch Summerfield Birm 57-60; Oldbury (in c of St John Langley) 60-63; V of St Marg Short Heath Dio Birm from 63. *St Margaret's Vicarage, Somerset Road, Erdington, Birmingham B23 6NQ.* (01-373 6989)

POWER, Arthur Lyle. St Jo Coll Morpeth. **d** 55 Bp Storrs for Graft **p** 56 Graft. C-in-c of Ulmarra 55-56; V 56-59; R of Eureka 59-62; C of Murwillumbah w Condong 62-64; R of Bribbaree 64-65; Perm to Offic Dio Brisb 65-66; R of Cleveland 66-68. *c/o Church House, 417 Ann Street, Brisbane, Queensland, Australia.*

POWER, David Michael. b 56. Oak Hill Coll BA 81. **d** 81 Portsm. C of Warblington w Emsworth Dio Portsm from 81. *30 St James Road, Emsworth, Hants, PO10 7DW.* (Emsworth 71503)

POWER, Ivor Jonathan. b 43. TCD 66. **d** 69 **p** 70 Down. C of Drom Cathl 69-71; Enniscorthy 71-74; R of Youghal (w Castlemartyr and Ballycotton from 78) 74-81; Athlone U Dio Meath from 81. *Rectory, Athlone, Co Westmeath, Irish Republic.* (0902-8350)

POWER, Canon Norman Sandiford. b 16. Worc Coll Ox BA 38, MA 42. Ripon Hall Ox 38. **d** 40 **p** 41 Birm. C of Ch Ch Summerfield 40-43; C-in-c of All SS Birm 43-45; V of Immanuel Highter's Heath 45-52; St John Ladywood Dio Birm from 52; Hon Can of Birm from 65. *Ladywood Vicarage, Birmingham 16.* (021-454 1293)

POWER, Robert Lloyd. b 50. K Coll NS BA 72. Atlantic Sch of Th Halifax 72. **d** 74 NS. C of Petite Riviere Dio NS from 75. *c/o The Rectory, Petite Riviere, New Dublin, NS, Canada.*

POWERS, Beaumont Ward. Univ of NSW BComm 61. Univ of Syd BA 65. BD (1st cl) Lon 63. Moore Th Coll Syd ACT ThL (2nd cl) 57. **d** 59 Bp Hilliard for Syd **p** 59 Syd. C-in-c of Provisional Distr Riverwood 59-64; Sec for External Studs Moore Th Coll Syd 64-68; R of Newtown 67-69 and 70-74; C of St Sav Ruskin Pk 69-70; L to Offic Dio Syd from 74. *259a Trafalgar Street, Petersham, NSW, Australia 2049.* (560-7603)

POWLES, Cyril Hamilton. Univ of McGill, BA 40. Trin Coll Tor STB 54. Harvard Univ MA Univ of BC PhD 68. Montr Th Coll LTh 43. **d** 43 **p** 44 Montr. C of St Matt Hampstead Montr 43-49; Dean of Res Montr Dioc Th Coll 45-47; Miss in Japan 49-71. *116 Rose Park Drive, Toronto, Ont., Canada.*

POWLES, Michael Charles. b 34. Univ of Reading BSc 56. Univ of Birm Dipl Th 60. Qu Coll Birm 58. **d** 60 **p** 61 Chelmsf. C of Goodmayes 60-65; St Matt Surbiton (in c of St Geo Tolworth) 65-78; Lect Woolwich Coll Further Educn from 79. *21 Tankerton Road, Tolworth, Surbiton, Surrey, KT6 7LF.* (01-391 1014)

POWLESLAND, Percy James. b 13. Kelham Th Coll 30. **d** 37 **p** 38 Sheff. C of St John Masbrough 37-38; H Trin Ilkeston 38-40; Wollaton (in c of Cossall) 40-45; Hasland 45-49; Blyth (in c of St Luke Langold) 49-53; C-in-c of St Luke's Eccles Distr Langold 53-56; V of St Barn Pleasley Hill Mansfield 56-65; R of Finningley Dio Southw from 65. *Finningley Rectory, Doncaster, DN9 3DA.* (Doncaster 770240)

POWLEY, Robert Mallinson. b 39. Fitzw Ho Cam 2nd cl Econ Trip pt i 59, BA (3rd cl Th Trip pt ii) 62, MA 65. Ridley Hall Cam 61. **d** 63 **p** 64 S'wark. C of Bermondsey 63-67; Hon C of St Anne Moseley 67-69; Perm to Offic Dio Man 72-78; Hon C of Walshaw Dio Man from 78. *9 Lowercroft Road, Bury, Lancs, BL8 2EX.*

POWNALL, Geoffrey Carr. b 06. St Edm Hall Ox BA 29. Wells Th Coll 29. **d** 31 **p** 32 Wakef. C of St John Wakef 31-33; Charlton Kings 33-38; St Marg Anfield 38-41; Minchinhampton 41-44; All SS Cheltm 44-47; St Nich Strood 47-53; Ashford Kent 53-60; Cheriton w Newington 60-64; R of Staple 64-76; Perm to Offic Dio Cant from 76. *4 St Nicholas Hospital, Harbledown, Canterbury, Kent.*

POWNALL, Tom Basil. b 19. Jes Coll Cam 2nd cl Hist Trip pt i 39, BA (2nd cl Th Trip pt i) 41, MA 44. Ridley Hall Cam 41. **d** 42 **p** 43 Chelmsf. C of St Mary Becontree 42-45; St John Deptford (in c of St Nich) 45-47; V of St Nich Deptford 47-52; St Mary Becontree 52-61; Surr 58-61; V of Felixstowe 61-68; Warden Mabledon Conf Centre Tonbridge 68-74; P-in-c of Fressingfield w Weybread (and Wingfield from 76) Dio St E from 74; Wingfield 76-79; RD of Hoxne from 81. *Vicarage, Fressingfield, Eye, Suff, IP21 5PE.* (Fressingfield 388)

POWNEY, Frank Rupert. b 10. Dorch Miss Coll 37. **d** 41 **p** 42 Lich. C of Ch Ch Wolverhampton 41-47; Palfrey Walsall 47-48; C-in-c of Ascen Conv Distr (Friar Pk) West Bromwich 48-54; V of Calton 54-57; Oakamoor w Cotton 57-60; Pampisford 60-62; V of Babraham 60-62; C-in-c of Hildersham 60-62; V of Quadring 62-68; St Barn Warrington 68-70; C ofAll SS Warwick 70-72. *6 Windsor Terrace, Douglas, IM.*

POWYS, Edwin Lionel Garrod. b 07. Late Exhib of St Edm Hall Ox BA (1st cl Mod Lang) 29, 2nd cl Th 31, MA 33. Wycl Hall Ox 29. **d** 31 **p** 32 S'wark. C of St Mary Magd Peckham 31-33; Miss Paraguayan Chaco Miss 33-37; C of All SS Shooters Hill 38-39; C-in-c of Ch Ch Chesterfield 39-43; V of St Thos-in-the-Moors Balsall Heath 43-49; Ch Ch Derby 49-55; PC (V from 69) of L Eaton 55-73; Perm to Offic Dio Derby from 74; Dio St D from 75. *Llain Fawr, Nebo, Llanon, Aberystwyth, SY23 5LN.* (Nebo 352)

POYNTING, Charles Robert Macvicar. b 23. Hertf Coll Ox BA (2nd cl Lit Hum) and MA 48. Wells Th Coll 48. **d** 50 **p** 51 Guildf. C of Gt Bookham 50-52; Ch Ch Epsom 52-55; V of H Trin Ashton L 55-62; Belfield Dio Man from 62. *St Ann's Vicarage, Milnrow Road, Rochdale, Lancs, OL16 5BT.* (Rochdale 46173)

✠ **POYNTZ, Right Rev Samuel Greenfield.** b 26. Trin Coll Dub BA (2nd cl Mod in Ment and Mor Sc) 48, 2nd cl Mod in Or Lang 49, Downes Pri (2nd) 49, (1st) 50, Robert King Mem Pri and Div Test (1st cl) 50, MA 51, BD 53, PhD 60. **d** 50 **p** 51 Dub. C of St Geo Dub 50-52; Bray 52-55; St Michan and St Paul Dub 55-59; I of St Steph Dub 59-78; V of St Ann Dub 67-78; Archd of Dub 74-78; Exam Chap to Abp of Dub 74-78; Cons Ld Bp of Cork, Cloyne and Ross in Ch Ch Cathl Dub 17 Sept 78 by Abp of Dub; Bps of Cash, Meath, Lim, Tuam, Kilm and Derry; and Abp Buchanan and Bp Stanistreet. *the Palace, Bishop's Street, Cork, Irish Republic.* (Cork 21214)

POZZI, Roy St Clair. Edin Th Coll 46. **d** 47 **p** 48 Glas. C of St Mary's Cathl (in c of St Pet) Glas 47-56; Ayr (in c of St Ninian Prestwich) 56-57; V of W Ashby 57-60; R of Belchford 57-60; V of Lidlington 60-67. *Bei Herrn Walter Rumer, Kranebitten 191a, Steinach in Tyrol, Austria.*

PRAGNELL, John William. b 39. ALCD 64. BD (Lon) 65. **d** 65 **p** 66 Win. C of Bitterne 65-68; Hatfield Hyde 68-73; Chap at Kuwait 73-75; Abbots Langley and Leavesden Hosps from 75. *78 The Crescent, Abbots Langley, Watford, Herts.*

PRANCE, Frederick Charles Victor. b 15. St Aid Coll 46. **d** 48 **p** 49 Chelmsf. C of Chadwell Heath 48-52; L Ilford 52-54; R of L Parndon 54-57; R of Netteswell 54-57; Tye Green w Netteswell 57-62; Surr from 55; R of Wickford 62-73; C-in-c of Rawreth 64-69; V of St Mich AA Westcliff-on-Sea Dio Chelmsf from 73. *5 Mount Avenue, Westcliff-on-Sea, Essex, SS0 8PS.* (Southend-on-Sea 78462)

PRANCE, Robert Penrose. b 47. Sarum Wells Th Coll 69. **d** 72 Bp MacInnes for Sarum **p** 73 Sarum. C of Gillingham 72-76; P-in-c of St Giles Wimborne 76-80; Woodlands 76-80; Edmondsham 76-80; Cranborne w Boveridge Dio Sarum 77-80; R (w Edmondsham, Wimborne and Woodlands) from 80. *Cranborne Rectory, Wimborne, Dorset, BH21 5PP.* (Cranborne 253)

PRASAD, James. d 67 Polyn. d Dio Polyn 67-72. *326 West 13th Avenue, Vancouver, Canada.*

PRASAD, Samuel Kampta. b 23. Ch Ch Coll 67. **d** 69 **p** 70 Auckld for Polyn. C of Ponsonby Auckld 70; St Mary's Cathl Auckld 71-72; St Alb Balmoral 73-75; New Lynn Dio Auckld from 75. *4 Marion Street, Mount Roskill, Auckland 4, NZ.* (675-486)

PRASADAM, Goruganthula Samuel. b 34. U Th Sem NY STM 68. **d** Ch of S India. In Ch of S India 62-74; C of Llanbeblig 75-76; Norbury Ches 76-77; V of Aberamam w Abercwmboi Dio Llan from 78. *Vicarage, Aberaman, Aberdare, Mid Glam.* (Aberdare 872871)

PRATER, Raleigh Brandon. b 09. ALCD 40. **d** 40 **p** 41 Lon. C of St Barn Holloway 40-44; St Luke Kilburn 44-48; V (w St Simon and St Jude from 52) 48-64; C-in-c of St Simon Paddington and St Jude Kensal Green 48-52; V of Ch Ch Roxeth Harrow 64-75. *13 Shirley Gardens, Rusthall, Tunbridge Wells, Kent.* (Tunbridge Wells 21724)

PRATT, Basil David. b 38. Ripon Hall Ox 64. **d** 67 **p** 68 S'wark. C of St Jo Bapt Southend Lewisham 67-68; Caterham Valley 68-70; CF from 70. *c/o Ministry of Defence, Bagshot Park, Bagshot, Surrey, GU19 5PL.*

PRATT, Benjamin John. b 42. TCD BA 63. Cudd Coll Ox 68. **d** 70 **p** 71 Connor. C of Ballymoney 70-72; Monaghan 72-74; Industr Chap Kirkby Dio Liv from 74. *39 Church Way, Kirkby, Liverpool, L32 1TQ.* (051-546 5670)

PRATT, Canon David George. b 10. St D Coll Lamp BA (1st cl Hist) and Trehearne Scho 32. Jes Coll Ox BA (2nd cl Th) 34, MA 38, BD 50. **d** 34 **p** 35 St D. C of Pembroke Dk 34-38; St Annes-on-the-Sea 38-40; V of St Gabr Blackb 40-53; St John Sandylands, Heysham 53-80; Surr 45-80; RD of Lanc 64-71; Hon Can of Blackb Cathl from 71. *30 Long Lands Lane, Heysham, Lancs.*

PRATT, Donald Russell. b 18. **d** and **p** 74 Bran. I of Sioux Miss Oak Lake Dio Bran from 74. *PO Box 162, Griswold, Manit., Canada.*

PRATT, Edward Andrew. b 39. Clare Coll Cam BA 61, MA 65. Clifton Th Coll 63. **d** 66 **p** 67 Lon. C of St John Southall 66-69; Drypool 69-71; V of Mackworth 71-78; R of Kirk Langley 71-78; C-in-c of Radburne 71-74; V of St Simon Southsea Dio Portsm from 78. *22 St Helen's Parade, Southsea, Hants, PO4 0QJ.* (0705-733068)

PRATT, Eric. Ridley Hall Cam. **d** 60 **p** 61 Carl. C of St Jas Denton Holme 60-63; All SS Cockermouth 63-65; Bredbury 66-69; V of Eaton w Hulme Walfield 69-75; Hollingworth Dio Ches from 75. *Hollingworth Vicarage, Hyde, Gtr Man, SK14 8HS.* (Mottram 2310)

PRATT, Jacob Ekundayo. d 66 **p** 67 Sier L. P Dio Sier L. *Vicarage, Lumley, Sierra Leone.*

PRATT, John Anthony. b 38. Selw Coll Cam 1st cl Math Trip pt i 59, BA (2nd cl Math Trip pt ii) 61, Math Trip pt iii 62, MA 65. Univ of Birm Dipl Th 66. Qu Coll Birm 64. **d** 66 **p** 67 Lon. C of Harrow Weald 66-69; St Pancras 69-74; Saffron Walden 74-75; Team V of Saffron Walden w Wendens Ambo and Littlebury 75-79; V of Harlow Dio Chelmsf from 79. *Latton Vicarage, The Gowers, Harlow, Essex, CM20 2JP.* (Harlow 24005)

PRATT, Very Rev John Francis Isaac. Keble Coll Ox BA (2nd cl Mod Hist) 34, MA 38. Wells Th Coll 34. **d** 36 Taunton for B & W **p** 37 B & W. C of All SS Weston Bath 36-39; Brighouse (in c of St Jas) 39-41; CF (EC) 41-46; Men in Disp 43; V of Rastrick 46-49; Wendover 49-59; Surr from 50; C-in-c of Halton 52-59; RD of Wendover 55-59; V of St Mary Virg w All SS, St Sav, St Mark and St Matt Reading 59-61; Chilton w Dorton 61-70; Archd of Buckingham 61-70; Provost and R of Southwell Minster 70-78; Provost (Emer) from 78; Exam Chap to Bp of Southw 71-78; C-in-c of Edingley w Halam 73-78. *42 Bickerton Road, Headington, Oxford, OX3 7LS.* (Ox 63060)

PRATT, Kenneth Wilfred. b 23. Open Univ BA 78. St Aid Coll 59. **d** 61 **p** 62 Lich. C of Bushbury 61-64; L Marlow 64-66; Chap Broadmoor Hosp Crowthorne 67-75; Chap HM Pris Nor from 75. *c/o HM Prison, Norwich.*

PRATT, Michael. b 42. Univ of Birm BSc (Pure Chem) 64. Univ of Leeds BA (2nd cl Th) 71. Coll of Resurr Mirfield 69. **d** 72 **p** 73 Ex. C of Barnstaple Dio Ex 72-78; Team V from 77. *Holy Trinity Vicarage, Barbican Road, Barnstaple, Devon.* (Barnstaple 5798)

PRATT, Robert James. St Chad's Coll Regina. **d** 59 Qu'App. I of Gull Lake 59-61; Strasbourg 61-63; Craik 63-68; R of Saltcoats 68-69; Maitland 69-72; I of Richibucto w Rexton 72-74; Hardwicke Dio Fred from 74. *Rectory, Bay du Vin, NB, Canada.*

PRATT, Ronald Arthur Frederick. G and C Coll Cam BA 09, MA 13. Ripon Cl Coll 10. **d** 10 **p** 11 Lon. C of Em W Hampstead 10-13; TCRN 17-19; C of St Matt Bethnal Green 13-21; PC of Ossington 21-23; Miss Dio Br Hond 30-31; PC of St John Long Eaton 23-33; St Barn Derby 33-35; P-in-c of St Jo Bapt Cathl Belize 35-38; Archd of Belize 35-46; Exam Chap to Bp of Br Hond 35-47; P-in-c of Guatemala and Salvador 38-43; St Jo Bapt Cathl Belize 43-46; L to Offic Dio Cant 47-62. *173 Old Dover Road, Canterbury, Kent, CT1 3EP.* (Canterbury 62702)

PRATT, Rupert Lionel William. b 13. St D Coll Lamp BA 35. Ripon Hall Ox 36. **d** 37 **p** 38 Birm. C of St Andr Bordesley 37-39; St Geo Ramsgate 39-40; St Alkmund Whitchurch 40-41; Chap RAF 41-68; R of Bildeston (w Wattisham from 77) 68-78; V of Wattisham 68-77. *59 Harefields, Long Melford, Sudbury, Suff.*

PRATT, Samuel Charles. b 40. Oak Hill Th Coll 69. **d** 71 **p** 72 Stepney for Lon. C of U Holloway 71-73; Bucknall w Bagnall 73-76; V of St Mich Liv 76-80; Chap R Liv Hosp from 80. *Vailima, 45 Queens Drive, Mossley Hill, Liverpool, L18 2DT.* (051-722 1625)

PRATT, Thaddeus Whitfield. b 35. Codr Coll Barb 74. **d** 76 **p** 77 Nass. P-in-c of St Phil Inagua 77-81; St Gregory I and Dio Nass from 81. *Box N-507, Nassau, Bahamas.*

PRATT, William Ralph. b 47. Keble Coll Ox BA 69, MA 73. Linc Th Coll 70. **d** 72 Lewes for Chich **p** 73 Chich. C of Ifield 72-78; Team V (in c of St Leon Langley Green) 78-79; C of St Pet Brighton Dio Chich from 79. *133 Ditchling Road, Brighton, BN1 4SE.*

PRATT-DOHERTY, Samuel William Olatunbosun. Im Coll Ibad 65. **d** 67 **p** 68 Lagos. P Dio Lagos. *c/o PO Box 13, Lagos, Nigeria.*

PRAX, Ronald Stuart. b 45. Univ of Dur BA 66, MA 72. Univ of Dur Dipl Th 68. St Chad's Coll Dur 63. **d** 69 **p** 70 Glouc. C of Charlton Kings 69-73; C-in-c of Horsley (and Newington Bagpath w Kingscote from 75) 73-78; Kingscote w Newington Bagpath 74-75. *c/o Horsley Vicarage, Stroud, Glos.* (Nailsworth 3814)

PREBBLE, Ven Albert Ernest. b 08. Univ of NZ BA (2nd cl Hist) 31, MA 32. St Jo Coll Auckld 32. **d** 32 **p** 33 Auckld. C of St Mark Remuera Auckld 32-35; V of Pukekohe 36-42; Exam Chap to Bp of Auckld 40-60; V of Whangarei 42-49; St Mark Remuera 49-63; Archd of Waimate 44-49; Manukau 49-56; Commiss Melan 45-61; VG and Archd of Auckld 56-63; Archd (Emer) from 76; V of St Jo Bapt Greenhill Harrow 63-72. *Pear Tree Cottage, Moreton Pinkney, Northants, NN11 6SG.* (Sulgrave 343)

PREBBLE, Frederick John. Sarum Th Coll. **d** 56 **p** 57 Roch. C of Bickley 56-58; St Silas Pentonville Islington 58-59; Clewer (in c of St Agnes Spital) 59-63; V of Saltley 63-75; R of Capel St Mary w L Wenham 75-80; Perm to Offic Dio Nor from 80. *1b Chamberlin Road, Norwich, NR3 3LZ.*

PREBBLE, Ven Kenneth Ralph. b 14. St Edm Hall Ox BA (3rd cl Mod Hist) 36, MA 48. Ripon Hall Ox 38. **d** 39 **p** 40 Chich. C of Horsham 39-43; CF (EC) 43-47; C of St Luke New Brompton Kent 47-48; V of Northcote 48-54; St Paul Auckld 54-74; Archd of Hauraki 65-75; Archd (Emer) from 76; V of Wellsford 74-79; Perm to Offic Dio Auckld 79-80. *c/o Box 82, Wellsford, NZ.*

PRECIOUS, John Robert. b 08. St Aid Coll 32. **d** 35 **p** 36 York. C of St Jude Hull 35-37; Guisborough w St Pet-in-Commondale 37-39; Chap Miss to Seamen Middlesbrough 39-45; Durban 45-52; Reg Sec for S Afr 48-52; R of Kensington W Austr 52-57; V of St Andr Leytonstone 57-59; Org Sec Miss to Seamen SE Area 59-61; Midl Area 63-66; Chap Port of Hong Kong 61-63; Yokohama 66-68; Hamburg and I of St Thos Becket Hamburg 68-71; Port of Lon 71-73. *12 St Olaves Road, Clifton, York, YO3 7AL.* (York 23945)

PREECE, Barry Leslie. b 48. Lich Th Coll 68. **d** 71 Dorking for Guildf. C of Ewell 71-74; Camberley 74-77; P-in-c of Ripley 77-80; Chap of HM Detention Centre Send 77-80; V of Cuddington Dio Guildf from 80. *Cuddington Vicarage, St Mary's Road, Worcester Park, Surrey.* (01-337 4026)

PREECE, Colin George. b 51. Chich Th Coll 72. **d** 75 Stafford for Lich **p** 76 Lich. C of St Pet U Gornal 75-78; St Paul Wednesbury 78-81; V of Oxley Dio Lich from 81.

Vicarage, Lymer Road, Oxley, Wolverhampton. (Wolverhampton 783342)

PREECE, Gordon Robert. b 54. Univ of Syd MA. Moore Th Coll Syd BD, ThL. **d** 81 Syd. C of St Paul Seaforth Dio Syd from 81. *1 French's Forest Road, Seaforth, NSW, Australia.*

PREECE, Harry Manning. Carleton Univ Ott BA 55. Bp's Univ Lennox LST 57. Trin Coll Tor STB 58. **d** 58 **p** 59 Ott. C of Trin Ott 58-61; I of Ashton 61-64; R of Long Sault 65-70; St John Nepean Ott 71-73; on leave. *363 Delaware Avenue, Burlington, Ont., Canada.*

PREECE, Canon James Derick. b 13. Lich Th Coll 37. **d** 40 **p** 41 Sheff. C of Tankersley 40-42; Eastwood (in c of St Sav) 42-46; V of Dalton Yorks 47-53; Chap at Port Louis Mauritius and sub-Dean of St Jas Cathl 53-55; Chap at Port Vic Seychelles, Sub-Dean of St Paul's Pro-Cathl Mahè, Archd of Seychelles and Can of St Jas Cathl Maur 55-60; V of St Matt Sheff 60-80; Hon Can of Sheff 73-80; Can (Emer) from 80; Surr from 72; RD of Ecclesall 74-80; Can of Sey from 80. *113 Nursery Crescent, North Anston, S Yorks, S31 7BR.* (Dinnington 562748)

PREECE, Joseph. b 23. Univ of Wales (Bangor) BA 50. N-W Ordin Course 73. **d** 73 Stockport for Ches **p** 74 Ches. C of Claughton 73-74; Barnston 74-75; R of Aldford and Bruera 75-80; V of Wincle w Wildboarclough Dio Ches from 80. *Vicarage, Wincle, Macclesfield, Cheshire.* (Wincle 234)

PREECE, Richard Benjamin. Lich Th Coll 30. **d** 30 **p** 31 Lich. [f Methodist Min] C of Brierley Hill 30-32; St Mary Kingswinford (in c of Ascen Wall Heath) 32-34; Ripley (in c of St John) 34-36; V of S Wingfield 36-47; R of Norton Fitzwarren 47-57; C-in-c of Ash Priors 51-52; Chap of Tonevale Hosp 52-57; V of Compton Bp 57-63; Chap of Shute Shelve Hosp 57-64. *Address temp unknown.*

PREECE, Robert James. b 44. St Steph Ho Ox 72. **d** 75 **p** 76 York. C of Middlesbrough 75-78; St Giles w St Sav Reading 78-81; V of St Luke Reading Dio Ox from 82. *St Luke's Vicarage, Erleigh Road, Reading, RG1 5LH.* (Reading 62372)

PREECE, Ronald Alexander. b 29. Univ of Lon BD 56. ALCD 55. **d** 56 **p** 57 Man. C of H Trin Platt Rusholme 56-59; Chap at Pernambuco 60-63; Asst Master Abp's Sch Cant and Perm to Offic 64-70; on Staff of Overseas Miss Fell from 70; Perm to Offic Dio Bris from 76. *203 Redland Road, Bristol, BS6 6YS.*

PREIST, Philip Brian Patrick. Univ of Liv BA 57. St Steph Ho Ox 58. **d** 60 **p** 61 Ex. C of St Pet Plymouth 60-65; St Mary Magd Paddington 65-74; E Wickham 74-75; Chap O of the H Paraclete Whitby 77-79; C of All SS Middlesbrough Dio York from 79; St Aid w St Alb Mart Middlesbrough Dio York from 79. *c/o All Saints' Centre, Church House, Grange Road, Middlesbrough, TS1 2LR.* (Middlesbrough 245035)

PRENDERGAST, Ross William. Montr Dioc Th Coll. **d** 62 **p** 63 Montr. Sec and Chap Andr Home Montr 62-65; I of Hemmingford 65-66; St Geo Hamilton 66-77; R of Greenfield Pk Dio Montr from 77; Hon Can of Niag 76-77. *321 Empire Avenue, Greenfield Park, PQ, Canada.* (671-6000)

PRENTICE, Hugh Kenneth. b 42. Univ of Melb BA 65. ACT Th Scho 68. Melb Coll of Div BD 70. **d** 70 **p** 71 Melb. C of Caulfield 70-71; H Trin Adel 71-74; Perm to Offic Dio Melb 74; CMS Miss Dio Moro from 74; Lect St Phil Th Coll Kongwa from 75. *Box 26, Kongwa, Tanzania.*

PRENTICE, Kenneth William. Trin Coll Melb BA (1st cl Cl Phil) 34, MA 36. ACT ThL 35. **d** 36 **p** 37 Melb. C of Surrey Hills 36-38; CMS Miss at Buwalasi Tr Coll 38-39; Mbale 39-41; Kabwangasi 41-45; Ngora 46-63; Hon Can of U Nile 54-63; Archd of Teso and Karamoja 61-62; V of Ch Ch Hawthorn 63-71; Wattle Pk 71-80; Exmouth Dio NW Austr from 80. *Kennedy Street, Exmouth, W Australia.*

PRENTICE, Michael Charles. b 35. Bps' Coll Cheshunt 59. **d** 62 **p** 63 Lon. C of St Pet Lon Dks w St John of Wapping 62-66; St Dunstan Cranford 66-70; St Jas Gt w St Jude Bethnal Green 70-71; Walsingham 71-73; Ch the Redeemer Southall 73; V of St Thos Acton Vale 73-78; P-in-c of Stow Bardolph w Wimbotsham 78-80; R of Woodford w Twywell Dio Pet from 80. *Woodford Rectory, Kettering, Northants, NN14 4HS.* (Thrapston 2478)

PRENTICE, Peter Stanley. Ridley Coll Melb ACT ThL 51. **d** 51 **p** 52 Bal. C of Warrnambool 51-55; V of Merino 55-57; Dir of Youth and Relig Educn Dio Wang 57-59; Sec Gen Bd of Relig Educn Dio Melb and Perm to Offic Dio Melb 59-66; Chap Trin Gr Sch Melb 66-78; Camberwell Gr Sch Melb from 78. *4 Montague Street, Hawthorn, Vic, Australia 3122.* (818 2139)

PRENTICE, Walter Gordon. b 07. Nor Ordin Course 73. **d** 75 Nor **p** 76 Lynn for Nor (APM). Hon C of Swanton Morley 75-78; P-in-c of Scarning w Wendling 76-78; Perm to Offic Dio Nor from 78; St E from 80. *65 St Nicholas Walk, Brandon, Suffolk, IP27 0DL.* (Thetford 810898)

PRENTICE, William Edward. b 51. Univ of Manit BA 72. Trin Coll Tor MDiv 75. **d** 75 **p** 77 Rupld. C of St Aid Winnipeg 75-77; St Mary Richmond Hill Dio Tor from 78. *10003 Yonge Street, Richmond Hill, Ont, L4C 1T8, Canada.*

PRENTIS, Richard Hugh. b 36. Ch Coll Cam BA 60, MA 64. Sarum Th Coll 69. **d** 71 Taunton for B & W **p** 72 B & W. C of St Mary Bathwick Bath 71-75; Dom Chap to Bp of Lich 76-80; V of St Mary and St Chad Longton Dio Lich from 80. *Presbytery, Anchor Road, Longton, Stoke-on-Trent, Staffs, ST3 5DH.* (S-on-T 313142)

PRENTIS, Thomas David. b 02. Kelham Th Coll 23. **d** 29 **p** 30 Lon. C of St Alphage Hendon 29-31; St Andr Bethnal Green 31-34; R of Bowen Queensld 34-39; C of Upton w Chalvey (in c of St Pet Chalvey) 39-44; Offg Chap RAF 44-46; V of Langley-Marish 44-48; R of Horton 48-77. *79 Hawkeridge Park, Westbury, Wilts.* (Westbury 822512)

PRESCOTT, Canon Alwyn Walker. Univ of Syd BEng (1st cl) 41. ACT ThL 45. Moore Th Coll 42. **d** and **p** 43 Syd. C of St John Beecroft 43-45; C-in-c of Pennant Hills and Thornleigh 45-49; R of Austinmer w Clifton Thirroul 49-51; Berrima w Moss Vale 51-63; Pittwater 63-67; Avalon w Palm Beach 67-71; Milsons Point Dio Syd from 71; Can of Syd from 73. *4 Parkes Street, Kirribille, NSW, Australia 2061.* (929-2363)

PRESCOTT, Anthony John. b 34. K Coll Lon and Warm AKC and Barry Pri 59. **d** 60 **p** 61 Bris. C of St Mark Swindon 60-66; PC of St Aid Small Heath Birm 66-68; V 68-72; L Publ Pr Dio Birm from 72; Hon C of Washwood Heath Dio Birm from 72; Asst Sec ACS 72-74; Gen Sec from 74. *264a Washwood Heath Road, Birmingham, B8 2XS.*

PRESCOTT, David. Wollaston Th Coll W Austr. **d** 63 Perth for Kalg **p** 64 Kalg. C of St John's Cathl Kalg 63-66; P-in-c of Quairading 66-68; R 68-70; Morawa 70-75; Kwinana Dio Perth from 75. *55 Medina Avenue, W Australia 6167.* (99 2065)

PRESCOTT, James Thomas. Worc Ordin Coll 60. **d** 61 **p** 62 Roch. C of Wigmore w Hempstead Conv Distr 61-63; Headless Cross 63-65; R of Kington w Dromston 65-73. *232 Bredhurst Road, Wigmore, Gillingham, Kent.*

PRESLAND, Robert Norman. **d** 80 **p** 81 Melb. C of St Barn Balwyn Dio Melb from 80. *86a Balwyn Road, Balwyn, Vic, Australia 3103.*

PRESSLY, George Nevil. Rhodes Univ Grahmstn BA 47. St Paul's Coll Grahmstn LTh 49. **d** 50 **p** 51 Kimb K. C of St Aug Kimb 50-53; L to Offic Dio Kimb K 53-54; P-in-c of Ulco 54-56; Barkly W Dio Kimb K 56-64 and from 66; R of S Kimb 64-66; Can of St Cypr Cathl Kimb 64-73. *Box 567, Kimberley, CP, S Africa.* (Kimb 25462)

PRESSWELL, John Lawrence Rowley. b 28. K Coll Lon and Warm AKC 51. Univ of Southn BEducn 79. **d** 52 **p** 53 S'wark. C of St Andr Surbiton 52-55; All SS Battersea Pk 55-57; Horley 57-61; Chap St Jo Coll York 61-62; V of St Faith Wandsworth 62-69; St Bart Battersea 69-71; C-in-c of St Luke Southn 71-73; C of Lymington 73-79; Chap and Asst Master Crookham Court Sch Newbury 79-81; Stanbridge Earls Sch Romsey from 81; L to Offic Dio Ox 79-81; Dio Win from 81. *2 South Drive, Stanbridge Earls School, Romsey, Hants, SO5 0HE.* (Romsey 516986)

PREST, Canon Walter. b 09. St Chad's Coll Dur BA 33, Dipl Th 34, MA 36. **d** 34 Carl **p** 35 Barrow-F for Carl. C of H Trin Millom 34-35; Min Can of Carl Cathl 35-39; C of Cantley 39-42; V of All SS w St Pet Weasenham 42-45; Bude Haven 45-69; RD of Stratton 48-63; Hon Can of Truro from 61; Can Missr 70-79; Preb and R of St Endellion 69-81. *30 Kings Avenue, Falmouth, Cornwall.*

PRESTON, Charles Franklyn. Univ of Tor MA 50, PhD 62. Wycl Coll Tor LTh 52, BD 54. **d** 52 **p** 53 NS. C of St Paul Halifax 52-54; St Paul Tor 54-55; C of St John Kingston 57-58; Miss at Mukono 58-60; Bp Tucker Coll Mukono 61-65; Hon C of Waterloo 66-68; L to Offic Dio Newfld from 68. *Box 21, St John's, Newfoundland, Canada.*

PRESTON, David Francis. b 50. BNC Ox BA 72, MA 78. St Steph Ho Ox 72. **d** 74 Roch **p** 75 Tonbridge. C of St Jas Elmers End Beckenham Dio Roch from 74. *6 Lloyds Way, Beckenham, Kent.* (01-650 1987)

PRESTON, Donald George. b 30. St Alb Ministerial Tr Scheme 77. **d** 80 St Alb **p** 81 Hertf for St Alb. Hon C of Elstow Dio St Alb from 80. *106 Putnoe Street, Bedford, MK41 8HJ.*

PRESTON, Preb Edwin Dewhurst. b 06. Univ of Liv BSc (1st cl Chem) 28, MSc 29. **d** 38 **p** 39 Liv. C of Sephton 38-43; St Pet Aintree 43-44; V of Fownhope w Fawley 44-47; Brockhampton 44-47; Lect and Asst Chap Culham Coll and L to Offic Dio Ox 47-51; Min Can of Heref Cathl 51-66; Chap and Asst Master of Heref Cathl Sch 51-66; RD of Heref S 66-72; Heref Rural 72-77; C-in-c of Hampton Bp 66-77; Woolhope 67-70; Preb of Heref Cathl from 72. *1 The Cloisters, Hereford.*

PRESTON, Preb Frederick Arnold. MBE 53. Univ of Leeds BA (3rd cl Lat) 42. Coll of Resurr Mirfield 42. **d** 44 Lon **p** 45 Stepney for Lon. C of H Cross Greenford 44-51; CF

51-61; R of W Hackney Dio Lon from 61; Preb of St Paul's Cathl Lon from 75. *306 Amhurst Road, N16.* (01-254 3235)

PRESTON, Frederick John. b 32. MBE 72. ALCD 67 (LTh from 74). Oak Hill Th Coll. **d** 57 **p** 58 Chich. C of Bp Hannington Mem Ch Hove 57-60; St Jo Bapt Woking (in c of H Trin Knaphill) 60-62; CF (TA) 58-62; CF 62-69; and from 71; V of Otterton 69-71. *c/o Ministry of Defence, Bagshot Park, Bagshot, Surrey.*

PRESTON (formerly PEANO), John. b 26. St Aid Coll 58. **d** and **p** 52 RC Bp of Milan. Rec into Angl Commun 57. C of Ch Ch Chadderton 58-59; Ch Ch W Didsbury 59-63; R of St Jo Evang Cheetham Dio Man from 63. *St John's Rectory, Brideoak Street, Cheetham, Manchester, M8 7AY.* (061-205 2005)

PRESTON, John Baker. b 23. Univ of Lon BA 49. Oak Hill Th Coll 46. **d** 51 **p** 52 Liv. C of Em Ch Fazakerley 51-55; H Trin Eastbourne 55-57; V of St Jo Evang Blackheath 57-65; Chairman Internat Studs Ho S from 65. *6 Frinstead Walk, Maidstone, Kent.*

PRESTON, John Martyn. b 13. Late Scho of St Jo Coll Cam 2nd cl Hist Trip pt i 34, BA (2nd cl Th Trip pt i) 35, MA 42. Qu Coll Birm 35. **d** 36 **p** 37 Birm. C of Langley 36-39; Actg C of Spennymoor w Whitworth 40-41; C-in-c of St Jas Ashted 41-44; C of St Mary Plaistow 44-45; CF (EC) 45-47; C of Falmouth 47-48; R of Marston Morteyne 48-50; C of Sutton Coldfield 50-57; King's Norton 57-59; St Columba Scarborough 59-60; Bunbury 60-62; St Pet Anlaby 62-63; Perm to Offic Dio York 63-68; C of St Paul Masborough 68-72; Howden 73-75; St Thos Bedford-Leigh 75-76; Ashton-under-Lyne 76-78. *Top Flat, 17 Granville Road, Scarborugh, N Yorks.*

PRESTON, John Michael. b 40. K Coll Lon and Warm BD and AKC 63. Univ of Lon BA Psychol 81. **d** 65 **p** 66 Lon. C of Heston 65-67; St Mary (in c of St Hugh) Northolt 67-72; Chap St Mich Sch Diego Martin 72-74; Hon C of St Mich Diego Martin Trinid 72-74; P-in-c of Aveley Dio Chelmsf 74-78; V from 78. *Vicarage, Mill Road, Aveley, South Ockendon, Essex, RM15 4SR.* (Purfleet 4865)

PRESTON, Joseph Arthur. b 11. Bps' Coll Cheshunt 60. **d** 61 **p** 62 St Alb. C of Bp's Hatfield Dio St Alb from 61; Hd Master Newtown Sch Hatfield 52-72; L to Offic Dio Nor from 72; C-in-c of Gt w L Snoring 76-77. *Unicorn House, Great Snoring, Fakenham, Norfolk.* (Walsingham 407)

PRESTON, Leonard. b 1898. St Aid Coll 32. **d** 34 **p** 35 Man. C of St Jas Gorton 34-36; Mottram-in-Longdendale (in c of Broadbottom) 36-41; CF (EC) 41-42; Hon CF 42; L to Offic Dio Ches 42-43; V of Kingsley Chesh 43-55; Morden w Almer and Charborough 55-64. *91 Agnew Road, Fleetwood, Lancs.*

PRESTON, Leonard Arthur. b 09. Univ of Leeds BA (2nd cl Hist) 32, Dipl Educn (1st cl) 48. Knight of the Order of Orange Nassau w Swords (Dutch) 46. Coll of Resurr Mirfield 34. **d** 34 **p** 35 Ches. C of St Columba Egremont 34-36; Penarth w Lavernock (in c of St Paul) 36-40; CF (EC) 40-46 (twice Men in Disp 45); Chap of St Alb Engl Ch Copenhagen 46-47; L to Offic Dio Lon 48-76; Asst Master Strode's Sch Egham 48-75; Chap Laleham Abbey 56-76; Perm to Offic Dio Cant from 76. *Underhill, Mountain Street, Chilham, CT4 8DG.* (Chilham 266)

PRESTON, Maurice. b 25. Dipl Th (Lon) 69. BD (Lon) 77. St Aid Coll. **d** 57 **p** 58 Southw. C of Stapleford 57-59; Wombwell (in c of St Geo Jump) 59-62; V of Thorpe Hesley Dio Sheff from 62. *Thorpe Hesley Vicarage, Rotherham, Yorks, S61 2RP.* (Sheff 467977)

PRESTON, Michael Christopher. b 47. Hatfield Coll Dur BA 68. Ripon Coll Cudd 75. **d** 78 **p** 79 Guildf. C of St Martin Epsom Dio Guildf from 78. *12 Worple Road, Epsom, Surrey, KT18 5EE.* (Epsom 20088)

PRESTON, Canon Percival Kenneth. b 16. Ch Ch Ox BA 38, MA 48. Cudd Coll. **d** 40 **p** 45 Win. C of St Helier Jersey 40-46; SS Phil and Jas Ox 46-48; Westbury-on-Trym 48-50; C-in-c of Lawrence Weston Conv Distr 50-55; V of St Greg Horfield 55-81; Hon Can of Bris from 74; RD of Horfield 76-80. *56 Gloucester Road, Rudgeway, Bristol, BS12 2RT.* (Almondsbury 612794)

PRESTON, Canon Ronald Haydn. b 13. Univ of Lon BSc (2nd cl Econ) 35. St Cath S Ox BA (1st cl Th) 40, MA 44. Ripon Hall Ox 38. **d** 40 **p** 41 Sheff. C of St John Park Sheff 40-43; Study Sec SCM and Ed *The Student Movement* 43-48; Warden of St Anselm Hall Univ of Man 48-63; Lect in Chr Ethics Univ of Man 49-70; Exam Chap to Bp of Man from 48; L to Offic Dio Man 48-50; C of St Chrys Vic Pk Dio Man 50-57; Can of Man 57-71; Sub-Dean 70-71; Hon Can 71-80; Can (Emer) from 80; Select Pr Univ of Cam 63; Univ of Ox 76 and 80; Exam Chap to Bp of Sheff 71-80; Prof of Social and Pastoral Th Univ of Man 70-80; Prof (Emer) from 80. *161 Old Hall Lane, Manchester, M14 6HJ.* (061-225 3291)

PRESTON, Thomas Leonard. b 27. Tyndale Hall Bris. **d** 64 Hulme for Man **p** 65 Man. C of St Jas Moss Side 64-66; Urmston 66-68; V of Thornham 68-76; Chap to the Deaf St Wilfrith Hastings 76-80; Chap for Deaf and Team V of All SS Pavement City and Dio York from 80. *St Denys Vicarage, Glenfield, Bull Lane, Heworth, Yorks, YO3 0TS.*

PRESTON, William. b 25. St Cath Coll Cam BA 46, MA 50. Oak Hill Th Coll. **d** 50 **p** 51 Southw. C of St Paul Hyson Green Nottm 50-52; Lenton (in c of St Barn) 52-55; Asst Master CMS Sch Maseno and L to Offic Dio Momb 55-59; Asst Master Thika High Sch 59-62; Perm to Offic Dio Momb 59-61; Dio Ft Hall 61-62; Asst Master Bethany Sch Goudhurst 62-69; Cranbrook Sch from 69; Perm to Offic Dio Cant from 64; Dio Roch from 66. *29 Orchard Way, Horsmonden, Tonbridge, Kent.*

PRESTON-THOMAS, Canon Colin Barnabas Rashleigh. b 28. Edin Th Coll 51. **d** 53 Edin **p** 54 St Andr. C of St D Dep Miss Pilton Edin 53-54; Chap St Ninian's Cathl Perth Dio St Andr 54-55; Prec 55-60; Chap HM Pris Perth 55-60; R of St Andr and St Geo Rosyth 60-72; P-in-c of Inverkeithing 60-72; Can of St Ninian's Cathl Perth from 68; Synod Clk Dio St Andr from 68; R of St Jo Evang Forfar Dio St Andr, Dunk and Dunbl from 72; Dioc Sec Dio St Andr, Dunk and Dunbl from 80. *24 St James Road, Forfar, Angus.* (Forfar 63440)

PRETORIA, Lord Bishop of. *See* Kraft, Right Rev Richard Austin.

PRETORIA, Lord Bishop Suffragan of. *See* Stevenson, Right Rev Hugh George.

PRETORIA, Dean of. (Vacant)

PRETTY, Arthur James Calvin. K Coll NS 60. **d** 63 **p** 64 NS. I of Ecum Secum 63-67; Lockeport 67-70; R of New Ross 70-75; St Mark Halifax Dio NS from 75. *5515 Russell Street, Halifax, NS, Canada.* (429-0469)

PREWER, Dennis. b 30. Kelham Th Coll 50. **d** 54 **p** 55 Ches. C of St Thos Stockport 54-58; St Mary and St Jas Grimsby 58-62; V of St John Gt Harwood 62-64; Scarcliffe 64-70; Clerical Org Sec CECS Dios Liv; Ban; and St A 70-78; Ches from 70; Man from 78; L to Offic Dio Ches from 70. *40 Oakfield Road, Davenport, Stockport, SK3 8SG.* (061-487 1632)

PRICE, Alastair Edwin. Univ of NZ BA 57, MA 58. Selw Coll Dun 59. **d** 59 **p** 60 Dun. C of Invercargill 59-62; V of Bluff 62-63; L to Offic Dio Dun 63-66; Dio Wai 67-68; Dio Auckld 69-74. *PO Box 28, Ngatia, NZ.*

PRICE, Alec Henry. b 14. Chich Th Coll 73. **d** 74 **p** 75 Portsm (APM). C of Portsdown Dio Portsm from 74. *31 Cranborne Road, Cosham, Portsmouth, PO6 2BG.*

PRICE, Alec John. b 32. Univ of Wales LLB 55. St Deiniol's Libr Hawarden 77. **d** 79 **p** 80 St A. C of Cathl Ch of St A from 79. *Plas Penucha, Caerwys, Mold, Clwyd, CH7 5BH.* (Caerwys 210)

PRICE, Anthony Ronald. b 49. Linc Coll Ox BA 71. St Jo Coll Dur BA 78. **d** 79 **p** 80 St Alb. C of St Paul St Alb 79-81; Wootton Dio St Alb from 81. *2 The Crescent, Stewartby, Bedford, MK43 9NQ.*

PRICE, Arnold James. b 11. Lon Coll of Div 37. **d** 40 **p** 41 Man. C of St John Facit 40-41; St Pet Levenshulme 41-43; C-in-c of St Jas Hope 43-45; Chap of City of Salford Hosps 45-47; C of Townstal Dartmouth 47-48; R of St Thos Lower Crumpsall 48-57; Chap Springfield Hosp Crumpsall 50-57; R of Dittisham 57-81. *Fairwinds, Hyne Town, Strete, Dartmouth, S Devon.* (Stoke Fleming 485)

PRICE, Barry. b 34. **d** 77 Nel. C of Greymouth Dio Nel from 77. *7 Cowper Street, Greymouth, NZ.*

PRICE, Benjamin. Coll Ho Ch Ch. **d** 47 **p** 48 Ch Ch. C of Timaru 47-52; V of Mount Somers 52-59; Temuka 59-66; Southbridge 66-72; L to Offic Dio Ch Ch from 72. *7 Masham Road, Christchurch, 4, NZ.*

PRICE, Benjamin Albert John. b 25. **d** 70 **p** 79 Newc. Hon C of Gosford 70-78; C of Wyoming Dio Newc from 79. *RMB 3290, Somersby, NSW, Australia 2251.* (043-72 1277)

PRICE, Cecil Johnston. Trin Coll Dub BA (2nd cl Mod in Ment and Mor Sc) 48, MA 52, Div Test (2nd cl) 49. **d** 50 **p** 51 Lim. C of Tralee 50-53; St Ann w St Luke Shandon Cork 53-56; I of Desertserges 56-58; St Mich Lim 58-67; Can and Preb of St Munchin in Lim Cathl 63-67; R of Bandon 67-69; Delgany Dio Glendal from 69. *Rectory, Delgany, Co Wicklow. Irish Republic.* (Dublin 874515)

PRICE, Clive Stanley. b 42. ALCD 69. **d** 69 **p** 70 Ox. C of Chenies w L Chalfont 69-75; R of Upper Stour 75-79; Min of Panshanger Conv Distr Digswell Dio St Alb from 79. *69 Hardings, Panshanger, Welwyn Garden City, Herts.* (W-G-City 33272)

PRICE, David. b 27. Wycl Hall Ox 61. **d** 63 **p** 64 Lich. C of Bucknall w Bagnall 63-67; Abingdon (in c of Ch Ch Northcourt) 67-75; Warden Stella Carmel Conf Centre Haifa 76-80; Sec Israel Trust of the Angl Ch from 80. *Box 191, Jerusalem, Israel.*

PRICE, David Douglas. b 16. Univ of Wales (Ban) BA (2nd cl Gr) 38. St Mich Coll Llan 38. **d** 39 **p** 41 St A. C of Llansilin 39-40; Rhos Wrexham 40-42; Colwyn Bay 42-43; Llangefni

43-46; Dwygyfylchi w Penmaenmawr 46-47; St Alkmund Shrewsbury 47-50; V of Hadnall Dio Lich from 50; V of Astley Dio Lich from 51; Asst Master Wem Gr Sch from 57. *Hadnall Vicarage, Shrewsbury, Salop.* (Hadnall 241)

PRICE, David Rea. b 39. St Aid Coll 61. **d** 63 **p** 64 Roch. C of Green Street Green 63-66; Gillingham Kent 66-69; N Windsor 69-72; V of Winkfield 72-80; Sunningdale Dio Ox from 80; RD of Bracknell from 77. *Sunningdale Vicarage, Ascot, Berks, SL5 0NL.* (Ascot 20061)

PRICE, David Rufus. b 08. St D Coll Lamp BA 32. **d** 32 Malmesbury for Bris **p** 33 Bris. C of St Lawr Bris 32-40; Westbury-on-Trym 40-41; St Mary Magd Stoke Bp 41-43; V of All SS Fishponds 43-47; Bishop's Nympton 47-50; Ottery St Mary 50-77; PC of Alfington 50-68; V 68-77; Surr 51-77; RD of Ottery 55-59. *Address temp unknown.*

PRICE, David Trevor William. b 43. Late Scho of Keble Coll Ox BA (2nd cl Mod Hist) 65, MA 69. FRHistS 79. Sarum Wells Th Coll 72. **d** 72 **p** 73 St D. Lect St D Coll Lamp from 70; Chap 79-80; Publ Pr Dio St D from 72. *65 Bridge Street, Lampeter, Dyfed, SA48 7AB.* (Lampeter 422707)

PRICE, Canon Derek William. b 27. St Pet Hall Ox BA 51, MA 55. Qu Coll Birm 51. **d** 53 **p** 54 Lon. C of St Mark St Marylebone 53-57; Stevenage 57-63; R of Linstead w Bogwalk Ja 63-67; R of E Harling w W Harling and Bridgham w Roudham 67-80; Hon Can of Nor from 75; RD of Thetford and Rockland from 76; Team R of Thetford Dio Nor from 80; R of Kilverstone and of Croxton Dio Nor from 80. *6 Redcastle Road, Thetford, Norf.* (Thetford 62291)

PRICE, Desmond. b 23. St D Coll Lamp BA 50. **d** 51 **p** 52 Llan. C of Llwynypia w Tonypandy 51-55; Ch Ch Watford 55-56; Chap RAF 56-64; Sen Chap 64-68; R of Dinas w Llanllawer 68-72; V of Llandeilo Fawr Dio St D from 72. *Vicarage, Llandeilo, Dyfed.* (Llandeilo 822421)

PRICE, Dewi Emlyn. b 09. St D Coll Lamp BA 32. **d** 33 **p** 34 Llan for Mon. C of Llanhilleth 33-35; St Nich w St Pet Droitwich 35-39; CF (EC) 39-45; Hon CF 45; C-in-c of St Mark's Conv Distr Worc 45-50; CF 50-63; Asst Master Cradley Secondary Sch 63-64; C of E Dereham 64-67; Hadzor w Oddingley 67-69; C-in-c 70-73; Tibberton w Bredicott and Warndon 70-73; Perm to Offic Dio Worc from 73. *25 Longfellow Road, Worcester, WR3 8DY.* (Worc 53384)

PRICE, Edward Glyn. b 35. St D Coll Lamp BA 55. Ch Div Sch of the Pacific, Berkeley, Calif BD 58. **d** 58 **p** 59 St A. C of Denbigh 58-65; V of Llanasa 65-76; Buckley Dio St A from 76. *Vicarage, Church Road, Buckley, Clwyd.* (Buckley 542645)

PRICE, Eric. Bps' Coll Cheshunt 42. **d** 44 **p** 45 Lich. C of St Paul Wednesbury 44-47; St Andr W Bromwich 47-48; Asst Master and Chap Harborne Colleg Sch 48-56; V of Ashford Carbonell w Ashford Bowdler 56-61; C-in-c of Brimfield 60-61; V of St Mich Handsworth Dio Birm from 61; Gen Sec Angl Assoc from 77. *Vicarage, Soho Avenue, Handsworth, Birmingham, B18 5LB.* (021-554 3521)

PRICE, Ernest Cyril Courtney. b 11. Sarum Th Coll. **d** 49 **p** 50 S'wark. C of Ch of the H Spirit Clapham 49-51; Beddington 51-53; Eltham 53-56; R of Upper w Nether Swell 56-59; Kemerton 59-63; Chap Commun of H Family Holmhurst St Mary and L to Offic Dio Chich 65-66; R of Denbury 66-80. *10 Meadow Close, Ottery St Mary, Devon.*

PRICE, Frank Watkin. b 22. St D Coll Lamp BA 45. ALCM 37. St Mich Coll Llan 45. **d** 47 **p** 48 St D. C of Cwmamman 47-50; Llanelly 50-52; Chap RAF Spitalgate 52-53; Leeming 53-55; Kuala Lumpur 55-58; Tern Hill and Mkt Drayton 58-60; Halton 60-61; Far E 61-62; Locking 62-63; S Cerney 63-64; Gibraltar 64-66; Chap and Lect RAF Chaps Sch Andover 66-68; Asst Master, Hd of Lower Sch, Amman Valley Sch from 68. *Caritas, Church Lane, Llanedi, Pontardulais, W Swansea.* (P'lais 882125)

PRICE, Frederick Leslie. b 30. Oak Hill Th Coll 59. **d** 61 **p** 62 Cant. C of Ch Ch Dover 61-64; R of Plumbland w Gilcrux Dio Carl from 64. *Gilcrux Rectory, Carlisle, Cumb.* (Aspatria 20255)

PRICE, Canon George. b 04. Men in Disp 44. FRAI 36. Ripon Hall Ox 44. **d** 34 **p** 36 Argent. [f Lay Missr SAMS] Asst Chap Paraguayan Chaco Miss 34-37; C of St Chad York 37-38; Morden 38; R of Bulmer w Welburn and Castle Howard 38-43; Chap RAFVR 40-46; R of Chipping Warden w Edgcote 45-50; RD of Brackley i 48-50; Pet 68-74; V of St Mark Pet 50-74; Dioc Chap from 50; Can of Pet 63-74; Can (Emer) from 74; Perm to Offic Dio York from 77. *15 Malton Way, Clifton, York.* (York 54128)

PRICE, Henry. b 14. St D Coll Lamp BA 39. Ely Th Coll 49. TD 68. **d** 49 **p** 50 Ox. Chap K Alfred's Gr Sch Wantage 49-77; C of Ridgeway Dio Ox from 77. *Glebe House, Childrey, Wantage, Oxon.* (Childrey 678)

PRICE, Very Rev Hilary Martin Connop. b 12. Qu Coll Cam BA 33, MA 37. Ridley Hall, Cam 34. **d** 36 Bp Golding-Bird for Guildf **p** 37 Guildf. C of Hersham 36-40; Cathl Ch Portsm 40-41; H Trin Cam 41-46; Chap RAFVR 43-46; PC of St Gabr Bp Wearmouth 46-56; Proc Conv Dur and Hon Sec Dur Dioc Conf 54-56; R and RD of Newcastle L 56-67; Proc Conv Lich 64-67; Preb of Bobenhull in Lich Cathl 64-67; Provost and R of Chelmsf 67-77; Provost (Emer) from 77. *98 St James Street, Shaftesbury, Dorset.* (Shaftesbury 2118)

PRICE, Ivor John. b 25. Univ of Wales BA 51. Univ of Lon BD 56. STh (Lambeth) 62. Linc Th Coll 79. **d** 80 **p** 81 Bradf. C of Addingham Dio Bradf from 80. *8 St Christopher's Drive, Addingham, Nr Ilkley, W Yorks, LS29 0RJ.*

PRICE, John Allan. Keble Coll Ox BA 30, MA 35. Wycl Hall, Ox 38. **d** 39 Dorch for Ox for Syd **p** 40 Syd. C of St John Parramatta 40-42; Ho Master Jun Ho The K Sch Parramatta Dio Syd 42-55; Hd Master Prep Sch 55-66; Chap K Sch 67-72; L to Offic Dio Syd from 72. *Condaford, Glen Road, Castle Hill, NSW, Australia 2154.* (634-2212)

PRICE, John Anthony Webb. St Francis Coll Brisb ACT ThDip 74. **d** 75 **p** 76 Brisb. C of St Matt Grovely 75-77; P-in-c of St Paul E Brisb 77-81; C of St D Cathl Hobart Dio Tas from 81. *83 Princes Street, Sandy Bay, Tasmania 7005.*

PRICE, John Francis. b 32. Qu Coll Cam 3rd cl Mus Trip pt i 53, BA 54, 3rd cl Th Trip pt ii 55. Ridley Hall Cam 54. **d** 56 **p** 57 Leic. C of H Ap Leic 56-60; V of St Mark Forest Gate 60-71; St Geo Harold Hill Romford 72-79; R of St Mary Loughton Dio Chelmsf from 79. *St Mary's Rectory, Loughton, Essex.* (Loughton 3643)

PRICE, John Richard. b 34. Mert Coll Ox BA (2nd cl Mod Lang) 58, MA 62. Westcott Ho Cam 58. **d** 60 **p** 61 Man. C of St Aid Langley 60-63; Bramley 63-67; V of All H w St Simon Leeds 67-74; C-in-c of Wrangthorn 73-74; V of Claughton w Grange 74-78; Mottram-in-Longdendale w Woodhead Dio Ches from 78; RD of Mottram from 79. *Mottram Vicarage, Mottram-in-Longdendale, Hyde, Gtr Man.*

PRICE, John Richard James. St Columb's Hall Wang 47. **d** 51 **p** 52 Wang. C of Milawa 51-52; Shepparton 52; R of Bright 52-62; Broadford 62-66; Nathalia 66-79; Shepparton Dio Wang from 79. *Box 471, Shepparton, Vic, Australia 3630.*

PRICE, Canon John Wheatley. b 31. Em Coll Cam 3rd cl Nat Sc Trip pt i, 53, BA 54, 3rd cl Th Trip pt ii, 55, MA 58. Ridley Hall, Cam 54. **d** 56 **p** 57 York. C of St Andr w St Pet Drypool 56-59; CMS Miss 59-76; Exam Chap to Bp of Soroti 61-74; Dom Chap 61-65; V of Soroti 63-67; Dioc Regr and Sec Dio Soroti 66-71; Warden St Pet Commun Centre Soroti 69-74; Archd of Soroti 72-74; Maseno N 74-76; Exam Chap to Bp of Maseno N 74-76; Surr from 76; V of Clevedon Dio B & W from 76; Hon Can of Soroti from 78. *St Andrew's Vicarage, 10 Coleridge Road, Clevedon, Avon, BS21 7TB.* (Clevedon 872982)

PRICE, Lawrence Robert. b 43. St Jo Coll Dur 76. **d** 78 **p** 79 Lich. C of Harlescott 78-80; Cheddleton Dio Lich from 80. *42 Hollow Lane, Cheddleton, Leek, Staffs.* (Churnetside 360225)

PRICE, Martin Randall Connop. b 45. BSc (Lon) 71. Fitzw Coll Cam BA 75, MA 79. *f Solicitor.* Ridley Hall Cam 73. **d** 76 B & W **p** 77 Taunton for B & W. C of Keynsham 76-79; V of Wortley Dio Sheff from 79; Industr Chap and M Sheff Industr Miss from 79. *Wortley Vicarage, Sheffield, S30 4DR.* (Sheff 882238)

PRICE, Norman Havelock. b 28. St D Coll Lamp BA 52. St Mich Coll Llan 52. **d** 54 **p** 55 Mon. C of St Jo Evang Maindee Newport 54-58; V of Llantilio-Crossenny and R of Llanfihangel-Ystern-Llewern 58-64; V of St Thos-over-Monnow (w Wonastow from 65 and Michel Troy from 71) City and Dio Mon from 64. *St Thomas's Vicarage, Overmonnow, Gwent, NP5 3ES.* (Mon 2869)

PRICE, Peter Bryan. b 44. Oak Hill Coll 72. **d** 74 **p** 75 Portsm. C of Portsdown 74-78; Chap Scargill Ho Yorks 78-80; Perm to Offic Dio Bradf 79-80; P-in-c of Addiscombe Dio Cant 80-81; V from 81. *Vicarage, Havelock Road, Croydon, Surrey, CR0 6QQ.* (01-654 3459)

PRICE, Peter Charles. b 27. Angl Th Coll BC 58, Dipl Th 61. **d** 61 **p** 62 New Westmr. C of Burnaby 61-62; St Edw Richmond 62-65; St Jas Vanc 65-66; Latton 66-68; Bearsted 68-74; V in R Benef of Ebbw Vale 74-77; Llanfihangel Crucorney w Cwmyoy, Llanthony and Oldcastle Dio Mon from 77. *Llanfihangel Crucorney Vicarage, Abergavenny, NP7 8DH.* (Crucorney 349)

PRICE, Philip. b 24. Tyndale Hall Bris 50. **d** 55 **p** 56 Momb. Miss at W Pokot 53-65 and 69-71; V of The Mau 65-69; V of Trans Nzoia Nak 71-75; R of Gt Horkesley Dio Chelmsf from 75. *Great Horkesley Rectory, Colchester, Essex, CO6 4HA.* (Gt Horkesley 242)

PRICE, Ven Philip Lewis Connop. b 09. Qu Coll Cam BA 32, MA 38. Westcott Ho Cam 32. **d** 33 Birm **p** 34 Bp Baynes for Birm. C of St Steph Selly Hill 33-36; Paignton (in c of St Mich) 36-40; V of St Thos Ex 40-48; Ilfracombe 48-52; Surr 49-52; R of Kingston Ja 52-56; Montego Bay Dio Ja 56-62; Archd of Cornw 56-72; Montego Bay 72-76; Archd (Emer) from 76; Dioc Sec Dio Ja 66-68; R of St Jas Montego Bay 68-76; Hon C of Honiton & Gittisham, Combe Raleigh and Awliscombe Dio Ex from 80. *St Michael's Cottage, Gittisham, Honiton, Devon EX14 0AH.*

PRICE, Philip Roger. b 09. Qu Coll Birm. **d** 57 **p** 58 B & W. C of Portishead 57-60; PC of St Faith w St Laur Harborne 60-68; C of Wraxall w Failand 68-72; V of Mark (w Allerton from 77) 72-79. *10 Stanchester Way, Curry Rivel, Langport, Somt, TA10 0PS.*

PRICE, Canon Ralph Emerson. Univ of Tor BA 47, LTh 50, BD 51. **d** 49 **p** 50 Niag. C of St Geo Guelph 49-52; R of Acton w Rockwood 52-54; Fonthill w Port Robinson 54-70; St Barn St Catherine's 70-77; St D and St Patr Guelph Dio Niag from 77; Hon Can of Niag from 77. *46 Balmoral Drive, Guelph, Ont, N1E 3N6, Canada.* (519-824 2452)

PRICE, Raymond Francklin. b 30. Wycl Hall Ox 61. **d** 62 Stafford for Lich **p** 63 Shrewsbury for Lich. C of Bilston 62-67; Keighley 67-70; V of Mangotsfield 70-79; Industr Chap Birm from 79. *25 Silver Birch Road, Erdington, Birmingham, B24 0AR.*

PRICE, Richard Philip. b 38. Edin Th Coll 60. **d** 63 **p** 64 Edin. C of St Aid Miss Niddrie Mains Edin 63-65; Old St Paul Edin 65-68; R of St Marg Aber 68-77; P-in-c of St Ninian Edin 77-81; V of Carnforth Dio Blackb from 81. *Vicarage, North Road, Carnforth, Lancs, LA5 9LJ.* (Carnforth 732948)

PRICE, Robert David. b 44. Acadia Univ BA 68. K Coll NS 68. **d** 70 Bp Arnold for NS. R of Arichat 72-75; Summerside Dio NS from 75. *Box 101, Summerside, PEI, Canada.*

PRICE, Roderick Joseph. b 45. St Mich AA Coll Llan 71. **d** 75 **p** 76 Mon. C of Fleur-de-Lys Dio Mon from 75. *30 Twynyffald Road, Fleur-de-Lys, Blackwood, Gwent.* (933 225308)

PRICE, Roy Ernest. AKC 38. **d** 38 Taunton for B & W **p** 39 B & W. C of Ilminster w Whitelackington 38-40; CF (EC) 40-47; CF 47-59; V of S Stoke w Woodcote 59-79. *74a London Road, Whitchurch, Hants, RG28 7LY.* (025-682 2581)

PRICE, Samuel. b 01. Vic Coll Man 27. **d** 31 **p** 32 Sheff. C of Ecclesall-Bierlow 31-36; V of H Trin Wicker Sheff 36-42; St Jas Hatcham 42-45; Hazlemere 45-70; Surr from 51; C-in-c of Glympton 73; Perm to Offic Dio Ox from 73. *30 Lewis Road, Chipping Norton, Oxon, OX7 5SJ.* (Chipping N 3163)

PRICE, Victor John. b 35. Oak Hill Th Coll 62. **d** 65 Barking for Chelmsf **p** 66 Chelmsf. C of Rainham 65-70; V of St Martin Dover 70-78; C-in-c of Ch Ch Dover 73-75; V of Madeley Dio Heref from 78. *Vicarage, Madeley, Telford, Salop, TF7 5BN.* (Telford 585718)

PRICE, William Haydn. b 20. Sarum Wells Th Coll 77. **d** 80 **p** 81 Portsm (APM). C of Alverstoke Dio Portsm from 80. *6 Beech Grove, Alverstoke, Hants, PO12 2EJ.*

PRICE, William Joseph. St Aid Coll 45. **d** 46 **p** 47 Mon. C of Mynddyslwyn 46-68; Penhow w St Bride 48-52; V of Raglan w Llandenny 52-58; Chap HM Pris Leyhill 58-64; Cardiff 64-67; V of Cinderford 67-74; L to Offic Dio Mon from 75. *13 Berkley Road, Bassaleg, Gwent.*

PRICE, William Kenneth. b 22. Keble Coll Ox BA (3rd cl Th) 44, MA 48. St Mich Coll Llan 44. **d** 46 **p** 47 St D. C of Llanwnda w Manorowen 46-48; St D Carmarthen 48-53; Pontypridd 53-56; C-in-c of Crynant Conv Distr 56-60; V 60-65; St Fagan Aberdare 65-71; Ilston w Pennard 71-79; Morriston Dio Swan B from 79; Warden of Readers from 77. *Vicarage, Morriston, Swansea, W Glam, SA6 6DR.* (Swansea 71329)

PRICE, William Trevor. b 17. Univ of Wales BA 43. St Mich Coll Llan 44. **d** 45 **p** 46 Llan. C of Port Talbot 45-50; Cymmer w Porth 50-56; C-in-c of Graig Pontypridd 56-68; V 68-72; St Fagan Aberdare Dio Llan from 72. *St Fagan's Vicarage, Aberdare, Mid Glam.* (Aberdare 2539)

PRICHARD, Edward Cowles. b 1896. Or Coll Ox Liddon Stud 21, BA (1st cl Th) 21, MA 22. Wells Th Coll 22. **d** 22 **p** 23 Bris. C of Corsham 22-24; St Mary de Lode w H Trin Glouc and Dom Chap to Bp of Glouc 24-26; PC of St Steph (St Luke L) Glouc 26-35; R of St Mich w St Jo Bapt Glouc 35-52; St Mary de Crypt w St Jo Bapt Glouc 52-62; Surr from 35; Exam Chap to Bp of Glouc 30-60; Glouc Dioc Chap 46-62; Perm to Offic Dio Lich from 62. *8 Mayfield Park, Mayfield Drive, Shrewsbury, Salop.* (Shrewsbury 62939)

PRICHARD, Lewis David. b 16. St Mich Coll Llan. **d** 65 **p** 66 Mon. C of Fleur-de-Lys 65-68; R of Llanhilleth Dio Mon from 68; RD of Blaenau Gwent from 74; Surr from 76. *Llanhilleth Rectory, Abertillery, NP3 2DA.* (Abertillery 41236)

PRICHARD, Canon Owen Pierce. Univ of Tor BA 38. Wycl Coll Tor LTh 41. **d** 41 **p** 42 Montr. C of St Jas Ap Montr 41-43; I of Papineauville 43-48; R of Ch of Advent Tor 48-54; Ch of Redeemer City and Dio Tor from 54; Can of Tor from 64. *3 Conrad Avenue, Toronto, Ont., Canada.* (416-922 4948)

PRICHARD, Canon Thomas John. b 16. Univ Coll of N Wales BA (2nd cl Welsh) 38, MA 72. Chich Th Coll 38. **d** 39 **p** 40 Ban. C of Blaenau Festiniog 39-41; Machynlleth 41-42; Llanfabon 42-44; Ystradyfodwg 44-50; V of Dinas w Penygraig 50-69; RD of Rhondda from 64; Can of Thos Jones in Llan Cathl from 66; Surr from 68; R of Neath w Llantwit Dio Llan from 69; Exam Chap to Bp of Llan from 71; Warden of Readers from 71. *Rectory, Neath, W Glam.* (Neath 4612)

PRIDDIS, Anthony Martin. b 48. CCC Cam BA (Biochem) 69, MA 73. New Coll Ox BA (by incorp 70), Dipl Th 71, MA 75. Cudd Coll 69. **d** 72 **p** 73 Cant. C of New Addington 72-75; Coll Chap Ch Ch Ox 75-80; L to Offic Dio Ox 76-80; Select Pr Univ of Ox 78; Team V of High Wycombe Dio Ox from 80. *St John's Vicarage, 136 Desborough Avenue, High Wycombe, HP11 2SU.* (High Wycombe 29586)

PRIDEAUX, Brian Kenneth. b 43. Sir Geo Williams Univ BA 65. McGill Univ BD 68, MA 73. Montr Dioc Th Coll LTh 68. **d** 68 **p** 69 Montr. I of Mascouche 69-72; R of Huntingdon w Ormstown 72-76; Otterburn Pk Dio Montr from 76. *221 Prince Edward Avenue, Otterburn Heights, PQ, Canada.* (514-467 7110)

PRIDEAUX, Humphrey Grevile. b 36. CCC Ox BA (2nd cl Th) 60, MA 63. Linc Th Coll 59. **d** 61 Pet **p** 62 Portsm. C of St Matt Northn 61-62; St Jas Gt Milton Hants 62-65; Asst Master Qu Mary's Gr Sch Walsall 66-69; Lect St Martin's Coll Lanc and L to Offic Dio Blackb 69-80; Lect Prices Coll Fareham from 80. *30 East Street, Fareham, Hants, PA16 0BY.*

PRIDHAM, Peter Arthur George Drake. b 16. Ely Th Coll 62. **d** 64 **p** 65 Newc T. C of St Aid Newc T 64-67; Berwick-on-Tweed 67-71; V of Sleekburn 71-77; P-in-c of Cambois 73-77; Otterburn w Elsdon and Horsley w Byrness 76-80; Team V of Bellingham-Otterburn Dio Newc T from 80. *Otterburn Vicarage, Newcastle upon Tyne, NE19 1NP.* (Otterburn 20212)

PRIDMORE, John Stuart. b 36. Univ of Nottm BA (1st cl Th) 62, MA 67. Ridley Hall Cam 62. **d** 65 **p** 66 Truro. C of Camborne 65-67; Tutor Ridley Hall Cam 67-68; Chap 68-71; Asst Chap K Edw Sch Witley Surrey 71-75; Chap from 75. *King Edward's School, Witley, Godalming, Surrey.* (Wormley 3336)

PRIEBE, Charles Martin. b 18. Houghton Coll NY BA 48. Kenyon Coll Ohio MDiv 50. **d** and **p** 50 Roch (USA). In Amer Ch 50-76; R of Ch Ch Maracaibo Dio Venez from 77. *Apt 10160, Maracaibo, Venezuela.*

PRIEST, Alexander Gary. b 41. St Jo Coll Morpeth 70. **d** 70 **p** 72 River. C of Leeton 70-74; P-in-c of Balranald 74-79; R of Broken Hill 79-81; Broken Hill S from 81. *214 Morish Street, Broken Hill, NSW, Australia 2880.* (4402)

PRIEST, David. b 44. Chich Th Coll 69. **d** 73 Willesden for Lon **p** 74 Lon. C of St Paul S Harrow 73-76; St Steph Glouc Rd Kens Dio Lon from 76. *66 Cornwall Gardens, SW7 4BD.* (01-937 0318)

PRIEST, Douglas Hamilton. b 04. Chich Th Coll 31. **d** 33 **p** 35 Win. C of St Mark Woolston 33-38; St Jas (in c of St Anne) Colchester 38-40; CF (EC) 40-46; V of St Bart Charlton-by-Dover 46-53; Ch Ch w St Jo and St Luke I of Dogs Poplar 53-57; Dom Chap to Abp of Capetn 57-58; Hon Chap 58-63; R of St Mark Capetn 58-65; V of St Alb Mart Holborn w St Pet Saffron Hill 65-79. *182 Eastern Road, Brighton, BN2 5BA.* (0273-605856)

PRIESTLEY, Alan Charles. b 41. BD (Lon) 69. William Temple Coll Rugby 64. **d** 65 **p** 66 Birm. C of St Aug Edgbaston 65-68; C (Team V from 72) of St Andr Chelmsley Wood 68-75; V of Hazelwell Dio Birm from 76. *316 Vicarage Road, Birmingham, B14 7NH.* (021-444 4469)

PRIESTLEY, John Christopher. b 39. Trin Coll Ox BA (3rd cl Th) 60. Wells Th Coll 61. **d** 68 Blackb **p** 69 Burnley for Blackb. C of All SS Habergham Burnley 68-70; Padiham w Higham 70-75; V of Ch Ch Colne Dio Blackb from 75. *Vicarage, Keighley Road, Colne, Lancs, BB8 7HF.* (Colne 863511)

PRIESTMAN, John Christopher. b 22. K Coll Lon BSc (2nd cl Geog) 51. Linc Th Coll 57. **d** 58 Maidstone for Cant **p** 59 Cant. C of Croydon 58-62; Folkestone 62-64; V of Loose 64-72; Ch Ch S Ashford 72-80; Team V in Beaminster Area 80-82; RD of Beaminster 81-82; R of Marnhull Dio Sarum from 82. *Rectory, New Street, Marnhull, Sturminster Newton, Dorset, DT10 1PZ.* (Marnhull 820247)

PRIESTNALL, Reginald Hayward. b 22. Jes Coll Cam 2nd cl Engl Trip pt i 43, BA (2nd cl Th Trip pt i) 44, MA 47. Ridley Hall Cam 44. **d** 45 **p** 46 S'wark. C of Im Streatham Common 45-48; Barking 48-51; R of Bonsall 51-53; C-in-c of St Francis Mackworth 53-54; PC 54-67; Chap Kingsway Hosp Derby 61-67; R of Rockingham w Caldecote 67-71; V of St Mich AA Northn 71-77; M Gen Syn from 75; V of Ketton Dio Pet from 77. *St Mary's Vicarage, Edmonds Drive, Ketton, Stamford, Lincs.* (Stamford 720228)

PRIESTNER, Hugh. b 45. Univ of Nottm BTh 75. Linc Th Coll 71. **d** 75 **p** 76 Newc T. C of Seaton Hirst 75-78; St Bart

Long Benton Dio Newc T from 78. *St Andrew's House, Whitfield Road, Forest Hall, Newcastle upon Tyne, NE12 0LJ* (Newcastle upon Tyne 665202)

PRIESTNER, James Arthur. b 14. Univ of Leeds, BA 39. Coll of Resurr Mirfield, 39. **d** 41 **p** 42 Leic. C of Wigston Magna 41-44; CF (EC) 44-47; Hon CF 47. C of Amersham 47-51; V of L Lever 51-60; St Aid Newc T 60-70; Longhoughton w Howick 70-79. *54 Cauldwell Avenue, West Monkseaton, Whitley Bay, Tyne & Wear, NE25 9RW.*

PRIME, Geoffrey Daniel. b 12. Lich Th Coll 32. **d** 35 **p** 36 Lich. C of Uttoxeter w Bramshall 35-42; C-in-c of Newborough w Needwood 42-43; V of Pattingham 43-55; PC of Longstone 55-62; Publ Pr Dio Derby from 62; Cler Org Sec CECS Dios Derby; Linc; Sheff; and Southw 62-65. *Dove Cottage, Hartington, Buxton, Derbys.* (Hartington 220)

PRIMMER, Dalba John. **d** and **p** 65 C & Goulb. C of Queanbeyan 65-67; Junee 67-68; P-in-c of Lyons w Chitley Provisional Distr 68-71; R of Holbrook 71-75; E Pilbara 75-78; P-in-c of Queanbeyan 78-79; R of Bega Dio C & Goulb from 79. *Box 50, Bega, NSW, Australia 2550.*

PRIMROSE, Thomas. St Jo Coll Morpeth. ACT ThL 44. **d** 40 **p** 42 River. C of Griffith 40-44 and 48-51; Chap AIF 44-48; R of Ganmain 51-64; Can Res and R of St Paul's Pro-Cathl Hay 64-74; R of Ariah Pk Dio River from 74. *Rectory, Pitt Street, Ariah Park, NSW, Australia 2684.* (Ariah Park 37)

PRINCE, David Albert Edward. **d** 81 Bel (NSM). C of St Mary City and Bel from 81. *2 Eyre Street, Belize City, Belize.*

PRINCE, Dennis Alan Ford. AKC 48. **d** 48 **p** 49 Chelmsf. C of Prittlewell 48-50; L to Offic at St Steph Conv Distr Prittlewell 50-54; V of Golcar 54-60; R of Slinfold 60-73; Sedlescombe w Whatlington Dio Chich from 73. *Sedlescombe Rectory, Battle, Sussex.* (Sedlescombe 233)

PRINCE, Garnet Donald Douglas. **d** 55 **p** 56 C & Goulb. C of Albury 55-58; St Geo Reservoir 58-60; V of Epping 60-62; R of Tongala 62-69; Echuca 69-79; Can of All SS Cathl Bend 77; Prov Sec ABM S Austr from 79. *6 Sydney Street, Ridgehaven, S Australia 5097.* (267 1411)

PRINCE, Glenbert Ballintine. United Th Coll of W Indies 65. **d** 67 **p** 68 Ja. C of Halfway Tree 67-72; R of Montpelier 72-76. *Rectory, Port Antonio, Jamaica, W Indies.*

PRINCE, Hugh. b 12. St Cath S Ox BA 34, MA 38. Wycl Hall Ox 34. **d** 36 **p** 37 Carl. C of St Mark Barrow-F 36-40; Actg C of H Trin Millom 40-42; C 42-44; R of Asby w Ormside 44-47; C of All SS Bingley (in c of St Lawr Eldwick) 47-49; V of St Sav Harden Bingley 49-53; Windhill 53-58; R of Kirkby Thore w Temple Sowerby 58-67; V of Isel w Setmurthy 67-72; R of Bowness-on-Solway 72-76. *Hillside, Temple Sowerby, Penrith, Cumb, CA10 1SD.* (Kirkby Thore 629)

PRINCE, John Frederick Lewis. Bp's Univ Lennox BA 62, MA 74. Trin Coll Tor STB 65. **d** 65 **p** 66 Caled. C of Terrace 65-66; Prec of Cathl Ch of Redeemer Calg 67-68; I of Blackfoot Miss Calg 68-70; Willow Creek Pastoral Distr 72-73; R of Claresholm w Nanton 73-76; White Rock Dio New Westmr from 76. *15751 Thrift Avenue, White Rock, BC, Canada.*

PRING, Althon Kerrigan. b 34. K Coll Lon and Warm AKC 58. **d** 59 **p** 60 Lon. C of Limehouse 59-61; L Stanmore 61-64; Langley Marish (in c of St Francis) 64-68; P-in-c of Radnage 68-72; Missr of Gayhurst w Stoke Goldington 72-75; Ravenstone w Weston Underwood Dio Ox 72-75; R of Gayhurst w Ravenstone, Stoke Goldington & Weston Underwood Dio Ox from 75; RD of Newport 78-80. *Stoke Goldington Rectory, Newport Pagnell, Bucks, MK16 8LL.* (Stoke Goldington 221)

PRINGLE, Cecil Thomas. b 43. Trin Coll Dub BA 65, Div Test 66. **d** 66 **p** 67 Down. C of St Donard Belf 66-69; R of Cleenish 69-80; Mullaghdun 78-80; Rossory Dio Clogh from 80. *Rossory Rectory, Kinarla, Enniskillen, Co Fermanagh, N Ireland.* (Enniskillen 2874)

PRINGLE, Charles Derek. b 46. TCD BA 69, Div Test 71. **d** 70 **p** 71 Dub. C of Raheny 70-73; St Geo St Catharines 73-76; R of St Phil Grimsby Beach 76-81; St D Welland Dio Niag from 81. *369 Thorold Road West, Welland, Ont, Canada.* (416-788 0569)

PRINGLE, John. b 05. OBE (Mil) 50. St Geo Windsor 56. **d** 56 **p** 57 Sarum. C of Wareham 56-59; R of Steeple w Tyneham 59-65; R of Church Knowle 59-65; PC of Kimmeridge 59-65; V of Owslebury w Morestead 65-73. *2 Abbot's Quay, Wareham, Dorset, BH20 4LW.* (Wareham 2092)

PRINGLE, John Richard. b 55. AKC 76. Chich Th Coll 78. **d** 78 **p** 79 Pet. C of St Matt Northampton 78-81; Delaval (in c of St Mich AA New Hartley) Dio Newc T from 81. *St Michael's Parsonage, New Hartley, Whitley Bay, Northumb, NE25 0RP.* (Seaton Delaval 371150)

PRINGLE, Neville Richard. St Paul's Coll Grahmstn. **d** 64 **p** 67 Zulu. C of Empangeni 64-69; R of Piet Retief 69-71; C of Clanwilliam 71-73; R of All SS Lansdowne 73-76; Caledon Dio Capetn from 76. *Box 25, Caledon, CP, S Africa.* (Caledon 97)

PRINGLE, Victor. b 45. St Barn Coll Adel 72. **d** 73 **p** 75 Murray. d Dio Murray 73-74; C of Murray Bridge 75-76; O'Halloran Hill 76; Perm to Offic Dio Adel 77-78; R of Clarence Town Dio Newc from 78. *Rectory, Queen Street, Clarence Town, NSW, Australia 2321.* (96 4135)

PRINS, Stanley Vernon. b 30. TD 76. Univ of Dur BSc 54, MA 69. Ripon Hall Ox 56. **d** 58 **p** 59 Newc T. C of St Jas Benwell Newc T 58-61; Asst Chap K Coll Newc T 61-65; CF (TA) from 64; C-in-c of H Nativ Chap Ho Estate Whorlton Newc T 65-72; Team V of Whorlton Dio Newc T 73-76; V of Humshaugh Dio Newc T from 76. *Humshaugh Vicarage, Hexham, NE46 4AA.* (Humshaugh 304)

PRINT, Norman George. b 38. Cudd Coll 64. **d** 66 **p** 67 Ox. C of Banbury 66-69; Ch Ch Reading 69-75; P-in-c of Shiplake Dio Ox 75-77; V (w Dunsden) from 77. *Shiplake Vicarage, Henley-on-Thames, Oxon.* (Wargrave 2967)

PRIOR, Ven Christopher. b 12. CB 68. Keble Coll Ox BA (2nd cl Th) 37, MA 41. Cudd Coll 37. **d** 38 **p** 39 York. C of Hornsea 38-41; Chap RN 41-69; Chap of the Fleet and Archd for the RN 66-69; Hon Chap to HM the Queen 66-69; M Gen Syn 66-70 and 75-77; Archd of Portsm 69-77; Archd (Emer) from 77; Perm to Offic Dio Sarum from 75. *Ponies End, West Melbury, Shaftesbury, Dorset, SP7 0LY.* (Fontmell Magna 811239)

PRIOR, David Clement Lyndon. b 40. Late Scho of Trin Coll Ox 2nd cl Cl Mods 61, BA (3rd cl Lit Hum) 63, MA 66. Ridley Hall Cam 65. **d** 67 **p** 68 S'wark. C of Reigate 67-72; Wynberg Dio Capetn 72-75; R 76-79; Can of Capetn 76-79; C of St Aldate City and Dio Ox from 79. *23 Leckford Road, Oxford.* (Ox 512563)

PRIOR, David Henry. b 42. Chich Th Coll 67. **d** 70 Pontefract for Wakef **p** 71 Wakef. C of S Kirkby 70-73; Barnsley 73-76; V of Middlestown w Netherton Dio Wakef from 76. *19 Wood Mount, Overton, Wakefield, W Yorks, WF4 4SB.* (Horbury 276159)

PRIOR, Ian Graham. b 44. Univ of Lon BSc (Econ) 71. Oak Hill Coll 78. **d** 80 **p** 81 Roch. C of Ch Ch Luton Dio Roch from 80. *11 Fallowfield, Downsview, Chatham, Kent, ME5 0DU.*

PRIOR, Ian Roger Lyndon. b 46. St Jo Coll Dur BA 68. Lon Coll Div 68. **d** 70 **p** 71 Cant. C of Em S Croydon 70-73; Perm to Offic Dio S'wark from 73; Dep Dir Tear Fund from 79. *40 Cambridge Avenue, New Malden, Surrey, KT3 4LE.* (01-949 0912)

PRIOR, John Gilman Leathes. b 15. Qu Coll Cam BA 37, MA 41. Ridley Hall, Cam 37. **d** 39 **p** 40 St E. C of St Marg Ipswich 39-41; CF (EC) 41-46; V of H Trin Springfield 46-49; Ch Ch Guildf 49-63; St Paul w St Mary Camberley 63-74; Crondall (and Ewshot from 77) 74-80. *Address temp unknown.*

PRIOR, John Miskin. b 27. Univ of Lon BSc (2nd cl Econ) 48. Westcott Ho Cam. **d** 51 **p** 52 Bris. C of St Francis Ashton Gate 51-55; Sherston Magna w Easton Grey 55-57; C of Yatton Keynell, of Castle Combe and of Biddestone w Slaughterford 57-61; V of Bishopstone w Hinton Parva 61-66; Marshfield w Cold Ashton 66-82; C-in-c of Tormarton w W Littleton 68-82; RD of Bitton 73-79; R of Trull w Angersleigh Dio B & W from 82. *Rectory, Wild Oak Lane, Trull, Somt, TA3 7JT.* (Taunton 72832)

PRIOR, Kenneth Francis William. b 26. Univ of Dur BA and LTh 49. Oak Hill Th Coll 46. **d** 49 **p** 50 Lon. C of Ch Ch Barnet (Mymms) 49-52; H Trin Eastbourne 52-53; V of St Paul Onslow Square Lon 53-65; Bp Hannington Mem Ch w H Cross Hove 65-70; R of Sevenoaks Dio Roch from 70. *Rectory, Sevenoaks, Kent.* (Sevenoaks 53628)

PRIOR, Canon Kenneth George William. b 17. Univ of Bris BA 39. BC Coll Bris 35. **d** 40 **p** 41 Liv. C of St Clement Toxt Pk 40-43; St Cypr Edge Hill 43-45; St Mich Garston 45-48; V of St Jude Plymouth 48-55; PC (V from 69) of Longfleet Dio Sarum from 55; Chap Poole Gen Hosp 55-76; RD of Poole 75-80; Can and Preb of Sarum Cathl from 77. *Longfleet Vicarage, Poole, Dorset.* (Poole 3791)

PRIOR, Nigel John. b 56. Univ of Bris BA 78. Westcott Ho Cam 79. **d** 81 Man. C of All SS & Marts Langley Dio Man from 81. *241 Rowrah Crescent, Langley, Middleton, Manchester, M24 4WL.*

PRISTON, David Leslie. b 28. Oak Hill Th Coll 66. **d** 66 **p** 67 Heref. [f Lay Miss 54-62] C of St Pet w St Owen Heref 66-71; V of Gaddesby w S Croxton Dio Leic from 71; R of Beeby Dio Leic from 71. *South Croxton Rectory, Leicester, LE7 8RJ.* (Gaddesby 245)

PRITCHARD, Brian James Pallister. b 27. CCC Cam 2nd cl Hist Trip pt i 50, BA (2nd cl Th Trip pt ia) 51. MA 66. Westcott Ho Cam 51. **d** 53 **p** 54 Sheff. C of Attercliffe w Carbrook Sheff 53-58; V of New Bentley 58-60; Manor Group of Parishes 60-72; Chap to Park Hill Flats Sheff 60-67;

C-in-c of St Swith Manor Sheff 67-72; V of Welton St Mary Dio Linc from 72. *Vicarage, Welton, Lincoln, LN2 3JP.* (0673-60264)

PRITCHARD, Colin Ivor. b 44. Chich Th Coll 66. **d** 69 Bp Graham-Campbell for Pet **p** 70 Pet. C of St Mary Kettering 69-72; Chap Clayesmore Sch Blandford 72-74; Asst Chap Ellesmere Coll 74-77; C of Duston 77-79; V of St Andr Wellingborough Dio Pet from 79. *Vicarage, Berrymoor Road, Wellingborough, Northants.* (Wellingborough 222692)

PRITCHARD, Colin Wentworth. b 38. K Coll Lon and Warm. **d** 63 **p** 64 S'wark. C of St Marg Putney 63-67; St Matt Brixton 67-70; C of Milton (in c of St Patr Southsea) 70-74; V of St Mark Mitcham 74-81; R of Long Ditton Dio S'wark from 81. *Rectory, St Mary's Road, Long Ditton, Surrey, KT6 5HB.* (01-398 1583)

PRITCHARD, Desmond Albert. St Jo Coll Morpeth ACT ThL 63. **d** 63 **p** 64 C & Goulb. C of St Jo Bapt Canberra 63-65; Yass 65-66; R of Gunning 66-70; Asst Master Canberra Gr Sch 70-73; R of Atherton Dio N Queensld from 74. *Box 218, Atherton, Queensland, Australia 4883.* (070-911051)

PRITCHARD, Donald Oliver. b 22. Qu Coll Birm 73. **d** 75 Bp Parker for Cov **p** 76 Bp McKie for Cov. C of Dunchurch Dio Cov from 75. *110 Norton Leys, Rugby, Warwicks.*

PRITCHARD, Glenn Lawrence. Univ of Tor BA 59. Trin Coll Tor 59. **d** 61 **p** 62 Tor. C of Epiph Scarborough 61-64; Ch of Advent Montr 64-66; Chap McGill Univ 66-69; on leave 70-75; Hon C of St Jas Cathl Tor 76-77; R 77-81; St Martin-in-the-Fields City and Dio Tor from 81. *151 Glenlake Avenue, Toronto, M0P 1E8, Ont, Canada.*

PRITCHARD, Gregory Parsons. K Coll NS LTh 62. **d** 62 **p** 63 NS. R of La Have and of Blue Rocks Dio NS from 62. *Bridgewater, RR3, NS, Canada.* (543-4860)

PRITCHARD, John Lawrence. b 48. St Pet Coll Ox BA 70 (2nd cl Law), MA 73, Dipl Th 70, Ridley Hall Cam 70. **d** 72 **p** 73 Birm. C of St Martin Birm 72-76; Youth Chap and Asst Dir of Educn Dio B & W 76-79; P-in-c of Wilton Dio B & W from 80. *Wilton Vicarage, Taunton, Somt.* (Taunton 84253)

PRITCHARD, John Richard. b 21. St Mich Coll Llan 46. **d** 48 **p** 49 Ban. C of Amlwch 48-51; Llandudno 51-53; Ripler 53-57; V of Lepton 57-69. *13 Wood Green, Chester Road, Mold, Clwyd.*

PRITCHARD, Kenneth John. b 30. Univ of Liv BEng 51. N-W Ordin Course 72. **d** 74 **p** 75 Ches. C of Ches Team Parish 74-78; V of St Jo Evang Weston Runcorn Dio Ches from 78; Hon Chap Miss to Seamen Runcorn Area from 78. *Weston Vicarage, Runcorn, Chesh, WA7 4LY.* (Runcorn 73798)

PRITCHARD, Michael Owen. b 49. St Mich Coll Llan 71. **d** 73 Bp Vaughan for Ban **p** 74 Ban. C of Conwy w Gyffin 73-76; V in R Benef of Dolgellau w Llanfachraeth and Brithdir w Bryncoedifor (w Llanelltud from 77) 76-78; Children's Officer Dio Ban from 77; V of Betws-y-Coed w Capel Curig Dio Ban from 78; CF (TA) from 79. *Vicarage, Betws-y-Coed, Gwyn.* (Betws-y-Coed 313)

PRITCHARD, Michael Robert. b 42. Lich Th Coll 70. **d** 71 **p** 72 Leic. C of Em Loughborough 71-74; Team V of Wolverton 74-78; P-in-c of Harpsden Dio Ox from 78. *Harpsden Rectory, Harpsden Way, Henley-on-Thames, Oxon, RG9 1NL.* (Henley 3401)

PRITCHARD, Canon Neil Lawrence. b 15. St Jo Coll Dur BA (3rd cl Th) 39, MA 45. **d** 39 **p** 40 Man. C of Ch Ch Harpurhey 39-40; St Matt Stretford 40-44; R of St Clem Ordsall Salford 44-50; Prin CA Tr Coll Reading 50-52; Lon 52-53; L to Offic Dio Ox 50-52; Dio Lon 52-58; Dep Chief Sec CA 53-58; V of H Trin S Shore Blackpool 58-73; Surr from 58; Hon Chap to Bp of Blackb 61-66; Hon Can of Blackb 66-81; Can (Emer) from 81; RD of Blackpool 66-73; V of Salesbury 73-80; Dioc Dir of Ordin Blackb from 73; Dom Chap to Bp of Blackb from 78; L to Offic Dio Blackb fcrom 81. *46 Harrington Avenue, South Shore, Blackpool, FY4 1QE.* (0253-44794)

PRITCHARD, Peter Benson. b 30. Late Scho of St D Coll Lamp BA (1st cl Hist) 51. St Cath S Ox Dipl Th 57. LCP 68. Univ of Liv MEducn 74, PhD 81. Ripon Hall Ox 55. **d** 58 Warrington for Liv **p** 59 Liv. C of Wavertree 58-60; Sefton (in c of Thornton) 60-61; C-in-c of St Frideswyde Conv Distr Thornton 61-64; Chap Liv Coll 64-70; Lect C F Mott Coll of Educn Liv 70-74; Sen Lect City of Liv Coll of Higher Educn from 74; C of St Bridget Wavertree Dio Liv from 70. *7 The Vineries, Woolton, Liverpool, L25 6EU.* (051-428 5653)

PRITCHARD, Robert Edmond. b 08. Trin Coll Dub BA (Resp) 38, MA 44. **d** 41 Bp Hind for Connor **p** 42 Connor. C of St Andr Belf 41-43; Chap RAFVR 43-46; C-in-c of Annahilt 46-51; I of St Andr Belf 51-68; Chap Belf City Hosp 51-68; R of Dunfanaghy 68-77. *16 Cathedral Close, Armagh City, N Ireland.* (Armagh 524601)

PRITCHARD, Canon Stephen Edward. b 08. MC 42. TD 63. Univ Coll Dur BA 32, MA 35. **d** 33 **p** 34 Dur. C of Jarrow Grange 33-36; Jesmond 36-39; CF (TA) from 37; V of Dalton-le-Dale 39-47; St Paul Newc T 47-55; Chap Elswick Lodge Dioc Mor Welfare Home 47-52; V of H Trin War Mem Ch Jesmond Newc T 55-69; Slaley 69-76; Ed Newc T Dioc Cal 61-68; Hon Can of Newc T from 70; L to Offic Dio Newc T from 76. *19 Redburn Crescent, Acomb, Hexham, Northumb, NE46 4QZ.* (Hexham 4931)

PRITCHARD, Thomas. b 14. Ch Ch Ox 2nd cl Cl Mods 35, BA (3rd cl Lit Hum) 37, MA 40. Westcott Ho Cam 37. **d** 38 **p** 39 Cov. C of St Andr Rugby 38-45; SPG Miss and Civ Chap Dio Maur 45-49; V of All H Ipswich 49-61; Surr 51-61; Hon Can of St E 58-61; Commiss Maur 59-81; V of St D Ex 62-81. *3 Mill Cottages, Exton, Nr Exeter, Devon.*

PRITCHARD, Thomas William. b 33. Univ Coll of N Staffs BA (2nd cl Hist and Pol) 55. St Mich Coll Llan. **d** 57 **p** 58 St A. C of Holywell 57-61; Ruabon 61-63; R of Pontfadog 63-70; Llanferres w Nercwys and Erryrys 71-77; V of Ruabon w Penylan Dio St A from 77. *Vicarage, Ruabon, Wrexham, Powys.* (097-881 3853)

PRITCHARD, Canon Wallace Jack. St Jo Coll Newc. **d** 27 **p** 28 Armid. C of Moree 27-33; P-in-c of Boggabilla 33-34; C of Tamworth 34-35; P-in-c of Pilliga 35-38; Dioc Commiss Dio Armid 38-45; Hon Can of Armid 42-45 and 58-68; Can (Emer) from 68; V of Werris Creek 45-58; Guyra 58-68; L to Offic Dio Armid from 69. *18 Edinburgh Street, West Tamworth, NSW 2340, Australia.*

PRITT, Stephen. b 06. AKC (1st cl) Knowling Pri and Barry Pri 31. **d** 31 **p** 32 Blackb. C of St Mark Witton 31-34; St Annes-on-the-Sea 34-37; PC of Ennerdale 37-40; V of Amblecote 40-45; Surr 44-45; Wolverley 46-48; H Trin w St Luke Warrington 48-55; Thornham All SS w Titchwell 55-58; Cl Org Sec CECS Dios Cant Chich Roch and Win 58-60; R of Helhoughton w Raynham 60-80. *65 Manor Lane, Charfield, Wotton-under-Edge, Glos.* (Falfield 260145)

PRIVETT, Ven Arthur Leonard. Wycl Coll Tor STh 46. **d** 46 **p** 47 Alg. Miss at Garden River 46-53; R of St Mark Sktn 53-57; Whitehorse 57-70; Can of Yukon 63-65; Archd of the Klondike 65-70 and 73-79; Hon C of Ch Ch Cathl Whitehorse 70-73 and from 79; I of Alaska Highway 74-79. *21 Oak Street, Whitehorse, Yukon, Canada.* (403-633 2664)

PRIVETT, Peter John. b 48. Qu Coll Birm 75. **d** 78 **p** 79 Birm. C of St Agnes Moseley 78-81; V of Kingsbury w Hurley Dio Birm from 81. *Kingsbury Vicarage, Tamworth, Staffs, B78 2LR.* (Tamworth 873500)

PROBART, Raymond. b 21. Sarum Th Coll 49. **d** 51 **p** 52 Blackb. C of Padiham w Higham 51-54; St Pet Burnley 54-56; V of Heyhouses (or Sabden) 56-60; Ch Ch Douglas-in-Parbold Dio Blackb from 60. *Douglas Vicarage, Parbold, Wigan, Lancs.* (Parbold 2350)

PROBERT, Christopher John Dixon. b 54. Univ of Wales (Cardiff) Dipl Th 77. St Mich AA Coll Llan 74. **d** 78 Bp Reece for Llan **p** 79 Llan. C of St Fagan Aberdare 78-79; Cadoxton-Juxta-Barry 79-81; R of Llanfynydd Dio St A from 81. *Llanfynydd Rectory, Wrexham, Clwyd, LL11 5HH.* (Caergwrle 760489)

PROBETS, Canon Desmond. b 26. AKC 50. St Bonif Coll Warm 50. **d** 51 **p** 52 Lon. C of St Clem City Road Lon 51-52; Kenton 52-62; Sub Warden St Pet Th Coll Siota 62-64; Hd Master All H Sch Pawa Ugi 64-69; Hon Can of All SS Cathl Honiara from 67; Dean of St Barn Cathl Honiara 69-72; V of Timperley Dio Ches from 72; Commiss Prov Melan from 76; RD of Bowdon from 77. *12 Thorley Lane, Timperley, Chesh.* (061-980 4330)

PROCKTER, Anthony John. b 37. Chich Th Coll 59. **d** 62 **p** 63 Lich. C of Wolverhampton 62-65; Digswell 65-70; V of St Ippolyts 70-75; R of Narborough Dio Leic from 75. *46 Leicester Road, Narborough, Leicester, LE9 5DF.* (Leicester 863232)

PROCKTER, Canon Basil Sydney. Univ of Sask BA (w distinc) 30. Em Coll Sktn LTh 32, BD 40. **d** 30 Athab for Caled **p** 31 Yukon for Caled. Miss at Vanderhoof 30-36; C of St Geo Sheff 37-38; I of Williams Lake 38-40; Macklin 41-45; R of St Andr Cathl Prince Rupert 46-57; Exam Chap to Bp of Caled 45-52; Hon Can Caled 49-57; R of St Matt Regina 57-59; Swift Curent 70-71; Archd of Moose Jaw and Regina 60-68; Hon Can of Qu'App 68-72; Can (Emer) from 77; I of St Mich Regina 77-78. *2058 Francis Street, Regina, Sask, Canada.*

PROCTER, Andrew David. b 52. St Jo Coll Ox BA 74. Trin Coll Bris 74. **d** 77 **p** 78 Bradf. C of H Trin Barnoldswick 77-80; P-in-c of Kelbrook Dio Bradf from 80. *Kelbrook Vicarage, Nr Colney, Lancs, BB8 6TQ.* (Earby 2984)

PROCTER, Herbert Oliver Hayward. b 1892. St Mich Coll Llan 56. **d** 56 **p** 57 Swan B. C of Oystermouth 56-57; Ch Ch Swansea 57-59; V of Beguildy w Crugbyddor (w Heyope from 64) 59-66. *8 Grange Court, Boundary Road, Newbury, Berks, RG14 7PH.*

PROCTER, Kenneth Stuart. b 1895. Univ Coll Dur LTh 21, BA 22, Capel Cure Pri 23, MA 26. Lon Coll of Div 19. **d** 23 **p** 24 Win. C of Ch Ch Woking 23-26; Chap Bassein (and Oilfields to 27) 26-29; St Phil E Rang 29-31; C of H Trin

Upper Tooting 31-34; Chap and Vice-Prin Fairbridge Farm Sch Pinjarra 34-36; C of H Trin W Greenwich 37-39; Chap Gordon Boys' Home Woking and LPr Dio Guildf 39-43; Chap to William Baker Tech Sch Goldings and L Pr Dio St Alb 43-46; Sub-Warden Aberlour Orph and LPr Dio Mor 46-48; C of Putney 48-52; V of St Phil Battersea 52-61; R of Walgrave w Hannington and Wold 61-65; C-in-c of Scaldwell 61-62; Perm to Offic Dio Ex 65-78. *23 Golden Park Avenue, Barton, Torquay, Devon.* (Torquay 36180)

PROCTOR, Cyril George Charles. b 03. Late Scho and Exhib of Clare Coll Cam 1st cl Cl Trip pt i 23, BA and LLB 24, MA 29. Westcott Ho Cam 38. **d** 38 **p** 39 Derby. Asst Master Repton Sch 27-61; Sen Master 61-63; Chap from 39; Perm to Offic Dio Derby from 39; Hon Chap to Bp of Derby 56-59. *Little Croft, Repton, Derby.* (Burton-on-Trent 703356)

PROCTOR, Hugh Gordon. b 08. Keble Coll Ox BA (2nd cl Th) 30. Cudd Coll 31. **d** 32 **p** 33 Derby. C of St John Long Eaton 32-36; L to Offic Dio Dur 49-50; V of Forest and Frith w Harwood Dio Dur from 50. *Forest and Frith Vicarage, Barnard Castle, Co Durham, DL12 OXW.*

PROCTOR, Ven Jesse Heighton. b 08. Univ of Lon BA 29, MA 32. St Andr Coll Whittlesford, 34. **d** 35 **p** 36 Ely. C of Whittlesford 35-38; St Phil Leic 38-39; V of S Wigston w Glen Parva 39-46; Prec of Cov Cathl 46-58; Hon Can of Cov 47-54; Can Th 54-59; Exam Chap to Bp of Cov 48-67; Dir of Ordin Cands and Post-Ordin Stud 48-65; Chap Gulson Hosp 53-58; Archd of Warw 58-74; Archd (Emer) from 74; V of Sherbourne 58-69; Perm to Offic Dio Heref from 75. *Dilkusha, Bank Crescent, Ledbury, Herefs, HR8 1AA.*

PROCTOR, Kenneth Noel. b 33. St Aid Coll 61. **d** 63 Hulme for Man **p** 64 Man. C of St Paul Oldham 63-66; Davyhulme 66-69; V of Norden w Ashworth Dio Man from 69. *Norden Vicarage, Rochdale, Lancs.* (Rochdale 41001)

PROCTOR, Michael Thomas. b 41. Ch Ch Ox BA 65, MA 67. Westcott Ho Cam 63. **d** 65 **p** 66 Newc T. C of Monkseaton 65-69; in Ch of Pakistan 69-72; P-in-c of Battle Hill 72-76; Team V of Willington Team Parish 76-79; P-in-c of Roxwell Dio Chelmsf from 79; Ed Sec of Nat Soc for Promoting Relig Educn from 79. *Roxwell Vicarage, Chelmsford, Essex.* (Roxwell 644)

PROCTOR, Noel. b 30. St Aid Coll 62. **d** 64 **p** 65 Dur. C of Haughton-le-Skerne 64-67; R of Byers Green 67-71; Chap HM Pris Eastchurch 72-74; HM Pris Dartmoor 74-79; Man from 79. *HM Prison, Southall Street, Manchester, M60 9AH.* (061-834 8626)

PROCTOR, Canon Thomas David. Em Coll Sask LTh 17. **d** 19 **p** 20 Sask. I of Lashburn 19-22; Miss at Hazelton 22-28; Pouce Coupe 28-42; Sec of Caled Synod 27-32; RD and Supt of Peace River Distr 29-42; Hon Can of Caled 30-42; V of Windermere 42-50; R of Salmon Arm 50-53; Hon Can of Koot 46-54; Can (Emer) from 54; V of Campbell River 54-62; L to Offic Dio BC from 62. *Box 548, Campbell River, BC, Canada.*

PROCTOR, William Cecil Gibbon. b 03. Late Scho of TCD BA (2nd cl Mod Math and Exper Sc) and Brooke Pri 25, Abp King Pri and Bp Forster Pri 26, 1st cl Th Exhib Pri and BD 28, MA 59. **d** 27 **p** 28 Dub. C of All SS Grangegorman 27-30; Ch Ch Leeson Pk 30-36; Asst Lect to Abp King's Prof Trin Coll Dub 30-63; I of Harold's Cross 36-46 and 47-63; Actg Sec CMS Ceylon and Actg I of Ch Ch Galle Face Colom 46-47; Can and Preb of Dunlavin in St Patr Cathl Dub 62-63; Sec C of I Jews' S 65-71; Chap St John's and Glenindare Dub 74-81. *20 Crannagh Park, Dublin 14, Irish Republic.* (Dub 905821)

PROFIT, David Hollingworth. Univ of Man BA 38. Cudd Coll Ox 40. **d** 41 **p** 42 Birm. C of All SS King's Heath 41-44; St Mark Athlone 44-48; P-in-c of Silvertown Dio Capetn from 48; Can of Capetn 67-72. *St George's Rectory, Calendula Road, Silvertown, Athlone, CP, S Africa.* (67-6886)

PRONGER, Canon Clifford Douglas. b 10. AKC 31. **d** 33 **p** 34 Cant. C of H Trin Margate 33-36; Kew 36-39; PC of Belper 39-50; C-in-c of Milford 44-46; V of Kew 50-80; RD of Richmond and Barnes 59-74; Hon Can of S'wark 68-80; Can (Emer) from 80. *65A The Avenue, Kew, Richmond, Surrey.* (01-948 2900)

PRONGER, Canon Kenneth Daniel. St Pet Coll Ja. **d** 38 **p** 39 Bp Sara for Ja. C of Cathl Ch Spanish Town 38-39; Mandeville 39; R of St Ann's Bay 40-46; P-in-c of H Cross Knightswood Glas 46-51; R of Rio Bueno w Clarkstown 51-75; Can of Ja 71-75; Can (Emer) from 76. *Duncans PO, Clark's Town, Jamaica, W Indies.*

PROPHET, Canon John Roy Henderson. b 10. ALCD 34. Univ of Dur LTh 48, BA 49. **d** 34 **p** 35 Chelmsf. C of Leyton 34-37; Canvey I 37-38; C-in-c of St Andr Walthamstow 38-39; V 39-44; H Trin Jesmond 44-48; St Jas w St Basil Newc T 48-61; Surr 48-61 and 65-80; R of Blaby 61-73; Hon Can of Leic Cathl 70-80; Can (Emer) from 80; R of Ch Langton w Tur Langton and Thorpe Langton 73-80. *29 Glebe Way, Oakham, Leics.*

PROSSER, David George. b 33. St D Coll Lamp BA 55. St Mich Coll Llan 59. **d** 60 **p** 61 Llan. C of Caerphilly 60-64; St Jo Bapt Moordown Bournemouth 64-65; Chap RN 65-81; V of St Barn Morecambe Dio Blackb from 81. *St Barnabas Vicarage, Regent Road, Morecambe, LA3 1AG.* (Morecambe 411283)

PROSSER, James Arthur. St Jo Coll Morpeth ACT ThL 67. **d** 67 Rockptn for Brisb **p** 68 Rockptn. C of St Steph Coorparoo Brisb 67-68; St Luke Wandal 69; Longreach 69-70; R of Aramac 70-72; V of Springsure 72-73; Inglewood 73-77; C of St Jas Toowoomba Dio Bris from 77. *69a Anzac Avenue, Toowoomba, Queensland, Australia 4350.*

PROSSER, Canon Kendall Frederick Evans. b 01. Late Scho of St D Coll Lamp BA 21, BD 38. Jes Coll Ox BA (3rd cl Th) 24, MA 37. **d** 24 **p** 25 Swan B. C of All SS Kilvey 24-28; Tormohun 28-30; Clevedon 30-31; Offg Chap Nat Nautical Sch Portishead 31-34; V of Norton (w The Leigh and Evington from 53) 34-81; V of The Leigh 47-52; Hon Can of Glouc Cathl 49-81; Can (Emer) from 81; Exam Chap to Bp of Glouc 49-81; RD of Glouc N 52-73; Dir of Relig Educn Dio Glouc 55-58. *24 Libertus Road, Cheltenham, Glos.*

PROSSER, Malcolm George. St D Coll Lamp BA 44. St Mich Coll Llan 44. **d** 45 **p** 46 Llan. C of Llantwit Fadre 45-49; Roath 49-58; V of Trealaw 58-66; High Littleton Dio B & W from 66. *High Littleton Vicarage, Bristol.* (Timsbury 70411)

PROSSER, Nicholas Wallace. Univ of Dur BA 49, LTh 47. Univ of Chicago MTh 55. Trin Coll Tor 47. **d** 40 **p** 41 Newfld. Miss at Lark Harbour 40-42; I of Tacks Beach 42-45; R of Belleoram 45-47; Harbour Breton 49-56; Aylesford 56-58; Glace Bay 58-63; St Jude St John 63-76. *284 Sherbrooke Street, St John, NB, Canada.*

PROSSER, Peter Edward. b 46. Univ of Montr BTh 75. **d** 75 **p** 76 Montr. C of St Matt Montr 75-77; on leave 77-78; P-in-c of Lakefield 78; I of Mascouche Dio Montr from 78. *1003 St Louis Street, Terrebonne, PQ, Canada,* (514-471 8858)

PROSSER, Rhys. b 51. Counc for Nat Acad Awards BA 74. Sarum Wells Th Coll 77. **d** 80 **p** 81 S'wark. C of Wimbledon Dio S'wark from 80. *9 Thornton Road, Wimbledon, SW19.*

PROSSER, (Keble) Richard Hugh. Trin Coll Cam BA 53, MA 57. Cudd Coll. **d** 57 **p** 58 Liv. C of Wigan 57-60; M CR from 62; L to Offic Dio Mashon 64-81; R of St Aug Penhalonga Dio Mutare from 81. *St Augustine's Mission, Penhalonga, Zimbabwe.*

PROSSER, William Stanley. b 04. St D Coll Lamp LDiv 35. **d** 35 **p** 36 Swan B. C of Ystalyfera 35-38; C-in-c of Llanddewi Ystradenny 38-41; R of Llandefalle 41-47; V of Falfielq and R of Rockhampton 47-58; V of Badgeworth w Shurdington 58-67; V of Upleadon w Pauntley 67-73; Perm to Offic Dios Glouc and Heref from 73. *23 Merrivale Lane, Ross-on-Wye, Heref.*

PROTHERO, Cecil Charles. b 15. BSc (2nd cl Econ) (Lon) 47. Univ of Bris MEd 74 **d** 68 **p** 69 Ex. C of St Mary Arches Ex 68-70; Chap St Luke's Coll Ex 70-78; Dep PV Ex Cathl from 79. *31 Cofton Hill, Cockwood, Starcross, Exeter, Devon.* (Starcross 890707)

PROTHERO, David John. b 43. St Pet Coll Ox BA 66, MA 70. St Steph Ho Ox 68. **d** 70 **p** 71 Warrington for Liv. C of Kirkby Liv 70-72; St Marychurch Torquay 72-74; V of Marldon Dio Ex from 74; Chap HM Pris Channings Wood from 78. *Marldon Vicarage, Paignton, Devon, TQ3 1NH.* (Paignton 57294)

PROTHERO, John Elwynne. b 20. Roch Th Coll 61. **d** 63 **p** 64 Truro. C of Redruth 63-68; V of Talland 68-73; R of Lansallos 68-73; V of Torpoint Dio Truro from 73; Surr from 73. *Vicarage, Torpoint, Cornw, PL11 2BW.* (Torpoint 812418)

PROTHERO, John Martin. b 32. Oak Hill Th Coll 64. **d** 66 **p** 67 Lich. C of St Martin Tipton 66-69; H Trin Wolverhampton 69-72; Distr Sec BFBS Nottm from 72; Hon C of Gedling 73; Perm to Offic Dios Derby from 73; Southw 73-74; Leic from 76; Linc from 78; Publ Pr Dio Southw from 74. *12 Blackhill Drive, Carlton, Nottingham, NG4 3FT.*

PROTHEROE, Rhys Illtyd. b 50. St D Coll Lamp Dipl Th 74. Bp Burgess Hall Lamp 70. **d** 74 **p** 75 St D. C of Pembrey w Llandyry 74-76; St D Carmarthen 76-78; V of Llanegwad (w Llanfynydd w Maesteilo from 79) Dio St D from 78. *Llanegwad Vicarage, Nantgaredig, Dyfed.* (Nantgaredig 327)

PROTHEROE, Robin Philip. b 33. St Chad's Coll Dur BA (2nd cl Engl) 54, Lightfoot Scho 54, Dipl Th 56, MA 60. Univ of Nottm MPhil 75. **d** 57 Swan B for Wales **p** 58 Llan. C of Roath 57-60; Asst Chap and Lect in Div Culham Coll 60-64; Lect in Div Nottm Coll of Educn from 64; Perm to Offic Dio Ox 61-64; Dio Southw 64-66; L to Offic from 66; C-in-c of Barton-in-Fabis 70-73; Thrumpton 70-73; L to Offic Dio

Southn from 74. *145 Perry Road, Sherwood, Nottingham.* (Nottm 605532)

PROTT, Neil Edmund. Moore Th Coll Syd ACT ThL 63. **d** 63 **p** 64 Syd. C of Caringbah 63-66; Albion Pk 67-68; C-in-c of St Matt Provisional Distr Oak Flats 68-72; R of Kurrajong Dio Syd from 72. *Grose Vale Road, Kurrajong, NSW, Australia 2578.* (045-73 1239)

PROUD, Andrew John. b 54. AKC and BD 79. Linc Th Coll 79. **d** 80 Chelmsf **p** 81 Colchester for Chelmsf. C of Stansted Mountfitchet Dio Chelmsf from 80. *43 Gilbey Crescent, Stanstead Mountfitchet, Essex, CM24 8DT.*

PROUD, Clyde Douglas. b 09. St Aid Coll 35. **d** 37 Pontefract for Wakef **p** 38 Wakef. C of St Andr Wakef 37-39; H Trin Wallington 39-43; R of Postwick 43-62; Chap St Andr Hosp Thorpe 43-62; Cane Hill Hosp Coulsdon 62-69; V of Withernwick 69-72; R of Rise 69-72; C of Bankfoot 72-79. *239 Queensgate, Bridlington, N Humb, YO16 5RG.*

PROUDMAN, Colin Leslie John. Univ of Lon BD (2nd cl) 60. MTh (Lon) 63. Wells Th Coll 60. **d** 61 **p** 62 St Alb. C of Radlett 61-64; Chap Qu Coll St John's 64-67; Assoc Sec Par and Dioc Services Angl Ch of Canada 67-73; Prin Em and St Chad Coll Sktn 73-78; L to Offic Dio Sktn 73-78; Exam Chap to Bp of Sktn 74-76; to Bp of Tor from 78; I of Mono 78-80; All S Lansing City and Dio Tor from 80. *15 Clairtrell Road, Willowdale, Ont, Canada M2N 5J7.*

PROUDMAN, John Henry Islaub. Univ of Syd BA 51. Moore Th Coll Syd. **d** 50 **p** 51 C & Goulb. C of St John Canberra 50-52; R of Delegate 52-54; on leave 54-55; Chap RAF 55-58; R of Kens Dio Perth 58-60. *55 Boomerang Street, Haberfield, NSW, Australia.*

PROUT, David William. b 47. St Steph Ho Ox 71. **d** 74 Lon **p** 75 Kens for Lon. C of All SS Hanworth 74-77; Chap Westmr City Sch 77-78; Hon C of St Pet Eaton Square Lon 77-78; Chap and Succr of Roch Cathl 78-81; Prec of St Alb Cathl from 81. *c/o 41 Holywell Hill, St Albans, AL1 1HE.*

PROUT, Hubert Douglas. b 18. St D Coll Lamp BA 38. **d** 41 Barking for Chelmsf **p** 42 Chelmsf. C of Leyton 41-44; CF (EC) 44-47; C of Wanstead 47-50; Perm to Offic in deanery of Gro-Neath 51-56; C of Wirksworth w Carsington and of Idridgehay 56-58; V of Kirk Hallam Dio Derby from 58. *Kirk Hallam Vicarage, Ilkeston, Derbys, DE7 4NF.* (Ilkeston 322402)

PROVINCE, William John. Trin Coll Tor. **d** 26 **p** 28 Tor. C of Ch of the Incarnation Tor 26-27; I of E Mono 27-30; Miss St Geo Medonte w St Luke Prince's Corners Dio Tor 30-40; RD of E Simcoe 38-40; Chap RCAF 40-46; I of Mulmur 46-48; Streetsville 48-63; Hon C of St Crispin Scarborough Tor 63-66; St Clem Riverdale City and Dio Tor from 69. *56 Wareside Road, Etobicoke, Ont, Canada.*

PROWSE, George David. **d** 66 **p** 67 Edmon. I of Manville w Vegreville 66-69; on leave 69-70; C of Prince George 70-73; CF (Canad) from 73. *10 Melfa Avenue, Petawana, Ont., Canada.*

PRUDOM, William Haigh. b 26. Lambeth STh 79. St D Coll Lamp 60. **d** 62 **p** 63 Roch. C of Aylesford 62-63; Margate 63-66; V of Long Preston 66-73; C of St Cuthb (in c of St Columba) Darlington 73-75; V of Ticehurst (and Flimwell from 79) 75-81; P-in-c of Flimwell 78-79; R of Spennithorne w Finghall and Hauxwell Dio Ripon from 81. *Spennithorne Rectory, Leyburn, N Yorks.* (Wensleydale 23010)

PRUEN, Edward Binney. b 56. AKC and BD 77. St Jo Coll Nottm 78. **d** 79 **p** 80 Worc. C of Kidderminster Dio Worc from 79. *90 Stoney Lane,* (off Stourbridge Road), *Kidderminster, Worcs.* (515195)

PRUEN, Hugh Barrington. b 18. AKC (2nd cl) 50. St Bonif Coll Warm 47. **d** 50 **p** 51 Lon. C of St Steph w St John Westmr 50-53; R of Didmarton w Oldbury-on-the-Hill and Sopworth 53-56; V of St Jo Bapt Ches 56-64; R of Skegness 64-71; Surr from 64; V of Heckington w Howell 71-79; R of Ashley w Weston-by-Welland and Sutton Bassett Dio Pet from 79. *Ashley Rectory, Market Harborough, Leics, LE16 8HF.* (Medbourne Green 827)

PRUEN, Hugh George. b 30. Worc Coll Ox BA 53, MA 62. Ely Th Coll 55. **d** 58 B & W **p** 59 Taunton for B & W. C of St Jo Bapt Bridgwater 58-63; St Thos Tor 63-64; P-in-c 64-65; Selsey 66-75; Belbroughton w Fairfield 76-82; Ed Worc Dioc News 76-81; V of S w N Bersted Dio Chich from 82. *121 Victoria Drive, Bognor Regis, W Sussex.*

PRYCE, Donald Keith. b 35. Univ of Man BSc (Tech). Linc Th Coll 69. **d** 71 Man **p** 72 Hulme for Man. C of St Jas Heywood Dio Man 71-74; C-in-c 74-75; V from 75. *46 Bury Old Road, Heywood, OL10 3JD.* (Heywood 69754)

PRYCE, James Taylor. Bp's Univ Lennox BA 61, LST 62. **d** 62 **p** 63 Tor. C of Ch of Ascen Tor 62-65; P-in-c of St Thos Brooklin Tor 65-66; R 66-70; Lorne Park 70-76; Ch Ch Scarborough City and Dio Tor from 76; Exam Chap to Bp of Tor from 77. *165 Markham Road, Scarborough, Ont., Canada.*

PRYCE, William Charles. ACT ThL 61. **d** and **p** 57 C & Goulb. C of Temora 57-59; St Paul Canberra 59-62; Warialda 62-65; Warden Ho of Peace Delungra 65-68; C of Young 68; P-in-c 68-69; R of Delegate 69-73; Moruya 73-76; N Albury 76-78; Junee Dio C & Goulb from 78. *Box 30, Junee, NSW, Australia 2593.* (Junee 110)

PRYCE, William Robert. b 28. **d** 79 St Alb **p** 80 Hertf for St Alb. C of H Trin Leverstock Green 79-81. *3 Birchitt Close, Bradway, Sheffield, S17 4QJ.*

PRYDE, Derek Weston. Ch Coll Hobart 62. **d** 63 **p** 64 Tas. C of St Steph Hobart 63-64; P-in-c of Geroka 65-66; C of St John's Pro-Cathl Port Moresby 66-67; St Andr Indooroopilly Brisb 68; V of H Spirit Kenmore Brisb 68-71; R 71-75; Coolangatta 75-77; V of Burleigh Heads Dio Brisb from 77. *18 West Street, Burleigh Heads, Queensland, Australia 4220.* (075-35 6066)

PRYKE, Edward John. b 20. K Coll Lon BD 51, AKC 51. St Cath S Ox BA (2nd cl Th) 53, MA 57, BLitt 63. Univ of Lon PhD 71. Wycl Hall Ox 51. **d** 53 **p** 54 Heref. C of Ross-on-Wye 53-56; Chap Brasted Place Westerham 56-60; Research Stud Univ of Ox 60-62; Asst Chap and Sen Lect Coll of St Mark and St John Chelsea 62-73; Plymouth from 74; R of E Portlemouth 74-76; C-in-c of S Pool w Chivelstone 74-75; P-in-c of Offord D'Arcy w Offord Cluny Dio Ely from 76; R from 78; P-in-c of Gt Paxton Dio Ely from 76; V from 78. *Offord D'Arcy Rectory, Huntingdon, Cambs.* (Huntingdon 810400)

PRYOR, Derek John. b 29. Univ of Lon Dipl Th 57, BD 63. Univ of Birm MEducn 74. Chich Th Coll 79. **d** 80 Repton for Derby **p** 81 Derby. Hon C of Youlgreave w Middleton Dio Derby from 80; Birchover w Stanton-in-Peak Dio Derby from 80; Asst Master Bp Grosseteste Coll Linc from 81. *Welsh House, Station Road, Darley Dale, Matlock, Derbys, DE4 2EQ.*

PRYOR, Henry Christopher. b 25. St Jo Coll Auckld 73. **d** 75 **p** 76 Auckld. C of Manurewa Dio Auckld from 75. *Kerrs Road, Wiri, S Auckland, NZ.*

PRYOR, John Wesley. BD (Lon) (2nd cl) 68. Fitzw Coll Cam BA (1st cl Th Trip pt iii) 70. Moore Th Coll Syd 65. **d** 70 **p** 72 Graft. C of Lismore 70-73; CMS Miss in India 73-76; C of Cronulla 76-77; R of Brighton-le-Sands 77-79; Miss in Fiji 79-81; Perm to Offic Dio Melb from 81. *Bible College, Albert Hill Road, Lilydale, Vic, Australia.*

PRYOR, William Lister Archibald. b 39. Trin Coll Cam BA 67, MA 69. St Steph Ho Ox 72. **d** 75 Ox (APM). C of Wolvercote w Summertown City and Dio Ox from 75. *Elm Tree Cottage, Summer Fields, Oxford.* (Oxford 55102)

PRYTHERCH, David. b 30. Down Coll Cam BA 54, MA 58. Coll of Resurr Mirfield, 54. **d** 56 **p** 57 Blackb. C of St Steph Blackpool 56-61; R of Matson 61-65; Chap and Asst Master St Elphin's Sch Darley Dale from 65; LPr Dio Derby from 65. *87 Chesterfield Road, Matlock.* (Matlock 55083)

PUDDEFOOT, John Charles. St Pet Coll Ox BA 74. New Coll Edin BD 78. Edin Th Coll 76. **d** 78 **p** 79 Dur. C of H Trin Darlington Dio Dur from 78. *79 Orchard Road, Darlington, Co Durham.*

PUDDY, Kenneth Wilfred. b 15. Late Exhib of Hatf Coll Dur BA 36, Dipl Th 38. St Aug Coll Cant 37. **d** and **p** 39 Taunton for B & W. C of Em Weston-s-Mare 39-41; Yeovil w Preston Plucknett 41-46; V of Meare 46-55; Kingsbury Episcopi w E Lambrook Dio B & W from 55; RD of Ilminster 59-71. *Kingsbury Episcopi Vicarage, Martock, Somt.* (Martock 3378)

PUGH, David. b 22. Univ of Wales (Abth) BA 48. St D Coll Lamp 48. **d** 50 St D **p** 51 Bp R W Jones for Llan for St D. C of Llanllwchaiarn 50-58; R of Bangor Teifi w Henllan (and Llanfair Orllwyn from 70) (and Llangynllo from 81) Dio St D from 58; RD of Emlyn from 73. *Rectory, Henllan, Llandyssul, Dyfed.* (Velindre 370463)

PUGH, Canon David Alun Richards. Lon Coll of Div. **d** 39 Lon for Col **p** 40 Willoch. C of Dowlais 39-40; M of Bush Bro Port Pirie 40-41; C of Cowell 41-44; I of Cummins 44-48; Cowell 48-56; P-in-c of Franklin Harbour Miss 56-57; Edwardstown Miss 57-59; R of Port Augusta 59-71; Hon Can of Willoch 68; Can 68-78; Can (Emer) from 78; Willoch Dioc Regr 71-78. *PO Box 96, Gladstone, Australia 5473.* (086-62 2055)

PUGH, David Bligh. b 16. Bps' Coll Cheshunt 50. **d** 53 **p** 54 B & W. C of H Trin Taunton 53-56; All SS Clevedon 56-59; V of Alderminster 59-75; C-in-c of Atherstone-on-Stour 59-65; Newbold-on-Stour w Halford 73-74; Halford 74-75; Longford 75-78; Hon C of St-Martin-by-Looe 78-79; Par Dio Truro from 79. *19 Trenovissick Road, St Blazey Gate, Par, PL24 2DX.* (Par 4683)

PUGH, Dilwyn. b 11. Late Exhib and Scho of St D Coll Lamp BA 35. **d** 35 **p** 37 Swan B. C of Ystradgynlais 35-41; Pontardawe 41-43; R of Aberedw w Llandeilo Graban 43-53; V of Hardwicke 53-70; R of Dorstone 53-70; V of Dixton w Wyesham 70-79. *15 The Willows, Raglan, Gwent, NP5 3EB.*

PUGH, Ernest William. AKC 41. **d** 41 **p** 42 Liv. C of H

Spirit Knotty Ash 41-44; St Mary W Derby 44-59; Asst Master Ormskirk Gr Sch 59-81; Commiss Nass from 62; Hon P-in-c of St Steph Mart Edgehill w St Cath Abercromby Square Dio Liv from 73. *54 Derwent Road, Liverpool 13.* (051-228 4022)

PUGH, Frank William. b 19. Roch Th Coll 62. **d** 64 **p** 65 Guildf. C of Oatlands 64-67; R of Hilton w Cheselbourne and Melcombe Horsey 67; St Geo Fordington 70-73; Team V of Dorchester 73-78; R of Stalbridge Dio Sarum from 78. *Rectory, Stalbridge, Dorset, DT10 2LR.* (Stalbridge 210)

PUGH, Canon George Humphrey. Qu Coll Ox BA 28, MA 32. Cudd Coll 28. **d** 29 **p** 30 Man. C of St Chrys Victoria Pk 29-32; SPG Miss Gatooma w Hartley 32-43; C of St John Bulawayo 43-47; R of Hillside Bulawayo 47-69; St Cuthb Gwelo 69-75; Hon Can of Matab 53-62 and from 75; Can 69-75; Archd of Bulawayo 62-69; Perm to Offic Dio Syd from 80. *1 Karimbla Road, Miranda East, NSW, Australia 2228.*

PUGH, Canon Harold John Lawrence David. Codr Coll Barb 53. **d** 53 Barb **p** 54 Nass. C-in-c of St Anne I and Dio Nass 53-55; R from 55; Hd Master St Anne's Sch Nass from 55; Dir of Educn Dio Nass from 63; Archd of the Bahamas 66-70; Can of Nass from 70. *PO Box N-1569, Nassau, Bahamas, W Indies.* (42037)

PUGH, Harry. b 48. BD 70. AKC 71. St Aug Coll Cant 71. **d** 72 Man **p** 73 Middleton for Man. C of Milnrow 73-75; C-in-c of Good Shepherd Rochdale 75-78; Team V of Rochdale 78-79; Asst Master Fairfield Girls' Secondary Sch Liv from 79; Perm to Offic Dio Liv from 79; Dio Man from 80. *12 Bedford Street, Heywood, Gtr Manchester.*

PUGH, Canon John. b 18. St D Coll Lamp BA 40. **d** 42 **p** 43 St A. C of Minera 42-46; Mold 46-51; V of Whitford 51-61; Bagillt 61-73; RD of Holywell 71-73; Wrexham from 77; V of Rossett Dio St A from 73; Hon Can of St A from 79. *Vicarage, Rossett, Wrexham, Clwyd.* (Rossett 570498)

PUGH, Raymond Ashton. b 26. Ch Coll Cam BA 53; MA 75. St Aug Coll Cant 53. **d** 54 **p** 55 Chich. C of Good Shepherd Preston Brighton 54-57; Brighton 57-60; V of St Pet (w St Paul from 63) St Leonards-on-Sea 60-81; Pevensey Dio Chich from 81. *Vicarage, Pevensey, Sussex.* (Eastbourne 762247)

PUGH, Ronald Keith. b 32. Late Scho of Jes Coll Ox Gladstone Mem Pri 53, BA (1st cl Mod Hist) 54, Liddon Stud 56, MA and DPhil 57. Ripon Hall Ox 56. **d** 59 **p** 60 Win. C of St Mich AA Bournemouth 59-61; Asst Master Ringwood Gr Sch 59-61; Asst Chap Bryanston Sch 61-66; Chap Cranleigh Sch 66-68; Lect in Th and Relig K Alfred Coll Win 68-74; Sen Lect in Hist 74-79; Prin Lect from 79; L to Offic Dio Win from 68; Perm to Offic Dio Portsm from 73. *6 Windermere Gardens, Alresford, Hants, SO24 9NL.* (Alresford 3252)

PUGH, Wilfrid Daniel. b 31. Lich Th Coll 63. **d** 64 **p** 66 Pet. C of St Andr Kettering 64-66; St Mich AA Northn 66-69; Asst Chap HM Pris Pentonville 69-70; Chap HM Borstal Dover 70-75; HM Pris Cardiff 75-78; V in R Benef of Ystradyfodwg 78-79; Team V of Cannock Dio Lich from 79. *St Chad's Vicarage, Cannock Road, Chadsmoor, Cannock, WS11 2TA.* (Cannock 79381)

PUGH, William Bryan. b 34. Univ of Man Certif Th 59. Ridley Hall Cam. **d** 61 **p** 62 Lon. C of St Luke Oseney Crescent w St Paul Camden Square St Pancras Lon 61-64; N Wembley 64-67; CF from 67. *c/o Williams & Glyn's Bank, Holt's Branch, Whitehall, SW1.*

✠ **PUGH, Right Rev William Edward Augustus.** b 09. Univ of Leeds BA (2nd cl Phil) 32, MA 34. LRAM 37. Coll of Resurr Mirfield 32. **d** 34 Derby **p** 35 Bp Crick for Derby. C of Staveley 34-37; Edwinstowe 37-38; R of Bestwood Pk 38-44; Surr from 44; V of Sutton-in-Ashfield 44-55; E Retford 55-59; Hon Can of Southw 54-59; Proc Conv Southw 55-59; RD of E Retford 58-59; C-in-c of Grove 55-59; R of Harrington 59-61; Hon Can of Carl from 59; Archd of W Cumb 59-70; V of Cockermouth 61-70; Cons Bp Suffr of Penrith 29 Sept 70 in York Minster by Abp of York; Bps of Blackb; Carl; Ches; Liv; Sheff; S & M; Wakef; Win; and others; res 79; Hon Asst Bp of Carl from 79. *25 Brigham Road, Cockermouth, Cumb, CA13 0AX.* (Cockermouth 3240)

PUGMIRE, Alan. b 37. Dipl Th (Lon) 63. Tyndale Hall Bris 61. **d** 64 **p** 65 Lon. C of St Steph w St Bart and St Matt Islington 64-66; St Mark Cowley Hill St Helens 66-71; R of St Bride Stretford Dio Man from 71. *Rectory, Clifton Street, Old Trafford, Manchester, M16 7PU.* (061-226 3047)

PUGSLEY, Ernest William Osmond. b 31. Univ of Natal BA 50. Univ of S Africa BA (Hist) 52. St Paul's Coll Grahmstn LTh 54. **d** 54 **p** 55 Natal. C of St Thos Durban Natal 54-56; L to Offic Dio Natal 69-72; R of St Jo Div Durban Dio Natal from 72. *220 Clark Road, Durban, Natal, S Africa.* (Durban 347076)

PULE, Robert. BEM 80. St Pet Coll Siota. **d** 54 **p** 64 Melan. P Dio Melan 54-75; Dio Ysabel 75-76; Dio Centr Melan from 76. *Ade, Gela, Solomon Islands.*

PULE, Simon Moshane. b 37. **d** 77 **p** 80 Bloemf (APM). C of St Mary Brandfort Dio Bloemf from 77. *886 Brandfort Location, Brandfort, OFS, S Africa.*

PULESTON, Derrick Carr. b 08. St Cath Coll Cam BA 33, MA 37. Wycl Hall Ox 34. **d** 34 **p** 35 Roch. C of St Jas Tunbridge Wells 34-36; Temple Ewell 36-38; Falmouth 38-39; E Grinstead 39-40; V of Quatford 40-45; Horspath 45-52; Warfield 52-55; Ringmer 56-68; High Hurstwood 68-71; Perm to Offic Dio B & W from 72. *White House, Chew Magna, Avon.*

PULESTON, Mervyn Pedley. b 35. K Coll Lon and Warm BD and AKC 60. **d** 61 **p** 62 Ox. C of Gt Marlow 61-65; Missr of Blackbird Leys Conv Distr 65-70; V of Kidlington Dio Ox 70-77; R from 77; R of Hampton Poyle Dio Ox from 70. *Kidlington Vicarage, Oxford.* (Kidlington 2230)

PULFORD, Shirley Walter John. b 31. Jes Coll Cam BA 55, MA 59. Cudd Coll. **d** 57 **p** 58 Blackb. C of St Steph Blackpool 57-60; P-in-c of Bancroft N Rhod 60-61; R 61-63; V of St Paul Newington 63-68; C of Seacroft 68-70; Asst Chap HM Pris Liv 70-71; Chap HM Pris Lincoln 71-73; Stud Counsellor at Linc Colls of Art and Tech 73-79; Counsellor Cam Univ Counselling Service from 79. *98 Malvern Road, Cherry Hinton, Cambridge, CB1 4LD.* (0223-243514)

PULFORD, Stephen Ian. b 25. Clifton Th Coll 53. **d** 56 **p** 57 Heref. C of St Jas Heref 56-58; R of Coberley w Cowley Dio Glouc from 58; P-in-c of Colesbourne Dio Glouc from 75. *Coberley Rectory, Cheltenham, Glos.* (Coberley 232)

PULKER, Edward Alfred. b 16. Univ of Tor BA 40. Trin Coll Tor BD 47. Qu Univ Ont BEducn 71. Univ of Ott MA 66, PhD 74. **d** and **p** 42 Niag. C of Ch Ch & St Steph Niag Falls w St Sav Queenston 42-44; I of Acton 44-47; C of St Jo Ott 47-50; R of N Gower & Dominion Supt of Ch Boys League 50-53; Probation Officer Prov of Ont 53-57; R of March 57-61; St Chris Ott 61-65; St Paul Ott 65-67; On leave 67-75; R of Gravenhurst 75-79. *Box 5, Bayshore Village, RR3, Brechin, Ont, Canada.*

PULKINGHAM, William Graham. b 26. Univ of W Ont BA 48. Episc Sem of th SW Texas BD 57 (MDiv from 76). **d** 56 **p** 57 Texas. In Amer Ch 56-74 and from 80; Provost of H Spirit Cumbrae and R of Millport 75-80. *4411 Dallas Avenue, Houston, Texas 77023, USA.*

PULLAN, Ben John. b 43. **d** 77 **p** 78 Bris (APM). C of St Alb Westbury Park Dio Bris from 77. *52 Druid Stoke Avenue, Stoke Bishop, Bristol, BS9 1DQ.*

PULLAN, Lionel Stephen. b 37. Keble Coll Ox BA (3rd cl Mod Hist) 58, MA 62. ARCO 58. **d** 60 **p** 61 Ches. C of S Tranmere 60-63; Higher Bebington 63-64; Perm to Offic Dio Ches 64-70; Dio St Alb from 70; Asst Master Park High Sch Birkenhead 64-66; Aigburth Vale High Sch Liv 66-68; Beech Hill High Sch 68-71; Shefford Sch 71-72; Hitchin Sch from 72; Hon C of H Sav Hitchin 72-73; Welwyn 73-78; Kimpton w Ayot St Lawr Dio St Alb from 79. *5 Balcombe Close, Luton, Beds, LU2 8HT.* (Luton 20679)

PULLAR, David Murray. St Jo Coll Morpeth. **d** 66 **p** 67 Newc. C of Singleton 66-68; P-in-c of Dampier w Mt Tom Price 69-70; R of Boulder 70-72; C of Gosford 72-75; P-in-c of Bulahdelah 75-76; Hon Chap to Bp of Bal 76-77; V of Kaniva 77-79; R of Hopetoun Dio Bal from 81. *Rectory, Hopetoun, Vic, Australia 3396.*

PULLAR, Douglas Arthur. Univ of NZ BSc 50. NZ Bd of Th Stud LTh (2nd cl) 66. Coll Ho Ch Ch 51. **d** 53 **p** 54 Wel. C of Karori 53-55; V of Hunterville 55-60; Eltham 60-64; Tinui 64-69; Silverstream 69-78; Hawera Dio Wel from 78. *202 Princes Street, Hawera, NZ.* (5467)

PULLEN, Canon George Alfred. **d** 43 Knaresborough for Ripon for Kimb K **p** 44 Kimb K. C of St Cypr Cathl Kimb 43-47; R of Vryburg 47-52; St Alb and St Barn Kimb 52-64; Archd of Mafeking 61-66; R of St Jo Evang Mafeking 64-66; Dean and R of St Cypr Cathl Kimberley 66-75; Hon Can of Kimb K Cathl from 75; R of Roodebloem 75-80; L to Offic Dio Capetn from 80. *44 Roodebloem Road, Woodstock, CP, S Africa.* (47-4894)

PULLEN, Laurence Archibald. Moore Th Coll 42. ACT ThL 42. **d** 43 **p** 44 Syd. C of Port Kembla 43; St Mary E Balmain 43-44; St Steph Port Kembla 44-45; CMS Miss India 45-72; R of St Cuthb S Carlton Dio Syd from 73. *34 Park Road, Carlton, NSW, Australia 2218.* (529-6141)

PULLEN, Roger Christopher. b 43. Univ of Lon BSc (3rd cl Physics) 65. Wells Th Coll 65. **d** 67 **p** 68 Portsm. C of S w N Hayling 67-69; Farlington 69-73; V of Farington 73-80; All SS Chorley Dio Blackb from 80. *All Saints' Vicarage, Moor Road, Chorley, Lancs, PR7 2LR.* (Chorley 63496)

PULLENAYEGUM, Ilex Frederick Malcolm. Edin Th Coll. [f Solicitor] **d** 62 **p** 63 S'wark for Lon for Col Bp. C of Richmond 62-65; V of St Luke Reigate Dio S'wark from 65. *Vicarage, Church Road, Reigate, RH2 8HY.* (Reigate 46302)

PULLIN, Andrew Eric. b 47. Linc Th Coll 71. **d** 73 **p** 74 Worc. C of Pershore w Pinvin Wick and Birlingham 73-77; Team V of Droitwich 77-80; V of Woburn Sands Dio St Alb from 80. *Vicarage, Church Road, Woburn Sands, Milton Keynes, Bucks, MK17 8TA.*

PULLIN, Arthur. b 18. St Jo Coll Dur LTh 39, BA 40, MA 45. ALCD 39. **d** 41 **p** 42 Ox. Asst Chap Kingham Hill Sch 41-43; C of St Jo Evang Penge 43-45; Chap St Lawr Coll Ramsgate 45-50; Ch Hosp Horsham 50-64; V of Midhurst Dio Chich from 64; R of Woolbeding Dio Chich from 64; RD of Midhurst from 81. *Vicarage, Midhurst, Sussex.* (Midhurst 3339)

PULLIN, Christopher. b 56. St Chad's Coll Dur BA 77. Ripon Coll Cudd 79. **d** 80 Kingston T for S'wark **p** 81 S'wark. C of All SS Tooting Dio S'wark from 80. *29 Avoca Road, London SW17.*

PULLIN, Norman Alfred. St Jo Coll Morpeth. ACT ThL 38. **d** 39 **p** 40 Newc. C of Ch Ch Cathl Newc 39-40; Mayfield 40-41; P-in-c of Clarence Town 41-45; R of Paterson 45-50; Raymond Terrace 50-52; Cessnock 52-56; Gosford 56-64; Mayfield 64-72; Can of Newc 72-74; Perm to Offic Dio Newc from 74. *139 Soldiers Point Road, Soldiers Point, NSW, Australia 2301.*

PULLIN, Stephen Robert. b 52. Univ of Newc BA, ThL 81. St Jo Coll Morpeth 77. **d** and **p** 81 Newc. C of Woy Woy Dio Newc from 81. *65 Dunalban Avenue, Woy Woy 2256, NSW, Australia.*

PULMAN, Edgar James. b 17. Selw Coll Cam BA 48, MA 53. ALCD 50. **d** 50 **p** 51 S'wark. C of Good Shepherd Lee 50-52; Stoke-sub-Hamdon 52-54; V 54-58; C of Norton-sub-Hamdon 52-54; R 54-58; Chap Summerlands Hosp Yeovil 54-58; Chap Bangkok 58-62; V of H Trin E Finchley 63-76. *Manor House, Norton-sub-Hamdon, Somt.* (Chiselborough 521)

PULMAN, John. b 34. E Midl Min Tr Course 78. **d** 81 Sherwood for Southw (NSM). C of SS Pet & Paul Mansfield Dio Southw from 81. *3 Wynndale Drive, Mansfield, Notts, NG18 3NY.*

PUMA, Yona. St Phil Coll Kongwa. **d** 60 Bp Wiggins for Centr Tang **p** 61 Centr Tang. P Dio Centr Tang. *Dabalo, Dodoma, Tanzania.*

PUMFREY, John Lawrence. b 06. Bps' Coll Cheshunt 48. **d** 49 **p** 50 Lich. C of W Bromwich 49-54; V of Birchfield 54-62; Hamstead 62-71. *18 Highfields, Callow End, Worcester, WR2 4TP.* (Worc 830609)

PUMPHREY, Norman John Albert. b 21. Nor Ordin Course 76. **d** 77 Nor (APM) **p** 78 Lynn for Nor. C of Aylsham Dio Nor from 77. *14 Buxton Road, Aylsham, NR11 6JD.* (Aylsham 3207)

PUMUNG NAW, David. Em Div Sch Mohnyin. **d** 63 Rang. d Dio Rang 63-70; Dio Mand from 70. *St Mark's Church, Nansiaung, Myitkyina District, Burma.*

PUN, James Shiu-Wah. Univ of Huachung BA 46. Stanford Univ MA 49. **d** 51 Bp Moyung Yin for Hong **p** 52 Hong. P Dio Hong 51-63; Dio Jess 63-65; L to Offic Dio Hong 65-68; in Amer Ch from 70. *1430 Mason Street, San Francisco, USA.*

PUNCHARD, Herbert Oliver. b 01. **d** 34 **p** 35 Sheff. C of Wadsley 34-37; C-in-c of Dunscroft Conv Distr 37-38; C of Whittlesford 38-40; Chap and Tutor St Andr Tr Ho for Ordinands 38-46; Warden 46-48; V of Pampisford 40-48; Babraham 47-48; Litlington w Abington Pigotts 48-68; RD of Shingay 52-67; Surr 53-68; V of Wendy w Shingay 55-68; Hon Can of Ely 62-68; R of Croydon 66-68; L to Offic Dio Lim from 68. *6 Kingston College, Mitchelstown, Co Cork, Irish Republic.* (025-24196)

PUNGWAYO, Augustine. **d** 42 **p** 43 Zulu. P Dio Zulu 42-59 and 61-68; Dio Swaz 68-74. *PO Box 1060, Mbabane, Swaziland.*

PUNSHON, George Wilson. b 30. Ripon Coll Ox 71. **d** 73 **p** 74 Leic. C of St Mary Knighton 73-76; V of Donisthorpe (w Stretton-en-le-Field from 78) Dio Leic from 76. *Donisthorpe Vicarage, Burton-on-Trent, Staffs, DE12 7PX.*

PUNSHON, Keith. b 48. Jes Coll Cam 3rd cl Econ Trip pt i 67, BA (2nd cl Econ Trip pt ii) 69, MA 73. Univ of Birm Dipl Th 73, MA 77. Qu Coll Birm 71. **d** 73 **p** 74 Birm. C of Yardley 73-75; Chap Eton Coll Windsor 75-78; V of Hill Dio Birm from 78. *61 Mere Green Road, Four Oaks, Sutton Coldfield, W Midl, B75 5BW.* (021-308 0074)

PUNTANG, Canon Arnold. Ho of Epiph Kuching, 52. **d** 55 **p** 56 Borneo. P Dio Borneo 55-63; Dio Jess 63-68; Dio Sabah from 68; Hon Can of Sabah from 70; Warden Angl Bible Tr Centre Sabah from 81. *PO Box 881, Tongud, Sabah, Malaysia.*

PUNTIS, Henry Alexander. b 20. Univ of Lon BSc 45. Coll of Resurr Mirfield 46. **d** 47 **p** 48 Guildf. C of St Mark S Farnborough 47-52; CF 52-55; C of St Nich Guildf 55-58; V of St Francis Honicknowle Devonport 58-65; Styvechale 65-75; C-in-c of Baginton 70-72; V of Chesterfield 75-81. *29 St George's Road, Babbacombe, Torquay, Devon.*

PURBRICK, Allan Louis. b 11. **d** 71 **p** 72 Melb. C of Surrey Hills Melb 71-72; P-in-c of All S Kallista 72-74; I 74-75; St Geo Monbulk 75-78; Perm to Offic Dio Melb from 78. *Hollyoak, Everest Crescent, Olinda, Vic, Australia 3788.*

PURCELL, Canon Borden Conrad. Bp's Univ Lennox BA 51. Trin Coll Tor LTh 54. **d** 53 **p** 54 Niag. C of Grace Ch Hamilton 53-54; R of Ch Ch St Catherine's 54-59; St Hilda Oakville 59-63; Thorold 63-68; St John City and Dio Ott from 69; Can of Ott from 73. *154 Somerset Street West, Ottawa 4, Ont, Canada.* (1-613-232-4500)

PURCELL, Stanley Thomas. b 08. AKC 41. **d** 41 **p** 42 Leic. C of Hugglescote 41-43; Hinckley 43-47; P-in-c of Eroro New Guinea 47-49; C of Dogura Cathl 49-50; P-in-c of Taupota New Guinea 50-52; C of S Wigston 52-53; V of Fridaythorpe w Fimber and Thixendale 53-57; Kexby w Wilberfoss 57-59; R of Denmark W Austr 59-62; Carl W Austr 62-66; V of Bushley 66-77; Chap for Mentally Handicapped Worc 68-77. *49 Arundel Road, Mitton, Tewkesbury, Glos.*

PURCELL, Canon William Ernest. b 09. Univ of Wales BA (2nd cl Engl) 34. Keble Coll Ox BA (2nd cl Engl) 36, MA 43. Qu Coll Birm 36. **d** 37 Bp Mounsey for Bradf **p** 38 Bradf. C of Ingrow w Hainworth 37-40; St Mary Virg Dover 40-43; V of St Pet Maidstone w Allington 43-47; Ed of Cant Dioc Journal and Press Sec 47-54; V of Sutton Valence w E Sutton 47-54; Chap HM Borstal Inst East Sutton Pk 49-54; Relig Broadcasting Org for Midl Region 54-66; Publ Pr Dio Birm 54-66; Can Th of Cov 59-66; Can Res of Worc 66-76; Can (Emer) from 76. *Eversley House, Stretton on Fosse, Moreton in Marsh, Glos.* (Shipston on Stour 61732)

PURCELL, Canon William Henry Samuel. b 12. Fitzw Ho Cam BA 36 3rd cl Th Trip pt i 37, MA 41. Westcott Ho Cam 36. **d** 37 **p** 38 Ripon. C of St Mich AA Headingley 37-40; Min Can and C of Ripon Cathl 40-43; V of St Matt Holbeck 43-47; PC of Chapel Allerton 47-63; Proc Conv Ripon 61-63; Hon Can of Ripon 62-63; Guildf from 68; V of Epsom 63-68; RD of Epsom 65-68; Archd of Dorking 68-82. *55 Windfield, Epsom Road, Leatherhead, Surrey.* (Leatherhead 75708)

PURCHAS, Canon Alban Alexander. St Jo Coll Auckld 49. LTh (NZ) 54. **d** 51 **p** 53 Ch Ch. C of Timaru 51-54; V of Fairlie 54-60; CF (NZ) from 54; V of Linwood-Aranui 60-66; Motueka 66-79; Hon Can of Nel 78-79; Chap Ch Coll Ch Ch from 79. *72 Rolleston Avenue, Christchurch 1, NZ.* (791-688)

PURCHAS, Canon Alban Charles Theodore. Univ of NZ BA 12, MA 14. LTh 16. **d** 14 **p** 15 Ch Ch. C of Geraldine 14-17; Chap at Ch Coll Ch Ch 17-19; C of Hokitika 19-21; V of Hokitika w Kumara 21-24; Akaroa 24-28; Lyttelton 28-32; Exam Chap to Bp of Ch Ch 28-53; V of Rangiora 32-39; Cashmere Hills 39-45; Archd of Rangiora and Westland 34-44; Ch Ch 44-49; Dioc Youth Org and Miss Dio Ch Ch 45-47; V of Fendalton 47-51; Methven 51-55; Hon Can Ch Ch Cathl 49-58; LPr Dio Ch Ch 55-58 and from 63; Chap St Geo Hosp Ch Ch 58-60; Perm to Offic Dio Ex 60-63. *48 Cholmondeley Avenue, Christchurch 2, NZ.* (35-055)

PURCHAS, Thomas. b 35. Qu Coll Birm 59. **d** 62 **p** 63 St Alb. C of Bp's Hatfield (in c of St Mich from 64) 62-71; R of Blunham (w Tempsford and L Barford from 78) 71-80; P-in-c of Tempsford and L Barford 71-78; R of Wheathampstead Dio St Alb from 80. *Wheathamstead Rectory, St Albans, Herts.* (Wheathampstead 3144)

PURCHASE, James Henry. Dalhousie Univ BA 63. **d** 64 **p** 65 NS. L to Offic Dio NS 64-65; I of New Germany 65-72; R of Tangier 72-74; Neil's Harbour 74-79; Trenton Dio NS from 79. *201 Temperance Street, New Glasgow, NS, Canada.* (752-4026)

PURCHASE, Roger Bentley. b 30. SS Coll Cam BA 51, MA 55. Westcott Ho Cam 53. **d** 55 **p** 56 St E. C of Newmarket 55-57; Portchester 57-60; V of Brading w Yaverland 60-63; Asst Master Cottesmore Sch Crawley 63-64; Thorpe Gr Sch Nor 64-66; Wymondham Coll 66-72; Hewett Sch Nor 73-76; Hon C of St Pet Mancroft Nor 67-77; Dep Hd Harlington Comprehensive Sch 76-79; Perm to Offic Dio Ox 76-79; Hd Master Nacton Heath Comprehensive High Sch Ipswich from 79. *c/o Nacton Heath Comprehensive High School, Ipswich, Suff.*

PURDIE, Anthony Watson. b 08. Univ of Glas MB, ChB 31, FRCP 68, FRCS 65. BD and AKC 76. **d** 76 Barking for Chelmsf **p** 77 Chelmsf. Hon C of Waltham Abbey 76-77; St Paul Goodmayes 77-80; Perm to Offic Dio Ex from 82. *Shearwater, Pope's Lane, Colyford, Devon, EX13 6QR.* (Colyton 53206)

PURDIE, Keith Maxwell. b 46. Monash Univ Vic BA 68. **d** 77 Bp Muston for Melb **p** 78 Melb. C of St Andr Brighton 77-80; St Mark Balnarring Dio Melb from 80. *2 Beach Street, Balnarring, Vic, Australia 3926.*

PURDY, Dean Kingsbury. Bp's Univ Lennox BA 64. Trin Coll Tor STB 67. **d** 67 **p** 68 Ott. C of Smith's Falls 67-71; I of Russell 71-72; Chap Lakefield Coll Sch Ont 72-75; C of St Steph Ott 75; I of Huntley 75-80; on leave. *Lakefield College School, Lakefield, Ont, Canada.*

PURDY, George William. b 13. Late Exhib and Scho of Hatf Coll Dur BA (2nd cl Cl Lit) and Thorpe Scho 35. BA

(2nd cl Engl) (Lon) 58. Ripon Hall Ox 36. **d** 36 **p** 37 Dur. C of St Jas Stockton-on-Tees 36-38; All SS Southampton 38-40; St Luke Kingstanding 40-42; PC of St Mark Londonderry 42-56; R of Morcott w S Luffenham 56-59; Asst Master D Challoner's Gr Sch Amersham 59-67; Lect in Div Newland Pk Coll Chalfont St Giles 67-76; Perm to Offic Dio Ox from 59. *7 London Road, Great Missenden, Bucks.* (Great Missenden 3589)

PURDY, John David. b 44.Univ of Leeds BA 65, Dipl Th 74. MPhil 76. Coll of the Resurr Mirfield 72. **d** 75 **p** 76 York. C of Marske-in-Cleveland 75-78; Marton-in-Cleveland 78-80; V of St Mark Newby, Scarborough Dio York from 80. *77 Green Lane, Newby, Scarborough, N Yorks.*

PURDY, Reginald. d and **p** 65 Athab. I of Wabasca 65-68; Lillooet 68-69; L to Offic BC from 71. *25 Newcastle Avenue, Nanaimo, BC, Canada.*

PURDY, Canon Reginald Robert. Univ of BC BA 59. Angl Th Coll Lth 61, STB 68. **d** 62 **p** 63 Caled. I of Ocean Falls Miss 62-63; C of St Andr Cathl Prince Rupert 63-66; I of Stewart 66-67; V of Ch K Burnaby 67-75; I of Trail Dio Koot from 75; Can of Koot from 79. *1347 Pine Avenue, Trail, BC, Canada.* (368-5581)

PURSER, Alan Gordon. b 51. Univ of Leic BSc 73. Wycl Hall Ox 74. **d** 77 **p** 78 Roch. C of Ch Ch Beckenham 77-81; Team V of Barking Dio Chelmsf from 81. *Christ Church Parsonage, Bastable Avenue, Barking, Essex.* (01-594 1976)

PURSER, Herbert Richard. b 05. ALCD 34. **d** 34 **p** 35 Blackb. C of St Mark Preston 34-37; St Phil Liv 37-40; St Marg Burnage 41; Org Sec CPAS for NW Distr and L to Offic Dio Man 41-44; V of Constable Lee 44-46; Parwich w Alsop-en-le-Dale 46-52; R of Scole w Billingford and Thorpe Parva 52-57; V of Llanyblodwell 57-62; R of Elford 62-65; Chap Crowhurst Home of Healing 65-67; C-in-c and Seq of Crowhurst 67-74; R 74-75. *16 St Peter's Crescent, Bexhill-on-Sea, Sussex, TN40 2EH.* (Bexhill 216833)

PURSER, John Arnold. Univ of Tor BA 48. Wycl Coll Tor. **d** 50 **p** 51 Tor. C of St Edm Tor 50-51; Peterborough Tor 51-53; I of Incarnation Ch Tor 53-56; Ch of Ap Tor 57-68; R of Lakefield 68-77; I of St Dunstan City and Dio Tor from 77. *1226 Lansdowne Avenue, Toronto 4, Ont, Canada.* (416-531 6783)

PURTELL, Michael Edward. St Jo Coll Morpeth. ACT ThL 59. **d** 59 **p** 60 Armid. C of Quirindi 59-61; Tamworth 61-62; V of Stratford 63-69; R of Leongatha 69-76; Dom Chap to Bp of Gippsld 73-81; Perm to Offic Dio Gippsld 76-80 and from 81. *Box 206, Traralgon, Vic, Australia 3644.*

PURVES, Noel. d 64 **p** 65 Perth. C of Narembeen 64-65; R 65-67; L to Offic Dio Perth 67-68; R of Cunderdin 68-71; Perm to Offic Dio Perth 71-76. *c/o 8th Avenue, Armadale, W Australia 6112.* (97 2164)

PURVIS, Colin. b 19. Kelham Th Coll 37. **d** 44 **p** 45 Dur. C of St Cuthb Hebburn 44-47; Sunderland 47-50; Darlington (in c of All SS Blackwell) 50-53; C-in-c of Conv Distr of St Mary Humbledon 53-58; St Mary Virg w St Pet Bp Wearmouth 58-62; V of Heworth 62-76; RD of Gateshead 69-76; R of Egglescliffe Dio Dur from 76. *Egglescliffe Rectory, Stockton-on-Tees, Cleve, TS16 9BT.* (Egglescliffe 780185)

PURVIS, Stephen. b 48. AKC 70. **d** 71 Dur **p** 72 Jarrow for Dur. C of Peterlee 71-75; Dioc Recruitment Officer Dur 75-79; V of All SS Stevenage Dio St Alb from 79. *418 Archer Road, Stevenage, Herts, SG1 5HW.* (Stevenage 3612)

PUSAN, Lord Bishop of. *See* Choi, Right Rev William Chul-Hi.

PUSEY, Ian John. b 39. Sarum Th Coll 69. **d** 71 Barking for Chelmsf **p** 72 Chelmsf. C of Waltham Abbey 71-75; Team V of Stantonbury 75-80; P-in-c of Bletchley Dio Ox from 80. *75 Church Green Road, Bletchley, Milton Keynes, MK3 6BY.* (Milton Keynes 73357)

PUSEY, Robert Guy. b 09. St Edm Hall Ox BA 36, MA 51. Linc Th Coll 36. **d** 38 **p** 39 Worc. C of Bromsgrove 38-43; R of Fallowfield 43-51; V of St Thos Stourbridge 51-59; St Pet Cowleigh Worc 59-73; Team V of Malvern Link w Cowleigh 73-75. *206 Wells Road, Malvern, Worcs, WR14 4HD.* (Malvern 3716)

PUTMAN, Stanley Wayne. b 53. Univ of Windsor Ont BA 76. Huron Coll Lon Ont MDiv 79. **d** 80 **p** 81 Alg. R of Trin St Alb Bala Dio Alg from 80. *PO Box 244, Bala, Ont, Canada, P0V 1A0.*

PUXLEY, Canon Herbert Lavallin. Yale Univ MA 31. BNC Ox MA 34. Trin Coll Tor LTh 48, Hon DD 55. Acadia Univ NS Hon DCL 62. Univ of Windsor NS Hon DD 63. St Mary's Univ NS Hon DLitt 65. Wycl Coll Tor Hon DD 66. **d** 47 **p** 48 Tor. I of Holland Landing 47-49; Gen Sec SCM of Canada and Hon C of Streetsville 49-54; Pres of KCNS 54-63; Can of NS 54-63; Hon Can from 63; Dir Canad Sch of Miss and Ecumenical Inst 63-73. *RR1, Claremont, Ont., Canada.* (649-2537)

✠ **PWAISHIHO, Right Rev Willie.** b 48. Bp Patteson Th Centre Kohimarama 71. **d** 74 **p** 75 Melan. P Dio Melan 74-75; Malaita 75-77; Dio Auckld 77-79; Dean of Honiara 80-81; Cons Ld Bp of Malaita in St Barn Cathl Fiu 28 June 81 by Abp of Melan; Bps of Ysabel, Vanuatu, Temotu and Graft. *Bishop's House, Auki, Malaita, Solomon Islands.*

PYATT, Noel Watson. b 34. K Coll Lon and Warm AKC 57. **d** 58 **p** 59 Ches. C of Prenton 58-61; Cheadle Hulme 61-63; C-in-c of Hattersley 63-66; V 66-70; St Paul City and Dio Ches from 70. *St Paul's Vicarage, Chester.* (Chester 25877)

✠ **PYATT, Right Rev William Allan.** Univ of NZ BA 38, MA (2nd cl Hist) 39. Westcott Ho Cam 45. **d** 46 **p** 47 Lich. C of Cannock 46-48; V of Brooklyn Wel 48-52; Hawera 52-58; St Pet Wel 58-62; Dean of Ch Ch 62-66; Cons Ld Bp of Ch Ch in Ch Ch Cathl 24 Aug 66 by Abp of NZ; Bps of Wel; Waik; Dun; Auckld; and Nel; and Bps Warren; McKenzie; and Monteith. *Bishopscourt, 100 Park Terrace, Christchurch 1, NZ.* (62-653)

PYAW BWA, James. d 56 Bp Ah Mya for Rang. d Dio Rang 56-70; Dio Pa-an from 70. *c/o St David's Church, Toungoo, Burma.*

PYBURN, Alan. b 29. G and C Coll Cam BA 51, MA 55. Westcott Ho Cam 53. **d** 55 Dur **p** 56 Jarrow for Dur. C of Barnard Castle 55-57; Chap G and C Coll Cam 57-60; V of St Mary Dallington Northn 60-72; St Giles Ox 72-79; R of Henley-on-Thames Dio Ox from 79; Remenham Dio Ox from 79. *15 Blandy Road, Henley-on-Thames, Oxon, RG9 1QB.* (Henley 77340)

PYBUS, Antony Frederick. b 54. Univ of Birm BA 77. St Jo Coll Dur 78. **d** 81 Ches. C of H Trin City and Dio Ches from 81. *114 Saughall Road, Blacon, Chester, CH1 5EZ.* (Ches 373955)

PYE, Allan Stephen. b 56. St D Coll Lamp BA (th) 78. Westcott Ho Cam 79. **d** 81 Blackb. C of Scotforth Dio Blackb from 81. *10 Lawnswood Avenue, Scotforth, Lancaster, LA1 4NZ.*

PYE, Joseph Terence Hardwidge. b 41. AIQS 65. Trin Coll Bris 70. **d** 73 **p** 74 Blackb. C of Ch Ch Blackb 73-77; Miss in Korea from 77. *PO Box 20, Masan, Republic of Korea.*

PYECROFT, Eric Stanley. b 26. Hatf Coll Dur BA 50. St Chad's Coll Dur Dipl Th 53. **d** 53 Bp Hollis from Cant **p** 54 Leic. C of St Mich AA Belgrave 53-54; St Paul Leic 54-57; R of Cole Orton 57-60; UMCA Area Sec Wales Glouc and Heref 60-62; E Counties 62-65; L to Offic Dio Ely 62-64; Chap St Gabr Sch Newbury 64-68; Perm to Offic Dio Glouc 68-72; P-in-c of Oakridge 72-79; V of Bisley w Oakridge Dio Glouc from 79. *Winsley Cottage, Oakridge Lynch, Stroud, Glos, GL6 7NZ.* (Frampton Mansell 260)

PYKE, Gordon Earl. d 58 **p** 59 NS. I of Hantsport 58-63; C of St Thos St John's 63-66; I of Glace Bay 66-74; N Syd Dio NS from 74. *28 King Street, North Sydney, NS, Canada.* (794-3392)

PYKE, William John. Univ of Tor BA 56. Trin Coll Tor. **d** 61 Hur **p** 62 Bp Townshend for Hur. I of Ayr Ont 61-67. *118 Yardley Avenue, Toronto 16, Ont, Canada.*

PYLE, John Alan. b 31. Qu Coll Birm **d** 69 **p** 70 Newc T. C of St Jas w St Basil Newc T 69-72; St Pet Monkseaton 72-74; Morpeth (in c of St Aidan) 74-78; R of Bothal Dio Newc T from 78. *Rectory, Longhirst Road, Pegswood, Morpeth, Northumb, NE61 6XF.* (Morpeth 56292)

PYM, David Pitfield. b 45. Univ of Nottm BA (2nd cl Th) 65. Ex Coll Ox DPhil 68. Ripon Hall Ox 66. **d** 68 **p** 69 Southw. C of Nottm 68-72; Chap RN 72-76; Worksop Coll 76-79; Chap RN from 79. *c/o Ministry of Defence, Lacon House, Theobald's Road, WC1X 8RY.*

PYM, Francis Victor. b 24. St Jo Coll Dur 75. **d** 76 **p** 77 Bradf. C of Keighley Bradf 76-79; Chap to Bethany Fellowship Commun Dio Chich from 79. *The Hyde, Handcross, Haywards Heath, W Sussex, RH17 6EZ.* (Handcross 400231)

PYM, Gordon Sydney. b 19. Worc Ordin Coll 59. **d** 61 **p** 62 Ex. C of Highweek 61-63; Em Plymouth 63-66; V of Kilnhurst 66-69; Owston 69-72; C-in-c of Moss 69-70; V of Hensall w Heck 72-75. *48 Castlegate, Tickhill, Doncaster, DN11 9QU.*

PYNE, Robert Leslie. b 51. Lanchester Poly Cov BA 72. Dipl Th (Leeds) 78. Coll of the Resurr 76. **d** 79 **p** 80 Bris. C of All SS w St Jo Evang Clifton 79-81; Dom Chap to Bp of Ox from 81. *c/o Diocesan Church House, North Hinksey, Oxford, OX2 0NB.*

PYNE-O'CALLAGHAN (formerly O'CALLAGHAN), Philip Homan. AKC 13. **d** 13 St Alb **p** 23 Lon. C of Much Hadham 13-14; Asst Master Orley Farm Harrow 14-16; Hill Brow Eastbourne 16-18; Kingmeads Seaford 18-20; Harborne Hall Worcs 20-22; C of St Jas Norlands Kens 22-24; Perm to Offic at Ch Ch S Hackney 24-25; C of St Bart Bethnal Green 25-29; H Trin Hoxton 29-31; H Trin Reading 31-33; Perm to Offic Dio Win 35-42; St Aug Southn 36-37; C of Binfield (in c of St Mark) 38-39; Perm to Offic Dio Pet 39-46; C-in-c of St John Clevedon 46; H Trin Bath 46-47; St

Pet Goldhanger 47-48; St Pet Gt Totham 48; St Mary Virg Broxted 48-49; C of Upminster 49-52. *Address temp unknown.*

PYNN, Robert Tilley. E Nazarene Coll Mass BA 63. Episc Th Sch Mass BD 66. **d** 66 **p** 67 Ott. C of St John Ott 66-70; Ch Ch Cathl Vanc 70-77; I of St Pet City and Dio Calg from 77. *919 75th Avenue SW, Calgary, Alta, Canada.* (255 1301)

✠ **PYTCHES, Right Rev George Edward David.** b 31. Univ of Bris BA 54. Tyndale Hall Bris 51. **d** 55 Roch for Ox **p** 56 Ox. C of St Ebbe Ox 55-58; Wallington Surrey 58-59; Asst Chap SAMS Cholchol 59-61; Chap Valparaiso 61-70; Cons Bp Suffr of Valparaiso 20 Dec 70 in St Paul's Ch Valparaiso by Bp in Chile; Bps Flagg and Bazley; VG of Chile 71-72; Apptd Bp in Chile, Bolivia and Peru 72; res 77; V of St Andr Chorleywood Dio St Alb from 77. *Vicarage, Quickley Lane, Chorleywood, Rickmansworth, Herts.* (Chorleywood 2391)

PYTCHES, Peter Norman Lambert. b 32. BD (Lon) 57. Univ of Bris MLitt 67. Univ of Southn PhD 81. STh (Lambeth) 74. Tyndale Hall Bris 53. **d** 57 **p** 58 Sarum. C of St Jo Evang Heatherlands Parkstone 57-61; Cromer 61-63; PC of St Jude Plymouth 63-71; V of St Jo Evang Heatherlands Parkstone 71-76; Dir of Pastoral Tr Oak Hill Coll 76-81; Publ Pr Dio Lon 77-81; V of Ch Ch Finchley Dio Lon from 81. *Christ Church Vicarage, Woodside Park Road, North Finchley, N12.* (01-445 2377)

PYWELL, Alan Baron. b 23. St Jo Coll Auckld. **d** 50 **p** 51 Waik. C of St Pet Cathl Hamilton 50-51; V of Mokau 51-53; Stratford 53-58; W New Plymouth 58-60; Chap Borstal Inst Invercargill and L to Offic Dio Dun 61-63; V of Riverslea 63-72; St Andr Napier Dio Wai from 72. *1 Alfred Street, Westshore, Napier, NZ.* (59-924)

PYWELL, Ven Arthur Baron. b 1892. St Aid Th Coll Bal ThL 16. **d** 16 **p** 17 Bal. C-in-c of Jeparit 16; P-in-c of Jeparit and Rainbow 17-20; Alvie 20-21; V 21-27; V of Dunstan w Pembroke 27-34; Port Chalmers 34-35; Caversham 35-52; Can of St Paul's Cathl Dun 46-52; Archd of Centr Otago 50-66; Archd (Emer) from 66; Chap of Dun Publ Hosps 52-61; Dept VG 57-66; L to Offic Dio Dun 66-73; Hon C of All SS w Port Chalmers Dio Dun from 77. *773 Great King Street, Dunedin, NZ.* (Dunedin 770-019)

Q

QABAZI, McLenen Stanley Dilika. St Pet Coll Rosettenville 52. **d** 54 **p** 55 Capetn. P Dio Capetn. P-in-c of Kaya Mandi 63-76; Guguletu Dio Capetn from 76. *Box 8, Guguletu, CP, S Africa.* (77-4167)

QANAFIIA, Martin. **d** 41 **p** 46 Melan. P Dio Melan 41-75; Dio Malaita from 75. *Ata'a, Malaita, Solomon Islands.*

QEALAV, Frank Bollen. Patteson Th Coll Kohimarama. **d** 72 Melan. d Dio Melan 72-75; Dio New Hebr from 75. *Merelava, Banks Islands, New Hebrides.*

QENGQA, Sydney Vuyisile. St Pet Coll Alice. **d** 68 **p** 69 Grahmstn. Miss O of Ethiopia Dio Grahmstn 68-70 and from 75; Dio Port Eliz 70-75. *24 Victoria Road, Grahmstn, CP, S Africa.*

QILIO, Apimeleki Nadoki. St Francis Coll Brisb 67. **d** 68 **p** 69 Polyn. P Dio Polyn. *PO Box 25, Levuka, Fiji.*

QOBO, John Mangaliso Fancy. St Pet Coll Rosettenville 56. **d** 58 **p** 59 Grahmstn. P Dio Grahmstn. *Box 227, Mdantsane 5219, CP, S Africa.*

QUANCE, John David. b 42. Kelham Th Coll 61. **d** 67 Lon **p** 68 Willesden for Lon. c of Ch Ch Southgate 67-70; St Phil Norbury 70-73; Asst Chap Middx Hosp Lon 73-80; R of Failsworth Dio Man from 80. *Rectory, Pole Lane, Manchester, M35 9PB.* (061-681 2734)

QU'APPELLE, Lord Bishop of. *See* Peers, Right Rev Michael Geoffrey.

QU'APPELLE, Dean of. *See* Wallace, Very Rev Duncan Douglas.

QUARCOOPOME, Percy Rodger. Trin Coll Legon. **d** 72 **p** 73 Accra. C of Bolgatanga 72-75; I of Bp Aglionby Ch Tamale 75-81; St Andr Kaneshie Dio Accra from 81. *Box 114, Kaneshie, Accra, Ghana.*

QUARMBY, David John. b 43. Univ of Dur BA (2nd cl Th) 64. Ridley Hall Cam 65. **d** 67 Birm **p** 68 Aston for Birm. C of Bournville 67-71; V of St Chad Erdington 71-73; L to Offic and Asst Master Norden Co High Sch Rishton Dio Blackb from 73. *11 Lyndon Avenue, Great Harwood, Blackburn, Lancs, BB6 7TP.* (Gt Harwood 887011)

QUARRELL, John Beck. b 39. Chich Th Coll 67. **d** 70 **p** 71 Pontefract for Wakef. C of Horbury 70-71; Sowerby 71-73; V of Brotherton 73-80; Staincliffe Dio Wakef from 80. *Vicarage, Staincliffe Hall Road, Batley, W Yorks.* (Batley 473343)

QUARTERMAIN, Henry Clifton. KCNS. **d** 39 NS for Arctic **p** 39 Fred for Arctic. Miss at Eskimo Point 39-40; Lake Harbour 40-49; R of Falmouth 49-53; New Waterford 53-64; P-in-c of Dominion 53-64; Annapolis Royal 64-68; Canso w Queensport 68-70. *Berwick, NS, Canada.*

QUARTEY, Canon John Kpakpa. St Aug Coll Kumasi. **d** and **p** 31 Accra. P Dio Accra; Hon Can of Accra 56-72; Can (Emer) from 72. *PO Box 491, Accra, Ghana.*

QUAYLE, Canon James Orry. St Jo Coll Morpeth. **d** 33 **p** 34 Armid. C of St Pet Cathl Armid 33-35; P-in-c of Wee Waa 35-41; V of Walgett 41-50; Urulla 50-61; Manilla 61-67; Chap AIF 43-46; Can of Armid 61-69. *29 Lock Avenue, Springfield, NSW, Australia.*

QUEBEC, Lord Bishop of. *See* Goodings, Right Rev Allen.

QUEBEC, Dean of. *See* James, Very Rev John Paul.

QUEE, Allen William. Moore Th Coll Syd 51. **d** 54 **p** 56 Gippsld. C of Yallourn 54-55; Prec of St Paul's Cathl Sale 56-57; R of Stratford 57-59; C-in-c of Mascot 59-63; R of Waterloo w Mascot and Eastlakes 62-65; Gen Sec S Austrn CMS 65-72; C of Magill 65-69 and 70-71; Perm to Offic Dio Adel 69-70; C of Kensington 71-72; R of Beverly Hills Dio Syd from 72. *121 Morgan Street, Beverly Hills, NSW, Australia 2209.* (50-8179)

QUEENSLAND, NORTH, Lord Bishop of. *See* Lewis, Right Rev Hurtle John.

QUEENSLAND, NORTH, Assistant Bishop of. (Vacant)

QUELCH, Aubrey Alfred. b 07. Univ of Dur LTh 37. ALCD 37. **d** 37 **p** 38 S'wark. C of H Redeemer Streatham Vale 37-41; St Mark Lyncombe Bath 41-46; Ottery St Mary 46-49; V of Kilmington Devon 49-55; Bp's C of Teampolna-Mbocht (or Altar) 55-59; I of Rathclaren U 59-64; Fermoy U 64-78. *30 Kingston College, Mitchelstown, Co Cork, Irish Republic.*

QUELCH, Canon Leslie William. b 1891. Univ of Lon BSc (2nd cl Chem) 12. Univ of Dur LTh 16. Univ of Glas MB ChB 25. Edin Th Coll 14, Luscombe Scho 16. **d** 16 **p** 17 Glas. C of Ch Ch Glas (w c of St Cuthb from 17) 16-20; Asst Dioc Super and Hosp Chap Glas 21-25; C of St Cuthb and Med Miss in c of St Lucy's Hosp Tsolo 26-27; Med Miss at Ensikeni 27-29; All SS Engcobo 29-43; P-in-c of Maclear 43-45; St Andr Lusikisiki 45-54; Warden St Jo Coll Umtata 54-60; Hon Can of St Jo Kaffr 57-60; C of Ampthill Millbrook and of Steppingley 60; Prec of St Ninian's Cathl Perth 62-63; R of H Trin Dunoon 63-69; Hon C of Stourport 69-73; Hon Can of Cumbrae from 70. *College of St Barnabas, Blackberry Lane, Lingfield, Surrey, RH7 6NJ.*

QUENNELL, Brian Michael. b 19. **d** 74 **p** 75 Pet. C of All SS Oakham w Hambleton and Egleton 74-78; V of Denford w Ringstead Dio Pet from 78. *Ringstead Vicarage, Kettering, Northants, NN14 4DF.* (Wellingborough 624627)

QUIBELL, George. Wycl Coll Tor LTh 74. **d** 74 **p** 75 Alg. C of Nipigon, Red Rock & Dorion 74-75; I 75-77; Port Edward 77-78; on leave. *1710 Isabella Street, Thunder Bay, BC, Canada.*

QUICK, Edward Keith. b 1889. St Jo Coll Cam BA 10, MA 14. Ridley Hall Cam. **d** 14 **p** 15 Chich. C of St Leonards-on-Sea 14-19; TCF 15-18; Hon CF 21; Asst Chap Bedford Sch 21-22; Master and Asst Chap St Steph Coll Hong Kong 22-26; LPr Dio Carl 26-28; Hd Master Cathl Sch Shanghai 29-36; Chap Ch Hosp Horsham 37-43; V of Monk Sherborne w Pamber 43-48; Long Sutton 48-54; R of Ellisfield w Farleigh Wallop 54-60. *Bernardine, Letchmore Heath, Watford, Herts.* (Radlett 7289)

QUIGLEY, John Molesworth. b 21. BNC Ox BA 43, MA 47. Wycl Hall Ox 43. **d** 44 **p** 45 Lon. C of St Jo Wembley 44-46; Hon C of Ellesmere Port 75-76; Bromborough 76-79; Prenton Dio Ches from 79. *21 Egerton Road, Birkenhead, Merseyside, L43 1UJ.*

QUIGLEY, Thomas Molesworth. ALCD 41. Univ of Lon BD 45. **d** 42 S'wark **p** 43 Kingston T for S'wark. C of St Sav Herne Hill 42-45; CF 45-58 (Men in Disp 52); C of Upperby Carl 58-62; Accrington 62-70. *1/42 Hampden Road, Artarmon, Sydney, NSW 2064, Australia.*

QUILL, John Stephen. b 51. Linc Th Coll 76. **d** 79 **p** 80 St Alb. C of Sawbridgeworth 79-81; Ch Ch Watford Dio St Alb from 81. *77 Northfield Gardens, Watford, Herts.* (Watford 25411)

QUILL, Walter Paterson. b 35. **d** 60 Derry **p** 66-81; C of Glendermott 60-63; R of Kilbarron 63-66; Kilcronaghan w Ballynascreen 66-81; Derg w Termonamongan Dio Derry from 81. *Rectory, Castlederg, Co Tyrone, N Ireland.*

QUIN, Charles William Cosslett. b 07. TCD 1st cl Cl Mod 29, BA 30, Div Test 31, BD 37. **d** 31 Down **p** 32 Meath for Down. C of St Mark Dundela 31-36; C-in-c of U Moville 36-40; Asst Master St Columba's Coll Rathfarnham 40-42; C-in-c of Drumlane 42-44; I of Killinagh w Kiltyclogher

44-50; Narraghmore w Fontstown 50-55; Exam Chap to Bp of Kilm 49-50; Chap of St John Cork and Dean of Residence for C of I Students at Cork Univ 55-60; I of Billis U 60-65; Prof Trin Coll Dub 62-66; I of Dunganstown w Redcross 65-72; Can and Preb of Swords in St Patr Cathl Dub 65-71. *67 South Park, Foxrock, Dublin 18, Irish Republic.* (Dublin 894921)

QUIN, Eric Arthur. b 22. Magd Coll Cam BA 46, MA 48. BD (Lon) 56. Bps' Coll Cheshunt 46. **d** 48 **p** 49 St Alb. C of St Andr Luton 48-50; Barnoldswick w Bracewell 50-52; V of St Sav Fairweather Green 52-57; C-in-c of St Ippolyts w Gt Wymondley 57-58; V of St Ippolyts 58-70; RD of Hitchin 68-70; V of Haynes Dio St Alb from 70. *Haynes Vicarage, Bedford.* (Haynes 235)

✠ **QUIN, Right Rev George Alderson.** b 14. TCD Carson Bibl Pri and Eccles Hist Pri (2nd) 36, BA and Div Test (2nd cl) 37, MA 40. **d** 37 **p** 38 Down. C of St Jude Ballynafeigh Belf 37-39; Dean's V of St Anne's Cathl Belf 39-41; Holywood 41-43; I of Magheralin or Maralin 43-51; V of Ballymacarrett 51-58; Can of St Anne's Cathl Belf 55-56; Archd of Down 56-70; Exam Chap to Bp of Down and Drom 57-70; R of Bangor 58-70; Cons Ld Bp of Down and Drom in Belf Cathl 6 Jan 70 by Abp of Arm; Bps of Cashel; Connor; Kilmore; res 80. *20 Kensington Park, Bangor, Co Down, N Ireland.*

QUIN, John James Neil. b 31. Late Scho of St Jo Coll Ox, Heath Harrison Trav Scho 52, BA (2nd cl Mod Lang) 53, MA 58. Qu Coll Birm 61. **d** 63 **p** 64 Lich. C of Cannock 63-68; V of Sneyd Green 68-78; Forebridge Dio Lich from 78. *St Paul's Vicarage, Lichfield Road, Stafford.* (Stafford 51683)

QUIN, Thomas Rothwell. b 15. OBE 80. Men in Disp 45. TCD BA and Div Test 39, MA 49. **d** 39 Tuam for Down **p** 40 Down. C of St Patr Ballymacarrett 39-41; Chap RAFVR 41-46; Chap RAF 46-70; Hon Chap to HM the Queen 67-70; Chap at Zurich 70-80; RD of Switzerland 76-79; Archd in Switzerland 79-80; Perm to Offic Dio Sarum from 80. *New Rushford, Walnut Close, Sutton Veny, Warminster, Wilts BA12 7AW.* (Sutton Veny 794)

QUINE, Christopher Andrew. b 38. St Aid Coll 61. **d** 64 **p** 65 Liv. C of Hunts Cross 64-67; Farnworth (in c of St John) 67-71; V of Clubmoor 71-78; H Trin Formby Dio Liv from 78. *47 Freshfield Road, Formby, Liverpool, L37 3HL.* (Formby 73642)

QUINE, David Anthony. b 28. Qu Coll Cam BA 52, MA 59. Ridley Hall Cam 53. **d** 55 **p** 56 Roch. C of Ch Ch Beckenham 55-59; Normanton-by-Derby 59-60; V of St Steph Newc T 60-66; Houghton 66-68; L to Offic Dio York 68-71; Chap Monkton Combe Jun Sch Bath from 71. *Treetops, Beechwood Road, Combe Down, Bath, Som.*

QUINE, Canon Ernest Kendrick Leigh. b 21. St Jo Coll Dur BA 50, Dipl Th (w distinc) 51, MA 55. Univ of Nottm DPhil 68. **d** 51 Liv **p** 52 Lich. C of St Mary Grassendale 51-52; St Akmund Shrewsbury 52-54; Min of St Chris Conv Distr Leic 54-61; V of Belgrave City & Dio Leic from 61; Ed Leic Dioc Leaflet from 60; Proc Conv Leic from 65; Hon Can of Leic from 67; Surr from 74. *St Peter's Vicarage, Belgrave, Leicester.* (Leicester 61401)

QUINLAN, Canon Alan Geoffrey. Kelham Th Coll 54. **d** 58 **p** 59 Man. C of St Thos Bedford Leigh (Lancs) 58-61; R of St Marg Bloemf 62-68; V of St Phil Miss Bloemf 63-64; R of Sasolburg 68-70; Parys 70-72; Warden CR and Chap Teachers Tr Coll Grahmstn 72-76; Exam Chap to Abp of Capetn from 76; P-in-c of Tr in Min Dio Capetn from 76; R of All SS Plumstead Dio Capetn from 76; Can of Capetn from 80. *6 Brent Road, Plumstead 7800, CP, S Africa.* (77-3668)

QUINLAN, Dermot William Allen. b 10. Trin Coll Dub BA 30, Div Test 31, MA 38. **d** 33 **p** 34 Down. C of Bangor 33-36; St Jas Belf 36-40; CF 40-62; R of Barwell w Stapleton and Potters Marston 62-71; V of Billesdon w Rolleston and Goadby 71-80; *13 Poplar Close, Ayston Road, Uppingham, Leics, LE15 9RQ.* (057-282 3918)

QUINN, Arthur Hamilton Riddel. b 37. Trin Coll Dub BA (2nd cl Hebr and Or Lang Mod) 60, Div Test 61, MA 64, BD 67. **d** 61 **p** 62 Connor. C of H Trin Belf 61-63; St Mary Magd Belf 63-64; Abp of York's Chap Univ of Hull 64-69; Chap Univ of Keele 69-74; L to Offic Dio Lich 69-72; C-in-c of Keele 72-74; V of Shirley Dio Cant from 74. *47 Shirley Church Road, Croydon, Surrey, CR0 5EF.* (01-654 1013)

QUINN, Cecil Hugh. b 24. Oak Hill Coll 73. **d** 76 St Alb **p** 77 Hertf for St Alb. C of St Jo & St Leon Bedford 76-80; R of Tyrella w Rathmullen Dio Down from 80. *10 Ballydonnell Road, Downpatrick, Co Down, BT30 8EN.* (Ballykinlar 237)

QUINN, Ven Harry Clement. Univ of Tor BA 54. Wycl Coll Tor. **d** 55 **p** 56 Tor. C-in-c of Washago 55-56; I of Cavan 56-58; R of St Luke St John Dio Fred from 58; Can of Ch Ch Cathl Fred from 71; Archd of St John from 80. *369 Main Street, St John, NB, Canada E2K 1J1.*

QUINN, John James. b 46. TCD 70, PhD 76. Univ of Nottm Dipl Th 80. St Jo Coll Nottm 79. **d** 81 Nor. C of Gorleston Dio Nor from 81. *8 Half Moon, Cliff Park, Gorleston, Gt Yarmouth, NR31 6TE.*

QUINNEY, William Elliott. b 33. Linc Th Coll 62. **d** 64 **p** 65 Leic. C of Coalville 64-68; C-in-c of Ibstock 68-69; R of Nailstone w Carlton (and Shackerstone from 79) Dio Leic from 69. *Nailstone Rectory, Nuneaton, Warws.* (Ibstock 60281)

QWELANE, Israel Pani. Kelham Th Coll 62. **d** 67 **p** 68 C of St Aug Miss Thaba 'Nchu 67-70; St Pet Miss Sasolburg 70-72; Dir 73-75; St Aug Thaba 'Nchu 75-81. *37 Lakhinpur Road, Merebank, Natal, S Africa.*

R

RABAN, Canon James Peter Caplin Priaulx. b 18. TED 50. **d** 54 **p** 55 Win. C of Weeke 54-59; V of Pennington 59-66; Maybush 66-80; RD of Southn from 70; Chap Countess Mountbatten Ho Southn from 80; Hon Can of Win from 73. *37 Northbrook Road, Southampton.* (Southn 27256)

RABAN, Matthew. b 45. Ho of Epiph Kuch 73. **d** and **p** 75 Kuch. P Dio Kuch. *c/o Bishop's House, PO Box 347, Kuching, Sarawak, Malaysia.*

RABBETTS, Reginald Douglas Cyprian. AKC 38. Sarum Th Coll 38. **d** 38 **p** 39 Wakef. C of Lightcliffe 38-43; Fordingbridge w Ibsley 43-50; V of Kingsclere Woodlands w Headley Dio Win from 50. *Woodlands Vicarage, Ashford Hill, Newbury, Berks.* (Headley 217)

RABE, Ose. b 40. St Aug Coll Mahanoro 69. **d** 73 Tam. d Dio Tam 73-79; Dio Toa from 79. *Mission Anglicane, Vavatenina, Tamatave, Madagascar.*

RABEFARITANY, Jean Marc. b 37. **d** 73 **p** 74 Antan. P Dio Antan 73-75 and from 77; Dio Tam 75-77. *Morarano, Ambohimandry, Malagasy Republic.*

RABENIRINA, Remi Joseph. Lich Th Coll 64. **d** 67 **p** 68 Madag. P Dio Madag 67-69; Dio Diego-S 69-72; Dio Antan from 73. *Ambohimangakely, Antananarivo, Madagascar.*

RABJOHNS, Alan. b 40. Univ of Leeds BA (2nd cl Hist) 62. Coll of Resurr Mirfield 62. **d** 64 **p** 65 Newc T. C of Ashington 64-67; Upton w Chalvey Slough 67-76; V of St Sav Roath Dio Llan from 76. *115 Splott Road, Cardiff, CF2 2BY.* (Cardiff 32203)

RABOTO, Georges. b 41. St Aug Coll Mahanoro 69. **d** 73 Tam. d Dio Tam. *Mission Anglicane, Ambodiharina, Mahanoro, Madagascar.*

RABVUKWA, Benjamin. St Jo Coll Lusaka 70. **d** 72 **p** 73 Mashon. C of Marlborough 72; C-in-c of Dzivarisekwa 72-74; C of Mazoe Valley Dio Mashon from 74. *PO Box 186, Bindura, Rhodesia.*

RABY, Canon Alfred Charles. b 04. Late Exhib of St Jo Coll Ox BA 27, MA 30. Wells Th Coll 27. **d** 28 **p** 29 S'wark. C of Lambeth 28-33; St Sav Raynes Park (in c of H Cross) 33-36; V of Ch Ch Shooter's Hill 36-39; St Mark Woodcote Purley 39-54; R of Clapham 54-74; Hon Can of S'wark 57-75; Can (Emer from 75) RD of Clapham and Brixton 63-74; Perm to Offic Dio St E from 75. *134b Southgate Street, Bury-St-Edmunds, Suffolk.*

RABY, Charles John. b 17. Clifton Th Coll 40. **d** 42 **p** 43 Wakef. C of St Geo Lupset 42-46; Thornhill 46-50; V of Dewsbury Moor 50-57; Claverley Dio Heref from 57. *Claverley Vicarage, Wolverhampton, Staffs.* (Claverley 268)

RABY, Percival Sydney. b 01. Lich Th Coll 21. **d** 24 Bp Hamilton Baynes for Birm **p** 25 Birm. C of Handsworth 24-26; Northwood 26-30; St Pet Dunstable 30; R of Ingworth 30-44; V of Calthorpe 31-44; C-in-c of Alby w Thwaite 43-48; R of Erpingham w Calthorpe 44-62; C-in-c of Colby 53-54; Perm to Offic Dio Nor from 62. *College of St Barnabas, Blackberry Lane, Lingfield, Surrey, RH7 6NJ.*

RACE, Alan. b 51. Univ of Bradf BTech 73. Cudd Coll Dipl Th 75. **d** 76 **p** 77 Heref. C of Tupsley 76-79; Asst Chap Univ of Kent from 79. *c/o University of Kent, Canterbury, CT2 7NZ.*

RACE, Christopher Keith. b 43. St Paul's Coll Grahmstn Dipl Th 78. **d** 78 **p** 80 Capetn. R of H Trin Kalk Bay Dio Capetn from 78. *42 Main Road, Kalk Bay, Cape, S Africa.*

RACE, Robert. b 09. **d** 52 Jarrow for Dur **p** 53 Dur. C of Easington Colliery 52-54; V of Tanfield 54-61; R of St Jas Gateshead 61-76; Perm to Offic Dio Dur from 76. *19 Lilywhite Terrace, Easington Lane, Houghton-le-Spring, T & W.*

RACHIER, Hezron. St Paul's Dioc Div Sch Limuru 46. **d** 49 **p** 51 Momb. P Dio Momb 49-61; Dio Maseno 61-70; Dio Maseno S from 71. *PO Box 373, Yala, Kenya.*

RACKSTRAW, Geoffrey William Arthur. St Paul's Coll Grahamstn 54. **d** 56 **p** 58 Capetn. C of Silverton 56-59; R of Clanwilliam 59-65; Hout Bay 65-79; P-in-c 79-80; R of Wellington Dio Capetn from 80. *4 Milner Street, Wellington 7655, CP, S Africa.*

RACTLIFFE, Dudley John. b 38. Univ of Man BA 62. Ridley Hall Cam 63. **d** 66 Bp McKie for Cov **p** 67 Cov. C of St Nich Radford 66-68; Haslemere 69-73; V of Perry Beeches 73-78; Worle Dio B & W from 78. *Worle Vicarage, Weston-super-Mare, Avon.* (W-s-M 513425)

RADCLIFFE, Alan Frederick. St Paul's Coll Grahmstn 66. **d** 68 **p** 70 Kimb K. C of St Steph Vryburg 68-70; St Mary Kuruman 71-73; Germiston 73-77; R of Alberton Dio Johann from 77. *504 Estuary Height, New Redruth, Johannesburg, S Africa.* (011-869 5619)

RADCLIFFE, Albert Edward. b 34. BD (Lon) 63. St Aid Coll. **d** 62 Calif **p** 63 Liv. C of St John Knotty Ash 62-64; St Nich Blundellsands 64-66; Chap St Luke Haifa 66-69; V of Tonge w Alkrington 69-77; Exam Chap to Bp of Man from 72; R of Ashton-u-Lyne Dio Man from 77. *Rectory, Caroline Street, Ashton-under-Lyne, Gtr Man, OL6 6NS.* (061-330 1172)

RADCLIFFE, Jeffrey. b 52. Linc Th Coll 77. **d** 79 Lanc for Blackb **p** 80 Blackb. C of Poulton-Le-Fylde Dio Blackb from 79. *60 Hodder Way, Poulton-Le-Fylde, Blackpool, Lancs, FY6 8AQ.*

RADCLIFFE, Jim. b 23. Univ of Liv BEng 43, MEng 46. St Jo Coll Dur 76. **d** 78 Penrith for Carl **p** 79 Carl. C of Penrith 78-80; P-in-c of Barton w Pooley Bridge Dio Carl from 81. *Barton Vicarage, Penrith, Cumb, CA10 2LR.* (Pooley Bridge 220)

RADCLIFFE-COX, Henry Richard Radcliffe. b 06. Selw Coll Cam BA 32, MA 36. Wells Th Coll 32. **d** 33 **p** 34 Bris. C of St Jo Div Fishponds 33-36; Stoke Bp 36-38; Brinkworth 38-41; Dom Chap to Bp of Malmesbury 38-41; CF (EC) 41-45; Chap Bris Gen Hosp Annexe 45-46; V of Almondsbury 46-62; Chap of Hortham Hosp and of Almondsbury Mem Hosp 46-61; Oaklands Home of Rest 55-58; V of Lechlade 62-76. *6 Folly View Road, Faringdon, Oxon, SN7 7DG.* (Faringdon 20194)

RADEBE, Ben Bubana. St Pet Coll Rosettenville 56. **d** 58 **p** 59 Natal. P Dio Natal 58-65 and from 79; Dio Johann 65-79. *29 Beatrice Street, Durban 4001, S Africa.*

RADFORD, Andrew John. b 44. Trin Coll Bris 72. **d** 74 **p** 75 Bris. C of Shirehampton 74-78; Producer Relig Programmes BBC Radio Bris and L to Offic Dio Bris 78-80; V of St Barn Southdown w Englishcombe Dio B & W from 80. *Vicarage, Mount View, Southdown, Bath, Avon.* (Bath 21838)

RADFORD, Arthur John. b 11. Oak Hill Th Coll 32. **d** 36 **p** 37 Lon. C of St Sav Tollington Pk 36-39; St Pet Paddington 39-41; CF (EC) 41-46; Hon CF 46; PC of E Stonehouse 46-53; C-in-c of St Paul Stonehouse 46-53; PC of St Barn Devonport 53-59; V of Okehampton (w Inwardleigh from 63) 59-74; RD of Okehampton 60-66; Surr 60-74; Perm to Offic Dio Ex from 76. *11 Langhill Road, Mutley, Plymouth, Devon, PL3 4JH.* (Plymouth 25586)

RADFORD, Derrell Ambrose. **d** 61 Bp Redding for Melb **p** 62 Melb. C of Belmont 61-63; Sunshine 63-64; V of Deer Pk w St Alb 64-72; I of Noble Pk Dio Melb from 72. *39 Wallarano Drive, Noble Park, Vic, Australia 3174.* (03-798 3838)

RADFORD, Donald George. b 16. Lich Th Coll 55. **d** 56 Bp Hawkes for Cant **p** 57 Guildf. C of Ch Ch Guildf 56-58; Stoke-next-Guildf (in c of St Pet Bellfields) 58-60; Min of Conv Distr of St Pet Stoke Hill 60-69; L to Offic Dio Glouc from 79. *384 London Road, Charlton Kings, Cheltenham, Glos, GL52 6YX.*

RADFORD, Maurice Frederick. b 06. Bps' Coll Cheshunt 60. **d** 60 **p** 61 St E. C of Brandon w Wangford Santon and Santon Downham 60-63; R of Glemsford 63-71; C-in-c of Somerton 63-71; L to Offic Dio St E from 71. *12 Mill Lane, Felixstowe, Suff, IP11 7RN.* (Felixstowe 5985)

RADFORD, Samuel. b 17. Kelham Th Coll. **d** 45 **p** 46 Dur. C of St Mary Tyne Dk 45-49; Good Shepherd Conv Distr Ford Estate Bp Wearmouth 49-50; Tynemouth (in c of St Faith) 50-52; C-in-c of Holywell 52-57; V of Metheringham 57-66; Asst Chap HM Pris Wormwood Scrubs 66-67; Chap HM Pris Camp Hill IW 67-69; C of Barton-on-Humber 69-71. *50 Pippins Green Avenue, Kirkhamgate, Wakefield, Yorks.*

RADI, Musa Mamour. Bp Gwynne Coll Mundri 61. **d** 62 **p** 63 Sudan. P Dio Sudan 62-76; Dio Rumbek from 76. *ECS, Bangolo, Sudan.*

RADICE, Anthony Alister Hutton. b 14. Late Exhib of Ex Coll Ox BA (2nd cl Mod Hist) 36, 2nd cl Th 37, MA 45. Cudd Coll 37. **d** 38 **p** 39 Ox. C of Newbury 38-42; CF (EC) 42-49; Perm to Offic at St Phil and St Jas Ox 49-51; Chap Eastbourne Coll and L to Offic Dio Chich 51-54; Woodbridge Sch and L to Offic Dio St E 54-56; R of Hepworth 56-81; P-in-c of Thelnetham 56-81; Wattisfield 58-81; Perm to Offic Dio St E from 81. *35 Maltings Garth, Thurston, Bury St Edmunds, Suffolk, IP3 3PP.* (Pakenham 30146)

RADLEY, Peter. b 31. Bps' Coll Cheshunt 60. **d** 62 Bp McKie for Cov **p** 63 Cov. C of Lillington 62-63; Nuneaton 63-67; P-in-c of Skillington 67-68; V of Waltham St Lawr Dio Ox from 68. *Waltham St Lawrence Vicarage, Reading, Berks.* (Shurlock Row 249)

RADLEY, Roy Taylor. Edin Th Coll 47. **d** 50 **p** 51 Edin. C of Ch Ch Morningside Edin 50-53; Asst Chap Miss to Seamen S Shields and Tyne and L to Offic Dio Dur 53-55; Area Sec Miss to Seamen Greater Lon Area and LPr Dio Chelmsf 55-57; Chap Miss to Seamen Colom 57-58; Area Sec NW Midls and LPr Dio Derby 59-68; Perm to Offic Dios Lich, Sheff and Southw from 59; Dios Leic and Linc from 68; Midl Reg Secr Leprosy Miss from 68. *200 Broadway, Derby, DE3 1BP.* (Derby 43109)

RADLOFF, Michael Thomas Eckard. b 54. St Paul's Coll Grahmstn Dipl Th 77. **d** 77 Grahmstn. C of St Alb E Lon 77-78. *c/o The Registrar, 86 High Street, Grahamstown, CP, S Africa.*

RADUA, Maikali. b 35. St Jo Bapt Th Coll Suva 66. **d** 69 **p** 70 Polyn. C of H Trin Cathl Suva 70-72; Glen Innes 72-73; P-in-c of Nadi, Viti Levu W 74-76; C of H Trin Cathl Suva Dio Polyn from 77. *Box 275, Suva, Fiji.*

✠ **RAFANOMEZANA, Right Rev Samuel.** Chevalier de l'Orde National de la République Malgache, 64. **d** 42 **p** 46 Madag. P at Anjanaminovola 42-45; P-in-c of Ambinanindrano 45-49; Mahanora 49-75; Exam Chap to Bp of Madag 54-69; Archd of E Madag 61-69; Tam 69-75; Exam Chap to Bp of Tam 70-75; Cons Ld Bp of Tam (Toa from 79) in St Laur Cathl Antan Madag 15 Oct 75 by Abp of Prov of the Indian Ocean; Bps of Diego S and Sey; and Bp Marcel. *La Mission Anglicane, Rue de la Fraternité, Toamasina, Malagasy Republic.*

RAFE, Levi. Bp Patteson Th Centre Kohimarama 68. **d** 70 **p** 72 Melan. P Dio Melan 70-75; Dio Centr Melan from 75. *Kolina, Guadalcanal, Solomon Islands.*

RAFF, Kenneth Brandreth Eglinton. Ridley Coll Melb ACT ThL 48. **d** 48 **p** 49 Gippsld. C-in-c of Bass 48; V 49-51; Trafalgar 51-54; R of Morwell 54-56; Chap Melb R Hosp 56-61; I of Beaumaris Dio Melb from 61. *26 Dalgetty Road, Beaumaris, Vic, Australia 3193.* (03-99 2239)

RAFF, Canon Kenneth William. Univ of Queensld BCom 72. St Francis Coll Brisb. **d** 59 **p** 60 Rockptn. C of St Paul's Cathl Rockptn 59-62; V of Miriam Vale 62-63; R of Longreach 63-68; Chap and Sec St John's Hosp City and Dio Rockptn from 68; Hon Can of Rockptn from 71; Dioc Regr and Sec Dio Rockptn from 72. *89 William Street, Rockhampton, Queensland, Australia.* (079-27 3188)

RAFIDIMANANA, Paul. St Paul's Coll Ambat. **d** 38 **p** 42 Madag. P Dio Madag 38-64; Dio Antan from 69; Bp's Chap 55-64. *Ankadifotsy, Tananarive, Madagascar.*

RAFUTHO, Ven Justin James. St Bede Coll Umtata. **d** 63 **p** 65 Basuto. P Dio Les; Archd of N Les from 77. *Box 38, Leribe, Lesotho, S Africa.*

RAGG, Edward Stanley. b 1900. Univ of Dur BA 22. Wells Th Coll 53. **d** 54 **p** 55 Win. C of Odiham w S Warnborough 54-58; R of Bow w Broad Nymet 58-63; Wolverton w Ewhurst and Hannington 63-67. *15 Windermere Avenue, Barrow-in-Furness, Cumb, LA14 4LN.*

RAGG, Harold Ivor Groves. Univ of BC BA 50. Trin Coll Tor LTh 53. **d** 52 **p** 53 Bp Ragg for Bran. C of St Simon Tor 52-55; I of The Pas 55-59; Castlegar 59-61; St Luke Vancouver 61-66; Lakeshore 66-73; Ch Ch Lon Dio Hur 73-75;

Duncan Dio BC from 75. *466 St Julian Street, Duncan, BC, Canada.* (604-746 6726)

✠ **RAGG, Right Rev Theodore David Butler.** Trin Coll Tor BA 47, BD 51. Hur Coll Ont Hon DD 75. **d** 49 **p** 50 Calg for Tor. C of St Mich AA Tor 49-51; I of Nokornis 51-53; Wolseley 53-55; St Clem Lynn Valley N Vancouver 55-57; R of St Luke Cedar Hill 57-62; Bp Cronyn Mem Ch Lon 62-67; Owen Sound 67-74; Exam Chap to Bp of Hur 64-68; Archd of Saugeen 67-74; Cons Ld Bp Suffr of Hur in St Paul's Cathl Lon Ont 25 Jan 74 by Abp of Alg; Bps of Hur, Moos, Niag, Ont and Tor; Bps Suffr of Moos and Tor; and others; Apptd Ld Bp of Hur May 74. *4-220 Dundas Street, London, Ont., N6A 1H3, Canada.* (519-434 6893)

RAGGETT, Geoffrey Francis. b 22. Lon Coll of Div 60. **d** 62 **p** 63 Guildf. C of Stoughton 62-66; V of St Paul E Ham 66-72; Chap to Woking Group Ministry 72-76; Long Grove Hosp Epsom from 76. *3 Long Grove House, Long Grove Hospital, Epsom, Surrey, KT19 8PU.* (Epsom 40330)

RAGGETT, John Parton. **d** 52 **p** 53 Waik. C of Te Awamutu 52-54; P-in-c of Kawhia Conv Distr 54-57; V of Ohura 57-59; Ngaruawahia 59-63; Otorohanga 63-65; Chap New Plymouth Hosp 65-71; Chap Tokanui Psychiatric Hosp Dio Waik from 71. *63 Hall Street, Kihikihi, NZ.*

RAHOVAII, Ezrona. b 34. **d** 77 **p** 78 Diego S. P Dio Diego S 77-79; Dio Antsir from 79. *Ambahatra-Bemanevika, Ambanja, Antsiranana, Madagascar.*

RAIKES, Canon Myles Kenneth. b 23. New Coll Ox BA 47, MA 51. Wells Th Coll 47. **d** 49 **p** 50 Chelmsf. C of St Mary's Cathl Chelmsf 49-51; St John Stratford 51-53; C-in-c of Hockerill 53-55; PC 55-63; Chap Herts and Essex Gen Hosp 56-63; V of Bushey Heath 63-70; R of Digswell 70-77; P-in-c of Meare 77-81; W Coker Dio B & W from 82; Hon Can of St Alb 76-77; Can (Emer) from 77. *West Coker Rectory, Yeovil, Somerset.* (W Coker 2328)

RAIKES, Peter. b 37. St Mich AA Llan 78. **d** 80 **p** 81 Llan. C of Roath Dio Llan from 80. *18 Sandringham Road, Roath, Cardiff, CF2 5BJ.*

RAIKES, Robert Laybourne. b 32. Wells Th Coll 59. **d** 61 **p** 62 Lon. C of Poplar 61-66; Swan Group (Barton Hartshorne w Chetwode, Grendon Underwood w Edgcott, Marsh Gibbon, Preston Bissett and Twyford) 66-71; V of Whitchurch Canonicorum w Stanton and Wootton Fitzpaine (and Monkton Wyld from 75) 71-80; P-in-c of St Aldhelm Branksome Dio Sarum from 80. *Vicarage, St Aldhelm's Road, Branksome, Poole, Dorset, BH13 6BT.* (Bournemouth 764420)

RAILSTON-BROWN (formerly BROWN), William Robert. b 1891. Selw Coll Cam BA 14, MA 19. Cudd Coll 18. **d** 19 **p** 21 Lich. C of St Mary Shrewsbury 19-23; St Mich AA Penkridge 23-24; R of Willersey (w Saintbury from 34) 24-39; V of Bishopthorpe York 39-45; Acaster Malbis 39-45; Chap to Abp of York 39-42; V of Bisham 45-57; Amberley 57-61. *Coombe Cottage, Chearsley Road, Long Crendon, Aylesbury, Bucks.* (Long Crendon 314)

RAINBOW, Preb Gerald Anton Hayward. b 15. St Edm Hall Ox 3rd cl Cl Mods 36, BA (3rd cl Th) 38, MA 41. Linc Th Coll 38. **d** 39 **p** 40 Dur. C of St Andr Monk Wearmouth 39-43; Chap RAFVR 43-47; V of Claverley 47-57; Leominster 57-80; RD of Leominster 60-80; Preb of Heref Cathl from 67; P-in-c of Eyton 69-80; *65 King's Acre Road, Hereford, HR4 0QL.*

RAINBOW, Henry David. b 10. Ripon Hall, Ox 64. **d** 65 Ox **p** 66 Reading for Ox. C of St Luke Reading 65-67; Asst Chap HM Pris Wormwood Scrubs 67-68; Chap HM Pris Cardiff 68-71; Chap HM Pris Pentonville 71-74; HM Pris Cant 74-78; Perm to Offic Dio Cant from 79. *21 Cavendish Road, Herne Bay, Kent.* (Herne Bay 2606)

RAINE, Patrick John Wallace. b 21. Sarum Wells Th Coll 72. **d** 74 **p** 75 Win. C of Chandlers Ford 74-76; R of Highclere w Ashmansworth and Crux Easton Dio Win from 76. *2 Flexford Close, Highclere, Newbury, Berks.* (Highclere 253991)

RAINES, William Guy. b 46. Univ Lon BSc 69, MSc 70. Univ of Ox BA (Th) 80. Ripon Coll Cudd 78. **d** 81 Willesden for Lon. C of W Drayton Dio Lon from 81. *31 Swan Road, West Drayton, Middx.* (W Drayton 42503)

RAINEY, William. Hur Coll. **d** 58 **p** 59 Tor. C of Ch Ch Deer Pk Tor 58-61; R of St Simon Highland Creek Tor 61-70; R of Port Hope Dio Tor from 70. *42 South Street, Port Hope, Ont., Canada.* (416-885 5276)

RAINSBERRY, Edward John. b 24. Trin Coll Dub BA (2nd cl Hist and Pol Sc) 48, Div Test 49, MA 58. **d** 49 **p** 50 Cork. C of Abbeystrawry U and Castlehaven 49-52; Chap RAF 52-58; V of Long Compton Dio Cov from 58; R of Whichford Dio Cov from 58. *Long Compton Vicarage, Shipston-on-Stour, Warws.* (Long Compton 207)

RAINSBURY, Albert Wolfe. b 15. TCD BA 35, Div Test 37, MA 39. **d** 38 Down **p** 39 Bp Kennedy for Down. C of Ballywillan 38-40; CF (EC) 40-46; Trav Sec Inter-Varsity Fellowship Scotld 46-51; V of Em S Croydon 51-69; Prin Belf Bible Coll 69-70; R of Knossington w Cold Overton 73-78; C-in-c of Owston w Withcote 73-78; Perm to Offic Dio Roch from 79. *20a Hillside Avenue, Frindsbury, Rochester, ME2 3DB.*

RAINSFORD, Barry Vere. Univ of Syd BEng 55. Moore Th Coll Syd ACT ThL 63. **d** 63 **p** 64 Syd. C of Ryde 63-64; Penrith 64-65; C-in-c of Pendle Hill 67-71; P-in-c of Coober Pedy 70-75; Cann River 76-80; R of Yarram Dio Gippsld from 80. *Rectory, Yarram, Vic, Australia 3971.*

RAINSFORD, Peter John. b 31. FCP 72. Qu Coll Birm 75. **d** 77 **p** 78 Lich. Hon C of St Chad City and Dio Lich 77-82; C from 82. *42 Brownsfield Road, Lichfield, Staffs, WS13 6BX.* (Lich 24375)

RAITH, Robert. b 31. Univ of Edin MA 61. Coll of Resurr Mirfield 57. **d** 59 **p** 60 Edin. C of St Jas Leith 59-61; St Mary Dalmahoy 61-65; Asst Prov Youth Org for Episc Ch in Scotld 61-65; C of Portobello 66-76; P-in-c of St Jas L Leith 76-77; Hon Dioc Super Dio Edin 77-78; P-in-c of Wester Hailes and Baberton 78-79. *6 Abercorn Avenue, Edinburgh, EH8 7HP.* (031-661 1387)

RAITT, Derek. b 41. K Coll Lon and Warm BD (2nd cl) and AKC (2nd cl) 63. **d** 64 Blackb **p** 65 Burnley for Blackb. C of St Jas Blackb 64-67; Burnley 67-69; V of Foulridge 69-74; Euxton Dio Blackb from 74. *Euxton Vicarage, Chorley, Lancs.* (Chorley 62102)

RAJARISON, Jean Harson. b 03. St Paul's Coll Ambatoharanana 71. **d** 71 Antan. d Dio Antan. *Santa Laurent, Ambohimanoro, Antananarivo, Madagascar.*

RAJARISON, Jean Harison. **d** 72 Antan. d Dio Antan. *Misiona Anglikana, Avaratr'anjoma, Avenue Marcel Olivier, Antananarivo, Madagascar.*

RAJARISON, Ralph Tesson. St Paul's Coll Ambat 57. **d** 61 **p** 62 Madag. P Dio Madag 61-69; Dio Antan from 69. *Ramainandro, Faratsiho, Madagascar.*

RAJIT, Frederick. St Francis Coll Brisb 58. **d** 59 **p** 60 Borneo. P Dio Borneo 59-62; Dio Kuch from 62. *St Mark's Church, Limbang, Sarawak, Malaysia.* (Limbang 2340)

RAJIT, Simon. b 51. Ho of Epiph Kuch 71. **d** 75 Kuch. d Dio Kuch. *St Augustine's Church, Betong, Sarawak, Malaysia.*

RAKAMBANA, Jean. St Paul's Coll Ambat. **d** 55 **p** 57 Madag. P Dio Madag 55-69; Dio Tam 69-79; Dio Toa from 79. *Befotaka, Malagasy Republic.*

RAKATOBE, Andre. St Paul's Coll Ambat. **d** 51 **p** 53 Madag. P Dio Madag 51-69; Dio Antan from 69. *Anjanaminovola, Antananario, Madagascar.*

RAKE, David John. b 47. Univ of Nottm BA 68, PhD 73. Wycl Hall Ox Dipl Th 73. **d** 74 **p** 75 Southw. C of Radcliffe-on-Trent 74-77; P-in-c of Upwell St Pet 77-79; P-in-c of Outwell 77-79; Chap Univ of Warw from 79. *92 De Montfort Way, Coventry, CV4 7DT.* (0203 411854)

RAKIONO, Mitchell. b 50. Bp Patteson Th Centre Kohimarama 70. **d** 73 **p** 74 Melan. P Dio Melan 73-75; Ysabel from 75. *Yandina, Russell Islands, Solomon Islands.*

RAKOENA, David Moeketsi. b 41. **d** 77 **p** 80 Bloemf (APM). C of St Mary Brandfort Dio Bloemf from 77. *599 Brandfort Location, Brandfort, OFS, S Africa.*

RAKOTOARIMANANA, Bery. **d** 77 **p** 78 Diego S. P Dio Diego S 77-79; Dio Antsir from 79. *Ampobibitaka, Malagasy Republic.*

RAKOTOARISON, Etienne. St Paul's Coll Ambat. **d** 54 **p** 55 Madag. P Dio Madag 54-69; Dio Antan 69-71. *Andranonanahary, Faratsiho, Madagascar.*

RAKOTOARIVONY, Celestin. St Andr Th Coll Marodimaka, 60. **d** 64 Bp Seth for Madag **p** 67 Madag. P Dio Madag 64-69; Dio Diego S 69-73; Dio Tam 73-79; Dio Toa from 79. *Anglican Mission, Fianarantsoa, Malagasy Republic.*

RAKOTOMALALA, Martin. **d** 75 **p** 77 Antan. P Dio Antan. *Andreba, Ambatondrazaka, Malagasy Republic.*

RAKOTOMALALA, Petera. **d** 76 Antan. d Dio Antan. *Avaratrakoholahy, Faratsiho, Malagasy Republic.*

RAKOTOMANGA, Thomas. St Paul's Coll Ambat. **d** 56 **p** 58 Madag. P Dio Madag 56-69; Dio Antan 69-76. *Morarano, Ambohmandry, Madagascar.*

RAKOTOMAVO, Elie Jean. St Paul's Coll Ambat. **d** 63 **p** 65 Madag. P Dio Madag 63-69; Dio Antan from 69. *Place d'Anjohy, Anjohy, Antananarivo, Madagascar.*

RAKOTONDRAMBONONA, Jean-Baptiste. St Paul's Coll Ambat 53. **d** and **p** 61 Madag. P Dio Madag 61-69; Dio Antan from 69. *Anjazafohy, Ambohidratrimo, Madagascar.*

RAKOTONIAINA, Emile Josefa. St Paul's Coll Ambatoharanana 65. **d** 70 **p** 72 Tam. P Dio Tam 72-79; Dio Toa from 79. *Ampahomanitra, Nosy Varika, Mananjary, Malagasy Republic.*

RAKOTOVAO, Petera. **d** 54 **p** 55 Madag. P Dio Madag 54-69; Dio Antan 69-76. *Ambohimanoro, Antananarivo, Madagascar.*

RAKOTOZAFY, Joseph. St Paul's Coll Ambat. **d** 54 **p** 55 Madag. P Dio Madag 55-69; Dio Diego-S 69-79; Dio Antsir from 79. *Perinet, Malagasy Republic.*

RALANE, Philip Mzoli. b 52. St Bede's Coll Umtata 77. **d** 78 **p** 80 St John's. P Dio St John's. *PO Box 1, Nqamakwe, Transkei.*

RALAWE, Douglas Roy. St Pet Coll Alice, 63. **d** 65 **p** 66 Kimb K. C of Upington 65-68; R 68-70; Hon Chap to Bp of Kimb 68-70; P-in-c of St Phil Graaff Reinet Dio Geo from 70. *463 Sobukwe Street, Graaf Reinet, CP, S Africa.* (Graaff Reinet 118)

RALISON, Jean. St Paul's Coll Ambat. **d** 45 **p** 47 Madag. C Dio Madag 45-47; P-in-c 47-62. *Ramainandro, Faratsiko, Madagascar.*

RALPH, Barrie Lawrence. Hur Coll 66. **d** 68 **p** 69 Tor. C of St Clem Eglinton Tor 68-72; R of Ajax 72-77; I of Collingwood Dio Tor from 77. *75 Ontario Street, Collingwood, Ont., Canada.* (705-445 2143)

RALPH, Charles. Trin Coll Dub BA 47, MA 58. **d** 47 **p** 48 Down. C of Kilmegan 47-49; Drumcree 49-50; I of Arboe 50-51; C of Armagh 51-53; I of Durrus 53-54; Kilcooley 54-58; V of St Cleopas Toxt Pk 58-62; I of Kilscoran U 62-64; R of Theberton Dio St E from 64; R of Middleton w Fordley Dio St E from 64. *Theberton Rectory, Leiston, Suff.* (Leiston 830692)

RALPH, Wilfred Francis. Qu Coll Newfld. **d** 39 **p** 40 Newfld. I of White Bay 40-44; Harbour Buffett 44-47; R of Petty Harbour 47-58; Thamesville 58-70; I of St D Windsor 70-73; Parkhill 73-78. *Box 361, Wheatley, Parkhill, Ont, Canada.*

RALPH-BOWMAN, Murray Peter. b 13. Qu Coll Cam BA 35, MA 45. Wells Th Coll 36. **d** 37 **p** 38 Chelmsf. C of Romford 37-41; Thorpe St Andr 41-45; R of Ashbrittle 45-57; W Camel 57-78; V of Qu Camel 57-78; C of Bryngwyn w Newchurch and Llanbedr Paincastle w Llanddewi Fach Dio Swan B from 78. *Rhos-Goch Rectory, Painscastle, Builth Wells, Powys.* (04975 260)

RALPHS, John Eric. b 26. St Cath S Ox BA 52, MA 56. Wycl Hall Ox. **d** 53 **Ox p** 54 Reading for Cant. C of Wolvercote 53-55; Asst Chap Radcliffe Hosp Ox 54-62; HM Pris Ox 58-61; Chap Dragon Sch Ox 55-68; Jun Chap Merton Coll Ox 59-62; Chap St Hugh's Coll Ox 62-66; L to Offic Dio Ox 55-66. *209 Woodstock Road,* (Psycho-Therapy Practice), *Oxford.* (Oxford 55550)

RALPHS, Robert Brian. b 31. Qu Coll Birm 75. **d** 78 **p** 79 Lich. C of St John Evang Wednesbury 78-80; St Paul Wednesbury Dio Lich from 80. *St Luke's House, Oldbury Street, Wednesbury, W Midl.*

RALSTON, Alexander James. **d** and **p** 59 Bath. C of Coonamble 59-60; Dubbo 60-65; R of Warren 65-68; Kandos w Portland 68-73; Chap Miss to Seamen Hobart Dio Tas from 73. *Hunter Street, Hobart, Tasmania 7000.* (002-34 6016)

✠ **RAMADHANI, Right Rev John Acland.** b 32. Univ of Birm Dipl Th 75. Univ of Dar-S BA 67. Qu Coll Birm 73. **d** 75 Birm **p** 76 Dar-S. Asst Chap Qu Coll Birm 75-76; Warden St Mark's Th Coll Dar-S 76-80; Cons Ld Bp of Zanz T at Tanga 27 Jan 80 by Abp of Tanzania; Bps of Dar-S, Ruv, S W Tang and Vic Nyan; Asst Bps of Centr Tang and Zanz T; and Bp Jumaa. *Bishop's Lodge, PO Box 35, Korogwe, Tanzania.* (Korogwe 22)

RAMAGE, John Eric. Univ of Wales, BA (2nd cl Hist) 28. St Mich Coll Llan. **d** 30 **p** 31 Ban. C of Llanllyfni 30-33; Llandegfan w Beaumaris 33-38 (and Llanfaes V from 50); R 38-76; RD of Tindaethwy 48-76; Surr 51-77; Can of Ban 55-77; Preb of Ban Cathl 59-77; Perm to Offic Dio Ban from 77. *Eryl Mor, Menai Bridge, Anglesey, Gwyn.*

RAMANAMBOLA, Philippe. **d** 28 **p** 32 Madag. P Dio Madag 28-62. *Mananjary, Madagascar.*

RAMANITRERA, Stefana. b 25. St Aug Coll Mahanoro 63. **d** 70 **p** 72 Tam. P Dio Tam 72-79; Dio Toa from 79. *Ambinanindrano, Mahanora, Malagasy Republic.*

RAMAROKOTO, Jakoba. St Paul's Coll Ambat 51. **d** 60 **p** 61 Madag. P Dio Madag 60-69; Dio Diego-S 69-71; Dio Antan from 71. *Faratsiho, Gare-Sambaina, Madagascar.*

RAMASAMY, Canon Nathaniel Seenuvassen. St Paul's Coll Maur. **d** and **p** 24 Maur. P Dio Maur from 24; Can of Maur 63-76; Can (Emer) from 76; Dom Chap to Bp of Maur 64-74. *23 Mallac Street, Rose Hill, Mauritius.* (4-2134)

RAMATALOU, David. St Pet Coll Siota. **d** 57 **p** 60 Melan. P Dio Melan 57-75; Dio Malaita from 75. *Bio, Malaita, Solomon Islands.*

RAMDEEN, Paul Mootiram. **d** 67 **p** 76 Trinid. C of San Fernando 67-76; P-in-c of Toco Dio Trinid from 76. *St David's Rectory, Toco, Trinidad, W Indies.*

RAMELL, Arthur Lewis. b 05. Cudd Coll 50. **d** 51 **p** 52 Bris. C of St Mark Swindon 51-56; R of Colerne 56-76; C-in-c of N Wraxall 68-76. *4 Tatlings Road, Steventon, Abingdon, Oxon.*

RAMELL, John Edwin. b 25. Univ of Bris BA 55. Tyndale Hall Bris. **d** 56 **p** 57 Cov. C of New Milverton 56-60; V of Wombridge 60-70; Chell Dio Lich 70-80; Team R from 80. *Chell Vicarage, Stoke-on-Trent, Staffs, ST6 6JT.* (Stoke-on-Trent 88708)

RAMILSON, Léon. St Paul's Coll Ambat. **d** 38 **p** 44 Madag. P Dio Madag 38-69; Dio Tam from 69. *Vatomandry, Madagascar.*

RAMM, Norwyn MacDonald. b 24. Linc Coll Ox BA (4th cl Th) 60, MA 64. St Pet Coll Jamaica 49. **d** 51 **p** 52 Jamaica. C of Montego Bay 51-53; R of Stony Hill w Mount James 53-57; C of St Mich City and Dio Ox 57-61; V from 61; C-in-c of St Martin and All SS Ox 61-71; Chap HM Pris Ox from 75. *24 St Michael's Street, Oxford, OX1 2EB.* (Oxford 42444)

RAMOABI, Bennett Tsokolo. **d** 65 **p** 66 Johann. P Dio Johann. *PO Box 19, Orlando 1804, Transvaal, S Africa.*

RAMOLEHE, Ernest Pule Charles. St Pet Coll Rosettenville 58. **d** 60 **p** 68 Bloemf. P Dio Bloemf. *Box 2027, Zamdela, OFS, S Africa.*

RAMOLEHE, Jeremiah Mohanoe. St Bede's Coll Umtata 59. **d** 60 **p** 62 Bloemf. P Dio Bloemf. *Box 2, Brandpan 9471, S Africa.*

RAMOSIE, Ernest Charles. St Pet Coll Rosettenville LTh 56. **d** 53 **p** 54 Basuto. P Dio Les. *Mohales Hoek, Lesotho, S Africa.*

RAMOSIME, Cyprian Lucas Nkokoto. b 27. **d** 78 Bp Stanage for Johann **p** 79 Johann (NSM). C of Pimville Dio Johann from 78. *PO Box 147, Kliptown, S Africa 1812.*

RAMPAI, Petrose Lesege. St Pet Coll Rosettenville 59. **d** 61 **p** 62 Bloemf. P Dio Bloemf 61-74; Dio Kimb K 74-77. *PO Box 103, Barkly West, CP, S Africa.*

RAMPTON, Paul Michael. b 47. St Jo Coll Dur BA 69, Dipl Th 70, MA 73. Wycl Hall Ox 72. **d** 73 **p** 74 Cant. C of H Trin w Ch Ch Folkestone 73-77; P-in-c of Ringwould w Oxney 77-79; Kingsdown 77-79; R of Ringwould w Kingsdown Dio Cant from 79. *Kingsdown Rectory, Upper Street, Kingsdown, Deal, Kent, CT14 8BJ.* (Deal 3951)

RAMSAY, Alan Burnett. b 34. K Coll Lon and Warm AKC (2nd cl) and Barry Prize 62. **d** 63 **p** 64 S'wark. C of Clapham 63-67; Warlingham w Chelsham and Farleigh 67-71; Parish Pr of Stockwell 71-78; V of Lingfield Dio S'wark from 78. *Vicarage, Vicarage Road, Lingfield, Surrey, RH7 6HA.* (Lingfield 832021)

RAMSAY, Jack. b 05. ALCD 33. **d** 33 **p** 34 Lon. C of St Andr Thornhill Square Islington 33-35; St Luke Southsea 35-38; V of St Mary, Birkenhead 38-40; St Paul Walcot Bath 40-51; R of Cucklington w Stoke Trister and Bayford 51-57; V of Portbury 57-70; R of Easton-in-Gordano (w Portbury and Clapton-in-Gordano from 70) 57-80. *10 Priory Gardens, Easton-in-Gordano, Bristol, BS20 0PF.* (Pill 2380)

RAMSAY, James. Moore Th Coll Syd ACT ThL 69. **d** 69 **p** 70 Syd. C of Dundas 69-70; Gladesville 70-72; Beverly Hills 72-75; C-in-c of Bexley N Dio Syd 75-79; R from 79. *366 Bexley Road, Bexley North, NSW, Australia.* (50-5949)

RAMSAY, Canon James Ancil Hugh. Codr Coll Barb 47. **d** 53 **p** 54 Ja. C of St Luke Cross Roads 53-55; C-in-c of St Margaret's Bay and of Hope Bay 55-57; P-in-c of Snowdon 57-63; Asst Master and Asst Chap Kingston Coll Ja 63-64; Chap from 64; C of Spanish Town Cathl Dio Ja from 67; Can of Ja from 80. *25 Knightsdale Drive, Kingston 8, Jamaica, W Indies.* (093-53547)

RAMSAY, John Leslie. Linc Th Coll 54. **d** 56 **p** 57 Linc. C of L Coates 56-59; V of Colton 59-62; Keelby 62-71; V of Riby 62-71; Hogsthorpe and Mumby 71-76; Perm to Offic Dio Linc from 76. *61 Clive Avenue, Boultham Park, Lincoln, LN6 7UR.* (Lincoln 36081)

RAMSAY, Kenneth William. b 18. ALCD 48. **d** 52 **p** 53 Lon. C of St John Southall 52-57; Asst Chap Lee Abbey Lynton 57-60; Perm to Offic Dio S'wark 60-69; Dio Portsm from 69; Dio Sarum from 77. *57 Dorchester Road, Lytchett Minster, Poole, Dorset, BH16 6JE.*

RAMSBOTHAM, George Haviland. **d** 67 **p** 68 Bom. P Dio Bom 67-71; Perm to Offic Dio Melb from 71. *17 St Huberts Road, Glenhuntly, Vic, Australia 3163.* (211-9261)

✠ **RAMSBOTHAM, Right Rev John Alexander.** b 06. Late Choral Scho of CCC Cam 2nd cl Hist Trip pt i 26, BA (1st cl Th Trip pt i) 28, MA 32. DD (Lambeth) 58. Wells Th Coll. **d** 29 **p** 30 Lon. C of All H Lombard Street Lon 29-32; Miss Sec SCM 30-32; PV of Wells Cathl 33-36; Chap Wells Th Coll 33-34; Vice-Prin 34-36; Warden of Coll of Ascen Selly Oak 36-41; R of Ordsall 41-42; V of St Geo Jesmond Newc T 42-50; Exam Chap to Bp of Newc T 47-50; to Bp of Dur 50-58; Archd of Auckld and Can of Dur 50-58; Cons Ld Bp Suffr of Jarrow in York Minster 2 February 50 by Abp of York; Bps of Dur; Sheff; Newc T; Man; and Wakef; Bps Suffr of Whitby; Grantham; Selby; and Pontefract; and Bps Weller, Hubbard, and Dunlop; Trld to Wakef 58; res 67; Asst Bp of Newc T 68-76. *13 Hextol Terrace, Hexham, Northumb, NE46 2DF.* (Hexham 602607)

RAMSBOTTOM, Albert Ernest. b 16. Univ of Lon BD 39. ALCD 39. **d** 39 **p** 40 Birm. C of Hall Green Birm 39-50; Bromley 50-51; L to Offic at St Pet Conv Distr Bexleyheath 51-55; Min 55-57; V 57-62; H Trin Beckenham 62-75; R of Mereworth w W Peckham Dio Roch from 75. *Mereworth Rectory, Maidstone, Kent.* (Maidstone 812214)

RAMSBURY, Lord Bishop Suffragan of. *See* Neale, Right Rev John Robert Geoffrey.

RAMSDEN, Arthur Stuart. b 34. Kelham Th Coll 56. **d** 61 **p** 62 Wakef. C of Featherstone 61-63; St Pet Barnsley 63-67; V of St Thos Halifax 67-70; Middlestown w Netherton 70-76; Purston w S Featherstone Dio Wakef from 76; M Gen Syn from 80. *Purston Vicarage, Pontefract, W Yorks, WF7 5EZ.* (Pontefract 792288)

RAMSDEN, Preb Francis Samuel Lloyd. b 12. Univ of Cam 28. Lon Coll of Div 31. **d** 35 **p** 37 S'wark. C of St Jas W Streatham 35-37; Bushbury 37-41; St Bart Wednesbury 41-45; V of Brown Edge 45-50; Stretton w Wetmoor 50-58; Surr 54-77; V of Trentham 58-77; RD of Trentham 63-77; Preb of Lich Cathl 69-77; Preb (Emer) from 77; Team V of St Helen Solihull 77-80; Perm to Offic Dio Birm from 80. *72 Northdown Road, Solihull, W Midl, B91 3ND.* (021-705 8923)

RAMSDEN, Peter Stockton. b 51. Univ of Lon BSc 74. Dipl Th (Leeds) 76. Coll of Resurr Mirfield 74. **d** 77 **p** 78 Dur. C of Houghton-le-Spring 77-80; W Harton Dio Dur from 80. *c/o All Saints Vicarage, West Harton, South Shields, T & W NE34 0NF.*

RAMSDEN, Raymond Leslie. b 49. Oak Hill Lon 75. **d** 78 Lon **p** 79 Willesden for Lon. C of St Jo Bapt Greenhill Harrow Dio Lon from 78. *20 Manor Court, Bonnersfield Lane, Harrow, Middx.*

✠ **RAMSEY of CANTERBURY, Right Rev and Right Hon Lord Arthur Michael.** b 04. PC 56. Late Scho of Magd Coll Cam 2nd cl Cl Trip pt i 25, BA (1st cl Th Trip pt i) 27, MA 30, BD 50, Hon DD 57. Univ of Dur Hon DD 51. Univ of Edin Hon DD 57. Univ of Leeds Hon DD 57. Univ of Hull Hon DD 57. Univ of Ox Hon DCL 60. Univ of Man Hon DD 61. Univ of Lon Hon DD 62. Gen Th Sem NY Hon DST 62. Columbia Univ Hon DST 62. Occidental Coll Calif Hon LLD 62. Virginia Th Sem Hon DD 62. Hur Coll Hon DD 63. Trin Coll Tor Hon DD 63. Univ of Cant NZ Hon LLD 65. Univ of Kent Hon DCL 66. Mem Univ of Newfld Hon DLitt 66. K Coll NS Hon DD 66. Univ of Keele Hon DLitt 67. Institut Catholique Paris Hon DTh 67. Pacific Lutheran Univ USA Hon DD 67. Episc Th Sch Cam USA Hon DD 67. Yonsei Univ Korea Hon DD 73. D of Humanities St Paul's Univ Tokyo 73. Univ of Salamanca Hon DTh 77. Univ of the South Tenn Hon DD 78. Cudd Coll 27. **d** 28 **p** 29 Liv. C of St Nich Liv 28-30; Sub-Warden of Linc Th Coll 30-36; Exam Chap to Bp of Ches 32-38; to Bp of Dur 40-50; to Bp of Linc 51-52; Lect of Boston 36-38; V of St Benedict Cam 38-40; Can of Dur Cathl 40-50; Prof of Div Univ of Dur 40-50; Regius Prof of Div Univ of Cam and Fell of Magd Coll Cam 50-52; Hon Fell from 52; Preb and Can of Caistor in Linc Cathl 51-52; Select Pr Univ of Cam 34, 40, 48, 59, 64 and 70; Ox 45-47; Cons Ld Bp of Dur in York Minster 29 Sept 52 by Abp of York; Bps of Sheff, Newc T, Southw, Blackb, Carl, Man, Wakef, Edin, Linc, and Ely; Bps Suffr of Grimsby, Whitby, Selby, Lanc, Warrington, Knaresborough, Pontefract, and Jarrow; and Bps Hubbard, Gerard, and Weller; Trld to York 56; to Cant (Abp, Primate of All England, and Metrop) 61; res Nov 74; Created Life Baron 74. *16 South Bailey, Durham.*

RAMSEY, Canon Frederick Arthur. Bp's Univ Lennox LST 23. **d** 22 Niag for Koot **p** 23 Koot. V of U Arrow Lake 23-26; Alberni 26-28; C of Ch Ch Cathl Vic 28-31; R of St Steph W Vancouver 31-41; Chap CASF 41-45; R of St Geo Vancouver 45-50; Chap Shaughnessy Mil Hosp Vancouver 50-62; Hon Can of New Westmr 59-62. *Apt 4, 2970 Oak Street, Vancouver 9, BC, Canada.*

✠ **RAMSEY, Right Rev Kenneth Venner.** b 09. Late Scho of Univ Coll Ox 1st cl Cl Mods 29, BA (1st cl Th) and Liddon Stud 31, MA 34. Univ of Man Sen Bp Lee Pri 32, BD (w distinc) and Scho in Th 33. **d** 33 **p** 34 Man. C of Stretford 33-35; Lect Univ of Man and Vice-Prin Egerton Hall Man 35-38; Vice-Prin of Bp Wilson Th Coll IM 38-39; Prin of Egerton Hall Man 39-41; V of Peel 41-48; R of Em Didsbury 48-55; Exam Chap to Bp of Man 41-53; Surr from 49; Hon Can of Man 50-53; Proc Conv Man 50-55; RD of Heaton 50-53; Cons Ld Bp Suffr of Hulme in York Minster 28th October 53 by Abp of York; Bps of Southw; Ripon; Man; and Wakef; Bps Suffr of Penrith; Pontefract; and Middleton; res 75; Hon Asst Bp of Man from 75. *41 Bradwell Drive, Heald Green, Cheadle, Chesh SK8 3BX.* (061-437 8612)

RAMSEY, Stuart John Andrew. b 46. St Jo Coll Dur BA 69. Wycl Hall Ox 69. **d** 74 Stepney for Lon **p** 75 Lon. C of Stoke Newington 74-77; Hersham 77-79; Hon C of Thames Ditton Dio Guildf from 79. *23 New Row, Covent Garden, WC2.* (01-836 2217)

RAMSEY, Thomas Alfred. Univ of Tor BASc 45. McGill Univ Montr BD 54. Montr Dioc Th Coll LTh 54. **d** 54 **p** 55 Montr. C of Trin Mem Ch Montr 54-58; P-in-c of Otterburn Pk (w St Bruno 58-66) 58-66; I 66-67; R of Chambly 67-80; I of St Marg and St Cypr City and Dio Montr from 80. *8535 De Teck Street, Montreal, PQ, Canada.* (514-352 9080)

RANAIVOJAONA, Jaona. **d** 48 **p** 49 Madag. P Dio Madag 48-69; Dio Tam 69-73; Dio Antan from 73. *Malaza, Ambohimanga, Antananarivo, Madagascar.*

RANDALL, Bryson. Univ of BC BA 68. Vanc Sch of Th 71. **d** 71 Qu'App. C of Pipestone 71-73; I of Notukeu 73-76; Wadena 76-77; CF (Canad) from 77. *c/o CFH Dept National Defence, Ottawa, Ont, Canada.*

RANDALL, Clarence Clifton. b 10. Mem Univ Newfld BA 54. **d** and **p** 68 Newfld. C of Corner Brook 68-71; I of Bay D'Espoir 71-74; Bell Island 73-76. *Terrace Apts, 64 Grand Falls, Newfoundland, Canada.*

RANDALL, Colin Michael Sebastian. b 50. Univ of Aston in Birm BSc 72. Qu Coll Birm 72. **d** 75 Man **p** 76 Hulme for Man. C of Tonge w Alkrington 75-78; Elton Dio Man from 78. *St Francis House, Hebburn Drive, Throstle Grove, Bury, Lancs, BL8 1EB.* (061-764 4817)

RANDALL, David William. b 47. Sarum Th Coll 68. **d** 71 **p** 72 Stepney for Lon. C of Poplar 71-75; Lect and Youth Chap at St Botolph's Aldgate 75-77; Team V of Notting Hill Dio Lon from 77. *St Clement's House, Sirdar Road, W11 4EQ.* (01-727 5450)

RANDALL, Canon Edmund Laurence. Late Sch of CCC Cam BA 40, 1st cl Th Trip pt i 47, MA 47. Wells Th Coll 47. **d** 49 **p** 50 Win. C of St Luke Bournemouth 49-52; L to Offic Dio Ely 52-59; Fell and Lect Selw Coll Cam 52-57; Chap 53-57; Exam Chap to Bp of Lich 53-60; Prin Ely Th Coll and Can Res of Ely 57-59; Select Pr Univ of Cam 57; Chap St Francis Coll Brisb 60-64; Warden St Barn Th Coll Belair Dio Adel from 64; Commiss N Queensld from 67; Hon Can of Adel from 79. *St Barnabas's Theological College, Belair, S Australia 5052.* (08-278 3418)

RANDALL, Harold Frederick George. Univ of Newc BA 67. St Francis Coll Nundah ACT ThL (2nd cl) 39. **d** 39 **p** 40 Bath. C of Cowra 39-41; R of Trundle 41-44; Coonamble 44-50; Port Moresby 50-58; Sub-Dean and Can Res of Pro-Cathl Port Moresby 55-58; R of Adamstown 58-72; Perm to Offic Dio Melb from 72. *Unit 6, 9-11 Radcliffe Avenue, Cheltenham, Vic, Australia 3192.*

RANDALL, Ian Neville. b 39. Late Sch of Or Coll Ox 2nd cl Cl Mods 60, BA (3rd cl Lit Hum) 62, 2nd cl Th 64, MA 65. St Steph Ho Ox 62. **d** 65 **p** 66 Lon. C of Perivale 65-68; St Jo Div Walham Green Fulham 68-73; Cowley (in c of St Francis) Dio Ox 73-79; Team V from 79. *St Francis House, Hollow Way, Headington, Oxford.* (Oxford 779179)

RANDALL, James Anthony. b 36. AIB 69. Univ of Kent Dipl Th 80. Ridley Hall Cam 68. **d** 70 **p** 71 Roch. C of Rusthall 70-74; V of Shorne 74-79; Bexleyheath Dio Roch from 79. *Christ Church Vicarage, Bexleyheath, Kent.* (01-303 3260)

RANDALL, John Randall. b 28. Univ of Lon BD 64. ALCD 60 (LTh from 74). **d** 60 **p** 61 Guildf. C of St Jo Bapt Woking 60-62; High Wycombe (in c of St Andr) 62-65; V of Patchway 65-73; P-in-c of Olveston w Aust 73-80; Warden Roch Dioc Conf and Retreat Ho Chislehurst from 80; Hon Chap to Bp of Roch from 81. *c/o Diocesan Registrar, The Precinct, Rochester, Kent.*

RANDALL, John Terence. b 29. St Cath Coll Cam BA 52, MA 59. Ely Th Coll 52. **d** 54 **p** 55 St Alb. C of Ch Ch Luton 54; Dunstable 54-57; H Trin w St Mary Ely (in c of St Pet) 57-60; St John March 60-62; Area Sec UMCA S Midls 62-64; USPG Dios Cov and Birm 65-76; Publ Pr Dio Cov 62-76; Perm to Offic Dio Birm 62-76; P-in-c of Fenny Compton 76-78; Avon Dassett w Farnborough 76-78; R of Avon Dassett w Farnborough & Fenny Compton Dio Cov from 78. *Avon Dassett Rectory, Leamington Spa, Warws, CV33 0AR.* (029 589305)

RANDALL, Kelvin John. b 49. AKC and BD 71. St Jo Coll Nottm 73. **d** 74 **p** 75 S'wark. C of Peckham 74-78; Ch Ch Portsdown Dio Portsm from 78; Commun Chap Crookhorn Ch Centre Purbrook from 79. *10 Crookhorn Lane, Purbrook, Hants.* (Waterlooville 2429)

RANDALL, Martin Trevor. b 51. St Jo Coll Dur BA 74. Trin Coll Bris 74. **d** 77 **p** 78 Ches. C of St Mary Ashton-on-Mersey 77-80; St Sav w St Cuthb Everton Dio Liv from 80. *26 Heyes Street, Liverpool, L5 6SG.* (051-264 8071)

RANDALL, Philip Joseph. b 10. St Bonif Coll Warm 57. **d** 58 **p** 59 Pet. C of St Mark Pet 58-61; V of Eye 61-77. *104 Deerleap, Bretton, Peterborough, PE3 6YD.*

RANDALL, Thomas Augustus Alexander. Fourah Bay Coll. **d** 43 **p** 45 Sier L. Miss at Mano 46-48; Bauya 48-50; Bonthe 50-57; I of St Patr Kissy 57-66. *c/o PO Box 128, Freetown, Sierra Leone.*

RANDALL, William Alfred. b 14. Univ of Lon BD (2nd cl) 41. AKC (2nd cl) and Jun McCaul Hebr Pri 41. **d** 41 **p** 42 Chelmsf. C of Laindon w Basildon 41-44; V of H Trin Harrow Green 44-50; R of Goldhanger w L Totham 50-61; V of Aveley 61-73; R of Wickford 73-79; P-in-c of Runwell 75-79. *43 Tunbridge Crescent, Liphook, Hants.*

RANDELL, John Harrison. b 35. BD (Lon) 62. Chich Th Coll 77. **d** and **p** 78 Blackb. C of Ribbleton 78-81; V of St Lawr Barton Dio Blackb from 82. *St Lawrence Vicarage, Garstang Road, Barton, Preston, Lancs.* (Broughton 8602020)

RANDELL, Murray Gordon. Qu Coll Newfld 56. **d** 60 **p** 61 Newfld. C-in-c of Brooklyn 60-62; St Mary Virg St John's 62-66; Chap Mem Univ Newfld 66-80; I of Mt Pearl Dio E Newfld from 80. *149 Park Avenue, Mount Pearl, Newfoundland, Canada.*

RANDELL, Phillip John. b 45. Dipl Th (Lon) 68, BD (Lon) 73. Linc Th Coll 67. **d** 68 **p** 69 Bris. C of Henbury w Hallen 68-71; C of Summertown 71-73; Liskeard w St Keyne 73-75; Chap Coll of St Mark and St John Plymouth 75-79; L to Offic Dio Ex 76-79; Tutor St Mark's Th Coll Dar-S from 80. *Box 25017, Dar-es-Salaam, Tanzania.*

RANDERSON, John Richard. Univ of Otago, NZ BA 61, MA (2nd cl Gr) 62, BD 65. St Jo Coll Auckld 62. **d** 64 **p** 65 Auckld. C of Papakura 64-68; in Amer Ch 69-70; C of Egglescliffe 70-71; Dir Inter-Ch Trade and Ministry Miss Auckld 71-78; Exam Chap to Bp of Auckld 72-78; Hon C of St Alb Balmoral 73-78; V of St Pet City and Dio Wel from 78. *327 The Terrace, Wellington, NZ.* (843-250)

RANDLE, Barry Edward. b 53. McMaster Univ Ont BA 74. Hur Coll Lon MDiv 77. **d** 77 Bp Robinson for Hur **p** 77 Ott. C of St Matt Ott 77-80; I of Kazabazua and Danford Lake Dio Ott from 80. *Box 52, Kazabazua, PQ, Canada.*

RANDLE, Canon Howard Stanley. St Jo Coll Dur LTh 34, BA 35. St Aid Coll 30. **d** 35 **p** 36 Bradf. C of St John Gt Horton Bradf 35-38; St Jas New Brighton 38-41; CF (EC) 41-45; R of Mobberley 46-80; Proc Conv Ches 59-64; RD of Knutsford 65-80; Hon Can of Ches 69-80; Can (Emer) from 80. *c/o Rectory, Mobberley, Chesh.* (Mobberley 3218)

RANDOLPH, Ven Thomas Berkeley. b 04. Late Scho of Qu Coll Ox BA (2nd cl Th) 27, MA 32. Cudd Coll 27. **d** 28 **p** 29 Portsm. C of St Mary Portsea 28-33; Chap (Eccles Est) St Paul's Cathl Calc 34-37; furlough 37-38; V of Eastleigh 38-46; St Mary Virg w All SS St Sav and St Mark Reading 46-59; Proc Conv Ox 50-55; Hon Can of Ch Ch Ox 57-59; Archd of Heref 59-70; Archd (Emer) from 70; V of Wel 59-61; Preb of Heref Cathl 59-70; Can Res of Heref 61-70. *14 Heatherwood, Midhurst, Sussex.* (Midhurst 2765)

RANDRIAMANANTENA, Wilson. St Paul's Coll Ambat. **d** 53 **p** 54 Madag. P Dio Madag 54-69; Dio Diego S 69-79; Antsir from 79; VG of Diego S 77-79; Antsir from 79. *Box 169, Mahajanga, Malagasy Republic.*

RANDRIAMISAINA, Samuel. St Paul's Coll Ambat. **d** 50 **p** 53 Madag. P-in-c Dio Madag 50-69; Dio Antan 69-74. *Ankadiefajoro, Antananarivo, Malagasy Republic.*

RANDRIANARISOA, Joseph. St Paul's Coll Ambat 56. **d** 58 **p** 59 Madag. P Dio Madag 58-69; Dio Antan from 69. *c/o La Mission Anglicane, Antananarivo, Madagascar.*

RANDRIANASOLO, Alfred. St Paul's Coll Ambat. **d** 45 **p** 47 Madag. P Dio Madag 45-69; Dio Antan from 69. *Anglican Mission, Ambanidia, Antananarivo, Madagascar.*

RANDRIANASOLO, Jean-Baptiste. b 40. St Aug Coll Mahanoro 63. **d** 70 **p** 72 Tam. P Dio Tam 72-79; Dio Toa from 79. *Soanierana, Toamasina, Malagasy Republic.*

✠ **RANDRIANOVONA, Right Rev Ephraim.** St Paul's Coll Ambat. **d** 45 **p** 47 Madag. P Dio Madag 45-69; Dio Antan 69-75; Sub-Dean of St Laur Cathl Antan 73-75; Dean from 75; VG Dio Antan 74-75; Cons Ld Bp of Antan in St Laur Cathl Antan 5 Oct 75 by Abp of Prov of the Indian Ocean; Bps of Diego S and Sey; and Bp Marcel. *Eveche Anglican, Ambohimanoro, Tananarive, Malagasy Republic.*

RANFORD, Redvers John. b 1900. Lich Th Coll. **d** 65 Shrewsbury for Lich **p** 66 Lich. C of Wem Dio Lich from 65. *14 Tilley Road, Wem, Shrewsbury, Shropshire.* (Wem 32230)

RANGIIHU, Hamiora. MBE 78. St Jo Coll Auckld. **d** 36 **p** 37 Wai. C Dio Wai 36-37; V 37-40; Tekaha 40-45; Taupo 45-47; Ohinemutu 47-53 and 55-57; CF Korea 53-55; V of Wairoa-Mohaka Maori Distr 57-68; Hon Can of Wai 58-74; Can 74-78; V of Waipatu-Moteo Past 68-77; P-in-c 77-78; Perm to Offic Dio Wai from 78. *c/o Hukarere Hostel, Napier Terrace, Napier, NZ.*

RANGOON, Lord Bishop of. *See* Hla Gyaw, Most Rev Gregory.

RANKEN, John Peter. Univ of Leeds BA 57. Coll of Resurr Mirfield. **d** 59 **p** 60 York. C of St Aid Middlesbrough 59-62; St Osw Middlesbrough 62-65; Industr Chap Dio York 62-67; w Mindolo Ecumen Found Kitwe 68-75. *c/o Regional Health Authority, Randolph House, Croydon.*

RANKEN, Michael David. b 28. Univ of Man BSc Tech 49. SOC 76. **d** 79 **p** 80 Guildf (APM). C of St Martin Epsom Dio Guildf from 79. *9 Alexandra Road, Epsom, Surrey, KT17 4BH.*

RANKIN, Dennis. b 29. Keble Coll Ox BA 53, MA 62. St Steph Ho Ox 53. **d** 55 **p** 56 Liv. C of St Steph w St Cath Liv 55-57; Boxmoor 57-59; St Martin Brighton 59-62; C-in-c of St Richard's Conv Distr Langney Eastbourne 62-69; V of St Thos Hove Dio Chich from 69. *18 Nizells Avenue, Hove, Sussex.* (Hove 736389)

RANKIN, John Cooper. b 24. Univ of Glas MA 44. Univ of Lon BD 53. Edin Th Coll 48. **d** 50 **p** 51 Brech. C of St Mary Magd Dundee 50-52; Chap R Merchant Navy Sch Bear Wood 53-60; Asst Master Bris Cathl Sch and Min Can of Bris Cathl 60-66; L to Offic Dio Bris 61-66; Dio Lich 66-69; Sen Lect Madeley Coll 66-69; Prin Lect Bp Otter Coll Chich from 69. *28 Worcester Road, Chichester, Sussex.*

RANKIN, Richard Barraclough. b 03. St Jo Coll Dur BA and Van Mildert Scho 36, MA 39. **d** 37 **p** 38 Dur. C of Gateshead Fell 37-45; V of St Silas Byker Newc T 45-73. *27 Broomlee Road, Killingworth, Newcastle upon Tyne.*

RANKIN, Robert Paterson. b 11. Edin Th Coll 46. **d** 48 **p** 49 Arg Is for Glas. C of St Jo Evang Greenock 48-50; CF 50-58; V of Woodhouse Eaves Dio Leic from 58; C-in-c of Woodhouse Dio Leic 58-61; V from 61. *Woodhouse Eaves Vicarage, Loughborough, Leics.* (Woodhouse Eaves 890226)

RANKIN, William David. Univ of Tor Wycl Coll Tor LTh 66. **d** 66 **p** 67 Calg. C of Lethbridge 66-68; I of Mayo 68-70; on leave 71-74; I of Porcupine Plain Dio Sktn rom 75. *Box 5, Porcupine Plain, Sask, Canada.*

RANKIN, William John Alexander. b 45. Univ of Dur BA 68. Fitzw Coll Cam BA (Th) 73, MA 77. Westcott Ho Cam 71. **d** 74 **p** 75 Lon. C of St John's Wood 74-78; Asst Master & Chap Clifton Coll Bris from 78. *6 College Fields, Clifton, Bristol.* (Bris 738490)

RANN, Harry Harvey. b 18. Sarum Th Coll 47. **d** 50 Barking for Chelmsf **p** 51 Chelmsf. C of Ascen Vic Dks 50-52; Christchurch 52-56; John Keble Ch Mill Hill 56-57; V of St Jas Woolfold Bury 57-62; Dean's Chap and PV of Ex Cathl 62-77; Sacr 65-77; Succr 73-77; V of Colyton Dio Ex from 77. *Vicarage, Colyton, Devon.* (Colyton 52307)

RANSOM, Ivan Frederick. b 41. Moore Coll ACT ThL 68. **d** and **p** 70 Armid. C of Inverell 70-73; V of Boggabilla 73-80. *c/o Vicarage, Boggabilla, NSW, Australia 2409.*

RANSOME, Arthur. b 21. St Jo Coll Nottm 71. **d** and **p** 72 Jer. Chap and Warden Stella Carmel Conf Centre Haifa 72-76; C of Virginia Water 76-79; P-in-c of Shackleford Dio Guildf from 79; Peper Harow Dio Guildf from 79. *Shackleford Rectory, Godalming, Surrey, GU8 6AE.* (Godalming 21423)

RANSON, Arthur Frankland. b 50. St Jo Coll Dur BA 73. Wycl Hall Ox 73. **d** 75 Burnley for Blackb **p** 76 Blackb. C of Bare Morecambe 75-78; Scotforth 78-81; V of St Ambrose Leyland Dio Blackb from 81. *St Ambrose Vicarage, Moss Lane, Leyland, Preston, Lancs.* (Leyland 21150)

RANSON, Terence William James. b 42. K Coll Lon and Warm AKC (2nd cl) 64. **d** 65 Warrington for Liv **p** 66 Liv. C of Walton-on-the-Hill 65-69; St Mary-le-Tower Ipswich 69-71; Chap Mersey Miss to Seamen 71-74; V of St Thos N Keyham Devonport 74-79; Chap RNR 78-79; Sen Chap Miss to Seamen Fremantle and State Sec Miss to Seamen W Austr from 79; Perm to Office Dios Bunb and Perth from 79. *12 Pannell Street, Bateman, W Australia 6153.* (332-4846)

RANSON, William John Robert. b 49. Univ of Tor LTh 78. Wycl Coll Tor 76. **d** 78 **p** 79 Fred. C of St Paul St John 78-80; I of Andover Dio Fred from 80. *Box 1076, Perth-Andover, NB, Canada E0J 1V0.*

RANTISI, Audeh. **d** 68 **p** 69 Jordan. P Dio Jordan 68-76; Dio Jer from 76. *PO Box 142, Ramallah, via Israel.*

RANWELL, Reginald Frederick. St Columb's Hall, Wang ACT ThL 28, Th Scho 59. **d** 28 **p** 29 Wang. C of Cobram 28-29; Albury 29-31; P-in-c of Dawson w Callide Valleys 32-33; St Mich AA Kingaroy 33-35; St Mary Kilcoy 35-41; R of Inglewood 41-44; St Alb Gatton 44-50; V of Coolangatta 50-52; R 53-74; Perm to Offic Dio Brisb from 75. *Karen Street, Jacobs Wells, Queensland, Australia 4207.* (Gold Coast 46 2360)

RANYARD, Michael Taylor. b 43. Univ of Nottm BTh 74. Linc Th Coll 72. **d** 74 **p** 75 Southw. C of Sutton-in-Ashfield 74-76; Hon C of St Mary Lewisham 76-77; Rushmere 77-79; R of Hopton-by-Thetford w Mkt Weston and Barningham w Coney Weston Dio St E from 79. *Hopton Rectory, Diss, Norf.* (Garboldisham 210)

RAPHAEL, Timothy John. b 29. Univ of Leeds BA 53. Coll of Resurr Mirfield. **d** 55 **p** 56 Lon. C of St Steph w St John Westmr 55-60; V of St Mary Welling 60-63; St Mich AA

Ch Ch 63-65; Dean and V of St Paul's Cathl Dun 65-72; V of St John's Wood Ch Dio Lon from 72; Commiss Waik from 73; Auckld from 75; Dun from 76. *St John's House, St John's Wood, NW8 7NE.* (01-722 4378)

RAPHOE, Bishop of. *See* Derry.

RAPHOE, Archdeacon of. *See* Moore, Ven Edward Alexander.

RAPHOE, Dean of. *See* Reede, Very Rev Samuel William.

RAPKIN, Kevern. St D Coll Lamp BA (2nd cl Mod Hist) 62. Lich Th Coll. **d** 65 **p** 66 Lich. C of Hanley 65-68; Woodchurch 68-70; Abbots Langley 70-73; R of Mt Pleasant 73-80; Rockingham w Safety Bay Dio Perth from 80. *8 Baralda Court, Rockingham, W Australia 6168.* (095-27 1417)

RAPLEY, Frederick Arthur. b 27. Roch Th Coll 67. **d** 69 **p** 70 Cant. C of Tenterden w Small Hythe 69-75; C-in-c of H Trin Sittingbourne Dio Cant from 75. *11 London Road, Sittingbourne, Kent.* (Sittingbourne 72724)

RAPP, William Basil. b 56. St Bede's Coll Umtata Dipl Th 80. **d** 79 **p** 80 Kimb K. P Dio Kimb K. *38 Green Street, Kimberley, S Africa.*

RAPSEY, Peter Nigel. b 46. K Coll Lon and Warm BD and AKC 68. **d** 69 Dorking for Guildf **p** 70 Guildf. C of Walton-on-Thames 69-73; Fleet 73-77; P-in-c of The Collingbournes and Everleigh 77-79; Team V of Wexcombe Dio Sarum from 79. *Collingbourne Ducis Rectory, Marlborough, Wilts, SN8 3EL.* (Collingbourne Ducis 279)

RAROA, Apirana Kopua. b 24. **d** 77 Aotearoa for Wai. C of Turanga Past Dio Wai from 77. *162 Disraeli Street, Gisborne, NZ.*

RASHBROOK, Alan Victor. b 42. FRICS 72. SOC 72. **d** 75 **p** 76 Guildf (APM). Hon C of St Mary-of-Bethany Woking Dio Guildf from 75. *78 York Road, Woking, Surrey, GU22 7XR.*

RASHIDI, Barnaba. b 35. St Cypr Coll Rondo 69. **d** 72 **p** 73 Abp Sepeku for Masasi. P Dio Masasi. *Box 92, Newala, Mtwara Region, Tanzania.*

RASHIDI, Canon John Wordsworth. **d** 45 **p** 49 Nyasa. P Dio Nyasa 49-52 and 53-64; Dio SW Tang 52-53; Dio Malawi from 64; Can of Malawi from 64; Archd of Fort Johnston 67-70. *PO Karonga, Malawi.*

RASHIDI, Paul Matthew. b 34. **d** 73 **p** 74 S Malawi. P Dio S Malawi 73-74; Lake Malawi from 75. *Forestry College, P/Bag Dedza, Malawi.*

RASHIDI, Stefano. St Cypr Th Coll Tunduru. **d** 57 **p** 60 Masasi. P Dio Masasi. *Box 92, Newala, Mtwara Region, Tanzania.*

RASMENI, Jacob. St Bede's Coll Umtata 59. **d** 60 **p** 63 Bloemf. P Dio Bloemf. *PO Box 5034, Location, Bethlehem, OFS, S Africa.*

RASMENI, Ven Kiewiet Meitheki. Dipl Th (S Afr) 68. **d** 67 **p** 68 Bloemf. P Dio Bloemf; Archd of Bethlehem and R of St Paul Ficksburg Dio Bloemf from 80. *Box 166, Ficksburg 9730, S Africa.*

RASMUSSEN, Kenneth Niels Peter Redfern. Trin Coll Dub BA 47. **d** 47 Chelmsf **p** 51 Roch. C of W Ham 47-48; St Mark Victoria Dks 48-50; Actg C of Swanley 50-53; C of Stowmarket 56-58; St Pet Paddington 59-61; Houghton Regis Dio St Alb from 61. *14 Vicarage Road, Houghton Regis, Dunstable, Beds.*

RASOLOFONJATOVO, Pierre. St Paul's Coll Ambat. **d** 56 **p** 57 Madag. P Dio Madag 57-69; Dio Diego S from 69. *Vohemar, Madagascar.*

RASOLOHARIVONY, Michael. **d** 47 **p** 49 Madag. P Dio Madag 47-69; Dio Antan 69-75. *Rue Dupleix, Antsirabe, Madagascar.*

RASOLOMANANA, Jean. St Paul's Coll Ambat. **d** 51 **p** 53 Madag. P Dio Madag 51-69; Dio Antan from 69. *Belanitra, Ambohidratrimo, Madagascar.*

RASOLONDRAIBE, Louis Edouard Joelson. St Paul's Coll Ambat. **d** 53 **p** 54 Madag. P Dio Madag 53-69; Dio Antan from 69. *Mahitsy, Madagascar.*

RASON, Frederick George. b 26. Qu Coll Birm 68. **d** 69 Sherborne for Sarum **p** 70 Sarum. C of H Trin Weymouth 69-72; P-in-c of Yatesbury 72-73; Cherhill 72-73; R of Oldbury 73-76; W Parley Dio Sarum from 76. *250 New Road, West Parley, Wimborne, Dorset.* (Ferndown 873561)

RASTALL, Thomas Eric. b 19. St Aid Coll 62. **d** 63 Shrewsbury for Lich **p** 64 Stafford for Lich. C of St Luke Leek 64-67; V of Brown Edge 67-74; Denstone (w Ellastone and Stanton from 81) Dio Lich from 74; P-in-c of Croxden 74-78; Ellastone 78-81. *Denstone Vicarage, Uttoxeter, Staffs, ST14 5HF.* (Rocester 263)

RATCLIFF, David William. b 37. K Coll Lon Edin Th Coll 59. **d** 62 **p** 63 Cant. C of St Aug Croydon 62-65; Selsdon 65-69; V of St Mary Milton Regis 69-75; Asst Dir of Educn (Parish Adult Educn) Dio Cant from 75; Hon Min Can of Cant Cathl from 75. *1 Lady Wootton's Green, Canterbury, Kent, CT1 1TL.* (Cant 59401)

RATCLIFF, Richard Charles. b 09. Late Scho of Univ Coll Ox 2nd cl Cl Mods 30, BA (1st cl Lit Hum) 32, 1st cl Th 33. St Steph Ho Ox 33. **d** 33 **p** 34 S'wark. C of St Andr Stockwell Green 33-35; St Matt Westmr 35-40; St Martin Brighton 40-41; Tormohun 41-45; R of Rumboldswyke Chich 45-61; Surr 53-61; Proc Conv Chich 54-55; Chap and Master St Marg Sch Bushey 61-65; V of Boxgrove 65-75; R of Tangmere 66-75; P-in-c of Apuldram Dio Chich from 77. *135 Birdham Road, Chichester, W Sussex.* (Chich 784870)

RATCLIFFE, Ernest Henry. b 09. Late Scho of Ch Coll Cam 2nd cl Hist Trip pt i 31, BA (2nd cl Hist Trip pt ii) 32, MA 36. Ripon Hall Ox 66-68; **d** 34 **p** 35 Bp Baynes for Birm. C of St Jas Handsworth 34-38; Luton (in c of St Anne Hart Hill) 38-41; L to Offic Dio Bradf 41-46; Asst Master Trin Sch of John Whitgift [f Whitgift Middle Sch] 46-73. *41 South Norwood Hill, SE25.* (01-653 4448)

RATCLIFFE, Harry. b 13. St Chad's Coll Dur BA and Jenkyns Scho 36, MA 39. **d** 37 **p** 38 Ches. C of Ch Ch Ches 37-39; St Olave w St Giles and St Mich-le-Belfrey York 39-43; Chap RAF 43-46; R of Skelton 46-61; V of Willerby (w Ganton and Folkton from 74) 61-77; R of Folkton 61-74; C-in-c of Ganton 72-74. *11 St Olave's Road, York, YO3 7AL.*

RATCLIFFE, Michael David. b 43. BSc (Lon) 65, BA (Lon) 75. Univ of Dur Dipl Th 77. Cranmer Hall Dur 75. **d** 77 Burnley for Blackb **p** 78 Blackb. C of St Thos Blackpool 77-81; V of St Paul Oswaldtwistle Dio Blackb from 81. *71 Union Road, Oswaldtwistle, Accrington, Lancs, BB5 3DD.* (Accrington 31038)

RATCLIFFE, Peter William Lewis. b 30. Univ of Birm BSc 55. BD (Lon) 58. Tyndale Hall Bris 55. **d** 58 **p** 59 Ely. C of St Andr L Cam 58-61; R of Wistow 61-74; Bury 61-74; Wennington Dio Chelmsf from 74; V of Rainham Dio Chelmsf from 74. *Vicarage, Broadway, Rainham, Essex.* (Rainham 52752)

RATCLIFFE, Sydney. AKC (1st cl) 34. **d** 34 **p** 35 Blackb. C of St Paul Scotforth 34-36; All SS Habergham 36-39; V of Cambo 39-45; Chap RNVR 41-44; V of St Thos Blackb 45-49; Bicker 49-54; R of Tansor w Cotterstock 54-56; V of Fotheringhay 54-56; Chap Abbey Sch Malvern 56-64; Qu Marg Sch Escrick from 66; V of Kirkwhelpington 64-66. *34 Hill Meadows, High Shincliffe, Durham.* (Durham 63640)

RATHBONE, Bruce Alistair. b 29. Univ of Manit BA 55. St Jo Coll Winnipeg. **d** 56 **p** 57 Rupld. C of St Matt Winnipeg 56-58; R of Stonewall 58-61; Chap RCAF 61-65; R of Rocky Mountain Ho Calg 65-69; I of Athab 69-75; Hon Can of Athab 74-81; I of Fort McMurray 75-81; St Jas City and Dio Sktn from 81. *607 Dufferin Avenue, Saskatoon, Sask, Canada.*

RATHBONE, John David. Univ of Tor LTh 59. **d** 57 **p** 58 Niag. R of Glen Williams 57-60; St Bart Hamilton Ont 60-63; Orangeville 63-69; Hannon 69-71; V of Ch Ch Cathl Hamilton 71-80; Hon Can of Niag 73-80; Exam Chap to Bp of Niag 74-80; P-in-c of Ch Ch Wainfleet Dio Niag from 81. *1122 Upper Wellington Street, Unit 3, Hamilton, Ont., Canada.*

RATHBONE, Very Rev Norman Stanley. b 14. Late Tancred Stud of Ch Coll Cam BA and Scho 35, 1st cl Th Trip pt i 37, MA 39. Westcott Ho Cam 37. **d** 38 **p** 39 Cov. C of St Mary Magd 38-45; V 45-59; Exam Chap to Bp of Cov 44-59; Can Th of Cov 54-59; Chan and Can and Preb of Welton Beckhall in Linc Cathl 59-69; Select Pr Univ of Cam 62; Dean of Heref from 69; V of St Jo Bapt City and Dio Heref from 69. *Deanery, Hereford.* (Hereford 2525)

RATHBONE, Paul. b 36. BNC Ox BA 58, MA 62. Wycl Hall, Ox 58. **d** 60 Penrith for Carl **p** 61 Carl. C of St Jo Evang Carl 60-63; H Trin Heworth (in c of Ch Ch) York 63-68; V of Thorganby w Skipwith and N Duffield Dio York from 68; Commun Officer Dio York from 74. *Skipwith Vicarage, Selby, N Yorks, YO8 7SQ.* (Bubwith 403)

RATHBONE, Royston George. b 37. St D Coll Lamp 58. **d** 60 **p** 61 Mon. C of Risca 60-63; St Mark Newport 63-65; V of St John Ebbw Vale 65-68; Chap HM Pris Coldingley 68-73; HM Pris Linc 73-77; CF (TAVR) 64-73; Chap HM Pris Man 77-79; HM Borstal Everthorpe from 79. *c/o 6 Jobsons Road, South Cave, Brough, N Humb.* (N Cave 3254)

RATHGEN, David Guy Stanley. b 43. Univ of Cant BA 67. St Jo Coll Auckld LTh 70. **d** 69 **p** 70 Ch Ch. C of Highfield 69-71; Linwood 71-73; on staff of CMS 74; Chap at Bordeaux 74-77; V of Hoon Hay Dio Ch Ch from 79. *212 Hoon Hay Road, Christchurch 2, NZ.* (384-277)

RATINGS, John William. b 37. St Pet Coll Ox BA (3rd cl Th) 62, MA 71. Cudd Coll 62. **d** 64 **p** 65 Man. C of All SS and Marts Langley 64-68; Easthampstead 68-71; V of Wargrave Dio Ox from 71. *Wargrave Vicarage, Reading, RG10 8EU.* (Wargrave 2202)

RATLEDGE, Canon Ernest David. b 11. Univ of Man BA (2nd cl Engl Lit and Lang) 32, MA 33, BD 52. Bps' Coll Cheshunt, 33. **d** 34 **p** 35 Man. C of St Jas E Crompton 34-36; St Marg Whalley Range 36-42; Chap RAFVR 42-46; R of St John Moston 46-52; Chorlton-cum-Hardy 52-67; Prestwich

67-78; RD of Stretford 55-67; Radcliffe and Prestwich 67-78; Hon Can of Man 62-78; Can (Emer) from 78. *22 Abbot's Walk, Cerne Abbas, Dorchester, Dorset, DT2 7JN.*

RATSIMBA, Joseph. St Paul's Coll Ambat **d** 30 **p** 35 Madag. P Dio Madag 30-69; Dio Antan 69-75. *Ankadiefajoro, Antananarivo, Malagasy Republic.*

RATSIMBA, Victor. St Paul's Coll Ambatoharanna 67. **d** 71 **p** 72 Antan. P Dio Antan. *Soavinandriana, Itasy, Malagasy Republic.*

RATTERAY, Alexander Ewen. b 42. Codr Coll Barb 61. **d** 65 Berm **p** 66 Wakef. C of S Kirkby 66-68; Sowerby 68-71; V of Airedale w Fryston 71-80; Pembroke Dio Berm from 80. *Box 544, Hamilton 5, Bermuda.* (2-3261)

RATTRAY, James Malcolm Charles. ACT ThL 56. **d** and **p** 47 Armid. C of Narrabri 47-49; V of Mungindi 48-50; Foster 50-53; CF Austr 53-56; P-in-c of Woomera 56-60; Min of Warburton 60-63; Asst Sec ABM Vic 63-66; C of St Paul's Cathl Melb 63-66; R of Moama 66-71; Perm to Offic Dio Melb from 71. *Flat 1, 23 Williams Road, Windsor, Vic, Australia 3181.* (529-5196)

RAUMATI, Tikituterangi. St Jo Coll Auckld **d** 65 **p** 66 Waik. C of Morrisville 65-66; Taumarunui 66-67; P-in-c of Taranaki Maori Past 67-69; C of Hastings 69-70; V of Opotiki 70-74; Mt Maunganui 75-78; Paeroa 78-81; P-in-c of Waik Maori Past Dio Waik from 81. *39 River Road, Ngaruawahia, NZ.* (8649)

RAURELA, Canon Lester. St Aid Th Coll Dogura 38. **d** 40 **p** 42 New Guinea. P Dio New Guinea 40-71; Dio Papua from 71; Can of New Guinea 68-71; Papua from 71. *Anglican Church, Gona, via Popondota, Papua New Guinea.*

RAVELONORANA, Flaurent. b 51. **d** 75 **p** 76 Diego S. P Dio Diego S 75-79; Dio Antsir from 79. *BP 278, Antsiranana, Malagasy Republic.*

RAVEN, Barry. b 48. Sarum Wells Th Coll 69. **d** 72 **p** 73 Bris. C of Henbury w Hallen 72-76; P-in-c of S Marston w Stanton Fitzwarren 76-78; Team V (w Stratton St Margaret) 78-80; P-in-c of Coalpit Heath Dio Bris from 80. *Vicarage, Coalpit Heath, Bristol.* (Winterbourne 775129)

RAVEN, Geoffrey Earle. b 1893. MC 17. Late Exhib of CCC Cam BA 19, MA 34. Westcott Ho Cam 33. **d** 34 **p** 36 Lich. C of Whitchurch 34-37; V of Osmaston-by-Ashbourne w Edlaston 37-42; Ed Derby Dioc Year Bk 40-47; R of Breadsall 42-47; V of Higham w Merston 47-58; Goodnestone-next-Wingham w Chillenden and Knowlton 58-64; RD of E Bridge 62-63; Perm to Offic Dio Pet from 64. *Hermitage, Lyddington, Oakham, Leics, LE15 9LN.* (Uppingham 2338)

RAVEN, Thomas Denys Milville. b 22. Lon Coll of Div 65. **d** 66 **p** 67 Ox. C of Bradfield w Buckhold 66-71; V of Otterton 71-74; Wadhurst Dio Chich from 74; Tidebrook Dio Chich from 74. *Vicarage, Wadhurst, Sussex.* (Wadhurst 2083)

RAVENS, David Arthur Stanley. b 30. Late Exhib of Jes Coll Ox BA (2nd cl Chem) 54, MA 61. BD (Lon) 63. Wells Th Coll 61. **d** 63 Knaresborough for Ripon **p** 64 Ripon. C of Seacroft 63-70; Team V 70-73. *Address temp unknown.*

RAVENSCROFT, Raymond Lockwood. b 31. Univ of Leeds BA 53. Coll of Resurr Mirfield 54. **d** 55 **p** 56 Capetn. C of Goodwood 55-57; St Jo Cathl Bulawayo 57-59; R of Francistown 59-62; C of St Ives Cornw 62-64; V of All SS Falmouth 64-68; St Steph-by-Launceston (w St Thos Launceston from 73) 68-74; C-in-c of St Thos Launceston 68-73; R of Probus, Ladock and Grampound w Creed Dio Truro from 74; RD of Powder 77-81. *The Sanctuary, Probus, Truro, Cornw.* (Grampound Road 882746)

RAVENSDALE, Canon Victor Andrew Joseph. b 14. OBE 73. **d** 66 **p** 67 Nam. Prin Buloba Coll 66-70; Chap Kampala and Entebbe 70-73; R of Stilton w Denton and Caldecote 73-76; C-in-c of Folksworth w Morborne 73-74; R 74-76; Chap St Geo Lisbon Dio Gibr (Gibr in Eur from 80) from 77; Can of Gibr Cathl from 81. *Rua da Estrela 4, Lisbon, Portugal.* (66 3010)

✠ **RAWCLIFFE, Right Rev Derek Alec.** b 21. OBE 71. Univ of Leeds BA (1st cl Engl) 42. Coll of Resurr Mirfield. **d** 44 **p** 45 Worc. C of St Geo Claines Worc 44-47; Asst Master All H Sch Pawa 47-53; Hd Master 53-56; Hd Master St Mary's Sch Maravovo 56-58; Archd of S Melan 59-74; Cons Asst Bp of Melan in St Paul's Ch Lolowai New Hebrides 25 Jan 74 by Abp of NZ; Bps of Melan and Polyn; and Asst Bps of Melan; Apptd Bp of New Hebr 75; res 80; Elected Bp of Glas and Gall 81. *Bishop's House, 48 Drymen Road, Bearsden, Glasgow, G61 2RH.* (041-943 0612)

RAWDON-MOGG, Timothy David. b 45. St Jo Coll Dur BA 76. Cudd Coll 75. **d** 77 **p** 78 Glouc. C of H Trin Longlevens 77-80; Ascot Heath Dio Ox from 80. *The Parsonage, King Edward's Road, Ascot, Berks, SL5 8PD.* (Winkfield Row 5500)

RAWE, Alan Charles George. b 29. ALCD 56. **d** 56 **p** 57 Lon. C of St Luke w St Simon and St Jude W Kilburn 56-59; Lect of Watford 59-61; R of Ore 61-69; Moreton 69-80; V of Coppull Dio Blackb from 80. *Vicarage, Chapel Lane, Coppull, Chorley, Lancs, PR7 4NA.* (Coppull 791218)

RAWLING, Stephen Charles. b 43. Univ of Man BSc 64. Univ of Bris MSc 71. Dipl Th 73. Sarum Wells Th Coll 71. **d** 73 **p** 74 Bris. C of Hartcliffe 73-76; Westlands 76-78; R of Darlaston Dio Lich from 78. *Darlaston Rectory, Victoria Road, Wednesbury, Staffs, WS10 8AA.* (021-526 2240)

RAWLINGS, David Ewart. b 35. Ex Coll Ox BA 58, MA 62. Cudd Coll 58. **d** 60 **p** 61 Dur. C of St Columba Southwick 60-66; C-in-c of St Jas Conv Distr Owton Manor 67-81; M Gen Syn 73-80. *c/o Warden of Co. of Mission Priests, St Helen's Rectory, Hemsworth, Nr Pontefract, W Yorks.*

RAWLINGS, John Dunstan Richard. b 25. Worc Coll Ox 43. Oak Hill Th Coll 62. **d** 64 **p** 65 Guildf. C of Farnborough 64-66; Wisley w Pyrford 66-68; Perm to Offic Dio Guildf from 69; Chap R Aircraft Est Farnborough 69-80; P-in-c of Wenden Lofts w Elmdon 80-81; Strethall 80-81; R of Elmdon w Wenden Lofts and Strethall Dio Chelmsf from 81. *Elmdon Vicarage, Saffron Walden, Essex, CB11 4NQ.* (Chrishall 255)

RAWLINGS, John Edmund Frank. b 47. K Coll Lon AKC 69. St Aug Coll Cant 69. **d** 70 **p** 71 Roch. C of Rainham 70-73; Tattenham Corner and Burgh Heath 73-76; Chap RN from 76. *c/o Ministry of Defence, Lacon House, Theobalds Road, WC1X 8RY.*

RAWLINS, Douglas Royston. OBE 68. Univ of Wales BSc 39. St Steph Ho Ox 39. **d** 41 **p** 42 Llan. C of St Bride's Minor w Bryncethin 41-45; St Aug Penarth w Lavernock 45-47; Chap RNVR 47-49; Asst Master St Thos Sch Kuching 50-51; Asst Prin Batu Lintang Tr Coll 52-56; Prin 63-73; Hd Master Tanjong Lobang Sch Miri 57-58; Kanowit Sch 59-62; L to Offic Dio Borneo 52-62; Dio Kuch 62-73; V of St Andr Bandar Seri Begawan Dio Kuch from 74. *Box 126, Bandar Seri Begawan, Brunei, Malaysia.* (Brunei 2768)

RAWLINS, Geoffrey Ernest Francis. Pemb Coll Cam BA 54. Ridley Hall Cam 54. **d** 56 **p** 57 Lon. C of All S Langham Place Dio Lon 56-66; Hon C 66-67. *Room 248, 475 Riverside Drive, New York 10027, USA.*

RAWLINS, George Edward. Rhodes Univ Coll Grahmstn BA 28, B Educn (S Afr) 48, M Educn (S Afr) 61. St Paul's Coll Grahmstn LTh (S Afr) 34. **d** 34 Grahmstn **p** 38 Capetn. C of Cathl Ch Grahmstn 34-35; Chap of St Matt Coll Cp 36-37; C of St Mary Colleg Ch Port Eliz 37-38; Asst Master Zonnebloem Coll 38-39; C of St Paul Rondebosch 40; CF (S Afr) 40-45; Chap and Hd Master St Faith's Sch 46-47; L to Offic Dio Grahmstn 47-48; R of Bredasdorp 48-53; St Marg Parow 53-67; P-in-c of St Phil Port Eliz 71-74. *2 Hamilton House, Pearson Street, Port Elizabeth, S Africa.*

RAWLINS, Patrick Allister. b 54. Univ of WI BA. Codr Coll Barb 77. **d** 79 **p** 80 Antig. C of St John's Cathl Dio Antig from 79. *East Gate House, Church Street, St John's, Antigua.*

RAWLINSON, Curwen. b 32. MBE 73. Open Univ BA 80. Sarum Th Coll 59. **d** 61 **p** 62 Liv. C of St Mich Wigan 61-63; CF from 63; DACG Berlin 78-80; ACG NE Distr York from 80. *c/o Ministry of Defence, Bagshot Park, Bagshot, Surrey.*

RAWLINSON, Rowland. b 20. Open Univ BA 74. **d** 80 Ches **p** 81 Birkenhead for Ches. C of Barnston Dio Ches from 80. *18 Winston Grove, Moreton, Wirral, Merseyside, L46 0PQ.*

RAWSON, Canon Harold. Moore Th Coll Syd ACT ThL 48. **d** and **p** 49 Syd. C of Springwood 49-51; C-in-c of St Pet Glenbrook 51-57; R 57-61; Windsor 61-80; Can of St John's Prov Cathl Parramatta 69-80; Can (Emer) from 80; L to Offic Dio Syd from 80. *Claremont Lane, Windsor, NSW, Australia 2756.* (045-772573)

RAWSTORNE, Richard Atherton. b 1893. Ch Ch Ox BA 19, MA 24. Cudd Coll 25. **d** 27 **p** 28 York. C of St Mary Whitby 27-32; R of Croston 32-60. *1 Tanners Court, Haslemere, Surrey.*

RAWSTORNE, Canon Robert Gwillym. b 07. Ch Ch Ox BA (3rd cl Mod Hist) 29, Dipl Th 30, MA 39. Westcott Ho Cam 32. **d** 39 **p** 40 B & W. C of Norton St Phil 39-43; V of Thornbury 43-76; Chap Thornbury Hosp 46-76; RD of Hawkesbury 48-65; Hon Can of Glouc 63-76; Can (Emer) from 76. *Wearne House, Langport, Somt, TA10 0QQ.* (Langport 250454)

✠ **RAY, Right Rev Chandu.** Wycl Coll Tor DD (*hon causa*) 58, Hur Coll DD (*hon causa*) 63. **d** 42 **p** 43 Lah. CMS P Dio Lah 42-49; Sec BFBS Punjab 49-57; Can of Lah 54-57; Cons Asst Bp of Lah in Lah Cathl 27 Jan 57 by Bp of Calc (Metrop); Bps of Chota N; Kurun; Bom; Luckn; Colom; Assam; Rang; Amrit; B'pore; E Bengal; Bhag; Lah; and Delhi; and Bp Partridge; Trld to Kar 63; res 69; Archd of Sind and Baluchistan 57-59; Kar 59-63; Dean of H Trin Cathl Ch Karachi 63-69; Commiss Rang from 70; L to Offic Dio Sing

70-80; Perm to Offic Dio Perth from 80. *10/46 Davies Road, Claremont, W Australia 6010.* (384-1181)

RAY, Douglass Ellicott. b 48. Wm's Coll Mass BA 73. Montr Th Coll LTh 76. **d** 74 **p** 76 Queb. On study leave 74-76; C of St Jas Kingston 76-78; on leave. *c/o 1335 Asylum Avenue, Hartford, CT 06105, USA.*

RAY, Robert John. b 52. Univ of Adel BSc 77. St Barn Th Coll Adel 78. **d** 81 Adel. C of St Francis Edwardstown Dio Adel from 81. *10 Seventh Avenue, Ascot Park, S Australia 5043.*

RAY, Robin John. b 44. Sarum Wells Th Coll 72. **d** 74 Sarum **p** 75 Ramsbury for Sarum. C of Bourne Valley Team Min 74-78; P-in-c of Dilton Marsh Dio Sarum from 78. *Dilton Marsh Vicarage, Westbury, Wilts, BA13 4BU.* (Westbury 822560)

RAY, Stanley Evan. ACT ThL 49. Ridley Coll Melb. **d** 49 **p** 50 Bend. V of Raywood 50-52; P-in-c of Eroro 52-55; H Trin Bend 55-57; Kaniva 57-62; V of Casterton 62-67; R 67-73; Stawell Dio Bal from 73. *Rectory, Stawell, Vic., Australia 3380.* (053-58 2081)

RAY, William Gordon Duncan. **d** and **p** 66 Tor. P-in-c of Apsley 66-72; R of Uxbridge Dio Tor from 72. *Box 673, Uxbridge, Ont., Canada.* (416-852 6892)

RAY, Canon William Robert. OBE 65. Univ of Adel BA 33. St Barn Coll Adel 34. **d** and **p** 36 Adel. C of St Pet Glenelg 36-38; P-in-c of Koolunga Miss 38-40; Asst Chap St Pet Colleg Sch Adel 40-47; Hd Master Pulteney Gr Sch Adel 47-72; Exam Chap to Bp of Adel from 57; Can of Adel from 64; Bp's V and Prec of St Pet Cathl Adel from 73. *12 Leroy Street, Glenunga, S Australia 5064.* (08-79 2163)

RAYBOULD, Norman William. b 18. Lich Th Coll 51. **d** 54 **p** 55 Lich. C of Bloxwich 54-57; Tettenhall Wood (in c of Good Shepherd Castlecroft) 57-60; Stoke-on-Trent (in c of St Paul Mt Pleasant) 60-61; PC of St Luke Wel Hanley 61-67; V of St Martin 67-76; Sheriffhales w Woodcote Dio Lich from 76. *Vicarage, Sheriffhales, Shifnal, TF11 8RA.* (Telford 460606)

RAYMENT, Andrew David. b 45. St D Coll Lamp BA 68. Univ of Wales (Abth) MA 70. Ridley Hall Cam 78. **d** 80 **p** 81 Nor. C of Costessey Dio Nor from 80. *St Helen's House, Gurney Road, New Costessey, Norwich, Norfolk, NR5 0HH.* (Nor 746637)

RAYMENT, Thomas Alleyne. Em Coll Sktn BA and LTh 56. **d** 56 **p** 57 Edmon. C of All SS Cathl Edmon 56-58; Ch Ch Edmon 58-60; R of St D w H Trin Prince Albert 60-63; Wetaskiwin 63-66; Hon C of St Jo Evang City and Dio Edmon from 66. *11424 71st Avenue, Edmonton, Alta, Canada.*

RAYMOND, Geoffrey Austin. b 23. Univ of Bris BSc 44. Qu Coll Birm. **d** 55 **p** 56 Wakef. C of Sandal Magna 55-58; V of Warley 58-64; Lupset 64-76; Upavon w Rushall Dio Sarum from 76; RD of Avon from 80. *Upavon Vicarage, Pewsey, Wilts.* (Upavon 248)

RAYMOND, George William. b 07. Wycl Hall Ox. **d** 67 Cant **p** 68 Croydon for Cant. C of W Wickham Dio Cant from 67. *58 Gates Green Road, West Wickham, Kent.*

RAYMOND, Laurence Clarke. Univ of Tor BA 48. Hur Th Coll LTh 52. **d** and **p** 52 Niag. C-in-c of Glanford 52-57; R of St Columba St Catherines 57-63; Assoc Sec GBRE Div of Coll Work 63-71; Executive Dir of Program from 71; Hon C of Ch Ch Cathl Hamilton Dio Niag from 76. *600 Jarvis Street, Toronto, Ont., M4Y 2J6. Canada.* (416-924 9192)

RAYMOND, William Ober. Univ of NB BA 02. Montr Dioc Coll LTh 05. Univ of Mich MA 12, PhD 17. Bp's Univ Lennox Hon DCL 50. FRS Canad 50. **d** 05 **p** 06 Fred. Miss at McAdam Junction NB 05-07; in Amer Ch 07-31; Prof of Engl Bp's Univ Lennox 31-50. *61 Forest Hill Road, Toronto 7, Ont, Canada.*

RAYNER, Brian Anthony. Ch Coll Tas ThL 65. **d** 66 **p** 67 Tas. C of St Steph Hobart 66-67; St Geo Launceston 67-70; Channel w Brunny 70; P-in-c of Cygnet 70-72; R of King Is 72-76; Oatlands 76-79; St Leonards Dio Tas from 79. *Rectory, St Leonards, Tasmania 7205.* (003 391195)

RAYNER, David. b 49. Trin Hall Cam BA 72, MA 75. Westcott Ho Cam 75. **d** 78 **p** 79 Man. C of St Clem Chorlton-cum-Hardy 78-81; St Mary Gt Cam Dio Ely from 81. *95 Windsor Road, Cambridge, CB4 3JL.* (Cam 357807)

RAYNER, George. b 1896. Univ Coll Dur BA (2nd cl Engl and Hist) 23, MA 26. Can Scho Linc 23. **d** 25 **p** 26 Ripon. C of St John w St Barn Holbeck Leeds 25-27; Leeds 27-31; C-in-c of St Martin's Conv Distr Whinney Banks Middlesbrough 31-36; Epiphany Conv Distr Gipton Leeds 36-38; V of St Silas Hunslet 38-47; Startforth 47-56; RD of Richmond N 52-56; Surr 53-62; R of Swillington 56-62; Perm to Offic Dio Ripon from 62. *3 Old Deanery Close, Ripon, N Yorks, HG4 1LZ.* (Ripon 4375)

RAYNER, George Charles. b 26. Bps' Coll Cheshunt 50. **d** 52 **p** 53 B & W. C of St Andr Rowbarton Taunton 52-56; V of H Trin Taunton 56-63; Chap Taunton and Somt Hosps 60-63; V of St Jo Evang Sandown 63-69; R of Wootton Dio Portsm from 69. *Rectory, Church Road, Wootton Bridge, IW.* (Wootton Bridge 882213)

✠ **RAYNER, Most Rev Keith.** Univ of Queensld BA (1st cl Hist) 51, PhD 63. St Francis Coll Brisb. ACT ThL (1st cl) 52. **d** and **p** 53 Bris. Miss Chap Dio Brisb 53-54; Chap St Francis Coll Milton 54; M Bro of St John Dalby 55-58; Vice-Warden St Jo Coll Brisb 58-59; V of St Barn Sunnybank 59-63; R of St Pet Wynnum Brisb 63-69; Exam Chap to Abp of Brisb 68; Cons Ld Bp of Wang in St Paul's Cathl Melb 24 June 69 by Abp of Melb; Abp of Brisb; Bps of St Arn; Bend; Gippsld; Bal; and River; Coadj Bps of Melb; and Asst Bp of Bal; Trld to Adel (Abp and Metrop of Prov of S Austr) 75; Chairman Internat Angl Th and Doctrinal Comm from 80. *Bishop's Court, 45 Palmer Place, N Adelaide, S Australia 5006.* (08-267 2364)

RAYNER, Paul Anthony George. b 39. Univ of Dur BA 60. Univ of Capetn MA 79. BD (2nd cl) Lon 68. Lon Coll of Div 65. **d** 68 **p** 69 Sheff. C of St Thos Crookes 68-72; Wynberg (in c of St Luke Diep River) 72-79; P-in-c of S Shoebury Dio Chelmsf from 80. *42 Church Road, Shoeburyness, Essex, SS2 9EU.* (Shoeburyness 2778)

RAYNER, Richard Noel. b 24. Univ of Lon BD 51. Oak Hill Th Coll 50. **d** 52 **p** 53 Ex. C of St Jude Plymouth 52-55; V of St Luke Walthamstow 55-61; Ch of Good Shepherd Romford 61-65; PC of St Paul Slough 65-68; V 68-72; V of H Trin Heworth (w St Cuthb Peaseholme to 75) York 72-81; Okehampton w Inwardleigh Dio Ex from 81. *Vicarage, Okehampton, Devon.* (Okehampton 2731)

RAYNER, Ronald James. St Paul's Coll Grahmstn 73. **d** 73 **p** 74 Port Eliz. Chap Miss to Seamen Port Eliz from 73. *Box 1769, Port Elizabeth 6001, CP, S Africa.* (041-23922)

RAYNER, Stewart Leslie. b 39. Univ of Dur BA 61, Van Mildert Exhib 64, Dipl Th 66, MA 73. Cranmer Hall Dur. **d** 67 **p** 68 Sheff. C of Whiston 67-70; Prec of Doncaster 70-74; R of Adwick-le-Street Dio Sheff from 74. *Adwick-le-Street Rectory, Doncaster, S Yorks, DN6 7AD.* (Doncaster 723224)

RAYNES, Frank Lloyd. b 29. Bps' Coll Cheshunt 56. **d** 59 **p** 60 S'wark. C of St Laur Catford 59-60; St Jo Evang Caterham 60-63; Gt Yarmouth (in c of St Paul) 63-65; V of Woodford Bridge Dio Chelmsf from 65. *4 Cross Road, Woodford Bridge, Essex.* (01-504 3815)

RAYNOR, Charles Hamblyn. NZ Bd of Th Stud LTh 65. **d** 64 **p** 65 Wel. C of Paraparaumu 64-66; V of Opunake 66-71; Seatoun-Strathmore Wel 71-78; Brooklands Dio Waik 78; Min from 78. *6 Tokomaru Street, New Plymouth, NZ.*

RAYNOR, Robert Ernest. b 14. Univ of Lon BA (1st cl Cl) 36. TCD BA (Resp) and Div Test (1st cl) 49, MA and BD 55. **d** 49 **p** 50 Derry. C of Ch Ch Londonderry 49-51; R of Mevagh 51-54; C of St Anne's Cathl Belf (in c of Cathl Miss) 54-59; C of St John Malone Belf 59-60; R of Portglenone 60-63; Kilbride 63-68; V of Drummaul 68-72; Lect and Chap Stranmillis Coll Belf from 72; C of St Bart Belf Dio Connor from 72. *32 Downshire Road, Cregagh, Belfast, N Ireland.*

RAYNOR, Ronald James. St Paul's Coll Grahmstn 73. **d** and **p** 73 Port Eliz. Chap Miss to Seamen Port Eliz from 73. *PO Box 1769, Port Elizabeth, S Africa.* (2-3922)

RAYNOR-SMITH, Charles Alfred Walter. b 12. Sarum Th Coll. **d** 55 Bris for Sarum **p** 56 Sarum. C of Oakdale 55-58; Swanage 58-62; PC of Colehill 62-68; V 68-81. *19 Tatnam Road, Poole, Dorset.* (Poole 71510)

RAYSON, Canon Robert Spencer. Late Scho and Pri of Qu Univ Kingston, Ont MA (1st cl Cl) 18. Gen Th Sem NY STB 27. Angl Th Coll BC DD (*jure dig*) 49. Trin Coll Tor DD 60. **d** 25 S Dakota for Qu'App **p** 25 Qu'App. Sub-Warden St Chad's Coll Regina 25-26; C of St Thos Tor 26-32; R of St Mark W Tor 32-43; St Martin-in-the-Fields Tor 43-47; R and Dean of St John's Cathl Newfld 47-55; I of Dorval w Strathmore Montr 55-58; Prin Cant Coll Windsor 58-65; Can of St Paul's Cathl Lon Ont 61-65; Can (Emer) from 65. *Apt 1212, 1209 Richmond Street North, London 11, Ont., Canada.*

RAZAFIMANANTSOA, Ven Bernard. **d** 42 **p** 44 Madag. P Dio Madag 42-69; Dio Antan from 69; Exam Chap to Bp of Madag 65-69; Archd of Antan from 72. *Avaratr, Anjoma, Avenue Marcel Oliver, Antananarivo, Madagascar.* (Tananarive 250 80)

RAZMARA, Khalil. Univ of Shiraz BLitt 62. United Th Coll Bangalore 63. **d** 65 **p** 66 Iran. P Dio Iran 65-80; Dio Melb from 80. *56 Gillies Street, Fairfield, Vic, Australia 3078.*

RAZZALL, Charles Humphrey. b 55. Worc Coll Ox BA 76, MA 81. Qu Coll Cam BA (Th) 78. Westcott Ho Cam 77. **d** 79 **p** 80 S'wark. C of Catford (Southend) and Downham Dio S'wark from 79. *59 Southend Lane, Catford, SE6.* (01-698 3600)

RAZZELL, James Bertram. AKC 35. **d** 35 **p** 36 Lich. C of St Mich Brierley Hill 35-38; Asst Miss at St Mich Herschel 38-39; Miss 39-48; P-in-c of St Alb Vincent 48-55; V 55-60; P-in-c of Findon 60-63; R of Narracoorte 63-65; Victor

Harbour 65-67; Chap Commun of H Name Cheltm 67-70; R of Toorak Gdns 70-74; L to Offic Dio Adel from 74. *5-534 Brighton Road, Brighton, S Australia 5048.*

REA, Walter Edgar. Trin Coll Dub BA 28, MA 32. **d** 29 **p** 31 Dub. C of Sandford 29-32; Chap RN 32-53; Chap Michaelho Sch 54-59; V of Umkomaas 59-60; L to Offic Dio Natal from 60. *PO Box 33, Hilton, Natal, S Africa.* (Pmbg 31376)

✠ **READ, Right Rev Allan Alexander.** Trin Coll Tor BA 45, LTh 48. **d** 48 **p** 49 Tor. I of Mono Mills 48-54; R of Trin Ch Barrie 54-72; Can of Tor 57-61; Archd of Simcoe 61-72; Cons Ld Bp Suffr of Tor in St Jas Cathl Tor 6 Jan 72 by Abp of Alg; Bps of Tor, Niag, Hur, Ont, Ott and The Arctic; Bp Suffr of Tor and Others; Trld to Ont 81. *90 Johnson Street, Kingston, Ont, Canada K7L 1X7.* (613-544 4774)

READ, Andrew Gordon. b 40. ARICS 63. Univ of Nottm BA 69. Cudd Coll 70. **d** 70 **p** 71 Southw. C of E Retford 70-72; St Mark Woodthorpe Nottm 72-76; P-in-c of St Leon Newark-on-Trent 76-78; L of Offic Dio Roch from 79. *13 Clevedon Road, Penge, SE20 7QQ.* (01-778 9545)

READ, Christopher Holditch. b 19. Qu Coll Birm 50. **d** 53 Taunton for B and W **p** 54 B and W. C of Portishead 53-56; Walton-on-Trent 56-58; R of Bonsall 58-63; V of Cromford 58-63; R of Grangemouth 63-72; V of Parwich w Alsop-en-le-Dale Dio Derby from 72; P-in-c of Tissington (and Fenny Bentley from 78) Dio Derby from 77. *Parwich Vicarage, Ashbourne, Derbys, DE6 1QD.* (Parwich 226)

READ, Canon Christopher John. b 07. Late Exhib of Worc Coll Ox 3rd cl Cl Mods 27, BA (3rd cl Lit Hum) 29, MA 32. K Coll Lon 29. **d** 30 **p** 31 Ex. C of St Marychurch 30-32; St Jas Ex 32-34; R of Combe-in-Teignhead 34-39; Gen Sec ACS 35-74; C of Flamstead 39-74; Hon Chap to Bp of St Alb 56-74; Hon Can of Llan Cathl from 64; Perm to Offic Dio Ex from 75. *8 Park Road, Torquay, TQ1 4QR.* (Torquay 36061)

READ, David Raymond. b 09. AKC 37. **d** 37 **p** 49 Lon. C of St Andr Kingsbury 37-38; St Alb Golders Green 49-53; Welwyn Garden City 53-56; C-in-c of St Osw Conv Distr Croxley Green 56-57; Min 57-61; V of Nazeing 61-77. *19 The Birches, Thames Road, Goring, Berks.*

READ, Francis Richard Waller. b 18. Selw Coll Cam BA 40, 2nd cl Th Trip pt i 41, MA 44. Ridley Hall Cam 40. **d** 42 **p** 43 Bris. C of Stratton St Marg 42-46; Walcot 46-47; H Trin Cheltm 47-49; R of Kingswood 49-60; C-in-c of Charfield 55-58; V of H Trin Bris 60-66; C-in-c of St Phil and St Jacob Bris 60-64; V of St Budeaux Devonport 66-80. *54 Shorton Valley Road, Preston, Paignton, TQ3 1RB.*

READ, George Arthur. b 04. BEM 42, MBE 62. Wycl Hall Ox 62. **d** 63 **p** 64 St E. C of Brandon w Santon Downham 63-65; R of Barking w Darmsden (and Gt Bricett from 68) 65-73. *Crowley Cottage, Barrett's Lane, Barking, Ipswich, Suffolk.*

READ, Ian. b 34. Selw Coll Cam BA 57. Linc Th Coll 57. **d** 59 **p** 60 Birm. C of Shard End 59-63; P Dio Lebom 64-71; Dean of Cathl Ch of St Aug Maciene 71-76; Distr Supt of Maciene 72-74; Lourenço Marques 74-76; P-in-c of St Germain Edgbaston 76-80; V of Warndon Dio Worc from 80. *Vicarage, Cranham Drive, Warndon, Worc.* (Worc 57806)

READ, Jack. b 19. Qu Coll Birm 67. **d** 68 **p** 69 Bradf. C of Tong 68-70; Baildon 70-72; V of Queensbury Yorks Dio Bradf from 72. *Vicarage, High Street, Queensbury, Bradford, Yorks.* (Bradford 880573)

READ, John. b 33. Worc Coll Ox BA (3rd cl Mod Hist) 56, MA 60. Chich Th Coll 56. **d** 58 **p** 59 Ex. C of Babbacombe 58-60; Heavitree Ex 60-63; PC of Swymbridge w Traveller's Rest and Gunn 63-69; V of St Matt Ex 69-80; Dep PV of Ex Cathl from 69; P-in-c of St Sidwell City and Dio Ex 79-80; R (w St Matt) from 80. *St Matthew's Vicarage, Spicer Road, Exeter, Devon.* (Exeter 71882)

READ, John Allan. b 53. Univ of Tor BA 76. Trin Coll Tor MDiv 79. **d** 79 Bp Read for Tor **p** 80 Tor. C of St Jude Wexford Dio Tor from 79. *10 Howarth Avenue, Scarborough, Ont, Canada, M1R 1H4.*

READ, John Charles. Late Exhib of Keble Coll Ox (2nd cl Hist) 29, Th 31 BA, MA 35. Scho of St D Coll Lamp 24. St Steph Ho Ox 29. **d** 31 **p** 32 Llan. C of Merthyr Tydfil 31; St Martin Roath 31-35; V of Abercwmboi 35-43; St Luke Canton Cardiff 43-77; Can of Llan Cathl 72-79; Perm to Offic Dio Llan from 79. *1 Palace Road, Llandaff, Cardiff, CF5 2AF.* (0222 568806)

READ, John du Sautoy. **d** 66 **p** 67 Derry. V Cho of St Columb Cathl Derry 66; Dean's V 67; St Geo Cathl Capetn 69-71; Chap St Cypr Sch Capetn 71; Peter Ho Mashon 72-77; Univ of Capetn from 77; L to Offic Dio Capetn from 77. *Cambria, Stanley Road, Rondebosch, CP, S Africa.* (652686)

READ, John Hanson. b 17. St Jo Coll Ox BA 49, MA 53. Qu Coll Birm 49. **d** 50 **p** 51 Chich. C of Eastbourne 50-53; Horsham (in c of St Mark) 53-57; V of St Wilfrid Brighton 57-61; R of Beddington 61-78; Surr 62-78; RD of Sutton 65-70; R of Guestling w Pett Dio Chich from 78. *Rectory, Pett, Hastings, Sussex.* (Pett 3234)

READ, John Ronald James. b 39. St D Coll Lamp BA 62, Dipl Th 63. **d** 63 **p** 64 St A. C of Mold 63-65; P-in-c of Sefoa New Guinea 66-70; C of Cheshunt 70-72; Chap RAF from 72. *c/o Ministry of Defence, Adastral House, WC1.*

READ, John Samuel. b 33. Fitzw Ho Cam BA 56. Clifton Th Coll 62. **d** 64 **p** 65 Southw. C of St Chris Sneinton 64-67; St Geo Huyton 67-70; L to Offic Dio Blackb 70-72; V of Mold Green Dio Wakef from 72. *Mold Green Vicarage, Huddersfield, Yorks.*

READ, Peter James. St Aid Coll 59. **d** 61 Bris for Graft **p** 62 Graft. C of St Andr Lismore 61-62; P-in-c of Coraki 63-65; Kingscliff 65-73; R of Sorell w Tasman Peninsula and Richmond 73-75; Tumut 75-79; Perm to Offic Dio C & Goulb from 79. *Box 182, Tumut, NSW, Australia, 2720.*

READ, Robert Edgar. b 47. Kelham Th Coll 66. **d** 70 Jarrow for Dur **p** 71 Dur. C of W Harton 70-75; Wilmslow 75-80; Asst Chap HM Pris Styal 78-80; V of Gatley Dio Ches from 80. *11 Northenden Road, Gatley, Cheadle, Chesh, SK8 4EN.* (061-428 4764)

READ, Victor. b 29. ALCD 57. BD (Lon) 58. **d** 58 **p** 59 S'wark. C of Wimbledon 58-61; L Marlow 61-64; V of Ulceby 64-67; V of Wootton 64-67; R of Croxton 64-67; V of St Pet-in-Eastgate Linc 67-73; Ch Ch W Wimbledon Dio S'wark from 73. *16 Copse Hill, SW20 0HG.* (01-946 4491)

READ, William Harvey. Codr Coll Barb. **d** 17 **p** 19 Gui. C of St Phil Georgetn 17-22; Miss P Bartica 22-25; V of St Clem and St Swith Barb 25-26; St Phil L Barb 26-28; St Bart Barb 28-29; St Martin Barb 29-31; R of St Andr Barb 31-49; Can of St Mich Cathl Barb and RD of St Pet 48-71; Hon Can 71-75; V of St Bart Barb 57-65. *40 Blue Waters, Barbados, W Indies.*

READE, Nicholas Stewart. b 46. Univ of Leeds BA 70, Dipl Th 72. Coll of Resurr Mirfield 70. **d** 73 **p** 74 Lich. C of St Chad Coseley 73-75; Codsall (in c of H Cross Bilbrook) 75-78; V of U Gornal 78-82; St Dunstan Mayfield Dio Lich from 82. *Vicarage, High Street, Mayfield, E Sussex.* (Mayfield 873180)

READER, John. b 53. Trin Coll Ox BA 75, MA 79. Ripon Coll Cudd 76. **d** 78 Ely **p** 79 Huntingdon for Ely. C of H Trin w St Mary Ely 78-80; Brooklands Dio Man from 80. *39 Dalebrook Road, Sale, Cheshire.* (061-973 0189)

READER, Nelson Frederick. Univ of Dur LTh 20. **d** and **p** 20 Jamaica. C of St Mich Kingston 20-22; Halfway Tree 22-23; R of Grange Hill 23-25; Gilnock w St Albans 25-28; May Pen (w Hayes from 35) 28-66; RD of Clarendon 46-66; Can of Jamaica 63-67. *May Pen PO, Jamaica, W Indies.*

READER, Sidney Herbert. b 03. Wycl Hall Ox 39. **d** 39 **p** 40 Lich. [f Methodist Min] C of St Geo Newc-L 39-41; V of Kidsgrove 41-50; Surr 43-73; St Luke Leek 50-61; Chap Moorlands Hosp and Mem Hosp Leek 51-61; RD of Leek 56-61; V of Wigginton 61-68; Chap St Editha's Hosp Tamworth 61-69. *75 Telford Road, Coton Lane Estate, Tamworth, Staffs.* (Tamworth 65156)

READER, Thomas Richard Andrew. b 47. Ball Coll Ox BA 70, MA 73. St Steph Ho Ox 70. **d** 73 **p** 74 Ox. C of Clewer 73-76. *c/o The Students' Union, 20 Bedford Way, WC1H 0AL.*

READING, Bishop Suffragan of. *See* Foley, Right Rev Ronald Graham Gregory.

READING, Albert Edward. b 16. **d** 68 **p** 69 St A. C of Newtown w Llanllwchaiarn and Aberhafesp 68-71; Colwyn Bay 71-73; V of Penycae 73-80. *61 Primrose Way, Maesgwyn, Wrexham, LL11 2AT.*

READING, Laurence John. b 14. DSC 44. AKC 39. Univ of Lon BD 39. **d** 39 **p** 40 Chelmsf. C of Prittlewell 39-42; Chap RNVR 42-46; C-in-c of St Pet Conv Distr Prittlewell 46-51; Min 51-60; V of All SS Shrub End Colchester 60-64; Tr Officer C of E Bd of Educn Adult C'tte 64; Sec 65-72; Development Officer Dio Heref 72-82; Can of Heref Cathl 72-82. *11 Wakelin Way, Witham, Essex.* (0376 513251)

REAGON, Darrol Franklin. b 46. Univ Coll Cardiff Dipl Th 76. St Mich AA Llan 74. **d** 76 **p** 77 St A. C of Llandrillo-yn-Rhos 76-78; Hawarden 78-81; V of H Trin & St Luke Northwick Dio Ches from 81. *Vicarage, Winnington, Northwick, Cheshire, CW8 4DN.* (Northwick 74362)

REAKES-WILLIAMS, John Michael Reakes Andrew. b 30. St Francis Coll Brisb 69. **d** 70 **p** 71 Brisb. C of Warwick Queensld 70-73; St Laur Northfield 73-74; C of Penarth w Lavernock 74-76; V of Llanbradach 76-78; Llanfabon 78-79; H Trin Oswestry Dio Lich from 79. *Holy Trinity Vicarage, Oswestry, Salop.* (Oswestry 2540)

REANEY, Harold Eaton Ivan. **d** 63 **p** 64 Wai. St Jo Coll Auckld. C of Gisborne 63-66; V of Tolaga Bay 66-68; Manaia 68-75; Wanganui Par Distr 75-78; Offg Min Dio Wel from 79. *361 Kennedy Road, Napier, NZ.*

REANEY, Joseph Silvester. b 13. Selw Coll Cam 2nd cl

Hist Trip pt i 34, BA 35, 2nd cl Hist Trip pt ii 36, MA 42. Wells Th Coll 36. **d** 37 **p** 38 S'wark. C of St John Southend Lewisham 37-40; St Dunstan Bellingham 40-42; Chap RAF-VR 42-46; V of Gt Barr Dio Lich from 47. *Vicarage, Great Barr, Birmingham, B43 7BD.* (021-357 1390)

REAR, Michael John. b 40. Lich Th Coll 61. **d** 64 **p** 65 York. C of St Alb Hull 64-69; Goldthorpe 69-73; V of Thornbury Dio Bradf from 73. *St Margaret's Vicarage, Thornbury, Bradford, Yorks, BD3 7HX.* (Bradford 664702)

REARDON, Bernard Morris Garvin. b 13. Keble Coll Ox BA 35, MA 38. Ripon Hall, Ox 35. **d** 37 **p** 38 Chelmsf. C of Saffron Walden 37-38; Shenfield 38-40; C-in-c 40-41; CF (EC) 41-46; V of H Cross Hornchurch 46-47; R of Kelly w Bradstone 47-59; Hulsean Pr Univ of Cam 58-59; R of Parham w Wiggonholt and Greatham 59-63; Lect in Div Univ of Newc T from 63. *2 The Grove, Newcastle upon Tyne 12.* (Newc T 661574)

REARDON, Kenneth Nash. Ridley Coll Melb ACT ThL (2nd cl) 55. Univ of Tas BA 64. **d** 56 **p** 57 Tas. C of H Trin Hobart 56-57; Asst P St D CAthl Hobart 57-59; P-in-c of Claremont w Chigwell 59-64; R of Cressy 64-66; Dir of Promotion Dio Bath 66-71; Dir Chr Educn Coun Dio Wel 71-74; Org Sec Dept of Chr Educn Dio Brisb from 75. *8 Kosma Street, Aspley, Queensland, Australia 4034.* (263 3429)

REARDON, Canon Martin Alan. b 32. Selw Coll Cam BA 54, MA 58. Cudd Coll 56. **d** 58 **p** 59 Cov. C of Rugby 58-62; H Trin Wicker w Neepsend Sheff 62-65; L to Offic Dio Sheff 65-71; LPr Dio Linc from 71; Sub-Warden Linc Th Coll 71-78; Sec Gen Syn Bd for Miss and Unity from 78; Can and Preb of Linc Cathl from 79. *c/o BMU, Church House, Dean's Yard, Westminster, SW1P 3NZ.* (01-222 9011)

REASON, Jack. b 28. St Alb Min Tr Scheme 77. **d** 80 St Alb **p** 81 Hertf for St Alb. C of St Hugh Lewsey, Luton Dio St Alb from 80. *110 Shelley Road, Luton, Beds, LU4 0JA.*

REAUME, Roy Lloyd. Univ of Ott BA 59. Bp's Univ Lennox LST 61. **d** 61 **p** 62 Ott. C of Smith's Falls 61-64; R of Bearbrook 64-69; Buckingham 69-73; St John Nepean Ott 73-77; on leave. *14 Oakview Avenue, Ottawa, Ont., Canada.*

REAY, David John. Moore Coll Syd ACT BTh 77. **d** and **p** 79 Syd. C of St Mark Darling Point 79-81; St Swith Pymble Dio Syd from 81. *15 Telegraph Road, Pymble, NSW, Australia 2073.* (44-1477)

REAY, John. Ely Th Coll. **d** 60 Penrith for Carl **p** 61 Carl. C of Workington 60-62; V of Crosscrake 62-71; H Trin and The Hill Chapel Millom 71-75; Thwaites 71-75; L to Offic Dio Carl from 75. *Woodland, Drovers' Lane, Penrith, Cumb.*

RECORD, John. b 47. St Chad's Coll Dur BA 71. Westcott Ho Cam 71. **d** 73 Kens for Lon **p** 74 Lon. C of St Jo Evang w St Mich AA Paddington 73-75; Witney 75-78; P-in-c of L Compton w Chastleton Dio Ox 78-80; V (w Cornwell, Little Rollright and Salford) from 80. *Little Compton Vicarage, Moreton-in-Marsh, GL56 0SE.* (060-874313)

REDDEN, Wilfred John. St Jo Coll Morpeth, 61. **d** 63 **p** 64 Newc. C of Wyong 63-66; Mayfield 66-69; Maitland 69-70; R of Kendall 70-75; Dir Dept of Social Work and L to Offic Dio Newc 75-79; R of Kotara S Dio Newc from 79. *Rectory, Melissa Avenue, Adamstown Heights, NSW, Australia 2289.* (43 0103)

REDDINGTON, Gerald Alfred. b 34. SOC 76. **d** 79 Bp Woollcombe for Lon **p** 79 Lon. C of St Vedast Foster Lane City and Dio Lon from 79. *9 Willow Road, NW3.* (01-435 3532)

REDDROP, Bruce Herbert. Trin Coll Melb BA (Hons) 48. ACT ThL (2nd cl) 49. **d** 50 **p** 51 Melb. C of St Paul's Cathl Melb 50-52; Min of Flinders 52-56; Sunshine 56-61; I of Deepdene 61-64; Dir of Marriage Guidance Dio Melb from 61. *26 Moorehouse Street, Camberwell, Vic, Australia 3124.* (03-82 4269)

REDDY, Christian Nelson. b 25. Univ of S Africa BA 50, BEducn 58. Univ of W Cape MEducn 70, DEducn 72. **d** 71 **p** 72 Bp Wade for Capetn (APM). C of Grassy Park Dio Capetn from 71. *Content, First Road, Grassy Park, Cape Town, S Africa.* (72-5569)

REDFEARN, John William Holmes. Univ of Sheff BA (1st cl Hist) and Gladstone Mem Pri 30, MA and Dipl Educn (w distinc Th and Prac) 31. **d** 33 **p** 34 Dur. C of Bp Wearmouth 33-35; Asst Master Bede Coll Sch Sunderland 31-45; L to Offic Dio Dur 35-45; Perm to Offic Dio York 39-44; Chap and Asst Master Berkhamsted Sch 45-55; Haberdashers' Aske's Sch Elstree 56-72; L to Offic Dio Lon 56-61; Perm to Offic Dio Lon from 61. *1 Greenbank Place, Edinburgh, EH10 6EW.* (031-447 1077)

REDFEARN, Michael. b 42. Open Univ BA 78. St Aid Coll 64. **d** 68 **p** 69 Man. C of St Pet Bury 68-71; Swinton 71-74; M Social and Industr Team Bris Cathl 75-81; M of N Humberside Industr Chap from 81. *c/o Registrar, Diocesan Registry, 5 New Street, York.*

REDFERN, Alastair Llewellyn John. b48. Trin Coll Cam BA 74. Ch Ch Ox MA 74. Qu Coll Birm 75. **d** 76 **p** 77 Lich. C of Tettenhall Regis 76-79; Tutor Ripon Coll Cudd & Dir of Ox Inst for Ch & Society from 79. *c/o Ripon College, Cuddesdon, Oxford.*

REDFERN, Ronald Henry. b 15. Univ of Birm LLB (1st cl) 35, LLM 36. Coll of Resurr Mirfield 36. **d** 38 Stafford for Lich **p** 39 Lich. C of St John West Bromwich 38-39; St Mich AA Walsall 39-42; R of St Kiaran Campbeltown 42-46; Org Sec W Distr Miss to Seamen 46-48; Cler Youth Sec and Lit Sec Miss to Seamen and LPr Dio S'wark 48-54; Sen Chap Miss to Seamen Port of Lon 54-60; R of Chingford 60-63; V of Kingswear 63-71; St Matthias Torquay (w St Mark and H Trin from 79) 71-80. *36 Torr Road, Hartley, Plymouth, Devon, PL3 5TF.* (Plymouth 778337)

REDGERS, Brian. b 42. Late Exhib of Univ of Dur BA (2nd cl Th) 65. Westcott Ho Cam 65. **d** 67 Dunwich for St E. C of Rushmere 67-73; L to Offic Dio St E from 73. *44 Belvedere Road, Ipswich, Suff.*

REDGRAVE, Cecil Goulden. b 14. Oak Hill Th Coll 37. **d** 41 **p** 42 Man. C of St Clem Higher Openshaw 41-43; St Jas Ashton-under-Lyne 43-44; Ch Ch Chadderton 44-46; V of Thornton w Bagworth 46-49; Fairlight 49-60; New Milverton 60-76; P-in-c of Tredington w Darlingscott and Newbold-on-Stour Dio Cov 76-77; R from 77. *Tredington Rectory, Shipston-on-Stour, Warws.* (Shipston 61264)

REDGRAVE, Hyma Goulden. Hatf Coll Dur BLitt 07, BA 09, MLitt 10, LTh and MA 12. Hon CF 18. **d** 14 **p** 15 Chelmsf. C of St Andr Walthamstow 14-18; TCF 16-18; C of Woodford 18-21; V of St Paul Woodford Bridge 21-28; St Jas Clacton-on-Sea 28-58; Surr 36-58; RD of St Osyth 49-55. *31 Southcliff Park, Clacton-on-Sea, Essex.* (Clacton 21155)

REDHEAD, Edward. **d** 63 **p** 64 Ches. C of Mottram-in-Longdendale 63-67; V of Rivington 67-72; Bloxwich 72-75. *2 Seedy Mill, Elmhurst, Lichfield, Staffs, WS13 8HQ.*

REDHEAD, Francis Edward. b 34. G and C Coll Cam 3rd cl Engl Trip pt i, 57, BA (3rd cl Engl Trip pt ii) 58. Chich Th Coll 58. **d** 60 **p** 61 Ripon. C of Adel 60-69; V of Rothwell (w Lofthouse from 76) Dio Ripon from 69; C-in-c of Lofthouse 74-76; RD of Whitkirk from 78. *Holy Trinity Vicarage, Beech Grove, Rothwell, Leeds, LS26 0EL.* (Leeds 822369)

REDHEAD, Stephen. b 03. **d** and **p** 74 Keew. C of Shamattawa Dio Keew from 74. *St John's Church, Shamattawa, via Ilford, Manitoba, Canada.*

REDHEAD, Stephen Harry. St Francis Coll Brisb ACT Dipl Th 71. **d** 72 **p** 73 Brisb. C of St Luke Ekibin Brisb 72-74; Maryborough 74-75; St Andr Lutwyche Brisb 75-76; V of Miles 76-80; R of Hervey Bay Dio Brisb from 80. *Box 35, Pialba, Queensland, Australia 4655.* (28 1028)

REDMAN, Arthur Thomas. b 28. Univ of Dur BA 52. Ridley Hall Cam 62. **d** 63 **p** 64 Bradf. C of Heaton 63-66; Hitchin 66-70; Asst Master Stopsley High Sch Luton 66-70; Hewett Sch Nor 70-72; Perm to Offic Dio Nor 70-72; P Missr Hitchin 72-75; V of Swanwick w Pentrich 75-80; Allestree Dio Derby from 80; Warden of Readers Dio Derby from 78; P-in-c of Morley Dio Derby from 82. *Allestree Vicarage, Derby, DE3 2FN.* (Derby 57396)

REDMAN, Douglas Stuart Raymond. b 35. Roch Th Coll 66. **d** 68 **p** 69 Roch. C of Shortlands 68-71; R of Kingsdown w Mappiscombe 71-76; Chatham 76-80; Surr from 79; V of Shortlands Dio Roch from 80. *37 Kingswood Road, Bromley, Kent, BR2 0HG.* (01-460 4989)

REDMAN, William Arthur. St Francis Coll Brisb. **d** 80 Brisb. C of St Pet Wynnum Dio Brisb from 80. *18 Roseberry Parade, Wynnum North, Qld, Australia 4178.* (396 9526)

REDMAYNE, John. OBE (Mil) 44. ACA 36. Qu Coll Birm Dipl Th 49. **d** 49 **p** 50 Guildf. C of Esher 49-51; R of Mandeville Ja 52-57; Girton 57-60; SPG Sec for Afr and WI 61-64; USPG Sec for S Afr and WI 65-68; Sec for Overseas Grants 68-70; Prec of St Paul's Cathl Wel 70-74; V of Miramar 74-77; Perm to Offic Dio Wel from 77. *31 Kotare Street, Waikanae, NZ.*

REDMOND, Ernest Wilkinson. b 10. TCD Kyle Pri 34 and 35, Bedell Scho 34, BA and Div Test (2nd cl) 36. **d** 36 **p** 37 Clogh. C of Clones 36-38; Muckrow Crossduff and Broomfield 38-40; C-in-c of Errigal Trough w Errigal Shanco 40-43; Asst Chap Miss to Seamen Belf 33-46; C-in-c of Trillick 46-51; I of Augher (w Errigal-Portclare to 65; Newtownsaville from 65) 51-73; RD of Clogher 58-73; Preb of Clogh Cathl 67-78; Chan 78-79; R of Monaghan 73-79. *c/o Rectory, Monaghan, Irish Republic.* (Monaghan 136)

REDMOND, Maxwell Lindsay. St Jo Coll Morpeth ACT ThL 50. **d** 51 **p** 52 River. C of Griffith 51-55; P-in-c of Urana 55-60; Chap Geelong Hosp 60-65; Geelong Gaol 60-65; Dir Tas Marriage Guidance Coun and L to Offic Dio Tas from 65. *6 Antill Street, Hobart, Tasmania 7000.*

REDMOND, Terence John. b 43. ACT BTh 77. Ridley Coll Melb 75. **d** 78 **p** 79 Melb. C of H Trin Kew 78-79; St Jas Dandenong 79-81; Newcomb w Whittington Dio Melb from 81. *59 Hibiscus Crescent, Newcomb, Vic, Australia 3219.*

REDPATH, Stewart Rosbotham. b 11. Trin Coll Dub BA

39. **d** 39 Bp Kennedy for Down **p** 40 Down. C of Shankill 39-41; Drumcree 41-43; I of Kildress 43-46; Donaghendry w Ballyclog 46-47; R of Camlough w Killeavy 47-62; Loughgall 62-80. *22 Rosemount Park, Armagh, BT60 1AX.* (Armagh 522698)

REDRUP, Robert John. b 38. Univ of Leeds BA (2nd cl Phil and Hist) 65. Oak Hill Th Coll 65. **d** 69 **p** 70 Ox. C of Maidenhead 69-74; St Keverne 74-78; P-in-c of St Kea Dio Truro 78-80; V from 80; P-in-c of Baldhu Dio Truro from 80. *8 Strathmore Avenue, Dunblane, Perthshire, FK15 9HX.* (Dunblane 824678)

REDSHAW, Horace George. St Francis Coll Brisb 30. ACT ThL 32, Th Scho 41. **d** 33 N Queensld **p** 36 Graft. C of Innisfail 33-35; C-in-c of Nymboida Distr 35-36; P-in-c 36-38; V of Burringbar 38-42; R of Nimbin 42-47; C of St Andr Lutwyche 47-48; R of St John Biggenden 48-51; Inglewood 51-53; Narromine 53-77. *Dundaloo Street, Narromine, NSW, Australia 2821.*

REDWAY, John Alfred George. Univ of Adel BEng 55. St Mich Th Coll Crafers 55. **d** 58 **p** 59 Bunb. C of St Paul's Pro-Cathl Bunb 58-61; R of Boyanup 61-66; C of Port Headland 66-67; Carnarvon 67-68; P-in-c 68-69; Hon Chap to Bp of Bunb 62-66; L to Office Dio NW Austr 70-73; C of Geraldton Dio NW Austr from 74. *24 Jove Street, Geraldton, W Australia 6530.* (099-211756)

REDWOOD, David Leigh. b 32. Edin Th Coll 57. **d** 59 **p** 60 Edin. C of H Trin Stirling 59-61; Ch Ch Glas 61-64; P-in-c of Ascen Mosspark Glas 64-66; R 66-69; St Mary Virg Hamilton 69-74; Callander w Lochearnhead and Killin 74-76; P-in-c of Callander 76-77; Doune 76-77; C of Aberfoyle, Callander and Doune Dio St Andr from 78. *8 Strathmore Avenue, Dunblane, Perthshire, FK15 9HX.* (Dunblane 824678)

REECE, Arthur. b 13. OBE 64, DSO 44, DFC 42, AFC 43. St Deiniol's Libr Hawarden 77. **d** 79 **p** 80 Ches. C of Lache-cum-Saltney 79-81; V of Tilstone Fearnall w Wettenhall Dio Ches from 81. *Tilstone Fearnall Vicarage, Tarporley, Chesh, CW6 9NP.* (Tarporley 2449)

✠ **REECE, Right Rev David.** b 13. G and C Coll Cam BA 34, MA 38. St Mich Coll Llan 35. **d** 36 **p** 37 St D. C of St Mich Aberystwyth 36-41; Llanelly 41-49; V of Pembroke (St Mary Virg w St Mich) 49-56; Port Talbot 56-71; RD of Margam 66-71; Can of Llan Cathl 69-71; Archd of Margam 71-81; Cons Asst Bp of Llan in St Deiniol's Cathl Ban 29 Sept 77 by Abp of Wales; Bps of St A, St D, Mon, Llan and Swan B; Bp Suffr of Birkenhead; and others. *75 Merthyrmawr Road, Bridgend, Mid Glam, CF31 3NS.* (Bridgend 3115)

REECE, Donald Malcolm Hayden. b 36. CCC Cam BA 58, MA 62. Cudd Coll 58. **d** 60 **p** 61 Ches. C of St Jas Latchford 60-63; Matlock w Tansley 63-67; Min of Ch Ch Eccles Distr Hackenthorpe Beighton 67-70; C of Salisbury Cathl Mashon 70-73; V of St Pet w St Hilda City and Dio Leic from 74. *2 St Peter's Road, Leicester.* (Leic 542011)

REECE, John Henry. b 19. Va Th Sem USA 47. **d** 49 **p** 50 W Va (USA). In Amer Ch 49-75; R of St Phil Inagua 75-77; St Marg I and Dio Nass from 77. *Box ES-5695, Nassau, Bahamas.* (32-704)

REED, Alan Ronald. b 44. Sarum Th Coll 66. **d** 68 **p** 70 Chich. C of Ifield w Langley Green and Gossops Green 68-71; Perivale 71-72; St Martin Ruislip 72-75; Burgess Hill 75; V of Shoreham Beach 78-80; Roffey Dio Chich from 80. *Roffey Vicarage, 52 Shepherds Way, Horsham, RH12 4LX.* (Horsham 65333)

REED, Albert. b 36. Univ of Wales BA 58, BD 63. St Mich Coll Llan 58. **d** 61 **p** 62 Mon. C of Rhymney 61-64; Chap St Woolos Cathl Newport 64-66; R of Aberystruth (Blaina) 66-67; Hon C of St Edm Dudley Dio Worc from 72. *21 Tanfield Road, Dudley, W Midl, DY2 8XF.*

REED, Allan Norman. b 31. Keble Coll Ox BA 55, MA 59. Wycl Hall Ox. **d** 57 **p** 58 York. C of Beverley Minster 57-60; Marfleet 60-64; R of St Andr Levenshulme 64-71; L to Offic Dio Man from 72. *6 Lawton Road, Stockport, Chesh, SK4 2RG.* (061-432 9806)

REED, Allan Rupert. Univ of Manit BA 67. Hur Coll 67. **d** 69 **p** 71 Rupld. C of St Jo Cathl Winnipeg 71-72; River N Angl Pars 72-76; Dioc Sec and Exec Asst to Bp of Rupld 72-76; I of St Mary Winnipeg Dio Rupld from 76. *3820 Roblin Boulevard, Winnipeg, Manit, Canada.*

REED, Canon Arthur. b 13. Late Scho and Exhib of St D Coll Lamp BA (2nd cl Engl) 35. St Mich Coll Llan 36. **d** 36 **p** 37 St A. C of Rhosddu 36-41; Hawarden (in c of St Francis Sandycroft) 41-46; R of Gladestry w Colva 46-54; Llangattock (w Llanbedr Ystradyw and Patricio from 61) 54-73; RD of Crickhowell from 71; R of Llanbedr Ystradyw and Patricio Dio Swan B from 73; Llangenny Dio Swan B from 79; Hon Can of Brecon Cathl from 81. *Llangenny Rectory, Crickhowell, Powys.* (Crickhowell 810348)

REED, Brian. b 43. Univ of Bris BSc 65. Univ of Nottm Dipl Th 76. Linc Th Coll 73. **d** 76 **p** 77 Cant. C of Ch Ch S Ashford 76-78; All SS Spring Pk Croydon Dio Cant from 78. 76. *45 Bushey Road, Spring Park, Shirley, Croydon, Surrey, CR0 8EW.* (01-776 0959)

REED, Bruce Douglas. b 20. Moore Th Coll Syd ACT ThL 45. Fitzw Ho Cam BA 52, MA 56. **d** 46 Syd **p** 46 Bp Pilcher for Syd. C of St Paul Wahroonga 46-47; St Clem Mosman 47-49; Chap Fitzw Ho Cam 50-54; C of St Paul Cam 53-54; Dir Ch Teamwork from 57; Chairman Grubb Inst Behavioural Stud from 69. *Grubb Institute, Cloudesley Street, N1 0HU.* (01-278 8061)

REED, Christopher John. b 42. Selw Coll Cam BA 64, MA 68. Univ of Dur Dipl Th 66. Cranmer Hall Dur. **d** 67 Barking for Chelmsf **p** 68 Chelmsf. C of St Andr Gt Ilford 67-70; P-in-c of St Andr Bordesley 70-72; V 72-80; Crofton, Kent Dio Roch from 80. *2 Oakwood Road, Orpington, Kent, BR6 8JH.* (Farnborough 52939)

REED, Colin Charles Gilmour. Dipl Th (Lon) 69. LCP 75. Tyndale Hall Bris 67. **d** 69 **p** 70 B & W. C of Ch Ch Weston-s-Mare 69-71; Asst Master St Andr Sch Turi and L to Offic Dio Nak 71-79; Chap Brighton Coll Jun Sch 79-80; R of Corrimal Dio Syd from 80. *121 Main Road, Corrimal, NSW, Australia 2518.* (Wollongong 844113)

REED, Denys Adrian. b 25. St Jo Coll Cam 2nd cl Mod Lang Trip pt i 43, BA (3rd cl Econ Trip pt i) 48, MA 51. Wells Th Coll 53. **d** 54 **p** 55 Dur. C of St Luke W Hartlepool 54-56; Prin of Schlenker Sec Sch Port Loko Sier L 56-60; R of Berrynarbor 60-63; Rep World Coun of Churches and Asst Chap St Geo Tunis 63-67; Warden Jerome Ho Kens 67-68; V of Starcross 68-74; Hon C of St Matt Ex 76-81; P-in-c of Martindale Dio Carl from 81. *Martindale Vicarage, Howtown, Penrith, Cumb, CA10 2NF.* (Pooley Bridge 500)

REED, Canon Douglas Victor. b 19. AKC 41. Middlebury Coll USA Hon DD 51. St Steph Ho Ox 41-42. **d** 42 Ox for Lon **p** 43 Lon. C of St Sav Poplar 42-44; St Paul Bedford 44-45; Asst Org Sec SPCK and L to Offic Dio Chich and Perm to Offic Dios Cant and Roch 46-47; V of St Aug Belvedere 47-52; Ed Roch Dioc Chron 48-55; Proc Conv Roch 50-70; V of The Annunc Chislehurst Dio Roch from 52; Hon Can of Roch Cathl from 81. *Annunciation Vicarage, Chislehurst, Kent.* (01-467 3606)

REED, Duncan Esmond Bousfield. b 51. AKC 74. St Aug Coll Cant 75. **d** 76 **p** 77 Dur. C of Houghton le Spring 76-79; St Pet Stockton-on-Tees Dio Dur from 79. *4 Hartburn Lane, Stockton-on-Tees, Cleve, TS18 3QH.*

REED, Ernest James. Carleton Univ Ott BA 61. Trin Coll Tor STB (Hons) 64. Westcott Ho Cam. **d** 64 **p** 65 Ott. C of St Lambert 64-67. *c/o Trinity College, Hoskin Avenue, Toronto, Ont, Canada.*

REED, Florence Patricia. b 20. Vanc Sch of Th 75. **d** and **p** 76 Carib. C-in-c of St Jo Quesnel Dio Carib from 76. *264 Roddie Avenue, Quesnel, BC, Canada.*

REED, Geoffrey Martin. b 51. Univ of Wales (Cardiff) BA 73. Oak Hill Coll 73. **d** 76 **p** 77 Swan B. C of St Nich-on-the-Hill Swansea 76-78; Sketty Dio Swan B from 78. *10 Sketty Park Close, Sketty, Swansea, W Glam.* (Swansea 24086)

REED, Jack. b 23. Univ of Bris BA 49. Univ of Lon BD 51. Tyndale Hall Bris. **d** 51 **p** 52 Sheff. C of St Thos Crookes Sheff 51-54; St Mark Cheltm 54-56; V of Elmdon w Bickenhill 56-60; Sparkbrook 60-66; Drypool Dio York 66-80; Team R from 80; Area Dean E Hull from 72. *139 Laburnum Avenue, Hull, N Humb, HU8 8PA.* (Hull 74257)

REED, John Mervyn. Univ of NZ BSc 47. St Jo Coll Auckld LTh 55. **d** 55 **p** 56 Wai. C of Tauranga 55-58; V of Waipiro Bay 58-63; Waipawa 63-68; Miss at Mwanza 68-80; C of Levin Dio Wel from 81. *8 Clark Street, Levin, NZ.* (84926)

REED, John Peter Cyril. b 51. AKC and BD 78. Ripon Coll Cudd 78. **d** 79 **p** 80 Cant. C of St Jo Bapt Croydon Dio Cant from 79. *8 The Ridgeway, Croydon, Surrey, CR0 4AB.* (01-688 3275)

REED, John Robert. Univ of Manit BSc 55. St Jo Coll Winnipeg LTh 58. **d** and **p** 58 Rupld. V of Rathwell 58-62; R of Lynn Lake 62-66; St Geo City and Dio Bran 66-80; Exam Chap to Bp of Bran 75; Hon Can of Bran 76-80; I of St Luke City and Dio Calg from 80. *55 Penworth Crescent South East, Calgary, Canada T2A 4C5.* (248-7339)

REED, Roger William. b 39. Wycl Hall Ox 65. **d** 68 **p** 69 Portsm. C of St Cuthb Copnor 68-71; St Jas Enfield 71-74; P-in-c of St Thos Becontree 74-78; R of Debden w Wimbish and Thunderley Dio Chelmsf from 78. *Rectory, Debden, Saffron Walden, Essex, CM11 3LB.* (Saffron Walden 40285)

REED, Stanley John. b 14. Clifton Th Coll 48. **d** 50 **p** 51 Ex. C of Ottery St Mary 50-52; Stoke Damerel Devonport (in c of St Bart) 52-55; R of Beaford w Roborough 55-60; V of St Aug Plymouth 60-76; Upottery, Luppitt and Monkton 76-81. *10 Lamb Park, Chagford, Newton Abbot, Devon.*

✠ **REED, Most Rev Thomas Thornton.** Trin Coll Melb BA (2nd cl Eng and Phil) 25, MA 27. Univ of Adel MA ([ad eund]) 29, DLitt 54. St Barn Coll Adel ACT ThL (1st cl) 26, ThD 55. **d** 26 Adel **p** 27 Bp White for Adel. C of St Aug Unley 26-28; P-in-c of Berri Miss 28-29; Tutor St Mark's Coll Adel Chap Toc H (S Austr) and L to Offic Dio Adel 29-31; Asst Chap C of E Gr Sch Melb and L to Offic Dio Melb 32-36; P-in-c of Henley Beach 36-43; R 43-44; St Theodore Rose Park 44-54; Ed Adel Ch Guardian 40-44; Chap AMF 39-57; AIF 44-45; Can of Adel 47-49; Exam Chap to Bp of Adel 48-57; Archd of Adel 49-53; Sen Chap AMF 4MD 53-57; Dean of Adel 53-57; Bp's V 55-56; Admin (*sede vacante*) 56-57; Cons Ld Bp of Adel in St Pet Cathl Adel 30 May 57 by Abp of Syd; Abp of Perth; Bps of Geelong; Willoch; Bunb; Gippsld; Kalg; and Bal; Sub-Prelate O of St John of Jer from 65; Elected Abp and Metrop of Prov of S Austr 73; res 74. *44 Jeffcott Street, North Adelaide, S Australia 5006.*

REED, William Harvey. b 47. K Coll Lon AKC and BD 69. St Aug Coll Cant 66. **d** 70 **p** 71 Jarrow for Dur. C of St Mark Conv Distr Stockton-on-Tees 70-72; St Cuthb Billingham 72-76; S Westoe 76-79; V of Chilton Moor Dio Dur from 79. *Chilton Moor Vicarage, Houghton-le-Spring, T & W.* (Fence Houses 852468)

REED, William Henry Grist. b 1900. St Cath Coll Cam BA 21, MA 26. MRCS and LRCP 26. St Geo Windsor. **d** 50 **p** 51 Bris. C of Chippenham 50-53; R of Iron Acton 53-56; Frenchay 56-61; Christian Malford 61-66; V of Bishopstone w Hinton Parva 66-70. *6 The Garlings, Aldbourne, Marlborough, Wilts.*

REEDE, Very Rev Samuel William. b 24. TCD BA 48, Div Test 50, MA 52, BD 55. **d** 50 **p** 51 Cash. C of Waterf 50-54; St Finnian Cregagh Belf 54-59; Hd of S Ch Miss Ballymacarrett 59-67; Chap Stranmillis Coll Belf 64-68; I of Raphoe w Raymochy Dio Raph from 67; Clonleigh Dio Raph from 68; Can of Raph from 67; Dean of Raphoe from 80. *Raphoe Rectory, Lifford, Co Donegal, Irish Republic.* (074 45226)

REEDER, Canon Aubrey Provost. d and **p** 44 Bath. C of All SS Cathl Bath 44-46; R of Trundle 46-51; Coolah 51-57; Dioc Dir of Youth Dio Bath 57-63; Dom Chap to Bp of Bath 57; Dir of Dioc Conf Centre 57-63; Member GBRE 57-63; Nat Treas YAF Austr 57-67; R of Cudal 63-64; Coonamble 64-70; Mudgee Dio Bath from 71; Can of All SS Cathl Bath from 72. *Rectory, Market Street, Mudgee, NSW, Australia 2850.* (72-1126)

REEDY, Pona Patukia. b 26. **d** 80 Wai. Hon C of Wairoa Mokaka Dio Wai from 80. *PO Box 172, Wairoa, HB, NZ.*

REES, Anthony John. b 49. St Jo Cll Dur BA 72, Dipl Th 73, MA 77. **d** 74 **p** 75 Birm. C of St Matt w St Chad Smethwick 74-77; Lect of Bolton-le-Moors 77-80; R of St Mark Cheetham Hill City and Dio Man from 80. *6 Cheltenham Crescent, Higher Broughton, Salford, M7 0FE.* (061-792 7161)

REES, Arthur Winnington. b 16. Late Scho of Jes Coll Ox BA 39, MA 43. St Mich Coll Llan 38. **d** 39 **p** 40 Llan. C of St Anne Ynyshir 39-43; St Marg Mountain Ash 43-53; V of Ystrad Rhondda 53-68; Pentyrch Dio Llan from 68. *Pentyrch Vicarage, Cardiff, S Glam.* (Pentyrch 890318)

REES, Brian Allison. b 48. McGill Univ Montr BA 74. Univ of St Andr Scotld BD 76, PhD 80. Montr Inst of Min 76. **d** 80 Montr. C of St Jas Ap City and Dio Montr from 80. *1439 St Catherine Street West, Montreal, Que, Canada, H3G 1S6.*

REES, Brynley Mervyn. b 18. Univ of Wales BA (1st cl German) 38, 2nd cl French 39. Lon Coll of Div 40. **d** 41 **p** 42 Chelmsf. C of St Luke Walthamstow 41-43; Bp Ryder Birm 43-46; V of St Paul W Bromwich 46-52; Handforth 52-60; PC of Ch Ch City and Dio St Alb 60-68; V from 68. *5 High Oaks, St Albans, Herts, AL3 6DJ.* (St Albans 57592)

REES, Brynmor. b 1900. St D Coll Lamp 27. Tyndale Hall Bris 29. **d** 31 **p** 32 Lich. C of Cobridge 31-34; Chasetown 34-36; V 36-39; V of Cobridge 39-49; High Offler 49-56; R of Norbury 49-56; Surr from 50; R of Standon 56-70; Chap Standon Orth Hosp 56-70. *25 Meadow Court, Old Road, Barlaston, Stoke-on-Trent, Staffs.*

REES, Christopher John. b 40. Univ of Dur BA 62. Ridley Hall Cam 62. **d** 64 **p** 65 Ches. C of Wilmslow 64-69; St Pet Birkenhead 70-75; Team V of Birkenhead Priory 75; V of Lostock Gralam Dio Ches from 75. *Lostock Gralam Vicarage, Northwich, Chesh.* (Northwich 3806)

REES, Daniel Brynmor. St D Coll Lamp 59. **d** 60 **p** 61 St D. C of Aberayron 61-63; R of Llanfihangel-Penbedw w Capel Colman 63-71; R of Clydey Penrhydd and Castellan 63-71; V of Brawdy w Hayscastle and Llandeloy (and Llanreithian 71-77) Dio St D from 71. *Brawdy Vicarage, Pencwym, Haverfordwest, Dyfed.* (Solva 298)

REES, David Aylwin. b 14. St D Coll Lamp BA 46. **d** 47 **p** 48 St D. C of Eglwysnewydd 47-50; Pembroke 50-53; V of Spittal w Trefgarne 53-75; Dale Dio St D from 75; R of St Bride's w Marloes Dio St D from 78. *Dale Vicarage, Haverfordwest, Dyfed.* (Dale 255)

REES, David Elwyn. b 37. Univ of Wales BA (2nd cl Mod Hist and Pol) 60. Ripon Hall Ox 63. **d** 65 **p** 66 Swan B. C of St Thos Swansea 65-69; Sketty 69-73; V of Clyro w Bettws and Llowes and All SS Glasbury 73-80; St Thos Swansea w Kilvey Dio Swan B from 81. *Vicarage, St Thomas, Swansea, W Glam, SA1 8BP.* (Swansea 52891)

REES, Canon David Frederick. b 21. SS Coll Cam BA 48, MA 52. Sarum Th Coll 48. **d** 50 **p** 51 Blackb. C of St Luke Blackb 50-53; St Thos St Annes-on-the-Sea 53-55; V Cho and Chamberlain of York Minster 55-62; V of St Mary Penwortham Dio Blackb from 62; RD of Leyland from 70; Hon Can of Blackb Cathl from 79. *St Mary's Vicarage, Cop Lane, Penwortham, Preston, Lancs PR1 0SR.* (Preston 743143)

REES, David Grenfell. b 18. St D Coll Lamp BA 40. Qu Coll Birm. **d** 43 **p** 44 Llan. C of Llangeinor 43-47; Cadoxton-juxta-Barry 47-53; St Andr Major 53-60; V of Dyffryn Dio Llan from 60. *Dyffryn Vicarage, Neath, W Glam.* (Skewen 814237)

REES, David John. 76-81; 44. BD (Lon) 66. St Aug Coll Cant 72. **d** 73 St Alb **p** 74 Bedford for St Alb. C of Goldington 73-75; w USPG 76; V of St Geo Penang 76-80; Milton-Ernest Dio St Alb from 81; Thurleigh Dio St Alb from 81. *Milton-Ernest Vicarage, Bedford.* (Oakley 2885)

REES, David Philip Dunn Hugh. b 38. Jes Coll Ox BA (2nd cl Th) 60, MA 64. Westcott Ho Cam 62. **d** 64 **p** 65 Man. C of St Phil w St Steph Salford 64-66; Perm to Offic Dio St A from 66; Asst Master Long Eaton Gr Sch and Perm to Offic Dio Derby 67-74; Chap St Marg C of E High Sch Aigburth Liv from 74. *16 Allangate Road, Liverpool, L19 9BZ.* (051-427 8248)

REES, Edgar Verdun. b 16. St D Coll Lamp BA 38. **d** 40 **p** 41 Llan. C of St Marg Aberaman 40-43; Neath w Llantwit 43-47; Cadoxton-juxta-Neath 47-54; V of Seven Sisters 54-66; Llwynypia 66-78; RD of The Rhondda 73-78; R of Eglwysbrewis w St Athan 78-81; Flemington w Gileston w St Hilary 78-81. *Emcote, Drove Road, Chilbolton, Nr Stockbridge, Hants.*

REES, Emlyn Meredith. b 06. Univ of Wales BA 37. St Mich Coll Llan 37. **d** 38 **p** 40 Llan. C of St Matthias Treharris 38-41; Gellygaer 41-47; V of Ystrad-Rhondda 47-53; Garw Valley w Blaengarw 53-62; Pontypool 62-74; Perm to Offic Dio Llan from 75. *Address temp unknown.*

REES, Eric Vernon. b 19. St Jo Coll Dur BA 41, MA 44. St Andr Coll Pampisford 43. **d** 43 **p** 44 Lon. C of Poole's P 43-51; Edmonton 51-66; Gospel Oak 66-68; P-in-c of St Giles Conv Distr Enfield 68-80; C of All SS Edmon Dio Lon from 80. *102 Mendip House, The Market Square, Edmonton, N9 0TA.* (01-807 4329)

REES, Frederick Llewellyn Forsaith. b 1891. Hatf Hall Dur LTh 13. Chich Th Coll 19. **d** 21 **p** 22 Southw. C of Long Eaton 21-24; St John w St Jas Nottm 24-31; V of St Matthias Sneinton 31-55; St Mich AA Sutton-in-Ashfield 55-61. *Molesfield, Thorgill, Rosedale Abbey, Pickering, N Yorks.* (07515 415)

REES, Gruffydd Nicholas. b 23. Late Exhib St D Coll Lamp BA 46. Wycl Hall Ox 46. **d** 48 **p** 49 Llan for St D. C of Fishguard 48-51; Bettws w Ammanford 51-53; St D Carmarthen 53-57; Epsom (in c of St Steph) 57-62; V of Llanbister w Llanbadarn Fynydd and Llananno 62-75; R of New Radnor w Llanfihangel Nantmelan and Evancoyd Dio Swan B from 75; Gladestry w Colva Dio Swan B from 79. *Rectory, New Radnor, Presteigne, Powys.* (New Radnor 258)

REES, Henry. b 08. Univ of Wales (Abth) BA 36. Ch Hostel Ban. **d** 40 **p** 41 St A. C of Gwersyllt 40-53; V of Cilcain 53-65; R of Llanddulas 65-74. *71 Bryn Avenue, Old Colwyn, Clwyd.*

REES, Hugh Lorimer Octavius. b 06. Magd Coll Ox BA 29, MA 39. St Steph Ho Ox 29. **d** 30 **p** 31 Lon. C of St Mary Somers Town 30-38; Asst Missr Magd Coll Miss Somers Town 32-38; R of E Bridgford 38-46; Chap RAFVR 41-46; Chap RAF BAFO Hamburg 46-48; Staff Chap Air Min 49-50; Asst Chap-in-Chief 50-53; AHQ Malta 53-55; Sen Chap Yatesbury 55-59; Res Chap St Clem Danes Lon 59-60; V of St Mary Abbots Kens 60-77; RD of Kens 64-77; M Gen Syn 73-77. *32 Inner Park Road, SW19 6EG.* (01-788 0625)

REES, James Arthur. b 04. Qu Th Coll Newfld 25. **d** 28 **p** 29 Newfld. C of Bonne Bay 28-29; P-in-c 29-33; Perm to Offic (Col Cl Act) at St Luke Cam 33-35; C 35-45; R of Elton 45-47; St Marg Fletton 47-58; Ed Ely Dioc Gazette 51-58; Surr from 52; RD of Yaxley 54-58; R of W Tarring 58-75; RD of Worthing 75-80; Chap Worthing Hosp from 80. *11 Bath Road, Worthing, W Sussex, BN11 3NU.*

REES, John Elwyn. St D Coll Lamp BA 31. **d** 33 **p** 34 St A. C of Newtown w Llanllwchaiarn 33-37; Machen 37-42; V of Dinas w Penygraig 42-50; R of St Jo Bapt Whittington 50-74. *Whaddon House, Holbache Road, Oswestry, Salop.*

REES, John Harold. b 15. St Mich Coll Llan 53. **d** 54 **p** 55 Swan B. C of St Thos Swansea 54-55; Llansamlet 55-58; V of Llanfihangel-y-Creuddyn 58-66; Llanarthney w Llanddarog

Dio St D from 66. *Vicarage, Llanddarog, Dyfed.* (Llanddarog 268)

REES, Very Rev John Ivor. b 26. Univ of Wales (Abth) BA 50. Westcott Ho Cam 50. **d** 52 **p** 53 St D. C Of Fishguard w Llanychaer 52-55; Llangathen w Llanfihangel Cifargen (in c of St Mary Court Henry) 55-57; C-in-c of Uzmaston w Boulston 57-59; V of Slebech w Uzmaston and Boulston 59-65; Llangollen w Trevor 65-74; RD of Llangollen 70-74; R of Wrexham 74-76; Chap O of St John 74-76; and from 81. Can of St A Cathl 75-76; Dean of Ban from 76; Surr from 78; V of Ban Cathl from 79. *Deanery, Bangor, Gwyn.* (0248-351693)

REES, John Martin Rawlins Gore. St D Coll Lamp BA 53. **d** 55 **p** 57 St A. C of Mold 55-56; Broughton 56-59; Newtown 59-61; V of Penycae 61-73; Northop Dio St A from 73. *Northop Vicarage, Mold, Clwyd, CH7 6BS.* (Northop 235)

REES, John Philip Walford. b 41. St D Coll Lamp BA (2nd cl Phil) 62. BD (Univ of Wales) 72. Linacre Ho Ox BA (3rd cl Th) 64, MA 68. Wycl Hall Ox 62. **d** 64 **p** 65 Ox. C of St Jo Evang w St Steph Reading 64-67; V of Kirk Patrick 67-68; C of Pontypool 68-70; Area Sec of the CMS Dios Glouc Worc and Heref 70-75; V of Bream Dio Glouc from 75. *Vicarage, Bream, Lydney, Glos, GL15 6ES.* (0594 562376)

REES, John Tyssul. b 09. St D Coll Lamp. **d** 65 **p** 66 St D. C of Henfynyw w Aberaeron and Llanddewi Aberath 65-67; V of Llandyssilio-Gogo 67-72; Trelech-a'r-Betts w Abenant 72-78. *c/o Trelech Vicarage, Penybont, Dyfed.* (Maddox 335)

REES, John Van der Horst. b 05. K Coll Lon 30. **d** 33 **p** 34 Chelmsf. C of St Pet Upton Cross 33-35; Twerton-on-Avon (in c of St Pet E Twerton) 35-40; Chap RAFVR 40-46; V of Hexton 45-48; R of Higham Gobion 45-48; Org Sec Miss to Seaman W Distr 48-52; LPr Dio Bris 48-50; Dio Sarum 50-52; Perm to Offic Dios B & W and Glouc 48-52; C-in-c of Canford Cliffs Conv Distr w Sandbanks 52-56; Min 56-65; V of Canford Cliffs and Sandbanks Dio Sarum from 65. *3 Chaddesley Glen, Poole, Dorset.* (Canford Cliffs 707435)

REES, Canon John Wynford Joshua. b 24. Late Scho of St D Coll Lamp BA 52. **d** 53 **p** 54 St D. C of Aberystwyth 53-60; V of Llanyre w Llanfihangel-Helygen an Disserth (and Llanwrthwl 60-71) Dio Swan B from 60; RD of Maelienydd from 74; Hon Can of Brecon Cathl 77-79; Can from 79; Dir of Educn Dio Swan B from 78. *Llanyre Vicarage, Llandrindod Wells, Powys.* (Llandrindod Wells 2530)

✠ **REES, Right Rev Leslie Lloyd.** b 19. Kelham Th Coll 36. **d** 42 **p** 43 Llan. C of St Sav Roath and Asst Chap HM Pris Cardiff 42-45; L to Offic Dio Dur 45-48; Chap HM Pris Durham 45-48; V of Princetown w Postbridge and Huccaby Chapels and Chap HM Pris Dartmoor 48-55; Chap HM Pris Win 55-62; Chap Gen of Prisons 62-80; Hon Can of Cant 66-80; Lich from 80; Chap to HM the Queen 71-80; Cons Ld Bp Suffr of Shrewsbury in Westmr Abbey 1 Nov 80 by Abp of Cant; Bps of Lon, Dur, Lich, Derby, Ely, Heref, Nor and Roch; Bps Suffr of Southn, Stafford and Wolverhampton; and Bps Allenby, Bulley and E J Roberts; and others. *Athlone House, London Road, Shrewsbury, SY2 6PG.* (Shrewsbury 56410)

REES, Llewelyn Phillip. St D Coll Lamp LDiv 02. **d** 03 **p** 04 Llan. C of Pentrebach 03-05; St Paul Llanelly 05-10; Sketty (w c of St Martin Dunvant) 10-14; R of Ciliau Aeron 14-20; St Lawrence (w Ford from 27) 20-36; V of Llanddarog 36-48. *26 Victoria Road, Llanelli, Dyfed.*

REES, Lloyd Clifford. Qu Th Coll Ont 49. **d** 52 **p** 53 Newfld. C of St Anthony 52-53; I of Lamaline 53-59; R of Salvage 59-66; Lewisporte 66-69; Bell I 69-70. *4985 53rd Avenue, Laval West, Montreal, PQ, Canada.*

REES, Michael Lloyd. b 51. St D Coll Lamp Dipl Th 74. Bp Burgess Hall Lamp 72. **d** 74 **p** 75 St D. C of Cardigan and Mwnt w Ferwig 74-77; Min Can of St D Cathl 77-81; V in R Benef of Abth Dio St D from 81. *Vicarage, Penparcau, Aberystwyth, Dyfed.* (Abth 617819)

REES, Canon Owain Peredur Dyfed. b 18. St D Coll Lamp BA 46. TD 67. **d** 47 **p** 48 Llan. C of Aberdare 47-51; Llanishen w Lisvane 51-58; CF (TA) 55-67; (ACF) from 67; Sen Chap from 74; C-in-c of All SS Cardiff 58-64; Chap HM Pris Cardiff 58-64; Dep Chap 64-76; R of Llanedeyrn w Cyncoed Dio Mon from 64; Can of Mon from 78. *Rectory, Cyncoed Road, Cardiff, CF2 6RU.* (Cardiff 752138)

REES, Chan Owen Geoffrey. b 14. Late Scho of St D Coll Lamp BA (2nd cl Hist) 35. Jes Coll Ox BA (1st cl Th) 37, MA 42. St Steph Ho Ox 37. **d** 38 **p** 39 Swan B. C of Llangyfelach w Morriston 38-43; Chap CF (EC) 43-46; Men in Disp 45; Lect and Sub-Warden St Mich Coll Llan 46-51; V of Llanbadarn Fawr 51-56; Surr from 51; V of Aberdare 56-57; RD of Aberdare 56-57; Warden St Mich Coll Llan 57-76; Lect in Th Univ Coll of S Wales and Mon Cardiff 58-76; Can of Warthacwm in Llan Cathl from 69; Chan of Llan Cathl from 71; R of Bonvilston w St Nich and St Geo-super-Ely Dio Llan from 76. *Rectory, Ger-y-Llan, St Nicholas, Cardiff, S Glam, CF5 6SY.* (Peterston-s-Ely 760728)

REES, Percival Antony Everard. b 35. Pemb Coll Ox 2nd cl Mods 54, BA (2nd cl Engl) 56, MA 59. Clifton Th Coll 58. **d** 60 **p** 61 Sarum. C of St Jo Evang Heatherlands Parkstone 60-65; P-in-c of Mahableshwar of Panchgani and of Satara 65-69; C of St Jo Evang Heatherlands Parkstone (in c of Good Shepherd) 69-70; V of St Luke w Hampstead Dio Lon from 70. *12 Kidderpore Avenue, NW3.* (01-794 2634)

REES, Peter Duncan. b 47. St D Coll Lamp BA 69. Ripon Hall Ox 70. **d** 72 **p** 73 S'wark. C of Putney 72-75; Ross-on-Wye 75-80; P-in-c of Dilwyn w Stretford Dio Heref from 80. *Dilwyn Vicarage, Hereford, HR4 8HW.* (Weobley 556)

REES, Peter Frederick Ransom. Univ of Lon BA 47. Linc Th Coll 47. **d** 49 **p** 50 Man. C of Leigh 49-52; St Thos Bedford Leigh 52-53; V of Laneside Dio Blackb from 53. *Laneside Vicarage, Haslingden, Rossendale, Lancs, BB4 4BG.* (Rossendale 213838)

REES, Richard John Edward William. St D Coll Lamp BA 58. St Mich Coll Llan 58. **d** 60 **p** 61 St D. C of St Issell 60-64; Llanedy 64-67; V of Whitchurch w Solva and St Elvis Dio St D from 67; RD of Dewisland and Fishguard from 73. *Whitchurch Vicarage, Solva, Dyfed.* (Solva 281)

REES, Richard Michael. b 35. St Pet Hall Ox BA 57, MA 61. Tyndale Hall Bris 57. **d** 59 Lewes for Chich **p** 60 Chich. C of Crowborough 59-62; Ch Ch Clifton (w Em Ch Clifton from 63) 62-64; V of Ch Ch Clevedon 64-72; Chap St Brandon's Sch Clevedon 71-72; V of H Trin Cam Dio Ely from 72; M Gen Syn from 75. *1 Selwyn Gardens, Cambridge, CB3 9AX.* (0223-354774)

REES, Sidney. b 12. St D Coll Lamp BA 34. St Mich Coll Llan 35. **d** 37 **p** 38 St D. C of Llandilofawr w Llandyfeisant 37-40; Pembrey w Burry Port 40-47; V of St Ishmael w Llansaint and Ferryside 47-65; RD of Kidwelly 64-65; V of Eglwys-Fair-Glyntaf (or Whitland) w Kiffig 65-79; Can of St D Cathl 77-79; *10 Morfa Lane, Carmarthen, Dyfed.*

REES, Thomas George. Moore Th Coll Syd ThL (2nd cl) 43. **d** and **p** 43 Syd. C of St Barn Syd 43-46; Syd Dioc Evang 46-54; R of Ryde W 54-65; Newtown 65-67. *16 Percival Road, Stanmore, NSW 2048, Australia.*

REES, Tudno. Moore Th Coll Syd ACT ThL 60. **d** and **p** 61 Syd. C of St John Darlinghurst Syd 61-63; Liverpool 63-64; C-in-c of Hillview 64-65; Chap Ld Howe I 66-69; Home Miss S Rep for S Coast 69-72; Perm to Offic Dio Syd from 76; Asst Master and Chap Illawarra Gr Sch from 79. *Illawarra Grammar School, West Wollongong, NSW, Australia 2500.*

REES, Vivian John Howard. b 51. Univ of Southn LLB 72. Univ of Ox BA 79. [f Solicitor]. Wycl Hall Ox 76. **d** 79 Knaresborough for Ripon **p** 80 Ripon. C of Moor Allerton Dio Ripon from 79. *409 Harrogate Road, Leeds 17.*

REES, William David Cledwyn. b 25. Qu Coll Cam 2nd cl Hist Trip pt i 48, BA (2nd cl Geog Trip pt i) 49, MA 51. Univ of Wales MA 75, PhD 81. **d** 65 **p** 66 St A. Hon C of Rhyl 65-72; Chap and Lect St Mary's Coll Ban 72-77; L to Offic Dio Ban from 72; Lect in Counselling and Chap Univ Coll of N Wales Ban from 77. *Anwylfa, Fron Park Avenue, Llanfairfechan, Gwyn.* (Gwyn 680054)

REES, Canon William Elfyn. b 17. St D Coll Lamp BA 37. Wycl Hall Ox 38. **d** 40 **p** 45 Ripon. C of Richmond 40-41; serving w RAF 41-45; C of St Geo Leeds 45-46; Emsworth w Warblington 46-50; R of Blendworth (w Chalton and Idsworth from 54) 50-62; Alverstoke Dio Portsm from 62; Hon Can of Portsm from 74. *Alverstoke Rectory, Gosport, Hants.* (Gosport 81979)

REES, Ven William Hugh. b 05. Late Scho of St D Coll Lamp BA 26. Westcott Ho Cam 28. **d** 28 **p** 29 St D. C of St Pet Carmarthen 28-31; St Phil Georgetn 31-34; C-in-c of Uzmaston w Boulston 34-35; Bp's Messenger Dio St D 35-39; V of St Mary Haverfordwest (w St Thos from 42) 39-50; Colwyn Bay 50-74; Surr 48-74; RD of Rhos 60-70; Can of Ricardi Harrison in St A Cathl 60-69; Preb of Faenol and Prec 69-70; Archd of St A 70-74; Archd (Emer) from 74. *11 Hesketh Road, Colwyn Bay, Clwyd.*

REES, William Trevor. Bp Wilson Th Coll IM 25. **d** 27 **p** 28 S and M. C of St Matt Douglas 27-29; Bickley 29-38; V of St Andr Orpington 38-50; Chap RAFVR 42-46; V of St Andr Bromley 50-64. *Address temp unknown.*

REES-DAVIES, Hamlyn Llewellyn. b 11. Selw Coll Cam 2nd cl Hist Trip pt i 33, BA 34, 3rd cl Th Trip pt i 35, MA 45. MBE (Mil) 47. Ridley Hall Cam 34. **d** 36 **p** 37 Heref. C of Much Wenlock 36-45; CF 40-65. *Gwynnon Villa, Llanarthney, Dyfed.*

REES-JONES, John Francis Howard. b 09. Peterho Cam 2nd cl Hist Trip pt i 30, BA (2nd cl Engl Trip pt i) 31, MA 37. St Steph Ho Ox 31. **d** 33 **p** 34 Ex. C of St Pet Plymouth 33-36; All SS Tooting 36-38; St Clem Bournemouth 38-46; CF (EC) 40-45; Hon CF 45; V of St Alb Southn 46-67; V of Charlestown 67-79; Surr 71-79; Perm to Offic Dio Sarum from 80.

258 Frome Road, Trowbridge, Wilts, BA14 0DS. (Trowbridge 66618)

REES-JONES, Stephen Idris Dynevor. b 11. Bp Wilson Th Coll IM 39. **d** 39 Chelmsf **p** 40 Barking for Chelmsf. C of St Jo Evang N Woolwich 39-40; C-in-c 40-41; St Mark Vic Dks 40-41; Godstone 41-45; Shepton Mallet 45-49; R of Watton-at-Stone 49-56; C-in-c of Sacombe 49-54; R of Curry Mallet (w Curland 56-60) 56-78; C-in-c of Fivehead w Swell 75-78; Perm to Offic Dio B & W from 79. *Little Curry, Hastings, Thickthorn Lane, Ashill, Somt, TA19 9LR.* (Hatch Beauchamp 480521)

REESE, Hobart Lawrence. b 23. Ohio State Univ BA 48, MA 49. Virginia Th Sem MDiv 58. Episc Th Sem in Virginia 56. **d** and **p** 58 Bp of Washington. In Amer Ch 58-73; Dir of Programme Dio Niag 73-74; R of Woodburn 74-76; P-in-c of St Mark Hamilton 76-78; R of Ch Ch Niag Falls Dio Niag from 78. *4750 Zimmerman Avenue, Niagara Falls, Ont, Canada.* (416-354 0772)

REESE, John David. b 49. Cudd Coll 73. **d** 76 **p** 77 Worc. C of St Mary & All SS Kidderminster 76-81; V of St Chris Johore Bahru Dio W Mal from 81. *St Christopher's Vicarage, Jalan Mustapha, Johore Bahru, Malaysia.*

REEVE, Brian Charles. b 36. BSc (Lon, 1st cl Gen) 57, BD (Lon) 60. Tyndale Hall Bris 58. **d** 61 Warrington for Liv **p** 62 Liv. C of St Luke Eccleston 61-63; Overchurch (or Upton) 63-65; St Mark Newtown Pemberton (in c of St Barn Marsh Green) 65-68; V of Ch Ch Macclesfield 68-74; Ch Ch Stone Dio Lich from 74; RD of Trentham from 77. *Christ Church Vicarage, Stone, Staffs, ST15 8DA.* (Stone 812669)

REEVE, Canon Charles Edward. Bp's Univ Lennox BA (1st cl Th) 31. **d** 31 **p** 32 Calg. C of Rocky Mountain House Distr 31-33; I of Delburne Miss 33-34; Mirror 34-36; Innisfail w Penhold Bowden and Ridgewood 36-41; St Mich AA Calg 41-55; Hon Can Calg 53-55; R of Vernon 55-71; Can of Koot 64-71; Can (Emer) from 71. *8572 109B Street, N Delta, BC, Canada.*

REEVE, David Michael. b 44. St Cath Coll Cam BA 67, MA 71. Coll of Resurr Mirfield 68. **d** 70 Lewes for Chich **p** 71 Chich. C of Willingdon 70-73; Hove 73-76; Moulsecoomb 76-80; R of Singleton Dio Chich from 80; V of E Dean Dio Chich from 80; W Dean Dio Chich from 80. *Singleton Rectory, Chichester, Sussex.* (Singleton 213)

REEVE, James Lawrence. Univ of Melb BA 50. Trin Coll Melb ThL 51. **d** 52 **p** 53 Melb. C of Ivanhoe 52-54; Min of Lorne 54-58; Bacchus Marsh 58-63; Em Oakleigh S 63-70; I of St Mark E Brighton 70-75; St Geo Ivanhoe Dio Melb from 75. *46 Warncliffe Road, E Ivanhoe, Vic, Australia 3079.* (03-49 5904)

REEVE, John David Genge. b 14. Em Coll Cam BA 36, MA 40. Westcott Ho Cam 38. **d** 39 **p** 40 Cant. C of Birchington w Acol (in c of Hersden Conv Distr from 46) 39-48; V of Lynsted (w Kingsdown from 55) 48-56; C-in-c of Kingsdown 53-55; R of St Andr Deal 56-60; V of St Sav Folkestone 60-65; Worth 65-80. *62 Sycamore Close, Lydd, Romney Marsh, Kent, TN29 9LE.* (Lydd 20438)

REEVE, Kenneth Robert. b 23. St Cath Coll Ox BA 49, MA 53. Sarum Th Coll 64. **d** 68 **p** 69 B & W. C of Farleigh-Hungerford w Tellisford 68-71; Perm to Offic Dio Virgin Is (Amer Ch) 71-72; Norton St Philip 72-74; Hinton Charterhouse 72-74; L to Offic Dio Sey 74-76; Perm to Offic Dio B & W 77; Dio Chich from 78. *31 Lucastes Avenue, Haywards Heath, W Sussex, RH16 1JU.* (H Heath 412015)

REEVE, Roger Patrick. b 42. Fitzw Coll Cam 2nd cl Hist Trip pt i 63, BA (2nd cl Th Trip pt ii) 65, MA 68. Coll of Resurr Mirfield. **d** 67 Crediton for Ex **p** 68 Ex. C of St Pet w H Trin Barnstaple 67-74; V of St Aid Ernesettle Plymouth 74-78; Braunton w Saunton and Knowle Dio Ex from 78. *Vicarage, Braunton, Devon.* (Braunton 813367)

REEVE, Ronald Ernest. St Pet Hall Ox BA (2nd cl Th) 48, MA 52, BD 54. Univ of Ox DPhil 76. Wycl Hall Ox 48. **d** 50 **p** 51 Roch. C of Bexleyheath 50-52; V of New Hythe 52-54; Lect Bp's Univ Lennox and I of E Sherbrooke 54-59; Vice-Prin Cranmer Hall Dur 60-62; St Jo Coll Dur 62-63; L to Offic Dio Dur 60-63; Prof of Dogmatic and Moral Th Univ of K Coll NS 63-68; Prof of Relig Bp's Univ Lennox from 68; Exam Chap to Bp of Queb 77-79. *Bishop's University, Lennoxville, PQ, Canada.*

REEVES, Arthur Jordan Jerome. b 21. Cudd Coll 67. **d** 68 Pet **p** 69 Bp Graham-Campbell for Pet. C of Kingsthorpe 68-73; R of Barby 73-81; V of Kilsby 73-81; Warmington Dio Pet from 81; P-in-c of Tansor w Fotheringhay Dio Pet from 81. *Warmington Vicarage, Peterborough, PE8 6TE.* (Elton 263)

REEVES, Christopher. b 30. Univ of Nottm BA (2nd cl Engl) 53. Wells Th Coll 53. **d** 55 Taunton for B & W **p** 56 B & W. C of St Andr Taunton 55-59; St Greg Gt City and Dio Cant 59-61; Chap Miss to Seamen Schiedam 61-67; V of Barkingside Dio Chelmsf from 67. *Vicarage, Mossford Green, Barkingside, Ilford, Essex.* (01-550 2669)

REEVES, David Eric. b 46. Sarum Th Coll 68. **d** 71 Dorking for Guildf **p** 72 Guildf. C of H Trin Guildf 71-74; St Pet Warmsworth Doncaster 74-78; V of Herringthorpe Dio Sheff from 78. *493 Herringthorpe Valley Road, Rotherham, S Yorks, S60 4LB.* (Rotherham 63526)

REEVES, Donald St John. b 34. Qu Coll Cam 2nd cl Engl Trip pt i 56, BA (2nd cl Engl Trip pt ii), 57, MA 61. Cudd Coll 62. **d** 63 **p** 64 Cant. C of Maidstone 63-65; Dom Chap to Bp of S'wark 65-68; Hon Chap from 68; V of St Pet St Helier Morden 68-80; Dir of Urban Min Project from 68; R of St Jas Piccadilly Dio Lon from 80. *197 Piccadilly, W1V 9LF.* (01-734 0956)

REEVES, Ernest William. Univ of S Afr. **d** 52 **p** 54 Johann. C of Parkview 52-53; St Mary Virg Cathl Johann 53-59; R of Umvukwes 59-68; L to Offic Dio Mashon from 68. *122 Jameson Avenue West, Salisbury, Rhodesia.*

REEVES, James Lacey. b 23. FCIS 58. SOC 60. **d** 74 **p** 75 Horsham for Chich (APM). C of Wisborough Green 74-81; St Mary Horsham Dio Chich from 81. *8 South Grove, Horsham, W Sussex, RH13 5BZ.* (Horsham 2795)

REEVES, James William. ACT ThL 65. **d** 64 **p** 65 Wang for Brisb. C of Redcliffe 64-66; Shepparton 66-69; R of Violet Tn 69-71; Myrtleford 71-74; P-in-c of Corryong 75-76; R of Rutherglen 76-79; Nathalia Dio Wang from 79; Dom Chap to Bp of Wang from 77. *Rectory, Muntz Avenue, Nathalia, Vic, Australia 3638.*

REEVES, John Graham. b 44. Kelham Th Coll 64. **d** 69 Sheff **p** 71 Burnley for Sheff. C of Aston w Aughton 69-71; Ribbleton 72-74; St Andr Cleveleys 74-75; P-in-c of Huncoat Dio Blackb 75-77; V from 77. *Huncoat Vicarage, Accrington, Lancs.* (Accrington 33346)

REEVES, Ven John Hastings. ACT ThL 42. **d** 42 **p** 43 Bath. M of Bro of Good Shepherd Dubbo 42-44; Gilgandra 44-47; R of Nyngan 47-48; C of Cowra 48-50; Coonable 50-53; R of Cowra 53-61; Parkes Dio Bath from 61; Archd of Camidge from 71. *Rectory, Parkes, NSW, Australia 2870.* (068-62 2083)

REEVES, Canon Joseph Wilfred. b 02. Univ of Birm BSc 26, MSc 40. Bps' Coll Cheshunt 31. **d** 33 Southw for Chich **p** 34 Chich. C of St Sav Preston Sussex 33-35; Good Shepherd Preston 35-39; CF (R of O) 39-45; V of Ferring 45-73; RD of Worthing 58-71; Can and Preb of Hova Villa in Chich Cathl from 63. *6 Penland Road, Bexhill-on-Sea, Sussex, TN40 2JG.* (Bexhill 215559)

REEVES, Kenneth William. b 38. TCD 67. **d** 69 Kilm for Derry **p** 70 Derry. C of Killowen 69-70; I of Ardara 70-76; Team V of Quidenham 76-81; V of Swaffham Dio Nor from 81. *Vicarage, Swaffham, Norf.* (Swaffham 21373)

REEVES, Nicholas John Harding. b 44. ALCD 69. **d** 69 **p** 70 Ches. C of Overchurch (or Upton) 69-72; All SS Woodlands 72-74; St Luke Eccles Distr Cranham Park Dio Chelmsf 74-79; V from 79. *201 Front Lane, Cranham, Upminster, Essex.* (Upminster 22562)

✠ **REEVES, Most Rev Paul Alfred.** Univ of NZ BA 55, MA 56. St Pet Coll Ox BA 61. MA 65. St Jo Coll Auckld LTh (1st cl) 58. **d** 58 Waik **p** 60 Ox for Waik. C of St Francis Tokoroa 58-59; St Mary Virg Ox 59-61; Kirkley Lowestoft 61-63; St Mary Lewisham 63-64; V of Okato 64-66; Lect St Jo Coll Auckld 66-69; Dir Educn Dio Auckld 70-71; L to Offic Dio Auckld 66-71; Cons Ld Bp of Wai 25 Mar 71 in St Jo Cathl Napier by Bp of Wel; Bps of Polyn, Waik, Auckld, Nel, Ch Ch and Dun; Bps Mackenzie, Monteith and Aotearoa; Trld to Auckld 79; Elected Primate and Abp of NZ 80. *Bishop's House, 2 Arney Crescent, Remuera, Auckland 5, NZ.* (543-473)

REEVES, William Graham. b 05. OBE 59. Sarum Th Coll 28. **d** 31 **p** 32 Lich. C of St John W Bromwich 31-34; St Pet Wolverhampton 34-37; SSC Dio Lich 38-39; C of St Jo Bapt Cov 39-43; Chap RAF 43-58; V of St Paul Foleshill Cov 59-75. *8b Cliff Road, Bridgnorth, Salop.*

REGISFORD, Sylvanus Hermus Alonzo. BD (Lon) 65. Codr Coll Barb. **d** 65 **p** 66 Windw Is. C of Carriacou 65-66; St Geo Grenada 66-69; P-in-c of Carriacon 69-72; R of Layou 73; Grand Turk 73-74; St Steph Grand Bahama 74-78; Riviere Doree St Lucia 78-80. *c/o Grace Church Rectory, Riviere Doree, St Lucia, WI.*

REGLAR, Canon Gerald John. Univ of Melb BA 33. Kelham Th Coll 34. St Cath S Ox BA and MA 48. **d** 37 **p** 38 Ox. C of Cowley St John 37-40; Sub-Warden St Geo Coll Crawley Perth 40-43; Chap RAAF 43-46; P-in-c of St John Salisbury 46-58; R 58-81; Chap Yatala Pris (w Morris Hosp and Northfield 46-58) 46-81; Can of Adel from 66; L to Offic Dio Adel from 81. *113 Bennowie Street, Ingle Farm, S Australia 5098.*

REHA, Phillip. b 29. **d** 80 Wai. Hon C of Ruatoki Whakatane Dio Wai from 80. *94 Domett Street, Kawerau, NZ.*

REID, Adam Alexander. Univ of Glas MA 27. **d** 42 Hull for York **p** 43 York. C of St Barn Linthorpe Middlesbrough

42-46; Stockton-on-Tees 46-47; St Pet Redcar 47-49; PC of St Jas Stockton-on-Tees 49-57; PC of Castleside 57-61; R of St Steph S Shields 61-72; L to Offic Dio Carl from 72. *Glebe Cottage, Low Wiend, Appleby, Westmd.*

✠ **REID, Right Rev Alfred Charles.** Episc Th Sem Mass BD 72. Boston Coll Mass MEducn 76. St Pet Th Coll Ja 47. **d** 60 Ja **p** 61 Kingston for Ja. C of Montego Bay 60-66; on leave 66-67; R of Vere w Race Course 67-71; Stony Hill 71-78; Exam Chap to Bp of Ja 69-76; CF (Ja) 78-80; Cons Bp Suffr of Montego Bay in Ch of St Jas Ap Montego Bay 26 July 80 by Abp of WI; Bps of Antig, Trinid, Nassau, Barb, Ja, Guy, Bel and Virgin Is (Amer Ch); Bp Suffr of Mandeville; and Bp H Edmonson. *Box 346, Montego Bay, Jamaica, W Indies.* (095-22933)

REID, Andrew Sutherland. b 56. Univ of Lon BD. Moore Th Coll Syd ThL. **d** 81 Syd. C of St Bede Beverly Hills Dio Syd from 81. *2 Sackville Street, Hurstville, NSW, Australia 2220.*

REID, Anthony Meredith. Univ of Tor. **d** 57 **p** 58 Montr. C of Cartierville Montr 57-60; I 60-61; R of Montebello 61-66. *1487 Briarwood Crescent, Oakville, Ont, Canada.*

REID, Colin Guthrie. b 30. **d** 56 **p** 57 Carl. C of St Thos Kendal 56-59; St Kentigern Crosthwaite 59-60; R of Caldbeck w Castle Sowerby (and Sebergham from 76) Dio Carl from 60; RD of Wigton 69-70; C-in-c of Sebergham w Welton 75-76. *Caldbeck Rectory, Wigton, Cumb.* (Caldbeck 233)

REID, David Collins. Acadia Univ NS BA 62, BEducn 64. K Coll NS BST 69. **d** 68 **p** 69 NS. L to Offic Dio NS 68-70; R of Neil's Harbour 70-73; Annapolis 73-78; Granville 73-78; Kentville Dio NS from 78; Exam Chap to Bp of NS from 75. *14 Highland Avenue, Kentville, NS, Canada.*

REID, Canon Douglas William John. b 34. Edin Th Coll. **d** 63 **p** 64 Glas. C of H Trin Ayr 63-68; R of St Jas Springburn Glas 68-74; St Ninian City and Dio Glas from 74; Synod Clk and Can of Glas from 79. *32 Glencairn Drive, Glasgow, G41 4PW.* (041-423 1247)

REID, Duncan Stuart Warren. b 50. Monash Univ Melb BA 72. Trin Coll Melb 76. **d** 78 Melb for Gippsld. C of St John Maffra 78-80. *2 Elm Street, N Melbourne, Vic, Australia 3051.*

REID, Frank. **d** 55 Newfld **p** 56 NS for Newfld. R of Rose Blanche 55-62; Porte de Grave 62-69; Bay d'Espoir 69-70; C of St Mary Virg St John's 70-76; R of Arichat Dio NS from 76. *Box 591, Port Hawkesbury, NS, Canada.*

REID, Frederick Alfred. Moore Th Coll Syd. **d** 35 **p** 36 Graft. C of Casino 35-37; Lismore 37-38; Kempsey 38; R of Centr Macleay 38-41; Chap AIF 41-45; I of Smithtown 42-52; R of Coonabarabran 52-57; Perm to Offic Dio Graft from 61. *Elizabeth Street, South West Rocks, NSW, Australia.*

REID, Gavin Hunter. b 34. K Coll Lon BA 56. Oak Hill Th Coll 58. **d** 60 **p** 61 Chelmsf. C of St Paul E Ham 60-63; Rainham 63-66; Publication Sec CPAS 66-71; L to Offic Dio Roch 66-68; Hon C of St Barn Cray 68-71; St Jo Bapt Woking Dio Guildf from 72; Ed Sec of United Society for Chr Lit 71-74; Sec for Evang w Ch Pastoral Aid Society from 74. *138 St John's Road, Woking, Surrey.* (Woking 5589)

REID, Herbert Alan. b 31. K Coll Lon and Warm AKC 55. **d** 56 **p** 57 Blackb. C of Penwortham 56-59; C-in-c of Conv Distr of St Leon Penwortham 59-63; V of Brierfield 63-72; St Paul Warton 72-79; Read-in-Whalley Dio Blackb from 79. *Vicarage, Read, Nr Burnley, Lancs. BB12 7RQ.* (Padiham 71361)

REID, Hugh Gamble. b 33. Roch Th Coll 63. **d** and **p** 64 Linc. C of Thornton w Martin 64-66; Alford w Rigsby 66-69; Chap HM Borstal Everthorpe 69-71; Chap HM Pris Dur 71-74; Wakef 74-77; V of Northowram 77-79. *c/o Northowram Vicarage, Halifax, HX3 7HH.* (Halifax 22551)

REID, Ian Davison. b 37. Univ of Liv BA (2nd cl Geog) 61, MA 63. Clifton Th Coll 63. **d** 65 Warrington for Liv **p** 66 Liv. C of Edge Hill 65-68; H Trin Heworth (w St Cuthb Peaseholme to 75) York 68-76; V of St Barn Linthorpe Dio York from 76. *5 Park Road South, Linthorpe, Middlesbrough, Cleve.* (Middlesbrough 817306)

REID, James Maxwell. Qu Th Coll Ont 49. **d** 52 **p** 53 Newfld. I of Battle Harbour Labrador 52-55; C of St Jo Bapt Cathl St John's 55-58; R of Fogo 58-63; Bay of Is 64-70; Gander Miss Dio Newfld (Centr Newfld from 76) from 70. *Rectory, Lindberg Road, Gander, Newfoundland, Canada.* (709-256-3838)

✠ **REID, Right Rev John Robert.** Univ of Melb BA 52. Moore Th Coll Syd ACT ThL 54. **d** and **p** 55 Syd. C of St Matt Manly 55-56; R of Gladesville 56-69; Commiss Centr Tang from 66; Exam Chap to Abp of Syd from 68; Archd of Cumb 69-72 and 75-79; Can of Syd 70-72; Cons Asst Bp of Syd in St Andr Cathl Syd 25 July 72 by Abps of Syd and Brisb; Bps of Armid, Bath, C & Goulb, Graft, Newc and River; and others. *33 Fairfax Road, Bellevue Hill, NSW, Australia 2023.* (36 3320)

REID, Peter Ivor. b 30. Qu Coll Cam BA 53, MA 70. St Mich AA Coll Llan 78. **d** 80 **p** 81 Llan. C of Llantwit Major w St Donats Dio Llan from 80. *Walton House, Station Road, Llantwit Major, S Glam.*

REID, Preb Samuel Henry. b 14. Trin Coll Dub BA 38, MA 46. **d** 40 **p** 41 Connor. C of St Luke Belf 40-42; Ballymena 42-45; C-in-c of H Trin Belf 45-61; I 61-70; C-in-c of Glynn w Raloo and Templecorran and Warden of Readers Dio Connor from 70; Preb of Connor Cathl from 81. *15 Rectory Road, Glynn, Larne, Co Antrim, BT14 3HH.*

REID, Stewart Thomas. b 45. Oak Hill Th Coll 66. **d** 70 **p** 71 Repton for Derby. C of Normanton-by-Derby 70-73; St Andr Leyland 73-78; V of St Luke Halliwell Dio Man from 78. *St Luke's Vicarage, Chorley Old Road, Bolton, Gtr Manchester, BL1 3BE.* (Bolton 43060)

REID, Theodore John Gerald Lockhart. b 22. **d** and **p** 77 Capetn (APM). C of Transfig Bellville Dio Capetn from 77. *5 Wiersma Road, Kuils River 7580, CP, S Africa.* (33-3695)

REID, Thomas Brangwin. b 04. AKC 34. **d** 34 **p** 35 Blackb. C of Barrowford 34-36; Thornton-le-Fylde 36-38; C-in-c of Ascen Conv Distr Torrisholme 38-47; CF (EC) 40-45; V of St Mich Whitewell 47-74; L to Offic Dio Blackb from 74. *36a Station Road, Thornton, Thornton-Cleveleys, Lancs.* (Cleveleys 867133)

REID, Wallace Melville. **d** 68 Bp Hunt for Tor. C-in-c of Price's Corners Orillia S Dio Tor from 68. *400 Bayview Parkway, Orillia, Ont, Canada.*

REID, William Alexander. Univ of Melb BA 48. ACT ThL 50. **d** 51 **p** 52 Melb. C of Malvern Dio Melb 51-52; C of St Jo Div Kennington 53; St Matt Westmr 53-56; St Pet Balkwell 56-57; Min of Lilydale 58-62; Can of St Arn 62-68 and 69-71; R of St Arn Cathl 62-68; Charlton 68-71; Exam Chap to Bp of St Arn 64-71; Chap Dioc Th Coll Kuch 71-76; Newton Th Coll Popondetta 77-81; I of St Anselm Middle Pk Dio Melb from 81. *39 Park Road, Middle Park, Vic, Australia 3206.*

REID, Canon William Frederick. b 22. Trin Coll Dub Div Test and BA (2nd cl Phil) 45, MA 53. **d** 46 **p** 47 Connor. C of Ardoyne Belf 46-49; Finaghy 49-52; Donnybrook 52-54; I of Carbury 54-59; C of St Steph Walbrook Lon 59-67; Chap Netherne Hosp Coulsdon 67-76; P-in-c of St Luke's Conv Distr Netherne Merstham 67-76; Sec and Dir of Training Hosp Chap Coun from 76; Publ Pr Dio S'wark from 77; Hon Can of Newc T Cathl from 79. *Hospital Chaplaincies Council, Church House, Deans Yard, Westminster, SW1P 3NZ.* (01-222 9011)

REID, William Gordon. b 43. Univ of Edin MA 63. Keble Coll Ox BA (2nd cl Th) 66. Cudd Coll 66. **d** 67 **p** 68 Edin. C of St Salvador Stenhouse Edin 67-69; Chap Sarum Th Coll 69-72; R of St Mich and All SS City and Dio Edin from 72. *15 Leven Terrace, Edinburgh, EH3 9LW.* (031-229 6104)

REILLY, Frederick James. b 29. Div Hostel Dub 70. **d** 73 **p** 74 Connor. C of Agherton 73-75; Ballymena Dio Connor from 75. *19 Deramore Avenue, Ballymena, Co Antrim, N Ireland.* (Ballymena 43953)

REILLY, Percival Trevor. Trin Coll Dub BA 41. **d** 41 **p** 42 Arm. C of Errigal Keerogue w Ballygawley and Killeshill 41-44; Drumcree 44-49; R of Altedesert (w Pomeroy from 52) Dio Arm from 49. *Altedesert Rectory, Pomeroy, Co Tyrone, N Ireland.* (Pomeroy 217)

REILLY, Thomas Gerard. b 38. **d** and **p** by RC Bp of Pamplona (Spain). In RC Ch 64-73; Rec into Angl Commun by Archd of Hackney for Bp of Lon (APM). Hon C of All S Clapton Pk 73-75; All SS Haggerston 75-81. *Address temp unknown.*

REIMER, John Walter. Univ of NSW BEng 61. BD (Lon) 67. Moore Th Coll Syd ACT ThL 67. **d** 68 **p** 69 Syd. C of Sans Souci 68-70; Nowra 70-72; C-in-c of Provisional Par Northmead 72-75; R 75-81; St E Pagewood Dio Syd from 81. *18 Holden Street, Pageword, NSW, Australia 2035.* (344-7559)

REIMERS, Alfred Gustav. Univ of Wisconsin BA 49. Nashotah Ho. **d** 51 **p** 52 Hur. C-in-c of Merlin and Ouvry 51; Muncey 52; in Amer Ch 53-57; R of Nipigon 57-61; Ascen Sudbury 61-66; Hon C of St Eliz Tor 66-67; Ch of Incarnation City and Dio Tor from 67. *97 Dentonia Park Avenue, Toronto, 13, Ont, Canada.*

✠ **REINDORP, Right Rev George Edmund.** b 11. Trin Coll Cam 2nd cl Mor Sc Trip pt i 34, BA (3rd cl Th Trip pt i) 36, MA 39. DD (Lambeth) 61. Westcott Ho Cam 35. **d** 37 **p** 38 Lon. C of St Mary Abbots Kens 37-46; Chap RNVR 38-48; V of St Steph Rochester Row w St Mary Virg Vinc Sq Westmr 46-50; C-in-c of St John Smith Square Lon 48-50; St Andr Ashley Place Westmr 48-53; V of St Steph w St Jo Evang Westmr 50-57; Commiss Natal 48-61; New Guinea 56-61; Capetn 58-61; Provost of S'wark and R of St Sav w All H S'wark 57-61; Cons Ld Bp of Guildf in S'wark Cathl 25 Mar 61 by Abp of Cant; Bps of Lon; Win; Chich; Leic;

S'wark; Roch; Ches; and Johann; and others; Trld to Salisbury 73; res 81. *28a Clarendon Gardens, W9 1AZ.* (01-286 6350)

REINDORP, Michael Christopher Julian. b 44. Trin Coll Cam BA 67, MA 70. Cudd Coll Ox. **d** 69 Stepney for Lon **p** 70 Lon. C of Poplar 69-74; V of St Wm Chatham Dio Roch from 74. *Vicarage, Marion Close, Walderslade, Chatham, Kent.* (Medway 61975)

REINHARDT, Theodore Charles Cameron. d 65 **p** 67 Sask. C of H Trin Prince Albert 65-67; I of John Smith's Reserve 67-68; MacDowall 69-71; H Trin Prince Albert 69-71; Chaleur Bay 71-73; Navan 73-74; Ingleside 74-77; Chaleur Bay Dio Queb from 77. *CP 67, Port Daniel, PQ, Canada.*

REISS, Robert Paul. b 43. Trin Coll Cam 2nd cl Econ Trip pt i 65, BA (2nd cl Th Trip pt ii) 67, MA 71. Westcott Ho Cam 67. **d** 69 **p** 70 Lon. C of St John's Wood 69-73; Rajshahi Miss Dacca 73; Chap Trin Coll Cam 73-78; Selection Sec ACCM from 78. *ACCM, Church House, Dean's Yard, SW1P 3NZ.* (01-222 9011)

REITH, Charles Martin. b 27. Univ of Edin MA (2nd cl Geog) 52. Edin Th Coll. **d** 57 **p** 58 Edin. C of St Cuthb (in c of St Hilda Colinton Mains) Edin 57-64; P-in-c of St Hilda's Miss Colinton Mains City and Dio Edin 64-66; R 66-71; Dioc Chap Dio Moray 71-77; Hon C of H Trin Stirling Dio Edin 78-80. *Apple Grove Cottage, Well Road, Scotlandwell, Kinross, KY13 7JB.*

REITH, Ivor Stuart Weston. b 16. Ridley Hall, Cam 65. **d** 66 **p** 67 Chich. C of H Trin Eastbourne 66-69, R of Angmering w Ham and Bargham 69-82. *147 Hornsey Road, N7 6DU.* (01-607 7113)

REKERAHO, John. b 31. **d** and **p** 73 Rwa. P Dio Rwa 73-75; Dio Kiga from 75. *c/o Shyogwe, BP 27, Gitarama, Rwanda.*

REMPEY, Philip Roland. b 19. GOC 74. **d** 76 Glouc **p** 76 Tewkesbury for Glouc. C of Charlton Kings Dio Glouc from 76. *87 Ravensgate Road, Charlton Kings, Cheltenham, GL53 8NS.*

RENDALL, John Albert. b 43. Ripon Hall, Ox 65. **d** 68 **p** 69 Portsm. C of St Simon Southsea 68-71; Wallington 71-76; P-in-c of Rufforth w Moor Monkton Dio York 77-79; V (w Hessay) from 79; P-in-c of Long Marston Dio York 77-79; V from 79. *Rufforth Vicarage, York, YO2 3QB.* (Rufforth 262)

RENDELL, Peter Vivian. b 26. K Coll Lon and Warm. **d** 52 **p** 53 Newc T. C of St Luke Wallsend 52-55; Sugley 55-60; Chap RNR 57-62; V of Kirknewton 60-68; Felton 68-77; St Paul Cullercoats (or Whitley Bay) Dio Newc T from 77. *53 Grosvenor Drive, Whitley Bay, T & W.* (W Bay 524916)

RENDELL, Roy Richard Neville. b 12. Nashdom Abbey Bucks. **d** 37 **p** 38 Ox. C of Newport Pagnell 37-41; Waltham Cross 41-45; R of Lavendon w Cold Brayfield 45-49; V of Wolverton St Geo 49-54; Surr 50-54 and 62-66; R of Sandiacre 54-58; Exam Chap to Bp of Derby 56-60; V of St Anne Derby 58-66; R of St Dominic 66-78; Landulph 73-78; RD of E Wivelshire 76-78; Perm to Offic Dios Pet and Ox from 78. *3 Astrop Road, King's Sutton, Banbury, Oxon.* (Banbury 811608)

RENDELL, Stanley James. b 1899. Ex Coll Ox BA 28, MA 32. Ripon Hall Ox 60. **d** 63 **p** 64 Chelmsf. C of Wethersfield 63-64; St Mary Virg Loughton 64-66; Perm to Offic Dio Ripon 66-69; L to Offic 69-75; Perm to Offic Dio Sarum 75-76; Dio Ex from 80. *92 Clifford Avenue, Kingsteighnton, Newton Abbot, TQ12 3NU.* (0626-4728)

RENDLE, Canon Charles Arthur. Ridley Hall Cam. **d** 46 **p** 47 Ugan. CMS Miss Mboga 46-60; Dio Momb 60-61; L to Offic Dio Nel from 63; Hon Can of Boga-Z from 79. *50 Muritai Street, Tahunanui, Nelson, NZ.*

RENFREY, Edward Donald John Baptist. b 53. St Barn Coll Adel 75. **d** 76 **p** 77 Murray. C of Naracoorte 76-78; P-in-c of Kingston-Robe 78-81; R of Kingston-Robe Dio Murray from 81. *Rectory, Agnes Street, Kingston, S Australia 5275.* (087-67 2590)

✠ **RENFREY, Right Rev Lionel Edward William.** Univ of Adel BA (1st cl Eng) 38. St Barn Coll Adel 39. ACT ThL (2nd cl) 40. **d** 40 Bp Thomas for Adel **p** 41 Adel. C of St Cuthb Prospect 40-43; Miss Chap Mid Yorke Peninsula 43-44; Warden of Bro of St Jo Bapt and P-in-c of Murray Bridge Pinnaroo Tailem Bend and Tatiara Miss 44-47; P-in-c of Berri w Barmera 48-50; Kens Gardens 50-57; Chap R Hosp Adel 50-55; R of St Jas Mile End 57-63; Ed Adel Ch Guardian 61-65; Org Chap Bp's Home Miss S Dio Adel 64-66; Archd of Adel 65-66; Exam Chap to Bp of Adel from 65; Dean of Adel from 66; Bps's V 66-69; Cons Asst Bp of Adel in St Pet Cathl Adel 1 May 69 by Abp of Brisb; Bps of Adel; Willoch; and St Arn; Coadj Bp of Melb (Arnott); Abp Fisher of Lambeth; and Bp Redding; Dioc Admin P-in-c of Two Wells-Mallala Dio Adel from 81. *40 Pennington Terrace, N Adelaide, S Australia 5006.* (08-267 2597)

RENNARD, Edward Lionel. b 51. Univ of Nottm BTh 80. Linc Th Coll 76. **d** 80 Linc **p** 81 Grimsby for Linc. C of Old Brumby Dio Linc from 80. *3 Glanville Avenue, Scunthorpe, S Humberside, DN17 1DF.*

RENNISON, Eric David Robert. b 1888. TCD BA and Div Test 12, MA 20. **d** 12 **p** 13 Meath. C of Kilbride w Lynally 12-20; TCF 15-20; Asst Chap (Eccles Est) at Karachi 21-22; Lah 22-24; Chap Kingsway 25-27; Dagshai 27-29 and 33; Karachi 29-31; Jullundur 24-25, 32 and 33-35; Razmak 35; Karachi 36-37; V of Willoughby w Grandborough 38-44; R of Blymhill 44-59. *c/o 29 Old Rectory Close, Bramley, Surrey.*

RENNISON, Walter Patrick. b 18. MBE 52. TCD BA (Mod Hist and Pol Sc) 40, Div Test 42, MA 45. **d** 42 Tuam for Down **p** 43 Down. C of Ballymacarrett 42-45; CF 45-73; V of Milland Dio Chich from 73. *Milland Vicarage, Harting Coombe, Rake, Hants.* (Liss 2774)

RENOUF, Peter Mark. b 30. Down Coll Cam BA 55, MA 59. Ridley Hall Cam. **d** 58 **p** 59 Chelmsf. C of Rainham 58-61; Asst Chap Wellington Coll Crowthorne 61-63; Chap 63-69; V of All SS Eastbourne 69-78; R of Farnborough Hants Dio Guildf from 78. *Rectory, Church Avenue, Farnborough, Hants.* (Farnborough 44754)

RENOWDEN, Very Rev Charles Raymond. b 23. Late Scho Powys Exhib and Dillwyn Llewelyn Stud of St D Coll Lamp BA (1st cl Phil) 44. Late Scho and Pri of Selw Coll Cam BA (1st cl Th Trip pt i, 2nd cl pt iii) 50, MA 53. Ridley Hall Cam 50. **d** 51 Llan for St D **p** 52 St D. C of Hubberston 51 55; Publ Pr Dio St D 55-71; Lect in Phil St D Coll Lamp 55-59; Hd of Dept of Phil 59-67; Sen Lect in Phil and Th 68-71; Dean of St Asaph from 71; Exam Chap to Bp of St A from 71. *Deanery, St Asaph, Clwyd.* (St A 583597)

RENOWDEN, Glyndwr Rhys. b 29. St D Coll Lamp BA (2nd cl Welsh) 49, LTh 52. **d** 52 **p** 53 St D. C of Tenby w Gumfreston 52-55; Chepstow w St Arvans and Penterry 55-58; Chap RAF from 58; Asst Chap in Chief from 75; Hon Chap to HM the Queen from 80. *c/o Ministry of Defence, Adastral House, Theobalds Road, WC1 8RU.*

RENSHAW, Peter Selwyn Kay. b 29. Late Squire Scho and Taylor Exhib at Keble Coll Ox BA 52, MA 64. St Steph Ho Ox 52. **d** 64 **p** 65 Ox. L to Offic Dio Ox 64-66; Chap RN 66-71; Chap Br Embassy & St Paul Athens 71-74; Chap St Andr Gothemburg 74-75; Chap and Asst Master R Sch of RN Haslemere from 75. *Ryde House, Angel Street, Petworth, W Sussex.*

RENWICK, Colin. St Aid Coll. **d** 59 **p** 60 York. C of Drypool 59-62; St Cath Wigan 62-64; C-in-c of St Frideswyde (Conv Distr to 77) Thornton Dio Liv 64-77; V from 77. *Vicarage, Thornton, Liverpool, L23 1TB.* (051-931 4676)

RENWICK, George Robert. b 07. K Coll Lon Relton Pri 35, AKC (2nd cl), Knowling Pri, Barry Pri and Jelf Pri 36. **d** 36 **p** 37 Dur. C of Shadforth 36-45; Offg C-in-c of Thornley 39-45; V of Tudhoe Grange 45-50; PC of Grangetown 50-52; St Nich Dunston 52-57; Asst Master S Shields Gr Sch 57-64; Goole Gr Sch 59-64; Hendon Co Gr Sch 64-68; Weston Park Sch Southn 68-73; L to Offic Dio Sheff 59-64; Dio Dur 62-64; Publ Pr Dio Win 68-73; C of St Mary Finchley 64-68; Burghclere w Newtown 73-79. *28 Glebe Avenue, Harrogate, HG2 0LT.* (Harrogate 57065)

RENWICK, Ivan. b 27. St Jo Coll Dur 70. **d** 72 Penrith for Carl **p** 73 Carl. C of St Herbert w St Steph Carl 72-74; Tettenhall Wood 74-76; V of Newsome 76-81; P-in-c of Brigham Dio Carl from 81. *Brigham Vicarage, 1 High Brigham, Cockermouth, Cumb, CA13 0TE.* (0900-825383)

RENYARD, Paul Holmwood. b 42. K Coll Lon and Warm BD and AKC 65. **d** 66 **p** 67 Cant. C of St Aug Croydon 66-69; Farnham 69-72; V of Capel 72-78; Asst Dir of Relig Educn Dio Guildf 72-78; Dio Roch from 78; Youth Tr Adv Dio Roch 78-80; Hon C of Roch Dio Roch from 78. *31 The Ridgeway, Chatham, Kent.* (Medway 407234)

REPATH, George David. b 43. St D Coll Lamp Dipl Th 68. **d** 68 **p** 69 Llan. C of St Jo Bapt Cardiff 68-73; Gt Stanmore 73-77; V of Stratfield Mortimer Dio Ox from 77. *Vicarage, Mortimer, Berks, RG7 2JX.* (Mortimer 332404)

REPATH, John Richard. b 48. Univ of Wales (Cardiff) Dipl Th 75. St Mich Coll Llan 72. **d** 75 **p** 76 Llan. C of St Jo Canton 75-79; Burghclere w Newton & Ecchinswell w Sydmonton Dio Win from 79. *Oakside, Ecchinswell, Newbury, Berks, RG15 8UA.* (Kingsclere 297107)

REPTON, Lord Bishop Suffragan of. *See* Verney, Right Rev Stephen Edmund.

REREMAN, William. d and **p** 77 New Hebr. P Dio New Hebr 77-80; Dio Vanuatu from 80. *Wosaga, Vanua Lava, Banks Islands, Vanuatu.*

RESEIGH, Herbert. AKC 41. **d** 41 **p** 42 Lon. C of St Anne Poole's Pk Holloway 41-43; Perm to Offic at St Paul S Harrow 43-44; St Paul (in c of St Luke) St Alb 44-47; R of Chesterton w Haddon 47-48; V of Ch Ch Stratford 48-52; L Amwell 52-55; St Patr Barking 55-60; St Simon Hammersmith 60-73; Mancetter 73-81. *Address temp unknown.*

RESTALL, Gerald Dalton. b 22. AKC (1st cl) and BD (1st cl) 50. St Bonif Coll Warm 50. **d** 51 **p** 52 Chelmsf. C of Grays Thurrock 51-55; Min of St Aug Conv Distr Rush Green Romford 55-58; Bp's Chap for Youth 58-62; Publ Pr Dio Chelmsf 58-62; CF (TA) 58-65; SCF (TA) 65-67; CF (TAVR) 67-69; CF (R of O) 69-77; V of St Eliz Becontree 62-71; C-in-c of St Geo Becontree 62-65; V of St Mary Virg (w St Laur from 77) Reading Dio Ox from 72; Dir St Mary's Centre Reading from 72. *39 Downshire Square, Reading, Berks, RG1 6NH.* (Reading 51738)

RETTER, John David. Univ of W Ont BA 62. Trin Coll Tor STB 65. **d** 65 **p** 66 Caled. C of Port Edward 65-67; I of Kincolith 67-71; I of Greenville 67-77; Hon Can of Caled 76-77. *c/o 692 Burrard Street, Vancouver, BC, Canada.*

REUSS, David Edward. Univ of BC BA 60. Wycl Coll Tor 64. **d** 68 **p** 69 Yukon. C of Fort St John 68-70; I of Cassiar 70-72; R of St Geo Rossland 72-74; on leave. *13674 Coldicutt Avenue, White Rock, BC, Canada.*

REUSS, Harold Leslie. b 45. ACT ThL 72. St Barn Coll Adel 67. **d** 69 Bp Porter for Bal **p** 70 Bal. C of Horsham 69-73; Lillington 73-75; R of Nhill 75-79; Portland Dio Bal from 79. *St Stephen's Rectory, Portland, Vic, Australia 3305.*

REUSS, John Christopher Edward. Lon Coll Div 36. **d** 38 **p** 39 S'wark. C of H Trin Sydenham 38-39; Chap RAF 39-45; R of Longhope Dio Glouc 45-46; P Dio Qu'App 46-48; in Amer Ch 48-52; V of Vulcan 52-56; Chap Vancouver Gen Hosp 56-59; R of Ladner 59-66; St Edw Richmond 66-68. *14627 Marine Drive, White Rock, BC, Canada.*

REVELL, Patrick Walter Millard. b 32. Wells Th Coll 65. **d** 67 Bp T Smith for Leic **p** 68 Leic. C of St Jas Gtr Leic 67-74; V of Quorn Dio Leic from 74. *Quorn Vicarage, Loughborough, Leics.* (Quorn 42593)

REVELL, Stanley. b 15. AKC 38. **d** 38 **p** 39 Blackb. C of St Thos Preston 38-44; St Sav Chorlton-on-Medlock 44-46; V of St Mary Magd Wiggenhall 46-60; St Barn York 60-63; R of Elvington 63-69. *Cartref, Sykehead Lane, Nawton, York.* (Kirkdale 201)

REVETT, Graham Francis. b 40. K Coll Lon and Warm AKC 63. **d** 64 **p** 65 Dur. C of St Thos Conv Distr Pennywell Bp Wearmouth 64-68; St Aid Hartlepool 68-71; V of Shiney Row 71-80; Herrington 73-80; RD of Houghton-le-Spring 76-80; R of St Geo Cullercoats Dio Newc T from 80. *St George's Vicarage, Cullercoats, N Shields, T & W, NE30 4NS.* (Whitley Bay 521817)

REVITT, Michael. Seagar Hall, Ont 58. **d** 57 **p** 59 Keew. I of Keewatin 57-59; Gillam 59-61; Rocanville 61-66; C of Queensbury Yorks 66-68; R of Last Mountain 68-78. *3902 Castle Road, Regina, Sask, Canada.* (528 2016)

REX, Keith Leslie Herbert. K Coll Lon and Warm AKC 53. **d** 55 **p** 56 Taunton for B & W. C of Shepton Mallet 55-58; Cheshunt 58-60; PC of Bournville Weston-s-Mare 60-67; R of Charlton Adam w Charlton Mackrell 67-69. *Address temp unknown.*

REYNISH, David Stuart. b 52. BEducn (Nottm) 75. Linc Th Coll 72. **d** 77 Grantham for Linc **p** 78 Linc. C of Boston 77-80; Chalfont St Pet (in c of All SS) Dio Ox from 80. *All Saints Parsonage, Oval Way, Chalfont St Peter, Gerrards Cross,*

REYNOLDS, Alan Martin. b 53. Sarum Wells Th Coll 73. **d** 77 **p** 78 Llan. C of Glan Ely Dio Llan from 77; Dep Chap HM Pris Cardiff from 81. *386 Grand Avenue, Ely, Cardiff.* (0222 591897)

REYNOLDS, Alan Thomas William. b 43. Univ of Lon BSc 64. Linc Th Coll 64. **d** 66 Bp Horstead for Leic **p** 67 Leic. C of St Pet Leic 66-70; Huntington York 70-72; R of Darliston Ja 72-76; V of Stechford Dio Birm from 76. *Stechford Vicarage, Albert Road, Birmingham, B33 8UA.* (021-783 2463)

REYNOLDS, Alfred George. Ridley Coll Melb ACT ThL 39. **d** 39 **p** 40 Melb. C of St Geo Malvern 39-40; Actg Chap Vic Miss to Seamen 40-42; I of Inverleigh and Meredith 42-44; V of Ch Ch Brunswick 45-47; Min of Vermont 47-52; R of St Geo Hobart 52-71. *8 Agnes Street, Margate, Tasmania 7153.*

REYNOLDS, Alfred Stanley. b 18. Univ of Birm BSc 39. St Deiniol's Libr Hawarden. **d** 70 **p** 71 Truro. Hon C of St Illogan Dio Truro from 70. *17 Castle Meadows, St Agnes, Cornw, TR5 0UB.* (St Agnes 2939)

REYNOLDS, Arthur Williams. St Paul's Coll Grahmstn 55. **d** 58 **p** 59 Natal. C of St Thos Durban 58-61; V of Harding 61-64; R of Queensburgh 64-68; Klip River 68-70; Tugela River 70-71; R of Blyvooruitzicht 71-77; Regent Hill 77-80; H Trin Upington Dio Kimb K from 80. *Box 514, Upington, CP, S Africa.*

REYNOLDS, Cecil Edward Arthur. **d** 26 Syd for Tas **p** 27 Tas. C of St Geo Hobart 27-28; Mortdale w Penshurst 28-29; All S Leichhardt 29-35; R of St Pet Syd 35-37; St Paul Wentworthville 37-50; St John Willoughby 50-69; L to Offic Dio Syd 69-73; Perm to Offic Dio Newc from 73. *Hopetoun Village, Castle Hill NSW, Australia 2154.*

REYNOLDS, David Hammerton. b 39. St Jo Coll Dur BA 62. Qu Coll Birm Dipl Th 63. **d** 65 **p** 66 York. C of N Ormesby 65-68; Hessle 68-71; V of Sherburn-in-Elmet w Barkston 71-79; St Osw Fulford City and Dio York from 79. *Fulford Vicarage, Fulford Park, York, YO1 4QE.* (York 33261)

REYNOLDS, David James. b 48. St Jo Coll Dur BA 72, Dipl Th 73. Cranmer Hall Dur 69. **d** 73 Warrington for Liv **p** 74 Liv. C of H Trin Formby 73-77; P-in-c of St Paul Widnes 77-80; V of St Paul Southport Dio Liv from 80. *St Paul's Vicarage, Aughton Road, Southport, Mer, P28 2AJ.* (0704 60005)

REYNOLDS, Dennis John. b 45. Univ of W Austr BA 66, BEducn 76. Trin Coll Melb BD 78. **d** and **p** 78 Perth. C of Kalgourlie/Boulder 78-80; R of S Cross Dio Perth from 80. *82 Antares Street, Southern Cross, W Australia 6426.* (090-49 1038)

REYNOLDS, Derrick Wilfrid. b 15. St Paul's Th Coll Grahmstn 47. **d** 49 **p** 50 St Jo Kaffr. C of All SS Engcobo 49-50; P-in-c of Indawana 50-54; R of Idutywa 54-61; V of Sparkwell 62-73; Ilsington Dio Ex from 73. *Ilsington Vicarage, Newton Abbot, Devon.* (Haytor 245)

REYNOLDS, Edward Thomas Selwyn. ACT ThL 36. **d** 37 **p** 38 Melb. C of St Cuthb Brunswick 37-46; V of Murrayville 46-49; Manangatang 49-55; LPr Dio St Arn 55-56; V of Bass 56-64; Bunyip 64-74. *Tucker Memorial Homes, Carrum Downs, Vic., Australia 3200.*

REYNOLDS, Gordon. b 42. Sarum Wells Th Coll 71. **d** 72 **p** 73 Lich. C of Tunstall 72-75; P-in-c of Fiwila Dio Centr Zam from 77. *P Bag 52XK, Kabwe, Zambia.*

REYNOLDS, Graham William. b 50. ACT ThL 74. St Barn Coll Adel 73. **d** and **p** 75 Gippsld. C of Bairnsdale 75-77; Traralgon Dio Gippsld from 77. *4 Lyndon Crescent, Traralgon, Vic, Australia 3844.*

REYNOLDS, Henry Parker. **d** and **p** 41 Goulb. C of St Sav Cathl Goulb 41-44; Dioc Commiss Dio Goulb 45-48; R of Yass 48-66; Can of St Sav Cathl Goulb 57-66; L to Offic Dio Syd from 66. *45 Essilia Street, Collaroy Plateau, NSW, Australia 2098.* (982-1305)

REYNOLDS, Hugh Justus Armiger. Univ of W Ont BA 50. Hur Coll LTh 50. Selw Coll Cam MLitt 60. **d** 50 Hur **p** 51 Ely for Col. L to Offic Dio Ely 50-51; C of Fen Ditton 51-53; Ch Ch Cathl Montr 53-55; R of Stanbridge E 55-60; St Jas Humber Bay Tor 60-67; Asst Master Sheridan Coll Brampton from 67. *68 Navy Street, Oakville, Ont, Canada.*

REYNOLDS, Ian Granville. b 15. Univ of Cant NZ BCom 50. ACA (NZ) 51. Ch Ch Coll 49. **d** and **p** 72 Ch Ch. Hon C of Spreydon Dio Ch Ch from 72. *17 Hewlings Street, Christchurch 1, NZ.* (859-133)

REYNOLDS, James Henry. LRAM 45. ARCM 59. St Jo Coll Morpeth 62. **d** 63 **p** 64 Melb. C of All SS St Kilda 63-65; P-in-c of St Jas Syndal 65-70; I 70-71; Nunawading 71-77; R of Wodonga 77-80; Bellarine Dio Melb from 80. *45 Collins Street, Drysdale, Vic. Australia 3222.*

REYNOLDS, Canon John Lionel. b 34. Chich Th Coll 58. **d** 61 **p** 62 Ripon. C of Whitkirk 61-64; Tong w Holme Wood 64-68; V of Chiseldon w Draycot Foliat 68-74; RD of Marlb 74-76; Calne from 76; R of Ridgeway 74-76; V of Calne w Blackland Dio Sarum from 76; Can and Preb of Sarum Cathl from 80. *10 Mill Street, Calne, Wilts, SN11 8DR.* (Calne 812340)

REYNOLDS, John Stewart. b 19. St Edm Hall, Ox BA 42, MA 45, BLitt 50. Ridley Hall, Cam 42. **d** 44 **p** 45 Ox. C of St Clem Ox 44-46; C-in-c of St Martin and All SS Ox 46-49; R of Easton-on-the-Hill 49-56; Besselsleigh w Dry Sandford and Cothill Dio Ox from 56; Lect Wycl Hall Ox 72-78. *Dry Sandford Rectory, Abingdon, Oxon.* (Frilford Heath 390403)

REYNOLDS, Percy Gatley. **d** 27 **p** 29 Ont. I of Augusta 27-29; Madoc 29-33; Miss Sharbot Lake 33-37; R of Leeds Rear 37-47; Lombardy 47-58. *Box 446, Perth, Ont, Canada.*

REYNOLDS, Raymond Ernest. b 29. Chich Th Coll 58. **d** 60 **p** 61 Ripon. C of St Marg Leeds 60-62; Beeston Notts 62-64; R of Farnley 64-76; Higham-on-the-Hill w Fenny Drayton Dio Leic from 76; P-in-c of Witherley Dio Leic from 81. *Rectory, Old Forge Road, Fenny Drayton, Nuneaton, Warws, CV13 6BD.* (Atherstone 4638)

REYNOLDS, Rex Wonder. Univ of S Afr BA 47. Univ of Syd BD 55. Trin Coll Dub BA 57, MA 68. ACT ThL (2nd cl) 50. Moore Th Coll Syd. **d** and **p** 51 Syd. C of Campsie 51-53; Dulwich Hill 53-54; Carlow 54-56; Kilmurry 56-60; V Cho and Min Can of St Mary's Cathl Lim 56-60; C of Attenborough w Bramcote (in c of St Pet Toton) 60-61; St Mich AA Queenstn 61-63; R of St Barn Bluff Durban 64-65; V of Tugela River 65-66; L to Offic Dio Johann 66-68; Dio Pret 68-80; Lect Univ of S Africa 69-80. *31 Dely Road, Hazelwood, Pretoria, Transvaal, S Africa.* (78-8631)

REYNOLDS, Richard Michael. b 42. St Steph Ho Ox 65. **d** 67 **p** 68 Worc. C of St Mary & All SS Kidderminster 67-70;

St Geo Cathl Georgetown 70-71; V of Skeldon w Leeds Dio Guy from 71; Chap Paramaribo 71-73; Team V of Woolfardisworthy E w Cheriton Fitzpaine 73-80; R of Holsworthy w Cookbury & Hollacombe Dio Ex from 80. *Rectory, Bodmin Street, Holsworthy, Devon, EX22 6BH.* (Holsworthy 253435)

REYNOLDS, Stanley Kenneth. b 14. Bps' Coll Cheshunt, 47. **d** 50 Derby **p** 51 Bp O'Ferrall for Derby. C of St Andr Derby 50-57; PC of Stonebroom 57-64; St Phil Chaddesden 64-70; V of Greenhill 70-81; P-in-c of Burghwallis w Skelbrooke Dio Sheff from 81. *St Helen's Rectory, Burghwallis, Doncaster, S Yorks.* (Donc 700227)

REYNOLDS, Stephen James. b 51. Univ of New Hampshire BA 73. Trin Coll Tor MDiv 78. **d** and **p** 78 E Newfld. C of St John's Cathl St John's Dio E Newfld from 78. *9 Cathedral Street, St Johns, Nfld A1C 3Y4. Canada.*

REYNOLDS, Canon Wilfrid James. b 14. Late Scho of St Jo Coll Cam 1st cl Cl Trip pt i 35, BA (1st cl Cl Trip pt 11) 36, 2nd cl Th Trip pt 1 37, MA 40. Ridley Hall Cam 37. **d** 38 **p** 39 Worc. C of Lower Mitton (or Stourport) 38-41; St Nich w St Pet Droitwich 41-42; Priv Chap to Bp of Worc 43; L to Offic at Wollaston 43-46; V of White Ladies Aston w Churchill and Spetchley 46-49; Hallow 49-79; RD of Martley and Worc W 72-79; Hon Can of Worc Cathl 74-79; Hon Can (Emer) from 79. *29 Bramley Avenue, Worcester.*

RHAM, Canon John Theodore. b 27. Magd Coll Cam BA 50, MA 65. Sarum Th Coll 50. **d** 52 **p** 54 Birm. C of Harborne 52-54; St Pet and St Paul Coleshill 54-56; Falmouth 56-59; R of St Ewe 59-68; RD of St Austell 65-68; V of St Budock Dio Truro from 68; RD of S Carnmarth from 77; Hon Can of Truro from 80. *St Budock Vicarage, Falmouth, Cornw.* (Penryn 2227)

RHAM, Robert Clifford. b 01. AKC 21. Univ of Lon BD 26. **d** 24 **p** 25 S'wark. C of Newington 24-25; Wimbledon 25-31; V of S Stoneham w Swaythling 31-46; St Andr Bournemouth 46-54; Sec Win Dioc Conf 46-54; Hon Can of Win 52-54; V of Madron w Morvah 54-63; R of Minstead 63-70. *Fairways, Feock, Truro, Cornwall.*

RHODES, Adrian Michael. b 48. AKC and BD 71. Qu Coll Birm 71. **d** 72 Man **p** 73 Middleton for Man. C of St John Bury 73-75; St Matt (w St Mary from 76) Crumpsall 75-77; Chap Walsall Manor and Bloxwich Hosps from 77; Walsall Gen from 81. *Chaplain's Office, Manor Hospital, Moat Road, Walsall, WS2 9PS.* (Walsall 28911)

RHODES, Anthony John. b 27. Mert Coll Ox BA 50, MA 53, Dipl Th 53. St Steph Ho Ox 52. **d** 54 **p** 55 Pet. C of St Alb Mart Northn 54-57; Oakham 57-60; P-in-c of St Mary S Queensferry 60-74; V of St Olave Mitcham 74-81; Owston Ferry Dio Linc from 81; W Butterwick Dio Linc from 81. *Vicarage, Owston Ferry, Doncaster, Yorks, DN9 1RG.* (Owston Ferry 305)

RHODES, Arthur. b 31. Univ of Dur BA 58. Cranmer Hall, Dur 57. **d** 59 **p** 60 Liv. C of St Lawr Kirkdale 59-61; Litherland 61-64; V of St Matt Thatto Heath 64-67; V of Samlesbury 67-80; L to Offic Dio Blackb from 80. *9 Craven Close, Fulwood Preston, Lancs.* (Preston 774147)

RHODES, Canon Cecil. b 10. St Pet Hall, Ox BA (3rd cl Hist) 34, MA 38. Wycl Hall, Ox 34. **d** 36 **p** 37 Birm. C of St Steph Selly Hill 36-38; Asst Ed and Youth Sec *The Pathfinder* 38-39; Birm Dioc Chap (in c of St Mary Pype Hayes) 39-44; V of St Luke Tunbridge Wells 44-49; St Aug Edgbaston 49-64; Dioc Adv on Chr Stewardship 60-64; Hon Can of Birm 61-64; Can Res of St E 64-80; Can (Emer) from 80; Commiss Willoch from 60; Perm to Offic Dio St E from 80. *College Gate House, Bury St Edmunds, Suff.*

RHODES, David. b 34. St Chad's Coll Dur BA 60. **d** 61 **p** 62 Worc. C of St John Dudley 61-64; C-in-c of St Mich AA Eccles Distr Norton 64-68; V of Astwood Bank w Crabbs Cross 69-78; Ecumen Officer Dio Worc 73-78; Team R of Hackney Dio Lon from 78. *Rectory, Mare Street, E8.* (01-985 5374)

RHODES, David Grant. b 43. Univ of Ex BA (2nd cl Pol) 66. Sarum Wells Th Coll 69. **d** 72 Pontefract for Wakef **p** 73 Wakef. C of Mirfield Dio Wakef 72-75; V of St Thos Batley 75-81. *c/o St Thomas' Vicarage, Rutland Road, Batley, W Yorks.*

RHODES, Geoffrey David. b 34. Univ of Birm BSc 55. Ridley Hall Cam 68. **d** 70 **p** 71 Bradf. C of Sedbergh 70-76; Firbank w Howgill and Killington 73-76; R of Carleton-in-Craven 76-78; C-in-c of Lothersdale 76-78; R of Carleton and Lothersdale Dio Bradf from 78. *Rectory, Carleton-in-Craven, Skipton, N Yorks.* (Skipton 2789)

RHODES, Canon James Tattersall. Univ of Tor BA 34. Wycl Coll Tor LTh 34. **d** 33 **p** 34 Tor. C of St Pet Tor 33-34; St Mark Vancouver 34-35; H Trin Halifax NS 35-36; St Thos St John's 36-42; I of Holland Landing 42-47; Newmarket 47-73; Can of Tor from 56. *Apt 1068, 100 Gowan Avenue, Toronto, Ont., Canada.*

RHODES, Canon John Lovell. b 33. MBE 81. BD (Lon) 59. St Aid Coll. **d** 59 **p** 60 Bradf. C of St Clem Bradf 59-61; Heeley Sheff 61-66; Industr Chap to Bp of Linc from 66; L to Offic Dio Linc from 66; RD of Grimsby and Cleethorpes from 77; Hon Can of Linc Cathl from 77; Industr Chap Dio Linc from 81. *St Luke's Vicarage, Heneage Road, Grimsby, S Humb, DN23 9DZ.* (Grimsby 43167)

RHODES, Leslie Howard. b 04. St Jo Coll Dur BA 27. **d** 28 **p** 29 Bradf. C of H Trin Idle 28-31; Tutor St Barn Sch Manmad 31-34; Prin 34-42; Prin Ahmadnagar Tr Coll 42-45; V of Tonge Fold 46-52; R of St Matt Crumpsall 52-57; V of Urmston 57-73; Surr 60-73; C of Much Birch 73-79; Perm to Offic Dio Man from 80. *84 Red Lane, Bolton, Lancs, BL2 5EL.*

RHODES, Maurice Arthur. b 27. Ridley Hall Cam. **d** 69 **p** 70 Bradf. C of Ch Ch Skipton-in-Craven 69-71; Brierley Hill 71-74; V of Walsall Wood Dio Lich from 74. *2 St John's Close, Walsall Wood, Walsall, WS9 9LD.* (Brownhills 2284)

RHODES, Peter Stuart. b 26. Coll of the Resurr Mirfield 77. **d** 78 Repton for Derby **p** 79 Derby (APM). C of Newbold w Dunston Dio Derby from 78. *42 Westbrook Drive, Brookside, Chesterfield, S40 3PQ.*

RHODES, Robert George. b 41. Univ of Man BSc 62. Ripon Hall Ox Dipl Th 73. **d** 74 Dorchester for Ox **p** 75 Ox. C of Banbury 74-77; Team V of Banbury 77-81; P-in-c of Longhorsley Dio Newc T from 81. *Vicarage, Longhorsley, Morpeth, NE65 8UU.* (067 088218)

RHODES, Trevor Martin. b 38. Qu Coll Birm 70. **d** 70 Birm **p** 70 Aston for Birm. C of St Osw Bordesley 70-72; Chap St Basil's Ch Centre Birm 72-73; C of Padiham w Higham 73-75; P-in-c of St Osw Preston 76-78; Chap HM Borstal Hindley 78-80; V of Blackhill Dio Dur from 80. *Vicarage, Blackhill, Co Durham.* (Consett 502155)

RHODES, William James. b 28. **d** 67 Tor **p** 67 Bp Hunt for Tor. R of Richvale 67-69; Dunbarton 69-72; Team V of Grantham 72-74; R of Gunness w Burringham 74-77; Assoc P of St Giles Barrie and St Thos Shanty Bay 77-81; St Hilda Fairbank City and Dio Tor from 81. *300 Mill Road, C41, Etobicoke, M9C 4W7, Ont., Canada.*

RHODES-WRIGLEY, James. b 35. K Coll Lon and Warm AKC 59. **d** 60 **p** 61 Lon. C of St Paul S Harrow 60-66; V of Ch Ch Hendon 66-71; St Barn Northolt Pk Dio Lon from 71. *Vicarage, Raglan Way, Northolt, Middx.* (01-422 3775)

RHYDDERCH, David Huw. b 48. Univ of Wales (Cardiff) Dipl Th 73. St Mich AA Coll Llan 70. **d** 73 **p** 74 Llan. C of Gelligaer 73-76; All SS Penarth 76-78; V of Resolven 78-81; Ystrad Rhondda Dio Llan from 81. *St Stephen's Vicarage, Ystrad Rhondda, Mid-Glam, CF41 7RR.* (Tonypandy 434426)

RHYMES, Canon Douglas Alfred. b 14. Univ of Birm BA (2nd cl Phil) 39. Ripon Hall, Ox 39. **d** 40 **p** 41 Chelmsf. C of Dovercourt 40-43; CF (EC) 43-46; C of Romford (in c of St Thos and St Geo) 46-49; C-in-c of Ascen Distr Chelmsf 49-50; PV of S'wark Cathl (in c of All H S'wark) 50-54; Sacr 52-54; V of All SS Eltham 54-62; Proc Conv S'wark 59-64; Can Res and Libr of S'wark Cathl 62-69; Hon Can from 69; Dir of Lay Tr Dio S'wark 62-68; V of Camberwell 68-76; M Gen Syn 75; and from 80; R of Woldingham Dio S'wark from 76. *Rectory, Woldingham, Surrey, CR3 7DD.* (905-2192)

RHYS, David Edwin. b 37. Peterho Cam BA 61. MA 65. Univ of Lon BA 74. St Steph Ho Ox. **d** 63 **p** 64 Lich. C of St Mich Tividale Tipton 63-65; Eltham (in c of St Francis Horn Pk) 65-72; Chap and Warden Lady Marg Hall Settlement Dio S'wark 72-75; Hon C of St Jo Bapt Eltham 75-81; R of Woolwich Dio S'wark from 81. *2 Ruskin Court, Wythfield Road, Eltham, SE9 5TQ.*

RHYS, Canon Edwin Vernon. b 02. Peterho Cam BA 26, MA 30. Linc Th Coll 26. **d** 28 **p** 29 Birm. C of St Francis Bournville 28-32; Chap of Erdington Ho and Homes 32-37; V of St Mary Aston Brook 37-43; St Jo Evang w All SS Waterloo Rd 43-72; Hon Can of S'wark 72; Can (Emer) from 72. *14 Ormond Avenue, Hampton-on-Thames, Middx, TW12 2RU.* (01-979 1373)

RHYS, Trevor William. b 11. Kenyon Coll USA BA 35. Sarum Th Coll 35. **d** 38 **p** 39 Bris. C of Avonmouth 38-40; Frome Selwood 40-45; PC of Woodlands 45-53; R of Charlton Adam w Charlton Mackrell 53-67; Asst Master K Sch Bruton 49-56; V of Stogumber 67-76; Perm to Offic Dio B & W from 78. *81 Ash Lane, Wells, Somt, BA5 2LW.* (Wells 74921)

RHYS, Canon Wendell. b 05. Late Scho of Univ of Birm BA (2nd cl Phil) 26. Ripon Hall Ox 26. **d** 29 **p** 30 Birm. C of St Benedict Bordesley 29-31; Temple Balsall 31-39; V of St Benedict Bordesley 39-71; Commiss Br Hond 44-45; Hon Can of Birm 64-72; Can (Emer) from 72. *21 Keresley Close, Solihull, W Midl, B91 2AD.* (021-705 6504)

RHYS, William Raymond. b 10. Univ of Wales BSc 34. St Mich Coll Llan 35. **d** 39 **p** 41 Swan B. C of Ystalyfera 39-46; Cwmbwrla 46-48; Llanguicke 48-52; R of Whitton w Pilleth and Bleddfa 52-57; C of Llandilo Talybont 57-59; V of

Penallt 59-78. *3 St Paul's Court, Heol Fair, Llandaff, Cardiff, CF5 2ES.*

RIA, Alfred. b 48. Patteson Th Centre Kohimarama Dipl Th 80. **d** 80 Centr Melan. d Dio Centr Melan. *c/o Church of Melanesia, PO Box 19, Honiara, Solomon Islands.*

RIAK, Henry Cuir. Bp Gwynne Coll Mundri, 63. **d** 67 N Ugan. d Dio N Ugan 67-76; Dio Rumbek from 76. *ECS, Wau, Sudan.*

RIANGA, Ven Matia Lemi. Bp Gwynne Coll Mundri 57. **d** 59 **p** 61 Sudan. P Dio Sudan; Hon Can of Sudan from 71; Archd of Bari from 73; Exam Chap to Bp of Sudan from 73. *c/o Yei Parish Church, Juba, Equatoria, Sudan.*

RIBAGA, Jeremie. b 20. **d** 76 **p** 77 Kiga. P Dio Kiga. *c/o BP 17 Kibungo, Rwanda.*

RICE, Brian Keith. b 32. Peterho Cam BA 55, MA 59. Seabury-Western Sem USA BD 57, STM 67, MDiv 79. Linc Th Coll. **d** 57 **p** 58 Lon. C of Winchmore Hill 57-60; St Werburgh Derby 60-63; Bp's Chap and Dioc Adv for Chr Stewardship Dio Derby 60-66; C of St Francis Mackworth 63-66; Chap Kingsway Ment Hosp 63-66; L to Offic Dio Derby 65-66; Proc Conv Derby 64-70; S'wark 70-72; Educn Sec USPG 66-72; Perm to Offic Dio S'wark 66-72; Birm from 72; Dir of Educn Dio Birm from 72; M Gen Syn Birm 75-80; Chap St Chad's Hosp Birm from 77. *44 Vernon Road, Edgbaston, B16 9SH.* (021-454 5559)

RICE, Brian Thomas. b 46. Univ of Wales (Cardiff) BD 77. St Mich AA Coll Llan 75. **d** 77 **p** 78 St D. C of Llanelli 77-79; P-in-c of Llandygwydd w Cenarth and Cilrhedyn Dio St D 79-80; V from 80. *Vicarage, Cenarth, Newcastle Emlyn, Dyfed.* (Newc Emlyn 710755)

RICE, Franklin Arthur. b 20. FRICS 49. St Alb Ministerial Tr Scheme 77. **d** 80 **p** 81 St Alb. Hon C of Hoddesdon Dio St Alb from 80. *4 Appleford Close, Hoddesdon, Herts, EN11 9DE.* (Hoddesdon 69794)

RICE, Frederick James William. Moore Th Coll Syd 43. **d** 43 **p** 44 Syd. Asst Chap Miss to Seamen 43-45; C-in-c of Port Kembla 45-46; Willoughby 46-47; Kingsgrove w Bexley N 47-50; R of Corrimal 50-54; Clovelly 54-59; Enfield 60-67; Dir C of E Homes Dio Syd 67-76; L to Offic Dio Syd from 67. *15/18 Essex Street, Epping, NSW, Australia 2121.* (869-2285)

RICE, John Leslie Hale. b 38. E Midl Jt Ordin Tr Scheme 73. Univ of Lon BSc 60, BD 68. **d** 76 Repton for Derby **p** 77 Derby. C of St Nich Allestree Dio Derby from 76. *14 Gisborne Crescent, Allestree, Derby, DE3 2FL.*

RICE, Leslie Frank. b 07. Em Coll Cam 3rd cl Hist Trip pt i 27, BA 3rd cl Geog Trip pt i 28, 2nd cl Th Trip pt 11 29, MA 32. **d** 32 **p** 33 Chelmsf for Egypt. Teacher Engl Miss Coll Cairo 32-34; Chap and CMJ Miss at Tunis 34-36; C of St Jas Tunbridge Wells 36-40; Hon C of St Mich AA Mill Hill Dio Lon from 73. *46 Flower Lane, NW7 2JL.* (01-959 1278)

RICE, William. b 37. **d** 73 Bp Legge for Newfld **p** 73 Newfld. C of Grand Falls 73-75; I of Gander Bay 75-80; C of St Thos, St John's Dio E Newfld from 80. *5 Diefenbaker Street, St John's, Newfoundland, Canada.*

RICE-OXLEY, John Richard. b 44. Keble Coll Ox BA 66, MA 69. Lon Coll of Div 68. **d** 70 Sherwood for Southw **p** 71 Southw. C of Eastwood 70-73; CMS Youth Adv 73-78; V of St Jo Evang Mansfield Dio Southw from 78. *Vicarage, St Jonn Street, Mansfield, Notts, NG18 1QH.* (Mansfield 25999)

RICH, Christopher Robin. b 49. Sarum Wells Th Coll 72. **d** 74 **p** 75 Win. C of Sholing 74-76; Maybush 76-79; R of Fawley Dio Win from 79. *Rectory, Church Lane, Fawley, Southampton.* (0703-893552)

RICH, Canon Clifford William. Moore Th Coll Syd ACT ThL 51. **d** and **p** 52 Syd. C of Dulwich Hill 52; Kembla 52-54; R of St Jas S Cant 54-56; Mt Magnet 56-59; Org Sec Bush Ch Aid S in NSW 59-63; Federal Sec for Austr 63-69; L to Offic Dio Syd 61-69; Dio Adel 63-69; Hon Can of H Cross Cathl Geraldton Dio NW Austr from 66; R of Orange 69-72; Org Sec Angl Miss Coun W Austr 72-78; Rector of Subiaco-Leederville Dio Perth from 78. *257 Barker Road, Subiaco, W Australia 6008.* (381 1130)

RICH, Harold Reginald. b 22. **d** 79 **p** 80 Truro (APM). C of St Austell Dio Truro from 79. *31 Bucklers Lane, St Austell, Cornwall, PL25 3JN.*

RICH, Paul Michael. b 36. Sarum Th Coll 62. **d** 65 Dunwich for St E **p** 66 St E. C of Woodbridge 65-68; W Wycombe (in c of St Birinus) 68-70; CF from 70. *c/o Ministry of Defence, Bagshot Park, Bagshot, Surrey.*

RICH, Peter Geoffrey. b 45. Oak Hill Coll 74. **d** 77 **p** 78 S'wark. C of St John Blackheath 77-80; St Matt Surbiton Dio S'wark from 80. *127 Hamilton Avenue, Tolworth, Surbiton, Surrey.* (01-397 4294)

RICH, Roger Fenner. ACT ThDip 71. St Jo Coll Morpeth. **d** 70 **p** 71 St Arn. C of Maryborough 71-75; V of Dunolly 75-77; C of St Paul Malvern 78-80; I of St Jas Pakenham Dio Melb from 80. *Vicarage, Main Street, Pakenhan, Vic, Australia 3810.*

RICHARD, David Thomas. b 16. St D Coll Lamp BA 39. **d** 40 **p** 41 St D. C of Llandeilo Fawr 40-43; Llanstadwell 43-45; Cardigan (in c of Mount w Verwick) 45-54; R of Bangor Teifi w Henllan 54-57; PC of H Trin Runcorn 57-58; R of Stoney Stanton 58-62; V of St Geo Darlaston 62-70; Hon Chap Miss to Seamen from 70; Mostyn Dio St A from 70. *Mostyn Vicarage, Holywell, Clwyd, CH8 9EJ.* (Mostyn 513)

RICHARD, Eldie. b 30. Atlantic Sch of Th Halifax NS 73. 1 76 NS. On study leave. *5959 Spring Garden Road, Apt No 508, Halifax, NS, Canada.*

RICHARDS, Alan Grenville. b 41. Kelham Th Coll 64. **d** 69 Lon **p** 70 Kens for Lon. C of Northolt 69-75; V of Fatfield Dio Dur from 75. *49 Larchwood, Harraton, Washington, T & W, NE38 9AN.* (0632 463134)

RICHARDS, Albert George Granston. b 06. Univ of Lon BSc 30. Wycl Hall Ox. **d** 55 Kens for Lon for St Alb **p** 60 St Alb. Hon C of Watford 55-67; Hon C of St Pet St Alb 67-69; V of Offley w Lilley 69-74; RD of Hurst 75-80; R of Poynings 80-82; Edburton 80-82; Hon C of Clayton w Keymer Dio Chich from 82. *East Coombe, North Bank, Hassocks, Sussex.* (Hassocks 2203)

RICHARDS, Alexander James. d 57 **p** 58 Armid. C of Narrabri 57-59; P-in-c of Baradine 60-63; R of Mulgoa 64-64; S Kogarah 64-72; L to Offic Dio Syd 72-77; Perm to Offic Dio Newc from 78. *76 Eric Street, Bundeena, NSW, Australia 2230.* (523-5208)

RICHARDS, Andrew David Thomas. b 55. St Jo Coll Dur BA 76. St Steph Ho Ox 76. **d** 78 **p** 79 Birm. C of Shirley 78-81; Cowley St John (in C of St Alb Mart) City and Dio Ox from 81. *c/o 60 Percy Street, Oxford, OX4 3AF.* (Oxford 722784)

RICHARDS, Anthony Francis. b 26. Wadh Coll Ox BA 51, MA 54. Ridley Hall Cam 50. **d** 52 **p** 53 Lon. C of Ch Ch North Finchley 52-55; Maidenhead 55-59; V of Ch Ch High Wycombe 59-63; C-in-c 63-67; V of Terriers 63-73; St Steph Cinderford 73-80; St Paul Clacton-on-sea Dio Chelmsf from 80. *St Paul's Vicarage, Clacton-on-Sea, Essex.* (Clacton 24760)

RICHARDS, Basil Ernest. b 18. Lich Th Coll 51. **d** 53 **p** 54 Worc. C of Kidderminster 53-55; Northfield Birm 55-56; Hon C of Malvern Dio Worc from 78. *137 Madresfield Road, Malvern, Worcs, WR14 2HD.*

RICHARDS, Bernard Oxland. St Jo Coll Auckld LTh 51. **d** 51 **p** 52 Ch Ch. C of Ashburton 51-54; Berkswich w Walton Dio Lich 54-55; V of Methven 55-59; Lyttleton 59-62; Barrington Street 62-69; Hon C of St Alb Dio Ch Ch from 70. *c/o Church House, 84 Gloucester Street, Christchurch 1, NZ.* (66-169)

RICHARDS, Brian Gordon. b 21. Sarum Wells Th Coll 71. **d** 73 **p** 74 Win. C of Milton 73-78; P-in-c of Hook w Greywell Dio Win from 78. *Hook Rectory, Basingstoke, Hants.* (Hook 2268)

RICHARDS, Canon Brian Murley. b 09. Late Symes Exhib and Squire Scho of Ex Coll Ox 3rd cl Cl Mods 30, BA (3rd cl Th) 32, MA 35. Cudd Coll 33. **d** 34 **p** 35 Glouc. C of H Trin Minchinhampton 34-36; St Steph Glouc 36-40 and 45-46; Offg C-in-c of Badminton w Acton Turville 40-45; PC of Stone w Woodford 46-56; V of Hill 46-56; R of Avening 56-74; RD of Tetbury 61-73; Surr 63-74; Hon Can of Glouc Cathl from 65. *99 Slad Road, Stroud, Glos, GL5 1QZ.* (Stroud 2539)

RICHARDS, Charles Dennis Vincent. K Coll Lon and Warm AKC 61. **d** 62 **p** 63 St Andr. Chap of St Ninian's Cathl Perth 62-64; C of St Mary Virg Pimlico 64-66; Ch Ch St Marylebone 66-68; St Mich Wood Green 68-69; Min S Kenton Conv Distr 69-77; C-in-c of Wembley Park 70-73; Hon C of St Jo Evang w St Mich AA Paddington Dio Lon from 76. *48a Kendal Street, W2.* (01-262 5633)

RICHARDS, Charles Edmund Nicholas. b 42. Trin Coll Cam BA 64, MA 68. Westcott Ho Cam 64. **d** 66 Bp McKie for Cov **p** 67 Cov. C of Rugby 66-72; C-in-c of St Pet Basingstoke Dio Win from 71; Team V of Basingstoke 72-77; R of Rotherhithe Dio S'wark from 77; RD of Bermondsey from 81. *Rectory, St Marychurch Street, SE16 4JE.* (01-231 2465)

RICHARDS, Christopher Mordaunt. b 40. New Coll Ox BA 63, MA 72. Univ of Bris MB, ChB 72. Cudd Coll 63. **d** 65 Bris **p** 81 B & W (NSM). C of St Mary Redcliffe w Temple Bedminster 65-66; Hon C of Keynsham Dio B & W from 81. *43 Charlton Road, Keynsham, Bristol, BS18 2JG.*

RICHARDS, Daniel. b 1892. St D Coll Lamp LDiv 15, BA, BD and Mathews Scho 29. Dipl Th (Lambeth) 81. **d** 15 **p** 16 St D. C of Llangathen w Llanfihangel Cilfargen 15-18; Pembrey (in c of St Mary Burry Port) 18-24; R of Llangeitho 24-31; V of Llangynwyd w Baiden and Maesteg (w Troedrhiw Garth 50-60) 31-65; Surr from 31; RD of E Upper Groneath 42-65; Can of St Dubritius in Llan Cathl 48-61; Prec of Llan Cathl 61-67; S Wales Sec SPCK 66-78; C-in-c of Merthyr Mawr 68-78; Ewenny 68-78; Perm to Offic Dio Llan from 78. *26 Brynteg Avenue, Bridgend, Mid Glam.* (Bridgend 5117)

RICHARDS, Daniel James. b 40. St D Coll Lamp Dipl Th 66. **d** 66 **p** 67 Lich. C of H Trin Kingswinford 66-69; Banbury w Neithrop 69-71; Aylesbury (in c of St Pet) 71-73; Missr St Jo Bapt Manor Pk Stoke Poges 73-78; Team R of W Slough 78-80; R of Ilchester w Northover, Limington, Yeovilton and Podymore Dio B & W from 80; RD of Ilchester from 81. *Rectory, Ilchester, Somt, BA22 8LJ.* (Ilchester 840296)

RICHARDS, David. b 30. Univ of Bris BA (2nd cl Gen) 52. St Mich Coll Llan. **d** 54 **p** 55 Llan. C of Llangynwyd w Maesteg 54-56; Miss Isfahan Iran 57-58; Kerman 58-61; C of Skewen 61-62; Chap of Khuzistan Oil Fields 62-66; V of Cwmbach 66-76; Chairman CMS Dio Llan from 76; Warden of Ordins Dio Llan 71-77; R of Coity w Nolton Dio Llan from 76. *Rectory, Merthyrmawr Road North, Bridgend, Mid Glam, CF31 3NH.* (Bridgend 2247)

RICHARDS, David Arnold. b 56. Wycl Hall Ox 76. **d** 81 Llan. C of Skewen Dio Llan from 81. *Manod, Drummau Road, Neath Abbey, Neath, W Glam.* (Skewen 813734)

RICHARDS, David Idris Thomas. b 07. St D Coll Lamp BA 29. **d** 30 **p** 31 Man. C of St Luke Miles Platting 30-32; St Marg Cwmamman 32-35; R of Troedyraur 35-50; Trefilan (w Nantcwnlle from 68) 50-73. *4 Bro-Llan, Llanwnen, Lampeter, Dyfed.*

RICHARDS, David Robert Lloyd. b 48. St D Coll Lamp Dipl Th 70. Bp Burgess Hall Lamp 67. **d** 71 **p** 72 Llan. C of Skewen 71-73; Neath w Llantwit 73-76; Chap Miss to Seamen Southn 76-77; V of Pontlottyn w Fochriw Dio Llan from 77. *Vicarage, Pontlottyn, Mid-Glam.* (Rhymney 841322)

RICHARDS, David Victor. St Mich Coll Llan. **d** 23 **p** 24 Llan. C of Neath w Llantwit 23-27; Llanedy (in c of Hendy) 27-34; R of Eglwys-Cymmin 34-54; Llanddowror 54-68; Surr from 65. *23 Picton Terrace, Carmarthen, Dyfed.*

RICHARDS, Derek Gordon. b 31. St D Coll Lamp BA 54. **d** 69 Bp T Hughes for Llan **p** 70 Llan. C of Neath w Llantwit 69-73; V of Llangeinor 73-77; Arthog w Fairbourne 77-80; R of Llanaber and Barmouth w Caerdeon and Bontddu Dio Ban from 80. *Rectory, Barmouth, Gwyn, LL42 1RL.* (Barmouth 280516)

RICHARDS, Donald Gera. Roch Th Coll. **d** 65 **p** 66 Truro. C of Liskeard w St Keyne 65-67; C-in-c of N Tamerton 67-70; Botus Fleming 70-72; V of Landrake w St Erny (w Botus Fleming from 73) Dio Truro from 70. *Landrake Vicarage, Saltash, Cornwall.* (Landrake 314)

RICHARDS, Edwin Thomas. Univ of Leeds, BA (Hist) 41. St D Coll Lamp 46. **d** 48 **p** 49 Llan. C of Llangwynd w Maesteg 48-50; St Mary Port Eliz 51-53; R of Alexandria 52-62; C of St Mich and St Geo Cathl Grahmstn 63-66; R of All SS E Lon 66-72; St Paul Port Alfred 72-75; Bath Grahmstn 72-75; V of Tonyrefail 75-77; R of Komga Dio Grahmstn from 77. *Rectory, Komga, CP, S Africa.* (Komga 54)

RICHARDS, Eric. b 36. Ely Th Coll 62. **d** 63 **p** 64 Ely. C of Fen Ditton 63-65; Woodston 65-68; V of St Pet Fort Colom 68-71; Publ Pr Dio Colom 68-71; Dio Kurunegala 69-71; Chap Miss to Seamen Colom 68-71; Tilbury 71-73; Publ Pr Dio Chelmsf 72-73; R of Roos w Tunstall-in-Holderness (and Garton-in-Holderness, Grimston and Hilston from 74) 73-79; C-in-c of Garton-in-Holderness w Grimston and Hilston 73-74; CF (TAVR) from 73; V of Wykeham & Hutton Buscel Dio York from 79; CF (TA) from 79; RD of Pickering from 80. *Vicar's House, Hutton Buscel, Scarborough, N Yorks. YO13 9LL.* (0723 862945)

RICHARDS, Fitzroy Ivan. K Coll NS LTh 62. **d** 62 NS for Koot **p** 62 Koot. C of Vernon 62-63; I of Kaslo-Slocan 63-65; Arrow Lakes 65-68; Salmon Arm 68-73; St Laur City and Dio Calg from 73. *6219 Lakeview Drive SW, Calgary, Alta., Canada T3E 5S9.* (249 6401)

RICHARDS, The Hon Fraser Arthur Richard. *See* Milverton, The Lord Fraser Arthur Richard

RICHARDS, Gregory Norman. b 46. St Mich Ho Crafers ThL 70. **d** 70 **p** 71 Bath. C of Parkes 70-73; Dubbo 74-76; Bedfont 76-79; Asst Chap HM Pris Wormwood Scrubs 79-80; Chap HM Pris Camp Hill 80-82; HM Pris Chelmsf & HM Borstal Bullwood Hall from 82. *c/o HM Prison, Chelmsford, Essex.*

RICHARDS, Gwynfryn. b 02. Univ of Wales BSc 21. Jes Coll Ox BA (1st cl Nat Sc) 23, MA 28. Boston Univ STB (1st cl) and Frank D Howard Fell 28. St Mich Coll Llan 29. **d** 30 **p** 31 St A. C of Eglwysrhos 30-34; Aberystwyth 34-38; R of Llanllyfni w Talysarn and Penygroes 38-49; V of Conwy w Gyffin 49-56; Can of Ban 43-62; Treas of Ban Cathl 43-57; Exam Chap to Bp of Ban 44-71; RD of Arllechwedd 53-57; Surr 53-71; R of Llandudno 56-62; Archd of Ban 57-62; Dean of Ban Cathl 62-71; Pantyfedwen Lect Univ Coll Aberystwyth 67. *Llain Werdd, Llandegfan, Anglesey, Gwyn, LL59 5LY.* (Menai Bridge 713429)

RICHARDS, Harold George. Ridley Coll Melb ACT ThL 50. **d** 51 **p** 52 Melb. C of St Luke S Melb 51-52; Min of St John Cranbourne 52-57; Mt Dandenong 57-60; V of Loddon 60-64; R of Roch 64-73; Cohuna Dio Bend from 73. *Rectory, King Edward Street, Cohuna, Vic, Australia.* (054-56 2225)

RICHARDS, Harold John Thomas. b 16. St D Coll Lamp BA 39. St Mich Coll Llan 45. **d** 47 **p** 48 Llan. C of Fochriw w Deri 47-50; Pontnewynydd 50-53; Panteg w Llanddewi Fach 53-56; V of Garndiffaith w Varteg 56-69; R of Goetre (w Llanfair Kilgeddin 69-72) Dio Mon from 69. *Goetre Rectory, Abergavenny, NP7 9DW.* (Nantyderry 378)

RICHARDS, Iorwerth. Late Scho of St D Coll Lamp BA 41. K Coll Lon. **d** 43 **p** 44 Swan B. C of St Mary Swansea 43-53; C-in-c of Llanddewi-Ystradenny 53-55; V (w Abbey Cwmhir from 55) 55-60; R of Penmaen w Nicholaston (and Oxwich from 72) Dio Swan B from 60; RD of W Gower from 71. *Penmaen Rectory, Swansea, W Glam.* (Penmaen 241)

RICHARDS, Irving St Clair. b 40. Coll of Resurr Mirfield 72. **d** 74 **p** 75 Leic. C of Wigston Magna 74-78; P-in-c of St Steph City and Dio Leic from 78. *214 East Park Road, Leicester, LE5 5FD.* (Leic 736752)

RICHARDS, Jack. Moore Coll Syd ThL 44. **d** and **p** 43 Syd. C of All SS Parramatta 43-44; St Silas Waterloo 44-45; St Luke Clovelly Syd 45; C-in-c of Berowra w Asquith 46-47; R of Wingecarribee 47-48; W Wollongong 48-54; Rockdale 54-76; Rose Bay Dio Syd from 76. *94 Newcastle Street, Rose Bay, NSW, Australia 2029.* (371-9723)

RICHARDS, James Harcourt. b 30. Oak Hill Th Coll. **d** 63 Warrington for Liv **p** 64 Liv. C of Ch Ch Norris Green 63-66; Em Fazakerley 66-68; C-in-c of St Cath Edge Hill 68-73; V of St Matt Thatto Heath St Helens Dio Liv from 73. *Vicarage, St Matthew's Grove, Thatto Heath, St Helens, Mer. WA10 3SE.* (St Helens 24644)

RICHARDS, John. b 20. St D Coll Lamp BA 40. Keble Coll Ox BA 42, MA 46. Westcott Ho Cam 43. **d** 43 **p** 44 St A. C of Chirk 43-47; St Jo Bapt Bollington 47-50; V of St Pet Macclesfield 50-56; Dioc Insp of Schs 53-56; Asst Master Macclesfield Tech Coll 53-56; Wel Sch 61-64; V of All SS New Brighton 56-67; Hoylake Dio Ches from 67; CF (TA) from 62; Surr from 67. *Hoylake Vicarage, Wirral, Chesh, L47 1HW.* (051-623 3897)

RICHARDS, Ven John. b 33. SS Coll Cam 2nd cl Hist Trip pt i, 54, BA (2nd cl Th Trip pt i) 55, MA 59. Ely Th Coll 57. **d** 59 **p** 60 Ex. C of St Thos Ex 59-64; R of Holsworthy w Cookbury 64-74; R of Hollacombe 64-74; RD of Holsworthy 70-74; V of Heavitree Ex 74-78; R (w St Paul) 78-81; RD of Christianity 78-81; Can Res of Ex Cathl from 81; Archd of Ex from 81. *12 The Close, Exeter, EX1 1EZ.* (Exeter 75745)

RICHARDS, John Ballantyne. Univ of Dur (Codr Coll Barb) Dipl Th 62. **d** 43 **p** 44 Windw Is. C of St Geo Grenada 43-47; V of St Clem w St Swithun Barb 47-53; C of Montego Bay 53-56; P-in-c of Gilnock and Santa Cruz 56-62; on leave. *c/o Church House, Cross Roads, Jamaica, W Indies.*

RICHARDS, John Francis. b 37. Univ of Dur BA 61. Wells Th Coll. **d** 63 **p** 64 Southw. C of Sherwood 63-67; Bp Wearmouth 67-69; Egg Buckland 69-75; V of St Jas L Ham Plymouth Dio Ex from 75. *St James's Vicarage, Ham Drive, Plymouth, Devon.* (Plymouth 362485)

RICHARDS, John Henry. b 34. CCC Cam BA 57, MA 75. St Mich AA Coll Llan BD 77. **d** 77 Llan **p** 78 Bp Reece for Llan. C of Llangynwyd 77-79; St Jo Bapt Cardiff Dio Llan from 79. *St Andrew, High Street, Llandaff, Cardiff, CF5 2DX.*

✠ **RICHARDS, Right Rev John Richards.** b 01. Univ of Wales BA (2nd cl Mod Lang) 22, MA 55, Hon LLD 71. DD (Lambeth) 56. St Mich Coll Llan. **d** 24 **p** 25 St D. C of Pembrey 24-27; CMS at Shiraz 27-37; Yezd 37-42; Isfahan 42-45; Archd in Iran 37-45; V of Skewen 45-52; Surr 46-54; Can of St Andr in Llan Cathl 49-54; Can Res of Ban Cathl 54-55; Dean 55-56; V of Pontypridd 52-54; St Jas Ban 54-55; Cons Ld Bp of St D in Cathl Ch of St Jo Evang Brecon 30 Nov 56 by Abp of Wales; Bps of Mon; Swan B; St A; Heref; and Ches; res 71; Chap and Sub-Prelate O of St John of Jer from 61; Pres St D Univ Coll Lamp 71-77. *Lluest Wen, Llanbadarn Road, Aberystwyth, Dyfed, SY23 iEY.*

RICHARDS, Canon John Stanley. **d** 21 **p** 23 Ban. C of Nyah 21-24; Manangatang 24-27; V of Charlton 27-29; R of Rylstone 29-31; Narromine 31-36; Rylstone 36-38; Condobolin 38-42; Canowindra 42-46; E Orange 46-56; Oberon 56-62; Can of All SS Cathl Bath 53-66. *57 Icely Road, Orange, NSW, Australia.*

RICHARDS, John Stanley. b 39. St Jo Coll Dur BA 60. Ridley Hall Cam 61. **d** 64 Southn for Win **p** 65 Win. C of Fordingbridge w Ibsley 64-67; CF (TA) 64-68; Bitterne Pk 67-68; All SS Southbourne Bournemouth 68-70; Res F Qu Coll Birm 70-71; C of St Andr Chesterton 71-73; Asst Chap Canford Sch and L to Offic Dio Sarum 73-77; Assoc Dir Fountain Trust 77-80; Perm to Offic Dio Guildf from 77. *Renewal Servicing Box 366, Addlestone, Weybridge, Surrey, KT15 3UL.*

RICHARDS, John William. b 29. Univ of Southn BSc 55.

Sarum Wells Th Coll 78. **d** 81 Guildf (NSM). C of St Mary-of-Bethany Woking Dio Guildf from 81. *15 Bonners Close, Westfield, Woking, Surrey, GU22 9RA.*

RICHARDS, Julian. b 25. Wycl Hall Ox 71. **d** 73 **p** 74 York. C of Hessle 73-76; C-in-c of Rowley Dio York from 76; Chap HM Pris Hull from 79. *Rowley Rectory, Little Weighton, Hull, HU20 3XR.* (Hull 843317)

RICHARDS, Keith John. Selw Coll Cam 3rd cl Hist Trip pt i 56, BA (3rd cl Hist Trip pt ii) 57, MA 61. Westcott Ho Cam 59. **d** 61 **p** 62 Man. C of Moss Side 61-66. *115 Gordon Hill, Enfield, Middx.*

RICHARDS, Lionel Caswall. b 44. Univ of WI Ja BA 70. Codr Coll Barb 67. **d** 71 Ja **p** 73 Antig. Asst Master St Jago High Sch Ja from 70. *Lot 385, Janet Crescent, Edgewater, St Catherine, Jamaica.*

RICHARDS, Llewelyn. b 15. St Deiniol's Libr Hawarden 73. **d** 75 **p** 76 St A (APM). C of Corwen Dio St A from 75; Gwyddelwern Dio St A from 78. *120 Maes Afallen, Corwen, Clwyd.*

RICHARDS, Ven Maurice Neville. b 14. **d** 41 **p** 42 Waik. C of St Geo Frankton 41-43; C-in-c of Par Distr of Ch Ch Tanmarunui 43-45; V 45-50; Fitzroy 50-56; Matamata 56-70; Paeroa 70-78; Can of Waik 57-66; Archd of Piako 66-76; Archd (Emer) from 77; Perm to Offic Dio Waik from 78. *2 Fitzgerald Avenue, Matamata, NZ.* (6256)

RICHARDS, Noel Thomas. b 47. St Jo Coll Morpeth 70. **d** 73 Gippsld **p** 74 Melb for Gippsld. C of Leongatha 73-75; R of Omeo 75-80; Cowes Dio Gippsld from 80. *Rectory, Cowes, Vic., Australia 3922.*

RICHARDS, Norman William. b 12. **d** 77 Ox **p** 78 Reading for Ox (APM). C of Epwell w Sibford, Swalcliffe and Tadmarton Dio Ox from 77. *The Cottage, Park Lane, Swalcliffe, Banbury, Oxon OX15 5ES.*

RICHARDS, Peter Garth. b 30. Univ of Lon BA (2nd cl Engl) 51. St Chad's Coll Dur Dipl Th 55. **d** 55 **p** 56 Ripon. C of Manston 55-57; Adel 57-62; V of Holbeck 62-66; C of Clyst St Geo 66-75; Team V of Clyst Valley 75-81. *3 Brooklands Orchard, Ottery St Mary, Devon.*

RICHARDS, Peter Lane Campling. St Cath S Ox BA (2nd cl Mod Hist) 51, MA 55. Wells Th Coll 51. **d** 53 Glouc **p** 54 Bp Barkway for Cant. C of St Paul Cheltm 53-56; Stonehouse 56-58; Tutor Bps' Coll Cheshunt 58-60; Chap 60-61; Vice Prin 61-64; L to Offic Dio St Alb 58-64; R of Marston Morteyne 64-75; P-in-c of Sharpness w Purton and Brookend 75-80; R of Dumbleton w Wormington and Toddington Dio Glouc from 80. *Rectory, Dumbleton, Evesham, Worc, WR11 6TG.* (Evesham 881410)

RICHARDS, Philip Llewelyn. b 11. St Pet Hall Ox BA 33, Dipl Th 34, MA 38. Wycl Hall Ox 33. **d** 35 Ex **p** 36 Crediton for Ex. C of St Andr Plymouth 35-39; All SS Highfield 39-40; CF (EC) 40-46; V of St Jo Evang Meads Eastbourne 46-65; St Aug Edgbaston 65-77. *4 Dharma Court, East Hill Road, Oxted, Surrey.*

RICHARDS, Robert Graham. b 42. St Jo Coll Nottm 77. **d** 80 Sarum **p** 81 Bp Henderson for Sarum. C of Radipole Dio Sarum from 80. *10 Lyndhurst Road, Weymouth, Dorset, DT4 7QR.*

✠ **RICHARDS, Right Rev Ronald Edwin.** Trin Coll Melb BA (2nd cl Phil) 32, MA 37, Hon ThD 60. **d** 32 **p** 33 Bal. C of Rokewood 32-33; P-in-c 34; P-in-c of Lismore 34-41 and 45-46; Chap AIF 41-45; V of Warrnambool 46-50; Archd of Bal 50-57; Exam Chap to Bp of Bal 50-57; VG 52-57; Cons Ld Bp of Bend in St Paul's Cathl Melb 1 May 57 by Abp of Melb; Bps of Bal; Wang; Centr Tang; St Arn; Gippsld; and Geelong; and Bps Baker; Stephenson; and Redding; res 74; Perm to Offic Dio Melb from 75. *119 Dare Street, Ocean Grove, Vic., Australia 3226.* (052-55 2116)

RICHARDS, Ronald Jervis. b 16. St D Coll Lamp BA 37. St Mich Coll Llan 38. **d** 39 **p** 40 St A. C of Minera 39-43; Chap RAF 43-71; Asst Chap-in-chief 66-71; Hon Chap to HM the Queen 70-71; R of Quendon w Rickling 71-75; V of Dedham Dio Chelmsf from 75. *Dedham Vicarage, Colchester, CO7 6DE.* (Colchester 322136)

RICHARDS, Simon Granston. b 47. Univ of Nottm BTh and ALCD 72. St Jo Coll Nottm 68. **d** 72 **p** 73 Chelmsf. C of Waltham Abbey 72-77; Team V of Basildon w Laindon (and Nevendon from 78) 77-80; V of Grayshott Dio Guildf from 80. *Grayshott Vicarage, Hindhead, Surrey, GU26 6NH.* (Hindhead 4540)

RICHARDS, Thomas Frank Oluwole. **d** 59 Sier L. d Dio Sier L. *Church House, York, Sierra Leone.*

RICHARDS, Thomas John Wynzie. b 25. St D Coll Lamp BA 49. **d** 51 Swan B for St D **p** 52 St D. C of Llandebie 51-53; Llandegai 53-56; R of Llanymawddwy 56-57; Chap Nat Nautical Sch Portishead 57-71; Hon Chap Miss to Seamen from 58; V of Llandebie Dio St D from 71; RD of Dyffryn Aman from 78. *Vicarage, Llandybie, Ammanford, Dyfed.* (Llandybie 850337)

RICHARDS, Thomas Malcolm Hart. **d** 33 **p** 34 Worc. C of Bromsgrove 33-38; Feckenham (in c of Astwood Bank) 38; CF (TA-R of O) 39-46; Hon CF 46; Min of Astwood Bank and Crabbs Cross Conv Distr 48-49; Chap Bromsgrove Sch 49-52; V of St Jo Bapt-in-Bedwardine Worc 52-75; C-in-c of Crown E 74-75. *Wayfarers, Park Road, West Malvern, Worcs.* (Malvern 5758)

RICHARDS, Trevor Thomas. b 09. Univ of Wales BSc 30, MSc 39. St Deiniol's Libr Hawarden 70. **d** 70 **p** 71 Bris. C of Charlton 70-73; Publ Pr Dio Bris from 73. *Mill Leaze, Upper Minety, Malmesbury, Wilts.* (Minety 323)

RICHARDS, Victor John Richard. AKC 48. St Bonif Coll Warm. **d** 48 Sherborne for Sarum **p** 49 Sarum. C of Bridport 48-51; CF 51-56; V of Hale 56-64; R of Chulmleigh Dio Ex from 64; RD of Chulmleigh and Surr from 69; P-in-c of Webworthy Dio Ex from 75; Chawleigh w Cheldon 77; Eggesford Dio Ex from 77. *Rectory, Chulmleigh, Devon.* (Chulmleigh 266)

RICHARDS, William Antony. b 28. Ex Coll Ox BA (3rd cl Mod Lang) 52, MA 56. St Steph Ho Ox 52. **d** 54 **p** 55 Lich. C of Fenton 54-55; St Mary Kingswinford 55-60; V of Meir 60-64; R of Warmington w Shotteswell 64-75; RD of Dassett Magna 70-74; Cler Org Sec CECS Dios Cov, Leic and Pet 75-81; V of Bidford-on-Avon Dio Cov from 81. *Bidford-on-avon Vicarage, Alcester, Warws, B50 4BQ.* (Bidford 772217)

RICHARDS, William Hughes. b 37. St D Coll Lamp BA 58. **d** 60 **p** 61 St D. C of Llandyssul 60-63; Llanelly 63-65; V of Llanddewi-Brefi w Llanbadarn Odwyn 65-73; Pembrey w Llandyry Dio St D from 73. *Vicarage, Pembrey, Burry Port, Dyfed.*

RICHARDS, Preb William Lloyd. b 17. Univ of Man BA 39, BD 41. Cudd Coll 47. **d** 48 **p** 49 Lich. C of Shifnal 48-50; C-in-c of St Thos Pennywell Conv Distr 51-56; R of Burford 2nd Portion (Whitton) w Greete and Hope Bagot 56-66; V of Holme Lacy w Dyndor 66-73; Dom Chap to Bp of Heref from 66; R of Stretton Sugwas Dio Heref from 73; Preb of Heref Cathl from 76. *Rectory, Stretton Sugwas, Hereford, HR4 7PT.* (Hereford 4640)

RICHARDS, Canon William Neal. b 38. ALCD 63. **d** 63 **p** 64 Bradf. C of Otley 63-65; St Mary Leamington 65-67; CMS Miss 67-69; V of Momb Cathl 69-71; Nai Cathl 71-74; Can Res 71-74; Can (Emer) from 74; V of Gt Malvern Dio Worc from 74. *Priory Vicarage, Clarence Road, Malvern, Worcs, WR14 3EN.* (Malvern 61020)

RICHARDS, Winfrid James Kirby. b 09. St Jo Coll Morpeth ACT ThL 36. **d** 35 **p** 36 Newc. C of Singleton 35-39; Mayfield 39-40; C-in-c of Wollombi w Ellalong 40-42; P-in-c of Belmont 42-44; Chap AIF 44-46; Asst Master C of E Boys' Sch Morpeth 46-47; V of Boggabri 47-53; Tywardreath w Tregaminion Cornw 53-59; R of Beaconsfield w Exeter Tas 59-61; P-in-c of Beresfield 61-69; C-in-c of Ludford 69-75; Ashford Carbonell w Ashford Bowdler 73-75; Perm to Offic Dios Lich and Heref from 75. *12 Burnell Close, Bayston Hill, Salop.* (Bayston Hill 3747)

RICHARDSON, Alan Brickell. b 11. K Coll Lon and Warm 47. **d** 50 Dover for Cant **p** 51 Cant. C of Selsdon 50-54; R of Biddenden 54-59; V of St Mich Sutton Court Chiswick 59-66; R of Barham 66-75; C of Boxgrove 75-78; Tangmere 75-78; Oving & Merston 75-78; Westbourne and of Forestside w Stansted 78-81. *4 Blenheim Gardens, Chichester, W Sussex, PO19 2XE.*

RICHARDSON, Anthony William. Moore Th Coll Syd ACT ThL 67. **d** 68 **p** 69 Syd. C of Beverly Hills 68-69; Dural 69-72. *Pitt Town Road, Kenthurst, NSW 2154, Australia.*

RICHARDSON, Arthur Athol. **d** and **p** 75 Melb. C of Box Hill 75-77; I of Hopper's Crossing 77-81; St Aid Strathmore Dio Melb from 81. *24 Williamson Avenue, Strathmore Vic., Australia 3041.*

RICHARDSON, Brian William. Moore Th Coll Syd ACT ThL 53. **d** and **p** 54 Syd. C of St Matt Manly 54-55; C-in-c of Pittwater 54-58; P-in-c of Penola 58-60; R of Carlingford 60-66; Manly 66-77; St Jas Turramurra Dio Syd from 77. *15 King Street, Turramurra, NSW, Australia 2074.* (44-1021)

RICHARDSON, Canon Charles. b 13. AKC 35. Linc Th Coll 35. **d** 36 **p** 37 S'wark. C of St Barn Eltham 36-40; St Pet St Helier (in c of Bp Andrewes' Ch) 40-45; Chap RNVR 45-47; Min of Legal Distr of the Ascen Mitcham 47-53; PC 53-54; R of Rawmarsh (w Parkgate from 60) 54-76; Surr from 60; RD of Rotherham 74-76; Hon Can of Sheff from 75; R of Harthill 76-80. *41 Nether Green Road, Sheffield, S11 7EH.* (Sheff 304699)

RICHARDSON, Charles Leslie. b 54. St Jo Coll Dur BA 76. Coll of Resurr Mirfield 76. **d** 79 **p** 80 Cant. C of Folkestone Dio Cant from 79. *6 Copthall Gardens, Folkestone, Kent, CT20 1HF.* (56440)

RICHARDSON, David Anthony. b 41. Kelham Th Coll 57. **d** 66 **p** 67 Bradf. C of Tong w Holme Wood 66-68; Richmond Surrey 68-71; C of Sanderstead (in c of St Edm Riddlesdown)

71-74; Team V 74-78; R of Beddington Dio S'wark from 78. *300 Croydon Road, Wallington, Surrey, SM6 7LQ.* (01-647 1973)

RICHARDSON, David Gwynne. b 39. K Coll Lon and Warm. **d** 64 **p** 65 Dur. C of Birtley 64-67; Soc and Industr Adv to Bp of Dur 67-77; Team V of Brayton w Barlow and Chap Selby Coalfield Dio York from 78. *20 Mayfield Drive, Brayton, Selby, YO8 9JZ.*

RICHARDSON, David John Leyburn. b 46. Univ of Queensld BA 69. St Barn Coll Adel ACT ThL 70. Melb Coll of Div BD 75. **d** 70 **p** 71 Brisb. C of Maryborough 71-74; St Paul Ipswich Brisb 74-75; St Mary Gt w St Mich Cam and Chap Girton Coll 76-79; Res Tutor St Barn Th Coll Adel from 79; Sub-Warden from 80. *St Barnabas Theological College, Belair, S Australia 5052.* (267 3417)

RICHARDSON, David John Thomas. St Francis Coll Brisb ACT ThL 38. **d** and **p** 39 Brisb. C of Angl Miss Brisb 39-40; S Andr S Brisb 40-45; Chap AIF 40-45; R of St Mark Eidsvold 45-47; Milton Brisb 47-52; Brisbane Valley 52-58; Gatton Dio Brisb from 58. *72 Railway Street, Gatton, Queensland 4343, Australia.*

RICHARDSON, Douglas Stanley. b 23. Bps' Coll Cheshunt. **d** 57 **p** 58 Lon. C of Hampton 57-61; V of W Twyford 61-69; St Pet Kens Pk Rd Notting Hill Lon 69-78; St Pet Staines Dio Lon from 78; P-in-c of St Mary Staines Dio Lon from 81. *14 Thames Side, Laleham Road, Staines, Middx, TW18 2HA.* (Staines 53039)

RICHARDSON, Duncan Stanley. Moore Th Coll Syd ACT ThL 59. **d** and **p** 60 Syd. C of Parramatta 60-61; St Mary's 61-64; P-in-c of Northmead 64-69; Chap Ld Howe I 69; C-in-c of Berala 70-74; Chap R Prince Alfred and R Alexandra Hosps Syd from 74; L to Offic Dio Syd from 74. *10/7 Tintern Road, Ashfield, NSW, Australia 2131.* (798-0719)

RICHARDSON, Canon Edward James Aubin. b 10. Ex Coll Ox BA 33, MA 39. Wycl Hall Ox 36. **d** 38 Ripon for Bradf **p** 39 Bradf. C of Cathl Ch Bradf 38-40; Succr 40-42; V of Denholme Gate 42-47; R of St Ouen Jersey 47-76; Vice-Dean of Jersey 66-76; Hon Can of Win Cathl 71-76; Can (Emer) from 76. *1 Farm Cottage, Snailbeach, Shrewsbury, Salop, SY5 0LP.* (Minsterley 489)

RICHARDSON, Edward John. b 39. Lich Th Coll 62. **d** 65 **p** 66 Guildf. C of Chessington 65-70; V in Trunch Par Group 70-75; Stoneleigh 75-79. *c/o 59 Stoneleigh Park Road, Stoneleigh, Surrey, KT19 0QU.*

RICHARDSON, Edward Sunderland. **d** 58 Bp Rich for Wel **p** 59 Wel. C of Hawera 59-61; V of Otaki 61-67; Hosp Chap Dio Wel 67-69; Perm to Offic Dio Auckld 69-73; C of Kaitaia 73-74; Hon C of Wellsford Dio Auckld from 74. *11 Davies Road, Wellsford, NZ.* (Wellsford 8977)

RICHARDSON, Edwin Thomas John. St Mich Ho Crafers ACT LTh 64.**d** and **p** 65 Melb. C of St Mich AA Broadmeadows 65; Coburg 65-67; Dept of Evangelism and Ex and P-in-c of Templestowe 67-71; I of Mt Duneed 71-77; R of Mansfield Dio Wang from 77. *Rectory, Mansfield, Vic, Australia 3722.*

RICHARDSON, Canon Emerson Cromwell. **d** 68 **p** 69 Antig. C of St John's Cathl Antig 68-69; R of St Pet w St John Montserrat 69-76; St Mary I and Dio Antig from 76; Can of Antig from 80. *St Mary's Rectory, Urlings, Antigua, W Indies.*

RICHARDSON, Ven Eric Hatherley Humphrey. Qu Coll Ox BA (3rd cl Mod Hist) 35. Westcott Ho Cam 35. **d** 36 **p** 37 Lon. C of St Mary Stoke Newington 36-39; St Mary's Cathl Johann 39-40; CF (S Afr) 40-46; R of Ermelo 46-50; Van der Bijl Pk 50-52; Orange Grove Johann 52-59; Hd of St Geo Home City and Dio Johann from 60; L to Offic Dio Johann 65-77; Can of Johann 67-75; Hon Can from 75; Archd of Germiston 77-78; Johann S from 78; Chap St Pet Sch Johann from 81. *44 Frere Road, Kensington B, Randburg, Johannesburg, S Africa.*

RICHARDSON, Frank Herbert. b 07. St Chad's Coll Dur BA 32, Dipl Th 33, MA 35. **d** 33 **p** 34 Dur. C of Silksworth 33-36; Greenside (in c of Crawcrook) 36-41; Staindrop w Cockfield 41-42; V of St Alb Heworth 42-54; R of Southwick 54-74. *60 Sidecliff Road, Sunderland, T & W, SR6 9JR.*

RICHARDSON, Geoffrey Stewart. b 47. St Jo Coll Ox BA (Maths) 69, MA 73. St Steph Ho Ox 70. **d** 72 **p** 73 Willesden for Lon. C of St Andr S Harrow 72-75; St Barn Woodford 75-80; V of St Paul Goodmayes Dio Chelmsf from 80. *20 Eastwood Road, Goodmayes, Ilford, Essex.* (01-590 6596)

RICHARDSON, Gerald. b 24. Chich Th Coll 54. **d** 56 **p** 57 Lon. C of Northolt 56-59; Caversham 59-63; V of Snibston 63-67; St Steph Smethwick 67-72; St Jas Aylestone Pk City and Dio Leic from 72. *38 Park Hill Drive, Leicester, LE2 8HR.* (Leic 832003)

RICHARDSON, Canon Jack Cyril. b 11. Univ of Leeds BSc 36. Coll of Resurr Mirfield 35. **d** 35 **p** 36 S'wark. C of St Andr Mottingham 35-38; St Mary Virg Port Eliz 38-40; CF (S Afr) 40-45; C of Farnham Royal 45-53; V of S Stoneham w Swaythling 53-65; U Clatford w Goodworth Clatford 65-77; RD of Andover 67-75; Hon Can of Win 73-77; Can (Emer) from 77; Perm to Offic Dio St Alb from 78. *Robin Cottage, The Street, Braughing, Ware, Herts.* (Ware 822020)

RICHARDSON, James Aidan. Late Scho of St Chad's Coll Dur BA (3rd cl Th) 51, Dipl Th 54. **d** 54 **p** 55 Dur. C of Ferryhill 54-56; Stirling 56-58; P-in-c of St Cath Bo'ness w St Mildred Linlithgow 58-64; V of Linthwaite 64-79; Clifton Dio Wakef from 79; RD of Blackmoorfoot 77-79. *Clifton Vicarage, Brighouse, Yorks.* (Brighouse 3290)

RICHARDSON, James Arthur. b 19. MC 44. ARICS 53. Univ of Lon BSc 51. Ridley Hall Cam 60. **d** and **p** 62 S'wark. C of Wandsworth 62-65; V of St Alb Streatham Pk Dio S'wark from 65. *5 Fayland Avenue, SW16.* (01-769 5415)

RICHARDSON, James Horner. b 19. Ch Coll Cam BA (Hist & Th) 42, MA 45. Ridley Hall Cam 41. **d** 43 **p** 44 Derby. C of St Giles Normanton-by-Derby 43-47; Far Headingley Leeds 47-48; St Pet Harrogate 48-50; CF 50-53; Hon CF 53; V of Em Chadderton 53-59; Surr 57-81; V of Huyton 59-70; Ormskirk 70-80; Giggleswick Dio Bradf from 80; P-in-c of Rathmell-in-Craven w Wigglesworth Dio Bradf from 80. *Giggleswick Vicarage, Settle, N Yorks, BD24 0AP.* (Settle 2425)

RICHARDSON, James John. b 41. Univ of Hull BA (2nd cl Law and Pol Stud) 63. Cudd Coll 66. **d** 69 **p** 70 Lich. C of Wolverhampton 69-72; P-in-c of All SS Hanley 72-75; R of Nantwich Dio Ches from 75. *Rectory, Nantwich, Chesh.* (0270-65268)

RICHARDSON, John. b 15. OBE 70. VRD 58, and Bar 68. St Aid Coll 46. **d** 48 **p** 49 Dur. C of Chester-le-Street 48-51; R of Burnmoor 51-54; Chap RN 54-58; RNR from 58; V of Bishopton w Gt Stainton 58-66; Mitford Dio Newc T from 66; Org Sec Miss to Seamen S Shields 59-68; Lect Northumb Tech Coll from 69. *Mitford Vicarage, Morpeth, Northumb.* (Morpeth 512527)

RICHARDSON, John. b 41. Qu Coll Birm 69. **d** 72 Warrington for Liv **p** 73 Liv. C of Ormskirk 72-74; Doncaster 74-76; R of Hemsworth 76-79; V of Penallt Dio Mon from 79. *Penallt Vicarage, Monmouth, NP5 4SE.* (Monmouth 2330)

RICHARDSON, John. b 47. Linc Th Coll 78. **d** 80 **p** 81 Bradf. C of Keighley Dio Bradf from 80. *10 Oakbank Drive, Keighley, W Yorks, BD22 7DX.*

RICHARDSON, Ven John Farquhar. b 05. Trin Hall Cam 2nd cl Hist Trip pt i 25, BA (2nd cl Hist Trip pt ii) 26, MA 30. Westcott Ho Cam. **d** 29 **p** 30 Ely. C of H Trin Cam 29-32; Publ Pr Dio Derby and Chap Repton Sch 32-35; C of St Martin-in-the-Fields Trafalgar Sq 35-36; V of Ch Ch Hampstead 36-41; R of Bp Wearmouth 41-52; RD of Wearmouth 47-52; Proc Conv Dur 50-52; Hon Can of Dur 50-52; Derby 52-55; 1st Can Resid 55-73; Archd 52-73; Archd (Emer) from 73; Exam Chap to Bp of Derby 52-73; Chap to HM the Queen 52-75. *474 Kedleston Road, Allestree, Derby, DE3 2NE.* (Derby 559135)

RICHARDSON, John Hedley. b 45. Univ of Leeds BA 72. Qu Coll Birm 72. **d** 74 **p** 75 Derby. C of St Phil Chaddesden 74-76; Perm to Offic Dio Derby from 76. *23 Milton Street, Long Eaton, Nottingham.*

RICHARDSON, John Henry. b 37. Trin Hall Cam 2nd cl Th Trip pt i 59, BA (3rd cl Th Trip pt ii) 61, MA 65. Cudd Coll 61. **d** 63 **p** 64 St Alb. C of Stevenage 63-66; Eastbourne 66-68; V of Chipperfield 68-75; Rickmansworth Dio St Alb from 75; RD of Rickmansworth from 77. *Vicarage, Rickmansworth, Herts.* (Rickmansworth 72627)

RICHARDSON, John Humphrey. b 33. Univ of Dur BA (2nd cl Psychol 57. Chich Th Coll 57. **d** 59 Lewes for Chich **p** 60 Chich. C of St Barn Bexhill 59-61; Moulsecomb w Stanmer and Falmer 61-64; Ifield 64-70; R of Earnley w E Wittering and Almodington 70-79; V of All SS w St Pet (and St Jo Bapt from 81) Stamford Dio Linc from 79; R of St Jo Bapt w St Clem Stamford 79-81; RD of Aveland and Ness w Stamford from 80. *All Saints Vicarage, Stamford, Lincs.* (Stamford 2163)

RICHARDSON, John Paul. b 44. St Steph Ho Ox 74. **d** 76 Lon **p** 77 Willesden for Lon. C of St Andr Kingsbury 76-78; St Steph Blackpool 78-79; Marton 79-81; V of Newchurch-in-Pendle Dio Blackb from 81. *Newchurch-in-Pendle Vicarage, Burnley, Lancs.* (Nelson 63535)

RICHARDSON, John Peter. b 50. Univ of Keele BA 72. St Jo Coll Nottm 73. **d** 76 Birm **p** 77 Bp Aston for Birm. C of Blackheath 76-81; P-in-c of Sparkbrook Dio Birm from 81. *34 Grantham Road, Sparkbrook, Birmingham, B11 1LU.* (021-772 6558)

RICHARDSON, John Stephen. b 50. Univ of Southn BA 71. St Jo Coll Nottm 72. **d** 74 **p** 75 Southw. C of Bramcote 74-77; Radipole and Melcombe Regis (in c of Em Ch Centre) 77-80; P-in-c of Stinsford, Winterbourne Came w Whitcombe and Winterbourne Monkton Dio Sarum from 80. *10 Treves Road, Dorchester, Dorset, DT1 2HD.*

RICHARDSON, John Stuart. b 46. Trin Coll Ox BA 68, MA 71, DPhil 73. **d** 79 **p** 80 St Andr. C of St Andr City and Dio St Andr from 79; Chap St Andr Univ from 80. *60 North Street, St Andrews, Fife, KY16 9AH.*

RICHARDSON, Joseph Edmund. b 27. St Chad's Coll Dur BA 49. Sarum Th Coll 51. **d** 52 Knaresborough for Ripon **p** 53 Ripon. C of Far Headingley 52-56; Hoylake 56-58; V of Halton 58-65; R of Davenham 65-76; V of Sale Dio Ches from 76. *Vicarage, Church Road, Sale, M33 3HB.* (061-973 4145)

RICHARDSON, Canon Kenneth Sinton George. Hur Coll LTh 50. **d** 50 **p** 51 Niag. C of Welland 50-51; I of Jarvis w Nanticoke 51-54; Georgetown (w Glen Williams to 58) 54-61; Chap Hamilton Hosps 62-66; R of Woodburn w Tapleytown 65-66; St Steph Niagara Falls Dio Niag from 67; I of Queenston 67-75; Hon Can of Niag from 73; R of Epiph Oakville Dio Niag from 75. *161 Bronte Road, Oakville, Ont., Canada.* (416-358 7775)

RICHARDSON, Maurice. b 12. **d** 66 **p** 67 Southw. C of Hawksworth w Scarrington 66-69; V of Lowdham w Gunthorpe and Caythorpe 69-77. *Old Orchard, Granby, Nottingham, NG13 9PR.* (Whatton 50860)

RICHARDSON, Michael Arkley. b 38. Univ of Bris BSc (2nd cl) 59. Clifton Th Coll 61. **d** 63 **p** 64 Chich. C of St Pancras w St Jo Evang Chich 63-68; V in Winfarthing Par Group 68-77. *Hebron, Heywood Road, Shelfanger, Diss, Norf.* (Diss 3144)

RICHARDSON, Neil. b 46. Sarum Wells Th Coll 71. **d** 74 **p** 75 Man. C of Oldham 74-77; C-in-c of St Hugh Conv Distr Holts Dio Man from 77. *St Hugh's Vicarage, Covert Road, Holts, Oldham, OL4 5PH.* (061-633 1387)

RICHARDSON, Paul. b 47. Qu Coll Ox BA (Mod Hist) 68, BA (Th) 70. Cudd Coll 71. **d** 72 **p** 73 S'wark. C of St John Earlsfield 72-75; Asst Chap of Oslo 75-77; R of Nambaiyufa 77-78; Lect Newton Th Coll Dogura 78-80; Prin from 81. *Newton College, Dogura, Papua New Guinea.*

RICHARDSON, Canon Robert Douglas. b 1893. Hertf Coll Ox BA (*sc* Th w distinc) 21, MLitt 23, MA 26, BD and DD 52. Ripon Hall Ox. **d** 23 **p** 24 Worc. C of Stourport (or Mitton Lower) 23-26; Cathl Ch Birm 26-29; V of Four Oaks 29-34; Lect Univ of Birm 28-47; Exam Chap to Bp of Birm 32-53; Select Pr Univ of Cam 34; V of Harborne 34-47; Hon Can of Birm 38-52; Can (Emer) from 53; L to Offic Dio Ox and Prin of Ripon Hall Ox 47-52; R of Boyton w Sherrington 52-67. *Corton Parva, Warminster, Wilts.* (Codford St Mary 286)

RICHARDSON, Robert Trevor. b 34. St Mich Coll Llan. **d** 60 **p** 61 Llan. C of Cymmer w Porth 60-62; Worsley w Ellenbrook 62-65; V of Waterfoot Dio Man from 65. *Waterfoot Vicarage, Rossendale, Lancs.* (Rossendale 215959)

RICHARDSON, Ronald Harold. b 29. St Paul's Coll Grahmstn 70. **d** 72 **p** 73 Natal. C of All SS Ladysmith 72-75; R of Port Shepstone 75-77; V of St Geo Windsor Brisb 77-80; Hosp Chap Dio Brisb from 80. *32 Wyndham Street, Herston, Queensland, Australia 4006.* (52 2941)

RICHARDSON, Stephen. b 1899. Worc Ordin Coll 57. **d** 58 **p** 59 B & W. C of S Lyncombe 58-61; R of Meysey Hampton w Marston Meysey 61-73. *The Lee, Church Street, Meysey Hampton, Cirencester, Glos GL7 5JU.* (Poulton 407)

RICHARDSON, Thomas Charles. b 15. **d** 78 Graft. C of Ballina Dio Graft from 78. *10 Hamilton Street, Ballina, NSW, Australia 2478.*

RICHARDSON, Thomas Warner. b 11. Late Scho St Jo Coll Dur BA (2nd cl Th) 38, MA 44. Westcott Ho Cam 38. **d** 38 **p** 39 Southw. C of St Marg Aspley 38-45; CF (EC) 40-46; V of All SS Nottm 46-50; PC of St Marg Aspley 50-57; V of Radcliffe-on-Trent 57-65; V of Shelford 57-65; Surr 58-65; RD of Bingham 58-62; V of St Austell 65-72; C-in-c of Teversal 72-76. *1 Glencross Court, Doctors Lane, Liskeard, Cornw.* (0579-43897)

RICHARDSON, Thomas Wood. b 16. Cranmer Hall Dur 65. **d** 66 **p** 67 Newc T. C of Rothbury 66-70; Hexham 70-75; V of Chevington Dio Newc T from 75. *Chevington Vicarage, Morpeth, Northumb, NE61 5AH.* (Red Row 760273)

RICHARDSON, Trevor Charles. b 37. Keble Coll Ox BA (Th) 60, MA 64. Westcott Ho Cam 78. **d** 78 **p** 79 Edmon for Lon. C of St Jas W Hampstead Dio Lon from 78. *2 St James's House, Sherriff Road, NW6.* (01-624 9221)

RICHARDSON, Warren Edward. Northwestern Univ Ill BSc 49. Seabury Western Th Sem Ill BD 61. **d** and **p** 61 Bp Street for Chicago. [F in Amer Ch] P-in-c of Ch K Grand Bahama I Dio Nass from 68. *Box 87, Freeport, Grand Bahama Island, W Indies.*

RICHARDSON, Canon William. b 11. Late Scho of Qu Coll Ox 1st cl Cl Mods 32, BA (2nd cl Lit Hum) and Liddon Stud 34, Jun Hall-Houghton Gr Test Pri and 2nd cl Th 35, Sen Hall-Houghton Gr Test and Jun Denyer and Johnson Th Sch 36, MA 37, BD 52. Ripon Hall Ox 35. **d** 36 **p** 38 Lich. C of Bilston St Leon 36-37; Wem 37-39; Tutor Ripon Hall Ox 39-43; Chap 40-43; LPr Dio Ox 39-43; Asst Master Stamford Sch 43-48; L to Offic Dio Pet and Actg C-in-c of St Martin Stamford Baron 43-46; LPr Dio Linc 43-46; R of Careby w Holywell and Aunby 46-48; Asst Chap and Asst Master at Oundle Sch 48-51; Chap and Asst Master Malvern Coll 51-52; V of Whitgift w Adlingfleet 52-59; Lect in Th at Hull Univ 54-72; V of Waghen Dio York 59-61 and 69-71; C-in-c 61-69; R of Routh 59-61; V of St Jas Sutton-in-Holderness 61-71; Team R of Sutton-in-Holderness w Wawne (or Waghen) 71-78; Select Pr Univ of Cam 61; Can and Preb of York Minster from 70. *1 Precentor's Court, York, YO1 2EJ.*

RICHENS, Geoffrey Roger. b 23. ALCD 52. **d** 52 **p** 53 Liv. C of St Helens (in c of St Mary's Miss) 52-56; V of Widnes 56-80; Skelmersdale Dio Liv from 80. *Vicarage, Skelmersdale, Lancs, WN8 8ND.* (Skelmersdale 22087)

RICHERBY, Glynn. b 51. BD and AKC 73. St Aug Coll Cant 73. **d** 74 **p** 75 Pet. C of Weston Favell 74-78; Prec of St Martin's Cathl Leic 78-81; V of Glen Parva w S Wigston Dio Leic from 81. *1 St Thomas Road, S Wigston, Leicester, LE8 2TA.* (Leic 782830)

RICHES, Claude Christopher. b 25. Westcott Ho Cam 70. **d** 72 **p** 73 St E. C of Woodbridge 72-75; R of Whitton and Thurleston w Akenham 75-78; R of Ashdon w Hadstock Dio Chelmsf from 78. *Ashdon Rectory, Saffron Walden, CB10 2HN.* (Ashdon 200)

RICHES, John Kenneth. b 39. CCC Cam 2nd cl Mod Lang Trip pt i 59, BA (2nd cl Th Trip pt ii) 61, 2nd cl Th Trip pt iii 63, MA 65. **d** 65 Nor **p** 66 Lynn for Nor. C of Costessey 65-68; Chap and Fell and Dir of Th Studs SS Coll Cam 68-73; Lect Glas Univ from 73. *Viewfield, Balmore, Glasgow, G64 4AE.* (Balmore 254)

✠ **RICHES, Right Rev Kenneth.** b 08. CCC Cam 2nd cl Hist Trip pt i 29, BA (1st cl Th Trip pt i) 31, MA 35. Gen Th Sem NY Hon STD 56. DD (Lambeth) 57. Hon Fell SS Coll Cam 58. Cudd Coll 32. **d** 32 **p** 33 Portsm. C of St Mary Portsea 32-35; St Jo Evang E Dulwich 35-36; Chap SS Coll Cam 36-42; Select Pr Univ of Cam 41 and 48; Exam Chap to Bps of Bradf and Wakef 36-44; L to Offic Dio Bradf 36-44; Dir of Service Ordination Cands 42-45; R of Bredfield w Boulge 42-44; Prin of Cudd Coll Ox 44-52; V of Cuddesdon 44-52; Commiss Zanz 44-54; Hon Can of Portsm 50-52; Archd of Ox and Can of Ch Ch Ox 52-56; Cons Ld Bp Suffr of Dorchester in St Paul's Cathl 25 July 52 by Abp of Cant; Bps of Lon; Win; Ox; S Rhod; Brech; and Zanz; Bps Suffr of Reading; and Buckingham; Bps Allen; and Vernon; Trld to Lincoln 56; res 74; Select Pr Univ of Ox 54 and 55; Univ of Cam 61; Hon Fell of CCC Cam, SS Coll Cam and Linc Coll Ox from 75. *Little Dingle, Dunwich, Saxmundham, Suff, IP17 3EA.*

RICHES, Lance Robert Alfred. B 45. **d** 78 **p** 79 Waik. Hon C of Taumarunui Dio Waik from 78. *Hikumutu, RD 2, Taumarunui, NZ.*

RICHEY, Herbert Grant David. Trin Coll Tor LTh 52. **d** 52 Ott **p** 58 Tor. C of Smith Falls 52; All H Tor 58-61; P-in-c of H Trin Oshawa 61; Hon C of All H City and Dio Tor from 61. *9 Humewood Drive, Toronto, 347, Ont, Canada.*

RICHEY, Canon Robert Samuel Payne. b 23. Late Th Exhib of TCD BA 46. **d** 48 **p** 49 Arm. C of Moy 48-50; I of Killinagh and Kiltyclogher (w Innismagrath from 60 and Killargue from 72) Dio Kilm from 50; Dioc Sec Kilm from 72; Can of Kilm from 80. *Killinagh Rectory, Blacklion, Co Cavan, Irish Republic.* (Blacklion 10)

RICHMOND, Archdeacon of (Dio Ripon). *See* Burbridge, Ven John Paul.

RICHMOND, Arnold. b 19. Sarum Wells Th Coll 77. **d** 80 **p** 81 Ex (NSM). C of Axminster Dio Ex from 80. *Tytherleigh House, Tytherleigh, Axminster, Devon, EX13 7BE.*

RICHMOND, Canon Francis Henry Arthur. b 36. TCD BA 59, MA 66. Univ of Strasbourg BTh 60. Linacre Coll Ox BLitt 64. Wycl Hall Ox 60. **d** 63 **p** 64 Sheff. C of Woodlands 63-66; Research Fell Univ of Sheff and Chap Sheff Cathl 66-69; V of St Geo Sheff 69-77; Chap Univ of Sheff 74-77; Warden Linc Th Coll from 77; Can and Preb of Linc Cathl from 77; Exam Chap to Bp of Linc from 77; M Gen Syn from 80. *Warden's House, Lincoln Theological College, Drury Lane, Lincoln, LN1 3BP.* (Linc 25879)

RICHMOND, Gordon Hazlewood. b 33. Launde Abbey Leic 77. **d** 79 Bp Garrett for Leic **p** 80 Leic. C of St Paul Leic 79-81; Shepshed Dio Leic from 81. *c/o Woodlands Drive, Shepshed, Loughborough, Leics, LE12 9SD.*

RICHMOND, Paul Ernest. b 15. Linc Th Coll 46. **d** 48 **p** 49 Liv. C of St Mich AA Wigan 48-51; All SS U Norwood (in c of St Marg) 52-56; V of Milton Regis-next-Sittingbourne 56-66; Chap Milton Regis Hosp 56-66; Court Regis Old People's Home 63-66; R of Cold Norton w N Fambridge 66-72; C-in-c of Stow Maries 71-72; R of Cold Norton w

Stow Maries 72-77; Gt Bromley w L Bromley 77-80. *Little Hayes, Lewes Road, Ringmer, E Sussex, BN8 5ER.*

RICHMOND, Peter James. b 54. St Jo Coll Nottm LTh 80. **d** 80 **p** 81 Lich. C of Ogley Hay w Brownhills Dio Lich from 80. *50 Lichfield Road, Brownhills, Walsall, W Midl.* (Brownhills 78542)

RICHTER, Murray Clifford. Moore Th Coll Syd. **d** 56 **p** 57 Armid. C of Moree 56-57; V of Baradine 58-59; R of Kilkivan 59-62; V of Epping 62-69; St Luke Frankston E 69-74; Chap Brighton Gr Sch Melb from 74. *273 New Street, Brighton, Vic, Australia 3186.* (92-8612)

RICKARD, George Frederick. Selw Coll Cam BA 32, MA 37. Wycl Hall Ox. **d** 48 **p** 49 Roch. L to Offic at St Marg Roch 48-54; Asst Master and Chap K Sch Roch 43-54; R of Chevening 54-60; Knockholt 60-65; V of Ugborough Dio Ex from 65; Chap Moorhaven and Moorfield Hosps from 65. *Ugborough Vicarage, Bittaford, Ivybridge, Devon, PL21 0ER.* (Ivybridge 2866)

RICKARD, Philip Alfred. Univ of Tor BASc 27. Wycl Coll Tor 30. **d** 30 Athab **p** 35 Edmon. C of Fairview 30-32; Colinton w Boyle 30-31; on Univ of Tor Staff 31-35; and 42-48; V of Clandonald 35-37; Wainwright 37-39; I of St Pet w St Mark Edmon 39-40; Princeton w Drumbo and Ayr 40-42; Kerrwood 42; Belmont 48-50; Hon C of St Jas Cathl City and Dio Tor from 50. *119 Balmoral Avenue, Toronto, Ont, Canada.*

RICKARDS, Peter Thomas Gisborne. b 42. Ridley Coll Melb 66. **d** 69 Melb for Gippsld **p** 69 Gippsld. C of Traralgon 69-71; Moe 71-79 St Pet Melb 79-80; C in Dept of Chap Dio Melb from 80. *46 Myrnong Crescent, Ascot Vale, Vic, Australia 3032.*

RICKARDS, Raymond Robert. Univ of NZ MA (3rd cl Phil and Psych) 50. Coll Ho Ch Ch LTh (2nd cl) 63. **d** 49 **p** 50 Wel. C of Palmerston N 49-52; V of Kiwitea 52-55; R and Dir of Nongoma 55-60; Perm to Offic Dio Cant 60-61; Chap and Tutor Ch Ch Coll 61-65; V of NE Valley 65-69; Perm to Offic Dio Melb 70-74; Dio Polyn from 74. *Box 1114, Suva, Fiji.*

RICKETTS, Allan Fenn. b 46. Cranmer Hall Dur 68. **d** 71 **p** 72 Birm. C of Rowley Regis 71-72; The Quinton 72-74; Brierley Hill (in c of St Paul Hawbush) 74-77; Team V of Chelmsley Wood 77-81; C of Brampton Abbotts 81-82; Team V of Ross-on-Wye Dio Heref from 82. *Brampton Abbots Rectory, Ross-on-Wye, Herefs, HR9 7JD.* (0989 64876)

RICKETTS, Peter William. b 28. M.IEE, CEng 60. **d** 79 St Alb **p** 80 Bedford for St Alb. Hon C of All SS Hertford Dio St Alb from 79. *38 Fordwich Rise, Hertford, Herts, SG14 2BL.*

RIDDEL, Robert John. b 37. Trin Coll Dub. **d** 68 **p** 69 Arm. C of Derryloran 68-74; R of Keady w Armaghbreague and Derrynoose 74-80; Cleenish Dio Clogh from 80; Mullaghdun Dio Clogh from 80. *Cleenish Rectory, Bellanaleck, Co Fermanagh, N Ireland.* (Florence Court 259)

RIDDELL, Morris Stroyan. b 34. BD (Lon) 69, Dipl Th (Lon) 59. Tyndale Hall, Bris 57. **d** and **p** 60 Capetn. C of Mowbray 60-62; V of Ch Ch Addington Durban 62-63; N Grimston w Wharram Percy and Wharram-le-Street 63-67; V of Kirby Grindalythe 63-67; C-in-c of Weaverthorpe w Helperthorpe and Luttons Ambo 65-67; C-in-c of Settrington 65-67; R of St Jo Bapt w St Mary-le-Port Bris 67-70; Chap HM Pris Long Lartin 71-74; Sen Chap HM Pris Brixton 74-78; Chap Cane Hill Hosp from 78. *Cane Hill Hospital, Coulsdon, Surrey, CR3 3YL.* (Downland 52221)

RIDDELSDELL, Canon John Creffield. b 23. Selw Coll Cam BA 47, MA 52. BD (Lon) 70. Ridley Hall Cam. **d** 49 **p** 50 Lon. C of St Mary Kilburn 49-52; CMS Coast Miss Adviser Dio Momb 52-59; V of Malindi Miss Distr 59-62; Prin of St Phil Bible Sch Maseno 62-71; Exam Chap to Bp of Maseno 64-71; Tutor St Paul's Th Coll Limuru 71-74; Prin 74-76; Can (Emer) of Momb Cathl from 77; V of St Andr Ilford Dio Chelmsf from 77. *St Andrew's Vicarage, Ilford, Essex, IG1 3PE.* (01-554 3858)

RIDDING, George. b 24. Or Coll Ox BA 50, MA 57. Wells Th Coll 60. **d** 61 **p** 62 Ex. C of Countess Weir 61-62; Chap Ex Sch 62-64; Prin John Connon Sch Bom 64-68; Hd Master W Buckland Sch and L to Offic Dio Ex 68-78; USPG Miss from 78. *St Luke's Church, Teluk Anson, Lower Perak, Malaysia.*

RIDDLE, John Charles. Univ of W Ont BA 65. Hur Coll BTh 68. **d** 68 Bp Appleyard for Hur **p** 69 Hur. C of Chatsworth 68-72; I of La Salle 72-76; New St Paul Woodstock Dio Hur from 76. *19 Wellington Street South, Woodstock, Ont., Canada.* (519-537 3921)

RIDDLE, Kenneth Wilkinson. b 20. St Cath S Ox BA (3rd cl Eng Lang and Lit) 42, MA 46. Ripon Hall, Ox 42. **d** 43 **p** 44 Nor. C of St Marg Lowestoft 43-47; Luton 47-49; R of Sundon w Streatley 49-52; Pakefield 52-59; Surr from 53; V of St Pet Mancroft Nor 59-60; R of E w W Harling 60-65; C-in-c of Bridgham w Roudham 60-61; R 61-65; Ed *Norwich Churchman* 60-68; R of Lowestoft 65-68. *Old Post Office, East Lyng, Taunton, Somt, TA3 5AU.* (Burrow Bridge 427)

RIDEOUT, Gordon Trevor. b 38. Lon Coll Div 58. **d** 62 **p** 63 Chich. C of St Mary Crawley 62-65; Chap Dr Barnardo's Homes Barkingside and Woodford Bridge 65-67; CF 67-73; V of Nutley 73-79; All SS Eastbourne Dio Chich from 79. *All Saints Vicarage, Grange Road, Eastbourne, E Sussex, BN21 4MG.* (Eastbourne 21133)

RIDER, Arthur William. b 10. BSc (Lon) 45. SOC 70. **d** 70 **p** 71 S'wark. C of Felbridge 70-74; P-in-c of Ballachulish 74-76; Glencoe 74-76; Chap to Bp and Itin P Dio Arg Is 78-79; Chap of St Andr Kyrenia Dio Cyprus from 80. *Box 171, Girne, Mersin 10, Turkey.* (Kyrenia 52196)

RIDER, Dennis William Austin. b 34. Dipl Th (Lon) 61. St Aid Coll 58. **d** 61 **p** 62 Derby. C of St Aug Derby 61-64; Sutton Lancs 64-67; V in Blakeney Par Group 67-71; R of Lammas w Hautbois 71-79; V of Buxton w Oxnead 71-79; R of Gaywood w Bawsey and Mintlyn Dio Nor from 79. *Gaywood Rectory, King's Lynn, Norf.* (King's Lynn 4662)

RIDER, Geoffrey Malcolm. b 29. Selw Coll Cam BA 53, MA 57. Coll of Resurr Mirfield 53. **d** 55 **p** 56 Wakef. C of S Elmsall 55-60; Barnsley 60-63; V of St Jo Evang Cleckheaton 63-67; Publ Pr Dio S'wark from 68; L to Offic Dio Lon from 75. *58 Melbury Gardens, SW20 0DJ.*

RIDER, James Clifford. Dorch Miss Coll 28. **d** 31 **p** 32 Birm. C of St Mark Washwood Heath 31-34; Miss P-in-c at Port Limon Costa Rica and Bocas del Toro Panama 34-36; Solihull 36-38; Stirchley 38-40; V of St Luke Holbeach Hurn 40-45; Chap of All SS Hosp Eastbourne 45-53; R of Kedington 53-59; V of Stirchley 59 66; R of Newbold-on-Stour w Halford 66-73; L to Offic Dio Sarum from 73; Chap Costa Del Sol E Dio Gibr from 73. *28 Ballard Estate, Swanage, Dorset, BH19 1QZ; and Edificio Mendiru , Spain.*

RIDER, Neil Wilding. b 35. St Jo Coll Dur BA 59, Dipl Th 61. Cranmer Hall Dur 59. **d** 62 **p** 63 Blackb. C of St Barn Blackb 62-64; Em Chadderton 64-69; Deane 69-72; V of H Trin Coldhurst Oldham 72-75; Perm to Offic Dio Ely 76-78; C of Ch Ch W Didsbury 78-79. *Haulfryn, Creuddyn Bridge, Lampeter, Dyfed, SA48 8AS.*

RIDGE, Aubrey. b 25. Oak Hill Th Coll 67. **d** 68 Thetford for Nor **p** 69 Nor. C of Gorleston 68-70; Hamworthy 70-75; P-in-c of Pitsea 75-77; R 77-81; P-in-c of Thorndon w Rishangles Dio St E from 81; Stoke Ash w Thwaite and Wetheringset Dio St E from 81. *Rectory, Wetheringsett, Stowmarket, Suffolk, IP14 5PP.* (Mendlesham 7720)

RIDGE, Haydn Stanley. b 24. St D Coll Lamp BA 51. Univ of Bris Cert Educn 52. Qu Coll Birm 56. **d** 56 **p** 57 Birm. C of St Paul Blackheath 56-60; Perm to Offic Dio Win 60-62; L to Offic Dio Win 62-70; Asst Master Guernsey Gr Sch 60-74; C of St Martin Guernsey 70-74; Dep Hdmaster St Pet Port Sch 74-80; Hon C of St Steph Guernsey Dio Win from 74; Hdmaster St Sampsons Secondary Sch from 80. *St David, Les Cherfs, Cobo, Castel, Guernsey.* (Guernsey 56209)

RIDGEWAY, Eric Victor. b 04. Wycl Hall, Ox. **d** 66 **p** 67 Southw. C of W Bridgford 66-69; Perm to Offic Dio Nor from 69. *21 Mary Warner Homes, Boyton, Woodbridge, Suffolk.*

RIDGEWELL, Kenneth William. b 39. Lich Th Coll 56. **d** 59 **p** 60 Lich. C of St Jas Gt Wednesbury 59-63; St Mary S Ruislip 63-65; R of Osgathorpe 65-69; Chap at Dubai Dio Jer 69-71; C of H Trin Northwood Lon 71-73; Asst Hosp St Bart's Hosp 73-80. *c/o 6 Charterhouse Square, EC1M 6ET.* (01-600 9000)

RIDGWAY, David. b 28. Trin Hall Cam BA 54, MA 58. Westcott Ho Cam 54. **d** 56 **p** 57 Portsm. C of St Jas Milton 56-59; CF 59-63; R of Gosforth 63-70; V of Walney I 70-76; P-in-c of Irthington Dio Carl 76-78; V (w Crosby-on-Eden) from 79; P-in-c of Crosby-on-Eden 77-78. *Edenway Vicarage, Crosby-on-Eden, Carlisle, CA6 4QN.* (Crosby-on-Eden 282)

RIDGWAY, Gilbert George Clifford. b 11. St Aug Coll Cant 37. **d** 39 **p** 40 York. C of St Jo Bapt Newington 39-41; St Mary w St Nich Beverley 41-43; Chap RAFVR 43-47; C of Em Ch Compton Gifford Plymouth 47-49; V of Newington Yorks 49-55; R of Sampford Spiney w Horrabridge 55-76; RD of Tavistock 61-66; Publ Pr Dio Ex from 77. *9 Merrivale View Road, Dousland, Yelverton, Devon.* (Yelverton 3987)

RIDGWAY, Canon Maurice Hill. b 18. St D Coll Lamp BA 40. Westcott Ho Cam 40. **d** 41 **p** 42 Ches. C of Grappenhall 41-44; St Pet Hale 44-49; V and Pr of Bunbury 49-62; Sec Ches Dioc Miss Coun 47-63; Surr from 53; V of Bowdon Dio Ches from 62; Hon Can of Ches from 66; Dioc Ecumen Officer 66-67; Commiss Yukon and Chairman Yukon Dioc Assoc from 66; Chairman Overseas C'tte Dioc Bd of Miss and Unity 67-71; St A Bp's Advisory Council from 79; Chap St Anne's Hosp Altrincham 80-81. *Vicarage, Church, Brow, Bowdon, Altrincham, Cheshire.* (061-928 2468)

RIDING, EAST, Archdeacon of. *See* Vickers, Ven Michael Edwin.

RIDING, Ian Terence. b 44. Univ of Lon BSc (2nd cl Econ)

68. Selw Coll Cam BA (2nd cl Th Trip pt ii) 70. Westcott Ho 68. **d** 71 Warrington for Liv **p** 72 S'wark. C of Maghull 71-72; Oxted Dio S'wark from 72. *30 Westerham Road, Oxted, Surrey.*

RIDLER, Cyril Herbert Buller. b 07. MBE 41. St Jo Coll Dur BA 29, Dipl Th 30, MA 32. Univ of Man BD 44. **d** 30 **p** 31 Birm. C of Aston-juxta-Birm 30-33; Rugby (in c of St Phil) 33-38; R of St John Old Trafford 38-47; St Mary Stoke Ipswich 47-57; C-in-c of Belstead 47-57; V of Aspley 57-65; Surr 60-65; R of Burton Bradstock w Shipston Gorge and Chilcombe 65-73; Waterkloof Pret 73-80; Perm to Offic Dio Sarum from 80. *3 The Esplanade, West Bay, Bridport, Dorset.*

RIDLER, Gordon Harold. b 17. ALCD 50. **d** 50 **p** 51 Ex. C of Em Plymouth 50-53; St Luke S Lyncombe 53-57; PC (R from 69) of Ashwick and Oakhill (w Binegar from 69) 57-75; V of Evercreech w Chesterblade (and Milton Clevedon from 76) Dio B & W from 75; Milton Clevedon 75-76; RD of Bruton from 78. *Evercreech Vicarage, Shepton Mallet, Somt, BA4 6HU.* (Evercreech 830322)

RIDLEY, Alfred Forbes. b 34. Bps' Coll Cheshunt, 62. **d** 65 Barking for Chelmsf **p** 66 Chelmsf. C of Prittlewell 65-69; R of Paulerspury 69-73; C-in-c of Wicken 71-73; V of W Haddon w Winwick Dio Pet from 73; RD of Brixworth from 80. *5 Sandy Close, Bollington, Macclesfield, Cheshire, SK10 5DT.*

RIDLEY, Andrew Roy. b 55. St Pet Coll Ox BA 77. Ripon Coll Cudd 78. **d** 79 **p** 80 Ches. C of St Jo Bapt Bollington Dio Ches from 79. *36 Church Street, Bollington, Macclesfield, Cheshire, SK10 5PY.*

RIDLEY, Christopher Robert. b 08. Em Coll Cam BA 31, MA 35. Ely Th Coll 31. **d** 32 **p** 33 Man. C of All SS Stand 32-37; C-in-c of St Geo Conv Distr Farnworth 37-41; C of Lanc (in c of Ch Ch) 41-44; PC of Finsthwaite 44-45; V of Ch Ch Lancaster 45-59; Thursby 59-69; RD of Wigton 68-69; R of Kirklinton w Hethersgill 69-74. *3 Rosebery Road, Carlisle, CA3 9HU.* (Carl 29322)

RIDLEY, Derek. b 40. Univ of Newc T BSc 74. St Jo Coll Dur 75. **d** 78 Penrith for Carl. C of St Jo Bapt Upperby Carl 78-81; Penrith & Newton Reigny Dio Carl from 81. *61 Croft Avenue, Penrith, Cumbria, CA11 7RL.* (Penrith 67053)

RIDLEY, Jay. b 41. Univ of Birm BA (2nd cl Cl) 63. St Steph Ho Ox 63. **d** 65 Barking for Chelmsf **p** 66 Chelmsf. C of Woodford 65-67; Prittlewell 67-70; C-in-c of Ch Ch Conv Distr Dunscroft 70-75; Chap HM Pris Wormwood Scrubs Lon 75-77; HM Remand Centre Ashford Middx from 77. *HM Remand Centre, Woodthorpe Road, Ashford, Middx, TW15 3JS.* (Ashford 41041 ext 219)

RIDLEY, John Sidney. b 15. Trin Coll Cam BA 37, MA 43. Chich Th Coll 37. **d** 39 **p** 40 Lon. C of St Sav Pimlico 39-42; St Wilfrid Brighton 42-44; Goring-by-Sea 44-45; St Geo Hanover Square 45-46; Chap St John's Coll Hurstpierpoint 46-47; R Wanstead Sch 47-49; C of H Cross w St Jude St Pancras 49-56; Asst Master Ullenwood Sch and L to 63-82; Dio Glouc 56-62; Asst Master Shrewsbury Ho and L to Offic Dios Guildf and S'wark 62-64; Chap Emscote Lawn Sch Warw 64-72; Asst Master St Dunstan's Coll Catford 72-81; L to Offic Dio S'wark from 72. *Flat 4, 4 Morden Road, SE3 0AA.*

RIDLEY, Canon Laurence Roy. b 19. St Pet Hall Ox BA (2nd cl Th) 41, MA 45. Wycl Hall Ox 41. **d** 42 **p** 43 Liv. C of St Sav Everton 42-44; Roby (in C of St Andr) 44-51; St Mary Virg (in c of All SS) Reading 51-57; V of Middlewich 57-69; Higher Bebington Dio Ches from 69; RD of Middlewich 66-69; Wirral N form 79; Hon Can of Ches from 80. *Vicarage, King's Road, Higher Bebington, Mer, L63 8LX.* (051-608 4429)

RIDLEY, Michael Edward. b 37. K Coll Lon and Warm AKC 62. **d** 63 **p** 64 Ripon. C of Chap Allerton 63-67; Epsom 67-70; C in Claxby Group 70-72; V of Leake 72-75; R of Harlaxton w Wyville and Hungerton 75-80; Stroxton 75-80; Dioc Stewardship Adv Dio Portsm from 80; P-in-c of Rowlands Castle Dio Portsm from 80. *Rectory, Manor Lodge Road, Rowlands Castle, Hants.* (Rowlands Castle 2605)

RIDLEY, Peter John. b 39. Keble Coll Ox BA (3rd cl Th) 61. Tyndale Hall Bris 61. **d** 63 **p** 64 Bris. C of Ch Ch w Em Clifton Bris 63-67; St Andr w St Thos Lambeth 67-69; V of St Cuthb W Hampstead 69-77; Eynsham Dio Ox from 77. *Eynsham Vicarage, Oxford, OX8 1JX.* (Oxford 881323)

RIDLEY, Simon. b 33. Late Cho Scho of Magd Coll Ox BA 54, MA 58, BD 66. Linc Th Coll. **d** 57 **p** 58 Lon. C of St John's Wood Ch Lon 57-60; Dom Chap to Abp Cant 60-61; V of N Wootton 61-66; Lect Wells Th Coll 61-65; Proc Conv B & W 64-66; V of Ch Ch Kowloon 66-70; R of Basingstoke 70-73. *Fordbrook, Burnt Oak, Crowborough, E Sussex.*

RIDLEY, Stewart Gordon. b 47. AKC 72. St Aug Coll Cant 72. **d** 73 **p** 74 Ripon. C of Armley w New Wortley 73-77; Hawksworth Wood in-c of Moor Grange 77-79; Rothwell w Lofthouse 79-81; R of Whitwood Dio Wakef from 81. *Rectory, Whitwood Lane, Whitwood, Castleford, W Yorks.* (Castleford 554760)

RIDLEY, Thomas George. b 10. Bede Coll Dur LTh 32, BA 33. Lich Th Coll 29. **d** 33 **p** 34 Newc T. C of St Ann Newc T 33-35; All SS W Bromwich 35-40; Stoke-on-Trent (in c of St Paul) 40-44; V of Cresswell 44-55; Delaval 55-67; Ellingham w S Charlton 67-79. *16 Eastfield Avenue, Monkseaton, Whitley Bay, T & W, NE25 8LT.*

RIDOUT, Christopher John. b 33. K Coll Lon and Warm BD and AKC 57. **d** 58 **p** 59 Lon. C of Ch Ch Roxeth Harrow 58-62; CMS 62-63; V of Nyeri 63-66; Tutor St Paul's Th Coll Limuru 67-70; CMS Repr Kenya 70-75; Chap of Gt Malvern 75-79; R of Bredon w Bredon's Norton Dio Worc from 79. *Bredon Rectory, Tewkesbury, Glos, GL20 7LF.* (Bredon 72237)

RIDSDALE, Leonard Gordon. St Francis Coll Brisb. **d** 80 Brisb. C of St Nicholas Sandgate Dio Brisb from 80. *14 21st Avenue, Brighton, Qld, Australia 4017.*

✠ **RIDSDALE, Right Rev Philip Bullen.** b 15. Trin Coll Cam BA (2nd cl Geog Trip pts i and ii) 37, MA 45. Ridley Hall Cam 45. **d** 47 **p** 48 Liv. C of St Helens Liv 47-49; Miss Dio Ugan 49-60; Archd of Ruw 61-64; Hon Can of Ruw from 63; R of Bramfield w Stapleford (and Waterford from 66) 64-72; C-in-c of Waterford 64-66; RD of Hertford 70-72; Cons Ld Bp of Boga-Z in Boga Ch 9 July 72 by Abp of Ugan, Rwa, Bur and Boga-Z; Bps of W Bugan, Nam, Kig and Ruw; res 80; Commiss Dios Kisangani & Boga-Z from 80. *3 Pemberton Terrace, Cambridge, CB2 1JA.*

RIDYARD, John Gordon. b 33. St Aid Coll 59. **d** 62 Lanc for Blackb **p** 63 Blackb. C of Lanc 62-65; C of Bushbury 65-68; V of All SS Darlaston 68-76; Res Min of Wolverhampton (in c of St Mark) Dio Lich 76-78; Team V & Missr from 78. *20 Tettenhall Road, Wolverhampton.* (Wolverhampton 771375)

RIDYARD, Malcolm Charles. b 32. St D Coll Lamp BA 54. Wycl Hall Ox 54. **d** 56 **p** 57 Liv. C of St Paul Widnes 56-59; St Thos Ashton-in-Makerfield (in c of St Luke Stubshaw Cross) 59-61; CMS Ind and L to Offic Dio Bom 62-67; V of Ahmedabad 67-71; CMS Area Sec Dios B & W, Bris and Sarum 71-80; P-in-c of Coniston Dio Carl from 80; Torver Dio Carl from 80. *Vicarage, Coniston, Cumbria, LA21 8DB.* (Coniston 262)

RIEHL, Thurston Leon. Penn State Univ BA 64. Codr Coll Barb. **d** 66 Barb for Guy **p** 66 Stabroek for Abp of W Indies. C of St Phil Georgetn 66-68; V 68-73; St Sav Georgetn 70-73; Perm to Offic Dio Guy 73-74; V of Belladrum Dio Guy from 74. *Vicarage, Belladrum, Berbice, Guyana.*

RIEN, David Willoughby. St Jo Coll Morpeth 63. **d** 64 **p** 65 Tas. C of St Jas Newtown 64-67; P-in-c of Bothwell w Kempton 67; R of Buckland 67-71; C of Temora 71-74; P-in-c of Koorawatha 74; C of Cooma 74-76; Perm to Offic Dio Syd from 80. *39 Gerrish Street, Gladesville, NSW, Australia 2111.*

RIESBERRY, James Clarence. Univ of Tor BA 56. Trin Coll Tor LTh and STB 59. **d** 59 **p** 60 Ont. C of St Thos Belleville 59-61; I of New Boyne and of Westport 61-65; R of Edwardsburg 65-79; Lansdowne Rear Dio Ont from 79. *Box 55, Athens, Ont, Canada, K0E 1B0.* (613-924 2108)

RIESBERRY, William Watts. Trin Coll Tor BA 47, LTh 50, BD 51, MTh 59. **d** 50 **p** 51 Tor. C of St Cuthb Tor 50-52; St Jo Bapt Norway Tor 53-55; R of St Geo City and Dio Tor from 55. *205 John Street, Toronto 26, Canada.* (416-364 5874)

RIET, Petrus Kgangetsile. St Bede's Coll Umtata. **d** 70 **p** 71 Bp Makhetha for Les. P Dio Les. *PO Box 4, Peka, Lesotho.*

RIGBY, Edward. Univ of Tor BA 36. Wycl Coll Tor LTh 37, BD 44. **d** 37 Bp Beverley for Tor **p** 38 Tor. L to Offic Dio Tor 37; C-in-c of Coboconk w Victoria Road 37-41; R of Omagh w Palermo and Bronte 41-46; Sec Niag 46-73; Treas Dio Niag 46-76; Regr 46-63 and 75-76; Can of Ch Ch Cathl Niag 52-64; Archd 64-76. *775 Hyde Road, Burlington, Ont, Canada.*

RIGBY, George Austin. St Columb's Hall Wang 64. **d** 65 **p** 66 Wang. C of Shepparton 65-66; R of Myrtleford 66-71; Rutherglen 71-73; C of H Trin Cathl City and Dio Wang from 73. *22 Warren Street, Wangaratta, Vic., Australia.* (061-21 5196)

RIGBY, Gordon Blandford. b 35. Atlantic Sch of Th Halifax NS BTh 77. **d** 76 Bp Hatfield for NS. Perm to Offic Dio NS from 76. *c/o 5732 College Street, Halifax, NS, Canada.*

RIGBY, Harold. b 34. Univ of Nottm BA (2nd cl Th) 56. St Cath S Ox BA (2nd cl Th) 58, MA 62. Ripon Hall Ox 56. **d** 58 **p** 59 Man. C of Em Ch Didsbury 58-61; St John Bury 61-64; C-in-c of Lostock Conv Distr Bolton 64-76; C of Davyhulme Dio Man from 76. *95 Davyhulme Road, Urmston, Manchester, M31 2BU.* (061-748 3535)

RIGBY, John Basil. b 19. Sarum Th Coll 46. **d** 48 **p** 49 Ripon. C of Horsforth 48-50; Baldock w Bygrave and Clothall 50-53; PC of Rye Pk 53-61; V of Boreham Wood 61-72; Sandbach Dio Ches from 72. *Vicarage, Offley Road, Sandbach, Ches.* (Sandbach 2379)

RIGBY, Joseph. b 37. Open Univ BA 72. **d** 78 Reading for Cant for Ox **p** 79 Buckingham for Ox. C of St Pet Earley 78-80; Penzance Dio Truro from 80. *9 Carminowe Crescent, Penzance, TR18 2RH.* (Penzance 3901)

RIGBY, Ronald Robert Pierpoint. b 13. Univ of Bris BA 34. St Cath S Ox BA (2nd cl Th) 36, MA 41. Wycl Hall Ox 34. **d** 36 **p** 37 Bris. C of St Mich Bris 36-39; H Trin Bris 39-40; St Mich AA (in c of St Mich Less) Windmill Hill Bris 40-44; V of Lemsford 44-49; Chilvers Coton (w Astley from 60) 49-65; Chap Geo Eliot Hosp Nuneaton 49-65; V of Kirk Michael IM 65-72; Hon C of German Dio S & M from 72. *Hope Cottage, Poortown, Nr Peel, IM.* (Peel 2822)

RIGBY, Stephen Stanley. b 39. Univ of Queensld BAgrSc 61. Melb Coll of Div BD 70. **d** 70 **p** 71 Melb. C of Balwyn 70-71; Moorabbin 71-73; C-in-c of St Jas Pakenham and U Beaconsfield 73-75; R of Blackwater Dio Rockptn from 75. *Rectory, Blackwater, Queensld, Australia 4728.*

RIGG, Alexander Letham. b 10. Univ of Edin MA 36. Edin Th Coll 36. **d** 39 Ely **p** 40 Bp Eyre Price for Ely. C of Welney 39-40; St Phil Cam 40-41; Eyke w Bromeswell 41-44; R of Copdock w Washbrook 44-52; Chap Ellerslie Sch Malvern 52-53; R of Stradishall w Denston 53-61; Kelsale w Carlton 61-70; V of Wingfield w Syleham 70-76; Perm to Offic Dio St E 76-78; Dio Worc from 79. *Davenham Lodge, Graham Road, Malvern, Worcs.*

RIGG, Arthur Neville. b 17. St Jo Coll Dur 45. St Aid Coll 49. Univ of Lanc MA 69. **d** 51 **p** 52 Man. C of Walkden Moor 51-54; St Marg Whalley Range 54-55; V of Allhallows 55-62; Egton w Newland 62-70; Kirkby Stephen w Mallerstang 70-80. *Nab Barn, South Dyke, Great Salkeld, Penrith, Cumb, CA11 9LL.* (Lazonby 762)

RIGG, John Foster. **d** 44 Glouc **p** 46 Bris. [f Bapt Miss] C of Northleach w Hampnett Stowell and Yanworth 44-46; St Barn Knowle 46-47; St Mary Redcliffe Bris 47-52; V of Wigtoft 52-58; R of Althorpe w Keadby 58-69; Bawdrip Dio B & W from 69. *Bawdrip Rectory, Bridgwater, Somt.* (Puriton 683421)

RIGGS, Sidney James. b 39. Bps' Coll Cheshunt 62. **d** 63 **p** 64 S'wark. C of St Geo Mart S'wark 63-66; Ascen Crownhill Devonport 66-69; Asst Youth Chap Dio Glouc 69-71; Hon Minor Can of Glouc Cathl 71-74; Min Can 74-76; Org Sec Glouc Co AYC 71-74; Dioc Ecumen Officer from 74; V of St Mary-de-Lode w St Nich City and Dio Glouc from 76; Hon Min Can of Glouc from 76. *38 St Mary's Square, Gloucester, GL1 2QT.* (Gloucester 412679)

RIGHTON, Sidney Lawrence. b 13. Bps' Coll Cheshunt 46. **d** 48 **p** 49 Lich. C of Cannock (in c of Huntington) 48-50; V of Linthwaite 50-58; Outwood 58-67; Dewsbury Moor 67-76; Darrington w Wentbridge 76-79. *Flat 3, Chad Cote, 14 Ripon Road, Harrogate, HG1 2JB.*

RIGLER, Edgar Henry. b 18. St Jo Coll Dur BA 50. Wycl Hall Ox 48. **d** 50 **p** 51 Lon. C of Southall 50-53; St Jas Muswell Hill 53-56; V of St Luke Hackney 56-67; St John W Ealing 67-80; St Luke Portsea, Southsea Dio Portsm from 80; P-in-c of St Jas W Ealing 77-80. *Vicarage, Greetham Street, Portsmouth, Hants PO5 4LH.* (Portsm 26073)

RILEY, Anne Elisabeth Thornton. b 42. **d** 79 **p** 80 Waik. Hon C of St Pet Cathl Hamilton 79-81; V of Orakau Dio Waik from 81. *4 Leslie Street, Kihikihi, NZ.* (6130)

RILEY, Geoffrey William. b 34. Univ of Dur BSc 58. N-E Ordin Course 76. **d** 79 **p** 80 Newc T (APM). C of St Geo Jesmond City and Dio Newc T from 79. *26 Berkeley Square, Gosforth, Newcastle-upon-Tyne, NE3 2JB.*

RILEY, Harold. b 03. Late Exhib of Univ of Birm BA (2nd cl Engl Lang and Lit) 24. Coll of Resurr Mirfield 25. **d** 27 Ripon for Birm **p** 28 Birm. C of St Mark Washwood Heath 27-31; St Marg Roath 31-37; R of Our Lady of Mercy and St Thos of Cant Gorton 37-44; Gen Sec Ch U 44-55; Proc Conv Lon 51-73; V of St Aug w St John Kilburn 55-75; Synod Sec Conv of Cant 58-70; M Gen Syn Cant 70-73; Preb of Neasden in St Paul's Cathl Lon 68-78; RD of Westmr (Paddington) 69-72; C-in-c of St Mary Aldermary City and Dio Lon from 76. *49 Delaware Mansions, W9 2LH.*

RILEY, Harold Collier. b 15. Selw Coll Cam BA 37, MA 43. Linc Th Coll 37. **d** 39 **p** 40 Dur. C of St Mary Heworth 39-47; Chap RNVR 43-47 and 50-55; C of Crawley w W Crawley 47-49; R of Wiston 49-55; Ashington 50-55; Chap RAF 55-63; R of Alvescot w Black Bourton and Shilton 63-82; (w Westwell and Holwell from 80) 63-82; C-in-c of Westwell w Holwell 76-80. *8 Lyster Road, Fordinbridge, Hants, SP6 1QY.* (0425 55326)

RILEY, Harold Winston. Codr Coll Barb BA 49. **d** 51 Barb for Gui **p** 52 Gui. C of St Phil Georgetn 52-55; L to Offic Dio Barb 55-56 and from 64; C of St Alb Cheetwood Man 58-60. *c/o Residence, Boscobel Boys' School, St Peter, Barbados, W Indies.*

RILEY, James Foster. b 34. Kenyon Coll Ohio BA 56. Gen Th Sem NY STB 59 (MDiv from 72). **d** 59 **p** 60 W Missouri (USA). In Amer Ch 59-75; V of Heathcote-Mt Pleasant Ch Ch 75-79; Executive Officer Dioc Bd of Chr Educn Dio Ch Ch from 79; Exam Chap to Bp of Ch Ch from 79. *Box 2698, Christchurch, NZ.* (795-950)

RILEY, John Graeme. b 55. St Jo Coll Dur BA 78. Trin Coll Bris 79. **d** 81 Carl. C of Hensingham Dio Carl from 81. *36 Muncaster Road, Hensingham, Whitehaven, Cumbria, CA28 8RS.*

RILEY, John Martin. b 37. St D Coll Lamp BA 62. **d** 63 **p** 64 Ban. C of Conway w Gyffin 63-68; C-in-c of Llanfachraeth 68-70; Team V of Dolgellau w Llanfacreth and Brithdir w Bryncoedifor 70-72; Dioc Youth Chap Dio Ban 72-78; V of Beddgelert 72-78; Tywyn Dio Ban from 78. *Vicarage, Tywyn, Meirionydd, Gwyn, LL36 9DD.* (Tywyn 710295)

RILEY, Kenneth Joseph. b 40. Univ of Wales BA (2nd cl Mus) 61. Linacre Ho Ox BA (2nd cl Th) 64. Wycl Hall Ox 61. **d** 64 Warrington for Liv **p** 65 Liv. C of Em Fazakerley 64-66; Chap and Lect Brasted Place Coll 66-69; Chap Oundle Sch 69-74; Liv Cathl 74-75; Univ Chap Dio Liv from 74; V of Mossley Hill Dio Liv from 75. *Vicarage, Mossley Hill, Liverpool, L18 8DB.* (051-724 2650)

RILEY, Lawrence William. G and C Coll Cam BA 38, MA 42. ACT ThL 42. **d** and **p** 42 Perth. C of St Andr Subiaco 42-43; Chap AIF 43-46; R of Dalwallinu 46-51; Applecross 51-68; St Mary W Perth 68-71; Hon Can of Perth 67-78; R of City Beach 71-78; Perm to Offic Dio Perth from 79. *23 Harvey Road, Shenton Park, W Australia 6008.* (381 8384)

RILEY, Leslie Daniel Burfitt. St Barn Coll Adel ACT ThL 15. **d** 15 **p** 16 Adel. C of Enfield Miss 15-16; All SS Hindmarsh w Bowden S Austr 16-17; Miss P for NW Austr distr 17-18; P-in-c of Meadows Miss 18-22; Waikerie 22-24; Pinnaroo Miss 24-27; Penola Miss 27-33; R of St Jude Port Elliot 33-37; Burnside 37-57; Chap AMF 44-46; LPr Dio Adel from 57. *Helping Hand Centre, Buxton Street, Adelaide, S Australia 5006.*

RILEY, Malcolm Gell. b 1899. Late Scho of Univ of Wales BSc 22, 1st cl Physics 23. St Mich Coll Llan 27. **d** 28 **p** 29 Mon. C of Usk 28-33; St German Roath 33-36; St Mary Mon 36-37; V of H Trin Abergavenny 37-60; Chap St Cath Home Ventnor 60-71; Perm to Offic Dio Ban from 73. *18 Maeshyfryd Road, Holyhead, Anglesey, LL65 2AL.*

RILEY, Patrick John. b 39. Univ of Leeds BA 62. Coll of Resurr Mirfield 62. **d** 64 **p** 65 Taunton for B & W. C of St Andr Taunton 64-72; C-in-c of Farleigh-Hungerford w Tellisford 72-73; Rode w Rode Hill and Woolverton 72-73; R of Rode Major Dio B & W from 73; RD of Frome from 78. *Tellisford Rectory, Bath, Somt, BA3 6RL.* (Frome 830251)

RILEY, Peter Arthur. Kelham Th Coll 40. **d** 51 **p** 52 Sheff. C of Aston w Aughton 51-53; Ch Ch Doncaster 53-55; H Trin Cathl Port of Spain 55-59; Min of St Chad's Eccles Distr Leic 59-62; R of Marley Ja 62-66; Chap De Carteret Coll Mandeville 66-69; R of St Marg Bay Ja 69-77; V of Abertillery Dio Mon from 77. *St Michael's Vicarage, Abertillery, NP3 1DA.* (Abertillery 212246)

RILEY, Peter Norman. St Barn Coll Adel 66. **d** 69 **p** 70 Adel. C of Naracoorte 69-70; Ch Ch N Adel 70-71; R of Berri w Barmera 72-77; P-in-c of Christies Beach Dio Murray from 77. *24 O'Halloran Hill Road, Christies Beach, S Australia 5165.* (08-382 1410)

RILEY, Reuben Cecil. b 17. St Pet Hall Ox BA 39, MA 43. Wycl Hall Ox. **d** 50 **p** 51 Worc. C of Hartlebury 50-52; Chap Embley Pk Sch Romsey 52-68; Hd Master 56-68; V of St Luke Blackb 68-71; Tunstall Dio Blackb from 71. *Tunstall Vicarage, Carnforth, Lancs.* (Tunstall 228)

RILEY, Sidney David. b 43. Univ of Birm BA (2nd cl Th) Ridley Hall Cam 69. **d** 71 **p** 72 Cant. C of Herne Bay 71-74; St Sav Croydon 74-77; P-in-c of Aylesham Dio Cant 77-78; V from 78. *Vicarage, Aylesham, Canterbury, Kent, CT3 3BL.* (0304 840266)

RILEY, Stanley Robert. b 29. **d** 74 **p** 75 Ont. I of Lansdowne Front 74-76; Land O'Lakes 76-79; Tweed w Roslin Dio Ont from 79. *Box 825, Tweed, Ont, Canada.* (613-478 2303)

RILEY, William. St Aid Coll 48. **d** 51 **p** 52 Liv. C of St Dunstan Edgehill 51-53; Halsall 53-57; V of Prestolee 57-62; C-in-c of Ringley 60-62; R of Tarleton Dio Blackb from 62. *Tarleton Rectory, Preston, Lancs.* (Hesketh Bank 2614)

RIMMER, Anthony Robert Walters. b 41. Univ of Hull BA (French and Th) 63. Coll of Resurr Mirfield 64. **d** 66 **p** 67 Ripon. C of All SS Leeds 66-69; Kippax w Gt Preston 69-72; Preston (in c of St Pet w St Geo) Dio Blackb 72-76; Team V from 76. *6 Hastings Road, Ashton-on-Ribble, Preston, PR2 1EU.* (Preston 729577)

RIMMER, David Henry. b 36. Ex Coll Ox BA (3rd cl Th) 60, MA 67. Linc Th Coll 62. **d** 64 Warrington for Liv **p** 65 Liv. C of Our Lady and St Nich Liv 64-66; Daybrook 66-69; Chap St Mary's Cathl Edin 69-71; R of Kirkcaldy 71-78; H Trin

Haddington Dio Edin from 78. *Rectory, Haddington, E Lothian, EH41 3EX.* (Haddington 2203)

RIMMER, John Clive. b 25. Oak Hill Th Coll 63. **d** 65 Warrington for Liv **p** 66 Liv. C of Earlestown 65-69; P-in-c of St Mark's Conv Distr Dallam Warrington 69-74; V of St Simon and St Jude Southport Dio Liv from 74. *128 Roe Lane, Southport, Mer.* (Southport 27095)

RIMMER, Paul Nathanael. b 25. Jes Coll Ox BA (3rd cl Engl Lit) 48, MA 50. Wycl Hall Ox 48. **d** 50 **p** 51 S & M. C of St Thos Douglas 50-52; Windermere 52-55; Ch of S India 55-59; V of Marston Dio Ox from 59; RD of Cowley 69-73. *Marston Vicarage, Oxford.* (Oxford 47034)

RIMMER, Roy Malcolm. b 31. Fitzw Ho Cam BA 58, MA 62. Tyndale Hall Bris. **d** 59 **p** 60 Ox. C of St Clem Ox 59-62; Perm to Offic Dio Ox 66-70; C of St Paul Portman Square St Marylebone 70-75; R of Rougham Dio St E from 75; P-in-c of Rushbrooke Dio St E from 78. *Rougham Rectory, Bury St Edmunds, Suff, IP30 9JJ.* (Beyton 70250)

RIMMINGTON, Gerald Thorneycroft. b 30. Univ of Lon BSc 56, PhD 64. Univ of Leic MA 59. Univ of Nottm MEd 72, PhD 75. **d** 76 **p** 78 Fred. C of Sackville & Dorchester and Prof of Educn Mt Allison Univ 76-79; L to Offic Dio Leic 79-80; R of Paston Dio Pet from 81. *Paston Rectory, Fulbridge Road, Peterborough, PE4 6SN.* (Pet 71943)

RINGROSE, Brian Sefton. b 31. Clare Coll Cam BA 54, MA 58. Tyndale Hall Bris 56. **d** 58 **p** 59 Ox. C of St Ebbe Ox 58-60; St Paul Northumberland Heath Erith 60-61; In Indian Ch 61-75; P-in-c of St Matt Grandpont w St Luke Ox 75-78; Gen Sec Scotld Bible and Med Miss Fellowship from 78. *12 Elm Avenue, Lenzie, Glasgow, G66 4HJ.* (041-776 2943)

RINGROSE, Hedley Sidney. b 42. Open Univ BA 79. Sarum Th Coll 65. **d** 68 **p** 69 Bris. C of Bishopston 68-71; Easthampstead 71-75; V of St Geo City and Dio Glouc from 75. *Vicarage, Grange Road, Gloucester.* (Glouc 20851)

✠ **RINGTHO, Right Rev Remelia.** Buwalasi Th Coll 60. **d** 62 **p** 63 N Ugan. P Dio N Ugan 62-69; Dio M & W Nile 69-77; Cons Asst Bp of M & W Nile in Em Cathl Mvara 27 June 76 by Abp of Ugan; Bps of M & W Nile, Kara, Bunyoro, Bukedi and Lango; Apptd Bp 77. *Box 370, Arua, Uganda.* (Arua 150)

RINGWOOD, Arthur George. b 07. Univ of Bris BA (2nd cl Engl) 29. AKC 32. **d** 34 **p** 35 Bris. C of St Chris Brislington 34-39; St Edyth Sea Mills 39-48; V of St Aug Swindon 48-58; St Andr w St Bart Bris 58-65; Chap Sisters of Love of God Burwash 65-74. *5 St Monica Court, Cote Lane, Westbury-on-Trym, Bristol.*

RINKER, Donald Engelbert. Angl Th Coll BC. **d** 67 Koot **p** 68 Qu'App. I of Pipestone 67-68; Gull Lake w Cabri 68-70; Wadena 71-73. *4820 - 47th Street, Lloydminster, Sask., Canada.*

RINTOUL, Canon Keith Richard Scott. b 17. Keble Coll Ox BA (3rd cl Mod Hist) 39, MA 44. Cudd Coll 39. **d** 40 **p** 41 Glouc. C of Stow-on-the-Wold w Broadwell 40-42; St Mary the Virgin Reading 42-44; St Francis Ashton Gate 44-47; Whitchurch Canonicorum (in c of Marshwood) 47-49; V of Collingbourne-Kingston 49-54; PC of H Trin Trowbridge 54-64; W Fordington 64-73; P-in-c of St Swith Allington 73-79; RD of Lyme Bay 79-82; Team V of Bridport 79-82; Can and Preb of Sarum Cathl from 80. *Park House, Allington Park, Bridport, Dorset, DT6 5DD.*

RIO PONGAS, *See* Gambia and the Rio Pongas.

RIPLEY, Geoffrey Alan. b 39. Univ of Dur BA 62. St Aid Coll. **d** 64 **p** 65 Dur. C of E Herrington 64-67; Hon C and Youth Leader of St Phil and St Jas Eccles Distr Hodge Hill 68-70; Youth and Commun Officer Liv 70-75; Chap Liv Cathl 70-78; Chap to Bp of Liv 75-78; V of St Bridget Wavertree Dio Liv from 78; Dioc Clergy Tr Officer Dio Liv from 78. *St Bridget's Vicarage, Cheltenham Avenue, Liverpool, L17 2AR.* (051-733 1117)

RIPLEY, Lloyd Harold. St Mary's Univ NS BA 72. Univ of K Coll NS MDiv 73. **d** 72 **p** 73 NS. C of Clements Dio NS from 72. *The Anglican Rectory, Box 80, Clementsport, NS, Canada.*

RIPLEY, Robert Charles Sims. Univ of Tor BA 49, MA 50. Bp's Coll Lennox LST 52. Angl Th Coll Vanc BD 54. **d** 51 Niag **p** 53 New Westmr. Sec SCM Univ of BC 52-55; R of N Kamloops 55-60; Thompson River Miss 57-59; Keremeos 60-62; Kerwood and Adel 62-67; Asst Prof of Phil Lakehead Univ Ont from 67. *94 Winnipeg Avenue, Thunder Bay, Ont., Canada.* (807-344 1365)

RIPON, Lord Bishop of. *See* Young, Right Rev David Nigel de Lorentz.

RIPON, Dean of. *See* Le Grice, Very Rev Frederick Edwin.

RIPPENGAL, Michael John. b 20. K Coll Lon and Warm AKC BD 50. **d** 50 Dover for Cant **p** 51 Cant. C of W Wickham 50-54; St Pet-in-Thanet (in c of St Andr) 54-61; Chap and Master Bedstone Sch and Perm to Offic Dio Heref 61-65; Sen Chap Bancroft's Sch Woodford Green 66-72; Asst Master Oakmeeds Sch Burgess Hill 72-79; Perm to Offic Dio Chich from 72. *30 Janes Lane, Burgess Hill, Sussex.* (Burgess Hill 3667)

RIPPER, Sydney Richard. Codr Coll Barb 47. **d** 49 **p** 50 Barb. C of St John Barb 49-50; St Mich Cathl Barb 50-52; St Matthias w St Lawr Barb 52-54; I of Portneuf 54-58; R of Magog 58-75. *661 Dufferin Street, Toronto, Ont, Canada.*

RIPPIN, Ronald John. b 27. Huron Coll Ont BMin 71. **d** 70 Hur for Fred **p** 72 Fred. C of Canning and Chipman 70-71; R 71-76; Oromocto Dio Fred from 76. *60 Broad Road, Oromocto, NB, Canada.*

RIPPINGALE, Denis Michael. b 29. Univ of Leeds BA (Engl Lang) 52. Coll of Resurr Mirfield 52. **d** 54 **p** 55 Wakef. C of S Kirkby 54-58; K Cross Halifax 58-60; St Thos Derby 60-63; V of Altofts 63-71; S Elmsall Dio Wakef from 71. *South Elmsall Vicarage, Pontefract, Yorks.* (S Elmsall 2861)

RIPPON, William. **d** 50 **p** 51 NS. C of Arichat 50-53; I of French Village 53-68. *1 Boutiliers Point, Halifax, NS, Canada.* (826-2727)

RIRIKA, Albert Maclaren. Newton Th Coll Dogura. **d** 55 **p** 58 New Guinea. P Dio New Guinea 55-71; Dio Papua from 71. *Box 26, Popondota, Papua New Guinea.*

RIROPO, Andrew. St Pet Coll Siota. **d** 53 **p** 57 Melan. P Dio Melan 53-75; Dio Centr Melan from 75. *Tulagi, Gela, Solomon Islands.*

RISBY, John. b 40. Univ of Lon Dipl Th 66. Oak Hill Th Coll 64. **d** 67 **p** 68 Lon. C of Ch Ch Fulham 67-68; Ealing 68-70; Chitts Hill 70-73; Bp Hannington Mem Ch (in c of H Cross) Hove 73-76; V of St Jude Mildmay Grove Isl Dio Lon from 76; P-in-c of St Paul Canonbury Dio Lon from 78. *Vicarage, Mildmay Grove, N1 4PL.* (01-254 2996)

RISDON, Edward Mark. St Bonif Coll Warm 29. **d** 29 **p** 30 Wakef. C of Almondbury 29-31; Asst P S Afr Ch Rly Miss Dio Johann 31-33; Prec of Cathl Ch Salisbury 33-39; R and Supt of Selukwe 39-41; Prec of St Mary's Cathl Johann 41-46; R of Randfontein 46-51; St Andr Kens Johann 51-63; R of Umkomaas w Scottburgh 63-72. *PO Box 38, Doonside, Natal, S Africa.*

RISDON, John Alexander. b 42. Dipl Th (Lon) 66. Clifton Th Coll 66. **d** 68 Lon **p** 69 Kens for Lon. C of St John Ealing 68-72; St Pet w St Owen Heref 72-74; Ordin Cand Sec CPAS 74-77; Hon C of Ch Ch Bromley 74-77; Team V of H Trin Cheltm Dio Glouc from 77. *100 Hewlett Road, Cheltenham, Glos, GL52 6AR.* (Cheltenham 23920)

RISING, Sidney Frederick. b 28. E Midl Jt V Tr Scheme 73. **d** 76 Sherwood for Southw **p** 77 Southw. C of W Bridgford 76-82; V of Whatton w Aslockton Dio Southw from 82; Hawksworth w Scarrington Dio Southw from 82; Orston w Thoroton Dio Southw from 82. *Whatton Vicarage, Nottingham, NG13 9EJ.* (Whatton 50539)

RISK, John Paterson. Univ of York Ont Ba 74. Trin Coll Tor MDiv 79. **d** and **p** 79 Qu'App. I of Good Shepherd Dio Qu'App from 79. *Box 247, Avonlea, Sask, Canada, S0H 0C0.*

RISLEY, Ronald Lewis. b 34. Wycl Coll Tor LTh 71. **d** 70 Tor **p** 70 Keew. C of S Alb Cathl Kenora Dio Keew 70-73; I of Gillam 73-78; Thompson 78-80; St Jas Departure Dio BC from 80. *2866 Rock City Road, Nanaimo, BC, Canada.*

RITCHIE, Brian Albert. b 34. Qu Coll Birm 60. **d** 63 Bp McKie for Cov **p** 64 Cov. C of St Jo Bapt Leamington 63-67; C-in-c of St Steph Conv Distr Canley 67-70; Perm to Offic Dio Cov 71-80. *Address temp unknown.*

RITCHIE, Canon David Caldwell. b 20. Ex Coll Ox BA 42, MA 46. Wells Th Coll 45. **d** 47 Lon **p** 48 Stepney for Lon. C of All SS Poplar 47-52; C-in-c of St Mary The Boltons Kens 52-54; V 54-60; Norton Herts 60-65; Pinner 65-73; Commiss Papua from 67; C-in-c of Bradf-on-Avon 73-75; V 75-81; Winsley Dio Sarum from 81; RD of Bradf from 80; Can and Preb of Sarum Cathl from 81. *Winsley Vicarage, Bradford-on-Avon, Wilts, BA15 2LP.* (Limpley Stoke 2230)

RITCHIE, David John Rose. b 48. Univ of Dur BA 72, Dipl Th 74. St Jo Coll Dur 69. **d** 74 Barking for Chelmsf **p** 75 Chelmsf. C of St Pet Harold Wood Hornchurch 74-79; Team V of Ipsley Dio Worc from 79. *Matchborough Vicarage, Winward Road, Matchborough, Redditch, Worcs.* (Redditch 29098)

RITCHIE, John Brocket. b 12. Roch Th Coll 63. **d** 63 **p** 64 S'wark. C of Ch Ch Gipsy Hill 63-66; Alvechurch 66-68; Burnham-on-Sea 68-71; R of Otterhampton w Combwich and Stockland Dio B & W from 71. *Combwich Rectory, Bridgwater, Somt, TA5 2QR.* (Combwich 652678)

RITCHIE, John Young Wylie. b 45. Univ of Aber MA 69. Univ of Wales (Cardiff) BD 76. St Mich Coll Llan 73. **d** 76 **p** 77 Mon. C of Trevethin 76-78; Cwmbran Dio Mon 78-81; Team V from 81. *Vicarage, Steynton Path, Fairwater, Cwmbran, Gwent, NP44 4QJ.* (Cwmbran 62414)

RITCHIE, Lawrence Dudley. Angl Th Coll Vancouver LTh 59. **d** and **p** 53 Koot. Miss at Sorrento 53-54; R of

Rossland 54-57; C of St Jo Div Montr 57-60; R of St Alb Burnaby 60-68; Chap Haney Correctional Inst Dio New Westmr from 68; P-in-c of Whonnock 74-75; Chap Alouette River Unit and L to Offic Dio New Westmr from 75. *25121 117th Avenue, Maple Ridge, BC, V2X 7G3, Canada.*

RITCHIE, Peter. b 25. Cant Coll Univ of NZ BA 51, MA 54. Coll Ho Ch Ch. **d** 55 **p** 56 Wel. C of Masterton 55-58; Riversdale CP 58-60; R 60-61; Ladismith CP 60-61; V of Brooklyn Wel 62-71; Linwood Dio Ch Ch from 71. *11 Carnarvon Street, Christchurch, NZ.* (895-833)

RITCHIE, Robinson Lyndhurst Wadmore. b 14. Univ of Alberta BA 36. K Coll NS MDiv 64. **d** 63 **p** 64 NS. d Dio NS 63-64; V of St Phil Bloemf 64-67; C of St Anne S Lambeth 67-68; Chap Holyrood Hosp Witney 68-73; C of Topsham 73-79. *20 Monmouth Hill, Topsham, Exeter, Devon.* (Topsham 5341)

RITCHIE, Samuel. b 31. Lon Coll of Div 65. **d** 67 **p** 68 Lich. C of St Andr Westlands 67-70; V of H Trin Springfield Dio Chelmsf from 70. *61 Hill Road, Springfield, Chelmsford, Essex.* (Chelmsf 53389)

RITSON, Arthur William David. b 35. K Coll Lon and Warm AKC 58. **d** 59 **p** 60 Dur. C of Bishop Wearmouth 59-63; Chap RN 63-67; C of St Greg w St Pet Sudbury 67-69; R of L Hallingbury Dio Chelmsf from 69. *Little Hallingbury Rectory, Bishop's Stortford, Herts.* (Bp's Stortford 723341)

RITSON, Canon Gerald Richard Stanley. b 35. CCC Cam BA 59, MA 63. Linc Th Coll 59. **d** 61 **p** 62 St Alb. C of St Jo Bapt Harpenden 61-65; St Mary Goldington 65-69; R of Clifton Beds 69-76; P-in-c of Aldenham Dio St Alb from 76; Hon Can of St Alb Cathl and Hon Chap to Bp of St Alb from 80. *Aldenham Vicarage, Watford, Herts.* (Radlett 5905)

RIUSIA, Barnas. Bp Patteson Th Centre Kohimarama. **d** 72 Melan. d Dio Melan 72-75; Dio Centr Melan from 75. *Manahuki, San Christoval, Solomon Islands.*

RIVERINA, Lord Bishop of. *See* Hunter, Right Rev Barry Russell.

RIVERS, Arthur. b 20. Oak Hill Th Coll 52. **d** 53 **p** 54 Liv. C of St Cath Wigan 53-56; V of H Trin Parr-Mount 56-60; Burscough Bridge 60-79; Holmesfield Dio Derby from 79. *Holmesfield Vicarage, Sheffield, S Yorks.* (Holmesfield 890243)

RIVERS, John Arthur. b 21. E Anglian Min Tr Course 79. **d** 81 Nor (APM). Hon C of Cley-next-the-Sea Dio Nor from 81. *1 Beau Rivage, Cley, Holt, Norfolk, NR25 7RW.*

RIVERS, Louis Ernest. b 45. Sir Geo Wms Univ Montr BA 70. McGill Univ Montr BTh 72. **d** 72 **p** 73 Athab. C of Grande Prairie 72-73; R 73-79; H Trin Cathl City and Dio New Westmr from 79. *520 Third Street, New Westminster, BC, Canada V3L 2S8.*

RIVERS, Paul Tudor. b 43. St Steph Ho Ox 70. **d** 72 **p** 73 Cant. C of St Mich and All AA Croydon 72-75; C-in-c of Ch Ch W Bromwich 75-79; V of St Steph Wolverhampton Dio Lich from 79. *St Stephen's Vicarage, Springfield, Wolverhampton, WV10 0LF.* (0902-54662)

RIVETT, Albert Lewis Donald. St Aid Th Coll Bal 26. ACT ThL 36. **d** 28 **p** 29 Bal. C of Alvie 28-29; Swan Marsh 29; P-in-c 29-30; C of Warrnambool 30; P-in-c of Lismore 32-34; Natimuk 34-38; V of Quambatook 38-40; Red Cliffs 40-45; R and Can Res of Ch Ch Cathl St Arn 45-54; C of St Jas w St John (in c of Old Cathl 54-60) Melb 54-62; Min of Gisborne 62-67; I of St Mark Spotswood 67-71; Perm to Offic Dio Melb from 71. *13 Illoura Avenue, Ringwood E, Vic, Australia 3135.* (870-3230)

RIVETT, Leonard Stanley. b 23. St Jo Coll Dur BA 47. Dipl Th 49. **d** 49 **p** 50 Man. C of St Clem Chorlton-cum-Hardy 49-53; C-in-c of Wm Temple Conv Distr Woodhouse Pk 53-57; Area Chap for Toc H in E and W Yorks 57-62; LPr Dio York and Perm to Offic Dios Ripon, Sheff and Wakef 57-62; V of Norton 62-74; Warden Wydale Hall Dio York from 74. *Wydale Hall, Brompton by Sawdon, Scarborough, N Yorks, YO13 9DG.* (Scarborough 85270)

RIVETT, Peter Culmer. Carroll Coll Waukesha, BA 49. Nashotah Ho BD 52. **d** and **p** 52 Fond du Lac. Hd Master of St Jo Coll City and Dio Nass from 55. *Box 517, Nassau, Bahamas, W Indies.*

RIVETT, Peter John. b 42. St Jo Coll Dur BA (Gen) 71, Cranmer Hall Dur Dipl Th 72. **d** 72 Hull for York **p** 73 York. C of Newland Hull 72-76; Team V of Marfleet (in C of St Hilda) Dio York from 76. *256 Annandale Road, Great Field, Hull.* (Hull 799100)

RIVETT-CARNAC, Canon Thomas Nicholas. b 27. Westcott Ho Cam. **d** 63 **p** 64 S'wark. C of H Trin Rotherhithe 63-68; H Trin Brompton Kens 68-72; V of St Mark Kennington Dio S'wark from 72; RD of Lambeth from 78; Hon Can of S'wark Cathl from 80. *St Mark's Vicarage, Kennington Oval, SE11.* (01-735 1801)

RIVIERA, Archdeacon of the. *See* Matthews, Ven Brian Benjamin.

RIX, James Allen. Univ of Tor BA 57. Wycl Coll Tor BTh 60. **d** 60 **p** 61 Tor. C of Ch Ch Deer Pk 60-64; St Jas Cathl Tor 64-66; on leave. *40 Summerhill Ave, Toronto 7, Ont, Canada.*

RIX, Patrick George. b 30. Magd Coll Ox BA 54, MA 58. Ridley Hall Cam. **d** 60 **p** 61 Dur. C of St Nich Dur 60-62; Asst Chap Wrekin Coll and L to Offic Dio Lich 62-70; Asst Master Gresham's Sch Holt and Perm to Offic Dio Nor from 70; Chap Bloxham Sch and Perm to Offic Dio Ox from 80. *195 Earlham Road, Norwich, NR2 3RQ.*

ROACH, Brian Norman. d 67 **p** 68 Newc. C of Adamstown 67-70. *115 St James Road, New Lambton, NSW 2305, Australia.*

ROACH, Canon Cecil Hayward. Bp's Univ Lennox BA 25, MA 26. **d** 27 **p** 28 Ott. C of All SS Ott 27-32; I of Metcalfe Ont 32-36; R of St Matthias Ott 36-67; Can of Ch Ch Cathl Ott 52-67; Hon Can from 67. *158 Clarendon Avenue, Ottawa 3, Ont, Canada.*

ROACH, Charles Alan. b 08. SS Coll Cam 2nd cl Econ Trip pt i, 31, BA (3rd cl Th Trip pt i) 33, MA 37. Westcott Ho Cam 33. **d** 35 **p** 36 Linc. C of Boston 35-40; Lect 38-40; Chap at Baghdad and Hon Chap to HBM Embassy 40-46; Chap Iraq Petroleum Co Ltd 41-46; P-in-c of Goldington 46-47; V of Em W Dulwich 47-51; Archd of the Seychelles and Sub Dean of St Paul's Pro-Cathl Mahé 51-55; V of St Sav Croydon 55-62; Chap of R Masonic Hosp Hammersmith 62-66; St Michael's Mount Marazion 66-75; Perm to Offic Dios Cant and Lon 62-66; Dio Truro 66-69; L to Offic from 69. *Trehoward, Green Lane West, Marazion, Cornwall, TR17 0HH.* (Marazion 710514)

ROACH, Kenneth Thomas. b 43. Univ of St Andr BD 69. Fitzw Coll Cam 2nd cl Th Trip pt iii BA 71, MA 75. Westcott Ho Cam 69. **d** 71 **p** 72 Glas. C of St Marg Newlands 72-73; CF 73-76; R of St Jo Evang Johnstone Dio Glas from 76. *Rectory, Floors Street, Johnstone, Renfrews.* (Johnstone 20623)

ROACH, Canon Neil Eric. Codr Coll Barb. **d** 56 **p** 57 Nass. P-in-c of Andros 60-65; St Sav Cat I 65-66; Dioc Missr Dio Nass 66-68; Asst Master St Jo Coll 68-70; R of H Cross New Providence I and Dio Nass from 70; Can of Nass from 75. *PO Box N-5808, Nassau, Bahamas, W Indies.* (32003)

ROAKE, Anthony Richard. b 52. Keble Coll Ox BA (Th) 75, MA 80. Wycl Hall Ox 75. **d** 77 **p** 78 Southw. C of St Mary Clifton 77-80; V of Lapley w Wheaton Aston Dio Lich from 80. *Lapley Vicarage, Wheaton Aston, Stafford, ST19 9PD.* (Wheaton Aston 840395)

ROAN, Canon William Forster. b 21. St Chad's Coll Dur BA 47, Dipl in Th 49. **d** 49 **p** 50 Carl. C of St Jas Gt Barrow-F 49-52; C-in-c of St Mary Westfield Conv Distr Workington 52-58; V 58-61; R of Greystoke w Penruddock 61-69; Warden Greystoke Th Tr Coll 61-69; Seq of Matterdale 61-69; V of St John Workington Dio Carl from 69; Surr from 72; Hon Can of Carl from 72; RD of Solway from 77. *St John's Vicarage, Workington, Cumb.* (Workington 2383)

ROBARTS, Very Rev David Oswald. Univ of Melb BA 60. ACT ThL (2nd cl) 63. Trin Coll Melb 61. **d** 63 Bp Sambell for Melb **p** 64 Melb. C of H Trin Kew 63-64; Ringwood 64-66; V of St Mich AA Broadmeadows 66-69; R of Alice Springs 69-76; Chap St Mary Miss Alice Springs 71-76; Hon Can of N Terr 74-76; Exam and Dom Chap to Abp of Perth 76-79; Warden Wollaston Coll and Dioc Regr Dio Perth 76-79; Can of Perth 77-79; Dean from 79. *Deanery, St George's Terrace, Perth, W Australia 6000.* (325 5766)

ROBATHAN, Canon Frederick Norman. b 1896. OBE 45. St Edm Hall Ox BA 20, MA 21. Wycl Hall Ox 20. **d** 21 **p** 22 Lich. C of Quarry Bank 21-23; PV of Truro Cathl 23-25; of Linc Cathl 25-28; Chap HM Pris Linc 26-28; Offg Chap Guy's Hosp 30-31; Min Can of St Paul's Cathl 28-33; Sacr and Jun Cardinal 33-34; Min Can of Westmr Abbey 34-37; Chap 37-40; Chap Westmr Hosp 35-37; R of St John-at-Hackney 37-45; Offg Chap Eastern Hosp and Surr 37-45; CF (R of O) 28-39; CF 39-45 (Men in Disp 44); Hon CF 45; V of Brighton 45-53; Preb of Waltham in Chich Cathl 45-53; RD of Brighton 45-53; Proc Conv Chich 50-54; Can of Ely 53-59; Can (Emer) from 59; Treas and Libr of Ely Cathl 54-59; V of Cardington 59-62; R of Charleton w Buckland-tout-Saints 62-66; Hon PV of Truro Cathl from 68. *Myrtle Court, Mevagissey, Cornw.* (Mevagissey 842233)

ROBB, Ian Archibald. b 48. K Coll Lon 68. **d** 72 **p** 73 Barking for Chelmsf. C of E Ham w Upton Pk 72-74; St Phil & St Jas Leckhampton w St Jas Cheltm 74-79; P-in-c of St Mich Cheltm Dio Glouc from 79. *St Michael's Vicarage, Severn Road, Cheltenham, Glos.* (Cheltm 515500)

ROBBIN, Lionel Alphonso. d 60 **p** 61 Sier L. P Dio Sier L from 60. *Parsonage, Kent, Sierra Leone.*

ROBBINS, John James. Wycl Coll Tor. **d** 15 **p** 16 Tor. Miss at Young's Point w Warsaw Ont 15-18; R of Cartwright 18-20; Miss at Coldwater 21-25; R of Markham w Unionville and Stouffville 25-35; Bolton w Tullamore 36-51; P-in-c of

Emsdale 53-55. *Riverdale Hospital, St Matthew's Road, Toronto, 8, Ont, Canada.*

ROBBINS, Peter Tyndall. b 25. Late Exhib of Magd Coll Ox (3rd cl Mod Hist) BA 46, Dipl in Th 47, MA 51. Westcott Ho Cam 48. **d** 50 **p** 51 Man. C of St Paul Bury 50-53; Swinton 53-55; V of St Hilda Prestwich 55-59; Lower Halstow 59-63; Charing w L Chart 63-73; Old Basing Dio Win from 73. *Old Basing Vicarage, Basingstoke, Hants, RG24 0DJ.* (Basingstoke 3762)

ROBBINS, Richard Harry. Univ of Lon BD 47, ALCD 41. Keble Coll Ox Dipl Th 50. **d** 41 **p** 42 Lon. C of St Geo Enfield 41-44; CF (EC) 44-48; Perm to Offic Dio Ox 48-49; CF 49-55; Chap Antofagasta, Iquique and Bolivia Dio Argent 55-63; Dio Chile 63-71. *Casilla S/T, Antofagasta, Chile.*

ROBBINS, Stephen. b 53. AKC and BD 74. St Aug Coll Cant 75. **d** 76 **p** 77 Dur. C of Tudhoe Grange 76-80; P-in-c of St Ninian's Conv Distr Harlow Green Dio Dur from 80. *18 Lyndhurst Drive, Gateshead, T & W, NE9 6BB.* (0632-876685)

ROBBINS, Ven Walter. b 35. **d** 72 Parag **p** 73 N Argent. Miss in Salta 73-80; Archd Dio N Argent from 80. *Casilla 187, 4400, Salta, Argentina.*

ROBERT, Frederick James. Moore Th Coll Syd 48. **d** 49 E Szech **p** 52 Syd. Miss Dio E Szech 49-51; C of Castle Hill 52-53; S Perak 53-67; Peakhurst w Lugarno 68-69. *c/o Diocesan Church House, George Street, Sydney NSW, Australia.*

ROBERTON, Richard Arthur. St Jo Coll Auckld 64. NZ Bd of Th Stud LTh 68. **d** 65 **p** 66 Ch Ch. C of Linwood 65-67; Burwood 67-70; Chap to Twizel Dio Ch Ch 70-73; V of Linc 73-78; Avonhead Dio Ch Ch from 78. *244 Avonhead Road, Christchurch 4, NZ.* (588-780)

ROBERTON, Spencer. b 08. Late Exhib of St Jo Coll Cam 2nd cl Cl Trip pt i 29, BA (3rd cl Cl Trip pt ii) 30, MA 34. Univ of Lon BD (2nd cl) 38, MTh 43. **d** 31 **p** 32 Ex. C of St Andr w St Cath Plymouth 31-34; Old Radford 34-35; Rodbourne Cheney 35-36; Skipton-in-Craven 36-39; R of Norton Malreward 39-46; PC of Cudworth w Chillington 46-51; V of Wroxton w Balscote 51-60; R of Creed 60-73. *1 St Martin's Close, Tregurthen Road, Camborne, Cornw, TR14 7DY.* (Camborne 712072)

ROBERTS, Alan. b 39. St Jo Coll Nottm 77. **d** 79 **p** 80 Worc. C of St Jo Bapt Bromsgrove Dio Worc from 79. *6 Buckfast Close, Friarscroft, Bromsgrove, Worcs, B61 7PE.*

ROBERTS, Andrew Alexander. b 49. Open Univ BA 74. Sarum Wells Th Coll 76. **d** 80 Sarum **p** 81 Sherborne for Sarum (NSM). C of Dorchester Dio Sarum from 80. *37 Bridport Road, Dorchester, Dorset.*

ROBERTS, Arthur Clifford. b 34. Univ of Wales BA (3rd cl German) 56. Coll of Resurr Mirfield 56. **d** 58 **p** 59 St A. C of Hawarden 58-66; R of Llandysilio, Penrhos, Llandrinio and Criggion 66-74; V of Shotton Dio St A from 74. *Shotton Vicarage, Deeside, Clwyd, CH5 1QD.* (0244 812183)

ROBERTS, Arthur Frederick. b 09. St Bonif Coll Warm 38. **d** 39 **p** 40 Bris. C of St Agnes Bris 39-41; St Mary Redcliffe Bedminster 42 and 45-46; C-in-c 43-44; V of All SS Bris 46-49; Horsford 49-58; R of Felthorpe w Haveringland 49-57; V of Horsham St Faith 57-58; R of Blakeney w Langham Parva 58-62; RD of Walsingham 59-62; R of Shipdham 62-75. *Moatside, Pages Lane, Saham Toney, Thetford, Norf, IP25 7HJ.* (Watton 882405)

ROBERTS, Canon Arthur Stansfield. b 06. Bp Wilson Th Coll IM 35. **d** 38 **p** 39 Lon. C of St Aldhelm U Edmonton 38-40; C-in-c of Carbis Bay Conv Distr 40-48; V 48-80; RD of Penwith 54-57; Hon Can of Truro from 68. *Ashcroft, Longstone Close, Carbis Bay, St Ives, Cornw.* (Penzance 798183)

ROBERTS, Arthur Thomas. St Jo Coll Morpeth 30. ACT ThL 31. **d** 30 Bath for Newc **p** 31 Newc. C of Singleton 30-32; Morpeth 32; Scone 32-33; Miss Chap of Loxton 33-36; Plympton 36-37; P-in-c 37-39; C of St Cuthb E Brunswick 39-40; Min of Panton Hills and Eltham 40-49; V of E Brunswick 49-54; Black Rock 54-66. *319 Nepean Highway, Vic, Australia 3186.* (96-2710)

ROBERTS, Benjamin. Late Phillips Scho of St D Coll Lamp BA 18. **d** 21 Ban **p** 22 St A for Ban. C of Festiniog w Maentwrog 21-31; V of Trefeglwys 31-39; R of Langeinwen w Llangaffo and Llanfair-yn-y-Cwmmyd 39-49; Llanllyfni w Talysarn and Penygroes 49-54; Criccieth w Treflys 54-65; L to Offic Dio Ban from 66. *Brynhyfryd, Llwyngwril, Gwyn, LL37 2QB.* (Fairbourne 473)

ROBERTS, Brian Geoffrey. **d** 78 Syd **p** 78 Bp Short for Syd. C of Camden Syd 78-80; P-in-c of Zeehan w Rosebery Dio Tas from 81. *Rectory, Zeehan, Tasmania 7469.* (004 71 6355)

ROBERTS, Bryan Richard. b 55. Univ of Wales (Cardiff) Dipl Th 78, BD 80. St Mich AA Coll Llan 78. **d** 80 Bp Mckie for Cov **p** 81 Cov. C of Finham Dio Cov from 80. *145 Green Lane, Finham, Coventry, CV3 6EA.* (Cov 413674)

ROBERTS, Byam William. OBE 71. Univ of Brisb BA (2nd cl Ment and Mor Phil) 32. Brisb Th Coll. **d** 33 **p** 34 Brisb. C of Ch Ch Bundaberg 33-36; M of Bush Bro of St Paul Charleville 36-38; Hd Master Slade Sch Warwick 38-51; Mart Mem Sch Agenehambo 52-69; Archd of N Papua 54-68; Dioc Archd Dio Papua 68-76; Perm to Offic Dio Brisb from 76. *165 Hargraves Avenue, Chelmer, Queensland, Australia 4068.* (379 2624)

ROBERTS, Christopher Michael. b 39. Qu Coll Birm 62. **d** 64 **p** 65 Roch. C of Ch Ch Milton-next-Gravesend 64-68; Thirsk w S Kilvington 68-69; V of Castleton 69-74, Team V of Buxton Dio Derby from 75. *St James' House, Harpur Hill Road, Buxton, SK17 9LD.* (Buxton 6983)

ROBERTS, Colin Frederick John. St Mich Th Coll Crafers ACT ThL 59. **d** 60 Brisb for N Queensld **p** 61 N Queensld. C of Ingham 60-63; Cairns 63-68; R of Edge Hill Cairns Dio N Queensld from 68. *100 Woodward Street, Edge Hill, Cairns, Queensland, Australia.* (070-531135)

ROBERTS, David. b 44. Univ of Ex BA (3rd cl Th) 65. St Steph Ho Ox 65. **d** 67 **p** 68 Dur. C of St Columba Southwick 67-72; C-in-c of St Cuthb Conv Distr Southwick 72-79; R of Alyth Dio Dunk from 79; Blairgowrie Dio Dunk from 79; Coupar Angus Dio Dunk from 79. *Rectory, Forfar Road, Coupar Angus, Blairgowrie, PH13 9AN.* (Coupar Angus 347)

ROBERTS, David Alan. b 38. **d** 73 **p** 74 Southw. C of W Bridgford 73-77; V of Awsworth w Cossall Dio Southw from 77. *Awsworth Vicarage, Nottingham.* (Ilkeston 321274)

ROBERTS, David Donald. b 21. Univ of Wales BA 42. TD 69. St Mich Coll Llan 42. **d** 44 Abp of Wales **p** 45 St D. C of Steynton w Johnston 44-45; St Mary Cardigan 45-48; Holmer w Huntingdon 48-53; V of Ditton 53-59; CF (TA) from 55; V of St Pet Newton-in-Makerfield 59-70; St Jas Birkdale Dio Liv from 70. *St James Vicarage, Birkdale, Southport, Lancs.* (Southport 66255)

ROBERTS, David Henry. b 38. St Chad's Coll Dur BA (2nd cl Cl) 60. Qu Coll Birm Dipl Th 62. **d** 62 Tewkesbury for Cant **p** 63 Glouc. C of Stonehouse 62-65; Hemsworth 65-69; V of Newsome 69-76; R of Pontesbury (I and II) w Cruckton Dio Heref from 76. *The Deanery, Pontesbury, Shrewsbury, Salop, SY5 0PS.*

ROBERTS, David John. b 04. St D Coll Lamp BA 29. **d** 29 **p** 30 St D. C of Brynamman 29-32; Ch Ch Llanelly 32-37; V of Yspytty Cynfyn 37-41; Nevern w Cilgwyn and Bayvil 41-56; RD of Kemes 51-56; R and V of Llandyssul 56-65; V of Llangathen w Llanfihangel Cilfargen 65-72. *38 High Street, Abergili, Dyfed.*

ROBERTS, David John. Univ of Man BSc (Tech) 58. St D Coll Lamp 65. **d** 67 **p** 68 St A. C of Rhosllannerchrugog 67-70; R of Cerrigydrudion w Llangwm Llanfihangel-glyn-myfyr, Ysbyty Ifan and Pentrefoelas 70-75; Llanrwst w Llanddoget (w Capel Garmon from 77) Dio St A from 75; RD of Llanrwst from 77. *Rectory, Llanddoget Road, Llanrwst, Gwynedd, LL26 0DW.* (Llanwrst 640223)

ROBERTS, Ven Denis William. St Chad's Coll Regina LTh 67. **d** 51 **p** 52 Qu'App. C of All SS Weyburn 51-52; St Barn Medicine Hat 52-53; I of Kenaston 53-55; R of Neepawa and Gladstone 55-59; The Pas Dio Bran 59-69; Hon Can of Bran 65-67 and 69-76; Archd of The Pas 67-69; R of Killarney 69-78; Dauphin Dio Bran from 78; Archd of Bran from 76. *410-First Street SW, Dauphin, Manit., Canada.*

ROBERTS, Derek Francis Madden. b 16. Ch Ch Ox BA 46, MA 48. St Steph Ho Ox 46. **d** 48 **p** 49 Ox. C of Crowthorne 48-52; R of Compton 53-72; Chap Bp's Coll Sch Lennoxville 72-80; Perm to Offic Dio Ex from 80. *Court Cottage, North Bovey, Newton Abbot, TQ13 8RA.* (Moretonhampstead 464)

ROBERTS, Dilwyn Carey. b 38. St Deiniol's Libr Hawarden 74. **d** 76 **p** 77 Ban. C of Glanadda w Penrhosgarnedd 76-77; Team V of Amlwch and Rhosybol w Llandyfrydog and Llanwenllwyfo w Llaneilian (w Llanerchymedd, Coedana and Llangwllog from 78) 77-81; R of Llanllechid Dio Ban from 81. *Llanllechid Rectory, Half Way Bridge, Bangor, Gwyn.* (Bethesda 601859)

ROBERTS, Canon Edward Eric. b 11. St Aug Coll Cant 34. **d** 61 **p** 62 Southw. C of Nottm 61-65; Dioc Dir of Educn Dio Southw 61-68; Hon Can of Southw 65-68; Can Res 69-79; Can (Emer) from 80; Vice-Provost 69-79; Proc Conv Southw 65-69; Chap to Bp of Southw 69-79; Sec Nottm Coun of Chs from 80. *83 Woodbank Drive, Wollaton, Nottingham.* (Nottm 283997)

ROBERTS, Edward Henry. b 06. Univ of Man BA 33, BD 36. Ridley Hall Cam 64. **d** 65 Barking for Chelmsf **p** 66 Chelmsf. C of Gt Clacton w L Holland 65-67; R of High Laver w Magdalen Laver 67-77; C-in-c of Moreton w L Laver 73-77; Hon C of Chipping Ongar Dio Chelmsf from 77. *154 High Street, Chipping Ongar, Essex.*

✠ **ROBERTS, Right Rev Edward James Keymer.** b 08. CCC Cam BA (2nd cl Th Trip) 30, MA 35, Hon DD 65, Hon Fell 65. Cudd Coll 30. **d** 31 **p** 32 Lon. C of All SS Margaret Street Lon 31-35; Vice-Prin Cudd Coll 35-39; Exam Chap to

Bp of Portsm 36-39; and 42-56; to Bp of Bris 56-61; Commiss Johann 36-39; N Rhod 46-51; V of St Matt Southsea 40-45; C-in-c of St Bart Southsea 41-45; Proc Conv Portsm 44-49; Hon Can of Portsm 47-49; Archd of IW 49-52; Portsm 42-56; V of Brading w Yaverland 49-52; Cons Ld Bp Suffr of Malmesbury in S'wark Cathl 1 Nov 56 by Abp of Cant; Bps of Lon; S'wark; Bris; Portsm; Sarum; Truro; B & W; Ches; Glas; and Zanz; Bp Suffr of Kens; and Bp Crabbe; Trld to Kens 62; to Ely 64; res 77; Hon Asst Bp of Portsm from 77. *Garden House, Tyne Hall, Bembridge, IW.* (Bembridge 2645)

ROBERTS, Edward John Walford. b 31. **d** 79 **p** 80 St D (APM). Hon C of Burry Port w Pwll Dio St D from 79. *Llwynygog Cwm, Heul Gwscwm, Porth Tywyn, Burry Port, Dyfed SA16 0YR.*

ROBERTS, Edward Owen. K Coll Lon and Warm BD and AKC 63. **d** 64 **p** 65 Dur. C of St Andr w St Anne Bp Auckland 64-67; St Paul Cheltm 67-68; Asst Master Colne Valley High Sch Linthwaite 69-71; V of Meltham Mills 71-75; R of Emley Dio Wakef from 75; Rd of Kirkburton from 80. *Rectory, Grange Drive, Emley, Huddersfield, HD8 9SF.* (Wakef 848301)

ROBERTS, Edward Thomas. b 20. St D Coll Lamp BA 42. **d** 44 Ban **p** 45 St A for Ban. C of Conway w Gyffin 44-49; Machynlleth 49-51; Llanfaes w Llandefan w Beaumaris 51-55; R of Trefriw w Llanrhychwyn 55-58; V Cho and Min Can of Ban Cathl 58-62; V of St Jas Ban Dio Ban from 62. *St James's Vicarage, Bangor, Gwynedd, LL57 2EH.* (Bangor 2975)

ROBERTS, Chan Elwyn. b 31. Univ Coll of N Wales BA (1st cl Latin) 52. Keble Coll Ox BA (2nd cl Th) 54, MA 59. St Mich Coll Llan 54. **d** 55 Ban **p** 56 St A for Ban. C of Glanadda 55-57; Libr St Mich Coll Llan 57-66; Lect in Th Univ Coll of S Wales and Mon 58-66; Exam Chap to Bp of Ban from 61; V of Glanadda w Penrhosgarnedd 66-71; Dir of Post Ordin Tr Dio Ban from 70; R of Llandudno Dio Ban from 71; Can of Ban Cathl 77-78; Chan from 78. *Rectory, Church Walks, Llandudno, Gwynedd.* (Llandudno 76624)

ROBERTS, Elwyn. Univ Coll of N Wales Dipl Th 54. St Mich Coll Llan 54. **d** 55 **p** 56 Ban. C of Llanfairfechan 55-61; V of Capel Curig 61-69; Glanogwen Dio Ban from 69. *Glanogwen Vicarage, Bethesda, Gwynedd.* (Bethesda 600294)

ROBERTS, Eric David Austin. St Paul's Th Coll Grahmstn 62. **d** 63 **p** 64 Natal. C of St Paul Durban 63-67; R of Bellair 67-75; L to Offic Dio Natal from 76. *104 Windmill Road, Durban, Natal, S Africa.*

✠ **ROBERTS, Right Rev Eric Matthias.** b 14. Univ of Wales BA (2nd cl Gr) 35. St Edm Hall Ox BA (3rd cl Th) 37, MA 41. St Mich Coll Llan 38. **d** 38 Bp Wentworth-Shields for Ban **p** 39 Ban. C of Dwygyfylchi w Penmaenmawr 38-40; L to Offic Dio Llan 40-47; Chap St Mich Coll Llandaff 40-45; Sub-Warden 45-47; V of St Theodore Port Talbot 47-56; Exam Chap to Bp of Llan 48-67; to Bp of Swan B 54-57; V of Roath 56-65; Surr from 56; RD of Cardiff 61-65; Archd of Margam 65-71; Cons Ld Bp of St D in Cathl Ch of St Pet and St Paul Llan 28 June 71 by Abp of Wales; Bps of Ban, Swan B, Mon, St Asaph, Glouc; res 81. *2 Tudor Close, Westbourne Road, Penarth, S Glam.*

ROBERTS, Francis Frederick Claudius. b 19. Univ of Dur LTh 43. Oak Hill Th Coll 40. **d** 43 Kingston-T for S'wark **p** 44 S'wark. C of St Luke Deptford 43-46; H Trin Walton Aylesbury 46-50; V of L Missendon Dio Ox from 50. *Vicarage, Little Missenden, Bucks.* (Great Missenden 2008)

ROBERTS, Frederick Gordon. Montr Dioc Coll LTh 56. Laurentian Univ Ont BA 69. **d** and **p** 56 Alg. C of Blind River 56-59; R of Sudbury 59-69; R of Haileybury 69-74; St Matt Sault Ste Marie Dio Alg from 74. *183 Mark Street, Sault Ste Marie, Ont., Canada.* (705-254 1313)

ROBERTS, Frederick Henry. b 22. Univ of Wales (Ban) BA 49. Univ of Lon MA 60, PhD 68. Wycl Hall Ox 49. **d** 51 **p** 52 Liv. C of St Chad Kirkby 51-53; All SS Woodford Wells 53-56; V of Hatfield Heath 56-62; Dir St Giles' Centre Camberwell 63-66; Chap Maudsley Hosp Camberwell 64-75; Perm to Offic Dio Chelmsf from 76. *24 Churchgate Street, Old Harlow, Essex, CM17 0JT.* (0279 29372)

ROBERTS, Frederick William. St Jo Coll Armid ACT ThL (2nd cl) 23. **d** 23 **p** 24 Bath. C of Dubbo 23-24; Forbes 24-25; C-in-c 25-26; R of Eugowra 26-28; C of Ch Ch Battersea 31-35; Cathl Ch Bath 35-36; R of Carcoar 36-42; Chap AIF 42-48; L to Offic Dio Syd from 61. *6 Burroway Street, Neutral Bay, NSW 2089, Australia.*

ROBERTS, Geoffrey Thomas. b 12. ARCM 33. Worc Ordin Coll 64. **d** 65 **p** 66 Linc. C of All SS Stamford 65-67; PC (V from 69) of Edenham 67-79; P-in-c of Witham-on-the-Hill 76-79. *West Flat, The Riding School, Grimsthorpe, Bourne, Lincs PE10 0LY.* (Edenham 240)

ROBERTS, George. St Jo Coll Morpeth 47. **d** 47 **p** 48 Armid. C-in-c of Tambar Springs 48-53; R of Coopernook 53-58; Dungog 58-71; Perm to Offic Dio Newc from 71. *34 Lord Street, Dungog, NSW 2420, Australia.*

ROBERTS, George Edward. St Francis Coll Brisb ACT Dipl Th 70. **d** and **p** 72 Brisb. Hon C of Cleveland 72-75; St Paul Manly Brisb 76-78; Chap St Marg Sch Ascot Brisb 78-80; Perm to Offic Dio Brisb from 80. *Dart Street, Redland Bay, Queensland, Australia 4165.* (206 7298)

ROBERTS, Glyn. b 47. Kelham Th Coll 67. **d** 72 **p** 73 Lich. C of Wombourne 72-76; St Cecilia Parson Cross Sheff 76-79; New Bentley Dio Sheff from 79. *SS Philip & James Clergy House, Daw Wood, Bentley, Doncaster, DN5 0PU.* (Doncaster 873356)

ROBERTS, Harold Frederick. b 44. Richmond Coll Ont BA 70. Trin Coll Tor MDiv 73. **d** 73 **p** 74 Tor. C of All SS Kingsway 73-76; Ch Ch Deer Pk Tor 76-78; R of H Trin Guildwood City and Dio Tor from 78. *60 Regency Square, Scarborough, Toronto, Ont, Canada.* (416-261 9503)

ROBERTS, Harold William. b 22. Qu Coll Birm 49. **d** 51 **p** 52 Man. C of H Trin St Jo Bapt St Phil Hulme and All SS Chorlton-on-Medlock 51-54; St Jo Bapt Atherton 54-58; R of St Phil Gorton 58-64; V of Cloughfold 64-71; V of St Thos Dixon Green Farnworth Dio Man from 72. *St Thomas's Vicarage, Harrowby Street, Farnworth, Bolton, Lancs.* (Farnworth 72455)

ROBERTS, Canon Harry Benjamin. b 08. Late Exhib of Down Coll Cam BA (2nd cl Hist Trip) 30, MA 34. Ridley Hall, Cam 30. **d** 32 **p** 33 Southw. C of St Jude Mapperley Nottm 32-34; Gorton 34-37; CMS Miss in Nilgiris and Wynaad 37-44; Chap of Calicut and Cannanore 41-44; Furlough 45; C of Abbey Ch Bath 46-47; V of St Steph Lansdown Walcot 47-58; Heanor 58-70; Ed Derby Dioc News 63-73; V of Youlgreave w Middleton 70-77; Hon Can of Derby Cathl 74-77; Can (Emer) from 77; C-in-c of Stanton-in-Peak w Birchover 75-77. *12 Lowside Close, Calver, Sheffield.*

ROBERTS, Henry Douglas. Em Coll Sktn LTh 35. **d** 35 **p** 36 Bran. C of Deloraine 35-36; R 36-37; Killarney 37-42; I of Montague w Franktown 42-44; Lanark 44-49; Metcalfe 49-60; Beachburg 61-69; R of Antrim w Galetta (w Pakenham and Waba from 70) 69-75. *Box 168, Metcalfe, Ont., Canada.*

ROBERTS, Canon Henry Edward. b 28. Oak Hill Th Coll 53. **d** 56 **p** 57 Lon. C of Edgware 56-58; Bedworth 58-61; V of St Jas L Bethnal Green 61-78; St Mark Vic Pk 61-78; RD of Tower Hamlets 76-78; Can Res of Bradf Cathl from 78. *2 Cathedral Close, Stott Hill, Bradford, BD1 4EG.* (Bradf 32005)

ROBERTS, Canon Hugh Godfrey Lloyd. b 09. AKC (1st cl) 34. St Steph Ho Ox 34. **d** 34 **p** 35 S'wark. C of St Andr S Wimbledon 34-39; St Martin (in c of Whittington Chap) Worc 39-43; V of St Jo Bapt Kidderminster 43-52; Priv Chap to Bp of Worc 43; Proc Conv Worc 45-55; Pet 65-71; R of Kettering 52-69; Chap Kettering Hosps 54-69; Hon Can of Pet 57-79; Can (Emer) from 79; Surr 58-79; Commiss Korea 58-63; RD of Kettering 58-68; R of Ashley w Weston-by-Welland and Sutton Bassett 69-79; Perm to Offic Dio Pet from 80; L to Offic Dio Leic from 80. *4 Victoria Avenue, Market Harborough, Leics, LE16 7BQ.*

ROBERTS, Hugh Silyn. Univ of Wales BA 34. St Mich Coll Llan 34. **d** 35 **p** 36 St A. C of Brymbo 35-39; Colwyn Bay 39-42; C-in-c of Esclusham 42-45; M SSF from 45; LPr Dio Sarum 50-53; C of St Hilda S Shields 53-57; C-in-c of St Phil and St Jas Plaistow 59-62. *The Friary, Hilfield, Dorchester, Dorset.* (Cerne Abbas 345)

ROBERTS, Hughie Graham. b 28. St Mich Coll Llan. **d** 60 Llan **p** 62 Bp T M Hughes for Llan. C of Pontlottyn 60-62; Ystrad-Mynach 62-63; Tonge w Alkrington 63-65; Chap RN 65-69; V of Goldcliff w Whitson and Nash 69-73; Garndiffaith and Varteg 73-78; St Nich Monkton Pembroke Dio St D from 78. *Monkton Priory, Pembroke, Dyfed.* (Pembroke 2723)

ROBERTS, Jack Anthony. Trin Coll Tor BA 37, LTh 46. **d** 38 **p** 40 Qu'App. C of Milestone 38-40; I of Avonlea 40-41; Chap at Brentwood Coll Vic 41-42; I of Alert Bay 42-47; R of Mirror w Alix Bashaw and Rockling Bay 47-50; Blyth 50-52; Esquimalt 52-71; Chap to Bp of BC from 71. *2355 Richmond Road, Victoria, BC, Canada.* (604-592 1261)

ROBERTS, Jack Bradshaw. b 11. Keble Coll Ox BA 34, MA 64. Cudd Coll 35. **d** 36 **p** 37 Ox. C of St Mary Virg Reading 36-38; St Edm Hunstanton 38-40; St Mary Old Basing 40-41; Chap RNVR 41-46; C of St Mich Chester Sq 46-47; V of N Elmham 47-50; Chap HBM Embassy Madrid 50-52; V of St Pet Kens Pk Road Lon 52-58; Chap at Helsinki w Moscow 58-60; V of All SS Highgate 60-76. *Vine House, Front Street, Mendlesham, Suff, IP14 5RY.* (04494 565)

ROBERTS, Jack Ross. b 41. Trin Coll Tor BA 63, STB 66. **d** and **p** 66 Tor. C of St Mich AA Tor 66-68; I of St Barn Halton St Tor 68-71; R of St D Hardington Tor 71-79; St Marg West Hill City and Dio Tor from 79. *Box 26 West Hill, Toronto, Ont, M1E 4R4, Canada.*

ROBERTS, James Arthur. b 34. Univ of Lon BSc (Econ)

56. Bps' Coll Cheshunt, 58. **d** 60 Lon **p** 61 Kens for Lon. C of St Steph U Holloway 60-62; St John March 62-65; V of Coldham 65-70; V of Friday Bridge 65-70; Ridgeway 70-72; C-in-c of Gleadless 72-74; R 74-79; P-in-c of Catfield Dio Nor from 79; Ingham w Sutton Dio Nor from 79. *Rectory, Catfield, Great Yarmouth, NR29 5DB.* (Stalham 81808)

ROBERTS, James Michael Bradley. b 18. Wycl Hall Ox. **d** 55 **p** 56 Roch. C of St Mary w St Paulinus Cray 55-62; V of Clerkenwell Dio Lon from 62. *St James's Vicarage, Wyclif Street, Northampton Square, EC1V 0EN.* (01-253 1568)

ROBERTS, Jeffrey David. b 25. St Cath Coll Cam 3rd cl Nat Sc Trip pt i 45, BA 46, MA 50. BSc (1st cl) Lon 58. **d** 65 **p** 66 Lich. Hd Master Adams Gr Sch Newport Salop 59-74; C of Newport Salop 65-74; Hd Master of St Geo C of E Sch Gravesend from 74. *23 Ascot Road, Gravesend, Kent.* (Gravesend 66034)

ROBERTS, John Anthony Duckworth. b 43. K Coll Lon and Warm BD and AKC 65. **d** 66 **p** 67 Man. C of Woodhouse Pk 66-69; Bradf-on-Avon 69-72; Chap Dauntsey's Sch W Lavington 72-73; CF 73-77; P-in-c of Verwood Dio Sarum 77-81; V from 81. *Verwood Vicarage, Wimborne, Dorset.* (Verwood 822298)

ROBERTS, John Arthur. b 37. Univ of Man BSc 59. Cranmer Hall Dur Dipl Th 71. **d** 71 **p** 72 Lich. C of Wellington w Eyton 71-75; P-in-c of Newton Flowery Field 75-80; V of Dunham Massey Dio Ches from 80. *St Margaret's Vicarage, Dunham Road, Altrincham, Chesh, WA14 4AQ.* (061-928 1609)

ROBERTS, John Charles. b 50. Univ of Nottm BA (Th) 71. Westcott Ho Cam 71. **d** 73 **p** 74 Southw. C of Newark-on-Trent 73-77; Chap RAF from 77. *c/o Ministry of Defence, Adastral House, WC1.*

ROBERTS, John David. b 08. St D Coll Lamp BA 33. **d** 33 **p** 34 Llan. C of Eglwysilan 33-37; Festiniog w Maentwrog 37-41; R of Llanfihangel-y-Pennant (or Abergynolwyn) 41-45; Penegoes 45-51; C of St Clem Ipswich 51-52; R of Worlingham 52-62; Chap Miss to Seamen Falmouth from 62. *2 Restormel Terrace, Falmouth, Cornw.* (Falmouth 312415)

ROBERTS, John Edward. b 07. Linc Th Coll 30. **d** 33 **p** 34 Ches. C of H Trin Birkenhead 33-36; Grimsby (in c of St Martin Conv distr) 36-40; CF (EC) 40-45 (Men in Disp 45); PC of Old Brumby 45-52; V of Gainsborough 52-70; RD of Coringham 52-69; Surr 52-70; Preb and Can of Corringham in Linc Cathl from 52-70; C-in-c of Morton 62-69. *18 Cedar Road, Barton-under-Needwood, Burton-on-Trent, Staffs.*

ROBERTS, John Edward Meyrick. b 20. TD. Keble Coll Ox BA, MA 80. Nor Ordin Course 76. **d** 80 **p** 81 Nor (NSM). C of Mundford Dio Nor from 80. *Cae Moch, Mundford, Thetford, Norfolk.*

ROBERTS, John Elliott. b 14. Trin Coll Cam BA 36. Cudd Coll 36. **d** 38 **p** 39 Lon. C of St Cuthb Kens 38-40; L to Offic Dio B & W 40; C of H Trin Taunton 40-44; Chap RNVR 44-47; C of Minehead 47; V of St Jo Evang Taunton 47-56; Chap Musgrove Pk Hosp 54-56; V of Whitwell 56-75; Perm to Offic Dio Portsm from 75. *St Anne's, Blackgang Road, Niton, Ventnor, IW.*

ROBERTS, John Haywood Boyd. b 15. St Cath S Ox BA (3rd cl Th) 43, MA 48. Ripon Hall Ox 40. **d** 43 **p** 44 Roch. C of St Pet Roch 43-45; Kippington 45-49; St Jas and St Basil Newc T 49-53; V of St Mich Byker Newc T 53-57; Keysoe w Bolnhurst and L Staughton 57-69; Crockham Hill 69-80; RD of Riseley 66-69. *1 Park Mead, Mead Road, Edenbridge, Kent, TN8 5DD.* (Edenbridge 862188)

ROBERTS, John Hugh. b 42. Wells Th Coll 65. Open Univ BA 75. **d** 67 **p** 68 Sarum. C of Wareham 67-70; Twyford Win 70-72; Asst Master Rawlins Sch Quorn from 72; Perm to Offic Dios Southw and Leic 72-73; V of Nassington w Yarwell 73-77; Asst Master Sponne Sch Towcester from 78. *Pimlico House, Pimlico, Brackley, Northants, Nn13 5TN.*

ROBERTS, John Mark Arnott. b 54. AKC 75. Chich Th Coll 77. **d** 77 **p** 78 Cant. C of St Mary Ashford Dio Cant from 77. *14 Chiltern End, Ashford, Kent.* (Ashford 26234)

ROBERTS, John Robert. b 15. Chich Th Coll 47. **d** 49 **p** 50 Glouc. C of Coney Hill 49-52; H Trin Stroud 52-55; V of Clearwell 55-59; PC of Whiteshill 59-69; V 69-80. *1 Fairby, Paganhill Lane, Stroud, Glos, GL5 4JX.* (Stroud 70316)

ROBERTS, John Victor. b 34. St Edm Hall Ox BA (2nd cl Th) 58, MA 62. Tyndale Hall Bris. **d** 60 **p** 61 Liv. C of Ch Ch Southport 60-62; St Mark Newtown Pemberton (in c of St Barn Marsh Green) 62-65; V of Ch of Sav Blackb 65-71; Chap Blackb and Lancs R Infirm and Park Lee Hosp Blackb 65-71; R of Parr 71-80; Much Woolton Dio Liv from 80. *Wootton rectory, Wootton, Liverpool, L25.*

ROBERTS, John William. b 09. ALCD 38. **d** 38 **p** 39 Liv. C of St Lawr Kirkdale 38-40; Org Sec CMJ for N distr 40-44; V of St Bede Toxt Pk 44-48; H Trin Ulverston 48-54; CF (TA) 49-60; V of St Paul Widnes 54-60; R of Grappenhall 60-74. *3 The Drive, Heysham, Lancaster, LA3 2JS.* (0524-52448)

ROBERTS, John William. Wycl Coll Tor LTh 65. Waterloo Lutheran Sem MDiv 73, MA 75. **d** and **p** 66 Bp Wilkinson for Niag. Chap Hagersville Tr Sch 66-75; Ont Correction Inst Brampton from 75. *70 Lorne Scotts Drive, Milton, Ont., Canada.* (416-878 0400)

ROBERTS, John William Melton. b 32. St Deiniol's Libr Hawarden. **d** 69 **p** 70 St A. C of Rhos-y-Medre 69-72; Wrexham 72-74; Llanrhos 74-76; R of Montgomery w Forden (and Llandyssil from 78) Dio St A from 76. *Rectory, Montgomery, Powys.* (Montgomery 243)

ROBERTS, Joseph Aelwyn. b 18. St D Coll Lamp BA 40. St Mich Coll Llan 41. **d** 42 **p** 43 Ban. C of Llanllyfni 42-44; Min Can of Ban Cathl 44-52; V of Llandygai (w Tregarth to 67) Dio Ban from 52; Dir of Social Work Dio Ban from 73. *Llandygai Vicarage, Bangor, Gwyn, LL57 4LA.* (Bangor 53711)

ROBERTS, Kenneth William Alfred. b 26. Roch Th Coll 63. **d** 65 **p** 66 Portsm. C of Waterlooville 65-67; St Francis Honicknowle Devonport 67-68; Christchurch (in c of St Geo) 68-69; Shiphay Collaton Ex 70-71; CF 71-74; R of Bassingham 74-75; Aubourn w Haddington 74-75; Carlton-le-Moorland w Stapleford 74-75; Thurlby w Norton Disney 74-75; Chap R Hosp Sch Holbrook 75-78; P-in-c of Copdock w Washbrook and Belstead 78-79; Brandeston w Kettleburgh Dio St E from 79. *Brandeston Vicarage, Woodbridge, Suff.* (Earl Soham 327)

ROBERTS, Laurence James. b 51. Univ of Sussex BEducn 73. Sarum Wells Th Coll 75. **d** 78 **p** 79 S'wark. C of Rotherhithe Dio S'wark from 78; Industr Chap Dio S'wark from 81. *37 Ravensbourne Park, Catford, SE6 4XY.* (01-690 9608)

ROBERTS, Canon Llewellyn Edwin Lloyd. b 1889. St Jo Coll Dur BA 18, MA 23. **d** 18 **p** 19 Lon. C of St Paul Canonbury 18-21; St Mary Battersea 21-24; V of St Luke Deptford 24-29; Sec C of E Scripture Readers' Assoc 24-35; Chap RAFVR 41-42; V of St Andr Whitehall Pk 29-42; LPr Dio Lon 42-49; Gen Sec Nat Ch League 42-49; Prin Clifton Th Coll 49-57; Asst Sec of CPAS 57-58; V of New Malden w Coombe 58-68; Hon Can of S'wark 66-68; Can (Emer) from 68; C of Reigate 68-75; LPr Dio Guildf 75-78; Dio Win from 78. *18 Beechwood Avenue, Boscombe, Bournemouth, BH5 1LY.* (0202 36254)

ROBERTS, Llewelyn Cradock. b 1888. Ch Coll Cam BA 11, MA 15. Ripon Th Coll 11. **d** 12 **p** 13 St Alb. C of Ch Ch Gt Warley 12-14; TCF 15-19; Hon CF 19; St John Stratford E 14-23; R of Pitsea 23-24; V of Ch Ch Gt Warley 24-38; R of St Helen Ipswich 38-44; Horndon W w Ingrave 44-52; L Burstead 52-59. *209 Brentwood Road, Herongate, Brentwood, Essex.* (Brentwood 810304)

ROBERTS, Martin Vincent. b 53. Univ of Birm BA 76, MA 77. Ripon Coll Cudd 76. **d** 78 **p** 79 Birm. C of Perry Barr 78-81; Chap and Lect W Sussex Inst of Higher Educn from 81. *Bishop Otter College, College Lane, Chichester, W Sussex.* (0243-787911)

ROBERTS, Matthew Garnant. b 13. St D Coll Lamp BA 37. **d** 37 **p** 38 Llan. C of St Bride's Min 37-39; Iford 39-43; St Alb Bournemouth 43-46; Chap RAF 47-68; C-in-c of Hinton Ampner w Bramdean 68-70; R (w Kilmeston from 74) 70-78; C-in-c of Kilmeston 72-74; L to Offic Dio B & W from 79. *The Granary, Quaperlake Street, Bruton, Somt.*

ROBERTS, Matthew John. AKC 37. TCD BA 46, MA 49. Univ of Glas PhD 49. **d** 37 **p** 38 Lon. C of St Jas L Bethnal Green 37-39; Chap RAF 39-41; Perm to Offic at St Mary Montrose and St D Inverbervie 39-40; R of Stubton 41-43; V of H Trin Kilburn 43-44; R of Croglin w Renwick V 44-48; Harrington 48-53; V of St Paul Princes Pk Toxt Pk 53-57; Lect in Th St Aid Coll 54-57; R of Morpeth Ont 57-60; St Geo Georgina 60-73; on leave 73-77. *22 Beech Street, Uxbridge, Ont., Canada.*

ROBERTS, Matthew King. Qu Coll Newfld 39. **d** 42 **p** 43 Newfld. C of Bell Is 42-43; Miss at St Anthony 43-46; Change Is 46-61; CF Canada 51-67; Hon Can of Ott 67-72; C of Ch Ch Cathl Ott 67-72; R of Clarendon Shawville 72-77; Archd of W Queb 72-77. *5 Hadley Circle, Ottawa, Ont, Canada.*

ROBERTS, Michael Brian. b 46. Or Coll Ox BA (Nat Sc Geol) 68, MA 72. St Jo Coll Dur BA (Th) 73, Dipl Th 74. Cranmer Hall Dur 71. **d** 74 **p** 75 Liv. C of St Helen 74-76; St Paul Goose Green 76-78; Blundellsands 78-80; V of St Nath Fazakerley, Walton-on-the-Hill Dio Liv from 80. *65 Fazakerley Road, Liverpool, L9 2AJ.* (051-525 7720)

ROBERTS, Michael Graham Vernon. b 43. Keble Coll Ox BA 65. Ch Div Sch of Pacific, Berkeley, Calif MDiv 67. Cudd Coll 65. **d** 67 Crediton for Ex **p** 68 Ex. C of Littleham w Exmouth 67-70; L to Offic Dio Ely 70-74; Chap Clare Coll Cam 70-74; V of St Mark Bromley 74-79; Lect Qu Coll Birm from 79; L to Offic Dio Birm from 79. *c/o Queens College, Birmingham.*

ROBERTS, Myrfyn Wyn. b 35. Univ of Wales (Bangor) BA 57, BMus 60. SOC 74. **d** 76 Lon **p** 77 Stepney for Lon. C of St Dunstan w All SS Stepney 76-79; R of Crofton Dio

Wakef from 79. *Rectory, Hare Park Lane, Crofton, Wakefield, W Yorks WF4 1HW.* (Wakef 862373)

ROBERTS, Nicholas John. b 47. Univ of Lon BD and AKC 70, MTh 78. Univ of Cam MA 78. St Aug Coll Cant 70. **d** 71 **p** 72 Lich. C of Tividale 71-74; H Cross Cromer Street Lon 74-76; St Giles Camberwell 76-78; Chap Ch Coll Cam from 78. *Christ's College, Cambridge.*

ROBERTS, Oswald John Theodore. b 17. St Cath S Ox BA 40, MA 44. **d** 42 Glouc **p** 43 Tewkesbury for Glouc. C of Winchcombe w Gretton and Sudeley Manor 42-45; St John-in-Bedwardine Worc 45-47; R of Buckland w Laverton 47-48; Naunton 48-51; V of Basildon 51-53; R of Crowmarsh Gifford w Newnham Murren 53-77. *Milton Lodge, Bromyard Road, St John's, Worcester.* (Worc 425906)

ROBERTS, Peter. b 40. N-W Ordin Course 71. **d** 74 **p** 75 Ches. C of St Geo Stockport 74-77; V of Bickerton (w Bickley from 78) Dio Ches from 77. *Bickerton Vicarage, Malpas, Chesh, SY14 8AR.* (Broxton 266)

ROBERTS, Peter Gwilym. NOC 78. **d** 81 Liv (NSM). C of St Thos Seaforth Dio Liv from 81. *20 Lime Grove, Seaforth, Liverpool, L21 3TT.*

ROBERTS, Peter John. b 46. K Coll Lon and Warm BD and AKC 68. **d** 69 **p** 70 St Alb. C of Broxbourne 69-71; Youth Worker E Herts Coll of Further Educn 71-73; C of St Luke Leagrave 73; on study leave. *10 Summerwood Lane, Stubley, Dronfield, Sheffield.*

ROBERTS, Peter Reece. b 43. Chich Th Coll 73. **d** 75 **p** 76 Llan. C of Cadoxton-Juxta-Barry 75-79; Brixham w Churston Ferrers 79-81; Bexhill (in C of St Mich AA) Dio Chich from 81. *St Michael's House, Glassenbury Drive, Bexhill-on-Sea, E Sussex, TN40 2NY.* (Bexhill 219937)

ROBERTS, Philip Anthony. b 50. St Jo Coll Dur BA (Th) 73. Wycl Hall Ox 75. **d** 77 **p** 78 Liv. C of Roby 77-79; St John Ainsdale 79-80; Pershore Dio Worc from 80. *10 Redlands, Cherry Orchard, Pershore, Worcs.* (Pershore 553294)

ROBERTS, Philip John. b 20. **d** 74 Bris **p** 75 Malmesbury for Bris (APM). C of Downend Dio Bris from 74. *190a Overndale Road, Downend, Bristol.*

ROBERTS, Canon Phillip. b 21. Sarum Th Coll. **d** 57 **p** 58 Sarum. C of St Mich AA Sarum 57-60; V of St Mich Beaumaris 60-61; Mont Albert Vic 61-63; Westbury w Westbury Leigh and Dilton Sarum 63-73; R of Dorchester 73-80; Can of Sarum Cathl from 75; R of H Trin Chelsea Dio Lon from 80. *97a Cadogan Lane, SW1X 9DU.* (01-235 3383)

ROBERTS, Piran William Astley. Trin Coll Tor. **d** 14 **p** 15 Tor. Miss in c of Wyebridge 14-19; R of Alliston 19-21; King w Maple 21-28; C of Cavan 28-31; R of Trin Colborne w St Pet Lakeport 31-41; RD of Durham and Northumb 38-41; P-in-c of St Hilda Fairbank 41-45; R of Ch of the Incarnation Tor 45-52. *2886 Colquitz Avenue, Victoria, BC, Canada.*

ROBERTS, Ven Raymond Harcourt. b 31. Late Welsh Ch Exhib of St Edm Hall Ox BA (Engl Lang and Lit) 54, MA 58. St Mich Coll Llan 54. **d** 56 **p** 57 Mon. C of Bassaleg 56-59; Chap RNR 58-59; RN 59-80; Chap of the Fleet, Archd for the RN and Hon Chap to HM the Queen from 80; Hon Can of Gibr Cathl from 80. *c/o Ministry of Defence, Lacon House, Theobalds Road, WC1X 8RY.*

ROBERTS, Richard. b 23. Univ of Wales BA 48. St Mich Coll Llan 48. **d** 50 **p** 51 Ban. C of Pwllheli 50-53; Llangelynin (in c of Fairbourne) 53-57; V of Llanwnog w Penstrowed 57-68; R of Llanrwst w Llanddoget 68-75; RD of Llanrwst 73-75; Surr from 73; V of Llandrillo-yn-Rhos Dio St A from 75. *Vicarage, Llandudno Road, Rhos-on-Sea, Colwyn Bay, Clwyd.* (Colwyn Bay 48878)

ROBERTS, Richard Llewellyn. St Francis Coll Brisb ACT ThL 41. **d** and **p** 40 N Queensld. C of St Jas Cathl Townsville 40-43; P-in-c of Mirani [f Pioneer] 43-45; R 45-47; Chap Miss to Seamen Townsville 47-53; Brisb 53-62; R of Oakey 63-67; Home Miss Sec Dio Brisb 67-72; R of Woolloongabba City and Dio Brisb from 72. *70 Hawthorne Street, Woolloongabba, Queensland, Australia 4102.* (391 4076)

ROBERTS, Richard Stephanus Jacob. b 28. TCD BA and Div Test 51, MA 57. **d** 51 **p** 53 Down. C of St John Orangefield Belf 51-54; Chap Miss to Seamen and R of Beira 54-57; Chap Miss to Seamen and R of Lourenço Marques 57-65; Chap Miss to Seamen Colom 65-68; Dub 68-72; Southn from 72; Sen Chap Ch on High Seas from 72. *The Missions to Seamen, 12-14 Queen's Terrace, Southampton, SO1 1BP.* (Southampton 333106)

ROBERTS, Canon Robert David. b 12. Univ of Wales BA 39. St Mich Coll Llan 40. **d** 41 **p** 42 Ban. C of Llanengan w Llangian 41-43; Llanfairfechan 43-50; V of Clynnog Fawr 50-55; Surr 53-81; R of Llangelynnin w Fairbourne (w Rhoslefain from 69) 55-81; RD of Ystumanner 70-81; Hon Can of Ban Cathl from 78. *1 Lon-y-Wylan, Llanfair, Anglesey.*

ROBERTS, Robert Owen. b 13. Late Philips Scho Exhib and Hebr Pri of St D Coll Lamp BA (2nd cl Th) 36. Univ of Wales MA 77. St Mich Coll Llan 36. **d** 37 Ban **p** 38 Bp Wentworth-Shields for Ban. C of Nevin 37-40; Dwygyfylchi w Penmaenmawr 40-41; St John Portmadoc 41-46; R of Llanwenllwyfo 46-51; Pentraeth w Llanddyfnan 51-65; Criccieth (and Treflys 65-74; Perm to Offic Dio Ban from 77. *Highfield, Brynbras Estate, Llanfairpwll, Gwynedd, LL51 5PX.* (Llanfairpwll 778)

ROBERTS, Roger Lewis. b 11. CVO 73. Late Scho of Ex Coll Ox (1st cl Mods) BA 33, Chas Oldham Pri and 1st cl Lit Hum 33, MA 38. **d** 46 Ex **p** 48 St Alb. Hd Master of Blundell's Sch Tiverton 43-47; C of St Albans Abbey 48-49; V of Sharnbrook 49-54; Surr from 51; C-in-c of Knotting w Souldrop 53-54; V of All H Lon Wall Lon 54-58; C-in-c 58-61; Gen Sec C of E Men's S 54-57; Warden 57-61; Select Pr Univ of Ox 55; V of St Botolph Aldersgate Lon 58-61; Ed *Church Times* 60-68; Chap Qu Chap of the Savoy and Chap R Vic O 61-73; L to Offic Dio Lon from 62; Chap to HM the Queen 69-81. *97 Corringham Road, NW11 7DL.*

ROBERTS, Sydney Neville Hayes. b 19. Cudd Coll 45. **d** 47 **p** 48 Ox. C of Aylesbury (in c of St John from 49) 47-52; CF 52-69; R of Theale (w Englefield from 76) Berks Dio Ox from 69. *Theale Rectory, Reading, Berks, RG7 5AS.* (Reading 302759)

ROBERTS, Canon Thomas. Lon Coll of Div 61. **d** 63 Warrington for Liv **p** 64 Liv. C of Burscough Bridge 63-68; V of St Matt Thatto Heath Eccleston 68-73; Chap at Basel Dio (Gibr in Eur from 80) Lon (N and C Eur) from 73; Can of H Trin Cathl Brussels from 81. *Henri Petri Strasse 25, Basel 4051, Switzerland.* (061 235761)

ROBERTS, Canon Thomas Ewart. b 17. Univ of Liv BA 41. VRD 65. St Aid Coll 39. **d** 41 **p** 42 Ches. C of Bowdon 41-45; V of St Marg Dunham Massey 46-52; Chap RNVR 44-46 and 53-58; RNR 58-67; Industr Chap Dio S'wark and C-in-c of H Trin Conv Distr Woolwich 52-55; Chap R Arsenal Woolwich 52-55; Min 54-55; PC of Selsdon 55-59; V of Dover 59-71; RD of Dover 59-71; Surr 59-71 and from 75; Hon Can of Cant 67-71; V of Chesterfield 71-74; Tenterden w Small Hythe Dio Cant from 75; Surr from 75; RD of W Charing from 81; Hon Can of Cant Cathl from 81. *Vicarage, Tenterden, Kent.* (Tenterden 3118)

ROBERTS, Victor William. Moore Th Coll Syd ACT ThL (2nd cl) 58, Th Scho 68. **d** 59 Bp Hilliard for Syd **p** 60 Bp Loane for Syd. C of Lindfield 59-60; R of Dural 61-64; C of Bournemouth Hants 65; Dagenham 66; Gen Sec SAMS (Austr) and L to Offic Dio Syd 67-73; R of Northbridge 73-78; St Clem Mosman Dio Syd from 78. *144 Raglan Street, Mosman, NSW, Australia 2088.* (969-2448)

ROBERTS, Vivian Phillip. b 35. BD (Wales) 78. St D Coll Lamp 57. **d** 60 **p** 61 St D. C of Cwmamman 60-64; R of Puncheston 64-72; V of Brynaman Dio St D from 72; Cwmllynfell Dio St D from 77; Surr from 81. *23 Llandeilo Road, Brynamman, Dyfed, SA18 1BA.* (Amman Valley 822275)

ROBERTS, Wallace Lionel. St D Coll Lamp BA 58. **d** 59 **p** 60 Man. C of Rawtenstall 59; Astley Bridge 59-61; Chap Stand Gr Sch and Hon C of Stand 61-65; Chap at Qu Sch Rheindahlen Dio Lon (N and C Eur) from 71. *Queens School, Rheindahlen, Germany.* (2161-58275)

ROBERTS, William. b 19. St Mich Coll Llan 61. **d** 62 **p** 63 Ban. C of St Mary Ban 62-64; Llangefni w Tregaian 64-67; R of Llanfechell w Bodewryd Rhosbeirio and Llanfflewin (w Llanbadrig from 72) 67-78; Machynlleth w Llanwrin Dio Ban from 78; RD of Cyfeiliog and Mawddwy from 78. *Rectory, Machynlleth, Powys, SY20 8HE.* (Machynlleth 2261)

ROBERTS, William Arthur. b 54. Trent Univ Peterborough Ont BA 76. Episc Div Sch Cam Mass MDiv. **d** 79 **p** 80 Niag. C of St John Ancaster Dio Niag from 79. *274 Wilson Street, Ancaster, Ont, Canada L9G 2B9.* (416-648 2353)

ROBERTS, William Arthur. b 01. **d** 41 **p** 42 Honolulu. Amer Ch 41-47; C of St Sav Westgate-on-Sea 48-50; Cove Farnborough 50-55; C-in-c of St Geo Conv Distr Badshot Lea 55-65; C of Walmer 65-69; Perm to Offic Dio Cant from 69. *37 Gilford Road, Deal, Kent.* (Deal 4306)

ROBERTS, William Henry. b 30. Open Univ BA 78. SOC 66. **d** 69 Tonbridge for Roch **p** 70 Roch. C of St Paul Beckenham 69-72; Hd Master St Alb C of E Secondary Sch 72-77; Brentside High Sch Ealing from 77; C of Solihull 73-79; St Steph W Ealing Dio Lon from 79. *22 Ascott Avenue, W5 5QB.* (01-579 0903)

ROBERTSHAW, Jonathan Kempster Pickard Sykes. b 41. K Coll Lon and Warm AKC 65. **d** 66 **p** 67 Truro. C of Perranzabuloe 66-69; Chap Miss to Seamen Hong Kong 69-72; Walvis Bay from 73; L to Offic Dio Damar 73-76; Team V of Probus, Ladock and Grampound w Creed 76-80; P-in-c of Talland Dio Truro from 80; Lansallos Dio Truro from 80. *Talland Vicarage, 3 Claremont Falls, Looe, Cornw, PL13 2JQ.* (Polperro 72356)

ROBERTSHAWE, Ralph Bracken. Univ of NZ BA 57. ACT ThL (2nd cl) 61. St Jo Coll Auckld. **d** 60 Bp Rich for Wel **p** 61 Wel. C of Masterton 60-62; Cannock w Chadsmoor

62-65; V of Pongaroa 65-67; Chap Rathkeale Coll Masterton and C of Masterton 67-80; St Paul's Colleg Sch Hamilton from 80. *St Paul's Collegiate School, Hamilton, NZ.*

ROBERTSON, Alexander. Wycl Coll Tor LTh 66. **d** and **p** 66 Tor. C of St Cuthb Tor 66-67; I of N Essa 67-70; Pickering Dio Tor from 70. *7 George Street, N Pickering, Ont., Canada.* (416-683 7981)

ROBERTSON, Canon Arthur Charles. b 16. Late Organ Scho of St Jo Coll Dur BA 47, Dipl Th 49. **d** 49 **p** 50 Dur. C of Easington Colliery 49-52; PC All SS Lobley Hill Gateshead 52-62; Tutor K Coll Newc 57-62; V of Ilkeston Dio Derby from 62; RD of Ilkeston 66-78; Surr from 67; Hon Can of Derby from 78; P-in-c of H Trin Ilkeston Dio Derby from 72. *St Mary's Vicarage, Ilkeston, Derby.* (Ilkeston 324725)

ROBERTSON, Blair Scott. St Jo Coll Auckld 63. NZ Bd of Th Stud LTh 65. **d** 65 **p** 66 Dun. C of N Invercargill 65-69; V of Waimea Plains Lumsden 69-73; N Invercargill 73-77; Balclutha Dio Dun from 77. *18 Lanark Street, Balclutha, NZ.* (81-033)

ROBERTSON, Canon Clement Gordon Cumpper. b 07. St Steph Ho Ox 30. **d** 32 **p** 33 Lich. C of St Andr Walsall 32-34; St Paul Balsall Heath 34-38; V of Helpringham 38-48; CF (EC) 40-45; R of Hale Magna w Hale Parva 42-48; Harlaxton w Wyville and Hungerton 48-72; RD of S Grantham 53-64; Beltisloe 64-72; R of Stroxton 61-72; R of N and S Stoke w Easton 67-68; Surr 66-74; Can and Preb of Linc Cathl from 66-74; (Emer) from 74; R of L Ponton 68-72; Perm to Offic Dios Linc and Pet from 72. *Guash Cottage, Great Casterton, Stamford, Lincs.* (Stamford 51867)

ROBERTSON, David John. b 54. Univ of Sheff BA 76. Ridley Hall Cam 77. **d** 79 **p** 80 Bris. C of Ch Ch Downend Dio Bris from 79. *5 Queensholm Close, Downend, Bristol, BS16 6LD.*

ROBERTSON, Canon Donald Keith. b 07. St D Coll Lamp BA 36. **d** 36 **p** 37 Lich. C of Wednesfield 36-40; Petersfield (in c of Sheet) 40-43; V of St John The Pleck and Bescot Walsall 44-48; R of St Chad Lich 48-52; V of Cannock w Chadsmoor 52-60; RD of Rugeley 54-60; Preb of Ufton Cantoris in Lich Cathl 59-60; Can Res and Custos of Lich Cathl 60-76; Can (Emer) from 76; Dir of Post Ordin Tr Lich 61-76. *Hempgarth, Hayton, Carlisle, Cumbria.* (Hayton 293)

ROBERTSON, Edward Macallan. b 28. Univ of Aber MA (1st cl Ment Phil) 49. Qu Coll Ox BLitt 51. Coll of Resurr Mirfield 53. **d** 55 **p** 56 Bris. C of St Mark (in c of St Luke from 58) Swindon 55-60; R of St Cuthb Hawick 60-69; Alloa 70-74; L to Offic Dio Edin 74-77; P-in-c of Bathgate Dio Edin from 77; Linlithgow Dio Edin from 77. *Parsonage, Muir Road, Bathgate, West Lothian.* (Bathgate 52292)

ROBERTSON, Egbert. St Pet Coll Ja. **d** 66 **p** 67 Ja. C-in-c of Trinityville 66-69; R of St Anne's Bay 69-78. *PO Box 217, Mandeville, Jamaica.*

ROBERTSON, Ernest Ian. b 22. Bede Coll Dur BA 49. Wycl Hall, Ox 49. **d** 51 Dur **p** 52 Jarrow for Dur. C of Jarrow 51-54; Sedgefield (in c of St Cath Fishburn) 54-56; PC of Eighton Banks 56-60; Benfieldside Dio Dur from 60; Chap Shotley Bridge Hosp 60-81; HM Detention Centre Medomsley from 61. *Vicarage, Shotley Bridge, Consett, DH8 0NW.* (Consett 503019)

ROBERTSON, George. Angl Th Coll BC Dipl STh 56. **d** and **p** 53 Athab. Miss at Sexsmith 53-55; Berwyn 55-56; Wembley 56; Ashcroft 56-59; I of Robertson 59-61; C of Kamloops 62-63. *c/o 2103 Glenwood Drive, Kamloops, BC, Canada.*

ROBERTSON, George Edward. b 14. Rhodes Univ S Afr BA and MA (2nd cl Engl) 35. Stellenbosch Univ S Afr MA 48. Wells Th Coll 52. **d** 53 Taunton for B & W **p** 61 Capetn. C of Wells 53-54; Fort Beaufort 54-59; Plumstead 59-64; Pinelands 64-66; Goodwood 66-73; Perm to Offic Dio Melb 73-74; L to Offic Dio Capetn 74-80. *11 Trees Court, Selsey, W Sussez, PO20 0NA.*

ROBERTSON, Harry Lee. Moore Th Coll Syd ACT ThL 64. **d** 64 **p** 65 Syd. C of Chatswood 64-65; R of Wallerawang w Littleton and Hartley 65-66; Schs Sec Syd 67-74; L to Offic Dio Syd from 67; Chap St Catherine Sch Waverley 74-75. *58 Finlay Street, Roseville, NSW, Australia 2069.* (411-2806)

ROBERTSON, Very Rev Irvin Lawrence. Univ of W Ont BA 51. Hur Coll LTh 52, BD 63. **d** 52 **p** 53 Alg. C of Sudbury 52-54; I of St Steph Port Arthur 54-58; R of Wawa 58-67; Parry Sound 67-75; Exam Chap to Bp of Alg from 67; Dean and R of Sault Ste Marie Cathl Dio Alg from 75. *1560 Queen Street East, Sault Ste Marie, Ont, Canada.* (705-256 6491)

ROBERTSON, James Alexander. b 46. Sarum Wells Th Coll 72. **d** 75 **p** 76 Newc T. C of St Pet Monkseaton 75-78; Prudhoe 78-79; Team V of Brayton w Barlow Dio York from 79. *c/o 25 Fox Lane, Thorpe Willoughby, Selby, N Yorks, YO8 9NA.*

ROBERTSON, Canon James Smith. b 17. Univ of Glas MA (3rd cl Math and Nat Phil) 38. Edin Th Coll 38. **d** 40 **p** 41 Edin. C of St Martin Edin 40-41; St Salvador Stenhouse Edin 41-45; Miss P Dio N Rhod 45; Warden St Mark's Tr Coll Mapanza 50-55; Chalimbana Tr Coll Zam 55-65; Exam Chap to Bp of N Rhod 60-64; Zam 64-65; Blackb from 68; Lect Bede Coll Dur and L to Offic Dio Dur 65-68; Hon Can of Zam 66-70; Lusaka from 71; Commiss Zam 68-70; Sec Coun of Ch Colls of Educn 68-70; Gen Syn Bd of Educn from 70; Perm to Offic Dio Lon from 68; Commiss Lusaka 71-74; N Zam and Centr Zam from 71; Sec USPG Lon from 73; Chap to HM the Queen from 80. *USPG, 15 Tufton Street, SW1P 3QQ.* (01-222 4222)

ROBERTSON, John Edward. b 09. St D Coll Lamp BA (3rd cl Engl) 32. St Mich Coll Llan 32. **d** 33 **p** 35 Llan. C of Treharris 33-34; Roath (in c of St Phil) 35-38; St Paul-in-the-Blockhouse Worc and Chap of Laslett's Almshouses Worc 38-39; CF (TA) 35-39; CF 39-45; Hon CF 45; TD 50; C of St Mary Kidderminster (in c of St Barn) 45-46; V of St Barn Rainbow Hill Worc 46-51; St Geo Claines Worc 51-59; Pevensey 59-81; Perm to Offic Dios Chich and Roch from 81. *Bloomfield Lodge, Withyham Road, Groombridge, Tunbridge Wells, Kent.* (Groombridge 661)

ROBERTSON, John Malcolm. Rutgers Univ USA BA 62. Trin Coll Tor STB 65. **d** and **p** 65 New Jersey. [f in Amer Ch] I of Kitkatla 66-68; Chap St Geo Sch Vancouver and L to Offic Dio New Westmr 68-70; P-in-c St Monica Vancouver W Dio New Westmr from 69. *St Monica's Church, Horseshoe Bay, BC, Canada.*

ROBERTSON, Langton George Duncan. **d** 75 **p** 77 Ja (APM). C of Port R Dio Ja from 75. *Box 337, Kingston 10, Jamaica, WI.*

ROBERTSON, Leslie Robert. Wycl Coll Tor LTh 78. **d** 77 Bp Hatfield for NS **p** 78 NS. C of Pugwash Dio NS from 77. *Box 89, Pugwash, NS, Canada.*

ROBERTSON, Paul Struan. b 45. Univ of Dur BA 73. Univ of Newc NSW BEducn 79. St Jo Coll Dur 70. **d** 72 Dur for Newc **p** 73 Newc. C of Chester-le-Street 72-73; Hamilton 73-77; Cessnock 77-79; R of Scone Dio Newc from 79. *Rectory, Hill Street, Scone, NSW, Australia 2337.* (065-45 1246)

ROBERTSON, Stuart Lang. b 40. Univ of Glas MA 63. Dipl Th (Nottm) 74. St Jo Coll Nottm 72. **d** 75 **p** 76 Liv. C of St John & St Jas Litherland 75-78; St Thos Edin 78-81; St Pet Lutton Place City and Dio Edin from 81; Hon Chap Univ of Edin from 81. *125 Warrender Park Road, Edinburgh, EH9 1DS.* (031-229 9796)

ROBERTSON, Thomas John. b 15. Univ of Wales, BA 38. St Steph Ho Ox 38. Dipl Th (Lon) 64. **d** 40 **p** 41 St A. C of Welshpool 40-42; Shotton 42-45; Colwyn Bay 45-48; V Cho of St A Cathl 48-49; R of Newmarket Flints 49-53; V of St Jas Woolfold Bury 53-57; St Thos Bury 57-61; Hd of RE Bramhall Gr Sch and LPr Dio Man 61-74; V of Taddington w Chelmorton and Flagg 74-80; Perm to Offic Dio Derby from 80. *20 Midland Road, Bramhall, Nr Stockport, Cheshire, SK7 3DR.*

ROBERTSON, Vernon Patrick. Ely Th Coll 56. **d** 59 **p** 60 Ches. C of H Trin Ches 59-61; St Thos Stockport 61-62; Chap RN 62-64; Asst City Miss Dio Auckld 64-67; V of Wellsford 67-70; Titirangi 70-74; Meadowbank 74-77; Offg Min Dio Auckld from 77. *84 Celtic Crescent, Auckland 5, NZ.*

ROBERTSON-GLASGOW, John Nigel. b 13. Cudd Coll 46. **d** 47 **p** 48 Ox. C of Banbury 47-50; R of Chipping Warden w Edgcote (and Aston-le-Walls from 79) 50-79; RD of Culworth 63-70; Surr 63-79. *19 Hayes Lane, Fakenham, Norf, NR21 9EP.* (0328 3674)

ROBEY, Herbert William. Moore Th Coll Syd ACT ThL (2nd cl) 55. **d** and **p** 54 Syd. C of St Mich Flinders Street Syd 54-55; C-in-c of Helensburgh 55-57; R of Riverstone 57-60; Burringbar w U Tweed 60-65; Booval 65-77; P-in-c of Beenleigh Dio Brisb from 77. *Rectory, Tancey Street, Beenleigh, Queensland, Australia.* (287 2326)

ROBILLARD, Roger Manuel. b 42. McGill Univ Montr BTh 78. Montr Dioc Th Coll 76. **d** 80 Monr. C of St Barn Pierrefonds 80; St Matt Hampstead Dio Montr from 80. *3410 Kensington Avenue, Apt 12, Montreal, Que, Canada, H4B 2V6.* (514-487-7425)

ROBIN, Arthur de Quetteville. Fitzw Ho Cam BA (2nd cl Th Trip pt ii) 61, MA 65. Univ of Melb BA 58. Univ of W Aus PhD 71. Ridley Coll Melb ACT ThL 53. **d** 54 **p** 55 Melb. C of Ch Ch S Yarra 54-56; Min of Kallista 56-59; Perm to Offic Dio Cant 59; C of Fen Ditton 59-60; V of St John Croydon 61-65; Sub-Warden and Chap St Geo Coll Univ of W Austr 65-69; V of St Paul Geelong 69-78; I of H Trin Kew Dio Melb from 78. *1A Pakington Street, Kew, Vic, Australia 3101.* (86 7132)

ROBIN, John Bryan Carteret. b 22. Trin Coll Ox BA 48, MA 55. Cudd Coll Ox 49. **d** 77 Pontefract for Wakef **p** 78 Wakef. Chap Rishworth Sch Ripponden 77-81; Geelong C of E Gr Sch Corio Vic from 82. *Geelong Grammar School, Corio, Vic, Australia;* .

ROBIN, Peter Philip King. b 23. Trin Coll Cam BA (3rd cl Hist Trip pt I) 48, MA 81. Cudd Coll 49. **d** 51 **p** 52 Lon. C of St Matt Bethnal Green 51-54; H Cross Miss Gona 54-56; P-in-c of Sag Sag 56-58; Simbai 58-65; Koinambe Miss 65-72; Chap Balob Tr Coll Lae 73-74; Can of New Guinea 66-71; Papua 71-75; R of Lyng w Sparham Dio Nor from 76; Elsing w Bylaugh Dio Nor from 76. *Lyng Rectory, Norwich, NR9 5RA.* (Gt Witchingham 381)

ROBINS, Alan James. b 46. St Cath Coll Cam 1st cl Nat Sc Trip pt i 66, BA (1st cl Electrical Sc Trip) 67, MA (Incorp) 71. St Jo Coll Dur BA 71, Dipl Th 71. **d** 73 **p** 74 York. C of Eston w Normanby 73-76. *8 Myrddin Baker Road, Church Lane Estate, Eston, Cleve, TS6 9SX.*

ROBINS, Christopher Charles. b 41. St Mich Coll Llan 66. **d** 68 **p** 69 Ex. C of Bideford 68-71; Dawlish 71-74; V of Laira Plymouth 74-81; P-in-c of Dodbrooke Dio Ex from 81; E Allington Dio Ex from 81. *Dodbrooke Rectory, Kingsbridge, Devon, TQ7 1NW.* (Kingsbridge 6231)

ROBINS, Edwin Knox. Univ of Melb BA 52. Ridley Coll Melb. **d** 41 **p** 43 Bal. C of Heywood 41-42; Swan Marsh 42; P-in-c 43-44; Chap RAAF 44-45; P-in-c of Edenhope 44-48; V of Kaniva 48-51; Casterton 51-57; C of Melb Dioc Centre 57-64; Asst to Dir 59-61; Chap Univ of Melb 57-64; Warden Perry Hall Th Centre from 62; I of Camberwell 64-70; H Trin E Melb Dio Melb from 70. *193 Hotham Street, E Melbourne, Vic, Australia 3002.* (03-41 3341)

ROBINS, Henry Temple. b 02. Qu Coll Cam BA 24, MA 29. Cudd Coll 24. **d** 25 **p** 27 Lich. C of St Mary Market Drayton 25-29; Smethwick Old Ch 29-34; H Trin Holmfirth 34-38; V of Cross Roads w Lees 38-43; S Milton 43-55; RD of Woodleigh 54-55; R of Whimple 55-72; Perm to Offic Dio Ex from 73. *Flat 2, 1 Regent's Park, Exeter, Devon, EX1 2NT.*

ROBINS, Ian Donald Hall. b 28. Univ of Lanc MA 74. K Coll Lon and Warm AKC and BD 51. **d** 52 **p** 53 Blackb. C of St Anne's-on-the-Sea 52-55; Clitheroe 55-57; V of Trawden 57-67; Asst Master St Chris Sch Accrington 67-75; P-in-c of Ings and Asst Adv in Educn Dio Carl from 75. *Ings Vicarage, Kendal, Cumb, LA8 9PU.* (Staveley 821383)

ROBINS, Roger Philip. b 44. K Coll Lon and Warm AKC 68. **d** 69 Dorking for Guildf **p** 70 Guildf. C of Farncombe 69-73; Aldershot (in c of The Ascen) 73-78; V of New Haw Dio Guildf from 78. *149 Woodham Lane, New Haw, Weybridge, Surrey, KT15 3NJ.* (Byfleet 43187)

ROBINS, Ronald Peter. b 36. St Jo Coll Morpeth 59. ACT ThL 62. **d** 62 Melb **p** 63 Bp Sambell for Melb. C of Camberwell 62-63; St Phil W Heidelburg 63-64; Croydon 64-65; I of E Preston 65-71; V of St Mich AA Bennettswood 71-75; R of Zeehan-Rosebery 75-77; Derby NW Austr 77-79; Lower Macleay Dio Graft from 80. *Anglican Rectory, Russell Avenue, Smithtown, NSW, Australia 2440.*

ROBINSON, Alan Booker. b 27. Keble Coll Ox BA (3rd cl Th) 51, MA 56. Sarum Th Coll 51. **d** 53 **p** 54 Ripon. C of All S Leeds 53-56; St Marg Ilkley 57-59; V of Carlton Barnsley 59-66; Hooe Dio Ex from 66; RD of Plympton from 81. *9 St John's Drive, Hooe, Plymouth, Devon, PL9 9SD.* (Plymouth 43076)

ROBINSON, Alan John. St Jo Coll Morpeth. **d** 61 **p** 62 Newc. C of Adamstown 62-63; New Lambton 63-64; Cessnock 64-66; R of Clermont 66-75; L to Offic Dio Rockptn from 75. *Wattle Grove, Ocean Heights, Yeppoon, Queensland, Australia 4703.* (079-39 1855)

ROBINSON, Albert. b 15. Roch Th Coll 60. **d** 61 **p** 62 S'wark. C of Limpsfield 61-64; R of Grimston w Congham 64-73; C-in-c of All SS Roydon 64-73; V of G w L Plumstead 73-81. *63 Marleyfield Way, Churchdown, Glos, GL3 1JW.* (Glos 855178)

ROBINSON, Andrew Nesbitt. b 43. K Coll Lon and Warm AKC 67. **d** 68 Aston for Birm **p** 69 Birm. C of Balsall Heath 68-71; St Steph w St Jo Roch Row Westmr 71-75; Chap to Sussex Univ from 75; P-in-c of Stanmer w Falmer Dio Chich from 80. *St Laurence House, Park Street, Falmer, Brighton, BN1 9PG.* (B'ton 606928)

ROBINSON, Arthur Robert Basil. b 32. St Jo Coll Dur BA (3rd cl Mod Hist) 56. ACP 67. Wycl Hall Ox 56. **d** 58 Warrington for Liv **p** 59 Liv. C of St Mark Newtown Pemberton 58-62; CF 62-65; Asst Master Colne Valley High Sch Linthwaite 65-69; Asst Chap HM Pris Man 69; Chap HM Borstal Roch 69-74; Chap at Lima Peru 74-77; V of Golcar Dio Wakef from 77. *Vicarage, Golcar, Huddersfield, W Yorks, HD7 4PX.* (Huddersfield 654647)

ROBINSON, Arthur William. b 35. Univ of Dur BSc (2nd cl Physics) 60. Clifton Th Coll 60. **d** 62 **p** 63 Ox. C of St Clem Ox 62-65; Chap at Temuco 65-70; Santiago 71-74; Angl Ex Sem Santiago 73-77; V of Hoxton Dio Lon from 78. *St John's Vicarage, Crondall Street, N1 6PT.* (01-739 9823)

ROBINSON, Brian. b 39. St Aid Coll 62. **d** 64 Warrington for Liv **p** 65 Liv. C of Knotty Ash 64-68; Sutton Lancs 68-72; V of Hunts Cross 72-79; St Andr Livesey Blackb Dio Blackb from 79. *19 Gib Lane, Blackburn, Lancs, BB2 5BP.* (Blackb 21078)

ROBINSON, Brian John Watson. b 33. St Cath Coll Cam BA 56, MA 60. Westcott Ho Cam 57. **d** 58 **p** 59 Dur. C of Spennymoor w Whitworth 58-62; Miss at Itki 62-63; Ranchi 63-66; C-in-c of St Steph Preston 66-72; V of Ashton-on-Ribble 72-79. *27 Pear Tree Road, Clayton-le-Woods, Nr Preston, Lancs, PR6 7JP.*

ROBINSON, Bryan. b 32. Fitzw Ho Cam BA 56. Ely Th Coll 56. **d** 58 Blackb **p** 59 Burnley for Blackb. C of Fleetwood 58-65; V of St Andr w St Marg Burnley Dio Blackb from 65. *St Andrew's Vicarage, Colne Road, Burnley, Lancs, BB10 1LF.* (Burnley 23185)

ROBINSON, Cedric Henry. b 17. K Coll Lon and Warm. **d** 58 **p** 59 Birm. C of K Heath 58-62; V of St Mary and St John Shaw Hill Saltley 62-67; Norton w Whittington 67-79; P-in-c of Hanbury Dio Worc from 79. *33 Victoria Avenue, Droitwich, Worcs, WR9 7DF.* (Droitwich 3324)

ROBINSON, Canon Clifford. Ch Coll Hobart, 31. **d** 32 **p** 33 Tas. C of Deloraine 32-36; R of Smithton 36-37; P-in-c of Moonah 37-38; Sorell 38-40; R of Channel 40-42; Chap AMF 40; R of Cygnet 42-47; Brighton 47-58; St John Devonport 58-70; Can of Tas 64-77; Can (Emer) from 77; R of Evandale 71-77; Perm to Offic Dio Tas from 77. *42 Windsor Street, Kingston Beach, Tasmania 7151.* (002-29 5803)

ROBINSON, Colin Dennie. b 18. St Jo Coll Auckld 49. **d** 52 **p** 53 Wai. C of Hastings 52-55; Gisborne 55-56; V of Waikohu 56-60; Otane 60-64; Miramar 64-71; Waverley-Watatora 71-75; Epiph Masterton S 75-80; Perm to Offic Dio Wel from 80. *Box 429, Feilding, NZ.*

ROBINSON, Daffyd Charles. b 48. Qu Coll Birm 77. **d** 80 Pet. C of Abington Dio Pet from 80. *21 Lime Avenue, Abington, Northampton, NN3 2HA.*

ROBINSON, Daryl Joseph. Moore Th Coll Syd. **d** 59 **p** 60 Armid. C of W Tamworth 59-61; P-in-c of Tambar Springs 61-66; Ashford 66-72; Narrabri 72-79; R of Haberfield Dio Syd from 79. *6 Dickson Street, Haberfield, NSW, Australia 2045.* (798-8287)

ROBINSON, David Hugh. b 47. Linc Th Coll 76. **d** 79 McKie for Cov **p** 80 Cov. C of Bulkington Dio Cov from 79. *Glebe Cottage, Bulkington Vicarage, Nuneaton, CV12 8JB.*

ROBINSON, David Michael Wood. b 28. Univ of Glas BSc (2nd cl Naval Architecture) 50. BD (Lon) 54. **d** and **p** 57 Roch. C of Erith 57-58; CMS Miss in Japan 58-71; R of Holton w Waterperry Dio Ox from 71. *Holton Rectory, Oxford.* (Wheatley 2460)

ROBINSON, David Neil. Univ of BC BA 56. Angl Th Coll of BC LTh 58, BD 63. **d** 57 **p** 58 Koot. I of Sorrento 58-59; V of Fruitvale 59-66; Quamichan 66-74; R of St Phil Oak Bay Dio BC from 74. *2928 Eastdowne Road, Victoria, BC, Canada.* (604-592 7398)

ROBINSON, David William Clough. b 40. Univ of Wales BA (3rd cl Gr) 61, BD (w distinc) 67. Jes Coll Ox BLitt 71. St Mich Coll Llan 64. **d** 67 **p** 68 Ox for Llan. C of St Cath Canton 69-71; Libr and Lect St Mich Coll Llan and Lect in Th Univ of Wales (Cardiff) from 72; C of St Barn Woodside Park Finchley Dio Lon from 78; Consultant BFBS from 78. *12 Courthouse Road, N12 7PJ.* (01-445 3404)

ROBINSON, Denis Paul. b 46. Moore Coll Syd ACT ThL 69. **d** 70 **p** 71 Syd. C of H Trin Kingsford 70-72; Hunter's Hill 73-74; R of Chester Hill 74-78; Perm to Offic Dio Wang from 78. *Milpo, Bandiana, Vic, Australia 3694.* (644-4196)

✠ **ROBINSON, Right Rev Donald William Bradley.** Qu Coll Cam BA (2nd cl Th Trip pt i) 49, 2nd cl Th Trip pt iii 50, MA 54. ACT ThD 79. **d** 50 **p** 51 Syd. C of Manley 50-51; St Phil Syd 51-53; Lect at Moore Th Coll Syd 51-59; Vice-Prin 59-73; Perm to Offic Dio Ely 61; Can of Syd 64-73; Cons Asst Bp of Syd (Bp in Parramatta) in St Andr Cathl Syd 25 Jan 73 by Abp of Syd; Bps of C & Goulb, Graft and River; and others. *5 Keith Place, Baulkham Hills, NSW, Australia 2153.* (639-9878)

ROBINSON, Douglas. b 48. BD (Lon) 74. U Sem in Virginia MA 75. Univ of Nottm BEducn 70. Trin Coll Bris 71. **d** 75 Warrington for Liv **p** 76 Liv. C of Ch Ch Southport 75-79; V of Clubmoor Dio Liv from 79. *176 Queen's Drive, Liverpool, L13 0AL.* (051-226 1977)

ROBINSON, Dugald Clifford. b 23. Qu Coll Birm 69. **d** 70 Bp McKie for Cov **p** 71 Cov. C of Stratford-on-Avon 70-73; V of Allesley Park Dio Cov from 73. *St Christopher's Vicarage, Allesley Park, Coventry, Warws, CV5 9HF.* (Coventry 72879)

ROBINSON, Edward Ernest. St Jo Coll Melb 16. ACT ThL 18. **d** 18 **p** 19 Melb. C of St John Camberwell Vic 18-19; Cowes Phillip I 19-21; Min at Newport 21-28; Ringwood 28-34; Belgrave 34-38; Ormond 38-52; Kooyong 52-57. *85 Outer Crescent, Brighton, Vic, Australia 3186.* (92-9034)

ROBINSON, Ernest Yeomans. b 03. **d** 56 **p** 57 Dub. C of St Jas Dub 56-59; R of Dromod 59-64; I of Kilscoran U 64-68;

V of Hensall w Heck 68-72; R of Kilmoe U 76-78. *Ilen Lodge, Rath, Baltimore, Co Cork, Irish Republic.*

ROBINSON, Francis George. b 08. Cranmer Hall Dur 68. **d** 69 **p** 70 York. C of Haxby w Wigginton 69-71; V of Sherburn 71-75; Kexby w Wilberfoss 75-78. *20 Little Lane, Haxby, York, YO3 8QU.*

ROBINSON, Fred Vernon. b 08. St Chad's Coll Dur BA 30, MA 33. **d** 31 **p** 32 York. C of South Bank 31-33; Barnard Castle 33-37; V of Haswell 37-55; Wortley 55-73. *53 The Old Village, Huntington, York, YO3 9RA.*

ROBINSON, Frederick William. b 12. **d** 43 **p** 44 Bradf. C of St Steph West Bowling 43-46; Stokesley 46-48; Queensbury 48-51; V of Oakenshaw w Woodlands 51-54; C of Speke 54-59; Chilvers Coton and of St Mary Astley 59-66; St Mary Pype Hayes Erdington 66-78; Perm to Offic Dio Birm from 78; Dio Cov from 80. *18 Speedwell Lane, Baddesley, Ensor, Atherstone, N Warws CV9 2DU.*

ROBINSON, Geoffrey. b 28. Ely Th Coll 52. **d** 53 **p** 54 Ches. C of Prenton 53-58; V of Gt Saughall Dio Ches from 58. *Great Saughall Vicarage, Chester, CH1 6EN.* (Saughall 213)

ROBINSON, George. Oak Hill Th Coll 59. **d** 61 **p** 62 Sarum. C of St Clem Parkstone 61-64; C-in-c Oatley Provisional Par 64-67; R of St Steph Willoughby 67-80; L to Offic Dio Syd from 80. *18 Lucknow Street, Willoughby, NSW, Australia 2068.* (95-6021)

ROBINSON, George [illegible] McMaster Univ Ont BA 44. **d** 46 **p** 47 Niag. C of St Jo Evang Hamilton 46-49; St Faith Miss Edson 49-56; V of Jasper 56-61; Archd of Metlakatla 61-66; P-in-c of Port Edward 61-66; Perm to Offic Dio New Westmr from 81. *303 East Cordova Street, Vancouver 4, Canada.*

ROBINSON, Gordon Stanislaus. b 13. K Coll Lon BD and AKC (2nd cl) 37. **d** 37 **p** 38 Liv. C of St Phil Southport 37-39; H Spirit Knotty Ash 39-41; St Agnes Toxt Pk 41-44; C-in-c of St Marg Anfield 44; V of St Paul Princes Pk 44-53; Charlton Horethorne w Stowell 53-78; L to Offic Dio B & W from 79. *18 North Street, Stoke sub Hamdon, Somt.* (Martock 823742)

ROBINSON, Canon Gordon Victor Michael. b 18. Keble Coll Ox BA (3rd cl Mod Hist) 40, MA 46. Cudd Coll 40. **d** 41 **p** 42 Ches. C of Coppenhall 41-47; Warsop w Sookholm 47-48; R of Coppenhall (or Crewe) 48-55; V of Ellesmere Port 55-71; R 71-73; Tarporley 73-76; Hon Can of Ches from 62; R of Birkenhead Priory Dio Ches from 76. *124 Catheart Street, Birkenhead, Mer.* (051-647 6604)

ROBINSON, Harry Sholto Douglas. Wycl Coll Tor LTh and BTh 55. **d** 55 **p** 56 Ont. C of St John Kingston 55-56; I of Ch of Redeemer Kingston 56-63; Trin E Tor 63-78; Can of Tor 75-78; I of St John Vanc Dio New Westmr from 78. *1490 Nanton Avenue, Vancouver 9, BC, Canada.*

ROBINSON, Hugh Stanley. b 21. AKC 47. **d** 47 **p** 48 Ox. C of St Geo Tilehurst 47-50; CF 50-53; Hon CF 53; C of Farnham Royal 53-59; V of Wheatley 59-67; Chiddingly Dio Chich from 67; V of Laughton 67-77. *Chiddingly Vicarage, Lewes, Sussex.* (Chiddingly 313)

ROBINSON, Ian Cameron. b 19. OBE 72. Em Coll Cam BA (Mech Sc) 40, MA 46. Linc Th Coll 71. **d** 72 **p** 73 St E. C of St Aug of Hippo Ipswich 72-74; V of Westleton w Dunwich Dio St E from 74; Darsham Dio St E from 74; RD of Saxmundham from 79. *Westleton Vicarage, Saxmundham, Suff, IP17 3AQ.* (Westleton 271)

ROBINSON, Jim. b 23. Ridley Hall Cam 70. **d** 72 Wakef **p** 73 Pontefract for Wakef. C of H Nativ Conv Distr Mixenden Halifax 72-73; Carlton-in-Lindrick 73-74; Tuxford 74-77; Selston w Westwood Dio Southw from 77. *The Parsonage, Church Lane, Main Road, Jacksdale, Nottingham NG16 5HR.* (Leabrooks 2800)

✠ **ROBINSON, Right Rev John Arthur Thomas.** b 19. Late Exhib Jes Coll Cam 38, 2nd cl Cl Trip pt i 40, Lady Kay Scho and Burney Pri 41, Burney Stud 42-43, BA (1st cl Th Trip pt ii) 42. Stanton Stud Trin Coll Cam 43-45, MA 45, PhD 46, BD 62, DD 68. Univ of S Calif Hon LLD 80. Westcott Ho Cam 41. **d** 45 **p** 46 Bris. C of St Matt Moorfields Bris 45-48; Chap to Wells Th Coll 48-51; Fell and Dean of Clare Coll Cam 51-59; L to Offic Dio Ely 52-59; Exam Chap to Abp of Cant 53-59; Select Pr Univ of Cam 53; Asst Lect in Div Univ of Cam 53-54; Lect 54-59; Visiting Prof Harvard Univ 55; Union Th Sem Richmond Va 58; Select Pr TCD 56; Six Pr Cant Cathl 58-68; Cons Ld Bp Suffr of Woolwich in Cant Cathl 29 Sept 59 by Abp of Cant; Bp of S'wark; Bps Suffr of Kens; Willesden; Kingston T; Maidstone; Dover; and Tonbridge; Bps Simpson, Rose, Stannard, Sinker; and Bp of Madura; res 69; Proc Conv S'wark 60-70; Select Pr Univ of Ox 65; Asst Bp of S'wark 69-80; Fell, Dean of Chapel, and Lect in Th Trin Coll Cam from 69; Hulsean Lect Univ of Cam 70; Hulsean Pr Univ of Cam 71; Visiting Lect Univ of S Africa Pret 75; Univ of the Witwatersrand 77; Exam Chap to Bp of B & W from 76; Selw Lect St John's Coll Auckld 79; Asst Bp in Dio Bradf from 81. *Trinity College, Cambridge, CB2 1TQ.* (Cam 358201)

ROBINSON, John Chorley. b 22. **d** 77 **p** 78 Syd. C of All SS Hunter's Hill 77; Prec of St Andr Cathl Syd 78-80; R of St Pet E Lindfield Dio Syd from 81. *110 Tyron Road, East Lindfield, NSW, Australia 2070.* (46-5911)

ROBINSON, John Ellis. b 07. ALCD 30. **d** 30 **p** 31 Sheff. C of Conisborough 30-33; St Laurence 33-39; Herne 39-44; Chap Blean Inst 43-44; V of Wymonswold 44-51; C-in-c of Aylesham 44-51; R of Cheriton w Newington 51-60; CF (TA) from 51; V of Leeds w Broomfield 60-73; Asst Chap O of St John of Jer from 60. *27 Golf Road, Deal, Kent.*

ROBINSON, John Eric. Roch Th Coll 64. **d** 68 Bran **p** 69 Bp Anderson for Bran. C of Snow Lake 68; I of Melita w Deloraine and Napinka 68-71; I of Emerson 71-76; Kimberley 76-80; Gibsons Dio New Westmr from 80. *RR4 Chaster Road, Gibsons, BC, Canada.*

ROBINSON, John Francis Napier. b 42. St Edm Hall Ox BA 64, MA 68. Dipl Th (Lon) 68. Clifton Th Coll 65. **d** 68 Warrington for Liv **p** 69 Liv. C of Ch Ch Southport 68-71; Coleraine 71-74; Deputn Sec BCMS Ireland 74-76; Team V of Marfleet Hull 76-81; V of Yeadon Dio Bradf from 81. *St John's Vicarage, Yeadon, Leeds, LS19 7SE.* (Rawdon 502272)

ROBINSON, John Henry Whinfield. Angl Th Coll Vanc LTh 41. **d** 41 **p** 42 New Westmr. C of St Paul Vanc 41; Ch Ch Vanc 41-43; R of St Aug Marpole w St Luke Vanc 43-48; St Helen Vanc 48-74; Can of New Westmr 63-74. *205-1770 Davie Street, Vancouver, BC, Canada.*

ROBINSON, John Kenneth. b 36. K Coll Lon and Warm BD and AKC 61. **d** 62 **p** 63 Blackb. C of Poulton-le-Fylde 62-65; Lanc Priory 65-66; Chap HM Pris Lanc 65-66; St John's Sch Sing 66-68; V of H Trin Colne 68-71; C of St Geo Grenada 71-74; Dir of Educn Windw Is 71-74; Exam Chap to Bp of Windw Is 71-74; V of Skerton 74-81; Commiss Windw Is from 78; USPG Area Sec E Anglia from 81. *26 Oswyn Close, Bury St Edmunds.* (B St E 4154)

ROBINSON, John Leonard William. b 23. Univ of Lon BA 50. Bps' Coll Cheshunt 50. **d** 52 **p** 53 Chelmsf. C of Ch of Ascen Vic Dks 52-55; St Aug Kilburn 55-63; St Jas Piccadilly 63-81; V of Compton, The Mardens, Stoughton, Racton and Lordington Dio Chich from 81. *Compton Vicarage, Chichester, Sussex.* (Compton 252)

ROBINSON, John Michael. b 51. AKC and BD 79. St Steph Ho Ox 80. **d** 81 Ex. C of St Pet w All SS Plymouth Dio Ex from 81. *9 Clarence Place, Stonehouse, Plymouth, PL1 3JN.* (Plymouth 24873)

ROBINSON, Ven John Victor James. MBE 81. St Jo Coll Morpeth ACT ThL 38. **d** and **p** 38 Graft. C of Liston 38; Lismore 38-40; V of U Clarence 40-41; Chap AIF 41-46; V of Copmanhurst 46-47; Alstonville 47-49; R of Casino 49-51; Lismore 51-72; Hon Can of Graft 53-69; Archd 58-77; Archd (Emer) from 77; Perm to Offic Dio Newc from 78. *Trevallyn, Vacy, NSW, Australia 2421.*

ROBINSON, Jonathan William Murrell. b 42. Sarum Th Coll 65. **d** 68 **p** 69 S'wark. C of All SS Tooting Graveney 68-71; St Thos-on-the-Bourne 71-76; Perm to Offic Dio B & W from 77; Dir of Grail Trust Chr Commun Centre Burtle from 78; C of St Gabr Cricklewood Dio Lon from 78. *Grail House, Burtle, Bridgwater, Somt.*

ROBINSON, Joseph. b 27. K Coll Lon and Warm AKC (1st cl) and BD (1st cl) 51, FKC 73. Jun McCaul Hebr Pri 52, Knowling Sermon Pri 52, MTh 58. **d** 52 **p** 53 Lon. C of All H Tottenham 52-55; Min Can St Paul's Cathl Lon 55-68; Asst Master Choir Sch 55-58; Sacr 58-68; Sen Cardinal 58-65; Lect K Coll 59-68; Warden Coll of Min Can 65-68; Sub-Chap O of St John of Jer from 65; Can Res of Cant 68-80; Can (Emer) from 81; Exam Chap to Abp of Cant 68-80; Libr 68-73; Treas 72-80; Master of the Temple, Lon from 80. *Master's House, Temple, EC4.* (01-353 8559)

ROBINSON, Joseph Frederick. **d** 54 **p** 55 Ugan. Hon Chap at Masaka Dio Ugan from 54. *PO Box 227, Masaka, Uganda.*

ROBINSON, Keith. b 48. Univ of Lon BA 75. AKC and BD 77. Westcott Ho Cam 77. **d** 78 Lon **p** 79 Stepney for Lon. C of Bow w Bromley St Leon 78-81; Leighton Buzzard w Hockliffe, Egginton and Billington Dio St Alb from 81. *138 Brooklands Drive, Leighton Buzzard, Beds.* (L Buz 373167)

ROBINSON, Kenneth Arnold. **d** 52 **p** 53 Ch Ch. C of Avonside 52-53; V of Oxford 53-59; Mt Somers 59-63; Rakaia 63-69; Mt Herbert 69-71; L to Offic from 71. *35 D'Arcy Street, Leeston, Canterbury, N Zealand.*

ROBINSON, Kenneth Arnold. Univ of Tor BA 57. Trin Coll Tor LTh 60, STB 65. **d** 60 **p** 61 Alg. I of St Joseph's I 61-66; Tutor Trin Coll Tor 66-67; R of Wawa 67-70. *First Avenue, Brochville, Ont., Canada.*

ROBINSON, Kenneth Borwell. b 37. BA (Lon) 62. Ridley Hall Cam 68. **d** 70 **p** 71 Barking for Chelmsf. C of St Jo Evang

Walthamstow 70-74; P-in-c of St Alb Becontree 74-78; Heybridge w Langford Dio Chelmsf from 78. *1a Crescent Road, Heybridge, Maldon, Essex, CM9 7ND.* (Maldon 56938)

ROBINSON, Lance Brandon. b 28. Univ of NZ BSc 53. Coll Ho Ch Ch. **d** 56 Wel **p** 57 Bp Rich for Wel. C of Hawera 56-58; V of Berhampore 58-62; U Hutt 62-67; Porirua 67-73; Khandallah City and Dio Wel from 73. *35 Box Hill, Khandallah, Wellington, NZ.* (796-588)

ROBINSON, Leslie. b 31. St Aid Coll 56. **d** 59 **p** 60 Leic. C of Hugglescote 59-61; Greenside 61-63; C-in-c of New Cantley Conv Distr Doncaster 63-66; V Cho and Chap Heref Cathl 66-67; R of Easton-on-the-Hill 67-69; Hon Min Can of Pet 68-69; C of Weston-s-Mare 69-70; V of Winkleigh 70-72; Thorpe Acre w Dishley 72-78; Cloughton 78-79; Hedon w Paull 79-81; St Pet Bywell Dio Newc T from 81. *Bywell Vicarage, Meadowfield Road, Stocksfield, Northumb, NE43 7PY.* (Stocksfield 2272)

ROBINSON, Michael George. b 52. Moore Th Coll Syd ACT ThL 76. **d** 77 Bp Dain for Syd **p** 77 Syd, C of St Matt Manly 77-79; Dapto 79-81; R of Kingsgrove Dio Syd from 81. *3 Paterson Avenue, Kingsgrove, NSW, Australia 2208.* (50-9417)

ROBINSON, Michael John. b 45. Univ of Nottm BA 66. Linc Th Coll 78. **d** 79 **p** 80 Sheff. C of All SS Aston 79-80; All SS Rotherham Dio Sheff from 80. *Top Flat, 42 Godstone Road, Rotherham, S60 2PU.* (Rotherham 64729)

ROBINSON, Michael Sidney Mostyn. b 23. Selw Coll Cam 3rd cl Econ Trip pt i 42, BA 46, MA 48. Qu Coll Birm 46. **d** 48 **p** 49 Pet. C of St Mary Far Cotton Northampton 48-50; V of Long Buckby 50-55; CF 55-68; Perm to Offic Dios Ex and B & W 68-80; Publ Pr Dio Cov 68-80; Chap Warwick Sch 68-80; P-in-c of Staple-Fitzpaine w Bickenhall, Orchard Portman, Thurlbear and Stoke St Mary Dio B & W from 80. *Thurlbear Rectory, Taunton, Somt.* (Henlade 442359)

✠ **ROBINSON, Right Rev Morse Cyril.** Bp's Univ Lennox BA 43. **d** 43 **p** 44 Niag. C of Wainfleet w Dainville and St Geo Welland 43-46; Chap Toc H Tor 46-48; R of St Jas Hamilton 48-54; St Geo Lon Ont 54-60; Exam Chap to Bp of Hur 56-60; Hon Can of Hur 62-66; R of St Jo Evang Kitchener 66-69; Archd of Perth 66-69; Archd without territorial Jurisd 69-74; Dioc Programme Executive Officer Hur 69-74; Cons Ld Bp Suffr of Hur in St Paul's Cathl Lon Ont 21 Sept 74 by Abp of Moos and Abp E W Scott (Primate); Bps of Hur, Niag, Tor, Ont and Ott; Bps Suffr of Tor and Moos; and others. *4-220 Dundas Street, London, Ont., N6A IH3, Canada.* (519-434 6893)

ROBINSON, Neal Sydney. b 48. Worc Coll Ox BA 70, MA 75. Univ of Birm PhD 77. Qu Coll Birm 74. **d** 76 Dover for Cant **p** 77 Cant. C of St Sav Folkestone 76-79; Bp's Chap to Students Dio Bradf from 79. *68 Little Horton Lane, Bradford, BD5 0HU.* (Bradford 27034)

ROBINSON, Canon Neil. b 29. Late Van Mildert Exhib of St Jo Dur BA (2nd cl Social Stud) 52, Dipl Th 54. **d** 54 York **p** 55 Selby for York. C of H Trin Hull 54-58; V of Glen Parva w S Wigston 58-68; Hon Can of Leic from 68; R of Mkt Bosworth Dio Leic from 68; RD of Sparkenhoe I from 68; Surr from 73. *Market Bosworth Rectory, Nuneaton, Warws.* (Market Bosworth 290239)

ROBINSON, Norman Graham. Univ of Syd BA 55. Moore Th Coll Syd ACT ThL 51. **d** and **p** 52 Syd. C of St Luke Mosman 52-56; C-in-c of Belfield 56-57; R of St Paul Cant 57-66; Arncliffe Dio Syd from 66. *1 Pitt-Owen Avenue, Arncliffe, NSW, Australia 2205.* (59-1449)

ROBINSON, Norman Leslie. b 50. Univ of Liv BSc 71. Lon Bible Coll BA (Th) 78. Wycl Coll Ox 78. **d** 80 **p** 81 Ches. C of St Andr Bebington Dio Ches from 80. *8 Rolleston Drive, Bebington, Wirral, Merseyside, L63 3DB.*

ROBINSON, Paul Leslie. b 46. Univ of Dur BA 67. Univ of Nottm Dipl Th 73. Linc Th Coll 71. **d** 74 **p** 75 Ches. C of Poynton 74-76; Prenton 76-78; V of Seacombe Wallasey Dio Ches from 78. *5 Brougham Road, Wallasey, Mer.* (051-638 3677)

ROBINSON, Paul Thomas. Angl Th Coll BC 66. **d** 69 **p** 70 Koot. C of Kelowna 69-70; I 70-72; Fernie Dio Koot from 72. *Box 279, Fernie, BC, Canada.* (423-6517)

ROBINSON, Peter. b 42. St D Coll Lamp BA 63. Univ Coll Cardiff BD 71. NOC 78. **d** 81 Man C of St Chad Rochdale Dio Man from 81. *8 Higher Cleggswood Avenue, Littleborough, Lancs, OL15 0DJ.*

ROBINSON, Peter Edward Barron. b 40. Sarum Wells Th Coll 76. **d** 78 **p** 79 Portsm. C of Petersfield Dio Portsm from 78. *42 Heath Road, Petersfield, Hants, GU31 4EH.*

ROBINSON, Peter McCall. b 24. Worc Coll Ox BA 48, MA 50. Wells Th Coll 48. **d** 50 **p** 51 Natal. C of St Thos Durban 50-54; Stoke Poges Bucks 55-57; Asst Chap Michaelho Sch Natal 57-58; V of Ixopo 58-65; R of Margate 65-71; V of Payhembury 71-79; R of Cheriton w Tichborne and Beauworth 79-81; Perm to Offic Dio Natal from 81. *515 Currie Road, Durban, Natal, S Africa.*

ROBINSON, Peter Stanley. b 20. Univ of Lon BD 49. Univ of Nottm MA 55. Qu Coll Birm 53. **d** 53 **p** 54 Southw. C of Arnold 53-55; Sunninghill 55-56; R of Easton-on-the-Hill 56-60; Boyup Brook 60-63; Wagin 63-65; Mandurah 65-68; Exam Chap to Bp of Bunb 64-68; C of Poplar 69-71; Team V 71-73; V of Owston Ferry 73-81; W Butterwick 73-81; R of Earl Soham w Cretingham and Ashfield Dio St E from 81. *Rectory, Church Lane, Earl Soham, Woodbridge, Suff IP13 7SD.* (Earl Soham 329)

ROBINSON, Philip Charles. **d** and **p** 73 Carp. P Dio Carp 73-75; C of Caloundra 75-76; St Andr Lutwyche Brisb 76-77; P-in-c of Nanango Dio Brisb from 77. *18 Burnett Street, Nanango, Brisbane, Australia 4315.* (074-792 2156)

ROBINSON, Philip Henry. NZ Bd of Th Stud LTh 66. **d** 61 **p** 62 Wel. C of Taita 61-64; V of Featherston 64-69; L to Offic Dio Wel 73-77. *12 Fettes Crescent, Seatoun, Wellington 3, NZ.* (882-463)

ROBINSON, Phillip Lewis. b 45. St Jo Coll Auckld 69. **d** 69 **p** 70 Dun. C of Invercargill 69-73; V of Waimea Plains Lumsden 73-78; Gladstone Dio Dun from 78. *Vicarage, Hollywood Terrace, Gladstone, NZ.* (86-390)

ROBINSON, Raymonde Robin. b 43. St Jo Coll Dur BA 66. Chich Th Coll 67. **d** 70 **p** 71 Willesden for Lon. C of St Barn Ealing 70-72; Pinner 72-75; H Redeemer Clerkenwell 75-80; Team V of Kingsthorpe w St D Northn Dio Pet from 80. *St David's Vicarage, Eastern Avenue, Northampton, NN2 7QB.* (Northn 714536)

ROBINSON, Richard Albert. b 14. Trin Coll Dub BA 36. **d** 38 **p** 39 Clogh. C of Kilskeery 38-40; Dioc C Dio Clogh 40-43 and 44-46; C-in-c of Drummully 43-44; Dioc C Dio Kilm 46-54; I of Taunagh w Kilmactranny (w Ballysumaghan and Killery from 60) Dio Elph from 54. *Rectory, Riverstown, Co Sligo, Irish Republic.*

ROBINSON, Richard Malcolm. b 20. Ex Coll Ox BA (2nd cl Mod Hist) 42, Dipl Th 43, MA 46. Wycl Hall Ox 42. **d** 44 **p** 45 Bris. C of St Paul Bedminster 44-45; Chap to Bp of Malmesbury 45-46; C of Brinkworth 45-48; CMS Youth Org 48-52; V of St Luke Manningham 52-56; St Pet Shipley 56-64; R of Ch Ch Morningside Edin 64-76; V of Dent w Cowgill Dio Bradf from 76; RD of Ewecross from 80. *Dent Vicarage, Sedbergh, Cumb.* (Dent 226)

ROBINSON, Robert Arthur. b 46. Univ of Melb LTh 69. Univ of Cant NZ BA 70. BD (Lon) 72. Ridley Coll Melb 66. **d** and **p** 73 Ch Ch. C of Shirley 73-75; L to Offic Dio Melb 76-77; Dio Sing 77; C of Ch Ch Sing 77-78; V of St Geo Tanglin City and Dio Sing from 78. *11 Wilton Close, Singapore 5.*

ROBINSON, Robert Nesbitt. Univ of the South USA BA 59. Wycl Coll Tor BTh 64. **d** 64 Rupld **p** 67 Bran. C of St Geo Winnipeg 64-66; St Matt Cathl Bran 66-68. *c/o Philosophy Dept, Citadel Hill, Charleston, SC 20409, USA.*

ROBINSON, Canon Roger George. b 24. Qu Coll Cam BA 46, MA 50. Ridley Hall, Cam 46. **d** 48 **p** 49 Nor. C of Gorleston 48-51; St Andr w St Pet Drypool 51-54; C-in-c of St Aid Southcoates Hull 54-55; V 55-60; St Phil and St Jas Clifton 60-70; Chap Clifton Hosp 61-70; V of Far Headingley 70-81; RD of Headingley 72-81; Hon Can of Ripon Cathl 81; Can (Emer) from 81; R of Drayton w Felthorpe Dio Nor from 81. *Drayton Rectory, Norwich, NR8 6EF.* (Nor 868749)

ROBINSON, Ronald Frederick. b 46. Oak Hill Coll 73. **d** 76 Man **p** 77 Portsm. C of Ch Ch Pennington 76-77; Bedhampton 77-79; St Mark North End Portsea 79-82; R of Rowner Dio Portsm from 82. *Rowner Rectory, Rowner Lane, Gosport, Hants, PO13 9SU.* (Gosport 81834)

ROBINSON, Ronald Gordon. Moore Th Coll Syd ACT ThL 58. **d** 59 Bp Hilliard for Syd **p** 59 Syd. C of Willoughby 59-60; Erskineville 60-62; R 62-65; Bondi Dio Syd from 65. *34 Ocean Street, Bondi, NSW, Australia 2026.* (389-9634)

ROBINSON, Roy David. b 35. K Coll Lon and Warm AKC 59. **d** 60 **p** 61 Birm. C of Acock's Green 60-62; Shirley 62-65; Haslemere (in c of St Chris) 65-70; R of Headley Epsom (w Box Hill from 71) Dio Guildf from 70. *Headley Rectory, Epsom, Surrey.* (Leatherhead 77327)

ROBINSON, Simon John. b 51. Univ of Edin MA 72. Univ of Ox BA (Th) 77. Wycl Hall Ox 75. **d** 78 **p** 79 Dur. C of Haughton-le-Skerne Dio Dur from 78. *87 Hutton Avenue, Haughton, Darlington, Co Durham, DL1 2AH.*

ROBINSON, Canon Sydney Ernest Fisher. b 14. ALCD 38. **d** 38 **p** 39 Blackb. C of St Paul Blackpool 38-41; Chap RAFVR 41-46; R of Thorley (w H Trin Bp's Stortford from 73) 46-79; RD of Bp's Stortford 67-73; C-in-c of H Trin Bp's Stortford 71-73; Hon Can of St Alb 74-79; Can (Emer) from 79. *34 Fourth Avenue, Frinton-on-Sea, Essex.*

ROBINSON, Thomas Fisher. b 20. St Jo Coll Dur BA 49. **d** 50 **p** 51 Man. C of St Jo Evang Pendlebury 50-54; St Mary Virg Davyhulme 54-56; V of St Andr Litherland 56-62; St

Cath Wigan 62-67; Garston Dio Liv from 67. *Vicarage, Horrocks Avenue, Liverpool, L19 5NY.* (051-427 4204)

ROBINSON, Thomas Hugh. b 34. TCD BA 55, MA 71. **d** 57 **p** 58 Down. C of St Clem Belf 57-60; Miss to Seamen Dio Momb 61-64; I of Youghal U 64-66; CF from 66. *c/o Ministry of Defence, Bagshot Park, Bagshot, Surrey, GU19 5PL.*

ROBINSON, Thomas Irven. b 10. TCD BA 34, MA 45. **d** 34 **p** 35 Cant. C of St Paul Maidstone 34-36; St Paul Margate 36-39; Chap RAFVR 39-45; C of All H Barking-by-the-Tower 45-46; Chap RAF 46-62; V of Hilmarton w Highway 62-67; Chap at Bahrain 67-69; in the Gulf 69-71; P-in-c of Stourpaine (w Durweston and Bryanston 73-76) 71-77; Durweston and Bryanston 76-77; Perm to Offic Dio Ox from 77; Offg Chap RAF Coll Bracknell from 81. *1 Avon Court, Cressex Close, Binfield, Bracknell, Berks RG12 5DR.*

ROBINSON, Thomas Robinson. Wycl Coll Tor 52. **d** 56 Ont for Tor **p** 57 Tor. C of St Paul Bloor Street Tor 56-57; All S Langham Place St Marylebone 57-62; R of Oak Ridges 62-65; Trin Queb 66-76; Dom Chap to Bp of Queb 73-76; Can of Queb 75-76; I of St Mark, Saint John Dio Fred from 76. *87 Carleton Street, Saint John, NB, Canada.*

ROBINSON, Virgil Austin Anderson. b 38. Univ of S-W Louisiana BS 62. St Steph Ho Ox 77. **d** 79 Ox **p** 80 Buckingham for Ox (APM). C of Bicester Dio Ox from 79. *4 Portway Gardens, Aynho, Banbury, Oxon, OX17 3AR.*

ROBINSON, Wilfred Henry Fox. b 11. Lich Th Coll 32. **d** 35 Bp Crick for Derby **p** 36 Derby. C of St Jas Derby 35-37; Eckington 37-39; Chap RNVR 39-47; V of St Jas Pokesdown Bournemouth 47-53; Friskney 53-56; Bournemouth 57-67; Surr 57-67; Perm to Offic Dios Lon & Linc from 79. *Boothby Hall, Spilsby, Lincs, PE23 5TE.*

ROBINSON, Canon William David. b 31. Univ Coll Dur BA 54, Dipl Th 58, MA 62. Cranmer Hall. **d** 58 Burnley for Blackb **p** 59 Blackb. C of Standish 58-61; Lanc 61-63; V of St Jas Blackb 63-73; P-in-c of Shireshead and Dioc Stewardship Adv Dio Blackb from 73; Hon Can of Blackb from 75. *Shireshead Vicarage, Forton, Preston, Lancs.* (Forton 791355)

ROBINSON, William Eason. b 12. Hatf Coll Dur LTh 35, Wansbrough Scho 36, BA (2nd cl Th) 37, MA 40. Qu Coll Ox BA 53, MA 56. Edin Th Coll 32. **d** 37 **p** 38 Edin. C of St Cuthb Colinton w St Mungo Balerno 37-45; Lect Edin Th Coll 42-45; Chap 45-47; Vice-Prin 47-49; P-in-c of Priory Ch S Queensferry 49-50; L to Offic Dio Ox 50-52; Chap and Lect Lich Th Coll 52-59; C of St Jo Evang Greenock 59-60; Perm to Offic Dio Glas 60-61; Dio Chelmsf from 61; Asst Master Tom Hood Tech High Sch Leytonstone 61-68; Alexandra High Sch Tipton 69-75; L to Offic Dio Lich from 69. *9 Rosebery Road, Stanwix, Carlisle, Cumb.*

✠ **ROBINSON, Right Rev William James.** Bp's Univ Lennox BA 39. **d** 39 **p** 40 Ont. C of St Geo Trenton 40-41; R of Tweed and Madoc 41-46; Tweed and N Addington 46-47; R of Napanee 48-53; St Thos Belleville 53-55; St John Ott 55-62; Ch of Ascen Hamilton 62-67; St Geo Guelph 67-70; Can of Niag 63-67; Archd of Trafalgar 67-70; Cons Ld Bp of Ott in the Civic Centre Ott 24 June 70 by Abp of Alg; Bps of Tor; Niag; Moos; Ont; NS; Calg; Montr; and others; res 81. *c/o 71 Bronson Avenue, Ottawa, Ont, K1R 6G6, Canada.* (613-232 7124)

ROBINSON, William Pitchford. b 50. Univ of Nottm BTh 75. Kelham Th Coll 71. **d** 75 Lon **p** 76 Stepney for Lon. C of St Mary Bow 75-79; Chap Claybury Hosp from 79. *Claybury Hospital, Woodford Green, Essex. IG8 8BY.*

ROBINSON-JOICE, Neil Gregory. b 46. Counc for Nat Acad awards BA 80. Oak Hill Coll 77. **d** 80 **p** 81 St E. C of Stowmarket Dio St E from 80. *4 Gainsborough Road, Stowmarket, Suffolk, IP14 1LG.* (04492-4332)

ROBJOHNS, Canon Alfred John. St Barn Coll Adel 30. ACT ThL 33. **d** 33 **p** 34 Adel. C of St Aug Unley 33-37; Miss Chap Pinnaroo 37-39; P-in-c of Berri 39-40; LPr Dio Adel 40-44; Chap AIF 40-44; R of St Paul Naracoorte 44-49; Renmark 49-55 (all in Dio Adel) V of Luppitt 56-57; R of Sheldon 56-57; V of Holbeach Hurn Lincs 57-60; P-in-c of Edwardstown Miss 60-68; Chap Repatriation Gen Hosp Daw Pk 68-75; L to Offic Dio Adel from 75; Hon Can of Adel from 70. *55 Dudley Avenue, Daw Park, S Australia 5041.* (08-297 3280)

ROBLES, Juan. b 25. **d** 71 **p** 72 Parag for Argent. P Dio Argent 71-73; N Argent from 73. *Parsonage, Embarcación, N Argentina.*

ROBLES, Juan Luis. b 57. **d** 79 **p** 81 N Argent. Chap Formosa Ch Dio N Argent from 79. *Casilla 76, Formosa, Argentina.*

ROBLIN, Graham Henry. b 37. K Coll Lon and Warm AKC 61. **d** 62 **p** 63 S'wark. C of St Pet St Helier 62-66; CF from 66. *c/o Ministry of Defence, Bagshot Park, Bagshot, Surrey.*

ROBO, Meke. b 48. **d** 76 **p** 77 Polyn. P Dio Polyn. *PO Box 35, Suva, Fiji.*

ROBOTHAM, Eric William. Ex Coll Ox BA (2nd cl Hist) 30, 3rd cl Th 32, MA 35. Wycl Hall, Ox 30. **d** 32 **p** 33 Chelmsf. C of St Chad Chadwell Heath 32-34; St John Leytonstone 35-37; Chap RAF 37-46; R of W w E Putford 46-49; PC of Swymbridge w Gunn and Traveller's Rest 49-52; R of Boulder 53-59; P-in-c of Leonara-Gwalia 53-56; Archd of the Goldfields 56-60; R of Guildf Perth 60-77; Exam Chap to Bp of Kalg 59-73; Perm to Offic Dio Perth from 77. *38 North Road, Bassendean, W Australia 6054.* (279 1480)

ROBSON, Andrew. b 13. St Bonif Coll Warm 37. **d** 41 **p** 42 Newc T. C of St Ann Newc T 41-42; Whittingham 42-45; Alwinton w Holystone 45-46; R of Beaufort W 47-50; V of Edlingham 50-61; Lowick w Kyloe 61-79. *8 Ethal Vicarage, Cornhill on Tweed, Northumb, TD12 4TN.* (Crookham 362)

ROBSON, Angus William. b 13. Kelham Th Coll 32. **d** 38 **p** 39 Lon. C of St Pet Regent Square Lon 38-40; St Pet Mill End St Alb 40-45; CF (EC) 43-45; C-in-c of St Pet Luton 45; Perm to Offic Dio St Alb 45-46; V of Sark 46-50; St Jas Jersey 50-75; Chap HM Pris Jersey 60-75. *La Petite Carriere, Wellington Road, St Helier, Jersey, CI.*

ROBSON, Bernard John. b 33. Ch Ch Ox BA 56, MA 60. Tyndale Hall, Bris 57. **d** 60 **p** 61 Birm. C of Walmley 60-64; Stapenhill w Caldwell 64-68; SE Area Sec CPAS 68-71; E Area from 71; Perm to Offic Dio Ely from 79. *33 Nightingale Avenue, Cambridge CB1 4SG.* (Cambridge 248740)

ROBSON, Featherstone. b 30. Univ of Nottm Dipl Educn 74. Oak Hill Th Coll 55. **d** 58 **p** 59 Truro. C of St Illogan w Trevenson 58-60; Chap and Tutor Bedstone Sch and Perm to Offic Dio Heref 60-61; Asst Master Wycombe Technical High Sch 61-67; Beaufoy Sch Lambeth 67-68; Headington County Secondary Sch Ox 68-69; Larkmead County Secondary Sch Abingdon 69-71; Perm to Offic Dio Ox from 61; Asst Master at Dorking Gr Sch and Perm to Offic Dio Guildf 71-76; Asst Master Scarisbrick Hall Sch Ormskirk 77-78; Chap and Asst Master Dean Close Jun Sch Cheltenham and Perm to Offic Dio Glouc 78-79; Asst Master K Edw Sch Witley and Perm to Offic Dio Guildf 79-81. *71 Springfield Drive, Abingdon, Oxon, OX14 1JF.*

ROBSON, George. b 34. K Coll Lon and Warm AKC 58. **d** 59 Blackb **p** 60 Lanc for York. C of St Geo Chorley 59-62; Chap RAF from 62. *c/o Ministry of Defence, Adastral House, WC1.*

ROBSON, George Dowglass. b 16. **d** 44 **p** 45 Waik. C of St Pet Cathl Hamilton 44-45; All SS Uruti 45-46; New Plymouth 46-51. *5 Raylands Way, Belle Isle, Leeds, 10.*

ROBSON, Gilbert Alan. b 30. St Pet Hall, Ox BA (2nd cl Th) 53, MA 57. Linc Th Coll. **d** 57 **p** 58 Roch. C of St Mary Chatham 57-59; Asst Master Sir J Williamson's Math Sch Roch 57-59; Sub-Warden Roch Th Coll 59-62; Chap 62-64; Min Can of Roch Cathl 59-62; Chap to Bp of Roch 61-64; Exam Chap from 66; R of Wouldham 61-64; Chap Nor Coll of Educn 65-68; Sen Lect in Div 68-72; L to Offic Dio Nor 65-70; V of Bramerton Group 70-72; Shotwick 72-74; Dom and Exam Chap to Bp of Ches 72-74; Dir of Ordinands Dio Ches 72-74; Asst Master and Chap Eton Coll Windsor from 74. *23 High Street, Eton, Windsor, Berks.* (Windsor 60205)

ROBSON, Ian Leonard. b 32. Bps' Coll Cheshunt, 61. **d** 63 **p** 64 St Alb. C of Croxley Green 63-65; Harpenden (in c of All SS from 66) 65-68; V of Redbourn 68-72; Ashford 72-77; St Mary Abbots Kens Dio Lon from 77. *St Mary Abbots Vicarage, Vicarage Gate, W8 4HN.* (01-937 6032)

ROBSON, Ian Trevor. b 53. Univ of Leeds BA 76. St Steph Ho Ox 78. **d** 80 Willesden for Lon **p** 81 Lon. C of All S Harlesden Willesden Dio Lon from 80. *1 Station Road, Harlesden, NW10 4UJ.*

ROBSON, Irwin. b 20. **d** 63 **p** 64 Newc T. C of Long Benton 63-69; C-in-c of St Martin's Conv Distr Byker Newc T 69-74; V of Willington 75-76; R of Willington Team Parish Dio Newc T from 76. *Vicarage, Churchill Street, Willington, Wallsend, T & W.* (Wallsend 628208)

ROBSON, James Arnold. **d** 77 Sask. Hon C of St Timothy City and Dio Sask from 77. *1011 - 7th Street E, Saskatoon, Sask, Canada.*

ROBSON, Canon John Maurice. b 11. Keble Coll Ox BA (3rd cl Th) 34, MA 38. St Jo Coll Dur 30. **d** 34 **p** 35 Dur. C of Pelton 34-36; Ryton-on-Tyne 36-46; CF (TA - R of O) 39; CF (EC) 39-46; Hon CF 46; CF (TA) 48-62; TD 51; Two Clasps 63; Perm to Offic Dio Momb 39; Dio Sier L 42-44; R of Bamford-the-Peak 46-52; Brailsford 52-77; V of Shirley 52-77; RD of Ashbourne 57-77; Surr 58-77; Hon Can of Derby 75-77; Can (Emer) from 78; Perm to Offic Dios Glouc and Ox from 78. *Bristows Close, Southrop, Lechlade, Glos, GL7 3QA.* (Southrop 273)

ROBSON, John Phillips. b 32. K Coll Lon and Warm AKC 58. **d** 59 **p** 60 Wakef. C of Huddersfield 59-62; Asst Chap Ch Hosp Horsham 62-65; Chap from 65. *Christ's Hospital, Horsham, Sussex.*

ROBSON, John Wingate. Montr Dioc Th Coll. **d** 49 **p** 50 Montr. C of St Matt Hampstead 49; I of N Clarendon 50-51; in Amer Ch 51-61; C of St Thos Montr 61; I of Malbay 62-64. *81 Roxton Crescent, Montreal West, Montreal, PQ, Canada.*

ROBSON, Paul Coutt. b 37. Univ of Leeds, BA 60. Coll of Resurr Mirfield, 63. **d** 64 **p** 65 Heref. C of Stokesay 64-66; St Geo Cathl Capetn 66-69; R of Roodebloem Dio Capetn 69-70; Chap of HM Prison Man 70-71; HM Borstal Feltham 71-74; HM Borstal Hollesley 74-78; HM Pris Grendon and Spring Hill from 78. *HM Prison, Grendon and Spring Hill, Grendon Underwood, Aylesbury, Bucks.*

ROBSON, Peter Cole. b 45. Cho Exhib Clare Coll Cam, John Stewart of Rannoch Hebr Scho 65, 2nd cl Or Stud Trip pt i, BA (2nd cl Th Trip ia) 66, 2nd Win Pri 67, MA 70. Or Coll Ox BA (by incorp) 67, Houghton Syriac Pri 68, BLitt 69, MA 70, MLitt 79. Coll of Resurr Mirfield 70. **d** 71 Linc **p** 72 Linc. C of St Mary and St Jas, Grimsby 71-73; Chap BNC Ox 73-76; R of Timsbury 76-79; P-in-c of Blanchland w Hunstanworth Dio Newc T from 80. *Blanchland Vicarage, Consett, Co Durham, DH8 9ST.* (Blanchland 207)

ROBSON, Canon Reginald. b 09. Keble Coll Ox BA (2nd cl Th) 31, MA 35. **d** 32 **p** 33 Dur. C of Seaton Carew 32-35; Bp Wearmouth 35-37; V of Haverton Hill 37-44; Woodlands 44-53; St Andr Sharrow Sheff 53-74; RD of Ecclesall 65-74; Hon Can of Sheff 67-75; Can (Emer) from 75; M Gen Syn 70-75; L to Offic Dio Sheff from 74. *2 Oakburn Court, Broomhall Road, Sheffield, S10 2DR.* (Sheffield 669871)

ROBSON, Robert. b 10. St Andr Coll Pampisford, 43. **d** 45 **p** 46 Dur. C of H Trin Stockton 45-50; V of Carlton-in-Cleveland 50-75; V of Faceby 50-75. *Bonny Cliff, Faceby, Middlesbrough, Cleve, TS9 7BN.*

ROBSON, Thomas George Harry. Late Exhib of Jes Coll Ox 2nd cl Cl Mods 32, BA (3rd cl Lit Hum) 34, 3rd cl Th 35, MA 41. Wells Th Coll 35. **d** 36 **p** 37 St Alb. C of St Mich AA Watford 36-39 St Luke Bournemouth 39-41; Chap RAFVR 41-46; R of Selukwe 47-48; St Cuthb Gwelo 48-61; Hermanus 61-66; St Marg Bulawayo N 68-70; Shabani 71-75. *80 Enterprise Road, PO Highlands, Salisbury, Rhodesia.*

ROBSON, William. b 34. FCIS 66. Sarum Wells Th Coll 77. **d** 79 **p** 80 Win. C of Lymington Dio Win from 79. *Needles View, Kings Saltern Road, Lymington, Hants.*

ROCHDALE, Archdeacon of. (Vacant)

ROCHE, Barry Robert Francis. b 40. BD (Lon) 66. Univ of Dur Dipl Th 67. Clifton Th Coll 63. **d** 68 **p** 69 Roch. C of Ch Ch Beckenham 68-72; Chester-le-Street 72-74; P Missr N Bletchley 74-78; R of Luton Kent Dio Roch from 78. *Rectory, Capstone Road, Luton, Chatham, Kent.* (Medway 43780)

ROCHE, Harold John. Ripon Hall Ox 54. **d** 54 Liv **p** 55 Warrington for Liv. C of St Phil Southport 54-57; V of St Steph Whelley Wigan 57-63; R of Sutcombe 63-72; W w E Putford 64-72; C-in-c of Bradworthy 71-72; V of Sutcombe and Putford Dio Ex from 72; RD of Holsworthy from 80. *Sutcombe Rectory, Holsworthy, Devon.* (Bradworthy 298)

ROCHESTER, Lord Bishop of. *See* Say, Right Rev Richard David.

ROCHESTER, Assistant Bishop of. (Vacant)

ROCHESTER, Archdeacon of. *See* Palmer, Ven Derek George.

ROCHESTER, Dean of. *See* Arnold, Very Rev John Robert.

ROCKHAMPTON, Lord Bishop of. *See* Hearn, Right Rev George Arthur.

ROCKHAMPTON, Dean of. (Vacant)

ROCKLEY, Canon Thomas Alfred. b 06. Univ of Leeds, BA 29. Coll of Resurr Mirfield, 24. **d** 31 **p** 32 Southw. C of St Mary Magd Sutton-in-Ashfield 31-35; C-in-c of Ch Ch Bircotes Conv Distr 35-37; V of St Lawr Mansfield 37-45; All SS Acton 45-46; P-Lect (Vol Relig Educn) Nat S 46-49; Warden of Whan Cross Conf Ho 46-47; V of Oxton 49-55; RD of Birkenhead 53-55; Tait Missr Dio Cant 55-64; Six-Pr of Cant Cathl 55-64; Adv in Relig Educn Dio Cant 57-64; C-in-c of St Geo Preston 64-69; Can Res and Chan of Blackb 64-75; Can (Emer) from 75; Publ Pr Dio Blackb from 75. *32 Rutland Street, Blackburn, BB2 1UY.* (Blackburn 670897)

ROCKWOOD, Edmund John. Angl Th Coll BC 53. **d** and **p** 55 Yukon. R of Carmacks 55-59; P-in-c of Mayo and I of Elsa and of Keno City 59; R of Pushthrough 59-61; Meadows 61-64; C of Corner Brook 64-67; V of Princeton 67-68; R of St Nich N Burnaby Dio New Westmr from 68. *3865 Cambridge Street, Burnaby 2, BC, Canada.*

RODDA, William Reginald. b 09. Clifton Th Coll 35. **d** 36 **p** 37 Ox. C of St Matt Ox 36-39; C of Thame and Offg C-in-c of Towersey w Ashton Sandford 39-42; Chap RAFVR 42-46; R of Caundle Bishop w Caundle Marsh 46-53; V of Broadwindsor w Burstock Blackdown and Drimpton 53-59; R of Corfe Mullen 59-66; PC of St Mich AA 66-70; V of Leigh w Batcombe (and Chetnale from 55) 71-73. *115 York Road, Bradstone, Poole, Dorset.*

RODDICK, Reginald John Harmsworth. Ridley Hall Melb ACT ThL 41. **d** 41 Melb **p** 42 Geelong for Melb. C of St Thos Essendon (in c of St Jas Moonee Ponds) 41-44; Min of Cranbourne 44-47; Mitcham 47-52; I of Elwood 52-77; C of H Trin Oakleigh 77-79; Perm to Offic Dio Melb from 79. *29 Hambleton Street, Albert Park, Vic., Australia 3206.* (699-4673)

RODEN, Cyril John. b 20. **d** 81 Ely (APM). C of Clenchwarton Dio Ely from 81. *52 Jubilee Bank Road, Clenchwarton, Kings Lynn, Norf.*

RODEN, John Michael. b 37. Ripon Hall Ox 71. **d** 73 Selby for York **p** 74 York. C of Saltburn-by-the-Sea 73-77; Chap and Hd of Relig Educn St Pet Sch York from 77. *St Peter's School, York.* (York 794596)

RODERICK, Bertram David. b 22. SOC 63. **d** 66 **p** 67 S'wark. C of St Matt Surbiton 66-69; Horley (in c of St Francis) 69-72; V of St Barn Sutton New Town Dio S'wark from 73. *226 Carshalton Road, Sutton, Surrey.* (01-642 4848)

RODERICK, Charles Edward Morys. b 10. Trin Coll Ox BA 32, MA 51. Ripon Hall, Ox 38. **d** 39 **p** 40 Lon. C of St Luke Chelsea 39-46; CF (EC) 40-45; Hon CF 45; R of Denham 46-53; V of St Mich w St Phil Ches Square Lon 53-71; Chap to HM the Queen 62-80; R of Longparish w Hurstbourne Priors 71-80. *135 Little Ann, Abbotts Ann, Andover, Hants.*

RODERICK, Henry Hugh. Univ of Sask BA 59. Em Coll Sktn LTh 59, BD 68. **d** 59 **p** 60 Sask. I of Leask 59-64; Nipawin 64-69; St D Prince Albert 69-77; Fraser-Cheam Team Min Dio New Westmr from 77. *46098 Higginson Road, RR2, Sardis, BC, Canada.*

RODERICK, John Howard. b 12. St D Coll Lamp BA 33. St Mich Coll 33. **d** 35 **p** 36 Swan B. C of St Jude Swansea (for St Nich Town Hill) 35-37; St Nich-on-the-Hill Swansea 37-39; Llandilo Talybont 39-42; C-in-c of Penllergaer Conv Distr 42; St Mary Swansea 42-43; R of Cathedine 43-49; Llangyfelach w Morriston 49-58; V of Falfield 58-60; R of Rockptn 58-60; PC (V from 69) of Wotton St Mary Without (or Longlevens) 60-73; R of Bromsberrow 73-77. *24 Biddulph Way, Deer Park, Ledbury, Herefs.*

RODERICK, John Lancaster. Univ of Queensld BA 58. Gen Th Sem NY STB 62. St Mich Th Coll Crafers ACT ThL 52. **d** 51 N Queensld **p** 52 Carp for N Queensld. d Dio Adel 51-52; C of Ayr 52-54; Charters Towers 54-56; Chap St Jo Coll Brisb 56-58; R of Mareeba 58-61; Home Hill 65-67; Ingham 67-70; Burnside Dio Adel from 70. *496 Glynburn Road, Burnside, S Australia 5066.* (08-31 2940)

RODERICK, Philip David. b 49. Univ of Wales (Swansea) BA 70. United Th Coll Abth BD 77. Linc Th Coll 79. **d** 80 **p** 81 Ban. C of Llanfairisgaer w Llanddeiniolen Dio Ban from 80. *21 Menai Street, Port Dinorwic, Gwynedd, Wales.*

RODFORD, Brian George. b 50. **d** 79 **p** 80 St Alb. Hon C of St Steph City and Dio St Alb from 79; Asst Master The Leggatt's Sch Watford from 79-81; St Mary's Sch Hendon from 82; Perm to Offic Dio Lon from 82. *6 Trumpington Drive, St Albans, Herts, AL1 2JP.*

RODGER, John. b 10. Edin Th Coll 47. **d** and **p** 50 Aber. Asst Dioc Super Dio Aber 50-51; R of Meldrum 51-55; St Andr Dunmore w St Mary Grangemouth 55-60; P-in-c of St Mary Dalkeith 60-66; R of Insch 66-74; Folla Rule 66-74; Forgue 66-74; Inverurie 74-78; Alford 74-78; Auchindoir 74-78; P-in-c of Kemnay w Monymusk 74-78. *5 Park Crescent, Oldmeldrum, Aberdeen.*

RODGER, Leonard George Parman. St Paul's Th Coll Grahmstn 60. **d** 62 **p** 63 Natal. C of St Paul Durban 62-64; R of Harding 64-68; St Raph Durban 68-70; St Mary Greyville, Durban 70-73; Kingsburgh Dio Natal from 73. *Box 35 Warner Beach, Durham, Natal, S Africa.* (Kingsburgh 3854)

✠ **RODGER, Right Rev Patrick Campbell.** b 20. Late Sch of Ch Ch Ox BA 43, MA 47. Westcott Ho Cam 47. **d** 49 **p** 50 Edin. C of St Jo Evang Edin 49-51; Chap Angl Students in Edin 51-55; Study Sec SCM and Ed *Student Movement* 55-58; C of St Barn Woodside Pk 55-58; R of Kilmacolm w Bridge of Weir 58-61; Select Pr Univ of Cam 59; Executive Sec of Faith and Order World Coun of Chs 61-66; Can of Edin 66-67; Vice-Provost of Edin 66-67; Provost 67-70; Exam Chap to Bp of Edin 67-70; Cons Ld Bp of Man 24 June 70 in York Minster by Abp of York; Bps of Glas; Edin; St Andr; Dur; Ches; Blackb; Liv; Carl; Wakef; and others; Select Pr Univ of Ox 75; Trld to Ox 78. *Bishop's House, 27 Linton Road, Oxford, OX2 6UL.* (Oxford 50473)

RODGER, Raymond. b 39. Bps' Coll Cheshunt 62. **d** 63 Grimsby for Linc **p** 64 Linc. C of Frodingham 63-66; Asst Chap St Geo Hosp Lon 66-69; C of Waltham (in c of St Matt New Waltham) 69-73; V of Nocton w Dunston Dio Linc from 73; C-in-c of Potter Hanworth Dio Linc from 74; RD of

Graffoe from 81. *Nocton Vicarage, Lincoln, LN4 2BJ.* (Metheringham 20296)

RODGERS, Arthur Harold. Bp's Coll Calc. **d** 39 **p** 41 Lah. Asst Chap Lawr Mem Ghoragali Coll 38-42; IEE Chap Risalpur 42; CF (Ind) 43-47; Hon CF 46; Chap Lah Cathl 47-48; Chap to Cottesmore Sch Crawley and L to Offic Dio Chich 48-50; C of Cuckfield 50-51; R of Newtimber w Pyecombe 51-57; Trotton w Chithurst 57-73; Perm to Offic Dio Chich from 73. *Meadow Cottage, West Wittering, Chichester.*

RODGERS, Charles Burton. Angl Th Coll BC 55. **d** and **p** 58 BC. I of Alert Bay 58-61; R of Teslin 62-64; Leduc 64-68; Perm to Offic Dio BC from 76. *Box 1506, Ladysmith, BC, Canada.*

RODGERS, Cyril George Hooper. b 20. Qu Coll Birm 50. **d** 52 **p** 53 Glouc. C of Bp's Cleeve 52-56; V of Nailsworth 56-61; Chap Longford's Approved Sch Minchinhampton 56-57; CF (TA) 58-62; CF (TA-R of O) from 62; R of Upwell-Christchurch 61-66; V of Wiggenhall 66-76; RD of Lynn Marshland 68-76; Lavenham from 78; Surr 70-76; R of Woolpit Dio St E from 76. *Woolpit Rectory, Bury St Edmunds, Suff.* (Elmswell 40805)

RODGERS, David. b 26. Sarum Th Coll 63. **d** 65 Taunton for B & W **p** 66 B & W. C of Combe Down 65-68; V of Leigh Woods 68-76; R of Wellow w Foxcote and Shoscombe 76-79; C-in-c of Wookey w Henton Dio B & W from 79; C of Wells Dio B & W from 79. *Vicarage, Wookey, Wells, Somt.* (Wells 72098)

RODGERS, Frank. b 27. Linc Th Coll 69. **d** 71 Linc **p** 72 Linc. C of Alford 71-75; P-in-c of Gosberton Clough 75-80, V (w Quadring) 80-82; P-in-c of Quadring 75-80; R of S Kelsey w Holton-le-Moor Dio Linc from 80; P-in-c of Kirkby w Kingerby Dio Linc from 80; N Owersby w Thornton-le-Moor Dio Linc from 80; Usselby Dio Linc from 80. *Rectory, South Kelsey, Lincoln, LN7 6HP.* (N Kelsey 251)

RODGERS, Frank Ernest. b 46. Tyndale Hall Bris, 68. **d** 71 **p** 72 Heref. C of Madeley 71-74; Littleover 74-77; V of Clodock and Longtown w Craswall and Llanveynoe (w St Margaret's, Michaelchurch Escley and Newton from 79) Dio Heref from 77; P-in-c of St Margaret's w Michaelchurch Escley and Newton 77-79. *Longtown Vicarage, Hereford, HR2 0LD.* (Longtown Castle 289)

RODGERS, Frederic William. b 21. TCD BA 44, MA 51. **d** 45 **p** 46 Arm. C of Derryloran 45-47; Sligo 47-49; Cler V of Ch Ch Cathl Dub 49-52; Hd Master Ch Ch Cathl Choir Sch Dub 52-64; Area Sec SPG Prov of Dub 64-65; USPG 65-67; Asst Master Wesley Coll Dub from 67. *Pilot View, Dalkey, Co Dublin, Irish Republic.* (Dublin 809501)

RODGERS, John Terence Roche. Bps' Coll Cheshunt, TCD BA (Resp) 53, MA 57. **d** 57 **p** 58 Connor. C of Templecorran 57-60; Derriaghy 60-61; Antrim 61-64; R of St Steph Belf 64-79; Dunmurry Dio Connor from 79. *Rectory, Dunmurry, Belfast, N Ireland.* (Belfast 610984)

RODGERS, Richard Thomas Boycott. b 47. MRCS 70. LRCP 70. St Jo Coll Nottm Dipl Th 77. **d** 77 Repton for Derby **p** 78 Derby. C of Littleover Dio Derby from 77. *21 Shepherd Street, Littleover, Derby, DE3 6GA.* (Derby 765313)

RODGERS, Robert Harrison Grant. b 54. Univ of Sask BA 76. Em & St Chad's Coll Sktn MDiv 81. **d** 81 Qu'App. C of New Sumner Dio Qu'App from 81. *c/o 1501 College Avenue, Regina, Sask, Canada, S4P 1B8.*

RODLEY, Ian Tony. b 48. Qu Coll Birm 77. **d** 80 **p** 81 Bradf. C of Baildon Dio Bradf from 80. *9 Coach Road, Baildon, Shipley, BD17 5JE.*

RODWELL, Arthur Reginald Henry. b 21. BD (lon) 71. Westcott Ho Cam 72. **d** 72 Colchester for Chelmsf **p** 73 Chelmsf. [f Methodist Min 50 and CF 51-72]. C of Saffron Walden 72-74; V (w Wendens Ambo) 74-75; C-in-c of Littlebury 75; R of Saffron Walden w Wendens Ambo and Littlebury Dio Chelmsf from 75; RD of Saffron Walden from 78. *Rectory, Saffron Walden, Essex.* (Saffron Walden 23130)

RODWELL, Barry John. b 39. Ridley Hall Cam 67. **d** 70 **p** 71 St E. C of St Greg w St Pet Sudbury 70-73; Perm to Offic Dio Chelmsf 73-80; Asst Master Hedingham Sch 73-80; R of Sible Hedingham Dio Chelmsf from 80. *Sible Hedingham Rectory, Halstead, Essex, CO9 3LE.* (Hedingham 61118)

RODWELL, John Stanley. b 46. Univ of Leeds BSc 68. Univ of Ox Dipl Th 73. Univ of Southn PhD 74. Cudd Coll 71. **d** 74 Bris **p** 75 Blackb. Hon C of Horfield 74-75; C of Skerton 75-77; L to Offic Dio Blackb from 77. *17 Ulleswater Road, Lancaster, LA1 3PP.*

ROE, Alan Arthur. b 26. Kelham Th Coll 43. **d** 51 **p** 52 Ox. C of St Giles Reading 51-55; St Jo Evang Newbury 55-58; C-in-c of St Geo Conv Distr Wash Common Newbury 58-59; V of Gt Walsingham 59-69; V of L Walsingham w Houghton-in-the-Dale 59-69; Walsingham w Houghton-in-the-Dale 69-77; Perm to Offic Dio Nor from 77. *Waveney, Dereham Road, Colkirk, Fakenham, Norfolk, NR21 7NH* (0328-3805)

ROE, Frank Ronald. Westcott Ho Cam 55. **d** 57 **p** 58 Portsm. C of Hayling I 57-61; Chap of St John's Cathl Hong Kong 61-66; Asst Chap Miss to Seamen Hong Kong and L to Offic Dio Hong 66-76; Asst Chap St John's Cathl Hong Kong 77; R of Merredin Dio Perth from 77. *Rectory, Merredin, W Australia 6415.* (41-1086)

ROE, George Henry Edward Talbot. b 07. Selw Coll Cam BA 30, MA 35. Sarum Th Coll 30. **d** 32 **p** 33 Roch. C of H Trin Dartford 32-36; Farnham 36-40; Baldock w Bygrave (in c of Clothall) 40-46; R of Wheathampstead 46-79. *1 Owlstone Road, Cambridge.*

ROE, John Patrick. St Jo Coll Auckld LTh 64. **d** 63 **p** 64 Dun. C of Roslyn 63-66; V of Maniototo 66-71; Balclutha 71-76; Flagstaff-Brockville 76-79. *183 Shetland Street, Wakari, Dunedin, NZ.* (63-701)

ROE, Canon Joseph Thorley. b 22. AKC 49. St Bonif Coll Warm 49. Univ of Leeds Dipl Adult Educn 77. **d** 50 **p** 51 Ripon. C of Methley and Mickletown 50-53; Richmond Yorks 53-55; V of Epiph Gipton Leeds 55-60; C of E Youth Coun Tr Officer and Perm to Offic Dio Ripon 60-64; Sec Youth Dept Br Coun of Chs 64-67; Prin Lect and Sen Counsellor Bretton Hall Coll of Educn Wakef 67-73; Sec for Miss and Unity Dio Ripon 74-78; Dioc Missr and Dom Chap to Bp of Ripon 75-78; Dir of Post-Ordin Tr Dio Ripon 76-78; Can Res of Carl Cathl from 78; Dioc Dir of Tr from 78. *4 The Abbey, Carlisle, CA3 8TZ.* (Carlisle 35904)

ROE, Peter Harold. b 37. K Coll Lon and Warm AKC and BD 62. **d** 63 **p** 64 Bris. C of St Barn Knowle 63-65; Leckhampton 65-68; V of St Mary and St John Shaw Hill Saltley 68-73; St Mary Hob's Moat Dio Birm from 73. *30 Hob's Meadow, Solihull, B92 8PN.* (021-743 4955)

ROE, Robert Henry. b 22. LCP 57. Westcott Ho Cam 72. **d** 74 **p** 75 Chelmsf (APM). C of Saffron Walden Dio Chelmsf from 75. *6 Little Larchmount, Saffron Walden, Essex.*

ROE, Robin. b 28. MC 68. Trin Coll Dub BA 52, MA 55. **d** 53 **p** 54 Dub. C of Sandford Dub 53-55; CF 55-81; Hon Chap to HM the Queen 77-81; R of Merrow Dio Guildf from 81. *c/o Barclays Bank, High Street, Guildford, Surrey.*

✠ **ROE, Right Rev William Gordon.** b 32. Jes Coll Ox BA (2nd cl Mod Lang) 55, MA 57, Dipl Th (w distinc) 57, DPhil 62. St Steph Ho Ox 56. **d** 58 **p** 59 Win. C of Bournemouth 58-61; Abingdon (in c of St Mich) 61-69; Vice-Prin St Chad's Coll Dur 69-74; V of St Osw w St Mary-le-Bow & St Mary L Dur 74-80; RD of Durham 74-80; Hon Can of Dur Cathl from 79; Cons Ld Bp Suffr of Huntingdon in Westmr Abbey 1 Nov 80 by Abp of Cant; Bp's of Lon, Dur, Ely, Derby, Heref, Nor, Roch and Lich; Bp's Suffr of Stafford, Southn and Wolverhampton; and Bp's Allenby, Bulley and E J Roberts; and others. *Whitgift House, Ely, Cambs, CB7 4DP.* (Ely 2137)

ROEBUCK, Austin Vincent. b 06. Lich Th Coll 40. **d** 43 **p** 44 Sheff. C of Rossington 43-49; V of Denaby Main 49-56; Swinefleet 56-63; Lyddington w Stoke Dry (and Seaton from 66) 63-71; L to Offic Dio St A from 72. *49b Kensington Avenue, Old Colwyn, Colwyn Bay, Clwyd.*

ROEBUCK, John William. b 11. Keble Coll Ox BA 34. Cudd Coll 45. **d** 47 **p** 48 Sheff. C of St Mary w St Simon Sheff 47-49; H Trin Darnall Sheff 49-53; Miss Dio Hong 53-56; V of St Bart Sheff 57-59; Asst Master Willenhall Sch 59-61; V of Wales 61-69; R of Kirkwall w Stromness 69-77. *4 Litton Slack, Millers Dale, Buxton, Derbys.*

ROEMMELE, Michael Patrick. b 49. Univ of Dub BA 72. TCD MA 76. **d** 73 **p** 74 Arm. C of St Columba Portadown 73-77; Drumachose 77-80; Chap at Manama, Bahrain Dio Cyprus from 79. *Box 36, Manama, Bahrain.*

ROFF, Andrew Martin. b 42. Bede Coll Dur BSc 65. Westcott Ho Cam 65. **d** 70 **p** 71 Ches. C of St Mary Ches 70-73; Prec and Min Can of Blackb Cathl 73-76; C-in-c of St John Blackb 74-75; V of St Andr Longton 76-81; Chap Trin Coll Glenalmond from 81. *Trinity College, Glenalmond, Perth.*

ROFF, John Michael. b 47. St Chad's Coll Dur BSc (2nd cl Geol) 69. Westcott Ho Cam 70. **d** 72 **p** 73 Blackb. C of Lancaster 72-75; Dronfield 75-76; Team V 76-80; Team R of N Wingfield w Pilsley and Tupton Dio Derby from 80. *North Wingfield Rectory, Chesterfield, Derbys.* (Chesterfield 851181)

ROGAN, Very Rev John. b 28. Late Lightfoot and Jenkyns Scho of St Jo Coll Dur BA (2nd cl Hist) 49, MA 51, Dipl Th (w distinc) 54. Open Univ BPhil 81. **d** 54 **p** 55 Man. C of St Mich AA Ashton L 54-57; C of Sharrow and Industr Missr Dio Sheff 57-61; Sec C of E Industr C'ttee 61-66; V of Leigh 66-78; RD of Leigh 71-78; Hon Can of Man Cathl from 75; Provost of St Paul's Cathl Dundee Dio Brech from 78. *4 Richmond Terrace, Dundee, Angus.* (Dundee 68548)

ROGBITAN, Lawrence Adewole. Melville Hall, Ibad. **d** 53 **p** 54 Ibad. P Dio Ibad 54-68. *St Peter's Vicarage, Ifetedo, Ile-Ife, Nigeria.*

ROGERS, Alan Chad John. b 33. Vic. Coll Cam 2nd cl Hist Trip pt i, 55, BA (2nd cl Th Trip pt ia) 56, MA 60. Bps' Coll Cheshunt 58. **d** 60 **p** 61 Lon. C of Sudbury 60-62; R of St Barn Rodrigues 62-64; Vice-Prin St Paul's Th Coll Maur 64-66; Exam Chap to Bp of Maur 64-66; R of Rose Hill 64-66; V of St Alphege 66-71; Commiss Maur 66-67 and from 78; V of St Geo Enfield Dio Lon from 71. *706 Hertford Road, Enfield, EN3 6NR.* (Lea Valley 762581)

ROGERS, Alan David. b 24. K Coll Cam BA 47, MA 50. Cudd Coll 50. **d** 52 **p** 53 Chelmsf. C of Saffron Walden 52-54; St Mich AA Walthamstow 54-57; Lect St Paul's Coll Ambat 57-66; Commiss Antan from 69; Lect In Div Coll of Educn Weymouth 67-73; Hd of Dept of Th and Relig 73-76; Perm to Offic Dio Sarum 67-69; L to Offic from 69; Prin Lect Dorset Inst of Higher Educn from 76. *75a Buxton Road, Weymouth, Dorset, DT4 9PW.* (Weymouth 71630)

✠ **ROGERS, Right Rev Alan Francis Bright.** b 07. K Coll Lon 25. Univ of Leeds 27. MA (Lambeth) 59. Bps' Coll Cheshunt 28. **d** 30 **p** 31 Lon. C of St Steph Shepherd's Bush 30-32; H Trin (in c of St Chad) Twickenham 32-34; Chap of St Clem Curepipe 34-36; Exam Chap to Bp of Maur 35-48; Chap of St Paul Vacoas 36-44; Chap of St Andr Quatre Bornes w St John Reduit 44-48; Hon Can of St Jas Cathl. Maur 44-59; Warden of Dioc Sch Maur 43-47; Archd of Maur 46-49; V of Twickenham 49-54; Commiss Maur 48-59; Proc Conv Lon 51-59; Surr 51-59; V of Hampstead 54-59; RD of Hampstead 55-59; Cons Ld Bp of Maur in Cant Cathl 29 Sept 59 by Abp of Cant; Bp of S'wark; Bps Suffr of Kens; Willesden; Kingston T; Maidstone; Dover; and Tonbridge; Bps Simpson, Rose, Stannard and Sinker; and Bp of Madura (Ch of S India); Trld to Fulham (in c of the jurisd of N and C Eur) 66; to Edmonton (Dio Lon) 70; res 75; Asst Bp of Pet from 75; P-in-c of Wappenham w Abthorpe and Slapton 77-80; Abthorpe w Slapton Dio Pet from 80. *3 Collswell Lane, Blakesley, Towcester, Northants, NN12 8RB.* (Blakesley 502)

ROGERS, Brian Robert. b 36. Open Univ BA 80. St Jo Coll Nottm 70. **d** 72 **p** 73 Willesden for Lon. C of Ealing 72-74; Greenside 74-75; L to Offic Dio Dur from 75. *11 Edington Gardens, Clara Vale, Ryton, T & W, NE40 3SW.*

ROGERS, Brian Victor. b 50. Trin Coll Bris 75. **d** 78 **p** 79 S'wark. C of St Jo Bapt Plumstead Dio S'wark from 78. *34 Earl Rise, Plumstead, SE18.*

ROGERS, Cecil George. b 05. St D Coll Lamp BA 28. **d** 28 **p** 29 S'wark. C of St Barn Sutton 28-30; Actg C of St Mich Bournemouth 31-34; C 34-37; V of Collingbourne-Kingston 37-40; R of Okeford Fitzpaine 40-43; W Horsley 43-53; Actg Chap at Davos-Platz 46-48; C of St Mary Abbots Kens (in c of Ch Ch Victoria Rd) 75-76. *18 Hans Place, SW1.* (584 2418)

ROGERS, Charles Murray. Qu Coll Cam BA 38. Westcott Ho Cam 38. **d** 40 **p** 41 Ex. C of St Andr Plymouth 40-42; Perm to Offic Dio Ely 42; H Q Staff CMS Lon 43-46; CMS Miss Khatauli 46-47; Allahabad 47-51; Sevagram 52-53; Jyotiniketan Ashram 54-71; L to Offic Dio Luckn 67-71; Chap Interfaith and Ecumen Spirituality Dio Jer 71-80; Dio Hong from 80. *St Francis House, Tao Fong Shan, Shatin, NT, Hong Kong.*

ROGERS, Christopher. b 47. NOC 79. **d** 81 Repton for Derby. C of SS Aug Chesterfield Dio Derby from 81. *32 Davian Way, Walton, Chesterfield, S40 3JG.*

ROGERS, David. b 48. Univ Coll of N Wales (Bangor) BA (Bibl Stud) 69. Westcott Ho Cam 70. **d** 72 **p** 73 Worc. C of St Barn Rainbow Hill Worc 72-75; Ch Ch Tolladine Worc 72-75; Astwood Bank w Crabbs Cross 75-79; V of Cradley Dio Worc from 79. *9 Drews Holloway, Halesowen, W Midl, B63 2AF.* (Cradley Heath 66928)

ROGERS, Ven David Arthur. b 21. Ch Coll Cam BA 47, MA 52. Ridley Hall, Cam. **d** 49 **p** 50 Ches. C of St Geo Stockport 49-53; R of Levenshulme 53-59; V of Sedbergh (w Cautley and Garsdale from 74) 59-79; RD of Sedbergh 59-73; C-in-c of Cautley w Dowbiggin 59-60; V 60-74; C-in-c of Garsdale 59-60; V 60-74; Surr from 59; Hon Can of Bradf from 67; RD of Ewecross 73-77; C-in-c of Firbank w Howgill and Killington 73-77; Archd of Craven from 77. *'Brooklands', Bridge End, Long Preston, Skipton, BD23 4RA.* (Long Preston 334)

ROGERS, David Eland. b 17. Wycl Hall Ox 49. **d** 51 **p** 52 Pet. C of St Giles Northn 51-54; Wimbledon 54-59; V of St Pet Brockley 59-61; R of Hanworth 61-72; Chap of Whiteley Village, Walton-on-Thames from 72. *Chaplaincy, Whiteley Village, Walton-on-Thames, Surrey, KT12 4EJ.* (Weybridge 48260)

ROGERS, David Handley. McGill Univ Montr BSc (Agr) 57, BD 60. Montr Dioc Coll LTh 60. **d** and **p** 60 Montr. P-in-c of Hemmingford 60-64; R of Alert Bay 64-67; V of Golden 67-69; on leave 69-70; L to Offic Dio Calg 70-75; I of Big Country Miss Dio Calg from 75. *Box 186, Castor, Alta, Canada.*

ROGERS, David Martyn. b 56. St D Coll Lamp BA 77. AKC and BD 79. Chich Th Coll 79. **d** 80 **p** 81 St Alb. C of Hockerill Dio St Alb from 80. *17 Legion's Way, Bishops Stortford, Herts, CM23 2AU.* (0279 53915)

ROGERS, Dewi Glyndwr. b 16. St D Coll Lamp BA 37. **d** 39 **p** 40 B and W. C of Portishead 39-42; Res Warden Toc H Services Club Ox 42-43; Abth 43-44; C of Caverswall (in c of St Phil Werrington) 44-48; V of Oakamoor w Cotton 48-57; R of Mavesyn Ridware 57-81; R of Hamstall Ridware 57-81; V of Pipe Ridware 57-81. *Sumach, Ashbrook Lane, Abbots Bromley, Rugeley, Staffs WS15 3DW.*

ROGERS, Canon Donovan Charles Edgar. Clifton Th Coll 32. **d** 35 **p** 36 Chelmsf. C of Em Leyton 35-37; St Jo Evang N Woolwich 37-38; Chap RAF Manby 38-41; ME and SEAC 41-46; S Afr 47-49; ME and Halton 49-52; Chap Miss to Seamen Durban 52-57; S Afr Navy 57; Prin Chap SA Defence Force 62-73; Prov Can of Capetn from 65; R of Simonstown Dio Capetn from 73. *The Cottage, Beach Road, Noordhoek, CP, S Africa.* (8-9823)

ROGERS, Edward Lyon Beresford Cheselden. b 22. VRD 65. Keble Coll Ox BA 48, MA 51. Wells Th Coll. **d** 49 **p** 50 Leic. C of Hinckley 49-52; Knighton 52-54; Chap RNVR 53-58; RNR 58-74; V of St Mich AA Knighton 54-59; R of St Luke Old Street w St Mary Charterhouse and St Paul Clerkenwell City and Dio Lon from 59; St Giles Cripplegate St Bart Moor Lane and St Alphage London Wall City and Dio Lon from 66. *4 The Postern, Wood Street, Barbican, EC2Y 8BJ.* (01-606 3630)

ROGERS, Edwin Lyall. St Jo Coll Auckld LTh 66. **d** 65 **p** 66 Auckld. C of Devonport 65-67; Whangarei 67-71; V of Ruawai 71-74; C of H Trin Cathl Auckld 75-80; V of Sandringham Dio Auckld from 80. *38 Owairaka Avenue, Sandringham, Auckland 3, NZ.* (865-123)

ROGERS, Eric Walton. b 02. Univ of Dur 26. Qu Coll Birm 24. **d** 30 **p** 31 Lon. C of Ch Ch Clapton 30-34; Rickmansworth 34-38; Willesden (in c of St Raphael Neasden) 38-40; R of Stibbard 40-45; V of Gayton 45-55; R of Grimston 46-52; Suckley 55-61; C of Withycombe Raleigh w Exmouth 61-64; Perm to Offic Dio Ex from 65. *Red Croft, Sarlsdown Road, Exmouth, Devon, EX8 2HY.* (Exmouth 72829)

ROGERS, Eric Witham. b 1898. AKC (2nd cl) 31. **d** 31 **p** 32 Cant. C of Lydd 31-35; Chap (Eccles Est) Naini Tal 35; Luckn 35-36; Cawnpore 36-39; Chaubattia 39; Cawnpore 39-42; St D Allahabad 42-43; Agra 43-45; Jhansi 45-46; Naini Tal 46-49; Ed Luckn Dioc Chron 38-43; Hon CF 47; Archd of Luckn 47-49; R of W Dean w E Grimstead 49-61; Commiss Luckn from 49; C-in-c of W Grimstead 56-61; RD of Alderbury 59-63; V of Alderbury 61-63; Can and Preb of Ilfracombe in Sarum Cath 61-65; L to Offic Dio Nor from 66; Dio Truro 69-71. *14 Chestnut Avenue, Oulton Broad, Lowestoft, Suff.* (Lowestoft 63991)

ROGERS, Ven Evan James Gwyn. b 14. St D Coll Lamp BA 34. Wycl Coll Ox 35. **d** 37 **p** 38 Man. C of Ch Ch Walmersley 37-39; Rochdale 39-43; V of All SS Hamer 43-47; Bp's Messenger Dio Man 46; V of St Cath Wigan 47-54; St Sav Liv 54-56; Chap to Bp of Liv 54-59; Surr from 52; Proc in Conv and Mem of Ch Assembly 57-59 and 67-70; Can of Liv Cathl 58-59; Dioc Missr 54-59; V of Coniston Cold 60-67; Dir of Educn Dio Bradf 60-67; Dioc Insp of Schs Dio Bradf 60-67; Exam Chap to Bp of Sheff from 62; Hon Can of Bradf 64-67; Archd of Doncaster 67-79; Archd (Emer) from 79; V of Melton-on-the-Hill (w Barnburgh from 77) 67-78; P-in-c of Marr 67-77. *1a Spring Lane, Sprotborough, Doncaster, S Yorks, DN5 7QE.* (Doncaster 854005)

ROGERS, Canon Geoffrey John. b 04. St Cath Coll Cam 3rd cl Cl Trip pt i, 25, BA (3rd cl Cl Trip pt ii) 26, MA 33. Ridley Hall, Cam 26. **d** 27 **p** 28 Roch. C of St Jas Gravesend 27-29; CMS Miss at Isfahan 29-39; Sec CMS Iran Miss 35-39; Asst Home Sec CMS 40-41; Actg 41-42; CMS Men Cands Sec 42-50; Commiss Iran from 48; Warden of Lee Abbey Lynton 50-64; Hon Can of Cov 64-72; Can (Emer) from 72; Dioc Missr and R of Honiley w Wroxall 64-72; Perm to Offic Dio St E 73-77; P-in-c of Palgrave 77-79; RD of Hartismere 77-78; Perm to Offic Dio St E from 79. *Yew Trees, Palgrave, Diss, Norfolk.* (Diss 2443)

ROGERS, George Hutchinson. Univ of Windsor Ont B Social Work 75. Wycliffe Coll Tor MDiv 78. **d** 78 Bp M C Robinson for BC **p** 78 BC. C of St Matthias Vic 78-81; R of Cobble Hill Dio BC from 81. *1260 Chapman Road, Cobble Hill, BC, Canada.*

ROGERS, Preb George Thomas. b 1899. Keble Coll Ox BA (3rd cl Mod Hist) 21, MA 30. Bps' Coll Cheshunt 21. **d** 23 **p** 24 S'wark. C of St Bart Battersea 23-25; St Jo Evang E Dulwich 26-34; Chap (Eccles Est) 35; Cathl Ch Calc 35-36 and 39-41; Dinapur 36-37; Kidderpore 37-38; Darjeeling 38-39 and 41-43; Metrop Chap 43-48; Offg Archd of Calc

44-45; Archd 47-48; Chap of St John Calc 44-45 and 47-48; Hon CF 47; V of Hyde 48-52; H Trin Taunton 52-56; RD of Taunton 53-58; V of N Curry 56-64; Preb of Wells Cathl from 57. *35 Whitmore Road, Taunton, Somt, TA2 6DZ.* (Taunton 87729)

ROGERS, Glyndwr. b 12. St D Coll Lamp BA 35. **d** 35 **p** 36 Llan. C of Llanwonno 35-38; Barnstaple 38-42; Okehampton 42-45; V of Colebrook 45-57; R of Hittisleigh 46-57; Monk Okehampton w Broadwoodkelly 57-65; V of Kilmington (w Shute from 74) 65-77; C-in-c of Shute 73-74; Publ Pr Dio Ex from 79. *Flat A, The Berry, Thorverton, Exeter, Devon, EX5 5NT.* (Silverton 846)

ROGERS, Harold William. Moore Th Coll Syd ACT ThL 48. **d** and **p** 49 Syd. C of St Thos N Syd 49-51; P-in-c of Mukawa 51-53; C of St Jas Syd 53-55; P-in-c of Miri 55-60; C of Fulham 60-62; L to Offic Dio Syd 62-66; State Sec ABM NSW 62-66; R of Mt Hagen 66-70; V of Braybrook 70-76; P-in-c of Chiltern Dio Wang from 76. *Rectory, Albert Road, Chiltern, Vic, Australia 3683.*

ROGERS, Preb Henry Richard. Trin Coll Cam 2nd cl Th Trip pt i, 25, BA (2nd cl Th Trip pt ii) 26, MA 30. Westcott Ho Cam 25. **d** 27 **p** 28 S'wark. C of St Geo Camberwell 27-30; Dom Chap to Bp of S'wark and Publ Pr Dio S'wark 30-32; V of St Antholin Nunhead 32-35; C of H Trin Elgin (in c of St Michael) and Chap Gordonstoun Sch Elgin 35-37; C of Melksham (in c of St Andr) 38-40; CF (EC) 40-45; Asst Industr Adv to Bp of Bris and Publ Pr 62-63; Bp's Cathl Chap 64-67; R of Liddington 63-67; Preb of Lyddington from 65. *Ellary, Achahoish, Lochgilphead, Argyll.*

ROGERS, Ibrahim Mohammed Kalilu. Fourah Bay Coll. **d** 46 **p** 49 Sier L. P Dio Sier L from 46. *Makeni, Sierra Leone.*

ROGERS, Jack. St Jo Coll Manit BA and LTh 32. BD 36. **d** 32 **p** 33 Rupld. C-in-c of Snowflake 32-34; I 34-35; I of Carman 35-38; R of St Thos Winnipeg 38-45; Trail 45-56; Can of Koot 55-56; R of Royal Oak 56-66; St Matthias Vic BC 66-71. *963 Arundel Drive, Victoria, BC, Canada.*

ROGERS, Jacob. Mem Univ of Newfld BA 59. Qu Coll St John's LTh 59. **d** and **p** 58 Newfld. C of Flower's Cove 59-62; I 62-64; on leave 64-67; R of Petty Harbour 67-72; L to Offic Dio Newfld from 72. *Gould's, St John's, Newfoundland, Canada.*

ROGERS, James Andrew O'Brien. Trin Coll Dub BA and Div Test (2nd cl) 38. **d** 39 **p** 40 Down. C of Kilmegan w Maghera 39-44; Lisburn Cathl 44-46; R of Acton 46-51; C-in-c of Cleenish 51-56; R 56-59; R of Sallaghy 59-67 and from 74; Drumkeeran 67-73. *Sallaghy Rectory, Lisnaskea, Enniskillen, Co Fermanagh, N Ireland.* (Lisnaskea 372)

ROGERS, John. b 34. St D Coll Lamp BA (2nd cl Th) 55. Or Coll Ox BA (3rd cl Th) 58, MA 61. St Steph Ho Ox 57. **d** 59 **p** 60 Llan. C of St Martin Roath 59-63; St Sidwell Lodge 63-65; P-in-c of H Redeemer Ruimveldt 65-66; V 66-69; Wismar 69-71; Caldicot 71-77; Monmouth Dio Mon from 77; RD of Monmouth from 81. *Vicarage, The Parade, Monmouth, NP5 3PA.* (Monmouth 3141)

ROGERS, John Alfred Clarence. b 02. Late Exhib of Trin Coll Cam Hist Trip pt i, 25, BA 26, MA 30. **d** 27 Chelmsf for Roch **p** 27 Roch. C of St Alb Dartford 27-34; V of H Redeemer Lamorbey 34-48; R of Hunton 48-56; V of Hindhead 56-71; Perm to Offic Dio Sarum from 73. *St Alban's Cottage, Broadwindsor, Beaminster, Dorset, DT8 3QQ* (Broadwindsor 68407)

ROGERS, John Arnold. b 34. St D Coll Lamp BA 57. **d** 59 **p** 60 Mon. C of Blaenavon 59-62; Bassaleg (in c of St Anne) 62-67; St Paul w St Steph Old Ford Bow 67-73; C-in-c 73-75; V 75-79; Hampton Dio Lon from 79. *St Mary's Vicarage, Church Street, Hampton, Middx, TW12 2EB.* (01-979 3071)

ROGERS, John Coulson. b 07. Keble Coll Ox BA 30, MA 41. Chich Th Coll 40. **d** 41 **p** 42 Carl. [f Solicitor] C of St Jas Whitehaven 41-44; St Jo Bapt Upperby Carl 44-47; Dom Chap to Bp of Carl 44-47; R of Patterdale 47-60; RD of Penrith 60; Chap at Helsinki and Moscow 60-62; R of Rockingham w Caldecote 62-67; Patterdale 67-76; RD of Weldon 65-67; Chap to Sheriff of Northn 66. *Glenridding House, Glenridding, Nr Penrith, CA11 0PG.* (Glenridding 421)

ROGERS, John Iorweth. b 17. St D Coll Lamp BA (3rd cl Hist) 39. Ripon Hall, Ox 39. **d** 41 **p** 42 Wakef. C of Sandel Magna 41-44; LPr Dio Chelmsf 44; C of H Ap Leic 44-46; LPr Dio Derby from 59; Asst Master Normanton Sch Buxton 46-71; Hd Master from 71. *Normanton School, Buxton, Derbys.*

ROGERS, John Robin. b 36. St Alb Min Tr Scheme 78. **d** 81 St Alb (NSM). C of St Jo Digswell Dio St Alb from 81. *69 Oakdale, Welwyn Garden City, Herts, AL8 7QP.*

ROGERS, Canon Joseph Henry. CD 58. Hur Coll STh 60. **d** and **p** 60 Niag. R of Wainfleet 60-65; Good Shepherd Hamilton 65-74; St Andr Hamilton Dio Niag from 65; Dir St Matt Ho Hamilton from 74; Hon Can of Niag from 79. *130 Riverdale Avenue, Hamilton, Ont., Canada.* (416-561 6951)

ROGERS, Keith Frederick. b 10. Keble Coll Ox BA 33, MA 37. Chich Th Coll 34. **d** 36 **p** 37 Win. C of Milton 36-41; Alton 41-43; Charlton Kings 43-46; R of Taynton 46-54; R of Tibberton 46-54; Rodborough 54-61; V of Methwold 61-64; PC of Chalford 64-70; R of Chilthorne Domer w Yeovil Marsh and Thorne Coffin 71-75. *Address temp unknown.*

ROGERS, Kenneth. b 33. Cudd Coll 68. **d** 69 Truro **p** 70 Bp Lash for Truro. C of Perranzabuloe 69-71; St Paul Truro 71-74; P-in-c of St Geo Mart City and Dio Truro from 74; RD of Powder from 81. *St George's Vicarage, St George's Road, Truro, Cornw, TR1 3JE.* (Truro 2630)

ROGERS, Kenneth George. b 41. ACT ThL 73. Ridley Coll Melb 71. **d** 74 **p** 75 Melb. C of St Jas Ivanhoe 74-76; R of Ceduna Dio Willoch from 76. *Box 162, Ceduna, S Australia 5690.* (Ceduna 54)

ROGERS, Leslie Vernon. b 12. AKC 35. **d** 35 **p** 36 Pet. C of Woodford Halse 35-37; Min Can of Pet Cathl 37-42; C of St Mark Pet 37-42; V of Spratton w L Creaton 42-47; R of Irthlingborough 47-66; Orton Longueville w Botolph Bridge 66-81; L to Offic Dio Ely from 81. *478 Oundle Road, Orton Longueville, Peterborough, PE2 0DE.*

ROGERS, Leslie William George. d 56 **p** 57 Wel. C of Waiwhetu 56-59; V of Wainuiomata 59-62; Berhampore 62-68; Martinborough 68-75; Perm to Offic Dio Wel from 75. *Clareville, Wairarapa, NZ.*

ROGERS, Llewelyn. St D Coll Lamp BA 59. St Mich Coll Llan. **d** 61 **p** 62 St A. C of Holywell 61-64; Hawarden 64-70; R of Bodfari 70-73; V of Rhos-y-Medre 73-77; Llansantffraid-yn-Mechain Dio St A from 77. *Vicarage, Llansantffraid, Powys.* (Ll'ffraid 244)

ROGERS, Martin Stephen. b 28. St Edm Hall, Ox BA 50, MA. 54. Cudd Coll 50. **d** 52 **p** 53 Ox. C of St Mary Virg Reading 52-54; Buxton Derby 54-57; Perm to Offic Dio N Queensld 58; Chap Melb Dioc Centre 58-62; Dom Chap and Exam Chap to Abp of Melb 62-64; Chap Littlemore Hosp Ox 65-74; Lect Cudd Coll 65-73; M Dept of Educn Cam Univ 73-76; Chap Coll of Ripon and York St John from 76. *c/o The College, Lord Mayor's Walk, York, YO3 7EX.* (York 56771)

ROGERS, Maurice George Walden. b 23. K Coll Lon and Warm AKC 51. **d** 52 **p** 53 St Alb. C of All SS Bedford 52-56; Southfields 56-58; Chingford 58-61; V of St Luke Gt Ilford 61-72; St Barn Woodford Dio Chelmsf from 72. *127 Snakes Lane East, Woodford Green, Essex.* (01-504 4687)

ROGERS, Michael Hugh Walton. b 52. AKC and BD 73. St Aug Coll Cant 74. **d** 75 Chich **p** 76 Lewes for Chich. C of St Andr Eastbourne 75-78; Uppingham w Ayston Dio Pet from 78. *4 Johnson Road, Uppingham, Leics.* (Uppingham 2640)

ROGERS, Noel Desmond. b 26. TD 71. St D Coll Lamp BA 51. **d** 53 **p** 54 St A. C of Rhyl 53-58; V of St Geo Everton 58-64; Chap John Bagot Hosp 58-64; CF (TAVR) 59-75; CF (R of O) 75-81; R of Newton-in-Makerfield 64-74; V of Rostherne w Bollington Dio Ches from 74. *Rostherne Vicarage, Knutsford, Chesh.*

ROGERS, Percival Hallewell. b 52. b 12. MBE (Mil) and Men in Disp (twice) 45. St Edm Hall Ox BA 35, MA 46. Bps' Coll Cheshunt. **d** 46 **p** 47 St Alb. Asst Master Haileybury Coll 36-52; Chap 52-54; Hd Master Portora R Sch Enniskillen 54-73; Chap Gresham Sch Holt 74-75; Dean Internat Acad for Continuous Educn Sherborne 75-76; in Amer Ch 76-80. *Moyglass Old School, Springfield, Enniskillen, N Ireland.* (036-589200)

ROGERS, Philip Gordon. b 31. Lich Th Coll 62. **d** 64 Blackb **p** 65 Burnley for Blackb. C of St Barn Morecambe 64-67; Bingley (in c of St Lawr Eldwick) 67-70; V of Cross Roads w Lees 70-76; St Martin Heaton Dio Bradf from 76. *Vicarage, Haworth Road, Bradford, W Yorks, BD9 6LL.* (Bradford 43004)

ROGERS, Philip John. b 52. Univ of Nottm BTh 79. St Jo Coll Nottm 76. **d** 79 **p** 80 Man. C of St Bride Stretford Dio Man from 79. *3 Blair Street, Old Trafford, Manchester, M16 9AZ.* (061-226 8022)

ROGERS, Richard Anthony. b 46. Ex Coll Ox BA (2nd cl Th) 69. Univ of Birm Dipl Th 70. Qu Coll Birm 70. **d** 71 **p** 72 Birm. C of St Jas Shirley 71-74; Chap of Solihull Sch 74-78; Hon C of The Cotteridgr Dio Birm from 79. *51 Lomas Drive, Northfield, Birmingham, B31 5LR.*

ROGERS, Robert. b 42. Ridley Hall Cam 69. **d** 70 Warrington for Liv **p** 71 Liv. C of St D Childwall 70-73; Huntington York 73-76; R of Brayton Dio York from 76. *Brayton Rectory, Selby, N Yorks, YO8 9HE.* (Selby 703390)

ROGERS, Canon Robert Victor Allan. Trin Coll Tor 48. **d** 51 **p** 52 Ott. C of Perth 51-52; R of Bearbrook 52-53 and 55-58; C of St Pet w Merivale Ott 53-55; Fitzroy Harbour 58-65; R of Ch of Resurr Ott 65-67; Iroquois 67-74; St Paul Ott 74-78; Hon Can of Ott from 78; Chap Dio Ott from 78. *611-1081 Ambleside Drive, Ottawa, Ont., Canada* (613-828 7489)

ROGERS, Ronald James. Univ of Bris BA (2nd cl Gen) 56. St Cath S Ox BA (3rd cl Th) 58, MA 65. Wycl Hall, Ox 56. **d** 58 Nor **p** 59 Thetford for Cant. C of St Pet Gt Yarmouth 58-62; St Mary Newington 67-69; Asst Master Starcross Sch Islington 68-76; Burlington Danes Sch 76-78; C of Our Lady and St Nich City and Dio Liv from 78. *Parish Church, Old Churchyard, Liverpool, L2 8TZ.* (051-236 5287)

ROGERS, Sidney Roy. b 46. Univ of Natal BSc 69. Univ of Nottm Dipl Th 79. Linc Th Coll 78. **d** 80 **p** 81 Matab. C of Riverside Bulawayo Dio Matab from 80. *PO Box 2422, Bulawayo, Zimbabwe.*

ROGERS, Thomas Alan. b 42. Univ of Arizona BA 65. Trin Coll Tor STB 71. **d** and **p** 71 Niag. C of St Luke Burlington 71-73; Welland 73-76; on leave. *Apt 1218, 50 Mississauga Valle, Mississauga, Ont, Canada.*

ROGERS, Thomas George. St Francis Coll Brisb 63. **d** 64 **p** 65 Rockptn. C of St Paul's Cathl Rockptn 64-69; R of Mt Morgan 69-73; V of Keppel Dio Rockptn from 73. *PO Box 197, Yeppoon, Queensland, Australia 4703.* (079-39 1226)

ROGERS, Thomas More Fitzgerald. b 13. **d** 62 **p** 63 Cant. C of St Dunstan w H Cross Cant 62-64; Chap Rochdale Distr Adult Deaf and Dumb S 64-65; RADD West Ham 65-70; Redhill Surrey from 71; Perm to Offic Dio S'wark from 71; Chap to Deaf and Dumb Dio Guildf 69-72; Dio Cant 72-77. *417 Sedlescombe Road North, St Leonards-on-Sea, E Sussex, TN37 7PD.* (Hastings 751913)

ROGERS, Vernon Donald. b 12. Keble Coll Ox BA (2nd cl Mod Hist) 34, MA 40. Ely Th Coll 35. **d** 36 **p** 37 Liv. C of St Mich AA Wigan 36-38; Burford w Fulbrook 38-71; R of Combe-in-Teignhead w Stoke-in-Teignhead 71-77; Perm to Offic Dio B & W from 77. *14 North Road, Wells, Somt, BA5 2TJ.*

ROGERS, Victor Alvin. Codr Coll Barb 66. **d** 69 **p** 70 Barb. C of St Paul Barb 69-70; St Phil Barb 70-75. *c/o Massiah Street, St John, Barbados, W Indies.*

ROGERS, Vivian Francis Edward. b 27. Oak Hill Th Coll 61. **d** 63 **p** 64 Ox. C of Iver 63-68; R of Norton Fitzwarren 68-77; V of Grassendale Dio Liv from 77. *63 Salisbury Road, Cressington Park, Liverpool, L19 0PH.* (051-427 1474)

ROGERS, William Arthur. b 41. Univ of Lon BA 64. Chich Th Coll 79. **d** 81 Win. C of Chandler's Ford Dio Win from 81. *10 Trevose Close, Chandler's Ford, Eastleigh, Hants, SO5 3EB.* (Chandler's Ford 65581)

✠ **ROGERSON, Right Rev Barry.** b 36. Univ of Leeds, BA (2nd cl Th) 60. Wells Th Coll 60. **d** 62 **p** 63 Dur. C of S Shields 62-65; St Nich Bp Wearmouth 65-67; Lect Lich Th Coll 67-71; Vice-Prin 71-72; L to Offic Dio Lich 68-72; Lect Sarum and Wells Th Coll 72-74; V of Wednesfield 75-79; Team R 79; Visiting Lect Bp Patteson Th Centre Guadalcanal Solomon Is 78; Cons Bp Suffr of Wolverhampton in St Paul's Cathl Lon 25 April 79 by Abp of Cant; Bps of Lich, Glouc, Ox, Chich, Derby, Leic, Newc T, Nor and St E; Bps Suffr of Barking, Dorch, Dudley, Fulham and Gibr, Grantham, Grimsby, Hertf, Jarrow, Lewes, Stafford and Taunton; and others; Hon Can of Lich Cathl from 79. *61 Richmond Road, Wolverhampton, WV3 9JH.* (Wolverhampton 23008)

ROGERSON, Christopher John Donald. b 31. Bps' Coll Cheshunt 55. **d** 57 **p** 58 Newc T. C of St Pet Monkseaton 57-59; St Matt Newc T 59-60; Blakenall Heath (in c of St Chad Walsall) 60-62; R of Aberlour 62-64; V of Skirlaugh w Long Riston 64-69; S Bank 69-74; Surr 69-74; Sen Chap Newc T Gen Hosp 74-75. *180 Osborne Road, Newcastle-upon-Tyne, NE2.* (N-u-T 812379)

ROGERSON, Clarence Edward. b 16. Edin Th Coll 49. **d** 52 Lanc for Blackb **p** 53 Blackb. C of St Pet Fleetwood 52-54; Padiham w Higham 54-57; V of St Mich AA Blackb 57-66; Asst Master Gateacre Sch Liv 66-68; Rhodesway Gr Sch Bradf from 68. *20 West Bank Rise, Keighley, Yorks.*

ROGERSON, Colin Scott. b 30. Univ of St Andr MA 55. Edin Th Coll. **d** 57 **p** 58 Newc T. C of St Anthony Newc T 57-59; St Geo Newc T 59-63; Wooler 63-67; V of St Aug Tynemouth 67-75; C of St Marg (in c of St John Neville's Cross) City and Dio Dur from 75. *St John's Vicarage, The Avenue, Durham, DH1 4DX.* (Durham 44260)

ROGERSON, David George. b 38. St Chad's Coll Dur BA 60, Dipl Th 63. **d** 63 **p** 64 Newc T. C of St Luke Wallsend 63-67; Delaval (in c of St Mich AA New Hartley) 67-70; V of St Mary Magd Long Benton 70-80; N Sunderland Dio Newc T from 81; Warden Newc and Dur Dioc Youth Hostel from 81. *North Sunderland Vicarage, Seahouses, Northumb, NE68 7TT.* (Seahouses 720202)

ROGERSON, Derek Russell. b 23. Univ of Lon BA 51. Sarum Th Coll 51. **d** 53 **p** 54 S'wark. C of Ch of Ascen Balham Hill 53-56; Mottingham 56-60; R of Sapcote 60-64; St Steph Harpurhey 64-70; V of Good Shepherd, Rochdale 70-74; Asst Chap of HM Pris Strangeways Man 74-76; Kirkham from 76. *HM Prison, Kirkham, Lancs, PR4 2RA.* (0772-684343)

ROGERSON, John William. b 35. Late Pri of Univ of Man BD (1st cl) 61, DD 75. Linacre Ho Ox Pusey and Ellerton Hebr Scho 62, BA (2nd cl Or Stud) 63, Kennicott Hebr Fell and Mew Rabbinical Hebr Scho 63, MA 67. Ripon Hall Ox 61. **d** 64 **p** 66 Dur. C of St Osw Dur 64-67; Lect in Th Univ of Dur 64-75; Sen Lect 75-79; Prof of Bibl Stud Univ of Sheff from 79. *59 Marlborough Road, Sheffield, S10 2TN.*

ROHIM, Rudolph. b 28. Em & St Chad's Coll Sktn. **d** 71 **p** 72 Trinid. C of Plymouth Tobago 71-73; R of Rio Claro Trinid 74-75; Good Shepherd w Avonlea 75-79; Lakeside Dio Qu'App from 79. *Box 128, Outlook, Sask, Canada.*

ROKEBY, Richard Samuel Collinson. Univ of Tor BSA 54. Hur Coll BTh 65. **d** and **p** 65 Niag. C of Ascen Hamilton 65-68; R of Jordan 68-71; St Columba St Catharines, Dio Niag from 71. *12 Nancy Drive, St Catharine's, Ont., Canada.* (416-934 0361)

ROKEBY-THOMAS, Howard Rokeby. Wycl Coll Tor LTh 38. **d** 34 Arctic **p** 34 Tor for Arctic. Miss at Cambridge Bay 34-39; I of Walter's Falls w Bognor Beaverdale and Fairmount 39-41; Chap CASF 41-45; R of Wyoming w Camlachie and Wanstead 45-48; Ch Ch Port Stanley 48-60; Perm to Offic Dio Tor 61-69; R of Kirkton 69-72. *74 Jackson Avenue, Kitchener, Ont, Canada.*

ROLAND-SHRUBB, David John. b 38. Roch Th Coll 68. **d** 70 Bradwell for Chelmsf **p** 71 Chelmsf. C of Corringham 70-72; Burgh 72-74; CF 74-78; P-in-c of St Paul Eastthorpe Mirfield 78-81; R of Caister-on-Sea Dio Nor from 81; Hon Min Can of Nor from 82. *Caister Rectory, Norf, NR30 5EH.* (0493-720287)

ROLFE, Charles Edward. b 34. Wells Th Coll 68. **d** 70 **p** 71 B & W. C of Twerton-on-Avon Bath 70-79; Team V of Wellington and Distr Dio B & W from 79. *22 Dyers Close, West Buckland, Wellington, Somt.* (Wellington 4925)

ROLFE, Edgar James. St Jo Coll Morpeth, ACT ThL 52. **d** and **p** 53 C & Goulb. C of St Paul Canberra 53-54; R of Delegate 54-57; Binda 57-62; Chap RAN 62-78; L to Offic Dios C & Goulb and Syd 62-78; R of Moruya 78-80; Perm to Offic Dio C & Goulb from 81. *1 Broadby Close, Spence, ACT, Australia 2615.*

ROLFE, Joseph William. b 37. Qu Coll Birm 78. **d** 81 Cov. C of St Greg Tredington Dio Cov from 81. *35 Manor Lane, Shipston-on-Stour, Warws, CV36 4EF.*

ROLL, Sir James William Cecil Bt. b 12. Chich Th Coll 34. **d** 37 **p** 38 Lon. C of St Jas Gt Bethnal Green 37-40; St Matt Vic Dks 40-44; East Ham 44-58; V of St Jo Div Becontree Dio Chelmsf from 58. *34 Castle Road, Dagenham, Essex.* (01-592 5409)

ROLLE, Warren Harold. b 41. AKC & BD 73. Univ of W Indies, LTh 68. Codr Coll Barb. **d** 68 Barb for Nass **p** 69 Nass. C of St Agnes Nass 68-70 and from 73; Asst Master St Jo Coll Nass from 73. *PO Box N-3597, Nassau, Bahamas, W Indies.*

ROLLETT, Robert Henry. b 39. Univ of Leeds BA 61. Linc Th Coll 77. **d** 79 Huntingdon for Ely **p** 80 Ely. C of Littleport w Little Ouse Dio Ely from 79. *25 Victoria Street, Littleport, Cambs, CB6 1LU.* (Ely 861419)

ROLLINSON, Frederick Mark. b 24. **d** 71 **p** 72 Stepney for Lon. C of St Mary Bow 71-75; St Barn Bethnal Green Dio Lon 75-76; P-in-c from 76. *11 Vivian Road, E3.* (01-980 3568)

ROLLINSON, Canon John Knighton. b 14. Univ of Sheff BMus 36, FRCO 34, AKC 48. **d** 49 **p** 50 Derby. C of Ilkeston 49-53; Wirksworth w Carsington 53-55; PC of Dethick w Lea and Holloway 55-64; R of Whittington 64-81; P-in-c of New Whittington 78-81; Hon Can of Derby Cathl 80-81; Can (Emer) from 81; Perm to Offic Dio Derby from 81. *75 Yew Tree Drive, Somersall, Chesterfield, Derbys, S40 3NB.* (Chesterfield 68647)

ROLLS, Douglas Maurice. St Jo Coll Morpeth, 61. **d** 62 **p** 63 River. C of Broken Hill 62-65; Griffith 65-66; P-in-c of Urana 66-67; Ariah Pk 67-71; R of Hillston 71-74; Berrigan-Mulwala Dio River from 74. *Box 56, Berrigan, NSW, Australia 2712.* (Berrigan 57)

ROLLS, Robert Laidlaw. CD 64. Niag Univ MA 57. Moore Th Coll Syd ACT ThL 44. **d** and **p** 45 Syd. C of St Andr Summer Hill Syd 45; Chap Trin Gr Sch Syd 45-46; C of St Geo Kidderminster 47; Chap Hartlebury Gr Sch and Perm to Offic Dio Worc 47-48; C of St Clem Ox 48-49; St Geo Hamilton Ont 49-50; R of St Phil Hamilton and Chap Hamilton Gaol 50-53; L to Offic Dio Syd 51-53; I of St Martin Niag Falls 53-68; Fort Vermilion 72-73; Ignace 73-75; Dryden Dio Keew from 75. *50 Van Horne Avenue, Dryden, Ont., Canada.* (807-223 5592)

ROLPH, Michael John. b 47. Waterloo Lutheran Univ Ont BA 70. Hur Coll Lon MDiv 73. **d** and **p** 73 Niag. C of St Mary's Hamilton 73-74; Dir of Programme Dio Niag from 75; P-in-c of Good Shepherd Hamilton 75-77; I of Iroquois Falls Dio Moos from 77. *Box 47, Iroquois Falls, Ont, Canada.*

ROLPH, Reginald Lewis George. b 29. Open Univ BA 74.

Bps' Coll Cheshunt, 55. **d** 58 **p** 59 Lon. C of Perivale 58-61; Wokingham 61-63; Letchworth 63-78; Perm to Offic Dio St Alb from 78. *104 Kirkeby, Letchworth, Herts.* (Letchworth 4596)

ROLSTON, Cyril Willis Matthias. TCD 66. **d** 68 **p** 69 Arm. C of Portadown 68-71; I of Loughgilly w Clare 71-81; Moy w Charlemont Dio Arm from 81; Dioc Dir of Ordinands Dio Arm from 72. *Rectory, Moy, Co Tyrone, N Ireland.* (Moy 312)

ROLSTON, John Ormsby. b 28. TCD Bp Forster Pri (1st) 50, BA (Resp) 51, MA 59, Div Test (1st cl) 51, BD 63. **d** 51 Connor **p** 52 Kilm for Connor. C of St Mary Magd Belf 51-55; St Columba Knock 55-59; C-in-c of Gilnahirk 59-63; R 63-66; St Jas Belf Dio Connor from 66; St Silas Belf Dio Connor from 79; Priv Chap to Bp of Down 65-67; RD of N Belf from 71. *3 Cliftonville Road, Belfast, BT14 6JJ, N Ireland.* (Belfast 744836)

ROLT, Canon Eric Wilfrid. b 17. Pemb Coll Cam BA 39, MA 45. Ely Th Coll 39. **d** 40 **p** 41 Wakef. C of Elmsall 40-47; Camberwell 47-50; V of All SS Battersea Pk 50-56; St Jo Evang E Dulwich 56-69; R of Campsea Ashe w Marlesford Dio St E from 69; C-in-c of Parham w Hacheston Dio St E from 70; RD of Loes from 78; Hon Can of St E Cathl from 79. *Marlesford Rectory, Woodbridge, Suff.* (Wickham Market 746295)

ROLTON, Patrick Hugh. b 49. Sarum Wells Th Coll 71. **d** 74 Roch **p** 75 Tonbridge for Roch. C of St Pet and St Marg Roch 74-79; Edenbridge 79-80; R of N Cray Dio Roch from 80. *2 St James Way, Sidcup, Kent.* (01-300 1655)

ROM, Hugh. b 22. SOC 77. **d** 80 Willesden for Lon **p** 81 Lon. Hon C of Hanger Hill Dio Lon from 80. *187 Linden Court, Brunswick Road, W5 1AL.*

ROM, Norman Charles. b 24. SOC 63. **d** 66 **p** 67 Guildf. C of Leatherhead 66-71; Chap HM Pris Cant 71-74; Pentonville from 74. *Chaplain, HM Prison, Pentonville, N7 8TT.*

ROMANES, William. b 11. Magd Coll Cam BA 35, MA 39. Ripon Hall, Ox 35. **d** 36 **p** 37 Birm. C of St Barn (in c of St Chad) Erdington 36-40; Offg C-in-c of Water Orton 40-45; Dioc Chap (in c of St Sav Hockley) Birm 45-49; R of Newton Regis w Seckington 49-52; V of Em Sparkbrook 52-64; Bp Latimer Mem Ch Birm 64-71; R of Ringsfield w Redisham Beccles 71-76; Perm to Offic Dio Birm from 77. *10 Shireland Close, Handsworth Wood, Birmingham, B20 1AN.*

ROMANIS, John Espenett. Univ of Melb BA 33, MA 35. ACT ThL 34. **d** 34 **p** 36 Melb. C of St Mark E Brighton 34-38; Chap RAN 38-43; C of St Paul's Cathl Melb 43-45; I of St Mark E Brighton 45-59; H Trin Oakleigh 59-76; C in Dept of Evang and Ex Dio Melb from 76. *3 Quarry Road, Mitcham, Vic, Australia 3132.* (873-2827)

ROMANS, Philip Charles. b 06. Peterho Cam BA 28, MA 32. Ripon Hall, Ox 65. **d** 65 Ely **p** 66 Huntingdon for Ely. C of Haddenham 65-67; V of Waresley 67-73; C-in-c of Abbotsley Dio Ely 67-68; V 68-73. *61 Kent Road, Harrogate, Yorks.* (Harrogate 66331)

RONAYNE, Peter Henry. b 34. FCA 68. Oak Hill Th Coll 64. **d** 66 **p** 67 Ox. C of Chesham 66-69; H Trin w St Matt Worthing 69-74; V of Shoreditch Dio Lon from 74. *36 Hoxton Square, N1 6NN.* (01-739 2063)

RONCHETTI, Quentin Marcus. b 56. Ripon Coll Cudd 79. **d** 80 Chich **p** 81 Lewes for Chich. C of St Mary Eastbourne Dio Chich from 80. *6 Bay Pond Road, Eastbourne, E Sussex.* (Eastbourne 28680)

RONE, James. b 35. St Steph Ho Ox 79. **d** 80 Dorchester for Ox **p** 81 Ox. C of Stony Stratford Dio Ox from 80. *9 Bunsty Court, Galley Hill, Stony Stratford, Milton Keynes, MK11 1NJ.*

RONEY, John Alexander. Univ of Sask BSc 49. Trin Coll Tor. **d** 55 **p** 56 Tor. C of Wexford 55-56; St Clem Eglinton Tor 56-60; R of Brighton and of Colborne 60-63; I of St Giles Barrie 63-69; R of Whitby Dio Tor from 69. *200 Byron Street West, Whitby, Ont., Canada.* (416-668 5101)

RONO, Arthur. **d** 78 New Hebr **p** 80 Vanuatu. P Dio New Hebr 78-80; Dio Vanuatu from 80. *Alolgalato, Matwo, Vanuatu.*

ROOK, Canon William Noel. Moore Th Coll Syd. **d** 26 **p** 27 Syd. C of St Paul Chatswood 27-28; Asst P of Far West Miss 29-30; C of Hornsby 31-32; Lane Cove 32-33; Rockdale 33-37; R of Milton 33-37; St Paul Cant 37-49; Epping 49-69; Hon Can of Syd from 65; L to Offic Dio Syd from 69. *13 Langford Road, Wentworth Falls, NSW, Australia 2782.* (57-1173)

ROOKE, George William Emmanuel. b 12. Univ of Lon BA 33, BD 34. K Coll Lon Bp Robertson Pri 33, AKC 34. **d** 35 **p** 36 Roch. C of Milton-next-Gravesend 35-38; Walsall 38-44; V of L Drayton 44-54; R of St Chad Ladybarn 54-66; St Swith (St Martin from 76) Worc 66-77; C-in-c of St Paul Worc 67-74. *106 Church Road, Hereford, HR1 1RT.*

ROOKE, Henry John Warburton. b 10. Ch Ch Ox BA (4th cl Physics) 32, MA 45. Wycl Hall, Ox 34. **d** 35 **p** 36 Roch. C of Hayes 35-40; CF (EC) 40-46; Perm to Offic at St Geo Edgbaston Birm 48; C 49-51; V of Weobley w Sarnesfield 51-69; RD of Weobley 64-67; Hon Chap to High Sheriff of Herefs 66-67. *Hammer Vale Cottage, Hammer Vale, Haslemere, Surrey, GU27 1QG.* (Haslemere 51523)

ROOKE, John George Michael. b 47. St Jo Coll Dur BA 72, Dipl Th 74. Cranmer Hall Dur 71. **d** 74 Warrington for Liv **p** 75 Liv. C of Skelmersdale 74-78; Team V (Missr from 79) of Speke 78-81; Chap in Liv Industr Miss from 81. *47 Arklow Drive, Hale Village, Nr Widnes.*

ROOKE, Oliver James. SS Coll Cam 2nd cl Hist Trip pt i 30, BA (2nd cl Hist Trip pt ii) 31, MA 42. **d** 44 Chelmsf **p** 45 Barking for Chelmsf. C of Harlow 44-47; V of Westhall 47-51; Holkham w Egmere and Waterden R 51-55; Docking 55-61; V of Fring 56-61; R of Gt Massingham 61-77; R of Harpley 63-77; Perm to Offic Dio St E from 77. *Eastholme, Walberswick, Southwold, Suff.*

ROOKE, Patrick William. b 55. Sarum Wells Th Coll 75. **d** 78 **p** 79 Connor. C of Mossley 78-81; Ballywillan Dio Connor from 81. *17 Victoria Street, Portrush, Co Antrim, N Ireland.* (Portrush 82268)

ROOKE, Thomas Herbert. Univ of Tor McMaster Univ BA 59. Wycl Coll Tor LTh 56. **d** 55 **p** 56 Tor. C of St Leon Tor 55-56; Ascen Hamilton 56-59; I of Clarkson 59-75; Mississauga Dio Tor from 75. *1532 Wembury Road, Mississauga, Ont., Canada.* (416-822 0422)

ROOKWOOD, Colin John. b 40. TCD BA 64, MA 68. Univ of Lon Dipl Th 69. Clifton Th Coll 67. **d** 70 Warrington for Liv **p** 71 Liv. C of Eccleston 70-75; V of St Jo Evang Penge Dio Roch from 75; Surr from 79. *Vicarage, St John's Road, SE20 7EQ.* (01-778 6176)

ROOM, Canon Frederick John. b 24. St Jo Coll Ox BA 49, MA 53. Wells Th Coll 49. **d** 51 **p** 52 Man. C of Ch Ch Bradf Man 51-54; St Marg Halliwell 54-56; Farnham Royal 56-58; C-in-c of St Mich Conv Distr Farnham Royal 58-70; V in Thetford Group Dio Nor from 70; Sen Industr Missr Dio Nor from 75; Hon Can of Nor from 77. *20 White Hart Street, Thetford, Norfolk.* (Thetford 2338)

ROONEY, James. b 31. TCD BA 58. **d** 58 **p** 59 Connor. C of St Matt Belf 58-60; Coleraine 60-61; I of Ballintoy 61-66; C-in-c of Rathlin 62-66; I of Craigs w Dunaghy and Killagan 67-74; R of St Matt Shankill Belf Dio Connor from 74; RD of Mid-Belfast from 80. *51 Ballygomartin Road, Belfast, BT13 3LA.* (Belf 744325)

ROONEY, Leslie Francis. b 16. Univ of Lon BSc 36. BD 40, AKC 40. **d** 40 **p** 41 Dur. C of Harton 40-43; St Phil Georgetown 43-44; V of Bartica w Potaro and Mazaruni 44-50; Miss Dio Gui 50-53; Metrop Area Sec SPG 53-54; V of S Benfleet 54-61; Chap and Tutor St Mark's Coll Mapanza 61-64; Chap St Mary Magd Sch Richmond Surrey 64-66; Hostel of God S'wark 66-71; Cathl Sch Ex from 72; Publ Pr Dio Ex from 72; Dep P-V Ex Cathl from 73. *1A Tuns Lane, Silverton, Exeter, Devon, EX5 4HY.* (Exeter 860137)

ROOSE-EVANS, James Humphrey. b 27. St Benet's Hall Ox BA 52, MA 56. **d** and **p** 81 Heref (NSM). C of Kington Dio Heref from 81. *71 Belsize Park Gardens, NW3.*

ROOSE-FRANCIS, Leslie. b 18. Magd Coll Ox BA 48, MA 52. Westcott Ho Cam 48. **d** 49 **p** 50 Man. C of Rochdale 49-52; Odiham w S Warnborough 52-54; V of Awbridge (w Mottisfont from 55) 54-60; R of Mottisfont 54-55; V of Epiph Bournemouth 60-68; Hilmarton w Highway 68-78; R of Compton Bassett 68-78. *Trencoth, Cassacawn, Blisland, Bodmin, Cornwall.* (Bodmin 850772)

ROOT, Claude William Samuel. **d** 64 **p** 65 Hur. R of Ilderton 64-69; I of Walkerton 69-70; R of Watford 70-75; Thamesford w Lakeside 75-78; St D Sarnia 79-81. *724 Fanshawe Park Road, London, Ont, Canada.*

ROOT, Canon Howard Eugene. b 26. St Cath S Ox BA (2nd cl Th) 51. Liddon Stud and Sen Demy Magd Coll Ox 52, MA 70. Sen Denyer and Johnson Scho 63. Magd Coll Cam MA 53. Ripon Hall, Ox 49. **d** 53 **p** 54 Ely. C of Trumpington 53; Asst Lect in Div Univ of Cam 53-57; Lect 57-66; Wilde Lect Univ of Ox 57-60; Fell of Em Coll Cam and L to Offic Dio Ely 54-66; Chap 54-56; Dean 56-66; Select Pr Univ of Cam 57; Exam Chap to Bp of Ripon 59-76; to Bp of S'wark 64-80; to Bp of Bris 65-81; to Bp of Win 71-81; to Bp of Wakef 77-81; Hulsean Pr Univ of Cam 61; Proc Conv Univ of Cam 65-66; Prof of Th Univ of Southn and Publ Pr Dio Win 66-81; Hon Chap of Win Cathl 66-67; Can Th of Win 67-80; Bampton Lect Univ of Ox 72; Hon Can of Cant Cathl from 80; Abp of Cant Counsellor on Vatican Affairs from 81; Dir Angl Centre Rome from 81. *Anglican Centre, Palazzo Doria Pamphilj, Via Del Corso 303, 00186 Roma, Italy.* (67 80 302)

ROOT, John Brereton. b 41. Univ of Lon BA (1st cl Hist) 64. Em Coll Cam BA (2nd cl Th Trip pt II) 66, 2nd cl Th Trip pt iii 67. Ridley Hall, Cam 64. **d** 68 Lon **p** 69 Willesden for Lon. C of St Mark Harlesden 68-73; St Paul's Homerton 73-76; Chap Ridley Hall Cam 76; Vice Prin 76-79; V of

Alperton Dio Lon from 79. *Alperton Vicarage, Stanley Avenue, Wembley, Middx.* (01-902 1729)

ROPER, Graham. St Mich Th Coll Crafers, 63. ACT ThL 67. **d** 68 **p** 69 Adel. C of Croydon Adel 68-70; Largs 70-71; P-in-c of Kangaroo I 71-75; R of Largs Bay Dio Adel from 75. *38 Musgrave Street, Largs, S Australia 5015.* (08-49 6643)

ROPER, Jeffrey Richard. Moore Th Coll Syd ACT ThL 55. **d** 56 **p** 57 Syd. C of Ryde 56-58; Sec CMS Queensld and L to Offic Dio Brisb 57-66; R of Kensington 66-70; Dalby 70-75; Kenmore Dio Brisb from 75. *1036 Moggill Road, Kenmore, Queensland, Australia 4069.* (378 2923)

ROPER, Robert Killby. Late Scho of St Jo Coll Dur BA (2nd cl Th) and Lightfoot Scho 27, Jenkyns Scho 28, MA 30. **d** 29 **p** 30 S'wark. C of St Anne Wandsworth 29-32; H Trin Gainsborough 32-35; Chap Chigwell Sch 35-45; R of Thurlby w Norton Disney 45-58; C-in-c of Swinderby 45-47; RD of Graffoe 48-58; R of All SS Chardstock 58-63; V of St Andr Chardstock 58-63; Chap at Alassio Dio Gibr from 63. *Galliano, 2 Alassio, Italy.*

ROPER, Timothy Hamilton. b 34. Qu Coll Cam 2nd cl Cl Trip pt i 56, BA (2nd cl Th Trip pt ia) 57, MA 61. Sarum Th Coll 57. **d** 59 **p** 60 Pet. C of Kingsthorpe 59-62; Kirkby 62-65; Chap Rossall Sch Fleetwood and L to Offic Dio Blackb from 65. *Rossall School, Fleetwood, Lancs.* (Fleetwood 4453)

ROPER, Preb William Lionel. b 17. Univ of Leeds, BA 39. Coll of Resurr Mirfield, 39. **d** 41 **p** 42 Ex. C of S Molton 41-43; St Aubyn and St Jo Bapt Devonport 43-47; C-in-c 47-51; V of Exwick 51-61; V of S Molton w Nymet St Geo 61-71; R of High Bray w Charles 61-71; RD of S Molton 68-72; V of Paignton Dio Ex from 72; Preb of Ex Cathl from 77. *Vicarage, Paignton, Devon.* (Paignton 59059)

ROSCAMP, Alan Nicholas Harrison. b 12. Univ of Dur LTh 37, BA 39, MA 42. St Aid Coll 32. **d** 36 **p** 37 Ches. C of Ch Ch Latchford 36-38; Perm to Offic Dio Dur 38-39; C of Tarvin (in c of Kelsall) 39-44; C-in-c of St Mary Bowden 44-45; V of St Paul Macclesfield 45-51; Wadhurst 51-63; Tidebrook 52-63; RD of Etchingham 57-63. *Horton Green, Ruckinge, Ashford, Kent.* (Ham Street 2491)

ROSE, Canon Alaric Pearson. b 09. St Edm Hall, Ox BA (1st cl Phil Pol and Econ) and Sen Exhib 31, 3rd cl Th 33, MA 38. Ripon Hall, Ox 31. **d** 33 **p** 34 Dur. C of St Mary Gateshead 33-38; Chap St Jo Cathl Hong Kong 38-41; Dean 41-52; Exam Chap to Bp of Hong 51-61; Can Res of Hong 52-61; Can (Emer) from 61; V of Hall Green 61-66; R of Sutton Coldfield Dio Birm from 66; RD of Sutton Coldfield 71-76; Hon Can of Birm from 73. *16 Coleshill Street, Sutton Coldfield, B72 1SH.* (021-354 3607)

ROSE, Alfred Reginald Thomas. b 10. St Paul's Coll Grahmstn 53. **d** 54 **p** 55 Grahmstn. C of St Barn Port Eliz 54-57; Hale 57-61; V of St Aug Aldershot 61-73; Chap Ascot Priory, Berks from 73. *The Hermitage, Priory Road, Ascot, Berks.* (Winkfield Row 88259)

ROSE, Andrew David. b 45. Council for Nat Acad Awards BA (Th) 81. Oak Hill Coll 78. **d** 81 Willesden for Lon. C of Em Northwood Dio Lon from 81. *4 Church Close, Northwood, Middx, HA6 1SG.* (Northwood 23493)

ROSE, Anthony James. b 47. Trin Coll Bris BD 72. **d** 73 **p** 74 Man. C of St Pet Halliwell 73-76; CF from 76. *c/o Ministry of Defence, Bagshot Park, Bagshot, Surrey, GU19 5PL.*

ROSE, Arthur William. Univ of Dur BA 51. Oak Hill Th Coll. **d** 52 Croydon for Cant **p** 53 Cant. C of St Luke Ramsgate 52-54; St Geo Leeds 54-56; V of Slade Green 56-59; C of St John Woking (in c of St Sav Brookwood) 59-62; Chap Pathfinders Fellowship 59-62; Missr 63-75; V of St Jas W Teignmouth Dio Ex from 75. *Vicarage, Landscore Road, Teignmouth, Devon.* (Teignmouth 4148)

ROSE, Barry Ernest. b 35. Chich Th Coll 58. **d** 61 **p** 62 Chelmsf. C of St Edm Forest Gate 61-64; St Jo Cathl Antig 64-65; R of St Mary Antig 65-66; Dominica 66-69; V of Latton 69-78; Stanstead Mountfitchet Dio Chelmsf from 78; Commiss Antig 71-79. *Vicarage, Stanstead, Essex.* (Bp's Stortford 812203)

ROSE, Bernard Alexander Bridges. b 1897. **d** 60 **p** 61 Chelmsf. C of Wickham St Paul w Twinstead 60-63; V of Cricksea w Althorne 63-66; Shalford 66-70; Perm to Offic Dio Chelmsf from 70. *148 London Road, Clacton-on-Sea, Essex, CO15 4DR.* (Clacton 24569)

ROSE, Ernest John. Bp's Univ Lennox BA 63, LST 64. **d** 64 **p** 65 Alg. C of Epiph Sudbury 64-66; R of Bala 66-67; CF 67-71; Chap Ridley Coll St Catharines Dio Niag from 70. *Ridley College, St Catharines, Ont., Canada.* (416-682 5152)

ROSE, Glyn Clee. b 16. Jes Coll Ox BA 39, MA 42. Bps' Coll Cheshunt 49. **d** 51 **p** 52 Lon. C of St Pet De Beauvoir Square 51-54; St Luke Southn 54-58; SPCK Port Chap Southn 58-66; Miss to Seamen 66-73; R of Millbrook 73-81. *11 Collins Lane, Hursley, Nr Winchester.*

ROSE, Gordon Henry. b 23. St Cath S Ox BA (3rd cl Mod Hist) 48, MA 53. Wells Th Coll 49. **d** 50 Southn for Win **p** 51 Win. C of St Andr Bournemouth 50-55; R of Bishopstoke Dio Win from 55. *10 Stoke Park Road, Eastleigh, Hants.* (Eastleigh 2192)

ROSE, Harry Sandford. Univ of W Ont BA 64. Trin Coll Tor STB 67. **d** 66 **p** 67 Sask. I of Loon Lake 66-69; Touchwood Hills 69-73; CF (Canad) 73-79; L to Offic Dio Calg 76-79; I of Stettler Dio Calg from 79. *Box 699, Stettler, Alta, Canada.*

ROSE, James Edward. b 50. Selw Coll Cam BA 75. Trin Coll Bris 73. **d** 75 **p** 76 Bris. C of H Trin w St Gabr Easton Bris 75-77; Youth Work Dir at Greenhouse Trust Camberwell from 77. *Greenhouse Trust, 103 Cobourg Road, SE5.* (01-703 8419)

ROSE, John Clement Wansey. b 46. New Coll Ox BA (1st cl Chem) 69, (2nd cl Th) 71, MA 72. Ripon Hall Ox 70. **d** 72 **p** 73 Birm. C of Harborne 72-76; Team V of Kings Norton 76-81; V of St Pet Maney Dio Birm from 81. *Vicarage, Maney Hill Road, Sutton Coldfield, W Midl, B72 1JJ.* (021-354 2426)

ROSE, John Spencer. b 20. Univ of Wales, BA (2nd cl Gr) 42. St Mich Coll Llan 42. **d** 44 **p** 45 Llan. C of St John Penydarren 44-50; Llanharan w Peterston-s-montem 50-54; C-in-c of Barry Is Conv Distr 54-57; R of Vaynor w Capel Taffechan 57-65; V of Crickadarn w Gwenddwr and Alltmawr 65-73; R of Loughor Dio Swan B from 73. *Rectory, Loughor, W Glam.* (Gorseinon 892749)

ROSE, Leslie George Bootle. St Columb's Hall, Wang 42. **d** 42 **p** 43 Wang. C of Yackandandah 42-43; R of Bathanga 43-45; Numurkah w Cobram 45-48; Bright 48-50; Rutherglen 50-53; Stratford 53-54; Murchison w Rushworth 54-58; Chiltern and P-in-c of Rutherglen 58-62; R of Artarmon 62-64; C-in-c of Mortdale 64-69; R of Cumnock 69-71; Rockley w Geo Plains 71; L to Offic Dio Syd from 71. *5 Stephen Street, Lawson, NSW, Australia 2783.* (Lawson 471)

ROSE, Lionel Stafford. b 38. Wells Th Coll 69. **d** 71 **p** 72 Glouc. C of Minchinhampton 71-73; Thornbury 73-75; R of Ruardean 75-80; V of Whiteshill Dio Glouc from 80. *St Paul's Vicarage, Farmhill, Stroud, Glos.* (Stroud 4759)

ROSE, Paul Rosamond. b 32. Trin Hall Cam BA 56, MA 60. Westcott Ho Cam. **d** 59 **p** 60 S'wark. C of St Anne Wandsworth 59-61; Torquay 61-64; P-in-c of Daramombe Rhod 64-67; Min Can Prec and Sacr of Pet Cathl 67-72; V of St Jo Evang w St Mich AA Paddington 72-79; PV of Westmr Abbey 74-79; Prec and Sacr of Cant Cathl from 79. *19 The Precincts, Canterbury, CT1 2EP.* (0227-61498)

ROSE, Peter Charles. b 30. St Aug Coll Cant 70. **d** 72 Lon **p** 73 Kens Lon. C of St Martin-in-the-Fields Westmr 72-76; St Buryan w St Levan w Sennen 76-78; V of St Feock Dio Truro from 78. *St Feock Vicarage, Truro, Cornw, TR3 6SD.* (Devoran 862208)

ROSE, Reginald Charles. Wycl Coll Tor. **d** 57 Tor **p** 58 NS for Tor. C of St Paul Halifax 57-62; I of Manvers 62-65; Port Perry Dio Tor from 65; P-in-c of Cartwright Dio Tor from 66. *PO Box 645, Port Perry, Ont., Canada.* (416-985 7278)

ROSE, Roy. b 11. Worc Ordin Coll 63. **d** and **p** 64 Linc. C of N w S Hykeham 64-68; R of Hale Magna and Parva 68-77; V of Helpringham 68-77; P-in-c of Scredington 73-77; Perm to Offic Dio Linc from 77. *72 Lincoln Road, Ruskington, Sleaford, Lincs, NG34 9AB.* (Ruskington 832669)

ROSE-CASEMORE, John. b 27. Chich Th Coll. **d** 55 **p** 56 Guildf. C of Ch Ch Epsom 55-58; C of Hednesford (in c of St Sav) 58-60; V of Dawley Magna 60-65; R of Puttenham w Wanborough 65-72; Frimley Dio Guildf from 72; RD of Surrey Heath 76-81. *Frimley Rectory, Camberley, Surrey.* (Camberley 23309)

ROSENTHALL, Henry David. b 08. QUB BA (Eng Lit) 30. TCD 30. **d** 32 **p** 33 Clogh. C of Clones 32-34; St Andr Monk Wearmouth 35-37; Asst Chap to Bp of Hong 37-41; P-in-c of Ch Ch Kowloon 37-41; L to Offic Dio Wel 41-45; P-in-c of St Pet Wanganui NZ 41-45; Archd of Sing and V of St Andr Cathl Sing 45-48; Exam Chap to Bp of Sing 46-48; V of Atherton 48-57; E Kirkby w Miningsby R 57-72; PC of Hagnaby 57-72; R of Bolingbroke w Hareby 66-72; Willoughby w Sloothby and Claxby 72-76; Ulceby w Dexthorpe and Fordington 72-76; P-in-c of Salle 78-80. *Station Road, Reepham, Norwich, NR10 4LJ.* (Reepham 202)

✠ **ROSEVEAR, Right Rev William James Watson.** Univ of NZ MA 41, LTh (1st Cl) 46. Univ of Melb BD 47. Univ of Lon MTh 50. **d** 45 Wai **p** 46 Aotearoa. C of St Jo Cathl Napier 45-48; Hayes Lon 49; Tutor Oak Hill Th Coll and Perm to Offic Dio Lon 50-51; Chap Te Aute Coll Wai 51-59; Exam Chap to Bp of Wai 51-65; V of Taupo 59-65; Hon Can of Wai 63-65; Sub-Warden and Lect St Jo Coll Auckld 65-81; L to Offic Dio Auckld 65-70; Hon C of Tamaki 71-73; Glen Innes 73-81; Cons Asst Bp of Wel in St Paul's Cathl Wel 29 Sept 81 by Abp of NZ; Bps of Nel, Ch Ch, Wel, Dun, Wai,

Waik and Aotearoa; and others. *c/o 28 Eccleston Hill, Wellington 1, NZ.*

ROSHEUVEL, Siegfried Winslow Patrick. b 39. Codr Coll Barb. **d** 68 Barb for Guy **p** 68 Guy. C of Skeldon 68-70; R of Anna Regina 70-73; C of St Geo Cathl Georgetn 73-74; V of Ruimveldt 74-75; C of Worksop Priory 75-78; Area Sec USPG Dios Chelmsf and St Alb from 78. *c/o USPG, 15 Tufton Street, SW1P 3QQ.*

ROSHEUVEL, Terrence Winst. Codr Coll Barb. **d** 68 Barb for Guy **p** 68 Guy. C of St Geo Cathl Georgetn 68-71; V of Wismar Dio Guy from 71. *Vicarage, Wismar, Linden, Demerara River, Guyana.* (04-3442)

✠ **ROSIER, Right Rev Stanley Bruce.** Univ of W Austr BSc 48. Ch Ch Ox BA 52, MA 56. Westcott Ho Cam 53. Melb Coll of Div Dipl Relig Educn 63. **d** 54 **p** 55 Sheff. C of Ecclesall 54-57; R of Wyalkatchem 57-64; Exam Chap to Abp of Perth 59-67; R of Kellerberrin 64-67; Can of Perth 66-67; Archd of Northam from 67-70; Cons Asst Bp of Perth in St Geo Cathl Perth 2 Feb 67 by Abp of Perth; Bps of Kalg; Bunb; and NW Austr; Bp Coadj of Perth; and Bps Frewer; Riley; and West; Apptd Bp of Willoch 70. *Bishop's House, Box 96, Gladstone, South Australia 5473.* (086-62 2057)

ROSKILLY, John Noel. b 33. Univ of Man MB, ChB 58. St Deiniol's Libr Hawarden 74. **d** 75 Ches **p** 76 Stockport for Ches (APM). C of Bramhall Dio Ches from 75. *31 Bridle Road, Woodford, Stockport, SK7 1QH.* (061-439 3838)

ROSS, Archdeacon of. *See* Hutchinson, Ven John Desmond.

ROSS, Bishop of. *See* Cork.

ROSS, Bishop of. *See* Moray.

ROSS, Dean of. *See* Fleming, Very Rev John Robert William.

ROSS, Alastair Alexander. b 54. CCC Ox BA 75. St Jo Coll Nottm 76. **d** 79 **p** 80 Liv. C of St Mich AA Huyton Dio Liv from 79. *30a Oxford Road, Huyton, Liverpool, L36 1XQ.*

ROSS, Anthony McPherson. b 38. St D Coll Lamp BA (2nd Cl Th) 60. BD (Lon) 63. St Mich Coll Llan 60. **d** 61 **p** 62 Llan. C of Gabalfa 61-65; Chap RN from 65. *c/o Ministry of Defence, Lacon House, Theobalds Road, WC1X 8RY.*

ROSS, Antony Mark. b 37. Univ of Otago BA 70. **d** 80 Auckld. C of St Pet Onehunga Dio Auckld from 80. *35 Grey Street, Onehunga, Auckland 6, NZ.*

ROSS, Benjamin. b 06. Univ of Dur BA 27. Westcott Ho Cam 42. **d** 43 Kingston T for S'wark **p** 44 S'wark. C of Battersea 43-45; Epsom (in c of St Steph-on-the-Downs) 45-52; V of St Jo Bapt Clay Hill Enfield 52-81; *Claysmore Cottage, Clay Hill, Enfield, Middx, EN2 9JJ.* (01-363 5298)

ROSS, Canon Chris Watson. b 20. Univ of Natal BA 52. St Paul's Th Coll Grahmstn Dipl Th 69. **d** 69 **p** 70 Matab. C of Ascen Hillside 69-73; R of St Mary Famona, Bulawayo 73-81; Exam Chap to Bp of Matab 73-81; Can of Matab from 77; R of Pro-Cathl Gwelo Dio Lundi from 81. *3 Fortress Road, Gwelo, Zimbabwe.* (3308)

ROSS, Cleon Marion. Montr Dioc Th Coll 77. **d** and **p** 80 Newfld. I of Bay L'Argent Newfld Dio Centr Newfld from 80. *PO Box 100, Bay L'Argent, Newfoundland, Canada, A0E 1B0.*

ROSS, Canon Clifford Edwin. b 10. St Edm Hall, Ox BA 50, MA 54. Trin Coll Bris 42. **d** 45 **p** 46 Ex. C of Fremington 45-47; L to Offic Dio Ex 47-53; Dio Ox 49-54; Dio Cov 50-54; Admin Chap to Bp of Cov 50-54; V of Claverdon (w Preston-Bagot from 55) 54-81; RD of Warw 62-67; Hon Can of Cov 63-81; Can (Emer) from 81. *15 Brook Avenue North, New Milton, Hants.*

ROSS, David Alexander. b 46. Dipl Th (Lon) 73. Oak Hill Coll 73. **d** 75 Willesden for Lon **p** 76 Lon. C of Em Northwood 75-80; R of Eastrop Dio Win from 80. *Eastrop Rectory, Goat Lane, Basingstoke, Hants, RG21 1PZ.*

ROSS, David Ian. b 44. Univ of Bris BVSc 67. Univ of Leeds Dipl Th 75. Coll of Resurr Mirfield 73. **d** 76 Repton for Derby **p** 77 Derby. C of Chesterfield 76-79; Atherton Dio Man from 79. *31 Wardour Street, Atherton, Manchester, M29 0AR.* (Atherton 870440)

ROSS, Dean Ellwood. b 48. Bp's Univ Queb BA 75. **d** 74 Queb. C of St Geo Lennoxville 74-80; Ch of the Advent Sherbrooke Dio Queb from 80. *44 Gordon Street, Lennoxville, PQ, Canada, J1M 1C3.*

ROSS, Derek Leighton. b 11. Ex Coll Ox BA (3rd Cl Geog) 34, MA 38. Wycl, Hall Ox 34. **d** 36 **p** 37 Liv. C of St Helens Lancs 36-38; Offg Chap of St Lawr Coll Ramsgate 38-40; Asst Master Liv Coll 40-41; Asst Chap 41; C-in-c of Altcar 41-44; V 44-47; Chap and Asst Master Liv Coll 44-51; Hd Master Felsted Jun Sch 51-71; Asst Chap 54-71; V of Lindsell 71-73; Stebbing (w Lindsell from 73) 71-78. *66 Palmeira Avenue, Hove, Sussex, BN3 3GF.*

ROSS, Duncan Gilbert. b 48. Univ of Lon BSc 70. Westcott Ho Cam 75. **d** 78 Lon **p** 79 Stepney for Lon. C of St Dunstan & All SS Stepney Dio Lon from 78. *11 Le Moal House, Dempsey Street, Stepney Way, E1 3HQ.*

ROSS, Canon Frank Herbert. Qu Coll Newfld. **d** 28 **p** 29 Newfld. C of Bonavista 28-29; I of Tack's Beach 29-32; Lamaline 33-37; P Org Cathl Ch Dio Newfld 37-43; I of Lamaline 43; C of Paget 44-53; Berm Dioc C 53-54; R of Smith's 54-73; Synod Sec Dio Berm 56-70; Chap to Bp of Berm 57-60; Hon Can of Berm 60-73; Can (Emer) from 73. *Upland, King Street, Hamilton, Bermuda.*

ROSS, Frederic Ian. b 34. Univ of Man BSc (1st cl Eng) 56. Westcott Ho Cam 58. **d** 62 Man **p** 63 Hulme for Man. C of Oldham 62-65; Sec Th Colls Dept SCM 65-69; L to Offic Dio Man from 69; Asst Master Man Gr Sch from 69. *19 Chatham Road, Old Trafford, Manchester, M16 0DR.*

ROSS, Frederick. b 36. Qu Coll Birm. **d** 64 **p** 65 York. C of Hessle 64-68; V of Marlpool 68-73; P-in-c of Norbury w Snelston 73-74; R 74-81; C-in-c of Clifton 73-74; V 74-81; RD of Ashbourne 78-81; Melbourne from 81; V of Melbourne Dio Derby from 81. *Vicarage Church Square, Melbourne, Derby, DE7 1EN.* (Melb 2347)

ROSS, Geoffrey Maxwell. **d** 58 **p** 59 Bend. V of Eaglehawk 58-64; R of Traralgon 64-79; Archd of Latrobe Valley 73-81; VG Dio Gippsld 78-81. *St Silas, Cnr Osburn and Maud Street, N Balwyn, Vic, Australia 3104.*

ROSS, George Douglas William. b 15. Linc Th Coll 76. **d** 76 Grimsby for Linc **p** 77 Linc (APM). C of Barton-on-Humber 76-81; Perm to Offic Dio Linc from 81.

ROSS, Glen Francis. b 48. St Mich Ho Crafers. **d** 72 **p** 73 N Queensld. C of H Trin Mackay 73; St John Cairns 74-75; Perm to Offic Dio Brisb 75-81. *c/o 455 Main Road, Kangaroo Point, Australia 4169.*

ROSS, Graham Robert. ACT ThL (1st cl) 63. McGill Univ Montr BA 70. Rutgers Univ NJ MA 72. St Francis Coll Brisb. **d** 64 **p** 65 Brisb. C of St Andr Indooroopilly 64-65; St Clem Stafford Brisb 65-67; St Thos Montr 67-70; in Amer Ch 70-72; Lect Univ of Syd 73-76; Perm to Offic Dio Brisb 77; Chap St Paul's Sch Bald Hills 78-80; V of Pinc Rivers N Dio Brisb from 80. *83 Leone Street, Lawnton, Queensland, Australia 4501.* (205 4467)

ROSS, Henry Ernest. b 40. N-W Ordin Course 70. **d** 73 Warrington for Liv **p** 74 Liv (APM). C of Litherland 73-75; St Pet, Newton-in-Makerfield 75-77; P-in-c of St Luke Walton Dio Liv 77-79; V from 79. *St Luke's Vicarage, 136 Southport Road, Bootle, Mer, L20 9EH.* (051-523 5460)

ROSS, John. b 41. Wells Th Coll 66. **d** 69 Bp Ashdowne for Newc T **p** 70 Newc T. C of St Gabr Heaton 69-71; Prudhoe 71-75; C-in-c of Shotley Dio Newc T from 75; Whittonstall Dio Newc T from 75. *Snods Edge Vicarage, Shotley Bridge, Consett, Co Durham.* (Edmundbyers 55665)

ROSS, John. b 31. Edin Th Coll 69. **d** and **p** 71 St Andr. C of St Jo Bapt, Perth 71-74; P-in-c of H Name Cumbernauld 74-77; R of Ballachulish 77-78; Glencoe 77-78; St Marg City and Dio Aber from 78. *St Margaret's Clergy House, Gallowgate, Aberdeen.* (Aberdeen 24969)

ROSS, John Alexander. Moore Th Coll Syd ACT ThL 47. **d** 47 **p** 48 Syd. C of Waterloo 47-48; Kembla 48-50; R of Mulgoa 50-51; Emu Plains w Castlereagh 51-52; St Silas Waterloo 52-56; St Luke Liv 56-81; Chap Liv Hosp Dio Syd from 81. *7 Hindmarsh Road, Liverpool, NSW, Australia 2170.* (602-5289)

ROSS, John Paton. b 29. Or Coll Ox BA (2nd cl Lit Hum) 52, Liddon Stud 55, MA 55, 2nd cl Th 56. Univ of Cam MA (by incorp) 59. Univ of Edin PhD 73. Wycl Hall Ox. **d** 57 **p** 58 Chelmsf. C of Hornchurch 57-59; Tutor Ridley Hall Cam 59-62; Chap 62-63; L to Offic Dio Ely 60-67; Asst Lect in Th Univ of Cam 62-67; Sen Admin Officer Univ of Edin 67-81; Asst Sec from 81. *50 Grange Road, Edinburgh, EH9 1TU.* (031-667 2166)

ROSS, Lynn Curtis. Bp's Univ Lennox BA 66, STB 69. **d** 68 **p** 69 Queb. I of Schefferville 68-75; Chaleur Bay 75-77; Magog Dio Queb from 77. *290 Pine Street, Magog, PQ, Canada.*

ROSS, Malcolm Hargrave. b 37. Univ of Dur BSc (3rd cl Chem) 58. Westcott Ho Cam 63. **d** 64 **p** 65 Ripon. C of Armley 64-67; V of Naparima 67-71; New Rossington 71-75; Bp's Chap for Miss E Lon and P-in-c of All SS Haggerston Dio Lon from 75. *All Saints Vicarage, Livermere Road, E8 4EZ.* (01-254 0436)

ROSS, Canon Philip James. St Jo Coll Cam 3rd cl Math Trip pt i, 38, BA (3rd cl Th Trip pt i) 40, MA 44. Ridley Hall, Cam 40. **d** 41 **p** 42 Lon. C of St Mary Isl Lon 41-45; CMS Miss from 45; Prin Dennis Mem Gr Sch Onitsha 51-53; St Mark's Coll Awka 54-58; Tutor Trin Coll Umuahia 59-60; Prin 60-68; Exam Chap to Bp on Niger 60-68; to Bp of Nig Delta 63-68; to Bp of Ow 63-68; Can of The Nig Delta 67-69; Can (Emer) from 69; Can Missr Dio Sier L from 70; CMS Rep Dio Sier L from 70; Exam Chap to Bp of Sier L from 72; Dom Chap to Bp of Sier L 70-75; Warden of the Th Hall and

Ch Tr Centre Freetown from 75. *PO Box 719, Freetown, Sierra Leone.*

ROSS, Raymond John. b 28. Trin Coll Cam BA 52, MA 57. St Steph Ho Ox 52. **d** 54 **p** 55 Bris. C of All SS Clifton Bris 54-58; Solihull (in c of St Mary Hob's Moat) 58-66; Min of St Mary's Eccles Distr Hob's Moat) 66-67; V 67-72; R of Newbold w Dunston Dio Derby from 72; RD of Chesterfield from 78. *Newbold Rectory, St John's Road, Chesterfield, Derbys.* (Chesterfield 450374)

ROSS, Robert Wilson. b 28. Hur Coll 47. **d** 52 **p** 53 Moos. C of Calstock 52-53; Miss at Albany 53-55; Chibongamau 55-56; C of St Jas Lon Ont 56-57; R of Prince William 57-62; Grand Manan 62-66; C of Humberstone 66-71; V of St Eliz Nether Hall 72-73; R of Petersville and Greenwich 73-81; St Martins and Black River Dio Fred from 81. *RRI, St Martins, NB, Canada.*

ROSS, William Arthur. St Jo Coll Morpeth ACT ThL 63. **d** and **p** 65 C & Goulb. C of St Luke Canberra 65-66; Albury 66-69; P-in-c of Kununurra 69-73; R of W Pilbara 73-80; Bluff Point Dio NW Austr from 80. *369 Chapman Road, Bluff Point, W Australia 6530.*

ROSS, William David. St Francis Coll Brisb 73. **d** 75 **p** 76 Brisb. C of Ch Ch Bundaberg 75-77; St Matt Grovely Brisb 77-78; V of Wondai Dio Brisb from 78. *St Mary's Vicarage, Bramston Street, Wondai, Queensland, Australia 4606.* (074-79 2236)

ROSSDALE, David Douglas James. b 53. Chich Th Coll 80. **d** 81 Barking for Chelmsf. C of Upminster Dio Chelmsf from 81. *6 Gaynes Park Road, Upminster, Essex.* (Upminster 26004)

ROSSER, Canon Reginald Marker. b 1897. St D Coll Lamp LDiv 22. **d** 23 **p** 24 St D. C of Llannon 23-27; Llandilo Fawr 27-31; V of Cilcennin w Llanbadarn Trefeglwys 31-35; Dewi-Sant Cardiff 35-66; Surr 35-66; Hon Can of Llan Cathl from 57; L to Offic Dio Mon 66-73. *Rosehill, Cefullys Road, Llandrindod Wells, Powys.*

ROSSINGTON, John Antony. b 32. Hatf Coll Dur BA 54. Ripon Hall, Ox 56. **d** 58 **p** 59 Birm. C of St Jas Handsworth 58-62; V of H Trin Smethwick 62-68; Surr from 65; V of St Faith and St Laur Harborne Dio Birm from 68. *115 Balden Road, Birmingham, B32 2EL.* (021-427 2410)

ROSSITER, Donald William Frank. b 30. **d** 80 Mon **p** 81 Llan for Mon. L to Offic Dio Mon from 80. *10 Meadow Lane, Abergavenny, Gwent, NP7 7AY.*

ROSSITER, Raymond Stephen David. b 22. St Deiniol's Libr Hawarden 75. **d** 76 Ches **p** 77 Stockport for Ches (APM). C of St Anne Sale Dio Ches from 76. *75 Temple Road, Sale, Gtr Man, M33 2FQ.* (061-962 3240)

ROSSON, Canon Bertram Thomas. b 1886. Univ of Dur LTh 13, BA 16, MA 19. Prelim TE (1st cl) 13. Can Sch Linc 11. JP 39. **d** 13 St Alb **p** 14 Chelmsf. C of L Ilford 13-15; St Thos Mart Brentwood 16-20; Romford (in c of St John) 20-22; Deputn and Org Sec C of E Children's S for Dios Linc; Southw and Sheff 22-24; L to Offic Dio Linc 23-24; R of Bryanston w Durweston 24-43; R and V of Blandford Forum 43-58; R of Long Langton 51-58; RD of Milton 39-43; Blandford 43-54; Preb of Sarum Cathl from 43; Can (Emer) from 73. *68 Monmouth Road, Dorchester, Dorset.*

ROSTRON, Derek. b 34. St Mich Coll Llan 65. **d** 67 **p** 68 Blackb. C of St Barn Morecambe 67-70; Ribbleton 70-72; V of All SS Chorley 72-79; C of Woodchurch 80; V of Audlem w Burleydam Dio Ches from 80. *St James's Vicarage, Heathfield Road, Little Heath, Audlem, Crewe, Chesh.* (0270-811543)

ROSTRON, Malcolm Raymond. b 35. **d** 65 **p** 66 Llan. C of Gabalfa 65-68; Whitchurch 68-72; V of Penrhiwceiber w Matthewstown and Ynysboeth (from 72) 72-75; Bargoed and Deri w Brithdir 75-78; Industr Chap to Bp of Llan 78-81. *c/o 40 Glanwen Avenue, Newport, Gwent, NP1 9BW.*

ROTHERHAM, Eric. b 36. Clifton Th Coll 63. **d** 67 Warrington for Liv **p** 68 Liv. C of Gt Crosby 67-69; St Nich Sutton w St Mich St Helens 69-71; V of St Paul Warrington Dio Liv from 72. *7 Paul Street, Warrington, Lancs.* (Warrington 33048)

ROTHERY, Cecil Ivor. St Jo Coll Winnipeg, 50. **d** 53 **p** 54 Bran. R of Holland 53-55; Souris 55-60; Rivers 60-61; Dean of Res St Jo Coll Winnipeg 61-63; R of Killarney 63-66; Hon Can of Bran 65-72; R of Lynn Lake 68-69; Snow Lake 69-72; C of Gainsborough 72-74; R of Fleet 74-79; C of Brigg 79-80; P-in-c of Wrawby 79-80; Perm to Offic Dio Southw from 80. *125 Queen Street, Retford, Notts, DN22 7DA.* (0777-701551)

ROTHERY, Robert Frederick. b 34. Lon Coll of Div 67. **d** 69 Warrington for Liv **p** 70 Liv. C of Burscough Bridge 69-72; Chipping Camden 72-75; P-in-c of Didmarton w Oldbury-on-the-Hill and Sopworth 75-77; R of Boxwell w Leighterton, Didmarton w Oldbury-on-the-Hill and Sopworth Dio Glouc from 77. *Rectory, Leighterton, Tetbury, Glos, GL8 8UW.* (Leighterton 283)

ROTHEY, George Auguste Frederick. b 06. LSE BCom 32. Univ of Lon BSc (Econ) 33. Ely Th Coll 63. **d** 64 **p** 65 Chelmsf. C of Brentwood 64-68; Hockley 68-76. *Le Chalet, Kandlewood, Mount Avenue, Hutton, Brentwood, Essex.* (Brentwood 218616)

ROTHWELL, Canon Eric. b 12. Univ of Man BA (2nd cl Hist) 35. Lich Th Coll 35. **d** 37 **p** 38 Blackb. C of Padiham w Higham (in c of St Anne and St Eliz Padiham) 37-41; P-in-c of St Cath Burnley 41-42; C of H Trin Blackpool (in c of St Mary) 42-47; V of Warton 47-63; RD of Tunstall 55-63; Surr 56-77; Hon Can of Blackb from 61; R of Chorley 63-77; Perm to Offic Dios Blackb and Carl from 79. *The Coach House, Wood Broughton Hall, Cartmel, Cumbria, LA11 7SH.*

ROTHWELL, Harold. b 34. K Coll Lon and Warm AKC 58. **d** 59 **p** 60 Linc. C of Old Brumby 59-62; C-in-c of St Phil w St Anne (w St Steph from 64) Sheff 62-64; V 64-67; Caistor (w Holton-le-Moor to 74) and Clixby 67-77; C-in-c of Grasby w Owmby 74-77; Searby 74-77; Org Sec CECS Dio Ex and Archdeaconries of Wells and Taunton 77-78; Perm to Offic Dio Ex 77-78; P-in-c of Deeping St Nich and Tongue End 78-81. *3 Wrawby Road, Brigg, S Humb.* (Brigg 53156)

ROTHWELL, Michael John Hereward. b 46. Chich Th Coll 74. **d** 78. Colchester for Chelmsf **p** 79 Bradwell for Chelmsf. C of All SS City and Dio Chelmsf from 79. *54 Tennyson Road, Chelmsford, Essex.*

ROTHWELL, Robert Keith. b 44. Univ of Syd BA. Univ of Lon BD. Moore Th Coll ThL. **d** 81 Syd. C of St Mark Darling Point Dio Syd from 81. *21 Etham Avenue, Darling Point, NSW, Australia 2027.*

ROTHWELL-JACKSON, Christopher Patrick. b 32. St Cath S Ox BA 58. MA 62. St Steph Ho Ox 55. **d** 59 Taunton for B & W **p** 60 Taunton for Cant. C of All SS Clevedon 59-62; Midsomer Norton 62-65; Asst Master St Pet VC Primary Sch Portishead 66-68; Clevedon VC Jun Sch 68-75; L to Offic Dio B & W 68-75; Dio Derby from 76; Hd Master Bp Pursglove Sch Tideswell from 75. *Hardy House, Tideswell, Buxton, Derbys.* (Tideswell 871468)

ROTIMI, Canon Reuben Adekoya. b 11. **d** 44 **p** 45 Lagos. P Dio Lagos 44-52; Dio Ondo-B 52-57 and 59-62; Dio Benin 62-68; C of St Pet Blackey Man 57-59; Can of Benin 67-68; P Dio Ibad 68-76; Dio Lagos from 76; Can of Ibad 71-76; Hon Can of Lagos from 76. *Box 376, Yaba, Lagos, Nigeria.*

ROUCH, David Vaughan. b 36. Oak Hill Th Coll 67. **d** 69 Penrith for Carl **p** 70 Carl. C of St Jas Denton Holme Carl 69-74; V of St John and St Jas Litherland Dio Liv from 74. *175 Linacre Lane, Bootle, Mer, L20 6AB.* (051-922 3612)

ROUGHLEY, Kenneth Bruce. Moore Th Coll Syd ACT LTh 48. **d** and **p** 49 Syd. C of Ryde 49-50; Min of Miranda Prov Distr 50-53; R of Mittagong 53-56; Dep Regr Dio Syd 56-64; C of St Andr Cathl Syd 56-64; R of Drummoyne 64-69; w Home Miss S Syd from 69; L to Offic Dio Syd from 70. *18 Swannell Avenue, Chiswick, NSW, Australia 2046.*

ROUIKERA, Christian. **d** 46 **p** 54 Melan. P Dio Melan 46-75. *Wahere, Marau, Guadalcanal, Solomon Islands.*

ROUND, Malcolm John Harrison. b 56. Univ of Lon BSC 77. Coun for Nat Acad Awards BA 81. Oak Hill Coll 78. **d** 81 Guildf. C of St Sav City and Dio Guildf from 81. *5b Artillery Terrace, Guildford, Surrey.*

ROUNDHILL, Canon Jack. b 22. TCD (1st cl Ment and Mor Sc) BA 44, Div Test 45, MA 47, BD 47. **d** 45 **p** 46 Lon. C of St Jo Bapt Greenhill 45-49; Min Can of St Anne's Cathl and Dean of Residences Qu Univ Belf 49-51; V of St Paul S Harrow 52-58; Heston 58-63; V of Dorking w Ranmore 63-75; RD of Dorking 70-75; Hon Can of Guildf from 75; R of Cranleigh Dio Guildf from 76. *Rectory, Cranleigh, Guildford, GU6 8AS.* (Cranleigh 3620)

ROUNDHILL, (Peter) Stanley. b 14. Chich Th Coll 46. **d** 49 **p** 50 Win. M OSP from 39. *The Abbey, Alton, Hants.*

ROUNDS, Canon Philip Rigby. b 21. Wells Th Coll. **d** 52 Bris for Sarum **p** 53 Sarum. C of H Trin Weymouth 52-56; V of Laverstock 56-67; R of Wyke Regis Dio Sarum from 67; Can of Sarum Cathl from 77. *Rectory, Portland Road, Wyke Regis, Weymouth, Dorset, DT4 9ES.* (Weymouth 784649)

ROUNDTREE, Prec Samuel William. b 19. Trin Coll Dub BA 42, Div Test (1st cl) 43, MA 54. **d** 43 **p** 44 Cashel. C of Waterford Cathl 44-47; R of Tallow w Kilwatermoy 47-51; I of Kiltegan w Stratford (and Rathvilly from 60) 51-62; R of Dunleckney U Dio Leigh from 62; Can and Preb of Clonemery in St Canice's Cathl Kilkenny 62-78; RD of Maryborough from 62; Treas of Leigh Cathl 62-78; Chan of Oss and Leigh Cathls 78-80; Prec from 80. *Rectory, Bagenalstown, Co Carlow, Irish Republic.*

ROUNTHWAITE, Maurice. St Jo Coll Auckld 46. **d** 51 **p** 52 Auckld. C of Takapuna 51-54; V of Hauraki Plains 54-59; Warkworth 59-64; C of St Andr Epsom Auckld 64-66; P-in-c of Blockhouse Bay Miss Distr 66-69; V of St Alb Balmoral Auckld 69-80; Par Distr of Birkdale-Beachhaven Dio Auckld from 80. *93 Birkdale Road, Auckland 10, NZ.* (436-989)

ROUNTREE, Cecil John. b 19. Trin Coll Dub Hebr Pri 39, BA (1st cl Mod) 41, Div Test (1st cl) 42. **d** 42 Arm for Down **p** 43 Down. St Luke Belf 42-46; Hd of Trin Coll Dub Miss in Belf 46-50; R of Ardclinis w Tickmacrevan 50-55; I of Mothel w Bilbo 55-60; R of Ballintoy 60-61; Templeharry w Borrisnafarney 61-79; Preb of Killaloe Cathl 67-76; Treas 76-79; Chan 79-80; I of Creagh U 79-80; Tubbercurry and Achonry Dio Achon from 80. *Rectory, Tubbercurry, Co Sligo, Irish Republic.*

ROUNTREE, Richard Benjamin. b 52. Nat Univ of Ireland Dub BA 73. Div Sch Dub 76. **d** 76 **p** 77 Down. C of St John Orangefield Dio Down from 76. *412 Castlereagh Road, Belfast, BT5 6BH.*

ROUTLEDGE, Donald Eugene. b 45. Univ of Dalhousie BSc 67. Atlantic Sch of Th Halifax NS MDiv 75. **d** 75 Abp Davis for Fred **p** 76 Fred. I of Kent 75-80; Hampton Dio Fred from 80. *RR2, Hampton, NB, Canada.*

ROUTLEDGE, Canon Kenneth Graham. b 27. Univ of Liv LLB 51. Fitzw Coll Cam BA 65, MA 69. Westcott Ho Cam 63. **d** 66 **p** 67 Ches. C of St Geo Stockport 66-69; Dean of Chap CCC Cam 69-77; Fell from 69; Chan Dio Ely from 73; Dios Pet and Lich from 76; Res Can of Pet Cathl from 77. *Canonry House, Minster Precincts, Peterborough, PE1 1XX.* (Pet 62125)

ROUTLEY, Donald. d 59 **p** 60 Brib. C of St Steph Coorparoo Brisb 59-62; P-in-c of Monto 62-64; R 64-65; V of Pine Rivers 65-70; Perm to Offic Dio Brisb 70-80; C of Palmwoods Dio Brisb from 80. *20 Adelong Crescent, Buddina Beach, Queensland, Australia 4557.* (071-44 2185)

ROWCROFT, Kenneth George Caulfeild. b 19. Sarum Th Coll 48. **d** 50 **p** 51 Sarum. C of Bradf-on-Avon 50-53; Broadstone 53-55; Lyme Regis 55-64; R of Hawkchurch w Fishpond 64-74; PC of Monkton-Wyld 67-68; V 69-74; Perm to Offic Dios Ex and Sarum from 74. *Colway Rise, Colway Lane, Lyme Regis, Dorset.* (Lyme Regis 3349)

ROWDON, John Michael Hooker. Univ of Witwatersrand BA 52. Ridley Hall, Cam 52. **d** 54 **p** 55 Chich. C of Broadwater 54-56; Im w St Anselm Streatham Common 56-59; Chap to Bp of Lagos 60-62; C of All H Barking-by-the-Tower Lon 62-66; Warden Toc H Tower Hill Lon 64-66; Immigration Chap Prov of W Austr and L to Offic Dio Perth 66-72; Dir Angl Social Services Dio Perth 70-72; R of Merredin 72-77; Dir Richmond Fellowship W Austr and Perm to Offic Dio Perth from 77. *25 Crawshaw Crescent, Manning, W Australia 6152.* (450 3390)

ROWE, Andrew Gidleigh Bruce. b 37. K Coll Lon and Warm AKC 62. **d** 63 **p** 64 B & W. C of Midsomer Norton 63-68; Chap RN from 68. *c/o National Westminster Bank Ltd., 25 Fore Street, Taunton, Somt, TA1 1JE.*

ROWE, Canon Antony Silvester Buckingham. b 26. St Jo Coll Dur 53. **d** 55 **p** 56 Cov. C of St Luke Holbrooks 55-59; V of St Mary Magd City and Dio Cov from 59; RD of Cov S from 72; Hon Can of Cov from 76; M Gen Syn from 78. *Vicarage, Craven Street, Coventry, Warws, CV5 8DT.* (Coventry 75838)

ROWE, Arthur John. b 35. TCD 73, Div Test 76. **d** 76 **p** 77 Down. C of Bangor Abbey 76-78; R of Kilbarron (w Rossnowlagh from 79) Dio Raph from 78. *St Anne's Rectory, Ballyshannon, Co Donegal, Irish Republic.* (Bundoran 65140)

ROWE, Cecil Leonard. b 16. AKC 48. **d** 48 Guildf for Chich **p** 49 Lewes for Chich. C of Southwick 48-51; Seaford 51-54; Aldwick 54-55; Uckfield 55-59; V of Ashley Green 59-62; All SS Charlton 62-68; R of Girvan 68-72; Stratford St Mary Dio St E from 72; C-in-c of Higham St Mary Dio St E from 72. *Rectory, Stratford St Mary, Colchester, Essex, CO7 6LZ.* (Colchester 322128)

ROWE, Cyril Ashton. b 38. K Coll Lon and Warm AKC 62. **d** 63 **p** 64 Lon. C of St Matt Bethnal Green 63-68; P-in-c 68-74; V of St Matthias Stoke Newington Dio Lon from 74. *Vicarage, Wordsworth Road, N16 8DD.* (01-254 5063)

ROWE, David Harvey. b 27. St D Coll Lamp BA 52. **d** 54 **p** 55 Leic. C of St Phil Leic 54-57; Loughborough 57-58; C-in-c 58-59; V of St Aid Leic 59-68; Glen Magna w Stretton Magna 68-80. *c/o Great Glen Rectory, Leicester.* (Great Glen 2238)

ROWE, Douglas Winn. b 08. Hatf Coll Dur BA 30. Sarum Th Coll 31. **d** 32 **p** 33 Worc. C of St Jas Dudley 32-34; Ribbesford w Bewdley 34-39; V of Powick (or Powyke) 39-46; St Pet Cowleigh 46-59; Redditch 59-68; All SS Wyche 68-73; Surr 59-73; RD of Bromsgrove 66-68. *7 St Bernard Drive, Malvern, Worcs, WR14 3PY.* (Malvern 4200)

ROWE, Edward Nelson. b 05. Trin Coll Dub BA 29, MA 40. Bp's Coll Cheshunt. **d** 62 **p** 63 Clogh. Dean's V of Enniskillen 62-65; R of Lack 65-66; Drum w Currin and Newbliss 66-76; RD of Clones 72-76. *22 Old Rossory Road, Enniskillen, Co Fermanagh, N Ireland.*

ROWE, Ernest Arthur Paul. Univ of Tor BA (Hons) 59. Trin Coll Tor STB 65. **d** 64 Bp Snell for Tor **p** 65 Tor. C of St Pet Tor 64-66; I of Mortlach 66-69; L to Offic Dio Calg 72-76. *Box 3000, Drumheller, Alta., Canada.*

ROWE, Everhard James. b 05. Bp's Coll Cheshunt 28. **d** 28 **p** 29 Lon. C of St Mich AA Stoke Newington 28-30; St Paul Camden Square 30-32; Rusthall 32-34; Abbey Ch Bath 34-36; V of Englishcombe (or Inglescombe) 36-47; Chap RNVR 41-46; V of All SS Weston Bath 47-70. *13 The Avenue, Tiverton, Devon.*

ROWE, Henry Maurice. b 07. **d** and **p** 73 Tas. C of Swansea 73; P-in-c 73-77. *Gracedieu, Swansea, Tasmania 7275.* (002-578237)

ROWE, Ven Herbert Edward. ACT ThL 51. **d** 38 **p** 39 Nel. C of N Suburban 38-40; V of Granity 40-46; CF (NZ) 42-46; V of Amuri 46-50; Richmond w Appleby 50-57; Can of Nel 49-52; Archd of Waimea 52-55; Mawhera 55-57; CF (NZ) 57-62; V of St Aug Napier 62-73; Hon Can of St John's Cathl Napier 66-68; Archd of Hawkes Bay 68-79; Archd (Emer) from 79; Exam Chap to Bp of Wai from 68; VG 69-79; V of Waipawa 73-79; Perm to Offic Dio Wai from 79. *31 Argyle Crescent, Tamatea, Napier, NZ.* (430-103)

ROWE, John Gordon. Harvard Univ SB (Hist) 45. Episc Th Sch Mass BD (*cum laude*) 50. Univ of Tor MA 51, PhD 55. **d** 50 Massachusetts **p** 51 Tor. C of St Anne Tor 51-53; Chap Univ of Tor 53-55; Prof of Eccles Hist Hur Coll (Univ of W Ont) 55-66; Prof of Hist 67-69; Prof of Hist Sch of Graduate Stud Univ of W Ont 63-69. *470 Victoria Street, London 24, Ont, Canada.*

ROWE, John Goring. b 23. McGill Univ Montr BA (2nd cl Engl and 1st cl Phil) 48, BD 51. Selw Coll Cam BA 53. Montr Dioc Th Coll. **d** 51 Montr **p** 52 Ely. C of N Clarendon 51; Trumpington 51-53; St Paul w St Luke Bow Common Dio Lon from 53. *10 Cordelia Street, E14 6DZ.* (01-515 4681)

ROWE, John Nigel. b 24. Ball Coll Ox MA 52, BD 53. **d** 54 **p** 55 Linc. C of Grimsby 54-57; St John Ches 57-58; Perm to Offic at St Jas Birch-in-Rusholme 58-59; C of Gorton 59-60; V of Newchurch-in-Pendle 60-80; Denholme Gate Dio Bradf from 80. *Denholme Vicarage, Bradford, W Yorks.* (Bradf 832813)

ROWE, Leslie Vernon. b 25. Oak Hill Th Coll 63. **d** 65 Barking for Chelmsf **p** 66 Chelmsf. C of Woodford Wells 65-69; C-in-c of L Burstead 69-74; R of Frinton-on-Sea Dio Chelmsf from 74. *Rectory, Frinton-on-Sea, Essex.* (Frinton 4664)

ROWE, Michael Gordon. b 55. McGill Univ Montr BA 77. Univ of Ox BA 79. Montr Dioc Th Coll 79. **d** 80 **p** 81 Montr. C of St Matthias Westmount Dio Montr from 80. *6 Park Place, Apt 20, Westmount, Que, Canada, H3Z 2K5* (514-933-4295)

ROWE, Peter Farquharson. b 19. Selw Coll Cam 2nd cl Hist Trip pt i, 40, BA 41, 3rd cl Th Trip pt i, 42. Westcott Ho Cam. **d** 43 **p** 44 S'wark. C of Putney 43-47; St Jo Bapt Southend Lewisham 47-54; V of Ascen Mitcham 54-65; St Luke Eltham 65-77; Ravensthorpe w E Haddon and Holdenby Dio Pet from 77. *Ravensthorpe Vicarage, Northampton.* (East Haddon 382)

ROWE, Philip Charles. b 08. Late Exhib of St Cath Coll Cam 2nd cl Mod Lang Trip pt i, 27, BA (3rd cl Th Trip pt i) 29, MA 35. Cudd Coll 29. **d** 31 **p** 32 Cant. C of St Aug Croydon 31-34; St Clem City Road Lon 34-38; V 38-45; St Barn Pimlico 47-59; RD of Westmr 55-59; Centr Barnet 67-72; Sen Insp of Schs Dio Lon 59-66; V of All SS E Finchley 66-75. *81 Chelsea Gardens, Chelsea Bridge Road, SW1.* (01-730 2621)

ROWE, Ralph Knight Munck. b 39. Univ of Tor BA 70. Wycl Coll Tor MDiv 75. **d** 75 Tor for Keew. C of Wunnumun Lake 75-80; P-in-c of Big Trout Lake Dio Keew from 80. *Big Trout Lake, Ont, Canada.*

ROWE, Richard Nigel. b 41. St Steph Ho Ox 67. **d** 70 **p** 71 Willesden for Lon. C of St Pet Acton Green 70-74; Leigh 74-79; V of St Marg Leytonstone Dio Chelmsf from 79. *33 Wragby Road, Leytonstone, E11.* (01-534 4905)

ROWE, Robert William. Ch Ch Coll LTh 65. **d** 65 **p** 66 Ch Ch. C of New Brighton 65-67; Linwood 67-69; Asst to Dir of Chr Educn 69-70; V of Waikari (w Glenmark from 72) 70-74; Hokitika Dio Ch Ch from 74; RD of Westland from 74. *Vicarage, Stafford Street, Hokitika, NZ.* (Hok 591)

ROWE, Samuel Ernest Alan. TCD BA 39, MA 44. **d** 40 Bp Kennedy for Dub for Oss **p** 41 Oss. C of Wexford w Rathaspeck 40-43; CF 43-68; R of Newtown Fertullagh 68-72; Monart w Ballycarney and Templescobin Dio Ferns from 72. *Rectory, Monart, Enniscorthy, Co Wexford, Irish Republic.* (Enniscorthy 2171)

ROWE, Stanley Hamilton. b 18. St Pet Hall, Ox BA 48, MA 52. ALCD 50. **d** 50 **p** 51 Chelmsf. C of St Paul Leyton 50-53; CMS Miss Nigeria 53-64; Dio Lagos 53-56; Tutor at St Jo Coll Owo 57-59; Vice Prin and Chap 59-62; Prin 62-64; C-in-c of St Cedd Becontree 65-67; Asst Master The John Hampden Sch High Wycombe from 67; Perm to Offic Dio Ox from 67. *37 Greenwood Avenue, Chinnor, Oxford, OX9 4HW.* (Kingston Blount 51278)

ROWE, Canon Thomas Desmond. McGill Univ Montr BA 49, BD 52. Montr Dioc Th Coll Hon DD 74. **d** 52 Montr **p** 53 Athab for Montr. I of North Star 52-57; C of St Pet Mt Royal 57-60; R of Shawville 60-64; Greenfield Pk 64-68; Granby 68-74; Archd of Bedford 68-74; Hon Can of Montr from 74; R of Beaurepaire Dio Montr from 74. *84 Fieldfare Avenue, Beaurepaire, PQ, Canada.* (514-697 4064)

ROWE, William Alfred. Open Univ BA 73. Bps' Coll Cheshunt, 50. **d** 52 **p** 53 St E. C of St Marg Ipswich 52-54; V of Walsham le Willows 54-57; R of Boyton w Capel 57-62; C-in-c of Bawdsey 57-61; V of Ermington 62-72; R of Bratton Clovelly w Germansweek 72-76; Chap Livery Dole Ex 76-79. *Vicarage, Flat A, Forestreet, Northam, Bideford EX9 1AW.* (Bideford 4306)

ROWE, Ven William John. b 24. Em Coll Sktn 43. **d** and **p** 70 Sask. Hon C of St Alb Cathl, Dioc Regr and Exec Sec of Synod Dio Sask from 70; Hon Can of Sask from 75; Archd of Prince Albert from 77. *Synod Office, Box 1088, Prince Albert, Sask, Canada.*

ROWELL, Alan. b 50. Univ of Lon BSc 71. AKC 71. Trin Coll Bris Dipl Th 75. **d** 75 Edmon for Lon **p** 76 Lon. C of St Cuthb w Hampstead 75-78; Camborne 78-81; V of Pendeen Dio Truro from 81. *Vicarage, Pendeen, Penzance, Cornw, TR20 8YT.* (St Just 788777)

ROWELL, Canon Douglas Geoffrey. b 43. CCC Cam 2nd cl Th Trip pt i, 62, BA (1st cl Th Trip pt ii) 64, MA and PhD 68. Mere's Pr Univ of Cam 69. New Coll Ox MA and DPhil (by incorp) 68. Cudd Coll. **d** 68 Ox **p** 69 Win. Asst Chap New Coll Ox 68-72; L to Offic Dio Ox from 68; Fell and Chap Keble Coll Ox from 72; Exam Chap to Bp of Leic from 79; M Liturgical Comm from 81; Can and Preb of Chich Cathl from 81. *Keble College, Oxford.* (Ox 59201)

ROWELL, Frank. b 22. Chich Th Coll 50. **d** 52 St E **p** 53 Dunwich for Cant. C of All SS Ipswich 52-56; R of Earl Stonham 56-65; Clopton Dio St E from 65; R of Otley Dio St E from 65. *Clopton Rectory, Woodbridge, Suff.* (Grundisburgh 351)

ROWELL, Peter Sydenham. b 13. Hertf Coll Ox Bible Clk 34, BA (3rd cl Th) 35, MA 47. Cudd Coll 35. **d** 36 **p** 37 Newc T. C of St Jo Bapt Newc T 36-41; Cathl Ch St Alb 41-43; Chap RNVR 43-46; C of Grahmstn Cathl 46-48; St Thos St Annes-on-the-Sea 48-53; Market Drayton 54-55; C of Tenby w Gumfreston 56-57. *2 Ivy House, St Julian's Street, Tenby, Dyfed.* (Tenby 2674)

ROWELL, William Kevin. b 51. Univ Reading BSc 71. Linc Th Coll 78. **d** 80 **p** 81 Lich. C of Cannock Dio Lich from 80. *18 Queen Street, Cannock, Staffs, WS11 1AE.*

ROWETT, William Berkeley. b 09. BA 61 (Lon) Westcott Ho Cam. **d** 62 **p** 63 Lon. C of St Martin-in-the-Fields Westmr 62-66; Chap of the Isles of Scilly and V of St Mary's 66-71; V of St Madron w Morvah 71-80; Perm to Offic dio Guildf from 80; Dios Lon and S'wark from 81. *Three Ducks, The Island, Thames Ditton, Surrey, KT7 0SQ.* (01-398 7196)

ROWLAND, Charles Louis Gordon. Qu Univ Belf BA 49. Angl Th Coll BC BD 65. **d** 51 **p** 52 Down. C of Aghalee 51-54; St Polycarp Finaghy 54-57; Ch Ch Cathl Ott 57-59; I of Quesnel 59-65; St Alb Winnipeg 65-71; St Martin Lon Dio Hur from 71. *538 Oak Park Drive, London, Ont., Canada.* (519-471 4250)

ROWLAND, Christopher Charles. b 47. Ch Coll Cam BA 69, MA 73, PhD 75. Ridley Hall Cam 72. **d** 75 **p** 76 Newc T. C of St Jas Benwell Newc T 75-78; All SS Gosforth Dio Newc T from 78. *21 Kelso Gardens, Newcastle-upon-Tyne, NE15 7DB.* (Newc 743154)

ROWLAND, Derrick Edward. b 31. St D Coll Lamp BA (2nd cl Phil) 55. St Cath S Ox BA (3rd cl Th) 57. Wycl Hall, Ox. **d** 57 **p** 58 Ox. C of St John Reading 57-61; V of St Matt Smethwick 61-67; PC of Turnditch w Windley 67-69; V 69-74; Dir of Educn Dio Derby 67-78; Development Officer from 79. *3 The College, Derby, DE1 3DY.* (Derby 45984)

ROWLAND, Canon Edward John. Chich Th Coll 37. **d** 40 Lon **p** 41 Chich. C of St Mary Virg Somers Town 40-41; Ch Ch St Leonards-on-Sea 41-58; St Mark Capetn 58-59; R of Woodstock 59-75; Can of Capetn 65-68; Prov Hon Can from 80; L to Offic Dio Capetn 75; C of Athlone 75-80; Perm to Offic Dio Capetn from 80. *Disa House, Orange Street, Cape Town, S Africa.* (43-6173)

ROWLAND, Eric Edward James. b 35. Univ of Leeds, BA 62. Coll of Resurr Mirfield, 61. **d** 63 **p** 64 Wakef. C of S Kirkby 63-65; Headingley 65-70; V of Osmondthorpe Leeds 70-79; R of Sandy Dio St Alb from 79. *Rectory, Sandy, Beds, SG19 1AQ.* (Sandy 80512)

ROWLAND, Geoffrey Watson. b 17. **d** 55 **p** 56 Rang. BCMS Miss Dio Rang 55-65; C of St Mich AA Blackheath Pk 65-71; V of St Paul's Golds Hill W Bromwich 71-76; Chap Commun Relns Southall Dio Lon from 77. *30 Kenton Avenue, Southall, Middx.* (01-571 4907)

ROWLAND, Henry Rees. b 03. ACLD 32 (LTh from 74). **d** 32 Taunton for B & W **p** 33 B & W. C of St Luke S Lyncombe 32-34; St Paul Worthing 34-38; V of Ardsley 38-42; Ch Ch Win 42-50; St Mich AA Bournemouth 50-69; Surr 50-69; Chap Bournemouth and Distr Hosp 51-73; Publ Pr Dio Win from 69. *5 The Green, Welwyn, Herts, AL6 9EA.* (Welwyn 5372)

ROWLAND, Robert William. b 51. Univ of Birm BA 72. St Mich AA Llan 72. **d** 74 **p** 75 St A. C of Shotton 74-76; Llanrhos 76-81; V of Dyserth, Trelawnyd and Cwm Dio St A from 81. *Vicarage, Dyserth, Rhyl, Clwyd.* (Dyserth 570750)

ROWLAND-SMITH, Albert. b 07. Worc OTC 56. **d** 57 **p** 58 Cov. C of Styvechale 57-59; C-in-c of St Chris Eccles Distr Allesley Pk 59-60; V 60-66; Exhall 66-71. *49 Wharton Avenue, Solihull, W Midl.* (021-705 8855)

ROWLANDS, Edward. b 18. Kelham Th Coll 37. **d** and **p** 44 Liv. C of Upholland 44-47; Leigh 47-49; V of St Jude W Derby 49-52; SPG Sec Dios York; Bradf; Wakef; Ripon and Sheff 52-58; LPr Dio York 53-58; V of Winshill 58-64; Pemberton 64-74; R 74-75; V of St D Haigh and Aspull Dio Liv from 75. *Haigh Vicarage, Wigan, Lancs.* (Wigan 831255)

ROWLANDS, Emyr Wyn. b 42. Univ of Wales (Bangor) Dipl Th 70. **d** 70 **p** 71 Ban. C of Holyhead 70-74; V of Bodedern w Llechgyfarwy Dio Ban from 74; Llechylched w Ceirchiog Llanfihangel-yn-Nhywyn and Caergeiliog Dio Ban from 74. *Vicarage, Bodedern, Caergybi, Ynys Mon, Gwyn.* (Valley 340)

ROWLANDS, Frank Wilson. b 29. LCP 58. Univ of Lon BA 61. St Deiniol's Libr Hawarden 78. **d** 81 Stockport for Ches. C of All SS Weston Dio Ches from 81. *20 Springfield Drive, Wistaston, Crewe, Cheshire, CW2 2RA.*

ROWLANDS, Forrest John. b 25. Univ of Lon BSc (Econ) 51. Chich Th Coll 54. **d** 56 **p** 57 Chich. C of St Phil Hove 56-58; Haywards Heath 58-62; R of Kingston-by-Sea (Kingston Buci) 62-75. *45 Meadway Court, Kingston Lane, Southwick, Brighton, E Sussex.*

ROWLANDS, Graeme Charles. b 53. AKC and BD 74. St Aug Coll Cant 75. **d** 76 **p** 77 Pet. C of St Mary Virg Higham Ferrers 76-79; St Thos Gorton 79-81; H Trin Reading Dio Ox from 81. *28 Prospect Street, Reading, Berks, RG1 7YG.* (0734-54920)

ROWLANDS, John Henry Lewis. b 47. St D Univ Coll Lamp BA (2nd cl Hist) 68. Powis Exhib 68. Magd Coll Cam BA 2nd cl Th Trip pt ii 70, MA 74. Westcott Ho Cam 70. **d** 72 **p** 73 St D. C of Abth 72-76; Chap St D Univ Coll Lamp and Dioc Youth Chap Dio St D 76-79; Exam Chap to Bp of St D from 78; Dir of Acad Stud St Mich Coll Llan from 79. *St Michael's College, Llandaff, Cardiff, CF5 2YJ.*

ROWLANDS, Canon John Llewellyn. b 13. TD 55. St Chad's Coll Dur BA 35. **d** 36 **p** 37 Dur. C of St Aid W Hartlepool 36-46; CF (TA) 39-46; V of St Mich AA Norton 46-56; Heworth 56-62; R of Ryton-on-Tyne 62-74; RD of Chester-le-Street 64-74; Hon Can of Dur 72-78; Can (Emer) from 78; V of Kelloe 74-78. *7 Glebelands, Corbridge, Northumberland, NE45 5DS.* (971-2390)

ROWLANDS, Joseph Haydn. b 36. St D Coll Lamp BA 62, Dipl Th 63. **d** 63 **p** 64 Ban. C of Llanfairisgaer 63-68; R of Maentwrog w Trawsfynydd 68-75; V of Henfynyw and Aberaeron w Llandewi Aberarth 75-80; R of Trefraeth Dio Ban from 80. *Trefraeth Rectory, Bodorgan, Gwyn.* (Bodorgon 280)

ROWLANDS, Kenneth Albert. b 41. N-W Ordin Course 70. **d** 73 Stockport for Ches **p** 74 Ches. C of Hoylake 73-80; Oxton Dio Ches from 80. *77 Queens Avenue, Hoylake, Chesh.* (051-652 5846)

ROWLANDS, Percival Llewellyn Noel. Univ of Melb B Com 52. **d** 66 **p** 69 Bal. Regr Dio Bal from 62; Dom Chap to Bp of Bal from 66. *9 Morton Street, Ballarat, Vic, Australia 3350.* (053-32 1026)

ROWLANDS, Richard. St Mich Coll Llan 59. **d** 62 **p** 63 Ban. C of Towyn 62-65; Dwygyfylchi w Penmaenmawr 65-69; V of Carno w Trefeglwys 69-71; CF from 71. *Ministry of Defence, Berkeley Square, W1X 6AA.*

ROWLANDS, Evan Celyn. MBE 46. Late Scho and Exhib of St Jo Coll Cam 1st cl Trip pt i, 27, BA 1st cl Cl Trip pt ii 29, 2nd cl Th Trip pt ii 30, MA 34. St Mich Coll Llan 30. **d** 39 Malmesbury for Llan **p** 31 Llan for St D, C of St Andr Llwynypia 30-31; Lect St D Coll Lamp 31-46; CF (EC) 40-45; Exam Chap to Bp of Swan B 39-46; Lect univ of Lon from 46. *Stretton Vicarage, Warrington, Chesh.* (Norcott Brook 276)

ROWLANDS, Canon Roy Griffith. ACT ThL 62. **d** 58 **p** 59 Bal. C of Merino 58-59; P-in-C 59-60; C of Warrnambool 60-61; V of Beech Forest 61-66; R of Stawell 66-73; St Paul City and Dio Bal from 73; Can of Bal from 80. *St Paul's Rectory, Ballarat, Vic., Australia 3350.* (053-32 6479)

ROWLES, Rothmore William James. Univ of W Ont BA 54. Hur Coll LTh 54. **d** 54 **p** 55 Hur. R of Thamesford 54-56; I of St Clair Beach 56-58; Bronte 58-63. *Meaford, Ont, Canada.*

ROWLEY, Canon Arthur James D'Alessio. Univ of S Afr (Rhodes Univ Coll) BA 35. **d** 37 **p** 38 Natal. C of St Jas Durban 37-45; CF (S Afr) 40-45; V of Tugela River 45-50; Estcourt 50-60; Archd of Pmbg 60-73; R of Kirby-Hilton 60-74; Hon Can of Natal from 73; Hosp Chap and L to Offic Dio Natal from 75. *4 Chapter Close, Pietermaritzburg, Natal, S Africa.*

ROWLEY, Christopher Francis Elmes. b 48. St Jo Coll Dur BA 70. St Steph Ho Ox 76. **d** 78 Sarum **p** 79 Bp Tiarks for Sarum. C of Parkstone w Branksea Dio Sarum from 78. *14 Marlborough Road, Parkstone, Poole, Dorset, BH14 0HJ.* (Parkstone 732751)

ROWLEY, Edward Patrick. b 29. Univ of Dur BSc 52. Coll of Resurr Mirfield. **d** 57 **p** 58 York. C of Kirkbymoorside 57-59; Huntington 59-61; Miss Dio Borneo 61-62; Prin Sungei Pinang Farm Sch 62-65; V of Ampleforth w Oswaldkirk 65-73; Chap Yorks Residential Sch for Deaf Doncaster from 74. *130 Bawtry Road, Bessacarr, Doncaster, DN4 7BP.*

ROWLEY, William Frederick. b 01. **d** 29 **p** 30 Ex. C of Ottery St Mary (in c of Alfington) 29-31; St Jo Bapt Paignton 31-35; St Marg Cov 35-36; Hordle 36-37; V of Kenton w Ashfield and Thorpe 37-39; R of Withington Lancs 39-46 Chap Christie Cancer Hosp 39-46; V of Irchester 46-49; Kentchurch w Llangua 49-54; R of Glaston w Bisbrooke 54-72; RD of Uppingham 61-68. *54 Dolphin Court, Johnson Road, Uppingham, Leics, LE15 9SA.* (Uppingham 2843)

ROWLEY, Canon William George. b 12. Chich Th Coll 33. **d** 55 Guildf **p** 56 Bp Hawkes for Cant. C of Cuddington Surrey 55-58; St Paul Egham Hythe 58-61; Sherborne Abbey (in c of St Paul) 61-64; V of St Swith Allington 64-73; RD of Bridport 68-70; Lyme Bay 71-76; P-in-c of Powerstock w W Milton, Witherstone and N Poorton 73-78; Can and Preb of Sarum Cathl 74-78; Can (Emer) from 78; Perm to Offic Dio Sarum from 78; Bp's Chap for Retired Clergy and Widows Lime Bay from 80. *Hatton, King William Head, Bradpole, Bridport, Dorset, DT6 3EA.* (Bridport 56265)

ROWNEY, Dean Kingsley. Univ of Minnesota, MA 69. St Mich Th Coll Crafers, 49. **d** and **p** 53 Adel. C of St Columba Hawthorn 53-56; P-in-c of Kingston w Robe 56-60; Actg Vice-Prin St Aid Coll Dogura 60-62; R of All S Lae 62-67; in Amer Ch 67-69; Prec of St Pet Cathl Adel 70-72; Chap Flinders Univ Adel 70-72; Chap C of E Gr Sch Woodlands 72-73; R of All S St Peters Dio Adel from 73. *51 Fourth Avenue, St Peter's, Australia 5069.* (08-42 1581)

ROWNEY, Geoffrey Anselm. b 27. St Jo Coll Morpeth 72. **d** 72 **p** 73 Newc. C of Wyong 72-75; P-in-c of Exper Pastoral Distr of Toukley-Budgewoi 75-79; R of Birm Gardens Dio Newc from 79. *Rectory, Moore Street, Birmingham Gardens, NSW, Australia 2286.* (55 9350)

ROWNTREE, Peter. b 47. St D Coll Lamp BA 68. Univ of Wales (S Wales & Mon) MA 70. St Steph Ho Ox 70. **d** 72 **p** 73 Kens for Lon. C of Stanwell 72-75; Northolt 75-79; Chap Ealing Gen Hosp from 79. *c/o Ealing General Hospital, Uxbridge Road, Southall, Middx.*

ROWSE, John Ridley. b 47. Univ of Massey NZ BA 70. Ridley Coll Melb 70. **d** 74 Wel **p** 75 Bp McKenzie for Wel. C of St Mary Levin 74-76; Perm to Offic Dio Melb 77-78; P-in-c of Elsternwick Dio Melb from 78. *16 Stanley Street, Elsternwick, Vic, Australia 3185.* (53 2036)

ROWSELL, Clifford Sanders. b 1898. Ex Coll Ox 19. LTh (Rome) 34. **d** and **p** 34 RC Bp of Salisbury S Rhod for Birm. Rec into Angl Commun by Abp of Cant 61. C of Reddal Hill 61-63; St Andr Netherton Dudley 63-68; Saltley Dio Birm from 68. *160 Saviour's Road, Birmingham, B8 1HG.* (021-327 0919)

ROWSELL, John Bishop. b 25. Jes Coll Cam 2nd cl Hist Trip pt i, 48, BA (3rd cl Hist Trip pt ii) 49, MA 55. Ely Th Coll 49. **d** 51 **p** 52 Lon. C of St Mary of Eton Hackney Wick 51-55; Ch Ch w St John and St Luke I of Dogs 55-56; St Mary Virg Reading 56-59; V of Hightown 59-69; Haslingfield 69-81; R of Harlton 69-81; V of Methwold Dio Ely from 81; RD of Feltwell from 81. *Methwold Vicarage, Thetford, Norf, IP26 4PQ.* (Methwold 8892)

ROWSELL, Robert Frederick. Qu Coll Newfld. **d** 55 Newfld **p** 56 NS for Newfld. I of Harbour Breton 55-63; U I Cove 63-76; U Gullies Dio E Newfld from 76. *Upper Gullies, Newfoundland, Canada.*

ROWSTON, Geoffrey. b 34. Sarum Th Coll 59. **d** 62 **p** 63 Ex. C of Ashburton w Buckland-in-the-Moor 62-65; Basingstoke 65-68; V of Netley Marsh 68-78; West End Dio Win from 78. *West End Vicarage, Southampton, SO3 3BU.* (West End 2180)

ROWSWELL, Philip Fleming. Bp's Univ Lennox BA 56. Trin Coll Tor STB 62. **d** 62 Ott **p** 63 Caled for Ott. C of N Peace River 62-65; St Martin Ott 65-68; Bp's Commiss Ott 69-72; R of St Chris Ott 72-75; on leave. *Rideau Regional Centre, Smiths Falls, Ont., Canada.*

ROWTHORN, Jeffery William. Ch Coll Cam BA 57, MA 62. U Th Sem NY BD 61. Or Coll Ox BLitt 72. Cudd Coll 61. **d** 62 **p** 63 S'wark. C of Woolwich 62-65; R of Garsington 65-68; in Amer Ch from 69. *60 Town House Road, Hamden, Connecticut 06514, USA.*

ROWTON-LEE, Edwin. b 06. St Aug Coll Cant. [f Methodist Min] **d** and **p** 61 Portsm. C of E Cowes w Whippingham 61-66; V of Kingston Lacy w Shapwick 66-80. *Pamphill Manor, Kingston Lacy, Wimborne, Dorset.* (Wimborne 3477)

ROXBURGH, Ven James William. b 21. St Cath Coll Cam BA 42, MA 46. Wycl Hall, Ox. **d** 44 Dover for Cant **p** 45 Cant. C of Ch Ch and H Trin Folkestone 44-47; Handsworth 47-50; V of St Matt Bootle 50-56; Drypool 56-65; Proc Conv York 64-65; Chelmsf from 66; V of Barking (w St Patr Barking from 73) 65-75; R 75-77; C-in-c of St Patr Barking 65-73; Hon Can of Chelmsf from 72; Archd of Colchester from 77; Pro-Prolocutor Conv of Cant from 77. *Uplands, Powers Hall End, Witham, Essex, CM8 2HE.* (Witham 513447)

ROXBY, Gordon George. b 39. Univ of Lon BSc (2nd cl Phys) 61. Coll of Resurr Mirfield, 61. **d** 63 **p** 64 Blackb. C of Fleetwood 63-66; Kirkham 66-68; V of St Jo Evang Weston Runcorn 68-78; R of St Chad Moston Dio Man from 78. *30 Hawthorn Road, New Moston, Manchester, M10 0RH.* (061-681 3203)

ROYAL, Ian Morris. Univ of Adel BA 63. Ridley Coll Melb. **d** 65 **p** 66 Adel. C of Naracoorte 65-67; Toorak Gardens 67-69; P-in-c of Morphettville 69-70. *c/o Church Office, 18 King William Road, N Adelaide 5006, S Australia.*

ROYALL, Preb Arthur Robert. b 19. Qu Coll Birm 51. **d** 53 Lon **p** 54 Kens for Lon. C of St Matt w St Hilda Ashford 53-56; V of Heap Bridge 56-59; St Aug Whitton 59-64; C-in-c of St Mich AA Bromley by Bow 64-71; C-in-c of St Sav w St Gabr and St Steph Poplar 68-71; RD of Poplar 65-66; R of Poplar 64-73; Bow w Bromley St Leon 73-76; Proc Conv Lon 68-71; RD of Tower Hamlets 68-76; Preb of St Paul's Cathl Lon from 73; C-in-c of H Trin Tredegar Sq Stepney 73-76; St Barn Bethnal Green 73-75; Clergy Appointments Adv from 76; Publ Pr Dio Lon from 77; Perm to Offic Dio Nor from 77; Dio Ely from 78. *Fielden House, Little College Street, SW1P 3SH.* (01-222 9544)

ROYCROFT, Preb Francis Joseph. TCD BA (2nd cl Mod) 32, Div Test 34, MA 35. **d** 34 **p** 35 Oss. C of Kilnamanagh 34-35; I of Dingle w Ventry 35-44; Ballymacelligott w Ballyseedy 44-69; C-in-c of Castleisland w Ballycushlane 52-69; RD of Listowel 52-54; Tralee 54-69; Preb of Kilpeacon in St Mary's Cathl Lim 59-69. *Address temp unknown.*

ROYCROFT, James Gordon Benjamin. b 26. TCD. **d** 56 Down for Connor **p** 57 Connor. C of St Aid Belf 56-58; Crossmolina 58-63; ICM Sec in N Engl 63-67; I of Drung w Castleterra Dio Kilm from 67; Laragh w Lavey Dio Kilm from 67. *Vicarage, Drung, Co Cavan, Irish Republic.* (Cavan 38104)

ROYCROFT, Michael. b 17. TCD BA 39, MA 45. **d** 40 **p** 41 Down. C of Willowfield 40-43; Holywood 43-47; I of Drumgooland and Kilcoo 47-52; Saul w Inch 52-56; RD of Lecale 53-56; R of St Mary Magd Belf 56-69; Portrush (Ballywillan) Dio Connor from 69; RD of Coleraine from 76. *10 Coleraine Road, Portrush, Co Antrim, N Ireland.*

ROYDEN, Eric Ramsay. b 29. St Deiniol's Libr Hawarden 75. **d** 77 **p** 78 Ches. C of St Paul w St Luke Tranmere 77-80; St Mary Eastham 80; V of All SS New Brighton Dio Ches from 80. *2 Zetland Road, New Brighton, Mer, L45 0JX.* (051-639 2748)

ROYDEN, Ross Eric. b 55. Lon Bible Coll BA (Th) 77. Wycl Hall Ox 79. **d** 81 Ches. C of Moreton Dio Ches from 81. *21 Wimbrick Hey, Moreton, Wirral, L42 9RU.*

ROYDS, John Caress. b 20. Qu Coll Cam BA 47, MA 50. **d** 74 **p** 75 Pet. C of St Andr Kettering 74-76; C-in-c of Loddington w Cransley Dio Pet 76; R 76-81; Dioc Dir of Educn Dio Pet 76-81; V of St Jas Northn Dio Pet from 81. *St James Vicarage, Northampton, NN5 7AX.* (Northn 51164)

ROYLE, Antony Kevan. b 50. Univ of Lon BSc 71. Trin Coll Bris 76. **d** 79 **p** 80 Lich. C of Chell Dio Lich from 79. *161 Biddulph Road, Chell, Stoke-on-Trent, ST6 6TA.*

ROYLE, Preb Edward. b 04. St Edm Hall, Ox BA 26, MA 30. Westcott Ho Cam 27. **d** 28 **p** 29 S'wark. C of St Mark East Street Walworth 28-30; C of St Sav w St Pet S'wark and Offg Chap Guy's Hosp 30-35; Dom Chap to Bp of S'wark 33-35; PV of S'wark Cathl 30-34; Dean's V 34-35; V of Lady Marg Walworth 35-42; R of Sampford Spiney w Horrabridge V 42-45; Holsworthy 45-54; R of Hollacombe 47-54; RD of Holsworthy 50; V of Heavitree 54-73; Chap Ex City Hosp 55-73; Devon and Ex Home Office Approved Sch for Girls from 55; RD of Christianity 62-65; Preb of Ex Cathl from 64. *42 Fairpark Road, Exeter, Devon.* (Exeter 73817)

ROYLE, Canon Edward Cecil. Bp's Coll Lennox LST 35, STh (Canada) 39. **d** 36 Queb for Montr **p** 36 Montr. C of St Matthias Westmount Montr 36-40; I of Arundel 40-43; CF (Canad) 43-46; R of Vaudreuil 46-77; Hon Can of Ch Ch

Cathl Montr 70-77; Can (Emer) from 77. *Box 423, Hudson Heights, PQ, Canada.* (514-458 5372)

ROYLE, Frank Peace. Egerton Hall Man 35. **d** 36 **p** 37 Man. C of Gorton 36-39; C-in-c 39-40; V of St Ambrose Oldham 41-45; St John Farnworth w Kearsley 45-47; Surr from 45; CF (TA) from 45; V of Egloshayle 47-60; Perranzabuloe w Perranporth 60-77; Dioc Insp of Schs Dio Truro from 60; RD of Powder 64-69; Perm to Offic Dio Truro from 77. *3 Droskyn Way, Perranporth, Cornw.* (Perranporth 2671)

ROYLE, George Herbert Watson. AKC 28. **d** 28 Bp Shaw for Ox **p** 29 Ox. C of High Wycombe 28-31; V of Chearsley w Nether Winchendon 31-37; R of N Chapel w Ebernoe V 37-44; Pulborough 44-70; Perm to Offic Dio Chich from 70. *Vicarage Gate, Riders Lane, Leigh Park, Havant, Hants.* (Havant 475276)

ROYLE, Peter Sydney George. b 34. K Coll Lon and Warm AKC and BD 57. **d** 58 **p** 59 S'wark. C of St Helier 58-62; Alice Springs 62-63; R 63-68; BGS 62-65; Can of Ch Ch Cathl Darwin 68; Commiss N Terr from 69; C-in-c of St Phil Sydenham 69-72; V of Leigh Park Dio Portsm from 72; RD of Havant from 77. *Vicarage, Rider's Lane, Leigh Park, Havant, Hants.* (Havant 475276)

ROYLE, Roger Michael. b 39. K Coll Lon and Warm AKC 61. **d** 62 **p** 63 Portsm. C of St Mary Portsea 62-65; St Helier 65-68; PV and Succr of S'wark Cathl 68-71, C-in-c of Dorney 71-74; Hon Chap to Bp of S'wark from 71; Sen Chap Eton Coll from 74. *Eton College, Windsor, Berks.* (Windsor 65411)

ROYLE, Stanley Michael. b 43. Univ of Man MA (Th) 75. AKC and BD 69. St Aug Coll Cant 71. **d** 72 **p** 73 Ches. C of Timperley 72-75; Research Stud Univ of Man and Perm to Offic Dio Ches 76-81; R of Milton Abbas, Hilton w Cheselbourne and Melcombe Horsey Dio Sarum from 81. *Rectory, Ansty, Dorchester, Dorset, DT2 7PX.* (Milton Abbas 880372)

RUAKOA, Ven Levi. Yei Div Coll Sudan. **d** 49 **p** 51 U Nile. P Dio U Nile 49-61; Dio N Ugan 61-69; Dio M & W Nile from 69; Can of M & W Nile from 72; Archd of Moyo from 76. *PO Moyo, Uganda.*

RUBAGORA, Elias. b 45. St Phil Coll Kongwa 68. **d** 73 **p** 74 Vic Nyan. P Dio Vic Nyan. *Box 8, Sengerema, Tanzania.*

RUBALE, Ven Shem. Bp Tucker Coll Mukono, 57. **d** 58 Ugan **p** 60 Ruw. P Dio Ugan 58-60; Dio Ruw from 60; Sub-Dean of Ruw 69-75; Dean from 76; Archd of Toro 71-72. *Box 37, Fort Portal, Uganda.*

RUBAMBURA, Peter. d and **p** 79 W Ank. P Dio W ank. *Box 105, Bushenyi, Uganda.*

RUBANDA, George Wilson. d and **p** W Ank. P Dio W Ank. *PO Mitooma, Ruhinda, Uganda.*

RUBARUHO, Stanley. d and **p** 79 W Ank. P Dio W Ank. *Box 2011, Rwashamaire, Uganda.*

RUBAYIZA, Elisee. d 76 **p** 77 Kiga. P Dio Kiga. *c/o B.P. 17 Buyumba, Rwanda.*

RUBEGA, Joseph. d and **p** 75 Bunyoro. P Dio Bunyoro. *Box 138, Parajwooki, Hoima, Uganda.*

RUBIO, Angel. b 08. Univ of Madras BA 42. **d** 39 **p** 40 RC Bp. Rec into Angl Commun by Abp of York 58. C of Harton 58-62; St Giles w St Pet Cam 62-64; V of Shouldham w Shouldham Thorpe 64-68; R of Water Newton 68-75; Stibbington 68-75. *41 Windsor Road, Cambridge.*

RUBONDO, Ernest. Bp Tucker Coll Mukono. **d** 57 **p** 60 Ugan. P Dio Ugan 57-60; Dio Nam 60-72; Dio Kamp from 72. *PO Box 7051, Kampala, Uganda.*

RUBWIRIZA, Daniel. d 80 Kiga. d Dio Kiga. *BP 17, Kibungo, Rwanda.*

RUCH, Richard August Ernest. Univ of W Ont BA 34. Wycl Coll Tor. **d** and **p** 37 Athab. Miss at Fort McMurray 37-41; I of Morpeth 41-43; Wiarton 43-45; Chesley and Tara 45-48; Walkerton w Hanover 48-50; RD of Bruce 46-50; R of St Paul Stratford Ont 50-58; St Jude Brantford 58-69; I of St Martin Niag Falls 69-70; R of Epiph Oakville 70-75. *Apt 415, 50 Governor's Road, Dundas, Ont, Canada.*

RUCH, Richard Philip. b 48. Wilfred Laurier Univ Waterloo Ont BA 74. Wycl Coll Tor MDiv 80. **d** 79 Hur **p** 81 Bp Robinson for Hur. C of St Jo Evang Lon Dio Hur from 80. *284 St James Street, London, Ont, Canada, N6A 1X3.*

RUCK, Arthur Naunton. b 01. Late Exhib of Wadh Coll Ox 3rd cl Cl Mods 22, BA (1st cl Th) 24, MA 27. Wells Th Coll 24. **d** 25 **p** 26 Bris. C of Chippenham 25-29; Dalston w Cumdivock and Dom Chap to Bp of Carl 29-31; R of Sapperton w Frampton Mansell 32-68; Hon Chap to Bp of Glouc 46-68. *Elm Grove, Somerford Road, Cirencester, GL7 1TX* (Cirencester 68649)

RUCK, John. b 47. Univ of Bris BSc 68. **d** 80 Sing. C of All SS Jakarta Dio Sing from 80. *Jalan Let Jen Suprapto 28, Cempaka Putih, Jakarta Pusat, Indonesia.*

RUCK, William. b 28. Qu Coll Birm. **d** 58 **p** 59 Carl. C of St Pet Kells Whitehaven 58-61; R of Corrigin-Kondinin W Austr 61-64; V of Ingleton w Chapel-le-Dale 64-80; RD of Ewecross 78-80; Chap Highroyds Hosp Menston from 80. *50 Valley Drive, Ben Rhydding, Ilkley, W Yorks.*

RUCYAHANA, John. d 74 **p** 75 Bunyoro. P Dio Bunyoro. *Box 20, Hoima, Uganda.*

RUDASHOBOKA, Abel. d 80 Kiga. d Dio Kiga. *BP 26, Ruhengeri, Rwanda.*

RUDD, Charles Nelson. b 06. **d** 72 **p** 73 St Arn. Hon C of Mildura Dio St Arn (Dio Bend from 77) from 72. *53 Thirteenth Street, Mildura, Vic., Australia 3500.* (050-23 1107)

RUDD, Charles Robert Jordeson. b 34. TCD BA 56, MA and BD 65. **d** 57 **p** 58 Drom. C of Ch Redeemer Lurgan 57-61; Ch Ch Cathl Lisburn 61-62; Willowfield 62-66; I of Drumgooland w Kilcoo 66-75; Moira Dio Drom from 75. *Moira, Lurgan, Co Armagh, N Ireland.* (Moira 611268)

RUDD, Canon Julian Douglas. b 19. Univ of Leeds, BA 40. Coll of Resurr Mirfield, 40. **d** 42 **p** 43 St E. C of St Jo Evang Bury St Edms 42-45; St Alb Holborn 45-49; V of St Francis Bournemouth 49-60; Surr from 55; RD of Bournemouth 56-60; Alresford 60-70; R of Old Alresford 60-70; Hon Can of Win 62-70; Proc Conv Win 64-70; V of St Mary Warw Dio Cov 70-76; R (w St Nich) from 76; C-in-c of Sherbourne 70-75; Hon Can of Cov from 76; RD of Warwick 77-79. *Rectory, The College Garden, The Butts, Warwick.* (Warwick 491132)

RUDD, Robert Arthur. b 33. ALCD 60. **d** 60 Burnley for York **p** 61 Blackb. C of Ch of Sav Blackb 60-63; St Geo Huyton 63-65; V of Bickershaw 65-72; Asst Chap Walton Pris Liv 72-73; Chap HM Pris Birm 73-78; Chap HM Pris Parkhurst from 78. *The Elms, Horsebridge Hill, Newport, IW, PO30 5TJ.* (0983-524415)

RUDDELL, Ven Joseph Frith William. b 06. TCD BA 29, Div Test 30, MA 34. **d** 30 **p** 31 Oss. C of Enniscorthy 30-34; Chap (Eccles Est) Ghorpuri 34-36; Poona 36-37; Colaba 38-40; SM Waziristan and Poona 40-41; Colaba 41-43; Deolali 43-47; I of Killanne U 48-72; RD of Bannow 54-59; Preb of Toome and Kilrush in Ferns Cathl 58-59; Archd of Ferns 59-71; Archd (Emer) from 71; Exam Chap to Bp of Oss 62-72. *Lyre, Milehouse, Enniscorthy, Co Wexford, Irish Republic.* (054-2754)

RUDDLE, Donald Arthur. b 31. Linc Th Coll 64. **d** 66 **p** 67 Pet. C of Kettering 66-70; V of St Anne w St Eliz Earlham 70-79; E Malling Dio Roch from 79. *Vicarage, 21 High Street, E Malling, Maidstone, Kent.* (W Malling 843282)

RUDDOCK, Brian John. b 45. Univ of Dur BA 66. Westcott Ho Cam 67. **d** 69 **p** 70 Heref. C of Ross-on-Wye 69-72; Kettering 72-75; C-in-c of St Steph Colchester Dio Chelmsf 75-77; R (w St Leon and St Mary Magd) from 77. *31 Old Heath Road, Colchester, Essex, CO1 2ES.* (Colchester 63662)

RUDDOCK, Charles Cecil. d 57 **p** 58 Connor. C of St Mary Belf 57-59; Carnmoney 59-61; St Aid Belf 61-63; I of Kiltegan w Rathvilly 63-69; C of Newtownards 69-72; R of Beaconsfield w Exeter 72-77; Sandford Dio Tas from 77. *Rectory, Sandford, Tasmania 7020.* (002-489873)

RUDDOCK, Edgar Chapman. b 48. St Jo Coll Dur BA 70, Dipl Th 73, MA 77. **d** 74 **p** 75 Birm. C of St Geo City and Dio Birm 74-78; R from 78. *100 Bridge Street West, Newtown, Birmingham, B19 2YX.* (021-359 2000)

RUDDOCK, Joyce-lyn Ramona Ann. b 29. Angl Women's Tr Coll Tor STh 60. **d** 71 **p** 77 Bran. C of St Bede Kinosota 71-80; I of Boissevain Dio Bran from 81. *Box 84, Boissevain, Manit, Canada.*

RUDDOCK, Kenneth Edward. b 30. TCD BA 52, Div Test (1st cl) 53. **d** 53 **p** 54 Connor. C of Ballymena 53-56; St Thos Belf 56-60; R of Tomregan w Drumlane 60-68; I of St Luke Lower Falls Belf 68-80; Whitehead Dio Connor from 80. *Rectory, Cable Road, Whitehead, Co Antrim, N Ireland.* (Whitehead 73300)

RUDDOCK, Norman Trevor. b 35. TCD BA 57, Div Test 58, MA 60, **d** 58 **p** 59 Connor. C of St Steph Belf 58-60; Ch Ch Leeson Pk Dub 60-63; Perm to Offic Dio Dub 63-73; Asst Master St Andr Coll Dub 63-69; in Amer Ch 70-72; I of Killanne 73-81. *Dardistown Castle, Julianstown, Co Meath, Irish Republic.* (041-36176)

RUDDOCK, Reginald Arthur. b 07. Oak Hill Th Coll 61. **d** 62 **p** 63 S'wark. C of Reigate 62-64; Chap Redhill Gen R Earlswood and Smallfield Hosps 64-70; R of Holton w Bratton St Maur 70-76; M Camelot Team Min 76-77. *Freshford, Horsington, Templecombe, Somt, BA8 0EF.*

RUDDY, Canon Denys Henry. b 22. Late Squire Scho Jes Coll Ox BA (2nd cl Th) 48, MA 53. Linc Th Coll 48. **d** 50 **p** 51 Portsm. C of Petersfield 50-53; Grimsby (in c of St Hugh) 53-58; R of Longworth (w Hinton Waldrist from 62) 58-77; RD of Vale of White Horse 68-75; Abingdon 79-80; Warden of Readers Dio Ox from 77; Chap St Nich Abingdon Dio Ox from 77; Hon Can of Ch Ch Ox from 79. *3 Warwick Close, Abingdon, Oxon, OX14 2HN.* (Abingdon 29474)

RUDGARD, Ven Richard Cuthbert. b 01. OBE 44, TD 50.

St Aug Coll Cant 21. **d** 27 Roch for Melan **p** 28 Melan. Miss of Ugi 27-32- Prin all H Sch Pawa 32-34; Perm to Offic (Col Cl Act) at Heene 34-35; C 35-36; V of Newbold Pacey w Moreton Morrell 36-45; CF (TA) 39-56; DACG (TA) S Command 48-56; Men in Disp 41 and 44; R of Eversley 45-60; Commiss Melan 48-74; RD of Odiham 53-59; Hon Chap to HM the Queen 54-56; Archd of Basingstoke 58-71; Archd (Emer) from 71; R of Ellisfield w Farleigh Wallop 60-74; C-in-c of Dummer 68-72; R 72-74. *22 Christchurch Road, Winchester, Hants.* (Winchester 61419)

RUDGE, Percy William Humble. b 18. St Jo Coll Dur BA 40, Dipl in Th 41, MA 43. **d** 41 **p** 42 Newc T. C of St Luke Wallsend 41-47; C-in-c of St Aid Conv Distr Lynemouth 47-52; V of St Ann Newc T 52-62; Willington-on-Tyne 62-67; Alston w Garrigill Nenthead and Kirkhaugh Dio Newc T 67-70; Gosforth Dio Newc T from 70; Chap to City Sheriff 72; Chap to High Sheriff of Tyne & Wear 74. *17 Rectory Road, Newcastle upon Tyne, NE3 1XR.* (Gosforth 851326)

RUDGE, Peter Frederick. b 27. Univ of Tas BCom 48. Univ of Leeds PhD 66. St Mich Th Coll Crafers, 49. ACT ThL 53. **d** 53 Adel **p** 53 C & Goulb. C of St Jo Bapt Canberra 53-55; P-in-c of Tumbarumba 55-56; C of Wagga Wagga 56-60; P-in-c of St Luke Canberra 60-62; Berridale 62-63; L to Offic Dio C & Goulb 67-70 and from 76; Perm to Offic Dio Pet 70-76; Dio Ox 74-76; Sen Consultant Chr Organisations Research and Advisory Trust from 70. *Box 1, Aranda, ACT, Australia 2614.*

RUDKIN, Simon David. b 51. Univ of Bradf BA 74. AKC and BD 77. Coll of Resurr Mirfield 77. **d** 78 **p** 79 Man. C of Flixton 78-81; Atherton Dio Man from 81. *13 Blake Avenue, Atherton, Manchester, M29 5PB.*

RUDLAND, Patrick Ivor. b 20. ACP 62. Tyndale Hall, Bris 56. **d** 59 Roch **p** 60 Tonbridge for Cant. C of St Jas Tunbridge Wells 59-62; L to Offic Dio Roch 62-66; Asst Master Tonbridge Co Secondary Sch 63-66; Hildenborough Sch 66-69; Hon C of Sevenoaks 66-69; Asst Master Longmead Sch Tonbridge from 69; Hon C of Tonbridge from 69. *Flat 4, 12 Dry Hill Road, Tonbridge, Kent, TN9 1LY.* (Tonbridge 351694)

RUDMAN, David Walter Thomas. b 48. Dipl Th (Lon) 70. BD (Lon) 72. Oak Hill Th Coll 68. **d** 72 **p** 73 Ex. C of St Jude Plymouth 72-75; Radipole 75-77; Warden St Geo Ho and Perm to Offic Dio Ex from 78. *St George's House, Georgeham, Braunton, Devon.* (Croyde 890755)

RUDMAN, Thomas Peter William. b 22. Oak Hill Th Coll 60. **d** 62 **p** 63 Roch. C of St Barn Conv Distr St Paul's Cray 62-65; Morden 65-67; V of Ch Ch Lowestoft 67-73; Stapenhill w Caldwell 73-81; Sutton-le-Marsh Dio Linc from 81. *Sutton-on-Sea Vicarage, Mablethorpe, Lincs, LN12 2HR.* (Sutton-on-Sea 291)

RUEHORN, Eric Arthur. b 33. St Aid Coll 58. **d** 61 **p** 62 Man. C of Harpurhey 61-65; V of Roughtown Dio Man 65-74; St Mary Hawkshaw Lane Dio Man from 74. *Hawkshaw Vicarage, Tottington, Bury, Lancs.* (Tottington 2955)

RUFF, Brian Chisholm. b 36. BD (Lon) 66. FCA 71. Oak Hill Th Coll 63. **d** 67 **p** 68 Ches. C of Cheadle 67-71; Educn and Youth Sec CPAS 72-76; V of New Milverton Dio Cov from 76. *St Mark's Vicarage, New Milverton, Leamington Spa, Warws.* (Leam Spa 21004)

RUFF, Michael Ronald. b 49. AKC and BD 72. St Aug Coll Cant 72. **d** 73 Chich **p** 74 Lewes for Chich. C of Old w New Shoreham 73-76; Perm to Offic Dio Cant 76-77; Asst Chap Ellesmere Coll 77-81; Chap Grenville Coll Bideford from 81. *Grenville College, Bideford, Devon.*

RUFFLE, Preb Frederick William. b 06. AKC 32. **d** 32 **p** 33 Lon. C of St Giles-in-the-Fields 32-35; Ashford 35-38; V of St Matt Yiewsley 38-73; RD of Uxbridge 57-67; Preb of St Paul's Cathl Lon 60-73; Preb (Emer) from 73. *61 Hetherington Road, Charlton Village, Shepperton, Middx, TW17 0SL.* (Sunbury-on-Thames 87160)

RUFFLE, John Leslie. b 43. ALCD 66. **d** 66 **p** 67 Southw. C of Eastwood 66-72; Keynsham 72-75; C-in-c of Em Weston-super-Mare Dio B & W 75; Team V from 75. *5 Walliscote Road, Weston-super-Mare, Avon, BS23 1X3.* (W-s-M 21046)

RUFFLE, Leslie Norman. b 12. Tyndale Hall Bris 49. **d** 50 **p** 51 Bradf. C of St Mary Eastwood 50-51; Bucknall w Bagnall 51-52; R of Collyhurst 52-54; V of St Chris Sneinton 54-59; R of Heanton Punchardon 59-70; Chawleigh w Cheldon 70-77; Eggesford 70-77. *14 Underhill Drive, Uphill, Weston-super-Mare, BS23 4TL.* (0934 29978)

RUFFLE, Peter Cousins. b 19. Univ of Lon BD (2nd cl) 42. ALCD 42. **d** 42 **p** 43 Lon. C of Ch Ch Highbury Lon 42-46; CMS Miss in Bihar 46-52; CMS Youth Org 52-57; Hon C of St Jo Evang Bromley 54-57; V of Walton Breck 57-60; Aigburth 60-66; Prin CA Tr Coll Blackheath 66-74; Can Res of Blackb Cathl and Dioc Missr 74-78; V of Meole Brace Dio Lich from 78. *Meole Brace Vicarage, Shrewsbury, SY3 9EZ.* (Shrewsbury 4737)

RUGE, Colin David. b 50. Univ of Auckld BA 74. St Jo Coll Auckld LTh 76. **d** 76 **p** 77 Auckld. C of St Aid Remuera 76-79; V of Panmure Dio Auckld from 79. *Box 14-197, Auckland 6, NZ.* (576-341)

RUGGLE, Richard Edward. McMaster Univ BA 63. Univ of Sussex MA 67. Wycl Coll Tor BTh 67. **d** 68 Niag **p** 68 Bp Coleman for Niag. R of Glen Williams w Norval Dio Niag from 68. *537 Main Street, Glen Williams, Ont, Canada.* (416-877 3404)

RUGGLES, Donald Clare. K Coll NS BA 58, LTh 61. **d** 60 **p** 61 NS. C of Fort George 60-65; R of Londonderry w Bass River 65-68; Sydney Mines 68-71; Bridgetown 71-76; Liv Dio NS from 76. *Box 1369, Liverpool, NS, Canada.* (354-3110)

RUGHI, Mariano. TCD 41. **d** 31 **p** 32 RC Bp of Gubbio. Rec into Angl Commun 39. Perm to Offic Dio Dub 40-45; Perm to Offic (Col Cl Act) as C of St Jas Alperton 46; C 46-49; Broadwater 49-53; Deputn and Org Sec ICM 53-56; V of Halliwell 56-61; C of H Trin Tor 61-63; St Edm Tor 63-66; R of Malton 67-78; Hon C of Mississauga Dio Tor from 79. *7150 Joliette Crescent, Mississauga, Ont, Canada.*

RUGINA, Ven Andrea Ndyabarira. **d** and **p** 48 Centr Tang. P Dio Centr Tang 48-63; Dio Vic Nyan from 63; Archd of W Lake from 68. *Box 11, Mabawe, Ngara, Tanzania.*

RUGONGEZA, Japheth. Buwalasi Th Coll 63. **d** 66 Ruw. d Dio Ruw 66-72; Dio Bunyoro from 72. *PO Box 64, Masindi, Bunyoro, Uganda.*

RUGUNDANA, [illegible] **d** and **p** 70 W Ank. P Dio W Ank. *PO Kabwohe, Ruhinda, Uganda.*

RUGUNDU, Benyamini. **d** 54 **p** 55 Centr Tang. P Dio Centr Tang 54-64. *Shunga, PO Kasulu, Tanzania.*

RUHINDI, Geresomu. **d** 64 Ankole-K. d Dio Ankole-K 64-67; Dio Kig from 67. *PO Karuhinda, Kigezi, Uganda.*

✠ **RUHINDI, Right Rev Yustasi.** Bp Tucker Coll Mukono. **d** 57 **p** 60 Ugan. P Dio Ugan 57-60; Dio Nam 60-72; Exam Chap to Bp of W Bugan 69-72; Prin Bp Tucker Coll Mukona 71-72; Cons Ld Bp of Bunyoro in St Paul's Cathl Kampala 6 Aug 72 by Abp of Ugan; Bps of W Bugan, Nam, Ank, Kig, M & W Nile, Mbale, Soroti, Ruw. N Ugan, Boga-Z, and others; Trld to N Kigezi 81. *c/o Box 23, Rukungiri, Uganda*

RUHUZA, Christopher. b 22. **d** 71 W Tang. d Dio W Tang 71-72; Dio Vic Nyan from 72. *Box 1484, Mwanza, Tanzania.*

RUJOKI, Ven John. Buwalasi Th Coll 64. **d** 65 Ankole-K **p** 67 Ank. d Dio Ankole-K 65-67; P Dio Ank 67-76; Dio E Ank from 76; Archd of Ank 74-76; E Ank from 76; Dioc Regr and Sec Dio E Ank from 79. *Box 14, Mbarara, Uganda.*

RUKIKANSHURO, Yowash. Warner Mem Th Coll Ibuye 61. **d** 63 **p** 64 Rwanda B. P Dio Rwanda B 63-66; Dio Rwa 66-75; Dio Kiga from 75. *Mpanda, Rwanda.*

RUKIMBIRA, Ven Ezekiel. **d** 68 **p** 69 Rwa. P Dio Rwa 68-75; Dio Kiga from 75; Can of Rwa 74-75; Kiga from 75; Archd Dio Kiga from 79. *BP 26, Ruhengeri, Rwanda.*

RUKIMIRANA, Peter. **d** and **p** 75 Bunyoro. P Dio Bunyoro. *Box 103, Kyangwali, Hoima, Uganda.*

✠ **RUKIRANDE, Right Rev William.** Bp Tucker Coll Mukono 64. **d** 66 **p** 67 Ankole-K. P Dio Ankole-K 66-67; Dio Kig from 67; Dean of Kig Cathl 74-75; Cons Asst Bp of Kig (Kig S from 81) in St Pet Cathl Kabale 13 April 75 by Abp of Ugan; Bps of Ank, Bukedi, Busoga, Kig, Nam and N Ugan; and others. *Box 65, Kabale, Kigezi, Uganda.*

RULA, Lizo. St Bede's Coll Umtata. **d** 53 **p** 58 Grahmstn. P Dio Grahmstn 58-61; Dio Capetn 61-62; Dio St John's 62-70; Dio Grahmstn from 70. *Box 89, Mdantsane, CP, S Africa.*

RUMALSHAH, Inayat. **d** 37 **p** 38 Lah. CMS Dio Lah 37-63; Dio Kar 63-73; C of Hazlemere 74-76; Wooburn 76-79. *40 Highfield Road, Bourne End, Bucks, SL8 5BG.*

RUMALSHAH, Munawar Kenneth. b 41. Punjab Univ BSc 60. Serampore Coll BD 65. Univ of Karachi MA 68. Bp's Coll Calc 62. **d** 65 **p** 66 Kar. C of H Trin Cathl Kar 65-70; St Edm Leeds 70-73; CMS Area Sec Dios Ripon and York 73-74; Asst Home Sec N Prov 74-78; Publ Pr Dio York 73-78; Educn Sec BCC from 78; P-in-c of St Geo Southall Dio Lon from 81. *1 Lancaster Road, Southall, Middx.* (01-574 1876)

RUMANYWOHA, Abel. **d** and **p** 75 Bunyoro. P Dio Bunyoro. *Box 102, Kinogozi, Hoima, Uganda.*

RUMBALL, Frank Thomas. b 43. Sarum Wells Th Coll 72. **d** 74 **p** 75 Heref. C of Bromyard 74-78; Team V of Ewyas Harold 78-81; L to Offic Dio Heref from 81. *The Smithy, Acton Scott, Church Stretton, Salop.*

RUMBALL, William Michael. b 41. Univ of Birm BSc 63, PhD 66, BA 75. Wycl Hall Ox 78. **d** 80 **p** 81 Ex. C of S Molton Dio Ex from 80. *2 North Road, South Molton, Devon, EX36 3AZ.*

RUMBEK, Lord Bishop of. *See* Yugusuk, Right Rev Benjamina Wani.

RUMBLES, Douglas Geoffrey. b 19. Linc Th Coll 71. **d** 73

p 74 Pet. C of Oundle 73-77; V of Nassington w Yarwell Dio Pet from 77. *Nassington Vicarage, Peterborough, PE8 6QG.* (Stamford 782271)

RUMBOLD, Bernard John. b 43. **d** 73 Papua **p** 75 Kendall for Papua. Hon C of Alotau 73-76; C of Gt Burstead 76; Chap RAF from 77. *c/o Ministry of Defence, Adastral House, Theobalds Road, WC1.*

RUMBOLD, Graham Charles. b 44. Sarum & Wells Th Coll 76. **d** 79 **p** 80 Portsm. Hon C of Wymering 79-81. *6 North Priors Court, Lings, Northampton.*

RUMENS, Canon John Henry. b 21. K Coll Lon and Warm AKC 49. **d** 50 **p** 51 Sarum. C of Wareham w Arne 50-54; V of Alderholt 54-59; R of St Edm Sarum 59-72; RD of Salisbury 69-72; Can and Preb of Sarum Cathl from 72; V of H Trin Trowbridge 72-79; P-in-c of Sturminster Marshall Dio Sarum from 79. *St Mary's Vicarage, Sturminster Marshall, Dorset, BH21 4BT.* (Stur Marshall 857255)

RUMING, Gordon William. b 27. Kelham Th Coll 45. **d** 52 **p** 53 Bradf. C of Baildon 52-55; Prestbury 55-60; St Mary Penzance 60-61; R of Calstock Dio Truro from 61; Hon Can of Truro from 79. *Rectory, Calstock, Cornw, PL18 9QX.* (Tavistock 832518)

RUMSEY, Canon Gavin Montague. Univ of BC BA 57. Angl Th Coll BC LTh 59. **d** 58 **p** 59 Koot. C of Vernon 58-61; I of Windermere 61-65; C of Trail 65-67; Koot Boundary Regional Par 67-70; R of Cranbrook 71-81; Hon Can of Koot from 75; I of St Timothy City and Dio Edmon from 81. *8420-145 Street, Edmonton, Alta, T5R 0T2, Canada.*

RUMSEY, Canon Philip Charles. b 21. Bps' Coll Cheshunt, 59. **d** 61 **p** 62 S'wark. C of St Geo Mart S'wark 61-63; Norton (in c of St Thos) 63-66; R of Knebworth 66-76; V of Lewsey Luton 76-81; R of High Wych w Gilston and Eastwick Dio St Alb from 81; Hon Can St Alb Cathl from 81. *Rectory, High Wych, Sawbridgeworth, Herts.* (Sawbridgeworth 723346)

RUMSEY, Canon Stephen Henry. b 14. St Edm Hall, Ox BA (Mod Hist) 35, MA 41. Linc Th Coll 35. **d** 37 **p** 38 Leic. C of St Pet Leic 37-47; V of Whetstone 47-78; Hon Can of Leic 77-78; Can (Emer) from 78. *8 Cooden Avenue, Leicester.* (Leic 856609)

RUMSEY, Thomas Philip. b 14. Selw Coll Cam 3rd cl Th Trip pt i, 36, BA (3rd cl Th Trip pt ii) 37. MA 41. St Aug Coll Cant 33. **d** 38 **p** 39 S'wark. C of St Geo Camberwell 38-40; SPG Miss at Nandyal 40-50; C of Strood 50-52; V of Stratfield-Mortimer 52-70; Skelsmergh w Selside and Longsleddale 70-79. *Old School Cottage, Heversham, Milnthorpe, Cumbria.*

✠ **RUNCIE, Most Rev and Right Hon Robert Alexander Kennedy.** b 21. MC 45. PC 80. BNC Ox BA (1st cl Lit Hum) and MA 48; Hon DD 80. Univ of Keele Hon DLitt 81. Univ of Cam Hon DD 81. Univ of the S Sewanee Tenn Hon DD 81. Westcott Ho Cam 48. **d** 50 **p** 51 Newc T. C of All SS Gosforth 50-52; Chap Westcott Ho Cam 53-54; Vice-Prin 54-56; Fell and Dean of Trin Hall Cam 56-60; Hon Fell for 77; Select Pr Univ of Cam 57 and 74; Gen Sec Cam Miss to Delhi 57-60; Select Pr Univ of Ox 59 and 74; Prin Cudd Coll 60-70; V of Cuddesdon 60-70; Commiss Geo 61-66; Pret 61-75; Colom from 65; Exam Chap to Bps of Wakef and Nor 60-70; to Bp of Guildf 61-70; to Bp of Chelmsf 62-70; Can and Preb of Melton Ross w Scamblesby in Linc Cathl 69-70; Cons Ld Bp of St Alb on 24 Feb 70 in Westmr Abbey by Bps of Lon; Win; Dur; Ox; Edin; Nor; Linc; Chelmsf; Sarum; Ely; Birm; Glas; and others; Chairman Internat Comm for Anglican-Orthodox Conversation 73-80; Centr Relig Advisory Coun for BBC and IBA 73-79; Hon Fell BNC Ox from 78; Trld to Cant (Abp, Primate of All England, and Metrop) 80. *Lambeth Palace, SE1 7JU.* (01-928 8282); *and Old Palace, Canterbury, Kent, CT1 2EE.*

RUNCORN, David Charles. b 54. Council for Nat Acad Awards BA (Th) 77. St Jo Coll Nottm 77. **d** 79 Lon **p** 80 Willesden for Lon. C of H Trin Wealdstone Dio Lon from 79. *2 Earls Crescent, Wealdstone, Harrow, HA1 1XN.*

RUNCORN, Canon Dennis Brookes. b 22. Ch Coll Cam BA 47, MA 52. Ridley Hall, Cam. 47. **d** 49 **p** 50 Guildf. C of Ashtead 49-53; Chap and Asst Master St Paul's Coll Hong Kong 54-62; Prin of CMS Tr Coll Chislehurst 62-67; V of Shortlands 67-80; Shorne Dio Roch from 80; RD of Beckenham 73-80; Hon Can of Roch from 78. *Shorne Vicarage, Gravesend, Kent.* (Shorne 2239)

RUNDELL, Geoffrey Edmund. b 21. St Jo Coll Dur BA (Hons Th) 48, Dipl Th 49. **d** 49 **p** 50 Dur. C of St Andr Monkwearmouth 49-52; St Jo Evang Edin 52-55; R of H Trin Stirling 55-60; V of Alvanley w Manley 60-67; Tarvin w Duddon Dio Ches from 67. *Tarvin Vicarage, Chester.* (Tarvin 40354)

RUNDLE, Donald Peter. b 19. St Cath S Ox BA (2nd cl Th) 48. MA 53. St Steph Ho Ox 46. **d** 49 **p** 50 Ex. C of St Mary Virg Laira Plymouth 49-53; Babbacombe 53-55; Paignton (in c of St Mich) 55-59; L to Offic Dio Ex 59-67; Chap Companions of Jesus the Good Shepherd 59-67; V of St Jo Evang Clevedon Dio B & W from 67. *St John's Vicarage, Clevedon, Avon.* (Clevedon 872410)

RUPERT'S LAND, Metropolitan of Province of. *See* Crabb, Most Rev Frederick Hugh Wright.

RUPERT'S LAND, Bishop of. *See* Valentine, Right Rev Barry.

RUPERT'S LAND, Dean of. *See* Harrison, Very Rev William Edward.

RURATETEREZA, Canon Mark. Warner Mem Th Coll Ibuye, 61. **d** 63 Rwanda B. d Dio Rwanda B 63-66; Dio Bur 66-75; Dio Kiga from 75; Can of Buye from 77. *Buhiga, Bujambura, Burundi.*

RUSBRIDGER, Henry John Allen. b 04. St Edm Hall, Ox BA 26, MA 30. Wells Th Coll 27. **d** 28 **p** 29 Ex. C of St Simon Plymouth 28-30; Northam Devon 30-32; Chap S Afr Ch Rly Miss Dio Kimb K 32-38; V of Swymbridge w Travellers' Rest and Gunn 39-49; R of Morchard Bp 49-64; V of Ide 64-69; Perm to Offic Dio Ex from 69. *St Crispin's, Brampford Speke, Exeter, Devon.*

RUSBY, Frank Edward. b 31. St Edm Hall, Ox BA 54, MA 58. Linc Th Coll 54. **d** 56 **p** 57 Linc. C of Louth w Welton-le-Wold 56-59; R of Kingston Bagpuize 59-62; V of Fyfield w Tubney (w Kingston Bagpuize from 62) 59-78; R of Sutton Dio S'wark from 78. *34 Robin Hood Lane, Sutton, Surrey, SM1 2RG.* (01-642 3499)

RUSCOE, John. b 12. Univ of Man BA 35. Lich Th Coll 35. **d** 37 **p** 38 Man. C of St Luke Weaste 37; St Mary Wardleworth 37-39; C-in-c 39-42; CF (EC) 42-47; PC of Penwerris 47-57; R of Redruth 57-70; Chap Redruth Hosp 57-70; Surr 57-70; R of St Mawnan w St Michael's Dio Truro from 70. *The Rectory, Mawnan, Falmouth, Cornw.* (Mawnan Smith 250280)

RUSCOE, John Ernest. b 32. Univ of Dur BA 57. Qu Coll Birm 57. **d** 59 **p** 60 Dur. C of St Paul Jarrow 59-63; Whitburn 63-65; V of St Mary S Hylton Bp Wearmouth Dio Dur from 65. *South Hylton Vicarage, Sunderland, SR4 0QB.* (Hylton 2325)

RUSH, Colin William Edward. Melb Coll of Div LTh 59. ACT ThL 63. **d** 63 **p** 64 C & Goulb. C of All SS Canberra 63-66; P-in-c of H Cross Canberra 66-68; R 68-72; Chap RAAF from 72. *11 Hedley Street, Hackett, ACT, Australia.*

RUSH, Frank Walter. St Jo Coll Morpeth ACT ThL 31. Univ of Syd BA 33. **d** 32 **p** 33 Newc. C of Lochinvar 32-34; Hamilton 34-36; C-in-c of Clarence Town 36-37; R of Jerry's Plains 37-41; Gresford 41-52; Muswellbrook 52-57; Can of Newc 55-79; R of Stockton 57-62; St John Newc 62-79; Perm to Offic Dio Newc from 79. *5/50 Wolfe Street, Newcastle, NSW, Australia 2300.* (2 2374)

RUSHER, James Victor Francis. b 28. Ridley Hall, Cam 58. **d** 60 Lon **p** 61 Kens for Lon. C of St Helen w H Trin Kens 60-63; Edgbaston 63-66; V of Ch Ch Summerfield Birm 66-71; Knowle Dio Birm from 71. *Knowle Vicarage, Solihull, W Midl.* (Knowle 3666)

RUSHFORD, Harold Tilney. b 08. Qu Coll Birm 55. **d** 56 Jarrow for Dur **p** 57 Dur. C of All SS Monkwearmouth 56-59; V of Dawdon Dio Dur from 59. *Dawdon Vicarage, Seaham, Co Durham, SR7 7NG.* (Seaham 812317)

RUSHFORTH, Colin Stephen. b 53. Chich Th Coll 74. **d** 77 Chich **p** 78 Horsham for Chich. C of St Andr Moulsecoomb 77-80; Rumboldswyke Chich 80-82; V of Friskney Dio Linc from 82. *All Saints Vicarage, Friskney, Nr Boston, Lincs.*

RUSHFORTH, Richard Hamblin. b 40. Keble Coll Ox BA (3rd cl Th) 62, MA 71. Chich Th Coll 62. **d** 64 **p** 65 Chich. C of Ch Ch St Leonards-on-Sea 64-79; Org Sec Fellowship of St Nich 79-81; V of Portslade Dio Chich from 81. *Vicarage, South Street, Portslade, E Sussex, BN4 2LE.* (Brighton 418090)

RUSHTON, James David. b 39. Univ of Dur BA (2nd cl Psychology) 61, Dipl Th 64. Cranmer Hall, Dur 63. **d** 64 **p** 65 Ripon. C of Ch Ch U Armley 64-67; Ch Ch Blackpool 67-70; V of St Cuthb Preston 70-79; St Jas Denton Holme City and Dio Carl from 79. *St James's Vicarage, Dalston Road, Carlisle, Cumb, CA2 5NW.* (Carlisle 21705)

RUSHTON, John Arnold. Univ of BC BA 63. Angl Th Coll BC STB 65. **d** 65 Koot **p** 65 Bp Greenwood for Koot. C of Kelowna 65-66; P-in-c of Kimberley 66-67; P-in-c of Golden 66-67; Staff P Dio Koot 67-68; I of Onoway 69-75; Hon C of St Faith City and Dio Edmon from 75. *Box 537, Stony Plain, Alta., Canada.* (403-963 3117)

RUSHTON, Malcolm Leslie. b 47. Univ of Bris BSc 69. Univ of Birm PhD 72. Fitzw Coll Cam BA 74. Ridley Hall Cam 72. **d** 75 **p** 76 Ex. C of Cullompton 75-79; Chap Univ Coll Lon from 79. *13 Woburn Square, WC1H 0NS.* (01-636 8880)

RUSHTON, Peter Lawrence. St Jo Coll Morpeth 61. **d** 63 **p** 64 Newc. C of Cessnock w Bellbird 63-67; Wyong 67-68; R of Weston 68-73; Wallsend Dio Newc from 73; Commiss

Carp from 78. *11 Brown Street, Wallsend, NSW, Australia 2287.*

RUSHTON, Philip William. b 38. Clifton Th Coll 62. **d** 65 **p** 66 S'wark. C of St Paul Brixton 65-67; Aldridge 67-69; Bushbury 69-71; Chap of Nat Nautical Sch Portishead 71-72; Chap RAF 72-79; P-in-c of Bolton-on-Swale Dio Ripon from 79; The Cowtons Dio Ripon from 80. *East Cowton Vicarage, Northallerton, DL7 0BN.* (N Cowton 230)

RUSHWORTH, Canon Jack Broxholme. St Jo Coll Auckld. **d** 36 **p** 37 Auckld. C of All SS Ponsonby Auckld 36-38; V of Warkworth 39-46; Northcote 46-48; Seatoun-Strathmore Wel 48-58; Hawera 58-61; P of Rangitikei-Manawatu Maori Distr Dio Wel 61-77; C 77-80; Hon Can of Wel Cathl 71-80; Can (Emer) from 80; Perm to Offic Dio Wel from 80. *Awahuri, RDG, Palmerston North, NZ.* (Feilding 7007)

✠ **RUSIBAMAYILA, Right Rev John Oswald.** b 26. **d** and **p** 71 Vic Nyan. P Dio Vic Nyan 71-73; Cons Asst Bp of Vic Nyan in Mwanza Tanzania 17 June 73 by Abp of Tanzania; Bps of Vic Nyan, Centr Tang, Moro, W Tang and SW Tang; Apptd Bp of Vic Nyan 76. *PO Box 278, Mwanza, Tanzania.* (058 2494)

RUSK, Frederick John. b 28. QUB BA 50. **d** 53 Down for Connor **p** 54 Connor. C of Ballymoney 53-56; St Nich Belf 56-59; R of St Matt Broomhedge Lisburn 59-65; St Simon Belf 65-78; Insp of Relig Educn Dios Connor, Down and Drom 64-66; I of Ballymena Dio Connor from 78. *St Patrick's Rectory, Ballymena, Co Antrim, N Ireland.* (Ballymena 2253)

RUSKELL, George Arnold. TCD BA 41, MA 46. **d** 42 **p** 43 Cash. C of Clonmel w Innislonagh 42-44; Monkstown 44-45; Chap St Steph Miss Fort Chimo 46-49; Miss at Lake Harbour 49-51 C of St Thos Tor 52-54; R of Petrolia 54-56; All SS Windsor 56-63; Hon Can of Hur 58-63; I of St John Vancouver 63-78; Exam Chap to Bp of New Westmr 65-71; Chap Bp Strachan Sch Tor from 78. *56 Birch Avenue, Toronto, M4V 1C8, Canada.*

RUSKIN, Leslie Edgar. d 60 **p** 61 River. C-in-c of Urana 60-63; R of Cobram 63-69; C of Gordonvale 69-71; R of Heywood Dio Bal from 71. *Rectory, Heywood, Vic, Australia 3304.* (055-27 2211)

RUSOTA, Julias. d 76 **p** 77 W Tang. P Dio W Tang. *PO Box 16, Kasulu, Tanzania.*

RUSS, Timothy John. b 41. AKC 64. Sarum Th Coll. **d** 66 **p** 67 Chelmsf. C of St Pet Walthamstow 66-70; Epping 70-73; St Dunstan and All SS Stepney 73-75; Youth Officer Dio Lon 75-79; Tutor YMCA Nat Coll Lon from 79. *642 Forest Road, E17.* (01-520 5599)

RUSSELL, Adrian Camper. b 45. Chich Th Coll 79. **d** 81 Burnley for Blackb. C of Marton Dio Blackb from 81. *28 Finsbury Avenue, Marton, Blackpool, FY1 6QN.*

RUSSELL, Andrew Lobanow-Rostovsky. *See* Lobanow-Rostovsky Russell, Andrew.

RUSSELL, Canon Anthony John. b 43. St Chad Coll Dur BA 65. Trin Coll Ox DPhil 71. Cudd Coll 65. **d** 70 **p** 71 Nor. C in Hilborough Group 70-73; P-in-c of Preston-on-Stour and Whitchurch (w Atherstone-on-Stour from 76) Dio Cov 73-76; R from 76; Atherstone-on-Stour 73-76; Chap Nat Agr Centre from 73; Can Th of Cov Cathl from 77; M Gen Syn from 80. *Whitchurch Rectory, Stratford-upon-Avon, Warws.* (Alderminster 225)

RUSSELL, Brian Kenneth. b 50. Trin Hall Cam BA 73, MA 76. Univ of Birm MA 77. Cudd Coll 74. **d** 76 **p** 77 S'wark. C of St Matt Redhill 76-79; Dir of Stud NE Ordin Course and P-in-c of Merrington Dio Dur from 79. *Kirk Merrington Vicarage, South View, Co Durham, DL16 7JB.* (Spennymoor 816101)

RUSSELL, Calvin William. Mem Univ Newfld BA 63. Qu Th Coll Ont LTh 55. **d** 52 **p** 53 Newfld. C of Bay Is 52-54; I of Seal Cove 54-59; C of St Mary St John's 59-62; on leave 62-63; R of Stephenville 64-70; Bay Roberts 70-73; Port Dufferin 73-74; Stellarton Dio NS from 74. *Rectory, Stellarton, NS, Canada.* (752 7213)

RUSSELL, Campbell Alexander. Univ of Tor BA 58 Trin Coll Tor LTh 61, STB 62. **d** and **p** 61 Tor. C of H Trin Tor 61-62; Tutor in Div Trin Coll Tor 62-63; Chap Univ of Tor 63-68; R of Midl 68-72; St Steph City and Dio Tor from 72. *99 Bellevue Avenue, Toronto, Ont., Canada.* (416-921 6143)

RUSSELL, David Charles. b 42. Montr Dioc Th Coll. **d** 70 **p** 71 Niag. C of Guelph 71-73; R of St John St Catherines 73-78; Chap Dio Niag 78-80; R of Fort Erie Dio Niag from 80. *303 Niagara Boulevard, Fort Erie, Ont, Canada.* (416-871 6704)

RUSSELL, David Patrick Hamilton. Univ of Capetn BA 59. Univ Coll Ox BA 63. Coll of Resurr Mirfield, 63. **d** 65 **p** 66 Grahmstn. C of St Matt Miss Dio Grahmstn 65-71; St John's Miss Zwelitsha 70-74; L to Offic Dio Capetn 74-75; C of Nyanga 75-78; Chap Migrant Workers Dio Capetn from 78. *17 Bowood Gardens, Bowood Road, Claremont 7700, CP, S Africa.* (61-9619)

RUSSELL, David Robert. b 43. Sarum Th Coll 68. **d** 70 **p** 71 Heref. C of Leintwardine 70-73; Bridgnorth w Tasley 73-75; R of Lockridge-Eden Hill 75-80; Bellevue-Darlington Dio Perth from 80. *104 Darlington Road, Darlington, W Australia 6070.* (299 7274)

RUSSELL, Dennis Tudor. b 23. Trin Coll Ox BA 50, MA 53. Westcott Ho Cam 49. **d** 51 **p** 52 Linc. C of Barton-on-Humber 51-52; Bourne 52-55; R of Belton 55-59; PC of Manthorpe w Londonthorpe 55-59; V of S Littleton w N and Middle Littleton 59-77; P-in-c of Cleeve Prior 73-77; V (w The Littletons) 77-80. *24 Barony Street, Edinburgh, EH3 6NY.* (031-226 5850)

RUSSELL, Derek John. b 30. St Pet Hall, Ox BA (2nd cl Phil Pol and Econ) 54, MA 58. Qu Coll Birm 54. **d** 56 Dover for Cant **p** 57 Cant. C of Boxley 56-59; Whitstable 59-63; Chap HM Pris Wormwood Scrubs 63-65 and from 71; Stafford 65-69; Pentonville 70; HM Remand Centre Latchmere Ho 74-77; SE Reg Chap from 74; ACG S Reg from 81. *Prison Service Chaplaincy, Tolworth Tower, Surbiton, Surrey, KT6 7DS.*

RUSSELL, Eric. b 19. Oak Hill Th Coll 38. Univ of Dur LTh 42, BA 48, MA 53. Univ of Man BD 52. **d** 42 **p** 43 Man. C of H Trin Platt Rusholme 42-45; Cheadle (in c of St Andr) 45-47; Bispham 47-49; Org Sec NW Area CPAS 49-52; LPr Dio Man 49-52; V of St John and St Jas Litherland 52-57; Cler Asst Sec Ch Soc 57-59; Asst Master Broadway Sch Cheadle 59-61; Div Master Wilmslow Gr Sch 61-64; Sen Lect Relig Educn W Midl Tr Coll Walsall 64-67; L to Offic Dio Lich 65-67; Hd of Relig Stud City Coll of Educn Sheff 67-78; L to Offic Dio Sheff 67-78; Lect Liv Bible Coll from 78; Perm to Offic Dio Liv 78-80; Dio Derby from 80. *Pine Cottage, Baulk Lane, Hathersage, Nr Sheffield.* (Hope Valley 50559)

RUSSELL, Eric Watson. b 39. Clifton Th Coll 66. **d** 69 Bp A C MacInnes for Sarum **p** 70 Sarum. C of Kinson 69-73; Peckham 73-77; Team V of Barking Dio Chelmsf from 77. *St Patrick's Vicarage, Sparsholt Road, Barking, Essex, IG11 7YG.* (01-594 0220)

RUSSELL, Garwood George. Univ of W Ont BA 48, BD 53. Hur Coll LTh 50. **d** 50 **p** 51 Hur. C of Stratford 50-51; R of Paisley Cargill and Pinkerton 50-52; St Steph Stratford w Sebringville 52-56; Tilbury 56-60; St Mary's 60-64; Goderich 64-76; Can of Hur 73-80; I of St Andr Mem Lon, Ont 76-80; Atikokan 80; Ignace Dio Keew from 80. *Box 48, Ignace, Ont, Canada.*

RUSSELL, George Frederick Robert. b 29. SOC 62. **d** 65 **p** 66 S'wark. C of Catford 65-67; Malden 67-70; V of St Paul Wimbledon Pk 70-79; Hurst Green Dio S'wark from 79. *Hurst Green Vicarage, Church Way, Oxted, Surrey.* (Oxted 2674)

RUSSELL, George Lawrence. b 09. Univ of Edin MB ChB 32. Westcott Ho Cam 34. **d** 35 **p** 36 Vic. C of St Luke Pakhoi 35-37; Lect C of E Moral Welfare Coun 38-41; V of St Pet Harrow 42-45; Educn Sec C of E Moral Welfare Coun 45-50; Perm to Offic Dio S'wark 51-64; R of Bentley 72-79. *Cleeve Cottage, Fontmell Magna, Shaftesbury, Dorset, SP7 0NY.*

RUSSELL, Harold Ian Lyle. b 34. Univ of Lon BD 60. ALCD (1st cl) 59. **d** 60 **p** 61 Ox. C of Iver 60-63; Fulwood Sheff 63-67; V of Chapeltown 67-75; M Gen Syn 70-75; RD of Tankersley 73-75; V of St Jude Mapperley Nottm Dio Southw from 75. *St Jude's Vicarage, Woodborough Road, Mapperley, Nottingham, NG3 5HE.* (Nottm 604102)

RUSSELL, Harold Percy. b 1896. Westcott Ho Cam 31. **d** and **p** 32 Leic C of H Trin Leic 32; CMS Miss Aurangabad 33; Nasik 33; Chap of Igatpuri 34-36; Manmad 36-38; CMS Supt Miss Dio Nasik 35-38; V of Bottisham 38-51; C-in-c of Six Mile Bottom 47-51; V of W Farleigh 51-54; R of Sundridge 54-63; Perm to Offic Dio Ely from 63. *Black Horse Cottage, Houghton, St Ives, Hunts.* (St Ives 62107)

RUSSELL, Herbert Mark. b 12. Univ of Dur LTh 38. Trin Coll Bris 35. **d** 38 **p** 39 Cant. C of Ch Ch Dover 38-40; Dagenham 40-42; PC of St Geo Gt Yarmouth 42-45; V of Ch Ch Dover 45-51; St Andr Whitehall Park U Holloway 51-56; Chap Whittington Hosp 52-56; Warden of Mabledon Conf Centre and L to Offic Dio Roch 56-67; V of Danehill 67-77; C of Glynde w Firle and Beddingham 77-80. *3-47 Upperton Gardens, Eastbourne, BN21 2AF.* (Eastbourne 643106)

RUSSELL, Howard Castleton. St Aid Th Coll Bal ACT ThL 10. **d** 10 **p** 12 Bal. C of St Paul E Bal Vic 10-11; Rainbow 11-12; P-in-c of Rainbow 13-14; Birchip 14-16; Mildura 16-20; V 20-23; RD of St Arnaud 16-23; Org Sec Home and Foreign Miss Newc 23-29; R of Woy Woy 29; Cooma 30-47; Bothwell 49-52. *Station Street, Whitebridge, NSW, Australia.*

RUSSELL, John Arthur. b 29. K Coll Lon and Warm AKC 62. **d** 63 **p** 64 Portsm. C of H Trin Fareham 63-67; R of Greatham w Empshott 67-79; V of Ham Dio S'wark from 79.

Vicarage, Ham Common, Richmond, TW10 5HG. (01-940 9017)

RUSSELL, John Graham. b 35. G and C Coll Cam BA 58, MA 62. Westcott Ho Cam 59. **d** 61 **p** 62 B & W. C of St Mary Bridgwater w Chilton Trinity and of Durleigh 61-66; Far Headingley 66-72; C-in-c of St Matt L Lon Leeds 72-79; V of Rowley Regis Dio Birm from 79. *192 Hanover Road, Rowley Regis, Warley, W Midl, B65 9EQ.* (021-559 1251)

RUSSELL, Jonathan Vincent Harman. b 43. K Coll Lon and Warm 68. **d** 69 **p** 70 Cant. C of Addington 69-73; Buckland-in-Dover 73-76; P-in-c of Selling Dio Cant from 76; Throwley (W Stalisfield and Otterden from 79) Dio Cant from 77. *Vicarage, Selling, Faversham, Kent, ME13 9RD.* (Selling 221)

RUSSELL, Lloyd George Winkler. b 19. Hatf Coll Dur LTh 45, BA 49. **d** 45 **p** 46 Ja. C of St Mich Kingston 45-47; and 50; P-in-c of Lucea and Green Is 48; Perm to Offic at Chester-le-Street 48-49; Wheatley Hill 49-50; (last two in Dio Dur); All SS Kingston Ja 50; St Luke Cross Roads 50; R of Black River Kings and Lacovia w Whitehall 51-52; Perm to Offic Dio Lon 53-58; Dio S'wark 53-59; Dio Roch 58-81; Asst Master Kemnal Manor Sch 67-81; R of Port Maria Dio Ja from 82. *Rectory, Port Maria, Jamaica, W Indies.*

RUSSELL, Martin Christopher. b 48. St Jo Coll Dur BA 70. Coll of Resurr Mirfield 72. **d** 74 Pontefract for Wakef **p** 75 Wakef. C of Huddersfield 74-77; St Paul's San Fernando 78-81; St Mark Point Fortin Dio Trinid from 81. *St Mark's Rectory, Point Fortin, Trinidad, WI.*

RUSSELL, Michael John. b 38. Clifton Th Coll 68. **d** 68 Bradwell for Chelmsf **p** 69 Chelmsf. C of St Luke's Eccles Distr Cranham Pk 68-70; Bucknall w Bagnall 70-76; P-in-c of Tintwistle Dio Ches 77-79; V from 79. *Tintwistle Vicarage, Hadfield, Hyde, Chesh.* (Glossop 2575)

RUSSELL, Neil. b 47. E Midl Min Tr Course. **d** 81 Grantham for Linc (APM). C of Wyberton Dio Linc from 81. *15 Cavendish Drive, Wyberton, Boston, Lincs, PE21 7BP.*

RUSSELL, Morris Charles. AKC 36. **d** 37 **p** 38 Lon. C of St Phil Tottenham 37-39; H Trin Winchmore Hill Lon 39-41; CF (EC) 41-46; C-in-c of Burnham-Sutton w Overy 46; V of Thornham w Titchwell R 46-51; Org Dir ICF and L to Offic Dio St E 48-51; R of St Mary Newmarket 51-59; St Matt Ipswich 59-67; V of St Matt Auckld 67-79; Offg Min Dio Auckld from 79. *19 Paisley Street, Howick, NZ.* (43116)

RUSSELL, Norman Atkinson. b 43. Churchill Coll Cam 2nd Cl Mech Sc Trip pt i 64, BA 65, 2nd cl Econ Trip pt ii 66, MA 69. BD (Lon) 70. Lon Coll of Div 67. **d** 70 **p** 71 Bris. C of Ch Ch w Em Clifton Bris 70-74; Cockfosters 74-77; R of Harwell w Chilton Dio Ox from 77. *Harwell Rectory, Didcot, Oxon, OX11 0EW.* (Harwell 365)

RUSSELL, Paul Selwyn. ALCD 61. **d** 61 **p** 62 Roch. C of St Mark Gillingham 61-64; Chap at Concepcion 64-66; Hon Chap Miss to Seamen Valparaiso 66-70; Valparaiso Region from 70. *Casilla 20943, La Paz, Bolivia.*

RUSSELL, Philip John Seymour. b 1900. Univ of Lon 17. Wells Th Coll 22. **d** 23 **p** 24 York. C of Whitby 23-27; St Steph Lansdown Bath 27-30; V of Liverton 30-34; Lythe 34-45; Bishopthorpe 45-55; V of Acaster Malbis 45-55; Hon Chap to Abp of York 47-55; RD of Ainsty 50-55; V of N Elmham (w Billingford from 56) 55-58; Sec Nor Dioc Reorganization C'tte 58-67; Publ Pr Dio Nor 58-67; Sec Nor Dioc Bd of Patr 59-67; Warden of Readers Dio Nor 61-67. *High Portling, Dalbeattie, Kirkcudbrightshire.* (Rockliffe 359)

✠ **RUSSELL, Most Rev Philip Welsford Richmond.** MBE (Mil) 43. Univ of S Afr BA 48, LTh (w distinc) 50. **d** 50 **p** 51 Natal. C of St Pet Maritzburg 50-54; V of Greytown 54-57; Ladysmith 57-61; Kloof 61-66; Archd of Pinetown 61-66; Cons Ld Bp Suffr of Capetn in St Sav Cathl Pietermaritzburg 26 June 66 by Abp of Capetn; Bps of Natal; Bloemf; and St John's; and Asst Bp of Natal; Trld to Port Eliz 70; to Natal 74; to Capetn 81. *Bishops Court, Claremont 7700, CP, S Africa.* (71-2531)

RUSSELL, Ralph Geoffrey Major. b 19. Sarum Th Coll 48. **d** 50 Bp Willis for Cant **p** 51 Truro. C of Redruth 50-55; Hayes 55-56; W Wycombe 56-62; V of New Bradwell w Stantonbury 62-74; C-in-c of Gt Linford 62-64; R of Stantonbury 74; Linslade Dio Ox 74-75; V from 75. *Vicarage, Linslade, Leighton Buzzard, Beds, LU7 7LP.* (Leighton Buzzard 372149)

✠ **RUSSELL, Right Rev Robert Neil.** b 06. Univ of Edin MA 28. Cudd Coll 28. **d** 29 **p** 30 Edin. C of Old St Paul Edin 29-33; S Rhodesia 33-34; UMCA Miss Dio Zanz 34-68; P-in-c Masinde 36-42; Warden of Hegongo Th Coll 43-48; P-in-c of Kwa Mkono 48-50; Kideleko 50-57; Tanga 57-63; Cons Asst Bp in Zanz in Ch Ch Cathl Zanz 19 March 63 by Abp of E Afr; Bps of SW Tang and Zanz; Asst Bp in Centr Tang (Omari) and Bp Bengt Sundkler of Bukoba (Ch of Sweden); Chap St Andr Tr Coll Korogwe 66-68; Asst Bp of Edin from 68; Hon C-in-c of Rosslyn Chap 68-73; Can of St Mary's Cathl Edin from 69. *Community of the Transfiguration, 23 Manse Road, Roslin, EH25 9LF.*

RUSSELL, Roger Geoffrey. b 47. Worc Coll Ox BA (2nd cl Th) 69, MA 73. Cudd Coll 70. **d** 72 Hull for York **p** 73 York. C of St Mark Anlaby 72-75; St Paul Knightsbridge Dio Lon from 75. *33 Wilton Place, Knightsbridge, SW1X 8SH.* (01-235 3437)

RUSSELL, Rosemary Ann. b 33. **d** 76 **p** 77 Wai. C of Rotorua Dio Wai from 76. *48 Sunset Road, Rotorua, NZ.*

RUSSELL, Stephen Waldemar. b 25. Univ of Lon, BA (2nd cl Mod Lang). Coll of Resurr Mirfield, 48. **d** 50 **p** 51 S'wark. C of St Pet Streatham 50-53; Publ Pr Dio St E 53-56; Chap and Asst Master Framlingham Coll 53-56; Chap Prince Rupert Sch Wilhelmshaven 56-57; Asst Master Old Swinford Hosp 57-58; Chap and Asst Master R Masonic Sch Bushey 58-60; V of Thornhill Lees w Savile Town 60-67; Perm to Offic H Trin Clapham 70; Asst Master Saidya Boys' Sch Muscat 70-75; C of Havant 75-79. *9 Park Lodge, Dyke Road, Hove, E Sussex, BN3 6NF.* (0273-553689)

RUSSELL, William Douglas. b 16. LCP 72. Open Univ BA 73. Worc Ordin Coll 57. **d** 59 **p** 60 Portsm. C of Farlington 59-61; V of Stanton Drew Dio B & W from 61. *Vicarage, Stanton Drew, Bristol, BS18 4EH.* (Chew Magna 2475)

RUSSELL, William Warren. b 52. Qu Univ Belf BSocSc 74. Trin Coll Dub 74. **d** 77 **p** 78 Connor. C of Portstewart Agherton 77-79; Ch Ch Cathl Lisburn Dio Connor from 79. *c/o 3 Benford Park, Lisburn, Co Antrim, N Ireland.*

RUSSELL-SMITH, Mark Raymond. b 46. St Jo Coll Dur BA (Gen) 71. Cranmer Hall Dur Dipl Th 72. **d** 72 **p** 73 Ches. C of Overchurch (or Upton) 72-75; Deane 75-77; Trav Sec for Univ and Colls Chr Fellowship 77-80; BCMS Miss Dio Nak from 81. *Box 34, Kapenguria, Kenya.*

RUSSENBERGER, Alexander. b 11. Lon Coll of Div 36. **d** 38 Truro for Ex **p** 39 Ex. [f Solicitor] C of Ch Ch Paignton 38-40; H Trin Cheltm 40-41; Chap RAFVR 41-46; C of St Mary Portsea 46-49; Area Sec CMS for Dios Bris, Glouc and B & W 49-55; V of St Mark Bromley Kent 55-67; St Alb Golders Green 67-71; Perm to Offic Dio Ex from 72. *Fairhills, Seaway Lane, Cockington, Torquay, Devon.* (Torquay 605437)

RUSSON, Joseph Kenneth. b 21. St Aid Coll 56. **d** 59 Lanc for Blackb **p** 60 Burnley for York. C of Haslingden 59-62; St Matt Preston Blackb 62-65; V of St Jas Burnley Dio Blackb from 65. *Vicarage, March Street, Burnley, Lancs.* (Burnley 24758)

RUSTED, Very Rev Edward Charles William. b 19. OBE 60. Hatf Coll Dur BA 41, MA 44. St Bonif Coll Warm LTh 40. **d** 42 Bp Crotty for Lon **p** 43 Lon. C of St Gabr Bounds Green 42-44; Chap RNVR 44-47; C of St Mark N Audley Street 47-49; L to Offic at St Jo Div Kennington 49-50; Prin of All SS Sch Jesselton 50-68; Hon Can of Jess 62-68; Sabah 68-76; Can (Emer) from 76; VG Jess 64-65; P-in-c of Tuaran w Kota Belud 67-68; V of St Osw Norbury 68-77; Dean and R of St Jo Bapt Cathl St John's Dio E Newfld from 77. *22 Church Hill, St John's, Newfoundland, Canada.* (709-726 6386)

RUSTON, Canon Cuthbert Mark. b 16. Jes Coll Cam 2nd cl Hist Trip pt i, 37, Lady Kaye Scho 38, BA (2nd cl Th Trip pt i) 39, MA 42. Ridley Hall, Cam 39. **d** 40 **p** 41 Guildf. C of St Jo Bapt Woking 40-42; Chap Cheltm Coll 42-51; Jes Coll Cam 51-53; Em Coll Cam 53-54; C of St Paul Cam 54-55; V of H Sepulchre (with All SS from 73) Cam Dio Ely from 55; Exam Chap to Bps of Ely and Nor from 71; RD of Cam 74-80; Hon Can of Ely Cathl from 75; Chap to HM the Queen from 80. *37 Jesus Lane, Cambridge.* (Cambridge 357931)

RUSTON, Ven John Harry Gerald. SS Coll Cam 1st cl Cl Trip pt i, 51, BA (1st cl Cl Trip pt ii) 52, MA 56. Ely Th Coll 52. **d** 54 **p** 55 Leic. C of St Andr Leic 54-57; Cuddesdon 57-61; Tutor Cudd Coll 57-61; C of Sekhukhuniland 62-70; Prin St Francis's Coll Sekhukhuniland 67-70; Exam Chap to Bp of Pret 67-76; to Bp of Bloemf from 76; Kimb K from 77; Can of Pret 68-76; Sub Dean of St Alb Cathl Pret 71-76; Archd of Bloemf from 76; Warden and Chap St Mich Sch Bloemf from 76. *Box 12110, Tempe, Bloemfontein, S Africa.*

RUSTON, William Victor Fitz-Gerald. b 01. St Paul's Coll Burgh. **d** 28 Grantham for Linc **p** 29 Linc. C of St Nich Skirbeck 28-30; Perm to Offic at St Mary Magd Paddington 30-31; C of St Matt Nass 31; P-in-c of St Andr Exuma 32-34; C of St Matthias Earl's Court 34-38; St Jo Evang Holborn 38-41; R of Tattingstone 41-46; P-in-c of St Patr Governor's Harbour and St Mary Magd Waynes Bight Eleuthera Nass 47-51; C of H Innoc Hammersmith 51; R of Annotto Bay 51-53; Buff Bay w Birnam Ja 51-56; V of Tintinhull 56-66. *10 Grand Marine Court, Durley Gardens, West Cliff, Bournemouth, Dorset, BH2 5HS.*

RUTAARA, Selevasta. d 74 **p** 76 Ruw. P Dio Ruw. *Box 37, Fort Portal, Uganda.*

RUTABALENGYA, George. d 73 **p** 76 Ruw. P Dio Ruw.

Nyakasura School, Box 16, Fort Portal, Uganda.

RUTAGARUKAYO, Canon Erenesti. Warner Mem Th Coll Ibuye, 48. **d** 49 **p** 51 Ugan. P Dio Ugan 49-60; Dio Ankole-K 60-67; Dio Kig from 67; Hon Can of Kig Cathl from 70. *PO Karuhinde, Kinkizi, Kigezi, Uganda.*

RUTEBUKA, James. d 74 **p** 76 Ruw. P Dio Ruw. *Box 37, Fort Portal, Uganda.*

RUTEITSIRE, Esau. Bp Tucker Coll Mukono, 60. **d** 62 **p** 64 Ankole-K. P Dio Ankole-K 64-67; Dio Ank from 67-76. *PO Box 452, Mbarara, Uganda.*

RUTHERFORD, Graeme Stanley. Ridley Coll Melb ACT ThL 65. **d** 66 **p** 67 Bend. C of St Paul Bend 66-70; V of Pyramid Hill 70-73; C of St Nich City 73-78; R of Kyabram Dio Bend from 78. *St Andrew's Rectory, Church Street, Kyabram, Vic., Australia 3620.*

RUTHERFORD, Ian William. b 46. St D Coll Lamp BA 68. Cudd Coll 68. **d** 70 Bp Ramsbotham for Newc T **p** 71 Newc T. C of All SS Gosforth Dio Newc T 70-73; Prestbury 73-76; Chap RN from 76. *c/o Ministry of Defence, Lacon House, Theobald's Road, WC1X 8RY.*

RUTHERFORD, John Allarton Edge. b 10. SS Coll Cam 2nd cl Math Trip pt i, 30, BA (2nd cl Th Trip pt i) 32, MA 36. Westcott Ho Cam 32. **d** 33 **p** 34 Portsm. C of Cathl Ch Portsm 33-40; Chap St Jo Coll York and Chap Abp Holgate's Gr Sch York 40-42; Chap RAFVR 42-46; Asst Master and Chap Charterho Sch and Perm to Offic Dio Guildf 46-70; V of Walsham-le-Willows Dio St E from 70; P-in-c of Hinderclay Dio St E from 75. *The Priory, Walsham-le-Willows, Bury St Edmunds, Suff.* (Walsham-le-Willows 280)

RUTHERFORD, Canon John Bilton. b 23. Qu Coll Birm 49. **d** 52 **p** 53 Newc T. C of H Cross Fenham Newc T 52-57; Long Benton (in c of St Mary Magd) 57-60; V of St Phil Newc T 60-66; Walker 66-74; St Jas Benwell Newc T 74-80; Lesbury w Alnmouth Dio Newc T from 81; Hon Can of Newc T from 80. *Vicarage, Lesbury, Northumb.* (Alnmouth 281)

RUTHERFORD, John Christopher. b 47. ACT ThL 77. Moore Coll Syd 75. **d** 77 **p** 78 Armid. C of Moree 77-80; V of Tambar Springs Dio Armid from 80. *Vicarage, Tambar Springs, NSW, Australia 2381.*

RUTHERFORD, Peter George. b 34. Nor Ordin Course 73. **d** 76 Lynn for Nor **p** 77 Nor (NSM). C of Ch Ch New Catton Nor 76-78; Eaton 79-80; St Steph City and Dio Nor from 81. *30 The Close, Norwich, NR1 4DZ.* (Nor 24386)

RUTHERFORD, Thomas Thompson. b 13. Qu Coll Birm 75. **d** 76 Bp Daly for Cov **p** 77 Cov (APM). C of St Jas Southam Dio Cov from 76. *17 Elan Close, Leamington Spa, Warwicks.* (Leam Spa 29688)

RUTHERFORD, Thomas William Hardy. b 24. TCD BA 46, MA 49. Div Test 47. **d** 47 **p** 48 Down. C of Newtownards 47-50; St Dunstan and H Cross w St Pet Cant 50-53; R of Bewcastle 53-57; V of Bolton w Cliburn 57-67; Blackford w Scaleby 67-75; P-in-c of Clifton w Brougham Dio Carl from 75; R (w Cliburn) from 77; P-in-c of Cliburn 75-77. *Clifton Rectory, Penrith, Cumb, CA10 2EA.* (Penrith 64766)

RUTIHINDA, Gerevazi Kazobona. d and **p** 48 Centr Tang. P Dio Centr Tang 48-63; Dio Vic Nyan from 63; Archd of Sukumaland 68-79. *Box 93, Ngara, Tanzania.*

RUTLEDGE, Christopher John Francis. b 44. BSc (2nd cl Soc) (Lon) 67. Sarum Th Coll 67. **d** 70 **p** 71 Birm. C of St Peter Birm 70-73; Calne 73-76; P-in-c of Derry Hill 76-78; V 78-81; P-in-c of Talbot Village Dio Sarum from 81. *St Mark's Vicarage, Talbot Village, Bournemouth, Dorset.* (Bournemouth 529349)

✠ **RUTT, Right Rev Cecil Richard.** b 25. CBE 73. Pemb Coll Cam BA 54, MA 58. Confucian Univ of Seoul Hon D Litt 74. Kelham Th Coll 47. **d** 51 **p** 52 Ely. C of St Geo Chesterton 51-54; Seoul 54-56; P-in-c of Anjung 56-58; Warden St Bede's Univ Centre Seoul 59-64; R of St Mich Sem Oryu Dong 64-66; Archd of W Seoul 65-66; Cons Asst Bp of Taejon in St Mary and St Nich Cathl Seoul 28 Oct 66 by Bp of Seoul; Bps of Taejon; and Kuch; and Bp Chadwell; Apptd Bp of Taejon 68; res 74; Bp Suffr of St Germans 74; Trld to Leic 79; Hon Can (Can Missr from 77) of Truro from 74; Commiss Taejon from 74; Chap O of St John of Jer from 78. *10 Springfield Road, Leicester, LE2 3BD.* (Leicester 708985)

RUTT, Canon Denis Fredric John. b 17. Kelham Th Coll 34. **d** 41 **p** 42 St Alb. C of Ch Ch Luton 41-46; Bp's Chap for Youth and LPr Dio St Alb 46-48; R and Dir of Empangeni 48-54; R of Yaxham 54-61; R of Welborne 54-61; Kirkley 61-71; Proc Conv Nor 60-76; RD of Lothingland 65-71; Commiss Wai from 71; V of King's Lynn 71-76; Hon Can of Nor 72-76; Can Res and Prec of Lich Cathl from 76. *23 The Close, Lichfield, Staffs.* (Lichfield 23337)

RUTTER, Allen Edward Henry. Qu Coll Cam 2nd cl Nat Sc Trip pt i 51, BA 52, MA 56. Cranmer Hall Dur Dipl Th 58. **d** 59 **p** 60 B & W. C of Bath Abbey 59-60; E Dereham w Hoe 60-64; R of Cawston 64-69; C-in-c of Felthorpe w Haveringland 64-69; R of Gingindhlovu 69-73; P-in-c of Over Compton w Nether Compton Trent (w Sandford Orcas from 75) 73-80; Sandford Orcas 73-75; Oborne w Poyntington 79-80; RD of Sherborne from 77; R of Queen Thorne Dio Sarum from 80. *Nether Compton Rectory, Sherborne, Dorset.* (Yeovil 6421)

RUTTER, Canon Arthur Percival Langley. Moore Th Coll Syd. **d** and **p** 50 Bal. P-in-c of Buninyong 50-52; All SS Bal and Chap of Bal Base Hosp 52-59; V of Stawell 59-66; R of Camperdown 66-76; Hon Can of Bal 68-73; Can 73-75; Can (Emer) from 76; Perm to Offic Dio Bal from 76. *4 Bennet Street, Stawell, Vic, Australia 3380.*

RUTTER, Canon David Carter. Late Scho of Ex Coll Ox BA 46, MA 50. Cudd Coll Organist Scho 48. **d** 50 **p** 51 York. C of Thornaby-on-Tees 50-53; Sub-Warden and Lect St Deiniol's Libr Hawarden and L to Offic Dios Ches and St A 53-55; Min Can Jun Cardinal and Succr of St Paul's Cathl Lon and L to Offic Dio Lon 55-64; Can and Preb of Linc Cathl from 64; Prec from 65. *Precentory, Lincoln.* (Lincoln 23644)

RUTTER, Gerald Ernest. b 12. Bps' Coll Cheshunt. **d** 48 **p** 49 Derby. C of Staveley 48-54; Chesterfield 54-55; Worksop 55-57; Norton (in c of St Thos) 57-62; V of Chinley w Buxworth 62-66; Chap Commun of Sacred Passion and St Giles Leper Home E Hanningfield and Perm to Offic Dio Chelmsf from 66. *69 Kennel Lane, Fetcham, Leatherhead, Surrey, KT22 9PR.* (Bookham 56270)

RUTTER, Canon Kenneth George. d 51 **p** 52 Alg. C of Nipigon and Red Rock 51-52; I of St Mich Port Arthur 52-57; C of St Barn 57-59; R of St Aid Ott 59-66; The Advent Montr 66-70; Sec of Synod Dio Montr 69-70; R of St Mary Virg Belize 70-71; I of Valleyfield 71-73; Renfrew 73-79; Kanata Dio Ott from 79; Can of Ott from 80. *56 Glamorgan Drive, Kanata, Ont, Canada.*

RUTTER, Martin Charles. b 54. Wolverhampton Poly BSc 75. Univ of Southn BTh 81. Sarum Wells Th Coll 76. **d** 79 **p** 80 Lich. C of St Luke Cannock Dio Lich from 79. *44 Manor Avenue, Cannock, Staffs, WS11 1AA.*

RUTTER, William Ralph. b 1894. **d** 58 **p** 59 Pet. C of St Jas Northm 58-60; V of Mears Ashby 60-69; R of Hardwycke 60-69; L to Offic Dio Pet 70-79; Dio Ox from 80. *Ellesborough Manor, Butler's Cross, Aylesbury, Bucks.*

RUVUMA, Lord Bishop of. *See* Ngahyoma, Right Rev Maurice David.

RUVUZUMUTEGO, Leonard. d 68 **p** 69 Rwa. P Dio Rwa 68-75; Dio Kiga from 75. *EAR Gikonko, Butare, Rwanda.*

RUWENZORI, Lord Bishop of. *See* Kamanyire, Right Rev Eustace.

RUWENZORI, Assistant Bishop of. (Vacant)

RUZIKAMUNZIRA, Elisha. d 66 **p** 67 Vic Nyan. P Dio Vic Nyan. *Muruvyagira, Shanga, PO Ngara, Tanzania.*

RUZINDANA, Eric. Bp Tucker Coll Mukono, 64. **d** 66 Ankole-K. d Dio Ankole-K 66-67; Dio Kig from 67. *Church of Uganda, Kashenyi, PO Rukungiri, Kigezi, Uganda.*

RUZIRO, Laurence. b 46. **d** 79 **p** 80 W Tang. P Dio W Tang. *PO Box Muyama, Kasulu, Tanzania, W Africa.*

RWABIGONJI, John Patrick. b 43. Bp Tucker Coll Mukono 70. **d** 72 W Bugan. d Dio W Bugan 72-79 and from 80; on leave 79-80. *Box 102, Mityana, Uganda.*

RWABIHAIGA, Amos. Bp Tucker Coll Mukono, 49. **d** 51 Ugan **p** 53 Bp Balya for Ugan. P Dio Ugan 51-60; Dio Ankole-K 60-67; Dio Ank 67-77; Can of Ank 72-77; E Ank 77-79. *PO Ibanda, Mbarara, Ankole, Uganda.*

RWABUKOBA, Charles. d 78 **p** 79 Vic Nyan. P Dio Vic Nyan. *PO Katoke, Bukoba, Tanzania.*

RWABUSHAIJA, Canon Simei. Bp Tucker Coll Mukono, 60. **d** 61 **p** 63 Ankole-K. P Dio Ankole-K 61-67; Dio Ank (E Ank from 76) from 67; Can of Ank 70-76; E Ank from 76; Archd of Ank 70-76; E Ank 76-79. *PO Kihonzi, Ankole, Uganda.*

✠ **RWAKAIKARA, Right Rev Yonasani.** Clifton Th Coll 64. **d** 65 **p** 66 Ruw. P Dio Ruw and Chap Masindi Sch 65-66; Cons Asst Bp of Ruw in Nam Cathl 8 Jan 67 by Abp of Ugan; Bps of Ankole-K, Mbale, Nam, N Ugan, Soroti, Bur, Nak, W Bugan, and Rwa; and Asst Bp in Sudan; Apptd Ld Bp of Ruw 72; Trld to Bunyoro 81. *Box 20, Hoima, Uganda.* (Hoima 128)

RWAKATARE, Charles. b 50. Univ of Serampore BD 80. Yeotmal Sem 75. **d** 80 **p** 81 Vic Nyan. P Dio Vic Nyan. *PO Box 26, Kongwa, Tanzania.*

RWAMARAKI, Erisa. d 75 **p** 77 Ruw. P Dio Ruw. *Box 497, Fort Portal, Uganda.*

RWAMURINDA, Aaron. d 65 Rwanda B **p** 66 Rwa. P Dio Rwa 65-75; Dio Kiga from 75. *Post Box 29, Gitarama, Rwanda.*

RWANDA, BURUNDI and BOGA-ZAIRE, Metropolitan of Province of. (Vacant)

RWANFIZI, Ven KeziRONI. Bp Tucker Coll Mukono **d** 60 **p** 62 Ankole-K. P Dio Ankole-K 60-67; Dio Kig from 67; Can of Kig from 70; Archd from 74. *PO Box 1017, Kisoro, Kigezi, Uganda.*

RWANGOGA, Samusoni. d 80 Kiga. d Dio Kiga. *BP 89, Kigali, Rwanda.*

RWEBAKUZA, Yerimiya. d and **p** 79 W Ank. P Dio W Ank. *Box 143, Bushenyi, Uganda.*

RWEIZIRE, Shem. d 64 Ankole-K. d Dio Ankole-K 64-66; Dio Rwa 66-75; Dio Kiga from 75. *Anglican Church, Byumba, Kigali, Rwanda.*

RWINONGO, George. d 64 Ankole-K. d Dio Ankole-K 64-67; Dio Ank 67-77; Dio W Ank 77-79. *Rubaare, Rusheny, Uganda.*

RWOBUSISI, Geoffrey. b 47. Bp Tucker Coll Mukono 71. **d** 73 **p** 74 Ruw. P Dio Ruw. *Box 37, Fort Portal, Uganda.*

RYALL, John Francis Robert. b 30. New Coll Ox BA 52, MA 57. Westcott Ho Cam 52. **d** 54 **p** 57 Portsm. C of Petersfield w Sheet 54-56; St Mary Portsea 56-62; Warblington w Emsworth 62-65; Freshwater 65-67; R of Frating w Thorington 67-73; Gt (w L from 76) Yeldham 74-80; C-in-c of L Yeldham 75-76; P-in-c of Shalfleet Dio Portsm from 80; Thorley Dio Portsm from 80. *Shalfleet Vicarage, Newport, IW, PO30 4NF.* (Calbourne 238)

RYALL, Michael Richard. b 36. TCD BA 58, MA 65. **d** 58 **p** 59 Dub. C of St Geo Dub 58-62; CF 62-65 and from 68; CF (TAVR) 67-68; C of Rathmines Dub 65-66; Asst Master Dungannon Secondary Sch 66-68. *c/o Ministry of Defence, Bagshot Park, Bagshot, Surrey.*

RYAN, Allen Gerald. St Francis Coll Brisb 47. ACT ThL 49. **d** 49 **p** 50 Brisb. Miss Chap Dio Brisb 49-53; V of Palmwoods 53-56; R of Oakey 56-59; Wau 59-65; Chap Princess Alexandra Hosp Brisb 65-76; C of St Pet Southport 76-80. *13a Imperial Parade, Labrador, Queensland, Australia 4215.*

RYAN, Denis Blake. Moore Th Coll Syd ACT ThL (2nd cl) 65. **d** 65 **p** 66 Syd. C of Longueville 65-67; C-in-c of Blakehurst Provisional Distr 67-71; L to Offic Dio Syd 72-77; R of Ch Ch N Syd Dio Syd from 77. *28 Lavender Street, N Sydney, NSW, Australia 2060.* (92-1719)

RYAN, Edward Joseph. Keble Coll Ox PhD 66. St Steph Ho Ox. **d** 67 Lon **p** 68 Willesden for Lon. C of Northwood 67-70; L to Offic Dio Lon from 71. *29 Kewferry Road, Northwood, Middx.* (01-65 23324)

RYAN, Jock Lugton. Univ of Melb BA 65. Ridley Coll Melb 47. ACT ThL 49. **d** 50 **p** 51 Melb. C of Coburg 50-51; Min of Berwick 51-54; C of Melb Dioc Centre and P-in-c of St Jude Carlton 54-59; V of Doncaster 59-67; I of St Jas Glen Iris 67-78; Chap Caulfield Gr Sch Dio Melb from 78. *19 Merriwoola Street, East St Kilda, Vic, Australia 3183.* (528 6544)

RYAN, Michael Dennis George Conybeare. b 15. Qu Coll Birm 54. **d** 56 **p** 57 Portsm. C of St Francis Conv Distr Leigh Park 56-59; V of All SS Chorley 59-64; Greenhead 64-74; P-in-c of Gilsland w Over Denton 74; V of Cornhill w Carham 74-80; P-in-c of Branxton 74-80; Coldstream Dio Edin from 80. *Leitholm Mill, Leitholm, Berwicks, TD12 4JP.* (089-084289)

RYAN, Roger John. b 47. Lon Bible Coll BA (Th) 79. Oak Hill Coll 79. **d** 80 **p** 81 St Alb. C of St Francis Luton Dio St Alb from 80. *15 Lancing Road, Luton, Beds, LUT 8JN.* (Luton 20082)

RYAN, Stephen John. b 49. Univ of Wales 67. BA 70. Univ of Bris Dipl Th 73. Sarum Wells Th Coll 70. **d** 73 **p** 74 Llan. C of Llantrisant 73-77; V of Treherbert w Treorchy Dio Llan from 77; Dioc Youth Chap Dio Llan from 81. *Vicarage, John Street, Treherbert, Mid Glam, CF2 5HH.* (Treorchy 772241)

RYCROFT, Stanley. b 30. Open Univ BA 73, BA (Hons) 75. Univ of Bris MEducn 81. Sarum Th Coll 56. **d** 59 Reading for Ox **p** 60 Ox. C of St Bart Earley 59-62; Chap and Asst Master Whittlebury Sch Towcester 62-63; C of Christchurch w Mudeford 63-67; Chap and Asst Master Durlston Court Sch Barton on Sea 67-71; Millfield Jun Sch Somt 71-75; Chap and Asst Master Wel Sch Somt from 75. *9 Orchard Close, Westford, Wellington, Somt.* (Wellington 7100)

RYDER, Derek Michael. b 36. St Cath Coll Cam BA 60, MA 64. Tyndale Hall, Bris 61. **d** 63 **p** 64 Sarum. C of Hampreston 63-66; Asst Chap Brentwood Sch 66-72; Chap Ipswich Sch 72-77; Home Sec CMJ from 77. *12 Lichfield Road, Woodford Green, Essex.* (01-505 0046)

RYDER, Lisle Robert Dudley. b 43. Selw Coll Cam 3rd cl Hist Trip pt i 67, (3rd cl Th Trip pt ii) 69. Sarum Th Coll 69. **d** 71 **p** 72 Lynn for Nor. C in Lowestoft Group (C of St Marg Lowestoft 71-75; Asst Chap Oxon Area Health Authority 76-79; C of St Mary and St Jas Littlehampton Dio Chich from 79; All SS Wick Dio Chich from 79. *St James's Vicarage, Arundel Road, Littlehampton, BN17 7DF.* (Littlehampton 24844)

RYDER, Thomas Arthur. b 02. Univ of Bris BSc (1st cl) 24, PhD 27. K Coll Lon 29. **d** 29 **p** 30 Glouc. C of Lydney w Aylburton 29-33; Parkend 33-37; V of Cam 37-70. *2a Upthorpe, Cam, Dursley, Glos.*

RYDER, Tom. b 08. Worc Coll Ox BA 31, MA 41. Cudd Coll 30. **d** 32 **p** 33 Ripon. C of All S Leeds 32-34; St Martin Brighton 34-36; All SS Marg Street St Marylebone 36-41; Ch Ch Ealing 41-42; Asst Sec Lon Dioc Fund 42-43; Chap RAFVR 43-46; RAF Cranwell 46-49; Chap RAF 49-65; Asst Chap-in-Chief Fighter Coastal and Signals Commands 59-60; Res Chap St Clem Danes Westmr 60-65; Chap at Beaulieu-sur-Mer 66-69; Perm to Offic Dio Lon from 70. *27a Culross Street, Park Lane, W17 3HF.*

RYDER, Vivian Charles. OBE 76. Qu Coll Birm 63. **d** 64 Pet for Argent **p** 65 Argent. L to Offic Yelvertoft w Claycoton and Lilbourne 63-65; Prin Quilmes High Sch 65-74; Chap at All SS Quilmes 65-81; Chap St Geo Coll Quilmes Dio Argent 67-74; R, Can and Sub-Dean of St John's Cathl Buenos Aires 74-81; P-in-c of Horseheath Dio Ely from 81. *Rectory, Horseheath, Cambridge.*

RYDER-JONES, Preb William Henry. b 16. St D Coll Lamp BA 38. Ridley Hall, Cam 39. **d** 40 **p** 41 Ex. C of St Jude Plymouth 40-44; Paignton 44-48; V of Kingston Dorset 48-50; St Luke Torquay 50-77; Preb of Ex 68-80; Preb (Emer) from 80. *c/o Barclays Bank Ltd., 39 Fleet Street, Torquay, Devon.*

RYDINGS, Donald. b 33. Jes Coll Ox BA (2nd cl Th) 57, MA 61. Linc Th Coll 57. **d** 59 Lanc for Blackb **p** 60 Burnley for York. C of Poulton-le-Fylde 59-62; St Mary Virg Ox 62-66; Staff Sec SCM Ox 62-66; C-in-c of St Mark's Conv Distr Bourne End Wooburn 66-74; R of Hedsor and Bourne End 74-76; Exam Chap to Bp of Ox from 73; P-in-c of Gt Missenden Dio Ox from 76; RD of Wendover from 79. *Vicarage, Walnut Close, Great Missenden, Bucks, HP16 9AL.* (Gt Missenden 2470)

RYE, David Ralph. b 33. K Coll Lon and Warm AKC 59. **d** 60 **p** 61 St E. C of Rushmere 60-64; V in Barnham Broom Group Dio Nor 64-76; Team V 76-82; Team R from 82. *Vicarage, Barnham Broom, Norwich, NR9 4DB.* (Barnham Broom 204)

RYE, Ven john Hanington Brooke. Univ of BC BA 54. Trin Coll Tor STB 58. **d** 57 **p** 58 Niag. R of St Cuthb Oakville 57-67; Dom Chap to Bp of Niag 63-67; L to Offic Dio Accra from 68; Hon Can of Accra 73-77; Archd Dio Accra from 77. *Anglican Church Mission, PO Box 46, Bolgatanga, Ghana.*

RYE, Peter Harry. b 29. K Coll Lon and Warm AKC 52. **d** 53 **p** 54 Linc. C of Grantham 53-58; Lowestoft (in c of St Pet) 58-60; V of Martham 60-68; PC of W Somerton 60-68; Chap and Sec Dioc Coun for Deaf and L to Offic Dio Ox 68-73; V of Brize Norton (w Carterton to 77) 73-81; Carterton 77-81; Freeland and Cassington Dio Ox from 81. *Vicarage, Wroslyn Road, Freeland, Oxford, OX7 2HL.* (Freeland 881232)

RYECART, Cecil Ernest. b 04. MVO 56. King's Coll Lon 24. **d** 27 **p** 29 Br Hond. C of St Mary Virg Belize 27-29; St Mark Limon 29-32; Perm to Offic (Col cl Act) at Wymondham 32-33; C 33-35; C of Sneinton 35-39; R of Winthorpe 39-50; V of Langford w Holme-by-Newark 39-50; CF (EC) 40-45; C and Seq of Buxted 50-51; V of St Bart Chich 51-54; Chap St Richard's Hosp Chich 51-54; Chap at Stockholm 54-63; V of St Pet Eastbourne 63-71; Perm to Offic Dio S'wark 76-79; Dio Win from 79. *27 Church Street, Alton, Hants.*

RYECART, John Reginald. b 07. AKC and Wichelow Pri 32. St Steph Ho Ox 32. **d** 33 **p** 34 Southw. C of St Leon Newark-on-Trent 33-35; St Jo Bapt Sevenoaks 35-41; Chap RAFVR 41-46; V of Leek Wootton 47-49; R of Honiley and Wroxall Chap 49-53; Chap at St Luke Haifa 53-60; V of Gt Sampford w Hempstead 60-74. *100 Fronks Road, Dovercourt, Essex.* (Harwich 7370)

RYELAND, John. b 58. AKC and BD 80. Linc Th Coll 80. **d** 81 Edmon for Lon. C of St Jas Enfield Highway Dio Lon from 81. *170 Addison Road, Enfield, Middx.*

RYLAND, Colin William. b 16. TD 52. St Steph Ho Ox 61. **d** 62 **p** 63 Ex. C of Plymstock 62-66; R of Ch Brampton w Chap Brampton 66-73; V of St Barn Wellingborough Dio Pet from 73. *St Barnabas's Vicarage, Wellingborough, Northants, NN8 3HA.* (Wellingborough 226172)

RYLANDS, Canon Thomas Michael. b 18. CCC Cam BA 39, MA 46. Wells Th Coll. **d** 47 **p** 48 Ches. C of Nantwich 47-51; V of Wilton 51-56; R of Malpas (w Threapwood from 68) Dio Ches from 56; CF (TA) from 57; C-in-c of Threapwood 63-68; RD of Malpas from 70; Hon Can of Ches from 72. *Rectory, Malpas, Ches.* (Malpas 209)

RYLE, Denis Maurice. b 16. OBE 70. St Aid Coll 35. **d** 39 **p** 40 Liv. C of St Pet Parr St Helens 39-42; St Paul Widnes 42-44; Woolton (in c of St Hilda Hunt's Cross) 44-45; CF 45-63; SCF 63-66; DACG 66-73; C-in-c of Latimer w Flaunden Dio Ox from 73. *Latimer Rectory, Bucks, HP5 1UD.* (Little Chalfont 4698)

RYLEY, Patrick Macpherson. b 30. Pemb Coll Ox 3rd cl Cl

Mods 52, BA (3rd cl LitHum) 54. BD (Lon) 56. Clifton Th Coll. **d** 56 **p** 57 Ox. C of St Clem Ox 56-59; Miss Dio Rang 60-66; Dio Nak 68-75; V of St Jo Evang Kings Lynn Dio Nor from 76; RD of Lynn from 78. *St John's Vicarage, Kings Lynn, Norf.* (Kings Lynn 3034)

RYMER, David John Talbot. b 37. Chich Th Coll 63. **d** 66 Tewkesbury for Glouc **p** 67 Glouc. C of St Barn Tuffley Glouc 66-69; R of Mabelreign Mashon 69-78; V of St Jude S Kens Dio Lon from 79. *18 Collingham Road, SW5 0LX.* (01-370 1088)

RYMER, Very Rev John Oliver. Univ of Queensld BA 47, MA 52. ACT ThL 50, Th Scho (2nd cl) 59. Univ of Lon MA 62. **d** 46 Rockptn **p** 48 Armid. Asst Chap C of E Gr Sch Brisb 46-48; C of St Pet Cathl Armid 48-50; St Paul's Cathl Rockptn 50-51; Exam Chap to Bp of Rockptn 50-54; V of Biloela 51-54; Chap Univ of New Engl and Girls' Sch Armid 54-59; and 62-64; Exam Chap to Bp of Armid 59-64; C of N Wembley 60-61; Prin Ch Ch Coll Ch Ch 65-70; Hon Can of Ch 64-70; Exam Chap to Bp of Ch Ch 65-70; Dean of Auckld from 70; VG 76-78; Abp's Commiss from 79. *8 Stephen's Avenue, Parnell, Auckland 1, NZ.* (373-424)

RYMER, William Vernon. St Jo Coll Melb ACT ThL 13. **d** 16 Gippsld **p** 17 Melb. C of Yarram Vic 16-17; Hastings Vic 17-18; St John Malvern 18-20; R of Bowen Queensld 20-23; S Townsville 23-24; Innisfail 24-25; Bowen 25-29; Violet Town 29-31; Blackall 31-36; V of St Luke Rockptn 36-45; R 45-46; Hon Can of St Paul's Cathl Rockptn 45-46; Admin Dio Rockptn 46-47; V of St Mary Bundarra 47-51; Tenterfield 51-61; L to Offic Dio Armid from 61. *Tenterfield, NSW, Australia.*

RYND, Peter Alfred Tatham. St Jo Coll Auckld. **d** 48 **p** 49 Auckld. C of Devonport 48-49; Takapuna 49-51; Pukekohe 51-54; Chap Miss to Seamen Colom 54-58; Sing 58-60; Whyalla 60-61; V of Waikouaiti 61-62; P Dio Polyn 63-69; Perm to Offic Dio Auckld 69-70; Hon C of St Mark's Remuera 71-73; Chap Miss to Seamen and L to Offic Dio N Queensld 73-74; Dio Wel 74-78; V of Seatoun-Strathmore 78-80. *c/o 40 Ferry Street, Wellington, NZ.* (866-882)

S

SABA, Philip Nmadu. St Paul's Coll Awka 56. **d** 60 **p** 61 N Nig. P Dio N Nig 60-77; Can of N Nig 72-77. *Eshiti, PA Kataeregi, Nigeria.*

SABAH, Lord Bishop of. *See* Chhoa Heng Sze, Right Rev Luke.

SABAH, Dean Of. (Vacant)

SABAN, Ronald Graham Street. Bps' Coll Cheshunt, 60. **d** 62 **p** 63 Cant. C of St Martin Maidstone 62-66; St Sav Croydon 66-72. *Address temp unknown.*

SABELL, Michael Harold. b 42. Open Univ BA 78. Sarum Wells Th Coll 77. **d** 80 Southn for Win **p** 81 Win (APM). Hon C of Shirley Dio Win from 80; Dioc Chap for the Deaf from 81. *46 Dale Valley Road, Upper Shirley, Southampton, SO1 6QR.*

SABIBI, Adbeel Ndayagiwe. **d** 57 **p** 58 Centr Tang. P Dio Centr Tang 57-66; Dio W Tang from 66. *PO Box 74, Kasulu, Tanzania.*

SABINE, Percy Thomas William. b 19. Sarum Wells Th Coll 76. **d** 79 **p** 80 Ex. C of Ascen Crownhill Plymouth 79-81; Ivybridge Dio Ex from 81. *70 Cole Lane, Stowford Park Estate, Ivybridge, Devon.*

SABITE, Adao. **d** and **p** 75 Lebom. P Dio Lebom 75-79; Dio Niassa from 79. *CP 120, Maputo, Mozambique.*

✠ **SABITI, Most Rev Erica.** **d** 33 **p** 34 Ugan. P Dio Ugan 33-60; Can of Ugan 58-60; Cons Ld Bp Suffr of Toro-Bunyoro-Mboga in St Paul's Cathl Kampala 1 May 60 by Bp of Ugan; Bp on U Nile; and Bps Balya; Lutaya; Shalita; Wiggins; and Tomusange; Trld to Ruw 60; to Kamp 72; Elected Metrop of Prov of Ugan and Rwanda B (w Boga-Z from 72) 66; res 74; Dean of Ruw 60-72; Episc Can of St Geo Cathl Jer 66-74. *Box 134, Mbarara, Uganda.*

SABITI, Sezi. **d** 44 **p** 45. P Dio Ugan 44-61; Dio Ruw 61-63; Dio Bunyoro from 72. *PO Box 20, Hoima, Uganda.*

SABOURIN, Robert. b 21. TCD. **d** 52 **p** 53 Lon. C of Wembley 52-54; St Sampson Guernsey 54-57; V of St Matt Cobo, Guernsey 57-60; Publ Pr Dio Win from 80. *Hauteville House, 38 Hauteville, Guernsey, CI*

SABUNE, Andereya. **d** 49 **p** 50 Ugan. P Dio Nam. *PO Box 14257, Kampala, Uganda.*

SACKEY, Ven Edward Augustus Benjamin. **d** and **p** 48 Accra. P Dio Accra; Archd of Sekondi from 68. *Box 85, Sekondi, Ghana.* (Sekondi 6048)

SACKEY, Victor Ray Kofi. b 43. Kelham Th Coll 68. **d** 77 Kum. d Dio Kum. *PO Box 144, Kumasi, Ghana.*

SADDLETON, Stephen John. BA (Lond) 55. **d** 80 Qu'App. C of Estevan Dio Qu'App from 80. *1714 2nd Street, Estevan, Sask, Canada, S4A 0N3.*

SADEN, Chambers. Trin Th Coll Sing 60. **d** 63 **p** 64 Kuch. P Dio Kuch from 63. *St Luke's Church, Simanggang, Sarawak, Malaysia.*

SADGROVE, Michael. b 50. Ball Coll Ox BA 71, MA 75. Trin Coll Bris 72. **d** 75 **p** 76 Dorchester for Ox. L to Offic Dio Ox 75-77; Tutor Sarum Wells Th Coll from 77; Vice Prin from 80; Hon V Cho of Sarum Cathl from 78. *Salisbury and Wells Theological College, 19 The Close, Salisbury, Wilts, SP1 2EE.* (0722-332235)

SADLEIR, Ralph Raymond. Wycl Coll Tor. **d** 42 **p** 43 Bran. C of Bethany 42-45; I of Courtright w Corunna and Mooretown 45-48; Shelburne w Primrose 48-50; R of Wallaceburg 50-56; Riverside 56-63; Ingersoll 63-74; Stoney Lake 74-78; P-in-c of St Alb Pet Dio Tor from 78. *412 Highland Road, Peterborough, Ont, Canada.*

SADLER, Anthony Graham. b 36. Qu Coll Ox BA 60, MA 64. Lich Th Coll. **d** 62 **p** 63 Lich. C of St Chad Burton-on-Trent 62-65; V of Rangemore 65-72; Dunstall 65-72; Abbots Bromley 72-78; Pelsall Dio Lich from 78. *Pelsall Vicarage, Walsall, Staffs, WS3 4BJ.* (Pelsall 2261)

SADLER, Ernest Eldred. b 07. St Bonif Coll Warm 28-32. **d** 41 **p** 42 Bris. C of St Martin Knowle 41-44; PC of Whitchurch Bristol 44-53; R of Norton Malreward 47-53; C-in-c of Sticklepath Conv Distr Barnstaple 53-56; V 56-63; Em Ex 63-78; Chap Redhills Hosp Ex from 64. *63 Dorset Avenue, Exeter, Devon.* (Ex 50049)

SADLER, Francis Ambrose. b 04. St Chad's Coll Dur BA 31, Dipl Th 32, MA 34. **d** 32 **p** 33 Lon. C of St Mary Bromley St Leon 32-36; St Mark Noel Pk 36-37; St Mich Shoreditch 37-39; Chap RAFVR 40-46; R of Kirby Misperton 46-59; V of St Agnes Truro 59-72; Publ Pr Dio Truro from 73. *Rocky Lane, St Agnes, Cornwall.* (St Agnes 2702)

SADLER, Ven George Howard Landon. Qu Univ Kingston Ont BA 21. Bp's Univ Lennox LST 23. **d** 23 **p** 24 Ott. C of Fitzroy Harbour 23-24; Miss of Combermere 24-27; I of Cobden 27-37; RD of Pembroke 28-34; R of Eganville 37-40; Cornwall 40-45; St John Smiths Falls 45-66; Can of Ch Ch Cathl Ott 48-62; Archd of Lanark 62-66; Archd (Emer) from 66. *20 Strathcona Street, Smiths Falls, Ont, Canada.*

SADLER, John Ernest. b 45. Univ of Nottm BTh 78. Linc Th Coll 74. **d** 78 Repton for Derby **p** 79 Derby. C of St Thos Brampton 78-81; Team V of Caludon City and Dio Cov from 81. *St Catherine's House, 7 The Pondfield, Stoke Aldermoor, Coventry, CV3 1EH.* (Cov 454534)

SADLER, John Harvey. b 33. K Coll Lon and Warm Robertson Pri 56, AKC (2nd cl) 57. BD (Lon) 66. Univ of Warw MEd 79. **d** 58 Kingston T for Guildf **p** 59 Guildf. C of Addlestone 58-60; Hemel Hempstead 60-62; Sub-Warden St Matt Coll Port Eliz 62-66; C of St Matt Miss 62-66; Frimley 67-69; V of St Mary Virg Ewell 69-71; Asst Master Erdington Gr Sch Birm 72-74; Manor High Sch Wednesbury 74-79; Dyson Perrins Ch High Sch Malvern from 80; Perm to Offic Dio Worc from 80. *Little Queenswood, Stone Drive, Colwall, Malvern, Worcs.* (Colwall 40047)

SADLER, Michael Stuart. b 57. Wycl Hall Ox 79. **d** 81 St D. C of Henfynyw w Aberaeron and Llanddewi Aberarth Dio St D from 81. *Hillcrest, Vicarage Hill, Aberaeron, Dyfed, SA46 0DY.*

SADLIER, Thomas Henry. St Jo Coll Auckld NZ Bd of Th Stud LTh 62. **d** 53 **p** 54 Waik. C of New Plymouth 53-56; V of New Plymouth West 56-58; Taumarunui 58-64; Tokoroa 64-67; Melville 67-80; Perm to Offic Dio Waik from 80. *26 Sheridan Street, Hamilton, NZ.*

SADYA, Leonard. St Andr Coll Mponda's 64. **d** 66 **p** 67 Bp Mtekateka for Malawi. P Dio Malawi 66-71; Dio Lake Malawi from 71. *Box 39, Nkhata Bay, Malawi.*

SAGAR, Brian. b 39. Sarum Wells Th Coll 78. **d** 80 **p** 81 Man. C of St Thos & St John Radcliffe Dio Man from 80. *10 Rush Acre Close, Radcliffe, Manchester, M26 0RU.*

SAGE, Albert Francis. St Jo Coll Morpeth ACT ThL 66. **d** 66 **p** 67 Melb. C of St Barn Balwyn 66-68; Cheltm 68-70; P-in-c of St John Frankston w Carrum Downs 70-73; L to Offic Dio N Queensld 73-77; I of Springvale Dio Melb from 77. *7 Heather Grove, Springvale, Vic., Australia 3171.* (546-9649)

SAGE, Arthur Ross. b 02. Em Coll Sktn LTh 25. **d** 25 **p** 26 Sask. I of Edgerton 25-27; R of St Sav Vermilion 27-29; C of St Pet Southborough Kent 29-33; St John Wynberg 33-38; Org Sec CMJ for N Distr and L to Offic Dio Liv 38-40; V of Walton Suff 40-59; Standon 59-66; Perm to Offic Dio St E from 76. *19 Chester Road, Felixstowe, Suff, IP11 9AH.* (03942-70778)

SAGE, Colston William. b 03. St Andr Coll Pampisford. **d** 45 Wakef for Bradf **p** 45 Bradf. C of St Luke Manningham 45-48; V of Esholt w Hawkesworth 48-58; Frizinghall 58-68; L to Offic Dio Bradf from 68. *3 Oak Avenue, Burley-in-Wharfedale, Ilkley, W Yorks, LS29 7PH.* (Burley-in-Wharfedale 3354)

SAGE, Jesse. b 35. Trin Hall Cam BA 61, MA 65. Chich Th Coll. **d** 63 **p** 64 Lon. C of Feltham 63-67; St Mary's Colleg Ch Port Eliz 67; P-in-c of Ch K and St Mark Port Eliz 68-72; R of Abbas and Templecombe (w Horsington from 76) 72-77; Chap to Agr and Rural Society in Kent Dio Cant from 78. *Rectory, Pluckley, Ashford, Kent, TN27 0QT.* (Pluckley 232)

SAGE, John Arthur. b 32. BSc (Gen) 54, BSc (Phys) 55 (Lon). St Alb Min Tr Scheme. **d** 81 St Alb (NSM). C of St Mary Shephall Stevenage Dio St Alb from 81. *36 Shephall Green, Stevenage, Herts.*

SAGOVSKY, Nicholas. b 47. CCC Ox BA 69. Univ of Nottm BA 73. Univ of Cam PhD 81. St Jo Coll Nottm 71. **d** 74 **p** 75 Newc T. C of St Gabr Heaton Newc T 74-77; St Mary Gt w St Mich AA Cam 81. *78 York Street, Cambridge, CB1 2PY.*

SAGWETE, Cephas. b 38. **d** 76 **p** 77 Mashon. P Dio Mashon. *c/o Box UA7, Salisbury, Zimbabwe.*

SAHAYAM, John Ponsami. St Jo Bapt Coll Suva 62. **d** 65 **p** 67 Polyn. P Dio Polyn. *PO Box 117, Lautoka, Fiji.*

SAHAYAM, Samuel. b 35. St Jo Coll Auckld 66. **d** 68 Polyn **p** 69 Bp Halapua for Polyn. P Dio Polyn. *Box 29, Labasa, Fiji Islands.*

SAHU, Nelson. St Pet Coll Siota. **d** 56 **p** 59 Melan. P Dio Melan 56-75; Dio Malaita from 75. *Faiketo, Malaita, Solomon Islands.*

SAIDI, George. St Cypr Th Coll Tunduru 37. **d** 39 **p** 43 Masasi. P Dio Masasi. *KJT Chiwata, c/o Private Bag, PO Masasi, Tanzania.*

SAIDI, Iteku. b 21. **d** and **p** 76 Boga-Z. P Dio Boga-Z. *BP 861, Kisangani, Zaire.*

SAILENI, Jackson Joel Hadad. St Phil Th Coll Kongwa 65. **d** 67 **p** 68 Moro. P Dio Moro. *Tunguli, Berega, PO Kilosa, Tanzania.*

SAINA, Canon Abraham. d 59 Momb **p** 61 Nak. d Dio Momb 59-61; P Dio Nak from 61; Hon Can of Nak from 70; Exam Chap to Bp of Nak from 76. *PO Box 31, Kapsabet, Kenya.*

SAINA, Philip Kipsongok. b 33. St Phil Coll Maseno 69. **d** 69 Maseno **p** 71 Nak. P Dio Nak 69-75. *Lessos, via Eldoret, Kenya.*

SAINSBURY, Max Henry. d 60 **p** 61 Graft. C of S Graft 60-61; Murwillumbah 61-62; V of St Jas U Macleay 62-65; Mid-Clarence 65-67; Asst Chap Miss to Seamen City and Dio Syd from 67. *c/o 100 George Street, Sydney, NSW 2000, Australia.*

SAINSBURY, Roger Frederick. b 36. Jes Coll Cam BA 58, MA 62. Clifton Th Coll. **d** 60 **p** 61 Lon. C of Ch Ch w All SS Spitalfields 60-63; Missr Shrewsbury Ho Everton 63-74; C-in-c of St Ambrose w St Timothy Everton 67-74; Warden Mayflower Family Centre Canning Town 74-81; P-in-c of St Luke Vic Dks 78-81; V of Walsall Dio Lich from 81. *48 Jesson Road, Walsall, W Midl.* (Walsall 24012)

SAINT, Arthur James Maxwell. b 10. Late Exhib of St Jo Coll Ox. BA (2nd cl Eng Lang and Lit) 31, MA 35. Cudd Coll 34. **d** 35 **p** 36 Lich. C of Stoke-on-Trent 35-37; Prin of St Thos Sch Kuching 37-41; C of St Mary Shrewsbury 42-43; V of St Mary Shawbury 43-48; PC of St Steph Cheltm 48-60; Res Chap Guy's Hosp Lon 60-65; PC of St Phil and St Jas Ox 65-68; V 68-76; Catechist Ex Coll Ox 76-81. *65 Ramsay Road, Headington, Oxford, OX3 8AY.* (Ox 61241)

SAINT, David Gerald. b 45. Sarum Wells Th Coll 72. **d** 75 **p** 76 Pet. C of Wellingborough 75-79; R of Kislingbury w Rothersthorpe Dio Pet from 79. *Kislingbury Rectory, Northampton, NN7 4AG.* (Northn 830592)

St ALBANS, Lord Bishop of. *See* Taylor, Right Rev John Bernard.

St ALBANS, Archdeacon of. *See* Norfolk, Ven Edward Matheson.

St ALBANS, Dean of. *See* Moore, Very Rev Peter Clement.

St ANDREWS, DUNKELD and DUNBLANE, Lord Bishop of. *See* Hare Duke, Right Rev Michael Geoffrey.

St ANDREWS, DUNKELD and DUNBLANE, Dean of. *See* Irvine, Very Rev Thomas Thurstan.

St ARNAUD, Diocese of. Part of Diocese of Bendigo from 77.

St ASAPH, Lord Bishop of. (Vacant)

St ASAPH, Archdeacon of. *See* Jones, Ven John Jenkin.

St ASAPH, Dean of. *See* Renowden, Very Rev Charles Raymond.

St CLAIR, John James. Moore Th Coll ACT ThL 53. **d** and **p** 54 Syd. C of Miranda 54; C-in-c of W Kembla 54-58; S Granville 58-62; R of Mirboo N w Mardan S 62-68; C-in-c of St Mark's Provis Distr Sylvania 68-74; R of Orbost 74-75; Chap St Vinc and Lewisham Hosps Dio Syd from 75. *20 Vernon Avenue, Eastlakes, NSW, Australia 2018.* (669-6516)

St CLARE, Ann Lynette. b 44. St Jo Coll Auckld 77. **d** 78 **p** 79 Auckld. C of Otara Dio Auckld from 78. *73 Hill Road, Manurewa, Auckland, NZ.*

St DAVIDS, Lord Bishop of. *See* Noakes, Right Rev George.

St DAVIDS, Archdeacon of. *See* Lewis, Ven Benjamin Alec.

St DAVIDS, Dean of. *See* Bowen, Very Rev Lawrence.

St EDMUNDSBURY and IPSWICH, Lord Bishop of. *See* Waine, Right Rev John.

St EDMUNDSBURY and IPSWICH, Assistant Bishop of. (Vacant)

St EDMUNDSBURY and IPSWICH, Provost of. *See* Furnell, Very Rev Raymond.

St GERMANS, Lord Bishop Suffragan of. *See* Fisher, Right Rev (Michael) Reginald Lindsay.

St HELENA, Lord Bishop of. *See* Cannan, Right Rev Edward Alexander Capparis.

St JOHN, Andrew Reginald. b 44. Univ of Melb LLB 66. Trin Coll Melb ACT Th Scho 71. **d** 71 **p** 72 Melb. C of St Geo w All SS Footscray 71-72; on leave 73-75; Prec and Min Can of St Paul's Cathl Melb 75-78; I of Chadstone E Dio Melb from 78. *37 Mawarra Crescent, Chadstone, Vic, Australia 3148.* (277 4244)

St JOHN, Ferdinand Richard John. b 08. Ely Th Coll. **d** 47 Dover for Cant **p** 48 Cant. Hon CF 48. C of Margate 47-50; Croydon 50-53; V of Lyneham (w Tockenham 52-54) and Bradenstoke 53-61; RD of Avebury 55-61; Proc Conv Sarum 59-61; V of St Pet Chorley Lancs 61-67; R of Banff 67-70; Portsoy 67-70; Ashton w Hartwell Pet 70-74; Tinwell 74-77. *5 Stockerston Crescent, Uppingham, Leics, LE15 9UA.* (Uppingham 2452)

St JOHN'S, Lord Bishop of. *See* Ashby, Right Rev Godfrey William Ernest Candler.

St JOHN'S, Bishop Suffragan of. *See* Dlamini, Right Rev Jacob Zambuhle Bhekuyise.

St JOHN'S, Dean of. *See* Bashe, Very Rev Gideon Velile.

St LEDGER, Preb Robert Joseph. b 21. TCD BA (Mod) 44, Bp Forster and Abp King Pri (1st) 44. **d** 45 **p** 46 Down. C of Willowfield 45-50; C-in-c of Sallaghy 50-58; I of Lisbellaw Dio Clogh from 58; Can of Clogh 78-81; Preb from 81; Exam Chap to Bp of Clogh from 78. *Rectory, Lisbellaw, Enniskillen, Co Fermanagh, N Ireland.* (Lisbellaw 219)

ST JOHN-CHANNELL, Michael Alister Morrell. b 53. Univ of Bris BEd 76. Ripon Coll Cudd 76. **d** 78 **p** 79 Portsm. C of St Mary Portsea 78-82; V of St Mary-le-Wigford w St Mark City and Dio Linc from 82. *125 Yarborough Road, Lincoln, LN1 1HR.* (Linc 38117)

St JOHN NICOLLE (formerly NICOLLE), Michael George. b 29. St Jo Coll Dur BA 52. **d** 70 **p** 71 Leic. C of L Bowden 70; St Jo Bapt Knighton 71-74; R of Desford 74-81; Tarrant Valley Dio Sarum from 81. *Tarrant Hinton Rectory, Blandford Forum, Dorset, DT11 8JB.* (Tarrant Hinton 258)

SAJABI, Canon Blasiyo. d 37 **p** 39 Ugan. P Dio Ugan 37-61; Dio Nam 61-70; Can of Nam 62-70; Hon Can of Nam from 71. *Box 30139, Kampala, Uganda.*

SAJABI, Nasanairi. Bp Tucker Mem Coll Mukono. **d** 25 Ugan **p** 27 U Nile. CMS P Dio U Nile 26-35; Dio Ugan 25-26 and 35-56. *Saanga, Gomb ya Sabawali via Omw, Luzinda, PO Box 91, Kampala, Uganda.*

SAJALYABENE, Canon Yekasafati Kizive. Bp Tucker Coll Mukono. **d** 51 **p** 53 Ugan. P Dio Ugan 51-60; Dio W Bugan from 60; Can of W Bugan from 70. *Church of Uganda, Kakoma, PO Box 2531, Kyotera, Uganda.*

SAKA, Theophilus Henry Olayiwola. Fourah Bay Coll 58. **d** 61 **p** 62 Sier L. P Dio Lagos. *St Jude's Church, PO Box 45, Ebute Metta Lagos, Nigeria.*

SAKAYA, John Terta. St Phil Coll Kongwa 69. **d** and **p** 72 Nai. P Dio Nai. *Box 21, Kajiado, Kenya.*

SAKER, Sidney William. b 08. Univ of Dur 32. ALCD 35. **d** 35 **p** 36 Lon. C of St Andr Thornhill Square Isl 35-38; Bermondsey 38-39; L to Offic Dio Ox from 39; PC of St Mary Chap Castle Street Reading 39-46; Org Sec for Midl BCMS from 46; Perm to Offic Dios Birm Lich Leic Cov Pet Heref Linc and Southw from 46; Org Sec SAMS W Area 53-63;

Perm to Offic Dio Truro Ex B & W Sarum Bris and Glouc from 53; S & M from 61; S Area Sec SAMS 63-64; Metrop Area Sec CCCS 64-65; Asst Sec 65-71; Publ Pr Dio S'wark 64-73; Area Sec Leprosy Miss SW Lon 71-73; Hon Rep SAMS Dio Leic & Pet from 73. *397 Uppingham Road, Leicester, LE5 4DP.*

SAKWA, Safani. b 43. **d** and **p** 74 Mbale. P Dio Mbale. *Bugimotwa, PO Sipi, Mbale, Uganda.*

SAKYIAMA, Kofi Parri. d and **p** 31 Accra. P Dio Accra 31-55; Hon Can of Accra 55-60; Archd of Kumasi 61-65; Koforidua 65-68; Cape Coast 68-80; P-in-c of St Cypr Kumasi 61-68; Ch Ch Cape Coast Dio Accra from 68. *Box 38, Cape Coast, Ghana.* (Cape Coast 2018)

SAKYIAMA, Theophillus Odom. b 43. Trin Coll Legon. **d** and **p** 75 Accra. P Dio Accra. *Box 85, Sekoni, Ghana.*

SALAKA, Manfred Amos Michael. St Cypr Coll Ngala 60. **d** 62 **p** 64 SW Tang. P Dio SW Tang 62-75; Dio Ruv from 75. *Chiulu, PO Mbamba Bay, Tanzania.*

SALAMEH, Bassis Butrus. d 34 **p** 35 Jer. P Dio Jer 35-53; Dio Jordan 58-66. *c/o St George's Close, PO Box 1248, Jerusalem.*

SALE, Dean of. *See* Gibson, Very Rev Edward George.

SALE, Barton. St Pet Coll Siota 52. **d** 54 **p** 57 Melan. P Dio Melan 54-74. *Tam, Maewo, New Hebrides.*

SALE, Edward Timothy. Univ of Tor BSc 63. Trin Coll Tor STB 66. **d** 66 Rupld **p** 67 Bp Anderson for Rupld. C of St Paul Fort Garry Winnipeg 66-70; Commun Ecumen Min 70-71. *c/o Diocesan Registrar, 302-257 Smith Street, Winnipeg, Manit, Canada.*

SALEH, Houghton Oliver. St Paul's Th Coll Limuru. **d** 56 **p** 58 Momb. P Dio Momb 56-65 and from 67; C of St Mary Virg Bury 65-67; Exam Chap to Bp of Momb from 74. *PO Wusi, Mombasa, Kenya.*

SALENIUS, Richard Mark. b 57. AKC and BD 79. Linc Th Coll 79. **d** 80 **p** 81 Bp Woollcombe for Lon. C of St Marylebone Dio Lon from 80. *84 Clarence Gate Gardens, Glentworth Street, NW1 6QR.*

SALES, Patrick David. b 43. K Coll Lon and Warm AKC 68, BD 74. **d** 69 **p** 70 Cant. C of All SS w St Phil Maidstone 69-72; Chart Sutton 72-74; Birchington w Acol 74-76; V of Boughton-under-Blean w Dunkirk Dio Cant from 77. *Boughton Vicarage, The Street, Boughton, Faversham, Kent, ME13 9BG.* (Cant 751410)

SALIMU, Magnus Edward. Namasakata Th Coll 58. **d** 60 **p** 63 SW Tang. P Dio SW Tang 60-70; Ruv from 71. *Lundo, PO Liuli, Tanzania.*

SALISBURY, Lord Bishop of. *See* Baker, Right Rev John Austin.

SALISBURY, Assistant Bishop of. (Vacant)

SALISBURY, Archdeacon of. *See* Sarum

SALISBURY, Dean of. *See* Evans, Very Rev Sydney Hall.

SALISBURY, Dean of (Dio Mashon). *See* Da Costa, Very Rev John Robert.

SALISBURY, George Malcolm Owen. Bp's Coll Calc. **d** 43 **p** 44 Nagp. C of All SS Cathl Nagp 43-44; Ch Ch Jubbulpore 44-45; Chap Bilaspur 45-49; C of St Pet St Alb 49-61; V of Markyate 61-68; R of Shenley 68-81. *c/o Shenley Rectory, St Albans, Herts.*

SALISBURY, Harold Gareth. b 21. St Pet Hall Ox BA 42 MA 46. Wycl Hall Ox 42. **d** 44 **p** 45 Pet. C of St Mark Pet 44-46; CMS Tr Coll Blackheath 46-47; Lect Bp's Coll Calc 47-49; L to Offic Dio Nasik 49-52; Chap St Andr Cathl Nasik 49-51; H Trin Aurangabad 51-52; L to Offic Dio Bom 52-62; Chap at Thana 53-57; St Andr Agripada Bom 53-57; Exam Chap to Bp of Bom 56-62; U Th Coll Poona 58-62; V of Duddo 63-70; Norham 63-70; Norham and Duddo 70-78; V of Snaith Dio Sheff from 78; P-in-c of Cowick Dio Sheff from 78. *11 Beast Fair, Snaith, Goole, Humb, DN14 9JQ.* (Goole 860866)

SALISBURY, John Forbes. b 16. St Jo Coll Dur 46. **d** 50 **p** 51 Worc. C of Ch Ch Malvern 50-53; St John Dudley 53-57; V of St Luke Manningham 57-62; Riddlesden 62-67; Tosside 67-79; L to Offic Dio Bradf from 80. *8 Ash Grove, Skipton, BD23 1QP.* (Skipton 661380)

SALISBURY, Roger John. b 44. BD (Lon) 67. Lon Coll of Div 66. **d** 68 Bradwell for Chelmsf **p** 69 Chelmsf. C of St Pet Harold Wood Hornchurch 68-73; V of St Paul Dorking 73-82; R of Rusholme Dio Man from 82. *Holy Trinity Rectory, Platt Lane, Manchester, M14 5NF.* (061-224 1123)

SALISBURY, Tobias. b 33. Em Coll Cam BA 60. Ripon Hall Ox 60. **d** 62 **p** 63 S'wark. C of Putney 62-65; St Jo Evang Churchdown 65-67; V of Urchfont w Stert 67-73; R of Burton Bradstock w Shipton Gorge and Chilcombe 73-79; C-in-c of Long w L Bredy 75-79; Team R of Bride Valley Dio Sarum from 79. *Rectory, Burton Bradstock, Bridport, Dorset, DT6 4QS.* (Burton Bradstock 359)

SALKELD, Gerald Irving. b 35. St Jo Coll Dur 77. **d** 79 **p** 80 Carl. C of St Mark Barrow-F Dio Carl from 79. *31 Parade Street, Barrow-in-Furness, LA14 2LN.*

SALMON, Andrew Meredith Bryant. b 30. Jes Coll Cam BA 54, 2nd cl Th Trip pt ii 55, MA 58. Ridley Hall Cam 54. **d** 56 **p** 57 Lon. C of Ch Ch Cockfosters 56-58; Chap Monkton Combe Sch Dio B & W from 58-71; Milton Abbey Sch Dio Sarum from 71. *Milton Abbey School, Blandford, Dorset.* (Milton Abbas 880676)

SALMON, Anthony James Heygate. b 30. CCC Ox BA 53, Dipl Th 54, MA 57. Cudd Coll 54. **d** 56 Dover for Cant **p** 57 Cant. C of St Mark S Norwood 56-59; Usuthu 59-61; R of Gingindhlovu 61-69; Chap Coll of Ascen Selly Oak Birm 69-74; R of Harrietsham Dio Cant from 74; C-in-c of Frinsted 74-78; P-in-c of Ulcombe Dio Cant from 81. *Harrietsham Rectory, Maidstone, Kent.* (Maidstone 859466)

SALMON, Bernard Bryant. b 24. Trin Hall, Cam 2nd cl Hist Trip pt i 49, BA (3rd cl Th Trip pt i) 50, MA 54. Wells Th Coll 50. **d** 52 Jarrow for Dur **p** 53 Dur. C of St Pet Stockton-on-Tees 52-55; Long Benton 55-58; V of Cramlington 58-71; Winscombe Dio B & W from 71; RD of Locking from 78. *Vicarage, Winscombe, Avon, BS25 1DE.* (Winscombe 3164)

SALMON, Charles Walter John. d 50 **p** 51 Bran. C of Russell 50-51; R 51-52; Bethany w Clanwilliam 52-54; Pilot Mound 54-55; in Amer Ch 55-59; C of Pembroke Berm 59-65; R of Oxford Ont 65-66; Merrickville Dio Ont from 66; P-in-c of Acton Ont 69-70. *Box 104, Merrickville, Ont, Canada.* (613-269 4239)

SALMON, Canon Harry. Seager Hall Ont 61. **d** 62 Tor for Sask **p** 63 Sask. C of Arborfield 62-66; I of Spruce Lake 66-68; I of Turtleford 66-68; Meadow Lake 68-70; I of Loon Lake 68-70; Paddockwood w Christopher Lake 71-76; R of Spiritwood Dio Sask from 76; Hon Can of Sask from 77. *Box 478, Spiritwood, Sask, Canada.*

SALMON, Reuben Oliver Davis. d 41 Tor **p** 43 Bp Beverley for Tor. C of St Aid Tor 41-43; I of Mulmur West 43-45; Chatsworth 45-49; St Luke Windsor 49-50; Roseland 50-51; St D Windsor 51-52; St Clair Beach 53-56; R of Milverton 64-72. *Box 174 Milverton, Ont, Canada.*

SALMON, Richard Harold. b 35. Fitzw Ho Cam BA 57. Clifton Th Coll 57. **d** 59 **p** 60 S'wark. C of St Mich AA Blackheath Pk 59-62; St Paul St Alb 62-64; Miss OME 64-66; V of Kuantan Dio Sing 66-70; Dio W Mal 70-75; C-in-c of St Wendreda March Dio Ely 75-76; R from 76. *Rectory, March, Cambs, PE15 9QW.* (March 3377)

SALMON, Very Rev Thomas Noel Desmond Cornwall. b 13. Trin Coll Dub 1st Jun Hebr Pri 34, BA (2nd cl Mod Oriental Lang) 35, Wall Bibl Scho, 2nd Syriac and Aramaic Prize, 2nd Hebr Prize, and Div Test (1st cl) 36, Th Exhib 37, BD and Elrington Th Pr 42, MA 49. **d** 37 **p** 38 Down. C of Bangor 37-40; St Jas Belf 40-41; Larne 42-44; Cler V of Ch Ch Cathl Dub 44-45; Hon Cler V 45-63; C of Rathfarnham 45-50; Lect Trin Coll Dub from 45; Exam Chap to Abp of Dub from 49; R of Tullow 50-62; V of St Ann Dub 62-67; Can and Preb of Dunlavin in St Patr Cathl Dub 63-67; Dean of Ch Ch Cathl Dub from 67. *13 Merlyn Park, Ballsbridge, Dublin 4, Irish Republic.* (Dublin 694780)

SALMON, William John. b 50. Univ of Lon BSc 72. St Jo Coll Dur 77. **d** 79 **p** 80 S'wark. C of Summerstown 79-81; Hampreston Dio Sarum from 81. *Flat 2, Cliveden, 31 Beaufoys Avenue, Ferndown, Dorset, BH22 9RQ.* (0202-892852)

SALOP, Archdeacon of. *See* Jeffery, Ven Robert Martin Colquhoun.

SALT, Alfred Lewis. Bp's Coll Lennox BA 49, MA 51, LST 54, BD 60. **d** 51 **p** 52 Queb. C-in-c of Sawyerville 51-52; I of Portneuf and of Rivière du Loup 52-55; R of Stanstead 55-62; R of St Mich Sillery Queb 62-72; Dom Chap to Bp of Queb 62-72; Can of Queb 71-72. *15 Cross Hill Road, Millington, NJ, USA 07946.*

SALT, David Christopher. b 37. St D Coll Lamp BA 59. Sarum Th Coll 59. **d** 61 **p** 62 Worc. C of Kidderminster 61-66; Industr Chap Kidderminster 66-73; R of Knightwick w Doddenham, Broadwas (and Cotheridge from 77) Dio Worc from 73; P-in-c of Cotheridge 74-77; Chap Worc Coll of Higher Educn from 73. *Broadwas Rectory, Worcester, WR6 5NE.* (Knightwick 21248)

SALT, David Thomas Whitehorn. b 32. AKC 56, BD 57. **d** 57 Reading for Cant for Col Bp **p** 58 Melan. Chap Torgil Girls' Sch Aoba 57-59; Warden Catechist Coll Lolowai 59-63; Prin St Andr Coll Guadalcanal 63-66; C of Hawley 66-68; V of Shelf 68-73; R of Checkendon 73-81; RD of Henley from 78; Team R of Langtree Dio Ox from 81. *Checkendon Rectory, Reading, Berks, RG8 0QS.* (Checkendon 680252)

SALT, John William. Kelham Th Coll 61. Dipl Th (Lon) 65. **d** 66 **p** 67 Carl. C of St Matt Barrow-F 66-70; Mohales Hoek 70-71; Asst Chap and Master St Agnes Sch teyateyaneng 71-72; C of St Mary and St Jas Cathl Maseru 73-77; Prec of St Cypr Cathl Kimb 77-80; R of St Steph Vryburg Dio Kimb K from 80. *Box 150, Vryburg, Cp, S Africa.*

SALT, Leslie. b 29. Linc Th Coll 68. **d** and **p** 69 Linc. C of

Alford w Rigsby and Ailby 69-75; V of Torksey Marton Newton-on-Trent and Kettlethorpe Dio Linc from 75. *The Vicarage, Torksey, Lincoln.* (Torksey 249)

SALT, Richard John. b 51. Bp's Univ Lennoxville Queb BA 71. **d** 75 **p** 77 Queb. C of St Geo Lennoxville 75-77; I of St Aug Duplessis 77-80; C of N Hatley Dio Queb from 80. *RR3, Ayer's Cliff, PQ, Canada.*

SALTER, Arthur Thomas John. b 34. K Coll Lon and Warm AKC 60. **d** 61 **p** 62 Lon. C of St Pet Ealing 61-65; St Steph w St Thos Shepherd's Bush 65-66; St Alb Holborn w St Pet Saffron Hill 66-70; V of St Silas w All SS (and St Jas from 81) Pentonville Isl Dio Lon from 70; P-in-c of St Clem Barnsbury 70-77; St Mich Bingfield Street Isl 70-77; CF (TAVR) from 75; Gen Sec Angl and E Chs Assoc from 76; P-in-c of St Dunstan-in-the-West and St Thos City and Dio Lon from 79. *87 Richmond Avenue, N1.* (01-607 2865)

SALTER, Derek Sowerby. Angl Th Coll BC 51. **d** 54 **p** 55 Koot. I of Chase 54-62; Watrous 62-67; Keremeos 69-77; Hon Can of Koot 75-77; on leave. *Box 433, Okanagan Falls, BC, Canada.*

SALTER, Francis Bernard. b 44. St Jo Coll Cam BA 67, MA 70. ARCO 62. Ridley Hall, Cam 66. **d** 68 **p** 69 Lich. C of Cannock w Chadsmoor 68-73; Preston 73-76; V of Londonderry Dio Birm from 76. *15 St Mark's Road, Smethwick, Warley, W Midl, B67 6QF.* (021-429 1149)

SALTER, Canon George Alfred. b 25. TCD BA 47. **d** 49 **p** 50 Oss. C of Rathdowney 49-51; St Luke Cork 51-53; R of Fermoy w Kilworth 53-55; St Luke w St Ann (w St Mary from 73) Shandon City and Dio Cork from 55; Can of Desertmore in Cork Cathl and Can of Timoleague in Ross Cathl from 69; Can of Killanully in Cork Cathl from 77. *St Luke's Rectory, Cork, Irish Republic.* (Cork 501672)

SALTER, John Addison. Bp's Univ Lennox **d** 53 **p** 54 Ott. I of Montague 53-56; R of Stafford 56-70; Almonte 70-73; Archd of Lanark 70-73. *261 Bridge Street, Almonte, Ont., Canada.*

SALTER, John Frank. b 37. Univ of Dur BA (2nd cl Psychology) 62. Dipl Th 64. Cranmer Hall, Dur 62. **d** 64 **p** 65 York. C of Bridlington 64-67; Trav Sec Inter-Varsity Fellowship 67-70; V of Em Stoughton Dio Guildf from 70. *3 Shepherd's Lane, Stoughton, Guildford, Surrey.* (Guildford 61603)

SALTER, John Leslie. b 51. AKC 76. Coll of the Resurr Mirfield 77. **d** 78 Lon **p** 79 Edmon for Lon. C of St Paul Tottenham Dio Lon from 78. *60 Park Lane, N17 0JR.*

SALTER, Nigel Christopher Murray. b 46. Loughborough Univ of Tech BTech. Ripon Coll Cudd 79. **d** 81 Tewkesbury for Glouc. C of St Aldate City and Dio Glouc from 81. *181 Tredworth Road, Gloucester, GL1 4QZ.* (Glouc 423986)

SALTER, Richard. b 24. Edin Th Coll 46. **d** 48 **p** 49 Brech. C of St Salvador Dundee 48-51; St Andr Watford 51-54; St Matt Oxhey and St Jas Watford 54-58; V of Robert Town 58-62; St Jo Evang Watford Dio St Alb from 62. *9 Monmouth Road, Watford, Herts, WD1 1QW.* (Watford 36174)

SALTER, Roger John. b 45. Trin Coll Bris 75. **d** 79 **p** 80 Bris. C of St Mich AA Bedminster Dio Bris from 79. *1 Nutgrove Avenue, Bedminster, Bristol, BS3 4QE.* (Bris 779697)

SALTER, Samuel. b 22. St Edm Hall Ox BA 49, MA 53. St Steph Ho Ox. **d** 50 **p** 51 Chich. C of St Wilfrid Brighton 50-53; Felpham w Middleton 53-56; R of Barkston w Syston 56-59; Coningsby 59-65; Offg Chap RAF 59-65; PC of Tattershall w Thorpe 59-65; Asst Chap Cheltm Coll 65-70; Chap 70-81; LPr Dio Glouc 65-81; Team V of Grantham Dio Linc from 81. *Lindisse Cottage, The Drift, Syston, Grantham, Lincs, NG2 2BY.* (Honnington 693)

SALTMARSH, David James. Ch Coll Hobart 64. **d** 68 **p** 69 Tas. C of St John Devonport Tas 68-70; St Geo Launceston 70-71; P-in-c of Flinders I 71-74; R of Sheffield 74-79; Hamilton 79-81; Scottsdale Dio Tas from 81. *Rectory, Scottsdale, Tasmania 7254.* (003 52 2389)

SALVIN, Philip Henry. b 27. Perry Hall Melb 66. **d** 69 **p** 70 Melb. C of St Jo Camberwell 69-71; P-in-c of Ch Ch St Kilda 71-77; I of Gardenvale 77-81. *c/o 111 North Road, Gardenvale, Vic., Australia 3185.*

SALWAY, Donald Macleay. b 31. St Pet Hall Ox BA (3rd cl Hist) 54, MA 59. Oak Hill Th Coll 54. **d** 56 **p** 57 Lon. C of St Mary Magd Holloway 56-67; V of St Phil Cam 67-81; St Cath Mile Cross City and Nor from 81. *St Catherine's Vicarage, Aylsham Road, Mile Cross, Norwich, NR3 2RJ.* (Nor 46767)

SALWAY, Roy James. b 28. Melb Coll of Div LTh 52. **d** and **p** 77 C & Goulb. P-in-c of S Queanbeyan 78-81; R of H Cross Hackett Dio C & Goulb from 81. *165 Phillip Avenue, Hackett, ACT, Australia 2602.*

SAM, Eric Lyttleton. Codr Coll Barb BA (2nd cl Th) 53. **d** 53 **p** 54 WI. L to Offic Dio Gui 53; C of New Amsterdam 54-57; Grand Bahama 57-58; R of Grand Turk w Salt Cay and E Caicos 58-60; P-in-c of Cat I Nass 60-62; R of Suddie w Queenstn 62-65; East Bank Demerara 65-67; C of Grand Bahama 68-80; R of Ch of Ascen Grand Bahama Dio Nass from 80. *PO Box F-2651, Freeport, Grand Bahama, W Indies.*

SAM, Heron Aloysius. Codr Coll Barb 56. **d** 60 Barb for Gui **p** 61 Gui. C of St Geo Cathl Georgetn 60-64; V of Wismar 64-69; NE La Penitence 69-70. *75-16, 164th Street, Flushing, New York 11366, USA.*

SAM, John Kwesi Abrekum. St Aug Th Coll Accra, 56. **d** and **p** 58 Accra. P Dio Accra. *Box 25, Saltpond, Ghana.* (Saltpond 92)

SAMALABO, Tunja. b 32. Trin Coll Nai 74. **d** 74 **p** 75 Boga-Z. P Dio Boga-Z 74-76; Dio Bukavu from 76. *BP 322, Butembe, Nord-Kivu, Zaire.*

SAMAYIRA, Tito. **d** 69 Bur. d Dio Bur. *c/o PO Box 58, Ngozi, Burundi.*

SAMBANO, Mattiya. St Cypr Tunduru 64. **d** 66 Bp Soseleje for Masasi **p** 68 Masasi. P Dio Masasi 66-70; Dio Dar-S from 70. *PO Box 50178, Dar-es-Salaam, Tanzania.*

SAMBELL, David John. b 31. St Aid Coll 60. **d** 63 **p** 64 Ches. C of Sutton 63-67; Alsager 67-71; V of St Pet Crewe 71-81; Upton Priory Dio Ches from 81. *152 Presbury Road, Macclesfield, Chesh.* (Macclesfield 26257)

SAMBROOK, Ernest. b 16. Kelham Th Coll 36. **d** 42 **p** 43 Wakef. C of St Jo Bapt Barnsley 42-44; Castleford 44-45; St John Ches 49-52; V of Alvanley w Manley 52-58; St Sav Stockport 58-76; Brinnington w Portwood Dio Chesh from 76. *St Luke's Vicarage, Brinnington, Stockport, Chesh.* (061-430 4164)

SAMMAN, Peter Bryan. b 27. Trin Coll Dub BA 53. Coll of Resurr Mirfield, 53. **d** 55 **p** 56 Blackb. C of Adlington 55-57; Church Kirk 57-60; V of Briercliffe 60-67; Ch Ch Lanc 67-74; St Jas Lostock Hall Preston Dio Blackb from 74. *Lostock Hall Vicarage, Preston, Lancs.* (Preston 35366)

SAMMONS, John Trevor. b 22. Univ of Birm BA (2nd cl) 48. Ripon Hall Ox. **d** 50 **p** 51 Birm. C of The Quinton 50-55; V of St Luke Birm 55-70; Chap Birm Skin Hosp 56-70; R of Newton Regis w Seckington Dio Birm from 70; C-in-c of No-man's Heath Dio Lich from 70. *Newton Regis Rectory, Tamworth, Staffs.* (082-784 254)

SAMPAINA, Jean Christophe. St Paul's Coll Ambat. **d** 52 **p** 53 Madag. P Dio Madag 52-69; Dio Tam 69-72; Dio Antan 72-76. *Anosibe an'Ala, Moramanga, Madagascar.*

SAMPFORD, John Alfred. b 36. Lich Th Coll 58. **d** 61 **p** 62 S'wark. C of St Phil Lambeth 61-65; Beddington 65-69; V of Ch Ch Hampstead 69-79; St Mary Magd Enfield Dio Lon from 79. *30 The Ridgeway, Enfield, Middx, EN2 8QH.* (01-363 1875)

SAMPSON, Clive. b 38. St Jo Coll Cam BA 61, MA 64. Ridley Hall Cam 63. **d** 65 **p** 66 Roch. C of St Jo Div Tunbridge Wells 65-69; Trav Sec to Script U 69-79; V of St Luke Maidstone Dio Cant from 79. *St Luke's Vicarage, Park Avenue, Maidstone, Kent.* (Maidstone 54856)

SAMPSON, Courtney Dale. b 56. St Paul's Coll Grahmstn 77. **d** 79 **p** 80 Grahmstn. C of Ch of Resurr Bonteheuwel Dio Grahmstn from 79. *Priest's House, David Profit Street, Bonteheuwel, Athlone 7764, S Africa.*

SAMPSON, Desmond William John. b 25. FRICS 60. Roch Th Coll 63. **d** 65 **p** 66 Cant. C of Hythe Kent 65-70; V of Alkham w Capel-le-Ferne (and Hougham-by-Dover from 72) 70-76; C-in-c of Hougham-by-Dover 70-72; V of Wingham w Elmstone and Preston w Stourmouth Dio Cant from 76; RD of E Bridge from 81. *Wingham Vicarage, Canterbury, Kent.* (Wingham 219)

SAMPSON, Edward Stanley. b 25. **d** 72 **p** 73 Bp Wade for Capetn (APM). C of Moorder Paarl Dio Capetn from 72. *19 Field Street, Huguenot, Paarl, S Africa.* (Paarl 7044)

SAMPSON, Preb Everard Archbold. b 12. Keble Coll Ox BA (3rd cl Mod Hist) 33, MA 47. Linc Th Coll 33. **d** 35 Barrow-F for Carl **p** 36 Carl. C of Cleator Moor 35-41; V of St Bees 41-49; Holcombe Burnell 49-77; Asst Dir Relig Educn Dio Ex 49-56; Dir 56-77; Preb of Ex Cathl from 60. *11 Arundel Close, Alphington, Exeter, Devon.* (Exeter 38389)

SAMPSON, Canon Frank. b 11. Keble Coll Ox BA 38, MA 46. Cudd Coll 38. **d** 39 **p** 40 Liv. C of St Columba Anfield 39-43; St Aug Qu Gate Lon 43-46; V of St Jo Bapt Tue Brook Dio Liv from 46; Chap Park Hosp Liv from 54; Hon Can of Liv from 69. *Vicarage, Tue Brook, Liverpool.* (051-228 2023)

SAMPSON, Jeremy John Egerton. b 23. Univ of Dur BSc 45. Wells Th Coll 46. **d** 48 **p** 49 Newc T. C of Long Benton 48-51; V of N Perak 51-52; P-in-c of Johore Bahru 52-57; V of St John Ipoh 57-62; Killingworth 62-76; Consett Dio Dur from 76; RD of Lanchester from 80. *10 Aynsley Terrace, Consett, Co Durham, DH8 5NF.* (Consett 50 2235)

SAMPSON, Philip John. b 50. Univ of Vic Wel LLB 74. Melb Coll of Div BD 79. **d** 79 Bp Wiggins for Wel **p** 80 Wel. C of St Jas Lower Hutt Dio Wel from 79. *39 Penrose Street, Lower Hutt, NZ.*

SAMPSON, Richard Ian Colin. b 55. Codr Coll Barb BA (Th) 79. **d** 78 **p** 80 Trinid. C of H Trin Cathl Port of Spain Dio Trinid from 78. *Deanery Flats, 30a Abercromby Street, Port of Spain, Trinidad, WI.*

SAMPSON, Terence Harold Morris. b 41. FCA 75. Bps' Coll Cheshunt, 64. **d** 67 **p** 68 Carl. C of St Andr Penrith 67-72; V of St Barn Carl 72-76; R 76-80; H Trin and St Barn City and Dio Carl from 80. *St Barnabas's Rectory, Brookside, Carlisle, Cumb.* (Carlisle 22936)

SAMS, David Stevenson. b 27. Hertf Coll Ox BA (3rd cl Hist) 50, MA 54. Wycl Hall Ox 50. **d** 52 **p** 53 Man. C of St Paul Kersal Salford 52-55; Benchill 55-57; V of St Thos Dixon Green Farnworth 57-61; R of Em Didsbury 61-69; Sen Lect (Welfare Officer from 72) Stockport Coll of Tech and L to Offic Dio Man 69-80; Res Tutor Colchester Inst at Clacton from 80; Perm to Offic Dio Chelmsf from 80. *Colchester Institute, Marine Parade East, Clacton-on-Sea, Essex, CO15 6JQ.*

SAMUEL, David. Bp's Th Coll Tirumaraiyur, 27. **d** 48 **p** 50 Sing. P Dio Sing 48-70. *5 Lorong 12/8a, Petaling Jaya, Malaysia.*

SAMUEL, David. St Paul's Th Coll Ambat. **d** 57 **p** 58 Madag. P Dio Madag. *Anaborana, Antingana, Madagascar.*

SAMUEL, David Norman. b 30. Univ of Wales, Dipl Th 54, BA (2nd cl Phil) 58. Univ of Hull MA 74. Edin Th Coll 60. **d** 61 **p** 62 St Alb. C of Bp's Stortford 61-65; St Jo Bapt Bedford 65-68; R of Beelsby Dio Linc from 68; R of Ashby w Fenby and Brigsley Dio Linc from 68; R of E w W Ravendale and Hatcliffe Dio Linc from 68. *East Ravendale Rectory, Grimsby, Lincs.* (Grimsby 823154)

SAMUEL, Ieuan. b 09. Fitzw Ho Cam BA 32, MA 37. Lich Th Coll 34. **d** 37 Lich **p** 38 Stafford for Lich. C of St Edw Leek 37-41; St Osw Oswestry 41-42; St Geo Altrincham 42-44; PC of Tow Law 44-50; V of Thornley 47-50; PC of St Nich Bp Wearmouth 50-55; V of Gainford w Piercebridge 55-74. *37 Quaker Lane, Richmond, N Yorks, DL10 4BB.* (Richmond 2474)

SAMUEL, James Louis. Sarum Th Coll 60. **d** 61 Glouc **p** 62 Tewkesbury for Cant. C of Dursley 61-63; Matson 63-65; St Phil and St Jas Leckhampton 65-66; Blakenall Heath 67-69. *Address temp unknown.*

SAMUEL, John Charles Kumar. b 55. **d** 79 **p** 81 W Mal. P Dio W Mal. *159-A Jalan Spooner, Ipoh, Perak, Malaysia.*

SAMUEL, Paul Gurubadam Thangarag. Bp's Coll Calc. Serampore Coll Bengal BD 52. **d** 50 Calc **p** 51 Sing. P Dio Sing 50-70; Dio W Mal from 70; Hon Can of Sing 63-70. *St Mary's Church, Jalan Rata, Kuala Lumpur, Malaysia.*

SAMUEL, Stuart. b 48. AKC 70. St Aug Coll Cant 70. **d** 71 **p** 72 Wakef. C of Golcar 71-77; V of St Mark Brampton 77-79; P-in-c of Hathern Dio Leic from 79. *Hathern Rectory, Loughborough, Leics.* (Loughborough 842259)

SAMUEL, Theophilus. b 35. Oak Hill Coll 70. **d** 72 Ox **p** 73 Buckingham for Ox. C of Slough 72-73; Chap Commun Relns Dio Ox 73-78; Chap Brunel Univ from 78. *Brunel University, Kingston Lane, Hillingdon, Middx.*

SAMUEL, Victor Dorai. **d** 64 **p** 65 Sing. P Dio Sing 64-70; Dio w Mal from 70. *16 Jalan Pudu Lama, Kuala Lumpur, Malaysia.*

SAMUELS, Christopher William John. b 42. K Coll Lon and Warm AKC 66. **d** 67 **p** 68 Man. C of St Thos Kirkholt Rochdale 67-72; C-in-c of St Thos Ap Conv Distr Parkside Houghton Regis 72-76; R of Tarporley Dio Ches from 76. *Rectory, Tarporley, Chesh.* (Tarporley 2491)

SAMUELS, Peter. b 34. Open Univ BA 79. Kelham Th Coll 57. **d** 61 **p** 62 Lon. C of St Aug of Cant Whitton 61-65; Ch Ch Milton-next-Gravesend 65-67; C-in-c of Stand Lane Dio Man 67-69; V 69-72; R of St Andr Droylsden Dio Man from 72. *Rectory, Merton Drive, Droylsden, Manchester, M35 6BH.* (061-370 3242)

SAMUPINDI, Justin Martin. St Jo Sem Lusaka, 64. **d** 66 **p** 68 Mashon. P Dio Mashon. *Merrywood House, Chikwaka, Rhodesia.*

SAMWAYS, Denis Robert. b 37. Univ of Leeds BA (3rd cl Gen) 62. Coll of Resurr Mirfield 62. **d** 64 **p** 65 Heref. C of Clun w Chapel Lawn 64-69; C of Pocklington w Yapham Meltonby Owsthorpe and Kilnwick Percy 69-71; C of Millington w Gt Givendale 69-71; R of Hinderwell w Roxby 71-76; Hon C of Loftus-in-Cleveland 76-80; Hinderwell w Roxby Dio York from 80. *Ruby House, Staithes, Saltburn, Cleve, TS13 5BH.* (Whitby 840532)

✠ **SANANA, Right Rev Rhynold Ewaruba.** b 39. Newton Th Coll 62. **d** 67 **p** 67 New Guinea. P Dio New Guinea 67-71; Dio Papua 71-73; Perm to Offic Dio Adel 73-74; Archd of E Papua from 75; Dean of St Pet and St Paul Cathl Dogura 75-76; Cons Asst Bp of Papua in Cathl Ch of St Pet and St Paul Dogura 9 May 76 by Abp of Brisb; Bps of Papua, Polyn, Ysabel and Malaita; and Bps Ambo, Meredith, Uka and J Ashton; Apptd Bp of Dogura 77. *Bishop's House, PO Dogura, Papua New Guinea.*

SAN CI HTAY, Samuel. H Cross Coll Rang BA 65. **d** 67 **p** 68 Rang. P Dio Rang. *104a Inya Road, Rangoon, Burma.*

SANDARS, Keith Lindsay. Moore Th Coll Syd ACT ThL 51. **d** and **p** 52 Syd. C of St Andr Summer Hill 52; Chap Trin Gr Sch Summer Hill 53-64; L to Office Dio Syd from 64; Hd Master Trin Prep Sch Summer Hill from 65. *12 Llandilo Avenue, Strathfield, NSW, Australia 2135.* (642-3834)

SANDBERG, Kenneth Graham. b 1888. Bp's Coll Cheshunt 16. **d** 17 **p** 18 Lon. C of St Mary Virg Primrose Hill 17-19; C of Banstead 19-21; Hd Master Parkside Sch Ewell 21-27; R of Pudleston w Whyle and Hatfield V 28-30; Hd Master and Chap Choir Sch Sarum 30-33; R of Lolworth 34-37; V of Haddenham 37-47; Leverington 47-62. *Brambles, Middle Common Road, Pennington, Lymington, Hants.* (Lymington 72136)

SANDBERG, Peter John. b 37. Univ of Lon LLB (2nd cl) 59. [f Solicitor]. Lon Coll of Div 67. **d** 69 **p** 70 Chich. C of Hailsham 69-72; Billericay Dio Chelmsf 72-77; Team V from 77. *10 Chestwood Close, Billericay, Essex, CM12 0PB.* (Billericay 52659)

SANDEMAN, Arthur Alastair Malcolm. b 14. Chich Th Coll 37. **d** 39 **p** 40 Windw Is. C of St Geo Cathl Kingstown 39-40; All SS Cathl Halifax NS 40-42; H Trin Cathl Queb 42-43; St Dunstan Cranford St John Lon 43-46; Swanage w Herston (in c of St Mark) 46-49; St Luke Woodside Croydon 49-51; St Steph Glouc Road Lon 51-52; Perm to Offic at St Mary Abbots Kens 52-54; R of St Jo Evang Wick 54-56; V of St Aug Brinksway w Cheadle Heath 56-60; Cressing 61-75; Commiss Windw Is from 70; Hon Chap Cant Cathl 49-52; Perm to Offic Dio Ex from 75; Dio Chelmsf from 77. *20 Orient Road, Preston, Paignton, Devon, TQ3 2PB.* (Paignton 521385)

SANDERCOMBE, Percy Oliver. b 07. St Bonif Coll Warm 35. **d** 38 **p** 39 Portsm. C of Liss 38-43; H Trin Win 43-48; V of Netley Marsh 48-67; Burton and Sopley 67-73; Offg Chap RAF 68-73; Perm to Offic Dio Sarum from 73. *39 Daniell Crest, Warminster, Wilts, BA12 8NZ.* (Warminster 213131)

SANDERS, Alan Edwin. b 51. AKC 74. St Aug Coll Cant 74. **d** 75 Stepney for Lon **p** 76 Lon. C of St Matthias Stoke Newington 75-77; St Cecilia Parson Cross Sheff 77-81; V of All S Leeds Dio Ripon from 81. *All Souls Clergy House, Blackman Lane, Leeds, LS2 9EY.* (Leeds 453078)

SANDERS, Canon Frederick Alexander. b 05. Univ of Lon BSc 25. Wells Th Coll 33. **d** 34 **p** 35 Win. C of St Mary Extra Southampton 34-36; St Pet Bournemouth 36-41; Asst Dioc Insp of Schs Dio Win 37-41; V of Eastmeon 41-45; R of Newnham w Hook (w Nately Scures Mapledurwell w Rotherwick) 45-51; (w Greywell and Up Nately 46-51) R and V of Overton (w Laverstoke and Freefolk from 52) 51-72; RD of Whitchurch 57-72; Hon Can of Win 61-72; Can (Emer) from 72; Perm to Offic Dio Ex from 72. *Langmead, South Zeal, Okehampton, Devon, EX20 2JS.* (Sticklepath 563)

SANDERS, Frederick Alvin Oliver. b 06. Late Scho of CCC Cam BA 28, MA 37. Coll of Resurr Mirfield. **d** 30 Lon for Guildf **p** 31 Guildf. C of Epsom 30-33; St Cuthb Hebburn-on-Tyne 33-35; St Mark East Street Walworth and Asst Missr Wel Coll Miss 35-37; Chap and Lect Bede Coll Dur and L to Offic Dio Dur 37-39; CF (EC) 43-48; R of Landbeach 48-59; CFTA from 50; Mere Pr to Univ of Cam 49 and 54; RD of Quy 58-59; R of Stalbridge 59-78; L to Offic Dio Killaloe from 78. *Skehanagh Point, Coolbawn, Nenagh, Co Tipperary, Irish Republic.* (Coolbawn 7)

SANDERS, Graham Laughton. b 32. Kelham Th Coll 52. **d** 56 **p** 57 Glouc. C of St Paul Glouc 56-60; Chap St Paul's Cathl Ranchi 61-63; Chap Bp Westcott Schs Namkum 61-68; V of St Martin Heaton 68-76; Gt Waltham (w Ford End from 79) Dio Chelmsf from 76; P-in-c of Ford End 79. *Great Waltham Vicarage, Chelmsford, Essex, CM3 1AR.* (Chelmsf 360334)

SANDERS, Herbert. Clifton Th Coll 51. **d** 53 **p** 54 Bradf. C of Laisterdyke 53-56; Bingley 56-59; V of Oxenhope 59-66; L to Offic Dio Linc from 67. *Low Toynton Vicarage, Horncastle, Lincs.*

SANDERS, James Alexander. Moore Th Coll Syd Dipl Th 65. **d** 65 Syd **p** 66 Bp Loane for Syd. C of Marrickville 65-66; Seaforth 68-70; R of Annandale 70-78; Perm to Offic Dio Lon 78-81. *6 Old Sydney Road, Seaforth 2092, NSW, Australia.*

SANDERS, John Logan. b 35. St Jo Coll Auckld 77. **d** 79 **p** 80 Auckld. C of Devonport Dio Auckld from 79. *16 Owens Road, Devonport, Auckland 9, NZ.*

SANDERS, Michael Barry. b 45. Fitzw Coll Cam 2nd cl Econ Trip pt i 65, BA (2nd cl Econ Trip pt ii) 67, MA 71. BD 71 (Lon). St Jo Coll Nottm 70. **d** 71 Dorking for Guildf **p** 72 Guildf. C of Ashtead 71-74; Chap St John's Coll Cam 75-79;

V of Dorridge Dio Birm from 79. *6 Manor Road, Dorridge, Solihull, Warws.* (Knowle 2472)

SANDERS, Raymond Joseph. b 20. Univ of Lon BA 40, BD 49. Qu Coll Birm 65. **d** and **p** 65 Worc. C of Pershore w Pinvin and Wick 65-67; R of Headless Cross 67-73; Dunsfold Dio Guildf from 73. *Dunsfold Rectory, Godalming, Surrey, GU8 4LT.* (Dunsfold 207)

SANDERS, Robert James Kendrick. Coll Ho Ch Ch LTh (1st cl) 57. **d** 51 **p** 52 Wel. C of Paraparaumu 51-53; Palmerston North 53-56; V of Pongaroa 56-58; Maniototo 58-63; Waikouaiti 63-66; Gonville 66-69; Castlecliff 69-78; Chap Auckld Pris from 78. *Box 50-124, Albany, NZ.* (478-5635)

SANDERS, Robin Michael. b 49. Univ Coll Ox BA 71, MA 76. Univ of Bris MA 75. Sarum Wells Th Coll 72. **d** 74 **p** 75 Guildf. C of Esher 74-78; St Nicolas City and Dio Guildf from 78. *61 Wodeland Avenue, Guildford, Surrey, GU2 5LA.* (Guildf 504304)

SANDERS, Ven William Leslie. St D Coll Lamp 32. **d** 37 **p** 38 Graft. C of Ettrick 37-38; P-in-c of Condong 38-40; C of Lismore 40-46; C-in-c 46-47; in England 47-48; R of Woodburn 48-53; Tweed Heads 53-58; RD of Murwillumbah 55-58; R of Coff's Harbour 58-77; RD of The Bellinger 64-75; Can of Ch Ch Cathl Graft 64-77; Archd of Graft from 77. *Glais House, Leonard Street, Nambucca Heads, NSW, Australia 2448.* (68-6733)

SANDERSON, Cecil John Harry. b 1899. Ridley Hall, Cam. **d** 58 Nor **p** 59 Thetford for Cant. C of Morley 58-60; R of Mulbarton w Kenningham 60-78; Perm to Offic Dio Nor from 78. *Little Manor, Topcroft, Bungay, Suffolk, NR35 2BL.*

SANDERSON, Daniel. b 40. K Coll Lon and Warm AKC 66. **d** 67 **p** 68 Carl. C of St Jo Bapt Upperby 67-72; V of Addingham w Gamblesby 72-75; Ireleth w Askam Dio Carl from 75. *Ireleth Vicarage, Askam-in-Furness, Cumb, LA16 7DL.* (Dalton 62647)

SANDERSON, Francis Lundy. b 29. **d** 71 New Westmr. C of St D Vanc 71-72; St Matthias Vanc 72; St Alb Burnaby 73-76; on leave. *923 Thermal Drive, Coquitlam, BC, Canada.*

SANDERSON, Harold. b 26. St Aid Coll. **d** 61 Warrington for Liv **p** 62 Liv. C of St Mark Newtown Pemberton 61-64; V of St Ann Warrington 64-73; C-in-c of St Pet Warrington 70-73; V of Orrell 73-79; Scarisbrick Dio Liv from 79. *Vicarage, Scarisbrick, Ormskirk, Lancs, L40 9RF.* (Scarisbrick 317)

SANDERSON, Howard Walter. St Andr Th Coll Pampisford. **d** 45 **p** 46 Lich. C of St Paul Burslem 45-47; Bucknall w Bagnall (in c of St Chad) 47-48; PC of Chell 49-53; R of Corrigin Dio Perth 53-55; V of Cantley w Limpenhoe and Southwood 55-57; R of Wramplingham w Barford 57-62; V of St Jo Bapt Islington 62-66; Barling w Wakering 66-72. *Address temp unknown.*

SANDERSON, Norman. b 14. Univ of Leeds BA 35. Coll of Resurr Mirfield 35. **d** 37 **p** 38 Blackb. C of St Cath Burnley 37-39; H Trin Carl 39-44; Min Can of Carl Cathl 40-44; V of Hesket-in-the-Forest 44-58; St Mary w St Paul Carl 58-65; Haverthwaite 65-72; R of Skelton w Hutton-in-the-Forest (w Ivegill from 74) 72-79; C-in-c of Ivegill w High Head 72-74. *Noreli, Bowness-on-Solway, Carlisle, CA5 5AF.*

SANDERSON, Peter Oliver. b 29. St Chad's Coll Dur BA 52. **d** 54 **p** 55 Dur. C of Houghton-le-Spring 54-59; R of Linstead Ja 59-63; Chap RAF 63-67; C-in-c of Winksley w Grantley and Aldfield w Studley Dio Ripon 67-68; V 68-74; St Aid Leeds Dio Ripon from 74. *St Aidan's Vicarage, Vicar's Road, Shepherd's Lane, Leeds, LS8 5AD.* (Leeds 490861)

SANDERSON, Peter Richard Fallowfield. b 18. St Cath S Ox BA 41, MA 46. Chich Th Coll 41. **d** 42 B & W **p** 44 Taunton for B & W. C of St Jo Evang Taunton 42-48; St Paul Ox 48-49; Perm to Offic at St Jo Evang Plymouth 49-55; V of Poundstock 56-74; P-in-c of St Patr Hove 74-79; St Mary Buxted Dio Chich from 79; Hadlow Down Dio Chich from 79. *St Mary's Vicarage, Church Road, Buxted, Uckfield, Sussex, TN22 4LP.* (Buxted 3103)

✠ **SANDERSON, Right Rev Wilfrid Guy.** b 05. Mert Coll Ox BA 28, MA 31. Ely Th Coll 31. **d** 32 **p** 33 Guildf. C of St Mark S Farnborough 32-34; Aldershot (in c of St Aid) 34-37; V of Woodham 37-46; All SS Alton 46-54; Chap Treloar Orthopaedic Hosp Alton Morland Hall Hosp and St Mary's Home Alton 46-54; R of Silverton 54-59; Archd of Barnstaple 58-62; R of Shirwell w Loxhore 59-62; Cons Ld Bp Suffr of Plymouth in S'wark Cathl 30 Nov 62 by Abp of Cant; Bps of Ex; Lon; Ely; and Heref; Bps Suffr of Fulham; Crediton; Bedford; Lewes; and Buckingham; and others; res 72. *3 Hinton Close, Hinton St George, Somerset, TA17 8SH.* (Crewkerne 73846)

SANDFORD, Edward Noel Teulon. b 17. St Pet Hall, Ox BA 43, MA 44. Wycl Hall, Ox **d** 43 **p** 44 Roch. C of Ch Ch Tunbridge Wells 43-45; Chap to Asst Bp of Lagos 46-51; Miss at Wusasa 48-51 and 54-58; Fagge 51-53 and 58-59; Actg Sec CMS Dio N Nig 51-53; BFBS Distr Sec Devon and Cornw 59-66; Regional Sec SW Engl from 66; Perm to Offic Dio Truro from 59; Dio Ex 59-63; L to Offic 63-78; Perm to Offic Dios B & W, Bris, Sarum, and Glouc from 72. *3 Madeira Road, Clevedon, Avon, BS21 7TJ.* (Clevedon 874035)

SANDFORD, Jack. Ripon Hall Ox. **d** 60 **p** 61 Chelmsf. C of Eastwood 60-63; V of Mayland 63-66; V of Steeple 63-66; St Laur Barkingside 66-77; Perm to Offic Dio Chelmsf from 77. *15 Lyndhurst Road, Holland-on-Sea, Essex.* (0255-815294)

SANDFORD, The Rev and Rt Hon Lord (John Cyril Edmondson). b 20. DSC 43. Westcott Ho Cam 56. **d** 58 **p** 60 St Alb. C of Harpenden 58-63; Perm to Offic Dio St Alb from 63; Hon Chap to Bp of St Alb 65-68; Ch Comm from 82. *6 Smith Square, Westminster, SW1.* (01-222 5715)

SANDFORD, Paul Richard. b 47. Em Coll Cam BA 69, MA 73. Wycl Hall Ox 72. **d** 75 Stepney for Lon **p** 76 Lon. C of St Pet U Holloway 75-77; St Luke Finchley 77-81; Team V of Cramlington Dio Newc T from 81. *24 Lindsey Close, Cramlington, Northumb, NE23 8EJ.*

SANDHAM, Stephen McCourt. b 41. K Coll Lon and Warm BD and AKC 65. **d** 66 **p** 67 Dur. C of St Pet Stockton-on-Tees 66-69; Ch of Good Shepherd Bp Wearmouth 69-71; Bp Wearmouth 71-75; V of St Mark w St Paul Darlington Dio Dur from 75. *394 North Road, Darlington, Co Durham.* (Darlington 64681)

SANDIFORD, Richard Howarth. b 06. AKC 31. **d** 32 **p** 33 Cant. C of St Mary Virg Dover 32-34; Stoke Damerel 34-35; Guildf 35-38; St Thos-on-the-Bourne 38-42; V of Binsted 42-47; Whitchurch (w Tufton from 54) 47-60; Surr from 48; R of Temple Ewell w Lydden 60-72; Perm to Offic Dio Cant from 72. *13 River Street, River, Dover, Kent, CT17 0RB.* (Kearsney 4543)

SANDILANDS, Canon George. Wycl Coll Tor LTh 69. **d** 69 Montr. C of St Paul Lachine 69-71; I of Lasalle St Lawr 71-73; R of Bedford 73-79; Sec of Synod Dio Montr 75-78; on leave 79-80; Comptroller Dio Montr from 81; Hon Can of Montr from 81. *144 Union Avenue, Montreal, PQ, Canada, H3A 2B8.* (514-845 6211)

SANDS, Kirkley. b 44. Codr Coll Barb 64. **d** 68 **p** 69 Nass. C of St Geo w St Marg 68-69; R of Grand Turk 69-70; C of H Trin Kingsway 71-73; R of Exuma 73-74; St Mary 74-79; St Matt I and Dio Nass from 79. *Box N-963, Nassau, Bahamas.*

SANDS, Nigel Colin. b 39. Univ of Dur BA 64, MA 68. Oak Hill Th Coll 65. **d** 67 Warrington for Liv **p** 68 Liv. C of Skelmersdale 67-71; All SS Childwall 71-72; V of St Bridget Wavertree 72-78; R of Welford w Wickham and Gt Shefford Dio Ox from 78; Boxford w Stockcross and Speen Dio Ox from 80. *Wickham Rectory, Newbury, Berks, RG16 8HD.* (Boxford 244)

SANDS, Percy. b 01. Fitzw Hall Cam BA 23, MA 27. Ridley Hall, Cam 23. **d** 29 **p** 30 Cov. C of St Paul Leamington 29-32; Chap Toc H for E Midlds 32-35; for W Austr 35-38; R of S Perth 38-41; L to Offic Dio New Guinea 42-43; Chap RAAF 41-46; PC of Flushing 45-52; R of St Mary Magd w St James Upton Torquay 52-66; L to Offic Dio Ex from 66. *31 Lloyd Avenue, Shiphay, Torquay, Devon, TQ2 7DH.* (Torquay 63464)

SANDS, Ronald Wilby. b 37. Univ of BC BA 64. Angl Th Coll of BC STB 68. **d** 68 New Westmr **p** 69 Bp Somerville for BC. C of St James Vanc 69-74; I of Port Moody Dio New Westmr from 74. *2206 St John's Street, Port Moody, BC, Canada.*

SANDWITH, Canon John Fleming. b 02. Ridley Hall Cam 32. **d** 33 **p** 34 Lon. C of St Mary Bryanston Square 33-36; St Mark (in c of St Nich) Portsea 36-39; PC of Streetly 39-50; V of St Mark Harrogate 50-72; Hon Can of Ripon 68-72; Can (Emer) from 72. *Flat 1, 4 Park Avenue, Harrogate, HG2 9BA.*

SANDY, George. **d** 71 Windw Is. C of St Geo Cathl Kingstown Dio Windw Is from 71. *St George Cathedral, Kingstown, St Vincent, W Indies.* (61684)

SANDYS-WUNSCH, John William Kervyn. Ch Ch Ox BA 58, MA and D Phil 61. **d** 61 **p** 62 BC. I of W Coast Miss 61-65; C of St John Vic 65-66; Chap Qu Coll St John's Dio Newfld from 66. *Queen's College, Forest Road, St John's, Newfoundland, Canada.*

SANFORD, Charles. Em Coll Sktn 66. **d** 69 Athab. d Dio Athab. *c/o Synod Office, Peace River, Alta, Canada.*

SANFORD, James David. b 36. Nashotah Ho Wisc LTh 76. **d** 76 **p** 77 Qu'App. C of Big Country Dio Qu'App from 76. *Box 1704, Kindersley, Sask, Canada.*

SANFORD, (Gabriel) William Henry Steward. b 14. Univ of Lon BD 37. AKC 36. Westcott Ho Cam 37. M CR 57. **d** 37 **p** 38 Chelmsf. C of H Trin Barkingside 37-43; Chap RNVR 43-46; C of H Trin Barkingside 46-48; C-in-c of St Paul

Bermondsey w Charterho Miss 48-54; Ho of the Resurr Mirfield 54-59; St Paul's Priory Lon 59-61; H Cross Codr Barb 61-67; Lon Priory 67-69; St D Priory Barb 69-76; Ho of the Resurr Mirfield from 76. *House of the Resurrection, Mirfield, W Yorks WF14 0BN.*

SANG', Mark Kichwen. b 44. St Paul's Coll Limuru 70. **d** 72 **p** 73 Nak. P Dio Nak. *Box 58, Kapsabet, Kenya.*

SANGA, Canon Kenneth. d and **p** 73 Lake Malawi. P Dio Lake Malawi; Can of Lake Malawi from 75. *Box 1, Likoma, Island, Malawi.*

SANGAI, Reynold. b 25. **d** 64 **p** 67 New Guinea. C of Sakarina 64-68; P-in-c of Safia 68-74; Ambasi Dio Papua from 74. *Anglican Church, Ambasi, Papua New Guinea.*

SANGAYA, Robinson. b 52. Yeotmal Sem India BD 80. **d** Centr Tang. d Dio Centr Tang. *Box 264, Dodoma, Tanzania.*

SANGER, Reginald Stephen John. b 15. Wycl Hall Ox. **d** 57 **p** 58 Roch. C of St Paul Beckenham 57-60; Bp's Youth Chap Dio Roch 57-62; Warden and Chap Roch Dioc Conf Ho and Youth Centre 60-62; V of St Mildred Lee Dio S'wark from 62. *St Mildred's Vicarage, Lee, SE 12.* (01-857 5205)

SANGLIER, Arthur Osmond. b 12. Sarum Th Coll 65. **d** 66 **p** 67 Sarum. C of Wilton w Netherhampton 66-69; R of Thornford w Beer Hackett 69-80. *Polebridge Farmhouse, Caundle Marsh, Sherborne, Dorset, DT9 5JU.*

SANGSTER, Andrew. b 45. K Coll Lon and Warm BD 67, BA (Lon) 71, AKC 67. **d** 69 **p** 70 Roch. C of Aylesford 69-72; Shirley 73-76; V of Woolston 76-79; Prov Youth Chap Ch in Wales from 79. *8 Hickman Road, Penarth, S Glam.*

SANGSTER, Arthur John. Linc Th Coll 41. **d** 42 **p** 43 Pet. C of St Barn Wellingborough 42-44; Min of distr of St Columba Corby 44-45; R of St Paul Aber 45-51; PC of Holland Fen w Chapel Hill and St Jo Bapt Amber Hill 51-53; V of Frampton 53-58; Gosberton 58-81. *c/o Gosberton Vicarage, Spalding, Lincs.* (Gosberton 410)

SANGUINETTI, Ven Samuel Dudley. St Pet Coll Ja 23. **d** 26 **p** 27 Ja. C of St Geo Kingston 26-28; Christiana w Spaldings 28-30; R of Kew Park 30-35; Albert Town w Troy 35-77; Can of Spanish Town Cathl Ja 51; Archd of N Middx (Dio Ja) 51-73; Mandeville 73-77; Archd (Emer) from 77. *Albert Town PO, Jamaica, W Indies.*

SANHOO, Canon Stephen. d 37 **p** 38 Rang. P Dio Rang; Hon Can of Rang from 53; Exam Chap to Bp of Rang 66-77. *Holy Cross Theological College, Rangoon, Burma.* (Rangoon 30658)

SANINGA, Marko. b 33. St Phil Coll Kongwa 80. **d** 81 Centr Tang. d Dio Centr Tang. *c/o Box 799, Moshi, Tanzania.*

SANJA, Samwire. Bp Tucker Coll Mukono. **d** 56 **p** 57 U Nile. P Dio U Nile 56-61; Dio Mbale 61-72; Dio Bukedi from 72. *Tirinyi, Uganda.*

SANKEY, David Arthur. Univ of Melb BA 69. Ridley Coll Melb ACT ThL 57. **d** 58 **p** 59 Melb. C of St John Camberwell 58-62; I of St Matthias N Richmond 62-64; Prec and Min Can of St Paul's Cathl Melb 64-75; I of All SS St Kilda Dio Melb from 75. *Vicarage, Chapel Street, East St Kilda, Vic, Australia 3182.* (51-7689)

SANKOK, Jeremiah. d 63 Momb. d Dio Momb 63-64; Dio Nai from 64. *c/o PO Box 30333, Nairobi, Kenya.*

SANSBURY, Christopher John. b 34. Late Scho of Peterho and Lady Kay Scho of Jes Coll Cam 2nd cl Th Trip pt i 55, BA (1st cl Th Trip pt ii) 57, 2nd cl Th Trip pt iii 58. Westcott Ho Cam 58. **d** 59 **p** 60 Portsm. C of St Mark Portsea 59-63; Weeke (in c of St Barn) 63-71; V of N Eling (or Copythorne) 71-78; R of Long Melford Dio St E from 78. *Long Melford Rectory, Sudbury, Suff.* (Long Melford 8145)

✠ **SANSBURY, Right Rev Cyril Kenneth.** b 05. Late Scho of Peterho Cam 2nd cl Cl Trip pt i, 26, BA (1st cl Th Trip pt i) 27, 1st cl Th Trip pt ii 28, MA 31. Trin Coll Tor Hon DD 54. Wycl Coll Tor Hon DD 54. Westcott Ho Cam 27. **d** 28 **p** 29 S'wark. C of St Pet Dulwich Common 28-31; Perm to Offic at Wimbledon 31-32; SPG Miss at Numazu 32-34; Prof Centr Th Coll and Br Chap St Andr Tokyo 34-41; Exam Chap to Bp in S Tokyo 35-41; Chap Br Embassy Tokyo 38-41; Chap RCAF 41-45; Warden of Linc Th Coll 45-52; Exam Chap to Bp of Linc 46-53; to Bp of Edin 47-59; to Bp of Bradf 56-60; to Abp of Cant 59-61; Can and Preb of Asgarby in Linc Cathl 48-53; Proc Conv Linc 50-55; Cant 55-61; Warden of St Aug Coll Cant 52-61; Hon Fell from 61; Hon Can of Cant 53-61; Select Pr Univ of Cam 57; Cons Ld Bp of Sing in Cant Cathl 6 Jan 61 by Abp of Cant; Bps of Leic; Sarum; Birm; Pet; Bris; and Blackb; Bps Suffr of Aston; Croydon; and Dover; and Bps Rose; D J Wilson; Trapp; Bayne and others; res 66; Gen Sec Br Coun of Chs 66-73; Asst Bp in Dio Lon 66-73; C-in-c of St Mary-in-the-Marsh City and Dio Nor from 73; Hon Min Can of Nor Cathl from 73. *67 The Close, Norwich, NR1 4DD.* (0603-618808)

SANSOM, Charles Nesbitt. b 14. Trin Coll Dub BA 37, MA and Weir Pri 40, Div Test (2nd cl) and Eccles Hist Pri (2nd) 41. **d** 41 Down **p** 42 Tuam for Down. C of St Matt Belfast 41-45; St Jude Ballynafeigh 45-48; R of St Phil Belf 48-60; Chap R Vic Hosp Group Belf 48-60; R of St Mary Belf 60-81; Preb of Connor Cathl 78-81. *57 Killarney Road, Donaghadee, Co Down, N Ireland.*

SANSOM, George Frederick. b 38. Ridley Coll Melb 78. **d** 78 **p** 79 Melb. C of St Thos Essendon 78-79; St Paul Ascot Vale Dio Melb from 79. *99 Roxburgh Street, Ascot Vale, Vic, Australia 3032.*

SANSOM, John Reginald. b 40. St Jo Coll Nottm 73. **d** 75 **p** 76 St E. C of St Marg Ipswich 75-79; P-in-c of Emneth Dio Ely from 79. *Emneth Vicarage, Church Road, Wisbech, Cambs.* (Wisbech 3089)

SANSOM, Joseph Donald. Ridley Coll Melb 29, ACT ThL 31. **d** 31 **p** 32 Gippsld. C of St Paul's Cathl Sale 31-34; V of Blackwood Forest w Bass 34-35; R of Orbost 35-41; Commissioner for Bd of Relig Educn 41-47; R of Leongatha 41-43; Chap CMF 41; AIF 42; Res Can of St Paul's Cathl 43-49; R of Sale 43-50; Commiss Gippsld 43-45; Dean of Sale 49-50; I of Brighton Beach 51-55; H Trin Kew 55-68; Black Rock 68-72; Perm to Offic Dio Melb from 73. *40 Iona Street, Black Rock, Vic, Australia 3193.*

SANSOM, Michael Charles. b 44. Univ of Bris BA 66. St Jo Coll Dur PhD 74. **d** 72 Sheff **p** 73 Doncaster for Sheff. C of Ecclesall 72-76; Dir of Stud Ridley Hall Cam from 76; Vice-prin from 79. *Ridley Hall, Cambridge, CB3 9HG.*

SANSOM, Robert Arthur. St Aid Coll 60. **d** 62 Southw **p** 63 Bp Gelsthorpe for Southw. C of Sutton-in-Ashfield 62-65; PC of Holbrooke 65-70; R of Patricia Bay and Sidney Vancouver 70-71; N Saanich 71-80; St Mary Vic Dio BC from 80. *1701 Elgin Road, Victoria, BC, Canada.*

SANSOME, Geoffrey Hubert. b 29. Univ of Man BA 53. Univ of Birm Dipl Th 62. Qu Coll Birm 60. **d** 62 **p** 63 Ches. C of St Steph Prenton 62-68; P-in-c of St Thos Liscard Wallasey 68-72; V of Kingsley Dio Ches from 72. *Kingsley Vicarage, Warrington, Chesh.* (Kingsley 88386)

SANSUM, David Henry. b 31. Univ of Bris BA (2nd cl Hist) 52, MA 63. St Aid Coll 54. **d** 56 Bris **p** 57 Malmesbury for Bris. C of St Pet Henleaze 56-59; Stratton St Marg 59-60; Stoke Bp 60-64; V of Stechford 64-76; Ashbourne w Mapleton Dio Derby from 76; P-in-c of Thorpe Dio Derby from 77; Min of St Jo Bapt Ashbourne Dio Derby from 81. *Vicarage, Belle Vue Road, Ashbourne, Derbys, DE6 1AT.* (Ashbourne 43129)

✠ **SANTER, Right Rev Mark.** b 36. Qu Coll Cam BA 60, MA 64. Westcott Ho Cam. **d** 63 **p** 64 Ox. C of Cuddesdon 63-67; Tutor Cudd Coll 63-67; Dean and Fell of Clare Coll Cam 67-72; Tutor 68-72; Asst Lect in Div Univ of Cam 68-72; Prin Westcott Ho Cam 73-81; Exam Chap to Bp of St Alb 70-81; Select Pr Univ of Ox 75; Hon Can of Win Cathl 78-81; Cons Area Bp of Kens in St Paul's Cathl Lon 7 Jan 81 by Abp of Cant; Bps of Lon, Ely, Birm, Derby, Edin, Guildf, Iran, Lich, Liv, Man, Ox, Portsm, St Alb, St E, Sarum, S'wark and Truro; Bps Suffr of Aston, Bedford, Buckingham, Edmon, Hertf, Knaresborough, Huntingdon, Lynn, Maidstone, Malmesbury, St Germans, Stepney, Kingston T, Taunton, Tonbridge, Warwick and Willesden; and others. *19 Campden Hill Square, W8 7JY.* (01-727 9818)

SANTILLAN, Fausto. b 24. **d** 70 **p** 71 Parag for Argent. P Dio Argent 71-73; N Argent from 73. *Parsonage, Carboncito, N Argentina.*

SANTINEER, Albert Alexander. Bp's Coll Calc 60. **d** 58 **p** 61 Madras. in Ch of S India 58-65; V of Karagpur and St Jas Calc 65-71; Perm to Offic Dio Perth from 71. *45 Rugby Street, Bassendean, W Australia 6054.* (326 2646)

SANTRAM, Philip James. b 27. Univ of Delhi BSc 48. Serampore Univ BD 53. Bp's Coll Calc 49. **d** 52 **p** 54 Delhi. P Dio Delhi 54-60; Lect Bp's Coll Calc 61-65; Dio Calc 62-64; Dio Delhi 65-66; Ethiopia 66-68; C of All SS L Horton Bradf 68-71; Ch Ch Reading 71-72; P Missr St Mary Magd Conv Distr Tilehurst 72-76; V of St Mary Magd Tilehurst 76-78; I of Lakefield Dio Montr from 78. *Lakefield, PQ, Canada.*

SANYAOLU, Samuel Oke. Im Coll Ibad 66. **d** 67 **p** 68 Lagos. P Dio Lagos. *Ilushin, Abigi, Nigeria.*

SAPSFORD, Ven Alan Geoffrey. ACT ThL 59. M SSM. **d** and **p** 60 Rockptn. C of Gladstone 60-62; V of theodore 62-66; Seymour Dio Wang from 66; Archd Dio Wang from 79. *Christ Church Rectory, Box 259, Seymour, Vic, Australia 3660.*

SAPSFORD, John Garnet. b 38. **d** and **p** 76 Glouc. C of Whiteshill 76-78; Perm to Offic Dio Melb from 81. *Braemar College, Woodend, Vic, Australia.*

SAPSFORD, Laurence Wybrew. b 17. St D Coll Lamp BA 40. St Mich Coll Llan 40. **d** 41 **p** 42 St A. C of Shotton 41-43; Mold 43-46; Chepstow 46-52; R of Llandrinio w Criggion 52-61; V of St Thos Stafford 61-67; R of Swynnerton 67-71;

Colton 71-77; Blithfeld 71-77. *5 Sparrow Close, Little Haywood, Stafford.*

SARALIS, Christopher Herbert. b 34. Univ of Wales BA (2nd cl Hist) 54. St Cath S Ox BA (2nd cl Th) 56, MA 60. Wycl Hall Ox. **d** 57 **p** 58 Mon. C of Abergavenny 57-61; Bridgwater 61-65; V of Berrow (w Breane from 72) 65-76; RD of Burnham 72-76; Exmoor from 80; V of Minehead Dio B & W from 76. *Vicarage, Warden Road, Minehead, Somt.* (Minehead 3530)

SARELINA, Israel. St Paul's Coll Ambat 56. **d** 57 **p** 62 Madag. P Dio Tam. *La Mission Anglicane, Ambinanindrano, Madagascar.*

SARGANT, John Raymond. b 38. CCC Cam BA 61, MA 70. Westcott Ho Cam 64. Harvard Div Sch 66. **d** 67 **p** 68 Cant. C of Croydon 67-72; Sec Zambia Angl Coun 72-75; C-in-c of Ch Ch Bradf-on-Avon Dio Sarum 76-81; V from 81. *Christ Church Vicarage, Bradford-on-Avon, Wilts.* (Bradf-on-Avon 3262)

✠ **SARGANT, Right Rev Norman Carr.** b 09. Univ of Birm BA 31. *Methodist Min.* In Ch of S India 47-51; Cons Ld Bp in Mysore (Ch of S India) in St Mark's Cathl Bangalore 12 April 51; res 72; Hon Can of Bris 74-81; Can (Emer) from 81. *75 Lower Redland Road, Bristol, BS6 6SP.* (Bris 30497)

SARGEANT, Frank Hubert. b 1894. Trin Hall Cam 2nd cl Hist Trip pt i 22, BA (2nd cl Th Trip pt i) 23, MA 31. Bps' Coll Cheshunt 23. **d** 24 Guildf for Win **p** 25 Win. C of St Mark Portsm 24-26; H Trin Fareham 26-35; V of St Steph Buckland Portsea 35-49; R of Bp's Waltham 49-62; V of Saxthorpe w Corpusty 62-66; V of Oulton 62-66. *36 Henley Road, Taunton, Somt, TA1 5BJ.* (Taunton 84716)

SARGEANT, Ven Frank Pilkington. b 32. St Jo Coll Dur BA (3rd cl Th) 55, Dipl Th 58. Cranmer Hall Dur 57. **d** 58 **p** 59 Linc. C of Gainsborough 58-62; Gt Grimsby (in c of St Martin) 62-66; V of N w S Hykeham 66-73; Can Res of Bradf 73-77; Dir In-Service Tr Dio Bradf from 73; Archd of Bradf from 77. *11 Carlton Drive, Bradford, BD9 4DL.* (Bradford 45747)

SARGEANT, Kenneth Stanley. b 19. Lon Coll Div 68. **d** 70 **p** 71 Barking for Chelmsf. C of St Paul East Ham 70-73; Southborough 73-77; R of Greenhithe Dio Roch from 77. *Rectory, Greenhithe, Kent.* (Greenhithe 842031)

SARGEANT, Lennard Lionel. b 10. **d** 73 **p** 76 Windw Is. C of St D Grenada Dio Windw Is from 73. *St David's Rectory, Grenada, W Indies.* (6227)

SARGEANT, Philip Toswell. St Jo Coll Winnipeg. **d** 53 **p** 54 Bran. Itin P Dio Bran 53-58; R of The Pas 58-59; Grand Rapids 58-59; St Jas Flin Flon 59-64; Hon Can of Bran 61-70; R of St Steph Edmon 71-76; Chap St Jo Sch Alta from 76. *RR1, Stony Plain, Alta., Canada.*

SARGENT, Albert Francis. b 15. Kelham Th Coll 31. **d** 39 **p** 40 Lich. C of St Giles Willenhall 39-43; C-in-c of Conv Distr of Stone Cross West Bromwich 43-44; CF (EC) 44-48; V of Tilstock 48-50; Edensor 50-60; St Andr W Bromwich 60-77. *24 Padstow Way, Trentham, Stoke-on-Trent, Staffs, ST4 8SU.* (0782-642529)

SARGENT, Canon Alexander. b 1895. St Edm Hall Ox 3rd cl Cl Mods 16, BA (3rd cl Th) 18, MA 21. Cudd Coll 18. **d** 19 Ox for Cant **p** 20 Cant. C of St Marg-at-Cliffe 19-21; All SS Maidstone 21-23; Chap of Cudd Coll 23-27; Sub-Warden of St Paul's Coll Grahmstn 27-29; Chap to Abp of Cant 29-39; Commiss Grahmstn 32-45; Six Pr in Cant Cathl 33-39; Archd of Maidstone 39-42; Cant 42-68; Select Pr Univ of Ox 49-51; Can of Cant 39-68; Hon Can 68-74; Can (Emer) from 74. *1 Starr's House, The Precincts, Canterbury, Kent.*

SARGENT, Daniel Wayne. b 49. Univ of W Ont BA 71. Hur Coll Ont 68. **d** 74 **p** 75 Yukon. I of Teslin 74-77; Blyth Dio Hur from 77. *Box 32, Blyth, Ont, Canada.* (519-523 9334)

SARGENT, James Malcolm. Ex Coll Ox BA 49, MA 53. Coll of Resurr Rosettenville. **d** 51 **p** 52 Capetn. Asst Chap Dioc Coll Rondebosch 51-55; Chap 55-59; Michaelho Sch Natal 59-68; C of St Paul Durban 68-73; R of St Thos Durban 73-79; Perm to Offic Dio Ox from 80. *37 Rectory Crescent, Middle Barton, OX5 4BP.* (Steeple Aston 40622)

SARGENT, Richard Henry. b 24. Univ of Man BA 50. **d** 52 **p** 53 Man. C of Rusholme 52-54; Cheadle 54-59; V of St Andr Cheadle Hulme 59-67; Bushbury 67-73; Castle Church Dio Lich from 73; Surr from 67; M Gen Syn 70-80; RD of Stafford from 81. *Castle Church Vicarage, Stafford.* (Stafford 3673)

SARGENT, William Richard Gerald. b 26. Linc Th Coll. **d** 57 **p** 58 York. C of St Aug of Hippo Newland 57-60; V of H Trin Dalston 60-70; St Mark N End Portsea Dio Portsm from 70. *3a Wadham Road, Portsmouth, Hants, PO2 9ED.* (Portsmouth 662500)

SARGISON, Ronald Ragsdale. b 10. AKC (1st Cl) and Univ of Lon BD 31. Wells Th Coll 32. **d** 33 **p** 34 Southw. C of St Cath Nottm 33-36; Mansfield Woodhouse 36-40; St Martin Sherwood 40-42; CF (EC) 42-46; Hon CF 46; PC of Carrington 47-52; V of Kneesall 52-54; V of Ossington 52-54; Ryhill 54-56; Dean and R of St Geo Cathl Georgetn Br Gui 56-60; V of St Jo Div Balham 61-64; R of Hawthorn 64-69; V of Trimdon 69-74. *18 Montgomery Road, Up Hatherley, Cheltenham, GL51 5LB.* (Cheltm 24731)

SARGISSON, Conrad Ralph. b 24. Keble Coll Ox BA (3rd cl Engl) 46, MA 50. Wells Th Coll 48. **d** 50 **p** 51 Glouc. C of St Mary Charlton Kings 50-53; Prestbury 53-55; V of St Briavels and of Hewelsfield 55-58; Lanteglos-by-Fowey 58-62; PC of St Mary Penzance 62-68; V 68-73; Surr 62-73; Proc Conv Truro 69-73; RD of Penwith 72-73; V of Westbury-on-Trym 73-79; P-in-c of Blisland w St Breward Dio Truro from 79. *Blisland Rectory, Bodmin, Cornw.* (Bodmin 850249)

SARKIES, John Walter Robert Courtney. b 12. Univ of Lon MRCS, LRCP, DOMS, 36. Cudd Coll 57. **d** 59 Dover for Cant **p** 60 Cant. C of Bearsted 59-61; Chap Jane Furse Mem Hosp Pret 61-67; L to Offic Dio Pret 61-67; Dio Maur 67; R of Curepipe 68-69; Hon C of St Matt Douglas Dio S & M from 69. *2 Westminster Terrace, Douglas, IM.*

SARUM, Archdeacon of. *See* McCulloch, Ven Nigel Simeon.

SASAI, Samuel. St Luke's Coll Siota 33. **d** 34 **p** 38 Melan. P Dio Melan 34-75. *Fiu, Malaita, British Solomon Islands.*

SASKATCHEWAN, Lord Bishop of. *See* Short, Right Rev Hedley Vicars Roycraft.

SASKATCHEWAN, Dean of. *See* Lee, Very Rev Lorne Francis.

SASKATOON, Lord Bishop of. *See* Wood, Right Rev Roland Arthur.

SASKATOON, Dean of. (Vacant)

SATCHELL, Sydney Victor. St Jo Th Coll Morpeth ACT ThL 33. **d** 27 **p** 28 Newc. C of Singleton 27-32; P-in-c of St Albans 32-34; Wollombi 34-37; Wallsend 37-45; Scone 45-55; C of Randwick 55-56; R of Drouin 56-57; LPr Dio Newc 57-61; Dio Syd from 61. *4/40 Albert Street, Hornsby, NSW, Australia 2077.* (476-2687)

SATRE, Lowell Jacobson. b 47. St Olaf Coll Minn USA BA 68. Nashotah Ho Wisc USA MDiv 72. **d** 74 **p** 75 Moos. C of Mistassini Lake 74-75; I of Noranda 75-78; Melville Dio Qu'App from 77. *Box 328, Melville, Sask, Canada.* (728-5746)

SATTERFORD, Douglas Leigh. b 18. Men in Disp 41. DSC 42. Ripon Hall Ox 59. **d** 60 **p** 61 S'wark. C of Sanderstead 60-65; V of Lyminster Dio Chich from 65; Poling Dio Chich from 66. *Lyminster Vicarage, Littlehampton, Sussex.* (Arundel 882152)

SATTERLY, Gerald Albert. b 34. Univ of Ex BA (Lon) 56. Wycl Hall, Ox 58. **d** 60 **p** 61 Roch. C of St Pet w Ch Ch Southborough 60-63; S Lyncombe 63-66; V of St Barn Sheff 66-69; R of Adwick-le-Street 69-73; V of Awre w Blakeney Dio Glouc from 73; P-in-c of Newnham-on-Severn Dio Glouc from 80. *Vicarage, Blakeney, Glos, GL15 4DS.* (Blakeney 229)

✠ **SATTERTHWAITE, Right Rev John Richard.** b 25. Univ of Leeds BA 46. Coll of Resurr Mirfield 48. **d** 50 **p** 51 Carl. C of St Barn 50-53; Ch Ch w St Aid Carl 53-55; Asst Gen Sec of C of E Coun on Foreign Relations 55-59; Gen Sec 59-70; Gen Sec abp's Comm on RC Relations 65-70; C of St Mich Paternoster Royal Lon 55-59; C-in-c 59-65; Guild V of St Dunstan-in-the-W 59-70; Hon Can of Cant 63-70; Asst Chap O of St John of Jer 63-70; Chap from 71; Hon Can of Utrecht from 68; Cons Ld Bp Suffr of Fulham (in c of the Jurisd of N and C Eur) in Westmr Abbey 28 Oct 70 by Abp of Cant; Bp of Lon; Bps of Win; Pet; Linc; St E; Leic; Ox; Abp of Utrecht; and others; Bp of Gibr 71-80; Bp of Gibr in Eur from 80. *5A Gregory Place, W8 4NG.* (01-937 2796)

SATTHIANADHAN, Victor Samuel Davaratnam. Univ of Tor BA 33. Wycl Coll Tor BD 44. **d** 36 **p** 37 Colom. C of Ch Ch Galle Face 36-40; I of Tamil Past Dickoya 40-41; on leave in Tor Univ 41-45; I of St Mary Kopay 45; C of St Paul Bambalapitiya 46-57; Lect Div Sch Colom 49-68; I of St Thos Colom 57-69; Chundikuli 69-70; Exam Chap to Bp of Colom 65-70; Hon Can of Colom 69-70; Tutor at St Geo Coll Jer from 70. *St George's College, Jerusalem, Israel.*

SAU, Elias. d 32 **p** 34 Melan. P Dio Melan 32-62. *Melanesian Mission, British Solomon Islands.*

SAUBER, Neil Ernest. St Jo Coll Morpeth ThDip 80. **d** and **p** 81 Newc. C of Mayfield Dio Newc from 81. *Clergy House, Durham Street, Mayfield 2304, NSW, Australia.*

SAUERBREI, Mark. d 57 Alg. C of St John Port Arthur 57-66. *203-3911 Carrigan Court, Burnaby, BC, Canada, V3N 4J7.*

SAUL, Norman Stanley. b 30. St Aid Coll 51. **d** 54 Lancaster for Blackb **p** 55 Blackb. C of H Trin S Shore Blackpool 54-57; Poulton-le-Fylde 57-59; V of Freckleton 59-66; St Luke Blackb 66-68; St Lawr Barton 68-72; Foxdale 72-77;

Kirk Maughold Dio S & M from 77. *Maughold Vicarage, Ramsey, IM.* (Ramsey 812070)

SAULI, Marshall Gordon Peter. St Jo Sem Lusaka 60. **d** 62 **p** 63 Nyasa. P Dio Nyasa 62-64; Dio Malawi 64-71; Dio S Malawi 71; Dio Lake Malawi from 71. *P/A Liwaladzi, Nkhotakota, Malawi.*

SAUNDERS, Andrew Vivian. b 44. Univ of Leeds BA (2nd cl Engl and Hist) 65. Coll of Resurr Mirfield. **d** 68 Bradwell for Chelmsf **p** 69 Chelmsf. C of St Paul Goodmayes 68-71; Horfield 71-75; Oldland 75-77; P-in-c of Buckland Dinham 77-80; Industr Chap Dio B & W from 77; V of Westfield Dio B & W from 80. *Westfield Vicarage, Midsomer Norton, BA3 4BJ.* (0761 412105)

SAUNDERS, Brian Gerald. b 28. Pemb Coll Cam BA 49, MA 53. Cudd Coll 63. **d** 66 St Alb **p** 67 Bedford for St Alb. C of Gt Berkhamsted Dio St Alb from 66. *2 North Road, Berkhamsted, Herts.* (Berkh 73608)

SAUNDERS, Bruce Alexander. b 47. Late Choral Exhib of St Cath Coll Cam BA 68, MA 72. Univ of Ox Dipl Th 70. Cudd Coll 68. **d** 71 **p** 72 Bris. C of Westbury-on-Trym 71-74; Hon C of St Paul Clifton Dio Bris from 74; Asst Chap of Bris Univ 74-78; Team v of H Trin w St Columba Fareham Dio Portsm from 78. *21 Miller Drive, Fareham, Hants.* (Fareham 281518)

SAUNDERS, David. b 28. Keble Coll Ox BA 50, Dipl Th 51, MA 59. Cudd Coll 51. **d** 53 **p** 54 Sheff. C of Mexborough 53-56; St Cuthb Firvale Sheff 56-60; V of New Bentley 60-67; PC of All SS Gt Grimsby 67-69; V 70-77; Caistor and Clixby Dio Linc from 78; P-in-c of Grasby w Owmby and Searby Dio Linc from 78. *Vicarage, Caistor, Lincs, LN7 6UH.* (Caistor 851339)

SAUNDERS, David Anthony. b 48. Trin Coll Bris 76. **d** 78 **p** 79 B & W. C of Walcot Bath 78-81; Dioc Youth Chap & Asst Dir of Educn Dio B & W from 81. *Old Deanery, Wells, Somt, BA5 2UE.* (Wells 72446)

SAUNDERS, David Roy. Bp's Univ Lennox BA 64, STB 66. **d** 65 New Jersey for Ont **p** 66 Ont. R of Lansdowne Front 65-66; Marmora 67-70; CF (Canad) from 71. *Kapyong Barracks, Depot M, Winnipeg, Manit, Canada.*

SAUNDERS, Edward George Humphrey. b 23. St Jo Coll Cam BA 48, MA 50. Ridley Hall Cam. **d** 50 **p** 51 Ox. C of St Ebbe Ox 50-52; Cands Sec for CPAS 52-54; Cler Asst Sec 54-58; V of Ch Ch Finchley 58-64; Proc Conv Lon 59-64; V of Chipping Campden 64-69; C-in-c of Ebrington 66-69; Warden Lindley Lodge Nuneaton and L to Offic Dio Leic 69-71; V of St Mich w St Phil Ches Sq Dio Lon from 71; P-in-c of Ch Ch Down Street Westmr Dio Lon from 80. *4 Chester Square, SW1.* (01-730 8889)

SAUNDERS, Ernest John. b 11. Clifton Th Coll 46. **d** 48 **p** 49 Truro. C of Illogan 48-50; V of Laneast w St Clether 50-54; St Keverne 54-63; St Feock 63-77; RD of Powder 74-77. *Trussel Cottage, Lamellion, Liskeard, Cornw, PL14 4JX.*

SAUNDERS, Francis Alfred. St Jo Coll Auckld LTh 48. ACT ThL 51. **d** 47 **p** 48 Waik. C of Te Awamutu 47-50; V of Pio Pio 50-57; Te Kauwhata 57-60; L to Offic Dio Waik 60-63; Dio Auckld 61-63; Dio Wel 63-69; Hon C of St Matt Masterton 68-74; Perm to Offic Dio Wel from 75. *41 Daniell Street, Featherston, NZ.* (89-709)

SAUNDERS, George Arthur. b 18. Kelham Th Coll 35. **d** 41 Kingston T for S'wark **p** 42 S'wark. C of St Barn Eltham 41-42; Camberwell 42-45; C-in-c of Em Camberwell 46-52; V 52-57; Ascen Plumstead Dio S'wark from 57. *Ascension Vicarage, Thornhill Avenue, Plumstead, SE18 2HS.* (01-854 3395)

SAUNDERS, Guy. b 27. K Coll Lon and Warm AKC 51. **d** 52 **p** 53 Lon. C of Highgate 52-55; Hurstpierpoint 55-59; V of Aldingbourne 59-65; Whitehawk 65-69; C-in-c of Duncton 69-81; Burton w Coates 69-81; Up Waltham 69-81; P-in-c of Bolney Dio Chich from 81. *Bolney Vicarage, Haywards Heath, Sussex, RH17 5QR.* (Bolney 301)

SAUNDERS, Henry Wilfred. b 19. St Steph Ho Ox 48. **d** 51 **p** 52 Newc T. C of St Anthony Newc T 51-52; St Gabr Heaton Newc T 52-54; St Matt Newc T 54-55; V of Kwakwani and Berbice River Miss Dio Gui 55-56; C of Hereford 56-57; St Teath w Michaelstow (in c of Delabole) 58-60; R of St Tudy 60-70; RD of Bodmin 68-70; Asst Chap HM Pris Pentonville 70-71; Chap HM Pris Holloway 71-76; HM Pris Haverigg from 76. *c/o HM Prison, Haverigg, Millom, Cumb, LA18 4NA.* (Millom 2131)

SAUNDERS, John Michael. b 40. Clifton Th Coll 68. **d** 70 **p** 71 Stepney for Lon. C of St Luke Hackney 70-74; SAMS Miss from 74. *CP 275, Petropolis, Rio de Janeiro, Brazil.*

SAUNDERS, Kenley Frederick. Moore Th Coll Syd 27. **d** 27 **p** 28 Syd. C of Wollongong 27-29; Mortdale w Penshurst 29-31; Min of Lord Howe I 31-35; C of St Andr Lakemba 35-36; C-in-c of St John Wilberforce 36-37; V 37-40; Chap AIF 40-46; C-in-c of Dee Why 46-49; R 49-54; St Luke Concord 54-66; L to Offic Dio Syd from 66. *185 Donington Court, Flinders Village, Castle Hill, NSW, Australia 2154.* (680-1227)

SAUNDERS, Kenneth John. b 35. Linc Th Coll 73. **d** 75 **p** 76 Linc. C of Boultham 75-79; V of Swinderby Dio Linc from 79. *Vicarage, Station Road, Swinderby, Lincs.* (Swinderby 673)

SAUNDERS, Leonard Ashton. **d** 75 **p** 77 Ja (APM). C of Morant Bay Dio Ja from 75. *19 Church Street, Morant Bay, Jamaica, WI.*

SAUNDERS, Malcolm Walter Mackenzie. b 35. Em Coll Cam 2nd cl Cl Trip pt i 57, BA (2nd cl Th Trip pt ia) 58, MA 62. Wycl Hall Ox 58. **d** 60 **p** 61 Pet. C of St Giles Northn 60-63; St Alb Northn and Lect Northn Coll of Tech 63-66; V of St Columba Corby Dio Pet from 66. *157 Studfall Avenue, Corby, Northants.* (Corby 4158)

SAUNDERS, Martin Paul. b 54. AKC and BD 76. Westcott Ho Cam 77. **d** 78 **p** 79 Newc T. C of Seaton Hirst 78-81; Asst Chap Miss to Seamen Hong Kong 81; C of Egglescliffe Dio Dur from 81. *1 Springfield Close, Eaglescliffe, Stockton-on-Tees, Cleveland.* (0642-782193)

SAUNDERS, Michael. b 35. K Coll Lon and Warm AKC 61. **d** 61 and **p** 62 Portsm. C of St Francis Leigh Pk 61-66; V of Weston, Surrey 66-73; C of Cathl and Abbey St Alb 73-75; C-in-c of Eversholt 76-79; Ridgmont 76-79; Warden Old Alresford Place and P-in-c of Old Alresford Dio Win 79-80; R (w Bighton) from 80. *Rectory, Old Alresford, Hants.* (Alresford 2780)

SAUNDERS, Phillip Warwick. Univ of NSW BSc 62. ACT ThL 70. BD (Lon) 71. Ridley Coll Melb 68. **d** 72 **p** 74 Melb. C of All SS Greensborough 72-74; H Trin Doncaster 74-76; P-in-c of Glen Waverley Dio Melb from 76. *3 Dubbo Court, Glen Waverley, Vic, Australia 3150.*

SAUNDERS, Reginald Frederick. b 15. **d** and **p** 79 St Andr (APM). C of St Ninian's Cathl Perth Dio St Andr from 79. *31 Muirend Road, Perth, PH1 1JU, Scotland.*

SAUNDERS, Richard Charles Hebblethwaite. b 17. Qu Coll Ox BA 40, Dipl Th 41, MA 42. Westcott Ho Cam 41. **d** 42 **p** 43 Sheff. C of H Trin Darnall Sheff 42-45; Chap of St Paul Agra and Tutor St Jo Coll Agra 46-49; V of Thornton-le-Street w Otterington Thornton-le-Moor and Thornton-le-Beans 49-52; Eastwood 52-62; St Ambrose Bris 62-75; C-in-c of All H Easton Bris 65-68; R of E Bris 75-77; P-in-c of Colerne Dio Bris from 77; N Wraxall Dio Bris from 77; RD of Chippenham from 80. *Colerne Rectory, Chippenham, Wilts.* (Box 742742)

SAUNDERS, Roan George. b 09. AKC 36. **d** 36 **p** 37 Chelmsf. C of St Eliz Becontree 36-39; St John Buckhurst Hill 39-40; H Trin Bramley 40-42; All SS Edmonton 42-45; V of St Mich Cricklewood 45-49; LDHM of St Alphege Edmonton 49-51; V 51-53; PC of E Huntspill 53-60; V of Draycott 60-75; R of Rodney Stoke 60-75. *Stokewood Cottage, Rodney Stoke, Cheddar, Somt.* (Priddy 344)

SAUNDERS, Ronald. b 37. ACP 67. Sarum Th Coll. **d** 68 **p** 70 Malawi. L to Offic Dio Malawi 68-70; C of Blantyre 71-72; St Mary Abbots Kens 72-73; St Francis Bournemouth 73-75; I of Twillingate 76; L to Offic Dio E Newfld 77-81; C of Gt Marlow Dio Ox from 81. *c/o Vicarage, Marlow, Bucks.*

SAUNDERS, Ross Hallett. Moore Th Coll ACT ThL 51. **d** and **p** 54 Syd. C-in-c of Wilberforce 54-56; R of Delegate 56-60; Adelong 60-63; Hon C of Five Dock 63; L to Offic Dio Syd 64-77; Asst Dir Relig Broadcasts Austrn Broadcasting Comm 67-71. *14 Richards Avenue, Drummoyne, NSW, Australia 2047.* (81-1192)

SAUNDERS, William Rolleston. b 04. Univ of Wales BSc 22. St Cath Coll Ox BLitt 25. Bps' Coll Cheshunt 34. **d** 37 **p** 39 St A. C of Llanychan 37-42; R of Mt Bures 42-56; V of White Colne 49-56; R of Kenchester w Bridge Sollars 56-73; R of Bishopstone 56-73. *Brynonnen, Llanarth, Dyfed, SA47 0NG.* (Llanarth 473)

SAUNT, James Peter Robert. b 36. Chich Th Coll 73. **d** 75 **p** 76 Sarum. C of Portland 75-79; P-in-c of Bratton Dio Sarum 78-81; V from 81; Chap HM Pris Erlestoke from 80. *Vicarage, Bratton, Westbury, Wilts. BA13 4SN.* (Bratton 830374)

SAUSBY, John Michael. b 39. **d** 63 **p** 64 Wakef. C of Crosland Moor 63-65; Halifax 65-67; V of St Cuthb Birkby Huddersfield 67-77; Holmfirth w Thongsbridge Dio Wakef from 77. *Holmfirth Vicarage, Huddersfield, HD7 1HG.* (Holmfirth 3285)

SAVAGE, Arthur Mellish. St Jo Coll Morpeth ACT ThL 64. **d** 65 **p** 66 Adel. C of Toorak Gardens 65-66; Whyalla W 66-69; Warrnabool 69-71; R of Skipton 70-75; V of Creswick w Clunes 76-80; R of Colac Dio Bal from 80. *St John's Rectory, Colac, Vic, Australia 3250.*

SAVAGE, Christopher Marius. b 46. Qu Coll Birm 68. **d** 70 **p** 71 S'wark. C of St Luke Battersea 70-75; Team V of St Nicolas Newbury 75-80; R of St Mich w St Mary City and

Dio Lich from 80. *St Michael's Rectory, Lichfield, Staffs, WS13 6EE.* (Lich 22420)

SAVAGE, David. b 1894. Lich Th Coll. **d** 55 Ely **p** 56 Bp Walsh for Cant. C of H Trin w St Mary Ely 55-58; R of Northwold 58-70. *Church House, Lawshall, Bury St Edmunds, Suff.*

✠ **SAVAGE, Right Rev Gordon David.** b 15. St Cath S Ox BA 49, MA 51. Tyndale Hall, Bris 39. **d** 40 **p** 41 Bris. Chap Tyndale Hall Bris 40-44; Tutor and Libr 41-44; LPr Dio Lon 45-52; Commiss N Afr 46-54; C of St Martin and All 55 Ox 48-52 Gen Sec Ch S and Ch S Trust 45-52; Proc Conv Ox 51-59; V of St Nich Marston Ox 52-57; Chap St Mich Ho Ox 52-55; V of Whitchurch w Creslow and Archd of Buckingham 57-60; Cons Ld Bp Suffr of Buckingham in St Paul's Cathl 18 Oct 60 by Abp of Cant; Bps of Lon; Ely; Ox; Linc; Birm; Lich; and Leic; and others; Trld to Southw 64; res 70. *Hinton House, Peterchurch, Hereford, HR2 0SH.*

SAVAGE, Leslie Walter. b 15. Cranmer hall, Dur 63. **d** 65 **p** 66 Carl. [f Methodist Ch]. C of Stanwix 65-69; V of Bolton w Cliburn 69-74; Holme-in-Cliviger Dio Blackb from 74. *Holme-in-cliviger Vicarage, Burnley, Lancs, BB10 4SU.* (Burnley 22467)

SAVAGE, Michael Atkinson. b 33. St Pet Hall Ox BA (2nd cl Th) 57, MA 61. Tyndale Hall Bris 57. **d** 59 **p** 60 Cov. C of St Matt Rugby 59-62; St Jo Evang Welling 62-66; V of St Steph Bowling 66-73; Ben Rhydding Dio Bradf from 73. *Ben Rhydding Vicarage, Ilkley, W Yorks, LS29 8PT.* (Ilkley 607363)

SAVAGE, Roderick. d 69 Papua. d Dio Papua 69-72; Perm to Offic Dio Brisb from 78. *42 Collard Street, Slacks Creek, Queensland, Australia 4127.*

SAVAGE, Rowland James Alexander. b 02. TCD BA 38, Div Test 40, MA 45. **d** 40 **p** 41 Oss. C of Killermogh 40-43; St Anne's Miss Distr Belf 43-46; C-in-c of Ch Ch Ardkeen 46-57; V 57-65; C of Dundonald 65-66; St Brendan Belf 66-69; Hon C of St Columba Knock Belf 69-78. *c/o 37 Beechill Park South, Saintfield Road, Belfast 8, N Ireland.*

SAVAGE, William. b 05. ACIS 31. Worc Ordin Coll 66. **d** 66 **p** 67 York. C of Sutton-in-Holderness 66-69; St Martin Middlesbrough 69-73; Hon C of West Acklam Dio York from 78. *8 Kimmerton Avenue, Acklam, Middlesbrough, Cleveland.*

SAVAGE, William Francis. b 42. ACT ThL 71. Moore Coll Syd 69. **d** 72 **p** 73 Tas. C of Burnie 72-73; Roseville 74-75; Palmwoods 76-78; P-in-c of Goodna Dio Brisb from 78. *96 Alice Street, Goodna, Queensland, Australia 4300.* (288 2667)

SAVAGE, William Humphrey. b 15. Worc Ordin Coll 63. **d** 65 **p** 66 Ex. C of St Thos Ex 65-68; V of Thorverton 68-73; V of Cadbury 68-73; R of Alphington 73-79; C of St Matt and of St Sidwell City and Dio Ex from 79. *77 Athelstan Road, Exeter, Devon.* (Exeter 72115)

✠ **SAVARIMUTHU, Right Rev John Gurubatham.** b 25. Serampore Coll Madras BD 52. Tamilnad Th Coll S Ind 48. St Aug Coll Cant Dipl Th 63. **d** 51 Colom **p** 52 Sing. C of Seremban 52-55; V of Negri Sembilan 56-62; C of St Geo Cathl Kingston Ont 63; V of S Johore 64-70; Exam Chap to Bp of Sing 65-70; Archd of W Mal from 70; Cons Ld Bp of W Malaysia in St Mary's Ch Kuala Lumpur 7 March 73 by Abp of Cant; Bps of Sing, Kuch and Sabah. *Rumah Bishop, 14 Pesiaran Stonor, Kuala Lumpur, 04-08, W Malaysia.* (03-22 426)

SAVARY, Reginald Neve. Univ of Tor BA 34, BD 39. Wycl Coll Tor LTh 35. **d** 35 **p** 36 Tor. C of Ch of Messiah Tor 35-37; Miss Dio Mid-Japan 37-41; R of Elizabethtown and Ballycanoe 41-42; Bd of Oriental Missions Dio Koot 42-46; I of Slocan 44-46; Miss to Japanese Prov Ont 46-47; R of Tyendinaga Dio Ont 47-52; service in Japan 52-62; I of Ch Ch Delaware 62-67; R of St Matt Lon 67-73; Kirkton 73-75. *RR3, Weymouth, NS, Canada.*

SAVEKA, George. d 81 N Queensld (NSM). C of All SS Gordonvale Dio N Queensld from 81. *c/o PO Box 181, Gordonvale, Qld, Australia 4865.*

SAVIGE, John Sydney. b 24. **d** 73 **p** 74 Leic. C of St Pet w St Hilda Leic 73-75; P-in-c of Harby (w Stathern from 76) Dio Leic 75-77; R from 77; RD of Framland I from 80; P-in-c of Long Clawson w Hose Dio Leic from 81. *Harby Rectory, Melton Mowbray, Leics, LE14 4BA.* (Harby 60269)

SAVILE, Ian Keith Wrey. b 26. Trin Hall Cam BA 51, 2nd cl Th Trip pt IA 52. Ridley Hall Cam 51. **d** 53 Liv **p** 54 Warrington for Liv. C of St Matt Bootle 53-56; St John Birkdale 56-57; V of St Mark Barrow-F 57-64; Wandsworth 64-74; RD of Wandsworth 70-74; V of H Trin Southw 74-80; Canford Magna Dio Sarum from 80; Bp of Southw's Adv on Evang 74-80. *Canford Magna Vicarage, Wimborne, Dorset.* (Wimborne 883382)

SAVILL, David. b 27. Em Coll Cam BA 49, MA 52. Ridley Hall Cam 50. **d** 52 **p** 53 St E. Chap of St E Cathl 52-54; C of St Martin-in-the-Fields 54-57; V of Sunbury-on-Thames 57-67; Heston 67-73; Asst Master Denes High Sch Lowestoft from 73; P-in-c of Mettingham 74-80; Chap Felixstowe Coll from 80. *63 Looe Road, Felixstowe, Suffolk.*

SAVILL, Richard Rodney. b 14. St Jo Coll Dur BA 37, MA 40, Dipl Th 38. **d** 38 **p** 39 Roch. C of Shortlands 38-40; Aylesford 40-41; C-in-c of St Jas Gravesend 41-42; C of St Jo Bapt Croydon (in c of St Geo Waddon) 43-47; V of Charing Heath 47-53; Rolvenden 53-61; Langdale 61-72; Perm to Offic Dio York from 72; Dio Ripon from 79. *12 Park Place, Harrogate, N Yorks.* (Harrogate 64348)

SAVILLE, David James. b 39. Ch Ch Ox BA 60, MA 64. Clifton Th Coll 61. **d** 63 **p** 64 Sheff. C of Darfield 63-66; St Leonards-on-Sea 66-68; Cands Sec CPAS 69-74; V of St Jas Taunton 74-80; Chorleywood Dio St Alb from 80; RD of Taunton N 78-80. *Christ Church Vicarage, Chorleywood, Rickmansworth, Herts.* (Chorleywood 2149)

SAVILLE, George Edward. d 42 **p** 43 Lich. C of St Mary and St Chad Longton 42-44; Carlton 44-46; Mary L Lambeth 46-49; St Mich AA Barnes 49-50; St Luke w St Paul Old Charlton 50-52; V of H Trin New Charlton 52-56; PC of H Trin Ilkeston 56-63. *Fernecumbe House, King's Coughton, Alcester, Warws.*

SAVILLE, Jeremy David. b 35. Late Squire Scho of Or Coll Ox BA (2nd cl Th) 59, MA 62. Chich Th Coll 58. **d** 60 **p** 61 Newc T. C of St Paul Cullercoats (or Whitley Bay) 60-63; Hexham 63-65; Chap Cudd Coll Ox 65-68; L to Offic Dio Ox 65-68; R of Holt 68-73; C-in-c of Kelling w Salthouse 68-71; R of Edgefield 71-73; V of E Dereham (w Hoe 73-78) 73-81; R of Scarning w Wendling 78-81; Beckenham Dio Roch from 81. *14 The Knoll, Beckenham, Kent, BR3 2JW.* (01-650 0983)

SAVINS, Thomas George. b 13. Univ of Bris BA (2nd cl Engl Lit and Phil) 36. St Bonif Coll Warm 36. **d** 38 **p** 39 Lon. C of St John w St Sav Fitzroy Square 38-39; St Mary Magd S Bersted 39-42; C of Hurstpierpoint 42-48; C-in-c of St Geo Mart Brighton 48-53; R of Hastings 53-57; V of Heathfield 57-66; R of St Clem (w All SS from 70) Hastings 66-81; RD of Dallington 61-65. *33 Park Lane, Eastbourne, Sussex.*

SAWANDA, Paul. d 67 **p** 68 Nak. P Dio Nak. *c/o PO Box Kapsabet, Kenya.*

SAWARD, Michael John. b 32. Univ of Bris BA 55. Tyndale Hall, Bris. **d** 56 Dover for Cant **p** 57 Cant. C of Ch Ch Croydon 56-59; Edgware 59-64; Warden H Trin Inter Ch Centre Liv and Sec Liv Coun of Chs 64-67; Radio and Television Officer Ch Information Office 67-72; Hon C of St Jo Bapt Beckenham 70-72; V of St Matt Fulham 72-78; Ealing Dio Lon from 78; M Gen Syn from 75; Ch Comm Dio Lon from 78; Area Dean of Ealing E from 79; Surr from 80. *11 Church Place, W5 4HN.* (01-567 0414)

SAWLE, Ralph Burford. b 14. Lich Th Coll 34. **d** 37 **p** 38 Derby. C of Sawley 37-40; St Barn Walthamstow 40-43; Offg C-in-c of All SS Hanley 43-46; V of Hanford 46-52; Malins Lee 52-57; St Mark Ocker Hill Tipton 57-61; PC of Werrington 61-68; V 68-72; V of N Petherwyn 62-68; RD of Trigg Major 66-72; R of St Giles-in-the-Heath w Virginstowe 68-72; V of St Neot 72-79; Perm to Offic Dio Win from 79. *32 Cavendish Close, Romsey, Hants, SO5 8HT.*

SAWLE, William John. b 16. Univ of Lon BD (2nd cl) 39. Tyndale Hall Bris 34. **d** 39 **p** 40 Bris. Chap Tyndale Hall Bris 39-41; C of St Mary Wakef 41-43; St Steph Wandsworth 43-45; Asst Sec Nat Ch League 45-46; Ch Assoc (Prov York) 46-49; Ch S 49-50; V of St Thos Crookes Sheff 50-57; Leyland 57-81; RD of Leyland 64-70. *8 Queensdale Close, Walton-le-Dale, Preston, Lancs, PR5 4JU.*

SAWREY, Harold. b 14. Edin Th Coll. **d** 60 Penrith for Carl **p** 61 Carl. C of Kirkby Stephen 60-63; V of Orton 63-80; P-in-c of Tebay 77-80. *8 Atkinson Court, Fell Foot, Newby Bridge, Nr Ulverston, Cumb.*

SAWYER, Andrew William. b 49. AKC 71. St Aug Coll Cant 71. **d** 72 **p** 73 Dorking for Guildf. C of Farnham 72-75; Dawlish 75-78; R of Colkirk w Oxwick, Whissonsett and Horningtoft Dio Nor from 78; P-in-c of Brisley Dio Nor from 80. *Colkirk Rectory, Fakenham, Norf, NR21 7NU.* (Fakenham 3890)

SAWYER, Charles. b 13. St Paul's Coll Grahmstn 50. LTh (SAfr) 53. **d** and **p** 51 Zulu. C of Usuthu Miss 51-52; R of Douglas and Dir of Douglas and Hopetown Miss 52-53; Prin of St Mich Sch Bremersdorp 53-60; Chap Brookland Hall Sch 61-64; C of Worksop 64-67; V of Blidworth Dio Southw from 67. *Blidworth Vicarage, Mansfield, Notts.* (Blidworth 2306)

SAWYER, Derek Claude. b 33. ALCD 58. **d** 58 **p** 59 Leic. C of Kirby Muxloe 58-60; Braunstone 60-65; R of St Paul Vacoas Maur 65-68; V of St Mich AA Knighton City and Dio Leic from 68. *St Michael's Vicarage, Scott Street, Knighton, Leicester, LE2 6DW.* (Leic 708033)

SAWYERR, Albert Weah. Im Coll Ibad 66. **d** 65 **p** 66 Sier

L. P Dio Sier L. *PO Box 5, Kenema, Sierra Leone.* (Kenema 244)

SAWYERR, Canon Harry Alphonso Ebun. MBE 54. CBE 63. Fourah Bay Coll BA 34, MA 36, MEd 40. **d** 43 **p** 45 Sier L. Tutor Fourah Bay Coll 33-45; Lect and Chap 48-52; Sen Lect and Chap 52-56; St Jo Coll Dur 45-48; Exam Chap to Bp of Sier L from 48; Vice-Prin Fourah Bay Coll 56-58 and 64-68; Prin 68-75; Can of St Geo Cathl Freetown from 61. *Codrington College, St John, Barbados, WI.*

SAWYERR, O'Brien Alphonso Dandison. **d** 19 **p** 25 Sier L. P Dio Sier L. C-in-c of H Innoc Freetown 43-48; C of Ch Ch Freetown 48-52. *Freetown, Sierra Leone.*

SAWYERS, Thomas Adam Barton. **d** 61 **p** 62 Derry. C of Drumragh 61-63; I of Tamlaght O'Crilly 63-69; Lissan Dio Arm from 69. *Lissan Rectory, Cookstown, Co Tyrone, N Ireland.* (Cookstown 3498)

SAXBEE, John Charles. b 46. Univ of Bris BA 68. Cranmer Hall Dur Dipl Th 69. PhD 74. **d** 72 **p** 73 Ex. C of Em Plymouth 72-77; P-in-c of St Phil Weston Mill Devonport 77-80; V 80-81; Team V of Ex Centr Dio Ex from 81; Jt Dir of Ex-Truro Min Tr Scheme from 81. *c/o 32 Barnfield Road, Exeter, EX1 1RX.*

SAXBY, Harold. b 11. St Chad's Coll Dur BA 37, MA 40. **d** 38 **p** 39 S'wark. C of St John Southend Lewisham 38-41; C-in-c of H Trin Hartlepool 41-45; PC of Williton 45-52; Chap Williton Hosp for Aged 47-52; PC of Highbridge 52-61; Cockerton 61-64; R of Jarrow 64-76; C-in-c of St Pet Jarrow 64-69; St Mark Jarrow 64-68; Hosp Chap Dio Dur 64-76; Perm to Offic Dio York 76-78; C of Wrington w Redhill & Butcombe Dio B & W from 79. *Parsonage, Redhill, Bristol, BS18 7SL.* (Wrington 862398)

SAXBY, Martin Peter. b 52. St Jo Coll Dur BA 77, Dipl Th 78. Cranmer Hall Dur 74. **d** 78 **p** 79 S'wark. C of St Mary Peckham 78-81. *Address temp unknown.*

SAXON, Canon Eric. b 14. Univ of Man BA (Admin) 35, MA 80. Univ of Lon BD (1st cl) 40. ALCD 40. O St John 73. **d** 40 **p** 41 Man. C of St Mary Droylsden 40-44; Davyhulme 44; Hon C of Ch Ch Heaton Norris 44-47; BBC Relig Broadcasting Org (N of Engl) 44-51; Hon C of St Ann City and Dio Man 47-51; R from 51; RD of Man Cathl 51-77; Surr from 52; Hon Can of Man Cathl from 58; Chap to HM the Queen from 67. *St Ann's Rectory, Kinnaird Road, Withington, Manchester, M20 9QL.* (061-445 1181)

SAXTON, George Albert. b 1896. Univ of Dur LTh 26. BA (Hatf) 26. St Aug Coll Cant 21. **d** 27 Man for Col Bp **p** 28 St Jo Kaffr. C of St Steph Matatiele 27-32; Almondbury 32-39; V of St Jo Bapt Dewsbury 39-49; Milnsbridge 49-57; Ryhill 57-65; Hoyland-Swaine 65-68; L to Offic Dio Wakef from 68. *14 George Street, Wakefield, W Yorks.*

✠ **SAY, Right Rev Richard David.** b 14. Ch Coll Cam BA 38, MA 41. DD (Lambeth) 61. Ridley Hall Cam 38. **d** 39 **p** 40 Cant. C of St Jo Bapt Croydon 39-43; St Martin-in-the-Fields Lon 43-50; Asst Sec C of E Youth Coun 42-44; Gen Sec 44-47; Gen Sec Br Coun of Chs 47-55; L to Offic Dio Lon 50-55; Select Pr Univ of Cam 54; R of Bp's Hatfield 55-61; Surr 55-61; Dom Chap to Marq of Salisbury and Chap Welfield Hosp 55-61; Hon Can of St Alb 57-61; Cons Ld Bp of Roch in Cant Cathl 6 Jan 61 by Abp of Cant; Bps of Sarum; St Alb; Birm; Pet; Worc; and Erie (USA); and others; Sub-Chap O of St John of Jer 58-61; Sub-Prelate from 61; Select Pr Univ of Ox 63; Lord High Almoner to HM the Queen from 70. *Bishopscourt, Rochester, Kent, ME1 1TS.* (Medway 42721)

SAYER, Cecil Albert. b 12. Univ of Leeds, BA (2nd cl Hist) 34. Coll of Resurr Mirfield 34. **d** 36 **p** 37 Worc. C of Malvern Link 36-39; R of Anna Regina 39-42; V of Kitty w Lodge Guyana 42-46; Exam Chap to Bp of Barb 46-55; Prin of Codrington Coll Barb 46-55; V of Urchfont w Stert 56-59; Chap St Mary's Sch Wantage 59-66; C-in-c of Clifton 66-73; Asst Master Qu Eliz Gr Sch Ashbourne from 73. *Queen Elizabeth Grammar School, Ashbourne, Derbys.*

SAYER, Derek John. b 32. St Steph Ho Ox 55. **d** 58 **p** 59 Lon. C of All H Tottenham 58-61; Letchworth 61-63; Chap RADD W Ham 63-64; C of St Mich AA Lancing 64-66; Chap RADD from 66. *49 Ruxley Lane, Ewell, Surrey, KT19 0JF.* (01-394 0428)

SAYER, Harold John. b 15. CCC Cam 2nd cl Hist Trip pt i, 35, BA (2nd cl Law Trip pt ii) 36. **d** 67 **p** 68 Glouc. C of St Jo Evang Churchdown 67-71; C-in-c of Dodington w Wapley and Codrington 71-73; R of Highnam w Lassington and Rudford 73-82. *c/o Highnam Rectory, Gloucester.*

SAYER, John Martin. Univ of Bris BA (3rd cl Th) 57. Clifton Th Coll 59. **d** 61 **p** 62 Sarum. C of Hamworthy 61-64; CMJ Area Sec N England Glas Edin and S & M 64-66; R of Andover 66-72; Dalhousie 72-77; on leave. *Box 307, Dalhousie, NB, Canada.*

SAYER, Canon Russell Arthur. Trin Coll Tor BA 49, LTh 52, STB 53. **d** 51 **p** 52 Edmon. C of Fort Sask 51-53; I 53-54; Westlock 55-61; R of St D City and Dio Edmon from 61; Can of Edmon from 66; Dom Chap to Bp of Edmon from 69. *7751 85th Street, Edmonton, Alta., Canada.* (403-469 7220)

SAYER, Wharton Allinson. **d** 54 Taunton for B & W **p** 55 B & W. C of Crewkerne 54-57; R of Seaborough and of Wayford 57-58; Mooi River 58-67; L to Offic Dio Natal from 67. *High Rising, PO Box 89, Greytown, Natal, S Africa.*

SAYER, William Anthony John. b 37. St Mich Coll Llan 60. **d** 64 **p** 65 Nor. C of Gorleston 64-67; V of Bacton w Edingthorpe 67-71; C-in-c of Honing w Crostwight 67-71; C-in-c of Witton w Ridlington 67-71; CF from 71. *c/o Barclays Bank, The Market Place, North Walsham, Norfolk.*

SAYERS, Guy Anthony. b 10. Ex Coll Ox BA 35, MA 37. Ely Th Coll 34. **d** 36 **p** 37 S'wark. C of St Pet Vauxhall 36-41; CF (EC) 41-46; CF (TA) 49-65; Men in Disp 44; C of St Aug Kilburn 46-50; V of Ch Ch Doncaster 50-58; St Mary Kettering 58-68; R of Empingham 68-81. *57 Radcliffe Road, Stamford, Lincs, PE9 1AU.* (Stamford 55191)

SAYLE, Gordon. b 03. St Edm Hall Ox BA 25, MA 45. Wells Th Coll 29. **d** 29 **p** 30 York. C of St Chad York 29-31; St Paul Middlesbrough (in c of H Cross) 31-34; V of Fylingdales 34-38; Chap of Qu Marg Sch Scarborough and C of St Martin Scarborough 38-39; V of Lezayre 39-47; CF (TA-R of O) 39-45; V of S Ramsey 47-52; Goathland 52-61; Leake (w Over and Nether Silton from 67) 61-71; V of Over w Nether Silton 61-67; C-in-c of Cowesby 67-71; Hon C of All SS Friern Barnet 78-81. *The Bernard Sunley Home, College Road, Maybury Hill, Woking, Surrey, GU22 8BT.* (04862-65427)

SAYWELL, Philip. b 33. Linc Th Coll 58. **d** 60 **p** 61 Lon. C of Stepney 60-63; Calstock 63-66; V of Lanteglos-by-Fowey 66-73; Chap at Khuzestan (Ahwaz) Iran 73-77; R of Hilborough Group (Cockley Cley w Gooderstone, Oxburgh w Foulden, Hilborough w Bodney, Gt w L Cressingham and Threxton, and Didlington) 78-80; Chap H Trin Dubai and St Martin Sharjah Dio Cyprus from 80. *Box 7415, Dubai, Arabian Gulf.*

SAYWELL, Sydney Wells. b 1896. **d** 40 **p** 41 Lich. C of Hodnet w Weston-under-Redcastle (in c of Peplow) 40-43; Actg C of Market Drayton and L Drayton 43-44; V of Quarnford 44-47; Wetley Rocks 47-61; Coven 61-68; Perm to Offic Dio Lich 68-75; Dio Ex 70-75; Llan 72-75. *22 Carlton Drive, Putney, SW15.*

SCAIFE, Andrew. b 50. Ex Coll Ox BA LitHum 73, BA (Th) 76, MA 76. Wycl Hall Ox 74. **d** 77 **p** 78 Liv. C of St Geo Everton 77-81; Team V of St Mich City and Dio Liv from 81. *St Michael's Vicarage, Upper Pitt Street, Liverpool, L1 5DB.* (051-709 7464)

SCAMMELL, Canon John James Frank. AKC 32. St Paul's Coll Burgh 32. **d** 32 **p** 33 Lon. C of St Cath Coleman Hammersmith 32-34; Frome-Selwood 34-39; LDHM of K Chas Mart S Mymms 39-47; V of All SS St Marg-on-Thames 47-54; Leighton Buzzard 54-80; V of Egginton 54-80; RD of Dunstable 58-77; Hon Can of St Alb 63-80; Can (Emer) from 80; C-in-c of Billington 65-80. *49 Heath Court, Plantation Road, Leighton Buzzard, Beds, LU7 7JR.* (0525-381380)

SCAMMELL, John Richard Lyn. b 18. Univ of Bris LLB 45. Wycl Hall, Ox 46. **d** 48 **p** 49 Bris. C of Bishopston 48-50; Stoke Bishop 50-52; CF 53-73; C-in-c of Bicknoller (w Crowcombe from 75) 73-78; R of Bicknoller w Crowcombe and Sampford Brett 78-81. *2A Ellenborough Park South, Weston-super-Mare, Avon, BS23 1XW.* (Weston-super-Mare 416488)

SCANDINAVIA, Archdeacon of. *See* Horlock, Ven Brian William

SCANDRETT, Canon John James. St Chad's Coll Regina. **d** 43 **p** 44 Qu'App. C of St Pet Regina 43-44; St Alb Regina 44-45; I of Ogema 45-52; R of Swift Current 52-55; V of St Jas Regina 55-65; Dom Chap to Bp of Qu'App 62-64 and 70-79 I of Melville 65-70; Moose Jaw 70-79; Hon Can of Qu'App 77-79; Can (Emer) from 79. *162 Coteau Street West, Moose Jaw, Sask, Canada.*

SCANLON, Geoffrey Edward Leyshon. b 44. Coll of Resurr Mirfield 74. **d** 76 **p** 77 Dur. C of Beamish 76-79; St Mary w St Pet Bp Wearmouth 79-81; in Amer Ch from 81. *Church of the Epiphany, PO Box 875, Laurens, S Carolina, 29360, USA.*

SCANLON, Canon James Philip. Qu Univ Kingston Ont BA 51, MA 54. Wycl Coll Tor LTh 55. **d** 55 Ont **p** 56 Moos. C of St John Kingston 56; R of Chapais Chibougamau 56-65; Moose Factory 65-69; Archd of James Bay 65-69; R of St John Kingston Dio Ont from 69; Can of Ont from 80. *176 Mowat Avenue, Kingston, Ont, Canada.* (613-548 7260)

SCANLON, Canon Thomas Henry. Trin Coll Dub BA 15, Div Test 16, MA 18. **d** 16 **p** 17 Down. C of Seagoe 16-18; Enniskillen 18-19; R of Tempo 19-29; Rynagh w Gallen 29-41; Dunshaughlin Ballymaglasson and Ratoath 41-58; RD of Ratoath 41-58; Ed of Meath Dioc Mag 50-58; Can of

Meath from 57. *Kinalee, Hillcrest Road, Sandyford, Co Dublin, Irish Republic.*

SCANTLEBURY, Gavin Stratton. Ridley Coll Melb 77. **d** 78 **p** 79 Willoch. C of Port Pirie 78-80; R of Streaky Bay Dio Willoch from 80. *27 Wells Street, Streaky Bay, S Australia, 5680.*

SCARAMANGA, George Ambrose. b 11. Oak Hill Th Coll 63. **d** 64 **p** 65 Chich. C of Hailsham 64-66; Crowborough 66-68; R of Abbotts Ann (w Monxton from 69) 68-75; C-in-c of Monxton 68-69; Perm to Offic Dio Ox from 77. *Cherry Tree House, Westfield, Medmenham, Bucks, SL7 2HE.* (049166-223)

SCARBOROUGH, John Richard Derek. b 32. BA (Lon) 54. Cudd Coll. **d** 69 **p** 70 Linc. C of Fulbeck 69-72; Bassingham 73-74; Asst Master Carre's Gr Sch Sleaford 69-76; L to Offic Dio Linc 74-76; V of Wellingore w Temple Bruer 76-78; R of Navenby 76-78; Boothby Graffoe 76-78; Gaffoe 77-78; Asst Master Carre's Gr Sch Sleaford from 78; L to Offic Dio Linc from 78. *10 Wansbeck Road, Leasingham, Sleaford, Lincs.* (Sleaford 304100)

SCARTH, John Robert. b 34. Univ of Leeds, BSc 55. St Jo Coll Dur Dipl Th 65. Cranmer Hall Dur 63. **d** 65 **p** 66 Wakf. C of Dewsbury 65-68; V of Shepley 68-72; Asst Master Kingston-upon-Hull Gr Sch 72-78; St Mary's C of E Sch Hendon Lon 78-81; V of Ossett Dio Wakef from 81. *Vicarage, Ossett, Yorks, WF5 9ET.* (Ossett 274068)

SCATTERGOOD, William Henry. **d** 56 **p** 57 Bath. C of Gilgandra 56-57; Bourke 57-60; P-in-c of Cobar 61-64; V of Miriam Vale 64-67; R of Balranald 67-74; Hillston 74-76. *c/o Diocesan Registry, Cathedral Buildings, Bathurst, Australia 2795.*

SCEATS, David Douglas. b 46. Ch Coll Cam 2nd cl Geog Trip pt i 67, BA (2nd cl Th Trip pt ia) 68, MA 72. Univ of Bris MA 71. Clifton Th Coll 68. **d** 71 **p** 72 Ely. C of St Paul Cam 71-74; Lect Trin Coll Bris and Publ Pr Dio Bris from 74. *Trinity College, Stoke Hill, Bristol, BS9 1JP.*

SCHAFFTER, James Haslam. Univ of Tor BA 48. Trin Coll Tor LTh 51. **d** 51 Hur **p** 51 Panama for Hur. Hon Asst C of St Jude Brentford 51; R of Good Shepherd San José Costa Rica 51-57; Leeds Rear 57-59; Glanfford 59-69; Hon C of Ch Ch Brampton Dio Tor from 70. *10 Roberts Crescent, Brampton, Ont, Canada.*

SCHARF, Brian Howard. Univ of Alta BA 60. Coll of Resurr Mirfield, 61. **d** 63 New Westmr **p** 65 Cant. C of St Faith Vancouver 63-65; Broadstairs 65-68. *3687 W 16th Avenue, Vancouver, BC., Canada.*

SCHARF, George Walter. 77. **d** and **p** Ott. C of St John Ott 77-80; CF (Canad) from 80. *c/o 6-134 Somerset Street East, Ottawa, Ont, Canada, K1N 6W2.*

SCHARF, Ulrich Eduard Erich Julian. b 35. Univ of Melb BA (1st cl Germanic Langs) 59, MA (2nd cl Germanic Langs) 67. Linacre Coll Ox BA (1st cl Th) 67, MA 72. Univ of Lon PhD 81. Ripon Hall Ox 65. **d** 67 Lon **p** 68 Stepney for Lon. C of Hackney 68-71; Chap to Bp of Stepney from 71; L to Offic Dio Lon 71-75; P-in-c of St Paul Shadwell w St Jas Ratcliffe 75-79; R of St Geo-in-the-E Stepney Dio Lon from 79. *St George-in-the-East Church, Cannon Street Road, E1 0BH.* (01-481 1345)

SCHAUFELBERGER, Johan Henry. b 16. Univ of Lon BA (3rd cl Hist) 38. Coll of Resurr Mirfield 38. **d** 40 **p** 41 S'wark. C of St Pet Vauxhall 40-42; St Kath Southbourne-on-Sea 42-46; C of All SS w St Columb Notting Hill 46-52; PC of St Jo Div Stamford Hill 52-61; V of Wantage w Charlton Dio Ox from 61. *Vicarage, Wantage, Oxon, OX12 8AQ.* (Wantage 2214)

SCHIBILD, Nigel Edmund David Shields. b 47. Co for Nat Acad Awards BA 81. Oak Hill Coll 78. **d** 81 Liv. C of Ch Ch Eccleston Dio Liv from 81. *34 Daresbury Road, Eccleston, St Helens, Mer, WA10 5DS.*

SCHIFF, Canon Leonard Maro. b 08. Ex Coll Ox BA (1st cl Th) 29, MA 34. Westcott Ho Cam 32. **d** 32 **p** 33 Ripon. C of Ch Ch Leeds 32-33; Vice-Prin Qu Coll Birm 33-35; Asst Chap 34-35; C of St Clem Barnsbury 35-37; SPG Miss at Cawnpore 38-41; Asst Chap Calc Cathl 41-43; V of Whitworth w Spennymoor 43-47; Warden of International Centre Sheff 47-49; L to Offic Dio Sheff 47-50; Chap of All S Kanpur 49-53; SPG Miss in Ch of S India 53-59; Fell of St Aug Coll Cant 59-65; L to Offic Dio Cant 59-65; Select Pr Univ of Cam 62; Prin Coll of Ascen Selly Oak Birm 65-69; Chap to Overseas Peoples Dio Birm from 69; Hon Can of Birm 69-75; Can (Emer) from 75; Guild Chap Univ of Aston 72-75; Perm to Offic Dio Carl from 75. *6 Victoria Street, Millom, Cumb.*

SCHIFFMAYER, Jeffrey Paul. **d** and **p** 64 Milwaukee. Chap Malosa Sec Sch Dio Malawi from 64. *Malosa School, PO Kasupe, Malawi.*

SCHILD, John. b 38. ALCD (1st cl) 64. **d** 64 **p** 65 Glouc. C of Ch Ch Cheltenham 64-67; CMS Area Sec Dios Sheff and Southw 67-73; Dios Chelmsf and St Alb 73-76; Publ Pr Dio St Alb 73-76; V of L Heath Dio St Alb from 76. *Little Heath Vicarage, Potters Bar, Herts.* (Potters Bar 54414)

SCHLOSS, Egbert Nathaniel. b 28. **d** 70 **p** 73 Bp Clark for Ja. C of Whitfield Town Dio Ja from 70. *121 Molynes Road, Box 151, Kingston, Jamaica.* (092-42092)

SCHMIDT, Theodore George Martin. b 35. St Paul's Coll Grahmstn 68. **d** 70 Bp Carter for Johann **p** 71 Johann. C of Dunstan Benoni 70-73; R of Standerton w Evander 73-77; Waterberg Dio Pret from 78. *PO Box 102, Nylstroom 0510, S Africa.*

SCHNEIDER, Canon Herman Peter. b 28. Fitz Ho Cam BA 52, MA 56. Ridley Hall Cam 53. **d** 54 **p** 55 S'wark. C of St Matthias U Tulse Hill 54-56; Chap Fitzw Ho Cam 56-60; L to Offic Dio Ely 58-60; Chap St Luke Haifa 60-63; Adv to Abp in Jer 64-73; Can Res of Bethany in St Geo Colleg Ch Jer 70-73; Hon Can 73-80; Can (Emer) from 80; C of St Greg w St Pet Sudbury 73-76; V of Burpham Dio Chich from 76; Sec of Consultants to Abps of Cant and York on Interfaith Relns from 76. *Burpham Vicarage, Arundel, W Sussex.* (Arundel 882948)

SCHOFIELD, Andrew Thomas. b 47. AKC 71, BD 70. St Aug Coll Cant 70. **d** 81 Huntingdon for Ely. C of St Andr & St Mary Whittlesey Dio Ely from 81. *34 Bellmans Road, Whittlesey, Peterborough, Cambs.*

SCHOFIELD, David. b 43. Linc Th Coll 74. **d** 75 **p** 76 Linc. C of Gainsborough 75-78; R of Bolingbroke w Hareby (and E Kirby w Miningsby, Hagnaby, Hagworthingham, Asgarby, Lusby and Mavis Enderby from 79) 78-81; P-in-c of Hagworthingham w Asgarby and Lusby 78-79; Mavis Enderby 78-79; East Kirkby w Miningsby 78-79; Hagnaby 78-79; P-in-c of Ch Ch Conv Distr Stamford Dio Linc from 81. *14 Queens Street, Stamford, Lincs, PE9 1QS.* (Stamford 2990)

SCHOFIELD, Douglas Lloyd. St Franics Coll Brisb. **d** 66 Brisb. C of Ingham 66-69. *c/o Rectory, Ingham, Queensland, Australia.*

SCHOFIELD, Edward Denis. b 20. **d** 61 **p** 62 Cant. C of St Mildred Addiscombe 61-63; C-in-c of St Jas Croydon 63-64; V 64-66; Boughton-under-Blean (w Dunkirk from 75) 66-76; C-in-c of Dunkirk 73-75; V of Sandgate Dio Cant from 76. *Sandgate Vicarage, Folkestone, Kent.* (Folkestone 38231)

SCHOFIELD, John Barry. Moore Th Coll Syd ACT ThL 52. **d** and **p** 53 Syd. C of Liverpool 53-54; C-in-c of Hammondville 54-56; R of Picton Dio Syd from 56. *223 Argyle Street, Picton, NSW, Australia 2571.* (77-1436)

SCHOFIELD, John Martin. b 47. Selw Coll Cam BA (Th) 69, MA 73. St Steph Ho Ox 70. **d** 72 **p** 73 Edmon for Lon. C of Palmers Green 72-75; Friern Barnet 75-80; V of Limbury Dio St Alb from 80. *215 Icknield Way, Luton, LU3 2JR.* (Luton 52415)

SCHOFIELD, John Verity. b 29. Late Scho of Jes Coll Ox BA 52, Dipl Th 53, MA 56. Cudd Coll 53. **d** 55 **p** 56 Glouc. C of Cirencester 55-59; R of Stella 59-67; Ed *Target* and *Lengo* (Ch Coun of Kenya and Tanzania) 67-69; Asst Chap St Paul's Sch Barnes 69-70; Chap 70-80; Chap Melb C of E Gr Sch 81; Cathl Gr Sch Bunbury 82. *59 Lowther Road, SW 13.* (01-748 4018)

SCHOFIELD, Neville John. b 47. Univ of Queensld BD 72. St Jo Coll Morpeth 67. **d** 71 **p** 72 Newc. C of Cardiff 72-76; Prec of Ch Ch Cathl Newc 76; P-in-c of Southlakes Dio Newc from 77. *Rectory, Newcastle Street, Morisset, NSW, Australia 2264.* (73 1204)

SCHOFIELD, Richard Wyndham. Or Coll Ox BA (2nd cl Mod Hist) 32, MA 38. Ripon Hall Ox 36. **d** 37 B & W **p** 38 Taunton for B & W. C of St Mary Taunton 37-39; Perm to Offic at St Thos (in c of St Christopher) Derby 39-40; C of Stanford-in-the-Vale 40-45; St Jas Haydock 45-46; St Giles (in c of St Andr) Newcastle-under-Lyme 48-52; St Steph w St Luke Paddington 52-58; R of Grundisburgh w Burgh Dio St E from 58. *Grundisburgh Rectory, Woodbridge, Suff.* (Grundisburgh 244)

SCHOFIELD, Rodney. b 44. St Jo Coll Cam BA 64, MA 68. St Pet Coll Ox BA 70, MA 74. St Steph Ho Ox 69. **d** 71 **p** 72 Pet. C of St Mary Northn 71-76; V of Irchester Dio Pet from 76. *Irchester Vicarage, Wellingborough, Northants, NN9 7EH.* (Rushden 2674)

SCHOLEFIELD, John. b 27. Univ of Leeds BSc 50. Wells Th Coll 51. **d** 53 **p** 54 Wakef. C of Ossett 53-56; Hebden Bridge 56-58; V of St Geo Sowerby 58-64; Darton 64-70; Stoke-Gabriel Dio Ex from 70. *Stoke-Gabriel Vicarage, Totnes, Devon.* (Stoke-Gabriel 307)

SCHOLER, Douglas William. b 23. Chich Th Coll 47. **d** 50 **p** 51 B & W. C of St Jo Evang Taunton 50-58; V of H Trin Bridgwater 58-69; W Pennard w W Bradley and Lottisham 70-81; P-in-c of Bleadon Dio B & W from 81. *Bleadon Rectory, Weston-super-Mare, Avon.* (Bleadon 812297)

SCHOLEY, Donald. b 38. Lich Th Coll 69. **d** 72 **p** 73 Leic. C of Blaby 72-75; Team V of Daventry w Norton 75-78; R of Wootton w Quinton and Preston Deanery Dio Pet from 78.

Wootton Rectory, Northampton, NN4 0LG. (Northampton 61891)

SCHOLFIELD, Peter. b 35. Sarum Th Coll 64. **d** 66 **p** 67 Wakef. C of S Kirkby Yorks 66-69; C-in-c of Carlton Barnsley Dio Wakef from 69. *2 Spring Lane, Carlton, Barnsley, Yorks.* (Barnsley 722086)

SCHOLLAR, Kenneth. Univ of NZ BA 30. NZ Bd of Th Stud LTh 30. **d** 30 **p** 31 Ch Ch. C of Avonside 30-32; St Luke Ch Ch 33-34; P-in-c of New Brighton 34-35; V 35-45; CF (NZ) 42-46; V of Fairlie 46-47; Prebbleton 47-50; Chap RNZAF 50-62; V of Malvern 62-66; L to Offic Dio Ch Ch 65-70; Chap Ch Ch Cathl Gr Sch 67-73; Hon C of St Mich AA City and Dio Ch Ch from 73. *473 Manchester Street, Christchurch 1, NZ.*

SCHOOLING, Bruce James. b 47. Rhodes Univ Grahmstn BA 74. St Paul's Coll Grahmstn 76. **d** 76 **p** 77 Capetn. C of St Thos Rondebosch 76-78; St Geo Cathl City and Dio Capetn from 79. *24 Maynard Street, Gardens, Cape Town 8001, S Africa.* (45-2221)

SCHOOMBEE, Nicholaas James. b 45. St Paul's Coll Grahmstn 76. **d** 78 Bp Ndwandwe for Johann **p** 79 Johann. C of Standerton w Evander Dio Johann from 78. *PO Box 163, Standerton, S Africa 2430.*

SCHOTTELVIG, Rolf. b 16. Univ of Wales (Swansea), BA (3rd cl Gr) 39. St Mich Coll Llan 39. **d** 41 **p** 42 Swan B. C of St Mary Brecon and St Cynog Battle 41-43; Min Can of Brecon 43-46; V of Whixall 46-49; Castlechurch 49-64; Bp's Wood Dio Lich from 64; V of Brewood Dio Lich from 64. *Brewood Vicarage, Stafford.* (Brewood 850368)

SCHRAM, Keith Lee. b 48. Trent Univ Ont BA 69. McGill Univ Montr BTh 78. **d** 79 **p** 80 Rupld. C of St Patr & St Jude Winnipeg Dio Rupld from 79. *849 Minto Street, Winnipeg, Manit, Canada, R3G 2R6.*

SCHREUDER, Andrew James. Ridley Coll Melb ACT ThL 51. **d** 52 **p** 53 Gippsld. C of St Paul's Cathl Sale 52-55; Dioc Youth and Sunday Sch Org Dio Tas 55-57; Gen Sec of E Boys' Soc Dio Melb from 57; Perm to Offic Dio Melb 57-59; Asst P St Paul Cant 59-61; V of Chadstone E 61-69; Ringwood E 69-80; Chap C of E Gr Sch Tintern from 80. *29 Alexander Road, Ringwood East, Vic, Australia 3135.* (03-870 1000)

SCHRODER, Edward Amos. Univ of Cant BA 64. Univ of Dur Dipl Th 66. Cranmer Hall Dur 64. **d** 67 Lon **p** 68 Willesden for Lon. C of All S Langham Place St Marylebone 67-71. *Gordon College, Wenham, Mass, 01984, USA.*

SCHROEDER, Robert Lee. b 45. Univ of W Ont MA 71. Hur Coll Lon MDiv 77. **d** 77 Bp Robinson for Hur **p** 78 E Newfld. C of St Aug St John's 77-79; I of H Trin Kitchener Dio Hur from 79. *100 Byron Avenue, Kitchener, Ont, Canada N2C 1Z8.*

SCHROEDER, William Fridolf. Univ of Notre Dame Indana MSc 64. St Jo Coll Auckld 72. **d** 72 **p** 74 Nel. Hon C of Greymouth 72-75; C of All SS Nel 75-77; V of Kaikoura Dio Nel from 77. *Vicarage, Kaikoura, NZ.*

SCHULTZ, Very Rev Bruce Allan. St Jo Coll Morpeth ACT, ThL 61. **d** 59 **p** 60 River. C of Broken Hill 59-63; C-in-c of Ariah Pk 64-67; R of Denilquin 67-73; Gladstone 75-79; Archd of Rockptn 75-79; Dean and R of Ch Ch Cathl Graft from 79. *2 Duke Street, Grafton, NSW, Australia 2460.* (42 2072)

SCHURR, Edmund Owen Proctor. St Paul's Coll Grahmstn. **d** 61 **p** 62 Capetn. C of Clanwilliam 61-64; Stellenbosch 64-68; P-in-c St Helena Bay 68-71; R of H Trin Paarl 71-76; L to Offic Dio Capetn 77-78; R of Ficksburg 78-80; Durbanville Dio Capetn from 80. *Rectory, Baxter Lane, Durbanville 7550, CP, S Africa* (96-1254)

SCHURR, Geoffrey Harold. NZ Bd of Th Stud LTh 29. **d** 24 **p** 25 Nel. C of Suburban N Nel 24-25; V of Collingwood 25-28; C of Cathl Ch Nel 28-29; V of Awatere w Seddon and Ward 30-33; Picton 33-38; Westport 38-39; Te Ngawai 39-46; CF (NZ) 42-43; V of Hokitika 46-49; RD of Westland 46-49; C of Ashburton 49; V of Waikari 49-53; Shirley 53-59; Oxford Cust 59-63; Perm to Offic Dio Ch Ch from 63. *26 Perceval Street, Rangiora, NZ.*

✠ **SCHUSTER, Right Rev James Leo.** Keble Coll Ox 2nd cl Cl Mods 33, BA (2nd cl Hist) 35, 2nd cl Th 36, MA 44. St Steph Ho Ox 35. **d** 37 **p** 38 S'wark. L to Offic in Clare Coll Miss Rotherhithe 37-38; Chap of St Steph Ho Ox 39-49; L to Offic Dio Ox 39-49; CF (EC) 40-46; Men in Disp 43; Prin St Bede's Coll Umtata 49-56; Cons Ld Bp of St John's in Umtata Cathl 16 Dec 56 by Abp of Capetn; Bps of Grahmstn; Natal; Zulu; Kimb K; and Bp Fisher; res 79; Asst Bp of Geo from 80; Archd of Riversdale from 80; R of Swellendam Dio Geo from 80. *Rectory, Andrew Whyte Street, Swellendam, CP, S Africa.* (Swellendam 64)

SCHWABACHER, Kurt Frederick. b 12. Chich Th Coll 36. **d** 39 **p** 40 S'wark. C of St Mark Plumstead 39-44; St Laur Catford 44-51; C-in-c of St Paul Forest Hill 51-63; V 63-68; L to Offic Dio Roch from 68. *Flat 1, Raleigh Court, 21a The Avenue, Beckenham, Kent BB3 2DL.*

SCHWARTZ, Gordon Grant. Univ of Sask BA 59. St Chad's Coll Regina LTh 62. **d** 62 **p** 63 Qu'App. I of Wadena 62-67; on leave 68-78; Chap Whitby Hosp Dio Tor from 78. *4 Belton Court, Whitby, Ont, Canada.*

SCHWEERS, Thomas Benedict. b 12. St Francis Coll Brisb 77. **d** 78 **p** 79 Brisb. Hon C of Ch Ch Bundaberg Dio Brisb from 78. *41 Avoca Street, Bundaberg, Queensld, Australia 4670.*

SCLATER, John Edward. b 46. Univ of Nottm BA (2nd cl Th) 68. Cudd Coll 69. **d** 71 **p** 72 Bris. C of St Mary Redcliffe Bris 71-75; Chap to Sisters of the Love of God from 75. *Bede House, Staplehurst, Kent.* (Staplehurst 891995)

SCOBIE, Geoffrey Edward Winsor. b 39. Univ of Bris BSc (2nd cl Psychology) 62, MSc 68. Univ of Birm MA 70. Univ of Glas PhD 78. Tyndale Hall Bris 62. **d** 65 **p** 66 Birm. C of Ch Ch Summerfield Birm 65-66; St Anne Moseley 66-67; Lect in Psychology Univ of Glas from 67; Hon C of St Silas City and Dio Glas from 71. *3 Norfolk Crescent, Bishopbriggs, Glasgow, G64 3BA.*

SCOGINGS, Very Rev Frank. Univ of Dur LTh 1914. St Paul's Coll Burgh 12. **d** 14 Linc for Cant **p** 15 S Rhod. C of St Aug Penhalonga 14-16; St Mich Salisbury 16-21; St John Bulawayo 21-26; P-in-c of St Mich Miss Salisbury 27-28; St Faith's Native Miss Durban 28-36; V of St Sav Cathl Pietermaritzburg 36-59; Sub-Dean 36-46; Can of Natal 44-59; Dean 46-59; Dean (Emer) from 60; VG 48-59; L to Offic Dio Natal from 60. *Chapter Close, 6 Taunton Road, Pietermaritzburg, Natal, S Africa.* (2-8969)

SCOONES, James Mansell. b 24. Univ of Birm Dipl Th 56. Qu Coll Birm 53. **d** 56 **p** 57 St Alb. C of Luton 56-61; V of Bordesley 61-64; Perm to Offic Dio Worc from 77. *46 Western Road, Hagley, W Midl.* (Hagley 882358)

SCORER, Denys Gould Seton. Tyndale Hall, Bris 35. **d** 39 Cant **p** 40 S'wark. C of St Luke Ramsgate 39-40; St Matt Surbiton 40-44; St Pet and St Paul Bromley 44-46; V of St Jo Evang Hollington 46-55; R of Newhaven 55-59; I of St Hilda St Thos 59-62; R of Strathroy 62-74; St Chad Winnipeg Dio Rupld from 74; H Trin Headingley Dio Rupld from 77. *3390 Portage Avenue, Winnipeg, Manit., Canada.*

SCORER, John Robson. b 47. Westcott Ho Cam 73. **d** 75 **p** 76 Dur. C of Silksworth 75-78; Newton Aycliffe Dio Dur from 78. *99 Winterburn Place, Newton Aycliffe, Co Durham, DL5 7ET.*

SCOTLAND, Primus of the Episcopal Church in. *See* Haggart, Most Rev Alastair Iain Macdonald.

SCOTLAND, Nigel Adrian Douglas. ALCD 66 (LTh from 74). McGill Univ Montr MA 71. Univ of Aber PhD 75. Gordon-Conwell Th Sem Mass USA MDiv 70. **d** 66 Barking for Chelmsf **p** 67 Chelmsf. C of St Pet Harold Wood Hornchurch 66-69; in Amer Ch 69-70; R of Lakefield 70-72; L to Offic Dio Aber 72-75; Chap and Lect St Mary Coll of Educn Cheltm 75-78; Sen Lect 78-79; Chap and Sen Lect Coll of St Paul and St Mary Cheltm from 79. *67 Hall Road, Leckhampton, Cheltenham, Glos.* (Cheltenham 29167)

SCOTT, Adam. b 47. TD 78. Ch Ch Ox BA 68, MA 72. City Univ Lon MSc 79. SOC 73. **d** 75 **p** 76 S'wark. C of St Mich AA Blackheath Park Dio S'wark from 75. *40c Lee Park, Blackheath, SE3 9HZ.* (01-852 3286)

SCOTT, Adrian John Allan. Univ of Melb BA 58. ACT ThL 58. **d** and **p** 59 Bend. C Worc. St Paul Bend 59; V of Mooroopna 60-62; L to Offic Dio Syd 63-65; Chap St Pet Coll Siota 65; Prin St Andr Coll Kohimarama 65-69; L to Offic Dio Newc 69-71; I of Mulgrave 72-76; Mont Albert N Dio Melb from 76. *38 Bundoran Parade, Box Hill, Vic, Australia 3129.* (89-2019)

SCOTT, Alfred Thomas. b 19. St Steph Ho Ox 78. **d** 81 Buckingham for Ox (NSM). C of S Ascot Dio Ox from 81. *Brook House, Station Road, Bagshot, Surrey, GU19 5AS.*

SCOTT, Allan George. b 39. Univ of Man BA 61. Coll of Resurr Mirfield 61. **d** 63 Middleton for Man **p** 64 Man. C of Ch Ch Bradf 63-66; C-in-c 66-72; Hon C of Bramhall 72-74; St Jo Bapt Tottenham 74-76; St Steph Bush Hill Pk 76-79; R of Stoke Newington Dio Lon from 79. *Rectory, St Mary's Church, Stoke Newington Church Street, N16.* (01-254 6072)

SCOTT, Andrew Charles Graham. b 28. Merton Coll Ox BA (2nd cl Th) 57. Wells Th Coll 57. **d** 59 **p** 60 Cov. C of Rugby 59-64; Chap RN 64-68; C of Prenton 68-71; V of Tow Law 71-81; RD of Stanhope 77-81; V of Bampton Dio Ox from 81. *Vicarage, Bourton Road, Clanfield, Oxford, OX8 2PB.* (Clanfield 255)

SCOTT, Andrew James Hendry. b 33. Lich Th Coll 57. **d** 60 **p** 61 Ches. C of St Mary without-the-Walls Ches 60-65; V of Halton 65-73; Team V of E Runcorn w Halton 73-80; R of Bruera w Aldford Dio Ches from 80. *Vicarage, Middle Lane, Aldford, Chester.* (Aldford 281)

SCOTT, Arthur. b 07. Qu Coll Cam 3rd cl Hist Trip pt i 28, BA 29, MA 33. Ridley Hall Cam 29. **d** 30 **p** 31 Man. C of Ch

Ch Harpurhey 30-34; Bolton 34; Lect of Bolton 34-38; R of St Luke Miles Platting 38-42; V of Oakington 42-47; C of H Trin S Shore Blackpool (in c of St Mary) 47-49; PC of St Geo Darwen 49-53; V of Shuttleworth 53-55; R of Sheff Tas 55-58; V of Murtoa 58-61; R of Bend N 61-64; Robinvale 64-67; V of Welwick w Holmpton (and Hollym from 68) 67-72; Perm to Offic Dio Melb from 72. *St Laurence Court, Upper California Gully Road, Eaglehawk, Vic, Australia 3556.* (054-46 8719)

SCOTT, Arthur William. b 21. Linc Th Coll 69. **d** 71 **p** 72 Linc. C of St Mich Linc 71-73; Team V of L Coates 73-76; L to Offic Dio Linc 76-78; V of St Andr w St Luke Grimsby Dio Linc from 78. *St Andrew's House, Albion Street, Grimsby, S Humb, DN32 7DY.* (0472-56004)

SCOTT, Bernard de Sausmarez. b 1889. Late Squire Scho of Keble Coll Ox 3rd cl Cl Mods 10, BA (Th) 12, MA 55. Ely Th Coll 12. **d** 13 **p** 14 S'wark. C of St Mich Battersea 13-15; All SS W Dulwich 15; All S King's Heath 15-17; St Jo Evang Clevedon 20-21; St Mary Beaminster 39-42; C of Phillack w Gwithian 42-46 and 51-52; Newquay 47-51; V of St Colan 52-58; C-in-c of St Issey 58-64. *61 Queens Avenue, Dorchester, Dorset.*

SCOTT, Brian. b 35. CCC Ox BA (2nd cl Mod Hist) 58. Coll of Resurr Mirfield 59. **d** 61 Bp Graham for Carl **p** 65 Leic. C of Ch Ch w St Aid Carl 61-62; Asst Master Hutton Gr Sch Preston 63-65; City of Leic Sch 65-70; Perm to Offic Dio Leic 65-67; L to Offic 67-70; V of Lubenham 70-78; C-in-c of Theddingworth 71-78; Asst Chap of Oundle Sch from 78; Chap of Lawton Sch Oundle from 78. *85b West Street, Oundle, Northants.* (Oundle 73568)

SCOTT, Charles Geoffrey. b 32. St Jo Coll Cam BA 54, MA 58. Cudd Coll 56. **d** 58 **p** 59 Wakef. C of Brighouse 58-61; St Mary Bathwick 61-64; V of Ch Ch Frome 64-78; R of Winchelsea Dio Chich from 78. *Rectory, Winchelsea, Sussex.* (Winchelsea 254)

SCOTT, Christopher John Fairfax. b 45. Magd Coll Cam BA 67, MA 71. Westcott Ho Cam 68. **d** 70 **p** 71 Nor. C of St Pet Mancroft Nor 70-73; Chap Magd Coll Cam 73-79; V of Ch Ch Hampstead Dio Lon from 79. *10 Cannon Place, NW3.* (01-435 6784)

SCOTT, Christopher Michael. b 44. SS Coll Cam BA (2nd cl Th) 66, MA 70. Cudd Coll 66. **d** 68 **p** 69 Cant. C of New Addington 68-73; St Steph w St Jo Westmr 73-78; V of St Mich AA Enfield 78-81; Effingham and R of L Bookham Dio Guildf from 81. *Vicarage, Lower Road, Effingham, Surrey, KT24 5JR.* (Bookham 58314)

SCOTT, Christopher Stuart. b 48. Sarum Wells Th Coll 79. **d** 81 Edmon for Lon. C of St Mary Enfield Dio Lon from 81. *3 Chase Court Gardens, Enfield, Middx, EN2 8DH.* (01-366 5949)

SCOTT, Ven Claud Syms. b 01. Late Ford Stud of Trin Coll Ox BA (3rd cl Mod Hist) 23, 2nd cl Th 25, MA 27. Ridley Hall Cam 25. **d** 26 **p** 27 Bris. C of St Luke Bedminster 26-30; C-in-c of All H Conv Distr Ipswich 30-38; V of Exning w Landwade 38-54; RD of Newmarket 46-54; Surr 46-54; Hon Can St E from 52; R of Stradbroke w Horham and Athelington 54-58; St Mary Stoke Ipswich 58-61; RD of Ipswich 58-62; Archd of Suff 62-70; V of Hoxne w Denham 62-70; Archd (Emer) from 70; L to Offic Dio St E from 71. *68 Lowestoft Road, Reydon, Southwold, Suffolk.*

SCOTT, Clifford Wentworth. b 04. Univ of Lon BSc 25. Ridley Hall Cam 25. **d** 27 **p** 28 Liv. C of St Paul Prince's Pk Toxteth Park 27-29; Rotherham (in c of St Jas Clifton) 29-32; C-inc of Thurcroft Conv Distr 32-35; V of St Bart Sheff 35-41; CF (EC) 41-46; V of Ardsley 46-56; R of N Kilworth (w S Kilworth from 62) 56-64; Sapcote 64-72; Perm to Offic Dio Truro from 72. *4 Egerton Road, Padstow, Cornwall, PL28 8DJ.* (Padstow 532649)

SCOTT, Colin. b 32. Univ of Dur BA 54. Coll of Resurr Mirfield 58. **d** 60 **p** 61 Newc T. C of Wallsend 60-64; Seaton Hirst (in c of St Andr) 64-68; Long Benton (in c of St Mary Magd) 68-70; V of St Aid Newc T 70-77; Sleekburn Dio Newc T from 77; P-in-c of Cambois Dio Newc T from 77. *St John's Vicarage, North View, Bedlington Station, Northumb, NE22 7ED.* (Bedlington 822309)

SCOTT, Canon Colin John Fraser. b 33. Qu Coll Cam BA 56, MA 60. Ridley Hall Cam 56. **d** 58 **p** 59 S'wark. C of St Barn Clapham Common 58-61; St Jas Hatcham (in c of St Mich) 61-64; V of St Mark Kennington 64-71; Hon Chap to Bp of S'wark 67-80; RD of Lambeth 68-71; Vice-Chairman S'wark Dioc Past C'tte 71-77; Hon Can of S'wark Cathl from 73; M Gen Syn from 72; R of Sanderstead Dio S'wark from 77. *1 Addington Road, Sanderstead, S Croydon, Surrey, CR2 8RE.*

SCOTT, Cuthbert Le Messurier. b 13. Wells Th Coll 60. **d** 61 **p** 62 Lon. C of St Mich Highgate 61-64; V of St Jo Evang w St Mich Paddington 64-72; V of Shamley Green Dio Guildf from 72. *Shamley Green Vicarage, Guildford, Surrey.* (Guildf 892030)

SCOTT, Cyril Edgar. b 1898. **d** 59 Thetford for Nor **p** 60 Nor. C of Antingham w Thorpe Mkt 59-60; R 60-64; Bradfield 60-64; V of Mundham w Seething 64-70; C-in-c of Thwaite St Mary 64-70. *Cockleshells, Stocks Green, Castle Acre, Kings Lynn, Norfolk.*

SCOTT, Ven David. b 24. Trin Hall Cam BA 50, MA 54. Cudd Coll 50. **d** 52 **p** 53 Portsm. C of St Mark Portsea 52-58; Asst Chap Univ of Lon 58-59; PC of Old Brumby 59-66; V of Boston Lincs 66-75; RD of Holland East 71-75; Can and Preb of Linc Cathl from 71; Surr from 72; Archd of Stow from 75; V of Hackthorn w Cold Hanworth Dio Linc from 75; P-in-c of N w S Carlton Dio Linc from 78. *Hackthorn Vicarage, Lincoln, LN2 3PF.* (Welton 60382)

SCOTT, David. Rhodes Univ BA 63. St Paul's Coll Grahmstn LTh 65. **d** 65 **p** 66 Natal. C of St Pet Pmbg 65-68; R of Harding 68-70; H Trin Newcastle 70-76; Bellair 76-78. *c/o Box 12075, Port Elizabeth, S Africa.*

SCOTT, David Lamplough. Selw Coll Cam BA (2nd cl Th Trip pt i) 42, 3rd cl Th Trip pt ii, 43, MA 48. Ripon Hall Ox 42. **d** 44 **p** 45 York. C of St Jas Sutton-in-Holderness 44-47; Ch Ch Chelsea 47-49; R of Creeton w Counthorpe and Swinstead 49-55; Rippingale 55-74; C-in-c of Dowsby w Dunsby 60-63; R 63-74; V of St Mary Hale Dio Liv from 74. *Hale Vicarage, Liverpool, L24 4AX.* (051-425 3195)

SCOTT, David Lloyd Thomas. b 31. FCA. Jes Coll Cam BA (Th) 76, MA 80. Ridley Hall Cam 73. **d** 76 **p** 77 Bris. C of Ch Ch Swindon 76-79; R of Ripple Dio Worc from 79. *Rectory, Ripple, Tewkesbury, Glos, GL20 6HA.* (Upton-on-Severn 2655)

SCOTT, David Victor. b 47. St Chad Coll Dur BA (2nd cl Th) 69. Cudd Coll 69. **d** 71 Bradwell for Cant **p** 72 Chelmsf. C of Latton 71-73; Chap Haberdashers' Aske's Sch Elstree 73-80; V of Torpenhow Dio Carl from 80; Allhallows Dio Carl from 80. *Torpenhow Vicarage, Carlisle, Cumb, CA5 1HT.* (Low Ireby 295)

SCOTT, Edgar. b 12. Linc Th Coll 76. **d** and **p** 76 Sheff. C of Wombwell Dio Sheff from 76. *17 Wood Walk, Wombwell, Barnsley, S Yorks.*

SCOTT, Canon Edward Geoffrey Spencer. b 21. K Coll Cam 2nd cl Hist Trip pt i 46, BA (1st cl Hist Trip pt ii) 47, MA 49. Chich Th Coll 47. **d** 49 Man **p** 50 Blackb. C of Howe Bridge 49-50; St Pet Burnley 50-53; Dom Chap to Bp of Colom 53-57; P-in-c of St Pet Colom 54-57; V of Darton 58-63; Ch Ch Woodhouse 63-70; Surr 63-70; V of Honley w Brockholes 70-81; RD of Almondbury 80-81; Res Can of Wakef Cathl from 81. *31 Westfield Grove, Wakefield, W Yorks.* (Wakefield 361922)

✠ **SCOTT, Most Rev Edward Walter.** Univ of BC BA 40. Angl Th Coll BC LTh 42, DD 66. **d** 42 New Westmr **p** 43 Caled. V of St Pet Seal Cove 43-45; Gen Sec SCM at Univ of Manit 45-49; R of St Jo Bapt Fort Garry Winnipeg 49-55; St Jude Winnipeg 55-60; Hon Can of Rupld 60-66; Dioc Dir of Social Service Dio Rupld 60-64; Cons Ld Bp of Koot in Angl Th Coll Chap Vancouver 25 Jan 66 by Abp of BC (Metrop); Bps of New Westmr; Caled; Yukon; and Olympia USA; Asst Bp of Carib; and Bp Ragg; Res 71; Primate of Canada from 71. *600 Jarvis Street, Toronto, Ont., Canada.*

SCOTT, Eric Hammond. Univ of Dur LTh 37. St Aug Coll Cant 34. **d** 37 **p** 38 Lon. C of St Pet Hammersmith 37-39; Asst Chap at Penang 39-40; Butterworth 39-41; Actg Chap at Penang 42; War Service 43-45; V of Prov Wellesley and Kedah Dio Sing 45-52; P-in-c of Betong 52-56; Debak 56-57; Lundu 58-71; Abok 71-75; Can of Kuch 72-75. *Holy Angels Cottage, Kampong Rukan, Lundu, Sarawak, Malaysia.*

SCOTT, Eric Walter. St Jo Coll Cam BA 38, MA 43. Ridley Hall Cam 38. **d** 40 Ox **p** 41 Buckingham for Ox. C of St John Reading 40-43; H Trin Cam 43-45; C-in-c of St Mary Magd Tilehurst 45-49; R of Wasing w Brimpton 49-53; V of Midgham Dio Ox 50-53; R of Foothills Miss Dio Calg 53-56; St Geo City and Dio Edmon 56-57; V of Midgham (w Brimpton from 59) Ox 57-61; Chap of Shawnigan Lake Sch 61-67; I of Shawnigan Lake 64-67; St John Courtenay 67-81; Hon Can of Ch Ch Cathl BC 76-81; Perm to Offic Dio BC from 81. *c/o 1510 Dingwall Road, Courtenay, BC, Canada.* (604-724 0762)

SCOTT, George. b 1896. Scotl Episc Th Coll 19. Univ of Dur LTh 23. **d** 22 **p** 23 Aber. C of St Andr Cathl Ch Aber 22-24; St Martin Dundee 24-29; St Mary's Cathl Glas 29-31; R of St Jo Evang Wick 31-42; C of Montrose 42-46; R of Muthill 46-68. *Burn Brae, Muthill, Perth, PH5 2AR.* (Muthill 325)

SCOTT, George. b 21. Open Univ BA 74. St Aid Coll 48. **d** 51 **p** 52 Glas. C of St Columb Clydebank 51-52; St Mich Govan (in c of St Mark) Glas 52-53; V of Cloughfold 53-56; P-in-c of St Columba Grantown-on-Spey 56-58; R of Selkirk 58-62; Port Chap Miss to Seamen Hull 62-65; V of Lower Shiregreen 65-74; R of St Luke Downfield, Dundee Dio

Brech from 74. *Rectory, St Luke's Road, Downfield, Dundee, DD3 0LO.* (Dundee 825165)

SCOTT, George Alfred. b 04. **d** 40 E Szech **p** 42 Bp Roberts for E Szech. C of Shanghai Cathl 40-45; furlough 45; Deputn Dept CIM 46-47; Asst Home Dir 48-55; Home Dir 55-69; Perm to Offic Dio St A from 69. *Bryn Gwyn, Abbey Road, Rhuddlan, Clwyd, LL18 5RH.* (Rhuddlan 590410)

SCOTT, Gordon. b 30. Univ of Man BA (1st cl French) 51. St Jo Coll Dur 51. **d** 53 **p** 54 Dur. C of St Andr Monk Wearmouth 53-55; Stranton 55-56; Chester-le-Street 56-59; V of Marley Hill 59-62; Chap Forest Sch Snaresbrook 62-66; Dunrobin Sch Sutherland 66-72; Pocklington Sch York 72-74; V of Barton w Pooley Bridge 74-80; RD of Penrith from 78; R of Gt Salkeld w Lazonby Dio Carl from 80. *Rectory, Lazonby, Penrith, Cumbria, CA10 1BL.*

SCOTT, Canon Guthrie Michael. b 07. Gen Th Sem NY Hon STD 72. St Paul's Coll Grahmstn 27. Chich Th Coll 29. **d** 30 **p** 32 Chich. C of Slaugham 30-32; St Steph Gloucester Road Kens 32-34; Dom Chap to Bp of Bom 35-37; Chap (Eccles Est) St Paul's Cathl Calc 37-38; Kasauli 38-39; C of St Alb Coloured Miss Johann 43-46; L to Offic Dio Johann 46-50; Dio Chich from 50; Hon Can of Damar (Namibia from 80) from 76. *43 King Henry's Road, NW3.* (01-722 5787)

SCOTT, Harold James. b 05. Univ of Dur LTh 30. St Aug Coll Cant 26. **d** 30 **p** 31 Birm. C of All SS King's Heath 30-33; V of St Silas and St Alb Barb 33-37; St Leon Barb 37-40; C-in-c of St Bart Allen's Cross 40-45; V of Bourn 45-50; R of Kingston 45-50; RD of Bourn 47-50; Commiss Barb 50-71; V of Walpole St Andr 50-61; Swavesey 61-71. *44 Partridge Drive, Bar Hill, Cambridge, CB3 8EN.* (Crafts Hill 80242)

SCOTT, Hedley. b 36. Coll of Resurr Mirfield 68. **d** 70 **p** 71 Newc T. C of St Phil Newc T 70-73; Sleekburn (in c of Cambois) 73-76; V of Shilbotel Dio Newc T from 76. *Shilbotel Vicarage, Alnwick, Northumb, NE66 2XR.* (Shilbottle 247)

SCOTT, Hugh Raymond James. Moore Th Coll Syd ACT ThL (2nd cl) 58. **d** 59 Bp Hilliard for Syd **p** 59 Syd. C of Dapto 59-61; Ryde 61-62; Hartley 62-64; Chap CMF 64; R of St Sav Punchbowl 65-69; Supervisor Teacher Training Bd of Educn 69-71; L to Offic Dio Syd 69-71; C-in-c of Padstow Dio Syd 71-77; R from 77. *102 Iberia Street, Padstow, NSW, Australia 2211.* (77-6574)

SCOTT, Ian Michael. b 25. Univ of Bris BA (2nd cl Gen) 50. Bps' Coll Cheshunt 52. **d** 53 **p** 54 S'wark. C of Rotherhithe 53-55; Ascen Lavender Hill 55-59; St Mich and All S Camberwell 59-60; St Mary (in c of St John) Kettering 60-63; V of H Trin w St Barn St Pancras Dio Lon from 63. *70 Haverstock Hill, NW3 2BE.* (01-485 3791)

SCOTT, Irvine John. ACT ThDip 74. St Francis Coll Brisb. **d** and **p** 65 Brisb. C of St Andr Indooroopilly Brisb 65-68; Bundaberg 68-70; R of St Jo Bapt Murray Bridge 70-79; Regr Dio Murray 70-74; Hon Can of The Murray 73-74; Archd of The Murray 74-79; Hosp Chap Dio Brisb 79-80; R of St Paul Ipswich Dio Brisb from 80. *Box 168, Ipswich, Queensland, Australia 4305.* (281 4261)

SCOTT, James. b 37. Trin Coll Dub 63. **d** 66 **p** 67 Down. C of Ballynafeigh 66-71; Asst Sec Leprosy Miss Belf 71-74; Asst Master Ashfield Boys' Secondary Sch Belf from 74. *35 Glenholm Avenue, Belfast, BT8 4LU, N Ireland.* (Belfast 642538)

SCOTT, James Alexander Gilchrist. b 32. Linc Coll Ox BA 56, Dipl Th 57, MA 60. Wycl Hall Ox 56. **d** 58 **p** 59 Bradf. C of St Paul Shipley 58-61; Dom Chap to Abp of York 61-65; Chap Miss to Seamen Santos Brazil 65-68; Chap All SS Santos 65-68; V of Grassendale 68-77; Thorp Arch w Walton Dio York from 77; Chap HM Pris Thorp Arch from 77; RD of Tadcaster from 78. *Vicarage, Thorp Arch, Wetherby, LS23 7AE.* (Boston Spa 842430)

SCOTT, James George. b 30. Sarum Wells Th Coll 71. **d** 73 Southn for Win **p** 74 Win. C of Bitterne Park 73-78; V of N Eling (or Copythorne) 78-82; St Ambrose Bournemouth Dio Win from 82. *St Ambrose Vicarage, West Cliff Road, Bournemouth, BH4 8BE.* (Bournemouth 764957)

SCOTT, James McIntosh. b 12. Hertf Coll Ox BA 34, MA 38. Wycl Hall Ox 34. **d** 37 **p** 38 Dur. C of Stockton-on-Tees 37-38; Gateshead-on-Tyne 38-44; V of Monkwearmouth 44-48; Surr 44-48; V of Roundhay 48-64; R of Sutton Surrey 64-66; V of Disley 66-77. *23 College Road, Buxton, Derbys.*

SCOTT, John. b 54. Qu Univ Belf BD 79. Ch of Ireland Th Coll Dub 80. **d** 81 Down. C of Willowfield Dio Down from 81. *57 Blenheim Drive, Belfast, BT6 9GD.*

SCOTT, John. b 13. K Coll Lon Jelf Pri and AKC 37. **d** 37 Lon for NY **p** 40 St Alb. Perm to Office (Col Cl Act) from 37; at St Jas Bushey 38-40; C 40-42; P-in-c 42-43; Chap RAFVR 43-47; Chap to Bp of St Andr 47-48; R of St Sav Bridge of Allan 48-60; St Andr Fife 60-79; Can of St Ninian's Cathl Perth 63-79. *14 Argyle Street, St Andrews, Fife, KY16 9BP.* (St Andrews 72144)

SCOTT, John David. b 52. Late Scho of St Jo Coll Ox 2nd cl Mod Lang BA 74, MA 78. Leeds Univ BA (Th) 78. Coll of the Resurr Mirfield 76. **d** 78 **p** 79 Pet. C of Oundle Dio Pet from 78. *14 Lime Avenue, Oundle, Peterborough.*

SCOTT, John Edward. b 28. Worc Ordin Coll 66. **d** 68 Ban **p** 71 Derby. C of Llandudno 68-69; C of Winshill 70-73; V of Seaton Carew 73-74; Ellistown Dio Leic from 77. *Ellistown Vicarage, Leicester, LE6 1FE.* (Ibstock 60350)

SCOTT, John Eric. b 16. St Cath Coll Ox BA (3rd cl Mod Hist) 38, 3rd cl Th 40, MA 42. Ripon Hall, Ox 39. **d** 40 **p** 41 Dur. C of St Alb Heworth 40-43; Gateshead 43-45; Chap and Sacr Ch Ch Ox 45-47; Asst Master Forest Sch Snaresbrook 48-55; Ho Master 55-81; P-in-c of St Mich Cornhill w St Pet-le-Poer and St Benet Fink City and Dio Lon from 81. *St Michael's Vestry, Cornhill, EC3.* (01-626 8841)

SCOTT, John Gabriel. b 16. OBE (Mil) 68. St Chad's Coll Dur LTh 45. St Aug Coll Cant 39. **d** 42 **p** 44 Roch. C of St Alb Dartford 42-46; Chap RNVR 46; RN 47-71; Hon Chap to HM the Queen from 68; V of Hindon w Cricklade and Pertwood 71-73; Chap RN 73-75; C of Wymering 74-81. *Edge-o-Beyond, Catherington, Portsmouth, Hants.* (Horndean 592275)

SCOTT, John Gilbert Mortimer. b 25. St Edm Hall Ox BA (3rd cl Mod Hist) 49, MA 52. Bps' Coll Cheshunt. **d** 51 **p** 52 Ex. C of St Thos Ex 51-54; Wolborough 54-58; V of Clawton 58-66; R of Tetcott w Luffincott 58-66; RD of Holsworthy 65-66; V of Newton St Cyres Dio Ex from 66; RD of Cadbury from 81. *Newton St Cyres Vicarage, Exeter, Devon, EX5 5BN.* (Newton St Cyres 230)

SCOTT, John Harold. b 46. Univ of Wales (Cardiff) BSc (Maths) 68. St Steph Ho Ox 69. **d** 72 **p** 73 Llan. C of Skewen 72-74; Port Talbot 74-77; P-in-c of Bedlinog Dio Llan 77-78; V from 78. *St Cadoc's Vicarage, Oakland Street, Bedlinog, Treharris, Mid Glam, CF46 6TE.* (Bedlinog 236)

SCOTT, John Nicolson. Coates Hall Edin 45. **d** 46 **p** 47 Arg Is. Chap of Oban Cathl 46-49; V of Wroxham w Hoveton St John 49-54; C of St Bart Brighton 54-65; V of Clewer St Steph Dio Ox from 65. *Clewer St Stephen Vicarage, Vansittart Road, Windsor, Berks.* (Windsor 63955)

SCOTT, John Peter. b 47. Open Univ BA 78. STh 81. St Aug Coll Cant 74. **d** 75 Tonbridge for Roch **p** 76 Roch. C of St Alb Dartford 75-78; Goring (in c of St Laur) 78-81; Chap Mendip, Priory, Wells and Distr, and Meare Manor Hosps from 81. *c/o Mendip Hospital, Wells, Somt.* (Wells 72211)

SCOTT, John Trevor. b 25. Roch Th Coll 61. **d** 63 **p** 64 Ripon. C of Wetherby 63-66; Stevenage (in c of St Nich) 66-69; V of Collingham (w Harewood from 77) 69-78; C-in-c of Harewood 75-77; V of Pannal (w Beckwithshaw from 80) Dio Ripon from 78. *Pannal Vicarage, Crimple Meadows, Pannal, Harrogate, N Yorks, HG3 1EL.* (Harrogate 870202)

SCOTT, Kenneth James. b 46. Univ of Bris BA 68. Trin Coll Bris 71. **d** 73 **p** 74 Truro. C of Illogan 73-76; St Paul Camberley 76-81; R of Bradford Peverell w Stratton, Frampton and Sydling St Nich Dio Sarum from 81. *Stratton Rectory, Dorchester, Dorset.* (Dorchester 63617)

SCOTT, Kenneth MacDowall. b 09. St Jo Coll Dur 72. **d** 72 **p** 73 Dur. C of Newton Aycliffe 72-75; Hon C of St Thos Brampton Dio Derby from 75. *Rose Cottage, Cotton Mill Hill, Holymoorside, Chesterfield, Derby.* (Chesterfield 69106)

SCOTT, Kenneth William. Wycl Coll Tor. **d** 52 **p** 53 Tor. C of St Paul Bloor Street Tor 52-54; R of Port Perry 54-60; C of St Paul Bloor Street Tor 60-63; I of St Edw Confessor Scarborough Tor 63-65; St Alb-the-Mart Tor 65-75. *120 Howland Avenue, Toronto, Ont., Canada.*

SCOTT, Canon Malcolm Kenneth Merrett. b 30. ACA 53, FCA 64. Clifton Th Coll 56. **d** 58 **p** 59 Lon. C of Ch Ch Highbury 58-60; CMS 60-62; Chap to Bp of Ruw 62-65; L to Offic Dio Ruw 62-65; Tutor Bp Usher Wilson Coll 65-66; Archd of Toro 67-71; Hon Can of Ruw from 72; CMS Rep Uganda and Tutor Bp Tucker Th Coll Mukono 73-74; V of Sunnyside w Bourne End Dio St Alb from 74. *Vicarage, Sunnyside, Berkhamsted, Herts, HP4 2PP.* (Berkhamsted 5100)

SCOTT, Matthew da Costa. Codr Coll Barb Dipl Th 75, LTh 76. **d** 75 **p** 77 Trinid. C of H Trin Cathl Port of Spain 75-81; R of St Thos Chaguanas Dio Trinid from 81. *St Thomas's Rectory, Chaguanas, Trinidad.*

SCOTT, Canon Maurice Woodforde. b 12. St Edm Hall Ox BA 33, MA 48. Wells Th Coll 46. **d** 48 **p** 49 Win. C of Sholing 48-52; V of Chilworth 52-59; Fair Oak 59-80; Hon Can of Win Cathl 75-80; Can (Emer) from 80; Chap St Cross Hosp Win from 80. *Chaplain's Lodge, St Cross, Winchester, Hants.*

SCOTT, Michael Bernard Campion. b 29. Or Coll Ox BA 52, MA 56. Edin Th Coll. **d** 54 St Andr **p** 55 Edin for St Andr. C of St Pet Kirkcaldy 54-58; H Sav Hitchin (in c of St Faith) 58-61; R of St Mary and Ch Ch St Kitts 61-66; C of St Mary Virg (in c of St Mark) Reading 66-72; Missr of St Mark Conv Distr Reading 72-76; C of Orton Longueville (in c of Orton

Tn) 76-80; Chap to Glouc Centre for Mentally Handicapped from 77. *c/o 85 Lythemere, Orton, Malborne, Peterborough.* (Pet 233624)

✠ **SCOTT, Most Rev Moses Nathaniel Christopher Omobiala.** CBE 70. Univ of Dur DD (*hon causa*) 62. Lon Coll of Div Dipl Th 52. Fourah Bay Coll. **d** 43 **p** 46 Sier L. C of Lunsar 43-44; Bullom 44-47; Miss-in-c of Makeni 47-48; Bo 48-51; C of Grappenhall Chesh 51-56; Archd of Missions Sier L 56-59; Bonthe and Bo 59-61; Cons Ld Bp of Sier L in St Geo Cathl Sier L 12 Nov 61 by Bp on Niger; Bp of Gambia and Rio Pongas; and Asst Bp of Sier L; Elected Abp and Metrop of W Afr 69; res 81. *c/o Bishopscourt, Box 128, Freetown, Sierra Leone.* (Freetown 22555)

SCOTT, Noel Joseph Alexander. Trin Coll Dub BA 59, Div Test 60, MA 64, BD 67. **d** 60 **p** 61 Down. C of Ballymacarrett 60-64; Shankill Lurgan 64-67; Ascen Hillside Bulawayo Dio Matab 67-69; R from 69. *PO Box 9010, Hillside, Bulawayo, Zimbabwe.* (881184)

SCOTT, Canon Norman Brian. St Jo Coll Dur BA (Th) 47, Dipl Th 48. **d** 48 **p** 49 Newc T. C of Walker 48-51; V of Brigham 51-57; Kirkby Stephen w Mallerstang 57-70; RD of Appleby and Kirkby Stephen 66-70; V of Hawkshead w Low Wray 70-81; M Gen Syn Carl 70-80; Hon Can of Carl Cathl from 71; M Pensions Bd from 76; P-in-c of Orton, Ravenstonedale & Newbiggin-on-Lune Dio Carl from 81. *The Haven, Ravenstonedale, Kirkby Stephen, Cumbria, CA17 4NQ.* (Newbiggin-on-Lune 628)

SCOTT, Patrick Henry Fowlis. b 25. Jes Coll Cam BA 51, MA 55. Wells Th Coll 51. **d** 53 **p** 54 Roch. C of Milton-next-Gravesend 53-54; V of New Hythe 54-57; CF from 57; DACG 70-71 and from 74; SCF 72-74; Perm to Offic Dios York, Dur, Newc T, Wakef, Bradf, Sheff and Southw 74-77; Dios Ches, Carl, Man and Blackb from 77. *c/o Barclays Bank Ltd., King Street, Gravesend, Kent.*

SCOTT, Peter Crawford. b 35. Ch Ch Ox BA (2nd cl Mod Hist) 56, MA 61. Cudd Coll 60. **d** 62 **p** 63 Heref. C of Broseley w Benthall 62-66; P-in-c of Hughenden 66-71; C of N w S Hykeham 71-73; P-in-c of Stottesdon and of Farlow 73-76; R of Willaura Dio Bal from 80. *Rectory, Willaura, Vic, Australia 3291.*

SCOTT, Peter Lawrence. b 20. St Cath Coll Cam BA 43, MA 46. Ely Th Coll. **d** 47 Cant for Chich **p** 48 Chich. C of Bognor 47-50; Forest Row 50-53; R of Withyham w Blackham Dio Chich from 53. *Withyham Rectory, Hartfield, Sussex.* (Hartfield 241)

SCOTT, Peter Lindsay. b 29. Keble Coll Ox BA 54, MA 58. Linc Th Coll 54. **d** 56 B & W **p** 57 Taunton for B & W. C of St Sav Weston-s-Mare 56-59; C of H Nativ Knowle 59-61; P-in-c of St Pet Glas 61-63; V of Heap Bridge 63-73; Oakenrod Dio Man from 73. *13 Brooklands Court, Rochdale, Lancs, OL11 4EJ.* (Rochdale 39743)

SCOTT, Philip Maxwell. b 49. Univ of Auckld MSc 70. Univ of Otago BD 77. St Jo Coll Auckld 75. **d** 77 Bp Spence for Auckld **p** 78 Auckld. C of Manurewa 77-80; Henderson Dio Auckld from 80. *7 Dellwood Avenue, Henderson, Auckland, NZ.*

SCOTT, Reginald Eldon. b 1898. AKC 22. St Aug Coll Cant 23. **d** 23 **p** 24 Wakef. C of St Mich AA Wakef 23-26; Miss P at Inhambane Lebom 26-30; C of St Matthias Stoke Newington 30-41; Felpham (in c of Middleton) 41-53; V of Flimwell 53-56; Scaynes Hill 56-66; Perm to Offic Dio Chich from 66. *2 St Augustine's Close, Cooden Drive, Bexhill-on-Sea, Sussex, TN39 3AZ.* (Bexhill 215411)

SCOTT, Reginald Walter. b 24. St Paul's Coll Grahmstn 76. **d** 76 **p** 77 Capetn. C of All SS Durbanville 76-78; R of Hoetjes Bay Dio Capetn from 78. *2 Plein Street, Vredenburg, CP, S Africa.* (3-1318)

SCOTT, Robert Edward. Univ of NZ BA 60. Ch Ch Coll **d** 61 **p** 62 Wel. C of St Pet Palmerston N 61-64; Cuddington Surrey 64-66; St Pet Wel 66-77; Dir Inner City Ministry Wel 72-77; On leave. *c/o Box 12046, Wellington, NZ.*

SCOTT, Ronald Lawrence. b 46. State Univ of NY at Albany BA 68. Qu Univ at Kingston Ont MA 70. Trin Coll Tor MDiv 75. **d** 75 Niag **p** 76 Bp Read for Tor. C of St Paul Fort Erie 75-76; C of All SS Pet 76-79; I of Apsley Dio Tor from 79. *Box 89, Apsley, Ont, Canada.*

SCOTT, Terence. b 56. Qu Univ Belf BSc 77. Div Hostel Dub 77. **d** 80 **p** 81 Connor. C of Ballymena Dio Connor from 80. *19 Deramore Avenue, Ballymena, Co Antrim, N Ireland.*

SCOTT, Canon Thomas Alfred. Seager Hall Ont. **d** 60 Hur **p** 61 Bp Luxton for Hur. I of Lion's Head 61-64; St Thos Owen Sound 64-71; Wiarton w Lion's Hd 71-76; Can of Hur 75-76; Can (Emer) from 76. *Allenford, Ont., Canada.*

SCOTT, Vernon Malcolm. b 30. TCD BA 57, Div Test (2nd cl) 58, MA 60. Ridley Hall Cam. **d** 58 **p** 59 Lon. C of St Anne Limehouse 58-62; All H Gospel Oak St Pancras 62-66; V of St Mich AA Enfield 66-77; R of Tansor w Cotterstock and Fotheringay 77-81; Barby Dio Pet from 81; V of Kilsby Dio Pet from 81. *Barby Rectory, Rugby, Warws.* (Rugby 890252)

SCOTT, Vernon Washington. St Pet Th Coll Ja 59. **d** 62 **p** 63 Ja. C of St Jago de la Vega Cathl Spanish Town 62-66; P-in-c of St Marg Bay 66-68; R of Annotto Bay Dio Ja from 68. *Rectory, Annotto Bay, Jamaica.* (099-62242)

SCOTT, Walter David Craig. Selw Coll Cam BA 49, MA 53. Sarum Th Coll 49. **d** 51 **p** 52 Jarrow for Dur. C of Shildon 51-55; Min of Cleadon Pk 55-67; V 67-71; Bulkington Dio Cov from 71; Actg RD of Bedworth 76-79. *Bulkington Vicarage, Nuneaton, Warws.*

SCOTT, Walter John. b 30. Bps' Coll Cheshunt 58. **d** 60 **p** 61 Lon. C of St Sav Paddington 60-64; Southgate 64-66; H Trin Mile End 66-70; V of Ch of Ch and St John w St Luke I of Dogs Poplar 70-77; R of Whippingham w E Cowes Dio Portsm from 77. *Rectory, East Cowes, IW, PO32 6AH.* (Cowes 2130)

SCOTT, William. Coll of Resurr Mirfield. **d** 60 **p** 61 Ex. C of Wolborough 60-63; Chap St Cath Sch Bramley 63-66; St Mary and St Anne Sch Abbots Bromley 72-76; Perm to Offic Dio Cant from 79. *42 Westgate Court Avenue, Canterbury, CT2 8JR.* (Cant 56277)

SCOTT, William John. b 46. Div Hostel Dub. TCD BA 70. **d** 71 **p** 72 Down. C of Bangor 71-74; Holywood 74-80; I of St Gall Carnalea Dio Down from 80. *Rectory, Crawfordsburn Road, Bangor, Co Down, N Ireland.* (Helen's Bay 853366)

SCOTT, William Sievwright. b 46. Edin Th Coll 67. **d** 70 **p** 71 Glas. C of St Ninian Glas 70-73; St Francis Bridgwater 73-77; C-in-c of Shepton Beauchamp w Barrington, Stocklynch, Puckington and Bradon 77; R 77-81; Perm to Offic Dio B & W from 81. *Rectory, Timsbury, Bath, BA3 1HY.* (Timsbury 70153)

SCOTT-BRANAGAN, Andrew Jamieson. b 32. Univ of Melb BA 65. **d** and **p** 79 Gippsld. Perm to Offic Dio Gippsld 79-81; C of H Trin Kew Dio Melb from 81. *10 Lytton Street, Kew, Vic, Australia 3101.*

SCOTT-BUCCLEUCH, Ian Lascelles. Univ Coll of Southn BSc (Lon) 41. Trin Coll Tor LTh 57. **d** 56 **p** 57 Tor. C of St John Pet 57-60; I of St Barn Pet Tor 60-65; V of Ch Ch Cathl Montr 65-67; R of Layou 68-72. *77 Davisville Avenue, Toronto, Ont., Canada.*

SCOTT-DEMPSTER, Colin Thomas. b 37. Em Coll Cam 2nd cl Th Trip pt i, BA (3rd cl Th Trip pt ii) 64, MA 68. Cudd Coll 64. **d** 66 **p** 67 Ox. C of Caversham 66-69; Chap Coll of St Mark and St John Chelsea 69-73; V of Chieveley w Winterbourne and Oare Dio Ox from 73; RD of Newbury from 77. *Chieveley Vicarage, Newbury, Berks.* (Chieveley 341)

SCOTT-JOYNT, Canon Michael Charles. b 43. K Coll Cam 2nd cl Cl Trip pt i 63, BA (1st cl Th Trip pt ii) 65, MA 68. Cudd Coll 65. **d** 67 Dorch for Ox **p** 68 Ox. C of Cuddesdon 67-70; Tutor Cudd Coll 67-71; Chap 71-72; Team V of Newbury 72-75; C-in-c of Bicester 75-79; Caversfield 75-79; Bucknell 76-79; RD of Bicester 76-81; R of Bicester w Bucknell, Caversfield and Launton 79-81; Can Res of St Alb Cathl and Dir of Ordinands Dio St Alb from 81. *c/o Holywell Lodge, 41 Holywell Hill, St Albans, AL1 1HD.*

SCOTT-OLDFIELD, Ivor Erroll Lindsay. b 21. Univ Coll Dur BA 49. Sarum Th Coll 49. **d** 51 Sherborne for Sarum **p** 52 Sarum. C of St Jas Trowbridge 51-54; St Paul Haggerston 54-58; V of St Pet and St Paul Enfield 58-61; St Benet and All SS St Pancras 61-68; Dir Gen RADD from 68. *1e Prior Bolton Street, Canonbury, N1.*

SCOVIL, Canon George Charles Coster. Trin Coll Tor BA 39, LTh 41, BD 43, MA 45, DD (*hon causa*) 50. **d** 41 Tor **p** 42 Niag. Sch of Chinese Studies and C of Grace Ch on the Hill Tor 43-44; I of Stoney Creek 45-46; Miss Dio Honan 46-48; Warden of St Chad's Coll Regina 48-55; C of Ascen Hamilton 55-56; R of St Alb Tor 56-61; Dean and R of St Matt Cathl Timmins and Exam Chap to Bp of Moos 61-74; R of Strathroy Dio Hur from 74; Dom Chap to Bp of Hur 78-80; Can of Hur from 80. *22 Head Street North, Strathroy, Ont., Canada.* (519-245 2131)

SCRACE, David Peter. b 46. Sarum Wells Th Coll 79. **d** 81 St Alb. C of Abbots Langley Dio St Alb from 81. *5a Tibbs Hill Road, Abbots Langley, Watford, WD5 0EE.* (Kings Langley 64039)

SCRAGG, Michael John. b 39. ACT Th Dipl 73. St Francis Coll Brisb 69. **d** 74 **p** 75 Brisb. C of Ch of Annunc Camp Hill Brisb 74-77; Good Shepherd Chesterton 77-79; St Paul Maryborough 79-80; V of Biggenden Dio Brisb from 80. *Vicarage, Edward Street, Biggenden, Queensland, Australia 4621.*

SCRASE, Canon Archer James Wimble. Univ of Sask BA 34. Em Coll Sktn LTh 35. Coll of Em & St Chad Sktn Hon DD 77. **d** 34 **p** 35 Bran. C of Reston 34-35; P-in-c 35; Moose Lake 35-40; C of St Geo Brandon 40-43; Chap RCAF 43-46; R of Minnedosa 46-49; Prin All SS Ind Sch Prince Albert 49-56; Prin Mackay Ind Sch Dauphin 56-73; Hon Can of Bran 59-73; Can (Emer) from 73; P-in-c of Amaranth and of

Kinosota 60-67. *25 Kirby Street East, Dauphin, Manit., Canada.*

SCRATCH, Gordon Clare. **d** and **p** 70 Queb. I of St Paul's River 70-73; SSJE Bracebridge 73-77; C of St Steph City and Dio Ott from 77. *930 Watson Street, Ottawa, Ont, Canada.*

SCREECH, Royden. b 53. AKC and BD 74. St Aug Coll Cant 75. **d** 76 **p** 77 S'wark. C of St Cath Hatcham 76-79; V of St Antony Nunhead Dio S'wark from 79. *St Antony's vicarage, Carden Road, SE15 3PT.* (01-639 4261)

SCRINE, Ralph. b 19. Univ of Bris BA (2nd cl Engl) 40. Fitzw Ho Cam BA (2nd cl Th Trip pt i) 46, MA 60. Inst of Educn Lon MPhil 81. Westcott Ho Cam 45. **d** 46 **p** 47 Bris. C of St Matt Moorfields 46-51; C-in-c of Biddestone 51-52; Conv Distr of St Mary and St Francis Lockleaze 52-60; V of St Jas L and Chap Eliz Coll Guernsey 60-65; Lect in Div Ch Ch Coll Cant 65-68; Sen Lect from 68; Chap 68-75. *Stray Lees, Blean, Canterbury, Kent.* (0227 77361)

SCRIVEN, Henry William. b 51. Univ of Sheff BA 72. St Jo Coll Nottm 73. **d** 75 Lon **p** 76 Willesden for Lon. C of Wealdstone 75-79; Chap in Salta Dio N Argent from 80. *Casilla 187, 4400, Salta, Argentina.*

SCRIVEN, Stanley William. ALCD 41. **d** 41 **p** 42 Chelmsf. C of St Mary Becontree 41-44; Kinson Bournemouth 44-45; St Martin Tipton 45-47; St Pet Upper Holloway 47-49; Alperton 49-51; Asst Sec Ch S 51-52; C of W Teignmouth 52-54; R of Worting 54-66; V of St Nich w H Trin Dunkeswell 66-68; C of Disley 68-71; Whitton w Thurleston and Akenham 71-76; Perm to Offic Dio St E 76-78; Dio Sarum from 78. *7 Franklin Road, Wastham, Weymouth, Dorset.*

SCRIVENER, Robert Allan. b 54. Univ of Nottm BEducn 78. Linc Th Coll 79. **d** 80 Southw **p** 81 Sherwood for Southw. C of Sherwood Dio Southw from 80. *10 Costock Avenue, Sherwood, Nottingham, NG5 3AR.* (Nottm 620208)

SCRIVENS, Ernest. Wycl Hall, Ox. **d** 62 **p** 63 Ox. C of St Mary Chesham 62-64; CF (S Rhod) 64-67; V of Ardington w Lockinge 68-69; Chap Miss to Seamen Bunb 69-79; V of Yeadon 79-80; C of Randwick Dio Syd from 81. *7 The Avenue, Randwick, NSW, Australia 2031.*

SCRUBY, Allington Frank Collard. Univ of Dur 32. AKC 35. **d** 35 **p** 36 Lon. C of St Mich AA Stonebridge 35-39; St Paul Wel NZ 39-41; Actg V of Kaitaia 41-44; V of N Wairoa 44-54; Avondale 54-60; Chap Green Lane and Cornw Hosps Auckld 60-72; Sen Hosp Chap Auckld 72; Hon C of Orewa Dio Auckld from 73. *49 Brightside Road, Stanmore Bay, Whangaparaoa, NZ.*

SCRUBY, Ven Ronald Victor. b 19. Trin Hall Cam BA 48, MA 52. Cudd Coll. **d** 50 **p** 51 Chich. C of Rogate 50-53; Chap King Edw V11 Hosp Midhurst 50-53; Chap Saunders-Roe Osborne E Cowes 53-58; V of Eastney 58-65; RD of Portsm 60-65; Archd of IW 65-77; Portsm from 77; Exam Chap to Bp of Portsm from 65. *Victoria Lodge, Osborn Road, Fareham, Hants, PO16 7DS.* (Fareham 280101)

SCUFFHAM, Canon Frank Leslie. b 30. K Coll Lon and Warm AKC 56. **d** 57 **p** 58 Pet. C of Kettering 57-59; Industr Missr Dio Sheff 60-61; Industr Chap Dio Pet from 61; Can of Pet Cathl from 71; M Gen Syn 75-80; P-in-c of Stoke Albany w Wilbarston Dio Pet 79; R from 79. *Stoke Albany Rectory, Market Harborough, Leics.* (Dingley 213)

SCUPHOLME, Albert Cooper. b 11. Late Scho of Em Coll Cam BA (2nd cl Math Trip pt ii) 33, MA 37. Coll of Resurr Mirfield 33. **d** 35 **p** 36 York. C of Redcar 35-37; Helmsley 37-39; V of Ugthorpe 39-50; R of Thurcaston w Cropston 50-76; RD of Sparkenhoe iii from 69. *5 Town Close, Holt, Norf.* (Holt 2676)

SCUSE, Harvey James. Trin Coll Tor LTh 44. **d** 44 **p** 45 Tor. C of St John Norway Tor 44-45; St Geo Cathl Kingston Ont 45-49; I of Cannington 49-51; R of St Geo Peterborough 51-61; St John Weston 61-70; R of St Timothy Agincourt City and Dio Tor from 70. *4125 Sheppard Avenue East, Agincourt, Ont., Canada.* (416-293 5711)

SCUSE, Paul Donald. b 53. Univ of Tor BSc 75. Wycl Coll Tor MDiv 79. **d** 79 Bp Read for Tor **p** 80 Tor. C of Ch Mem Ch Oshawa 79-80; I of Ch of the Advent City and Dio Tor from 79. *81 Delemere Avenue, Toronto, Ont, Canada, M6N 1Z8.*

SCUTT, John Melville. b 07. St Edm Hall Ox BA (3rd cl Phil Pol and Econ) 29, Dipl Th 30, MA 33. Wycl Hall Ox 29. **d** 31 **p** 32 Sarum. C of St John Weymouth 31-33; Ch Ch Brixton Rd 33-36; R of Worting 36-39; Chap RAF 39-45; V of Ch Ch Worthing 45-49; R of Edgware 49-60; V of Woodford Wells 60-72; C of Colney Heath 72-73; C-in-c of Elveden 75-77; Perm to Offic Dio St Alb from 77. *3 Greyfields, Welwyn Garden City, Herts.*

SCUTTER, James Edward. K Coll Lon and Warm AKC 59. **d** 60 **p** 61 Chelmsf. C of St Jo Bapt Tilbury Dks 60-63; Miss at St Pet Miss Madinare 63-65; Serowe 65-68; P-in-c of Que Que 68-70; C of Whangarei 70-74; Chap RNZAF from 74; L to Offic Dio Ch Ch 74-77; Dio Nel 77-79; Dio Wel 79-82. *RNZAF Station, SE Asia, Singapore.*

SCYNER, Lawrence Anthony. Selw Coll Cam BA 61, MA 65. McGill Univ BD 63. Montr Dioc Th Coll LTh 63; **d** 62 **p** 63 Montr. C of Ch Ch Cathl Montr 62-65; R of St Ignatius Montr 65-66; Chap Douglas Hosp Montr 66-72; Dir Group Services Dio Montr 72-74; Social Services Montr 74-76; L to Offic Dio NS from 76. *Crowfield, Crapaud, PEI, Canada.*

SEABORN, Francis Vincent. b 15. Kelham Th Coll 33. **d** 39 **p** 40 Ripon. C of St Hilda Leeds 39-43; St Edm the K Northwood Hills 43-45; Kelham Th Coll 46; C of St Clem City Road Lon 47-48; H Trin Reading 48-49; V of St Agnes Kennington Park 49-54; R of Willey w Barrow 54-56; C of St Mary Magd Bridgnorth 56-59; V of St Steph Wolverhampton 59-64; St Mary and St Chad Longton 64-80; Perm to Offic Dio Lich from 80. *60 Kirkup Walk, Longton, Stoke-on-Trent, ST3 2SD.* (0782-324092)

✠ **SEABORN, Most Rev Robert Lowder.** Trin Coll Tor BA 32, MA 34, BD 39, DD (*jure dig*) 48. Bp's Univ Lennox Hon DCL 62. **d** 34 **p** 35 Tor. C of St Simon Tor 34-36; St Jas Pro-Cathl Tor 37-41; R of Cobourg 41-48; CF (Canad) 42-45; Dean and R of H Trin Cathl Queb 49-56; Immigration Chap Queb 52-56; R of St Mary Kerrisdale Vancouver 56-58; Exam Chap to Bps of Yukon and New Westmr 56-58; Cons Asst Bp of Newfld in H Trin Cathl Queb 25 April 58 by Abp of Queb; Bps of Alg, NS, Newfld, Montr, Fred, Ont, Ott; and Bp Davis; Can of Newfld 58-65; Apptd Ld Bp of Newfld 65; E Newfld and Labrador 76; res 80; Elected Abp and Metrop of Prov of Canada 75; res 80; Bp Ord to Canad Armed Forces from 80. *67 Portugal Cove Road, St John's, Newfoundland, Canada.* (709-726 9447)

SEABROOK, Alan Geoffrey. b 43. ALCD 65. (Ludlow 66 **p** 67 Stepney for Lon. C of St Jas L Bethnal Green 66-70; Madeley 70-73; V of Girlington 74-80; R of Bitterley w Middleton Dio Heref from 80; P-in-c of Hopton Cangeford Dio Heref from 80; Cold Weston Dio Heref from 80; Stoke St Milburgh Dio Heref from 80; Clee St Marg Dio Heref from 80. *Bitterley Rectory, Ludlow, Shropshire.* (Ludlow 890239)

SEABROOK, Geoffrey Barry. b 45. Open Univ BA 77. Chich Th Coll 66. **d** 69 **p** 70 Lon. C of Tottenham 69-72; H Trin Winchmore Hill 72-74; V of St Geo Hornsey Dio Lon from 74; P-in-c of St Mary Hornsey Dio Lon from 80. *140 Cranley Gardens, N10 3AH.* (01-883 6846)

SEACH, Terrence Neil. b 52. St Bede's Coll Umtata 78. **d** 79 Bp Ndwandwe for Johann **p** 80 Johann. C of Rosebank Dio Johann from 79. *PO Box 52139, Saxonwold, S Africa 2132.*

SEACOME, Michael Owen. b 19. Wadh Coll Ox BA and MA 47. ARCM 50. Sarum Th Coll 47. **d** 49 **p** 50 Glouc. C of Tewkesbury 49-54; V of Forthampton w Chaceley 54-58; Barnwood Dio Glouc from 58. *27a Barnwood Avenue, Gloucester, GL4 7AB.* (Gloucester 66265)

SEAFORD, John Nicholas. b 39. Univ of Dur BA 67, Dipl Th 68. St Chad's Dur 68. **d** 68 Willesden for Lon **p** 69 Lon. C of St Mark Bush Hill Pk 68-71; St Luke Stanmore, Win 71-73; V of N Baddesley 73-76; Chilworth (w N Baddesley from 76) 75-78; Highcliffe w Hinton Admiral Dio Win from 78; Exam Chap to Bp of Win from 79. *33 Nea Road, Highcliffe, Christchurch, Dorset, BH23 4NB.* (Highcliffe 72767)

SEAGER, Ven Edward Leslie. Late Found Scho of Hatf Coll Dur BA (3rd cl Hist) and Jenkyns Scho 26, Capel Cure Pri 27, Dipl Th 28, MA 31. **d** 28 **p** 29 Newc T. C of St Cuthb Newc T 28-31; Chap Wel Sch Somt 31-39; Asst Master 31-36; Ho Master 36-39; CF (TA) 37-39; TCF 39-46; DACG 45-46; Hon CF 46; V of Gillingham w E and W Stour and Milton 46-79; Surr 46-79; C-in-c of Fifehead Magdalen 51-66; V 66-79; RD of Shaftesbury 51-56; Can and Preb of Sarum Cathl 54-79; Archd of Dorset 55-74; Archd (Emer) from 74; C-in-c of Stour Provost w Stour Row and Todbere 65-70; Exam Chap to Bp of Sarum 68-79; Team V of Gillingham 79. *c/o Vicarage, Gillingham, Dorset.* (Gillingham 435)

SEAGER, Roland Douglas. b 08. St Bonif Coll Warm 32. **d** 33 **p** 34 Man. C of St Mary Wardleworth 33-36; Asst P Korogwe 37-38; Zanz 38-39; C of St Steph SneiNton 39-41; C-in-c of Olney 41-43; V of Barlby 43-48; R of Beaconsfield CP 48-54; St Pet Port Eliz 54-59; N Midl Area Sec SPG 59-64; V of Kirkby Woodhouse 64-71; C-in-c of St Cath Nottm 71-73; Perm to Offic Dio Southw from 74. *22 Willow Road, Carlton, Nottingham, NG4 3BH.*

SEAGO, Canon Jesse Edward Charles. b 06. ALCD 37. **d** 37 **p** 38 Chelmsf. C of St Paul Leyton 37-40; St Paul St Alb 40-44; V of St Paul Leyton 44-67; RD of Leyton 61-67; Hon Can of Chelmsf 66-74; Can (Emer) from 74; V of St Sav Westcliff-on-Sea 67-74. *10a Nelson Road, Leigh-on-Sea, Essex, SS9 3HU.* (Southend 712483)

SEAGRAM, James William. b 51. Qu Univ at Kingston Ont BA 74. Wycl Coll Tor MDiv 77. **d** 77 **p** 78 Hur. C of St Geo Lon Ont 77-79; I of Wiarton, Lion's Head and Tobermory Dio Hur from 79. *Box 306, Wiarton, Ont, Canada N0H 2T0.*

SEAL, Edward Hugh. b 10. ARCM 31. Univ of Lon BMus 36. Wells Th Coll 46. **d** 48 **p** 49 B & W. C of Midsomer Norton 48-50; V of Churt 50-57; Pemberton 57-63; R of Morecambe (Poulton-le-Sands) 63-78; Surr 73-78. *3 Fern Bank, Scotforth, Lancaster, LA1 4TT.*

SEAL, Philip Trevor. b 32. K Coll Lon and Warm AKC 55. **d** 56 Bp Hawkes for Cant **p** 57 Guildf. C of Godalming 56-60; Tamworth 60-61; R of St Chad Lich 61-73; Chap HM Detention Centre Swinfen Hall 66-73; R of Shere Dio Guildf from 73; RD of Cranleigh 76-81. *Shere Rectory, Guildford, Surrey.* (Shere 2394)

SEAL, Ronald Frederick. b 28. Lich Th Coll. **d** 61 **p** 62 Portsm. C of Bedhampton 61-65; R of N w S Kilworth 65-71; Barwell w Stapleton and Potters Marston 71-80; P-in-c of U Stour Dio Sarum from 80. *Upper Stour Rectory, Zeals, Warminster, Wilts.* (Bourton 840221)

SEAL, William George. b 27. Dipl Th (Lon) 71. Oak Hill Th Coll. **d** 70 **p** 71 S'wark. C of St Jo Bapt Plumstead 70-73; All SS Camberwell 73-80; V of St Matt Luton Dio St Alb from 80. *Vicarage, Wenlock Street, Luton, Beds, LU2 0NQ.* (Luton 32320)

SEALE, Robert Lionel. b 04. Univ of Lon BD and AKC (1st cl) 29, Scho in Th 31. Diplômc d'Études de Civilisation Française Sorbonne 35. **d** 29 **p** 30 S'wark. C of St Luke Battersea 29-32; St Jo Evang Caterham Valley 32-34; SPG Miss at Tananarive 35-39; C-inc of Weeke 40-42; R of Millbrook 42-47; CF Western Command 47-48; BAOR 48-50; Hon CF 50; Chap to Sarum Tr Coll and to Salisbury Gen Hosp 50; R of Uplyme 50-72; RD of Honiton 59-62; Perm to Offic Dio Roch 73-80; Dio Ex from 81. *15 Fosseway Court, Seaton, Devon.*

SEALY, Daniel O'Neill. b 21. Oak Hill Th Coll 62. **d** 64 B & W **p** 65 Taunton for B & W. C of Walcot 64-67; Chap RN 67-73; V of St Andr Zaria 73-79; Chap at Tripoli w All SS Benghazi Dio Egypt from 79. *Box 6626, Tripoli, Libya.*

SEALY, Gordon William Hugh. b 27. Univ of Leeds, BA (Econ) 53, MA 64. Coll of Resurr Mirfield, 53. **d** 55 **p** 56 Lon. C of H Cross Greenford 55-58; R of Stan Creek and P-in-c of Stan Creek Valley and St Matt Pomona 58-68; Exam Chap to Bp of Br Hond 67-68; R of Tarrant Gunville 68-74; Tarrant Hilton 68-74; V of Tarrant Monkton w Tarrant Launceston 68-74; St Paul City and Dio Leic from 74; M Gen Syn from 80. *St Paul's Vicarage, Kirby Road, Leicester.* (Leic 28062)

SEALY, Pelham Roy Kenneth. b 27. Em & St Chad's Coll Sktn 68. **d** 74 **p** 75 Skin. I of Watrous 74-79; R of Grace Ch New Grant Dio Trinid from 79. *Rectory, New Grant, Princes Town, Trinidad, W Indies.*

SEAMAN, Alfred Jonathan. *See* Nix-Seaman, Alfred Jonathan

SEAMAN, Canon Arthur Roland Mostyn. b 32. TCD BA 54. Div Test 55, MA 58. Westcott Ho Cam 58. **d** 58 **p** 59 Man. C of St Pet Blackley 58-61; Sanderstead 61-62; V of St Luke Heywood 62-70; Dir of Relig Educn Dio Man from 70; Hon Can of Man from 74. *24 Darley Avenue, West Didsbury, Manchester, M20 8YD.* (061-445 4994)

SEAMAN, Brian Edward. b 35. Univ of Dur BA 59. Cranmer Hall, Dur 59. **d** 61 **p** 62 Man. C of Burnage 61-65; Chap Mayflower Family Centre Canning Town 65-75; V of St Paul Elswick City and Dio Newc T 75. *Vicarage, Park Close, Elswick, Newcastle upon Tyne, NE4 6SB.* (Newc T 734705)

SEAMER, Stephen James George. b 50. AKC 71. Ridley Hall Cam 74. **d** 75 **p** 76 Chich. C of Rustington 75-78; St Jo Div Bulwell 79-80; P-in-c of Camber and E Guldeford 79-80; Team V of Rye Dio Chich from 80. *Vicarage, Lydd Road, Camber, E Sussex, TN31 7RN.* (Camber 386)

SEAR, Peter Lionel. b 49. Univ of Ex BA 72. Linc Th Coll 72. **d** 74 **p** 75 Birm. C of Sheldon 74-77; Caversham (and Mapledurham from 81) Dio Ox from 77. *33 Grove Road, Emmer Green, Reading, Berks.*

SEARIGHT, Mervyn Warren. b 26. **d** 59 **p** 60 Dub. C of St Mary Crumlin Dub 59-63; All SS Grangegorman Dub 63-65; Miss to Lepers Purulia W Bengal 65-66; C of St Steph Dub 67-68; R of Killermogh 68-77; Aughaval Dio Tuam from 77. *Rectory, Newport Road, Westport, Co Mayo, Irish Republic.* (Westport 123)

SEARLE, Charles Peter. b 20. Selw Coll Cam BA 48, MA 53. Ridley Hall Cam. **d** 50 **p** 51 Chelmsf. C of St Mary Becontree 50-53; C-in-c of St Jo Bapt Bedford 53-56; R 56-60; V of Ch Ch Weston-s-Mare 60-70; Ch Ch Woking Dio Guildf from 70. *Christ Church Vicarage, Heathside Road, Woking, Surrey.* (Woking 62100)

SEARLE, Hugh Douglas. b 35. St Cath Coll Cam BA 59, MA 63. Oak Hill Th Coll 59. **d** 61 Kens for Lon **p** 62 Lon. C of H Trin Cloudesley Square Islington 61-64; Chap HM Pris Lewes 64-65; HM Borstal Roch 65-69; Hollesley 70-74; HM Pris Parkhurst 74-78; P-in-c of Barton Dio Ely from 78; Coton Dio Ely from 78; RD of Bourn from 81. *Barton Vicarage, Cambridge, CB3 7BG.* (Comberton 2218)

SEARLE, Michael Owen. b 26. Sarum Wells Th Coll 76. **d** 78 **p** 79 Basingstoke for Win. C of St Luke Stanmore Win 78-82; Team V of Seacroft Dio Ripon from 82. *51 St James Approach, Seacroft, Leeds, LS14 6JJ.*

SEARLE, Michael Westran. b 47. Univ of Leeds LLB 68. Univ of Nottm Dipl Th 69. Cudd Coll 69. **d** 71 **p** 72 Dur. C of St Mary Virg Norton 71-74; Westbury-on-Trym 74-77; V of St Osw Bedminster Down Dio Bris from 77. *St Oswald's Vicarage, Cheddar Grove, Bedminster Down, Bristol, BS13 7EN.* (Bristol 642649)

SEARLE, Wilfred Rees. St D Coll Lamp BA 32. St Mich Coll Llan 32. **d** 33 **p** 35 Liv. C of St Jas Wigan 33-36; Ashton-in-Makerfield 36-37; Perm to Offic at Upholland 38-47; R of Stanford-on-Teme w Orleton 47-54; Woolstone w Oxenton and Gotherington 54-57; Acton Beauchamp and Evesbatch w Stanford Bp 57-58. *Cherry Orchard, Newton, Martley, Worcs.*

SEARLE-BARNES, Albert Victor. b 28. Univ of Sheff BA 48. Univ of Lon BD 53. ALCD 53. **d** 53 Ox **p** 54 Buckingham for Cant. C of Iver 53-55; Attenborough w Bramcote and Chilwell (in c of St Barn Inham Nook) 55-59; V of Cratfield w Heveningham and Ubbeston 59-64; Wick w Doynton 64-70; Asst Master Thornbury Gr Sch Bris 70-72; Perm to Offic Dio Bris 70-72; V of Downend 73-78; Market Rasen Dio Linc from 78; Legsby Dio Linc from 78; R of Linwood Dio Linc from 78. *Vicarage, Market Rasen, Lincs.* (Market Rasen 843424)

SEARLE-BARNES, Canon Charles William James. b 20. St Cath Coll Cam BA 42, MA 46. Ridley Hall Cam. **d** 44. **p** 45 S'wark. C of Morden 44-46; CIM Miss E Szech 47-51; Dom Chap to Bp of E Szech 49-51; C of Em S Croydon 51-53; V of Rainham 53-60; C-in-c of Wennington 53-54; R 54-60; Chap S Ockendon Hosp 55-60; V of Cromer 60-70; C-in-c of Gresham 68-70; Chap Cromer Distr Hosp 60-70; V of Tonbridge Dio Roch from 70; RD of Tonbridge from 70; Hon Can of Roch Cathl from 75. *Vicarage, Tonbridge, Kent.* (Tonbridge 352867)

SEARS, Derek Lynford. b 25. St Jo Coll Cam 2nd cl Hist Trip pt i 48, BA (2nd cl Hist Trip pt ii) 49, MA 53. Wycl Hall Ox 49. **d** 51 **p** 52 Blackb. C of St Steph Blackb 51-53; St Paul Preston 53-56; V of St Jas Burnley 56-62; Tutor St Pet Coll Kingston 62-64; Sen Tutor 64-66; L to Offic Dio Ja 62-66; Exam Chap to Bp of Ja 64-66; V of Freckleton 66-74; R of Morant Bay Dio Ja 74-78; V of St Mich AA Ashton-on-Ribble Dio Blackb from 78; P-in-c of St Mark Preston Dio Blackb from 82. *St Michael's Vicarage, Ashton-on-Ribble, Preston, Lancs, PR2 1AJ.* (Preston 726157)

SEARS, Eric John. b 47. Univ of Cant NZ BSc 72. Ridley Coll Melb ACT LTh 76. **d** and **p** 77 Nel. C of Richmond 77-78; P-in-c of Havelock Dio Nel from 78. *The Vicarage, Havelock, NZ.*

SEARS, Frank. b 29. Wycl Hall Ox 62. **d** 64 **p** 65 Guildf. C of Ashtead 64-72; V of St Luke Finchley Dio Lon from 72; C-in-c of St Paul Finchley Dio Lon from 76. *64 Mountfield Road, N3 3NP.* (01-346 2979)

SEARS, Michael Antony. b 50. Univ of Birm BSc 71. Linc Th Coll 78. **d** 80 **p** 81 Lich. C of Short Heath Dio Lich from 80. *13 Wesley Road, Willenhall, W Midl, WV12 5QT.*

SEARS, Wilwood Aloysius. Codr Coll Barb LTh 31. Dorch Miss Coll 29. **d** 31 **p** 32 Guy. C of St Geo Cathl Georgetown 31-35; Miss of NW Distr Gui 35-39; V of Enmore 39-46; Kitty w Lodge 46-60; Can of Guy 49-71; Dioc Regr Guy 59-71; V of Ch Ch Georgetn 60-71; L to Offic Dio Guy from 71. *615/616 South Ruimveldt Gardens, Georgetown, Guyana, S America.* (02-718 38)

SEATON, James Bradbury. b 29. Ch Coll Cam 2nd cl Geog Trip pt i, 52, BA (2nd cl Geog Trip pt ii) 53, MA 57. Westcott Ho Cam 53. **d** 55 **p** 56 Derby. C of St Werburgh Derby 55-58; Darlington (in c of All SS Blackwell) 58-64; V of All SS Preston-on-Tees 64-72; Team V of Central Stockton 72-75; R of Anstey Dio Leic from 75; RD of Sparkenhoe 3 from 81. *190 Bradgate Road, Anstey, Leicester, LE7 7FD.* (Leic 362176)

SEATREE, Eric Joseph. MC 43. Moore Th Coll Syd ACT ThL 40. **d** 40 **p** 41 Syd. C of St Silas Waterloo 40-41; Chap AIF 41-45; R of Prospect Seven Hills and Blacktown 45-46; Botany 46-48; Blackheath 48-51; Graft Dioc Comm 52-55; P-in-c of Neutral Bay 55-57; R of Concord N 57-60 and 62-66; Centennial Pk 66-70; Perm to Offic Dio Cant 60-62; L to Offic Dio Syd from 70. *14 Panorama Crescent, Wentworth Falls, NSW, Australia 2782.* (047-57 1936)

SEAVER, Donald Vanor. b 39. Boston Univ BA 64. Boston Coll MSW 66. Nashotah Ho 76. **d** 76 Bp of Milwaukee **p** 77 Bran. C of St John's Miss Moose Lake 76-78; St Lambert 78-81; R of All SS Ridgeway w Bertie Dio Niag from 81. *Box 555, Ridgeway, Ont, Canada L0S 1N0.*

SEBADUKA, Yerimiya. **d** 39 **p** 41 Ugan. P Dio Ugan

39-61; Dio Nam 61-65; Dio W Bugan 65-69. *Katende, Uganda.*

SEBARUNGU, Nathanaeli. d 80 Kiga. d Dio Kiga. *BP 20, Nyamata, Rwanda.*

SEBATINDIRA, Mizulaimu. Bp Tucker Coll Mukono. **d** 56 Ugan **p** 58 Bp Balya for Ugan. P Dio Ugan 56-61; Dio Nam 61-65; Dio W Bugan 65-71; Dio Nam from 71. *Lutete, PO Bamunanika, Uganda.*

SEBAZUNGU, John William. d 64 Ankole-K. d Dio Ankole-K 64-67; Dio Kig from 67. *PO Box 1049, Kisoro, Kigezi, Uganda.*

SEBBOWA, Ezera Kateregga. Bp Tucker Coll Mukono. **d** 60 Ugan for Nam **p** 62 Nam. P Dio Nam. *Jungo, PO Box Kakiri-Kampala, Uganda.*

SEBEKO, Elliot Mathealira. b 29. **d** 76 Les. d Dio Les. *St John's Rectory, PO Box 11, Mafeteng, Lesotho, S Africa.*

SEBER, Derek Morgan. b 43. Oak Hill Coll 71. **d** 73 **p** 74 Man. C of The Saviour Collyhurst Man 73-75; St Thos and St John Radcliffe 75-77; P-in-c of St Geo Hulme City and Dio Man from 77; Industr Chap and M Gtr Man Industr Miss Team from 77. *6 St Austell Road, Manchester, M16 8WQ.* (061-881 3517)

SEBUNNYA, Mesusera Sekajugo. Bp Tucker Coll Mukono. **d** 48 **p** 50 Ugan. P Dio Ugan 48-61; Dio Nam from 61. *Church of Uganda, PO Kasawo, Masaka, Uganda.*

✠ **SEBUNUNGURI, Right Rev Adoniya. d** 54 **p** 56 Bp Brazier for Ugan. P Dio Ugan 54-60; Dio Rwanda B 60-65; Can of Rwanda B 64-65; Cons Asst Bp of Rwanda B (for Rwanda) in Em Ch Kigeme 6 June 65 by Abp of Ugan; Rwanda B; Bps of Rwanda B; and Ruw; Trld to Rwa (Kiga from 75) 66. *Anglican Church, Post Box 61, Kigali, Rwanda.* (Kigali 6687)

SEBURIMBGA, Simon. Warner Mem Th Coll Ibuye 56. **d** 58 **p** 59 Bp Brazier for Ugan. P Dio Ugan 58-60; Dio Rwanda B 60-66; Dio Rwa 66-75; Archd of N Rwa 68-75. *BP22, Kigali, Rwanda.*

SEBUSHISHI, Denis. d 65 Rwanda B **p** 66 Rwa. P Dio Rwa 65-75; Dio Kiga from 75. *Post Box 135, Butare, Rwanda.*

SECCOMBE, David Peter. b 46. Univ of New Engl Armid BSc 68. BD (Lon) 72. Em Coll Cam PhD 78. Moore Th Coll Syd ACT ThL 71. **d** and **p** 73 Perth. C of Claremont 73-75; on leave 75-79; L to Offic Dio Perth 79; R of Rosalie-Shenton Pk Dio Perth from 79. *74 Keightley Road, Subiaco, W Australia 6008.* (381 1240)

SECCOMBE, Marcus John. b 34. Oak Hill Th Coll 60. **d** 63 Bp Gelsthorpe for Southw **p** 64 Southw. C of Woodthorpe 63-67; St Mary Doncaster 67-72; V of Owston Dio Sheff from 72. *Owston Vicarage, Askern, Doncaster, Yorks, DN6 9JF.* (0302-723309)

SECKER, Brian. Qu Coll Birm 62. **d** 65 **p** 66 Sheff. C of Goldthorpe 65-68; V of New Bentley 68-75; St Paul City and Dio Pet from 75; P-in-c of St Barn Pet 75-80. *St Paul's Vicarage, Peterborough, PE12 2PA.* (Peterborough 3746)

SECKER, Herbert Charles. Montr Dioc Th Coll LTh 35. **d** 31 **p** 32 Ont. C of St Thos Belleville 31; I of New Boyne 34-37; Amherst I 37-41; R of Westport 41-43; Adolphustown 43-51; Stirling and Frankford w Glen Miller 51-57; St Luke Kingston 57-74; RD of Frontenac 69-74; Can of St Geo Cathl Kingston 69-74. *1 Oakridge Avenue, Kingston, Ont, Canada.*

SECOMBE, Preb Frederick Thomas. b 18. St D Coll Lamp BA (2nd cl Hist) 40. St Mich Coll Llan 40. **d** 42 **p** 43 Swan B. C of St Mark Swansea 42-44; St Edw Knighton 44-46; Machen 46-49; St Woolos Newport 49-52; Chap to St Woolos Hosp 49-52; V of Llanarth w Clytha Llansantffraed and Bryngwyn 52-54; R of Machen w Rudry 54-59; V of St Pet Cockett Swansea 59-69; R of Hanwell Dio Lon from 69; RD of Ealing W from 78; Preb of St Paul's Cathl Lon from 81. *91 Church Road, W7.* (01-567 6185)

SECORD, Joseph Alward. K Coll NS BA 49. **d** 45 Fred **p** 50 Queb. I of Inverness and Leeds 50-53; Bury 53-55; Grand Manan 55-58; R of Canning 58-64; St Geo w Pennfield 64-70; Shediac 71-81; Upham Dio Fred from 81. *RR3, Hampton, NB, Canada.*

SECRETAN, Philip Buckley. b 09. TD 50. Pemb Coll Ox BA 32, MA 46. FLAS (FRICS from 70) 46. Roch Th Coll 62. **d** 63 **p** 64 Chich. C of Aldwick 63-66; R of Folkington 66-79; V of Wilmington 66-79. *70 Newick Drive, Newick, Lewes, Sussex, BN8 4PB.* (Newick 2857)

SECRETT, Ian Russell. b 27. Clare Coll Cam 2nd cl Hist Trip pt i 47, BA (2nd cl Hist Trip pt ii) 48, MA 52. Westcott Ho Cam 73. **d** 73 **p** 74 Bris. C of St Andr w St Bart Bris 73-75; C-in-c of Burwell Dio Ely 75; V from 76. *Burwell Vicarage, Cambridge.* (Newmarket 741262)

SEDDON, Ernest Geoffrey. b 26. St Deiniol's Libr Hawarden 80. **d** 80 Ches **p** 81 Stockport for Ches. C of St Marg Dunham Massey Dio Ches from 80. *6 Longcroft Drive, Dunham Park, Altrincham, WA14 4RA.*

SEDDON, Fred. b 07. Fitzw Ho Cam BA 37, MA 41. Ridley Hall Cam 38. **d** 38 **p** 39 Man. C of St Bart Westhoughton 38-41; St Jude Nottm 41-42; C of H Trin Leic 42-45; Actg Chap HM Pris Leic 42-45; V of St Nich Baddesley 45-51; St Pet Preston 51-60; PC of Longton 60-75. *3 Hastings Place, Lytham, Preston, Lancs.*

SEDDON, James Edward. b 15. Univ of Dur LTh 39. Tyndale Hall Bris 36. **d** 39 **p** 40 Liv. C of St Chrys Everton 39-41; St Philemon Toxt 41-43; St Simon and St Jude Southport 43-45; BCMS Missr Tangier 45-50; Demnat Marrakesh 50-55; Home Sec BCMS 55-67; R of Hawkwell 67-74; P-in-c of Peldon 74; P-in-c of Gt and L Wigborough 74; R of Peldon w Gt and L Wigborough 75-80; Perm to Offic Dio Chelmsf from 80. *45 Byron Avenue, Lexden, Colchester, CO3 4HG.*

SEDDON, John Richard. Moore Th Coll Syd 58. ACT ThL (2nd cl) 60. **d** 61 Syd **p** 61 Bp Kerle for Syd. C of St Alb Epping 61-65; R of Ashfield 66-73; St Luke Mosman Dio Syd from 73. *Ourimbah Road, Mosman, NSW, Australia 2088.* (969-6910)

SEDDON, Philip James. b 45. Jes Coll Cam BA 68, MA 71. Ridley Hall Cam 67. **d** 70 **p** 71 Man. C of Tonge w Alkrington 70-74; Lect Trin Th Coll Umuahia 74-78; Exam Chap to Bp on The Niger 75-78; Lect St John's Th Coll Nottm 78-79; Chap Magdalen Coll Cam from 79. *Magdalen College, Cambridge, CB3 0AG.*

SEDE, Daudi. d 64 **p** 65 Mbale. P Dio Mbale 64-72; Dio Bukedi from 72. *Butaleja, PO Box 241, Tororo, Uganda.*

SEDGLEY, Timothy John. b 42. St Jo Coll Ox BA (2nd cl Engl) 63, Dipl Th 64, MA 68. Westcott Ho Cam 64. **d** 66 **p** 67 Nor. C of St Pet Mancroft Nor 66-70; V of Costessey 70-79; RD of Nor N 75-79; V of Walton-on-Thames Dio Guildf from 79. *Vicarage, Ashley Park Avenue, Walton-on-Thames, Surrey, KT12 1EU.* (Walton-on-Thames 27184)

SEDGMORE, Evan. b 09. St D Coll Lamp 47. **d** 50 **p** 51 Llan. C of Neath w Llantwit 50-54; Garw Valley w Blaengarw 54-59; V of Fochriw and Deri 59-71; Llanbradach 71-76; Perm to Offic Dio Llan from 76. *52 Hookland Road, Newton, Porthcawl, Mid Glam, CF36 5SG.* (Porthcawl 8991)

SEDGWICK, Peter Humphrey. b 48. Trin Hall Cam BA 70. Westcott Ho Cam 71. **d** 74 Lon **p** 75 Stepney for Lon. C of Stepney 74-77; P-in-c of Pittington 77-79; Hon C of The Lickey (in c of Blackwell) 79-82; Lect at Univ of Birm 79-82. *c/o 12 Station Road, Blackwell, Near Bromsgrove, Worcs.*

SEED, Leslie. b 27. Jesus Coll Cam BA 50, MA 55. Coll of Resurr Mirfield. **d** 71 Blackb **p** 72 Burnley for Blackb. C of St Mich AA Blackpool 71-72; Haslingden 72-75; P-in-c of Church Kirk Dio Blackb 75-78; R from 78. *434 Blackburn Road, Accrington, Lancs, BB5 0DE.* (Accrington 36946)

SEED, Richard Murray Crosland. b 49. Edin Th Coll 69. **d** 72 Ripon for Bradf **p** 73 Bradf. C of Ch Ch Skipton 72-75; Baildon 75-77; Team V of Kidlington 77-80; Chap HM Detention Centre Kidlington 77-80; V of Boston Spa Dio York from 80. *Vicarage, Boston Spa, W Yorks, LS23 6AL.* (Boston Spa 842454)

SEEDS, Colin Wilfred. b 39. Univ of Man BSc Tech 60. Linacre Coll Ox BA 67. Ripon Hall Ox 65. **d** 67 **p** 68 Derby. C of Frecheville 67-70; Publ Pr Dio Derby 71-75; C-in-c of Milford 75-76; Ch Ch Belper and Milford 75-76; Asst Master Staveley Netherthorpe Sch and Publ Pr Dio Derby from 77. *Vicarage Flat, High Street, Bolsover, Chesterfield, Derbys.*

SEEGMILLER, Harold Adam. Univ of W Ont BA 43. Hur Th Coll LTh 44, BD 59. **d** 42 **p** 44 Hur. I of Huntingford and Zora 42-44; Pelee I 44-48; R of Geraldton 48-50; Prin Ind Resid Sch and Miss James Bay 50-52; CF (Canad.) 52-54; I of Louisburg 54-58; R of Parrsboro 58-60; I of Hubbards 60-63; R of Windsor 63-67; Exeter 67-69; St John Halifax 69-75; Exam Chap to Bp of NS 71-75; I of Ft Simpson 76-77; Prin Arthur Turner Tr Sch Pangnirtung 77-81. *c/o Arthur Turner School, Pangnirtung, NWT, Canada.*

SEELEY, John Frederick. b 36. K Coll Lon and Warm AKC 61. **d** 62 Hulme for Man **p** 63 Man. C of Ascen Lower Broughton Salford 62-64; St Paul Grove Park Chiswick 64-66; St Mary S Ruislip 66-67; St Jude Hampstead Garden Suburb 67-69; C-in-c of All SS St John's Wood 69-71; C of St Bart Stamford Hill 74-80; V of Harringay Dio Lon from 80. *Vicarage, Wightman Road, N4 1RW.* (01-340 5299)

SEELEY, Martin Alan. b 54. Jes Coll Cam BA 76. U Th Sem NYC STM 78. **d** 78 Grimsby for Linc **p** 79 Linc. C of Bottesford w Ashby Dio Linc from 78. *The Lodge, St Paul's Road, Ashby, Scunthorpe, S Humb, DN16 3DL.*

SEERS, Brian John. Ridley Coll Melb **d** and **p** 64 Brisb. C of St Steph Coorparoo Brisb 64-66; Booval 66-68; Pine Rivers 68-70; Chap Miss to Seamen Port Kembla 70-76; C-in-c of Merrylands W Dio Syd from 76. *11 Ridge Street, Merrylands West, NSW, Australia 2160.* (637-4497)

SEFTON, Thomas Albert. Kelham Th Coll 38. **d** 45 **p** 46 S'wark. C of St Paul w St Mark Deptford 45-47; St Jo Bapt Southend Catford 47-48; CF 48-55; V of St Paul Tottenham Dio Lon 55-58; R of Pemberton 59-60; Wagin 60-63; Tuart

Hill w Mt Yokine 63-70. *27 Frape Avenue, Yokine, W Australia.*

SEGAL, Michael Bertram. b 20. Univ of Lon BA 44. Cudd Coll 46. **d** 48 **p** 49 S'wark. C of St Jo Bapt Southend Catford 48-53; St Andr Coulsdon 53-61; V of St Pet S Wimbledon 61-71; Crofton Park w Brockley 71-82; Gt Doddington Dio Pet from 82. *Vicarage, Great Doddington, Wellingborough, Northants, NN9 7TQ.*

SEGOBIA, Demetrio. b 34. **d** 77 **p** 78 Bp Leake for N Argent. P-in-c of Juarez Dio N Argent from 77. *Casilla 19, Ing GN Juarez, Provincia de Formosa, Argentina.*

✠ **SEGUN, Right Rev Festus Oluwole.** b 15. Fourah Bay Coll BA (Dur) 50. U Th Sem NY BD 56. **d** 51 **p** 52 Lagos. P Dio Lagos 51-60; Syn Sec Dio Lagos 57-70; Provost of Ch Ch Cathl Lagos 60-70; Cons Bp of N Nig 5 April 70 in Ch Ch Cathl Lagos by Abp of W Afr; Bps of Accra; Benin, Ekiti, Enugu; Ibadan; Lagos; Niger; Ow; and Bp Afonya; Trld to Lagos 75. *Bishopscourt, Box 13, Lagos, Nigeria.* (25647)

SEHAU, Lawrence Ntoebe. b 49. St Bede's Coll Umtata Dipl Th 79. **d** 79 **p** 80 Bleomf. C of Bernard the Martyr Witsicshoek Dio Bloemf from 79. *PO Box 5542, Phuthaditjhaba 9866, S Africa.*

SEHUME, Ambrose Orapeleng. St Pet Coll Rosettenville 48. **d** 51 Johann for Kimb K **p** 52 Kimb K. C of St Matt Kimberley 51-53; Glen Red 54-56; P-in-c of Good Shepherd Gatlhose 56-57; St Steph Rustenbeug E 58-60; Serowe 61-63; C of Mpopoma 64-65; P-in-c of Tonota 66-76; Mmadinare 77-78; R of St Mark's Lobatse Dio Botswana from 79. *Box 359, Lobatse, Botswana.*

SEHUME, Joseph Mongane. St Pet Coll Resettenville 51. **d** 53 **p** 54 Bloemf. C of St Patr Miss Bloemf 53-56; P Dio Bloemf from 56. *Box 560, Senekal, OFS, S Africa.*

SEIGNIOR, James Frederick. b 1897. Univ Coll Lon 19. TD 46. **d** 46 **p** 47 St A. C of Hawarden 46-49; V of Bruera 49-69; Perm to Offic Dio Melb 69-79; Dio Glouc 79-80; Dio Guildf from 80. *12 Chase Road, Epsom, Surrey, KT19 8TL.* (Epsom 20611)

SEIN HU, d 78 **p** 79 Akyab. P Dio Akyab. *St Mark's Church, Chang-Ki, Burma.*

SEIN PU, David. d 31 **p** 32 Rang. P Dio Rang. *Church of Christ the King, Myitkyina, Kachin State, Burma.*

SEIN TUN, Justin. d 74 **p** 75 Akyab. P Dio Akyab. *St John's Church, Paletwa, Akyab, Burma.*

SEIPHEMO, Benjamin Philip Selebogo. St Pet Coll Rosettenville 49. **d** 52 **p** 53 Johann. P Dio Johann. *All Saints' Rectory, 241 Khuma Township, Stilfontein, Transvaal, S Africa.*

SEITLHEKO, Benjamin Thabo Ezekiel. b 18. **d** 72 **p** 74 Les. P Dio Les. *St Peter's Mission, Mopeli, PO Mohalkoanas, via Quthing, Lesotho, S Africa.*

SEITLHEKO, Joseph Ezekiel. St Bede's Coll Umtata. **d** 53 Basuto. d Dio Basuto 53-56; Dio Les from 66. *PO Box 17, Qacha's Nek, Lesotho, S Africa.*

SEITLHEKO, Peter. St Bede's Coll Umtata. **d** 58 **p** 60 Basuto. P Dio Basuto 58-66; Dio Les from 66. *St Peter's Mission, Mopeli, Lesotho.*

SEIVEWRIGHT, Robert Taylor. b 1887. Univ of Aber MA 09. Edin Th Coll O9. Luscombe Scho 11. **d** 11 **p** 12 Glas. C of St John Greenock 11-13; All S Clapton Pk 13-17; St Jas Ap Islington 17-18; V of Barkestone w Plungar 18-28; R of Houghton-on-the-Hill 28-48; V of Scalford (w Wycombe and Chadwell 54-72) 48-72; Chap of Chadwell 51-54. *The School House, Scalford, Melton Mowbray, Leics.*

SEIWARI, Joseph Dan. b 25. **d** 73 **p** 74 Nig Delta. P Dio Nig Delta. *St James's Parsonage, Ekowe, via Ahoada, River State, Nigeria.*

SEKABEMBE, Yusufu. d 45 Ugan. d Dio Ugan 45-60; Dio W Bugan from 60. *Kyamukasa, RCM Naluggi, PO Box 12, Mityana, Singo Uganda.*

SEKAZIGA, Danieri. Bp Tucker Coll Mukono. **d** 61 Ruanda-Urundi **p** 63 Nam for Rwanda B. P Dio W Bugan. *Church of Uganda, Njeru, PO Box 2084, Kalisizo, Uganda.*

SEKELENI, Leopold Horatius Tokozile. St Bede's Coll Umtata 65. **d** 66 **p** 67 St John's. P Dio St John's. *Box 165, Mount Frere, Transkei, S Africa.*

SEKGAPHANE, Canon Zachariah. St Pet Coll Rosettenville LTh 39. **d** 39 **p** 40 Johann. P Dio Johann 39-72; Can of St Mary Virg Cathl Johann 65-72; Hon Can from 72; P-in-c of St Mary Parys 74-78; L to Offic Dio Johann from 78. *Box 79, Lichtenburg, TVL, S Africa.*

SEKGOMA, Haskins. d 37 **p** 39 S Rhod. P Dio Matab. *PO Box 140, Serowe, Botswana.*

SEKHOTO, Simon. d 26 **p** 30 Bloemf. LPr Dio Johann 28-30; Dio Bloemf 26-28 and 30-35; Miss Vrede 35-58. *PO Box 88 Vrede, OFS, S Africa.*

SEKIMPI, Erenesiti. Bp Tucker Coll Mukono. **d** 56 Ugan **p** 58 Bp Balya for Ugan. P Dio Nam. *Box 222, Mukono, Uganda.*

SEKONDI, Lord Bishop of. *See* Annobil, Right Rev Theophilus Samuel Anyanya.

SEKU, William Mzwamdile. b 43. St Bede's Coll Umtata 77. **d** 78 St John's. d Dio St John's. *St Andrew's Mission, Lusikisiki, Transkei.*

SEKWAO, Hosea. d 39 **p** 41 Centr Tang. P Dio Centr Tang 35-65; Dio Moro 65-74. *Box 124, Kilosa, Tanzania.*

SELBY, Lord Bishop Suffragan of. *See* Maddocks, Right Rev Morris Henry St John.

SELBY, Fraser Geoffrey. b 10. CBE 57. FCA 60. Cudd Coll 58. **d** 60 **p** 61 Lon. C of St Andr Willesden Green 60-64; Bursar of Cudd Coll from 64; C of Cuddesdon 71-75; Hon Chap to Bp of Ox from 75; Hon C of Wheatley Dio Ox from 80. *Weylands, Ladder Hill, Wheatley, Oxon.*

SELBY, Canon George Raymond. b 22. Univ of Nottm BA (1st cl Th) 53. Univ of Lon PhD 67. Wells Th Coll. **d** 57 **p** 58 Sarum. C of Talbot Village 57-59; V of St Justus Roch 59-63; Sub-Warden Roch Th Coll 63-67; Min Can of Roch Cathl 63-67; C-in-c of Em Leeds 67-70; Sen Chap Univ of Leeds 67-70; Exam Chap to Bp of Ripon from 68; Hon Can of Man Cathl 70-79; Prin NW Ordin Course 70-77; Perm to Offic Dios Blackb, Ches and Liv 70-77; Exam Chap to Bp of Bradf from 77; Consulting P Dio N Carolina 77-78; Res Can St Asaph Cathl 79-81; in Amer Ch. *c/o Box 17025, Raleigh, NC 27609, USA*

SELBY, John Holmes. b 21. BEM 46. St Mich Coll Llan. **d** and **p** 69 Mon. C of Trevethin 69-73; Abergavenny 73; V of Llantilio Crossenny R of Llanvihangel-Ystern-Llewern (and V of Penrhos from 74) Dio Mon from 73. *Vicarage, Llantilio Crossenny, Abergavenny, NP7 8SU.* (Llantilio 240)

SELBY, Canon Peter Stephen Maurice. b 41. Late Scho of St Jo Coll Ox 2nd cl Cl Mods 62, BA (1st cl Psychol and Phil) 64, MA 67. Episc Th Sch Cam USA BD (*cum laude*) 66. K Coll Lon PhD 75. Bps' Coll Cheshunt 66. **d** 66 **p** 67 Lon. C of Queensbury 66-69; Limpsfield w Titsey 69-77; Assoc Dir of Training Dio S'wark 69-72; Vice-Prin SOC 70-72; Asst Missr Dio S'wark 73-77; Can Res of Newc T and Dioc Missr from 77. *208 Osborne Road, Newcastle upon Tyne, NE2 3LD.* (Newc T 810714)

SELBY, Canon Sydney Arthur. b 17. K Coll Lon 41. **d** 48 **p** 50 Bradf. C of Menston-in-Wharfedale w Woodhead 48-53; V of Kildwick 53-74; RD of S Craven 73-74; Bowland from 79; Hon Can of Bradf from 73; V of Gisburn Dio Bradf from 74. *Gisburn Vicarage, Clitheroe, Lancs, BB7 4HR.* (Gisburn 214)

SELF, David Christopher. b 41. Univ of Tor BSc 62, MA 64. K Coll Lon and Warm BD and AKC 68. **d** 69 Bp Partridge for Heref **p** 70 Heref. C of Tupsley 69-73; Chap Univ of Durham 73-78; Team V of Southn (City Centre) Dio Win from 78. *St Matthew's Vicarage, Kings Park Road, Southampton, SO1 2AT.*

SELF, David William. b 33. St Jo Coll Auckld. **d** 70 **p** 71 Wel. Hon C of Manaia Dio Wel from 71. *16 Tauhuri Street, Manaia, NZ.*

SELL, Harold Claude. Ripon Hall Ox 45. **d** 45 **p** 46 Nor. C of Gt Yarmouth (in c of St Luke) 45-48; CF 48-54; Hon CF from 54; R of Humber 54-57; PC of Stoke Prior 54-57; Seq of Docklow 54-57; V of Fownhope w Fawley 57-70; Brockhampton 57-70; Weobley w Sarnesfield 70-81; C-in-c of Norton Canon 74-81. *43 Avondale Road, Gorleston-on-Sea, Gt Yarmouth, Norfolk.*

SELL, John. b 1897. Edin Th Coll 28. **d** 31 **p** 32 Brech. C of St Mary Magd Dundee (in c of All SS) 31-35; P-in-c of St Martin Miss Dundee 35-42; R of St Marg Leven 42-50; V of Crosthwaite Kendal 50-62; C-in-c of Crook 50-51; PC of Cartmel Fell 51-62; R of Burnmoor 62-67; Perm to Offic Dio Dur from 68. *42 Newcastle Road, Chester-le-Street, Co Durham.*

SELL, John Lewis. b 10. Univ Coll Dur LTh 37, BA 40. New Coll Ox BA (3rd cl Th) 43, MA 47. St Bonif Coll Warm 30. **d** 35 **p** 36 Blackb. C of St Mary Nelson 35-37; Perm to Offic Dio Heref 37-39; C of All SS Heref 39-41; Leonard Stanley 41-43; P-in-c of Painswick 43-44; Min Can and Sacr of Glouc Cathl 44-50; R of Coln St Denys w Coln Rogers 50-75; RD of Northleach 60-67; Surr 65-75; V of Sandhurst 75-80. *79 Calton Road, Tuffley, Glos, GL1 5DT.* (Glos 416906)

SELL, Noel Lightfoot. b 15. St Cath Coll Cam 3rd cl Mod Lang Trip pt i 37, BA (3rd cl Archaeol and Anthrop Trip pt i) 38, MA 44. **d** 41 **p** 42 Chelmsf. C of West Ham 41-43; Ch Ch Radlett 43-46; Chap of Shenley Hosp St Alb 46-51; R of Hotham 51-54; Sec SCM in Schs NE area 51-54; V of St Pet Abbeydale Sheff 54-64; Kingston St Mary 64-77; V of Broomfield 64-77. *The Bell House, Bushy Cross Lane, Rushton, Taunton, Somt, TA3 5JT.*

SELLARS, Charles Harold. b 18. Univ of Leeds BA (2nd cl Hist) 40. Coll of Resurr Mirfield 37. **d** 42 **p** 44 Linc. C of Clee w Cleethorpes 42-46; Chap De Aston Gr Sch Market Rasen 46-47; Chap and Tutor, Barnard Castle Sch Dur

47-49; Chap RAF 49-52; Chap Solihull Sch 52-56; CF 56-61; Chap at Qu Sch Rheindahlen 61-70; V of Hampton 70-78; R of Nuthurst Dio Chich from 78. *Nuthurst Rectory, Horsham, Sussex.* (Lower Beeding 279)

SELLER, James Stoddart. b 16. St Jo Coll Dur LTh 45. TD 64. Tyndale Hall Bris. **d** 44 **p** 45 Ely. C of St Andr L Cam 44-47; St Geo Mart w H Trin Holborn Lon 47-48; Whitby 48-50; V of St Hilda Ravenscar w Stainton Dale 51-53; Sledmere 53-60; C-in-c of Huttons Ambo w Cowlam 57-60; R of Londesborough Dio York from 60; Nunburnolme Dio York from 60; Burnby Dio York from 60; P-in-c of Shiptonthorpe w Hayton Dio York from 78. *Londesborough Rectory, York.* (Market Weighton 3251)

SELLER, Russell Desmond. b 38. **d** 78 Bp Stanage for Johann **p** 79 Johann (NSM). C of Randfontein Dio Johann from 78. *12 Buffel Street, Greenhills, Randfontein, S Africa 1760.*

SELLERS, Warren John. b 43. Sarum Th Coll 65. **d** 68 **p** 69 Guildf. C of H Trin w St Mary Guildf 68-72; Epping 73-76; Asst Master Easebourne Par Sch and C of Pulborough Dio Chich from 76. *110 Glebelands, Pulborough, W Sussex, RH20 2JL.* (Pulborough 3732)

SELLGREN, Eric Alfred. b 33. K Coll Lon and Warm AKC 61. **d** 62 Warrington for Liv **p** 63 Liv. C of Ditton 62-66; V of Hindley Green 66-72; Lay Tr Officer Dio Liv 70-73; Tr Officer Charismatic Min 73-78; V of St Paul Southport 72-80; Warden of Barnabas Fellowship Whatcombe Ho, Blandford Forum from 80. *Whatcombe House, Winterborne Whitechurch, Blandford Forum, Dorset, DT11 0PB.*

SELLIX, Martin Gordon. b 45. Ridley Hall Cam 74. **d** 76 **p** 77 Roch. C of Crofton 76-80; R of Rayne Dio Chelmsf and Industr Chap Braintree and Bocking from 80. *19 Shalford Road, Rayne, Braintree, Essex.*

SELLORS, John. b 1886. Keble Coll Ox BA (3rd cl Th) 14, MA 18. St Aug Coll Cant 08. Cudd Coll 15. **d** 16 **p** 17 Ox. C of St Luke Maidenhead 16-17; TCF 17-19; R of St John Capetn 20-26; V of White Colne 26-29; Shepley 29-34; Bruntcliffe 34-42; Mossley 42-52; PC of Swallowcliffe w Ansty 52-56. *99 Pear Tree Lane, Bexhill-on-Sea, Sussex.* (Cooden 2719)

SELLORS, Michael Harry. b 36. K Coll Lon and Warm 60. **d** 61 **p** 62 Lon. C of Willesden 61-64; Aldershot 64-67; V of Hale Surrey Dio Guildf from 67. *Hale Vicarage, Farnham, Surrey, GU9 0NX.* (Farnham 716469)

SELLS, Charles Hastings. Hur Coll. **d** 64 **p** 65 Bran. R of Carberry and of McGregor 64-66; Boissevain 66-71; I of Russell 71-73; Fort Qu'App Dio Qu'App from 73. *Box 667, Fort Qu'Appelle, Sask, Canada.* (332-5201)

SELLS, Graeme Arthur. b 39. Ridley Coll Melb 59. **d** 78 Bp Grant for Melb **p** 79 Melb. C of St John Blackburn 78-81; St Alfred N Blackb Dio Melb from 81. *19 Davison Street, Mitcham, Vic, Australia 3132.*

SELLWOOD, William John. McGill Univ Montr Dioc Th Coll. **d** 55 **p** 56 Montr. I of Clarenceville 55-61; P-in-c of Lacolle 59-61; R of St Aid Montr 61-67; Rawdon Dio Montr from 67. *PO Box 263, Rawdon, PQ, Canada.* (514-834 2234)

SELMAN, Cyril Allen. b 25. Wycl Hall Ox 64. **d** and **p** 65 Ox. [f Methodist Min] C of Thame 65-69; V of Beedon Dio Ox from 69; R of Peasemore Dio Ox from 69. *Beedon Vicarage, Newbury, Berks, RG16 8SW.* (East Ilsley 244)

SELMAN, Michael Richard. b 47. Univ of Sussex BA 68. Univ of Bris MA 70. Coll of Resurr Mirfield 71. **d** 73 Chich **p** 74 Lewes for Chich. C of Hove 73-74; Horfield 74-78; C-in-c of Landkey 78-79; Team V of Barnstaple Dio Ex from 79. *Vicarage, Landkey, Barnstaple, Devon.* (Swimbridge 677)

SELMES, Brian. b 48. Univ of Nottm BTh 74. Linc Th Coll 70. **d** 74 Warrington for Liv **p** 75 Liv. C of Padgate 74-77; Sydenham 77-80; Chap Darlington Hosps from 80. *56 West Crescent, Darlington, Co Durham.*

SELTZER, Jacob Adam. b 1900. **d** 66 Bp Wilkinson for Niag. On leave; C of St Mark Orangeville Dio Niag from 76. *258 Broadway Street, Orangeville, Ont, Canada, L9W 1K7.*

SELVARATNAM, Anton John Candiah. Univ of Lon BA 47. Gen Th Sem NY STB 55, MDiv 72. Bp's Coll Calc 39. **d** 42 **p** 43 Colom. C of Ch Ch Jaffna 42-43; Chap St Jo Coll Chundikuli 43-45; C of St Paul Kandy 45-56; St Paul Colom 46-47; Milagiriya 47-48; Chap St John Coll Jaffna 45-50; C of Ch Ch Galle Face 50-57; Tutor Chr Coll Kotte 50-61; C of Ch Ch Cathl Colom 56-58; Actg Chap Univ of Ceylon 58-60; P-in-c of Kelani Valley 60-61; I of Mt Lavinia 61-65; Warden St Thos Coll Mt Lavinia 65-69; Exam Chap to Bp of Colom 65-75; I of ch Ch Cathl Colom 69-71; St Jo Bapt Jaffna 71-76; Hon C of All SS W Samoa 76; R of Frenchville Frenchville Rockptn 77-80; Marysville Dio Wang from 80. *Rectory, Buxton Road, Marysville, Vic, Australia 3779.*

SELVEY, John Brian. b 33. Univ of Dur BA 54. Cudd Coll 56. **d** 58 **p** 59 Blackb. C of Lanc Priory 58-61; St Mary Virg Cathl Blackb 61-65; Cathl Chap Blackb 64-65; V of Foulridge 65-69; V of Walton le Dale 69-82; Cleveleys Dio Blackb from 82; Commiss Bloemf from 79. *Cleveleys Vicarage, Blackpool, Lancs, FY5 2BD.* (Cleveleys 852153)

SELVINI, John Claude Gaston. b 46. St Steph Ho Ox 72. **d** 75 Repton for Derby **p** 76 Derby. C of St Luke Derby 75-78; St Osw of Worc Bordesley 78-80; Shrewsbury Dio Lich from 80. *All Saints Vicarage, Severn Bank, Shrewsbury.* (0743-63046)

SELWOOD, Ven Francis Neville. Selw Coll Dun 62. **d** 62 **p** 63 Dun. C of Roslyn 62-64; V of Balclutha 64-70; NE Valley 70-75; Mornington Dio Dun from 75; Archd of Dun from 75; VG from 75. *32 Whitby Street, Mornington, Dunedin, NZ.* (36-091)

SELWOOD, Robin. b 37. ALCD 61. **d** 61 **p** 62 Southw. C of Lenton 61-63; Norbury Chesh 63-66; V of Newton Flowery Field 66-75; Kelsall Dio Ches from 75. *St Philip's Vicarage, Chester Road, Kelsall, Tarporley, Chesh.*

SELWYN, David Gordon. b 38. Clare Coll Cam 1st cl Th Trip pt i 60, BA (1st cl Th Trip pt ii) 62, MA 66. New Coll Ox MA (by incorp) 66. Ripon Hall Ox 62. **d** 64 **p** 65 Sheff. Stephenson Fell Univ of Sheff and C of Ecclesall 64-65; Asst Chap New Coll Ox 65-68; Lect St D Univ Coll Lamp from 68. *19 Penbryn, Lampeter, Dyfed.* (Lampeter 422748)

SEMAHIMBO, Andrea. Hegongo Th Coll 43. **d** 44 **p** 48 Zanz. P Dio Zanz T 44-72. *PO Box 80, Muheza, Tanzania.*

SEMAKULA, Livingstone Ssalongo. b 46. **d** 77 Nam. d Dio Nam. *Kirema Church of Uganda, c/o Kalasa Church of Uganda, PO Box 156, Bombo, Uganda.*

SEMAKULA, Canon Seminoni. Bp Tucker Coll. **d** 49 **p** 50 Ugan. P Dio Ugan 49-60; Dio W Bugan from 60; Can of W Bugan from 70. *Church of Uganda, Misanvu, PO Box 261, Mpigi, Uganda.*

SEMAKULA, Stanley. Bp Tucker Coll Mukono, 57. **d** 57 **p** 58 Ugan. P Dio Ugan 58-60; Dio W Bugan from 60. *Madudu, PO Box 73, Mubende, Uganda.*

SEMAYIRA, Tite. **d** 70 **p** 71 Bur. P Dio Bur 70-75; Dio Buye from 75. *BP 58 Ngozi, Burundi.*

SEMBONI, Peter. b 34. St Cypr Coll Rondo 62. **d** 64 **p** 66 Zanz T. P Dio Dar-S. *Box 30170, Kibaha, Dar-es-Salaam, Tanzania.*

SEMBWANA, Isaac Kibwembwele. b 40. St Mark's Coll Dar-S. **d** 80 Dar-S. d Dio Dar-S. *PO Box 25017, Dar es Salaam, Tanzania.*

SEMHANDO, Harold. **d** 76 **p** 77 Zanz T (APM). P Dio Zanz T. *PO Muheza, Tanga Region, Tanzania.*

SEMPALA, Baker. Bp Tucker Coll Mukono 54. **d** 56 Ugan. d Dio Ugan 56-60; Dio W Bugan from 60. *Lakayi, Uganda.*

SEMPAR, Yafesi. St Aug Coll Cant. **d** 56 Ugan **p** 58 Bp Balya for Ugan. P Dio Ugan 56-61; Dio Nam from 61. *Box 14123, Kampala, Uganda.*

SEMPER, Cecil Michael. Late Organ Scho of St D Coll Lamp BA 51. Late Exhib of Fitzw Ho Cam BA 53, MA 57. St Mich Coll Llan 53. **d** 54 **p** 55 St A. C of Hawarden 54-60; R of Montgomery (w Forden from 66) 60-76; RD of Pool 65-76; V of Gresford Dio St A from 76. *Gresford Vicarage, Wrexham, Clwyd.* (Gresford 2236)

SEMPER, Canon Colin Douglas. b 38. Keble Coll Ox BA 62. Westcott Ho Cam 61. **d** 63 **p** 64 Guildf. C of H Trin City and Dio Guildf 63-66; Hon C from 75; Sec ACCM and Perm to Offic Dio Guildf 67-69; Producer Relig Dept BBC 69-75; Overseas Relig Broadcasting Org BBC 75-79; Hd of Relig Programmes BBC Radio from 79; Hon Can of Guildf Cathl from 80. *BBC, Broadcasting House, W1A 1AA.*

SEMPIGA, Simon. Stanley-Smith Th Coll Gahini 65. **d** 67 **p** 68 Rwa. P Dio Rwa 67-75; Dio Kiga from 75. *BP 61 Kigali, Rwanda.*

SEMPLE, Alan Joseph. BP's Univ Lennox BA 59. Hur Coll BTh 62. **d** and **p** 61 Ont. C of Brockville Trin 61-62; R of Ameliasburg 62-65; Merrickville 65-67. *184 Whitney Avenue, Sidney River, NS, Canada.*

SEMPLE, Patrick William. b 45. Univ of Sussex BA 66. Univ of Bris Dipl Th 70. Sarum Wells Th Coll 68. **d** 72 Lon **p** 73 Kens for Lon. C of Ch Ch Lanc Gate Lon 72-75; P-in-c of Woodbastwick (w Panxworth to 77) 75-79; Industr Chap Dio Nor 75-79; V of St Barn Kens Dio Lon from 79. *23 Addison Road, W14 8LH.* (01-602 2615)

SEMPLE, Studdert Patrick. b 39. TCD BA 66, Div Test 67. **d** 67 **p** 68 Down. C of St Jo Evang Orangefield 67-70; I of Stradbally Dio Leigh from 71. *Rectory, Stradbally, Portlaoise, Co Laois, Irish Republic.*

SEMPUNGU, Mulindwa Samwiri. b 50. **d** 77 Nam. d Dio Nam. *c/o Namirembe Cathedral, PO Box 14297, Kampala, Uganda.*

SEMTAMU, Richard. b 35. St Cypr Th Coll Ngali 62. **d** 64 Bp Lukindo for Zanz T **p** 66 Bp Russell for Zanz T. P Dio Zanz T. *Box 65, Pangani, Tanzania.*

SEMUHUTU, Nikodemu. **d** 66 **p** 67 Bur. P Dio Bur. *Gifunzo, DS 12, Bujumbura, Burundi.*

SEMURUNGA, Enos. Warner Mem Th Coll 61. **d** 63

Rwanda B. d Dio Rwanda B 63-66; Dio Bur from 66. *Matana, Burundi.*

SEMWENDA, Canon Alfeji. St Paul's Dioc Div Sch Limuru. **d** and **p** 53 Centr Tang. P Dio Centr Tang 53-65; Dio Moro from 65; Hon Can of Moro from 65; Dioc Regr Moro from 65. *PO Turiani, Morogoro, Tanzania.*

SENADA, Jamal. b 52. Ho of Epiph Kuch 71. **d** 75 **p** 76 Kuch. P Dio Kuch. *St Boniface Church, Mamut, Sarawak, Malaysia.*

SENAR, Canon Howard. b 15. St Chad's Coll Dur BA (2nd Cl Hist) 37, Dipl Th 38, MA 40. BD (Lon) 58. **d** 38 **p** 39 Liv. C of Wigan 38-46; V of Haigh w Aspull 46-56; Offley 56-58; C-in-c of Lilley 56-58; Surr from 52; V of Offley w Lilley 58-62; RD of Hitchin 60-62; R of L Gaddesden Dio St Alb from 62; Dir of Ordinands Dio St Alb 63-76; Exam Chap to Bp of St Alb 66-78; Hon Can of St Alb from 68. *Little Gaddesden Rectory, Berkhamsted, Herts, HP4 1PA.* (Little Gaddesden 2274)

SENDALL, George Edward. Univ of BC BA and BD 47. **d** and **p** 60 Olympia. [f in Amer Ch] I of N Delta w Colebrook 63-78. *6512 Knight Drive, Delta, BC, Canada.*

SENDEGEYA, Fareth. b 52. Yeotmal Sem India BTh 79. **d** and **p** 79 Vic Nyan. P Dio Vic Nyan. *PO Box 278, Mwanza, Tanzania.*

SENDIWALA, Ven Esau Kiwanuka. Bp Tucker Coll Mukono. **d** 51 **p** 54 Ugan. P Dio Ugan 51-60; Dio W Bugan from 60; Archd of W Bugan from 68. *Church of Uganda, Kasaka, PO Kanoni-Mpigi, Uganda.*

SENGENDO-ZAKE, Very Rev Justin Gustavus. b 15. Amer Univ in Cairo BA 48. Univ of Chicago AM 51. Virginia Th Sem 67. **d** 69 **p** 70 Nam. Dioc Sec Nam 70-74; Archd of Nam 73-74; Dean and Can of St Paul's Cathl Kamp from 74. *Mamirembe Diocesan Offices, Box 14297, Kampala, Uganda.*

SENGI, Semu. Bp Tucker Coll Mukono 56, **d** 56 Bp Balya for Ugan **p** 58 Ugan. P Dio Ugan 56-60; Dio Ruw from 60; Can of Ruw 72-73; Archd of Bumandu 73-75. *Box 1108, Bundibugyo, Fort Portal, Uganda.*

✠ **SENGULANE, Right Rev Dinis Salomao.** Sarum Wells Th Coll 71. **d** and **p** 74 Lebom. P Dio Lebom 74-76; Cons Bp Suffr of Lebom in St Cypr Ch Maputo 25 March 76 by Bp of Lebom and Bps of Pret and Swaz; Apptd Ld Bp of Lebom 76. *CP 120, Maputo, Mozambique.* (73-4364)

SENGULANE, Jossias. **d** 78 **p** 80 Lebom (APM). P Dio Lebom. *CP 57, Maputo, Mozambique.*

SENG'UNDA, Dan Alfeji. **d** 39 **p** 41 Centr Tang. P Dio Centr Tang 39-65; Dio Moro 65-74. *Box 18, Kimamba, Tanzania.*

SENIOR, David Geoffrey Christopher Murray. Magd Coll Ox BA 40, MA 42. K Coll Cam and Westcott Ho Cam 40. **d** 41 **p** 42 S'wark. C of St Antholin Nunhead 41-44; Eltham 44-48; V Cho and Chamberlain of York Minster and C of St Mich-le-Belfrey York 48-55; V of Helmsley w Sproxton Carlton and Rievaulx Dio York from 55; V of Pockley w Eastmoors 55-77; RD of Helmsley from 75. *Helmsley Vicarage, York, YO6 5AQ.* (Helmsley 70236)

SENIOR, James Robertson. **d** 79 **p** 81 Gippsld. P Dio Gippsld. *8 Sandy Mount Avenue, Inverloch, Vic, Australia 3995.*

SENIOR, John Peter. b 23. BSc (2nd cl Eng) (Lon) 48. Edin Th Coll 63. **d** 65 Blackb **p** 66 Lanc for Blackb. C of Marton 65-68; Heysham 68-71; V of St Mich AA Blackpool 71-79; Heddon-on-the-Wall Dio Newc T from 79. *St Andrew's Vicarage, Heddon-on-the-Wall, Newcastle-upon-Tyne, NE15 0DT.* (Wylam 3142)

SENIOR, Kenneth Norman. b 23. Univ of Leeds BSc 45. Ridley Hall Cam 55. **d** 57 **p** 58 Cant. Asst Chap St Lawr Coll Ramsgate 57-60; Chap Dean Close Sch Cheltm 60-62; Prince Rupert Sch Wilhelmshaven 62-67; Chap and Master City of Lon Sch 67-71; Hon C of New Malden w Coombe 67-71; Hd Master of Elmbridge Sch Cranleigh 71-73; Perm to Offic Dio Guildf 74; V of White Waltham w Shottesbrooke Dio Ox from 74. *Vicarage, White Waltham, Maidenhead, Berks, SL6 3JD.* (Littlewick Green 2000)

SENOGA, Jellico Eccles. **d** 77 Nam. d Dio Nam. *Bunnamwaya Church of Uganda, PO Box 31250, Kampala, Uganda.*

SENOGA, Ven Yowasi. Bp Tucker Coll Mukono 55. **d** 56 Ugan **p** 58 Bp Balya for Ugan. P Dio Ugan 56-61; Dio Nam from 61; Archd of Mukono from 74. *Box 39, Mukono, Uganda.*

SENOKOANE, Thakadu Enoch. b 36. **d** 80 **p** 81 Bloemf. d Dio Bloemf. *House 481, Motsethabong, Welkom 9463, S Africa.*

SENTAMA, Stephano. Stanley-Smith Th Coll Gahini 65. **d** 67 **p** 68 Rwa. P Dio Rwa 67-75; Dio Kiga from 75. *BP 135, Butare, Rwanda.*

SENTAMU, John Mugabi. **d** 79 S'wark for Ugan. Chap HM Remand Home Ham from 79. *99 Barnfield Avenue, Kingston, KT2 5EG.*

SENTANCE, Cecil Leslie. b 23. BSc (Econ) 1st cl Lon 58. SOC 64. **d** 67 Lon **p** 68 Willesden for Lon. C of Finchley 67-73; V of St Pet-le-Poer Muswell Hill 73-75; Feltham Dio Lon from 75. *Vicarage, Cardinal Road, Feltham, TW13 5AL.* (01-890 6681)

SENTSHO, Lucas Jacob Rammui. St Pet Coll Alice 66. **d** 68 Bp Carter for Johann **p** 69 Johann. C of Mohlakeng 68-70; St Cypr Sharpeville 71-72; R of Wolmaransstad Dio Johann from 72. *Box 38, Wolmaransstad, Transvaal, S Africa.*

SENYAGWA, Enoch Ayubu. St Phil Th Coll Kongwa, 62. **d** 65 Bp Madinda for Centr Tang **p** 65 Centr Tang. P Dio Centr Tang. *TTC, Mawapwa, Tanzania.*

SENYAGWA, Nathaneli Lemunga. St Phil Coll Kongwa. **d** 60 Bp Wiggins for Centr Tang **p** 61 Centr Tang. P Dio Centr Tang. *Sagala, Tanzania, E Africa.*

SENYAGWA, Yunus. St Phil Coll Kongwa 66. **d** 68 Bp Madinda for Centr Tang **p** 68 Centr Tang. P Dio Centr Tang. *Zoissa, Box 27, Kongwa, Tanzania.*

✠ **SENYONJO, Right Rev Christopher Disani.** Buwalasi Th Coll 61. **d** 63 **p** 64 Nam. P Dio Nam 63-74; Cons Ld Bp of W Bugan in St Paul's Cathl Nam 20 Jan 74 by Abp of Ugan and Abp Scott (Primate of Canada); Bps of N Ugan, Bunyoro, Busoga, Nam, M & W Nile, Mbale, Bukedi, Ruw, Ank and Soroti. *Box 242, Masaka, Uganda.* (Masaka 2178)

SENYONYI, Mesusera. b 36. **d** 77 Nam. d Dio Nam. *c/o Namirembe Cathedral, PO Box 14297, Kampala, Uganda.*

SENZIA, Simon. b 37. **d** and **p** 75 Vic Nyan. P Dio Vic Nyan. *PO Box 144, Shinyanga, Tanzania.*

SEOKA, Johannes. b 48. St Bede Coll Umtata 72. **d** 74 **p** 76 Natal. C of St Andr Newc 74-77; Umlazi 77-78; R of St Pet Greytown 78-80; Senaoane Dio Johann from 80. *Box 120, Tchiawelo 1818, S Africa.*

SEOUL, Lord Bishop of. *See* Lee, Right Rev Paul.

✠ **SEPEKU, Right Rev John.** Hegongo Th Coll 36. **d** 38 **p** 40 Zanz. C Dio Zanz 38-55; P-in-c 55-60; Can of Zanz 57-60; Archd of Magila 60-63; VG of Zanz 63-65; Cons Asst Bp of Zanz in St Nich Ch Dar-es-Salaam 24 March 63 by Abp of E Afr; Bps of Centr Tang; and Zanz; Asst Bp of Centr Tang (Omari); and Bp Thorne; Apptd Bp of Dar-S 65; Dean of Dar-S from 45; Elected Abp and Metrop of Prov of Tanzania 70; res 78. *PO Box 25016, Ilala, Dar-es-Salaam, Tanzania.* (051-29560)

SEPHTON, Ven Arthur. b 1894. Ch Ch Ox BA 20, MA 24. Cudd Coll 20. **d** 21 Ox for Goulb **p** 22 Goulb. C of St Mary Redcliffe Bris 21-22 and 23-24; St Sav Cathl Goulb NSW 22-23; St Luke Woodside Croydon 24-25; St John Hove 25-28; Ch Ch Harrogate 28-29; V of Holmfirth 29-33; Kirkburton 33-43; R of Skipton-in-Craven 43-64; Hon Can of Bradf Cathl 44-72; RD of Skipton 43-56; Surr 43-64; Proc Conv Bradf 45-56; Archd of Craven 56-72; Archd (Emer) from 72; Exam Chap to Bp of Bradf 56-72. *4 Abbeyfield, Woodlands Drive, Gargrave Road, Skipton, N Yorks.* (Skipton 4848)

SERCOMBE, Theodore Friend. b 27. Ch Coll Cam BA 47, MA 51. Univ of Ox Dipl Th 70. Wycl Hall Ox 68. **d** 70 **p** 71 Ex. C of St Andr Plymouth 70-73; New Plymouth 73-76; V of Inglewood 76-80; Waihi Dio Waik from 80. *Vicarage, Rata Street, Waihi, NZ.* (Waihi 8864)

SEREMBA, David. Bp Tucker Coll Mukono 57. **d** 58 **p** 60 Ugan. P Dio Ugan 58-60; Dio Nam from 60. *PO Box 18508, Kajjansi, Uganda.*

SERFONTEIN, Henry Reginald. b 46. St Pet Coll Alice Dipl Th 76. **d** and **p** 76 Port Eliz. C of St Jas Cradock Dio Port Eliz from 76. *PO Box 427, Cradock 5880, CP, S Africa.*

SERGEANT, Canon Claud Edmund. Wells Th Coll 28. **d** 29 **p** 30 Truro. C of Falmouth 29-31; St Aldhelm Branksome 31-33; P-in-c of Liuli 34-43; Songea 43-52; Dioc Treas SW Tang 52-62; Can of SW Tang 59-65; Hon Can 66-70; P-in-c of Linda 64-65; C of H Cross Cathl Liuli 71-80; Hon Can of Ruv from 71. *c/o PO Liuli, Tanzania.*

SERGEANT, Ernest Noel Copland. b 11. Linc Coll Ox BA (2nd cl Th) 32, 1st cl Mod Lang (Russian) 34, MA 36. Nubar Pasha Armenian Schol 50-53. **d** 34 **p** 35 Lon. C of H Trin Northwood 34-37; R of St Martin and All SS Ox 38-43; V of Twyford w Poundon and Charndon 43-46; CMS Miss Dio Jer 46-49; V of Gt and L Tew 49-57; Perm to Offic Dio Ox 57-60; Dio B & W 57-76; Chap Millfield Sch 57-76. *7 South Street, Walton, Nr Street, Somt.*

SERGEANT, John Middlemore. b 13. Wadh Coll Ox BA (2nd cl Mod Hist) 34, Dipl Th 35, MA 38. Wycl Hall, Ox 34. **d** 36 **p** 37 Chelmsf. C of W Ham 36-39; St Pet Battersea 39-43; V of St Sav Battersea Pk 43-51; Keelby 51-54; R of Gt Coates 54-59; PC of Aylesby 52-59; V of E Peckham 59-67; R of Fringford w Hethe Newton Purcell and Shelswell 68-78; C-in-c of Hardwick w Tusmore 68-78; Cottisford 68-78; L to

Offic Dio Ox from 78. *37 Rectory Crescent, Middle Barton, Oxford, OX5 4BP.* (Steeple Aston 40622)

SERGEL, Clement Stuart. Clare Coll Cam BA 35, MA 52. Wycl Hall Ox 35. **d** 37 **p** 38 Guildf. C of St Mary Oatlands 37-39; Ch Ch Crouch End 39-41; St John Bulawayo 41-42; Salisbury Cathl 42-47; R of Umtali 47-52; Prec of St Geo Cathl Capetn 52-55; R of Bulawayo Cathl and Hon Can of Matab 55-62; Dean 61-62; R of Rosebank w Bryanston 62-67; Bellville 67-71; St Thos Rondebosch 71-75; Can of Capetn 72-79; R of Athlone 74-75; Green Point 75-79; C of Somerset W Dio Capetn from 79. *Box 905, Somerset West, CP, S Africa.*

SERGEL, Canon Paul Clement Scott. St Jo Coll Auckld. **d** 32 **p** 33 Waik. Chap of Southwell Sch 32-41; C of St Pet Cathl Hamilton 32-40; Dom Chap to Bp of Waik 40-41; CF (NZ) 41-45; Amer Silver Cross 46; Chap Southwell Sch Hamilton 46-75; Hon Can of Waik from 61; Perm to Offic Dio Waik from 76. *River Road, Horsham Downs, RDI, Hamilton, NZ.* (294-850)

SERJEANT, Frederick James. b 28. K Coll Lon And Warm AKC 53. **d** 54 **p** 55 Chelmsf. C of St Marg w St Columba Leytonstone 54-57; Parkstone 57-59; V of St Luke Reigate 59-65; St Pet Battersea 65-71; C-in-c of St Paul Battersea 67-71; V of W Mersea 71-73; C-in-c of E Mersea 71-73; R of W Mersea w E Mersea 73-75. *Address temp unknown.*

SERJEANT, John Frederick. b 33. K Coll Lon and Warm 55. **d** 56 **p** 57 Ches. C of Over w Winsford Chap 56-59; C-in-c of St Luke's Conv Distr Brinnington 59-63; V 63-69; Gatley 69-79; Team V of Halesworth Dio St E from 79. *Vicarage, Beccles Road, Holton St Peter, Halesworth, Suff, IP19 8NG.* (Halesworth 2984)

SERJEANTSON, Eric William. b 09. St Jo Coll Ox BA 32, MA 40. St Bonif Coll Warm 30. **d** 32 **p** 33 Heref. C of Ch Stretton 32-35; SPG Chap Ranchi 35-36; Dhanbad 36-37; Kamdara 37-38; Jamshedpur 38; Adra 38-40; Chap to Bp of Chota N 35-38; C of Holmer w Huntingdon 40-42; CF (EC) 42-46, V of Cleeton w Silvington 46-50; Longborough w Seizencote and Condicote 50-54; Leebotwood w Longnor 54-74; C-in-c of Stapleton 72-74; Dorrington 72-74; L to Offic Dio Heref from 74. *6 Chartwell Close, Church Stretton, Salop, SY6 6ES.*

SERJEANTSON, John Cecil Mylles. b 36. Bp's Univ Lennox BA 63. McGill Univ Montr BD 66. Montr Dioc Th Coll. **d** 66 **p** 67 Montr. C of St Matthias Westmount Montr 66-68; R of Huntingdon w Ormstown Montr 68-72; C of Gt w L Driffield 72-76; V of Bilton-in-Holderness 76-79; R of Brome Dio Montr from 79. *Box 17, Brome, Quebec, Canada, JOE 1KO.* (514-243 6096)

SEROCOLD, Ralph Edward Pearce. b 16. Trin Coll Cam BA 38, MA 45. Bps' Coll Cheshunt 57. **d** 58 **p** 59 St E. C of St Jas Cathl Bury St Edm 58-61; V of Long Sutton 61-69; Chap Ld Wandsworth Coll Win 61-69; RD of Odiham 65-69; R of N Stoneham w Bassett 69-75; V of Hamble Dio Win from 75. *Hamble Vicarage, Southampton.* (Southn 452148)

SERONGOANE, Theophilus Molifi. St Pet Coll Rosettenville 49. **d** 49 **p** 50 Johann. P Dio Johann 49-66; Dio St John's 75-79; L to Offic Dio Johann from 80. *A19 Cape Stands, Thokoza 1421, S Africa.*

SERTIN, John Francis. b 22. Late Exhib of Fitzw Ho Cam 3rd cl Hist Trip pt i 49, BA (2nd cl Hist Trip pt ii) 50, MA 54. Tyndale Hall, Bris. **d** 45 **p** 46 Roch. C of Ch Ch Sidcup 45-47; Fitzw Ho Cam 47-50; Perm to Offic Dios Ely and Pet 47-50; Min of Conv Distr of St Barn Cray 50-59; PC of St Cuthb Chitts Hill Wood Green 59-62; Sec Ch S 62-67; R of St Geo Mart Qu Square w H Trin and St Bart Gray's Inn Road Holborn 67-80; Donyatt w Horton, Broadway and Ashill Dio B & W from 80; C-in-c of Ch Ch Woburn Square 67-77. *Broadway Rectory, Ilminster, Somt.* (Ilminster 2559)

SERTIN, Peter Frank. b 27. Fitzw Ho Cam BA 50, MA 55. Ridley Hall Cam 50. **d** 52 **p** 53 Roch. C of Ch Ch Beckenham 52-55; Chap K Edw Sch Witley 55-62; V of St Paul Woking 62-69; Chorley Wood 69-80; Chap of St Mich Paris Dio Gibr in Eur from 80. *5 rue d'Aguesseau, 75008 Paris, France.* (742 70 88)

SERUBOYO, Amoni. b 31. Bp Tucker Coll Mukono 71. **d** 73 Ruw. d Dio Ruw. *Box 1104, Bundibugyo, Bwamba, Uganda.*

SERUCACA, Zefaniya. Ibuye Coll 57. **d** 58 **p** 60 Bp Shalita for Ugan. P Dio Ugan 58-61; Dio Ankole-K 61-67; Dio Kig from 67. *Kabindi, PO Box 1049, Kisoro, Uganda.*

SERUWAGI, Christopher. Bp Tucker Coll Mukono. **d** 52 **p** 53 Ugan. P Dio Ugan 52-60; Dio Nam from 60. *Ndeeba, PO Box 18014, Kayunga, Uganda.*

SERVANTE, Kenneth Edward. b 29. K Coll Lon and Warm AKC 55. **d** 56 **p** 57 Derby. C of St Phil Chaddesden 56-58; St Thos Brampton 58-61; Whitfield 61-63; V of St Paul Derby 63-70; Elmton w Creswell 70-81; P-in-c of South Darley and of Elton and of Winster Dio Derby from 81. *Winster Vicarage, Matlock, Derbys.*

SERVICE, Donald Thomas McKinlay. b 26. Trin Coll Cam BA 51, MA 53. Ridley Hall, Cam 51. **d** 53 Lon **p** 54 Kens for Lon. C of St John W Ealing 53-57; Farnborough 57-61; Asst Chap Kingham Hill Sch and Perm to Offic Dio Ox 62-79; Chap 77-79; V of Mayfield Dio Lich from 79. *Mayfield Vicarage, Nr Ashbourne, Derbys, DE6 2JR.* (0335-42855)

SERWADDA, Isiraeri. b 19. **d** 74 **p** 75 Nam. P Dio Nam. *Kasubi, Box 14128, Kampala, Uganda.*

SERWANGA, Daniel. St Paul's Coll Lim. **d** 70 **p** 70 Nai. P Dio Nai. *Box 53012, Nairobi, Kenya.*

SESSANGA, Efulayimu. b 26. Bp Tucker Coll Mukono 68. **d** 70 W Bugan. d Dio W Bugan. *Box 21514, Mitalo Malia, Uganda.*

SESSFORD, Alan. b 34. Bps Coll Cheshunt 65. **d** 66 Southn for Win **p** 67 Win. C of Highcliffe w Hinton Admiral 66-69; Minehead 70; Chandler's Ford 70-73; V of Burton w Sopley Dio Win from 73. *Burton Vicarage, Christchurch, Dorset.* (Christchurch 484471)

✠ **SESSFORD, Right Rev George Minshull.** b 28. Univ of St Andr MA 51. Linc Th Coll. **d** 53 **p** 54 Glas. C of St Mary's Cathl Glas 53-58; Chap Angl Studs Univ of Glas 55-58; P-in-c of H Name Cumbernauld 58-66; Lect Jordanhill Coll of Educn Glas 58-62; R of St John Forres 66-70; Cons Ld Bp of Moray, Ross and Caithness 8 Dec 70 in St Andr Cathl Inverness by Bp of Glas (Primus); Bps of Aber; Arg Is; Brech; Edin; and St Andr; Bps Howe; Russell; and Abp of Utrecht. *Spynie House, 96 Fairfield Road, Inverness.* (Inverness 31059)

SETCHELL, Alan William. Moore Th Coll Syd 31. ACT ThL 35. **d** 34 Bp Kirkby for Syd **p** 36 Syd. C of St Mary w Rooty Hill 34; Dulwich Hill 34-36; St John Parramatta 36-37; C-in-c of Harris Park w Rose Hill 37-40; R of Guildford w Merrylands 40-41; Chap on the Hawkesbury River 41-47; R of Ashbury 47-54; St Pet Neutral Bay 54-64; Hornsby 64-76; L to Offic Dio Syd from 76. *10 Pearl Parade, Pearl Beach, NSW, Australia 2256.* (043-41 9202)

SETH, Andre. b 42. St Paul's Coll Ambat 70. **d** 73 **p** 74 Tam. P Dio Tam 73-79; Dio Toa from 79. *Vohitsara, Toamasina, Malagasy Republic.*

SETLHABI, Samuel. St Bede's Coll Umtata 56. **d** 58 **p** 59 Kimb K. P Dio Kimb K 58-77. *Box 412, Hartswater, CP, S Africa.*

SETON, Christopher Cariston. b 50. Macquarie Univ BA 72. Trin Coll Melb 75. **d** 78 Melb **p** 79 Wang for Melb. C of Shepparton 78-79; I of Benalla 79-80; St Geo Malvern Dio Melb from 80. *1/296 Glenferrie Road, Malvern, Vic, Australia 3144.*

SETPAW, d 36 **p** 38 Rang. P Dio Rang 36-56. *c/o St Paul's Diocesan School, Myitkyina, Burma.*

SETTEE, Jack. d 74 Sask. C-in-c of St Mich AA Molonosa w Weyakwin Dio Sask from 74. *La Ronge, Sask, Canada.*

SETTER, Ven James Ernest. Univ of Manit BA 58. St Jo Coll Winnipeg LTh 62. **d** 62 **p** 63 Bp Anderson for Rupld. C of St Luke Winnipeg 62-65; V of Morden 65-67; I of Manitou 67; C of Epsom 67-69; R of St Mark Winnipeg 69-71; on leave 71-74; Actg Chap St Jo Coll and Univ of Manit 74-76; I of All SS Winnipeg Dio Rupld from 76; Archd of Winnipeg from 80. *175 Colony Street, Winnipeg, Manit, Canada.*

SEVARU, Emmanuel Baro. Newton Coll Dogura. **d** 74 Bp Ambo for Papua **p** 75 Papua. P Dio Papua. *Anglican Church, Wanigela, Papua New Guinea.*

SEWAGABA, Yowasi. Bp Tucker Coll Mukono. **d** 33 **p** 34 Ugan. P Dio Ugan; RD of Bulemezi 43-48. *Mukono, Uganda.*

SEWAGUDE, Yosamu Bosa. Bp Tucker Coll Mukono. **d** 50 **p** 51 Ugan. P Dio Ugan 50-60; Dio W Bugan from 60. *Anglican Church, Mayungwe, PO Mpenja, Uganda.*

SEWANNYANA, William Epaphras. Bp Tucker Coll Mukono 66. **d** 68 **p** 70 W Bugan. P Dio W Bugan. *Bulamu, PO Box 44, Mityana, Uganda.*

SEWARD, Francis Ian. b 36. Chich Th Coll 60. **d** 63 **p** 64 B & W. C of St Mich AA Yeovil 63-67; Chap RAF 67-69; R of Chedzoy 69-78; C-in-c of H Trin Taunton Dio B & W from 78. *Holy Trinity Vicarage, Holway Avenue, Taunton, Somt.* (Taunton 87890)

SEWELL, Edward James. d and **p** 65 Niag. C of Erin 65-70; R of St Mark Hamilton 70-76; Hosp Chap St Catharines Ont from 76; V of St Geo Homer Dio Niag from 78. *Unit 704, 5 Carriage Road, St Catharines, Ont, Canada.* (416-684 8941)

SEWELL, Godfrey John. St D Coll Lamp BA 59. **d** 60 **p** 61 Mon. C of Llangattock-juxta-Caerleon 60-63; H Trin Cathl Port of Spain 63-68; R of Toco 68-69; La Brea Dio Trin from 72. *St Augustine's Rectory, La Brea, Trinidad, W Indies.*

SEWELL, John. b 10. MBE 46. Tyndale Hall Bris 60. **d** 61 **p** 62 Chelmsf. C of Dagenham 61-63; L Burstead 63-69; Chap

New Lodge Billericay 64-69; R of Yelvertoft w Clay Coton and Lilbourne 69-74. *Flat 6, Alstone Lodge, 23 Queens Road, Cheltenham, GL50 2LX.*

SEWELL, Richard Michael Blackwood. b 50. Moore Th Coll Syd 76. **d** 77 Bp Dain for Syd **p** 77 Syd. C of St Mark Darling Point 77-79; Nowra Dio Syd from 79. *12 Tarawal Street, Bomaderry NSW, Australia 2540.*

SEWELL, Canon William. Univ of W Ont BA 49. Hur Th Coll LTh 50, DD 61. **d** 50 **p** 51 Hur. C of Glencoe w Newbury and Wardsville 50-51; R 51-53; St Jo Evang Edmon 53-61; Dean and R of St Paul's Pro-Cathl Regina 61-69; R of Ascen Hamilton Dio Niag from 69; Hon Can of Niag from 73. *Church of Ascension, John Street and Forest Avenue, Hamilton, Ont., Canada.* (416-520 6004)

SEWO, Canon Emanuel Oluwayemi. Im Coll Ibad 58. **d** 60 **p** 61 Lagos. P Dio Lagos; Hon Can of Lagos from 77. *St Andrew's Vicarage, Okepopo, Lagos, Nigeria.*

SEXBY, Canon Arthur James. St Paul's Coll Grahmstn LTh 36. **d** 39 S Rhod for Johann **p** 40 Johann. C of St Bonif Germiston 39-41; Benoni 41-45; R of Klerksdorp 45-47; Bezuidenhout Valley Johann 52-80; Hon Can of Johann from 80. *PO Kenton-on-Sea 6191, S Africa.*

SEXTON, Geoffrey Holroyd. St Jo Coll Morpeth 58. **d** 58 **p** 60 Adel. C of Mt Gambier 58-60; Henley Beach 60-62; P-in-c of Morphettville 62-66; H Trin Cathl Suva 67-68, Archd of Polyn 67-69; Suva 69-72; Dom Chap to Bp of Polyn 67-69; VG of Polyn 69-72; Exam Chap to Bp of Polyn 69-72; V of Samabula Par Distr 69-72; State Sec ABM Vic 72-76; C of St Paul's Cathl Melb 73-76; R of Corryong 76-79; Kilmore Dio Wang from 79. *Rectory, Union Street, Kilmore, Vic, Australia 3601.*

SEXTON, Henry Alfred. d 64 Bp Snell for Tor. C of St Giles Scarborough Dio Tor from 64. *49 Wye Valley Road, Scarborough, Ont, Canada.*

SEXTON, Martin Andrew. Univ of Leeds, BA (2nd cl Engl) 55. ACT ThL (2nd cl) 65. St Jo Coll Morpeth. **d** 64 Newc for New Guinea **p** 65 Brisb for New Guinea. C of Morpeth 64-65; Roma 65-66; P-in-c of Aiome Miss 67-68; R of Lae New Guinea 68-69; Chap Guildf Gr Sch Dio Perth 70-75; R of Mt Lawley Dio Perth from 75. *731 Beaufort Street, Mount Lawley, W Australia 6050.* (71 1654)

SEXTON, Michael Bowers. b 28. SS Coll Cam BA (2nd Cl Hist Trip) 52, MA 56. Wells Th Coll 52. **d** 54 **p** 55 Man. C of St Luke Miles Platting Man 54-57; Ch Ch Bradf Man 57-58; C-in-c of St Chad Conv Distr Limeside Oldham 58-62; R of Filby w Thrigby and Mautby 62-72; C-in-c of Runham 67-72; C-in-c of Stokesby w Herringby 68-72; R of Hethersett w Canteloff Dio Nor from 72; V of Ketteringham Dio Nor from 73; RD of Humbleyard from 81. *Hethersett Rectory, Norwich, NR9 3AR.* (Norwich 810273)

SEYCHELLES, Lord Bishop of. *See* Chang-Him, Right Rev French Kitchener.

SEYCHELLES, Dean of. *See* Celestin, Very Rev Louis Dickens.

SEYMOUR, David. b 43. Kelham Th Coll 60. **d** 68 Ox **p** 69 Francis for Ox. V of Cowley Ox 68-73; Team V of Lynton 73-77; Min of Princes Park Conv Distr Chatham 77-79; V of Rosherville Dio Roch from 79. *Rosherville Vicarage, Gravesend, Kent, DA11 9NH.* (Gravesend 4430)

SEYMOUR, David Raymond Russell. b 56. Keble Coll Ox BA (Th) 79. St Steph Ho Ox 79. **d** 81 Reading for Ox. C of St Mich Tilehurst Dio Ox from 81. *2 Church Cottages, New Lane Hill, Tilehurst, Reading, RG3 4JW.*

SEYMOUR, John Charles. b 30. Oak Hill Th Coll 55. **d** 57 **p** 58 Lon. C of St Andr w St Thos Islington 57-60; St Geo Worthing 60-63; V of Thornton w Bagworth 63-70; Kirby Muxloe Dio Leic 70-80; Team R from 80. *6 Station Road, Kirby Muxloe, Leicester, LE9 9EJ.* (Leic 386822)

SEYMOUR, Keith. b 28. Oak Hill Th Coll 48. **d** 51 **p** 52 Lich. C of St Julian Shrewsbury 51-53; Chap RN 53-61; C of Chapeltown 61-62; V of W Thurrock w Purfleet 62-65; Bilston 65-69; R of Thorndon w Rishangles and Chap Kerrison Approved Sch 69-74; P-in-c of Bedingfield 74; V of Bedgrove, Aylesbury 74-81. *c/o Bedgrove Vicarage, Camborne Avenue, Aylesbury, Bucks, HP21 7UE.* (Aylesbury 22214)

SEYMOUR, Kenneth Norman. Ridley Coll Melb ThL 48. **d** and **p** 49 Bal. C of St Jo Horsham 49-50; P-in-c of Otway Forest 50-54; St Mary N Melb 54-56; V of Rupanyup 57-59; Min of Emerald 59-65; I of Prahran 65-73; Mentone Dio Melb from 73. *88 Como Parade, Mentone, Vic, Australia 3194.* (03-93 2057)

SEYMOUR, Ven Laurence Esmond. St Jo Coll Morpeth. **d** 54 **p** 55 Armid. C of W Tamworth 54-56; P-in-c of Delungra 56-59; Emmaville 59-61; V of Tenterfield 61-66; Boggabri 66-74; Kootingal Dio Armid from 74; Can of Armid 74-77; Archd of New Engl from 77. *Vicarage, Kootingal, NSW, Australia 2352.* (67-3361)

SEYMOUR, Ralph. b 05. Cudd Coll 73. **d** 73 Bedford for St Alb **p** 73 St Alb. Hon C of Tring Dio St Alb 73-80; Perm to Offic Dio St Alb from 80. *44 Grove Park, Tring, Herts, HP23 5JW.* (Tring 2223)

SEYMOUR, Samuel Maxwell. Univ of Melb BA 62. **d** 61 **p** 62 Melb. C of Glen Iris 61-67; Perm to Offic Dio Melb 68-74; Dio Brisb from 74. *Somerville House, Vulture Street, S Brisbane, Australia 4101.*

SEYMOUR, Sidney Maxwell. d 61 **p** 62 Perth. C of St Mary S Perth 61-64; Wembley-Floreat Pk 64-66; R of Rockingham w Safety Bay 66-71; E Fremantle w Palmyra 72-76; Northam Dio Perth from 76. *11 Wellington Street, Northam, W Australia 6401.* (096-22 1016)

SEYMOUR, Warwick James. Univ of Witwatersrand BA 53. St Paul's Coll Grahmstn LTh 54. **d** 54 **p** 55 Johann. C of Krugersdorp 54-56; Rosettenville 57-58; R of Blyvooruitzicht (w Carletonville from 65) 59-71; St Jo Bapt Fort Beaufort w Seymour and Winterberg 71-74; H Trin City and Dio Port Eliz from 74. *152 Cape Road, Port Elizabeth, CP, S Africa.* (041-338617)

SEZIBERA, Salatiel. b 48. Butare Th Coll 71. **d** 74 Rwa. d Dio Rwa. *E.N.I. Shyogwe, BP 27, Gitarama, Rwanda.*

SHAAMENA, Jeremiah. b 34. **d** 71 Damar **p** 72 Bp Wade for Capetn for Damar. P Dio Damar 71-80; Dio Namibia from 80. *c/o St Mary's, Odibo, PO Oshikango, Ovamboland, SW Africa.* (Oshikango 5)

SHACKELL, Kenneth Norman. b 26. SOC. **d** 69 **p** 70 S'wark. C of Greenwich Dio S'wark from 69. *48 Crooms Hill, SE10 8HD.* (01-858 3458)

SHACKLETON, Alan. b 31. Univ of Sheff BA 53. Wells Th Coll 54. **d** 56 **p** 57 Man. C of St Chad Ladybarn 56-58; Lect St Pet Bolton 58-61; V of Middleton Junction 61-70; St Luke Heywood Dio Man from 70. *Vicarage, York Street, Heywood, Lancs, OL10 4NN.* (Heywood 60182)

SHACKLETON, Arnold. b 08. BA (Lon) 31. Chich Th Coll 75. **d** 75 **p** 76 Roch. C of Annunc Chislehurst Dio Roch from 75. *54 High Street, Chislehurst, Kent.* (01-467 6759)

SHACKLETON, Bernard. b 35. St Chad's Coll Dur BA (3rd cl Math) 58, Dipl Th 60. BD (Lon) 65. **d** 60 Tonbridge for Cant **p** 61 Roch. C of Annunc Chislehurst 60-67; V of Higham w Merston Dio Roch from 67. *Higham Vicarage, Rochester, Kent.* (Medway 77360)

SHACKLETON, Ian Roderick. b 40. St Francis Coll Brisb ACT ThL 71. **d** and **p** 72 Brisb. C of St Jas Toowoomba 72-74; P-in-c of Millmerran 74-75; R 75-77; C of Maryborough 78-79; Birch-in-Rusholme 79-80; P-in-c of St Wilfrid & St Anne Newton Heath Dio Man from 80. *St Wilfrid's Rectory, Oldham Road, Newton Heath, Manchester 10.* (061-205 1235)

SHACKLOCK, David Peter Riley. B 36. CCC Cam BA 60, MA 64. Ridley Hall Cam 60. **d** 62 **p** 63 Leic. C of St Chris Conv Distr Leic 62-66; CF 66-71; R of Northiam 71-80; V of St Mary Hammersmith Road, Fulham Dio Lon from 80. *2 Edith Road, W14.* (01-602 1996)

SHAFEE, Kenneth Harold. b 30. Ex/Truro Min Tr Scheme. **d** 81 Ex (NSM). C of Littleham w Exmouth Dio Ex from 81. *40 Capel Lane, Exmouth, Devon, EX8 2QZ.*

SHAI, Ernest Koena. St Pet Coll Rosettenville 56. **d** 58 **p** 59 Grahmstn. P Dio Grahmstn; Can of Grahmstn 70-81. *Box 76, Sterkspruit, CP, S Africa.*

SHAIL, Canon Harold Manford. d and **p** 53 Moos. I of Schumacher 53-60; Dom Chap to Bp of Moos from 54; Dioc Sec Dio Moos 54-61; Dioc Treas 55-61; Hon Can of Moos from 60; I of Kapuskasing Dio Moos from 60. *3 Stewart Avenue, Kapuskasing, Ont., Canada.* (705-335 2921)

SHAIL, William Frederick. b 15. Kelham Th Coll. **d** 41 **p** 42 S'wark. C of St Paul w St Mark Deptford 41-44; Lewisham 44-47; Christchurch 47-52; R of N Stoneham w Bassett 52-68; V of St Alb Bournemouth 68-78; Burley Ville Dio Win from 78. *Burley Vicarage, Ringwood, Hants.* (Burley 2303)

SHAKESPEARE, Daniel. b 19. E Angl Min Tr Course 79. **d** 81 Nor (NSM). C of Hethersett Dio Nor from 81. *23 Central Crescent, Hethersett, Norwich, NR9 3EP.*

SHALITA, Ven Ernest Munyambazi. b 36. Bp Tucker Coll Mukono 65. **d** 65 Ankole-K **p** 67 Kig. d Dio Ankole-K 65-67; P Dio Kig from 67; Dioc Regr and Sec Dio Kig from 73; Can and Archd of Kig from 75. *PO Box 3, Kabale, Kigezi, Uganda.*

✠ **SHALITA, Right Rev Kosiya. d** 33 **p** 34 Ugan. P Dio Ugan 34-57; Cons Asst Bp of Ugan at Mbarara 5 May 57 by Bp of Ugan; Bp on the U Nile; and Bp of Momb; and Bps Balya; Lutaya; Brizier; Tomusange; and Omari; Trld to Ankole-K 61; to Ank 67; res 70. *Box 14, Mbarara, Uganda.*

SHALLARD, John Sidney Dillon. b 39. St Jo Coll Auckld 79. **d** 80 Bp Bennett for Wai. C of Rotorua Dio Wai from 80. *115 Otanga Road, Rotorua, NZ.*

SHALLCROSS, John Robin. b 37. Univ of Cant BA 60, MA 62. Univ of Chicago MA 68. St Jo Coll Auckld 76. **d** 76 **p** 77 Ch Ch. C of Cashmere Hills 76-78; Merivale 78; V of

Temuka Dio Ch Ch from 78. *St Peter's Vicarage, 32 Allnatt Street, Temuka, NZ.* (Temuka 104)

SHALLCROSS, Martin Anthony. b 37. FRICS 70. Sarum Wells Th Coll 75. **d** 78 **p** 79 (NSM). Hon C of Landford w Plaitford 78-81; Bramshaw 78-81; Tisbury Dio Sarum from 81. *Wallmead Farm, Tisbury, Salisbury, SP3 6RB.*

SHALLCROSS, Mary-Lloyd. b 41. Univ of Chicago MA 70. **d** 78 **p** 79 Ch Ch. C of Temuka Dio Ch Ch from 78. *St Peter's Vicarage, Dyson Street, Temuka, NZ.* (104)

SHAMASH, Albert Saul. b 11. Bp's Coll Calc Dipl Th 42. **d** 41 Calc **p** 43 Bom. Asst Chap Dio Calc 41-43; Ch Ch Byculla 43-45; C of St Mary Rawtenstall 45-46; Ch Ch Harpurhey 46-49; Org Sec CMJE Distr 49-51; L to Offic Dio St E 49-51; Perm to Offic Dio Nor 50-51; C of Normanton by Derby (in C of St Steph Sinfin) 51-52; C-in-c of Wormhill w Peak Dale Dio Derby 52-53; PC (w Peak Forest from 57) 53-68; V 68-71; V of Brackenfield w Wessington 71-76. *The Coppice, Broadway, Swanwick, Derby, DE5 1AJ.* (Leabrooks 5547)

SHAMMAS, Ven Adeeb. Wycl Hall Ox 30. **d** 34 **p** 35 Egypt. CMS P Dio Egypt 34-37; I of Old Cairo 37-71; Bp's Rep in Egyptian Angl Ch 49-71; Archd in Egypt 53-71; Archd (Emer) from 71; C of Old Cairo Dio Egypt from 71; Hon Can of All SS Cathl Cairo from 71. *PO Box 1427, Cairo, Egypt.*

✠ **SHAND, Right Rev David Hubert Warner.** Univ of Queensld BA (2nd cl Phil) 52. St Francis Th Coll Brisb ACT ThL (2nd cl) 48. **d** 48 **p** 49 Brisb. C of St Andr Lutwyche 48-52; V of St Mary Moorooka Brisb 52-53; R of Inglewood 53-55; Nambour 55-60; Org Sec Home Miss Fund Dio Brisb 60-63; R of St Paul Ipswich 63-66; Ch Ch S Yarra 66-69; St Andr Brighton Melb 69-73; Cons Ld Bp of St Arn in St Paul's Cathl Melb 30 Nov 73 by Abp of Melb (primate); Bps of Bal, Gippsld, River and Wang; Coadj Bps of Melb and Brisb; and others: res 76; Bp Coadj of Melb from 78; V of St Steph Mt Waverley 76-78. *5 Bates Street, East Malvern, Vic, Australia 3145.* (211 8760)

SHANGE, Azariah. St Pet Coll Rosettenville, LTh. **d** 43 **p** 44 Zulu. P Dio Zulu 43-76. *PB 122, Nkandhla, Zululand.*

SHANKAWNG, Zau Gawng. **d** 55 **p** 56 Rang. P Dio Rang. *c/o BCMS, Mohnyin, Burma.*

SHANKS, Robert Andrew Gulval. b 54. Ball Coll Ox BA 75. Caius Coll Cam BA (Th) 79. Westcott Ho Cam 77. **d** 80 Ripon **p** 81 Knaresborough for Ripon. C of Potternewtown Dio Ripon from 80. *Flat 1, 33 Cowper Street, Leeds 7.* (Leeds 628967)

SHANLEY, Beverley Joan. b 39. Angl Women's Tr Coll Tor STh 59. **d** 71 Tor **p** 76 Niag. C-in-c of Lowville w Nassagaweya 76 R 76-80; Dom Chap to Bp Suffr of Niag from 80; R of St Bart Hamilton Dio Niag from 80. *435 Mohawk Road West, Hamilton, Ont, Canada.* (416-389 1942)

SHAN LONE, John. H Cross Coll Rang. **d** 60 Rang. d Dio Rang. *St Michael's Church, Hmawbi, Burma.*

SHANNON, Brian James. b 35. St Chad's Coll Dur BA 59. Univ of Dur Dipl Th 61. **d** 61 Kens for Lon **p** 62 Lon. C of St Jo Evang Palmers Green 61-65; St Mary Virg Kenton (in c of H Spirit) 65-70; V of St Andr Roxbourne Harrow 70-81; Thorpe-le-Soken Dio Chelmsf from 81. *Vicarage, Thorpe-le-Soken, Essex, CO16 0ED.* (Clacton-on-Sea 861234)

SHANNON, Chan Francis Thomas. b 16. Trin Coll Dub BA 39. **d** 39 **p** 40 Oss. C of Rathdowney 39-41; I of Mothel (w Bilbo from 50) 41-51; RD of Fiddown 50-52; I of Aghade w Ardoyne 51-61; Carnew and Kilrush Dio Ferns from 61; RD of Wexford from 68; Preb of Ferns Cathl 71-80; Treas 80-81; Chan from 81. *Rectory, Carnew, Co Wicklow, Irish Republic.*

SHANNON, Canon John. b 05. TD 52. St Paul's Coll Burgh 33. **d** 35 **p** 36 Dur. C of W Pelton 35-45; CF (TA) 38-45; Hon CF 45; CF (TA) from 48; PC of W Pelton 45-50; R of Winlaton 50-58; Chap of Gibside Chap 50-58; Surr 50-78; Master of Greatham Hosp 58-78; V of Greatham 58-78; Hon Can of Dur 59-79; Can (Emer) from 79. *South Cottage, 2 West Row, Greatham, Hartlepool, Cleve, TS25 2HS.*

SHANNON, Malcolm James Douglas. b 49. TCD BA 72, Div Test 75, MA 75. Sch of Div Dub 72. **d** 75 **p** 76 Derry. C of Clooney 75-78; R of Kilcolman Dio Ardf from 78. *Kilcolman Rectory, Miltown, Co Kerry, Irish Republic.* (Miltown 2)

SHANNON, Robert. Trin Coll Tor. **d** 43 **p** 44 Ott. I of Metcalfe 43-49; Ellwood 49-52; I of Lanark w Balderson 53-61; Chap RCN 61-66; Col Belcher Hosp Calg 66-68; L to Offic Dio Calg 68-73 and from 75; on leave 73-75. *804, 1209-6th Street SW, Calgary, Alta, Canada.* (262-1970)

SHANNON, Trevor Haslam. b 33. Selw Coll Cam BA 57, MA 61. BD (Lon) 69. Westcott Ho Cam. **d** 59 **p** 60 Man. C of Moss Side 59-62; V of St Jas Woolfold Bury 62-66; Chap Forest Sch Snaresbrook 66-72; Asst Master from 72. *Forest School, Snaresbrook, E17.*

SHANNON, Canon William Patrick. b 09. Univ of Glas MA 31. Edin Th Coll 31. ARCO 34. **d** 33 **p** 34 Edin. Chap of St Mary's Cathl Edin 33-39; Succr 33-38; Prec 38-39; R of Haddington 39-46; P-in-c of Tranent Miss Edin 39-46; R of H Trin Elgin 46-55; Can of St Andr Cathl Inverness 53-55; R and Prov of St Andr Cathl Aber 55-65; Hon Can of Connecticut (USA) 56-71; V of Kington w Huntington 65-75; RD of Kington and Weobley 72-75; Preb of Heref Cathl 74-75; Hon Can of St Andr's Cathl Aber from 76; Perm to Offic Dio Glouc from 76. *1 Abbey Cottage, Tewkesbury, Glos, GL20 5SR.* (Tewkesbury 295330)

SHANTZ, Gerald Samuel. Wilfrid Laurier Univ BA 65. Univ of W Ont MA 67. Ch Ch Ox BA 70. **d** 76 Bp Bothwell for Niag **p** 81 Bp Mitchell for Niag. C of St Jo Elora Dio Niag from 76. *Apt 24, 122 David Street, Milton, Ont, Canada, N0B 1S0.* (519-846 5940)

SHAPIRO, Ivor. b 53. St Bede's Coll Umtata BTh 80. **d** 78 **p** Kimb K. P Dio Kimb K. *Box 369, Kimberley, S Africa.*

SHAPLAND, David Edward. b 26. St Cath Coll Cam BA (2nd cl Hist Trip pt i) 51, MA 56. Cudd Coll 51. **d** 53 Dover for Cant **p** 54 Cant. C of Cranbrook 53-55; Chap St Cath Coll Cam and L to Offic Dio Ely 55-61; Select Pr Univ of Cam 59; R of Fittleworth 62-65; L to Offic Dio Cant and Perm to Offic Dio Chich 65-69; Warden Bede House Staplehurst 65-69; L to Offic Dio Swan B 70-78. *Address temp unknown.*

SHAPRE TANG, Mohnyin Div Sch. **d** 61 **p** 63 Rang. P Dio Rang 61-71. *Lawa Naya Village, Kamaing PO, Myitkyina District, Rangoon, Burma.*

SHARE, David James. b 30. Sarum Th Coll 56. **d** 58 **p** 59 Ex. C of Whipton 58-63; C-in-c of St Andr Eccles Distr Tiverton 63-69; V 69-79; RD of Tiverton 67-74; P-in-c of St Thos City and Dio Ex 79-80; Team R (w Em) from 80. *St Thomas's Vicarage, Exeter, Devon.* (Ex 55219)

SHARIFIAN, Nusratullah. U Th Coll Bangalore 63. **d** 65 **p** 66 Iran. C of St Andr Kerman Iran 65-70; St Luke Isfahan Dio Iran from 70. *St Andrew's Church, Kerman, Iran.* (0341-3800)

SHARLAND, Alan John. St Paul's Coll Grahmstn LTh 53. **d** 53 **p** 54 Johann. C of Germiston 53-56; Benoni 56-58; R of Standerton 58-62; Malvern 62-69; C of Orange Grove 70-71; P-in-c of St Mark Krugersdorp 71; W Rand 71-76. *7 Carnation Road, Primrose, Transvaal, S Africa.*

SHARLAND, Canon Charles Thomas. b 08. Wycl Hall Ox 45. **d** 45 Ox for Bp in Egypt and Sudan **p** 46 Sudan. Miss CMS Loka 45-50; Lainya Dio Sudan 50-53; V of St Bede Toxt Pk Dio Liv 53-61; R of H Trin Heigham 61-75; Hon Can of Nor from 73. *101 Trafford Road, Norwich, NR1 2QT.*

SHARLAND, William James. St Paul's Miss Coll Burgh, 28. Univ of Dur LTh 35. **d** 32 **p** 33 Glouc. C of All SS Cheltm 32-34; St Mary Magdalene Chiswick 34-35; St Leon Hythe 35-39; R of St Mary-in-the-Marsh 39-42; Actg C of St Luke Woodside 42-43; V of Hernhill 43-49; Twyning 49-75. *Three Ways, Churchend, Twyning, Tewkesbury, Glos.*

SHARMAN, Harry David Howard. b 40. Ridley Coll Melb ThDip 80. **d** 81 Tas. C of Kingston & Channel Dio Tas from 81. *125 Beach Road, Kingston, Tasmania 7150.*

SHARMAN, Herbert Leslie John. b 27. St Aid Coll 60. **d** 62 Carl **p** 63 Penrith for Carl. [f CA] C of Stanwix 62-66; Brandon w Santon Downham Dio St E from 66. *18 Princes Close, Brandon, Thetford, Norf.* (Thetford 811163)

SHARMAN, Hilary John. b 32. Univ of Leeds BA 58. Coll of Resurr Mirfield 58. **d** 60 **p** 61 St Alb. C of St Andr Hertford 60-64; Harpenden 64-72; V of High Cross and of Thundridge Dio St Alb from 72. *7 Ducketts Wood, Thundridge, Ware, Herts.* (Ware 5561)

SHARMAN, Stephen Clifford. b 51. Brandon Univ Manit BA 72. Univ of Vic BC MA 74. Univ of tor MA 74. St Jo Coll Winnipeg MDiv 78. **d** 78 **p** 79 Rupld. C of Ch Ch Selkirk 78-81; R of Woodlands Area Dio Rupld from 81. *Woodlands, Manit, R0C 3H0, Canada.*

SHARP, Alfred James Frederick. b 30. Oak Hill Th Coll 62. **d** 64 **p** 65 Lon. C of St Sav w St Paul Holloway 64-68; C-in-c of Leverton Dio Linc 68-82; R from 82. *Leverton Rectory, Boston, Lincs.* (Boston 870550)

SHARP, Arthur Thomas. **d** 63 **p** 64 Sask. I of Macdowall 63-66; Meadow Lake 66-68; Mortlach 68-70; Pipestone 70-74; Oyen 74-77. *Box 408, Bentley, Alta, Canada.* (748-4025)

SHARP, Bernard. b 03. AKC (1st cl) and Knowling Pri 30. **d** 30 **p** 31 Sheff. C of St Cuthb Sheff 30-34; V of Gleadless 34-71. *80 Ecclesall Road South, Sheffield, S11 9PG.*

SHARP, Cyril Harry. b 07. MBE 63. St Aug Coll Cant 38. **d** 39 Dorch for Ox for Col Bp **p** 40 Brisb. C of St Aug Hamilton Brisb 40; St Andr S Brisb 40-41; Chap AMF 41-42; AIF 42-46; C of St Botolph (in c of St Steph) Colchester 46-48; V of Bures 49-55; Chap Miss to Seamen and I of St Thos à Becket Hamburg 55-64; V of St Thos Ap Hanwell 64-75. *20 Chrisdory Road, Portslade, Brighton, BN4 2WQ.*

SHARP, David Malcolm. b 33. Late Scho of Hertf Coll Ox 2nd cl Cl Mods 54, BA (2nd cl Lit Hum) 56, MA 59. Cudd Coll 56. **d** 58 **p** 59 Bris. C of St Mary Redcliffe w Temple Bris

58-65; V of Henleaze 65-75; St Pet Mancroft City and Dio Nor from 75; M Gen Syn from 80. *37 Unthank Road, Norwich, NR2 2PB.* (Nor 27816)

SHARP, Donald Douglas McLeod. **d** 64 **p** 65 Fred. C of Upham 64-65; I of Restigouche 65-68; R of clementsport 69-73; Seaforth Dio NS from 73. *Millside Drive, RR1, Porters Lake, NS, Canada.* (827-2582)

SHARP, John. b 54. K Coll Lon BA (Hist) 74, MTh 76. Cudd Coll Ox 74. **d** 77 Kens for Lon **p** 78 Lon. C of St Mich AA Ladbroke Grove Kens 77-80; Chap and Fell Qu Coll Cam from 80. *Queen's College, Cambridge, CB3 9ET.* (0223 65511)

SHARP, Louis. **d** 66 **p** 68 Pret. C of Potgietersrus Dio Pret from 66. *PO Box 182, Potgietersrus, Transvaal, S Africa.* (1083)

SHARP, Michael William Hamilton. Ch Ch Ox (2nd cl Cl Mods 2nd cl Lit Hum 1st cl Th) BA 49, MA 52. Qu Th Coll Birm 50. **d** 52 **p** 53 Lon. C of St Jo Bapt Greenhill Harrow 52-55; Chap Ripon Hall Ox 55-58; V of Brockley Hill 58-64; R of Kidbrooke 64-72; Exam Chap to Bp of S'wark 64-81; R of Streatham 72-81. *Tunstall Old School, Tunstall, Woodbridge, Suff.*

SHARP, Canon Nevill Maurice Granville. b 02. Selw Coll Cam BA 24, MA 29. Westcott Ho Cam 24. **d** 25 **p** 26 Roch. C of St Geo Bickley 25-29; All SS Maidstone 29-35; V of Birchington w Acol 35-55; RD of Thanet 52-55; Hon Can Cant 54-79; Can (Emer) from 79; V of Ashford 55-72; RD of E Charing 55-72; L to Offic Dio Cant from 73. *7 Orchard Drive, Wye, Ashford, Kent.* (Wye 812496)

SHARP, Ralph Norman. 1896. Qu Coll Cam BA 21, MA 24. Ridley Hall, Cam 21. **d** 22 **p** 23 S'wark. C of Ch Ch Gipsy Hill 22-24; CMS Miss at Yazd 24-37; Shiraz 37-62; Exam Chap to Bp of Iran 35-65; Lect Shiraz Univ 59-67. *7 Hungerford Road, Chippenham, Wilts.* (Chippenham 2659)

SHARP, Canon Reuben Thomas George. b 27. ALCD 57. **d** 57 **p** 58 Bradf. C of Pudsey 57-60; Bradf Dioc Youth Chap 60-63; V of Cononley w Bradley 60-63; Youth Officer Dio Wakef 63-68; V of Dewsbury Dio Wakef from 68; RD of Dewsbury from 68; Surr from 68; Hon Can of Wakef from 76. *25 Oxford Road, Dewsbury, Yorks, WF13 4LN.* (Dewsbury 465491)

SHARP, Richard Lloyd. b 16. St Edm Hall Ox BA (2nd cl Engl Lit) 38, MA 42. Sarum Th Coll 38. **d** 40 **p** 41 Sarum. C of H Trin Weymouth 40-44; PC of Portland St John 44-49; Hon Chap to Bp of Sarum 46-49; V of Wootton Bassett 49-55; PC of Broad Town 51-55; V of St Mark Sarum 55-64; H Trin Weymouth 64-75; Can and Preb of Sarum Cathl from 68; RD of Weymouth 71-74; Archd of Dorset 75-82. *269 Verity Crescent, Canford Heath, Poole, Dorset, BH17 7UB.*

SHARP, Robert. b 36. FLCM 58. St Aid Coll 64. **d** 67 **p** 68 Bradf. C of Shipley 67-70; C-in-c of St Barn Conv Distr Thwaites Brow Keighley 70-74; V of Thwaites Brow 74-77; Ford Dio Heref from 77; P-in-c of Alberbury w Cardeston Dio Heref 77-78; V from 78. *Ford Vicarage, Shrewsbury, Shropshire.* (Shrewsbury 850254)

SHARP, Ronald Arthur. Wycl Coll Tor. **d** 56 Suffr Bp for Tor **p** 57 Tor. I of St Matt Oshawa Dio Tor from 56. *522 King Street East, Oshawa, Ont., Canada.* (416-725 9841)

SHARP, Thomas Crawford. b 15. St Chad's Coll Regina. **d** 49 **p** 51 Qu'App. V of Ituna 49-51; Kisbey 51-53; C-in-c of Milngavie 53-55; C of Redruth 55-58; R of St Enoder 58-74. *154 Killyvarder Way, St Austell, Cornw.*

SHARPE, Alan Brian. b 39. Lich Th Coll 64. **d** 67 **p** 68 Cant. C of St Luke Woodside Croydon 67-70; Portsea (in c of St Faith) 70-75; V of Sheerness Dio Cant from 75. *241 High Street, Sheerness, Kent.* (Sheerness 662589)

SHARPE, Bruce Warrington. b 41. St Steph Ho Ox 64. **d** 65 **p** 66 S'wark. C of St Pet Streatham 65-67; Castries St Lucia 67-68; L to Offic Dio Leic 69; Hon C of Catford 69-70; Youth Leader Riverside Youth Club Deptford 70-75; Youth and Commun Officer Bexley from 75; Hon C of Deptford 70-75; H Redeemer Lamorbey Dio Roch from 76; Commiss Dio Windw Is from 77. *16 Beverley Avenue, Lamorbey, Sidcup, Kent, DA15 8HE.* (01-300 0695)

SHARPE, Cecil Frederick. b 23. Edin Th Coll 52. **d** 54 **p** 55 Edin. C of Ch Ch Falkirk 54-56; King's Norton 56-58; V of Wythall 58-80. *57 Blythsford Road, Hall Green, Birmingham, B28 0UP.* (021-744-8838)

SHARPE, David Francis. b 32. Ex Coll Ox BA 56, Liddon Stud 57, MA 59. St Steph Ho Ox 57. **d** 60 **p** 61 Ripon. C of St Mary Hunslet 60-63; St Jo Evang Notting Hill Kens 63-68; V of Haggerston Dio Lon from 68; C-in-c of St Aug w St Steph Haggerston 73-78. *St Chad's Vicarage, Dunloe Street, E2 8JR.* (01-739 3878)

SHARPE, David Robert Scott. b 31. Keble Coll Ox BA 54, MA 66. Ely Th Coll 54. **d** 56 **p** 57 Lon. C of St John Bethnal Green 56-59; St Ives 59-61; V of Carnmenellis w Pencoys 61-65; Penwerris 65-70. *16 Privett Place, Gosport, Hants, PO12 3SQ.*

SHARPE, Geoffrey. Worc Ordin Coll 58. **d** 59 **p** 60 Chelmsf. C of St Thos Becontree 59-62; R of Gt Yeldham 62-68; C-in-c of Ashen 62-68; R of Ashen w Ridgewell 68-74. *Cooksferry Cottage, Poole Street, Great Yeldham, Essex.*

SHARPE, Gerard John. b 23. Westcott Ho Cam. **d** 64 Thetford for Nor **p** 65 Nor. C of St Cuthb Thetford 64-70; V of Holme (w Conington from 75) Dio Ely from 70; R of All SS Conington 70-75; Glatton Dio Ely from 73. *Holme Vicarage, Peterborough.* (Ramsey 830622)

SHARPE, Harold Dudley. b 18. Ch Coll Cam BA 40. St Andr Coll Whittlesford. **d** 41 **p** 42 Roch. C of Ch Ch Luton Kent 41-44; Keston 44-46; Chap RN 46-73; Perm to Offic Dio S'wark 73-74; Dio B & W from 75; Asst Master Brooklands Commun Home Langport from 74. *44 Kingsdon, Nr Somerton, Somt.* (Ilchester 840384)

SHARPE, John Edward. b 50. Univ of Dur BSc 72. St Jo Coll Dur Dipl Th 75. **d** 76 Barking for Chelmsf **p** 77 Chelmsf. C of Woodford Wells 76-79; St Mary Ealing Dio Lon from 79. *59 Ranelagh Road, W5 5RP.* (01-567 6454)

SHARPE, John Leslie. b 33. Open Univ BA 75. Kelham Th Coll 54. **d** 58 Woolwich for Cant **p** 59 S'wark. C of Old Charlton 58-63; P-in-c of Eiwo Distr 63-68; R of Popondetta 68-70; Archd of N Papua 68-70; C-in-c of St Pet and St Paul w All SS Southn 71-73; Team V of Southn (City Centre) 73-76; Chap Psychiatric Services Southn and SW Hants from 76. *50 Holly Grove, Fareham, Hants, PO16 7UP.* (Fareham 287903)

SHARPE, John Thomas. b 43. Ch Army Coll Tor 66. **d** 70 **p** 73 Fred. C of Westmorland 70-71; Moncton 71-74; R of Salisbury w Havelock Dio Fred from 74. *Rectory, Petitcodiac, NB, Canada.*

SHARPE, Canon Kenneth Henry. Roch Th Coll. **d** 60 U Nile **p** 61 Chich for Mbale. P Dio U Nile 60-61; Dio Mbale 61-64; Dioc Sec Mbale 61-64; Prov Treas Ugan and Rwanda B 62-69; L to Offic Dio Nam 64-69; V of the Mau 69-78; Dioc Treas and Exam Chap to Bp of Nak 72-78; Can of Nak 73-78; Hon Can from 78; Commiss Mbale 73-78; V of Coley Dio Wakef from 78. *Coley Vicarage, Hipperholme, Halifax, Yorks, HX3 7SA.* (Halifax 202292)

SHARPE, Kenneth William. b 40. St D Coll Lamp BA 61. Sarum Th Coll 61. **d** 63 St D **p** 64 Swan B for St D. C of Hubberston 63-71; Team V of Croesyceiliog in Rectorial Benef of Cwmbran 71-74; V of Dingestow w Llangovan and Pen-y-Clawdd Dio Mon from 74; Youth Chap and Children's Adv Dio Mon from 74. *Dingestow Vicarage, Monmouth, Gwent, NP5 4DY.* (Dingestow 206)

SHARPE, Kevin James. b 50. Univ of Cant NZ BSc 71. La Trobe Univ Vic Aus PhD 75. Episc Div Sch Mass MDiv 76. **d** and **p** 76 Waik. C of St Pet Cathl Hamilton 76-78; Andersons Bay 78-80; Chap Univ of Auckld from 80. *2 Takutai Street, Parnell, Auckland 1, NZ.*

SHARPE, Richard Gordon. b 48. Univ of Birm BA 69. Univ of Nottm BA (Th) 74. St Jo Coll Nottm 72. **d** 75 **p** 76 Leic. C of H Trin Hinckley 75-78; Hull Dio York from 78. *69 Adelaide Street, Hull, HU3 2EZ.* (Hull 24483)

SHARPE, Robert Nelson. Trin Coll Dub 64. **d** 65 **p** 66 Clogh. C of Enniskillen 65-67; I of Sallaghy 67-73; I of Clogher w Errigal-Portclare 73-80; Augher 73-80; Preb of Clogh Cathl 76-80; C of Bangor Abbey Ch 81. *22 Sherwood Road, Bangor, Co Down, BT19 2DJ, N Ireland.* (Bangor 54890)

SHARPE, Roger. b 35. TCD BA 60, MA 63. Qu Coll Birm 60. **d** 62 **p** 63 Dur. C of H Trin Stockton-on-Tees 62-64; Oakdale 64-68; V of Redlynch w Morgan's Vale Dio Sarum from 68. *Redlynch Vicarage, Salisbury, Wilts.* (Downton 20439)

SHARPE, Sydney Harold. b 06. Kelham Th Coll 25. **d** 31 **p** 32 Portsm. C of St Jo Bapt Rudmore Portsea 31-35; Perm to Offic Dio S'wark 35; Chap Ellesmere Coll 36-44; Min Can of Ripon Cathl 44-47; Succr 45-47; Prec 47-53; V of Boroughbridge (w Roecliffe from 57) 53-59; Surr 54-59; C of Methley 59-61; Haywards Heath 61-69; St Mary w St Geo Rumboldswyke Chich 69-72. *Flat 3, 50 Rowlands Road, Worthing, Sussex.* (Worthing 36881)

SHARPE, William Lyndsie. Univ of Tor BASc 55, MCom 58. Bp's Univ Lennox LST 63. **d** 63 Bp Snell for Tor **p** 64 Tor. C of St Jo Bapt Norway Tor 63-64; I of Campobello 64-66; R of Westfield 66-69; Chap Appleby Coll Oakville 69-75; C of St Chris Burlington 74-75; P-in-c of Nelson 76; Asst Chap Ridley Coll St Catharines Ont from 76. *42 McDonald Street, St Catharines, Ont, Canada.* (416-682 5682)

SHARPLES, Canon Alfred Cyril. b 09. Univ of Man BA 33. Linc Th Coll 33. **d** 35 **p** 36 Man. C of Rochdale 35-39; Ashton L 39-42; R of St Mark Cheetham Man 42-46; V of Tonge w Alkrington 46-51; Hope 51-76; Hon Can of Man Cathl 74-76; Can (Emer) from 76; Perm to Offic Dios Man and Ches from 77. *30 Greenbank Drive, Bollington, Macclesfield, Chesh.*

SHARPLES, David. b 41. Linc Th Coll 71. **d** 73 **p** 74 Man.

C of St Elis Reddish 73-75; Prestwich 75-78; V of St Jas Ashton L Dio Man from 78. *St James's Vicarage, Union Street, Ashton-under-Lyne, Lancs.* (061-330 2771)

SHARPLES, John Gregson. Univ of Dur BA 55. Wells Th Coll. **d** 62 **p** 63 Leic. C of Bottesford w Ashby 62-65; V of Aukborough w Whitton 65-67; C-in-c of W Halton 65-67; Lect in Div Bede Coll dur 67-72. *Address temp unknown.*

SHARPLES, John Stanley. BA (1st cl Phil) Lon 54, MA 64. Tyndale Hall Bris 33. **d** 37 **p** 38 Lon. C of St Pet U Holloway 37-39; St Paul Dorking 39-41; Dep Gov and Chap William Baker Technical Sch Goldings 41-42; R of St Phil Man 42-44; V of Hatherden w Tangley 44-52; R of Durham w Egremont 52-54; Delhi Ont 54-67; Seaforth 67-69; Clinton 69-77. *563 Ontario Street, Beamsville, Ont., Canada.*

SHARPLEY, Ven Roger Ernest Dion. b 28. Ch Ch Ox BA 52, MA 56. St Steph Ho Ox 52. **d** 54 **p** 55 Dur. C of St Columba Southwick 54-60; V of All SS Middlesbrough 60-81; C-in-c of St Hilda w St Pet Middlesbrough 64-72; RD of Middlesbrough 70-81; Can and Preb of York Minster 74-81; P-in-c of St Aid Middlesbrough 79-81; V of St Andr Holborn City and Dio Lon from 81; Archd of Hackney from 81. *5 St Andrew Street, EC4A 3AB.* (01-353 3544)

SHARR, Roger Thomas. b 44. Univ of Melb BA 69. Univ of Syd MA 73. St Mich Th Coll Crafers ACT ThL 66. **d** 68 **p** 69 Melb. C of E Malvern 68-70; St Jas Syd 70-72; Tutor Univ of Nottm 72-73; Perm to Offic Dio Ely 73-75; Chap Trin Coll Melb from 75; Perm to Offic Dio Melb 77-79; P-in-c of Burwood E Dio Melb from 79. *378 Blackburn Road, Burwood East, Vic, Australia 3151.* (232 4863)

SHARWOOD, Alexander Livingstone. Univ of Melb BA (Hons) 27, MA 29. Keble Coll Ox Dipl Th 29. Brisb Th Coll ACT ThL (1st cl) 32, ThD 55. **d** 32 **p** 33 Brisb. C of All SS Brisb 32-37; V of Taringa 37-40; Lect St Jo Coll Brisb 36-59; Lect Univ of Queensld from 39; R of St Colomb Clayfield Brisb 40-56; Exam Chap to Abp of Brisb 51-77; Can Res of Brisb 52-77; Warden of St Jo Coll Brisb 56-72; Chap S of the Sacred Advent Brisb 59-61; Warden 61-77. *46 Coolum Terrace, Coolum Beach, Queensland, Australia.* (071-46 1293)

SHARWOOD, Robert Francis. Cudd Coll Ox 72. **d** 72 **p** 73 Brisb. C of Sherwood Brisb 72-76; St Jas Syd 76-77; R of Dorrigo Dio Graft from 78. *Rectory, Dorrigo, NSW, Australia 2453.*

SHASHA, Agrippa Mputumi. St Bede's Coll Umtata 66. **d** 67 **p** 69 St John's. P Dio St John's. *St Thomas's Mission, Tabankulu 4860, Transkei, S Africa.* (Tabankulu 12)

SHAULA, Crispo Tuluwene. St Cypr Coll Ngala 73. **d** 72 **p** 74 SW Tang. P Dio SW Tang. *Box 32, Njombe, Tanzania.*

SHAURI, Stanford Abraham. b 29. St Mark's Coll Dar-S. **d** 78 Ruv **p** 80 Bp Wood for Dar-S. d Dio Ruv 78-80; P Dio Dar-S from 80. *PO Box 2537, Dar es Salaam, Tanzania.*

SHAVE, Charles Richard. b 47. Univ of Wisc (Platleville) BSc 70. Moore Th Coll Syd ThL 80. **d** 80 Armid. C of Narrabri Dio Armid from 80. *6 Mealee Street, Narrabri, NSW, Australia 2391.*

SHAW, Alan. b 24. Univ of Man BSc (2nd cl Chem) 44, MSc 48, PhD 51. Ely Th Coll 55. **d** 57 **p** 58 Liv. C of Orford 57-59; Bury 59-61; Perm to Offic Dio Liv 61-70; V of St John Beckermet 71-76; L Leigh w Nether Whitley 76-80; Latchford Dio Ches from 80; Dioc Social Responsibility Officer from 78. *Christ Church Vicarage, Wash Lane, Latchford, Warrington, WA4 1HT.* (Warrington 30846)

SHAW, Alexander Martin. b 44. AKC and Warm 67. **d** 68 **p** 69 Glas. C of St Osw King's Pk 68-70; Old St Paul Edin 70-75; Chap K Coll Cam 75-77; C of All SS Marg Str St Marylebone Lon 77-78; Prin Inst Chr Stud Lon 77-78; R of H Trin Dunoon 78-81; Succr of Ex Cathl from 81. *6a The Close, Exeter, Devon, EX1 1EZ.* (Ex 58892)

SHAW, Anthony Keeble. b 36. Ex/Truro Ordin Course. **d** 81 Ex (NSM) C of E Teignmouth Dio Ex from 81. *62 St Leonard's Road, Newton Abbot, Devon.*

SHAW, Basil Earle. b 06. Late Colquitt Exhib of BNC Ox BA (3rd cl Lit Hum) 28, Dipl Th 29, MA 32. Wells Th Coll 29. 1 30 **p** 31 Ripon. C of Leeds 30-33; Chap RN 33-37; V of Sheriff Hutton 38-40; Thorne 40-45; Dringhouses York 45-47; C of Guisborough 47-50; Beverley Minster 50-60; V of N Frodingham 60-73; Perm to Offic Dio York from 74. *21 Cranbrook Avenue, Hull, Yorks.*

SHAW, Bruce William. b 44. Monash Univ BA 67. Melb Coll of Div BD 74. Trin Coll Melb 70. **d** 73 Melb **p** 73 Bp Grant for Melb. C of St Paul Bend 73-75; M SSF from 75; Perm to Offic Dio Brisb from 75. *Friary, Brookfield Road, Brookfield, Queensland, Australia 4069.* (378 2160)

SHAW, Very Rev Charles Allan. Late Scho of Ch Coll Cam and Tancred Stud 2nd cl Mod Lang Trip 46, BA (2nd cl Th Trip pt i) 48, MA 52. Westcott Ho Cam 49. **d** 51 **p** 52 Man. C of Swinton 51-54; Asst Master and Chap Malvern Coll 54-58; L to Offic Dio Worc 56-58; V of St Ambrose Pendleton 58-62; Dom Chap to Bp of Birm and Succr of Birm Cathl 62-67; Dean and R of St Jo Bapt Cathl Bulawayo 67-75; Dean (Emer) from 75; Archd of Bulawayo 69-75; VG of Matab 72-75; Can Res and Preb of Heref Cathl from 75; Prec from 75; Commiss Matab from 77. *The Canon's House, Hereford.*

SHAW, Charles Edward. b 10. Univ of Man BA 33. Egerton Hall Man 33. **d** 35 **p** 36 Man. C of St Matt w St John Deansgate Man 35-38; Worsley 38; Moston 38-43; V of St Jo Evang Wingates 43-57; Waterhead Dio Man from 57. *Vicarage, Church Street East, Waterhead, Oldham, Lancs OL4 2JQ.* (061-624 4011)

SHAW, Colin Clement Gordon. b 39. Linc Th Coll 65. **d** 67 **p** 68 Lich. C of Tettenhall Regis 67-70; St Pet Tile Cross Birm 70-72; V of Edstaston 72-75; Whixall 72-75; Hosp Chap to Aylesbury Distr from 75; C of Aylesbury Dio Ox from 75. *69 Oxford Road, Aylesbury, Bucks.* (Aylesbury 748383)

SHAW, Colin Martin. b 21. [f CA 52-68] Oak Hill Th Coll 68. **d** 69 Middleton for Man. C of St Pet Halliwell 69-72; V of Tonge Fold 72-78; Ch Gresley w Linton Dio Derby from 78. *Gresley Vicarage, Linton, Burton-on-Trent, Staffs, DE12 6PZ.* (B-on-T 761441)

SHAW, Joseph Charles Matthew. Kelham Th Coll 36. Univ of Lon BA (3rd cl Phil) 49. CCC Cam BA (2nd cl Mor Sc Trip pt ii) 51. M. SSM 43. **d** 43 **p** 44 Sheff. C of Parson Cross Sheff 43-48; L to Offic Dio Southw 48-60; Perm to Offic Dio Ely 49-51; Chap and Tutor Kelham Th Coll 51-60; Tutor St Mich Th Coll Crafers 60-63; Sub Prior 63-65; L to Offic Dio Adel 60-65; Chap Univ of Lanc 65-74. *Brook Cottage, Whitmore Vale, Hindhead, Surrey.*

SHAW, David George. b 40. BD (Lon) 64. Tyndale Hall Bris 58. **d** 65 Warrington for Liv **p** 66 Liv. C of St Lawr Kirkdale 65-68; Bebington 68-70; V of Swadlincote 70-75; R of Eyam Dio Derby from 75. *Eyam Rectory, Sheffield, S30 1QH.* (Hope Valley 30821)

SHAW, David Parlane. b 32. **d** 69 Kilm for Derry **p** 70 Derry. Bp's C of Langfield 69-75; R of Chedburgh w Depden and Rede (and Hawkedon from 79) Dio St E from 75; P-in-c of Hawkedon 76-79. *Rede Rectory, Bury St Edmunds, Suff, IP29 4BE.* (Hawkedon 342)

SHAW, Denis. b 26. Westcott Ho Cam. **d** 59 **p** 60 Lon. C of St Matt Bethnal Green 59-63; R of St Wilfrid Newton Heath Man 63-71; St Andr Clewer Dio Ox from 71. *Clewer Rectory, Windsor, Berks, SL4 5EN.* (Windsor 65185)

SHAW, Canon Denis Walter. b 16. Sarum Th Coll 65. **d** 67 **p** 68 Sarum. C of Bridport 67-70; R of Tarrant Rushton 70-76; Tarrant Keynston and Tarrant Crawford 70-76; RD of Milton and Blandford 73-81; C-in-c of Bere Regis Dio Sarum 76-78; V (and Affpuddle w Turnerspuddle) from 78; Can of Sarum Cathl from 77. *Bere Regis Vicarage, Wareham, Dorset, BH20 7HQ.* (Bere Regis 262)

SHAW, Dennis Alfred Arthur. b 24. Wells Th Coll 64. **d** 65 **p** 66 Worc. C of St Steph Redditch 65-70; R of Addingham Dio Bradf from 70. *Rectory, Addingham, Ilkley, Yorks. LS29 0QP.* (Addingham 830276)

SHAW, Ernest Ronald. b 16. K Coll Lon BA (2nd cl German) 38. Chich Th Coll 72. **d** 72 **p** 73 Cov (APM). Asst Chap to the Commun at Cov Cathl 72-78; Perm to Offic Dio Sarum from 79. *Rectory, Semley, Shaftesbury, Dorset, SP7 9AU.* (East Knoyle 362)

SHAW, Frank Ernest. b 04. Wells Th Coll 50. **d** 50 **p** 51 Ex. C of Okehampton 50-52; V of Paparoa 52-54; C of Umtali 54-56; Warden Fairfield Ho Dawlish 59-69; Perm to Offic Dio Ex from 69; Commiss W Tang from 69; Hon C of St Marychurch Dio Ex from 73; Stoke-in-Teignhead w Combe-in-Teignhead Dio Ex from 78. *The Bourne, Hampton Avenue, St Marychurch, Torquay, Devon, TQ1 3LA.* (Torquay 37326)

SHAW, Frederick Allen Seymour. Univ of Syd BA 31. Moore Th Coll Syd ACT ThL 29. **d** 29 **p** 30 Syd. C of St John Ashfield 29-32; St Clem Marrickville 32-34; Dom Chap to Abp of Syd 34-35; R of Picton w The Oaks and Yerranderie 35-49; Ashfield 49-65; Chap Prince Henry Hosp Little Bay 66-74; L to Offic Dio Syd from 74. *12 St Michael's Flat, 71 Hunter Street, Sydney, Australia 2000.* (221-2986)

SHAW, Frederick Hugh. b 16. Univ of Dur BSc 49. Univ of Dur MSc 66. **d** 76 Repton for Derby **p** 77 Derby. C of Wingerworth Dio Derby from 76. *1 Frances Drive, Wingerworth, Chesterfield, S42 6SJ.*

SHAW, Geoffrey Norman. b 26. Jes Coll Ox (2nd cl Th) BA 50. MA 54. Wycl Hall, Ox. **d** 51 **p** 52 Pet. C of St Mary Rushden 51-54; Ch Ch Woking 54-59; V of St Paul Woking 59-62; R of St Leonards-on-Sea 62-68; Asst Master Ecclesfield Gr Sch and L to Offic Dio Sheff 68-69; Asst Master Silverdale Sch Sheff 69-72; Tutor and Vice-Prin Oak Hill Coll 72-79; L to Offic Dio St Alb from 72; Dio Lon from 73; Dio Ox from 79; Prin Wycl Hall Ox from 79. *Wycliffe Hall, Oxford, OX2 6QB.* (Oxford 57539)

SHAW, George Peter. St Mich Th Coll Crafers ACT ThL 58. **d** 57 **p** 59 Brisb for Rockptn. C of St Luke Wandal Rockptn 57-60; Longreach 60; V of St Hugh Inala Brisb 60-65; Perm to Offic Dio Brisb 65-66 and from 71; Dio C &

Goulb 67-70; Lect Univ of Queensld 70. *5 Yarawa Street, Kenmore, Queensland, Australia 4069.* (378 4125)

SHAW, Gerald Keith Gregg. St Jo Coll Winnipeg, LTh 68. **d** 67 Edmon. I of Hinton w Edson 68-70; Sec and Treas Dio Calg 70-71; R of Ch of Ascen Ott 72-74; on leave 75-78 and from 80; R of Gaspé 78-80. *Box 130, Bat Cave, N Carolina 28710, USA.*

SHAW, Gerald Oliver. b 32. K Coll Lon and Warm 56. **d** 60 Lanc for York **p** 61 Blackb. C of St Cuthb Burnley 60-62; Heysham 62-65; C-in-c of All SS Conv Distr Oswaldtwistle 65-66; V 66-69; Chap Leavesden Hosp 69-75; Broadmoor Hosp Crowthorne from 75. *Redwoods, Eastern Lane, Crowthorne, Berks.* (Crowthorne 3111)

SHAW, Gordon Alfred Raymond. b 26. **d** 78 Waik. Hon C of New Plymouth 78-80; on leave. *St John's College, St John's Road, Auckland 5, NZ.*

SHAW, Graham. b 44. Late Scho of Worc Coll Ox BA (2nd cl Mod Hist) 65, 2nd cl Th 67. Cudd Coll. **d** 69 Dorking for Guildf **p** 70 Guildf. C of Esher 69-73; R of Winford 73-78; Chap of Ex Coll Ox from 78. *Exeter College, Oxford.*

SHAW, Grahame David. b 44. Lich Th Coll 65. **d** 68 **p** 69 Ches. C of St Andr Grange Runcorn 68-73; Team V of E Runcorn w Halton 73-74; Thamesmead 75-79; V of St Paul Lorrimore Square Newington Dio S'wark from 79. *St Paul's Vicarage, Lorrimore Square, SE17.* (01-735 2947)

SHAW, Jack Firth. Dorch Miss Coll 35. **d** 38 **p** 39 Derby. C of Bolsover 38-41; St Sav Walthamstow 41-42; W Midl Dir ICF and C of St Paul Bridgtown 42-45; PC of Barrow Hill 46-50; Chap St Aug Hosp Chartham Down 50-52; V of H Trin Maidstone 52-57; Surr from 52; Chap Springfield Hosp Tooting 57-59 and 61-64; V of Brabourne w Monks Horton and Smeeth 59-61; St Jo Div Merton 64-76; Perm to Offic Dio Cant from 79. *37 The Crescent, St Stephen's, Canterbury, Kent.* (Cant 51963)

SHAW, James Alan. b 20. Keble Coll Ox BA 42, MA 47. Linc Th Coll 42. **d** 44 **p** 45 Carl. C of Egremont 44-49; Redditch 49-50; Sacr and C of Wakef Cathl 50-54; Asst Master Qu Eliz Gr Sch Wakef 54-56; V of N Bradley w Southwick and Brokerswood 56-65; R of Flax Bourton 65-80; V of Barrow Gurney 77-80; Chap and Lect St Deiniol's Libr Hawarden 80-81. *27 Parc Sychnant, Conwy, Gwyn, LL32 8SB.* (0492 63 6758)

SHAW, John. b 20. K Coll Lon and Warm 57. **d** 59 **p** 60 Newc T. C of Monkseaton 59-62; St Jas Benwell Newc T 62-63; V of St Cuthb Burnley 63-74; Goosnargh Dio Blackb from 74; RD of Garstang from 79. *Goosnargh Vicarage, Preston, Lancs, PR3 2BN.* (Goosnargh 274)

SHAW, John Jeremy. St Jo Coll Auckld LTh (1st cl) 64. **d** 62 **p** 63 Auckld. C of St Helier's Bay 62-65; St Mary's Cathl Auckld 65-67; Lect in Pastoral Th St Jo Coll Auckld from 67; Hon C of Meadowbank 71-73; St Aid Remuera City and Dio Auckld from 73. *11 Ascot Avenue, Auckland 5, NZ.*

SHAW, John Reginald Derek. b 32. Sarum Th Coll 57. **d** 59 **p** 60 Bradf. C of Thornbury 59-61; Tong w Tong Street 62-63; Clifford 63-65; V of Bramham Dio York from 65. *Bramham Vicarage, Wetherby, W Yorks, LS23 6QG.* (Boston Spa 843631)

SHAW, John Richard Astley. b 24. St Jo Coll Dur 46. ACT ThL 53. **d** 51 Liv for Gippsld **p** 53 Gippsld. C of Yallourn 51-52; Bairnsdale 52-55; C (Col Cl Act) of Braunstone 55-57; R of Ratcliffe-on-the-Wreake w Rearsby 57-65; Ste Marguerite de la Forêt (Forest Ch) Guernsey Dio Win from 65. *Forest Rectory, Guernsey, CI.* (Guernsey 38392)

SHAW, Michael Howard. b 38. Univ of Leeds, BSc (2nd cl Chem) 61. Linc Th Coll 64. **d** 66 **p** 67 Dur. C of St Paul Hartlepool 66-68; Asst Master Stockbridge Co Secondary Sch 68; Totton Coll 69; Gravesend Boys' Gr Sch 70-72; Maidstone Gr Sch from 72. *2 Bredgar Close, Maidstone, Kent.* (Maidstone 673415)

SHAW, Peter Haslewood. b 17. Pemb Coll Cam BA 39, MA 65. Worc Ordin Coll 65. **d** 67 Lon **p** 68 Kens for Lon. C of St Jude S Kens 67-69; V of St Anne Alderney 69-78; Disley Dio Ches from 78. *Disley Vicarage, Stockport, Chesh.* (Disley 2068)

SHAW, Ralph. b 38. Univ of Man MEducn 70. Sarum Wells Th Coll 78. **d** 80 **p** 81 Dur. C of Consett Dio Dur from 80. *Church House, Aynsley Terrace, Consett, Co Durham, DH8 5LX.*

SHAW, Ralph Michael. b 45. Lich Th Coll 68. **d** 70 Pontefract for Wakef **p** 71 Wakef. C of Dewsbury 70-75; Team V of Redcar w Kirkleatham 75-76; Dioc Youth Officer Dio St Alb from 76. *All Saints House, 7c Hall Grove, Welwyn Garden City, Herts, AL7 1813)*

SHAW, Richard Tom. b 42. AKC 69. St Aug Coll Cant 69. **d** 70 Jarrow for Dur **p** 71 Dur. C of St Nich Dunston 70-73; Maidstone 73-75; Chap RN 75-79; V of Barrow-on-Humber w New Holland Dio Linc from 79. *Vicarage, Barrow-on-Humber, S Humb, DN19 7AA.* (B-on-H 30357)

SHAW, Robert William. b 41. Lich Th Coll 62. **d** 65 **p** 66 Man. C of Westhoughton 65-69; Abington 69-73; R of Teigh w Whissendine 73-77. *c/o Whissendine Vicarage, Oakham, Leics.* (Whissendine 333)

SHAW, Robert William. b 46. Univ of Lon BD 69. St Aug Coll Cant 69. **d** 70 **p** 71 Ripon. C of Hunslet 70-74; Hawksworth Wood 74-76; R of Stanningley Dio Ripon from 76. *Rectory, Stanningley Road, Stanningley, Pudsey, W Yorks, LS28 6HP.* (Pudsey 573460)

SHAW, Ronald Forbes. b 16. RIBA 47. FRICS 55. SOC 67. **d** 70 **p** 71 S'wark. C of Belmont 70-73; V of St Mich AA Sydenham Dio S'wark from 73. *Vicarage, Champion Crescent, SE26 4HJ.* (01-778 7196)

SHAW, Stephen Albert. b 42. Univ of Cant BEng 64. St Jo Coll Auckld. **d** 78 Wel. C of Lower Hutt Dio Wel from 78. *39 Penrose Street, Lower Hutt, NZ.* (661-343)

SHAW, Tom. Ch Coll Cam BA 41, MA 44. **d** 41 Bp Duppuy for Worc **p** 42 Worc. C of Old Hill 41-49; V of N Frodingham 49-59; R of Ilmington w Stretton-on-Fosse 59-63; Drayton 63-80. *24 Greenfields Close, Shipston-on-Stour, Warws.*

SHAW, Vernon Graham Havergal. b 1887. Late Scho of Clare Coll Cam BA (2nd cl Cl Trip) 09, MA 14. Ridley Hall Cam 12. **d** 14 Lon for Col Bp **p** 16 Luckn. Warden of Ox and Cam Hostel Allahabad 15-18 and 21-22; St John's Coll Agra 19-21; Engl Presbyterian Miss Bengal 23-27; C of St John Rouding 27-30; V of St Barn Mossley Hill 30-33; St Luke Walton 33-39; Keynsham 39-45; Qu Charlton 39-45; Chap and Lect St Paul's Coll Calc 45-48; R of Sampford Brett 49-60; L to Offic Dio Sarum 62-72; Dio Chelmsf from 72. *21 Ventnor Gardens, Barking, Essex, IG11 9JY.* (01-594 3568)

SHAW, Canon Victor Charles Campbell. St Paul's Coll Grahmstn LTh 29. Westcott Ho Cam 30. **d** and **p** 31 York. C of St John Middlesbrough 31-35; St Thos Durban 35-38; P-in-c of Bulwer w Himeville 38-45; CF (S Afr) 40-45; V of St Martin Durban N 46-53; St Thos Durban 61-73; Can of St Sav Cathl Pmbg 68-75; Hon Can from 75; C of Karkloof 73-75; Perm to Offic Dio Natal 75-76. *PB Howick, Natal, S Africa.*

SHAW-HAMILTON, Robert Jemmett. b 02. Wycl Hall Ox. **d** 49 **p** 50 Sarum. C of Radipole 49-52; V of Fordcombe 52-57; R of N Cray 57-65; V of Barkestone w Plungar and Redmile 65-70. *17 Churchill Way, Painswick, Glos, GL6 6RQ.*

SHAWINIMASH, Charles. b 45. **d** and **p** 74 Keew. C of Fort Hope Dio Keew from 74. *St James Church, Fort Hope, via Nakina, Ont., Canada.*

SHAXTED, Edwin Douglas John. Ridley Coll Melb ACT ThL 32. **d** 33 Bend for Melb **p** 34 Melb. C of St Bart Burnley Melb 33-35; Perm to Offic (Col Cl Act) at St Simon Southsea 35-36; C of St Faith Maidstone 36-38; St Simon Southsea 38-40; W Preston Melb 40; Vic Sec BCA 41-43; V of All SS Northcote Melb 43-45; R of St Luke Adel 45-53; Commiss (in Austr) Centr Tang 46-53; V of Charing Heath 53-57; C-in-c of Boughton Malherbe 53-57; R of All Cannings w Etchilhampton 57-61; SW Area Sec CCCS 61-65; L to Offic Dio Ex 61-65; V of W Ashton 65-81; V of Heywood 65-81. *Manormead, Filford Road, Hindhead, Surrey.*

SHAYLOR, Denis Freke. Sarum Th Coll 68. **d** 69 **p** 70 Ox. C of Caversham 69-75; L to Offic Dio Ox 76-79; Perm to Offic Dio Win from 80. *12 Emery Hill, Alton, Hants.*

SHEA, David Tak-Shun. b 44. Union Coll Hong 68. **d** 71 **p** 73 Hong. C of All SS Sheng Kung Hui 71-73; St Paul City and Dio Hong from 74. *St Paul's Church, Hong Kong.* (5-254165)

SHEA, Derwyn Spencer. Laurentian Univ Ont BA 69. Univ of Tor MA 71. Hur Coll Dipl Th 66. **d** 66 **p** 67 Sask. I of Macdowall 66-69; L to Offic Dio Tor 71-73; P-in-c of St Clem Riverdale City and Dio Tor from 73. *29 Grenadier Heights, Toronto, Ont, Canada.*

SHEA, Guy Roland John. b 33. Trin Coll Connecticut BA 55. Ch Ch Ox BA (3rd cl Th) 58, MA 62. Coll of Resurr Mirfield 60. **d** 60 **p** 61 S'wark. C of Kennington 60-63; St Mark N Audley Street Westmr 63-67; St Sav Hammersmith 67-70; C-in-c of St Jas Gunnersbury 70-75; C of St Jo Div Kennington 75-77; Perm to Offic Dio Lon from 77. *5c Collier House, 163-169 Brompton Road, SW3.*

SHEAD, John Frederick Henry. b 38. ACP 74, FCP 81. Westcot Ho Cam 72. **d** 74 **p** 75 Colchester for Chelmsf (NSM). C of Thaxted Dio Chelmsf from 74; Hd Master of Thaxted County Primary Sch from 70. *Bluegates, Watling Lane, Thaxted, Dunmow, Essex, CM6 2QX.* (Thaxted 830687)

SHEAF, John Gale. b 49. Univ of Cant NZ BSc 71. St Jo Coll Auckld LTh 73. **d** 73 **p** 74 Ch Ch. C of Linwood 73-75; Ashburton 75; Papanui 75-78; V of Ross and S Westland Dio Ch Ch from 78. *Box 15, Hari Hari, South Westland, NZ.*

SHEARD, Ernest. b 29. Linc Th Coll 73. **d** 74 Leic **p** 75 Bp Mort for Leic. Hon C of Birstall Dio Leic from 74. *21 Orchard Road, Birstall, Leicester, LE4 4GD.*

SHEARER, Ven John. b 26. Late Pri of Trin Coll Dub BA (Resp) 48, Th Exhib 50, MA and BD 53. **d** 50 **p** 51 Down. C of Maralin 50-52; Ballymacarrett 52-59; R of Magheradroll 59-64; Seagoe Dio Drom from 64; Archd of Drom from 70; Exam Chap to Bp of Down from 70. *Seagoe Rectory, Upper Church Lane, Portadown, Co Armagh, N Ireland,*

SHEARER, John Frank. b 35. Univ of Ex BSc (Geog) 60. Tyndale Hall Bris 62. **d** 63 **p** 64 S'wark. C of St Jo Evang Blackheath 63-67; R of Nuffield 67-82; Chap HM Borstal Huntercombe from 67; V of St Pet Woking Dio Guildf from 82. *Vicarage, Turnock Avenue, Old Woking, Surrey, GU22 0AJ.* (Woking 62707)

SHEARING, Michael James. b 39. Univ of Lanc BA 71. Linc Th Coll. **d** 66 **p** 67 Dur. C of St Paul W Hartlepool 66-76; Asst Master Dyke Ho Comprehensive Sch Hartlepool from 76. *29 Eastfield, Peterlee, Co Durham.* (Peterlee 864023)

SHEARING, Victor Ingram. b 07. **d** 70 **p** 71 Mashon. Hosps' Chap Salisbury Dio Mashon from 71. *15 Baines Avenue, Salisbury, Rhodesia.*

SHEARLOCK, Very Rev David John. b 32. Univ of Birm BA (Geog) 55. Westcott Ho Cam 56. **d** 57 **p** 58 York. C of Guisborough 57-60; Christchurch 60-64; V of Kingsclere 64-71; Romsey 71-82; Surr 71-82; Dioc Dir of Ordinands Dio Win 77-82; Hon Can of Win from 78; Dean of Truro and R of St Mary Truro from 82. *Deanery, Lemon Street, Truro, Cornw.* (Truro 2661)

✠ **SHEARMAN, Right Rev Donald Norman.** OBE 78. St Jo Coll Morpeth ACT Thl 50. **d** 50 **p** 51 Bath. C of Dubbo 50-52; Forbes 52-57; R of Coonabarabran 57-59; Can of Bath 62; Archd of Mildura 62-64; R of Mildura 62-64; Cons Ld Bp of Rockptn in St Jo Cathl Brisb 24 Feb 64 by Abp of Brisb; Bps of New Guinea; N Queensld; Carp; Bath; Graft; and Newc; Bp Coadj of Brisb; Asst Bps of New Guinea (Ambo); and Melan (Tuti); and Abp Moline; res 71; Chairman ABM Gen Syn 71-73; L to Offic Dio Syd 71-73; Apptd Bp of Graft 73. *Bishopsholme, PO Box 4, Grafton, NSW, Australia 2460.* (42 2070)

SHEARMAN, Michael Alan. b 22. Down Coll Cam BA 44, MA 48. Coll of Resurr Mirfield 46. **d** 48 **p** 49 Lon. C of Bounds Green 48-53; Wembley Pk 53-58; V of St Luke Enfield Dio Lon from 58. *St Luke's Vicarage, Browning Road, Enfield, Middx, EN2 0HG.* (01-363 6055)

SHEARS, Michael George Frederick. b 33. Pemb Coll Cam BA 57, 3rd cl Th Trip pt 1a, 57, MA 68. St Steph Ho Ox 57. **d** 59 **p** 60 Linc. C of Grantham 59-68; R of Waltham w New Waltham 68-80; Barnoldby-le-Beck 73-80; RD of Haverstoe 78-80; V of Soham w Barway Dio Ely from 80. *Soham Vicarage, Ely, Cambs.* (Ely 720423)

SHEARWOOD, Alexander George Dobbie. b 21. New Coll Ox BA (3rd cl Th) 48. Wells Th Coll 49. **d** 50 **p** 51 S'wark. C of St John Walworth 50-52; Kennington Cross 52-57; St Paul Nork 57-59; Asst Chap Beecholme Resid Sch 57-59; R of Wickenby w Friesthorpe Dio Linc from 59; V of Lissington w Holton-le-Beckering Dio Linc from 59; R of Snelland w Snarford Dio Linc from 63; C-in-c of Faldingworth w Buslingthorpe Dio Linc from 73. *Wickenby Rectory, Lincoln.* (Wickenby 256)

SHEASBY, Adrian. St Aid Coll 54. **d** 57 **p** 58 cov. C of St Paul Foleshill 57-60; St Jo Bapt Pet 60-65; V of Maxey w Northborough Dio Pet from 65. *Maxey Vicarage, Peterborough.* (Market Deeping 343329)

SHEEHAN, Patrick Edward Anthony. b 37. **d** 67 RC Bp of Lisbon **p** 69 RC Bp of Westmr. In RC Ch 67-73; Rec into Angl Commun 74 by Bp of S'wark; C of Clapham S'wark 74-75; Wimbledon (in c of St Matt) 75-76; R of Balga 77-80; Melville Dio Perth from 80. *9 Williams Court, Melville, W Australia 6156.* (330-1550)

SHEEHY, Jeremy Patrick. b 56. Magd Coll Ox BA 80. St Steph Ho Ox 78. **d** 81 Birm. C of Erdington Dio Birm from 81. *74 Spring Lane, Erdington, Birmingham, W Midl, B24 9EB.* (021-382 3071)

SHEEKEY, Raymond Arthur. b 23. Chich Th Coll 51. **d** 53 Dover for Cant **p** 54 Cant. C of Ramsgate 53-56; Birchington 56-61; R of Smeeth 61-62; V of Brabourne (w Monks Horton 61-62; w Smeeth from 62) 61-79; Lenham w Boughton Malherbe Dio Cant from 79; RD of N Lympne 75-78. *Lenham Vicarage, Maidstone, Kent.* (Maidstone 858245)

SHEEN, John Harold. b 32. Qu Coll Cam 3rd cl Th Trip pt i, 52, BA (2nd cl Th Trip pt ii) 54, MA 58. Cudd Coll 56. **d** 58 **p** 59 Lon. C of St Dunstan Stepney 58-62; PC of St Jo Bapt Tottenham 62-68; V of St Mich Wood Green Lon 68-78; P-in-c of St Mich-at-Bowes Bowes Pk Lon 76-78; R of Kirkbride Dio S & M from 78; V of St Olave Ramsey Dio S & M from 80. *Rectory, Kirkbride, Ramsey, IM.* (Kirk Andreas 351)

SHEEN, Canon Victor Alfred. b 17. Tyndale Hall, Bris 47. **d** 49 Lon **p** 51 U Nile. Miss Dio U Nile 49-56; C of St Mark Cheltm 56-58; V of St Jas W Streatham 58-65; St Jas Clapham Pk Dio S'wark from 65; RD of Clapham and Brixton from 75; Hon Can of S'wark Cathl from 80. *1 Rodenhurst Road, SW4 8AE.* (01-674 3973)

SHEERAN, Canon Ernest William. b 17. St Aid Coll 47. **d** 50 **p** 51 Southw. C of Aspley 50-52; W Bridgford 52-55; V of Edwalton Dio Southw from 55; RD of S Bingham from 68; Surr from 72; Hon Can of Southw from 72. *Edwalton Vicarage, Nottingham, NG12 4AB.* (Nottingham 232034)

SHEFFIELD, Lord Bishop of. *See* Lunn, Right Rev David Ramsay.

SHEFFIELD, Assistant Bishop of. (Vacant)

SHEFFIELD, Archdeacon of. *See* Paton, Ven Michael John Macdonald.

SHEFFIELD, Provost of. *See* Curtis, Very Rev Wilfred Frank.

SHEFFIELD, Arthur Edward. b 52. McGill Univ Montr BA 74, BTh 76. Montr Dioc Th Coll 76. **d** 78 **p** 79 Montr. C of St Geo Ste Anne de Bellevue 78-81; R of Good Shepherd Cartierville City and Dio Montr from 81. *12235 Somerset Road, Montreal, PQ, Canada, H4K 1S1.* (514-334 7050)

SHEFFIELD, Michael Julian. b 53. Sarum Wells Th Coll 76. **d** 79 **p** 80 Portsm. C of Locks Heath Dio Portsm from 79. *11 Laurel Road, Locks Heath, Southampton, Hants.* (Locks Heath 2699)

SHEGOG, Eric Marshall. b 37. Lich Th Coll 64. **d** 65 **p** 66 S'wark. C of Benhilton 65-68; Asst Youth Adv Dio S'wark 68-70; V of St Mich AA Abbey Wood Plumstead 70-75; Chap of Bp Wearmouth Dio Dur from 75. *19 Thornhill Terrace, Sunderland, T & W.* (Sunderland 75570)

SHEHADEH, Shehadeh. **d** 68 **p** 69 Jer. P Dio Jer. *PO Box 10, Shefa'amr, Israel.*

SHEILD, Canon Edward Oscar. b 10. Univ of NZ LLB 33. Qu Coll Ox BA (2nd cl Th) 36, MA 40. **d** 36 **p** 37 Man. C of H Innoc Fallowfield 36-39; Lyall Bay Wel 39-40; C-in-c of U Hutt 40-42; TCF (NZ) 42-46; Tutor Cudd Coll 46-49; L to Offic Dio Ox 46-58; LPr Dio Man 49-58; Dioc Miss Dio Man 49-58; Hon Can of Man 54-58; Can (Emer) from 58; Commiss Waik 57-58; Sing 64-72; Dean of Sing Cathl 58-64, V of St Andr Cathl Sing 58-64; Exam Chap to Bp of Sing 59-64; V of Chapel Allerton 64-75; L to Offic Dio Carl from 75; P-in-c of Coldstream 77-79. *Midtown Cottage, Askham, Penrith, CA10 2PF.* (Hackthorpe 427)

SHEK, Pauline. b 30. U Th Coll Hong 69. **d** 71 **p** 73 Hong. C of Kei Oi Ch Kowloon Dio Hong from 71. *607 Block 5, Jordan Valley, Kowloon, Hong Kong.* (3-427291)

SHELDON, John Gordon. b 22. Trin Coll Cam BA (3rd cl Hist Trip Pts i and ii) 43, MA 47. Ridley Hall Cam 43. **d** 45 **p** 46 S'wark. C of Morden 45-49; L to Offic Dio Guildf and Cands Sec CPAS 49-51; V of St Jo Bapt Beckenham 51-57; St Geo Worthing 57-62; Lindfield 62-80; P-in-c of Cowden 80-81; R of Cowden w Hammerwood Dio Chich from 81. *Cowden Rectory, Edenbridge, Kent.* (Cowden 221)

SHELDRAKE, Christopher Wray. b 45. Sarum Wells Th Coll 72. **d** 75 Lon **p** 76 Stepney for Lon. C of Poplar 75-79; E Ham (in c of St Bart) Dio Chelmsf from 79. *Fellowship House, The Cottage, St Bartholomew's Road, East Ham, E6 3AG.* (01-552 5082)

SHELFORD, Gordon Hope McNeill. b 16. Westcott Ho Cam 41. **d** 42 **p** 43 Blackb. C of Ch Ch Accrington 42-44; St Pet Frimley (in c of St Andr) 44-45; Min of Conv Distr Frimley Green 45-48; V 48-49; R of Haslemere 49-55; Surr 49-58; V of Hemel Hempstead 55-58; C-in-c of St Paul Hemel Hempstead 56-58; Perm to Offic Dio Bris 75-78; Publ Pr Dio Bris 78; P-in-c of Nettleton w Littleton Drew Dio Bris from 79. *The Glebe House, Grittleton, Chippenham, Wilts.* (Castle Combe 782409)

SHELL, Canon Harry Arnold. Angl Th Coll BC. **d** 58 **p** 59 Edmon. R of Mannville 58-63; Ponoka 63-69; St Luke City and Dio Edmon from 69; Can of Edmon from 75. *8119 96th Avenue, Edmonton, Alta., Canada.* (403-469 7220)

SHELLEY, Derrick Sydney David. b 38. Univ of Lon LLB 60. AKC 65. Linc Th Coll. **d** 68 **p** 69 Guildf. C of Weybridge 68-72; Chap of Red Bank Sch Newton-le-Willows 72-77; Hon C of Lytham Dio Blackb from 81. *21 Agnew Street, Lytham St Annes, Lancs.*

SHELLEY, George. b 18. Qu Coll Birm 56. **d** 57 **p** 58 Win. C of St Andr Boscombe 57-60; Org Sec Ox C'tte for Famine Relief 61-66; Chap Miss to Seamen Gt Yarmouth 67-71; R of Gt Ringstead 71-77; C-in-c of Sedgeford w Southmere 71-77; P-in-c of St Jas Gateshead 77-78; R 78-81. *18 Burnt Hills, Cromer, Norf, NR27 9LW.*

SHELLOCK, Norman Stanley. b 15. Univ of Dur LTh 38. ATCL 53. St Aug Coll Cant 34. **d** 38 St Alb **p** 39 Bedford for St Alb. C of Biscot 38-41; All SS New Amsterdam Berbice 41-44; R of Canje 44-49; St Matt Providence and E Bank Demerara Dio Guy 49-59; Area Sec SPG (USPG from 65) Dios Nor, Ely and St E 59-80; L to Offic Dio St E from 59. *24 Runnymede Green, Bury St Edmunds, Suff, IP33 2LH.* (Bury St E 703506)

SHELLS, Charles Harry. b 15. St Chad's Coll Dur BA 38, MA 43. **d** 39 **p** 40 Wakef. C of Almondbury 39-42; St Geo Camberwell 42-47; V of St Paul Newington 47-54; St Anne Wandsworth 54-65; RD of Wandsworth 63-65; R of Trunch w Swafield 65-71; Bradfield 65-71; C-in-c of Gimingham 65-71; Trimingham 65-71; Antringham W Thorpe Mkt 65-71; Felmingham 65-68; Suffield 65-68; Gunton 65-71; RD of Tunstead 65-68; Can Res of Bris Cathl 71-81; L to Offic Dios B & W, Bris and Sarum from 81. *Welcot, Wellow, Nr Bath, Avon, BA2 8QE.* (Combe Down 837116)

SHENNAN, Maxwell Cassels. St Jo Coll Auckld LTh 66. **d** 65 **p** 66 Auckld. C of Grey Lynn 65-68; Panmure 68-70; on leave 71-72; Chap Auckld Hosp 72-74; Assoc Dir of Chr Educn Dio Auckld 75-76; C of St Andr Epsom Auckld 77-78; Chap Waik Publ Hosp from 78. *27 Lake Crescent, Hamilton, NZ.* (80466)

SHENTON, Brian. b 43. Chich Th Coll 73. **d** 75 Lon **p** 76 Edmon for Lon. C of John Keble Ch Mill Hill 75-78; New Windsor 78-81; Team V 81-82; R of Cherbury Dio Ox from 82. *Rectory, Longworth, Abingdon, Oxon, OX13 5DX.* (Longworth 820213)

SHENTON, John Snelson. b 1890. Jes Coll Cam BA (2nd cl Th Trip pt i) 12, Lady Kay Scho (2nd cl Th Trip pt ii) 13, MA 16. **d** 14 **p** 15 Ex. C of Tavistock 14-17; TCF 17-19; Hon CF 21; C of Appledore 19-21; Tiverton 21-25; V of Winkleigh 25-31, R of Templeton w Loxbeare 31-35; RD of Tiverton 35; V of St Kew 35-61; RD of Bodmin 47-50. *Hallowed Mead, Hatch, Tisbury, Wilts.*

SHEPHARD, Allan George. St Jo Coll Morpeth 59. **d** 61 **p** 62 Graft. C of Coffs Harbour 61-62; Lismore 63-66; R of Dorrigo 66-70; Chap Miss to Seamen Syd 70-72; R of Kyogle 72-77; Lismore Dio Graft from 77. *Box 378, Lismore, NSW, Australia 2480.*

SHEPHARD, Brian Edward. b 34. Magd Coll Cam 2nd cl Cl Trip pt i 55, BA (1st cl Th Trip pt ia) 56, MA 60. Magd Coll Ox MA (by incorp) 60. Wycl Hall Ox 58. **d** 60 **p** 61 Liv. C of St Cath Wigan 60-62; St Geo Kidderminster 62-65; Lect CA Tr Coll 65-70; Hamilton Coll of Educn 70-78; Perm to Offic Dio Glas 70-77; Chap Buchan Sch Castletown from 77; Perm to Offic Dio S & M from 77. *The Shieling, Howe Road, Port St Mary, IM.*

SHEPHEARD, Denis Arthur. b 28. Oak Hill Th Coll 56. **d** 59 Dover for Cant **p** 60 Cant. C of St Jo Bapt Folkestone 59-64; St Pet w Ch Ch Southborough 64-66; All S Langham Place St Marylebone 66-72; V of Loudwater 72-81; Staff Evang (CPAS) Miss at Home from 81. *14 College Road, Reading, Berks.* (Reading 661268)

SHEPHEARD-WALWYN, John. b 16. Or Coll Ox BA 38, MA 44. Wells Th Coll 38. **d** 41 **p** 43 Roch. C of St Pet Roch 41-44; H Redeemer Lamorbey 44-49; Edenbridge 49-56; V of Rosherville 56-61; Westleigh 61-78; R of Horwood 61-78; P-in-c of Harberton w Harbertonford Dio Ex from 78. *Harberton Vicarage, Totnes, Devon, TQ9 7SA.* (Totnes 865200)

SHEPHERD, Anthony Michael. b 50. Em Coll Cam BA 72, MA 76. Westcott Ho Cam 72. **d** 74 dover for Cant **p** 75 Cant. C of Folkestone 74-79; Dom Chap to Bp of Ripon and Dioc Communications Officer from 79. *c/o Bishop Mount, Ripon, HG4 5DP.* (Ripon 2045)

SHEPHERD, Canon Charles Lawton. b 15. St Aid Coll 42. **d** 45 **p** 46 Ches. C of Sandbach 45-49; V of Sandbach Heath 49-54; R of Brereton w Smethwick 54-71; C-in-c of Swettenham 59-71; RD of Congleton 64-74; Hon Can of Ches 69-81; Can (Emer) from 81; R of Brereton w Swettenham 71-81. *8 St Tudwals Estate, Mynytho, Pwllheli, Gwyn, LL53 7RU.*

SHEPHERD, Christopher Francis Pleydell. b 44. St Steph Ho Ox 68. **d** 69 **p** 70 Ex. C of Milber 69-72; St Thos Ex 72-74; Team V of Ilfracombe w Lee and W Down 74-80; P-in-c of Tregony w St Cuby and Cornelly Dio Truro from 80. *Rectory, Tregony, Truro, Cornw, TR2 5SE.* (Tregony 392)

SHEPHERD, David. b 42. Univ of Dur BA 65, MA 68, MLitt 76. Edin Th Coll 66. **d** 68 **p** 69 Brech. Chap of St Paul's Cathl Dundee 68-79; Chap to Univ of Dundee 73-79; R of St Mary Magd Dundee Dio Brech from 79. *14 Albany Terrace, Dundee, DD3 6HR.* (0382-23510)

SHEPHERD, Donald Milton. **d** 58 C & Goulb **p** 61 Bp Arthur for C & Goulb. C of Albury 58-60; Cootamundra 60-61; Temora 61-63; Wagga Wagga 63-66; Dioc Centre (in c of St Luke N Fitzroy 66-72) 66-76; P-in-c of St Mary and St Alb N Melb, St Geo Flemington and H Trin Kens 72-76; I of Sunbury Dio Melb from 76. *Vicarage, O'Shanassy Street, Sunbury, Vic, Australia 3429.* (744 1347)

SHEPHERD, Ernest John Heatley. b 27. TCD BA 48, BD 53. 1 50 **p** 51 Connor. C of St Mary Magd Belfast 50-54; R of Whitehouse Dio Connor from 54. *St John's Rectory, Whitehouse, Newtownabbey, Co Antrim, N Ireland.* (Whitehouse 2622)

SHEPHERD, Frederick John. b 32. Lich Th Coll 54. **d** 57 **p** 58 Nor. C of Walsingham 57-59; St Jo Div Balham 59; St Agnes Kennington Pk 67-68; St Barn Southfields 68-70; C-in-c of St Jo Div Vartry Road Tottenham 70-74; V of St Pet and St Paul Enfield Lock Dio Lon from 74; Bp of Edmon Chap for Post-Ordin Tr 75-79; Treas Gen S of H Cross from 79. *177 Ordnance Road, Enfield, Middx, EN3 6AB.* (Lea Valley 719770)

SHEPHERD, Ivan John. b 33. **d** 75 **p** Graft. C of Casino 76-80; Coffs Harbour Dio Graft from 80; P-in-c of Sawtell Dio Graft from 80. *29 Dirrigeree Crescent, Sawtell, NSW, Australia 2452.*

SHEPHERD, John Donald. b 33. Univ of Dur BA 59, Dipl Th 61. Cranmer Hall Dur 59. **d** 61 **p** 62 Wakef. C of Dewsbury 61-63; Chapelthorpe 63-66; V of Stainland 66-70; Youth Chap Dio Truro 70-74; V of Newquay Dio Truro from 74; RD of Pydar from 81. *Vicarage, Pentire Road, Newquay, Cornw, TR7 1NX.* (Newquay 2724)

SHEPHERD, John Harley. b 42. Univ of Melb BA 65. ACT ThL 67. U Th Sem NY MSacMus 72. Trin Coll Melb 60. **d** 67 **p** 68 Melb. C of St Geo Footscray 67-69; Brunswick 69-70; St Matt Stretford 71; in Amer Ch 72-77; C of Cherry Hinton 77-80; Chap Ch Ch Ox from 80. *Christ Church, Oxford.*

SHEPHERD, John Michael. b 42. BNC Ox BA (2nd cl Th) 63, MA 72. Coll of Resurr Mirfield 64. **d** 66 **p** 67 S'wark. C of H Spirit Clapham 66-69; Kingston T 69-72; V of H Trin U Tooting 73-79; St Paul Wimbledon Pk Dio S'wark from 80. *St Paul's Vicarage, Augustus Road, SW19 6EW.* (01-788 2024)

SHEPHERD, John William. b 20. SOC 67. **d** 70 **p** 71 St Alb. C of Leighton Buzzard 70-77; C-in-c of Studham w Whipsnade Dio St Alb 77-80; R from 80. *Parsonage, Studham, Dunstable, Beds.* (Whipsnade 872223)

SHEPHERD, Canon Maurice Alfred. b 09. St Chad's Coll Dur BA and Van Mildert Exhib 33, Dipl Th 34, MA 36, BCL 44. **d** 34 **p** 35 Dur. C of Tudhoe Grange 34-37; S Moor (in c of Holmside from 39) 37-41; V of Coxhoe 41-54; Proc Conv Dur 50-70; R of Easington 54-74; Hon Can of Dur 72-78; Can (Emer) from 78. *4 The Green, Greatham, Hartlepool, Cleveland, TS25 2HG.* (Hartlepool 870600)

SHEPHERD, Norman Edward. b 07. Univ of Dur LTh 30. St Jo Coll Dur BA 36, MA 39. St Aid Coll 27. **d** 31 **p** 32 Carl. C of St John Barrow F 31-34; Maryport 34-35; V of St Cuthb Holme Cultram 36-40; R of Brougham 40-42; V of Frosterley 42-46; Distr Sec BFBS for SW Midls 46-59; Perm to Offic Dios Heref Worc and Glouc 46-52; Dios Glouc Birm and Cov 52-56; Dio Lich 57-59; R of Weston-sub-Edge w Aston-sub-Edge 59-64; V of Ravenstonedale w Newbiggin-on-Lune 64-68; Sproxton w Saltby and Coston 68-72. *Heanor, Shenington, Banbury, Oxon, OX15 6NA.* (Edge Hill 330)

SHEPHERD, Peter James. b 38. Univ of Dur BA 64. Ridley Hall, Cam 64. **d** 66 **p** 67 Roch. C of Luton Kent 66-70; Belvedere 70-71; Wisley w Pyrford 71-75; V of Thorney Abbey w Wrydecroft Knarr Fen Dio Ely from 75. *Thorney Abbey Vicarage, Peterborough, Cambs.* (Peterborough 270388)

SHEPHERD, Peter William. b 48. Univ of Reading BA 71. Univ of Lon BD 80. Chich Th Coll 77. **d** 80 Chich **p** 81 Lewes for Chich (NSM). C of St Sav w St Pet Eastbourne Dio Chich and Asst Master Chailey Comprehensive Sch from 80. *3 Bakewell Road, Eastbourne, E Sussex, BN21 1PX.* (Eastbourne 35476)

SHEPHERD, Philip Reginald. b 07. Keble Coll Ox BA 29, MA 36. Cudd Coll 29. **d** 30 Ox for Ches **p** 31 Ches. C of Wybunbury 30-33; All S Leeds 33-37; St Luke Southampton 37-39; V of Bramham 39-54; Chap HM Pris Askham Grange 49-54; V of St Marg Leeds 54-63; R of Shepton Beauchamp 64-72. *3 Coles Lane, South Petherton, Somt.* (S Petherton 40809)

SHEPHERD, Very Rev Ronald Francis. Univ of Br Columb BA 48. AKC 52. **d** 52 **p** 53 Lon. C of St Steph w St Jo Evang Westmr 52-57; C-in-c of Glanford 57-59; R of All SS Winnipeg 59-65; Exam Chap to Abp of Rupld 62-65; Dean and R of All SS Cathl Edmon 65-69; Ch Ch Cathl City and Dio Montr from 70. *1440 Union Avenue, Montreal 111, PQ, Canada.* (514-288 6421)

SHEPHERD, Stewart Reginald. Qu Coll Newfld. **d** 24 **p** 25 Newfld. C of Whitbourne 24-25; Bonavista 25-26; I of Random 26-29; Whitbourne 29-43; Upper Island Cove 43-53; Petite Riviere 53-55; Chester 55-62; Granville 62-67. *Bridgewater, NS, Canada.* (543-5752)

SHEPHERD, Thomas Eric. **d** 61 Bp Snell for Tor. C of St Geo Scarborough City and Dio Tor from 61. *87 Scarborough Heights Boulevard, Scarborough, Ont, Canada.*

SHEPHERD, Timothy Roy. b 34. Selw Coll Cam 3rd cl Cl Trip pt i, 57, BA (2nd cl Th Trip pt ia) 58. Linc Th Coll 62. **d** 64 Aston for Birm **p** 65 Birm. C of Selly Oak 64-67; Stockland Green 67-72; V of Perry Common 72-76; Holton-le-Clay Dio

Linc from 76. *Vicarage, Holton-le-Clay, Grimsby, DN36 5AN.* (Grimsby 824082)

SHEPHERD, William Harry Edwin. b 55. Univ of Montr BA 77, MA 78. Montr Dioc Th Coll 79. **d** 81 Montr. C of St Mich AA Thorndale-Pierrefonds Dio Montr from 81. *15560 Cabot Street, Pierrefonds, Que, Canada, H9H 1R5.*

✠ **SHEPPARD, Right Rev David Stuart.** b 29. Trin Hall Cam BA 53, MA 56. Ridley Hall Cam 53. **d** 55 **p** 56 Lon. C of Islington 55-58; Warden and Chap Mayflower Family Centre Canning Town 58-69; Cons Ld Bp Suffr of Woolwich in S'wark Cathl 18 Oct 69 by Abp of Cant; Bps of Lon; Chich; Chelmsf; S'wark; and Southw; Bp Suffr of Kingston T; and Bps Boys, Stannard, Houghton, Robinson, Sansbury and Gough; Trld to Liv 75. *Bishop's Lodge, Woolton Park, Liverpool, L25 6DT; and Church ool, L1 3DW.* (051-708 9480)

SHEPPARD, Desmond Eric. b 23. MBE (Mil) 61. TCD BA 46, MA 61. **d** 47 **p** 48 Connor. C of Templecorran 47-50; Chap RAF from 50; Asst Chap-in-Chief from 70; Hon Chap to HM the Queen from 76; Chap at Ahmadi Kuwait Dio Cyprus from 78. *c/o Northern Bank, Whitehead, Co Antrim, N Ireland.*

SHEPPARD, Elliott Alton. Sir George Williams Univ Montr BA 60. Montr Dioc Th Coll LTh 63. **d** 63 Bp Clarke for Moos **p** 64 Moos. I of Mistassini 63-66; Chapais 66-68; Red Lake Miss 69-71; Turtleford 71-76; Wainwright Dio Edmon from 76. *Box 447, Wainwright, Alta, Canada.* (403-842 3176)

SHEPPARD, Elwyn Derais Moxey. Moore Th Coll ThL 62. **d** 62 **p** 63 Syd. C of Guildf 62-64; Bondi 64-65; C-in-c of Jannali w Como 65-71; Regents Pk w Birrong 71-77; R 77-78; Rooty Hill Dio Syd from 78. *24 Westminster Street, Rooty Hill, NSW, Australia 2766.* (625-8527)

SHEPPARD, Iliffe Dwight. b 49. Mem Univ of Newfld BA 71. Qu Coll St Jo Newfld LTh 73. **d** and **p** 73 Newfld. R of White Bay 73-77. *Box 42, Burin, Newfoundland, Canada.*

SHEPPARD, Martin. b 37. Hertf Coll Ox BA (2nd cl Engl) 61, Squire Scho 61, 3rd cl Th 63, Ellerton Pri and MA 65. Chich Th Coll 63. **d** 65 **p** 66 York. C of St Mich AA Hull 65-68; St Jo Bapt Hove 68-71; V of St Richard Heathfield 71-77; Surr 75-77 and from 81; V of Old w New Shoreham Dio Chich from 77. *Vicarage, Church Street, Shoreham-by-Sea, Sussex, BN4 5DQ.* (Shoreham-by-Sea 2109)

SHEPPARD, Patrick Ashton Gregg. b 08. TCD BA 31. **d** 31 Down **p** 32 Meath for Down. Head of Trin Coll Miss Belfast 31-36; C of Derriaghy 36-41; Offg C-in-c of Inver 41-46; I of Derriaghy 46-60; Ballydehob 60-78; Aghadown w Kilcoe 60-78; Can of Kilbrittain in Cork Cathl and of Donoughmore in Cloyne Cathl 76-78. *Kielbronogue, Ballydehob, Schull, Co Cork, Irish Republic.* (028-28157)

SHEPPARD, Ven Ralph Samson. **d** 34 **p** 35 Newfld. C-in-c of Joe Batt's Arm 34-35; P-in-c 35-38; R 38-42; R of Trinity 42-47; Harbour Breton 47-49; RD of Fortune Bay 47-49; C of Grand Falls 52-55; R 55-68; Can of Newfld 65-76; Archd of Avalon 68-76; Archd (Emer) from 77; Regr Sec (and Treas to 74) of Syn Dio Newfld 68-76; P-in-c of Petty Harbour 72-76. *7 Whiteway Place, St John's, Nfld, Canada.*

SHEPPARD, Stanley Gorton. b 18. St Jo Coll Dur. **d** 62 **p** 63 Leic. C of St Mark Leic 62-65; R of Cole-Orton 65-75; V of Ashby Folville w Twyford and Thorpe Satchville Dio Leic from 75. *Vicarage, Ashby Folville, Melton Mowbray, Leics, LE14 2TA.* (Gaddesby 276)

SHEPPARD, William. b 48. Mount Allison Univ NB BA. Dalhousie Univ NS BEducn. Wycl Coll Tor MDiv 80. **d** 80 Fred. C of Kent Dio Fred from 80. *PO Box 446, Richibucto, NB, Canada, E0A 2M0.*

SHEPPARD-JONES, James Gurney Sheppard. Ch Coll Cam BA 17, MA 22. **d** 18 **p** 19 Llan. C of Caerphilly 18-20; Chepstow 21-22; Penmaen 23-27; Trevethin 27-30; St Lawr Bris 30-32; R of St Devereux w Wormbridge 32-36; V of Llangattock-Vibon-Avel w Llanfaenor and St Maughan 36-48; C of Tamworth 48; V of Sutton-on-the-Hill 49-55; V of Ch Broughton w Barton (and Sutton-on-the-Hill from 55) 51-65; L to Offic Dio Derby 66-81. *Address temp unknown.*

SHEPTON, Robert Leonard McIntire. b 35. Jes Coll Cam BA 58, MA 62. Oak Hill Th Coll 59. **d** 61 **p** 62 Sarum. C of St Jo Evang Weymouth 61-63; Dept Hd Cam Univ Miss Bermondsey 63-66; Warden Oxford-Kilburn Club W Kilburn Lon 66-69; Perm to Offic Dio Lon 66-69; Chap St D Coll Llan 69-78. *Lever House, Old Town, Onich, Nr Fort William, Inverness-shire.*

SHERBORNE, Lord Bishop Suffragan of. *See* Kirkham, Right Rev John Dudley Galtrey.

SHERBORNE, Archdeacon of. *See* Ward, Ven Edwin James Greenfield.

SHERGOLD, Alexander Hedley. b 02. Tyndale Hall Bris 30. **d** 31 **p** 32 Lon. C of St John U Holloway 31-33; St Steph Hounslow 33-37; St Dunstan E Acton 37-38; Charlwood (in c of Lowfield Heath) 38-47; V of All SS N Beddington 47-55; Sidlow Bridge 55-71; Perm to Offic Dio Chelmsf from 72. *5 Madrisa Court, New Street, Lymington, Hants.*

SHERGOLD, William Frank. b 19. St Chad's Coll Dur BA (2nd cl Mod Hist) 40, MA 47. Coll of Resurr Mirfield, 40. **d** 42 **p** 43 Lon. C of All SS Poplar 42-49; Min of All SS Conv Distr Hanworth 49-51; PC 51-59; V of St Mary of Eton w St Aug Hackney Wick and Hd of Eton Coll Miss 59-64; V of St Mary Paddington Green 64-69; St Bart Dover 69-72; C-in-c of St Pet and St Paul Charlton Dover 70-72; R 72-78; Tunstall Dio Cant from 78; V of Rodmersham Dio Cant from 80. *Rectory, Tunstall, Sittingbourne, Kent.* (Sittingbourne 23907)

SHERI, Jonayi Seth. Ch Tr Centre, Kapsabet, 62. **d** 63 **p** 65 Nak. P Dio Nak. *Box 6021, Rongai, Kenya.*

SHERLEY-PRICE, Lionel Digby. b 11. SS Coll Cam BA 32, MA 36. Chich Th Coll 33. **d** 34 **p** 35 Portsm. C of All SS Ryde 34-36; Chap RN 36-63; R of Thurlestone 63-69; RD of Woodleigh 65-69; V of Dawlish 69-74; R of Manaton 74-78; N Bovey 74-78; Publ Pr Dio Ex from 78; RD of Moreton from 80. *Laira, Smokey Lane, Haytor, Newton Abbot, Devon,*

SHERLOCK, Charles Henry. b 45. Univ of Syd BA 67. BD (Lon) 71. Austrn Nat Univ MA 73. Ridley Coll Melb 72. **d** 77 Melb. C of St Aug Moreland Dio Melb from 77. *2 McKenzie Street, Brunswick, Vic, Australia 3056.*

SHERLOCK, Canon Charles Henry. Moore Th Coll ACT THL 40. **d** 41 **p** 42 Syd. C of St Faith Narrabeen 41-42; Hon C 42-46; Chap RAAF 42-47; R of Denmark Paroch Distr 47-49; R of St Pet Milton 49-52; Campbelltown w Appin 52-56; Granville 56-62; R of Hunter's Hill 62-81; Hon Can of Syd from 69; on leave. *2 Ambrose Street, Hunter's Hill, NSW, Australia 2110.* (89-2167)

SHERLOCK, Charles Patrick. b 51. New Coll Ox BA 73, MA 76. Ripon Coll Cudd 75. **d** 77 **p** 78 Guildf. C of Ashtead 77-80; Asst Chap of St Matt Addis Ababa Dio Egypt from 80. *Box 109, Addis Ababa, Ethiopia.* (Addis Ababa 112623)

SHERLOCK, Desmond. b 31. K Coll Lon and Warm BD and AKC 60. **d** 61 **p** 62 S'wark. C of Ascen Mitcham 61-64; St Luke Reigate (in c of St Pet Doversgreen) 64-67; V of Aldersbrook 67-76; Witham Dio Chelmsf from 76; RD of Redbridge 72-76. *Vicarage, Chipping Dell, Witham, Essex.* (Witham 2056)

SHERLOCK, Eric William. b 15. Worc Ordin Coll 64. **d** 66 **p** 67 Ex. C of Highweek 66-68; Asterby 68-71; V of Hoxne w Denham 71-74. *The Perch, Wessington Court, Woolhope, Hereford.*

SHERLOCK, Ewart Templeman. AKC 31. **d** 30 **p** 31 Lon. C of St Ethelreda Fulham 30-33; H Trin Paddington 34-36; St Steph Hampstead 36-43; St Nich Stevenage 43-44; V of Stowe 44-47; R of Croft w Yarpole 47-48; C-in-c of Lucton 47-48; V of TreverbyN 48-51; CF 51-56; R of Risby 56-60; V of Dorney 60-70. *11 Fairview Road, Taplow, Maidenhead, Berks, SL6 0NQ.*

SHERLOCK, George Henry Kenneth. b 02. Or Coll Ox BA 26, MA 29. Wells Th Coll 29. **d** 30 **p** 31 Lon. C of St Dunstan Stepney 30-36; PC of All SS Hampton Lon 36-46; Chap RNVR 40-45; DSC 42; V of St Gabriel Bounds Green Lon 46-51; R of Boyton w Capel and Chap Mary Warner Almshos 51-56; C-in-c of Bawdsey 51-56; RD of Wilford 55-73; R of Sudbourne w Orford 56-72; Perm to Offic Dio St E from 73. *Twitchett's End, Fornham All Saints, Bury St Edmunds, Suff.*

SHERLOCK, John James. St Jo Coll Morpeth ACT ThL 39. **d** 40 **p** 41 Newc. C of St Mark Islington Newc 40-41; Hamilton 41-43; Actg R of Lochinvar w S Maitland 43-45; C of Waratah 45-47; P-in-c of The Entrance 47-51; R of Coopernook 51-53; S Bath 53-69; Molong 69-75; P-in-c of W Wallsend 75-79; Perm to Offic Dio Newc from 79. *231 New England Highway, Rutherford, NSW, Australia 2320.* (32 6280)

SHERLOCK, Robert Edward. Moore Th Coll Syd ThL 47. **d** 47 Bp Pilcher for Syd **p** 47 Syd. C of Randwick 47-48; C-in-c of Glen Davis 48-51; R of Millthorpe 51-57; Coonamble 57-59; Coonabarabran 59-74; Cumnock 75-77; Robinvale Dio Bend from 77. *St Peter's Rectory, Bromley Road, Robinvale, Vic, Australia 3549.*

SHERRATT, Allan Dennis. Chich Th Coll 78. **d** 79 Chich **p** 80 Lewes for Chich. C of Seaford 79-81; Chap Eliz Coll Guernsey from 81. *Elizabeth College, Kings Road, St Peter Port, Guernsey, CI.*

SHERRELL, Sidney Edgar Alban. b 09. Bp's Univ Lennox BA (3rd cl Cl) 33. AKC 37. **d** 37 **p** 38 Chelmsf. C of H Cross Hornhcurch 37-41; Royston and Kelshall 41-45; St Mark Talbot Village (in c of St Thos Ensbury Pk) 45-48; St Mary Stoke Ipswich 48-51; Warminster (in c of St John Boreham) 51-55; V of E and W Orchard w St Marg Marsh and Farrington 55-74. *17 Vicarage Close, Grove, Wantage, Oxon.* (02357-4717)

SHERREN, Douglas Henry. K Coll NS STh 49. **d** 49 **p** 50 NS. R of Liscomb 49-51; Blandford 51-53; Guysboro 53-68;

Antigonish and of Country Harbour Dio NS from 68. *Box 85, Antigonish, NS, Canada.* (863-3507)

SHERRIFF, Donald Gordon. b 16. Univ of Lon BD 37, MTh 39. ALCD 37. **d** 39 Willesden for Lon **p** 40 Lon. Tutor Lon Coll Div 39-42; C of St John Bexley 42-45; CMS Miss 46-68; Tutor N Ind Div Sch Khatauli 46-50; I of Saharanpur 47-50; Bulandshahr 50-56; U Th Sem (N Ind Th Coll from 65) Bareilly 56-68; I of Shahjahanpur 58-68; I of Bareilly 64-68; V of St Mary w St Paulinus Cray 69-73; Linton w Hunton Dio Roch from 73. *Hunton Rectory, Maidstone, Kent.* (Hunton 242)

SHERSBY, Brian Alfred. b 41. Clifton Th Coll 68. **d** 71 Dorking for Guildf **p** 72 Guildf. C of Em Stoughton 71-74; St Jas and of St Pet w St Owen Heref 74-79; V of Earlham Dio Nor from 79. *St Mary's Vicarage, Douglas Haig Road, Norwich, NR5 8LD.* (Norwich 54742)

SHERWIN-WHITE, Esmond Verinder. b 10. AKC 33. St Steph Ho Ox 33. **d** 34 **p** 35 Lon. C of All SS Poplar 34-36; St Mary Magd Munster Square Lon 36-42; St Paul Brighton 42-52; St Martin Brighton 52-55; V of St Osmund Parkstone 55-69; Chap Burford Priory Dio Ox from 69. *Priory of Our Lady, Burford, Oxford.* (Burford 3071)

SHERWOOD, Lord Bishop Suffragan of. *See* Darby, Right Rev Harold Richard

SHERWOOD, Canon Charles Purvis. b 10. Trin Coll Melb 33. Wycl Hall Ox 37. **d** 38 Leic **p** 39 Bp Willis for Leic. C of St Barn New Humberstone Leic 38-40; St Alb Bournemouth 40-41; C-in-c St Nich Leic 41-42; Chap RAFVR 42-46; C of St Mary Virg Reading 46-48; V of Mapledurham 48-54; R of Bladon w Woodstock 54-58; Sec Ox Dioc Coun of Educn 55-62; Chap HM Pris Campsfield Ho 55-62; R of Launton 58-62; Dir of Relig Educn Dio Man 62-69; Hon Can of Man 64-76; Can (Emer) from 76; R of Em Didsbury 69-75; Hon P-in-c of St Pet Leck 75-77. *Flat 5, Holt House, Dene Road, Didsbury, Manchester M20 8ST.*

SHERWOOD, Denys Charles. b 20. Univ of Lon BA 49. Oak Hill Th Coll. **d** 51 **p** 52 Lon. C of St Mary Hornsey Rise 51-54; Dagenham 54-56; V of St Luke w St Silas Bedminster 56-63; St Barn Lenton Abbey 67-77; Org Sec CPAS SE Area 63-67; Perm to Offic Dio Portsm 63-67; V of Basford Dio Lich from 77. *St Mark's Vicarage, Lower Oxford Road, Basford, Newcastle-under-Lyme, -Lyme 619045)*

SHERWOOD, Edwin Frank. b 1893. Linc Th Coll 25. **d** 27 **p** 28 Sheff. C of St Mary Worsborough 27-29; CF (Res) from 28; C-in-c of New Edlington Conv Distr 29-31; C of Kewstoke Milton 31-35; V of Burrowbridge 35-54; Puxton w Hewish and Wick St Lawr 54-64. *44 Courtwick Road, Wick, Littlehampton, Sussex, BN17 7NP.*

SHERWOOD, Gordon Frederick. b 29. Sarum Wells Th Coll 77. **d** 80 **p** 81 Southn for Win. C of Weeke Dio Win from 80. *104 Teg Down Meads, Weeke, Winchester, Hants, SO22 5NN.*

SHERWOOD, Michael Colin Gordon. b 20. Magd Coll Ox BA (3rd cl Th) 47, MA 51. Cudd Coll. **d** 49 Bedford for St Alb **p** 50 St Alb. C of Sandridge 49-52; Cirencester w Watermoor 52-57; R of Colne 57-61; Surr from 58; V of Tetbury w Beverston Dio Glouc from 61; RD of Tetbury from 73; C-in-c of Shipton Moyne Dio Glouc 72-75. *Vicarage, Tetbury, Glos, GL8 8DN.* (Tetbury 52333)

SHEUMACK, Ven Colin Davies. Moore Th Coll ACT ThL 51. **d** 52 **p** 53 C & Goulb. C of St Jo Bapt Canberra 52-54; R of Kameruka 54-59; Kyabram 59-67; Dom Chap to Bp of Bend 63-67; Archd of Bend from 67; VG of Bend from 68. *12 Rowan Street, Bendigo, Vic, Australia.* (054-43 7992)

✠ **SHEVILL, Right Rev Ian Wotton Allnutt.** b 18. Univ of Syd BA 39, MA 45. ACT ThD 53. Moore Th Coll Syd 39. **d** 40 **p** 41 Syd. C of St Paul Burwood 40-45; Org Sec of ABM for Prov of Queensld 46-47; Sec For Educn SPG 48-51; L to Offic Dio Lon 49-51; Dio Syd 51-53; Home Sec ABM 51-53; Cons Ld Bp of N Queensld in Brisb Cathl 19 Apr 53 by Abp of Brisb; Abp of Syd; Bps of N Guinea; Rockptn; Carp; C & Goulb; and Graft; and Bps Dixon; Collins; and Ash; res 70; Sec USPG Lon 70-73; Asst Bp in Lon 71-73; Apptd Ld Bp of Newc 73; res 77; Commiss Taejon 71-73. *13 Cottesmore Street, Fig Tree Pocket, Brisbane, Queensland, Australia 4069.* (07-378 7856)

SHEWAN, Alistair Boyd. b 44. Open Univ BA 79. Edin Th Coll 63. **d** 67 **p** 68 Moray. Prec of St Andr Cathl Inverness 67-69; Bp's Chap Dio Moray 70; C of St Steph Uxbridge Rd Hammersmith 70-73; St Mich and All SS Edin 73-75; Perm to Offic Dio Edin 75-78; C of Old St Paul City and Dio Edin from 80. *3 Castle Wynd North, Edinburgh 1.* (225-6537)

SHEWAN, James William. b 36. Sarum Th Coll 61. **d** 63 Worc **p** 64 Dur. C of St Barn Worc 63-64; Newton Aycliffe 64-66; St Pet Harton (in c of St Lawr) 66-69; V of S Moor 69-72; CF 72-77; P-in-c of St Aid Newc T 77-79; V of Longhoughton w Howick Dio Newc T from 79. *Longhoughton Vicarage, Alnwick, Northumb, NE66 3AG.* (Longhoughton 664)

SHEWARD, Canon Cyril Godfrey. b 1900. Univ of Man BD 22. **d** and **p** 42 Carl. [f Methodist Min] C of St John Barrow-F 42-44; V of St Jas Whitehaven 44-71; Chap Meadow Ho Hosp Whitehaven 47-64; Hon Can of Carl 69-71; Can (Emer) from 71; L to Offic Dio Carl from 71. *Cedar Garth, Burgh-by-Sands, Carlisle.*

SHEWELL, Edward Charles Beaudon. b 12. St Pet Hall, Ox 3rd cl Cl Mods 33, BA 36, MA 46. Ridley Hall, Cam 36. **d** 37 **p** 38 Ex. C of St Andr Plymouth 37-41; Offg C-in-c of St Jo Bapt Devonport 41-42; C of St Mark Torquay 42-44; Chap RNVR 44-47; C of St Luke Wimbledon Park 47-51; Cheam (in c of St Osw) 51-54; V of Berry Pomeroy w Bridgetown 54-77; RD of Totnes 63-66; R of L Hempston 69-77; P-in-c of Clawton 77-81; Tetcott w Luffincott 77-81. *3 Dreva Road, Broughton, Peeblesshire.*

SHEWRING, Derek Ivan Gordon. b 15. Univ of Birm BA 50. Qu Coll Birm 46. **d** 50 **p** 51 S'wark. C of Ch Ch E Greenwich (w St Andr and St Mich from 51) 50-57; V of St Jo Evang Angell Town Brixton 57-63; R of Bilborough w Strelley 63-77; RD of Beeston 67-77; C-in-c of Broxtowe 74-75; V of E Retford Dio Southw from 77; P-in-c of Grove Dio Southw from 77; RD of Retford from 77. *1 Chapelgate, Retford, Notts, DN22 6PL.* (Retford 702696)

SHEZI, Cyril Cyprian Vincent. St Pet Coll Alice, 63. **d** 65 Bp Cullen for Zulu **p** 66 Zulu. P Dio Zulu 65-76; Dio St John's 76-80; Dio Natal from 80. *P Bag 518, Impendle, Natal, S Africa.*

SHIBAOKA, Atsushi. b 52. Univ of Syd ACT BTh 77. Ridley Coll Melb 75. **d** 77 **p** 78 Gippsld. P-in-c of Omeo Dio Gippsld from 77. *Rectory, PO Box 27, Omeo, Vic, Australia 3898.*

SHIELD, Douglas Farnham. St Jo Coll Morpeth ACT ThL 55. **d** 55 Adel **p** 57 Carp for Adel. C (332 8459) of St Mary Magd Adel 55-56; Chap Elizabeth Miss 56-57; C of Ch Ch Mt Gambier 57-60; P-in-c of Cummins 60-62; Berri w Barmera 62-66; CF (Austr) 66-75; P-in-c of Newman 75-76; Chap R Adel Hosp Dio Adel from 76. *9/14 Tusmore Avenue, Leabrook, S Australia 5068.*

SHIELD, Ian Thomas. b 32. Late Scho of Hertf Coll Ox BA 56, MA and BLitt 60. Westcott Ho Cam 59. **d** 61 York for Bradf **p** 62 Bradf. C of Shipley 61-64; Tutor Lich Th Coll 64-71; Chap 67-71; V of Dunston w Coppenhall 71-79; Team V of Wolverhampton Dio Lich from 79. *176 Crowther Road, Wolverhampton, WV6 0HY.* (Wolverhampton 751911)

SHIELDS, Christopher Charles. Ridley Coll Melb ACT ThL 69. **d** 70 Bp Dann for Melb. **p** 71 Melb. C of St Silas N Balwyn 70-71; St Geo Malvern 71-72; P-in-c of Ch Ch Melton 73-74; Perm to Offic Dio Melb from 74. *51 Brunel Street, E Malvern, Vic, Australia 3145.* (25-7462)

SHIELDS, John Holdsworth. d 42 **p** 45 St Arn. C of Wedderburn 42-45; Boort 45-48; R of Sea Lake 48-55; Avoca 55-56; Beechworth 56-58; Cohuna 58-66; Cobden 66-70; Perm to Offic Dio Bend from 70; Dio St Arn 70-76. *47 Sullivan Street, Inglewood, Vic, Australia 3519.* (054-38 2211)

SHIELDS, Michael Penton. b 30. Bps' Coll Cheshunt. **d** 64 Lon **p** 65 Willesden for Lon. C of St Andr Kingsbury 64-67; All SS Friern Barnet 67-69; V of St Matthias Colindale Hendon 69-76; St Jo Bapt Sevenoaks Dio Roch from 76. *62 Quakers Hall Lane, Sevenoaks, Kent, TN13 3TX.* (Sevenoaks 51710)

SHIELDS, Peter Anderson. b 22. St Jo Coll Auckld 70. **d** 70 **p** 71 Ch Ch. C of Hornby 70-73; P-in-c of Waihao Downs 73-74; V of New Brighton 74-78; Wakatipu Dio Dun from 78. *Vicarage, Earl Street, Queenstown, NZ.* (330)

SHIELDS, William Gordon. b 41. Bp's Univ Lennoxville BA 68. Trin Coll Tor MDiv 71. **d** 71 **p** 72 Tor. CF (Canad) from 71; Hon C of Ch Ch Winnipeg 76-77; St Pet Winnipeg Dio Rupld from 77. *CFB Kapyong Barracks, Depot M, Winnipeg, Manit, Canada.*

SHIELLS, Robert Thornton. b 03. Univ of Lon BSc 23, MSc 54. **d** 36 **p** 37 Wakef. Asst Master Gr Sch Hemsworth 25-39; C of Hemsworth 36-39; Chap Nautical Coll Pangbourne 39-47; V of Taynton w Gt and L Barrington 47; Asst Chap and Master Brentwood Sch 47-54; Perm to Offic Dio Lon 47-54; R of Shenfield 54-70; Chap Brentwood Distr Hosp 54-70; Perm to Offic Dio Ox from 71. *Lincolns Inn, Hook Norton, Oxon.* (Hook N 244)

SHIELS, Donald Allan Patterson. b 15. Selw Coll Cam BA 38, 2nd cl Th Trip pt i 38, MA 42. Wycl Hall Ox 38. **d** 39 **p** 40 B & W. C of St Mary Magd Taunton 39-42; Bermondsey 42-45; St John Redhill 45-47; V of St Jo Evang Brownswood Pk 47-62; Stoke Gifford 62-80. *20 Westbourne Drive, Cheltenham, GL52 2QQ.* (Cheltm 41537)

SHIER, John Michael. b 42. St Chad's Coll Dur BA 64. **d** 66 **p** 67 Lon. C of St Mary Virg Kenton 66-72; St Mary Pimlico 72-77; V of St Clem w St Barn and St Matt Finsbury

Dio Lon from 77. *Vicarage, King Square, EC1V 8DA.* (01-253 9140)

SHIKONGO, Jafet Hafeni. **d** 66 **p** 69 Damar. P Dio Damar 66-80; Dio Namibia from 80. *c/o St Mary's Mission, Odibo, PO Oshikango, Ovamboland, SW Africa.* (Oshikango 5)

SHILIMI, Charles. Buwalasi Th Coll 60. **d** 61 **p** 62 Mbale. P Dio Mbale; Hon Can of Mbale 69-78. *Box 902, Mbale, Uganda.*

SHILL, Kenneth Leslie. b 49. Univ of Leic BA 70. BD (Lon) 73. Ridley Hall Cam 75. **d** 77 **p** 78 Birm. C of St Jo Bapt Harborne Dio Birm from 77. *53 Station Road, Harborne, Birmingham B17 9LP.*

SHILLAKER, John. K Coll Lon and Warm BD and AKC 60. **d** 61 **p** 62 Lon. C of Bush Hill Pk 61-65; St Mary Magd Milton 65-69; C-in-c of St Luke's (Conv Distr to 78) Moulsham Dio Chelmsf 69-78; V from 78. *St Luke's Church, Lewis Drive, Chelmsford, CM2 9EF.* (Chelmsf 354479)

SHILLIDAY, Ven Errol Joseph. Hur Coll 54. **d** 54 **p** 55 Hur. I of Kerwood 54-57; R of St Mark Windsor 57-62; R of St John St Thomas 62-69; St Bart Sarnia 69-75; St Steph City and Dio Calg from 75; Can of Hur 73-75; Hon Can of Calg 78-79; Archd of Bow Valley from 79. *514-40th Street SW, Calgary, Alta, Canada.*

SHILLINGFORD, Brian. b 39. Lich Th Coll. **d** 68 S'wark **p** 69 Bp Boys for S'wark. C of St Swith Hither Green 68-71; Godstone (in c of St Steph S Godstone) 71-75; Team V of St Geo Croydon 75-81; Woolfardisworthy E w Cheriton Fitzpaine (in C of Morchard Bp, Down, Clannaborough and Washford Pyne) Dio Ex from 81. *Morchard Bishop Rectory, Crediton, Devon.* (Morchard Bp 221)

SHILONGO, Ven Philip Hangula. **d** 66 **p** 67 Damar. P Dio Damar 66-68; Dio Namibia from 80; Archd of Odibo from 70. *c/o St Mary's Church, Odibo, PO Oshikango, SW Africa.* (Oshikango 5)

SHILTON, Jack Henry. Ridley Coll Melb ThL 48. **d** 49 **p** 50 Gippsld. C of Warragul 49; V of St John Cann River 50-51; Blackwood Forest w Bass 51-55; N Carlton 55-57; I of E Geelong 57-64; V of Ivanhoe 65-77; I of Greensborough Dio Melb from 77. *Vicarage, Church Street, Greensborough, Vic., Australia 3088.* (435-1162)

SHILTON, Very Rev Lancelot Rupert. BA (Melb) 54. BD (Lon) 56. Ridley Coll Melb ThL (2nd cl) 49. **d** 49 **p** 50 Melb. C of Hawthorne 49-51; Min of Carlton 51-54; Melb Dioc Centre 51-54; Comm for Ridley Coll Appeal 54-55; Perm to Offic Dios Cant and Ely 55-57; R of H Trin Adel 57-73; P-in-c of Kidman Pk 58-64; Dean of Syd from 73. *2 Wallace Parade, Lindfield, NSW, Australia 2070.* (46-4777)

SHILVOCK, Geoffrey. b 47. St D Coll Lamp BA (Th) 69. Sarum Wells Th Coll 70. **d** 72 **p** 73 Worc. C of Kidderminster (in c of St Barn Franche from 76) 72-78; P-in-c of Malvern Dio Worc from 78. *8 Christchurch Road, Malvern, Worcs, WR14 3BE.* (Malvern 4106)

SHIMBODE, Stephen Hilukilua. **d** 64 **p** 65 Damar. P Dio Damar. *c/o St Mary's Mission, Odibo, PO Oshikango, Ovamboland, SW Africa.* (Oshikango 5)

SHIMWELL, Robert John. b 46. Univ of Lon Dipl Th 68. Trin Coll Bris 75. **d** 78 S'wark **p** 79 Ex. C of H Trin Richmond 78-79; Kentisbeare w Blackborough and of Cullompton 79-81; V of S Cave & Ellerker w Broomfleet Dio York from 81. *10 Station Road, South Cave, Brough, N Humb, HU15 2AA.* (N Cave 3693)

SHIN, Andrew. **d** 69 **p** 70 Taejon. P Dio Taejon 69-73; on leave. *c/o Box 22, Taejon 300, Korea.*

SHINER, Michael Joseph. b 21. Chich Th Coll 51. **d** 53 Ox for Sarum **p** 54 Sarum. C of H Trin Weymouth 53-56; V of Stanbridge w Tilsworth 56-63; Chap Worc R Infirm 63-67; V of Powerstock w W Milton Witherstone and N Poorton 67-73; St Cross Knutsford 73-75; Area Sec for Age Concern Cornwall from 75; Co Org W Sussex from 80. *26 Southgate, Chichester, W Sussex, PO19 1ES.* (Chich 775588)

SHINN, William Raymond. b 22. Sarum Wells Th Coll 71. **d** 73 St Alb **p** 74 Bedford for St Alb. C of St Paul Letchworth 73-75; Dunstable 75-78; Team V 78-80; V of Round Green, Luton Dio St Alb from 80. *33 Felix Avenue, Luton, Beds.* (Luton 24754)

SHINZE, Meshak. **d** 68 **p** 69 W Tang. P Dio W Tang. *Box 161, Kigoma, Tanzania.*

SHIPLEY, Preb Cecil Gange. MBE 73. Lon Coll of Div 34. **d** 36 **p** 37 Sheff. C of St Barn Sheff 36-38; Wombwell 38; Hemingfield 39; Warden Imp Services Inst Bris 40-42; Sec YMCA Weston-super-Mare 42-49; LPr Dio B & W 43-49; C of Portishead 49-53; R of Foxcote w Shoscombe 53-59; V of H trin Frome Selwood 59-76; Preb of Wells Cathl from 70. *5 The Homes, Langford, Bristol, BS18 7HU.* (Wrington 862624)

SHIPLEY, Christopher John. b 44. Univ of Leeds BSc 65, MSc 70, BA 72. Coll of Resurr Mirfield 70. **d** 73 **p** 74 Blackb. C of Preston 73-77; Chap Preston Poly 75-77; V of St Mich AA w St Jo Evang (and H Trin from 81) Blackb Dio Blackb from 77; P-in-c of H Trin Blackb 78-81. *St Michael's Vicarage, Whalley New Road, Blackburn, Lancs, BB1 6LB.* (Blackb 57121)

SHIPMAN, Canon Eric Arthur. b 16. AKC 40. **d** 40 **p** 41 Chelmsf. C of St Jo Bapt Leytonstone 40-42; V of St Andr (w St Phil and St Jas from 77) Plaistow 42-81; Chap Mansfield Ho Univ Settlement Plaistow Dio Chelmsf 49-61; Warden from 61; RD of W Ham 64-65; Newham 65-75; Hon Can of Chelmsf 66-81; Can (Emer) from 81. *The Residence, Mansfield House, 30a Avenons Road, E13 8AT.* (01-476 2375)

SHIPTON, Don Robert. b 44. K Coll NS BA 67, STB 71. Atlantic Sch of Th Halifax NS MTh 77. **d** 70 NS. C of Herring Cove 70-72; on leave. *36 Kelly Street, Apt 404, Armdale, Halifax, NS, Canada.* (454-0493)

SHIRE, William Stanley. b 17. TCD BA and Div Test 39, MA 43. **d** 40 **p** 41 Arm. C of Dundalk Arm 40-43; St Mark Portadown 43-45; C-in-c of Mullaglass 45-51; I 51-57; C of Attenborough w Bramcote and Chilwell 57-58; V of Lowdham w Gunthorpe 58-66; R of Pilton w Wadenhoe and Stoke Doyle (and Aldwincle w Thorpe Achurch from 70) Dio Pet from 67. *Rectory, Aldwincle, Kettering, Northants.* (Clopton 613)

SHIREHAMPTON, William John Prankerd. Qu Coll Cam BA 34, MA 38. Lon Coll of Div 34. **d** 36 **p** 37 S'wark. C of New Malden w Coombe 36-39; H Trin Eastbourne 39-40; Chap RAFVR 40-47; Chap Kingham Hill Sch Ox 47; L to Offic Dio Ox 47-49; Dio Mon from 49; Warden of Mon Sch 49-80; Almshos from 49. *Larne, Highfield Close, Monmouth, Gwent.* (Monmouth 2082)

SHIRES, Alan William. b 36. BA (Lon) 60. Oak Hill Th Coll 57. **d** 61 **p** 62 York. C of St Paul York 61-64; St Mary Southgate Crawley Sussex 64-67; V of St Mary Doncaster 67-75; Stud Counsellor Portsm Poly from 75. *Portsmouth Polytechnic, Town Mount, Hampshire Terrace, Portsmouth, PO1 2QG.*

SHIRESS, David Henry Faithfull. b 27. St Cath Coll Cam BA 49, MA 53. Ridley Hall Cam 51. **d** 53 **p** 54 Liv. C of Ch Ch Southport 53-55; St Mark St Helens 55-58; V of St Julian Shrewsbury 58-67; St Mich AA Blackheath Pk Dio S'wark from 67. *2 Pond Road, SE3 9JL.* (01-852 5287)

SHIRLEY, Timothy Francis. b 25. Univ Coll Ox BA (2nd cl Mod Hist) and MA 49. Qu Coll Birm. **d** 51 **p** 52 Lon. C of St Gabr Warwick Square Pimlico 51-56; C-in-c of St Edm Yeading Hayes Middx 56-65; V of St Etheldreda (w St Clem from 68) Fulham Dio Lon from 65. *Vicarage, Doneraile Street, SW6 6EL.* (01-736 3809)

SHIRRAS, Edward Scott. b 37. Univ of St Andr BSc 61. Clifton Th Coll 61. **d** 63 **p** 64 S'wark. C of Ch Ch Surbiton Hill 63-66; Jesmond Newc T 66-68; Hon C H Trin Wallington 69-75. Youth Sec CPAS 68-71; Publications Sec 71-74; Asst Gen Sec 74-75; V of Ch Ch Roxeth Harrow Dio Lon from 75; M of Abp's Coun of Evang 77-80. *Christ Church Vicarage, Roxeth Hill, Harrow, Middx, HA2 0JN.* (01-422 3241)

SHOESMITH, Brian Edward. b 46. McMaster Univ BA 68. Huron Coll Ont BTH 71. **d** and **p** 71 Niag. C of St Chris Burlington 71-73; R of W Flamboro 73-80; Leduc Dio Edmon from 80. *Box 1220, Leduc, Alta, Canada.*

SHOLE, Mophalane Manasseh Reuben. St Pet Coll Rosettenville. **d** 64 **p** 66 Johann. P Dio Johann 64-77; L to Offic from 78. *Box 798, Potchefstroom 2520, S Africa.*

SHOLL, Preb Ernest Redfern. b 09. AKC 33. **d** 33 **p** 34 S'wark. C of St Mark Walworth 33-34; St Luke Camberwell 34-38; L to Offic Dio Cant 38; Perm to Offic Dio B & W 39-44; R of Holford w Dodington 44-53; RD of Quantoxhead 53-68; V of Stoke Courcy (or Stogursey) 53-74; V of Stockland Bristol 55-70; Preb of Easton-in-Gordano in Wells Cathl from 57; C-in-c of Fiddington 60-64; R 64-74. *Egypt Cottage, Beattock, Moffat, Dumfries.*

SHONE, Canon John Terence. b 35. Selw Coll Cam BA 58, MA 62. Linc Th Coll. **d** 60 Lon **p** 61 Kens for Lon. C of St Pancras 60-62; Chap Angl Studs in Aber 62-68; St Andr Cathl Aber 62-65; Exam Chap to Bp of Aber 66-68; Lect Aber Coll of Educn 66-68; PC St Andr w St Luke Grimsby 68-69; R of Bridge of Allan Dio St Andr from 69; Chap Univ of Stirling 69-80; P-in-c of Alloa Dio St Andr from 77; Dollar Dio St Andr from 81; Can of St Ninian's Cathl Perth from 80. *Rectory, Fountain Road, Bridge of Allan, Stirlingshire, FK9 4AT.* (Bridge of Allan 832368)

SHONE, Raymond. b 21. Late Exhib of St Jo Coll Dur BA (Hons Th) 47, MA 54. Linc Th Coll 48. **d** 48 **p** 49 Lich. C of Penn 48-50; Warblington w Emsworth 50-58; R of Monks Risborough 58-61; Chap and Lect Bp Otter Coll Chich 61-66; Perm to Offic Dio Chich from 61; Sen Lect Eastbourne Coll of Educn 66-76; E Sussex Coll of Higher Educn 76-79; Brighton Poly 79-80. *15 Fennell's Close, Eastbourne, E Sussex, BN21 2RJ.* (Eastbourne 36139)

SHONE, Robert Alan. b 16. Qu Coll Cam BA 38, MA 42. St Steph Ho Ox 39. **d** 39 **p** 40 Liv. C of Good Shepherd W

Derby 39-41; Wigan 41-42; Birch-in-Rusholme 42-45; St Mary Wardleworth 45-47; R of St Chris Withington 47-56; V of St Paul Morley 56-63; St Mary (w St Jas from 73) Wardleworth Rochdale 63-81; V of St Jas Wardleworth 66-73. *172 Bar Terrace, Whitworth, Rochdale, Lancs.* (Rochdale 344405)

SHONE, William Leslie. b 07. St Aid Coll 30. **d** 33 **p** 34 Sheff. C of Woodlands 33-37; Bucknall (in c of St Chad Bagnall) 37-41; V of Rawcliffe Goole 41-44; St Steph Newc T 44-51; All SS Tufnell Pk 51-59; H Trin Sydenham 59-69; Nutley 69-73; Perm to Offic Dio Cant from 73. *42 Alder Road, Folkestone, Kent, CT19 5DA.* (Folkestone 52904)

SHONGWE, Benjamin. b 30. **d** 80 Swaz. d Dio Swaz. *PO Box 36, Mbabane, Swaziland.*

SHONGWE, Londoloza Percy. St Bede's Coll Umtata 76. **d** 78 **p** 79 Swaz. P Dio Swaz. *St Anne's Parish, PO Box 57, Piggs Peak, Swaziland.*

SHONGWE, Majawonkhe Joseph. St Bede's Coll Umtata 76. **d** 78 **p** Swaz. P Dio Swaz. *PO Box 40, Tshanani, Swaziland.*

SHORROCK, John Musgrave. b 29. TCD BA (Mod in Ment and Mor Sc) 54, MA 58. Bps' Coll Cheshunt 54. **d** 56 **p** 57 Blackb. C of St Pet Fleetwood 56-59; Lanc 59-61; C-in-c of Eccles Distr of St Wilfrid Mereside Blackpool 61-65; V 65-67; Sacr and Min Can of Cant Cathl 67-70; V of St Geo Chorley 70-78; Bredgar w Bicknor and Hucking Dio Cant from 78; Frinsted w Wormshill and Milstead Dio Cant from 78. *Bredgar Vicarage, Sittingbourne, Kent, ME9 8HA.* (Wormshill 387)

SHORT, Brian Frederick. b 29. St Jo Coll Nottm 70. **d** 72 **p** 73 St E. C of Walton 72-75; P-in-c of Ringshall w Battisford 75-78; Barking w Darmsden and Gt Bricett 75-78; Team V of Parmentergate Team Min City and Dio Nor from 78. *31 Bracondale, Norwich, NR1 2AT.* (0603-24827)

✠ **SHORT, Right Rev Hedley Vicars Roycraft.** Univ of Tor BA 41, LTh (1st cl) 43. Trin Coll Tor BD (1st CL) 45, Hon DD 64. **d** Bp Beverley for Tor **p** 44 Tor. C of St Mich Tor 43-46; St Mich Cathl Cov 46-47; Lect Trin Coll Tor 47-49; Actg Dean 49-51; R of Cochrane Ont 51-56; St Barn St Catharines 56-63; Exam Chap to Bp of Moos 51-57; to Bp of Niag 61-63; to Bp of Sask 66-70; Can of Niag 62-63; Dean and R of St Alb Cathl Prince Albert 63-70; Archd of Prince Albert 66-70; Cons Bp of Sask 29 Nov 70 in Ind Stud Res Auditorium Prince Albert by Abp of Qu'App; Bps of Athab; Calg; Keew; Bran; Pres of Coun of Em and St Chad Coll Sask 74-80; Hon Fell from 80; Chan Univ of Em Coll 75-80. *427 21st Street West, Prince Albert, Sask, Canada.* (306-763 2455)

SHORT, James. d 81 Calg. Hon C of H Nativ City and Dio Calg from 81. *424 Canterbury Place SW, Calgary, Alta, Canada, T2W 2B6.*

SHORT, John Sinclair. b 33. Oak Hill Th Coll 64. **d** 66 **p** 67 Lon. C of St Mary Islington 66-70; V of St Mary Becontree 70-75; New Malden w Coombe Dio S'wark from 76; RD of Kingston from 79. *93 Coombe Road, New Malden, Surrey, KT3 4RE.* (01-942 0915)

SHORT, John Timothy. b 43. Dipl Th (Lon) 67. Kelham Th Coll 63. **d** 68 Lon **p** 69 Willesden for Lon. C of Ch Ch w St Barn St Marylebone 68-70; Ch Ch Southgate 70-72; P-in-c of Mosser 72-78; R of Heyford w Stowe Nine Churches Dio Pet from 78. *Heyford Rectory, Northampton, NN7 3LQ.* (Weedon 40487)

SHORT, Kenneth Arthur. b 33. Tyndale Hall Bris 64. **d** 67 **p** 68 Lon. C of St Steph E Twickenham 67-71; Paddock Wood 71-74; SE Area Sec BCMS from 74; Hon C of Ch Ch Sidcup Dio Roch from 74. *12 Sandhurst Road, Sidcup, Kent, DA15 7HL.* (01-300 5213)

✠ **SHORT, Right Rev Kenneth Herbert.** Moore Th Coll Syd ThL 51. **d** and **p** 52 Syd. C of St Clem Mosman 52; C-in-c of Pittwater Provisional Distr 52-55; Miss at Kongwa 55; Tabora 55-56; Mwanza 56-59; Berega 60-61; Prin of Msalato Bible Sch Dodoma 61-64; Gen Sec CMS in NSW and L to Offic Dio Syd 64-71; Can of Syd 70-75; R of Vaucluse 71-75; Exam Chap to Abp of Syd from 72; Cons Asst Bp of Syd (Bp in Wollongong) in St Andr Cathl Syd 1 April 75 by Abp of Syd; Bps of Armid, Bath and C & Goulb; and others; Archd of Wollongong 75-79; Chap Gen (Austr) from 79; Bp to Austr Forces from 79. *49 Market Street, Wollongong, NSW, Australia 2500.* (042-28 8487)

SHORT, Martin Peter. b 54. Peterho Cam BA 77. Wycl Hall Ox 77. **d** 79 **p** 80 Bradf. C of St Pet Shipley Dio Bradf from 79. *43 George Street, Shipley, W Yorks, BD18 4PT.*

SHORT, Michael John. b 38. St D Coll Lamp BA 59. Sarum Th Coll 59. **d** 61 **p** 62 Swan B. C of St Nich-on-the-Hill Swansea 61-64; Oystermouth 64-69; V of Merthyr Vale Dio Llan from 69; RD of Merthyr Tydfil from 76. *Vicarage, Merthyr Vale, Mid Glam.* (Ynysowen 690249)

SHORT, Terence. K Coll Lon and Warm AKC 63. **d** 64 **p** 65 Ripon. C of Seacroft 64-68; Mansfield 68-69; C-in-c of St Mich AA Sutton-in-Ashfield 69-75; V of St Jo Bapt Carlton Dio Southw from 75. *261 Oakdale Road, Carlton, Nottingham.* (Nottm 246051)

SHORTEN, Richard Deering. b 08. Qu Coll Cam BA 30, MA 48. Westcott Ho Cam 30. **d** 32 **p** 33 Ripon. C of St Wilfrid Leeds 32-35; V of St Silas Hunslet 35-38; Kirkby Wharfe w Ulleskelf 38-56; Chap RAFVR 43-47; V of Preshute 56-75; Asst Chap of Marlb Coll 56-75; RD of Marlb 64-74. *Throg Cottage, Preshute Lane, Marlborough, Wilts, SN8 4HQ.* (0672-52447)

SHORTHOUSE, Mervin. b 14. Edin Th Coll. **d** 47 **p** 48 Dur. C of Greenside 47-50; St Marg (in c of St John Nevilles Cross) Dur 50-52; PC of Chopwell 52-55; V of Cornforth 55-75; Chap Winterton Hosp 60-66; Industr Tr Centre 68-74; V of Aycliffe 75-79. *122 Salutation Road, Darlington, Co Durham.* (Darlington 50647)

SHORTHOUSE, Raymond Trevor. b 34. Ridley Hall Cam 68. **d** 70 **p** 71 Barking for Chelmsf. C of St Andr, Gt Ilford 70-73; Ludlow 73-75; P-in-c of Cressage w Sheinton 75-79; Harley 75-79; Denby and Adult Educn Officer Dio Derby from 79. *Vicarage, Denby Village, Derby, DE5 2PH.* (Derby 880262)

SHORTHOUSE, Canon Stephen Arthur. b 20. Trin Coll Cam 3rd cl Math Trip pt i, 39, BA (3rd cl Physics Trip pt ii) 41, MA 45. Westcott Ho Cam 41. **d** 43 **p** 44 Birm. C of St Paul Balsall Heath 43-47; Actg C-in-c of Perry Beeches Conv Distr 47-49; PC 49-57; V of Yardley Wood 57-75; Bartley Green Dio Birm from 75; Hon Can of Birm from 76. *Vicarage, Romsley Road, Bartley Green, Birmingham, B32 3PS.* (021-475 1508)

SHORTLAND, Charles Brown. Coll Ho Ch Ch NZ 53. **d** 56 Wel **p** 57 Bp Rich for Wel. C of Wanganui 56-58; Wel Maori Past 58-60; Waik Maori Past 60-62 and 64-66; Frankton 62-64; P-in-c of Aotea-Kuruhaupo Maori Past 66-73; C of Rangiatea Maori Past 73-76; P-in-c of Wairarapa Maori Past Dio Wel from 76. *131 Cole Street, Masterton, NZ.* (6297)

SHORTT, John Buckley. Linc Coll Ox BA (2nd cl Mod Hist) 28, MA 32. St Aug Coll Cant. **d** 29 **p** 30 Ripon. C of Richmond w H Trin 29-32; St Mary's Cathl Johann 32-39; R of Brakpan 39-42; CF (S Afr) 42-45; L to Offic Dio Johann 45-55; Hd of St Geo Home Johann 45-55; R of W Wickham 55-63; V of River 63-74; RD of Dover 71-74; Hon C of Walmer Dio Cant from 75. *8 Herschell Road, Walmer, Deal, Kent.*

SHORTT, Noel Christopher. b 36. Open Univ BA 76. Bps' Coll Cheshunt. **d** 63 **p** 64 Connor. C of St Mary Belf 63-66; Agherton 66-68; Chap RAF 68-69; I of Duneane w Ballyscullion 69-79; St Steph Belf Dio Connor from 79; St Luke Belf Dio Connor from 80. *92 Lansdowne Road, Belfast, N Ireland.* (Belfast 779064)

SHOTLANDER, Lionel George. b 27. Cant Univ Coll BA 49, MA 51. **d** 51 **p** 52 Wel. C of Petone 51-53; Marton 53-54; V of Eketahuna 54-58; C of St Pet Southsea 58-60; V of U Hutt 60-62; Petone 62-68; Henderson Auckld 68-74; V of Curdridge Dio Portsm from 74; P-in-c of Durley Dio Portsm 78; R from 78. *St Peter's Vicarage, Curdridge, Southampton, SO3 2DR.* (Botley 2795)

SHOTTER, Preb Edward Frank. b 33. St D Coll Lamp BA 58. St Steph Ho Ox 58. **d** 60 **p** 61 Ex. C of St Pet Plymouth 60-62; Inter Colleg Sec SCM Lon 62-66; Perm to Offic Dio Lon (N & C Eur 64-66) 62-69; Dir of Stud Lon Med Group 66-74; S for Study of Med Eth from 74; Chap Univs in Lon from 69; M of Abp of Cant's Counsellors on Foreign Relns and BCC E-W Relns Advisory C'tee Preb of St Paul's Cathl Lon from 77; Perm to Offic Dio Nor from 80. *7 Seaford Court, 222 Great Portland Street, W1.* (01-387 2129)

SHOTTER, Eric James Barrie. b 30. **d** 77 Aotearoa for Wai. C of Turanga Past Dio Wai from 77. *74 Stout Street, Gisborne, NZ.*

SHOZAWA, John Motoki. Angl Th Coll BC Dipl Th 65. **d** 64 **p** 65 New Westmr. I of H Cross Japanese Miss Vancouver 64-78; in Amer Ch. *c/o Box 2164, Los Angeles, CA 90051, USA.*

SHREEVE, David Herbert. b 34. St Pet Hall Ox BA 57, MA 61. Ridley Hall Cam 57. **d** 59 **p** 60 Ex. C of St Andr Plymouth 59-64; V of St Anne Bermondsey 64-71; V of Eccleshill Dio Bradf from 71; M Gen Syn Dio Bradf from 77; RD of Calverley from 78. *Vicarage, Fagley Lane, Eccleshill, Bradford, BD2 3NS.* (Bradf 636403)

SHREWSBURY, Lord Bishop Suffragan of. *See* Rees, Right Rev Leslie Lloyd.

SHREWSBURY, Michael Buller. b 30. St Jo Coll Dur BA 54. Linc Th Coll 54. **d** 56 **p** 57 Man. C of St Phil and of St Steph Salford 56-60; Chap RN 60-63; HM Pris Pentonville 64-67; Dioc C Dio Berm 67-70; Chap to Bp of Berm 68-70; V of H Trin w St Phil Dalston Dio Lon from 70; RD of Hackney from 79. *89 Forest Road, E8 3BL.* (01-254 5062)

SHRIMPTON, Canon Aner Clive. b 14. Univ of Lon BD (2nd cl) 39. ALCD 39. **d** 39 Bris for Chich **p** 40 Chich. C of Ch Ch Ore 39-41; Battle 42-46; C-in-c of S Patcham Conv Distr 46-52; V of Ruddington Dio Southw from 52; Hon Can of Southw Minster from 78. *Ruddington Vicarage, Notts.* (Nottingham 212116)

SHRIMPTON, George Roderick. b 33. Selw Coll Cam BA 56, MA 60. Bp's Hostel Linc 56. **d** 58 Lich **p** 59 Stafford for Lich. C of Bilston 58-63; High Wycombe 63-67; V of Dalton 67-74; Milborne Port w Goathill Dio B & W from 74. *Vicarage, Milborne Port, Sherborne, Dorset, DT9 5AN.* (Milborne Port 250248)

SHRISUNDER, David Shripat. b 29. Osmania Univ Hyderabad BA 52. Serampore Univ BD 59; Shivaji Univ Kolhapur MA 69. Bp's Coll Calc 54. **d** 57 **p** 58 Bom. P Dio Bom 57-70; Dio Kolhapur 70-74; C of Batley 71-72; Skegness 75-77; on Leave 77-80; C of Ascen Hull 80; SS Pet & Paul Grays 81-82; Team V desig of Grays. *St Clement's Vicarage, London Road, W Thurrock, Essex.*

SHRIVE, Canon Francis Gordon. M SSJE. **d** 50 **p** 51 St Jo Kaffr. C of St Cuthb Tsolo 50-57; Hon C of Cowley St John Ox 57-58; P-in-c of Tsolo 58-62; C of St Cuthb Miss 62-70; Upper Mjika 70-81; Hon Can of St John's from 72. *St Edward's House, 22 Great College Street, SW1p 3QA.*

SHRIVES, Austen Geoffrey. b 28. BD (2nd cl) Lon 68, MTh Lon 77. SOC. **d** 64 **p** 65 S'wark. C of St Mich AA Lower Sydenham 64-68; Chap Miss to Seamen Port of Lon 68-69; Sen Chap Hong 69-74; L to Offic Dio Hong 69-74; V of Epsom Dio Guildf from 74. *30 St Martin's Avenue, Epsom, Surrey.* (Epsom 23845)

SHUFFLEBOTHAM, Alastair Vincent. b 32. Lich Th Coll 63. **d** 65 **p** 66 Ches. C of W Kirby 65-69; V of St Paul (w St Luke from 71) Tranmere 69-78; Neston Dio Ches from 78; M Gen Syn 75-80. *Vicarage, Neston, Wirral, Chesh, L64 6QQ.* (051-336 4544)

✠ **SHUKAI, Right Rev Butrus Tia.** b 30. Bp Gwynne Coll Mundri. **d** 56 **p** 58 Sudan. P Dio Sudan 56-71; Hon Can of Sudan 69-71; Archd of N Sudan 69-76; Exam Chap to Bp in Sudan 69-76; Cons Asst Bp in the Sudan 24 Jan 71 in All SS Cathl Khartoum by Abp in Jer; Bps of Sudan; Iran; Jordan; Mt Kenya; and Asst Bp in Jer; Apptd Bp of Omdurman 76. *Box 65, Omdurman, Sudan.* (Omdurman 50182)

SHULER, Jon Christopher. b 45. US Mil Acad W Point BSc 67. St Jo Coll Dur Dipl Th 71. **d** 72 Dur **p** 73 Bp Krumm (S Ohio) for Dur. C of St Marg City and Dio Dur from 72. *Gatehouse Flat, Hatfield College, Durham.*

SHURVIN, Ven Howard. St Chad's Coll Regina 54. **d** 54 **p** 55 Qu'App. C-in-c of Lucky Lake 54-56; Shaunavon 56-60; I of Whitewood 60-71; Estevan 71-79; Maple Creek Dio Qu'App from 79; Archd of Swift Current from 79. *Box 1568 Maple Creek Sask, Canada.* (667-2311)

SHUTE, Ronald Archie. b 06. St D Coll Lamp BA 32. **d** 32 **p** 33 S'wark. C of St Paul Clapham 32-34; St Pet Walworth 34-37; Cheam (in c of St Alb) 37-39; Min of Ascen Conv Distr Mitcham 39-47; V of St Cath Hatcham 47-55; R of Rotherhithe 55-63; V of Bourton w Silton 63-71; Heytesbury w Tytherington and Knook 71-75. *66 High Street, Heytesbury, Warminster, Wilts, BA12 0ED.* (Sutton Veny 320)

SHUTT, Rowland James Heath. b 11. Univ of Dur Found Scho 30, C Schol 32. St Chad's Coll Dur De Bury Scho and BA (1st cl Cl) 33, PhD and MA 36, Gabbett Pri 37. **d** 35 Dur **p** 36 Jarrow for Dur. Jun Fell St Chad's Coll Dur 34-36; Fell 36-39; C of Farnham Royal 39-45; R of Rampisham w Wraxall 45-47; Shaston St Rumbold (or Cann) 47-53; Lect and Tutor Sarum Th Coll 47-53; R of Cadeleigh 53-57; Chap Univ of Ex 54-63; R of St Martin St Steph St Lawr w All H and St Paul Ex 57-64; Warden Worc Ordin Coll 64-69; Hon Min Can of Worc Cathl 64-78; Lect in Div Worc Coll of Educn 69-76. *7 Greenhill, Bath Road, Worcester, WR5 2AT.* (Worc 355410)

SHWE DAUNG, Canon Joseph. **d** 33 **p** 34 Rang. P Dio Rang 33-74; Hon Can of Rang from 72. *St Paul's Church, Kyaiklat, Rangoon, Burma.*

SHYOGOTERA, Dandi Kazebe. Kongwa Coll 46. **d** 47 **p** 48 Centr Tang. P Dio Centr Tang 48-63; Dio Vic Nyan from 63. *Box 52, Ngara, Tanzania.*

SIBA, Walter. b 49. Bp Patteson Th Centre Kohimarama 70. **d** 73 **p** 74 Melan. P Dio Melan 73-75; Centr melan 75-76; On leave. *Pacific Theological College, Suva, Fiji.*

SIBANDA, Isaiah. b 30. **d** 76 **p** 77 Matab. C of Gwelutshena Dio Matab from 76. *c/o Box 2422, Bulawayo, Zimbabwe.*

SIBENDA, Alfred. **d** 78 **p** 79 Ruw. P Dio Ruw. *c/o Box 1108, Bundibugyo, Uganda.*

SIBISI, Lawrence Ndabezinhle. b 55. St Bede's Coll Umtata 77. **d** 79 **p** 80 Natal. C of St Gabriel Wentworth Dio Natal from 79. *c/o 28 Essex Street, Jacobs 4026, S Africa.*

SIBIYA, James Mnjunju. St Bede's Coll Umtata 61. **d** 63 **p** 64 Zulu. P Dio Zulu *Box 49, Mandini, Zululand.*

SIBIYA, Paul Sostin. St Bede's Coll Umtata 57. **d** 58 Zulu **p** 60 St John's for Zulu. P Dio Zulu. *Box 346, Vryheid, Natal, S Africa.* (Vryheid 1194)

SIBLEY, Barrie Noel Benedict. St Mich Coll Crafers 61. **d** 67 **p** 68 Adel. Perm to Offic Dio Adel 67-69; on leave 69-70; Chap Chas Gairdner Hosp Perth from 71. *23-38 Onslow Road, Shenton Park, W Australia 6008.* (81 3372)

SIBLEY, Harold William. Qu Coll Newfld. **d** 51 **p** 52 Newfld. C of Corner Brook 51-55; R of Trinity 55-56; C of St Mary St John's 56-58; Corner Brook 58-60; R of Burgeo 60-61; Metchosin 61-62; Miss at Sturgeon Lake Reserve 62-64; Hon C of Portage la Prairie 71-73. *c/o Synod Office, 66 St Cross Street, Winnipeg, Manit., Canada.*

SIBLEY, Peter Linsey. b 40. Selw Coll Cam BA 61, MA 63. Oak Hill Coll 79. **d** 81 Portsm. C of H Rood Crofton Dio Portsm from 81. *11 Oakdown Road, Stubbington, Fareham, Hants, PO14 2QR.* (Stubbington 2113)

SIBLY, Geoffrey Dean. St Jo Coll Morpeth 55. **d** 57 **p** 60 Adel. C of Mt Gambier 57-58; Henley Beach 58-60; Prospect 60-61; P-in-c of Whyalla W 61-64; R of Burra 64-68; C of Hawthorn 68-70; St Paul Canberra 70-73; R of Braidwood 73-77; H Cross Hackett 77-80; Chap RAAF from 80. *RAAF, Butterworth, Malaysia.*

SIBLY, Mark Maslin. b 48. St Barn Coll Adel ThDip 73. **d** 74 Adel **p** 75 Bp Renfrey for Adel. C of Henley Beach 74-75; Modbury 75; Tea Tree Gully 75-76; R of Jamestown Dio Willoch from 77. *Box 3, Jamestown, S Australia 5491.* (086-64 1090)

SIBSON, Edward John. b 39. St Aid Coll 63. **d** 65 Barking for Chelmsf **p** 66 Chelmsf. C of Gt Parndon 65-69; Saffron Walden 69-72; C-in-c of St Leon Colchester 72-77; Team V (w St Mary Magd and St Steph) 77-80; Industr Chap Colchester 72-80; V of Layer-de-la-Haye Dio Chelmsf from 80. *45 Malting Green Road, Layer-de-la-Haye, Colchester, Essex.* (L-de-la-H 243)

SIBSON, Robert Francis. b 46. Sarum Wells Th Coll 78. **d** 80 **p** 81 St Alb. C of St Mich AA Watford Dio St Alb from 80. *57 Whippendell Road, Watford, Herts, WD1 7LY.* (Watf 48739)

SIBTHORP, Ronald Ellwood. b 11. Keble Coll Ox BA (3rd cl Nat Sc) 32, MA 36. Linc Th Coll 34. **d** 35 **p** 36 Linc. C of Boston 35-39; Min Can Prec and Sacr of Pet Cathl 39-45; R of St Pet w Upton Northampton 45-47; PV and Succr of Truro Cathl 47-57; Prec V and Subchanter of Lich Cathl 57-63; V of Farley w Pitton 63-81. *2 St George's Close, West Harnham, Salisbury, Wilts.*

SIDAWAY, Geoffrey Harold. b 42. Kelham Th Coll 61. **d** 66 **p** 67 Derby. C of Beighton 66-70; Chesterfield 70-72; C-in-c of St Bart Derby 72-74; V 74-77; St Martin Maidstone Dio Cant from 77. *St Martin's Vicarage, Northumberland Road, Maidstone, Kent.* (Maidstone 52504)

SIDDALL, Arthur. b 43. ALCD 67 (LTh from 74). Univ of Lanc MA 81. **d** 67 Warrington for Liv **p** 68 Liv. C of H Trin Formby 67-70; Childwall 70-72; Perm to Offic Dio Birm 73-74; Chap Ch Ch Chittagong 74-76; V of St Paul Low Moor Clitheroe 77-82; St Gabr City and Dio Blackb from 82. *St Gabriel's Vicarage, Pleckgate Road, Blackburn, Lancs, BB1 8QU.* (Blackb 48430)

SIDDELL, John. St Francis Coll Nundah. **d** 48 **p** 49 Melb for Armid. C of Tenterfield 48-50; C-in-c of Emmaville 50-51; C of Tamworth 51-52; V of Boggabilla 52-53; Chap of Alfred Hosp Melb 53-58; Min of Dingley 58-60; Kingston-Robe 60-61; C of Elizabeth 61-65; P-in-c of Auburn 66-69; Perm to Offic Dio Adel 69-75; L to Offic from 75. *124a Augusta Street, Glenelg East, S Australia 5045.* (295-5828)

SIDDENS, William John. Moore Th Coll Syd ACT ThL 23. **d** 23 Syd **p** 24 Bp Langley for Syd. C of Golden Grove Darlington 23-25; C-in-c 25-29; R of Mortdale w Penshurst 29-45; St Thos N Syd 45-70; Commiss (in Austr) for River from 63; Hon Can of Syd 63-73. *1339 Anzac Parade, Chifley, NSW, Australia 2036.*

SIDDLE, Michael Edward. b 33. Univ of Dur BA 54. St Aid Coll 55. **d** 57 Liv **p** 58 Warrington for Liv. C of Fazakerley 57-59; Farnworth 59-62; PC of Swadlincote 62-70; Distr Sec (Northumb & Dur) BFBS 70-72; Yorks from 72. *46 North Park Avenue, Leeds, LS8 1EJ.* (Leeds 661369)

SIDEBOTHAM, Arthur George. b 13. Selw Coll Cam BA 34, MA 38. Wells Th Coll 35. M CR 48. **d** 36 **p** 38 Lich. C of All SS Bloxwich 36-39; Cathl Ch Salisbury S Rhod 39-41; CF (S Rhod) 41-45; L to Offic Dio Wakef 47; Vice-Prin Coll of Resurr Mirfield 48-49; P-in-c of Sophiatown Miss Distr 49-56; Rosettenville 56-62; L to Offic dio Barb 62-64; Commiss Windw Is 64-69; Master R Found of St Kath 75-82. *House of the Resurrection, Mirfield, W Yorks, WF14 0BN.* (0924-494318)

SIDEBOTHAM, Very Rev Stephen Francis. Qu Coll Cam 3rd cl Cl Trip pt i 57, BA (2nd cl Th Trip pt ia) 58. Linc Th Coll. **d** 60 **p** 61 Win. C of Ascen Bitterne Pk 60-64; St John's

Cathl Hong 64-69; Prec 69-70; V of Ch Ch Kowloon 70-76; Dean of Hong Kong from 76. *26 Garden Road, Hong Kong.* (5-234157)

SIDEBOTTOM, Andrew John. b 54. Univ of Wales (Abth) BMus 76. FRCO 75, FTCL 76. Sarum Wells Th Coll 79. **d** 81 St D. C of Tenby w Gumfreston Dio St D from 81. *Rest Harrow, Cresswell Street, Tenby, Dyfed, SA70 7HJ.*

SIDEBOTTOM, Ernest Malcolm. b 21. Univ of Dur BA 49, MLitt 56. Qu Coll Birm 49. **d** 51 Dur **p** 52 Jarrow for Dur. C of St John Greenside 51-54; Seaton Carew (in c of St Jas Owton Manor) 54-57; R of Hart w Elwick Hall 57-63; Grindleton 63-81; RD of Bolland 68-70. *17 Riversway, Gargrave, Nr Skipton, N Yorks, BD23 3NR.*

SIDEBOTTOM, George. b 16. TCD 43. **d** 49 **p** 50 Derry. C of Drumholm w Rossnowlagh 49-52; Maghera 52-53; St Mary-without-the-Walls Ches 53-56; I of Achill w Dugort U 56-60; V of Felmersham (w Bletsoe 62-79) 60-81; R of Bletsoe 60-62. *11 Cody Road, Clapham, Bedford.* (Bedford 56189)

SIDES, James Robert. b 37. TCD BA 66, Div Test 68. **d** 67 **p** 68 Down. C of St Clem Belf 67-70; All SS Antrim 70-73; R of Tomregan w Drumlane 73-80; Killesher Dio Kilm from 80. *Killesher Rectory, Florencecourt, Enniskillen, Co Fermanagh, N Ireland.* (Florencecourt 235)

SIERRA LEONE, Lord Bishop of. *See* Thompson, Right Rev Prince Eustace Shokehu.

SIERWALD, John Wedgwood. St Paul's Coll Grahmstn 53. **d** and **p** 54 Zulu. P Dio Zulu 54-63; C of Upton-cum-Chalvey Slough 63-65; R of Douglas 65-70; St Phil Capetn 71-73; Caledon Capetn 73-76; Hon C of St Thos Leigh 76-77; Rowlands Castle 77-80; Perm to Offic Dio Roch from 80. *52 High Street, Chislehurst, Kent, BR7 5AQ.*

SIGECA, Willie. St Jo Coll Lusaka. **d** 53 **p** 54 Matab. P Dio Matab 53-79. *P Bag 5414, Bulawayo, Zimbabwe.*

SIGEL, Henry. b 05. ALCD 29 (LTh from 74). **d** 29 **p** 30 Lon. C of St Mary Acton 29-31; Darfield (in c of Gt Houghton) 32-35; St Cuthb Wells 35-40; R of Rode w Rode Hill and Woolverton 40-54; PC (V from 68) of Easton 54-73; L to Offic Dio B & W from 73. *13 Somerleaze Close, Wells, Somt.* (Wells 74049)

SIGGINS, Ian Dudley Kingston. Univ of Melb BA 56. Yale Univ PhD 64. Ridley Coll Melb 59. **d** 60 **p** 61 Melb. Tutor Ridley Coll Melb and C of Moreland 60-61. *409 Prospect Street, Newhaven, Connecticut, USA.*

SIGRIST, Richard Martin. b 46. Sarum Th Coll 68. **d** 71 Taunton for B & W **p** 72 B & W. C of St Mich AA Yeovil 71-74; Chap RN from 74. *c/o Ministry of Defence, Lacon House, Theobalds Road, WC1X 8RY.*

SIJUADE, Michael Josian Adeyeye. Melville Hall, Ibad 37. **d** 38 **p** 40 Lagos. P Dio Lagos 38-52 and 55-64; Dio Ibad 52-55 and from 64; Hon Can of Lagos 56-61. *Ijomu, Nigeria.*

SIKANA, Dickson. b 31. St Phil Coll Kongwa 68. **d** 69 Madinda for Centr Tang **p** 69 Moro. P Dio Centr Tang. *Box 38, Babati, Tanzania.*

SIKUKU, Festus Henry. b 41. **d** 74 **p** 76 Maseno N. P Dio Maseno N. *Box 80, Bungoma. Kenya.*

SIKUNDLA, Ven Isaac Tobigunya Nyamekile. Univ of S Afr BTh. St Bede's Coll Umtata, 65. **d** 66 **p** 67 St John's. P Dio St John's; Archd of St Mark's from 77; P-in-c of Nqamakwe and Willowvale Dio St John's from 77. *Box 1, Nqamakwe, Republic of Transkei, S Africa.* (Nqamakwe 26)

SILANGA, Canon Martin. b 24. **d** 72 **p** 73 Lake Malawi. P Dio Lake Malawi; Hon Can of Lake Malawi from 80. *Box 62, Mponela, Malawi.*

SILARSAH, Simon Ronald. St Paul's Th Coll Maur LTh 67. **d** 65 **p** 66 Maur. C of St Pet Cassis 65-67; St Paul Vacoas 67-69; Rose-Hill 70-73; Beau-Bassin Dio Maur from 73. *20 Blackburn Lane, Rose Hill, Mauritius.* (4-4835)

SILBERBAUER, Eitel Raymond. Univ Coll Ox BA 30, MA 33. Wycl Hall Ox 29. **d** 31 **p** 32 S'wark. C of H Trin Tulse Hill 31-33; L to Offic Dio Calc 34-37; Perm to Offic Dio Johann 38; C of St Mary's Cathl Johann 38-39; St Jas Sea Point 40-41; Army Educl Scheme U Defence Force 42-46; Perm to Offic Dio Guildf 51-54; V of St Mark Nairobi 54-59. *PO Box 11021, Johannesburg, S Africa.*

SILBERMAN, Robert David. b 43. Univ of Wollongong BA 77. Canberra Coll of Min BTh 81. **d** 80 C & Goulb. C of St Matt Albury Dio C & Goulb from 80. *760 Riverview Terrace, Albury, NSW, Australia 2640.*

SILCOCK, Donald John. b 30. K Coll Lon and Warm AKC 59. **d** 60 **p** 61 Lon. C of Hackney 60-63; Min of William Temple Ch Conv Distr Abbey Wood 63-68; C of Felpham w Middleton 68-74; R of Ightham Dio Roch from 74. *Ightham Rectory, Sevenoaks, Kent.* (Borough Green 4176)

SILCOX, Canon Bertram Allanmore. Univ of W Ont BA 40. Hur Coll Ont LTh 41, DD 68. **d** 40 **p** 41 Hur. C of Otterville w Dereham and Culloden 40-42; I of St Paul and St Jas Brantford 42-45; R of St Paul Windsor Dio Hur from 45; Can of Hur from 56. *1518 Victoria Avenue, Windsor 12, Ont., Canada.* (519-254 3601)

SILK, Claude Whitehall. Angl Th Coll BC LTh 16. McGill Univ MD CM 26. **d** 17 Br Columb for New Westmr **p** 18 New Westmr. I of St Jo Div Maple Ridge 17-19; Lytton Indian Miss 19-29; in Amer Ch 29-36; LPr Dio Lon 37-39; Chap and Lect Hockerill Tr Coll 39-43; R of Eckington w Renishaw 43-53; Surr 45-53; R of Bimini Bahamas 53-59; L to Offic Dio N Rhod 62-64; Dio Zam 64-67. *c/o Barclays Bank, PO Box 923, Durban, Natal, S Africa.*

SILK, John Arthur. b 52. Selw Coll Cam BA 73, MA 77. K Coll Lon MTh 80. **d** 77 **p** 78 Guildf. C of Banstead 77-80; Dorking w Ranmore Dio Guildf from 80. *79 Ashcombe Road, Dorking, Surrey, RH4 1LX.* (Dorking 884378)

SILK, Ven Robert David. b 36. Univ of Ex BA (3rd cl Th) 58. St Steph Ho Ox. **d** 59 Bp Stannard for Roch **p** 60 Tonbridge for Cant. C of St Barn Gillingham 59-62; H Redeemer Lamorbey (in c of Good Shepherd Blackfen from 67) 63-69; R of Swanscombe 69-75; C-in-c of All SS Swanscombe 69-71; M Gen Syn from 70; R of Beckenham 75-80; Archd of Leic from 80; Prolocutor of Conv of Cant from 80; Team R of H Spirit City and Dio Leic from 82. *13 Stoneygate Avenue, Leicester, LE2 3HE.* (Leic 704441)

SILKSTONE, Harry William James. b 21. St D Coll Lamp BA 48. **d** 49 **p** 50 Llan. C of Dowlais 49-51; St Fagan Aberdare 51-53; Southall 53-56; V of St Paul Stratford 56-63; R of Debden 63-72; V of St Pet Bocking 72-78; R of Gt Hallingbury Dio Chelmsf from 78. *Great Hallingbury Rectory, Bishop's Stortford, Herts.* (Bp's Stortford 54365)

SILKSTONE, Thomas William. St Edm Hall Ox BA 51, MA 55, BD 68. Wycl Hall Ox 51. **d** 53 Bp Linton for Cant **p** 54 Birm. C of St Pet and St Paul Aston 53-56; Asst Master Merchant Taylors' Sch Crosby 56-62; Lect K Alfred's Coll Win from 62; Asst Chap 62-70; L to Offic Dio Win from 62. *19 Cheriton Road, Winchester, Hants.*

SILLAR, David William. b 08. Trin Hall Cam BA 31, MA 36. Westcott Ho Cam 31. **d** 33 **p** 34 Newc T. C of St Gabr Newc T 33-37; Area Org Bedlington RD Northumb Assoc of Boys' Clubs 37-39; V of St Phil Newc T 39-46; Haltwhistle 46-56; Surr from 46; PC of Armley 56-62; R of Richmond 62-73. *64 Barleyfields Road, Wetherby, Yorks, LS22 4PT.* (Wetherby 64786)

SILLER, James Robert William. b 44. Pemb Coll Ox BA 65, MA 70. Westcott Ho Cam 67. **d** 70 **p** 71 Kens for Lon. C of St Mary Osterley Isleworth 70-73; Leeds (in c of St Mary Quarry Hill) 73-77; V of Gilling and Kirkby Ravensworth w Dalton Dio Ripon from 77; P-in-c of Melsonby Dio Ripon from 78. *Gilling West Vicarage, Richmond, N Yorks, DL10 5JG.* (Richmond 4466)

SILLIS, Eric Keith. b 41. N-W Ordin Course 75. **d** 78 Burnley for Blackb **p** 79 Blackb. C of St Stephen-on-the-Cliffs Blackpool (in-c of St Anne Greenlands from 79) Dio Blackb from 78. *The Parsonage House, Salmesbury Avenue, Bispham, Blackpool, FY2 0PR.* (Blackpool 53900)

SILLIS, Graham William. b 46. SOC 73. **d** 76 Edmon for Lon **p** 77 Lon. C of Palmers Green 76-79; Dawlish 79-81; V of St Thos Ipswich Dio St E from 81. *St Thomas's Vicarage, Norwich Road, Ipswich, IP1 5DU.* (Ipswich 41215)

SILLITOE, William John. b 37. Lich Th Coll 67. **d** 69 **p** 70 Shrewsbury for Lich. C of Ettingshall 69-71; St John March 72-74; V of Fordham 74-77; St Clem Castle Bromwich Dio Birm from 77; C-in-c of Kennett 74-77. *Vicarage, Lanchester Way, Castle Bromwich, Birmingham, B36 9JG.* (021-747 4460)

SILLS, Alfred Oswald. b 17. Jes Coll Cam BA 38, MA 42. Westcott Ho Cam 38. **d** 40 **p** 41 St E. C of All SS Ipswich 40-41; St Sav Croydon 41-44; Chap RNVR 44-46; C of Croydon 46-48; Chap of King's Sch Ely and Min Can of Ely Cathl 48-55; L to Offic Dio Ely 48-55; V of Lee-on-the-Solent 55-65; R of Farlington 65-74; Commiss Maur 68-76; V of St Mary Virg Shipley Dio Chich from 74. *Shipley Vicarage, Horsham, W Sussex.* (Coolham 238)

SILLS, John. b 49. St Jo Coll Dur BA 71. Univ of Bris MA 74. Trin Coll Bris 71. **d** 73 Bp McKie for Cov **p** 74 Cov. C of Bedworth 73-76; Perm to Offic Dio Derby 77; Asst Chap H Trin Sch Halifax and Perm to Offic Dio Bradf from 77. *5 Bridgehouse Lane, Haworth Lane, Keighley, W Yorks.*

SILLS, Peter Michael. b 41. Univ of Nottm BA 63, LLM 68. [f Barrister] 76. SOC 78. **d** 81 S'wark. C of Ch Ch W Wimbledon Dio S'wark from 81. *Copse Hill, SW20 0NA.* (01-946 1275)

SILVA, Peter John. Univ of Rhodes Grahmstn BA 74. St Paul's Coll Grahmstn 68. **d** and **p** 74 Bloemf. C of Cathl Ch of Bloemf 74-75; Chap Dioc Sch for Girls Grahmstn 75-79. *c/o Diocesan Girl's School, Worcester Street, Grahamstown, S Africa.*

SILVER, (Gregory) George William. Keble Coll Ox BA (3rd cl Th) 53. St Steph Ho Ox 53. M OSB 58. **d** 55 **p** 56 Lon.

C of H Trin Hoxton 55-58. *St Gregory's Priory, Box 330, Three Rivers, Michigan 49093, USA.*

SILVERSIDES, Mark. b 51. BD (Lon) 73. St Jo Coll Nottm 74. **d** 76 Chelmsf **p** 77 Barking for Chelmsf. C of St Andr Hornchurch (in c of St Geo) 76-79; P-in-c of Becontree Dio Chelmsf from 79. *Vicarage, Burnside Road, Dagenham, Essex, RM8 2JN.* (01-590 6190)

SILVERTHORN, Alan. b 37. St Mich Coll Llan 62. **d** 65 **p** 66 Swan B for Mon. C of Machen w Rudry 65-71; V of New Tredegar Dio Mon from 71. *Vicarage, New Tredegar, Mid-Glam.* (Bargoed 834267)

SILVERWOOD, Thomas. Wollaston Coll W Austr 67. **d** 68 Bunb. P-in-c of Pemberton 68-70; Williams 70-72; Donnybrook 72-74; R of Boyup Brook 74-77; Collie 77-78; on leave. *199 Marine Terrace, Busselton, W Australia 6280.*

SILVERWOOD, Canon William James. Dorch Miss Coll. AKC 22, BSc 45. **d** 22 **p** 24 Calg. C of Bassano w Brooks 22-24; R 24-25; Togo 25; V of Bonnington w Fruitvale 25-27; V of Grand Forks 28-32; Ch of Redeemer Nelson 32-63; RD of W Koot 45-63; Hon Can of Koot 49-63; Can (Emer) from 63; L to Offic Dio BC from 64. *Apt 104 Parklyon Apts, 110 Douglas Street, Victoria, BC, Canada.*

SILVESTER, Henry. Angl Th Coll BC 64. **d** 65 **p** 66 BC. C of W Coast Miss 65-68; I of Metchosin Dio BC from 68. *587 Wootton Road, RR1, Victoria, BC, Canada.* (604-478 1337)

SIM, David Hayward. b 29. Qu Coll Birm 57. **d** 59 **p** 60 Cov. C of Foleshill 59-62; Kenilworth 62-64; V of Devenport 64-69; Frampton 69-74; St Geo w H Trin Gainsborough Dio Linc from 74. *St George's Vicarage, Gainsborough, Lincs.* (Gainsborough 2717)

SIM, Glenn Arthur. b 42. York Univ BA 69, MDiv 72. Wycl Coll Tor 71. **d** 72 **p** 73 Tor. C of St John York Mills Tor 72-74; I of Apsley 74-78; Craighurst Dio Tor from 78. *Rectory, Minesing, Ont., Canada.* (705-728 4379)

SIMALENGA, John. b 53. Univ of Nai BA 77. St Mark's Coll Dar-S 78. **d** 77 **p** 79 SW Tang. P Dio SW Tang. *c/o St Mark's Theological College, Dar-es-Salaam, Tanzania.*

SIMBABURE, Webster. d 70 **p** 71 Mashon. P Dio Mashon 70-81; Dio Mutare from 81. *St Mary Magdalene's Mission, PB 2005, Inyanga, Zimbabwe.*

SIMBIRI, George Nixon. Newton Th Coll 55. **d** 59 **p** 62 New Guinea. P Dio New Guinea 59-71; Dio Papua from 71. *PO Box 34, Popondetta, Papua.*

SIMBIZI, Joel. d 72 **p** 73 Bur. P Dio Bur 72-75; Dio Buye from 75. *c/o Buhiga D/S 127, Bujumbura, Burundi.*

SIMBIZI, Philippe. d 74 Bur **p** 75 Buye. P Dio Buye. *c/o Buhiga D/S 127, Bujumbura, Burundi.*

SIMCOCK, Canon James Alexander. b 1897. Egerton Hall Man 19. **d** 22 **p** 23 Man. C of St Luke Weaste 22-24; Milnrow 24-27; I of St Mark Chadderton 27-31; R of St Mark Newton Heath 31-33; Org Sec C of E Children's S for Dios B & W Ex and Truro and C of St Martin Exminster 33-36; R of Calstock 36-43; Surr from 39; V of St Gluvias w Penryn 43-52; RD of S Carnmarth 46-49; Hon Can of St Germoe in Truro Cathl 48-52; Can Res and Treas 52-74; Can (Emer) from 74. *25 Kemp Close, Truro, Cornw, TR1 1EF.* (Truro 79277)

SIMCOCK, Michael Pennington. Qu Coll Cam BA 50, MA 52. Bps' Coll Cheshunt, 50. **d** 52 **p** 53 Win. C of Andover 52-55; Eastleigh 55-57; Min of Tadley St Mary Conv Distr 57-67; V of Altarnon 67-70; C-in-c of Bolventor 67-70; V of Treleigh Dio Truro from 70. *Treleigh Vicarage, Redruth, Cornwall.* (Redruth 5242)

SIME, John Alexander. b 1897. MBE 46. St D Coll Lamp BA 21. **d** 24 St D **p** 25 Swan B for St D. C of Milford Haven 24-27; Perm to Offic at St Andr S Croydon 27-28; St Andr Nottm 28-30; V of Madeley 30-36; Org Sec CMS for Liv Ches and N Wales 36-38; V of Billesdon w Rolleston and Goadby 38-41; Gt w L Dalby 41-46; CF (EC) 43-46; Hon CF 46; V of Cosby 46-54; Chap Carlton Hayes Hosp 47-54; CF (TA) 49-53; RD of Guthlaxton I 50-54; V of H Trin Torquay 54-59; PC of Starcross 59-68; Chap RWC Hosp Starcross 59-68; Perm to Offic Dio Ex from 68. *3 The Drive, Exeter Road, Dawlish, Devon.* (Dawlish 3455)

SIMELANE, Barnabas. St Pet Coll Rosettenville. **d** 39 **p** 40 Zulu. C at Mapopoma 39-40; P-in-c of Ingwavuma 40-47; C of Mahashini Miss 47-51; Nongoma 51-56; Gingindhlovu Miss 56-58; Kwamagwaza 58-69. *PO Isandhlwana, via Dundee, Natal, S Africa.*

SIMIONE, Harry Tabanoa. b 32. **d** 71 **p** 72 Polyn. P Dio Polyn. *Box 18, Savusavu, Fiji Islands.*

SIMISTER, Charles Arnold. b 19. MM 44. Edin Th Coll 49. **d** 52 **p** 53 Glas. C of Ch Ch Glas 52-57; Worsley 57-60; V of Downton 60-63; P-in-c of Kirkcudbright w Gatehouse Dio Glas 63-67; R from 67. *Rectory, High Street, Kirkcudbright.*

SIMISTER, Thomas Brocklehurst. b 19. Keble Coll Ox BA (2nd cl Th) 48, MA 53. St Steph Ho Ox. **d** 50 **p** 51 Lich. C of St Pet Wolverhampton 50-55; V of Rushall Dio Lich from 55. *10 Tetley Avenue, Walsall, WS4 2HE.* (Walsall 24677)

SIMMONDS, Clement. b 05. Late Exhib of K Coll Lon AKC (2nd cl) 30. BD (Lon) 59. **d** 30 **p** 31 S'wark. C of St Mich AA S Beddington 30-34; St Luke Eltham 34-40; R of Hunworth w Stody 40-48; Chap RAFVR 43-46; Asst Master Sutherland Ho Sch Cromer 46-61; R of Spixworth w Crostwick 48-59; Heigham Dio Nor 59-74; C from 74. *7 Queen Elizabeth Close, Norwich, NR3 1RY.* (Nor 26483)

SIMMONDS, David Brian. b 38. Selw Coll Cam 2nd cl Th Trip pt i 60, BA (3rd cl Th Trip pt ii) 62, MA 66. Ridley Hall Cam. **d** 65 **p** 66 Lich. C of Newc L 65-69; V of Branston Dio Lich from 69. *Branston Vicarage, Burton-on-Trent, Staffs.* (Burton-on-Trent 68926)

SIMMONDS, Edward Leslie. Univ of Tor BA 37, MA 38. Wycl Coll Tor LTh 39. **d** and **p** 39 Niag. C of Ch of Ascen Hamilton 39-40; R of Elora w Fergus and Alma 40-44; I of N Essa 48-50; R of St Jas Orillia 50-54; Prin Tor Bible Coll 54-77; Hon C of Ch of Messiah Tor 55-77. *55 Hillhurst Boulevard, Toronto, Canada.*

SIMMONDS, Herbert John. St Jo Coll Auckld LTh 56. **d** and **p** 57 Auckld. C of St Mark Auckld 57-59; R of Ruawi 59-63; Papakura 63-73; V of Tamaki Dio Auckld from 73. *368 Kohimarama Road, Auckland 5, NZ.* (582-697)

SIMMONDS, John. b 24. Univ of Sheff BA 50. Ridley Hall Cam 50. **d** 52 **p** 53 Portsm. C of Portsdown 52-55; H Trin Fareham (to Offic in St Jo Evang) 55-56; Min of St Jo Evang Eccles Distr Fareham 56-65; V of St Jas Streatham 65-73; Congresbury (w Puxton and Hewish St Ann from 75) Dio B & W from 73; C-in-c of Puxton w Hewish St Ann and Wick St Lawr 73-75. *Vicarage, Congresbury, Bristol, BS19 5DX.* (Yatton 833126)

SIMMONDS, Paul Andrew Howard. b 50. Univ of Nottm BSc 73. Dipl Th (Lon) 78. Trin Coll Bris 75. **d** 78 **p** 79 Bp Mort for Leic. C of H Trin City and Dio Leic from 78. *15 Northcote Road, Knighton, Leicester, LE2 3FH.* (0533 703135)

SIMMONDS, Paul Richard. b 38. K Coll Lon and Warm AKC 63. **d** 64 **p** 65 S'wark. C of Newington 64-67; Cheam 68-73; C-in-c of Stockwell Green Dio S'wark from 73. *St Andrew's Vicarage, Moat Place, Stockwell, SW9 0TA.* (01-274 7531)

SIMMONDS, Robert William. b 52. Univ of Nottm BTh 77. Linc Th Coll 72. **d** 80 **p** 81 S'wark. C of Roehampton Dio S'wark from 80. *35 Holmsley House, Tangley Grove, SW15.*

SIMMONDS, Russell John. b 44. St Barn Th Coll Adel. **d** 71 **p** 72 Adel. C of St Jude, Brighton 71-73; Perm to Offic Dio Adel 74-79; C of Walkerville Dio Adel from 79. *19 Smith Street, Walkerville, S Australia 5081.*

SIMMONDS, William Hugh Cyril. b 08. **d** 37 **p** 38 E Szech. CIM Miss Dio E Szech 31-51; C of Normanton-by-Derby 52-54; V of St Jude Wolverhampton 54-67; S Malling 67-78. *79 Grange Close, Horam, E Sussex.* (Horam 2743)

SIMMONS, Alvin Edward. Codr Coll Univ of Dur LTh 32, BA 33. **d** and **p** 34 Barb. C of St Mich Cathl 34-40; V of St Leon Barb 40-50; R of St Lucy Barb 50-51; St John Barb 51-61; V of St Paul Barb 61-66; Can of Barb 62-66; Gen Hosp Chap 62-66; Archd of Barb 64-66. *Bay Street, Bridgetown, Barbados, W Indies.*

SIMMONS, Barry Jeremy. b 32. Univ of Leeds BA 54, MA 62. Ridley Hall Cam 61. **d** 63 **p** 64 Bradf. C of St Aid Buttershaw 63-65; P-in-c of Swallowfield w Havendale and Padmore Ja 65-68; V of Earby 68-73; Chap St John's Cathl Hong Dio Hong 73-74; Perm to Offic Dio Bradf 74-75; Chap at Bahrain 75-79; Luxembourg Dio Gibr in Eur from 80; Hon Chap Miss to Seamen Bahrain from 75. *La Chapelle du Convict, 5 Avenue Marie-Therese, Luxembourg.*

SIMMONS, Brian Dudley. b 35. St Steph Ho Ox 62. **d** 64 **p** 65 Win. C of Bournemouth 64-67; Chap Miss to Seamen Gravesend 67-70; Sen Chap 70-71; Hon C of Gravesend 67-71; V of Lamorbey Dio Roch from 71. *Holy Trinity Vicarage, Hurst Road, Sidcup, Kent, DA15 9AE.* (01-300 8231)

SIMMONS, Eric. b 30. Univ of Leeds BA (2nd cl Phil) 51. Coll of Resurr Mirfield 51. M CR 63. **d** 53 **p** 54 Ely. C of St Luke Chesterton 53-57; Chap Univ Coll of N Staffs 57-61; L to Offic Dio Wakef 63-65 and from 67; Dio Ripon 65-67; Warden and Prior Hostel of Resurr Leeds 66-67; Supr Commun of Resurr Mirfield from 74. *House of the Resurrection, Mirfield, W Yorks, WF14 0BN.* (Mirfield 494318)

SIMMONS, Geoffrey Basil. Moore Th Coll Syd ACT ThL 54. **d** and **p** 45 Syd. C of Kangaroo Valley 45-50; Chap of Hawkesbury River Distr 50-53; C-in-c of Wiseman's Ferry 51-53; Padstow NSW 53-58; C of Lenton Notts 58; R of Cammeray 59-66; Chap Parramatta Psychiatric Centre 66-77; Dir of Chaps HMS from 77. *76 Houison Street, Westmead, NSW, Australia 2145.* (635-8778)

SIMMONS, Godfrey John. b 39. Open Univ BA 77. Edin Th Coll 77. **d** and **p** 74 St Andr. Perm to Offic Dio St Andr 74-75; C of Aberfeldy w Strathtay and Dunkeld 75-76; Bridge of Allan and of Alloa 77-80; St Columba Crieff Dio St Andr 80-81; R from 81; C of Comrie Dio St Andr 80-81; R from 81;

C of Muthill Dio St Andr 80-81; R from 81; Chap Stirling Univ 79-80; HM Pris Perth from 80. *St Columba's Rectory, Perth Road, Crieff, Perthshire, PH7 3EB.*

SIMMONS, Gordon John Joseph. b 44. Univ of W Ont BA 72. Hur Coll Ont MDiv 75. **d** 75 **p** 76 Hur. C of St Jo Evang Kitchener 75-77; I of Tryconnell Dio Hur from 77. *RR2 Wallacetow, Ont., Canada.* (519-762 3247)

SIMMONS, Harrie Wilson Scott. Ridley Coll Melb ACT ThL 42. **d** 43 **p** 44 Melb. C of H Trin Kew 43-44; St Andr Brighton 44-46; Asst to Dean of Melb 46-47; in Ch of S India 47-63; Chap Caulfield Gr Sch 63-71; C of St Geo Bentleigh 71-75; Asst Chap Ridley Coll Melb from 75. *26 Glendearg Grove, Malvern, Vic, Australia 3144.* (03-509 3806)

SIMMONS, John Orrie. d 62 **p** 63 Tor. C of St Jo Bapt Norway Tor 62-65; I of St Cypr City & Dio Tor from 65. *58 Rameau Drive, Willowdale, Ont., Canada.* (416-494 2442)

SIMMONS, Canon Maurice Samuel. b 27. St Chad's Coll Dur BA 50, Dipl Th 52. **d** 52 Jarrow for Dur **p** 53 Dur. C of St Hilda S Shields 52-58; Dioc Youth Chap Dio Dur 56-60; R of Croxdale 58-81; Social and Industr Adv to Bp of Dur 61-70; Gen Sec Dioc Social Responsibility Group Dur 70-75; Hon Can of Dur from 71; Hon Sec NE Ecumen Group from 71; Sec Dioc Bd for Miss and Unity Dio Dur 75-82; V of Norton Dio Dur from 81. *Vicarage, Norton Cleveland, TS20 1EL.* (Stockton 558888)

SIMMONS, Norman. b 11. Wycl Hall Ox 49. **d** 49 **p** 50 Sheff. C of All SS Rotherham 49-53; V of St Leon and St Jude Doncaster 53-74; R of Burghwallis w Skelbrooke 74-81. *c/o St Helen's Rectory, Burghwallis, Doncaster, S Yorks.* (Doncaster 700227)

SIMMONS, Peter Watherston. b 53. St Barn Coll Adel 73. **d** 77 **p** 78 Adel. C of Ch of Good Shepherd Plympton 77; Campbelltown 77-70; R of Minlaton Dio Willoch from 80. *23 First Street, Minlaton, S Australia 5575.* (53 2093)

SIMMONS, Raymond Agar. b 35. Linc Th Coll 69. **d** 71 **p** 72 Dur. C of St Luke Hartlepool 71-74; P-in-c of Purleigh and Industr Chap Maldon 74-81; P-in-c of Cold Norton w Stow Maries 81; Chap Rampton Special Hosp from 81. *c/o Rampton Special Hospital, Retford, Notts.*

SIMMONS, Richard Andrew Cartwright. b 46. Trin Coll Bris 73. **d** 75 **p** 76 Southn for Win. C of Worting 75-80; R of The Six Pilgrims Dio B & W from 80. *Rectory, North Barrow, Yeovil, BA22 7LZ.* (Wheathill 230)

SIMMONS, Robert John Andrew. St Bonif Coll Warm 07. Univ of Dur LTh 10. **d** 10 St Alb for Cant for Melan **p** 12 Melan. Miss for NW Mala Melan 10-18; C of Wargrave 18-20; Miss P Dio Melan 1920-21; C of Fielding NZ 21-22; Tidenham 22-24; Cockfield w Staindrop 24-28; V of Mattersey 28-43; E and W Wellow 43-52. *C/o National Provincial Bank, 105 High Street, Winchester, Hants.*

SIMMS, Alan Reginald. Univ of Manit BA 61. St Jo Coll Winnipeg LTh 63. **d** 63 **p** 64 Rupld. C of St Matt Winnipeg 63-65; V of Poplar Point 65-67; L to Offic Dio Rupld 67-70; Chap of Ch for the Deaf Winnipeg Dio Rupld from 70. *68 Primrose Crescent, Winnipeg, 17, Manit, Canada.*

SIMMS, Ernest Desmond Ross. b 25. Late Scho of Trin Coll Dub BA 48, MA 51, BD 51, Th Exhib (1st cl) 51. **d** 51 Connor **p** 52 Kilm for Connor. C of Ballymena 51-53; St Mary Belf 53-55; Carnmoney (in c of Rathcoole) 55-62; Exam Chap to Bp of Connor 60-62; CF 62-81; R of Cheriton w Tichborne & Beauworth Dio Win from 81. *Cheriton Rectory, Alresford, Hants.* (Bramdean 226)

✠ **SIMMS, Most Rev George Otto.** b 10. Late Scho of TCD BA (2nd cl Mod Cl and Hist and Pol Sc) 32, Elrington Th Pri 34, MA 35, BD 36, PhD 50, DD (*jure dig*) 52, MRIA 57. Hur Coll DD (*hon causa*) 63. Univ of Kent Hon DCL 78. New Univ of Ulster Hon DLitt 81. **d** 35 **p** 36 Dub. C of St Bart Dub 35-38; Hon Cler V of Ch Ch Cathl Dub 35-52; Chap Linc Th Coll 38-39; Dean of Res TCD 39-52; Asst Lect to Abp King's Prof of Div in Dub Univ 39-52; Chap Sec to Ch of Ireland Tr Coll Dub 43-52; Dean of Cork 52; Cons Ld Bp of Cork, Cloyne and Ross in Cathl Ch of St Fin Barre Cork 28 Oct 52 by Abp of Dub; Bps of Oss, Cash, Killaloe and Nyasa, Trld to Dub 56; to Arm 69 (Primate of All Ireland); res 80; Preb of Cualaun in St Patr Cathl Dub 57-69; Select Pr Univ of Ox 59 and 72; Univ of Leeds 62; Hon Fell of TCD 78. *62 Cypress Grove Road, Templeogue, Dublin 6, Irish Republic.*

SIMON, d 68 **p** 69 Rang. P Dio Rang 69-70; Dio Mand from 70. *St Paul's Church, Pang Long, SSS Burma.*

SIMON, Christopher Richard. Univ of New Engl BA 75, BLitt 77. St Jo Coll Morpeth 65. **d** 68 **p** 69 C & Goulb. C of Coostamundra 68-71; R of Batlow 71-74; Tarcutta 74-77; R of Bodalla Dio C & Goulb from 77. *12 Montague Street, Narooma, NSW, Australia 2546.*

SIMON, Frederick Fairbanks. b 42. Ripon Coll Cudd 75. **d** 77 **p** 78 Lich. C of Cheddleton 77-79; Woodley Dio Ox from 79. *8 Caldbeck Drive, Woodley, Reading, RG5 4LA.* (Reading 692981)

SIMON, Oliver. b 45. Univ of Dur BA 67. Univ of Sussex MA 68. Univ of Ox Dipl Th 71. Cudd Coll 69. **d** 71 Reading for Ox **p** 72 Ox; C of Kidlington 71-74; Bracknell 74-78; V of Frodsham Dio Ches from 78. *Frodsham Vicarage, Warrington, Chesh, WA6 7DU.* (0928-33378)

SIMON, Ulrich Ernst. b 13. AKC and BD (2nd cl) 38, Caldicott Pri 42, MTh 43, DD 59. Linc Th Coll 38. **d** 38 **p** 39 S'wark. C of St Pet St Helier 38-42; Upton w Chalvey 42-45; Lect in Hebrew and OT K Coll Lon 45-59; L to Offic as C of Blechingley 50-52; C-in-c of Millbrook 52-55; L to Offic Dio St Alb 55-72; Fell of K Coll Lon from 57; Reader in Th Univ of Lon 59-71; Prof of Chr Lit from 71; Exam Chap to Bp of Pet 62-72; to Bp of Chelmsf 72-80; Dean of K Coll Lon 78-80. *11 Anson Road, N7 0RB.* (01-607 8665)

SIMONDSON, Geoffrey William. Ridley Coll Melb 46. ACT ThL 48. **d** 50 **p** 51 Melb. C of Melb Dioc Centre 50-52; Min of Hastings 52-56; Doncaster 56-59; I of Heidelberg 59-78; St Jas Glen Iris Dio Melb from 78. *1461 High Street, Glen Iris, Vic, Australia 3146.* (25 6654)

SIMONS, John. b 10. Qu Coll Cam BA 33, MA 40. Ely Th Coll 33. **d** 34 **p** 35 S'wark. C of St Pet St Helier 34-38; St Aug Wisbech 38-40; R of Felsham w Gedding 40-76. *22 Fairmile, Fleet, Hants.*

SIMONS, John MacMillan. b 46. Bp's Univ Lennoxville BA 66. Trin Coll Tor STB 69. Georgetn Univ Washington DC PhD 80. **d** and **p** 69 Edmon. Chap Univ of Alberta 69-73; P-in-c of St Geo Edmon 69-73; V of Ch Ch Cathl Montr 73-75; on leave 75-81; Chap Trin Coll Tor from 81. *Trinity College, Toronto, Ont, Canada, M5S 1H8.*

SIMONS, John Trevor. b 34. ALCD 66. BD (Lon) 67. **d** 67 Barking for Chelmsf **p** 68 Chelmsf. C of St Mary Becontree 67-71; V of St Luke Cranham Pk 71-78; C-in-c of Nailsea Dio B & W from 78. *Nailsea Rectory, Bristol.* (Nailsea 853227)

SIMONS, Lewis Christmas. Univ of Wales BA (2nd cl Hist) 10, MA 14. Ridley Hall Cam 15. **d** 15 **p** 16 Llan. C of Llanfabon 15-17; St Cath Pontypridd 17-20; Eglwysilan 20-21; Chap of Cardiff U 21-22; V of Cwmaman 22-23; Treherbert 23-31; R of Merthyr Mawr 31-68; V of Ewenny 31-68; Surr 24-68. *30 Newbridge Gardens, Bridgend, Mid-Glam.* (Bridgend 2615)

SIMONS, Mark Anselm. b 38. ARCM 62. Oak Hill Th Coll. **d** 65 **p** 66 Southw. C of St Ann Nottm 65-68; N Ferriby 68-75; P-in-c of Sherburn 75-78; V of Gt w L Driffield Dio York from 78. *Vicarage, Driffield, York, YO25 7DU.* (Driffield 43394)

SIMONS, Rodney Marlow Francis. b 39. Chich Th Coll 73. **d** 75 Stepney for Lon **p** 76 Lon. C of H Trin w St Mary Hoxton 75-78; Kidbrooke Dio S'wark from 78. *27 Teleman Square, SE3.* (01-856 2003)

SIMONS, William Angus. b 18. Keble Coll Ox BA 39, MA 47. Cudd Coll 40. **d** 41 **p** 42 Lon. C of All SS Poplar 41-44; and 47-48; CF 44-47; C of Ch Ch I of Dogs 48-54; V of St Jas Fulham 54-62; Industr Chap Dio Worc 62-63; Industr Missr R Found of St Kath Ratcliffe Lon 63-65; Chap Hammersmith Hosp 65-68; Gen Hosp Northn 68-72; St Edm Hosp Northn from 68; C-in-c of St Lawr Northn 72-76; C of H Sepulchre w St Andr and St Lawr Northn 76-81. *54 Park Avenue North, Northampton.* (Northn 713767)

SIMONS, William James. b 54. St Thos Univ Fred NB BA 75. Univ of Ott BTh 79. St Paul's Univ Ott STB 79. **d** 80 Ott. C of St Matt City and Dio Ott from 80. *214 First Avenue, Ottawa, Ont, Canada, K1S 2G5.*

SIMONSEN, Dallas George Hill. d 81 N Queensld (NSM). C of St Luke Sarina Dio N Queensld from 81. *c/o PO Box 74, Sarina, Qld, Australia 4737.*

SIMONSON, Canon Juergen Werner Dietrich. b 24. Univ of Lon BD 52. ALCD 52. **d** 52 **p** 53 Lon. C of St Luke W Kilburn 52-56; Tutor Im Coll Ibad 57-63; Chap CMS Tr Coll Chislehurst 64-65; Vice-Prin 65-67; Prin 67-69; V of St Marg Putney 69-81; Exam Chap to Bp of S'wark from 72; RD of Wandsworth 74-81; Hon Can of S'wark Cathl from 77; R of Barnes Dio S'wark from 81. *25 Glebe Road, SW13 0DZ.* (01-876 9669)

SIMONSON, Werner Siegmund Moritz. b 1889. Univ of Leipzig LLD 21. Ridley Hall Cam 40. **d** 42 **p** 43 Lon. C of Ch Ch Fulham 42-49; V of St Mark Dalston (w St Bart from 53) 49-56; St Luke W Hampstead 56-65; Hon C of All SS Harrow Weald Dio Lon from 73. *25 Ashdale Grove, Stanmore, Middx.* (01-954 4480)

SIMPANDE, Joseph Dunestan. b 39. **d** 75 Lusaka (APM). d Dio Lusaka. *Shampande Primary School, Box 402, Choma, Lusaka, Zambia.*

SIMPER, Allan Frederick. b 32. G and C Coll Cam 2nd cl Hist Trip pt i 54, BA (2nd cl Th Trip pt ii) 56, MA 59. Cudd Coll 56. **d** 58 **p** 59 Liv. C of Wigan 58-61; Kirkby (in c of St Chad) 61-64; Chap Dover Coll 64-70; V of New Addington

70-79; Selsdon Dio Cant 79-81; Team R from 81. *Rectory, Upper Selsdon Road, Selsdon, S Croydon, Surrey CR2 8DD.* (01-657 2343)

SIMPER, Terence Ernest. b 27. Qu Coll Birm 53. **d** 56 **p** 57 Bris. C of St Mary Fishponds 56-59; Shirehampton 59-61; P-in-c of St Pet Lowden Conv Distr Chippenham 61-69; C of Cairns 69-71; R of Mirani 71-75; V of Lockleaze 75-79; P-in-c of St Anne Brislington Dio Bris from 79. *Vicarage, First Avenue, Bristol, BS4 4DU.* (Bris 776667)

SIMPKIN, Frederick George. b 25. Univ of Man BA (2nd cl Engl) 46. Ripon Hall Ox. **d** 55 **p** 56 Man. C of Ch Ch W Didsbury 55-58; V of Bardsley Dio Man from 58. *Bardsley Vicarage, Oldham, OL8 2TJ.* (061-624 9004)

SIMPKINS, Frank Charles. b 19. Oak Hill Coll 72. **d** 75 Willesden for Lon **p** 76 Lon. C of St Mich AA Harrow Weald 75-78; P-in-c of Oxgate 78-80; Perm to Offic Dio Lon 80-81; C of St Mich AA Harrow Weald Dio Lon and Chap Northwick Pk Hosp from 81. *7 Milne Field, Hatch End, Middx.* (01-428 2477)

SIMPKINS, Lionel Frank. b 46. Univ of E Anglia BSc 68. ALCD 72 (LTh from 74). Lambeth STh 77. St Jo Coll Nottm 70. **d** 73 **p** 74 Leic. C of H Ap Leic 73-77; Bushbury 77-80; V of Sudbury w Ballingdon and Brundon Dio St E from 80. *All Saints Vicarage, Sudbury, Suff, CO10 6BL.* (Sudbury 72400)

SIMPLICIO, Centeno. b 18. **d** 66 **p** 67 Argent. P Dio Argent 66-73; N Argent from 73. *Parsonage, [illegible] N Argentina.*

SIMPSON, Alexander. b 31. Oakhill Coll 74. **d** 76 **p** 77 Stepney for Lon. C of St Paul Homerton Dio Lon from 76. *84 Roding Road, E5 0DS.*

SIMPSON, Anthony Cyril. b 30. K Coll Lon and Warm BD and AKC (2nd cl) 55. **d** 56 **p** 57 Glouc. C of Bp's Cleeve 56-59; E Grinstead 59-62; R of E w W Barkwith 62-76; V of Hainton w Sixhills 63-76; R of E w W Torrington 63-76; R of S Willingham 63-76; Barkwith Group Dio Linc from 76; RD of W Wold from 78. *Barkwith Rectory, Wragby, Lincoln, LN3 5RY.* (Wragby 858291)

SIMPSON, Athol. Lich Th Coll 41. **d** 44 **p** 45 Newc T. C of All SS Gosforth 44-48; Benwell 48-52; V of Mickley 52-57; R of St Pet Man 57-60; C of All SS Gosforth (in c of Ascen Kenton) 60-63; V of Amble Dio Newc T from 63. *Amble Vicarage, Morpeth, Northumb, NE65 0DY.* (Alnwick 710273)

SIMPSON, Bertram Douglas Cyril. St Jo Th Coll Morpeth. **d** 27 **p** 29 Newc. Supt St Geo Tr Farm for Boys Oakhampton 27-28; LPr Dio Newc 28-30; C of Scone 30-32; P-in-c of Aberdare 32-34; R of Tumbarumba 34-39; Adelong 39-41; Bombala 41-44; Gunning 44-45; L to Offic Dio C and Goulb 45-55. *c/o PO Box 266, Goulburn, NSW, Australia.*

SIMPSON, Brian Shepherd Tinley. Linc Th Coll 38. **d** 40 **p** 41 St Andr. Chap of St Ninian's Cathl Perth 40-45; Perm to Offic Dio York 45-47; Itin P Dio Moray 47-64; C-in-c of Everdon w Farthingstone and Chap St John's Sch Tiffield 65-66; C of Jeppe Johann 67; L to Offic Dio Bunb 68; P-in-c Alice Springs 68; C of Caversham NZ 69; R of Duror w Portnacrois and Glencreran 70-80; Can of St John's Cathl Oban 77-80. *Tigh na Crois, Appin, Argyll.*

SIMPSON, Charles Porter. b 16. Linc Th Coll 68. **d** 70 Lynn for Nor **p** 71 Thetford for Nor. C of St Mary Virg Diss 70-72; V of Dersingham 72-76; I of Drumholm (w Rossnowlagh to 79 and Laghey from 79) 76-81. *246 Kilkeel Road, Annalong, Newry, BT34 4TW, N Ireland.*

SIMPSON, Clarence. b 13. Bps' Coll Cheshunt. **d** 40 **p** 41 Glouc. C of St Aldate Glouc 40-43; St Paul Glouc 43-48; St Geo L Tuffley 48-52; R of Eastington w Frocester 52-65; Hon Ed Glouc Dioc Year Book 54-65; PC of Bicknoller 65-71; Chap St Audries Sch W Quantoxhead 71-74; C-in-c of Port Isaac 74-77; Hon C of Welsh Newton w Llanrothal 77-80. *Amberley Cottage, Hasfield, Glos.* (Tirley 233)

SIMPSON, David Stanley. b 44. St Jo Coll Morpeth ACT ThL 70. **d** 69 **p** 70 Newc. C of Charlestown 70-74; P-in-c of Swansea 74-77; R 77-79; Denman 79-81; Warden Conf Centre Morpeth from 81. *Conference Centre, Morpeth, NSW, Australia 2321.*

SIMPSON, Derrick. b 27. N-W Ordin Course 72. **d** 75 **p** 76 Ches. C of Disley 75-80; St Geo Stockport 80-81; R of Wistaston Dio Ches from 81. *44 Church Lane, Wistaston, Crewe, CW2 8HA.* (Crewe 67119)

SIMPSON, Edward. b 16. TD 67. Univ of Leeds BCom (2nd cl) 38. Bps' Coll Cheshunt 46. **d** 48 Pontefract for York **p** 49 Wakef. C of Mount Pellon 48-51; Dewsbury 51-52; Normanton 52-55; H Trin w St Mary Ely 55-57; CF (TA) from 56; V of Witcham w Mepal 57-70; Armitage Bridge 70-80; C-in-c of Lockwood 71-73; R 73-80; V of Hartshead Dio Wakef from 80. *Hartshead Vicarage, Liversedge, Yorks.* (Cleckheaton 873605)

SIMPSON, Francis Haldane. b 06. Late Exhib of CCC Cam 2nd cl Cl Trip pt i 26. BA (2nd cl Th Trip pt i) 28. Cudd Coll 28. **d** 29 Southn for Win **p** 30 Win. C of St Barn Southn 29-32; Miss Dio Shantung 32-45; C of St Francis Bournemouth 46; R of Talaton 47-57; V of Kingsclere 58-64; C of Romsey Dio Win 64-71; Hon C from 71. *4 St Clement's Close, Romsey, Hants, SO5 8FF.*

SIMPSON, Frederic Louis. **d** 71 **p** 72 St John's. C of St Jo Evang Cathl Umtata Dio St John's from 71. *101 Alexandra Road, Umtata, 7SA. S Africa.*

SIMPSON, Geoffrey Sedgwick. b 32. Gen Th Sem NY STB 57. Pemb Coll Cam PhD 70. **d** and **p** 57 Bp Hallock (Milwaukee). in Amer Ch 57-77; Chap Univ of Birm 77-80; V of Shoreham Dio Roch from 80. *Shoreham Vicarage, Sevenoaks, Kent, TN14 7SA.* (Otford 2363)

SIMPSON, George William. b 18. **d** 76 **p** 77 Reading for Ox (NSM). C of All SS Didcot Dio Ox from 76. *80 Lydalls Road, Didcot, Oxon.* (Didcot 812950)

SIMPSON, Godfrey Lionel. b 42. Sarum Th Coll 63. **d** 66 **p** 67 Heref. C of Leintwardine 66-70; Leominster 70-73; C-in-c of Whitbourne 73-79; V of Barlaston Dio Lich from 79. *Barlaston Vicarage, Stoke-on-Trent, Staffs.* (Barlaston 2452)

SIMPSON, Graham McGregor. Univ of Syd BA 69. BD (Lon) 71. Moore Coll Syd ThL 70. **d** and **p** 72 Syd. C of Randwick 72-73; Roseville E 73-74; Eastwood 74-76; CMS Miss from 76. *c/o 93 Bathurst Street, Sydney, Australia 2000.*

SIMPSON, Harry Eckersall. b 12. TD 56. Univ of Lon BD (2nd cl) [illegible] AKC (1st cl) 38. **d** 38 **p** 39 Blackb. C of St Paul Preston 38-40; Colne 40-41; on active service 41-46; Hon CF 46; Men in Disp 45; C of Lancaster (in c of St Anne) 46-48; CF (TA) 48-59; SCF 59-62; TA (R of O) from 62; V of St Pet Chorley and Chap Eaves Lane Hosp 48-60; Area Insp of Schs Dio Blackb 53-60; V of Billingham 60-71; Chief Insp of Schs Dio Dur 61-68; Perm to Offic Dio Dur from 71. *10 Woodlands, Barnard Castle, Co Durham.* (Teesdale 37595)

SIMPSON, Henry Herbert. **d** 21 **p** 22 Lagos. P at Lokoja 21-24; P-in-c of Belfield Woodside and Bromley 25-32; R of Lluidas Vale 32-51; Arthur's Seat and Croft's Hill 51-67. *69 Coral Way, Harbour View, Kingston 17, Jamaica.*

SIMPSON, Ian. b 52. Univ of N Wales (Bangor) BSc 75. St Jo Coll Nottm 76. **d** 79 **p** 80 Liv. C of Huyton Dio Liv from 79. *St Michael's Vicarage, Huyton, Liverpool, Mer.*

SIMPSON, John Andrew. b 44. Ridley Coll Melb 75. **d** 76 **p** 77 Melb. C of St John Croydon 76-78; P-in-c of Deer Pk w St Alb Dio Melb from 78. *835 Ballarat Road, Deer Park, Vic, Australia 3023.* (363 1458)

SIMPSON, Ven John Arthur. b 33. Keble Coll Ox BA (2nd cl Mod Hist) 56, MA 60. Clifton Th Coll 56. **d** 58 **p** 59 Chelmsf. C of Leyton 58-59; Ch Ch Orpington 59-62; Tutor Oak Hill Th Coll 62-72; Publ Pr Dio St Alb 62-72; V of Ridge 72-81; Exam Chap to Bp of St Alb 74-81; Dir of Ordinands and Post Ordin Tr Dio St Alb 75-81; Hon Can of St Alb Cathl 77-79; Can Res 79-81; Archd of Cant from 81. *29 The Precincts, Canterbury, Kent.* (Cant 63036)

SIMPSON, John Barrie. Ridley Coll Melb 54. **d** 58 **p** 60 Melb. C of St Mark E Brighton 58-61; Greensborough 61-62; I of Montmorency 62-69; CF (Austr) from 70; Perm to Offic Dio Brisb 70-75 and from 79. *19 Casula Street, Arana Hills, Qld, Australia 4054.* (07-355 5797)

SIMPSON, John Lawrence. b 33. SS Coll Cam BA 55, MA 59. Wells Th Coll 63. **d** 65 **p** 66 Win. C of St Bart Hyde Win 65-69; Chap Win Cathl 65-66; Chap Repton Sch 69-71; Asst Master Helston Sch and L to Offic Dio Truro 71-78; Res Gov Trelowarren Fellowship 75-78; P-in-c of Curry Rivel Dio B & W 79-80; R (w Fivehead and Swell) from 80; P-in-c of Fivehead and Swell 79-80. *Vicarage, Curry Rivel, Langport, Somt, TA10 0HQ.* (Langport 231375)

SIMPSON, John Peter. b 39. ALCD 66. **d** 66 Ripon **p** 67 Knaresborough for Ripon. C of Woodside 66-69; Burnage 69-72; V of St Luke Deeplish Rochdale 72-80; Lamplugh w Ennerdale Dio Carl from 80. *Ennerdale Vicarage, Kinniside, Cleator, Cumb, CA23 3AG.* (Lamplugh 310)

SIMPSON, John Raymond. b 29. Univ of Man BA (2nd cl Phil) 57. Kelham Th Coll 50. **d** 57 **p** 59 Southw. Lect St Mich Ho Crafers 57-59; C of Bawtry w Austerfield 59-61; St Mary Virg w All SS St Sav and St Mark Reading (in c of St Matt) 61-66; Southn 67-68; V of Moulsford 68-73; Hurley 73-75. *c/o Hurley Vicarage, Maidenhead, Berks, SL6 5LT.* (Littlewick Green 4261)

SIMPSON, John Raymond. b 41. Chich Th Coll 65. **d** 67 **p** 68 York. C of St Martin Scarborough 67-71; Grangetown 71-72; H Trin Hamilton 72-73; Youth Chap Dio Berm 72-75; C of Lewisham 75; Albany 76-78; R of Carey Pk Dio Bunb from 78. *17 Molloy Street, Bunbury, W Australia 6230.* (097 214648)

SIMPSON, Preb Leigh. b 04. Keble Coll Ox BA 30, MA 34. **d** 30 **p** 31 Swan B. C of Landore (in c of St Alb Treboeth from 32) 30-33; Leominster and Eyton 33-36; V of Hope-under-Dinmore w Ford 36-39; Cleobury Mortimer 39-46; Bromyard 46-60; Surr from 41; RD of Stottesdon 41-46;

Bromyard 46-60; L to Offic Brockhampton Chap 47-60; Chap of Bromyard Hosp 46-60; C-in-c and Seq of Much Cowarne w Moreton Jeffries 51-54; Preb of Hinton in Heref Cathl 56-65; Preb (Emer) from 65; R of Tedstone Delamere w Edvin Loach and Tedstone Wafer 60-65. *16 Heath Gardens, Walton Stone, Staffs.* (Stone 818712)

SIMPSON, Michael Anthony Rattray. b 46. St Paul's Th Coll Grahmstn 76. **d** 78 Bp Ndwandwe for Johann **p** 79 Johann. Chap St Geo Home for Boys Dio Johann from 78. *PO Box 40004, Cleveland, S Africa 2022.*

SIMPSON, Patrick Verrant. b 26. Fitzw Ho Cam BA 49, MA 54. Ridley Hall Cam 49. **d** 51 **p** 52 S'wark. C of St Jo Evang Redhill 51-54; Handsworth 54-55; R of Stifford 55-59; Chap St Aid Coll Birkenhead 59-62; V of Green Street Green 62-67; Exam Chap to Bp of Roch 63-67; Chap and Asst Master Prince Rupert Sch Wilhelmshaven 67-71; Northfleet Girls' Sch 71-81; Hon C of Meopham w Nurstead 71-81; P-in-c of Weare Giffard w Landcross Dio Ex from 81; Monkleigh Dio Ex from 81; Littleham Dio Ex from 81. *Weare Giffard Rectory, Bideford, Devon, EX39 4QP.* (Bideford 2017)

SIMPSON, Peter. b 28. Trin Hall Cam 3rd cl Th Trip pt i 54, BA (2nd cl Th Trip pt ii) 56, MA 60. **d** 57 **p** 58 Chich. C of St Mark Kemp Town Brighton 57-60; St Pet Walthamstow 60-64; V of St Anne Chingford 64-75; C-in-c of Widdington 75; Perm to Offic Dio Win 76-79; Chap Princess Eliz Hosp Guernsey 77-79; R of St Michel du Valle Guernsey Dio Win from 79. *St Michel du Valle Rectory, Guernsey, CI.* (Guernsey 44088)

SIMPSON, Peter Wynn. b 32. Univ of Birm BA (2nd cl Hist) 53. Ripon Hall Ox 55. **d** 57 **p** 58 Cov. C of H Trin Leamington 57-60; Croydon 60-63; V of Foleshill 63-70; St Nich Radford Cov 70-79; Finham Dio Cov from 79; RD of Cov N 76-79. *Vicarage, Green Lane, Coventry, CV3 6EA.* (Coventry 418330)

SIMPSON, Raymond James. b 40. ALCD 63 (LTh from 74). **d** 64 **p** 65 Lich. C of Longton 64-68; H Trin U Tooting 68-71; Distr Sec BFBS E Anglia 71-77; L to Offic Dios Nor, Ely and St E 71-77; Pet 75-77; Min of Bowthorpe Conv Distr Dio Nor from 77. *Church House, Waldegrave, Bowthorpe, Norwich, NR5 9AW.* (Nor 745698)

SIMPSON, Preb Reginald Ernest. Univ of Lon BA (2nd cl Hist) 38, BD (2nd cl) 41. ALCD 41. **d** 41 **p** 42 Lon. C of St Matt Fulham 41-44; CF (EC) 44-47; V of St Matt W Ham 47-56; St Mary Magd Holloway 56-81; C-in-c of St D W Holloway 59-77; Preb of St Paul's Cathl Dio Lon from 81. *c/o St Paul's Cathedral, EC4.*

SIMPSON, Ven Rennie. b 20. MVO 74. MA (Lambeth) 70. Kelham Th Coll 39. **d** 45 **p** 46 Wakef. C of S Elmsall 45-49; Succr Blackb Cathl 49-52; Min Can and Sacr of St Paul's Cathl Lon 52-58; Hon Min Can from 58; Jun Cardinal 54-55; Sen Cardinal 55-58; Chap RNVR 53-55; Dep P-in-Ord to HM the Queen 56-67; P-in-Ord 67-74; Asst Chap O of St John of Jer 56-64; Chap from 64; Sub-Prelate from 73; Chap Gt Ormond Street Hosp for Sick Children 54-58; V of John Keble Ch Mill Hill 58-63; Prec of Westmr Abbey 63-74; Can Res of Ches Cathl 74-78; Vice-Dean 75-78; Archd of Macclesfield from 78; R of Gawsworth Dio Ches from 78; Chap to HM the Queen from 82. *Gawsworth Rectory, Macclesfield, SK11 9RP.* (026-03201)

SIMPSON, Richard Andrew. NZ Bd of Th Stud LTh 67. Coll Ho Ch Ch 55. **d** 57 Bp Rich for Wel **p** 57 Wel. C of Karori Wel 57-60; V of Patea 60-63; Chap RNZAF 63-78; Perm to Offic Dio Wel 70-75; Dio Sing 75-78; Chap Huntley Sch Marton 78-79; V of Lyall Bay Dio Wel from 79. *67 Freyberg Street, Lyall Bay, Wellington 3, NZ* (879-269)

SIMPSON, Canon Richard James George. b 15. Qu Coll Birm 54. **d** 54 **p** 55 Birm. C of Warley Woods 54; Erdington 54; V of Langley Birm 57-80; Hon Can of Birm Cathl from 80. *c/o 33 Moat Road, Oldbury, Warley, Worcs.* (Broadwell 1809)

SIMPSON, Robert. Univ of Leeds, BA 42. Coll of Resurr Mirfield, 42. **d** 44 **p** 45 Ox. C of Cowley St John 44-46; Bladon w Woodstock 46-49; St Paul Thornaby 49-51; Marske-in-Cleveland 51-53; Wensley 53-56; V of Woodhouse (w Buslingthorpe to 75) Dio Ripon from 56. *Vicarage, St Mark's Avenue, Woodhouse, Leeds 2.* (Leeds 458694)

SIMPSON, Robert McGregor. Moore Th Coll Syd ACT ThL 60. **d** 61 Syd **p** 61 Bp Kerle for Syd. C of Lithgow 61-63; C-in-c of Ermington w Rydalmere 63-69; L to Offic Dio Syd from 70. *42 Endeavour Street, Seven Hills, NSW, Australia 2147.* (621-5081)

SIMPSON, Robert Theodore. Linc Coll Ox BA (2nd cl Th) 58, MA 62. Chich Th Coll 58. M CR 66. **d** 60 **p** 61 Ches. C of Ellesmere Port 60-63; Vice-Prin of St Pet Th Coll Alice 68-76; P-in-c of Manzini Dio Swaz from 76. *PB Kwaluseni, Swaziland.*

SIMPSON, Roger Westgarth. b 51. Univ of Lon BSc 72. St Jo Coll Nottm 77. **d** 79 **p** 80 Lon. C of All S Langham Place St Marylebone Dio Lon from 79. *32 Maple Street, W1P 5GD.* (01-637 0449)

SIMPSON, Canon Samuel. b 26. TCD BA 55, Div Test 56, MA 69. **d** 56 **p** 57 Connor. C of Coleraine 56-60; I of Donagh U 60-64; Ballyscullion 64-81; RD of Maghera from 75; Can of St Columb Cathl Derry from 78; R of Errigal w Desertoghill Dio Derry from 81. *Rectory, Station Road, Garvagh, Co Londonderry, BT51 5LA.* (Garvagh 226)

SIMPSON, Thomas Eric. b 31. St Chad's Coll Dur BA 55. Ely Th Coll 55. **d** 57 **p** 58 Dur. C of Jarrow 57-61; St Mary Virg w St Pet Conv Distr Bp Wearmouth 61-62; PC (V from 68) of Chopwell Dio Dur from 62. *Vicarage, Chopwell, Newcastle upon Tyne.* (Chopwell 248)

SIMPSON, Ulric George Williams. b 29. **d** 64 Bp McKenzie for Wel **p** 65 Wel. C of Masterton 64-68; V of Mangaweka 68-69; Bulls w Rongotea 69-76; Carterton Dio Wel from 76. *185 High Street South, Carterton, NZ.* (8371)

SIMPSON, William. b 1889. Univ of W Ont BA 30. Hur Th Coll LTh 30. **d** 30 **p** 31 Hur. I of Otterville Dereham and Culloden 30-33; Hespeler 33-40; RD of Waterloo 38-40; C of Saltney 40-43; V of St Nich Wallasey 43-58; RD of Wallasey 56-58; V of Ingleton w Chapel-le-Dale 58-64. *The Lilacs, Lancaster Road, Slyne, Lancaster.* (Hest Bank 822611)

SIMPSON, William Henry. Wycl Coll Tor 39. **d** 39 **p** 40 Tor. C of Dur 40-49; R of Dur w Egremont and Allan Pk 49-52; St Jo Evang Stamford 52-59; St Steph Hamilton 59-73; Hon Can of Niag 70-73; I of Collingwood 73-77; St Matt First Avenue Tor 77-81. *10 Davidson Street, Barrie, Ont, Canada.*

SIMPSON, William Michael. b 45. Univ of Leeds BA 66. St Jo Coll Nottm 75. **d** 77 **p** 78 Pet. C of Desborough 77-80; P-in-c of Arthingworth 79-80; Chap St Steph Coll Stanley and St John's Cathl Hong Kong from 80. *1 St Stephen's College, Stanley, Hong Kong.* (H Kong 5-930308)

SIMPSON, William Thomas. St Chad's Coll Dur BA and Van Mildert Exhib 35, Dipl Th 36, MA 38. **d** 36 **p** 37 Portsm. C of St Cuthb Copnor 36-46; V of St Agnes Kennington Pk 46-49; St Matt Sheff 49-59; R of Week St Mary 59-81; R of Whitstone 62-81. *Waverley, Under Road, Gonnislake, Cornw, PL18 9JL.* (Tavistock 833396)

SIMPSON, William Vaughan. b 16. Worc Ordin Coll. **d** 57 **p** 58 Glouc. C of Charlton Kings 57-61; R of Willersey w Saintbury 61-73; RD of Campden 69-73; C-in-c of Cherington 73-76; Rodmarton 73-76; V of Clearwell 76-79. *Little Glebe, Cidermill Lane, Chipping Campden, Glos, GL55 6HU.*

SIMS, Christopher Sidney. b 49. Wycl Coll Ox 74. **d** 77 **p** 78 Birm. C of Walmley 77-80; V of Hay Mill Dio Birm from 80. *164 Waterloo Road, Birmingham, B25 8LD.* (021-706 0509)

SIMS, David John. St Aug Cant Coll 50. **d** and **p** 56 Barb. [f Methodist Min] C of St Mich Cathl Barb 56-57; V of St Jo Bapt Barb 57-59; R of St Jas Annotto Bay 60-62; Christiana and P-in-c of Alston w Sanquiretti 62-63; V of Haxey 63-73; in Amer Ch from 73. *Hugo, Oklahoma, USA.*

SIMS, Leonard Charles. b 15. Oak Hill Th Coll 62. **d** 63 **p** 64 Derby. C of H Trin Chesterfield 63-67; R of St Clem w St Matthias and St Simon Salford 67-71; P-in-c of H Trin Conv Distr Hove 72-81; Perm to Offic Dio Chich from 81. *74 Hill Rise Avenue, Sompting, Lancing, W Sussex, BN15 0LT.*

SIMS, Peter George Russell. b 36. Univ of Wales BA (2nd cl Engl) 57. St Mich Coll Llan 63. **d** 65 **p** 66 Swan B. C of Brecon w Battle and Min Can of Brecon Cathl 65-72; R of Llanfrynach w Cantref and Llanhamlach Dio Swan B from 72. *Llanfrynach Rectory, Brecon, Powys.* (Llanfrynach 667)

SIMS, Roland Eric. b 17. **d** 71 Bp Garnsworthy for Tor **p** 72 Bp Read for Tor. L to Offic Dio Tor 71-73; R of Bridgenorth-Omemee Dio Tor from 73. *Box 33, Bridgenorth, Ont., Canada.* (705-292 7104)

SIMS, Sidney. b 20. Wycl Hall Ox. **d** 64 **p** 65 Southw. C of Attenborough w Bramcote and Chilwell 64-67; V of Ramsey St Mary w Pondsbridge 67-70; St Matt Cam Dio Ely from 70. *St Matthew's Vicarage, Cambridge, CB1 2LU.* (Cam 350775)

SIMS-WILLIAMS, Leofric Temple Sims. b 1900. Late Scho of Trin Hall Cam BA (2nd cl Mech Sc Trip) 23, MA 27. Westcott Ho Cam 36. **d** 37 **p** 38 Lewes for Chich. C of Barcombe 37-39; Chap RNVR 39-46; Chap Westmr Sch 46-49; V of Bembridge 49-65; Thorncombe 65-69; Perm to Offic Dio Sarum 70-75; Hon C of Whitchurch Canonicorum Dio Sarum from 75. *St Francis Lodge, Morcombelake, Bridport, Dorset.*

SIMS-WILLIAMS, Michael Vernon Sims. b 09. Trin Hall Cam 3rd cl Engl Trip pt i, 29, BA (3rd cl Th Trip pt i) 30, MA 34. Westcott Ho Cam 32. **d** 33 **p** 35 Win. C of Eastleigh 33-35; Freemantle 35-36; St Thos and St Clem w St Mich and St Swith Win 36; C-in-c of Testwood 36-38; PC 38-43; Chap Trin Hall Cam 43-46; Regional Sec Midl Distr of SCM in Schs 46-48; V of Upnor 48-55; Chap TS *Arethusa* 49-60; LPr Dio Roch 56-60; Dio Cant 60-73; Asst Master St John's Boys' Sch Sittingbourne 60-73; Perm to Offic Dio Cant from 73.

Broumfield, Borden, Sittingbourne, Kent, ME9 8JH. (Sittingbourne 72014)

SIMULAI, Gerald Maibani. d 68 Bp Ambo for New Guinea. d Dio New Guinea 68-70; Dio Papua from 71. *PO Dogura, via Boroko, Papua New Guinea.*

SIN, Andrew Hyonsam. b 42. **d** 69 **p** 70 Taejon. P Dio Taejon 69-73; and from 77; on leave 74-76. *114-11, Onchonri, Onyangeup, Chungnam, Korea.*

SINABULYA, George. d 77 **p** 78 Mityana. P Dio Mityana. *Box 102, Mityana, Uganda.*

SINAHANUE, James Gordon. St Pet Th Coll Siota 55. **d** 57 **p** 60 Melan. P Dio Melan 57-75; Dio Malaita from 75. *Oloha, S Malaita, Solomon Islands.*

SINCLAIR, Allan John. St Jo Coll Auckld LTh 68. **d** 68 Auckld. C of St Luke Mt Albert Auckld 68-70; Auckld Cathl 70-72; V of Waiuku Dio Auckld from 72. *PO Box 41, Waiuku, NZ.* (Waiku 40)

SINCLAIR, Charles Horace. b 19. Keble Coll Ox BA (2nd cl Th) 40, MA 44. Linc Th Coll 41. **d** 42 **p** 43 Cant. C of St Jo Evang Upper Norwood 42-45; Chap K Coll Auckld 46-50; Asst Chap Haileybury Coll 51; Hd Master Prebendal Sch Chich PV and Succr of Chich Cathl 51-53; Chap and Sen Tutor Brookland Hall Welshpool 53-57; Hd Master St Aid Sch Denby Dale 57-64; Perm to Offic Dio Wakef 58-64. *94 Harbour Way, Folkestone, Kent.* (Folkestone 50882)

SINCLAIR, Constantine. b 1898. **d** 31 **p** 32 Edin. C of St [illegible] 34-36; Foots Cray 37; St Geo Perry Hill 37-40; R of Chale 40-73. *2 The Precinct, Bembridge, IW.* (Bembridge 3502)

SINCLAIR, David William. Qu Univ Ont BA (2nd cl Hist) 59. Wycl Coll Tor BTh 62. **d** 61 Ont **p** 62 Bp Snell for Tor for Ont. C of St Thos Belleville 61-64; R of Tweed 64-67; St Paul Kingston 67-71; N Addington 71-74; N Frontenac 71-74; on leave 75-76; C of St Geo Cathl Kingston 76-78; R of Hornby Dio Niag from 78. *c/o 1480 Steeles Avenue, RR2, Hornby, Ont, Canada.* (416-878 4762)

SINCLAIR, John Malcolm. b 36. Univ of Leeds BSc 62. Linc Th Coll. **d** 64 **p** 65 S'wark. C of St Faith N Dulwich 64-69; P-in-c of St Andr Conv Distr Holmfield 69-73; R of Banket 74-78; V of Davyhulme Dio Man from 78. *Davyhulme Vicarage, Manchester, M31 3TP.* (061-748 2210)

SINCLAIR, Malcolm Robert. Bp's Univ Lennox BA 58, LST 60. **d** 60 **p** 61 Tor. C of Ch of Epiph Scarborough 60-63; Mono Mills 63; Ascen Hamilton 63-65; R of Wainfleet 65-69; St Hilda Oakville 69-74; Hosp Chap Hamilton and Hon C of St Jo Evang Hamilton 74-77; I of Penetanguishene Dio Tor from 77. *9 Robert Street East, Penetanguishene, Ont, Canada.* (705-549 2223)

SINCLAIR, Canon Maurice Walter. b 37. Univ of Nottm BSc 59. Tyndale Hall, Bris 62. **d** 64 Southn for Win **p** 65 Win. C of St Jo Evang Boscombe 64-67; Miss SAMS 67-79; Overseas Sec SAMS from 79; Hon Can of N Argent from 80. *Allen Gardiner House, Pembury Road, Tunbridge Wells, Kent, TN2 3QU.*

SINCLAIR, Robert Charles. b 28. Univ of Liv LLB 49. QUB LLM 69. Ely Th Coll 58. **d** 60 **p** 61 Connor. C of Glenavy 60-63; Chap RN 63-67; C of Cregagh 67-68; Lect Belf Tech Coll 69-76; Waterford Reg Coll 76-79; Coll of Commerce Rathmines from 79; Perm to Offic Dio Connor from 69. *Juniper Cottage, Glen Road, Glenavy, Co Antrim, N Ireland.* (Crumlin 53126)

SINCLAIR, Robert Michael. Edin Th Coll 63. **d** 66 **p** 67 St Andr. C of Dunfermline 66-69; Old St Paul Edin 69-72; P-in-c of St D of Scotld 72-77; Hon C from 77. *143 Greenbank Road, Edinburgh 10.* (031-447 5068)

SINCLAIR, Ronald Yelverton. d 75 **p** 76 Wai (APM). Hon C of Dannevirke Dio Wai from 75. *Te Rehunga, R.D., Dannevirke, NZ.*

SINCLAIR, Stanley Robert. Univ of Calif Berkeley BA 53. Ch Div Sch of the Pacific BD 56. **d** and **p** 56 San Joaquin (Calif). In Amer Ch 56-74; R of St Mary Regina Dio Qu'App from 74. *15th and Montague Streets, Regina, Sask, Canada.*

SINCLAIR, Thomas. b 04. Edin Th Coll 32. **d** 35 **p** 36 Glas. C of St Mary's Cathl Glas 35-37 and 38-40; Arthuret 37-38; Corbridge 40-41; St Michel AA Helensburgh 41-43; Offg R of H Trin Ayr 43-44; R of St John Johnstone 45-49; Sen Chap at St Mary's Cathl Edin 49-51; V of Gilsland w Over Denton 51-55; Chap St Geo Hosp Lon 55-56 and 58-61; V of Crosby-on-Eden 56-58; Ch Ch Mayfair Westmr 61-69. *33 Etterby Street, Stanwix, Carlisle.*

✠ **SINDAMUKA, Right Rev Samuel.** b 28. **d** 73 **p** 74 Bur. P Dio Bur 73-75; Cons Ld Bp of Buj in Nat Stadium of Bur 26 Oct 75 by Abp of Ugan; Bps of Rwa and Mbale; and Bps Rukirande and Shalita. *Bp 1300, Bujumbura, Burundi.*

SINDEN, Philip Rodney. Univ of NSW BCom 72. Moore Coll Syd ThL 77. BD (Lon) 78. **d** and **p** 79 Syd. C of St Bede Beverley Hills 79-82; St Andr Lane Cove Dio Syd from 81. *69 Tambourine Bay Road, Lane Cove, NSW, Australia 2066.* (428-1995)

SINDEN, (Gilbert) Richard Albert. b 29. Univ of Nottm BA 57. Kelham Th Coll 49. M SSM 54. **d** 78 Adel. Perm to Offic Dio Adel 78-79; Dir of Stud St Geo Coll Jer from 80. *Box 1248, Jerusalem.*

SINDON, Oscar. Ho of Epiph Kuching, 52. **d** 55 **p** 56 Borneo. P Dio Borneo 55-62; Dio Kuch from 62. *c/o Box 347, Kuching, Sarawak, Malaysia.*

SINEGOGONA, Wilfrid. Patteson Th Centre Kohimarama. **d** 72 Melan. P Dio Melan 72-75; Dio New Hebr from 75. *Lombaha, Aoba, New Hebrides.*

SINFIELD, George Edward. b 16. E Midl Jt Ordin Tr Scheme 73. **d** 76 Sherwood for Southw **p** 77 Southw. C of Radcliffe-on-Trent 76-79; P-in-c of St Oswald-in-Lee w Bingfield and Wall Dio Newc T from 79. *St Oswald-in-Lee Vicarage, Wall, Hexham, Northumb, NE46 4DU.* (Humshaugh 354)

SINGANO, Eliya. b 49. St Cypr Coll Ngala 75. **d** 77 Zanz T. d Dio Zanz T 77-79. *Box 25017, Dar-es-Salaam, Tanzania.*

SINGAPORE, Lord Bishop of. *See* Chiu, Right Rev Ban It.

SINGAPORE, Dean of. *See* Chiu, Right Rev Ban It.

SINGER, Very Rev Samuel Stanfield. b 20. TCD BA (1st cl Resp) 42, Div Test (1st cl) 43, MA 61. **d** 43 **p** 44 Down. C of [illegible] 43-45; Min Can of Down Cathl and C of Down 45-46; C of Wirksworth (in c of Alderwasley) 46-49; V of Middleton-by-Wirksworth 49-52; R of St Geo Maryhill Glas 52-62; All SS Jordanhill Glas 62-75; Synod Clk and Can of Glas from 66; Dean of Glas and Gall from 74; R of H Trin Ayr w St Osw Maybole Dio Glas from 75. *12 Barns Terrace, Ayr, Scotland.* (Ayr 262482)

SINGH, Daniel. b 22. Oak Hill Coll 75. **d** 77 Stepney for Lon **p** 78 Lon. C of St Mary Islington Dio Lon from 77. *15 Peabody Estate, Farringdon Road, EC1R 3BQ.* (01-251 2803)

SINGH, Jagdutt. b 48. St Jo Coll Auckld 71. **d** 73 **p** 74 Polyn. P Dio Polyn 73-80; C of St Jo Evang City and Dio Edmon from 80. *11111-57 Avenue, Edmonton, Alta, Canada.*

SINGH, Canon Santa. St Jo Coll Auckld 71. **d** 74 **p** 75 Auckld for Polyn. C of St Thos Tamaki 74-76; Hon C of Samabula 76-78; H Trin Cathl Suva Dio Polyn from 78; Can of H Trin Cathl Suva from 78. *c/o Box 240, Suva, Fiji.*

SINGH, Vivian Soorat. b 30. Trin Coll Cam BA (3rd cl Nat Sc Trip) 53, MA 60. Westcott Ho Cam 54. **d** 55 **p** 56 Birm. C of Yardley Wood 55-57; St Paul w St Mark Birm 57-59; L to Offic Dio St E from 59; Chap Framlingham Coll 60-72; Wymondham Coll from 72; L to Offic Dio Nor from 72; Dep Hd Master Litcham High Sch from 75. *Manor Cottage, Wendling Road, Longham, Dereham, Norf.*

SINGIRANKABO, Samusoni. Warner Th Coll Buye 67. **d** 69 Bur **p** 70 Ruw. P Dio Bur 69-70; Dio Ruw from 70. *PO Kabujogera, Fort Portal, Uganda.*

SINGLETON, Aubrey Winter. Univ of Melb BA 40. Ridley Coll Melb ACT ThL (2nd cl) 38, Th Scho 48. **d** 39 **p** 40 Melb. C of H Trin Surrey Hills 39-41; Chap RAAF 41-47; C of St Silas N Balwyn Melb 47-49; Min of Bacchus Marsh 49-51; V of St Paul E Kew 51-58; Min of Wattle Pk 58-64; I of Alphington 64-72; C in Dept of Chaps Dio Melb 72-80; Perm to Offic Dio Melb from 80. *32 Lantana Street, Ivanhoe, Vic, Australia 3079.* (03-49 2836)

SINGLETON, Ernest George. b 15. St Aug Coll Cant 38. **d** 41 **p** 42 Portsm. C of St Mark Portsea 41-46 (in c of St Francis Hilsea 43-46); Hendon (in c of St Mary Magd) 46-48; M CR 48-68; L to Offic Dio Wakef 49-51; Dio Lon 52-56; Dio Johann 56-60; Dio Llan 61-68; Miss P at Sophiatown Johann 56-60; Prior of Priory of St Teilo Cardiff 61-68; Perm to Offic Dio Lon from 68. *4 Eyot Lodge, Cross Deep, Twickenham, Middx, TW1 4QH.* (01-892 5496)

SINGLETON, John Douglas. St Jo Coll Morpeth, 62. **d** 63 **p** 64 Gippsld. C of Morwell 62-65; V of Foster 65-71; Lang Lang 71-73; R of Yallourn (w Newborough from 75) Dio Gippsld from 73. *Box 62, Newborough, Vic., Australia 3828.*

SINGLETON, Robert William. b 13. Univ of Dur LTh 41. St Aid Coll 38. **d** 40 **p** 41 Man. C of St Mary Virg Davyhulme 40-43; Ch Ch Pennington 43-49; I of St Mark Chadderton 49-55; V of Simon and St Jude Anfield 55-80. *29 Hampton Road, Southport, PR8 6SR.*

✠ **SINKER, Right Rev George.** b 1900. Late Colquitt Exhib of BNC Ox BA (3rd cl Mod Hist) 21, MA 30. Wycl Hall Ox 23-24. **d** 24 Lon for Col Bp **p** 25 Lah. CMS Miss Dio Lah 24-35; Hd Master Bp Cotton Sch Simla 35-45; Exam Chap to Bp of Lah 35-46; Can of Lah Cathl 44-49; Gen Sec Bible S of Ind and Ceylon 46-49; Cons Ld Bp of Nagp in All SS Cathl Nagp 2 Feb 49 by Bps of Calc; Bhag; Nasik; Bom; Chota N; Delhi; Luckn; Colom; and Rang; and Bps Tarafdar and De Mel; res 54; Asst Bp and Hon Can of Derby 54-62; Proc Conv

Derby 55-72; V of Elvaston w Thurlaston and Ambaston 54-55; Bakewell 55-62; Provost and Asst Bp of Birm 62-72; Provost (Emer) from 72; Commiss Kar 63-71; Nagp 65-71; UK Rep of Ch of N India from 73. *5 Vicars' Close, Lichfield, Staffs, WS13 7LE.* (Lich 53947)

SINKER, Canon Michael Roy. b 08. Clare Coll Cam BA 30, MA 34. Cudd Coll 31. **d** 32 **p** 33 Carl. C of Dalston 32-34; Miss S Afr Ch Rly Miss Alicedale 35-38; C of Bp's Hatfield 38-39; V of Dalton-in-Furness 39-46; Hon Chap to Bp of Carl 42-46; Surr 42-63; V of Saffron Walden 46-63; RD of Saffron Walden 48-63; Hon Chap to Bp of Chelmsf 51-61; Hon Can of Chelmsf 55-63; Exam Chap to Bp of Chelmsf 62-63; V of Hackthorn w Cold Hanworth 63-67; Archd of Stow 63-67; Can and Preb of Leic St Marg in Linc Cathl 63-67; R of St Matt Ipswich 67-77; Can (Emer) of Linc from 70. *8 White Horse Way, Westbury, Wilts.*

SINNAMON, William Desmond. b 43. TCD BA 65, Div Test (2nd cl) 66. **d** 66 **p** 67 Down. C of Seapatrick 66-70; St Mark Arm 70-74; V Cho of Arm Cathl 73-74; I of Ballinderry 75-80; V of St Patr Cathl Group Min Dio Dub from 80. *c/o 248 South Circular Road, Dublin 8, Irish Republic.*

SINNICKSON, Charles. b 21. Univ of Princeton BA 43. Cudd Coll 60. **d** 63 **p** 64 Lon. C of St Anne Soho 63-67; St Luke Chelsea 67-72; St Jude S Kens 73-81. *Flat 4, Cranley Mansion, 160 Gloucester Road, SW7 4QF.* (01-373 2767)

SINTON, John Charles William. b 16. MBE 77. St Deiniol's Libr Hawarden 74. **d** 74 Lon for Trinid **p** 75 Trinid. C of H Trin Cathl Port of Spain 74-77; Chap Miss to Seamen Port of Spain 74-77; Shoreham-by-Sea Dio Chich from 78. *29 Roman Crescent, Southwick, Brighton, BN4 4TV.* (Brighton 592003)

SIRMAN, Allan George. b 34. BA (Lon) 58. Oak Hill Th Coll. **d** 59 Taunton for B & W **p** 60 Taunton for Cant. C of Uphill 59-61; Morden 61-65; R of Chadwell St Mary 65-75; V of Wandsworth Dio S'wark from 75. *11 Rusholme Road, SW15.* (01-788 7400)

SIRR, Canon John Maurice Glover. b 42. TCD BA (3rd cl Hebr and Or Lang Mod) 63, Div Test 65. **d** 65 **p** 66 Connor. C of St Mary Belf 65-68; Finaghy 68-69; I of St Columba Drumcliffe Dio Elph from 69; RD of S Elph from 75; Dioc Sec Dios Elph and Ard from 78; Can from 81. *Rectory, Drumcliffe, Co Sligo, Irish Republic.* (Sligo 73125)

SIRR, William James. b 1889. Wall Scho and 2nd Th Exhib Pri of Trin Coll Dub, Wray Pri, Sen Mod Phil and BA 10, Hebrew Pri (1st) 11, BD 14. **d** 12 Meath **p** 13 Down. C of Shankill 12-15; St Mary Magd Belf 15-23; C-in-c of Cooneen w Mullaghfad 23-31; Cleenish 31-37; I of Ematris w Rockcorry 37-67; Can of Clogh and Exam Chap to Bp of Clogh 37-67; L to Offic Dio Down from 67. *6 Wellington Gardens, Bangor, Co Down, N Ireland.* (Bangor 63832)

SIRR, William James Douglas. b 40. TCD BA (2nd cl Hebr and Or Lang Mod) 62, Div Test (1st cl) 64. **d** 65 **p** 66 Connor. C of H Trin Belf 65-68; Chap RAF from 68. *c/o Ministry of Defence, Adastral House, Theobalds Road, WC1.*

SISLEY, Frederick Herbert. b 25. Oak Hill Th Coll 48. **d** 52 **p** 53 Roch. C of Gravesend 52-54; Normanton-by-Derby 54-58; V of St Paul Brixton 58-63; Chap HM Pris Man 63-64; Stoke Heath 64-69; Stafford 69-75; Wandsworth 75-81; LPr Dio Man 63-64; Dio Lich 64-75; Dio S'wark 75-81; Chap HM Pris Maidstone from 81. *60 Bower Street, Maidstone, Kent, ME16 8SD.* (0622-55611)

SISSMORE, David. b 34. Univ of Tor BA 67, Wycl Coll Tor BTh 70. **d** 70 Bp Hunt for Tor **p** 71 Bp Garnsworthy for Tor. I of Craighurst 70-74; C of Cavan 74-78; I of Stoney Lake Dio Tor from 78. *Young's Point, Ont, Canada.*

SISSON, Trevor. b 54. St Jo Coll Dur 76. **d** 79 **p** 80 Southw. C of Rainworth Dio Southw from 79. *89 Sherwood Road, Rainworth, Mansfield, Notts, NG21 0LP.* (Blidworth 6972)

SITCH, Keith Frank. b 40. Univ of Ex BA 63. SOC 72. **d** 75 Chelmsf **p** 76 Barking for Chelmsf. C of Romford 75-78; Kidbrooke Dio S'wark from 78. *92 Kidbrooke Park Road, SE3 0DX.*

SITHOLE, Archibald Barnabas. St Peter Th Coll Rosettenville, 59. **d** 61 **p** 62 Johann. P Dio Johann 61-76; Dio Swaz 76-80; Dio Natal from 80. *c/o Box 147, Eshowe, Natal, S Africa.*

SITHOLE, David Christopher. b 39. St Pet Coll Alice 69. **d** 72 Zulu. d Dio Zulu. *St Augustine's Rectory, PO St Augustine's, via Dundee, Zululand.*

SITHOLE, Ezekiel Mzimkulu. St Bede's Coll Umtata. **d** 53 **p** 54 Kimb K. P Dio Kimb K 53-73; Dio Grahmstn from 73. *Box 569, Queenstown, CP, S Africa.*

SITOTOMBE, Edwin. St Pet Coll Rosettenville LTh 51. **d** 50 **p** 51 S Rhod. P Dio S Rhod 50-52; Dio Matab 52-81. *26 Orange Grove Road, Northend, Bulawayo, Zimbabwe.*

SITSHEBO, Wilson Timothy. St Bede's Coll Umtata Dipl Th. **d** 78 **p** 80 Matab P Dio Matab 78-81; Dio Lundi from 81. *Box 1047, Gwelo, Zimbabwe.*

SITTICHINLI, James Edward. **d** 43 **p** 60 Arctic. C of All SS Cathl Aklavik 43-61; I 61-68; Tuktoyaktuk 69-74. *Anglican Mission, Tuktoyaktuk, NWT, Canada.*

SIUTA, Noel. **d** 72 Papua **p** 73 Bp Kendall for Papua. P Dio Papua. *Awaiama, via Dogura, Papua New Guinea.*

SIVITER, Cecil Isaac Hill. b 11. Tyndale Hall Bris 36. **d** 41 **p** 42 Lon. C of St Paul Ealing 41-43; H Trin Frogmore (in c of St Luke Bricket Wood) 43-46; R of Pettaugh w Winston 46-48; Markfield w Stanton-under-Bardon 48-55; Chap Markfield Sanat 48-55; V of St Mark Vic Pk 55-60; Pott-Shrigley 60-74; Ch Ch Alsager 74-79; Perm to Offic Dio Ches from 79. *193 South Parade, West Kirby, Wirral, Mer, L48 3HX.* (051-625 6676)

SIVITER, Hugh Basil. b 21. St Pet Hall, Ox MA 47. Wycl Hall, Ox 46. **d** 48 **p** 49 Nor. C of Gt Yarmouth (in c of St John) 48-52; V of Birkdale 52-59; Gateacre 59-66; V of Knotty Ash Dio Liv from 66. *St John's Vicarage, Thomas Lane, Liverpool, L14 5NR.* (051-228 2396)

✠ **SIYACHITEMA, Right Rev Jonathan.** b 32. Sarum Th Coll 69. **d** 70 **p** 71 Matab. C of St Andrew W Commonage Dio Matab 70-71; P-in-c 71-75; R 75-78; Archd of Matab 73-78; P-in-c of H Cross Luveve 75-78; Dean and R of St Jo Bapt Cathl Bulawayo 78-81; VG 78-81; Cons Ld Bp of the Lundi 4 Oct 81. *St Cuthbert's Church, Selukwe Road, Gwelo, Zimbabwe.*

SKEET, Edward Kenneth Walter. b 27. Univ of Southn BEducn 70. Chich Th Coll 79. **d** 81 Portsm. C of Denmead Dio Portsm from 81. *76 Whichers Gate Road, Rowlands Castle, Hants, PO9 6BB.*

SKEGG, Kenneth Bruce. ACT ThL 46. Univ of Tas BA 62. **d** 46 River **p** 47 Tas. Chap Ch Coll Hobart 46-47; C of Deloraine 47-48; P-in-c 48-52; R of H Trin Hobart 52-66; Cressy 66-68; Perm to Offic Dio Adel 68-76; Dio Tas 77-79; P-in-c of Cygnet Dio Tas from 79. *24 Cutana Road, Snug, Tasmania 7154.* (002-67 9385)

SKEGGS, John Charles McKerrow. b 48. Univ of Birm BA (Th) 70. St Steph Ho Ox 71. **d** 73 **p** 74 Barking for Chelmsf. C of St Cedd Canning Town 73-76; Asst Chap at St Geo Paris 76. *Astveitskoten 14a, 5084 Tertnes, Norway.*

SKELDING, Donald Brian. b 23. Trin Coll Cam BA 47, MA 52. Cudd Coll. **d** 50 **p** 51 Lich. C of All SS Sedgley 50-54; All SS W Bromwich 54-56; V of Tong 56-61; St Jo Evang Walton-on-the-Hill 61-65; St Paul Southport 65-72; R of Norton Canes 72-81; Hinstock and Sambrook Dio Lich from 81. *Rectory, Ellerton Road, Hinstock, Shropshire.* (Sambrook 532)

SKELHORN, Joseph Roy. Bp Wilson Th Coll IM 32. **d** 36 S & M **p** 38 Sheff. C of St Barn Douglas IM 36-37; Goole 37-39; Ince-in-Makerfield (in c of Belle Green) 39-40; Perm to Offic as C-in-c of Foxdale 40-43; C of St Jude Blackb 43-44; Moreton 44-48; V of Newton Flowery Field 48-54; R of Garveston w Thuxton 54-59; Barnham Broom w Bixton Kimberley and Carleton Forehoe 59-62; Mettingham w Ilketshall St John 62-73. *36 Grace Jarrold Court, Golden Dog Lane, Norwich, Norf.*

SKELLETT, Barrington John. Univ of Syd BA 56. Moore Th Coll Syd ACT ThL 59. **d** and **p** 60 Syd. C of Gladesville 60-61; CMS Miss Dio Centr Tang 62-71; R of St John Bishopthorpe City and Dio Syd from 71. *138a Glebe Road, Glebe Point, NSW, Australia 2037.* (660-1818)

SKELTON, Beresford. b 52. St Chad's Coll Dur BA 74. Chich Th Coll. **d** 76 **p** 77 Newc T. C of St Anthony Byker City and Dio Newc T from 76. *St Anthony's Vicarage, Enslin Gardens, Newcastle-upon-Tyne, NE6 3ST.*

SKELTON, David. b 37. Univ of Lon MB, BS 63, MRCS 63. LRCP 63. **d** and **p** 79 Rupld. L to Offic Dio Edmon from 80. *9906-144 Street, Edmonton, Alta, Canada*

SKELTON, Dennis Michael. b 33. K Coll Lon BSc 55. N-E Ordin Course 76. **d** 79 **p** 80 Dur (AFM). Lect Sunderland Poly and C of St Thos Conv Distr Pennywell Bp Wearmouth Dio Dur from 79. *74 Broadmayne Avenue, High Barnes, Sunderland, T & W, SR4 8LU.*

SKELTON, Frank Seymour. b 20. DFC and Bar 44. DSO and bar 45. Trin Hall Cam BA 48, 2nd cl Th Trip pt i 49, MA 52. Ridley Hall Cam 48. **d** 50 **p** 51 Liv. C of Ormskirk 50-52; Chap of Clare Coll Cam Charles Simeon Chap to Univ and L to Offic Dio Ely 52-59; R of Bermondsey 59-69; C-in-c of St Luke Bermondsey 59-65; Hon Chap to Bp of S'wark from 63; RD of Bermondsey 65-69; Clk Lambeth Endowed Charities 69-75; Dir from 75. *127 Kennington Road, SE11 6SF.* (01-735 1925)

SKELTON, Canon Henry John Nugent. b 13. Linc Th Coll 37. **d** 40 **p** 41 Linc. C of Grantham Chap RAFVR 43-47; V of Heckington w Howell & E Heckington 47-56; Holbeach 56-73; RD of E Elloe 68-73; Can & Preb Linc Cathl 70-73; Can (Emer) from 73. *Upton Castle, Pembroke Dock, Dyfed.*

✠ **SKELTON, Right Rev Kenneth John Fraser.** b 18. CBE 72. Late Scho of CCC Cam 1st cl Cl Trip pt i 39, BA (1st cl Th

Trip pt i) 40, MA 44. Wells Th Coll 40. **d** 41 **p** 42 Derby. C of Normanton-by-Derby 41-43; Bakewell 43-45; Bolsover 45-46; PV of Wells Cathl and Lect Wells Th Coll 46-50; V of Howe Bridge 50-55; R of Walton-on-the-Hill 55-62; Exam Chap to Bp of Liv 57-62; Cons Ld Bp of Matab in Bulawayo Cathl 25 July 62 by Bp of Mashon; Bps of N Rhod; and Nyasa; res 70; Asst Bp of Dur and R of Bp Wearmouth 70-75; RD of Wearmouth 70-75; Select Pr Univ of Cam 71 and 73; Commiss Matab 71-75; Apptd Ld Bp of Lich 75. *Bishop's House, The Close, Lichfield, Staffs, WS13 7LG.* (Lichfield 22251)

SKELTON, Melvyn Nicholas. b 38. St Pet Coll Ox BA 61, MA 65. Selw Coll Cam BA 63, MA 68. Ridley Hall, Cam 62. **d** 64 **p** 65 Ex. C of St Mary Church 64-66; St Mary Bury St Edmunds 66-69; Hon C 69-78; Perm to Offic Dio St E from 78. *Milburn House, The Street, Moulton, Newmarket, Suff.*

SKEMP, Canon Stephen Rowland. Wadh Coll Ox BA 34, MA 62. Cudd Coll 34. **d** 35 **p** 36 Lon. C of St John Hendon 35-39; Chap S Afr Ch Rly Miss Bulawayo 39-42; CF (S Afr) 42-46; PC of Pensford w Publow 47-50; V of Hornsea w Goxhill 50-62; V of Atwick w Nunkeeling and Bewholme 50-62; RD of N Holderness 52-62; R of Gt Stanmore 62-71; Chap Br Embassy Ankara 71-74; St Paul Athens 74-77; Archd of the Aegean 71-77; Can of Malta from 80. *6 Karneadou Street, Athens, Greece.* (714906)

SKEOCH, David Windsor. b 37. Ch Ch Ox BA 58, MA 62. Westcott Ho Cam 73. **d** 74 **p** 75 Lon (APM). C of St Mary Pimlico 74-79; Dom Chap to Bp of Truro from 79; to Bp of Lon from 81. *9 Strutton Court, 54 Great Peter Street, SW1P 2HH.* (01-222 2170)

SKEPPER, Robert. b 25. **d** 67 **p** 68 Bp T G S Smith for Leic. C of Loughborough 67-71; V of Shelthorpe (w Good Shepherd Loughborough from 74) Dio Leic from 71. *2 Bramcote Road, Loughborough, Leics.* (Loughborough 61377)

SKETCHLEY, Edward Sydney. b 20. Qu Coll Birm. **d** 49 **p** 50 Derby. C of Bakewell 49-53; PC of Ridgeway 53-57; Abbeydale 57-65; V of Walsgrave-on-Sowe 65-73; Hound w Netley Abbey Dio Win from 73. *Netley Abbey Vicarage, Southampton.* (Hamble 2209)

SKEY, William Trevor Fortescue. St Jo Coll Auckld LTh 25. **d** 24 **p** 25 Wai. C of Rotorua 24-28; P-in-c of Taumarunui 28-29; V of Raglan 29-34; Maori Miss K Co Dio Waik 34-42; RD of Te Kuiti 35-42; V of Woodville 42-47; Tolaga Bay 47-53; P-in-c of Taupo Maori Distr 53-59. *c/o The Pines, Carterton RD2, NZ.*

SKIDMORE, Walton Sudbury. b 09. Univ of Leeds, BA (2nd cl Hist) 32. Coll of Resurr Mirfield, 28. **d** 34 Derby **p** 35 Bp Crick for Derby. C of Long Eaton 34-37; Chap RN 37-64; Perm to Offic Dio Sarum 64-71; Dio Glouc 73-75; Dio Ex 75-79. *New Forge, Blacksmith Road, Rede, Bury St Edmunds, Suff, IP29 4BE.*

SKILLICORN, Walter Stanley. Univ of Syd BA 56. Moore Th Coll Syd ACT ThL (1st cl) 61. **d** 58 **p** 59 Medak. [f in Ch of S India] C-in-c of Yagoona 68-70; R 71-72; Eastwood Dio Syd from 72. *25 Clanalpine Street, Eastwood, NSW, Australia 2122.* (85-1610)

SKILLINGS, Martyn Paul. b 46. St Chad Coll Dur BA 68. Linc Th Coll 68. **d** 70 **p** 71 Warrington for Liv. C of St Anne Stanley Liv 70-72; Warrington 72-75; Industr Chap Warrington Dio Liv 75-76. *32 Uffington Road, Barnack, Peterborough.*

SKILTON, Christopher John. b 55. Magd Coll Cam BA 76. MA 80. Wycl Hall Ox 77. **d** 80 Willesden for Lon **p** 81 Lon. C of St Mary Ealing Dio Lon from 80. *38 Airedale Road, W5 4SD.* (01-567 6926)

SKILTON, Joseph Laurence. b 41. Univ of Wales (Cardiff) Dipl Th 70. St Mich Coll Llan. **d** 70 **p** 71 Ox. C of Bicester 71-73; St Chad Shrewsbury 73-76; V of St Phil W Bromwich 76-80; R of Kenwick-Thornlie Dio Perth from 80. *1 Ravenhill Road, Thornlie, W Australia 6108.* (459-2298)

SKINNER, Basil Garnet. b 23. Univ Coll Ex BSc (1st cl Chem) (Lon) 42, MSc (Lon) 45. BD (2nd cl) (Lon) 60. Ball Coll Ox DPhil 51. Univ of Ex MA (Th) 73. Chich Th Coll 54. **d** 54 **p** 55 Guildf. C of Gt Bookham 54-57; Wolverhampton 57-59; V of Beckwithshaw 59-64; Chap Harrogate Gen Hosp 59-64; Exam Chap to Bp of Ripon 62-72; Sec CACTM 64-66; ACCM 66-69; Perm to Offic Dios Cant and Roch 64-69; V of Brixham 69-75; Surr 74-75; Asst Master Torquay Girls Gr Sch from 75; Perm to Offic Dio Ex from 75. *23 Vicarage Hill, Cockington, Torquay, Devon, TQ2 6HZ.* (Torquay 607021)

✠ **SKINNER, Right Rev Brian Antony.** Univ of Reading BSc (Agr) 60. Tyndale Hall Bris 66. **d** 67 **p** 68 Guildf. C of Woking 67-70; P at Quilpue 70-77; Archd of Valparaiso 76-77; Cons Asst Bp in Chile (Bp of Valparaiso) in St Paul's Ch Valparaiso 14 Aug 77 by Bp of Chile; Bps Flagg and Morrison. *Casilla 561, Vina del Mar, Chile.*

SKINNER, David Malcolm. b 26. CCC Cam 2nd cl Hist Trip pt i, 54, BA (2nd cl Th Trip pt ia) 55, MA 59. Wells Th Coll 55. **d** 57 **p** 58 Bris. C of Lockleaze 57-60; Executive Officer of C of E Radio and Television Coun 60-64; Ch Information Office and Sec of Abps' Advisers on Radio and Television 64-67; L to Offic Dio S'wark 60-67; V of Ston Easton w Farrington Gurney 67-70. *Glasha, Cromane, Killorglin, Co Kerry, Irish Republic.*

SKINNER, Donald John. b 52. Univ of Alta BA 75. Vanc Sch of Th 79. **d** 80 **p** 81 Sktn. I of St Mark City and Dio Sktn from 80. *1911 Alexandra Avenue, Saskatoon, Sask, Canada, S7K 3C8.*

SKINNER, Canon Frederick Arthur. b 08. **d** 35 W China **p** 37 E Szech. CIM Miss Dio W China 29-46; Tahsien 36-46; V of St Cuthb W Hampstead 46-51; R of Bidborough 51-81; Hon Can of Roch 70-80; Can (Emer) from 81. *10 Faraday Ride, Tonbridge, Kent, TN10 4RL.*

SKINNER, John Cedric. b 30. Univ of Bris BA (Econ) 55. Dipl Th (Lon) 57. Tyndale Hall Bris 55. **d** 57 **p** 58 Ex. C of St Leon Ex 57-62; Univ Sec Inter-Varsity Fellowship 62-68; V of St Sav Guildf 68-76; R of Stoke-next-Guildf (w St Sav from 76) City and Dio Guildf from 74. *Rectory, Wharf Road, Guildford, Surrey, GU1 4RP.* (Guildford 61867)

SKINNER, John Timothy. b 55. Linc Th Coll 79. **d** 81 Dur. C of Newton Aycliffe Dio Dur from 81. *51 Shafto Way, Newton Aycliffe, Co Durham, DL5 5QN.*

SKINNER, Canon John Victor. b 16. Univ of Wales BA 38. St Steph Ho Ox 38. **d** 40 **p** 41 Llan. C of St Dyfrig Cardiff 40-41; Portishead 41-44; King's Norton 44-50; Chap Monyhull Hall Hosp and Resid Sch 47-50; V of St Alb Rochdale 50-53; St Jas Pokesdown Bournemouth 53-70; Dir Educn and LPr Dio Sarum from 70; Can and Preb Sarum Cathl from 73. *Audley House, Crane Street, Salisbury, Wilts.* (Sarum 28648)

SKINNER, Leonard Harold. b 36. K Coll Lon and Warm BD and AKC 62. **d** 63 **p** 64 Lon. C of St Mary of Eton Hackney Wick 63-66; St Jo Evang Palmers Green 66-69; V of Grange Pk 69-80; Team V of St Mark Shelton Dio Lich from 80. *45 The Parkway, Hanley, Staffs, ST1 3BB.* (Stoke/T 266066)

SKINNER, Michael Thomas. b 39. SOC 73. **d** 78 **p** 79 Roch. Hon C of St Andr Orpington 78-81; All SS Orpington Dio Roch from 82. *80 Spur Road, Orpington, Kent, BR6 0QN.* (Orpington 25322)

SKINNER, Raymond Frederick. b 45. St Jo Coll Dur BA 67. Cranmer Hall Dur. **d** 70 **p** 71 Newc T. C of St Paul Elswick Newc T 70-75; V of Newbottle Dio Dur from 76; M Gen Syn from 80. *Newbottle Vicarage, Houghton-le-Spring, T & W.* (Houghton-le-Spring 843244)

SKINNER, Raymond Geoffrey. b 24. CCC Ox 1st cl Cl Mods 43, 2nd cl Lit Hum 49, BA and MA 50, 2nd cl Th 51. Linc Th Coll 51. **d** 53 **p** 54 S'wark. C of Mitcham 53-57; Sprowston (in C of St Francis Heartsease) 57-58; Hawley (in c of All SS) 58-65; V of St Barn Pleasley Hill Mansfield Dio Southw from 66. *Vicarage, Church Street, Pleasley Hill, Mansfield, Notts, NG19 7SZ.* (Mansfield 810277)

SKINNER, Preb Robert William Murray. b 27. St Edm Hall Ox BA (2nd cl Mod Hist) 51, MA 55. Ridley Hall Cam 51. **d** 53 **p** 54 B & W. C of Bath Abbey 53-56; Mottingham (in c of St Alb) 56-59; R of Withington w Westhide 59-62; CF (TA) 60-62; CF (TA-R of O) 62-63; Chap RNR from 63; R of H Trin Ayr w St Osw Maybole and St Ninian Prestwick 62-75; P-in-c of Condover 75-80; RD of Condover 78-80; Preb of Heref Cathl from 79; R of Tarrington w Stoke Edith, Aylton w Pixley, Munsley and Putley Dio Heref from 80; RD of Ledbury from 81. *Tarrington Rectory, Hereford, HR1 4EU.* (Tarrington 314)

SKIPP, Arthur John. b 18. Late Open Exhib of Em Coll Cam BA (2nd Cl Engl) 41, MA 44. Wells Th Coll 52. **d** 53 Ox **p** 54 Buckingham for Cant. C of High Wycombe 53-58; L to Offic Dio Ox 58-60; Chap R Gr Sch High Wycombe from 60. *School House, Royal Grammar School, High Wycombe, Bucks.* (High Wycombe 26019)

SKIPPER, Joseph Allen. b 17. Lich Th Coll 58. **d** 59 **p** 60 Worc. C of Halesowen 59-61; Wareham w Arne 61-64; R of Bishopstrow and Boreham 64-72; Fleet 72-74; V of Sutterton (w Wigtoft from 78) Dio Linc from 74; P-in-c of Wigtoft 77-78. *Sutterton Vicarage, Boston, Lincs.* (Sutterton 285)

SKIPPER, Kenneth Graham. b 34. St Aid Coll 65. **d** 68 **p** 69 York. C of St Aug Newland 68-71; St Mark Newby 71-74; V of Dormanstown 74-78; Aldbrough and Mappleton w Goxhill and Withernwick Dio York from 78. *Mappleton Vicarage, Hornsea, N Humb.* (Hornsea 3499)

SKIPPER, Canon Lawrence Rainald. b 17. St Pet Hall Ox BA (Th) 39, MA 43. Wycl Hall Ox 39. **d** and **p** 41 Guildf. C of H Trin Aldershot 41-44; Ch Ch Paignton (in c of St Paul Preston) 44-48; V of St Paul Preston Paignton 48-50; Chap of Trent Coll Nottm 50-56; LPr Dio Derby 51-56; V Claughton w Grange Birkenhead 56-65; R of Christleton 65-72; RD of

Ches 69-78; 69; P-in-c of Eccleston Dio Ches 72; R (w Pulford from 73) from 72; Hon Can of Ches from 74. *Rectory, Eccleston, Chester.* (Chester 674703)

SKIPPER, William Stanley. St Paul's Coll Grahmstn. **d** 71 **p** 72 Bloemf. C of St Marg Bloemf 71-74; Welkom 74-75; R of Alexandria 75-79; St Barn Sydenham City and Dio Port Eliz from 79. *7 Rhodes Street, Sydenham, Port Elizabeth, CP, S Africa.*

SKIPPON, Kevin John. b 54. St Steph Ho Ox 78. **d** 81 Nor. C of Gt Yarmouth Dio Nor from 81. *90 Lawn Avenue, Great Yarmouth, NR30 1QW.*

SKIPWITH, Osmund Humberston. b 06. New Coll Ox BA 28, MA 33. Cudd Coll 29. **d** 30 **p** 31 Leic. C of St Pet Leic 30-35; UMCA Miss Dio Masasi 35-41; CF (EC) 41-47; CF 47-54; Perm to Offic Dio Momb 44-54; R of Maperton 54-66; C-in-c 66-71; R of N Cheriton 54-66; C-in-c 66-71; RD of Cary 60-71; C-in-c of Compton Pauncefoot w Blackford 63-71; C-in-c of Yarlington 63-71; Preb of Wells Cathl 64-74; R of N Cadbury 66-71; C of Worle 71-74; L to Offic Dio Ox from 74. *16 Kingswood Court, Southcote Road, Reading, RG3 2AU.* (Reading 51246)

SKIRVING, Canon Archibald Howard. Univ of W Ont BA 55. Hur Coll BTh 58. Wycl Coll Tor MTh 72. **d** 57 **p** 58 Hur. I of St Mich AA Riverside 57-62; St Timothy Lon Ont 62-66; R of Ch of Transfig Lon 66-71; St John Cam Ont 71-81; Ch Ch Chatham Dio Hur from 81; Can of Hur from 77. *Box 502, Chatham, Ont., Canada.*

SKLIROS, Michael Peter. b 33. Clare Coll Cam BA 57, MA 62. Ridley Hall Cam 57. **d** 59 Barking for Chelmsf **p** 60 Chelmsf. C of Hornchurch 59-61; Asst Chap Denstone Coll 61-65; L to Offic Dio Lich 62-65; Chap RAF 65-77; P-in-c of Stowmarket Dio St E 77-78; Hon C from 78. *56 Crown Street, Stowmarket, Suff.* (Stowmarket 5050)

S'KOSANA, Philip. b 41. **d** 80 Swaz. d Dio Swaz. *PO Box 162, Mbabane, Swaziland.*

SKOULDING, Peter Arthur. b 32. Clifton Th Coll 63. **d** 66 **p** 67 Bradf. C of St John Bowling 66-69; Rushden w Newton Bromswold 69-72; St Mary Crawley 72-77; R of Flixton w Homersfield and S Elmham Dio St E from 77. *Flixton Vicarage, Bungay, Suff.* (Bungay 3588)

SKOWRONSKI, Don Roy. Univ of Santa Clara Calif BA 69. Penn State Univ MA 70. Univ of Tor MA 73. Trin Coll Tor MDiv 78. **d** 78 **p** 79 Ont. C of Ch Ch Belleville 78-79; I of Merrickville Dio Ont from 79. *104 Merrickville, Ont, K0G 1N0, Canada.*

SKOYLES, Douglas Hardie. b 45. Univ of Windsor BA 66. Trin Coll Tor STB 69. **d** 69 **p** 70 Calg. C of St Barn Calg 69-71; Ch Ch Calg 71-74; R of Banff 74-78; St Mark City and Dio Calg from 78; Exam Chap to Bp of Calg from 78. *1816-33rd Avenue SW, Calgary, Alta, Canada T2T 1Y9.* (244-3211)

SKRINE, William Napier. b 1898. Late Scho of G and C Coll Cam BA (2nd cl Th Trip pt i) 22, MA 26. Ridley Hall Cam 22. **d** 22 **p** 23 Bris. C of H Trin Clifton 22-24; St Luke S Lyncombe Bath 24-26; Ch Ch Weston-s-Mare 26-30; PC of Longcot w Fernham 30-31; R of Middleton w Fordley 31-38; Hockwold w Wilton V 38-43; Otterhampton w Combwich 43-71. *Rose Cottage, Shovel Lane, North Petherton, Bridgwater, Somt.*

SKUBLICS, Ernest. b 36. Univ of Ott LTh 64. **d** 73 Tor **p** 73 Qu'App. C of Whitewood 73-76; Chap St Jo Coll Winnipeg from 76. *c/o St John's College, Winnipeg, Manit, Canada.*

SKUCE, Ven Francis John Leonard. b 26. TCD BA 48. **d** 50 **p** 51 Drom. C of Warrenpoint w Clonallan 50-53; I of Innishmacsaint Dio Clogh from 53; Dioc Sec Clogh from 67; Preb of Clogh Cathl 70-73; Archd of Clogh from 73; Exam Chap to Bp of Clogh from 73. *Rectory, Derrygonnelly, Enniskillen, Co Fermanagh, N Ireland.*

SKUES, Eric. b 1899. Univ of Leeds BA 22. Coll of Resurr Mirfield 19. **d** 24 Sheff for Shantung **p** 26 Shantung. Miss at Yenchow 24-28; Pingyin 29-34; Chap and Miss at Weihaiwei 35-40; Tsing-tao 40-45; SPG Area Sec Dio Cov 47-53; Dios Glouc and Worc 47-65; Dio Heref 53-65; USPG Area Sec Dios Heref and Worc 65-70; Perm to Offic Dio Cov 47-53; Dio Glouc 47-65; Dio Heref 53-70; L to Offic Dio Worc 47-70; Dio S'wark 70-81. *Juxon, Lollards Tower Chambers, Lambeth Palace Road, SE 1.*

SKUES, John Anthony. b 30. Qu Coll Cam BA 52, MA 56. Coll of Resurr Mirfield, 52. **d** 55 Linc **p** 56 Grimsby for Cant. C of Boston 55-58; Stroud 58-59; Cirencester w Watermoor 59-62; CF (R of O) from 60; Hosp to St Thos Hosp Lon 62-69; Chap Walsgrave Hosp Cov from 69. *8 Shirley Road, Walsgrave, Coventry, CV2 2EN.* (Coventry 614193)

SKUSE, Canon Frank Richard. b 18. TCD BA 42. **d** 42 **p** 43 Clogh. C of Monaghan 42-45; Drumcondra w N Strand 45-50; C-in-c Clonaslee and Rosenallis 50-54; I of Kinneigh w Ballymoney 54-68; Kilgarriffe (w Castleventry to 76 and Timoleague and Lislee from 76) Dio Ross from 68; Can of Kilbrittain and H Trin in Cork Cathl and of Donoughmore in Cloyne Cathl from 78. *Rectory, Clonakilty, Co Cork, Irish Republic.* (Bandon 43357)

SLACK, Canon Ellis Edward. b 23. Univ of Birm BA (2nd cl Th) 51, MA 53. Qu Coll Birm 51. **d** and **p** 53 Ripon. C of Halton 53-56; R of Stanningley 57-64; V of St Faith N Dulwich 64-72; St John Bethnal Green 72-78; R (w St Bart) 78-79; Exam Chap to Bp of Stepney 72-79; Can Res of Portsm Cathl from 79. *44 St Thomas's Street, Old Portsmouth, PO1 2EZ.*

SLACK, Preb William Wynne. b 09. TCD BA (1st cl Resp) 35, MA 39, Div Test (1st cl) 41. **d** and **p** 42 Kilm. C of Urney 42-45; I of Elph Dio Elph from 45; Hd Master Elph Gr Sch 45-76; Preb of Elph Cathl from 46; Exam Chap to Bp of Kilm from 50. *Deanery, Elphin, Co Roscommon, Irish Republic.* (Elphin 20)

SLADDEN, Duncan Julius Edward. b 25. K Coll Cam BA (2nd cl Hist) 50, MA 54. Cudd Coll 51. **d** 53 **p** 54 Wakef. C of Huddersfield 53-55; St Mary Virg Reading (in c of St Matt Southcote) 55-61; R of Largs 61-65; C of Stevenage (in c of St Pet Broadwater) 65-70; R of St Jo Evang Johnstone 70-76. *31 Laburnum Grove, Stirling.*

SLADDEN, Harry Eversley. b 1892. Late Found Scho and De Bury Scho of St Chad's Coll Dur BA 14, MA 17. **d** 17 **p** 18 Dur. C of St Hilda S Shields 17-20; St Mary Magd Sutton-in-Ashfield 20-25; St Mary Scarborough 25-27; V of Parkgate 27-58. *Dulverton Hall, St Martin's Square, Scarborough, Yorks.*

SLADDEN, Canon John Cyril. b 20. Late Postmaster of Mert Coll Ox BA 42, MA 46, 1st cl Th 47, Ellerton Th Essay Pri 48, BD 66. Wycl Hall Ox 46. **d** 48 **p** 49 Lich. C of Oswestry 48-51; Tutor St Aid Coll Birkenhead 51-53; Exam Chap to Bp of Sheff 53-59; Sec Dio Tr C'tte 53-57; R of Todwick 53-59; PC (V from 68) of Lower Peover Dio Ches from 59; Exam Chap to Bp of Ches 63-73; RD of Knutsford from 80; Hon Can of Ches Cathl from 80. *Lower Peover Vicarage, Knutsford, Ches, WA16 9PZ.* (Lower Peover 2304)

SLADE, Adrian Barrie. b 47. Univ of Nottm BTh 73. St Jo Coll Nottm 69. **d** 73 **p** 74 S'wark. C of Im w St Anselm Streatham 73-76; Chipping Barnet 76-80; V of Sundon Dio St Alb from 80. *St Mary's Vicarage, Selina Close, Sundon Park, Luton, Beds.* (Luton 583076)

SLADE, Alfred Laurence. b 12. Roch Th Coll 67. **d** 69 Maidstone for Cant **p** 70 Cant. C of St Paul Cliftonville 69-71; St Jas Westgate-on-Sea 71-75; Perm to Offic Dio Sarum 75-81; Dio Cant from 81. *82 Ingoldsby Road, Minnis Bay, Birchington, Kent, CT7 9PJ.*

SLADE, Canon Frank James Arthur. Qu Coll Newfld 43. Univ of Dur LTh 46, BA 50. **d** 46 **p** 47 Newfld. C of Bonavista Newfld 46-49; C-in-c of Brooklyn 49-50; L to Offic Dio Dur 50-51; C of St Jo Bapt Cathl St John's 51-55; R 55-76; Can from 57; R of Harbour Grace Dio E Newfld from 76. *Rectory, Harbour Grace, Newfoundland, Canada.* (709-596 6041)

SLADE, Herbert Edwin William. b 12. Univ of Lon BA (3rd cl Engl) 33. Dorch Miss Coll 34. M SSJE 39. **d** 35 **p** 36 Glouc. C of St Barn Tuffley 35-39; Perm to Offic Dio Ox 39-48; CF (EC) 42-46; V of St Pet Mazagon Bom 48-53; Prin St Pet Sch Mazagon and Perm to Offic Dio Bom 48-56; L to Offic Dio Lon 56-59 and 66-71; Dio Ox 59-66; Dio Chich from 71. *The Anchorhold, Paddockhall, Haywards Heath.* (Haywards Heath 52468)

SLADE, Canon William Clifford. b 24. St Jo Coll Dur BA 47, Dipl Th 49, MA 53. **d** 49 Whitby for York **p** 50 York. C of Northallerton 49-52; Eston w Normanby 52-54; V of St Mark Anlaby 54-60; Brompton w Snainton 60-67; R of Stokesley 67-71; Kirkby Knowle Dio York from 71; V of Felixkirk w Boltby Dio York from 71; Can and Preb of York Minster from 79. *Felixkirk Vicarage, Thirsk, N Yorks, YO7 2DP.* (0845-537215)

SLADEN, Philip. b 50. Fitzw Coll Cam BA 71, MA 75. Ripon Hall Ox 72. **d** 75 **p** 76 St Alb. C of Bushey Heath 75-78; Chap RAF from 78. *c/o Ministry of Defence Adastral House, Theobalds Road, WC1X 8RU.*

SLADER, William Basil. b 16. Sarum Th Coll 55. **d** 57 **p** 58 Win. C of Overton w Laverstoke and Freefolk 57-60; V of N Eling (or Copythorne) 60-70; St Mary Bourne w Woodcott 70-81. *12 Hazel Close, Chandler's Ford, Eastleigh, Hants, SO5 1RF.*

SLATER, Gilbert Leonard. Selw Coll Cam BA 31, MA 35. Wells Th Coll 31. **d** 32 **p** 34 Lich. C of Shelton 32-35; Tamworth (in c of Hopwas) 35-39; SSC Dio Lich 39-42; V of St Jo Evang W Bromwich 42-60; Gt w L Dalby Dio Leic from 60. *Great Dalby Vicarage, Melton Mowbray, Leics.* (Melton Mowbray 2458)

SLATER, Canon James Douglas. Univ of Tor BA (Sc) 52. Oak Hill Th Coll 55. **d** 58 **p** 59 Carib. R of St Paul's Cathl Kamloops 58-63; I of Thomson River Miss 60-64; C of St Jas Kingston Ont 64-67; R of St Marg Winnipeg Dio Rupld from 67; Exam Chap to Bp of Rupld from 76; Can of Rupld from

79. *160 Ethelbert Street, Winnipeg, Manit, Canada.*

SLATER, John. b 11. St D Coll Lamp BA 35. **d** 35 **p** 36 Blackb. C of All SS Blackpool 35-38; St Mark Witton 38-40; St Jo Evang Sparkhill 40-45 V of St A Birm 45-49 St Matt Smethwick 49-51; Chap Parkstone Sea Tr Sch 51-56; R of Halstock 56-76; R of W w E Chelborough 56-76. *5 Brit View Road, West Bay, Bridport, Dorset.* (Bridport 56381)

SLATER, John. b 45. K Coll Lon BA (1st cl Hist) and AKC 67. Fitzw Coll Cam BA (2nd cl Th Trip pt ii) 69. U Th Sem NY STM 70. Westcott Ho Cam 67. **d** 70 **p** 71 Lon. C of All SS Marg Str St Marylebone 70-77; Prin Inst Chr Stud Lon 73-77; V of St Sav Paddington Dio Lon from 77. *42 Warwick Avenue, W9 2PT.* (01-286 4962)

SLATER, John Albert. b 25. Univ of Lon BA (2nd cl) 52. Oak Hill Th Coll 47. **d** 52 **p** 53 Liv. C of Em Everton 52-55; V of St Paul Kirkdale; 55-61; St Sav Bacup 61-69; St Thos Blackpool Dio Blackb from 69. *Vicarage, Devonshire Road, Blackpool, Lancs.* (Blackpool 32544)

SLATER, John Allen. b 20. St Aid Coll. **d** 62 **p** 63 York. C of Ch Ch Bridlington 62-65; V of Welton w Melton Dio York from 65. *St Helen's Vicarage, Welton, Brough, N Humb, HU15 1ND.* (0482-666677)

SLATER, John Ralph. b 38. Linc Th Coll 71. **d** 73 Stepney for Lon **p** 74 Chelmsf. C of St Mich AA w St Paul's Haggerston 73-74; St Marg w St Columba Leytonstone 74-77; Whitstable 77-80; V of St Alb Gt Ilford Dio Chelmsf from 80. *St Alban's Vicarage, Albert Road, Ilford, Essex, IG1 1HS.* (01-478 2428)

SLATER, Keith Francis. b 49. ACT ThL 74. St Francis Coll Brisb 73. **d** and **p** 75 Rockptn. C of Gladstone 75-78; P-in-c of Springsure Dio Rockptn from 78. *Box 33, Springsure, Qld, Australia 4722.*

SLATER, Percy William. b 06. Armstrong Coll Dur BA (2nd cl Hist) 28, MA 31. St Jo Coll Dur 28. **d** 29 **p** 30 Dur. C of All SS Stranton 29-32; St Cuthb Bensham 32-35; V of Tow Law 35-40; Blackhall 40-55; R of Winston 55-72; Perm to Offic Dio Carl from 80. *11 Penrith Road, Keswick, Cumbria, CA12 4HF.*

SLATER, Philip David. b 27. K Coll Lon and Warm 58. **d** 60 **p** 61 Portsm. C of St Faith Havant 60-67; Leigh Pk Portsm 68-69; Co Adv in Relig Educn Hants 69-74; Educn Adv Officer Gosport and Fareham from 74; Hon C of Bp's Waltham Dio Portsm from 76. *Woodfidley, New Road, Swanmore, Hants.*

SLATER, Robert Adrian. b 48. St Jo Coll Nottm 76. **d** 79 McKie for Cov **p** 80 Cov. C of Bedworth Dio Cov from 79. *38 Gallagher Road, Bedworth, Coventry, CV12 8SD.*

SLATER, Canon Robert Henry Lawson. Em Coll Cam 2nd cl Hist Trip pt i, 21, BA (2nd cl Hist Trip pt ii) 22, Members' Pri (Engl) 22, 1st cl Th Trip pt ii 24, MA 29. Univ of Columb PhD 48. Sir Geo Williams Univ Mon LLD (*hon causa*) 69. Lady Kay Scho of Jes Coll Cam 22, Wordsworth Stud 24. Westcott Ho Cam 22. **d** 24 Bp Wood for Newc T **p** 25 Newc T. C of Benwell 24-28; Chap Toc H N Area 25-29; L to Offic Dio Dur 28-29; Chap Kokine 29-36; Cathl Ch Rang 36-38; Maymyo 38-41; Taunggyi Rang 41-48; Exam Chap to Bp of Rang 36-43; CF (Ind) 43-47; Hon CF 46; Chap to Bp of Rang 47-48; Lect Union Th Sem New York 47; Prof of Ch Hist Hur Coll 48-49; Prof of Systematic Th McGill Univ Montr 49-58; Prin Montr Dioc Th Coll 51-58; Exam Chap to Bp of Montr 51-58; to Bp of Queb 76-80; Hon Can Ch Ch Cathl Montr 55-64; Can (Emer) from 65; Prof of World Religions Harvard Univ 58-64; P-in-c of Georgeville 71-72. *Box 75, Georgeville, PQ, Canada.* (819-843 3868)

SLATER, Ronald George. b 11. Fitzw Coll Cam 2nd cl Hist Trip pt i 32, BA (3rd cl Engl Trip pt ii) 33, MA 48. Qu Coll Birm 38. **d** 40 **p** 41 Blackb. C of St Jo Bapt Gannow 40-41; SPG Miss at Cawnpore 41-59; Prin Ch Ch Coll Cawnpore 43-57; SPG Rep Luckn 41-46 and 54-59; P-in-c of Kanpur 57-59; R of Crofton 59-68; RD of Wakef 66-68; Asst Chap HM Pris Wandsworth 68; Win 68-75; P-in-c of Ampfield 75-79; Perm to Offic Dio Ox from 80. *98 Shinfield Road, Reading, Berks.*

SLATER, Ronald Spencer. Univ of Man BA 36. Lich Th Coll 36. **d** 38 **p** 39 Blackb. C of St Cuthb Fulwood Preston 38-41; St Paul Scotforth 41-43; CF (EC) 43-47; V of St Jo Bapt Baxenden 47-53; V of St Erth 53-70; Ed of Truro Dioc Year Book 56-70; RD of Penwith 67-70; R of Wetheral w Warw 70; V of Mabe 71-76. *1 Col-Moor Close, Off Guildford Road, Hayle, Cornw.*

SLATER, Thomas Ernest. b 37. BD (Lon) 71. **d** 67 Warrington for Liv **p** 68 Liv. C of Ch Ch Bootle 67-72; Stapleford 72-75; Supt of Tower Hamlets Miss 75-77; Hon C of St Pet w St Benet Mile End Stepney 78-79; Asst Chap Whitechapel and Mile End Hosp from 79. *22 Cephas Street, Stepney, E1 4AX.* (01-790 0578)

SLATOR, Edward Douglas. b 18. TCD BA 41, MA 47. Univ of Hull BPhil 75. **d** 43 **p** 44 Dub. C of Dundrum 43-46; Chap St Columba's Coll Rathfarnham 46-60; I of Dunmore E w Killea 60-73; C of Dundrum 74-80; Bp's C of Rathmolyon U Dio Meath from 80. *Rathmolyon House, Rathmolyon, Co Meath, Irish Republic.* (Rathmolyon 67)

SLATOR, William Thompson Howard. b 09. TCD BA 31, MA 34. **d** 33 **p** 34 Down. C of Ballywillan 33-35; C-in-c of Mullaghdun 35-38; R of Boyle w Aghanagh 38-52; Clonbroney w Killoe 52-66; RD of Edgeworthstown 58-66; Fenagh 67-81; I of Kiltoghart 66-81; Preb of Elph Cathl 66-81. *1 Glenageary Terrace, Dunlaoghaire, Dublin, Irish Republic.*

SLATTERY, Canon Humphrey Oswald. **d** 51 Knaresborough for Fred **p** 52 Fred. C of Trin Ch St John 51-54; R of Prince William 54-55; C of St Jo Evang Montr 55-58; R of Farnham 58-63; St Steph Lachine 63-68; St Columba Montr 68-71; St Jo Evang City and Dio Montr from 71; Hon Can of Montr from 74. *6 Redpath Place, Montreal 109, PQ, Canada.* (514-844 7761)

SLAUGHTER, Clive Patrick. b 36. St Paul's Coll Grahmstn. **d** 77 **p** 78 Natal. C of St John Pinetown 77-79; I of Bluff Dio Natal from 80. *936 Bluff Road, Bluff, Natal, S Africa.*

SLAUGHTER, Frederick. b 05. TD 50. Ridley Coll Melb 29. ACT ThL 31. **d** 31 **p** 32 Gippsld. C of St Geo Wonthaggi 31-33; C-in-c of Korumburra 33; V of Alberton 33-36; C of Gt Yarmouth 36-38; CF (TA) 39-49; TA (R of O) from 49; V of Sheringham 46-56; R of Stratton St Mary w Stratton St Mich 57-71; Gt w L Wacton 57-71. *22 Arundel Road, Wymondham, Norf.* (W'ham 2089)

SLAUGHTER, Canon Maurice Basil. b 20. Univ of Leeds BA 42. Coll of Resurr Mirfield 42. **d** 44 **p** 45 Lich. C of St Mary Kingswinford 44-46; St Nich Roch 46-47; Ch Ch (in c of St Pet) Luton 47-50; V of Marg Ladywood Birm 50-52; Newsome 52-60; Queensbury 60-63; Ch Ch Skipton-in-Craven 63-78; Hon Can of Bradf from 67; RD of Skipton from 73; P-in-c of Bolton Abbey w Barden Dio Bradf from 78; Rylstone Dio Bradf from 78; Arncliffe w Halton Gill Dio Bradf from 78. *Hewitt Gate, Threshfield, Skipton, BD23 5HB. N Yorks.* (Grassington 752158)

SLEDGE, Ven Richard Kitson. b 30. Peterho Cam BA 52, MA 57. Ridley Hall, Cam 52. **d** 54 **p** 55 Ex. C of Em Plymouth 54-57; St Martin (in c of St Steph) Ex 57-63; V of Dronfield w Unstone 63-76; R 76-78; RD of Chesterfield 72-78; Archd of Huntingdon from 78; R of Hemingford Abbots Dio Ely from 78; Hon Can of Ely Cathl from 78. *Hemingford Abbots Rectory, Huntingdon, PE18 9AN.* (St Ives 69856)

SLEE, Canon Colin Bruce. b 45. AKC and BD 69. St Aug Coll Cant 69. **d** 70 Lynn for Nor **p** 71 Thetford for Nor. C of St Francis Heartsease Nor 70-73; St Mary Gt w St Mich AA Cam 73-76; Chap Girton Coll Cam 73-76; Chap and Tutor K Coll Lon 76-82; Can and Sub-Dean of St Alb Cathl from 82. *Old Rectory, Sumpter Yard, St Albans, Herts.* (St Albans 54827)

SLEGG, John Edward. b 36. St Pet Coll Ox BA (3rd cl Th) 62, MA 66. Ridley Hall, Cam 62. **d** 64 **p** 65 Truro. C of Perranzabuloe 64-66; CF from 66. *c/o Ministry of Defence, Lansdowne House, Berkeley Square, W 1.*

SLEIGHT, Gordon Frederick. b 47. AKC 69. St Aug Coll Cant 69. **d** 70 **p** 71 Linc. C of St Botolph Boston 70-74; C-in-c of St Mich Louth 74-75; Stewton 74-75; Team V of Louth 75-81. *87 Ferry Road, Scunthorpe, Lincs, DN15 8LY.*

SLEIGHT, Roland Arthur. b 16. Univ of Leeds BA 37. Coll of Resurr Mirfield 37. **d** 39 Linc **p** 40 Grimsby for Linc. C of H Trin Gainsborough 39-43; Chap RNVR 43-47; V of Elsham 47-49; Worlaby 47-49; C of St Nich Sutton 49-52; Chap of Sutton and Cheam Hosp 50-52; C of St Mary Magd Wandsworth Common 52-55; UMCA Area Sec for NW Engl and N Wales 55-58; V of Whitworth 58-67; P-in-c of Gt Horwood 67-81; C-in-c of Middle w E Claydon 67-71. *28 Church Lane, Balderton, Newark, Notts.*

SLIGO, Bruce James. St Francis Coll Brisb ACT ThDip 74. **d** 75 **p** 76 Brisb. C of Stafford 75-76; Drayton 76-77; Warwick 77; P-in-c of Millmerran 77-81; C of St John Darlinghurst Dio Syd from 81. *45 Surrey Street, Darlinghurst, NSW, Australia 2010.*

SLIGO, Charles Edsall Alexander. Univ of Melb LTh 52, BA 53. **d** 53 **p** 54 Melb. C of St Andr Brighton 53-55; Chap Brighton Gr Sch Dio Melb 55-62; Hd Master Brighton Jun Sch 63-69; Perm to Offic Melb 70-74; Dio Gippsld from 74; Hd Master Gippsld Gr Sch 70; Prin 71-75; Hon C of St Paul's Cathl Sale 70-75; Exam Chap to Bp of Gippsld 71-81; Hd Master Ivanhoe Gr Sch and L to Offic Dio Melb from 75. *Box 91, Ivanhoe, Vic, Australia 3079.* (03-49 1590)

SLOAN, Geoffrey Keith. b 29. St Jo Coll Morpeth 69. **d** 70 **p** 72 River. C of Deniliquin 70-73; The Rock 73-75; P-in-c 75-77; L to Offic Dio Melb from 77. *Aird Street, Camberwell, Vic, Australia 3124.* (83-5632)

SLOANE, Isaac Reburn. TCD BA and Div Test 41, MA 60. **d** 42 **p** 43 Kilm. C of Kinawley and 42-44; I of Gleneely w Culdaff 44-54; Baronscourt w Drumclamph 54-76; Drumclamph w Drumquin 76-78. *40 Rawdon Place, Moira, Craigavon, Co Armagh, N Ireland.*

SLOCOMBE, Frederick Steed. **d** 68 **p** 69 Ott. C of Pembroke 69-70; I of Win 70-72. *58 Promenade Avenue, Ottawa, Ont., Canada.*

SLOCOMBE, Peter Ralph. b 45. Sarum Wells Th Coll 71. **d** 73 **p** 74 Taunton for B & W. C of H Trin Bridgwater 73-75. *1 Ashleigh Avenue, Bridgwater, Somerset.*

SLOUGH, Colin Richard. b 40. AKC 66. Ripon Hall Ox. **d** 68 Bp Sinker for Birm **p** 69 Birm. Hon C of St Luke Birm and Asst Master Lea-Mason Sch 68-69; Hon Chap Portsm Cathl (in c of St Geo Ch Centre Portsea) 70-72; Lect Culham Coll of Educn 72-75; RE Adv Dio Ox 72-75; Dep Hd Master St Luke Comprehensive Sch Southsea 75-80; V of St John Evang and of Ch Ch Sandown Dio Portsm from 80. *Vicarage, 26 Nunwell Street, Sandown, IW, PO36 9DE.* (Sandown 402548)

SLOW, Leslie John. b 47. Univ of Liv BSc 68, MSc 69. N Ordin Course 77. **d** 80 **p** 81 Bradf. Dir of Stud Bradf Gr Sch and Hon C of St Jo Evang Gt Horton City and Dio Bradf from 80. *19 Dale Croft Rise, Allerton, Bradford, W Yorks, BD15 9AT.*

SLUMAN, Richard Albert. b 02. Univ of Wales BSc 23. St Mich Coll Llan 23. **d** 25 **p** 26 Swan B. C of St Mark Swansea 25-27; Chepstow 27-35; Tredegar (in c of Dukestown) 35-36; V of Llantilio-Crossenny w Llanfihangelystern-Llewern 36-47; Blaenavon w Capel Newydd 47-58; Surr from 48; R of Whitchurch w Ganarew 58-77; Perm to Offic Dio Heref from 78. *Grayfoot House, Livesey Road, Ludlow, Salop.*

SLUMAN, Richard Geoffrey Davies. b 34. St Jo Coll Ox BA and MA 68. Sarum Th Coll 68. **d** 70 Lynn for Nor **p** 71 Thetford for Nor. C of Gt Yarmouth 70-73; V of Churchdown Dio Glouc from 73. *Vicarage, Vicarage Close, Churchdown, Gloucester.* (Churchdown 713203)

SLY, Christopher John. Selw Coll Cam 2nd cl Th Trip pt i 56, BA (3rd cl Th Trip pt ii) 58, MA 62. Wycl Hall Ox. **d** 60 **p** 61 Chelmsf C of St John Buckhurst Hill 60-64; V of Berechurch 64-75; St Sav Westcliff-on-Sea Dio Chelmsf from 75. *33 King's Road, Westcliff-on-Sea, Essex.* (Southend-on-Sea 42920)

SLY, Canon Harold Kenneth. b 15. Kelham Th Coll 34. **d** 38 Leic **p** 39 Bp Willis for Leic. C of Wigston Magna 38-41; St Edm Dudley 41-43; St Steph Redditch 43-49; R of St Swith Worc 49-57; V of Hampton-in-Arden Dio Birm from 57; Chap Midl Hosp Hampton-in-Arden 58-76; Hon Can of Birm Cathl from 78. *Hampton-in-Arden Vicarage, Solihull, W Midl, B92 0AE.* (Hampton-in-Arden 2604)

SLYFIELD, John David. b 32. TD 67. Roch Th Coll 66. **d** 68 **p** 69 Cant. C of St Mary-in-the-Marsh Cant 68-71; P-in-c of Middle w E Claydon and Steeple Claydon 71-76; The Claydons 76-78; RD of Claydon 73-78; V of S Westoe, S Shields Dio Dur from 78. *South Westoe Vicarage, South Shields, Co Durham.* (S Shields 2132)

SMAIL, Thomas Allan. b 28. Univ of Glas MA 49. Univ of Edin BD 52. New Coll Edin 49. **d** 79 Kens for Lon **p** 79 Southw. [f in Ch of Scotld]. C of St Steph E Twickenham 79; Vice-Prin & Lect St Jo Coll Nottm from 79. *7 The Close, Beeston, Nottingham, NG59 5DF.* (Nottm 259328)

SMAILES, Robert Anthony. b 44. Linc Th Coll 79. **d** 81 York. C of Stokesley Dio York from 81. *25 Riversdene, Stokesley, Cleveland.*

SMALE, Frederick Ronald. b 37. K Coll Lon and Warm BD and AKC 60. **d** 61 **p** 62 Cant. C of Bearsted 61-64; Fishponds 64-69; V of Hartlip (w Stockbury from 71) 69-74; C-in-c of Stockbury 69-71; V of River Dio Cant from 75. *23 Lewisham Road, River, Dover, Kent.* (Kearnsey 2037)

SMALL, David Binney. b 39. Westcott Ho Cam 63. **d** 65 **p** 66 Portsm. C of St Jas Milton 65-77; CF from 77. *c/o Ministry of Defence, Bagshot Park, Bagshot, Surrey.*

SMALL, Edwin James. b 15. Univ of Lon BA 44. AKC 48. **d** 67 **p** 68 B & W. C of Cannington 67-70; St Thos Wells 71-75; R of Rodney Stoke w Draycott 75-80; Sec Dioc Advisory C'tte Dio B & W from 80. *69 St Thomas Street, Wells, Somt.*

SMALL, Gordon Frederick. b 41. St Jo Coll Nottm 77. **d** 79 repton for Derby **p** 80 Derby. C of St Pet Belper Dio Derby from 79. *11 Openwood Gate, Belper, Derbyshire, DE5 0SD.*

SMALL, James MacPherson. Wycl Coll Tor LTh 66. **d** and **p** 66 Tor. C of St Geo-on-the-Hill Tor 66-70; I of Bay Ridges 70-73; Newmarket 73-80; Mono E Dio Tor from 80. *53 Simcoe Street, Mono Hills, Ont, Canada.*

SMALL, John. **d** 68 C & Goulb. L to Offic Dio C & Goulb from 68. *72 Scrivener Street, O'Connor, ACT, Australia.*

SMALL, Canon Kenneth Roland Robinson. Univ of NZ. **d** 34 **p** 35 Waik. C of St Bride Otorohanga 34-35; P-in-c 35-37; V 37-39; P-in-c of Papatoetoe 40-41; V of Bombay 42; Thames 42-48; Mt Roskill 48-53; Commiss Auckld 53-56; Asst Chief Org Sec SPCK Lon and Gen Perm to Offic 53-57; Dioc Chap Auckld 57-60; V of Meadowbank 60-74; Can of Auckld 67-78; Can (Emer) from 78; Hon C of H Trin Cathl City and Dio Auckld from 74. *1264 Whangaparaoa Road, Whangaparaoa, NZ.* (Whang 8966)

SMALL, Leonard Norman. b 09. AKC 32. **d** 32 **p** 33 S'wark. C of St Thos Old Charlton 32-35; Sutton Surrey 35-40; CF (EC) 40-46; Hon CF from 46; C of St Swith London Stone 46-48; C-in-c of St Ethelburga Bishopsgate Lon 48-54; V 54-76; C-in-c of St Swith London Stone w St Mary Bothaw London 51-53; CF (TA) 52-60; (TA-R of O) 60-65. *13 Kingston Avenue, Leatherhead, Surrey, KT22 7HY.*

SMALL, Seibert Dacosta. b 45. Univ of WI BA 76. Codr Coll Barb LTh 73. **d** 72 **p** 73 Barb. C of St John Barb 72-75; R of All SS I and Dio Barb from 75. *All Saints Rectory, Maynard's Road, St Peter, Barbados, WI.*

SMALLBONE, Ven Denys George. Worc Ordin Coll 65. **d** 66 Tewkesbury for Glouc **p** 67 Glouc. C of Bourton-on-the-Water w Clapton 66-69; Prec St Paul's Cathl Sale 69-71; R of Yarram 71-80; Exam Chap to Bp of Gippsld from 75; Hon Can of Gippsld 79-81; Archd from 81. *6 Bruce Street, Leongatha, Vic, Australia 3953.*

SMALLDON, Keith. b 48. Open Univ BA 76. Univ of Wales (Cardiff) Dipl Th 71. St Mich Coll Llan 68. **d** 71 **p** 72 Mon. C of Cwmbran 71-73; Chepstow 73-75; Dioc Youth Adv Dio Bradf from 75. *115 Ashbourne Way, Bradford, BD2 1ER.* (Bradf 20861)

SMALLEY, David. b 15. Univ of Man BA 62, BD (2nd cl) 65. FCA 60. Clifton Th Coll 64. **d** and **p** 65 Warrington for Liv. C of H Trin Warrington 65-66; Finance Sec BCMS 66-80. *4 Paragon House, Blackheath, SE3.* (01-852 4108)

SMALLEY, Canon Stephen Stewart. b 31. Late Found Scho of Jes Coll Cam BA 55, MA 58. Eden Th Sem USA BD 57. Ridley Hall Cam. **d** 58 **p** 59 Lon. C of St Paul Portman Square St Marylebone 58-60; Chap Peterho Cam 60-63; Actg Dean 62-63; Select Pr Univ of Cam 63-64; Lect Relig Stud Univ of Ibad 63-69; L to Offic Dio Man 70-77; Lect in Th (and Warden St Anselm Hall from 72) Univ of Man 70-77; Exam Chap to Bp of Nor from 71; Can Res and Prec of Cov Cathl from 77; M C of E Doctrine Comm from 81. *35 Morningside, Coventry, CV5 6PD.* (Coventry 75446)

SMALLFIELD, Geoffrey Mandeno. Coll Ho Ch Ch. Univ of NZ BA 48. **d** 48 **p** 49 Wel. C of St Pet Wel 48-51; V of Pohangina 51-56; Foxton 56-63; Te Atatu 63-71; Glen Edin Dio Auckld from 71. *10a Clayburn Road, Glen Eden, NZ.* (818-6756)

SMALLHORNE, William Joseph. b 14. TCD 38. **d** 40 Bp Duppuy for Worc **p** 41 Worc. C of Reddal Hill 40-42; St Luke Nor 42-44; served in HM Forces 44-47; Booterstown 47-48; I of St Kevin City and Dio Dub from 48. *258 South Circular Road, Dolphin's Barn, Dublin, Irish Republic.*

SMALLWOOD, Canon Graham Marten. b 19. St Pet Hall Ox BA 48, MA 52. Cudd Coll. **d** 50 **p** 51 Linc. C of Spalding 50-54; V of Wyken 54-60; St Nich Warw 60-69; Cannock 69-77; R 77-78; RD of Rugeley 72-78; Surr from 72; P-in-c of Gailey w Hatherton 76-78; Can Res and Custos of Lich Cathl from 78. *20 The Close, Lichfield, WS13 7LD.* (Lichfield 28777)

SMART, Alfred Ernest. b 14. Univ of Leeds BA 35, MA 42. Coll of Resurr Mirfield 35. **d** 37 **p** 38 S'wark. C of St Jo Evang E Dulwich 37-40; Oxted w Hurst Green 40-43; C-in-c 43-44; V of St Mark Mitcham 44-55; PC (V from 68) of St Mark Talbot Village 55-80. *8 Oakdene Close, Wimborne, Dorset.*

SMART, Clifford Edward James. b 28. Kelham Th Coll 48. **d** 53 **p** 54 Blackb. C of St Pet Blackb 53-56; Miss at Seoul 56-57; P-in-c of Suwon 57-62; Seoul 62-65; C of St Aid Small Heath 65-66; Warden Catechists' Sch Ch'ongju 66-68; VG Dio Taejon 68-70; Chap St Mich Sem Seoul 68-72; H Cross Conv Seoul from 72. *CPO Box 5865, Seoul 100, Korea.* (75-7480)

SMART, Canon Edward Rogers. b 01. Univ of Leeds BA 24. Coll of Resurr 24. **d** 26 **p** 27 Bris. C of Horfield 26-31; V of St Dunstan Bedminster Down 31-35; St Anne Brislington 35-49; Actg RD of Bedminster 43-44; V of St Martin Knowle 49-68; Commiss Bunb from 58; Surr 58-68; Hon Can of Bris 60-68; Hon Can of Bunb from 60; RD of Bedminster 62-68; R of Belstone w Sticklepath Chap 68-74; Perm to Offic Dio Ex from 74. *Sunnymede, Ford Cross, South Zeal, Okehampton, Devon.*

SMART, Canon Eric Roy. b 29. Kelham Th Coll. **d** 55 **p** 56 Ches. C of Ellesmere Port 55-58; Farnham-Royal 58-66; C-in-c of St Geo Conv Distr Britwell Farnham-Royal 67; C-in-c of St Thos Ap Derby 67-73; V 74-75; Dudley Dio Worc from 75; Surr from 76; Hon Can of Worc Cathl from 81. *Vicarage, King Street, Dudley, W Midl, DY2 8QB.* (Dudley 52015)

SMART, Harry Robert. ALCD 36. **d** 36 **p** 37 Lich. C of St Jude Wolverhampton 36-39; BCMS Miss at Algiers 39; Casablanca 39-42; Chap of St Andr Tangier 42-46; R of Danby Wiske W Yafforth 47-54; C-in-C of Hutton Bonville 47-54; V of Hammerwood W Holtye 54-81. *4a St Wilfrid's Green, Hailsham, E Sussex, BN27 1DR.* (0323-846332)

SMART, Haydn Christopher. b 38. Wells Th Coll 66. **d** 69 Bp J D McKie for Cov **p** 70 Cov. C of Hillmorton 69-72; Duston (in c of St Francis) 72-75; V of Woodford Halse Dio Pet 75-78; R (w Eydon) from 78. *Woodford Halse Vicarage, Daventry, Northants, NN11 6RE.* (Byfield 60551)

SMART, Isaac Probyn Daniel. Fourah Bay Coll. **d** 55 Bp P J Jones for Sier L **p** 57 Sier L. P Dio Sier L. *PO Box 21, Bo, Sierra Leone.* (Bo 451)

SMART, John Francis. b 36. Keble Coll Ox 3rd cl Cl Mods 57, BA (3rd cl Lit Hum) 59, MA 69. Cudd Coll 59. **d** 61 Lich **p** 66 Stafford for Lich. C of Cannock 61-63; Hon C of Gt Wyrley 63-66; C (in c of Ashmore Park) of Wednesfield 66-70; V of Brereton Dio Lich from 70. *Brereton Vicarage, Rugeley, Staffs.* (Rugeley 2466)

SMART, Joseph Oliver. b 04. Wycl Hall Ox 44. **d** 44 **p** 45 Glouc. C of St Paul Cheltm 44-46; H Trin Folkestone 46-50; V of S Bersted (w N Bersted from 51) 50-57; Cuckfield 57-64; V of St Francis Nai 64-69; C-in-c and Seq Shermanbury 69-73; V of Wymeswold 73-76. *2 Trinity Mansions, 14 Atlantic Road, Weston-super-Mare, BS23 2DQ.* (0934 418904)

SMART, Malcolm Graham. b 43. Lon Coll of Div. **d** 66 Bp Horstead for Leic **p** 67 Leic. C of Blaby 66-68; Selby 68-71; R of St Alb Cheetwood Man 71-75; Gt Greenford Dio Lon from 75. *Rectory, Oldfield Lane, Greenford, UB6 9JS.* (01-578 1543)

SMART, Ven Michael Rawson. Ch Ch Coll LTh 62. **d** 62 **p** 63 Nel. C of Motueka 62-65; All SS Nel 65-66; V of Reefton 66-69; Chap Nel Hosps 69-73; Exam Chap to Bp of Nel 71-73; V of Dannevirke 73-77; Whakatane Dio Wai from 77; Archd of Tauranga from 77. *Box 164, Whakatane, NZ.* (88123)

SMART, Peter James. Moore Th Coll Syd ACT ThL (2nd cl) 63. **d** 62 **p** 63 Armid. C of Merewether 62-65; V of Emmaville 65-68; P-in-c of St Pet S Tamworth 68-76; Prin C of E Gr Sch Tamworth from 76; VG Dio Armid from 76. *Brisbane Street, Tamworth, NSW, Australia.*

SMART, Richard Henry. b 22. Clifton Th Coll 48. **d** 52 **p** 53 Ripon. C of St Geo Leeds 52-54; Asst Chap and Prec of All SS Cathl Nairobi 54-56; C of New Addington 56-59; V of Awsworth w Cossall 59-63; Distr Sec BFBS E Anglia 63-70; Perm to Offic Dios Ely Nor and St E 63-70; L to Offic Dio Ely 71-74; Dioc Officer for Miss Dio Ely 70-74; Ecumen Adv to Bp of Ely 71-81; P-in-c of Dry Drayton 74-81; Madingley 80-81; V of St John Sandylands, Heysham Dio Blackb from 81. *St John's Vicarage, 2 St John's Avenue, Morecambe, Lancs, LA3 1EU.* (Morecambe 411299)

SMART, Richard Henry. b 23. Univ of Lon BA 51. Oak Hill Th Coll. **d** 53 **p** 54 Cov. C of Bedworth 53-56; New Malden w Combe 56-59; V of St Sav w St Paul Holloway 59-71; All SS Shooter's Hill Dio S'wark from 71. *106 Herbert Road, SE18 3PU.* (01-854 2995)

SMART, Robert Edward. b 27. St Mich Coll Llan 59. **d** 61 **p** 62 St A. C of Shotton 61-67; V of Llanarmon-yn-Ial w Treuddyn 67-79; Warden and R of Ruthin w Llanrhydd Dio St A from 79; RD of Dyffryn Clwyd from 79. *The Cloisters, Ruthin, Clwyd, LL15 1BL.* (Ruthin 2068)

SMART, Canon Sydney. Late Scho and Exhib of TCD Bernard Pri 36, BA (1st cl Ment and Mor Sc) and Wray Pri 37, Gold Med and Mod Pri 37, Toplady Pri and Bp Forster Pri 38, Downes Pri Warren Pri and Div Test (1st cl) 39, MA 43. **d** 39 Tuam for Down **p** 40 Down. C of St Mich Belf 39-42; C-in-c of St Barn Belf 42-46; R 46-60; All SS Belf Dio Connor from 60; RD of S Belf 65-73; Can of St Anne's Cathl Belfast from 76; Exam Chap to Bp of Connor 78. *25 Rugby Road, Belfast 7, N Ireland.* (Belfast 23327)

SMARTT, Frederick Adolphus Augustine. d 49 **p** 51 Antig. C of St Geo Dominica 49-51; P-in-c of St Patr and St D St Vincent 51-55; R of Riviere Doree St Lucia 55-64; St D w St Paul Grenada 64-71; L to Offic Dio Windw Is 71-72. *Mount Pleasant, Carriacou, via Grenada, W Indies.*

SMEATON, Archibald John. b 1899. Ho of Resurr Mirfield 51. **d** and **p** 51 Cov. [f Methodist Min] C of St Nich Radford Cov 51-54; St Mary Virg Loughton 54-59; R of Wivenhoe 59-60; V of St Laur Barkingside 60-66; Perm to Offic Dio Chelmsf from 66. *1 Uplands Court, Uplands Road, Clacton-on-Sea, CO15 1BB.* (0255 28340)

SMEATON, William Brian Alexander. b 37. Div Hostel Dub 69. **d** 71 **p** 72 Connor. C of St Luke Lower Falls Belfast 71-81; R of Tullyaughnish, Kilmacrennan & Killygarvon Dio Raph from 81. *Rectory, Ramelton, Letterkenny, Donegal, Irish Republic.*

SMEDLEY, Canon Frank. b 17. Kelham Th Coll 35. **d** 40 **p** 41 Worc. C of St Steph Redditch 40-42; Swinton 42-48; C-in-c of New Maltby Conv Distr 48-52; V of Bolton-upon-Dearne 52-57; Overton w Fyfield and E Kennett 57-64; PC of H Trin Trowbridge 64-68; V 68-71; Wool w E Burton and Coombe Keynes (and E Stoke from 76) Dio Sarum from 71; C-in-c of E Stoke 75-76; RD of Purbeck from 76; Can and Preb of Sarum Cathl from 80. *Wool Vicarage, Wareham, Dorset.* (Bindon Abbey 215)

SMEDLEY, Leonard Sydney. b 05. Univ of Sheff BA 26, MA 42. Linc Th Coll. **d** 45 **p** 46 Southw. C of St Mich AA Radford 45-48; St Paul Leic 48-52; Chap Kent and Sussex Hosp Tunbridge Wells 52-61; Sunderland Hosps and L to Offic Dio Dur 61-68; C of Llandrillo-yn-Rhos 68-75. *Ty'n Refail, Llanbedrog, Pwllheli, Gwyn.* (Llanbedrog 320)

SMEE, Gordon Harvey. Moore Th Coll Syd 33. ACT ThL 35. **d** 36 **p** 37 Syd. C of Mortdale w Penshurst Oatley and Peakhurst 36-39; Chap at Children's Court Syd 40-43; R of St John Woolwich NSW 43-50; St Luke Liverpool w Holsworthy 50-52; Orange 52-58. *Orange, NSW, Australia.*

SMELLIE, Donald William. b 27. Qu Univ Kingston Ont BSc 50. Univ of BC MSc 51. Austrn Nat Univ Canberra PhD 61. Vanc Sch of Th 72. **d** 73 Ott. d Dio Ott 73-74; on leave. *32 Phillip Drive, Ottawa, Ont., Canada.*

SMERDON, Stanley William. b 19. Oak Hill Coll 72. **d** 74 Basingstoke for Cant for Win **p** 75 Southn for Win (APM). C of St Paul Bournemouth 74-81; Hd Master St Paul's Sch Bournemouth 65-81; P-in-c of Luccombe Dio B & W from 81. *Parsonage, Luccombe, Minehead, Somt.* (Porlock 862834)

SMETHURST, David Alan. b 36. BD (Lon) 60. Tyndale Hall Bris 57. **d** 61 **p** 62 Man. C of St Marg Burnage 61-64; St Marg Whalley Range 64-65; R of St Mary Virg Haughton 65-74; Ulverston Dio Carl from 74. *Rectory, Ford Park, Ulverston, Cumb, LA12 7JR.* (Ulverston 54331)

SMETHURST, Gordon McIntyre. b 40. Univ of Man BA 62, BD 69. **d** 70 Pontefract for Wakef **p** 71 Wakef. C of Sandal Magna 70-72; C-in-c of St Mich Castleford 72-75; Whitwood Mere (Whitwood from 74) 74-75; Asst Master Goole Gr Sch from 75; Hon C of Howden Dio York from 77. *27 The Meadows, Howden, N Humberside.*

SMETHURST, John Brian. b 20. TD 50. Sarum Th Coll 59. **d** 60 Blackb **p** 61 Lanc for Blackb. C of Fulwood 60-64; Lanc 64-66; V of Charnock Richard Dio Blackb from 66; Asst Chap O of St John of Jer from 66. *Charnock Richard Vicarage, Chorley, Lancs, PR7 5NA.* (Coppull 791385)

SMETHURST, John Michael Benedict. St Pet Coll Ox BA (2nd cl Th) 66, MA 70. St Steph Ho Ox 66. **d** 68 Lon **p** 69 Willesden for Lon. C of St Francis Gladstone Pk Lon 68-71; H Cross w St Jude and St Pet, St Pancras 71-73; Hendon 73-76; Chap and Lect S Devon Tech Coll 76-79; V of St Thos N Keyham Devonport Dio Ex 79-80. *90 Royal Navy Avenue, Keyham, Plymouth, Devon, PL2 2AJ.* (Plymouth 51102)

SMETHURST, Leslie Beckett. b 22. CEng. N-W Ordin Course 72. **d** 75 Man **p** 76 Hulme for Man. C of Brooklands 75-78; Team V of Droylsden 78-81; V of St Martin Droylsden Dio Man from 81. *St Martin's Vicarage, Greenside Lane, Droylsden, Manchester, M35 7SJ.* (061-370 9833)

SMITH, Alan. b 38. Tyndale Hall, Bris 63. **d** 65 Bp McKie for Cov **p** 66 Cov. C of New Milverton 65-68; Cheadle (in c of All H) 68-71; V of Handforth 71-78; Asst Chap HM Pris Wormwood Scrubs 78-79; Chap HM Borstal Wellingborough from 79. *HM Borstal, Wellingborough, Northants.*

SMITH, Alan Gregory Clayton. b 57. Univ of Birm BA 78, MA 79. Wycl Hall Ox 79. **d** 81 Bradf. C of St Lawr Pudsey Dio Bradf from 81. *1 Somerset Road, Pudsey, W Yorks, LS26 7LN.*

SMITH, Alan Pearce Carlton. b 20. Trin Hall Cam BA 40, MA 45. LLB 46. Westcott Ho Cam 76. **d** 78 Ely **p** 79 Huntingdon for Ely. C of St Jo Evang Cam Dio Ely from 78. *38 Alpha Road, Cambridge, CB4 3DG.*

SMITH, Albert Austin. Univ of Melb BA (Hons) 52. Ridley Coll Melb. **d** and **p** 44 Goulb. Asst Master Canberra Grammar Sch 44-45; C of St John Young 45-47; Perm to Offic Dio Melb 47-48; C of Canberra 48; P-in-c of Thuddungra 48-51; R of Boorowa 51-55; Braidwood 55-56; Macksville 56-61; V of Niddrie 61-65; Burnley 65-72; I of Coburg 72-78; Em Oakleigh 78-80; Perm to Offic Dio Melb from 80. *21 McIlwraith Street, Bundaberg, Qld, Australia 4670.*

SMITH, Albert Joseph. ACT Th Scho 10. **d** 06 **p** 07 Gippsld. Min of Lang Lang Vic 06-07; Poowong w Loch Vic 06-09; Yarragon Vic 09-12; Foster 12-18; R of Morwell 18-28; Eureka 28-40; Mid-Clarence 40-42; I of H Trin Concord West 42-46; R of St Mary Balmain 46-53; Chap of Gladesville Ment Hosp and LPr Dio Syd 53-63. *137 Lyons Road, Drummoyne, NSW, Australia.*

SMITH, Albert Rowland. *See* Rowland-Smith, Albert.

SMITH, Alec John. b 29. K Coll Lon and Warm AKC (1st cl) 53. **d** 54 Bp Barkway for Cant **p** 55 Glouc. C of Charlton Kings 54-57; Findon 57-58; V of Viney Hill 58-65; St Jo Evang Churchdown 65-66; Bp's Cannings 66-69; CF from 69. *c/o Ministry of Defence, Bagshot Park, Bagshot, Surrey.*

SMITH, Alexander Montgomery. b 36. TCD BA (2nd cl Or

Lang Mod) 59, MA 64, BD 65. **d** 61 **p** 62 Down. C of St Columba Knock Belf 61-64; St Thos Belf 64-66; Lect St Kath Coll Liv 66-69; Sen Lect from 69; Asst Chap 66-69; Chap 69-80. *14 Lynnbank Road, Liverpool, L18 3HF.* (051-722 8254)

SMITH, Alfred Cecil. ACT ThL 37. **d** 38 **p** 39 Rockptn. M of St Andr Bush Bro Dio Rockptn 38-42; C of N Rockptn 38-40; P-in-c of Biloela 40-42; Chap AIF 42-45; R of Springsure 46-48; Darwin 48-51; Peak Hill 51-54; Kandos 54-57; Prin St Paul's Training Sch for Boys Phillip I 57-61; V of Willaura 61-67; R 67-71; Nhill 71-74; L to Offic Dio N Queensld from 74. *69 Juliet Street, Mackay, Qld, Australia.*

SMITH, Alfred James. **d** 63 Newc. Hon C of The Entrance 63-76. *8 Willow Street, Long Jetty, NSW, Australia 2262.* (043-32 2263)

SMITH, Ven Alfred John. K Coll Lon and Warm AKC 59. **d** 60 **p** 61 Ex. C of Crediton 60-63; R of Litlington w W Dean 63-70; Bp's Chap for Youth 63-70; R of Bridgetown 70-76; Busselton 76-81; P-in-c of Augusta 78-80; Can of Bunb Cathl 79-80; Archd Dio Bunb from 80, Bp's Commiss from 80. *27 College Row, Bunbury, W Australia 6230.* (097-216 906)

SMITH, Alfred William. Sir Geo Williams Univ Montr BA 66. Trin Coll Tor STh 50, LTh 55. Montr Dioc Coll. **d** 31 **p** 32 Montr. I of Boscobel w N Ely 31-37; Poltimore 37-38; C of St Luke Ecclechill 38-39; V of St Jo Evang Bradf 39-47; Madoc 47-50; Perrytown 50-53; Omemee 53-56; Ch of Redeem Montr 56-73. *18 Sinclair Street, Belleville, Ont., Canada.*

SMITH, Preb Alfred William Webster. b 10. St Chad's Coll Dur BA 32, Dipl Th 33, MA 35. **d** 33 **p** 34 S'wark. C of St Jas Riddlesdown 33-36; UMCA Miss Dio Masasi 36-39; Hd Master Centr Sch Chidya 39-44; P-in-c of Mindu 44-48; Masasi 48-51; Asst Gen Sec UMCA 51-59; LPr Dio S'wark 51-59; Hon Can of Masasi from 57; R of Lusaka 59-66; Dean 62-66; Can of N Rhod 60-62; Can (Emer) from 66; R of Pontesbury (1st and 2nd Portions) w Cruckton 66-76; RD of Pontesbury 66-76; M Gen Syn 70-76; Preb of Heref Cathl 73-81; Preb (Emer) from 81; L to Offic Dio Heref 76-80; Perm to Offic Dio S'wark from 81. *6 Frederick Gardens, Cheam, Sutton, Surrey, SM1 2HX.*

SMITH, Andrew John. b 37. Univ of Leeds, BA (2nd cl Phil) 61. Coll of Resurr Mirfield. **d** 63 **p** 64 Lon. C of W Hackney 63-65; L to Offic Dio Wakef 65-72; Warden of The Ox Ho Lon 72-78; Dir Target Tr Centre Lon from 78; L to Offic Dio Lon from 72. *18 Chisenhale Road, Bow, E3.* (01-981 4655)

SMITH, Andrew John. b 46. Univ of Lon BSc 67, PhD 71. Trin Coll Ox Dipl Th 74. Coll of Resurr Mirfield 74. **d** 76 **p** 77 Bris. C of St Mark New Swindon 76-78; Southmead 78-79. *44 Fremantle Road, Cotham, Bristol.*

SMITH, Canon Anthony Cecil Addison. Keble Coll Ox (3rd cl Engl Lang and Lit) 47, BA 48, MA 53. Linc Th Coll. **d** 49 **p** 50 Newc T. C of H Trin Berwick 49-52; V of St Chad Middlesbrough 52-58; Saltburn-by-the-Sea 58-64; R of Long Marston 64-66; V of Easingwold w Raskelfe 66-78; RD of Easingwold 70-77; Can and Preb of York Minster from 76; V of Abbey Ch of St Mary & St German Selby Dio York from 78. *The Abbey Vicarage, Selby, Yorks.* (Selby 703123)

SMITH, Anthony Cyril. b 40. K Coll Lon and Warm 65. **d** 69 **p** 70 B & W. C of Crewkerne 69-74; Team V of Hemel Hempstead 74-76; Asst Chap K Coll Taunton 76-81; Sen Chap from 81. *c/o King's College, Taunton, Somt, TA1 3DX.*

SMITH, Anthony Grahame. b 29. ALCD 54. **d** 54 **p** 55 Chelmsf. C of St Paul Stratford 54-56; All SS Woodford Wells 56-58; R of Simonds Dio Fred 58-60; C of St Andr Ilford 60-62; V of St Andr Chelmsf 62-69; R of Mistley w Manningtree 69-81; RD of Harwich 75-81; R of Fordham Dio Chelmsf from 81. *Rectory, Wood Lane, Fordham Heath, Colchester, Essex.* (Colchester 240221)

SMITH, Ven Anthony Michael Percival. b 24. G and C Coll Cam BA 48, MA 53. Westcott Ho Cam. **d** 50 **p** 51 Cov. C of H Trin Leamington 50-53; Dom Chap to Abp of Cant 53-57; V of All SS w St Marg U Norwood 57-66; Chap Norwood and Distr Hosp 57-66; V of Yeovil w Preston Plucknett and Kingston Pitney 66-72; RD of Merston 68-72; Preb of Wells Cathl 70-72; V of St Mildred Addiscombe 72-79; Archd of Maidstone from 79; Dir of Ordinands Dio Cant from 80; Hon Can of Cant from 80. *Archdeacon's House, Charing, Ashford, Kent, TN27 0LU.* (Charing 2294)

SMITH, Antony Adam Dalziel. b 42. Qu Coll Birm 65. **d** 68 **p** 69 Dur. C of Peterlee 68-71; Tilehurst (in c of St Birinus) 71-76; V of Wootton Dio Ox from 76. *Wootton Vicarage, Boars Hill, Oxford, OX1 5JL.* (Oxford 735661)

SMITH, Arthur. b 1896. St D Coll Lamp LDiv 27. **d** 27 **p** 28 Sheff. C of Heeley 27-32; V of Aldbrough w Colden Parva R 32-68. *The Mamelons, New Ellerby, Hull, Yorks.*

SMITH, Ven Arthur Cyril. b 09. VRD 55. Univ of Sheff BA (2nd cl Cl and Hist) 34, MA 50. St Jo Coll Manit 29. Westcott Ho Cam 33. **d** 34 **p** 35 Bradf. C of Keighley 34-37; Bp's Hatfield 37-41; Chap RNVR 40-76; R of S Ormsby w Ketsby Calceby and Driby 46-60; C-in-c of Harrington w Brinkhill 50-52; R 52-60; C-in-c of Somersby w Bag Enderby 50-52; R 52-60; C-in-c of Tetford and Salmonby 51-52; R 52-60; RD of Hill N 56-60; Holland W 65-69; R of Oxcombe 58-60; R of Ruckland w Farforth and Maidenwell 58-60; C-in-c of Worlaby 58-60; R of Algarkirk 60-76; Archd of Linc 60-76; Archd (Emer) from 77; Can and Preb of Linc Cathl 60-77; Can (Emer from 77) Ch Comm 68-73. *Farthings, Church End, Great Rollright, Chipping Norton, Oxon, OX7 5RX.* (Hook Norton 737769)

SMITH, Canon Arthur Eric. b 08. Late Exhib of St Edm Hall, Ox BA 2nd cl Mod Hist 29, 1st cl Th 31, MA 33. Wycl Hall, Ox 29. **d** 31 **p** 32 Roch. C of H Trin Beckenham 31-34; St Mary Battersea (in c of G and C Coll Miss) 34-36; Seaford w Sutton 36-37; V of St Pet Norbiton 37-45; Chap Kingston Co Hosp and Centr Relief Inst 38-45; R of Hayes Kent 45-65; Hon Can of Roch Cathl 59-74; Can (Emer) from 74; Proc Conv Roch 59-70; RD of Bromley 61-65; R of Knockholt 65-74; Perm to Offic Dio Chich from 75. *Lowesden, Burpham, Arundel, Sussex, BN18 9RH.* (Arundel 882303)

SMITH, Austin John Denyer. b 40. Worc Coll Ox BA (2nd cl Th) 62. Cudd Coll 64. **d** 66 Kens for Lon **p** 67 Lon. C of St Steph w St Thos Hammersmith 66-69; W Drayton 69-72; Angl Chap to Univ of Sussex 72-78; V of Caddington Dio St alb from 79. *Vicarage, Collings Wells Close, Caddington, Luton, Beds, LU1 4BG.* (Luton 31692)

SMITH, Axel Christian. **d** 64 **p** 65 Sask. Treas Dio Sask 63-69; I of Sturgeon Valley 64-68; John Smith Reserve 68-72; Macdowall 73-77; R of St Cath Prince Albert 73-77; Perm to Offic Dio Koot from 78. *RRI, Nelson, BC, Canada.*

SMITH, Barry. b 41. St D Coll Lamp BA (2nd cl Hist) 62. Fitzw Ho Cam BA (3rd cl Th) 64, MA 68. Ridley Hall, Cam 62. **d** 65 **p** 66 St A. C of Rhyl 65-70; Chap of Scargill Ho Skipton 70-72; C of Flint 72-74; V of Broughton Dio St A from 74. *Broughton Vicarage, Wrexham, Clwyd.* (Wrexham 756210)

SMITH, Brian. b 44. Sarum Wells Th Coll 71. **d** 74 **p** 75 Dur. C of St Thos Conv Distr Pennywell Bp Wearmouth 74-77; Chap RAF from 77. *c/o Staff Chaplain, Ministry of Defence, Adastral House, Theobalds Road, WC1.*

SMITH, Canon Brian Arthur. b 43. Univ of Edin MA (2nd cl Phil) 66. Late Exhib Fitzw Coll Cam 1st cl Th Trip pt iii BA 68, MA 72. Lady Kay Scho Jes Coll Cam 71, Burney Stud 72, MLitt 73. Westcott Ho Cam 66. **d** 72 Dorchester for Ox **p** 73 Ox. C of Cudd 72-79; Tutor and Libr Cudd Coll 72-75; Dir of Stud Ripon Coll Cudd 75-78; Sen Tutor 78-79; P-in-c of Cragg Vale Dio Wakef from 79; Dir of In-Service Tr Dio Wakef from 79; Hon Can of Wakef Cathl from 81; Dir Post-Ordin Tr Dio Wakef from 80; Ministerial Tr Dio Wakef from 81; Warden of Readers Dio Wakef from 82. *Vicarage, Cragg Vale, Hebden Bridge, W Yorks, HX7 5TB.* (Halifax 882571)

SMITH, Brian Godfrey. Chich Th Coll 63. **d** 65 **p** 66 Newc T. C of H Cross Fenham Newc T 65-68; Redcar 68-72; C of Kirkleatham 68-72; V of Wortley 72-76; Chap at Costa Del Sol E 76-81; Estoril Dio Gibr in Eur from 81. *St Paul, Av Voluntarios Bombeiros, Estoril, Portugal.*

SMITH, Ven Brian John. b 33. Sarum Th Coll 62. **d** 65 Cant **p** 66 Dover for Cant. C of All SS Whitstable 65-69; V of Woodford w Wilsford 69-74; P-in-c of Durnford 74; V of Woodford Valley 74-76; Mere w W Knoyle and Maiden Bradley 76-80; RD of Heytesbury 78-80; Archd of Wilts from 80; V of Bp's Cannings w All Cannings and Etchilhampton Dio Sarum from 80; Can and Preb of Sarum Cathl from 80. *Bishop's Cannings Vicarage, Devizes, Wilts.* (Cannings 650)

SMITH, Brian Michael. b 42. Kelham Th Coll 69. **d** Willesden for Lon 69 **p** 70 Lon. C of St Mary Virg St Pancras 70-74; St Jo Div Stamford Hill Dio Lon from 74; St Bart Stamford Hill Dio Lon from 74. *St John's Church, Vartry Road, N15 6PU.* (01-800 2116)

SMITH, Brian Norrell. St Mich Ho Crafers, 47. ACT ThL 60. **d** 59 **p** 60 Adel. C of Ch Ch N Adel 59-61; Miss Chap of Campbelltown 61-64; R of Woodville 64-74; P-in-c of Woodville Gdns 69-74; R of Toorak Gdns 74-79; Chap Hillcrest Hosp Dio Adel from 79. *10 Beaven Street, Broadview, S Australia 5083.* (266 0707)

SMITH, Bruce Leslie. Moore Th Coll Syd ACT ThL 54, Th Scho 59. BD Lon 59. **d** and **p** 56 Syd. Lect Moore Th Coll Syd from 55; C of Chatswood 56-58; Willoughby 58-59; Beecroft 60-62; St Andr L Cam 63-64; L to Offic Dio Ely 64-66; C of St Jas S Cant 66-68; St Barn Broadway 69; Darlinghurst 70-72; Northbridge 73; St Pet Syd 74-75; Asst Master Syd Gr Sch and L to Offic Dio Syd from 75. *37 Queen Street, Newtown, NSW, Australia 2042.* (51-8380)

SMITH, Canon Cecil Knowles. b 01. Univ of Leeds, BA (2nd cl Cl) 23, MA 28. Univ of Lon BD 32, 2nd cl Th (Ch Hist) 34. Coll of Resurr Mirfield, 19. **d** 25 **p** 26 Mon. C of St Mary Mon 25-30; St Paul Daybrook 30-31; R of Llanfair

Kilgeddin (w Llanfihangel Gobion from 35) 31-37; V of Llanfrechfa Upper (or H Trin Pontnewydd) 37-43; Rumney (w St Hilary 59-69) 43-71; Surr from 47; RD of Bassaleg 55-67; Can of Mon from 56. *12 Yew Tree Court, St Nicholas Close, Barry, CF6 8RS.* (Barry 737724)

SMITH, Canon Cecil William. b 09. St Steph Ho Ox 45. **d** 47 **p** 48 Ox. C of All SS Marlow 47-49; St Steph Cheltm 49-52; C-in-c of Conv Distr of St Geo L Tuffley Glouc 52-59; V of Up Hatherley 59-79; Hon Can of Glouc Cathl from 77. *23 Arden Road, Leckhampton, Cheltenham, Glos.*

SMITH, Charles. b 1890. Univ of Dur LTh 26. St Aid Coll 23. **d** 26 **p** 27 Liv. C of Ch Ch Liv 26-28; Org Sec CMJ for NW Distr 28-30; L to Offic Dio Liv 29-30; V of St Clem Toxt Pk 30-66; Offg Chap Sefton Gen Hosp Liv 30-66. *16 Fell View, Cockermouth, Cumb.*

SMITH, Canon Charles. b 11. Late Exhib of St Jo Coll Dur BA (1st cl Th) and Fell 39, MA 42. **d** 39 **p** 40 Dur. Chap, Tutor and Bursar St Jo Coll Dur 39-45; C of St Mary le Bow Dur 39-45; V of Grindon 46-48; PC of Heatherycleugh Dio Dur from 48; V of Westgate-in-Weardale Dio Dur from 57; V of St John's Chap-in-Weardale Dio Dur from 57; Angl Adv Tyne Tees Television from 62; RD of Stanhope 72-77; Hon Can of Dur Cathl from 79. *Heatherycleugh Vicarage, Cowshill, Co Durham, DL13 1DA.* (Wearhead 260)

SMITH, Canon Charles David. b 15. St Cath S Ox BA (2nd cl Th) 36, MA 43. St Steph Ho Ox 36. **d** 38 **p** 39 Taunton for B & W. C of H Trin Bath 38-41; St Mark Swindon (in C of St Sav) 41-49; V of St Pet Streatham 49-68; Exam Chap to Bp of S'wark 61-68; Hon Can of S'wark 62-68; Can (Emer) from 68; RD of Streatham and Mitcham 64-68; Proc Conv S'wark 65-70; L to Offic Dio Nor from 68; RD of Burnham & Walsingham 71-72; M Gen Syn Nor 70-72; C-in-c of Barsham 68-72; V of St Mary Magd City and Dio Ox from 72; M Gen Syn Ox 75-80; RD of Ox from 76. *15 Beaumont Street, Oxford, OX1 2NA.* (Ox 47836)

SMITH, Charles Edward. Moore Th Coll Syd. **d** 02 **p** 03 Bal. C of Carisbrook Vic 02-03; V 03-08; I of Alvie 08-16; V of Clunes 16-24; Koroit 24-31; Terang 31-42; I of St Mark W Preston 42-44; Doncaster 44-46; P-in-c of Lorne 49-54. *The Nook, Bay Street, Lorne, Vic, Australia.*

SMITH, Charles Frederick. St Aid Coll 54. **d** 56 **p** 58 Carl. C of Stanwix 56-58; Hoddesdon 58-60; R of Everleigh 60-74; R of Manningford Bruce w Manningford Abbas 67-74; V of Burneside 74-79; Perm to Offic Dio Chich from 80. *7 Manor Road, Seaford, BN25 4NL.* (Seaford 890433)

SMITH, Canon Charles Henry Neville. b 31. Univ of Nottm BA (2nd cl French) 52, MA 65. Sarum Th Coll 55. **d** 57 **p** 58 York. C of Thirsk w S Kilvington 57-60; St Barn (in c of St Jas) Linthorpe Middlesbrough 60-61; V of Danby w Castleton and Fryup 61-66; Chap United Cam Hosps 66-76; Lanc Moor Hosp from 76; Hon Can Blackb from 81. *Lancaster Moor Hospital, Lancaster, LA1 3JR.* (0524-65241)

SMITH, Canon Charles Percy. b 22. Westcott Ho Cam 44. **d** 46 Lon **p** 47 Vic. Chap St Paul's Coll Hong Kong 46-47; V of Ch Ch Kowloon Tong Hong Kong 47-53; R of Hawkchurch 54-59; Warden of Pilsdon Ho Dio Sarum from 59; Can and Preb of Sarum Cathl from 71. *Pilsdon House, Bridport, Dorset.* (Broadwindsor 308)

SMITH, Charles Reginald. b 1896. M CR 33. **d** 23 **p** 24 Wakef. C of Dewsbury 23-26; M of Bush Bro Bunb 26-30; Miss P St Aug Penhalonga Dio S Rhod 34-62; Dio Mashon 52-62. *Community of the Resurrection, Mirfield, W Yorks, WF14 0BN.*

SMITH, Charles Rycroft. b 46. Sarum Wells Th Coll 76. **d** 78 **p** 79 Heref. C of St Martin Heref 78-81; Maybush Dio Win from 81. *St Peters House, Lockerley Crescent, Maybush, Southampton, SO1 4BP.* (Southn 775014)

SMITH, Charles Septimus. b 24. Bris & Glouc Dioc Sch of Min 75. **d** 79 **p** 80 Bris (APM). Hon C of St Agnes City and Dio Bris from 79. *485 Stapleton Road, Bristol, BS5 6PQ.* (0272 512235)

SMITH, Charles Whadcoat. b 1886. Qu Coll Cam BA 08, MA 12. Can Scho Linc 09. Hon CF 19. **d** 09 **p** 10 Wakef. C of Almondbury 09-13; M of Abp's Miss to W Canada in S Alta 13-17; TCF 17-19; C of Attleborough 19-20; N Walsham 20-21; Coddington 21-22; V of Metheringham 22-41; R of Gt Ponton 41-43; Halton Holgate 43-71. *Eresby Hall, Spilsby, Lincs.*

SMITH, Christopher Francis. b 46. BD and AKC 68. St Aug Coll Cant 69. **d** 70 **p** 71 Cant. C of All SS U Norwood 70-72; Asst Chap Marlborough Coll 72-76; C of St Leon Deal (in c of St Richard) 77-81; P-in-c of Benenden Dio Cant from 81. *Benenden Vicarage, Cranbrook, Kent.* (Benenden 658)

SMITH, Christopher John. b 55. Univ of Bris BSc (Soc Sc) 76. St Steph Ho Ox 78. **d** 81 Birm. C of St Jas Shirley Dio Birm from 81. *392 Priory Road, Shirley, Solihull, W Midl.*

SMITH, Christopher Milne. b 44. Selw Coll Cam 3rd cl Th Trip pt i, 64, BA (3rd cl Th Trip pt 11) 66. Cudd Coll 67. **d** 69 Warrington for Liv **p** 70 Liv. C of Our Lady and St Nich Liv 69-73; Team V of Kirkby 74-81; R of St Mary Walton-on-the-Hill Dio Liv from 81. *Walton Rectory, Liverpool, L4 6TJ.* (051-525 3130)

SMITH, Clifford. b 31. Dipl Th (Lon) 60. St Aid Coll 59. **d** 61 Kens for Lon **p** 62 Lon. C of St Anne Limehouse 61-63; Ashtead 63-66; R of All H Bromley 66-76; V of Hillsborough and Wadsley Bridge Dio Sheff from 76. *218 Fox Hill Road, Sheffield, S6 1HJ.* (Sheffield 311576)

SMITH, Canon Clifford Hoole. b 11. St Pet Hall Ox BA 34, MA 42. Wycl Hall Ox 34. **d** 35 **p** 36 Lon. C of St Mary Islington 35-38; Chap to Bp of Ugan and CMS Miss Ugan 38-40; CF (EC) 40-46; Hon CF 46; Men in Disp 46; V of Ch Ch Tunbridge Wells 46-50; St Jas w St Jo Bapt and St Lawr Bris 50-53; Chap Bris Eye Hosp 50-53; V of St Werburgh Derby 53-61; RD of Derby 57-61; V of Wimbledon 61-73; Broadway 73-77; Hon Can of S'wark Cathl 71-74; Can (Emer) from 74. *3 Glendale Avenue, Eastbourne, E Sussex, BN21 1UT.* (Eastbourne 28878)

SMITH, Clive Leslie. b 50. Univ of Leeds BA 72. Coll of Resurr Mirfield 75. **d** 77 **p** 78 St Alb. C of Goldington 77-81; Cheshunt (in c of St Clem Turnford) Dio St Alb from 81. *St Clement's House, Hill View Gardens, Cheshunt, Herts, EN8 0PE.* (Waltham Cross 25098)

SMITH, Colin Ian McNaughton. b 28. St Jo Coll Dur BA 53. **d** 55 **p** 56 Dur. C of Consett 55-59; L to Offic Dio Dur 59-60; Chap Miss to Seamen S Shields 59-60; Port Sudan 60-63; C of Wilton-in-Cleveland 63-67; V of Weaverthorpe w Helperthorpe Luttons Ambo (and Kirby Grindalhythe from 76) Dio York from 67; C-in-c of Kirby Grindalhythe 74-76; RD of Buckrose 75-76. *Helperthorpe Vicarage, Malton, N Yorks, YO17 8TJ.* (West Lutton 213)

SMITH, Colin Sambrook. b 09. Wycl Hall Ox 54. **d** 56 **p** 57 Chelmsf. C of Chingford 56-59; V of St Andr Leytonstone 59-67; Chap Whipps Cross Hosp 59-65; R of Gt Hallingbury 67-77; Warden Yetts Ho Eastbourne and Perm to Offic Dio Chich from 77. *29 The Goffs, Eastbourne, E Sussex.*

SMITH, Cyril Laurence. b 1893. Ch Ch Ox BA 15, MA 19. Cudd Coll 15 and 19. **d** 19 Lon for S'wark **p** 21 S'wark. C of St Jo Evang E Dulwich 19-22; St Alb Holborn 22-23; St Aug Vic Pk 24-26; Beckenham 26-35; V of St Mich AA Beckenham 35-62; Chap to the Benedictine Commun St Mary's Abbey W Malling 62-66; Perm to Offic Dio Guildf from 66. *36 The Riding, Woodham, Woking, Surrey, GU21 5TA.* (Woking 72588)

SMITH, Daryll Michael. b 41. St Jo Coll Morpeth Dipl Th 71. **d** and **p** Bath. C of Wellington 72-73; Cowra 74-76; Blayney 76-78; R of Cumnock 78-80; Mortdale Dio Syd from 80. *112 Morts Road, Mortdale, NSW, Australia 2223.* (57-6852)

SMITH, David Alan. b 48. Alfred Univ NY BA 69. Episc Th Sch Harvard MDiv 72. **d** 72 Albany (USA) **p** 73 B & W. C of St Jo Bapt Keynsham 72-75; Gt Marlow 75-80; V of Wing w Grove Dio Ox from 80. *25 Aylesbury Road, Wing, Bucks.* (Wing 496)

SMITH, Ven David Arthur Pritchard. Trin Coll Tor BA 55, LTh 58. **d** and **p** 58 Alg. C of Sault Ste Marie 58-60; I of Cobalt 60-63; Chap Trin Coll Tor 64-68; I of W Thunder Bay 68-72; R of St Brice North Bay Dio Alg from 72; Archd of Muskoka 75-76; Temiskaming from 76. *1225 Cassells Street, North Bay, Ont., Canada.* (705-474 2589)

SMITH, David Charles Stuart. Oak Hill Th Coll 61. **d** 61 Bp Kerle for Syd **p** 62 Syd. Org Sec Crusader U of NSW 61; L to Offic Dio Syd 61-64; Asst Chap and Ho Master Caulfield Gr Sch Melb 65-66; Asst Master King's Sch Parramatta 66-67; Shore Sch N Syd 68-76; L to Offic Dio Syd 70-76; Chap Caulfield Gr Sch Melb 76-79; I of St Paul Glen Waverley Dio Melb from 79. *25 Kirstina Road, Glen Waverley, Vic., Australia 3150.* (560 7494)

SMITH, David Earling. b 35. K Coll Lon and Warm AKC 60. **d** 61 **p** 62 St Alb. C of Knebworth 61-63; Chipping Barnet 64-66; S Ormsby 66-69; R of Claxby w Normanby-le-Wold 69-74; Nettleton 69-74; S Kelsey 69-74; N Owersby w Thornton-le-Moor 69-74; Stainton-le-Vale w Kirmond-le-Mire 69-74; V of Ancaster 74-79; Warden of St Anne Bedehouses and C of Minster City and Dio Linc from 79. *St Anne's Lodge, 29 Sewell Road, Lincoln, LN2 5RY.* (Linc 28354)

SMITH, David Gordon. b 15. Wycl Hall, Ox 63. **d** 65 Cant **p** 66 Dover for Cant. C of St Pet Croydon 65-70; Team V of the Isle of Dogs 70-72; P-in-c of St Pet w St Thos Bethnal Green 72-78; V 78-81; P-in-c of St Jo Bapt Hove Dio Chich from 81. *209 Elm Drive, Hove, E Sussex, BN3 7JD.* (Brighton 731950)

SMITH, David Graham. b 08. MBE 46. Wadh Coll Ox 4th cl Cl Mods 29, BA (4th cl Lit Hum) 31, MA 34. Cudd Coll 31. **d** 32 **p** 33 S'wark. C of Wimbledon 32-37; St Geo Camberwell 37-39; C-in-c of St Alb Cheam 39; CF (R of O) 39-45; Actg Miss in c of St Jas Conv Distr Merton 45-47; Min 47-48; V of

H Trin S Wimbledon 48-59; R of Woldingham 59-76. *10 Kersey Crescent, Newbury, Berks.*

SMITH, Ven David James. b 35. K Coll Lon and Warm AKC 58. **d** 59 **p** 60 Newc T. C of All SS Gosforth 59-62; C of St Francis High Heaton Newc T 62-64; C-in-c of St Mary Magd Long Benton 64-68; V of Longhirst w Hebburn 68-75; M Gen Syn 73-80; V of Monkseaton 75-82; Felton Dio Newc T from 82; RD of Tynemouth 80-81; Archd of Lindisfarne from 81. *Felton Vicarage, Morpeth, Northumb, NE65 9HP.* (Felton 263)

SMITH, David John. b 42. Oak Hill Coll 75. **d** 77 Bp McKie for Cov **p** 78 Cov. C of New Milverton 77-81; V of Hartshill Dio Cov from 81. *Hartshill Vicarage, Nuneaton, Warws, CV10 0LY.* (Chapel End 392266)

SMITH, David John. b 32. Univ of Lon BA (Psychol) 76, MSc (Soc Psychol) 79. Lon Coll of Div 68. **d** 70 **p** 71 Lon. C of St Jas Clerkenwell 70-73; P-in-c of St Paul Penge Dio Roch 74-78; V from 78. *Vicarage, Hamlet Road, Upper Norwood, SE19.* (01-653 0978)

SMITH, Preb David Lloyd. b 17. TD 63. AKC 39. **d** 39 **p** 40 Lich. C of U Gornal 39-43; Stoke-on-Trent 43-49; V of St Andr Wolverhampton 49-58; Cross Heath 58-66; R of Brierley Hill 66-77; Surr 66-77; RD of Himley 68-77; Preb of Lich Cathl 71-77; Preb (Emer) from 77; P-in-c of Chaddesley Corbett Dio Worc from 77; Stone Dio Worc from 77. *Chaddesley Corbett Vicarage, Kidderminster, Worcs.* (Chaddesley Corbett 425)

SMITH, David Roland Mark. b 46. Univ of Dur BA 68. ACP 78. Edin Th Coll 68. **d** 70 Jarrow for Dur **p** 71 Dur. C of St Columba Southwick 70-74; Asst Chap Univ Coll Cardiff 74-76; Hon C of E Bris 76-78; St Pet Filton 78-79; Youth Filton High Sch 76-79; P-in-c of St Andr Conv Distr Leam Lane Heworth 79-81; Hon C of St Columba Southwick Dio Dur from 81; Co-ordinator Sunderland Poly Chap Service from 81. *St Columba's Cottages, Southwick, Sunderland, T & W, SR5 1RU.*

SMITH, David Sidney. b 54. Univ of Bris BEducn 76. Cudd Coll 77. **d** 79 Glouc **p** 80 Tewkesbury for Glouc. C of Wotton-u-Edge Glouc from 79. *3a Long Street, Wotton-under-Edge, Glos.* (W-u-E 3415)

SMITH, David Watson. b 31. Sarum Th Coll 63. **d** 65 **p** 66 S'wark. C of Ch Ch Wimbledon 65-69; Cheam (in c of St Osw) 69-74; V of Haslington Dio Ches from 74. *163 Crewe Road, Haslington, Crewe, Chesh, CW1 1RL.* (Crewe 582388)

SMITH, David William. b 46. Sarum Th Coll 70. **d** 72 **p** 73 York. C of Stokesley 72-75; St Mich & All SS Edin 75-77; R of Galashiels Dio Edin from 77. *Rectory, Galashiels, Selkirks.* (Galashiels 3118)

SMITH, Denis Gilbert. b 15. AKC 37. Relton Pri 37. **d** 38 **p** 39 Sheff. C of Warmsworth 38-42; Bucksburn (in c of All SS Dep Miss Hilton) 42-46; Warden of Ho of Bethany Aber 45-64; Youth Organizer of SE Church 46-49; R of St Salvador Dundee 49-59; V of Owston 59-69; C-in-c of Moss 59-69; V of St Jas (w St Hilda 69-79) Darlington Dio Dur from 69. *St James Vicarage, Vicarage Road, Darlington, Co Durham, DL1 1JW.* (Darlington 65980)

SMITH, Ven Denison Guy. St Paul's Coll Grahmstn. **d** 55 **p** 56 Johann. C of Boksburg 55-58; P-in-c of N Rand Johann 58-63; Chap Edenvale Hosp 60-66; R of Edenvale and Kempton Pk 63-66; Vereeniging 66-73; St Aug Kimberley Dio Kimb K from 73; Archd of Kimberley from 76. *46 Green Street, Kimberley, CP, S Africa.* (Kimb 24733)

SMITH, Dennis Austin. b 50. Univ of Lanc BA 71. N-W Ordin Course 74. **d** 77 **p** 78 Liv (APM). C of St Faith Gt Crosby Dio Liv from 77. *16 Fir Road, Waterloo, Liverpool, L22 4QL.*

SMITH, Derek Arthur. Chich Th Coll 63. **d** 66 **p** 67 Lich. C of Cheadle 66-70; Blakenall Heath 70-72; V of Knutton 72-76; C-in-c of Blakenall Heath Dio Lich 76-77; R from 77. *Blakenall Heath Rectory, Walsall, Staffs.* (Bloxwich 76276)

SMITH, Derek Arthur Byott. b 26. Sarum Wells Th Coll 78. **d** 81 Sarum (NSM). Hon C of Wimborne Minster and Holt St Jas Dio Sarum from 81. *4 Badbury View, Wimborne, Dorset, BH21 1DH.*

SMITH, Derek Arthur Douglas. b 26. Univ of Dur BA (2nd cl Hist) 51. Qu Coll Birm 58. **d** 60 **p** 61 Worc. C of Evesham 60-63; St Jo Bapt Bollington 63-68; V of Thelwall 68-78; Whitegate w L Budworth Dio Ches from 78. *Whitegate Vicarage, Northwich, Chesh.* (Sandiway 882151)

SMITH, Derek George. b 39. Univ of BC BA 64. Harvard Univ MA 65. **d** 69 **p** 74 Ott. P Dio Ott from 69. *75 Laurentian Place, Ottawa, Ontario, Canada.*

SMITH, Derek Graham. b 52. St Cath Coll Cam BA 74, MA 77. Westcott Ho Cam 74. **d** 76 **p** 77 Sarum. C of H Trin Weymouth 76-79; P-in-c of Bradpole 79; Team V of Bridport Dio Sarum from 79. *Bradpole Vicarage, Bridport, Dorset, DT6 3JA.* (Bridport 56635)

SMITH, Desmond. b 37. St Jo Sem Lusaka 70. **d** 70 Bp Mataka for Zam. M SSF. d Dio Centr Zam 70-73; Dio N Zam from 73. *PO Box 1993, Kitwe, Zambia.* (022-66431)

SMITH, Donald. b 44. Univ of Man BSc 70. **d** and **p** 79 Dun. Hon C of St Matt City and Dio Dun from 79. *44 Spencer Street, Dunedin, NZ.* (45-819)

SMITH, Ven Donald John. b 26. Clifton Th Coll 50. **d** 53 **p** 54 Lon. C of Edgware 53-56; St Marg Ipswich 56-58; V of St Mary Hornsey Rise 58-62; R of Witton w Thurleston and Akenham 62-75; Hon Can of St E Cathl 73-75; Archd of Suff from 75; R of Redgrave w Botesdale and Rickinghall 75-79. *Starlings, Yoxford Saxmundham, Suffolk.* (Yoxford 387)

SMITH, Canon Donald Westwood. Edin Th Coll 54. **d** 54 **p** 55 Aber. Asst Super Dio Aber 54-55; Chap of Aber Cathl 55-56; C of Brantford Ont 56-57; R of St Jo Evang Longside 57-65; St Barn Rodrigues 65-80; Can of Maur from 75. *Holy Trinity Rectory, Moka Road, Rose Hill, Mauritius.*

SMITH, Douglas David Frederick. b 28. Univ of Lon BD 53. ALCD 53. **d** 53 Lon **p** 54 Kens for Lon. C of Ch Ch Fulham 53-57; St Jo Evang Heatherlands Parkstone 57-61; V of Hyson Green Nottm 61-66; Area Sec CPAS NE Distr 66-69; L to Offic Dio York 66-69; R of St Clem Higher Openshaw 69-80; Ch Brampton w Chap Brampton (and Harlestone from 81) Dio Pet from 80. *Brampton Rectory, Northampton.* (Northampton 842235)

SMITH, Douglas James. b 29. Univ of Lon BSc (2nd cl Soc) 63. Chich Th Coll 54. **d** 57 **p** 58 Lich. C of St Mary Virg Shrewsbury 57-60; St Anne Brookfield 60-63; Asst Master Pk Sch Dagenham 63-70; Warden Sir John Cass Found and Red Coat Sch Stepney 70-74; Sen Master from 74. *Address temp unknown.*

SMITH, Edmund Hastings. b 1886. Qu Coll Cam BA 09, MA 13. **d** 10 **p** 12 Man. C of Em Bolton 10-13; St Martin Norris Bank Stockport 13-15; H Trin Habergham Eaves 16-17; Warmfield w Sharlston 17-22; Honley w Brockholes 22-25; V of St Jo Div Thorpe Yorks 25-32; Harleywood 32-48; R of Kirk Smeaton 48-55; R of L Massingham 57-62. *Ramsay Hall, Byron Road, Worthing, Sussex.*

SMITH, Edward Charles. Ridley Coll Melb ACT ThL 64. **d** and **p** 64 Melb. C of St Geo Bentleigh 64-65; Berwick 65-67; V of Ferntree Gully Dio Melb 67-74; Dromana Dio Melb from 74. *Box 99, Dromana, Vic, Australia 3936.* (059-87 2856)

SMITH, Edward Leonard Richard. b 27. SOC 74. **d** 77 Lon **p** 78 Willesden for Lon (APM). C of St Cuthb N Wembley Dio Lon from 77. *5 Holt Road, North Wembley, Middx, HA0 3PT.* (01-904 9042)

SMITH, Elmer James. b 15. Temple Univ Phil BSc 40, STB 41. Reformed Episc Sem Phil BD 41. Nashotah Ho Sem Wisc STM 46. **d** 43 Penn **p** 45 Bp Roberts of China for Penn. In Amer Ch 43-60; R of Prince William Dio Fred from 69. *Route No 2, Prince William, NB, Canada.*

SMITH, Elvyn Garston. b 09. St Pet Hall, Ox BA (2nd cl Mod Hist) 36, MA 40. Wycl Hall, Ox 36. **d** 37 **p** 38 Lon. C of St John Ealing Dean 37-40; Org Sec CPAS for SW Distr and L to Offic Dio Bris 40-45; R of H Trin Chesterfield 45-55; Chap Scarsdale Hosp 45-55; V of Patcham 55-75; RD of Preston 73-75. *45 Sheridan Road, Broadwater, Worthing, W Sussex, BN14 8EU.* (Worthing 208611)

SMITH, Eric Alfred Norman. b 25. St D Coll Lamp BA 51, LTh 53. **d** 53 Bp Hollis for Cant **p** 54 Leic. C of Em Loughborough 53-56 St Mark Leic 56; Asst Master Hanson Boys' Gr Sch Bradf 56-59; Thornton Boys' Gr Sch Bradf 60-61; Asst Lect Bradford Tech Coll 62-63; Hon C of St Jude Manningham 62-63; V 63-65; Asst Master Tyldesley Secondary Sch Blackpool 65-69; J H Whitley Sch Halifax 70-81; C of Stocksbridge (in c of Deepcar) Dio Sheff from 81. *41 Carr Road, Deepcar, Sheffield, S Yorks.* (Sheff 883187)

SMITH, Eric Frederick. b 19. ALCD 38. Univ of Lon BA 40, BD 42. **d** 42 **p** 43 Sarum. C of St Mark Talbot Village 42-44; St Jude S'wark 44-48; Missr of St Edw Conv Distr Mottingham 48-52; Min 52-56; V of Good Shepherd (w St Pet from 60) Lee 56-67; Chap Sir Robert Gefferey's Almshos Mottingham 56-67; R of Long Ditton 67-81; V of St Geo Mart Deal Dio Cant from 81. *Vicarage, St George's Road, Deal, Kent.* (Deal 2587)

SMITH, Eric Harold. St Francis Coll Brisb ACT ThL 43. **d** 41 **p** 44 Brisb. C of St Alb Auchenflower 41-43; St Andr S Brisb 44-46; V of Caboolture 47-52; R of Noosa 52-57; V of St Pet W End Brisb 57-60; R 60-79; Perm to Offic Dio Brisb from 79. *31 Mapleleaf Street, Eight Miles Plains, Queensland, Australia 4123.* (341 4643)

SMITH, Ernest Ambrose. b 02. Edin Th Coll. **d** 62 Blackb **p** 63 Burnley for Blackb. C of Brierfield 62-65; L Marsden 65-66; C-in-c of St Alb w St Paul Eccles Distr Burnley 66-69; V 69-76; Perm to Offic Dio Bradf from 76. *Reader's House, Waddington, Clitheroe, Lancs.* (Clitheroe 22348)

SMITH, Ernest Harry Quibell. b 13. Linc Th Coll 40. **d** 42 **p** 43 Lich. C of Tettenhall Wood 42-44; St Barn Melksham 44-48; St Edm Dudley 48-51; V of Amblecote 51-57. *24 Goldthorn Avenue, Wolverhampton, W Midl, WV4 5AB.*

SMITH, Ernest John. b 24. ARICS 49. Oak Hill Th Coll 59. **d** 61 **p** 62 Chelmsf. C of Leyton 61-64; Bp Hannington Mem Ch w H Cross Hove 64-72; V of H Trin Hampstead Dio Lon from 72. *4 Netherhall Gardens, NW3 5RR.* (01-794 2975)

SMITH, Errol Gordon Stewart. St Jo Coll Auckld LTh 65. **d** 58 **p** 59 Waik. C of New Plymouth 58-60; V of Kawhia 60-61; Katikati 61-64; Chap Publ Hosp Hamilton 64-72; Perm to Offic Dio Waik 73-80; Hon C of Frankton Dio Waik from 80. *60 Northolt Street, Hamilton, NZ.* (52-439)

SMITH, Esmond Ernest Carrington. b 22. Mert Coll Ox BA 43, MA 47. Westcott Ho Cam 46. **d** 46 **p** 47 Birm. C of Aston 46-51; V of St Jas E Crompton 51-57; PC of Ripley, Derby 57-65; V of Aston-juxta-Birm 65-75; RD of Aston 71-75; Asst Master Staniforth Sch Thetford 75-78; Perm to Offic Dio St E from 79. *The Saltings, Broad Street, Orford, Woodbridge, Suffolk.* (Orford 234)

SMITH, Eustace. b 20. St Pet Hall, Ox BA 43, MA 46. Wycl Hall, Ox 43. **d** and **p** 46 Ex. C of St Pet Tiverton 46-47; Lenton 47-49; Aston-juxta-Birm 49-53; V of St Anne Bermondsey 53-59; Buckminster w Sewstern (and Sproxton and Coston from 74) Dio Leic from 59. *Buckminster Vicarage, Grantham, Lincs.* (Buckminster 284)

SMITH, Francis Armand. Sarum Th Coll 59. **d** 61 **p** 62 Sarum. C of Marlborough 61-63; V of Upavon w Rushall 63-76; Perm to Offic Dio S'wark from 76; Dio Roch from 77; Dio Chich from 78. *15 High Street, Cowden, Edenbridge, Kent.* (Cowden 484)

SMITH, Francis Christian Lynford. b 36. Cudd Coll 72. **d** 74 **p** 75 S'wark. C of St Laur Catford 74-79; P-in-c of St Paul Vacoas Dio Maur from 79. *St Paul's Vicarage, La Caverne, Vacoas, Mauritius, Indian Ocean.*

SMITH, Francis James Prall. b 22. Nor Ordin Course 73. **d** 76 Lynn for Nor **p** 77 Thetford for Nor (APM). Hon C of Gunthorpe w Bale Dio Nor from 76. *Uplands, Bale, Fakenham, Norfolk, NR21 0QS.*

SMITH, Frank. b 39. Open Univ BA 76. Cudd Coll 69. **d** 69 Hulme for Man **p** 70 Middleton for York. C of St Mary Davyhulme 69-72; V of Peak Forest and Wormhill w Peakdale 72-78; R of W Hallam w Mapperley Dio Derby from 78. *Rectory, West Hallam, Derby, DE7 6GR.* (Ilkeston 0602-324695)

SMITH, Fred Hilton. b 13. St Jo Coll Dur LTh 45, BA 46, MA 52. Oak Hill Th Coll 35. **d** 39 **p** 40 Lon. C of Kentish Town 39-41; Perm to Offic at St Bart Wednesbury 41-42; C of Heston Middx 42-45; L to Offic Dio Dur 45-48; C-in-c of St Herbert's Conv Distr Darlington 48-53; C of Gt Yarmouth (in c of St Paul) 53-55; V of Ludham 55-81. *28 Trendull Road, Sprowston, Norwich, Norf.* (Nor 410258)

SMITH, Frederick Arthur. Trin Coll Tor BA 24. **d** 26 **p** 27 Ont. Miss at Roslin 26-31; R of Athens 31-32; Trenton 32-40; CF (Canad) 40-45; R of St Thos Belleville 45-53; Archd of Ont 48-53; R of Ch Ch Deer Park Tor 53-66; Can of Tor 56-66. *260 Poplar Drive, Oakville, Ont, Canada.*

SMITH, Frederick Thomas William. b 12. Kelham Th Coll 28. **d** 36 **p** 37 Brech. C of St Marg Lochee 36-38; All SS Edin 38-40; R of St Jo Evang Coatbridge 40-46; St Mary Hamilton 46-51; St Salvador Edin 51-62; Chap HM Pris Edin 51-62; V of Whittlebury w Silverstone Dio Pet from 62. *Whittlebury Vicarage, Towcester, Northants, NN12 8XS.* (Silverstone 857333)

SMITH, Geoffrey. b 45. Sarum Th Coll 66. **d** 69 Sheff **p** 70 Bp Gerard for Sheff. C of Hatfield 69-71; St Pet Bolton 71-75; V of L Hulton 75-78; P-in-c of St Andr City and Dio Newc T from 78; Adv for Social Responsibility Dio Newc T from 78. *50 High Street, Gosforth, Newcastle upon Tyne, NE3 1LX.* (0632-845495)

SMITH, Geoffrey Cobley. b 30. Bps' Coll Cheshunt, 63. **d** 65 **p** 66 St Alb. C of Hockerill 65-68; Evesham 68-72; V of Walberswick w Blythburgh Dio St E from 72; RD of Halesworth from 81. *Walberswick Vicarage, Southwold, Suff, IP18 6UN.* (Southwold 722118)

SMITH, Geoffrey Keith. b 37. Lon Coll of Div 57. **d** 60 **p** 61 Lich. C of St Luke Leek 60-63; Trentham 63-66; V of Lilleshall Dio Lich from 66. *Lilleshall Vicarage, Newport, Salop, TF10 9HE.* (Telford 604281)

SMITH, Geoffrey Raymond. b 49. AKC 71. St Aug Coll Cant 71. **d** 72 **p** 73 Edmon for Lon. C of St Alphage Hendon 72-76; St Mich AA Ladbroke Grove (in c of St Francis) 76-78; P-in-c of St Francis Isleworth Dio Lon from 78. *865 Great West Road, Isleworth, Middx.* (01-560 4839)

SMITH, George Aelbert. b 15. Sarum Wells Th Coll 77. **d** 80 **p** 81 Ex (NSM). C of Milton Abbot Dio Ex from 80. *St Mary's, Milton Abbot, Tavistock, Devon, PL19 0NX.*

SMITH, George Albert. b 15. Chich Th Coll 76. **d** and **p** 77 Gibr. Chap St Jo Menton Dio Gibr from 77. *Av du Pigautier, 06500 Menton, France.*

SMITH, George Frederic. b 35. K Coll Lon and Warm AKC 59. **d** 60 **p** 61 Cov. C of St Nich Radford Cov 60-64; Kenilworth 64-67; V of Burton Dassett 67-71; CF 71-74; V of Lapley w Wheaton Aston 74-80; Gt Wyrley Dio Lich from 80. *Great Wyrley Vicarage, Walsall, WS6 6LJ.* (Cheslyn Hay 414309)

SMITH, Canon George Moore Wauchope. Univ of Tor BA 32. **d** 34 **p** 35 Niag. C of St Alb Hamilton 34-39; I of Port Maitland S Cayuga and Byng 39-48; R of St Matthias Tor 48-67; Can of Tor Cathl from 58; C of St Mich AA Tor 69-70; Mandeville 70-72; R of Christiana 72-76. *c/o Box 15, Christiana, Jamaica, WI.* (096-42274)

SMITH, Canon George Robert Henry. b 24. Chich Th Coll 49. **d** 52 **p** 52 Glouc. C of St Steph Glouc 52-56; V of Parkend 56-65; C-in-c of Clearwell 60-62; PC of St Barn Tuffley 65-69; V 69-82; M Gen Syn Dio Glouc from 75; Hon Can of Glouc from 81; R of Leckhamtpon Dio Glouc from 82. *Leckhampton Rectory, Cheltenham, Glos, GL51 5XX.* (Cheltm 513647)

SMITH, Gerald. b 36. Sarum Th Coll 61. **d** 63 **p** 64 Bradf. C of Menston-in-Wharfedale 63-66; Chap RAF 66-70; C of Hoylake 70-72; R of St Mary Inverurie 72-74; Monymusk w Kemnay and Monymusk Aber 72-74; Team V of St Pet and St Paul Hucknall Torkard 74-75; R of the Falkld Is 75-78; V of Luddenden w Luddendenfoot Dio Wakef from 79. *St Mary's Vicarage, Luddenden, Halifax, Yorks, HX2 6PR.* (Halifax 882127)

SMITH, Gilbert. b 14. BD (Lon) 64. St Bonif Coll Warm 39. **d** 40 **p** 41 Lich. C of Brierley Hill 40-42; CF (EC) 42-48; CF 48-51; R of Wrockwardine Wood 51-58; V of Codsall Dio Lich from 58; RD of Penkridge from 73. *Codsall Vicarage, Wolverhampton, Staffs.* (Codsall 2168)

SMITH, Godfrey Declan Burfield. b 42. TCD BA (2nd cl Mod Lang) 64, MA 67. Sarum Th Coll. **d** 69 Zam **p** 70 Bp Mataka for Zam. P Dio N Zam 70-75; S Reg Sec CMS Ireland and L to Offic Dio Dub from 81. *Overseas House, 3 Belgrave Road, Rathmines, Dublin 6, Irish Republic.* (970931)

SMITH, Gordon. Angl Th Coll BC LTh 43. **d** and **p** 43 Caled. C of Dawson Creek 43-50; CF (Canad) 50-55; Chap RCAF from 55. *RCAF Headquarters, Ottawa 4, Ont, Canada.*

SMITH, Gordon Ewen. St Chad's Coll Regina. **d** 54 **p** 55 Qu'App. C-in-c of Mortlach 54-58; I of Lumsden 58-60; Gull Lake 60-67; Notukeu 67-73; Hon Can of Qu'App 68-78; I of Craik 73-78; R of Farnham Rougemont Dio Montr from 78. *430 Main Street, Farnham, PQ, Canada.* (293-4614)

SMITH, Gordon Walter. b 25. **d** 78 **p** 79 Moray. Hon C of Forres Dio Moray from 78. *66 High Street, Forres, Moray, IV36 0PQ.*

SMITH, Graham Charles Morell. b 47. St Chad's Coll Dur BA 74. Westcott Ho Cam 74. **d** 76 **p** 77 S'wark. C of All SS Tooting 76-80; Team V of Thamesmead Dio S'wark from 80. *50 Malthus Path, Thamesmead, SE28 8AM.* (01-310 6557)

SMITH, Graham David Noel. b 37. Oak Hill Coll 72. **d** 73 Tonbridge for Roch **p** 74 Roch. C of St Pet w Ch Ch and St Matt Southborough 73-76; Bedworth 76-79; R of Treeton Dio Sheff from 79. *Treeton Rectory, Rotherham, S Yorks, S60 5QP.* (Sheffield 696542)

SMITH, Graham Francis. b 27. BD 2nd cl (Lon) 57. Wells Th Coll 51. **d** 54 **p** 55 Man. C of Howe Bridge 54-57; Hatfield Hyde 57-63; V of St Jo Evang Angell Town Brixton 63-73; St Anne Wandsworth Dio S'wark from 73; P-in-c of St Faith Wandsworth 75-78; RD of Wandsworth from 81. *2 St Ann's Crescent, SW18 2LR.* (01-874 2809)

SMITH, Graham John. b 31. **d** 75 **p** 76 Ex. C of St Mark Ford Devonport 75-81; Plympton St Maurice Dio Ex from 81. *15 Abingdon Road, North Hill, Plymouth, Devon.*

SMITH, Grahame Clarence. Lich Th Coll 58. **d** 60 **p** 61 Linc. C of New Sleaford 60-63; R of Tydd St Mary 63-76; Uffington Dio Linc from 76; V of Barholme w Stow Dio Linc from 76; Tallington Dio Linc from 76; P-in-c of W Deeping Dio Linc 76-81; R from 81. *Uffington Rectory, Stamford, Lincs.* (Stamford 2430)

SMITH, Gregory William. b 53. Univ of W Ont BA 75. Hur Coll Lon Ont MDiv 78. **d** 78 **p** 79 Hur. C of St Jo Evang Lon 78-80; R of Kirkton Dio Hur from 80. *Rectory, Kirkton, Ont, Canada, N0K 1K0.*

SMITH, Ven Guy Howard. b 33. Univ of Man BA (2nd cl Hist) 54. Trin Hall, Cam 55. Coll of Resurr Mirfield, 60. **d** 62 **p** 63 Lich. C of H Trin Oswestry 62-66; Chap RNR from 63; Prin St Aug Sch Betong Sarawak 66-69; V of St Anne Willenhall 69-79; P-in-c of St Steph Willenhall 75-79; Exam Chap to Bp of Lake Malawi from 79; R of St Pet Lilongwe Dio Lake Malawi from 79; Archd Dio Lake Malawi from 80. *Box 30106, Lilongwe 3, Malawi.*

SMITH, Harold. b 20. Qu Coll Birm 77. **d** 80 **p** 81 Birm (NSM). C of All SS Gravelly Hill Erdington Dio Birm from 80. *37 Dovey Tower, Duddeston Manor Road, Nechells, Birmingham, B7 4LE.*

SMITH, Harold George. b 19. Sarum Wells Th Coll 74. **d**

76 Sarum **p** 77 Bp Tiarks for Sarum (APM). Hon C of Bridport 76-79; Pastoral Care of Litton Cheney and Puncknowle w Swyre and Long & Little Bredy 79; Team V of Bride Valley Dio Sarum from 79. *Rectory, Litton Cheney, Dorchester, Dorset.* (Long Bredy 302)

SMITH, Harold John. b 15. Ridley Hall, Cam 49. **d** and **p** 51 Leic. C of All SS Loughborough 51-53; PC of Knotty Ash 53-63; Chap CA from 63; R of St Marg Lothbury City and Dio Lon from 73. *9a Ironmonger Lane, EC2V 8EY.* (01-606 8688)

SMITH, Harold Willmot. b 07. St Andr Coll Whittlesford 43. **d** and **p** 45 Honolulu. Amer Ch 45-51; C of St Jas (in c of St Geo) New Bury Farnworth 51-52; V of Tonge Fold 52-57; Walshaw 57-67; R of Colton 67-73; V of Easton 67-73; Perm to Offic Dio Nor 73-76; Hon C of Mirfield Dio Wakef from 76. *12 Lady Heton Drive, Mirfield, W Yorks, WF14 9DZ.* (Mirfield 497082)

SMITH, Harry Colin. b 15. **d** 69 **p** 71 Willesden for Lon. C of All SS Harrow Weald 69-72; St Alb N Harrow Dio Lon from 72. *24 Abbey Close, Cuckoo Hill, Pinner, HA5 2AW.* (01-868 2964)

SMITH, Harvey Jackson. St Jo Coll Auckld LTh 68. **d** and **p** 68 Wai. C of St Jo Cathl Napier 68-70; Laindon w Basildon 71; St Steph Shepherd's Bush 72-73; V of Waikohu 74-76; Edgecumbe-Kawerau Dio Wai from 76. *4 Galway Street, Kawerau, NZ.* (8630)

SMITH, Henry John. Worc Ordin Coll 62. **d** 64 **p** 65 Worc. C of Fladbury w Throckmorton 64-67; St Geo Kidderminster 67-69; R of Eversholt w Milton Bryan 69-74; V of Bagshot Dio Guildf from 74. *Vicarage, Bagshot, Surrey.* (Bagshot 73348)

SMITH, Henry Neville. b 25. Chich Th Coll 53. **d** 54 **p** 55 Man. C of Oldham 54-56; St Olave Mitcham 57-59; Succr of Leic Cathl 59-60; Chap St Jas Hosp Balham and St Benedict Hosp Tooting 60-63; V of Ivinghoe w Pitstone 63-73; Chap Qu Anne's Sch Caversham from 73. *Queen Anne's School, Caversham, Reading, Berks.*

SMITH, Henry Robert. b 41. Council for Nat Acad Awards (Lanchester Poly) BSc 66. Qu Coll Birm 75. **d** 78 Bp McKie for Cov **p** 79 Cov. C of Hillmorton 78-81; Publ Pr Dio Southw from 81. *3 Lamcote Gardens, Radcliffe-on-Trent, Nottingham, NG12 2BS.* (06073 2753)

SMITH, Canon Herbert Gordon. K Coll NS BA 42, BLitt 44. **d** 42 **p** 44 Fred. C of Cant NB 42-56; I of St Jas Moncton 56-63; R of Newcastle 63-69; Ch Ch St Anne's City and Dio Fred from 69; Can of Ch Ch Cathl Fred from 71. *245 Westmorland Street, Fredericton, NB, Canada.*

SMITH, Herbert Newton. Wycl Coll Tor LTh 17. **d** 16 **p** 17 Niag. Miss at Erin Ont 16-18; Omagh w Palermo and Nelson 18-22; R of York 22-25; Arthur w Damascus 25-28; Wainfleet 28-32; All SS Hagersville 32-36; Chippawa 36-41; I of St Marg W Hamilton 41-55; Hannon 55-58. *429 Taylor Mille Drive North, Richmond Hill, Ont, Canada.*

SMITH, Howard Alan. b 46. St Jo Coll Dur BA 73, Dipl Th 74. **d** 74 Lewes for Chich **p** 75 Chich. C of St Matthias Preston 74-77; Henfield 77-80; R of Northiam Dio Chich from 80. *Northiam Rectory, Rye, E Sussex, TN31 6NH.* (Northiam 3118)

SMITH, Howard Charles. St Jo Coll Morpeth. **d** and **p** 69 Bath. C of All SS Cathl Bath 69-70; C of Wellington 70-72; Dubbo 72-73; R of Oberon Dio Bath from 74. *Rectory, Oberon, NSW, Australia 2787.* (3621 64)

SMITH, Howard Charles. b 08. St Steph Ho Ox. **d** 70 **p** 71 Kens for Lon. C of St Mary Abbots Kens 70-72; John Keble Ch Mill Hill 72-78; St Alphage Hendon 78-79; Perm to Offic Dio Chich from 80. *8 Camden Road, Eastbourne, BN21 4SU.*

SMITH, Howard Gilbert. b 48. Univ of Leeds BA (Pol) 69. St Steph Ho Ox BA (Th) 71 (Linacre Coll). Ridley Hall Cam 72. **d** 73 **p** 74 Newc T. C of St Luke Wallsend 73-76; Farnworth 76-77; P-in-c of All SS Farnworth 77-78; Team V of E Farnworth and Kearsley Dio Man from 78. *17 Station Road, Kearsley, Bolton, BL4 8ED.* (Farnworth 76470)

SMITH, Ian Charles. b 39. Lich Th Coll 65. **d** 68 Aston for Birm **p** 69 Birm. C of Kingshurst 68-71; Chap RAF from 72. *c/o Ministry of Defence, Adastral House, WC 1.*

SMITH, Ian Maxwell. b 54. Univ Coll Lon BA (Cl) 77. Univ of Leeds BA (Th) 79. Coll of the Resurr Mirfield 77. **d** 80 **p** 81 Wakef. C of Monk Bretton Dio Wakef from 80. *12 Coronation Street, Monk Bretton, Barnsley, S Yorks, S71 2ES.*

SMITH, Ian Walker. b 29. Univ of Leeds BA 52. Coll of Resurr Mirfield 52. **d** 54 **p** 55 Chich. C of Moulsecomb 54-61; Chap K Sch Cant 61-62; C of Crawley 62-79; Team V 79-81; R of Clenchwarton Dio Ely from 81. *Clenchwarton Rectory, King's Lynn, Norf, PE34 4DT.* (King's Lynn 2089)

SMITH, Ivan Charles. Univ of Waik BSc 80. St Jo Coll Auckld LTh 66. **d** 65 **p** 66 Auckld. C of Kaitaia 65-68; Kohimarama 68-73; St Andr Epsom Auckld 73; V of Bombay 73-76; Chap Southw Sch Hamilton from 76. *Box 14-015, Enderley, Hamilton, NZ.* (55-162)

SMITH, Jack Douglas. b 37. Down Coll Cam BA 60, MA 64. Westcott Ho Cam 78. **d** 80 **p** 81 Ely. C of Fincham Dio Ely from 80. *Rectory, Barton Bendish, King's Lynn, Norf, PE33 9DP.* (Fincham 363)

SMITH, Jack Winston. AKC 31. Chich Th Coll 27. **d** 31 **p** 32 S'wark. C of H Trin New Charlton 31-34; St Faith Wandsworth 34-36; St Bart Battersea 36-39; Actg C of St Matt Brixton 39-46; V of Chipperfield 46-48; Thames 49-56; LPr Dio Auckld 56-61; Dio Dun 61-69; V of Reefton 69-73; L to Offic Dio Dun from 73. *12 Chelmer Street, Oamaru, NZ.*

SMITH, Jacques. Montr Dioc Th Coll 63. **d** 63 Bp Dixon for Montr **p** 64 Montr. I of St Mary Montr 63-67; C-in-c of L'Eglise du Redempteur Montr 63-67; R of Neil's Harbour 67-70; New London 70-76; Lakefield 76-78. *447 Begin Street, Granby, PQ, Canada, J2G 5R2.*

SMITH, James. b 26. St Jo Coll Dur 78. **d** 79 **p** 80 Newc T (APM). C of Seaton Hirst Dio Newc T from 79. *140 Pont Street, Ashington, Northumberland, NE63 0PX.*

SMITH, James Athelston. St Jo Coll Newc ACT ThL 27. **d** 27 **p** 28 Newc. C of Aberdare 27-28; P-in-c 28-32; R of Weston 32-35; Jerry's Plains 35-37; Denman 37-41; Gloucester 41-45; Merriwa 45-50; Islington 50-58; Murrurundi 58-64. *21 Judith Street, Kotara South, NSW 2288, Australia.*

SMITH, James Edward. b 30. Chich Th Coll 57. **d** 58 **p** 59 Ches. C of Ellesmere Port 58-61; W Bromwich 61-63; Chap RN 63-65; V of St Jo Evang Walton-on-the-Hill Liv 65-71; St Columba Anfield 71-79; Altcar Dio Liv from 79. *St Michael's Vicarage, Lord Sefton Way, Gt Altcar, Lancs, L37 5AG.* (Formby 72670)

SMITH, James Harold. Ch Coll Tas ACT ThL 61. **d** and **p** 61 Tas. C of St John Newtn 61-62; Queenstn 62-64; P-in-c of Bothwell 65-67; Chap R Hobart Hosp 69-76 and from 77. *11 Swan Street, North Hobart, Tasmania 7000.* (002-344539)

SMITH, James Henry. b 32. St Aid Coll. **d** 65 Warrington for Liv **p** 66 Liv. C of St Cath Wigan 65-68; V of Parkfield 68-77; Breightmet Dio Man from 77. *Breightmet Vicarage, Roscow Avenue, Bolton, BL2 6HU.* (Bolton 25640)

SMITH, James Hoseason Sydney. St Jo Coll Morpeth. **d** 45 Armid for New Guinea **p** 47 New Guinea. Miss 46-47; P-in-c of Isivita 47-50; Miss P at Arawe New Britain 50-51; P-in-c of Kandrian Pugi 51-68; Mamba 68-70; Manau 70-73; R of Samarai Dio Papua from 74. *Box 25, Samarai, Papua New Guinea.* (Samarai 313)

SMITH, James Huia. Cant Univ Coll BA 51. **d** 51 **p** 52 Wel. C of St Pet Palmerston N 51-53; V of Aramoho 53-59; Ohakune 59-63; Wairarapa Maori Past 63-71; City Missr Dio Wel 71-74; Perm to Offic Dio Wel from 74. *100 Mortimer Terrace, Wellington, NZ.* (71-149)

SMITH, James Thomas. b 14. **d** 79 **p** 80 Bloemf. C of St Mich Sasolburg Dio Bloemf from 79. *28 Waterson Street, Sasolburg 9570, S Africa.*

SMITH, James William. b 47. Chich Th Coll 78. **d** and **p** 80 Truro. C of Kenwyn w Trgavethan 80-82; Haslemere Dio Guildf from 82. *Church Cottage, Chatsworth Avenue, Haslemere, Surrey.* (Haslemere 2045)

SMITH, Jeffery Donald Morris. b 23. **d** 53 Lon for Col Bp **p** 54 Matab. C of St Cuthb Gwelo 53-57; St Patr 57-59; P-in-c 59-61; R of St Drostan Old Deer 61-63; St Pet Fraserburgh 63-68; C of St Cypr Cathl Kimberley 68-70; R and Dir of Upington Dio Kimb K 70-73; R of Twyford w Guist (and Bintry w Themelthorpe from 76 and Wood Norton from 80) 73-81; C-in-c of Bintry w Themelthorpe 73-76; RD of Sparham 80-81; R of Hempnall Dio Nor from 81. *Rectory, The Street, Hempnall, Norwich, Norfolk, NR15 2AD.* (Hempnall 8157)

SMITH, Jeffrey Drew. b 22. Univ of Dur BSc 46, MSc 57. Coll of Em & St Chad Sktn 73. **d** 75 **p** 76 Sktn. L to Offic Dio Sktn from 75. *306 Egbert Avenue, Saskatoon, Sask, Canada.*

SMITH, Jeffrey Howard. b 28. Trin Coll Cam BA 50, MA 56. Wells Th Coll 55. **d** 57 Bedford for St Alb **p** 58 St Alb. C of Ch Ch Luton 57-59; Ch Ch Epsom 59-63; Asst Master Gt Houghton Hall Prep Sch Northn 65-80; K Wm's Coll Castletown IM from 80. *Ballagorry Beg, Glen Mona, Maughold, IM.* (0624 781101)

SMITH, Jerry William. b 51. Hur Coll Lon MDiv 76. **d** 76 **p** 77 Alg. C of H Trin Sault Ste Marie 76-78; I of Manitowaning Dio Alg from 78. *Box 212, Manitowaning, Ont, P0P 1N0, Canada.*

SMITH, John. Univ of NZ BA 44. NZ Bd of Th Stud LTh 45. **d** 45 **p** 46 Ch Ch. C of Timaru 45-47; Ashburton 47-48; V of Waimea Plains 48-53; Wyndham 53-56; Tuapeka 56-60; C of Melb Dioc Centre and Hosp Chap 60-70; L to Offic Dio Bal 60-66; Chap Bal Gr Sch 70-74; Perm to Offic Dio Bal 74-76; R of Camperdown Dio Bal from 76. *Rectory, Camperdown, Vic, Australia 3260.* (055-931160)

SMITH, Canon John. b 14. Qu Coll Birm 47. **d** 50 **p** 51 Lich. C of Tettenhall Regis 50-52; St Mary Kingswinford 52-56; V of St John Dudley 56-62; R of Weston Favell 62-72; Uppingham w Ayston Dio Pet from 72; Master St Jo Hosp Weston Favell 66-72; P-in-c of Wardley w Belton Dio Pet from 76; Can (Non-Res) of Pet from 76; RD of Rutland from 77; Surr from 78. *Rectory, Uppingham, Leics, LE15 9TJ.* (Uppingham 3381)

SMITH, John Alec. b 37. ALCD (1st cl) 62. BD (Lon) 63. **d** 63 **p** 64 Nor. C of Cromer 63-66; Barking 66-69; V of Attercliffe w Carbrook Sheff 69-75; P-in-c of St Barn Highfield City and Dio Sheff 75-78; V (w St Mary) from 78; RD of Ecclesall from 80. *4 Thornsett Road, Sheffield, S7 1NA.* (Sheff 51396)

SMITH, John Bartlett. b 50. St Chad's Coll Dur BA 73. Cudd Coll 73. **d** 76 **p** 77 Heref. C of St Martin Heref Dio Heref from 76. *27 Web Tree Road, Hereford.*

SMITH, John David Elliott. b 39. Univ of Dur BA 61. Cranmer Hall Dur 61. **d** 64 Bp McKie for Cov **p** 65 Cov. C of Stratford-on-Avon 64-70; P-in-c of Tredington w Darlingscott 70-76; Newbold-on-Avon w Long Lawford Dio Cov 76-81; V from 81. *Newbold-on-Avon Vicarage, Rugby, CV21 1HH.* (Rugby 3055)

SMITH, John Denmead. b 44. Keble & St Jo Coll Ox BA 65, MA 69, DPhil 71. Coll of the Resurr Mirfield 72. **d** 75 **p** 76 Win. Hon C of St Lawr w St Swith Win 75-80; Asst Master Win Coll from 75. *16 College Street, Winchester, Hants, SO23 9LX.* (Win 61820)

SMITH, John Douglas. b 20. Roch Th Coll 63. **d** 65 **p** 66 Guildf. C of Byfleet 65-69; Hersham 69-72; V of Churt 72-80; Cobham Dio Guildf from 80. *Vicarage, St Andrew's Walk, Cobham, Surrey, KT11 3EQ.* (Cobham 2109)

SMITH, John Eckersley. Wycl Hall Ox 53. **d** 55 **p** 56 Man. C of St Jas Heywood 55-57; Atherton 57-59; R of All SS W Gorton 59-65; C of Northenden 73-75; V of St Geo w St Barn Charlestown Salford Dio Man from 75. *Vicarage, St George's Way, Salford, M6 6SW.* (061-736 1549)

SMITH, John Edward Allin. b 29. K Coll Lon BA 52. Ridley Hall Cam 52. **d** 54 **p** 55 S'wark. C of H Trin U Tooting 54-57; St Luke w All SS Weaste 57-58; Min of St Phil Conv Distr Reigate 58-65; V of St Swith Hither Green 65-71; R of Wexham Dio Ox from 71. *Rectory, Church Lane, Wexham, Slough, SL3 6LL.*

SMITH, John Ernest. b 52. Univ of St Andr MTh 77. Wycl Hall Ox 78. **d** 79 **p** 80 S'wark. C of St Mary Magd Bermondsey Dio S'wark from 79. *107 Grange Road, SE1 3BW.*

SMITH, John Graham. b 32. **d** 78 **p** 79 Win. C of Hordle Dio Win from 78. *3 Marryat Road, New Milton, Hants, BH25 5LW.* (0425 615701)

SMITH, John Hamilton. **d** 38 **p** 39 Brisb. C of St Jas Toowoomba 38-41; R of St Luke Rosewood 41-49; Bulimba 49; St Paul E Brisb 55-71; Perm to Offic Dio Brisb from 71. *38 Wardle Street, Mount Gravatt, Queensland, Australia 4122.* (49 8258)

SMITH, John Lawrence. b 43. Univ of Birm BSc 65. Linc Th Coll 67. **d** 70 **p** 71 Linc. C of St Laur Fordingham 70-74; Team V of Gt Grimsby Dio Linc from 75. *54 Scartho Road, Grimsby, Lincs.* (Grimsby 77450)

SMITH, John Leslie. b 44. Trin Coll Cam BA 65, MA 71. Ripon Coll Cudd 79. **d** 81 Southw. C of Ollerton Dio Southw from 81. *The Glebe House, Church Road, Boughton, Newark, Notts, NG22 9JR.*

SMITH, John Macdonald. b 29. Ch Coll Cam 2nd cl Math Trip pt i 50, BA (2nd cl Physics Trip pt ii) 52, MA 56. Wells Th Coll 56. **d** 58 **p** 59 Bris. C of Westbury-on-Trym 58-60; St Giles Reading 60-63; V of Kidmore End Dio Ox from 63. *Kidmore End Vicarage, Reading, Berks.* (Kidmore End 2160)

SMITH, John Oswald Salkeld. b 32. Oak Hill Th Coll 57. **d** 60 **p** 61 S'wark. C of St Mary Magd Peckham 61-63; Rodbourne-Cheney 63-67; V of St Aug Bradf 67-74; C-in-c of St Simon Hammersmith 74-76; V of St Jo Evang w St Andr Chelsea Dio Lon from 76. *43 Park Walk, SW10 0AU.* (01-352 1675)

SMITH, Canon John Reginald. b 15. TCD BA 39, MA 42. Wycl Hall Ox 40. **d** 41 **p** 42 Man. C of Ch Ch Heaton Norris 41-44; St Matt Stretford 44-47; R of All SS Stretford 47-49; V of St Thos Radcliffe 49-59; Sutton Lancs 59-66; R of Bury Dio Man from 66; RD of Bury from 66; Hon Can of Man Cathl from 72. *Rectory, Bury, Lancs.* (061-764 2452)

SMITH, John Roger. b 36. Univ of Dur BA 59. Tyndale Hall Bris 59. **d** 61 **p** 62 Derby. C of Chaddesden 61-63; Ch Gresley w Linton 63-66; V of Ch Ch Burton-on-Trent 66-75; St Mary Doncaster Dio Sheff from 76. *St Mary's Vicarage, Doncaster, DN1 2NR.* (Doncaster 62565)

SMITH, Canon John Stewart. b 18. St Cath S Ox BA 42, MA 46. Ripon Hall, Ox 42. **d** 43 **p** 44 Birm. C of Ch Ch Oldbury 43-46; Ch Ch Hengrove 46-49; C-in-c of St Chad Conv Distr Patchway 49-58; V of Shirehampton 58-72; St Alb Westbury Park Dio Bris from 72; RD of Clifton 73-79; Hon Can of Bris Cathl from 77. *21 Canowie Road, Bristol 6.* (0272 35844)

SMITH, John Thompson. b 30. Wycl Hall Ox 64. **d** 66 **p** 67 Lich. C of Walsall 66-69; V of Stoke Prior 70-75. *c/o Stoke Prior Vicarage, Bromsgrove, Worcs.* (Bromsgrove 72398)

SMITH, John Trevor. b 47. GGSM 69. Coll of Resurr Mirfield 74. **d** 77 Barking for Chelmsf **p** 78 Chelmsf. C of St Jo Bapt Loughton 77-80; St Martin Ruislip Dio Lon from 80. *5 North Drive, Ruislip, Middx, HA4 8HA.* (Ruislip 33788)

SMITH, Jonathan Peter. b 55. AKC and BD 77. Westcott Ho Cam 79. **d** 80 Newc T **p** 81 Bp Gill for Newc T. C of All SS Gosforth Dio Newc T from 80. *All Saints' House, West Avenue, Gosforth, Newcastle-upon-Tyne, NE3 4ES.* (0632 857864)

SMITH, Julian. b 48. Linc Th Coll 71. **d** 73 **p** 74 B & W. C of St Pet Lyngford Taunton 73-76; Team V of Wellington and Distr 76-81; R of Axbridge w Shipham and Rowberrow Dio B & W from 81. *Rectory, Axbridge, Somt, BS26 2BN.* (Axbridge 732261)

SMITH, Julian Rodney Victor. b 46. Univ of Southn BA (2nd cl Engl) 67, MA 69. Fitzw Coll Cam BA (2nd cl Th Trip pt ii) 70. Qu Coll Birm 70. **d** 71 Hulme for Man **p** 72 Man. C of All SS Newton Heath 71-74; All SS Stretford Man 74-75. *102 Lilac Court, Salford, Gtr Man, M6 5AH.* (061-737 8459)

SMITH, Keith. b 32. **d** 69 **p** 70 St Arn. Hon C of Maryborough Dio St Arn (Dio Bend from 77) from 69. *Box 1, Carisbrook, Vic, Australia 3464.* (054-64 2220)

SMITH, Kenneth Harry. b 21. St Chad's Coll Dur BA 49, Dipl Th 50. Linc Th Coll 51. **d** 51 **p** 52 Ches. C of Nantwich 51-52; St Pet Hale 52-54; V of Lindal-in-Furness w Marton 54-60; St Andr Dacre Dio Carl from 60. *Vicarage, Dacre, Penrith, Cumb, CA11 0HH.* (Pooley Bridge 232)

SMITH, Kenneth Robert. b 48. AKC and BD 75. St Aug Coll Cant 75. **d** 76 **p** 77 Dur. C of Birtley 76-80; V of Lamesley Dio Dur from 80. *Lamesley Vicarage, Gateshead, Co Durham.* (Low Fell 876490)

SMITH, Kenneth Victor George. BD (Lon) 62. ALCD 61. **d** 62 **p** 63 Roch. C of St Aug Bromley 62-66; Streatham W 66-68; Perm to Offic Dio S'wark 68-78; C of Sanderstead Dio S'wark from 78. *72 Beechwood Road, S Croydon, Surrey, CR2 0AA.* (01-657 0436)

SMITH, Laurence Kenneth Powell. b 17. ALCD 41 (LTh from 74). **d** 41 **p** 42 S'wark. C of H Redeem Streatham Vale 41-44; St Matt Surbiton 44-51; V of St Matt Southn 51-57; Iford 57-72; R of Stockbridge w Houghton Dio Win from 72; RD of Romsey from 79. *Rectory, Houghton Road, Stockbridge, Hants.* (Stockbridge 810)

SMITH, Laurence Sidney. b 37. Sarum Wells Th Coll 70. **d** 73 **p** 74 S'wark. C of St Matt Surbiton 73-76; St Bart Horley (in c of St Wilfrid Horley Row) 76-81; V of W Ewell Dio Guildf from 81. *Vicarage, Church Road, West Ewell, Surrey, KT19 9QY.* (01-393 4357)

SMITH, Lawrence Paul. b 51. Univ of Southn BTh 81. Chich Th Coll 76. **d** 79 **p** 80 Cant. C of St Jo Bapt Margate Dio Cant from 79. *173 Ramsgate Road, Margate, Kent, CT9 4EY.* (Thanet 294621)

SMITH, Leonard Charles Ralph. Univ of Syd BA 34 Dipl Educn 42, MA 45. ACT ThL 54. **d** 52 **p** 53 C & Goulb. C of St Sav Cathl Goulb 52-54; R of Barmedman 54-57; L to Offic Dio Borneo 57-59; C of Wagga Wagga 59-62; L to Offic Dio Newc 62-79; Perm to Offic from 80; P-in-c of Gresford 79-80. *39 Tomago Road, Tomago, NSW, Australia 2322.* (049-87 2850)

SMITH, Leslie Percival Gordon. St Barn Coll Adel 39. ACT ThL 47. **d** 41 **p** 43 NW Austr. C of Greenough 41-42; R 43-44; C of St Aug Unley 44-45; R of St John Wentworth 45-49; V of Te Kuiti 49-51; Stratford 51-53; R of Longreach 53-56; Kapunda 56-59; Merbein 59-69; Inglewood 69-76; L to Offic Dio Willoch 76-79; Dio Murray from 79. *74 O'Sullivan Beach Road, Morphett Vale, S Australia 5162.* (382 0517)

SMITH, Leslie Philip. b 04. Univ of Lon BA (2nd cl Engl) 25. Ripon Hall, Ox 31. **d** 35 **p** 36 Win. C of Stoneham 35-36; Chap of St Julien French Ch Southn 36-44; Asst Master Taunton Sch 30-44; Chap and Asst Master Oakham Sch 44-48; Lect in Div Alsager Tr College and L to Offic Dio Ches 48-51; Lect and Asst Chap Culham Coll 51-69; Chap St Nich Abingdon 60-72; Perm to Offic Dio Ox 70-71; L to Offic from 71. *6 Norman Avenue, Abingdon, Oxon, OX14 2HQ.*

SMITH, Lewis Shand. b 52. Univ of Aber MA 74. Univ of Edin BD 78. Edin Th Coll 74. **d** 77 **p** 78 Glas. C of H Trin Motherwell and of St Andr Wishaw 77-80; R of Lerwick Dio Aber and Ork from 80; Burravoe Dio Aber and Ork from 80. *St Magnus Rectory, Lerwick, Shetland, ZE1 0AQ.* (Lerwick 3862)

SMITH, Lloyd Burton. Fred Dioc Th Sch 60. **d** 64 **p** 65 Fred. I of Musquash 64-68; Harcourt w Weldford 68-72; I of Richibucto w Rexton 68-72; R of Andover 72-80; Shediac Dio Fred from 80. *Box 1017, Shediac, NB, Canada.*

SMITH, Lorin Ambrose Cope. Univ of Manit BA 28. St Jo

Coll Manit LTh 30. **d** 30 Rupld **p** 31 Bp Matheson for Rupld. Asst Lect St Jo Coll Winnipeg 31-35; I of St Aid Winnipeg 32-34; R of Emerson 35-37; I of Merritt Miss 37-41; Exam Chap to Bp of Carib 39-40; R of Trail 41-45; Western Field Sec of Gen Bd of Relig Educn 45-48; R of Vernon 48-54; Can of Koot 54-55; R of St Mark Vanc 54-60; St Jo Evang N Vanc 60-67; Woodsdale 67-71; Can of Ch Ch Cathl Vanc 64-67. *PO Box 39, Oyama, BC, Canada.*

SMITH, Louis Robert. b 12. St Bonif Coll Warm 65. **d** 66 **p** 67 Leic. C of St Mark Leic 66-69; R of Bruntingthorpe 69-75; C of Mkt Harborough 75-77; L to Offic Dio Leic 77-80; Perm to Offic Dio Linc from 80. *300 Hainton Avenue, Grimsby, DN32 9LS.*

SMITH, Malcolm. b 46. SSM ACT ThL 75. **d** 76 Bp Renfrew for Adel **p** 77 Adel. C of Henley Beach 76-77; Christies Beach 77-79; P-in-c of Maylands-Firle Dio Adel from 79. *54 Phillis Street, Maylands, S Australia 5069.* (42 4991)

SMITH, Malcolm Peter. b 48. Bp Burgess Hall Lamp 69. **d** 74 **p** 75 St D. C of Llanelli 74-76; Betws w Ammanford 76-78; V of Llwynhendy 78-81. *Address temp unknown.*

SMITH, Mark Gordon Robert Davenport. b 56. St Jo Coll Dur BA (Th) 77. Ridley Hall Cam 78. **d** 80 **p** 81 Sheff. C of St Jo Evang Park City and Dio Sheff from 80. *261 Granville Road, Sheffield, S2 5EA.* (Sheff 25534)

SMITH, Canon Martin Barry. Ridley Coll Melb 60. ACT ThL 64. **d** 64 **p** 65 Melb. C of St Mark Sunshine 64; St Phil W Heidelberg 64-66; Tennant Creek 67; V of St Silas Geelong 68-72; I of Brighton Beach 72-77; E Thornbury Dio Melb from 77; Can of Melb from 80. *68 Pender Street, Thornbury, Vic, Australia 3071.* (44-1762)

SMITH, Martin David. b 52. Univ of Hull BA 75. Cudd Coll 75. **d** 78 Chelmsf **p** 79 Bradwell for Chelmsf. C of Brentwood 78-80; St Giles w St Sav Reading Dio Ox from 80. *St Saviour's House, Holybrook Road, Reading, RG1 6DG.* (Reading 595280)

SMITH, Martin Lee. b 47. Worc Coll Ox BA (1st cl Th) and Can Hall Jnr Gk NT Pri 68, MA 72. Cudd Coll 68. **d** 70 **p** 71 St Alb. C of Digswell 70-71; Cheshunt 71-73; Perm to Offic Dio Ox 74-80; In Amer Ch from 81. *980 Memorial Drive, Cambridge, Mass 02138, USA.*

SMITH, Martin William. b 40. K Coll BD and AKC 63. **d** 64 **p** 65 Lon. C of St Hilda's Conv Distr Ashford 64-67; R of Labuan Sabah 67-69; Likas Sabah 69-71; V of St Mark Lakenham Dio Nor from 71. *St Mark's Vicarage, 2 Conesford Drive, Lakenham, Norwich, NR1 2BB.* (Nor 22579)

SMITH, Martyn. b 52. Oak Hill Coll 78. **d** 81 Man. C of St Pet Halliwell (in c of St Andr Montserrat) Dio Man from 81. *29 Tattersall Avenue, Montserrat, Bolton, BL1 5TE.* (Bolton 42444)

SMITH, Maurice Jeffrey. b 18. Bps' Coll Cheshunt 56. **d** 56 **p** 57 Lon. C of St Jas Muswell Hill 56-58; V of H Trin Springfield 58-70; Chap HM Pris Chelmsf 65-70; R of Wickham Bishops Dio Chelmsf from 70; RD of Witham from 76. *Rectory, Church Road, Wickham Bishops, Witham, Essex CM8 3LA.* (Maldon 891360)

SMITH, Mervyn Gilbert Morris. b 18. Ripon Hall Ox 56. **d** 58 **p** 59 Roch. C of Strood 58-61; V of Burham 61-67; Rosherville 67-79; R of Horsmonden Dio Roch from 79. *Horsmonden Rectory, Horsmonden, via Tonbridge, Kent.* (Brenchley 2521)

SMITH, Michael Anthony. b 47. Univ of Wales (Abth) MA 73. **d** 78 **p** 79 St D (APM). C of Llandingat w Myddfai Dio St D from 78; Chap Llandovery Coll from 81. *Ty Teilo, Llandovery College, Llandovery, Dyfed.*

SMITH, Michael George. Late Scho of Univ Coll Ox BA (2nd cl Mod Hist) 57 2nd cl Th 59, MA 61, BD 65. St Steph Ho Ox 57. **d** 60 **p** 61 Ex. C of St Thos Ex 60-63; St Mary Virg Ox 63-65; in Amer Ch 65-70; Chap Qu Marg Sch Escrick 70-74; Pocklington Sch from 74. *11a Barmby Road, Pocklington, York.*

SMITH, Michael James. b 47. AKC 69. St Aug Coll Cant 70. **d** 71 **p** 72 Pet. C of St Columba Corby 71-78; V of Collierley (w Annfield Plain from 80) Dio Dur from 78. *Collierley Vicarage, Front Street, Annfield Plain, Co Durham.* (Stanley 36254)

SMITH, Michael John. b 47. Dipl Th (Lon) 71. Kelham Th Coll 65. **d** 71 **p** 72 Cov. C of St Mary Magd Cov 71-75; Chap RN from 75. *c/o Ministry of Defence, Lacon House, Theobald's Road, WC1X 8RY.*

SMITH, Michael Raymond. b 36. Qu Coll Cam BA 59, MA 63. ARCM and ARCO 56. Cudd Coll 64. **d** 65 **p** 66 York. C of Redcar 65-70; V of Dormanstown 70-73; Prec of Worc Cathl 73-77; R of St Barn Rainbow Hill w Ch Ch Tolladine City and Dio Worc from 77; RD of Worcester E from 79. *St Barnabas Vicarage, Church Road, Rainbow Hill, Worcester, WR3 8NX.* (Worc 23785)

SMITH, Michael Robin. b 34. Sarum Th Coll 59. **d** 62 **p** 63 S'wark. C of St Geo Perry Hill 62-65; Streatham 65-68. *10 Wiseton Road, SW17.*

SMITH, Neil Reginald. b 47. Qu Coll Birm 70. **d** 72 Ripon **p** 73 Bradf. C of All SS L Horton Bradf 72-75; New Mills 75-80. *Whaley Hall, Reservoir Road, Whaley Bridge, Derby.* (Whaley Bridge 2495)

SMITH, Neville Arthur. St Jo Coll Auckld LTh 65. **d** 59 **p** 60 Waik. C of Taumarunui 59-60; New Plymouth 60-63; V of Waihi 63-68; Morrinsville 68-73; Perm to Offic Dio Waik from 73. *33 Macky Street, Waihi, NZ.* (Waihi 8287)

SMITH, Nicholas Victor. b 54. St Jo Coll Dur BA 76. St Steph Ho Ox 76. **d** 78 Birm. C of St Sav Saltley Dio Birm from 78. *8 Langton Road, Saltley, Birmingham, B8 3DG.* (021-327 4595)

SMITH, Noel. **d** 55 **p** 57 C & Goulb. C of Wagga Wagga 55-57; R of Taralga Dio C & Goulb from 57. *Taralga, NSW, Australia.* (0485211 12)

SMITH, Norman. b 11. Lich Th Coll 54. **d** 55 **p** 56 Pet. C of Rothwell and of Desborough Thorpe Malsor and Rushton 55-58; R of Barrowden w Wakerley 58-66; V of Beer 66-77. *44 Newlands Park, Seaton, Devon.*

SMITH, Norman Bach. Univ of Otago BA 49, MA 50. **d** 51 **p** 52 Wel. C of Palmerston N 51-54; C (Col Cl Act) of St Jas w Ch Ch Clapton 55-56; Harrow Weald 56-57; P-in-c of Maori Past Wel 57-58; V of Waverley-Waitotara 58-62; Gonville 62-70; C of Palmerston N 70-75; V of Manaia 75-81; Featherston Dio Wel from 81. *Bell Street, Featherston, NZ.* (89-589)

SMITH, Norman George. b 27. K Coll Lon and Warm BD 52. AKC 52. **d** 53 **p** 54 Man. C of Ch Ch Pennington 53-56; Chorlton-cum-Hardy 56-57; V of St Jas Heywood 57-63; R of Bedhampton 63-81; V of St Bart Hyde City and Dio Win from 81. *1 Abbey Hill Close, Winchester, Hants, SO23 7AZ.* (Win 2032)

SMITH, Norman Jordan. Sarum Th Coll 57. **d** 60 Glouc **p** 61 Chich. C of Parkend and of Clearwell 60-61; W Tarring 61-65; Asst Chap Geelong Gr Sch 65-66; Chap Geelong C of E Gr Sch Timbertop 67-68; V of Chidham Dio Chich from 68. *Chidham Vicarage, Chichester, Sussex.* (Bosham 573147)

SMITH, Paul Andrew. b 55. St Chad's Coll Dur BA 76. Chich Th Coll 78. **d** 80 Burnley for Blackb **p** 81 Blackb. C of St Matt Habergham Eaves Burnley Dio Blackb from 80; H Trin Habergham Eaves Burnley Dio Blackb from 80. *19 Durban Grove, Burnley, Lancs.*

SMITH, Paul Gregory. b 39. Univ of Ex BA (2nd cl Th) 61. St Steph Ho Ox 61. **d** 63 **p** 64 Chelmsf. C of St Mich AA Walthamstow 63-66; St Mark Ford Devonport 66-69; Hemel Hempstead (in c of St Barn, Team V from 71) Dio St Alb from 69. *St Barnabas Vicarage, Everest Way, Adeyfield, Hemel Hempstead, HP2 4HY.* (Hemel Hempstead 53681)

SMITH, Paul Wilfrid Lee. Univ of Manit BA 58, LTh 58. **d** 57 **p** 58 Bran. C of St Matt Cathl Bran 57-59; R of St Pet Flin Flon 59-64; Selkirk 64-69; Dynevor 69-70; I of St Jas Winnipeg Dio Rupld from 71. *195 Collegiate Street, St James, Winnipeg 12, Manit, Canada.*

SMITH, Canon Percival McDonald. MBE 80. **d** 26 **p** 27 Brisb. C of All SS Charleville 26-30; St John Dalby 31-32; St Francis Nundah 32-33; P-in-c of Alice Springs 32-42; R 42-45; Supt St Francis Home Semaphore Adel and Miss Chap and Surr Dio Carp 45-49; Archd of N Territory and Surr 49-54; Supt of St Mary's Hostel Alice Springs 49-54; R of Alice Springs 52-54; Biloela 54-56; V of Callide Valley 56-58; R of Auburn 58-62; P-in-c of Kilburn 62-67; Perm to Offic Dio Adel 67-69; L to Offic from 69; Hon Can of N Terr from 71. *Flat 8, Kingslea, 3 Darwin Street, Glenelg North, S Australia 5045.* (294-3760)

SMITH, Percy George. b 10. **d** 55 **p** 56 Ox. C of Stokenchurch 55-57; Wooburn 57-59; V of Ascott-under-Wychwood Dio Ox from 59; V of Leafield Dio Ox from 59. *Leafield Vicarage, Oxford.* (Asthall Leigh 638)

SMITH, Peter. b 36. Keele Univ BA 60. Cudd Coll 73. **d** 75 **p** 76 Lich. C of St Chad Shrewsbury 75-80; Commiss Swaz from 76; V of St Chad Burton-on-Trent Dio Lich from 80. *St Chad's Vicarage, Burton-on-Trent, Staffs.* (B-on-T 64044)

SMITH, Peter Albert. b 26. Keble Coll Ox BA (2nd cl Th) 51, MA 55. Wells Th Coll 51. **d** 53 **p** 54 Ripon. C of Leeds 53-55; Kingswinford 55-59; Chap of Lich Th Coll 59-62; Vice-Prin 62-67; L to Offic Dio Lich 60-67; Bp's Chap to Studs and L to Offic Dio Bradf 67-73; Dio Glouc from 81; V of Madeley 73-77. *The Almshouses, Newland, Coleford, Glos, GL16 8NL.*

SMITH, Peter Anson Stewart. b 16. AKC (2nd cl) 37. **d** 39 **p** 40 S'wark. C of St Luke W Norwood 39-41; S Ossett 41-44; C-in-c of Conv Distr of St Francis Broadfield 44-49; V of Leavesden 49-73; St Jo Bapt Greenhill Harrow 73-81; Dioc Dir of Ordins Willesden Episc Area 73-81; ACCM Selector 75-81; Perm to Offic Dio Chich from 81. *3 West Drive, Brighton, Sussex, BN2 2GD.* (Brighton 605042)

SMITH, Peter Edward Harold. b 47. St Mich Ho Crafers 76. **d** 76 **p** 77 Willoch. C of Port Linc 76-79; P-in-c of Orroroo Dio Willoch from 79. *Fourth Street, Church, Orroroo, S Australia 5431.*

SMITH, Peter Francis Chasen. Univ of Leeds, BA 54. Coll of Resurr Mirfield, 54. **d** 56 **p** 57 S'wark. C of St Clem E Dulwich 56-59; Sutton 59-62; C-in-c of Wrangbrook w N Elmsall Conv Distr 62-68; Asst Master and Chap St Aid C of E High Sch Harrogate from 68. *28 Mallinson Oval, Harrogate, N Yorks, HG2 9HH.* (Harrogate 871238)

SMITH, Peter Howard. b 55. Univ of St Andrews MTh 78. Trin Coll Bris 78. **d** 79 **p** 80 Ches. C of Handforth Dio Ches from 79. *28 Pickmere Court, Handforth, Cheshire.*

SMITH, Peter James. b 23. K Coll Lon and Warm 49. **d** 53 **p** 54 Man. C of Atherton 53-55; Wokingham 55-56; Doncaster 56-59; V of Whitgift w Adlingfleet 59-62; Chap Highcroft Hosp Birm 62-71; C of Wolborough 71-74; St Pet Maidenhead 74-78; Trav Sec Ch Coun for Health and Healing from 78. *73 Kidwells Close, Maidenhead, Berks.* (Maidenhead 23164)

SMITH, Canon Peter James. Hur Coll LTh 59. **d** and **p** 59 Niag. R of Palmerston 59-64; St Jas St Catherines Niag 64-72; Can Res of Ott from 72. *439 Queen Street, Ottawa, Ont., Canada.* (1-613-236-9149)

SMITH, Peter Michael. b 28. Open Univ BA 75. K Coll Lon and Warm 52. **d** 56 **p** 57 Win. C of St Jas Pokesdown Bournemouth 56-59; Weeke (in c of St Barn) 59-63; V of Hutton Roof w Lupton 63-69; St Aid Barrow-F 69-72; Preston-Patrick Dio Carl from 72. *Preston Patrick Vicarage, Milnthorpe, Cumb, LA7 7NY.* (Crooklands 235)

SMITH, Peter William. b 31. GOC 74. **d** and **p** 77 Glouc. C of St John Coleford Dio Glouc from 77. *41 Coalway Road, Coleford, Glos, GL16 7HQ.* (Dean 32518)

SMITH, Philip Lloyd Cyril. b 22. Ch Coll Cam BA 47, MA 49. Wycl Hall, Ox 47. **d** 49 **p** 50 Liv. C of St Helens (in c of St Mary's Miss) 49-52; St John Woking (in c of Brookwood) 52-56; R of Burslem Dio Lich from 56. *190 Waterloo Road, Burslem, Stoke-on-Trent, Staffs, ST6 3HF.* (Stoke-on-Trent 84026)

SMITH, Canon Philip Morell. b 10. Wadh Coll Ox BA 33, MA 36. Wells Th Coll 33. **d** 34 **p** 35 S'wark. C of Streatham 34-39; CF (R of O) 39; C of Putney (in c of All SS) 39-46; Lee 46; V of St Mary Balham 47-54; Chap Weir Hosp Balham 52-54; Surr from 53; V of St Mark Woodcote Purley 54-64; R of Streatham 64-72; RD of Streatham 68-72; Hon Can of S'wark 68-72; Hon Can (Emer) from 72; R of Puttenham w Wanborough 72-78. *50 Wooteys Way, Alton, Hants.* (0420-85325)

SMITH, (Luke) Philip Sydney Bellman. b 11. St Cath S Ox BA 35, Dipl Th 36, MA 46. St Steph Ho Ox 35. M CR 51. **d** 37 **p** 38 Bris. C of Highworth 37-39; Storrington 39-42; Chap RNVR 43-46; C of Banbury 47-48; Sekhukhuniland Native Miss Pret 52-62. *House of the Resurrection, Mirfield, Yorks.*

SMITH, Ralph William. Fred Dioc Th Sch 60. **d** 64 **p** 65 Fred. C of St Luke St John 64-67; I of Gladstone 67-76; St Geo w Pennfield Dio Fred from 76. *St George, NB, Canada.*

SMITH, Ralph Willingdon. **d** 52 **p** 53 Ott. C of St Pet Carlington Ott 52; I of Iroquois 52-59; C of Ch Ch Cathl Ott 59-65; R of Fitzroy Harbour 65-72; St Luke Ott 72-76; Ch of Resurr City and Dio Ott from 76. *3191 Riverside Drive, Ottawa, Ont., Canada.*

SMITH, Ralston Antonio. St Pet Coll Kingston, 53. **d** 56 **p** 57 Ja. C of Montego Bay 57-60; St Thos Ex 60-62; Withycombe Raleigh w Exmouth 63-68; V of Exwick 68-72; P-in-c Ch of Transfig Havendale and St Jo Meadow Brook Dio Ja from 72; Exam Chap to Bp of Ja from 76. *3 Meadowbrook Main, Meadowbridge, Jamaica.* (092-42964)

SMITH, Ven Raymond Bruce. St Francis Coll Brisb ACT ThL 62. **d** and **p** 62 Rockptn. C of Longreach 62-63; V of St Matt Pk Avenue Rockptn 63-68; R of Blackall 68-69; Asst Chap C of E Gr Sch Brisb 70-72; R of Callide Valley 72-75; W Mackay Dio N Queensld from 75; Archd of Mackay from 78. *PO Box 559, Mackay, Queensland, Australia 4740.*

SMITH, Raymond Charles. b 24. AKC 49. Bps' Coll Cheshunt, 49. **d** 50 **p** 51 Chelmsf. C of St Alb Mart Westcliff-on-Sea 50-53; Caversham (in c of St Barn) 53-55; Wooburn (in c of St Mark Bourne End) 55-56; R of St Leon Colchester 56-63; V of St Francis of Assisi Barkingside 63-73; Surr from 67; R of Leigh-on-Sea Dio Chelmsf from 73. *St Clement's Rectory, Leigh-on-Sea, Essex.* (Southend-on-Sea 75305)

SMITH, Raymond Charles William. b 56. AKC and BD 78. Coll of the Resurr Mirfield 79. **d** 80 Dorchester for Ox **p** 81 Ox. C of Iffley City and Dio Ox from 80. *Church House, The Oval, Rose Hill, Oxford, OX4 4SE.*

SMITH, Canon Raymond Douglas. b 31. TCD BA 53, BD and MA 56. **d** 54 **p** 55 Connor. C of St Mich Belf 54-56; St Patr Ballymacarrett 56-58; CMS Tr Coll 58-60; C of Weithaga 60-61; Tutor St Paul's Th Coll Limuru 61-71; L to Offic Dio Ft Hall 61-65; Mt Kenya 65-71; Asst Gen Sec Hibernian CMs 71-74; Gen Sec (CMS Ireland from 76) from 74; Hon Can of Maseno N from 78. *Overseas House, 3 Belgrave Road, Rathmines, Dublin 6, Irish Republic.*

SMITH, Raymond Frederick. b 28. Univ of Lon BSc 51. Univ of Leeds MA 65, Oak Hill Th Coll 51. **d** 53 **p** 54 Liv. C of St Philemon Toxt Pk 53-56; St Pet Halliwell 56-58; V of Denton Yorks 58-66; V of Weston Yorks 58-66; Adviser on Christian Stewardship Dio Bradf 61-66; V of Normanton 66-81; RD of Chevet 73-81; M Gen Syn 75-80; R of Moreton Dio Ches from 81. *Rectory, Dawpool Drive, Moreton, Wirral, Mer L46 0PH.* (051-677 3540)

SMITH, Ven Raymond George. Moore Th Coll Syd ACT ThL (2nd cl) 58. **d** 58 **p** 60 Armid. C of Barraba 58-60; Moree 60-61; P-in-c of Ashford 61-66; V of Uralla 66-69; Dir Christian Educn Dio Armid from 69; Chap New Engl Sch Armid 70-73; Archd of Namoi from 77. *Box 40, South Tamworth, NSW, Australia 2340.*

SMITH, Raymond Horace David. b 30. Lon Coll of Div 64. **d** 67 **p** 68 Lon. C of St Leon Shoreditch 67-70; Miss S Amer Miss Soc Santiago 71-73; Chap Santiago Commun Ch 73-80; P-in-c of Castle Hedingham Dio Chelmsf from 80. *Castle Hedingham Vicarage, Halstead, Essex.* (Hedingham 60274)

SMITH, Raymond Keith. b 48. St Mich Ho Crafers ACT ThDip 76. **d** and **p** 77 Perth. C of Scarborough 77-78; Perm to Offic Dio Adel 79-81; C of Coleambally and Darlington Dio River from 81. *Rectory, Coleambally, NSW, Australia 2707.*

SMITH, Richard. b 47. St D Coll Lamp Dipl Th 75. Bp Burgess Hall Lamp 73. **d** 75 **p** 76 Llan. C of Aberavon 75-78; Industr Chap Dio Llan 78-81; Team V of St Swithun Bournemouth Dio Win from 81. *St Swithun's Vicarage, Gervis Road, Bournemouth, BH1 3ED.* (Bournemouth 22740)

SMITH, Richard Arthur. b 44. Chich Th Coll 71. **d** 74 Edmonton for Lon **p** 75 Lon. C of St Jude-on-the-Hill Hampstead Garden Suburb 74-78; St Mark Noel Pk Wood Green Dio Lon from 78. *29b Lymington Avenue, Noel Park, N22 6LJ.* (01-888 5541)

SMITH, Richard Geoffrey. b 46. St Jo Coll Dur BA 68. St Steph Ho Ox BA (Th) 74, MA 78. **d** 75 **p** 76 Chelmsf. C of Brentwood 75-78; Corringham 78-81; R of Shepton Beauchamp w Barrington, Stocklinch, Puckington and Bradon Dio B & W from 81. *Shepton Beauchamp Rectory, Ilminster, Somt, TA19 0LQ.* (S Petherton 40338)

SMITH, Richard Harwood. b 34. Sarum Th Coll 57. **d** 59 **p** 60 Heref. C of Kington 59-62; St Phil Georgetn 62-64; Kitty 64-65; V of Mackenzie 65-69; C of Broseley w Benthall 69-70; Sec USPG from 70; L to Offic Dio Heref 70-76; R of Wigmore Abbey Dio Heref from 76. *Leintwardine Rectory, Craven Arms, Salop.* (Leintwardine 235)

SMITH, Richard Ian. b 46. Jes Coll Ox BA (2nd cl Th) 69. Ripon Hall Ox 69. **d** 70 **p** 71 York. C of Eston 70-75; Team V of E Ham 75-80; R of Crook Dio Dur from 80. *Rectory, Crook, Co Durham.* (Crook 2588)

SMITH, Canon Robert. b 13. Wycl Hall, Ox 52. **d** 52 Sheff for W Afr **p** 53 N Nig. P Dio N Nig 52-58; V of Withnell 58-61; NW Area Sec SAMS 61-63; NE Area Sec 79-81; Home Sec 63-71; Hon Can of N Argent from 70; V of Ch Ch Pennington 71-78; Min of St John Downshire Hill Hampstead Dio Lon from 81. *64 Pilgrim's Lane, NW3 1SN.* (01-435 8404)

SMITH, Robert Benjamin. Sir Geo Williams Univ Montr BA 58. K Coll NS STB 62, BD 64. Univ of Ex PhD 69. **d** 62 **p** 63 Fred. C of St Luke St John 62-64; R of St Clem Milledgeville St John 64-66; C of Crediton 66-68; Perm to Offic Dio Ex 68-69; R of Westfield 69-76; Renforth Dio Fred from 76. *90 Wiljac Street, Saint John, NB, Canada.*

SMITH, Robert Harold. b 23. Univ of Lon BA 49. Oak Hill Th Coll. **d** 50 **p** 51 Southw. C of St Ann Nottingham 50-52; C-in-c of Elburton Conv Distr Plymstock 52-57; V of Ch Ch Lowestoft 57-67; R of St Mary Magd w St Jas Upton Torquay 67-80; (R of Bressingham and P-in-c of Fersfield and N Lopham w S Lopham) 80-81; R of Bressingham w N and S Lopham and Fersfield Dio Nor from 81. *Bressingham Rectory, Diss, Norf, IP22 2AT.* (Bressingham 762)

SMITH, Canon Robert James. b 09. Univ of Dur LTh 37. St Aid Coll 34. **d** 37 **p** 38 Liv. C of St Cath Edge Hill 37-39; St Anne Aigburth 39-41; CF (EC) 41-46; Prescot 46-47; V of Ditton 47-52; Burscough Bridge 52-60 Surr from 53; Proc Conv Liv 58-64; V of Highfield 60-74; Can Dioc of Liv Cathl 68-74; Can (Emer) from 74. *Highfield, Crank Road, Crank, St Helens, Merseyside, WA11 7RZ.* (Rainford 4761)

SMITH, Robert Raymond. St Francis Coll Brisb. **d** 60 **p** 61 Brisb. C of H Trin Fortitude Valley 60-61; Maryborough 61-64; P-in-c of Goondiwindi 64-65; R 66-69; St Pet Wynnum Bris 69-74; Southport Dio Brisb from 74. *87 Nerang Street, Southport, Queensland, Australia 4215.* (Gold Coast 31 1702)

SMITH, Robert William. b 16. Fitzw Ho Cam BA 46, MA 51, Ripon Hall Ox. **d** 49 **p** 50 Birm. C of Hay Mill 49-51; All SS Northn 51-56; R of Kislingbury w Rothersthorpe 56-64; Toft w Caldecote (and Childerley from 72) 64-73; R of

Hardwicke 64-73; C-in-c of Childerley 64-72. *36 Shelford Road, Trumpington, Cambridge.*

SMITH, Robin Handley Stockley. NZ Bd of Th Stud LTh 65. Coll Ho Ch Ch 53. **d** 56 Wel **p** 57 Bp Rich for Wel. C of Marton 56-58; V of Pongaroa 58-61; Taita-Stokes Valley 61-64; Stokes Valley 64-69; Eltham 69-74; Geraldine Dio Ch Ch from 74. *PO Box 28, Geraldine, NZ.* (Ger 409)

SMITH, Robin Jonathan Norman. b 36. Worc Coll Ox BA (3rd cl Th) 60, MA 64. Ridley Hall, Cam 60. **d** 62 **p** 63 Chelmsf. C of Barking 62-67; Chap Lee Abbey Ex 67-72; V of Chesham 72-80; RD of Amersham from 79; R of Gt Chesham Dio Ox from 80. *St Mary's Rectory, Church Street, Chesham, Bucks.* (Chesham 783629)

SMITH, Roderick Henry. Univ of Natal BA 69. St Paul's Coll Grahmstn Dipl Th 69. **d** 69 Natal **p** 70 Bp Hallowes for Natal. C of St Sav Cathl Pmbg 69-71; R of St Columba Durban 71-74; St Paul Geo 74; L to Offic Dio Natal 77-80; R of Richmond Dio Natal from 80. *Box 171, Richmond, Natal, S Africa.*

SMITH, Rodney John Boughton. b 19. AKC 41. Sarum Th Coll 41. **d** 42 **p** 43 Taunton for B & W. C of St John Frome Selwood 42-44; Perm to Offic Dio B & W 44; C of St Andr Eastbourne 45-48; St Aug Belvedere 48-49; Horsham 49-55; V of King's Bromley 55-60; Porthill 60-68; E Meon Dio Portsm from 68; Langrish Dio Portsm from 75. *East Meon Vicarage, Petersfield, Hants, GU32 1NL.* (East Meon 221)

SMITH, Roger Douglas St John. b 12. TD 56, w clasp 62. Selw Coll Cam BA 37, MA 41. Jes Coll Ox BA (3rd cl Th) 39, MA 43. Univ of Man BD 51. Ripon Hall Ox 37. **d** 39 **p** 40 Man. C of St Paul Kersal 39-42; CF (EC) 42-46; Hon CF 46; CF (TA) 48-62; R of St Thos Lower Crumpsall 46-48; V of Crawshawbooth 48-53; Astley Bridge 53-63; R of Darley (w S Darley from 64) 63-77; PC of S Darley 63-64. *28 Ffordd Penrhwylfa, Prestatyn, Clwyd, LL19 8AG.* (Prestatyn 7307)

SMITH, Roger Stuart. b 41. Chich Th Coll 65. **d** 66 Ripon **p** 67 Knaresborough for Ripon. C of Garforth 66-70; C in Hilborough Group 70-73; V 73-78; V of Mendham w Metfield and Withersdale Dio St E from 78. *Metfield Vicarage, Harleston, Norf.* (Fressingfield 488)

SMITH, Ronald. ALCD 56. **d** 56 **p** 57 Roch. C of St Jas Gravesend 56-59; Min of Istead Rise Conv Distr 59-79; V of Istead Rise Dio Roch from 79. *Vicarage, Upper Avenue, Istead Rise, Northfleet, Kent.* (Southfleet 2403)

SMITH, Ronald. b 29. St Jo Coll Auckld LTh 80. **d p** 81 Auckld. C of Whangarei Dio Auckld from 80. *22 Mill Road, Whangarei, NZ.*

SMITH, Ronald Anthony. b 24. **d** 73 **p** 75 (APM). C of St Ann's Bay Dio Ja from 73. *2 Park Avenue, St Ann's Bay, Jamaica, WI.*

SMITH, Ronald David Roy. b 42. **d** 72 **p** 73 Queb. C of Fitch Bay 72-73; Team Min of Gtr Coaticook Dio Queb 73-80; I from 80; Dom Chap to Bp of Queb from 78. *54 Cutting Street, Coaticook, PQ, Canada.*

SMITH, Ronald Deric. BA (2nd cl Hist) Lon 46. Bps' Coll Cheshunt 59. **d** 61 **p** 62 Roch. C of Crayford 61-67; in Amer Ch 67-68; C of W Malling w Offham 68-71; V of Slade Green 71-78; St Luke Bromley Common Dio Roch from 78. *St Luke's Vicarage, Bromley Common, Bromley, Kent, BR2 9PD.* (01-464 2076)

SMITH, Ronald George. b 34. Univ of Dur BA and Van Mildert Exhib 56, Dipl Th 58. Cranmer Hall Dur 57. **d** 58 **p** 59 Win. C of St Jas Shirley Southn 58-60; Basingstoke 60-63; R of Wolviston 63-74; L to Offic Dio Dur 74-78; Asst Master Loughton Co High Sch for Girls and Perm to Offic Dio Chelmsf 78-80; V of St Geo Harold Hill, Romford Dio Chelmsf from 80. *St George's Vicarage, Chippenham Road, Harold Hill, Romford, RM3 8HX.* (Ingrebourne 43415)

SMITH, Ronald James. b 36. Linc Th Coll 73. **d** 75 **p** 76 Southw. C of St Jo Bapt Bilborough 75-78; P-in-c of Netherfield Dio Southw 78-81; V from 81; Colwick Dio Southw 78-81; R from 81. *St George's Vicarage, Victoria Road, Netherfield, Nottingham.* (Nottm 248532)

SMITH, Ronald William. b 16. ACIS 40, FCIS 61. Worc Ordin Coll 63. **d** 65 **p** 66 Heref. C of Colwall 65-68; V of Stretton Grandison w Ashperton and Canon Frome (w Yarkhill from 71) 68-81; P-in-c of Yarkhill 68-71. *17 Knapp Close, Ledbury, Herefs.*

SMITH, Ronald William. b 45. Chich Th Coll 70. **d** 73 **p** 74 York. C of St Martin Scarborough 73-76; Stainton-in-Cleveland 76-80; V of Coatham E Dio York from 80. *9 Blenheim Terrace, Redcar, Cleve.* (Redcar 482870)

SMITH, Rowan Quentin. K Coll Lon and Warm AKC 66. **d** 67 Bp Russell for Capetn **p** 68 Capetn. C of Matroosfontein 67-69; Bonteheuwel 70; All SS Plumstead 71-72; P-in-c of Grassy Park 72-77; MCR 80; Chap St Martin's Sch Rosettenville from 80. *Box 49027, Rosettenville 2130, Johannesburg, S Africa.*

SMITH, Roy Leonard. b 36. Clifton Th Coll 63. **d** 66 **p** 67 S'wark. C of St Jas Clapham Pk 66-70; St Mark Kennington 70-74; Min of Emmanuel Conv Distr Southall Dio Lon from 74. *93 Dormers Wells Lane, Southall, Middx.* (01-843 9556)

SMITH, Royston Burleigh. b 26. St Deiniol's Libr Hawarden 76. **d** 79 **p** 80 St A. C of Prestatyn Dio St A from 79. *111 High Street, Prestatyn, Clywd, LL19 9AR.*

SMITH, Russell Howard. b 51. Univ of Melb BA 73. ACT BTh 78. St Jo Coll Morpeth 76. **d** 79 Melb for Bend. C of H Trin City and Dio Bend from 79. *14 Keck Street, Bendigo, Vic, Australia 3550.*

SMITH, Samuel Donald. St Francis Coll Brisb ACT ThL 49. **d** 50 Melb for Carp **p** 51 Carp. C of Darwin 50-52; Alice Springs 52-55; Miss Chap Seacombe Pk 55-57; LPr Dio Adel 57-59; C of St Sav w St Gabr and St Steph Poplar Lon 59; St Jas Mile End 60-62; R of Auburn Adel 62-65; P-in-c of Morphettville 66-69. *Glengowrie Court, Bell's Road, Glengowrie, S Australia.*

SMITH, Sidney Arthur. b 1884. **d** 54 Bp Hubback for Guildf **p** 54 Guildf. C of Abinger (w Coldharbour from 61) 54-65; Perm to Offic Dio Guildf from 65. *The Dene, Abinger Hammer, Dorking, Surrey.*

SMITH, Sidney Frank. b 10. AKC 40. **d** 30 **p** 41 Ox. C of St Mary Virg Henley-on-Thames 40-47; St John Windsor 47-51; PC (V from 68) of Prestwood 52-77. *4 Riverway, Barry Avenue, Windsor, Berks.*

SMITH, Stanley. St D Coll Lamp BA (3rd cl Th) 35. **d** 35 **p** 36 Dur. C of Beamish 35-37; Asst Chap Miss to Seamen Southn and LPr Dio Win 37-38; Chap Durban 38-45; Org Sec Miss to Seamen in S Afr 45-49, L to Offic Dio Johann 45-49; Chap Miss to Seamen S Shields and Tyne and L to Offic Dio Dur 49-54; New Westmr 54-75; Hon Can of New Westmr 63-75. *204-1270 Nicola Street, Vancouver, BC, Canada.*

SMITH, Stanley Roland. **d** 56 **p** 57 Hur. C of Ascen Windsor 56-58; I of La Salle 58-67; R of St Geo Walkerville 67-69; St Geo Windsor 69-78; Dom Chap to Bp of Hur 75-78. *133 Quellette Avenue, Apt 1208, Windsor, Ont, Canada.*

SMITH, Stephen John. b 46. Kelham Th Coll 65. **d** 69 Sherwood for Southw **p** 70 Southw. C of Warsop w Sookholme 69-73; Ch Ch Heaton 73-75; V of St Bede Morris Green Bolton 75-78; R of Bilborough w Strelley Dio Southw from 78. *St Martin's Rectory, St Agnes Close, Bilborough, Nottingham, NG8 4BJ.*

SMITH, Stephen John. b 55. BD (Lon) 80. Trin Coll Bris 77. **d** 81 Kens for Lon. C of St Matt Fulham Dio Lon from 81. *2a Clancarty Road, Fulham, SW6 3AB.*

SMITH, Ven Stuart Meldrum. Univ of Adel BA 49. St Mich Ho Crafers ACT ThL 54. **d** 53 **p** 54 Adel. C of Glenelg 55-57; Dom Chap to Bp of Adel 57-58; Prec 57-58; P-in-c of Kilburn 58-61; R of St Barn Clare 61-65; Coromandel Valley 65-69; Belair 69-72; Unley Dio Adel from 72; Exam Chap to Bp of Adel from 70; Can of Adel from 74; Archd of Sturt from 76. *86 Edmund Avenue, Unley, S Australia 5061.* (08-74 1321)

SMITH, Sydney John. b 21. St D Univ Coll Lamp BA 48. **d** 49 Whitby for York **p** 50 York. C of Scarborough 49-53; V of St Paul Middlesbrough 53-59; St Luke Scarborough Dio York from 59. *37 Woodland Ravine, Scarborough, Yorks.* (Scarborough 72831)

SMITH, Sydney Robert. b 17. ALCD 39. St Jo Coll Dur LTh 39, BA 40. **d** 40 **p** 41 York. C of St Paul York 40-46; Darfield and C-in-c of Gt Houghton 46-48; PC of Ch Ch Chesterfield 48-55; St Chad Derby 55-64; V of St Nath Fazakerley Walton-on-the-Hill 64-75; Westhead Dio Liv from 75. *St James' Vicarage, Westhead, Ormskirk, Lancs, L40 6HG.* (Ormskirk 72276)

SMITH, Terence. b 38. Dipl Th (Lon) 69. Tyndale Hall Bris 67. **d** 69 Bp Daly for Cov **p** 70 Cov. C of Ch Ch Cov 69-71; St Paul Leamington Priors 71-74; V of St Luke Halliwell Bolton 74-75; Chap Brunel Univ Uxbridge from 75. *50 The Greenway, Uxbridge, Middx.*

SMITH, Terrence Gordon. b 34. St Mich Coll Llan 68. **d** 70 **p** 71 Llan. C of Gelligaer 70; Aberavon 73; V of Pontlottyn w Fochriw 75-76; Kenfig Hill Dio Llan from 76. *Vicarage, High Street, Mid-Glam, CF33 6DR.* (0656-740856)

SMITH, Thomas Armstrong. TCD BA (Resp) 52, Div Test (1st cl) 54, LLB 57, MA 57. **d** 54 **p** 55 Down. C of Newcastle 54-57; St Jo Evang Kitchener 57-60; I of Pine Falls Keew 60-63; R of Aghalurcher w Colebrook and Tattykeeran 63-67; Hampton Fred 67-72; St Mary York City and Dio Fred from 72; Exam Chap to Bp of Fred from 71. *770 McEvoy Street, Fredericton, NB, Canada.*

SMITH, Canon Thomas Eldridge. **d** 41 **p** 42 Newfld. C of Grand Falls 42; St Thos St John's 42-48; R of Salvage 48-53; C of Corner Brook 53-56; R of Bell I 56-64; Portugal Cove 64-73; Bay Roberts Dio Newfld (E Newfld from 76) from 73; Can of E Newfld from 79. *PO Box 202, Bay Roberts, Conception Bay, Newfoundland, Canada.* (709-786-3024)

SMITH, Thomas Francis. b 08. Linc Th Coll 37. **d** 38 Southw **p** 39 Dub. C of St Mary Magd Sutton-in-Ashfield 38-39; St Paul Glenageary 39-40; St Ann Dub 40-42; I of

Kilgobbin Killiney and Ballynacourty 42-46 and 49-51; St Mich Lim 46-49; Leigh w Grange Silvae and Shankill 51-62; Preb of Tecolme in Leigh Cathl 55-60; Tascoffin in St Canice's Cathl Kilkenny 55-62; Treas of Leigh Cathl 60-62; I of Kells 62-76; Ennisnag 62-76; Preb of Kilkenny 62-76; RD of St Canice 69-76; Preb of Leigh 70-76; I of Dromod U 76-81. *Lough Gill House, Castlegregory, Co Kerry, Irish Republic.*

SMITH, Thomas Robert Selwyn. b 12. Bps' Coll Cheshunt 35. **d** 37 **p** 38 Carl. C of Workington 37-40; St Paul Wilton Place 40-41; Cheshunt (in c of St Clem Turnford) 41-44; V of Dalston w Cumdivock 44-55; Box (and Sinecure R of Hazelbury) Dio Bris from 55. *Vicarage, Box, Wilts.* (Box 742405)

SMITH, Thomas Roger. b 48. Cant Sch of Min 77. **d** 80 **p** 81 Cant. C of St Sav Folkestone Dio Cant from 80; Asst Master Wyndgate Sch Folkestone from 80. *Wellington House, Lydden, Dover, Kent.*

SMITH, Tony. b 23. Roch Th Coll 62. **d** 64 **p** 65 Roch. C of Frindsbury 64-67; V of Hadlow 67-78; R of Wrotham Dio Roch from 78; RD of Shoreham from 80. *Rectory, Wrotham, Kent.* (Fairseat 822464)

SMITH, Trevor Bernard. Oak Hill Th Coll 61. **d** 64 **p** 65 Blackb. C of Bispham 64-66; Chesham 66-68. *23 Darrell Way, Abingdon, Oxon, OX14 1HG.*

SMITH, Trevor Lindsay. St Jo Coll Morpeth 66. **d** 68 **p** 69 Newc. C of Singleton 68-72; Perm to Offic Dio Brisb 72-79; Dioc Educn Consultant Dio Newc from 81. *13 Robert Street, Tenambit, NSW, Australia 2323.*

SMITH, Canon Ulric LeRoy. Codr Coll Barb. **d** 63 **p** 64 Windw Is. C of Georgetown St Vincent 63-69; P-in-c of H Cross Codr Barb 69-78; Can, R and Sub-Dean of St Geo Cathl St Vincent Dio Windw Is from 78. *Box 128, St Vincent, W Indies.*

SMITH, Vivian Hamilton. **d** 73 **p** 74 Johann. C of Evaton w Sebokeng 73-80; Lenasia w Grasmere Dio Johann from 80. *418 2nd Avenue, Mid-Ennerdale, Grasmere 1828, S Africa.*

SMITH, Walter. b 04. St Chad's Coll Regina 29. **d** 32 **p** 33 Qu'App. C of St Pet Regina 32-33; I of Sceptre (w Cabri from 35) 33-36; Perm to Offic (Col Cl Act) at St Mary Cottingham 36-38; C of St Mary w St Nich Beverley 38-41; V of Leake w Over and Nether Silton 41-45; St Paul Sculcoates 46-48; St Jas Scarborough 48-59; Ruswarp w Sneaton 59-64; Nether w U Poppleton 64-68. *23 Rimington Way, Scarborough, Yorks, YO11 3QN.* (Scarboro 582812)

SMITH, Walter. b 37. Westcott Ho Cam 67. **d** 69 **p** 70 York. C of St Mich AA Hull 69-72; All SS Whitby 72-74; V of Newington w Dairycoates 74-77; C-in-c of Baldersby 77-78; Skipton-on-Swale 77-78; Team V of Thirsk Dio York from 78; P-in-c of Topcliffe w Dalton and Dishforth Dio York from 81. *Baldersby Vicarage, Thirsk, N Yorks.* (Melmerby 471)

SMITH, Walter Asbury. b 1895. Univ of Lon 28. Ridley Hall, Melb 23. ACT ThL 24. **d** 25 **p** 26 Bend. C of Sebastian Melb 25-27; Perm to Offic at St Jas Teignmouth 27-28; ACS Chap Ch Ch Cawnpore 28-30; C of St Luke Thornaby-on-Tees 30-31; R of Wattisfield 31-36; C of Cove 36-39; Chap Mariners' Ch Glouc 39-48; R of Peldon 48-50; Perm to Offic at All SS Leyton 50-54; C of St Paul Old Ford 54-55; St Andr Stoke Newington 55-62. *c/o 49 Cambridge Road, Aldershot, Hants.*

SMITH, Weldon Samuel. **d** and **p** 59 NS. R of Neil's Harbour 59-66; P-in-c of Baddeck 62-66; R of Coxheath Dio NS from 66. *46 Coxheath Road, Sydney, NS, Canada.* (564-6674)

SMITH, William Carrington. b 16. Selw Coll Cam BA 40, MA 44. SOC 63. **d** 66 **p** 67 S'wark. C of Nunhead Dio S'wark from 66. *49 Woodwarde Road, SE22.* (01-693 1009)

SMITH, William Dundas. Univ of Manit BA 27. **d** 62 **p** 63 Bran. R of Hamiota 62-63; Shoal Lake 63-70; Souris 70-74; Reston 70-74. *Souris, Manit, Canada.*

SMITH, William Edwin. b 05. Clifton Th Coll 31. **d** 34 Derby **p** 35 Bp Crick for Derby. C of Ripley 34-38; V of St Gabr Walthamstow 38-60; St Mich AA Westcliff-on-Sea 60-72. *48 Buxton Avenue, Gorleston-on-Sea, Norfolk, NR31 6HF.* (Great Yarmouth 61128)

SMITH, William Herbert. St Aid Coll 61. **d** 64 **p** 65 York. C of Tadcaster 64-66; Cross Roads Dio Ja from 66. *8 Caledonia Road, Kingston 5, Jamaica, W Indies.*

SMITH, Canon William Ivan Doersam. Univ of Tor BA 38. Wycl Coll Tor LTh 39, Hon DD 77. **d** 39 **p** 40 Tor. C of Stanhope 39-41; R of St Geo Haliburton 41-44; Chap CASF 44-46; C of St John Tor 46-48; R of Georgina and Sutton W 48-52; I of Ap Ch Tor 52-55; St Luke Tor 55-60; St Pet Calg 60-77; Hon Can of Calg 73-77; Can (Emer) from 77. *335 Mill Road, Apt 904, Etobicoke, Ont, M9C 1Y6, Canada.*

SMITH, William Joseph Thomas. b 20. Chich Th Coll 54. **d** 55 **p** 56 Chelmsf. C of Laindon w Basildon 56-61; R of Stifford 61-65; V of Boreham Dio Chelmsf from 65. *Boreham Vicarage, Chelmsford, Essex, CM3 3EG.* (Chelmsford 467281)

SMITH, William Lyndon. Ch Ch Ox BA 30. Univ of Tor BA 27, MA 28. **d** 31 Ott for Tor **p** 32 Niag for Tor. C of St Thos Tor 31-40; Chap Trin Coll Tor from 40. *Trinity College, Toronto, Ont, Canada.*

SMITH, William Melvyn. b 47. AKC and BD 69. St Aug Coll Cant 70. **d** 71 **p** 72 Lich. C of H Trin Kingswinford 71-73; Hon C of Ch Ch Coseley 73-74; C of St Paul Wednesbury 74-78; V of St Chad Coseley Dio Lich from 78. *St Chad's Vicarage, Oak Street, Coseley, Bilston, Staffs, WV14 9TA.* (Sedgley 2285)

SMITH, William Wilmot. St Jo Coll Auckld LTh (2nd cl) 66. **d** 65 **p** 66 Auckld. C of Takapuna 65-69; R of Dongara w Greenough-Walkaway 69; Mt Magnet w Murchison Distr 69-73; V of Coromandel 73-81; Marsden-Waipu Miss Distr Dio Auckld from 81. *Vicarage, Waipu, NZ.*

SMITH, Willie Ernest. b 1900. Univ of Leeds MA (Phil) 34. LRCP (Lon) 44. MRCS (Engl) 44. St Aid Coll 33. **d** 33 **p** 34 York. C of St Andr Drypool 33-36; PC of Gateforth w Hambleton 36-46; L to Offic Dio Ripon from 46. *Ryder Cottage, East Keswick, Leeds.* (Collingham Bridge 3483)

SMITH-CAMERON, Canon Ivor Gill. b 29. Madras Univ BA 50, MA 52. Coll of Resurr Mirfield. **d** 54 **p** 55 Chich. C of Rumboldswyke Chich 54-58; Chap Univ of Lon and L to Offic Dio Lon from 58; M Gen Syn 70-80; Can Res of S'wark Cathl and Dioc Missr from 72. *25 The Chase, SW4 0NP.* (01-622 1909)

SMITHEN, James Rudolph. b 42. Qu Th Coll Ont BTh 73. **d** 73 Ont **p** 73 Antig. C of St John's Cathl Antig 73-75; R of Anguilla 75-78; St Geo Basseterre Dio Antig from 78; Exam Chap to Bp of Antig from 80. *St George's Rectory, Basseterre, St Kitts, WI.*

SMITHERS, Edward Hampden. Rhodes Univ Grahmstn BA 56. St Paul's Coll Grahmstn 57. **d** 57 **p** 58 Grahmstn. C of Walmer 57-60; St Hugh Port Eliz 61-62; R of Alexandria 62-67; St Paul Port Eliz 68-78; Archd of Port Eliz 72-78. *c/o Box 745, Pretoria, S Africa.*

SMITHIES, Edwin Henry. b 23. **d** 60 **p** 61 Wakef. C of Ossett 60-68; Chap Highfields Gr Sch Ossett 60-62; Hd Master 62-73; L to Offic Dio Wakef 69-73; C of St Mary Beeston 73-79; Perm to Offic Dio Ripon 79-81; L to Offic from 81. *8 Noster View, Leeds, LS11 8QQ.* (Leeds 770154)

SMITHSON, Alan. b 36. Qu Coll Ox 2nd cl Cl Mods 60, BA (2nd cl Lit Hum) 62. Univ of Birm Dipl Th 64. Qu Coll Birm 62. **d** 64 **p** 65 Bradf. C of Ch Ch Skipton-in-Craven 64-68; St Mary Virg Ox 68-72; Chap Qu Coll Ox 69-72; Chap Reading Univ 72-77; Exam Chap to Bp of Ox 73-82; V of Bracknell Dio Ox from 77. *26 Park Road, Bracknell, Berks, RG12 2LU.* (Bracknell 23869)

SMITHSON, Michael John. b 47. Univ of Newc T BA 68. BD (Lon) 79. Trin Coll Bris 76. **d** 79 Lon **p** 80 Edmon for Lon. C of Ch Ch Mymms Barnet 79-81; Support & Publ Relns Sec for UCCF from 82. *45 St Leonards Road, Leicester, LE2 1WT.*

SMITHSON, Sidney George. b 48. Waterloo Univ Ont BA 71. Wycl Coll Tor MDiv 79. **d** 79 Bp Robinson for Hur **p** 80 Hur. C of St Geo Lon Dio Hur from 79. *227 Wharncliffe Road N, London, Ont, Canada, N6H 2B6.*

SMITS, Eric. **d** 61 **p** 62 York. C of Thornaby-on-Tees 61-66; R of Brotton Parva Dio York from 66. *Brotton Parva Rectory, Saltburn-by-Sea, Yorks.* (Brotton 275)

SMOUT, Michael John. b 37. St Pet Coll Ox BA (3rd cl Hist) 61. MA 75. Dipl Th 62. BD (Lon) 64. Lon Coll of Div 62. **d** 64 Warrington for Liv **p** 65 Liv. C of St Philemon w St Silas Toxt Pk 64-69; C of St Sav w St Cuthb Everton 69-70; V 74-78; Missr E Everton Group of Chs 70-74; R of St Mich Aughton Dio Liv from 78. *Rectory, Church Lane, Aughton, Ormskirk, Lancs.* (Aughton Green 423204)

SMURTHWAITE, William. b 25. **d** 57 **p** 58 Dur. C of St Simon S Shields 57-59; Chap Miss to Seamen Lagos 59-63; Trinid 63-65; Immingham and L to Offic Dio Linc 65-72; R of St Jas Cupar Dio St Andr from 72. *Rectory, Castlebank Road, Cupar, Fife.* (Cupar 2372)

SMYE, Frank Hasell. Trin Coll Tor 23, DD (*jure dig*) 44. McGill Univ BA 28. St Chad's Coll Regina, DD (*hon Causa*) 43. **d** 25 Montr **p** 27 Queb for Montr. Miss S Shore Montr 25-27; C of St Jo Evang Montr 28-34; Miss of Milestone 34-40; Can Missr Dio Qu'App 40-42; Warden of St Chad's Coll Regina 40-42; Perm to Offic (Col Cl Act) at All SS Fulham 42-43; R of Pro-Cathl and Dean of Calg 43-47; Exam Chap to Bp of Calg 43-47; V of St Luke New Kentish Town 47-55; V of H Trin Haverstock Hill 48-53; Hon C of St Anne City and Dio Tor from 59. *270 Gladstone Avenue, Toronto, Ont, Canada.*

SMYTH, Anthony Irwin. b 40. TCD BA (3rd cl Mod) 63, MA 66. Clifton Th Coll 64. **d** 66 **p** 67 Chich. C of St Geo Worthing 66-69; SAMS Dio Chile 70-75; Dir of Th Educn Valparaiso 72-75; Exam Chap to Bp of Chile 72-75; C of Woodley 75-80; V of St Ethelburga St Leonards-on-Sea Dio

Chich from 80. *31 St Saviour's Road, St Leonards-on-Sea, E Sussex, TN38 0AS.* (Hastings 421488)

SMYTH, Benjamin Pinkerton. Wycl Coll Tor LTh 31. **d** 27 Tor for Keew **p** 31 Tor. Miss at Baker Lake 27-30; C of All SS Tor 31-33; I of Innisfil 33-41; Alliston 41-45; Chap RCAF 41-45; I of Woodbridge 45-47; C of All SS Tor 47-49; R 49-53; Exam Chap to Bp of Arctic 52-55; Miss at Pangnirtung 53-56; R of Loughboro 57-63; Dunbarton 63-67; Hon C of Lindsey Dio Tor from 69. *41 Regent Street, Lindsay, Ont, Canada.*

SMYTH, Canon Charles Hugh Egerton. b 03. CCC Cam 1st cl Hist Trip pt i 23, BA (1st cl Hist Trip pt ii) 24, Thirlwall Med and Gladstone Pri 25, MA 28. Wells Th Coll 29. **d** 29 **p** 30 Derby. Fell of CCC Cam 25-32 and from 37; Tutor and Lect in Hist Harvard Univ USA 26-27; Univ Lect in Hist Cam 29-32 and 44-46; Perm to Offic at St Clem Barnsbury 33-34; C of St Sav Chelsea 34-36; St Giles w St Pet Cam 36-37; Dean of Chap CCC Cam 37-46; Hon Can of Derby and Hon Chap to Bp of Derby at Univ of Cam 38-46; Commiss Colom 38-47; Birkbeck Lect Trin Coll Cam 37-38; Select Pr Univ of Ox 41-43 and 65; Bp Paddock Lect in Gen Th Sem NY 53; Can of Westmr and R of St Marg Westmr 46-56; Proc Conv Westmr 50-56; Select Pr Univ of Cam 59-60; Hon Can of Linc Cathl 65-79; Can (Emer) from 79; Can (Emer) of Derby Cathl from 77. *Corpus Christi College, Cambridge.*

SMYTH, Francis George. b 20. Ridley Hall Cam 64. **d** 65 Warrington for York **p** 66 Liv. C of Ormskirk 65-70; V of Bicton Dio Lich from 70; Chap HM Pris Shrewsbury Dio Lich from 71. *Vicarage, Bicton, Shrewsbury.* (850260)

SMYTH, James Desmond. b 12. TCD BA 36, MA 39. **d** 36 **p** 37 Worc. C of Pershore 36-44; Priv Chap to Bp of Worc 42; L to Offic Dio Worc 44-46; V of Eldersfield 46-54; CF 51-58; R of Wappenham w Abthorpe and Slapton 58-77; L to Offic Dio Glouc from 77. *The Ferns, Vicarage Lane, Frampton-on-Severn, Glos.*

SMYTH, Canon John. b 08. Ch Coll Cam 2nd cl Hist Trip pt i 29, BA (3rd cl Histp Trip pt ii) 30, MA 34. Ridley Hall Cam 30. **d** 32 **p** 33 Worc. C of St John Dudley 32-34; Chipping Camden 34-35; Asst Master Malvern Coll and L to Offic Dio Worc 35-40; R of Elmsett and Dir of Relig Educn Dio St E 41-45; V of E and W Looe 45-51; St John Truro 51-64; Surr 49-64; Hon Can Truro 55-64; Can (Emer) from 64; Asst Sec Dioc Educn C'tte Dio Bris 64-68; R of Westonbirt w Lasborough and Chap Westonbirt Sch 68-75. *88a Albert Road South, Malvern, Worcs, WR14 1RR.*

SMYTH, Kenneth James. b 44. TCD BA 67, MA 72. **d** 68 **p** 69 Down. C of Bangor Abbey 68-71; Holywood 71-74; I of Gilnahirk Dio Down from 74. *237 Lower Braniel Road, Belfast, N Ireland, BT5 7QN.* (Belf 791748)

SMYTH, Thomas William. Univ of Tor BA 60, MA 63. Wycl Coll Tor BTh 63. **d** 64 Bp Snell for Tor **p** 65 Tor. C of St Marg N Tor 64-65; I of S Orillia 65-67; R of St Theodore Tor 67-70. *Elora, Ont., Canada.*

SMYTH, Trevor Cecil. b 45. Chich Th Coll 66. **d** 69 **p** 70 Ripon. C of H Trin Cookridge Adel 69-73; St Mary Virg Middleton 73-75; Felpham w Middleton 75-78; P-in-c of Ch Ch Wellington Dio Lich 78-80; V from 80. *Christ Church Vicarage, Wellington, Telford, Salop.* (Telford 3185)

SMYTH, William Ernest. b 23. Sarum Wells Th Coll 77. **d** 77 Plymouth for Ex **p** 78 Ex. C of St Mary Plympton 77-80; R of Beaford w Roborough and St Giles-in-the-Wood Dio Ex from 80. *Rectory, Beaford, Winkleigh, Devon, EX19 8NN.* (Beaford 213)

SMYTH-KING, Richard Stafford. Moore Th Coll Syd. **d** 78 Bp Cameron for Syd **p** 78 Syd. C of Narrabeen 78-79; Ch Ch Blacktown Dio Syd from 80. *61 Joseph Street, Blacktown, NSW, Australia 2148.* (621-7261)

SMYTHE, Canon Audley Hugh. St Pet Coll Ja. **d** 42 **p** 43 Ja. C of St Geo Kingston 43-47; R of Balaclava w Siloah 47-51; C of St Mich w Ch Ch Vineyard Town Kingston Dio Ja 51-52; R 52-62; Can of Ja from 71. *17 Belmont Road, Kingston 5, Jamaica, W Indies.* (093-66946)

SMYTHE, Harry Reynolds. Univ of Syd BA 45. Moore Th Coll Syd ACT ThL (1st cl), Hey Sharp Pri 44. St Pet Hall Ox BA (1st cl Th) and Sen Scho of Ch Ch Ox 48, MA and DPhil 51. **d** 51 **p** 53 Ex. C of Tavistock 51-53; St Mary Arches City and Dio Ex 53-54; Vice-Warden of St Jo Coll Morpeth 54-60; V of St Jas E St Kilda 60-70; Lect in NT Ridley Coll Melb 60-63; Tutor in Th Univ of Melb 60-69; Commiss Polyn 65-69; Dir Angl Centre Rome 69-81. *Address temp unknown.*

SMYTHE, Paul Rodney. b 05. Late Postmaster of Mert Coll Ox 2nd cl Cl Mods 26, BA (2nd cl Lit Hum) 28, MA 31, BD 37. Ripon Hall Ox 34. **d** 35 Liv **p** 36 Warrington for Liv. C of St Nich Blundellsands 35-37; St Giles Ox 37-39; Perm to Offic at Colwall 39-40; C-in-c of Gt Warley 40-41; C of H Trin Sutton Coldfield 41-44; PC (V from 68) of Horningsea Dio Ely from 44. *Vicarage, Horningsea, Cambridge, CB5 9JG.* (Cam 860392)

SMYTHE, Peter John Francis. Univ of Lon LLB 56. Wells Th Coll 56. **d** 58 Croydon for Cant **p** 59 Cant. C of Maidstone 58-62; V of St Jo Evang Barrow F 62-65; Billesdon w Rolleston and Goadby 65-71. *36 Rogers Hill, Worcester.*

SMYTHE, Ronald Ingoldsby Meade. b 25. Qu Coll Ox BA 46, MA 51. Ely Th Coll 51. **d** 54 **p** 55 Chelmsf. C of Wanstead 54-56; Min of All SS Eccles Distr Belhus Pk 56-62; V of Hatfield Heath 62-78; Select Pr Univ of Ox 63; Ed *Essex Churchman* 64-68; Sen Counsellor, Lect and Supervisor Westmr Pastoral Found from 78; Hon C of Writtle Dio Chelmsf from 78. *27 The Green, Writtle, Chelmsford, Essex.*

SNAITH, Bryan Charles. b 33. Univ of Wales BSc 55. St Mich Coll Llan 61. **d** 61 Llan **p** 62 Bp Hughes for Llan. C of Bargoed 61-62; Llanishen w Lisvane 62-71; Chap Teesside Industr Miss Dur 71-77; C of Stone and of Chaddesley Corbett 77-81; Industr Chap Kidderminster 77-81; Colchester from 81; Team V of St Leon w St Mary Magd and St Steph Colchester Dio Chelmsf from 81. *2 Colvin Close, Colchester, Essex, CO3 4BS.* (0206 47744)

SNAPE, Bernard Reginald Roy. b 08. OBE (Mil) 56. Sarum Th Coll 69. **d** 69 **p** 70 Portsm. C of W Leigh Conv Distr Havant 69-71; V of Arreton 71-75; Perm to Offic Dio Portsm from 76. *Church House, Whippingham, IW.*

SNAPE, Harry. b 21. Qu Coll Birm 76. **d** 78 **p** 79 Birm. C of Highters Heath Dio Birm from 78. *4 Mulberry Drive, St Agnes Road, Moseley, Birmingham, B13.*

SNAPE, Henry Currie. b 02. CCC Ox 2nd cl Cl Mods 22, BA (3rd cl Lit Hum) 24, MA 31, Dipl Th 32. Ripon Hall Ox. **d** 32 **p** 33 Newc T. C of H Sav Priory Tynemouth 32-34; Rothbury 34-36; PC of Clay Cross 36-38; R of Skelton (w Hutton in the Forest from 45) 38-51; V of Whalley 51-67; Chap Calderstones Hosp 51-67; Surr 61-67. *Corner House, Bampton, Oxford.* (Bampton Castle 850338)

SNASDELL, Antony John. b 40. St Chad's Coll Dur BA 63, Dipl Th 65. **d** 65 **p** 66 Linc. C of Boston 65-70; Worksop Priory Dio Southw from 70. *31 Victoria Road, Worksop.* (Worksop 2180)

SNEARY, Michael William. b 38. Open Univ BA 81. Ely Th Coll 62. **d** 64 **p** 65 Chelmsf. C of Loughton 64-69; Youth Chap Dio Chelmsf 69-71; C of Gt Waltham 71-72; Asst Master Bedfords Pk Sch 72-75; Ivybridge Sch 75-77; Coombe Dean Sch Plymouth from 77. *Coombe Dean School, Plymouth, Devon.*

SNEATH, Canon Sidney Dennis. b 23. Univ of Leeds BA 50. Bps' Coll Cheshunt 50. **d** 52 **p** 53 Cov. C of St Mary Virg Nuneaton 52-59; Min of Camp Hill Eccles Distr w Galley Common Dio Cov 59-68; V from 68; Hon Can Cov Cathl from 80. *Vicarage, Edinburgh Road, Camphill Estate, Nuneaton, Warws.* (Chapel End 392523)

SNELGAR, Douglas John. DSC and Men in Disp 45. Trin Hall Cam BA 48, MA 53. Westcott Ho Cam. **d** 50 **p** 51 Portsm. C of St Pet and St Paul Fareham 50-53; C of St Cath and of H Trin Ventnor 53-57; V of Steep Dio Portsm from 57. *Steep Vicarage, Petersfield, Hants.* (Petersfield 4282)

✠ **SNELGROVE, Right Rev Donald George.** b 25. TD 72. Qu Coll Cam BA 48, MA 53. Ridley Hall,Cam. **d** 50 **p** 51 Lon. C of St Thos Oakwood 50-53; Hatch End 53-56; V of Dronfield w Unstone 56-62; CF (TA) 60-73; V of Hessle 63-70; RD of Kingston-upon-Hull 67-70; Can and Preb of York Minster 69-81; Proc Conv York from 69; R of Cherry Burton 70-78; Archd of E Riding 70-81; Cons Ld Bp Suffr of Hull in York Minster 28 May 81 Abp of York; Bps of Southw, Blackb, Ripon, Man, Sheff, Bradf, Derby and Bloemf; Bps Suffr of Stockport, Selby, Sherwood, Hulme, Whitby, Doncaster, Jarrow, Grimsby, Grantham and Plymouth; and others. *Hullen House, Woodfield Lane, Hessle, N Humb, HU13 0ES.* (Hull 649019)

SNELGROVE, Harold Beaconsfield. b 04. Bps' Coll Cheshunt 47. **d** 50 **p** 51 Sarum. C of Sturminster Newton 50-53; CF 53-56; R of Kington Magna (w Buckhorn-Weston from 58) 56-74; C-in-c of Buckhorn-Weston 56-58. *35 Shreen Way, Gillingham, Dorset.*

SNELL, (Antony) Alfred. Late Scho of New Coll Ox 22, 1st cl Cl Mods 24, Jun LXX Pri 25, BA (2nd cl Lit Hum) and Liddon Stud 26, 2nd cl Th 27, MA 29. St Steph Ho Ox 26. M SSM 34. **d** 28 **p** 29 Portsm. C of St Jo Bapt Rudmore 28-31; Tutor Kelham Th Coll 31-46; and 53-56; Perm to Offic Dio Southw 32-46; Tutor St Mich Ho Crafers and Perm to Offic Dio Adel 47-52 and 56-79; Perm to Offic Dio C & Goulb from 79. *Box 421, Woden, ACT, Australia 2606.*

SNELL, Ven Basil Clark. b 07. Qu Coll Cam 2nd cl Hist Trip pt i 27, BA (3rd cl Hist Trip pt ii) 28, MA 32. Chich Th Coll 32. **d** 33 **p** 34 Carl. C of Crosthwaite 33-35; Chap Aldenham Sch 35-40; Chap Loretto Sch 40-46; R of Tattingstone 46-55; Dir and Sec of Relig Educn Dio St E and Insp of Schs Dio St E 47-58; Can Res of St E 55-58; Proc Conv St E 55-58; Archd of Bedford 58-62; Dir of Relig Educn Dio St Alb 58-68; Archd of St Alb 62-73; Archd (Emer) from 73. *Glebe Cottage, Melbourn, Royston, Herts.*

✠ **SNELL, Right Rev Geoffrey Stuart.** b 20. St Pet Coll Ox BA (2nd cl Phil, Pol and Econ) 50, MA 53. Called to Bar Inner Temple 57. Lon Coll of Div 61. **d** 62 Willesden for Lon **p** 62 Lon. C of Em Northwood 62-63; Fell of St Aug Coll Cant 63-75; Chap HM Pris Cant 63-66; Dir Chr Org Research and Adv Trust (UK) 68-75; and (Afr) 75-77; Cons Ld Bp Suffr of Croydon in Cant Cathl 1 Nov 77 by Abp of Cant; Bps of Guildf and Roch; Bps Suff of Dover, Maidstone and Stockport; and Bps Warner, Cragg and Howe; and others. *52 Selhurst Road, South Norwood, SE25 5QD.* (01-689 0767)

✠ **SNELL, Right Rev George Boyd.** Trin Coll Tor BA 29, MA 30, PhD 37, DD 48. Wycl Coll Tor Hon DD 59. Hur Coll Hon DD 68. **d** 31 Tor **p** 32 Niag for Tor. C of St Mich AA Tor 31-39; R 40-48; Priv Chap to Bp of Tor 45-48; R of Pro-Cathl Calg and Dean of Calg 48-51; Exam Chap to Bp of Calg 48-51; R of St Clem Eglinton Tor 51-56; Archd of Tor 53-56; Exam Chap to Bp of Tor 53-55; Cons Ld Bp Suffr of Tor in St Jas Cathl Tor 25 Jan 56 by Abp of Alg; Bps of Tor; Niag; Ont; Ott; Moos; Arctic; W New York; and Erie; Bp Suffr of Hur; Asst Bp of Hur; Abp Renison; and Bps Beverley, Wells, White and Zielinsky; elected Bp Coadj of Tor 59; Apptd Bp of Tor 66; res 72. *1210 Glen Road, Mississauga, Ont., Canada.*

SNELL, Guy Stuart. b 49. Univ of W Ont BMin 78. Hur Coll Lon 76. **d** 78 Bp Parke-Taylor for Koot. C of Kelowna Dio Koot from 78. *608 Sutherland Avenue, Kelowna, BC, Canada, ViY 5X1.*

SNELL, Canon Herbert Bruce. **d** 39 **p** 40 Ont. Min of N Frontenac w N Addington 39-40; Kitley 40-41; St Mary Virg Tor 41-43; St Chad Tor 43-44; I of Agincourt 44-48; R of St Luke Tor 48-54; St Aid 54-70; Can of Tor 58-70; Archd of Tor E 65-70; R of St Marg New Tor 70-79; Can of Tor from 72. *42 Hilldowntree Road, Islington, Ont, Canada M9A 2Z8.*

SNELL, James Osborne. b 13. Selw Coll Cam BA 35, MA 39. Ely Th Coll 35. **d** 36 **p** 37 Ox. C of Summertown 36-38; Fenny Stratford 38-43; Rugeley 43-47; V of Dawley Parva 47-52; Stantonbury w New Bradwell 52-61; C-in-c of Gt Linford 55-61; R of St Pet and St Paul Charlton Dover 61-69; H Trin Ramsgate 69-78; Perm to Offic Dio Cant from 79. *Small Downs, Sea Street, St Margaret's Bay, Dover, Kent, CT15 6DG.* (Dover 852210)

SNELL, Robert Stanley. St Francis Coll Brisb ACT ThL 62. **d** 61 **p** 63 Brisb. C of St Mary Redcliffe 62-63; St Andr Indooroopilly Brisb 63-66; St Paul Ipswich 66-67; R of Millmerran 67-73; Perm to Offic Dio Brisb from 74. *Lot 42, Summer Street, Deception Bay, Queensland, Australia 4508.* (203 1727)

SNELL, William Graham Brooking. b 14. Lon Coll of Div 36. **d** 39 **p** 40 Lich. C of Ch Ch Burton-on-Trent 39-41; St Pet Rushden 41-46; St Paul W Ealing 46-48; St Mark (in c of St Barn) Cheltm 48-51; V of Beckford w Ashton-under-Hill 51-54; St Polycarp Everton 54-57; R of Ashby w Oby Thurne and Clippesby 57-79. *Arden, Main Road, Rollesby, Gt Yarmouth, NR29 5EH.*

SNELLGROVE, Frederic Mortimer. b 06. Univ of Lon BSc 28. Ridley Hall Cam 28. **d** 29 **p** 30 S'wark. C of St Luke W Norwood 29-32; St Pet Harrogate 32-33; Tutor Fourah Bay Coll 33-36; Chap to Bp of Sier L 35-36; C of St John Sparkhill 36-40; V of H Trin Knaresborough 40-45; CMS Miss Freetown 45-47; Tutor Fourah Bay Coll and Sec CMS Dio Sier L 47-51; V of St Andr Lower Streatham 51-60; Commiss Sier L 55-70; R of Bergh Apton w Yelverton 60-72. *64 Rugby Road, Worthing, Sussex, BN11 5NB.*

SNELLING, Brian. b 40. Dipl Th (Lon) 68. Oak Hill Th Coll 66. **d** 69 **p** 70 Ox. C of St Paul Slough 69-72; All SS Hoole 72-76; V of Millbrook 76-80; St Luke Hackney Dio Lon from 80. *23 Cassland Road, E9 7AL.* (01-985 2263)

SNELLING, Ven Robert Wilfred. **d** 60 **p** 61 Niag. I of Hannon 60-63; C of St Jude Oakville 65-68; R of Glanford 68-73; Grace Ch St Cath Dio Niag from 73; Exam Chap to Bp of Niag from 73; Archd of Linc from 77. *7 Spruce Street, St Catharines's, Ont., Canada.* (416-685 7533)

SNELLING, Stanley Alfred. b 03. Lich Th Coll 54. **d** 55 **p** 56 St E. C of Cathl Par Bury St E 55-57; V of Thurston 57-62; Furneux Pelham w Stocking Pelham 62-76. *Old School House, Furneux Pelham, Buntingford, Herts.* (Brent Pelham 418)

SNELSON, William Thomas. b 45. Ex Coll Ox BA 67. Fitzw Coll Cam BA 69, MA 75. Westcott Ho Cam 67. **d** 69 Dorking for Guildf **p** 70 Guildf. C of Godalming 69-72; Leeds 72-75; V of Chapel Allerton 75-81; Bardsey w E Keswick Dio Ripon from 81. *Vicarage, Bardsey, Leeds, LS17 9DG.* (Collingham Bridge 72243)

SNEYD, Sidney Colin. b 27. St Aid Coll 67. **d** 69 **p** 70 Ches. C of Claughton w Grange 69-72; Walsall 72-75; CMS Area Sec Dios Heref and Glouc 75-81; V of Weobley w Sarnesfield Dio Heref from 81; P-in-c of Norton Canon Dio Heref from 81; Letton w Staunton-on-Wye, Byford, Mansel Gamage and Mornington-on-Wye Dio Heref from 81. *Weobley Vicarage, Hereford.* (Weobley 415)

SNIDER, Canon Kenneth Cober. Em Coll Sktn. **d** 67 **p** 68 Yukon. R of St Paul Dawson City 67-78; Can of Yukon from 75; R of Ch Ch Cathl Whitehouse Dio Yukon from 78. *Box 4489, Whitehorse, Yukon, Canada.* (403-667 2392)

SNOOK, Eric Quintin. b 03. Richmond Coll 26. **d** and **p** 72 Portsm. C of Locks Heath Dio Portsm from 72. *5 Raley Road, Locks Heath, Southampton, SO3 6PA.*

SNOOK, Walter Currie. b 39. Dipl Th (Lon) 66. Tyndale Hall Bris 64. **d** 67 Nor **p** 68 Lynn for Nor. C of Cromer 67-70; Macclesfield 70-74; R of Postwick Dio Nor from 74. *Postwick Rectory, Norwich, NR13 5HL.* (Norwich 33420)

SNOW, Alexander Elijah. **d** 66 **p** 67 Newfld. C of Fogo 66-67; Flower's Cove 67-68; I of Kings Cove 69-71; R of Bay L'Argent 71-76. *11 Steer Street, St John's, Newfoundland, Canada.*

SNOW, Arthur Cluney. K Coll NS. **d** 50 **p** 51 NS. C of Maitland 50-55; I of Port Wallis 55-61; R of Dartmouth 61. *60 Raymor Drive, Dartmouth, NS, Canada.* (434-5186)

SNOW, Ven Brian. b 22. **d** 65 **p** 66 Cork. C of H Trin w St Paul St Pet and St Mary Shandon Cork 65-67; Dun Laoghaire 67-72; Hon Cler V of Ch Ch Cathl Dub from 69; I of Rathkeale 72-77; Kilmallock U Dio Lim from 77; Archd of Lim from 81. *Rectory, Kilmallock, Co Limerick, Irish Republic.* (Kilmallock 334)

SNOW, Campbell Martin Spencer. b 35. Roch Th Coll 65. **d** 67 **p** 68 Cant. C of Dover 67-72; Birchington w Acol 72-74; V of Reculver 74-80; New Addington Dio Cant from 80. *Vicarage, Cleves Crescent, New Addington, Croydon, CR0 0DL.* (Lodge Hill 45588)

SNOW, Glyn Francis. b 53. St Chad's Coll Dur BA 74. St Steph Ho Ox 76. **d** 78 **p** 79 Mon. C of Pontnewynydd Dio Mon from 78. *All Saints House, Mount Pleasant, Pontnewynydd, Pontypool, Gwent.*

SNOW, Peter David. St Jo Coll Cam 3rd cl Th Trip pt i 60, BA (3rd cl Th Trip pt ii) 62, MA 66. Ridley Hall, Cam 62. **d** 64 **p** 65 Birm. C of Kingshurst 64-66. *76 Humphrey Road, Santa Barbara, Calif, USA.*

SNOW, Peter Normington. b 23. St Jo Coll Ox BA (2nd cl Th) 48, MA 52. Ely Th Coll. **d** 50 **p** 51 Lich. C of Lower Gornal 50-52; Solihull 52-56; V of All SS Emscote Warwick Dio Cov from 56; RD of Warw 67-77. *All Saints' Vicarage, Warwick.* (Warwick 492073)

SNOW, Canon Philip. b 13. Late Exhib of Ch Ch Ox 2nd cl Cl Mods 35, BA (2nd cl Lit Hum) 37, 2nd cl Th 38, MA 40. Cudd Coll 38. **d** 39 **p** 40 York. C of Hornsea w Goxhill 39-43; Wakef Cathl 43-46; V of Chippenham w Tytherton Lucas (and St Pet Lowden 46-55) 46-78; Chap to Chippenham Hosps 49-78; Hon Chap to Bp of Bris 53-64; Hon Can of Bris Cathl 58-78; Can (Emer) from 78. *2 Horwood Close, Headington, Oxford, OX3 7RF.* (Oxford 68407)

SNOW, William George Sinclair. b 08. Univ of Edin MA (2nd cl Hist) and Elliott Pri 31, PhD 40. Edin Th Coll 32. **d** 33 **p** 34 Glas. C of St John Dumfries 33-35; P-in-c of St Gabr Govan 35-39; R of St Mungo Alexandria 39-42; V of Elmley Castle w Bricklehampton 42-52; Bognor 52-76; Surr 52-76; Hon C of Rustington Dio Chich from 79. *25 Merton Avenue, Rustington, W Sussex.* (Rustington 71610)

SNOWDEN, Canon William Harvey. b 13. Univ Coll Dur BA and LTh 36, MA 39. Qu Coll Birm 32. **d** 36 **p** 37 Southw. C of St Mary Virg Bulwell 36-38; Edwinstowe 38-48; CF (EC) 43-47; Hon CF from 47; V of Laxton w Moorhouse 48-54; St Lawr Mansfield 54-61; N and S Muskham 61-78; R of Cromwell 61-78; RD of Norwell 65-78; Hon Can of Southw Cathl 71-78; Can (Emer) from 78; Surr from 75; C-in-c of Caunton 76-78; Perm to Offic Dio Southw from 79. *Grange Lodge, Caunton, Newark, Notts, NG23 6AB.* (Caunton 382)

SNOWBALL, Michael Sydney. b 44. Univ of Dur BA 70, MA 72. St Jo Coll Dur Dipl Th 72. **d** 72 Bp Skelton for Dur **p** 73 Dur. C of St Pet Stockton 72-75; St Nich Dunston 75-78; St John (in c of St Herbert) Darlington 78-81; V of St Aid Chilton Dio Dur from 81. *Vicarage, New South View, Chilton, Durham.* (Bp Auckld 720243)

SNOWDEN, John Ernest William. **d** 33 **p** 35 Qu'App. C of Fleming 34-35; I of Wawota 35-41; Grenfell 41-44; V of Gibson's Landing 44-46; R of St Martin N Vanc 46-51; V of Sorrento 51-52; Okanagan Miss 52-65. *373 Battle Street, Kamloops, BC, Canada.*

✠ **SNOWDEN, Right Rev John Samuel Philip.** Angl Th Coll Vanc LTh 51. **d** 51 **p** 52 Koot. C of Kaslo-Kokanee 51-53; Oak Bay 53-57; Nanaimo 57-60; I of St Timothy Vanc 60-65; C of Ch Ch Cathl Vanc 65-67; R of St Timothy 67-71; Dean and R of St Paul's Cathl Ch Kamloops 71-74; Dom Chap to Bp of Carib 71-73; Cons Ld Bp of Carib at Kamloops Sen Secondary Auditorium 20 Dec 74 by Bp of Yukon (Actg Metrop of Prov of BC) and Abps E W Scott (Primate) and G P Gower; Bps of Caled, Koot, BC and Edmon; Vice-Pres Canad Coun of Chs from 80. *133 West Battle Street, Kamloops, BC, Canada.*

SNOWSELL, Raymond Ernest Elijah. b 15. Wycl Hall Ox 67. **d** 68 **p** 69 Leic. C of St Pet w St Hilda 68-71; V of Oaks-in-Charnwood (w Copt Oak from 79) 71-80. *Charnwood, Castle Street, Keinton Mandeville, Somerton, Somt, TA11 6DX.*

SNYMAN, Very Rev Robin Roy. St Paul's Coll Grahmstn 54. LTh (S Afr) 57. **d** 57 **p** 58 Grahmstn. C of St Sav E Lon 57-60; St Mich and St Geo Cathl Grahmstn 60-64; Heston Middx 65-66; R of Good Shepherd E Lon 66-68; Chap Rhodes Univ 68-71; R of Germiston 71-77; Dean and R of St Cypr Cathl Kimberley Dio Kimb from 78. *Deanery, Park Road, Kimberley, CP, S Africa.* (Kimb 5697)

SO, Athanasius Yong-p'ill. St Mich Sem Oryudong. **d** 68 **p** 70 Taejon. P Dio Taejon. *6 Dong, 1 Danzi, Hyo Ja Dong Apt, Chonju, Korea.*

SO, Peter Pyongo. b 38. Univ of Hanyang Seoul. St Mich Coll Seoul 67. **d** and **p** 71 Taejon. P Dio Taejon. *639 Kyodong, Eusong, Ch'ungbuk, Korea.*

SOADY, Francis Benney. b 1894. TCD BA 21, MA 24. **d** 21 **p** 22 Cash. C of Clonmel 21-24; St Luke Ramsgate 24-26; St Paul Rusthall 26-32; V of Tamerton Foliott 32-45; R of Cheriton Bishop 45-51; Port Isaac 51-54; V of Millbrook 54-64. *Tower Cottage, Cremyll, Torpoint, PL10 1HY.* (Plymouth 822396)

SOAR, Canon Reginald Herbert. b 05. Univ of Lon BSc (2nd cl Chem) 26. K Coll Lon Plumptre Pri 30. **d** 31 **p** 32 Roch. C of St Luke Bromley Common 31-34; Min of St Aug Peel Distr Bromley Common 34-39; V of St Jo Evang Bexley 39-44; Wateringbury 44-62; CF (R of O) from 39; Hon Can of Roch 53-71; Can (Emer) from 71; Dir of Relig Educn Dio Roch 57-65; V of St Mary Virg Platt 62-71; C-in-c of Trottiscliffe 64-66. *Spray's Bridge, Sedlescombe, Battle, Sussex.* (Hastings 751172)

SOARES, Alan Deas. St Francis Coll Brisb ACT ThL (2nd cl) 57. **d** 57 Rockptn **p** 59 Brisb for Rockptn. C of N Rockptn 57-59; V of Winton 59-63; R of Raymond Terrace 63-70; Perm to Offic Dio Brisb from 70. *6 Jupetta Street, Aspley, Queensland, Australia 4034.* (263 2005)

SOBEY, Haydn Norman. b 28. Late Sen Scho of St D Coll Lamp BA 52. Qu Coll Cam BA 54, MA 58. St Mich Coll Llan 54. **d** 55 **p** 56 Llan. C of Port Talbot 55-58; C of Trinid Cathl 58-60; P-in-c of Siparia 60-65; Prin St Steph Coll Princes Town Trinid 67-78; Hon Can of Trinid 71-78; V of St Agnes Port Talbot Dio Llan from 78. *St Agnes Vicarage, Ynys Street, Port Talbot, W Glam, SA13 1YW.*

✠ **SOBUKWE, Right Rev Ernest Archibald.** St Pet Coll Rosettenville. **d** 58 **p** 60 Geo. P Dio Geo 58-69; Can of St John's from 69; Cons Ld Bp Suffr of St John's in St Mary Virg Cathl Johann 16 Nov 69 By Abp of Capetn; Bps of Bloemf, Damar, Geo, Grahmstn, Johann, Kimb K, Natal, St John's, Swaz, Zulu, and others; Asst Bp of Grahmstn from 79; P-in-c of St Barn Alice and Chap Fort Hare Univ from 79. *Box 336, Alice 5700, CP, S Africa.*

SODIPE, Samson Sunday Olusanya. b 43. Univ of Ibad BA 68, Univ of Ox BA 73. Wycl Hall Ox 70. **d** 73 **p** 74 Lagos. P Dio Lagos. *Cathedral Church of Christ, Lagos, Nigeria.* (26542)

SODIPE, Stephen Akiwumi. Fourah Bay Coll **d** 54 **p** 55 Lagos. P Dio Lagos 53-59. *c/o St Peter's Vicarage, Ake, Abeokuta, Nigeria.*

SODOR AND MAN, Lord Bishop of. *See* Nicholls, Right Rev Vernon Sampson.

SOGA, Christopher Philip Mayamezeli. b 24. St Bede's Coll Umtata 72. **d** 73 Grahmstn **p** 74 St John's. O of Ethiopia. C of St Bart's Miss Dio St John's from 74. *St Bartholomew's Mission, PO Askheaton 5413, Transkei, S Africa.*

SOK, Mark Kyun-u. St Mich Sem Oryudong. **d** 67 **p** 68 Taejon. P Dio Taejon. *237 Wonsungsong, Chonan 330, Chungnam, Korea.*

SOKALE, Emmanuel Oluyemi Jokotade. b 26. Fourah Bay Coll Freetown Sier L BA 60. **d** 69 **p** 70 Ibad. P Dio Ibad. *Aiyedade Grammar School, Box 29, Ikire, via Ibadan, Nigeria.*

SOKEFUN, Gabriel Babafunmilola. b 39. Im Coll Ibad BA 68. **d** 70 **p** 71 Lag. P Dio Lagos 70-73. *Immanuel College, Ibadan, Nigeria.*

SOKEFUN, Joseph Akinbowale. **d** 41 **p** 43 Lagos. P Dio Lagos 41-52; Dio Ibad from 52; Hon Can of Ibad 64-70. *Olana, Ibadan, Nigeria.*

SOKHELA, Edmund Mcitheka. St Bede's Coll Umtata, 60. **d** 61 **p** 62 Natal. P Dio Natal 62-70. *c/o Dumakude Store, PO Dannhauser, Natal, S Africa.*

SOLOMON, Alexander Mackertich. b 14. Serampore Coll LTh (2nd cl) 32, BD 34. St Aug Coll Cant 36. **d** 38 **p** 39 S'wark. C of St Geo Camberwell 38-42; Chap at Asansol 42-45; Chap at Victoria and Dow Hill Schs Kurseong Dio Calc 45-50 and 51-53; Actg C of St Jas L Westminster Lon 50-51; C of Fletton 53-55; C-in-c of St Nich Perivale 55-58; R of St Geo-in-the-E (w St Paul Dock Str from 71) Stepney 58-79; C-in-c of St Paul Dock Str w St Mark Whitechapel 68-71; C of W Tarring 79-80. *11 Bath Road, Worthing, BN11 3NU.* (Worthing 207820)

SOLOMON, Arthur Creagh. b 33. ACT ThL Ch Coll Hobart. **d** 62 **p** 63 Tas. C of St Steph Hobart 62-63; Smithton 63-64; R of Avoca-Fingal 64-67; C of St Mildred Addiscombe 67-68; on Study Leave 68-69; Chap Pierrepont Sch Frensham 69-72; R of Clifton Camville w Chilcote Dio Lich from 72; Thorpe Constantine Dio Lich from 72. *Clifton Camville Rectory, Tamworth, Staffs.* (Clifton Camville 257)

SOLOMON, George Harry Frederick. **d** 77 Geo. C of St Luke Swellendam Dio Geo from 77. *c/o PO Box 169, Swellendam, CP, S Africa 6740.*

SOLOMON, Gerald Tankerville Norris. b 12. Univ of Lon BA (2nd cl Phil) 36. Sarum Th Coll 37. **d** 39 **p** 40 Sarum. C of Broadstone 39-42; CF 42-63; R of Corsley w Chapmanslade 63-78. *The Old Forge, Hindon, Salisbury, Wilts, SP3 6DR.* (Hindon 255)

SOLOMONA, Seme Luate. Bp Gwynne Coll Mundri 61. **d** 64 Bp Dotiro for Sudan **p** 68 Sudan. P Dio Sudan 64-76; Provost of All SS Cathl Juba 72-76. *Box 110, Juba, Sudan.*

SOLTAU, Bernard Alick. b 08. Trin Coll Ox BA 32, MA 50. St Bonif Coll Warm. **d** 50 **p** 51 Guildf. Asst Chap St John's Sch Leatherhead and L to Offic Dio Guildf 50-53; PC (V from 68) of Stubbings Dio Ox from 53. *Stubbings Vicarage, Henley Road, Maidenhead, Berks.* (Littlewick Green 2966)

SOMAILI, Daudi. St Cypr Th Coll Tunduru 50. **d** 52 **p** 55 Masasi. P Dio Masasi 52-59; Dio Zanz 59-60; Dio Masasi from 60. *USPG, Mindu, Tanzania.*

SOMERS-EDGAR, Carl John. b 46. Univ of Otago BA 69. St Steph Ho Ox 72. **d** 75 Willesden for Lon **p** 76 Lon. C of Northwood 75-79; All SS St Marylebone Dio Lon from 79. *c/o All Saints Vicarage, Margaret Street, W1N 8JQ.*

SOMERS-SMITH, Leslie John. b 17. **d** 61 Gippsld **p** 63 River. C of Korumburra 61-62; Stratford 62-63; P-in-c of Urana 63-64; R of Dunolly 64-70; Perm to Offic Dio Chich 70-71; Dio Win from 72; C of Monmouth 71-72. *6 Broadwater Road, Worthing, W Sussex, BN14 8AE.*

SOMERVILLE, Francis Marshall. St Jo Coll Morpeth 61. **d** 63 **p** 64 Graft. C of Tweed Heads 63-65; R of Eureka 65-70; Chap Prince Henry and Caulfield Hosps Dio Melb from 70. *17 Carawatha Avenue, Doncaster, Vic, Australia 3108.* (03-84 85231)

SOMERVILLE, John Arthur Lewis. Ja Th Coll. **d** 11 **p** 12 Ja. C of Vaughansfield 11-12 and associated stations in Ja Dio 12-14; R of Pedro Plains 14-16; Woburn Lawn and Trinity Ville 16-20; Siloah 20-26; Old Harbour 26-29; Buff Bay 29-33; Montpelier w Chich 33-45; Bog Walk and Linstead 45-50; Guy's Hill 50-54; P-in-c of The Grove 54-56. *Farquharson House, Cross Roads, Jamaica, W Indies.*

SOMERVILLE, John William Kenneth. b 38. St D Coll Lamp 60. **d** 63 **p** 64 St A. C of Rhosllanerchrugog 63-67; Llangystennin 67-70; V of Gorsedd (w Brynford and Ysceifiog from 77) Dio St A from 70. *Vicarage, Gorsedd, Holywell, Clwyd,* (Holywell 711675)

✠ **SOMERVILLE, Most Rev Thomas David.** Univ of BC BA 37. Angl Th Coll BC LTh 39, BD 51, Hon DD 69. **d** 39 **p** 40 New Westmr. C of St Mary Kerrisdale Vanc 39-40; I of Princeton 40-44; Sardis w Rosedale 44-49; C of St Jas Vanc 49-52; R 52-60; Can of New Westmr 57-69; Dean of Residence Angl Th Coll Vanc 60-65; Gen Sec Bd Relig Educn Gen Synod Angl Ch Canada 65-66; Dir of Planning and Research 66-69; Cons Bp Coadj of New Westmr in Vanc Cathl 26 Jan 69 by Abp of BC; Bp of Yukon; Bp Suffr of Tor; and Abp Sexton; Apptd Ld Bp of New Westmr 71; res 80; Elected Abp and Metrop of Prov of BC 75; res 80; Chap Vanc Sch of Th from 81. *3102-1011 Beach Avenue, Vancouver, BC, V6E 1T8, Canada.*

SOMES, Arthur Marston. b 1897. **d** 46 **p** 47 Ex. C of Meeth w Huish 46-48; R of Newton St Petrock w Abbots Bickington and Bulkworthy 48-49; Monk Okehampton w Broadwood Kelly 49-54; V of Gt w L Oakley 54-67. *Old Rectory, Little Oakley, Corby, Northants, NN18 8HA.* (0536-742423)

SOMHLAHLO, Isaiah. St Bede's Th Coll Umtata. **d** 48 **p** 50 St Jo Kaffr. P Dio St Jo Kaffr 48-65; L to Offic Dio St John's from 65. *Mgobozi, PO Kentani, Transkei, S Africa.*

SOMKENCE, Ven Oliver. MBE 61. St Jo Coll Lusaka, 51. **d** 53 **p** 54 Matab. P Dio Matab 53-63; Hon Can of Matab from 62; P-in-c of W Commonage Bulawayo 63-66; St Patr Miss Gwelo 66-68; Archd of Bembesi 63-66; Gwelo 66-78; Archd (Emer) from 78; L to Offic Dio Matab from 78. *c/o Box 2087, Bulawayo, Zimbabwe.* (02130)

SOMNER, Ernest William. b 1889. Edin Th Coll 25. **d** 27 Barrow-F for Carl **p** 28 Carl. C of St Mary Ulverston 27-29; Gt Broughton (in c of St Columba Broughton Moor) 29-34;

V of Gilsland w Over Denton 34-42; St Jo Bapt Upperby Carl 42-49; Rocliffe w Cargo 49-58; L to Offic Dio Carl from 59. *Rocliffe Cottage, Ambleside Road, Windermere, Westmd.* (Windermere 2504)

SONDIYAZI, Goodwin Ngwenyana. **d** 68 **p** 69 Grahmstn. C of St Mich AA Herschel 68-81; R of St Phil City and Dio Grahmstn from 81. *Box 107, Grahamstown 6140, CP, S Africa.*

SONG, James. b 32. Lon Coll of Div 57. **d** 60 **p** 61 Guildf. C of Virginia Water 60-63; St Paul Portman Square St Marylebone 63-66; PC of Matlock Bath 66-69; V 69-76; St Jo Bapt Woking Dio Guildf from 76. *St John's Vicarage, Woking, Surrey, GU21 1RQ.* (Woking 61253)

SONGELWA, Jacob Mabalarana. St Bede's Coll Umtata, 64. **d** 64 **p** 65 St John's. P Dio St John's 64-78. *Box 233, Umtata, Transkei, S Africa.*

SONJE, Gerard. St Cypr Th Coll Tunduru, 30. **d** 32 **p** 37 Masasi. Miss Dio Masasi 32-72. *PO Chuingutwa, Tanzania.*

SONN, Peter Graham Douglas. St Paul's Coll Grahmstn. **d** 64 Capetn for Johann **p** 65 Johann. C of Parkview 64-66; Krugersdorp 66-70; R of Salt River 70-76; Perm to Offic Dio Capetn from 76. *10 Lovers Walk, Rondebosch, CP, S Africa.* (69-5783)

SONNERS, Nat Lewis. **d** 55 **p** 63 Tas. C of Moonah 55-64; P-in-c of Ross 64-69; R of Oatlands 69-73; Actg R Geeveston Dio Tas from 74. *21 Kendall Street, East Moonah, Tasmania 7009.* (002-28 2168)

SONTI, Garlic Weaver Hlathi. b 38. **d** and **p** 74 Les. P Dio Les. *PO Box MS 127, Maseru, Lesotho, S Africa.*

SOO, Mishek. b 36. **d** 74 Mt Kenya **p**75 Mt Kenya E. P Dio Mt Kenya E. *Nyangwa Parish, Box 158, Embu, Kenya.*

SOO, Thomas. b 41. Chinese Univ of Hong Kong BA 69. Trin Coll Tor 78. **d** 78 Hong. d Dio Hong. *Chung Chi College, Shatin, NT, Hong Kong.*

SOOLI, Alikupasadi. b 47. **d** 77 Nam. d Dio Nam. *Kasawo Church of Uganda, PO Box 21002, Kasawo, Uganda.*

SOON, Soo Kee. b 48. Univ of Tas BA 74. **d** 76 **p** 77 Sing. C of St John w St Marg Sing 76-77; St Hilda Katong City and Dio Sing from 77. *41 Ceylon Road, Singapore 15.*

SOPAMANA, Richard. b 45. Bp Patteson Th Centre Kohimarama 71. **d** 74 Melan **p** 74 Ysabel. P Dio Ysabel. *Russell Island, Santa Ysabel, Solomon Islands.*

SOPER, Brian Malcolm. b 31. Univ of Lon BSc 53. Mansfield Coll Ox. Ripon Hall, Ox. **d** 63 **p** 64 Roch. C of St Mary Virg Platt 63-72; Chap K Sch Roch 64-72; Repton Sch Derby 72-75; Bennett Mem Sch Tunbridge Wells from 75; Perm to Offic Dio Can from 79. *Mount le Hoe, Benenden, Kent, TN17 4BW.* (Rolvenden 583)

SORENSEN, Arthur Frank. b 29. SOC 66. **d** 69 **p** 70 Chich. C of Broadwater Down 69-71; P-in-c of Shenley 72-75; R of Loughton (w Bradwell to 73) 72-75; P-in-c of Thornborough 75-77; Nash w Thornton, Beachampton (and Thornborough from 77) Dio Ox from 75. *Nash Rectory, Milton Keyes, Bucks, MK17 0ES.* (Whaddon 273)

SORENSEN, Errol Dannemand. St Jo Coll Morpeth. **d** 60 Newc for Bal **p** 61 Bal. C of Beech Forest 61-62; Warrnambool 63-65; V of Condah 65-66; C in Dept of Chaps Dio Melb 66-74; L to Offic Dio Bend 74-77; R of Charlton 77-81; Murchison Dio NW Austr from 81. *Attwood Street, Mount Magnet, W Australia 6638.*

SORFLEET, Douglas Roy. b 23. St Mich & AA Llan 73. **d** 75 **p** 76 St A. C of Denbigh 75-77; R of Cerrigydrudion w Llangwm, Llanfihangel Glyn-Myfyr, Ysbyty Ifan, Pentrefoelas, Betws Gwerfil Goch and Dinmael 77-80; V of Abbotsley Dio Ely from 80; Waresley Dio Ely from 80; Everton w Tetworth Dio Ely from 80. *Everton Vicarage, Sandy, Beds.* (Sandy 80538)

SOROTI, Lord Bishop of. *See* Ilukor, Right Rev Geresom.

✠ **SOSELEJE, Right Rev Maurice.** St Cypr Th Coll Tunduru, 52. **d** 54 Zanz for Masasi **p** 57 Masasi. P Dio Masasi 54-63; Cons Asst Bp of Masasi in Cathl Ch of St Mary and St Bart Masasi 11 June 63 by Abp of E Afr; Bps of Zanz, SW Tang and Masasi; Asst Bp of Zanz (Sepeku); and Bp Street (Amer Ch); res 69; L to Offic Dio Dar-S from 81. *Box 25017, Dar-es-Salaam, Tanzania.*

SOTI, Yoeli. **d** 67 **p** 68 W Tang. P Dio W Tang. *Gihwahuru, c/o Box 74, Kasulu, Tanzania.*

SOTIMEHIN, Samson Oladipo. b 25. **d** 71 **p** 74 Lagos. P Dio Lagos 71-76; Dio Ijebu from 76. *St John's Vicarage, Itele, Box 136, via Ijebu-Ode, Nigeria.*

SOTUNDE, Canon Victor Olufowora. Im Coll Ibad 59. Dipl Th (Lon) 61. St Aid Coll. **d** 61 Liv for Ondo-B **p** 63 Ondo-B. P Dio Ondo 63-70; Dio Lagos 71-76; Dio Egba from 76; Can of Egba from 76. *PO Box 182, Abeokuta, Nigeria.*

SOULSBY, Michael. b 36. Univ of Dur BSc 57. Westcott Ho Cam 61. **d** 62 **p** 63 Birm. C of Selly Oak 62-66; King's Norton 66-72; Team V 72-76; Team R of Sutton Mer Dio Liv from 76. *Sutton Rectory, New Street, St Helens, Mer, WA9 3XE.* (Marshalls Cross 812347)

SOUPER, Patrick Charles. b 28. K Coll Lon and Warm AKC and BD 55. **d** 57 **p** 58 Derby. Chap of Derby Cathl 57-62; Derby City Hosp 57-62; Asst Chap Univ of Lon 62-64; C of St Marylebone w H Trin 64-65; Chap St Paul's Sch Barnes 65-70; Lect in Educn Univ of Southn from 70; LPr Dio Win from 70. *11 Underwood Road, Southampton, SO1 7BZ.*

SOUTH, James Walter. Moore Th Coll Syd ACT ThL 67. **d** 67 **p** 68 Syd. C of St Matt Manly 67-68; Port Kembla 69-71; C-in-c of Greenacre Provisional Distr 71-73; R of Emu Plains Dio Syd from 73. *Short St, Emu Plains, NSW, Australia 2750.* (047-21 2128)

SOUTH, Keith Leonard. b 45. **d** 73 **p** 74 Gippsld. C of Nowa Nowa 73-76; R of Lang Lang Dio Gippsld from 76. *Rectory, Lang Lang, Vic, Australia 3984.*

SOUTH, Canon Thomas Horsman. b 06. Qu Coll Ox BA (3rd cl Th) 31, MA 35. Cudd Coll 31. **d** 32 **p** 33 Ox. C of Banbury 32-34; Warden of St Anselm Hall Man and Publ Pr Dio Man 34-39; V of Adderbury w Milton 39-47; R of Amersham w Coleshill 47-62; Chap of Amersham Hosp 47-62; Surr 53-67; R of Latimer w Flaunden 62-73; RD of Amersham 65-70; Hon Can of Ch Ch Cathl Ox from 66. *Folly Cottage, Deddington, Oxford.* (Deddington 38464)

SOUTHALL, Colin Edward. b 36. Lich Th Coll 63. **d** 65 Aston for Birm. C of Wylde Green Dio Birm 65-67; Perm to Offic Dio Birm 67-73; Dio Pet 73-81; Dio Linc from 81. *Hawthorns, 3 Albion Crescent, Lincoln, LN1 1EB.*

SOUTHALL, Peter Blackburn. b 44. Dipl Th (Lon) 71. Cudd Coll 68. **d** 71 Warrington for Liv **p** 72 Liv. C of Our Lady and St Nich Liv 71-75; C-in-c of St Jo Evang Walton-on-the-Hill 75-77; V 77-81. *Address temp unknown.*

SOUTHAM, Edward Adnet. b 01. Lich Th Coll 57. **d** and **p** 57 Birm. C of Erdington 57-60; V of Barnt Green 60-72; Perm to Offic Dio B & W from 74. *Flat 2, Oaklands, Elton Road, Clevedon, Somt.* (Clevedon 6833)

SOUTHAMPTON, Lord Bishop Suffragan of. *See* Cavell, Right Rev John Kingsmill.

SOUTHCOMBE, Hector George. b 07. Clare Coll Cam BA 29, MA 33. Westcott Ho Cam 67. **d** 69 Taunton for B & W **p** 70 B & W. C of Congresbury 69-73; V of Crimplesham w Stadsett 73-80; RD of Fincham 75-80. *5 Church Close, Yatton, Bristol, BS19 4HG.* (Yatton 834163)

SOUTHCOTT, Canon Harvey Frank. Univ of W Ont BA 48. Hur Coll LTh 50. Waterloo Lutheran Univ BD 63. **d** 50 **p** 51 Hur. R of Dover and Mitchell's Bay 50-55; Blenheim 55-56; Waterloo 56-62; Dioc Comm Ott 63-67; Hon Can of Ott 63-67; R of Trin Ch Ott 67-81; I of Carleton Place Dio Ott from 81. *225 Edmund Street, Carleton Place, Ont., Canada.*

SOUTHEARD, Alfred Gordon. b 22. Univ Coll of S Wales, BA 54. Ely Th Coll 49. **d** 51 **p** 52 Nor. C of Wymondham 51-53; Leamington 53-57; V of St Thos Cov 57-67; Wootton-Wawen Dio Cov from 67; Ed *Shire and Spire* 57-59; RD of Alcester 69-78. *Wootton-Wawen Vicarage, Solihull, Warws.* (Henley-in-Arden 2659)

SOUTHEND, Archdeacon of. *See* Bailey, Ven Jonathan Sansbury.

SOUTHERDEN, John Edward. Univ of Queensld BCom 58. Qu Coll Ox Lucas Tooth Scho 65, BA (2nd cl Th) 67, MA 71 St Francis Coll Brisb ACT ThL (2nd cl) 61. **d** 60 Brisb **p** 62 C and Goulb. C of Redcliffe 60-62; Wagga Wagga 62-64; Yass 64-65; P-in-c of Lake Bath 67-68; Belconnen Provisional Distr 68-71; R of N Albury 71-76; Vice-Prin St Jo Coll Morpeth 76-79 and 80-81; Actg Prin 79-80; Exam Chap to Bp of Newc from 79; R of Belmont Dio Newc from 81. *24 Church Street, Belmont, NSW, Australia 2280.*

SOUTHERN, Gerald Holte Bracebridge. b 1889. St Steph Ho Ox. **d** 12 **p** 13 Trinid. C of Tunapuna w St Jos 12-15; All SS Trinid 15-16; TCRN 17-19; C of St Mary Scarborough 16-22; Chap (Eccles Est) Luckn Canton 22-23; Ranikhet 23-24; Benares 24-25 Chaubattia 25; Meerut 25-26; Roorkee 26-28; Muttra 28-31; Landour 31; Luckn Canton 32-33; Allahabad Canton 33-36; Agra 37-38; Perm to Offic at St Lawr Northn 38-39; V of Flore 39-45; Monkleigh 45-48. *c/o National Westminster Bank, Wrexham, Clwyd.*

SOUTHERN, John Abbott. b 27. Univ of Leeds BA 47. Coll of Resurr Mirfield. **d** 51 **p** 52 Man. C of St Mary Leigh 51-55; Grimsby 55-58; V of St Jas Oldham 58-60; St D Haigh 60-75; R of Pemberton Dio Liv from 75. *148 Orrell Road, Wigan, Gtr Man, WN5 8HJ.* (Wigan 222237)

SOUTHERN, John Roy. b 05. Late Exhib of St Jo Coll Cam BA 28, MA 33. Egerton Hall Man 29. **d** 30 **p** 31 Man. C of St Jas Gorton 30-33; St Jas Birch-in-Rusholme 34-36; R of St Laur Denton 36-39; Black Notley 39-45; V of E Ham 45-47; R of Holt 47-61; C-in-c of High Kelling 55-61; R of Felbrigg w Metton and Sustead 61-78; Perm to Offic Dio Nor from 78. *129 Overstrand Road, Cromer, Norf.*

SOUTHERTON, Peter Clive. b 38. St D Coll Lamp BA

59. Qu Coll Birm. **d** 61 **p** 62 St A. C of Llandrillo-yn-Rhos 61-68; Pembroke Dio Berm 68-71; V of Esclusham Dio St A from 72. *Vicarage, Rhostyllen, Wrexham, Clwyd.* (Wrexham 54438)

SOUTHEY, Richard Mellon. Trin Coll Melb BA 32. Ridley Coll Melb 31. ACT ThL 35. **d** 32 **p** 36 Gippsld. C of Buchan 32-34; Paynesville 34-36; V of Foster 36-39; R of Omeo 39-43; Chap AIF 40-43; R of Leongatha 43-52; Exam Chap to Bp of Gippsld 50-58; RD of Toora 52-58; R of Yarram w Alberton 52-58; Hon Can of Gippsld 56-58; Min of Kingsville 58-61; I of Box Hill Melb 61-66; R of Ch Ch N Adel 66-73; P-in-c of St Cypr Adel 66-73; L to Offic Dio Adel from 73. *18 Gordon Avenue, Clearview, S Australia 5085.* (62 6176)

SOUTHGATE, Geoffrey Trevor Stanley. b 28. K Coll Lon and Warm AKC 56. **d** 57 **p** 58 Man. C of Tonge Moor 57-60; St Pet w St John Wapping Lon Dks 60-62; V of St Matt U Clapton 62-67; Fleetwood Dio Blackb from 67. *Vicarage, Fleetwood, Lancs, FY7 7DJ.* (Fleetwood 4402)

SOUTHGATE, Herbert Ernest. b 1884. St Andr Coll Pampisford, 46. **d** 46 **p** 48 Truro. C of Saltash 46-54; C-in-c of Tideford 59-64. *Springbank, Tideford, Saltash, PL12 5LH.*

SOUTHGATE, Ven John Eliot. b 26. St Jo Coll Dur BA 53, Dipl Th 55. **d** 55 **p** 56 Leic. C of S Wigston 55-59; Good Shepherd w St Pet Lee 59-62; V of Plumstead 62-66; R of St Luke Old Charlton 66-72; RD of Greenwich 69-72; Hon Can of S'wark 70-72; Sec for Miss and Evangelism Dio York 72-81; V of Harome 72-76; Can and Preb of York Minster from 72; Archd of Cleveland from 74. *79 Middleton Road, Pickering, YO18 8NQ.* (Pickering 73605)

SOUTHGATE, Norman Frederick. b 12. AKC 39. **d** 39 **p** 40 Chelmsf. C of Ascen Collier Row 39-41; St Andr Romford 41-42; Saffron Walden 42-46; R of Birchanger 46-48; V of Gt Wakering 48-51; R of Hopton-by-Thetford w Mkt Weston 51-56; Worlingworth w Tannington 56-60; C-in-c of Southolt 59-60; R of Dumbleton w Wormington 60-71; Perm to Offic Dio Glouc from 71. *Rosevine, Wormington, Broadway, Worcs, WR12 7NL.* (Stanton 343)

SOUTHWARD, Canon Douglas Ambrose. b 32. ALCD 57 (LTh from 74). **d** 57 **p** 58 Bradf. C of Otley 57-61; Sedbergh w Cautley and Garsdale 61-63; PV of Lich Cathl 63-65; V of Hope 65-72; Crosby Ravensworth Dio Carl from 72; P-in-c of All SS Bolton Dio Carl from 74; RD of Appleby from 78; Sec Dioc Pastoral and Redundant Chs C'tte Dio Carl from 78; Hon Can of Carl Cathl from 81; C of Asby w Ormside Dio Carl from 81. *Crosby Ravensworth Vicarage, Penrith, Cumb.* (Ravensworth 226)

SOUTHWARK, Lord Bishop of. *See* Bowlby, Right Rev Ronald Oliver.

SOUTHWARK, Assistant Bishops of. *See* Knapp-Fisher, Right Rev Edward George; and Capper, Right Rev Edmund Michael Hubert.

SOUTHWARK, Archdeacon of. *See* Whinney, Ven Michael Humphrey Dickens.

SOUTHWARK, Provost of. *See* Frankham, Very Rev Harold Edward.

SOUTHWELL, Lord Bishop of. *See* Wakeling, Right Rev John Dennis.

SOUTHWELL, Assistant Bishop of. (Vacant)

SOUTHWELL, Provost of. *See* Irvine, Very Rev John Murray.

SOUTHWELL, Canon Eric Medder Baden. b 02. St Cath Coll Cam BA 24, MA 28. Westcott Ho Cam 25. **d** 26 Liv for Ches **p** 27 Ches. C of H Trin Hoylake 26-29; St Helen Witton (Northwich) 29-33; V of Wharton 33-38; Ellesmere Port 38-51; R of Nantwich 51-75; Hon Can of Ches 63-75; Can (Emer) from 75. *1 Eastern Road, Wistaston, Nr Nantwich, Chesh.*

SOUTHWELL, Peter John Mackenzie. b 43. New Coll Ox BA (Th) 64, (Or Stud) 66, Pusey-Ellerton Scho 64, Sen Hebr Pri 66, Houghton Syriac Pri 67, MA 68. Wycl Hall Ox 66. **d** 67 **p** 68 Sheff. C of St Thos Crookes Sheff 67-70; Lect Univ of Sheff 67-70; Sen Tutor Wycl Hall Ox from 70; L to Offic Dio Ox from 71. *Wycliffe Hall, Oxford, OX2 6PW.* (Oxford 53829)

SOUTHWELL, Ven Roy. b 14. AKC 42. **d** 42 **p** 43 Liv. C of St Mich AA Wigan 42-44; St Jo Div Kennington 44-48; V of Ixworth 48-51; C-in-c of Ixworth Thorpe 48-51; V of St Jo Evang Bury St Edms 51-56; R of Bucklesham w Brightwell and Foxhall 56-59; Asst Dir of Relig Educn Dio St E 56-58; Dir 59-67; Hon Can of St E 59-68; V of Hendon 68-71; Archd of Northolt 70-80; Archd (Emer) from 80. *397 Sprowston Road, Norwich.* (Norwich 405977)

SOUTHWELL-SANDER, Peter George. b 41. G and C Coll Cam BA 64, MA 67. Westcott Ho Cam 63. **d** 65 Cant **p** 66 Dover for Cant. C of All SS w St Phil Maidstone 65-68; St Mary Gt Cam 68-71; Chap Girton Coll Cam 69-73; V of St Paul Clapham 73-76; Merton Dio S'wark from 76. *Merton Vicarage, Church Path, SW19 3HJ.* (01-542 1760)

SOUTHWOOD, Robert Alfred. b 31. Sarum Wells Th Coll 72. **d** 74 **p** 75 Win. C of Christchurch 74-76; Fordingbridge w Ibsley 76-79; P-in-c of St Aid Ernesettle, Plymouth 79-80; V from 80. *Vicarage, Rochford Crescent, Ernesettle, Plymouth.* (Plymouth 361703)

SOUTTAR, Preb Edward Herbert. b 16. Bps' Coll Cheshunt. **d** 46 **p** 47 Ex. C of St Pet Plymouth 46-52; R of Lynton (w Brendon from 54) 52-64; C-in-c of Brendon 52-54; V of Sidmouth 64-73; R (w Woolbrook and Salcombe Regis) 73-79; Team R of Sidmouth, Woolbrook, Salcombe Regis and Branscombe 79-81; RD of Ottery 71-77; Preb of Ex from 72. *20 Fosseway Close, Axminster, Devon, EX13 5LW.* (Axminster 34382)

SOUTTAR, John. b 12. Qu Coll Ox BA 34, MA 44. Westcott Ho Cam 34. **d** 36 **p** 37 Lon. C of H Cross Greenford 36-39; Cathl Ch Bloemf 39-40; L to Offic Dio Capetn 40-41; P-in-c of Hermanus 41-42; R of H Redeemer Sea Point Capetn 42-48; Somerset W 48-55; V of Carisbrooke 55-63; St Nich-in-Castro Carisbrooke 55-63; R of Bramshott w Liphook 63-81. *Old Vicarage, St John's Close, Rudmore, Portsmouth, Hants, PO2 8EH.*

SOUTTER, James Morris Grieve. Montr Dioc Th Coll LTh 57. **d** 57. **d** 57 **p** 58 Ont. I of Maynooth 57-61; Deseronto 61-64; Wel 65-70; C of H Trin Castries, St Lucia and Bp's Youth and Stewardship Adv 70-73; on leave. *c/o 90 Johnson Street, Kingston, Ont, Canada.*

SOWALE, Samuel Olubayo. b 51. Im Coll Ibad 74. **d** 77 **p** 78 Ibad. P Dio Ibad. *c/o Box 3075, Ibadan, Nigeria.*

SOWDON, Henry Lewis Malcolm. b 37. Bp's Coll Cheshunt. **d** 64 **p** 65 Lich. C of Newport w Longford 64-66; Caverswall 66-69; Chap Clayesmore Sch 69-72; Asst Master St D Sch Hornsey 72-80; Hon C of Ch Ch Crouch End Hornsey Dio Lon from 72; Chap and Asst Master Gordon Boys' Sch from 80. *1 Monkridge, Crouch End Hill, N8.*

SOWERBUTTS, Alan. b 49. Univ of Sheff BSc 70, PhD 73. Qu Coll Cam BA 75, MA 79. Westcott Ho Cam 74. **d** 76 Burnley for Blackb **p** 77 Blackb. C of Salesbury 76-80; V of Lower Darwen Dio Blackb from 80. *St James Vicarage, Stopes Brow, Lower Darwen, Lancs, BB3 0QP.* (Blackburn 53898)

SOWERBY, Geoffrey Nigel Rake. b 35. St Aid Coll 56. **d** 60 **p** 61 Ripon. C of Armley 60-63; Succr and Min Can of Ripon Cathl 63-65; V of Thornthwaite w Darley and Thruscross 65-69; All SS w St Alb Leeds 69-73; Leyburn w Bellerby 73-81; R of Old St Paul City and Dio Edin from 81. *Lauder House, Jeffrey Street, Edinburgh, EH1 1DH.* (031-556 3332)

SOWTER, Richard Francis. b 46. Univ of Lon BSc. Sarum Wells Th Coll 79. **d** 81 Kens for Lon. C of Shepperton Dio Lon from 81. *Flat 1, The Rectory, Church Square, Shepperton, Middx, TW17 9JY.*

SOYANNWO, Moronfolu Olatunde. b 40. Univ of Ibad BSc (Agric). Im Coll Ibad 78. **d** 79 **p** 80 Ijebu. P Dio Ijebu. *Zonal Education Office; Abeokuta, Nigeria.*

SPACKMAN, Murray Leonard. St Jo Coll Auckld LTh 66. **d** 66 **p** 67 Auckld. C of Takapuna 66-70; Manurewa 70-71; V of Clevedon 71-75; Paparoa 75-81; Devonport Dio Auckld from 81. *20 Church Street, Devonport, NZ.*

SPACKMAN, Peter John. b 37. Univ of Southn BSc (3rd cl Chem) 60. Westcott Ho Cam 65. **d** 66 St Alb **p** 67 Bedford for St Alb. C of Boxmoor 66-69; St Paul Alnwick and of Edlingham w Bolton 69-72; Brown's Town (in c of Stewart Town and Gibraltar) 72-75; Asst Master St Hilda's Sch Brown's Town Ja 72-75; I of Seven Is 75-77; Baie Comeau Dio Queb from 77. *30 Carleton Avenue, Baie Comeau, PQ, Canada.*

SPAFFORD, Very Rev Christopher Garnett Howsin. b 24. St Jo Coll Ox BA (2nd Cl Mod Hist) 48, MA 54. Wells Th Coll. **d** 50 **p** 51 Wakef. C of Brighouse 50-53; Huddersfield 53-55; V of Hebden Bridge 55-61; R of Thornhill 61-69; V of St Chad Shrewsbury 69-76; Provost and V of Newc T Cathl from 76. *23 Montague Avenue, Newcastle upon Tyne, NE3 4HY.* (Gosforth 853472)

SPALDING, Hubert John. b 10. AKC (2nd cl) 34. **d** 34 **p** 35 Man. C of St Jas Hope 34-38; St Marg Hollinwood 38-40; C-in-c of St Cuthb Conv Distr Herringthorpe 40-42; V of St Phil and St Anne Sheff 42-49; Offg C-in-c of St Mich Neepsend Sheff 42-48; V of St Cuthb Firvale Sheff 49-59; Asst Chap City Gen Hosp 49-59; V of St Cecilia Parson Cross Sheff 59-65; Surr 61-78; RD of Ecclesfield 64-65; PC of Abbeydale 65-67; V 68-78. *4 Roxton Road, Beauchief, Sheffield, S8 0BD.* (Sheffield 746321)

SPALDING, Reginald Augustine. b 15. Clare Coll Cam 3rd cl Nat Sc Trip pt i 35, BA (2nd cl Geog Trip pt i) 36, MA 40. LRCP Edin 48. Cudd Coll 38. **d** 39 **p** 40 York. C of St John Middlesbrough 39-43; St Geo Maryhill Glas 43-44; St Mich AA Helensburgh 44-46; C-in-c of H Trin Riddrie 46-49; Holy Cross E Pondoland 49-52; Med Miss at Hosp of Div Compassion St Matthews and LPr Dio Grahmstn 52-62; Med Miss Holy Cross and LPr Dio St John's 62-67; V of Babraham 67-80; V of Pampisford 67-80. *72 Ecton Lane, Sywell, Northampton, NN6 0BA.* (0604-45429)

SPALDING, Wilfrid Frank. b 20. Sarum Th Coll. **d** 57 **p** 58 Blackb. C of St Mary Magd Clitheroe 57-60; V of St Paul Accrington 60-68; R of Hoole Dio Blackb from 68. *Much Hoole Rectory, Preston, Lancs.* (Longton 612267)

SPANNER, Douglas Clement. b 16. Univ of Lon BSc 46, PhD 51, DSc 72. **d** 73 Edmon for Lon **p** 75 Willesden for Lon. C of Ealing 73-78; Eynsham Dio Ox from 79. *7 Foxburrow Lane, Hailey, Witney, Oxon, OX8 5UN.* (Witney 4684)

SPARGO, George. Ch Ch Coll NZ 58. **d** 58 **p** 59 Nel. C of Ahaura-Brunnerton 58-61; V of Motupiko 61-64; Cobden w Runanga 64-66; C of Blenheim 66-71; V of Granity w Waimangaroa 71-73; Tinui 73-76; Petone Dio Wel from 76. *12 Brittania Street, Petone, NZ.* (685-309)

SPARGO, Peter Frederick Duncan. b 21. Kelham Th Coll 47. **d** 51 **p** 52 S'wark. C of St Mark Camberwell 51-52; Catford 52-55; W Molesey 55-57; V of Castletown Dio Dur from 57. *St Margaret's Presbytery, Hylton Castle Road, Sunderland, T & W, SR5 3ED.* (Hylton 2319)

SPARHAM, Anthony George. b 41. St Jo Coll Dur BA (2nd cl Psychol) 69. Cranmer Hall Dur 66. **d** 71 **p** 72 Linc. C of Bourne 71-74; Team V of Tong 74-76; V of Windhill 76-81; Dioc Dir of Educn and Adult Adv Dio St E from 81. *c/o Diocesan Registrar, 22 Museum Street, Ipswich, Suffolk.*

SPARKES, Colin Anthony. b 37. Univ of Surrey MSc 68. St Steph Ho Ox 78. **d** 81 Buckingham for Ox (NSM). Perm to Offic Dio Ox from 81. *7 Martens Close, Shrivenham, Swindon, SN6 8BA.*

SPARKES, Donald James Henry. b 33. Dipl Th (Lon) 59. Oak Hill Th Coll 56. **d** 59 **p** 60 Lon. C of St Jo Evang Southall 59-63; C-in-c (V from 70) of Ch Ch Pitsmoor (w H Trin from 73) 63-79; H Trin Wicker Sheff 70-73; V of Pitsmoor w Ellesmere Dio Sheff from 79. *257 Pitsmoor Road, Sheffield, S3 9AQ.* (Sheffield 27756)

SPARKS, Christopher Thomas. b 29. St D Coll Lamp BA 53. Lich Th Coll 53. **d** 55 **p** 56 Ches. C of St Mich Macclesfield 55-59; W Kirby 59-61; V of St Jo Evang Altrincham 61-68; L to Offic Dio Blackb 69-79; C of St Mary Lanc (in-c of St Geo Marsh) Dio Blackb from 79. *The Hollies, Littlefell Lane, Lancaster, LA2 0RG.* (Lanc 67507)

SPARKS, Hedley Frederick Davis. b 08. Late Colquitt Exhib of BNC Ox BA (1st cl Th) and Sen Hulme Scho 30, Liddon Stud and Jun Hall Gr Test Pri 31, Jun Denyer and Johnson Scho and Sen Hall Gr Test Pri 33, MA and Sen Hall-Houghton LXX Pri 34, BD 37, DD 49. Univ of Birm MA (*ex offic*) 47. Univ of St Andr Hon DD 63. FBA 59. Ripon Hall Ox 30. **d** 33 **p** 34 Ox. C of St Martin and All SS Ox and Chap Ripon Hall Ox 33-36; Lect in Th Univ of Dur 36-46; Prof of Th Univ of Birm 46-52; Dean of Arts Univ of Birm 49-52; L to Offic Dio Ox 38-54; Dio Birm 46-52; Perm to Offic Dio Cant 53-69; L to Offic from 69; Select Pr Univ of Cam 49; Ox 79; Or Prof of Interpretation of H Script and Fell Or Coll Ox 52-76; Hon Fell from 80; R of Wytham 61-68; Exam Chap to Bp of Dur 68-72. *14 Longport, Canterbury, Kent, CT1 1PE.* (0227-66265)

SPARKS, Herbert Francis. K Coll Lon and Warm AKC (2nd cl) 49. **d** 50 **p** 51 York. C of St Osw Middlesbrough 50-53; Whitby (in c of St Mich) 53-58; C of St Mary Newington Surrey 58-59; V of St Paul Middlesbrough 59-64; Chap HM Pris Leyhill 64-69; Leic 69-73; Kirkham 73-76; Liv 76-79; Long Lartin from 79. *c/o HM Prison, Longlartin, Worcs.* (0386-830101)

SPARKS, Norman Robert. St Chad's Coll Regina STh 56. **d** 52 **p** 53 Qu'App. I of St Mich Regina 52-54; V of St D Barb 54-56; R of Ecum Secum 56-59; Shelburne NS 59-63; V of Silverdale Staffs 63-66; R of Alderley w Tresham and Hillesley 66-78. *3 Wellfields Drive, Bridport, Dorset.* (Bridport 24637)

SPARKS, Roger Tadwell Walsh. b 40. Univ of Natal BA 62. Wycl Hall Ox 78. **d** 80 **p** 81 Natal. C of St Jo Bapt Pinetown Dio Natal from 80. *7 Lytton Crescent, Pinetown, Natal 3600, S Africa.*

SPARKS, William Henry. b 10. Sarum Th Coll. **d** 56 **p** 57 Dur. C of S Westoe 56-59; V of Haswell Dio Dur from 59. *Haswell Vicarage, Durham.* (Hetton-le-Hole 261333)

SPARLING, Arthur Cecil. b 16. TCD BA 40. Div Test 40, MA 44. **d** 41 **p** 42 Man. C of St Steph Elton 41-45; St Paul Rusthall 45-51; V of Spelsbury (w Chadlington from 63) 51-81; RD of Chipping Norton 65-74. *Parkfield, Mill Lane, Lower Slaughter, Cheltenham, Glos, GL54 2HX.* (Bourton-on-the-Water 20987)

SPARLING, Harold William. b 19. Univ of Lon BD (2nd cl) 40. AKC 40. Bps' Coll Cheshunt 40. **d** 41 **p** 43 Cant. C of St Mark S Norwood 41-43; C-in-c of Bradfield 43-46; R of Langham 46-55; Min Can of St Paul's Cathl 54-56; Succr 55; L to Offic Dio Lon 55; R of Cranham 56-60; Asst Master Brentwood High Sch 59-60; R of U Hardres w Stelling 60-78; Asst Master Wye High Sch from 79; Perm to Offic Dio Cant from 79; Dio St E from 80. *3 Station Road, Lyminge, Nr Folkestone, Kent.*

SPARLING, Ven James Wallace. Montr Dioc Th Coll LTh 66. **d** 66 **p** 67 Montr. C of Greenfield Pk 66-68; R of Bedford 68-73; St Mark, St Laurent Montr 73-79; Cowansville Dio Montr from 79; Archd of Bedford from 79. *104 Bruce Boulevard, Cowansville, PQ, Canada.* (514-263 0431)

SPARROW, Michael Kenneth. b 47. St Jo Coll Dur BA 74. Coll of Resurr Mirfield 74. **d** 75 Dorchester for Ox **p** 76 Ox. C of N Hinksey 75-78; Portsea (in c of St Faith) Dio Portsm from 78. *St Faith's House, Fyning Street, Landport, Portsmouth, PO1 1JS.* (Portsmouth 823451)

SPARROW, Wilfred Aubrey. St Chad's Coll Regina. **d** 61 **p** 62 Calg. I of Elnora Miss 61-63; Castor 63-65; R of Olds 65-68; Miss Carib Lakes 68-69; L to Offic Dio Koot from 70. *Box 435, Summerland, BC, Canada.*

SPEAK, Geoffrey Lowrey. OBE 70. Selw Coll Cam BA 49, MA 53. Ridley Hall, Cam 49. **d** 51 **p** 52 Wakef. C of Sandal Magna 51-54; Asst Master St Paul's Coll Hong Kong 54-59; Hd Master 59-67; LPr Dio Hong from 54; Prin I Sch Hong Kong 67-78; Sec Engl Schs Found Dio Hong from 78. *Island School, Bowen Road, Hong Kong.* (5-248497)

SPEAKMAN, Anthony Ernest. b 43. St D Coll Lamp Dipl Th 71. Bp Burgess Hall Lamp. **d** 71 **p** 72 St A. C of Newtown 71-72; Holywell 72-74; St Marylebone w H Trin Lon 74-77; V of St Phil w St Mark Camberwell 77-80. *c/o St Philip's Vicarage, Avondale Square, SE1.* (01-237 3239)

SPEAKMAN, Charles Francis. Wycl Coll Tor LTh 52. **d** 51 Tor for Sask **p** 52 Sask. C-in-c of Sturgeon Valley 51-52; I of Fort Pitt 52-54; Arborfield 54-58; In Amer Ch 59-61; I of St Geo Scarborough Tor 62-74; Craighurst 74-78. *c/o Rectory, Minesing, Ont., Canada.* (705-728 4379)

SPEAKMAN, Herman Daniel. b 1895. K Coll Lon AKC (Law and Th) and Whichelow Pri 21. **d** 21 **p** 22 Lon. C of St Luke Enfield 21-24; Perm to Offic at St Alb Mart Bordesley Birm 24-25; C of St Andr Grimsby 25-27; Grimsby (in c of St Hugh) 27-30; V of Moulton St Jas 30-42; Perm to Offic Dio Leic 34-42; V of Crowle 42-78; R of Wroot 59-78; RD of I of Axholme 51-69; Surr 51-78; Perm to Offic Dio Nor from 78. *St Anthony, Horstead, Norwich.* (Norwich 738614)

SPEAKMAN, Joseph Frederick. b 26. N-W Ordin Course 75. **d** 78 **p** 79 Ches. C of Wallasey Dio Ches from 78. *12 Curzon Avenue, Wallasay, Merseyside, L45 5AX.*

SPEAKMAN, Walter Davidson. b 13. St Aid Coll. **d** 46 **p** 47 Man. C of H Trin Bury 46-49; St Mary Prestbury 49-52; V of Ruishton w Thorn Falcon 52-60; R of Rosalie W Austr 60-61; V of Brompton-Regis w Withiel Florey 61-65; Min of All SS Eccles Distr Halcon Taunton 65-67; V 67-76; R of H Trin Bath 76-78; Min of Ch Ch Bath 76-78; Perm to Offic Dio B & W from 79. *Cloud Cottage, Stogumber, Nr Taunton, Somt, TA4 3DT.*

SPEAR, David Grahame. b 44. Em & St Chad's Coll Sktn BA 69, MDiv 72. **d** and **p** 72 Bran. I of Wabowden 72-74; Carman Dio Rupld from 75; Elm Greek Dio Rupld from 78. *Box 575, Carman, Manit., Canada.*

SPEAR, John Cory. b 33. Ridley Hall Cam 68. **d** 70 **p** 71 Ox. C of Gerrards Cross 70-73; Team V of Washfield (Exe Valley Group) 73-79; P-in-c of Instow Dio Ex 79; R from 79; P-in-c of Westleigh Dio Ex 79; V from 79. *Rectory, Quay Lane, Instow, Bideford, Devon.* (Instow 860346)

SPEAR, John Forrest Yeoman. St Jo Coll Auckld. **d** 59 **p** 60 Waik. C of Stratford 59-60; St Andr Cam 60-61; V of Kawhai 61-63; Melville 63-67; Pio Pio w Aria 67-74; Tirau 74-76; Te Kauwhata 76-81; Perm to Offic Dio Auckld from 81. *Hahei RD, Whitianga, NZ.*

SPEAR, Kenneth Robert. b 50. Univ of W Ont BMusA 78. Trin Coll Tor MDiv 81. **d** 81 Ott. C of Trin Ch Cornwall Dio Ott from 81. *105 Second Street West, Cornwall, Ont, Canada, K6J 1G4.*

SPEARS, Reginald Robert Derek. b 48. Trin Coll Ox BA 72, MA 75. Cudd Coll 72. **d** 75 Kens for Lon **p** 76 Lon. C of All SS Hampton 75-79; Caversham (and Mapledurham from 81) Dio Ox from 79. *25 Ilkley Road, Caversham, Reading, RG4 7BD.* (Reading 472070)

SPECK, Peter William. b 42. Univ of Wales BSc 64. Univ of Birm BA (2nd cl Th) 66. MA 71. Qu Coll Birm 64. **d** 67 **p** 68 St A. C of Rhosddu 67-71; Wrexham 71-72; Asst Chap United Sheff Hosps 72-73; Chap N Gen Hosp Sheff 73-79; R Free Hosp Lon from 79. *1 Ellington Road, N10 3DD.* (01-883 3386)

SPECK, Raymond George. b 39. Oak Hill Th Coll 64. **d** 67 **p** 68 Man. C of St Bride Stretford 67-70; Ch Ch Roxeth Harrow 70-74; V of St Jo Evang Woodbridge Dio St E from 74. *St John's Vicarage, Woodbridge, Suff, IP12 1HS.* (Woodbridge 2083)

SPEDDING, Geoffrey Osmond. b 46. Univ of Hull BA (2nd cl Th) 67. Fitzw Coll Cam BA (2nd cl Th Trip pt iii) 69. **d** 70 **p** 71 Bradf. C of St Pet Cathl Bradf 70-73; Sutton-in-Holderness 73-76; Team V of Preston (in c of St Sav w St Jas)

Dio Blackb from 76. *St James Vicarage, Larkhill Road, Preston, Lancs.* (Preston 54112)

SPEDDING, William Granville. b 39. BD (Lon) 60. Tyndale Hall Bris 57. **d** 62 Hulme for Man **p** 63 Man. C of Albert Mem Ch Man 62-65; Perm to Offic Dio Man from 65; Asst Master Whitecroft High Sch Bolton 65-71; Hayward Green High Sch Bolton from 71; Hon C of St Jas New Bury Farnworth 69-78; St Paul w Em Ch Bolton Dio Man from 78. *26 Milverton Close, Lostock, Bolton, Lancs, BL6 4RR.*

SPEED, Alfred Blenkarn. b 06. K Coll Lon and Warm AKC 48. **d** 48 **p** 49 Guildf. C of Frimley Green and Chap Burrow Hill Sch 48-50; Farncombe 50-52; C-in-c of All SS Conv Distr Lightwater 52-57; CF (TA) 53-74; Hon CF from 74; V of Gt Gaddesden 57-72; Perm to Offic Dio St Alb from 72. *5 Moore Road, Northchurch, Berkhamsted, Herts, HP4 3PX.* (Berkhamsted 5568)

SPEED, Patrick William Andrew. St Francis Coll Brisb. **d** 80 Brisb. C of St Andr Indooroopilly Dio Brisb from 80. *50 Dixon Street, Auchenflower, Qld, Australia 4064.*

SPEED, Richard Vernon. St Jo Coll Morpeth ACT ThL 63. **d** 63 **p** 64 St Arn. C of Maryborough 63-66; Mildura 66; R of Robinvale 66-68; C of Swan Hill 68-69; Regr Dio St Arn 69-76; Asst Regr and Bp's Chap Dio Bend from 77; Dom Chap to Bp of St Arn 74-76; R of Heathcote Dio Bend from 77. *Rectory, High Street, Heathcote, Vic, Australia 3606.*

SPEED, Thomas Edward. Univ of BC BA 52. Angl Th Coll BC LTh 53. **d** 53 **p** 54 New Westmr. C-in-c of Fort Langley 54-60; Good Shepherd Miss Vancouver 60-66; Chap BC Penit 66-80; Correctional Services of Canada from 80. *Box 1500, Agassiz, BC, Canada.*

SPEEDY, Darrel Craven. b 35. St Chad's Coll Dur BA 57. Wells Th Coll 57. **d** 59 **p** 60 Linc. C of Frodingham 59-63; V of Heckington w Howell 63-71; Barton-on-Humber 71-79; R of St Andr Tain Dio Ross from 79; Exam Chap to Bp of Moray from 81. *St Andrew's Rectory, Tain, Ross-shire, IV19 1HE.* (Tain 2193)

SPEER, James Dunbar. b 50. Univ of Puget Sound Wash BA 73. Vanc Sch of Th MDiv 79. **d** 79 **p** 80 Yukon. I of St Aid Telegraph Creek Dio Yukon from 79. *Telegraph Creek, BC, Canada V0J 2W0.*

SPEERS, Canon Albert Edward. Wycl Hall Ox. **d** and **p** 44 Roch. C of Dartford 44-47; R of Snodland 47-54; V of St Paul Chatham 54-67; Barnehurst Dio Roch from 67; Hon Can of Roch Cathl from 74. *St Martin's Vicarage, Erith Road, Barnehurst, Bexleyheath, Kent.* (Crayford 523344)

SPEERS, John. b 15. TCD BA 38, MA 41. **d** 39 **p** 40 Chelmsf. C of St Giles Colchester 39-41; CF 41-65; R of Flixton w S Elmham 65-76; P-in-c of Toppesfield w Stambourne Dio Chelmsf from 77. *Toppesfield Rectory, Halstead, CO9 4DZ.* (Gt Yeldham 306)

SPEERS, John Cunningham. ACT ThL 57. St Jo Coll Morpeth. **d** and **p** 57 Newc. C of E Maitland 57-58; R of Weston 58-61; Lambton 61-65; Branxton 65-76; C of Coolangatta Dio Brisb 76-77; V from 77. *135 Mallawa Drive, Palm Beach, Queensland, Australia 4221.* (35 4048)

SPEERS, Canon John Edward. Univ of Tor BA 50. LTh 53. **d** 52 Bp Wells for Tor **p** 53 Tor. C of St Clem N Tor 53-55; R of Georgina 55-60; Aurora 60-68; St Steph Tor 68-72; Trin Ch Barrie Dio Tor from 72; Can of Tor from 77. *Box 641, Barrie, Ont., Canada.* (705-728 2691)

SPEERS, John Stevenson. Ripon Hall, Ox. **d** and **p** 43 Roch. C of St Mark New Brompton 43-45; V of St Matt Borstal 45-50; R of Luton Kent 50-66. *13 Rodway Road, Bromley, Kent.*

SPEERS, Samuel Hall. b 46. Univ of Dub BA 70. Cudd Coll 70. **d** 73 **p** 74 St Alb. C of Borehamwood 73-77; Vice-Prin of St Paul's Coll Ambatoharanana, Antananarivo, Malagasy 77-79; Prin from 79. *St Paul's College, Ambatoharanana, Antananarivo, Malagasy.*

SPEIGHT, Philip Henry. b 1887. Coll of Resurr Mirfield 05. Univ of Leeds BA (1st cl Engl Lang and Lit) and Ripon Pri 10. M CR 24. **d** 12 Ban for St A **p** 13 St A. C of Hawarden 12-21; L to Offic Dio Wakef 21-25; Asst Master St Jo Coll and Miss P Commun of Resurr Johann 25-35; Perm to Offic Dio Lon 36-44; Dio Wakef from 44; L to Offic Dio Llan 46-52; Miss P Rossettenville 52-59; Ho of Resurr Mirfield 59-60; Priory of St Paul Lon 60-69; R Found of St Kath 69-80; L to Offic Dio Lon 60-80; Ho of Resurr Mirfield from 80. *House of the Resurrection, Mirfield, W Yorks, WF14 0BN.* (Mirfield 494318)

SPELLER, George. Univ of Lon BD 40. **d** 53 **p** 54 Birm. C of Hall Green 53-56; V of Ingrow 56-67; Coniston Cold 67-80. *c/o Coniston Cold Vicarage, Skipton, Yorks.* (Gargrave 265)

SPENCE, Ahab. Univ of Sask BA 52, LLD (*hon causa*) 64. Em Coll Sktn LTh 37. **d** 37 **p** 38 Sktn for Sask. C of Stanley 37-43; Miss at Little Pine Ind Reserve 43-47; I of Maidstone w Paynton 47-56; Miss at L Pines 55-56; Can of Sktn 55-62; I of Wilkie 56-59; Commiss for Ind Miss 58-63; Miss at Red Pheasant 59-63; Archd of Sktn 59-63; Prin of Pelican Lake Sch 63-67; L to Offic Dio Qu'App 67-71; Hon Asst C of Fairford 71-81; P-in-c of Indian and Metis Min Dio Qu'App from 81. *27 Dolphin Bay, Regina, Sask, Canada.*

SPENCE, Brian Robin. b 39. St Chad's Coll Dur BA (3rd cl Geog) 61 Dipl Th 63. **d** 63 **p** 64 Guildf. C of All SS Weston 63-67; Miss P at Leribe Miss 67-68; C of Chobham 68-71; Gt Yarmouth 71-74; V of Warnham 74-81; St Mary Virg E Grinstead Dio Chich from 81. *Vicarage, Windmill Lane, East Grinstead, W Sussex, RH19 2DS.* (E Grinstead 23439)

SPENCE, Canon David Ralph. Wycl Coll Tor LTh 68. **d** 68 Niag **p** 68 Bp Coleman for Niag. C of St Geo Guelph 68-70; R of St Bart Hamilton 70-74; Thorold Dio Niag from 74; Hon Can of Niag from 80. *38 Claremont Street, Thorold, Ont., Canada.* (416-227 1298)

SPENCE, Edward. b 10. **d** and **p** 74 Keew. C of Webequie Dio Keew from 74. *Church of the Messiah, Webequie, via Nakina, Ont., Canada.*

SPENCE, Gerald William. **d** 61 **p** 63 Sask. I of Paddockwood 61-64; Leask 64-68; R of Innisfail 68-76; Turtleford 76-79; Birch Hills Dio Sask from 79. *Box 278, Birch Hills, Sask, Canada.*

SPENCE, Herman Victor. St Pet Th Coll Ja, 59. **d** 62 **p** 63 Ja. C of Half Way Tree 62-67; R of Highgate 67-69; Half Way Tree Dio Ja from 69. *14 Ottawa Avenue, Kingston 6, Jamaica, W Indies.* (093-77687)

SPENCE, James Knox. b 30. Worc Coll Ox BA 55, MA 58. Ridley Hall Cam. **d** 57 **p** 58 Lon. C of H Trin Hampstead 57-60; St Ebbe Ox 61-64; Cands Sec CPAS 64-68; V of Greyfriars Reading 68-78; C of St Helen Bishopsgate City and Dio Lon from 79. *St Helen's Vestry, Great St Helen's, EC3A 6AT.* (01-283 2231)

SPENCE, James Timothy. b 35. St Jo Coll Cam BA 59, MA 63. Wycl Hall Ox 59. **d** 61 Bp McKie for Cov **p** 62 Cov. C of St Mich Stoke Cov 61-64; H Trin Cam 64-67; R of Tarrington w Stoke Edith and Dioc Youth Officer Heref 67-72; L to Offic Dio Win 73-75; R of Falstone 75-80; Team V of Bellingham-Otterburn 80-82; V of Dinnington Dio Newc T from 82. *Vicarage, East Acres, Dinnington, NE13 7NA.* (Ponteland 71377)

SPENCE, John Edis. b 24. St Edm Hall Ox BA 46, MA 48. Westcott Ho Cam 47. **d** 48 York **p** 49 Whitby for York. C of Newland Yorks 48-50; V of Winton Dio Rockptn 50-54; C of Uckfield 54-55; Chap RN 55-59 and 60-65; V of Thornton-le-Street w N Otterington Thornton-le-Moor and Thornton-le-Beans 59-60; V of St Germans 65-73; PC of Tideford Dio Truro 65-58; V 68-73; C-in-c of Sheviock 69-70; Perm to Offic Dio Truro from 73; Dioc Chap to Bp of Truro 76-78; Bp's Asst Chap for the Maintenance of the Min 78-81; Chap from 81. *Gwarnick Cottage, St Allen, Truro, TR4 9QU.* (Zelah 377)

SPENCE, Philip Arthur. b 39. Univ of Lon Dipl Th 67, BD 71. Open Univ BA 76. Westcott Ho Cam 78. **d** 78 Colchester for Chelmsf **p** 79 Barking for Chelmsf. [f in Methodist Min]. C of St Pet Walthamstow 78-80; P-in-c of Greensted Dio Chelmsf from 80. *Greensted Rectory, Ongar, Essex.* (Ongar 2630)

✠ **SPENCE, Right Rev Selby Norman.** St Jo Coll Auckld. **d** 33 **p** 35 Auckld. C of St Mary's Cathl Auckld 33-36; CMS Miss at Kar Dio Lah 36-63; Dio Kar 63-70; Archd of Sind and Baluchistan 49-56; Hon Can of Lah 56-63; Can (Emer) from 63; Warden Selwyn Ho 59-70; Cons Bp of Kar in St Paul's Cathl Calc 1 Jan 70 by Bp of Calc (Metrop); Bps of Bom, Luckn, Nasik, Nagp, Delhi, Amrit, B'pore, Chota N, A & N, Assam, Kurun, Patna, Dacca, Lah, Nand and Colom; and others; Appt Bp of Kar in Ch of Pakistan 30 Nov 70; res 72; Asst Bp of Waik 72-76; Auckld 77-79; C of Te Awamutu 72-76; Fell of St Jo Coll Auckld 73; L to Offic Dio Auckld 76-77 and from 79. *c/o 4b The Glebe, Howick, Auckland, NZ.* (47-957)

SPENCE, Very Rev Walter Cyril. b 19. TCD Hebr Pri 39, BA 40, MA 43, BD 43, Eccles Hist Pri 41, 1st Th Exhib 42, Elrington Pri 43. **d** 42 **p** 43 Derry. C of Maghera 43-48; Roscommon 48-50; I of Ballysumaghan w Killery 50-55; Tubbercurry w Kilmactigue (w Achon from 60) 55-66; Surr from 60; RD of Dromard 61-66; Preb of Killaraght and Kilmovee in Achon Cathl 62-66; Exam Chap to Bp of Tuam 62-70; Asst Dioc Regr Dios Tuam Killala and Achon 64-66; Regr from 66; Dean and R of Tuam 66-81; Dean (Emer) from 81; Can and Preb of St Patr Cathl Dub from 67; RD of Omey 77-81; I of Kilmoremoy Dio Killala from 81. *Rectory, Ballina, Co Mayo, Irish Republic.* (096-21654)

SPENCELEY, Malcolm. b 40. St Jo Coll Dur 78. **d** 80 **p** 81 York. C of Redcar Dio York from 80. *34 Ings Road, Redcar, Cleveland.* (Redcar 480426)

SPENCER, Preb Christopher John Edward. b 16. AKC 41. **d** 41 **p** 42 Lon. C of St John Walham Green 41-45; K Chas Mart S Mymms 45-47; All S St Marg-on-Thames 47-49; Asst

Chap Lon Dioc Coun for Youth and Further Educn 49-50; R of Ch Ch St Marylebone (w St Barn from 52) 50-58; V of Ch Ch Hendon 58-66; R of L Stanmore Dio Lon from 66; RD of Harrow 72-77; Preb of St Paul's Cathl Lon from 79. *Whitchurch Rectory, St Lawrence Close, Edgware, Middx, HA8 6RB.* (01-952 0019)

SPENCER, David Stanley. Ohio Univ BA 43. Seabury-Western Th Sem LTh 45. **d** and **p** 45 Bp Conkling. In Amer Ch 45-67; R of Gracechurch Trinid 68-77; R of St Paul San Fernando 77-81; Rio Claro Dio Trinid from 81. *St Faith's Rectory, Rio Claro, Trinidad, WI.*

SPENCER, David William. b 43. E Angl Min Tr Course 80. **d** 81 Ely (NSM). C of St Aug Wisbech Dio Ely from 81. *5 Frinton Way, Wisbech, Cambs, PE13 3ST.*

SPENCER, Douglas Gordon. **d** 37 **p** 38 Nel. C of Murchison 37-38; V 38-44; Takaka 44-55; Brightwater w Waimea 55-60; Can of Nel 52-57; Archd of Mawhera 57-60. *Brightwater, NZ.*

SPENCER, Edwin Thomas. Univ of NB BA 51. Trin Coll Tor LTh 54. **d** 54 **p** 55 Fred. R of Ludlow and Blissfield 54-59; I of Richmond 59-67; P-in-c of St Marg City and Dio Fred from 67. *329 Southampton Drive, Forest Hill, Fredericton, NB, Canada.*

SPENCER, George Ernest. Qu Coll Newfld 59. **d** and **p** 61 Newfld. R of Pushthrough 61-64; Bonne Bay 64-73; Gander Bay 74-75. *Victoria Cove, Gander Bay, Newfoundland, Canada.*

SPENCER, Gilbert Hugh. b 43. BD (Lon) 67. ALCD 66. **d** 67 **p** 68 Roch. C of Bexleyheath 67-73; St Jo Evang Bexley 73-76; P-in-c of St Jo Evang Bromley 76-78; V 78-81; R of Chatham Dio Roch from 81. *Rectory, Maidstone Road, Chatham, Kent, ME4 6DP.* (Medway 43632)

SPENCER, Gordon Charles Craig. b 13. Oak Hill Th Coll 35. **d** 38 **p** 39 Southw. C of Attenborough w Bramcote 38-41; Heanor 41-45; Offg C-in-c of Eastwood 45-46; R of W Hallam 46-66; PC of Mapperley 51-66; RD of Ilkeston 62-66; V of Bathampton 66-81; P-in-c of Ditteridge Dio Bris from 81. *Rectory, Ditteridge, Nr Box, Corsham, Wilts.* (Box 742852)

SPENCER, John. b 42. Mem Univ Newfld BA 68, LTh 69. **d** 68 Bp Legge for Newfld **p** 69 Newfld. C of St Thos St John's 68-70; I of Twillingate 70-75; St Mich AA Lon Ont 75-80; St Mark Brantford Dio Hur from 80. *141 Memorial Drive, Brantford, Ont, Canada.*

SPENCER, John Edward. b 36. Univ of Bris BA (2nd cl Th) 60. Tyndale Hall, Bris 57. **d** 61 **p** 62 Liv. C of St Mark St Helens 61-64; CMS Miss Japan 65-70; Area Sec CMS Dios Leic and Pet 70-71; L to Offic Dio Leic 70-71; Warden & Chap Rikkyo Japanese Sch Rudgwick 71-73; L to Offic Dio Guildf 71-73; Dio Chich from 73; Hd Master Pennthorpe Sch from 73. *Pennthorpe School, Rudgwick, Horsham, Sussex.* (Rudgwick 2391)

SPENCER, John Leslie. b 09. St Cath S Ox BA 30, MA 34. St Aid Coll 31. **d** 32 **p** 33 S'wark. C of St Luke Wimbledon Pk 32-34; H Ap Leic 34-37; Org Sec S Amer MS 37-43; R of Peckleton 39-43; Sec S Amer Miss S for Metrop Area 43-48; V of Em Stoughton Guildf 48-53; St Luke Wimbledon 53-65; R of St Matt St Leonards-on-Sea 65-69; V of Bramfield w Walpole 69-74; L to Offic Dio Chich from 80. *Flat 3, 6 Enys Road, Eastbourne, E Sussex.* (Eastbourne 638108)

SPENCER, John Roland. b 16. **d** 58 **p** 59 Glouc. C of St Jo Evang Coleford 58-60; V of Ch Ch Coleford 60-72; C-in-c of English bicknor 63-72; V of Dean Forest Ch Ch w English Bicknor from 72. *Christ Church Vicarage, Forest of Dean, Coleford, Glos, GL16 7NS.* (Coleford 32334)

SPENCER, Norman Ernest. b 07. FCIS 70. **d** 74 **p** 75 Bris (APM). Hon C of Olveston w Aust Dio Bris from 74. *26 Park Crescent, Frenchay, Bristol, BS16 1NZ.*

SPENCER, Peter Cecil. b 30. Lich Th Coll 58. **d** 61 **p** 62 Win. C of Alton 61-63; St Luke Winton Bournemouth 63-66; St Anne Nass 66-67; West End Hants 67-70; St Mary Virg (in c of St Matt) Reading 70-72; Missr of St Matt Conv Distr Reading 72-76; V of St Matt Reading 76-78; Team V of Sidmouth, Woolbrook and Salcombe Regis (and Branscombe from 79) Dio Ex from 78. *St Francis Vicarage, Woolbrook, Sidmouth, Devon, EX10 9XH.* (Sidmouth 4522)

SPENCER, Peter Lane. St Jo Coll Cam BA 40, MA 45. Linc Th Coll 41. **d** 43 **p** 44 St Alb. C of St Matt Oxhey 43-46; St Mary's Miss Hunyani 46-47; Avondale 47-48; R of Selukwe 48-52; C of Umtali 52-54; R of Hatfield (f St Martin S Salisbury) 54-60; Archd of Salisbury 60-66; Chap and Lect Univ of Natal from 66; L to Offic Dio Natal from 71. *32 Davdon, 42 Musgrave Road, Durban, S Africa.* (Durban 346893)

SPENCER, Peter Roy. b 40. Sarum Wells Th Coll 72. **d** 74 **p** 75 Pet. C of St Alb Mart Northampton 74-77; Team V of Cov E Dio Cov from 77. *St Anne's Vicarage, London Road, Coventry, CV1 2JQ.* (Cov 23381)

SPENCER, Richard Alan. b 42. Vanc Sch of Th LTh 72. **d** and **p** 72 New Westmr. C of Fraser-Cheam 72-75; R of Comox Dio BC from 75. *218 Church Street, Comox, BC, Canada.*

SPENCER, Richard William Edward. b 33. Qu Coll Birm 78. **d** 81 Birm (NSM). C of The Lickey Dio Birm from 81. *8 Tanglewood Close, Blackwell, Bromsgrove, Worcs, B60 1BU.*

SPENCER, Robert. b 27. St Aid Coll 48. **d** 51 **p** 52 Ches. C of St Paul Crewe 51-53; St Jo Bapt Bollington 53-56; V of Lower Tranmere 56-62; St Alb Stockport 62-71; St Paul Coppenhall Crewe 71-81; Over Dio Ches from 81. *Vicarage, Over Hall Drive, Over, Winsford, Chesh, CW7 1EY.* (06065-3222)

SPENCER, Robert John. b 08. Linc Th Coll 39. **d** 40 Linc for Southw **p** 41 Southw. C of Ordsall 40-43; Blyth (in c of St Luke Langold) 43-47; V of Forest Town 47-55; R of Fledborough 55-74; V of Dunham-on-Trent w Darlton and Ragnall 55-74; Perm to Offic Dio Southw from 75. *49 High Street, Sutton-on-Trent, Newark, Notts.*

SPENCER, Roy Primett. b 26. Oak Hill Th Coll. **d** 53 **p** 54 St Alb. C of St Pet Bedford 53-55; Ch Ch Luton 55-58; Nottm 58-60; V of Middlestown w Netherton 60-61; Chap Crumpsall Hosp 61-66; R of Fleet Lincs 66-69; V of St Paul Accrington 69-78; Woodplumpton Dio Blackb from 78. *Woodplumpton Vicarage, Preston, Lancs.* (Catforth 690355)

SPENCER, Stanley. b 11. Clifton Th Coll 32. **d** 36 **p** 37 Chelmsf. C of St Mark Forest Gate 36-39; St Jas Muswell Hill 39-43; V of St Andr w St Mary Maidenhead 43-51; Surr for Archd of Berks 44-51; V of H Trin Southall 51-61; St Anselm Belmont 61-67; R of Monken Hadley 67-77. *27 Chestnut Avenue, Holbeach, Spalding, Lincs, PE12 7NE.*

SPENCER, Walter. Ridley Coll Melb ACT ThL (2nd cl) 48, Th Scho 53. **d** 48 **p** 49 Gippsld. C-in-c of Foster 48-49; V of Mirboo N 49-55; Org Sec CMS for W Austr and LPr Dio Perth 55-58; Min of St Geo Bentleigh 58-62; Dioc Missr and L to Offic Dio Syd 62-66; R of Mittagong 66-72; Chap HMS Pris Long Bay 72-75; R of St Sav Punchbowl Dio Syd from 75. *1363 Canterbury Road, Punchbowl, NSW, Australia 2196.* (709-3815)

SPENCER, Canon William Lowbridge. Keble Coll Ox BA 38, MA 46. Wells Th Coll 46. **d** 47 **p** 48 Bris. C of St Aldhelm Bedminster 47-50; St Mark Swindon 50-51; P-in-c of Mindu 52-58; Tunduru 59-63; Nachingwea Dio Masasi from 64; Can of Masasi from 75. *Box 19, Nachingwea, Lindi Region, Tanzania.*

SPENCER-LEE, Donald. b 16. Univ of Nottm BSc 37. **d** and **p** 77 Ont. C of Oxford Mills Dio Ont from 77. *Rectory, Oxford Mills, Ont, Canada.* (613-258 5117)

SPENCER-THOMAS, Owen Robert. b 40. Univ of Lon BSc (Soc) 70. Westcott Ho Cam 70. **d** 72 **p** 73 Kens for Lon. C of St Luke Kens 72-76; Lect Fulham and S Kens Inst 73-76; Dir of Lon Chs Radio Workshop and Relig Producer BBC Lon 76-78; L to Offic Dio Lon from 76; w Anglia TV from 78. *52 Windsor Road, Cambridge, CB4 3JN.* (0223-358446)

SPERRING, Clive Michael. b 43. Oak Hill Coll 71. **d** 75 **p** 76 Chelmsf. C of Hawkwell 75-78; Gt Baddow Dio Chelmsf from 78. *9 Winchelsea Drive, Great Baddow, Chelmsford, Essex.* (Chelmsf 55720)

✠ **SPERRY, Right Rev John Reginald.** Coll of Em & St Chad Sask Hon DD 73. Wycl Coll Tor Hon DD 79. K Coll NS. **d** 50 **p** 51 Arctic. Miss at Coppermine NWT 50-69; Hon Can of Arctic 57-59; Archd of Coppermine 59-69; Miss at Ft Smith (Mack Episc Distr from 71) 69-74; Exam Chap to Bp of Mack Distr 71-74; Cons Ld Bp of The Arctic in St Jude Pro-Cathl Frobisher Bay 31 March 74 by Abp of Rupld; Bps of Athab and Edmon. *Diocese of the Arctic, 1055 Avenue Road, Toronto, Ont, Canada.* (416-481 2263)

SPEYER, Nicholas Anthony. Univ of Syd BE 70. Moore Coll Syd ThL 77. Univ of Lon BD 78. **d** and **p** 79 Syd. C of St Paul Wahroonga 79-81; St Luke Dapto Dio Syd from 81. *95 Byamee Street, Dapto, NSW, Australia 2530.* (611-0147)

SPICER, David John. b 49. Univ of Lon BEducn 71. Linc Th Coll 76. **d** 78 Chelmsf **p** 79 Barking for Chelmsf. C of Upminster 78-80. *c/o 6 Gaynes Park Road, Upminster, Essex, RM14 2HH.*

SPICER, David John. b 52. Sussex Univ BA 76. Univ of Lon MTh 78. Westcott Ho Cam 77. **d** 79 **p** 80 S'wark. C of St Jo Evang E Dulwich Dio S'wark from 79. *11 Hinckley Road, E Dulwich, SE15.*

SPICER, Leigh Edwin. b 56. Sarum Wells Th Coll 78. **d** 81 Birm. C of Harborne Dio Birm from 81. *21 Vicarage Road, Harborne, Birmingham, B17 0SN.*

SPIERS, Cyril Douglas. St Andr Coll Pampisford. **d** 45 **p** 46 Lich. C of St Paul Stafford 45-46; Cannock w Chadsmoor 46-48; St Steph Ealing 48-50; V of St Jo Bapt Hoxton (w Ch Ch from 53) 50-54; St Luke Hammersmith 54-62; C-in-c Groombridge 62-65. *17 Oval Way, Ferring, Worthing, Sussex.* (Worthing 42156)

SPIERS, Ven Graeme Hendry Gordon. b 25. ALCD 52. **d**

52 Croydon for Cant **p** 53 Cant. C of Addiscombe 52-56; Succr of Bradf Cathl 56-58; V of Speke 58-66; Aigburth 66-80; RD of Childwall 75-79; Hon Can of Liv Cathl from 78; Archd of Liv from 79. *40 Sinclair Drive, Liverpool, L18 0HW.* (051-722 6675)

SPIKIN, Simon John Overington. b 48. Linc Th Coll 70. **d** 75 **p** 76 St Alb. C of Sawbridgeworth 75-79; Odiham, S Warnborough and Long Sutton 79-81; R of Dickleburgh w Langmere, Thelveton, Frenze and Shimpling Dio Nor from 81; P-in-c of Rushall Dio Nor from 81. *Dickleburgh Rectory, Diss, Norf.* (Dickleburgh 313)

SPILLER, David Roger. b 44. St Jo Coll Dur BA 70. Fitzw Coll Cam 2nd cl Th Trip pt ii BA 72, MA 76. Ridley Hall Cam 70. **d** 73 **p** 74 Bradf. C of Cathl Ch Bradf 73-77; Stratford-on-Avon (in c of All SS Luddington) 77-80; V of Chilvers Coton w Astley Dio Cov from 80. *Chilvers Coton Vicarage, Nuneaton, CV11 4NJ.* (Nuneaton 383010)

SPILLER, George Dennis. b 30. TD. St Jo Coll Dur BA 55. **d** 57 **p** 58 Lich. C of Newc L 57-62; R of Armitage 62-65; Ch Lawford w K Newnham 65-73; CF (TA) from 63; Publ Pr Dio Cov 73-81; Team R of Stratford-on-Avon Dio Cov from 81. *Rectory, Old Town, Stratford-upon-Avon, CP37 6PG.* (Stratford/Avon 3098)

SPILMAN, Derrick Geoffrey. Roch Th Coll. **d** 63 **p** 64 Cant. C of Dover 63-67; CF 67-70; Chap Miss to Seamen and Port Chap New Westmr 71-75; I of St Marg of Scotld Burnaby Dio New Westmr from 75. *6771 Napier Street, Burnaby, BC, V5B 2C5, Canada.*

SPILMAN, John. b 28. Wells Th Coll 65. **d** 66 Jarrow for Dur **p** 67 Dur. C of Norton 66-70; Min Newton Hall Ecumen Experiment Dio Dur 70-75; R of Crick Dio Pet from 75. *Crick Rectory, Northampton, NN6 7TU.* (Crick 822223)

SPILSBURY, Stephen Ronald Paul. b 39. Univ of Nottm BSc 69, MPhil 72. Linc Th Coll 71. **d** 64 **p** 65 Northn (RC). rec into Angl Commun by Bp of Southw 71. C of Cricklade w Latton 72-75; P-in-c of All SS Swindon 76-81; V of Lawrence Weston Dio Bris from 81. *335 Long Cross, Lawrence Weston, Bristol.* (Avonmouth 825863)

SPINK, Canon George Peter Arthur. b 26. Oak Hill Th Coll 54. **d** 56 **p** 57 Leic. C of Thurnby 56-58; C-in-c of Ch Ch Distr Thurnby Lodge 58-59; CMS 59; Chap to Br Embassy at Bonn and Cologne 59-62; Vienna w Prague and Budapest 62-68; Chap Cov Cathl 68-70; Can Res of Cov 70-77; Can (Emer) from 77; Commiss of the Episc Ch of Brazil from 71; Warden of Burrswood Groombridge 77-81; Perm to Offic Dio Roch from 81. *Kent House, Camden Park, Tunbridge Wells, Kent.* (Tunbridge Wells 36709)

SPINKS, Bryan Douglas. b 48. St Chad's Coll Dur BA (Th) 70, Dipl Th 71, BD 79. K Coll Lon MTh 72. **d** 75 Chelmsf **p** 76 Colchester for Chelmsf. C of Witham 75-78; St Jas Clacton-on-Sea 78-79; Asst Master St Pet Sch Huntingdon from 80; P-in-c of the Chap Churchill Coll Cam from 80. *Churchill College, Cambridge, CB3 0DS.* (0223-61200)

SPINNEY, Giles Martin. b 16. Ch Coll Cam Econ Trip pt i 37, BA (Law Trip pt ii) 39, MA 43. Wycl Hall Ox 39. **d** 41 **p** 42 Lon. C of St Thos Oakwood 41-46; V of Ch Ch Roxeth 46-50; R of St Paul Kersal 50-54; Brixton Deverill (The Deverills from 71) 54-81; R of Kingston Deverill w Monkton Deverill 55-71. *17 Chancery Lane, Warminster, Wilts, BA12 9JS.*

SPITTLE, Ralph Edward. b 23. Qu Coll Birm 75. **d** 77 Bp McKie for Cov **p** 78 Cov (NSM) C of Caludon Team Min 77-81; St Paul Foleshill Dio Cov from 81. *227 Tennyson Road, Coventry, CV2 5JE.* (Cov 440612)

SPIVEY, Colin. b 35. Oak Hill Coll 74. **d** 76 **p** 77 Guildf. C of St Jo Bapt Egham 76-79; Edgware (in c of St Andr) Dio Lon from 79. *1 Beulah Close, Edgware, Middx, HA8 8SP.* (01-958 9730)

SPIVEY, Canon Peter. b 19. Edin Th Coll 46. **d** 48 Pontefract for Wakef **p** 49 Wakef. C of Dewsbury Moor 48-50; Mirfield 50-53; R of Whitwood Mere 53-61; Chap Castleford Normanton and Distr Hosp 53-61; V of Meltham Dio Wakef from 61; Chap Moorview Hosp Meltham 61-68; Surr from 61; Press and Publicity Officer Dio Wakef 68-71; RD of Blackmoorfoot from 79; Hon Can of Wakef Cathl from 81. *Vicarage, Meltham, W Yorks, HD7 3HR.* (Huddersfield 850479)

SPOHR, Neville Keith Charles. St Jo Coll Morpeth ACT ThL 57. **d** and **p** 56 Newc. C of Largs 56; Mayfield 56-59; P-in-c of W Wallsend 59-70; R of Toronto Dio Newc from 71. *146 Brighton Avenue, Toronto, NSW, Australia 2283.* (59-1106)

SPONG, Terence John. Roch Th Coll 63. **d** 66 **p** 67 Portsm. C of Forton 66-68; St Jo Bapt Cathl Bulawayo 68-69; Chap Midl Area Prisons Gwelo 70-73; Matab Area Prisons Bulawayo 73-75; R of St Marg Bulawayo N 75; L to Offic Dios Mashon and Matab from 77; CF Gwelo 77; SCF Bulawayo from 78. *25 Livingstone Road, Suburbs Box 698, Bulawayo, Zimbabwe.* (61974)

SPOONER, Anthony Patrick David. b 45. BA (Lon) 68. Univ of Nottm Dipl Th 72. Linc Th Coll 71. **d** 74 **p** 75 Lewes for Chich. C of Glynde w Firle & Beddingham 74-77; Hillside 77-78; R of Que Que 78-80; Belvedere Dio Mashon from 80. *14 Clarendon Circle, Belvedere, Salisbury, Zimbabwe.*

SPOWART, John. b 04. Cranmer Hall Dur 64. **d** 65 **p** 66 Newc T. C of Long Benton 65-68; L to Offic Dio Newc T from 68; P-in-c of Cambois 69-73. *24 Ferneybeds, Widdrington, Morpeth, Northumb.* (Ulgham 790522)

SPRACKLING, Frederick Phillips. BC Coll Bris 37. **d** 40 **p** 41 Lon. C of Ch Ch Spitalfields 40-46; R of Botus Fleming 46-49; V of All SS Caledonian Road Islington 49-57; St Mary Stamford Brook Dio Lon from 57. *St Mary's Vicarage, Stamford Brook Road, W6.* (01-743 4362)

SPRACKLING, William Henry. b 09. Sarum Th Coll 67. **d** 68 **p** 69 Sarum. C of Wyke Regis 68-79; Perm to Offic Dio Sarum from 80. *5 Bourne Valley Road, Branksome, Poole, Dorset BH12 1DS.*

SPRATLEY, Deryck Edward. b 30. Oak Hill Th Coll 62. **d** 64 **p** 65 Cant. C of St Luke Ramsgate 64-67; St Mary Magd (in c of St D) Holloway 67-72; V of St Pet U Holloway (w St John from 79) Dio Lon from 73. *2 Anatola Road, N19 5HN.*

SPRATT, Laurence Herbert. b 28. Linc Th Coll 76. **d** 78 Doncaster for Sheff **p** 79 Sheff. C of Mexborough 78-80; R of Wrentham w Covehithe and Benacre and Frostenden w S Cove Dio St E from 80. *Rectory, Wrentham, Beccles, Suff, NR34 7LX.* (Wrentham 208)

SPRAY, Charles Alan Francis Thomas. b 27. Univ of Lon BSc 51. Ridley Hall Cam 57. **d** 59 Lewes for Chich **p** 60 Chich. C of St Pancras w St John Chich 59-63; PC of St Mary Virg Shipley 63-69; R of Ore Dio Chich from 70. *St Helen's Rectory, Elphinstone Road, Hastings, Sussex.* (Hastings 425172)

SPRAY, John William. b 29. Sarum Wells Th Coll 71. **d** 73 **p** 74 Lich. C of Clayton 73-76; V of Hartshill Dio Lich from 76. *Hartshill Vicarage, Stoke-on-Trent, Staffs, ST4 7NJ.* (Newcastle 616965)

SPREAD, John Henry Seymour. b 14. MC 46. Univ of Lon BA 37. Chich Th Coll 38. **d** 39 **p** 41 Portsm. C of St Steph Portsea 39-42; West Hyde 42-44; CF (EC) 44-47; CF (TA) 47-54; CF (R of O) 54-69; C of Willian 47-49; R and V of Hulcote w Salford 49-53; V of Ridgmont 49-53; Sundon w Streatley 53-79; C of Brent Pelham w Meesden and Anstey Dio St Alb from 79. *Hillside House, Anstey, Buntingford, Herts.* (Barkway 351)

SPRENT, Michael Francis. b 34. Ex Coll Ox BA (Th) 58, MA 62. Kelham Th Coll 58. M SSF 61. **d** 61 **p** 62 Chelmsf. C of St Phil and St Jas Plaistow 61-63; Koke Miss Port Moresby 65-69; Novice Master Engl Prov SSF 69-73; Guardian Alnmouth Friary 74-75; Team V of High Stoy 76-77; Guardian Harbledown Friary from 78. *St Nicholas Friary, Harbledown, Canterbury, Kent, CT2 9AD.*

SPRIGGS, Harold. b 1899. Dorch Miss Coll 29. **d** 31 **p** 32 Lich. C of St Paul (in c of St Luke) Wednesbury 31-34; St Jas Cathl Ch Townsville 34-35; R of Herberton N Queensld 35-39; Kingsley Staffs 39-47; Chap and Dir Garvald Sch Dolphinton 47-48; C of Old St Paul Edin 48; V of St Aid Shobnall 48-60; Mountfield Dio Chich from 60; Netherfield Dio Chich from 60. *Parson's Patch, Church Cottages, Mountfield, Robertsbridge, Sussex.* (Robertsbridge 880261)

SPRIGGS, John David Robert. b 36. BNC Ox BA 58, MA 63. SOC 73. **d** 75 Ox **p** 76 Reading for Ox (APM). L to Offic Dio Ox from 75. *Windward, Pangbourne College, Pangbourne, Berks., RG8 8JL.* (Pangbourne 4101)

SPRINGBETT, John Howard. b 47. Pemb Coll Cam BA 70, MA 74. Ridley Hall Cam 70. **d** 72 **p** 73 Carl. C of Ulverston 72-76; V of Dewsbury Moor Dio Wakef from 76. *St John's Vicarage, Boothroyd Lane, Dewsbury, W Yorks, WF13 2LP.* (Dewsbury 465698)

SPRINGER, James Levi. Codr Coll Barb 56. **d** 60 **p** 61 Barb. C of St Mich Cathl Barb 60-65; V of St Bart I and Dio Barb from 65. *St Bartholomew's Vicarage, Barbados, W Indies.*

SPRINGETT, Geoffrey William James. b 27. K Coll Lon and Warm AKC 53. **d** 54 **p** 55 S'wark. C of H Trin S Wimbleton 54-58; Chalfont St Pet 58-61; V of Balderton 61-74; Ed Southw Dioc Directory from 67; V of Bawtry w Austerfield Dio Southw from 74; Misson Dio Southw from 74; RD of Bawtry from 74. *Bawtry Vicarage, Doncaster, Yorks, DN10 6NJ.* (Doncaster 710298)

SPRINGETT, Simon Paul. b 56. Univ of Warwick LLB 78. Wycl Hall Ox 78. **d** 81 Barking for Chelmsf. C of Harlow Dio Chelmsf from 81. *129 Guilfords, Old Harlow, Essex, CM17 0HY.* (Harlow 413850)

SPRINGFORD, Frank George. b 05. Dorch Miss Coll 28. **d** 31 **p** 32 Heref. C of Ross 31-34; St Phil Georgetn 34-39; R of St Patr Canje 39-43; Hd Master of Govt Boys' Sch Essequibo and L to Offic Dio Gui 43-47; C of Cuckfield 47-49; V of Stonehouse 49-54; Surr 51-72; V of St Andr Kingsbury

54-69; S Mymms 69-73; Commiss to Abp of W Indies 56-78. *21 Tanqueray Avenue, Clophill, Beds, MK45 4AW.* (Silsoe 60859)

SPRINGFORD, Patrick Francis Alexander. b 45. Wycl Hall Ox 71. **d** 74 Lon **p** 75 Edmon for Lon. C of Ch Ch Finchley 74-79; CF from 79. *c/o Minstry of Defence, Bagshot Park, Bagshot, Surrey, GU19 5PL.*

SPRINGHAM, Desmond John. b 32. Univ of Bris BA (2nd cl Th) 56. Oak Hill Th Coll 56. **d** 58 **p** 59 St Alb. C of St Paul St Alb 58-61; St Jo Evang w St Steph Reading 61-66; R of Worting 66-80; V of St Andr Jersey Dio Win from 80. *St Andrew's Vicarage, First Tower, Jersey, CI.* (Central 34975)

SPRINGTHORPE, David Frederick. b 47. AKC 72. St Aug Coll Cant 72. **d** 73 **p** 74 Roch. C of St Alb Dartford 73-77; Biggin Hill 77-80; R of Ash w Ridley Dio Roch from 80. *Ash Rectory, Sevenoaks, Kent.* (Ash Green 872209)

SPROSTON, Bernard Melvin. b 37. St Jo Coll Dur 77. **d** 79 **p** 80 Lich. C of Westlands Dio Lich from 79. *10 Melrose Avenue, Westlands, Newcastle, Staffs, ST5 3PE.*

✠ **SPROTT, Right Rev John Chappell.** b 03. Univ of Glas MA (2nd cl Hist) 25. Univ of St Andr Hon DD 65. Edin Th Coll 25. **d** 27 Edin **p** 28 Arg for Edin. Chap and Succr of St Mary's Cathl and Chap-in-c of Water of Leith Miss 27-29; Lect in Mus Edin Th Coll 28-29; C of All SS Jordanhill (in c of St D Miss Scotstoun) Glas 29-33; St Geo Mart w H Trin Holborn 33-37; R of W Hackney 37-40; Provost of St Paul's Cathl Dundee 40-59; Exam Chap to Bp of Brech 50-59; Cons Ld Bp of Brech in St Paul's Cathl Dundee 6 May 59 by Bp of Arg Is (Primus); Bps of Glas, St Andr, Aber, Moray and Edin; and Bp Burrows; res 75; Hon C of Troon 75-81. *29 Bruntsfield Gardens, Edinburgh, 10.*

SPROULE, David Norman. Wycl Coll Tor LTh 66. **d** 66 **p** 67 Tor. C of Ascen Tor 66-68; P-in-c of St Gabr Richmond Hill 69-74; I of St Jas Humber Bay City and Dio Tor from 74. *190 Park Lawn Road, Toronto, Ont., Canada.* (416-251 8711)

SPROULE, Gerald Norman. b 26. **d** 60 **p** 61 Clogh. C of Monaghan 60-62; I of Cleenish 62-68; Magheracross 68-73; Admin Sec BCMS Ireland 73-79; I of St Aid Belf Dio Connor from 79. *35 Eglantine Avenue, Belfast, N Ireland, BT9 6DN.* (Belfast 666741)

SPROULE-JONES, Canon Henry Rees. b 09. St D Coll Lamp BA 32. St Mich Coll Llan 32. **d** 33 **p** 34 Mon. C of Pontnewynydd 33-39; R of Grosmont (w Skenfrith V from 48) 39-50; V of Tredegar 50-54; All SS Newport 54-62; St Mary Abergavenny and R of Llanwenarth Citra 62-77; Can of Mon from 63. *25 Merthyr Road, Abergavenny, Gwent, NP7 5PR.*

SPRUYT, John Harry. b 29. St Edm Hall Ox BA 56, MA 57. Wycl Hall Ox 56. **d** 56 **p** 57 Win. C of St Mark Southn 56-58; Kidlington 58-61; V of Lockerley w E Dean 61-68; Thornton-le-Street w Thornton-le-Moor and Thornton-le-Beans 68-70; Milborne St Andrew w Dewlish 71-77; All SS Jersey Dio Win from 77; C-in-c of St Simon Jersey Dio Win from 77. *All Saints' Vicarage, Savile Street, St Helier, Jersey CI.* (Jersey Central 24885)

SPURGIN, Canon Basil Layton. b 08. SS Coll Cam BA 31, MA 44. Sarum Th Coll 31. **d** 32 **p** 33 Roch. C of St Aug Gillingham 32-35; St Barbara Earlsdon 35-38; Wyken 38-39; V 39-45; Chap RAFVR 41-45; V of Market Drayton 45-52; RD of Hodnet 45-51; Gen Sec C of E Youth Coun 53-58; V of St Mary-le-Tower Ipswich 58-72; Hon Can of St E 59-72; RD of Ipswich 62-72; Can (Emer) from 72. *The Hills, Llanfarian, Aberystwyth, Dyfed.*

SPURIN, Richard Mark. b 28. Peterho Cam 3rd cl Th Trip pt i 50, BA (3rd cl Th Trip pt ii) 52, MA 60. Wycl Hall Ox 54. **d** 55 **p** 56 Cov. C of Foleshill 55-58; Atherstone 58-60; CMS 60-61; Chap to Bp of Maseno 61-65; Relig Educn Adv Dio Maseno 65-73; P-in-c of St Paul's Conv Distr Howell Hill Ewell Dio Guildf from 73. *St Paul's Church House, Northey Avenue, Cheam, Surrey.* (01-643 3838)

SPURLING, Cuthbert Terence. b 04. AKC 28. Wells Th Coll 28. **d** 28 **p** 30 Guildf. C of Ashtead 28-33; Farnham 33-35; Faversham 35-44; R of Otham w St Jo Evang Maidstone 44-64; Elmstone w Preston-next-Wingham and Stourmouth 64-71. *Goldspur Cottage, Peasmarsh, Rye, Sussex.*

SPURR, Antony. b 12. St Jo Coll Dur BA 33, MA 36. **d** 36 **p** 37 Linc. C of Wildmore 36-38; Coll of Chinese Stud Peking 39-40; CMS Miss Hangchow 40-52; Chap National Chekiang Univ Kweichow Prov 42-45; Chekiang Prov 47-52; CMS Miss Spinagar 52-57; Dio Amrit 53-57; Dios Nel and Ch Ch 58; R of Chester-le-Street 59-71; V of Barrow-on-Humber w New Holland 71-79. *9 Fauchelle Avenue, Richmond, Nelson, NZ.* (Richmond 6756)

SPURRELL, John Mark. b 34. CCC Ox BA 57, Dipl Th 58, MA 61. Linc Th Coll 58. **d** 60 **p** 61 Chelmsf. C of Tilbury Dks 60-65; Lect and C of Boston 65-76; R of Stow w Sturton Dio Linc from 76; P-in-c of Willingham-by-Stow Dio Linc from 76; Coates Dio Linc from 76. *Stow Rectory, Lincoln.* (Gainsborough 788251)

SPURRIER, Richard Patrick Montague. Univ of Bris BA 59. Wycl Hall, Ox 59. **d** 61 **p** 62 B & W. C of St Luke S Lyncombe 61-63; St Jo Evang Weston Bath 63-64. *158 Whiteladies Road, Bristol, BS8 2XZ.*

SPURRY, Canon Bernard David Allison. b 28. Univ of Wales BA (2nd cl Hist) 48. BD (2nd cl) (Lon) 54. St Mich Coll Llan 48. **d** 50 **p** 52 Llan. C of Merthyr Tydfil 50-55; St Marg Roath 55-62; V of Wheelock 62-67; St Jas Birkenhead (w St Bede from 72) 67-74; C-in-c of All SS Birkenhead 71-72; R of Delamere Dio Ches from 75; Hon Can of Ches Cathl from 79. *Delamere Rectory, Northwich, Chesh, CW8 2HS.* (0606-882184)

SPYKER, John Edward. St Paul's Coll Grahmstn 53. **d** 55 **p** 56 Johann. C of Mayfair Johann 55-58; Klerksdorp 58-60; R of Ermelo 60-63; Roodepoort 63-67; St Dunstan Benoni 68-73; Orchards 73-79; St Kath Uitenhage Dio Port Eliz from 79. *Box 486, Uitenhage, CP, S Africa.*

SQUAREY, Gerald Stephen Miles. b 36. Lich Th Coll 59. **d** 62 **p** 63 Lon. C of Poplar 62-64; Heston 64-67; V of Bradford Abbas w Clifton Maybank 67-74; P-in-c of Corfe Castle Dio Sarum 74-78; R from 78; Steeple w Tyneham, Church Knowle and Kimmeridge Dio Sarum from 78. *Rectory, Corfe Castle, Wareham, Dorset.* (Corfe Castle 480257)

SQUIBB, John Herbert. Univ of Lon ALCD (1st cl) 54, BD (2nd cl) 55. **d** 55 **p** 56 Nor. C of Gorleston 55-60; V of Ch Ch New Catton 60-74; R of Overstrand Dio Nor from 74. *Overstrand Rectory, Cromer, Norf.* (Overstrand 350)

SQUIRE, David George Mitchell. b 31. Worc Coll Ox BA 54, MA 58. Qu Coll Birm Dipl Th 66. **d** 67 **p** 68 Glouc. C of Dursley 67-70; V of Cam 71-77; Cler Org Sec CECS Dios Heref, Lich and Worc from 77. *Woodland View, Crundalls Lane, Bewdley, Worcs, DY12 1ND.*

SQUIRE, Herbert Walter. St Barn Th Coll Adel 65. **d** 66 **p** 67 Adel. C of Salisbury 66-70; Elizabeth 70-73; Salisbury 74-78; L to Offic Dio Adel from 78. *212 Main North Road, Elizabeth Grove, S Australia 5112.* (08-255 6724)

SQUIRE, Humphrey Edward. b 29. St Chad's Coll Dur BA 55. Coll of Resurr Mirfield. **d** 57 **p** 58 Derby. C of Newbold 57-59; Thorpe Episcopi 59-61; Chap St Andr Coll Minaki Zanz 61-63; C of Whittington 63-64; R of Drayton 64-75; Chap to Dover Coll from 75. *24 Folkestone Road, Dover, Kent.*

SQUIRE, Preb John Brinsmead. b 16. Late Exhib of St Edm Hall Ox BA (2nd cl Engl Lit) 38, MA 43. Linc Th Coll 38. **d** and **p** 40 Bris. C of St Martin Knowle 40-41; St Jo Bapt Bathwick 41-45 and 48-51; St Andr Walsall 45-46; St Jas Lower Gornal 47-48; V of H Trin Bridgwater 51-57; St Andr Taunton 57-81; Preb of Wells Cathl from 77. *Xanadu, 1 St Mary Street, Nether Stowey, Bridgwater, Somt.*

SQUIRE, William Joseph. St Columb's Hall Wang. ACT ThL 64. **d** 64 **p** 65 Wang. C of Benalla 64-65 and 67-68; Shepparton 66-68; S Yarra 69-70; Miss at Panguna Dio New Guinea 70-71; Dio Papua 71-72; Perm to Offic Dio Wang 72-78; Dio Melb from 78. *13 Bay Road, Mount Martha, Vic, Australia 3934.* (059-74 2472)

SQUIRES, Frank Spence. b 54. Univ of Tor BA, MDiv. Wycl Coll Tor. **d** 79 **p** 80 Bran. C of Birch River, Mafeking and Shoal River Dio Bran from 79. *Box 273, Birch River, Man, Canada, R0L 0E0.*

SQUIRES, John Wallace Howden. Univ of Syd BA 67. Moore Coll Syd ACT ThL 74. BD (Lon) 75. **d** and **p** 76 Syd. C of St Steph Normanhurst 76-78; St Mary Luton 78-79; Chap Dio Chich 79-80; C-in-c of St Chad Putney Dio Syd from 80. *1 Delange Road, Putney, NSW, Australia 2112.* (80-3598)

SQUIRES, Malcolm. 46. St Chad's Dur BA 72. Cudd Coll 72. **d** 74 **p** 75 Ripon. C of Headingley 74-77; Stanningley (in c of Ch The Sav) 77-80; V of Bradshaw, Halifax Dio Wakef from 80. *Vicarage, Bradshaw, Halifax, Yorks, HX2 9UU.* (Halifax 244330)

SQUIRES, Sidney James. b 1898. St Cath Coll Cam BA 23, MA 33. Ridley Hall Cam 24. **d** 25 **p** 26 St E. C of St Mary Stoke Ipswich 25-27; Cathl Ch Bury St E 27-29; CF Cant 29-30; Chatham 30-33; Dover 33-36; Plymouth 36-39; Arborfield 39-40; Singapore 40-41; Hong Kong 41-45; Bordon 46-47; DACG Home Cos Distr 47-48; CF N Ireland Distr 48; DACG Br Forces in Austria 48-50; R of Bootle (w Corney from 57) 50-57; RD of Gosforth 66-67; L to Offic Dio Carl from 67. *Mount Rivers, Bootle, Cumb.*

SQUIRES, Trevor Alexander. b 43. St Jo Coll Auckld 69. **d** 71 **p** 72 Nel. C of Blenheim 71-74; Ch Ch Cathl Nel 74-75; V of Granity-Karamea (w Murchison from 77) 75-78; Chap RNZAF from 79. *RNZAF Base, Ohakea, NZ.*

STABLER, Arthur. b 22. Coll of Resurr Mirfield. **d** 74 **p** 75 Ripon. C of Rothwell 74-76; P-in-c of Kelbrook 76-78; V 78-80. *8 Pilmoor Close, Richmond, Yorks.*

STABLES, Courtley Greenwood. b 13. Keble Coll Ox (2nd cl Th 48), BA 49, MA 54. St Steph Ho Ox. **d** 50 **p** 51 Ox. C of Watlington 50-51; Bracknell w Chavey-Down 51-55; Hd Master St Mich Coll Belize Br Hond 55-57; C of H Trin Cathl Ch w St Mary Guildf 57-61; Chap Bedford Modern Sch 62-63; Lect All SS Coll Tottenham 63-72; C of St Andr Undershaft w St Mary Axe Lon 64-72; Hon C of Uckfield Isfield and Horsted Parva Dio Chich from 73. *Framland, Easons Green, Framfield, Uckfield, Sussex, TN22 5RE.* (Halland 228)

STABROEK, Lord Bishop Suffragan of. (Vacant)

STACEY, Edward Alan. b 28. Cant Sch of Min 77. **d** 80 **p** 81 Cant (APM). C of Preston-next-Faversham 80-81; Chap of St Mary of Charity Jun Sch Faversham from 81. *32 London Road, Faversham, Kent, ME13 8RY.* (Faversham 2423)

STACEY, John Roderick. b 33. Univ of Bris BA (2nd cl Phil and Engl) 54. St D Coll Lamp LTh 56. **d** 56 **p** 57 Mon. C of Bedwellty 56-57; St Mary Mon 57-62; V of New Tredegar 62-66; CF 66-69; Men in Disp 68; V of St John Ebbw Vale 69-74; SCF (TAVR) from 73; R of Mamhilad w Llanvihangel Pontymoile 74-77; Pontynewynydd Dio Mon from 77. *Pontnewynydd Vicarage, Pontypool, Gwent, NP4 8LW.* (Pontypool 2938)

STACEY, Nicolas David. b 27. St Edm Hall, Ox BA 51, MA 55. Cudd Coll 52. **d** 53 **p** 54 Portsm. C of St Mark N End Portsea 53-58; Dom Chap to Bp of Birm 58-59; L to Offic Dio Birm 58-59; R of Woolwich 59-68; RD of Greenwich 65-68; Perm to Offic Dio Ox 68-71; Dio Cant from 79; Dep Dir of Oxfam 68-70. *The Old Vicarage, Selling, Faversham.* (Selling 833)

STACEY, Robert George Hugh. b 12. Sarum Wells Th Coll 74. **d** 76 Sarum **p** 77 Sherborne for Sarum (APM). C of Swanage Dio Sarum from 76. *59 Bay Crescent, Swanage, Dorset, BH19 1RB.* (Swanage 4138)

STACEY, Victor George. b 44. Univ Coll Dub BA 69. TCD Div Test 72. **d** 72 **p** 73 Connor. C of Derriaghy 72-76; St Columba Knock Belf 76-79; Hd of S Ch Miss Ballymacarrett Dio Down from 79. *7 Greenwood Park, Belfast, BT4 3NJ, N Ireland.*

STACKHOUSE, Canon Reginald Francis. Univ of Tor BA 46, MA 51. Wycl Coll Tor LTh 50, BD 54. Yale Univ PhD 62. **d** 49 **p** 50 Tor. C of Isl 49-52; I 52-56; R of St John W Tor 56-60; Assoc Prof Wycl Coll Tor 63-65; Prof from 65; Vice Prin 74-75; Prin from 75; Can of Tor from 78. *Wycliffe College, Hoskin Avenue, Toronto, Ont., Canada.*

STACY, Bernard Howard. b 09. **d** 60 **p** 61 Bran. C of Kelwood 60-66; R and RD of Minnedosa 66-69; C of W Tarring 70-75. *64 Robson Road, Goring-by-Sea, Sussex, BN12 4EF.*

STADNYK, William Robert. Trin Coll Tor LTh 58. **d** 57 **p** 58 Alg. I of Manitouwadge 59-63; Elliot Lake 63-71; H Trin Sault Ste Marie Dio Alg from 71. *1389 Queen Street East, Sault Ste Marie, Ont., Canada.* (705-253 6379)

STAFF, George Denis. b 29. Qu Coll Birm. **d** 56 Carl **p** 60 Ox. C of St Geo Barrow-F 56-57; Headington Ox 59-62; Banbury 62-66; V of Cropredy w Gt Bourton 66-73; Wooburn Dio Ox from 73. *Wooburn Vicarage, High Wycombe, Bucks, HP10 0JA.* (Bourne End 20030)

STAFFORD, Lord Bishop Suffragan of. *See* Waller, Right Rev John Stevens.

STAFFORD, Bertram Leyland. b 14. Lich Th Coll 40. **d** 65 **p** 66 Leic. C of Wigston Magna 65-69; V of St Hugh L Bowden Dio Leic from 69. *St Hugh's Vicarage, Northampton Road, Market Harborough, Leics.* (Market Harborough 63182)

STAFFORD, David George. b 45. Qu Coll Birm 75. **d** 77 Repton for Derby **p** 78 Derby. C of SS Aug Chesterfield 77-80; C of Ranmoor City and Dio Sheff from 80. *301 Lydgate Lane, Sheffield, S10 5FR.* (Sheff 662800)

STAFFORD, Dennis George. b 18. Worc Ordin Coll. **d** 69 Truro **p** 70 Bp Lash for Truro. C of St Columb Minor (in c of St Colan from 77) Dio Truro from 69. *Old Vicarage, St Columb Minor, Newquay, Cornw.* (Newquay 2625)

STAFFORD, John Ingham Henry. b 31. TCD BA 52, MA 58. **d** 53 **p** 55 Down. C of Clonallon 53-56; St John Malone Belf 56-59; M Bush Bro of St Barn 59-64; Min Can of Down Cathl 64-68; Commiss N Queensland from 66; Hd of S Ch Miss Ballymacarrett 68-73; R of Ballee w Bright and Killough Dio Down from 73; Hon Min Can of Down from 76; Exam Chap to Bp of Down from 80. *Bright Rectory, Downpatrick, Co Down, N Ireland.* (Ardglass 841268)

STAFFORD, John James. b 31. Linc Th Coll 69. **d** 71 **p** 72 Southw. C of All H Ordsall 71-73; V of St Paul Manton Worksop 73-78; R of Nuthall Dio Southw from 78. *Nuthall Rectory, Nottingham.* (Nottm 278680)

STAGG, Charles Roy. G and C Coll Cam 1st cl Cl Trip pt i, 39, BA 45, 2nd cl Th Trip pt i and MA 47. Ripon Hall, Ox. **d** 48 **p** 49 Dur. Chap Dur Sch 48-54; C of The Lickey 54-55; Chap Kampala Tech Inst 55-58; Aldenham Sch 59-64; Kenya High Sch 64-66; Hd Master Kenton Coll Nai from 66. *Box 30017, Nairobi, Kenya.* (Nairobi 553003)

STAGG, Michael Hubert. b 39. St Chad's Coll Dur 58. **d** 63 **p** 64 B & W. C of St Sav Weston-s-Mare 63-66; C-in-c of Fosdyke 66-70; V of Brompton Regis w Upton and Skilgate 70-78; V of St Jo Bapt Kidderminster 78-80; C-in-c of Cannington Dio B & W from 80. *Vicarage, Brook Street, Cannington, Bridgwater, Somt, TA5 2HP.* (Combwich 652953)

STAGGS, Kenneth William. b 30. STh (Lambeth) 76. **d** 61 **p** 62 Wakef. C of Lindley 61-64; V of St Phil Dewsbury 64-66; S Ossett Dio Wakef from 66. *South Ossett Vicarage, Ossett, Yorks.* (Ossett 273421)

STAINER, John. Magd Coll Ox BA 38, MA 42. **d** 51 **p** 52 Br Columb. C of St Paul Nanaimo 51-52; I of French Creek 52-61; R of Oliver 61-64; S Okanagan 64-71; Arrow Lakes 71-77; Windermere Dio Koot from 77. *Box 700, Invermere, BC, Canada.*

STAINES, Edward Noel. b 26. Late Scho of Trin Coll Ox BSc 50, MA 52. Chich Th Coll 57. **d** 57 **p** 58 Chich. C of Eastbourne 57-61; V of Amberley w N Stoke 61-70; Forest Row 70-75; St Aug Bexhill 75-79; Team R of Ovingdean w Rottingdean and Woodingdean Dio Chich from 79. *Rectory, Steyning Road, Rottingdean, Brighton, BN2 7GA.* (Brighton 309216)

STAINES, Michael John. b 28. Trin Coll Ox BA 52, MA 56. Wells Th Coll 62. **d** 64 **p** 65 Chich. C of Southwick 64-67; Team V in Harling Group 67-73; P Missr in S Chilterns Group 74-75; R of W Wycombe w Bledlow Ridge, Bradenham and Radnage Dio Ox from 76. *Rectory, Church Lane, West Wycombe, Bucks, HP14 3AH.* (High Wycombe 29988)

✠ **STAINTON, Right Rev Thomas William.** Hatf Coll Dur LTh 21, Barry Scho 23, BA (3rd cl Th) 24, MA 30. St Paul's Coll Burgh 19. **d** 24 **p** 25 S'wark. C of Camberwell 24-27; Hlamankulu 27-30; P-in-c of Inhambane 30-33; Masiyene Dio Lebom 33-41; VG Dio Lebom 35-41; Archd of Lebom 38-41; Cons Asst Bp of Bloemf in Bloemf Cathl 27 April 41 by Abp of Capetn; Bps of Natal; Kimb K; Grahmstn; Pret; Bloemf; Zulu; and Lebom; res 50; Archd of Basuto 41-51; VG 50; R and Dir of Miss Mafeteng 41-47; Exam Chap to Bp of Bloemf 45-50; V of Umzinto 51-53; R of Knysna 53-71; Archd of Geo 54-71; VG of Geo 60-61; 65-66; and 68-71; Asst Bp of Natal from 71. *9 Cherodene, PO Umtentweni, Natal, S Africa.* (Port Shepstone 1506)

STALEY, John Colin George. b 44. Wycl Hall Ox 68. **d** 71 **p** 72 Sheff. C of St Lawr Tinsley 71-73; Slaithwaite w E Scammonden 73-75; V of St Andr w St Mary Wakef 75-80; Warden Scargill Ho Kettlewell from 80. *Scargill House, Kettlewell, Skipton, N Yorks, BD23 5HU.* (Kettlewell 234)

STALLARD, Frederick Hugh. b 11. Pemb Coll Cam 3rd cl Hist Trip pt i, 32, BA (3rd cl Th Trip pt i) 33, MA 37. Cudd Coll 33. **d** 34 **p** 35 Pet. C of St Matt Northn 34-40; CF (EC) 40-45; V of All SS Pet 45-81; RD of Pet 52-68; Can (Non-res) of Pet 57-81. *3 Fridaybridge Road, Elm, Wisbech, Cambs.*

STALLARD, John Charles. b 34. Selw Coll Cam BA 58, MA 62. Ripon Hall Ox 62. **d** 64 **p** 65 Birm. C of Hall Green 64-66; Sutton Coldfield 66-68; Min of St Bede's Eccles Distr Brandwood 68-71; Chap and Asst Master Dame Allan's School Newc-T 71-74; V of Warley Woods Dio Birm from 74. *Vicarage, Abbey Road, Smethwick, Warley, B67 5NQ.* (021-429 1384)

STALLARD, Michael Frederick. b 39. Pemb Coll Cam BA 62, MA 66. Linc Th Coll 74. **d** 76 **p** 77 Lich. C of St Chad Shrewsbury 76-78; Youth Chap Bedford and C of St Pet de Merton w St Cuthb 78-80; R of Cawston and Chap Cawston Coll Dio Nor from 80. *Cawston Rectory, Norwich.* (Cawston 282)

STALLARD, Ronald Edward. St Jo Coll Manit LTh 16. **d** 66 **p** 67 Bp J O Anderson for Rupld. I of Hodgson 66-71; I of Peguis Reserve 66-71; Mapleton 71-73; Manitou 73-77; St Thos Winnipeg 77-80; Cardston Dio Calg from 80. *Box 302, Cardston, Alta, Canada.*

STALLEY, Brian Anthony. b 38. Oak Hill Th Coll 60. **d** 63 **p** 64 S'wark. C of St Mary Summerstown 63-70; Sec BFBS Surrey Distr 70-73; Manager Action Centre BFBS 74-76; L to Offic Dios Cant, Guildf and Lon 70-76; Dio Roch 73-76; Publ Pr Dio S'wark 70-76; R of Branston Dio Linc from 76. *Rectory, Abel Smith Gardens, Branston, Lincoln, LN4 1NN.* (Linc 791296)

STALLEY, Canon Frank Ernest. b 11. Univ of Reading BA (2nd cl Engl) 31. Bps' Coll Cheshunt 35. **d** 36 **p** 37 Cov. C of St Thos Cov 36-38; V of Ryton-on-Dunsmore 38-44; St Marg Cov 44-57; Market Rasen 57-78; R of Linwood 57-78; Exam Chap to Bp of Linc from 61; RD of Walshcroft W 63-69; W Wold 69-78; Surr 64-78; Can and Preb of Linc Cathl 66-78; Can (Emer) from 78; C-in-c of Legsby 74-78. *Braeside, Monyash Road, Bakewell, Derbys.* (Bakewell 2499)

STALLY, Arthur James. b 32. K Coll Lon and Warm 55. **d** 59 **p** 60 Cov. C of St Nich Radford Cov 59-62; R of Sandakan 62-66; Alcester w Arrow Oversley and Weethley Dio Cov from 66; Sec Borneo Miss Assoc 67-77; RD of Alcester from 79. *Rectory, Alcester, Warws, B49 5AL.* (Alcester 762639)

STALTER, David Kennedy. Hur Coll LTh 65. **d** 65 Hur for Ott **p** 66 Ott. I of S March 65-67; Maberly-Lanark 67-68; R of Ashton 68-72; St Marg Vanier Ott 72-78; St Mark City and Dio Ott from 78. *1606 Fisher Avenue, Ottawa, Ont, Canada.* (1-613-224 6675)

STAMMERS, Robert Andrew. b 46. St Jo Coll Dur BA 70, Dipl Th 76. **d** 77 Chich **p** 78 Horsham for Chich. C of St Mary Crawley 77-78; St Richard Haywards Heath 78-80; St Wilfrid Haywards Heath 80; Old Basing Dio Win from 80. *19 Petty's Brook Road, Chineham, Basingstoke, Hants.* (Hackwood 4280)

STAMP, Andrew Nicholas. b 44. Univ of Ex BA (2nd cl Th) 67. Sarum Th Coll. **d** 69 Stepney for S'wark **p** 70 S'wark. C of St Mich AA S Beddington 69-73; Tutor Sarum and Wells Th Coll 73-76; Chap RN 76-81; P-in-c of St Alb W Leigh, Havant Dio Portsm from 81. *St Alban's Parsonage, Martin Road, West Leigh, Havant, Hants, PO9 5TE.* (Havant 451751)

STAMP, Ewen Campbell Morrell. b 16. Cranmer Hall Dur 71. **d** 72 **p** 73 Newc T. C of Gosforth 72-76; Chap City Centre Newc T 76-81. *c/o St Andrew's Church, Newgate Street, Newcastle-on-Tyne, NE1 5SS.* (0632-27935)

STAMP, Harold William Tremlett. b 08. St Aug Coll Cant 30. **d** 35 Colchester for Chelmsf **p** 36 Chelmsf. C of St Jo Bapt Tilbury Dk 35-37; Colyton 37-39; C-in-c of Burnt House Lane Conv Distr 39-43; V of Kilmington 43-49; R of Hemyock w Culm Davy 49-58; V of Trull 58-61; R of Newton Ferrers w Revelstoke 61-69; Farway w Northleigh and Southleigh 69-72; V of Branscombe 72-76; Publ Pr Dio Ex 77 and from 81; C-in-c of Coldridge (or Coleridge) 77-81. *Jasmine Cottage, Coldridge, Crediton, Devon.*

STAMP, Richard Mark. St Chad's Coll Dur BA 60, Dipl Th 62. **d** 62 Dur for Bath **p** 63 Bath. Bro of Good Shepherd 62-67; C of Bourke 63-66; Tottenham NSW 66-67; Chap Dept of Home Missions Dio Melb 67-68; C of St Jo Bapt Greenhill Harrow 69-72; Chap Bath Cathl 72-76; All SS Coll Bath from 76. *251 Howick Street, Bathurst, NSW, Australia 2795.* (31-3207)

✠ **STANAGE, Right Rev Thomas Shaun.** Pemb Coll Ox BA 56, MA 60. Cudd Coll 56. **d** 58 **p** 59 Liv. C of St Faith Gt Crosby 58-61; Orford (in c of St Andr) 61-63; V of St Andr Orford 63-70; Commiss Kimb K 68-70; R of Somerset W 70-75; Dean and R of St Cypr Cathl Kimberley 75-78; Exam Chap to Bp of Kimb K 77-78; Archd of Germiston from 78; Cons Ld Bp Suffr of Johann in St Mary Virg Cathl Johann 19 May 78 by Abp of Capetn; Bps of Johann, Natal, Bloemf, Port Eliz, Swaz, Pret and Kimb K; and Bp Nye. *Box 1131, Johannesburg, 2000, S Africa.*

STANBRIDGE, Ven Leslie Cyril. b 20. St Jo Coll Dur BA 47, Dipl Th 49, MA 54. **d** 49 **p** 50 Roch. C of Erith 49-51; Tutor St Jo Coll Dur and L to Offic Dio Dur 51-55; Chap 52-55; Hon Chap to Bp of Leic 53-72; V of St Martin Hull 55-64; Exam Chap to Abp of York from 63; R of Cottingham 64-72; Can and Preb of York Minster from 68; RD of Kingston-upon-Hull 70-72; Archd of York from 72. *14 St George's Place, York, YO2 2DR.* (York 23775)

STANBROOK, Harry. b 05. Kelham Th Coll 27. **d** 33 **p** 34 Wakef. C of Cudworth 33-36; St Hilda S Shields 36-44; St Anselm Kennington Cross 44-46; Perm to Offic at Windsor 47-51; C of Windsor (in c of All SS from 52) 51-58; Perm to Offic Dio Ox from 59; Sub-Warden Commun of St Jo Bapt Clewer 61-63; Asst Chap 63-69. *81 Springfield Road, Windsor, Berks, SL4 3PR.* (Windsor 65566)

STANCLIFFE, Canon David Staffurth. b 42. Trin Coll Ox BA 65, MA 68. Cudd Coll 65. **d** 67 Ripon **p** 68 Knaresborough for Ripon. C of Armley 67-70; Chap Clifton Coll 70-77; Res Can of Portsm Cathl from 77; Dir of Ordinands Dio Portsm from 77. *50 Penny Street, Old Portsmouth, PO1 2NL.* (Portsm 730792)

STANCLIFFE, Very Rev Michael Staffurth. b 16. Trin Coll Ox BA 38, Dipl Th 39, MA 43. Linc Th Coll 39. **d** 40 **p** 41 Sarum. C of St Jas Southbroom 40-43; C-in-c of Ramsbury 43-44; C of Cirencester w H Trin Watermoor 44-49; Chap Westmr Sch 49-57; L to Offic Dio Guildf 53-57; Pr at Lincoln's Inn 54-57; Can of Westmr 57-69; Steward 59-69; R of St Marg Westmr 57-69; Chap to Speaker of Ho of Commons 61-69; Select Pr Univ of Ox 60 and 73; Univ of Cam 62; Dean of Win from 69; M Gen Syn 70-80. *Deanery, Winchester, Hants.* (Winchester 3738)

STANCOMBE, Ronald Douglas. d 64 Tas. C of St Mark-on-the-Hill Launceston Dio Tas from 64. *22 Weedon Avenue, Launceston, Tasmania.*

STANDBROOK, Harold Alfred. b 12. St Paul's Th Coll Grahmstn 46. **d** 47 **p** 48 Capetn. C of Good Shepherd Kensington Capetn 47-49; St Phil Capetn 49-50; Chap of St Ninian's Cathl Perth 50-52; CF 52-55; R of St Aid Clarkston Glas 55-59; Prec of St Paul's Cathl Dundee 59-63; R of Faldingworth w Buslingthorpe 63-72; Toft w Newton-by-Toft 63-72; R of Spridlington w Saxby and Firsby 63-72; Gordon Chap Fochabers 72-74; P-in-c of Aberlour 72-74; C of E Preston w Kingston 74-75; St Mary Dover 75-77. *6 Bramwell Lodge, Woodmancote, Henfield, Sussex.*

STANDEN, David Ian. b 57. AKC and BD 78. St Steph Ho Ox 80. **d** 81 Lich. C of St Francis Friar Park W Bromwich Dio Lich from 81. *207 Hydes Road, West Bromwich, W Midl, B71 2EF.* (021-556 0713)

STANDEN, Frederick George. Moore Th Coll Syd ACT ThL 31. **d** 31 **p** 32 Syd. C of St Phil Syd 31-35; St Aug Neutral Bay 35-36; R of Kurrajong 36-38; Narrabeen and Pitt Water 38-42; Mittagong 42-47; Dir of Youth Org and L to Offic Dio Newc 47-52; Chap RAAF 52-55; R of Merewether 55-69; Terrigal 69-72; Perm to Offic Dio Newc from 72. *10 Hall Street, Belmont, NSW, Australia 2280.*

STANDEN McDOUGAL, John Anthony Phelps. b 33. K Coll Lon and Warm AKC 58. **d** 59 **p** 60 St E. C of St Marg Ipswich 59-63; St Mary's Bury St Edmunds 63-65; Wadhurst and of Tidebrook 65-70; R of Tollard Royal w Farnham Dio Sarum from 70; C-in-c of St Mich Gussage Dio Sarum 71-76; R (w All SS) from 76; Ashmore Dio Sarum from 81; Chettle Dio Sarum from 81; RD of Milton and Blandford from 81. *Farnham Rectory, Blandford, Dorset, DT11 8DE.* (Tollard Royal 221)

STANDIDGE, Arthur William McPherson. b 03. BA (Lon) 46. FRCO 31. Ely Th Coll. **d** 57 Lon **p** 58 Willesden for Lon. C of All SS Friern Barnet 57-61; PC of St Pet-le-Poer Friern Barnet 61-66; R of Islip Pet 66-78. *110 Willingdon Road, Eastbourne, E Sussex.*

STANDING, Victor. b 44. Univ of Lon BMus 66, FRCO 67. Univ of Ox Dipl Th 77. Ripon Coll Cudd 75. **d** 78 Sarum **p** 79 Sherborne for Sarum. C of Wimborne Minster Dio Sarum 78-80; Team V (w Holt St Jas) from 80. *Vicarage, Holt, Wimborne, Dorset, BH21 7DJ.* (0202-882437)

STANDISH, Derrick Edgar. b 41. St D Coll Lamp BA 67. Wycl Hall, Ox 67. **d** 68 **p** 69 Swan B. C of Brynmawr 68-70; Llangyfelach w Morriston 70-71; Morriston 71-74; V of Merthyr Cynog w Duffryn Honddu 74-76; R of Llanwenarth Ultra Dio Mon from 76. *Govilon Rectory, Abergavenny, Gwent, NP7 9PT.*

STANDISH, Canon Granville Nelson. McGill Univ Montr BA 41. Montr Dioc Th Coll **d** 42 Fred for Montr **p** 43 Queb for Montr. C of St Steph Westmount Montr 42-43; I of Mirror w Alix and Bashaw 43-47; R of Grande Prairie 47-50; Can of Athab 48-50; R of Dunham w St Armand 50-52; P-in-c of E Farnham 52-54; I of Merriton 54-58; R of Port Colborne 58-69; St John Stamford Niag Falls 69-80; Hon Can of Ch Ch Cathl Hamilton 67-75; Dom Chap to Bp of Niag 71-74; Archd of Brock 76-80; Hon Can of Niag from 80; P-in-c of St Sav Queenston Dio Niag from 81. *4480 Philip Street, Niagara Falls, Ont., Canada.* (416-356 6219)

STANDLEY, Leslie Gordon. b 19. St Chad's Coll Dur BA 42, Dipl Th 43, MA 45. **d** 43 **p** 44 Linc. C of Gainsborough 43-47; St Jo Evang Spitalgate Grantham 47-50; R of Wyberton 50-54; V of Middleton Junction 54-56; Brothertoft w Kirton Holme 56-59; PC of H Trin Gainsborough (w St Geo from 64) 59-67; C-in-c of St Geo Conv Distr Gainsborough 59-64; V of Ulceby 67-70; V of Wootton 67-70; R of Croxton 67-70; V of Forest Town 70-76; Swineshead Dio Linc from 76; RD of Holland W from 79. *c/o Swineshead Vicarage, Boston, Lincs.* (Boston 820271)

STANDLEY, Robert Henry. b 21. Univ of Lon BD (2nd cl) 42. Linc Th Coll **d** 44 Grimsby for Linc **p** 45 Linc. C of Grimsby (in c of St Hugh) 44-51; V of Morton 51-59; V of E Stockwith w Walkerith 52-59; Hd Master All H Sen Sch Pawa Ugi 59-64; V of Coleby 65-74; Harmston 65-74; Skirbeck Quarter Dio Linc from 74; RD of Holland E from 80. *St Thomas's Vicarage, Linley Drive, Boston, Lincs.* (Boston 67380)

STANES, Ian Thomas. b 39. Univ of Sheff BSc 62. Linacre Coll Ox BA 65, MA 69. Wycl Hall Ox 63. **d** 65 **p** 66 Leic. C of H Ap Leic 65-68; V of Broom Leys 68-76; Warden Marrick Priory Centre Dio Ripon from 76. *Marrick Priory, Richmond, N Yorks., DL11 7LD.* (Richmond 84434)

STANESBY, Derek Malcolm. b 31. Univ of Leeds BA 56. Univ of Man MEducn 75. Coll of Resurr Mirfield. **d** 58 **p** 59 Thetford for Cant. C of Lakenham 58-60; St Mary Virg Welling 60-62; V of St Mark Bury 62-67; Chap Bury Gen Hosp 62-67; R of Ladybarn Dio Man from 67. *St Chad's Rectory, Withington, Manchester, M20 9WH.* (061-445 1185)

STANFORD, Ronald John. b 02. Late Minor Scho of Trin Coll Ox BA (2nd cl Nat Sc w distinc in Crystallography) 24, MA 28. Ripon Hall Ox 32. **d** 33 **p** 34 Ox. Asst Chap Culham

Coll and L to Offic Dio Ox 33-35; C of N Wingfield 35-37; V of Pilsley 37-45; CF (R of O) from 39; R of Darley-in-the-Dale (w S Darley from 55) 44-63; RD of Bakewell 55-63; Surr 55-63; Proc Conv Derby 59-64; V of Snape w Friston 63-73; RD of Saxmundham 67-72; Perm to Offic Dio St E from 73. *c/o Bowling Green, Friston, Saxmundham, Suff.* (Snape 358)

STANGER, Charles Thomas. St Jo Coll Winnipeg Div Test 50. **d** 50 Yukon **p** 51 Edmon for Yukon. C of Ch Ch Whitehorse 50-51; R of St Sav Carcross 51-54; Prin of Chooutla Ind Res Sch 51-56; Miss at Peigan Miss 56-59; C of Ascen Hamilton 59-62; I of All SS Ridgeway 62-68; R of St Jas Hamilton 68-70. *Box 14, Beachburg, Ont, Canada.*

STANGER, William Hursthouse. b 02. Univ of Syd BA 23, MA 26. ACT ThL 24. Moore Th Coll Syd 23. **d** 25 **p** 26 Syd. C of St Pet Hornsby 25-28; St Aug Neutral Bay 28-34; R of St John Milson's Point 34-39; Asst Sec for Ireland CCCS 39-40; Chap RAFVR 40-48; RAF 48-57; R of Wittering w Thornhaugh and Wansford 57-64; V of Wilstead 64-70. *Huntly, Bishopsteignton, Teignmouth, Devon, TQ14 9SJ.*

STANHAM, Charles Taylor. St Jo Coll Cam BA 14, MA 19. Bps' Coll Cheshunt. **d** 21 **p** 22 Lon. C of St Simon Zelotes Bethnal Green 21-22; St Jas Fulham 22-24; St Jo Evang E Lon CP 24-27; St Jas Stamford Hill Durban 27-29; V of Tugela Rivers 29-32; Umzinto 32-37; Karkloof 37-42; Mooi River 42-46; Verulam Dio Natal 46-52, R of Palmyra 52-56; Bicton 56-58; Perm to Offic Dio Perth 58-63 and from 66; P-in-c of St Mary N Freemantle 63-66. *12 Ranelagh Crescent, South Perth, W Australia 6151.*

STANIFORTH, John Hamilton Maxwell. b 1893. Late Scho and Exhib of Ch Ch Ox 2nd cl Cl Mods 14, BA 19, MA 42. Chich Th Coll 37. **d** 38 Lewes for Chich **p** 38 Chich. C of Woolavington w Graffham 38-40; Felpham w Middleton 40-41; V of Flimwell 41-45; Chap and Tutor St Mich Sch Petworth 45-47; Beehive Sch Bexhill 47-52; L to Offic Dio Chich 48-52; V of Pentridge w Handley 52-63; Dioc Insp of Schs 54-57; RD of Blandford 55-63. *Five Chimneys, Pilley Hill, Lymington, Hants.*

STANLEY, Alfred. b 1891. Trin Coll Tor LTh 21. St Chad's Coll Regina LTh (*ad eund*) 23. **d** 21 Tor **p** 22 Qu'App. C of Togo Sask 21-22; I 22-25; C of Rodney Stoke 25-26; I of Outlook 26-29; Gull Lake 29-34; C of Cannock (in c of St Paul Bridgtown) 34-38; R of Draycott-le-Moors 38-49; V of Dilhorne 49-57; R of Trefonen 57-64. *1 Burn Hall Crescent, Burn, Selby, Yorks.* (Burn 679)

STANLEY, Arthur Patrick. b 32. TCD BA 54, MA 63. **d** 55 **p** 56 Cash. C of Waterford 55-58; CF from 58; DACG Wales 74-75; Gibr 75-77; Aldershot 77-78; Cyprus 78-80; Bulford from 80. *c/o Williams & Glyns Bank, Holts Branch, Farnborough, Hants.*

STANLEY, Bernard Leslie. b 32. St Steph Ho Ox 75. **d** 76 **p** 77 Reading for Ox (APM). C of Thame Dio Ox from 76. *65 Seven Acres, Thame, Oxon, OX9 3JQ.* (Thame 3748)

STANLEY, Douglas Arnold Bruce. Univ of Tor BA 59. Wycl Coll Tor BTh and LTh 62. **d** 62 Keew **p** 63 Arctic. C of Fort Chimo 62-63; I of Tuktoyaktuk Dio Arctic 63-66; Dio Athab 66-69. *487 Shannon Road, Sault Ste Marie, Ont., Canada.* (705-253 9241)

STANLEY, Ven Eric William. b 22. Trin Coll Dub BA 45, MA 58 **d** 45 **p** 46 Oss. C of Carlow w Killishin 45-48; C-in-c of Seir-Kyran and Aghancon w Kilcolman 48-53; I of Bourney Corbally and Dunkerrin 53; C-in-c of Seir-Kyran and of Aghancon w Kilcoman 54-66; Can and Preb of Killaloe Cathl from 65; Chan 72-79; I of Nenagh w Ballymackey 66-68; Nenagh w Templederry and Killodiernan Dio Killaloe from 68; Ballinaclough w Templederry Dio Killaloe from 68; Dioc Sec Killaloe from 73; Archd of Killaloe and Kilfen from 79; Preb of St Patr Cathl Dub from 81. *St Mary's Rectory, Nenagh, Co Tipperary, Irish Republic.* (Nenagh 31399)

STANLEY, Frank John. St Paul's Coll Grahmstn 61. **d** 61 **p** 62 Kimb K. C of St Cypr Cathl Ch Kimb 61-65; R of Cathcart 65-66; C of Hooton 66-68; Ouyen 68-71; R of Charlton 71-72; Heathcote 73-77; Rochester 77-80; Perm to Offic Dio Melb from 80. *15 Nutter Crescent, St John's Park, Mooroolbark, Vic, Australia.*

STANLEY, George Rolf. Univ Coll Tor BA 42, LTh 45. Wycl Coll Tor 45. **d** 43 Tor **p** 44 Moos. C of Ch of Transfig Tor 43-44; I of Kapukasing 44-54; Can of Moos 50-54; R of Midland 54-57; St Clem E Tor 57-68. *55 Chevron Crescent, Scarborough 703, Ont, Canada.*

STANLEY, John Alexander. b 31. Tyndale Hall Bris 51. Dipl Th 56. **d** 56 Blackb **p** 57 Ches for Blackb. C of All SS Preston 56-60; St Mark St Helens 60-63; V of St Cuthb Everton 63-70; C-in-c of St Sav Everton 69-70; V of St Sav w St Cuthb Everton 70-74; Huyton Dio Liv from 74; M Gen Syn from 73. *Huyton Vicarage, Liverpool, L36 7XE.*

STANLEY, Joseph. b 12. Chich Th Coll 37. **d** 39 **p** 40 Chelmsf. C of Canvey I 39-41; The Ascen Collier Row Romford 41-44; Chap RNVR 44-46; C-in-c of St Paul Walthamstow 47-51; V of Swaffham 51-60; Surr 51-60. *Hillside Lodge, Milton-under-Wychwood, Oxford.*

STANLEY, Keith William. b 23. **d** 79 **p** 80 Bal. Perm to Offic Dio Bal 79; C of Horsham Dio Bal from 80. *14 Andrew Street, Horsham, Vic, Australia 3400.*

STANLEY, Robert John. TCD BA 50, MA 54. **d** 50 **p** 51 Connor. C of TCD Miss Belf 50-52; St Matt Belf 52-54; R of Tamlaghtard w Aghanloo 54-60; Donaghheady 60-63; CF 63-79; V of St Steph Prittlewell Dio Chelmsf from 79. *213 Manners Way, Prittlewell, Southend, Essex.*

STANLEY, Simon Richard. b 44. Wells Th Coll 66. **d** 69 Bp J D Mackie for Cov **p** 70 Cov. C of Foleshill 69-71; Hessle 71-75; C-in-c of Flamborough 75-80; R of Dunnington Dio York from 80. *Rectory, Dunnington, York, YO1 5PW.* (York 489349)

STANLEY, Thomas Derby. St Jo Coll Auckld. **d** 59 **p** 69 Wel. C of Lower Hutt 59-69; St Pet Palmerston N Dio Wel from 69. *c/o St Peter's Vicarage, Palmerston North, NZ.*

STANNARD, Canon Colin Percy. b 24. TD 66. Selw Coll Cam BA 47, MA 49. Linc Th Coll 47. **d** 49 **p** 50 St E. C of St Jas Cathl Bury St Edms 49-52; C-in-c of St Martin Conv Distr Nunsthorpe 52-55; CF (TA) 53-67; V of St Jas Barrow-F 55-64; St Jo Bapt Upperby Carl 64-70; RD of Calder 70-75; Kendal from 75; R of Gosforth 70-75; Hon Can of Carl from 74; P-in-c of Natland Dio Carl 75-76; V from 76. *Natland Vicarage, Kendal, Cumb, LA9 7QQ.* (Sedgwick 60355)

STANNARD, Derek Raymond Ouseley. Em Coll Sktn 53. **d** 56 **p** 57 Sktn. I of Rosthern 56-59; R of Wetaskiwin 59-63; Chap RN (Canad) 63-67; I of Cortes I 67-68; R of Alert Bay 68-72; I of Chemainus Dio BC from 72. *Box 463, Chemainus, BC, Canada.* (604-246 9067)

✠ **STANNARD, Right Rev Robert William.** b 1895. Late Sch of Ch Ch Ox BA (sc Lit Hum w Distinc) 20, 1st cl Th Liddon Stud and MA 21. Cudd Coll Ox 21. **d** 22 **p** 23 S'wark. C of St Mary Magd Bermondsey 22-24; Putney (in c of St Mary) 24-27; V of St Jas Barrow-F 27-34; RD of Dalton 34; Wearmouth 36-41; R of Bp Wearmouth 34-41; Archd of Doncaster 41-47; V of Melton-on-the-Hill 41-47; RD of Doncaster 45-47; Chap to HM the King 44-47; Cons Ld Bp Suffr of Woolwich in S'wark Cathl 25 July 47 by Abp of Cant; Bps of S'wark; Sheff; Sarum; and Albany; Bps Suffr of Kingston T; and Burnley; and Bp Heaslett; res 59; Archd of Lewisham 47-55; Exam Chap to Bp of S'wark 47-59; Dean of Roch 59-66. *Dendron, Reading Road North, Fleet, Hants.* (Fleet 4059)

STANSBURY, Alan David. Ridley Hall Cam 59. **d** 61 **p** 62 S'wark. C of St Mark Kennington 61-63; Wynberg (in c of St Luke Diep River 63-68; Em Ch from 68) 63-73; R of Clanwilliam Dio 73-79; St Pet and St Jas Cradock w All SS Somerset E Dio Port Eliz from 79. *Box 427, Cradock 5880, CP, S Africa.*

STANTON, Canon Eric Edwin. b 11. SS Coll Cam 2nd cl Hist Trip pt i, 32, BA (3rd cl Geog Trip pt ii) 33, MA 37. Wells Th Coll 34. **d** 35 **p** 36 Newc T. C of Ponteland 35-38; All SS W Southbourne Bournemouth 38-39; Croydon 39-43; V of Wingham 43-48; Faversham 48-55; Chap of HM Pris Cant 46-48; Surr 48-55; R of Saltwood 55-68; Hon Can of Cant 62-79; Can (Emer) from 79; V of Goudhurst 68-74; RD of W Charing 71-74; Perm to Offic Dio Cant from 75. *9 Eastgate Road, Tenterden, Kent.* (Tenterden 4295)

STANTON, John Maurice. b 18. Univ Coll Ox BA (2nd cl Nat Sc) 45, MA 45. Wycl Hall, Ox 51. **d** 52 **p** 53 Roch. C of Tonbridge 52-54; Asst Chap Tonbridge Sch 52-59; Publ Pr Dio Roch 54-59; Hd Master Blundell's Sch 59-71; Publ Pr Dio Ex 71-72; C of St Matt Ex 72-73; R of Chesham Bois Dio Ox from 73. *Rectory, Chesham Bois, Bucks, HP6 5NA.* (Amersham 6139)

STANTON, Ven Mervyn Richard. Ch Coll Tas ACT ThL (2nd cl) 49. **d** 50 **p** 51 Tas. C of H Trin Hobart 50-52; C-in-c of Zeehan 52-54; R of Beaconsfield w Ex 54-58; New Norf 58-64; St Geo Invermay Launceston 64-66; Dir of Overseas Dept Dio Tas 66-71; R of All SS Hobart 71-73; Burnie Dio Tas from 73; Can of Tas from 77; Archd of Darwin from 79. *24 View Road, Burnie, Tasmania 7320.* (004-31 2315)

STANTON, Ronald Geoffrey. b 14. Univ of Leeds, BA 48. Wells Th Coll. **d** 50 **p** 51 Cov. C of St Barbara Cov 50-53; H Trin Cov 53-58; V of Willenhall w Whitley 58-61; Wellesbourne 61-72; R of Walton D'Eivile 61-72; V of Finham 72-79. *8 Margetts Close, Kenilworth, W Midl, CV8 1EN.* (Kenilworth 511036)

STANTON, (Timothy) Thomas Hugh. Trin Coll Cam BA 38, MA 45. Coll of Resurr Mirfield 46. **d** 47 **p** 48 S'wark. C of St Geo Camberwell 47-49; M CR from 52; Vice-Prin Coll of Resurr Rosettenville 54-62; Miss P Priory of Ch K Alice 62-69; P-in-c of Alice 69-77; L to Offic Dio Johann from 80. *Box 49027, Rosettenville, Johannesburg, S Africa.*

STANTON-SARINGER, Maurice Charles. b 49. Univ of

Bris BSc 71. Fitzw Coll Cam BA 77, MA 81. Ridley Hall Cam 75. **d** 78 Reading for Cant for Ox **p** 79 Buckingham for Ox. C of Gerrard's Cross 78-80; Bletchley Dio Ox from 80. *1 Ashburnham Close, Bletchley, Milton Keynes, MK3 7TR.* (Milton Keynes 642749)

✠ **STANWAY, Right Rev Alfred.** Ridley Coll Melb ACT ThL 34. MA (Lambeth) 51. **d** 34 **p** 36 Melb. C of St Alb 34-36; St Jas and St John Melb 36-37; CMS Miss Kaloleni 37-44; Maseno 44-45; RD of Nyanza 45-47; Exam Chap to Bp of Momb 45-51; Gen Sec Afr Coun 48-51; Archd of Kenya and Can of Momb 49-51; Commiss Momb 49-51; Cons Ld Bp of Centr Tang in Westmr Abbey 2 Feb 51 by Abp of Cant; Bps of Lon; Nor; Worc; Glouc; S & M; and Man; Bp Suffr of Kens; and Bps Heywood, Chambers, and Ridsdale; Dean of Dodoma Cathl 51-71; res 71; Dep Prin Ridley Coll Melb 71-75; on leave 75-78; Perm to Offic Dio Melb from 79. *1/7 Elm Grove, Mount Waverley, Vic, Australia 3149.* (233 8425)

STANWAY, John David. Montr Dioc Th Coll. **d** 65 **p** 66 Montr. C of All SS Verdun (in c of Lasalle Miss) 65-71; I of St Bruno 71-74; R of Knowlton-Masonville Dio Montr from 74. *Box 315, Knowlton, PQ, Canada.* (514-243 6061)

STANWAY, Peter David. b 48. K Coll Lon BD 71. St Aug Coll Cant 72. **d** 73 **p** 74 Cant. C of Maidstone 73-77; I of Leask Dio Sask from 77. *Box 433, Leask, Sask, Canada.*

STAPLE, David Randall. St Paul's Coll Grahmstn 49. **d** 52 **p** 53 Grahmstn. C of Vincent 52-57; St Mich AA Queenstown 57-60; R of Barkly E 60-67; Aliwal N Dio Grahmstn from 67; R of Burgersdorp 67-74; Stutterheim Dio Grahmstn from 74. *Box 118, Stutterheim, CP, S Africa.*

STAPLEFORD, Michael Henry Mark. b 55. St Chad's Coll Dur BA 77. St Steph Ho Ox 78. **d** 80 **p** 81 Dur. C of St Ignatius Hendon Bp Wearmouth Dio Dur from 80. *St Ignatius Clergy House, Mowbray Road, Sunderland, T & W.*

STAPLES, Canon Charles Edward. **d** 51 Bp W C White for Ont **p** 52 Ont. C of N Frontenac 51-52; R 52-55; C of Kingston Cathl 55-59; R of Edwardsburg 59-63; Assoc Sec Gen Bd of Relig Educn 63-70; R of Stirling 71; St Luke Kingston 74-80; St Pet Brockville Dio Ont from 80; Archd of Kingston 78-80; Can of Ont from 80. *46 Park Street, Brockville, Ont, Canada.*

STAPLES, Canon David. b 35. Jes Coll Ox BA (3rd cl Th) 59, MA 63. Linc Th Coll 59. **d** 61 **p** 62 Pet. C of St Andr Kettering 61-64; Doncaster 64-66; Dioc Youth Chap Sheff 66-71; V of Mexborough Dio Sheff from 71; RD of Wath from 77; Hon Can Sheff from 80. *Vicarage, Mexborough, S Yorks.* (Mexborough 2321)

STAPLES, David Richard. b 50. Univ of New Brunswick MA 73. Atlantic Sch of Th MDiv 76. **d** 76 Fred **p** 77 Tor. On leave 76-77; C of Kingsclear & Newmaryland 77-80; R of St Pet Kingsclear Dio Fred from 80. *RR No 6, Fredericton, NB, Canada. E3B 4X7.*

STAPLES, Canon Edward Eric. b 10. CBE 77. OBE 73. Chich Th Coll 46. **d** 48 **p** 49 S'wark. C of Wallington 48-51; Dom Chap to Bp of Portsm and L to Offic Dio Portsm 51-55; Dioc Youth Chap 52-58; V of Shedfield 55-64; Hon Chap to Bp of Portsm 55-59; Dioc Insp of Schs Dio Portsm 55-58; Perm to Offic Dio Lon (N and C Eur) 64-66; Chap at Helsinki w Moscow 66-80; Chap to HM the Queen 73-80; Hon Can of Gibr from 74; Perm to Offic Dio B & W from 81. *Coombe Cottage, Templecombe, Somt, BA8 0QH.*

STAPLES, John Wedgwood. b 42. Hertf Coll Ox BA (3rd cl Th) 64. Wycl Hall Ox 64. **d** 66 **p** 67 Birm. C of Yardley 66-69; Knowle 69-74; R of Barcombe 74-81; V of Old Windsor Dio Ox from 81. *Vicarage, Church Road, Old Windsor, Berks, SL4 2PQ.* (Windsor 65778)

STAPLES, Peter. Jes Coll Ox BA (2nd cl Th) 59, MA 63. Univ of Nottm PhD 70. Ripon Hall Ox 59. **d** 62 **p** 64 Derby. C of Fairfield 62-63; Dore 63-66; Wilne w Draycott and Breaston 66-71; Sen Asst (Ch Hist) Univ of Utrecht from 71; Ecumen Adv to Archd of NW Eur from 81. *Doldersweg 390, Huis Ter Heide, The Netherlands.* (030 531940)

STAPLES, Peter Brian. b 38. Bps' Coll Cheshunt 66. **d** 68 Warrington for Liv **p** 69 Liv. C of St Jas Birkdale 68-71; St Jo Bapt Sevenoaks 71-74; V of Treslothan 74-80; St Paul and St Clem City and Dio Truro from 80. *41 Tregoll's Road, Truro, TR1 1LE.* (Truro 2576)

STAPLETON, Derrick Adolphus. Codr Coll Barb 63. **d** 67 **p** 68 Antig. C of St Anthony Montserrat 67-68; R of St Bart w St Martin Antig 68-75; St Mary Antig 75-76. *St Mary's Rectory, Urlings, Antigua, WI.*

STAPLETON, Canon Henry Edward Champneys. b 32. Pemb Coll Cam 2nd cl Cl Trip pt i, 53, BA (2nd cl Th Trip pt i) 54, MA 58. Ely Th Coll 54. **d** 56 **p** 57 York. C of St Olave w St Giles York 56-59; Pocklington 59-61; V of Seaton Ross w Everingham Harswell and Bielby 61-67; RD of Weighton 66-67; R of Skelton 67-75; V of Wroxham w Hoveton 75-81; P-in-c of Belaugh 76-81; Hoveton St Pet 79-81; Can Res of Roch Cathl from 81. *2 King's Orchard, The Precinct, Rochester, Kent, ME1 1TG.* (Medway 41491)

STAPLETON, Canon Kenneth Hargrave. b 11. St Pet Hall Ox BA (3rd cl Th) 38, MA 42. Wells Th Coll 38. **d** 39 **p** 40 Ripon. C of St Bart Armley 39-43; C-in-c of St Pet Bramley Leeds 43-45; CF (EC) 46-47; V of Holbeck 47-62; V of New Wortley 52-57; Surr from 61; St Wilfrid Halton 62-78; RD of Whitkirk 69-70; Hon Can of Ripon 74-78; Can (Emer) from 78; Lect Leeds Par ch from 78. *146 Tinshill Road, Leeds, LS16 7PN.* (Leeds 676669)

STAPLETON, Leonard Charles. b 37. Chich Th Coll 75. **d** 77 **p** 78 Roch. C of Crayford 77-81; H Redeemer Lamorbey Dio Roch from 81. *34 Ronaldstone Road, Sidcup, Kent, DA15 8QU.* (01-859 4058)

STAPLETON, Robert Michael Vorley. b 25. ALCD 51. **d** 51 **p** 52 Ex. C of St Andr w St Cath Plymouth 51-56; Chap RN 56-60; C of St Matt Surbiton (in c of St Geo Tolworth) 60-64; R of Chenies and L Chalfont Dio Ox from 64. *Chenies Rectory, Rickmansworth, Herts.* (Chorley Wood 4433)

STAPLETON, Robert Vauvelle. b 47. St Jo Coll Dur BA 70, Dipl Th 71. **d** 71 **p** 72 Ches. C of Ch Ch Moreton 71-73; Monk Wearmouth 73-76; Stranton 76-79; P-in-c of Kelloe Dio Dur from 79. *Vicarage, Church Villas, Kelloe, Co Durham, DH6 4PT.* (Durham 770263)

STARBUCK, Francis Tony. b 36. Kelham Th Coll 56. **d** 61 **p** 62 Southw. C of St Mark Mansfield 61-64; Didcot 67-71; C-in-c St Jo Conv Distr California Wokingham 71-75; R of Barkham 74-75; V of Hagbourne Dio Ox from 75. *Hagbourne Vicarage, Didcot, Oxon, OX11 9LR.* (Didcot 815047)

STARES, Brian Maurice William. b 44. St Deiniol's Libr Hawarden 74. **d** 74 **p** 75 Mon. C of Risca 74-77; V of St Steph w H Trin Newport Dio Mon from 77. *15 Clytha Square, Newport, NPT 2EF.* (Newport 65192)

STARK, Preb Edwin George John. b 20. Ex Coll Ox 3rd cl Mod Hist 47, BA 48, MA 52. Wells Th Coll **d** 49 **p** 50 Cant. C of St Jo Evang U Norwood 49-52; Chap Hurstpierpoint Coll 52-54; C of Stepney and Chap Lon Hosp 54-56; V of St Mary Magd Paddington 56-64; St Mary of Eton Hackney Wick 64-77; All SS Falmouth 77-80; Mylor w Flushing Dio Truro from 80; Preb of St Endellion Dio Truro from 81. *Mylor Vicarage, Falmouth, Cornw, TR11 5UD.* (Penryn 74408)

STARK, John Jordan. b 40. Univ of Hull BA (2nd cl Hist and Th) 62. St Chad's Coll Dur Dipl Th 64. **d** 64 **p** 65 Derby. C of Buxton 64-67; Wolborough w Newton Abbot (in c of St leon) 67-74; R of Belstone w Sticklepath Chap 74-79; P-in-c of St Gabr Plymouth Dio Ex 79-80; V from 80. *Vicarage, Peverell Terrace, Peverell, Plymouth, Devon.* (Plymouth 63938)

STARK, Michael. b 35. Univ of Dur BSc 56. Chich Th Coll. **d** 60 **p** 61 York. C of St Paul Middlesbrough 60-64; S Bank 64-66; R of Skelton-in-Cleveland 66-74; C-in-c of Upleatham 66-67; V 67-74; Asst Chap HM Pris Wormwood Scrubs 75-76; Chap HM Pris Featherstone, Wolverhampton from 76. *c/o HM Prison, Featherstone, Wolverhampton, WV10 7PU.* (Standeford 790991)

STARKEY, Ernest Walter Josiah Stanley. b 1892. AKC (1st cl) 22, BD 24. **d** 23 **p** 24 Lon. C of St Laur Brondesbury 23-25; St Gabr Bounds Green 25-38; V of St Mark Bush Hill Park 38-63; Chap Conv of H Rood Findon 63-67; Lindfield 67-70. *College of St Barnabas, Dormans, Lingfield, Surrey.*

STARKEY, John Douglas. b 23. St Chad's Coll Dur BA (2nd cl Th) 47, Lightfoot Scho 47, Univ Hebr Scho 47, Dipl Th 48. **d** 48 **p** 49 Lich. C of Horninglow 48-52; Lower Gornal 52-55; C-in-c of Ascen Conv Distr West Bromwich 55-57; PC of Coseley 57-66; V of Freehay Dio Lich from 66; P-in-c of Oakamoor Dio Lich from 78. *Freehay Vicarage, Cheadle, Stoke-on-Trent, ST10 1TS.* (Tean 2287)

STARKEY, Patrick Robin. b 37. St Pet Hall, Ox BA (2nd cl Th) 60, MA 64. Wycl Hall, Ox 60. **d** 64 **p** 65 Roch. C of Tonbridge 64-68; Asst Chap Sherborne Sch 68-72; C of Mill Hill 72-73; on Staff of Script U from 73. *c/o Scripture Union, 130 City Road, EC1V 2NJ.*

STARKEY, Simon Mark. b 36. Univ of Liv BA 78. Clifton Th Coll. **d** 66 **p** 67 Ox. C of St Ebbe w St Pet-le-Bailey Ox 66-72; Commun Chap CPAS Kirkdale Dio Liv from 72; P-in-c of St Bede Toxt Pk Dio Liv from 77; RD of Toxteth from 81. *76a Hartington Road, Liverpool, L8 0SQ.* (051-733 6843)

STARLING, Cyril James. St D Coll Lamp 63. **d** 65 **p** 66 Mon. C of St Andr Liswerry 65-67; R of H Trin Newport 67-70; Chap Basingstoke Hosp 70-73; Perm to Offic Dio Melb 74-77; Dio Gippsld from 77. *Macalister Street, Sale, Vic, Australia 3850.*

STARR, Ven Charles Murray. Trin Coll Tor BA 48, LTh 51. **d** 51 Tor for Calg **p** 52 Calg. C of St Martin w St Mark Calg 51-53; I of Hanna 53-61; Hon Can of Calg 58-69; R of St Mich AA Calg 61-68; Red Deer 68-74; Archd of Rocky

Mountain 69-75; R of St Jo Evang City and Dio Edmon from 75; Exam Chap to Bp of Edmon 78-80; Archd of Cold Lake from 80. *5507-113th Street, Edmonton, Alta, T6H 3K7, Canada.*

STARR, John Michael. b 50. Sarum Wells Th Coll 71. **d** 74 **p** 75 Win. C of Basingstoke 74-78; Maybush 78-79; Milton Dio Win from 79. *25 Ashley Common Road, New Milton, BH25 5AJ.* (New Milton 612644)

STARR, Michael Richard. b 43. Sarum Th Coll 65. **d** 68 **p** 69 Ex. C of St Pet Plymouth 68-72; St Paul Blackpool 72-74; V of St Cuthb Burnley 74-79; C of St Mary Eastbourne Dio Chich from 79. *20 Motcombe Road, Eastbourne, BN21 1QT.* (Eastbourne 29667)

STARTUP, Edward Williams. **d** 46 **p** 47 Waik. C of St Pet Cathl Hamilton 46-48; P-in-c of Torkoroa w Mangakino 48-50; C of St Pet Ap Cathl Hamilton 50-52; C of Tamaki W 52-55; V of Panmure Auckld 55-57; Asst City Miss Auckld 57-58; C of St Alb Holborn Lon 59; Chap Conv of Mich Ham Common 59-67. *81 Charles Street, Christchurch, NZ.*

STATHAM, Brian Edward. b 55. AKC 76. St Steph Ho Ox 77. **d** 78 **p** 79 Ches. C of H Trin Ches 78-81; Birkenhead Priory Dio Ches from 81. *1 Ashville Road, Birkenhead, Mer, L41 8AU.* (051-652 1309)

STATHAM, John Francis. b 31. Kelham Th Coll 51. **d** 56 **p** 57 Derby. C of St Mary Ilkeston 56-58; St Geo New Mills 58-59; Newbold w Dunston 59-62; PC of Ridgeway 62-69; V of New Mills 69-81; RD of Glossop 78-81; P-in-c of Matlock Dio Derby from 81. *Rectory, Matlock, Derbys, DE4 3BZ.* (Matlock 2199)

STATON, Geoffrey. b 40. Wells Th Coll 64. **d** 66 **p** 67 Lich. C of Wednesfield 66-69; Cannock 69-72; V of Cheddleton Dio Lich from 72; RD of Leek from 77. *Cheddleton Vicarage, Leek, Staffs.* (Churnet Side 360226)

STAUNTON, Richard Steedman. b 25. Wadh Coll Ox BA 49, MA 50, BSc 51. Cudd Coll 63. **d** 64 Bp McKie for Cov **p** 65 Cov. C of Wyken 64-68; V of Tile Hill 68-76; Hillmorton Dio Cov from 76. *Hillmorton Vicarage, Hoskyn Close, Rugby, Warws.* (Rugby 76279)

STAVELEY, Dennis Frank. b 21. Open Univ BA 75. SOC 77. **d** 80 Bradwell for Chelmsf **p** 81 Chelmsf. C of Danbury Dio Chelmsf from 80. *15 Landisdale, Danbury, Chelmsford, CM3 4QR.* (Danbury 3250)

STAVELEY-WADHAM, Robert Andrew. b 43. Ridley Hall Cam 79. **d** 81 Colchester for Chelmsf. C of Saffron Walden Dio Chelmsf from 81. *17 Saxon Way, Saffron Walden, Essex.*

STAVERT, Canon Alexander Bruce. Bps' Univ Lennox BA 61. Trin Coll Tor STB 64, MTh 76. **d** 64 **p** 65 Queb. I of Schefferville 64-69; Fell and Tutor in Div Trin Coll Tor 69-70; Chap 70-76; P-in-c of St Clem Miss, St Paul River Dio Queb 76-81; I from 81; Hon Can of Queb from 80; Chap Bp's Univ Lennoxville from 81. *Chaplain's Office, Bishop's University, Lennoxville, PQ, Canada J1M 1Z7.*

STEAD, Canon George Christopher. b 13. Late Scho of K Coll Cam 1st cl Cl Trip pt i, 33, Pitt Scho 34, BA (1st cl Mor Sc Trip pt ii) 35, MA 38, LittD 78. New Coll Ox BA 35. Keble Coll Ox MA 49. FBA 80. Cudd Coll 38. **d** 38 Grimsby for Linc **p** 41 Linc. Perm to Offic Dio Newc T 38-39; Fell K Coll Cam 38-48; Lect in Div 44-48; Prof Fell 71-80; Asst Master Eton Coll 40-44 and from 80; Fell and Chap Keble Coll Ox 49-71; Exam Chap to Bp of Heref from 51; to Bp of Win from 58; Commiss Colom 48-65; Select Pr Univ of Ox 58-59 and 61; Ely Prof of Div Univ of Cam 71-80; Can of Ely 71-80; Can (Emer) from 81. *13 Station Road, Haddenham, Ely.*

STEAD, Leslie Cawthorn. b 11. Oak Hill Th Coll 58. **d** 59 Stafford for Lich **p** 60 Lich. C of Bucknall w Bagnall 59-62; V of St Marg Collier Street 62-71; C of Ashburnham w Penshurst Dio Chich from 71. *The Pound Cottage, Ashburnham, Battle, TN33 9NR.* (Ninfield 892580)

STEADMAN, Fred. b 11. Univ Coll Ox BA (Nat Sc) 34, MA 65. **d** 65 **p** 66 Ches. C of Timperley 65-69; V of Willaston 69-79; C-in-c of Capenhurst 71-79. *24 Glan Aber Park, Chester, CH4 8LF.*

STEADMAN, Norman Neil. b 39. Qu Univ Belf BSc 61. TCD Div Test 63. **d** 63 Down **p** 64 Tuam for Down. C of Newtownards 63-65; Whiterock 65-67; Asst Dean of Residences QUB 67-71; Perm to Offic Dio St Alb 71-76; Youth Officer Dio St Alb 73-76; C-in-c of H Sav Hitchin Dio St Alb 76; Team V from 77. *1 Wymondley Close, Hitchin, Herts.* (Hitchin 56140)

STEADMAN-LEWIS, Arthur Edward. **d** 39 **p** 40 Lon. C of St Jas Hampton Hill 39-41; C-in-c of St Andr Conv Distr Uphill and St Sav and St Paul Weston-s-Mare 41-55; R of Walton 55-76. *11 Beach Court, Beach Road, Weston-super-Mare, Somt.* (Weston-s-Mare 27899)

STEAR, Michael Peter Hutchinson. b 47. Wycl Hall Ox 71. **d** 74 **p** 75 S'wark. C of Streatham Vale 74-78; St Luke Ramsgate (in c of St Mark) Dio Cant from 78. *7 Highfield Road, Ramsgate, CT12 6QH.* (Thanet 55832)

STEARN, Alfred John Steed. b 1888. St Cath Coll Cam BA 11, MA 15. Cl Tr Sch Cam 11. **d** 12 **p** 13 Ex. C of Barnstaple 12-15; Asst Chap H Trin Cathl Shanghai and Chap Miss to Seamen 16-19; Chap and Asst Master Dioc Sch Hong Kong 19-24; LPr Dio Ely 24-25; C of Fletton 25-29; R of Broughton and Ripton Regis 29-35; V of Swaffham Bulbeck 35-55; Shepreth 55-59; Perm to Offic Dio Ely from 59. *6 Allen Court, Hauxton Road, Trumpington, Cambridge.* (Trumpington 3197)

STEARN, Peter Reginald. b 38. Linc Th Coll 75. **d** 77 **p** 78 St Alb. C of St Pet St Alb 77-79; Bushey Dio St Alb from 79. *Trinity House, Bushey Mill Lane, Bushey, Herts.* (Waltham 20565)

STEBBING, Michael Langdale. b 46. BA (Lon) 68. Coll of the Resurr Mirfield 73. **d** 74 **p** 76 Mashon. C of Borrowdale 74-76; P-in-c of Chikwaka Dio Mashon from 76. *c/o Box UA7, Salisbury, Zimbabwe.*

STEDMAN, David Algernin. St Pet Coll Ja. **d** 65 **p** 66 Ja. C of Halfway Tree 65-69; R of Porus 69-73; Bartons Dio Ja from 73. *Rectory, Bartons, Jamaica, W Indies.*

STEDMAN, Michael Sydney. b 34. ARICS 58. Clifton Th Coll 62 **d** 65 **p** 66 Chich. C of Lindfield 65-68; Gt Baddow 68-73; Team V in Bramerton Group Dio Nor 73-75; R from 75; RD of Loddon from 78. *Rectory, Bergh Apton, Norwich, NR15 1BP.* (Brooke 50217)

STEDMAN, Robert Alfred. b 24. Qu Coll Birm 50. **d** 52 **p** 53 Portsm. C of Portchester 52-55; V of St Anne Brighton 55-61; Salehurst 61-76; R of Bodiam 64 75; RD of Etchingham 67-76; R of Newhaven Dio Chich from 76. *St Michael's Rectory, Second Avenue, Newhaven, E Sussex.* (Newhaven 5251)

STEDMOND, William. b 1894. Lancashire Coll Man 14. **d** 31 Win **p** 31 Southampton for Win. [f Congregational Min] C of All SS Pokesdown 31-34; St Helier Jersey 34-39; V of Holdenhurst w Throop 39-65. *17 Elmwood Avenue, Fordingbridge, Hants.* (Fordingbridge 52309)

STEED, Herbert Edward. b 23. St Jo Coll Dur BA 51, Dipl Th 52. **d** 52 **p** 53 Liv. C of Stoneycroft 52-55; H Trin w Ch Ch Folkestone 55-57; V of St Jas Croydon 57-63; St Francis Strood 63-64; R of E Barnet Dio St Alb from 64. *Rectory, East Barnet, Herts.*

STEEDMAN, Aubrey Wyld. b 11. Univ of Dur BA 40, MA 43. St Aid Coll 34. **d** and **p** 38 Southw. C of St Mary Magd Sutton-in-Ashfield 38; Bulwell 38-39; C of Blyth (in c of Langold) 41-42; V of Swaton w Spanby R 42-49; Chap RAFVR 43-47; R of Beckingham w Fenton Dio Linc from 49. *Beckingham Rectory, Lincoln, LN5 0RF.* (Fenton Claypole 298)

STEEL, Anthony Lincoln. Em Coll Sktn. **d** 64 **p** 65 Edmon. I of Sedgewick 64-67; L to Offic Dio Edmon 67-71; C of H Trin Edmon 71-73; R of Hinton 73-76; I of Fort Sask Dio Edmon from 76. *10021-99th Avenue, Fort Saskatchewan, Alta, Canada.* (403-998 3620)

STEEL, Frederick George. TCD BA (2nd cl Phil Mod) 38, Div Test 39, MA 42. **d** 39 **p** 40 Guildf. C of Em Stoughton 39-43; St Paul S Harrow (in c of St Andr) 43-45; R of St Barn Paisley 45-50; PC of St Matthias Canning Town 50-61; C-in-C of St Gabr Canning Town 50-56; H Trin Barking Road Canning Town 53-61; V of Canning Town 61-75; R of Sheering Dio Chelmsf from 75. *Sheering Rectory, Bishop's Stortford, Herts.* (Sheering 237)

STEEL, George Barradale. b 09. MBE 75. **d** 75 **p** 78 Glas. C of Cambuslang Dio Glas from 75; Dioc Chap Dio Glas from 81. *33 Southhill Avenue, Burnside, Rutherglen, G73 3TB.* (041-647 4026)

STEEL, Kenneth Jack. St Jo Coll Morpeth. **d** 47 **p** 48 Armid. C of W Tamworth 47-50; C-in-c of Baradine 50-53; V of Walcha 53-59; Supt Ohio Boys' Home Walcha 59-60; R of Wickham 60-61; Nabiac 62-66; Glouc Dio Newc from 66. *St Paul's Rectory, Ravenshaw Street, Gloucester, NSW, Australia 2422.* (Gloucester 65)

STEEL, Ven Leslie Frederick. Univ of NZ LTh (2nd cl) 65. St Jo Coll Auckld 57. **d** 59 **p** 60 Dun. C of Roslyn 59-62; V of Waimea Plains 62-68; CF 68-74; Hon C of Taihope 70-71; V of Dunstan Roxburgh Dio Dun from 74; Archd of Otago from 77. *17 Bantry Street, Alexandra, NZ.* (Alexandra 8327)

STEEL, Thomas Molyneux. b 39. Univ of Man BA (Th) 61. Ripon Hall Ox. **d** 63 **p** 64 Newc T. C of H Cross Fenham Newc T 63-66; C-in-c of St Aid Man 66-71; R of Failsworth 71-79; P-in-c of Farnham R Dio Ox 79-81; R (w Hedgerley) from 81; Hedgerley 80-81. *Rectory, Farnham Common, Slough, SL2 3NJ.* (Farnham Common 3233)

STEELE, Charles Edward Ernest. b 24. Cudd Coll 72. **d** 74 **p** 75 Birm. C of Rubery 74-77; P-in-c of St Mary and St John Shaw Hill Alum Rock Dio Birm 77-79; V from 79. *52 Couchman Road, Birmingham, B8 3SP.* (021-327 0529)

STEELE, Clive Norman. Moore Th Coll Syd ACT ThL 42. **d** and **p** 43 Syd. C of St Andr Summer Hill 43; C-in-c of St

Luke Mascot w St Steph Eastlakes 43-45; R of Canley Vale w Cabramatta 45-49; St Steph Newtown 49-55; Burwood E 55-59; Sutherland 59-76; Can of St Mich Pro Cathl Wollongong 73-77; R of Sutton Forest 76-77; Katoomba 77-81; L to Offic Dio Syd from 81. *371 Great Western Highway, Bullaburra, NSW, Australia 2784.*

STEELE, David Robert. b 29. Peterho Cam BA 53, MA 57. Oak Hill Th Coll 53. **d** 56 **p** 57 Lond. C of St Paul Portman Square 56-59; Sevenoaks 59-62; Navigators' Rep in Kenya 63-65; Chap Steward's Trust Lon 65-72; Jt Gen Sec Intercontinental Ch S from 73. *c/o ICS, 175 Tower Bridge Road, SE1 2AQ.* (01-407 4588)

STEELE, Edward Harry. b 02. Ref Episc Th Coll 26. **d** 38 **p** 39 Roch. [f Min of Ref Episc Ch] C of Stone 38-40; R of Farmborough 40-45; Trent 45-50; V of St Paul Stratford 50-56; St Alb Becontree 56-60; St Gabr Walthamstow and Chap Thorpe Coombe Hosp 60-63; R of N Ockendon 63-74; Perm to Offic Dio Chelmsf from 74. *34 Dulverton Avenue, Westcliff-on-Sea, Essex, SS0 0HR.* (Southend 524690)

STEELE, Edward Robert. St Francis Coll Brisb 59. **d** 61 **p** 62 N Queensld. C of Ayr 61-62; Mount Isa 62-65; Mundingburra 65-67; Colac 67-68; R of Hopetoun 68-72; V of H Trin Sebastopol 72-78. *c/o Box 1244, Townsville, Queensland, Australia.*

STEELE, Canon Gerald Arthur. Univ of Tor BASc 48. Trin Coll Tor STB 69. Wycl Coll Tor LTh 54. **d** 54 Tor **p** 54 Bp Wilkinson for Tor. C of Ch Redeemer Tor 54-56; I of Wynyard 56-62; R of Biggar 62-70; Hon Can of Sktn 63-67 and 70-74; Archd of Sktn 67-70; Chap Univ of Sask 70-74; R of Tisdale Dio Sask from 74; Hon Can of Sask from 77. *Box 1225, Tisdale, Sask., Canada.*

STEELE, Gerald Robert. b 25. St D Coll Lamp BA 49. **d** 51 **p** 52 Llan. C of St Mary Glyntaff Pontypridd 51-63; V of Llangeinor 63-73; R of Cadoxton-juxta-Barry Dio Llan from 73. *Cadoxton Rectory, Rectory Road, Cadoxton, Barry, S Glam CF6 6QB.* (Barry 733041)

STEELE, John Durno. Or Coll Ox BA (Mod Hist) 21. MA 25. Wells Th Coll 34. **d** 35 **p** 36 S'wark. C of E Wickham 35-37; St Mark Bexhill 37-38; R of Thurlby w Norton Disney 39-44; Asst Dioc Insp of Schs Linc 40-44; Ox 45-49; R of Farnborough w W Isley 44-49; Chap and Actg Hd Master of St Geo Coll Quilmes Buenos Aires and L to Offic Dio Argent 50-51; Chap of Ch Ch Cathl Port Stanley 51-53; R of Plymtree 54-63. *Quinta Maori, Quequen, FCGR, Buenos Aires, Argentina.*

STEELE, John Gladstone. Univ of Queensld BSc 60, PhD 65. St Francis Coll Brisb ACT ThL 58. **d** 58 **p** 59 Brisb. Miss Chap Brisb 58-60; Chap St Jo Coll Brisb 60-65; Hon C of St Geo Cathl Kingston Ont 66-67; Ch Ch St Lucia Brisb 67-74; Lect in Physics Univ of Queensld 67-74; in Amer Ch 74-75; Miss Chap Dio Brisb from 76. *48 Dunmore Terrace, Auchenflower, Queensland, Australia 4066.* (377 3422)

STEELE, John Leonard. Univ of NSW BSc 65, PhD 70. Moore Coll Syd ThL 79. **d** 80 Syd **p** 80 Bp Robinson for Syd. C of St Steph Penrith Dio Syd from 80. *32 Bringelly Road, Kingswood, NSW, Australia 2750.* (31-6680)

STEELE, John Thomas Robson. b 02. Late Exhib of Qu Coll Ox 3rd cl Cl Mods 22, BA (3rd cl Th) 24. **d** 32 **p** 33 Bradf. C of St Paul Manningham 32-34; Wensley w Leyburn 34-37; St Cypr Hay Mill 37-39; V of Hardraw w Lunds 39-46; Askrigg w Stalling Busk 46-53; R of Kirkandrews-on-Esk 53-70; L to Offic Dio Carl from 70. *4 Lonsdale Terrace, Cumwhinton, Carlisle.* (Wetheral 61289)

STEELE, John William Jackson. b 05. OBE 43. CBE 45. Men in Disp 45. St Aid Coll 26. **d** 29 **p** 30 Ches. C of St Paul Stalybridge 29-31; TCF Aldershot 31-34; CF 34-51; Hon Chap to HM the King 48-51; R of Breamore 51-55; Tarrington w Stoke Edith 55-61; Powderham 61-79. *c/o Powderham Rectory, Exeter, Devon.* (Starcross 229)

STEELE, Keith Atkinson. b 28. CEng, MIMechE. Oakhill Coll 80. **d** 81 St Alb. C of Westoning Dio St Alb from 81. *Mariners Lodge, Church Road, Westoning, Beds, MK45 5JW.*

STEELE, Ronald Frank. d 37 **p** 38 Willoch. C of St Paul Port Pirie 37-41; P-in-c of Gladstone 41-44; Offg R of Port Augusta 44-46; C of St Aug Unley 46-47; R of S Yorke Penin 47-51; Strathalbyn 51-56; Col Light Gardens 56-76; L to Offic Dio Adel from 76. *Unit 5, 89 Princes Road, Mitcham, S Australia 5062.* (71 8961)

STEELE, William Oliver. b 21. Univ of Lon BA (3rd cl Geog) 51. Lon Coll of Div 64. **d** 65 **p** 66 Nor. C of H Trin Heigham 65-69; R of W Winch 69-73; V of St Francis Heartsease Nor 73-79; N Walsham w Antingham Dio Nor from 79. *Vicarage, Yarmouth Road, North Walsham, Norf, NR28 9AT.* (0692-402069)

STEELE-PERKINS, Richard de Courcy. b 36. Clifton Th Coll 61. **d** 64 **p** 65 Ex. C of Stoke Damerel Devonport 64-65; Washfield (in c of Rackenford and Loxbeare) 65-68; P-in-c of Wimbledon 68-70; Asst Chap St Thos Hosp Lon and Chap Lambeth Hosp 70-74; P-in-c of Tawstock 74-75; R 75-81; Sticklepath 74-75; R 75-81; V of Buckfastleigh w Dean Prior Dio Ex from 81. *Vicarage, Buckfastleigh, Devon.* (Buckfastleigh 2213)

STEEP, Colin Leslie. d 62 **p** 63 Graft. C of Upper Hastings 62-64; V of Copmanhurst 64-70; R of Mid-Clarence 68-70; R of Bowraville Dio Graft from 70. *Rectory, Bowraville, NSW, Australia.* (Bowraville 15)

STEER, Frederick Arthur. b 06. Hatf Coll Dur BA and LTh 38. St Bonif Coll Warm 34. **d** 38 Ox **p** and Bourne End 44-51; R of Wokingham 51-69; Surr 51-69; V of Aldermaston w Wasing 69-73; Perm to Offic Dio Chich from 76. *2 Edensor Road, Eastbourne, E Sussex. BN20 7XR.* (Eastbourne 26345)

STEER, Herbert Philip. b 04. Univ of Lon BA (2nd cl Med and Mod Hist) 25, AKC 27 (1st cl Th). Ely Th Coll 27. **d** 27 **p** 28 S'wark. C of St Luke w St Paul Charlton 27-35; V of St Aug S Bermondsey 35-44; R of Abington 44-48; V of Westbury-on-Trym 48-61; Chap St Monica's Home of Rest Westbury-on-Trym and of Brentry Hosp 61-71; Perm to Offic Dio Heref from 72. *Briar Cottage, Hinton, Peterchurch, Herefs, HR2 0SH.* (Peterchurch 370)

✠ **STEER, Right Rev Stanley Charles.** Univ of Sask BA (1st cl Gr and Phil) and Univ and Copland Scho 28. Em Coll Sktn LTh 29, BD 37. St Cath S Ox BA (2nd cl Th) 33, MA 37. Wycl Coll Tor DD (*hon causa*) 46. Em Coll Sktn DD (*hon causa*) 52. St Chad's Coll Regina DD (*hon causa*) 64. **d and p** 29 Caled. Miss at Vanderhoof w Chilco 29-30; L to Offic Dio Ox and Chap Univ Coll Ox 32-33; L to Offic Dio Lon 33-41; Lect Lon Coll of Div 33-36; Vice-Prin 36-41; Commiss Caled 36-41; Offg Chap Mercer's Co 37-41; Prin of Em Coll Sktn 41-50; Hon Can of Sktn 43-50; CF (R of O) 44-46; Cons Ld Bp of Sktn in St Jo Cathl Sktn 25 July 50 by Abp of Rupld; Bps of Sask; and Edmon; Res 70. *2383 Lincoln Road, Victoria BC, Canada.*

STEER, Canon William George Reginald Kitto. Ridley Hall, Cam 34. **d** 36 **p** 37 Truro. C of Liskeard 36-38; R of Duloe w Herodsfoot 38-48; St Pinnock 41-46; RD of Wivelshire 43-46; V of Launceston Dio Truro from 46; Surr from 44; RD of Trigg Major from 51; Hon Can of Truro from 52. *St Mary's Vicarage, Launceston, Cornw.* (Launceston 2878)

STEERS, Ronald Cornelius. Univ of Tor BA 60. Wycl Coll Tor LTh and BTh 63. **d** 63 **p** 64 Edmon C of All SS Cathl Edmon 63-65; I of Jasper 65-73. *Box 664, Jasper, Alta, Canada.*

STEGEMANN, William Charles. St Francis Coll Brisb ACT ThL (2nd cl) 67. **d** 67 **p** 68 Brisb. C of Toowoomba 67-70; R of Kameruka 70-71; Berridale 71-76; Perm to Offic Dio C & Goulb 76-78; Hon C of Ainslie Dio C & Goulb from 78. *18 Brennan Street, Hackett, ACT, Australia 2602.*

STEGEN, George Albert. d 53 **p** 54 Koot. C of Kelowna 54-55; Chap Vanc Gen Hosp 55-56; C of Ch Ch Cathl Vanc 56-58; R of Powell River 58-62; St Geo Winnipeg 62-68; Can of St Jo Cathl Winnipeg 66-68. *202-733 Johnson Street, Victoria, BC, Canada.*

STEGGALL, John Alexander. b 17. Down Coll Cam Hist Trip pt i 37. BA (Th Trip pt ii) 38, MA 42. Sarum Th Coll 38. **d** 40 **p** 41 Dur. C of St Pet Stockton 40-48; R of St Jas Gateshead 48-60; St Mary Arbroath 60-65; Perm to Offic Dio Dur 65-67; V of Easby w Brompton-on-Swale Dio Ripon from 67. *Easby Vicarage, Richmond, N Yorks, DL10 7EU.* (Richmond 2621)

STEINBURG, Howard. Seager Hall, Ont. **d** 62 Bp Appleyard for Hur **p** 63 Hur. C of New Hamburg 62-64; I of Warwick 64-66; St D Windsor 66-70; St Paul and St John Chatham 70-74; Waterford Dio Hur from 74. *Rectory, Waterford, Ont., Canada.* (519-443 8375)

STEINKE, Roger Alan. b 47. Concordia Sen Coll Ind USA BA 69. Concordia Sem Mo USA MDiv 73. **d** and **p** 76 Ott. C of St Thos Ott 76-78; R of Blackb w Navan Dio Ott from 78. *41 Beechmont Crescent, Ottawa, Ont., Canada.*

STELL, Peter Donald. b 50. Sarum Wells Th Coll 78. **d** 81 Knaresborough for Ripon. C of Rothwell w Lofthouse Dio Ripon from 81. *4 Green Lane, Lofthouse, Nr Wakefield, W Yorks, WF2 2LH.*

STENHOUSE, William Douglas. b 11. ALCD 35. **d** 36 **p** 37 Cant. C of Ch Ch Ramsgate 36-38; St Martin Dover and St Lawr Hougham 38-40; C-in-c of Georgeham 40-41; R of Gt w L Moulton and Aslacton 41-47; V of Martham 47-53; V of W Somerton 47-53; Tamerton Foliot 53-58; Lamerton w Sydenham Damerel 58-76. *Cranmere, Burrator Road, Dousland, Yelverton, Devon.*

STENNETT, John Allan. b 43. Em & St Chad Coll Sktn LTh 76. **d** 76 **p** 77 Moos. C of St Thos Moose Factory 76-77; I of Rupert's Ho Dio Moos from 78. *Rupert's House, via Moosonee, Ont, Canada.* (418-895 8820)

STEPHEN, David Allan. b 07. Lon Coll of Div 45. **d** 47 **p** 48 S'wark. C of St Jo Evang Blackheath 47-49; Chorley Wood 49-51; V of St Luke Deptford 51-59; R of Alfold 59-75.

4 Porlock Gardens, Nailsea, Bristol, Avon, BS19 2QX. (Nailsea 6416)

STEPHEN, Donald James. b 45. St Paul's Coll Grahmstn 68. **d** 70 Capetn. C of St Marg Parow 70-73; Namaqualand 73-75; P-in-c of Huguenot 75-78; R of Namaqualand 78-80; Kraaifontein Dio Capetn from 80. *Rectory, Fourth Avenue, Kraaifontein 7570, CP, S Africa.* (9024648)

STEPHEN, Gregory Lawrence. b 53. Univ of WI BA (Th) 76. Codr Coll Barb 72. **d** 77 **p** 78 Windw Is. C of St Mary Bequia Dio Windw Is from 77. *Port Elizabeth, Bequia, St Vincent, W Indies.*

STEPHEN, John Newton. Univ of Syd BA 10. Ridley Hall, Cam 11. **d** 12 **p** 13 Lon. C of St Jas L Bethnal Green 12-15; All SS Woollahra 15-16; R of H Trin Erskineville 16-22; St Aid Longueville 22-24; St Matthias Centennial Pk (Paddington) 24-65; L to Offic Dio Syd from 65. *264 Mowbray Road, Chatswood, NSW 2067, Australia.*

STEPHEN, Kenneth George. b 47. Univ of Strathclyde BA (2nd cl Soc) 69. Univ of Edin BD 72. Edin Th Coll 69. **d** 72 **p** 73 Glas. C of Ayr 72-75; R of Renfrew 75-80; Motherwell Dio Glas from 80; Wishaw Dio Glas from 80. *Rectory, Crawford Street, Motherwell, Lanarks.* (Motherwell 62634)

STEPHENI, Frederick William. b 28. TD 73. Qu Coll Birm 54. **d** 55 **p** 56 Southw. C of Arnold 55-57; C-in-c 57-58; Hucknall Torkard 58-59; Chap Stoke-on-Trent Hosp and N Staffs R Infirm 59-62; CF (TA) from 60; Chap King's Coll Hosp 62-63; R of Cotgrave 63-76; V of Owthorpe 63-76; Sen Chap Addenbrooke's Hosp Cam from 76. *13 Tunwells Lane, Great Shelford, Cambridge, CB2 5LJ.* (Cam 842914)

STEPHENS, Alan Reginald. b 28. St Deiniol's Libr Hawarden 70. **d** 73 Truro **p** 74 St Germans for Truro (APM). C of St Geo Truro 73-79; P-in-c of St Allen 79-81. *Address temp unknown.*

STEPHENS, Alec Miller. b 03. Univ of Dur LTh 25. Edin Th Coll. **d** 26 **p** 27 Glas. C of St Mary's Cathl Glas 26-29; St Jas W Hartlepool 29-34; V of Birtley 34-56; PC of St Jo Bapt Stockton-on-Tees 56-78; Perm to Offic Dio B & W from 78. *51 Crofton Park, Yeovil, Somt, BA21 4EB.* (0935-21497)

STEPHENS, Canon Archibald John. b 15. Selw Coll Cam BA 37, MA 44. Wells Th Coll 46. **d** 47 **p** 48 Worc. C of St Mary and St Mich Malvern 47-50; CMS Miss Dio Lagos 50-52; Dio Ondo-B 52-60; Manager and Chap of Ado-Ekiti Hosp 50-55; Missr Dio Ondo 55-58; Prin Bp Phillips Hall Owo 58-60; Hon Can of St Steph Cathl Ondo 57-71; Lit Sec Christian Coun of Nigeria 60-68; L to Offic Dio Ibad 64-68; C of Swindon 68-70; Missr Dio Ow 70-71; Hon Can of Ow from 71; C-in-c of Ash Vale Conv Distr 71-72; V 72-77; Commiss Ilesha from 74; Ijebu from 77; C-in-c of Thursley Dio Guildf and Personal Asst to Bp of Guildf from 77. *Thursley Vicarage, Godalmng, Surrey.* (Elstead 702276)

STEPHENS, Charles Herbert. Univ of Lon BA 41, AKC 42. **d** 42 **p** 43 Lich. C of St Mich Chell 42-44; Asst Chap Denstone Coll 44-45; Asst Master Nottm High Sch from 45; Perm to Offic Dio Southw from 73. *96 Grassington Road, Nottingham*

STEPHENS, Eric Alexander. b 31. United Th Coll of WI Ja 74. **d** 70 Bp Clark for Ja **p** 73 Bp Edmondson for Ja (APM). Perm to Offic Dio Ja 70-76; R of Porus Dio Ja from 76. *Rectory, Porus, Jamaica, W Indies.*

STEPHENS, Francis William. b 21. SOC 67. **d** 70 **p** 71 Edmonton for Lon. C of St Mary Virg Primrose Hill Dio Lon from 70. *14 St Edmund's Close, NW8 7QS.* (01-722 7931)

STEPHENS, Frederick William. b 10. Egerton Hall Man 32. **d** 34 **p** 35 Man. C of H Trin Horwich 34-36; St Paul Stalybridge 36-39; V of Ch Ch Dukinfield (or Stalybridge) 39-48; Liscard 48-61; Commiss Ja 56-61; R of Kingston Ja 61-62; V of Witton 62-80. *25 East Park Road, Blackburn, Lancs.* (Blackburn 51989)

STEPHENS, Geoffrey Elford. b 19. St Jo Coll Dur BA 41, MA 58. Ripon Hall Ox 41. **d** 43 **p** 44 Man. C of St Thos Werneth 43-45; St Marg Whalley Range (in c of St Geo Miss) 45-46; Douglas-in-Parbold (in c of Appley Bridge) 46-53; CF (TA) 48-54; CF (TA-R of O) 54-68; CF (RARO) 68-74; V of Whitechapel Lancs 53-55; Ch Ch Preston 55-58; Asst Master R Gr Sch Clitheroe 58-60; Perm to Offic Dio Blackb 58-60; R of Mawdesley w Bispham Dio Blackb from 60; Visiting Lect Edge Hill Coll Ormskirk 70-71. *Mawdesley Rectory, Ormskirk, Lancs.* (Mawdesley 203)

STEPHENS, Geoffrey Henry. Univ of Melb BA (2nd cl Hist) 62. Linacre Ho Ox BA (2nd cl Th) 65. St Steph Ho Ox 63. **d** 65 **p** 66 Melb. C of Glenroy 65-66; Chap and Asst Master Melb Gr Sch 67-68; V of St Phil Heidelberg W 71-72; Chap Perth Coll 72-74; Hutchins Sch Sandy Bay from 74. *Hutchins School, Sandy Bay, Tasmania 7005.* (002-25 2544)

STEPHENS, Grahame Frederick. Ridley Coll Melb ThL 68. **d** 68 **p** 69 Melb. C of Greensborough 68-70; Berwick 70; C-in-c of Winchelsea 70-71; I 71-73; Springvale 73-76; C of Dalby 76-79; R of St John U Mt Gravatt City and Dio Brisb from 79. *2142 Logan Road, Upper Mount Gravatt, Queensland, Australia 4122.* (349 6149)

STEPHENS, Grosvenor Humphrey Arthur. b 04. Keble Coll Ox BA (2nd cl Phil, Pol and Econ) 26, 2nd cl Th 28, MA and BLitt 31, MLitt 80. St Steph Ho Ox 26. **d** 29 **p** 30 Mon. C of Risca 29-34; St Aug Penarth w Lavernock 34-40; V of St Martin Roath 40-47; Surr from 40; Exam Chap to Bp of Llan 44-64; R of Penarth w Lavernock 47-64; V of Chislet w Hoath 64-71; Perm to Offic Dio Cant from 72. *9 Leasingham Gardens, Bexhill-on-Sea, E Sussex.*

STEPHENS, Humphrey John Lewis. b 10. Keble Coll Ox BA 32. St Steph Ho Ox 32. **d** 33 **p** 34 Lon. C of St Jo Evang Limehouse 33-37; C of St Mich AA (in c of St Francis) N Kens 37-41; C-in-c of All SS Hanley 41-43; V of St Jo Evang Hammersmith 43-53; Burnham Essex 53-57; PC of St Pet Folkestone 57-70; V of St Bart Herne Bay Dio Cant from 70. *25 Dence Park, Herne Bay, Kent, CT6 6BQ.* (Herne Bay 2040)

STEPHENS, John James Frederick. QUB BA 34. Lon Coll of Div 34. **d** 37 **p** 38 Worc. C of St Mark Stambermill 37-40; CF (EC) 40-46; C of Seapatrick (Banbridge) 46-47; Wollaston 47-48; R of Shelsley Beauchamp w Shelsley Walsh 48-51; V of Broadheath 51-82. *c/o Vicarage, Lower Broadheath, Worcester.* (Worcester 640244)

STEPHENS, John Michael. b 29. ARICS 52. Lich Th Coll 62. **d** 64 **p** 65 Cant. C of Birchington w Acol 64-70; V of Tovil 70-79; Brabourne w Smeeth Dio Cant from 79. *Smeeth Rectory, Ashford, Kent.* (Sellindge 2126)

STEPHENS, Joseph George. AKC 36. **d** 36 **p** 37 Lon. C of St John Chelsea 36-37; All SS Edmonton 37-41; V of St Mark Vic Dks 41-74. *72 De Vere Gardens, Ilford, Essex.*

STEPHENS, Joseph Gwynfor. b 08. Univ of Wales (Swansea) BA 36. St Mich Coll Llan 36. **d** 38 **p** 39 St D. C of Conwyl Cayo w Llansawel 38-40; Llandilo Fawr 40-46; R of Cilrhedyn (w Cenarth from 53) 46-71; RD of Emlyn 62-70. *22 Heol Morfa Brenin, Johnstown, Carmarthen, Dyfed.*

STEPHENS, Keith. Moore Th Coll Syd ACT ThL 64. **d** 63 **p** 65 C & Goulb. C of All SS Canberra 63-66; R of Lake Bathurst 66-67; C of Pearce Torrens Provis Distr 69-71; P-in-c of Weston Creek 71-74; R of Pambula Dio C & Goulb from 74. *PO Box 43, Eden, NSW, Australia 2551.* (Eden 6 1251)

STEPHENS, Lance. Angl Th Coll BC 67. **d** 67 **p** 68 New Westmr. C of St Laur Coquitlam 67-68; R of St Alb Burnaby 68-74; Terrace Dio Caled from 74. *4818 Olson Avenue, Terrace, BC, Canada.* (604-635 5855)

STEPHENS, Marcus James Treacher. b 11. BA (Lon) 59. Kelham Th Coll 32. **d** 37 **p** 38 Bris. M SSM 37-72; C of Bedminster 37-46; Asst Tutor Th Coll of SSM Crafers and L to Offic Dio Adel 48-54; LPr Dio Southw 54-64; Miss at St Aug Miss Modderpoort 64-72; Prov of SSM in S Afr 67-72; Can of Bloemf 67-72; Chap All SS Beirut 73-75; V of St Phil w St Bart Battersea 75-78; Chap Commun of the Epiph Truro 79-81. *10 Wheal Golden Drive, Holywell, Newquay, TR8 5PE.*

STEPHENS, Patrick. b 14. **d** 77 **p** 78 Lim (APM). Perm to Offic Dio Ard 77-78; P-in-c of Dingle U Dio Ard from 78. *Maharabeg, Castlegregory, Co Kerry, Irish Republic.*

STEPHENS, Peter John. b 42. Late Scho of Or Coll Ox BA 64, MA 67. Clifton Th Coll 63. **d** and **p** 68 Southw. C of Lenton 68-71; St Sav Brixton Hill 71-73; P-in-c 73-82; Team V of Barnham Broom Group Dio Nor from 82. *Garveston Rectory, Norwich, Norf, NR9 4QR.* (Dereham 858377)

STEPHENS, Peter Stanley. b 33. ALCD (1st cl) 59. **d** 59 Ex **p** 60 Crediton for Ex. C of St Paul Preston Paignton 59-64; V of Buckland Monachorum 64-74; RD of Tavistock 70-74; V of Em Plymouth Dio Ex from 74. *Emmanuel Vicarage, Lockington Avenue, Hartley, Plymouth, PL3 5QS.* (0752-774447)

STEPHENS, Richard William. b 37. Univ of Dur BSc 62, Dipl Th 64. Cranmer Hall, Dur 62. **d** 64 Penrith for Carl **p** 65 Carl. C of Hensingham 64-67; Norbury 67-71; V of Elworth w Warmingham 71-79; St Matt Bootle Dio Liv from 79. *418 Stanley Road, Bootle, Lancs.* (051-922 3316)

STEPHENS, Ronald John. b 13. Sarum Th Coll. **d** 57 **p** 58 Sarum. C of Calne 57-61; V of Stanstead Abbotts 61-82. *c/o Stanstead Abbotts Vicarage, Ware, Herts.* (Ware 870115)

STEPHENS, Simon Edward. b 41. Bps' Coll Cheshunt 63. **d** 67 Bp McKie for Cov **p** 68 Cov. C of St Mark Cov 69-71; Lillington 71-75; P-in-c of St Steph Canley 76-79; V 79-80. *c/o St Stephen's Vicarage, Glebe Close, Canley, Warws.* (Cov 469016)

STEPHENS, William Robert. TCD BA 55. **d** 57 **p** 58 Arm. C of St Mark Arm 57-63; R of Keady w Armaghbreague 63-67; St Phil Dunbar Heights Vancouver Dio New Westmr from 67. *3691 West 27th Avenue, Vancouver, BC, Canada.*

STEPHENS-HODGE, Lionel Edmund Howard. b 14. Selw Coll Cam 2nd cl Cl Trip pt i 35, BA 36, 1st cl Th Trip pt i 37, MA 40. Ridley Hall, Cam 36. **d** 38 **p** 39 York. C of H Trin

Hull 38-40; Heworth and St Mary Castlegate w St Mich Spurriergate York 40-41; Offg C-in-c of Bulmer w Welburn 41-43; R 43-44; Chap of Trin Coll Cam and Libr of Tyndale Ho Cam 44-45; R of Hatch Beauchamp w Beercrocombe 45-51; St Silas Engl Episc Ch Glas 51-54; V of Rosedale 54-56; Lect Lon Coll of Div 56-64; LPr Dio Lon 63-64; R of Brindle 64-74; Exam Chap to Bp of Blackb 65-79; M of Liturgical Comm 69-75; LPr Dio Blackb 74-79; Perm to Offic Dio Ex from 79. *14 Markers, Uffculme, Cullompton, Devon.*

STEPHENSON, Alan Malcolm George. b 28. Late Lady Kay Sch of Jes Coll Cam 2nd cl Cl Trip pt i 50, BA (1st cl Th Trip pt ia) 52, 1st cl Th Trip pt iii 54, MA 55. St Cath S Ox BA (by incorp) 55, MA 60, BLitt 60, DPhil 64, Sen Denyer and Johnson Scho 65. Ripon Hall Ox. **d** 56 **p** 57 Ripon. C of Knaresborough 56-58; Tutor, Lect, and Libr Lich Th Coll 58-62; Vice-Prin Ripon Hall Ox 62-71; Exam Chap to Bp of Lich 63-75; Dir of Abp of Cant's Examn in Th (Lambeth Dipl) from 70; Tutor St Steph Ho Ox from 70; R of Steventon (w Milton from 73) Dio Ox from 71; Hulsean Lect Cam 79-80. *Rectory, Vicarage Road, Steventon, Abingdon, Oxon.* (Abingdon 831243)

STEPHENSON, Ven Edgar. b 1894. MM 18. TD 50. Univ of Man BA (2nd cl Hist) 22, BD 25, MA 29. **d** 24 **p** 25 Man. C of Sacr Trin Salford 24-26; Worsley (in c of Ellenbrook) 26-29; V of Peel 29-30; St Luke Weaste 30-37; St Mary Rochdale 37-42; CF (EC) 39-42; CF (TA) 33-50; Hon Chap to Bp of Man 34-46; Hon Can Man 46-51; V of Swinton 42-47; Oldham 47-55; RD of Oldham 47-51; Surr from 47; Archd of Rochdale 51-62; Archd (Emer) from 62; Proc Conv Man 51-62; Dir of Relig Educn Dio Man 55-62. *College of St Mark, Audley End, Saffron Walden, Essex, CB11 4JD.*

STEPHENSON, Eric George. Univ of Birm Dipl Th 65. Qu Coll Birm 63. **d** 66 Wakef **p** 67 Pontefract for Wakef. C of St Jo Bapt Wakef 66-69; Seaham w Seaham Harbour 69-73; Cockerton 73-75; Asst Master Haughton Sch Darlington from 75. *5 Swaledale Avenue, Darlington, Co Durham, DL3 9AJ.* (Darlington 66734)

STEPHENSON, Geoffrey Alexander. Ridley Coll Melb 63. **d** 63 **p** 64 St Arn. C of Ch Ch Cathl St Arn 63-65; Swan Hill 65-67; V of H Trin Wedderburn 67-70; R of Wedderburn w Boort 70-76; Charlton 76-77; Woodend Dio Bend from 77. *Rectory, Owen Street, Woodend, Vic, Australia 3442.*

STEPHENSON, Ian Clarke. Tyndale Hall Bris 52. Lon Dipl Th 69. **d** 56 **p** 57 Cov. C of Bedworth 56-58; Edgware 58-65; R of Biddulph Moor 65-70; L to Offic Dio Lich from 70; Perm to Offic Dio Ches from 75. *58 Park Lane, Knypersley, Stoke-on-Trent, Staffs, ST8 7AU.* (Stoke-on-Trent 512416)

STEPHENSON, John. b 46. St Barn Coll Adel ACT ThDip 76. **d** 77 **p** 78 Adel. C of Hawthorn 77-79; P-in-c of Ingle Farm-Pooraka Dio Adel from 79. *6 Brecon Drive, Ingle Farm, S Australia 5098.* (264-2153)

STEPHENSON, John Henry. St Mich Th Coll Crafers, 56 ACT ThL 61. **d** 61 **p** 62 Adel. C of Glenelg 61-65; P-in-c of Minipa Miss 65-68; R of Burra 68-74; Brighton Dio Adel from 74. *14 Beach Road, Brighton, S Australia 5048.* (08-296 7669)

STEPHENSON, John Joseph. b 35. St Jo Coll Dur BA 74. Qu Coll Birm 75. **d** 76 **p** 77 Dur. C of Spennymoor w Whitworth 76-79; V of Eppleton Dio Dur from 79. *Vicarage, Eppleton, Houghton-le-Spring, T & W.* (Hetton-le-Hole 267412)

STEPHENSON, Martin Woodard. b 55. St Cath Coll Cam MA 81. Westcott Ho Cam 78. **d** 81 Win. C of Eastleigh Dio Win from 81. *St Francis House, Nightingale Avenue, Eastleigh, Hants, SO5 3JB.*

STEPHENSON, Michael James. b 29. St Steph Ho Ox 54. **d** 56 **p** 57 Lon. C of H Trin w St Mary Hoxton 56-64; V of St Mary Magd Paddington Dio Lon from 64. *Clergy House, Woodchester Street, W2 5TF.* (01-289 1818)

STEPHENSON, Michael Paul. Univ of Queensld BD 70. St Francis Coll Brisb 69. **d** 72 **p** 73 Brisb. C of All SS Chermside Brisb 72-75; Hosp Chap Chermside Dio Brisb from 75. *Box 199, Chermside, Queensland, Austraia 4032.* (263 6245)

STEPHENSON, Nicolas William. b 22. Ely Th Coll 60. **d** 62 **p** 63 Dur. C of S Westoe 62-65; M CR from 68; L to Offic Dio Wakef from 74. *5 Dudfleet Lane, Horbury, Wakefield, W Yorks, WF4 5EX.* (Wakefield 270864)

STEPHENSON, Richard Frederick. Trin Coll Tor BA 49, LTh 52, STB 53. **d** 51 Arctic **p** 52 Edmon from Bran. P-in-c of Oak Lake and Sioux Miss 52-54; Devon Miss 54-56; R of Lynn Lake 56-57; Chap Shawnigan Lake Sch Cobble Hill 57-63; R of Duncan 63-64; L to Offic Dio BC from 64. *PO Box 201, Shawnigan Lake, BC, Canada.*

STEPHENSON, Robert. b 36. St Chad's Coll Dur BA (2nd cl Th) 58, Dipl Th 60. **d** 60 **p** 61 Dur. C of Whickham 60-63; Gateshead 63-65; PC of St Paul Gateshead 65-67; R of Stella 67-74; V of Comberton Dio Ely from 74. *Comberton Vicarage, Cambridge.* (Comberton 2793)

STEPHENSON, Canon Robert Ommanney. b 09. St Cath Coll Cam BA 32, MA 36. Cudd Coll 32. **d** 33 Win **p** 34 Southampton for Win. C of St Jas Westend 33-37; St Aug Tonge Moor 37-41; V of Horton w Cowpen and New Delaval 41-47; PC of Ascen Ch Bitterne Pk 47-70; Surr from 59; Hon Can of Win 67-79; Can (Emer) from 79; R of E Woodhay w Woolton Hill 70-79; RD of Whitchurch 72-79; Perm to Offic Dio B & W from 79. *Fairlawn, Witcombe Lane, Ash, Martock, Somt, TA12 6AH.* (Martock 824330)

STEPHENSON, Simon George. b 44. St Jo Coll Dur BA 67. Trin Coll Bris 74. **d** 76 **p** 77 Roch. C of Hildenborough Dio Roch from 76. *96 Brookmead, Hildenborough, Kent, TN11 9EX.*

STEPNEY, Lord Bishop Suffragan of. *See* Thompson, Right Rev James Lawton.

STERLING, John Haddon. b 40. Pemb Coll Cam 2nd cl Th Trip pt i, 60, BA (3rd cl Th Trip pt ii) 62, MA 66. Cudd Coll 63. **d** 65 Bris for Pret **p** 66 Pret. C of St Alb Cathl Pret 65-69; L to Offic Dio Natal 69-70; C of St Thos Mart Bedminster 71-74; M Dioc Social and Industr Team Bris and Bp's Cathl Chap 71-74; Industr Chap to Bp of Linc and M of S Humb Industr Miss from 74. *25 Park Avenue, Grimsby, Lincs, DN32 0DG.* (Grimsby 70320)

STERRY, Christopher. b 54. AKC and BD 77. St Jo Coll Nottm 79. **d** 80 **p** 81 Wakef. C of St Jo Evang Huddersfield Dio Wakef from 80. *4 King Cliff Road, Huddersfield, W Yorks, HD2 2RR.*

STERRY, Timothy John. b 34. Or Coll Ox BA (3rd cl Jurispr) 58, MA 62, Dipl Th 60. Wycl Hall, Ox 58. **d** 60 **p** 61 Nor. C of Cromer 60-64; Chap Oundle Sch Pet 64-72; Cheam Sch Newbury 72-75; Hd Master Temple Grove Sch Uckfield 75-80; Scripture U Schs Staffs from 81. *1 The Close, Chart Lane, Reigate, Surrey, RH2 7BN.* (Reigate 44370)

STEVART, Edward Thomas. b 14. Worc Ordin Coll 64. **d** 66 Colchester for Chelmsf **p** 67 Chelmsf. C of Romford 66-69; C-in-c of St Paul's Conv Distr Parkeston 69-72; V of St Barn Colchester 72-78; Toc H Padre SE Essex from 80. *67 Waverley Road, South Benfleet, Essex.* (Benfleet 55225)

STEVEN, David Bowring. b 38. K Coll Lon and Warm AKC 64. **d** 64 **p** 65 Linc. C of Grantham 64-68; St Cypr Kimb 69-71; R of Mafeking 71-74; C of Bramley 75-77; V of Sutton Valence w E Sutton and Chart Sutton 77-82; Commiss Kimb K from 79; V of Littlebourne Dio Cant from 82; Warden of Readers Dio Cant from 82. *Vicarage, Littlebourne, Kent, CT3 1UA.* (Littlebourne 233)

STEVEN, James Gordon. Univ of Birm BA 31. ALCD 35. **d** 35 **p** 36 Liv. C of St Mary Bootle 35-37; Childwall 37-39; CF (TA - R of O) 37-38; CF (TA) 38-44; Hon CF 44; C of All SS Bedworth 44-45; R of Wolverton w Norton Lindsey and Langley 45-49; Chap RAF 16 MU Stafford 49-50; MEAF 50-53; Radio Sch 53-58; Gibr 58-60; Cottesmore 61-62; V of Greatham w Stretton and Clipsham 62-63; R of Penicuik 64-70; Gt w L Bealings 70-74; V of Playford w Culpho 70-74. *75 Langer Road, Felixstowe, Suff, IP11 8HR.* (Felixstowe 5076)

STEVEN, James Malcolm. b 31. St Andr ordin Course 71. **d** 73 **p** 74 St Andr. Perm to Offic Dio St Andr 73-77. *Northcliff Cottage, North Queensferry, Fife, KY11 1HA.*

STEVEN, Peel Othmar. b 20. Montr Dioc Th Coll 70. **d** and **p** 73 Montr. C of St Paul Lachine 73-74; I of St Ignatius Montr 74-78; Granby Dio Montr from 78. *124 Main Street, Granby, PQ, Canada.* (514-372 2197)

STEVENETTE, John Maclachlan. St Pet Coll Ox MA 60. Ripon Hall Ox 60. **d** 61 **p** 62 Chich. C of Newhaven 61-66; R of Lynch w Iping Marsh 66-74; Birdham w W Itchenor 74-78; Byfleet Dio Guildf from 78. *Rectory, Byfleet, Surrey, KT14 7LX.* (Byfleet 42374)

STEVENS, Arthur Edward Geary. b 14. Lon Coll of Div 34. **d** 37 **p** 38 Lon. C of St Barn Woodside Pk Finchley 37-40; Actg C of St Luke Hampstead 40-41; St Sav Herne Hill 41-42; V of St Cuthb W Hampstead 42-46; H Trin Southw 46-50; St Jo Evang Sheff 50-54; H Trin Guernsey 54-67; Chap Castel Hosp Guernsey 60-67; State Pris Guernsey 61-67; V of Bitterne 67-72; Duffield Dio Derby from 72. *Vicarage, Duffield, Derby.* (Derby 841168)

STEVENS, Brian Henry. b 28. Oak Hill Th Coll. **d** 69 **p** 70 Chelmsf. C of St Mary Chadwell 69-75; V of Ch Ch w H Trin Penge Dio Roch from 75. *234 Anerley Road, SE20.* (01-778 4800)

STEVENS, Bruce Allen. b 50. ACT LTh 76, BTh 78, MTh 81. **d** 81 C & Goulb. C of St John Canberra Dio C & Goulb from 81. *7 Amaroo Street, Reid, ACT, Australia 2601.*

STEVENS, Cyril David Richard. b 25. NZ Bd of Th Stud LTh 66. **d** 59 **p** 60 Wai. C of Wairoa 59-61; Tauranga 61-62; V of Gate Pa 62-65; Playford w Culpho and Tuddenham Suff 65-67; Belfast-Styx 67-68; R of Rendham w Sweffling (and Cransford to 73) Dio St E from 69; RD of Saxmundham

72-74. *Sweffling Rectory, Saxmundham, Suff, IP17 2BG.* (Rendham 495)

STEVENS, Canon David Alan John. b 16. Univ of Aber MA (2nd cl Hist) and Gladstone Mem and Caithness Pri 36. St Steph Ho Ox 37. **d** 39 **p** 40 Lich. C of Meir 39-42; CF (EC) 42-46; C-in-c of St Mich Cross Heath 46-52; Chap Univ Coll of N Staffs 51-53; PC 52-57; V of Horninglow 57-66; Proc Conv Lich 64-71; R of Uppingham w Ayston 66-72; RD of Uppingham 68-69; Rutland 69-77; M Gen Syn from 70; R of Market Overton w Thistleton 72-77; Can of Pet 74-81; Can (Emer) from 81; V of Staverton w Helidon and Catesby 77-81; RD of Daventry 78-81; Pro-Prolocutor Conv of Cant from 80. *3 Chapel Street, Belton, Uppingham, Leics.*

STEVENS, David Charles. b 31. Keble Coll Ox BA (2nd cl Engl) 55, Dipl Th 56, MA 59. Wycl Hall Ox 55. **d** 57 Plymouth for Ex **p** 58 Ex. C of Plymouth 57-60; Chap Falcon Coll Essexvale S Rhod 61-66; Asst Chap Bryanston Sch 66-70; Chap 70-73; P-in-c of Shillingstone 73-76; Chap Chigwell Sch from 76. *Grange Court, High Road, Chigwell, Essex, IG7 6PX.*

STEVENS, David George. b 12. Univ of Wales BA 34. St Bonif Coll Warm 36. **d** 36 **p** 37 St D. C of H Trin Aberystwyth 36-39; CMS Miss Nasik 39-40; Aurangabad 40-54; Archd of Aurangabad 47-53; Nasik 53-56; Asst Master Barnes Sch Deolali 54-63; Can of Nasik 56-60; Exam Chap to Bp of Nasik 54-63; CMS Rep for Ch of India and Chap St Thos Cathl Bom 60-63; V of Pemb Dk 63-77; Can of St D Cathl 63-77; Treas of St D Cathl 75-77. *c/o Vicarage, Pembroke Dock, Dyfed.* (Pembroke 2943)

STEVENS, David John. b 45. Univ of Bris BA 67. Dipl Th (Lon) 69. Clifton Th Coll. **d** 70 **p** 71 Ex. C of St Leon Ex 70-75; C-in-c of L Burstead 75-77; Team V of Billericay and L Burstead Dio Chelmsf from 77. *Rectory, Little Burstead, Billericay, Essex.* (Billericay 22977)

STEVENS, Canon David Johnson. b 13. St Cath S Ox BA 51, MA 55. Wycl Hall Ox 49. M SSF. **d** 52 **p** 53 Liv. C of St Cath Wigan 52-54; C-in-c of St Paul Hatton Hill Litherland 54-57; Industr Chap to Bp of Liv from 57; V of St Paul Warrington 61-70; Guardian of Franciscan Ho Liv from 70; Hon Can of Liv 71-78; Can (Emer) from 78; SSF from 78. *The Friary of St Francis, Alnmouth, Alnwick, Northumb, NE66 3NJ.* (066-573 213)

STEVENS, David Leonard. b 28. St Edm Hall Ox BA 51, MA 57. Cudd Coll 60. **d** 62 **p** 63 Linc. C of Old Brumby 62-67; Chap St Alb Sch Chorley 67-71; V of St Faith w St Martin City and Dio Linc from 72. *St Faith's Vicarage, Carholme Road, Lincoln, LN1 1RU.* (Linc 31477)

STEVENS, Douglas George. b 47. BA (Lon) 69. Westcott Ho Cam 69. **d** 72 **p** 73 Portsm. C of St Geo Conv Distr Portsea 72-75; Hon Chap Portsm Cathl 73-79; C of St Mark North End Portsea 75-79; Chap NE Lon Poly from 79. *4 Mathews Park Avenue, Stratford, E15 4AE.* (01-555 1753)

STEVENS, Douglas John. b 41. Ridley Coll Melb ACT ThL 70. **d** 69 **p** 70 St Arn. Perm to Offic Dio St Arn 69; C of E Malvern 70; Swan Hill 70-72; V of Charlton 72-76; C of St Pet Melb 76-79; I of St Geo and All SS Footscray Dio Melb from 79. *Vicarage, Clive Street, Footscray, Vic, Australia 3012.* (68 3011)

STEVENS, Douglas Robert. b 52. Univ of Newc BTh 79. St Jo Coll Morpeth 76. **d** and **p** 79 Newc. C of Toronto Newc 79-81; Merriwa Dio Newc from 81. *40 Gooch Street, Merriwa 2329, NSW, Australia.*

STEVENS, Edward. b 28. Qu Coll Ox BA 52, Dipl Th 53, MA 56. Ridley Hall Cam. **d** 55 **p** 56 Lon. C of St Mary Fulham 55-58; SW Area Sec BCMS 58-59; Miss BCMS in Burma 59-64; India 64-75; I of Brooklin Dio Tor from 76. *c/o BCMS, 157 Waterloo Road, SE1.*

STEVENS, Frank Hayman. b 11. Univ Coll Ox BA 32, MA 38. Linc Th Coll 64. **d** 65 **p** 66 B & W. C of Burnham Somt 65-68; V of Kenn (w Kingston Seymour from 69) 68-74; C-in-c of Kingston-Seymour 68-69; C-in-c of Cossington 74-76. *c/o Rectory, Cossington, Bridgwater, Somt.* (Chilton Polden 228)

STEVENS, Frederick Crichton. b 42. AKC and BD 78. St Steph Ho Ox 78. **d** 79 St Germans for Truro **p** 80 Truro. C of Newquay 79-81; St Martin-in-the-Fields Westmr Dio Lon from 81. *5a St Martin's Place, WC2N 4JJ.*

STEVENS, George Henry. b 11. Univ of Lon BD 34, MTh 44. ALCD 34. **d** 34 **p** 35 S'wark. C of St Mary Magd Peckham 34-38; Miss (CMJ) and Asst Chap Bucharest 38-40; Perm to Offic Dio S'wark 40-41; V of St Sav Herne Hill Road 41-45; Gen Sec Irish Aux CMJ and Hd of Ch of Ireland Jews' S 45-49; L to Offic Dio Dub 45-49; V of Normanton-by-Derby 49-57; RD of Derby 52-57; Ed Sec CMJ 57-62 and 63-71; Publ Pr Dio S'wark 57-62; Ed *Jewish Miss News* 57-62; *CMJ News* 62-68; V of All H Twickenham 62-76; Lect Univ of Lon 66-76; Hon C of H Trin Eastbourne Dio Chich from 76; St Botolph Aldgate Dio Lon from 76. *St Botolph's Vestry, Aldgate, EC3N 1AB.* (01-283 1670)

STEVENS, Hubert Emerald. b 31. **d** 79 Caled. C of Ch Ch Kincolith Dio Caled from 79. *Kincolith, BC, Canada, V0V 1B0.*

STEVENS, Hugh Leslie. b 1888. Qu Coll Cam BA 10, MA 14. Ridley Hall Cam 10. **d** 11 **p** 12 Nor. C of St Marg Ipswich 11-14; Ch Ch w Good Shepherd Sandown 14-17; Ch Ch Barnet 17-23; Org Sec for CPAS E Distr 23-27; V of St Mary Hornsey Rise 27-34; H Trin Torquay 34-43; Chudleigh 43-54; Chap of Torbay Hosp 54-60; Perm to Offic Dio Ex 60-64; Dio Ely from 70. *Selborne, Cae Mair, Beaumaris, Anglesey, Gwyn, LL58 8YN.* (0248-810586)

STEVENS, James Anthony. b 47. Worc Coll Ox MA 69. Trin Coll Bris 78. **d** 80 **p** 81 Heref. C of St Pet w St Owen & St Jas City and Dio Heref from 80. *6 Ledbury, Hereford, HR1 2SY.* (Heref 69944)

STEVENS, John David Andrew. b 44. Wycl Hall Ox. **d** 68 **p** 69 Blackb. C of Standish Blackb 68-71; Stonehouse Glos 71-76; Team V of Yeovil (in c of Barwick and Closworth) 76-80; R of Chewton Mendip w Ston Easton, Litton and Emborough Dio B & W from 80. *Chewton Mendip Vicarage, Bath, Somt, BA3 4LL.* (Chewton Mendip 333)

STEVENS, Joseph. St Paul's Coll Grahmstn LTh 48. **d** 48 **p** 49 Natal. C of St Jas Durban 48-50; V of Tugela River 50-59; R of All SS Stanger Dio Natal from 59. *Box 3, Stanger, Natal, S Africa.* (Stanger 300)

STEVENS, Leslie Walter. b 08. Wycl Hall Ox. **d** 64 **p** 65 Chelmsf. C of Eastwood 64; St Jo Bapt Southend-on-Sea 68-71; St Thos-on-the-Bourne 72-77; Perm to Offic Dio Guildf from 77. *11 Sampson's Cottages, West Street, Farnham, surrey, GU9 7AW.*

STEVENS, Martin Leonard. b 35. Univ of Dur BA 60, MA 72. Oak Hill Th Coll 60. **d** 62 **p** 63 Newc T. C of St Steph Newc T 62-65; Em Croydon 65-69; S Engl Sec ICM 69-74; Perm to Offic Dios Ex, Lon, Guildf, Nor, St E, Roch, St Alb, Ox and Win 70-74; Hon C of Em S Croydon 70-74; V of Felling 74-78; S Engl Dep Sec ICM 78; Perm to Offic Dio St Alb from 78. *93 Avondale Road, South Croydon, Surrey.*

STEVENS, Michael John. b 37. St Cath Coll Cam 3rd cl Th Trip pt i, 61, BA (3rd cl Th Trip pt ii) 63. Coll of Resurr Mirfield, 63. **d** 65 **p** 66 Lon. C of Poplar 65-71; Asst Chap Lon Hosp 71-75; Chap St Thos Hosp from 75. *2 Walcot Square, SE11 4TZ.* (01-735 7362)

STEVENS, Neville. Clare Coll Cam BA 52, MA 54. Or Coll Ox BA (by Incorp.) 53, MA 54, Dipl Th (w distinc.) 54. Wycl Hall, Ox 52. **d** 54 **p** 55 Bris. C of Bishopsworth 54-56; Chap Leeds Gr Sch from 56; Perm to Offic Dio Wakef from 71. *Westwood, Park Avenue, Morley, Leeds, LS27 0JW.* (Morley 538038)

STEVENS, Norman William. b 38. St Chad's Coll Dur BA 61, Dipl Th 63. **d** 63 Dur. C of Wingate 63-64; Asst Master Kenilworth Gr Sch 64-66; Libr Lyng Hall Comprehensive Sch Cov 66-67. *67 Knightsbridge, SW1X 7RA.*

STEVENS, Peter David. b 36. ARICS. Oak Hill Coll Dipl Higher Educn 81. **d** 81 Sarum. C of St Clem Branksome Dio Sarum from 81. *17 Manor Avenue, Parkstone, Poole, Dorset, BH12 4LB.*

STEVENS, Canon Ralph. b 11. Selw Coll Cam BA 36, MA 40. Qu Coll Birm 36. **d** 38 **p** 39 Southw. C of E Retford 38-40; Perm to Offic at St Paul Harringay 40-41; C of Finchley 41-43; LPr (as C-in-c of Ch Ch West Green Tottenham) 43-46; Surr 46-49; V of St Thos Becontree 46-49; R of Lambourne 49-65; St Mary-at-the-Walls (Ch Ch w St Mary Virg from 77) Colchester 65-79; Hon Can of Chelmsf Cathl 71-79; Can (Emer) from 79; Perm to Offic Dio St E from 79; P-in-c of N Cove w Barnby Dio Nor from 81. *9 York Road, Southwold, Suffolk, IP18 6AN.* (Southwold 723705)

STEVENS, Canon Ralph Samuel Osborn. b 13. Univ of Birm BSc 34. St Cath S Ox BA (2nd cl Th) 36, MA 41. Ripon Hall, Ox 34. **d** 36 **p** 37 Birm. C of Aston-juxta-Birm 36-45; Dioc Chap in c of St Paul and St Mark City and Dio Birm 45-50; V from 50; RD of Centr Birm 46-58; Birm City 58-73; Hon Chap to Bp of Birm from 48; Hon Can of Birm from 52; Dir of Bp of Birm Industr Miss and Industr Chap to Bp 54-78; Proc Conv Birm 65-70; Chap to HM the Queen from 67. *68 Westfield Road, Edgbaston, Birmingham, B15 3QQ.* (021-454 1907)

STEVENS, Canon Reginald Charles. ALCD 35. **d** 35 **p** 36 Sheff. C of Walkley 35-39; Handsworth Yorks 39-40; V of St Luke Dyer's Hill (Sale Mem Ch) Sheff 40-47; C-in-c of St Aid Sheff 41-47; V of St Andr Netherton Dudley 47-79; RD of Dudley 56-79; Hon Can of Worc from 67. *29 Birch Avenue, Evesham, Worcs, WR11 6YJ.* (Evesham 48652)

STEVENS, Richard William. b 36. K Coll Lon and Warm AKC 59. **d** 60 **p** 61 Lon. C of St Jo Bapt Greenhill Harrow 60-63; Chap RAF 63-79; CF from 79. *c/o National Westminster Bank Ltd, 315 Station Road, Harrow, Middx, HA1 2AD.*

STEVENS, Robin George. b 43. Univ of Leic BA 65. Cudd Coll 74. **d** 74 **p** 75 St Alb. C of Hemel Hempstead 74-80; Chap

K Coll Sch Wimbledon from 80. *329 Wimbledon Park Road, SW19.*

STEVENS, Canon Rupert John. b 13. Univ of Dur LTh 39. BA 43. Oak Hill Th Coll 35. **d** 38 **p** 39 Ex. C of Cullompton 38-40; Bramcote w Attenborough 40-47; V of Kirklington w Hockerton 47-56; N Collingham (w S Collingham from 72) Dio Southw from 56; Ed Southw Dioc Directory 51-72; Southw Dioc News 63-72; C-in-c of S Scarle (w Besthorpe 56-68) Dio Southw from 56; S Collingham 68-72; Hon Can of Southw from 63; Surr from 69; RD of Newark from 75. *North Collingham Vicarage, Newark, Notts.* (Newark 892317)

STEVENS, Stephen Robert. b 14. **d** 66 **p** 67 Glouc. C of Cirencester w Watermoor 66-70; Bourton-on-the-Water 70-75; V of Bussage Dio Glouc from 75. *Bussage Vicarage, Stroud, Glos, GL6 8BB.* (Brimscombe 3556)

STEVENS, Thomas Walter. b 33. Bps' Coll Cheshunt. **d** 65 **p** 66 Newc T. C of St Matt w St Mary Virg Newc T 65-69; St Luke Wallsend 69-70; Cranford Dio Lon from 70. *St Dunstan's Clergy House, 133 Roseville Road, Hayes, Middx, UB3 4RA.* (01-573 3211)

STEVENS, Timothy John. b 46. Selw Coll Cam BA 68, MA 72. Ripon Coll Cudd 75. **d** 76 Chelmsf **p** 77 Barking for Chelmsf. C of E Ham w Upton Pk 76-79; Team V of 79-80; Team R of Canvey I Dio Chelmsf from 80. *210 Long Road, Canvey Island, Essex, SS8 0JR.* (Canvey Island 683192)

STEVENSEN, Albert. b 24. Wycl Hall Ox 61. **d** 62 **p** 63 Ox. C of Trin Aylesbury 62-64; Chap HM Pris Brixton 64-70; Wandsworth 70-71; V of St Steph Wandsworth Dio S'wark from 71. *2a Oakhill Road, SW15 2QU.* (01-874 5610)

STEVENSON, Alastair Rice. b 42. Open Univ BA 78. Ripon Coll Cudd. **d** 80 Chich **p** 81 Lewes for Chich. C of Bexhill Dio Chich from 80. *137 Dorset Road, Bexhill-on-Sea, E Sussex.* (Bexhill 215115)

STEVENSON, Brian. b 34. N-W Ordin Course 76. **d** 79 **p** 80 Blackb. C of Padiham Dio Blackb from 79. *12 Moore Drive, Higham, Burnley, Lancs.*

STEVENSON, Christopher James. b 43. Late Exhib and Sizar of Trin Coll Dub BA (2nd cl Cl) 65, MA 73. Em Coll Cam BA (2nd cl Th Trip pt ii) 69, MA 73. Westcott Ho Cam 68. **d** 70 S'wark for Newc T **p** 71 Newc T. C of H Cross Fenham 70-72; Armagh 72-73; Crumlin 73-76; Hon Cler V of Ch Ch Cathl Dub 75-76; C-in-c of All SS Conv Distr Appley Bridge Dio Blackb from 76. *154 Appley Lane North, Appley Bridge, Wigan, WN6 9DX.* (Appley Bridge 2875)

STEVENSON, Derick Neville. b 36. Open Univ BA 76. Ridley Hall Cam 79. **d** 80 **p** 81 Portsm. C of St Lawrence Dio Portsm from 80. *Rectory, St Lawrence, Ventnor, IW.*

STEVENSON, Frank Beaumont. b 39. Duke Univ Durham NC BA 61. Episc Th Sch Harvard MDiv 64. **d** and **p** 64 Bp of S Ohio. In Amer Ch 64-66; M Chr Educn Team Zambia 66-68; Bp's Tr Officer Dio Ox 69-70; Chap Keble Coll Ox 71-72; Bp of Ox Commun Health Chap from 68; Lect in Past Tr Ox Th Colls from 68; Chap Isis Group of Hosps Ox 73-75; Littlemore and Assoc Hosps from 75. *c/o Chaplain's Office, Littlemore Hospital, Oxford.* (Ox 778911)

STEVENSON, Frederick Robert. b 14. RIBA 38. Univ of Edin PhD 66. **d** 76 **p** 77 Edin (APM). C of St Anne Dunbar Dio Edin from 76; Haddington Dio Edin from 80. *Monks Orchard, East Linton, E Lothian, EH42.*

✠ **STEVENSON, Right Rev Hugh George.** MBE 45. Univ of S Afr BA 33. Univ of Witwatersrand LLB 38. St Paul's Coll Grahmstn 54. **d** 54 **p** 55 Johann. C of Malvern 54-56; R of Ermelo 56-60; St Pet Brakpan 60-64; Turffontein 64-66; Hon Can of Johann 67-68; Chap Tara Hosp Johann 67-68; R of Nelspruit 68-78; Irene Dio Pret from 78; Archd of E Transv 72-78; Cons Ld Bp Suffr of Pret in St Mary Virg Cathl Johann 19 May 78 by Abp of Capetn; Bps of Pret, Johann, Swaz, Kimb K, Natal, Port Eliz and Bloemf. *Box 1032, Pretoria, S Africa.*

STEVENSON, James Frederick. b 42. Carleton Univ Ott BA 67. Episc Th Coll Cam USA MDiv 73. **d** 73 Ott **p** 73 Bp Greenwood for Ott. C of Smith's Falls 73-75; I of Campbell's Bay Dio Ott from 75. *Box 68, Campbell's Bay, PQ, JOX 1KO, Canada.* (819-648 5685)

STEVENSON, James Jackson. b 14. TCD BA 36, MA 44. **d** 39 Tuam for Down **p** 40 Down. C of Newtownards 39-43; St Mary Belf 43-48; C-in-c of Stoneyford 48-51; R 51-53; St Lawr Denton 53-56; Donagh w Tyholland 56-60; I of Clogher (w Errigal-Portclare from 65) 60-73; Preb of Donacavey in Clogh Cathl 61-67; Prec 67-82; I of Carrickmacross 73-82. *Glebe Cottage, Tullynaskeagh, Carrickmacross, Co Monaghan, Irish Republic.*

STEVENSON, James Sherwood. Montr Dioc Th Coll LTh 67. **d** 66 **p** 67 Hur. C of All SS Windsor 69-71; R of Hespeler 71; St Jas Cam 71-75; Kingsville Dio Hur from 75. *Rectory, Kingsville, Ont., Canada.* (519-733 4394)

STEVENSON, John. Lich Th Coll. **d** 54 **p** 55 Lich. C of Walsall 54-58; V of Knutton 58-72. *16 Kings Avenue, Wolstanton, Newcastle, Staffs, ST5 8DA.*

STEVENSON, John Charles. b 22. St Jo Coll Dur LTh 48. Oak Hill Th Coll 45. **d** 49 **p** 50 Man. C of Davyhulme 49-51; Thornham w Gravel Hole 51-54; V of Steeple Claydon 54-58; RD of Claydon 58; Chap HM Pris Grendon Hall 57-58; R of Stowell Mem Ch Salford 58-64; V of St Bede Bolton 64-75; Asst Chap HM Pris Wandsworth 75-77; Chap HM Pris Linc 77-80; R of Fiskerton w Reepham Dio Linc from 80. *Fiskerton Rectory, Lincoln, LN3 4EZ.* (Linc 750577)

STEVENSON, Keith Charles. b 02. Clifton Th Coll 37 **d** 38 Carl **p** 39 Penrith for Carl. C of St Jas Denton Holme Carl 38-40; High Wycombe 40-42; R of Vange 42-44; Fyfield 44-55; V of Berners Roding 45-46; Ch Ch Camberwell 55-59; Tulse Hill 59-68; L to Offic Dio Chelmsf from 68. *10 Cedar Close, Walton-on-the-Naze, Essex.* (Frinton 3414)

STEVENSON, Keith Robin Norman. St Francis Coll Brisb ACT ThL 66. **d** and **p** 66 Brisb. C of Annunc Camp Hill Brisb 66-67; Warwick 67-69; R of Bright 70-74; Rutherglen 74-75; Chinchilla Dio Brisb from 75. *52 Middle Street, Chinchilla, Queensland, Australia 4413.* (Chinchilla 45)

STEVENSON, Kenneth William. b 49. Univ of Edin MA 70. Univ of Southm PhD 75. Sarum Wells Th Coll 70. **d** 73 **p** 74 Linc. C of Grantham 73-76; Lect Linc Th Coll 75-80; St Botolph Boston 76-80; Chap and Lect Univ of Man from 80; Team V of Whitworth Dio Man from 80. *38 Sandleigh Avenue, Withington, Manchester, M20 9LW.* (061-445 6833)

STEVENSON, Lawrence Todd. b 30. St Jo Coll Auckld 68. **d** 70 Polyn **p** 72 Auckld. C of H Trin Cathl Auckld 70-72; St Aid Remuera 72-73; R of Trafalgar Dio Gippsld from 76. *Rectory, Trafalgar, Vic, Australia 3824.* (056-34 1211)

STEVENSON, Ven Richard Clayton. b 22. TCD BA Div Test Downes Oratory Prize 48, MA 56. **d** 48 **p** 49 Connor. C of St Mary Magd Belfast 48-51; Bangor Co Down 51-54; R of Comber 54-60; St Barn Belf 60-70; St Nich Belf Dio Connor from 70; Archd of Connor from 79. *42 Malone Heights, Belfast, BT9 5PG.*

STEVENSON, Richard Hugh. b 45. Univ of Ex BA Th) 68. Westcott Ho Cam 68. **d** 70 Gerard for Sheff **p** 71 Sheff. C of H Trin, Millhouses 70-74; Chap St John's Cathl Hong from 74. *St John's Cathedral, Hong Kong.* (5-234157)

STEVENSON, Robert Brian. b 40. QUB BA (2nd cl Mod Hist) 61. Late Scho of Cam. Qu Coll Cam BA (2nd cl Th Trip pt ii) 67, MA 71. Pemb Coll Ox BA (by incorp) 69, BD 76, MA 76. Univ of Birm PhD 70. Cudd Coll 69. **d** 70 S'wark **p** 71 Newc T for S'wark. C of St Jo Bapt Southend Lewisham 70-73; Catford (Southend) and Downham 73-74; Lect Chich Th Coll 74-81; Dir of Pastoral Stud 74-81; Actg Vice-Prin 81; V of W Malling w Offham Dio Roch from 81. *138 High Street, West Malling, Kent.* (W Malling 842245)

STEVENSON, Canon Ronald. b 17. Univ of Leeds BA (3rd cl Hist) 38. Coll of Resurr Mirfield. **d** 40 **p** 41 Wakef. C of All SS Pontefract 40-44; C-in-c of Lundwood Conv Distr 44-47; Area Sec Miss to Seamen 47-49; Perm to Offic Dios Linc, Ches, Man, Blackb, Carl, Leic, Derby, Pet and Chap of Lancaster Moor Hosp 49-65; N Lancs and S Westmd Hosps from 65; Hon Can of Blackb 71-75; Can (Emer) from 75. *28 Slyne Road, Torrisholme, Morecambe, Lancs.* (Morecambe 410957)

STEVENSON, Thomas. b 15. Worc Ordin Coll 60. **d** 61 **p** 62 Ripon. C of Belle Isle 61-64; Garforth 64-65; V of St Mich Castleford 65-68; Shouldham w Shouldham Thorpe 68-71; C of Wellingborough (in c of Hemingwell Estate) 71-73; R of Stoke Albany w Wilbarston 74-78. *25 Brignall Croft, Leeds, LS9 7EU.*

STEVINSON, Harold John Hardy. b 34. Selw Coll Cam BA 57, MA 61. Qu Coll Birm. **d** 59 **p** 60 Bris. C of St Mary Redcliffe Bedminster 59-63; Caversham 63-73; Social Responsibility Officer Sunderland 74-82; P-in-c of Croxdale Dio Dur from 82. *Rectory, Croxdale, Durham, DH6 5HB.* (Durham 780273)

STEWARD, Donald John. b 10. K Coll Lon Sen Th Exhib 31 and 32, AKC 33. St Steph Ho Ox 33. **d** 33 **p** 34 Dur. C of H Trin Sunderland 33-37; St Bart Brighton 37-43; V of All SS Sidley 43-66; Perm to Offic Dio Lon 66-68; C of Old St Pancras w St Matt Oakley Square Lon 69-75; Perm to Offic Dio Cant from 79. *4 Bramley Hill, Croydon, Surrey.* (01-681 1283)

STEWARD, Robert Edward Alan. Late Exhib of BNC Ox BA 57, MA 61. Ridley Hall Cam 57. **d** 59 **p** 60 Guildf. C of Ashtead 59-62; Chap Bourne Sch Kuala Lumpur 63-65; Asst Chap Tonbridge Sch 65-70; L to Offic Dio Lich 70-71; Chap Haileybury Coll from 71; Chap (TAVR) from 74; Chap to Sheriff of City of Lon 75-76. *c/o Haileybury College, Herts.*

STEWARDSON, Ian Joseph. b 28. Ex Coll Ox BA (2nd cl Eng) 52, Dipl Th 54, MA 56. Wycl Hall Ox 52. **d** 54 **p** 55 Liv. C of St Luke Farnworth 54-57; Mossley Hill 57-60; V of St Jas New Barnet 60-72; C-in-c of Potton w Cockayne-Hatley and Sutton Dio St Alb 72-73; R from 73. *Potton Vicarage, Sandy, Beds.* (Potton 260261)

STEWART, Canon Alexander Butler. b 25. **d** 58 **p** 59 Down. C of Holywood 58-61; Chap Miss to Seamen Beira 61-64; I of Donagh 64-65; Helen's Bay 65-72; R of Donegal Dio Raph from 72; RD of Donegal from 79; Can of Raph from 81. *Rectory, Donegal, Irish Republic.* (Donegal 75)

STEWART, Alexander Charles. b 1892. Late Scho of Peterho Cam 1st cl Math Trip pt i, 12, BA (Wrangler Math Trip pt ii) 14, MA 28. K Coll Lon 49. **d** 49 **p** 50 Ches. C of Neston 49-51; V of Hooton 51-59; Thornham w Titchwell 59-65; Perm to Offic Dio Nor from 65. *c/o Barclay's Bank, Hunstanton, Norf.*

STEWART, Ven Alexander John. Univ of NZ LLB 37. St Jo Coll Auckld LTh 39. **d** and **p** 40 Wel. C of Khandallah Wel 40-43; C-in-c of Ohakune and Raetihi 43-47; V of Tinui 47-51; St Luke Wadestown Wel 52-55 Invercargill 55-65; Waikouaiti 65-77; Archd of Southland 63-66; N Otago 66-77; Archd (Emer) from 77; L to Offic Dio Dun from 77. *11 Pratt Street, Waikouaiti, NZ.* (Waikouaiti 134)

STEWART, Very Rev Charles Cuthbert. St Paul's Miss Coll Burgh. **d** 21 Brech for Glas for St Jo Kaffr **p** 22 St Jo Kaffr. C of Ch Ch Glas 21-22; P-in-c of Mt Ayliff Griquald E 22-23; C of St Barn Miss Ntlaza 23-25; P-in-c of Clydesdale 25-40; Dean of St John's 40-65; Dean (Emer) from 65. *Flat 101, Harae Centre, Church Street, Somerset West, CP, S Africa.*

STEWART, Douglas Dutholt. **d** 55 **p** 56 Rupld. C of St Jo Cathl Winnipeg and I of Stonewall 55-58; St Pet Winnipeg 58-65; V of St Chad Winnipeg 65-73; Can of Rupld 68-73; R of St Timothy Edmon 73-81; St Chris W Vanc Dio New Westmr from 81. *1068 Inglewood Avenue, West Vancouver, BC Canada.*

STEWART, Douglas Robert. St Jo Coll Morpeth ACT ThL 41. **d** 41 **p** 42 Newc. C of Hamilton 41-47; R of Hill End 47-50; C of Ch Ch Cathl Newc 50-54; R of Cardiff 54-58; V of Warracknabeal 58-62; R of Colac 62-73; Can of Bal 68-73; R of Rabaul 73-77; St Geo Mart Cathl Rabaul 77-80; VG and Exam Chap to Bp of New Guinea Is 77-80; R of Victor Harbor Dio Murray from 80. *14 Burke Street, Victor Harbour, S Australia 5211.* (085-52 1076)

STEWART, Fletcher Jeremy. Univ of Tor BA 64. Trin Coll Tor STB 68. **d** 68 **p** 69 Tor. C of Vespra (in c of Minesing) 68-70; I of Hastings 71-74; Univ Chap Dio Edmon 74-79; Hon C of St Geo Edmon 79-80; R of Ch Ch The Pas Dio Bran from 80. *Box 125, The Pas, Manit, Canada.*

STEWART, George William. b 23. **d** 69 Wel. Hon C of Lower Hutt 68-73; L to Offic Dio Wel from 73. *94 Peel Place, Wainuiomata, NZ.*

STEWART, Canon Harold Cowley. Univ of Leeds, BA 31. Coll of Resurr Mirfield, 31. **d** 33 **p** 34 Liv. C of St Faith Gt Crosby 33-36; St Pet Colleg Ch Wolverhampton 36-39; V of H Trin Carl 39-49; St Mich Appleby 49-51; Murton w Hilton 49-51; St Luke Barrow-F 51-65; Hon Can of Carl 57-71; Can (Emer) from 71; RD of Dalton 58-65; V of Penrith 65-71; R of Newton Reigny 66-71; L to Offic Dio Carl 71-80. *Address temp unknown.*

STEWART, James. b 32. **d** 69 **p** 70 Down. C of St Donard Belf 69-72; Dundonald 72-74; R of Tyrella w Rathmullen 74-80; St Clem Belf Dio Down from 80. *80a Sandown Road, Belfast, BT5 8GU.* (Belf 657345)

STEWART, Jeffrey John. Moore Th Coll Syd ACT ThL 67. **d** 68 **p** 69 Syd. C of Drummoyne 68; Panania 68-71; Dapto 71-72; Perm to Offic Dio Papua from 75. *PO Box 18, Goroka, Papua New Guinea.*

STEWART, John. b 09. Late Exhib of St Cath Coll Cam 1st cl Math Trip pt i 29, BA (2nd cl Th Trip pt i) 31, MA 35. Cudd Coll 31. **d** 32 **p** 33 York. C of St Jo Evang Middlesbrough 32-35; St Martin Scarborough 35-37; V of Ugthorpe 37-39; St Mary Lowgate Hull 39-47; St Martin Middlesbrough 47-51; Exam Chap to Abp of York 42-51; R of Hilborough w Bodney 51-57; V of Lastingham 57-74; Appleton-le-Moors 57-74; RD of Helmsley 58-74; Hon Chap to Bp of Kimb K 62-66; Proc Conv York 64-70; Chap Qu Mary's Sch Helmsley from 75. *Bodney Cottage, Buckingham Square, Helmsley, York, YO6 5DZ.* (Helmsley 70517)

STEWART, John. b 39. Oakhill Th Coll 75. **d** 77 Lanc for Blackb **p** 78 Blackb. C of Ch Ch Accrington 77-79; Team V of Darwen w Hoddlesden Dio Blackb from 79. *St Paul's Vicarage, Johnson New Road, Hoddlesden, Nr Darwen, Lancs.*

STEWART, Canon John. **d** 38 **p** 40 Alg. C-in-c of St Joseph's I 38-40; C of St Mary Magd Tor 40-42; CF (Canad) 42-46; I of Eastview 47-56; R of St Columba Ott 56-72; Hosp Chap Ott 72-81; Can of Ott from 73. *342-515 Saint Laurent, Ottawa, Ont., Canada.*

STEWART, John Edward Craig. Ridley Coll Melb ACT ThL 64. **d** 65 **p** 66 Adel. C of Prospect 65-67; Mt Gambier 67-68; Crawley 68-70; I of Parkdale 70-74; Frankston E 74-79; Gen Sec CMS Vic and L to Offic Dio Melb from 79. *35 Robert Street, North Balwyn, Vic, Australia 3104.* (857 7401)

STEWART, John Roberton. b 29. Sarum Th Coll 63. **d** 65 **p** 66 Sarum. C of Gillingham 65-70; R of Langton Matravers Dio Sarum from 70. *Langton Matravers Rectory, Swanage, Dorset, BH19 3HB.* (Swanage 2559)

STEWART, John Vernon. b 36. Late Scho of BNC Ox BA (1st cl Th) 57, MA 66. Coll of Resurr Halki 59. **d** 61 **p** 62 Accra. Lect Fell and Chap Univ of Ghana 61-64; L to Offic Dio Accra 61-64; Miss USPG Dio Madag 64-66; V of Balsall Heath 66-70; Commiss Diego S 69-79; Antsir from 79; V of Sibford Gower w Sibford Ferris and Epwell 70-75; R of Northolt Dio Lon from 75. *Northolt Rectory, Middx, UB5 6AA.* (01-841 5691)

STEWART, John Walter. b 46. St Jo Coll Morpeth ThL 72. **d** 73 **p** 74 Melb. C of H Trin Surrey Hills 73-74; Swan Hill 74-75; V of Merbein 75-79; Wantirna S Dio Melb from 79. *St John's Vicarage, Burwood Highway, Wantirna, Vic, Australia 3152.* (221 2165)

STEWART, John Wesley. b 52. Qu Univ Belf BD 76. TCD 76. **d** 77 **p** 78 Down. C of Seagoe 77-79; Ch Ch Lisburn Dio Connor from 79. *6 Woodland Park, Lisburn, Co Antrim, N Ireland.* (Lisburn 6658)

STEWART, Chan Maurice Evan. TCD BA (Mod) 50, MA 53, BD 67. Univ of Belf PhD 75. **d** 52 Kilm for Connor **p** 53 Connor. C of St Jas Belf 52-55; Chap Bps' Coll Cheshunt 55-58; Hd of Trin Coll Miss Belf 58-61; I of Newcastle 61-69; Tutor Ch of Ireland Th Coll from 69; Vice-Prin 80; Lect TCD from 72; Centr Dir of Ordinands for Ch of Ireland from 75; Chan of St Patr Cathl Dub from 80. *99 Landscape Park, Dublin 14, Irish Republic.*

STEWART, Raymond John. b 55. TCD BA 79. **d** 79 **p** 80 Derry. C of All SS Clooney Dio Derry from 79. *c/o 8 Clooney Terrace, Waterside, Londonderry, N Ireland.*

STEWART, Norman Andrew. Edin Th Coll 54. **d** 58 Edin for Glas **p** 59 Glas. C of Ch Ch Glas 58-59; H Trin Paisley 59-60; St Marg Newlands Glas 60-62; Kingsthorpe Pet 62-64; R of Balaclava Ja 64-67; Chap and Asst Master Bp's High Sch Mandeville 64-67; Chap RAF 67-71. *Address temp unknown.*

STEWART, Canon Robert Henry. Trin Coll Tor BA 55. **d** 55 **p** 56 Rupld. C of H Trin Winnipeg 55-56; Ch Ch Cathl Vanc 56-59; V of Sardis 59-63; R of Marmora 63-67; Picton 67-79; Prescott Dio Ont from 79; Can of Ont from 77. *Box 576, Prescott, Ont, Canada.* (613-925 2748)

STEWART, Preb Robert Stevenson. b 15. TCD BA (2nd cl Mod) 38, Div Test (1st cl) 39. **d** 39 **d** 39 **p** 40 Dub. C of Ch Ch Leeson Pk Dub 39-43; St Donard Belf 43-45; I of Ahoghill 45-59; Ballymoney Dio Connor from 59; Preb of Connor Cathl from 78. *Rectory, Ballymoney, Co Antrim, N Ireland.* (Ballymoney 62149)

STEWART, Thomas Adam Gardiner Bruce. b 15. New Coll Edin 31. **d** and **p** 74 Edin (APM). Hon C of St Andr Niddrie 74-77; St Aid Niddrie Mains Edin 76-77; Dalkeith and of Lassawade Dio Edin from 77. *2 Glebe Street, Dalkeith, EH22 1JG.* (031-663 1231)

STEWART, Thomas Alexander. TCD BA 38. **d** 38 **p** 39 Dub. C of St Thos Dub 38-41; C-in-c of Kilnahue and Kilpipe 41-44; I of Fertagh w Eirke and Clonmantagh 44-54; RD of Fiddown 52-54; R of York W Austr 54-57; C-in-c of Offerlane (w Borris-in-Ossory and Aghavoe from 58) 57-58; I 58-80; Seir-Kyran 57-80; Preb of Mayne in St Canice's Cathl Kilkenny 58-62; Treas 62-78; Prec of Oss and Leigh Cathls 78-80. *Offerlane Rectory, Mountrath, Leix, Irish Republic.*

STEWART, William Allen. b 43. Trin Coll Cam BA (2nd cl Hist) 65. MA 69. Cranmer Hall Dur Dipl Th 68. **d** 68 **p** 69 Sheff. C of Ecclesall 68-72; Cheltm 72-74; V of St Jas Glouc 74-80; P-in-c of All SS Glouc 78-80; R of St Mary Magd w St Jas Upton Torquay Dio Ex from 80. *8 Shirburn Road, Torquay, Devon.* (Torquay 37065)

STEWART, William Jones. b 32. Trin Hall, Cam BA (2nd cl Cl) 55, MA 59. Edin Th Coll 67. **d** and **p** 69 St Andr. Chap of St Ninian's Cathl Perth 69-71; Dom Chap to Bp of Ox 71-75; V of Lambourn Dio Ox from 75; Hon Chap to Bp of Ox from 75. *Vicarage, Lambourn, Berks.* (Lambourn 71546)

STEWART-HARGREAVES, Ian. b 37. Wells Th Coll 69. **d** 70 Lanc for Black **p** 71 Blackb. C of St Mary Lanc 71-74. *27 St Oswald Street, Lancaster.*

STEWART-MAUNDER, Canon David George Brian. b 30. TCD 60. **d** 60 **p** 61 Connor. C of Ballymoney 60-63; R of Ardara 63-70; I of Clondehorkey Dio Raph from 70; RD of Kilmacrennan W from 78; Kilmacrennan E from 81; Can of Raph Cathl from 79. *Ballymore Rectory, Port-na-Blagh, Co Donegal, Irish Republic.* (074-36185)

STEWART-SMITH, Canon David Cree. b 13. K Coll Cam BA 39, MA 42. Cudd Coll 40. **d** 41 **p** 42 Pet. C of St Matt Northn 41-43; St Steph Cheltm 43-44; V Cho and Sacr at York Minster 44-49; Sub-Chanter 48-49; Chap Qu Marg Sch Castle Howard 45-49; LPr Dio York 44-49; V of Shadwell

49-52; Warden Brasted Place Coll 52-63; Dean and Admin St Geo Colleg Ch Jer 64-67; Commiss Jer 67-77; Hon Can of Roch 67-69 and 76-78; Can (Emer) from 78; Res Can 69-76; Archd of Bromley 68-69; Roch 69-76; C of E Pensions Bd from 69; Home Sec Jer and Middle E Ch Assoc 76-78; Ch Comm 73-78; Perm to Offic Dio Ex from 76. *Flat 3, 7 Fortfield Terrace, Sidmouth, Devon, EX10 8NT.* (Sidmouth 4440)

STEYNOR, Victor Albert. b 15. SOC 68. **d** 71 Horsham for Chich **p** 72 Chich. C of Bognor Regis 71-75; V of Debenham (w Aspall and Kenton from 81) 75-82; P-in-c of Aspall 75-81; Kenton 75-81. *74 Elmhurst Drive, Ipswich, IP3 0PB.* (Ipswich 78922)

✠ **STIBBARD, Right Rev Leslie.** St Aug Coll Cant 35. **d** 37 Cant for Melan **p** 38 Melan. Miss at Maravovo 37-38; Hd Master Maravovo Boys' Sch 38-42; R of Eugoura 42-44; Adamstown 44-51; Commiss Melan in Australia from 43; Abp's Gen Perm to Offic in Engl 47-48; R of Hamilton 48-62; Hon Can of Newc 58-62; Archd of Newc 62-74; Dom Chap to Bp of Newc 62-73; Cons Asst Bp of Newc in St Andr Cathl Syd 19 May 64 by Abp of Syd; Bps of Newc; Bath; Graft; C & W Goulb; and Tas; and Bps Kerle, Loane and A W G Hudson; res 74; Perm to Offic Dio Newc from 74. *62 Kemp Street, Hamilton, NSW, Australia 2303.*

STIBBS, Wilfrid James. b 12. Linc Th Coll 67. **d** 40 **p** 41 RC Asst bps of Westmr. Rec into Angl Commun by Rev S R Birchnall 67; C of Hessle 68-69; R of W & E Rounton and Welbury 69-72; Master of Charterho Hull 73-76; Perm to Offic Dio York from 76. *62 Front Street, Sowerby, Thirsk, N Yorks.* (0845-23371)

STICKLAND, Geoffrey John Brett. b 42. St D Coll Lamp Dipl Th 66. **d** 66 **p** 67 Llan. C of H Trin Aberavon 66-69; C-in-c of Llanrumney 69-72; C of Tetbury 72-75; V of Hardwicke Dio Glouc from 75. *Vicarage, Hardwicke, Glos.*

STIDOLPH, Robert Anthony. b 54. St Steph Ho Ox 77. **d** and **p** 80 Chich. C of All SS Hove Dio Chich from 80. *Church House Flat, Wilbury Road, Hove, E Sussex, BN3 3PB.* (0273 736643)

STIEVENARD, Alphonse Etienne Arthur. b 13. Selw Coll Cam BA 36, MA 40. Lon Coll of Div 36. **d** 37 **p** 38 Lon. C of Em Northwood 37-40; St Pet Southborough 40-44; V of Ch Ch Leyton 44-51; St Matt Millbrook Jersey 51-78. *Anapausis, Route Orange, La Moye, Jersey, CI.*

STIFF, Derrick Malcolm. b 40. Lich Th Coll 69. **d** 72 **p** 73 Cov. C of St Geo Cov 72-75; R of Benhall w Sternfield 75-79; C-in-c of Snape 75-79; V of Cartmel Dio Carl from 79. *Cartmel Priory, Grange-over-Sands, Cumbria, LA11 6PU.* (Cartmel 261)

✠ **STIFF, Right Rev Hugh Vernon.** Univ of Tor BA 50. Trin Coll Tor BD 57, LTh 58, DD 69. **d** 52 **p** 53 Tor. C of St Mary Magd Tor 52-53; St Aid Tor 53-55; Miss at Lintlaw 55-58; R of All SS Sktn 58-63; Dom Chap to Bp of Sktn 58-63; Hon Can of Sktn 61-63; R of Cathl Ch of the Redeemer Calg 63-69; Dean 65-69; Cons Ld Bp of Keew in St John's Cathl Winnipeg 24 June 69 by Abp of Rupld (Primate); Bps of Sktn; Athab; Sask; Qu'App; Edmon; BC; and Calg; Bp Coadj of New Westmr; Bps Suffr of Hur (Appleyard); and Athab; and Bps P F McNairy (USA) and J Nieminski (Polish Nat Catholic Ch in Canada); res 74; Dean (R 74-77) of St Jas Cathl Tor from 74; Asst Bp of Tor from 77. *65 Church Street, Toronto, M5C 2E9, Ont, Canada.* (416-364 7865)

STILEMAN, John William Hampson. b 1896. Jes Coll Cam BA 22, MA 28. Clifton Th Coll 52. **d** 52 **p** 53 Roch. C of Penge 52-53; Chap Mariners' Ch Glouc 53-61; R of Corscombe w Toller Whelme 61-69. *St Nicholas Hospital, Salisbury, SP1 2SW.* (Salisbury 25328)

STILL, Canon Colin Charles. b 35. Selw Coll Cam BA 67, MA 71. Univ of Dur Dipl Th 68. United Th Sem Dayton Ohio STM 69. Cranmer Hall Dur 67. **d** 69 **p** 70 York. C of Drypool 69-72; Dom Chap to Abp of York 72-75; P-in-c of Ockham w Hatchford Dio Guildf 76-80; R from 80; Recruitment Sec ACCM 76-80; Can Missr & Ecumen Officer Dio Guildf from 80. *Rectory, Ockham, Woking, Surrey, GU23 6NP.* (Guildford 22358)

STILLINGS, Tom Atkinson. b 33. Univ of Wales Dipl Th 61. St Mich Coll Llan 58. **d** 61 **p** 62 St A. C of Rhos-y-Medre 61-67; Minera 67-70; R of Llanfynydd 70-74; V of Bagillt Dio St A from 74. *Vicarage, Bagillt, Clwyd.* (Flint 2732)

STIMPSON, Graham George. b 40. MB, BS (Lon) 65. Cudd Coll 69. **d** 70 **p** 71 Bris. Hon C of Redcliffe Dio Bris from 70. *5 Fernleigh Court, Redland Road, Bristol, BS6 6YE.*

STINSON, William Gordon. b 29. Univ of Lon BSc (2nd cl Chem) 50. Ely Th Coll 51. **d** 52 York **p** 53 Selby for York. C of St Alb Hull 52-56; V of St Sav Georgetn Br Gui 56-61; R of E w W Ravendale and Hatcliffe 61-67; R of Beelsby 61-67; C-in-c of Ashby w Fenby and Brigsley 62-66; R 66-67; PC of St Aid New Cleethorpes 67-69; V 69-76; RD of Grimsby and Cleethorpes 73-76; C-in-c of Dovercourt Dio Chelmsf from 76. *51 Highfield Avenue, Dovercourt, Harwich, Essex.* (Harwich 2033)

STIRK, Peter Francis. b 24. Linc Coll Ox BA (3rd cl Th) 49, MA 53. Qu Coll Birm 49. **d** 50 **p** 51 Ripon. C of St Mary Beeston 50-68; C-in-c of Kirby-on-the-Moor Dio Ripon 68-71; V from 71; C-in-c of Cundall w Norton-le-Clay Dio Ripon 73-81; V from 81. *Vicarage, Kirby Hill, Boroughbridge, York, YO5 9DS.* (Boroughbridge 2551)

STIRRUP, Roger. b 34. St Cath Coll Cam 2nd cl Hist Trip pt i 57, BA (2nd cl Th Trip pt ia) 58, MA 62. Linc Th Coll 58. **d** 60 **p** 61 Birm. C of St Mary Selly Oak 60-63; Battersea 63-65; Chap Univ of St Andr 65-68; Chap and Asst Master Nottm High Sch 68-80; Asst Chap & Master Rugby Sch from 80. *Rugby School, Rugby, Warwick.*

STIRTON, Canon Horace Albert. d 58 Bp McKie for Bend **p** 59 Bend. C of Maldon 58-59; V 59-62; R of Kangaroo Flat 62-68; Kyneton 68-77; Can of Bend from 70; R of H Trin City and Dio Bend from 77. *Rectory, Keck Street, Bendigo, Vic, Australia 3550.*

STOCK, Basil Lievesley. Ch Coll Cam BA 28, MA 62. **d** 61 **p** 62 Melb. C of S Yarra 61-62; Min of Belgrave 62-69; on leave 69-75; Perm to Offic Dio Tas 76-78. *44 Wellesley Street, South Hobart, Tasmania 7000.*

STOCK, Canon Kenneth Lawrence. b 28. Univ of Leeds BA 49. Coll of Resurr Mirfield. **d** 51 **p** 52 Lon. C of St Aug Haggerston 51-54; St Alb Bordesley 54-66; PC (V from 68) of St Columba Southwick Dio Dur from 66; Hon Can of Dur Cathl from 80. *St Columba's Clergy House, Southwick, Sunderland, Tyne & Wear, SR5 1RU.* (Sunderland 487037)

STOCK, Victor Andrew. b 44. K Coll Lon and Warm AKC 68. **d** 69 Willesden for Lon **p** 70 Lon. C of Pinner 69-73; Chap Univ of Lon 73-79; R of Friern Barnet Dio Lon from 79; M Gen Syn from 80. *147 Friern Barnet Lane, N20 0NP.* (01-445 7844)

STOCK, William Nigel. b 50. Univ of Dur BA 72. Univ of Ox Dipl Th 75. Ripon Coll Ox 75. **d** 76 **p** 77 Dur. C of St Pet Stockton-on-Tees 76-78; Lae (in c of Taraka Distr) Dio Aipo from 79. *Box 31, Lae, Papua New Guinea.* (42-1089)

STOCKALL, Reginald Bruce. K Coll Halifax NS LTh 59. **d** 59 **p** 60 Fred. I of Ludlow 59-65; R of St Mary York Fred 65-72; St Jo Bapt, St John Dio Fred from 72. *815 Millidge Avenue, St John, NB, Canada.*

STOCKBRIDGE, Alan Carmichael. b 33. Keble Coll Ox BA 55, MA 62. Wycl Hall Ox 66. **d** 68 Ox **p** 69 Croydon for Cant. CF 68-78; Chap Reading Sch from 78. *c/o 54 Crawshay Drive, Emmer Green, Reading, Berks.*

STOCKDALE, Anthony John Norman. Univ of Bris BSc 56. St Jo Coll Auckld LTh 67. **d** 66 **p** 67 Waik. C of Morrinsville 66-67; Stratford 67-69; V of Eketahuna 69-73; C of Lower Hutt 73-80; Devonport City and Dio Auckld from 80; Chap RNZN from 80. *17 Mirovale Place, Glenfield, Auckland, NZ.*

STOCKDALE, Richard John. St Columb's Hall, Wang ACT ThL 47. **d** 47 **p** 48 Wang. C of Milawa 47-49; R of Yackandandah 49-54; Warragul 54-63; I of St Mark E Brighton 63-69; Min of Deepdene 69-73; R of Cudal Dio Bath from 75. *Rectory, Cudal, NSW, Australia 2864.* (64-2062)

STOCKDALE, Robert Edward. b 1888. St Jo Hall Dur LTh 10, BA 11, MA 14. St Aid Coll 08. **d** 11 **p** 12 Newc T. C of St Steph Newc T 11-13; Ch Stretton 13-16; Bunbury Chesh 16-18; TCF 18-20; C of Bolsover 20-22; Neath 22-25; Asst Dioc Missr Dio Llan 25-28; Dioc Insp of Schs 26-28; C of St Aug Penarth w Lavernock 28-29; R of Llandough w Leckwith and Cogan 29-47; C-in-C of St Jo Bapt Whitchurch 47-49; V of Granborough 49-61. *16 Richmond Hill, Clifton, Bristol 8.*

STOCKDALE, William John Douglas. Moore Th Coll ACT ThL 50. **d** 51 **p** 52 Melb. C of Melbourne Dioc Centre 51-52; P-in-c of Wilcannia 53-61; Sec Bush Ch Aid S Vic 61-68; Perm to Office Dio Melb 61-62; C of Doncaster 62-69; I of H Trin Thornbury Dio Melb from 69. *28 Shaftesbury Parade, Thornbury, Vic, Australia 3071.* (03-44 3884)

STOCKER, David William George. b 37. Univ of Bris BA (2nd cl Gen) 58. Qu Coll Birm 59. **d** 60 **p** 61 Birm. C of Sparkhill 60-64; Keighley (in c of Utley) 64-66; V of Grenoside Dio Sheff from 66. *87 Main Street, Grenoside, Sheffield.* (Sheff 467513)

STOCKLEY, Michael Ian. b 41. Lon Coll of Div 66. **d** 69 Warrington for Liv **p** 70 Liv. C of St Mark St Helens 69-74; Fazakerley Dio Liv 74; Team V from 74. *St Paul's House, Formosa Drive, Liverpool 10.*

STOCKLEY, Roland. b 23. St Jo Coll Dur BA 47, Dipl Th 49. **d** 49 **p** 50 Worc. C of St Barn Rainbow Hill Worc 49-52; CF 52-57; V of Broadwaters 57-66; Himbleton w Huddington

66-68; R of Pedmore Dio Worc from 68. *Rectory, Pedmore Lane, Pedmore, Stourbridge, W Midl, DY9 0SW.* (0652-884856)

STOCKPORT, Lord Bishop Suffragan of. *See* Strutt, Right Rev Rupert Gordon.

STOCKS, John Cedric Hawkesworth. Em Coll Cam 2nd cl Hist Trip 35, BA (3rd cl Engl Trip) 37, MA 40. Westcott Ho Cam. **d** 40 **p** 41 Wakef. C of St Geo Barnsley 40-43; St Barn Crosland Moor 43-45; Whitby (in c of St Mich and St Hilda) 45-46; Guiseley 46-49; V of St Bridget Beckermet 49-52; V of Ponsonby and Chap Pelham Ho Approved Sch 49-52; V of Fewston w Blubberhouses 52-55; R of Bentham 55-57; Whitestone 57-60; PC of Oldridge 57-60; V of Ellerton Priory w Aughton and E Cottingwith 60-65; Sheriff Hutton 65-80. *c/o Sheriff Hutton Vicarage, York, YO6 1PY.* (Sheriff Hutton 336)

STOCKS, Norman. b 01. St Aid Coll 29. **d** 30 **p** 31 Down. C of Coleraine 30-39; V of Cononley w Bradley 39-60; R of Oldbury-on-Severn Dio Glouc from 60. *Oldbury-on-Severn Rectory, Thornbury, Bristol.* (Thornbury 3281)

STOCKTON, Ian George. b 49. Selw Coll Cam BA 72, MA 76. St Jo Coll Nottm 73. **d** 75 **p** 76 Lich. C of Chell 75-78; Trentham 79-80; R of Dalbeattie Dio Glas from 80. *Rectory, Blair Street, Dalbeattie, Kirkcudbright, DG5 4DZ.* (0556-610420)

STOCKTON, Wilfred. b 32. Roch Th Coll 63. **d** 65 **p** 66 Derby. C of Shirebrook 65-67; Boulton 67-69; V of Ault Hucknall 69-73; R of Pinxton Dio Derby from 73. *Pinxton Rectory, Nottingham, NG16 6HH.* (Ripley 810278)

✠ **STOCKWOOD, Right Rev Arthur Mervyn.** b 13. Ch Coll Cam BA 35, 2nd cl Hist Trip pt i 34, 2nd cl Th Trip pt i 36, MA 39. DD (Lambeth) 59. Univ of Sussex Hon DLitt 63. Hon DD Bucharest 78. Westcott Ho Cam 35. **d** 36 **p** 37 Bris. C of St Matt Moorfields Bris and Blundell's Sch Missr 36-41; V 41-55; Commiss Sing 46-49; Proc Conv Bris 51-55; Hon Can Bris 53-55; V of St Mary Gt Cam (The Univ Ch) 55-59; Select Pr Univ of Cam 53; Exam Chap to Bps of Man and S & M 55-59; Cons Ld Bp of S'wark in S'wark Cathl 1 May 59 by Abp of Cant; Bps of Lon, Win, Ely, Sarum, Roch, Truro, Guildf, Cov, Ex, Chich, Portsm, St E, Chelmsf, Linc, Leic, Pet, Bris, Carl, Man, Ches, and Lebom; Bps Suffr of Colchester, Woolwich, Kingston T, Tewkesbury, Maidstone, Warrington, Stepney, and Tonbridge; and Bps Rawlinson and Cockin; res 80. *15 Sydney Buildings, Bath, Avon.* (Bath 63978)

STOKE-ON-TRENT, Archdeacon of. (Vacant).

STOKER, William Kenneth. b 29. **d** 73 Bp Monteith for Auckld **p** 74 Auckld. Hon C of Birkdale-Beachhaven Miss 73-76; Devonport Auckld 76-78; Milford 78-80; P-in-c of Is Dio Auckld from 80. *17 Church Bay Road, Oneroa, Waiheke Islands, NZ.*

STOKES, Canon Albert Edward. b 21. Late Scho of TCD BA (1st cl Mod Hist) 43, MA 46, BD 46. Th Exhib 46. **d** 46 **p** 47 Dub. C of Monkstown 46-51; Hon Cler V of Ch Ch Cathl Dub 47-63; Lect in Hist Ch of Ireland Coll of Educ 49-79; C of Grangegorman 51-56; I of Powerscourt (w Kilbride Bray from 57) Dio Glendal from 56; Can of Ch Ch Cathl Dub from 70. *Powerscourt Rectory, Enniskerry, Bray, Co Wicklow, Irish Republic.* (Dublin 01-863534)

STOKES, Andrew John. b 38. G and C Coll Cam 2nd cl Mod Lang Trip pt i 58, BA (2nd cl Th Trip pt ii) 60, MA 64. Ripon Hall Ox 60. **d** 62 **p** 63 Pet. C of All SS Northn 62-65; St Aug Sheff 65-68; Industr Missr (Sen Chap from 69) Sheff 65-74; C-in-c of Bridport Dio Sarum 74-79; Team R 79-80. *c/o Bridport Rectory, Dorset.* (Bridport 22138)

STOKES, David Lewis. b 49. Keble Coll Ox BA 74. Westcott Ho Cam 73. **d** 75 **p** 76 Chelmsf. C of St Edw Romford Dio Chelmsf from 75. *22 Carlton Road, Romford, Essex.*

STOKES, Donald Roy. b 30. AKC and BD 79. **d** 80 Stepney for Lon **p** 81 Lon. C of St Geo-in-the-East w St Paul Dock St Whitechapel Dio Lon from 80. *Old Rectory, St George's-in-the-East, Cannon Street Road, E1 0BH.* (01-481 2345)

STOKES, George Smithson Garbutt. b 13. Univ of Leeds, BA 35. Coll of Resurr Mirfield, 35. **d** 37 **p** 38 Dur. C of St Francis S Shields 37-39; St Mich AA Summertown Ox 39-41; CF 41-68; DACG 61-68; C-in-c of Amport 68-69; Grately w Quarley 68-69; V of Amport w Grately and Quarley 69-74; Sonning Dio Ox from 74. *Sonning-on-Thames Vicarage, Reading, Berks, RG4 0UR.* (Reading 693298)

STOKES, Godfrey Julian Fenwick. b 04. SS Coll Cam BA 26, MA 31. Wescott Ho Cam 29. M OSB 42. **d** 30 **p** 31 Derby. C of St Jo Bapt Staveley 30-34 and 40-42; CUM Miss at Delhi 34-40. *Nashdom Abbey, Burnham, Slough, SL1 8NL.* (Burnham 3176)

STOKES, John Raymond. Bp's Univ Lennox BA 58. Hur Coll BTh 60 BD 63. **d** and **p** 60 Niag. C of Stoney Creek (in c of Our Sav) 60-62; Ascen Hamilton 62-63; St Jude Oakville 63-65; I of St Pet Winnipeg 65-67. *Crest Wood, Kirk's Ferry, PQ, Canada.*

STOKES, Canon John Whitley. Univ of BC BA 48. **d** 60 **p** 61 Caled. I of Fort St John 60-64; Smithers 64-71; Terrace 71-74; Hon Can of Caled from 71; NW Development Liaison Officer Dio Caled from 74; Dir of Camping Min from 78. *Box 2848, Smithers, BC, Canada.*

STOKES, Joseph Keith. Trin Coll Tor BA 58; STB 61. **d** 61 **p** 62 Calg. C of Hanna 61-62; I of Rimbey 62-65; Walpole I 65-70; Blyth 70-73; Leamington 73-79; St Andr Mem Lon Dio Huron from 79. *49 Foxbar Road, London, Ont., Canada.*

STOKES, Leonard Peter Norton. b 21. Jes Coll Cam 1st cl Cl Trip pt i, 42, BA 2nd cl pt ii, 43, 2nd cl Th Trip pt i, 44, MA 47. Wescott Ho Cam 44. **d** 45 **p** 46 Portsm. C of St Mary Portsea 45-48; Chap of Jes Coll Cam from 48; L to Offic Dio Ely 49-50; Select Pr Univ of Cam 50; C of H Trin St Marylebone 50-51; Leverstock Green 51-59; C-in-c of the Adeyfield Distr Hemel Hempstead 51-59; R of Wolborough w Newton Abbot Dio Ex from 59; Chap Newton Abbot Hosp from 59; Surr from 59; Chap Forde Park Sch from 59. *Wolborough Rectory, Forde Park, Newton Abbot, Devon.* (Newton Abbot 4700)

STOKES, Leslie. b 27. Bps' Coll Cheshunt. **d** 59 **p** 60 Dur. C of Hebburn-on-Tyne 59-62; W Harton 62-64; PC of Hedgefield 64-69; V 69-75; Dipton Dio Dur from 75. *Vicarage, Dipton, Stanley, Durham.* (Dipton 570226)

STOKES, Michael John. b 34. Lich Th Coll 63. **d** 65 **p** 66 Guildf. C of Worplesdon 65-68; Chap RAF from 68. *c/o Ministry of Defence, Adastral House, WC1.*

STOKES, Peter. b 31. Qu Coll Birm 68. **d** 69 **p** 70 St Alb. C of Norton (in c of St Thos from 73) 69-77; V of Harlington Dio St Alb from 77; P-in-c of Chalgrave Dio St Alb from 80. *Harlington Vicarage, Dunstable, Beds, LU5 6LE.* (Toddington 2413)

STOKES, Richard Spencer. b 29. TCD 66. **d** 68 Connor. C of Ch Ch Lisburn 68-71; St Geo and St Thos Dub 71-75; Rathfarnham 75-79; I of Blessington w Kilbridge Dio Glendal from 79. *Rectory, Blessington, Co Wicklow, Irish Republic.* (Naas 65178)

STOKES, Roger Sidney. b 47. Clare Coll Cam 2nd cl Math Trip pt ia 66, BA (3rd cl Nat Sci Trip pt ii) 68, MA 72. Sarum Th Coll 69. **d** 72 Ripon for Bradf **p** 73 Bradf. C of Keighley 72-74; St Jas w St Chrys Bolton Bradf 74-78; V of Hightown Dio Wakef from 78. *Highton Vicarage, Liversedge, W Yorks.* (Cleckheaton 873786)

STOKES, Terence Harold. b 46. Sarum Wells Th Coll 71. **d** 73 **p** 74 Lich. C of Blakenall Heath 73-75; Walsall Wood 75-78; Northn St Alb 78-81; Team V of Swinton Dio Man from 81. *38 Moss Bank Road, Wardley, Swinton, Manchester, M27 3UY.*

STOKES, Terence Ronald. b 35. Linc Th Coll. **d** 69 Knaresborough for Ripon **p** 70 Ripon. C of Bramley 69-72; Osbournby w Scott Willoughby 72-74; N w S Hykeham 74-77; V of Birchwood Dio Linc from 77. *St Luke's Vicarage, Jasmin Road, Birchwood, Lincoln, LN6 0YR.* (Lincoln 683507)

STOKES, Terence Walter. b 34. Bps' Coll Cheshunt, 62. **d** 64 **p** 65 Chelmsf. C of Wanstead 64-67; St Alb Abbey 67-70; Asst Dir of Relig Educn Dio B & W and Bp's Youth Chap 70-75; C-in-c of H Trin Yeovil 75-76; Team V of Yeovil Dio B & W from 76. *Holy Trinity Vicarage, Yeovil, Somt.* (Yeovil 23774)

STOKES, Thomas Hartley. b 47. **d** 78 Bp Grant for Melb **p** 80 Melb. C of St Paul Ringwood 78-80; St Andr Rosanna Dio Melb from 80. *21 Lascelles Avenue, Rosanna, Vic, Australia 3084.*

STOKOE, Rodney James Robert. St Jo Coll Dur BSc 46, BA 48, Dipl Th 49. Crozer Th Sem ThM 67. **d** 49 **p** 50 Dur. C of St Paul Hartlepool 49-53; R of Ch Ch Leith 53-57; PC of St Gabr Bp Wearmouth 57-60; Prof of Div K Coll NS from 60. *King's College, Halifax, NS, Canada.* (423-4990)

STOKREEF, Hendrik Bart. d and **p** 56 Niag. C of St Thos Hamilton 56-58; R of Acton 58-61; St Jas Hamilton 61-65; Ch Ch Niag Falls 65-69; on leave 69-77; Hon C of St Mark Niagara-on-the-Lake Dio Niag from 77. *Box 996, Niagara-on-the-Lake, Ont, Canada.*

STONE, Alexander Edward Hepburn. Univ of Melb BA 74. St Mich Th Coll Crafers ACT ThL 58. **d** 57 Bal **p** 60 Bend for Bal. C of Warrnambool 57-60; P-in-c of St Luke, St Steph and St Mark Bal 61-65; V of Coleraine 65-69; Perm to Offic Dio Melb 69-70; P-in-c of St Geo Flemington 70-76; Woodend 76-77; Chap Launceston Gr Sch Tas 78-81; St Pet Coll Adel from 82. *St Peter's College, Adelaide, S Australia.*

STONE, Ven Alvin Emanuel. Howard Univ Washington MDiv 74. St Pet Th Coll Ja 57. **d** 60 Kingston for Ja **p** 61 Ja. C of St Matt Kingston 60-62; R of Porus 62-69; Highgate 69-74; St Luke Cross Roads Dio Ja from 74; Archd of

Kingston from 78. *6 West King's House Road, Kingston 10, Jamaica, W Indies.* (092-65382)

STONE, Andrew Francis. b 43. K Coll Lon and Warm AKC 65. **d** 66 Colchester for Chelmsf. **p** 67 Kens for Lon. C of St Mich AA Walthamstow 66-67; St Barn Ealing 67-70; E Grinstead 70-74; C-in-c of St Pet Conv Distr Hydneye Hampden Park 74-81; R of Denton w S Heighton and Tarring Neville Dio Chich from 81. *Denton Rectory, Newhaven, E Sussex, BN9 0RB.* (Newhaven 4319)

STONE, Christopher John. b 49. Linc Th Coll 78. **d** 81 Roch. C of St Mark Bromley Dio Roch from 81. *4 Pinewood Road, Bromley, Kent.*

STONE, Ernest Arthur. VRD 60. AKC (2nd cl) and Plumptre Pri 34. Open Univ BA 81. **d** 34 **p** 35 Chelmsf. C of Saffron Walden 34-37; Dioc Insp of Schs 36-46 and 48-74; V of Clavering w Langley 37-46; Chap RNVR 44-64; V of Clymping 46-54; St Aug Bexhill 54-74; Dioc Adv in Relig Educn Dio Chich 74-80. *56 Manor Road, Worthing, W Sussex, BN11 4SQ.* (Worthing 35120)

STONE, Godfrey Owen. b 49. Ex Coll Ox BA 71, MA 75, BA (Th) 78. Wycl Hall Ox 80. **d** 81 Pet. C of Rushden Dio Pet from 81. *49 Manor Road, Rushden, Northants, NN10 9EX.*

STONE, Hector Marcus. St Cath Coll Cam BA 33, MA 52. Wells Th Coll 33. **d** 34 Worc **p** 36 Glouc for Worc. C of St John-in-Bedwardine 34-44; R of St Nich Peopleton w Naunton Beauchamp 44-64; RD of Pershore 52-64; R of Rochford w Eastham 64-70; C-in-c of Hanley William 64-70; RD of Lindridge 64-70. *Grafflydd, Carno, Caersws, Powys, SY17 5JR.*

STONE, John Anthony. b 46. St Chad's Coll Dur BA 68, Dipl Th 69. **d** 69 **p** 70 Cant. C of New Addington 69-72; Tewkesbury 72-76; C-in-c of All SS Conv Distr Dedworth Clewer Dio Ox 76-78; P Missr from 78. *229 Dedworth Road, Windsor, Berks, SL4 4JW.* (Windsor 64591)

STONE, John Geoffrey Elliot. b 20. Ch Coll Cam BA 41, MA 45. Ridley Hall, Cam. **d** 49 **p** 50 Pet. C of St Barn Wellingborough 49-51; Bexhill (in c of St Mich) 51-56; Ifield (in C of St Leon Langley Green) 56-59; V of Southwater 59-70; V of Thornham w Titchwell 70-74; R of Copdock w Washbrook and Belstead 74-77; P-in-c of Therfield Dio St Alb from 77; Kelshall Dio St Alb from 77. *Therfield Rectory, Royston, Herts, SG8 9QD.* (Kelshall 364)

STONE, John Wesley. TCD BA 44, Div Test 45. **d** 45 **p** 46 Chelmsf. C of St Jo Bapt Leytonstone 44-50; V of St Jo Evang Seven Kings Ilford 50-56; R of Woodham Ferrers Dio Chelmsf from 56. *Woodham Ferrers Rectory, Chelmsford, Essex.*

STONE, Michael John. b 33. Trin Hall Cam MA 56, LLB 57. E Anglian Min Tr Course 78. **d** 80 **p** 81 St E (APM). C of Whitton Dio St E 80. *60 Westerfield Road, Ipswich, Suffolk, IP4 2XN.*

STONE, Noel Alfred William. b 32. St Jo Coll Morpeth. **d** 62 **p** 63 Melb. C of Glen Iris 62-63; Pascoe Vale 63-65; R of Katherine 65-66; C of St Luke E Frankston 66-69; C of The Quinton Birm 74-75; Chap Miss to Seamen Hong 75-78; Wel from 78. *25 Upland Road, Kelburn, Wellington, NZ.* (757-293)

STONE, Peter James. b 54. Univ of Leic BA 75. Qu Coll Cam BA (Th) 77, MA 81. Westcott Ho Cam 76. **d** 78 Sarum **p** 79 Ramsbury for Sarum. C of Bradford-on-Avon from 78. *126 Trowbridge Road, Bradford-on-Avon, Wilts, BA15 1EW.*

STONE, Reginald Peter. b 32. Ex Coll Ox BA (3rd cl Th) 56, MA 61. St Steph Ho Ox 56. **d** 58 Croydon for Cant **p** 59 Cant. C of St Jo Evang U Norwood 58-62; Hon C 62-67; Master Kingsdale Comprehensive Sch 62-63; Abp Tenison's Gr Sch Kennington Oval 63-75; Perm to Offic Dio S'wark 67-75; Chap Highgate Sch Lon from 75; L to Offic Dio Lon from 75. *15a Bishopswood Road, N6 4PB.* (01-348 9211)

STONE, Richard Anthony. b 46. Hatf Coll Dur BA 68. Univ of Nottm Dipl Th 71. Linc Th Coll 70. **d** 73 Selby for York **p** 74 York. C of Marske-in-Cleveland 73-78; Team V of Haxby w Wigginton Dio York from 78. *Vicarage, Back Lane, Wigginton, York, YO3 8ZH.* (York 768178)

STONE, Rodney Cameron. b 32. Sarum Th Coll 67. **d** 69 **p** 70 Portsm. C of Milton 69-74; CF (TAVR) from 72; R of Rowlands Castle 74-80; V of St Mich Tividale 80-81; C of Weeke (in c of St Barn) Dio Win from 81. *Parsonage, Fromond Road, Weeke, Winchester, SO22 6DY.* (0962-882728)

STONE, Rodney Milton (Robertson). b 25. Ely Th Coll 51. **d** 53 **p** 54 St Alb. C of Stopsley 53-55; S Ormsby 55-57; R of Gunthorpe w Bale 57-70; C-in-c of Sharrington 62-70; R of Newport w Tayport Dio St Andr from 70. *Rectory, Newport-on-Tay, Fife.* (Newport-on-Tay 543311)

STONE, Ronald Francis. ACT ThL 63. **d** 62 **p** 63 C & Goulb. C of Junee 62-66; P-in-c of Kameruka 66-69; R of Kerang Dio Bend from 69. *70 Wyndham Street, Kerang, Vic, Australia.* (054-52 1170)

STONE, Ross Young. b 15. Keble Coll Ox BA 36, MA 40. Ely Th Coll 36. **d** 38 **p** 39 Willesden for Lon. C of St Francis Isleworth 38-40; St Mary Bideford 40-44; St Mary Thatcham 44-45; Caversham (in c of St Barn Emmer Green) 45-53; PC of Spencer's Wood Dio Ox 53-68; v 68-73; C-in-c of Aldermaston w Wasing 73-76; V (w Brimpton) 76-80; Woolhampton 73-76; Midgham w Brimpton 75-76. *28 The Garstons, Great Bookham, Surrey, KT23 3DS.* (Bookham 52279)

STONE, Walter Percival. b 04. Hatf Coll Dur LTh 25, BA 27, MA 32. Edin Th Coll 23. **d** 27 **p** 28 Glas. C of Bearsden (in c of St Andr Milngavie) 27-30; St Cuthb Dur (in c of St Aid Framwellgate Moor) 30-33; V of St John Hebburn-on-Tyne 33-36; Yeddingham and Knapton 36-40; PC of Evenwood 40-46; CF (EC) 42-46; C of St Jo Bapt Stockton 46-49; V of Monkhesleden 49-54; PC of Coxhoe 54-58; V of Ingleton w Denton 58-67. *3a Harewood Grove, Darlington, Co Durham.* (Darlington 65818)

STONEBANKS, David Arthur. b 34. Coll of Resurr Mirfield 64. Abp's P-Stud Louvain Univ 68-70; Lic Sc Mor et Rel 70. **d** 66 **p** 67 Chich. C of Burgess Hill 66-68; Chap City Univ Lon 70-73; Strasbourg, Stuttgart and Heidelberg Dio Lon (N and C Eur) from 73; L to Offic Dio Lon 70-73; Chap at Geneva Dio Gibr in Eur from 80. *59 rue de Lyon, Geneva, Switzerland.* (45 53 32)

STONEHOUSE, Hector George. b 41. **d** 80 Auckld. C of New Lynn Dio Auckld from 80. *59 Sheridon Drive, New Lynn, Auckland 7, NZ.*

STONEHOUSE, John Herman. b 1895. **d** 18 **p** 19 Plymouth (RC). Rec into Angl Commun by Abp of Cant 40. C-in-c of Pulham 40-42; C of Beaminster 42-45; Br and Amer Chap in S Amer 45-49; C of Ch Ch Sutton 49-55; C-in-c of All SS S Merstham 55-58; V 58-62; Perm to Offic Dio Chich from 62. *44b Marine Drive, Goring-by-Sea, Worthing, Sussex.* (Worthing 45525)

STONEHOUSE, Joseph Christopher. b 48. Chich Th Coll 68. **d** 71 **p** 72 Dur. C of Beamish 71-76; St Leon and St Jude Doncaster 76-80; V of Copmanthorpe Dio York from 80. *Vicarage, Sutor Close, Copmanthorpe, York, YO2 3TX.* (York 706280)

STONEHOUSE, Canon Julius Courteen. Univ of Syd BA 47. Univ of New Engl Armid BLitt 67. Ridley Coll Melb ACT ThL 51. **d** 52 **p** 53 River. P-in-c of Barham Dio River 52-70; R from 70; Hon Can of St Paul's Pro-Cathl Hay from 68. *PO Box 129, Barham, NSW, Australia 2739.* (054-53 2158)

STONELEY, Herbert. Bp Wilson Coll IM 31. **d** 34 **p** 36 Man. C of St Phil Bradford Rd Man 34-35; St Paul Oldham 35-36; Cromer 36-38; V of Ince-in-Makerfield 38-65; Surr 49-65; L to Offic Dio Carl from 65. *52 Plantation Avenue, Arnside, Carnforth, Lancs, LA5 0HX.*

STONEMAN, Edwin Greek. b 01. K Coll Lon and Warm. **d** 54 **p** 55 S'wark. C of Stockwell Green 54-56; V of St Anne S Lambeth 56-60; PC of Cleeve-in-Yatton 60-63; R of Cranham 63-71; Perm to Offic Dio Ex from 79. *Cleavelands Cottage, Weir Quay, Bere Alston, Yelverton, Devon.* (Bere Alston 256)

STONESTREET, George Malcolm. b 38. K Coll Lon and Warm AKC 61. **d** 62 **p** 63 Ripon. C of Leeds 62-64; Far Headingley 64-67; V of Askrigg w Stalling Busk 67-81; Bramley Dio Ripon from 82. *8 Hough Lane, Bramley, Leeds, LS13 3NE.* (Pudsey 571827)

STONEY, Thomas Vesey. b 34. Late Scho of Or Coll Ox BA (3rd cl Mod Hist) 56, MA 60. TCD Abp King Bp Forster and Downes Oratory Comp and Liturgy Prizes 57, Div Test (1st cl) 58. **d** 58 **p** 59 Connor. C of Ballywillan 58-61; Carrickfergus 61-66; I of Skerry w Rathcavan and Newtowncrommelin Dio Connor from 66. *Rectory, Broughshane, Co Antrim, N Ireland.* (Broughshane 215)

STONHOUSE, Michael Philip. b 48. Univ of Alta BA 74. Wycl Coll Tor LTh 77. **d** 77 Calg. C of St Pet Calg 77-80; I of Parkland Miss Dio Calg from 80. *Box 539, Elnora, Alta, Canada, T0M 0Y0.* (773-3594)

STONIER, Alfred James Arthur. Ridley Coll Melb 62. **d** 63 Bp Hudson for Brisb **p** 63 Brisb. C of Booval 63-66; P-in-c of Monto 66-68; R 68-72; Asst Chap Southport Sch Queensld 72-73; Chap from 73. *Southport School, Surch Avenue, Southport, Queensland, Australia 4215.* (31 3927)

STONIER, Peter John. b 53. St Jo Coll Dur BA 75. St Steph Ho Ox 76. **d** 79 **p** 80 Wakef. C of St Jo Evang Huddersfield Dio Wakef from 79. *35 Clough Road, Birkby, Huddersfield.*

STOPFORD, Eric. b 08. Tyndale Hall Bris 31. **d** 34 **p** 35 Man. C of St Clem Lower Broughton 34-37; H Trin Horwich 37-39; R of St Mark Newton Heath 39-46; V of St Simon and St Jude Bolton 46-48; R of Whitmore 48-79. *38 Glasgow Road, Blanefield, Glasgow, G63 9PB.*

STOPPARD, Henry. b 16. Worc Ordin Coll 60. **d** 61 **p** 62 Derby. C of Ripley 61-63; V of Blackwell Dio Derby from 63. *Blackwell Vicarage, Derby.*

STOREY, Edward John. Moore Th Coll. **d** 47 **p** 48 Nel.

C-in-c of Granity w Karamea 47-48; V 49; V of Motupiko 49-52; R of Byron Bay 52-55; C of Dulwich Hill 55-56; Eastwood 56-58; R of St Mary's w Rooty Hill 58-62; Hurlstone Park 62-70; C-in-c of Flemington w Homebush 70-76; L to Offic Dio Syd from 76. *4 Slade Avenue, Mowll Memorial Village, Castle Hill, NSW, Australia 2154.* (634-6794)

STOREY, George. b 21. Clifton Th Coll 61. **d** 63 Warrington for Liv **p** 64 Liv. C of Much Woolton 63-67; V of Ch Ch Accrington Dio Blackb from 67. *3 Bentcliffe Gardens, Accrington, Lancs.* (Accrington 36347)

STOREY, Michael. b 36. Chich Th Coll 73. **d** 75 **p** 76 Wakef. C of St Mary Illingworth Halifax 75-78; V of St Jo Div Rastrick Dio Wakef from 78. *102 Huddersfield Road, Rastrick, Brighouse, Yorks.* (Brighouse 2529)

STOREY, Thomas William. Clifton Th Coll 50. **d** 52 **p** 53 Wakef. C of Sowerby Bridge w Norland 52-54; Northowram 54-57; V of Brownhill 57-64; Cler Org Sec CECS Dios S'wark and Guildf 64-73; C of St Mary Beddington 73-80. *Address temp unknown.*

STOREY, William Leslie Maurice. Oak Hill Th Coll 67. **d** 69 Lon **p** 70 Willesden for Lon. C of Wembley 69-71; St John W Ealing 71-75; V of St Luke W Derby 75-80; Hunts Cross Dio Liv from 81. *Hunts Cross Vicarage, Kingsmead Drive, Woolton, Liv, L25 0NG.* (051-486 1220)

STORR, John Hugh. Keble Coll Ox BA 36, MA 40. Cudd Coll 37. **d** 38 **p** 39 Cov. C of St John Leamington 38-42; Bridport 42-43; Chap RAFVR 43-49; RAF 49-67: Tangmere 43-44; Kinloss 44-46; Ismailia 46; L Rissington 47-48; Gütersloh 48-50; Lüneburg 50-51; St Eval 51-54; Ismailia 54-55; Khormaksar 55-56; Hemswell 56-58; Scampton 58-60; AHQ Hong Kong 60-62; Cottesmore 62-64; Nocton Hall Hosp 64-65; Binbrook 65-67. *Church Races, Upton Cliffs, Bude, Cornw, EX23 0LZ.*

STORREY, Reuben Archer. d and **p** 46 Georgia. In Amer Ch 46-57; R of St Mich Sem Seoul 57-64; Jesus Abbey, Husami Dio Taejon from 65. *Jesus Abbey, PO Box 17, Hwangji, Kangwon 241-11, Korea.*

STORTON, Charles Edward. Trin Coll Tor 66. **d** and **p** 69 Tor. C of Willowdale Dio Tor from 69. *24 Edith Vale Drive, Willowdale, Ont, Canada.*

STORY, Charles William Herbert. b 04. Men is Disp 45. Univ of Leeds, BSc (1st cl Chem) 25, MSc 26, PhD 28. Wycl Hall, Ox 32. **d** 33 **p** 34 Leic. C of St Jo Div Leic 33-35; CF 35-59; R of W Grinstead 59-68; C-in-c of Cleeton w Silvington 72-76. *Lower Harcourt, Chorley, Bridgnorth, Salop.* (Stottesdon 603)

STOTE, Philip Raymond. Montr Dioc Th Coll LTh 37. **d** 37 **p** 40 Montr. C of St Luke Montr 37-41; I of N Clarendon 41-49; R of St Matt Grenville 49-60; Ormstown w Huntingdon 60-68; Lachute 68-75; P-in-c of Valleyfield 75-78. *141 Larch Drive, Beaconsfield, Quebec, Canada.*

STOTE-BLANDY, Canon Gordon Blandy. G and C Coll Cam BA (3rd cl Nat Sc Trip pt i) 33, MA 38. Westcott Ho Cam 33. **d** 35 Guildf **p** 36 Bp Golding Bird for Guildf. C of Epsom 35-38; C-in-c of Hawera 38-40; V of Foxton w Shannon 40-43; Levin 43-52; Brooklyn Wel 52-57; Feilding 55-63; Patea 63-68; Hon Can of Wel 65-78; Can (Emer) from 78; Chap Porirua Hosp 68-78; Offg Min Dio Wel from 78. *2 Huia Street, Waikanae, NZ.* (5219)

STOTER, David John. b 43. K Coll Lon and Warm AKC 66. **d** 67 **p** 68 Ox. C of St Giles Reading 67-71; St Hugh Lewsey 71-73; Chap Westmr Hosp Lon 73-79; Nottm Univ Hosp from 79. *105 Julian Road, West Bridgford, Nottingham.* (Nottm 862678)

STOTT, Antony. b 21. Bps' Coll Cheshunt 53. **d** 55 St Alb for Cant for Col Bp **p** 56 Perth. C of Northam 55-57; R of Como 57-62; V of Longbridge Deverill w Crockerton and Hill Deverill 62-66; PC (V from 69) of Bratton 66-74; R of Marnhull 74-81; P-in-c of Broadchalke w Bowerchalke and of Ebbesbourne Wake w Fifield Bavant & Alvediston and of St Jo Berwick Dio Sarum 81-82; V from 82. *Broadchalke Vicarage, Salisbury, Wilts.* (Broadchalke 262)

STOTT, Christopher John. b 45. BD (Lon) 68. Tyndale Hall Bris. **d** 69 **p** 70 Cant. C of Ch Ch Croydon 69-72; CMJ Miss Ethiopia 73-76; S W Area Sec BCMS 76-78; Perm to Offic Dio Ex 76-78; BCMS Miss and V of Ch Ch Arusha Dio Centr Tang from 78. *Christ Church Vicarage, Arusha, Tanzania.*

STOTT, Eric. b 36. ALCD 62. **d** 62 **p** 63 Lich. C of Penn Fields 62-65; Normanton-by-Derby 65-71; R of St Clem w St Matthias and St Simon Salford 71-79; V of Em Chadderton Dio Man from 79. *Emmanuel Vicarage, 15 Chestnut Street, Chadderton, Oldham, Lancs.* (061-681 1310)

STOTT, John Robert Walmsley. b 21. Late Scho of Trin Coll Cam BA 43, 1st cl Th Trip pt i 44, MA 47. Trin Evang Div Sch Deerfield Ill Hon DD 71. Ridley Hall Cam. **d** 45 **p** 46 Lon. C of All S Langham Place St Marylebone Dio Lon 45-50; R (w St Pet Vere Str) 50-75; R (Emer) from 75; Select Pr Univ of Cam 55; Chap to HM the Queen from 59; Dir Lon Inst for Contemporary Christianity from 82. *13 Bridford Mews, W1N 1LQ.* (01-580 1867)

STOTT, Wilfrid. b 04. Univ of Lon BA 26, BD 27. Linc Coll Ox BLitt 62, DPhil 66. Lon Coll of Div 26. **d** 27 Malmesbury for Bris **p** 28 Bris. C of St Matt Kingsdown and Tutor Tyndale Hall Bris 27-29; BCMS Miss at Nanning 29-44; Sec S China Miss 30-42; R of Rishangles w Bedingfield 44-45; Vice-Prin Tyndale Hall Bris 45-46; BCMS Miss 46-51; R of Dowdeswell 51-63; Lect St Mich Ho Ox 56-63; V of St Phil Cam 63-66; Vice-Prin St Paul's Th Coll Limuru Dio Mt Kenya 66-67; Prin 68-71; P-in-c of Croxton w Eltisley Dio Ely from 71. *Eltisley Vicarage, Huntingdon.* (Croxton 252)

STOUT, Arthur Graham. ACT ThL Ridley Coll Melb 54. **d** 55 **p** 56 Melb. C of Box Hill 55-56; St John E Malvern 56-57; P-in-c of Sefoa 57-66; V of Pascoe Vale 66-75; Supt of Child Care St John's Homes Cant Dio Melb from 75. *10 Sycamore Street, Box Hill South, Vic, Australia 3128.* (288-7527)

STOUT, Trevor. b 24. Qu Coll Birm 77. **d** and **p** 77 Worc. C of Stourport Dio Worc from 77. *9 Ullswater Avenue, Burlish Park, Stourport-on-Severn, Worcs, DY13 8QP.* (Stourport 3348)

STOUTE, Douglas Andrew. b 43. Univ of Waterloo Ont BA 73, MA 75. Univ of Cam PhD 79. Ont Bible Coll BTh 71. Wycl Coll Tor MDiv 80. **d** 81 Bp Read for Ont. C of St Paul Bloor Street City and Dio Tor from 81. *227 Bloor Street E, Toronto, Ont, Canada, M4W 1C8.*

STOVES, Ernest. b 17. Bps' Coll Cheshunt. **d** 64 **p** 65 Dur. C of H Trin Darlington 64-68; V of Evenwood Dio Dur from 68. *Evenwood Vicarage, Bishop Auckland, Co Durham.* (Bp Auckland 832348)

STOVOLD, Ven Kenneth Ernest. b 09. MBE 74. Univ Coll Ox BA 31, MA 36. Wycl Hall Ox 38. **d** 39 **p** 40 Carl. C of Crosthwaite (Cumb) 39-41; Prin Kaloleni Normal Sch 41-42; Miss Rabai 42-45; Mombasa 45-46; Maseno 47-51; RD of the Coast 45-46; RD of Nyanza 47-50; Centr and S Nyanza 51; Miss Adviser Nyanza 51-53; Can of Momb and Archd of W Kenya 53-55; Metrop Sec (South) CMS 55-58; Archd and VG of Momb 58-61; Exam Chap to Bp of Momb 59-61; to Bp of Maseno 61-71; Archd of W Kenya 61-71; Archd of Nai 70-76; Archd (Emer) from 76; Exam Chap to Bp of Nai 72-76; Hon Can of Maseno N from 72; Nai from 77; Perm to Offic Dio Guildf from 76; Bursar of Kenya Chr Homes (Barnardo's) Nai 77-80. *Chandlers Cottage, Weybourne Road, Farnham, Surrey, GU9 9EN.* (0252 716087)

STOW, Archdeacon of. *See* Scott, Ven David.

STOW, John Mark. b 51. Selw Coll Cam BA 73, MA 77. Linc Th Coll 76. **d** 78 **p** 79 St Alb. C of St Jo Harpenden 78-82; Team V of Beaminster Area Dio Sarum from 82. *Vicarage, South Perrott, Dorset.*

STOWE, Brian. b 32. Trin Coll Cam BA 55, 2nd cl Th Trip pt ii 56, MA 59. Ridley Hall Cam. **d** 57 **p** 58 Nor. C of New Catton 57-59; Chap R Masonic Sch 59-70; Alleyn's Sch Dulwich 71-76; C of St Barn Dulwich 71-76; Chap Ellerslie Sch Malvern from 76. *65 Abbey Road, Malvern, Worcs, WR14 3HN.* (Malvern 3382)

STOWE, Nigel James. b 36. Univ of Bris BSc (2nd cl Geog) 57. Clifton Th Coll 59. **d** 61 **p** 62 St Alb. C of Ch Ch Ware 61-64; Reigate 64-67; V of St Jude Mildmay Pk Islington 67-75; Penn Street w Holmer Green Dio Ox from 75. *Penn Street Vicarage, Amersham, HP7 0PX.* (High Wycombe 712194)

STRACHAN, Donald Philip Michael. b 37. St D Coll Lamp 57. **d** 62 **p** 63 Aber. C of St Mary Aber 62-64; C-in-c of St Paul Aber 64-66; Chap St Andr Cathl Aber 66-68; Itin P Dio Moray 68-73; R of Coatbridge Dio Glas from 73. *Rectory, Dunbeth Road, Coatbridge, Lanarks, ML5 3ES.* (Coatbridge 23562)

STRACHAN, Canon Kenneth Archibald Gibson. b 08. Univ Coll Dur LTh 30. **d** 31 **p** 32 Brech. C of St Salvador Dundee 31-35; Perm to Offic at St Jude Peckham 36-37; C of St Marg Aber 37-44; Chap Sisterhood of St Marg of Scotl 37-68; R of St Marg Aber 44-68; Can of St Andr Cathl Aber 50-68; Hon Can from 78; Hon Chap of St Mary Cathl Edin from 69; Lect Edin Th Coll 70-77; Hon Can of St Andr Cathl Aber from 78. *Dunnet Head House, Dunnet, Thurso, Caithness.* (Barrock 637)

STRACHAN, Canon Nehemiah Willrow Dudley. Univ of Dur (Codr Coll) BA 58. **d** 57 **p** 59 Nass. C of St Agnes and Asst Master St Jo Coll Nass 57-62; St Anne and Asst Master St Anne's Sch Nass 62-66; R of Bimini 66-70; Hd Master St Jo Coll Nass 70-79; Can of Nass from 78; R of St Geo City and Dio Nass from 79. *PO Box N-1103, Nassau, Bahamas.*

STRADLING, Ivor Llewellyn. b 10. St D Coll Lamp BA 33. St Steph Ho Ox 33. **d** 35 **p** 36 Llan. C of St Brides Minor 35-37; Ross 37-41; Chap RAFVR 41-47; V of Walsgrave-on-Sowe 47-50; Bisley w Lypiatt and Eastcombe 50-59; C of Tenby w Gumfreston 62-64; V of Carew 64-77. *Mellaston, Hundleton, Pembroke.*

✠ **STRADLING, Right Rev Leslie Edward.** Late Scho of Qu Coll Ox 3rd cl Cl Mods 28, BA (2nd cl Lit Hum) 30, MA 31. Bp's Univ Lennox Hon DCL 68. Westcott Ho Cam 32. **d** 33 **p** 34 S'wark. C of St Paul Newington 33-38; V of St Luke Camberwell 38-43; Chap Camberwell Ho 39-43; V of St Anne Wandsworth 43-45; Cons Ld Bp of Masasi in Westmr Abbey 25 July 45 by Abp of Cant; Bps of S'wark; Ely; and Gambia and the Rio Pongas; Bps Suffr of Fulham; Kingston T; Woolwich; and Kens; Trld to SW Tang 52; to Johann 61; res 74; Perm to Offic Dio Capetn from 75. *197 Main Road, Kalk Bay, S Africa.* (85588)

STRAKER, Ernest Leonard. Wycl Coll Tor LTh 67. **d** 67 **p** 69 Tor. C of Ch Ch Oshawa 67-71; R of Babcaygeon and Dunsford Dio Tor from 71. *Box 133, Bobcaygeon, Ont., Canada.* (705-738 2415)

STRANACK, David Arthur Claude. b 43. Chich Th Coll 65. **d** 68 Colchester for Chelmsf **p** 69 Chelmsf. C of St Edm Forest Gate 68-69; St Jas Gt Colchester 69-74; V of St Geo Brentwood Dio Chelmsf from 74. *28 Robin Hood Road, Brentwood, Essex, CM15 9EN.* (Brentwood 213618)

STRANACK, John Robert Shuckburgh. b 1897. MC 19. Late Organist Scho of Or Coll Ox BA (3rd cl Mod Hist) 22, MA 27. Bps' Coll Cheshunt 23. **d** 24 **p** 25 Lon. C of St Martin W Acton 24-27; Basingstoke 27-32; V of All SS Alton 33-46; RD of Alton 40-46; R of N Stoneham w Bassett 46-52; V of St Kath Southbourne 52-59; Surr from 40; V of Ch Ch Emery Down 59-65. *Rectory, The College Garden, The Butts, Warwick.* (0926-496680)

STRANACK, Richard Nevill. b 40. Univ of Leeds, BA 63. Coll of Resurr Mirfield, 63. **d** 65 **p** 66 Lon. C of Bush Hill Park 65-68; St Martin Brighton 68-72; V of Hempton w Pudding Norton 72-81; P-in-c of Toftrees w Shereford 72-74; V 74-81; P-in-c of Pensthorpe 72-74; V 74-81; RD of Burnham and Walsingham 78-81; V of Par Dio Truro from 81. *Vicarage, Vicarage Road, Tywardreath, Par, Cornw, PL24 2PH.* (Par 2775)

STRANEX, Alan. Oak Hill Th Coll 63. **d** 65 **p** 66 Southw. C of Stapleford 65-68; R of York w Ravensworth 68-74; Org Sec Bible S of S Afr and Perm to Offic Dio Capetn from 74. *Box 6446, Roggebaai 8012, CP, S Africa.*

STRANEX, Douglas. St Jo Coll Dur BA 39, Dipl in Th 40, MA 42. **d** 40 **p** 41 Down. C of St Phil Belf 40-43; St Mary Belf 43-50; St Andr Belf 50-53; I of Stoneyford 53-78. *25 Ruskin Park, Sprucefield Heights, Lisburn, Co Down, BT27 5QN, N Ireland.* (Lisburn 77729)

STRANGE, Bryan. b 26. Sarum Wells Th Coll 73. **d** 75 Basingstoke for Win **p** 76 Southn for Win. C of King's Worthy w Headbourne Worthy 75-79; Wilton 79-80; V of Kewstoke w Wick St Lawr Dio B & W from 80. *Vicarage, Kewstoke, Weston-super-Mare, Avon.* (W-s-M 29449)

STRANGE, Peter Robert. b 48. Univ of Lon BA (Hist) 69. Ex Coll Ox BA (Th) 71, MA 76. Cudd Coll 71. **d** 72 Bp Ramsbotham for Newc T **p** 73 Newc T. C of Denton Newc T 72-74; St Jo Bapt Newc T 74-79; R of Wallsend Dio Newc T from 79. *Rectory, Wallsend, T & W, NE28 6PY.* (Wallsend 623852)

STRANGE, Robert Lewis. b 45. Sarum Wells Th Coll 72. **d** 74 Barking for Chelmsf **p** 75 Chelmsf. C of St Barn w St Jas Gtr Walthamstow 74-77; Wickford and of Runwell 77-80; P-in-c of Treverbyn Dio Truro from 80. *Vicarage, Treverbyn, St Austell, Cornw, PL26 8TA.* (St Austell 850335)

STRANGEWAYS, David Inderwick. b 12. DSO 43. OBE and Legion of Merit (US) 44. Trin Hall Cam BA 33, MA 36. Wells Th Coll 58. **d** 59 Portsm **p** 59 Bp Robin for Cant. C of St Faith Lee-on-Solent 59-61; R of Symondsbury W Eype and Broadoak 61-65; V of Bradf-on-Avon 65-73; Surr 71-73; Chap at Stockholm 73-77; Chan of St Paul's Cathl Valetta 77-81. *c/o St Paul's Anglican Cathedral, Valetta, Malta.*

STRANGEWAYS, Thomas Gerald German. b 07. Trin Hall, Cam BA 28, MA 32. St George's, Windsor. **d** 54 **p** 55 Portsm. C of Alverstoke 54-58; V of H Trin Fareham 58-64; RD of Alverstoke 62-64; Bp's Waltham 67-69; R of Droxford 64-69. *Bosney Farm House, Iden, Rye, Sussex.* (Iden 349)

STRANRAER-MULL, Canon Gerald Hugh. b 42. AKC 69. St Aug Coll Cant 69. **d** 70 Bp Ramsbotham for Newc T **p** 71 Newc T. C of Hexham 70-72; Corbridge 72; R of Ellon Dio Aber from 72; Cruden Dio Aber from 72; Can of St Andr Cathl Aber from 81. *Rectory, Ellon, Aberdeens.* (Ellon 20366)

STRAPPS, Robert David. b 28. St Edm Hall, Ox BA 52, MA 56. Wycl Hall, Ox 52. **d** 54 **p** 55 Chelmsf. C of Leyton 54-57; St Aldate Ox 57-60; V of Sandal Magna w Newmillerdam Dio Wakef from 60; RD of Chevet from 81. *Sandal Magna Vicarage, Barnsley Road, Wakefield, Yorks, WF2 6TJ.* (Wakefield 255441)

STRATFORD, Ven Ralph Montgomery. b 30. TCD BA 53, Div Test 53, MA 67. **d** and **p** 54 Waterf. Dioc C Dio Waterf 54-55; C of Waterf Cathl 55-56; I of Collooney w Ballysodare Dio Achon from 56; Dom Chap to Bp of Tuam 58-69; RD of Straid 61-66; Dromard 66-69; Archd of Killala and Achon from 69. *Rectory, Ballysodare, Co Sligo, Irish Republic.* (071 71260)

STRATFORD, Terence Stephen. b 45. Chich Th Coll 67. **d** 69 **p** 70 Chich. C of Old w New Shoreham 69-73; Uckfield Horsted Parva and Isfield 73-75; C-in-c of Waldron 75-80; R 80-82; V of Ch Ch Blacklands Hastings Dio Chich from 82; St Andr Hastings Dio Chich from 82. *Vicarage, Laton Road, Hastings, E Sussex.* (Hastings 421821)

STRATFORD, William Anthony. b 23. Roch Th Coll 64. **d** 66 **p** 67 Sheff. C of Conisborough 66-68; Doncaster 68-71; V of Arksey 71-75; R of Armthorpe 75-80; Harthill Dio Sheff from 80. *Harthill Rectory, Sheffield, S31 8YG.* (Worksop 770279)

STRATHERN, Francis Michael. b 23. St Paul's Coll Grahmstn 74. **d** 75 Bp Carter for Johann **p** 76 Johann. C of St Mary's Cathl Johann 75-78; R of Brakpan Dio Johann from 78. *Box 386, Brakpan 1540, S Africa.*

STRATTON, Ven Basil. b 06. Hatf Coll Dur BA 29, MA 32. **d** 30 **p** 31 Linc. Tutor St Paul's Coll Burgh 30; C of St Steph Grimsby 30-32; SPG Miss at Moradabad 32-34; Chap at Allahabad 34-35; Chap (Eccles Est) Luckn 35-36; Naini Tal 36; Agra 36-37; Luckn 37; Jhansi 37-38; Luckn 39-41; CF (Ind) 41-47; Men in Disp 46; Hon CF 47; V of Figheldean w Milston 48-53; Market Drayton 53-59; R of Adderley 56-59; RD of Hodnet 53-59; Archd of Stafford 59-74; Archd (Emer) from 74; Can Res and Treas of Lich Cathl 60-74; Chap to HM the Queen 65-76. *Woodlands Cottage, Rook Street, Mere, Wilts.* (Mere 235)

STRATTON, Geoffrey Frederick. b 25. ARICS 52. Oak Hill Coll 78. **d** 81 St Alb. C of St Jo Bapt Chipping Barnet Dio St Alb from 81. *40 Fitzjohn Avenue, Barnet, Herts, EN5 2HW.*

STRATTON, Ian Herbert Shearing. b 27. St Jo Coll Dur BA (2nd cl Th) 52, Dipl Th 53, MA 78. **d** 53 **p** 54 Win. C of St Jas Shirley 53-58; Succr of Bradf Cathl 58-60; Tutor St Aid Coll 60-62; Vice-Prin 62-65; Perm to Offic Dio Sarum 61-72; Actg C-in-c of Chettle 69-72; C of St Francis Sarum 72-80; Harnham Dio Sarum from 81. *c/o Harnham Vicarage, Old Blandford Road, Salisbury, SP2 8DQ.*

STRATTON, John Jefferies. b 27. Bps' Coll Cheshunt, 53. **d** 55 **p** 56 St Alb. C of St Mich AA Watford 55-60; Stevenage (in c of St Pet Broadwater) 60-65; R of Cottered w Broadfield and Throcking Dio St Alb from 65; RD of Buntingford from 75. *Cottered Rectory, Buntingford, Herts.* (Cottered 218)

STRATTON, Canon Leslie Verdun. b 16. Edin Th Coll 36. **d** 39 **p** 40 Brech. C of St Mary Magd Dundee 39-45; P-in-c of St Cath Bo'ness w Linlithgow and Blackness 45-50; St Jo Bapt Dundee 50-81; Can of St Paul's Cathl Dundee 70-81; Hon Can from 81; Syn Clk Dio Brech 70-81; Hon Dioc Chap from 81. *16 Argyle Street, Dundee, Scotland.*

STRAW, Leonard Arthur. St Aid Coll 64. **d** and **p** 66 Man. C of Middleton 66-69; V of Coramba 69-72; R of Rose Bay 72-76; French's Forest w Belrose Dio Syd from 76. *Rectory, Bantry Bay Road, French's Forest, NSW, Australia 2086.* (451-1873)

STRAW, Ven William Oliver. Hur Coll LTh 54. **d** and **p** 54 Niag. C of St Jas Hamilton 54-55; I of Guelph 55-58; R of Lac du Bonnet 58-60; I of Norway Ho 60-63; Jarvis 63-65; R of St Jas Hamilton 65-68; Fort Erie 68-74; Hon Can of Niag 72-80; R of Port Colborne Dio Niag from 74; Archd of Brock from 80. *55 Charlotte Street, Port Colborne, Ont., Canada.* (416-835 8540)

STREATER, David Arthur. Oak Hill Th Coll 67. **d** 68 **p** 69 Chich. C of Lindfield 68-71. *Bible Institute of South Africa, Main Road, Kalk Bay, Cape, S Africa.*

STREATFEILD, Francis Richard Champion. b 22. Qu Coll Cam BA 48, MA 59. Cudd Coll 48. **d** 50 **p** 51 Dur. C of Houghton-le-Spring 50-53; Miss at Murhu Chota Nagpur 54-56; Manoharpur Chota N 56-70; V of Sacriston 70-80; Area Sec USPG Dio Carl from 80. *Fenton Lane Head, How Mill, Carlisle, CA4 9LD.*

STREATFEILD, Gerald Champion. b 02. Trin Coll Ox BA (3rd cl Mod Hist) 24, Dipl Th 25, MA 28. Cudd Coll 27. **d** 28 **p** 29 Chelmsf. Asst Missr Trin Coll Ox Miss Stratford 28-31; Asst P Cathl Ch Salisbury S Rhod 31-33; V of Colden Common 33-36; Sec for Youth Work for SPG 36-39; L to Offic Dio Lon 37-39; C of St John Bulawayo 39-43; R of Plumtree; w Francistown 43-45; Can of S Rhod 44-46; Dir S Afr Ch Inst 45-51; Commiss Capetn Pret Bloemf St Jo Kaffr Lebom 45-51; S Rhod 46-52; Mashon 52-72; Matab from 53; Zulu and S Afr Ch Rly Miss 47; Grahmstn 49-60; Ed *Cape to Zambezi* 46-51; R of St Thos and St Clem w St Mich-in-the-Soke and St Swith upon Kingsgate Win 51-61; Surr 54-61; R of Binfield 61-67; V of Emery Down 67-73; L to Offic Dio Sarum from 73; Dio Win from 78. *16 Priors Way, Oliver's Battery, Winchester, Hants.* (Winchester 61945)

STREATFEILD-JAMES, Eric Cardew. b 04. OBE (Mil) 45. RN Coll Greenwich 39. **d** 62 **p** 63 Cant. C of New Romney w Hope 62-66; V of Hernhill 66-75; Perm to Offic Dio Guildf from 75. *Arden, Headley Hill Road, Headley, Hants.* (0428-712248)

STREEK, Stanley James. b 11. Univ of Man BD 42. Wycl Hall, Ox **d** 42 **p** 43 Ripon. C of St Marg Horsforth 42-47; V of Warmfield 47-51; Holmbridge 51-76. *Bridgend Cottage, Laurieston, Castle Douglas, Kirk.*

STREET, David Grover. b 24. St Aid Coll 49. **d** 54 **p** 55 Liv. C of St Ambrose Everton 54-56; Miss of Shrewsbury Sch Miss Liv 56-62; Chap Cotswold Sch Ashton Keynes 62-63; Abingdon Sch 64-68; Warden Rugby Clubs Notting Hill 68-70; Chap Milton Abbey Sch 70; St Lawr Coll Ramsgate 71; Warden Boys Welfare Club Hartlepool from 74. *77 Thornhill Gardens, Hartlepool, Cleve.*

STREET, Canon Frederick William. b 07. St D Coll Lamp BA 31. St Mich Coll Llan 31. FIGCM 43. **d** 32 **p** 33 St A. C of Gwersyllt 32-34; St Cath Coleman N Hammersmith 34-37; Seacombe (in c of St Pet) 37-41; RAFVR 41-48; L to Offic Dio Momb 44-45; C-in-c of Bramshaw 46; C of Lancaster (in c of St Anne) 48-51; Hon CF 48-54; V of Feniscliffe 51-78; Succr of Blackb Cathl 52-78; Prec from 78; Hon Can 71-78; Can (Emer) from 78; L to Offic Dio Blackb from 78. *105 Yew Tree Drive, Blackburn, Lancs, BB2 7DH.* (0254-50545)

STREET, Kenneth Thomas. Univ of Dur LTh 30, BA 40, MA 55. St Aug Coll Cant 26. **d** 30 **p** 31 S'wark. C of St Luke Well Hall Eltham 30-34; St Mary Wimbledon 34-37; P-in-c of Copper Belt N Rhod 37-39; Actg C of St Marg Dur (in c of St John Neville's Cross) 40-44; R of Navenby 44-55; Skinnand 50-55; Chap Wellingore Open Pris 53-54; CF 55-59; V of Aslackby w Kirkby Underwood Dio Linc from 59. *Aslackby Vicarage, Sleaford, Lincs.* (Dowsby 281)

STREET, Peter Ernest. b 17. Oak Hill Th Coll 37. **d** 40 **p** 42 Chelmsf. C of Waltham Abbey 40-43; H Trin Heigham 43-44; Chap RAF VR 44-48; C of St Andr L Cambridge 48; Min of Conv Distr of St Steph Cambridge 48-52; V of Ch Ch Lowestoft 52-57; St Jas Denton Holme Carl 57-68; St Andr Cheadle Hulme 68-73; Evang on Staff CPAS 74-78. *Rosemary, Church Way, Tydd St Mary, Wisbech, Cambs PE13 5QY.* (094-576 638)

STREET, Peter Jarman. b 29. K Coll Lon and Warm BD (2nd cl) and AKC 59. **d** 59 Aston for Birm **p** 60 Birm. C of Highter's Heath 59-60; Shirley 60-62; Lect Chesh Coll of Educn 62-66; St Pet Coll of Educn Birm 66-70; Relig Educn Adv Essex Co Coun from 70; Hon C of Gt Dunmow Dio Chelmsf from 70; Sen Insp RE and Humanities Subjects from 74. *Rectory, Great Easton, Dunmow, Essex.* (Gt Easton 202)

STREET, Philip. b 47. Univ of Lon BPharm 68. N-W Ordin Course 75. **d** 78 **p** 79 Bradf. C of Heaton 78-82; St Denys Evington City and Dio Leic from 82. *15 Millersdale Avenue, Leicester, LE5 6PR.* (Leic 415605)

STREETER, David James. b 42. Pemb Coll Cam 2nd cl Cl Trip pt i, 63, BA (2nd cl Th Trip pt ia) 64, MA 68. Qu Coll Birm 65. **d** 67 Barking for Chelmsf **p** 68 Chelmsf. C of Saffron Walden 67-71; Shrub End 71-73; R of Rayne 73-79; V of All SS Highams Pk 79-82; P-in-c of Stradbroke w Horham and Athelington Dio St E from 82. *Rectory, Stradbroke, Eye, Suffolk, IP21 5HU.* (037-984363)

STREETING, Laurence Storey. b 14. St Jo Coll Dur BA 39, Dipl Th 40, MA 42. VRD 65. **d** 40 **p** 41 Dur. C of St Gabr Bp Wearmouth 40-46; Chap RNVR 42-46; Hd Master St Mark's Dioc Sch George 46-48; Asst Chap Miss to Seamen Capetn 48-49; Chap to Garden City Woodford Bridge and Village Home Barkingside 49-51; L to Offic Dio Chelmsf 49-51; Chap RAF 51-56; Asst Chap Eliz Coll Guernsey 56-60; Perm to Offic Dio Win 56-60; Chap RNR from 56; Chap and Ho Master Eshton Hall Sch Gargrave 60-64; Perm to Offic Dio Bradf 60-64; Dio Cant 64-65; R of St Sampson Guernsey 65-71; Actg Prin Bp's Coll Kingstown and L to Offic Dio Windw Is 72-76; Chap H Trin Madeira 77-80; Perm to Offic Dio Win from 80. *L'Amarrage, La Marette, St Sampson, Guernsey, CI.*

STRETCH, Jerome Bates. b 38. **d** 70 Bp Persell for Albany **p** 71 Keew. I of St Paul's Churchill 71-76. *Box 57, Churchill, Manitoba, Canada.* (204-675-2459)

STRETTON, George Peter. b 22. MBE. **d** 70 Sabah **p** 71 Hong for Sabah. P Dio Sabah 70-78; V of Shireoaks Dio Southw from 79. *Vicarage, Shireoaks, Worksop, Notts.* (Worksop 5258)

STRETTON, Robert John. b 45. Dipl Th (Lon) 69. Kelham Th Coll 62. **d** 69 **p** 70 Dur. C of St Ignatius Hendon Bp Wearmouth 69-73; St Thos Middlesbrough 73-76; M OSB 77; V of Brandon Dio Dur from 78. *Clergy House, Sawmill Lane, Brandon, Durham, DH7 8NS.* (Durham 780845)

STREVENS, Brian Lloyd. b 49. St Jo Coll Dur BA 70. Ripon Hall Ox 70. **d** 73 **p** 74 Man. C of St Jo Evang Old Trafford 73-76; Bolton-le-Moors Dio Man from 76; Org Sec Southn Coun of Commun Service from 78. *49 Westridge Road, Portswood, Southampton.* (Southampton 557174)

STREVENS, Richard Ernest Noel. b 34. Univ of Nottm BA (3rd cl Th) 60. Linc Th Coll 60. **d** 62 **p** 63 Lon. Lect of St Botolph Aldgate w H Trin Minories Lon 62-66; C of St Steph Ealing 66-68; Hon C of St Botolph without Bishopsgate Lon 68-76; Perm to Offic Dio Ex from 69; V of Clent Dio Worc from 76. *Clent Vicarage, Stourbridge, W Midl, DY9 9QT.* (0562-882675)

STRICKLAND, Derek. b 26. Bps' Coll Cheshunt 64. **d** 66 Ox **p** 66 Buckingham for Ox. C of Bray 66-67; Hall Green 67-70; V of St Bernard Hamstead 70-76; Industr Chap Herts and Beds Industr Miss Team from 76; L to Offic Dio St Alb from 76. *55 Crofts Path, Leverstock Green, Hemel Hempstead, Herts, HP3 8HD.* (Hemel Hempstead 54185)

STRICKLAND, Canon Douglas John. b 13. St Jo Coll Cam BA 35, MA 39. Westcott Ho Cam 36. **d** 37 **p** 38 Birm. C of Aston-juxta-Birm 37-43; C-in-c of Dorridge Conv Distr 43-47; V of St Jas Handsworth 47-53; R of Sheldon 53-66; RD of Coleshill 58-66; Hon Can of Birm 64-66; V of Wimborne Minster 66-80; Team R (w Holt) 80-81; RD of Wimborne 68-73; Can and Preb of Sarum Cathl 70-81; Can (Emer) from 81. *15 Peveril Heights, Swanage, Dorset.*

STRICKLAND, Ernest Armitage. b 24. Ch Coll Cam BA 49, MA 54. Wycl Hall Ox 49. **d** 51 **p** 52 Man. C of St Paul Bolton 51-53; St Paul Hyson Green Nottm 53-55; C-in-c of St Mary's Conv Distr Wollaton Pk 55-57; V 57-64; St Phil Southport 64-76; R of Broughton Dio Linc from 76; RD of Yarborough from 81. *Broughton Rectory, Brigg, S Humb, DN20 0DG.* (Brigg 52506)

STRICKLAND, Francis Evelyn Petterson. **d** 66 **p** 67 Melb. C of Frankston 66-72; Perm to Offic Dio Melb from 72. *Wooralla Drive, Mount Eliza, Vic, Australia 3930.* (787 2005)

STRICKLAND, George Henry. b 15. Kelham Th Coll 33. **d** 38 **p** 39 Cov. C of St Luke Holbrooks 38-41; St Aug Tonge Moor 41-45; Supt Ind Miss Labasa Dio Polyn 45-51; Hd Master All SS Sch Labasa 47-49; Deputation Pr SPG 51-52; SPG Area Sec SW Area 52-64; USPG 65-68; L to Offic Dio B & W 52-65; Publ Pr Dio Ex and L to Offic Dio Truro 52-68; Commiss Polyn 54-70; R of Exton and Winsford (and Cutcombe w Luxborough from 77) 68-80; C-in-c of Cutcombe w Luxborough 75-77. *8 Delhi Avenue, Foleshill, Coventry.*

STRICKLAND, Canon Paul Lowndes. b 21. Linc Th Coll 46. **d** 49 **p** 50 Guildf. C of Oatlands Weybridge 49-52; St Jo Evang Huddersfield 52-54; V of Carlton 54-58; Offton w Willisham and Nettlestead 58-61; CF (TA) 59-67; V of Debenham 61-75; PC of Aspall 61-75; Lakenheath Dio St E from 75; Hon Can of St E from 81. *Lakenheath Vicarage, Brandon, Suff.* (Thetford 860250)

STRIDE, Desmond William Adair. b 15. Ch Coll Cam BA (2nd cl Th Trip pt i) 37, 3rd cl Th Trip pt ii 38, MA 41. Ridley Hall Cam 38. **d** 39 Willesden for Lon **p** 40 Lon. C of St Jas Alperton 39-41; Actg C of All S Langham Place Lon 41-42; C of Milton 42-45; Chap Dover Coll and L to Offic Dio Cant 45-57; Warden of St Mich Coll Tenbury and PC of St Mich AA Tenbury Wells 57-65; Asst Master Tre-Arddur Ho Sch and L to Offic Dio Ban 65-67; Chap Heathfield Sch Ascot 67-80; Hon C of St Mary Finchley Dio Lon from 80. *16 Asmuns Hill, NW11 6ET.* (01-455 5037)

STRIDE, Edgar George. b 23. Tyndale Hall Bris 47. **d** 51 Dover for Cant **p** 52 Cant. C of Ch Ch W Croydon 51-55; V of W Thurrock w Purfleet 55-61; St Mary Becontree 61-70; Proc Conv Chelmsf 65-70; R of Ch Ch w All SS Spitalfields Dio Lon from 70; M Gen Syn from 80. *Rectory, Fournier Street, E1.* (01-247 7202)

STRIDE, John Michael. b 48. Oak Hill Coll 77. **d** 80 **p** 81 Edmon for Lon. C of All SS Edmon Dio Lon from 80. *1 Bury Street, Edmonton, N9.* (01-804 2650)

STRINGER, Alfred William. **d** 74 **p** 75 Adel. Asst Chap St Pet Coll St Peters Dio Adel 74-78; Chap from 78. *St Peter's College, St Peters, S Australia 5069.* (08-42 3455)

STRINGER, Harold John. b 36. Peterho Cam BA 58. St Cath S Ox BA (by incorp) 58. Ripon Hall Ox 62. **d** 64 **p** 65 Lon. C of Hackney 64-68; Roehampton 68-71; C-in-c of St Mich w H Rood, St Lawr, St John and St Jas Southn 71-73; Team V of Southn (City Centre) Dio Win from 73; Chap S Hants Industr Miss from 77. *55 Bugle Street, Southampton.* (Southn 24242)

STRINGER, Henry Richard. b 12. AKC 40. **d** 40 **p** 41 Lon. C of St Jas Ap Islington 40-41; H Trin Dalston 41-45; St Jo Evang Ladbroke Grove Lon 45-51; Hayes (in c of St Nich) 51-55; V of St Steph w St Luke Paddington 55-73; Gen Sec Angl and E Ch Assoc 57-64; R of Outwell 73-77. *130 Carr Road, Walthamstow, E17 5EW.* (01-531 3530)

STRINGER, James Philip. b 05. Lich Th Coll 53. **d** 53 **p** 54 Bradf. C of Skipton 53-56; V of Oakworth 56-64; Hubberholme 64-66; Horton-in-Ribblesdale 66-72. *17 Castle Road, Whitby, Yorks, YO21 3NQ.* (Whitby 4238)

STRINGER, John Roden. b 33. K Coll Lon and Warm AKC 61. **d** 62 **p** 63 Dur. C of St Helen Bp Auckld 62-63; Hebburn-on-Tyne 63-67; V of Cassop-cum-Quarrington Dio

Dur from 67. *Vicarage, Bowburn, Co Durham DH6 5DL.* (Durham 770347)

STRINGER, Leonard Gordon. b 14. Westcott Ho Cam 64. **d** 66 **p** 67 B & W. C of Bath Abbey 66-80. *69 Michel Dene Road, East Dean, E Sussex, BN20 0JZ.* (E Dean 2356)

STRINGER, Canon Stanley Padbury. b 11. Univ of Lon BD 36. ALCD 36. **d** 36 **p** 37 Lon. C of Ch Ch Fulham 36-38; St Paul St Alb 38-41; Harlington (in c of Ch Ch) 41-45; Hitcham 45-49; R of Occold w Redlingfield 49-79; C-in-c of Bedingfield 59-60; RD of N Hartismere 65-73; Hon Can of St E Cathl from 76; Perm to Offic Dio St E from 80. *7 Dove Close, Debenham, Stowmarket, Suff.* (Debenham 524)

STRINGER, William Eric. Em Coll Sktn. **d** 61 **p** 62 Sktn. I of Sturgeon Valley and Canwood 61-62; Hudson Bay 62-66; on leave 66-76; Hon C of Markdale Dio Hur from 77. *Box 629, Markdale, Ont, Canada.*

STRINGER, William Randall. Wycl Coll Tor. Univ of Manit BSc in Electrical Eng 34. **d** 38 **p** 39 Tor. C of Ch Ch N Oshawa 38-39; I 39-42; Selkirk 42-46; R of St Paul's Cathl Dawson 46-52; R of Westview 52-59; High River 59-67; Brooks 67-74; Foothills Miss 74-78. *Box 2111, Pincher Creek, Alta., Canada T0K 1W0.* (627-2656)

STROMBERG, Charles Walsham. St Chad's Coll Dur BA (Hons Th) 48. Ely Th Coll 48. **d** 49 **p** 50 Newc T. C of St Jo Bapt Newc T 49-52; Seaton Hirst 52-56; V of St John Wallsend 56-62; C of St Jo Bapt Cathl Bulawayo 62-64; R of St Francis Bulawayo 64-67; V of St Paul Preston Lancs 67-68; C-in-c of St Mary Virg w St Pet Conv Distr Bp Wearmouth 68-73; Chap Harperbury Hosp Shenley from 73. *Gate Lodge, Harper Lane, Shenley, Radlett, Herts.* (Radlett 4861)

STRONG, Donald Frederick. b 18. Oak Hill Th Coll. **d** 50 **p** 51 Liv. C of St Mark Haydock 50-52; St Philemon Toxt Pk 52-53; Org Sec CPAS Midl Area 53-57; Publ Pr Dio Birm 54-57; V of St Lawr Kirkdale 57-61; R of St Jo Bapt (and St Leon from 75) Bedford 61-81. *West Grove, Wilden Road, Renhold, Beds.* (0234-771047)

STRONG, George Ian Mossman. b 27. Chich Th Coll 53. **d** and **p** 56 Man. C of St Marg Hollinwood 56-57; St Mary Port Eliz 57-58; R of Port Alfred 58-60; V of St Marg Burnley 60-65; CF 65-74; R of Narborough w Narford 74-79; C-in-c of Pentney w W Bilney 74-79; P-in-c of Corsenside 79-80; Team V of Bellingham-Otterburn Dio Newc T from 80. *Rectory, West Woodburn, Hexham, NE48 2SG.* (N Woodburn 60235)

STRONG, Canon George Noel. b 1897 Late Found Scho St Chad's Coll Dur BA (2nd cl) and Lightfoot Scho 21, Dipl Th 22, MA 24. **d** 22 **p** 23 Liv. C of St Dunstan Edge Hill Liv 22-26; on Staff of Bp in Kobe 26-28; P-in-c Shimonoseki and of Matsuyama 28-40; Exam Chap to Bp in Kobe 35-40; Deputn Staff SPG 42-44; V of Hoar Cross 44-64; Commiss to Bp of Kobe from 48; Hon Can of Kobe Cathl from 58; RD of Tutbury 61-64; Master St John's Hosp Lich 64-81; Ed Lich Dioc Mag 64-76; Dioc Directory from 65. *4 Fecknam Way, Lichfield, Staffs, WS13 6BY.* (Lich 24976)

STRONG, Jack. b 16. St Aid Coll. **d** 54 **p** 55 Man. C of St Thos Radcliffe 54-58; V of St Mark Chadderton 58-66; Burgh-by-Sands w Kirkbampton Dio Carl from 66. *Burgh-by-Sands Vicarage, Carlisle, Cumb.* (022876 324)

STRONG, Jack Sargent. b 15. AKC 38. Lich Th Coll 37. **d** 38 **p** 39 S'wark. C of St Phil Cheam Common 38-42; St Steph Battersea 42-45; St Sav Raynes Pk (in c of H Cross Miss) 45-47; Streatham 47-48; Deptford 48-51; L to Offic at Eythorne 51-55; Industr Worker and Founder M of Worker Ch Group 51-67; at Ch Ch Luton 55-56; C-in-c of Harlington 56-62; Perm to Offic Dio Blackb 62-64; L to Offic Dio Ox 64-67; R of Marsh Baldon and Toot Baldon (w Nuneham Courtenay from 72) from 67-81; L to Offic Dio Sarum from 81. *Southover, Morcombelake, Bridport, Dorset.*

STRONG, John David. b 34. Cudd Coll 59. **d** 61 **p** 62 Newc T. C of All SS Gosforth 61-65; Chap Malvern Coll 65-71; R of Welford-on-Avon w Weston-on-Avon 72-79; V of Nailsworth w Inchbrooke and Shortwood Dio Glouc from 79. *Nailsworth Vicarage, Stroud, Glos, GL6 0PJ.* (Nailsworth 2181)

STRONG, Neil. b 34. Bps' Coll Cheshunt 57. **d** 61 **p** 62 Ripon. C of Hunslet w Stourton 61-65; Claxby 65-67; R of Buckie 67-69; C of Ludlow 69-71; C-in-c of Withern, N w S Reston and Castle Carlton, Strubby w Woodthorpe, Gayton le Marsh, and Authorpe w Tothill 71-74; Swaby w S Thoresby 73-74; Belleau w Claythorpe Aby and Greenfield 73-74; R of Stanningley 74-76; P-in-c of Bp Wilton 76-79; Full Sutton 76-79; V of Holme-on-Spalding Moor Dio York from 79. *Holme-on-Spalding Moor Vicarage, York, YO4 4AG.* (H-on-S Moor 248)

STRONG, Owen Trevor. b 47. St Francis Coll Brisb 75. **d** and **p** 77 Brisb. C of Bundaberg 77-78; Toowoomba 78-80; P-in-c of St John Munduberra Dio Brisb from 80. *Rectory, Mundubera, Queensland, Australia 4626.*

✠ **STRONG, Most Rev Philip Nigel Warrington.** KBE 70. CMG 58. Selw Coll Cam BA 21, MA 25, ThD 45, Hon Fell 67. Fell ACT 36. DD (Lambeth) 68. Bps' Coll Cheshunt 21. **d** 22 **p** 23 Dur. C of St Mary Tyne Dk 22-26; V of Ch Ch Meadow Lane Leeds 26-31; St Ignatius Hendon Dur 31-36; Proc Conv Dur 35; Cons Ld Bp of New Guinea in St Paul's Cathl 28 Oct 36 by Abp of Cant; Bps of Lon; Linc; Derby; Guildf; Centr Tang; and others; Dean of St Pet and St Paul Cathl Dogura 36-62; Trld to Brisb 62; elected Primate of Austr and Tas 66; res 70; Sub-Prelate O of St John of Jer 67-70; L to Offic Dio Wang from 70. *11 Cathedral Close, Wangaratta, Victoria, Australia.*

STRONG, Rowan Gordon William. b 53. Univ of Vic (Wel) BA 76. St Jo Coll Auckld. **d** 77 **p** 78 Wel. C of Kapiti 77-79; St Pet Palmerston N 79-81; V of Shannon Dio Wel from 81. *34 Stout Street, Shannon, NZ.*

STRONG, Preb Stephen Charles. b 16. Em Coll Cam BA 38, MA 43. Lon Coll of Div 38. **d** 40 **p** 41 Birm. C of St Jo Bapt Harborne 40-43; St Kevin Dub 43-45; Hd of Cam Univ Miss Bermondsey and LPr Dio S'wark 45-52; V of St Matthias U Tulse Hill 52-57; Egham 57-66; St Pet w St Owen (and St Jas from 79) Heref 66-82; P-in-c of St Jas Heref 78-79; Preb of Heref Cathl from 78. *27 Westcroft, Leominster, Herefs.*

STRONGE, Canon John Stafford Cecil. b 17. TCD BA 41, MA 68. **d** and **p** 42 Oss. C of Rathdowney 42-44; C-in-c of Corbally 44-46; R of Aughrim 46-53; Preb of Kilteskill and Can of Kinvara in Clonf Cathl 50-53; I of Dunlavin w Hollywood 53-64; Celbridge w Straffan and Newc Lyons Dio Glendal from 64; Can of Dub Cathl from 74. *Celbridge Rectory, Co Kildare, Irish Republic.* (Celbridge 288231)

STROPLE, Beverley Cecil. K Coll NS STh 45. **d** 43 **p** 44 NS. I of Spryfield 43-52; R of Ches 52-54; Exam Chap to Bp of NS from 52; R of Spryfield 54-65; H Spirit Dartmouth 65-71; Sackville Dio NS from 70. *RR2, Bedford, NS, Canada.* (865-2458)

STROUD, Ernest Charles Frederick. b 31. St Chad's Coll Dur BA (Th) 59, Dipl Th 60. **d** 60 **p** 61 Wakef. C of S Kirkby 60-63; Whitby (in c of St Ninian) 63-66; Min of All SS Eccles Distr Chelmsf 66-69; V of All SS Chelmsf 69-75; St Marg Leigh Dio Chelmsf from 75; RD of Hadleigh from 79; M Gen Syn from 80. *1465 London Road, Leigh-on-Sea, Essex, SS9 2SB.* (Southend 76062)

STROUD, Robert Owen. b 29. K Coll Lon and Warm AKC 56. **d** 57 **p** 58 Ox. C of Aylesbury (in c of St Pet Distr Quarrendon from 58) 57-60; Bexhill (in c of Good Shepherd) 60-64; All SS Gosforth (in c of Ascen Kenton) 64-66; V of St Phil Newc T 66-72; V of St Paul Cullercoats (or Whitley Bay) 72-77; R of Orlestone w Ruckinge and Warehorne 77-81; RD of Lympne N from 79; V of H Trin w Ch Ch Folkestone Dio Cant from 81. *21 Manor Road, Folkestone, CT20 2SA.* (Folkestone 53831)

STRUDWICK, Canon Donald Frank. b 12. Univ of Leeds BA 33. Coll of Resurr Mirfield 33. **d** 35 **p** 37 S'wark. C of St Anne Wandsworth 35-39; Ascen Plumstead 39-44; V of St Luke Camberwell 44-49; St Clem E Dulwich Dio S'wark from 49; RD of Dulwich 57-67; Hon Can of S'wark from 73. *140 Friern Road, SE22.* (01-693 1890)

STRUDWICK, Vincent Noel Harold. b 32. Univ of Nottm BA 59. Kelham Th Coll. M SSM 56. **d** 59 **p** 60 Southw. Tutor Kelham Th Coll 59-63; Sub-Warden 63-70; C of Crawley (in c of St Eliz from 71) 70-73; R of Fittleworth 73-77; Dioc Adv in Adult Educn Dio Chich 73-77; Educn Min Milton Keynes and N Bucks 77-80; Dir of Educn Dio Ox from 80. *Diocesan Church House, North Hinksey, Oxford, OX2 0NB.* (Oxford 44566)

STRUGNELL, John Richard. BA (3rd cl Engl) Lon 52. Wells Th Coll 54. **d** 56 **p** 57 Ripon. C of St Wilfrid Halton 56-59; Moor Allerton 59-62; Lect Univ Coll Townsville 62; Univ of Queensld 65; Perm to Offic Dio Brisb from 65. *161 Grandview Road, Pullenvale, Queensland, Australia 4069.* (374 1776)

STRUTHERS, Neil Campbell. b 50. NZ Bible Coll Auckld LTh 76. **d** and **p** 77 Nel. C of All SS Nel 77-78; P-in-c of Cobden-Runanga Dio Nel from 78. *93 Ward Street, Cobden, NZ.* (Grey 7667)

✠ **STRUTT, Right Rev Rupert Gordon.** b 12. Univ of Lon BD (2nd cl) 42. Wycl Hall Ox 41. **d** 42 **p** 43 Southw. C of Carlton-in-the-Willows 42-43; CF (EC) 43-45; R of Normanton-on-Soar 45-48; V of H Trin Leic 48-52; C-in-c of St Jo Div Leic 49-52; Chap HM Pris Leic 48-52; V of Addiscombe 52-59; Commiss Sktn 58-81; Archd of Maidstone 59-65; Can of Cant Cathl 59-65; Prior Hosp of St John Cant 59-65; Proc Conv Cant 61-65; Cons Ld Bp Suffr of Stockport in Ches Cathl 7 Nov 65 by Abp of York; Bps of Dur; Liv; Ches; Blackb; Southw; Bps Suffr of Warrington; Pontefract; Bps Crick and Barry. *Bishop's Lodge, Macclesfield Road, Alderley Edge, Chesh, SK9 7BH.* (Alderley Edge 582074)

STUART, Alan Leigh. BA (1st cl Ment and Mor Sc) and

Wray Pri 29, MA 34, PhD 44. **d** 34 **p** 35 Sheff. C of St Phil Sheff 34-36; Chap St Geo Sch Harpenden 36-37; C-in-c of Cashel w Rathcline 37-39; R of Athboy w Kildalkey and Girley 39-45; Sen Lect Gordon Mem Univ Coll Khartoum 45-51; I of Drumshambo Kilronan and Kiltubride 51-53; Perm to Offic Dio Lon 53-54; C of Putney 54-55; V of Dormansland 55-58; Stalisfield w Otterden 58-64; Lect W Kent Coll of Further Educn Tunbridge Wells from 64. *White Walls, Cornwallis Avenue, Tonbridge, Kent.* (Tonbridge 2770)

✠ **STUART, Right Rev Cyril Edgar.** b 1892. St Jo Coll Cam BA 14, MA 20. Ridley Hall Cam. **d** 20 **p** 21 Lon. C of St Mary Hornsey Rise 20-21; Chap and Lect Ridley Hall Cam 21-25; Asst Master Govt Coll Achimota and L to Offic Dio Accra 25-30; CMS Miss Dio Ugan 31-32; Cons Asst Bp in Dio of Ugan in Lambeth Palace Chap 25 July 32 by Abp of Cant; Bps of Roch; and Leic; and Bp Suffr of Croydon Elected Bp 34; res 52; Commiss Ugan 52-60; Nam from 60; Asst Bp of Worc 53-65; R of All SS w St Andr and St Helen Worc 53-57; Hon Can Worc 53-56; Can Res 56-65. *4 Eddystone Court, Churt, Farnham, Surrey.*

STUART, Francis David. b 32. Univ of Lon BA 54, AKC 57. Ridley Hall Cam 62. **d** 64 **p** 65 Cant. C of St Mildred Addiscombe 64-67; Chap RN 67-71; L to Offic Dio Liv 76-80. *Address temp unknown.*

STUART, Ven Herbert James. b 26. TCD BA (Ment and Mor Sc Mod) 48, Div Test 49, MA 55. **d** 49 Meath for Kilm **p** 50 Kilm. C of St John Sligo 49-53; Rathmines Dub 53-55; Chap RAF from 55; Asst Chap-in-Chief 73-80; Chap-in-Chief and Archd from 80; Hon Chap to HM the Queen from 78; Can and Preb of Linc Cathl from 81. *c/o Ministry of Defence, Adastral House, Theobalds Road, WC1X 8RU.*

STUART, Canon Ian Duke. ACT ThL 51. St Barn Coll Adel 49. **d** 51 **p** 52 Adel. C of St Marg Woodville 51-54; Miss Chap Woodville Gdns 54-55; Miss P at Port Moresby 55-56; P-in-C of Eroro 56-62; Gen L Dio Adel 58-62; P-in-c of St Martin Boroko Port Moresby 62-64; R of Port Moresby Dio New Guinea (Papua from 71, Port Moresby from 77) from 64; Can of New Guinea (Papua from 71 S Papua from 77) from 64; Regr Dio New Guinea Is from 77; Dio Port Moresby from 78. *Box 6, Port Moresby, Papua New Guinea.* (24-2042)

STUART, Ian George Charles. d 64 **p** 65 Bp Snell for Tor. C of St Simon Tor 64-66; on leave 67-71; Hon C of Appleby Coll Chap Oakville Dio Niag from 71; Chap Appleby Coll Oakville from 75. *Appleby College, Oakville, Ont, Canada.* (416-844 0715)

STUART, John Ramsay. d 57 **p** 58 Edmon. I of Bon Accord 57-61 and 65-74; L to Offic Dio Edmon 61-65; Hon C of H Trin Edmon 75-79; P-in-c of Westlock 79-80; R of Edson Dio Edmon from 80. *Box 157, Edson, Alta, Canada.*

STUART, Peter Alan. Univ of NZ BA 56, MA (1st cl Hist) 59. Trin Coll Ox BA (2nd cl Th) 62, MA 67. Coll of Resurr Mirfield 62. **d** 63 Lon for Ch Ch **p** 63 Ch Ch. C of St Pet U Riccarton 63-65; Chap Vic Univ Wel 65-71; V of Eastbourne Dio Wel from 71; Exam Chap to Bp of Wel from 73. *11 Ngaio Street, Eastbourne, NZ.* (Eastbourne 7304)

STUART-BURNETT, Raymond Frank. St Francis Th Coll Nundah, ACT ThL (2nd cl) 24. **d** 32 Bal **p** 38 Melb. C of All SS Bal 32-34; Ch Ch Essendon 35-36; St Paul Ascot Vale 36-37; Actg Chap Ivanhoe Gr Sch 37-38; C-in-c of Merlynston 38-40; Chap AIF 40-47; V of Belgrave 47-50; Min of Mont Albert North 50-58; Perm to Offic Dio Melb from 58. *70 Crisp Street, Hampton, Vic, Australia 3188.* (598-3102)

STUART-FOX, Ven Desmond. Selw Coll Cam BA 33, MA 37. Bps' Coll Cheshunt, 33. **d** 34 **p** 35 Leic. C of St Pet w St Hilda Leic 34-37; St Mich Lich 37-40; Treas v and Sacr of Lich Cathl 37-40; CF (EC) 40-46; V of St Andr W Bromwich 46-49; R of St Jo Morialta 49-53; Charters Towers 53-62; Exam Chap to Bp of N Queensld 53-71; Hon Can of N Queensld 56-62; R of Cairns N Queensld 62-74; Archd of Cairns 62-74; Archd (Emer) from 75; R of Gresford 74-79. *11 Hovell Street, Goulburn, NSW, Australia 2580.*

STUBBINGS, Frank Edward. b 20. Fitzw Ho Cam BA 48, MA 53. Worc Ordin Coll. **d** 61 **p** 62 B & W. C of St Andr Taunton 61-64; PC (V from 68) of Catcott 64-74; PC (V from 68) of Burtle 64-74; Chap St Cath Sch Bramley from 74. *St Catherine's School, Bramley, Guildford, Surrey, GU5 0DF.* (Guildford 893736)

STUBBS, (Aelred) Anthony Richard Peter. b 23. Ball Coll Ox BA (2nd cl Engl) 49. M CR 54. Coll of Resurr Mirfield, 51. **d** and **p** 54 Wakef. L to Offic Dio Wakef 54-57; Dio Llan 57-59; Prin Coll of Resurr Rosettenville 60-62; St Pet Coll Alice 63-72; R of St Pet Rosettenville 72-75; Dir Dept Th Educn Dio Johann 75-77; Perm to Offic Dio Les from 77. *House of the Resurrection, Mirfield, Yorks.*

STUBBS, Ian Kirtley. b 47. Kelham Th Coll. **d** 70 Southn for Win. **p** 71 Win. C of Chandlers Ford 70-75; Farnham Royal 75-80; Industr Chap Burnham Deanery 75-80; Industr Miss Dio Man from 80; Team V of Oldham Dio Man from 80. *192 Windsor Road, Oldham, OL8 1RG.* (061-624 2684)

STUBBS, John Pattinson. b 27. SS Coll Cam BA (2nd cl Cl) 48. St Cath S Ox BA (2nd cl Th) 52, MA 67. Wycl Hall Ox 50. **d** 53 **p** 54 Cov. C of Wyken 53-54; Stoke St Mich Cov 54-56; Minehead 56-59; R of Brushford 59-64; V of Doulting w E and W Cranmore and Downhead 64-78. *The Friary, Hilfield, Dorchester, Dorset.*

STUBBS, John Philip. St Chad's Coll Dur BA 65. Wells Th Coll 65. **d** 66 Dover for Cant. C of St Martin w St Paul Cant 66-68. *Address temp unknown.*

STUBBS, Stanley Peter Handley. b 23. Univ of Lon BD 52. Ely Th Coll 55. **d** 55 Ely **p** 56 Bp Walsh for Cant. C of Fletton 55-58; Hon Min Can Pet Cathl 56-58; C of St Paul Hounslow Heath (in c of Good Shepherd) 58-63; CF (TA) 59-78; V of St Alb Mart Northn 63-76; R of Ch Ch w St Laur Brondesbury from 76. *Rectory, Chevening Road, Brondesbury Park, NW6 6DU.* (01-969 5961)

STUBBS, Trevor Noel. b 48. AKC 70. St Aug Coll Cant 73. **d** 74 **p** 75 Wakef. C of Heckmondwike 74-77; St Mark Warwick Queensld 77-80; V of St Cross Middleton Dio Ripon from 80. *Vicarage, Middleton Park Avenue, Leeds, LS10 4HT.* (Leeds 716398)

STUBENBORD, Jess William. b 48. Coun for Nat Acad Awards BA 72. Trin Coll Bris 75. **d** 78 **p** 79 Nor. C of Cromer Dio Nor from 78. *St Helen's, Park Road, Cromer, Norfolk.*

STUBER, Richard Leonard. b 33. Angl Th Coll BC 68. **d** 71 **p** 72 Yukon. C of St Mary Magd Fort Nelson 71-72; I 72-77; R of Ch Ch Cathl Whitehorse 77-78; in Amer Ch. *3423 South Poplar, Casper, WY 82601, USA.*

STUBLEY, Peter Derek. b 28. K Coll Lon & Warm AKC 57. Univ of Dur MA 79. **d** 58 **p** 59 Dur. C of St Chad Stockton-on-Tees 58-61; V of St Osw W Hartlepool 61-66; Chap Teesside Industr Miss from 66. *South View, Montrose Street, Saltburn-by-Sea, Cleveland, TS12 1LH.* (Guisborough 23985)

STUBLEY, Ronald James. Trin Coll Tor. **d** 55 **p** 56 Tor. C of St Aid Tor 55-57; R of Belmont and of Norwood 57-60; Glen Williams w Norval 60-65; W Flamboro 65-67; P-in-c of Port Maitland 74-78; on leave. *Apt 1102, 550 Jarvis Street, Toronto, Ont., Canada.*

STUCHBERY, Ian. Selw Coll Cam BA 58, MA 62. McGill Univ Montr BD 60. Montr Dioc Th Coll 58. **d** 60 Montr **p** 61 Chelmsf. C of Wanstead 61-63; V of Latton 63-69; Ch Ch Cathl Montr 69-73; R of St Phil Montr W 73-78; I of St Matt Winnipeg Dio Rupld from 78. *641 St Matthew's Avenue, Winnipeg, Manit., Canada.*

STUCKEY, Frederick Walter. b 04. **d** 76 Sarum **p** 77 Sherborne for Sarum (APM). C of Wareham (in c of St Nich Arne) Dio Sarum from 76. *16 Shirley Road, Wareham, Dorset, Bh20 4QE.*

STUDD, Allan Wilfred. b 51. Qu Univ Kingston Ont BA 73, MDiv 76. **d** and **p** 79 Ott. P-in-c of Maniwaki 79-81; I of Petawawa Dio Ott from 81. *46 Victoria Street, Petawawa, Ont, Canada.*

STUDD, Christopher Sidney. b 25. SOC. **d** 68 **p** 69 Chelmsf. C of Shenfield 68-73; R of Stifford Dio Chelmsf from 73. *Stifford Rectory, Grays, Essex.* (Grays Thurrock 2733)

STUDD, John Eric. b 34. Clare Coll Cam BA 58, MA 62. Coll of Resurr Mirfield 58. **d** 60 **p** 61 Kens for Lon. C of St Steph w St John Westmr Lon 60-65; Chap R Perth Hosp 65-67; C of Mosman Park 67-69; Hon C of St Mary Abbotts Kens and Chap to Bp of Kens 70-71; P-in-c of Monks Risborough 72-77; Gt Kimble w L Kimble 72-77; P-in-c of St Pet Quarrendon Estate Aylesbury 78; Ox Dioc Chap to the Deaf from 78. *Ardenham Lane House, Ardenham Lane, Aylesbury, Bucks.*

STUDDERT, Michael John de Clare. b 39. Trin Coll Cam BA 64, MA 67. Cudd Coll 64. **d** 66 **p** 67 Man. C of Langley 66-69; Fleet (in c of SS Phil and Jas) 69-73; Perm to Offic Dio Guildf 73-77; Chap Eagle House Sch Sandhurst from 77. *Southlands, Churt Road, Hindhead, Surrey.* (Hindhead 4620)

STUDDERT, Richard Charles Guy. Lon Coll of Div 26. **d** 28 **p** 30 Cashel. C of Clonmel 28-32; C-in-c of Kilnaboy w Kilkeedy 32-34; I of Tullow 34-78; Aghade w Ardoyne 62-75; Preb of Timaloe Aghour and Killamery in Oss Cathl 47-70; RD of Baltinglass 47-62; Preb of Tecolme in Leigh Cathl 47-55; Treas 55-60; Chan 60-63; Prec 62-78; Dom Chap to Bp of Oss 62-78. *Station House, Tullow, Co Carlow, Irish Republic.*

STUDDERT-KENNEDY, Canon Christopher John. b 22. BNC Ox 3rd cl Pol Phil and Econ 48, BA 49, MA 53. Wells Th Coll. **d** 51 **p** 52 S'wark. C of Bermondsey 51-54; Chap Ox and Bermondsey Club 51-54; C of Clapham 54-56; V of St Marg Putney 56-66; R of Godstone Dio S'wark from 66; RD of Godstone from 76; Hon Can of S'wark Cathl from 80. *Rectory, Godstone, Surrey.* (Godstone 842354)

STUDDERT-KENNEDY, Patrick Gerald. Westcott Ho Cam 40. **d** 41 **p** 42 Worc. C of St Francis Dudley 41-45; Chap RAFVR 45-46; R of Puckington w Stocklynch 46-49; V of W Pennard 49-54; CF 54-55. *Address temp unknown.*

STUDDS, William John. Univ of Syd BA 46. St Cath S Ox ACT ThL 49. Ripon Hall Ox 53. **d** 54 Man for Tas **p** 55 Man. C of Bradf w Beswick 54-57; Vauxhall S'wark 57-59; Moonah Tas 59-60; I of Zeehan 60-61; Msoro 61-62; P-in-c of Fort Jameson 62-63; Miss P at Chipili 63-65; Chingola 65-68; L to Offic Dio Syd 69; and from 71; P-in-c of Culcairn 70-71. *38 Eureka Crescent, Sadleir, NSW, Australia 2168.*

STUNZNER, Horst Friedrich. b 36. **d** 79 Auckld. C of Howick Dio Auckld from 79. *19 Trelawn Place, Howick, Auckland, NZ.*

STURCH, Richard Lyman. b 36. Late Scho of Ch Ch Ox 3rd cl Cl Mods 56, BA (1st cl Lit Hum) 58, MA 61, DPhil 70. Ely Th Coll. **d** 62 **p** 63 Chich. C of Hove 62-65; Burgess Hill 65-66; St Mich Ox 68-69; Tutor Ripon Hall Ox 67-71; Lect Univ of Nigeria 71-74; Lon Bible Coll 75-80; L to Offic Dio Lon 75-80; Team V of Wolverton Dio Ox from 80. *74 Trinity Road, Milton Keynes, MK12 5PB.* (M Keynes 318731)

STURDY, Canon John Brian. b 10. Late Exhib of Trin Coll Cam BA 31, MA 36. Ridley Hall Cam 31. **d** 33 **p** 34 Sheff. C of St Geo Sheff 33-37; Offg Chap Newton Coll 37-38; CMS Miss at Buwalasi Tr Coll 38-48; Educn Sec Gen for Prot Miss Ugan 48-57; Ed Sec 57-59; Can (Emer) of U Nile from 59; Commiss N Ugan 61-69; PC of Barrow Gurney 60-66; Perm to Offic Dio Ex 67-71; Dio Truro 68-71; V of St Goran w Caerhays 71-75. *Mirembe, Cliff Road, Gorran Haven, St Austell, Cornw, PL26 6JW.*

STURDY, John Vivian Mortland. b 33. Late Scho of Ch Ch Ox 1st cl Cl Mods 52, BA (2nd cl Lit Hum), Sen Scho and Liddon Stud 54, Hall-Houghton Sen Septuagint Pri and 1st cl Th 56, Houghton Syriac Pri and MA 57. Trin Coll Cam BA (2nd cl Or Lang Trip pt ii) 58, MA 62. Westcott Ho Cam 56. **d** 58 **p** 59 St Alb. C of Hitchin 58-62; Ampthill w Millbrook and Steppingley 62-63; Tutor Wells Th Coll 63-65; Fell and Dean of G and C Coll Cam from 65. *Gonville and Caius College, Cambridge, CB2 1TA.*

STURDY, Philip Hugh Francis. b 20. AKC 47. **d** 47 **p** 48 Southw. C of Warsop w Sookholm 47-50; Blyth (in c of St Barn Ranskill and Barnby Moor) 50-52; Min of Good Shepherd Eccles Distr Bp Wearmouth 52-55; V of H Trin S Shields 55-62; Area Sec Miss to Seamen NE Area 62-67; Chap at Swansea 67-73; Dubai 73-78; Chap Miss to Seamen Lon 78-79; Cardiff 79-80; V of Norton Cuckney w Holbeck Dio Southw from 80. *Cuckney Vicarage, Mansfield, Notts, NG20 9SR.* (Mansfield 842443)

STURDY, Thomas Oswald. b 12. TCD BA 36, Div Test 39. **d** 40 **p** 41 Newc T. C of Bedlington 40-42; Jesmond 42-43; CF (EC) 43-45; CF 45-66; R of Mohill 67-73; Clonfert 73-76. *Gertlaskey, Donegal Town, Irish Republic.*

STURDY, William David Mark. b 28. Late Tancred Stud of Ch Coll Cam BA 52, 3rd cl Th Trip pt ii 53, MA 56. Qu Coll Birm. **d** 55 **p** 56 Leic. C of Lutterworth w Cotesbach 55-59; Em Loughborough 59-61; V of Thorpe Acre w Dishley 61-71; R of Kegworth Dio Leic from 71. *Kegworth Rectory, Derby.* (Kegworth 2349)

STURMAN, Geoffrey. b 25. Late Dykes Scho and Holwell Stud of Qu Coll Ox BA (2nd cl Phil Pol Econ) 46, 3rd cl Th 48, MA 50. Wycl Hall Ox 47. **d** 49 **p** 50 Liv. C of All H Allerton 49-52; Prescot 52-55; Bridlington 55-56; V of Carnaby 56-61; V of Bessingby 56-61; R of Preston-in-Holderness 61-68; R of Sproatley 62-68; Industr Chap Dio York and L to Offic Dio York from 68; Course Dir Hull Univ from 78; Lect from 82. *605 Holderness Road, Hull, Yorks.* (Hull 781964)

STURMAN, Jeffrey. Univ of W Austr BEng 68. Melb Coll of Div BD 78. **d** and **p** 79 Perth. C of H Cross Cathl Geraldton Dio NW Austr from 79. *Lot 97, Abraham Street, Rangeway, W Australia 6530.* (099-21 2967)

STURMAN, Leslie George. b 16. Chich Th Coll 44. **d** 46 **p** 47 Roch. C of St Barn Beckenham 46-47; Ch of the Annunc Chislehurst 47-50; R of S Pickenham 50-57; R of N Pickenham w Houghton-on-the-Hill 50-57; RD of Swaffham 54-57; Repps 63-69; V of Sheringham 57-69; Surr from 59; Proc Conv Nor 64-70; R of Ampthill w Millbrook and Steppingley Dio St Alb from 69. *Ampthill Rectory, Bedford.* (Ampthill 402320)

STURMAN, Robert George. b 50. Univ of Nottm BTh 79. Linc Th Coll 75. **d** 79 **p** 80 Glouc. C of Cainscross w Selsley Dio Glouc from 79. *Church House, Upper Church Road, Cainscross, Stroud, Glos, GL5 4JF.* (04536 77966)

STURRUP, Samuel Franklyn James. b 45. Sarum Th Coll. **d** 70 **p** 71 Nass. C of Ch K Gr Bahama 71-74; P-in-c of St Thos Grand Turk 74-76; Ch K I and Dio Nass from 76. *Box 1054, Nassau, Bahamas.* (36822)

STURT, Graeme Leslie. St Barn Coll Adel 75. **d** and **p** 77 River. C of Griffith 77-80; P-in-c of Urana w Jerilderie Dio River from 80. *St Philip's Rectory, Urana, NSW, Australia 2645.*

STURT, Napier Pitfield. b 02. Chich Th Coll 25. **d** 28 **p** 29 Lon. C of St Andr Bethnal Green 28-30; St Mary Magd Paddington 30-38; All SS Notting Hill 38-45; V of H Cross w St Jude (and St Pet from 54) St Pancras 45-69; Commiss Antig 47-52; Chap St Sav Priory Haggerston Lon 55-73; Perm to Offic Dio Chich from 79. *Alexian Nursing Home, Twyford Abbey, Park Royal, NW10 7DP.*

STYCH, Brian John. St Jo Coll Auckld LTh 56. **d** 56 **p** 57 Auckld. C of St Aid Auckld 56-58; V of Coromandel 58-62; Waiuku 62-68; Northcote 68-81; Kamo Hikurangi Dio Auckld from 81. *Box 4054, Kamo, Whangarei, NZ.*

STYLER, Geoffrey Marsh. b 15. Late Scho of CCC Ox Craven Scho 34, 1st cl Cl Mods 35, BA of cl Lit Hum) and Liddon Stud 37, 1st cl Th 38, MA 40, Commonwealth Fell (in Th) 38. Union Th Sem NY STM (*magna cum laude*) 39. Univ of Cam MA (by incorp) 44. Cudd Coll 40. **d** 41 **p** 42 Wakef. C of Heckmondwike 41-44; Vice Prin Westcott Ho Cam 44-48; LPr Dio Ely from 44; Exam Chap to Bp of Man 47-54; to Bp of Heref 49-80; Fell CCC Cam from 48; Univ Lect in Th 53-82; Select Pr Univ of Ox 55-57; Select Pr Univ of Cam 58 and 63; Proc Conv Univ of Cam 60-64. *Corpus Christi College, Cambridge.* (Cambridge 59418)

STYLER, James Cuming. b 36. Sarum Wells Th Coll 70. **d** 72 **p** 73 Ex. C of Whipton 72-75; Paignton 75-78; V of Topsham Dio Ex from 78. *Vicarage, Globefield, Topsham, Exeter, Devon.* (Topsham 4504)

STYLER, Leslie Moreton. b 08. Late Scho of CCC Ox 1st cl Cl Mods 28, BA (1st cl Lit Hum) 30, MA 33. Cudd Coll 36. **d** 36 **p** 37 Ox. L to Offic Dio Ox from 36; Asst Master St Edw Sch Ox 36-47; Chap and Fell BNC Ox 47-73; Sen Tutor 65-72; Vice-Prin 66-69; Fell (Emer) from 73; Chap to Bp of Ox 47-73; Hon Chap from 73; Select Pr Univ of Ox 57-59; Lect in Th Univ of Ox 65-73. *1a Charlwood Place, SW1V 2LX.* (01-834 9380)

STYLES, James. Em Coll Sktn LTh 58. **d** 58 Sktn for Caled **p** 59 Cariboo for Caled. C-in-c of Cassiar 58-59; I of Boundary Bay 59-62; R of St Mary Virg Vancouver 62-66; St John St Catharines 66-73; Ridgeway 73-77; St Geo Hamilton Dio Niag from 77. *69 Paisley Avenue South, Hamilton, Ont, Canada.* (416-523 1690)

STYLES, John Ernest Fredric. Univ of Bris BA 34. Ch Ch Ox BA (3rd cl Th) 49, MA 53. FLCM 54. Ely Th Coll 36. **d** 36 **p** 37 Derby. C of Bakewell 36-40; Wirksworth w Carsington (in c of All SS Alderwasley) 40-45; Repton 45-47; Chap and Sacr Ch Ch Ox 47-51; Chap St Cuthb Coll Worksop 51-52; Chap Ch Ch Ox and Asst Master Cathl Choir Sch 52-54; C of Ilkeston 54-56; PC of Hadfield 56-60; Dioc Insp Schs Dio Derby 58-60; Prec of St Mary's Cathl Edin 60-69; Asst Master Choir Sch 60-69; Hd Master 69-73; Prec of H Trin Hull 73-78; Prin Vic Coll of Mus Lon from 77; Perm to Offic Dio York from 78. *45 Ash Grove, Beverly Road, Hull, HU5 1LT.* (0482-446138)

STYLES, Lawrence Edgar. Pemb Coll Cam BA 48, MA 52. Ridley Hall, Cam. **d** 50 Bedford for Cant **p** 51 St Alb. C of Bp's Stortford 50-53; V of Tyldesley 53-60; C of St Jas w St John (in c of St Jas Old Cathl) Melb 60; Industr Chap Dio Melb 60-62; Dir Dept of Industr Miss Dio Melb from 63. *Box 1868R, GPO, Melbourne, Vic, Australia.* (03-63 1837)

STYLES, Norman Paul. b 27. Trin Coll Dub. **d** 61 **p** 62 Connor. C of St Mary Magd Belf 61-63; R of Aghabog 63-64; C of Dun Laoghaire 64-66; I of Donoughmore w Donard Dio Glendal from 66. *Rectory, Donard, Co Wicklow, Irish Republic.* (Curragh 53631)

SUBRAMANI, Ven Edward Aramugam. NZ Bd of Th Stud LTh 67. **d** 62 **p** 64 Polyn. P Dio Polyn 62-66; and 67-70; L to Offic Dio Auckld 66-67; C of St Mark Wel 70-71; P-in-c of Ba, Viti Levu W 71; V of Samabula Dio Polyn from 72; Can of H Trin Cathl Suva from 74; Archd of Suva from 75; VG of Polyn from 75; Exam Chap to Bp of Polyn from 75. *Box 3718, Samabula, Fiji.* (382-483)

SUBULOYE, Solomon Ibikunle. b 31. **d** 75 **p** 76 Ilesha. P Dio Ilesha. *St Thomas's Church, Iwoye, via Ilesha, Nigeria.*

SUCH, Howard Ingram James. b 52. Univ of Southn BTh 81. Sarum Wells Th Coll 77. **d** 81 S'wark. C of Cheam Dio S'wark from 81. *77 Stoughton Avenue, Cheam, Surrey, SM3 8PH.*

SUDAN, Metropolitan of Province of. *See* Ngalamu, Most Rev Elinana Jabi.

SUDAY, Philemon. b 45. St Phil Coll Kongwa 68. **d** & **p** 70 Centr Tang. P Dio Centr Tang 70-77; on leave. *PO Mudemu, Tanzania.*

SUDBURY, Archdeacon of. *See* Child, Ven Kenneth.

SUDBURY, Peter John. b 41. Open Univ BA 80. Sarum Wells Th Coll 78. **d** 79 Tewkesbury for Glouc **p** 80 Glouc. C of SS Phil & Jas Leckhampton w St Jas Cheltm 79-81; CF (R of O) from 81; R of Siddington w Preston Dio Glouc from 82.

Rectory, Preston, Cirencester, Glos, GL7 5PR. (Cirencester 4187)

SUDI, Canon William Bishop. Hegongo Th Coll 29. **d** 30 **p** 34 Zanz. C Dio Zanz 30-33; Asst P 34-43; CF (E Afr) 43-46; P Dio Zanz T 46-78; Can of Zanz T from 61 Archd of Zanz 66-74. *Box 5, Zanzibar, Tanzania.*

SUDWORTH, Frank. b 43. Oak Hill Th Coll 76. **d** 78 **p** 79 Man. C of Deane 78-81; St Jo Evang Worksop Dio Southw from 82. *17 Westminster Close, Worksop, Notts.* (Worksop 475842)

SUFFOLK, Archdeacon of. See Smith, Ven Donald John.

SUFFRIN, Arthur Charles Emmanuel. b 09. Selw Coll Cam 3rd cl Th Trip pt i 29, BA (2nd cl Th Trip pt ii) 30, MA 34. Qu Coll Birm 34. **d** 35 **p** 36 Lon. C of H Trin Winchmore Hill 35-39; Abbots Langley 39-42; CF (EC) 42-44; LPr Dio St Alb 44-47; Min of Conv Distr of St Chris Round Green 47-53; V of Croxley Green 53-63; Hexton 63-68; Pirton 68-74; Insp Schs Dio St Alb 63-68; Hon Can of St Alb 65-75; Can (Emer from 75); RD of Hitchin 71-74; Perm to Offic Dio Sarum from 74. *32 St Michael's Road, Melksham, Wilts, SN12 6HN.* (0225-708041)

SUGDEN, Andrew Neville Burn. b 14. Men in Disp 40. ERD 54. TD 60. St Pet Hall Ox BA (3rd cl Hist) 37, MA 41. Wycl Hall Ox 37. **d** 46 **p** 47 Ripon. C of Ch Ch Harrogate 46-48; CF (TA) 48-68; CF (ACF) 68-70; Chap Army Apprentices' Sch Harrogate 47-48; V of St Paul Chatham 48-54; Shortlands 54-66; St Pet Harrogate Dio Ripon from 66; Surr 54-66; OCF RAF from 67. *13 Beech Grove, Harrogate, N Yorks.* (Harrogate 503554)

SUGGIT, Canon John Neville. Worc Coll Ox BA (2nd cl Lit Hum) 45, Liddon Stud 45, 1st cl Th 46, MA 49. **d** 48 Bp Etheridge for Grahmstn **p** 48 Grahmstn. C of Grahmstn Cathl 48-53; V of St Hugh Port Eliz 53-60; Can of Grahmstn Cathl from 57; Chan from 69; R of Queenstn 60-6 Archd of Queenstn 62-64; Warden of St Paul's Coll Grahmstn 65-75; Exam Chap to Bp of Grahmstn from 69; Prof of New Test Stud Rhodes Univ from 75. *69 Hill Street, Grahamstown, CP, S Africa.* (Grahmstn 2670)

SULLIVAN, Andrew Gray. Univ of NZ BA 50. Selw Coll Dun 56. **d** 57 **p** 58 Dun. C of Omaru 57-60; V of Tuapeka 60-64; Waikari 64-66; Hokitika 66-70; RD of Westland 66-70; Chap St Marg Coll Ch Ch 70-74; C of Fendalton 75-79; V of Chatham Is Dio Ch Ch from 76; Chap Cathl Gr Sch Ch Ch from 79. *22 Park Terrace, Christchurch 1, NZ.* (62-530)

SULLIVAN, Bernard George. b 24. St Jo Coll Dur BA 50. **d** 51 **p** 52 Worc. C of St Thos Dudley 51-54; Braunstone 54-55; Chap RAF 55-58; Ascham Ho Sch Gosforth Newc T 59-63; V of Stannington Dio Newc T from 63. *Stannington Vicarage, Morpeth, Northumb, NE61 6HL.* (Stannington 222)

SULLIVAN, John Louis Grant. St Jo Coll Morpeth ACT ThL 53. **d** 47 **p** 48 Armid. C of Glen Innes 48-49; Armid Cathl 49-50; V of Walgett 50-52; Warialda 52-56; C of Parkes 57-59; R of Carcoar 59-63; Portland 63-64; Asst Master C of E Gr Sch Wentworth Falls and L to Offic Dio Syd 65-69. *30 Jersey Avenue, Leura, NSW, Australia.*

SULLIVAN, Trevor Arnold. b 40. Div Hostel Dub 69. **d** 70 **p** 71 Down. C of Shankill, Lurgan 71-72; Ballymacelligott Ardf and Agh 72-75. *School of Ecumenics, Dublin, Irish Republic.*

SULLIVAN, William. b 1897. Coll of Propaganda Fide Rome BD 20. Gregorian Univ Rome STL 22. **d** 21 Philippi **p** 22 Velletri. Rec into Angl Commun 29. Perm to Offic (Col Cl Act) Dio Chelmsf 30; C of Ch Ch Brondesbury 30-34; V of Tolleshunt D'Arcy 34-39; Asthall w Asthalleigh 39-62; Perm to Offic Dio Sarum from 67. *St John's Hospital, Flat 10, Heytesbury, Warminster, Wilts.* (Sutton Veny 363)

SULSTON, Canon Arthur Edward Aubrey. b 07. St Edm Hall, Ox BA (2nd cl Th) 30, MA 34. Wycl Hall, Ox 30. **d** 31 **p** 32 Ox. C of Ch Ch Reading 31-33; Fell of St Aug Coll Cant 33-41; CF (EC) 40-46; Overseas Sec of SPG 46-60; of USPG 68-73; L to Offic Dio St Alb from 46; Dep Sec SPG (USPG from 65) 60-73; Sec Asia and Pacific Is SPG (USPG from 65) 60-68; Hon Can of Kuch from 66; Commiss Kuch from 76. *6 The Close, Rickmansworth, Herts, WD3 2AZ.* (Rickmansworth 74167)

SULTER, Edwin Alexander. Rhodes Univ BA 42, MA 47. St Paul's Coll Grahmstn LTh 49. **d** 49 **p** 50 Kimb K. C of St Cypr Cathl Kimberley 49-52; Chap at St Jo Coll Johann 53-73 and from 75; L to Offic Dio Johann 65-73; R of Krugersdorp 73-75. *St John's College, Houghton Estate, Johannesburg, S Africa.* (011-43 1451)

SULULU, Joao. St Bart Th Coll Msumba. **d** 60 **p** 63 Lebom. P Dio Lebom 60-79; Dio Niassa from 79. *Nampula, CP 507, Mozambique.*

SUMMERELL, Philip John. b 38. St Jo Coll Morpeth 79. **d** and **p** 81 Newc. C of The Entrance Dio Newc from 81. *6 Jean-Albion Place, Long Jetty 2261, NSW, Australia.*

SUMMERELL, Wilfred Herbert George. b 02. Chich Th Coll. **d** 28 **p** 29 Leic. C of St Geo Leic 28-32; Wolborough (in c of St Leon Newton Abbot) 32-42; PC of Woodbury Salterton 42-54; R of Woodleigh (w Loddiswell from 56) 54-68; L to Offic Dio Ex from 68. *14 Stonelands Park, Dawlish, Devon, EX7 9BJ.* (Dawlish 863723)

SUMMERGOOD, Gerard. b 20. Clare Coll Cam BA 48, MA 53. Cudd Coll 48. **d** 50 **p** 51 Lich. C of St Luke Cannock w Chadsmoor (in c of Chadsmoor from 52) 50-55; Seaford 55-58; V of Chiddingly 58-64; Seq and V of Laughton 58-64; V of St Elis Eastbourne 64-68; C of S w N Bersted (in c of N Bersted) 68-75; V of Ch K Patcham Dio Chich from 75. *10 Church Close, Brighton, BN1 8HS.* (brighton 502385)

SUMMERHAYES, Stuart Frederick. Trin Coll Tor 58. **d** 59 **p** 60 Edmon. C of All SS Cathl Edmon 61-63; I of St Agnes Tor 63-68; St Jo Bapt Norway Tor 68-74; Hon C of St Jas Dundas Dio Niag from 80. *263 Main Street East, Cambridge, Ont, Canada.*

SUMMERS, Ernest Charles. Late Th Exhib and Scho of Dur Univ LTh (2nd cl) 04, BA (3rd cl Cl) 06, MA 09. Serbian O of St Sava 20. **d** 06 **p** 07 Win. C of Basingstoke 06-14; Org Sec SPCK for S Midl Distr 14-23; Perm to Offic Dios Win, Sarum, Worc and Birm 14-23; Cov 19-23; Lon 25-27; L to Offic Dio Ox 17-23; Chief Sec of SPG for N Prov 23-25; Res Chap Middx Hosp Lon 25-28; L to Offic Dio Lon 27-28; Res Chap Nautical Sch Portishead 28-29; L to Offic Dios Lon and Chelmsf 30; C of H Trin Sloane Street (in c of St Jude Upper Chelsea) 30-31; R of Ch Ch Kincardine O'Neil 31-36; Itteringham w Mannington 36-68. *Kincardine, Itteringham, Norwich, NOR 17Y.*

SUMMERS, John Ewart. b 35. MIMechE 66. ALCD (2nd cl) 69. **d** 69 **p** 70 Kens for Lon. C of St Matt Fulham 69-72; Chap RN 72-80; V of St Barn Devonport Dio Ex from 80. *10 De-la-Hay Villas, Stoke, Plymouth, Devon.* (Plymouth 666544)

SUMMERS, Paul Anthony. b 53. Coll of Ressur Mirfield 77. **d** 80 Ripon **p** 81 Knaresborough for Ripon. C of Manston Dio Ripon from 80. *2 Manston Avenue, Crossgates, Leeds, LS15 8BT.* (Leeds 641301)

SUMMERS, Raymond John. b 41. Open Univ BA 75. **d** 77 **p** 78 Mon (APM). C of Mynyddyslwyn Dio Mon from 77. *19 Bryngwyn Road, Newbridge, Gwent, NP1 4GX.*

SUMMERS, Thomas Gresley. b 25. Worc Coll Ox BA (3rd cl Th) 53, MA 57. Cudd Coll 53. **d** 55 **p** 56 S'wark. M OGS. C of St Mich AA S Beddington 55-59; C-in-c of H Trin Charlton 59-63; V of St Luke Chesterton 63-81; St Jo Evang Brownswood Pk Dio Lon from 81. *St John's Vicarage, Gloucester Drive, N4 2LW.* (01-800 7875)

SUMNER, John Gordon. b 46. CCC Cam BA 68, MA 72. Ridley Hall Cam 69. **d** 72 **p** 73 Truro. C of Liskeard 72-75; Caversham 75-81; V of Swallowfield and Farley Hill Dio Ox from 81; Asst Chap Univ of Reading from 81. *Swallowfield Vicarage, Reading, Berks, RG7 1QY.* (Reading 883786)

SUMNER, Mark Darryl. b 56. Trin Coll Melb BTh 80. **d** 79 **p** 80 Bal. C of St Paul Bal 79-80. *c/o 2 Princes Street, Truro, Cornwall, TR1 2EZ.*

SUMNER, Thomas. b 24. Univ Coll Dur LTh 49. St Aid Coll 42. **d** 50 Ches **p** 51 Liv. C of Middlewich 50-51; Walton-on-the-Hill 51-55; PC of Clifton-in-Workington 55-60; V of Dearnley 60-63; Perm to Offic Dio Man 63-72; Dio Blackb from 72. *9 Glendale Drive, Mellor, Nr Blackburn, Lancs.*

SUMPTON, Henry Thomas James. St Barn Coll Adel 48. **d** 49 **p** 50 Perth. C of St Pet Mt Hawthorn 49-52; Northam 52-55; R of Bencubbin 55-59; Trayning 59-65; C of Cottesloe and Mosman Pk 65-66; P-in-c of N Beach 66-68; C of Mundaring 68-71; P-in-c of Gingin w Chiltering 71-75; Perm to Offic Dio Perth from 75. *Parrie House, Lesmurdie, W Australia 6076.* (291 8379)

SUNAONE, Francis. b 51. Bp Patteson Th Centre Kohimarama 70. **d** 73 **p** 74 Melan. P Dio Melan 73-75; Centr Melan from 75. *Arosi, San Cristoval, Solomon Islands.*

SUNDERLAND, Charles Edward. b 05. Wells Th Coll 45. **d** 47 **p** 48 Sheff. C of Goole 47-50; St Cuthb Firvale Sheff 50-52; V of St Bart Sheff 52-56; St Cath Woodthorpe Sheff 56-74. *206 Halifax Road, Sheffield, S6 1AA.* (Sheff 341835)

SUNDERLAND, Preb Geoffrey. b 21. St Edm Hall Ox 2nd cl Mod Lang 42, BA 43, MA 47. St Steph Ho Ox Dipl Th 47. **d** 48 **p** 49 Bris. C of All SS Clifton 48-51; Chap All SS Sch Clifton 50-51; C of Elland (in c of All SS) Dio Wakef 52-54; St Mark Ford Devonport (in c of St Anne Swilly) 55-56; C-in-c of St Jas L Conv Distr Ham Plymouth 56-59; V 59-63; Chap K Coll Taunton 63-65; C of All SS Clifton w St Mary Tyndall's Pk 65-68; V of Plymstock Dio Ex from 68; RD of Plympton 76-81; Preb of Ex Cathl from 81. *Vicarage, Plymstock, Plymouth, Devon, PL9 9BQ.* (Plymouth 43126)

SUNDUA, Elkana. **d** 63 **p** 66 Momb. P Dio Momb. *Anglican Church, Rongé, PO Voi, Kenya.*

SUNG, Khi Fong. **d** 30 **p** 32 Lab. C Dio Lab 30-32; P-in-c 32-34; C of Sandakan 34-52. *PO Box 376, Sandakan, Sabah, Malaysia.*

SUNYANIKAMALA, Lord Bishop of. *See* Dadson, Right Rev Joseph Kobina.

SUPA, Ezekiel Vilasa. b 51. Bp Patteson Th Coll Kohimarama 74. **d** 77 Ysabel. d Dio Ysabel. *Tasia Training Centre, Maringe Lagoon, Santa Ysabel, Solomon Islands.*

SURDIVALL, Hope Wrixon. Punjab Univ BA 42. Wycl Coll Tor LTh 50. **d** 50 **p** 51 Tor. I of Mulmur W 50-51; P-in-c of St D Hardington 51-53; I of St D Lawr Ave Tor 53-60; St Luke Tor 60-70; Atonement Ch Tor 70-74; Erindale 74-78; C of St Paul Fort Erie 79-80; P-in-c of St Matt Guelph Dio Niag from 80. *99 Woolwich Street, Guelph, Ont, Canada.* (519-836 4925)

SURI, Ellison. **d** 78 **p** 79 Centr Melan. P Dio Centr Melan. *St Nicholas Training Centre, Honiara, Solomon Islands.*

SURMAN, Malcolm Colin. b 48. Sarum Wells Th Coll 76. **d** 78 **p** 79 Win. C of Basingstoke 78-81; P-in-c of All SS Alton Dio Win from 81. *Vicarage, Queen's Road, Alton, Hants.* (Alton 83458)

SURREY, Archdeacon of. *See* Barber, Ven Paul Everard.

SURREY, Christopher Arthur. b 13. Selw Coll Cam BA 35, MA 39. Ely Th Coll 35. **d** 36 **p** 37 S'wark. C of St Paul Bermondsey 36-39; St Mark Cov 39-41; St Francis W Bromwich 41-42; St Mich AA Walsall 42-45; V of St Columba Wanstead Slip 45-51; R of Hemington w Luddington-in-the-Brook 51-52; Luddington w Hemington and Thurning 52-58; St Matt Ardwick Man 58-63; V of All S Castleton Heywood 63-78; Perm to Offic Dio Blackb from 78. *34 Black Bull Lane, Fulwood, Preston, Lancs.* (Preston 716179)

SURTEES, Cecil Vivian de Leybourne. b 1896. Trin Coll Ox BA 21, MA 25. Westcott Ho Cam. **d** 24 **p** 25 Dur. C of St Andr Auckld 24-26; CTA 25; CF 27-30; R of Clopton w Thurning 30-32; V of Roxby w Risby 32-45; R of Asterby w Goulceby V 45-50; Donington-on-Bain 45-50; Roughton w Haltham 50-57; R of Kirkby-on-Bain 50-57; Preston w Ridlington 57-62; Shipham w Rowberrow 62-65. *Church Cottage, Chedzoy, Bridgwater, Somt.* (Bridgwater 424039)

SURTEES, Geoffrey. b 06. St Chad's Coll Dur BA 33, Dipl Th 34, MA 36. **d** 34 **p** 35 Dur. C of St Jo Evang Hebburn-on-Tyne 34-36; St Nich Gosforth 36-39; V of St Andr Nether Hoyland 39-57; C-in-c of St Pet Hoyland 56-57; V of Ch Ch Belper 57-75; Chap Commun of St Laur Belper 57-75; RD of Duffield 57-70; Surr 57-75; Perm to Offic Dio Derby from 75. *28 Penn Lane, Melbourne, Derby.* (Melbourne 2381)

SURTEES, Timothy John de Leybourne. b 31. G and C Coll Cam 2nd cl Hist Trip pt i 53, BA (2nd cl Hist Trip pt ii) 54, MA 58. Westcott Ho Cam 54. **d** 56 **p** 57 York. C of Guisborough 56-59; Grantham (in c of Ascen Harrowby) 59-61; V of Cayton w Eastfield 61-72; R of Cheam Dio S'wark from 72; M Gen Syn S'wark 75-80. *Rectory, Cheam, Surrey, SM3 8QD.* (01-644 9110)

SUTCH, Christopher David. b 47. AKC 69. St Aug Coll Cant 69. **d** 70 Malmesbury for Bris **p** 71 Bris. C of Hartcliffe 70-75; St Paul Covingham Swindon 75-77; Team V of Dorcan Swindon 77-79; P-in-c of Alveston Dio Bris from 79. *Alveston Vicarage, Bristol, BS12 2QT.* (Thornbury 414810)

SUTCH, Christopher Lang. b 21. Or Coll Ox BA and MA 47. Cudd Coll 47. **d** 49 **p** 50 Bris. C of Westbury-on-Trym 49-53; V of St Osw Bedminster Down 53-58; Hanham w Hanham Abbots 58-74; R of Brinkworth w Dauntsey Dio Bris from 74; RD of Malmesbury from 79. *Brinkworth Rectory, Chippenham, Wilts.* (Brinkworth 207)

SUTCH, Douglas Reginald. b 19. Wells Th Coll 64. **d** and **p** 66 Wakef. C of Royston Yorks 66-69; Woodbridge 69-72; R of Haughley w Wetherden Dio St E from 72. *Vicarage, Haughley, Stowmarket, Suff, IP14 3NS.* (Haughley 467)

SUTCLIFFE, Allen. b 1899. St Aid Coll 30. **d** 32 **p** 33 Man. C of Ch Ch Heaton Norris 32-35; St Thos Hyde (in c of St Andr) 35-44; V of St Anne Birkenhead 44-74; Perm to Offic Dio Ches from 74. *48 Manor Way, Crewe, Chesh.* (0270-212244)

SUTCLIFFE, Crispin Francis Henry. b 48. Keble Coll Ox BA 69. Sarum Wells Th Coll 73. **d** 74 **p** 75 Truro. C of St Paul Truro 74-77; St Jo Evang Cathl Umtata 77-80; P-in-c of Treslothan Dio Truro from 80. *Vicarage, Troon, Camborne, Cornw, TR14 9ES.*

SUTCLIFFE, David. b 29. ALCD 56. BD (Lon) 57. **d** 57 **p** 58 Lich. C of Penn 57-61; V of St Pet Ashton L 61-65; Eccleshill 65-71; Asst Master Crashaw Pudsey 71-74; L to Offic Dio Bradf 71-74; V of Manningham 74-79; St Jas Bolton w St Chrys City and Dio Bradf from 79. *1056 Bolton Road, Bradford, W Yorks, BD2 4LH.* (Bradford 637193)

SUTCLIFFE, Geoffrey Alan. b 32. St Jo Coll Dur BA (3rd cl Th) 54. Cranmer Hall Dur Dipl Th 57. **d** 58 Lanc for Blackb **p** 59 Blackb. C of Cleveleys 58-61; Colne 61-63; V of Good Shepherd Rochdale 63-70; Tottington Dio Man from 70. *Tottington Vicarage, Bury, Lancs.* (Tottington 3713)

SUTCLIFFE, Harold Winward. b 14. Oak Hill Th Coll 34. **d** 37 **p** 38 Man. C of St Clem Broughton 37-39; St Sav Chorlton-on-Medlock 39-41; St Bede Toxt Pk 41-44; Org Sec CPAS NW Area and LPr Dio Man 44-49; V of St Luke Halliwell Bolton 49-73; Perm to Offic Dio Man from 74. *647 Chorley New Road, Horwich, Lancs, BL6 6LH.* (Horwich 66049)

SUTCLIFFE, Howard Guest. b 44. Fitzw Coll Cam BA 66, MA 70. Westcott Ho Cam 73. **d** 74 Man. C of Chorlton-cum-Hardy 74-77; Chap of Chetham's Hosp Sch Man 77-80; Publ Pr Dio Man 77-80; V of St Paul Oldham Dio Man from 80. *33 Belgrave Road, Oldham, Lancs.* (061-624 1068)

SUTCLIFFE, Ian. Univ of Surrey BSc (Human Relns) 69. Qu Coll Birm 61. **d** 63 **p** 65 S'wark. C of Ch Ch Wimbledon 63-65; St Phil Battersea 65-66; St Paul Kingston Hill 71-74; L to Offic Dio Carl from 75. *Ashlands, Church Walk, Ulverston, Cumb.*

SUTCLIFFE, John Leslie. b 35. Univ of Liv BA 56. Sarum Th Coll 58. **d** 60 Lanc for York **p** 61 Blackb. C of Lytham 60-62; Altham w Clayton-le-Moors 62-65; C-in-c of St Leon Conv Distr Penwortham 65-71; Industr Chap Warrington 71-74; V of St Andr Orford 74-79; St Cuthb Burnley Dio Blackb from 79. *St Cuthbert's Vicarage, Melville Street, Burnley, Lancs, BB10 3EN.* (Burnley 24978)

SUTCLIFFE, Lance Edward. ACT ThL (2nd cl) 63. St Mich Th Coll Crafers 58. **d** 63 **p** 64 Adel. C of Walkerville 63-65; P-in-c of Tailem Bend 65-69; R of Auburn 69-75; Riverton 69-75; C of Crafers Dio Adel from 75. *1 Arkaba Road, Aldgate, S Australia 5154.* (08-339 1274)

SUTCLIFFE, Maurice. b 13. St Aug Coll Cant 39. **d** 42 **p** 43 Man. C of New Bury 42-44; St Jo Bapt Atherton 44-49; V of St Jas Bolton 49-58; Barnacre Dio Blackb from 58. *Barnacre Vicarage, Garstang, Preston, PR3 1GL.* (Garstang 2117)

SUTCLIFFE, Canon Thomas Henry. b 07. Qu Coll Cam BA (2nd cl Th Trip pt i) 30, MA 34. Westcott Ho Cam 30. **d** 31 **p** 32 Blackb. C of Adlington 31-33; Ch Ch Accrington 33-36; Asst Chap Deaf and Dumb W Lon Distr (St Sav Acton) 36-37; Chap SE Lon Distr (St Barn Deptford) 37-42; N and E Lancs Distr and Dio Blackb 42-52; Org Sec C of E Coun for Deaf 52-74; Hon Can of Cant from 66. *10 Blenheim Drive, Oxford, OX2 8DG.* (Oxford 57871)

SUTCLIFFE, William Norman. b 09. Lich Th Coll. **d** 57 **p** 58 Lich. C of Leek 57-59; Portishead 59-60; PC of Burrowbridge 60-69; PC of Northmoor Green 60-69; Perm to Offic Dio Sarum 69-72 and from 80; LPr 72-80. *The Bungalow, Hollis Hill, Broadwindsor, Beaminster, Dorset.* (Broadwindsor 476)

SUTER, Canon Martin Edward Hayles. b 17. Cudd Coll 46. **d** 47 **p** 48 Lon. C of All SS S Acton 47-50; All SS Friern Barnet 50-53; V of St Mark Noel Pk Wood Green 53-68; R of Downham L w Pymoor 68-72; V of Good Shepherd Chesterton Camb Dio Ely from 72; Hon Can of Ely Cathl from 79. *51 Highworth Avenue, Cambridge, CB4 2BQ.* (Cam 51844)

SUTER, Richard Alan. b 48. Rhodes Univ Grahmstn BA 72. St Jo Coll Dur BA 74. Cranmer Hall Dur 72. **d** 75 **p** 76 Dur. C of H Trin Darlington 75-77; Wrexham Dio St A from 77. *6 Chanticleer Close, Wrexham, Clywd.*

SUTHERLAND, Alan. b 55. Sarum Wells Th Coll 77. **d** 80 **p** 81 York. C of Hessle Dio York from 80. *29 Seaton Road, Hessle, N Humb.*

SUTHERLAND, Alexander. **d** 76 **p** 77 Edin (APM). C of St Jas L Leith Dio Edin from 76. *99 Lochend Road, Edinburgh, EH6 8BY.*

SUTHERLAND, Alistair Campbell. b 31. BSc (Lon) 50. Univ of Ex BA 77. Wycl Hall Ox 77. **d** 78 **p** 79 Southw. C of St Jude Mapperley Nottm 78-81; R of Barton-in-Fabis Dio Southw from 81; V of Thrumpton Dio Southw from 81. *Barton Rectory, Church Lane, Barton-in-Fabis, Nottingham, NG11 0AG.* (Nottm 830252)

SUTHERLAND, Donald Frederick Alexander. b 19. SOC. **d** 67 Barking for Chelmsf **p** 68 Chelmsf. C of W Ham 67-73; V of St Aid Leigh Dio Chelmsf from 73. *Vicarage, Moor Park Gardens, Fairway, Leigh-on-Sea, Essex.*

SUTHERLAND, Douglas Milton. St Barn Coll Adel ACT ThL 49. **d** 50 **p** 51 Adel. C of St Andr Walkerville 50-52; Brighton 52; Chap of Broadview 53-54; Mitchell River Miss 54-60; P-in-c of Normanton w Croydon 54-56; C of Longreach 60-61; V of Dawson Valley 61-62; R of All SS Clermont 62-64; St Jas Mile End Adel 64-67; Chap St Geo Miss Palm I 67-73; R of Ch Ch Killarney 73-74; St Phil Thompson Estate City and Dio Brisb from 74. *115 Cornwall Street, Annerley, Queensland, Australia 4103.* (391 3915)

SUTHERLAND, Eric. b 54. AKC 76. Sarum Wells Th Coll 76. **d** 77 **p** 78 S'wark. C of Roehampton Dio S'wark from 77. *35 Holmsley House, Tangley Grove, Roehampton, SW15 4HE.*

SUTHERLAND, Canon George William. Univ of Tor BA 46, BD 50. Trin Coll Tor LTh 49. **d** 49 **p** 50 Alg. C of St Geo Port Arthur 49; St Luke's Pro-Cathl Sault Ste Marie 49-51; I of Wa Wa 51-54; R of Huntsville Dio Alg from 54; Exam Chap to Bp of Alg 57-67; Hon Can of Alg 64-67 and from 75;

Archd of Muskoka 67-75. *Box 248, Huntsville, Ont., Canada.* (705-789 2216)

SUTHERLAND, Graham Russell. b 39. Univ of Dur BA (3rd cl Mod Hist) 60. Bps' Coll Cheshunt 61. **d** 66 **p** 67 Win. C of Yateley 66-69; Caterham 69-70; Odiham (in c of S Warnborough and Long Sutton) 70-77. *Olive Tree Christian Bookshop, 18 London Street, Basingstoke, Hants.* (Basingstoke 28199)

SUTHERLAND, Canon Lorne Reginald Arthur. Trin Coll Tor LTh 47. **d** 47 Qu'App for Alg **p** 50 Alg. C of Sudbury 47-49; I of Capreol 49-53; Gore Bay 53-65; Coniston 65-71; Espanola Dio Alg from 71; Hon Can of Alg from 76. *Box 666, Espanola, Ont., Canada.* (705-869 1244)

SUTHERN, William. b 08. St Chad's Coll Dur BA (2nd cl Hist) and De Bury Scho 29, Dipl Th 31, MA 32. **d** 31 **p** 32 Dur. C of St Jude S Shields 31-35; St Paul W Hartlepool 35-38; V of Burnopfield 38-46; Newsome 46-52; Hampsthwaite 52-73; RD of Nidderdale 65-70. *Flat 2, 14 Ripon Road, Harrogate, Yorks.*

SUTHERST, Frederick Charles. Univ of Tor BA 40. Wycl Coll LTh. **d** and **p** 42 Niag. C of Ch of Good Shepherd St Cath 42-46; I of Wainfleet 46-48; C of St Pet Hamilton 48-51; P-in-c of W Flamboro 51-53; R of Mount Forest w Riverstown 53-59. *546 Hillside Street, Peterborough, Ont, Canada.*

SUTTERS, Herbert John. b 15. Late Scho of St Jo Coll Ox 2nd cl Cl Mods 35, BA (1st cl Lit Hum) 37, 1st cl Th 38, Liddon Stud 38, Jun Denyer and Johnson Scho 39, MA 40. St Steph Ho Ox 37. **d** 39 Buckingham for Ox **p** 40 Ox. C of St Thos Mart Ox 39-41; Lect St Steph Ho Ox and L to Offic Dio Ox 41-43; C of Fenny Stratford 43-49; Min Can of Ripon Cathl 49-52; Chap St Mary's Hosp Ripon and Asst Master Ripon Gr Sch 49-52; Chap St Jo Hosp Ripon 50-52; PV of Wells Cathl and Chap Wells Th Coll 52-54; L to Offic Dio B & W 53-54; V of Coleford 54-61; Highbridge 61-73; Asst Master K Alfred Sch Highbridge 61-71; Select Pr Ox 66; V of St Marg-on-Thames 73-81. *c/o 30 Ailsa Road, Twickenham, Middx, TW1 1QW.* (01-892 4171)

SUTTLE, Neville Frank. b 38. Univ of Reading BSc 61. Univ of Aber PhD 64. **d** 76 **p** 77 Edin (APM). C of Penicuik Dio Edin from 76. *44 St James Gardens, Penicuik, Midlothian.*

SUTTON, Anthony William. Univ of NZ LLB 52. Westcott Ho Cam 53. **d** 55 **p** 56 Wel. C of Palmerston N 55-57; V of Taita 57-61; Kilbirnie Wel 61-64; Haitaitai-Kilbirnie 64-70; Gisborne 70-76; Hillcrest Dio Waik 76; Min from 77. *3 Eton Drive, Hillcrest, Hamilton, NZ.* (67-960)

SUTTON, Charles Alfred. b 10. St Paul's Coll Burgh 31. St Chad's Coll Regina LTh 37. **d** 35 **p** 36 Qu'App. C of Gainsboro 35-36; I 36-39; I of Whitewood 39-41; P-in-c of N Saanich w Sidney 41-43; Chap RCAF 43-45; C of St Paul Bow Common 46; Asst Sec CCCS (Irish Aux) 46-48; Asst Chap Miss to Seamen Belf 48; Chap Cardiff 48-49; Brentwood Ment Hosp 49-51; I of St Mich Schander Township Port Elizabeth 51-52; Chap to SA Ch Rly Miss Naauwpoort 52-55; Hon C of Romford 62-65; St John Moulsham Chelmsf 65-67; Downham 67-70; C-in-c of Stapleford Tawney w Theydon Mt 70-74; V of Bradworthy 74-76; Hon C of Bengeo 76-80. *Address temp unknown.*

SUTTON, Charles Edwin. b 53. Univ of Bris BEducn 77. Ripon Coll Cudd 77. **d** 80 Penrith for Carl **p** 81 Carl. C of Stanwix Dio Carl from 80. *12 Etterby Street, Stanwix, Carlisle, CA3 9JB.*

SUTTON, Christopher Hope. b 06. St Edm Hall Ox BA (3rd cl Phil Pol and Econ) 31, Dipl Th 32, MA 43. Wycl Hall Ox 27 and 31. **d** 32 **p** 33 S'wark. C of St Crispin Bermondsey 32-35; Ch Ch Mitcham 35-37; H Trin Hull 38-40; Willian 40-42; C-in-c 42-45; Asst Org Sec (Metrop Area) SAMS 45-46; Chap of Araucanian Miss Dio Argent 46-51; C-in-c of Ardingly 51-52; R of Longfield 52-60; Chap RADD SW Lon Area 60-63; R of Aldbury 63-78. *1 The Twitten, Southwick, Sussex, BN4 4DB.*

SUTTON, Colin Phillip. b 51. Univ of Birm BA 73. Chich Th Coll 73. **d** 75 **p** 76 Llan. C of All SS Penarth 75-77; Roath 77-80; Caerau w Ely Dio Llan from 80. *92 Bishopston Road, Ely, Cardiff.* (Cardiff 566297)

SUTTON, David Robert. b 49. Univ of Birm BA (2nd cl Th) 69. St Steph Ho Ox 70. **d** 72 **p** 73 Blackb. C of Clitheroe 72-75; Fleetwood 75-78; V of Calderbrook Dio Man from 78. *Calderbrook Vicarage, Littleborough, Lancs.* (Littleborough 78414)

SUTTON, Harry Chamberlain. b 15. St D Coll Lamp BA 41. **d** 41 **p** 42 Sheff. C of Bentley 41-43; Clifton Rotherham 43-47; C-in-c of St Pet Conv Distr Whinney Hill Rotherham 47-50; V of St Geo Sutton 50-54; Surr from 53; V of Over w Winsford Chap 54-60; St Steph Congleton 60-63; Chap HM Pris Liv 64; Preston 64-70; V of Childs Ercall 70-73; R of Stoke-on-Tern 70-73; V of St Thos Preston 73-80. *27 Garstone Croft, Fulwood, Preston, Lancs, PR2 3WY.*

SUTTON, Henry. b 16. Tyndale Hall Bris 38. **d** 41 **p** 42 Liv. C of Em Fazakerley 41-43; St Philemon Toxt Pk 43-45; St Andr Bebington 45-46; V of Ch Ch Lowestoft 46-51; St Mark Layton Blackpool 51-59; Gen Sec SAMS 59-74; Can Miss 74-78; Hon Can of Argent 64-78; Publ Pr Dio Chelmsf 74-78; V of St Paul Portman Square Marylebone 78-81. *3 Starling Close, Buckhurst Hill, Essex, IG9 5TN.* (01-504 0663)

SUTTON, James William. b 50. Univ of Sask BA 70. Hur Coll Lon Ont MDiv 78. **d** 78 Bp Robinson for Hur **p** 79 Hur. C-in-c of St D Cam Dio Hur from 78. *c/o 20 Elgin Street N, Cambridge, Ont, Canada, N1P 5G7.*

SUTTON, John. b 47. St Jo Coll Dur BA 70. Ridley Hall Cam 70. **d** 72 Man **p** 73 Middleton for Man. C of St Lawr Denton 72-75; C-in-c 75-77; R 77-82; V of High Lane Dio Ches from 82. *High Lane Vicarage, Stockport, SK6 8DX.* (Disley 2627)

SUTTON, John Parker. b 02. Worc Ordin Coll 62. **d** 63 **p** 64 Worc. C of Ribbesford w Bewdley and Dowles 63-65; Madron w Morvah 65-68; C-in-c of North Hill 68-71; R 71-73; V of Lewannick Dio Truro 71-73. *20 Daniell Street, Truro, TR1 2DN.* (Truro 70648)

SUTTON, John Stephen. b 33. Em Coll Cam BA 57, MA 61. Wycl Hall Ox 57. **d** 59 **p** 60 Chelmsf. C of Dagenham 59-62; St Gabr Bp Wearmouth 62-63; V of Over Kellett 63-67; St Barn Over Darwen 67-74; St Jo Evang Walthamstow Dio Chelmsf from 74. *Vicarage, Brookscroft Road, E17 4LH.* (01-527 3262)

SUTTON, John Wesley. b 48. **d** 76 Bp Flagg for Chile **p** 77 Peru. Miss Dio Chile 76-77; P Dio Peru from 77. *Apartado 1424, Arequipa, Peru.*

✠ **SUTTON, Right Rev Keith Norman.** b 34. Jes Coll Cam BA 58, MA 62. Ridley Hall Cam. **d** 59 Ex **p** 60 Crediton for Ex. C of St Andr Plymouth 59-61; Chap St Jo Coll Cam 62-67; Tutor and Chap Bp Tucker Coll Mukono 68-72; Prin Ridley Hall Cam 73-78; Exam Chap to Bp of Nam 70-72; to Bp of Nor 73-78; to Bp of Bradf 75-78; Cons Ld Bp Suffr of Kingston T 29 Sept 78 in S'wark Cathl by Abp of Cant; Bps of Lon, Win, Derby, S'wark, Birm, Bradf, Ely, Leic, Liv, Nor, Portsm, Ripon, Roch, St E, St Alb and Southw; Bps Suffr of Dorking, Edmon, Kens, Maidstone, Taunton, Tonbridge, Willesden and Woolwich; and others. *173 Kew Road, Richmond, Surrey.* (01-940 3531)

SUTTON, Canon Malcolm David. b 26. Selw Coll Cam 2nd cl Mod Lang Trip pt i 46, BA (2nd cl Mod Lang Trip pt ii) 47, MA 52. Ridley Hall Cam 48. **d** 50 **p** 51 Sheff. C of Owlerton 50-52; Kew 52-54; Hornchurch 54-56; V of Ch Ch Roxeth 56-63; R of Beccles Dio St E from 63; RD of Beccles 65-73; Hon Can of St E from 70. *Rectory, Beccles, Suff.* (Beccles 712213)

SUTTON, Peter. Ely Th Coll 60. **d** 62 **p** 63 Ripon. C of Kippax w Gt Preston 62-64; R of Hamerton 64-77; V of Winwick 64-77; R of Upton w Copmanford 69-77; V of Bradworthy Dio Ex from 77. *Bradworthy Vicarage, Holsworthy, N Devon, EX22 7RJ.* (Bradworthy 200)

✠ **SUTTON, Right Rev Peter Eves.** Univ of NZ BA 45, MA (2nd cl Hist) 47 NZ Bd of Th Stud L Th 48. **d** 47 **p** 48 Wel. C of Wanganui 47-50; St Jo Evang Bethnal Green 50-51; Bp's Hatfield 51-52; V of St Cuthb Berhampore 52-58; Whangarei 58-64; Archd of Waimate 62-64; Dean of St Paul's Pro-Cathl Dun 64-65; Cons Ld Bp of Nel in Ch Ch Cathl Nel 24 Aug 65 by Abp of NZ; Bps of Wel; Ch Ch; Dun; Melan; and Auckld; Bp Suffr of Aotearoa; Asst Bps of Wel; and Auckld. *Bishopdale, Nelson, NZ.* (Nelson 88991)

SUTTON, Richard Alan. b 39. Univ of Reading BSc (Hort) 61. Wycl Hall Ox 70. **d** 72 **p** 73 Chelmsf. C of Galleywood 72-76; in Ch of Pakistan 76-79; C of St Matt Walsall (in c of St Martin) Dio Lich from 79. St Matt *St Martin's House, Daffodil Road, Walsall, WS5 3DQ.* (Walsall 23216)

SUTTON, Ronald. b 27. N-W Ordin Course 76. **d** 79 **p** 80 Ches. C of Helsby 79-81; R of Ch Lawton Dio Ches from 81. *Rectory, Liverpool Road West, Church Lawton, Stoke-on-Trent, Chesh.* (Alsager 2103)

SUTTON, Thomas. Wollaston Th Coll W Austr. **d** and **p** 67 Perth. C of City Beach 67; Nedlands 67-70; on Leave 71; Applecross 72; R of Dianella 72-77; Spearwood-Willagee Dio Perth from 77. *12 Holmes Place, Hilton Park, W Australia 6163.* (337 5969)

SUTTON, Wray Welburn. St Aid Coll 31. **d** 33 **p** 34 Lich. C of Bucknall w Bagnall 33-35; Uttoxeter w Bramshall 35-39; V of Allerton 39-40; St Bart w St Luke Broomfields 40-46; Thrandeston w Stuston 47-50; R of Finningham 50-53; Westhorpe 51-53; V of St Jo Bapt Portland 53-57; Husthwaite w Carlton and Birdforth 57-58. *6 Welney Road, Old Trafford, Manchester 16.*

SUUNORUA, Samuel. St Pet Th Coll Siota 59. **d** 62 **p** 64 Melan. P Dio Melan 62-75; Dio Malaita from 75. *Fauabu, N Malaita, Solomon Islands.*

SUUZA, Acleo. **d** 78 **p** 79 Ruw. P Dio Ruw. *PO Kayarusozi, Uganda.*

SUVA, Dean of. (Vacant)

SWABEY, Henry Sandys. b 16. Late Found and Cl Scho of Univ Coll Dur BA (2nd cl Cl) 37, MA 40, BD 50. Chich Th Coll 37. **d** 39 **p** 40 Derby. C of St John Long Eaton 39-41; Bolsover 41-45; V of Lindsell 45-51; R of Port Perry and Brooklin Dio Tor 51-54; V of Tathwell w Haugham 54-58; R of Raithby and Withcall 55-58; PC (V from 68) of Deeping St Nich and Tongue End 58-78; R of Rippingale Dio Linc from 78; Dowsby w Dunsby Dio Linc from 78. *Rippingale Rectory, Bourne, Lincs.* (Dowsby 380)

SWABY, Canon John Edwin. b 11. Late Scho of St Jo Coll Dur BA (2nd cl Hist) 32, Gladstone Mem Pri 31 and 33, Jenkyns Scho 33, Dipl Th (w distinc) 34, MA 35. **d** 34 **p** 35 Linc. C of Louth w Welton-le-Wold 34-40; V of Scunthorpe 40-53; R of Mablethorpe w Stane 53-60; C-in-c of Theddlethorpe All SS w St Helen and Mablethorpe St Pet 53-54; V 54-60; RD of E Louthesk 57-61; Yarborough 69-70; Surr from 59; V of Barton-on-Humber 60-70; Can and Preb of Linc Cathl 69-77; Can (Emer) from 77; R of Uffington 71-76; V of Tallington 71-76; Barholme w Stowe 71-76. *Farrendon, Southorpe, Stamford, Lincs.* (Stamford 740496)

SWABY, Keith Graham. b 48. Univ of Southn BA (Th) 75. St Steph Ho Ox 75. **d** 77 Willesden for Lon **p** 78 Lon. C of L Stanmore 77-80; All SS Hove Dio Chich from 80. *10 Cornwall Court, Wilbury Avenue, Hove, BN3 6GJ.* (Brighton 734474)

SWAGA, Fenekasi. **d** 52 **p** 54 U Nile. P Dio U Nile 52-61; Dio Mbale 61-72; Dio Bukedi 72-76. *Box 543, Mbale, Uganda.*

SWAIN, David Noel. b 36. Univ of Wel BA 63, MA 66. Coll of Resurr Mirfield. **d** 67 **p** 68 S'wark. C of Clapham 67-70; Paraparaumu 70-72; Chap Vic Univ Wel 72-75; Commiss Wel from 74; P-in-c of Hermitage (V w Hampstead Norreys from 76) 75-80; Hampstead Norreys 75-76; Team R of Hermitage and Hampstead Norreys, Cold Ash and Yattendon w Frilsham Dio Ox from 80. *Rectory, High Street, Hermitage, Newbury, Berks RG16 9ST.* (Hermitage 200448)

SWAIN, Graham Edgar. Univ of Dur BA 65. Ripon Hall Ox 66. **d** 68 S'wark **p** 69 Woolwich for S'wark. C of Woolwich 68-72; Asst Chap Univ of Bris 72-74; Hon C of St Paul Clifton 72-74. *c/o 14 Linden Road, Bristol 6.* (Bristol 44566)

SWAIN, John Edgar. b 44. Lich Th Coll 67. **d** 69 Thetford for Nor **p** 70 Nor. C of E Dereham w Hoe and Dillington 69-73; R of S Ormsby w Ketsby Calceby and Driby 73-74; Harrington w Brinkhill 73-74; Oxcombe 73-74; Ruckland w Farforth and Maidenwell 73-74; Somersby w Bag Enderby 73-74; Tetford w Salmonby 73-74; Belchford 73-74; W Ashby 73-74; V of Haugh 73-74; C of Attleborough 74-78; Besthorpe 74-78; R of Ox Centre Dio Hur from 78. *Anglican Rectory, RR4, Woodstock, N4S 7V8, Ontario, Canada.* (519-537 7797)

SWAIN, John Herbert. b 35. Atlantic Sch of Th Halifax 71. **d** 73 NS **p** 73 Bp Arnold for NS. C of Ecum Secum Dio NS from 74. *Box 3, General Delivery, Moser River, Halifax, NS, Canada.* (4 R 6)

SWAIN, John Roger. Fitzw Ho Cam BA 55, MA 59. Bps' Coll Cheshunt. **d** 57 **p** 58 Ripon. C of Headingley 57-60; Moor Allerton (in c of St Steph Moortown) 60-65; V of Ven Bede Wyther Leeds 65-76; Horsforth Dio Ripon from 76. *St Margaret's Vicarage, Horsforth, Leeds, LS18 5LA.* (Leeds 582481)

SWAIN, Ronald Charles Herbert. b 08. Univ of Dur LTh 32, BA 42, MA 50. St Aug Coll Cant. **d** 32 **p** 33 S'wark. C of H Trin S Wimbledon 32-34; SPG Miss N China 34-40; Perm to Offic Dios Dur and Newc T 41-42; C-in-c of Padgate 42-46; Perm to Offic Dio S'wark 46-47; Chap RAF 47-54; CF 54-62; V of Walsham-le-Willows 62-70; St Mary Virg Shipley 70-74; Perm to Offic Dio St E from 74. *81 Westley Road, Bury St Edmunds, Suff.*

SWAIN, William Allan. b 38. Kelham Th Coll 63. **d** 68 **p** 69 St Alb. C of Welwyn Garden City 68-72; Romsey 72-74; Weeke (in c of St Barn) 74-78; V of H Epiph Muscliff Bournemouth Dio Win from 78. *81 Castle Lane West, Bournemouth, Dorset, BH9 3LH.* (Bournemouth 512481)

SWAINE, John Arthur. b 45. St Steph Ho Ox 68. **d** 71 **p** 72 Lon. C of St Aug Kilburn 71-74; Lavender Hill 74-77; Warden St Mark Commun Centre and Hon C of Deptford 77-80; V of St Chad City and Dio Leic from 80. *145 Coleman Road, Leicester, LE5 4LM.* (Leic 766062)

SWAINSON, Norman. Univ of Salford MSc 79. St Jo Coll Nottm 77. **d** 79 **p** 80 Man. C of Levenshulme Dio Man from 79. *49 Forest Range, Levenshulme, Manchester, M19 2ES.* (061-224 5470)

SWAKA, Canon Jebedayo Jada. **d** 47 **p** 50 Bp Allison for Sudan. P at Rokon 50-61; Juba 61-67; Hon Can of All SS Cathl Khartoum from 61. *c/o Church Office, Juba, Sudan.*

SWALLOW, Canon Allan Whittaker. b 09. Univ of Man BSc 34. Ely Th Coll 34. **d** 35 **p** 36 Chelmsf. C of Halstead 33-38; V of Canvey I 38-45; Halstead 45-74; RD of Halstead and Hedingham 55-74; Hon Can of Chelmsf 61-74; Can (Emer) from 75. *The Glebe House, Takeley, Bishops Stortford, Herts, CM22 6QH.*

SWALLOW, Arnold Birkett. b 04. Late Exhib of SS Coll Cam 2nd cl Cl Trip pt i 25, BA (2nd cl Cl Trip pt ii) 27, MA 30. Westcott Ho Cam 37. **d** 38 **p** 39 Sheff. C of St Mark Sheff 38-41; Chap RAFVR 41-46; V of St Jas Clifton 46-57; R of Fulbourn 57-76; RD of Quy 66-73. *40 Pierce Lane, Fulbourne, Cambridge.* (0223-880358)

SWALLOW, John Allen George. b 28. St Jo Coll Dur BA 53, Dipl Th 54. **d** 54 **p** 55 Chelmsf. C of Billericay 54-57; Bp's Stortford 57-59; V of Roxwell 59-64; S Weald 64-81; R of W w E Mersea Dio Chelmsf from 81. *69 Kingsland Road, West Mersea, Colchester, CO5 8QZ.* (W Mersea 2303)

SWALLOW, Robert Andrew. b 52. Univ of Leeds BA 73. Univ of Keele MA 76. Linc Th Coll 76. **d** 78 **p** 79 Lich. C of Gt Wyrley 78-81; Blakenall Heath Dio Lich from 81. *24 Blakenall Lane, Leamore, Walsall, WS3 1RG.*

SWAN, Canon Cecil William Edwin. Selw Coll Cam BA 12. **d** 13 Bp Wilson for Adel **p** 14 Adel. C of Ch Ch Mt Gambier 13-16; P-in-c of Penola 16-19; Mid Yorke's Peninsula Miss 19-25; R of Clare 25-36; RD 30-36; R of St Columb Hawthorn 36-57; Hon Can of Adel from 56; LPr Dio Adel from 57. *56 High Street, Grange, S Australia 5022.*

SWAN, Charles Martin. St Barn Coll Adel 34 ACT ThL 36. **d** and **p** 36 Adel. C of Ch Ch Adel 36-38; Miss Chap Loxton 38-40; P-in-c of Koolunga 40-43; Chap AMF 40-41 and 46-54; AIF 41-46; R of St Thos Balhannah (in c of St Jas Blakiston) 46-47 (all in S Austr); Asst Chap and Master Coll of St Pet Adel from 47; Chap Kennion Ho 54-59; Perm to Offic Dio Adel from 71; L to Offic Dio Murray from 72. *Ravensthorpe, Woodside, S Australia 5244.* (08-389 7024)

SWAN, Frederick. b 1887. Trin Coll Cam BA 09. **d** 30 **p** 31 Ripon. C of Moor Allerton 30-34; V of Burneston 34-47; Newton Hall 47-55. *Eachwick Red House, Dalton, Newcastle upon Tyne.*

SWAN, Ven John Alfred. St Francis Coll Brisb ACT ThL 39. **d** 40 **p** 41 Brisb. C of St Francis Nundah 40-42; St Paul Ipswich 42-43; V of St Mary Gin Gin 43-46; R of Inglewood 46-51; Childers 51-55; Woolloongabba Brisb 55-64; Camp Hill 64-68; St Andr Indooroopilly City and Dio Brisb from 68; Archd of Lilley 68-76; Brisb from 76. *Rectory, Lambert Road, Indooroopilly, Queensland, Australia 4068.* (370 7263)

SWAN, John Towler Maurice. Hur Coll LTh 50. **d** 51 Hur. C of Trin Ch Galt 50-52; R of St D Galt 52-58; Chap Ch Ex Areas Lon 58-59; I of St Alb Lon Hur 59-62; I of Hanover 62-74; Essex 75-77; St Phil Wingham Dio Hur from 77. *19 John Street East, Wingham, Ont., Canada.* (519-357 2634)

SWAN, Owen. b 28. ACP 71. Edin Th Coll. **d** 59 **p** 60 S'wark. C of St Jo Bapt Southend Lewisham 59-64; CF (TA) from 60; V of St Luke Richmond Dio S'wark from 64; Dioc Insp Schs Dio S'wark from 66. *St Luke's Vicarage, The Avenue, Kew, Surrey, TW9 2AJ.* (01-940 3170)

SWAN, Ronald Frederick. b 35. St Cath Coll Cam Geog Trip pt i 58, BA (Th Trip pt ia) 59. Coll of Resurr Mirfield. **d** 61 **p** 62 Derby. C of Stavely 61-66; Chap Univ of Lon 66-72; C of St Martin-in-the-Fields 72-76; V of St Barn Ealing Dio Lon from 76; St Steph Ealing Dio Lon from 81. *66 Woodfield Road, W5.* (01-998 0826)

SWAN, Thomas Hugh Winfield. New Coll Ox MA 62. Ridley Hall Cam 63. **d** 65 Ely **p** 66 Huntingdon for Ely. C of Yaxley 65-68; P-in-c of Sawtry 69; R 69-79; P-in-c of Southery Dio Ely from 79; Hilgay Dio Ely from 79; Fordham Dio Ely from 79. *Rectory Bungalow, Southery, Downham Market, Norf.* (Southery 320)

SWAN, Canon William John Minto. Wycl Coll Tor BA 22, BD 25. K Coll NS MA 24. Qu Univ Ont DD 62. **d** 23 **p** 24 Tor. C of St Olave Swansea 23; St John Tor 23-25; St Jas Cathl Tor 26-28; St John W Tor 28-29; R of Portage La Prairie Manit 29-31; RD 30-31; RD of Vancouver W 38-42; R of St Mark Vancouver 31-42; Chap RCAF 41-47; R of St John Kingston [f Portsmouth] 47-64; Dom Chap to Abp of Ont 49-52; Chap to Collins Bay Penit 50-64; Can of Ont 54-64. *302-160 Government Street, Victoria, BC, Canada.*

SWANBOROUGH, Alan William. b 38. Univ of Southn BEducn 75. Sarum Wells Th Coll 79. **d** 80 **p** 81 Portsm (APM). C of St Cath and of H Trin Ventnor Dio Portsm from 80. *1 St Boniface Terrace, Ventnor, IW, PO38 1PJ.*

SWANBOROUGH, Robert Charles. b 28. Sarum Wells Th Coll 75. **d** 77 Buckingham for Ox **p** 78 Reading for Ox. C of Woodley 77-79; Bray w Braywood 79-80; V of Gt Coxwell w Coleshill w Buscot and Eaton Hastings Dio Ox from 80. *Great Coxwell Vicarage, Faringdon, Oxon, SN7 7NG.* (Faringdon 20665)

SWANE, Peter. Ridley Coll Melb 60. **d** 63 **p** 64 Armid. C of Moree 63-66; Wee Waa 66-68; P-in-c of Collarenebri 68-72; V of Ashford 72-75; Delungra and Tingha 72-75; C of

S Tamworth Dio Armid 75-76; V from 76. *Vicarage, Vera Street, S Tamworth, NSW, Australia 2340.*

SWANEPOEL, David John. b 41. Rhodes Univ Grahmstn BA 62. **d** 75 Bp Nye for Pret **p** 76 Pret. Chap St Alb Coll Dio Pret from 75. *St Alban's College, Private Bag 1, Alkantrant 0005, S Africa.*

SWANN, Antony Keith. b 34. Dipl Th (Lon) 60. St Aid Coll 58. **d** 61 **p** 62 Lich. C of Bilston 61-66; CMS Miss Dio Sier L 66-70; V of St Phil W Bromwich 70-75; CMS Tr Officer Dio N Nig 76-79; R of Church Lench Dio Worc from 79. *Rectory, Church Lench, Nr Evesham, Worcs, WR11 4UB.* (Evesham 870345)

SWANN, David William Malcolm. b 31. **d** 80 Auckld. C of New Lynn Dio Auckld from 80. *199 Godley Road, Tihrongi, Auckland, NZ.*

SWANN, Edgar John. b 42. TCD BA (Hebr and Or Lang Mod) 66, Div Test 68, MA 70, BD 77. **d** 68 **p** 69 Dub. C of Crumlin 68-70; Howth 70-73; I of Greystones Dio Glendal from 73. *Rectory, Greystones, Co Wicklow, Irish Republic.*

SWANN, Frederick David. b 38. **d** 69 **p** 70 Down. C of Shankill (Lurgan) 69-77; R of Ardmore and St Sav Craigavon 77-79; Comber Dio Down from 79; Dom Chap to Bp of Down and Drom from 77. *Comber Rectory, Newtownards, N Ireland.* (Comber 872283)

SWANN, Robert Edgar. b 50. Univ of Salford BSc 72. Univ of Leeds Dipl Th 79. Coll of the Resurr Mirfield 77. **d** 80 Liv **p** 81 Warrington for Liv. C of H Trin Southport Dio Liv from 80. *80 St Luke's Road, Southport, Lancs.*

SWANNELL, George Alfred Roderick. b 20. St Edm Hall Ox BA 47, MA 51. Ridley Hall Cam. **d** 50 Lewes for Chich **p** 50 Chich. C of Crowborough 50-51; Chap K Edw Sch Witley 51-55; C of Sevenoaks 55-57; Chap at Nakuru 57-62; V 62-65; C of All S Langham Place St Marylebone 65-68; V of Hildenborough 68-80; Chap Kent & Sussex Hosp Tunbridge Wells from 80. *Kent & Sussex Hospital, Mount Ephraim, Tunbridge Wells, Kent.*

SWANSBOROUGH, Rodney Harry. b 47. Univ of New Engl NSW BA 78. Canberra Coll of Min BTh 81. **d** 79 **p** 80 Graft. Hon C of Hughes 79-80; C of Lismore Dio Graft from 81. *PO Box 378, Lismore, NSW, Australia 2480.*

SWANSEA AND BRECON, Lord Bishop of. *See* Vaughan, Right Rev Benjamin Noel Young.

SWANSON, Ven Cecil. Univ of Tor BA 11. St Jo Coll Manit Hon DD 35. Angl Th Coll of BC Hon DD 53. **d** 12 **p** 13 Yukon. Miss-in-c of Carmacks and L Salmon Miss 12-16; I of Whitehorse 16-20; C of Ch Ch Vancouver 20-22; R of St Aug Lethbridge 22-32; St Steph Calg 32-40; RD of Lethbridge 25-32; Archd of Lethbridge 27-32; Archd in Calg 32-40; Miss Archd 38-40; Dean of New Westmr 40-53; R of Ch Ch Cathl Vancouver and Exam Chap to Bp of New Westmr 40-53; R of St Paul Tor 53-60; Archd of Tor E 56-59; Archd (Emer) from 59; Dom Chap to Bp of Calg 61-67 and 70-72. *3040 Glencoe Road SW, Calgary, Alta., Canada.* (243-0193)

SWANSON, Raymond Powys St Clair. b 1894. Univ of Glas MA 15. **d** 22 **p** 23 Glas. C of St Mary's Cathl (in c of St Sav Miss Ch) Glas 22-31; L to Offic Dio St Jo Kaffr 31-32; Asst Chap St John Territet Switzerland 32-33; C of H Cross E Pondoland 33-34; P-in-c of St Andr Miss Lusikisiki 34-41; L to Offic Dio Capetn 42-44; Perm to Offic at Clydesdale Miss Dio St Jo Kaffr 47-50; Chap St Jo Evang Mentone 50-52; Palermo 52-56; All SS San Remo 58-65. *Address temp unknown.*

✠ **SWARTZ, Right Rev George Alfred.** Univ of Witwatersrand BA 50. Coll of Resurr Mirfield 52. **d** 54 **p** 55 Capetn. C of St Paul Capetn 52-56; C-in-c of St Helena Bay 56-60; R of St Phil Capetn 61-71; Can of Capetn 69-72; P-in-c of Bonteheuwel 71-72; Cons Ld Bp Suffr of Capetn in St Geo Cathl Capetn 12 Nov 72 by Abp of Capetn; Bps of Bloemf; Swaz; Natal, Kimb K, Grahmstn, St Hel and Johann; and others. *18 Rue Ursula, Glenhaven, Bellville, CP, S Africa.* (94-0184)

SWARTZ, Oswald Peter Patrick. b 53. St Paul's Coll Grahmstn Dipl Th 79. **d** and **p** 80 Bloemf. C of St Matt Welkom Dio Bloemf from 80. *Box 231, Welkom 9460, S Africa.*

SWAYNE, William Hope George. Trin Coll Tor 26. **d** 26 Tor for Ont **p** 27 Ont. C of Milford 26-28; St Geo Tor 28-31; I of Bannockburn 31-32; Tweed (w Madoc from 33) 32-39; R of Merrickville 39-43; Picton 43-55; Barriefield 55-66. *Box 2101, Picton, Ont, Canada.* (613-476 6788)

SWAZILAND, Lord Bishop of. *See* Mkhabela, Right Rev Bernard Lazarus.

SWEARS, Peter Hamlin. St Jo Coll Auckld LTh 67. **d** 66 Nel. C of Stoke 66-68; All SS Nel 68-71; V of Cobden 71-76; Golden Bay Dio Nel from 76. *Vicarage, Collingwood, NZ.*

SWEATMAN, John. b 44. Oak Hill Th Coll 68. **d** 71 Bradwell for Chelmsf **p** 72 Chelmsf. C of H Trin Rayleigh 71-73; St Leon Seaford 73-77; Chap RN from 77. *c/o Ministry of Defence, Lacon House, Theobalds Road, WC1X 8RY.*

SWEED, John William. b 35. Clifton Th Coll 59. **d** 62 Lich **p** 63 Shrewsbury for Lich. C of St Julian Shrewsbury 62-64; St Jo Evang Park Sheff 64-70; V of St Jas Doncaster 70-79; Hatfield, Doncaster Dio Sheff from 79. *Hatfield Vicarage, Doncaster, Yorks, DN7 6RS.* (Doncaster 840280)

SWEENEY, Robert Maxwell. b 38. Ch Ch Ox BA 63, MA 66. Univ of Birm MA 78. Cudd Coll. **d** 65 Glouc **p** 66 Tewkesbury for Glouc. C of Prestbury 65-68; St Andr Handsworth 68-70; Asst Chap Lancing Coll 70-73; V of Wotton St Mary Without (or Longlevens) 74-79; St Thos City and Dio Ox from 79; St Frideswide w Binsey City and Dio Ox from 79. *39 Helen Road, Osney, Oxford.* (Ox 43431)

SWEET, Canon John Philip McMurdo. b 27. New Coll Ox BA 49, MA 52. Selw Coll Cam MA (by incorp) 58. Westcott Ho Cam 53. **d** 55 **p** 56 Southw. C of St Mark Mansfield 55-58; Fell, Chap and Lect in Th Selw Coll Cam from 58; Asst Lect in Div Univ of Cam 60-63; Lect from 64; Exam Chap to Bp of Southw 58-64; to Bp of Lich 60-74; to Bp of Chich 62-74; Wiccamical Preb of Chich Cathl from 62. *Selwyn College, Cambridge, CB3 9DQ.* (Cambridge 62381)

SWEET, Reginald Charles. b 36. Open Univ BA 74. Ripon Hall Ox 61. **d** 62 **p** 63 Cov. C of Styvechale 62-65; Chap RN 65-69; R of Riddlesworth w Gasthorpe and Knettishall 69-75; Brettenham w Rushford and Shadwell 69-75; Chap RN from 75. *c/o Ministry of Defence, Lacon House, Theobald's Road, WC1X 8RY.*

SWEET-ESCOTT, Richard Mark. b 28. Late Scho of Hertf Coll Ox 2nd cl Cl Mods 48, BA (3rd cl Lit Hum) 51, MA 53. Westcott Ho Cam 56. **d** 58 **p** 59 Ripon. C of Leeds 58-62; Littlehampton 62-65; Seaford w Sutton (in c of St Luke) 65-72; C-in-c of St Mary Burpham 72-75; V of Easebourne 75-79; Crawley Down Dio Chich from 79. *Vicarage, Vicarage Road, Crawley Down, Crawley, RH10 4JJ.*

SWEETING, Philip James. b 32. Cudd Coll 75. **d** 75 Bris **p** 75 Malmesbury for Bris. C of St Greg Horfield 75-80; V of Airedale w Fryston Dio Wakef from 80. *Holy Cross Vicarage, Castleford, W Yorks, WE10 3JL.* (Castleford 553157)

SWEETLAND, Robert Bruce. Bp's Univ Lennox BA and LST 62. **d** 62 **p** 63 Newfld. C of Grand Falls 62-63; I of Carbonear 63-68. *Bay Robert's, Newfoundland, Canada.*

SWEETMAN, Denis Harold. b 22. Roch Th Coll 61. **d** 63 **p** 64 Roch. C of Riverhead 63-70; Dunton Green 67-70; Chap Sevenoaks Hosp 70-72; V of Eynsford w Lullingstone Dio Roch 71-73; R (w Farningham) from 73. *Rectory, Pollyhaugh, Eynsford, Kent.* (Farningham 863050)

SWEETMAN, Erskine Cuthbert. Univ of W Austr BA 37. St Barn Coll Adel ACT ThL 38. **d** 38 Bunb for Perth **p** 39 Perth. C of St Mary S Perth 38-40; Chap Forrest River Miss 40-42; R of Meckering-Quairading 42-44; Chap RAAF 44-46 and 51-67; Prin Chap 67-75; R of Palmyra 46-51; Pearce W Austr 51-54; 56-61 and 63-75; Japan 54-55; Darwin 55-56; Malaya 61-63; Archd in RAAF 69-75; Perm to Offic Dio Melb 75-78; Dio Perth from 78. *13 Unwin Avenue, Wembley Downs, W Australia 6019.*

SWENARTON, Preb John Creighton. b 19. Late Found Scho Trin Coll Dub BA (1st cl Mod w Gold Med Ment and Mor Sc) 41, Div Test 42, MA 45. **d** 42 **p** 43 Down. C of Lurgan 42-45; St Donard Belf 45-46; Donaghcloney w Waringstown 46-51; I of Tullylish 51-60; R of Donaghadee Dio Down from 60; Exam Chap to Bp of Down from 70; Preb of Down Cathl from 81. *Rectory, Donaghadee, Co Down, BT21 0PD, N Ireland.* (0247-882594)

SWIDENBANK, Stephen. b 37. Lich Th Coll 58. **d** 61 Penrith for Carl **p** 62 Carl. C of Penrith 61-64; Dalton-in-Furness 64-67; V of St Pet Kells Whitehaven 67-76; Staveley w Kentmere Dio Carl from 76. *Vicarage, Kentmere Road, Kendal, Cumb, LA8 9PD.* (Staveley 821267)

SWIFT, Christopher John. b 54. Linc Coll Ox BA 76, MA. Selw Coll Cam BA (Th) 80. Westcott Ho Cam 79. **d** 81 Portsm. C of St Mark Northend Portsea Dio Portsm from 81. *27 Hartley Road, Northend, Portsmouth, Hants, PO2 9HO.*

SWIFT, Francis Bernard. b 06. Lich Th Coll Univ of Dur LTh 32. **d** 31 **p** 32 Wakef. C of Ravensthorpe 31-35; V of Bromfield 35-40; St Cuthb Holme Cultram 40-50; Addingham w St John Gamblesby 50-58; Ireby w Uldale 58-72; L to Offic Dio Carl from 72. *5 Westhaven, Thursby, Carlisle, CA5 6PH.* (Dalston 710099)

SWIFT, James Theodore. b 11. Ripon Hall Ox 67. **d** 68 **p** 69 Ox. C of Highfield Ox 68-72; V of Lyford w Charney-Basset 72-78; Denchworth 72-78; R of Cherbury 78-81; L to Offic Dio Ox from 81. *5 Cedar Road, Faringdon, Oxon, SN7 8AY.* (Faringdon 21158)

SWIFT, John Russell. K Coll Lon. **d** 33 **p** 34 Chelmsf. C of Thundersley 33-35; Stansted Mountfitchet 35-38; CF 38-57; V of Healey 57-81. *c/o Healey Vicarage, Rochdale, Lancs.* (Rochdale 48940)

SWIFT, Richard Barrie. b 33. Selw Coll Cam BA 58, MA 64. Ripon Hall Ox. **d** 60 **p** 61 Lon. C of Stepney 60-64; Sidmouth 64-72; V of Mill End and Heronsgate (w West Hyde from 77) Dio St Alb from 72; C-in-c of West Hyde 72-77. *Mill End Vicarage, Rickmansworth, Herts.* (Rickmansworth 72785)

SWIFT, Selwyn. b 41. Trin Coll Bris 73. **d** 76 Sarum **p** 77 Ramsbury for Sarum. C of Melksham 76-79; Team V 79-81; Whitton Dio Sarum from 81. *Vicarage, Aldbourne, Marlborough, Wilts.*

SWIFT, Stanley. b 47. Univ of Nottm Dipl Th 73. ACIS 71. Linc Th Coll 71. **d** 74 **p** 75 Bradf. C of Heaton 74-77; Bexhill (in c of St Mich AA) 77-81; R of Croyland or Crowland Dio Linc from 81. *Abbey Rectory, Crowland, Peterborough, PE6 0EN.* (Peterborough 210499)

SWIFT, Canon Thomas William. b 17. **d** 57 **p** 58 Blackb. C of St Matt Preston 57-60; V of St Osw Preston 60-64; Chap Deepdale Hosp 60-64; HM Pris Preston 63-64; V of Tuxford 64-80; W Markham w Bevercotes 64-80; P-in-c of Weston Notts 66-80; RD of Tuxford 70-80; Surr from 72; P-in-c of E Drayton w Stokenham 74-78; Headon w Upton 74-76; Hon Can of Southw Minster from 78; V of Wellow Dio Southw from 80. *Wellow Vicarage, Newark, Notts.* (Mansfield 861161)

SWIFT, William Arthur. b 02. St Jo Coll Dur LTh 32, BA 33. St Aid Coll 29. **d** 33 **p** 34 Liv. C of St Athanasius Kirkdale 33-36; St Luke Gt Crosby 36-39; V of St Cleopas Toxt Pk Liv 39-49; V of St Phil Griffin Blackb 49-58; Yealand Conyers 58-68. *119 Church Street, Milnthorpe, Cumb, LA7 7DZ.* (Milnthorpe 2254)

SWINBANK, John Beecroft. b 20. Peterho Cam BA 42, MA 46. Ridley Hall Cam. **d** 43 **p** 44 Roch. C of St Jo Bapt Beckenham 43-45; Chap Bradfield Coll Dio Ox from 46. *Applegarth Bradfield College, Berks.* (Bradfield 379)

SWINBANK, Peter. b 19. Linc Coll Ox BA 41, MA 47. Ridley Hall Cam. **d** 43 **p** 44 Derby. C of Chaddesden 43-45; Ch Ch Southport 45-47; Lect of Watford 47-50; V of St Paul Northumberland Heath Erith 50-56; H Trin Hampstead 56-72; R of Hinton St Geo w Dinnington 72-78; V of Stebbing w Lindsell Dio Chelmsf from 78. *Vicarage, Stebbing, Dunmow, Essex, CM6 3SP.* (Stebbing 468)

SWINBURN, Roderick Neville. b 34. Roch Th Coll 65. **d** 68 **p** 69 B & W. C of H Trin Taunton 68-72; Wraxall w Failand 72-74; C-in-c of Monksilver (and Elworthy to 75) w Brompton Ralph and Nettlecombe Dio B & W from 74; Stogumber Dio B & W from 77. *Monksilver Rectory, Taunton, Somt.* (Stogumber 221)

SWINBURNE, Harold Noel. Univ of Lon BA (Geog) 49. St Chad's Coll Dur 51. **d** 53 **p** 54 Dur. C of Cockerton 53-57; St Aug Wisbech 57-59; PC of Chilton Moor 59-71; Lect in Relig Stud New Coll Dur from 71. *39 Durham Moor Crescent, Framwellgate Moor, Durham.* (Durham 62603)

SWINDELL, Anthony Charles. b 50. Selw Coll Cam BA (Th) 73, MA 77. Univ of Leeds MPhil 77. Ripon Hall Ox 73. **d** 75 **p** 76 York. C of Hessle 75-78; Adult Educn Adv E Sussex and P-in-c of Litlington w W Dean 78-80; Chap Univ of York 80-81; Team V of Heslington 80-81; R of Harlaxton, Denton, Stroxton, and Wyville w Hungerford Dio Linc from 81. *Rectory, Harlaxton, Grantham, Lincs, NG32 1HD.* (Grantham 75019)

SWINDELLS, Philip John. b 34. St Edm Hall Ox BA (3rd cl Th) 56, MA 60. Ely Th Coll 56. **d** 58 **p** 59 Ox. C of St Mary Slough 58-62; St Jo Evang Taunton 62-66; Stevenage (in c of St Francis) 66-71; V of St Francis (All S from 75) Stevenage 71-78; R of Clophill Dio St Alb from 78. *Rectory, Great Lane, Clophill, Bedford, MK45 4BQ.* (0525-60792)

SWINDELLS, Stephen Seel Sherwood. b 17. Mert Coll Ox BA 38, MA 43. Wycl Hall Ox 38. **d** 40 **p** 41 Bris. C of St Paul Bedminster 40-42; St Gabr E Bris 42-44; Stoke Bp 44-46; Prec of Bris Cathl 46-50; V of Rennington w Rock 50-55; St Cuthb Blyth 55-66; Dioc Insp of Schs Dio Newc T 55-61; R of Whitfield 66-75; V of Ninebanks (w Carrshield from 68) 66-75; V of Carrshield 66-68; P-in-c of Bolam 75-79; Whalton 77-79; R of Bolam w Whalton 79-82. *36 Fountain Head Bank, Seaton Sluice, Whitley Bay, Northumb, NE26 4HV.* (Seaton Delaval 373598)

SWINDLEHURST, Michael Robert Carol. b 29. Worc Coll Ox BA 52, MA 56. Cudd Coll 61. **d** 63 **p** 64 Portsm. C of Havant 63-66; Hellesdon 66-69; V of Brightlingsea Dio Chelmsf from 69; Surr from 72. *Vicarage, Richard Avenue, Brightlingsea, Essex, CO7 0LP.* (Brightlingsea 2407)

SWINDLEY, Geoffrey. b 25. St Mich Coll Llan 59. **d** 61 **p** 62 St A. C of Flint 61-68; V of Buttington w Pool Quay 68-77; Welshpool w Castle Caereinion Dio St A from 77; RD of Pool from 77. *Vicarage, Welshpool,Powys.* (Welshpool 3164)

SWINDON, Archdeacon of. (Vacant)

SWINFIELD, David Frederick Ebenezer. Moore Th Coll Syd ACT ThL (2nd cl) 63. **d** 63 **p** 64 Syd. C of St Luke Mosman 63-64; C-in-c of Moorebank Dio Syd 65-74; R 74-75; St Andr Abbotsford Dio Syd from 75. *81 Byrne Avenue, Abbotsford, NSW, Australia 2046.* (83-8059)

SWINGLER, Preb Jack Howell. b 19. Late Scho of St Jo Coll Cam 1st cl Cl Trip pt i 40, BA 41, MA 47. Ridley Hall Cam. **d** 48 **p** 49 B & W. C of Yeovil w Preston Plucknett 48-53; V of Henstridge (and Charlton Horethorn w Stowell from 79) Dio B & W from 53; RD of Merston from 75; P-in-c of Charlton Horethorne w Stowell 78-79; Preb of Wells Cathl from 79. *Henstridge Vicarage, Templecombe, Somt, BA8 0QE.* (Stalbridge 62266)

SWINGLER, Canon Leslie Ronald. b 12. Lich Th Coll 35. **d** 38 Grantham for Linc **p** 39 Linc. C of Flixborough w Burton-on-Stather 38-44; V of Whaplode 44-49; Sempringham w Pointon Pointon Fen and Birthorpe and of Billingborough 49-58; St Faith Linc 58-62; R of Finmere w Mixbury 62-74; Sec Ox Dioc Coun of Educn 62-78; Hon Can of Ch Ch Ox from 73; Perm to Offic Dio Nor from 78. *54 Folly Road, Wymondham, NR18 0QR.*

SWINGLER, Phillip Frank. b 45. Keble Coll Ox BA 67, MA 71. Westcott Ho Cam 68. **d** 70 **p** 71 St Alb. C of Aldenham 70-72; Asst Master Aldenham Sch 70-72; Eton Coll 72-75; Sen Chap Oundle Sch from 75. *Oundle School, Peterborough, Northants.* (Oundle 72338)

SWINGLER, Reginald Walter. b 11. St Aug Coll Cant 39. **d** 42 **p** 43 St Alb. C of St Andr Luton 42-45; CF (EC) 45-46; CF 46-51; Hon CF 51; Min of St Pet Conv Distr Watford 51-55; R of Thurlaston 55-65; C of Bodiam 65-67; Perm to Offic Dio Chich from 67. *21 Arlington Road, Eastbourne, Sussex.* (Eastbourne 29870)

SWINN, Gerald Robert. b 40. Univ of Leeds BSc (Math) 60. Univ of Lon BD 70. Oak Hill Th Coll 63. **d** 66 **p** 67 B & W. C of Ch Ch Weston-s-Mare 66-69; Harefield 70-72; Perm to Offic Dio Sarum from 72; Asst Master Weymouth Gr Sch 72-75; Wyke Regis Jun Sch 76-79; Lockyer's Middle Sch Corfe Mullen from 79. *16 Heddington Drive, Blandford, Dorset.* (Blandford 51637)

SWINNERTON, Brian Thomas. b 31. LCP 62. State Univ of NY BA 74. Lich Th Coll 67. **d** 69 **p** 70 Lich. C of Swynnerton 69-71; Eccleshall 71-74; Croxton w Broughton 74-80; CF (TAVR) from 70; Lect Stafford Coll from 81. *c/o Stafford College, Tenterbanks, Stafford, ST16 2QR.* (Staff 42361)

SWINNERTON, Edward. b 26. St Aid Coll 62. **d** 64 Warrington for Liv **p** 65 Liv. C of Prescot 64-67; H Trin S Shore (in c of St Chris) Blackpool 67-69; V of Hambleton Dio Blackb from 69. *Hambleton Vicarage, Blackpool, Lancs.* (Hambleton 700231)

SWINNERTON, Ernest George Francis. b 33. Clare Coll Cam BA 54, MA 59. Linc Th Coll 56. **d** 58 **p** 59 Man. C of St Thos Kirkholt Rochdale 58-61; Swindon 61-67; C-in-c of St Andr Conv Distr Walcot Swindon 67-75; Chilton Foliat 76; Froxfield Dio Sarum from 76; Team V of Whitton Dio Sarum from 76. *Chilton Foliat Rectory, Hungerford, Berks, RG17 0TF.* (Hungerford 2470)

SWINNEY, Fergus William Henry. b 37. Edin Th Coll 67. **d** 69 Bp Ramsbotham for Newc T **p** 70 Newc T. C of St Jas Benwell Newc T 69-72; Willington-on-Tyne 72-75; V of Longhirst w Hebron 75-81. *c/o Longhirst Vicarage, Morpeth, Northumb, NE61 3LU.* (Ulgham 253)

SWINNEY, Thomas. b 14. Kelham Th Coll 32. **d** 38 **p** 39 Dur. C of St Aid Gateshead 38-41; Bolden 41-42; Winlaton (in c of Rowlands Gill) 42-48; V of St Jas W Hartlepool 48-54; PC of Ch Ch W Hartlepool 53-54; Dawdon 54-59; V of Witton-le-Wear (and Fir Tree from 79) 59-79; C-in-c of Firtree 72-79. *18 Lambton Drive, Bishop Auckland, Co Durham, DL14 6LG.*

SWINSON, Kenneth Anthony. b 41. Chich Th Coll 66. **d** 69 **p** 70 Derby. C of SS Aug Chesterfield 69-73; St Chad Kirkby 73-76; V of Boosbeck w Moorsholm Dio York from 76. *Boosbeck Vicarage, Saltburn, Cleve, TS12 3AY.* (Guisborough 50360)

SWINTON, William Alan. **d** 55 **p** 56 Edmon. C of H Trin Edmon 55-56; R of Drayton Valley 56-60; Lac la Biche 60-63; Mannville 63-66; L to Offic Dio Calg from 66. *General Delivery, Sylvan Lake, Alta, Canada, T0M 1Z0.*

SWITHINBANK, Kim Stafford. b 53. SS Coll Cam BA 77, MA 80. Cranmer Hall Dur 78. **d** 80 **p** 81 Nor. C of H Trin Heigham Dio Nor from 80. *14 Trinity Street, Norwich, NR2 2BQ.*

SWITZER, Peter Allen. b 42. Vanc Sch of Th STB 72. **d** 72 **p** 73 BC. C of St Jo Div Vic 72-74; R of All SS Port Alberni Dio BC from 74. *730 Brown Road, Port Alberni, BC, Canada.* (604-724 0762)

SWITZERLAND, Archdeacon in. *See* Nind, Ven Anthony Lindsay.

SWORN, Geoffrey Ernest. St Jo Coll Auckld LTh 57. **d** 58 **p** 59 Auckld. C of Whangarei 58-61; H Trin Devonport Auckld 61-62; V of Hokianga 62-66; Paparoa 66-70; Kaitaia

70-77; C of Whangarei Dio Auckld from 77. *51a Kamo Road, Whangarei, NZ.*

SYDENHAM, Canon Herbert Reginald. b 04. OBE 58. New Coll Ox BA (2nd cl Hist) 26, Dipl Th (w distinc) 27, MA 31. St Steph Ho Ox 26. **d** 27 **p** 28 S'wark. C of St Paul Newington 27-30; Stockwell Green 30-33; CF (R of O) 29-33; UMCA Miss Dio Zanz 33-35; P-in-c of Korogwe 35-43; Archd of Korogwe 37-61; Can of Zanz 37-74; Hon Can from 74; VG 52-63; Treas 59-64; Admin Sec Dio Dar-S 65-67; Tropical Afr Sec USPG 67-68; Personnel Sec (Overseas) 68-74; Commiss Malawi 67-75; SW Tang 67-75; Ruv 71-78. *St Matthew's Clergy House, 20 Great Peter Street, SW1P 2BU.* (01-222 3704)

SYDNEY, Lord Archbishop of, and Metropolitan of Province of NSW. (Vacant)

SYDNEY, Assistant Bishops of. *See* Right Revs A J Dain; D W B Robinson; J R Reid; K H Short; E D Cameron.

SYDNEY, Dean of. *See* Shilton, Very Rev Lancelot Rupert.

SYER, Canon George Vivian. b 11. AKC (2nd cl) and Jelf Prize 39. ACT ThL 56. **d** 39 Guildf for Col Bp **p** 42 Cant. C of St Paul's Cathl Rockptn 39-40; serving w RAAF 40-42; Chap RAFVR 42-45; R of Didmarton w Oldbury-on-the-Hill and Sopworth 44-47; R of Bothwell Dio Tas 47-49; Coberley w Cowley and Colesbourne 49-54; Kirby Cane 54-59; V of Whitchurch Canonicorum w Stanton S Gabr 59-71; R of Wootton Fitzpaine 66-71; RD of Lyme Bay 62-71; Can Sarum Cathl 70-71; Can (Emer) from 71; R of Chagford 71-76. *Ryes Cottage, Diptford, Totnes, Devon.*

SYEUNDA, Jonathan. d 71 **p** 72 Maseno N (APM). P Dio Maseno N. *Box 49, Bungoma, Kenya.*

SYKES, Albert. b 08. Egerton Hall Man 33. **d** 35 **p** 36 Man. C of St Pet Levenshulme 35-41; V of the Sav Bolton 41-46; R of St Denys 46-55; V of Lostwithiel 55-67; R of Lanreath 67-73; V of Pelynt 67-73; Publ Pr Dio Truro 73-76; Perm to Offic Dio Tas 76-78; Hon C of St Austell Dio Truro from 78. *32 Biscovey Road, Par, Cornw, PL24 2HW.*

SYKES, Arthur. b 14. BA (Lon) 34. St Deiniol's Libr Hawarden 77. **d** 77 **p** 78 Birkenhead for Ches. C of Birkenhead Priory Dio Ches from 77. *15 Village Close, Wallasey, Merseyside.*

SYKES, Colin George. b 30. Late Exhib of K Coll Cam 2nd cl Mod Lang Trip pt i 51, BA (2nd cl Mod Lang Trip pt ii) 52, MA 56. BD (Lon) 61, MTh (Lon) 65. **d** 61 **p** 62 Win. C of Bournemouth 61-64; St Pet and St Paul Cathl Llan 64-66; Exam Chap to Bp of Llan 65-70; Libr and Lect St Mich Coll Llan, Lect Univ Coll of S Wales and Mon, and Perm to Offic Dio Llan 66-70; Chap Bradfield Coll 70-75; R of Ewhurst 75-81; Bodiam 75-81; Chap St Mary and St Anne's Sch Abbots Bromley from 81. *St Mary and St Anne's School, Abbots Bromley, Staffs.*

SYKES, Frederick Drummond. b 11. CCC Cam BA 33, MA 37. Ely Th Coll 33. **d** 34 Southampton for Win **p** 36 Win. C of Ascen Bitterne Pk 34-37; St Jas Southbroom 37; H Trin Weymouth 37-40; CF (EC) 40-46; CF 46-54; C of St Jo Evang Huddersfield 54-56; V of W Vale 56-71; Hepworth Yorks 71-75. *4 West Lodge Crescent, Fixby, Huddersfield, W Yorks.*

SYKES, James Clement. b 42. Keble Coll Ox 52764) (3rd cl Th) 64, MA 71. Westcott Ho Cam 65. **d** 67 **p** 68 St Alb. C of Bp's Stortford 67-71; Chap of St Jo Sch Leatherhead 71-73; V of Smith's Berm 74-79; Northaw Dio St Alb from 79. *Northaw Vicarage, Vineyards Road, Northaw, Potters Bar, Herts.* (P Bar 52764)

SYKES, John. b 39. Univ of Man BA 62. Ripon Hall Ox 61. **d** 63 **p** 64 Man. C of St Luke Heywood 63-67; C-in-c of H Trin Bolton 67-71; Lect Bolton Inst of Technology 67-71; R of St Elisabeth Reddish 71-78; V of Saddleworth Dio Man from 78; M Gen Syn from 80. *Saddleworth Vicarage, Station Road, Uppermill, Oldham, OL3 6HQ.* (Saddleworth 2412)

SYKES, John Trevor. b 35. Lich Th Coll 60. **d** 62 Bp McKie for Cov **p** 63 Cov. C of Lillington 62-65; St Marg Cov 65-68; V of Ryton-on-Dunsmore (w Bubbenhall from 77) Dio Cov from 68; C-in-c of Bubbenhall 68-78. *Ryton-on-Dunsmore Vicarage, Coventry, CV8 3ET.* (Cov 303570)

SYKES, Kevin. b 35. St Barn Coll Adel 74. **d** 77 **p** 78 Adel. C of St Matt Kens 77-79; P-in-c of Para Hills Dio Adel from 79. *Box 29, Para Hills, S Australia 5096.* (258 9851)

SYKES, Nicholas John Geoffrey. d 75 Ja (APM). C of Manchester Dio Ja from 75. *Cross Keys PO, Jamaica, W Indies.*

SYKES, Patrick Carrington. b 38. Univ of Lon BA 81. Oak Hill Coll 78. **d** 81 Guildf. C of Ashtead Dio Guildf from 81. *1 Oakfield Road, Ashtead, Surrey, KT21 2RE.*

SYKES, Paul Carton. b 03. **d** 54 **p** 55 Natal. C of St Pet Pmbg 55-56; V of Margate Natal 56-65; Aymestrey and Leinthall Earles w Wigmore and Leinthall Starkes 65-72; Warden Dowty Ho 72-76; Vice-Chairman Retired Clergy Assoc from 78. *74 Harthurstfield Farm, Gloucester Road, Cheltenham, GL51 0TA.*

SYKES, Canon Stephen Whitefield. b 39. St Jo Coll Cam BA 61, 1st cl (w distinc) Th Trip pt iii 62, MA 65. Ripon Hall Ox 63. **d** 64 **p** 65 Ely. Fell and Dean St Jo Coll Cam 64-74; Asst Lect in Div Univ of Cam 64-68; Lect 68-74; Van Mildert Prof of Div Univ of Dur from 74; Exam Chap to Bp of Chelmsf from 70; Can of Dur Cathl from 74. *14 The College, Durham, DH1 3EQ.* (Durham 64567)

SYKES, William George David. b 39. Ball Coll Ox BA 63, MA 68. Wycl Hall Ox 63. **d** 65 **p** 66 Bradf. C of Bradf Cathl 65-69; Chap Univ Coll Lon 69-78; Chap and Fell Univ Coll Ox from 78. *University College, Oxford, OX1 4BH.* (0865-41661)

SYLVESTER, George Henry. LTh (S Afr) 49. **d** 48 Bp Lewis for Capetn **p** 49 Capetn. C of Rylands 48-51; Athlone 51-53; R of Hopefield 53-57; St Matt Claremont 57-61; Can of Capetn 62-76; R o Lower Paarl 61-65; Steenberg 65-76; Woodstock 76-77; Warden Zonnebloem Coll from 76; Archd of The Cape 76-80; R of St Bart Walmer Estate Dio Capetn from 77. *Zonnebloem College, Cambridge Street, Cape Town, S Africa.* (45-1083)

SYMCOX, Canon Kenneth George. b 05. Univ of Birm BA 27. Lich Th Coll 27. **d** 29 **p** 30 Lich. C of St Giles Willenhall 29-34; Wotton-under-Edge 34-35; Stoke-on-Trent 35-38; V of St Andr w St Mich W Bromwich 38-45; L to Offic Dio Lon from 46; Metrop Sec SPG Dios Lon, S'wark and Chelmsf 45-50; Ed Sec 50-55; Warden SPG Fellowship 55-64; Friends of USPG 65-71; Hon Can of Gambia from 70. *10 Midholm Road, Shirley, Croydon, Surrey.* (01-776 0650)

SYMES, Collin. Univ of Birm BA (2nd cl Engl) 47, MA 48. Bps' Coll Cheshunt. **d** 58 **p** 59 Lon. C of St Mich AA Enfield 58-60; St Anne Brondesbury w H Trin Kilburn 60-62; R of Scaldwell 62-66; R of Maidwell w Draughton 62-66; R of Yardley Hastings 66-68; V of Denton 66-68; Hon C of Rusthall Dio Roch from 68. *2 Berkeley Road, Tunbridge Wells, Kent.* (T Wells 32283)

SYMES, Percy Peter. b 24. Univ of Leeds BA 50. Coll of Resurr Mirfield 50. **d** 52 **p** 53 Ox. C of St Barn Ox 52-54; Headington Ox 54-56; Abingdon 56-61; PC (V from 68) of St Luke Reading 61-81; Drayton Dio Ox from 81. *Drayton Vicarage, Abingdon, Oxon.* (Drayton 374)

SYMES-THOMPSON, Hugh Kynard. b 54. Peterho Cam BA 76; MA 81. Univ of Dur Dipl Th 79. St Jo Coll Dur 77. **d** 79 **p** 80 Birm. C of Ch Ch Summerfield City and Dio Birm from 79. *13b Gillott Road, Birmingham, B16 0EU.*

SYMINGTON, Canon Alexander Aitken. b 02. Late Scho of Hertf Coll Ox 1st cl Cl Mods 24, Liddon Stud 26, BA (2nd cl Lit Hum) 26, MA 29. **d** 29 **p** 30 Southw. C of St Mary and St Cuthb Worksop 29-38; V of St Ippolyts w Gt Wymondley 39-57; RD of Hitchin 48-53; R of Pertenhall w Swineshead 57-71; RD of Riseley 57-64; Hon Can of St Alb 58-71; Can (Emer) from 71. *8 Field House Drive, Oxford.*

SYMON, Canon John Francis Walker. b 26. Univ of Edin MA 50. Edin Th Coll 50. **d** 52 **p** 53 Edin. C of St Cuthb Colinton Edin 52-56; CF 56-59; R of St Jo Evang Forfar 59-68; St Mary Dunblane Dio St Andr from 68; Can of St Ninian's Cathl Perth from 74. *St Mary's Rectory, Dunblane, FK15 0HQ.* (Dunblane 824225)

SYMON, John Walker. b 1895. Univ of Aber MA 19. Coates Hall Edin 19. **d** 21 Brech for Glas **p** 22 Glas. C of St Marg Newlands (in c of St Aid Clarkston) Glas 21-31; R of St Jas Stonehaven 31-38; P-in-c of Catterline 31-38; R of St Jo Evang New Pitsligo 38-44; St Andr Ardossan 44-45; Kirriemuir 55-65. *South View, Gellymill Street, Macduff, Banff.*

SYMON, Roger Hugh Crispin. b 34. St Jo Coll Cam 3rd cl Hist Trip pt i 58, BA (3rd cl Hist Trip pt ii) 59. Coll of Resurr Mirfield 59. **d** 61 Kens for Lon **p** 62 Lon. C of St Steph w St Jo Evang Westmr 61-66; Chap Univ of Surrey 66-74; C-in-c of Hascombe 66-68; V of Ch Ch Lanc Gate Lon 74-78; St Jas Paddington 78-79. *c/o 1 Porchester Gardens, W2 3LA.* (01-229 5089)

SYMONDS, Edward George. b 03. **d** 59 **p** 60 Leic. C of S Wigston 59-64; V of All S Leic 64-74; Surr 69-74. *17 Victoria Square, Penarth, S Glam, CF6 2EJ.*

SYMONDS, James Henry. b 31. Ripon Hall Ox 67. **d** 69 **p** 70 Win. C of Southn 69-71; CF 71-78; P-in-c of Orwell 78; V 78-80; P-in-c of Arrington 78; V 78-80; P-in-c of Wimpole 78; V 78-80; P-in-c of Croydon w Clapton 78; V 78-80. *Officers Mess, Mercian Depot, Whittington Barracks, Lichfield, WS14 9PY.* (Whittingtin 43334 ext 227)

SYMONDS, Canon Robert Pinder. b 10. Late Exhib of CCC Cam BA 32, MA 37. Linc Th Coll 32. **d** 34 **p** 35 Lon. C of All SS Hampton 34-36; Willoughby and Skendleby 36-38; Hawarden (in c of St Francis Sandycroft) 38-42; L to Offic at Crowland 42-46; M OGS from 44; Tutor Linc Th Coll 46-51; Chap 51-56; V of St Mary de Castro Leic 56-74; Chap Trin Hosp Leic and Pr at the Newarke 56-74; Exam Chap to Bp of Leic 58-78; Surr 59-74; Hon Can of Leic 73-74; Can (Emer) from 74; Sub-Warden of St Deiniol's Libr Hawarden 74-78; Chap H Trin Hosp Retford from 78; Perm to Offic Dio Southw from 80. *Rectory Farm, Rectory Road, Retford, Notts, DN22 7AY.* (Retford 700774)

SYMONDS, Thomas Powell. b 03. Sarum Th Coll 28. **d** 30 **p** 32 Lich. C of St Osw Oswestry 30-33; Huntingdon 33-35; V of St Mary Huntingdon and Chap Hunts Co Hosp 35-37; Chap of Ch Ch Yokohama 37-42; Chap Br Embassy Tokyo 41-42; Chap RNVR 43-46; Men Candidates' Sec SPG 46-49; Chap Ardingly Coll Dio Chich 49-54; V of Beeley w Edensor 54-71; Exam Chap to Bp of Derby 56-70; RD of Bakewell 63-70. *Parkside, Baslow, Bakewell, Derbys.* (Baslow 2349)

SYMONDS, Walter Herbert. b 04. Qu Coll Cam BA 27, MA 30. Lon Coll of Div 27. **d** 29 **p** 30 St Alb. C of St Paul St Alb 29-32; St Luke Portsea 32-34; Hillsborough w Wadsley Bridge 34-37; St Faith Maidstone 38-41; St Edw Leyton 41-43; V of N Shoebury 43-75. *9 Hemel Hempstead Road, Redbourn, Herts.*

SYMONDSON, Anthony Nigel. b 40. Cudd Coll 74. **d** 76 Lon **p** 77 Stepney for Lon. C of St Aug Kilburn 76-77; St Pet De Beauvoir Town 77-80; P-in-c of St Anne Hoxton Dio Lon from 80. *78 De Beauvoir Road, N1 5AT.* (01-254 7945)

SYMONS, Fernley Rundle. b 39. Peterho Cam BA 61, MA 71. St Steph Ho Ox 61. **d** 64 **p** 65 Ely. C of St Geo Chesterton 64-67; Henleaze 67-72; V of Shirehampton Dio Bris from 72. *St Mary's Vicarage, Priory Gardens, Shirehampton, Bristol, BS11 0BZ.* (Avonmouth 822737)

SYMONS, James Edward. b 28. K Coll Lon and Warm AKC 57. **d** 58 **p** 59 Newc T. C of St Jas Benwell Newc T 58-62; Alnwick 62-65; Prudhoe 65-67; V of Mickley Dio Newc T from 67. *Mickley Vicarage, Stocksfield, Northumb.* (Stocksfield 3342)

SYMONS, Peter Henry. b 25. K Coll Lon and Warm AKC 51. **d** 52 **p** 53 Ex. C of St Matt Ex 52-55; Brixham 55-59; Braunton 59-61; PC of Woolacombe 61-68; V 68-75; Kingsteignton Dio Ex from 75. *Kingsteignton Vicarage, Newton Abbot, Devon, TQ12 3BA.* (Newton Abbot 4915)

SYMONS, Stewart Burlace. b 31. Keble Coll Ox BA (3rd cl Physics) 55, MA 59. Clifton Th Coll. **d** 57 **p** 58 Lon. C of Hornsey Rise 57-60; St Geo Gateshead 60-61; Patcham 61-64; R of St Bride Stretford 64-71; V of St Jo Div Waterloo Dio Liv from 71. *16 Adelaide Terrace, Liverpool, L22 8QD.* (051-928 3793)

SYMONS, William Rex. Univ of Tor BA 38. Wycl Coll Tor LTh 39. **d** 38 **p** 39 Niag. C of St Pet Hamilton 38-42; R of Homer w Virgil and McNab 42-45; Caledonia w York 45-52; Lloydstown 52-63; Alliston 63-77. *Box 567, Penetanguishene, Ont, Canada.*

SYMS, Richard Arthur. b 43. Ch Coll Cam 2nd cl Engl Trip pt i 64, BA (2nd cl Th Trip pt ii) 66, MA 69. Wycl Hall Ox 66. **d** 68 **p** 69 S'wark. C of All SS New Eltham 68-72; Arts and Recreation Chap Dio Dur 72-73; C of St Mary (in c of St Mark) Hitchin 73-76; Team V 77-78. *27 Haygarth, London Road, Knebworth, Herts.* (Stevenage 811933)

SYNGE, Edward Francis. b 1900. Keble Coll Ox Hon Scho and 1st cl Cl Mods 21, Liddon Stud 23, BA (2nd cl Lit Hum) 23, 2nd cl Th 24, MA 32. St Steph Ho Ox 23. **d** 25 Calc for Chota N **p** 26 Chota N. Miss at Kamdara 25-32; Murhu 32-34; Lohardaga 35; Itki 37; Murhu 38-48; Exam Chap to Bp of Chota N 36-48; Treas Chota N Dioc Coun 37-39; in c of Vernacular Th Sch 39-40 and 46-47; Archd of Chota N 40-48; Chap of St Paul's Cathl Ranchi 45-46; R of Albury w St Martha Dio Guildf 48-59; Commiss to Bp of Chota N 48-70; RD of Cranleigh 55-59; V of Butleigh 59-69; Perm to Offic Dio Ox 69-80; Dio Chich from 80. *College of St Barnabas, Dormans, Lingfield, RH7 6NJ.*

SYNGE, Francis Charles. Selw Coll Cam Stewart of Rannoch Hebr Scho 1st cl Th Trip pt i 23, BA (2nd cl Th Trip) 24, MA 28. Wells Th Coll 26. **d** 27 **p** 28 B & W. C of St Andr Taunton 27-30; Chap S Afr Ch Rly Miss Dio S Rhod 30-33; R of Tostock 33-35; Vice-Prin Qu Coll Birm and Publ Pr Dio Birm 35-39; Dom Chap to Bp of Lon 39-45; Dep P-in-Ord to HM the King and L to Offic Dio Lon 40-45; Warden of St Paul's Coll Grahmstn 45-54; Dean and R of St Mark's Cathl Geo 54-59; Exam Chap to Bp of Geo 46-59; Prin of Ch Ch Coll Dio Ch Ch 59-64; Hon Can of Ch Ch 59-64; Exam Chap to Bp of Ch Ch 59-64; R of St Geo Kroonstad 65-68; Exam Chap to Bp of Bloemf 65-68; Archd of Kroonstad 65-68; L to Offic Dio Capetn 68-80; Perm to Offic from 80. *19 Oldbridge West, Somerset Oaks, Somerset West, CP, S Africa.*

SYNGE, Canon Michael Henry Randall. b 08. Late Chor Scho of K Coll Cam BA 30, MA 35. Cudd Coll 30. **d** 31 **p** 32 Derby. C of St Mary and All SS Chesterfield 31-34; Cirencester 34-37; V of Parkend 37-43; Chap RNVR 40-46; V of St Nich Strood 46-49; Spalding 49-59; Can and Preb of Linc Cathl 55-70; Can (Emer) from 70; Prec of Linc Cathl 59-64; V of Ditchling 64-70; Chap to Commun of Epiph Truro 70-73; Perm to Offic Dio Chelmsf 76-78. *5 Downsview, Small Dole, Henfield, W Sussex, BN5 9YB.*

SYNNOTT, Canon Patrick Joseph. b 18. **d** 52 **p** 54 Down. C of Ballymacarrett 52-55; Shankill 55-60; R of Scarva 60-63; I of Magheralin 63-74; RD of Shankill 70-74; I of St Donard Belf Dio Down from 74; Can of Down Cathl from 80; Dom Chap to Bp of Down from 80. *44 Cyprus Avenue, Belfast, BT5 5NT.* (Belf 659070)

SYRIA, *See* Jerusalem.

SYSON, Stanley Harvey. Ex Coll Ox BA (3rd cl Hist) 34, Dipl in Th 35. Wycl Hall Ox 34. **d** 36 **p** 37 Lon. C of St John Highbury Vale 36-38; CMS Miss Momb 38-39; CF (E Afr) 40-46; CMS Miss Buhiga 47-53; R of High Halstow w Hoo 53-56; C of St John Wynberg 56-62; Maputaland 62-63; Dir 63-73; R of Tugela Rivers 74-80. *Box 16, Kwambonambi, Natal, S Africa.*

SYTHES, George Paul Sutcliffe. b 07. TCD BA 29, MA 34. **d** 32 **p** 33 Kilm. C of Kinawley 32-35; C-in-c of Innishmagrath w Dowra 35-55; Derrylane 55-65. *5 Church Row, Belturbet, Co Cavan, Irish Republic.*

T

TAAGA, Balisasa Erisa. b 22. **d** and **p** 77 Boga-Z. P Dio Boga-Z. *BP 154, Bunia, Zaire.*

TA'AI, Abel. St Pet Coll Siota 66. **d** 68 **p** 70 Melan. P Dio Melan 68-75; Dio Centr Melan 75-76; on leave. *Pacific Theological College, Suva, Fiji.*

TABAARO, Eriasaph. d and **p** 79 W Ank. P Dio W Ank. *Box 25, Bushenyi, Uganda.*

TABERN, James. b 23. St Aid Coll 57. **d** 59 **p** 60 Liv. C of Garston 59-61; V of St Paul Hatton Hill Litherland 61-72; St Mark Gillingham 72-79; Lindow Dio Ches from 79. *Lindow Vicarage, Wilmslow, Ches.* (Alderley Edge 583251)

TABERNACLE, Peter Aufrère. b 22. SOC 72. **d** 74 Edmonton for Lon **p** 75 Lon. C of St Geo Enfield 74-80; St Jo Bapt w Epiph Corby Dio Pet from 80. *29 Pages Walk, Corby, Northants.* (Corby 3666)

TABI, Haggai. d 77 **p** 79 New Hebr. P Dio New Hebr 77-80; Dio Vanuatu from 80. *Lamalana, Central Pentecost, Vanuatu.*

TABIA, Yepeta. St Paul's Th Coll Limuru 66. **d** 67 **p** 69 N Ugan. P Dio N Ugan 67-76; Dio Yambio from 76. *ECS, Yambio, Sudan.*

TABO, Nagai. St Paul's Coll Moa I. **d** 69 **p** 70 Carp. P Dio Carp; Prec of Carp Cathl 76; P-in-c of Murray I Dio Carp from 77. *Box 79, Thursday Island, Queensland, Australia 4875.*

TABOR, John Tranham. b 30. Ball Coll Ox BA 56, MA 58. Ridley Hall Cam 55. **d** 58 Chich **p** 59 Lewes for Chich. C of Lindfield 58-62; Tutor Ridley Hall Cam 62-63; Chap 63-68; Warden Scargill Ho 68-75; R of Northchurch Dio St Alb from 75. *80 High Street, Northchurch, Berkhamsted, Herts, HP4 3QW.* (Berkhamsted 5312)

TABOR, Leonard Frank. St Steph Ho Ox 47. **d** 50 **p** 51 Chelmsf. C of St Thos of Cant Brentwood 50-55; V of Bobbing w Iwade 55-58; H Innoc S Norwood 58-66; All SS Westbrook Margate Dio Cant from 66. *All Saints' Vicarage, Hartsdown Road, Westbrook, Margate, Kent.* (Thanet 20795)

TABORN, John Selwyn. Keble Coll Ox BA (3rd cl Th) 31, MA 35. Wells Th Coll 31. **d** 32 **p** 33 Sheff. C of St Jas Doncaster 32-36; St Aug Sheff 36-40; V of St Thos Ap Werneth Oldham 40-44; Hook Surrey 44-61; R of Goodleigh 61-67; R of Stoke Rivers 61-67; V of Bampton Proper w Bampton Lew 67-74; Bampton Aston w Shifford 67-74; Perm to Offic Dio Ex from 74. *2 Wilbarn Road, Paignton, Devon.*

TABRAHAM, Canon Albert John. b 14. Univ of Birm Dipl Th 71. Coll of Resurr Mirfield 55. **d** 56 **p** 57 Birm. C of Oldbury 56-59; V of Stockland Green 59-70; RD of Aston from 68; V of Acocks Green 70-80; RD of Yardley 74-77; Hon Can of Birm Cathl from 78; Hon C of Stechford Dio Birm from 80. *221 Flaxley Road, Birmingham 33.*

TABUSE, Peter. d 78 **p** 79 Vic Nyan. P Dio Vic Nyan. *Box 93, Ngara, Tanzania.*

TADMAN, John Christopher. b 33. Lon Coll of Div 54. **d** 58 **p** 59 S'wark. C of St Jo Evang Blackheath 58-61; Ch Ch Surbiton Hill 61-64; V of Cratfield w Heveningham and Ubbeston 65-70; R of Kelsale w Carlton 70-74; Ashurst w Fordcombe 74-76; C-in-c of Penshurst Dio Roch 76-77; R (w Fordcombe) from 77. *Rectory, Penshurst, Tonbridge, Kent.* (Penshurst 316)

TAEJON, Lord Bishop in. *See* Pae, Right Rev Mark.

TAEJON, Assistant Bishop of. (Vacant)

TAFENI, Josiah David. St Bede's Coll Umtata 78. **d** and **p** 79 St John's. P Dio St John's. *PO Box 17, Umtata, Transkei.*

TAGG, Kenneth. b 09. AKC 34. **d** 34 **p** 35 Lon. C of St Thos Hanwell 34-37; Saltash 37-41; Offg C-in-c of Wembury 41-45; V 45-54; Hungerford w Denford 54-75; Surr 54-75; L to Offic Dio Win from 75. *17 East View Road, Ringwood, Hants, BH24 1PP.* (Ringwood 6858)

TAGGART, Charles Scott Lindsay. b 38. QUB BA (3rd cl German) 60. TCD Div Test (2nd cl) 62, **d** 62 **p** 63 Down. C of Knockbreda 62-64; Succr of St Patr Cathl Dub and Warden Cathl Gr Sch 64-70; R of Castledermot 70-73; Asst Master Gymnasium in den Pfarrwiesen, Sindelfinoen from 74. *D-7031 Nufringen, Alleenstr, W Germany.*

TAGGART, Geoffrey Marmaduke. b 11. Qu Coll Birm 54. **d** 56 **p** 57 Man. C of Astley Bridge 56-58; V of St Jas Bolton 58-60; St Steph and All Marts Lower Moor Oldham 60-71; Denshaw 71-76. *4 Pilling Lane, Lydiate, Merseyside, L31 4HF.*

TAGGART, Canon Justin Paul. b 11. Linc Th Coll 32. **d** 34 **p** 35 Linc. C of St Jo Evang-in-Spitalgate Grantham 34-40; St Nich w St John Newport Linc 40-45; V of Morton w Hacconby 45-52; St Andr w St Pet Langton-by-Horncastle (or Woodhall Spa) 52-76; R of Langton-by-Horncastle w Woodhall 52-76; C-in-c of Kirkstead 52-76; RD of Gartree 59-64; Can and Preb of Linc Cathl 68-77; Can (Emer) from 77. *Reedsbeck, Droghadfayle Road, Port Erin, IM.*

TAGGART, Thomas Reginald. b 04. Linc Th Coll 25. **d** 27 **p** 28 Linc. C of St John New Clee Grimsby 27-29; Asst P at Likoma Nyasa 29-30; P-in-c of Malindi 30-32; C of Horley 32-34; St Barn Hove 34-37; V of Walberton 37-44; CF (EC) 40-45; Hon CF 45; V of St Richard Haywards Heath 45-53; Org Sec SPCK Dio Chich 51-62; V of St Jo Div W Worthing 53-69; Chap Courtlands Hosp Worthing 54-69; Perm to Offic Dio Ox 69; Sarum from 79. *30 Talbot Road, Lyme Regis, Dorset.*

✠ **TAH, Right Rev Preh Paw.** **d** 31 **p** 34 Rang. P Dio Rang 31-66; Cons Asst Bp of Rang in H Trin Cathl Rang 13 Feb 66 by Bp of Rang; Bps Ah Mya and Aung Hla; Apptd Bp of Pa-an 70; res 72. *c/o St Peter's Cathedral, Bishops Kone, Pa-an, Kawthoolei, Burma.*

TAHERE, Te Wheoki Rahiri. St Jo Coll Auckld LTh 60. **d** 60 **p** 61 Auckld. C of Ellerslie 60-63; St Thos Auckld 63-65; Hokianga 65-67; V 68-72; Te Atatu Dio Auckld from 73; Exam Chap to Bp of Auckld 73-78; Perm to Offic Dio Auckld from 78. *14 Eddowes Street, Manurewa, Auckland, NZ.*

TAHI, John. **d** 77 **p** 79 New Hebr. P Dio New Hebr 77-80; Dio Vanuatu from 80. *Labultamwata, N Pentecost, Vanuatu.*

TAHIREVE, Barton. St Paul's Coll Lolowai 37. **d** 39 **p** 44 Melan. P Dio Melan 44-47; Can 57-70. *Dui Dui, Aoba, New Hebrides.*

TAILBY, Ian Renton. b 25. Univ of Otago BDS 50. **d** 77 Bp Spence for Auckld **p** 78 Auckld. Hon C of Kaitaia Dio Auckld from 77. *Box 58, Kaitaia, Auckland, NZ.*

TAILBY, Mark Kevan. b 36. K Coll Lon and Warm 60. **d** 64 Bp McKie for Cov **p** 65 Cov. C of Newbold-on-Avon 64-67; Stratford-on-Avon 67-70; CF 70-76; P-in-c of S Shoebury 76-79; Stambridge Dio Chelmsf from 79. *Stambridge Rectory, Rochford, Essex.* (Canewdon 272)

TAIT, Henry Alexander. b 30. St Chad's Coll Dur 65. **d** 66 **p** 67 Newc T. C of Hexham 66-69; R of Elmsett w Aldham 69-75; Educn Adv Dio St E 69-74; P-in-c of Kersey w Lindsey 74-75; R of Sandiacre 75-81; V of East Dereham Dio Nor from 81; P-in-c of Scarning Dio Nor from 81; Surr from 82. *Vicarage, Dereham, NR20 3AS.* (Dereham 3143)

TAIT, James Laurence Jamieson. b 47. St Jo Coll Dur 78. **d** 80 **p** 81 Man. C of Heyside 80-81; Westhoughton Dio Man from 81. *81 Wigan Road, Westhoughton, Bolton, Gtr Man.* (Westhoughton 812377)

TAIWO, Augustus Omotunde. Im Coll Ibad 60. **d** 62 **p** 63 Lagos. P Dio Lagos. *St Paul's Vicarage, Ilese, Ijebo-Ode Nigeria.*

TAKENS, Hendrik Jan. Coll Ho Ch Ch. **d** 55 **p** 56 Ch Ch. C of St Alb 55-56; Avonside 56-59; P-in-c 59-60; V of Ross w S Westland 60-64; Tuapeka 64-71; Hon C of Roslyn 71-72; P-in-c of Flagstaff 72-73; V of Bluff w Stewart I 73-78; Hon C of Mornington Dio Dun from 78. *23 Carnarvon Street, Dunedin, NZ.* (36-274)

TAKILMA, Comins. b 50. Bp Patteson Th Centre Kohimarama 70. **d** 73 **p** 74 Melan. P Dio Melan 73-75; Centr Melan from 75. *Reef Islands, Solomon Islands.*

TAKIRIMA, Benson. b 28. **d** 71 **p** 72 Lake Malawi. P Dio Lake Malawi. *PB Katimbira, Bua Court, Nkhotakota, Malawi.*

TAKURUA, Anaru Kingi. b 33. St Jo Coll Auckld. **d** 58 **p** 59 Wai. C of Gisborne 58-63; V of Waipawa Maori Past 63-68; Waiapu Maori Past 68-75; Turanga 75-78; C of Wel Maori Past Dio Wel from 78. *74 Wyndrum Avenue, Lower Hutt, NZ.* (699-694)

TALABI, Very Rev Samuel Bolaji. Melville Hall Ibad. **d** 56 **p** 57 Lagos. P Dio Lagos 56-58 and 59-76; C of St Alb Clifton Glos 58-59; Hon Can of Lagos 72-75; Archd of Ijebu 75-76; Provost of St Sav Cathl Ijebu from 77; Exam Chap to Bp of Ijebu from 77. *St Saviour's Cathedral, Box 16, Ijebu-Ode, Nigeria.* (Ijebu-Ode 49)

TALASA, Ven Ignatio. St Cypr Coll Tunduru 54. **d** 55 **p** 58 Masasi. P Dio Masasi; Dioc Archd of Masasi from 74; Can of Masasi from 74. *PO Box 92, Newala, Mtwara Region, Tanzania.*

TALAZO, Solomon Tamsanqa. St Pet Coll Rosettenville 57. **d** 60 Bp Paget for Johann **p** 61 Johann. P Dio Johann. *Box 5, Sebokeng, Johannesburg, S Africa.*

TALBOT, Alan John. b 23. BNC Ox BA (3rd cl Phil Pol and Econ) 49, MA 55. Coll of Resurr Mirfield 49. **d** 51 **p** 52 Lon. C of St Mary of Eton Hackney Wick 51-54; St Sav Portsea 54-63; Chap St Jo Coll Chidya 63-65; P-in-c of Namakambale 65-68; V of St Aug w St Phil Stepney 69-78; All H Twickenham Dio Lon from 78. *All Hallows Vicarage, Chertsey Road, Twickenham, TW1 1EW.* (01-892 1322)

TALBOT, Allan Peter Surman. b 09. Worc Coll Ox BA 30, MA 69. St Andr Coll Pampisford 46. **d** 46 **p** 47 Lich. C of Uttoxeter 46-48; Cheddleton 48-50; W Bromwich 50-52; V of Stonnall 52-55; V of Wal 52-55; Pattingham 55-62; Midgham w Brimpton 62-75. *14 Midgham Green, Reading, Berks.* (Woolhampton 3154)

TALBOT, Edgar White. b 21. TCD BA 43, MA 64. **d** 44 **p** 45 Oss. C of Enniscorthy 44-46; Killaloe 46-48; L to Offic Dio Dub 50; C of Ferns 51-53; I of Bannow 53-63; C-in-c of Inniscaltra 63-75; RD of Drumcliffe from 65; Dom Chap to Bp of Killaloe from 69; R of Aughrim U Dio Clonf from 75; Kilmacdaugh Group Dio Kilmac from 75. *Aughrim Rectory, Ballinsaloe, Galway, Irish Republic.* (0905-3735)

TALBOT, George Brian. b 37. Qu Coll Birm 78. **d** 80 **p** 81 Heref. C of St Martin City and Dio Heref from 80. *27 Webb Tree Avenue, Hereford.*

TALBOT, Jack. b 21. Lon Coll of Div 56. **d** 58 **p** 59 Man. C of St Jo Evang Old Trafford 58-61; V of St Thos Dixon Green Farnworth 61-71; Min of Tadley St Mary Conv Distr 71-73; V of N Tadley Dio Win from 73. *St Mary's Vicarage, Bishopswood Road, Tadley, Basingstoke, Hants RG26 6HQ.* (Tadley 4435)

TALBOT, James Edward. b 03. St Jo Coll Dur BA 26, Dipl Th 27, MA 29. **d** 27 **p** 28 Dur. C of St Geo Gateshead 27-30; H Trin Stockton-on-Tees 30-33; V of Dunston-on-Tyne 33-37; Chilton 37-48; Consett 48-59; Surr 48-59; R of Edmundbyers w Muggleswick 59-68; Perm to Offic Dio Dur from 68; Perm to Offic Dio Liv from 69. *18 Chantry Walk, Bryn, Wigan.*

TALBOT, John Frederick Gordon. Chich Th Coll. **d** 50 **p** 51 Lich. C of Ch Ch Wolverhampton 50-57; R of St Jo Evang Wednesbury 57-73; W Felton Dio Lich from 73. *West Felton Rectory, Oswestry, Salop.* (Queen's Head 228)

TALBOT, Canon John George Beamish. St Jo Coll Auckld LTh 37. **d** 38 Aotearoa for Wai **p** 38 Wai. C of St Aug Napier 38-40; Wairoa 40-43; CF (NZ) 43-46; V of Waerenga-a-Hika 46-54; Rotorua 54-65; St Pet Palmerston N 65-78; Can of Wai 58-65; Hon Can of Wel 74-78; Can (Emer) from 78; Offg Min Dio Wel from 78. *16 Dickson Street, Wanganui, NZ.*

TALBOT, John Herbert Boyle. b 30. TCD BA 51, MA 57. **d** 53 Cork for Dub **p** 54 Dub. C of St Pet Dub 53-57; Zion Ch Rathgar Dub 57-61; Chan V of St Patr Cathl Dub 56-61; Asst Hosp St Thos Hosp Lon 61-64; Min Can and Sacr of Cant Cathl 64-67; R of Brasted Dio Roch from 67. *Brasted Rectory, Westerham, Kent.* (Westerham 63491)

TALBOT, John Michael. b 23. SOC 75. **d** 78 **p** 79 Cant. Hon C of Em Ch S Croydon Dio Cant from 78. *2b Harewood Road, S Croydon, Surrey, CR2 7AL.* (01-688 9104)

TALBOT, Martin Robertson. b 20. Keble Coll Ox BA (2nd cl Phil Pol and Econ) 48, MA 48. Cudd Coll 48. **d** 49 **p** 50 Dur. C of St Pet Stockton-on-Tees 49-52; Chap and Lect at Qu Coll Birm and Publ Pr Dio Birm 52-56; V of Esh 56-66; PC of Hamsteels 56-66; Harton 66-67; V 68-80; R of Ewelme and Britwell Salome Dio Ox from 80; P-in-c of Brightwell Baldwin and of Cuxham w Easington Dio Ox from 80. *Ewelme Rectory, Oxford, OX9 6HP.* (Wallingford 37823)

TALBOT, Very Rev Maurice John. b 12. TCD BA and Div Test (2nd cl) 35, MA 43. **d** 35 **p** 36 Lim. C of Rathkeale w Nanenan 35-43; I 43-52; RD of Croom 48-52; I of Killarney 52-54; Dean and R of St Mary's Cathl Lim 54-71; Dean (Emer) from 71; Can and Preb of St Patr Cathl Dub 59-73; C of Kilmallock 71-73; L to Offic Dio Lim 75-80; R of Drumcliffe Dio Killaloe from 80. *Rectory, Ennis, Co Clare, Irish Republic.*

TALBOT, Reginald George. b 1900. G and C Coll Cam 2nd cl Hist Trip pt i 26, BA (2nd cl Th Trip pt i) 27, MA 31. St Aug Coll Cant. **d** 28 **p** 29 Lich. C of St Luke Leek 28-30;

Hednesford 30-37; Chap of Highcroft Hall and Erdington Children's Homes 37-45; V of Em Sparkbrook 45-51; Bordesley 51-55; Cotes Heath 55-60; R of Chawleigh w Cheldon 60-69; RD of Chulmleigh 64-69; LPr Dio Ex 70-80. *Southover House, Rusper Road, Ifield, Crawley, W Sussex RH11 0LN.* (0293 33795)

TALBOT, Richard Allen. b 06. MC 40. St D Coll Lamp Scho and Th and Hebr Pri 31, BA (1st cl Th) and Th and Hebr Pri 32, BD 45. **d** 32 **p** 33 Man. C of St Clem Ordsall Salford 32-35; St Jo Bapt Knaresborough 35-39; Min of Epiph Conv Distr Gipton Leeds 39; PC 39-43; CF (EC) 39-45; PC of St Pet Bramley 45-51; Surr 46-61; C-in-c of Knaresborough 51-53; V 53-65; Proc Conv Ripon 54-59; R of Hunsingore w Cowthorpe 65-74. *25 Boroughbridge Road, Knaresborough, N Yorks, HG5 0LY.* (Harrogate 863164)

TALBOT, Richard Henry. b 01. Selw Coll Cam 3rd cl Hist Trip pt i 24, BA 25, MA 42. Ridley Hall Cam 25. **d** 27 **p** 28 Dur. C of St Luke Darlington 27-29; Ch Ch W Hartlepool 29-33; C-in-c of St Nich Conv Distr Bp Wearmouth 33-37; Min 37-39; PC 39-49; V of St Edm Roundhay 49-67; CF (TA) 39-46; Hon CF 46; R of Thornton Watlass 67-75. *Manor House, Tunstead, Norwich, NR12 8AH.*

TALBOT-PONSONBY, Andrew. b 44. Univ of Leeds Dipl Th 66. Coll of Resurr Mirfield 66. **d** 68 **p** 70 St Alb. C of Radlett 68-70; St Martin Sarum 70-73; P-in-c of Acton Burnell w Pitchford 73-80; Cound 73-80; Frodesley 73-80; Kimbolton w Middleton-on-the-Hill and Hamnish Dio Heref 80-81; V from 81; P-in-c of Bockleton w Leysters Dio Heref 80-81; V from 81. *Kimbolton Vicarage, Leominster, Herefs.* (Leominstr 2024)

TALBOTT, Anthony Alexander. b 25. **d** 79 **p** 80 Waik. Hon C of St Andr Cam Dio Waik from 79. *113 Thornton Road, Cambridge, NZ.*

TALBOTT, Brian Hugh. b 34. RD 78. St Pet Hall Ox BA (3rd cl Th) 57, MA 64. Westcott Ho Cam. **d** 59 **p** 60 Newc T. C of H Cross Fenham Newc T 59-61; St Jo Bapt Newc T 61-64; Chap RNR from 63; Chap Barnard Castle Sch 64-71; Chap Bp's Stortford Coll and Hon C of Bp's Stortford Dio St Alb from 71; Sen Chap RNR Lon from 77. *96 Hadham Road, Bishops Stortford, Herts.* (Bps Stortford 51845)

TALENT, Canon Jack. AKC 49. St Bonif Coll Warm. **d** 50 **p** 51 Linc. C of St Wulfram Grantham 50-59; R of Corsley w Chapmanslade 59-62; R and Dir of Vryburg 62-67; P-in-c of H Cross Miss St John's 67-72; Archd of Kuruman 72-81; R of St Mary Kuruman 72-81; St John Mafeking Dio Kimb K from 81; Hon Can of Kimb K from 81. *Box 129, Mafeking, Bophuthatswana, CP, S Africa.*

TALU, Daniel. Patteson Th Centre Kohimarama. **d** 72 Melan. d Dio Melan 72-75; Dio Ysabel from 75. *Toelegu, Havulei District, Solomon Islands.*

TAMA, Jeremiah. b 48. St Paul's Coll Limuru 73. **d** and **p** 75 Nai, P Dio Nai. *Box 17174, Nairobi, Kenya.*

TAMAHORI, Canon John Thornton. Te Aute Coll LTh 47. **d** 39 **p** 40 Wai. C Dio Wai 39-40; V of Ohinemutu Past 40-43; Wairoa and Mohaka Past 43-53; Tonga-Nukualofa 53-60; Chap Te Aute Coll 61-67; Can of Wai 63-71; Can (Emer) from 72; Lect of St Jo Coll Auckld from 71; Hon C of Maori Miss Dio Auckld from 77. *St John's College, Meadowbank, Auckland 5, NZ.* (581-856)

TAMARAPA, Wi Mauri. b 38. **d** 74 **p** 76 Wai. Hon C of Gate Pa 74-77; L to Offic Dio Nel 77; Hon C of Hokitika 77-80; Perm to Offic Dio Waik from 80. *Box 55, Katikati, NZ.*

TAMATAVE, Diocese of. *See* Toamasina.

TAMBLING, Peter Francis. b 20. St Pet Hall Ox BA (3rd cl Th) 47. Westcott Ho Cam. **d** 49 **p** 50 Ches. C of Stockport 49-51; Westbury 52-56; R of Bishopstrow and Boreham 56-64; Zeals w Stourton 64-73; C-in-c of Bourton w Silton 71-73; R of Upper Stour 73-74; Glenfield Dio Leic from 74; RD of Sparkenhoe III 76-81. *Glenfield Rectory, Leicester, LE3 8DG.* (Leicester 871604)

TAMBLYN, Anthony John. b 47. St Barn Coll Adel 71. **d** 74 Adel **p** 75 Bp Renfrey for Adel. C of Burnside 74-77; R of Warracknabeal Dio Bal from 78. *c/o Rectory, Warracknabeal, Vic, Australia 3393.*

TAME, Walter James. **d** 27 **p** 28 Bal. C of Beeac 27-28; P-in-c of Harrow w Outstations 28-30; Natimuk 30-34; V of Rupanyup 34-36; Beaufort 36-47; Coleraine 47-60; Can of Bal 57-60; Perm to Offic Dio Bal 60; Dio Melb from 60. *Unit 3, Strathallan Village, Coleraine, Vic., Australia 3315.* (055-75 2491)

TAMMIK, Robert. b 52. St Jo Coll Auckld 74. **d** 75 **p** 76 Wai. C of St Geo Whakatane Dio Wai from 75. *6 Churchill Street, Whakatane, NZ.* (5502)

TAMPLIN, Francis William St John. b 1891. TCD BA 15, MA 18. **d** 16 **p** 17 Clogh. C of Clones 16-18; Portarlington 18-25; C-in-c of Ballycommon w Killaderry 25-28; Coolbanagher 28-33; I of Dunganstown w Redcross 33-53; Killiskey and RD of Rathdrum 53-62; Can of Ch Ch Cathl Dub 50-62; Treas 59-62. *c/o Milfield, Shankill, Co Dublin, Irish Republic.* (854249)

TAMPLIN, Peter Harry. b 44. Sarum Wells Th Coll 71. **d** 73 **p** 74 St Alb. C of Digswell 73-76; St Luke Chesterton (in c of St Aug) Dio Ely from 76. *40 Eachard Road, Cambridge, CB3 0HY.* (Cam 54850)

TAMPLIN, Roger Ian. b 41. K Coll Lon and Warm BD and AKC 63. **d** 64 **p** 65 S'wark. C of St Helier 64-68; Camberwell 68-72; Miss Dio Zanz T 73-74; P-in-c of Anstey 74-78; Brent Pelham w Meesden 74-78. *39 Benslow Lane, Hitchin, Herts.* (Hitchin 4156)

TAN, James Choon Kwan. Trin Th Coll Sing BD 79. **d** 79 **p** 80 Sing. C of St Pet City and Dio Sing from 79. *St Peter's Church, 1 Tavistock Avenue, Singapore 1995.*

TAN, John Teng Wai. Univ of Malaya BA 60. **d** and **p** 80 (NSM). P Dio Sing. *St Andrew's Junior College, Singapore.*

TAN, Pek Hua. Trin Th Coll Sing 71. **d** 75 **p** 76 Sing. C of St Pet Sing 75-81; P-in-c of Good Shepherd City and Dio Sing from 81. *2 Dundee Road, Singapore 0314.*

TAN, Wee Chong. b 30. Univ of Louisville BSc 58. Butler Univ MSc 63. Univ of Indiana PhD 66. Lon Coll of Div 68. **d** 70 **p** 71 Lon. C of St Jas Paddington 70-71. *Hormel Institute, Austin, Minnesota 55912, USA.*

TANBURN, John Walter. b 30. Jes Coll Cam BA (2nd cl Law Trip pt ii) 53, MA 57. Clifton Th Coll 54. **d** 56 **p** 57 Roch. C of Ch Ch Orpington 56-59; Min of St Barn Eccles Distr St Paul's Cray 59-64; V of St Barn Cray 64-67; Chap Stowe Sch 67-72; Wymondham Coll from 72; R of Morley Dio Nor from 72. *Morley Rectory, Wymondham, Norf.* (Wymondham 603217)

TANDA, Athamasius Mdoda. b 27. **d** 79 St John's (APM). d Dio St John's. *PO St Cuthbert's, Transkei.*

TANDWA, Absalom Vusumzi. St Bede's Coll Umtata 64. **d** 68 **p** 71 St John's. P Dio St John's. *PO Nqamakwe, Transkei, S Africa.*

TANDY, Kenneth Edward. Univ of Windsor Ont BA 71. Wycl Coll Tor LTh 74. **d** 74 Qu'App. C of Pipestone 74-76; I of Notukeu 71-79. *Box 274, Hodgeville, Sask, Canada.* (677-2339)

TANE, Craven. St Jo Coll Auckld 57. **d** 61 **p** 63 Auckld. C of St Mark Remuera 61-62; New Lynn 62-64; L to Offic Dio Auckld 65-69; Hon C of Maori Miss Dio Auckld from 77. *106, Avondale Road, Avondale, Auckland 7, NZ.*

TANGAERE, Honaara Waikari. b 19. **d** 76 Wai (APM). Hon C of Turangi Past Dio Wai from 76. *5 Argyle Street, Gisborne, NZ.*

TANGANYIKA, CENTRAL, Lord Bishop of. *See* Madina, Right Rev Yohana.

TANGANYIKA, CENTRAL, Assistant Bishop of. *See* Mohamed, Right Rev Alpha Francis.

TANGANYIKA, SOUTH-WEST, Lord Bishop of. *See* Mlele, Right Rev Joseph Williard.

TANGANYIKA, WESTERN, Lord Bishop of. *See* Kahurananga, Most Rev Musa.

TANGI, Salesi. b 22. **d** 76 **p** 77 Polyn. P Dio Polyn. *PO Box 31, Nukualofa, Tonga, Pacific Ocean.*

TANGO, Patteson. **d** 79 **p** 80 Centr Melan. P Dio Centr Melan. *Savo Islands, Guadalcanal Region, Solomon Islands.*

TANGOHAU, Harry Hauwaho. b 14. St Jo Coll Auckld 48. **d** 51 **p** 52 Wai. C of St Aug Napier 51-54; Rotorua and Taupo 54-59; V of Te Ngae Maori Past 59-70; Ruatoki Maori Past 70-72; L to Offic Dio Wai 72-78; Hon C of Turanga Past 78-80; Offg Min Dio Wai from 80. *Box 108, Tolaga Bay, NZ.*

TANKARD, Reginald Douglas Alan. b 37. Sarum Th Coll 60. **d** 62 **p** 63 York. C of Howden 62-65; Heckmondwike 65-67; CF 67-70; Hon C of St Marg Thornbury Dio Bradf from 81. *1 Grenfell Terrace, Bradford, BD3 7EJ.*

TANN, David John. b 31. K Coll Lon and Warm BD and AKC 57. **d** 58 **p** 59 S'wark. C of St Anne Wandsworth 58-60; Sholing (in c of St Francis) 60-64; Asst Chap Univ of Lon 64-65; C of All SS Fulham 65-68; Hon C from 72; L to Offic Dio Lon from 68. *77 Parkview Court, Fulham High Street, SW6 3LL.* (01-736 6018)

TANNAR, Norman Edgar. Angl Th Coll Vancouver, LTh 48. **d** 47 **p** 48 New Westmr. C of St Phil Vancouver 47-49; Miss at Selkirk 49-51; R of Whitehorse 51-53; V of St Andr Vancouver 53-61; R of Summerland 61-71; V of Creston Dio Koot from 71. *Box 781, Creston, BC, Canada.* (428-4248)

TANNER, Alan John. b 25. SS Coll Cam 43. Linc Coll Ox BA 52, MA 65. Coll of Resurr Mirfield, 52. **d** 54 Kens for Lon **p** 55 Lon. C of Hendon 54-58; V of St Paul S Harrow 58-60; Dir Coun for Christian Stewardship Dio Lon 60-65; Dir of Lay Training Dio Lon 65-71; Sec Coun for Miss and Unity Dio Lon from 65-80; V of St Nich Cole Abbey Lon 66-78; Pr to The Charterhouse from 73; Sec Gtr Lon Chs Coun from 76; M BCC from 76; R of St Botolph without Bishopsgate City and Dio Lon from 78; P-in-c of St Ethelburga within Bishopsgate City and Dio Lon from 78; All H Lon Wall City and Dio Lon from 80; Bp of Lon Ecumen Officer from 81. *St Botolph's Vestry, Bishopsgate, EC2M 3TL.* (01-588 1053)

TANNER, Bernard William. b 1894. Keble Coll Ox BA 19, MA 20. Bps' Coll Cheshunt 19. **d** 20 **p** 21 Lon. C of St Mary of Eton Hackney Wick 20-24; St Phil Kens 24-26; M of Bush Bro Busselton 26-30; P-in-c of Bo-allia 30; C-in-c of N Aldrington Conv Distr 31-38; V of Portfield 38-50; C-in-c of St Aug Preston Pk Brighton 50-53; V of Wartling Dio Chich 54-70; Seq of Bodle Street Green 54-58; R 58-70; Perm to Offic Dio Chich from 70. *Ramsay Hall, Byron Road, Worthing, BN11 3HN.*

TANNER, Carl Errington. Univ of NZ BA 28. NZ Bd of Th Stud LTh 29. **d** 29 **p** 30 Auckld. C of St Mary's Cathl Parnell Auckld 29-33; Hastings 33-35; V of Reefton 35-38; Amuri 38-44; C-in-c of Picton 43; V of Riccarton 44-55; Geraldine 55-60; Waihao Downs 60-65. *24 Selwyn Road, Napier, NZ.*

TANNER, Frank Hubert. b 38. St Aid Coll. **d** 66 **p** 67 St E. C of St Marg Ipswich 66-69; St Pet Mansfield 69-71; V of Huthwaite 71-79; Chap to the Deaf Dio Southw from 79. *28 Alexandra Avenue, Mansfield, Notts.* (Mansfield 23847)

TANNER, Frederick James. b 24. **d** 64 **p** 65 Mbale. Prin of Kabwangasi Tr Coll 65-69; Hd Master Summerhill Jun Mixed Sch Bris from 69; Hon C of Chew Magna w Dundry Dio B & W from 81. *Four Winds, Wells Road, Dundry, Bristol, BS18 8NE.* (Bristol 644568)

TANNER, Canon Laurence Ernest. b 17. Late Crabtree Exhib and Welsh Ch Exhib of St Cath Coll Cam 2nd cl Hist Trip pt i 38, BA (2nd cl Hist Trip pt ii) 39, MA 43. St Mich Coll Llan. **d** 40 **p** 41 Llan. C of Pentyrch 40-42; Chap of Cranleigh Sch and LPr Dio Guildf 42-64; V of Shamley Green 64-71; RD of Cranleigh 68-71; Res Can of Guildf Cathl and Dir of Ordinands from 71; Sub-Dean from 72; Exam Chap to Bp of Guildf from 74. *4 Cathedral Close, Guildford, Surrey.* (Guildford 75140)

TANNER, Richard Charles. b 51. York Univ Ont BA 73. Wycl Coll Tor MDiv 76. **d** 76 Bp Read for Tor **p** 77 Tor. C of St Timothy Tor 76-78; I of Coldwater-Medonte 78-80; C of Woodbridge Dio Tor from 80. *2850 Jane Street, Downsview, Ont, Canada.*

TANNOCK, David Alexander. b 40. St Jo Coll Auckld 70. **d** 72 Bp McKenzie for Wel **p** 73 Wel. C of St Matt Masterton 72-76; V of Bulls Rongotea 76-80; Tinui Dio Wel from 80. *Vicarage, Tinui, NZ.*

TANSILL, Canon Derek Ernest Edward. b 36. St D Coll Lamp BA 61. Ripon Hall, Ox 61. **d** 63 **p** 64 Lon. C of St Luke Chelsea 63-67; P-in-c of St Nich Conv Distr Saltdean 67-69; V of Saltdean 69-73; Billingshurst Dio Chich from 73; RD of Horsham from 77; Can and Preb of Chich Cathl from 81. *Vicarage, Billingshurst, Sussex.* (Billingshurst 2332)

TANSLEY, Romney. b 41. K Coll Lon and Warm BD (3rd cl) and AKC 64. **d** 65 Hulme for Man **p** 66 Man. C of St Anne Longsight Royton 65-68; Chap St Hilda's Coll Belize 68-70; R of Stann Creek and Chap Stann Creek High Sch 70-71; V of St Pet Westleigh 72-77. *99 Dursley Road, Eastbourne, Sussex.*

TANSWELL, Duanne Le Roy Hughes. b 42. Atlantic Sch of Th 76. **d** 78 Bp Hatfield for NS. On leave. *20 Coupar Terrace, Truro, NS, Canada, B2N 5L3.*

TANTON, Ven George Stavert. K Coll NS BA 45, LTh 38, Hon DD 67. **d** 38 **p** 39 NS. C of Ch Ch Dartmouth 38-44; Chap RCAF 43-44; R of Tangier 44-58; St Mark Halifax 58-67; St Pet Cathl Charlottetown 67-74; Hon Can of NS 60-63; Can 63-67; Archd of PEI 67-74; Archd (Emer) from 74. *Bridmote, Boutilier's Point, Halifax, NS, Canada.* (826-2562)

TANZANIA, Metropolitan of Province of. *See* Kahurananga, Most Rev Musa.

TAPLIN, John. b 35. St Alb Min Tr Scheme 78. **d** 81 St Alb. C of Knebworth Dio St Alb from 81. *4 Oak Road, Woolmer Green, Knebworth, Herts, SG3 6LS.*

TAPLIN, Stewart Tennent Eaton. b 46. Ridley Coll Melb ThL 69. **d** 72 Melb. C of St Geo Reservoir 72-74; St Luke Stocking Farm Leic 74-76; Chap Yarra Valley Sch Dio Melb from 78. *1/30 Mount Dandenong Road, East Ringwood, Vic, Australia 3135.* (870 9729)

TAPSFIELD, Alan Charles. b 27. Selw Coll Cam BA 51. Linc Th Coll 51. **d** 53 **p** 54 Guildf. C of Hindhead 53-55; St Paul Egham Hythe 55-58; Ash w Ash Vale 58-63; V of Newborough w Ch Ch on Needwood 63-76; P-in-c of Trysull Dio Lich from 76. *Trysull Vicarage, Wolverhampton, WV5 7HR.* (Wombourne 892647)

TARAI, William. St Pet Coll Siota 62. **d** 64 **p** 65 Melan. P Dio Melan 64-75; Dio Centr Melan from 75; Dioc Sec Dio Centr Melan from 76. *Taroaniara, Gela, Solomon Islands.*

TARALATO, Remigius. St Aid Coll Dogura. **d** 46 **p** 51 New Guinea. P Dio New Guinea 46-71; Dio Papua from 71. *Anglican Church, Boianai, Samarai, Papua, New Guinea.*

TARATIBU, Vincent. **d** 75 **p** 76 Zanz T. P Dio Zanz T. *Box 35, Korogwe, Tanzania.*

TARDY, Lorne Randolph. b 56. McGill Univ Montr BTh 78. Montr Dioc Th Coll 75. **d** 79 **p** 80 Montr. C of St Mich AA Pierrefonds 79-81; St Geo, St Anne-de-Bellevue Dio Montr from 81. *262 Maple Drive, Pincourt, Queb, Canada.*

TARENYIKA, Douglas Tarambgwa. b 20. **d** and **p** 72 Mashon (APM). P Dio Mashon. *PO Daramombe, via Enkeldoorn, Rhodesia.*

TARGETT, Clifford. b 29. K Coll Lon and Warm AKC 56. **d** 57 **p** 58 S'wark. C of St Jo Evang E Dulwich 57-60; Glastonbury 60-62; Alverstoke 62-65; R of Binstead 65-72; V of Shorwell w Kingston 72-80. *51 Collingwood Road, Shanklin, IW, PO37 7LP.*

TARI, Christopher. **d** 79 New Hebr **p** 81 Vanuatu. P Dio New Hebr 79-80; Dio Vanuatu from 80. *Waileni, Longana, Aoba, Vanuatu.*

TARI, Frank Bollen. Bp Patteson Th Centre Kohimarama 75. **d** 78 **p** 79 New Hebr. P Dio New Hebr 78-80; Dio Vanuatu from 80. *Lolowai, Vanuatu.*

TARIAMBARI, Reuben. Newton Coll Dogura 68. **d** 71 **p** 72 Bp Ambo for Papua. P Dio Papua 71-77; Dio Aipo from 77. *Box 340, Madang, Papua New Guinea.*

TARIFA, Enosa. **d** 72 **p** 73 Sudan. P Dio Sudan 72-76; Dio Yambio from 76. *ECS, Nadiangere, Yambio, Sudan.*

TARILEO, Richard Paley. b 22. **d** 73 **p** 74 Bp Rawcliffe for Melan. P Dio Melan 73-75; Dio New Hebr 76-80; Dioc Sec New Hebr 77-80. *Lolowai, Longana, Vanuatu.*

TARIVUTI, Levi. Patteson Th Centre Kohimarama. **d** 71 Melan. d Dio Melan 71-75; Dio New Hebr 75-80; Dio Vanuatu from 80. *Lovuibakagoromaraga, Aoba, Vanuatu.*

TARLETON, Denis Reginald. b 12. TCD BA 35, Div Test (2nd cl) 36, MA 45. **d** 36 **p** 37 Lim. C of St Mary's Cathl Lim 36-38; St John Egremont 38-40; CF (EC) 40-46; CF (R of O) 50-61; I of Kilcornan w Ardcanny 46-49; Tullyaughnish w Milford 49-51; R of Dromore 51-59; Devenish w Boho 59-63; Priv Chap to Bp of Clogh 60-63; Perm to Offic Dio Down from 67; Hon P Bangor Abbey 71-79. *14a Knockdene Park, Knock, Belfast, BT5 7AD, N Ireland.*

TARLETON, Peter. b 46. Univ of Dub BA 72, (Div Test) 73, MA 80. TCD 69. **d** 73 Cork. C of St Luke w St Ann Shandon 73-75; Drumcondra 75-78; V of St Mich Lim 78-82; R of Drumgoon Dio Kilm from 82. *Rectory, Cootehill, Co Cavan, Irish Republic.*

TARLETON, Canon Terrence Anthony. Wycl Coll Tor LTh 67. **d** 67 Tor. C of St Paul Bloor Street 67-70; R of Cobourg Dio Tor from 70; Can of Tor from 77. *118 King Street East, Cobourg, Ont., Canada.* (416-372 3442)

TAROHOAISI, Matthias. Bp Patteson Th Centre Kohimarama. **d** 71 Melan. d Dio Melan 71-75; Dio Centr Melan from 75. *Pamua, San Cristoval, Solomon Islands.*

TARR, James Robert. b 39. Bps' Coll Cheshunt 64. **d** 67 **p** 68 Ripon. C of Wortley 67-69; Hunslet 70-73; V of Moor Ends 73-77; Cross Stone Dio Wakef from 77. *Cross Stone Vicarage, Todmorden, Yorks. Lancs.* (Todmorden 3516)

TARRANT, John Michael. b 38. Late Scho of St Jo Coll Cam Sen Opt 58, BA (2nd cl Mor Sc Trip pt ii) 59. MA 63. Ball Coll Ox BA (3rd cl Th) 62. Ripon Hall Ox 60. **d** 62 **p** 63 Lon. C of Chelsea Old Ch 62-65; Chap and Lect St Pet Coll of Educn Saltley 66-70; M of Ecumen Centre Belmopan Bel 70-75; V of Forest Row Dio Chich from 75. *Vicarage, Forest Row, E Sussex, RH18 5AF.* (Forest Row 2595)

TARRIS, Canon Geoffrey John. b 27. Em Coll Cam BA (3rd cl Mus Trip pt i) 50, MA 55. Westcott Ho Cam 51. **d** 53 **p** 54 St Alb. C of Abbots Langley 53-55; Prec of St Jas Cathl Ch Bury St Edms 55-59; V of Bungay 59-72; Surr from 63; RD of S Elmham 65-72; V of St Mary-le-Tower (w St Lawr and St Steph from 78) Ipswich 72-81; Hon Can of St E Cathl 74-81; Can Res of St E from 81. *1 Abbey Precincts, Bury St Edmunds, Suffolk, IP33 1RS.*

TASIE, Christian. Trin Coll Umuahia 80. **d** 81 Ow. d Dio Ow. *St Mary's Church, PO Box 35, Oguta, Imo State, Nigeria.*

TASKER, Harry Beverley. b 41. Wycl Hall Ox 64. **d** 67 **p** 68 Man. C of St Paul Withington 67-71; All SS Bingley 71-72; Chap RAF 72-76; R of Publow w Pensford, Compton Dando and Chelwood Dio B & W from 76. *Rectory, Compton Dando, Bristol.* (Compton Dando 221)

TASKER, Peter John. Moore Th Coll Syd ACT ThL (2nd cl) 63. **d** 63 **p** 64 Syd. C of W Wollongong 64-65; Chatswood 65-66; Engadine w Heathcote 67-69; CMS Miss 69-70; V of St Geo Penang 70-76; Asst Gen Sec CMS for NSW 77-78; Gen Sec from 78; L to Offic Dio Syd from 77. *93 Bathurst Street, Sydney, Australia 2000.* (267-3711)

TASKER, Reginald Oscar. b 11. St D Coll Lamp BA (3rd cl Engl) 34. St Mich Coll Llan 35. **d** 36 **p** 37 Llan. C of Tonyrefail 36-38; Dowlais 38-43; Chap RAFVR 43-47; PC of the Ascen Derringham Bank 47-49; Chap of Ch Ch Amsterdam 49-50; C-in-c of Llanllowell w Llanbadoc 50-55; CF (TA) from 51; R of Blaina Aberystruth 55-65; Llanwern w

Bishton 65-81; RD of Netherwent 72-80; Surr 76-81. *Address temp unknown.*

TASMANIA, Lord Bishop of. (Vacant)

TASMANIA, Assistant Bishop of. *See* Jerrim, Right Rev Henry Allingham.

TASMANIA, Dean of. *See* Parsons, Very Rev Jeffrey Michael Langdon.

TASSELL, Albert Henry. St Francis Coll Brisb ACT ThL 37. **d** 37 Perth **p** 38 Bunb for Perth. C of St John Fremantle 37-39; Chap Forrest River Miss 39-40; Harvey 40-42; Chap AIF 42-46; R of Manjimup 46-52; Commiss Bunb 52-54; Can Res and R of Bunb 54-58; R of Subiaco 58-59; L to Offic Dio C & Goulb 63-64; CF (Austr) 59-65; R of Beverley w Brookton 65-78; Hon Can of Perth 73-78; Perm to Offic Dio Perth from 78. *Parry House, Lesmurdie, W Australia 6076.*

TASSELL, Douglas Rene. b 15. St Edm Hall, Ox BA (3rd cl Fr) 37. MA 52. Wycl Hall, Ox 37. **d** 39 **p** 40 Worc. C of St Geo Kidderminster 39-46; Chap RAFVR 42-46; C of St Bart Wilmslow 46-49; PC of Lower Peover 49-59; R of Lexden 59-65; Asst RD of Colchester 65; R of Tattenhall 65-69; Delamere 69-74; RD of Middlewich 69-74; P-in-c of Welland 74-79; Chap of St Jas Sch W Malvern 77-81. *Fairfield, Castlemorton, Malvern, Worcs, WR13 6JB.* (Birtsmorton 263)

TASSELL, Canon Dudley Arnold. b 16. K Coll Lon and Warm BD (2nd cl) and AKC (1st cl) 49. **d** 49 **p** 50 S'wark. C of All SS New Eltham 49-55; V of St Andr Catford 55-63; R of Rotherhithe 63-76; RD of Bermondsey 69-76; Hon Can of S'wark 72-76; Can (Emer) from 76; V of All SS Spring Pk Croydon Dio Cant from 76; RD of Croydon Addington 81. *All Saints' Vicarage, Bridle Road, Shirley, Croydon, CRO 8HD.* (01-777 4447)

TASSINARI, Frederick Leonard. Dalhousie Univ NS BA 66. K Coll NS. **d** 67 NS. R of Falkland 67-69; St Paul Halifax 69-70; R of St Martins 70-76; Bridgetown Dio NS from 76. *Box 341, Bridgetown, NS, Canada.* (665-4319)

TATCHELL, Canon David Donald George. Univ of Sask BA 57. Em Coll Sktn LTh 56. **d** 56 **p** 57 Sktn. R of St Timothy Sktn 56-66; Ch Ch Calg 66-80; Can St John's Cathl Sktn 65-66; Hon Can of Calg from 73; on staff of WCC from 80. *150 Route de Ferney, 1211 Geneva 20, Switzerland.*

TATE, Andrew. d 75 **p** 76 New Hebr. P Dio New Hebr 75-80; Dio Vanuatu from 80. *Point Cross, S Pentecost, Vanuatu.*

TATE, Harold Richard. b 24. St Jo Coll Dur BA 50. **d** 51 **p** 52 Man. C of St Jas Moss Side 51-54; C-in-c of Langley Conv Distr 54-60; R of St Pet Blackley 60-79; Chap Booth Hall Hosp 60-79; V of Ch Ch Alsager Dio Ches from 79. *Christ Church Vicarage, Church Road, Alsager, Stoke-on-Trent, ST7 2HS.* (Alsager 3727)

TATE, Henry Charles Osmond. K Coll Lon. **d** 65 **p** 66 Win. C of St Andr Boscombe Bournemouth 65-68; R of Winfrith Newburgh w Chaldon Herring 68-78; V of Chardstock Dio Ex from 78. *Vicarage, Chardstock, Axminster, Devon, EX13 7BY.* (0460-20005)

TATE, John Alexander. b 13. Selw Coll Cam BA 37, MA 43. Cudd Coll 37. **d** 39 **p** 40 Newc T. C of St Mary Newc T 39-41; Seaton Hirst 41-46; V of St Phil Newc T 47-50; St Jo Div Kennington 50-62; Commiss Korea 53-54; Zanz T 54-68; Sub-Warden Commun St Mary Virg Wantage 62-76; Chap N Foreland Lodge from 76; L to Offic Dio Win from 76. *North Foreland Lodge, Sherfield-on-Loddon, Basingstoke, Hants.* (Basingstoke 882431)

TATE, John Robert. b 38. Univ of Dur BA 61, Dipl Th 69, MA 71. Cranmer Hall Dur 67. **d** 70 **p** 71 Blackb. C of Bare 70-73; V of St Jas Darwen 73-81; Caton w Littledale Dio Blackb from 81. *Caton Vicarage, Brook House, Lancaster, LA2 9NX.* (Caton 770300)

TATE, Robert John Ward. b 24. St Jo Coll Morpeth ACT ThL 48. **d** 49 **p** 50 Newc. C of Hamilton 49-52; Mayfield 52-53; Chap RN 53-79; Hon Chap to HM the Queen 76-79; Perm to Offic Dio Newc from 80. *119 Sunshine Parade, Sunshine, NSW, Australia 2264.*

TATHAM, Joseph George Tatham. b 1888. Hertf Coll Ox BA 11, MA 14. Ely Th Coll 12. **d** 13 **p** 14 Ripon. C of St Hilda Leeds 13-19; St Sav Ealing 19-32; Ch Ch Ealing 34-39; Perm to Offic Dio Lon 39-45; R of Stock Harvard (w Ramsden Bellhouse to 64) 45-68; L to Offic Dio Chelmsf from 69. *1 Rectory Close, Stock, Ingatestone, Essex CM4 9BP.*

TATKEY, Nehemiah Kipsambu. Ch Tr Centre Kapsabet 62. **d** 63 **p** 65 Nak. P Dio Nak 63-79. *Box 988, Eldoret, Kenya.*

TATNALL, Alec James. b 09. Codr Coll Barb 51. **d** 52 **p** 53 Guy. C of St Phil Georgetown 53-55; V of Morawhanna 55-62; Chap at Paramaribo and V of Skeldon w Leeds Guy 62-67; C of St Andr Catford 68-69; R of St Pet Orange Walk 69-71; R of St Mary Virg Bel 71-75; C of Hale 75-79; Chap at Livery Dole Ex from 79. *9 Livery Dole, Exeter, EX2 5DT.* (0392-79027)

TATTERSALL, Canon George Neville. b 10. Late Cho Exhib of Em Coll Cam 2nd cl Math Trip pt i, 30, BA (Math Trip pt ii, Aegr) 32, MA 36. Ridley Hall, Cam 32. **d** 33 **p** 34 Man. C of St Paul Kersal 33-37; St Mich Flixton 37-39; R of St Mark Cheetham Hill Man 39-42; Bucklesham w Brightwell and Foxhall 42-50; V of Batley Dio Wakef from 50; Hon Can of Wakef from 68. *Vicarage, Batley, Yorks.*

TATTERSALL, Robert Edward. b 1900. Ely Th Coll 27. **d** 29 **p** 30 Blackb. C of St Marg Burnley 29-31; Miss P St Cypr Native Miss Capetn 31-34; C of St Paul Capetn 34-36; L to Offic Dio Capetn 36-37; R of St John Capetn 37-50; St Mary Jeppestown Johann 50-52; St John Belgravia Johann 52-55; H Trin Paarl 55-56; H Redeem Sea Point 56-60; Newlands 61-66; L to Offic Dio Blackb 66-69. *Address temp unknown.*

TATTON-BROWN, Simon Charles. Qu Coll Cam BA 70, MA 78. Coll of the Resurr 78. **d** 79 **p** 80 Man. C of St Mich AA Ashton-u-Lyne Dio Man from 79; Bp's Chap & P-in-c of St Gabr Prestwich Dio Man from 82. *St Gabriel's Vicarage, Bishops Road, Prestwich, Manchester, M25 8HT.* (061-773 8839)

TATTRIE, John William. b 46. Dalhousie Univ BA 68. K Coll NS MSLitt 72. **d** 71 NS **p** 72 Bp Arnold for NS. I of New Germany Dio NS from 71. *Box 116, New Germany, Lun Co, NS, Canada.* (644-2260)

TAUDIN-CHABOT, Henri Cornelis Marie. Angl Th Coll Vancouver DTh 58. **d** 61 **p** 62 New Westmr. C of St John Shaughnessy Heights 61-64; St Chad Vancouver Dio New Westmr from 64. *2362 Oliver Crescent, Vancouver 8, BC, Canada.*

TAUHARA, Waha. St Jo Coll NZ 46. **d** 51 **p** 52 Auckld. C of Paroch Distr of St Thos Auckld 51-53; N Wairoa 53-55; Whangarei 55-59; Kaitaia 60-68; P-in-c of Waimate N 68-71; C of St Aug Napier 71-76; Rangiatea Maori Past Dio Wel from 76. *150 Waerenga Road, Otaki, NZ.* (7443)

TAUKEREI, Augustine. Bp Patteson Th Centre Kohimarama. **d** 71 Melan. d Dio Melan 71-75; Dio Centr Melan from 75. *Taroaniara, Solomon Islands.*

TAUMOMOA, Suckling. Newton Coll Dogura 67. **d** 71 **p** 72 Papua. P Dio Papua 71-77; Dio Port Moresby from 77. *Boroko, Papua, New Guinea.*

TAUNO, Samuel. Newton Coll Dogura 69. **d** and **p** 72 Papua. P Dio 72-77; Dio Aipo 77-78. *PO Box 340, Madang, Papua New Guinea.*

TAUNTON, Lord Bishop Suffragan of. *See* Nott, Right Rev Peter John.

TAUNTON, Archdeacon of. (Vacant)

TAVERNOR, James Edward. b 23. St D Coll Lamp BA 49. Lich Th Coll 41. **d** 50 **p** 51 Mon. C of St Mary Mon 50-52; Prestbury 52-53; Newbold w Dunston 53-55; Buxton 67-69; Perm to Offic Dio Derby 70-75; Dio Heref from 76. *The Old Rectory, Willey, Broseley, Salop, TF12 5BT.* (Telford 882894)

TAVERNOR, William Noel. b 16. Lich Th Coll 37. **d** 40 **p** 41 Heref, C of Ledbury 40-43; St Mary Kidderminster 43-46; V of Bettws-y-Crwyn w Newcastle 46-50; Upton Bishop 50-57; Aymestrey w Leinthall Earles 57-65; C-in-c of Shobdon 58-65; V of Canon Pyon w King's Pyon and Birley Dio Heref from 65. *Canon Pyon Vicarage, Hereford.* (Canon Pyon 268)

TAVOA, Michael Henry. Bp Patteson Th Centre Kohimarama 71. **d** 73 Melan **p** 75 New Hebr P Dio Melan 73-75; New Hebr from 75. *Pacific Theological College, PO Box 388, Suva, Fiji.*

TAWAMBA, Fabian. d 74 **p** 75 Mashon. P Dio Mashon. *Kambazuma Chapelry, Box 46, Norton, Zimbabwe.*

TAWHAI, Koro Ranqi Poua. b 30. **d** 80 Wai. Hon C of Te Kaha Dio Wai from 80. *Omaio PO, via Opotiki, NZ.*

TAW MWA, Gabriel. d 63 **p** 64 Rang. P Dio Rang 64-70. *Kwambi, Burma.*

TAY, John Sin Hock. Univ of Lon BD 71. Univ of Sing MMed 73, MD 77. **d** 79 **p** 80 Sing (NSM). Sen Lect Univ of Sing from 79; C of St Matt City and Dio Sing from 79. *St Matthew's Church, 184 Neil Road, Singapore 0208.*

TAY, Louis Seng Kong. b 49. Univ of Sing BDS 72. **d** 76 **p** 77 Sing. C of Ch of Good Shepherd Sing 76-81; Succr of St Andr Cathl City and Dio Sing from 81. *St Andrew's Cathedral, Singapore 0617.*

TAY, Moses Leng Kong. Univ of Malaya MB, BS 62. Univ of Lon BD 71. Univ of Sing MMed 72. **d** 77 **p** 78 Sing (NSM). Med Supt Alexandra Hosp 78; C of St Andrew Cathl City and Dio Sing from 78. *St Andrew's Cathedral, Coleman Street, Singapore 0617.*

TAYLER, Michael Frederick. b 20. Fitzw Ho Cam BA 50, MA 55. Linc Th Coll. **d** 52 **p** 53 Newc T. C of Sugley 52-55; M Cam Bro of Ascen Delhi 55-61; C of Alverstoke 61-69; Testwood 69-70; R of Chawton w Farringdon Dio Win from 70; RD of Alton 74-80. *Rectory, Farringdon, Alton, Hants.* (Tisted 398)

TAYLER, William Henry Stuart. b 1897. Dorch Miss Coll 20. **d** 22 **p** 23 Lon. C of St Matt Westmr 22-34; St Mark (in c of St Luke) Swindon 34-36; V of Tue Brook 36-46; St Matt Gt Pet Street Westmr 46-49; Chap Conv Sisters of Charity Knowle 49-68; L to Offic Dio Bris 50-68; Perm to Offic 68-77. *2 Holway Cottages, The Mall, Swindon, Wilts, SN1 4JB.* (Swindon 29881)

TAYLOR, Alan Cecil. b 34. Keble Coll Ox BA (3rd cl Math) 57, MA 63. Cudd Coll 58. **d** 60 Lanc for York **p** 61 Blackb. C of St Steph Blackpool 60-63; Chorley 63-65; V of St Mark Burnley Dio Blackb from 65. *9 Rossendale Road, Burnley, Lancs.* (Burnley 28178)

TAYLOR, Alan Clive. b 48. Univ of Southn BTh 79. Sarum Wells Th Coll 69. **d** 74 **p** 75 St Alb. C of St Pet Watford 74-78; Broxbourne w Wormley Dio St Alb from 78. *1 The Oval, Wormley, Broxbourne, Herts.* (Hoddsden 42356)

TAYLOR, Alan Gerald. b 33. St Aid Coll 61. **d** 63 **p** 64 Southw. C of W Bridgford 63-66; Barkwith Group 66-69; V of Morton w E Stockwith 69-76; Countryside Officer Dio Linc from 69; R of Willoughby w Sloothby and Claxby Dio Linc from 76; Ulceby w Dexthorpe and Fordington Dio Linc from 76. *Willoughby Rectory, Alford, Lincs.* (Alford 2343)

TAYLOR, Alan Leonard. b 43. Chich Th Coll 67. **d** 69 Warrington for Liv **p** 70 Liv. C of Walton-on-the-Hill 69-73; St Marg Toxteth 73-75; V of St Anne Stanley Dio Liv from 75. *St Anne's Vicarage, Derwent Square, Liverpool, L13 6QT.* (051-228 5252)

TAYLOR, Alfred Edgar. b 16. Wycl Hall Ox 55. **d** 55 **p** 56 Leic. C of S Wigston 55-58; Hon CF from 56; V of H Trin Loughborough 58-68; Earl Shilton w Elmesthorpe Dio Leic from 68. *Earl Shilton Vicarage, Leicester, LE9 7BA.* (Earl Shilton 43961)

TAYLOR, Alfred Harry Bryant. b 17. St Deiniol's Libr Hawarden 77. **d** 79 **p** 80 Ches. C of Woodchurch Dio Ches from 79. *111 New Hey Road, Woodchurch, Wirral, Merseyside, L49 7NE.*

TAYLOR, Alfred Peter. b 08. Keble Coll Ox BA (3rd cl Engl Lang and Lit) 30, MA 34. Cudd Coll 34. **d** 35 **p** 36 S'wark. C of St Pet Clapham 35-39; Min Can of Worc Cathl 39-48; Chap Worc R Infirm 39-41; C of St Pet Gt Worc 40-41 and 46-47; Chap RNVR 41-46; Asst Master KS Worc 46-47; R of St Martin w Whittington 47-60; RD of Worc 56-60; V of St Mary The Boltons Kens 60-70; Chap R Marsden Hosp 60-70; R of Barford St Martin and C-in-c of Baverstock 70-75; Dinton 73-75. *45 Grosvenor Road, Shaftesbury, Dorset, SP7 8DP.* (Shaftesbury 3823)

TAYLOR, Very Rev Anthony James. St Jo Coll Morpeth. **d** 56 **p** 57 Bal. C of Warrnambool 56-57; V of Dimboola 57-61; P-in-c of All SS Bal w Sebastopol 61-63; Findon W and Seaton Pk 63-67; Mile End 67-72; R of Belair 72-78; Sub-Dean of St Bonif Cathl Bunb 78; Dean of Bunb from 78. *Deanery, Oakley Street, Bunbury, W Australia 6230.* (21 3970)

TAYLOR, Anthony William Harold. b 35. Keble Coll Ox 3rd cl Cl Mods 58, BA (2nd cl Th) 60. Coll of Resurr Mirfield 60. **d** 62 **p** 63 Lon. C of St Aug Whitton 62-67; St Steph w St Thos Shepherd's Bush 67-70; St Luke Chesterton 70-75; V of St Mich AA Stonebridge Willesden Dio Lon from 75. *Vicarage, Hillside, Stonebridge, NW10 8LB.* (01-965 7443)

TAYLOR, Arthur John. b 17. Univ of Lon BD (2nd cl) 39. ALCD 39, BA 52. **d** 40 **p** 41 Chelmsf. C of St Andr Walthamstow 40-42; Asst Master Alleyne's Gr Sch Stevenage and Perm to Offic Dio St Alb 42-45; C of H Sav Hitchin 44-45; Asst Master Felsted Sch 45-46; St Mich Sch Ingoldisthorpe 46-47; Alleyne's Gr Sch Stevenage 47-56; K S Ely 56-80; Sen Tutor 60-76; Admissions Tutor 76-80; Hon Min Can of Ely Cathl and Perm to Offic Dio Ely from 56. *27 Histon Road, Cambridge.* (Cam 61952)

TAYLOR, Arthur Robert. b 26. ACIS 59. Oak Hill Th Coll 67. **d** 68 **p** 69 Roch. C of Wilmington 68-71; Polegate 71-73; R of Chesterton w Haddon 73-80; P-in-c of Alwalton 73-75; R 75-80; Sawtry Dio Ely from 80. *Sawtry Rectory, Huntingdon, PE17 5TD.* (Ramsey 830215)

TAYLOR, Brian. b 42. St Deiniol's Libr Hawarden 78. **d** 80 **p** 81 St A. C of Mold Dio St A from 80. *2 Harrowby Road, Mold, Clwyd, CH7 1DN.* (0352 3624)

TAYLOR, Brian. b 29. Keble Coll Ox BA 52, MA 56. Linc Th Coll. **d** 57 **p** 58 Linc. C of St Jo Bapt Spalding 57-60; PC 60-61; Asst Master Spalding Gr Sch 54-61; Chap 57-61; Perm to Offic Dio Leic 58-62 and 68-69; L to Offic Dio Borneo 62; Dio Kuch 62-68; Prin St Columba's Sch Miri Sarawak 62-65; Chap and Tutor Batu Lintang Coll Kuch 65-68; w USPG 68-69; V of St Gabr Leic 69-74; R of St Nicolas Guildf and Dioc Insp of Schs Dio Guildf from 75; Commiss Sabah from 77. *Rectory, The Flower Walk, Guildford, Surrey, GU2 5EP.* (Guildf 504895)

TAYLOR, Brian. b 38. Univ of Bris BA 60. Univ of Liv Ba 70. Ridley Hall Cam 60. **d** and **p** 66 Ondo. Chap Vic Coll and L to Offic Dio Ondo 66-72; Publ Pr Dio Derby 74-78; Sen Lect Newbury Coll from 79; Hon C of Bucklebury w Marlston Dio Ox from 81. *Ramblers, Little Lane, Bucklebury, Reading, RG7 6QX.* (0635 64359)

TAYLOR, Brian John Chatterton. b 30. Trin Hall Cam BA 53, MA 57. Westcott Ho Cam 53. **d** 55 **p** 56 Man. C of St Pet Leigh 55-57; Ashton L 57-58; Chap Miss to Seamen Port Melbourne 58-59; Hobart 59-60; Lect Vic State Coll from 72. *Box 224, Malvern, Vic, Australia 3144.*

TAYLOR, Brian Valentine. b 34. St Deiniol's Hawarden 69. **d** 71 Penrith for Carl **p** 72 Carl. C of Workington 71-72; St Aid w Ch Ch and St Andr Carl 73-74; Asst Chap St Mary Rotterdam and Chap Miss to Seamen Rotterdam 74-75; Madrid 75-76; Chap at Marseilles 77-78; Alassio w H Ghost Genoa Dio Gibr (Gibr in Eur from 80) from 78. *Cardellino 21, Alassio, Italy.* (42885)

TAYLOR, Bryan. Ridley Hall, Cam. **d** 60 **p** 61 Bris. C of St Barn Knowle 60-63; V of Corston w Rodbourne Dio Bris from 63; R of Foxley w Bremilham Dio Bris from 63. *Corston Vicarage, Malmesbury, Wilts.* (Malmesbury 3245)

TAYLOR, Bryan George. b 41. Univ of Auckld BSc 64. **d** 78 Bp Spence for Auckld **p** 79 Auckld. Hon C of Mt Roskill 78-80; Hillsborough Dio Auckld from 80. *48 Glenveagh Drive, Mount Roskill, Auckland 4, NZ.* (695-651)

TAYLOR, Charles Derek. b 36. Trin Hall Cam BA 59, MA 62. Ripon Hall Ox 59. **d** 61 **p** 62 Southw. C of All SS Nottm 61-64; Binley w Coombe Fields 64-67; St Mich Stoke 67-70, R of Purley 70-74; V of Milton Dio B & W from 74. *461 Locking Road, Weston-super-Mare, Avon.* (W-s-M 25651)

TAYLOR, Charles John. ACT ThL 62. St Jo Coll Morpeth. **d** 60 **p** 62 Newc. C of Wyong 60-63; Cessnock 64; Cardiff 64-66; Waratah 66-69; P-in-c of Paterson 69-75; C of Maitland 75-77; P-in-c Exper Area of Telarah-Rutherford 77-79; Prov Distr of Telarah-Rutherford Dio Newc from 80. *Rectory, Gillies Street, Rutherford, NSW, Australia 2320.* (32 8604)

TAYLOR, Charles William. b 53. Selw Coll Cam BA (Th) 74, MA 78. Cudd Coll 74. **d** 76 Lich **p** 77 Shrewsbury for Lich. C of St Pet Wolverhampton 76-79; Chap of Westmr Abbey from 79. *6 Little Cloister, Westminster Abbey, SW1P 3PL.* (01-222 2065)

TAYLOR, Preb Clive Cavanagh. b 28. Cranmer Hall, Dur 61. **d** 63 **p** 64 Lon. C of Wembley 63-66; Edmonton 66-68; V of St Jo Bapt Tottenham 68-76; RD of E Haringey 73-76; V of St Barn Temple Fortune Dio Lon and Chap Metrop Police Coll Hendon from 76; Dir Ordin Tr Dio Lon from 76; Preb of St Paul's Cathl Lon from 78; Area Dean of W Barnet from 79. *7 Oakfields Road, NW11 0JA.* (01-458 7828)

TAYLOR, Canon Cyril Vincent. b 07. Ch Ch Ox BA 29, MA 35. Westcott Ho Cam 30. **d** 31 **p** 32 Leic. C of St Mary Hinckley 31-33; St Andr Kingswood (in c of Lower Kingswood) 33-36; Prec and Sacr of Bris Cathl 36-39; Asst to Hd of Relig Broadcasting BBC 39-53; Fell of St Mich Coll Tenbury 43; Warden and Chap of R Sch of Ch Mus and Perm to Offic Dio Cant 53-58; V of Cerne Abbas w Upcerne 58-69; PC of Nether Cerne 58-69; R of Godmanstone 58-69; R of Minterne Magna 58-69; Can Res and Prec of Sarum Cathl 69-75; Can (Emer) from 75. *15 The Spain, Petersfield, Hants, GU32 3JZ.* (Petersfield 3604)

TAYLOR, David Mortimer. Univ of NZ BA 32, MA 33, LTh 34, BD 40. Univ of Melb BD (Hons) 44. **d** 33 **p** 34 Ch Ch. C of Timaru 34-37; V of Chatham Is 37-39; Fairlie 39-43; P-in-c of Akaroa 43-46; V of Hinds 46-48; Belfast w Burwood NZ 48-51; Exam Chap to Bp of Ch Ch 45-59; Exam Bd of Th Stud 43-48 and 56-59; Asst Lect Coll Ho Ch Ch 48-51; Vice-Prin Ch Ch Coll 48-59; Asst Gen Sec Austr Coun of Chs and L to Offic Dio Syd 59-62; Assoc Gen Sec Nat Coun of Chs in NZ 63-64; Gen Sec 64-74; Perm to Offic Dio Waik 63-74; Dio Ch Ch 75-78; Dio Wai from 78. *141 Darraghs Road, Tauranga, NZ.*

TAYLOR, Denis Erskine. Univ of Glas MA 27. Edin Th Coll 33. **d** 34 **p** 35 Glas. C of St Mary's Cathl Glas 34-36; R of St John Pittenweem 36-39; St Pet Kirkcaldy 39-44; Youth Org Scot Episc Ch 42-46; Youth Sec Br Coun of Ch 46-48; Dir of Austr Gen Bd of Relig Educn of C of E 48-52; Perm to Offic Dio Melb 49-52; Dean of Brisb 53-58; V of Churston Ferrers w Goodrington 58-62; Home Sec ABM 63-64; Perm to Offic Dio Syd 63-64; Dio Brisb 64-74. *104 Windermere Road, Ascot, Brisbane, Queensland, Australia 4007.* (68 2841)

TAYLOR, Dennis James. b 31. ACIS 62. Ripon Hall, Ox. **d** 68 **p** 69 Lich. C of Berkswich 68-77; P-in-c of H Trin Hastings Dio Chich 77-81; V from 81. *72 Priory Avenue, Hastings, Sussex, TN34 1UG.* (Hastings 441766)

TAYLOR, Derek John. b 31. St D Coll Lamp BA 52. Fitzw Ho Cam BA (3rd cl Th Trip pt ii) 54, MA 58. St Mich Coll Llan 55. **d** 55 **p** 56 Mon. C of St Paul Newport 55-59; CF (TA) 57-59 and 62-64; CF 59-62; R of Henllys w Bettws 62-64; V of Exminster 64-70; Asst Master Heathcoat Sch Tiverton 70-71; Chap and Asst Master Prince Rupert Sch Wilhelmshaven 71-75; Chap R Russell Sch Croydon 75-79; V of St Andr

Croydon and Chap St Andr Sch Dio Cant from 79. *St Andrew's Vicarage, 6 St Peter's Road, Croydon, Surrey, CR0 1HD.* (01-688 6011)

TAYLOR, Ven Edward. AKC 48. St Bonif Coll Warm. **d** 49 **p** 50 Nor. C of Diss 49-51; V of Stockingford 51-57; St Nich Radford Cov 57-64; Surr from 60; Proc in Conv Cov 60-80; R of Spernall (w Oldberrow and Morton Bagot from 72) 65-74; Oldberrow w Morton Bagot 65-72; C-in-c (V from 70) of Coughton w Sambourne 65-74; Hon Can of Cov 69-74; Archd of Warw from 74; V of Sherbourne 75-77. *The Archdeacon's House, Sherbourne, Warwick, CV35 8AB.* (Barford 624344)

TAYLOR, Edward Frank. b 23. Univ Coll of Hull 41. Univ of Lon BSc (2nd cl Zoology) 44. Chich Th Coll 50. **d** 52 Knaresborough for Ripon **p** 53 Ripon. C of Manston 52-55; Chap Chich Th Coll 55-59; PV of Chich Cathl 57-59; C of Ifield 59-63; PC of Hangleton 63-68; V 68-73; Wivelsfield Dio Chich from 73. *Wivelsfield Vicarage, Haywards Heath, Sussex.* (Wivelsfield Green 227)

TAYLOR, Edward Norman. b 43. Wycl Coll Tor LTh 72. **d** 72 **p** 73 Sktn. C of Watson 72-75; in Amer Ch from 75. *803 State, Emmetsburg, IA 50536, USA.*

TAYLOR, Canon Edwin Norman. b 24. Trin Coll Ox BA and MA 50. Ripon Hall, Ox 49. **d** 51 **p** 52 Man. C of Benchill 51-55; V of High Crompton 55-59; St Thos Radcliffe 59-71; R of Heaton Moor Dio Man from 71; RD of Heaton Dio Man from 71; Hon Can of Man from 75. *42 Lea Road, Heaton Moor, Stockport, SK4 4JU.* (061-432 1227)

TAYLOR, Edwin William. b 44. McMaster Univ Ont BA 67. Yale Univ MPhil 70. St John's Coll Cam BA 73. Trin Coll Tor MDiv 74. **d** 75 Yukon **p** 78 New Westmr. C of Ch Ch Cathl Whitehorse 75; I of Carcross Whitehorse 75-76; on leave 76-78; CF (Canad) from 78. *Military College, FMO Victoria, BC, Canada.*

TAYLOR, Egbert Donald Ignatius. St Pet Coll Ja 56. **d** 59 **p** 60 Ja. P Dio Ja 60-71; P-in-c St Mary's Maverley Dio Ja from 71. *44 Lorraine Avenue, Kingston 8, Jamaica, W Indies.*

TAYLOR, Eric Hargreaves. Oak Hill Th Coll 47. **d** 51 **p** 52 Ches. C of St Cath Higher Tranmere 51-54; V of Constable Lee 54-62; W Seaton 62-71; V of Ch Ch Ramsgate Dio Cant from 71. *8 Crescent Road, Ramsgate, Kent.* (Thanet 52806)

TAYLOR, Eric William. b 17. St Jo Coll Dur BA 40, Dipl Th 41, MA 43. **d** 41 **p** 42 Dur. C of St Columba Southwick 41-48; Ferryhill 48-51; Surr from 51; V of Wingate 51-63; C-in-c of Hutton Henry Conv Distr 60-63; V of Wingate Grange Dio Dur from 63. *Wingate Grange Vicarage, Wingate, Co Durham, TS28 5BW.* (Wingate 8338)

TAYLOR, Eustace Lovatt Hebden. Trin Hall Cam 2nd cl Hist Trip pt i 48, BA (2nd cl Hist Trip pt ii) 49, MA 53. Angl Th Coll BC LTh 52. **d** 52 New Westmr for Yukon **p** 52 Yukon. R of Teslin 52-54; C of St Matt Montr 54-55; I of Temiskaming 55-59; Fenelon Falls w Coboconk 59-61; R of Caledon E 61-62; C of Langley Marish 62-64; V of Greengates 64-68. *c/o Dordit College, Sioux Centre, Iowa 51250, USA.*

TAYLOR, Francis Nicholas John. Univ of Bris (1st cl Chem) 59. Clifton Th Coll 59. **d** 61 **p** 62 S'wark. C of St Jas Clapham Pk 61-65; Cheadle (in c of St Cuthb) 65-71; V of H Trin (and Ch Ch from 77) Richmond Dio S'wark from 71; C-in-c of Ch Ch Richmond 75-77; RD of Richmond and Barnes from 77. *Vicarage, Sheen Park, Richmond, Surrey, TW9 1UP.* (01-940 3995)

TAYLOR, Francis Oswald. b 10. Chich Th Coll 37. **d** 40 **p** 41 Dur. C of St Mary Heworth 40-42; St Ignatius Bp Wearmouth 42-45; Ch Ch St Leonards-on-Sea 45-65; V of St Mich AA w All SS Brighton 65-67; C-in-c of Flimwell 67-78. *12 St Richard's House, Pevensey Road, St Leonards on Sea, E Sussex, TN38 0JX.*

TAYLOR, Frank. b 02. Kelham Th Coll 22. **d** 28 **p** 29 Lon. C of St John Hendon 28-33; St Mellitus Hanwell 33-37; LDHM at St Mary Virg E Hounslow 37-43; V of St Anne Brondesbury 43-53; St Jo Evang Hammersmith 53-61; Lambourn 61-69; Perm to Offic Dio Ox from 74. *18 Bertie Road, Cumnor, Oxford.* (Cumnor 3239)

TAYLOR, Frank Alfred. b 10. Linc Th Coll 80. **d** 80 **p** 81 Linc. [f Bapt Min]. C of Louth Dio Linc from 80. *5 Upgate, Louth, Lincs, LN11 9ER.*

TAYLOR, Frank Leslie. b 05. Late Scho of St Jo Coll Ox BA 27, Dipl Th (w distinc) 28, MA 30. Wycl Hall, Ox 27. **d** 29 Roch **p** 30 Bp King for Roch. C of St Pet Tunbridge Wells 29-33; CMS Miss at Pathra 33-38; Barharwa 43-61; Archd of Bhag 57-61; R of E Hoathly 62-72. *4 Penn Mead, Church Road, Penn, High Wycombe, Bucks HP10 8NY.* (Penn 2268)

TAYLOR, Garry Kenneth. b 53. Univ of Edin BMus 75. Sarum Wells Th Coll 76. **d** 79 **p** 80 Portsm. C of H Spirit Southsea Dio Portsm from 79. *219 Fawcett Road, Southsea, Hants, PO4 0DH.* (Portsmouth 812128)

TAYLOR, Geoffrey Albert. Moore Th Coll Syd ACT ThL (2nd cl) 59. **d** 60 **p** 61 Bp Loane for Syd. C of Kingsgrove 60-61; Lithgow (in c of Wallerawang) 61-62; R of Wallerawang (w Littleton and Hartley from 65) 63-66; Youth Dir Syd 66-69; L to Offic Dio Syd 66-69 and 72-74; R of Lithgow 69-72; R of Lalor Pk 74-76; C of Mt Druitt Dio Syd from 76. *44 Callagher Street, Mt Druitt, NSW, Australia 2770.* (625-8028)

TAYLOR, Geoffrey James. Melb Coll of Div LTh 53. **d** 51 **p** 52 Melb. C of St Kilda 51-52; Min of W Footscray 52-58; Hon C of St Mary Magd Munster Sq Lon 59; C of St Pet Melb 59-64; I 64-79; R of Albany Dio Bunb from 79. *Rectory, Albany, W Australia 6330.* (098-41 1228)

TAYLOR, George Davidson. St Aid Coll 60. **d** 62 **p** 63 Man. C of Urmston 62-65; V of Shuttleworth 65-71; V of St Phil Litherland Dio Liv from 71. *St Philip's Vicarage, Litherland, Liverpool 21.* (051-928 3902)

TAYLOR, Canon George Downham Row. b 05. **d** 44 **p** 45 St E. C of St Clem Ipswich 44-46; R of Bedingfield 46-50; Rishangles 46-50; Otley 50-65; C-in-c of Clopton 50-51; R 51-65; RD of Carlford 59-73; R of Martlesham 65-75; Hon Can of St E 70-75; Can (Emer) from 75; C-in-c of Tuddenham St Martin 68-70; Perm to Offic Dio St E from 76. *12 Hilly Fields, Woodbridge, Suff, IP12 4DX.* (Woodbridge 4666)

TAYLOR, George Edward. b 28. Atlantic Sch of Th Halifax NS BTh 78. **d** 77 **p** 78 NS. C of Lower Sackville Dio NS 77-78; R of Seaforth Dio NS from 78. *c/o The Rectory, Millside Drive, Route No 2, Porter's Lake, NS, Canada.*

TAYLOR, George James Trueman. b 36. Ripon Hall Ox 66. **d** 69 Warrington for Liv **p** 70 Liv. C of Wavertree 69-73; V of All SS Newton-in-Makerfield 73-79; Stoneycroft Dio Liv from 79. *Vicarage, Oakhill Park, Stoneycroft, Liverpool, L13 4BW.* (051-228 3581)

TAYLOR, Gerald Hamer. Univ of Queensld BA (3rd cl Math) 48. ACT ThL 54. St Francis Coll Brisb. **d** 55 **p** 56 Brisb. C of Wynnum 55-56; Southport 56-57; Bundaberg 57-59; P-in-c of Aiome 59-60; Sag Sag New Guinea 60-62; C of St Luke Ekibin Brisb 62-64; P-in-c of Biggenden 64-70; V of Gin Gin 70-73; Perm to Offic Dio Brisb from 73. *c/o Station 4ZR, Roma, Queensland, Australia 4455.*

TAYLOR, Gilbert George. Trin Coll Tor BA 54, LTh 57. **d** 57 **p** 58 Koot. C of Vernon 57-59; Redeemer Cathl Calg 59-62; R of All SS Medicine Hat 62-63; Esterhazy 63-65. *515 210 Woolner Avenue, Toronto 9, Ont, Canada.*

TAYLOR, Gordon. b 46. AKC 68. St Aug Coll Cant 69. **d** 70 Bp Gerard for Sheff **p** 71 Sheff. C of Rotherham 70-74; P-in-c of St Thos Brightside Sheff 74-79; St Marg Brightside Sheff 77-79; V of St Thos and St Marg City and Dio Sheff from 79. *Brightside Vicarage, Beacon Road, Sheffield, S9 1AD.* (Sheff 386640)

TAYLOR, (Kevin) Gordon. b 38. TCD 71. **d** 73 **p** 74 Connor. M SSF from 60. C of St Luke Lower Falls Belf 73-75; Guardian Belf Friary 75-80; In Amer Ch from 80. *207a Baltimore Avenue, Huntington Beach, Calif 92648, USA.*

TAYLOR, Gordon Clifford. b 15. VRD 56, and bar 66. Ch Coll Cam 2nd cl Engl Trip pt i 36, BA (2nd cl Geog Trip pt ii) 37, MA 41. Ripon Hall Ox 37. **d** 38 **p** 39 Lon. C of St Steph Ealing 38-40; Chap RNVR 40-58; RNR 58-70; Asst Master Eton Coll 46-49; R of St Giles-in-the-Fields Dio Lon from 49; RD of Finsbury and Holborn 54-67. *15a Gower Street, WC1.* (01-636 4646)

TAYLOR, Henry. St Jo Coll Morpeth 46. ACT ThL 50. **d** 49 **p** 50 Armid. C of W Tamworth 49-52; P-in-c of Baradine 52-55; V of Emmaville 55-59; Boggabri 59-66; Barraba 66-69; Glen Innes 69-74; R of St Pet Wynnum City and Dio Brisb from 74. *81 Charlotte Street, Wynnum Central, Brisbane, Australia 4178.* (396 1913)

TAYLOR, Henry. b 46. St Cath Coll Ox BA 69, MA 73. Cudd Coll 70. **d** 73 **p** 74 Lich. C of Tettenhall Regis 73-76; Walsall 76-80; V of Witton-le-Wear & Firtree Dio Dur from 80. *Witton-le-Wear Vicarage, Bishop Auckland, Co Durham, DL14 0AN.* (Witton-le-Wear 346)

TAYLOR, Henry Gordon. DSO 43. OBE (Mil) 54. Univ of NZ BA 31. **d** 32 **p** 33 Auckld. C of St Barn Mt Eden NZ 32-34; V of Bom and Chap St Steph Sch Bom NZ 35-37; Perm to Offic (Col Cl Act) at St Simon Zelotes w St Anthony Bethnal Green 37; V of Kaitaia 37-44; CF (NZ) 40-49; Chap RNZ Navy 49-68; St Steph Sch Bombay Auckld 68-75; L to Offic Dio Auckld 51-70; V of Patea 75-77; Perm to Offic Dio Wel from 77. *26 Richmond Road, Carterton, NZ.* (7381)

TAYLOR, Herbert Bindley. Codr Coll Barb BA 43. **d** 35 **p** 38 Trinid. Chap of Publ Insts Dio Trinid 35-38; V of St John Speyside 38-46; St Clem Naparima 46-64; Exam Chap to Bp of Trinid 52-62. *c/o Naparima, Trinidad, W Indies.*

TAYLOR, Canon Herbert Cyril. b 06. Em Coll Cam BA 29, MA 34. Ridley Hall, Cam 29. **d** 31 **p** 32 S'wark. C of Ch Ch Surbiton Hill 31-42; V of Ch Ch Orpington 42-73; Hon Can of Roch 64-73; Can (Emer) from 73. *Bishop Mann Flat, Mabledon, London Road, Southborough, Tunbridge Wells Kent.* (Tonbridge 357495)

TAYLOR, Herbert Elmo. CD 63. Hur Coll STh 53. **d** 49 **p**

50 Moos. R of St Matt Hearst w Calstock and Mattice 50-53; C of Ascen Hamilton 53-54; R of Kirkland Lake 55-60; Hon Can of Moos 57-60; I of Punnichy 60-64; Supt Ind Miss Dio Qu'App from 61; R of St Geo Moose Jaw 64-72; RD of Moose Jaw 69-72; L to Offic Dio Qu'App from 74. *1053 Clifton Avenue, Moose Jaw, Sask., Canada.* (693-4543)

TAYLOR, Humphrey John. **d** 43 **p** 44 Waik. C of St Pet Cathl Hamilton 43-44 and 55-60; P-in-c of Ngaruawahia 44-47; I of Saguenay Miss 47-48; C of St Jo Evang Montr 48-51; R of St Paul's Cathl Dawson 51-54; C of S Ormsby 54-55; V of Te Kauwhata 60-64; Chap Tokanui Psychiatric Hosp 64-71; Hon C of Porirua 71-73; Perm to Offic Dio Wel from 79. *2 Huia Street, Waikanae, NZ.*

TAYLOR, Humphrey Vincent. b 38. Pemb Coll Cam BA 61, MA 66. Univ of Lon MA 70. Coll of Resurr Mirfield 61. **d** 63 **p** 64 Lon. C of St Kath N Hammersmith 63-64; St Mark Notting Hill Kens 64-66; R of Lilongwe Malawi 67-71; Chap Bp Grosseteste Coll Linc 72-74; Sec for Chaplaincies in Higher Educn C of E Bd of Educn 75-80; Perm to Offic Dio S'wark from 75; Commiss S Malawi from 78; Lake Malawi from 80; Sec Miss Programmes USPG from 80. *15 Tufton Street, SW1P 3QQ.* (01-222 4222)

TAYLOR, James Alfred. b 1886. **d** 56 Jarrow for Dur **p** 57 Dur. C of St Barn Hendon Bp Wearmouth 56-59; L to Offic Dio St Alb 59-64; C of St Sav Wood Green 64-67; Perm to Offic Dio Lon from 67; Hon C of St Paul Harringay Dio Lon from 72; St Geo Hornsey Dio Lon from 78. *11 Barratt Avenue, N22 4EZ.* (01-889 1077)

TAYLOR, James Arnold. Moore Coll Syd ThL 58. **d** 58 Syd **p** 58 Bp Hilliard for Syd. C of Ryde 58-60; Chap at Groote Eylandt Miss 60-74; Asst Gen Sec CMS in NSW 74-77; R of Nightcliff Dio N Terr from 77. *Box 39304, Winnellie, NT, Australia 5789.* (089-85 1820)

TAYLOR, James M'Murray. b 16. TCD BA 38. **d** 39 Bp Kennedy for Down **p** 40 Down. C of St Mary Belf 39-43; CF (EC) 43-47; C-in-c of U Moville 47-48; Tamlaght O'Crilly Lower 49-53; Derrybrusk 53-55; R 55-57; Castle Archdale and Killadeas 57-80; Ed Clogh Dioc Mag 58-70. *Hollybank House, Lisbellaw, Co Fermanagh, N Ireland.* (Lisbellaw 259)

TAYLOR, John Alfred. b 25. **d** 62 **p** 63 Win. C of Basingstoke 62-65; Chap RN from 65. *c/o Ministry of Defence, Lacon House, Theobald's Road, WC1X 8RY.*

TAYLOR, Canon John Ambrose. b 19. Coll of Resurr Mirfield 49. **d** 50 **p** 51 York. C of Helmsley 50-55; V of Nether w Upper Poppleton 55-63; St Osw (w Little St John from 68) Ches 63-72; C-in-c of Little St John Ches 63-68; Team V of Ches 72-74; V of St Jo Evang Withyham Dio Chich from 74; Commiss N and C Eur and Gibr 74-80; Gibr in Eur from 80; Hon Can of Gibr from 74; RD of Rotherfield from 77. *St John's Vicarage, Crowborough, E Sussex, TN6 1ST.* (Crowborough 4660)

TAYLOR, John Andrew Wemyss. b 27. LDS RCS 51. PhD 62. Sarum Wells Th Coll 70. **d** 72 **p** 73 Ex. C of Ashburton w Buckland-in-the-Moor 72-76; P-in-c of E Portlemouth Dio Ex 76-79; R (w S Pool and Chivelstone) 79-81; P-in-c of S Pool w Chivelstone 76-79; V of Salcombe Dio Ex from 81. *Vicarage, Devon Road, Salcombe, Devon.* (Salcombe 2626)

✠ **TAYLOR, Right Rev John Bernard.** b 29. Late Scho of Ch Coll Cam 1st cl Cl Trip pt i 49, BA (2nd cl Th Trip pt ia) 50, MA 54. Lady Kay Scho of Jes Coll Cam 1st cl Th Trip pt iii 52. Ridley Hall Cam 55. **d** 56 **p** 57 S'wark. C of Morden 56-59; V of Henham 59-64; V of Elsenham 59-64; Exam Chap to Bp of Chelmsf 62-80; Sen Tutor Oak Hill Th Coll 64-65; Vice-Prin 65-72; Publ Pr Dio St Alb 64-72; V of Woodford Wells 72-75; Dioc Dir of Ordinands 72-80; Archd of W Ham 75-80; Cons Ld Bp of St Alb in Westmr Abbey 1 May 80 by Abp of Cant; Bps of Chelmsf, Cov, Derby, Ely, Guildf, Portsm, Roch, S & M and Truro; Bps Suffr of Barking, Bedford, Bradwell, Colchester, Hertford and Stepney; and others. *Abbey Gate House, St Albans, Herts, AL3 4HD.* (St Albans 53305)

TAYLOR, John Denys. St Bonif Coll Warm 35. **d** 36 Man for Col Bp **p** 38 S Rhod. Miss of St D Bonda 37-52; Dio Mashon 52-76. *Bonda Hospital, Post-Box J7187, Umtali, Rhodesia.*

TAYLOR, John Denys. Univ of Leeds, BA 49. Coll of Resurr Mirfield. **d** 51 **p** 52 Ripon. C of St Marg of Antioch Leeds 51-54; Chap of St Paul's Cathl Calc 54-56; Seamen's Chap Calc 5b-59; C of Grimsby 59-66; V of Tuakau 66-69; Asst Master Northcote Coll and Perm to Offic Dio Auckld from 69. *155 Queen Street, Northcote, Auckland, NZ.* (486-545)

TAYLOR, John Edward. b 16. Keble Coll Ox BA 38, MA 47. St Steph Ho Ox 38. **d** 41 **p** 42 Bris. C of All H Easton 41-45; St Paul Ox 45-49; W Wycombe 49-54; V of Wolverton St Geo 54-62; Frickley w Clayton 62-65; Barlby 65-74; Micklefield 74-81; Perm to Offic Dio Ex from 81. *Ground Floor Flat, 23 Church Road, Dartmouth, Devon, TQ6 9HQ.* (0884 34170)

TAYLOR, Canon John Frederick. b 20. St Chad's Coll Dur Ely Th Coll 59. **d** 61 **p** 62 York. C of Grangetown 61-64; V of St Cuthb Middlesbrough 64-71; Skipsea w Ulrome (and Barmston w Fraisthorpe from 79) 71-82; P-in-c of Barmston w Fraisthorpe 77-79; Can and Preb of York Minster from 79; V of Hemingbrough Dio York from 82. *Vicarage, Hemingbrough, Selby, N Yorks, YO8 7QS.* (Selby 638528)

TAYLOR, John Howard. Univ of Tor BA Sc 53. Wycl Coll BD 58. **d** 56 **p** 57 Tor. C of All SS Tor 56-58; St Timothy Tor 58-59; R of Haliburton 59-62; Tisdale 62-68; I of Aborfield 65-68; Haney Dio New Westmr from 68. *12071-221st Street, Mapleridge, BC, Canada.*

TAYLOR, Canon John Michael. b 30. St Aid Coll 56. **d** 59 Lanc for Blackb **p** 60 Burnley for York. C of St Jas Chorley 59-62; Broughton Preston Lancs 62-64; Chap St Bonif Coll Warm 64-67; V of Altham w Clayton-le-Moors 68-76; RD of Accrington 71-76; Can Res of Blackb Cathl from 76. *22 Billinge Avenue, Blackburn, BB2 6SD.* (Blackburn 61152)

TAYLOR, Canon John Mitchell. b 32. Univ of Aber MA 54. Edin Th Coll. **d** 56 **p** 57 Aber and Ork. C of St Marg Aber 56-58; C-in-c of H Cross Knightswood Glas 58-59; R 59-64; St Ninian Glas 64-73; Dumfries Dio Glas from 73; Can of St Mary's Cathl Glas from 79. *St John's Rectory, Newall Terrace, Dumfries, Scotland.* (Dumfries 4126)

TAYLOR, John Ralph. b 48. Univ of Nottm BTh 74. St Jo Coll Nottm 70. **d** 74 **p** 75 Blackb. C of St Jas Clitheroe 74-77; Kidsgrove 77-79; Hawkwell Dio Chelmsf from 79. *94 Rectory Road, Rochford, Essex, SS4 1UG.*

TAYLOR, Canon John Rowland. OBE 74. St Mich Coll Llan. **d** 58 **p** 59 Llan. C of Caerau St Cynfelin 58-59; Aberdare 59-61; Chap Miss to Seamen Dar-S Dio Zanz 61-65; Dio Dar-S 65-73; Archd of Dar-S 65-73; VG of Dar-S 67-73; Hon Can of Dar-S from 73; V of Ch Ch Bangkok Dio Sing from 73; Chap British Embassy Bangkok from 74. *11 Convent Road, Bangkok, Thailand.* (234-3634)

✠ **TAYLOR, Right Rev John Vernon.** b 14. Late Exhib of Trin Coll Cam 2nd cl Engl Trip pt i 35, BA (2nd cl Hist Trip pt ii) 36. St Cath S Ox BA (2nd cl Th) 38, MA 41. Wycl Coll Tor Hon DD 64. Wycl Hall Ox 36. **d** 38 Lon **p** 39 Willesden for Lon. C of All S Langham Place St Marylebone 38-40; St Helens (in c of St Andr) Lancs 40-43; CMS Miss at Bp Tucker Mem Coll Mukono and Exam Chap to Bp of Ugan 45-55; Commiss to Bp of Ugan 55-60; Nam from 60; Ondo 64-71; M Internat Miss Coun 55-59; CMS Afr Sec 59-63; Gen Sec 63-74; Hon Can of St Paul's Cathl Kampala from 63; Exam Chap to Bp of Truro 74; Cons Ld Bp of Win in Westmr Abbey 31 Jan 75 by Abp of Cant; Bps of Ox, Nor, Sarum, Worc, Derby, Wakef, Heref, Chelmsf, Linc, Bris, St E and Nam; Bps Suffr of Kens, Edmon, Basingstoke, Southn, Woolwich and Lewes; and others; Prelate of Most Noble Order of Garter and Prov Chan of Cant from 75; Chairman Doctrine Comm from 77. *Wolvesey, Winchester, Hants.* (Winchester 4050)

TAYLOR, John Waldron. Ridley Coll Melb ACT ThL (2nd cl) 65. **d** 65 **p** 66 Melb. C of Doncaster 65-66; Essendon 66-67; Dioc Centre (in c of St Jude Carlton) Dio Melb 67-70; Perm to Offic Dio Melb 70-72; C of St Jas w St John's Miss Melb 72-76; L to Offic Dio Melb 76-81. *583 Ferntree Gully Road, Glen Waverley, Vic, Australia 3150.*

TAYLOR, Joseph Henry. b 04. Linc Th Coll 44. **d** 46 **p** 47 Linc. C of Barton-on-Humber 46-48; Frodingham 48-50; V of Appleby 50-63; PC of Shiney Row 63-69; R of Wrabness 69-73. *1 St James Close, Kissing Tree Lane, Alveston, Stratford-on-Avon, Warwicks, CV37 7RH.*

TAYLOR, Joseph Robin Christopher. b 34. St Aid Coll 58. **d** 61 **p** 62 Guildf. C of Aldershot 61-64; Fleet (in c of SS Phil and Jas) 64-68; R of Manaton 69-73; N Bovey 69-73; V of Dawlish Dio Ex from 73. *Vicarage, West Cliff Road, Dawlish, Devon.* (Dawlish 862204)

TAYLOR, Joseph Wolfrey. Qu Coll Newfld. **d** 40 **p** 41 Newfld. C of St Mary St John's 41-42; R of Badger's Quay 42-46; I of Cow Head 46-50; R of Smith's Sound 50-52; I of Random 52-56; R of Harbour Buffett 56-60; Gander Bay 60-69; Port de Grave 69-71; Hosp Chap Dio E Newfld from 76. *St Luke's Homes, Topsail Road, St John's, Newfoundland, Canada.*

TAYLOR, Kenneth Charles. b 24. St Deiniol's Libr Hawarden 76. **d** 76 **p** 77 Ches. C of Wilmslow 76-79; V of Willaston Dio Ches from 79. *Vicarage, Willaston, Wirral, Merseyside.* (051-327 4737)

TAYLOR, Kenneth Gordon. Selw Coll Cam BA 54, MA 58. Chich Th Coll 54. **d** 56 **p** 57 Nor. C of All SS King's Lynn 56-60; Holbeck 60-62; Moor Allerton 62-71; R of Northwold 71-81; P-in-c of Haslingfield and of Harlton Dio Ely from 81.

Haslingfield Vicarage, Cambridge, CB3 7JF. (Cambridge 870285)

TAYLOR, Leslie. b 09. BD (Univ of Lon) 51. Kelham Th Coll 26. **d** 33 **p** 34 Bradf. C of Ch Ch Windhill 33-36; St Jo Bapt Bridgwater 36-40; St Jo Evang Taunton 40-42; St Mich Yeovil 42-47; R of Ansford 47-58; C-in-c of Alford w Hornblotton 54-58; V of All SS Rockwell Green Wellington w Thorne St Marg 58-76; Team V of Wellington and Distr 76-79. *4 Rosebank Gardens, Milverton, Taunton, Somt.*

TAYLOR, Lloyd Hopeton. b 42. Univ of the WI BA 74. U Th Coll of WI 70. **d** 74 **p** 75 Bel. Chap St Mich Coll Bel from 74; R of All SS City and Dio Bel from 75. *111 Albert Street, Belize City, Belize.* (02-3161)

TAYLOR, Marcus Beresford. b 13. TCD 1st cl Ment and Mor Sc 33, BA 35, Div Test 36, MA 43. **d** 36 **p** 37 Dub. C of St Paul Glenageary 36-39; St Jas Dub 39-47; I of Stillorgan Dio Dub from 47; Can of Ch Ch Cathl Dub from 71; V of All SS Blackrock Dio Dub from 78. *Rectory, Stillorgan, Co Dublin, Irish Republic.* (Stillorgan 881091)

TAYLOR, Mark Edward. b 54. St Jo Coll Auckld 76. **d** 78 **p** 79 Waik. C of Claudelands 78-80; Taumarunui 80-81; V of Te Aroha Dio Waik from 81. *Box 23, Te Aroha, NZ.* (48-728)

TAYLOR, Michael Alan. b 47. Trin Coll Bris 72. **d** 76 **p** 77 Southw. C of Ch Ch Chilwell 76-79; Chap RAF from 79. *c/o Ministry of Defence, Adastral House, Theobalds Road, WC1 8RU.*

TAYLOR, Michael Allan. b 50. Univ of Nottm BTh 80. St Jo Coll Nottm 76. **d** 80 **p** 81 Bradf. C of St Jo Evang Bowling Dio Bradf from 80. *15 West View, Bowling, Bradford, W Yorks, BD4 7ER.*

TAYLOR, Michael Barry. b 38. Bps' Coll Cheshunt 63. **d** 65 **p** 66 Ripon. C of Harehills 65-68; Stanningley 68-70; V of St Pet w St Cuthb Hunslet Moor 70-78; Starbeck Dio Ripon from 78. *78 High Street, Starbeck, Harrogate, Yorks.* (Harrogate 883036)

TAYLOR, Michael Frank Chatterton. b 30. St Aid Coll 59. **d** 61 **p** 62 Leic. C of St Jo Bapt Knighton 61-65; R of Melton Constable w Swanton Novers Dio Nor from 65; V of Briningham Dio Nor from 65. *Swanton Novers Rectory, Melton Constable, Norfolk, NR24 2RB.* (Melton Constable 860329)

TAYLOR, Michael Laurence. b 43. Ch Coll Cam BA 66, MA 70. Cudd Coll 66. **d** 68 **p** 69 Bris. C of Westbury-on-Trym 68-72; Asst Chap Wellington Coll Crowthorne 72-76; C of St Helier Morden (in c of Bp Andrewes' Ch) 76-78; Team V of Bedminster Dio Bris from 78. *St Paul's Vicarage, Southville Road, Bristol, BS3 1DG.* (Bristol 663189)

TAYLOR, Neil Hamish. b 48. Linc Th Coll 72. **d** 75 **p** 76 Sheff. C of Rotherham 75-78; Doncaster Dio Sheff from 78. *St Edmund's House, Anchorage Lane, Sprotbrough, Doncaster.* (Doncaster 781986)

TAYLOR, Nicholas James. b 46. St Chad's Coll Dur BA 67, Dipl Th 68. **d** 69 **p** 70 Dur. C of Beamish 69-74; Styvechale 74-77; C-in-c of Wilmcote w Billesley 77-79; Aston Cantlow 77-79; V of Aston Cantlow and Wilmcote w Billesley Dio Cov from 79. *Vicarage, Wilmcote, Stratford-on-Avon, Warws, CV37 9XD.* (S-on-A 292376)

TAYLOR, Norman. b 26. Late Scho of CCC Cam BA 49, MA 52. Cudd Coll 49. **d** 51 **p** 52 Blackb. C of St Mary Magd Clitheroe 51-54; Pontesbury 54-55; R of L Wilbraham w Six Mile Bottom 55-71; L to Offic Dio Ely from 72; Chap St Faith's Cam from 71. *46 Highsett Hills Road, Cambridge, CB2 1NZ.* (Cam 357922)

TAYLOR, Norman Adrian. b 48. St D Univ Coll Lamp Dipl Th 73. Bp Burgess Hall Lamp 70. **d** 73 **p** 74 Mon. C of Fleur-de-Lys 73-75; W Drayton 75-79; C-in-c of St Edm Conv Distr Yeading Hayes Dio Lon from 79. *St Edmund's Vicarage, Edmunds Close, Hayes, Middx, UB4 0HA.* (01-573 6913)

TAYLOR, Norman Wentworth. b 18. Ely Th Coll 46. **d** 49 **p** 50 Newc T. C of Ashington 49-53; C-in-c of Shiremoor Conv Distr 53-59; V of St Anthony Byker Newc T 59-66; N Sunderland 66-74; H Sav Priory Ch Tynemouth Dio Newc T from 74; Surr from 77; RD of Tynemouth from 81. *1 Crossway, Tynemouth, T & W, NE30 2LB.* (N Shields 571636)

TAYLOR, Norman Wyatt. b 23. Wells Th Coll 58. **d** 60 **p** 61 Bris. C of Lawrence Weston 60-63; V 63-69; Bp's Cannings (w All Cannings and Etchilhampton from 77) 69-80; V of W Moors Dio Sarum from 80. *Vicarage, Glenwood Road, West Moors, Wimborne, Dorset.* (Ferndown 893197)

TAYLOR, Paul Latham. b 11. **d** 49 **p** 50 Newc T. C of St Pet Monkseaton 49-52; St Barn Epsom 52-54; V of Milford 54-72; Chap K Geo V Hosp Godalming 54-70; Milford Chest Hosp 70-72; Warden Homes of St Barn Lingfield 72-77. *14 Church Street, Chipping Norton, OX7 5NT.* (Chipping Norton 3216)

TAYLOR, Paul Wright. b 47. Univ of W Ont BA 70. Hur Coll Lon MDiv 73. **d** and **p** 73 Niag. C of Ancaster 73-75; R of St Monica Niag Falls 75-78; Queenston 75-78; Hagersville Dio Niag from 78. *Box 365, Hagersville, Ont, Canada.* (416-768 3526)

TAYLOR, Peter. b 51. St Jo Coll Cam BA 72, MA 76. Ridley Hall Cam 73. **d** 76 **p** 77 Roch. C of St Pet w St Marg Roch 76-79. *52 High Street, Landbeach, Cambridge, CB4 4DT.* (Cam 861908)

TAYLOR, Peter. b 35. Univ of Sussex MA 72. Wells Th Coll 58. **d** 60 **p** 61 Guildf. C of Godalming 60-62; Epsom 62-65; R of W Clandon 65-75; E Clandon 65-75. *7 Westbrooke, Worthing, W Sussex.*

TAYLOR, Peter David. b 38. FCA. N Ordin Course 77. **d** 80 **p** 81 Blackb. C of Penwortham Dio Blackb from 80. *11 The Grove, Penwortham, Preston, PR1 0UU.*

TAYLOR, Peter David. b 47. Univ of Liv BEducn 74. Univ of Man MEducn 78. NOC 78. **d** 81 Liv. C of H Trin Formby Dio Liv from 81. *19 Hampton Road, Formby, Mer, L37 6EJ.*

TAYLOR, Peter Flint. b 44. Qu Coll Cam BA 65, MA 69. BD (Lon) 70 Lon Coll of Div 67. **d** 70 **p** 71 Stepney for Lon. C of St Aug Highbury 70-73; St Andr Plymouth 73-77; V of Ironville Dio Derby from 77. *Ironville Vicarage, Nottingham, NG16 5PH.* (Leabrooks 602241)

TAYLOR, Peter John. b 40. Oak Hill Th Coll 62. **d** 65 **p** 66 Roch. C of St Barn Cray 65-69; St Jo Bapt Woking 69-77; R of Necton w Holme Hale Dio Nor from 77. *Necton Rectory, Swaffham, Norf.* (Swaffham 22021)

TAYLOR, Peter John. Ridley Coll Melb ACT ThL 65. **d** 65 **p** 66 Nel. C of All SS Nel 65-68; V of Collingwood (w Takaka from 70) 68-73; Golden Bay 73-75; Chap Dilworth Sch Auckld from 76; Hon C of St Mark Remuera 77-79; C of Papakura Dio Auckld from 79. *14 Gollan Road, Mount Wellington, Auckland 6, NZ.*

TAYLOR, Peter John. b 46. Trin Coll Bris 71. **d** 73 **p** 74 Man. C of Walshaw 73-75; Rodbourne-Cheney 75-78; Asst Chap HM Pris Pentonville 78-79; Chap HM Borstal Roch from 79. *H.M. Borstal, Rochester, ME1 3NE.* (Medway 44215)

TAYLOR, Peter Joseph. b 41. Bps' Coll Cheshunt 66. **d** 68 **p** 69 Southw. C of Wollaton 68-71; Cockington w Chelston 71-74; V of Broadhembury (w Payhembury from 79) 74-81; Gt Staughton Dio Ely from 81; Chap HM Borstal Gaynes Hall from 81. *Vicarage, Great Staughton, Cambs, PE19 4BA.* (Kimbolton 252)

TAYLOR, Peter Lindsay. Univ of Syd BA 64. Univ of Lon BD 77. Moore Th Coll Syd ThL 76. **d** and **p** 78 Syd. C of S Turramurra 78-80; Chap Macquarie Univ from 78. *22 Saddington Street, Turramurra, NSW, Australia 2074.*

TAYLOR, Peter Tyson. b 20. St Aid Coll 58. **d** 60 Bradf **p** 61 York for Bradf. C of St Aid Buttershaw 60-62; V of Cross Roads w Lees 62-70; V of Oakenshaw w Woodlands Dio Bradf from 70. *Oakenshaw Vicarage, Bradford, Yorks.* (Bradford 679686)

TAYLOR, Philip Francis. Ridley Th Coll Melb 41. ACT ThL 44. **d** 45 **p** 46 Gippsld. C of St Paul's Cathl Sale Vic 45-47; CMS Miss Iran 47-54; Sukkur Lah 54-63; V of Rosedale 63-70; Chap of Oenpelli Miss N Terr 70-76; R of Umbakumba 76-78; Perm to Offic Dio Brisb from 80. *Banyula, Mary Cairncross Drive, Maleny, Queensld, Australia 4552.*

TAYLOR, Preb Philip Mountford. b 1887. Trin Coll Cam BA 09, MA 13. Ely Th Coll 09. **d** 11 **p** 12 B & W. C of Furnham Chard 11-15; Lenham 15-20; Chap of K Coll Taunton 20-27; Div Chap of S of St Mary and St Andr Taunton 27-30; Hd Master K Coll Taunton 30-34; C of All SS Brighton 34-35; V of St Jo Bapt Bridgwater 35-62; Surr 59 RD of Bridgwater 60-62; Preb of Wells Cathl from 62. *17 King Edward Road, Minehead, Somt.* (Minehead 3991)

TAYLOR, Raymond. b 34. Lon Coll of Div 62. **d** 65 **p** 66 Man. C of Pennington Leigh 65-70; P-in-c of Wombridge 70-80; R of S Normanton Dio Derby from 80. *South Normanton Rectory, Derbys, DE5 5BY.* (Ripley 811273)

TAYLOR, Raymond Montgomery. b 43. Oak Hill Coll 77. **d** 80 **p** 81 Edmonton for Lon. C of St Pet Cricklewood Dio Lon from 80. *25 Rowan Drive, Hendon, NW9 5JL.*

TAYLOR, Reginald Reynolds. Angl Th Coll BC Dipl Th 66. **d** 66 **p** 67 Koot. C of Koot Boundary Regional Par 66-68; R of Armstrong 68-73; N Surrey BC 73-78. *10919 - 141st Street, Surrey, BC, Canada.*

TAYLOR, Richard. b 46. Univ of Reading BA (Hist) 68. Sarum Wells Th Coll 70. **d** 73 **p** 74 Bris. C of Swindon 73-76; P-in-c of Charlton w Brokenborough and Hankerton 76-79; St Matt Croydon Dio Cant from 79. *St Matthew's Vicarage, Stanhope Road, Croydon, CR0 5NS.* (01-688 5055)

TAYLOR, Richard David. b 44. Late Scho of Worc Coll Ox 2nd cl Cl 65, BA (2nd cl Th) 67, MA 70. Coll of Resurr Mirfield, 67. **d** 69 Penrith for Carl **p** 70 Carl. C of St Geo w St Luke Barrow F 69-73; All SS Gosforth (in c of St Mary Virg Fawdon) 73-80; Team R of The Epiph City and Dio Newc T from 80. *St Mary's Vicarage, 7 Fawdon Lane, Newcastle-upon-Tyne, NE3 2RR.* (0632 855403)

TAYLOR, Preb Richard John. b 21. Kelham Th Coll 38. **d** 45 **p** 46 Lich. C of Ch Ch Tunstall 45-48; Uttoxeter 48-52; V of Croxden w Hollington 52-57; Short Heath 57-68; R of Edgmond 68-77; V of Streetly Dio Lich from 77; Preb of Lich Cathl from 78. *2 Foley Church Close, Streetly, Sutton Coldfield, W Midl, B74 3JX.* (021-353 2292)

TAYLOR, Robert Noel. b 48. Sir Geo Wm's Univ Montr BA 72. Trin Coll Tor MDiv 76. **d** 76 **p** 77 Calg. C of St Aug Lethbridge 76-78; Chap Univ of Calg 78-81; I of Beddington Area Dio Calg from 81. *910-19th Avenue NW, Calgary, Alta, Canada, T2M 0Z5.* (282-0287)

✠ **TAYLOR, Right Rev Robert Selby.** St Cath Coll Cam BA 30, MA 34. Rhodes Univ Hon DD 66. Cudd Coll 30. **d** 32 **p** 33 York. C of St Olave w St Giles York 32-34; UMCA Miss P at Msoro 35-37; Fiwila 38-39; Kakwe Lesa 39-41; Cons Ld Bp of N Rhod in Lik Cathl 29 Sept 41 by Bp of Zanz for Abp of Cant; and Bps of Masasi; Ugan; Nyasa; and Lebom; Trld to Pret 51; to Grahmstn 59; to Capetn 64; res 74; Sub-Prelate O of St John of Jer from 60; Hon Fell St Cath Coll Cam from 64; Perm to Offic Dio Capetn 75-79; Apptd Bp of Centr Zam 79. *PO Box 70172, Ndola, Zambia.*

TAYLOR, Roger. b 21. Birkbeck Coll Lon BA (2nd cl) 50. Univ of Leeds, MA 59. Oak Hill Th Coll 47. **d** 51 **p** 52 Man. C of Ch Ch Chadderton 51-55; V of St Steph Bowling 55-63; SW Area Sec CPAS 63-68; V of Felixstowe 68-81; P-in-c of Gt w L Thurlow & L Bradley Dio St E from 81. *Vicarage, The Street, Little Thurlow, Haverhill, Suffolk, CB9 7LA.* (Thurlow 360)

TAYLOR, Roger Patrick. Univ of NZ BA 31. NZ Bd of Th Stud LTh 34. **d** 35 Abp Julius for Ch Ch **p** 36 Nel for Ch Ch. C of Fendalton 35-38; St Anne Wandsworth 38-39; Avonside 39-41; V of Kumara 41-44; P-in-c of Sydenham 44-45; Lyttleton 45-46; V of Kaiapoi 46-52; Caversham 52-62; V of U Cluther 62-65; Flagstaff 65-71; St Kilda 71-77; Perm to Offic Dios Ch Ch and Dun from 77. *22 Wingate Street, Redwood, Christchurch 5, NZ.*

TAYLOR, Canon Roland Haydn. b 29. St Chad's Coll Dur BA 53, Dipl Th 55. **d** 55 **p** 56 Newc T. C of St Columba N Gosforth 55-58; C of Barnsley Yorks 58-61; V of Brotherton 61-68; Purston w S Featherstone 68-76; RD of Pontefract from 74; R of Badsworth Dio Wakef from 76; Hon Can of Wakef Cathl from 81. *Badsworth Rectory, Pontefract, W Yorks, WF9 1AF.* (S Elmsall 43642)

TAYLOR, Ronald Enfield Bissett. CCC Cam BA 54, MA 59. Cudd Coll 54. **d** 56 Nor for Cant for Col Bp **p** 57 Bp Lavis. C of St Paul Rondebosch 56-59; Chap St Paul's Coll Grahmstn 60-62; R of Nelspruit (w White River from 64) 62-65; St Jo Bapt Walmer 65-80; Can of Port Eliz 75-80; Archd Dio Port Eliz 77-80; R of St Sav Claremont Dio Capetn from 80. *St Saviour's Rectory, Bowwood Road, Claremont, CP, S Africa.*

TAYLOR, Ronald John. Univ of NZ BA 55, MA 60. NZ Bd of Th Stud ThL (2nd cl) 62. Coll Ho Ch Ch 54. Ridley Coll Melb 56. **d** 57 Bp Rich for Wel **p** 57 Wel. C of Lower Hutt 57-58; Masterton 58-60; V of Martinborough 60-64; Chap H Spirit Cathl Dodoma 64-66; on leave 66-68; V of Ch Ch Arusha 68-72; Can of Centr Tang 71-75; Chap Dar-S Univ and Prov Sec Tanzania 72-75; Perm to Offic Dio Dar-S 72-75; Chap St Marg Coll Ch Ch 75-77; V of Sumner-Redcliffs Dio Ch Ch from 77. *48 Wakefield, Christchurch 8, NZ.* (Sumner 6251)

TAYLOR, Canon Rowland Wilfred. b 09. AKC 34. **d** 34 Buckingham for Ox **p** 35 Ox. C of Chalfont St Pet 34-36; St Mary Virg Kenton Middx 36-39; C of Tewkesbury Abbey 39-42; St Alb Holborn 42-47; V of St Mary Wellingborough 47-52; Archd of Bel and VG Br Hond 52-59; R of St Mary Stamford 59-62; Commiss Br Hond (Bel from 73) from 59; V of St Barn Tunbridge Wells 62-74; Surr 64-74; Can of Br Hond (Bel from 73) from 72; RD of Tunbridge Wells 73-74; Perm to Offic Dio Chich from 75. *5 Montpelier Crescent, Brighton, Sussex, BN1 3JF.*

TAYLOR, Roy William. b 37. Ch Coll Cam BA 61, MA 65. Clifton Th Coll 61. **d** 63 **p** 64 Blackb. C of Ch of the Sav Blackb 63-66; Hensingham 66-69; Warden St Mich Ho Taiwan 71-79; Team V of Bushbury Dio Lich from 79. *131 Taunton Avenue, Fordhouses, Wolverhampton.* (Wolverhampton 782030)

TAYLOR, Stanley Richard. Hur Coll LTh 68. **d** 68 **p** 69 Fred. P-in-c of Prince William Dio Fred from 68. *Prince William, NB, Canada.*

TAYLOR, Stephen Gordon. b 35. Univ of Bris BA 60. Ridley Hall Cam 60. **d** 62 **p** 63 Chelmsf. C of Gt Baddow 62-65; Portsdown 65-69; C-in-c of Elveden 69-70; R 70-75; C-in-c of Icklingham 69-70; R 70-75; C-in-c of Eriswell 69-70; R 70-75; Chap St Felix Sch Southwold 75-76; R of L Shelford w Newton Dio Ely from 77. *Little Shelford Rectory, Cambridge.* (Cam 843710)

TAYLOR, Stephen James. b 48. Chich Th Coll 70. **d** 73 Edmon for Lon **p** 74 Lon. C of St Paul Tottenham 73-76; P-in-c of Biabou Dio Windw Is from 78. *Rectory, Biabou, St Vincent, West Indies.*

TAYLOR, Stewart. b 51. St Jo Coll Dur 74. **d** 77 **p** 78 S'wark. C of W Norwood 77-81; Surbiton Hill (in c of Em Tolworth) Dio Southwark from 81. *181 Elgar Avenue, Tolworth, Surrey.* (01-399 1503)

TAYLOR, Stuart Bryan. b 40. St Chad's Coll Dur BA 64. **d** 66 Grantham for Linc for Portsm **p** 67 Portsm. C of St Mark N End Portsea 66-70; Epsom 70-76; Chap Clifton Coll Bris from 76. *7 College Fields, Bristol, BS8 3HP.* (Bris 738605)

TAYLOR, Thomas. b 42. Univ of Dur BA 64. Linc Th Coll 64. **d** 66 Lanc for Blackb **p** 67 Blackb. C of Clitheroe 66-69; Skerton 69-71; C-in-c of St Leon Conv Distr Penwortham 71-72; V 72-78; R of Morecambe (Poulton-le-Sands) 78-81; P-in-c of St Laur Morecambe 79-81; R of Holy Trin Poulton-le-Sands w St Laur Morecambe Dio Blackb from 81. *Rectory, Morecambe, Lancs, LA4 5PR.* (Morecambe 410941)

TAYLOR, Thomas. b 33. Sarum Wells Th Coll 77. **d** 80 Sarum **p** 81 Bp Maddock for Sarum (NSM). C of St John Heatherlands Parkstone Dio Sarum from 80. *31 Turbary Road, Parkstone, Poole, Dorset.*

TAYLOR, Thomas Fish. b 13. Univ of Glas MA 2nd cl Hist 46. Kelham Th Coll 30. **d** 36 **p** 37 Dur. C of St Mary Magd Millfield 36-38; All SS Middlesbrough 38-41; R of St Martin Polmadie Glas 41-48; Chap to The Priory Burford 48-50; Distr Hosp Mount Ephraim Tunbridge Wells and L to Offic Dio Roch 50-52; V of Chalford 52-58; R of Over Compton w Nether Compton 58-65; P-in-c of Trent 62-65; Poughill w Stockleigh English 67-69; Rattery 69-79; Perm to Offic Dio Ex from 79. *6 Times Mews, Totnes, Devon.*

TAYLOR, Thomas Ronald Bennett. b 23. TCD MA 54. **d** 47 **p** 48 Connor. C of Inver (Larne) 47-49; Chap RAF 49-65; Cranwell 49-51; Gibr 51-53; Catterick 53-55; Ceylon 55-58; Stafford 58-61; Wildenrath 62-64; Ballykelly 64-65; I of Narraghmore w Fontstown and Timolin 65-68; R of Tynan w Middletown Dio Arm from 68. *Rectory, Tynan, Co Armagh, N Ireland.* (Caledon 619)

TAYLOR, William Austin. b 36. Linc Th Coll 65. **d** 67 **p** 68 Man. C of Tyldesley 67-71; R of St Mark Cheetham Hill Man 71-79; V of Peel Dio Man 79-80; Team R from 80. *122 Peel Lane, Little Hulton, Worsley, Manchester, M28 6FL.* (061-790 4202)

TAYLOR, William Henry. b 1897. Wycl Hall Ox. **d** 63 **p** 64 Chelmsf. C of Hornchurch 63-65; V of Chrishall 65-79. *The Brewhouse, Boscastle, N Cornwall, PL35 0HD.*

TAYLOR, William James. b 29. St Aid Coll. **d** 59 Stafford for Lich **p** 60 Lich. C of Bushbury 59-62; V of St Mark Millfield Bp Wearmouth 62-74; R of Gateshead Fell Dio Dur from 74. *St John's Rectory, Shotley Gardens, Low Fell, Gateshead, T & W,*

TAYLOR, William Richard de Carteret Martin. b 33. CCC Cam Ba 57, MA 61. Westcott Ho Cam 58. **d** 59 Bp Robin for Cant **p** 60 Portsm. C of St Marg Eastney 59-63; Chap RN 63-67; and from 70; R of Childe Okeford 67-70; R of Manston w Hammoon 67-70. *c/o Ministry of Defence, Lacon House, Theobalds Road, WC1X 8RY.*

TAYLOR, William Walter Joseph. b 11. ALCD 42 (LTh from 74). **d** 41 **p** 42 Lon for Argent. C of St Bart Grays Inn Rd 41-43; Org Sec S Amer MS Dios St Alb and Roch 43-45; S Amer MS Youth Sec 43-45; Chap Cordoba Distr Argent and Dir Allen Gardiner Homes Los Cocos Cordoba 45-48; C of St Jas Gravesend 48-50; V of Haddenham 50-64; Surr from 50; V of Kingsey 53-64; R of Fulmer 64-75; Perm to Offic Dio Ex from 76. *1 Nash Gardens, Dawlish, Devon, EX7 9RR.* (Dawlish 863922)

TEAGE, Alan Dixon. b 17. Ripon Hall, Ox 59. **d** 61 **p** 62 Ex. C of Dartmouth 61-63; V of Blackawton (w Stoke Fleming from 76) Dio Ex from 63; P-in-c of Stoke Fleming 76; RD of Woodleigh from 80. *Blackawton Vicarage, Totnes, Devon, TQ9 7AY.* (Blackawton 222)

TEAGUE, Gaythorne Derrick. b 24. Univ of Bris MB, ChB 49. **d** 74 Bris **p** 75 Malmesbury for Bris (APM). C of Hartcliffe Dio Bris from 74; Perm to Offic Dio B & W from 79. *40 Flaxbourton Road, Failand, Bristol, BS8 3UN.* (Long Ashton 2912)

TEAGUE, Robert Hayden. b 15. **d** 63 **p** 64 St A. C of Rhosddu 63-65; Llanrhos 65-66; V of Llangernyw w Llanddewi and Gwytherin 66-77; Meliden and Gwaenysgor Dio St A from 77; RD of Llanrwst 75-77. *St Melyd's Vicarage, Meliden, Prestatyn, Clwyd.* (Prestatyn 6220)

TEAL, Canon John. VRD 78. Univ of NZ BSc 45. Univ of Otago BTh 77. Coll Ho Ch Ch. **d** 46 **p** 47 Ch Ch. C of Sydenham NZ 46-49; Leeds (in c of St Jo Bapt) 49-51; V of Temuka 51-59; Hornby 59-62; Caversham Dio Dun from 62; CF 54-64; Chap RNZNVR 64-78; Exam Chap to Bp of Dun from 76; Hon Can of Dun from 79. *57 Baker Street, Caversham, NZ.* (Dunedin 53-961)

TEALE, Adrian. b 53. Univ of Wales (Abth) BA 74, MA 80. Wycl Hall Ox 78. **d** 80 **p** 81 St D. C of Bettws w Ammanford Dio St D from 80. *32 Tirydail Lane, Ammanford, Dyfed,* (Ammanford 3590)

TEALE, Ernest Burdett. b 20. Keble Coll Ox BA (2nd cl Mod Hist) 42, MA 46. Westcott Ho Cam 42. **d** 43 **p** 45 Portsm. C of Havant 43-48; Melksham 48-54; R of Bradf Peverell w Stratton 54-61; Asst Dir of Relig Educn Dio Sarum 61-64; R of Morton 64-69; C-in-c of Radbourne Derby 69-70; L to Offic Dio Lon from 70; Adv for Relig Educn Dio Lon from 70. *103 Sandringham Gardens, North Finchley, N12.* (01-445 2037)

TEANAKEI, Francis. Bp Patteson Th Centre Kohimarama. **d** 72 **p** 74 Melan. P Dio Melan 72-75; Dio Centr Melan from 75. *Lord Howe Island, Santa Cruz, Solomon Islands.*

TEAPE, Canon Thomas William. St Jo Coll Manit BA and LTh 31. **d** 31 **p** 32 Edmon. C of Westlock 31-32; V of St John Kitscoty 32-38; I of Tofield 38-40; Perm to Offic (Col C Act) at H Trin Heref 40-41; C of St John Hackney 41-44; R of Cadomin 44-46; Vermilion 46-52; Can of Edmon 49-60 and 65-71; Hon Can from 71; St Pet Edmon 52-55; C of All SS Cathl Edmon 55-60; Archd of Edmon N 56-60; Exam Chap to Bp of Edmon 58-69; Dean and R of All SS Cathl Edmon 60-65; R of Ft Sask 65-71. *3 Greenwood Way, Sherwood Park, Alta., Canada.* (403-467 6779)

TEAPE-FUGARD, Theodore Charles William Cooper. b 04. Ball Coll Ox 3rd cl Cl Mods 25, BA (4th cl Lit Hum) 27, MA 32. Médaille D'Argent de la Reconnaissance Française 45. Sarum Th Coll 30. **d** 30 **p** 31 Ches. C of H Ascen Upton Ches 30-32; Offg Chap KS Ches 31-48; PC of L St John (or St John Without the Northgate) Ches 32-48; Chap Blue Coat Hosp Ches 32-48; R of Blunham 48-54; Asst Insp Schs Archd of Bedford 51-54; V of Crambe w Whitwell 54-63; V of Huttons Ambo 54-63; RD of Malton 58-63; Proc Conv York 58-63; Chap of Stockholm Dio Lon (N & C Eur) 63-69; I of Hacketstown 69-71. *The Old Deanery, Killala, Co Mayo, Irish Republic.*

TEARE, Robert John Hugh. b 39. Univ of Bris BSc 62. Univ of Leeds Dipl Th 69. Coll of Resurr Mirfield 67. **d** 70 **p** 71 Portsm. C of Fareham 70-73; Chap K Alfred's Coll Win 73-78; Exam Chap to Bp of Win from 76; V of St Jas Pokesdown Bournemouth Dio Win from 78; M Gen Syn from 80. *12 Harewood Avenue, Boscombe East, Bournemouth, Dorset, BH7 6NQ.* (Bournemouth 425918)

TEARNAN, John Herman Janson. b 37. Univ of Bris BSc (Mech Eng) 59. Kelham Th Coll 62. **d** 66 **p** 67 Pet. C of Kettering 66-71; L to Offic Dio Pet from 71. *40 Headlands, Kettering, Northants, NN15 7HR.* (Kettering 81420)

TEBBOTH, Alfred Thomas Henderson. b 09. Qu Coll Birm 51. **d** 52 **p** 53 Sheff. C of Ecclesfield 52-56; V of Kilnhurst 56-66; C of Royston 66-69; R of Therfield 69-76; Kelshall 69-76. *2 Priory Close, Royston, Herts.* (Royston 42276)

TEBBOTH, John Arthur. b 17. Univ of Lon BSc (2nd cl Chem) 40, PhD (Lon) 45. **d** 60 **p** 61 Lich. C of Walsall 60-63; V of St Nich Strood 63-67; Crofton Kent 67-79; RD of Orpington 76-79; C of Speldhurst w Groombridge & Ashurst Dio Roch from 79. *Somerden, Groombridge, Tunbridge Wells, Kent.* (Groombridge 303)

TEBBS, Richard Henry. b 52. Univ of Southn BTh. Sarum Wells Th Coll 75. **d** 78 **p** 79 Southw. C of Cinderhill Dio Southw from 78. *22 Overdale Road, Stockhill Estate, Cinderhill, Nottingham, NG6 0LQ.* (Nottm 789000)

TEDMAN, Alfred. b 33. K Coll Lon and Warm AKC 59. **d** 60 **p** 61 S'wark. C of Newington 60-64; St Jas Milton (in c of St Patr) 64-68; R of Bonchurch Dio Portsm from 68; RD of E Wight from 78; P-in-c of St Lawr, I W Dio Portsm from 79. *Bonchurch Rectory, Ventnor, IW.* (Ventnor 852357)

TEE, Ven Cecil Lindsay. Univ of S Afr BA 63. St Paul's Coll Grahmstn LTh 54. **d** 54 **p** 55 Johann. C of Klerksdorp 54-57; Benoni 58-59; R of Ladybrand 60-61; Odendaalsrus 61-63; Sasolburg 63-64; Parys 64-70; Witbank Dio Pret from 72; Archd of E Transvaal from 78. *PO Box 182, Witbank, Transvaal, S Africa.* (Witbank 3095)

TEED, Daniel Williamson. St Jo Coll Morpeth, 60. **d** 61 **p** 62 Gippsld. C of Morwell 61-64; V of Bass 64-68; P-in-c of Boianai 68-71; Sag Sag 71-74; R of Tongala Dio Bend from 75. *7 St James' Street, Tongala, Vic, Australia.* (058581-153)

TE HAARA, Waiohau Rui. St Jo Coll Auckld 58. **d** 61 **p** 62 Auckld. C of St Barn Mt Eden Auckld 62-64; N Wairoa 64-67; V of Coromandel 67-71; P in Mangere Team Ministry 71-80; in Maori Miss Auckld 80-82; V of Ohinemutu Dio Wai from 82. *Vicarage, Ohinemutu, NZ.*

TEITEH, Godfrey Ampin. b 36. **d** and **p** 75 Accra. P Dio Accra. *Box 491, Korle Gonno, Accra, Ghana.*

TEKERE, Zacharia. St Jo Sem Lusaka. **d** 53 **p** 54 Mashon. P Dio Mashon from 53. *c/o Box UA7, Salisbury, Zimbabwe.*

TEKYI-MENSAH, Canon Henry. St Aug Coll Cant LTh 41. **d** 42 **p** 43 Gambia. Hd Master St Mary's Sch Bath Gambia 42-46; Perm to Offic as C of Ch of Our Lady and St Nich Liv 46-47; P-in-c of All SS Conakry 47-55; Chap Conv of Our Lady Mampong 55-58; P-in-c of Nsawam 58-60; Tarkwa 60-64; Adabraka 64-68; Sunyani 68-75; Dom Chap to Bp of Accra 64-68; Archd of Sunyani 68-75; Can (Emer) from 75. *c/o Box 2795, Accra, Ghana.*

TELEMAQUE, Harold Milton. b 10. **d** 80 Trin. C of St Aug La Brea Dio Trin from 80. *Bungalow 11, 22 Road, Crest Camp, Fyzabad, Trinidad, WI.*

TELFER, Canon Frank Somerville. b 30. Trin Hall Cam 2nd cl Hist Trip pt i, 52, BA (2nd cl Hist Trip pt ii) 53, MA 58. Ely Th Coll 53. **d** 55 **p** 56 Liv. C of Our Lady and St Nich Liv 55-58; Chap at Down Coll Cam 58-62; Dom Chap to Bp of Nor 62-65; Chap Univ of Kent 65-73; Six Pr in Cant Cathl 66-72; Can Res of Guildf from 73; Exam Chap to Bp of Guildf from 74; M Gen Syn from 80. *2 Cathedral Close, Guildford, Surrey.* (Guildford 60329)

TELFER, Robert Brian. Moore Th Coll Syd ACT ThL (2nd cl) 62. BD (Lon) 63. **d** 63 **p** 64 Syd. C of Mittagong 63-66; V of Coramba 66-68; C of Gunnedah 69-70; Chap K Sch Parramatta 72-76; R of Gladesville Dio Syd from 76. *4 Jordan Street, Gladesville, NSW, Australia 2111.* (89-2631)

TELFORD, Cyril Harry. St D Coll Lamp. **d** 54 **p** 55 Liv. C of St Faith Gr Crosby 54-57; Our Lady and St Nich Liv 57-60; V of L Lever Dio Man from 60. *Little Lever Vicarage, Bolton, BL3 1HH.* (Farnworth 73574)

TELFORD, Canon Edward Cecil. b 17. Selw Coll Cam BA 47, MA 52. Linc Th Coll 47. **d** 49 **p** 50 Chelmsf. C of Laindon w Basildon 49-52; P-in-c of St Aug Miss Leytonstone 52-59; R of Langdon Hills 59-70; Exam Chap to Bp of Chelmsf from 66; R of Shenfield Dio Chelmsf from 70; Hon Can of Chelmsf Cathl from 75; RD of Brentwood from 76. *Rectory, Shenfield, Essex.* (Brentwood 220360)

TELFORD, John Edward. TCD BA 40, Div Test 40, MA 46. **d** 41 **p** 42 Liv. C of St Mark St Helens 41-44; St Matt Irishtown and Chap Miss to Adult Deaf and Dumb Dub Area 44-60. *12 Woodbine Avenue, Blackrock, Co Dublin, Irish Republic.* (Dublin 691187)

TELFORD, Richard Francis. b 46. K Coll Lon and Warm. **d** 69 Colchester for Chelmsf **p** 70 Chelmsf. C of Barkingside 69-72; Wickford 72-77; P-in-c of St Jo Div Mawneys Romford Dio Chelmsf 77-79; V from 79. *Vicarage, Mawney Road, Romford, Essex.* (Romford 42265)

TELLINI, Gianfranco. b 36. Gregorian Univ Rome Doctor (Or Stud) 65. **d** RC Abp of Trent **p** 61 RC Abp of Trieste. Rec into Angl Commun by Bp of Willesden 66. C of John Keble Ch Mill Hill 66; St Andr Harrow 66-67; Lect Sarum Th Coll 67-69; Sen Tutor 69-74; Vice Prin of Edin Th Coll from 74. *Theological College, Rosebery Crescent, Edinburgh 12.* (031-337-4537)

TEMBY, Richard Desmond. b 46. Ridley Coll Melb 77. **d** 78 **p** 79 Melb. C of Templestowe 78-79; St John Camberwell Dio Melb from 79. *503 Camberwell Road, Camberwell, Vic, Australia 3124.*

✠ **TEMENGONG, Right Rev Basil.** Bps' Coll Calc. **d** 41 Bp Tarafdar for Calc for Lah **p** 43 Calc. Asst Chap St Thos Calc 41-43; Asansol 43-46; Hd Master Betong Sch 46-53; P-in-c of Saratok 56-62; Can of Borneo 60-62; Kuching 62-68; P-in-c of Simanggang 62-68; Archd of Kuching 65-68; Cons Ld Bp of Kuch in St Thos Cathl Kuch 6 Dec 68 by Bp of Taiwan (USA) for Cant; Bps of Sing; and Sabah. *Bishop's House, Kuching, Sarawak.* (Kuching 20187)

TEMPLE, Donald Hubert. b 08. **d** 41 **p** 42 E Szech. Miss Dio E Szech 41-51; Dio Upper Nile 52-54; Dio Sing and Malaya 55-67; Bp's Chap Dio M & W Nile 68-72; V of Kericho Kenya 72-75; Perm to Offic Dio Ex from 77. *7 Arkendale, Whittington College, Felbridge, E Grinstead, Sussex RH19 2QU.*

✠ **TEMPLE, Right Rev Frederick Stephen.** b 16. Ball Coll Ox 2nd cl Mods 37, BA (2nd cl Hist) 39, MA 45. Trin Hall, Cam BA 47, MA 52. Westcott Ho Cam. **d** 47 **p** 48 Southw. C of Arnold 47-49; Newark 49-51; R of St Agnes Birch-in-Rusholme 51-53; Dean of Hong 53-59; Sen Chap to Abp of Cant 59-61; V of St Mary Portsea 61-70; Proc Conv Portsm 64-70; Hon Can of Portsm 65-69; Archd of Swindon 70-73; Hon Can of Bris from 70; Exam Chap to Bp of Bris from 70; Cons Ld Bp Suffr of Malmesbury in St Paul's Cathl 1 Nov 73 by Abp of Cant; Bps of Lon, Birm, Bris, Chich, Derby, Linc, Nor, Ox and Portsm; Bps Suffr of Dorking, Dorch, Doncaster, Huntingdon, Taunton and Croydon; and others. *Morwena, Mill Lane, Swindon, SN1 4QH.* (Swindon 35798)

TEMPLE, Ven George Frederick. b 33. Wells Th Coll 66. **d** 68 **p** 69 Guildf. C of Gt Bookham 68-70; St Mary Penzance 70-72; V of St Just-in-Penwith 72-74; Sancreed 72-74; St Gluvias 74-81; Archd of Bodmin from 81; Hon Can of Truro from 81. *Archdeacon's House, St Catherine's Hill, Launceston, Cornw, PL15 7EJ.* (Launceston 2714)

TEMPLE, Iris Evelyn. b 37. St Jo Coll Auckld LTh 78. **d** 78 **p** 79 Wai. V of Takapau Dio Wai from 78. *Vicarage, Nancy Street, Takapau, NZ.*

TEMPLE, John Vincent. d 26 **p** 27 Montr. C of Glen Sutton 26-27; R of Shawville 27-32; Temaskaming 32-37; I of Mille Isles 37-41; R of All SS w St Hilda and St Ignatius Montr 41-48; I of Thessalon 48-49; Fort Frances 49-61; Hon Can of Keew 59-61; Miss at Tyendinaga 61-67. *8 Highland Avenue, Belleville, Ont, Canada.* (613-968 5297)

TEMPLE-HILL, Lionel Novinger. McGill Univ Montr BA 35 Montr Dioc Th Coll LTh 37. **d** 38 **p** 39 Montr. PQ, Canada. C of St Jo Div Verdun Montr 38-44; P-in-c of St Thos Montr 44-45; C of St Matt Montr 45-46; I of Arundel 46-49; R of St John's (in c of Iberville) 49-64; Chap Sailors' Inst Montr 64-69; R Vic Hosp Montr 69-78. *476 Mortlake Avenue, St Lambert, PQ., Canada.* (514-671 1020)

TEMPLEMAN, Peter Morton. b 49. Ch Ch Ox BA (Jurispr) 71, BA (Th) 75, MA 75. Wycl Hall Ox 73. **d** 76 **p** 77 Glouc. C of St Mary w St Matt Cheltm 76-79; Chap of St Jo Coll Cam from 79. *St John's College, Cambridge, CB2 1TP.*

TEMPLER, Canon John Merson. NZ Bd of Th Stud LTh 49. **d** 31 **p** 32 Waik. C of Cambridge NZ 31-33; P-in-c of Uruti 33-35; C of St Mary New Plymouth 35-37; V of Dunstan w Pembroke 37-41; CF (NZ) 41-45; P-in-c of Hororata 45-46; V 46-52; Otorohanga 52-59; Huntly 59-65; St Andr Ohura 65-68; Can of St Pet Cathl Hamilton from 60; P-in-c of Ohura Miss Distr 68-70; Kawhia Miss Distr Dio Waik from 70. *PO Kawhia, NZ.* (Kawhia 719)

TEMPLETON, Basil William. b 29. **d** 75 Bp Carter for Johann **p** 76 Johann. C of Krugersdorp Dio Johann from 75. *18 Tara Road, Kenmare 1740, S Africa.*

TEMPLETON, John Herbert. TCD Downes Pri Essay (2nd) and Oratory Pri 24, BA Downes Pri Essay (1st) Liturgy Pri and Div Test 25, Elrington Th Pri (1st) 28, MA and BD 36, BLitt 43, PhD 46. MLitt 61. **d** 25 **p** 26 Down. C of Derriaghy 25-31; St Mary Newry w Donaghmore 31-34; C-in-c of Dunseverick 34-64; R 64-78; Preb of Connor in Connor Cathl 58-61; Treas 61-65; Chan 65-73. *2 Chichester Court, Antrim Road, Belfast, BT15 5DS.* (Belfast 771806)

TENAI, Philemon. d 77 **p** 78 Nak. P Dio Nak. *PO Kapcheni, Kapsabet, Kenya.*

TENNANT, Charles Roger. b 19. Open Univ PhD 75. Linc Th Coll. **d** 51 **p** 52 Leic. C of St Pet Belgrave Leic 51-54; Miss S Korea 54-62; V of Bitteswell Dio Leic from 62; Commiss Seoul 68-73; P-in-c of Misterton Dio Leic from 80. *Bitteswell Vicarage, Lutterworth, Leics.*

TENNANT, Cyril Edwin George. b 37. Keble Coll Ox BA 59, MA 63. BD Lon 61. Clifton Th Coll 59. **d** 62 Southw **p** 63 Bp Gelsthorpe for Southw. C of Stapleford 62-65; Felixstowe 65-68; V of Ch Ch Gipsy Hill Dio S'wark from 69. *1 Highland Road, SE19 1DP.* (01-670 0385)

TENNANT, Osmond Roy. b 21. Worc Ordin Coll 62. **d** 63 **p** 64 Ex. C of S Molton w Nymet St Geo 63-67; R of Talaton Dio Ex from 67; V of Escot Dio Ex from 67; P-in-c of Clyst Hydon 74-81; Clyst St Lawr 74-81; R of Plymtree, Clyst Hydon and Clyst St Lawr Dio Ex from 81. *Talaton Rectory, Exeter, Devon.* (Whimple 822256)

TENNICK, Edward. b 10. St Aid Coll 38. **d** 40 **p** 41 Sheff. C of Worsborough 40-43; Frodingham 43-46; PC of Belton-in-the-I of Axholme 46-49; V of E Farleigh 49-62; St Thos Southborough 62-75; Warden Yetts Ho Eastbourne 75-77; Warden Michell Ho Eastbourne from 77. *Michell House, 6 Chatsworth Gardens, Eastbourne, E Sussex.* (Eastbourne 638688)

TENYWA, Yokana. Bp Tucker Mem Coll 42. **d** 44 **p** 45 Ugan. P Dio Ugan 44-60; Dio W Bugan from 60. *Kaboyo, PO Box 553, Masaka, Uganda.*

TEOH, Keat Seng. b 44. Trin Th Coll Singapore 66. **d** 71 Sabah. d Dio W Mal. *Lorongi, Yong Peng, Johor, Malaysia.*

TER BLANCHE, Harold Daniel. St Paul's Coll Grahmstn 61. **d** 63 **p** 64 Natal. C of St Pet Pietermaritzburg 63-65; St Thos Durban 65-72; R of Gingindlovu 73-78; Dioc Missr Dio Zulu from 78. *Box 566, Richards Bay, Natal, S Africa.*

TERRELL, Richard Charles Patridge. b 43. Wells Th Coll 69. **d** 71 B & W **p** 72 Bp Wilson for B & W. C of Shepton Mallet 71-76; C-in-c of Drayton 76-78; Muchelney 76-78; Team V of Langport Dio B & W from 78. *Vicarage, Drayton, Langport, Somt, TA10 0JX.*

TERRETT, Mervyn Douglas. b 43. K Coll Lon and Warm AKC 65. **d** 66 **p** 67 Pet. C of St Mary Pet 66-69; Sawbridgeworth 69-74; V of H trin Stevenage Dio St Alb from 74. *Vicarage, Letchmore Road, Stevenage, Herts.*

TERRIS, John James. St Jo Coll Auckland. **d** 70 **p** 71 Wel. C of St Jas Lower Hutt 70-71; L to Offic Dio Ch Ch 71-72; Dio Wel from 74. *206 Waterloo Road, Lower Hutt, Wellington, NZ.* (698-076)

TERRY, Geoffrey Ronald. ACT ThDip 74. St Jo Coll Morpeth. **d** 73 **p** 74 River. C of Denilquin 73-76; Echuca Dio Bend from 76; Moama 76-78; R of St Cuthb Yarrawonga Dio Wang from 79. *Rectory, Yarrawonga, Vic, Australia 3730.*

TERRY, Ian Andrew. b 53. Univ of Dur BA 74. Coll of the Resurr Mirfield 78. **d** 80 Dorchester for Ox **p** 81 Ox. C of Beaconsfield Dio Ox from 80. *Old Rectory, Windsor End, Beaconsfield, Bucks, HP9 2JW.* (Beaconsfield 4506)

TERRY, John Arthur. b 32. SOC. **d** 66 **p** 67 S'wark. C of All SS Shooter's Hill Plumstead 66-69; Peckham (in c of St Paul) 69-72; V of H Redeemer Streatham Vale 72-80; R of Benhall w Sternfield and Snape Dio St E from 80. *Sternfield Rectory, Saxmundham, Suff.* (Saxmundham 2200)

TERRY, Stephen John. b 49. K Coll Lon BD 72, AKC 74. St Aug Coll Cant 74. **d** 75 Willesden for Lon **p** 76 Lon. C of Tokyngton 75-78; St Steph w All H Hampstead 78-81; V of St Jo Ap Whetstone Dio Lon from 81. *1163 High Road, N20 0PG.* (01-445 4569)

TESKEY, Ernest. Qu Univ Kingston BA 11. Trin Coll Tor LTh 13. **d** 13 **p** 14 Ont. Miss at Westport 13-17; R of Oxford Mills 17-26; Elizabethtown w Lyn 26-34; St Paul Kingston 34-54; Hon Cl Sec Dio Ont 50-54; Can of Ont 50-55. *Newboro, Ont, Canada.* (613-272 4135)

TESTER, Clarence Albert. b 20. Qu Coll Birm 47. **d** 50 **p** 51 Bris. C of Southmead 50-53; St Barn Knowle 53-55; Chap Ham Green Hosp Winford Orthopaedic Hosp and Leigh Court 55-70; V of Halberton w Ash Thomas Dio Ex from 70. *Vicarage, Halberton, Tiverton, Devon. Peverell* (Tiverton 820320)

TESTER, Francis Edward. b 24. Univ of Leeds, BA 46. Coll of Resurr Mirfield, 45. **d** 47 **p** 48 Lon. C of St Pet Lon Dks 47-51; St Mary Bourne Street Pimlico 51-58; V of St Pet Acton Green 58-64; Hockerill 64-71; Brentwood Dio Chelmsf from 71. *91 Queen's Road, Brentwood, Essex, CM14 4EY.* (Brentwood 225700)

TETLOW, James. d 55 **p** 58 C & Goulb. C of Albury 55-59; R of Moruya 59-64; Adelong 64-74; Perm to Offic Dio C & Goulb from 74. *16 Jumut Street, Adelong, NSW, Australia 2729.*

TETLOW, John. b 46. St Steph Ho Ox 73. **d** 76 Lon **p** 77 Kens for Lon. C of Stanwell 76-77; All SS Hanworth 77-80; St Mary Virg Somers Town St Pancras Dio Lon from 80. *Leonard Day House, Athlone Street, NW5.*

TETT, Peter McDonald. Bp's Coll Lennox BA 54. McGill Univ BD 57. **d** 56 **p** 57 Ont. C of Trenton 56-59; R of Parham and of Sharbot Lake 59-63; Edwardsburg 63-65; N Hastings 65-69; Belleville 69-77; Can of Ont 74-76; Archd of Ont 76-77; I of St Aid Lon Dio Hur from 77; Dom Chap to Bp of Hur from 80. *1242 Oxford Street West, London, Ont, Canada.* (519-471 1434)

TETT, Robert George. d 80 **p** 81 Melb. C of St Andr Brighton Dio Melb from 80. *7 James Street, Brighton, Vic, Australia 3186.*

TEULON, Austin Harvey. Univ of NZ BA 42, LTh (NZ) 48. Fitzw Ho Cam BA 49, MA 54. **d** 43 **p** 44 Ch Ch. C of Fendalton 43-45; C-in-c of Kensington Otipua 45-46; C of Lithgow NSW 46-47; St Matt Cambridge 47-49; St Martin Birm 49-50; V of Hokitika 52-57; Highfield 57-71; Cashmere Hills Dio Ch Ch from 71. *3 Cracroft Terrace, Cashmere Hills, Christchuch 2, NZ.* (326-627)

TEVEMIDE, David. St Pet Coll Maka. **d** 41 **p** 46 Melan. P Dio Melan 41-74. *Tasvaron, Pentecost, Solomon Islands*

✠ **TEVI, Right Rev Harry Sevehi.** St Pet Coll Siota. **d** 69 **p** 70 Melan. P Dio Melan 69-73; Lect Bp Patteson Th Centre Kohimarama 73-74; Warden 74-78; Exam Chap Prov of Melan 73-79; Can of St Barn Cathl Honiara 77-79; I of Lombaha 78-79; Cons Asst Bp of New Hebr at Godden Mem Hosp Lolowai 4 Feb 79 by Abp of Melan; Bps of Ysabel; Malaita, New Hebr, Aipo Rongo and Poly; and Bp Uka; Apptd Bp of New Hebr (Vanuatu from 80) 80. *Bishop's House, Box 238, Santo, Vanuatu.* (631)

TEWKESBURY, Lord Bishop Suffragan of. *See* Deakin, Right Rev Thomas Carlyle Joseph Robert Hamish.

TEWKESBURY, Alec. b 13. Univ of Lon 30. ALCD 36. Univ of Dur LTh 38. **d** 36 **p** 37 Chelmsf. C of All SS Leyton 36-39; Ch of Mart Leic 39-42; C-in-c of St Chris Conv Distr Leic 42-48; V of Earl Shilton w Elmesthorpe R Dio Leic 48-53; Chap British Families Educn Service Germany 54-61; Thos Bennett Sch Crawley 61-70; Perm to Offic Dio Chich 61-65; and from 79; C of Crawley (in c of St Mich Lowfield Heath) 65-70; V of Loxwood 70-78. *1 Stonefield Close, Southgate, Crawley, RH10 6AU.* (Crawley 34420)

TEWKESBURY, Noel. b 44. Univ of Hull BA (Th) 67. Wycl Hall Ox 70. **d** 72 **p** 73 Portsm. C of Bp's Waltham 72-76; Havant 76-77; Filey 77-79; V of Monk Fryston Dio York from 79; Hambleton w Gateforth Dio York from 79. *Monk Fryston Vicarage, Leeds, Yorks.* (S Milford 682357)

THA SAY, Gabriel. b 52. **d** 74 **p** 75 Pa-an. P Dio Pa-an.

c/o Church of the Resurrection, Mawchi Mines, via Loikaw, Kayah State, Burma.

THACKER, Charles Kent. K Coll Cam 2nd cl Hist Trip pt i 30, BA (3rd cl Hist Trip pt ii) 31, MA 35. Ely Th Coll 31. **d** 32 **p** 34 Lich. C of St Jas Wednesbury 32-36; Chap Denstone Coll 36-42; V of St Paul Wood Green Wednesbury 42-48; Rugeley 48-55; Surr from 49; R of St Pet Jersey 55-63; Chap Vic Coll Jersey from 63; C of St Clem Jersey Dio Win from 73. *Sea Court, Bel Royal, Jersey, CI.*

THACKER, Eric Lee. b 23. Coll of Resurr Mirfield 76. **d** and **p** 76 Man. [f Methodist Min]. C of St Jas Birch-in-Rusholme and of H Innoc Fallowfield 76-78; Team V of Seacroft 78-82; V of Womersley Dio Wakef from 82; P-in-c of Kirk Smeaton Dio Wakef from 82. *Womersley Vicarage, Doncaster, Yorks, DN6 9BG.* (Pontefract 620436)

THACKER, Jonathan William. b 53. Univ of Lon BA 74. Univ of Nottm Dipl Th 78. Linc Th Coll 76. **d** 79 **p** 80 Heref. C of Bromyard Dio Heref from 79. *7 Highwell Avenue, Bromyard, Herefs, HR7 4EL.*

THACKER, Kenneth Ray. b 31. Tyndale Hall Bris 56. Open Univ BA 73. **d** 59 **p** 60 Lich. C of Penn Fields 59-62; St Martin Tipton 62-64; V of Moxley 64-71; R of Leigh Dio Lich from 71. *Leigh Rectory, Stoke-on-Trent, ST10 4PT.* (Field 237)

THACKER, Roger Ailwyn Mackintosh. b 46. CCC Cam BA 68, MA 73. Westcott Ho Cam 68. **d** 70 Willesden for Lon **p** 71 Lon. C of St John's Wood Ch 70-74; C-in-c of Hammersmith 74-78; V from 78. *20 Luxemburg Gardens, Hammersmith, W6.* (01-603 4303)

THACKERAY, Bernard John Martin. b 05. Chich Th Coll 31. **d** 34 **p** 35 Lon. C of Friern Barnet 34-38; St Sav Luton 38-43; V of Thatcham 43-69; Gt Coxwell 69-74; Coleshill 69-74; L to Offic Dios Glouc and Mon 74-82. *Makepeace Cottage, Staunton, Coleford, Glos, GL16 8NX.*

THACKRAY, Peter Michael. b 29. Univ of Leeds, BA 52. Coll of Resurr Mirfield, 52. **d** 54 **p** 55 S'wark. C of St Mary L Lambeth 54-57; St Mary Virg Primrose Hill and of St Paul Hampstead 57-59; Min of Annunc Conv Distr S Kenton Wembley 59-61; Chap Pierrepont Sch Frensham 61-67; Windsor Girls' Sch Hamm 67-73; CF from 73; Hdmaster British Embassy Sch Ankara from 78; L to Offic Dio Gibr in Eur from 78. *British Embassy, Ankara, Turkey.*

THACKRAY, William Harry. b 44. Chich Th Coll 70. **d** 73 Doncaster for Sheff. **p** 74 Sheff. C of St Cuthb Firvale 73-78; Stocksbridge (in c of St John Deepcar) 76-78; P-in-c of St Leon Newark-on-Trent 78-80; Team V of Newark w Hawton, Cotham and Shelton Dio Southw from 80. *St Leonard's Vicarage, Lincoln Road, Newark, Notts, NG24 2DQ.* (Newark 703691)

THAIN, Ven Albert Edwin. Angl Th Coll BC LTh 33. **d** 33 **p** 34 New Westmr. I of Gibson's Landing 33-37; S Westmr w Port Kells and Colverdale 37-39; Alert Bay 39-42; R of Fairford 42-44; Sturgeon Creek 44-51; R and Dean of Athab Cathl 51-58; R of Camrose 58-63; Exam Chap to Bp of Edmon 61-75; Can of Edmon 61-72; R of St Pet Edmon 63-75; Archd of Edmon 72-75; Archd (Emer) from 75; Admin Asst to Primate of Canada 75-79; Hon C of All SS Cathl City and Dio Edmon from 79. *305, 10039-103 Street, Edmonton, Alta, T5J 3G4, Canada.*

THAKE, Terence. b 41. ALCD 65. **d** 66 **p** 67 Ox. C of Faringdon 66-70; Aldridge 70-73; V of Werrington, Staffs Dio Lich from 73. *360 Ash Bank Road, Werrington, Stoke-on-Trent, Staffs, St9 0JS.* (Ash Bank 2441)

THALE, Zacharia Ramolete. b 33. **d** 74 **p** 75 Johann. C of Dobsonville Dio Johann from 74. *Box 244, Roodepoort Tvl 1725, S Africa.*

THAN, Phillip. Trin Th Coll Sing BTh 47. **d** 67 **p** 68 Kuch. P Dio Kuch. *Box 79, Seria, Brunei, Malaysia.* (Brunei 2768)

THAN LWIN, David. **d** 68 **p** 69 Rang. P Dio Rang. *446 Bogyoke Aung San Road, Rangoon, Burma.*

THANJI, Frederick. b 47. **d** 71 **p** 72 Mt Kenya. P Dio Mt Kenya 71-75; Dio Mt Kenya S from 75. *Box 214, Thika, Kenya.*

THAN PE, Joseph. H Cross Coll Rang. **d** 59 **p** 60 Rang. P Dio Rang. *Church of the Resurrection, Syriam, Burma.*

THA NU, d 78 **p** 79 Akyab. P Dio Akyab. *St John's Church, Kyaukpyu, Burma.*

THATCHER, John Farler. BSc (Eng) Lon (2nd cl) 37. McGill Univ Montr BD 64. Montr Dioc Th Coll LTh 64. **d** 64 **p** 65 Montr. C of St Matt Montr 64-66; I of S Shore Extension 66-71; R of Ascen City and Dio Montr from 70. *780 Wilder Avenue, Montreal 154, PQ, Canada.* (514-738 8792)

THATCHER, Kenneth Arthur. Univ of Capetn BSc (Mech Eng) 36. Trin Coll Tor 64. **d** and **p** 63 Bp Snell for Tor. P-in-c of Richvale 63-67; Minden 67-68. *c/o Synod Office, 135 Adelaide Street East, Toronto 1, Ont, Canada.*

THAUNG TIN, Stephen. H Cross Coll Rang. **d** 59 **p** 60. P Dio Rang. *St Paul's Church, Kyaiklat, Burma.*

THAWLEY, Very Rev David Laurie. St Edm Hall, Ox BA 47, 2nd cl Th and MA 49. Cudd Coll 49. **d** 51 **p** 52 Win. C of Ascen Bitterne Pk 51-56; C-in-c of St Mich AA Conv Distr Andover 56-60; Vice-Prin St Francis Coll Brisb 60-65; Chap S of Sacred Advent Brisb 61-72; St Marg Sch Brisb 65-69; Univ of Queensld 69-72; Can Res of Brisb 64-72; Dean of H Trin Cathl Wang from 72; Exam Chap to Bp of Wang from 77. *Deanery, Cathedral Close, Wangaratta, Vic., Australia.* (061-21 3719)

THAYER, Michael David. b 52. Sarum Wells Th Coll 77. **d** 80 B & W **p** 81 Taunton for B & W. C of Minehead Dio B & W from 80. *28 Paganel Road, Minehed, Somerset.*

THEAKER, David Michael. b 41. Wells Th Coll 65. **d** 68 **p** 69 Linc. C of Folkingham 68-71; St Aid New Cleethorpes 71-74; P-in-c of St Andr w St Luke Grimsby 74-77; Thurlby 77-79. *c/o Thurlby Vicarage, Bourne, Lincs, PE10 0EH.* (Bourne 2475)

✠ **THEAUNG HAWI, Right Rev Barnabas.** **d** 69 Rang **p** 71 Akyab. D Dio Rang 68-70; P Dio Akyab 71-78; Archd 76-78; Cons Asst Bp of Akyab in H Trin Cathl Rang 24 Sept 78 by Abp of Burma and Abp Ah Mya; Bps of Rang and Mand; and Bp Kumsaung Tu; Apptd Bp of Akyab 80. *St John's Church, Paletwa, Akyab, Burma.*

THEIN MYINT, John. **d** 68 **p** 69 Rang. P Dio Rang. *All Saints Church, Gayan, Rangoon, Burma.*

THEIN MAUNG, Peter. St Aug Coll Cant 61. **d** 63 Cant for Rang **p** 64 Rang. P Dio Rang. *120-142 St John's Road, Rangoon, Burma.*

THEKISO, Ven Joseph. Coll of Resurr Johann. **d** 54 **p** 55 Kimb K. C of Mafeking Miss 54-59; St Matt Kimberley 59-61; Dir of Batlharos Miss 61-67; Hon Chap to Bp of Kimb K 63-67; Archd of Kuruman 65-67; R of Wolmaransstad 68-73; St Paul and St Jas Kimberley 73-76; All SS Mafeking Dio Kimb K from 76; Archd of Kimberley 73-76; Mafeking from 76. *Box 87, Mafeking, CP, S Africa.* (014442)

THELEJANE, Sidwell Sydney Mokhele. St Bede's Coll Umtata. **d** 55 **p** 57 St Jo Kaffr. C of St Cuthb, St John's 56-58; Mt Fletcher 58-59; All SS, St John's 59-60; Chap and Lect St Bede Th Coll 61-64; Perm to Offic Dio S'wark 64-67; Dio Ely 68; Chap St Bede Th Coll 68-71; Vice-Prin 72-74; C of St Martin-in-the-Veld 75-77; Rosebank 77-78; R of H Cross Orlando Dio Johann from 78. *Box 192, Orlando, Johannesburg, S Africa.*

THELWALL, George de Crespigny. b 05. St John's Coll Morpeth 37. ACT ThL 38. **d** 38 **p** 39 Bath. M of Bro of Good Shepherd Dubbo 38-44; C of Gilgandra 38-39; P-in-c of Cobar 39-44; R of Stuart Town 44-46; C of St Botolph Northfleet 46-48; R of Burrough-on-the-Hill 48-54; V of Ellistown 54-65; R of Brushford 65-75. *Flat 1, Harbour Court, Minehead, Somt., TA24 5QS.*

THELWALL, Canon Robert Champion de Crespigny. St Paul's Coll Grahmstn 48. **d** and **p** 48 S Rhod. C of Avondale 48-50; St Jo Bapt Bulawayo 50-52; R of St Marg of Scotland Bulawayo 52-67; St Mary Famona Bulawayo 67-73; Hon Can of Matab from 73. *2 - 18th Avenue, Famona, Bulawayo, Zimbabwe.* (19-63132)

THELWELL, John Berry. b 49. Univ of Wales (Bangor) BD 72. Qu Coll Birm 73. **d** 73 **p** 74 St A. C of Minera 73-80; Youth Chap Dio St A from 78; V of Gwernaffield Dio St A from 80; Llanferres Dio St A from 80. *Gwernaffield Vicarage, Mold, Clwyd.* (Mold 740205)

THEM, Canon Barnaba Dhiath. Bp Gwynne Coll Mundri 57. **d** 59 **p** 61 Sudan. P Dio Sudan 59-76; Dio Rumbek from 76; Can of Rumbek from 77. *ECS Tonj, Bahrel Ghazal, Sudan.*

THEMA, Zacchaeus Hezekiah. St Pet Coll Rosettenville. **d** 41 **p** 42 Pret. P Dio Pret. *2624, Zone 2, Seshego, Transvaal, S Africa.*

THEOBALD, Graham Fitzroy. b 43. ALCD 63. **d** 67 **p** 68 Guildf. C of Crookham 67-71; St Mich Yorktown Camberley Guildf 71-74; V of Wrecclesham Dio Guildf from 74. *2 Kings Lane, Wrecclesham, Farnham, Surrey, GU10 4QB.* (Farnham 716431)

THEOBALD, Henry Charles. b 32. **d** 63 **p** 64 S'wark. C of St Phil Battersea 63-65; Caterham 65-68; St Luke Reigate (in c of St Pet Doversgreen) 68-73; Chap St Jas Hosp Balham and S Lon Hosp for Women from 73. *c/o St James' Hospital, Sarsfeld Road, Balham, SW12 8HW.* (01-672 1222)

THEOBALD, John Walter. b 33. St Aid Coll. **d** 65 Warrington for Liv **p** 66 Liv. C of Hindley 65-68; Beverley Minster 68-71; R of Loftus-in-Cleveland Dio York from 71; C-in-c of Carlin How w Skinningrove Dio York from 73. *Rectory, Loftus, Cleveland.* (Loftus 40738)

THEODOSIUS, Hugh John. b 32. Trin Coll Cam BA 56, MA 60. Cudd Coll. **d** 58 **p** 59 Win. C of Milton 58-62; Romsey 62-64; Maybush Shirley (in c of Redbridge) 64-70; V of Malden 70-81; Billingborough Dio Linc from 81; Sempringham w Pointon and Birthorpe Dio Linc from 81; Horbling

Dio Linc from 81. *Billingborough Vicarage, Sleaford, Lincs.* (Billingborough 7750)

THEODOSIUS, Richard Francis. b 35. Fitzw Coll Cam BA 59. Lich Th Coll 69. **d** 71 Lich. Chap Bluecoat Sch Walsall 71-73; Ranby Ho Sch Retford from 73; C of Bloxwich 71-73. *Ranby House School, Retford, Notts.*

THEOTAHIGNA, William. b 49. Bp Patteson Th Coll Kohimarama 72. **d** 75 **p** 76 Ysabel. P Dio Ysabel. *Tasia Training Centre, Maringe District, Santa Ysabel, Solomon Islands.*

THERIAULT, Serge André. b 47. Univ of Ott PhD 78. **d** and **p** 77 Ott. On leave 77-78; P-in-c of St Bernard de Clairvaux, Hull Dio Ott 78-79; I from 79. *47-F Woodfield Drive, Ottawa, Ont, Canada, K2G 3Y7.*

THETFORD, Lord Bishop Suffragan of. *See* Dudley-Smith, Right Rev Timothy.

THEW, John Michael Harden. b 46. Moore Th Coll Syd 69. **d** and **p** 73 Armid. C of W Tamworth Dio Armid from 73. *43 Edinburgh Street, West Tamworth, Armidale, Australia 2340.* (65-7289)

THEWLIS, Brian Jacob. Univ of Melb BA (Hons) 49. Ridley Coll Melb 45. Coll of Resurr Mirfield 52. **d** 53 Stafford for Cant **p** 54 Lich. C of St Jas Gt Wednesbury 53-57; Chap K Coll Auckld 57-58; C of All SS Sidley Bexhill 59-60; V of St Geo Reservoir 61-68; St Paul Malvern Dio Melb from 68. *2 Glenfernie Street, Caulfield, Melbourne, Vic, Australia 3161.* (03-509 6024)

THEWLIS, John Charles. b 49. Van Mildert Coll Dur BA 70, PhD 75. NOC 78. **d** 81 York. Hon C of St Mary Sculcoates Hull Dio York from 81. *7 Beech Grove, Beverley Road, Hull, HU5 1LY.*

THEYISE, Gordon. St Bede's Coll Umtata. **d** 66 **p** 67 Kimb K. P Dio Kimb K 66-76; R of Springfontein 76-78; C of Thaba'Nchu 78-80; P-in-c of St Matt Virginia Dio Bloemf from 80. *PO Box 150, Virginia, OFS, S Africa.*

THEYISE, William Christopher Sipho. Coll of Resurr and St Pet Johann. **d** 48 **p** 49 Johann. C of Brakpan Miss Distr 48-50; Germiston 50-54; P-in-c of Roodepoort Miss 54-63; R of Dobsonville Dio Johann from 63. *Rectory, Dobsonville, Transvaal, S Africa.*

THICKE, James Balliston. b 43. Sarum Wells Th Coll 74. **d** 77 Sarum **p** 78 Sherborne for Sarum. C of Wareham Dio Sarum 77-80; Team V from 80. *9 Keysworth Drive, Sandford, Wareham, Dorset.*

THICKITT, John Laurence. b 16. St Jo Coll Dur BA 38, Dipl Th 39, MA 41. **d** 39 **p** 40 Southw. C of St Jas Porchester Nottm 39-41; Old Radford 41-45; V of Peasenhall Dio St E from 45; RD of S Dunwich 65-72; P-in-c of Sibton Dio St E from 76. *Peasenhall Vicarage, Saxmundham, Suff.* (Peasenhall 256)

THICKNESSE, Ralph. b 21. Trin Coll Ox BA 46, MA 51. Cudd Coll 45. **d** 47 **p** 48 Win. C of St Faith Win 47-50; Christchurch w Mudeford 50-54; V of Old Basing 54-59; Waresley 59-67; V of Abbotsley 59-67; R of Doddington 67-74; R of Benwick 70-74; V of Clare w Poslingford 74-76; St Mich AA w St Edm Northn Dio Pet from 77. *19 St Michael's Avenue, Northampton.* (Northampton 37928)

THIEME, Paul Henri. b 22. **d** and **p** 50 Haarlem. C of St Aug Newland 58-63; V of St Sav and St Mark Wilmington 63-73; St Aid Middlesbrough 73-79. *Molenstraat 48, The Hague, Netherlands.*

THIERING, Barry Bernard. Univ of Syd BA 53, MA 67. Moore Th Coll Syd ACT ThL 53. **d** and **p** 54 Syd. C of W Manly 54-56; R of Mittagong 56-59; Chap Cranbrook Gr Sch Bellevue Hill Dio Syd from 59. *16 Wyong Road, Mosman, NSW, Australia 2088.* (960-1167)

✠ **THIRD, Right Rev Richard Henry McPhail.** b 27. Em Coll Cam BA 50, MA 55. Linc Th Coll 50. **d** 52 **p** 53 S'wark. C of Mottingham 52-55; Sanderstead 55-59; V of H Trin (w St Paul from 63) Sheerness 59-67; Orpington 67-76; Surr 67-76; RD of Orpington 73-76; Hon Can of Roch Cathl 74-76; M Gen Syn Roch 75-76; Cons Ld Bp Suffr of Maidstone in Cant Cathl 30 Nov 76 by Abp of Cant; Bps of Lon, B & W, Birm, Chelmsf, Chich, Heref, Lich, Nor, Roch, Sarum and Ely; Bps Suffr of Barking, Bradwell, Dover, Croydon, Dorchester, Grantham, Ramsbury, Shrewsbury, Southn and Tonbridge; and Bps Ramsey, Isherwood, Betts, Sansbury and others; Apptd Bp Suffr of Dover 80. *Upway, St Martin's Hill, Canterbury, Kent.* (Canterbury 64537)

THIRKELL, Edward William Hylton. b 10. **d** 56 **p** 58 Accra. P Dio Accra 56-63; Dom Chap to Bp of Accra 58-63; Perm to Offic Dio Portsm 63-65; Dio Pet 65; C of St Mary Wellingborough 65-67; Higham Ferrers 67-70; Perm to Offic Dio Wakef 70-71; C of St Mary Virg Bulwell 71-73; Perm to Offic Dio Portsm from 73. *32 Argyll Street, Ryde, IoW, PO33 3BY.* (Ryde 62016)

THIRKELL, Frederick William. Angl Th Coll BC LTh 54. **d** 54 **p** 55 New Westmr. C of St Mary Vancouver 54-56; I of Newport 56-59; R of Westview 59-61; I of New Germany 61-63; Glace Bay 63-66; R of St Jo Evang N Vanc 72-79; on leave. *1014 Clements Avenue, North Vancouver, BC, Canada.*

THIRLWELL, Philip John. Univ of Syd LLB 57. St Jo Coll Morpeth ACT ThL 59. **d** 57 **p** 59 C & Goulb. C of St Jo Bapt Canberra 57-59; Albury 59-61; Labasa 62-64; Viti Levu W 64-68; P-in-c of Ba, Viti Levu W 68-70; Nadi 70-74; Chap Miss to Seamen Newc and Perm to Offic Dio Newc from 74. *Mission to Seamen, Hannell Street, Wickham, NSW, Australia 2293.*

THISELTON, Anthony Charles. b 37. BD (Lon) 59, MTh (Lon) 64. Univ of Sheff PhD 77. Oak Hill Th Coll 58. **d** 60 **p** 61 S'wark. C of H Trin Sydenham 60-63; Tutor Tyndale Hall Bris 63-67; Sen Tutor 67-70; L to Offic Dio Bris 63-70; Lect Univ of Sheff from 70; Sen Lect in Bibl Stud from 79; L to Offic Dio Sheff from 71; Exam Chap to Bp of Sheff 77-80; to Bp of Leic from 79; Visiting Fell Calvin Coll Mich 82. *Dept of Biblical Studies, The University, Sheffield, S10 2TN.*

THISTLE, John Gaston Cornell. b 16. AKC and Jelf Pri 46. Cudd Coll 46. **d** 46 **p** 47 S'wark. C of Wimbledon 46-50; Limpsfield (in c of Good Shepherd and St Silvan) 50-52; CF 52-69; Area Sec USPG Dios Liv and Man 69-70; Grants Sec 70-80; LPr Dio S'wark 71-80; Commiss SW Tang from 75; P-V Westminster Abbey from 75; Perm to Offic Dio Ox from 80. *The Ryeneck, Fisherman's Retreat, St Peter Street, Marlow, Bucks, SL7 1NH.* (06284-6194)

THISTLE, William Roberts. St Chad's Coll Regina 54. **d** 54 **p** 55 Qu'App. C of Weyburn 54-56; I of Wolseley 56-57; Sturgeon Falls 57-60; R of Gravenhurst 60-71; Ch Ch St Catharines 70-76; St Mich Hamilton Dio Niag from 76; Dom Chap to Bp of Niag from 80. *1188 Fennell Avenue East, Hamilton, Ont, Canada.* (416-385 5694)

THISTLETHWAITE, Nicholas John. b 51. Selw Coll Cam BA 73, MA 77, PhD 80. Univ of Ox BA 78. Ripon Coll Cudd 76. **d** 79 **p** 80 Newc T. C of St Gabr Heaton City and Dio Newc T from 79. *33 Swindon Terrace, Heaton, Newcastle-on-Tyne 6.* (0632 655738)

THISTLEWOOD, Michael John. b 31. Late Tancred Stud of Ch Coll Cam 2nd cl Cl Trip pt i 52, BA (2nd cl Th Trip pt ia) 53, MA 57. Linc Th Coll 54. **d** 56 **p** 57 York. C of St Mich AA N Hull 56-59; Scarborough 59-61; V of St Jude w St Steph Hull 61-67; St Aug Newland 67-72; Asst Master Bemrose Sch Derby 72-80; V of St Andr w St Osmund City and Dio Derby from 80. *St Osmunds Vicarage, London Road, Derby, DE2 8UW.* (Derby 71329)

THOM, James. b 31. St Chad's Coll Dur BA 53, Dipl Th 57. **d** 57 **p** 58 York. C of St Thos Middlesbrough 57-60; Hornsea 60-62; S Bank 62-63; V of Copmanthorpe 63-75; Coxwold (and Husthwaite from 77) Dio York from 75; RD of Easingwold from 77. *Vicarage, Coxwold, N Yorks, YO6 4AD.* (Coxwold 253)

THOM, Thomas Kennedy Dalziel. b 29. Pemb Coll Cam BA 53, MA 57. St Steph Ho Ox 60. **d** 61 **p** 62 Chelmsf. C of St Jas w All SS St Nich and St Runwald Colchester 61-65; P-in-c of Bolgatanga 65-70; Chap Univ of Essex 73-80; Sec for Chaplaincies in Higher Educn C of E Bd of Educn from 81. *Church House, Dean's Yard, SW1P 3NZ.* (01-222 9011)

THOMAS, Adrian Leighton. b 37. St D Coll Lamp BA 62. **d** 63 **p** 64 Llan. C of Port Talbot 63-70; V of Troedrhiw Garth 70-73; Warden Youth Centre and C of Sandhurst 73-77; P-in-c of Streatley Dio Ox 77-79; V from 79; P-in-c of Moulsford Dio Ox from 81. *Streatley Vicarage, Reading, Berks, RG8 9HX.* (Goring-on-Thames 872191)

THOMAS, Alan. b 42. Univ of Wales BA 66. St Mich Coll Llan 65. **d** 67 Llan **p** 68 Bp T M Hughes for Llan. C of St Pet Fairwater 67-69; Llanishen w Lisvane 69-73; V of Troedyrhiw 73-77; Pemb Dk Dio St D from 77. *Vicarage, Pembroke Dock, Dyfed.* (Pembroke 2943)

THOMAS, Alan William Charles. b 19. Univ of Liv BA (3rd cl Cl) 41, Archd Madden Pri 43, Pilkington Pri 44. St Aid Coll 42. **d** 43 Liv **p** 44 Warrington for Liv. C of Em Everton 43-45; Em Fazakerley 45-50; V of St Benedict Everton 50-56; PC of Tipton 56-67; V of St Jude Wolverhampton Dio Lich from 67. *St Jude's Vicarage, St Jude's Road, Wolverhampton, Staffs.* (Wolverhampton 753360)

THOMAS, Albert. b 19. St Aid Coll 57. **d** 59 **p** 60 Pet. C of St Andr Kettering 59-61; Childwall 61-64; V of Parr Mt 64-72; Ch Ch Toxt Pk Dio Liv from 72. *Vicarage, Linnet Lane, Liverpool, L17 3BE.* (051-727 2827)

THOMAS, Albert Kenneth. b 18. Late Scho and Pri of St D Coll Lamp BA (2nd cl Hist) 40. St Mich Coll Llan 40. **d** 42 **p** 43 Mon. C of Griffithstown 42-47; CF 47-67; R of Charlton Musgrove (w Cucklington and Stoke Trister from 80) Dio B & W from 67; RD of Bruton 71-77; P-in-c of Cucklington w Stoke Trister 79-80. *Rectory, Charlton Musgrove, Wincanton, Somt.* (Wincanton 33233)

THOMAS, Alexander Robert. Univ of Manit BA 61. Em Coll Sktn LTh 63, BD 68. **d** 63 **p** 64 Sask. I of Spiritwood

63-66; R of Carman 66-70; L to Offic Dio Calg 70-72; I of Ch of Good Shepherd Calg 72-74; R of Carbon-Acme 74-77; on staff of Ch Ho Tor 77-78; R of Killarney Dio Bran from 78. *Box 623, Killarney, Manit, Canada.*

THOMAS, Alfred James Randolph. b 48. St D Coll Lamp Dipl Th 71. **d** 71 **p** 72 St D. C of Kidwelly 71-74; St D Carmarthen 74-76; Team V of Abth 76-81; V of Bettws w Ammanford Dio St D from 81. *Vicarage, College Street, Ammanford, Dyfed.* (Ammanford 2084)

THOMAS, Andrew Herbert Redding. b 41. Lon Coll of Div. **d** 69 **p** 70 Nor. C of Cromer 69-73; Chap Dio Nor 73-76; R of Grimston w Congham and of Roydon Dio Nor from 76. *Grimston Rectory, Kings Lynn, Norf, PE32 1BQ.* (Hillington 600335)

THOMAS, Arthur George. b 19. Univ of Wales (Swansea), BA (2nd cl Hist) 40 St Mich Coll Llan 40. **d** 42 **p** 43 Swan B. C of Landore 42-44; Ch Ch Swansea 44-45; St Mary Virg Cardiff 45-47; St Andr Netherton (in c of St Pet Darby End) Dudley 47-51; Milford Haven 51-54; R of Moora 54-60; RD of Moora 58-60; Bassendean 60-62; Maesmynis w Llangynog and Llanynis 62-65; Newbridge-on-Wye w Llanfihangel Brynpabuan 65-69; R of Llanganten w Llanafan Fawr, w Maesmynis, LLanynys and Llangynog 69-79; Llanganten w Llanafan Fawr; Llangammarch, Llanfechan and Llanlleonfel Dio Swan B from 79. *Vicarage, Llanganten, Builth Wells, Powys, LD2 3NT.* (Builth Wells 2269)

THOMAS, Arthur Norman. b 17. St Aid Coll 54. **d** 56 **p** 57 Ripon. C of Chap Allerton 56-59; V of Ven Bedf Wyther Leeds 59-65; Seacroft 65-70; R 70-77; Thornton Watlass w Thornton Steward and E Witton Dio Ripon from 77. *Thornton Watlass Rectory, Ripon, N Yorks.* (Bedale 2737)

THOMAS, Arthur Roy. b 25. St Steph Ho Ox 55. **d** 58 **p** 59 Linc. C of Boston 58-60; Lect 60-63; N Group Org SPCK 63-64; Executive Officer Feed the Minds Campaign 64-67; Regional Officer SPCK 67-72; St Antholin Lect at St Mary Aldermary 66-72; V of St Cedd Canning Town 72-79; P-in-c of Vic Dks 78-79; P-in-c of Wickford Dio Chelmsf 79-80; Team R of Wickford & Runwell Dio Chelmsf from 80. Runwell 79-80. *Rectory, Southend Road, Wickford, Essex.* (Wickford 3147)

THOMAS, Austin George. b 23. Wells Th Coll 65. Open Univ BA 75. **d** 67 **p** 68 Bris. C of St Luke Brislington 67-73; C-in-c of St Geo Bris 73-74; St Leon Redfield Bris 74-75; Team V of E Bristol 75-80; R of Lyddington w Wanborough Dio Bris from 80. *19 Church Road, Wanborough, Swindon, Wilts, SN4 0BZ.* (Wanborough 242)

THOMAS, Barry Wilfred. b 41. Univ of Wales (Cardiff) BD 75. St Mich AA Coll Llan 72. **d** 75 Bp Vaughan for Ban **p** 76 Ban. C of Porthmadog 75-78; V of Llanegryn and Llanfihangel-y-Pennant w Talyllyn Dio Ban from 78; Sec Dioc Coun for Miss & Unity Ban from 81. *Llanegryn Vicarage, Tywyn, LL36 9SS.* (Tywyn 710447)

THOMAS, Canon Basil James. St Jo Coll Morpeth, 41. **d** 42 **p** 44 River. C of Hay 42-44; Leeton 44-46; P-in-c of Balranald 46-51; R of Lake Cargelligo and of Hillston 51-58; Coolamon 58-66; Leeton Dio River from 66; Hon Can of St Paul's Pro-Cathl Hay from 68. *PO Box 336, Leeton, NSW, Australia 2705.* (069-53 2107)

THOMAS, Benjamin Lewis. b 10. St George's Windsor, 55. **d** 56 **p** 57 B & W. C of Crewkerne 56-58; V of Ettington 59-63; V of Loxley 59-63; Kineton 63-69; Combroke w Compton Verney 63-69; Cutcombe w Luxborough 70-75; Perm to Offic Dio Ex 75-78; Dio Truro from 78. *4 St Martin's Close, Tregurthen Road, Camborne, Cornwall.* (Camborne 714446)

THOMAS, Ven Brian. St Jo Coll Morpeth, ACT ThL 47. **d** and **p** 48 Armid. C of Moree 48-50; V of Mungindi 50-53; Boggabri 53-58; Barraba 58-66; R of Casino Dio Graft from 66; Archd of Graft from 76. *Rectory, Casino, NSW, Australia 2470.* (61 21120)

THOMAS, Bryan. b 36. Univ of Wales (Abth) BA (2nd cl Welsh) 59. St Deiniol's Libr Hawarden 68. **d** 70 **p** 71 Llan. C of Llangynwyd w Maesteg 70-72; V of Cwmllynfell 72-76; Gorslas Dio St D from 76. *Gorslas Vicarage, Llanelly, Dyfed.* (Cross Hands 842561)

THOMAS, Cedric Blake. Moore Th Coll Syd 35. **d** 60 **p** 61 Tas. C of Burnie 60-52; R of St Paul E Davenport 62-72; St Helens Tas 72-78. *Goodwin Village, Woollahra, NSW, Australia 2025.*

THOMAS, Charles Edward. b 27. St D Coll Lamp BA 51 Coll of Resurr Mirfield, 51. **d** 53 Taunton for B & W **p** 54 B & W. C of Ilminster 53-56; Chap and Asst Master St Mich Coll Tenbury 56-57; C of St Steph St Alb 57-58; V of St Mich AA Boreham Wood 58-66; R of Monksilver w Elworthy (w Brompton Ralph and Nettlecombe 69-74) 66-74; C-in-c of Nettlecombe 68-69; V of S Petherton (w The Seavingtons from 80) Dio B & W from 74; RD of Crewkerne from 77. *Vicarage, South Petherton, Somt.* (South Petherton 40377)

THOMAS, Canon Charles Elliott. St Jo Coll Morpeth ThL 43. **d** 43 Newc for Graft **p** 44 Graft. C of Lismore 43-44; Ch Ch Cathl Graft 44-47; V of U Clarence 47-49; Byron Bay 49-52; R of St Matt Groveley Brisb 52-58; Millmerran 58-60; Pittsworth 60-67; St Alb Wilston Brisb 67-72; St Jas Toowoomba Dio Brisb from 72; Hon Can of Brisb from 75. *145 Mort Street, Toowoomba, Queensland, Australia 4350.* (32 3436)

THOMAS, Charles Moray Stewart Reid. b 53. BNC Ox BA 74. Wycl Hall Ox 75. **d** 78 **p** 79 Bradf. C of St Pet Cathl Ch Bradf 78-81; St Andr w H Trin Isl Dio Lon from 81. *149 Naish Court, Bemerton street, N1 0BP.* (01-837 0720)

THOMAS, Cheeramattathu John. b 26. Univ of Travancore BA 46, Serampore Univ BD 55, Andover Newton Th Sch Mass MA 66. **d** 55 **p** 57 Sing. P Dio Sing 55-61; Dio Kuch 61-65; C of Eastham 66-74; V of Gt Sutton Dio Ches from 74. *Great Sutton Vicarage, Wirral, Chesh.*

THOMAS, Christopher Nutter. Pemb Coll Cam 2nd cl Cl Trip pt i, 33, BA (2nd cl Th Trip pt i) 35, MA 41. Linc Th Coll 35. **d** 36 **p** 37 St Alb. C of Bp's Hatfield 36-39; Leeds 39-42; Chap RNVR 42-46; C of H Trin Kew Melb 46-47; V of Croydon 47-58; Austrn Sec SPCK from 57; I of Glenhuntly 58-66; Box Hill Dio Melb from 66; Can of Melb 65-80; Perm to Offic Dio Melb from 80. *42 Asbury Street West, Ocean Grove, Vic, Canada 3226.*

THOMAS, Colin Norman. b 41. Open Univ BA 78. Trin Coll Bris 72. **d** 74 **p** 75 Ches. C of Handforth 74-77; Bucknall w Bagnall Dio Lich 77-80; Team V from 80. *52 Dawlish Drive, Bentilee, Stoke-on-Trent, ST2 0HZ.* (Stoke/Trent 260876)

THOMAS, Cuthbert William. Wycl Coll Tor STh 52. **d** 50 Tor **p** 50 Athab. C of Fort Chipewyan 50-53; I of Glenmore and of Sarcee Miss 53-55; Cannington and Sunderland 55-59; R of Mulmur 59-67; on leave. *357 Belsize Drive, Toronto 7, Ont, Canada.*

THOMAS, Canon Cyril. b 15. Univ of Wales, BA (2nd cl Phil) 38 Ex Coll Ox BA (3rd cl Th) 40, MA 45. **d** 41 **p** 42 St D. C of St Mich Aberystwyth 41-48; C-in-c of Newchurch 48-58; V of Llandingat w Llanfair and Myddfai Dio St D from 58; Can of St D from 72. *Vicarage, Llandovery, Dyfed, SA20 0EH.*

THOMAS, David. b 42. Keble Coll Ox 2nd cl Cl Mods 62, BA (3rd cl Lit Hum) 64, 1st cl Th 66, MA 67 St Steph Ho Ox 64. **d** 67 Swan B for St A **p** 68 St A. C of Hawarden 67-69; Lect St Mich Coll Llan 69-70; Chap 70-75; Sec of Ch in Wales Liturgical Comm 70-75; Vice-Prin St Steph Ho Ox 75-79; V of Chepstow Dio Mon from 79. *Vicarage, Beech Grove, Chepstow, Gwent, NP6 5BD.* (Chepstow 70980)

THOMAS, David Edgar. St Aid Coll 47. **d** 49 **p** 50 Wakef. C of All S Halifax 49-52; H Trin Hull 52-53; V of Luddendenfoot 53-72. *Address temp unknown.*

THOMAS, Canon David Geoffrey. b 24. AKC 48. St Bonif Coll Warm 48. **d** 49 St D **p** 50 Llan for St D. C of St Kath Milford Haven 49-52; Chap Miss to Seamen Cardiff 52-53; C of Pembroke 53-54; R of Rhoscrowther w Pwllcrochan 54-68; V of Milford Haven Dio St D and Chap Miss to Seamen 68-81; Can of St D Cathl from 77. *Address temp unknown.*

THOMAS, David Geoffrey. b 37. Univ of Wales (Cardiff) BA 58. Launde Abbey 71. **d** 71 **p** 72 Leic. Hon C of Fenny Drayton 71-75; Chap Commun of H Family Baldslow from 75. *Vicarage, Precincts, Burnham, Slough, SL1 7HU.* (Burnham 4173)

THOMAS, David Glynne. b 41. Univ of Dur BSc (2nd cl Gen) 63. Westcott Ho Cam. **d** 67 Willesden for Lon **p** 68 Lon. C of St John's Wood 67-70; St Alb Abbey 70-72; St Mary Virg Ox 72-75; Chap Wadham Coll Ox 72-75; Chap to Bp of Ox 75-78; P-in-c of Burnham Dio Ox from 78; Hitcham Dio Ox from 81. *Vicarage, Burnham, Slough, SL1 7HU.* (Burnham 4173)

THOMAS, David Godfrey. b 50. St Chad's Coll Dur BA 71. Fitzw Coll Cam BA 74, MA 78. Westcott Ho Cam 72. **d** 75 Warrington for Liv **p** 76 Liv. C of St Andr E Kirkby 75-78; Team V of Cov E Dio Cov from 78. *55 St Paul's Road, Coventry, CV6 5DE.* (Cov 88264)

THOMAS, David Harradence Bond. b 23. Ch Coll Cam BA 44, MA 51. **d** 59 **p** 60 Ox. C of Langley Marish 59-62; Earley (in c of St Nich 68-71) 62-71; P-in-c of Middleton Stoney 71-77; Bucknell 71-76; Weston-on-the-Green 72-76; Chesterton (w Middleton Stoney 77) and Wendlebury Dio Ox 76-77; V from 77. *Chesterton Vicarage, Bicester, Oxon, OX6 8UW,* (Bicester 2387)

THOMAS, David Martin Luther. St D Coll Lamp BA 23. **d** 23 St D **p** 24 Swan B. C of St Mark Swansea 23-25; St Edw Knighton 25-28; Llansamlet 28-31; V of Llangammarch 31-35; St Barn Swansea 35-68; Surr from 44; Can of Melineth in Brecon Cathl 53-69; Treas 58-59; RD of Swansea 58-59; Archd of Gower 59-69. *35 Sketty Road, Uplands, Swansea, W Glam.* (Swansea 56549)

THOMAS, David Noel. b 08 Univ of Wales, BA 30. St Mich Coll Llan 31. **d** 32 **p** 33 Llan. C of St John Penydarren

32-33; Porthkerry w Barry 33-37; Chap Miss to Seamen Hull 37-38; Santos 38-44; Southn 44-49; LPr Dio Win 44-49; V of Kingsclere 49-57; Chap Supt of Mersey Miss to Seamen 57-61; V of Harwich 61-74. *The Old School House, Birdbrook, Halstead, Essex, 9CO 4BX.* (Ridgewell 222)

THOMAS, David Richard. b 48. BNC Ox BA 71, MA 74. Fitzw Coll Cam BA 75, MA 80. Qu Coll Birm 79. **d** 80 Liv **p** 81 Warrington for Liv. C of St Columba Anfield Dio Liv from 80. *51 Anfield Road, Anfield, Liverpool, L4 0TG.*

THOMAS, David Ronald Holt. b 28. Lich Th Coll 55. **d** 58 **p** 59 Lich. C of Uttoxeter 58-61; Hednesford 61-66; R of Armitage Dio Lich from 66. *Rectory, Hood Lane, Armitage, Rugeley, Staffs.* (Armitage 490278)

THOMAS, David Thomas. b 44. St Cath Coll Cam BA 66, MA 70. St Jo Coll Dur Dipl Th 68. **d** 71 **p** 72 Man. C of Chorlton-cum-Hardy 71-74; Chap Salford Coll of Tech 74-80; P-in-c of Pendleton 74-77; V 77-80; Team R of Gleadless Dio Sheff from 80. *245 Hollinsend Road, Sheffield, S12 2EE.* (Sheffield 390757)

THOMAS, Ven David Trefor. St Pet Coll Ja. **d** and **p** 39 Ja. C of Halfway Tree 39-41; R of Comb Cure Stony Hill and Brandon Hill 41-46; C of Hayling I Hants 46-47; Actg R of Guy's Hill 47-50; P-in-c of Moneague 47-56; Claremont 48-56; Can of Ja 67-76; R of Brown's Tn Dio Ja from 56; P-in-c of Stewart Tn Dio Ja from 56; Archd of Montego Bay from 76. *Rectory, Brown's Town, Jamaica, W Indies.* (097-52276)

THOMAS, Canon David William. b 17. St D Coll Lamp BA 38. Univ of Wales, BA 63, MA 67. St Mich Coll Llan 39. **d** 41 **p** 43 St D. C of Cynwyl Gaeo w Llansawel 41-46; Llandysul 46-48; V of Clydau U 48-55; Llanfihangel-Genau'r-Glyn U (w Llangynfelyn 58-62) 55-67; Pontyberem 67-76; Llanilar w Rhostie w Llangwyryfon and Llanfihangel-Lledrod Dio St D from 76; Hon Can of St D Cathl from 78. *Llanilar Vicarage, Aberystwyth, Dyfed.* (Llanilar 659)

THOMAS, David William Wallace. b 51. St Chad's Coll Dur BA 72. St Mich Coll Llan 72. **d** 75 **p** 76 Llan. C of Bargoed and Deri w Brithdir Dio Llan from 75. *7 Llancayo Street, Bargoed, Mid Glam.*

THOMAS, David Wynford. b 48. Univ Coll of Wales (Abth) LLB 70. Qu Coll Birm 76. **d** 79 **p** 80 Swan B. C of St Mary Swansea Dio Swan B from 79. *22 Glebe Road, Lougher, Swansea, W Glam, SA4 2QS.*

THOMAS, Derek. b 51. Mem Univ of Newfld BA 72, AKC 75. **d** and **p** 75 Newfld. C of Flower's Cove Dio Newfld (E Newfld from 76) from 75. *Plum Point, St Barbe, Newfoundland, Canada.*

THOMAS, Dillwyn Morgan. b 26. St D Coll Lamp BA 50. Qu Coll Birm 50. **d** 52 **p** 53 Llan. C of Dowlais 52-59; Pontypridd 59-63; V of Llanwonno 63-68; Bargoed w Brithdir (and Deri from 74) 68-75; All SS Penarth Dio Llan from 75. *2 Lower Cwrt-y-Vil Road, Penarth, S Glam, CF6 2HQ.* (Penarth 708952)

THOMAS, Donald George. b 22. DFC 44. Qu Coll Cam BA 47, MA 52. Ridley Hall Cam 47. **d** 49 **p** 50 York. C of Drypool 49-51; St Illogan 51-52; Cheltm 52-55; V of St Steph Cinderford 55-61; Runcorn Dio Ches from 61. *Vicarage, Highlands Road, Runcorn, Ches, WA7 4PS.* (Runcorn 73709)

THOMAS, Douglas Graham. b 13. **d** 45 Calc **p** 46 Derby. C of St Thos Derby 45-48; Perm to Offic Dio Ripon 49-50; C of St Mary Hunslet (in c of St Silas) 50-51; St Alb Dartford 53-55; Bp's Chap to Seamen Dio Roch 55-60; C of Gravesend 54-56; St Nich Roch 56-58; V of Grayne 58-60; C-in-c of Darenth Dio Roch 60-65; V from 65. *Darenth Vicarage, Dartford, Kent.* (Dartford 23367)

THOMAS, Edward Bernard Meredith. Univ of Leeds BA 44. Univ of Queensld BEducn 68, BD 72. Coll of Resurr Mirfield, 47. **d** 49 **p** 50 S'wark. C of St Mary L Lambeth 49-54; St Mark Portsea 54-56; V of All SS Portsea 56-64; R of Woolloongabba Brisb 64-72; Perm to Offic Dio Brisb 72-78; Miss Chap Dio Brisb from 78. *33 Highfield Street, Oxley South, Queensland, Australia 4075.* (372 3517)

THOMAS, Canon Edward Maldwyn. b 12. Univ of Wales, BA 34, 2nd cl German 35, 2nd cl Econ 36, St Mich Coll Llan 37. **d** 38 Llan **p** 39 Swan B for Llan. C of H Trin Tylorstown 38-41; St Mark Gabalfa 41-43; Kingsbury (in c of Dosthill) 43-49; Dioc Chap Birm (in c of St Anne Duddeston and St Cath Nechells) 49-51; V of St Matt Duddeston Dio Birm from 51; Hon Can of Birm from 72. *St Matthew's Vicarage, Duddeston Manor Road, Nechells Green, Birmingham 7.* (021 359 1609)

THOMAS, Edward Owen Alban. b 02. Keble Coll Ox BA (3rd cl Th) 24, MA 28. Wells Th Coll. **d** 29 **p** 30 Ches. C of St Sav Oxton 29-33; St Mary Disley 34-38; V of Bidston 38-62; RD of Birkenhead 55-62; R of More w Lydham 62-70; R of Snead 62-70. *1 High Street, Bishop's Castle, Salop.* (Bishop's Castle 369)

THOMAS, Edward Walter Dennis. b 32. St Mich Coll Llan 61. **d** 63 **p** 64 Swan B. C of Loughor 63-69; V of Ystradfellte w Pontneathvaughan 69-74; St Mark and St Luke Dukinfield Dio Ches from 74. *Vicarage, Church Street, Dukinfield, SK16 4PR.* (061-330 2783)

THOMAS, Eirwyn Wheldon. b 35. St Mich Coll Llan 58. **d** 61 Ban **p** 62 Llan for Ban. C of Glanadda w Penrhosgarnedd 61-67; R of Llanddeusant w Llanbabo Llantrisant and Llanllibio 67-75; V of Nefyn w Morfa Nefyn Pistyll, Edern Tudweiliog and Llandudwen Dio Ban from 75. *Morfa Nefyn Vicarage, Pwllheli, Gwyn.* (Nefyn 494)

THOMAS, Elwyn Bernard. b 45. Univ of Wales BSc 68, BD 71. St Mich Coll Llan. **d** 71 **p** 72 Llan. C of St Fagan Aberdare 71-74; Merthyr Dyfan 74-76; R of Dowlais Dio Llan from 76. *Rectory, Dowlais, Mid Glam, CF48 3NA.* (Merthyr Tydfil 2118)

THOMAS, Canon Elwyn Lloyd. b 08. Univ of Wales, BA (2nd cl Engl) 30, MA and Morgan Evanson Scho 32. St Steph Ho Ox 32. **d** 33 **p** 34 St D. C of St Pet Carmarthen 33-38; St Mich Aberystwyth 38-44; V of Pontyberem 44-62; Surr from 44; V of St D w Ch Ch Carmarthen 62-79; Can of St D Cathl from 62; Chan 75-79. *3 St Mary Street, Carmarthen, Dyfed.* (Carmarthen 7662)

THOMAS, Ernest Keith. b 49. Univ of Wales (Cardiff) Dipl Th 76. St Mich AA Coll Llan 73. **d** 76 **p** 77 Swan B. C of St Gabr Swansea 76-79; Killay Dio Swan from 79. *The Parsonage, Ash Grove, Killay, Swansea, W Glam.* (Swansea 20031)

THOMAS, Erwin Arthur. b 09. Univ of Boston, BA 42. Nashotah Ho BD 46. **d** and **p** 45 Milwaukee (USA). M SSJE from 42; L to Offic Dio Ox 56-79; Dio Lon from 79. *St Edward's House, 22 Great College Street, Westminster, SW1P 3QA.*

✠ **THOMAS, Right Rev Eryl Stephen.** b 10. St Jo Coll Ox BA (2nd cl Th) 32, MA 38, Wells Th Coll 32. **d** 33 **p** 34 St A. C of Colwyn Bay 33-38; Hawarden (in c of Ewloe) 38-43; V of Risca 43-48; Warden of St Mich Coll Llan 48-54; Dean of Llan 54-68; Cons Ld Bp of Mon in St A Cathl 29 March 68 by Bp of St A; Bps of Llan; St D; Ban; Swan B; and Heref; and Bps A E Morris and T M Hughes; Trld to Llan 71; res 75. *17 Orchard Close, Gilwern, Abergavenny, Gwent.*

THOMAS, Euros Lloyd. b 53. Bris Poly BA 75. St Mich Coll Llan Dipl Th 79. **d** 79 **p** 80 St D. C of Llanelli Dio St D from 79. *17 Sunny Hill, Llanelli, Dyfed.*

THOMAS, Frank Lowth. b 22. Lon Coll of Div 64. **d** 66 Barking for Chelmsf **p** 67 Chelmsf. C of Walthamstow 66-68; Bickenhill w Elmdon 68-71. R of Carlton Colville 71-81; Smallburgh w Dilham and Honing w Crostwight Dio Nor from 81. *Honing Vicarage, North Walsham, Norf, NR28 9AB.* (Smallburgh 466)

THOMAS, Frederick Eric. Bps' Coll Cheshunt, 57. **d** 59 **p** 60 Leic. C of Lutterworth 59-61; V of Dunton Bassett 61-67; C of Alverstoke 72-78; P-in-c of Webheath 79-81; Chap Hewell Grange Open Borstal from 79; Team V of The Ridge, Redditch Dio Worc from 81. *The Vicarage, Church Road, Webheath, Redditch, Worcs.* (Redditch 41210)

THOMAS, Geler Harries. b 28. St D Coll Lamp BA 55. St Mich Coll Llan. **d** 57 **p** 58 St D. C of Ch Ch Llanelly 57-62; V of Llandyssilio w Egremont 62-69; R of Llanedy Dio St D 69-81; Llangennech Dio St D from 81. *Vicarage, Mwrwg Road, Llangennech, Llanelli, Dyfed.* (Llanelli 820324)

THOMAS, Geoffrey Brynmor. b 34. Univ of Lon BA (2nd cl Engl) AKC and Barry Pri 56. Ridley Hall, Cam 58. **d** 60 **p** 61 Chelmsf. C of Harlow New Town w L Parndon 60-65; V of All SS Leyton 65-74; All S Haley Hill Halifax Dio Wakef from 74. *All Souls Vicarage, 10 Elm View, Halifax, W Yorks, HX3 6DR.* (Halifax 52098)

THOMAS, Geoffrey Charles. b 30. ALCD 64. **d** 64 **p** 65 York. C of St Paul Holgate York 64-67; Ch Ch Cheltm 67-70; V of Whitgift w Adlingfleet 70-74; C-in-c of Eastoft 72-74; V of Mortomley Dio Sheff from 74. *Mortomley Vicarage, High Green, Sheffield, Yorks, S30 4HS.* (High Green 8231)

THOMAS, Geoffrey Heale. St Mich Coll Llan 58. **d** 60 **p** 61 Swan B. C of Llansamlet 60-63; V of St Piran Jos 63-67; St Nich-on-the-Hill Swansea 67-80; Oystermouth Dio Swan B from 80. *Oystermouth Vicarage, Swansea, W Glam.* (Swansea 66710)

THOMAS, Geoffrey Oswald. St Francis Coll Brisb 65. **d** 67 **p** 68 Brisb. C of St Andr Indooroopilly 67-70; St Jas Toowoomba 70; V of Surat 70-73; R of Drayton 73-76; St Andr Lutwyche City and Dio Brisb from 76. *Rectory, Lutwyche, Queensland, Australia 4030.* (57 5734)

THOMAS, George. b 46. Univ of Leeds BEducn 69. St Jo Coll Dur 75. **d** 78 **p** 79 Liv. C of Highfield Dio Liv from 78. *32 Melrose Drive, Winstanley, Wigan, Lancs, WN3 6ER.*

THOMAS, Canon George Emanuel. Episc Th Sch Cam Mass MDiv 74. St Pet Coll Ja. **d** 63 **p** 64 Ja. C of Cross Roads 63-66; Spanish Town Cathl 66-67; P-in-c of Guy's Hill 67-69; R of Port Antonio 69-76; R and Can of Cathl Ch of St Jago de la Vega Dio Ja from 76. *Cathedral Rectory, Spanish Town, Jamaica, W Indies.* (098-42300)

THOMAS, George Henry. Moore Th Coll Syd ACT ThL 63. **d** 63 **p** 64 Syd. C of Nowra 63-65; Liverpool 66-67; P-in-c of Franklin Harbour 67-68; R of Cleve 68-72; Streaky Bay 72-80; Balaklava Dio Willoch from 80. *Rectory, May Terrace, Balaklava, S Australia 5461.* (088-62 1427)

THOMAS, George William Curtis. b 04. Keble Coll Ox BA (2nd cl Engl Lang and Lit) 29, Dipl Th 30, MA 37. Wycl Hall Ox 29. **d** 30 **p** 31 Leic. C of St Marg Leic 30-32; Maidenhead 33-35; V of St Steph-by-Saltash 35-37; Org Sec CMS Dio Man and LPr Dio Man 37-38; Org Sec CMS Dios Blackb; Bradf and Carl 39-42; S & M 38-39; V of Hillsborough w Wadsley Bridge 42-47; St Giles Northn 47-55; St John w St Mark Southend-on-Sea 55-72. *Tudor Lodge, Robertsbridge, Sussex.* (Robertsbridge 880342)

THOMAS, Gordon Wallace. **d** 60 C & Goulb **p** 61 Bp Arthur for C & Goulb. C of St Jo Bapt Canberra 60-61; Kew 61-62; Waterloo w Mascot 63-64; R of Blackheath 64-69; Roseville E 69-72; S Cross 72-75; Kelmscott-Roleystone Dio Perth from 75. *4 River Road, Kelmscott, W Australia 6111.* (390 5351)

THOMAS, Gwilym Ivor. b 20. St D Coll Lamp BA 41. **d** 43 **p** 44 St D. C of Llansadwrn w Llanwrda 43-47; Llanedy 47-53; V of Ambleston w St Dogwells 53-62; Llansantffraed (w Llanbadarn-Trefeglwys from 70, w Llanrhystyd from 80) Dio St D from 62; RD of Glyn Aeron from 78. *Vicarage, Llanon, Cards, Dyfed.* (Llanon 394)

THOMAS, Gwyn Aubrey. b 12. St D Coll Lamp BA 35. **d** 35 **p** 36 Llan. C of Gilfach Goch 35-37; Sowerby Bridge w Norland 37-42; CF (EC) 42-48; V of Rashcliffe 48-50; C of E Org Sec Dr Barnardo's Homes SW Area and L to Offic Dio Truro 50-54; V of Hilton w Cheselbourne and Melcombe Horsey 54-66; R of S Perrott w Mosterton and Chedington 66-79. *c/o South Perrott Rectory, Beaminster, Dorset.* (Corscombe 281)

THOMAS, Gwynfor. b 13. St D Coll Lamp BA 40. **d** 46 **p** 47 Mon. C of Ebbw Vale 46-47; Beaufort 47-48; Blaenavon w Capel Newydd 48-51; Trevethin 51-52; V of Abercarn 52-61; R of Ilchester w Northover 61-69; C-in-c of Limington 61-65; R 65-69; V of Wookey (w Henton from 74) 69-78; L to Offic Dio B & W from 79. *Crieff, New Street, Somerton, Somt, TA11 7NT.* (Somerton 72549)

THOMAS, Harold Heath. b 08. Univ of Man BA 32. AKC 47. Linc Th Coll 47. **d** 47 **p** 48 Ches. C of St Paul Tranmere 47-53; V of Low Marple 53-75. *102 Hollins Lane, Marple Bridge, Stockport, SK6 5DA.* (061-449 8176)

THOMAS, Herbert. Univ of Wales, BA 27. St Mich Coll Llan 27. **d** 29 Mon for Ban **p** 30 Ban. C of Llanaber w Barmouth 29-31; Llanfairfechan 31-38; R of Llannor w Llanfihangel Bachellaeth (w Bodfuan from 49) 38-77; SPCK Dioc Sec from 49; RD of Lleyn 63-76. *c/o Rectory, Llannor, Pwllheli, Gwyn, LL53 6DL.* (Pwllheli 2300)

THOMAS, Herbert John. AKC 42. **d** 42 Bp Sara for B & W **p** 43 Taunton for B & W. C of H Trin Yeovil 42-44; Street 44-48; C-in-c of St Barn Conv Distr Southdown 48-57; Min 57-58; PC of St Barn Bath 58-62; V of St Jo Bapt Bridgwater 62-73; R of Compton Martin w Ubley 73-79. *25 Delmore Road, Frome, Somt, BA11 4EG.* (Frome 63762)

THOMAS, Howard Donald Lewis. b 19. Chich Th Coll 46. **d** 49 **p** 50 Ripon. C of Bramley Leeds 49-52; Armley 52-54; Sedbergh 54-57; Min of St Geo Statutory Distr Bury St E 57-61; V of Kersey w Lindsey 61-67; R of Hanborough Dio Ox from 67. *Rectory, Swan Lane, Long Hanborough, Oxford, OX7 2BT.* (Freeland 881270)

THOMAS, Hugh. b 14. St D Coll Lamp BA 36. **d** 37 **p** 38 St A. C of Llanrhaiadr-yn-Mochnant 37-41; Ruthin w Llanrhydd 41-50; R of Clocaenog (w Gyffylliog from 55) 50-79; RD of Dyffryn Clwyd 70-79. *The Nook, Llanfair-DC, Ruthin, Clwyd, N Wales.*

THOMAS, Hugh. Bro of St Paul Bardfield 33. **d** 40 **p** 41 Graft. C of Lismore 40-44; Llangelynin 47-49; Arthog 49-52; V of Brithdir w Bryncoedifor 52-64. *Address temp unknown.*

THOMAS, Hugh. St D Coll Lamp BA 50. **d** 51 Bp R W Jones for Llan **p** 52 St D. C of Pembrey w Llandyry 51-55; C-in-c of Moylgrove w Monnington 55-63; V of Llanfynydd 63-74; Pontyates Dio St D from 74; Llangyndeyrn Dio St D from 80. *Vicarage, Pontyates, Llanelly, Dyfed.* (Pontyates 860451)

THOMAS, Hugh Meredith. b 39. St D Coll Lamp BA 61. St Mich Coll Llan 61. **d** 63 **p** 64 St D. C of Llandeilo Fawr w Llandefeisant 63-70; V of Gwynfe w Llanddeusant 70-74; Llanpumpsaint Dio St D from 74. *Llanpumpsaint Vicarage, Dyfed.* (Llanpumpsaint 205)

THOMAS, Huw Glyn. b 42. St D Coll Lamp BA 62. Linacre Coll Ox BA 65. MA 69. Wycl Hall Ox 62. **d** 65 **p** 66 Swan B. C of Oystermouth 65-68; Asst Chap Solihull Sch 68; Chap 69-73; Selection Sec ACCM 73-78; C of Loughton 74-76; V of St John Bury Dio Man from 78; Dioc Dir of Ords from 82. *6 Arley Avenue, Bury, Lancs, BL9 5HD.* (061-764 3412)

THOMAS, Ian Fyffe. St Jo Coll Morpeth, 64. **d** 66 **p** 67 Melb. C of St John E Malvern 66-67; St Paul Ringwood 68-70; C of Beddington 71-72; P-in-c of St Phil Heidelberg W 72-75; R of Bothwell and Kempton 75-80; Moonah Dio Tas from 80. *1 Springfield Avenue, Moonah, Tasmania 7009.* (002 72 9823)

THOMAS, Ian Melville. b 50. Jes Coll Ox BA 71. St Steph Ho Ox 71. **d** 73 **p** 74 St D. PV of St D Cathl Dio St D from 73. *Pembroke Cottage, Glasfryn Lane, St Davids, SA62 6ST.*

THOMAS, Idris. b 48. Burgess Hall Lamp Dipl Th 71. **d** 71 **p** 72 Ban. C of Llanbeblig w Caernarfon and Betws Garmon w Waenfawr 71-75; P-in-c of Llanaelhaiarn w Trefor Dio Ban 75-77; R from 77; Clynnog Fawr from 77. *Rectory, Trefor, Caernarfon, Gwynedd.* (Clynnog Fawr 547)

THOMAS, Canon Ilar Roy Luther. b 30. Late Griffiths Scho of St D Coll Lamp BA 51. St Mich Coll Llan 51. **d** 53 **p** 54 Swan B. C of Oystermouth 53-56; Gorseinon 56-59; R of Llanbadarn Fawr w Llandegley (w Llanfihangel Rhydithon from 60) 59-66; CF (TA) 62; V of Knighton w Norton 66-79; RD of Knighton 66-79; Can of Brecon from 75; V of Sketty Dio Swan B from 79. *Sketty Vicarage, Swansea, W Glam.* (Swansea 22767)

THOMAS, Iorwerth. Univ of Wales, BSc 35. St Mich Coll Llan 38. **d** 38 Bp Wentworth Shields for Ban **p** 40 Ban. C of Amlwch 38-45; V of Llandrygarn w Bodwrog 45-52; R of Llanfihangel Ysgeifiog w Llanffinnan Dio Ban from 52. *Gaerwen Rectory, Anglesey.* (Gaerwen 665)

THOMAS, Very Rev James. St D Coll Lamp BA 41. Selw Coll Cam BA (3rd cl Th Trip pt i) 46, MA 51. **d** 42 **p** 43 St D. C of Amroth 42-44; Laugharne w Llansadwrnen 44; CF (EC) 46-49; Hon CF 48; C of Braunton (in c of Saunton) 49-51; V of Thornthwaite w Darley and Thruscross 51-54; Kensington-Otipua 54-60; U Riccarton 60-62; St Mark Remuera Auckld 62-78; Archd of Waitemata 72-78; Dean and V of St Paul's Cathl City and Dio Wel from 78; Exam Chap to Bp of Wel from 79. *Deanery, Bolton Street, Thorndon, Wellington, NZ.* (721-568)

THOMAS, James Christopher. b 43. St Chad's Coll Dur Dipl Th 68; PhD 74. Selw Coll Cam MA 71. **d** 70 Bp of Jarrow for Accra **p** 71 Accra. Lect Univ of Ghana from 70; Chap from 72. *University of Ghana, PO Box 66, Legon, Ghana.*

THOMAS, Canon James Godfrey Tansley. b 13. Univ of Leeds, BA 34, MA 40, BD 47. Coll of Resurr Mirfield, 34. **d** 36 **p** 37 Llan. C of St Martin Roath 36-38; Llanishen (in c of Lisvane) 38-41; Publ Pr Dio Nor and Actg C-in-c of Winterton 41-46; R of Morley 46-53; RD of Hingham 52-61 and 66-70; V of Wymondham 53-73; Chap Wicklewood Hosp 61-73; RD of Humbleyard 72-73; Hon Can of Nor from 72; R of L Massingham 78-81. *6 Lowick Close, Toftwood, Dereham, Norf.*

THOMAS, James Morris. b 02. **d** 37 **p** 38 Kalg. C of Norseman 37-38; R of Southern Cross 38-43; C of St Geo Cathl Perth 43-44; R of Wiluna 44-47; C of Mynyddyslwyn 48-51; R of Henllys w Bettws 51-57; Tintern Parva w Chapel Hill 57-73; L to Offic Dios Mon, Heref and Glouc from 74. *Green Acres Farm, Broadoak, Newnham-on-Severn, Glos.*

THOMAS, James Owen. b 1895. Worc Coll Ox BA 17, MA 22. Ridley Hall Cam 17. **d** 31 **p** 32 Ox. C of H Trin Wolverton 31-34; St Pet Bayswater 34-36; V of Framsden w Cretingham 36-40; R of Trimley St Mary 40-65; Actg R of Trimley St Martin 43-46. *30 Brook Lane, Felixstowe, Suff.* (Felixstowe 2670)

THOMAS, John Albert. b 13. **d** 51 Ripon for Col Bp **p** 52 Puerto Rico for WI. C of St Anthony Montserrat 51-54; P-in-c of St Thos St Kitts 54-61; R of Dominica 61-62; C of H Sav Hitchin 62-65; V of Walesby 65-74; R of Kirton 65-74; V of Sutton w Lound 74-78; Hon Asst Chap Trin Hosp Retford from 78. *2 Trinity Hospital, Retford, Notts, DN22 8PT.* (Retford 707333)

THOMAS, John Alun. b 1896. Univ of Wales, BA 23. Univ of Liv MA 51. Univ of Sheff PhD 56. FR Hist S 57, St Mich Coll Llan. **d** 24 **p** 25 Ban for St A. C of Brymbo 24-27; Llangystenyn 27-30; R of Gwaenysgor 30-33; Sen V Cho of St A Cathl and V of St A 33-39; V of Penycae 39-52; Surr 33-65; M Governing Body of Ch in Wales 47-65; Dioc Insp of Schs Dio St A 48-65; V of Llangollen w Trevor 52-65; RD of Llangollen 55-65; Can of St A Cathl 57-60; Preb of Llanefydd and Chan of St A Cathl 59-65; Perm to Offic Dio Ex from 75. *164 Northfield Lane, Brixham, Devon, TQ5 8RH.*

THOMAS, John Bowden. Linc Coll Ox BA (2nd cl Mod Hist) 21, MA 25. **d** 21 **p** 22 St D. C of Ch Ch Llanelly 21-26; Pembrey (in c of St Mary Burry Port) 26-29; V of St Matt Borth 29-50; St Mary (w St Thos 50-65) Haverfordwest 50-66; Surr from 53; Can of St D 57-70. *185 Haven Road, Haverfordwest, Dyfed.*

THOMAS, John Bryn. b 37. Lich Th Coll 63. **d** 66 **p** 67

Lich. C of Stoke-on-Trent 66-71; R of Wotton (and Holmbury St Mary from 80) Dio Guildf from 71; P-in-c of Holmbury St Mary 78-80. *Wotton Rectory, Dorking, Surrey.* (Dorking 5335)

THOMAS, Canon John Degwel. b 11. Univ of Wales, BSc (2nd cl Metallurgy) 33. St Steph Ho Ox 34. **d** 36 **p** 37 Llan. C of St Jo Bapt Cardiff 36-43; St Mary Virg Bathwick 43-47; V of Haddenham 47-51; PC of St Geo Chesterton 51-74; Surr from 52; Ed Ely Dioc Gazette 58-70; R of Rampton 74-81; Communications Officer Dio Ely from 74; Commiss Pusan (Busan) from 74; Hon Can of Ely 77-81; Can (Emer) from 81. *17 King Street, Over, Cambridge, CB4 5PS.* (Swavesey 31198)

THOMAS, John Elwern. b 14. Univ of Wales, BA (2nd cl Welsh) 35. Coll of Resurr Mirfield, 35. **d** 37 Ban **p** 38 Bp Wentworth-Shields for Ban. C of Conway w Gyffin 37-41; Llandrillo-yn-Rhos 41-47; V of St Fagan Aberdare 47-55; R of Dollgellau 55-70; C-in-c of Brithdir w Bryncoedifor 65-70; RD of Ystumaner 58-70; Can Res of Ban Cathl 69-70; Warden and R of Ruthin w Llanrhydd 70-79; Can of St A Cathl 77-79; Surr from 77. *Fron Deg, Ffordd Goch, Llandyrnog, Denbigh, Clwyd LL16 4LE.* (Llandyrnog 445)

THOMAS, John Herbert Samuel. b 34. Pemb Coll Cam 3rd cl Th Trip pt i, 55, BA (2nd cl Th Trip pt ii) 57, MA 64. St Mich Coll Llan 57. **d** 58 **p** 59 Llan. C of Port Talbot 58-60; Llantwit Major 60-67; C-in-c of Duffryn Conv Distr 67-74; V of Dinas and Penygraig Dio Llan from 74. *Vicarage, Penygraig, Rhondda, Mid Glam, CF40 1TA.* (Tonypandy 433304)

THOMAS, John Iorwerth. b 17. St D Coll Lamp BA 40. **d** 40 **p** 41 St D. C of Laugharne w Llansadwrnen 40-44; C-in-c of Dale 44-46; Chap RNVR 46-47; C of Pembroke Dock 47-53; C-in-c of Uzmaston w Boulston 53-56; R of Stackpole Elidor w St Petrox Dio 56-72; V of Laugharne w Llansadwrnen and Llandawke Dio St D from 72; Surr from 72. *Laugharne Vicarage, Dyfed.* (Laugharne 218)

THOMAS, John James. b 1900. St D Coll Lamp BA 23. **d** 24 **p** 25 Llan. C of Ch Ch Ferndale 24-26; Llangynwyd 26-28; Coity w Nolton 28-30; C-in-c of Conv Distr of Cymmer w Abercregan 30-33; V of Blaengarw 33-39; R of Cilybebyll 39-46; Llantrisant 46-56; Surr from 40; V of Ystradowen w Welsh St Donats 56-71; RD of Cowbridge (w Llantwit Major from 67) 62-70; Perm to Offic Dio Llan from 71. *Cilrhedyn, Aberthyn, Cowbridge, CF7 7HB.*

✠ **THOMAS, Right Rev John James Absalom.** b 08. Univ Coll of Wales BA (1st cl Phil) 29. Keble Coll Ox 1st cl Th 31, BA and MA 36. DD (Lambeth) 58. **d** 31 **p** 32 Swan B. C of Llanguicke 31-34; Sketty 34-36; Bp's Messenger 36-40; Exam Chap to Bp of Swan B 36-40; to Bp of Ban 40-44; Warden of Ch Hostel Lect in Th Univ Coll Ban and L to Offic Dio Ban 40-44; V of Swansea 45-58; Surr 45-58; Chap to Bp of Swan B 45-58; Hon Can of Hay in Brecon Cathl 46-53; Can and Prec 53-54; Hon Sec Swan B Dioc Conf 49-54; RD of Swansea 52-54; Archd of Gower 54-58; Cons Ld Bp of Swan B 25 Jan 58 in Cathl Ch of St Woolos Newport by Abp of Wales; Bps of B & W; St A; St D; Llan; and Ban; res 76; Sub-Prelate O of St John of Jer from 65. *Woodbine Cottage, St Mary's Street, Tenby, Dyfed.* (Tenby 2013)

THOMAS, Canon John Keble Holliday. b 09. St D Coll Lamp BA 31. **d** 32 **p** 33 St D. C of St Ishmael 32-39; Old Swinford 39-43; R of Stoke Bliss w Kyre Wyard 43-52; Ripple 52-78; RD of Bredon from 73; Hon Can of Worc from 75. *Brook House, Wyre Piddle, Pershore, Worcs.*

THOMAS, John Roland Lloyd. b 08. Late Sen Scho of St D Coll Lamp BA (1st cl Hist) 30, Hon LLD 76. Late Scho of Jes Coll Ox 2nd cl Th 32, BA and MA 36. **d** 32 **p** 33 Llan. C of St Jo Bapt Cardiff 32-40; CF (EC) 40-44; Hon CF 52; R of Canton 44-49; Surr 44-75; V of St Mark Newport 49-52; St Woolos Cathl Ch Newport 52-53; Dean of Mon 52-53; Exam Chap to Bp of Mon 52-58; Prin of St D Coll Lamp 53-75; Can of Llangan in St D Cathl 56-63; Llawhaden 63-75; Chan 63-75. *1 Rock House, St Julian Street, Tenby, Dyfed, SA70 7BD.* (Tenby 2679)

THOMAS, Joseph Neville. b 33. St D Coll Lamp BA 57. St Mich Coll Llan. **d** 59 **p** 60 Ban. C of Portmadoc 59-62; St Jo Bapt Cardiff 62-65; CF from 65. *c/o Ministry of Defence, Chaplains* (Army), *Bagshot Park, Bagshot, GU19 5PL.*

THOMAS, Very Rev Kalluzhathill Thomas. **d** and **p** 61 Centr Tang. P Dio Centr Tang 61-65; Dio Moro 65-71; Dio Dar-S 71-76; Dio Centr Zam from 76; Dean of Centr Zam Cathl from 80. *Box 70172, Ndola, Zambia.*

THOMAS, Leonard Glynne. b 04. Late Exhib of St D Coll Lamp BA 28. **d** 28 **p** 29 St A. C of Denbigh 28-30; V Cho and V of St A Cathl 30-35; C of Stoke Lacy 35-36; PC of Llanfair Waterdine 36-45; CF (R of O) 39-42; Hon CF 42; V of Capel Garmon 45-50; Thurgoland 50-55; Minsterley and R of Habberley 55-59; V of All SS Princes Pk Toxt Pk 59-72; Chap R Infirm Liv 59-71; St D Liv 72-74; Perm to Offic Dio Nor from 74 *9 Hillside Close, Swardeston, Norwich, NR14 8DY.* (Mulbarton 594)

THOMAS, Leslie Richard. b 45. Lon Coll of Div 65. **d** 69 Warrington for Liv **p** 70 Liv. C of Knotty Ash 69-72; Sutton (in c of St Mich AA) 72-74; Team V 74-77; Banks Dio Liv from 77. *Banks Vicarage, Southport, Mer, PR9 8ET.* (Southport 28985)

THOMAS, Lewis Llewellyn. b 21. St D Coll Lamp BA 41. Selw Coll Cam BA 44, MA 48. Westcott Ho Cam 44. **d** 45 **p** 46 Lich. C of Wednesbury 45-48; Wymondham 48-51; V of Cantley w Limpenhoe and Southwood 51-55; St Mary Bilston 55-75; Perm to Offic Dio Lich 75-81; Hon C of St Jo Evang Wolverhampton Dio Lich from 80. *10 Richmond Avenue, Finchfield, Wolverhampton, WV3 9JB.* (Wolverhampton 711087)

THOMAS, Lewis Madoc. b 12. St D Coll Lamp BA 33. St Mich Th Coll Llan 34. **d** 35 St D **p** 36 Swan B for St D. C of St Issels 35-37; Dafen 37-38; Min Can and C of St D Cathl 38-41; R of St Nicholas w Grandston 41-51; V of Llansantffraed 51-61. *16 Coedcae Road, Llanelli, Dyfed.* (Llanelli 4720)

THOMAS, Llewellyn. b 17. St D Coll Lamp BA 40. **d** 42 **p** 43 St D. C of Llangeler 42-46; Llannon 46-61; V of Llawhaden w Bletherston 61-80; Llanycefn 79-80. *Cross Hill, Eglwyswrw, Crymych, Pembs, Dyfed.* (Boncath 527)

THOMAS, Malcolm Andrew. **d** 80 **p** 81 Melb. C of St Steph Belmont Dio Melb from 80. *c/o 42 Regent Street, Belmont, Vic, Australia 3216.*

THOMAS, Mark Wilson. b 51. Univ of Dur BA 72. Ripon Coll Cudd 76. **d** 78 **p** 79 Wakef. C of Chapelthorpe 78-81; Seaford w Chyngton Dio Chich from 81. *5 Chyngton Gardens, Seaford, E Sussex.* (Seaford 893876)

✠ **THOMAS, Right Rev Maxwell McNee.** Univ of Syd BA 46, BD 50, MA 59. Gen Th Sem NY DTh 64. **d** 50 **p** 52 Newc. Lect in Th St Jo Coll Morpeth 50; C of E Maitland 50-52; Richmond Surrey 52-54; Singleton 55; P-in-c of The Entrance 55; R 55-59; Fell and Tutor Gen Th Sem NY 59-64; Tutor Trin Coll Melb 64-68; Chap to Angl Studs Univ of Melb 64-68; Lect in Div Trin Coll Melb 69-75; Abp's Consultant Theologian 69-75; Cons Ld Bp of Wang in St Paul's Cathl Melb 17 Dec 75 by Abps of Melb, Brisb and Adel; Bps of St Arn, Bend, Bal and Gippsld; Coadj Bps of Melb; and Asst Bp of Newc; and others. *Bishop's Lodge, Wangaratta, Vic., Australia 3677.* (061-21 3643)

THOMAS, Melvyn. b 04. St D Coll Lamp BA 32. **d** 33 **p** 34 St D. C of Llanedy 33-35; Llandebie 35-38; V of Elerch 38-48; Llangain 48-60; Llangadock 60-74. *Brodeg, Pontfaen Road, Lampeter, Dyfed.*

THOMAS, Michael. b 37. Univ of Birm BA 58. Wells Th Coll. **d** 60 **p** 61 Birm. C of Kingshurst 60-63; Bp's Cleeve 63-66; PC (V from 69) of Ripley 66-73; P-in-c of Dilwyn w Stretford 73-79; V of Much Wenlock w Bourton 79-81; P-in-c of Easthope w Stanton Long and of Shipton and of Hughley w Ch Preen 79-81; Kenley 79-81; Team R of Wenlock Dio Heref from 81. *Vicarage, Much Wenlock, Shropshire, TF13 6BN.*

THOMAS, Michael Edward. b 37. Oak Hill Th Coll 62. **d** 65 Burnley for Blackb **p** 66 Blackb. C of Bispham 65-68; St Mark Cheltenham 68-75; Camborne 75-78; H Trin Hinckley Dio Leic from 80. *27 Lochmore Drive, Hinckley, Leics. LE10 0TZ.* (Hinckley 610589)

THOMAS, Michael Edward Randolph. b 17. **d** 74 **p** 75 Accra. P Dio Accra. *Box 1628, Accra, Ghana.*

THOMAS, Michael Longdon Sanby. b 34. Trin Hall, Cam BA 55, MA 60. Wells Th Coll 56. **d** 58 **p** 59 Wakef. C of Sandal 58-60; Chap Portsm Cathl 60-64; V of Shedfield 64-69; Portchester Dio Portsm from 69. *164 Castle Street, Portchester, Hants.* (Cosham 76289)

THOMAS, Michael Paul. b 29. **d** 52 Lon for Col Bp **p** 53 Alg. I of Mindemoya 53-62; C of Bushey 62-67; V of Ardeley Dio St Alb from 67. *Ardeley Vicarage, Stevenage, Herts.* (Walkern 286)

THOMAS, Ven Owen. b 17. Selw Coll Cam 3rd cl Math Trip pt i, 38, BA (3rd cl Th Trip Sect A) 40, MA 58. St Mich Coll Llan 40. **d** 41 **p** 42 St A. C of Rhyl 41-44; V Cho of St A Cathl 44-48; C of Welshpool 48-53; R of Llanferres 53-65; V of Welshpool and R of Castle Caereinion 65-77; RD of Pool 76-77; Archd of Montgomery from 77; V of Berriew (w Manafon from 80) Dio St A from 77; Preb of St A Cathl from 77. *Vicarage, Berriew, Powys, SY21 8PL* (Berriew 223)

THOMAS, Owen James. b 17. Univ of Wales, BA 38. Tyndale Hall, Bris 38. **d** 40 **p** 41 S'wark. C of St Steph Wandsworth 40-43; Dagenham 43-46; R of St Silas Glas 46-51; C-in-c of Ch Ch Woburn Sq 51-52; Tutor Lon Bible Coll 51-62; Chap and Lect 62-76; Perm to Offic Dio Lon 52-76; Hon C of Em Northwood 70-76; V of St Steph Canonbury Road Dio Lon from 76. *9 River Place, N1 2DE.* (01-226 7526)

THOMAS, Owen William. Univ of Syd BA 62, BD (Lon) 66. Moore Th Coll Syd ACT ThL 65. **d** 66 Bp Loane for Syd **p** 67 Syd. C of Epping 66-69; R of S Hurstville 69-76; L to Offic Dio Syd from 76. *276 Old Canterbury Road, Summer Hill, NSW, Australia 2130.* (799-4552)

THOMAS, Patrick Hungerford Bryan. b 52. Late Exhib of St Cath Coll Cam BA 73, MA 77. Univ of Leeds BA (Th) 78. Coll of the Resurr Mirfield 76. **d** 79 **p** 80 St D. C of Aberystwyth 79-81; Carmarthen Dio St D from 81. *Clergy House, The Parade, Carmarthen, Dyfed.*

THOMAS, Paul Wyndham. b 55. Oriel Coll Ox BA (Hist) 76, BA (Th) 78. Wycl Hall Ox 77. **d** 79 **p** 80 Llan. C of Llangynwyd w Maesteg Dio Llan from 79. *The Old Vicarage, Llangynwyd, Maesteg, Mid Glam.*

THOMAS, Peter George Hartley. b 38. K Coll Lon and Warm AKC 63. **d** 64 **p** 65 Portsm. C of Leigh Pk Conv Distr 64-69; V of Cosham 69-77; R of Hayes Dio Roch from 77. *Hayes Rectory, Bromley, Kent.* (01-462 1373)

THOMAS, Peter James. b 53. Univ of Lon BSc 75. Trin Coll Bris 77. **d** 80 **p** 81 Glouc. C of Hucclecote Dio Glouc from 80. *3 Millfields, Hucclecote, Gloucester.* (Glouc 60010)

THOMAS, Peter Rhys. b 37. TCD BA 59, MA 72. **d** 72 **p** 73 Dub. C of Cong Dio Tuam 73-75; R 75-77; C of All SS Bingley 77-79; V of Shelf Dio Bradf from 79. *St Michael's Vicarage, Carr House Lane, Shelf, Halifax, Yorks, HX3 7RH.* (Bradford 677413)

THOMAS, Philip Edward. b 13. Univ of Lon BA 35. K Coll Lon AKC 36. **d** 36 **p** 37 S'wark. C of St Sav Brixton Hill 36-39; St Andr Newington 39-40; St Pet St Alb 40-47; PC of H Trin Leverstock Green 47-53; Perm to Offic Dio St Alb from 53; Asst Master Friern Barnet Gr Sch 53-54; Hd Master 54-60; Asst Master Queenswood Sch from 60. *Flat 8, 36 Barnard Hill, N10.*

THOMAS, Philip Harold Emlyn. Univ of Cant BA 64. Ridley Coll Melb 66. **d** 68 **p** 69 Adel. C of H Trin 68-71; L to Offic Dio Ch Ch 71-78; on leave. *101 Waimairi Road, Christchurch 4, NZ.* (486-473)

THOMAS, Philip Sewell. Late Cl Scho of Linc Coll Ox 2nd cl Mods 30, BA (2nd cl Th) 32, MA 38. Ely Th Coll 32. **d** 33 Win **p** 34 Southn for Win. C of Odiham 33-36; Midsomer Norton 36-42; PV and Sacr Wells Cathl 42-46; C of Easton 42-46; St Jo Bapt Bridgwater 46-49; V of Barton St David w Kingweston Dio B & W from 49. *Barton St David Vicarage, Somerton, Somt, TA11 6BN.* (Baltonsborough 50257)

THOMAS, Ralph. ED 64. St Barn Coll Adel ACT ThL 36. **d** 36 **p** 37 Perth. C of Ch Ch Claremont 36-40; R of Wiluna 40-42; Chap AMF 39-42; AIF 42-46; CMF 49-50; Sen Chap 50-69; R of Victoria Pk 46-64; St John Fremantle 64-74; Archd of Fremantle 64-74; Chap Dept of Corrections Fremantle 74-79; L to Offic Dio Perth 79-80; Perm to Offic from 80. *16 Solomon Street, Fremantle, W Australia 6160.* (335 1113)

THOMAS, Ralph Pilling. b 23. St D Coll Lamp BA 49. Wycl Hall, Ox 49. **d** 51 **p** 52 Blackb. C of H Trin S Shore Blackpool 51-53; St Geo Chorley 53-59; R of Wellow 59-63; C-in-c of Hinton Charterhouse 59-63; V of St Jo Div Coppull 63-68; Asst Chap HM Pris Wandsworth 68-69; Chap HM Pris Leeds 69-73; R of Kirklington w Burneston and Wath Dio Ripon from 73. *Kirklington Rectory, Bedale, N Yorks, DL8 2NJ.* (Thirsk 567429)

THOMAS, Richard. b 45. Bp Burgess Coll Lamp 68. **d** 71 **p** 72 St D. C of St Paul Llanelly Dio St D from 71. *59 Queen Victoria Road, Llanelly, Dyfed.*

THOMAS, Richard Evans. b 11. MPS 35. **d** 68 **p** 69 Ban. Hon C of Llandudno 68-80; Perm to Offic Dio Ban from 81. *2 Park Avenue, Craig-y-don, Llandudno, Gwynedd, LL30 1EZ.* (Llandudno 75539)

THOMAS, Richard Frederick. b 24. Qu Coll Cam 3rd cl Mech Sc 44, BA 45, MA 49. Ridley Hall Cam 47. **d** 49 Dover for Cant **p** 50 Cant. C of Em S Croydon 49-51; Chap Haileybury Coll 51-67; Ho Master 57-67; Publ Pr Dio St Alb 52-67; Hd Master Angl Ch Sch Jer 67-73; L to Offic Dio Jer 67-73; Ho Master Bp Luffa Sch Chich 74-81; L to Offic Dio Chich 75-81; Hon C of St Pancras and St John Chich 78-81; V of N Mundham w Hunston Dio Chich from 81. *Hunston Rectory, Chichester, W Sussex.* (Chich 782003)

THOMAS, Richard Paul. b 50. Wycl Hall Ox 74. **d** 76 Dorchester for Ox **p** 77 Ox. C of Abingdon 76-79; R of All SS w St Andr Chilcomb and St Pet Chesil City and Dio Win from 79. *Rectory, Petersfield Road, Winchester, Hants.* (Win 3777)

THOMAS, Robert Stanley. b 31. Univ of Lon BD 65. Sarum Th Coll 66. **d** 67 **p** 68 Sheff. C of Maltby 67-70; L to Offic Dio St Alb 70-72; Asst Master Eliz Allen Sch Barnet 70-72; Knowl View Sch Bamford 72-80; Perm to Offic Dio St A from 80. *Brynaber, Cerrigydrudion, Corwen, Clwyd.* (049-082220)

THOMAS, Roger James. b 37. Univ of Bris BA 59. Wells Th Coll 59. **d** 61 **p** 62 Bris. C of Henbury 61-64; Stapleton 64-69; P-in-c of Hardenhuish 69-71; R 71-75; P-in-c of St Mich Kington 69-71; V 71-75; Hartcliffe 75-81; RD of Bedminster 79-81; P-in-c of Frenchay Dio Bris from 81; Winterbourne Down Dio Bris from 81. *Frenchay Rectory, Bristol, BS16 1NB.* (Bristol 567616)

THOMAS, Ronald Maurice. St D Coll Lamp BA 37. **d** 46 **p** 47 Swan B. C of Ystalyfera 46-50; St Pet Swansea 50-55; R of Llanfihangel-Cwmdu w Tretower 55-60; Bishopston 60-73. *c/o Bishopston Rectory, Swansea, W Glam.* (Bishopston 238)

THOMAS, Ronald Stuart. Univ of Wales, BA (2nd cl Latin) 35. St Mich Coll Llan 35. **d** 36 **p** 37 St A. C of Chirk 36-40; Hanmer (in c of Talarn Green) 40-42; R of Manafon 42-54; V of Eglwysfach 54-67; Aberdaron w Bodferin (and Rhiw w Llanfaerlrhys from 72) 67-78. *Sarn-y-Plas, Rhiw Pwllheli, Gwyn.*

THOMAS, Canon Rosser Elwyn. b 13. St D Coll Lamp BA 42. Lich Th Coll 43. **d** 46 **p** 47 Swan B. C of Loughor 46-50; Llanguicke 50-55; R of Penderyn Dio Swan B from 55; Hon Can of Brecon Cathl from 81. *Rectory, Penderyn, Aberdare, Mid-Glam.* (Hirwain 410)

THOMAS, Royston. b 31. **d** 59 **p** 60 Llan. C of Aberaman 59-64; Llanishen w Lisvane 64-69; V of Ynyshir 69-79. *6 Upper Colliers Road, Merthyr Tydfil, Mid Glam.*

THOMAS, Russen William. b 30. Late Organ Scho of St D Coll Lamp BA 55. St Mich Coll Llan 55. **d** 57 **p** 58 Mon. C of St Jo Bapt Newport 57-59; Pembroke Dk w Nash and Upton 59-62; R of St Florence w Redberth 62-69; V of St Julian Newport 69-79; Stratton Dio Truro from 79. *Vicarage, Diddies Road, Stratton, Bude, EX23 9DW.* (Bude 2254)

THOMAS, Simon Jonathan Franklin. b 51. Univ of Sheff BA (Psych) 72. Univ of Nottm BA (Th) 79. St Jo Coll Nottm 77. **d** and **p** 80 Peru. P Dio Peru. *Apartado 5152, Lima, Peru.*

THOMAS, Stephen Blayney. b 35. St D Coll Lamp BA 62, Dipl Th 63. **d** 63 **p** 64 Heref. C of Ledbury 63-67; Bridgnorth 67-68; Clun w Chapel Lawn, Bettws-y-Crwyn w Newcastle, Clungunford, Bedstone w Hopton Castle 68-73; V of Worfield Dio Heref from 73; RD of Bridgnorth from 81. *Worfield Vicarage, Bridgnorth, Salop.* (Worfield 698)

THOMAS, Sydney. b 09. Bp Wilson Th Coll IM 32. **d** 35 **p** 36 Heref. C of Madeley 35-38; H Trin Heref 38-39; Clun w Chapel Lawn 39-46; CF (EC) 40-46; R of Rochford 46-49; St Anne Newton Heath 49-53; V of Chipping Sodbury (w Old Sodbury from 57) 53-61; R of St Jo Evang Old Trafford 61-69; V of Woodford Halse 69-74; Perm to Offic Dio B & W from 79. *22 Parkfield Gardens, Bishops Sutton, Bristol, BS18 4XF.* (Chew Magna 2144)

THOMAS, Sydney Robert. b 44. Univ of Wales, BA (2nd cl Mod Hist and Pol) 65. St D Coll Lamp LTh 67. **d** 67 **p** 68 St D. C of Llanelli 67-77; V of Pontyberem Dio St D from 77. *Pontyberem Vicarage, Llanelli, Dyfed.* (Pontyberem 345)

THOMAS, Sydney Weswel. b 26. Codr Coll Barb 71. **d** 71 Starbroek for Guy **p** 72 Guy. C of New Amsterdam 71-74; V of Port Mourant Dio Guy from 74. *Vicarage, Port Mourant, Berbice, Guyana.*

THOMAS, Telford Ifano. b 17. Univ of Wales, BA 38. St D Coll Lamp 38. **d** 40 **p** 41 St D. C of Llanegwad 40-45; Llanddowror 45-46; Ch Ch Llanelly 46-52; V of Llansadwrn w Llanwrda and Capel Dewi Sant 52-61; Llangennech 61-79; Llanstephan Dio St D from 79. *Vicarage, Llanstephan, Carmarthen, Dyfed.* (Llanstephan 293)

THOMAS, Theodore Eilir. b 36. St D Coll Lamp BA (2nd cl Th) 58. Sarum Th Coll 58. **d** 60 **p** 61 Lich. C of Fenton 60-63; Stourport 63-67; V of H Trin w St Matt Worc 67-74; St Francis Dudley Dio Worc from 74. *St Francis Vicarage, Dudley, Worc.* (Dudley 53123)

THOMAS, Theodore Glenn. b 32. **d** 76 **p** 77 Port Eliz. C of St Paul City and Dio Port Eliz from 76. *11 Aubrey Street, Gelvan Street, Gelvan Park, Port Elizabeth, 6016, CP, S Africa.*

THOMAS, Thomas Alan. b 37. K Coll Lon and Warm BD and AKC 60. **d** 61 **p** 62 Dur. C of Washington 61-65; St Mary Virg w St Pet Conv Distr Bp Wearmouth 65-70; V of Ruishton w Thornfalcon Dio B & W from 70. *Vicarage, Church Lane, Ruishton, Taunton, Somt. TA3 5JW.* (Henlade 442269)

THOMAS, Thomas Hugh. Open Univ BA 77. St D Coll Lamp 59. **d** 60 **p** 61 St D. C of Cwmamman 60-63; V of Martletwy w Lawrenny and Minwear 63-80; R of Narberth w Robeston Wathen, Mounton and Crinow Dio St D from 80. *Rectory, Narberth, Dyfed.* (Narberth 860370)

THOMAS, Thomas John. b 15. St D Coll Lamp BA 37. St Mich Coll Llan 37. **d** 38 **p** 39 St D. C of Conwil Elvet w Abernant 38-41; St Mary Cardigan (in c of Mount w Verwick) 41-45; C-in-c of Taliaris 45-48; I of Talley w Taliaris 48-51; C-in-c of St Mary's Conv Distr Burry Port w Pwll 51-59; I 59-64; V of St Benet Paul's Wharf City and Dio Lon from 64; C-in-c of St D Welsh Ch Paddington Dio Lon from 64. *St David's Vicarage, St Mary's Terrace, W2 1SJ.* (01-723 3104)

40. St Aug Coll Cant 37. **d** 40 **p** 41 Pet. C of Ch Ch Northn 40-44; All SS Maidstone 44-46; Chap St John Trichinopoly 46-48; Ch of S India 47-51; Chap All S Kanpur 52-57; SPG Area Sec Dios Birm and Lich 57-64; V of Tutbury 64-80. *90 Finnemore Road, Little Bromwich, Birmingham 9.*

✠ **THOMPSON, Right Rev Geoffrey Hewlett.** b 29. Trin Hall, Cam 2nd cl Hist Trip pt i, 51, BA (2nd cl Th Trip pt ia), 52, MA 56. Cudd Coll 52. **d** 54 **p** 55 Pet. C of St Matt Northn 54-59; V of St Aug Wisbech 59-66; St Sav Folkestone 66-74; Cons Ld Bp Suffr of Willesden in Westmr Abbey 24 Jan 74 by Abp of Cant; Bps of Lon, Ox, Ely, Glouc, Worc, Pet, Birm, Guildf, Bradf and Derby; Bps Suffr of Kens, Edmon, Tonbridge, Dorking, Basingstoke and Sherborne; and others. *173 Willesden Lane, NW6 7YN.* (01-451 0189)

THOMPSON, George Harry Packwood. b 22. Late Scho of Qu Coll Ox 2nd cl Mods 42, BA (2nd cl Lit Hum) and MA 48, 1st cl Th 49. Qu Coll Birm 50. **d** 51 **p** 52 Birm. C of Coleshill and Lect Qu Coll Birm 51-53; Chap and Lect at Sarum Th Coll 53-55; Vice-Prin 55-64; Publ Pr Dio Sarum 56-64; PC of Combe Longa Dio Ox 64-68; V from 68. *Combe Longa Vicarage, Combe, Oxford, OX7 2NG.* (Stonesfield 249)

THOMPSON, George Henry. McGill Univ Montr BA 40. Montr Dioc Th Coll LTh 42. Columbia Univ NY MA 47. **d** 42 Fred for Montr **p** 43 Queb for Montr. C of Valois 42-43; P-in-c of St Edw Montr 43-45; Prof of Relig Educn Trin Coll Tor 49-57; R of St Leon Tor 57-64; on leave. *9520 Windsor Street, Chilliwack, BC, Canada.*

THOMPSON, Canon George Robert. Wycl Coll Tor LTh 51. **d** 30 **p** 31 NS. I of Ecum Secum 30-32; R of Kentville 32-42; Truro (in c of Clifton and Kemptown from 48) 42-54; I of Ch of Ascen Tor 55-73; Can of Tor from 64. *4657 Dundas Street West, Islington, Ont., Canada.*

THOMPSON, Gerald George. b 17. TCD BA and Div Test (1st cl) 40. **d** 41 **p** 42 Down. C of St Bart Belf 41-43; St Mich Belf 43-45; I of Lorrha 45-49; Sec for N Ireland ICM from 49; L to Offic Dio Down 51-78. *17 Knockeden Park, Belfast, BT6 0JG, N Ireland.* (Belfast 641567)

THOMPSON, Ven Gilbert. Univ of W Ont BA 29. Hur Coll LTh 30. **d** 30 **p** 31 Hur. C of Merlin w Ouvry 30-31; Chap Columbia Coast Miss 31-33; I of St Thos and Prin Indian Res Sch Moose Fort 33-45; Gore Bay 45-50; R of St John Copper Cliff 50-71; Archd of Nipissing 57-71; Archd (Emer) from 72. *116 McNabb Street, Elora, Ont., Canada.*

THOMPSON, Gilbert. Codr Coll Barb. Lambeth STh 61. **d** 60 Barb for Nass **p** 61 Nass. C of Long I 60-68; P-in-c of St Barn I and Dio Nass from 68; Dioc Regr Dio Nass from 73. *PO Box N-1258, Nassau, Bahamas, W Indies.* (35995)

THOMPSON, Gordon George. b 37. Edin Th Coll 66. **d** 68 **p** 69 Ches. C of St Jo Bapt Ches 68-72; in Hackney Team Ministry Lon 72-76; P-in-c of Craghead Dio Dur 76-77; V 77-79; Warden Pembroke Ho Dio S'wark from 79; Team V of Walworth Dio S'wark from 79. *Pembroke House, 80 Tatum Street, SE17 1TR.*

THOMPSON, Gordon Henry Moorhouse. b 41. K Coll Lon and Warm 63. **d** 67 **p** 68 Heref. C of Leominster 67-70; Tenbury Wells Dio Heref 70-74; Team V from 74; C of Burford iii w L Hereford Dio Heref 70-74; Team V from 74; C of Burford ii w Greete and Hope Bagot Dio Heref 70-74; Team V from 74; Team V of Burford i Dio Heref from 74. *Burford Rectory, Tenbury Wells, Worcs, WR15 8HG.* (Tenbury Wells 810678)

THOMPSON, Grahame Charlton. b 54. Univ of Tor BA 77. Wycl Coll Tor MDiv 80. **d** 80 Bp A.A.Read for Ont. I of Lansdowne Front Dio Ont from 80. *PO Box 192, Lansdowne, Ontario, Canada, K0E 1L0.*

THOMPSON, Henderson Aaron Fitzroy. Codr Coll Barb. **d** 68 **p** 69 Barb. C of Ch Ch Barb 68-71; V of St Mark I and Dio Barb from 71. *St Mark's Vicarage, Barbados, W Indies.*

THOMPSON, Henry. b 03. B Com (Lon) 29. **d** 67 Birm **p** 68 Aston for Birm. C of Perry Barr 67-73. *65 Grange Road, Erdington, Birmingham, B24 0DQ.* (021-373 1083)

THOMPSON, Ishmael Dionysius Lemuel. **d** 35 **p** 39 Sier L. Miss Dio Sier L 35-47; C of H Trin Freetown 47; St Andr Gloucester 48-51; P-in-c Kissy 51-53; R of Ch Ch Freetown 53-59; Can of Sier L 53-67; R of H Trin Freetown 59-67. *14 Tarleton Lane, Freetown, Sierra Leone.*

THOMPSON, James. b 30. Wycl Hall Ox 66. **d** 66 **p** 67 Sheff. [f Congregational Min]. C of Woodlands 66-69; R of Firbeck w Letwell 69-71; V of Milnsbridge 71-81; L to Offic Dio Wakef from 81. *54 Calder Terrace, Longcauseway, Dewsbury, W Yorks.*

THOMPSON, James. b 37. Coll of Resurr Mirfield, 64. **d** 67 **p** 68 Newc T. C of Ch Ch Shieldfield Newc T 67-69; St Ignatius Hendon Bp Wearmouth 69-74; V of St Chad Bensham Gateshead Dio Dur from 74. *St Chad's Vicarage, Gateshead, NE8 4QL.* (Gateshead 771964)

THOMPSON, Canon James Henry. **d** 64 Ont. I of Madoc 64-79; Can of Ont from 77; R of Collins Bay Dio Ont from 79. *62 Cambridge Crescent, Kingston, Ont, Canada.* (613-389 7584)

✠ **THOMPSON, Right Rev James Lawton.** b 36. Em Coll Cam BA 64, MA 71. ACA 59, FCA 70. Cudd Coll 64. **d** 66 Barking for Chelmsf **p** 67 Chelmsf. C of E Ham 66-68; Chap Cudd Coll 68-70; L to Offic Dio S'wark 70-72; R of Thamesmead 72-78; Exam Chap to Bp of S'wark 72-78; Cons Area Bp of Stepney in S'wark Cathl 29 Sept 78 by Abp of Cant; Bps of Lon, Win, St Alb, Birm, Bradf, Derby, Ely, Leic, Liv, Nor, Portsm, Ripon, Roch, St E, S'wark and Southw; Bps Suffr of Dorking, Edmon, Kens, Maidstone, Taunton, Tonbridge, Willesden and Woolwich; and others. *400 Commercial Road, E1 0LB.* (01-790 4382)

THOMPSON, John Albert. b 37. Univ of Tor BA 58, MEducn 78. Trin Coll Tor LTh 61, STB 62, MTh 70. **d** 61 **p** 62 Tor. C of Ch Ch Deer Park Tor 61-62; Endako 62-64; Relig Educn Adv and L to Offic Dio Nai 65-72; Bp's Tr Chap Dio S Malawi 72-74; Lect Bp Tucker Th Coll Ugan 74-76; Dir APM Clergy Tr Dio Les from 77. *Box 87, Maseru, Lesotho, S Africa.*

THOMPSON, John Carver. St Francis Coll Brisb ACT ThL 64. **d** and **p** 65 Brisb. C of All SS Chermside 65-66; St Matt Grovely Brisb 67-68; V of Taroom 68-71; R of Willaura 71-74; Ararat 74-77; Redcliffe Dio Brisb from 77. *73 Sutton Street, Redcliffe, Queensland, Australia 4020.* (284 2393)

THOMPSON, John David. b 40. Univ of Lon BD (2nd cl) 65. Ch Ch Ox DPhil 69. St Steph Ho Ox 65. **d** 67 **p** 68 Birm. C of Solihull 67-71; Yatton Keynell 71-73; Castle Combe 71-73; Biddestone w Slaughterford 71-73; Lect Wells Th Coll 71-72; V of Braughing 74-77; R of Digswell Dio St Alb from 77. *354 Knightsfield, Welwyn Garden City, Herts, AL8 7NG.* (Welwyn Garden 26677)

THOMPSON, John Henry. b 03. St Cath S Ox BA (2nd cl Th) 32, MA 44. Wycl Hall, Ox 32. **d** 33 **p** 34 Lich. C of Cheadle Staffs 33-36; Battersea (in c of G and C Coll Miss from 37) 36-39; V of St Mary Kingswinford 39-46; Publ Pr Dio Roch 46; Dio Ex 46-47; V of St Osw Bordesley Birm 47-52; R of Swan Perth 52-54; St Paul W Perth 54-56; Tuart Hill w Mt Yokine 56-63; V of Croxden w Hollington 63-70. *Slade Cottage, Slade Hollow, Stanton, Ashbourne, Derbys, DE6 2BY.*

THOMPSON, John Michael. b 47. Univ of Nottm BTh 77. Linc Th Coll 73. **d** 77 **p** 78 Linc. C of Old Brumby 77-80; Grantham Dio Linc 80-81; Team V from 81. *Vicarage, Edinburgh Road, Harrowby, Grantham, NG31 9QR.* (Grantham 4781)

THOMPSON, John Miller. b 26. **d** 63 **p** 64 St A. C of Hawarden 63-66; Connah's Quay 66-67; V of Askern 67-72; St Marg Brightside Sheff 72-77; Chap Sheff Industr Miss from 72; P-in-c of St Silas City and Dio Sheff from 77. *Vicarage, Hanover Street, Sheffield, S3 7WT* (Sheff 25300)

THOMPSON, Canon John Richard. Univ of W Ont BA 31, BD 35. Hur Coll. **d** 31 **p** 32 Hur. C of St Geo Sarnia 31-33; R of Durham w Egremont 34-36; Point Edward Perche and Sarnia Tn 36-39; St Paul Stratford 39-43; Trin Ch St Thomas 43-51; RD of Elgin 48-52; R of St Andr Windsor 51-52; St Geo Willowdale Tor 52-72; Can of Tor from 62; P-in-c of Erin Dio Niag from 72. *PO Box 99, Erin, Ont, Canada.* (519-833 2226)

THOMPSON, (Nathanael) Kenneth. b 29. St Deiniol's Libr Hawarden 76. M SSF 62. **d** 78 **p** 79 Ban. C of Llanbeblig 78-80. *Ty'r Brodyr, Llanrhos, Llandudno, Gwyn.*

THOMPSON, Kenneth Charles. b 04. Late Scho of Jes Coll Ox 2nd cl Cl Mods 24, BA 2nd cl Lit Hum) 26, 1st cl Th 27, MA 34. St Steph Ho Ox 26. **d** 27 **p** 28 Lon. C of All SS Notting Hill 27-29; St German Roath 29-31; St Cuthb Philbeach Gardens Kens 31-36; Asst Chap and Master Lancing Coll 36-38; L to Offic Dio Chich Libr and Tutor Chich Th Coll 38-40; Chap RNVR 40-46; Vice-Prin of Ely Th Coll 46-47; Asst Master Blackfriars Sch 49-50; Stoneyhurst Coll 51-53; Harrow Sch 54; Perm to Offic Dios Chich and Lon 54-55; C of Ch Ch Swansea 55-56; Headington Quarry Ox 57-62; R of Gt Haseley (w Albury Tiddington and Waterstock from 65) 62-75. *4 Blackthorn Close, Headington, Oxford, OX3 9JF.* (Oxford 61119)

THOMPSON, Kevin Craig. Univ of NZ BA 61. NZ Bd of Th Stud LTh 64. Selw Coll Dun. **d** 64 **p** 65 Dun. C of Anderson's Bay 64-67; Oamaru 67-69; V of Wyndham 69-74; Milton-Tuapeka 74-76; P-in-c of Waimate N 76-77; C of Whangarei Dio Auckld from 77. *22 Mills Road, Whangarei, NZ.*

THOMPSON, Laurence John. b 1897. Angl Th Coll BC LTh 26. **d** and **p** 26 Koot. I of U and Lower Arrow Lakes 26-28; Surrey 28-30; V of White Rock BC 30-32; C of St Mary Pet 32-35; V of Duston 35-42; R of Yardley Hastings 42-58; Boughton 58-66; L to Offic Dio Pet from 66. *St Christopher's Home, Abington Park Crescent, Northampton, NN3 3AD.*

THOMPSON, Canon Leslie. b 09. Univ Coll Dur LTh 36. St Aid Coll 38. **d** 38 **p** 39 Sheff. C of Laughton-en-le-Morthen w St John Thorpe 38-41; Witton Gilbert 41-43; Staindrop w Cockfield 43-47; V of Satley 47-51; R of Middleton-in-Teesdale 51-81; RD of Barnard Castle 72-80; Hon Can of Dur from 74. *c/o Rectory, Middleton-in-Teesdale, Co Durham.* (Middleton-in-Teesdale 267)

THOMPSON, Lester. Moore Th Coll Syd 60. **d** 63 **p** 64 Graft. C of Coff's Harbour 63-64; Ch Ch Cathl Graft 64-65; CF (Austr) from 65; Perm to Offic Dio Brisb 65-67; Dio C & Goulb 67-69; Dio Graft 70-73; Dio Sing 73-75; Dio Brisb from 75. *Lot 16, Mandy Street, Wishart, Queensland, Australia 4122.* (355 8253)

THOMPSON, Lionel Arthur. b 14. Lich Th Coll. **d** 57 **p** 58 Ches. C of Oxton 57-60; V of Frankby 60-73; Gt Meols Dio Ches from 73. *Vicarage, Birkenhead Road, Meols, Wirral, Mer, L47 0LT.* (051-632 1661)

THOMPSON, Mark William. b 52. St Jo Coll Nottm 77. **d** 81 Stepney for Lon. C of St Andr w H Trin Isl Dio Lon from 81. *45 Cloudesley Mansions, Cloudesley Street, Islington, N1.*

THOMPSON, Melvyn Rodney. b 46. AKC BD 69. Univ of Lon MPhil 73. St Aug Cant 69. **d** 70 Bradwell for Chelmsf **p** 71 Chelmsf. C of Tye Green w Netteswell 71-73; St Mary The Boltons Kens 73-76. *66 Fulham Park Gardens, SW6 4LB.* (01-736 0019)

THOMPSON, Michael James. b 55. Univ of St Andr MTh 78. St Mich AA Coll Llan 78. **d** 79 **p** 80 Llan. C of Aberavon 79-81; St Mary Abbots Kens Dio Lon from 81. *c/o St Mary Abbots Vicarage, Vicarage Gate, W8 4HN.* (01-937 2364)

THOMPSON, Michael Reginald. b 34. Roch Th Coll 66. **d** 68 **p** 69 Chich. C of Aldrington 68-70; R of Litlington w W Dean 70-78; Dioc Youth Officer for E Sussex 70-78; RD of Seaford (and Lewes from 77) from 75; P-in-c of Bishopstone 77-78; V of Seaford w Sutton Dio Chich from 78. *Vicarage, Seaford, E Sussex.* (Seaford 893508)

THOMPSON, Neil Hamilton. b 48. Ven Bede Coll Dur BEducn 72. Univ of Leic MA 75. SOC 77. **d** 80 **p** 81 S'wark. C of St Mary Merton Dio S'wark from 80. *St Mary's House, Church Path, Merton, SW19 3HJ.*

THOMPSON, Patrick Arthur. b 36. Univ of Dur BA (3rd cl Th) 59. Univ of Birm Dipl Th 61. Qu Coll Birm 59. **d** 61 **p** 62 Cant. C of St Francis of Assisi W Wickham 61-65; Portchester 65-68; Birchington 68-71; V of St Mark S Norwood 71-77; St Osw Norbury Dio Cant from 77. *220 Norbury Avenue, Thornton Heath, CR4 8AJ.* (01-764 2853)

THOMPSON, Paul Noble. b 54. Univ Coll Cardiff BMus 77. Univ of Leeds Dipl Th 79. Coll Of Resurr Mirfield 77. **d** 80 **p** 81 Llan. C of Bargoed & Deri w Brithdir Dio Llan from 80. *61 Park Road, Bargoed, Mid Glam, CF8 8SR.* (Bargoed 837271)

THOMPSON, Peter Homer. b 17. Keble Coll Ox 37. Chich Th Coll 39. **d** 41 **p** 42 Lon. C of St Mich AA w Ch Ch N Kens 41-44; St Pet Fulham 44-47; Perm to Offic Amer Ch 47-50; C of St Jo Bapt Holland Road Kens 50-53; Min of St Mary's Distr Ruislip 53-59; V 59-81; Mullion Dio Truro from 81; Commiss Venez from 76. *Mullion Vicarage, Helston, Cornw.* (Mullion 325)

THOMPSON, Peter Kerr. Kelham Th Coll. **d** 56 Blackb for Melan **p** 57 Adel for Melan. Master at All H Sch Pawa 57-59; P Dio Melan 60; Supt of Melan Clergy Dio Melan 60-70; Archd of Malaita and Outer E Solomons 62-68; N Melan 68-70; L to Offic Dio Melan 71-74; Dio Centr Melan 75-76; P-in-c of Normanton 76-78; R of Port Hedland Dio NW Austr from 78. *Rectory, Port Hedland, W Australia 6721.*

THOMPSON, Peter Ross. b 26. St Jo Coll Cam BA 47, MB BChir 50. Tyndale Hall, Bris. **d** 60 **p** 61 S'wark. C of New Malden w Coombe 60-61; BCMS Miss Burma 61-66; R of Slaugham w Handcross 66-72; V of Polegate Dio Chich from 72. *Vicarage, Polegate, Sussex.* (Polegate 3259)

✠ **THOMPSON, Right Rev Prince Eustace Shokehu.** Univ of Dur (Fourah Bay Coll) BA 51, Dipl Th 53. **d** 55 Sier L **p** 56 Dur for Sier L. C of H Trin Freetown 55-56; C of Stella Co Dur 58; St Pet Stockton 59-62; Chap Univ Coll of Sier L 62-81; Can of Sier L 75-81; Cons Ld Bp of Sier L 81. *Bishopscourt, Box 128, Freetown, Sierra Leone.* (Freetown 22555)

THOMPSON, Randolph. b 25. Lich Th Coll 63. **d** 65 **p** 66 Linc. C of Boultham 65-68; V of Paddock 68-69; C-in-c of Cornholme 69-71; V 71-72; Chap Barnsley Hall and Lea Hosps Bromsgrove 72-81. *Address temp unknown.*

THOMPSON, Reginald Clifford. b 04. St Chad's Coll Regina 29. **d** 32 **p** 33 Qu'App. C of Balcarres 32; Ogema 32-33; H Trin Medicine Hat 33-34; Cabri 34-35; I of Imperial 35-37; Perm to Offic (Col Cl Act) at St Jo Bapt Tilbury Dks 37-38; C of St John New Clee 38-42; Harborough w Immingham 42-43; V of E Halton 43-45; C-in-c of St D Conv Distr Hale 45-48; R of Amcotts 48-54; PC of St Jas Moulton 54-68; V 68-75; Perm to Offic Dio Linc from 76. *Woodlands, Moulton Eaugate, Spalding, Lincs.*

THOMPSON, Robert. K Coll Lon and Warm AKC 61. **d** 62 **p** 63 Dur. C of Cockerton 62-65; St Marg (in c of St John Neville's Cross) Dur 65-70; V of St John Wallsend 70-79; V of Norham and Duddo Dio Newc T from 79. *Templeharry Rectory, Cloughjordan, Co Tipperary, Irish Republic.* (0505 42237)

THOMPSON, Robert McLean. b 48. United Th Coll of WI LTh 73. **d** 73 **p** 74 Ja. C of St Mary's Kingston Dio Ja from 73. *25 Petunia Way, Kingston 6, Jamaica, WI.*

THOMPSON, Robert Stanley. b 03. TCD BA 31. **d** 33 **p** 34 Oss. C of Ferns w Camolin 33-36; C-in-c of Drinagh 36-51; Timahoe 51-61; Dioc C Ardf 61-65; I of Bourney 65-79; RD of Ikerrin 73-79. *Templeharry Rectory, Cloughjordan, Co Tipperary, Irish Republic.* (0505 42237)

THOMPSON, Roger Frederick Norton. NZ Bd of Th Stud LTh 37. Cant Coll. **d** 37 **p** 38 Ch Ch. C of Sumner 37-41; V of Woodend 41-46; Spreydon 46-61; Chap Sunnyside Ment Hosp 46-54; V of Motueka 61-66; C of St Jo Bapt Ch Ch 66-69; V 69-77; RD of Centr Ch Ch 75-77; Perm to Offic Dio Ch Ch 77-78; Warden Latimer Ho Ch Ch from 78. *101 Waimairi Road, Christchurch 4, NZ.*

THOMPSON, Ronald. b 10. DFC 43. Linc Th Coll 59. **d** 60 **p** 61 Nor. C of E Dereham 60-65; R of Saham-Toney 65-78. *169 Earlham Green Lane, Norwich, NR5 8RG.*

THOMPSON, Canon Ronald Cooper. b 02. Hertf Coll Ox BA (3rd cl Mod Hist) 24, Dipl Th 25, Ellerton Th Pri 26, MA 28. Wycl Hall, Ox 24. **d** 26 **p** 27 Liv. C of St Helens 26-27; Chap Wycl Hall Ox and L to Offic Dio Ox 27-31; Chap Toc H Lon Area and L to Offic Dio Lon 31-32; C of Cathl Ch Sheff 33-36; Chap and Prec 36-37; V of Ch Ch Toxt Pk Liv 37-44; R of Woolwich 44-59; RD of Woolwich 46-59; Surr 50-59; Can Res of Southw Cathl 59-71; Can (Emer) from 71; Southw Dioc Missr 59-68; Exam Chap to Bp of Southw and Dir of Post-Ordin Tr 62-71; Publ Pr Dio Southw from 71. *85 London Road, Newark, Notts, NG24 1SR.* (Newark 71017)

THOMPSON, Ross Edwards. b 42. Univ of Otago BA 63. Coll of Resurr Mirfield, 66. **d** 68 **p** 69 Portsm. C of Fareham 68-71; St Barn W Hackney 71-72; Northolt (in c of St Richard) 72-75; C-in-c of St Thos Wells w Horrington 75-80; V 80-81; Team R of Cowley Dio Ox from 81. *St Luke's House, Temple Road, Cowley, Oxford, OX4 2EX.* (Oxford 778333)

THOMPSON, Royce Dundas. b 48. ACT ThL 74. Ridley Coll Melb 72. **d** 75 **p** 76 Melb. C of St John Bentleigh 75-77; R of Kununurra Dio NW Austr from 77. *Box 60, Kununurra, W Australia 6743.* (81254)

THOMPSON, Stephen Cuthbert. b 04. Univ of Lon BA (2nd cl Hist) 24, Teacher's Dipl 25, BD 28, AKC (Arts) 25, AKC (1st cl Th) and Jun McCaul Pri 28. **d** 28 **p** 29 Lon. C of Ch Ch Hampstead 28-33; St Paul Winchmore Hill (in c of St Thos) 33-35; V of H Trin Haverstock Hill 35-42; Charing 42-46; R of L Chart 42-46; Chap of St Jas Hosp Balham 46-51; V of All S Hampstead 51-62; St Barn Temple Fortune 62-71; Perm to Offic Dio S'wark from 71; Asst Chap Br Home and Hosp for Incurables 78-80. *55 Warrior Square, St Leonards-on-Sea, E Sussex, TN37 6BG.* (0424-715438)

THOMPSON, Treas Thomas John. b 12. TCD BA 34, Div Test 35. **d** 36 **p** 37 Oss. C of Castlecomer 36-39; Dioc C Dio Leigh 39-48; Dios Oss and Leigh from 48; Dioc Sec Dio Leigh (and Dio Oss from 74) from 59; Can of Oss from 62-80; Can of Leighlin 71-80; Treas of Oss and Leigh Cathls from 80. *Ballywilliamroe, Bagenalstown, Co Carlow, Irish Republic.* (0503-27153)

THOMPSON, Thomas Oliver. b 27. TCD 61. **d** 63 **p** 64 Connor. C of Ch Ch Lisburn 63-68; Chap Ch of Ireland Miss to Deaf and Dumb 68-76; I of Glenavy Dio Connor from 76. *Glenavy Vicarage, Crumlin, Co Antrim, N Ireland.* (Crumlin 52361)

THOMPSON, Timothy. b 34. Fitzw Ho Cam Th Trip BA 59, MA 64. Cudd Coll 59. **d** 61 **p** 62 Lon. C of St Mark Noel Pk Wood Green 61-64; All SS Shrub End 64-67; V of Mt Somers NZ 67-70; R of Tolleshunt Knights w Tiptree 70-81; St Jas w All SS, St Nich and St Runwald Colchester Dio Chelmsf from 81; Commiss Ch Ch from 77. *St James's Rectory, East Hill, Colchester, Essex, CO1 2QW.* (Colchester 866802)

THOMPSON, Timothy Charles. b 51. Univ of Lon BSc 73. Westcott Ho Cam 75. **d** 78 **p** 79 St E. C of St Mary Stoke Ipswich 78-81; Industr Chap in the Lowestoft Area Nor Industr Miss from 81. *149 Spashett Road, Lowestoft, Suff.* (Lowestoft 511622)

THOMPSON, Tom Malcolm. b 38. Univ of Dur BA (2nd cl Th) 60. Bps' Coll Cheshunt 60. **d** 62 **p** 63 Blackb. C of Standish 62-65; Lancaster 65-67; V of All SS Chorley 67-72; Barrowford 72-78; RD of Pendle 75-78; King's Norton from 79; R of Northfield Dio Birm from 78. *Northfield Rectory, Birmingham, B31 2NA.* (021-477 3111)

THOMPSON, Canon William Edward. Univ of Dur BA (2nd cl Th) 57, MA 68. Codr Coll Barb. **d** 56 **p** 57 Nass. C of Exuma 56-62; St Agnes Nass 63-65; Master St Jo Coll Nass 62-65; Dom Chap to Bp of Nass 65-66; P-in-c of Long I 66-67; St Agnes I and Dio Nass from 67; Exam Chap to Bp of Nass from 68; Can of Nass from 73. *PO Box N-1221, Nassau, Bahamas, W Indies.* (52640)

THOMPSON, William George. b 32. Univ of Leeds, BA 54. Coll of Resurr Mirfield, 54. **d** 56 Warrington for Liv **p** 57 Liv. C of St Luke Southport 56-60; R of St Aid Man 60-64; V of Bradshaw Dio Man from 64. *New Vicarage, Bolton Road, Bradshaw, Bolton, BL2 3EU.* (Bolton 54240)

THOMPSON-McCAUSLAND, Marcus Perronet. b 31. Trin Coll Cam BA 54, MA 60. Coll of Resurr Mirfield, 57. **d** 59 **p** 60 Birm. C of Perry Barr 59-65; V of Rubery 65-72; R of Cradley 71-82; C-in-c of Mathon 72-82; Storridge 72-82; Fromes Hill 72-82. *c/o Mathon Vicarage, Malvern, Worcs, WR13 5PW.* (Ridgway Cross 206)

THOMPSTONE, John Deaville. b 39. BNC Ox BA 63, MA 67. Ridley Hall Cam 63. **d** 65 **p** 66 Ches. C of All SS Hoole 65-68; Fulwood Sheff 68-71; V of H Trin Skirbeck 71-77; St Pet Shipley Dio Bradf from 77. *2 Glenhurst Road, Shipley, Yorks.* (Bradford 584488)

THOMSON, Alexander Keith. b 38. Univ of Dur BA 63. Cranmer Hall, Dur 62. **d** 64 **p** 65 Man. C of Middleton 64-68; Chap Rannoch Sch 68-72, C-in-c All SS Kinloch Rannoch 68-72; Asst Chap Oundle Sch Northants Dio Pet from 72. *34 Kings Road, Oundle, Peterborough, PE8 4AY.* (Oundle 73416)

THOMSON, Canon Alvin James. b 19. Univ of Tor BA 44. Trin Coll Tor LTh 47. **d** 46 **p** 47 Alg. C of St John (in c of St Mich) Port Arthur 46-47; I of St Mich Port Arthur 47-52; R of Bracebridge 52-57; St John's Thunder Bay 57-73; Hon Can of Alg from 62; Chap Miss to Seamen Thunder Bay 74-79; Hon Chap from 79. *201 Woodside Street, Thunder Bay, Ont., Canada.* (807-767 2828)

THOMSON, Andrew Maitland. **d** 79 **p** 80 Mashon. P Dio Mashon. *c/o Anglican Diocesan Offices, PO Box UA7, Salisbury, Zimbabwe.*

THOMSON, Clarke Edward Leighton. b 19. TD 65. Pemb Coll Ox BA 41, MA 45. Wycl Hall Ox 44. **d** 45 **p** 46 Roch. C of H Trin Anerley 45-47; Chap of St Mark w All SS Alexandria Egypt 47-50; C of Chelsea 50-51; V of Chelsea Old Ch (All SS) Dio Lon from 51; CF (TA) 52-67; CF (TAVR) 67-69; Commiss Egypt from 75. *4 Old Church Street, SW3 5DQ.* (01-352 5627)

THOMSON, Cyril. b 18. Wells Th Coll. **d** 60 **p** 61 Wakef. C of Almondbury 60-63; V of Thurgoland 63-70; Chap of Stainborough 63-70; V of Paddock Dio Wakef from 70. *Paddock Vicarage, Huddersfield, Yorks, HD1 4UD.* (Huddersfield 30814)

THOMSON, Cyril Raby. b 12. Serampore Coll BD 60. Dipl Th (Lon) 64. Tyndale Hall Bris 32. **d** 36 **p** 37 S'wark. C of St John Deptford 36-38; BCMS Miss at Saugor 38-40; serving w Ind Army 40-46; Chap Old Miss Ch Calc 46-48; C of St Jo Evang Weymouth 49; BCMS Miss at Jaunpur 49-52; Ch of S India 52-61; and 64-67; Educn Sec CCCS 62-64; C of St Jo Evang Bromley 62-63; Southborough 63-64; Ch of S India 64-67; V of H Trin Southw 67-73; C of St John Southall 73-76; Wimbledon (in c of Em) Dio S'wark from 76. *2 Coppice Close, SW20.* (01-540 7748)

THOMSON, David. b 52. Keble Coll Ox MA, D Phil 78. Selw Coll Cam BA 80. Westcott Ho Cam 78. **d** 81 Sheff. C of Maltby Dio Sheff from 81. *86 Braithwell Road, Maltby, Rotherham, S Yorks, S66 8JT.*

THOMSON, David MacMillan Garth. b 24. Trin Coll Tor BA 49, LTh 52. **d** 52 **p** 53 Ott. C of All SS Ott 52-56; R of Deep River 56-62; St Martin Ott 62-70; All SS City and Dio Ott from 71. *18 Blackburn Avenue, Ottawa 2, Ont., Canada.* (1-613-238-2895)

THOMSON, David William. b 1900. Edin Th Coll 60. **d** 61 **p** 62 St Andr. C of All SS St Andr 61-63; Prec of St Ninian's Cathl Perth 63-66; Chap HM Pris Perth 63-66; V of Stanford w Swinford 66-72; Perm to Offic Dio St Alb from 72. *28 Bridge End, Bromham, Bedford.* (Oakley 4015)

THOMSON, Douglas Walter. **d** 58 **p** 59 Melb. C of Sunshine 58-60; Ashburton 60-61; R of Rutherglen 61-65; CF (Austr) 65-70; L to Offic Dio Brisb 65-70; V of St John's Enoggera 70-78; Chap Wolston Pk Hosp Wacol from 78. *Wolston Park Hospital, Wacol, Queensland, Australia 4076.* (372 2211)

THOMSON, Canon Duncan. b 24. CCC Ox BA 46, MA 50. Univ of Lon BD 49. **d** 51 **p** 52 Glouc. C of Northleach w Hampnett and Stowell w Yanworth 51-53; Min Can of Ripon Cathl 53; Succr 53-54; Prec 54-57; Chap St Mary and St John Hosp Ripon 53-57; Chap and Asst Master Aysgarth Sch 57-60; L to Offic Dio Ripon from 57; Min Can and Hon Prec of Ripon Cathl from 60; Hd Master Cathl Choir Sch from 60; C of Ripon w Littlethorpe Dio Ripon from 60; Hon Can of Ripon from 78. *Cathedral Choir School, Ripon, Yorks.* (Ripon 2134)

THOMSON, George. b 28. St Jo Coll Nottm 70. **d** 72 **p** 73 Carl. C of St Paul Newbarns w Hawcoat Barrow-F 72-75; V of Wingates Dio Man from 76. *95 Chorley Road, Wingates, Bolton, BL5 3PG.* (0942-812119)

THOMSON, George Ian Falconer. b 12. Ball Coll Ox BA (3rd cl Mod Hist) 34, Ellerton Th Essay Pri 36. Hertf Coll Ox MA 38. Westcott Ho Cam 34. **d** 36 **p** 37 Lon. C of St Luke Chelsea 36-37; Chap Hertf Coll Ox 37-46; Tutor and Jun Dean 39-42; Chap Ox Past 38-42; Chap RAFVR 42-46; R of Hilgay w Ten Mile Bank 46-51; Sec GOE 46-52; Asst Master Maidstone Gr Sch 51-62; Sen Ho Master 57-62; Chap and Lect St Paul's Coll Cheltm 62-66; L to Offic Dio Glouc from 62; Exam Chap to Bp of Glouc 64-75; Dir Conf Br Miss SS Research Project 66-68; Dir Bible Reading Fellowship 68-77; Select Pr Univ of Ox 73; L to Offic Dio Ox from 68; Chap All S Coll Ox from 81. *Jackson's Farmhouse, Yarnton, Oxford, OX5 1QD.*

THOMSON, George Miller McMillan. b 33. Edin Th Coll 59. **d** 62 **p** 63 Edin. C of Old St Paul Edin 62-64; in Amer Ch 64-68; C of St Mary Brookfield St Pancras 68-72; V of St Mark Noel Pk Wood Green 72-81; RD of E Haringey 77-81; Surr 78-81; R of Newark w Hawton, Cotham and Shelton Dio Southw from 81. *6 Bede House Lane, Newark, Notts, NG24 1PY.* (Newark 704513)

THOMSON, Heather Joan. b 52. Concordia Univ Montr BA 75. Montr Dioc Th Coll BTh 77. **d** 77 **p** 80 Queb. C of Lennoxville Dio Queb from 79. *Box 247, Waterville, PQ, Canada, J0B 3H0.*

THOMSON, Canon Henry Frederick. Univ of NZ BA 35. Selw Coll Dun 31. **d** 36 Nel for Ch Ch **p** 37 Ch Ch. C of Sumner 36-38; P-in-c 38-39; Lyttelton 39-40; V of Methven 40-46; Org Sec CSSM NZ 46-50; L to Offic Dio Ch Ch 46-50 and 61-71; V of Woolston 50-61; Gen Sec NZCMS 54-71; Hon Can of Vic Nyan from 71; V of Mt Herbert 71-77; Perm to Offic Dio Ch Ch from 77. *66 Heberden Avenue, Christchurch 8, NZ.* (Sum 5127)

THOMSON, Hugh Ernest. Univ of NZ BA 47. Coll Ho Ch Ch. **d** 48 Dun for Nel **p** 49 Nel. C of Ch Ch Cathl Nel 48-52; Miss at Katoke 52-54; Mwanza 54-57; Arusha 57-61; L to Offic Dio Ch Ch 61-62; P-in-c of Highfield 62-63; C of Riccarton 63-64; V of Avonhead 64-77; Mt Herbert Dio Ch Ch from 77. *45 Waipapa Avenue, Diamond Harbour, NZ.*

THOMSON, Jack George. St Mich Th Coll Crafers 60. **d** 64 **p** 65 Melb. C of H Trin Kew 64-67; Brunswick 67-69; V of Noble Pk 69-72; R of Yarrawonga 72-78; Carnarvon 78-81. *5 Glass Street, Carnarvon, W Australia 6701.* (099-41 1571)

THOMSON, James William. b 32. Moore Coll Syd ThL 71. **d** and **p** 73 Syd. C of French's Forest 73-74; Normanhurst 74-75; R of Albion Pk 75-77; C of Blacktown 78-79; R of Auburn Dio Syd from 79. *28 Hall Street, Auburn, NSW, Australia 2144.* (649-7228)

THOMSON, John Alexander. b 1898. Univ of Dur LTh 28. St Aid Coll 26. **d** 28 **p** 29 Liv. C of St Mary Wavertree 28-31; Org Sec BFBS for Midl Distr 31-36; Publ Pr Dio Birm and Perm to Offic Dios Cov, Worc and Glouc 31-36; V of Salford Priors 36-44; Offg C-in-c of Harvington 40-44; R of Arrow w Weethley 44-52; Ed Cov Dioc Gaz 44-48; Chap Alcester Publ Asst Inst 44-52; V of St Mich-on-Wyre 52-55; Kenilworth 55-66; RD of Kenilworth 58-63; Chap CECS and Perm to Offic Dio Cov 67-71. *15 Cherry Tree Crescent, Salford Priors, Evesham, Worcs.* (0789 772516)

THOMSON, John Colin Clunn. St Francis Th Coll Nundah 27. **d** 29 **p** 30 Rockptn. C of St Paul's Cathl Rockptn 29-32; P-in-c of Dawson and Callide Miss Distr 32-34; V of Keppel and Chap St Faith's Girls' Sch Rockptn 34-37; C of All S Brisb 37-38; V of Noosa 38-41; R of Sandgate 42-74; Perm to Offic Dio Brisb from 74. *23 Fahey Street, Zillmere, Queensland, Australia 4034.* (263 4857)

THOMSON, John Forbes. Univ of St Andr MA 35. St Steph Ho Ox 35. **d** 36 **p** 37 Lon. C of St Mary Magd Paddington 36-39; St Frideswide Poplar 39-40; Tong w St John Tong Street 40-45; V of St Marg Burnley 45-60; St Pet Blackb 60-63; R of Owmby w Normanby 63-70; R of Caenby w Glentham 63-70; Perm to Offic Dio Linc from 70; Dio Lon 73-75. *The Pantiles, Middle Street, Rippingale, Bourne, Lincs.* (Dowsby 218)

THOMSON, Julian Harley. b 43. AKC 70. St Aug Coll Cant 70. **d** 71 **p** 72 Pret. C of Wellingborough 71-74; Prec of Ely Cathl 74-80; C-in-c of Stuntney 74-80; V of Arrington Dio Ely from 80; Croydon w Clopton Dio Ely from 80; Orwell Dio Ely from 80; Wimpole Dio Ely from 80. *The New Rectory, Fisher's Lane, Orwell, Royston, Herts, SG8 5QX.* (Cam 20808)

THOMSON, Lawrence John. **d** 73 St Arn. Hon C of Ch Ch Cathl St Arn 73-76; Ch Ch Old Cathl St Arn Dio Bend from 77. *10 Inkerman Street, St Arnaud, Vic, Australia 3478.* (054-95 1516)

THOMSON, Malcolm Macmillan. b 1885. Univ of Lon BA (1st cl Phil) 10, BD 12. St Aug Coll Cant 58. **d** 58 **p** 59 Lon. C of Ch Ch Hampstead 58-64; E Coker 64-75; L to Offic Dio B & W from 75. *Herne Cottage, East Coker, Yeovil, Somt.* (West Coker 2207)

THOMSON, Oliver Miles. b 38. Magd Coll Cam BA 61, MA 65. Wycl, Hall Ox 61. **d** 63 **p** 64 Lon. C of All S w St Pet and St John St Marylebone 63-67; Fulwood (in c of St Luke Lodge Moor) 67-70; V of Wick w Doynton 70-74; St Pet Harold Wood Dio Chelmsf from 74. *Vicarage, Athelstan Road, Harold Wood, Romford, Essex.* (Ingrebourne 42080)

THOMSON, Peter Ashley. Ridley Coll Melb ACT ThL (2nd cl) 57, Th Scho 63. **d** 59 Bp McKie for Melb **p** 60 Melb. C of Melb Dioc Centre 59-61; Sunshine 61-62; Fen Ditton 62-63; V of Upwood w Gt and L Raveley 63-64; St Jas E Thornbury 64-65; C of St John E Malvern 68-69; Chap Timbertop C of E Gr Sch 69-72 and from 75; on leave 72-74; Perm to Offic Dio Wang from 76. *Timbertop, Mansfield, Vic, Australia 3722.* (Merrijig 3)

THOMSON, Peter Malcolm. b 44. Trin Coll Bris 75. **d** 78 **p** 79 Roch. C of St Steph Tonbridge 78-81; V of Cobham w Luddesdowne Dio Roch from 81. *Vicarage, Battle Street, Cobham, Gravesend, Kent, DA12 3DB.* (0474 814332)

THOMSON, Peter Somerville. b 51. St Mich Ho Crafers ThL 74. **d** 75 Bp Renfrey for Adel **p** 76 Adel. C of Unley 75-77; Goodwood 77; St D Burnside 77-79; P-in-c of Eliz 79; Assoc P 79-80; P-in-c of Modbury Dio Adel from 81. *6 Carsten Court, Modbury, S Australia 5096.*

THOMSON, Richard Irving. b 32. Oak Hill Th Coll 57. **d** 60 **p** 61 York. C of H Trin Hull 60-63; Em Croydon 63-66; V of Shoreditch 66-73; Chap at Vevey 73-77; V of Reigate Dio S'wark from 77. *Vicarage, Reigate, Surrey, RH2 0SP.* (Reigate 42973)

THOMSON, Robert Douglass. b 37. Univ of Dur BEducn 75. Crammer Hall Dur 76. **d** 79 **p** 80 Dur (NSM). C of Shincliffe Dio Dur from 79. *11 Hill Meadows, High Shincliffe, Durham, DH1 2PE.*

THOMSON, Canon Ronald. b 24. Univ of Leeds, BA 49. Coll of Resurr Mirfield. **d** 51 **p** 52 Jarrow for Dur. C of Sunderland 51-54; Attercliffe (in c of St Alb) Sheff 54-57; V of St Hilda Shiregreen 57-73; RD of Ecclesfield 72-73; V of Worsbrough Dio Sheff from 73; RD of Tankersley from 75; Hon Can of Sheff Cathl from 77. *St Mary's Vicarage, Worsbrough, Barnsley, S Yorks, S70 5LW.* (Barnsley 203113)

THOMSON, Ronald Arthur. b 29. G and C Coll Cam BA 53, MA 57. Ripon Hall, Ox. **d** 57 **p** 58 S'wark. C of Sanderstead 57-60; Kidbrooke 60-62; Chap RAF 62-68; C of Amersham 68; R of Watton-at-Stone Dio St Alb from 68. *Watton-at-Stone Rectory, Hertford, SG14 3RD.* (Ware 830262)

THOMSON, Russell. b 39. K Coll Lon and Warm AKC 62. **d** 63 **p** 64 Lon. C of Hackney 63-66; Wm Temple Conv Distr Abbey Wood Plumstead 66-69; Strood Team Ministry 69-75; V of Gillingham Dio Roch from 75. *27 Gillingham Green, Gillingham, Kent, ME7 1SS.* (Medway 50529)

THOMSON, Preb Sidney Seward Chartres. b 01. St George's Windsor 53. OBE (Mil) 44. **d** 54 Bp Sara for Heref **p** 55 Heref. C of Clun w Chapel Lawn 54-56; V of Worfield 56-72; RD of Bridgnorth 65-71; Preb of Heref Cathl from 70; Perm to Offic Dio Heref from 71; Lich from 73. *Hartlebury House, Worfield, Bridgnorth, Salop.* (Worfield 220)

THOMSON-GLOVER, William Hugh. b 28. Trin Hall, Cam BA 52, MA 56. Cudd Coll 52. **d** 54 **p** 55 Lon. C of St Dunstan and All SS Stepney 54-58; Tiverton 58-60; C-in-c of St Andr Eccles Distr Tiverton 60-63; Chap Clifton Coll and Publ Pr Dio Bris 63-69; V of St Mary Magd w St Francis, Lockleaze Bris 70-75; C-in-c of Sherston Magna w Pinkney and Easton Grey Dio Bris from 75; Luckington w Alderton Dio Bris from 75. *Sherston Magna Vicarage, Malmesbury, Wilts.* (Sherston 209)

THORBURN, Austin Noel. b 13. Trin Coll Cam BA 36, MA 40. Bps' Coll Cheshunt 36. **d** 38 **p** 39 Man. C of St Jas Hope 38-43; V of All S Castleton Heywood 43-48; Blackrod 48-51; Surr 48-51; Prin Cathl Sch Lah and Sub-Warden St Hilda's S 51-56; Exam Chap to Bp of Lah 55-56; L to Offic Dios Glouc Worc and Lich 63-67; C of Tettenhall Regis 67-69; C of Langley Marish 71-76; Team V 76-79; Perm to Offic Dio Carl from 79. *62 Holborn Hill, Millom, Cumb, LA18 5BJ.*

THORBURN, Peter Hugh. b 17. Worc Coll Ox Cl Exhib 38, 2nd cl Cl Mods 38, BA (Lit Hum) 41, MA 43. Wells Th Coll 46. **d** 47 **p** 48 Lon. C of John Keble Ch Mill Hill 47-51; LDHM of St Matthias Colindale 51; PC 51-54; V of St Mich Wigan 54-65; in Amer Ch 65-68; V of Chipping Sodbury w Old Sodbury 68-72; Chap Withington Hosp Man from 72. *13 Duke Street, Alderley Edge, Chesh, SK9 7HX.*

THORBURN, Simon Godfrey. b 51. Univ of Newc T BSC 73. Fitzw Coll Cam Ba 77, MA 81. Westcott Ho Cam 75. **d** 78 Lich **p** 79 Stafford for Lich. C of St Mary Stafford Dio Lich from 78. *1 Richmond Close, Rising Brook, Stafford, ST17 9BY.* (Stafford 40346)

THORLEY, Barry. b 44. Westcott Ho Cam 70. **d** 73 **p** 74 S'wark. C of Camberwell 73-76; Moseley 76-78; V of Birchfield Dio Birm from 78. *213 Birchfield Road, Birmingham, B20 3DG.* (021-356 4241)

THORLEY, Barry Allan. b 48. Atlantic Sch of Th Halifax NS BTh 77. **d** 76 **p** 77 Fred. C of Musquash 76-80; R of St Mary Coldbrook, St John Dio Fred from 80. *648 Westmorland Road, St John East, NB, Canada.*

THORMAN, Richard Hugh. b 06. SS Coll Cam BA 28, MA 32. Cudd Coll 28. **d** 29 **p** 30 Wakef. C of St Mary Barnsley 29-35; V of Airedale w Fryston 35-39; R of Garforth 39-53; V of Arncliffe w Halton Gill 53-75. *Heck Gill Cottage, Stumps Lane, Darley, Harrogate, HG3 2RS.*

THORN, Robert Anthony D'Venning. AKC 76. Chich Th Coll 75. **d** 77 **p** 78 Truro. C of Bodmin 77-80; Team V of North Hill Dio Truro from 80. *5 Hendra Tor View, Five Lanes, Launceston, PL15 7RG.* (Pipers Pool 579)

THORN, Timothy McLellan. Univ of Melb BCom 57. ACT ThL (2nd cl) 62. St Jo Coll Morpeth 60. **d** 62 Melb **p** 63 Bp Sambell for Melb. C of St Barn Balwyn 62-64; P-in-c of E Doncaster 64-67; Chap Camberwell Gr Sch 67-74; I of Carrum w Seaford Dio Melb from 74. *5 Poulson Street, Carrum, Vic, Australia 3197.* (03-772 2880)

THORNBER, John Edward. Egerton Hall, Man 37. **d** 39 **p** 40 Blackb. C of Adlington 39-43; V of St Jas Leyland 43-69; L to Offic Dio Blackburn from 70. *36 Hugh Barn Lane, New Longton, Preston, Lancs.* (Longton 614449)

THORNBURN, Christopher John Baade. b 51. AKC and BD 73. St Aug Coll Cant 73. **d** 74 **p** 75 S'wark. C of St Pet Streatham 74-76; Clapham 76-78; Clapham Old Town Team Min 78-81; Perm to Offic Dio Lon from 81. *St Francis Vicarage, Ellesmere Road, NW10.*

THORNE, Clifford Graham. b 16. St Jo Coll Cam BA 38, MA 50. Westcott Ho Cam 78 **d** 78 **p** 79 Newc T. C of Ponteland Dio Newc T from 78. *Dissington Old Hall, Dalton, Newcastle-on-Tyne.* (Ponteland 25258)

THORNE, George Stewart. Moore Th Coll Syd. **d** and **p** 57 Syd. C of Belmore 57-58; C-in-c of Villawood 58-61; P-in-c of Orroroo 61-64; Melrose w Wilmington and Wirrabra 65-67; R of Yorketown 67-74; Perm to Offic Dio Adel 75-76; Dio Syd from 76. *26 Caroline Crescent, Georges Hall, NSW, Australia 2198.*

THORNE, John Anthony Christopher. b 40. Univ of Syd BA 67. Wollaston Coll Perth ThL 67. **d** and **p** 77 Bath. C of Dubbo 77-78; Staff Officer ABM in NSW 78-79; R of St Pet Cremorne Dio Syd from 79. *29 Waters Road, Cremorne, NSW, Australia 2090.* (90-1050)

THORNE, Canon Ralph Frederick. b 14. St Jo Coll Dur LTh 36, BA 37. ALCD 36. **d** 37 **p** 38 Lon. C of All S Harlesden 37-41; St Thos Heigham 41-42; C-in-c of N and S Wootton 42-44; V of Middleton 45-49; Newhey 49-62; R of Heaton Reddish 62-80; RD of Ardwick 71-77; Hon Can of Man 74-80; Can (Emer) from 80. *9 Greenfield Road, Atherton, Manchester, M29 9LW.* (Atherton 873894)

THORNE, Robert Edward Earle. b 31. Bp's Univ Lennox LST 69. **d** 68 Queb for Ott **p** 69 Ott. R of Stafford 69-76; Ch Ch St Catharines 76-81; St Paul Dunnville Dio Niag from 81. *233 Lock Street West, Dunnville, Ont, Canada.* (416-774 7011)

THORNEWILL, Canon Mark Lyon. b 25. ALCD 56. **d** 56 **p** 58 Bradf. C of Bradf Cathl 56-59; Otley 59-62; R of Lifton 62-66; Kelly w Bradstone 62-66; Asst Chap Med Coll of Virginia 66-68; in Amer Ch from 66; Hon Can Louisville Cathl from 70. *2516 Top Hill Road, Louisville, Kentucky, USA.*

THORNHILL, Alan Edward Carlos. b 06. Hertf Coll Ox BA (2nd cl Mod Hist) 27, Dipl Th (w distinc) 29, MA 31, Sen Denyer and Johnson Scho 32. Wycl Hall Ox 27. **d** 29 **p** 30 S'wark. C of St Mary Magd Peckham 29-31; Chap Hertf Coll Ox 31-37; Fell 32-37; Exam Chap to Bp of Blackb 33-37; Chap Wycl Hall Ox 37-39; Perm to Offic Dio Lon from 39; Dio Chich from 68. *Maynards Mead, Rotherfield, Crowborough, Sussex.* (Rotherfield 2331)

THORNHILL, Francis William Philip. b 03. AKC 27. **d** 27 Cant **p** 28 Dover for Cant. C of St Bart Charlton-in-Dover 27-35; Banstead (in c of St Mary Burgh Heath) 35-37; V of Alderminster 38-51; R of Capel St Mary w L Wenham 51-63; V of St Matt Willesden 63-74. *31 Cedar Grove, Southall, Middx.* (01-575 0606)

THORNHILL, Raymond. b 16. Late Scho of St Chad's Coll Dur, Maltby Pri 37, Cl Scho Lightfoot Scho and BA (1st cl Cl) 38, Jenkyns Scho 39, 1st cl Th 40, MA 41. Univ Fell in Semitics 40-42. **d** 40 **p** 41 Dur. L to Offic Dio Dur from 40; Foreign Office 42-46; Perm to Offic at St Jo Bapt Old Malden 42-46; Asst Lect in Semitics Univ of Man 46-47; Lect in Hebr and Oriental Lang Univ of Dur 47-80. *6 Mayorswell Close, Durham, DH1 1JU.* (Durham 64856)

THORNLEY, Arthur Richard. b 15. Selw Coll Cam 3rd cl Econ Trip pt i 36, BA (3rd cl Th Trip pt ii) 38. Westcott Ho Cam 38. **d** 39 **p** 40 S'wark. C of Lambeth 39-44; Chap RNVR 44-47; RN 47-58; Chap at Malvern Coll 58-65; in Amer Ch 65-66; Chap RN 66-70; Chap London House, Mecklenburgh Sq Lon 70-75; PV of Truro Cathl and Chap Truro Cathl Sch 75-80. *Flat 1, Porthgwidden, Feock, Truro, TR3 6GS.* (Devoran 862659)

THORNLEY, David Howe. b 43. Wycl Hall Ox 77. **d** 79 Chich **p** 80 Horsham for Chich. C of Burgess Hill Dio Chich from 79. *21 Noel Green, Burgess Hill, W Sussex, RH15 8BS.* (Burgess Hill 3047)

THORNLEY, Geoffrey Pearson. b 23. Pemb Coll Cam BA 47, MA 52. Cudd Coll. **d** 50 **p** 51 Lon. C of St Dunstan and All SS Stepney 50-53; Chap RN 53-73; Dom Chap to Bp of Linc 73-75; Warden Dioc Ho Linc 73-75; P-in-c of Riseholme w Grange-de-Lings 73-82; V of Dunholme (w Scothern from 77) Dio Linc from 75. *Dunholme Vicarage, Lincoln, LN2 3QT.* (Welton 60132)

THORNLEY, Harold. b 29. Lich Th Coll. **d** 67 **p** 68 Lich. C of St Paul Wednesbury 67-71; V of Ogley Hay w Brownhills Dio Lich from 71. *Brownhills Vicarage, Walsall, Staffs.* (Brownhills 2187)

THORNLEY, Nicholas Andrew. b 56. Univ of Nottm BTh 81. St Jo Coll Nottm 77. **d** 81 Grimsby for Linc. C of Frodingham Dio Linc from 81. *66 Church Lane, Frodingham, Scunthorpe, S Humb.*

THORNTON, Canon Cecil. Tyndale Hall Bris 47. **d** 50 **p** 51 Down. C of Kilmegan 50-51; Drom Cathl 51-54; R of Magherahamlet 54-60; Dom Chap to Bp of Down 58-60; I of Inniskeel 60-65; Fahan w Inch Dio Derry from 65; I of Fahan Lower w Desertegney Dio Derry from 65; RD of Inishowen from 67; Exam Chap to Bp of Derry from 75; Can of Raph from 79. *Fahan Lower Rectory, Buncrana, Co Donegal, Irish Republic.*

THORNTON, Cecil Anderson Montagu. b 01. Clare Coll Cam BA 22, MA 26. **d** 63 **p** 64 Ches. C of Disley 63-68; V of Haslington 68-73. *25 Gingerbread Lane, Nantwich, Chesh, CW5 6NH.*

THORNTON, David John Dennis. b 32. Kelham Th Coll 52. **d** 56 **p** 57 S'wark. C of New Eltham 56-58; Stockwell Green 58-62; V of Tollesbury 62-74; C-in-c of Salcott-Virley 72-74; V of Kelvedon Dio Chelmsf from 74. *Kelvedon Vicarage, Colchester, Essex, CO5 9AL.* (Kelvedon 70373)

THORNTON, Harrison. b 10. Fell Exhib of Ch Ch Ox BA (3rd cl Hist) 33, MA 38. St Steph Ho Ox 33. **d** 35 Dur **p** 36 Jarrow for Dur. C of St Barn Hendon 35-36; St Mary Heworth 36-37; Rainton 37-40; CF (EC) 40-46; Men in Disp 45; V of Hawkhurst 46-51; Cleadon 51-68; Marcham w Garford 68-75. *42 Milton Gardens, Wokingham, Berks.*

THORNTON, James Charles. Univ of NZ BA 51, MA (1st cl Phil) 54. Coll Ho Ch Ch 49. **d** 54 **p** 55 Wel. C of St Paul's Cathl Wel 54-56; LPr Dio Ch Ch 56-57; V of Mangaweka 58-59; Chap and Tutor Ch Ch Coll 59-60; L to Offic Dio Ch Ch from 60. *44 Seven Oaks Drive, Christchurch, NZ.*

THORNTON, John. b 26. St Edm Hall Ox BA 53, MA 57. Westcott Ho Cam 53. **d** 55 **p** 56 Linc. C of Langton w Woodhall 55-58; St Steph Glouc 58-60; Longlevens 60-62; C-in-c of Gt Witcombe w Bentham Dio Glouc 62-63; R from 63. *Great Witcombe Rectory, Gloucester, GL3 4TS.* (Witcombe 2594)

THORNTON, Kenneth. b 27. Open Univ BA 77. ALCD 55. **d** 55 **p** 56 Liv. C of Em Fazakerley 55-61; V of St Paul Widnes 61-69; Childwall 69-81; Ormskirk Dio Liv from 82; RD of Childwall 79-81. *Ormskirk Vicarage, Ormskirk, L39 3AJ.* (Ormskirk 72143)

THORNTON, Louis Calvin. b 25. **d** 73 **p** 75 Rupld. Hon C of St Aid Winnipeg 73-78; I of Cobbie Hill 79-81; Chap Brentwood Coll BC from 81. *RR1, Mill Bay, BC, Canada, BC, Canada.*

THORNTON, Canon Martin Stuart Farrin. b 15. AKC 46. Ch Coll Cam BA (3rd cl Th Trip pt iii) 51, MA 55. Gen Th Sem NY STD 66. **d** 46 **p** 47 Nor. C of Gayton 46-48; Perm to Offic Dio Chelmsf 48-49; C of St Geo Chesterton 49-51; L to Offic Dio Ely 51-52; V of Swaffham Prior w St Cyriac and Reach 52-57; Select Pr Univ of Cam 57; C of Coppenhall 57-62; Sub-Warden St Deiniol's Libr Hawarden 62-68; Perm to Offic Dios St A and Ches 62-68; Exam Chap to Bp of Ban 67-71; V of Payhembury 68-71; Can Res and Chan of Truro Cathl from 75. *13 Kestle Drive, Truro, TR1 3PT.*

THORNTON, Peter Stuart. b 36. St Pet Hall Ox BA (2nd cl Th) 59, MA 67. Cudd Coll 59. **d** 61 **p** 62 York. C of E Coatham 61-64; St Martin Scarborough 64-67; R of Seaton Ross w Everingham Harswell and Bielby 67-81; Seaton Ross Group Dio York from 81; RD of Weighton from 76; P-in-c of Thornton w Allerthorpe and Melb 80-81. *Rectory, Everingham, York, YO4 4JA.* (0696 60346)

THORNTON, Ronald Charleton. b 07. Keble Coll Ox BA 30, MA 34. Wycl Hall Ox 31. **d** 31 **p** 32 Dur. C of St Paul Stockton-on-Tees 31-35; Norton 35-37; Ch Ch W Hartlepool 37-46; CF (EC) 40-46; V of Egglestone 46-75. *7 Cramond Close, Darlington, Co Durham.*

THORNTON, Ronald Edward William. b 14. Late Scho and Pri TCD BA (1st cl Mod Hist and Pol Sc) and Eccles Hist Pri 36, Higher Dipl Educn Brooke Exhib Abp King Pri (1st) and Bp Forster Pri (1st) 37, Div Test (1st cl) Div Comp Pri and Robert King Mem Pri 38, BD and 1st cl Th Exhib 39. **d** 39 **p** 40 Arm. C of Drumglass 39-42; Shankill 42-47; I of Aghalee 47-53; Exam Chap to Bp of Connor from 54; I of Lambeg 53-59; R of Larne (Inver) 59-68; V of Antrim 68-80; Exam Chap to Bp of Connor 68-80; Can of Connor Cathl 76-80; C of Kirkbride Dio S & M from 80; St Olave Ramsey Dio S & M from 80. *St Olave's Vicarage, Ramsey, IM.*

THORNTON, Stanley John. b 23. Ely Th Coll. **d** 58 **p** 59 Ripon. C of Armley 58-61; V of Allerton Bywater 61-68; Industr Chap to HM Dyd Devonport 68-76; V of Devonport 69-73; Team R 73-76; V of St Mary Virg Illingworth Halifax 76-81; R of Clayton W w High Hoyland Dio Wakef from 81. *Rectory, Clayton West, Huddersfield, Yorks, HD8 9LY.* (Huddersfield 862321)

THORNTON, Timothy Charles Gordon. b 35. Late Scho of Ch Ch Ox BA 58, MA 61. Linc Th Coll 60. **d** 62 Bp Hulme for Man **p** 63 Man. C of St Thos Conv Distr Kirkholt Rochdale 62-64; Tutor Linc Th Coll 64-68; Chap 66-68; L to Offic Dio Linc 65-68; Lect Pacific Th Coll Suva and L to Offic Dio Polyn 69-73, Chap Brasted Coll Westerham 73-74; L to Offic Dio Roch 74; Can Missr of Guildf 74-79; P-in-c of Hascombe 74-79; V of Chobham w Valley End Dio Guildf from 79. *Vicarage, Bagshot Road, Chobham, Surrey, GU24 8BY.* (Chobham 8197)

THORNTON, Timothy Martin. b 57. Univ of Southn BA 78. St Steph Ho Ox 78. **d** 80 **p** 81 Wakef. C of Todmorden Dio Wakef from 80. *15 Hammerton Terrace, Todmorden, Lancs, OL14 5HR.*

THORNTON-DUESBERY, Canon Julian Percy. b 02. Late Domus Exhib of Ball Coll Ox 21, Goldsmiths' Exhib 22, 1st cl Cl Mods 23, BA (1st cl Lit Hum) 25, 1st cl Th and Jun Gr Test Pri 26, MA Sen Denyer and Johnson Scho 28. Wycl Hall Ox 25. **d** 26 **p** 27 Ox. Chap Wycl Hall Ox and L to Offic Dio Ox 26-27; Vice-Prin of Wycl Hall Ox and Exam Chap to Bp of Blackb 27-33; Chap and Fell of CCC Ox 28-33; Hd Master of St Geo Sch Jer and Exam Chap to Bp in Jer 33-40; R of St Pet-le-Bailey Ox 40-45; Master of St Pet Hall Ox 40-45; Actg Prin of Wycl Hall Ox 43-44; Prin 44-55; Commiss Jer 43-63; Exam Chap to Bp of Worc 41-71; to Bp of Nor 43-61; to Bp of S & M from 43; to Bp of Ox 55-68; to Bp of Bradf 56-61; Select Pr Univ of Ox 43-45; Master of St Pet Coll Ox 55-68; R of St Pet-le-Bailey Ox 55-61; Can Th of Liv Cathl 68-78; Can (Emer) from 79; L to Offic Dio Liv from 69. *College of St Barnabas, Blackberry Lane, Lingfield, Surrey, RH7 6NO.* (Dormans Park 508)

THORNTON-WAKEFORD, David Blackstone. b 50. St Ho Crafers 67. **d** 73 **p** 74 Adel. C of Toorak Gardens 73-74; Edwardstown w Ascot Pk 74-76; P-in-c of Kidman Pk w Flinders Pk 76-79; Prec of St Geo Cathl City and Dio Perth from 79. *23 Griffin Crescent, Manning, Perth, W Australia 6152.* (450-1187)

THOROGOOD, Lionel Geoffrey. b 23. SOC 66. **d** 69 **p** 70 Roch. C of Bexley 69-71; Hayes 71-73; V of Sutton-at-Hone Dio Roch from 73. *Sutton-at-Hone Vicarage, Dartford, Kent, DA4 9HQ.* (Farningham 862253)

THOROLD, Henry Croyland. Ch Ch Ox 40. Cudd Coll 42. **d** 44 **p** 45 Brech. Chap of St Paul's Cathl Dundee and Dom Chap to Bp of Brech 44-46; Chap RNVR 46-48; RN 48-49; Asst Master and Chap Lancing Coll and LPr Dio Chich 49-68; Ho Master 54-68; Chap and Regr Summer Fields Ox 68-75; Regr from 75; L to Offic Dio Ox from 69. *Summer Fields, Nr Oxford; and Marston Hall, Grantham, Lincs.* (Honington 225)

THOROLD, John Robert Hayford. K Coll Cam Cl Trip (Aegr) 40, BA 43, MA 45. Cudd Coll Ox 42. **d** 42 Glouc **p** 43 Tewkesbury for Glouc. C of Cheltm 42-44; Perm to Offic at St Anne Limehouse 44-45; Asst Master Eton Coll 45-46; Tutor Ripon Hall and L to Offic Dio Ox 47-52; V of Mitcham Dio S'wark from 52; M OGS from 53. *Vicarage, Mitcham, Surrey.* (01-648 1566)*; and Marston Hall, Grantham, Lincs.* (Honington 225)

THOROLD, John Stephen. b 35. Bps' Coll Cheshunt 61. **d** 63 Linc **p** 64 Bp Dunlop for Linc. C of Cleethorpes (in c of St Francis from 65) 63-70; V of Cherry Willingham w Greetwell 70-77; V of Spilsby w Hundleby Dio Linc from 77; Gt Steeping w Firsby Dio Linc from 77; R of Aswardby w Sausthorpe Dio Linc from 77; Langton-by-Partney w Sutterby Dio Linc from 77; Halton Holgate Dio Linc from 77; L Steeping Dio Linc from 77; Raithby Dio Linc from 77. *Vicarage, Spilsby, Lincs.* (Spilsby 52526)

THORP, Adrian. b 55. Clare Coll Cam BA 77, MA 80. Univ of Lon BD 80. Trin Coll Bris 77. **d** 80 **p** 81 Carl. C of St

Thos Kendal Dio Carl from 80. *Curates House, Southview Lane, Kendal, Cumbria.*

THORP, Harold John. St Jo Coll Morpeth ACT ThL 39. **d** 39 **p** 40 Melb. C of St Cuthb E Brunswick 39-41; St Andr Brighton 41-44; Chap AIF 44-47; C of St Bart Burnley Melb 47; Min of W Footscray 47-52; I of Ormond 52-61; Balwyn 61-74; St Marg Caulfield Dio Melb from 74. *383 Glen Eira Road, Caulfield, Vic, Australia 3161.* (03-53 7440)

THORP, John David. MBE (Mil) 53. Bps' Coll Cheshunt 57. **d** 58 Nor **p** 59 Thetford for Cant. C of Sprowston 58-61; R of Spixworth w Crostwick 61-65; C-in-c of Frettenham w Stanninghall 62-65; All S Kanpur 65-67; R of Kilscoran 68-70; Armadale 71-75; Yokine Dio Perth from 75. *27 Frape Avenue, Yokine, W Australia 6060.* (49 1534)

THORP, Norman Arthur. b 29. Tyndale Hall Bris 63. **d** 65 **p** 66 Portsm. C of St Jude Southsea Portsea 65-68; Braintree (in c of St Paul) 68-73; P-in-c of Tolleshunt D'Arcy and Tolleshunt Major Dio Chelmsf from 73; V from 75. *Tolleshunt D'Arcy Vicarage, Maldon, Essex, CM9 8TS.* (Tolleshunt D'Arcy 521)

THORP, Robert Penfold. b 29. Chich Th Coll 54. **d** 57 **p** 58 Roch. C of St Jas Beckenham 57-60; Babbacombe 60-66; C-in-c of St Geo Conv Distr Goodrington Dio Ex from 66. *St George's House, Horseshoe Bend, Goodrington, Paignton, Devon, TQ4 6NH.* (Paignton 556476)

THORP, Roderick Cheyne. b 44. Ch Ch Ox BA 65, MA 69. Ridley Hall Cam 66. **d** 69 **p** 70 Ox. C of Greyfriars Reading 69-73; St Martin Hull 73-75; H Trin Heworth 75-79; P Missr in Conv Distr of N Bletchley Dio Ox from 79. *3 Braybrooke Drive, Furzton, Milton Keynes, MK4 1AE.* (Milton Keynes 501425)

THORP, Thomas Malcolm. b 49. St Aug Coll Cant 71. **d** 72 Repton for Derby **p** 73 Derby. C of St Bart City Derby 72-75; Newport Pagnell 75-79; Youth Officer in Archd of Bucks Dio Ox from 79. *93 Hivings Hill, Chesham, Bucks.* (Chesham 3717)

THORPE, Albert David. Nundah Th Coll. **d** 25 **p** 26 N Queensld. C of Mackay 25-30; P-in-c of Mareeba 30-34; Mirani 34-43; Bowen 43-51; Can of N Queensld 48-69; R of Ayr 51-67. *81 Carlingsford Road, Epping, NSW 2121, Australia.*

THORPE, Arthur. Univ of Alta BA 30. St Steph Th Coll Edmon 31. Wycl Hall Ox 52. **d** and **p** 53 Liv. C of Bootle 53-55; N Area Sec CCCS 55-57; R of Hawksworth w Scarrington 57-61; V of Clarborough w Hayton 61-68. *4 Blake Road, West Bridgford, Nottingham.*

THORPE, Ven Benjamin James. McGill Univ Montr BA 28, MA 32. Montr Dioc Coll L Th 30. **d** 30 **p** 31 Montr. I of N Clarendon 30-31; C of Ascen Montr 31-33; I of Pointe Claire 33-39; R of Goodwin 39-42; Lachute 42-44; CF (Canad) 44-46; Actg C-in-c of Valleyfield 46; I of Ch of Redeem Montr 46-50; R of St Mark St Laurent Montr 50-73; Hon Can of Montr 66-67; Archd of St Andr 67-73. *643 Sevilla Park Place, London, Ont., Canada.* (411-438 4243)

THORPE, Christian Leonard. d and **p** 67 Sier L. P Dio Sier L. *Bonthe, Sierra Leone.*

THORPE, Canon David Dumville. Univ of NZ BA 32, LTh (3rd cl) 33. **d** 32 **p** 33 Ch Ch. C of Timaru 32-34; V of Banks Peninsula 34-37; Hokitika 37-40; RD of Westland 38-40; CF (NZ) 40-43; Chap of Southwell Sch Hamilton 43-45; V of Cashmere Hills 45-54; St Jo Bapt Ch Ch 54-69; P-in-c of Phillipstown 63-69; Hororata 69-72; Hon Can of Ch Ch 64-72; Can (Emer) from 72; L to Offic Dios Ch Ch and Nel from 72. *Tree Tops, Hanmer Springs, NZ.*

THORPE, Donald Henry. b 34. St Aid Coll 57. **d** 60 **p** 61 Sheff. C of Mexborough 60-64; St Leon and St Jude Doncaster 64-67; V of Intake 67-74; H Trin Millhouses City and Dio Sheff from 74. *Holy Trinity Vicarage, Millhouses Lane, Sheffield, S7 2HB.* (Sheff 362838)

THORPE, Canon Harry Fletcher Cyprian. b 12. **d** 36 **p** 37 Bloemf. L to Offic Dio Bloemf 36-37; Miss P 37-52; CF 42-46; Dir Relig Educn Dio Basuto 50-52; Miss at St Mich Herschel 52-58; I of St Mark Port Eliz 58-60; Miss at Kwazakele Port Eliz 58-62; St Matt Miss and Warden of St Matt Coll 62-68; Archd of K William's Town 64-68; Hon Can of Grahmstn from 68; Dir Prov Dept of Miss in S Afr 68-73; R of Ecton and Warden of Ecton Ho 73-78; Prov Commiss S Afr 73-81; Commiss Les from 73. *9 Borough Hill, Petersfield, Hants, GU32 3LQ.*

THORPE, Harry Reginald Brodie. MBE 55. St Jo Coll Morpeth 35. ACT ThL 37. **d** 37 **p** 38 Bath. C of Orange 37-40; Eugowra 40; Dubbo 40-41; P-in-c Millthorpe 41; serving w AIF 41-45; Chap AIF 45-47; Comm Homes and Youth Dio Bath 47-57; Can of All SS Cathl Bath 55-72; Dioc Chap Dio Bath 59-74; Perm to Offic Dio Newc from 75. *155 Steyne Road, Saratoga, NSW, Australia 2251.*

THORPE, John Graham Anderson. d and **p** 64 Niag. C of St John Ancaster 64-66; R of Ch of Our Sav Stoney Creek Dio Niag from 66; R of Winona 66-78; St Brendan Port Colborne Dio Niag from 78. *44 Elmvale Crescent, Port Colborne, Ont, Canada.* (416-835 1028)

THORPE, John Wellburn. b 31. Lich Th Coll 55. **d** 58 **p** 59 Heref. C of St Martin Heref 58-61; St Francis Dudley 61-65; R of Gt w L Witley and Hillhampton 65-70; C of St Barn Glouc 70-73; P-in-c of Blaisdon w Flaxley (and Westbury-on-Severn from 76) Dio Glouc 73-77; V from 77. *Flaxley Vicarage, Newnham, Glos, GL14 1JR.* (Westbury-on-Severn 229)

THORPE, Kerry Michael. b 51. BD (Lon) 78. Oak Hill Th Coll Dipl Th 76. **d** 78 **p** 79 Ches. C of Overchurch (or Upton) Dio Ches from 78. *19 Church Road, Upton, Wirral, Merseyside, L49 6JZ.*

THORPE, Michael William. b 42. Lich Th Coll 67. **d** 70 Bradwell for Chelmsf **p** 71 Chelmsf. C of St Mich AA Walthamstow 70-71; St Andr Plaistow 71; C-in-c of St Mary Plaistow 72-74; Team V of Gt Grimsby 74-78; Chap Grimsby Distr Hosps from 78. *11 Sackville Street, Grimsby, South Humberside, DN34 4NX.* (Grimsby 57216)

THORPE, Trevor Cecil. b 21. Em Coll Cam BA (2nd cl Hist Trip pt i) 47, 2nd cl Th Trip pt i 49, MA 52. Ridley Hall Cam 48. **d** 50 **p** 51 Guildf. C of Farnborough 50-53; W Ham 53-56; V of N Weald Dio Chelmsf from 57. *North Weald Vicarage, Epping, Essex.* (North Weald 2246)

THREADGILL, Alan Roy. b 31. St Alb Ministerial Tr Scheme 77. **d** 80 St Alb **p** 81 Hertford for St Alb (NSM). C of St Andr Bedford Dio St Alb from 80; Asst Chap to the Deaf from 81. *30 Pipit Rise, Bedford, MK41 7JT.*

THRELFALL, Stanley Frederick. St Jo Coll Morpeth 55. **d** 57 **p** 58 Perth. C of Wembley 57-60; P-in-c of Osborne Pk Nollamara 60-64; C of St Bonif Cathl Bunb 64-68; R of Katanning 68-71; Narrogin 71-76; Archd of Albany 74-76; Dioc Archd 76-78; Sub-Dean and Can Res of St Bonif Cathl Bunb 76-78; R of Nedlands Dio Perth from 78. *58 Tyrell Street, Nedlands, W Australia 6009.* (386 1083)

THRIFT, Dudley Richard Moore. b 10. **d** 80 Newc. Hon C of Scone Dio Newc from 80. *Hazeldene, Parville, via Scone 2337, NSW, Australia.*

THROSSELL, John Julian. b 30. Univ of Nottm BSc 53. Univ of Syracuse PhD 56. Oak Hill Coll 72. **d** 75 **p** 76 St Alb (APM). C of Wheathampstead Dio St Alb from 75. *38 Dale Avenue, Wheathampstead, St Albans, Herts, AL4 8LS.*

THROWER, Clive Alan. b 41. Univ of Sheff BSc 62. E Midl Jt Ordin Scheme 76. **d** 79 **p** 80 Derby. C of All SS Cathl Ch Dio Derby from 79. *Prospect House, Park Road, Spondon, Derby, DE2 7LN.*

THROWER, George. b 06. St Paul's Miss Coll Burgh 26. **d** 30 **p** 31 Windw Is. C of St Geo Cathl St Vincent 30-34; Crosby 34-36; St Faith Linc 36-38; PC of Wildmore w Langrick and Thornton-le-Fen 38-44; V of Metheringham 44-49; St Marg Bentham 49-56; C-in-c of St Cuthb Wrose Bradf 56-59; V 59-63; Woodford Halse 63-68; Spratton 68-71. *12 St Leonards Gardens, Hove, Sussex, BN3 4QB.*

THROWER, Philip Edward. b 41. Kelham Th Coll 61. **d** 66 **p** 67 Lon. C of Hayes 66-69; Yeovil 69-71; St John Shirley 71-77; V of St Mark S Norwood Dio Cant from 77. *101 Albert Road, SE25.* (01-656 9221)

THRUSH, Alfred William Cyril. b 09. St Aid Coll 43. **d** 45 **p** 46 Lich. C of St Matt Tipton 45-48; St Paul Walsall 48-50; V of St Barn Hull 50-54; Min of St Steph Eccles Distr Prittlewell 54-59; V of Grays 59-79. *20 St George's Avenue, Grays, Essex.*

THUBRON, Thomas William. Edin Th Coll 62. **d** 65 Dur **p** 66 Jarrow for Dur. C of St Mary Gateshead 65-66; Shildon 66-68; Miss OMC Barisal 68-70; in Ch of Bangladesh 70-79; V of Wheatley Hill Dio Dur from 80. *Vicarage, Wheatley Hill, Durham, DH6 3RA.* (Thornley 496)

THUI PRENG, d 79 **p** 81 Akyab. P Dio Akyab. *St Peter's Church, La Kung, Burma.*

THULBORN, Neville John. ACT ThL 60. St Jo Coll Morpeth. **d** 59 **p** 61 Bal. C of Ararat 59-61; P-in-c of Dimboola 61-62; V 62-66; Miss at Tarakwaruru 66-68; Cape Vogal 68-69; R of Coleraine 70-71; Miss Dio Papua 71-74; R of St John Bal 74-78; Asst Sec ABM Brisb from 79. *25 Glenella Street, The Gap, Queensland, Australia 4061.* (30 1774)

THULO, Johannes Lesua. b 37. **d** 78 Bp Stanage for Johann **p** 79 Johann (NSM). C of Evaton w Sebokeng Dio Johann from 78. *547 Zone 13, Sebokeng, S Africa 1982.*

THUR, Hermann Alois Anton. b 1900. Univ of Vienna. **d** 22 Asst Bp of Vienna **p** 23 Abp of Vienna. Rec into C of E 39. C of St Sav Brockley Hill (Col Cl Act) 40-41; St Mary Magd Wandsworth Common 41-45; All SS Wandsworth 45-51; V of Paston w Knapton 51-80. *c/o Paston Vicarage, North Walsham, Norf.* (Mundesley 230)

THURBURN-HUELIN, David Richard. b 47. St Chads Coll Dur BA 69. Westcott Ho Cam 69. **d** 71 **p** 72 Stepney for Lon. C of Poplar 71-76; Chap Liddon Ho Lon 76-80; V of Harrold and R of Carlton w Chellington Dio St Alb from 81.

Rectory, Carlton, Bedford. (Bedf 720262)

THURGOOD, John William Voce. b 1896. Roch Th Coll. **d** 60 Linc **p** 60 Grantham for Linc. C of Wellingore w Temple Bruer Dio Linc 60-62; V 62-71; Perm to Offic Dio St E from 75. *182b High Road, Trimley St Mary, Felixstowe, Suff.*

THURLEY, Graham Douglas. Ridley Coll Melb ACT ThL (2nd cl) 68. **d** and **p** 69 Tas. C of Burnie 69-71; Launceston 71-73; R of Exmouth w Ashburton 73-76; S Pilbara 76-78; I of Hastings Dio Melb from 78. *Vicarage, Hastings, Vic, Australia 3915.* (059-79 1210)

THURLOW, Very Rev Alfred Gilbert Goddard. b 11. Selw Coll Cam BA (3rd cl Th Trip pt i) 32, MA 36. FRHistS 62. Cudd Coll 33. **d** 34 **p** 35 Ox. C of All SS Wokingham 34-39; Min Can of Nor Cathl 39-55; Prec 39-55; C of St Mary-in-the-Marsh Nor 39-45; R of St Clem w St Edm and St Geo Colegate Nor 43-52; V of St Andr Nor 52-55; R of St Mich at Plea w St Pet Hungate Nor 52-55; V of Gt Yarmouth 55-64; Hon Can of Nor 62-64; Can Res 64-72; Vice-Dean 69-72; Dean of Glouc from 72. *Deanery, Gloucester, GL1 2BP.* (Gloucester 24167)

THURLOW, Canon Tom. Univ of Manit LTh 50. St Jo Coll Winnipeg. **d** 50 **p** 51 Bran. R of Gilbert Plains 50-53; Hamiota and Shoal Lake 53-55; Elgin 55-57; C of St Mary Kerrisdale 57-59; V of St Marg of Scotld (Lochdale) N Burnaby 59-63; I of Outlook 63-64; St Paul Regina 64-67; R of Oxbow 67-71; Unity 71-81; Hon Can of Sktn from 80; I of Quill View Dio Sktn from 81. *Box 232, Wadena, Sask, Canada.*

THURMER, Canon John Alfred. b 25. Or Coll Ox BA (2nd cl Mod Hist) 50, MA 55. Linc Th Coll 50. **d** 52 **p** 53 Chelmsf. C of L Ilford 52-55; Chap and Lect Sarum Th Coll 55-64; L to Offic Dio Chelmsf 55-73; Dio Ex 64-73; Lazenby Chap Univ of Ex 64-73; Lect Univ of Ex from 64; Can Res and Chan of Ex Cathl from 73. *6 The Close, Exeter, Devon.* (Ex 72498)

THURSFIELD, John Anthony. b 21. Magd Coll Ox BA (2nd cl Mod Hist) 47, MA 51. Cudd Coll 47. **d** 49 **p** 50 Lich. C of Brierley Hill 49-51; Colwall 51-53; Chap Woodbridge Sch 53-54; C-in-c of Grundisburgh w Burgh 54; R 55-57; V of Chaddesley Corbett 57-60; Old Basing 60-72; Chap to Br Embassy Bonn and All SS Cologne 72-75; R of W Clandon 75-79; E Clandon 75-79; V of Reydon Dio St E from 79. *Reydon Vicarage, Wangford Road, Reydon, Southwold, Suff.* (Southwold 722192)

THURSFIELD, John Richard. b 22. Roch Th Coll 60. **d** 62 **p** 63 Win. C of St Andr Bournemouth 62-66; C-in-c of Frating w Thorington 66-67; USPG Kobe Japan 67-69; C of St Luke Battersea 69-71; St Mich Wandsworth Common 71-72; Chap St Ebba's Hosp Epsom from 72; Qu Mary's Hosp Carshalton and Henderson Hosps Sutton Surrey from 73. *c/o Queen Mary's Hospital for Children, Carshalton, Surrey, SM5 4NR.* (01-643 3300)

THURSFIELD, Preb Raymond John. b 14. St Aid Coll 43. **d** 45 **p** 46 Bris. C of H Trin Clifton w St Andr L and St Pet Bris 45-47; St Paul Weston-s-Mare (in c of Good Shepherd) 47-50; V of Mark 50-55; R of Yarlington 55-60; Dir of Relig Educn for Youth Work Dio B & W 55-60; V of Rudby-in-Cleveland w Middleton 60-62; R of Tarrington w Stoke Edith 62-67; Ross-on-Wye 67-79; C-in-c of Brampton Abbotts 67-72; Dir Youth Work Dio Heref 62-68; Hon Chap to Bp of Kimb K 63-67; Preb of Heref 65-80; Preb (Emer) from 81; Commiss Kimb K 68-76; RD of Ross 71-79; P-in-c of Watermillock 79-80. *7B Millers Green, Cathedral, Gloucester.*

THURSTON, Canon Leo Sydney. St Jo Coll Winnipeg. **d** 50 **p** 51 Edmon. I of Ashmont 50-53; V of Mayerthorpe 53-56; I of Barrhead 56-59; Rocky Mountain Ho 59-65; R of Lacombe 65-71; Can of Calg from 66; R of Banff 71-74; I of Taber 74-81; Strathmore Dio Calg from 81. *Box 553, Strathmore, Alta, Canada.*

THUU, Elijah Henry Morrison. b 39. **d** 73 bp Kuria for Nak. d Dio Nak. *Kapsabet Girls' High School, Box 320, Kapsabet, Kenya.*

THWAITS, Alan Russell. b 48. Trent Univ Ont BA 69. Trin Coll Tor MDiv 78. **d** 78 Alg. C of Ch of Epiph Sudbury 78-80; on leave. *21 Jalan Sultan Abdul, Kuala Lumpur, Malaysia.*

THWALA, Robert Elijah. b 21. St Bede's Coll Umtata 69. **d** 70 **p** 72 Natal. C of St Andr Springvale 70-76; R of St Phil Dundee Dio Natal from 76. *Box 259, Dundee, Natal, S Africa.*

THWALA, Selby Daniel. St Pet Coll Rosettenville LTh 54. **d** 53 **p** 54 Pret. P Dio Pret 53-65; Dio Natal from 65. *Box 46, Kwa Mashu, Natal, S Africa.*

TIAN, Leuben. b 15. **d** 78 Lango. d Dio Lango. *PO Chawente, Lira, Uganda.*

TIAN, Wilson. **d** 61 **p** 62 N Ugan. P Dio N Ugan. *PO Alemere, Uganda.*

✠ **TIARKS, Right Rev Geoffrey Lewis.** b 09. St Jo Coll Cam BA (2nd cl Engl Trip) 31, MA 35. Westcott Ho Cam 31. **d** 32 **p** 33 S'wark. C of St Sav w St Pet S'wark 32-33; Chap RN 34-47; Asst Chap Dioc Coll Rondebosch 48-50; R of St Paul Rondebosch 50-54; V of Lyme Regis 54-61; Archd of IW 61-65; Portsm 65-69; Cons Ld Bp Suffr of Maidstone in Westmr Abbey 25 Jan 69 by Abp of Cant; Bps of Lon, Ely, Portsm, Roch, and Sarum; Bps Suffr of Croydon, Lewes, Buckingham, Taunton, Dover, and Dunwich; and Bps Warner, Boys and Woolmer; res 76; Sen Chap to Abp of Cant 69-74; RD of Lyme Bay 76-79; Chap to Retired Clergy and Widows in Archd of Sherborne from 77. *Primrose Cottage, Netherbury, Bridport, Dorset.* (Netherbury 277)

TIBAGWA, Yefusa. **d** 74 **p** 75 Bunyoro. P Dio Bunyoro. *c/o Box 20, Hoima, Uganda.*

TIBAGWA, Yosia. Bp Tucker Coll Mukono 61. **d** 63 **p** 66 Ruw. P Dio Ruw. *PO Kiryandongo, Masindi, Uganda.*

TIBANYENDERA, Zephania. **d** and **p** 79 W Ank. P Dio W Ank. *Box 47, Bushenyi, Uganda.*

TIBANYURURWA, Asanasio. **d** and **p** 79 W Ank. P Dio W Ank. *PO Rubaare, Rwashamaire, Uganda.*

TIBATEGYEZA, William. Bp Tucker Coll Mukono 60. **d** 60 **p** 62 Ankole-K. P Dio Ankole-K 60-67; Dio Ank 67-77; Dio W Ank from 77. *PO Ruhinda, Bushenyi, Uganda.*

TIBBATTS, Canon George King. b 02. K Coll Cam 3rd cl Hist Trip pt i 23, BA (3rd cl Hist Trip pt ii) 24, Morton Exhib 24, MA 28. Ely Th Coll 25. **d** 26 **p** 27 Roch. C of St Luke New Brompton 26-31, UMCA Miss Masasi 31-32; Hd Master Centr Sch and Tr Coll Chidya 32-38; Select Pr Univ of Cam 38 44 and 58; Org Sec UMCA for E Cos 38-40; Chap of Magd Coll Cam 39-46; Exam Chap to Bp of Blackb 43-57; Commiss Masasi from 42; Zanz from 44; Johann 52-61; LPr Dio Ely 44-52; Chap and Sub-Libr of SS Coll Cam 46-52; M of the Oratory of the Good Shepherd from 26; Supr 50-66; Hon Can of Masasi from 51; V of St Luke Chesterton 52-63; L to Offic as Chap Neale Ho Cam 56-63; Candidates Sec UMCA 63-64; Commiss Centr Afr 63-72; USPG Sec for Europe Univs & Th colls 65-72; Commiss N Terr from 74; LPr Dio Lon 68-78; Dio Ely from 78; Perm to Offic Dio Pet 74-76; Dio Ely 76-78; Dio Lon from 78. *18 Partridge Drive, Bar Hill, Cambridge, CB3 8EN.* (0954 81101)

TIBBERT, Harry Leonard. b 07. Univ Coll Ex 26. Ripon Hall Ox. **d** 59 Ex **p** 60 Crediton for Ex. C of St Mark Ford Devonport 59-62; V of Heap Bridge 62-63; C-in-c of Good Shepherd W Hounslow 63-65; R and Arch P of Haccombe w Coffinswell 65-69; Perm to Offic Dio Ex from 75. *24 Peverell Terrace, Peverell, Plymouth, PL3 4JL.* (Plymouth 20041)

TIBBLES, Charles Mogford. b 10. St Aid Coll 53. **d** 55 **p** 56 S'wark. C of E Greenwich 55-58; Sprowston 58-60; Min of St Francis's Conv Distr Heartsease 60-65; V of H Trin Coldhurst Oldham 65-72; Scouthead 72-75. *79 Kiln Road, Fareham, Hants, PO16 7UL.* (Fareham 4036)

TIBBO, George Kenneth. b 29. Univ of Reading BA (2nd cl Mod Hist) 50, MA 54. Coll of Resurr Mirfield 55. **d** 57 **p** 58 Dur. C of St Aid W Hartlepool 57-61; V of St Mark (w St Paul from 74) Darlington 61-75; R of Crook 75-80; V of Stanley 76-80; St Chad Limeside, Oldham Dio Man from 80. *St Chad's Vicarage, Higher Lime Road, Limeside, Oldham, Lancs.* (061-624 0970)

TIBBO, Wilson Samuel. Qu Coll Newfld. **d** 54 **p** 55 Newfld. I of Sandwich Bay Labrador 54-59; Brooklyn 59-60; R of Lamaline 60-66; Grand Bank 66-67; I of Watrous 67-68; R of Colonsay 68-70; I of Weyburn 70-74; Whitbourne 74-77; Topsail Dio E Newfld from 77. *PO Box 70, Topsail, Newfoundland, Canada.*

TIBBOTT, Joseph Edwards. b 14. K Coll Lon. **d** 55 **p** 56 S'wark. C of St Jo Evang Caterham Valley 55-59; V of Stockwell 59-71; Cwmdauddwr w Nantgwyllt 71-75; Llanguicke (Pontardawe) 76-77; R of Llangammarch w Garth Llanfechan and Llanlleonfel 77-80. *Ochr Lon, Elan Valley Road, Cwmdeuddwr, Rhayadar, Powys.* (Rhayadar 810783)

TIBBS, Canon Howard Abraham Llewellyn Thomas. b 15. Univ of Wales BA 39. Coll of Resurr Mirfield 39. **d** 41 York **p** 42 Hull for York. C of St Osw Middlesbrough 41-44; Chap RAFVR 44-47; R of Dunnington 47-52; V of St Barn Balsall Heath 52-65; H Sepulchre w St Andr (and St Lawr from 76) Northn Dio Pet from 65; RD of Northn 70-79; Surr from 71; Can (Non-Res) of Pet from 74. *2 Langham Place, Northampton, NN2 6AA.* (Northampton 37106)

TIBBS, John Andrew. b 29. K Coll Lon and Warm AKC 53. **d** 54 **p** 55 Chich. C of Eastbourne 54-57; P-in-c of Jeppestown 57-62; Chap of St Martin's Sch Rosettenville 57-62; C of St Thos-on-The-Bourne Farnham 63-64; R and Dir of Mbabane 64-68; V of Sompting 69-73; Ifield Dio Chich 73-78; Team R from 78; M Gen Syn from 80. *Ifield Rectory, Crawley, Sussex, RH11 0NN.* (Crawley 20843)

TIBEESIGWA, George. **d** 76 **p** 77 Ank. P Dio Ank 76-77; Dio W Ank from 77; Dioc Regr and Sec from 78. *Box 140, Bushenyi, Uganda.*

TIBEKINGA, Laban. Bp Tucker Coll Mukono 42. **d** 44 **p** 46 Ugan. P Dio Ugan 44-60; Dio Ankole-K 60-67; Dio Ank from 67. *PO Box 103, Mbarara, Ankole, Uganda.*

TIBENDERANA, Eric. d 76 **p** 77 Ank. P Dio Ank 76-77; Dio W Ank from 77. *Box 4, Rubirizi, Uganda.*

TIBESASA, Lazalo. Bp Tucker Coll Mukono. **d** 31 **p** 34 Ugan. P Dio Ugan 31-60; Dio Ankole-K 60-65. *Rutooma, Kashari, PO Box 14, Mbarara, Uganda.*

TICEHURST, David. b 29. K Coll Lon and Warm 50. **d** 55 **p** 56 Roch. C of Gillingham w Upberry 55-57; Chap Brunswick Sch 57-60; C of St Jo Bapt Cove 60-63; Ch Ch Chelsea 63-64; Sen Master St Mich Sch Old Woking 65-67; Hd Master Hawley Place Camberley 67-76; Perm to Offic Dio Guildf 72-76; P-in-c of Bury w Houghton Dio Chich from 76. *Bury Vicarage, Pulborough, RH20 1PB.* (Bury 677)

TICKLE, Robert Peter. b 51. St Chad's Coll Dur BA 74. St Steph Ho Ox 74. **d** 76 **p** 77 York. C of St Alb Hull 76-80; St Chad City and Dio Leic from 80. *c/o 145 Coleman Road, Leicester, LE5 4LH.*

TICKNER, Colin de Fraine. b 37. Chich Th Coll. **d** 66 **p** 67 Wakef. C of Huddersfield 66-68; Dorking 68-74; V of Shottermill Dio Guildf from 74. *Shottermill Vicarage, Haslemere, Surrey.* (Haslemere 2057)

TICKNER, David Arthur. b 44. K Coll Lon and Warm AKC 67. **d** 69 Pontefract for Wakef **p** 70 Wakef. C of Thornhill Lees w Savile Town 69-71; St Aid Billingham 71-74; Team V 74-78; CF from 78. *c/o Ministry of Defence, Bagshot Park, Bagshot, Surrey GU19 5PL.*

TICKNER, John Frederick. b 05. Univ of Leeds BA (3rd cl Hist) 30. Coll of Resurr Mirfield 27. **d** 32 Malmesbury for Bris **p** 33 Bris. C of St Mark Swindon (in c of St Sav 37-40) 32-40; C-in-c 40-42; V of St Greg Gt Horfield 42-55; PC of St Pet Plymouth 55-63; Proc Conv Ex 59-64; Sub-Warden Commun of St Jo Bapt Clewer 63-68; C of Bramley Guildf 68-72; Perm to Offic Dio Chich from 72. *11 Guildford Place, Chichester, Sussex, PO19 4DU.* (Chich 782834)

TICQUET, Cyril Edward. b 11. Ripon Hall Ox 63. **d** 64 Birm **p** 65 Aston for Birm. C of Coleshill 64-68; C-in-c of St Clem Castle Bromwich 68-71; V 71-76; C of Stokenham w Sherford Dio Ex from 77. *Bay Trees, Slapton, Kingsbridge, Devon.*

TIDBALL, Reginald James. Moore Th Coll Syd ACT ThL 57. **d** 59 Bp Hilliard for Syd **p** 59 Syd. C of Ryde 59-61; Kensington 61-65; R of Thornleigh and Pennant Hills 65-79; St Simon and St Jude Bowral Dio Syd from 79. *34 Bendooley Street, Bowral, NSW, Australia 2576.* (048-611574)

TIDDY, Alastair James. St Paul's Coll Grahmstn Dipl Th. **d** 80 Capetn. C of St Martin Bergvliet Dio Capetn from 80. *55 Eksteen Avenue, Bergvliet 7800, CP, S Africa.*

TIDMARSH, Canon Peter Edwin. b 29. Keble Coll Ox BA 52, MA 56. St Steph Ho Ox 52. **d** 54 **p** 55 Lon. C of Stepney 54-58; St Pet Streatham 58-62; Chap Shiplake Coll Ox 62-64; C of All SS Margaret Street St Marylebone and Hd Master All SS Choir Sch 64-68; V of St Cubert Dio Truro from 68; Dir and Sec for Educn Dio Truro from 69; Hon Can of Truro Cathl from 73. *St Cubert Vicarage, Newquay, Cornw, TR8 5HA.* (0637 830301)

TIDMARSH, Philip Reginald Wilton. b 14. Late Chor Exhib of G and C Coll Cam BA 36, MA 40. Ridley Hall Cam 46. **d** 48 **p** 49 Guildf. C of Ashtead 48-51; Chap Dean Close Sch Cheltm 51-58; Prin Bp Willis Teacher Tr Coll Iganga 58-65; V of Odiham w S Wanborough 65-76; P-in-c of Long Sutton 72-76; Dogmersfield w Winchfield 73-76; RD of Odiham 74-76; P-in-c of Abbot's Ann 76-79. *Gravel Pit Bungalow, Broadheath, Presteigne, Powys.*

TIDWELL, Neville Leslie Arthur. Selw Coll Cam 1st cl Th Trip pt i 54, BA (1st cl Th Trip pt ii) and Barwell Scho 56, MA 60. Keble Coll Ox MA (by incorp) 61. St Steph Ho Ox 56. **d** 58 **p** 59 Dur. C of St Columba Southwick 58-60; Tutor St Steph Ho Ox 60-62; Chap 62-65; Vice-Prin 65-68; St Bede's Coll Umtata 68-70. *St Bede's College, Umtata, CP, S Africa.*

TIDY, John Hylton. b 48. AKC 71. St Aug Coll Cant 73. **d** 73 **p** 74 Dur. C of Newton Aycliffe 73-78; V of St Pet Bp Auckland Dio Dur from 78. *St Peter's Vicarage, Etherley Lane, Bishop Auckland, Co Durham, DL14*

TIERNAN, Paul Wilson. b 54. Univ of Man BA 76. Coll of the Resurr Mirfield 77. **d** 79 **p** 80 S'wark. C of Lewisham Dio S'wark from 79. *36d Clarendon Rise, Lewisham, SE13.* (01-318 3057)

TIFFEN, James Franklin. b 41. Newman Th Coll Edmon BTh 73. **d** 72 **p** 73 Edmon. L to Offic Dio Edmon 72-73; P-in-c of St Barn City and Dio Edmon from 73. *10712-159th Street, Edmonton, Alta., Canada.* (403-484 3779)

TIGWELL, Brian Arthur. b 36. SOC 74. **d** 77 **p** 78 S'wark. C of St Mark Woodcote Purley 77-80; Team V of U Kennet Dio Sarum from 80. *c/o Broad Hinton Vicarage, Swindon, SN4 9PA.*

TILBURY, Robert Edward Warneford. b 16. **d** 68 Bp Wilkinson for Niag **p** 76 Bp Bothwell for Niag. C of H Trin Hamilton 68-75; St Paul Hamilton Dio Niag from 75. *PO Box 68, Ancaster, Ont, Canada, L9G 3L3.*

TILEY, George Edward. b 13. St Jo Coll Dur LTh 35, BA 36, MA 39. Lon Coll of Div 32. **d** 36 **p** 37 Lon for Bris. C of St Mich AA Bishopston 36-38; Erdington 38-42; Oldbury 42-45; V of St Paul W Smethwick 45-51; Powick w Callow End 51-63; R of Honington w Idlicote and Whatcote 63-68; Sapperton w Frampton Mansell 68-74; V of Chewton Mendip w Emborrow 74-76; C-in-c of Ston Easton 74-76. *Old Rectory, Litton, Bath, Somt.*

TILFORD, Henry Norman Allan. Hur Coll. **d** 64 **p** 65 Hur. I of Alvinston 64-66; Princeton 66-69; St Mich AA Windsor 69-70; R of Oldcastle 70-75; St Mark Lon Dio Hur from 75. *539 Hale Street, London, Ont., Canada.* (519-455 0553)

TILL, Barry Dorn. b 23. Jes Coll Cam BA (1st cl Th Trip pt ii) and Lightfoot Scho 49, MA 49. Westcott Ho Cam 48. **d** 50 **p** 51 Man. C of Bury 50-53; Fell Jes Coll Cam and L to Offic Dio Ely 53-60; Chap 53-56; Dean 56-60; Select Pr Univ of Cam 56; Exam Chap to Bp of Lich 57-60; Dean of Hong Kong 60-64; Prin Morley Coll Lon from 65. *Morley College, Westminster Bridge Road, SE1.*

TILL, Kenneth James. b 12. Clifton Th Coll 33. **d** 36 **p** 37 Lon. C of St Geo Brentford 36-39; St Aldhelm Bedminster 39-40; CF from 40; DACG 47-62; ACG 62-68; Hon Chap to HM the Queen 65-68; V of Ryhall w Essendine 68-71; Walford w Bishopwood 71-78; Perm to Offic Dio B & W from 79; Dio Sarum from 80. *27 Springfield, Bradford-on-Avon, Wilts.* (B-on-A 5596)

TILL, Michael Stanley. b 35. Linc Coll Ox BA 60, MA 67. Westcott Ho Cam. **d** 64 **p** 65 Lon. C of St John St John's Wood 64-67; Chap K Coll Cam 67-70; Dean 70-81; V of Fulham Dio Lon from 81. *All Saints' Vicarage, Fulham High Street, SW6 3LG.* (01-736 6301)

TILLER, Canon Clifford George. St Aid Th Coll Bal 27. ACT ThL 30. **d** 30 **p** 31 Bal. C of Swan Marsh 31-32; P-in-c of Apollo Bay 32-33; R of Northampton 35-38; Mullewa 38-41; Chap AIF 41-45; R of Boulder 46-48; Katanning 48-58; Hon Can of Bunb 57-58; Can (Emer) from 58; L to Offic Dio Bunb 59-61; P-in-c of Donnybrook 61-65; R of Pingelly 65-68; L to Offic Dio Bunb from 68. *16 West Road, Bunbury, W Australia 6230.* (097-21 4725)

TILLER, Edgar Henry Vallentine. b 22. Open Univ BA 78. ACP 71. Wells Th Coll 57. **d** 59 Taunton for B & W **p** 60 Taunton for Cant. C of Weston-s-Mare 59-62; V of Leigh-on-Mendip 62-67; V of Stoke St Mich 62-67; Perm to Offic Dio Ex from 67; Asst Master Barnstaple Boys Co Sch 69-72; Pilton Sch Barnstaple 72-81. *3 Byron Close, Pilton, Barnstaple, EX31 1QH.* (Barnstaple 72483)

TILLER, James Douglas. Bp's Univ Lennox BA 49. **d** 50 **p** 51 Niag. C of St Thos St Catharines 50-51; R of Fergus 51-53; at Univ of Tor 53-55; R of Unionville w Stouffville 55-60; St Patr City and Dio Tor from 60. *12 Whitman Street, Willowdale, Ont., Canada.* (416-225 5151)

TILLER, Canon John. b 38. Late Scho of Ch Ch Ox BA (2nd cl Mod Hist) 60, MA 64. Univ of Bris MLitt 72. Tyndale Hall Bris 60. **d** 62 **p** 63 St Alb. C of St Cuthb Bedford 62-65; Widcombe 65-67; Tutor and Chap Tyndale Hall Bris 67-71; L to Offic Dio Bris 69-73; Lect Trin Coll Bris 72-73; C-in-c of Ch Ch Bedford 73-78; Chief Sec ACCM Westmr from 78; Hon Can St Alb from 80. *ACCM, Church House, Dean's Yard, SW1P 3NZ.* (01-222 9011)

TILLETT, John Edwin. b 14. Ely Th Coll 46. **d** 48 **p** 49 Carl. C of St Mich Workington 48-51; Prec of St Ninian's Cathl Perth 51-52; R of All SS Glencarse 52-59; Coates 59-65; Chap R Agr Coll Cirencester 59-68; PC of Stroud 65-68; V of Gt w L Tew 68-79. *14 Ledbury Road, Christchurch, Dorset, BH23 3LB.*

TILLETT, Leonard Wilfred. Selw Coll Cam 2nd cl Hist Trip pt i 31, BA 32, 2nd cl Th Trip pt i 33, MA 36. Wells Th Coll 33. **d** 34 **p** 35 Win. C of Milton Hants 34-37; Perm to Offic at St Marg King's Lynn 37-38; St Marg Lowestoft (in c of St Pet) 38-42; R of Rackheath 42-47; C-in-c of Salhouse 42-47; V of Ormesby St Marg w Ormesby St Mich and Scratby 47-57; RD of Flegg 55-57; Brooke 59-66; V of Trowse 57-66; PC of Arminghall 57-66; R of Roughton 66-75; Perm to Offic Dio Nor from 75. *4 Greenyard, Cromer Hall, Cromer, Norf.* (Cromer 3150)

TILLETT, Leslie Selwyn. b 54. Peterho Cam BA 75, MA 79. Univ of Leeds BA (Th) 80. Coll of the Resurr Mirfield 78. **d** 81 S'wark. C of All SS W Dulwich Dio S'wark from 81. *110 Turney Road, Dulwich, SE21.*

TILLEY, David Robert. b 38. Kelham Th Coll 58. **d** 63 **p** 64 Win. C of St Francis Bournemouth 63-67; St Andr Moulscoomb 67-70; Ifield (in c of St Alb Gossops Green) 70-75; Team V of Warwick Dio Cov from 76. *25 Sutherland Close, Woodloes Park, Warwick.* (Warw 42097)

TILLEY, Derise Ralph. b 21. Sarum Th Coll 55. **d** 57 **p** 58 Win. C of St Jo Bapt Moordown Bournemouth 57-61; St

Mary Penzance 61-64; V of Millbrook 64-80; St John w Millbrook Dio Truro from 80. *Millbrook Vicarage, Torpoint, Cornw, PL10 1BW.* (Plymouth 822264)

TILLEY, Peter Robert. b 41. Univ of Bris BA 62. Sarum Wells Th Coll 77. **d** 79 **p** 80 S'wark. C of St Paul Wimbledon Park Dio S'wark from 79. *65 Gartmoor Gardens, Southfields, SW19.* (01-788 1516)

TILLYARD, James Donald. b 16. St D Coll Lamp BA 38. Ripon Hall Ox 38. **d** 39 **p** 40 Wakef. C of Sandal Magna 39-42; Sowerby Bridge 42-43; CF (EC) 43-50; CF 50-71; Warden Sch of Relig Instruction Far East 50-52; DACG 62-65; V of Uffington w Woolstone and Baulking 71-81. *2 Chapel Lane, Uffington, Near Faringdon, Oxon.*

TILLYER, Desmond Benjamin. b 40. Ch Coll Cam BA 63, MA 67. Coll of Resurr Mirfield 64. **d** 66 Kens for Lon **p** 67 Lon. C of All SS Hanworth 66-70; Chap Liddon Ho Westmr 70-74; V of St Pet Eaton Square w Ch Ch Broadway Dio Lon from 74. *24 Chester Square, SW1W 9HS.* (01-730 4354)

TILNEY, Harold Arthur Rhodes. b 04. OBE 45. Linc Th 52. **d** 52 **p** 53 Nor. C of N Walsham 52-54; V of Hales w Heckingham 54-59; C-in-c of Raveningham 54-56; V 56-59; R of Southrepps 59-69. *Old Victoria House, Burnham Market, King's Lynn, Norfolk.*

TILNEY-BASSETT, Hugh Francis Emra. b 01. Keble Coll Ox BA 21, MA 26. Sarum Th Coll 24. **d** 26 **p** 27 Sarum. C of H Trin Dorch 26-29; Chap (Eccles Est) B'pore 29-31; St John Calc 31; Dinapore 34-35; Chap Lebong 31-33 and 35-36; Darjeeling 36-38; Dinapore 38-38; Kidderpore 40; Cuttack 40; Dinapore 40-46; Hon CF 47; Chap B'pore 47; R of How Caple w Sollers Hope 48-61; V of Hatherden w Tangley 61-65; Perm to Offic Dio Ex from 66. *Lychgate Cottage, Dittisham, Dartmouth, Devon.* (Dittisham 265)

TILSON, Alan Ernest. b 46. TCD. **d** 70 **p** 71 Derry. C of Ch Ch Londonderry 70-73; I of Inver w Mountcharles 73-79; Killaghtee 73-79; Dom Chap to Bp of Derry from 75; R of Leckpatrick w Dunnalong Dio Derry from 79. *1 Lowerton Road, Ballymagorry, Strabane, Co Tyrone, BT82 0LE.* (0504 883545)

TILSTON, Derek Reginald. b 27. N-W Ordin Course. **d** 73 Man **p** 74 Hulme for Man (APM). C of St Mark Bury 73-77; Em Holcombe Dio Man from 77. *50 Kendal Road West, Holcombe Brook, Ramsbottom, Bury, BL0 9SY.* (Tottington 3596)

TILSTON, John Sefton. b 31. K Coll Lon and Warm AKC 57. **d** 58 **p** 59 Liv. C of Pemberton 58-61; Kirkby (in c of St Martin Southdene) 61-70; R of Broseley w Benthall 70-80; P-in-c of Jackfield 70-80; Willey w Barrow 72-76; Linley (w Willey and Barrow from 76) 72-80; Surr 70-80; RD of Telford Severn Gorge 78-80; R of Tilehurst Dio Ox from 80. *Tilehurst Rectory, Routh Lane, Reading, RG3 4JY.* (Reading 27331)

TILTMAN, Alan Michael. b 48. Selw Coll Cam BA 70, MA 74. Cudd Coll 71. **d** 73 Huntingdon for Ely **p** 74 Ely. C of Good Shepherd Chesterton 73-77; St John Preston and Chap Preston Poly 77-79; Chap Univ of Man Inst of Sc & Tech from 79; Team V of Whitworth City and Dio Man from 79. *35 Torbay Road, Chorlton-cum-Hardy, Manchester, m21 2XE.* (061-861 9541)

TIMANYA, Emmanuel. **d** 78 **p** 79 Vic Nyan. P Dio Vic Nyan. *Box 87, Maswa, Tanzania.*

TIMBERLAKE, Neil Christopher. b 26. Kelham Th Coll. **d** 51 **p** 52 Man. C of St Benedict Ardwick Man 51-54; Ch Ch Moss Side 54-55; St Alb Stockport 55-57; St Jo Bapt Cov 57-60; V of Heath 60-68; R of Bridgetown W Austr 68-70; C of St Ambrose Leyland 70-72; Bilborough w Strelley 72-74; V of Langold Dio Southw from 74. *St Luke's Vicarage, Langold, Worksop, Notts.* (0909 730398)

TIMBRELL, Keith Stewart. b 48. Edin Th Coll 72. **d** 74 **p** 75 Blackb. C of St Pet Chorley 74-77; Altham w Clayton-le-Moors 77-79; Chap Whittingham Hosp Goosnargh from 79. *c/o Whittingham Hospital, Preston, Lancs.* (Goosnargh 531)

TIMBRELL, Maxwell Keith. St Jo Coll Morpeth ACT ThL (1st cl) 51. **d** 51 **p** 52 Bath. P-in-c of Bourke 52-57; C of Ch Ch St Lawrence Syd 57-58; All SS Hanworth 59-63; M Bush Bro of St Paul Brisb 63-67; Prin Bro of Good Shepherd Dubbo and R of Bourke 68-72; P-in-c of Par Distr of Cunnamulla 72-77; Weston Dio Newc from 77. *63 First Street, Weston, NSW, Australia 2326.* (37 1070)

TIMBUKA, Alfeji Crispo. St Cypr Coll Ngala 60. **d** 62 **p** 64 SW Tang. P Dio SW Tang. *Box 132, Njombe, Tanzania.*

TIMINS, John Francis Holmer. b 03. Clare Coll Cam 26, MA 29. Ely Th Coll 33. **d** 34 **p** 35 Southw. C of Thrumpton 34-36; R of Little Glemham w Gt Glemham 36-48; CF (EC) 40-45; Men in Disp 45; R of Long Newnton 48-52; Martlesham 52-59; Horringer w Ickworth 59-65; L to Offic Dio St E 67-75. *16 St Michael's Road, Worthing, Sussex, BN11 4SD.* (0903-206326)

TIMMONS, Edward Patrick Alfred. Univ of Sask BA 57. Em Coll Sktn LTh 51, BD 57. **d** and **p** 51 Arctic. Miss-in-c of Fort McPherson 51-56; C of St Matthias Westmount Montr 56-59; R of Hull 59-62; P-in-c of Chelsea PQ 59-62; Chap RCN 62-81; R of St Jo Moose Jaw Dio Qu'App from 81. *1124-1st Avenue North West, Moose Jaw, Sask, Canada, S6H 3N3.* (306-692 2198)

TIMMS, Ven George Boorne. b 10. St Edm Hall Ox BA (2nd cl Th) 33, MA 45. Coll of Resurr Mirfield 33. **d** 35 **p** 36 Cov. C of St Mary Magd Cov 35-38; St Bart Earley Reading 38-49; Gen Sec Angl S 38-54; Dioc Insp of Schs Ox 44-49; Pv and Sacr of S'wark Cathl 49-52; Succr 51-52; V of St Mary Virg Primrose Hill (w St Paul Hampstead from 57) 52-65; St Andr Holborn Lon 65-81; Proc Conv Lon 55-59, 64-70 and 74-81; RD of Hampstead 59-65; Preb of St Paul's Cathl Lon 64-71; Exam Chap to Bp and Dir of Ordin Tr Dio Lon 64-81; Archd of Hackney 71-81; Archd (Emer) from 81; Exam Chap to Bp of Stepney 72-81; Perm to Offic Dio Cant from 78. *Cleve Lodge, Minster-in-Thanet, Ramsgate, Kent, CT12 4BA.* (0843 821777)

TIMMS, Robert Newell. b 13. Dorch Miss Coll 33. Univ of Dur LTh 36. **d** 36 **p** 37 Lich. C of L Gornal 36-39; CF (TA-R of O) 39-46; V of Northwood Staffs 46-48; Lower Gornal 48-56; Cler Org Sec CECS Dios S'wark and Guildf 61-63; R of Watton-at-Stone 64-68; Perm to Offic Dio Glouc from 76. *30 Thrupp Lane, Stroud, Glos, GL5 2ER.* (Stroud 6992)

TIMOTHY, Gnanaraj. b 24. **d** 75 **p** 76 W Mal. P Dio W Mal. *414 England Gardens, Seremban, Malaysia.*

TIMPSON, Thomas Henry. Univ of Melb BA 36, MA 38, BEducn 52. ACT ThL 37. **d** and **p** 38 Goulb. Ho Master and Asst Chap Canberra Gr Sch 38-40; Lect Canberra Univ Coll 36-40; Chap RAAF 40-46; Chap Canberra Gr Sch 46-47; Uppingham Sch 48-50; Sen Master Canberra Gr Sch 50-54; Hd Master of Camberwell Gr Sch 55-66; Perm to Offic Dio Melb 66-72; C of H Trin Surrey Hills Dio Melb from 72. *13 Albany Crescent, Surrey Hills, Vic, Australia 3127.* (03-89 2511)

TIMS, Christopher Purefoy. b 34. St Jo Coll Auckld 70. **d** 71 **p** 72 Waik. C of Cambridge 71-73; Taumarunui 73-75; CMS Miss Dio Vic Nyan 75-77; Dio Centr Tang 77-78; V of Castle Cliff Dio Wel from 78. *34 Manuka Street, Wanganui, NZ.* (45-344)

TIN, Stephen. H Cross Coll Rang. **d** 65 **p** 66 Rang. P Dio Rang. *Kyaungdaw Gale, Daunggyi, Rangoon, Burma.*

TIN MAUNG, John. **d** 68 **p** 69 Rang. P Dio Rang. *Christ Church, Insein, Rangoon, Burma.*

TINDALE, Robert. b 1900. Linc Th Coll 28. **d** 31 **p** 32 Dur. C of Dawdon 31-34; Dursley 34-36; St Phil and St Jas Leckhampton 36-40; V of Hawkesbury 40-45; Maisemore 45-58; PC of Rangeworthy 58-66. *Inglenook, Success Road, Houghton-le-Spring, Co Durham, DH4 4TJ.*

TINDALL, David Nigel. b 14. St Chad's Coll Dur BA 41. Linc Th Coll 42. **d** 42 **p** 43 Linc. C of Bourne 42-45; Crosby 45-50; V of Elsham 50-57; V of Worlaby 50-57; Rillington 57-63; V of Scampston 57-63; C-in-c of Yedingham 57-63; PC of Fatfield 63-69; V 69-75; Trimdon 75-79; C-in-c of Deaf Hill w Langdale 75-77. *4 Linden Grove, Leadgate, Consett, Co Durham.* (Consett 508160)

TINDALL, Edward Frederick. b 08. St Andr Coll Pampisford 44. **d** 45 Knaresborough for Ripon **p** 46 Ripon. C of St Mary Beeston 45-48; All SS Leeds 48-51; Adel 51-56; V of Kippax w Gt Preston 56-66; PC (V from 69) of Arkengarthdale 66-75. *2 Mallard Road, Scotton, Catterick Garrison, N Yorks, DL9 3NP.* (0748 832345)

TINDALL, Canon Frederick Cryer. b 1900. AKC (1st cl) 22, Univ of Lon BD 23, McCaul Hebr Pri and Trench Gr Pri (Spec) 23, 2nd cl Phil of Relig 27. Ely Th Coll 23. **d** 24 **p** 25 Lon. C of St Cypr St Marylebone 24-28; Lect and Bursar Chich Th Coll 28-30; Vice-Prin 30-36; L to Offic Dio Chich 28-39; Perm to Offic Dios Win and Portsm; Warden of Connaught Hall and Lect in Th Univ Coll Southn and Hon Chap to Bp of Chich 36-39; V of St Aug Preston Pk Brighton 39-50; Proc Conv Chich 36-45 and 49-50; Proc Conv Sarum 50-75; Exam Chap to Bp of Chich 41-50; Can and Preb of Hampstead in Chich Cathl 48-50; Prin of Sarum Th Coll 50-65; Prin (Emer) from 65; Can and Preb of Sarum Cathl 50-81; Can (Emer) from 81; Fell K Coll Lon from 51; Pro-Prolocutor of Lower Ho of Conv of Cant 59-75; Cler Judge in Court of Arches 69-80. *16 The Close, Salisbury, Wilts, SP1 2EB.* (0722 22373)

TINDALL, Canon Robert. b 1893. Coll of Resurr Mirfield 12. **d** 21 **p** 22 Bradf. C of Heaton 21-26; V of Oakworth 26-32; St Wilfrid Lidget Green 32-40; St Andr Yeadon 40-56; St Marg Bentham 56-64; Hon Can of Bradf 53-64; Can (Emer) from 64; RD of Ewecross 61-64. *29 Littledale Road, Brookhouse, Lancaster.*

TINDYEEBWA, Stanley. Bp Tucker Coll Mukono 60. **d** 63 Ankole-K **p** 67 W Bugan. P Dio W Bugan. *PO Box 272, Masaka, Uganda.*

TINGAY, Kevin Gilbert Xavier. b 43. Univ of Sussex BA

79, Chich Th Coll 79. **d** 80 Chich **p** 81 Lewes for Chich. C of W Tarring Dio Chich from 80. *24 Upton Road, Worthing, W Sussex, BN13 1BX.*

TINGEY, Canon William Henry. St Chad's Coll Regina. **d** 41 **p** 42 Qu'App. C of Ogema 41-42; I 42-44; R of Cupar 44-50; Grenfell 50-56; Fernie and of Michel 56-61; I of St Luke Regina Dio Qu'App from 61; Hon Can of Qu'App from 74. *3240 Montague Street, Regina, Sask., Canada.* (306-586 8974)

TINGLE, Mangas Rosyn. **d** 78 **p** 79 New Hebr. P Dio New Hebr 78-80; Dio Vanuatu from 80. *Pentecost, Vanuatu.*

TINGLE, Michael Barton. b 31. Bps' Coll Cheshunt 65. **d** 67 **p** 68 St Alb. C of Totteridge 67-70; St Mary (in c of St Mark) Hitchin 70-73; V of Gt Gaddesden 73-78; St Anselm Belmont Dio Lon from 78. *St Anselm's Vicarage, Ventnor Avenue, Stanmore, Middx, HA7 2HU.* (01-907 3186)

TINKAMANYIRE, Philemon. Bp Tucker Coll Mukono 77. **d** 80 E Ank. d Dio E Ank. *PO Box 14, Mbarara, Uganda.*

TINKASIMIRE, Yusufu. **d** 78 **p** 79 Ruw. P Dio Ruw. *PO Kyegegwa, Uganda.*

TINKER, Preb Eric Franklin. b 20. Ex Coll Ox BA 42, MA 46. Linc Th Coll 42. **d** 44 Bp Heywood for St Alb **p** 45 St Alb. C of St Pet Gr Berkhamsted 44-46; Rugby 46-48; CF 48-49; Lon Sec SCM 49-51; C of E Chap to Univ of Lon and Chap to Cant Hall Lon 51-55; V of St Jas Handsworth 55-65; Enfield 65-69; Sen Chap Univs and Polys in Lon from 69; Preb of St Paul's Cathl Lon from 69: Dir of Educn Dios Lon & S'wark 72-80; Gen Sec Lon Dioc Bd of Educn from 80. *26 John Street, WC1N 2BL.* (01-242 8184)

TINKER, Michael Jonathan Russell. b 50. Univ of York BA 72. Qu Coll Birm Dipl Th 74. **d** 75 **p** 76 Birm. C of Castle Vale 75-78; Dom Chap to Bp of Birm 78-80; R of All SS Stretford Dio Man from 80. *233 Barton Road, Stretford, Manchester, M32 9RB.* (061-865 1350)

TINKLER, Ian Henry. Selw Coll Cam BA 57, MA 61. Westcott Ho Cam. **d** 60 **p** 61 Newc T. C of All SS Gosforth 60-65; Asst Chap at Brussels 65-68; R of S Ferriby Dio Linc from 68; V of Horkstow Dio Linc from 68; R of All SS Saxby Dio Linc from 72. *South Ferriby Rectory, Barton-on-Humber, Lincs.* (Saxby All Saints 258)

TINNE, Derek Ernest. b 08. Univ Coll Ox BA 31, MA 65. **d** and **p** 75 Tuam. C of Omey Dio Tuam from 75. *Emlaghmore Lodge, Ballyconneely, Co Galway, Irish Republic.*

TINNISWOOD, Robin Jeffries. b 41. K Coll Lon BSc (Eng) 64. Univ of Bris Dipl Th 69. Wells Th Coll 67. **d** 70 **p** 71 B & W. C of St Mich AA Yeovil 70-72; Gt Marlow 72-74; Christow w Bridford and Ashton w Trusham 74-77; P-in-c of St Paul's Burnt House Lane Ex 77-78; Team V (w Heavitree) 78-79; Ifield Dio Chich from 79. *10 Martyrs Avenue, Langley Green, Crawley, RH11 7RZ.* (Crawley 518419)

TINNISWOOD, William Robert. b 11. K Coll Lon and Warm AKC 57. **d** 57 **p** 58 S'wark. C of Barnes 57-59; V of Defford w Besford 59-62; Bp Auckland 62-67; L to Offic Dio St E from 67; Chap to Bp of St E 69-71. *The Links, Church Road, Elmswell, Bury St Edmunds, Suff, IP30 9DY.* (Elmswell 40382)

TINSLEY, Bernard Murray. b 26. Univ of Nottm BA 51. Westcott Ho Cam 51. **d** 53 **p** 54 Sheff. C of Rotherham 53-56; Goole 56-58; V of Thorpe Hesley 58-61; R of Alverdiscott w Huntshaw (w Newton Tracey, Horwood and Yarnscombe from 78) Dio Ex from 61; Newton Tracey 61-78; Beaford w Roborough 67-78; V of St Giles-in-the-Wood 67-78; V of Yarnscombe 67-78; RD of Torrington from 81. *Newton Tracey Rectory, Barnstaple, N Devon, EX31 3PL.* (Newton Tracey 292)

TINSLEY, Derek. N-W Ordin Course 73. **d** 76 **p** 77 Liv. C of St Faith Gt Crosby 76-80; V of St Anne Wigan Dio Liv from 80. *154 Beech Hill Avenue, Beech Hill, Wigan, WN6 7TA.* (Wigan 41930)

TINSLEY, Derek Michael. b 35. ALCD 66 (LTh from 74). **d** 66 Warrington for Liv **p** 67 Liv. C of Rainhill 66-68; Chalfont St Pet (in c of All SS Oval Way) 68-73; R of N Buckingham Dio Ox from 73; RD of Buckingham from 78. *Maids Moreton Rectory, Buckingham, MK18 1QD.* (Buckingham 3246)

✠ **TINSLEY, Right Rev Ernest John.** b 19. St Jo Coll Dur de Bury Scho and BA (1st cl Engl) 40, 1st cl Th 42, MA 43, BD 45. Fell of Dur Univ 42. Westcott Ho Cam 43. **d** 42 **p** 43 Dur. C of St Mary le Bow Dur 42-44; S Westoe 44-46; Lect in Th Univ Coll Hull 46-54; Sen Lect 54-61; Hd 61-62; C of St John Newland Hull 47-48; St Alb Hull 48-55; Lect of St Mary Lowgate Hull 55-62; Exam Chap to Abp of York 57-63; to Bp of Sheff 63-75; Prof of Th Univ of Leeds 62-76; L to offic Dio Ripon 62-75; Hon Can of Ripon 66-75; Cons Ld Bp of Bris in S'wark Cathl 6 Jan 76 by Abp of Cant; Bps of Derby, Ex, Sheff, Heref, Lich, Nor, Portsm, S'wark, Leic and Ely; Bps Suffr of Edmon, Huntingdon, Malmesbury and Doncaster; and others; Special Lect in Th Univ of Bris from 76; Chairman Gen Syn Bd of Educn & Nat Society from 79. *Bishop's House, Clifton Hill, Bristol, BS8 1BW.* (Bristol 30222)

TINSLEY, Canon John. b 17. K Coll Lon and Warm AKC (1st cl) and Jelf Pri 49. **d** 49 **p** 50 S'wark. C of St Marg Putney 49-56; Bp's Chap to Youth 51-56; V of St Paul Wimbledon Pk 56-70; RD of Wandsworth 69-70; V of St Jo Evang Redhill 70-80; RD of Reigate 76-80; Hon Can of S'wark Cathl 80; Can (Emer) from 80; P-in-c of Middlezoy 80-81; Othery 80-81; Moorlinch w Stawell and Sutton Mallet 80-81; V of Middlezoy and Othery and Moorlinch w Stawell & Sutton Mallet Dio B & W from 81. *Vicarage, North Lane, Othery, Bridgwater, Somt, TA7 0QG.* (Burrowbridge 700)

TINSLEY, Canon John Eaves. b 14. Late Scho of Univ Coll Dur BA (2nd cl Th) 36, MA 39. Wells Th Coll 36. **d** 37 **p** 38 York. C of St Paul Middlesbrough 37-40; Tutor and Lect Lich Th Coll 40-41; C of St Francis Dudley 41-42; C-in-c of Gt Ayton w Easby 42-45; St Chad York 45-47; Whitby 47-48; V of Hollym w Withernsea 48-66; St Mary Sculcoates Hull Dio York from 66; RD of S Holderness 60-66; M Gen Syn from 70; Can and Preb of York Minster from 72; M Crown Appts Comm from 77. *12 Eldon Grove, Beverley Road, Hull, Yorks.* (Hull 43417)

TIPLADY, Frederick Thomas. b 37. Sir Geo Williams Univ BA (Phil) 65. Trin Coll Tor STB 68. **d** 68 **p** 69 Montr. I of Arundel 70-73; R of Ch of Redeemer City and Dio Montr from 73. *5620 Angers Street, Montreal 205, PQ, Canada.* (514-769 4255)

TIPP, James Edward. b 45. Oak Hill Coll 73. **d** 75 Tonbridge for Roch **p** 76 Roch. C of Cray (w St Paul's Cray to 77) 75-78; Southborough 78-82; V of Snodland w Lower Birling Dio Roch from 82. *Vicarage, St Katherine's Lane, Snodland, Kent.* (0634 240232)

TIPPEN, Wallis Percival. b 1895. Lich Th Coll 22. **d** 24 **p** 25 Roch. C of E Farleigh 24-26; All SS Belvedere 26-27; East Malling (in c of H Trin New Hythe) 27-31; C-in-c of St Jo Evang Conv Distr Bexley 31-32; C of Redenhall w Harleston 32-34; R of Alby w Thwaite All SS 34-43; Tavenham 43-44; Chap Gt Yarmouth Inst 43-44; C-in-c of Drayton w Hellesdon 43-44; R of Baconsthorpe 44-46; V of St Marg Barb 46-47; R of Baconsthorpe w Plumstead 47-53; V of Hempstead-by-Holt 47-53; Dersingham 53-59; Cowlinge 59-63. *18 Offas Lane, Winslow, Bucks, MK18 3OS*

TIPPER, David Allen. b 21. Tyndale Hall Bris 54. **d** 56 **p** 57 Man. C of St Clem Higher Openshaw 56-59; V of Roughtown 59-65; Balderstone Rochdale 65-79; P-in-c of Linton w Upton Bp and Aston Ingham Dio Heref 79; R from 80. *Linton Rectory, Ross-on-Wye, Herefs.* (Gorsley 472)

TIPPER, Michael William. b 38. Univ of Hull BSc 59, MSc 61. Em & St Chad's Coll Sktn 72. **d** 73 **p** 74 Bran. **d** of MacGregor 73-75; Lynn Lake 75-77; R of Amcotts (w Garthorpe and Luddington from 79) 77-79; P-in-c of Luddington and Garthorpe 77-79; R of Sask-Gateway 79-80; V of Aycliffe Dio Dur from 80. *Aycliffe Vicarage, The Wynd, Darlington, Co Durham, DL5 6JT.* (Aycliffe 313395)

TIPPETT, Ernest James Latham. b 13. **d** 68 **p** 69 Bris. Hon C of St Paul Bedminster 68-73; Publ Pr Dio Bris from 73; P-in-c of Hankerton Dio Bris from 80; Long Newnton Dio Bris from 80. *35 Follyfield, Hankerton, Malmesbury, Wilts.* (Crudwell 254)

TIPPING, Angus Cornwell. Moore Th Coll Syd ACT ThL 45. **d** 47 Syd **p** 48 Bp C V Pilcher for Syd. C of St Luke Mosman 47-50; R of St Aug Stanmore 50-56; Campbelltown 56-66; St Anne Strathfield Dio Syd 66-78 and from 79. *42 Homebush Road, Strathfield, NSW, Australia 2135.* (76-6349)

TIPPING, John Henry. b 27. St Mich Coll Llan 63. **d** 65 **p** 66 Swan B. C of Clydach 65-68; Oystermouth 68-70; V of Llangynllo w Bleddfa 70-79; Cwmdeuddwr w Nantgwyllt, St Harmon and Llanwrthwl 79-80; R of Ashton Gifford Dio Sarum from 80. *Codford Rectory, Warminster, Wilts.*

TIPPING, John Woodman. b 42. K Coll Lon and Warm AKC 65. **d** 66 **p** 67 Cant. C of St Sav Croydon 66-70; St Mary Bromley Kent 70-72; V of Brockley Hill Dio S'wark from 72. *5 Lowther Hill, SE23.* (01-690 2499)

TIPPING, Murray Jesse Rushton. Hur Coll Ont LTh 73. **d** and **p** 53 Alg. C of Sault Ste Marie 53-59; I of Ch Ch N Bay 59-63; CF (Canad) from 63. *c/o A G Branch, Army HQ, Ottawa, Ont, Canada.*

TIRRELL, Canon Leslie Burditt. b 07. Univ of Lon BSc (Spec) 27. Sarum Th Coll 28. **d** 30 **p** 31 Leic. C of Em Ch Loughborough 30-34; Alnwick 34-37; V of Ulgham 37-41; Chap Tynemouth Sch and V of Tynemouth Priory 41-49; Surr 43-49; Newc T Dioc Insp of Schs 44-48; Dir of Relig Educn Dios Lon and S'wark 49-71; LPr Dio S'wark from 49; Hon Can of S'wark 51-71; Can (Emer) from 71; Proc Conv S'wark 59-64; Dep Gen Sec NS 71-75; Perm to Offic Dio Guildf from 72; Schs Inspector Dio Guildf 77-80. *Fairwinds, Park Corner Drive, East Horsley, Surrey.* (048-65 3376)

TIRUGURWA, Amos. **d** 74 **p** 75 Ank. P Dio Ank. *PO Ibanda, Mbarara, Uganda.*

TISANI, Ezra Vuyisile Kenton. b 41. St Pet Coll Alice. **d** 68 **p** 69 Grahmstn. P Dio Grahmstn 68-79; Dioc Dir of Relig Educn Grahmstn 76-78; Publ Pr Dio Southw from 79. *26 Station Road, Lowdham, Nottingham, NG14 7DW.* (Lowdham 4330)

TISCH, Gerald Winston. Ch Ch Coll LTh 65. **d** 64 **p** 66 Ch Ch. C of Shirley 64-66; Spreydon-Hoon Hay 66-69; V of Tinui 71-72; Featherstone 72-74; Woolston 74-77. *10 St John Street, Christchurch 6, NZ.* (841-737)

TISDALL, Charles Gordon St Clair. b 14. Wadh Coll Ox BA (3rd cl Th) 36, MA 40. Wycl Hall Ox 36. **d** 37 **p** 38 Sarum. C of St Mary Weymouth 37-39; Perm to Offic Dio Sarum 39-43; CMS Miss Palestine 43-44; Iran 44-50; C of Lah Cathl 50-51; P-in-c of Gojra 51-54; P-in-c of Clarkabad 55-58; V of H Trin Ashby-de-la-Zouch 59-68; R of Earl Soham w Cretingham 68-80; P-in-c of Ashfield 77-80; Perm to Offic Dio St E from 80. *8 Pembroke Road, Framlingham, Woodbridge, Suff, IP13 9HA.* (0728 723437)

TISDALL, Douglas Michael. Trin Coll Tor BA 58, MA 61. FTCL 59. Wycl Coll Tor LTh 65. **d** 65 Bp Snell for Tor **p** 65 Tor. C of St Matthias Tor 65-67. *99 Gloucester Street, Toronto 5, Ont, Canada.*

TISDALL, Geoffrey Michael. b 43. Monash Univ Melb BA 64. Trin Coll Melb ACT Th Schol 71. **d** 71 **p** 72 Melb. C of St Steph Belmont 71-72; Kenilworth 73-76; P-in-c of Bundoora 76-80; I of St Pet Box Hill Dio Melb from 80. *Vicarage, Whitehorse Road, Box Hill, Vic, Australia 3128.*

TITCHENER, Neville Cecil Knox. St Jo Coll Auckld. **d** 40 **p** 41 Nel. C of Cathl Ch Nel 40-42; CF 40; Chap RNZAF 41-42; V of Havelock 42-47; Actg V of Sounds 42-47; C of Ch Ch Wanganui 47-48; V of Kitwitea 48-52; Porirua 52-58; Khandallah Wel 58-73; Perm to Offic Dio Wel from 73. *10 Burnham Street, Seatoun, Wellington, NZ.* (881-353)

TITFORD, Richard Kimber. b 45. Univ of E Anglia BA 67. Ripon Coll Cudd 78. **d** and **p** 80 Man. C of St Leon Middleton Dio Man from 80. *206 Rochdale Road, Middleton, Manchester, M24 2GH.* (061-643 4913)

TITLER, Stanley George. St Columb's Hall Wang ACT ThL 34. **d** 32 **p** 33 Wang. C of Longwood 32-35; R of Kiewa 35-38; Yackandandah 38-40; Nathalia 40-42; Chap CMF 42-44; V of St Paul Myrtleford 44-63; L to Offic Dio Wang from 63. *Wangaratta, Vic, Australia.*

TITTENSOR, Sidney. b 10. St Aid Coll 60. **d** 62 **p** 63 Lich. C of Blurton 62-65; V of Fazeley 65-71; Alstonfield 71-76; V of Wetton 71-76; C-in-c of Ch Ch Burton-on-Trent 76-79. *22 Wissage Lane, Lichfield, WS13 6DF.*

TITTERINGTON, Canon John Milne. b 23. St Cath S Ox BA 49, MA 53. Linc Th Coll 49. **d** 51 **p** 52 Man. C of St Pet Westleigh 51-55; Newton Heath 55-56; R 56-68; V of All SS and Marts Langley 68-72; R of Newchurch-in-Rossendale (St Nich w St Jo Newchurch from 73) 72-80; RD of Rossendale 72-80; M Gen Syn Man 74-80; Hon Can of Man 76-80; Can (Emer) from 80; Lect Newton Th Coll Popondetta from 81. *Box 162 PO, Popondetta, OP, Papua New Guinea.*

TITTERINGTON, Mark. b 24. St Aid Coll 66. **d** and **p** 67 Blackb. C of Chorley Blackb 67-71; St Steph (in c of St Anne) Blackpool 71-75; V of Woodplumpton 75-78; St Matt Preston Dio Blackb from 78. *20 Fishwick View, Preston, Lancs, PR1 4YA.* (Preston 794312)

TITTERTON, Harold Graham. NZ Bd of Th Stud LTh 61. **d** 59 **p** 60 Wai. C of Havelock N 59-61; Hastings 61-62; V of Mahora 62-67; Otumoetai Par Distr 67-74; Te Puke Par Distr Dio Wai from 74. *28 Tui Street, Te Puke, NZ.*

TITTLEY, Donald Frank. b 22. ACP 70, LCP 74. St Jo Coll Dur 78. **d** 80 Newc T **p** 81 Bp Gill for Newc T (APM). C of St Paul Cullercoats Dio Newc T from 80. *4 Waterford Crescent, Whitley Bay, T & W, NE26 2EA.*

TITUS, David Vincent. St Pet Coll Alice. **d** 71 **p** 72 Capetn. C of Matroosfontein 71-76; P-in-c of Steenberg 76-80; R of St Helena Bay Dio Capetn from 80. *Box 14, Laaiplek 7370, CP, S Africa.*

TITUS, John David. b 21. **d** 72 Bp Wade for Capetn **p** 72 Capetn. C of Robertson Dio Capetn from 72. *Aster Avenue, Bergsig, Montagu 6720, S Africa.* (Montagu 86)

TITUS, Joseph. b 47. **d** 71 **p** 72 Geo. C of All SS Mossel Bay 71-77; P-in-c of Oudtshoom 77-80; R of Lenasia w Grasmere Dio Johann from 80. *Box 992198, Odin Park 1825, Johannesburg, S Africa.*

TITUS, Joseph George. Univ of Tor BA 54. Wycl Coll Tor LTh 54. **d** 54 New Westmr **p** 55 BC. Chap Columbia Coast Miss 54-59; I of Petersville w Greenwich 59-62; Chap RCN 62-71; R of Colwood Dio BC from 71. *520 Mountview Avenue, Victoria, BC, Canada.* (604-478 4330)

TITUS, Julian John Claude. b 46. St Pet Coll Alice 67. **d** 69 Capetn **p** 71 Bp Wade for Capetn. C of Bonteheuwel 69-72; Lansdowne 72-74; R of Hopefield 74-78; Huguenot Dio Capetn from 78. *5 Maasdorp Street, Huguenot 7645, CP, S Africa.* (Paarl 28327)

TITUS, Macdonald Atwell. **d** 45 **p** 46 St Jo Kaffr. P Dio St John's 45-67. *PO Coghlans, Transkei, CP, S Africa.*

TITUS, Matthew Mgubuli. b 16. **d** 79 **p** 80 St John's (APM). P Dio St John's. *PO All Saints, Transkei.*

TITUS, Noel Fitzallan. St Chad's Coll Dur BA (2nd cl Th) 63. Univ of W Indies MA (Hist) 68. **d** 63 **p** 64 Trinid. C of San Fernando 63-66; R of St Jos w San Juan 66-71; Vice Prin and Tutor Codr Coll Barb 72-75; P-in-c of St Lawr I and Dio Barb 75-77; R from 77. *St Lawrence Rectory, Christ Church, Barbados, WI.*

TIU JO, **d** 61 Bp Ah Mya for Rang **p** 62 Rang. P Dio Rang 61-70; Dio Akyab from 70; Hon Can of Akyab from 77. *St Paul's Church, Nkakuseaung, Paletwa, Arakan, Burma.*

TIYO, Herbert Tillard Mjuza. St Bede's Coll Umtata 49. **d** 50 Grahmstn for St Jo Kaffr **p** 53 St Jo Kaffr. P Dio St John's. *Box 52, Qumbu 5180, Transkei, S Africa.*

TIZZARD, David John. b 40. Sarum Th Coll 65. **d** 68 **p** 69 Worc. C of H Innoc Kidderminster 68-70; Chap Miss to Seamen Gravesend 70-72; Hon C of St Geo Gravesend 70-73; Nat Sec Flying Angel League of Miss to Seamen 72-73; PV of Truro Cathl 73-75; Team V of Bemerton 75-79; Adv on Social Responsibility and Chap to the Deaf Dio Sarum from 79. *48 Bouverie Avenue, Salisbury, Wilts.* (Sarum 332500)

TIZZARD, Dudley Frank. b 19. Roch Th Coll 63. **d** 65 **p** 66 Cant. C of Bearsted 65-68; St Martin w St Paul Cant 68-71; Chap HM Prison Cant 68-71; V of Petham w Waltham 71-75; C-in-c of Elmsted w Hastingleigh 71-74; Lower Hardres w Nackington 73-75; C of St Jo Bapt Sevenoaks 75-78; Perm to Offic Dio Cant from 78. *12 Fullers Close, Bearsted, Kent.* (Maidstone 39518)

TO, Albany Shiu-kin. St Pet Hall Sing BTh 61. Trin Th Coll Sing. **d** 61 Sing **p** 62 Kuala Lumpur for Sing. P Dio Sing from 61; Commiss Jess from 67. *St Hilda's Church, Ceylon Road, Katong, Singapore 15.*

TO, Paul Chung Fong. **d** 54 Hong **p** 56 Maur. Chinese Missr Dio Maur. *c/o Bishop's House, Phoenix, Mauritius.*

TOA, Oscar Arthur. St Pet Coll Siota 59. **d** 62 **p** 63 Melan. P Dio Melan 62-75; Dio New Hebr 75-80; Dio Vanuatu from 80. *Labultamwata, Pentecost, Vanuatu.*

TOAMASINA, Lord Bishop of. *See* Rafanomezana, Right Rev Samuel.

TOASE, Richard Whiteside. Trin Coll Dub BA 59. **d** 60 **p** 61 Down. C of Glencraig 60-62; St Thos Montr 62-64; R of Dunham 64-78; P-in-c of Johore Bharu 78-80. *5 Jalan Mustapha, Johore Bharu, W Malaysia.*

TOBIAS, Edwin John Rupert. b 16. TCD BA 40, MA 59. **d** 40 Down **p** 41 Dub. C of Donaghadee 40-41; Drumcondra N Strand 41-44; St Fin Barre's Cathl Cork 44-47; I of Durrus 47-49; Lislee w Timoleague 49-55; C of Rathmines 55-59; Hon Cler V of Ch Ch Cathl Dub 55-59; I of Kilbixy 59-77; Killucan Dio Meath from 77; RD of Loughseudy and Mullingar from 68. *Rectory, Killucan, Westmeath, Irish Republic.*

TOBIAS, William Trevor. b 10. St Steph Ho Ox 62. **d** 63 **p** 64 Lon. C of Perivale 63-69; P-in-c of St Mark Hanwell 69-80. *58 Claremont Road, W13 0DG.* (01-997 6023)

TOBIN, Gregory Francis. b 51. Univ of Syd BSc 72. Moore Th Coll Syd ThL 80. BD. **d** and **p** 80 Armid. C of Armid Dio Armid from 80. *40 Proctor Street, Armidale, NSW, Australia 2350.*

TOBIN, Richard Francis. b 44. Chich Th Coll 76. **d** 78 Portsm **p** 79 Chelmsf. C of St Alb West Leigh Conv Distr Havant 78-79; Halstead Dio Chelmsf from 79. *47 Tidings Hill, Halstead, Essex, CO9 1BL.*

TOBIN, Vincent McBain. b 42. Dalhousie Univ Halifax NS BA 63, MA 65. Atlantic Sch of Th Halifax NS MDiv 75. **d** 75 NS **p** 76 Bp Hatfield for NS. C of St Mark Halifax Dio NS from 76. *6238 Lawrence Street, Halifax, NS, Canada.*

TODD, Alastair. b 20. CMG 71. CCC Ox BA 45. Dipl Th (Lon) 65. Sarum Wells Th Coll 71. **d** 73 Chich **p** 74 Lewes for Chich. C of Willingdon 73-77; P-in-c of St Aug Preston Dio Chich 77-78; V from 78. *32 Florence Road, Brighton, Sussex, BN1 6DJ.* (Brighton 561755)

TODD, George Robert. b 21. Sarum Wells Th Coll 74. **d** 76 **p** 77 B & W. C of Wellington & Distr Dio B & W from 76. *15 John Grinter Way, Wellington, Somt.*

TODD, John Lindsay. b 22. Univ of Wales (Ban) BA 49. St Mich Coll Llan. **d** 51 **p** 52 St A. C of Chirk 51-53; Eglwysrhos 53-58; V of Guilsfield Dio St A from 58. *Guilsfield Vicarage, Welshpool, Powys.* (Welshpool 3879)

TODD, Leslie Alwill. b 15. St Aid Coll 46. **d** 48 B & W for Gui **p** 49 Gui. C of St Phil Georgetn 48-52; R of St Patr Canje 52-56; Barrouallie 56-58; P-in-c of St Serf Shettelston Glas 58-59; C of St Faith Stoke Newington 59-60; R of Carriacou Grenadines 60-67; V of St Geo Bris 67-70; P-in-c of Good Shepherd Pinder's Point Grand Bahama 70-72; R of Biabou 72-73; C of H Redeemer Clerkenwell 73-74; Chap Nat Hosp for Nervous Diseases Lon 74-81. *Calle de Flor 7, Gualchos Prov de Granada, Spain.*

TODD, Leslie James. b 08. ALCD 31. **d** 31 **p** 32 Southw. C of St Ann Nottm 31-35; St Luke Ramsgate 35-38; V of St Thos Crookes 38-42; St Paul Chatham 42-48; Sec Young People's Dept CCCS 48-53; V of St Paul Ap Gatten Shanklin 53-64; Lon Sec Irish Ch Miss and L to Offic Dio Guildf 64-65; Dio Portsm 65-79; Dio Win 79-81. *Calle de Flor 7, Gualchos, Prov de Granada, Spain.*

TODD, Norman Henry. b 19. Univ of Lon BPharm 42. Fitzw Ho Cam BA 50, MA 55. Univ of Nottm PhD 78. Westcott Ho Cam 50. **d** 52 **p** 53 Southw. C of St Marg Aspley 52-54; Chap Westcott Ho Cam 55-58; Exam Chap to Bp of Cov 56-59; V of Arnold 58-65; Rolleston w Fiskerton and Morton 65-69; Can Res of Southw Cathl 65-69; R of Elston 71-76; V of E Stoke w Syerston 71-76; C-in-c of Sibthorpe 71-76; Bp's Adv on Tr Dio Southw from 76; C of Averham w Kelham 76-80; V of Rolleston w Fiskerton and Morton Dio Southw from 80; P-in-c of Upton Dio Southw from 80. *Rolleston Vicarage, Newark, Notts.*

TODD, Roy Charles. St Mich Ho Adel 54. ACT ThL 61. **d** 58 **p** 59 Kalg. C of Boulder 58-59; C of St Jo Cathl Kalg and P-in-c of Leonora-Gwalia 59-60; P-in-c of Norseman 60-64; Gooa 64-68; R of Mt Pleasant 68-72; Mt Hawthorn 72-79; Cummins w Tumby Bay Dio Willoch from 79. *5 Phyllis Street, Tumby Bay, W Australia 5605.* (88-2175)

TODD, Rupert Granville. ALCD 61. **d** 61 **p** 62 Ely. C of Wisbech 61-64; Seagoe 64-66; R of Lissan 66-69; Dioc C Dio Arm from 70. *47 Abercorn Park, Portadown, Co Armagh, N Ireland.*

TODD, William Andrew Hankins. Qu Coll Cam BA 53, MA 58. Westcott Ho Cam 53. **d** 55 **p** 56 Lon. C of St Luke Chelsea 55-58; Min of St Hugh's Eccles Distr Eyres Monsell Leic 58-66; C of Vaudreuil 75-77; I of Valois Dio Montr from 77. *31 Prince Edward Avenue, Pointe Claire, PQ, Canada.* (514-697 0381)

TODD, William Colquhoun Duncan. K Coll Lon and Warm AKC 53. **d** 54 **p** 55 Lon. C of St Steph w St Jo Evang Westmr 54-59; C-in-c of Leigh Pk Conv Distr 59-72; R of Bp's Hatfield Dio St Alb from 72. *Rectory, Fore Street, Hatfield, Herts.* (Hatfield 62072)

TODD, William Moorhouse. b 26. Lich Th Coll 54. **d** 57 Warrington for Liv **p** 58 Liv. C of W Derby 57-61; V of Norris Green Dio Liv from 61. *St Christopher's Vicarage, Norris Green, Liverpool 11.* (051 226 1637)

TODHUNTER, Frank. b 14. Edin Th Coll 37. **d** 41 Penrith for Carl **p** 42 Carl. C of St John Workington 41-42; Ch Ch Falkirk 42-44; St Paul w St Geo (in c of St Barn Miss) Edin 44-47; CF 47-52; V of Clifton-in-Workington 52-54; R of Cranbrook W Austr 54-56; Margaret River 56-58; Wagin W Austr 58-59; St Congan Turriff 59-60; R of St Luke Cuminestown 59-60; C of St Gabr (in c of All SS) Pimlico 60-63; R of Baxterley 63-80; V of Merevale w Bentley 63-80. *2 Church House Mews, Sheepy Magna, Atherstone, Warws, CV9 3QS.* (Tamworth 880690)

TOFT, Canon Charles. Peterho Cam BA 13, MA 17. **d** 14 **p** 15 Birm. C of St Paul Balsall Heath 14-16; Northfield 17-22; R of Wiveton w Glandford 22-56; R of Cley-next-the-Sea 35-58; RD of Holt 47-65; Hon Can of Nor from 55; V of Weybourne w U Sheringham 58-66; Perm to Offic Dio Nor from 66. *Glandford, East Avenue, Brundall, Norwich, NOR 86Z.*

TOFTS, Jack. b 31. Roch Th Coll 66. **d** 68 Ripon **p** 69 Knaresborough for Ripon. C of Richmond Yorks 68-71; St Jo Bapt Croydon 71-74; C-in-c of Upwell Christchurch 74-78; Welney 74-78; R of Newton-in-the-Isle Dio Ely from 78; Tydd St Giles Dio Ely from 78; V of Gorefield Dio Ely from 78. *Newton Rectory, Wisbech, Cambs, PE13 5EX,* (Newton 205)

TOGORO, Ephraim. St Pet Coll Siota 62. **d** 64 **p** 65 Melan. P Dio Melan 64-75; Dio New Hebr from 75. *Bwatnapni, Pentecost, New Hebrides.*

TOHI, Viliami Tavakefai'ana. b 37. Pacific Th Coll Suva BD 72. **d** 72 **p** 73 Polyn. C of St Matt Samabula 72-75; Labasa 76; P-in-c of W Samoa Dio Polyn 77-78; V from 78. *Box 16, Apia, Western Samoa.*

TOKE, Frank Bollen. d 37 **p** 46 Melan. P Dio Melan 37-75. *Verahue, Guadalcanal, Solomon Islands.*

TOKOTA, Sipho Aubrey. b 50. St Bede's Coll Umtata Dipl Th 78. **d** 78 **p** 79 Port Eliz. C of H Spirit Ch Kwazakele Dio Port Eliz from 78. *c/o PO Box 42, Kwazakele, Port Elizabeth 6205, S Africa.*

TOLEY, Robin David. b 44. Ex Coll Ox BA (2nd cl Phil Pol and Econ) 66. Clifton Th Coll 66. **d** 68 **p** 69 Ex. C of St Jude Plymouth 68-72; St Jo Bapt Harborne 72-74; Vocation Sec CPAS 74-79; V of Shenstone Dio Lich from 79. *Shenstone Vicarage, Lichfield, Staffs, WS14 0JB.* (Shenstone 480286)

TOLL, Brian Arthur. b 35. Linc Th Coll 64. **d** 65 **p** 66 Linc. C of St Aid Cleethorpes 65-68; Hadleigh w Layham and Shelley 69-72; R of Claydon and Barham Dio St E from 72. *Claydon Rectory, Ipswich, IP6 0EB.* (Ipswich 830362)

TOLLEMACHE (formerly WRIGLEY), Harry Norman. Linc Th Coll 33. **d** 34 **p** 35 Liv. C of St Geo Wigan 34-35; R of W Leake w Ratcliffe-on-Soar and Kingston-on-Soar 35-38; V of Sutton-in-Ashfield 38-44; Surr 38-44; R of Liss 44-53; Binstead 53-58; L to Offic Dio St E from 58. *Bentley House, Ipswich, Suff.* (Copdock 220)

TOLLEY, Canon George. b 25. Univ of Lon BSc 45, MSc 48, PhD 52. Linc Th Coll 66. **d** 67 **p** 68 Sheff. C of St Andr Sharrow City and Dio Sheff from 67; Hon Can of Sheff from 76. *74 Furniss Avenue, Dore, Sheffield, S17 3QP.*

TOLLIT, Denis Fitzwilliam. b 11. St Chad's Coll Dur BA 34. **d** 35 Liv **p** 36 Warrington for Liv. C of St Columba Anfield 35-38; Spalding 38-47; CF (EC) 40-45; V of Messingham w E Butterwick 47-54; Gosberton 54-58; The Sav Bolton-le-Moors 58-66; R of Bolton (w Ireby and Uldale from 75) Cumb 66-81; C-in-c of Ireby w Uldale 72-75. *Jacky Garth, Threlkeld, Keswick, CA12 4RX.*

TOLO, Walter Edwin. St Paul's Th Coll Limuru 64. **d** 67 **p** 68 Maseno. P Dio Maseno 67-70; Dio Maseno S from 70. *PO Box 121, Kisii, Kenya.*

TOLWORTHY, Colin. b 37. Chich Th Coll 64. **d** 67 **p** 68 Man. C of St Phil Hulme 67-70; Lawton Moor 70-72; Hangleton Dio Chich 72-76; V of St Phil Eastbourne Dio Chich from 76. *Vicarage, St Philip's Avenue, Eastbourne, BN22 8LU.* (Eastbourne 32381)

TOMALIN, William Patrick. b 39. Univ of Sask BA 69. Em Coll Sask BTh 71. **d** 71 **p** 71 Qu'App. R of Ox Bow 71-76; Pipestone Dio Qu'App from 76. *Box 117, Grenfell, Sask, Canada.*

TOMBLING, Arthur John. b 32. St Jo Coll Cam BA 54, MA 58. Ridley Hall Cam. **d** 57 **p** 58 Pet. C of Rushden 57-59; Asst Chap Repton Sch and L to Offic Dio Derby 59-61; C of Reigate 61-64; V of St Sav Battersea Pk Dio S'wark from 64; C-in-c of St Geo w St Andr Battersea Dio S'wark from 74. *7 Alexandra Avenue, SW11 4DZ.* (01-622 4526)

TOMES, Stanley George. Hur Coll LTh 59. **d** 59 Hur for Keew **p** 60 Keew. C of Kenora 59-61; I of Trout Lake 61-68; R of Hammond River 68-74; Grand Manan 74-79. *Grand Harbour, Grand Manan, NB, Canada.*

TOMKINS, Canon Clifford Vernon. Hur Coll LTh 39. **d** 35 **p** 36 Hur. C of Trin Ch Chelsea Green Lon Ont 35; Ayr 35-36; Merlin w Ouvry and Erieau 36-39; St Geo Walkerville 39-40; I of Princeton w Ayr and Drumbo 40; C-in-c of St Geo Walkerville 40-42; Chap RCAF 42-47; I of St Luke and St John Brantford 47-75; Can of St Paul's Cathl Lon Ont 64-75; Can (Emer) from 76. *Box 149, St George, Ont., Canada.*

✠ **TOMKINS, Right Rev Oliver Stratford.** b 08. Ch Coll Cam 2nd cl Hist Trip 30, BA (2nd cl Th Trip) 32, Win Reading Pri 33, MA 35. Hon DD (Edin) 53. Univ of Bris Hon LLD 75. Westcott Ho Cam 32. **d** 35 **p** 36 Chelmsf. C of St Mary Prittlewell 35-39; Sec SCM 35-40; LPr Dio Lon 39-40; V of H Trin Millhouses 40-45; Select Pr Univ of Cam 41 and 55; Univ of Ox 63 and 65; Assoc Gen Sec and Sec C'ttee on Faith and Order World Coun of Chs 45-52; Warden of Linc Th Coll 53-58; Preb and Can of Asgarby in Linc Cathl 53-58; Exam Chap to Bp of Sheff 40-45; Hon Chap 46-53; Exam Chap to Bp of Linc 53-58; Cons Ld Bp of Bris in Westmr Abbey 6 Jan 59 by Abp of Cant; Bps of Man; Lon; Sarum; B & W; Linc; Pet; Ox; Bps Suffr of Grantham; Malmesbury; Grimsby; Bps T Sherwood Jones and Cockin; and Bps of Madura and Mysore (Ch of S India); res 75. *14 St George's Square, Worcester, WR1 1HX.* (Worcester 25330)

TOMKINSON, Frank. Univ of Wales BA (1st cl Hebr) 30, MA 32. St Mich Th Coll Llan 32. **d** 33 **p** 34 Llan. C of Penrhiwceiber 33-41; C-in-c of Cymmer w Abercregan Conv Distr 41-49; V of Penydarren 49-53; R of Paisley w Pinkerton and Cargill 53-56; I of Mitchell 56-62; R of St Steph Stratford 62-69; Woodhouse 69-74. *47 Chestnut Street, Stratford, Ont., Canada.*

TOMLIN, Henry Alfred. b 14. Worc Ordin Coll 62. **d** 64 **p** 65 Lich. C of Oxley 64-68; V of Smallthorne 68-80. *c/o Smallthorne Vicarage, Stoke-on-Trent, Staffs.* (Stoke-on-Trent 85941)

TOMLIN, Keith Michael. b 53. Univ of Lon BSc 75. Ridley Hall Cam 77. **d** 80 **p** 81 Man. C of St Jas Heywood Dio Man from 80. *14 Kelsey, Meadow Close, Heywood, Ol10 1ES.* (Heywood 623803)

TOMLINE, Stephen Harrald. b 35. Univ of Dur BA 57, Dipl Th 61. Cranmer Hall Dur 59. **d** 61 **p** 62 Man. C of St Pet Blackley 61-66; V of Audenshaw Dio Man from 66. *176 Stamford Road, Audenshaw, Manchester, M34 5WW.* (061-370 1863)

TOMLINSON, Arthur John Faulkner. b 20. Clare Coll Cam BA 41, MA 45. Ridley Hall Cam 46. **d** 48 Lon **p** 49 Stepney for Lon. C of Em W Hampstead 48-50; St Helen w H Trin Kens 50-54; V of Furneux Pelham w Stocking Pelham

54-62; R of Sarratt Dio St Alb from 62. *Sarratt Rectory, Rickmansworth, Herts, WD3 6BP.* (Kings Langley 64377)

TOMLINSON, Barry William. b 47. Clifton Th Coll Bris 72. **d** 72 Man **p** 73 Middleton for Man. C of Pennington 72-76; SAMS Miss 76-80; Dioc Treas Admin Dio Chile 77-80; V of St Mary Magd Gorleston Dio Nor from 80. *Vicarage, Nuffield Crescent, Gorleston, Great Yarmouth, Norf, NR31 7LL.* (Gt Yarmouth 61741)

TOMLINSON, Eric Joseph. b 45. Qu Coll Birm 70. **d** 73 **p** 74 Lich. C of Cheadle 73-77; Sedgley 77-79; V of Ettingshall Dio Lich from 79. *Ettingshall Vicarage, Wolverhampton, W Midl.* (Sedgeley 4616)

TOMLINSON, Canon Geoffrey. b 15. Linc Coll Ox BA (3rd cl Mod Hist) 37, MA 47. Westcott Ho Cam 37. **d** 39 **p** 40 Dur. C of Spennymoor 39-43; Chap RNVR 43-47; C-in-c of Murton w Dalton-le-Dale 47; Dom Chap to Bp of Linc and LPr Dio Linc 47-50; V of Mkt Rasen 50-56; Surr from 50; C-in-c of Linwood 52-53; R 53-56; V of St Alb Westbury Pk Clifton 56-66; Lanc 66-81; Overton Dio Blackb from 81; RD of Clifton 61-66; Lanc from 71; Hon Can of Blackb from 67. *St Helen's Vicarage, Overton, Morecambe, Lancs, LA3 3HU.* (Overton 234)

TOMLINSON, Ian James. b 50. AKC 72. St Aug Coll Cant 72. **d** 73 Selby for York **p** 74 York. C of Thirsk w S Kilvington 73-76; St Wilfrid Harrogate 76-79; R of Appleshaw and Kimpton and Thruxton and Fyfield Dio Win from 79. *Vicarage, Ragged Appleshaw, Andover, Hants, SP11 9HX.* (Weyhill 2414)

TOMLINSON, John Coombes. b 34. Univ of Nottm Dipl Adult Educn 76. Lich Th Coll 60. **d** 62 **p** 63 Lich. C of Cheadle Staffs 62-66; Alstonfield 66-68; Warden Lich Dioc Tr Centre from 66; C-in-c of Ilam Dio Lich 68-73; Youth Tr Officer Lich 68-73; Dioc Youth Officer and Publ Pr Dio Derby 73; Dioc Dep Dir of Educn Dio Derby 78; Dir from 79. *Farriers, Ilam Moor Lane, Ilam, Ashbourne, Derbys.* (Thorpe Cloud 385)

TOMLINSON, Peter Robert Willis. b 19. Linc Th Coll 53. **d** 55 **p** 56 Derby. C of Matlock w Tansley 55-57; R of Risley 57-60; PC of Repton 60-68; V 68-70; PC of Foremark 60-68; V 68-70; V of Barrow Gurney 70-77; C-in-c of Langport w Aller 77-78; Team V 78-80; R of Flax Bourton Dio B & W from 80; V of Barrow Gurney Dio B & W from 80. *Flax Bourton Rectory, Bristol, BS19 3QJ.* (Flax Bourton 2582)

TOMLINSON, Reginald William Alexander. b 07. **d** 69 **p** 70 Mon. C of Usk 69-72; Pontypool 72-73; V of Crumlin 73-77; L to Offic Dio Mon from 78. *4 Brynhyfryd Close, Little Mill, Pontypool, Gwent, NP4 0HS.* (Little Mill 538)

TOMLINSON, Robert Herbert. b 12. Univ of Lon BD 38, ALCD 38. **d** 38 Ripon **p** 39 Knaresborough for Ripon. C of Farnley 38-41; CF (EC) 41-46; R of Brancaster 45-56; CF (RA - R of O) 50-67; Hon CF from 67; RD of Heacham 53-56; R of Wolferton w Babingly 56-62; RD of Rising 59-62; V of Docking 62-78; R of Gt Bircham w Bircham Newton and Tofts 62-66; C-in-c of Stanhoe 63-66; C-in-c of Bagthorpe 63-66; V of Fring 66-78; R of Stanhoe Dio Nor 71-78; C-in-c from 78. *The Chantry, Stanhoe, King's Lynn, Norf.* (Docking 456)

TOMLINSON, Vincent Bellini. b 11. Bps' Coll Cheshunt 66. **d** 67 Dunwich for St E **p** 68 St E. C of All SS Ipswich 67-70; H Trin Ipswich 70-73; R of Westerfield w Tuddenham St Martin 73-77; Perm to Offic Dio Guildf 77-79. *11 Edward Terrace, Sun Lane, Alresford, Hants, SO24 9LY.*

TOMPKINS, Barnett Alfred. b 1899. **d** 29 **p** 30 Argent. Miss (SAMS) Chaco Miss 29-45; Chap All SS Quilmes 45-51; Dom Chap to Bp in Argent 48-51; Hon Can St John's Pro-Cathl Buenos Aires 49-51; Org Sec S Amer MS 52-53; R of Yelvertoft w Clay Coton and Lilbourne 54-69; C-in-c of Cold Ashby 60-69; Perm to Offic Dio York 69-73; Dio Southw from 73. *20 Moorgate Park, Retford, Notts.* (Retford 704026)

TOMPKINS, David John. b 32. Oak Hill Th Coll 55. **d** 58 **p** 59 Pet. C of St Giles Northn 58-61; St Jo Evang Heatherlands Parkstone 61-63; V of St Jas Ap Selby 63-73; V of Wistow 63-73; St Sav Retford Dio Southw from 73. *St Saviour's Vicarage, Retford, Notts.* (Retford 702437)

TOMPKINS, Francis Alfred Howard. b 26. St Jo Coll Dur BA 50, Dipl Th 52. **d** 52 **p** 53 Lon. C of St Mary Magd Islington 52-55; Chap Argent Chaco SAMS 55-61; Field Supt 61-65; V of Donington 65-79; Silloth Dio Carl from 79; RD of Holland W 69-78. *Vicarage, Skinburness Road, Silloth, Carlisle, CA5 4QF.* (Silloth 31413)

TOMPKINS, Canon James Charles Harrison. b 20. Peterho Cam BA 41, MA 45. Westcott Ho Cam 45. **d** 47 **p** 48 Cov. C of St Andr (in c of St Phil) Rugby 47-51; Commiss Sing 49-56; Chap and Asst Master Eton Coll 51-55; R of Handsworth Dio Birm from 55; Lect Qu Coll Birm from 57; Hon Can of Birm from 76; RD of Handsworth from 77. *Handsworth Rectory, Hamstead Road, Birmingham, B20 2RB* (021 554 3407)

TOMPKINS, Stanley James. b 03. **d** 71 **p** 71 Argent. R of Los Cocos, Dio Argent from 71. *Cruz Chica, Cordoba, Argentina.*

TOMPSETT, David James. b 54. Grey Coll Dur BA 76. Ridley Hall Cam 76. **d** 79 **p** 80 Bradf. C of St Jas Bolton City and Dio Bradf from 79. *66 Myers Lane, Bradford, BD2 4HB.*

TOMSETT, James. b 08. SOC 61. **d** 64 **p** 65 S'wark. C of Surbiton 64-68; Wells 68-70; V of Compton Bp (w Loxton and Christon from 79) 70-80. *9 St Andrew's Road, Cheddar, Somt.*

✠ **TOMUSANGE, Right Rev Stephen Salongo.** K S Budo 23. Buwalasi Th Coll 34. **d** 36 **p** 38 U Nile. P Dio U Nile 36-52; Cons Asst Bp on U Nile in Pro-Cathl of St Phil Evang Ngora 25 April 52 by Bp of Ugan; Bp on U Nile; and Bps Balya, Beecher, and Carey; Archd of Teso 56-61; Trld to Soroti 61; to W Bugan 65; res 74; Dean of W Bugan 65-74; Prov of Ugan and Rwanda B (and Boga-Z from 73) 67-74. *PO box 3245, Kampala, Uganda.*

TONBRIDGE, Lord Bishop Suffragan of. (Vacant)

TONBRIDGE, Archdeacon of. *See* Mason, Ven Richard John.

TONG, Gad Kelaotswe. **d** 68 **p** 69 Kimb K. P Dio Kimb K. *P Bag 813, Vryburg, CP, S Africa.*

TONG, Herbert Siak Kong. b 50. Ridley Coll Melb 74. **d** 77 **p** 78 Sabah. P Dio Sabah. *PO Box 217, Labuan, Malaysia.*

TONG, Paul Hin-Sum. Univ of Hong Kong BA 63. Westcott Ho Cam 63. **d** 66 **p** 67 Hong. C of All SS Homuntin Kowloon 66-70; L to Offic Dio Hong from 70. *St John's College, Hong Kong.* (5-877102)

TONG, Peter Laurence. b 29. Univ of Lon BA 50. Oak Hill Th Coll 52. **d** 54 **p** 55 Liv. C of St Chrys Everton 54-56; C-in-c of St Sav Liv 56-59; Chap Blackb and E Lancs R Infirm and Park Lee Hosp 63-65; V of Ch of the Sav Blackb 59-65; St Andr w St Matthias Isl 65-75; Welling Dio Roch from 75; Surr from 80. *Vicarage, Danson Lane, Welling, Kent.*

TONGA, Sione Tauanga'a. b 41. St Jo Bapt Coll Suva 66. **d** 69 Polyn **p** 70 Bp Halapua for Polyn. C of Viti Levu W 69-71; Labasa 71-72; St Luke Par Distr Dio Polyn from 73. *PO Box 35, Suva, Fiji.*

TONGASAONA, Johnson. b 44. **d** 73 **p** 74 Antan. P Dio Antan. *Misiona Anglikana, Anosibe An'Ala, Malagasy Republic.*

TONGE, Brian. b 36. Univ of Dur BA (2nd cl French) 58. Ely Th Coll 59. **d** 61 **p** 62 Blackb. C of Fleetwood 61-65; Chap Ranby Ho Sch Retford 65-69; C of St Andr w St Marg Burnley Dio Blackb from 69. *61 Colne Road, Burnley, Lancs.* (Burnley 23185)

TONGE, David Theophilus. b 30. Wells Th Coll 68. **d** 70 **p** 71 Worc. C of Kidderminster 70-75; P-in-c of Finstall dio Worc from 76. *Finstall Vicarage, Bromsgrove, Worcs.* (Bromsgrove 72459)

TONGE, Lister. b 51. AKC 74. St Aug Coll Cant 74. **d** 75 **p** 76 Liv. C of Our Lady & St Nich Liv 75-78; St Mary's Cathl Johann 78; L to Offic 79; M CR from 79. *House of the Resurrection, Mirfield, W Yorks, WF14 0BN.* (0924-494318)

TONGE, Malcolm Wallace. b 09. Univ of Man BA 33. Wycl Hall Ox. **d** 63 **p** 64 Roch. Hon C of Swanley 63-69; V of Chiddingstone Causeway (w Chiddingstone from 73) 69-74. *Maranatha, Halley Road, Broad Oak, Heathfield, E Sussex.*

TONGUE, Denis Harold. b 15. Em Coll Cam 3rd cl Th Trip pt i 36, BA (2nd cl Th Trip pt ii) 37, MA 41. Tyndale Hall Bris 37. **d** 38 **p** 39 Birm. C of Bp Ryder's Ch Birm 38-40; Wigtoft and Bicker 40-42; St Mary w St Pet Bury St E 42-46; R of Clapton-in-Gordano 46-53; NT Lect Tyndale Hall (Trin Coll from 72) Bris 46-77; V of Locking 53-67. *Eaglehurst, St John's Road, Exmouth, Devon.* (Exmouth 4695)

TONGUE, Paul. b 41. St Chad's Coll Dur BA (2nd cl Th) 63, Dipl Th 64. **d** 64 **p** 65 Worc. C of St Edm Dudley 64-69; Sedgley 69-70; V of Amblecote Dio Worc from 70. *Amblecote Vicarage, Stourbridge, W Midl.* (Stourbridge 4057)

TONGUE, Ross Taaffe. St Jo Coll Morpeth 66. ACT ThL 68. **d** 68 **p** 69 River. C of Broken Hill 68-72; Griffith 72-73; N Albury 74-75; R of Callide Valley Dio Rockptn from 75. *Box 69, Biloela, Queensland, Australia 4715.*

TONJENI, Hemming Zama. b 39. St Bede's Coll Umtata 70. **d** 71 **p** 73 St John's. C of H Cross 71-77; Tsomo 77-81; P-in-c of St Francis Kokstad Dio St John's from 81. *Box 136, Kokstad 4700, S Africa.*

TONKIN, David Graeme. Univ of NZ LLB 56, LLM 57. Coll of Resurr Mirfield 57. **d** 59 **p** 60 Lon. [F Barrister-at-Law] C of St Mary of Eton Hackney Wick 59-61; Asst Chap and Master Worksop Coll 62-63; Chap 63-68; L to Offic Dio Southw 63-68; Prin Bp's Sch Amman and Chap Dio Jordan 68-74; Hon C of Stratford Dio Waik from 74; Hd Master St Mary's Dioc Sch Stratford from 74. *St Mary's School, Stratford, NZ.* (Stratford 6690)

TONKIN, John Marshall. b 40. St Jo Coll Morpeth 76. **d**

and **p** 80 Newc. C of Wallsend 80-81; Merewether Dio Newc from 81. *104 Morgan Street, Merewether, NSW, Australia 2291.*

TONKIN, Richard John. b 28. Univ of Lon BD 60. ALCD 59. **d** 60 Bp Maxwell for Leic **p** 61 Leic. C of The Martyrs Leic 60-63; Keynsham 63-66; V of H Trin Hinckley 66-74; RD of Sparkenhoe II 71-74; Surr 73-77; V of Oadby Dio Leic from 74. *Oadby Vicarage, Leicester, LE2 5BD.* (Leic 712135)

TONKINSON, David Boyes. b 47. K Coll Lon AKC and BD 71. St Aug Coll Cant 71. **d** 72 **p** 73 S'wark. C of St Andr Surbiton 72-75; C-in-c of Selsdon (in c of St Francis S Croydon) 75-81; V of St Aug Croydon Dio Cant from 81. *23a St Augustine's Avenue, South Croydon, CR2 6JN.* (01-688 2663)

✠ **TONKS, Right Rev Basil.** Wycl Coll Tor Hon DD 81; Codr Coll Barb 51. **d** 54 **p** 55 Trinid. C of H Trin Cathl Port of Spain 54-56; P-in-c of Siparia 56-60; Chap Miss to Seamen Port of Spain Trinid 60-63; R of Scarborough Tobago 63-69; Hon C of St Aid and Asst Chap Miss to Seamen Tor 69-70; R of St Giles Barrie 70-81; Shanty Bay 70-81; Archd of Simcoe 72-80; Cons Ld Bp Suffr of Tor in St Paul's Ch Bloor Street E, Tor by Abp of Tor; Bps of Alg, Carib, Hur, Moos, Ott and W New York (USA); Bps Suffr of Tor, Niag, Hur and The Arctic; and others. *135 Adelaide Street East, Toronto, Ont, M5C 1L8, Canada.* (416-363 6021)

TONKS, Colin Robertson. Univ of NZ BA 57. Ridley Coll Melb ACT ThL 60. **d** 60 Dun for Ch Ch **p** 62 Ch Ch. C of Timaru 60-62; Spreydon-Hoon Hay 62-64; Shirley 64; V of Chatham Is 64-66; Ross w S Westland 66-70; St Martin's Ch Ch 70-79; Bishopdale-Harewood Dio Ch Ch from 79. *4 Chedworth Avenue, Christchurch 5, NZ.* (597-203)

TONKS, Denys. Codr Coll Barb. **d** 58 **p** 59 Barb. C of Ch Ch Barb 58-59; St Mich Cathl Barb 59-61; Gen L Dio Windw Is 61-62; C of H Cross Greenford Lon 62-64; R of St Patr Tobago 64-69; V of La Brea Trinid 69-71; R of St Agnes Port of Spain 71-73; Whitfords 73-76; Rupanyup 76-79; St John City and Dio Bal from 79. *8 Brougham Street, Ballarat, Vic, Australia 3350.* (053-32 4723)

TONTA, Jerome. St Aug Coll Ambinanindrano. **d** 48 **p** 50 Madag. C of Brickaville 48-50; P-in-c 50-52; Lohariandava 52-60; Fenerive w Soanierana 60-69. *Betambako, Moramanga, Madagascar.*

TOOBY, Derrick David Johnson. b 35. Lich Th Coll 66. **d** 68 Bp McKie for Cov **p** 69 Cov. C of Stratford-on-Avon 68-69; H Trin Leamington 69-71; V of Eastern Green Dio Cov from 71. *Eastern Green Vicarage, Coventry, Warws.* (Cov 466215)

TOOGOOD, Noel Hare. b 32. Univ of Birm BSc (2nd cl Maths-Phys) 54. Wells Th Coll 59. **d** 61 Sheff **p** 62 Bp Gerard for York. C of Rotherham 61-65; St Jo Evang Darlington (in c of St Herbert) 65-70; V of Burnopfield 70-81; P-in-c of Roche Dio Truro from 81; Withiel Dio Truro from 81. *Rectory, Fore Street, Roche, St Austell, Cornw, PL26 8EP.* (Roche 890301)

TOOGOOD, Robert Charles. b 45. AKC 70. St Aug Coll Cant 70. **d** 71 **p** 72 Kens for Lon. C of St Nich Shepperton 71-74; Kirk Ella 74-76; C-in-c of Levisham w Lockton 76-81; Ebberston w Allerston 76-81; R of Kempsey & Severn Stoke w Croome d'Abitot Dio Worc from 81. *Kempsey Vicarage, Worcester.* (Worc 820202)

TOOKEY, Christopher Tom. b 41. K Coll Lon and Warm AKC (2nd cl) 67. **d** 68 **p** 69 Dur. C of St Pet Stockton-on-Tees 68-71; Burnham-on-Sea 71-77; R of Clutton w Cameley (Temple Cloud) 77-81; V of St Thos Wells w Horrington Dio B & W from 81. *St Thomas's Vicarage, Wells, BA5 2UZ.* (Wells 72193)

TOOLE-MACKSON, Kenneth Toole. b 09. Late Sambrooke Exhib of K Coll Lon 34. **d** 38 **p** 39 Lon. C of St Mark Teddington 38-40; Royston 40-41; Isleworth 41-43; V of St Phil S Tottenham 43-45; Harefield 45-52; Chap Harefield Hosp 45-52; V of St Anselm Belmont 52-61; Lancing 61-74; R of Coombes 61-74; Perm to Offic Dios Lon and Chich from 74. *110 Sea Lane, Goring-by-Sea, Worthing, W Sussex, BN12 4PU.* (Worthing 42987)

TOOLEY, Charles Crouch. b 1896. TED and clasp 50. Univ Coll Dur BA 23, MA 37. **d** 23 **p** 24 Dur. C of St Ignatius Hendon Dur 23-26; All SS Newc T 26; Chap (Eccles Est) H Trin Bangalore 26-29; Bolarum 29-31; St Geo Cathl Madr 31-32; R of St John Arpafeelie w St Mary Highfield 32-37; C of St Mary Virg (in c of Ch Ch) Colchester 38-39; CF (TA - R of O) 39-47; V of Garstang 47-53; Perm to Offic Dio Liv 53-54; C of Warrington 54-66. *6 Rushmore Grove, Paddington, Warrington, Lancs.*

TOOLEY, Geoffrey Arnold. b 27. Lon Coll of Div 55. **d** 58 **p** 59 Roch. C of Chalk 58-60; Meopham 60-62; C-in-c of Snodland 62-68; Burham 68-76; C-in-c of Riverhead w Dunton Green 76-79; C of N and S Bersted Dio Chich from 79. *330 Chichester Road, Bognor Regis, W Sussex, PO21 5AU.* (Bognor Regis 23800)

TOOLEY, Norman Oliver. b 27. Roch Th Coll. **d** 65 **p** 66 Roch. C of St Mary Gravesend 65-68; Ormskirk 68-73; Chap Mersey Side Centre for the Deaf Liv 73-78; L to Offic Dio Liv 73-78; C of Ch Ch Bootle 78-80; All SS W Ham Dio Chelmsf from 80. *Flat 2, West Ham Church Hall, 25 Meath Road, E15.*

TOOMBS, Alan Trevor. b 33. Univ of Man BA (Th) 54. Ripon Hall Ox 54. **d** 56 **p** 57 Man. C of St Jas Hope Salford 56-61; R of Moston 61-74; V of St Luke w All SS Weaste, Salford 74-81; R of Newchurch Dio Man from 81. *Newchurch Rectory, Rossendale, Lancs, BB4 9HH.* (Rossendale 215098)

TOOMEY, Alfred James. b 06. Hatf Coll Dur LTh 29. St Aug Coll Cant 25. **d** 30 Dur **p** 31 Chich. C of St Andr Bp Auckld 30-31; Littlehampton 31-33; Camberwell 33-34; R of Three Springs w Coorow W Austr 34-39; C of St Nich Plumstead and Wilberforce Missr Dio S'wark 39-45; CF (EC) 41-45; Hon CF 45; R of Clifton Reynes w Newton Blossomville 45-49; Chap Mayday and Queen's Hosps Croydon and L to Offic Dio Cant 49-60; Chap U Chine Sch Shanklin and L to Offic Dio Portsm 60-64; Chap Horton Hosp Epsom and L to Offic Dio Guildf 64-73; Perm to Offic Dio Win from 73. *4 Montagu Court, Highcliffe, Christchurch, Dorset.* (Highcliffe 72703)

TOON, Norman. b 22. Launde Abbey Leic 75. **d** 76 **p** 77 Leic. C of Shepshed 76-80; P-in-c of Kimcote w Walton and Bruntingthorpe Dio Leic from 80. *Kimcote Rectory, Lutterworth, Leics.* (Lutterworth 2543)

TOON, Peter. b 39. K Coll Lon BD 65. MTh (Lon) 67. Univ of Liv MA 72. Ch Ch Ox DPhil 77. N-W Ordin Course 72. **d** 73 Warrington for Liv **p** 74 Liv. C of Skelmersdale 73-74; Libr Latimer Ho Ox 74-76; Hon C of St Ebbe Ox 74-76; Tutor Oak Hill Coll Southgate from 76; Hon Lect St Giles-in-the-Fields Lon from 79. *Oak Hill College, Chase Side, N14 4PS.* (01-449 0467)

TOONE, Lawrence Raymond. b 32. Open Univ BA 77. St Aid Coll 61. **d** 63 Middleton for Man **p** 64 Man. C of St Agnes Birch-in-Rusholme 63-66; Ch Ch W Didsbury 66-69; V of St Paul Oldham 69-79; St Mary Greenfield Dio Man from 79; RD of Oldham from 80. *St Mary's Vicarage, Park Lane, Greenfield, Oldham, OL3 7DX.* (Saddleworth 2346)

TOOP, William John. b 07. Univ of Lon BSc 27. K Coll Cam BA (2nd cl Nat Sc) 38, MA 42. **d** 41 **p** 42 Lah. Lect and Asst Chap Lawr Coll Ghora Gali 41-44; Chap Ind Eccles Est 44-47; Lahore Cathl 44; Rawalpindi 46; Offg Archd of Lahore 47; Rawalpindi 47; PC of Cofton St Mary 48-52; Chap R W Co Inst 50-52; R of St Mark Torwood Torquay 52-79; C-in-c of H Trin Torquay 74-79; Publ Pr Dio Ex from 80. *4 Seaton Close, Torbay Park, Babbacombe, Torquay, TQ1 3UH.*

TOOPE, Frank Morris. Qu Coll Newfld 42. **d** 45 **p** 47 Newfld. C of Channel 45-47; St Mary St John's 47-49; P-in-c of Burgeo 49-50; R of Change I 52-53; Stephenville 53-54; C of Guelph 54-56; St Matt Montr 56-58; R of Buckingham 58-65; St Jo Div Verdun Montr 65-68; Beaconsfield Dio Montr from 68. *110 Florida Drive, Beaconsfield, PQ, Canada.* (514-697 1453)

TOOTH, Nigel David. b 47. Sarum Wells Th Coll 71. **d** 74 **p** 75 S'wark. C of S Beddington 74-77; Whitchurch Dio Bris from 77. *127 Bristol Road, Whitchurch, Bristol, BS14 0PU.* (Whitchurch 834992)

TOOTH, William George Alexander. Moore Th Coll Syd ACT ThL 46. **d** and **p** 47 Syd. C of Ch Ch Gladesville 47-49; R of Jamberoo 49-54; Fairfield 54-59; Chap Sunshine Technical Sch 59-61; C of Braybrook 59-60; R of Berrigan 61-65; I of Elsternwick 65-78; Perm to Offic Dio Brisb 78-81. *4 Edenderry Street, Manly, Queensland, Australia 4179.*

TOOVEY, Graeme Charles. Univ of NSW BSc 70. Moore Coll Syd ThL 78. Univ of Lon BD 79. **d** and **p** 80 Syd. C of Ch Ch Gladesville Dio Syd from 80. *14 Pile Street, Gladesville, NSW, Australia 2111.* (89-4549)

TOOVEY, Kenneth Frank. b 26. K Coll Lon and Warm BD and AKC 51. **d** 52 **p** 53 Lon. C of St Mary Magd Munster Square 52-60; V of St Pet and St Paul Teddington 60-70; Ruislip Dio Lon from 70; RD of Hillingdon from 75. *53 Bury Street, Ruislip, Middx.* (Ruislip 33040)

TOPLEY, John Ernest Wilmot. b 21. Keble Coll Ox BA (2nd cl Th) 48. Ely Th Coll. **d** 49 **p** 50 Roch. C of Petts Wood 49-53; Earley 53-55; St Jas Cowley (in c of St Francis) Ox 55-61; V of Scropton w Boylestone 61-66; Chap Middlewood and Wharncliffe Hosps Sheff 66-72; R of Stowford 72-73; V of Broadwoodwidger 72-73. *c/o 6 South Lea Avenue, Hoyland, Barnsley, Yorks.*

TOPPING, David Gerald Victor. TCD BA 37, MA 60. **d** 39 Linc **p** 40 Grimsby for Linc. C of St Mary Mablethorpe and of St Helen w All SS Theddlethorpe 39-42; St Mary and St Jas Grimsby 42-47; I of Milestone 47-48; St Geo Moose Jaw 48-49; Wadena 49-50; C of St Paul's Pro-Cathl Regina 50-51; PC of New Clee 51-55; V of Sundays River Valley 55-60; R of

St Alb E Lon 60-74; St Mich AA Queenstn w St Mary Tarkastad 74-75; R of Ch Ch Arcadia Dio Pret from 75. *821 Church Street, Arcadia, Pretoria 0002, S Africa.* (74-4032)

TOPPING, Kenneth Bryan Baldwin. b 27. Bps' Coll Cheshunt 58. **d** 59 Blackb **p** 60 Lanc for York. C of Fleetwood 59-63; V of Ringley 63-70; Cleator Moor (w Cleator from 68) Dio Carl from 70. *Vicarage, Trumpet Road, Cleator, Cumb, CA23 3EF.* (Cleator Moor 810510)

TOPPING, Norman. b 32. N-W Ordin Course 73. **d** 76 Ches **p** 77 Birkenhead for Ches. C of Prenton 76-79; E Runcorn w Halton 79-80; Halton Dio Ches 80; P-in-c of Newton Flowery Field, Hyde Dio Ches 80-81; V from 81. *St Stephen's Vicarage, Bennett Street, Hyde, Gtr Man, SK14 4SS.* (061-368 3333)

TORAKASI, Paul. b 51. Bp Patteson Th Centre Kohimarama 70. **d** 73 **p** 74 Melan. P Dio Melan 73-75; Centr Melan from 75. *Haununu, San Cristoval, Solomon Islands.*

TORDOFF, Donald William. b 45. Univ of Nottm BA 69. Qu Coll Birm 69. **d** 71 **p** 72 Ripon. C of Ch Ch, High Harrogate 71-75; Moor Allerton (in c of Alwoodley) 75-80; V of Bilton Dio Ripon from 80. *Bilton Vicarage, Elm Tree Avenue, Harrogate, Yorks.* (Harrogate 65129)

TORLACH, Ven Charles Emil. Kelham Th Coll 23. **d** 27 **p** 28 Lon. C of St Mary Magd Munster Square Lon 27-29; M of St Barn Bush Bro Atherton 29-34; P-in-c of Mareeba 34-41; C of St Paul's Cathl Rockptn 41-43; I of Longreach 43-49; V of Winton 49-50; Yeppoon 50-54; Mount Morgan 54-69; Hon Can of Rockptn 56-65; Archd of Rockptn 65-69; Archd (Emer) from 69. *Whitman Street, Yeppoon, Queensland, Australia* (079-39 1844)

TORLEY, John. b 29. **d** 80 **p** 81 Calg. Hon C of St Jas City and Dio Calg from 80. *6395 Ranchview Drive NW, Calgary, Alta, Canada, T3G 1B5.*

TORO KIARIE, Hamuel. **d** and **p** 64 Mt Kenya. P Dio Mt Kenya 64-75; Dio Mt Kenya S from 75. *Githunguri, Box 301, Thika, Kenya.*

TORONTO, Lord Bishop of. *See* Garnsworthy, Most Rev Lewis Samuel.

TORONTO, Suffragan Bishops of. *See* Brown, Right Rev Arthur Durrant; Tonks, Right Rev Basil; Hunt, Right Rev Desmond Charles; and Parke-Taylor, Right Rev Geoffrey Howard.

TORONTO, Dean of. *See* Stiff, Right Rev Hugh Vernon.

TORRANCE, Edwin Ovendon. St Paul's Coll Grahmstn 32. LTh (S Africa) 34. **d** 34 **p** 35 Capetn. C of H Trin Caledon 35-37; All SS Plumstead 37-39; R of Robertson 39-50; Muizenberg 59-63; Groot Drakenstein 63-68; C of Robertson 68-71; L to Offic Dio Capetn 69-80; Perm to Offic from 80. *Box 152, Montagu, CP, S Africa.* (02341-3102)

TORRAVILLE, Arnold. Qu Th Coll St John's 48. **d** 51 **p** 52 Newfld. I of Sandwich Bay Miss 51-54; R of Greenspond 54-60; Smith's Sound 60-64; C of Grand Falls 64-68; R of Heart's Content 68-75; Catalina Dio Newfld (Centr Newfld from 76) from 75. *Box 29, Trinity Bay, Catalina, Newfoundland, Canada.* (709-496-2743)

TORRENS, John Herbert. b 10. St Edm Hall Ox BA (3rd cl Mod Hist) 31, MA 52. Cudd Coll 33. **d** 33 **p** 34 Worc. C of Stambermill 34-36; All SS W Ham 36-39; St Matt Hull 40-46; C-in-c of St Geo Conv Distr Marfleet Hull 46-50; Marfleet (St Giles) 49-50; Surr 50-72; V of Horley 50-65; H Trin U Tooting 65-72; Shalbourne w Ham 72-77. *51 St Martin's, Marlborough, Wilts, SN8 1AS.* (0672-53297)

TORRENS, Robert Harrington. b 33. Trin Coll Cam BA 56, 3rd cl Th Trip pt ii 57, MA 61. Ridley Hall Cam 56. **d** 58 **p** 59 Roch. C of Bromley 58-60; Aylesbury (in c of St Pet) 60-63; V of Eaton Socon 63-73; L to Offic Dio St Alb 73-75; V of All SS Cheltm Dio Glouc from 75. *66 All Saints' Road, Cheltenham, Glos.* (Cheltm 23341)

TORRES, Zebedeo. b 30. **d** 70 **p** 71 Parag for Argent. P Dio Argent 70-73; N Argent from 73. *Parsonage, Santa Maria, N Argentina.*

TORREY, Ven Reuben Archer. b 18. Davidson Univ N Carolina BA 39. Univ of the S Tenn BD 45. **d** 45 **p** 46 Bp of Georgia. In Amer Ch 45-64; Dir of Jes Abbey Dio Taejon from 64; Archd of Kangwon 74-76; S Kangwon from 76. *Box 17, Hwangji, Samch'ok Gun, Kangwondo 241-11, Korea.*

TORRINGTON, Norman Russell. b 17. Kelham Th Coll 37. **d** 43 **p** 44 S'wark. C of Malden 43-45; St Sav Raynes Pk 45-49; Putney 49-51; Leek 51-53; V of Tunstall 53-61; Rugeley 61-72; Cheswardine 72-78; Hales 73-78 Surr from 68; RD of Hodnet from 72; V of Hodnet w Weston-under-Redcastle and Peplow Dio Lich from 78. *Rectory, Hodnet, Salop, TF9 3NT.* (Hodnet 441)

TORRO, George H. **d** 80 **p** 81 Jer. P Dio Jer. *c/o PO Box 2211, Beirut, Lebanon.*

TORRY, Alan Kendall. b 33. **d** 77 **p** 79 Truro (APM). C of St Paul Truro 77-80; Team V of Probus, Ladock & Grampound w Creed Dio Truro from 80. *Rectory, Ladock, Truro, TR2 4PL.* (St Austell 882554)

TORRY, Malcolm Norman Alfred. b 55. St Jo Coll Cam BA 76, MA 80. BD (Lon) 78. K Coll Lon Mth 79. Cranmer Hall Dur 79. **d** 80 **p** 81 S'wark. C of H Trin w St Matt S'wark Dio S'wark from 80. *224 Ashenden, Deacon Way, SE17 1UB.*

TOSTEVIN, Canon Ronald Edwin. b 26. Selw Coll Cam BA 51, MA 56. Ely Th Coll 51. **d** 53 **p** 54 Man. C of Ascen L Broughton Salford 53-55; Dom Chap to Bp of Ely 55-57; V of St Paul Crewe 57-71; R of H Cross Woodchurch Dio Ches from 71; RD of Birkenhead from 74; Hon Can of Ches from 78. *Rectory, Woodchurch, Wirral, Chesh.* (051-677 5352)

TOTNES, Archdeacon of. *See* Hawkins, Ven Richard Stephen.

TOTTY, Canon Lawrence Harold. b 07. Tyndale Hall Bris 46. **d** 46 **p** 47 Momb. BCMS Miss Dio Momb 46-61; Dio Nak 61-64; R of Kingswood Glouc 65-72; Perm to Offic Dio Glouc from 73; Chap St Paul's Hosp Cheltm from 80; Hon Can of Nak from 81. *10 Kingscote Close, Up Hatherley, Cheltenham, Glos, GL51 6JU.* (Cheltenham 22809)

TOULSON, Frank Kinlay. b 14. BEM 52. Bps' Coll Cheshunt 64. **d** 66 Barking for Chelmsf **p** 67 Chelmsf. C of L Ilford 66-71; V of Goxhill 71-79; Thornton Curtis 72-79. *Address temp unknown.*

TOUTAIN, Philippe Roger Marcel. b 50. Univ of the Sorbonne BA 72, MA 74. Univ of Otago BD 77. St Jo Coll Auckld 77. **d** 77 **p** 78 Dun. C of Caversham 77-78; St John Invercargill 78-80; V of Winton-Otautau Dio Dun from 80. *53 Meldrum Street, Winton, NZ.*

TOUW, Dennis Frank Pieter. b 49. Chich Th Coll 77. **d** 80 **p** 81 Willesden for Lon. C of St Jo Bapt Pinner Dio Lon from 80. *16 Barrow Point Avenue, Pinner, Middx, HA5 3HF.*

TOVEY, John Hamilton. b 50. Univ of Cant NZ BA 72. St Jo Coll Nottm Dipl Th 78. **d** 80 **p** 81 Southw. C of St Paul Hyson Green Nottm Dio Southw from 80. *8 Austen Avenue, Forest Fields, Nottingham, NG7 6PE.*

TOVEY, Peter Hamilton. Univ of NZ BA 41. **d** 46 **p** 47 Roch. C of Ch Ch Beckenham 46-49; CMS Miss Dio Kar 49-64; L to Offic Dio Auckld 64-65; C of Bryndwr 65-70; V of Mt Somers 70-72. *Vicarage, Mayfield, Mid-Canterbury, NZ.*

TOVEY, Ven Ronald. K Coll Lon and Warm AKC 51. **d** 52 **p** 53 Derby. C of Glossop 52-55; St Phil and of H Trin and St Jo Bapt Hulme Man and of All SS Chorlton-on-Medlock 55-57; Miss at Mponda's 57-67; St Pet Cathl Likoma 67-69; R of Mohales Hoek Dio Les from 69; Archd of S Les from 77. *Box 22, Mohales Hoek, Lesotho.*

TOVUTU, Albert. **d** 76 **p** 78 New Hebr. P Dio New Hebr 76-80; Dio Vanuatu from 80. *Vuingalato, Nduindui, Omba, Vanuatu.*

TOWARD, Stanley. b 25. Cranmer Hall Dur 65. **d** 66 **p** 67 Dur. C of S Westoe 66-69; V of Swalwell 69-74; R of Ryton-on-Tyne Dio Dur from 74; Surr from 76. *Rectory, Barmoor House, Main Road, Ryton, T & W NE40 3AJ.* (Ryton 4592)

TOWELL, Geoffrey Leonard. b 37. K Coll Lon BA (2nd cl Hist) 59. Linc Th Coll. **d** 61 **p** 62 Derby. C of Ashbourne 61-65; Claxby w Normanby-le-Wold 65-67; V of Alkborough w Whitton (and W Halton w Winteringham from 80) Dio Linc from 67; R of W Halton 67-80; P-in-c of Winteringham 75-80. *Alkborough Vicarage, Scunthorpe, S Humb, DN15 9JJ.* (Scunthorpe 720341)

TOWELL, Canon John William. b 16. Late de Bury Exhib of St Jo Coll Dur 36, BA (2nd cl Cl) 38, Dipl Th 39, MA 41. **d** 39 **p** 40 Dur. C of St Paul Stockton-on-Tees 39-43; C-in-c of Evenwood 43-44; Chap RAFVR 44-47; C-in-c of H Trin S Shields 47-48; Tutor St Jo Coll Dur 48-50; Chap Actors' Ch Union 48-50; V of Ch of Ven Bede Gateshead 48-50; Cambo 50-59; C-in-c of Kirkheaton Newc T 50-52; Dioc Insp of Schs 51-59; Bp's Exam of Readers Newc T 52-70; Dioc Warden of Readers Newc T 55-59; V of Kirkharle 52-59; Chap and Asst Master Harrogate Coll 59-67; L to Offic Dio Ripon 59-67; R of Leathley w Farnley 62-67; Can Res of Bradf 67-77; Can (Emer) from 77; Dioc Insp of Schs Dio Bradf 68-73; Warden of Readers Bradf 72-75; Surr 77; Perm to Offic Dio Bradf from 77. *4 Ashfield Avenue, Shipley, W Yorks, BD18 3AL.* (Bradford 583905)

TOWERS, David Francis. b 32. G and C Coll Cam BA 56, MA 60. Clifton Th Coll 56. **d** 58 **p** 59 Derby. C of Ch Gresley 58-63; V of St Paul Brixton 63-74; Chatteris Dio Ely from 74. *Vicarage, Chatteris, Cambs.* (Chatteris 2173)

TOWERS, John Keble. b 19. Keble Coll Ox BA 41, MA 57. Edin Th Coll 41. **d** 43 **p** 44 Brech. Chap of St Paul's Cathl Dundee 43-47; Miss P Dio Nagp 47-62; R of St Jas Inverleith Row Edin 62-71; V of St Osw Little Horton Bradf 71-78; V of Holm Cultram Dio Carl from 78. *Holm Cultram Vicarage, Abbey Town, Carlisle, Cumb.* (Abbey Town 246)

TOWERS, Terence John. b 33. K Coll Lon and Warm AKC (2nd cl) 60. **d** 61 **p** 62 Dur. C of Ch of Good Shepherd Bp Wearmouth 61-65; R of Stokesby w Herringby 65-67; V of Runham 65-67; PC (V from 69) of Ushaw Moor Dio Dur from 67. *Vicarage, Ushaw Moor, Durham.* (Durham 730298)

TOWLER, David George. b 42. Cranmer Hall Dur 73. **d** 76 Penrith for Carl **p** 77 Carl. C of S Paul Barrow-F 76-80; V of St Geo Huyton Dio Liv from 80. *Vicarage, St George's Road, Huyton, Liverpool, L36 8BE.* (051-489 1997)

TOWLER, John Frederick. b 42. Bps' Coll Cheshunt 63. **d** 66 **p** 67 Nor. C of Lowestoft 66-71; R of Horstead 71-77; Warden Dio Nor Youth Centre 71-77; Prec of Worc Cathl from 77; Min Can of Worc from 78. *2 College Green, Worcester, WR1 2LH.* (Worc 24110)

TOWLSON, Arthur Stanley. b 20. Late Organ Exhib St Jo Coll Dur LTh 48, BA (2nd cl) 49. ALCD 48. **d** 50 **p** 51 Liv. C of All SS Southport 50-52; Chan V of Lich Cathl 52-57; R of Ingestre w Tixall and Chap to the Earl of Shrewsbury 53-57; Hon PV of Lich Cathl from 57; Blithfield 57-70; Colton 57-70; R of St Jas L Longton 70-71; L to Offic Dio Lich 71-78; P-in-c of Checkley Dio Lich from 78; Croxden w Hollington Dio Lich from 78. *Rectory, Church Lane, Checkley, Stoke-on-Trent, Staffs. ST10 4NJ.* (Tean 2225)

TOWNDROW, Ven Frank Noel. b 11. K Coll Cam 2nd cl Hist Trip pt i 33, BA (2nd cl Hist Trip pt ii) 34, MA 38. Coll of Resurr Mirfield, 35. **d** 37 **p** 38 Chelmsf. C of Chingford 37-40; Chap RAFVR 40-47; R of St Andr Dunmore 47-51; P-in-c of St Mary Grangemouth 47-48; R 48-51; V of Kirton-in-Lindsey 51-53; R of Manton 51-53; Gt Greenford 53-62; V of E Haddon 62-66; R of Holdenby 62-66; V of Ravensthorpe w Teeton and Coton 63-66; Proc Conv Pet 64-67; Chan and Libr of Pet Cathl 66-67; Can Res 66-77; Archd of Oakham 67-77; Archd (Emer) from 77; Exam Chap to Bp of Pet 67-81; Chap to HM the Queen 75-81. *2 Bourne Road, Swinstead, Grantham, Lincs.* (Corby Glen 422)

TOWNE, David William. b 34. St Jo Coll Dur BA 58, Dipl Th 60. Cranmer Hall Dur 58. **d** 60 Tonbridge for Cant **p** 61 Roch. C of St Jo Evang Bromley 60-63; Lect of Watford 63-66; V of Prestonville 66-73; R of Slaugham w Handcross 73-79; V of Wilmington Dio Roch from 79. *Vicarage, High Road, Wilmington, Dartford, Kent, DA2 7EG.* (Dartford 20561)

TOWNEND, George William Russell. Moore Th Coll Syd ACT ThL 57. **d** and **p** 57 Syd. C of Port Kembla 57-58; Chap at Norfolk I 58-59; CMS 59-61; C-in-c of Mona Vale 61-64; Chap RAAF 64-80; Perm to Offic Dio Adel 64-80; R of Loch 80-81. *91 Nelson Road, Valley View, S Australia.*

TOWNEND, John. b 24. Oak Hill Th Coll 70. **d** 71 **p** 72 Wakef. C of Kirkheaton Wakef 71-74; V of Sowerby Bridge w Norland Dio Wakef from 74. *c/o Vicarage, Sowerby Bridge, Yorks.* (Halifax 31253)

TOWNEND, Noel Alexander Fortescue. b 06. Selw Coll Cam BA 28, MA 32. Cudd Coll 29. **d** 30 **p** 32 Southn for Win. C of Freemantle 30-34; M of Bush Bro of St Barn Dio N Queensld 34-39; C of St Jas Cathl Townsville 39-40; Chap RAFVR 40-47; R of Week St Mary 47-55; PC (V from 68) Port Isaac 55-73; RD of Bodmin 65-68; Hon C of N Petherton Dio B & W from 73. *Rose Cottage, Clare Street, North Petherton, Bridgewater, Somt.*

TOWNER, Colin David. b 39. St Pet Coll Ox BA (2nd cl Mus) 61, MA 65. BD (Lon) 63. Tyndale Hall Bris 61. **d** 64 **p** 65 Portsm. C of St Simon Southsea 64-67; St Jo Evang Penge 67-70; V of St Chris Leic 70-74; Asst Master S Gr Sch Portsm 74-75; Springfield Sch Portsm 75-79; Hon C of St Jude Southsea 75-81. *142 Francis Avenue, Southsea, Portsmouth, PO4 0ER.*

TOWNER, Leslie Bernard. b 05. St Cath Coll Cam 2nd cl Engl Trip pt i, 25, BA (3rd cl Th Trip pt i) 27, MA 30. Westcott Ho Cam 27. **d** 28 **p** 29 Guildf. C of Gt Bookham 28-32; St Andr Handsworth 32-36; Camberley 36-39; V of Shottermill 39-50; R of Holmbury St Mary 50-70; RD of Dorking 67-70. *The Old Smithy, Queen Camel, Yeovil, Somt.*

TOWNER, Paul. b 51. Univ of Bris BSc 72. Co for Nat Acad Awards BA (Th) 81. Oak Hill Coll 78. **d** 81 Sherwood for Southw. C of Aspley Dio Southw from 81. *The Bungalow, St Margaret's Church, Aspley Lane, Nottingham, NG8 5GE.*

TOWNLEY, Peter Kenneth. b 55. Univ of Sheff BA 78. Ridley Hall Cam 78. **d** 80 **p** 81 Man. C of Ch Ch Ashton-u-Lyne Dio Man from 80. *33 Taunton Road, Ashton-under-Lyne, OL7 9DP.* (061-344 2372)

TOWNLEY, Robert Keith. b 44. St Jo Coll Auckld LTh 67. **d** 67 Auckld **p** 68 Bp Monteith for Auckld. C of H Trin Devonport Auckld 67-70; Ch Ch Lisburn 71-74; St Paul Portman Square St Marylebone Dio Lon from 75. *Flat 3, 18 Hans Crescent, SW1.* (01-935 5941)

TOWNLEY-SMITH, James William. Univ of Manit BA 67. **d** 68 Bran **p** 69 Rupld for Bran. I of Lynn Lake 68-71; Hon C of St Geo Transcona Winnipeg 71-75. *302-3450 Fieldgate Drive, Mississauga, Ont., Canada.*

TOWNROE, Canon Edward John. b 20. St Jo Coll Ox BA 42, MA 48. Fell K Coll Lon 59. Linc Th Coll 42. **d** 43 **p** 44 Dur. C of Good Shepherd Conv Distr Sunderland 43-48; Chap for K Coll Lon at St Boniface Coll Warm 48-56; Warden 56-69; L to Offic Dio Sarum from 48; Can and Preb of Teinton Regis in Sarum Cathl from 69. *St Boniface Lodge, Warminster, Wilts, BA12 8PG.* (Warminster 212355)

TOWNROE, Canon Michael Dakeyne. b 15. Linc Th Coll 35. **d** 38 Grantham for Linc **p** 39 Linc. C of Grantham 38-41; W Grinstead (in c of Partridge Green) 41-44; Pulborough 44-47; R of Graffham w Woolavington 47-59; Chap St Mich Sch Burton Pk 47-59; RD of Petworth 56-59; R of Bexhill Dio Chich from 59; Surr from 59; RD of Battle and Bexhill 64-77; Can and Preb of Chichester from 69. *Old Town Rectory, Bexhill-on-Sea, Sussex.* (0424-211115)

TOWNSEND, Christopher Robin. b 47. St Jo Coll Nottm LTh 74. **d** 74 **p** 75 Bradf. C of St Jo Evang Gt Horton Bradf 74-77; Heaton 77-78; Wollaton 78-80; V of Slaithwaite w E Scammonden Dio Wakef from 80. *Slaithwaite Vicarage, Huddersfield, W Yorks.* (Huddersfield 842748)

TOWNSEND, David Warren. ACT ThDip 61. **d** 61 **p** 72 Bp Redding for Melb. C of H Trin Coburg 61-62; Blackb 62-64; St Luke N Altona 64-68; Chap St Thos Coll Mt Lavinia 68-72; I of Heathmount 72-79; Frankston E Dio Melb from 79. *72 McMahon's Road, Frankston, Vic, Australia 3199.* (783 1561)

TOWNSEND, Canon John Clifford. b 24. St Edm Hall Ox BA 48, MA 49. Wells Th Coll. **d** 50 **p** 51 Mon. C of Machen 50-51; Usk 51-55; R of Melbury Osmond w Melbury Sampford 55-60; Chap RNR 57-75; V of St Aldhelm Branksome 60-69; Melksham 70-73; R 73-80; Can and Preb of Sarum Cathl from 72; RD of Bradf 73-80; V of Harnham Dio Sarum from 80; RD of Sarum from 80. *Harnham Vicarage, Salisbury, Wilts, SP2 8DQ.* (Salisbury 3564)

TOWNSEND, John Elliott. b 39. ALCD 63. **d** 64 **p** 65 Chelmsf. C of St Pet Harold Wood Hornchurch 64-68; Walton Suff 68-72; V of St Martin Kensal Rise Dio Lon from 72. *93 College Road, NW10 5EU.* (01-969 4598)

TOWNSEND, John Errington. b 20. St Aug Coll Cant 64. **d** 65 **p** 66 Portsm. C of Alverstoke 65-69; R of Droxford Portsm 69-74; Dioc Org for Social Work Portsm 74-78. *Little Meon House, Selworth Lane, Soberton, Hants, SO3 1PX.*

TOWNSEND, Noel Maxwell. Wollaston Th Coll W Austr 59. **d** 61 **p** 62 Perth. C of Moora 62; Cottesloe and Mosman Pk 63-65; R of Trayning 65-68; Bluff Point 69-80; Manjimup Dio Bunb from 80. *Box 114, Manjimup, W Australia.* (71-1015)

TOWNSEND, Peter. b 35. K Coll Lon and Warm AKC 63. **d** 64 **p** 65 Cant. C of St Osw Norbury 64-67; New Romney w Hope 67-69; St Francis Westborough Guildf 69-74; R of Paulerspury Dio Pet from 74; C-in-c of Wicken Dio Pet from 74. *Rectory, Tews End Lane, Paulerspury, Towcester, Northants, NN12 7NQ.* (Paulerspury 670)

TOWNSEND, Peter. b 37. Wells Th Coll 67. **d** 69 **p** 70 Pet. C of Desborough 69-72; Bramley Leeds 72-75; P-in-c of Newton Hall Ecumen Experiment 75-80; P-in-c of Newton Hall 80-81; V of St Luke Hartlepool Dio Dur from 81. *St Luke's Vicarage, Tunstall Avenue, Hartlepool, Cleve, TS26 8NF.* (Hartlepool 72893)

TOWNSEND, Philip Roger. b 51. Univ of Sheff BA 78. Trin Coll Bris 78. **d** 80 **p** 81 S'wark. C of St Jas W Streatham Dio S'wark from 80. *242 Mitcham Lane, Streatham, SW16 6NY.*

TOWNSHEND, Charles Hume. b 41. St Pet Coll Ox BA (2nd cl Th) 64, MA 69. Westcott Ho Cam 64. **d** 66 **p** 67 S'wark. C of Warlingham w Chelsham and Farleigh 66-75; R of Old Cleeve w Leighland and Treborough Dio B & W from 75. *Old Cleeve Rectory, Minehead, Somt.* (Washford 576)

TOWNSHEND, Ven Charles Robert. Univ of W Ont BA 61. Hur Coll BTh 63. **d** 62 **p** 63 Bp Townshend for Hur. d Dio Hur 62-63; C of St Geo Lon 63-64; R of Florence 64-67; I of St Jas Sarnia 67-71; H Trin Chatham 71-74; Dom Chap to Bp of Hur 71-74; R of Owen Sound Dio Hur from 74; Archd of Saugeen from 74. *412 11th Street, Owen Sound, Ont., Canada.* (519-376 3287)

TOWNSHEND, Edward George Hume. b 43. Pemb Coll Cam BA 66, MA 70. Westcott Ho Cam 68. **d** 70 Lynn for Nor **p** 71 Thetpord for Nor. C of Hellesdon 70-74; Industr Chap Lowestoft Dio Nor 74-81; Team V of Lowestoft Group 74-81; V of St Jo Bapt Stafford Dio Lich from 81; P-in-c of Ingestre w Tixall Dio Lich from 81. *St John's Vicarage, Westhead Avenue, Stafford.* (Stafford 53493)

TOWNSHEND, Canon Horace Lyle Hume. b 14. TCD BA 39, MA 46. Westcott Ho Cam 44. **d** 46 **p** 47 Lich. C of Alrewas w Fradley 46-48; R of Hethersett w Canteloff 48-50; Bucklesham w Brightwell and Foxhall 50-56; Dioc Adviser for Youth Work Dio St E 50-54; V of Rugeley 56-61; Cannock w Chadsmoor 61-68; RD of Rugeley 60-68; R of Lyng w Sparham 68-75; C-in-c (R 73-75) of Elsing w Bylaugh 71-75; RD of Sparham 70-73 and 75-79; Hon Can of Nor 73-80 Can (Emer) from 80; M Gen Syn 75-79; R of Bawdeswell w Foxley 76-79. *46 The Close, Norwich, Norfolk.* (Norwich 26049)

TOWNSHEND, Peter Thomas. b 55. Univ of W Ont Lon BA 77. Hur Coll Lon Ont MDiv 80. **d** 80 Hur **p** 81 Bp Townshend for Hur. C of St Jas (Westmr) Lon Dio Hur from 80. *112 Base Line Road W, Apt 1005, London, Ont, Canada, N6J 1V4.*

✠ **TOWNSHEND, Right Rev William Alfred.** Hur Coll LTh 21. Univ of W Ont DD *hon causa* 49, LLD 60. **d** 26 **p** 27 Hur. C of Bervie 26-27; R of Bervie Kingarf and Kinlough 27-29; Ch of The Redeemer Lon 29-39; RD of E Middx 35-38; Can of Hur 38-45; Dioc Comm Dio Hur 39-49; Archd of Hur 45-55; Hur Dioc Regr Sec and Treas 47-55; Cons Ld Bp Suffr of Hur in St Paul's Cathl Lon Ont 30 November 55 by Abp of Alg; Bps of Hur; Niag; Ont; Tor; Ott; W New York; Ohio; and Erie; Bps Suffr of Moos; and Michigan; Asst Bp of Hur; Abp Renison; Bps Lofthouse and Wells; and Bp Zielinski; res 67. *950 Colborne Street, London 11, Ont, Canada.*

TOWNSHEND-CARTER, Philip Alfred Grenville. b 24. Univ of BC BSc 46. McGill Univ Montr MComm 50. Trin Coll Tor MDiv 80. **d** 80 Edmon. Hon C of Ch Ch City and Dio Edmon from 80. *10975 - 126 Street, Edmonton, Alberta, Canada.*

TOWNSON, Eric James. b 34. St Aid Coll 60. **d** 62 Blackb **p** 63 Burnley for Blackb. C of Heysham 62-65; Preston Lancs 65-69; Miss Ruanda Miss 69-74; Dioc Youth Chap Rwa 69-74; C of Burley Dio Ripon from 74. *32 Park View Grove, Leeds 4.*

TOWNSON, Sania Guy. d 81 N Queensld. Perm to Offic Dio N Queensld from 81. *48 Twelfth Avenue, Railway Estate, Qld, Australia 4810.*

TOWNSON, Canon William Dixon. Bp's Univ Lennox LST 61. Hur Coll 59. **d** and **p** 61 Niag. C of Oakville 61-63; I of St Phil Burlington 63-65; C of St Mark Ott 65-66; Chap Renison Coll Waterloo 66-70; R of Kincardine 71-73; Trail 73-75; Lambeth 75-79; Trin Ch St Thomas Dio Hur from 79; Can of Hur from 80. *81 Wellington Street, St Thomas, Ont, Canada.*

TOWSE, Anthony Norman Beresford. b 21. Linc Coll Ox BA 48, MA 52. Westcott Ho Cam 48. **d** 50 **p** 51 Southw. C of St Jo Bapt Beeston 50-55; St Osw Norbury 57-60; Tenterden w Smallhythe 60-64; V of Appledore (w Stone-in-Oxney and Ebony from 72 and Kenardington from 75) Dio Cant from 64; C-in-c of Stone-in-Oxney and Ebony 69-72; Kenardington 74-75; RD of S Lympne from 81. *Vicarage, Appledore, Ashford, Kent, TN26 2DB.* (023-383 250)

TOY, John. b 30. Late Scho of Hatf Coll Dur BA (1st cl Th) 53, MA 62. Univ of Leeds PhD 82. Wells Th Coll 53. **d** 55 **p** 56 S'wark. C of St Paul Newington 55-58; S Sec SCM 58-60; Chap Ely Th Coll and L to Offic Dio Ely 60-64; Chap at Gothenburg 65-69; Lect and Asst Chap St Jo Coll York 69-72; Sen Lect 72-79; Prin Lect from 79; L to Offic Dio York from 69. *6 Whitby Avenue, Stockton Lane, YO3 0ET.* (York 53714)

TOYA, Ishmael. CMS Div Sch Limuru 43. **d** 44 **p** 45 Momb. P Dio Momb. *Bamba, PO Mariakani, Kenya.*

TOZER, Frank William. b 21. Wells Th Coll 61. **d** 63 **p** 64 Chich. C of St Mark Kemp Town Brighton 63-65; Crawley (in c of Three Bridges) 65-73; V of Heathfield Dio Chich from 73. *Old Heathfield Vicarage, Heathfield, E Sussex.* (Heathfield 2457)

TOZER, Reginald Ernest. b 25. St Aid Coll 57. **d** 59 **p** 60 Chelmsf. C of St Andr Plaistow 59-62; C-in-c of Clayton Conv Distr Newc L 62-69; V of E Ham w Upton Pk 69-75; Surr from 71; V of Hatfield Peverel w Ulting Dio Chelmsf from 75. *Vicarage, Hatfield Peverel, Chelmsford, Essex.* (Chelmsford 380958)

TRACEY, Arthur. b 01. BNC Ox BA 24. Wycl Hall Ox 50. **d** 51 **p** 52 Roch. C of Aylesford 51-53; R of Trottiscliffe 53-63; V of Mark Cross 63-66; Perm to Offic Dio Chich from 66. *Rothbury, Church Road, Crowborough, Sussex.* (Crowborough 61301)

TRACEY, Thomas Patrick. b 14. Sarum Th Coll 54. **d** 56 **p** 57 Worc. C of St Geo Claines Worc 56-59; St Jo Evang Newbury 59-61; V of Edlesborough w Northall and Dagnall 61-71; R of Rotherfield Peppard 71-75; P-in-c of Stadhampton w Chislehampton 75-78; Warborough 75-78; Team V of Dorchester 78-81. *14 Myrtle Close, Long Hanborough, Oxford, OX7 2DE.* (Freeland 882412)

TRACY, Roy Dixon. St Steph Ho and St Jo Coll Morpeth ACT ThL 30. **d** 30 **p** 31 Armid. C of Quirindi 30-33; St Pet Cathl Armid 33-34; P-in-c of Boggabilla 34-35; R of Aberdare 35-36; C of Morpeth 36-38; Bro of St Lawr Dio Melb 38-40; V of Charlton 40-43; Chap AMF 43-46; V of Birregurra 46-51; L to Offic Dio Wang 61-63. *Myrtleford, Vic, Australia.*

TRAFFORD, Canon Nelson. b 05. ALCD 32. **d** 32 **p** 33 Birm. C of Bp Latimer Mem Ch Birm 32-36; Warboys 36-42; R 42-73; RD of St Ives 55-69; Surr from 63; Hon Can of Ely from 65. *11 Westfield Road, Brundall, Norwich, Norf, NR13 5LF.* (0603-713645)

TRAILL, James Watson Corry. TCD BA 63, Div Test (2nd cl) 64. **d** 64 **p** 65 Derry. C of Maghera Dio Derry from 64. *21 Meetinghouse Avenue, Maghera, Co Derry, N Ireland.*

TRAIN, Clifford Walton. d 58 Tor **p** 64 Niag. C of St Mark W Tor 58-64; R of Hannon 64-69. *South River, Ont., Canada.* (705-386 2260)

TRAINER, James. Kelham Th Coll 33. **d** 40 S'wark **p** 41 Kingston T for S'wark. C of H Trin Lambeth 40-42; St Jo Evang w All SS Waterloo Road Lambeth 42-44; Chap Lambeth Hosp and R Waterloo Hosp 43-44; Chap RNVR 44-47; Chap Ardingly Coll 47-48; C of Eastbourne 48-50; Chap Guildf Gr Sch Perth 50-52; Chap R Austr Naval Coll Flinders 52-53; RAN 51-67; Commiss Rockptn 59-69; Wang 63-67; L to Offic Dio Syd 63-67; Perm to Offic from 77; P-in-c of Bethanga 67-70. *57 Kent Road, Epping, NSW 2121, Australia.*

TRAINOR, Ian James. d 79 **p** 81 N Queensld (NSM). C of St Jas Mt Isa Dio N Queensld from 79. *15 Hercules Street, Mount Isa, Qld, Australia 4825.*

TRANTER, John. Kelham Th Coll 36. **d** 43 **p** 44 Derby. C of Staveley 43-47; Bolsover 47-51; V of Denby 51-68; R of Aston-on-Trent w Weston-on-Trent Dio Derby from 68. *Aston-on-Trent Rectory, Derby.* (Derby 792658)

TRANTER, Paul Trevor William. b 10. Qu Coll Cam BA 32. Clifton Th Coll 34. **d** 34 Chelmsf **p** 35 Barking for Chelmsf. C of Leyton 34-37; V of St Edw Birm 37-41; St Jas Islington 41-49; R of Myland 49-61; V of Bere Regis (w Winterbourne Kingston 61-71) 61-76; RD of Bere Regis 64-73. *Green Bough, Gold Hill, Childe Okeford, Blandford, Dorset.*

TRAPNELL, Stephen Hallam. b 30. G and C Coll Cam BA 53, MA 57. Virginia Th Sem USA BD 56, MDiv 70. Ridley Hall Cam 53. **d** 56 **p** 57 S'wark. C of St Matthias U Tulse Hill 56-59; C of Reigate 59-61; V of Ch Ch Richmond 61-72; H Trin Sydenham 72-80; R of Worting Dio Win from 80. *Worting Rectory, Glebe Lane, Basingstoke, Hants.* (Basingstoke 22095)

✠ **TRAPP, Right Rev Eric Joseph.** b 10. Univ of Leeds BA (1st cl Phil) 32. Trin Coll Tor Hon DD 67. Coll of Resurr Mirfield 32. **d** 34 **p** 35 S'wark. C of St Olave Mitcham 34-37; Prin of Masite Tr Inst 37-38; Chap 38-40; Dir of Masite Miss Basuto 37-40; R of Bethlehem OFS 40-43; R and Dir of Maseru Basuto 43-47; Can of Bloemf Cathl 44-47; Cons Ld Bp of Zulu in Bloemf Cathl 2 Feb 47 by Abp of Capetn (Metrop); Bps of Natal; St Jo Kaffr; Grahmstn; Pret; Bloemf; Lebom; and Geo; Asst Bp (Stainton) of Bloemf; res 57; Sec of SPG 57-64; USPG 65-70; Commiss Zulu 58-68; Centr Afr 63-70; Apptd Bp of Bermuda 70; res 75; Perm to Offic Dio St Alb from 75; Hon Asst Bp of St Alb 76-80. *18 Sorrel Garth, Hitchin, Herts, SG4 9PS.* (Hitchin 4097)

TRASLER, Graham Charles George. b 44. Ch Ch Ox BA (2nd cl Th) 65, MA 69. Cudd Coll 66. **d** 68 **p** 69 Dur. C of St Mary Gateshead 68-71; P-in-c of St Pet Monkwearmouth 71-79; Bentley & Binsted Dio Win from 79. *Binsted Vicarage, Alton, Hants, GU34 4NX.* (Bentley 2174)

TRATHEN, John Vernon. d and **p** 62 Bloemf. C of St Marg Bloemf 62-64; R of Springfontein 64-67; Harrismith 67-68; Kroonstad 68-73; Archd of Kroonstad 68-73; L to Offic Dio Johann 73-75; C of Parkview Dio Johann from 75. *59 Galway Road, Park View, Johannesburg, Transvaal, S Africa.* (011-41 4863)

TRAVELL, Peter Valentine. b 23. Univ of Lon Dipl Th (external) 62. Sarum Wells Th Coll 75. **d** 77 **p** 78 Win (NSM). C of Romsey Abbey Dio Win from 77. *Kingswood, The Crescent, Romsey, Hants.*

TRAVERS, Colin James. b 49. St Pet Coll Ox BA 70, MA 74. Ridley Hall Cam 70. **d** 72 **p** 73 Barking for Chelmsf. C of Hornchurch 72-75; Aldersbrook 75-77; V of St Lawr Barkingside Dio Chelmsf from 77. *Vicarage, Donington Avenue, Barkingside, Ilford, Essex.* (01-554 2003)

TRAVERS, John William. b 48. Linc Th Coll 75. **d** 78 **p** 79 Ripon. C of Headingley 78-81; Team V of Louth Dio Linc from 81. *St Michael's Vicarage, Little Lane, Louth, Lincs.* (Louth 601340)

TRAVERSE, Ernest. b 28. Oak Hill Coll 73. **d** 75 **p** 76 Liv. C of Roby 75-77; Rainhill 77-78; V of St Barn Marsh Green 78-80; Team V of Bemerton Dio Sarum from 80. *Vicarage, St Michael's Road, Salisbury, Wilts.* (Sarum 3750)

TRAVIS, Robert Leonard. b 15. Sarum Th Coll 55. **d** 56 **p** 57 Portsm. C of Rowner 56-59; V of Em Ch Everton and Chap Mill Road Hosp 59-61; V of Weald 61-66; Perm to

Offic Dio Liv 67-80; Dio Wai 80; Dio Auckld from 80. *The Lodge, Selwyn Village, Target Street, Auckland, NZ.*

TRAYNOR, William Thomas. b 23. Univ Laval Queb BA 45, PhD 51. **d** and **p** 49 RC Abp of Tor. In RC Ch 49-78; Rec into Angl Commun 78 by Bp of Tor. Educn Adv Canadian Forces Tor from 79. *312 Simonstone Boulevard, Thornhill, Ont, Canada, L3T 4T5.*

TREADGOLD, Canon John David. b 31. Univ of Nottm BA 58. Wells Th Coll. **d** 59 **p** 60 Southw. V Cho of Southw Minster 59-64; CF (TA) 62-67; R of Wollaton 64-74; V of Darlington 74-81; CF (TAVR) 74-78; Surr 76-81; Can of Windsor and Chap to HM the Queen from 81. *Chaplain's Lodge, Windsor Great Park, Windsor, Berks.* (Egham 32434)

TREADWELL, Albert Frederick. K Coll Lon and Warm 55. **d** 57 **p** 58 Ox. C of Clewer 57-59; Chap Licensed Victuallers' Sch Slough and Hon C of St Mary Upton w Chalvey Slough 59-65; V of St Mich AA Barnes Dio S'wark from 65. *39 Elm Bank Gardens, SW 13.* (01-876 5230)

TREANOR, Canon Desmond Victor. b 28. St Jo Coll Dur BA (3rd cl Th) 53, Dipl Th 54, MA 59. **d** 54 Kens for Lon **p** 55 Lon. C of St Thos Oakwood 54-57; St Andr Sudbury 57-59; V of St Steph Lansdown Walcot 59-66; St Werburgh Derby 66-68; St Anne Leic 68-75; St Mary Humberstone City and Dio Leic from 75; Hon Can of Leic from 78; P-in-c of St Eliz Nether Hall City and Dio Leic from 81. *Humberstone Vicarage, Leicester, LE5 1EE.* (Leic 767281)

TREANOR, Terence Gerald. b 29. St Jo Coll Ox BA (3rd cl Hist) 52, MA 56. Wycl Hall Ox 52. **d** 54 Reading for Lon **p** 55 Lon. C of Ch Ch Crouch End 54-57; H Trin Cam 57-60; V of St Mary Doncaster 60-66; Chap Oakham Sch from 66. *Lincoln house, Oakham, Leics, LE15 6De.* (Oakham 3800)

TREASURE, Andrew Stephen. b 51. Oriel Coll Ox BA 73, MA 77. St Jo Coll Nottm BA 76. **d** 77 **p** 78 York. C of Beverley Minster 77-81; H Trin City and Dio Cam from 81. *42 Pretoria Road, Cambridge, CB4 1HE.* (0223 350511)

TREASURE, Canon Herbert John. b 16. Keble Coll Ox BA 37, MA 41. Cudd Coll 38. **d** 39 **p** 40 Sarum. C of Gillingham w Milton and E and W Stour 39-42; Asst Miss St Chris Hanwell 42-43; Bridport 43-47; V of Ramsbury w Axford 47-58; Broadchalke w Bowerchalke 58-69; Puddletown w Athelhampton and Burleston 69-75; RD of Chalke 64-69; C-in-c of Barford St Martin 75-80; Baverstock 75-80; Dinton 75-80; Compton Chamberlayne 75-80; Can and Preb of Sarum Cathl from 76; R of Barford St Martin, Dinton, Baverstock, Burcombe and Compton Chamberlayne Dio Sarum from 80. *Barford St Martin Rectory, Salisbury, Wilts., SP3 4AS.* (Wilton 3385)

TREASURE, Ronald Charles. b 24. Or Coll Ox BA (2nd cl Th) 48, MA 52. Cudd Coll. **d** 50 **p** 51 York. C of Whitby 50-54; Min of St Mich AA Distr N Hull 54-58; V 58-62; New Malton Dio York from 62; RD of Malton 63-75. *17 The Mount, Malton, Yorks, YO17 0ND.* (Malton 2089)

TREBBLE, Canon William Henry. b 09. Wadh Coll Ox BA (3rd cl Engl Lit) 30, MA 34. Wycl Hall Ox 32. **d** 33 **p** 34 Ox. C of Ch Ch Reading 33-35; Windsor 35-40; V of Woodley 40-45; R of Theale 45-54; Ed Ox Dioc Mag 49-65; RD of Bradfield 53-54; Bicester (w Islip from 57) 54-74; V of Bicester 54-74; V of Caversfield 54-74; C-in-c of Bucknell 55-65; Hon Can of Ch Ch Ox 63-79 Can (Emer) from 79; P-in-c of Fifield w Idbury 74-79; Perm to Offic Dio Ex from 79. *1 Willow Close, New Barnstaple Road Ilfracombe, EX34 9RP.*

TREBLE, Harry. b 06. AKC (1st cl) 32. Univ of Lon BD 55 BA (3rd cl Phil) 61. **d** 32 **p** 33 Lon. C of St Bart Stamford Hill 32-34; Ch Ch S Hackney 34-42; V of Epping Upland 42-49; C-in-c of St Cedd's Conv Distr Barkingside Dio Chelmsf 49-61; Min from 61; CF (EC) 43-46; Hon CF 46. *11 Summit Drive, Woodford Green, Essex, IG8 8QW.* (01-550 4662)

TREBY, Raymond Harold. b 14. **d** 74 **p** 75 Bris. C of H Trin (w St Gabr and St Lawr Easton from 75) Bris 74-81; P-in-c of St Luke w Ch Ch City and Dio Bris from 81. *65 Barton Hill Road, Barton Hill, Bristol, BS5 0AP.* (Bris 551660)

TREDENNICK, John Edwin Foster. b 06. St Jo Coll Dur LTh 33, BA 35. ALCD 33. **d** 36 **p** 37 Chelmsf. C of Good Shepherd Collier Row 36-40; St Paul Leyton 40-44; V of St Luke New Catton 44-55; C-in-c of St Thos Lambeth 55-56; V of St Andr (w St Thos from 56) Lambeth 55-75. *Roselle, Kenwyn Road, Truro, Cornw, TR1 3SH.* (Truro 2246)

TREDWELL, James Jeffery. St Jo Coll Morpeth ACT ThL 33. **d** 33 **p** 34 Bath. M of Bush Bro Dubbo 33-40; R of Coonabarabran 40-52; R of Baradine 42-49; Prin of St Cuthb Boys' Home Colac 52-55; R of Busselton 55-64; Can of Bunb 58-73; R of Bridgetown 64-65; Brunswick Junction 65-71; Bp of Bunb Commiss 68-73; R of Mandurah 71-73; Archd in Bunb 72-73; L to Offic Dio Bunb from 74. *Lot 104, Ewing Crescent, Mandurah, W Australia 6210.*

TREEBY, Stephen Frank. b 46. Univ of Man LLB 67. Univ of Nottm Dipl Th 69. Cudd Coll 69. **d** 71 Repton for Derby **p** 72 Derby. C of Ashbourne w Mapleton 71-74; Boulton 74-76; Chap Trowbridge Coll 76-79; Team V of Melksham Dio Sarum from 79. *Vicarage, Church Lane, Melksham, Wilts, SN12 7EF.* (Melksham 702310)

TREEN, Anthony Robert. b 37. Chich Th Coll 72. **d** 74 Lewes for Chich **p** 75 Horsham for Chich. C of St Richard Haywards Heath 74-77; Industr Chap Crawley 77-80; V of St John Burgess Hill Dio Chich from 80. *68 Park Road, Burgess Hill, RH15 8HG.*

TREEN, Preb Robert Hayes Mortlock. b 19. New Coll Ox BA 46, MA 46. Westcott Ho Cam 45. **d** 47 **p** 48 B & W. C of Bath Abbey 47-52; PC of Pill 52-61; R of St Sav Bath 61-76; Preb of Wells Cathl from 74; V of Bp's Hull Dio B & W from 76; RD of Taunton S 77-81; Taunton from 81. *Bishops Hull Vicarage, Taunton, Somt.* (Taunton 73032)

TREFTS, Todd Hubbard. Trin Coll Hartford BA 55. Virginia Th Sem. **d** 61 WNY (USA) **p** 62 Mbale. P Dio Nam 63-69. *Bishop Tucker College, PO Box 4, Mukono, Uganda.*

TREGEA, Canon James Lewis. ACT ThL 61. **d** 56 **p** 57 C & Goulb. C of Albury 56-59; Junee 59-61; R of Gunning 61-64; N Albury 64-71; All SS Canberra 71-80; Can of St Sav Cathl Goulb from 76; R of Cootamundra Dio C & Goulb from 81. *Box 37, Cootamundra, NSW, Australia 2590.*

TREGLOWN, Geoffrey Leonard. b 19. MBE (Mil) 44. Hon CF 44. Handsworth Coll Birm 38. **d** 60 Bris **p** 60 Malmesbury for Bris. [f Methodist Min] C of Ch Ch Hanham 60-63; V of Cricklade w Latton w Eisey 63-73; Perm to Offic Dio Glouc from 74. *36 Christchurch Road, Cheltenham, Glos.* (Cheltenham 512496)

TREHERNE, Alan Thomas Evans. b 30. Late Scho of St D Coll Lamp BA (2nd cl Phil) 53. Wycl Hall Ox. **d** 55 **p** 56 Heref. C of St Pet Heref 55-57. CMS Miss 57-72; Youth Miss Luckn 58-63; C of Sikandra 58-63; P-in-c of St Geo Agra 63-72; Min of Ch Ch Netherley 72-74; V of Gateacre Dio Liv 74-75; R from 75; RD of Farnworth from 81. *St Stephen's Rectory, Belle Vale Road, Liverpool, L25 2PQ.* (051-487 9338)

TREHERNE, Thomas. St. Francis Coll Brisb. **d** 57 **p** 58 Brisb. C of Maryborough 57-61; P-in-C of Gayndan 61-64; R of Millmerran 64-67; Dioc Youth Leadership Tr Officer Dio Brisb 67-71; Asst Sec ABM in Prov of Queensld 71-74; Chap St Marg Sch Albion Brisb 74-77; Perm to Offic Dio Brisb from 78. *3/18 Kent Street, Coorparoo, Queensland, Australia 4151.* (396 3965)

TRELLIS, Oswald Fitz-Burnell. b 35. Chich Th Coll 73. **d** 74 **p** 75 Chelmsf. C of All SS Chelmsf 74-78; Min of New Eccles Distr of N Springfield Dio Chelmsf from 79. *44 Golden Acres, North Springfield, Chelmsford, Essex.* (Chelmsf 466160)

TREMELLEN, Raymond Guy. b 04. Lich Th Coll 30. **d** 32 **p** 33 Lon. C of All SS Fulham 32-34; Saltwood 34-37; St Pet-in-Thanet (in c of St Andr Broadstairs) 37-38; Bexhill (in c of St Mich AA) 38-43; R of Dallington 43-46; V of St Luke Brighton 46-53; St Phil Eastbourne 53-55; Hadlow Down 56-61; Perm to Offic Dio Chich from 61. *85 Southwick Street, Southwick, Sussex.* (Brighton 593120)

TREMEWAN, Christopher Charles. b 51. Univ of Auckld BA 73, MA 76. St Jo Coll Auckld 74. **d** 75 **p** 76 Ch Ch. C of Ashburton 75-76; Geraldine 76-77; Hon C of Maori Miss Dio Auckld from 78. *10 Burleigh Street, Auckland 3, NZ.* (775-400)

TREMEWAN, Colin Wilkinson. Univ of NZ BSc 36. Ch Ch Coll 57. **d** 58 **p** 59 Ch Ch. C of Riccarton 58-60; Papanui 60-61; V of Waikari 62-64; Hornby 64-68; Rangiora 68-75; Oxford-Cust 75-78; RD of N Cant 74-78; Perm to Offic Dio Ch Ch from 78. *121 Elizabeth Street, Christchurch 4, NZ.* (45-254)

TREMLETT, Anthony Frank. b 37. Ex/Truro Min Tr Scheme 78. **d** 81 Ex. C of H Spirit Southway Plymouth Dio Ex from 81. *124 Beverston Way, Widewell, Roborough, Plymouth, PL6 7EG.*

✠ **TREMLETT, Right Rev Anthony Paul.** b 14. K Coll Cam 3rd cl Hist Trip pt i 35, BA (3rd cl Hist Trip pt ii) 36, MA 46. Cudd Coll 37. **d** 38 **p** 39 Lon. C of St Barn Wood End Northolt 38-41; CF (EC) 41-46; Men in Disp 45; Dom Chap to Bp of Trinid 46-50; Chap Trin Hall Cam and L to Offic Dio Ely 50-58; Commiss to Bp in Jer 52-74; Exam Chap to Bp of Linc 52-56; Commiss Trinid 53-62; Select Pr Univ of Cam 55 and 56; V of St Steph Roch Row w St Jo Evang Westmr 58-64; Exam Chap to Bp of Portsm 60-64; to Bp of Nor 60-64; to Bp of Guildf 61-64; Cons Ld Bp Suffr of Dover in Cant Cathl 30 Nov 64 by Abp of Cant; Bps of Nor; Pet; Ely; Roch; Guildf; and Glas; Bps Suffr of Dunwich; Croydon; Maidstone; Lynn; and Buckingham; and Bps Rose, Montgomery Campbell, Barry, Davis, Jackson, Boys, Clarke and Craske; res 80. *Doctors Commons, The Square, Northleach, Glos, GL54 3EH.* (N Leach 426)

TRENAM, Canon John Alfred. Dorch Th Coll. **d** 49 Barb for Windw Is **p** 50 Windw Is. C of St Geo Grenada 49-50; P-in-c of St D w St Paul Grenada 50-53; R 53-64; St Andr

Grenada 64-79; Can of St Geo Cathl Kingstown St Vincent from 69. *c/o Kent's Agencies, Grenville, St Andrew, Grenada, W Indies.*

TRENCHARD, Hugh. b 50. Univ of Wales (Cardiff) BD 75. St Mich Coll Llan 73. **d** 75 **p** 76 Mon. C of Llangattock-juxta-Caerleon 75-80; V of Llanarth w Clytha, Llansantffraed and Bryngwyn Dio Mon from 80. *Vicarage, Llanarth, Gwent, NP5 2AU.*

TRENCHARD, Paul Charles Herbert Anstiss. Univ of Liv LLB 76. St Steph Ho Ox 77. **d** 80 **p** 81 Ex. C of St Martin Barton Dio Ex from 80. *c/o St Martin's Vicarage, Beechfield Avenue, Barton, Torquay, Devon.*

TRENDALL, Peter John. b 43. Oak Hill Th Coll 66. **d** 69 **p** 70 Roch. C of Ch Ch Beckenham 69-73; Bedworth 73-76; V of Hornsey Rise Dio Lon from 76; P-in-c of St Steph U Holloway Dio Lon from 80. *73 Sunnyside Road, N19.* (01-272 1783)

TRENDER, Lawrence. b 37. Bps' Coll Cheshunt 64. **d** 66 **p** 67 S'wark. C of Petersham 66-71; Malden 71-73; R of Thornham Magna w Thornham Parva Dio St E from 73; P-in-c of Gislingham Dio St E 73-81; R from 81; Mellis Dio St E 73-81; R from 81. *Thornham Parva Rectory, Eye, Suffolk, IP23 8ET.* (Mellis 378)

TRENEER, Cyril George Howard. b 14. Univ of Leeds BA 36. Coll of Resurr Mirfield 36. **d** 38 **p** 39 Ex. C of St Pet Plymouth 38-45; St Jo Bapt Cov 45-46; C-in-c of St Mich AA Paignton 46-51; R of S Molton w Nymet St Geo 51-60; R of High Bray w Charles 55-60; V of St Gabr Plymouth 60-79; Perm to Offic Dio Ex from 79. *2 Headborough Road, Ashburton, Newton Abbot, Devon, TQ13 7QP.* (Ashburton 52159)

TRENGOVE, Harry Christopher. b 04. **d** 56 **p** 58 Bradf. C of Keighley 56-58; St Jo Bapt Southend-on-Sea (in c of St Mark) 58-60; R of Litton 60; R of Hinton Blewett 60; Croscombe 60-62; V of St Steph Colchester 62-64; Shalford 64-66; Perm to Offic Dio Chelmsf 66-70; Dio Ox 70-72; Dio Llan 72-76; Dio Pet 80-81. *Miles Court, Hereford Street, Brighton, BN2 1JT.* (0273 693204)

TRENGOVE, Leonard. b 17. Univ of Lon BD 47, BSc 51, MSc 54, PhD 57. Univ of Melb MA 68. Kelham Th Coll 37. **d** 42 S'wark **p** 43 Kingston T for S'wark. C of St Pet Walworth 42-45; South Molton 45-50; V of Yealmpton 50-55; C of Northwood Middx 55-58; Perm to Offic Dio Melb 59-70. *Emlyn, Lighthouse House, Portreath, Redruth, Cornwall.*

TRENIER, Robert Ernest. b 10. TCD BA 33, Div Test (2nd cl) 34. **d** and **p** 35 Clogh. C of Tydavenet Kilmore and Drumsnatt 35-38; Urney 38-39; I of Swanlinbar 39-44; R of Knockbridge w Sherock 44-56; I of Drumgoon w Ashfield 56-71; Can of Kilm Cathl 59-71; RD of Lurgan 64-71. *Hall House, Tonaghbarn, Cootehill, Co Cavan, Irish Republic.*

TRESS, Anthony Glennie. Moore Th Coll Syd ACT ThL 65. **d** 66 Bp Loane for Syd **p** 67 Syd. C of Beecroft 66-67; Lithgow 67-69; H Trin Adel 69-73; P-in-c of Woomera 73-76; R of Fairy Meadow Dio Syd from 77. *450 Princes Highway, Fairy Meadow, NSW, Australia 2519.* (042-844685)

TRETHEWAY, William Robert. b 05. St Bonif Coll Warm 35. **d** 35 Dur **p** 36 Jarrow for Dur. C of St Aid W Hartlepool 35-37; Bideford 37-40; Actg C of Townstal 40-42; Sprowston 42-44; V of Costessey (or Cossey) 44-62; St Phil Heigham 62-71. *6 Brentwood, Greenways, Eaton, Norwich, NR4 6PW.* (Nor 56925)

TRETHEWEY, Frederick Martyn. b 49. Univ of Lon BA 70, Dipl Th 77. STh (Lambeth) 79. Oak Hill Th Coll 75. **d** 78 Lon **p** 79 Stepney for Lon. C of St Mark Tollington Park Holloway Dio Lon from 78. *68b Tollington Park, N4 3RA.*

TREVELYAN, James William Irvine. b 37. Selw Coll Cam BA 64, MA 67. Cudd Coll 62. **d** 65 Lon **p** 66 Kens for Lon. C of Heston 65-68; St Sav Folkestone 68-72; V of Lenham w Boughton Malherbe 72-78; P-in-c of Honiton w Gittisham and Combe Raleigh Dio Ex 78-79; R from 79; P-in-c of Monkton Dio Ex from 81. *Rectory, Honiton, Devon, EX14 8AN.* (Honiton 2925)

TREVIVIAN, Roy. b 21. Lich Th Coll 54. **d** and **p** 55 Guildf. [f Methodist Min]. C of Burgh Heath 55-56; C-in-c of St Francis Conv Distr Westborough Guildf 56-58; V 58-64; Perm to Offic Dio Guildf 64-75; Producer BBC Relig Dept 64-73; Chap Mayflower Family Centre Canning Town from 75; Tutor Chs Radio and TV Tr Centre from 78. *23 Grena Road, Richmond, Surrey.* (01-940 3409)

TREVOR, Charles Frederic. b 27. Sarum Th Coll 54. **d** 56 **p** 57 Southw. C of St Mich AA Sutton-in-Ashfield 56-58; Birstall 58-61; PC of Prestwold w Hoton 61-66; V of Burton-in-Lonsdale 66-74; Thornton-in-Lonsdale 66-74; Kirkby in Malhamdale Dio Bradf from 74; P-in-c of Coniston Cold Dio Bradf from 81. *Kirkby Malham Vicarage, Skipton, N Yorks, BD23 4BS.* (Airton 215)

TREVOR, Colin Stuart. b 26. Sarum Th Coll 78. **d** 60 **p** 61 RC Bp of Birm. In RC Ch 60-67; L by Bp of Portsm 78; C of St Mary W Cowes 78-80; V of Paulsgrove Dio Portsm from 80. *St Michael's Vicarage, Hempsted Road, Paulsgrove, Portsmouth, PO6 4AS.*

TREVOR, Ian Cotterill. St Jo Coll Morpeth 54. **d** 56 Geelong for Adel **p** 57 Adel. C of Hawthorn 56-57; Gawler 57-59; Miss Chap Woodville Gardens 59; P-in-c of Waikerie 59-61; V of W Samoa 62-65; R of Emerald 66-69; Prec of St Paul's Cathl Rockptn 69-72; Org Sec ABM Adel 72-79; R of Tea Tree Gully Dio Adel from 79. *19 Perseverance Road, Tea Tree Gully, S Australia 5091.* (264 4085)

TREVOR-MORGAN, Basil Henry Trevor. b 27. St D Coll Lamp BA 51. Wells Th Coll 51. **d** 53 **p** 54 Mon C of Chepstow w St Arvans and Pentery 53-56; Halesowen w Hasbury 56-59; V of St Thos Stourbridge 59-76; CF (TA) from 59; Christchurch w Mudeford Dio Win from 76. *The Priory Vicarage, Christchurch, Dorset, BH23 1BU.* (0202 483102)

TREW, Alen Robert. b 30. Univ Coll Cardiff BD 77. St Mich AA Llan 74. **d** 77 **p** 78 Mon. C of Abergavenny Dio Mon from 77. *59 Park Crescent, Abergavenny, Gwent.*

TREWIN, Algernon Burney. RMC Sandhurst 03. Sarum Th Coll 33. **d** 34 **p** 35 Lon. C of St Mary Stoke Newington 34-36; V of Exminster 36-46; L to Offic Dio Geo 47-48; Dio Grahmstn 48-64; Dio Natal from 64. *23 St Aubyn Court, Musgrave Road, Durban, S Africa.* (33-6528)

TRIBE, Arthur John. Trin Coll Tor LTh 65. **d** 64 Bp Snell for Tor **p** 65 Tor. C of St Leon Tor 64-65; Rexdale 65-67; St leon 67-69; R of Jarvis 75-79; Acton Dio Niag from 79. *185 Jeffery Street, Hulton Hills, Acton, Ont, Canada.* (519-853 2694)

TRIBE, Arthur Wilfrid Newton. b 03. Trin Coll Ox BA 25, MA 31. Ridley Hall Cam 25. **d** 27 **p** 28 Lon. C of Ch Ch Spitalfields 27-32; St Matt Cam 32-35; CMS Miss Kabale 35-39; Chap RAFVR 39-46; Chap and Asst Master Seaford Coll 46-49; L to Offic Dio Chich 46-49; Dio Ely 49; C of St Lawr Morden 49-50; V of Shustoke w Bentley 50-52; Weald 52-61; R of High Ongar w Norton Mandeville 61-76. *19 Longfields, Marden Ash, Ongar, Essex.*

TRICKER, Russel. b 1891. Paton Congregational Coll Nottm 13. **d** 38 **p** 39 Sheff. C of St Jo Evang Sheff 38-40; Offg C-in-c of Bradfield 40-42; V of St Cath Richmond Road Sheff 42-56; R of Shimplingthorne w Alpheton 56-71. *11 Stratford Drive, City Road, Norwich, NR1 2EY.* (Nor 610407)

TRICKETT, Stanley Mervyn Wood. b 27. Lich Th Coll 64. **d** 66 **p** 67 Heref. C of Kington w Huntington 66-70; P-in-c of Old Radnor w Kinnerton 70-80; Knill 70-80; V of Shrewton and Rollestone Dio Sarum from 80; P-in-c of Winterbourne Stoke Dio Sarum from 80. *Vicarage, Chapel Lane, Shrewton, Salisbury, Wilts, SP3 4BX.*

TRICKEY, Frederick Marc. b 35. Univ of Dur BA (2nd cl Psychol) 62, Dipl Th 64. Cranmer Hall Dur. **d** 64 Southn for Win **p** 65 Win. C of Alton 64-68; R of St Jo Bapt w Winnall Win 68-77; St Martin Guernsey Dio Win from 77. *St Martin's Rectory, Guernsey, CI.* (Guernsey 38303)

TRIGG, John Alfred. b 29. Keble Coll Ox BA and MA 64. Ripon Hall Ox 64. **d** 65 Glouc **p** 66 Tewkesbury for Glouc. C of Dursley 65-67; St Geo Glouc 67-68; Swan Group 68-72; Missr-in-c of S Chilterns Group (C-in-c of Stokenchurch and Ibstone, (of Cadmor End, Lane End, and of Radnage to 76) Dio Ox from 72. *Vicarage, Stokenchurch, High Wycombe, Bucks.* (Radnage 3384)

TRIGG, Jeremy Michael. b 51. Ripon Coll Cudd 80. **d** 81 Knaresborough for Ripon. C of St Edm Rundhay Dio Ripon from 81. *8 Earlswood Avenue, Roundhay, Leeds, LS8 2BR.*

TRILL, Barry. b 42. Chich Th Coll 65. **d** 68 **p** 69 Lon. C of W Hackney 68-73; Team V of Ch of Ch and St John w St Luke, Isle of Dogs, Poplar 73-78; P-in-c of All S Hastings Dio Chich 78-79; V from 79. *All Souls Vicarage, 16 Berlin Road, Hastings, TN35 5JD.* (Hastings 421445)

TRILL, Victor Alfred Mansfield. b 21. St Deiniol's Libr Hawarden. **d** 81 Stockport for Ches. C of St Pet Prestbury Dio Ches from 81. *16 Alison Drive, Macclesfield, SK10 1PZ.*

✠ **TRILLO, Right Rev Albert John.** b 15. K Coll Lon Abp Robertson Pri 37, AKC (1st cl), Jun McCaul Hebr Pri and Trench Gr Test Pri 38, Fell 60. Clothworkers' Co Exhib of Univ of Lon BD (1st cl) 38, MTh 44, Box LXX Pri 45. **d** 38 Lon **p** 39 Willesden for Lon. C of Ch Ch Fulham 38-41; St Gabr Cricklewood (in c of St Mich) 41-45; Schs Sec SCM and L to Offic Dio Ripon 45-50; R of Friern Barnet and Lect at K Coll Lon 50-55; Prin of Bps' Coll Cheshunt and Exam Chap to Bp of St E 55-63; Publ Pr Dio St Alb 55-63; Hon Can of St Alb 58-63; Can Res 63-65; Cons Ld Bp Suffr of Bedford in Cant Cathl 2 Feb 63 by Abp of Cant; Bps of St Alb; St E; Leic; Glouc; and Roch; Bps Suffr of Willesden; Dover; and Tonbridge; and Bps Rose, Warner, Boys, and Craske; Exam Chap to Bp of St Alb from 63; Proc Conv St Alb from 64; Trld to Hertf 68; to Chelmsf 71; Chairman C of E Youth Coun 69-72; Chairman Executive Committee BCC 73-78;

Gen Syn Coun for RC Relns from 75. *Bishopscourt, Main Road, Margaretting, Ingatestone, Essex, CM4 0HD.* (Ingatestone 2001)

TRIMBLE, John Alexander. b 33. BD (Lon) 65. Edin Th Coll 55. **d** 58 **p** 59 Glas. C of St Mary's Cathl Ch Glas 58-60; St Jo Evang Edin 60-65; R of St John Baillieston 65-69; Ch Ch Falkirk Dio Edin from 69. *Christ Church Rectory, Falkirk, Stirlingshire.* (Falkirk 23709)

TRIMINGHAM, John Spencer. Late Nubar Pasha Armenian Scho 31. St Cath S Ox BA (2nd cl Or Lang) 34, MA 39. Univ of Glas D Litt 60. Wells Th Coll 35. **d** 36 **p** 37 S'wark. C of St Silas Nunhead 36-37; CMS Miss Omdurman 37-49; Cairo 49-52; Sec N Sudan Miss 41-49; Exam Chap to Bp Sudan 45-52; Lect in Islamic Univ of Glas 53-56; Sen Lect in Arabic 56-62; Reader 62-64; Prof of Hist Amer Univ of Beirut 64-70; CMS Miss Lebanon 64-70; Prof of Islamic Stud in Near East Sch of Th Beirut 70-78. *Address temp unknown.*

TRINDALL, Jack Alan. NZ Bd of Th Stud LTh 71. **d** 65 **p** 66 Wai. C of Hastings 65-68; V of Waipawa 68-73; Tauranga Dio Wai from 73. *13 Fourth Avenue, Tauranga, NZ.* (86-620)

TRINDER, John Derek. b 28. GOC 74. **d** 77 **p** 78 Glouc. C of Ch Ch Dean Forest 77-80; St Paul Newport Dio Mon from 81. *15 St Bride's Crescent, Newport, Gwent.*

TRINGHAM, Bernard. St Chad's Coll Dur BA 38. **d** 39 **p** 40 Liv. C of Seaforth 38-40; St Cath Liv 40-46; CF (EC) 41-46; Chap of Jamshedpur 46-53; C of Midsomer Norton 53-55; R of Gordonvale 55-58; St Matt Townsville 58-62; Mt Isa 62-64; Archd of the West 62-64; Dean and R of St Jas Cathl Townsville 64-69; R of All SS Brisb 69-75; Commiss N Queensland from 69; Perm to Offic Dio Brisb from 75. *PO Box 22, Cleveland, Queensland, Australia 4163.*

TRINIDAD, Lord Bishop of. *See* Abdulah, Right Rev Clive.

TRINIDAD, Dean of. *See* Harrison, Very Rev Alfred Tuke Priestman.

TRIPLOW, Keith John. b 44. Selw Coll Cam BA 66, MA 70. Chich Th Coll 70. **d** 72 **p** 73 St E. C of Ipswich 72-76; Dartford 76-78; V of Fyfield w Tubney and Kingston Bagpuize Dio Ox from 78. *Vicarage, Fyfield, Abingdon, Oxon, OX13 5LR.* (Frilford Heath 390803)

TRIPP, Richard Howard. Trin Ho Cam BA 55, MA 59. Coll Ho Ch Ch. **d** 57 **p** 59 Ch Ch. C of Sydenham 57-61; V of Bryndwr 61-63; Methven 63-70; Hoon Hay 70-73; L to Offic Dio Ch Ch from 73. *43 Opawa Road, Christchurch 2, N Zealand.*

TRIPPASS, Canon William Arthur. b 08. Univ of Birm BA (3rd cl Engl) 30. Wells Th Coll 30. **d** 31 **p** 32 Worc. C of St Mary Kidderminster 31-39; V of Lower Mitton (or Stourport) 39-47; R of St Nich w St Pet V Droitwich 47-52; RD of Droitwich 47-52; Kidderminster 58-60; Evesham 66-68; V of St Jo Bapt Kidderminster 52-60; Bengeworth 60-68; Bidford-on-Avon 68-73; Hon Can of Worc 66-68; Can (Emer) from 68; C of Alveston 73-81; Perm to Offic Dio Cov from 81. *19 Grange Road, Bidford-on-Avon, Alcester, Warws, B50 4BY.*

TRIPPENSEE, James Arthur. Wayne State Univ BA 60. Nashotak Ho BD 63. **d** 63 Bp Dewitt for Mich **p** 64 Windw Is. P-in-c of Georgetown Charlotte N 66-70. *St Andrews Memorial Episcopal Church, 920 Putnam Avenue, Detroit, Michigan 48202, USA.*

TRISKLE, Kenneth Carl. b 51. Wilfred Laurier Univ Waterloo Ont BSc 74. Univ of W Ont MDiv 76. Hur Coll Tor 76. **d** 76 **p** 77 Keew. C of St Alb Cathl & St Jas Ch Keew 76-81; P-in-c of Lamerton Miss Dio Calg from 81. *Box 479, Bashaw, Alta, Canada.*

TRISTRAM, Geoffrey Robert. b 53. K Coll Lon BA 76. Pemb Coll Cam BA 78. Westcott Ho Cam 77. **d** 79 **p** 80 Sarum. C of H Trin Weymouth Dio Sarum from 79. *65 Rodwell Road, Weymouth, Dorset.*

TRIVETT, Donald Frederick Lionel. K Coll Halifax NS BA 50, LTh 52. **d** 52 **p** 53 NS. C of Ch Ch Dartmouth 52-53; R of Weymouth 53-56; Sackville 56-65; Chap Univ of K Coll Halifax Dio NS from 65; Exam Chap to Bp of NS 71-78; and from 80. *2271 Macdonald Street, Halifax, NS, Canada.* (423-5707)

TRODDEN, Canon Hugh. b 20. St Chad's Coll Dur BA 48, Dipl Th 50. **d** 50 **p** 51 Sheff. C of Denaby Main 50-53; Gosforth Newc T 53-57; R of Gt w L Wratting 57-60; C-in-c of Barnardiston 57-60; All SS Conv Distr Bury St Edms Dio St E 60-63; V from 63; Hon Can of St E Cathl from 79. *18 West Road, Bury St Edmunds, Suff.* (Bury St Edmunds 2704)

TRODDEN, Michael John. b 54. AKC and BD 77. Wycl Hall Ox 79. **d** 80 Chelmsf **p** 81 Barking for Chelmsf. C of St Mary Woodford Dio Chelmsf from 80. *33 Elmshurst Drive, Woodford, E18.* (01-989 3958)

TROLLOPE, David Harvey. b 41. BSc (NCAA) 63. Lon Coll of Div 66. **d** 68 **p** 69 S'wark. C of St Jas w Ch Ch Bermondsey 68-71; CMS Miss Dio Nam 71-72; Dio Kamp 72-77; Dio Nai from 77. *Box 42493, Nairobi, Kenya.*

TROM, Theodoric. Coll of Resurr Rosettenville. **d** 46 **p** 49 Grahmstn. C of St Mich Herschel 46-53; Miss at Peddie 53-55; St Steph Port Eliz 55-56; Queenstown 56-59; Asst Miss St Phil Miss Grahmstn 59-65; R of St Luke's Miss Queenstn 65-66; R of St Phil Miss E Lon 65-67; C of St Pet Aliwal N 70-73; St Matt Miss Grahmstn 73-77; R of H Trin Ft Beaufort 77-78; St Mary Sterkspruit Dio Grahmstn from 78. *Box 76, Sterkspruit, CP, S Africa.*

TROOP, John Richard. b 37. Ely Th Coll 61. **d** 64 **p** 65 Linc. C of St Andr and St Swith Linc 64-66; St Andr w St Luke Grimsby 66-70; V of Wrangle 70-78; South Moor Dio Dur from 78. *St George's Vicarage, South Moor, Stanley, Durham, DH9 7EN.* (Stanley 32564)

TRORY, Alfred Henry. b 14. Chich Th Coll 47. **d** 49 **p** 50 Dur. C of Beamish 49-53; PC of St Simon Simonside S Shields 53-66; St Helen Low Fell Gateshead Dio Dur from 66. *St Helen's Vicarage, Gateshead, T & W, NE9 6DE.* (Low Fell 876510)

TROSS, Canon Julian Chamings. b 14. AKC 35. Bps' Coll Cheshunt 37. **d** 37 **p** 38 Lon. C of St Anne Limehouse 37-43; St Mary Finchley 43-46; V of H Trin Stepney 46-55; R of Datchworth (w Tewin from 77) 55-79; RD of Stevenage 71-75; Hon Can of St Alb from 72. *63 Colestrete, Stevenage, Herts.*

TROTMAN, Anthony Edward Fiennes. b 11. Ex Coll Ox BA (3rd cl Hist) 33, MA 56. Wycl Hall Ox. **d** 48 Connor **p** 49 Down. C of Ballymacarrett 48-51; Dundela 51-52; R of Corsley w Chapmanslade 52-59; Chilmark 59-76; C-in-c of Teffont Ewyas and Teffont Magna 73-75. *17 Estcourt Road, Salisbury, Wilts, SP1 3AP.* (Salisbury 24857)

TROTT, Boyd Wilfred. b 24. **d** and **p** 75 Bunb. P-in-c of Carey Park 75-76; R of Kondinin Dio Bunb from 76. *Rectory, Kondinin, W Australia 6367.* (Kondinin 12)

TROTTER, Harold Barrington. b 33. Sarum Th Coll 64. **d** 66 **p** 67 Sarum. C of St Francis Sarum 66-69; V of Horton w Chalbury 69-73; R of Frenchay 73-81; V of Henbury w Hallen Dio Bris from 81. *Vicarage, Station Road, Henbury, Bristol, BS10 7QQ.* (Bristol 500536)

TROTTER, Michael Frederick Charles. b 32. Fitzw Coll Cam BA (2nd cl Hist Trip pt ii) 56, MA 60. Cudd Coll 56. **d** 58 **p** 59 Ripon. C of Chap Allerton 58-61; Cowley Ox 61-65; V of St Mark Dukinfield 65-69; Team V of Bow w Bromley St Leon 69-75; L to Offic Dio S'wark from 75. *22a Malwood Road, SW12.* (01-673 8065)

TROTTER, Robert James Frederick. b 06. ALCD (1st cl) 41. Univ of Dur LTh 43. Univ of Liv MA 47. Univ of Lon BD 55. Univ of Leeds PhD 62. **d** 41 **p** 42 Man. C of St Mary Radcliffe 41-42; St John and St Jas Litherland 42-43; Sephton (in c of St Osw Netherton) 43-46; Chap Co Ment Hosp Rainhill 46-74. *12 Scarisbrick Road, Rainford, WA11 8JL.* (074 4883769)

TROTTER, Torrens James. b 31. St Jo Coll Dur BA 54. Westcott Ho Cam 54. **d** 56 **p** 57 Ripon. C of Leeds 56-58; Cheam 58-62; Asst Chap Marlborough Coll 62-65; V of Roby 65-68; Team V of St Aid Billingham 68-77; Commun Chap Gateshead Dio Dur from 77; Team V of Gateshead Dio Dur from 77. *9 Saltwell View, Gateshead, T & W, NE8 4JS.* (Gateshead 783569)

TROUGHTON, Canon Charles Reginald. b 1899. Keble Coll Ox BA 22, MA 26. Wells Th Coll 22. **d** 23 **p** 24 Ches. C of St Geo Stockport 23-26; St Hilary Wallasey 26-30; V of St Barn Crewe 30-37; St Luke Poolton 37-51; Ch Ch Willaston 51-69; Hon Can of Ches 58-69; Can (Emer) from 69; RD of Wirral S 59-69; Perm to Offic Dio Ches from 69. *57 Queen's Avenue, Meols, Wirral, Chesh.*

TROUNSON, Ronald Charles. b 26. Em Coll Cam 1st cl Cl Trip pt i 47, BA (2nd cl Cl Trip pt ii) 48, MA 52. **d** 56 **p** 57 Ex. Asst Master Plymouth Coll 53-58; C of St Gabr Plymouth 56-58; Chap of Denstone Coll Staffs 58-76; Asst Master 69-76; Bursar 76-78; Prin St Chad's Coll Dur from 78. *St Chad's College, Durham.* (Durham 64681)

TROWELL, Hubert Carey. b 04. OBE 54. Univ of Lon MB BS 28, MD 33. FRCP (Lon) 45. Wells Th Coll. **d** 59 **p** 60 Glouc. C of Cirencester 59-60; PC of Stratford-sub-Castle 60-69; Chap Sarum Gen Infirm 60-69. *Windhover, Brook Lane, Woodgreen, Fordingbridge, Hants.*

TROWER, Canon George Ernest. St Francis Coll Brisb 57. **d** 60 **p** 61 N Queensld. C of Cairns 60-65; P-in-c of Tully 65-69; C of Mackay 69-71; P-in-c of Hughenden 71-74; C of St Matt Mundingburra Dio N Queensld from 74; Can of N Queensld from 81. *c/o Rectory, Mundingburra, Queensland, Australia.* (077-795963)

TRUBRIDGE, George Ernest Samuel. b 11. ALCD 35. **d** 35 **p** 36 Blackb. C of St Thos Blackpool 35-37; H Trin w St Mark Nottm 37-41; PC of H Trin Derby 41-52; R of Broughton 52-76. *27 Clarendon Road, Broadstone, Dorset.*

TRUDGEON, Frank. Seager Hall Ont 60. **d** 66 Sktn. I of Macklin 66-69; R of Humboldt 69-74; Hon C of Mt Forest

Dio Niag from 75. *Box 535, Mount Forest, Ont., Canada.*

TRUDGILL, Harry Keith. b 25. Univ of Leeds Dipl Educn 49. LCP 54. St Deiniol's Libr Hawarden 76. **d** and **p** 76 Glas. C of St Marg Newlands Glas 76-78; R of Lenzie Dio Glas from 78. *1a Beech Road, Lenzie, Glasgow, G66 4HN.* (041-776 4149)

TRUEMAN, Reginald. b 24. K Coll Cam BA 47, MA 49. Univ of Man BD 54. St Jo Coll Winnipeg Hon DD 58. U Th Sem NY STM 50 Ely Th Coll 49. **d** 50 **p** 51 Man. Lect at St Pet Bolton 50-53; V of Ch Ch Hong Kong 53-57; Prin U Th Coll Hong Kong 57-61; L to Offic Dio Hong 57-61; Lect K Coll Lon 63-74; Commiss Hong Kong from 71; Lect N Counties Coll of Educn Newc T from 75. *Rebillion House, High Callerton, Newcastle-upon-Tyne, NE20 9TT.* (Ponteland 22138)

TRUEMAN, Whitley Alder. K Coll NS BA 51, BS Litt 53. **d** 53 NS. I of Arichat 53-56; New Germany 56-60; R of Yarmouth 60-68; Horton 68-72; St Paul Charlottetown 72-74; on leave 74-75; R of Parrsboro and Port Greville Dio NS from 76. *Rectory, Parrsboro, NS, Canada.* (254-2106)

TRUMAN, Canon Francis Cecil. Univ of NZ BA 27. St Jo Coll Auckld NZ LTh 29. **d** 27 **p** 28 Auckld. C of Otahuhu 27-31; Leeds (to Offic at St Edm) 31-33; V of Hauraki Plains 33-38; Northcote 39-46; Ellerslie 46-63; Can of Auckld 49-78; Can (Emer) from 78; V of Kohimarama Distr Auckld 63-66; C of Southgate 67-68; Chap at Santiago 68; C of All SS Ponsonby Auckld 69-72; L to Offic Dio Auckld 73-79; Perm to Offic from 80. *68 Atkin Avenue, Mission Bay, Auckland 5, NZ.* (583-516)

TRUMAN, Jack Vanstone. McGill Univ Montr BA 48. Trin Coll Tor STB 52. **d** 52 **p** 53 Ott. I of Newington 52-54; Lanark 54-58; C of St Jo Evang Ott 58-61; R of St Steph Winnipeg 61-73; Kars w Osgoode Dio Ott from 73. *Rectory, Kars, Ont., Canada.* (1-613-489-3981)

TRUMAN, John Malcolm. b 33. Cudd Coll 61. **d** 63 **p** 64 Dur. C of St Aid Billingham 63-65; Alnwick 65-68; R of Ford w Etal 68-75; V of St Jas and St Basil Fenham City and Dio Newc T from 75. *Vicarage, Wingrove Road, Newcastle-upon-Tyne, NE4 9EJ.* (Newc T 745078)

TRUMBLE, Francis Meredith. b 15. SOC 73. **d** 74 **p** 75 S'wark. C of H Trin Richmond 74-79; Maidenhead Dio Ox from 79. *18 Courtlands, Shoppenhangers Road, Maidenhead, Berks.* (Maidenhead 21975)

TRUMP, Leonard George. St Jo Coll Morpeth. **d** 62 Armid for Graft. C of S Graft 62-64; Inverell 64-65; P-in-c of Tingha 65-67; V of Mungindi 67-70; CF (Austr) 71-80; V of Uralla Dio Armid from 80. *Vicarage, Uralla, NSW, Australia 2358.*

TRUMPER, Roger David. b 52. Univ of Ex BSc 74. K Coll Lon MSc 75. Univ of Ox BA 80. Wycl Hall Ox 78. **d** 81 Roch. C of St Jo Div Tunbridge Wells Dio Roch from 81. *112 Stephens Road, Tunbridge Wells, Kent, TN4 9QA.*

TRUNDLE, Herbert Edward. b 11. Lich Th Coll 33. **d** 36 **p** 37 Chelmsf. C of St Jo Evang Gt Ilford 36-40; W Cheam (in c of St Alb) 40-44; V of St Steph Battersea 44-52; St Phil Cheam Common 52-76. *Westlands, Mappowder, Sturminster Newton, Dorset.*

TRUNDLEY, Frank Charles. b 09. Ridley Hall Cam 44. **d** 46 **p** 47 Southw. C of St Paul Carlton-in-the-Willows 46-48; C-in-c of Rainworth Mansfield 48-49; V of All SS Shooters Hill Plumstead 49-55; I of Em Wimbledon 55-61; V of Braintree 61-65; Chap Wm Julien Courtauld Hosp 61-65; Min of Ch Ch Conv Distr Westbourne Bournemouth 65-68; V of All S Eastbourne 68-72. *10 Mill Close, Pulham Market, IP21 4TQ.* (Pulham Market 409)

TRURO, Lord Bishop of. (Vacant)

TRURO, Assistant Bishop of. (Vacant)

TRURO, Dean of. *See* Shearlock, Very Rev John David.

TRUSS, Charles Richard. b 42. Univ of Reading BA (Pol Econ) 63. K Coll Lon MPhil 79. Linacre Ho Ox BA (2nd cl Th) 66, MA 69. Wycl Hall Ox 64. **d** 66 Bp Horstead for Leic **p** 67 Leic. C of H Ap Leic 66-69; Hampstead 69-72; V of St Pet Belsize Pk 72-79; St Mich Wood Green Dio Lon from 79. *39 Bounds Green Road, N22.* (01-888 1968)

TRUSTRAM, David Geoffrey. b 49. Pemb Coll Ox BA 71, MA 76. Qu Coll Cam BA 73, MA 77. Westcott Ho Cam 74. **d** 75 **p** 76 S'wark. C of Surbiton 75-78; Richmond Dio S'wark from 78. *14 Dunstable Road, Richmond, Surrey.* (01-940 7932)

TRUSWELL, Philip. Bp Wilson Th Coll IM 26. **d** 27 **p** 28 Liv. C of St Geo Everton 27-29; St Matt Blackb 29-32; V of St Steph Preston 32-34; R of Whicham and V of Whitbeck 34-38; Chap of Oldchurch Co Hosp Romford 38-42; V of Elsenham and Org Sec SPCK Chelmsf 42-45; V of St Paul Oswaldtwistle 45-53; Hensingham 53-59; PC of Over Peover 59-69; V 69-71; L to Offic Dio St A from 72; Perm to Offic Dio Ches from 72. *28 Wynn Avenue, Old Colwyn, Clwyd, LL29 9RF.* (Colwyn Bay 55322)

TRUTWEIN, Percy William. b 05. Bp's Coll Calc BA 25. **d** 33 Bp Pakenham Walsh for Nasik **p** 34 Nasik. C of St Paul Scott's Lane Calc 33-34; Chap Barnes High Sch Deolali 34-41; Chap St Jas Calc 42; Dacca 42-46; Kurseong 46-47; Darjeeling 47-52; C of Aylesbury 52-54; PC (V from 69) of Hurst 54-79. *209 Stowey Road, Yatton, Avon, BS19 4QU.*

TS'AI, Yung-ch'un. Univ of Yenching BA 30. U Th Sem and Univ of Columb MA 47, PhD 50. **d** 43 **p** 44 Hong. P Dio Hong. *School of Religion, Yenching University, Peking, China.*

TSANG, Kei Ngok. d 13 **p** 14 Hong. P Dio Hong 14-36; V 36-50; Archd of Pakhoi 46-50; V of Macao 52-54; LPr Dio Hong 54-78. *9/F Flat E, Kiu Wang Mansion, Waterloo Road Hill, Kowloon, Hong Kong.* (3-033833)

TSANG, Kowk-Wai. U Th Coll Hong Kong LTh 65. **d** 65 Hong. d Dio Hong. *Calvary Church, Kowloon, Hong Kong.* (3-201417)

TSANG, Paul Kai-Choy. U Th Coll Hong 66. **d** 68 **p** 69 Hong. P Dio Hong. *c/o All Saints' Church, Kowloon, Hong Kong.* (3-884798)

TSANG, Richard Ping-Sun. d 50 **p** 57 Hong. P Dio Hong. *St Simon's, Castle Peak, NT, Hong Kong.* (732413)

TSAWE, Victor Zama. b 53. St Bede's Coll Umtata 78. **d** 79 St John's. d Dio St John's. *St Bede's College, Umtata, Transkei.*

TSEBE, Asaph Mariri. St Francis Coll Sekhukhuniland. **d** 65 **p** 66 Pret. C of Potgietersrus 65-71; Mahwelereng Dio Pret from 71. *Box 60, Potgietersrus, Tvl, S Africa.*

TSEBE, Canon John Bartholomew Kgoale. d 41 **p** 42 Pret. P at Sekhukhuniland Native Miss 41-45 and 47-50; L to Offic Dio Johann 45-46; P Dio Pret from 56; Can of Pret 60-67 and from 72; Hon Can 67-72; Archd of E and W Transvaal 61-62; Pret 62-64; Pietersburg 64-67; R of Atteridgeville Dio Pret from 72. *PO Box 1, Atteridgeville, Pretoria, S Africa.* (79-2379)

TSHABALALA, Gilbert. d 78 **p** 79 Matab. P Dio Matab. *c/o Box 193, Barbourfields, Bulawayo, Zimbabwe.*

TSHABALALA, Samuel Godfrey Michael. Isandhlwana Th Coll. **d** 31 **p** 34 Zulu. P 31-46; Dio Natal 46-57; C of Springvale Miss 57-65. *c/o 2 West End, Mbokodo Drive, Sobantu Village, Pietermaritzburg, Natal, S Africa.*

TSHAZIBANE, Phakamile Solomon Mutuyedwa. b 48. St Bede's Coll Umtata 72. **d** 74 **p** 76 Kimb K. P Dio Kimb K 74-80; Dio Pret from 81. *P Bag X37, Soshanguve, 0152, S Africa.*

TSHENKENG, Isaac Drake Pule. b 46. St Pet Coll Alice 69. **d** 71 **p** 72 Johann. C of Evaton w Sebokeng 71-74; R of St Mary Orlando 75-80. *Box 19, Orlando East, Transvaal, S Africa.*

TSHINGWANA, Jacob. b 35. **d** 76 **p** 77 Matab. C of Gwelutshena Dio Matab 76-79; P-in-c from 79. *P Bag T5414, Bulawayo, Zimbabwe.*

TSHOBENI, Ven Joseph Galelani. St Bede's Coll Umtata 59. **d** 60 **p** 62 St John's. P Dio St John's; Archd of All SS from 80. *Box 35, Tsomo, Transkei, S Africa.*

TSILAILAY, Ambroise. b 38. **d** 76 **p** 78 Diego S. P Dio Diego S 76-79; Dio Antsir from 79. *Eklesia Episkopaly Malagasy, Ambanja, Antsiranana, Malagasy Republic.*

TSIMILANJA, Noa. b 38. St Paul's Coll Ambatoharanana 67. **d** 70 **p** 71 Diego-S. P Dio Diego-S 70-79; Dio Antsir from 79. *Misiona Anglikana, Ankaramy, Antsiranana, Malagasy Republic.*

TSIPOURAS, John George. b 38. Trin Coll Bris 76. **d** 78 **p** 79 Ches. C of St Andr Cheadle Hulme Dio Ches from 78. *36 Buckingham Road, Cheadle Hulme, Cheshire, SK8 5EG.*

TSIRY, Gabriel. St Paul's Coll Ambat 65. **d** 68 Madag. d Dio Tam 69-79; Dio Toa from 79. *Soanierana-Ivongo, Toamasina, Madagascar.*

TSIVERY, Nelson. St Paul's Coll Ambat 55. **d** 55 **p** 57 Madag. P Dio Madag 55-69; Dio Tam 69-79; Dio Toa from 79. *La Mission Anglicane, Ambodiharina, Madagascar.*

TSOSANE, Judah. b 47. **d** and **p** 74 Les. P Dio Les. *St Matthias Mission, PO Box PK4, Peka, Lesotho, S Africa.*

TSUBELLA, Joseph Mahapu. b 43. St Pet Coll Alice 68. **d** 71 **p** 72 Johann. C of Natalspruit 71-74; R of Standerton 74-76; Ikageng Dio Johann from 76. *Box 4010, Lesedi, Transvaal, S Africa.* (014-81 3478)

TSUI, Louis Tsan-Sang. b 43. U Th Coll Hong 70. **d** 73 **p** 74 Hong. P Dio Hong 73-76; on leave. *Yeuk Wing Primary School, Hong Kong.* (3-215588)

TUAM, KILLALA and ACHONRY, Lord Bishop of. *See* Duggan, Right Rev John Coote.

TUAM, Archdeacon of. *See* Grant, Ven William James.

TUAM, Dean of. *See* Grant, Very Rev William James.

TUBBS, Brian Ralph. b 44. K Coll Lon and Warm AKC (2nd cl) 66. **d** 67 **p** 68 Ex. C of St Thos Ex 67-73; Team V of Sidmouth Woolbrook and Salcombe Regis 73-77; R of St Jas w St Anne's Chap City and Dio Ex from 77; M Gen Syn from 80. *St James's Rectory, Old Tiverton Road, Exeter, EX4 6NG.* (Exeter 55871)

TUBBS, Christopher Norman. b 25. G and C Coll Cam BA 51, MA 54. Wycl Hall Ox. **d** 52 **p** 53 Bp Tubbs for Ches. C of Neston 52-55; St Pet Mancroft Nor 55-59; V of Scalby (w Ravenscar from 68) Dio York from 59; RD of Scarborough from 76. *Scalby Vicarage, Scarborough, N Yorks.* (Scarborough 62740)

TUBBS, Peter Alfred. b 22. G and C Coll Cam BA 48, MA 53. Linc Th Coll. **d** 57 Bp Tubbs for Lich **p** 58 Lich. C of Tettenhall Regis 57-60; Ch Ch Wel 60-64; Asst Chap Univ of Keele 65-69; V of Cardington Dio St Alb from 69; RD of Elstow from 77. *Cardington Vicarage, Bedford, MK44 3SS.* (Cardington 203)

TUBOKU-METZGER, Constant Ernest. Univ of Pittsburg, Pennsylvania 28. St Aug Coll Cant 60. **d** 60 Sier L **p** 64 Accra. P Dio Sier L 60-62; and from 65; L to Offic Dio Accra 62-64. *Bishop Crowther Memorial Church, Sierra Leone.*

TUBWOMWE, Joseph. Buwalasi Th Coll 64. **d** 65 **p** 67 Nam. P Dio Nam. *Box 30366, Kampala, Uganda.*

TUCK, Andrew Kenneth. b 42. Kelham Th Coll 63. **d** 68 **p** 69 Lon. C of Poplar 68-74; Team V 74-76; V of Walsgrave-on-Sowe Dio Cov from 76. *Walsgrave Vicarage, Coventry, Warws.* (Cov 613960)

TUCK, David John. b 36. St Cath Coll Cam BA 61, MA 65. Cudd Coll 61. **d** 63 **p** 64 Nor. C of Holt Kelling and Salthouse 63-69; Chap St Mark's Coll Mapanza 69-72; V of Sprowston Dio Nor from 73; R of Beeston Dio Nor from 73; RD of Nor from 81. *Sprowston Vicarage, Norwich, NR7 8TZ.* (Nor 46492)

TUCK, Edward Layton Harris. K Coll Halifax NS. **d** 60 **p** 61 NS. C of Melford 60-65; R of Parrsboro Dio NS from 65; R of Port Greville 65-72; Chester Dio NS from 72. *Chester, NS, Canada.* (275-3804)

TUCK, Canon Robert Critchlow. Univ of K Coll NS BA 48 St Mich Coll Llan 51. **d** 53 **p** 54 Mon. C of Risca 53-56; R of Canso w Queensport 56-62; C All SS Cathl Halifax 62-64; R of Summerside 64-75; Can of St Pet Cathl PEI from 72; R of Georgetn Dio NS from 75. *136 North River Road, Charlottetown, PEI, Canada.*

TUCK, Ronald James. b 47. SOC 75. **d** 78 Lon **p** 79 Stepney for Lon. C of St Pet U Holloway 78-81; P-in-c of Swanton Abbot w Skeyton Dio Nor from 81; P-in-c of Scottow Dio Nor from 81. *Rectory, Swanton Abbott, Norf.* (Swanton Abbott 212)

TUCKER, Alfred Kenneth. b 1895. Univ of Lon BA 17, MA 22, PhD 31. Wells Th Coll. **d** 61 **p** 62 Lon. C of Sunbury Dio Lon from 61. *1 Rooksmead Road, Sunbury-on-Thames, Surrey.* (Sunbury-on-Thames 88228)

TUCKER, Bryant Burgess. b 1895. McGill Univ Montr BSc 23. Ridley Hall Cam 29. **d** 31 **p** 32 Birm. C of St Geo Birm 31-33; Perm to Offic at St Sidwell Ex 34-35; SSC Dio Ex 35-36; Perm to Offic at St Leon Heston 36-38; C of All SS Highgate 38-40; R of Blyborough 40-41; CF (EC) 41-49; CF 49-55; Hon CF 56; C of St Pancras Pennycross Plymouth 56-58; C-in-c 58-59; Perm to Offic Dio Truro 60-62; Dio Ex 62-65; L to Offic from 65. *19 Effingham Crescent, Hartley, Plymouth, Devon.* (Plymouth 771011)

✠ **TUCKER, Right Rev Cyril James.** CBE 75. St Cath Coll Cam BA 33, MA 37. MA Ox (by incorp) 51. Ridley Hall Cam 33. **d** 35 **p** 36 Lon. C of St Mark Dalston (in c of Highgate Sch Miss) 35-37; St Barn Cam 37-38; Youth Sec BFBS 38-39; Chap RAFVR 39-46; Warden Mon Sch 46-49; Perm to Offic Dio Mon 46-49; Chap Ox Past 49-57; Chap Wadh Coll Ox 51-57; V of H Trin Cam 57-63; Cons Ld Bp in Argent and ES Amer w Falkld Is in Westmr Abbey 18 Oct 63 by Abp of Cant; Bps of Lon; Win; Ely; Leic; and S'wark; Bps Suffr of Kingston T; Maidstone; Stepney; Tonbridge; and others; res 75; Hon Executive Dir Argentine Dioc Assoc from 75; Perm to Offic Dio Ely from 77. *202 Gilbert Road, Cambridge, CB4 3PB.*

TUCKER, Douglas Greening. b 17. Univ of Lon Dipl Th 53. St Aid Coll 49. **d** 52 **p** 53 Newc T. C of Jesmond 52-56; St Jas and St Basil Newc T 56-58; V of St Pet Cowgate Newc T 58-62; Elsham Dio Linc from 62; Worlaby Dio Linc from 62; Bonby Dio Linc from 72. *Worlaby Vicarage, Brigg, S Humb, DN20 0NE.* (Saxby-all-Saints 386)

TUCKER, Canon Ernest Henry. b 09. Sarum Th Coll 34. **d** 37 Glouc **p** 38 Tewkesbury for Glouc. C of Dursley w St Mark Woodmancote 37-40; Coleford w Staunton 40-43; Almondbury 43-47; V of Marsden 47-53; Newland w Redbrook 53-59; H Trin Stroud 59-76; Hon Can of Glouc 74-78; Can (Emer) from 78; RD of Bisley 76-78. *5 Weyhouse Close, Bowbridge Lane, Stroud, Glos, GL5 4JJ.* (Stroud 6983)

TUCKER, Preb Gordon Elijah. b 1896. Kaisar-i-Hind Silver Med 47. Wells Th Coll 25. **d** 26 **p** 27 B & W. C of Ilminster 26-29; Chap (Eccles Est) at Risalpur Nowshera and Campbellpur 29; Quetta 29-33; Serampore 34-43; Organist Calc Cathl 41-43; Commiss Calc 38; Exam Chap to Bp of Calc 43-47; Dom Chap to Bp of Calc 34-43; Archd of Calc 43-49; Chap of St John Calc 43-47; R of Brushford 47-52; RD of Wiveliscombe 50-52; V of Ilminster w Whitelackington 52-62; RD of Ilminster 52-62; Surr from 51; Preb of Wells Cathl from 54; Proc Conv B & W 55-64. *Combe Cottage, Weacombe, West Quantoxhead, Taunton, Somt TA4 4EB.* (Williton 32526)

TUCKER, Graham Harold. Univ of Tor BASc 47, MASc 48. McGill Univ Montr BD and LTh 53. **d** 53 Montr **p** 64 Caled. I of Kitimat 53-63; Hon Can of Caled 63-70; Supervisor of Stewardship Gen Synod 63-67; Dir 67-72; Dir of Par Development and Conf Centre Dio Tor 73-77; Chap King Bay Dio Tor from 77. *88 Murray Drive, Aurora, Ont., Canada.*

TUCKER, Harold George. b 21. St Aug Coll Cant 48. Sarum Th Coll 50. **d** 51 **p** 52 Ex. C of S Molton 51-56; PC of Mariansleigh w Romansleigh (and Meshaw from 62) 56-64; R of Bratton Fleming 64-73; C-in-c of Goodleigh 67-73; C-in-c of Stoke-Rivers 67-73; C-in-c of Parracombe 69-73; C-in-c of Martinhoe 69-73; R of Whimple Dio Ex from 73. *Whimple Rectory, Exeter, Devon, EX5 2TF.* (Whimple 822317)

TUCKER, John Yorke Raffles. b 24. Magd Coll Cam BA 49, MA 56. Westcott Ho Cam 49. **d** 51 **p** 52 Lon. C of St Paul Shadwell 51-54; Ascen Wembley 54-58; V of St Mich AA Lon Fields Hackney 58-67; St Anselm Belmont 67-78; Sunbury-on-Thames Dio Lon from 78. *Vicarage, Thames Street, Sunbury-on-Thames, Surrey, TW16 6AA.* (Sunbury 85448)

TUCKER, Margaret Ansley. Univ of Ott BScN 75. Trin Coll Tor MDiv 78. **d** 80 **p** 81 Bp Read for Tor. C of St Nich Birch Cliff Dio Tor from 80. *1512 Kingston Road, Scarborough, Ont, Canada, M1N 1R7.*

TUCKER, Maurice Grahame. b 12. Univ of Bris BA (1st cl Mod Hist) and Gladstone Pri 34, MA 37. Coll of Resurr Mirfield 37. **d** 39 **p** 40 Bris. C of St Mich Two-Mile Hill Bris 39-42; Asst Master Magd Coll Sch Brackley and Perm to Offic Dio Pet 42-44; Chap of Dover Coll and Perm to Offic Dio Ex 44-45; Asst Master and Chap Colston's Sch Stapleton and Perm to Offic Dio Bris 45-63; C of Henbury (in c of St Mark Brentry) 63-74; P-in-c of St Anne Greenbank Bris 74-75; C of St Anne w St Thos Eastville Bris 75-79; Hon C from 79. *13 Camelford Road, Greenbank, Bristol, BS5 6HW.*

TUCKER, Nevil Francis. K Coll Lon 36. **d** 38 Taunton for B & W **p** 39 B & W. C of Ch Ch Bath 38-41; St Pet Bournemouth 41-44; Stratford-on-Avon (in c of St Andr Shottery w All SS Luddington) 44-47; V of Lower Shuckburgh w Wolfhampcote and Fleckinoe 47-49; C of St Geo Ramsgate 49-51; Gt Yarmouth (in c of St Jas) 51-52; I of Sawyerville 52-54; Coaticook 54-60; R of Danville 60-63; Cler Sec Queb Dioc Synod 60-74; R of Baie Comeau 63-74; Can of Queb 72-74; R of Waterloo 74-79. *18 Regent Stret, Amherst, NS, Canada, B4H 3S7.*

TUCKER, Stephen Reid. b 51. New Coll Ox MA 76, Dipl Th 76. Ripon Coll Cudd 75. **d** 77 **p** 78 Chich. C of All SS Hove 77-80; Lect Chich Th Coll from 80. *c/o Theological College, Chichester, PO19 3ES.*

TUCKETT, Christopher Mark. b 48. Qu Coll Cam BA 69, MA 74. Westcott Ho Cam 71. **d** 75 Burnley for Blackb **p** 76 Blackb. C of Lancaster 75-77; L to Offic Dio Ely 77-79; Perm to Offic Dio Man from 79. *7 Veronica Road, Didsbury, Manchester, M20 0ST.*

TUCKEY, John William Townsend. b 19. TCD BA (3rd cl Cl Mod) 41, Div Test 42, Th Exhib (1st cl) 43. **d** 43 **p** 44 Dub. C of Rathfarnham 43-45; Asst Miss of St Martin Ballymacarrett (S Ch Miss)45-47; Miss 47-50; C-in-c of St Ann Shandon 50-52; Chap Female Orph Ho Dub 52-59; Hon Cler V of Ch Ch Cathl Dub 55-59; C of Monkstown 59-60; St Paul Weston-s-Mare (in c of Good Shepherd) 60-63; Kewstoke (in c of St Jude Milton) 63-65; V of Milton Somt 65-74; C-in-c of E Brent (R w Lympsham from 75) 74-81. *10 Hill Head Close, Glastonbury, Somt, TA6 8AL.*

TUCKLEY, Laurence. b 05. Lich Th Coll 26. **d** 29 **p** 30 Lich. C of Ettingshall 29-31; Ch Ch Stafford 31-38; R of Dalbury w Long Lane (with Trusley from 52) 38-71. *Darley Dene, 17 Horwood Avenue, Derby.*

TUCKWELL, Christopher Howard. b 45. Chich Th Coll 70. **d** 73 Stepney for Lon **p** 74 Lon. C of St Matt U Clapton 73-76; R of H Trin Georgetn St Vinc Dio Windw Is from 76. *Holy Trinity Rectory, Georgetown, St Vincent, W Indies.* (86334)

TUCKWELL, Paul. b 12. Magd Coll Ox BA (2nd cl Lit Hum) 35, MA 38 Westcott Ho Cam 36. **d** 38 **p** 39 Derby. C of St Luke Derby 38-40; Whitwell 40-41; C-in-c of St Cypr Conv Distr Frecheville Beighton 41-43; Min 43-52; V 52-66; RD of Staveley 61-66; R of Appleton 66-79. *18 Canonbury Street, Berkeley, Glos, GL13 9BG.*

TUDBALL, Arthur James. K Coll Lon and Warm AKC 54. **d** 54 **p** 55 Lon. C of St Mary Magd Munster Square Lon 54-56; L to Offic Dio Borneo 56-59; P-in-c of Beaufort 59-61; R of Labuan 61-65; C of All SS Cathl Kota Kinabalu 65-67;

R of Kudat 67-68; C of St Thos Cathl Kuch 70-73; V of St Marg Seria 73-75; Chap Angl Commun Centre Kuch 76-79; Warden St Pet Hall, Sing 79-80; V of St Pet City and Dio Sing from 80; Exam Chap to Bp of Sing from 80. *1 Tavistock Avenue, Singapore, 1955.*

TUDDENHAM, Noel Archer. b 07. Lon Coll Div 49. **d** 51 **p** 52 Lon. C of Alperton 51-54; Harrow Weald (in c of St Barn) 54-55; V of St Luke Finchley 55-64; R of Weston-sub-Edge w Aston-sub-Edge 64-73. *20 Thornley Road, Felixstowe, Suffolk.* (Felixstowe 78655)

TUDGEY, Stephen John. b 51. Univ of Nottm BTh 81. St Jo Coll Nottm LTh. **d** 81 Bradwell for Chelmsf. C of SS Pet & Paul Grays Dio Chelmsf from 81. *Church House, West Street, Grays, Essex, RM17 6HR.*

TUDOR, David Charles Frederick. b 42. Sarum Wells Th Coll 70. **d** 73 Crediton for Ex **p** 74 Ex. C of St Pet Plymouth 73-75; St Elisabeth Reddish 75-78; C-in-c of All SS Hamer Rochdale 78-80; V of Goldenhill Dio Lich from 80. *Goldenhill Vicarage, Stoke-on-Trent, Staffs.* (Kidsgrove 2736)

TUDOR, David St Clair. b 55. AKC and BD 77. Cudd Coll Ox 77. **d** 78 **p** 79 S'wark. C of St Nich Plumstead 78-80; St Matt Redhill Dio S'wark from 80. *44 Ridgeway Road, Redhill, Surrey, Rh1 6PH.*

TUDOR, Canon Harold St Clair. Codr Coll Barb BA 42. Univ of Lon BD (2nd cl) 49, Junior McCaul Hebr Pri 49, MTh 52. **d** 42 **p** 43 Barb. C of St Mich Cathl Barb 42-45; V of St Mark Barb 45-46; C of St Mich AA Walthamstow 47-50; Chap Harrison Coll 50-66; Exam Chap to Bp of Barb from 59; L to Offic Dio Barb from 66; Can of Barb from 75. *Tudor Hall, My Lord's Hill, St Michael, Barbados, W Indies.*

TUDOR, Malcolm George Henry Booth. b 36. Univ of Nottm BA (Th) 71. Linc Th Coll 72. **d** 60 **p** 61 RC Abp of Birm. In RC Ch 60-71; Rec into Angl Commun 71 by Bp of Southw; C of Cinderhill 72-74; P-in-c of Broxtowe 74-78; V of E Markham w Askham Dio Southw from 78; P-in-c of E Drayton w Stokenham Dio Southw from 78; Headon w Upton Dio Southw from 78. *Vicarage, East Markham, Newark, Notts, NG22 0SA.* (Tuxford 870699)

TUFF, Harold. b 02. Men in Disp 45. TD 52. St Jo Coll Dur BA 30. **d** 30 **p** 31 Dur. C of All SS New Shildon 30-32; St Thos Bp Wearmouth 32-35; V of Sacriston 35-51; CF (TA - R of O) 39-45; CF (TA) 51-57; Hon CF from 57; V of Lindley 51-62; Darrington w Wentbridge 62-68. *14 Chapel Street, Grassington, Skipton, Yorks.*

TUFFEL, Kennedy Joseph. b 20. Worc Ordin Coll 64. **d** 66 Lon **p** 67 Willesden for Lon. C of Belmont 66-68; Goring 68-72; V of Barnham 72-78; Hon C of St Jo Div W Worthing 78-81; C of Goring (in c of St Laur) Dio Chich from 81. *192 Goring Road, Goring-by-Sea, Sussex.* (Worthing 48793)

TUFFIELD, Basil Thomas. b 23. Fitzw Coll Cam BA (3rd cl Hist Trip pt i) 49, 2nd cl Hist Trip pt ii 50, MA 54. Wells Th Coll. **d** 52 **p** 53 S'wark. C of St Luke w St Paul Old Charlton 52-58; Carshalton (in c of Good Shepherd) 58-65; V of Good Shepherd Carshalton 65-79; Cross Canonby Dio Carl from 79; P-in-c of Allonby Dio Carl from 81. *Cross Canonby Vicarage, Maryport, Cumb, CA15 6SJ.* (Maryport 2146)

TUFFIN, Allan Wilfred. Or Coll Ox BA (2nd cl Th) 60. Wells Th Coll 60. **d** 62 **p** 63 Lon. C of H Trin w St Phil Dalston Dio Lon from 62. *22 Horton Road, E8.*

TUFNELL, Edward Nicholas Pember. b 45. Churchill Coll Cam BA 68. Univ of Nottm BA (Th) 73. St Jo Coll Nottm 70. **d** 73 Willesden for Lon **p** 74 Lon. C of Ealing 73-76; BCMS Miss Dio Moro from 77. *Box 113, Morogoro, Tanzania.*

TUFT, Patrick Anthony. b 31. Selw Coll Cam BA 56, MA 60. Edin Th Coll 56. **d** 58 **p** 59 Bradf. C of Keighley 58-63; PV of Chich Cathl 63-68; Chap Prebendal Sch Dio Chich 63-68; Min Can (Succr 70-74; Sen Cardinal from 72) of St Paul's Cathl Lon 68-74; Lect St Mary Aldermary 71-73; Hon Min Can from 74; PV of Westmr Abbey 74-79; V of Chiswick Dio Lon from 74. *Chiswick Vicarage, The Mall, W4 2PJ.* (01-995 4717)

TUFTON, Canon Colin Charles Guy. b 24. Or Coll Ox BA 48, MA 53 Ely Th Coll 49. **d** 51 Dover for Cant **p** 52 Cant. C of St Jo Bapt Croydon 51-55; Rickmansworth 55-58; R of Deal 58-67; V of All SS w St Phil and H Trin Maidstone 67-74; RD of Sutton 67-74; Hon Can of Cant from 68; Tutor St Aug Coll Cant 74-76; R of St Pet and St Alphege w St Marg and St Mildred w St Mary de Castro City and Dio Cant from 76; Master of Eastbridge Hosp from 76. *Master's Lodge, St Peter's Street, Canterbury, Kent, CT1 2BE.* (Canterbury 62395)

TUFTS, Canon Karl Henry. K Coll NS BA 40. **d** 40 **p** 41 NS. R of Em dartmouth 41-44; St Clements 44-48; Ecum Secum 48-56; Sackville 56-67; Hosp Chap Halifax 67-75; Exam Chap to Bp of NS 66-75; Hon Can of All SS Cathl Halifax 69-72 and from 75; Can 72-75. *RR1, Granville Ferry, Anna Co, NS, Canada.*

TUHIWAI, Te Reo Tiopira. b 37. **d** 78 Wai. Hon C of Waipatu-Moteo Past Dio Wai from 78. *c/o Post Office, Clive, Hawkes Bay, NZ.*

TUHIWAI, Tiopira. St Jo Coll Auckld 48. **d** 51 **p** 52 Wai. C of Rotorua 51-56; V of Waipawa Past 56-63; Te Kaha Maori Past 63-68; V of Wairoa Mohaka Maori Past 68-75; Porangahau 75-76; P-in-c 76-79; Perm to Offic Dio Wel from 79. *55 Lyndhurst Street, Palmerston North, NZ.*

TU'INEAU, Iloa-i-Pangai. b 38. St Jo Coll Auckld 71. **d** 73 Bp Halapua for Polyn **p** 74 Polyn. P Dio Polyn. *Box 362, Nukualofa, Tonga.*

TUITT, Arnold Reginald Llewellyn. Codr Coll Barb 79. **d** and **p** 80 Antig. C of St Anthony Montserrat Dio Antig from 80. *Fort Barrington, Plymouth, Montserrat, WI.*

TUKUA, John. St Columb Hall Wang ACT ThL 68. **d** 69 **p** 70 Polyn. P Dio Polyn; Actg Dioc Sec Polyn 77-78; Dep VG 78-79; C of St Paul's Cathl City and Dio Wel from 79. *22 Selwyn Terrace, Wellington 1, NZ.*

TUKUAFU, Aleki Halamei. b 20. **d** 76 **p** 77 Polyn. P Dio Polyn. *PO Box 31, Nukualofa, Tonga, Pacific Ocean.*

TULL, Christopher Stuart. b 36. Hertf Coll Ox BA 60, MA 64. Oak Hill Th Coll 60. **d** 62 **p** 63 Ex. C of Washfield and of Stoodleigh 62-71; Team V of Exe Valley Group 71-75; RD of Tiverton from 74; V of Bishopsnympton w Rose Ash 75-77; Mariansleigh 75-77; R of Oakmoor Team Min Dio Ex from 77; RD of S Molton from 80. *Bishopsnympton Rectory, South Molton, Devon.* (Bishopsnympton 427)

TULLOCH, Alton Beresford. Univ of WI BA (Th) 73. United Th Coll of WI 73. **d** 73 Ja. C of St Geo Kingston 73-76; R of Claremont Dio Ja from 76. *Rectory, Claremont, Jamaica, W Indies.* (097-23228)

TULLOCH, Richard James Anthony. b 52. Wadham Coll Ox BA 74. Selw Coll Cam BA (Th) 79. Ridley Hall Cam 76. **d** 79 **p** 80 S'wark. C of Morden Dio S'wark from 79. *The Old School House, Central Road, Morden, Surrey, SM4 5SR.* (01-648 9653)

TULLOCH, Walter Harold. b 16. St Deiniol's Libr Hawarden 79. **d** 79 **p** 80 Liv (APM). Hon C of Maghull Dio Liv from 79. *8 Tailors Lane, Maghull, Mer, L31 3HD.*

TULLOCH, William Joseph. b 10. Univ of Liv BA 35, MA 45. St Aid Coll 35. **d** 36 Warrington for Liv **p** 37 Liv. C of Good Shepherd W Derby 36-40; Ch Ch Bootle 40-48; V of St Sav Everton 48-53; St Pet Aintree 53-80. *11 Hilton Grove, W Kirby, Wirral, L48 5HB.* (051-625 8570)

TULLY, Ross. b 22. Clare Coll Cam BA 44, MA 48. Ridley Hall Cam 47. **d** 49 **p** 50 Roch. C of Ch Ch Beckenham 49-52; CMS Miss at Quetta 53-61 and 69-73; V of H Trin Cathl Kar 61-69: Chap St Bernard's Hosp Southall 74-80; C of H Trin Eastbourne Dio Chich from 80. *Flat 1, 10 Trinity Trees, Eastbourne, BN21 3LD.*

TUMBARE, Ambrose Amon. St Pet Coll Rosettenville 50. **d** 51 **p** 52 S Rhod. P Dio S Rhod 51-52; Dio Matab 52-61; Dio Mashon from 61. *Mabvuka, Salisbury, Rhodesia.*

TUMKOU, Daniel. St Paul's Th Coll Limuru 59. **d** 61 **p** 63 Nak. P Dio Nak. *St Andrew's Church, Lityei, Kapenguria, Kenya.*

TUMONDE, Sylvanus. Newton Th Coll. **d** 59 **p** 62 New Guinea. P Dio New Guinea 59-71; Dio Papua from 71. *Anglican Church, Saga, via Kokoda, Papua New Guinea.*

TUMUTEGYEREIZE, Amos. **d** 65 Ankole-K. d Dio Ankole-K 65-67; Dio Ank 67-77; Dio W Ank from 77. *PO Kikagate, Uganda.*

TUMWESIGYE, Elijah. **d** and **p** 79 W Ank. P Dio W Ank. *PO Kabwohe, Mbarara, Uganda.*

TUN OO, Jacob. **d** 68 Rang **p** 71 Mand. d Dio Rang 68-71; P Dio Mand from 71. *Christ Church, Mandalay, Burma.*

TUNBRIDGE, Colin Geoffrey. Moore Th Coll Syd ACT ThL (2nd cl) 59. **d** and **p** 61 Adel. C of H Trin Adel 61-63; Chap at Cochabamba 66-68; Trujillo 68-70; La Paz 70-77; Perm to Offic Dio C & Goulb from 77. *10 Centaurus Street, Giralang, ACT, Australia 2617.*

TUNBRIDGE, John Stephen. b 31. Keble Coll Ox BA 54, MA 59 Ely Th Coll 54. **d** 56 Dover for Cant **p** 57 Cant. C of All SS U Norwood 56-57; Ramsgate 57-60; Folkestone 60-62; R of Gt Chart 62-67; V of Wymynswold 67-76; Min of Aylesham Conv Distr 67-76; P-in-c of Ramsgate Dio Cant from 76. *1 Grove Road, Ramsgate, Kent, CT11 0NB.* (Thanet 51192)

TUNBRIDGE, Lewis Roy Tilden. b 22. Trin Coll Tor S Th 62. **d** 70 Tor. C of Ch of the Atonement, City and Dio Tor from 70. *Box 909, Adullun Road, RR2, Stroud, Ont, Canada.*

TUNG-YEP, Ven George. St Francis Coll Brisb ACT ThL 54. **d** 54 **p** 55 N Queensld. C of Ayr 54-56; P-in-c of Cloncurry 56-59; St Pet Townsville 60-67; R of Ayr Queensld 67-74; Mundingburra 74-78; Cairns Dio N Queensld from 78; Archd of Townsville 74-78; Cairns from 78; Exam Chap to Bp of N Queensld from 76. *Rectory, Cairns, Queensland, Australia 4870.*

TUNGAY, Michael Ian. b 45. Oak Hill Coll 70. **d** 73 Kens for Lon **p** 74 Lon. C of St Mary Hammersmith Road, Fulham 73-79; St Simon Hammersmith Dio Lon 76-79; V from 79. *153 Blythe Road, W14 0HL.*

TUN HLA AUNG, Timothy. d 76 **p** 77 Rang. P Dio Rang. *St Paul's Church, Kyaiklat, Burma.*

TUNKS, Henry Roy Samuel. Ridley Coll Melb ACT ThL 42. **d** 40 Melb **p** 42 Geelong for Melb. C of Moorabbin 40-43; Min 43-65; Perm to Offic Dio Melb 65-72; P-in-c of Wynyard 73; St Paul Launceston 73-74. *c/o PO Sorrento, Vic, Australia 3943.* (059-88 8283)

TUNNADINE, Henry Christopher. b 1896. Keble Coll Ox BA 21, MA 25 Lich Th Coll 21. **d** 22 **p** 23 Lich. C of St Pet Walsall 22-26; St Andr Wolverhampton 26-33; V of U Gornal 34-55; Tutbury 55-63. *3 Hall Road, Rolleston, Burton-on-Trent, Staffs, DE13 9BX.* (Burton-on-Trent 812289)

TUNNICLIFFE, Martin Wyndham. b 31. Univ Coll of N Staffs BA (2nd cl Engl and French) 56. Qu Coll Birm 59. **d** 60 **p** 61 Birm. C of Castle Bromwich 60-65; V of Shard End 65-73; R of Over Whitacre w Shustoke 73-78; V of Tanworth-in-Arden Dio Birm from 78. *Tanworth-in-Arden Vicarage, Solihull, B94 5EB.* (05644 2565)

TUN SEIN, Canon Timothy. d 39 **p** 40 Rang. P Dio Rang 39-75; Hon Can of Rang from 73. *Church of The Resurrection, Htanbinkone Street, Syriam, Burma.*

TUNSTALL, Barry Anthony. b 29. Sarum Th Coll 53. **d** 55 **p** 56 St Alb. C of Croxley Green 55-58; Apsley End 58-63; V of N Mymms 63-81; R of Kirkby Overblow Dio Ripon from 81. *Kirkby Overblow Rectory, Harrogate, Yorks.* (Harrogate 81087)

TUNSTALL, John Josiah. St Francis Coll Brisb. **d** 44 **p** 45 Brisb. C of St Mark Warwick 44-47; P-in-c of Eidsvold w Muredubbera 47-50; R 50-51; Nanango 51-54; Drayton 54-57; Wondai 57-61; C of Bundaberg 61-64; R of Brisb Valley 64-74; Perm to Offic Dio Brisb 74-81. *7 Bank Street, Margate, Queensland, Australia 4019.*

TUNSTALL, Thomas Boulton. b 02. St Cath S Ox BA 30, MA 35 ACA 26, FCA 60 Ripon Hall, Ox 28. **d** 30 **p** 31 Birm. C of King's Norton 30-34; St Geo Edgbaston 34-36; V of St Luke Birm 36-45; St Agnes The Cotteridge 45-56; Surr 49-56; V of Bramley Hants 56-67; Perm to Offic Dio Chich from 67. *60 Singleton Crescent, Goring-by-Sea, Worthing, Sussex, BN12 5DQ.*

TUPPER, Martin Evelyn. Em Coll Cam 3rd cl Geog Trip pt i, BA (3rd cl Archaeol and Anthrop Trip) 30, MA 34 Wycl Hall Ox 30. **d** 32 **p** 33 S'wark. C of St Jas Hatcham 32-37; Albury w St Martha 37-40; R of Eaton Hastings 40-42; Reg Sec Fell of Reconciliation 42-46; R of Stedham 46-55. *Fantails, Albury, Guildford, Surrey.*

TUPPER, Michael Heathfield. b 20. St Edm Hall Ox BA 41, MA (2nd Cl Th) 46. Ridley Hall Cam 41. **d** 43 **p** 44 Win. C of Ch Ch Win 43-45; Chap Monkton Combe Sch 45-48; Asst Chap Shrewsbury Sch 48-59 and 60-79; Ho Master 62-72; Chap Kisumu Dio Momb 59-60; Hon C of Bayston Hill Dio Lich from 80. *23 Glebe Road, Bayston Hill, Shrewsbury, SY3 0PN.* (Bayston Hill 2674)

TUREI, William Brown. St Jo Coll NZ. **d** 49 **p** 50 Wai. C of Tauranga 49-52; V of Whangara Past 52-59; Te Puke Past 59-65; Ruatoki Past 65-70; Turianga Past 70-74; Phillipstown & Maori Missr 74-82; Waipatu-Moteo Past Dio Wai from 82. *Vicarage, Waipatu, Hastings, NZ.*

TURIC, Henry Mabor. Bp Gwynne Col Mundri 60. **d** 64 **p** 65 Bp Ngalamu for Sudan. P Dio Sudan. *ECS, Rumbek, Bahr el Ghazal Province, Sudan.*

TURKINGTON, Ivan. b 32. St Pet Hall Ox BA (Th) 53, MA 57. Westcott Ho Cam 53. **d** 55 **p** 56 Ripon. C of Ch Ch Harrogate 55-59; Asst Chap Peterhouse Mashon 59-63; Chap Geelong Gr Sch 63-67; Trin Coll Glenalmond 67-70; Asst Chap Dioc Coll Capetn 70-71; Chap Geelong Gr Sch 72-77; Succr of Leeds Par Ch 78-80; V of Goff's Oak Dio St Alb from 80. *Goff's Oak Vicarage, Waltham Cross, Herts,* (Cuffley 2328)

TURKINGTON, Very Rev Robert Christopher Howard. b 13. TCD Eccles Hist Pri (2nd) 35, BA and Div Test 37, MA 57. **d** 37 **p** 38 Kilm. C of Annagh w Quivvy and St Andr 37-40; C-in-c of Castleterra 40-47; I of Bailieborough 47-55; Kilmore w Ballintemple Dio Kilm from 55; Dom Chap to Bp of Kilm from 60; Can of Drumlease in Kilm Cathl 57-65; Dean of Kilm from 65. *Danesfort, Cavan, Co Cavan, Irish Republic.* (049-31918)

TURLEY, James Arthur. Ch Coll Hobart 62. **d** 62 **p** 64 Tas. Asst Chap Ch Coll Hobart 62-69; St D Cathl Hobart 69-70; Perm to Offic Dio Tas from 78. *884 Huon Road, Fern Tree, Tasmania 7101.*

TURLEY, Keith Edward. d 80 N Queensld (NSM). C of Ch of the Ascen Heatley Dio N Queensld from 80. *8 Daley Street, Heatley, Qld, Australia 4814.*

TURLEY, Lyall Alexander. St Jo Coll Morpeth ACT ThL 64. **d** 65 **p** 66 Melb. C of Pascoe Vale 65-67; ABM Miss 67-73; R of Cooma 73-77; Lae Dio Aipo from 77. *Box 31, Lae, Papua New Guinea.*

TURNBULL, Canon Allen Chorlton. b 06. Tyndale Hall Bris 30. **d** 33 **p** 35 Lich. C of St Paul Burslem 33-36; Bebington 36-41; V of St Cath Higher Tranmere 41-51; Surr 41-51; Chap St Cath Hosp Annex and Birkenhead Ment Hosp 45-51; R of March 51-75; Surr 70-75; Hon Can of Ely Cathl 73-75; Can (Emer) from 75; Perm to Offic Dio Guildf from 75. *2 The Beeches, Wych Hill Lane, Woking, Surrey, GU22 0AH.* (Woking 65654)

TURNBULL, Anthony Michael Arnold. b 35. Keble Coll Ox BA 58, MA 62. Univ of Dur Dipl Th 60. Cranmer Hall Dur 58. **d** 60 **p** 61 Man. C of Middleton 60-61; Luton 61-64; Lect 64-65; Dom Chap to Abp and L to Offic Dio York 65-69; Dir of Ordin York 65-69; V (R from 73) of Heslington 69-76; Chap Univ of York 69-76; Chief Sec CA from 76. *Church Army, Independents Road, Blackheath, SE3 9LG.*

TURNBULL, Arthur Donald. K Coll NS 63. **d & p** 66 NS. I of Arichat 66-69; CF (Canad) from 69. *c/o CFH Dept National Defence, Ottawa 4, Ont, Canada.*

TURNBULL, Brian Robert. b 43. Chich Th Coll 71. **d** 74 Croydon for Cant **p** 75 Cant. C of St Phil Norbury 74-76; St Sav Folkestone 76-78. *41 Oakley Street, Belle Vue, Shrewsbury, Salop.*

TURNBULL, Charles Philip. b 13. Ely Th Coll 37. **d** 38 Roch **p** 39 Bp Linton Smith for Roch. C of Pembury 38-42; St Mich AA N Kens 42-47; St Mary Ely 47-50; V of Gorefield 50-52; C-in-c of St Paul Camden Square Lon 52-54; R of Coveney 54-64; PC of St Pet Hornsey 64-69; V 69-76; Chap Commun of St Pet Laleham Abbey 76-79; Perm to Offic Dio Chich from 79. *3 Clarence Drive, East Preston, Littlehampton, W Sussex, BN16 1EH.* (09062 74043)

TURNBULL, Canon Colin. b 22. St Chad's Coll Dur BA 46. **d** 48 **p** 49 Newc T. C of Wallsend 48-52; N Gosforth 52-58; V of St Luke Wallsend 58-68; Monkseaton 68-75; RD of Tynemouth 70-75; V of Embleton w Craster and Newton and Rennington w Rock Dio Newc T from 75; Hon Can of Newc T Cathl from 79. *Embleton Vicarage, Alnwick, Northumb.* (Embleton 660)

TURNBULL, David Charles. b 44. Univ of Leeds BA 65. Chich Th Coll 67. **d** 69 Dur **p** 70 Jarrow for Dur. C of Jarrow 69-74; V of Carlinghow Batley Dio Wakef from 74. *Vicarage, Ealand Road, Carlingmow, Batley, Yorks WF17 8HT.* (Batley 472576)

TURNBULL, Donald Keith. d and **p** 65 C & Goulb. C of All SS Ainslie Canberra 65-66; R of Crookwell 66-71; P-in-c of Belconnen Provis Distr 71-77; R of Young Dio C & Goulb from 77. *Box 58, Young, NSW, Australia 2594.* (063-82 1811)

TURNBULL, Canon Eric Samuel. b 17. Clare Coll Cam BA 48, MA 52. Cudd Coll. **d** 48 **p** 49 Nor. C of St Pet Mancroft Nor 48-52; St Mary Virg Redcliffe Bedminster 52-54; C-in-c of Ascen Conv Distr Crownhill Devonport 54-58; V 58-62; King's Lynn 62-71; RD of Lynn 63-68; Can Res of Worc Cathl from 71. *9 College Green, Worcester, WR1 2LH.* (Worcester 24857)

TURNBULL, Canon Francis Charles. St Chad's Coll Regina 39. **d** 39 **p** 40 Qu'App. C of Hazenmore 39; St Matt Regina 39-40; I of Hemaruka 40-43; Ituna 43; Rockglen 43-47; Milden 47-53; RD of Rosstown 50-53; I of Moosonin 53-61; Hon Can of Qu'App from 56; I of St Pet Regina Dio Qu'App from 61. *1261 Garnet Street, Regina, Sask, Canada.* (306-523 4765)

TURNBULL, Ian Reginald. b 41. St Francis Coll Brisb 77. **d** 78 **p** 79 Brisb. C of Ch Ch Bundaberg 78-80; R of Gayndah Dio Brisb from 80. *Box 69, Gayndah, Queensland, Australia 4625.*

TURNBULL, James. b 19. St Aug Coll Cant. **d** 58 **p** 59 Chich. C of Brighton 58-61; V of Sayers Common 61-75; R of Twineham 61-75; P-in-c and Seq of Kingston Buci 75-81. *34 Hood Close, Chalybeate Springs, Glastonbury, Somt.* (Glastonbury 33796)

TURNBULL, John Desmond Stewart. b 20. Worc Coll Ox BA 42, MA 45. St Steph Ho Ox 41. **d** 44 **p** 45 Mon. C of St Mary Virg Mon 44-46; All SS Heref 46-51; St Jo Bapt Bathwick 51-57; V of Salcombe 57-70; Hurley 70-73; Hon C of Romsey 73-78; Perm to Offic Dio Win from 79. *Abbey Cottage, Church Street, Romsey, Hants, SO5 8BU.* (0794 515132)

TURNBULL, Canon John Smith Gardiner. b 13. Kelham Th Coll 30. **d** 36 **p** 37 Wakef. C of Whitwood Mere 36-38; Sunderland 38-43; PC of St Aid W Hartlepool Co Dur 43-51; R of Charters Towers Queensld 51-53; V of St Helen Bp Auckld 53-78; RD of Auckld 56-73; Hon Can of Dur 58-78; Can (Emer) from 78; Commiss N Queensld from 60; Newc 73-79. *32 Ridgeway, Mount Park Drive, Lanchester, Durham.*

TURNBULL, Kenneth Franklin. Univ of Manit BA 69, MA 74. Wycl Coll Tor MDiv 78. **d** 78 Tor for Rupld. On leave. *c/o The Registry, 400 University Avenue, Toronto 1, Canada.*

TURNBULL, Robert William. b 29. Late Exhib of Em Coll Cam 2nd cl Cl Trip pt i 51, BA 52, 2nd cl Th Trip pt ii 53, MA 56. Qu Coll Birm 52. **d** 54 **p** 55 Birm. C of Yardley 54-56; Edgbaston 56-58; Chap Univ of Birm 58-63; Warden of Chap 60-63; Asst Master and Chap Cheltenham Coll 63-65; Pastoral Consultant Clinical Th Centre Nottm and Perm to Offic Dio Southw 67-68; Chap Wakef City Centre 68-75; 68; Can Res of Wakef 69-75; V of Warmfield 75-79; C of Witney (in c of St Luke) 79-80; Asst Master Buckfast Abbey Sch from 80. *76 Oaklands Park, Buckfastleigh, S Devon, TQ11 0BP.* (03644 2548)

TURNBULL, Stephen. b 40. Univ of Nottm BTh 74. Linc Th Coll 70. **d** 74 **p** 75 Ripon. C of Kirkstall 74-76; Fairfield 76-79; Team V of Seacroft Dio Ripon from 79. *St Richards Vicarage, Ramshead Hill, Leeds, LS14 1BX.* (Leeds 656388)

TURNBULL, William George. b 25. Lich Th Coll 63. **d** 65 **p** 66 S'wark. C of St Silas Nunhead 65-69; Portishead 69-73; Holsworthy 73-75; P-in-c of Bridgerule 75-79; Pyworthy w Pancrasweek 77-79; R (w Bridgerule) 79-81; V of Otterton and Colaton Raleigh Dio Ex from 81. *Vicarage, Otterton, Budleigh Salterton, EX9 7JQ.* (Colaton Raleigh 68457)

TURNER, Alan James. b 40. Oak Hill Coll BA 81. **d** 81 Wakef. C of St Thos Bradley Dio Wakef from 81. *57 Bradley Road, Bradley, Huddersfield, W Yorks, HD2 1UZ.*

TURNER, Alfred Raymond. b 1898. St Aug Coll Cant. **d** 59 **p** 60 Lon. Hon C of John Keble Ch Mill Hill 59-81. *8 Delamere Gardens, NW7 3EB.* (01-959 2014)

TURNER, Antony Hubert Michael. b 30. Dipl Th (Lon) 56. FCA 63. Tyndale Hall Bris 54. **d** 56 **p** 57 Southw. C of St Ann Nottm 56-68; Cheadle (in c of St Cuthb) 58-62; PC of Ch Ch Macclesfield 62-68; Home Sec BCMS 68-74; Publ Pr Dio S'wark 68-75; V of St Jude Portsea Southsea Dio Portsm from 74; P-in-c of St Luke Portsea Southsea 75-80; RD of Portsm from 79; M Gen Syn 70-75 and from 80. *St Jude's Vicarage, Grove Road South, Southsea, Hants, PO5 3QR.* (Portsm 21071)

TURNER, Canon Arthur James Clement. b 06. Kelham Th Coll 26. **d** 32 **p** 33 Bloemf. C of Heilbron 32-37; Saltwood 37-40; Clewer (in c of All SS Dedworth) 41-42; R of Aston Somerville 42-52; V of Childswyckham 42-52; R of N Cerney 52-73; RD of Cirencester 61-73; C-in-c of Bagendon 62-73; Hon Can of Glouc from 65. *12a Abbey House, Cirencester, Glos, GL7 2QU.* (Cirencester 4307)

TURNER, Ashley Douglas. b 1895. AKC (1st cl) 21. Univ of Lon BD 21, Jun McCaul Hebr Pri 21. **d** 23 **p** 24 Lon. C of St John Westmr 23-24; St Jas L Bethnal Green 24-27; Barking (in c of St Paul) 27-29; Min of St Martin Dagenham 29-32; V 32-37; Min of Ch of Ascen Chelmsf 37-50; V of Pleshey 50-62; Hon Ed Chelmsf Dioc Chronicle 51-52; *Essex Churchman* 52-60; RD of Roding 52-62; Hon Can of Chelmsf 54-62; Chap Dioc Ho of Retreat Pleshey 56-62; V of Curdridge 62-66; Hon Chap Portsm Cathl 66-77. *5 East Street, Thame, Oxon, OX9 3JS.* (Thame 4889)

TURNER, Basil Ward. b 19. Trin Hall Cam BA 47, MA 50. Cudd Coll. **d** 50 **p** 51 Pet. C of All SS (in c of Dogsthorpe from 53) Pet 50-59; V of Apethorpe w Woodnewton Dio Pet from 59. *Woodnewton Vicarage, Peterborough.* (Kingscliffe 241)

TURNER, Brian Anthony. b 45. Canberra Coll of Min 74. **d** and **p** 77 C & Goulb. P-in-c of Batlow 77-80; on leave. *6 Woodside Park, South Norwood, SE25 5DW.*

TURNER, Charles Maurice Joseph. b 13. **d** 79 **p** 80 Bris. C of St Luke Brislington Dio Bris from 79. *31 Eagle Road, Brislington, Bristol, BS4 3LQ.*

TURNER, Christopher James Shepherd. b 48. Ch Ch Coll Ox BA 70, MA 74. Wycl Hall Ox 71. **d** 74 Man **p** 75 Middleton for Man. C of Rusholme 74-78; Chadderton Dio Man 78-80; V from 80. *Christ Church Vicarage, Chadderton, Oldham, Lancs OL9 7QB.* (061-624 2326)

TURNER, Colin Peter John. b 42. Clifton Th Coll 63. **d** 66 **p** 67 Sarum. C of Kinson 66-69; St Paul York 69-73; SE Area Sec CPAS 73-78; P-in-c of St Jo Evang Weymouth 78-79; Team V of Radipole and Melcombe Regis Dio Sarum from 79. *St John's Vicarage, 14 Carlton Road North, Weymouth, Dorset, DT4 7PX.*

TURNER, Cyril Donald. Moore Th Coll Syd ACT ThL (2nd cl) 60. **d** 61 Syd **p** 61 Bp Kerle for Syd. C of Ch Ch Blacktown 61-64; R of Riverstone 64-76; Guildf Dio Syd from 76. *2 Bolton Street, Guildford, NSW, Australia 2161.* (632-8545)

TURNER, David. b 40. Univ of St Andr BSc 63. Ridley Pri Cam 63. **d** 65 Warrington for Liv **p** 66 Liv. C of St Matt Bootle 65-68; St Mark Newtown Pemberton (in c of St Barn Marsh Green) 68-73; V of St Geo Huyton Simon Meltham Mills Dio Wakef from 79; Wilsham Dio Wakef from 79; P-in-c of Helme Dio Wakef from 81. *Meltham Mills Vicarage, Huddersfield, W Yorks, HD7 3AL.* (Huddersfield 850050)

TURNER, Donald. b 29. SOC. **d** 71 **p** 72 Kens for Lon. C of St Steph Hounslow 71-76; Hd Master St Lawr w St Paul Primary Sch 74-78; C of St John Isleworth 76-78; V of Brighton Dio Chich from 78. *41 Stanford Avenue, Brighton, Sussex, BN1 6GA.* (0273-554632)

TURNER, Douglas John. b 15. Ely Th Coll 45. **d** 47 **p** 48 St E. C of St Matt Ipswich 47-50; R of Shotesham All SS w St Mary St Botolph and St Martin 50-53; Blakeney w Langham Parva 53-58; RD of Walsingham 55-58; R of Beaconsfield Tas 58-59; Hethersett w Canteloff 59-66; V of Ketteringham 59-66; H Trin and St Cath Ventnor 66-72; Surr 66-81; V of Ryde 72-81; Perm to Offic Dio Chich from 81. *102 Wallace Avenue, Worthing, W Sussex, BN11 5QA.* (Worthing 46973)

TURNER, Canon Edward Robert. b 37. Em Coll Cam 2nd cl Th Trip pt i 62, BA 64, 2nd cl Th Trip pt iii 66, MA 67. Westcott Ho Cam 64. **d** 66 Hulme for Man **p** 67 Man. C of St Phil w St Steph Salford 66-69; Chap Tonbridge Sch and L to Offic Dio Roch 69-81; Dir of Educn Dio Roch and Can Res of Roch Cathl from 81. *1 King's Orchard, The Precinct, Rochester, ME1 1TG.*

TURNER, Edwin Alban. b 11. TD 52; Down Coll Cam 3rd cl Hist Trip pt, i 33, BA (3rd cl Th Trip pt i) 35, MA 44 Ridley Hall, Cam 34. **d** 36 **p** 37 Lon. C of H Trin Southall 36-39; CF (TA) 39-40; CF (EC) 40-46; Hon CF 46; C of H Trin Sloane Street 46-47; R of St Luke Miles Platting 47; Asst Chap HMTS *Mercury* 47-50; Chap 50-52; Chap HMS *Conway* and Perm to Offic Dio Ban 52-68; Perm to Offic Dio Ox 69-70; Asst Master Shrewsbury Ho Sch Surbiton 70-80; Perm to Offic Dio S'wark 70-80; Dio Southw from 80; Hon C of Long Ditton 72-80. *Ormonde Cottage, Normanton-on-Trent, Newark, Notts.* (Newark 821168)

TURNER, Canon Eric Gurney Hammond. b 11. St Edm Hall Ox BA 40, MA 44. Cudd Coll 40. **d** 41 **p** 42 Chelmsf. C of St Barn Woodford Green 41-45; Little Ilford 45-47; Northfield 47-49; C-in-c of ST Aug Conv Distr Rush Green Romford 49-55; V of St Edm Forest Gate w St Steph Upton Pk 55-69; Chap E Ham Mem Hosp 55-69; Surr 55-81; R of St Jas w All SS, St Nich and St Runwald Colchester 69-81; Hon Can of Chelmsf Cathl 74-81; Can (Emer) from 81; RD of Colchester 75-81. *D'arcy Cottage, Tolleshunt D'arcy, Nr Maldon, Essex.* (D'arcy 232)

TURNER, Ernest Edward. b 15. Late Th Exhib of K Coll Lon AKC (2nd cl) 49. St Bonif Coll Warm. **d** 49 **p** 50 Roch. C of St Barn Gillingham 49-53; St Jas Elmers End Beckenham 53-56; C-in-c of Foots Cray 56-60; R 60-67; Chap Qu Mary's Hosp Sidcup 59-67; R of Cuxton 67-73; V of St Barn Beckenham Dio Roch from 73. *St Barnabas's Vicarage, Beckenham, Kent.* (01-650 3332)

TURNER, Ernest Marshall. b 09. Univ of Sheff BA (2nd cl Engl) 30, MA 31. Or Coll Ox BLitt 35. Bps' Coll Cheshunt, 38. **d** 39 **p** 40 Sheff. C of Wath-upon-Dearne 39-41; Ecclesall 41-46; R of Eyam 46-75. *Pursglove Lodge, Tideswell, Nr Buxton, Derbys, SK17 8LD.* (Tideswell 871156)

TURNER, Eustace. b 18. Univ of Liv BA 40. St Cath Soc Ox BA 50, Dipl Th 51, MA 53. Wycl Hall Ox 46-48; Linc Th Coll 52. **d** 52 **p** 53 Liv. C of St Jo Evang Walton-on-the Hill 52-54; Chap Sir Roger Manwood's Gr Sch Sandwich Kent 54-57; Hd Master Port Howard Sch Falkland Is 57-60; Tutor Bida Tr Coll 60-62; Asst Master Plymouth High Sch for Girls 64-66; Perm to Offic Dio Ex 65-67; Dio Blackb from 68; Dio Liv from 69. *7 Lathom Road, Southport, Mer, PR9 0JA.* (Southport 38263)

TURNER, Francis Edwin. b 29. Sarum Th Coll 54. **d** 57 **p** 58 Cant. C of Cheriton Street 57-61; Willesborough 61-64; C-in-c of Betteshanger w Ham 64-65; R of Northbourne (w Betteshanger and Ham 65-74 and Tilmanstone 70-74) 64-74; V of Sittingbourne Dio Cant from 74; RD of Sittingbourne from 78. *St Michael's Vicarage, Valenciennes Road, Sittingbourne, Kent, ME10 1EN.* (Sittingbourne 72874)

TURNER, Frederick Charles Jesse. b 07. St Bonif Coll Warm. **d** 36 **p** 37 Lon. C of St Matt Ponders End 36-38; Hayes (in c of St Nich Grange Pk) 38-46; V of H Trin Tottenham 46-59; R of Linch (or Lynch) w Iping Marsh 59-65; Ninfield 65-74; V of Hooe 65-74. *1 Birchwood Road, Malvern, Worcs, WR14 1LD.*

TURNER, Frederick Glynne. b 30. St D Coll Lamp BA 52 St Mich Coll Llan 52. **d** 54 **p** 55 Llan. C of Aberaman 54-60; Oystermouth 60-64; V of Abercynon 64-71; Ton Pentre 71-73; Ystradyfodwg 73-77; R of Caerphilly 77-82; V of Whitchurch Dio Llan from 82. *Vicarage, Penlline Road, Whitchurch, Cardiff.* (Cardiff 66072)

TURNER, Geoffrey Arthur Edmund. ACT ThL (2nd cl) 51. **d** 50 **p** 51 Gippsld. C-in-c of St Thos Bunyip 50-51; V of Bruthen 51-55; R of Mirboo N 55-61; Trafalgar 61-68; Can of St Paul's Cathl Sale 62-68; V of Moreland 68-72; I of

Boronia Dio Melb from 72. *1 Henry Street, Boronia, Vic, Australia 3155.* (03-762 1794)

TURNER, Geoffrey Bruce. b 43. St Jo Coll Morpeth 68. **d** 71 **p** 72 Graft. C of Casino w Wyan-Rappville 71-76; R of Bangalow Dio Graft from 76. *Rectory, Bangalow, NSW, Australia 2479.*

TURNER, Geoffrey Edwin. b 45. Univ of Aston Birm BSc 68. Univ of Newc T MSc 69, PhD 72. Univ of Dur BA 74, Dipl Th 75. Cranmer Hall Dur 72. **d** 75 Bp Parker for Cov **p** 76 Bp McKie for Cov. C of St Chad Cov 75-79; V of St Gabr Huyton Quarry from 79. *Vicarage, Seel Road, Huyton Quarry, Liverpool, L36 6DT.* (051-489 2688)

TURNER, Geoffrey Martin. b 34. Oak Hill Th Coll 60. **d** 63 **p** 64 Roch. C of St Steph Tonbridge 63-66; St Jo Evang Heatherlands Parkstone 66-69; V of St Pet Derby 69-73; Ch Ch Chadderton 73-79; R of Bebington Dio Ches from 79. *Bebington Rectory, Wirral, Mer, L63 3EX.* (051-645 6478)

TURNER, Geoffrey Raymond. b 28. Sarum Wells Th Coll 71. **d** 73 Basingstoke for Win **p** 74 Win. C of All SS w Southbourne Bournemouth 73-76; R of N Waltham w Steventon, Ashe and Deane Dio Win from 76. *North Waltham Rectory, Basingstoke, Hants.* (Dummer 256)

TURNER, George Stanley Derington. b 01. Egerton Hall Man. **d** 28 **p** 30 Man. C of St Paul Royton 28-30; St Mark Cheetham 30-31; Loftus-in-Cleveland 31-33; R of Cowesby and V of Over w Nether Silton 33-39; V of Wykeham 39-47; Old Warden 47-53; Eaton 55-60; V of Troutbeck 60-70; L to Offic Dio Chich from 70. *9 Buttsfield Lane, East Hoathly, Sussex, BN8 6EE.* (Halland 314)

TURNER, Canon Gerald Garth. b 38. Late Scho of St D Coll Lamp BA 61. Late Squire Scho St Edm Hall, Ox BA 63, MA 67. St Steph Ho Ox 63. **d** 65 **p** 66 Lich. C of Market Drayton 65-68; PV of Chich Cathl, Chap Preb Sch and L to Offic Dio Chich 68-70; C of Forest Row (in c of Ashurst Wood) 70-72; V of Hope 72-78; Prec and Leasehold Can of Man Cathl from 78. *28 Rathen Road, Manchester, M20 9GH.* (061-445 3847)

TURNER, Graham Colin. Univ of Bradf BTech. Oak Hill Coll BA 81. **d** 81 Ripon. C of Ch Ch U Armley Dio Ripon from 81. *115a Heights Drive, Upper Armley, Leeds, LS12 3TG.*

TURNER, Canon Henry Ernest William. b 07. St Jo Coll Ox 1st cl Cl Mods 27, BA (1st cl Lit Hum) and Liddon Stud 29, 1st cl Th and Jun Gr Test Pri 30, Jun Denyer and Johnson Scho and Magd Coll Ox Sen Demyship 31, MA 33. Linc Coll Ox BD 40, DD 55. Wycl Hall Ox 31. **d** 31 **p** 32 Carl. C of Ch Ch Cockermouth 31-34; Wavertree 34-35; Fell, Chap and Tutor Linc Coll Ox 35-50; Chap RAFVR 40-45; Exam Chap to Bp of Bris 46-73; to Bp of Linc 47-50; to Bp of Dur 50-66 and 68-72; to Bp of Derby 70-73; Commiss U Nile 48-61; Lightfoot Prof of Div Univ of Dur 51-58; Can Res of Dur 51-73; Can (Emer) from 74; Actg Dean of Dur 73; Univ of Ox Bampton Lect 54; Van Mildert Prof of Div Univ of Dur from 58. *Realands, Eskdale, Holmbrook, Cumb, CA19 1TW.* (Eskdale 321)

TURNER, Henry John Mansfield. b 24. Magd Coll Cam BA 45, MA 48. Westcott Ho Cam 48. **d** 50 **p** 51 Linc. C of Crosby 50-52; St Ambrose Chorlton-on-Medlock and Intercolleg Sec SCM 52-55; C of Leigh Lancs 55-57; V of Good Shepherd Rochdale 57-62; Ch of S India 63-67; V of St Geo Becontree 67-71; R of Weeley 71-79; Chap and Lect St Deiniol's Libr Hawarden 79-80; Sub-Warden from 80; Perm to Offic Dio St A 79; L from 80. *St Deiniol's Library, Hawarden, Clwyd, CH5 3DF.* (0244-532350)

TURNER, Ivor Cuthbert William. b 09. MPS 30. Worc Ordin Coll 63. **d** 64 **p** 65 Bris. C of Horfield 64-67; Dartmouth 67-72; Tamworth 72-79; Perm to Offic Dio Ex from 79. *15 Townstal Road, Dartmouth, TQ6 9HT.* (Dartmouth 2057)

TURNER, James. **d** 52 **p** 53 Alg. I of Schreiber 52-56; R of Gravenhurst 56-59; St Geo Thunder Bay (f Port ArthurY 59-72; Dioc Sec Alg from 71; I of W Thunder Bay 72-77; Capreol Dio Alg from 77. *Box 302, Capreol, Ont., Canada.* (705-858 2550)

TURNER, John David Maurice. b 22. Keble Coll Ox BA 45, MA 48. Ripon Hall Ox 69. **d** 70 **p** 71 Ox. C of Crowthorne 70-73; V of Cropredy w Gt Bourton (and Wardington from 80) Dio Ox from 73. *Cropredy Vicarage, Banbury, Oxon.* (Cropredy 715)

TURNER, John Gilbert. b 06. **d** 66 **p** 67 Southw. C of Holme Pierrepont w Adbolton 66-69; Radcliffe-on-Trent 69-71; Colston Bassett and of Cropwell Bishop 71-77; Tythby w Cropwell Butler 71-77; Langar w Barnstone 71-77; Granby w Sutton and Elton-on-the-Hill 71-77; Perm to Offic Dio Southw from 78. *Landyke, Tythby Road, Cropwell Butler, Radcliffe-on-Trent, Nottingham.*

TURNER, John Jeffrey. Moore Th Coll Syd ACT ThL 54. **d** and **p** 55 Syd. C of Willoughby 55-57; P-in-c of Villawood 57-59; Dir of C of E Boys' S Syd 59-60; Chap for Youth Dio Syd 60-65; R of Kingsgrove 65-68; Commiss Moro from 66; C of Mosman 68-69; Chatswood 69; C-in-c of Mowbray Provis Par 69-73; Asst Gen Sec CMS Syd 73-74; Gen Sec 74-78; Perm to Offic Dio C & Goulb 77-78; R of Dapto Dio Syd from 78. *Rectory, Dapto, NSW, Australia 2530.* (042-61 1001)

TURNER, Ven John Thomas. K Coll NS 26. 1 27 **p** 28 NS. C of Tangier 27-28; I of Port Morien 28-33; R of Tangier 33-37; Melford 37-42; RD of St Geo 40-42; CF (Canad) 42-45; C of N Sydney NS 45-47 and 53-59; R 59-69; R of Louisburg 47-53; Archd of Cape Breton 65-69; Archd (Emer) from 70. *3 Oxford Avenue, Sydney Mines, NS, Canada.* (736-3390)

TURNER, Keith Howard. b 50. Univ of Southn BA 71. Wycl Hall Ox 72. **d** 75 Lon **p** 76 Edmon for Lon. C of Cockfosters 75-79; Chilwell Dio Southw from 79. *10 College Road, Chilwell, Nottingham.* (Nottm 256501)

TURNER, Lawrence John. b 43. Kelham Th Coll 65. **d** 70 **p** 71 Shrewsbury for Lich. C of Lower Gornal 70-73; St Paul's Wednesbury 73-74; Porthill 74-77; Wilton-in-Cleveland 77-80; P-in-c 80-82; R of St Martin Jersey Dio Win from 82. *Rectory, St Martin, Jersey, CI.* (0534 54294)

TURNER, Leslie. b 29. St Aid Coll. **d** 54 **p** 55 Blackb. C of St Cuthb Darwen 54-56; Haslingden 56-59; V of St Paul Oswaldtwistle 59-65; Chap Belmont and Henderson Hosps Sutton and St Ebba's Hosp Epsom 65-71; Qu Mary's Hosp for Children Carshalton 67-71; St Crisp & Princess Marina Hosp Northn from 71. *130 Park Lane, Duston, Northampton.*

TURNER, Leslie Philip. St Jo Coll Morpeth. **d** 61 **p** 62 Bath. C of Wellington 65-66; R of Geurie 66-69; R of Coolah, Dio Bath from 69. *Rectory, Coolah, NSW, Australia 2853.* (7722-9)

TURNER, Leslie William. St Jo Coll Morpeth. **d** 46 **p** 48 Graft. C of Kempsey 46-48; Ch Ch Cathl Graft 48; V of Copmanhurst 48-49; C of Toowoomba 49-52; R of Oakey 52-56; Pittsworth 56-60; Gympie 60-64; Fortitude Valley 64-68; Kingaroy 68-72; St Alb Wilston Brisb 72-78; St Matt Holland Pk City and Dio Brisb from 78. *Rectory, Alamine Street, Holland Park, Brisbane, Australia 4121.* (397 2300)

TURNER, Mark Richard Haythornthwaite. b 41. TCD MA 67. Linc Coll Ox BA (2nd cl Th) 68. Wycl Hall Ox 65. **d** 68 **p** 69 Dur. C of Birtley 68-71; St Mary the Great, Cam 71-74; Chap Loughborough Univ Colls 74-79; Univ of Keele from 80; P-in-c of Keele Dio Lich from 80. *5 Church Bank, Keele, Staffs, ST5 5AT.* (Newc-under-Lyme 627385)

TURNER, Martin John. b 34. Trin Hall Cam BA 55, 2nd cl Th Trip pt ia 56, MA 59. Cudd Coll. **d** 60 **p** 61 Cov. C of Rugby 60-65; St Mich Cathl Cov 65-68; in Amer Ch 68-70; V of Rushmere Dio St E from 70. *5 Thornley Drive, Ipswich, Suff, IP4 3LR.* (Ipswich 76785)

TURNER, Maurice William. b 27. Sarum Th Coll 53. **d** 56 **p** 57 Wakef. C of Thornhill 56-60; V of Gawber 60-71; Alverthorpe 71-74; Shelton w Oxon 74-81; Leaton Dio Lich from 81; P-in-c of Albrighton w Battlefield Dio Lich from 81. *Leaton Vicarage, Bomere Heath, Shrewsbury, SY4 3AP.* (Bomere Heath 290259)

TURNER, Michael Andrew. b 34. K Coll Cam 2nd cl Engl Trip pt i 57, BA (2nd cl Th Trip pt ii) 59, MA 62. Cudd Coll 59. **d** 61 **p** 62 St Alb. C of St Andr Luton 61-64; Northolt (in c of St Jos) 64-70; V of St Andr Luton 70-77; Commiss Gambia from 76; Publ Pr Dio St Alb from 77. *35 Culverhouse Road, Luton, Beds, LU3 1PY.* (Luton 391835)

TURNER, Michael John Royce. b 43. Univ of Dur BA 65. Chich Th Coll 65. **d** 67 Birm **p** 68 Aston for Birm. C of St Phil and St Jas Conv Distr Hodge Hill 67-71; Eling and Testwood 71-73; Team V (w Marchwood) 73-77; R of Kirkwall w Stromness Dio Aber and Ork from 77. *Rectory, Dundas Crescent, Kirkwall, Orkney, KW15 1JQ.* (Kirkwall 2024)

TURNER, Nicholas Anthony. b 51. Clare Coll Cam BA 73, MA 77. Keble Coll Ox BA (Th) 77, MA 81. Ripon Coll Cudd 78. **d** 78 Hulme for Man **p** 79 Man. C of St Matt Stretford 78-80; Tutor St Steph Ho Ox from 80. *St Stephen's House, Oxford, OX4 1JX.* (0865 47874)

TURNER, Nigel. b 16. Late Exhib of Univ Lon K Coll Lon Sen Wordsworth Lat Pri 35, Abp Robertson Pri 36, Plumptre Pri 37. AKC (2nd cl) 37. Univ of Lon BD (2nd cl) 39, MTh 49, PhD 53. Qu Coll Birm 38. **d** 39 **p** 40 Birm. C of St Mary Pype Hayes 39-42; Erdington 42-44; Aldridge 47-49; Battle 49-51; V of Diseworth 51-58; R of Milton 58-60; Select Pr Univ of Cam 59; Lect in Th Univ of Rhodesia from 72. *PO Box MP 167, Mount Pleasant, Rhodesia.*

TURNER, Noel Macdonald Muncaster. b 08. Ch Coll Cam BA 31. Ely Th Coll 32. **d** 32 **p** 33 Southw. C of Ollerton 32-35; Sutton-in-Ashfield 35-37; St Mary Southw 37-39; Dom Chap to Bp of Southw 38-45; V of Upton 39-41; R of Gonalston 41-73; Epperstone 41-73; Chap HM Borstal Inst Lowdham Grange 45-73; C-in-c of Oxton 67-73; Perm to Offic Dios Chich and Portsm from 73. *27 West Close, Fernhurst, Haslemere, Surrey.* (Haslemere 53542)

TURNER, Peter Carpenter. b 39. Oak Hill Th Coll 63. **d** 66 Barking for Chelmsf **p** 67 Chelmsf. C of St Mary Chadwell 66-69; Braintree 69-73; R of Fyfield Dio Chelmsf from 73; P-in-c of Moreton Dio Chelmsf from 77. *Fyfield Rectory, Ongar, Essex, CM5 0SD.* (Fyfield 255)

TURNER, Peter Robin. b 42. Open Univ BA 79. K Coll Lon and Warm AKC 65. **d** 66 **p** 67 Ex. C of Crediton 66-69; Perm to Offic Dio Ex 69-70; Chap RAF from 70. *c/o Ministry of Defence, Adastral House, WC1X 8RU.*

TURNER, Philip William. b 25. Worc Coll Ox BA 50, MA 62. Chich Th Coll 49. **d** 51 **p** 52 Ripon. C of St Bart Armley 51-56; Crawley 56-62; V of St Matt Northn 62-66; Relig Broadcasting Org for BBC Midl Region 66-70; Asst Master Droitwich High Sch Worcs 70-73; Chap & Asst Master Eton Coll Windsor 73-75; Malvern Coll from 76. *181 West Malvern Road, Malvern, Worcs.* (Malvern 63852)

TURNER, Phillip Sidney. b 29. Roch Th Coll 67. **d** 69 Grimsby for Linc **p** 70 Linc. C of L Coates Linc 69-72; Team V 72-73; R of Stickney 73-80; P-in-c of Stickford 73-80; Eastville and New Leake w Midville 77-80; V of Kilnhurst Dio Sheff from 80. *Kilnhurst Vicarage, Rotherham, S Yorks.*

TURNER, Raymond Keith. Univ of BC BA 59. Angl Th Coll BC LTh 63. **d** and **p** 63 Koot. C of Penticton 63-68; L to Offic Dio Koot from 69. *RR2, Oliver, BC, Canada.*

TURNER, Canon Robert Edgar. b 20. TCD BA 42, MA 51. Linc Th Coll 44. **d** 45 **p** 46 Birm. C of All SS King's Heath Birm 45-51; Dean of Stud Residences Qu Univ Belf 51-58; L to Offic Dio Connor 51-58; Min Can of Belf Cathl 51-63; Dom and Exam Chap to Bp of Down and Drom 56-67; R of St Geo Belf Dio Connor from 58; Can of St Anne's Cathl Belfast 71-76; Can and Preb of St Patr Cathl Dub from 76; Exam Chap to Bp of Connor from 74. *28 Myrtlefield Park, Belfast, N Ireland, BT9 6NF.* (Belfast 667134)

TURNER, Robin Edward. b 35. Selw Coll Cam BA 57, MA 63. Univ of Birm Dipl Th 63. Qu Coll Birm 61. **d** 63 **p** 64 Chelmsf. C of Aveley 63-67; Upminster 67-71; R of Goldhanger w L Totham 71-80; L Baddow Dio Chelmsf from 80. *Rectory, Colam Lane, Little Baddow, Chelmsford, Essex.* (Danbury 3488)

TURNER, Rodney David. St Jo Coll Morpeth 63. ACT ThL 65. **d** 66 **p** 67 Armid. C of St Pet Cathl Armid 66-68; Quirindi 68-71; V of Emmavile 71-74; P-in-c of Boggabri 74-78; Tamworth Dio Armid from 78. *Box 448, Tamworth, NSW, Australia 2340.*

TURNER, Roger Dyke. b 39. Trin Coll Bris 79. **d** 81 Taunton for B & W. C of St Andr Clevedon Dio B & W from 81. *23 Turner Way, Yeo Park, Clevedon, Avon, BS21 7YN.*

TURNER, St John Alwin. b 31. Univ of Dur BA 57, Dipl Th 58, MA 61. Cranmer Hall, Dur 57. **d** 59 **p** 60 Dur. C of St Paul W Hartlepool 59-62; H Trin S Shore Blackpool (in c of St Nich Marton Moss) 62-65; V of Huncoat 65-67; Area Sec CMS Dios Ripon and York 67-72; L to Offic Dio York 67-72; V of St Mark Harrogate Dio Ripon from 72. *13 Wheatlands Road, Harrogate, N Yorks, HG2 8BB.* (Harrogate 504959)

TURNER, Sydney Alfred. Moore Th Coll Syd Abbott Scho 17 ACT ThL 17. **d** 17 **p** 18 Syd. C of St John Bishopthorpe 17-21; St John Camden 21-22; Ch Ch N Syd 22; Kensington 22-23; St Thos N Syd 23-26; R of Milton 26-30; Bulli 30-38; Smithfield (w Fairfield 38-52) 38-67; L to Offic Dio Syd from 67. *21 Swadling Street, Long Jetty, NSW, Australia 2262.* (043-32 6531)

TURNER, Sydney Joscelyn. **d** 75 Ja (APM). C of Cathl Ch Spanish Town Dio Ja from 75. *Box 105, Spanish Town, Jamaica, WI.*

TURNER, Thomas Francis. Univ of Leeds, BA (2nd cl German Lang and Lit) 50. Chich Th Coll 52. **d** 54 **p** 55 Ripon. C of Holbeck 54-57; Moor Allerton 57-59; R of St Olaf Kirkwall 59-65; St Mary Aber 65-68. *3 Dundas Crescent, Kirkwall, Orkney.*

TURNER, Walter. b 21. Lich Th Coll 51. **d** 53 **p** 54 Carl. C of St Jas Barrow-F 53-56; Penrith 56-58; V of Haverthwaite 58-65; Frizington 65-70; Underbarrow w Helsington and Crook 70-77; Allithwaite 77-79; Team V of Kirkby Lonsdale Dio Carl from 79. *Vicarage, Kirkby Lonsdale, Carnforth, Lancs.* (K Lonsdale 71184)

TURNER, Preb Walter John. b 29. Univ of Bris BA (2nd cl Th) 53. Clifton Th Coll 49. **d** 54 **p** 55 Lich. C of W Bromwich 54-58; Min of Oxley Eccles Distr 58-60; V 60-65; Wednesfield 65-75; Surr from 68; V of Shifnal Dio Lich from 75; Boningale Dio Lich from 75; RD of Shifnal from 75; Preb of Lich Cathl from 80. *Vicarage, Shifnal, Salop.* (Telford 460625)

TURNER, William. MBE 57. Univ of Liv BA 31. Coll of Resurr Mirfield 34. **d** 36 **p** 37 Glas. C of St Martin Polmadie Glas 36-38; UMCA Miss Lik 39-40; Prin of St Mich Coll Likwenu 40-61; Can of Nyasa 53-61; Exam Chap to Bp of Nyasa 59-61; L to Offic Dio Kuch 61-65; V of St Agnes Toxt Pk 65-69; R of St Geo Montserrat 70-71; Anguilla 71-75; Hon C of St Paul Furzedown Streatham Dio S'wark from 75. *11 Mansard Beeches, Welham Road, SW17 9DA.*

TURNER, William Edward. b 41. Keble Coll Ox BA 63, MA 73. Linc Th Coll 76. **d** 78 **p** 79 Lich. C of St Chad Lich 78-80; Assoc Chap Trent Poly Nottm from 80. *2 Osborne Avenue, Sherwood, Nottingham, NG5 2HJ.* (0602 604494)

TURNEY, Preb Francis Irving. Univ of Liv BA 27. Wycl Hall, Ox 32. **d** 34 **p** 35 Liv. C of St John Birkdale 34-36; Ormskirk 36-40; St Nich Blundellsands (in c of St Steph Hightown) 40-41; V of Downton-on-the-Rock w Burrington 41-49; R of Aston w Elton 41-49; Brampton Bryan w Lingen 49-55; RD of Wigmore 47-55; V of Clehonger 55-59; R of Eaton Bp 55-59; V of Bridstow w Peterstow 59-73; Preb of Heref Cathl from 65; RD of Ross and Archenfield 67-71; Past Care of Pudleston, Hatfield and Humber 74-81. *Blanchland, Orchard Lane, Ryelands, Leominster, Herefs HR6 8PW.*

TURNEY, Thomas Henry. Trin Hall Cam BA (2nd cl Nat Sc Trip pt i) 23, 1st cl Nat Sc Trip pt ii 24, MA 27. Bps' Coll Cheshunt. **d** 27 **p** 28 Liv. C of Warrington 27-30; Succr of Ripon Cathl 30-40; V of Well w Snape and Chap Neville's Hosp 40-45; Asst Master Ripon Gr Sch 43-46; Skellfield Sch Thirsk 55-65; Hulme Gr Sch Oldham 65-68; Perm to Offic Dio Liv 68-71. *Les Terrasses, Grange-Pacot, Fribourg 1700, Switzerland.*

TURNHAM, Derek Lynn. b 52. Kelham Th Coll 71. **d** 75 **p** 76 Worc. C of St Martin w St Pet Worc 75-78; All SS Maidstone 78-81; V of New Rossington Dio Sheff from 81. *St Luke's Vicarage, New Rossington, Doncaster, DN11 0QP* (Doncaster 868288)

TURNQUEST, Addison. b 40. Sarum Wells Th Coll 69. **d** 71 **p** 72 Nass. C of Long I Dio Nass 71-75; P-in-c of All SS Calvary Hill Dio Nass from 76. *PO Box N9376, Nassau, Bahamas.* (35217)

TURP, Paul Robert. b 48. Oak Hill Coll BA 79. **d** 79 Willesden for Lon **p** 80 Lon. C of St John Southall Green Dio Lon from 79. *9 Derley Road, Southall, Middx, UB2 5EJ.*

TURPIN, John Richard. b 41. St D Coll Lamp BA (2nd cl Hist) 63. Magd Coll Cam BA (2nd cl Th Trip pt ii) 65, MA 70. Cudd Coll 65. **d** 66 **p** 67 Win. C of Tadley 66-71; V of St Chris Thornhill Southn Dio Win from 71. *402 Hinkler Road, Thornhill, Southampton.* (Southampton 448537)

TURPIN, Canon Reginald Matthew. Bp's Univ Lennox BA 37. Montr Dioc Th Coll Hon DD 78. **d** 42 **p** 43 Queb. C of Kenogami 42-44; Peninsula 44-45; I of Cookshire 45-52; R of Buckingham 52-59; I of St Mark Dorval Montr 59-69; Synod Executive Officer Montr 69-76; Hon Can of Montr from 69; Exam Chap to Bp of Montr 70-76; R of Longueuil Dio Montr from 76. *134 St Charles Street West, Longueuil, PQ, Canada.* (514-674 6618)

TURRALL, Albert Thomas George. b 19. Linc Th Coll 64. **d** 66 **p** 67 Birm. C of Rowley Regis 66-69; R of Astley Worc 69-74; V of Montford w Shrawardine (R w Fitz from 77) Dio Lich from 74; C-in-c of Fitz 75-77. *Montford Rectory, Shrewsbury, SY4 1AA.* (Shrewsbury 850519)

TURTLE, Malcolm. b 28. ACP (External) 66. Qu Coll Birm 77. **d** 80 **p** 81 Heref (APM). C of Worfield Dio Heref from 80. *School House, Worfield, Bridgnorth, Salop.*

TURTON, Arthur Bickerstaffe. b 19. Oak Hill Th Coll 46. **d** 48 **p** 49 Man. C of Rawtenstall 48-51; Islington 51-52; V of St Silas Lozells 52-56; St Alb Streatham Pk 56-60; Org Sec CPAS Metrop Area 60-64; V of St Pet w Ch Ch Southborough (w St Matt from 68) 64-76; C-in-c of St Matt Southborough 67-68; V of Histon Dio Ely from 76. *Histon Vicarage, Cambridge, CB4 4EP.* (Histon 2255)

TURTON, Douglas Walter. b 38. Univ of Kent at Cant BA 77. Oak Hill Coll 77. **d** 78 **p** 79 Cant. C of St Mary Bredin Cant 78-81; V of Thornton Heath Dio Cant from 81. *1 Norbury Avenue, Thornton Heath, Surrey, CR4 8AH.* (01-653 2762)

TURTON, Neil Christopher. b 45. Wycl Hall Ox 77. **d** 79 **p** 80 Guildf. C of Ch Ch City and Dio Guildf from 79. *23a Waterden Road, Guildford, GU1 2AZ.*

TURTON, Paul Edward. b 26. St Pet Hall Ox BA (3rd cl Phil Pol and Econ) 50, MA 55. Qu Coll Birm 50. **d** 52 Birm **p** 53 Bp Linton for Cant. C of Selly Oak 52-55; Ward End Birm 55-57; PC of St Osw Conv Distr Netherton 57-61; V 61-64; Dioc Visitor Ch Schs Dio Liv 59-64; V of Brockley Hill 64-68; Perm to Offic Dio S'wark 68-70; Dir of Relig Educn Dio Nor 70-75; Dep Dir Nat S Centre Camberwell 75-77; Dir Nat S Relig Educn Centre Kens from 78. *23 Kensington Square, Kensington, W8 5HN.* (01-937 4241)

TURVEY, Joseph Gordon. b 02. MBE 65. St Cath Coll Cam BA 24, MA 63. Westcott Ho Cam. **d** 65 **p** 66 St Alb. C of St Paul Letchworth 65-68; V of Langford 68-72; Hon C of Crewkerne w Wayford 72-76; Radlett Dio St Alb from 77. *Little Orchard, Radlett Park Road, Radlett, Herts.* (Radlett 5754)

TURVEY, Raymond Hilton. b 16. St Cath Coll Cam BA 38, MA 42. Ridley Hall Cam 38. **d** 40 **p** 41 Roch. C of H Trin

Brompton Chatham 40-43; Succr of St Pet Cathl Ch Bradf 43-47; V of Ch Ch N Finchley 47-58; St Geo Leeds 58-72; St Paul Onslow Sq Kens 72-78; H Trin Brompton Road Kens 76-80. *3 Peacock Road, Harberton Mead, Oxford, OX3 0DQ.* (0865 46898)

TURVEY, Warwick. St Jo Coll Morpeth. **d** 52 **p** 53 Newc for Melan. C of Largs 53-54; Singleton 54-55; P Dio Melan 55-57; R of Stroud 57-61; Merriwa 61-72; Adamstown Dio Newc from 72. *Rectory, Brunker Road, Adamstown, NSW, Australia 2289.* (57-1895)

TURYAGYENDA, Jackson Jack. Bp Tucker Coll Mukono 64. **d** 66 Ankole-K. d Dio Ankole-K 66-67; Dioc Treas and Sec Dio Kig 67-69; Sch Visitor Dio Kig from 69. *Box 3, Kabale, Kigezi, Uganda.*

✠ **TUSTIN, Right Rev David.** b 35. Late Cho Exhib of Magd Coll Cam 2nd cl Mod Lang Trip pt i, 55, BA (3rd cl Th Trip pt ii) 57, MA 61. Cudd Coll. **d** 60 **p** 61 Lich. C of Stafford 60-63; Asst Gen Sec C of E Coun on Foreign Relations and C of St Dunstan-in-the-W Lon 63-67; V of St Paul Wednesbury 67-71; Tettenhall Regis 71-79; RD of Trysull 76-79; Cons Ld Bp Suffr of Grimsby in Westmr Abbey 25 Jan 79 By Abp of Cant; Bps of Lon, Linc, St E, B & W, Heref, Nor, Portsm, Lich, Roch, Ox and Truro; Bps Suffr of Buckingham, Grantham, Hertford, Shrewsbury, Tonbridge, St Germans and Jarrow; and others; Can and Preb of Linc Cathl from 79. *43 Abbey Park Road, Grimsby, S Humb, DN32 0HS.* (Grimsby 58223)

TUTE, James Stanley. b 11. Bps' Coll Cheshunt. **d** 34 **p** 35 Lon. C of St Mich AA Stoke Newington Common 34-35; St Benet and All SS Kentish Town 35-46; PC of St Mark Hanwell 46-56; V of St Bart Stamford Hill 56-80; C-in-c of St Jo Div Stamford Hill 76-77. *c/o St Bartholomew's Vicarage, Craven Park Road, Stamford Hill, N15 6AA.* (01-800 1554)

TUTE, John Armytage. b 13. Lich Th Coll 37. **d** 40 Bp Tubbs for Ches **p** 41 Ches. C of St Thos Stockport 40; Neston 40-41; St Alb Stockport 41-55; V 55-62; Lower Tranmere 62-66; R of Hawkridge w Withypool 66-80. *Address temp unknown.*

✠ **TUTI, Right Rev Dudley.** OBE 74. St Jo Coll Auckld. **d** 46 Melan **p** 54 Auckld for Melan. P Dio Melan 46-63; Cons Asst Bp of Melan in All SS Cathl Honiara 30 Nov 63 by Abp of NZ; Bps of Melan; Nel; Carp; New Guinea; and Polyn; Bp Suffr of Aotearoa; and Bps Hudson and Ambo; Apptd Bp Suffr 68; Bp of Ysabel 75; res 81; Archd of Centr Solomons 68-75; VG 71-75. *c/o Bishop's House, Seleo, Santa Ysabel, Solomon Islands.*

TUTIN, Richard Brendon. b 53 . St Francis Coll Brisb 75. **d** 77 **p** 78 Brisb. C of St Luke Toowoomba 77-78; Ch Ch Bundaberg 78-79; V of St Mary Gin Gin Dio Brisb from 80. *43 Milden Street, Gin Gin, Queensland, Australia 4671.*

TUTT, Ernest Hedley. b 02. AKC (1st cl) Plumptre Pri in Engl Lit and Barry Div Pri 32. Bps' Coll Cheshunt, 32. **d** 33 **p** 34 Win. C of Eastleigh 33-36; St Mary Beverley (in c of St Nich) 36-38; Margate 38-40; St Steph Glouc 40-41; V of Malins Lee 41-48; St Mary Bilston 48-54; St Paul Wednesbury 54-67; R of Elford 67-72. *56 Roche Way, Wellingborough, Northants.*

TUTT, Kelvin Aubrey. Moore Th Coll Syd ACT ThL (2nd cl) 52. **d** and **p** 53 Syd. C of W Manly and C-in-c of Mobile Ch 53-54; Chap Norfolk I 54-56; V of Stoke NZ 56-60; Cobden 60-63; C-in-c of Peakhurst w Lugarno 63-72; R of Balgowlah Dio Syd from 72. *311 Sydney Road, Balgowlah, NSW, Australia 2093.* (94-2455)

TUTTON, John Knight. b 30. Univ of Man BSc (3rd cl Physics) 51. Ripon Hall Ox 53. **d** 55 **p** 56 Man. C of Tonge w Alkrington 55-57; Bushbury 57-59; R of Blackley 59-67; Ch Ch Denton Dio Man from 67. *1 Windmill Lane, Denton, Manchester, M34 3RN.* (061-336 2126)

TUTTY, Thomas James Robert. **d** 58 **p** 59 St Arn. C-in-c of Dunolly 58-60; V 60; Woomelang w Tempy 60-64; R of Avoca 64-70; V of Daylesford 71-72. *2/21 Belmont Avenue, Vic., Australia 3146.*

✠ **TUTU, Right Rev Desmond Mpilo.** Univ of S Afr BA 54. LTh (S Afr) 60. Univ of Lon BD (2nd cl) 65, MTh 66. Univ of Kent Hon DCL 78. Univ of Aber Hon DD 81. St Pet Coll Rosettenville, 58. **d** 60 Abp Paget for Johann **p** 61 Johann. P Dio Johann 61-62; Perm to Offic Dio Lon 62-65; Dio S'wark 65-66 and 74-75; Tutor St Pet Coll Alice and L to Offic Dio Grahmstn 67-70; Lect in Th Univ of Botswana, Les and Swaz 70-74; Dean and R of St Mary Virg Cathl Johann 75-76; Cons Ld Bp of Les in St Mary's Cathl Johann 11 July 76 by Abp of Capetn; Bps of Pret, Bloemf, Zulu, Swaz and Ja; Bps Suffr of Les and Johann; and others; res 77; Asst Bp of Johann from 78; Gen Sec S Afr Coun of Chs from 78. *Box 31190, Braamfontein, 2017, S Africa.*

TUWEI, Jacob Kiptalam. St Paul's Th Coll Limuru 61. **d** 63 **p** 65 Nak. P Dio Nak 63-78; on leave. *PO Box 381, Nakuru, Kenya.*

TUYAPENI, Michael Hituuashive. b 37. **d** 71 Damar **p** 72 Bp Wade for Capetn for Damar. P Dio Damar 71-80; Dio Namibia from 80. *c/o St Mary's, Odibo, PO Oshikango, Ovamboland, SW Africa.* (Oshikango 5)

TWADDELL, William Reginald. b 33. TCD 61. **d** 62 **p** 63 Connor. C of Whiterock 62-65; R of Loughgilly w Clare 65-71; Milltown Dio Arm from 71. *Rectory, The Birches, Portadown, Co Armagh, N Ireland.*

TWAHIRWA, Peter. **d** and **p** 75 Bunyoro. P Dio Bunyoro. *Box 214, Biizi, Masindi, Uganda.*

TWAMUGABO, Atanasi. b 29. **d** and **p** 73 Rwa. P Dio Rwa 73-75; Dio Kiga from 75. *BP 166, Gisenyi, Rwanda.*

TWEDDELL, Ian Henry. **d** 60 **p** 62 River. C of Tocumwal 60-64; V of Woodville 64-68; Petone 68-76; Taihape 76-78; Wanganui E Dio Wel from 79. *Vicarage, Wanganui East, NZ.*

TWEDDLE, David William Joseph. b 28. Univ of Dur BSc 50. Wycl Hall Ox 54. **d** 56 Jarrow for Dur **p** 57 Dur. C of H Trin Darlington 56-60; P-in-c of St Andr Prestonpans 60-63; PV of Linc Cathl 63-65; C of Peterborough 65-71; Hon Min Can of Pet from 68; V of Southwick w Glapthorne Dio Pet from 71; P-in-c of Benefield Dio Pet from 80. *Vicarage, Southwick, Peterborough, PE8 5BL.* (Cotterstock 226)

TWEEDIE, Andrew Stuart Rankin. b 09. Univ of Edin MA 33. **d** 74 **p** 75 Rupld. Hon C of St Pet Winnipeg Dio Rupld from 74; Dioc Sec Dio Rupld from 75. *511 Montrose Street, Winnipeg, R2W 3X8, Canada.*

TWEEDY, (Mark) Christopher Harold. b 12. Univ of Lon BD and AKC 36. M CR 41. **d** 36 **p** 37 Sarum. C of St Pet Parkstone w Branksea 36-38; L to Offic Dio Wakef 40-62; Vice Prin Coll of Resurr Mirfield 58-62; Coll of St Pet Alice 63-69; L to Offic Dio Grahmstn 63-69; Dio Lon from 70. *St Katherine's Foundation, 2 Butcher Row, E14 8DS.* (01-790 3540)

TWELL, Canon Alfred Maurice. b 04. AKC 32. St Steph Ho Ox 33. **d** 33 **p** 34 York. C of H Trin Goodramgate York 33-35; St John Middlesbrough 35-39; USPG (f UMCA) Miss at Chipili Dio Zam (f N Rhod; N Zam from 71) 39-44; 47-53 and 65-73; Mapanza 45-47 and 53-65; Hon Can of Lusaka 70-76; Can (Emer) from 76. *College of St Barnabas, Lingfield, Surrey, RH7 6NJ.*

TWENTYMAN, Trevor Lawrence Holme. b 35. Chich Th Coll 67. **d** 70 Dorking for Guildf **p** 71 Sheff. C of N Holmwood 70; St Cecilia Parson Cross Sheff 71; St Aug Qu Gate Kens Dio Lon from 76. *9 Gunterstone Road, W Kensington, W14.*

TWESIGYE, Emmanuel. b 42. Makerere Univ Kamp Dipl Th 69, BA 73. Bp Tucker Coll Mukono 67. **d** 69 **p** 71 P Dio Kig 71-72; Dio Kamp from 72. *Box 20012, Kampala, Uganda.*

TWIDELL, William James. b 30. St Mich Coll Llan 58. **d** 60 **p** 61 Man. C of Tonge w Alkrington 60-63; High Wycombe 63-65; Min of St Pet Conv Distr Larch Farm 65-66; V of St Thos Bury 66-72; St Jas Daisy Hill Dio Man from 72. *Daisy Hill Vicarage, Lower Leigh Road, Westhoughton, Bolton, Lancs,*

TWINING, John Sanford. Angl Th Coll of BC LTh 43, BA (Univ of BC) 52. **d** 43 **p** 44 New Westmr. C of Cloverdale w Port Kells 43-44; P-in-c All SS Alta Vista 44-45; C of Ch Ascen Montr 45-46; V of Squamish 46-48; I of St D Westview N Vancouver 48-51; P-in-c of Seal Cove 52-53; Ocean Falls 53-55; R 55-59; I of St Aug Ogden and St Luke Calg 59-63; R of Banff 63-66; I of Birch Hills 66-71; R of Arthur 71-78; St Jo Evang Hamilton Dio Niag from 78. *17 Beulah Avenue, Hamilton, Ont, Canada.* (416-522 4445)

TWINING-SMITH, Walter Edward. Wells Th Coll 47. **d** 48 **p** 49 Cov. C of Lillington 48-49; CF 49-58; S Command 49-50; BTA Austria 50-53; BAOR 53-54; Egypt 54-56; Cyprus 56-58; V of Cubbington 58-67; R of Beaudesert w Henley-in-Arden 67-75; C-in-c of Ullenhall 73-75; C of W Parley 75-77; Chap Poole Gen Hosp and St Annes Hosp Canford Cliffs from 77. *12 Pinebeach Court, Branksome Chine, Canford Cliffs, Poole, Dorset.* (Canford Cliffs 708361)

TWISLETON, John Fiennes. b 48. St Jo Coll Ox BA 70, MA 73, DPhil 74. Univ of Leeds Dipl Th 75. Coll of the Resurr Mirfield 74. **d** 76 **p** 77 Sheff. C of New Bentley 76-79; P-in-c of Moorends Dio Sheff 79-80; V from 80. *Vicarage, West Road, Moorends, Doncaster, Yorks.* (Thorne 812237)

TWISLETON-WYKEHAM-FIENNES, Very Rev The Hon Oliver William. b 26. New Coll Ox BA 54, MA 55. Cudd Coll 52. **d** 54 **p** 55 Win. C of Milton 54-58; Chap Clifton Coll Bris 58-63; L to Offic Dio Bris 59-63; R of Lambeth 63-69; RD of Lambeth 67-69; Dean of Linc from 69; Can and Preb of Linc Cathl from 69. *Deanery, Lincoln.* (Lincoln 23608)

TWOHIG, Brian. b 48. La Trobe Univ Vic BA 77. St Mich Ho Crafers 70. **d** 72 Adel **p** 73 C & Goulb. Perm to Offic Dio Adel 72-73; Dio C & Goulb 73-74; Dio Melb 74-75; C of W

Coburg 75-78; Leatherhead 78-80; Perm to Offic Dio Melb from 80. *1a Edwin Street, East Preston, Vic, Australia 3072.*

TWYCROSS, Christopher John. b 37. St Pet Coll Ox BA 59, MA 63. Wycl Hall Ox 60. **d** 64 **p** 65 Leic. C of Blaby 64-66; Em Loughborough (in c of Good Shepherd Shelthorpe) 66-69; V of Shelthorpe 69-71; R of Holbrook w Stutton 71-73; Asst Master & Hon Chap Wellesley Ho Broadstairs 73-78; Perm to Offic Dio St E from 77; Asst Master Chantry High Sch Ipswich from 78. *Ivy Cottage, Brown Street, Old Newton, Stowmarket, Suff.*

TWYCROSS, Peter David. b 51. Univ of Natal BA 74. Univ of Ox BA 77. Wycl Hall Ox 75. **d** 78 Bp Carter for Capetn. C of Wynberg 78-80; Stellenbosch Dio Capetn from 80. *Box 196, Stellenbosch 7600, CP, S Africa.* (02231-3173)

TWYCROSS, Stephen Jervis. b 33. Wycl Hall Ox 58. Univ of Nottm BEd 73. **d** 60 **p** 61 Leic. C of H Trin Hickley 60-64; V of Barlestone 64-71; Dioc Co-Ordinator Miss to Seamen from 69; Perm to Offic Dio Leic 71-73; L to Offic from 73; Asst Master Rawlins U Sch Leic 73-74; Mundella Girls Sch Leic from 74. *48 Laburnum Avenue, Newbold Verdon, Leicester, LE9 9LQ.* (Desford 2484)

TWYFORD, Canon Arthur Russell. b 36. ALCD 60. **d** 60 Liv **p** 61 Warrington for Liv. C of Speke 60-64; R of Maids Moreton w Foscott 64-72; Asst Youth Officer 64-70; C-in-c of Lillingstone Dayrell w Lillingstone Lovell 70-72; V of Desborough Dio Pet from 72; C-in-c of Braybrooke Dio Pet 73-77; C-in-c of Brampton Ash w Dingley Dio Pet 73-77; R (w Braybrooke) from 77; RD of Kettering from 79; Can Non-res of Pet Cathl from 81. *Desborough Vicarage, Kettering, Northants.* (Kettering 760324)

TWYMAN, George Charles William. b 12. ARICS 36. FRICS 73. SOC 71. **d** 72 **p** 73 S'wark. C of Wandsworth 72-75; P-in-c of Kings Nympton Dio Ex 75-79; C-in-c from 81; P-in-c of Romansleigh Dio Ex 75-79; C-in-c from, 81. *c/o Rectory, Kings Nympton, Umberleigh, Devon, EX37 9ST.* (Chulmleigh 457)

TYDEMAN, Richard. b 16. St Jo Coll Ox Ba (2nd cl Th) 39, MA 43. Hon GSM 75. Ripon Hall Ox 38. **d** 39 **p** 40 Birm. C of Langley 39-41; All SS Ipswich 41-45; C-in-c of St Helen Ipswich 45-46; V of St Jo Evang Woodbridge 46-53; Surr from 50; V of All SS Newmarket 53-63; RD of Newmarket 54-63; Hon Can of St E 59-63; R of St Sepulchre w Ch Ch Greyfriars and St Leon Foster Lane Lon 63-81; Dep Min Can of St Paul's Cathl Lon from 63; Pr at Lincoln's Inn 72-81; Sub-Chap O of St John of Jer from 77. *10 Colneis Road, Felixstowe, Suff, IP11 9HF.* (Felixstowe 3214)

TYE, Dominic Geoffrey Bernard. b 43. Univ of Lanc BA (2nd cl Engl) 70, PhD 75. Kelham Th Coll 61. M SSM 66-78. **d** 67 **p** 68 Blackb. C of Lancaster 67-70; Tutor Kelham Th Coll 70-73; LPr Dio Southw 70-73; Dio Ox 73-75; C of St Alb Canberra 75-76; Asst Master Skerton Sch Lanc 78-79; Our Lady's High Sch Lanc from 79. *72 North Road, Carnforth, Lancs, LA5 9NA.* (Carnforth 733137)

TYE, John Raymond. b 31. Stud Th (Lambeth) 64. Linc Th Coll 66. **d** 68 **p** 69 Ches. C of St Mich Coppenhall Crewe 68-71; Wednesfield 71-76; P-in-c of Petton w Cockshutt 76-79; Weston Lullingfield and of Hordley 78-79; R of Petton w Cockshutt and Weston Lullingfield w Hordley 79-81; V of Hadley Dio Lich from 81. *19 Manor Road, Hadley, Telford, Shropshire, TF1 4PN.* (Telford 54251)

TYE, Leslie Bernard. b 14. AKC 40. **d** 40 **p** 41 Lon. C of St Alphege Edmon 40-42; St Mary Hornsey 42-43; St John Whetstone 43-47; Hawarden (in c of St Francis Sandycroft) 47-52; Addlestone (in c of All SS New Haw) 52-59; V of Ault Hucknall 59-69; V of Ambergate 69-79. *31 Cromwell Drive, Swanwick, Derbys.*

TYERS, Gerald Seymour. b 22. St Pet Hall Ox BA 46, MA 49. Linc Th Coll 47. **d** 49 **p** 50 Roch. C of All SS Perry Street Northfleet 49-52; St Aug Gillingham 52-53; V of St Andr Orpington 53-60; St Aug Gillingham 60-67; Ch Ch Erith Dio Roch from 67; RD of Erith from 79. *Christ Church Vicarage, Erith, Kent.* (Erith 34729)

TYERS, John Haydn. b 31. Univ of Lon BSc 51. Ridley Hall Cam 53. **d** 55 **p** 56 Cov. C of Nuneaton 55-58; Rugby 58-62; V of St Anne Cov 62-71; V of Keresley w Coundon 71-78; Atherstone Dio Cov from 78. *40 Holte Road, Atherstone, CV9 1HN.* (Atherstone 3200)

TYLDESLEY, Douglas Wilfred. b 31. CCC Cam BA 54, MA 58. Oak Hill Th Coll 54. **d** 56 **p** 57 Linc. C of Skellingthorpe 56-58; Doddington Lincs 57-58; St Jo Bapt Beckenham 58-61; V of St Luke Walthamstow 61-66; PC of Prestwold w Hoton Leic 66-72; R of Sapcote Dio Leic from 72. *Rectory, Sharnford Road, Sapcote, Leicester, LE9 6JN.* (Sapcote 2215)

TYLER, Preb Frank Cecil. b 08. AKC 32. **d** 32 **p** 33 Lon. C of St Anne Limehouse 32-40; St Pet Hammersmith 40-42; St Marg Lothbury 42-49; Asst Dir Lon Dioc Coun for Youth 41-42; Sec 42-48; Gen Sec of Dioc Miss to Lon 48-49; V of Hillingdon 49-77; Chap Hillingdon Hosp 49-77; Preb of St Paul's Cathl Lon 61-77; Preb (Emer) from 77; Surr 61-77; Perm to Offic Dio Sarum from 79. *13 Wylye Road, Warminster, Wilts, BA12 9PE.* (0985-215275)

TYLER, Henry George. b 08. OBE (Mil) 63. St Chad's Coll Dur BA 35. **d** 35 Liv **p** 36 Warrington for Liv. C of St Mich Garston 35-38; St Bart Wilmslow 38-39; CF 39-63; V of Husthwaite w Carlton and Birdforth 63-77. *Emcott, Preston under Scar, Leyburn.* (Wensleydale 23671)

TYLER, John Arthur Preston. Em Coll Cam 3rd cl Engl Trip pt i 41, BA (2nd cl Hist Trip pt ii) 42, MA 46. Wycl Hall Ox 42. **d** 44 **p** 45 Bris. C of Rodbourne Cheney Swindon 44-47; Ch Ch Worthing 48-50; St Alb Streatham Pk 50-59; R of Wickhambreaux w Stodmarsh 59-65; Ickham w Wickhambreaux and Stodmarsh Dio Cant from 65. *Rectory, Wickhambreaux, Canterbury, Kent, CT3 1RX.* (Littlebourne 278)

TYLER, John Thorne. b 46. Selw Coll Cam 2nd cl Engl Trip pt i 67, BA 68, (2nd cl Th Trip pt ii) 69, MA 72. Sarum Wells Th Coll 70. **d** 72 **p** 73 B & W. C of Frome Selwood 72-74; Chap Huish Coll Taunton from 74; C-in-c of Lyng Dio B & W from 77. *56 Mountway Road, Bishops Hull, Taunton, TA1 5LS.*

TYLER, Leonard George. b 20. Univ of Liv BA 41. Ch Coll Cam BA (2nd cl Th Trip pt i) 46, MA 50. Westcott Ho Cam. **d** 43 **p** 44 Liv. C of Ch Ch Toxt Pk 43-44; Ch Coll Cam 44-46; Trin Coll Kandy 46-48; Prin Div Sch Colom 48-50; R of Ch Ch Bradford-w-Beswick 50-55; V of Leigh Lancs 55-66; RD of Leigh 57-62; Archd of Rochdale 62-66; Prin Wm Temple Coll Man 66-73; R of Easthamstead Dio Ox from 73. *Easthampstead Rectory, Bracknell, Berks, RG12 4ER.* (Bracknell 25205)

TYLER, Samuel John. b 32. Univ of Lon BD 57. Oak Hill Th Coll 57. **d** 58 **p** 59 Chelmsf. C of W Ham 58-61; V of Berechurch 61-64; R of Leaden Roding w Aythorpe Roding and High Roding 64-72; Perm to Offic Dio Chelmsf 73-74; P-in-c of St Jo Evang Seven Kings Dio Chelmsf 74-76; V from 76. *St John's Vicarage, St John's Road, Newbury Park, Ilford, Essex.* (01-590 5884)

TYLER, Thomas May. b 39. Selw Coll Cam 2nd cl Hist Trip pt i 63, BA (2nd cl Hist Trip pt ii) 64. Wells Th Coll 64. **d** 66 **p** 67 Guildf. C of Walton-on-Thames 66-69; Prin St Andr Catechist Coll Kohimarama 69-70; Hd Master of Selw Coll Br Solomon Is 70-71; C of Bexhill 71-77; V of Henfield (w Shermanbury and Woodmancote from 78) Dio Chich from 77; P-in-c of Shermanbury Dio Chich 77-78; P-in-c of Woodmancote Dio Chich 77-78. *Vicarage, Church Lane, Henfield, W Sussex, BN5 9NY.*

TYLER, William Stanley. b 12. Ripon Hall Ox 54. **d** 55 **p** 56 Ex. C of St Mary Magd Upton Torquay 55-58; PC of Stonehouse E 58-68; R of Woodleigh w Loddiswell 68-76; Perm to Offic Dio Ex 76-78; Publ Pr from 78. *71 Woolbrook Road, Sidmouth, Devon.* (Sidmouth 4573)

TYLER-WHITTLE, Michael Sydney. b 27. Peterho and Fitzw Ho Cam BA 49, MA 51. Wells Th Coll 53. **d** 55 **p** 56 Nor. C of Wymondham 55-58; PC of Old Buckenham 58-69; Chap Univ of E Anglia 65-67; L to Offic Dios Nor and Gibr 69-80; Chap of the Amalfi Coast 72-80; P-in-c of Forton and of Norbury Dio Lich from 80. *Forton Rectory, Newport, Salop, TF10 8BY.*

TYM, Malcolm Jeffrey. b 50. ACT ThL 76. Ridley Hall Melb 74. **d** 77 **p** 78 Melb. C of All SS Greesborough 77-79; St Matt Kens Adel 79-81; I of Epiph Hoppers Crossing Dio Melb from 81. *c/o Cathedral Buildings, Flinder's Lane, Melbourne, Australia 3000.*

TYMMS, Canon Wilfrid Widdas. b 18. Late Tancred Stud of Ch Coll Cam 2nd cl Th Trip pt i 39, BA 40, MA 44. Linc Th Coll 40. **d** 41 **p** 42 Dur. C of St Jas Gateshead 41-45; St Benedict Cam and Cam Sec SCM 45-47; C of St Pet and St Paul Springs 47-50; R of Brixton and Newlands Johann 50-53; Chap Univ of Witwatersrand 50-53; R of Stella 53-59; Surr from 54; V of St Pet Stockton-on-Tees 59-70; Chap Stockton and Thornaby Hosp 59-70; R of Middleton-S-Geo 70-78; Hon Can of Dur 72-78; Can Res from 78. *6a The College, Durham.*

TYNDALE-BISCOE, John Annesley. b 08. Univ of Cam BA 33, MA 61. Westcott Ho Cam 34. **d** 34 **p** 35 Worc. C of Bredon 34-38; Dom Chap to Bp of Rang 38-46; Perm to Offic Dio Lon 53-60; R of Gilston w Eastwick 60-76; Perm to Offic Dio Chelmsf from 76. *Woodham Mortimer House, Maldon, Essex, CM9 6SW.* (Danbury 2125)

TYNDALE-BISCOE, William Francis. Trin Coll Ox BA (3rd cl Th) 25, MA 29. Westcott Ho Cam 27. M SSF 37. **d** 28 **p** 29 S'wark. C of St Andr Catford 28-32; St Ives Hunts 32-37; V of St Chrys Peckham 38-45; L to Offic Dio Sarum 45-62; Miss P Chipili Miss 62-65; Fiwila Miss Zam 65-74; Perm to Offic Dio Brisb from 75. *PO Box 96, Kenmore, Queensland, Australia 4069.* (378-2160)

TYNDALL, David Bruce. Univ of Syd BA 71. Moore Coll Syd ACT ThL 75. **d** and **p** 76 Syd. C of St Clem Mosman

76-79; R of Willoughby E Dio Syd from 79. *25 Warrane Road, Willoughby, NSW, Australia 2068.* (95-2245)

TYNDALL, Jeremy Hamilton. b 55. Univ of Nottm BTh 81. St Jo Coll Nottm LTh 81. **d** 81 Lon. C of St Thos Oakwood Dio Lon from 81. *22 Curthwaite Gardens, Enfield, Middx, EN2 7LN.*

TYNDALL, Timothy Gardner. b 25. Jes Coll Cam 2nd cl Hist Trip pt i 49, BA (2nd cl Th Trip pt ia) 50. Wells Th Coll 50. **d** 51 **p** 52 Southw. C of Warsop w Sookholme 51-55; V of St Leon Newark 55-60; Sherwood 60-75; P-in-c of Bp Wearmouth Dio Dur from 75; RD of Wearmouth from 75. *21 Thornhill Terrace, Sunderland, T & W.*

TYNEY, James Derrick. b 33. TCD. **d** 62 **p** 63 Down. C of Ballynafeigh 62-64; Bangor 64-69; R of Clonallon w Warrenpoint 69-75; Groomsport Dio Down from 75. *31 Bangor Road, Groomsport, Co Down, BT19 2JF.*

TYRREL, John Cockett. Qu Coll Cam 2nd cl Hist Trip pt i, 37, BA (2nd cl Hist Trip pt ii) 38, MA 42. Ridley Hall, Cam 38. **d** 40 **p** 41 Lon. C of H Trin Southall 40-43; Chap RNVR 43-46; Chap Michaelho Sch Natal 46-50; Chap and Asst Master Gr Sch Canberra Dio C & Goulb 52-58; Sen Master and Dir of Stud from 58. *Canberra Grammar School, Canberra, ACT, Australia.*

TYRRELL, Charles Robert. b 51. Open Univ BA 80. Oak Hill Coll 74. **d** 77 **p** 78 Liv. C of Halewood Dio Liv from 77. *Old School House, Church Road, Liverpool, L26 6LA.* (051-487 0873)

TYRRELL, Frank Englefield. b 20. DSC 44. Qu Coll Birm 70. **d** 72 **p** 73 Roch. C of S Gillingham 72-76; Chap N Staffs R Infirm and City Gen Hosp Stoke-on-Trent 76-78. *Alnmouth, Thorpeness, Nr Leiston, Nr Alderburgh, Suffolk.*

TYRRELL, John James Armstrong. d 68 **p** 69 Ott. C of H Trin Pembroke 70-72; R of Win 72-74; CF (Canad) from 74. *Canadian Forces Station, Box 30, Pineimuta, Manit, Canada.*

TYRRELL, John Patrick Hammond. b 42. Cranmer Hall Dur 62. **d** 65 **p** 66 Edin. C of St Jo Evang Edin 65-68; Chap RN 68-72; Chap St John's Cathl Hong 72-74; V of St Francis Westborough 74-79; Chap of St John's Cathl Hong Dio Hong from 79. *St John's Cathedral. Garden Road, Hong Kong.* (5-234157)

TYRRELL, Stephen Jonathan. b 39. Univ of Sheff BA 62. Clifton Th Coll. **d** 65 **p** 66 Bris. C of Rodbourne Cheney 65-68; Lillington 68-73; C-in-c of Bp's Itchington Dio Cov 73-78; V from 78. *Bishop's Itchington Vicarage, Leamington, Warws.* (Harbury 612282)

TYSOE, James Raymond. b 19. Qu Coll Birm 70. **d** 75 Bp Parker for Cov **p** 76 McKie for Cov (APM). C of Cov E Team Min City and Dio Cov from 75. *Primrose Cottage, Norton Lindsey, Warwick.*

TYSON, George Arthur. b 1889. St Chad's Coll Regina, 14. **d** 17 **p** 18 Qu'App. C of Pelly 17-18; I 18-21; Foam Lake 21-28; P-in-c of Brock 28-31; V of Marton 31-38; R of Hameringham w Scrafield and Winceby 38-43; V of Deeping St Nich 43-46; R of Mavis Enderby w Raithby 46-51; Commiss Qu'App 47-69; V of Hemswell w Harpswell 51-56; V of Glentworth 51-56; Dunholme 56-59; LPr Dio Linc from 59. *Manormead, Tilford Road, Hindhead, Surrey, GU26 6RA.*

TYSON, Gordon David. b 35. Univ of Melb BD 68. **d** 75 **p** 77 Tas. Hon C of Beaconsfield & Ex Dio Tas from 75. *Deviot Road, Robigana, Exeter, Tasmania 7251.* (003-94 4453)

TYSON, Hugh Dawson. b 16. ALCD 40. **d** 40 **p** 41 S'wark. C of H Trin Wallington 40-46; H Ap Leic 46-53; R of Heather 53-55; Brome w Oakley 55-60; V of Weoley Castle 60-68; Westhall w Brampton and Stoven 68-81. *29 Badingham Road, Framlingham, Woodbridge, Suffolk.* (Framlingham 724123)

TYSON, John Wood Worsley. b 22. ACII 50. Ripon Hall, Ox 54. **d** 56 **p** 57 Southw. C of Worksop 56-59; V of Sneinton Dio Southw from 59; Surr from 69. *Vicarage, Windmill Lane, Sneinton, Nottingham.* (Nottingham 50508)

TYSON, Canon Ronald Desmond. Ch Coll Hobart ACT ThL 43. **d** 42 Tas **p** 43 Gippsld for Tas. C of H Trin Hobart w St John New Town 42-43; P-in-c of King I 43-47; Perm to Offic at Bothwell and Wynyard 47-48; R of Buckland 48-55; Scottsdale Tas 55-58; St Mark Launceston Dio Tas from 58; Can of Tas from 71. *3 Normanstone Road, Launceston, Tasmania.* (003-44 1256)

TYSON, William Edward Porter. St Cath Coll Cam BA 49, MA 52. Ridley Hall Cam 49. **d** 51 **p** 52 Ches. C of Wilmslow 51-54; Astbury 54-57; V of St Pet Macclesfield 57-62; V of Over Tabley 62-70; PC of High Legh 62-70; CF (TA) 64-67; CF (TAVR) from 67; V of Ch Hulme (Holmes Chapel) Dio Ches from 70. *Holmes Chapel Vicarage, Crewe, Chesh.* (0477-33124)

TYTE, Canon Keith Arthur Edwin. b 31. St D Coll Lamp BA 55. **d** 57 **p** 58 Mon. C of Mynyddyslwyn 57-61; Llanfrechfa 61-64; R of Henllys w Bettws 64-71; V of Griffithstown 71-77; RD of Pontypool 74-77; V of Malpas Dio Mon from 77; Can of Newport Cathl from 77. *Malpas Vicarage, Newport, NP7 6GQ.* (Newport 85204)

✠ **TYTLER, Right Rev Donald Alexander.** b 25. Late Scho of Ch Coll Cam BA 47, MA 52. Ridley Hall Cam 47. **d** 49 **p** 50 Birm. C of Yardley 49-52; SCM Sec Univ of Birm 52-55; Prec of Birm Cathl 55-57; Dir of Relig Educn Dio Birm 57-63; PC (V from 68) of Londonderry Birm 63-72; RD of Warley 63-72; Hon Can of Birm Cathl 71-72; Can Res 72-82; Archd of Aston 77-82; Cons Ld Bp Suffr of Middleton in York Minster 22 July 82 by Abp of York. *c/o Church House, 90 Deansgate, Manchester, M3 2GH.*

TYZACK, Clement. Bps' Coll Cheshunt 31. **d** 34 **p** 35 Ox. C of S Banbury 34-36; Calne 36-40; V of Membury 40-43; PC of Bratton 43-67; Perm to Offic Dio Sarum from 67; Dio B & W from 68. *Sharow, Greenhead, Sidbury, Sidmouth, Devon.*

TYZACK, Leonard George. b 37. Chich Th Coll. **d** 63 **p** 64 Cant. C of Folkestone 63-67; Dom Chap to Abp of Cant 67-69; Min of St Nich Conv Distr Buckland Valley Dover 69-72; R of Buckland-in-Dover (w Buckland Valley from 74) Dio Cant from 72; RD of Dover from 81. *St Andrew's Rectory, London Road, Dover, CT17 0TF.* (Dover 201324)

U

UADAMEVBO, Canon Higo Obakhena. Im Coll Ibad. **d** 63 **p** 64 Benin. P Dio Benin; Hon Can of Benin from 79. *St James's Vicarage, Jattu Uzairue, Nigeria.*

UAMUSSE, Zefanias. d and **p** 75 Lebom. P Dio Lebom. *CP 120, Maputo, Mozambique.*

UANACADIN, Juancito. d 68 **p** 69 Argent. P Dio Argent 68-73; N Argent from 73. *Parsonage, Toba, N Argentina.*

UBIA, Hilikiah. d 61 **p** 62 Soroti. P Dio Soroti 61-76; Dio Kara from 76. *c/o Karamoja Diocesan Office, PO Box 44, Moroto, Uganda.*

UBOCHI, Davidson Eziefule. b 40. Trin Coll Umuahia 71. **d** 74 Ow. d Dio Ow. *St Paul's Parsonage, Nkwerre, Nigeria.*

UBUN, Matthew. b 50. Ho of Epiph Kuch 71. **d** and **p** 75 Kuch. P Dio Kuch. *Box 126, Bandar Seri Begawan, Brunei, Malaysia.*

UCHEJI, Moses Onyeogadirinma. b 29. St Paul's Coll Awka 78. **d** and **p** 79 Aba. P Dio Aba. *St Mark's Parsonage, Obigbo, Rivers State, Nigeria.*

UDALI, Daudi Wesley. St Paul's Div Sch Limuru 49. **d** 49 **p** 51 Momb. P Dio Momb 49-61; Dio Maseno 61-63; Dio Nak 63-69; Dio N Maseno 70-76; Hon Can of N Maseno 71-76; Exam Chap to Bp of N Maseno 70-76. *Box 82, Maragoli, Maseno, Kenya.*

UDE, Humphrey Onyeneke. b 39. Trin Coll Legon 69. **d** 73 **p** 74 Enugu. P Dio Enugu. *Box 16, Nsukka, ECS, Nigeria.*

UDEZE, Eric Nwafor. d 75 **p** 76 Niger. P Dio Niger. *St Mark's Church, Nnewichi, Nigeria.*

UDOGWU, Canon Emmanuel Chukunonyelum. Melville Hall Ibad 57. **d** 57 **p** 58 N Nig. P Dio N Nig 57-68; Dio Benin 68-77; Dio Asaba from 77; Hon Can from 79. *St John's Parsonage, Agbor, Nigeria.*

UDOH, B. O.. Trin Coll Umuahia 74. **d** 76 Nig Delta. d Dio Nig Delta. *Holy Trinity Church, 81 Calabar Road, PO. Box 79, Calabar, Nigeria.*

UDY, John Francis. b 24. E Midl Min Tr Course 78. **d** 81 Grantham for Linc (APM). C of Kirton-in-Holland Dio Linc from 81. *6 Grosenover Road, Frampton, Boston, Lincs, PE20 1DB.*

UFFINDELL, David Wilfred George. b 37. Qu Coll Birm 72. **d** 75 **p** 76 Lich (APM). C of Harlescott Dio Lich from 75. *13 Kenley Avenue, Heath Farm, Shrewsbury, Salop., SY1 3HA.*

UGANDA, Metropolitan of Province of. *See* Wani, Most Rev Silvano Goi.

UGBEBOR, Gideon. b 37. **d** 73 **p** 74 Benin. P Dio Benin. *St Luke's Church, Ute-Okpu, via Agbor PO, Nigeria.*

UGBELASE, Emmanuel Chukwuemeka. b 24. St Paul's Coll Awka. **d** 73 **p** 74 Benin. P Dio Benin. *RTC Anwai-Asaba, Nigeria.*

UGOKWE, Godwin Ndubisi. Trin Coll Umuahia 61. **d** 63 **p** 64 Ow. P Dio Nig Delta 63-69; Dio Ow from 70. *Parsonage, Amaigbo, via Orlu, Nigeria.*

UGUNNAH, Joshua Ikpeama Nwokorie. St Paul's Coll Awka 60. **d** 60 **p** 61 Nig Delta. P Dio Nig Delta 60-72; Dio Aba 72-78; Archd of Aba 72-78. *c/o St Peter's Church, Ekenobizi, Umuahia, Nigeria.*

UGUZI, Canon Nehemia. St Phil Th Coll Kongwa. **d** and **p** 53 Centr Tang. P Dio Centr Tang 55-78; Can of Centr Tang from 76. *Buigiri, PO Chamwino, Tanzania.*

UGWUAYI, Ven Simon Odo. Trin Coll Umuahia 58. **d** & **p** 60 Niger. P Dio Niger 60-70; Dio Enugu from 71; Hon Can of Enugu 71-76; Archd of Nsukka from 76. *St Paul's Parsonage, Nsukka, Nigeria.*

UGWUNEBO, Silas Chukwunyere. **d** 60 **p** 61 Ow. P Dio Ow. *Amiagbo, Owerri, Nigeria.*

UHLIR, Frantisek. Univ of Prague. **d** 55 Hur for NS **p** 56 NS. Prof at K Coll Halifax 55-65. *RR 1, Gatineau Point, PQ, Canada.*

UHUMUAVBI, Ven Robert Aihobekun. **d** 55 **p** 56 Ondo-B. P Dio Ondo-B 55-62; Dio Ondo 62-69; Dio Benin from 69; Can 70-73; Archd from 73. *c/o PO Box 82, Benin City, Nigeria.*

✠ **UKA, Right Rev Caspar.** MBE 80. St Pet Coll Siota 59. **d** 62 **p** 64 Melan. P Dio Melan 62-75; Cons Asst Bp of Centr Melan in Prov Cathl of St Barn Honiara 8 Nov 75 by Abp of Melan; Bps of Ysabel, New Hebr and Malaita; res 80. *St Luke's Church, Poti-Siku, Tikopia, Solomon Islands.*

UKACHUKWU, Pius Ndubueze. b 30. Trin Coll Umuahia 65. **d** 68 Bishop Uzodike for Niger **p** 68 Niger. P Dio Niger. *St Matthew's Church, Nibo, Nr Awka, Nigeria.*

UKADIKE, Ramson Chinedu Obidugwu. Trin Coll Umuahia 49. **d** 52 **p** 53 Niger. P Dio Niger 52-76. *c/o St Jude's Church, Oraifite, Nigeria.*

UKECH, Aloni. Buwalasi Th Coll 49. **d** 51 **p** 53 U Nile. P Dio U Nile 51-61; Dio N Ugan from 61. *Paidha, PO Box 37, Arua, Uganda.*

UKELEGHARANYA, Canon Walter Maduako Okafor. b 34. Trin Coll Legon. **d** 72 **p** 73 Enugu. P Dio Enugu; Hon Can of Enugu from 81. *St Peter's Parsonage, Nachi, Nigeria.*

UKENNA, Timothy Chukuemeka. b 35. Trin Coll Umuahia 71. **d** 74 Ow. d Dio Ow. *St Paul's Parsonage, Umuobom, via Orlu, Nigeria.*

UKOHA, Jacob Ndimele. b 19. St Paul's Coll Awka 55. **d** 73 **p** 74 Aba. P Dio Aba. *St Stephen's Parsonage, Umuobasi-Amavor, Aba, Nigeria.*

UKPABIA, Charles Onwukne. **d** 60 **p** 61 Ow. P Dio Ow. *Parsonage, Ife-Ezinihitte, via Nbawsi, Nigeria.*

UKWUOMA, Theophilus Aba Onyekuru. Im Coll Ibad 58. **d** 61 **p** 63 Ibad. P Dio Ibad 63-69; Dio Ow 70-76. *Holy Trinity Church, Uratta, Owerri, Nigeria.*

ULANGA, Benjamin. **d** and **p** 77 Centr Tang. P Dio Centr Tang. *Nghaheleze, PO Mvumi, Tanzania.*

ULLATHORNE, Canon William Archer Clement. b 02. Qu Coll Ox BA 25, MA 29. Can Scho Linc 25. **d** 26 **p** 27 Liv. C of St Marg Anfield Liv 26-31; St Nich Brighton 31-32; Arundel w S Stoke and Tortington 32-36; St Jas Wednesbury 36-42; V of St Jo Evang Bury St Edms 42-51; St Bart Ipswich 51-64; Proc Conv St E 58-59; Hon Can of St E 62-74; Can (Emer) from 74; V of Lakenheath 64-74; RD of Mildenhall 68-73; Perm to Offic Dio Nor from 74; Dio St E from 74. *17 Gallants Lane, East Harling, Norf, NR16 2NQ.* (East Harling 717275)

ULLMER, Derek Sefton. b 35. St Jo Coll Dur BA (2nd cl Mod Hist) 55. Wells Th Coll 57. **d** 59 **p** 60 Leic. C of Wigston Magna 59-61; Brighton 61-65; V of Aldingbourne 65-70; C of St Clem (in c of all SS) Hastings 70-72; Asst Master Hastings Sec Sch for Boys from 72. *16 Godwin Road, Hastings, Sussex, Tn35 5JR.* (0424 433308)

ULLYETT, Basil Christopher. **d** 32 **p** 33 Antig. R of St Paul w St John St Kitts 34-40; St Geo w St Jas Nevis 40-46; V of St Steph I and Dio Barb from 46; Chap of Lazaretto 46-52; Mental Hosp Barb from 52; Dioc Sec Barb 54-62; Dom Chap to Bp of Barb 60-62; Dioc Regr 62-75; Can of Barb 64-75. *Curate's Lodge, St George, Barbados, W Indies.*

UMEGBOLU, Matthew Anyiam. b 25. Trin Coll Umuahia 63. **d** 65 **p** 66 Niger. P Dio Niger. *Parsonage, Ogidi, Nigeria.*

UMEIFEKWEM, Josiah Nwankwo Chukwueloka. b 37. Trin Coll Umuahia 66. **d** 68 Niger **p** 70 Niger. P Dio Niger. *Holy Trinity Parsonage, Abatete, Via Ogidi, East Central State, Nigeria.*

UMEJEI, Wilfred Okeke. Im Coll Ibad 57. **d** 58 **p** 59 N Nig. P Dio N Nig 58-68; Dio Benin 68-77; Dio Asaba 77-80; Hon Can 78-80. *Anglican Parsonage, Ubulu-Uku, Nigeria.*

UMEKWE, Canon Godwin Chukuledo Sam. b 31. **d** 76 **p** 77 Aba. P Dio Aba; Hon Can of Aba from 80. *St Peter's Parsonage, Amizi, Olokoro, Nigeria.*

UMESIE, Godfrey Enwerem Nkemakolam. b 48. Trin Coll Umuahia 74. **d** 76 **p** 77 Enugu. P Dio Enugu. *St Batholomew's Cathedral, Box 444, Enugu, Nigeria,*

UMEZINWA, Simon Ikebude. St Paul's Coll Awka. **d** 62 Nig Delta. d Dio Nig Delta 62-69; Dio Niger from 69. *St Stephen's Church, Osumenyi, Nigeria.*

UMI, Juda Edward. St Cypr Th Coll Tunduru 46. **d** 47 **p** 50 Masasi. P Dio Masasi 47-66. *c/o CPEA, Lulindi, PO Masasi, Tanzania.*

UMILA, John William Patrick. b 40. St Cypr Th Coll 67. **d** 69 **p** 70 Masasi. P Dio Masasi. *KJT Mkomaindo, PO Box 16 Masasi, Mtwara Region, Tanzania.*

UMOBI, Samuel Onyemalage. Trin Coll Umuahia. **d** 57 **p** 58 N Nig. P Dio N Nig 57-63; Dio Niger from 63. *Parsonage, Ezinifite, via Aguata, Nigeria.*

UMPHERVILLE, Daniel Robert. Wycl Coll Tor 53. **d** 54 **p** 57 Sask. Miss Thunderchild Reserve 54-60; Sturgeon Lake 60-63; Thunderchild 63-64; I of Pelican Lake 65-66; Onion Lake 66-74; Sturgeon Lake 74-80; Big Whitefish Dio Sask from 80. *111 Lindsay Drive, Saskatoon, Sask, Canada.*

UMUKORO, Timothy Onovorakpo. Trin Coll Umuahia. **d** 62 **p** 63 Benin. P Dio Benin. *St Luke's Parsonage, Box 3, Oleh, Nigeria.*

UMUNNA, Wilson Anaebom. b 48. Trin Coll Umuahia 75. **d** 78 Aba. d Dio Aba. *St Matthew's Parsonage, Aba, Nigeria.*

UNDERHILL, Cecil Howard. b 07. St Aid Coll 36. **d** 38 **p** 39 Lon. C of H Trin Haverstock Hill 38-40; Habrough w Immingham 40-42; Portchester 42-51; R of Holme Hale 51-57; V of Hadlow 57-60; Williams W Austr 60-62; V of St Cuthb Wrose Bradf 63-66; Buckland Brewer 66-73. *16 Bransgore Gardens, Bransgore, Christchurch, Dorset.*

UNDERHILL, Edward Mark Thomas. b 24. Univ Coll Dur BA 50. St Aid Coll 50. **d** 52 **p** 53 Roch. C of Meopham 52-54; Prin of Kigari Coll and LPr Dio Momb 55-57; PC of St Geo Gateshead Dio Dur 57-68; V from 68. *St George's Vicarage, Gateshead, Co Durham, NE9 5AJ.* (Low Fell 875587)

UNDERHILL, George Henry. **d** and **p** 60 Calg. C of St Barn Calg 60-66. *110 15th Street NW, Calgary, Alta., Canada.* (283-1150)

UNDERHILL, Harry Gordon. Paton Congr Coll 33. Linc Th Coll 41. **d** 41 **p** 42 Blackb. C of St Jo Bapt Burnley 41-42; St Geo Chorley 42-44; Ulverston 44-47; V of Dacre 47-50; Hogsthorpe 50-56; R of Croxton w Kirmington 56-60; V of Ulceby 56-63; Wootton 60-63; R of Croxton 62-63; V of Appleby 63-66; Gedney Hill 66-70; PC of Whaplode Drove 66-70; C of Deeping St Jas 71-72. *Address temp unknown.*

UNDERHILL, Mervyn Spenser. b 23. Univ of Dur BA 49 Chich Th Coll 49. **d** 51 **p** 52 Pet. C of St Mary Far Cotton Northn 51-56; All SS Southbourne Bournemouth 56-61; V of Hedge End Dio Win from 61. *Vicarage, Vicarage Drive, St John's Road, Hedge End, Southampton.* (Botley 2288)

UNDERHILL, Very Rev Michael Leeke. Qu Coll Ox BA 34, MA 38. Westcott Ho Cam 34. **d** 35 **p** 36 Carl. C of H Trin Millom 35-38; V of Ohakune w Raetihi 38-45; CF (NZ) 41-45; Men in Disp 45; Org Sec Peace Thank Offering Appeal Dio Wel 45-47; V of Addingham 47-49; St Jo Bapt Upperby 49-61; Commiss Waik 51-61; V of Fendalton 61-66; Dean of Ch Ch from 66; Exam Chap to Bp of Ch Ch from 66; Commiss Centr Tang from 69. *80 Bealey Avenue, Christchurch 1, NZ.* (70-272)

UNDERWOOD, Albert William. b 12. Qu Coll Birm. **d** 64 **p** 65 Bradf. C of Ilkley 64-67; V of St Jo Bapt Clayton 67-75; C-in-c of Seagrave w Walton-le-Wolds Dio Leic from 75. *Seagrave Rectory, Loughborough, Leics.* (Sileby 2610)

UNDERWOOD, Brian. b 35. Univ of Dur BA 57, MA 72. Clifton Th Coll. **d** 59 Lanc for Blackb **p** 60 Burnley for York. C of Ch Ch Blackpool 59-61; New Malden w Coombe 61-64; Trav Sec of Pathfinders 64-68; Chap Chantilly, Rouen and Le Havre 68-69; Home Sec CCCS 69-71; C-in-c of St Paul Gatten Shanklin 71-72; Chap Lyon, Grenoble and Aix-les-Bains 72-75; L to Offic Dio Derby 76-80; Dio Blackb from 80; Asst Chap Trent Coll Nottm 76-80; Chap Qu Eliz Gr Sch Blackb from 80. *63 Saunders Road, Blackburn, Lancs, BB2 6NP.* (0254-59489)

UNDERWOOD, Charles Brian. b 23. Univ of Leeds BA (2nd cl Phil) 48 Coll of Resurr Mirfield 48. **d** 50 **p** 51 Ox. C of St Mich Tilehurst 50-53; St Paul Leic 53-54; Dioc Youth Chap Dio Leic 54-61; V of St Geo Leic 57-59; R of Harby 59-61; C of St Aid Remuera 61-62; Chap K Sch Auckld 61-62; R of Carleton-in-Craven 63-75; Dioc Youth Chap Dio Bradf 63-72; V of Twyning Dio Glouc from 76; RD of Tewkesbury from 81. *Twyning Vicarage, Tewkesbury, Glos.* (Tewkesbury 292553)

UNDERWOOD, Jack Maurice. Univ of Leeds BA 36, Univ of Lon BD 41. Coll of Resurr Mirfield 36. **d** 38 **p** 39 Worc. C of Kidderminster 38-40; St Mary Hornsey 40-42; Chap RAFVR 42-46; Perm to Offic Dio Lich 46-47; Dio Birm 47-50; V of Middleton 50-53; Rep of Br Coun of Chs Refugee Service and Inter-Ch Aid 53-60; Prin Stroud Court Ox 60-71; Perm to Offic Dio Gibr from 73. *Le Corti, Castell 'Anselmo, Livorno, Italy.*

UNDERWOOD, Canon James Derrick. b 09. Trin Hall Cam 2nd cl Hist Trip pt i 32, BA 33, 3rd cl Th Trip pt i 34, MA 39. Linc Th Coll 34. **d** 35 **p** 36 S'wark. C of St John

Southend Lewisham (in c of St Luke Downham from 39) 35-42; R of Mottingham 42-50; V of Warlingham w Chelsham (and Farleigh from 57) 50-65; C-in-c of Farleigh 53-57; Hon Can of S'wark from 61; RD of Caterham 61-65; R of Oxted 65-71; RD of Godstone 66-71. *31 Woodlands Drive, South Godstone, Surrey.* (S Godstone 3185)

UNEGBU, Lawrence Ibeghulam. Univ of Lon Dipl Th (Extra Mural Stud) 65. Trin Coll Umuahia 60. **d** 62 **p** 63 Ow. P Dio Ow. *St John's Parsonage, Amumara, Mbaise, via Nbawsi, Nigeria.*

UNGGIN, McDonald. b 44. Ho of Epiph Kuch 73. **d** and **p** 75 Kuch. P Dio Kuch. *St Peter's Church, Saratok, Sarawak, Malaysia.*

UNGOED-THOMAS, Peter. Pemb Coll Ox BA 51, MA 67. St Mich Coll Llan. **d** 60 **p** 62 Llan. C of Llangeinor 60-64: St Mary Virg Leigh 70-74; Chap Leigh C of E Schs 70-74; Perm to Offic Dios St D and Birm from 75. *93 Hoel Felin-Foel, Llanelli, Dyfed, SA15 3JQ.*

UNSWORTH, Thomas Foster. b 28. BA (Lon) 56. Lich Th Coll 60. **d** 62 **p** 63 Birm. C of Northfield 62-64; The Lickey 64-66; V of Forcett 66-68; Leyburn 68-73; Bellerby 68-73; Chap Whittingham Hosp 73-79; V of Freckleton Dio Blackb from 79. *Vicarage, Sunnyside Close, Freckleton, Preston, PR4 1YJ.* (Freckleton 632209)

UNURHIERI, Ven Peter Ohwojenaga. Im Coll Ibad 56. **d** 57 Bp Awosika for Ondo-B **p** 58 Ondo-B. P Dio Ondo-B 57-62; Dio Benin 62-77; Dio Warri from 77; Archd of Warri from 81. *Box 52, Sapele, Nigeria.*

UNWIN, Christopher Michael Fairclough. b 31. Univ of Dur BA 57. Linc Th Coll 65. **d** 67 **p** 68 Dur. C of S Shields 67-73; R of Tatsfield 73-81; Adv Relig Educn to Ch Secondary Schs Dio S'wark 73-81; V of St Gabr Heaton Dio Newc T from 81. *St Gabriel's Vicarage, Heaton, Newcastle-upon-tyne, NE6 5QN.* (Newc T 655843)

UNWIN, Ven Christopher Philip. b 17. TD 63. Late Exhib of Magd Coll Cam BA 39, MA 63. Qu Coll Birm 39. **d** 40 **p** 41 Newc T. C of Benwell 40-44; Sugley 44-47; V of Horton w Cowpen and New Delaval 47-55; CF (TA) 50-63; V of St Jas Benwell Newc T 55-63; Proc Conv Newc T 59-63; RD of Newcastle W 62-63; Archd of Northumb and Can Res of Newc T from 63; Exam Chap to Bp of Newc T from 73. *80 Moorside North, Newcastle upon Tyne, NE4 9DU.* (Newcastle upon Tyne 738245)

UNWIN, Geoffrey William. b 25. Selw Coll Cam 2nd cl Th Trip pt i 47, BA 48, MA 52. Clifton Th Coll 48. **d** 49 **p** 50 Lich. C of St Jo Bapt Burslem 49-51; Boulton 51-53; Dagenham 53-54; R of Beeston-next-Mileham 54-58; Colney w Earlham 58-72; Earlham w Bowthorpe 72-78; Mulbarton w Kenningham Dio Nor from 78. *Mulbarton Rectory, Norwich, NR14 8JS.* (Mulbarton 70296)

UNWIN, Ven Kenneth. b 26. St Edm Hall, Ox BA (2nd cl Mod Lang) 48, MA 52. Ely Th Coll 49. **d** 51 **p** 52 Ripon. C of All SS Leeds 51-55; St Marg Dur (in c of St John Neville's Cross) 55-59; V of Dodworth 59-69; Royston Yorks 69-73; St Jo Bapt City and Dio Wakef from 73; Hon Can of Wakef Cathl from 80; RD of Wakef 80-81; Archd of Pontefract from 81. *St John's Vicarage, Bradford Road, Wakefield, Yorks, WF1 2AA.* (Wakefield 71029)

UNWIN, Percival Alexander. b 04. St Jo Coll Dur BA 28, MA 33. Dipl Th 29. **d** 29 **p** 30 Lich. C of St Giles Newc L 29-31; CMS Miss Dio U Nile 32-39; TCF (E Afr) 39-46; V of Okewood Surrey 47-50; Chap Ruzawi Sch Marendellas 50-53; V of Figheldean w Milston 53-61; Canford Magna 61-71. *58 Cannon Street, Winchester, Hants.* (Winchester 65481)

UNWIN, Reginald Christopher. b 02. TD 78. St Jo Coll Dur BA 24, Dipl Th 25, MA 29. **d** 25 **p** 26 Dur. C of St Gabr Bp Wearmouth 25-29; Aston 29-30; V of St A Birm 30-35; CF (TA) 34-39; R of All SS Birm 35-45; CF (EC) 39-45; R of Chilton Foliat 45-65; C-in-c of Baydon 54-57; R of Ousby w Melmerby 65-68; P-in-c of Bp Wearmouth 69; Perm to Offic Dio Dur from 69. *The Close, Sea View Park, Whitburn, Sunderland, Co Durham, SR6 7JS.* (Whitburn 293492)

UPHILL, Keith Ivan. b 35. Keble Coll Ox BA 70. MA 74. Wycl Hall Ox 67. **d** 70 **p** 71 Warrington for Liv. C of Maghull 70-73; V of Wroxall 73-77; Team V of Fareham Dio Portsm from 77. *Vicarage, Hillson Drive, Fareham, Hants, PO15 6PF.* (Titchfield 43705)

UPRICHARD, Horace Launcelot. b 17. TCD BA and Div Test 42, MA 47. **d** 42 **p** 43 Kilm. C of Manorhamilton 42-44; Chap RAFVR 44-50; Miss of St Martin Ballymacarrett 50-53; R of Drumbeg Dio Down from 53. *Drumbeg Rectory, Dunmurry, Belfast, N Ireland.* (Belfast 613265)

UPTON, Anthony Arthur. b 30. Wells Th Coll 61. **d** 63 **p** 64 Portsm. C of St Jas Milton 63-67; Chap RN from 67. *c/o Ministry of Defence, Lacon House, Theobalds Road, WC1X 8RY.*

UPTON, Charles Treyhern. b 09. Univ of Birm BSc 30. Linc Th Coll 46. **d** 47 Stafford for Lich **p** 48 Lich. C of Wolverhampton 47-52; St Geo Grenada Windw Is 52-53; PC of Oxley Statutory Distr 53-58; V of Kingstone w Gratwich 58-71; Warslow w Elkstone 71-79; RD of Alstonfield 74-79. *Old School House, Hawling, Cheltenham, Glos, GL54 5TA.*

UPTON, Donald George Stanley. Late Scho of Peterho Cam 1st cl Cl Trip pt i 37, BA (2nd cl Cl Trip pt ii) 38, 2nd cl Th Trip pt ii 40. MA 44. Westcott Ho Cam 39. **d** 40 **p** 41 Derby. C of Ashbourne 40-43; V of Mackworth 43-51; Chap to Bps' Coll Cheshunt 51-54; Haileybury Coll 54-58; Asst Master Qu Eliz Gr Sch Barnet 59-60; Alleyne's Gr Sch Stevenage 60-69; Asst Master and Chap St Alb High Sch for Girls 69-73; L to Offic Dio St Alb 69-80; Asst Master Ch Hosp Sch Hertf 73-80. *The Pump House, The Square, Braughing, Ware, Herts.*

UPTON, Kenneth Roy. b 19. K Coll Cam BA 40, MA 48. Oak Hill Th Coll. **d** 48 **p** 49. C of St John and St Jas Litherland 48-51; Darfield (in c of Gt Houghton) 51-54; V of Ch Gresley w Linton 54-65; V of St Chad City Dio Derby from 65. *12 Empress Road, Derby, DE3 6TD.* (Derby 43765)

UPTON, Michael Gawthorne. b 29. K Coll Lon and Warm AKC 53. **d** 54 **p** 55 Man. C of Middleton Lancs 54-57; St Andr Plymouth 57-59; Asst Dir of Relig Educn and L to Offic Dio Cant 59-63; Youth Chap Dio Roch and Hon C of Riverhead 63-70; Chr Aid Area Sec for Devon and Cornw and L to Offic Dio Ex from 70; SW Reg Co-Ordinator 73-80; Dioc Development Rep Dio Ex from 80. *Otter Dell, Harpford, Nr Sidmouth, Devon.* (Colaton Raleigh 68448)

UPTON, Rex Pitt. Moore Th Coll Syd. **d** 63 **p** 64 Tas. C of Deloraine 63-64; Perm to Offic Dio S'wark 65-66; Chap Miss to Seamen Buenos Aires 67-68; Rosario 68-70; R of St Bart Rosario 68-70; R of Ringaroona w Derby 70-72; Geo Tn 72-74; Admin Clarendon Home Kingston Beach 74-79; Western Port Miss of St Jas and St John Dio Melb 79-80; R of Oatlands Dio Tas from 80. *Rectory, Oatlands, Tasmania 7205.* (002 54 1133)

UPTON, Robert de Courcy Everard. b 26. Dipl Th (Lon) 57. St Aid Coll. **d** 57 **p** 58 Lich. C of Bushbury 57-61; L to Offic Dio Lich 61-62; C of Pensnett 62-65; Oswestry 65-67; Prees 67-69; C-in-c of Tilstock Dio Lich from 69. *Tilstock Vicarage, Whitchurch, Salop, SY13 3JL.* (Whixall 317)

UPTON, Ronald Alfred. b 21. **d** 76 **p** 77 Reading for Ox (APM). C of Cropredy Dio Ox from 76. *Sundridge, Creampot Close, Cropredy, Oxon.*

URANTA, Obediah Assisssi Egoni. b 40. **d** 76 **p** 77 Aba. P Dio Aba. *St Simon's Parsonage, Ohanku, Ndoki, Nigeria.*

URCH, Harold Henry. b 08. Roch Th Coll 59. **d** 60 Crediton for Ex **p** 61 Ex. C of Ch Ch Ellacombe Torquay 60-63; V of Sticklepath 63-73; Perm to Offic Dio Ex 74-77; Dio Cov from 77. *2 Margetts Close, Barrowfield Lane, Kenilworth, Warws, CV8 1EN.* (Kenilworth 56759)

UREN, Malcolm Lawrence. b 39. K Coll Lon and Warm AKC 63. **d** 64 **p** 65 Cant. C of St Martin w St Paul Cant 64-67; Falmouth 67-71; V of St Blazey 71-79; P-in-c of Tuckingmill Dio Truro from 79. *All Saint's Vicarage, Camborne, Cornw, TR14 8DG.* (Camborne 712114)

URQUHART, Colin. b 40. K Coll Lon and Warm AKC 62. **d** 63 **p** 64 St Alb. C of Cheshunt 63-67; Norton Herts 67-70; V of Lewsey Luton 70-76; Perm to Offic Dio Guildf 76-78; Dir Bethany Trust and L to Offic Dio Chich from 78. *The Hyde, Handcross, Haywards Heath, Sussex, RH17 6EZ.* (Handcross 400231)

URQUHART, Dennis John. St Jo Coll Auckld LTh (2nd cl) 68. **d** 68 Auckld. C of St Andr Epsom Auckld 68-71; Kaitaia 71-72; P-in-c of Parengarenga-Ahipara-Peria Maori Past Dio Auckld from 72. *3 Mission Place, Kaitaia, NZ.* (Kaitaia 412)

URQUHART, Edmund Ross. b 39. Univ Coll Ox BA (2nd cl Mod Lang) 62, Dipl Th 63, MA 68. St Steph Ho Ox 62. **d** 64 **p** 65 Win. C of Milton 64-69; Norton (in c of St John Hemsworth) 69-73; V of Bakewell Dio Derby from 73. *Vicarage, Bakewell, Derbys, DE4 1FD.* (Bakewell 2256)

URRA, Alberto. **d** 74 **p** 75 Bp Bazley for Chile. P Dio Chile *Casilla 4, Chol-Chol, Chile.*

URSELL, Philip Elliott. Late Exhib of Univ of Wales BA 66. St Steph Ho Ox 66. **d** 68 Bp T M Hughes for Llan **p** 69 Llan. C of Newton Nottage, Porthcawl 68-71; Asst Chap Univ Coll Cardiff 71-77; Chap Poly of Wales 74-77; Em Coll Cam from 77; Fell from 80; Prin of Pusey Ho Ox and Fell of St Cross Coll from 82. *Pusey House, Oxford, OX1 3LZ.* (Oxford 59519)

URWIN, Canon John Edwin Strutt. b 04. Coll of Ven Bede Dur BA 25, Long Pri and Dipl Educn 26. Wells Th Coll 30. **d** 31 **p** 32 Newc T. C of Seaton Hirst 31-35; Ch Ch Tynemouth 35-37; V of Warden w Newbrough 37-45; Dir of Relig Educn Dio Liv 45-62; L to Offic Dio Liv 45-52; Can Dioc of Liv 47-73; Can (Emer) from 73; Chap Huyton Coll 49-52 and 68-72; R of Winwick 52-68. *27 Grange Street, Bare, Morecambe, Lancs, LA4 6BW.*

URWIN, John Hope. b 09. Lich Th Coll 29. **d** 32 **p** 33 Lich. C of St Paul Wednesbury 32-33; St Steph Willenhall 33-35; St

Matt Walsall 35-37; Org Sec Miss to Seamen W Centr Distr and L to Offic Dio Lich 37-44; V of Ogley Hay w Brownhills 44-50; Hints 50-60; R of Weeford 50-60; Surr from 44; V of Trysull 60-74. *77 Fountain Fold, Gnosall, Stafford.* (Stafford 822601)

URWIN, Lindsay Goodall. Cudd Coll Ripon 77. **d** 80 **p** 81 S'wark. C of St Pet Walworth Dio S'wark from 80. *6 Liverpool Grove, SE17.* (01-703 7683)

URWIN, Roger Talbot. b 22. Ex Coll Ox BA 43, MA 47. 2nd cl Phil Pol and Econ 48. Sarum Th Coll 48. **d** 50 **p** 51 Sarum. C of H Trin Weymouth 50-53; V of Netheravon (w Fittleton from 54) 53-57; R of Fittleton 53-54; CF (R of O) 56-77; V of Townstal w St Sav Dartmouth 57-66; V of St Petrox w St Barn Dartmouth 58-66; Littleham w Exmouth Dio Ex 66-72; R from 72; RD of Ipplepen 61-66; Aylesbeare 69-73; C-in-c of Withycombe Raleigh w All SS Exmouth 72-74. *Rectory, Exmouth, Devon.* (Exmouth 2227)

USHER, George. b 30. Univ of Wales (Swansea) BSc 51. St Deiniol's Libr Hawarden 73. **d** 75 **p** 76 Heref (APM). C of Clun 75-80; St Giles Shrewsbury Dio Lich from 80. *18 Sutton Grove, Shrewsbury.* (Shrewsbury 64140)

USHER, Michael Hugh. b 25. St Jo Coll Dur 48. **d** 51 **p** 52 B & W. C of Clevedon 51-55; Newark 55-59; V of Everton w Mattersey 59-68; Scawby (and Redbourne from 79) Dio Linc from 68; P-in-c of Redbourne 72-79. *Scawby Vicarage, Brigg, S Humb, DN20 9LX.* (Brigg 53767)

USHER, Robin Reginald. b 50. AKC 74. St Aug Coll Cant 75. **d** 76 Man **p** 77 Middleton for Man. C of The Ascen Hulme Man 76-80; P-in-c of Newall Green Dio Man from 80. *Vicarage, Chalford Road, Newall Green, Manchester, M23 8RD.* (061-437 4605)

USHER, Thomas Gordon. b 12. St Chad's Coll Dur BA 35, Dipl Th 36, MA 38. **d** 36 **p** 37 Newc T. C of St Anthony Newc T 36-39; St Geo Cullercoats 39-41; CF (EC) 41-46; Hon CF 46; C-in-c of Newsham Conv Distr 46-50; V of St Cross Middleton 50-54; St Barn Derby 54-67; R of Fenny Bentley w Thorpe and Tissington 67-77; Perm to Offic Dio Derby from 78. *99 Windmill Hill Lane, Derby, DE3 3BN.* (Derby 371997)

USHER, William. b 05. Late Scho of St Jo Coll Dur BA Jenkyn's Exhib and Hebr Scho 26. **d** 28 **p** 29 Dur. C of St Gabr Bp Wearmouth 28-33; C-in-c of St Nich Conv Distr Dunston Co Dur 33-36; PC 36-40; V of St Paul Elswick Newc T 40-47; St Mich Newc T 47-53; St Mary Low Harrogate w Harlow Hill 53-71; Surr 40-71; RD of Knaresborough 66-71. *19 Birstwith Grange, Birstwith, Harrogate, HG3 3AH.* (Harrogate 770821)

USHER WILSON (formerly WILSON), Rodney Neville. St Aug Coll Cant 26. Univ of Dur LTh 31. **d** 30 **p** 31 Glouc. C of Stonehouse 30-33; Chap at Hubli 33-36; Miss Industr Settlement Hubli 26-43. *24 East 83rd Street, New York, NY 10028, USA.*

✠ **USHER-WILSON (formerly WILSON), Right Rev Lucian Charles.** b 03. CBE 61. Linc Coll Ox BA (3rd cl Phil and Pol) 25, MA 36. St Aug Coll Cant 21. **d** 27 Cant for Col Bp **p** 29 Ugan. Asst Master K Coll Budo 27-33; CMS Miss Jinja 33-36; Cons Bp on Upper Nile 28 Oct 36 in St Paul's Cathl Lon by Abp of Cant; Bps of Lon; Linc; Guildf; Derby; Centr Tang; and others; trld to Mbale 61; res 64; Apptd Asst Bp of Guildf 64; res 72; V of Churt 64-72; Hon Can of Bris 65-72. *58 The Dell, Westbury-on-Trym, Bristol, BS9 3UG.*

USSHER, Ven Clifford Edward. ACT ThL (1st cl) 32, Th Scho 52. **d** 33 **p** 34 Bath. C of Mudgee 33-34; All SS Cathl Bath 34-37; R of Oberon 37-40; Chap AIF 40-47; R of Tarcutta 47-54; Grenfell 54-69; S Bath 69-71; Can of Bath 61-65; Archd of Camidge 65-71; Archd without territorial jurisd 71-72; Archd of Marsden 72-74; Broughton from 74; Dioc Sec SPCK Dio Bath from 76. *PO Box 23, Bathurst, NSW, Australia 2795.* (31 2860)

USUMAE, Canon Lonsdale. St Pet Coll Siota 63. **d** 65 **p** 67 Melan. P Dio Melan 65-75; Dio Centr Melan from 75; Can of St Barn Cathl Honiara from 77. *Pamua Training Centre, San Cristoval, Solomon Islands.*

UTI, Johnson Achinike. b 34. Trin Coll Umuahia 79. **d** 81 Asaba. d Dio Asaba. *St Mark's Church, PO Box 8, Ubulu-Uku, Nigeria.*

UTLEY, Canon Edward Jacob. b 24. K Coll Lon and Warm AKC 52. **d** 53 **p** 54 Wakef. C of Pontefract 53-56; Bexhill 56-60; Chap Dudley Road and Summerfield Hosps Dio Birm from 60; RD of Birm City from 75; Hon Can of Birm Cathl from 80. *50 Wheatsheaf Road, Edgbaston, Birmingham, B16 0RY.* (021-454 2666)

UTTLEY, John Richard. Trin Coll Tor BSc 62. Linc Th Coll 64. **d** 66 **p** 67 Ont. R of Kitley 66-71; C of Ch Ch Belleville 71-76; I of Marysburgh 76-78; Newboro w Westport 78-81; C of St Thos Belleville Dio Ont from 81. *40 Applewood Drive, Belleville, Ont, Canada.* (613-962 5527)

UVUKA, Godwin Egbuna. b 40. Trin Coll Umuahia 72. **d** 74 Enugu. d Dio Enugu. *St Matthew's Church, Amechi, Awkunanaw, Box 445, Enugu, ECS, Nigeria.*

UWAOMA, John Emelike. b 36. Univ of Nigeria BA 65. **d** 76 **p** 77 Aba. P Dio Aba. *Ovom Girls High School, PO Box 807, Aba, Nigeria.*

UWARE, Andrew. d 57 New Guinea. d Dio New Guinea 57-71; Dio Papua from 71. *PO Box 36, Popondetta, Papua, New Guinea.*

UWOGHIREN, Canon Timothy Osarinmwian. Im Coll Ibad. **d** 59 **p** 60 Ondo-B. P Dio Ondo-B 59-62; Dio Benin 62-67; and from 74; Can of Benin from 75; Exam Chap to Bp of Benin from 79. *c/o Box 82, Benin City, Nigeria.*

✠ **UZODIKE, Right Rev Lucius Madubuko.** Dipl Th (Lon) 47. Wycl Hall Ox 44. **d** 45 Ox for Niger **p** 47 Niger. P Dio Niger 45-52; Hon Can of Niger 52-59; Archd of Jos 59-61; Ow 61-64; Cons Asst Bp to Bp on the Niger in All SS Cathl Onitsha 11 June 61 by Abp of W Afr; Bp on the Niger; Bps of Nig Delta; Ibad; Ow; Ondo-B; Lagos; N Nigeria; Accra; and Gambia and the Rio Pongas; and Bps P J Jones; Afonya; and Nkemena; Apptd Ld Bp on the Niger 69; res 74. *PO Box 8, Nnewi, Nigeria.*

V

VAIL, David William. Univ of Dur BA 56. Oak Hill Th Coll 56. **d** 58 Warrington for Liv **p** 59 Liv. C of St Bede Toxt Pk 58-61; Chap at Eldoret Kenya 62; V of Uasin Gishu Dio Nak 62-70; Chap Kenya High Sch 73-77; Asst Chap at Versailles Dio (Gibr in Eur from 80) Lon (N & C Eur) from 77. *17 rue de Peintre Lebrun, Versailles, France.*

VAINES, Samuel. b 09. Montr Dioc Th Coll LTh 68. **d** 67 **p** 68 Montr. C of St Hubert 67-68; St Mary Beeston 69-70; Streatham S'wark 70-73; Milton Regis-next-Sittingbourne 73-74; St Andr Luton 74-80. *101-120 Douglas Street, Victoria, BC, V8V 2N9, Canada.*

VAIZEY, Martin John. b 37. K Coll Lon and Warm AKC 64. **d** 65 **p** 66 Dur. C of Ch of Good Shepherd Bp Wearmouth 65-69; H Trin Darlington 69-72; V of Easington Colliery 72-80; St Mary Virg w St Pet Bp Wearmouth Dio Dur from 80. *Vicarage, Springwell Road, Sunderland, Co Durham, SR3 4DY.* (Sunderland 283754)

VAKA, Clement. b 52. Bp Patteson Th Centre Kohimarama 70. **d** 73 **p** 74 Melan. P Dio Melan 73-75; Centr Melan 75-80. *c/o Navigation Company, Honiara, Solomon Islands.*

VAKA, Melchior. Bp Patteson Th Centre Kohimarama 70. **d** 72 Melan. d Dio Melan 72-75; Dio Centr Melan from 75. *Vura, Honiara, Solomon Islands.*

VALADON, Zenas Samuel. d 49 **p** 50 Maur. Miss P Dio Maur. *Duperré Street, Quatre Bornes, Mauritius.*

VALE, David Phipps. b 37. Univ of Lon BSc 64. St Steph Ho Ox 64. **d** 66 **p** 67 Lon. C of Chiswick 66-70; Diego Martin Trinid 70-72; V of St Andr Huddersfield 72-73; Industr Chap for Huddersfield 72-73; Asst Chap and Master St Olaves Sch Orpington 73-75; Perm to Offic Dio St E 76-78; Hon C of St Clem w H Trin Ipswich 78-80; Team V of Wolstanton Dio Lich from 80. *St Barnabas Vicarage, Oldcastle Avenue, Bradwell, Newcastle, Staffs, ST5 8QG.* (Newc 566978)

VALENCIA, Antonio. d 64 **p** 66 Chile. P Dio Chile from 64; Archd of Valparaiso 72-76. *Casilla 561, Vina Del Mar, Chile.*

✠ **VALENTINE, Right Rev Barry.** St Jo Coll Cam BA 49, MA 52. McGill Univ Montr BD 51. St Jo Coll Winnipeg Hon DD 69 **d** 51 **p** 52 Montr. Bp's Miss Dio Montr 51-52; C of Ch Ch Cathl Montr 52-54; I of Beauharnois 54-57; Sec Dioc Bd Relig Educn Dio Montr 58-61; R of St Lambert 61-65; Executive Officer of Synod Dio Montr 65-69; Archd of Montr 66-69; Dean and R of Ch Ch Cathl Montr 68-69; Cons Bp Coadj of Rupld in St John's Cathl Winnipeg 24 June 69 by Abp of Rupld (Primate); Bps of Sktn; Athab; Sask; Qu'App; Edmon; BC; and Calg; Bp Coadj of New Westmr; Bps Suffr of Hur (Appleyard); and Athab; and Bps P F McNairy (USA) and J Nieminski (Polish Nat Catholic Ch in Canada); Apptd Ld Bp of Rupld 70. *935 Nesbitt Bay, Winnipeg, Manit, R3T 1W6, Canada.* (453-6248)

VALENTINE, Derek William. b 24. SOC 65. **d** 68 **p** 69 S'wark. C of St Luke Battersea 68-77; Hon C of Fenstanton Dio Ely from 77. *4 Bourdillon Close, Fenstanton, Huntingdon, Cambs.* (St Ives 67419)

VALENTINE, Jeremy Wilfred. b 38. N-W Ordin Course 76. **d** 79 **p** 80 Ripon. C of Cundall w Norton-le-Clay Dio

Ripon from 79. *Cundall Manor, Helperby, York, YO6 2RW.* (090 16200)

VALENTINE, Robin James. b 41. Lich Th Coll 63. **d** 66 **p** 67 St E. C of Ipswich 66-69; Staveley 69-73; P-in-c of Pleasley w New Houghton 74-81. *Address temp unknown.*

VALENTINE, William. MC 45. Univ of BC LTh 33. **d** 34 **p** 35 Yukon. Miss of Selkirk 34-36; Mayo 36-38; R of Dawson 39-42; Chap CASF 42-46; Hon CF from 46; R of Caulfeild 49-65; V of Aldergrove 66-72. *286 Tyee Drive, North Vancouver, BC, Canada.*

VALLANCE, Canon Cyril Roger. b 15. ALCD 43. **d** 43 **p** 44 Bradf. C of St Pet Shipley 43-47; Keighley (in c of St Mark Utley) 47-50; V of Thornton Yorks 50-57; Horton Kirby 57-80; Hon Can of Roch 77-80; Can (Emer) from 80. *75 Oaklands, South Godstone, Surrey, RH9 8HX.* (S Godstone 3415)

VALLINS, Christopher. b 43. Lich Th Coll 63. **d** 66 **p** 67 Guildf. C of Cuddington 66-70; Aldershot (in c of Ch of Ascen) 70-73; V of All SS W Ewell 73-81; R of Worplesdon Dio Guildf from 81. *Worplesdon Rectory, Guildford, Surrey, GU3 3RB.* (Worplesdon 234616)

VALLIS, Hubert. Dioc Th Coll Montr 47. **d** 50 **p** 51 Moos. Miss at Calstock 50-53; I of White River 53-55; R of Marathon 55-59; Thunder Bay 59-74; I of Magdalen Is 74-77; R of Murdochville 77-80; Eaton-Dudswell Dio Queb from 80. *Box 327, Cookshire, PQ, Canada.*

VAMPLEW, Peter Gordon. Jes Coll Cam BA 57. MA 61. Ridley Hall Cam 57. **d** 59 **p** 60 S'wark. C of St Nich Tooting Graveney 59-65; Poole 70-76. *c/o 10 Terrace Row, West Street, Poole, Dorset.* (Poole 3551)

VAN, Paul Ted Chon. Ho of Epiph Kuch 71. **d** and **p** 75 Kuch. P Dio Kuch. *St Thomas's Cathedral, POB 347, Kuching, Sarawak, Malaysia.*

VAN ALSTINE, Daniel Ross. b 50. Univ of Alta BA 73. Univ of Trin Coll Tor MDiv 78. **d** 78 **p** 79 Edmon. I of Edgerton Dio Edmon from 79. *10210-121st Street, Edmonton, Alta, Canada, T5N 1K7.*

VAN CARRAPIETT, Timothy Michael James. Chich Th Coll 60. **d** 63 **p** 64 Newc T. C of Sugley 63-65; St Francis High Heaton Newc T 65-69; C-in-c of Wrangbrook w N Elmsall Conv Distr Wakef 69-74; Flushing 74-75; St Day Dio Truro from 76. *St Day Vicarage, Redruth, Cornw.* (St Day 820275)

VAN DE KASTEELE, Peter John. b 39. Magd Coll Cam BA 61, MA 65. Clifton Th Coll 61. **d** 63 **p** 64 Chich. C of H Trin Eastbourne 63-66; N Pickenham w Houghton-on-the-Hill S Pickenham and of Ashill 66-70; R of Mursley w Swanbourne and L Horwood 70-81. *c/o Mursley Rectory, Milton Keynes, Bucks, MK17 0RT.* (Mursley 369)

VAN DER BYL, Canon Adrian Foster Pelham Voltelin. St Paul's Th Coll Grahmstn LTh 33. **d** 33 **p** 34 Capetn. C of St Geo Cathl Capetn 33-37; Portsea 37-41; Dean's V and C of St Geo Cathl Capetn 41-47; R of Maitland 47-52; Caledon 52-61; Can of Capetn 58-59; Can (Emer) from 72; R of Ceres 61-63; St Barn Capetn 63-74; Commiss Damar 63-70; Archd of Paarl 59-63; Cape N Suburbs 63-65; Capetn 65-72; C of St Sav Claremont Dio Capetn from 75. *33 Upper Bishopscourt Road, Claremont, CP, S Africa.* (61-7838)

VAN DER LEEST, Canon John Joseph. Angl Th Coll BC LTh 50. **d** 50 **p** 51 BC. C of Ch Ch Cathl Vic BC 50-52; R of Sandwick 52-59; St Jo Evang Calg 59-72; Dom Chap and Exam Chap to Bp of Calg from 68; Hon Can of Calg from 69; C of St Pet Calg 72-76; Hosp Chap Dio Calg from 76. *7716 7th Street SW, Calgary, Alta., Canada.* (253-4209)

VAN DER LINDE, Herbert John. b 43. Rhodes Univ Grahmstn BA 66. Coll of Resurr Mirfield. **d** 68 S'wark **p** 69 Kingston T for S'wark. C of St Luke Kingston T 68-75; Chipping Camden 75-78; V of St Pet Cheltm Dio Glouc from 78. *St Peter's Vicarage, Swindon Road, Cheltenham, Glos, GL51 9LB.* (Cheltm 24369)

VAN DIJK, James Johannes Cornelis. St Pet Coll Rosettenville. **d** 57 **p** 58 Johann. C of Springs 57-61; R of Bryanston 61-70; Asst Chap of The Hague Holland 71-79. *c/o Riouwstr 2, The Hague, Netherlands.* (55 33 59)

VAN DISSEL, Dirk. b 47. Univ of Adel BA 70. Univ of Melb MA 73. Melb Coll of Div BD 75. Trin Coll Melb 70. **d** 74 **p** 75 Melb. C of Moorabbin 74-76; All SS Geelong 76-78; P-in-c of Keith Dio Murray 78-79; R from 79. *Box 230, Keith, S Australia 5267.* (087 551527)

VAN EMMERIK, Johannes Adolph. Ch Coll Hobart. **d** 59 **p** 60 Tas. C of St Jas Newtown 59-65; CMS Kenya 65-71; Prin St Phil Bible Sch Maseno 71-75; Exam Ch to Bps of N and S Maseno 71-75: CMS Miss Dio Centr Tang 76-78; R of New Norf Dio Tas from 78. *Rectory, Bathurst Street, New Norfolk, Tasmania 7450.* (002-61 2223)

VAN GORDER, Lloyd Franklin. b 11. **d** 73 **p** 74 Win. C of Hartley Wintney w Elvetham 74-76; Perm to Offic Dio Chich 76-78; Dio Portsm from 79. *Hoxall Cottage, Hoxall Lane, Mottistone, IW, PO33 4EE.* (Brighstone 740235)

VAN HEERDEN, Charles Ernest. b 50. St Paul's Coll Grahmstn 71. **d** 73 **p** 74 Natal. C of St Martin Durban N 73-74; St Thos Berea 75-77; R of Prestbury Dio Natal from 77. *8 Adrian Road, Prestbury, Pietermaritzburg, S Africa.*

VAN MUSSCHENBROEK, Canon Samuel Gesbertho. St Paul's Coll Grahmstn. **d** 64 **p** 65 Bloemf. C of St Andr Cathl Bloemf 64-69; R of Harrismith 69-73; N Suburbs Pret 73-77; Archd of Pret 76-77; Pris Chap and L to Offic Dio Pret 77-80; Can of Pret from 80. *P Bag X2, PO Bryanston 2021, S Africa.*

VAN RENSBURG, Marthinus Phillippus. St Paul's Coll Grahmstn 63. **d** 64 **p** 65 Pret. C of N Suburbs Pret 64-66; R 66-69; Gezina Pret 69-71. *529 Jacobs Street, Gezina, Pretoria, Transvaal, S Africa.*

VAN SCHALKWYK, George Edward John. b 39. **d** 75 **p** 76 Capetn. C of St Andr Steenberg 75-78; Grassy Pk 79-80; R of Parkwood Estate Dio Capetn from 80. *Rectory, Acacia Way, Parkwood Estate, CP, S Africa.*

VAN SCHALKWYK, Harry Leslie. b 54. St Bede's Coll Umtata 75. **d** 76 St John's **p** 78 Bloemf. d Dio St John's 76-77; C of Heidedal 78-80; Good Shepherd E Lon Dio Grahmstn from 80. *c/o 19 Elton Street, Southernwood, East London, CP, S Africa.*

VAN STADEN, James Abel. b 49. St Pet Coll Natal Dipl Th 76. **d** 76 **p** 77 Capetn. C of St John Wynberg 76-80; Bredasdorp Dio Capetn from 80. *Box 187, Bredasdorp 7280, CP, S Africa.*

VAN WYK, Michael Stuart. b 40. St Paul's Coll Grahmstn 70. **d** 72 Capetn **p** 76 Johann. C of Ascen Huguenot Pk 72-74; Namaqualand 74-75; Klipton 75-78; R of Reiger Pk Dio Johann from 78. *PO Box 571, Boksburg 1460, Johannesburg, S Africa.*

VAN ZUYLEN, Roderick Neil. Rhodes Univ Grahmstn BA 69. St Paul's Coll Grahmstn. **d** 68 **p** 69 Capetn. C of Bellville 68-71; St Jas Morningside Durban 71-72; R of St Jas Dundee 72-77; St Cypr Durban Dio Natal from 77. *2 Payne Road Congella, Durban, Natal, S Africa.* (Durban 357318)

VAN ZYL, Willem Petrus. St Paul's Coll Grahmstn LTh 63. **d** 63 **p** 64 Mashon. P Dio Mashon 63-65 and 67-73; C of Eastcote 65-67; R of Parow 73-78; Groot Drakenstein Dio Capetn from 78. *Rectory, Groot Drakenstein 7680, CP, S Africa.* (Groot Drak 4120)

VAN-LANE, John Jeremy. Univ of Tor BA 57. Trin Coll Tor 60. **d** 63 **p** 64 Bran. C of St Matt Cathl Bran 63-66; I of Birtle 66-68; R of St Richard Tor 68-75; P-in-c of St Jo Bapt Norway City and Dio Tor from 75. *470 Woodbine Avenue, Toronto, Ont., Canada.*

VAN DER GOES, Deborah Helen. b 49. Univ of Sask BA 77. Coll of Em & St Chad Sktn MDiv 79. **d** and **p** 79 Rupld. C of Pembina Hills Dio Rupld from 79. *Box 73, Pilot Mound, Manit, Canada, R0G 1P0.*

VAN DER STOK, Albert Frederick. b 55. St Paul's Coll Grahmstn Dipl Th 80. **d** 80 **p** 81 Pret. C of St Alb Cathl Pret from 80. *237 Schoeman Street, Pretoria 0002, S Africa.*

VAN DER WEEGEN, Geoffrey Josephus Henricus Bernardus. b 50. Ridley Hall Cam 78. **d** 80 **p** 81 S'wark. C of St Jo Evang Waterloo Rd Lambeth Dio S'wark from 80; St Andr Lambeth Dio S'wark from 80. *17 Ospringe House, Wootton Street, Waterloo, SE1.* (01-261 9613)

VANDERWOLF, Dennis Arnold. b 50. ACT ThL 72. St Mich Ho Crafers 71. **d** 73 **p** 74 Rockptn. Asst C St Geo Homes Parkhurst 73; C of Park Ave Rockptn 71-74; Callide Valley 74; St Paul's Cathl Rockptn 75-76; P-in-c of Clermont 76; R of Moranbah Dio Rockptn from 77. *Mills Avenue, Moranbah, Queensld, Australia 4744.* (50-7216)

VAN de WEYER, Robert William Bates. b 50. Univ of Lanc BA 76. SOC 78. **d** 81 Ely (NSM). Warden of L Gidding Commun Dio Ely from 81. *The Community, Little Gidding, Huntingdon, PE17 5RJ.*

VANE, Walter Brian. b 21. Univ of Liv BSc (Maths) 46, MA (Social Sc) 50. Coll of Resurr Mirfield 51. **d** 53 **p** 54 Man. C of Leigh Lancs 53-56; St Pet Wolverhampton 56-58; R of St Geo Abbey Hey 58-62; V of St Hilda Prestwich 62-65; Asst Master Man Gr Sch from 65; Perm to Offic Dio Man 65-66; C of Heaton Norris 66-71; L to Offic Dio Man from 71; Dio Ches from 74. *Greenbank House, Albert Square, Bowdon, Chesh.* (061-928 2070)

VANIER, John George William. Codr Coll Barb BA 07. **d** 05 **p** 07 Antig. C of St Paul w H Cross St Croix 05; R of St Mary and St Aug Anguilla 12-13; St Paul and St Thos Nevis 13-19; St Paul St Kitts 19-21; Chap to Bp of Antig 16-37; R of St Mary Antig 21-34; C of St Jo Cathl Antig 34-36; Sec of Synod 14-33; Can of St Jo Cathl Antig 33-47; R of St Anthony Montserrat 36-45; Archd of St Kitts-Nevis 45-47. *Harbour View, Basseterre, St Kitts, Leeward Islands, W Indies.*

VANN, Lawson Edmund. b 1897. Qu Coll Ox BA 21, MA 25. **d** 21 **p** 22 Carl. C of Cleator Moor 21-25; Wigton 25-26; Lanc 26-27; CF 27-50; Hon CF from 50; V of Crewe Green 50-53; Inskip 53-62; Allhallows 62-66; L to Offic Dio Carl from 66. *The Stone House, Thursby, Carlisle, Cumb, CA5 6NU* (Dalston 710651)

VANN, Paul. b 41. St D Coll Lamp Dipl Th 65. **d** 65 **p** 66 Mon. C of Griffithstown 65-67; Llanfrechfa 67-71; Chap St Woolos Cathl Newport 71-72; C-in-c of Llanrumney Conv Distr Dio Mon 72-76; V from 76; Dep Chap HM Pris Cardiff 75-78. *Vicarage, Llanrumney, Cardiff, CF3 9RN.* (Cardiff 792761)

VANSTON, William Francis Harley. b 24. TCD BA 48, MA 52. **d** 48 **p** 49 Connor. C of St Mary Belf 48-51; Rathfarnham 51-58; I of Narraghmore w Fontstown and Timolin 58-65; Arklow Dio Glendal from 65; Kilbride Dio Glendal from 73; Inch Dio Glendal from 67; RD of Rathdrum from 77. *Rectory, Arklow, Co Wicklow, Irish Republic.* (Arklow 2439)

VANSTONE, Walford David Frederick. b. 38. ACK 69. Open Univ BA 81. St Aug Coll Cant 69. **d** 70 **p** 71 Kens for Lon. C of Feltham 70-75; Team V of E Runcorn w Halton 75-80; V of St Andr Grange, Runcorn Dio Ches from 80. *37 Lime Grove, Runcorn, Cheshire.* (0928 74411)

VANSTONE, Canon William Hubert. b 23. Ball Coll Ox BA (1st cl Cl Mods and 1st cl Lit Hum) 48. St Jo Coll Cam BA (1st cl Th Trip pt ii) 50. U Th Sem NY STM 50. Westcott Ho Cam 48. **d** 50 **p** 51 Man. C of St Thos Halliwell 50-55; C-in-c of St Thos Conv Distr Kirkholt 55-64; V 64-76; Exam Chap to Bp of Man 59-78; Hon Can of Man 68-76; Ches 78; Can Res from 78; Th Chap to Bp of Ches from 76; V of Hattersley 77-78. *14 Abbey Square, Chester.*

VANT, Thomas Neil. b 44. Univ of BC BA 72. Vanc Sch of Th 73. **d** 74 Caled **p** 75 Carib. I of Carib Highways Miss Dio Carib from 74. *Box 1079, 100 Mile House, BC, V0K 2E0, Canada.* (395-2397)

VANUATU, Diocese of. *See* Tevi, Right Rev Harry Sivehi.

VANVA, Walter. d 59 Melan **p** 80 Vanuatu. d Dio Melan 59-75; Dio New Hebr 75-80; P Dio Vanuatu from 80. *Box 238, Santo, Vanuatu.*

VARAH, Preb Edward Chad. b 11. OBE 69. Albert Schweitzer Gold Medal 72. Late Exhib of Keble Coll Ox BA 33, MA 46. Linc Th Coll 34. **d** 35 **p** 36 Linc. C of St Giles Linc 35-38; Putney 38-40; St Jo Evang Barrow-F 40-42; V of H Trin Blackb 42-49; St Paul Battersea 49-53; C-in-c of St Steph Walbrook w St Swithun Lon Stone, St Benet Sherehog, St Mary Bothaw and St Laur Pountney City and Dio Lon 53-54; R from 54; Dir The Samaritans 53-74; Preb of St Paul's Cathl Lon from 75; Hon Fell of Keble Coll Ox 81. *St Stephen's Church, Walbrook, EC4N 8BN.* (01-283 3400)

VARCOE, Connol Henry Rowe. b 28. St John Th Coll Morpeth ACT Th Dip 70. **d** 69 **p** 70 Newc. C of New Lambton 70-72; Maitland 72-75; P-in-c of Exper Area of Wyoming 75-79; R of Swansea Dio Newc from 79. *Rectory, Josephson Street, Swansea, NSW, Australia 2286.*

VARCOE, Donald Arthur. Wycl Coll Tor. **d** 61 **p** 62 Calg. R of Hanna 62-68; I of Oakville 68-69; I of Poplar Point 68-69; R of Virden Dio Bran from 69; R of Virden 69-73; Dauphin 73-80; St Alb Regina Dio Qu'App from 80. *60 McNaughton Avenue, Regina, Sask, Canada.*

VARDON, Denis Andrew. St Jo Coll Morpeth ACT ThL (2nd cl) 64. **d** 64 **p** 65 Gippsld. C of Bairnsdale 65-66; Traralgon 66-68; Perm to Offic Dio Melb from 68. *25 Fifth Street, Black Rock, Vic, Australia 3193.*

VAREY, Douglas Logan. Univ of Tor BA 56. Wycl Coll Tor LTh 58. **d** 58 **p** 59 Tor. C of Thornhill 58-60; St Paul Bloor Street Tor 61-63; R of St Bede and Ch of Incarnation Tor 63-65; St Andr Scarborough City and Dio Tor from 65. *47 Shandon Drive, Scarborough, Ont., Canada.* (416-447 1481)

VARGAS PALOMINO, Walter Pompeyo. b 35. **d** 77 Peru. d Dio Peru. *Apartado 5152, Av Santa Cruz 491, Miraflores, Lima 18, Peru.*

VARLEY, Ernest. b 46. Linc Th Coll 71. **d** 74 **p** 75 Wakef. C of Hanging Heaton 74-76; Brandon 76-79; Rekendyke 79-80; V of Shiney Row Dio Dur from 80; Herrington Dio Dur from 80. *Shiney Row Vicarage, Houghton-le-Spring, T & W, DH4 4JU.* (Fencehouses 852215)

VARLEY, Robert. b 36. St Jo Coll Cam BA 57, MA 64. N-W Ordin Course 71. **d** 74 **p** 75 Ches. C of Wallasey 74-77; V of Rock Ferry 77-81. *c/o Vicarage, St Peter's Road, Birkenhead, L42 1PY.*

VARNEY, Peter David. b 38. Univ of Dur BA 61, MA 64. Univ of Birm Dipl Th 63. Qu Coll Birm 61. **d** 64 **p** 65 S'wark. C of St Paul Newington 64-66; St Mich AA w All S Camberwell 66-67; Perm to Offic Dio Kuch 67-68; Hon C of Croxley Green 69; Perm to Offic Dio Roch 69-72 and from 73; Asst Sec Miss and Ecumen Coun of Ch Assembly 69-70; Miss and Ecumen Coun 70-71; Bd for Miss and Unity Gen Syn 71-72; Asst Chap Commun of St Jo Bapt Clewer 72-73; Asst Sec Chrs Abroad from 74. *4 The Glen, Bromley, Kent, BR2 0JB.* (01-464 4383)

VARNEY, Wilfred Davies. b 10. Sarum Th Coll 71. **d** 71 **p** 72 Glouc. C of St Paul Glouc 71-74; V of Lydbrook 74-77; Hon C of Felpham 77-80; Overbury Dio Worc from 80. *St Nicholas Cottage, Teddington, Tewkesbury, Glos, GL20 8JA.* (Alderton 435)

VARNEY, William James Granville. b 22. St D Coll Lamp 63. **d** 65 **p** 66 St D. C of Burry Port w Pwll 65-68; V of Strata-Florida 68-71; Llandyfriog w Llangynllo and Troedyraur 72-78; R of Aberporth w Tremaen Dio St D from 78. *Rectory, Aberporth, Dyfed.* (Aberporth 810217)

VARNHAM, Gerald Stanley. b 29. Sarum Wells Th Coll 74. **d** 77 **p** 78 Portsm. C of Portchester Dio Portsm from 77. *15 Southampton Road, Fareham, Hants, PO16 7DZ.* (Fareham 234182)

VARNISH, Michael Rowley. b 37. St Barn Coll Adel 73. **d** 75 Bp Renfrey for Adel **p** 76 Adel. C of Hawthorn 75-77; P-in-c of Warradale-Darlington Dio Adel from 77. *16a Dwyer Road, Oaklands Park, S Australia 5046.*

VARTY, John Eric. b 44. Tyndale Hall Bris 68. **d** 71 **p** 72 Carl. C of St Mark Barrow-in-Furness 71-74; Cheadle Dio Ches from 74. *172 Queens Road, Cheadle Hulme, Gtr Man.* (061-485 5792)

VASETHE, James. St Pet Th Coll Siota 59. **d** 62 **p** 64 Melan. P Dio Melan 62-75; Dio Ysabel from 75. *Kolotubi, Hograno District, Santa Ysabel, Solomon Islands.*

VASEY, Arthur Stuart. b 37. Qu Coll Birm 68. **d** 71 Bradf **p** 72 Ripon for Bradf. C of Shelf 71-73; Adel 74-76; Chap St John's Hosp Linc 76-79; P-in-c of Tanfield Dio Dur from 79. *Vicarage, Tanfield Village, Stanley, Co Durham, DH9 9PX.* (Stanley 32750)

VASEY, David. b 26. St Aid Coll 55. **d** 58 **p** 59 York. C of St Jo Bapt Hull 58-61; St Thos Middlesbrough 61-62; Fulford 62-64; V of Swinefleet 64-68; St Cypr w St Jas Leeds 68-78; St Columba Scarborough Dio York from 78. *St Columba Vicarage, Peasholm Drive, Scarborough, N Yorks, YO12 7NA.* (Scarborough 72249)

VASEY, Michael Richard. b 46. Ball Coll Ox BA 68, MA 71. Wycliffe Hall 68. **d** 71 **p** 72 Roch. C of Tonbridge Dio Roch 71-75; Tutor St John's Coll Dur from 75; L to Offic Dio Dur from 75. *St John's College, Durham, DH1 3RJ.* (Durham 69113)

VASULA, Henry. St Pet Coll Siota. **d** 53 **p** 57 Melan. P Dio Melan 53-75; Dio Ysabel 75-76. *Buala, Santa Ysabel, Solomon Islands.*

✠ **VAUGHAN, Right Rev Benjamin Noel Young.** St D Coll Lamp BA (1st cl Cl) 40. St Edm Hall Ox 2nd cl Th 42, BA 43, MA 46. Westcott Ho Cam 42. **d** 43 **p** 44 St D. C of Llannon 43-45; St D Carmarthen 45-48; Tutor Codr Coll Barb 48-52; Exam Chap to Bp of Barb 51-52; to Bp of Trinid 55-61; Commiss Barb 52-55; Lect in Th St D Coll Lamp and Publ Pr Dio St D 52-55; Dean and R of H Trin Cathl Port of Spain 55-61; Cons Ld Bp Suffr of Mandeville in Llan Cathl 29 June 61 by Abp of Wales; Bps of St A; Llan; St D; Ban; Swan B; Jordan; and Bp Wilson; R of Mandeville 61-64; Archd of S Middx 61-67; Apptd Ld Bp of Br Hond 67; res 71; Dean of Ban 71-76; Asst Bp of Ban 71-76; Apptd Ld Bp of Swan B 76. *Ely Tower, Brecon, Powys.*

VAUGHAN, Brian John. b 38. Lich Th Coll 65. **d** 68 **p** 69 Sarum. C of St Paul Fisherton Anger Sarum 68-70; Wareham w Arne 70-73; St Patr Perth 73; R of Dalwallinu 73-75; Morawa-Perenjori 75-78; Field Officer Bible S of W Austr and Perm to Offic Dio Perth from 78. *6 Otterden Street, Gosnells, W Australia 6110.* (398 7786)

VAUGHAN, Canon Edward Richard. Bp's Univ Lennox LST 64. **d** 64 **p** 65 Queb. I of Kenogami 64-67; R of La Tuque 67-72; Three Rivers Dio Queb from 72; Can of Queb from 78. *787 des Ursulines, Three Rivers, PQ., Canada.*

VAUGHAN, Canon George Ralph. b 15. TCD BA 48, MA 51. St Aid Coll 38. **d** 52 **p** 53 Down. C of Down w Hollymount 52-54; Min Can of Down Cathl 52-54; C of Carrickfergus 54-57; I of Mevagh 57-65; Milford 61-65; Castlebar U Dio Tuam from 65; Can of Tuam Cathl from 81. *Vicarage, Curragh, Castlebar, Co Mayo, Irish Republic.* (Castlebar 21319)

VAUGHAN, Gilbert Earl. Codr Coll Barb. **d** 55 **p** 56 Barb. V of St Phil I and Dio Barb from 55. *Boscobel Vicarage, St Peter, Barbados, W Indies.*

VAUGHAN, Herbert Clayton. Bp's Univ Lennox BA 29, LST 31. **d** 31 **p** 32 Ott. C of Lanark 31-40; R of Bell's Corners 40-47; St Geo Ott 47-54; Navan 55-65. *Apt 701, 1071 Ambleside Drive, Ottawa 14, Ont, Canada.*

VAUGHAN, Idris Samuel. b 46. Sarum Wells Th Coll 70. **d** 72 **p** 73 Carl. C of St Jo Workington 72-76; H Innoc Kidderminster 77-79; V of Hayton Dio Carl from 79. *Vicarage, Hayton, Nr Brampton, Cumb.* (Hayton 248)

VAUGHAN, Ivor Emlyn. b 16. **d** 79 Qu'App. C of Swift Current Dio Qu'App from 79. *1200 Dahl Street East, Swift Current, Sask, Canada, S9H 3Z3.*

VAUGHAN, John. b 30. Sarum Th Coll 53. **d** 56 **p** 57 Liv. C of St Andr Wigan 56-59; Katanning 59-61; R of Pingelly 61-64; PC of Riddings 64-71; R of Hasland 71-79; V of Temple-Normanton 71-79; Team V of Dronfield Dio Derby from 79. *11 Rothay Close, Dronfield Woodhouse, Sheffield, S18 5PR.*

VAUGHAN, John Harrington. Moore Th Coll Syd ACT ThL 31. **d** 32 Syd **p** 33 Bp Kirkby for Syd. C of Kiama w Gerringong 32-34; St John Ashfield 33-35; Vic Dept Sec BCA 35-36; Chap Hawkesbury River Distr 36-41; R of All SS Nowra and C-in-c of Provis Distr of H Trin Huskisson 41-44; Chap RAAF 44-47; R of Artamon 47-52; Springwood 52-54; LPr Dio Syd 54-58; C of Epping 68-70; L to Offic Dio Syd 70 and from 72; Chap Ld Howe I 71-72. *26 Coral Crescent, Pearl Beach, NSW, Australia 2256.* (043-415 110)

VAUGHAN, Joseph Charles Handley. b 07. TCD BA and Downes Div Pri 28, Div Test and Downes Div Pri (two) 29, MA 31. **d** 30 **p** 31 Down. C of St Aid Belf 30-32; Bangor 32-35; I of Ballywillan (Portrush) 35-46; Chap to Ch of I students at Stranmillis Tr Coll 39-44; Sec CMS Belf 46-58; V of Blackpool 58-73. *194 Warwick Avenue, Derby, DE3 6HP.* (Derby 760148)

VAUGHAN, Kenneth Macdonald. b 52. Dalhousie Univ Halifax NS BPhysEducn 75. Atlantic Sch of Th Halifax NS 75. **d** 77 Bp Hatfield for NS **p** 78 NS. C of N Syd Dio NS from 77. *Box 133, North Sydney, NS, Canada.*

VAUGHAN, Patrick Handley. b 38. Late Exhib and Pri of TCD, Wall Bibl Scho 59, BA (1st cl Hebr and Or Lang Mod) 60, BD 65. Selw Coll Cam BA (2nd cl Th Trip pt iii) 62, MA 66. Ridley Hall Cam 61. **d** 63 **p** 64 Bradf. Min Can of Bradf Cathl 63-66; Tutor Bp Tucker Th Coll Mukono 67-71; Exam Chap to Bp of Nam 70-71; Lect Makerere Univ Kampala 71-73; P-in-c of Hovingham 74-77; Slingsby 74-77; Tutor NW Ordin Course 74-77; Prin E Midl Min Tr Course from 77. *Old Vicarage, Derby Road, Beeston, Nottingham, NG9 2SN.* (Nottm 255535)

VAUGHAN, Peter Llewelyn. b 20. Wells Th Coll 47. **d** 49 **p** 50 Portsm. C of All SS Ryde 49-53; Sudbury w Somersal 53-56; L to Offic Dio Melan 56-58; R of Ingestre w Tixall 58-63; Westbere w Hersden 63-69; Perm to Offic Dio Cant from 70; Chap St Mary's Hosp Etchinghill Folkestone from 73. *Birchwood, Stodmarsh Road, Canterbury, Kent.* (Cant 61864)

VAUGHAN, Peter St George. b 30. Selw Coll Cam BA 55, MA 59. BNC Ox MA (by incorp) 63. Ridley Hall Cam. **d** 57 Birm **p** 58 Aston for Birm. C of St Martin Birm 57-63; Chap to Ox Past 63-67; Asst Chap BNC Ox 63-67; V of Ch Ch Galle Face Colom 67-72; Sec CMS in Ceylon 68-72; Prec H Trin Cathl Auckld 72-75; Prin Crowther Hall from 75. *Crowther Hall, Weoley Park Road, Selly Oak, Birmingham, B29 6QT.*

VAUGHAN, Richard John. b 09. MC and Men in Disp 45. St Edm Hall, Ox BA (1st cl Phil Pol and Econ) 34, Dipl Th (w distinc) 35, MA 38. Wycl Hall Ox 34. **d** 35 **p** 36 Bris. C of Kingswood 35-38; St Luke Redcliffe Sq Kens 38-40; Ch Ch Harlington Lon 40-41; CF 41-47; V of St Mich-within-Schonbrunn Vienna 46-47; PC of St Sav Alexandra Pk 47-55; Sec Dioc Miss Coun 59-66; St Geo Headstone 55-81; RD of Harrow 61-67. *3 Brookshill Avenue, Harrow Weald, Middx.* (01-954 7855)

VAUGHAN, Roger Maxwell. b 39. K Coll Lon and Warm AKC 62. **d** 63 **p** 64 Lich. C of W Bromwich 63-65; Wolverhampton 65-70; V of Tunstall 70-79; Abbots Bromley Dio Lich from 79; C-in-c of St Chad's Conv Distr Tunstall 70-79. *Vicarage, The Market Place, Abbots Bromley, Staffs.* (B-o-T 840242)

VAUGHAN, Ronald Alfred. b 38. SOC 78. **d** 81 Stepney for Lon. Hon C of St Pet w St Benet Mile End Stepney Dio Lon from 81. *14 Cephas Street, E1 4AX.*

VAUGHAN, Thomas Gareth. b 30. Sarum Th Coll 62. **d** 63 **p** 64 Bradf. C of All SS L Horton Bradf 63-66; Menston-in-Wharfedale w Woodhead 66-68; Chap Botleys Pk Hosp Chertsey 68-80; St Pet Distr Gen Hosp 78-80; Wearmouth Hosps Sunderland from 80. *2 Killingworth Drive, High Barnes, Sunderland, T & W.*

VAUGHAN, Trevor. b 41. Linc Th Coll 66. **d** 69 Bp McKie for Cov **p** 70 Cov. C of Wyken 69-72; Stratford-on-Avon 72-73; P-in-c of Wolvey w Burton Hastings and Stretton Baskerville 73-77; Monk's Kirby (to 75) w Copston Magna 73-77; V of Heyhouses (or Sabden) 77-80; St Geo Chorley Dio Blackb from 80. *St George's Vicarage, Letchworth Place, Chorley, Lancs, PR7 2HJ.* (Chorley 63064)

VAUGHAN, William Harold. Bp Wilson Coll IM. **d** 27 S & M for Liv **p** 28 Liv. C of Ch Ch Ince-in-Makerfield 27-29; St Thos Ashton-in-Makerfield 29-30; V of St Steph Wigan 30-34; Abram 34-44; St Mary Widnes 44-46; PC of Mapperley 46-51; V of Altcar 51-57. *2 The Limes, Mapperley, Derby.*

VAUGHAN-JAMES, Gwilym Vaughan. b 17. Lich Th Coll 39. **d** 42 **p** 43 Llan. C of Pentyrch 42-46; Heavitree 46-51; Chap RAF 51-60; RN 60-73; Sub-Warden and Chap Commun of St Denys Warm 73-78; V of Willerby w Ganton and Folkton Dio York from 78. *Willerby Vicarage, Scarborough, Yorks.* (Sherburn 364)

VAUGHAN-JONES, Frederick Edward Cecil. Selw Coll Cam BA 40, MA 44. Cudd Coll Ox. **d** 42 **p** 43 Chelmsf. C of St Marg Leigh-on-Sea 42-46; H Cross Miss E Pondoland 46-53; P-in-c 53-62; C of Gt w L Gransden 63-65; R of Cambridge 65-73; Can of Grahmstn 70-73; R of Benoni Dio Johann from 73. *11 Lakefield Avenue, Westdene, Benoni, Transvaal, S Africa.*

VAUGHAN-JONES, Geraint James. b 29. St Deiniol's Libr Hawarden. **d** 70 **p** 71 Ban. C of Llanaber 70-73; V in R Benef of Dolgellau 73-76; R of Mallwyd w Cemais and Llanymawddwy Dio Ban from 76. *Mallwyd Rectory, Machynlleth, Powys, SY20 9HJ.* (Dinas Mawddwy 217)

VAUGHAN-JONES, Canon John Paschal. b 18. Keble Coll Ox BA (3rd cl Th) 39, MA 43. St Steph Ho Ox 40. **d** 41 **p** 42 Chelmsf. C of Laindon w Basildon 41-49; CF (EC) 43-47; R of Chipping Ongar Dio Chelmsf from 49; R of Shelley Dio Chelmsf from 49; Surr from 55; RD of Ongar from 72; Hon Can of Chelmsf from 78. *Rectory, Chipping Ongar, Essex, CM5 9AD.* (Ongar 362173)

VAUGHAN-THOMAS, Harold Owen. Angl Th Coll BA 59. **d** 62 **p** 63 Carib. V of Chilcotin Miss 62-64; N Thompson River 64-69. *2265 Railway Street, Abbotsford, BC, Canada.*

VAVASOUR, David Ralph. b 52. Carleton Univ Ott BA 76. Huron Coll Lon Ont MDiv 79. **d** and **p** 79 Ott. C of St Steph Ott 79-81; St Martin City and Dio Ott from 81. *505-35 Woodridge Crescent, Nepean, Ont, Canada.*

VAVATE, Stephen. b 41. Bp Patteson Th Centre Kohimarama 70. **d** 73 **p** 74 Melan. P Dio Melan 73; Centr Melan from 75. *Pamua, Makira Region, Solomon Islands.*

VEAR, Frank Henry. b 12. K Coll Lon and Warm 67. **d** 68 Southn for Win **p** 69 Win. C of N Stoneham w Bassett 68-75; V of St Chris Southbourne Dio Win from 75. *81 Watcombe Road, Bournemouth, Dorset.* (Bournemouth 424886)

VEAZEY, Harry Christopher Hurford. b 11. Westcott Ho Cam 33. **d** 35 **p** 36 S'wark. C of St Barn Sutton New Town 35-38; St Mary Newington 38-41; V of St Silas Nunhead 41-57; Doddington w Wychling 57-80; V of Newnham 57-80; RD of Ospringe 78-80. *Five Oaks, Pluckley Road, Charing, Ashford, Kent.*

VEDIER, Derek. b 33. St Mich Ho Crafers 77. **d** 79 **p** 80 Tas. C of Kingston & Channel 79-80; P-in-c of Bothwell 80; Furneaux Is Dio Tas from 81. *Rectory, Whitemark, Flinders Island, Tasmania 7255.*

VEDY, Louis George. b 07. Univ of Lon BSc (1st cl) 27. Down Coll Cam 1st cl Nat Sc Trip pt i, 27, BA (1st cl Nat Sc Trip pt ii) 28, MA 32. FInstP 33. Wycl Hall Ox 52. **d** 52 **p** 53 Roch. C of St Nich w St Clem Roch 52-55; V of Bredhurst 55-58; Downe 58-69. *7 Copse Hill, Purley, Surrey, CR2 4LL.*

VEEL, William Tomkins. b 1881. CM Coll Isl 07. Univ of Dur LTh 10, BA 21, MA 26. **d** 10 Lon for Col Bp **p** 11 Bom. CMS Miss Poona 11-13; Prin of CMS Sch Nasik 13-16 and 23-26; Manmad 17-20 and 26-28; furlough 20-23; LDHM at St Paul Roxeth 28-29; Min 29-36; V of Em Maida Hill 36-51; C of St Jo Bapt Southend-on-Sea (in c of St Mark) 51-53; Thornton Heath 53-57; Surr 36-51; Perm to Offic Dio Chich 57-60; Dios S'wark and Lon from 60. *17 Boyne Park, Tunbridge Wells, Kent.*

VEITCH, Thomas. b 12. Univ of Glas MA 37. **d** 40 **p** 41 Glas. C of St Mary's Cathl Glas 40-41; H Trin Ayr (in c of Wallacetown 41-43; Prestwick from 43) 41-46; R of St John Girvan w Stranraer and Portpatrick 46-48; St Pet Peterhead 49-56; Chap HM Pris Peterhead 49-53; R of St Paul and St Geo (w St Vinc 60-71) City and Dio Edin from 56. *53 Albany Street, Edinburgh EH1 3QY.* (031-5563974)

VELO, Etienne. St Paul's Coll Ambat 37. **d** 38 **p** 42 Madag. P Dio Madag 38-69; Dio Tam from 69. *Andevoranto, Madagascar.*

VELPEL, Philip Maurice. b 44. Univ of Manit BSc 65. Wycl Coll Tor MDiv 73. **d** 73 **p** 74 Qu'App. C of Wolseley 73; Cupar 73-74; R 74-76; All SS Niag Falls Dio Niag from 76. *5856 Robinson Street, Niagara Falls, Ont., Canada.* (416-354 4355)

VENA, Nthetheleli Bethuell. St Bede's Coll Umtata 78. **d** 79 **p** 80 Grahmstn. C of St Columba Lady Frere Dio Grahmstn from 79. *PO Box 2, Lady Frere, CP, S Africa.*

VENABLES, Arthur Peter. b 20. **d** 49 **p** 50 Edmon. C of St Jo Evang N Vancouver 49-50; I of Vengreville and of Good Shepherd w St Jas Edmon 50-54; C of Beckenham 54-56; St Martin Brighton 56-58; St Mary Magd Paddington 58-59; St Silas Islington 59-61; St Andr Willesden Green 61-63; SS Aug Chesterfield 63-66; St Phil Earl's Court Road Kens 69-74; C-in-c of Uxbridge Moor Dio Lon from 74. *77 Cowley Mill Road, Uxbridge Moor, Middx.* (Uxbridge 32778)

VENABLES, Dudley James. b 17. Cant Sch of Min 77. **d** 80 **p** 81 Cant (APM). C of H Trin Ramsgate Dio Cant. from 80. *7 Queens Road, Ramsgate, Kent, CT11 8AG.* (Thanet 54393)

VENABLES, Francis Edmund Cyril. Angl Th Coll BC LTh 31. **d** and **p** 31 New Westmr. C of Maple Ridge w Whonnock and Haney 31-33; R of St Mary Virg (Bp Hill's Mem Ch) Vancouver 34-36; Chap Columb Coast Miss Distr 36-38; R of Ch Ch Alert Bay 38-39; on leave 39-40; C of St Mary Oak Bay 40-43; Maple Ridge 43-44; Perm to Offic Dio BC from 61. *900 Park Blvd, Victoria, BC, Canada.*

VENABLES, Francis Isaac. b 1900. Univ of Lon BA 22. Univ of Ox MA 53. **d** 70 Sarum [f Prin Culham Coll 46-61: Dir Inst Chr Educn 61-64; C of Wareham 70-75; P-in-c of E Stoke w E Holme 71-75; Perm to Offic Dio Bris from 81. *20 Hallen Road, Bristol BS10 7QX*

VENABLES, Stanley Paul. b 02. AKC (2nd cl) 32. **d** 32 **p** 33 Lon. C of St Mary Kilburn 32-35; Bourton-on-the-Water (in c of L Slaughter and Clapton-on-the-Hill) 35-46; V of Minsterworth 46-72. *37 St Mary's Square, Gloucester, GL1 2QT.* (Glouc 35043)

VENESS, David Roger. b 48. Brunel Univ Uxbridge Middx BTech 70. St Jo Coll Nottm 73. **d** 75 **p** 76 Birm. C of Selly Hill 75-80; V of Colney Heath Dio St Alb from 80. *Vicarage, Colney Heath, St Albans, Herts, AL4 0NQ.*

VENEZUELA, Lord Bishop in. *See* Jones, Right Rev Haydn Harold.

VENIMORE, Colin Whitby. **d** 51 **p** 52 Wel. C of Porirua 51-52; Kilbirnie 52-53; V of Opunake 53-56; Patea 56-60; Greytown 60-62; Wanganui E 62-69; Pohangina 69-72; C of Ch Ch Wanganui Dio Wel 72-78; Hon C from 78. *12 Lewis Avenue, Aramoho, Wanganui, NZ.* (Wanganui 37241)

VENIMORE, Ven Vincent Charles. Univ of NZ BA 32, MA 33. NZ Bd of Th Stud LTh 36. Melb Coll of Div BD 37. St Jo Coll Auckld 29. **d** 33 **p** 34 Wel. C of St Mark Wel 33-37; St Paul Thornton Heath 37-38; V of Gonville 39-52; CF (NZ) 42-46; V of Masterton 52-74; Hon Can of Wel 56-63; Archd of The Wairarapa 63-80; Archd (Emer) from 81; V of U Hutt 74-80; *4 Patete Place, Tawhero, Wanganui, NZ.*

VENN, Robert Thomas. b 1894. Linc Coll Ox BA 20, 3rd cl Th 21, MA 21. **d** 21 **p** 22 Chelmsf. Asst Master Forest Sch Walthamstow; 21-25; Chap RN 25-49; Hon Chap to HM the King 49; Chap Wellington Sch 49-52; Perm to Offic Dio B & W 49-56; Dio Ex 53-59; L to Offic Dio Ex from 59. *32 Richmond Road, Exeter, Devon, EX4 4JF.* (Exeter 38696)

VENNER, Stephen Squires. b 44. Univ of Birm BA (2nd cl Engl) 65. Linacre Coll Ox BA (3rd cl Th) 67, MA 71. St Steph Ho Ox 65. **d** 68 **p** 69 S'wark. C of St Pet Streatham 68-71; Streatham Hill 71-72; Balham Hill 72-74; Asst Master St Paul's Girls' Sch Hammersmith 72-74; V of St Pet Clapham 74-75; Chap Overseas Studs S Lon 74-75; P-in-c of Studley Dio Sarum 76; V from 76. *Studley Vicarage, Trowbridge, Wilts, BA14 0ED.* (Trowbridge 3162)

VENNING, Nigel Christopher. b 50. AKC and BD 75. St Aug Coll Cant 75. **d** 76 B & W **p** 77 Taunton for B & W. C of Minehead 76-80; Fawley Dio Win from 80. *21 Cedric Close, Blackfield, Southampton, SO4 1ZZ.* (Fawley 893379)

VENTER, Sarel Gerhardus. **d** 72 **p** 73 Pret. C of Pretoria W Dio Pret from 72. *Box 19028, Pretoria West, S Africa.*

VENTON, Bertram Ernest. b 1900. St Bonif Coll Warm. **d** 50 **p** 51 Ex. C of Petrockstowe 50-53; R of Martinhoe w Trentishoe 53-59; V of Molland 59-68; L to Offic Dio Ex from 68. *Champson Cottage, Molland, South Molton, Devon.*

VENUS, John Charles. b 29. K Coll Lon and Warm AKC 53. **d** 54 **p** 55 Portsm. C of Havant 54-59; Chap St Geo Gr Sch Capetn 60-65; RN 66-70; Trin Coll Glenalmond 70-78; Chap RN from 79. *c/o Ministry of Defence, Lacon House, Theobald's Road, WC1X 8RY.*

VENVILLE, Canon Francis Maurice Royston. St Jo Th Coll Auckld LTh 52. **d** 48 **p** 49 Auckld. C of Mt Albert 48-51; P-in-c of Henderson 51-54; V of Waimate North 54-59; C of Panmure 59-63; Chap Oakley Psychiatric Hosp from 63; Hon Can of Auckld from 78. *998 New North Road, Mount Albert, Auckland, NZ.* (867-199)

VEOGO, Douglas. **d** 64 New Guinea **p** 71 Bp Kendall for Papua. d Dio New Guinea 64-70; P Dio Papua from 71. *Cape Vogel, via Dogura, Papua New Guinea.*

VERAE, Rupert. b 20. **d** 76 Papua. d Dio Papua 76-77; New Guinea Is from 77. *St John's Church, Aisega, Sag Sag Private Bag, Kimbe WNBP, Papua New Guinea.*

VERCOE, Michael John. b 43. Melb Coll of Div LTh 74. **d** 73 **p** 74 C & Goulb. C of St John Canberra 73-76; P-in-c of Adaminaby 76-77; R of Braidwood Dio C & Goulb from 77. *62 Wilson Street, Braidwood, NSW, Australia 2622.*

✠ **VERCOE, Right Rev Whakahuihui.** MBE 70. Coll Ho Ch Ch 47. **d** 51 **p** 52 Wel. C of Feilding 51-53; P-in-c of Wairarapa Maori Distr 53-58; Rangitikei-Manawatu Maori Past 58-61; CF NZ 61-67; Chap and Prin Te Wai Pounamu Coll Ch Ch 67-76; Asst Maori Missr Ch Ch 71-73; V of Ohinemutu 76-78; P-in-c of Ruatoki-Whakatane Past 78-81; Te Kaha Past 78-81; Archd of Tairawhiti 78-81; VG Bishopric of Aotearoa 78-81; Cons Ld Bp of Aotearoa 81. *2 Maclean Street, Rotorua, NZ.*

VERCOE, William George. St Jo Th Coll Auckld LTh (2nd cl) 49. **d** 49 **p** 50 Auckld. C of Mt Roskill 49; Onehunga 49-53; V of Tuakua 53-61; C of Otahuhu 61-62; P-in-c of Mangere E 62-63; V 63-71; Te Atatu 71-73; Apia 73-76; Avondale Dio Auckld from 77. *27 Roberton Road, Avondale, Auckland, NZ.*

VERITY, Cecil Beaumont. b 01. Trin Coll Cam BA 22, MA 26. Ridley Hall Cam 24. **d** 25 Lewes for Chich **p** 26 Chich. C of H Trin Eastbourne 25-28; CMS Miss Uganda 28-30; Gahini Ruanda-Urundi 30-38; Chap RAF 39-58; V of Barton Stacey w Bullington 58-69; Surr 60-69. *9 Conyngham Lane, Bridge, Canterbury, CT4 5JX.* (Cant 830940)

VERITY, Harry William. b 20. Keble Coll Ox BA 42, MA 45. Westcott Ho Cam 42. **d** 43 Kingston-T for S'wark **p** 44 S'wark. C of Battersea 43-45; St Sav and St Pet w St Mich S'wark 45-47; Limpsfield 47-50; R of Port Rowan Hur 50-51; C of Deal 52-54; V of St Jo Evang Walton-on-the-Hill 54-60; Thorner 60-73; W Witton 73-81; R of Wensley 73-81; V of St Annes-on-Sea Dio Blackb from 81. *Vicarage, St David's Road North, St Annes-on-Sea, FY8 2DD.* (St Annes 722648)

✠ **VERNEY, Right Rev Stephen Edmund.** b 19. MBE 45. Ball Coll Ox BA and MA (2nd cl Lit Hum) 48. **d** 50 **p** 51 Southw. C of Gedling 50-52; C-in-c of New Clifton Conv Distr Nottm 52-57; V of St Francis Clifton 57-58; Surr from 58; Dioc Missr Cov 58-64; V of Leamington Hastings 58-64; Can Res of Cov Cathl 64-70; Proc Conv Cov 65-70; Can of St Geo Chap Windsor 70-77; Cons Ld Bp Suffr of Repton in Westmr Abbey 31 March 77 by Abp of Cant; Bps of Lon, Derby, Bradf, Ely, Glouc, Guildf, Lich, Portsm, Roch and Worc; Bps Suffr of Buckingham, Dorch, Edmon, Grimsby, Hertf, Horsham, Huntingdon, Jarrow, Kingston, Knaresborough, Malmesbury, Selby, Sherborne, Shrewsbury, Stafford, Tonbridge and Willesden; and others. *Repton House, Lea, Matlock, Derbys, DE4 5JP.* (Dethick 644)

VERNON, Bryan Graham. b 50. Qu Coll Cam BA 72, MA 76. Qu Coll Birm Dipl Th 74. **d** 75 **p** 76 Newc T. C of St Gabr Heaton Newc T 75-79; Chap Univ of Newc T from 79. *Chaplaincy, Claremont Buildings, Eldon Place, Newcastle-on-Tyne.* (Newc T 328511)

VERNON, Charles Harold. b 09. Univ of Lon 26, AKC 38. Westcott Ho Cam 38. **d** 39 **p** 40 S'wark. *f Solicitor* C of Malden 39-43; V of St Antholin Nunhead 43-47; Bream 47-52; Sherborne w Windrush 52-55; C of Stoke Newington 55-56; Northolt (in c of St Hugh) 59-62; C-in-c of St Matthias Eccles Distr Colindale Hendon 62-69; C-in-c of Bishopstone 69-70; V 70-76; RD of Seaford 72-75; Perm to Offic Dio Chich from 76. *Marecotte, Waldron, Heathfield, E Sussex.*

VERNON, John Christie. b 40. Univ of Lon BSc (Eng) 62. Linc Th Coll 63. **d** 65 Dur **p** 66 Jarrow for Dur. C of St Mary Barnard Castle 65-69; CF from 69. *c/o National Westminster Bank, 28 Market Place, Barnard Castle, Co Durham, DL12 8NB.*

VERNON, Michael Helm. b 33. G and C Coll Cam BA 56, MA 61. Clifton Th Coll 56. **d** 58 **p** 59 Man. C of St Clem Higher Openshaw 58-61; SAMS Miss Dio Argent 61-63; Chap of Hurlingham and Devoto 63-67; R of St Pet Flores Buenos Aires 67-69; C of St Geo Leeds 69-70; V of Skellingthorpe 70-76; R of St Pet Doddington 72-76; R of Marfleet 76-82; V of St John Newland Hull Dio York from 82. *St John's Vicarage, Newland, Hull, HU6 7PA.* (0482-43658)

VERNON, Reginald Joseph. b 08. Lon Coll Div 49. **d** 51 **p** 52 Ox. C of H Trin Aylesbury 51-54; Norbiton 54-59; V of Steeple Claydon w Calvert 59-71. *46 Blenheim Place, Aylesbury, HP21 8AQ.* (Aylesbury 84516)

VERNON, Robert Leslie. b 47. Sarum Wells Th Coll 73. **d** 76 **p** 77 Dur. C of St Luke Hartlepool Dio Dur from 76. *25 Tunstall Avenue, Hartlepool, Cleve, Ts26 8NF.*

VERNON, William Bradney. b 05. St Jo Coll Ox BA 28, MA 32. Wells Th Coll 28. **d** 29 **p** 30 B & W. C of St Jo Bapt Weston-s-Mare 29-33; St Jas Colchester 33-38; V of St Barn Woodford 38-44; Kilmersdon 44-51; R of Babington 44-51; RD of Midsomer Norton 46-51; V of St Phil and St Jas Ox 52-65; RD of Ox 59-65; R of Winterslow 65-70; L to Offic Dio B & W from 70; Dio Ex from 72. *Winterslow, Northmoor Road, Dulverton, Somt.*

VERRELLS, Canon Herbert Stuart. b 1900. Hatf Coll Dur BA 25. **d** 25 **p** 26 St E. C of Beccles 25-29; St Marg Ipswich 29-33; R of Ringsfield w Gt and L Redisham 33-70; C-in-c of Weston w Ellough 48-51; R 51-67; Hon Can of St E 59-70; Can (Emer) from 70; RD of Beccles 63-65. *9 Marsh Lane, Worlingham, Beccles, Suff.*

VERRYN, Canon Trevor David. Univ of S Afr BA 56. St Paul's Coll Grahmstn. **d** 57 **p** 58 Pret. C of Ch Ch and E Miss

Pietersburg 57-60; St Alb Cathl Pret 60-61; R of Waterburg and P-in-c of Waterburg Miss 61-66; C of Irene Dio Pret from 78. R of Pietersburg 66-69; Dir Ecumen Research Unit Pret 70-76; L to Offic Dio Pret from 70; Can of Pret from 72; Lect Univ of S Afr from 77; Sen Lect from 80. *PO Box 392, Pretoria, S Africa.*

VERSPAANDONK, Joseph Maria. Perry Hall Melb 65. **d** 65 **p** 66 Melb. C of Toorak 65-68; V of Emerald 68-75; R of Orbost 75-79; Rosedale Dio Gippsld from 79. *Rectory, Rosedale, Vic, Australia 3847.*

VESE, Felix Mark Ebago. d 69 Benin. d Dio Benin. *c/o Parsonage, PO Box 3, Oleh, via Ughelli, Nigeria.*

VESEY, Arthur Lawrence. b 05. RMA Woolwich Westcott Ho Cam 33. **d** 34 **p** 35 Portsm. C of St Mary Portsea 34-38; V of Alderbury 38-43; R of Wickham 43-50; S Brent 50-71; RD of Totnes 61-63; Perm to Offic Dio Ex 71-75; Dio Heref from 75. *Yew Tree House, Madley, Hereford, HR2 9JD.*

VESSEY, Peter Allan Beaumont. b 36. ALCD 65 (LTh from 74). **d** 64 **p** 65 Chelmsf. C of Rayleigh 64-67; H Trin Cam 67-71; V of St Aid Southcoates Drypool 71-80; Swanwick w Pentrich Dio Derby from 80. *Vicarage, Swanwick, Derbys.* (Leabrooks 60 2684)

VEVAR, Canon John Harvard. b 14. Univ of Wales BA 36. St Mich Coll Llan 37. **d** 38 Bp Wentworth-Sheilds for Ban **p** 40 Ban. C of Llanfechell w Bodewryd Rhosberio and Llanfflewin 38-42; Newtown w Llanllwchaiarn 42-46; P-in-c of Llanfairynghornwy w Llanrhwydrys 46-51; R of Mellteyrn w Botwnnog (w Llandygwnning and Llaniestyn from 55) Dio Ban from 51; P-in-c of Llandudwen 67-73; Surr From 70; Cursal Can of Ban Cathl from 78. *Botwnnog Rectory, Pwllheli, Gwyn, LL53 8PY.* (Botwnnog 663)

VEVE, Stephen. Maka Th Coll 36. **d** 38 **p** 41 Melan. P Dio Melan 38-75; Dio Centr Melan 75-76. *Suhu, Guadalcanal, Solomon Islands.*

VEVERS, Eric. Oak Hill Th Coll 54. **d** 56 **p** 57 Chelmsf. C of Dagenham 56-58; St Paul E Ham 58-60; V of Ch Ch Fulham 60-68; Ealing 68-78; All SS Sidmouth Dio Ex from 78. *All Saints' Vicarage, Sidmouth, Devon, EX10 8ES.* (Sidmouth 4116)

VEYSEY, John Norris. b 14. **d** 47 **p** 48 Cov. C of St Jo Bapt Cov 48-50; Chap Cov and Warws S for Deaf and Dumb 46-50; Somt (B & W from 75) Miss to Deaf from 50. *8 Richmond Place, Lansdown, Bath, BA2 4AL.* (0225 313965)

VICARS, David. b 22. Univ of Leeds BA 48. Coll of Resurr Mirfield 48. **d** 50 **p** 51 S'wark. C of St Paul Newington 50-54; St Luke Kingston-T 54-56; Cirencester w Watermoor 56-59; P-in-c of Seria Borneo 59-66; Area Sec USPG Dios Llan Mon St D and Swan B 67-77; R of Coychurch w Llangan and St Mary Hill Dio Llan from 77. *Coychurch Rectory, Bridgend, Glam, CF35 5HF.* (Bridgend 860785)

VICARY, Canon Douglas Reginald. b 16. Late Scho of Trin Coll Ox BA (1st cl Chem) 38, BSc 39, Dipl Th (w distinc) 40, MA 42, Wycl Hall Ox 39. **d** 40 **p** 41 Pet. C of Courteenhall 40-45; Asst Chap St Lawr Coll Ramsgate at Courteenhall 40-45; Chap Hertf Coll Ox 45-48; Tutor Wycl Hall Ox 45-47; Chap 47-48; L to Offic Dio Ox 45-48; Dir of Relig Educn Dio Roch 48-57; Publ Pr Dio Roch 48-52; Min Can of Roch Cathl 49-52; Can Res and Prec 52-57; Hon Can 57-75; Exam Chap to Bp of Roch from 50; Dir Post-Ordin Training 52-57; Hd Master K Sch Roch 57-75; Can Res and Prec of Wells Cathl from 75; Exam Chap to Bp of B & W from 75; Chap to HM the Queen from 77. *4 The Liberty, Wells, Somt., BA5 2SU.* (Wells 73188)

VICK, Canon Laurence John. b 18. BNC Ox BA 40, MA 45. Wycl Hall Ox 40. **d** 41 **p** 42 Roch. C of H Trin Penge 41-44; CF (EC) 44-47; C of Southborough 47-51; V of Felsted Dio Chelmsf from 51; RD of Braintree from 63; Hon Can of Chelmsf from 80. *Felsted Vicarage, Dunmow, Essex, CM6 3DQ.* (Gt Dunmow 820242)

VICK, Richard Arthur Edward. b 24. Univ Coll Ox BA 51, MA 55. Ridley Hall Cam 51. **d** 53 **p** 54 Chelmsf. C of St Mary Virg Loughton 53-55; Woolwich 55-58; St Mary Virg Plaistow Bromley 57-59; Putney (in c of St Jo Evang) 59-60; V of St Paul Westcliff-on-Sea 60-78; Publ Pr Dio Chelmsf from 78. *7 Brackendale Close, Hockley, Essex.*

VICK, Samuel Kenneth Lloyd. b 31. St D Coll Lamp BA 53. Linc Th Coll. **d** 55 **p** 56 St A. C of Shotton 55-56; Rhosddu 56-61; Knowle Bris 61-67; V of St Paul Eastthorpe Mirfield 67-78; Altofts Dio Wakef from 78. *Vicarage, Church Road, Altofts, Normanton, W Yorks, WF6 2QG.* (Wakef 892299)

VICKERMAN, John. b 42. Chich Th Coll 69. **d** 72 Pontefract for Wakef **p** 73 Wakef. C of Horbury 72-76; Elland 76-77; V of Glasshoughton Dio Wakef from 78. *Glasshoughton Vicarage, Castleford, WF10 4BW.* (Castleford 552018)

VICKERS, Allan Frederick. b 24. St Jo Coll Dur BA 50, Dipl Th 52. **d** 52 **p** 53 Lon. C of Gt Stanmore 52-57; Chap RAF 57-78; Asst Chap HM Pris Wandsworth 78-79; HM Pris Ford from 79. *4 Drake Grove, Burndell Road, Yapton, Arundel, BN18 0HX.* (Yapton 551454)

VICKERS, John David. d 62 **p** 63 BC. I of All SS View Royal w St Columba Strawberry Vale 62-67; R of St Phil Oak Bay 67-73. *701-831 Dunsmuir Road, Victoria, BC, Canada.*

VICKERS, Kenneth. St Chad's Coll Regina Testamur 49. **d** 49 Qu'App **p** 50 Edmon for Qu'App. I of Cabri 49-52; Rocanville 52-55; Craik 55-57; Wolseley 57-62; Assiniboia 62-68; St Barn Moose Jaw 68-71; I of Watrous 71-73; Russell 73-81. *Neepawa, Manit, Canada.*

VICKERS, Ven Michael Edwin. b 29. Worc Coll Ox BA and MA 56. Univ of Dur Dipl Th 59. **d** 59 **p** 60 Roch. C of Bexleyheath 59-62; Chap of Lee Abbey 62-67; V of St John Newland Hull 67-81; Area Dean in Hull RD 72-81; M Gen Syn Dio York from 75; Can of York from 81; Archd of E Riding from 81. *27 Molescroft Road, Beverley, HU17 7DX.* (Hull 881659)

VICKERS, Randolph. b 36. St Alb Ministerial Tr Scheme 77. **d** 80 St Alb. C of Hitchin Dio St Alb from 80. *4 Highbury Road, Hitchin, Herts, SG4 9RW.*

VICKERS, Roger. St D Coll Lamp 63. **d** 63 **p** 66 Mon. C of Abergavenny 65-67; P-in-c of Nantyglo 67-69; V (W Blaina 70-71) 69-74; St Teilo Newport Dio Mon from 74. *Vicarage, Ladyhill Road, Newport, Gwent, NPT 9RY.* (Newport 273593)

VICKERY, Charles William Bryan. b 38. Lich Th Coll. **d** 65 **p** 66 Chich. C of St Barn Hove 65-73; Chap Hostel of God Clapham Common 73-76; V of St Luke Kingston T Dio S'wark from 76. *4 Burton Road, Kingston Upon Thames, Surrey.* (01-546 4064)

VICKERY, David Christopher. b 23. Late Exhib of Jes Coll Ox BA (Th) 48, MA 49. St Steph Ho Ox 48. **d** 50 Asst Bp of Wales **p** 51 Llan. C of Newton Nottage 50-58; All SS St Marylebone 58-63; PC of St Pet w St Matt and w All SS Plymouth 63-68; V 68-78; Proc Conv Ex 65-70; V of Caldicot Dio Mon from 78; RD of Netherwent from 81. *Vicarage, Caldicot, Newport, Gwent, NP6 4HT.* (Caldicot 420221)

VICKERY, Ernest William. b 05. Kelham Th Coll 24. **d** 29 **p** 30 Liv. C of St Andr Wigan 29-32; Clee w Cleethorpes 32-33; St Luke Hornsey 33-36; Stoke-on-Trent (in c of St Barn) 36-40; V of Hanford 40-46; Longdon 46-81. *Address temp unknown*

VICKERY, Robin Francis. b 48. AKC 73. Univ of Lon BD 73. St Aug Coll Cant 73. **d** 74 **p** 75 S'wark. C of St Jo Evang Clapham 74-77; St Luke Reigate Dio S'wark from 78. *St Peter's House, Lynn Walk, Reigate, Surrey, RH2 7NZ.* (Reigate 45560)

VICKERY, Trevor Hopkin. b 17. Univ of Wales BA 39. St Mich Coll Llan 39. **d** 40 **p** 41 Ban. C of St Jas Ban 40-43; L to Offic Dio Ban 43-47; Chap HMS *Conway* 43-47; C of Heacham 47-48; Chap Cranbrook Sch and L to Offic Dio Cant 48-51; R of Staplehurst Dio Cant from 51; Chap HM Detention Centre Blantyre Ho Goudhurst from 54-80. *Staplehurst Rectory, Tonbridge, Kent.* (Staplehurst 891258)

VICTORIA NYANZA, Assistant Bishop of. (Vacant)

VICTORIA NYANZA, Lord Bishop of. *See* Rusibamayila, Right Rev John Oswald.

VIDAL-HALL, Roderic Mark. b 37. Univ of Sheff BSc (3rd cl Phys) 60. Lich Th Coll 62. **d** 64 **p** 65 Derby. C of Ilkeston 64-67; Nether w Over Seal 67-70; V of Chellaston Dio Derby from 70. *Chellaston Vicarage, Derby.* (Chellaston 701197)

VIDLER, Alexander Roper. b 1899. Late Exhib of Selw Coll Cam 20, BA (2nd cl Th Trip pt i) 21, MA 25, Norrisian Pri 33, BD 38. Univ of Edin DD 46. K Coll Cam Litt D 57. Univ of Tor Hon DD 61. Em Coll Sktn Hon DD 66. Wells Th Coll 21. **d** 22 **p** 23 Newc T. C of St Phil Newc T 22-24; St Aid Small Heath 25-31; M OGS from 27; on staff Oratory Ho Cam 31-38; Select Pr Univ of Cam 38, 40 and 59; Commiss New Guinea 36-63; Perm to Offic Dio St A 38-41; LPr 41-48; Warden of St Deiniol's Library Hawarden 39-48; Commiss N Rhod 41-48; Select Pr Univ of Ox 43-45; TCD 44 and 66; Hon Can of Derby 46-48; Can of Windsor 48-56; Ed *Theology* 39-64; Jt-Ed *The Frontier* 50-52; Birkbeck Lect in Eccles Hist Trin Coll Cam 52-53; Lady Marg Pr Cam 53; Fell and Dean of K Coll Cam 56-67; LPr of Univ of Cam from 57; Div Lect Univ of Cam 59-67; Sarum Lect Univ of Ox 68-69; Hon F K Coll Cam 72. *Friars of the Sack, Rye, Sussex, TN31 7HE.*

VIGAR, Charles Hatton. B 17. MRCS and LRCP 52, FDSRCS 62. Univ of Lon BD 77, MTh 80. **d** 66 **p** 67 Ches. C of Upton (or Overchurch) 66-69; Hon C of Reigate 69-77; V of Lower Nutfield 77-81; Perm to Offic Dio Chich from 81. *4 Upper Dukes Drive, Eastbourne, E Sussex, BN20 7XT.* (Eastbourne 26266)

VIGAR, Gilbert Leonard. b 12. Univ of Lon BD 46, BA (2nd cl Phil) 50, MA 53. Univ of Nottm MPhil 72; Kelham Th Coll 32. **d** 38 **p** 39 Sheff. C of St Cuthb Sheff 38-42; C-in-c of Herringthorpe 42-47; PC of Bradwell 47-52; V of Ault Hucknall 52-55; C-in-c of Heath 52-55; V of Winshill 55-57;

Madingley 57-61; Asst Dir of Relig Educn Dio Ely 57-61; Chap and Sen Lect in Div Dioc Teacher Tr Coll Linc 61-65; Hd of Relig Stud Bp Grosseteste Coll Linc 65-78; L to Offic Dio Linc 61-78; Pastoral Care of H Trin City and Dio Win from 78. *Rectory, Upper Brook Street, Winchester, Hants.* (Win 4133)

VIGARS, Anthony Roy. b 54. St Jo Coll Dur BA 75. Trin Coll Bris 77. **d** 78 Chelmsf **p** 79 Barking for Chelmsf. C of Barking 78-81; Littleover Dio Derby from 81. *4 Merridale Road, Littleover, Derby, DE3 7DJ.* (0332-766060)

VIGEON, Owen George. b 28. Peterho Cam 2nd cl Hist Trip pt i, 51, BA (2nd cl Hist Trip pt ii), 52, MA 57. Ely Th Coll 52. **d** 54 **p** 55 Carl. C of St Luke Barrow-F 54-58; Chap St John's Coll York 58-61; V of St Steph Burnley 61-69; Asst Dir of Educn Dio Blackb 69-73; V of Bilsborrow 69-73; St Thos St Annes-on-Sea Dio Blackb from 73; RD of Fylde from 80. *St Thomas's Vicarage, St Annes-on-Sea, Lancs.* (St Annes 723750)

VILAKAZI, Johann. b 39. St Bede's Coll Umtata 69. **d** 70 Bp Hallowes for Natal **p** 71 Natal. L to Offic Dio Natal 70-73; C of Kwa Mashu Durban 73-74; R of St Barn Estcourt Dio Natal from 74. *Rectory, Estcourt, Natal, S Africa.*

VILAKAZI, Canon Meshak Bhekinto. St Bede's Coll Umtata. **d** 61 **p** 62 Zulu. P Dio Zulu from 61; Can of Zulu from 79. *PO Box 79, Eshowe, Zululand.*

VILE, Canon Donald Arthur. b 15. Down Coll Cam 2nd cl Hist Trip pt i 36, BA (2nd cl Hist Trip pt ii) 37, MA 41. Cudd Coll 37. **d** 38 **p** 39 S'wark. C of Lewisham 38-40; C-in-c of St Jo Bapt Caversham 40-42; V of St Hilda Crofton Pk 42-49; St Geo Camberwell and Chap of St Giles's Hosp Camberwell 49-56; CF (TA) 55-67; V of St Jo Bapt Southend Lewisham 56-68; Caterham Valley 68-80; Hon Can of S'wark from 64. *1 Loxwood Close, Little Common, Bexhill-on-Sea, TN39 4LX.*

VILE, John Frederick. b 48. Univ of Wales (Cardiff) Dipl Th 74. St Mich AA Coll Llan 71. **d** 74 **p** 75 Llan. C of St German Roath 74-78; Newton Nottage 78-80; V of Landore Dio Swan B from 80. *Vicarage, Salem Road, Plasmarl, Swansea, SA6 8NN.*

VILJOEN, Christian Smuts. b 50. St Paul's Coll Grahmstn Dipl Th 76. **d** 76 **p** 77 Capetn. C of St Mary Stellenbosch 76-78; R of Worcester Dio Capetn from 78. *St James's Rectory, Waterloo Street, Worcester, CP, S Africa.* (Worc 3145)

VILLER, Allan George Frederick. b 38. E Anglian Min Tr Course 78. **d** Ely (NSM). C of St Mary City and Dio Ely from 81. *15 Church View, Witchford, Ely, Cambs, CB6 2HH*

VILLIERS, Tony. B 45. BD 69 (Lon). Univ of Bris MA 72. Univ of Lon MTH 80. Tyndale Lich Th Coll 59. **d** 62 **p** 63 Lich. C of Shifnal 62-65; St Paul Wednesbury 65-67; R of Llanymynech Dio Lich from 67; V of St Phil and St Jas Morton Dio Lich from 72. *Llanymynech Rectory, Pant, Oswestry, Shropshire, SY10 9RA.* (Llanymynech 830446)

VINCE, Edwin George. b 13. Univ of Leeds BA 36. Coll of Resurr Mirfield 36. **d** 39 **p** 40 Sarum. C of Wyke Regis 39-41; H Trin Taunton 41-43; Ho of Resurr Mirfield 43-45; C of St Marg Aber 45-66; St Aldate Glouc 67-74; Chap to the Commun of the Companions of Jesus the Good Shepherd W Ogwell 74-77. *The Grey House, Church Street, Chiseldon, Nr Swindon, Wilts.*

VINCE, Raymond Michael. b 45. BD 69 (Lon). Univ of Bris MA 72. Univ of Lon MTh 80. Tyndale Hall Bris 66. **d** 71 **p** 72 Portsm. C of St Jude Southsea Portsea 71-75; Chap N Lon Poly from 75; Hon C of Isl Dio Lon from 75. *123 Calabria Road, N5 1HS.* (01-226 4517)

VINCENT, Alfred James. b 30. Univ of Bris BA (2nd cl Th) 54. BD (Lon) 56. Tyndale Hall Bris 50. **d** 54 **p** 55 Lich. C of St Julian Shrewsbury 54-56; Camborne 56-59; V of Kenwyn w Tregavethan 59-68; Surr 65-68; Tutor Bps' Coll Cheshunt and L to Offic Dio St Alb 68; Lect Qu Coll Birm and L to Offic Dio Birm 68-70; Perm to Offic Dio Truro 68-70; V of St Osw Bordesley 70-76; S Shields Dio Dur from 76; Surr from 78. *72 Beach Road, South Shields, T & W, NE33 2QS.* (S Shields 561580)

VINCENT, Christopher Robin. b 30. Sarum Th Coll 57. **d** 60 Taunton for Cant **p** 61 B & W. C of Frome Selwood 60-64; V of Puxton w Hewish and Wick 64-70; Buckland Dinham w Elm (w Orchardleigh and Lullington from 71) 70-77; C-in-c of H Trin Frome Selwood Dio B & W from 77. *Holy Trinity Vicarage, Frome, Somt BA11 3BX* (Frome 62586)

VINCENT, David Cyril. b 37. Selw Coll Cam BA 60, MA 64. Coll of Resurr Mirfield, 60. **d** 62 **p** 63 Man. C of St Alb Cheetwood Man 62-65; St Mich AA Lawton Moor 65-67; V of St Mary Magd Wandsworth Common Dio S'wark from 67; RD of Tooting 75-80; Surr from 76. *291 Burntwood Lane, SW17 0AP.* (01-874 4804)

VINCENT, Edward Henry. Perry Hall Melb 65. **d** 67 **p** 68 Gippsld. C of Wonthaggi 67-68; V of Bruthen 68-72; Perm to Offic Dio Gippsld from 72. *c/o PO Beaconsfield, Vic., Australia 3807.* (059-44 3417)

VINCENT, George William Walter. ALCD 40. **d** 40 **p** 41 Lon. C of St Simon Hammersmith 40-44; Stowmarket 44-47; R of Earl Stonham 47-55; Alderton w Ramsholt (and Bawdsey from 61) Dio St E from 55. *Alderton Rectory, Woodbridge, Suff.*

VINCENT, Henry William Gordon. b 16. Univ of Leeds BA 42. Coll of Resurr Mirfield 42. **d** 44 Lon for B & W **p** 45 Taunton for B & W. C of St Jo Bapt Easton Bridgwater 44-46; H Redeem S Greenford 46-52; Teddington 52-55; V of St Kath N Hammersmith 55-64; St Aug Whitton 64-81. *21 West Mills Road, Dorchester, Dorset, DT1 1SR.*

VINCENT, Ian Humphrey. b 12. Ch Coll Cam 3rd cl Mod and Med Lang Trip pt i, 34, BA (3rd cl Th Trip pt i) 35, MA 43. Chich Th Coll 35. **d** 37 **p** 38 York. C of St Paul Sculcoates 37-39; St Aug Haggerston 39-41; RNVR 41-44; C of St Geo Wolverhampton 44-46; St Geo Grenada 46-49; R of St Patr and St D St Vincent 49-50; Bequia 51-54; St Andr Grenada 54-60; Can of St Geo Cathl Kingstown 58-66; R of Castries St Lucia 60-66; Archd of St Vincent and St Lucia 62-66; Chap St Mary's Conv Chiswick from 66. *St Mary's Convent, Burlington Lane, W4.* (01-994 4641)

VINCENT, Noel Thomas. b 36. Fitzw Ho Cam BA 60, MA 64. Ridley Hall Cam. **d** 63 **p** 64 Newc T. C of St Jas w St Basil Newc T 63-67; Prudhoe 67-70; V of Holbrook 70-74; C-in-c of L Eaton 73-74, P-in-c of Osmaston w Edlaston Dio Derby 74-78; Hon C from 78. *c/o Osmaston Vicarage, Ashbourne, Derbys, DE6 1LX.*

VINCENT, Canon Ronald John. St Jo Coll Morpeth. **d** 47 **p** 50 River. C of Hay 47-48; Leeton 48-51; C-in-c of Balranald 51-54; R 54-63; Producer and Dir Dioc Television Bath 63-75; Can of Bath from 69; R of Kelso Dio Bath from 75. *Rectory, Kelso, NSW, Australia 2795.* (31 3984)

VINCENT, Spencer William. **d** 52 **p** 53 Ch Ch. C of Sydenham 52-55; V of Southbridge 55-62; Lyttleton 62-65; Hon Chap Miss to Seamen 62-65; V of Waihao Downs 65-68; Hinds 68-69; C of Sumner-Heathcote 69; L to Offic Dio Ch Ch from 69. *14 Bayview Road, Christchurch 8, NZ.*

VINCENT, Canon William Alfred Leslie. b 11. Univ of Bris BA (2nd cl Hist) 33. St Edm Hall Ox BLitt 44, DPhil 68. **d** 39 **p** 40 Chelmsf. L to Offic Dio Mon 39-40; C of H Trin S Woodford 39-41; Asst Master R Wanstead Sch 35-41 (Asst Chap 39-41); St Edw Sch Ox 41-45; Perm to Offic Dio Ox 41-45; L to Offic Dio Mon from 42; Dio Ches from 52; Chap Ch Ch Ox and Hd Master Ch Ch Cathl Choir Sch 45-51; Chap and Lect Dioc Tr Coll Ches 51-64; Vice-Prin St Matthias Coll Bris 64-76; Can of Bris 74-77; Can (Emer) from 77; Perm to Offic Dio Sarum from 77. *Hunter's Moon, Tarrant Keyneston, Blandford Forum, Dorset.*

VINCENT, William Royce. St Jo Coll Winnipeg. **d** 67 Bp J O Anderson for Rupld **p** 68 Rupld. C of St Luke Winnipeg 68-71; I of Carman 71-74; St Bart Winnipeg Dio Rupld from 75. *881 Autumnwood Drive, Winnipeg, Manit., Canada.*

VINCER, Michael. b 41. Sarum Wells Th Coll 77. **d** 80 **p** 81 Ex. C of Littleham w Exmouth Dio Ex from 80. *5 Albion Hill, Exmouth, Devon, EX8 1JS.*

VINE, John. b 24. Keble Coll Ox BA (2nd cl Mod Hist) 45, MA 50. St Steph Ho Ox 45. **d** 48 Kens for Lon **p** 49 Lon. C of St Mary of Eton Hackney Wick 48-50; St Alb Holborn 50-53; Chap Ely Th Coll 53-56; Vice-Prin 56-60; Perm to Offic Ch Ch St Leonards Dio Chich 60-62; Chap Lich Th Coll 62-67; R of Wrington w Redhill 67-69; V of St Cuthb w St Matthias Kens Dio Lon from 69. *Clergy House, Philbeach Gardens, SW5.* (01-370 3263)

VINE, Michael Charles. B 51. Worc Coll Ox BA 73, MA 80. Cudd Coll 73. **d** 76 **p** 77 Newc T. C of St Luke Wallsend 76-79; H Spirit Denton 79-81; V of Sugley Dio Newc T from 81. *Sugley Vicarage, Sugley Villas, Lemington, Newcastle-upon-Tyne, NE15 8RD.* (Newc T 674633)

VINE, Michael Derek. b 35. Ch Ch Ox BA (Nat Sc) 58, MA 63. Ely Th Coll 58. **d** 60 **p** 61 Leic. C of Syston 60-63; S Ascot 63-66; Chap RN 66-70; Perm to Offic Dio Portsm from 71; Dio Lon from 74. *The Hall School, Crossfield Road, NW3 4NU.*

VINE, Michael Xavier. Ridley Coll Melb ACT ThL 59. **d** 60 **p** 61 Melb. C of Murrumbeena 60-62; P-in-c of Agenehambo 63-66; R of Goroka 66-68; V of Kingsville 69-72; R of Tallangatta 72-75; P Assoc of Warrnambool 75-76; Perm to Offic Dio Melb 76-78; C in Dept of Industr Miss Dio Melb from 78. *130 Como Parade, Mentone, Vic, Australia 3194.* (63 1837)

VINE, Neville Peter. b 54. AKC and BD 80. Linc Th Coll 80. **d** 81 Dur. C of Peterlee Dio Dur from 81. *33 Quantock Place, Peterlee, Co Durham, SR8 2LP.*

VINER, John Eckstein. b 11. Univ of Lon BSc 31. MICE 37. ALCD 48. **d** 48 **p** 49 Lon. C of All SS Queensbury 48-54; V of Branston 54-61; St Paul w St Barn Bris 61-75; Perm to

Offic Dio Bris from 76. *75 Malmesbury Road, Chippenham, Wilts.* (Chippenham 3656)

VINER, Canon Leonard Edwin. b 20. Univ Coll Dur LTh 41, BA 43. St Aug Coll Cant 38. **d** 43 Guildf **p** 44 Bp Golding-Bird for Guildf. C of St Pet W Molesey 43-45; Miss Likoma 46-52; Warden of St Andr Th Coll Likoma 52-56; and 58-60; C of St Andr Roxbourne Harrow 56-58; Chap St Mich Teacher Tr Coll Malindi 60-64; Warden St Andr Th Coll Mponda's 64-67; P-in-c Malindi 67-69; R of Zomba 69-71; Honing w Crostwight 71-75; Hon Can of S Malawi from 71; C-in-c (V from 73) of E Ruston 71-75; C-in-c (R from 73) of Witton and Ridlington 71-75; C of Epiph w St Jo Bapt Corby 75-79; V of Brigstock w Stanion Dio Pet from 79. *Vicarage, Brigstock, Kettering, Northants, NN14 3EX.* (Brigstock 371)

VINES, Hubert Harry. Em Coll Sktn 41. **d** 41 **p** 42 Bran. C of Kenville 41-42; I of Kenville 42; R of Bethany 46-49; R and RD of Virden and P-in-c of Kola 49-52; CF (Canad) 52-72; R of Barriefield w St Jas Pittsburg 72-75. *64 Carruthers Street, Kingston, Ont, Canada.* (613-544 7940)

VINEY, Brian Leslie. Ridley Coll Melb ACT ThL 58. **d** 58 Bal **p** 60 Tas. C of Beech Forest 58; Timboon 59-60; P-in-c of Tarraleah Miss Distr 60-63; Menindee 63-65; R of Derby 65-69; Mullewa 69-70; Sec Bush Ch Aid S and L to Offic Dio Perth 71-72; V of Hastings 72-78; I of Avondsale Heights 78-81; St John Footscray Dio Melb from 81. *Vicarage, Pickett Street, Footscray, Vic, Australia 3011.*

VINEY, Peter. b 43. **d** 76 Reading for Ox **p** 77 Buckingham for Ox (APM). C of High Wycombe Dio Ox from 76. *5 Avery Avenue, Downley, High Wycombe, Bucks, HP13 5UE.*

VINEY, Stafford Stanley. ACT ThL 28 Ridley Coll Melb 27. **d** 28 **p** 29 Bend. C of Moama w Turrumberry 28-30; St Paul Chatswood NSW 30-31; H Trin Erskineville NSW 31-32; P-in-c of Croajingolong 32-35; V of Raywood 35-38; Malmesbury 38-43; Emerald 43-48; I of St John W Brunswich 48-60; V of Springvale 60-72; Perm to Offic Dio Melb from 73. *8 Ahern Road, East Pakenham, Vic, Australia 3810.* (059-41 1961)

VIPOND, Canon John. b 17. Univ of Lon BD 48. ALCD 48. **d** 48 Lon **p** 49 Stepney for Lon. C of Ch Ch Roxeth 48-51; V 51-56; Chap Harrow Hosp 51-56; V of Pudsey 56-73; Exam Chap to Bp of Bradf from 66; Hon Can of Bradf 67-73; Can (Emer) from 73; V of St Austell Dio Truro from 73. *1 Carnsmerry Crescent, St Austell, Cornw.* (St Austell 3839)

VIRGIN, Alun John Morris. b 27. Late Scho of Ball Coll Ox BA 50, MA 57. Wycl Hall Ox 51. **d** 53 Chelmsf **p** 54 Birm. C of St Matthias Canning Town 53-54; Northfield 54-55; Acock's Green 55-56; Chap of Wellesbourne Sch 56-60; Perm to Offic Dio Birm 56-59; Publ Pr 59-60; Perm to Offic Dio Cov 58-60; V of Ingham w Cammeringham 60-71; R of Fillingham 60-71; Huntspill (w E Huntspill from 76) Dio B & W from 71; C-in-c of E Huntspill 76. *Rectory, Church Road, West Huntspill, Highbridge, Somt TA9 3RN.* (Burnham-on-Sea 783454)

VIRGO, Leslie Gordon. b 25. Linc Th Coll 56. **d** 58 **p** 59 S'wark. C of Hatcham Pk 58-61; Selsdon 61-65; Chap Warlingham Pk Hosp 65-73; Exam Chap to Bp of S'wark 69-74; R of Chelsfield Dio Roch from 74; Dioc Adv on Pastoral Care and Counselling Dio Roch from 74. *Rectory, Skibbs Lane, Chelsfield, Kent, RB6 7RH.* (Orpington 25749)

VIRTUE, Thomas James. b 32. QUB BA 56. TCD Div Test (2nd cl) 58. **d** 58 **p** 59 Connor. C of St Mich Belf 58-61; St Bart Belf 61-63; I of Tempo 63-66; R of Glynn 66-70; Team V of Ellesmere Port 70-74; Ches (Team Parish from 74) Dio Ches from 70. *St Oswald's Vicarage, Chester, CH1 4AG.* (Ches 371612)

VISSER, Pier Taeckele. St Paul's Grahmstn 68. **d** and **p** 69 Capetn. C of Durbanville 69-72; R of Turrontein 72-76. *PO Box 80, Mondeor, Transvaal, S Africa.* (011-59 1804)

VITNELL, Leslie George. Moore Th Coll Syd ACT ThL (2nd cl) 57. **d** 58 Syd **p** 59 Bp Hilliard for Syd. C of Lindfield 58; C-in-c of Harbord 59-63; Asquith w Mt Colah 63-69; R of Blackheath 69-72; Carlingford w N Rocks Dio Syd from 72. *9 Trigg Avenue, Carlingford, NSW, Australia 2118.* (871-6519)

VITTLE, Cyril Wilfrid. b 13. **d** 55 **p** 56 Bris. C of Bishopsworth 55-57; Henbury Glos 57-59; V of All SS Fishponds 59-69; St Cuthb Brislington 69-76; C of Thornbury 76-79; Chap Thornbury Hosp and Dep Chap HN Detention Centre Eastwood Pk from 79. *39 Hyde Avenue, Thornbury, Avon, BS12 1HZ* (Thornbury 415614)

VIVIAN, Adrian John. b 42. K Coll Lon and Warm BD and AKC 65. **d** 66 **p** 67 Roch. C of St Andr Bromley 66-69; Egg Buckland 69-73; Perm to Offic Dio Ex from 73. *22 Church Park Road, Torr, Yealmpton, Devon, PL8 2EY.*

VIVIAN, Thomas Keith. b 27. St Jo Coll Cam BA 48, MA 52. St Deiniol's Libr Hawarden 77. **d** 80 **p** 81 Heref (APM). Hdmaster Lucton Sch Leominster from 80. *Lucton School, Leominster, Herefs, HR6 9PL.*

VIZARD, Terence Robert. ACT ThL 30. **d** 32 **p** 33 Gippsld. C of Lang Lang 32-33; V 33-36; R of Leongatha 36-41; Belmont 41-50; V of Sunshine 50-56; Ascot Vale 56-65; Perm to Offic Dio Brisb from 65. *35 Olive Street, Hendra, Brisbane, Queensland, Australia 4011.* (268 2193)

VIZARD, William George. ACT ThL 25. **d** 24 Melb **p** 26 Bend. C of St Columb Hawthorn 24-26; Min-in-c of St Matt Long Gully 26-29; R of Milloo 29-32; C of Ch Ch Geelong 32-33; P-in-c of Tallangatta 33-34; V of St Mark Golden Sq 34-36; C of All SS Cathl Bend 36-37; V of Tongala 37-38; Min of Whittlesea 38-42; Drysdale w Portarlington 42-48; Melton 48-54; P-in-c of Maldon 54-56; LPr Dio Bend from 56. *30 Newstead Flat, Alexander Home, Castlemaine, Vic, Australia.*

VOAKE, Andrew James Frederick. b 28. Univ of Dur BA (3rd cl Th) 55. Oak Hill Th Coll 51. **d** 55 **p** 56 Lon. C of Uxbridge 55; St Matt Fulham 55-58; Bp Hannington Mem Ch Hove (in c of H 72-80; 58-61; V of St 77-80; Kirkdale 61-63; Chap Millfield Sch Street 63-71; V of Bp Latimer Mem Ch (w All SS and St Chrys 80. 73) Birm 71-80; Crondall and Ewshot Dio Guildf from 80. *Vicarage, Crondall, Farnham, Surrey, GU10 5RA* (Aldershot 850379)

✠ **VOCKLER, Right Rev John Charles.** b 24. Univ of Queensld BA (1st cl Hist) and Fulbright Scho 53. Gen Th Sem NY STB 54, STM 56, STD (*hon causa*) 61. ACT ThL 48, ThD (*jure dig*) 61. St Jo Coll Morpeth 48. **d** 48 Bath for Newc **p** 48 Newc. C of Ch Ch Cathl Newc 48-50; Vice-Warden St Jo Coll Brisb 50-52; Actg Vice-Warden and Lect in OT St Jo Coll Morpeth 53; Fell and Tutor Gen Th Sem NY 54-56; C of Singleton and Lect St Jo Coll Morpeth 56-59; Cons Bp Coadj of Adel (Bp of Mt Gambier) in St Pet Cathl Adel 30 Nov 59 by Bp of Adel; Bps of Newc; Willoch; and Bath; and Bp McKie; VG Dio Adel and Archd of Eyre Peninsula 59-62; Exam Chap to Bp of Adel 60-62; Elected Bp of Polyn 62; res 68; M SSF from 69; Perm to Offic Dio Sarum 69-72; Dio Lon 72-75; Hon Asst Bp of Worc 71-72; Asst Bp of Chelmsf 72-73; S'wark 73-75; Hon Can of S'wark 75; Can (Emer) from 75; Perm to Offic Dio Newc from 75; Dio Auckld from 76; Dio Brisb from 78; Hon Miss Chap Dio Brisb from 75; Guardian Brookfield Friary 75-77; Min Pacific Prov SSF from 76. *Box 96, Kenmore, Queensland, Australia 4069.* (Brisbane 5782160)

VODDEN, George Trevor. b 04. St D Coll Lamp BA 31. **d** 31 **p** 32 Llan. C of Pontlottyn 31-33; St Luke Canton Cardiff 33-36; Aberavon 36-41; C-in-c of St Bride's Minor 41-44; R 44-57; R of Cossington 57-70; C-in-c of Angersleigh 71-78. *4 Calway Road, Taunton, Somt.* (Taunton 82548)

VOGAN, Eric Lloyd. b 24. Univ of W Ont MSc 47. McGill Univ Montr PhD 52. **d** 75 Hur. d Dio Hur. *23 Gretna Green, London, Ont, Canada.*

VOGAN, George Douglas. Univ of W Ont BA 49, LTh 50. Hur Th Coll. **d** 50 **p** 51 Hur. I of Gorrie 50-53; La Salle 53-54; Thamesville 54-58; R of Leamington 58-62; St Matt Lon 62-67. *145 Windsor Crescent, London 17, Ont, Canada.*

VOGEL, Charles Edward. b 06. Trin Coll Ox BA 28, MA 31. Cudd Coll 64. **d** and **p** 65 Ox. C of L Missenden 65-69; C-in-c of Childrey 69-75; Sparsholt w Kingston Lisle 73-75. *Yew Tree Cottage, Kington Lisle, Wantage, Oxon.* (Uffington 270)

VOGEL, John Romaine. **d** 51 **p** 52 Johann. C of Springs 52-55; St Mary's Cathl Johann 55-59; R of All SS and Dir of St Paul's Miss Beaconsfield and Dir of De Beers Compounds Kimberley 59-61; Chap UDF Camp Wynberg Capetn 61-62 and 67-74; Prin Chap from 74; R of Voortrekkerhoogte 62-66; Perm to Offic Dio Pret 74-76. *420 Brink Drive, Military Base, Wynberg, CP, S Africa.*

VOGT, Robert Anthony. b 25. Jes Coll Cam BA 50, MA 54. SOC 60. **d** 63 **p** 64 S'wark. C of St Barn Sutton 63-67; Kidbrooke (in c of St Nich) 67-72; V of St Chad Cov 72-80; RD of Cov E 77-80; R of Kidbrooke Dio S'wark from 80. *Rectory, Kidbrooke Park Road, SE3 0DU.* (01-856 3438)

VOKES, Frederick Ercolo. b 10. Late Sizar and Scho of St Jo Coll Cam 1st cl Cl Trip 31, Naden Div Stud 32, BA (1st cl Th Trip) Carus Gr Test Pri and Jun Scholefield Pri 33, Geo Williams and Jeremie Hellenistic Pri 34, MA 46, BD 53. TCD MA 67. Westcott Ho Cam 33. **d** 34 **p** 35 Portsm. C of St Jas E Cowes 34-37; Asst Master Cranbrook Sch and LPr Dio Cant 37-42; Stamford Sch 42-43; K Edw VI Sch Retford 43-44; R of Thornhaugh w Wansford 44-47; Forncett St Mary w St Pet 47-55; Prof of Th and Hebr at St D Coll Lamp and LPr Dio St D 55-57; Abp King Prof of Div at TCD 57-80; Fell 74-80; Fell (Emer) from 80; Dean of Faculty of Arts 76-80 *97 Westbourne Road, Lancaster, LA1 5JY.*

VOKES, Robert Henderson. b 12. Oak Hill Th Coll 33. **d** 36 **p** 37 Man. C of St Geo Mart Daubhill 36-39; All SS Camberwell 39-40; V of St Paul Halliwell 40-47; Dunkeswell w Dunkeswell H Trin 47-54; Beckford w Ashton-under-Hill 54-62; R of Postwick 62-68; Chap St Andr Hosp Thorpe 62-68; RD of Blofield 65-68; Res Chap Pastures Hosp Mickleover 68-77; Perm to Offic Dio Derby from 77. *6 Heather Close, Somercotes, Derbys, DE55 1RU.* (Leabrooks 60 4061)

VOKES, William Alan. St Jo Coll Dur BA 55. **d** 56 **p** 57 Dur. C of All SS Stranton 56-58; CF from 58. *c/o Ministry of Defence, Lansdowne House, Berkeley Square, W1X 6AA.*

VOKES-DUDGEON, Preb Thomas Pierre. b 09. Univ of NZ BA 32. St Jo Coll Auckld 29. **d** 32 **p** 33 Auckld. C of St Thos Auckld 32-37; C of St Mich AA Woolwich 37-39; St Pet Vauxhall 39-46; CF (EC) 41-46; V of Ipplepen w Torbryan 46-51; St Marychurch 51-75; RD of Ipplepen 58-61; Proc Conv Ex 64-75; Preb of Ex 72-75; Preb (Emer) from 75; Perm to Offic Dio Ex from 75. *The Aster, Warren Road, Torquay, TQ2 5TR.*

VOLLER, David Albert. Ridley Coll Melb 55 ACT ThL 57. **d** 57 **p** 58 Adel. C of Kens 57-59; St Matt Groveley 59-62; C-in-c of Eidsvold w Mundubbera 62-63; C of St Andr S Brisb 63-64; Southport 64-68; V of Texas 68-74; C of Coorparoo Brisb 74-80; V of Ch Ch Imbil Dio Brisb from 80. *Box 2, Imbil, Queensld, Australia 4570.*

VOLLER, Henry. b 06. Wycl Hall Ox 50. **d** 52 **p** 53 Pet. C of St Andr Kettering 52-55; V of Long Buckby (w Brington from 60) 55-61; St Barn Wellingborough 61-68; Wingham (w Elmstone and Preston w Stourmouth from 74) 68-75; C-in-c of Elmstone w Preston-next-Wingham and Stourmouth 72-74; Chap St John Hosp Northgate Cant from 76. *40 Northgate, Canterbury, Kent, CT1 1BE.*

VOLLICK, Wilbert Edward Charles. Univ of W Ont BA 60. Hur Coll LTh 51. **d** 48 Moos **p** 49 Hur. I of Nakina 48-49; Ailsa Craig 49-52; R of Kincardine and Pine River 52-54; I of St Barn Lon Ont 54-57; R of Albion w Caledon 57-61; on leave 62; R of Lloydtown 62-67; P-in-c of Ch of Ap Tor 68-77. *RR1, Palgrave, Ont., Canada.*

VOLWANA, Daniel. b 35. **d** 80 St John's (APM). d Dio St John's. *PO Box 72, Engcobo, Transkei.*

VOMO, Theo. **d** 63 **p** 64 Bp Kahurananga for Centr Tang. P Dio Centr Tang 63-66; Dio W Tang from 66. *Gihwahuru, Box 13, Kasulu, Tanzania.*

VONBERG, Michael. b 27. Univ of Lon BA (3rd cl Engl) 51. Wells Th Coll 58. **d** 59 **p** 60 Win. C of St Andr Bournemouth 59-61; Milton (in c of St Pet Ashley) 61-64; V of St Geo Camberwell and Warden Trin Coll Cam Miss 64-74; V of Kenley Dio S'wark from 74. *3 Valley Road, Kenley, Surrey, CR2 5DJ.* (01-660 3263)

VOOGHT, Michael George Peter. b 38. St Pet Coll Ox BA (3rd cl Th) 61 MA 65. **d** 63 **p** 64 S'wark. C of St Jo Evang E Dulwich 63-66; Prestbury 66-72; R of Minchinhampton Dio Glouc from 72. *Minchinhampton Rectory, Stroud, Glos.* (Brimscombe 882289)

VOPNI, Roy Thomas. b 32. Wycl Coll Ont 74. **d** 74 **p** 75 Ont. I of Camden E Dio Ont from 74. *Vicarage, Camden East, Ont, Canada.* (613-378 6460)

VORLEY, Kenneth Arthur. b 27. Sarum Th Coll 65. **d** 67 Repton for Derby **p** 68 Derby. C of Ashbourne 67-71; R of W Hallam w Happerley 71-77; V of Hemingford Grey Dio Ely from 77. *Hemingford Grey Vicarage, Huntingdon, PE18 9BX.* (0480-67305)

VORSTER, John Peter Milton. b 22. **d** 77 **p** 78 Johann. C of Orchards 77-80; Bramley Dio Johann from 80. *24 - 13th Street, 2192, Orange Grove, S Africa.*

VOSS, Hugh Raymond. Moore Th Coll Syd. **d** 58 Bp Kerle for Syd **p** 58 Bp Hilliard for Syd. C of Katoomba 58-59; Belmore 59-61; C-in-c of Kembla W 61-64; SUM 64-66; R of Littleton 67-69; Balmain 69-77; Chap Parramatta Psychiatric Centre from 77. *1 Concord Road, Strathfield, NSW, Australia 2135.*

VOUSDEN, Alan Thomas. b 48. K Coll Lon BSc (Botany) 69. Univ of Birm Dipl Th 71. Qu Coll Birm 69. **d** 72 **p** 73 Roch. C of Orpington 72-76; Belvedere (in c of St Andr Bostall heath) 76-80; R of Cuxton and Halling Dio Roch from 80. *Cuxton Rectory, Rochester, Kent, ME2 1AF.* (Medway 77134)

VOUT, Victor Alan. b 25. BA (2nd cl Hist) Lon 53. Univ of Hull BA (1st cl Th) 56. Ripon Hall Ox 63. **d** 65 **p** 66 Sheff. C of Norton Lees 65-70; V of Clifton Dio Sheff from 70. *Clifton Vicarage, Rotherham, Yorks.* (Rotherham 63082)

VOWLES, Peter John Henry. b 25. Magd Coll Ox BA 50, MA 55. Westcott Ho 50. **d** 52 Birm **p** 53 Bp Linton for Cant. C of All SS King's Heath 52-56; Huddersfield 56-57; PC of Perry Beeches Dio Birm 57-64; V 64-72; R of Cottingham Dio York from 72. *Rectory, Hallgate, Cottingham, Hull, HU16 4AX* (Hull 847668)

VOYLE, Robert John. b 52. Univ of Auckld BEng 77. Melb Coll of Div BD 80. St Jo Coll Auckld. **d** 79 **p** 80 Waik. C of H Trin Fitzroy Dio Waik from 79. *21 Mangorei Road, New Plymouth, NZ.*

VOYSEY, Adrian Charles. St Cath S Ox BA 57, MA 61. Angl Th Coll BC LTh 54. **d** 54 New Westmr **p** 55 Ox for New Westmr. C of St Martin w All SS Ox 54-57; V of Deep Cove BC 57-59; C of Bicester 59-61; St Pet w St Hilda Leic 61-62; Headley 62-65; V of Ford 65-69; C-in-c of Alberbury 65-69; R of Fairview 69-70; on leave 70-72; R of Wadena 72-75; Exam Chap to Bp of Qu'App 72-80; Archd of Moose Mountain 74-80; I of Yorkton 75-80; St Mich Merritt Dio Carib from 80. *Box 1509, Merritt, BC, V0K 2B0, Canada.*

VUKI, Ratu Laione Qorere. St John's Th Coll Suva 63. **d** 66 Polyn **p** 68 Bp Halapua for Polyn. P Dio Polyn 66-74. *PO Box 29, Labasa, Fiji Islands.*

VUMBUCA, Noel Ellerton. St Aug Coll Maciene 63. **d** 66 **p** 68 Lebom. P Dio Lebom 66-79; Dio Niassa from 79. *Chiuanga, Lago, Niassa, Mozambique.*

VUN, Albert Cheong Fui. b 56. Sing Bible Coll BTh 81. **d** 81 Sabah. d Dio Sabah. *PO Box 17, Sandakan, Sabah, Malaysia.*

VUN, Robert Yee Hin. b 58. Sing Bible Coll BTh 81. **d** 81 Sabah. d Dio Sabah. *PO Box 279, Tawau, Sabah, Malaysia.*

VUN, William Yee Tshan. b 56. Sing Bible Coll Dipl Th 76. Ridley Coll Melb ThL 80. **d** 81 Sabah. d Dio Sabah. *PO Box 69, Kota Kinabalu, Sabah, Malaysia.*

VUNDLA, Jerome Tembenkosi. b 47. Univ of Zululand BA 71. St Pet Coll Alice CP Dipl Th 72. **d** 72 **p** 73 Natal. C of St Chad Klip River 72-78. *Box 228, Ladysmith, Natal, S Africa.*

VUNINGOMA, Meshach. **d** 54 **p** 55 Bp Brazier for Ugan. P Dio Ugan 54-60; Dio Rwanda B 60-65; Dio Ruw 65-80. *PO Box 1401, Kamwenge, Uganda.*

VYSE, Canon Jack Walter Miller. b 15. CCC Cam BA 37, Lightfoot Sch 39, MA 41. Westcott Ho Cam 38. **d** 39 **p** 40 Win. C of St Mary Southn 39-43; Clee w Cleethorpes 43-47; R of Gt Braxted 47-61; R of L Braxted 48-61; Exam Chap to Bp of Chelmsf 51-70; RD of Witham 55-61; V of St Mary Abchurch Lon 61-70; Asst Dir Cler Stud Dio Lon 61-70; Perm to Offic Dio Chelmsf 61-70; Sec of Gen Ord Examn 62-69; Vice-Prin SOC 66-70; V of Aylsham Dio Nor from 70; C-in-c of Alby w Thwaite 70-81; RD of Ingworth Dio Nor from 74; Hon Can of Nor Cathl from 81. *Vicarage, Aylsham, Norwich, NR11 6BY.* (Aylsham 2128)

VYVYAN, John Philip. b 28. New Coll Ox BA 51, MA 59. Cudd Coll 57. **d** 59 **p** 60 Lon. C of St Mark Notting Hill 59-61; SPG Borneo 61-64; V of Adderbury w Milton Dio Ox from 64. *Adderbury Vicarage, Banbury, Oxon, OX17 3EP* (Banbury 810309)

VYVYAN-JONES, Canon Frederick Charles. b 03. Univ of Wales 26. St Mich Coll Llan 26. **d** 27 **p** 28 Swan B. C of St Jude Swansea 27-30; St Ambrose Bris 30-31; Temple (or H Cross) Bris 31-35; R of St Mich-on-the-Mount without Bris 35-81; Hon Can of Bris from 80. *40 Seymour Avenue, Bishopston, Bristol, BS7 9HN.* (Bristol 427397)

W

WACHIRA, Gershom. Weithaga Bible Scho 60. **d** 61 **p** 62 Ft Hall. P Dio Mt Kenya 61-75; Dio Mt Kenya S from 75. *Box 70, Kagongo, Othaya, Kenya.*

WACIBIRA, Hociya Upio. Buwalasi Th Coll 58. **d** 60 **p** 61 N Ugan. P Dio N Ugan. *PO Box 42, Pakwach, Uganda.*

WACIBRA, Hosea. Buwalasi Th Coll 49. **d** 50 U Nile **p** 53 Bp Tomusange for U Nile. P Dio U Nile from 50. *Jonam, Uganda.*

WADDINGTON, Very Rev John Albert Henry. b 10. MBE 45. TD 50. Univ of Lon BCom 29. MA (Lambeth) 59. Lon Coll of Div 33. **d** 33 **p** 34 S'wark. C of St Andr L Streatham 33-35; St Paul Furzedown Streatham 35-38; CF (TA) from 35 (twice Men in Disp 44) R of Gt Bircham w Bircham Newton and Bircham Tofts 38-45; V of St Pet Mancroft Nor 45-58; Proc Conv Nor 50-59; Hon Can of Nor 51-59; Provost and V of St Jas Cathl Ch Bury St Edms 58-76; Provost (Emer) from 76; Proc Conv St E 59-70; Ch Comm 72-76; Perm to Offic Dio St E from 76. *Three Ways, Maypole Green, Bradfield St George, Bury St Edmunds, Suff.* (Sicklesmere 352)

WADDINGTON, Canon Reginald Guy Frushard. b 1888. TCD Downes Div Pri 11, BA 12, MA 15. **d** 12 **p** 13 Ripon. C of St Steph W Bowling Bradf 12-15; H Trin Idle 15-18; Kippax (in c of St Aid Gt Preston) 18-19; Org Sec CPAS for N Distr 19-21; V of Ch Ch (w St Thos from 35) Bradf 21-40; St John Idle 40-55; RD of Calverley 43-48; Hon Can of Bradf 50-70; V of Embsay w Eastby 55-58; Can (Emer) from 70. *6 Glen View, Harden, Bingley, W Yorks, BD16 1JE.* (Cullingworth 3985)

WADDINGTON, Canon Robert Murray. b 27. Selw Coll Cam BA (2nd cl Th Trip pt ii) 51. Ely Th Coll 51. **d** 53 **p** 54 Lon. C of St Jo Evang Bethnal Green 53-56; Chap Slade Sch

Warw and M of Bush Bro of St Paul Dio Brisb 56-59; C of St Luke Chesterton Dio Ely 59-61; Commiss Brisb 60-61; Hd Master St Barn Sch Ravenshoe and M of Bro of St Barn 61-71; Can Res of Carl Cathl and Bp's Adv for Educn 72-77; Hon Can from 77; Exam Chap to Bp of Carl from 77; Gen Sec NS from 77; Gen Sec Gen Syn Bd of Educn from 77. *Church House, SW1P 3NZ.* (01-222 1672)

WADDINGTON, Stanley Horton. **d** 61 Hur for Sktn **p** 62 Sktn. I of Raddison 61-67; R of St Mark 67-71; Yorkton 71-76; St Geo Prince Albert Dio Sask from 76. *1104 4th Street E, Prince Albert, Sask, Canada.*

WADDINGTON-FEATHER, John Joseph. b 33. Univ of Leeds BA 54. St Deiniol's Libr Hawarden 75. **d** 77 Bp Wood for Heref **p** 78 Heref. Hon C of Pontesbury Deanery Dio Heref from 77; Aux Chap HM Pris Shresbury from 77. *Fair View, Old Coppice, Lyth Bank, Shrewsbury, SY3 0BW.*

WADDLE, William. b 31. Linc Th Coll 64. **d** 66 **p** 67 Newc T. C of H Sav Priory Ch Tynemouth 66-69; Long Benton 69-75; V of Denton Newc T 75-81; Beadnell Dio Newc T from 81. *Beadnell Vicarage, Chathill, Northumb.* (Seahouses 223)

WADDLETON, Christopher Martindale. b 51. AKC 72. Univ of Lon BD 73. St Aug Coll Cant 73. **d** 74 Stepney for Lon **p** 75 Lon. C of St Barn w Hackney 74-77; Stockton Heath Dio Ches from 77. *25 Greenfields Avenue, Appleton, Warrington, Chesh.* (Warrington 601557)

WADDLETON, Edwin Henry. b 12. Men in Disp 46; Clifton Th Coll 37. **d** 39 **p** 40 Bris. C of St Phil and St Jacob Bris 39-42; CF (EC) 42-46; Hon CF 46; V of Bp Ryder Ch Birm 46-49; Tytherington 49-54; Chap HM Pris Falfield 51-54; Leyhill 51-53; V of Bishopsworth 54-65; R of St Paul Chippenham w Langley Burrell 65-77. *66 Sadlers Mead, Chippenham, Wilts.* (Chippenham 3721)

WADDY, Richard Patteson Stacy. b 04. Ball Coll Ox BA (3rd cl Engl Lit) 26, MA 30. Cudd Coll 26. **d** 27 **p** 28 Leic. C of St Pet Leic 27-30; SPG Miss Ahmadnagar 30-34; Chap St Thos Cathl Bom 34-37; Kirkee 38-42; Sen Pres Chap Bom 42-47; R of Ampthill 47-52; Commiss Bom 49-62; RD of Ampthill 51-52; Warden SPG Coll of Ascen Birm 52-59; Hon Can of Birm 54-59; R of Morley and Warden of Ch Ho Morley 59-67; Hon Can of Derby 63-67; Chap Qu Anne's Sch Caversham 67-72; Chap to the Community of All Hallows Ditchingham 72-79. *21 Cattistock Road, Maiden Newton, Dorchester, Dorset.* (0300 20778)

WADE, Anthony Austen. b 14. Univ of Leeds BA (2nd cl Gen) 36, MA 38. Coll of Resurr Mirfield 36. **d** 38 Lon **p** 39 Willesden for Lon. C of St Paul Ruislip Manor 38-45; V of Whitton 46-58; St Jo Evang Hendon 58-68; St Andr Sudbury 68-79; Perm to Offic Dio Bris from 80. *28 Claremont Road, Bishopston, Bristol, BS7 8DH.*

WADE, Arthur Claude. b 03. AKC 32. **d** 33 Stepney for Lon **p** 34 Lon. C of St Steph U Holloway 33-35; Welwyn (in c of Woolmer Green) 35-39; V of Edenhall w Langwathby 39-43; Pennington 43-51; Frizington 51-57; St Jo Evang Barrow-F 57-61; R of Aldingham 61-72; C-in-c of Bardsea 61-72. *Address temp unknown.*

WADE, Arthur Patrick. Moore Th Coll Syd 25. **d** 28 **p** 29 Syd. C of Five Dk 28-31; Enfield 31-34; C-in-c of Wentworthville 34-36; R of St Nich Coogee 36-65; L to Offic Dio Syd from 65. *55 Carr Street, Coogee, NSW, 2034, Australia.*

WADE, Canon Eustace Holland. b 01. Wadh Coll Ox BA 28, MA 29. Down Coll Cam BA (by incorp) 29, MA 31. Lon Coll of Div Wycl Hall Ox. **d** 28 **p** 29 Ely. Chap Down Coll Cam 28-34; Cam Past 31-34; V of Horningsea 30-34; Hildenborough 34-35; LPr Dio Ox Chap Ox Past and Wadh Coll Ox 35-38; Chap of Embassy Ch Paris 38-41; Metrop Sec CMS 41-42; V of H Trin Bournemouth 42-47; R of St Sav Claremont 47-51; V of St Paul Durban 51-60; Archd of Durban City 54-60; Durban 60-61; Can of Natal 54-61; Hon Can from 61; Commiss Natal from 61; N and C Eur from 68; Gen Sec United S for Christian Lit 61-71; Commiss Gibr 70-74. *Sharsted Court, Sittingbourne, Kent.* (Eastling 223)

WADE, John Martin. b 22. Wells Th Coll. **d** 54 **p** 55 St E. C of St Jo Bapt Felixstowe 54-57; C-in-c of All SS Conv Distr Bury St Edms 57-60; V of Nayland w Wissington 60-74; Chap Jane Walker Hosp Nayland 62-74; V of Shrivenham w Watchfield (and Bourton from 81) Dio Ox from 74. *Shrivenham Vicarage, Swindon, Wilts.* (Swindon 0793)

WADE, Very Rev Kenneth Ernest. b 14. K Coll Lon 37. Coll of Resurr Mirfield 40. **d** 41 **p** 42 Chelmsf. C of Chingford 41-47; Hd of Felsted Sch Miss and V of Ch of Ascen Vic Dks 47-64; C-in-c of St Matt Custom Ho Vic Dks 52-62; RD of W Ham 54-64; Dean and R of Bocking Dio Chelmsf from 64. *Bocking Deanery, Braintree, Essex.* (Braintree 24887)

WADE, Spencer. b 1888. Univ of Man BA 13, MA 34. **d** 13 **p** 14 Dur for Ex. C of Ellacombe 14-15; Barnard Castle 15-16; C-in-c of Bp Middleham 16-17; St Pet Bp Auckld 17-22; C of St Andr Monkwearmouth 22-24; V of St Matt Bolton 24-25; Lynesack 25-28; Gateshead Fell 28-31; R of Wark-on-Tyne 31-38; Whalton 38-46; Whickham 46-58; RD of Chester-le-Street 56-57; PC of Whorlton 59-70. *52 Galgate, Barnard Castle, Co Durham.* (Barnard Castle 3515)

WADE, Wakely Robert. Moore Th Coll Syd ACT ThL 52. **d** and **p** 53 Syd. C of St Luke Miranda 53; Wollongong 53-54; Corrimal 54-55; R of Mulgoa 55-58; Guildf 58-64; St Phil Auburn 64-69; Brighton-le-Sands 69-77; State Sec Bush Ch Aid S for NSW from 77-80; Federal Sec from 80; perm to Offic Dio Newc from 78; Dio C & Goulb from 79. *135 Bathurst Street, Sydney, Australia 2000.* (264-3164)

WADE, Walter. b 29. Oak Hill Th Coll 64. **d** 66 Penrith for Carl **p** 67 Carl. C of St Jas Denton-Holme Carl 66-69; V of H Trin War Mem Ch Jesmond Newc T 69-78; R of Moresby Dio Carl from 78. *Moresby Rectory, Whitehaven, Cumb.* (Whitehaven 3970)

WADE, Warren Laidley. St Francis Coll Brisb ACT ThL 64. **d** and **p** 61 Bath. C of Gilgandra 61-62; Bourke 62-63; R of Gulargambone 63-66; Peak Hill 66-73; Cudal 73-75; Perm to Offic Dio Syd from 75. *10/32 Frances Street, Lidcombe, NSW, Australia 2141.* (649-4476)

WADE, William Henry. b 07. ALCD 35. **d** 35 **p** 36 Liv. C of St Helens (in c of St Mary) 35-38; Speke 38-40; V 40-48; Childwall 48-69; Hon Can of Liv 65-69; RD of Childwall 66-68; R of Gt Oakley 69-75; V of Wix 69-75; C-in-c of Beaumont w Moze 69-75. *Address temp unknown.*

WADE-STUBBS (formerly STUBBS), Edward Pomery Flood. St Jo Coll Dur LTh 39, BA 40. Tyndale Hall Bris 36. **d** 40 **p** 41 Lich. C of St John Burslem 40-42; St Jas Handsworth 42-44; Hawkhurst 44-46; St Mark (in c of St Barn) Cheltm 51-53; R of Gt Witcombe w Bentham 53-62; Markdale Ont 62-63; Sutton Veny 63-66; V of Norton Bavant 63-66; *Address temp unknown.*

WADERO-NASIGE, Gibson William. Bp Usher-Wilson Coll Buwalasi. **d** 64 Mbale. d Dio Mbale. *PO Box 297, Mbale, Uganda.*

WADGE, Alan. b 46. Grey Coll Dur BA (2nd cl Th) 68. MA 72. St Chad Coll Dur Dipl Th 69. **d** 70 **p** 71 Dur. C of Cockerton 70-74; Whitworth w Spennymoor 74-75; P-in-c of Shipton Moyne and Westonbirt w Lasborough and Chap Westonbirt Sch 75-80; V of Drybrook Dio Glouc from 80. *Holy Trinity Vicarage, Drybrook, Glos, GL17 9JX.* (Drybrook 542232)

WADSWORTH, Michael Philip. b 43. Qu Coll Ox 1st cl Cl Mods 63, BA (2nd cl Lit Hum) 65, 2nd cl Or Stud 67, MA 68, DPhil 75. Univ of Cam PhD (by incorp) 78. Ripon Hall Ox 67. **d** 70 **p** 71 York. C of Sutton-in-Holderness 70-73; Lect Univ of Sussex 73-78; Hon C of St Jo Bapt Hove 75-78; Fell & Chap SS Coll Cam 78-81; Dir of Th Studies 79-81; CF (TAVR) from 80; C of Ditton (in c of St Thos) Dio Liv from 81. *22 Green Lane, Widnes, Cheshire, WA8 7HF.* (051 4206614)

WADSWORTH, Norman Charles. b 26. Bps' Coll Cheshunt 62. **d** 64 **p** 65 St Alb. C of Leighton Buzzard 64-69; C-in-c of Wing 69-73; St Mich AA Grove 69-73; Wingrave (w Rowsham Aston Abbots and Cublington from 74) 69-74; V of Wing w Grove 73-79; R of Didcot Dio Ox from 79. *Rectory, Lydalls Road, Didcot, Oxon.* (Didcot 813244)

WADSWORTH, Peter Richard. b 52. Qu Coll Ox BA 73, BA (Th) 76, MA 77. Cudd Coll 74. **d** 77 Buckingham for Ox **p** 78 Reading for Ox. C of High Wycombe 77-81; Farnham Royal w Hedgerley Dio Ox from 81. *St Mary's House, Rectory Close, Farnham Royal, Slough, SL2 3BG.* (Farnham Common 4293)

WAGADALA, Erukana. **d** 46 **p** 48 U Nile. P Dio U Nile 46-61; Dio Mbale 61-66. *Anglican Church, Mayuku, PO Box 297, Mbale, Uganda.*

WAGALANGA, Canon Bulasiyo. **d** 46 **p** 48 U Nile. Asst P Bolrugu 46-48; Kamuge 49-55; Bulutsekhe 55-61; P Dio Mbale from 61; Hon Can of Mbale from 69. *Church of Uganda, PO Box 984, Mbale, Uganda.*

WAGHORN, Geoffrey Brian. b 28. St Aid Coll 62. **d** 64 **p** 65 Roch. C of H Trin Twydall Gillingham 64-66; St Mary Cray w St Paul's Cray 66-68; Lenton 68-70; V of Messingham w E Butterwick 70-77; R of Fishtoft Dio Linc from 77. *Fishtoft Rectory, Boston, Lincs.* (Boston 63216)

WAGHORNE, Frederick Charles. b 07. St Jo Coll Dur BA 32, MA and Dipl Th 35. **d** 33 **p** 34 S'wark. C of St Geo Mart S'wark 33-37; All SS Tooting 38-41; V of St Mary of Nazareth W Wickham 41-63; Bearsted 63-73. *Townfield, Burleigh Road, Charing, Kent.*

WAGIDDO, Gideon William. **d** 64 **p** 65 Mbale. P Dio Mbale 64-81. *PO Box 473, Mbale, Uganda.*

WAGIRA, Moses. Buwalasi Th Coll. **d** 61 **p** 62 Mbale. P Dio Mbale 62-68. *PO Box 170, Tororo, Uganda.*

WAGLAND, John Frederick. **d** 44 Abp Owen for Montr **p** 45 Montr. C of Ch Ch Cathl Montr 44-46; St Columba Montr 46-52; R of Lucan w Clandeboye 52-56; St Martin-in-the-Fields Lon 56-61; Trin Ch St Thomas, Hur 61-72; St Paul w St Thos Nevis Dio Antig from 72; Exam Chap to Bp of Antig 74-80. *Box 193, Charlestown, Nevis, Antigua, W Indies.*

WAGNER, Charles William. b 49. Univ of St Mary Halifax NS BA 73, BEducn 73. Atlantic Sch of Th Halifax NS MDiv 77. **d** 76 NS. C of Lockeport Dio NS from 76. *Anglican Rectory, Lockeport, Shelburne Co, NS, Canada.*

WAGNER, Francis Henry. b 02. AKC 22. Hertf Coll Ox BA 26, MA 30. St Steph Ho Ox 26. **d** 26 **p** 27 S'wark. C of All SS Battersea Pk 26-29; Annunc Chislehurst 29-30; Weybridge 30-39; V of H Trin Newtown Bp's Stortford 39-56; Chap of Haymeads Inst 39-56; V of Ardeley 56-67; Perm to Offic Dio Ex from 67. *30 St Andrew's Road, Exmouth, Devon.* (Exmouth 72250)

WAGNER, James Albert Walter. **d** 66 Bp Elder for Guy. C of Wismar Dio Guy from 69. *St Aidan's Vicarage, Wismar, Demerara River, Guyana, S America.*

WAGNER, James Patrick. b 45. Univ of Calgary BA 71. Univ of Trin Coll Tor MDiv 76. **d** 77 Barb for Sask **p** 77 Sask. P-in-c of Kinistino w Meskanaw Dio Sask from 77. *Box 805, Kinistino, Sask, Canada.*

WAGNER, Peter Frederick. Univ of Lon BSc (2nd cl Chem) 56. Westcott Ho Cam. **d** 60 Birm **p** 61 Aston for Birm. C of Longbridge 60-64; V of Nechells 64-70; Warden St Barn Centre Dio Mashon from 72; L to Offic Dio Matab from 78; Exam Chap to Bp of Mashon from 80. *PO Box UA7, Salisbury, Zimbabwe.*

WAGNER, Wilfred Steadman. Em Coll Sktn 58. **d** 62 **p** 63 Athab. I of N Star 62-66; Chipewyan 66-70; L to Offic Dio Athab 70-72; R of Port Greville 72-76; Parrsboro 72-76; New Lon Dio NS from 76. *Box 68, Kensington, PEI, Canada.*

WAGSTAFF, Alan Robert Joseph. b 21. Univ of Lon Dipl Bibl and Relig Stud 69. SOC 67. **d** 70 **p** 71 Roch. C of St Barn Cray 70-76; V of Southborough Dio Roch from 76. *86 Prospect Road, Southborough, Tunbridge Wells, Kent, TN4 0EG.* (Tunbridge Wells 28534)

WAGSTAFF, Christopher John Harold. b 36. St D Coll Lamp BA 62, Dipl Th (w distinc) 63. **d** 63 **p** 64 Lon. C of All SS Queensbury 63-68; V of St Mich Tokyngton Wembley 68-73; Coleford w Staunton Dio Glouc from 73; RD of Forest South from 76. *40 Boxbush Road, Coleford, Glos, GL16 8DN.* (Dean 33379)

WAGSTAFF, Norman William. b 38. St Francis Coll Brisb 71. **d** 75 **p** 76 Rockptn. C of Park Ave Rockptn 75-77; P-in-c of Barcaldine Dio Rockptn from 77. *Box 50, Barcaldine, Queensland, Australia 4725.*

WAGSTAFF, Robert Hugh. b 22. Pemb Coll Ox BA 43, MA 47. Wycl Hall Ox 47. **d** 49 **p** 50 Liv. C of Burscough Bridge 49-52; C-in-c of St Nath Conv Distr Walton-on-the-Hill 52-57; V 57-58; St Mary Ince-in-Makerfield 58-75; Surr from 58; V of Glazebury Dio Liv from 75. *Glazebury Vicarage, Warrington, Ches, WA3 5LR.* (Culcheth 3163)

WAGSTAFF, Robert William. b 36. Edin Th Coll 61. **d** 63 **p** 64 Lon. C of Harringay 63-64; John Keble Ch Mill Hill 64-69; Perm to Offic Dio S'wark 76-81; Dio Worc from 81. *The Red House, Hartlebury, Worcs.* (Hartlebury 250883)

WAGSTAFFE, Eric Herbert. b 25. St Aid Coll 55. **d** 57 **p** 58 Man. C of Harpurhey 57-60; R 60-69; V of St Jo Evang Pendlebury Dio Man from 69. *St John's Vicarage, Pendlebury, Manchester.* (061-736 2176)

WAHOBO, Yeremiya. **d** 77 Nam. d Dio Nam. *c/o St Paul's Cathedral, Kampala, Uganda.*

WAI, George Fairly. **d** 79 New Hebr **p** 81 Vanuatu. P Dio New Hebr 79-80; Dio Vanuatu from 80. *Longana, Aoba, Vanuatu.*

WAIAPU, Lord Bishop of. *See* Matthews, Right Rev Ralph Vernon.

WAIAPU, Dean of. *See* Coles, Very Rev David John.

✠ **WAIARU, Right Rev Amos Stanley.** b 44. Bp Patterson Th Centre Kohimarama 69. **d** 72 Melan **p** 76 New Hebr. d Dio Melan 72-75; P Dio New Hebr 76-80; Chap Vureas High Sch Longana 77-80; Cons Ld Bp of Temotu at St Jas Naban, Santa Cruz 1 Jan 81 by Abp of Melan; Bps of Ysabel, Malaita and Vanuatu. *Bishop's House, Luejalo, Graciosa Bay, Eastern Outer Islands, Solomon Islands.*

WAIBALE, Ven Yokana. Bp Tucker Coll Mukono 33. **d** 35 **p** 37 Ugan P Dio Ugan 35-60; Dio Nam from 60; Can of Nam 62-65; Archd of Busoga 65-67; Jinja from 67. *PO Box 4013, bugembe, Uganda.*

WAIDA, Gideon Busira. Newton Coll 65. **d** and **p** 67 New Guinea. P Dio New Guinea 67-70; Dio Papua 71-77; Dio Aipo 77-79; Dio New Guinea Is from 79; VG Dio New Guinea Is from 80. *Box 198, Kimbe, Papua New Guinea.*

WAIGANA, Stanley Mark Giro. St Paul's Th Coll Moa I 58. **d** 63 **p** 64 Carp. Miss at Murray I 63-65; Saibai I 66-68; Yorke I 69-74; Darnley I Dio Carp from 74. *Darnley Island, via Thursday Island, Queensland, 4875, Australia.*

WAIGOLO, Sedulaki. Bp Tucker Coll Mukono. **d** 42 Ugan. d Dio Ugan 42-61; Dio Nam 61-64. *c/o Anglican Church, Vukula, PO Box 36, Kaliro, Uganda.*

WAIJUBA, Abusolomu. Bp Tucker Coll Mukono. **d** 56 Ugan **p** 58 Bp Balya for Ugan. P Dio Ugan 56-60; Dio Nam from 60. *Gadumire, PO Box 53, Kaliro, Uganda.*

WAIKATO, Lord Bishop of. *See* Davis, Right Rev Brian Newton.

WAIKATO, Assistant Bishop of. (Vacant)

WAIKATO, Dean of. *See* Dunningham, Very Rev Selwyn David Eden.

WAIMAGA, Boazi. Bp Tucker Coll Mukono. **d** 52 **p** 56 Ugan. P Dio Ugan 52-60; Dio Nam from 60. *Naminage, PO Box 4524, Bulopa, Uganda.*

WAIMI, Johnsford. **d** 71 New Guinea **p** 71 Papua. P Dio Papua from 71. *Anglican Church, Iaudari, via Ioma, Papua New Guinea.*

WAIMIRI, Samuel Wakagia. St Paul's Coll Limuru 69. **d** 71 Nak **p** 72 Bp Kuria for Nak. P Dio Nak. *Box 171, Molo, Kenya.*

WAIN, Frank. b 13. Univ of Leeds BA (2nd cl Lat) 35. Coll of Resurr Mirfield 35. **d** 37 Lich **p** 38 Stafford for Lich. C of H Cross Shrewsbury 37-39; St Andr Walsall 39-42; R of S Charlotte St Vincent BWI 42-48; P-in-c of St Paul Grenada 48-49; C of Rushall 49-51; Edgmond 51-53; Min of St Francis Eccles Distr N Radford 53-55; R of Kinwarton w Gr Alne and Haselor Dio Cov from 55. *Kinwarton Rectory, Great Alne, Alcester, Warw.*

WAIN, Frank Lonsdale. b 1900. Late Scho and Exhib of St Jo Coll Cam 2nd cl Nat Sc Trip pt i 21, BA (2nd cl Th Trip pt i) 22, MA 26. Cudd Coll 22. M SSJE 34. **d** 23 **p** 24 York. C of S Bank 23-29; All SS Middlesbrough 29-31; Miss P (SSJE) Mazagon Bom 34-37; Poona 37-67; Exam Chap to Bp of Bom 41-67; Archd of Poona 53-65; Perm to Offic Dio Leic from 80. *St John's House, 2 Woodland Avenue, Leicester, LE2 3HG.*

WAIN, John. b 15. Qu Coll Birm 57. **d** 58 **p** 59 York. C of Newland 58-62; V of Carnaby 62-75; Bessingby 62-75; Nafferton w Wansford Dio York from 75. *Nafferton Vicarage, Driffield, E Yorks, YO25 0JS.* (Driffield 84372)

WAIN, Norman. b 25. Univ of Bris BA (Th) 54. Tyndale Hall Bris 49. **d** 54 **p** 55 Ches. C of All SS Marple 54-58; St Thos Blackpool 58-59; V of Lower Darwen 59-65; C-in-c of Mascot Sydney 65-68; V of Tunstead 69-78; Ch Ch Pennington Dio Man from 78. *Vicarage, Pennington, Leigh, Lancs.* (Leigh 73619)

✠ **WAINE, Right Rev John.** b 30. Univ of Man BA (Th) 51. Ridley Hall Cam 53. **d** 55 **p** 56 Liv. C of W Derby 55-58; Sutton (in c of All SS) 58-60; V of Ditton 60-64; H Trin Southport 64-69; Kirkby 69-71; R 71-75; Cons Ld Bp Suffr of Stafford in St Paul's Cathl 24 June 75 by Abp of Cant; Bps of Lon, Lich, Derby, Nor, Chelmsf and Birm; Bps Suffr of Stepney, Kens, Willesden, Fulham & Gibr, Bradwell, Colchester, Shrewsbury, Warrington and Dudley; and others; Trld to St E 78; Hon Can of Lich Cathl 75-78. *Bishop's House, 4 Park Road, Ipswich, Suff, IP1 3ST.* (Ipswich 52829)

WAINWRIGHT, Alfred David. b 32. wycl Coll Tor LTh 78. **d** and **p** 78 Tor. C of Cavan & Manvers Dio Tor from 78. *The Rectory, Bethany, Ont, Canada.*

WAINWRIGHT, Barrington Herbert. b 09. St Cath Coll Cam 3rd cl Hist Trip pt i 30, BA (3rd cl Th Trip pt i) 31, MA 35. Men in Disp 45. Wycl Hall Ox 31. **d** 33 **p** 34 Ches. C of Bebington 33-35; Perm to Offic at Stoke-next-Guildf 35-36; C of St Mary Weymouth 36-37; St Mary Harrogate 38-40; Offg C-in-c of Em Leeds 40-41; CF (EC) 41-46; V of St Steph-by-Saltash 46-53; St Austell 53-65; RD of St Austell 61-65; V of St Mark Hamilton Terrace St John's Wood 65-79. *98 Bargates, Leominster, H & W.*

WAINWRIGHT, David Bernard Pictor. b 25. St Jo Coll Dur BA 50, MA 53. Chich Th Coll 50. **d** 51 **p** 52 Worc. C of St Geo Redditch 51-53; Aveley 53-55; C-in-c of All SS Conv Distr Belhus Pk 55-56; V of St Mary Magd Harlow 56-61; Dioc Adviser for Social Responsibility Dio Ripon 62-69; Lect St Jo Evang Leeds 65-69; V of Scouthead 69-72; Sen Social Worker Bd for Soc Resp Man 69-73; LPr Dio Man 72-73; Asst Sec Gen Syn Bd for Social Responsibility and Sec for Social Work and Services 74-78; Dep Sec 78-79; Dioc Officer for Social Responsibility and P-in-c of Charlton-on-Otmoor w Oddington Dio Ox from 79. *Charlton-on-Otmoor Rectory, Oxford, OX5 2UG.*

WAINWRIGHT, Frank Alan. b.18. Univ of Leeds BA 39. Coll of Resurr Mirfield 39. **d** 41 **p** 42 Glouc. C of St Paul Glouc 41-46; St Geo Perry Hill Catford 46-47; V 47-57; V of St Faith N Dulwich 57-64; Chap Maudsley Hosp 60-62; St Gabr Tr Coll Camberwell 62-64; V of Woodham 64-72. *Roydon, Pendoggett, St Kew, Bodmin Cornwall, PL30 3HH.* (Port Isaac 528)

WAINWRIGHT, Graham Leslie. **d** 63 **p** 64 Syd. C of Campbelltown 63-65; Randwick 66-68; C-in-c of Rooty Hill

Provisional Distr 68-69; C of Wyalong 69-70; R of Dunedoo 71-76; Gilgandra Dio Bath from 76. *Rectory, Gilgandra, NSW, Australia 2827.* (068-4716 64)

WAINWRIGHT, Ven Hastings Burnaby. K Coll NS BA 39, LTh 39. **d** 37 **p** 39 NS. C-in-c of Falkland 37-41; Chap CASF 41-46; R of Granville 46-49; Bedford 49-53; St Geo Syd 53-59; Ch Ch Windsor 59-63; Hon Can of NS 61-68; Can of All SS Cathl Halifax 68-70; R of St Phil Halifax 63-72; Archd of Halifax and E Shore 70-74; Archd (Emer) from 74; R of Falkland 72-77. *6847 Quinpool Road, Halifax, NS, Canada.*

WAINWRIGHT, John Pounsberry. b 42. St Steph Ho Ox 64. **d** 66 Lon **p** 67 Willesden for Lon. C of St Jo Evang Palmers Green 66-70; St Mary Virg Primrose Hill 70-71; C-in-c of All SS St John's Wood 71-73; V of All SS Childs Hill Dio Lon from 73. *Vicarage, Church Walk, NW2 2TJ.* (01-435 3182)

WAINWRIGHT, Joseph Allan. b 21. Univ of Lon BD (1st cl) 50. AKC (1st cl) 50. St Bonif Coll Warm 50. **d** 50 **p** 51 Linc. C of Boston 50-53; Chap and Lect to St Paul's and St Mary's Colls Cheltm 53-62; Perm to Offic Dio Linc 54-62; Educn Sec British Coun of Chs 62-66; L to Offic Dio Lon 62-66; Perm to Offic Dio Edin 66-79; Dio Chich from 79; Lect Moray Ho Coll of Educn Edin 66-78; Chap Southover Manor Sch Lewes 80-81. *Beggars Roost, Southway, Lewes, E Sussex, BN7 1LX.* (Lewes 77453)

WAINWRIGHT, Kennedy Barr. K Coll NS BA 34. **d** 33 **p** 34 NS. C of Baddeck 33; Conquerall 33-47; R of Aylesford and Berwick 47-54; Stewiacke 54-63; Seaforth 63-73. *St Stephen's New Vicarage, Kearsley Moor, Bolton, Lancs, BL4 8QP* (Farnworth 72535)

WAINWRIGHT, Kevin Frank. b 46. Linc Th Coll 72. **d** 75 **p** 76 Man. C of Stand 75-78; St Thos & St John Radcliffe 78-80; V of Kearsley Moor Dio Man from 80. *St Stephen's Vicarage, Kearsley Moor, Bolton, Lancs, BL4 8QP.* (Farnworth 72535)

WAINWRIGHT, Maurice Sidney. BSc (Econ) 2nd cl (Lon) 54. Bps' Coll Cheshunt 54. **d** 56 **p** 57 Lon. C of Twickenham 56-59; Caversham 59-61; LPr Dio Chelmsf from 61; Dep Warden Woodford Youth Centre 61-66; Lect East Ham Tech Coll from 66. *60 Eastwood Road, E18.* (01-989 1529)

WAINWRIGHT, Peter Anthony. b 45. K Coll Lon BD 73. ARICS 67. Ridley Hall Cam 73. **d** 75 **p** 76 Guildf. C of Ashtead 75-79; V of St Paul Woking Dio Guildf from 79. *St Paul's Vicarage, Pembroke Road, Woking, Surrey, GU22 7ED.* (Woking 72081)

WAINWRIGHT, Raymond Laycock. b 25. BD (Lon) 60. **d** 56 **p** 57 Bradf. C of All SS Bingley 56-58; Almondbury 58-60; V of Gawthorpe and Chickenley Heath 60-74; New Mill Dio Wakef from 74; Thurstonland Dio Wakef from 74. *New Mill Vicarage, Huddersfield, Yorks, HD7 7YE.* (Holmfirth 3375)

WAIPIRA, Dudley. b 51. Bp Patteson Th Centre Kohimarama 70. **d** 73 **p** 74 Melan. P Dio Melan 73-75; Centr Melan from 75. *Star Harbour, San Cristoval, Solomon Islands.*

WAISWA, Enoka. Bp Tucker Coll Mukono. **d** 56 Ugan **p** 58 Bp Balya for Ugan. P Dio Ugan 56-61; Dio Nam from 61; Can of St Paul's Cathl Kampala 63-76. *c/o Box 14297, Kampala, Uganda.*

WAIT, Alan Clifford. b 33. St Cath S Ox BA (2nd cl Geog) 58, MA 70. Coll of Resurr Mirfield. **d** 60 **p** 61 S'wark. C of Old Charlton 60-67; Caterham 67-72; V of St Faith N Dulwich S'wark from 72; RD of Dulwich from 78. *Vicarage, Red Post Hill, SE24.* (01-274 1338)

WAITE, Harry. b 21. Linc Th Coll. **d** 55 Linc **p** 56 Grimsby for Cant. C of Gainsborough 55-58; V of Dunholme 59-64; Youth Chap Dio Linc 58-69; Dio Pet from 69. *90 Harlestone Road, Northampton, NN5 7AG.*

WAITE, John Langton. b 10. Univ of Man 30. Wycl Hall Ox 37. ACP 37. **d** 39 **p** 40 Chich. [f Solicitor]. C of Bp Hannington Mem Ch Distr Hove 39-41; Walcot Bath 41-42; V of St Jo Evang Blackheath 42-48; St Geo w St Phil and of St Andr Leeds 48-58; V of St Jo Bapt Woking 58-76. *11 The Cresent, Alverstoke, Gosport, Hants, PO12 2DH.* (Gosport 21458)

WAITE, Julian Henry. b 47. Ridley Hall Cam 70. **d** 72 **p** 73 Southw. C of Wollaton 72-75; Herne Bay 75-79; P-in-c of Mersham Dio Cant from 79; Sevington Dio Cant from 79; Pastoral Care of Hinxhill Dio Cant from 79. *Rectory, Mersham, Ashford, Kent.* (Ashford 24138)

WAKABI, Erisa. Bp Tucker Coll Mukono 68. **d** 68 **p** 69 Nam. P Dio Nam. *Bishop Willis College, PO Box 150, Iganga, Uganda.*

WAKANYASI, Silvester. Buwalasi Th Coll 62. **d** 64 **p** 65 Mbale. P Dio Mbale from 65. *PO Box 1228, Mbale, Uganda.*

WAKE, Colin Walter. b 50. Oriel Coll Ox BA 72. Cudd Coll 74. **d** 75 **p** 76 Reading for Ox. C of Sandhurst 76-79; Faversham 79-80; Team V of High Wycombe Dio Ox from 80. *St Peter's House, Micklefield Road, High Wycombe, Bucks.* (High Wycombe 31141)

WAKE, Hugh. b 16. St Aug Coll Cant. **d** 62 **p** 63 St E. C of St Greg w St Pet Sudbury 62-67; R of Stanningfield w Bradfield Combust 67-74; V of Gt Finborough (w Onehouse and Harleston from 76) Dio St E from 74; R of Onehouse w Harleston 74-76. *Finborough Vicarage, Stowmarket, Suff.* (Stowmarket 3240)

WAKEFIELD, Lord Bishop of. *See* James, Right Rev Colin Clement Walter.

WAKEFIELD, Assistant Bishops of. *See* Wheeldon, Right Rev Philip William; and Cragg, Right Rev Albert Kenneth; and Harris, Right Rev Patrick Burnet.

WAKEFIELD, Provost of. *See* Lister, Very Rev John Field.

WAKEFIELD, Allan. b 31. Qu Coll Birm 72. **d** 74 **p** 75 Pet. C of Kingsthorpe 74-77; Team V of St Francis Clifton 77-81; V of St Jo Bapt Bilborough Dio Southw from 81. *Vicarage, Graylands Road, Bilborough, Nottingham, NG8 4FD.* (Nottm 293320)

WAKEFIELD, Andrew Desmond. b 55. AKC and BD 77. Coll of the Resurr Mirfield 77. **d** 78 **p** 79 S'wark. C of Ascen Mitcham 78-81; St Mary's w All SS Putney Dio S'wark from 81. *54 Clarendon Drive, SW15 1AM.* (01-789 6806)

WAKEFIELD, Canon Kenneth Eyles. b 25. St Jo Coll Dur BA 50, MA 56. Dipl Th 51. **d** 51 **p** 52 S'wark. C of H Trin Redhill 51-54; Attenborough w Bramcote 54-56; V of St Edw Leyton 56-59; Walton Dio St E from 59; RD of Colneys from 72; Hon Can of St E Cathl from 75; Surr from 76. *Walton Vicarage, Felixstowe, Suff.* (Felixstowe 4803)

WAKEFIELD, Peter. b 48. Univ of Nottm BTh and ALCD 72. St Jo Coll Nottm 68. **d** 72 **p** 73 Leic. C of H Trin Hinckley 72-75; Kirby Muxloe 75-78; V of Barlestone Dio Leic from 78. *Barlestone Vicarage, Nuneaton, Warws, CV13 0EP.* (Mkt Bosworth 290249)

WAKEFORD, Victor David. Ex Coll Ox BA 37, MA 41. Ripon Hall Ox 41. **d** 46 **p** 47 York. C of Scarborough 46-50; Chap to Oakham Sch 51-54; Chap and Sen Master Eshton Hall Sch Gargrave 54-58; Chap and Asst Master K Sch Glouc 58-71; Hon Min Can of Glouc 61-71. *Weavers Cottage, Waldron, Sussex, TN21 0NJ*

WAKELIN, Alan Frank. Late Scho of St D Coll Lamp BA (2nd cl Hist) 58. Coll of Resurr Mirfield 58. **d** 60 **p** 61 Pet. C of St Matt Northn 60-63; All SS Pet 63-65; Spalding 65-68; R of Skirbeck Dio Linc from 68. *Skirbeck Rectory, Boston, Lincs.*

WAKELING, Alexander Irwin. Sir Geo Williams Univ Montr BA 57. **d** 58 **p** 59 Ont. C of St John Kingston 58-60; I of Ameliasburg 60-62; L to Offic Dio Calg 62-65; CF (Canad) 62-65; R of St Laur Calg 65-67; CF (Canad) from 67. *CFB Esquimalt, Workpoint Barracks, Victoria, BC, Canada.*

WAKELING, Bruce. b 50. Univ of Lon BA 74. Westcott Ho Cam 74. **d** 77 Sarum **p** 78 Bp Tiarks for Sarum. C of H Trin Weymouth Dio Sarum from 77. *151 Chickerell Road, Weymouth, Dorset, DT4 0BP.*

WAKELING, Hugh Michael. b 42. Univ of Capetn BSc (Chem Eng) 63. Wycl Hall Ox 71. **d** 74 **p** 75 S'wark. C of St Mark Kennington 74-78; Surbiton Hill (in c of Em Tolworth) 78-80; Hon C of H Trin & Ch Ch Richmond Dio S'wark from 80. *12 St Mary's Grove, Richmond, Surrey, TW9 1UY.* (01-940 3442)

✠ **WAKELING, Right Rev John Denis.** b 18. MC 45. St Cath Coll Cam BA 40, MA 44. Ridley Hall Cam 46. **d** 47 **p** 48 Leic. C of Barwell w Stapleton and Potters Marston 47-50; Chap of Clare Coll Cam Chap of Cam Past and L to Offic Dio Ely 50-52; PC of Em Plymouth 52-59; Proc Conv Ex 56-59; Preb of Ex Cathl 57-59; Preb (Emer) from 59; V of Barking 59-65; C-in-c of St Patr Barking 60-65; Archd of W Ham 65-70; Cons Ld Bp of Southw in York Minster 29 Sept 70 by Abp of York; Bps of Ches; Blackb; Liv; Carl; Wakef; Win; and S & M; Bps Suffr of Knaresborough; Sherwood; Stockport; Pontefract; Barking; Bradwell; and Grantham; and Bps Way, Cockin, Betts, and T G S Smith; Chairman Abp's Coun for Evang 76-78. *Bishop's Manor, Southwell, Notts.* (Southwell 812112)

WAKELING, Ven Ronald. b 20. **d** 71 **p** 72 Johann. C of Linden 71-77; R of Sabie w Lydenburg Dio Pret from 77; Archd of Lowveld from 81. *Box 71, Sabie, Transvaal, S Africa.*

WAKELING, Stanley George. b 11. St Cath Coll Cam BA 35, MA 39. Wycl Hall Ox 35. **d** 37 **p** 38 Leic. C of H Ap Leic 37-39; H Trin Leic 39-42; Org Sec CMS for Midl Area 42-44; Publ Pr Dio Birm 42-44; V of St Francis Dudley 44-48; C of St John Wynberg 48-50; R 50-69; Hon Can of Capetn 61-69; V of Tulse Hill 69-73; S Nutfield 73-77; RD of Streatham 72-73; Hon C of Nether Stowey 77-80. *19 Stringers Drive, Rodborough, Stroud, Glos, GL5 3RA.*

WAKELY, John Edward Victor. b 14. QUB BA 34, TCD Div Test (1st cl) and Bibl Gr Pri (2nd) 37. **d** 37 **p** 38 Down. C of St Clem Belf 37-39; St Jude Ballynafeigh 39-42; I of All SS w Burt 42-46; Tullyaughnish and Milford 46-49; Drumragh and C-in-c of Mountfield 49-80; Can of St Columb's Cathl Derry 56-80; Preb of St Patr Cathl Dub 70-80; R of Ch Ch City and Dio Grahmstn from 80. *4 Grant Street, Grahamstown 6140, CP, S Africa.*

WAKELY, Roger. b 42. SOC 67. **d** 70 **p** 71 Willesden for Lon. C of Ealing 70-76; Chap Bp Wand's Sch Sunbury-on-Thames from 77. *49 Ashurst Drive, Shepperton, Surrey.*

WAKER, Anthony Francis. b 30. St Chad's Coll Dur BA (3rd cl Th) 56, Dipl Th 57. **d** 57 **p** 58 Ox. C of Stokenchurch 57-60; St Mich AA Summertown Ox 60-65; R of Iron Acton Dio Bris from 65. *Iron Acton Rectory, Bristol.* (Rangeworthy 412)

WAKER, William Joseph. b 1896. St Jo Coll Ox BA (*sc* Hist) 21, 2nd cl Th 23, MA 28. St Steph Ho Ox 21. **d** 23 **p** 24 Lon. C of St Andr W Kensington 23-25; St Mellitus Hanwell 25-32; Org Dir ICF for SE Area 32-39; PC of St Jo Bapt Stockton-on-Tees 39-56; R of Lillingstone Dayrell w Lillingstone Lovell 56-70; RD of Buckingham 63-70; L to Offic Dio Glouc from 70. *49 Shaw Green Lane, Prestbury, Cheltenham, GL52 3BS.*

WAKHONDOLA, Canon Yekoyada. CMS Tr Coll Buwalasi 38. **d** 39 **p** 41 U Nile. P Dio U Nile 39-61; Dio Mbale 61-69; Hon Can of Mbale 61-69. *[illegible], PO Box 984, Mbale, Uganda.*

WAKIBI, Enaka. Bp Tucker Coll. **d** 53 **p** 57 Ugan. P Dio Ugan 53-61; Dio Nam from 61. *PO Box 10, Kamuli, Uganda.*

WAKUBA, James. Bp Tucker Coll Mukono. **d** 64 **p** 65 Mbale. P Dio Mbale 64-72; Dio Bukedi from 72. *Church of Uganda, Busaba, PO Busolwe-Tororo, Uganda.*

WALAKIRA, Yokana. b 19. **d** 77 Nam. d Dio Nam. *c/o Namirembe Cathedral, PO Box 14297, Kampala, Uganda.*

WALDEGRAVE, Charles Tansey. b 48. Massey Univ NZ BA 70. Univ of Waikato BPhil 73. Univ of Cam BA 75. Westcott Ho Cam 75. **d** 75 **p** 76 Wel. C of St Jas Lower Hutt Dio Wel 75-78; Hon C from 79. *80 Waterloo Road, Lower Hutt, NZ.* (661-234)

✠ **WALDEN, Right Rev Graham Howard.** b 31. Univ of Queensld BA (1st cl Phil) 52, MA 54. Ch Ch Ox BLitt 59, MLitt 80. St Francis Coll Brisb ACT ThL 54. **d** 54 Brisb **p** 55 Lon for Col Bp. C of W Hackney 54-56; St Sav Poplar 57-58; Perm to Offic Dio Ox 58-59; M Bush Bro Good Shepherd 59-63; L to Offic Dio Carp 59-63; C of Gilgandra (in c of All SS Gulargambone) 60-63; Vice-Prin Torres Strait Miss Th Coll 63-65; R of Mudgee 65-70; Archd of Barker 68-70; Bal from 70; VG from 70; R of Hamilton Dio Bal from 81; Cons Asst Bp of Bal 25 March 81 by Abp of Melb; Bps of Bend, Gippsld, Bal, Wang, Murray and Graft; and others. *301 Gray Street, Hamilton, Vic, Australia 3300.* (055-72 4869)

WALDEN, John Edward Frank. b 38. Oak Hill Th Coll 67. **d** 69 Colchester for Chelmsf **p** 70 Chelmsf. C of Rainham 69-73; P-in-c of H Cross Inns Court Green Bris 73-78; Conf and Publicity Sec SAMS 78-81; Hon C of Southborough 78-81; Sec Spanish and Portuguese Ch Aid S from 81. *54 Douglas Road, Tonbridge, Kent.*

WALDEN, Samuel. b 15. Richmond Th Coll Surrey 45. **d** 57 **p** 58 Panama Canal Zone. [f Methodist Min] In Amer Ch 57-71; R of H Trin Blackley 71-74; Chap Prestwich Hosp & LPr Dio Man 74-80; Perm to Offic Dio Man from 80. *8 Brighton Road, Ben Rhydding, Ilkley, W Yorks, LS29 8PS.* (Ilkley 601860)

WALDEN-ASPY, Frederick Charles. Trin Hall Cam BA 26, MA 39. Univ of Lon MA 51. Bps' Coll Cheshunt 26. **d** 27 **p** 28 Lich. C of Ch Ch Tunstall 27-28; St Paul Burton-on-Trent 28-29; Witney (in c of H Trin Wood Green) 29-33; St Barn Bexhill 33-41; V of St Jas Littlehampton 41-64; RD of Arundel 53-64; Surr 53-68; Proc Conv Chich from 54; R of Jevington 64-68; L to Offic Dio Chich from 68. *3 Tresllian Gardens, Mount Pleasant Road, Exeter, EX4 7AJ.* (Ex 37005)

WALDOCK, Cecil Arnold Christie. **d** 34 **p** 35 Br Hond. Miss of Stann Creek 34-37; P-in-c of St Mark Bluefields 37-47; in Amer Ch 47-62; R of Gt Sutton 62-71; V of Shopland 62-71. *Broad Oaks, Rush Green Road, Clacton, Essex.*

WALDRON, Albert Ivan. Univ of Birm BA 33. Univ of Lon BD 39, MTh 42. **d** 55 **p** 56 Blackb. C of St Mich AA Ashton-on-Ribble 55-57; Asst Master Altrincham Gr Sch 58-59; Perm to Offic Dios Ches and Man 58-60; V of Ellel 60-63; Em Southport 63-67; R of Moreton Saye 67-69; Perm to Offic Dio Ches from 69; Lich 69-74; St A 69-71; L to Offic Dio St A from 71. *56 Haytor Road, Wrexham, Clwyd, LL11 2PU.* (Wrexham 51124)

WALDRON, Francis Herbert. Univ of NZ BA 36, MA 39. **d** and **p** 41 Dun. C of All SS Dun 41-42; Gore 42-47; V of Taieri w Green I Distr 47-50; Gladstone 50-78; Offg Min Dio Nel from 78. *Dorset Street, Richmond, NZ.*

WALDRON, Geoffrey Robert. b 15. Selw Coll Cam BA 37, MA 41. Ely Th Coll 37. **d** 38 Grimsby for Linc **p** 39 Linc. C of St Jo Div Gainsborough 38-41; PV and Sacr of S'wark Cathl and C of St Sav w St Pet S'wark 41-44; C-in-c of St Mich AA S'wark 42-44; C of Leamington (in c of St Alb) 44-48; St Alb Copnor Portsea 48-50; C-in-c of Combe-in-Teignhead w St Luke Milber 50-52; Milber (St Luke's Conv Distr) 52-55; Chap at Beaulieu-sur-Mer 55-57; V of Gt w L Gransden 57-63; R of Barwick 63-76; R of Closworth 63-76; C-in-c of Charlton Adam w Charlton Mackrell 76-78; C-in-c of Kingsdon 78; R of Charlton Adam w Charlton Mackrell and Kingsdon 78-80. *Roseland, Castle Street, Keinton Manderville, Somt, TA11 6DX.* (045 822324)

WALDRON, Laurence Charles. b 22. Bps' Coll Cheshunt 58. **d** 59 Aston for Birm **p** 60 Birm. C of All SS Gravelly Hill Erdington 59-63; C-in-c of St Richard Lea Hall Conv Distr 63-66; V 66-76; Wiggenhall Dio Ely from 77; St Mary Magd Wiggenhall Dio Ely from 77. *Wiggenhall St Germans Vicarage, King's Lynn, Norf.* (St Germans 371)

WALES, Lord Archbishop of. *See* Williams, Most Rev Gwilym Owen.

WALFORD, David. b 45. SOC 75. **d** 78 **p** 79 S'wark. Hon C of All SS N Beddington Dio S'wark from 78. *6 Senga Road, Hackbridge, Wallington, Surrey.* (01-669 1558)

WALFORD, David Gordon. b 49. Univ of BC BA 77. Vanc Sch of Th MDiv 81. **d** 81 Caled. I of Houston, Topley & Granisle Dio Caled from 81. *PO Box 1477, Houston, BC, Canada, V0J 1Z0.*

WALFORD, David John. b 47. AKC 71. St Aug Coll Cant 71. **d** 72 **p** 73 Ches. C of Oxton 72-77; Neston 77-80; V of Backford 80-81; Dioc Youth Officer Ches 80-81; C of Woodchurch 81-82; Chap Fulbourne Hosp Cam & Ida Darwin Hosp Fulbourne from 82. *c/o Fulbourne Hospital, Cambridge.*

WALFORD, David Sanderson. b 23. BEM 49. Chich Th Coll 78. **d** 79 **p** 80 Chich. Hon C of St Pet Gt City and Dio Chich 79-81; C of St Paul and St Pet Gt from 81. *84 Bowes Hill, Rowlands Castle, Hants, PO9 6BS.*

WALFORD, Frank Roy. b 35. Univ of Birm MB, ChB 58. Qu Coll Birm 78. **d** 80 **p** 81 Lich. Hon C of St John, The Pleck & Bescot Walsall Dio Lich from 80. *257 Broadway North, Walsall, WS1 2PS.*

WALFORD, Robin Peter. b 46. Qu Coll Birm 75. **d** 78 **p** 79 Bp Sherwood for Southw. C of Radcliffe-on-Trent 78-81; Team V of Newark w Hawton, Cotham and Shelton Dio Southw from 81. *All Saints House, Hawton, Newark, Notts, NG24 3RN.* (Newark 71705)

WALIMBWA, Cyprian. Bp Usher-Wilson Coll Buwalasi. **d** 64 Mbale. d Dio Mbale. *Butiru, PO Butiru-Mbale, Uganda.*

WALKER, Albert William John. b14. Linc Th Coll 43. **d** 45 **p** 46 Ches. C of St Mary-without-the-Walls Ches 45-48; Hoylake 48-51; V of St Luke L Tranmere 51-56; St Nich Plumstead 56-66; St Jas Merton 66-67; St Luke Kingston T 67-74; Mickleton 74-79; Chap Conv of St Mary at the Cross Edgware from 79. *St John's Lodge, 218 Hale Lane, Edgware, Middx.* (01-958 8900)

WALKER, Anthony Charles St John. b 55. Trin Coll Ox MA 80. Wycl Hall Ox 78. **d** 81 Bradf. C of Cathl Ch of St Pet City and Dio Bradf from 81. *Cathedral Clergy House, Berkerend Road, Bradford, W Yorks, BD3 9AF.* (Bradf 26987)

WALKER, Arthur Keith. b 33. Univ of Dur BSc 57. Fitzw Ho Cam BA 60, MA 64. Univ of Leeds PhD 68. Lich Th Coll 62. **d** 63 Wakef **p** 64 Pontefract for Wakef. C of Slaithwaite 63-66; V of N Wootton and Lect Wells Th Coll 66-71; Prec of Chich Cathl 71-80; Can Res 71-80; M Gen Syn 75-80; Team V of Basingstoke Dio Win from 81. *45 Beaconsfield Road, Basingstoke.* (Basingstoke 64616)

WALKER, Barry Donovan. b 28. Linc Coll Ox BA (2nd cl Th) 52, MA 56. Linc Th Coll 52. **d** 54 **p** 55 Lon. C of St Mich AA Enfield 54-58; Hornsey 58-61; V of Kensal Rise 61-71; St Jo Evang Palmers Green Dio Lon from 71. *Vicarage, Bourne Hill, N13 4DA.* (01-886 1348)

WALKER, Brian Cecil. b 28. FCA 62. Cranmer Hall Dur 68. **d** 70 **p** 71 York. C of Heworth w Peaseholme 70-73; Attenborough w Chilwell 73-75; Chilwell 75-78; R of Trowell Dio Southw from 78. *Rectory, Nottingham Road, Trowell, Nottingham, NG9 3PF.* (0602-321474)

WALKER, Cecil James. **d** 61 Bp Snell for Tor. C of St Timothy Agincourt City and Dio Tor from 61. *2014 Brimley Road, Agincourt, Ont, Canada.*

WALKER, Charles. b 24. Linc Th Coll 53. **d** 56 **p** 57 Liv. C of St Mich AA Wigan 56-59; Chap Mersey Miss to Seamen 59-62; Chap RN 62-66; C of Garston 66-68; V of Glazebury 68-75; Surr from 68; Perm to Offic Dio Liv 75-79; V of St Mich Wigan Dio Liv from 79. *Vicarage, Swinley Road, Wigan, Lancs.* (Wigan 42381)

WALKER, Charles Edward Cornwall. b 18. Selw Coll Cam BA 39, MA 43. Cudd Coll 40. **d** 41 **p** 42 Sarum. C of Gillingham w Milton and E and W Stour 41-46; Evesham 46-48; V of Gt Amwell (w St Marg from 81) Dio St Alb from 48; C-in-c of Stanstead St Marg 74-81. *Great Amwell Vicarage, Ware, Herts.* (Stanstead Abbots 139)

WALKER, Christopher John. b 52. Chich Th Coll 75. **d** 78 Buckingham for Ox **p** 79 Ox. C of All SS Reading Dio Ox from 78. *All Saints' House, Brunswick Street, Reading, RG1 6NZ.* (0734-584626)

WALKER, Christopher John Deville. b 42. St Jo Coll Dur BA 69. Westcott Ho 69. **d** 71 **p** 72 Portsm. C of Portsea 72-75; Saffron Walden 75-77; St Martin-in-the-Fields Trafalgar Square 77-80; V of Riverhead w Dunton Green Dio Roch from 80. *Vicarage, Riverhead, Kent.* (Sevenoaks 55736)

WALKER, Clark. b 30. **d** 81 Auckld. C of Auckld Angl Maori Miss Dio Auckld from 81. *10 Waterview Road, Papakura, NZ.*

WALKER, David. b 48. Linc Th Coll 71. **d** 74 **p** 75 Southw. C of Arnold 74-76; C of Crosby 77-79; V of Scrooby w Ranskill Dio Southw from 79. *Ranskill Vicarage, Retford, Notts, DN22 8NL.* (Retford 818476)

WALKER, David Andrew. b 52. Univ of St Andr MTh 75. Linc Th Coll 79. **d** 81 York. C of Hessle Dio York from 81. *21 Northolme Road, Hessle, N Humb, HU13 9HR.*

WALKER, Canon David Grant. b 23. Univ of Bris BA (1st cl Hist) 49. Ball Coll Ox DPhil 54. FRHistS 62. **d** 62 Swan B **p** 62 Llan for Swan B. Hon C of St Mary Swansea Dio Swan B from 62; Lect in Hist Univ Coll Swansea 53-63; Sen Lect from 63; Dean of Arts 69-71; Bp's Chap for Post-Ordin Tr Dio Swan B from 65; Dir Post-Ordin Tr from 77; Can of Brecon Cathl from 72; Prec from 79. *52 Eaton Crescent, Swansea, W Glam.*

WALKER, David Ian. b 41. Bps' Coll Cheshunt 65. **d** 68 Wakef **p** 69 Pontefract for Wakef. C of Todmorden 68-72; V of St Jo Div Rastrick 72-77; Crosland Moor Dio Wakef from 77. *Crosland Moor Vicarage, Huddersfield.* (Huddersfield 22381)

WALKER, David John. b 41. ACT Dipl Th 73. Ridley Coll Melb. **d** 78 **p** 79 Melb. C of Doncaster 78-80; I of Ch Ch Whittlesea Dio Melb from 80. *Christ Church Vicarage, Whittlesea, Vic, Australia.*

WALKER, Dennis Richard. b 25. Bp Gray Coll Capetn LTh 57. **d** 57 **p** 58 Capetn. C of Sea Point 57-59; Green Point 59-62; R of Observatory Capetn 62-73; V of Catterick w Tunstall 73-78; Manston Dio Ripon from 78. *Manston Vicarage, Church Lane, Leeds, LS15 8JB* (Leeds 645530)

WALKER, Derek Fred. b 46. Trin Coll Bris 71. **d** 74 **p** 75 Roch. C of St Barn Cray 74-78; Rushden w Newton Bromswold 78-80; R of Kirkby Thore w Temple Sowerby and Newbiggin Dio Carl from 80. *Kirkby Thore Rectory, Penrith, Cumb.* (Kirkby Thore 248)

WALKER, Douglas. b 36. Lich Th Coll 61. **d** 63 **p** 64 Bris. C of St Ambrose Bris 63-68; C-in-c of All H Easton 68-71; V of Penhill 71-79; Elmsted w Hastingleigh Dio Cant from 79; Crundale w Godmersham Dio Cant from 79. *Elmstead Vicarage, Hastingleigh, Ashford, Kent, TN25 5HP.* (Elmstead 414)

WALKER, Edward Charles. b 32. Trin Coll Cam BA 55, MA 59. Cudd Coll Ox 55. **d** 57 **p** 58 Win. C of Milton 57-61; St Alb Cathl Pret 61-62; R of Zoutpansburg w Louis Trichardt 62-66; C of Cowley (in c of St Jas) 66-75. *147 Divinity Road, Oxford, OX4 1LP.*

WALKER, (Dominic) Edward William Murray. b 48. K Coll Lon 70, AKC 73. **d** and **p** 72 S'wark. M CGA from 67; C of St Faith Wandsworth 72-73; Dom Chap to Bp of S'wark 73-76; Publ Pr Dio S'wark 73-76; Perm to Offic Dio B & W 76; Hon Chap to Bp of S'wark 76-80; R of Newington Dio S'wark from 76; RD of S'wark and Newington from 80. *Newington Rectory, Kennington Park Road, SE11 4KQ.* (01-735 1894)

WALKER, Eric Edward Rutter. ACT ThL 40. **d** 47 Goulb **p** 67 Newc. Hon C of Gundagai 47-49; Coonamble 49-52; Boorowa 52; Grenfell 52-64; C of Gosford 67-76. *Berenbel, Duffy Avenue, Thornleigh, NSW, Australia 2120.* (02-841699)

WALKER, Eric Henry. b 15. AKC 39. Univ of Lon BD 54. **d** 39 Willesden for Lon **p** 40 Lon. C of St Sav Paddington 39-42; All SS Sydenham 42-44; Chap RAFVR 44-47; RAF 47-51; V of St Barn Rotherhithe 50-56; C-in-c of St Kath Rotherhithe 53-56; RD of Bermondsey 55-65 and 78-80; V of St Kath w St Barn Rotherhithe 56-81; Asst Lect in NT Gr K Coll Lon 56-63. *10 Barton Road, Ely, Cambs, CB7 4DE.* (0353-5927)

WALKER, Ernest. b 26. Univ of Man BA (Com) 50. St Aid Coll 55. **d** 57 **p** 58 Man. C of Ch Ch Denton 57-60; Sen Master Audenshaw Gr Sch and L to Offic Dio Man from 60. *c/o Audenshaw Grammar School, Manchester.*

WALKER, Ernest Alwyn. Clifton Th Coll 54. **d** 56 **p** 57 S'wark. C of Ch Ch N Brixton 56-59; V of St Barn Hull 59-70; Shipton Thorpe w Hayton 70-77; St Geo Mart Daubhill Bolton Dio Man from 77. *Vicarage, Roseberry Street, Bolton, BL3 4AR.* (Bolton 61067)

WALKER, Frederick George. **d** 65 Bp McKenzie for Wel **p** 66 Wel. Hon C of Trentham 65-69; Silverstream Dio Wel from 69. *7 Glenrae Flats, Kiln Street, Silverstream, NZ.*

WALKER, Gavin Russell. b 43. FCA 78. Coll of Resurr Mirfield 76. **d p** 79 Wakef. C of St John Wakef 78-81; Northallerton w Kirby Sigston Dio York from 81. *37 Ainderby Road, Romanby, Northallerton, N Yorks, OL7 8HF.* (Northallerton 3431)

WALKER, Geoffrey Frederick. St Francis Coll Brisb 52. **d** 55 **p** 56 Brisb. C of St Pet Southport 55-56; Warwick 56-59; Bundaberg 59-61. *92 Burnett Street, Bundaberg, Queensland, Australia.*

WALKER, Geoffrey Frederick. b 23. Oak Hill Th Coll. **d** 59 **p** 60 Bradf. C of Clayton 59-62; V of Clapham w Keasden 62-66; R of Necton w Holme Hale 66-71; C-in-c of Mundham w Seething Dio Nor 71-73; V from 73; C-in-c of St Mary Thwaite Dio Nor 71-75; R from 75. *Vicarage, Seething, Norwich, NR15 1DJ.* (Brooke 582)

WALKER, George. St Pet Coll Rosettenville 55. **d** 57 **p** 58 Johann. P Dio Johann. *PO Box 4010, Lesedi, Johannesburg, S Africa.*

WALKER, Canon George Percival John. Univ of Dur LTh 38. St Bonif Coll Warm 35. **d** 38 **p** 39 Bris. C of St Anne Brislington 38-42; Chap and Asst Master Dioc Gr Sch Antig 42-50; Perm to Offic Dio Win 51; V of All SS and P-in-c of St Pet Antig 51-52; R of St Geo Basseterre St Kitts 52-78; Hon Can of Antig 55-78; Can (Emer) from 78; Archd of St Kitts 64-78. *St George's Rectory, Basseterre, St Kitts, W Indies.* (2167)

WALKER, Gerald Roger. b 41. K Coll Lon and Warm BD and AKC 67. **d** 68 **p** 69 Newc T. C of St Phil 68-70; Goring-by-Sea 70-75; R and V of Selsey 75-81; V of St Andr (Old Ch) Hove Dio Chich from 81. *17 Vallance Gardens, Hove, E Sussex, BN3 2DB.* (Brighton 734859)

WALKER, Glenn Hallet Lovis. Coll of Emporia BA 45. Nashotah Ho Wisconsin 46. **d** 50 Salina (US) for Gui **p** 50 Gui. C of Wismar 50-52; P-in-c of Demarara River Miss 52-55; R of Stann Creek 56-58; P-in-c of Punta Gorda 58-62. *Spearville, Kansas, USA.*

WALKER, Gordon Welby. Univ of Sask BA 62. St Chad's Coll Regina 60. **d** 61 **p** 62 Qu'App. d Dio Qu'App 61-62; I of Avonlea 62-64; Esterhazy 64-66; Sumner 66-68; Weyburn 68-70; C of Kingston Cathl St Vincent 70-73; R of St Geo Moose Jaw 73-80; St Phil Regina Dio Qu'App from 80. *29 Bond Crescent, Regina, Sask, Canada.*

WALKER, Graham. b 35. Ex Coll Ox BA (3rd Hist) 58, 3rd cl Th 60, MA 62. Univ of Leeds MPhil 80. Sarum Th Coll 60. **d** 61 **p** 62 Bradf. C of Guiseley 61-64; Ingrow 64-68; L to Offic Dio Bradf 68-80; V of Hellifield Dio Bradf from 80. *Hellifield Vicarage, Skipton, N Yorks, BD23 4HY.* (Hellifield 243)

WALKER, Harold Gordon. Univ of Manit BA 30, CD 54. St Jo Coll Manit LTh 33. **d** 33 **p** 34 Bran. C-in-c of Cartwright 33-34; I 34-35; R of BElmont 35-38; St Jas Neepawa 38-42; CF (Canad) 42-46; C of St Jas Winnipeg 46-48; R of St Thos Winnipeg 48-60; P-in-c of Stony Mountain 55-56; R of Cordova Bay 60-76. *1655 Richardson Street, Victoria, BC, Canada.*

WALKER, Canon Harvey William. b 26. Univ of Edin MA (2nd cl Hist) 52. St Steph Ho Ox 58. **d** 60 **p** 61 Newc T. C of St Matt Newc T 60-64; V of St Matt w St Mary Virg City and Dio Newc T from 64; Hon Can of Newc T Cathl from 80. *10 Winchester Terrace, Newcastle-upon-Tyne, NE4 6EH.* (Newc T 322866)

WALKER, Hugh. b 08. Bp Wilson Th Coll IM 36. **d** 37 **p** 38 S & M. C of Braddan (w c of St Luke Baldwin) 37-39; Bilton 39-44; R of Gt Smeaton w Appleton Wiske 45-68. *37 Carmel Road South, Darlington, Co Durham.*

WALKER, Ian Richard Stevenson. b 51. St D Coll Lamp BA 73. Univ of Birm Dipl Th 75. Qu Coll Birm 74. **d** 76 **p** 77 York. C of Stainton-in-Cleveland 76-79; Fulford York 79-81; Team V of Kidderminster Dio Worc from 81. *St Barnabas House, Franche, Kiderminster, Worcs.* (Kidderminster 2729)

WALKER, Jack. b 21. **d** 45 Dur for Newc T **p** 46 Newc T. C of Ch Ch Tynemouth 45-49; St Luke Wallsend 49-51; St Barn Linthorpe Middlesbrough 51-55; V of Sancton Dio York from 55; V of N Newbald Dio York from 55. *Vicarage, North Newbald, York.* (North Newbald 284)

WALKER, James Robert. b 07. K Coll Lon 30. Bp Wilson Th Coll IM 32. **d** 35 **p** 36 Lon. C of St Jas Moore Pk Fulham 35-38; Ch Ch Falkirk 38-42; P-in-c of H Trin Riddrie Glas 42-46; C of St Mary Magd Dundee 46-49; R of St Paul Rothsay 49-57; C of E Dereham 58-60; P Dio Trinid 60-61; Dio Brech 61-62; Dio Geo 62-63; C of St Jo Evang Bexley 63-65; St Jo Bapt Worc 65-67; St Cypr Cathl Kimb 67-68; Mansfield 68-72. *14 Overdale Avenue, Skegby, Sutton-in-Ashfield, Notts, NG17 3ES.*

WALKER, John. b 49. Univ of Sheff BSc 74. Univ of Birm Dipl Th 77. Qu Coll Birm 75. **d** 78 **p** 79 Leic. C of Em Ch Loughborough 78-81; All SS Nottm Dio Southw from 81. *96 Dryden Street, Nottingham.* (Nottm 412162)

WALKER, John. b 51. Univ of Aber MA 74. Edin Th Coll 75. **d** 78 **p** 79 Brech. C of Broughty Ferry 78-81; P-in-c of St Jo Bapt Dundee Dio Brech from 81. *16 Argyle Street, Dundee.* (Dundee 41013)

WALKER, John Cameron. b 31. Univ of St Andr MA 52. Edin Th Coll 63. **d** 65 **p** 66 Edin. C of H Cross Davidson's Mains 65-67; St Jo Bapt Perth 67-70; Chap to Angl Students in Glas 70-74; Youth Tutor Warw Co Coun 75-77; Officer Gen Syn Bd of Educn from 78; C of St John E Hendon Dio Lon from 79. *General Synod Board of Education, Church House, Dean's Yard, Westminster, SW1P 3NZ.*

WALKER, John David. b 44. St Jo Coll Dur BA 76, Dipl Th 77. **d** 77 **p** 78 York. C of H Trin Heworth 77-81; P-in-c of Barmby Moor w Fangfoss Dio York from 81; Allerthorpe Dio York from 81. *Barmby Moor Vicarage, York.* (Pocklington 2657)

WALKER, John David. b 38. Em Coll Sktn LTh 72. **d** 72 **p** 73 Athab. I of Wabasca Dio 73-76; on leave. *Wabasca, Alta., Canada* (891 3828)

WALKER, John Frank. b 53. Univ of Leeds BEducn 76. N Ordin Course 78. **d** 81 Knaresborough for Ripon. C of Whitkirk Dio Ripon from 81. *c/o 386 Selby Road, Leeds, LS15 0AA.* (Leeds 645790)

WALKER, John Frederick. b 21. St Jo Coll Dur BA 47, Dipl Th 49, MA 51. **d** 49 **p** 50 Wakef. C of Normanton 49-51; Northowram 51-53; V of Gawthorpe w Chickenley Heath 53-59; All S Haley Hill Halifax 59-74; Hampsthwaite Dio Ripon from 74; C-in-c of Killinghall Dio Ripon from 76. *Hampsthwaite Vicarage, Harrogate, Yorks, HG3 2HB.* (Harrogate 770337)

WALKER, John Howard. b 47. Clifton Th Coll 69. **d** 72 Ches **p** 73 Stockport for Ches. C of St Mary Upton Ches 72-76; Asst Chap Liv Univ 76-80; V of St Jo Chrys Everton Dio Liv from 80. *Vicarage, Chrysostoms Way, Liverpool, L6 2NF.* (051-263 3755)

WALKER, John Hugh. b 34. K Coll Lon and Warm BD and AKC 57, Jun McCaul Hebr Pri and Wordsworth Lat Pri 57. Univ of Lon MTh 75. **d** 58 **p** 59 Chelmsf. C of St Alb Mart Westcliff-on-Sea 58-61; V of St Alb Gt Ilford 61-67; Perm to Offic Dio Chelmsf 67-68; C of St Edm Forest Gate 68-74; Asst Master Woodford Co High Sch 68-74; St Aug Coll Cant 74-75; Folkestone Technical High Sch and Perm to Offic Dio Cant from 75. *Aberfeldy, Covet Lane, Kingston, Canterbury, Kent, CT4 6HU.* (Bridge 830818)

WALKER, John Michael. Qu Coll Birm. **d** 57 **p** 58 Southw. C of Ruddington 57-60; Horsham 60-64; Sullington and of Storrington 64-70; V of Peasmarsh 70-73; Washington (and Ashington w Buncton and Wiston from 77) Dio Chich from 73. *Ashington Rectory, Pulborough, W Sussex, RH20 3BX.* (Ashington 892304)

WALKER, John Percival. b 45. Div Hostel Dub 68. **d** 71 Down. C of St Clem Belf 71-74; Magheraculmoney 74-78; St Paul Lisburn 78-81; I of St Ninian Belf Dio Connor from 81. *Rectory, Whitewell Road, Newtownabbey, BT36 7EU, N Ireland.* (Belfast 777976)

WALKER, John Thomas. b 14. Univ of Wales BA (2nd cl Latin) 37. RD 70. Linc Th Coll 38. **d** 39 Llan for Mon **p** 40 Mon. C of Risca 39-42; Merthyr Dyfan 42-44; Chap RNVR 44-47; C of St Pet Leic 47-49; V of Snibston 49-57; St Sav Woolcott Pk Clifton 57-69; Chap RNR 58-70; V of St Anne Brislington 69-78; P-in-c of Bishopstone w Hinton Parva Dio Bris from 78. *Bishopstone Vicarage, Swindon, Wilts, SN6 8PW.* (0793 79475)

WALKER, John Wolfe. b 15. Trin Coll Cam BA 37, MA 47. LRAM 38. Cudd Coll 46. **d** 47 **p** 48 Pet. C of St Matt Northn 47-50; Frome Selwood 50-52; V of Kilmersdon 52-57; R of Babington 52-57; V of Pilton (w Wootton, North from 72) 57-80; RD of Shepton Mallet 75-80. *Eldermere, Old Wells Road, Shepton Mallet, Somt.* (Shepton Mallet 2662)

WALKER, Kenneth Donovan. St Jo Coll Auckld LTh 62. **d** 62 **p** 63 Waik. C of Te Aroha 62-63; Matamata 63-66; V of Orakau 66-72; Tokoroa 72-77; Otorohanga Dio Waik from 77. *PO Box 126, Otorohanga, NZ.* (7006)

WALKER, Kenneth Lewis. Moore Th Coll Syd ACT ThL 47. **d** and **p** 47 Syd. C of St Matt Manly 47-48; C-in-c of Wilberforce 48-50; Carlton 50-53; R 53-54; W Wollongong 55-57; Wahroonga 57-72; L to Offic Dio Syd from 72. *41 Yanco Avenue, Wentworth Falls, NSW, Australia 2782.* (047-57 1292)

WALKER, Kenneth Saxon Watkinson. b 21. Jes Coll Cam BA 47, MA 50. Westcott Ho Cam 67. **d** 68 **p** 69 Ches. Hon C of W Kirby 68-70; L to Offic Dio Ches 70-78; Dio Arg Is from 77. *Tigh an Allt, Dervaig, Tobermory, Isle of Mull, Argyll.*

WALKER, Kingsley. b 17. Univ of Dur BA 42, Dipl Th 43, MA 46. St Paul's Th Coll Grahmstn. **d** 47 **p** 48 Natal. C of St Paul Durban 47-48; P-in-c of Springvale 48-51; C of St Sav Cathl Pietermaritzburg (in c of St Alphege Scotsville) 51-53; Roehampton 53-54; V of Finham 54-60; Archd of Seychelles 60-63; Dean of St Paul's Pro-Cathl Mahe 61-63; C-in-c of Whitchurch w Preston-on-Stour 68-73; C-in-c of Atherstone-on-Stour 68-73; R of St D Prestbury 73-77; St Jas Morningside Dio Natal from 77. *115 Venice Road, Durban, Natal, S Africa.* (33-5606)

WALKER, Leslie. b 47. St Paul's Coll Grahmstn Dipl Th 78. **d** 78 **p** 79 Pret. C of St Mich AA Nelspruit 78-79; R of St Geo White River Dio Pret from 79. *PO Box 1151, White River, 1240, S Africa.*

WALKER, Martin Frank. b 39. St Jo Coll Nottm 71. **d** 73 **p** 74 Lich. C of Penn 73-78; V of Bentley Walsall Dio Lich from 78. *Bentley Vicarage, Walsall, Staffs, WS2 0HP.* (Walsall 24200)

WALKER, Martin John. b 52. Linc Coll Ox BA 73, MA 77. Univ of Dur BA (Th) 78. Cranmer Hall Dur 75. **d** 79 Barking for Chelmsf **p** 80 Chelmsf. C of St Paul Harlow New Town 79-81; Dorchester (in c of Berinsfield and Drayton St Leon) Dio Ox from 81. *Vicarage, Cherwell Road, Berinsfield, Oxon.* (OX 340460)

WALKER, Michael John. b 32. Late Colquitt Exhib BNC Ox BA (2nd cl Th) 55, MA 59. Clifton Th Coll 55. **d** 57 **p** 58 Chich. C of Patcham 57-61; V of Stapleford 61-66; R of Saxmundham 66-71; V of St Paul Beckenham 71-78; St Mary Bury St Edms Dio St E from 78, M Gen Syn from 80. *St Mary's Vicarage, Bury St Edmunds, Suff.* (Bury St E 4680)

WALKER, Michael John. b 39. St D Coll Lamp BA 61. St Aid Coll 61. **d** 63 **p** 64 York. C of St Phil and St Jas Clifton York 63-66; Marfleet 66-69; V of St Jude Salterhebble Halifax Dio Wakef from 69. *St Jude's Vicarage, Savile Park, Halifax, Yorks, HX1 2XH.* (Halifax 54842)

WALKER, Michael Sykes. b 10. Trin Hall Cam BA 33, MA 40. **d** 49 **p** 50 Wakef. C of Northowram 49-51; Castleford 51-53; R of Langton w Birdsall 53-61; Escrick 61-75; RD of Escrick 66-73; Hon C of Stillingfleet 75-81. *Ousefield, Riccall Lane, Kelfield, York, YO4 6RE.* (Riccall 577)

WALKER, Nigel Maynard. b 39. ALCD 66. **d** 67 **p** 68 Portsm. C of St Jude Southsea Portsea 67-70; Ch Ch Addington Durban 70-73; R 73-76; C of Abingdon (in c of Ch Ch) 76-80; V of Overchurch (or Upton) Dio Ches 80-81. *Address temp unknown.*

WALKER, Paul Garred. b 42. Univ of W Ont BA 65. Trin Coll Tor STB 68. **d** 68 **p** 69 Tor. C of St Timothy Tor 68-74; I of the Atonement Alderwood Tor 75-79; St Mark Port Hope Dio Tor from 79. *53 King Street, Port Hope, Ont, L1A 2R6, Canada.*

WALKER, Peter. b 14. Magd Coll Ox MA 75. Ripon Hall Ox 61. **d** and **p** 62 Ox. C of Abingdon w Shippon 62-72; P-in-c of S Leigh 72-79; Perm to Offic Dio Sarum from 80. *Orhard Rise, Highmore Road, Sherborne, Dorset, DT9 4BT.* (Sherborne 2516)

WALKER, Peter Anthony Ashley. b 46. Chich Th Coll 67. **d** 70 **p** 71 Lon. C of St Thos Clapton Common 70-74; Bethnal Green 74-77; V of St Mary w St Aug Hackney Wick Dio Lon from 77. *St Mary's House, Hackney Wick, E9 5JA.* (01-986 8159)

WALKER, Peter Jeffrey. b 46. Kelham Th Coll 65. **d** 70 **p** 71 York. C of All SS Middlesbrough 70-75; and 77-78; SSF 75-77; P-in-c of Wrangbrook Dio Wakef from 78. *Abingdon, New Lane, Upton, Pontefract, WF9 1HJ.* (S Elmsall 43638)

✠ **WALKER, Right Rev Peter Knight.** b 19. Late Scho of Qu Coll Ox 2nd cl Cl Mods 40, BA (1st cl Lit Hum) and MA 47. Hon Fell 81. Westcott Ho Cam 53. **d** 54 **p** 55 St Alb. Asst Master Merchant Taylors' Sch 50-56; C of Hemel Hempstead 56-58; Fell, Dean of Chap and Th Lect CCC Cam 58-62; Asst Tutor 59-62; Hon Fell 77; Mere's Pr Cam 59; Select Pr Cam 62 and 67 (Hulsean). Ox 75; and 80; Prin Wescott Ho Cam 62-72; Exam Chap to Bp of Portsm 61-72; Commiss Delhi 62-66; Hon Can of Ely 66-72; Can of Ch Ch Ox 72-74; Cons Bp Suffr of Dorchester in Ch Ch Cathl Ox 13 July 72 by Abp of Cant; Bps of Lon, Blackb, Ches, Chich, Derby, Linc, Ox, Pet, Portsm, St Alb, Ely and Edin; and others; Trld to Ely 77. *The Bishop's House, Ely, Cambs.* (Ely 2749)

WALKER, Peter Raymond. Univ of Tor BA 75. Univ of Ox BA (Th) 77. Trin Coll Tor MDiv 78. **d** 78 **p** 79 Tor. C of Ch Ch Deer Park City and Dio Tor from 78. *Christ Church, Deer Park, 1570 Yonge Street, Toronto, M4T 1Z8, Canada.*

WALKER, Peter Sidney Caleb. b 50. St Mich Ho Crafers 76. **d** 80 **p** 81 Tas. C of Sorell 80-81; Devonport 81; P-in-c of Fingal Valley Dio Tas from 81. *Rectory, Fingal, Tasmania 7214.*

WALKER, Philip Geoffrey. b 24. Univ Coll Leic BA (1st cl Engl) (Lon) 50. Sarum Th Coll 50. **d** 52 **p** 53 Southw. C of Bulwell 52-55; V of Forest Town 55-63; Greasley Dio Southw from 63; RD of Bulwell 64-70. *Greasley Vicarage, Newthorpe, Nottingham.* (Langley Mill 2509)

WALKER, Philip Geoffrey. b 47. St Jo Coll Dur BA 70. Or Coll Ox BA (Th) 72, MA 76. Ripon Hall Ox 70. **d** 74 **p** 75 Sheff. C of St Geo Sheff 74-77; St Mary Gt Cam 77-81; V of St Andr Roker Monk Wearmouth Dio Dur from 81. *St Andrew's Vicarage, Park Avenue, Sunderland, T & W, SR6 9PU.* (Sunderland 73697)

WALKER, Richard Bickersteth Roscoe. b 03. K Coll Lon BA (2nd cl) 31. Sarum Th Coll 47. **d** and **p** 49 Glouc. C of All SS Cheltm 49-51; Youth Chap Dio Glouc 51-64; V of Gt and L Barrington w Taynton 51-55; PC OF St Barn Tuffley Glouc 55-64; V of Northleach w Eastington and Hampnett 64-73; RD of Northleach 67-72. *17 Cecily Hill, Cirencester, Glos, GL7 2EF.* (Cirencester 4512)

WALKER, Robert Edward Lea. b 23. Qu Coll Ox MA 49. Wycl Hall Ox 49. **d** 51 **p** 52 Ox. C of Witney 51-61; V of Wroxton and Balscote (w Shenington and Alkerton from 80) Dio Ox from 61; P-in-c of Shenington w Alkerton 79-80. *Wroxton Rectory Banbury, Oxon, OX15 6QE* (Wroxton St Mary 344)

WALKER, Robert Harold. b 1899. Pemb Coll Cam BA 22, MA 26. **d** 27 **p** 28 Lon. C of Ch Ch Spitalfields 27-30; St Andr L Cam 30-32; V of Ch Ch N Brixton 32-36; Chudleigh 36-43; St Pet Tunbridge Wells 43-47; Moulsford 47-53; Virginia Water 53-59; Chap Fernhill Manor Sch 59-64; Perm to Offic Dio Guildf from 77. *5 Trotsworth Avenue, Virginia Water, Surrey.*

WALKER, Ven Robert Percival. Univ of Tor (Trin Coll) BA 26. STB Gen Th Sem NY. **d** 27 **p** 28 Niag. C of St Patr Guelph 27-29; St Simon Tor 29-34; R of Good Shepherd Mt Dennis Tor 34-41; St Geo Tor 41-50; RD of Tor Centre 47-50; R of St Mary Virg Tor 50-56; St Luke Pet 56-72; Can of Tor 56-62; Archd of Peterborough 62-72; Archd (Emer) from 72. *366 Briar Hill Road, Toronto, Ont., Canada.*

WALKER, Ronald Alfred. b 39. Univ of W Ont BA 77. Hur Coll Lon Ont MDiv 80. **d** 80 Hur **p** 81 Bp Parke-Taylor for Hur. C of St Anne Lon Dio Hur from 80. *1 Farm Manor Court, London, Ont, Canada, N6H 4J2.*

WALKER, Ronald Delwin. b 35. Atlantic Sch of Th Halifax 74. **d** 76 Bp Hatfield for NS. C of Martin's River Dio NS from 76. *St Martin's, Western Shore, Lunenburg County, NS, Canada.*

WALKER, Ronald Sydney. Moore Th Coll Syd 33. ACT ThL 35. **d** 36 **p** 37 Syd. C of All S Leichhardt 36-40; R of Denham Court w Rossmore 40-46; Chap RAAF 41-46; R of St Faith Narrabeen w Pittwater 46-49; Concord W Dio Syd from 49. *268 Concord Road, Concord West, NSW, Australia 2138.* (73-1189)

WALKER, Rudolf Edmund Ernest. b 08. Ex Coll Ox BA (Mod Hist Aegr) 32, MA 37. Ripon Hall, Ox 32. **d** 34 **p** 35 Bradf. C of H Trin Idle 34-36; Sedbergh 36-39; R of Whicham 39-46; V of Whitbeck 39-46; Chaplain RAFVR 42-46; V of Drigg 46-50; R of L Hallingbury 50-56; V of St Elis Becontree 56-58; C-in-c of St Phil and St Jas Conv Distr S Woodford 58-62; Min 62-65; R of Moulton 65-74; R of Kennett 65-74; Hon Asst P-in-c of Alloa 74-78; Perm to Offic Dio St Andr from 78. *19 Torry Drive, Alva, Clackmannanshire, FK12 5NQ.* (0259-61121)

WALKER, Canon Stephen. b 09. St Jo Coll Dur BA 30, Dipl Th (w distinc) 31, MA 33. **d** 32 **p** 33 Ripon. C of Horsforth 32-35; Perm to Offic at Ch Ch (in c of St Bede) U Armley 35-36; V of St Barn Birm 36-40; All SS Monkwearmouth 40-43; Bruntcliffe 43-50; N Ferriby 50-58; Proc Conv York 57-59; V of St Mary Beverley 58-77; Surr from 58; RD of Beverley 63-73; Can and Preb of York Minster 64-77; Can (Emer) from 77; Perm to Offic Dios Dur and York from 77. *Victoria Flat, Auckland Castle, Bishop Auckland, DL14 7NR.* (Bp Auckld 661740)

WALKER, Thomas. b 18. St Aid Coll 58. **d** 60 **p** 61 Bradf. C of St Phil Girlington 60-62; All SS L Horton Bradf 62-63; C-in-c of St Paul Pudsey 63-65; V of Lower Darwen 65-68; Wrightington Dio Blackb from 68. *Vicarage, Church Lane, Wrightington, Wigan, WN6 9SL.* (Eccleston 451332)

WALKER, Canon Thomas Overington. b 33. Keble Coll Ox BA 58, MA 61. Oak Hill Th Coll 58. **d** 60 **p** 61 Guildf. C of St Paul Woking 60-62; St Leonards-on-Sea 62-64; Trav Sec Inter-Varsity Fellowship 64-67; Succr Birm Cathl 67-70; V of St Jo Bapt Harborne Dio Birm from 70; Hon Can of Birm Cathl from 80. *99 Wentworth Road, Birmingham 17.* (021-427 3037)

WALKER, Trevor John. b 51. Univ of Southn BTh 80. Sarum Wells Th Coll 75. **d** 78 Blackb **p** 79 Lanc for Blackb. C of Standish 78-81; P-in-c of N and of S Somercotes Dio Linc from 81. *Vicarage, Keeling Street, North Somercotes, Louth, Lincs LN11 7QU.* (N Somercotes 456)

WALKER, Victor John. b 05. TCD BA 36, Carson Bibl Pri 37, Div Test (2nd cl) 38, MA 49. **d** 38 **p** 39 Dub. C of St Matt Irishtown Dub 38-43; C-in-c of Coolbanagher 43-49; C of Tooting Graveney 49-51; V of St Andr Toxt Pk 51-71; Hon C of Woolton Dio Liv from 81. *12 Menlove Court, Menlove Avenue, Liverpool, L18 2EP.*

WALKER, Walter. b 02. St Bonif Coll Warm 34. **d** 35 **p** 36 Wakef. C of Battyeford 35-39; Ch Ch Leeds 39-41; CF (EC) 41-46; V of Ch Ch Leeds w St John and St Barn Holbeck 46-51; Whorlton 51-55; All SS Middlesbrough 55-60; Clifford 60-69; R of Kirby Underdale w Bugthorpe 69-72. *8 Moorland Drive, Birkenshaw, Nr Bradford, W Yorks, BD11 2BU.*

WALKER, Canon Walter Ernest. Bp's Univ Lennox. **d** 38 **p** 39 Queb. C of Malbay 38-39; Miss at Leeds 39-42; I of Port Daniel Miss w Shigawake 42-48; Kingsey 48-50; Scotstown 50-60; P-in-c of Bury 60-65; R of Richmond 65-79; P-in-c of Windsor 70-79; Can of Queb 72-79; Hon Can from 79. *Apt 308, 2500 Benny Crescent, Montreal, PQ, Canada.*

WALKER, Canon Walter Stanley. b 21. AKC 42. Cudd Coll Ox 42. **d** 44 **p** 45 Liv. C of All SS Southport 44-47; Chap Mersey Miss to Seamen and L to Offic Dio Ches 47-48; C-in-c of St Phil Conv Distr Kelsall 48-53; V of Birkenhead 53-61; Surr from 54; R of Wistaston 61-66; Bromborough 66-77; Chap Barony Hosp Nantwich 61-66; R of Wallasey Dio Ches from 77; RD of Wallasey from 77; Hon Can of Ches from 80. *Rectory, St Hilary Drive, Wallasey, Mer, L45 3NH.* (051-638 4771)

WALKER, William. b 12. AKC 36. Knutsford Test Sch Hawarden 32. Bps' Coll Cheshunt 36. **d** 37 **p** 38 Lon. C of St Matt Westmr 37-42; H Redeemer Clerkenwell 42-48; St Pet Lon Dks 49-51; V of St Chris Hanwell Dio Lon from 51. *St Christopher's Vicarage, Bordars Road, Hanwell, W7.* (01-587 2796)

WALKER, William. b 10. Coll of Industr Management Birm FCIME 48. Stanford Coll Loughborough. **d** 51 **p** 52 Southw. C of Gotham 51-58; Chap, Lect and Tutor of Stanford Coll Loughborough 51-70; C-in-c of Normanton-on-Soar 58-65; V of Daybrook 70-80; L to Offic Dio Southw from 80. *278 Rutland Road, West Bridgford, Nottingham.* (Nottm 869353)

WALKER, William George. b 11. Late Exhib of St Jo Coll Cam and Welsh Ch Scho 3rd cl Cl Trip pt i 31, BA (3rd cl Th Trip pt i) 32, MA 36. St Mich Th Coll Llan 33. **d** 34 Mon for Llan **p** 35 Llan. C of Cyfarthfa 34-36; Glyntaff 36-38; Griffithstown 38-42; St Luke Canton Cardiff 42-45; Ystrad Mynach 45-49; C-in-c of Cymmer w Abercregan Conv Distr 49-53; V of Penydarren 53-55; Llanover (w Llanfair Kilgeddin from 72) 55-77; RD of Raglan 72-77; Surr 76-77; Perm to Offic Dio Bris from 78. *1 Lansdown Court, Mortimer Road, Clifton, Bristol, BS8 4EX.* (Bristol 739447)

WALKER, William George Leslie. Bibl Gr Pri and Brooke Exhib TCD BA and Div Test (1st cl) 39, Ma 42. **d** 39 **p** 40 Dub. C of St Kevin Dub 39-42; St Comgall Bangor 42-43; CF (EC) 43-46; I of Saul w Inch 46-52; Magheradroll 52-59; Surr 53-66; R of Knockbreda 59-78; RD of Hillsborough 66-70; Preb of Down Cathl 70-78. *160 Ballylesson Road, Belfast 8, N Ireland.*

WALKER, William John. b 20. **d** 80 Glas. Hon C of Ch Ch Lanark Dio Glas from 80. *17 Ridgepark Drive, Lanark, ML11 7PG*

WALKERDEN, Ernest Roy. St Francis Coll Brisb ACT ThL 53. **d** 53 **p** 54 Wang. C of Shepparton 53-56; R of Violet Town 56-58; Croydon 58-61; C of Melb Dioc Centre from 61; Chap Bal Gen Hosp 62-64; Alfred Hosp Melb 64-70; R of Winton 70-71; I of St Mary E Preston 71-74; Perm to Offic Dio Melb from 74. *255 Poath Road, Hughesdale, Vic, Australia 3166.* (579-1563)

WALKEY, Malcolm Gregory Taylor. b 44. Dipl Th (Lon) 68. Kelham Th Coll 63. **d** 68 Bp Horstead for Leic **p** 69 Leic. C of Oadby 68-72; Team V of St Pet and St Andr Corby w Gt and L Oakley 72-79; R of Ashton w Hartwell Dio Pet from 79. *Hartwell Vicarage, Northampton, NN7 2EZ.* (Roade 862600)

WALL, Charles William. b 20. Kelham Th Coll 39. **d** 44 **p** 45 Wakef. C of St John Cleckheaton 44-47; Banstead 47-53; Cobham (in c of Hatchford) 53-55; R of Ockham w Hatchford 55-63; V of St Silas Nunhead 63-71; R of Sidlow Bridge 71-76; Feltwell 76-78. *56 Barrack Road, Bexhill-on-Sea, E Sussex.*

WALL, Colin Edward. b 35. Open Univ BA 74. K Coll Lon and Warm 58. **d** 59 **p** 60 Newc T. C of Tynemouth 59-62; Cowley (in C of St Francis) 62-65; V of Syston Leics Dio Leic from 65; RD of Goscote ii from 75. *Syston Vicarage, Leicester, LE7 8GP.* (Leic 608276)

WALL, David Oliver. b 39. Bps' Coll Cheshunt 62. **d** 65 **p** 66 Chelmsf. C of L Ilford 65-68; CF 68-73; R of Sudbourne w Orford (and Chillesford w Butley from 76) 73-79; P-in-c of Chillesford w Butley 75-76; Iken 76-79; R of Rattlesden Dio St E from 79; Drinkstone Dio St E from 79. *Rattlesden Rectory, Bury St Edmunds, Suff, IP30 0RA.* (Rattlesden 7787)

✠ **WALL, Right Rev Eric St Quintin.** b 15. BNC Ox BA

(3rd cl Lit Hum) 37, MA 46. Wells Th Coll 37. **d** 38 Grimsby for Linc **p** 39 Linc. C of Boston 38-41; Chap RAFVR 41-45; V of Sherston Magna w Pinkney 44-53; RD of Malmesbury 51-53; V of Cricklade w Latton 53-60; Hon Chap to Bp of Bris 60-66; Dioc Adv in Chr Stewardship 60-66; Hon Can of Bris from 60; Proc Conv Bris 64-69; Cler Sec Bris Dioc Conf 65-66; V of St Alb Westbury Pk Clifton 66-72; RD of Clifton 67-72; Can of Ely 72-80; Cons Ld Bp Suffr of Huntingdon in S'wark Cathl 11 May 72 by Abps of Cant and York; Bps of Lon; Ely; Bris; Heref; Derby; Birm; Portsm; Nor; and others; res 80. *7 Peregrine Close, Diss, Norf.* (Diss 4331)

WALL, Gerald Robert. Ridley Coll Melb ACT ThL 56. **d** 57 **p** 58 Melb. C of St Barn Balwyn 57-59; Box Hill 59-60; V of Dingley 60-63; Boronia 63-72; I of Clayton 72-78; Hawthorn Dio Melb from 78. *2 Wood Street, Hawthorn, Vic, Australia 3122.* (818 6077)

WALL, James Leach. b 19. Univ of Leeds BA 40. **d** 64 Hong for Bradf **p** 65 Hong. C of Ch Ch Kowloon 64-66; C of Prenton 66-71; Bp Auckland 71-74; V of Hart w Elwick Hall 74-80; Chap Hartlepool Gen Hosp from 76. *191 Park Road, Hartlepool, Cleve.*

WALL, Martyn Philip Lucas. b 17. Hertf Coll Ox BA 38, MA 43. Wells Th Coll 69. **d** 71 **p** 72 Bris. C of Highworth w Sevenhampton and Hannington and Inglesham 71-74; V of Wick w Doynton Dio Bris from 74. *Vicarage, High Street, Wick, Bristol, BS15 5QQ.* (Abson [illegible])

WALL, Nicholas John. b 46. Trin Coll Bris 71. **d** 73 **p** 74 S'wark. C of Morden 73-78; R of St Nich Dunkeswell w H Trin Dunkeswell Abbey Dio Ex from 78; V of Sheldon Dio Ex from 78; P-in-c of Luppitt Dio Ex from 81. *Dunkeswell Rectory, Honiton, Devon, EX14 0RE.* (Luppitt 243)

WALL, Philip John. b 12. St Chad's Coll Dur BA (2nd cl Hist) and Jenkyns Scho 34, Dipl Th 35, MA 37. **d** 35 **p** 36 Mon. C of Fleur-de-Lys 35-38; St Sav Roath 38-39; St Jo Bapt Newport 39-41; Usk and Gwernesney w Llangeview 41-43; V of St Julians Newport 43-63; Chap HM Pris Holloway 63-68; C-in-c of Norwood-by-Southall 68-69; R 69-81; RD of Ealing W 74-78. *Precinct House, St Andrew's, Hillingdon Road, Uxbridge, UB10 0AE* (8905 53402)

WALL, William John St John Llewellyn. b 1885. **d** 15 **p** 16 Liv. C of St Luke the Evang Walton 15-18; Bp's Messenger Liv 18-19; C of St Geo w All SS Douglas IM 19-22; St Paul Widnes 22-25; St Mary Virg Prescot 25-27; V of Whiston 27-30; St Matt Bootle 30-36; St Barn Warrington 36-44; L Leigh 44-58; C of Stockton Heath Dio Ches from 58. *5 Carlton Street, Stockton Heath, Warrington, Lancs.* (Warrington 61391)

WALLACE, Alastair. b 10. Univ of Edin MA 38. St Paul's Coll Limuru 70. **d** 72 Bp Neill for Mt Kenya **p** 72 Mt Kenya. Chap St Mark's Teacher Tr Coll Kigari 72-76; C of St John W Ealing Dio Lon from 76. *4 Warwick Dene, W5 3JG.*

WALLACE, Alastair Robert. b 50. St Cath Coll Cam BA 71, MA 75, BD (Lon) 75. Trin Coll Bris 72. **d** 75 **p** 76 Ex. C of St Leon Ex 75-79; Chap Ridley Hall Cam 79-80; Research Stud St Cath Coll Cam from 80. *23 Belmore Close, Cambridge, CB4 3NN.*

WALLACE, Canon Albert Ferguson Whitelaw. b 13. Univ of Dur LTh 42. Edin Th Coll. **d** 42 **p** 43 Brech. C of St Salvador Dundee 42-45; P-in-c of St Clem Miss Aber 45-47; C of All S Leeds 47-48; Ch Ch Leeds 48-50; R of St Marg Leven 50-55; Belle Isle Dio Ripon from 55; Hon Can of ripon from 78. *Vicarage, Windmill Approach, Belle Isle, Leeds, LS10 3DT.* (Leeds 716193)

WALLACE, Alexander Ross. b 1891. Late Scho of CCC Cam BA (2nd cl Cl Trip pt i) 13, MA 24. **d** 38 **p** 39 Sarum. Hd Master of Sherborne Sch 34-50; Asst Chap 38-39; Chap 39-50; Can and Preb of Maj Pars Altaris in Sarum Cathl 43-50; Select Pr Univ of Cam 42; Dean and Preb of Ex 50-60. *Steeple Close, Hindon, Nr Salisbury, Wilts.*

WALLACE, Canon David Mayberry. ACT ThL 36. **d** 33 **p** 36 Bend. C of St Paul Bend 33-35; C-in-c of Bridgewater 35-36; R of Heathcote 36-41; St D Milloo 41-45; Tatura 45-52; Can of Bend 49-70; Can (Emer) from 70; R of Castlemaine 52-70; Chap Castlemaine Pris 56-70; L to Offic Dio Bend 70-72; Perm to Offic Dio Melb from 72; Dio Bend from 77. *32 Grant Street, Blairgowrie, Vic, Australia 3942.* (059-88 8628)

WALLACE, Derek George. b 33. Univ of Glas MA 55. Edin Th Coll 55. **d** 57 **p** 58 Edin. C of Ch Ch Falkirk 57-60; H Trin Ayr 60-62; Chap of Netherton Tr Sch Morpeth 62-67; V of St John Werneth Oldham 67-70; R of Lerwick and P-in-c of Burravoe 70-78; R of St Mary Virg Port Glas Dio Glas from 78. *St Mary's Rectory, Port Glasgow, PA14 5NL.* (Port Glasgow 41140)

WALLACE, Donald. Univ of Adel BA 39. ACT ThL 40. **d** 40 Bp Thomas for Adel **p** 41 Adel. C of St Columb Hawthorn 40-47; Chap Royal Adel Hosp 44-46; R of Pinaroo 46-48; Hd Master and Chap of All SS Sch Labasa Dio Polyn 48-53; R of Tatiara-Bordertown 53-57; Willunga 57-63; St John Adel 63-78; L to Offic Dio Adel 78-80; P-in-c of Kilburn Dio Adel from 80. *5a Fuller Street, Parkside, S Australia 5063.*

WALLACE, Very Rev Duncan Douglas. Univ of Manit BA 61. St Jo Coll Winnipeg BTh 65. **d** 64 Bp Anderson for Rupld **p** 65 Rupld. V of Fairford 65-71; I of St Ann Winnipeg 71-72; P Assoc of River N Pars 72-74; R of Milton 74-78; Dean and R of St Paul's Cathl Regina Dio Qu'App from 78. *1861 McIntyre Street, Regina, Sask, Canada.* (306-522 6439)

WALLACE, Edgar Walker. St D Coll Lamp BA 40. **d** 42 **p** 43 Llan. C of Llangynwyd 42-44; Downend Bris 44-46; C-in-c of St Chad's Conv Distr Patchway 46-49; H Cross Conv Distr Filwood Pk 49-56; V of Henleaze 56-65; Industr Chap Dio Chich from 65. *Red Tiles, Horsham Road, Crawley, Sussex.* (Crawley 22713)

WALLACE, Edward Hugh. Univ of Manit BA 48. Wycl Coll Tor LTh 52. **d** 51 Tor for Koot **p** 52 Koot. C of Trail 52-53; St Matt Winnipeg 53-54; R of Fergus 54-59; Miss at Williams Lake 59-64; R of St Martin 64-70; St Stephens W Vancouver Dio New Westmr from 70. *2242 Kings Avenue, West Vancouver, BC, Canada.*

WALLACE, Ernest Frederick Gordon. Lon Coll Div 20. Univ of Dur LTh 25. **d** 22 **p** 23 Chelmsf. C of St Mary Leyton 22-28; V of St Kath Northn 28-32; Em Holloway 32-44; Mettingham w Ilketshall St John 44-53; Surr 33-44. *Ingleside, Old Fishbourne, Chichester, Sussex.*

WALLACE, Godfrey Everingham. b 32. Univ of Bris BA (3rd cl Th) 57. Tyndale Hall Bris 53. **d** 58 **p** 59 Chich. C of Broadwater 58-61; V of S Tidworth w Shipton Bellinger 61-70; St Paul Bournemouth Dio Win from 70. *Vicarage, St Paul's Road, Bournemouth, Dorset,* (Bournemouth 25064)

WALLACE, Hugh Carlton. b 1900. Ch Ch Ox BA and MA 26. St Geo Windsor 53. **d** 54 **p** 55 Man. C of All SS Stand 54-57; V of Holme Cultram 57-65. *7 St Michael's Close, Hilperton, Trowbridge, Wilts.*

WALLACE, Hugo. Trin Coll Cam BA 54, MA 59. Ridley Hall Cam 54. **d** 56 **p** 57 Chelmsf. C of Hornchurch 56-58; CMS Ugan 58-59; Dioc Youth Organiser Dio Ugan 59-60; C of Bermondsey 61; Usuthu 61-66; Min of St Paul's Conv Distr Parkeston 67-69; C of Wynberg 69-76; Parow 76-78; P-in-c of Ravensmead 78-80; Perm to Offic Dio Capetn from 80. *Vagabond, Albert Road, Hout Bay 7800, CP, S Africa.* (70-8390)

WALLACE, Irene. b 13. Wycl Coll Tor LTh 50. **d** 74 **p** 77 Niag. C of St Pet Hamilton 74-77; Assoc R of St Pet Hamilton 77-79; P Assoc of Steph Hamilton Dio Niag from 79. *603-159 Prospect Street South, Hamilton, Ont, Canada, L8N 2Z5.* (416-544 6136)

WALLACE, Ven John Murdock. b 07. TCD BA and Div Test 30, MA 59. **d** 30 **p** 32 Tuam. C of St Nich Galway 30-33; R of Kilgrass w Enniscrone and Castleconnor 33-43; Chap (Eccles Est) Dio Madr 43-47; Hon CF 47; Dioc C Lim 49-52; I of Listowel U 52-59; Dioc Sec Ardf and Agh 54-72; Can of Lim from 59; I of Kilnaughtin and Listowel 59-79; Archd of Ardf and Agh 62-79; Archd (Emer) from 79; Preb of Effin in Lim Cathl 63-68; Treas 68-79. *c/o Rectory, Listowel, Co Kerry, Irish Republic.* (068-21466)

WALLACE, Martin William. b 48. K Coll Lon BD and AKC 70. St Aug Coll Cant 70. **d** 71 **p** 72 Sheff. C of Attercliffe Sheff 71-74; New Malden w Coombe 74-77; V of St Mark Forest Gate Dio Chelmsf from 77. *28 Godwin Road, E7.* (01-555 2988)

WALLACE, Raymond Sherwood. b 28. Selw Coll Dun. **d** 52 Ch Ch for Dun **p** 54 Dun. C of Roslyn 52-54; Invercargill 54-55; P-in-c of Waitaki 55-58; C of H Cross St Pancras 58-64; St Alb N Harrow 64-67; V of H Trin Stroud Green 67-79; Penwerris Dio Truro from 79. *12 Stratton Terrace, Falmouth, Cornw, TR11 2SY.* (Falmouth 314263)

WALLACE, Richard Colin. b 39. Mert Coll Ox BA 61, MA 64. St Chad's Coll Dur 69. **d** 71 Dur **p** 72 Jarrow for Dur. Tutor and Libr St Chad's Coll Dur 71-72; P-in-c of Kimblesworth 72-74; Bp's Chap to Studs Dio Bradf 74-79; C of Bingley Dio Bradf 79-80; Team V from 80. *Winston Grange, Otley Road, Eldwick, Bingley, BD16 3EQ.* (Bingley 2445)

WALLACE, Richard Ernest. ACT ThL 60. Ridley Th Coll Melb 58. **d** 61 Melb **p** 62 Bp Redding for Melb. C of St Barn Balwyn 61-62; Ch Ch S Yarra 62-64; Bentleigh 64-65; V of Ch of Epiph Northcote Austr 65-66; C of St Francis Ipswich 67-69; I of Belgrave 69-79; on leave. *PO Box 135, Belgrave, Vic, Australia 3160.* (03-754 2101)

WALLACE, Richard Samuel. b 17. TCD BA 39, MA 53. **d** 41 Down **p** 42 Bp Hind for Down. C of St Luke Belf 41-43; St Pet Hammersmith 43-44; Missr Dub Univ Miss at Hazaribagh 44-51; LDHM of St Nich Perivale 51-54; V of St Mark Notting Hill 54-60; Commiss Chota N 59-70; V of St Mark S Teddington Dio Lon from 60. *Vicarage, St Mark's Road, Teddington, Middx, TW11 9DE.* (01-977 4067)

WALLACE, Robert. b 52. Univ of Sussex BSc 73. Univ of Nottm Dipl Th 75. Linc Th Coll 73. **d** 76 **p** 77 Roch. C of St

Mary's Plaistow 76-79; Dartford Dio Roch from 79. *42 Dorchester Close, Dartford, Kent.* (Dartford 28648)

WALLACE, Thomas Raymond. b 37. Moore Th Coll Syd ACT ThL 63. **d** 61 **p** 62 Armid. C of Inverell 61-64; L to Offic Dio Syd 64-67; Chap Bd of Educn 64-67; Adult Educn Officer 67-70; Dir Relig Educn Dio Perth 71-74; L to Offic Dio Syd from 75; Assoc Dir Relig Educn Dio Syd 75; Actg Dir 75-76; Dir from 77. *St Andrew's House, Sydney Square, Sydney, NSW, Australia 2000.* (2-0642)

WALLACE, Victor Joseph Francis. d 63 **p** 64 Johann. C of Krugersdorp 64-66; R of Mayfair Dio Johann from 66. *Rectory, Park Drive, Mayfair, Transvaal, S Africa.* (011-35 1523)

WALLACE-HADRILL, David Sutherland. b 20. CCC Ox BA 41, MA 45. Univ of Man BD (w distinc) 44, DD 60. **d** 43 **p** 44 Man. C of St Mich Flixton 43-45; Walthamstow 45-47; V of H Cross Hornchurch 47-50; Chap Aldenham Sch 50-55; Ho Master 62-72; Asst Master from 72; V of Eston w Normanby 55-62; L to Offic Dio St Alb from 62. *Alden Cottage, New Road, Letchmore Heath, Watford, Herts.* (Radlett 6283)

WALLBANK, Preb Newell Eddius. b 14. Late Scho of Qu Coll Cam Stewart of Rannoch Scho BA and MusB 34, MA 40. TCD MusB (*ad eund*) and MusD 36. Univ of Lon BA (2nd cl Phil) 40, PhD 56. Ripon Hall Ox 35. **d** 37 **p** 38 Lon. C of St Bart Gt Lon 37-45; R 45-79; RD of City 58-63; Preb of St Paul's Cathl Lon 64-79; Preb (Emer) from 79; Select Pr Univ of Ox 68; Hon Chap Imperial S of Knights Bachelor 68-79. *Meldrum, Boveney Road, Dorney Common, Windsor, Berks, SL4 6QD.*

WALLER, Alfred Raymond. Angl Th Coll BC Dipl Th 62. **d** 62 **p** 63 New Westmr. I of S Burnaby 62-73; on leave 74-76; P-in-c of St Edw Richmond 76-77; I of St Pet and St Luke Vanc Dio New Westmr from 77. *4366 Winnifred Street, Burnaby, BC, Canada.*

WALLER, Arthur Henry Naunton. b 06. Selw Coll Cam BA 30, MA 34. Wycl Hall Ox. **d** 31 **p** 32 St E. C of St Jo Bapt Ipswich 31-35; Leiston w Sizewell 35-36; R 36-45; Frostenden w S Cove 45-74. *Mill Field, Waldringfield, Woodbridge, Suff.*

WALLER, Gordon Hamilton. b 18. AKC and Warm 49. **d** 49 Bedford for St Alb **p** 50 St Alb. C of Boreham Wood 49-56; Bp's Stortford 56-58; V of H Trin Bp's Stortford 58-62; Biscot 62-71; Asst RD of Luton 67-71; R of Meppershall and U w Lower Standon Dio St Alb from 71. *Meppershall Rectory, Shefford, Beds.* (Hitchin 813334)

WALLER, John Pretyman. b 41. Sarum Th Coll 68. **d** 71 Dunwich for St E **p** 72 St E. C of St Jo Bapt Ipswich 71-74; R of Waldringfield w Hemley (and Newbourn from 78) Dio St E from 74; P-in-c of Newbourn 74-78. *Waldringfield Rectory, Woodbridge, Suff.* (Waldringfield 247)

✠ **WALLER, Right Rev John Stevens.** b 24. Peterho Cam BA (2nd cl Hist Trip pt i) 48, MA 53. Wells Th Coll 48. **d** 50 **p** 51 Lon. C of Hillingdon 50-52; Twiverton 52-55; C-in-c of Conv Distr of St Andr Bournville Weston-s-Mare 55-57; Min of Eccles Distr 57-59; V 59-60; R of Yarlington and Dioc Youth Chap Dio B & W 60-63; Tr Officer C of E Youth Coun 63-67; V of Frindsbury w Upnor 67-72; P-in-c of St Nich w St Mary and St Francis Strood 67-72; Team R 72-73; RD of Strood 67-73; R of Harpenden 73-79; Commiss Zulu and Swaz from 78; Cons Ld Bp Suffr of Stafford in Westmr Abbey 25 Jan 79 by Abp of Cant; Bps of Lon, Lich, B & W, Heref, Nor, Portsm, Roch, Ox, Truro, Linc and St E; Bps Suffr of Hertford, Buckingham, Grantham, Shrewsbury, Tonbridge, St Germans and Jarrow; and others; Hon Can of Lich Cathl from 79. *Park Lodge, 3 Beech Court, Stone, Staffs, ST15 8QG.* (0785 816007)

WALLER, John Watson. b 35. Univ of Lon BSc (2nd cl Chem) 57. St Cath S Ox Dipl Th 60. Wycl Hall Ox 59. **d** 61 **p** 62 Bradf. C of Pudsey 61-65; V of Mortomley 65-74; Pudsey Dio Bradf from 74; M Gen Syn from 77. *Vicarage, Church Lane, Pudsey, W Yorks, LS28 7RL.* (Pudsey 577843)

WALLER, Richard Charles Eisdell. b 19. Or Coll Ox BA 50, MA 54. Linc Th Coll 50. **d** 51 **p** 52 St Alb. C of Cheshunt 51-56; PC of Biscot 56-62. *11 Black Butts Cottage, Sutton Road, Cookham, Berks.*

WALLER, Robin Timothy. b 49. Univ of Sask BA 74. Em & St Chad's Coll Sktn LTh 74, MDiv 75. **d** and **p** 74 Koot. C of Trail 74-76; on leave. *898 Moyer Road, Kelowna, BC, Canada.*

WALLER, Canon Trevor. b 04. Selw Coll Cam BA 27, MA 31. Ridley Hall Cam 27. **d** 29 **p** 30 St E. C of St Matt Ipswich 29-30; Newmarket 30-33; Leiston w Sizewell 33-35; V of Debenham 35-48; R of Hemley w Waldringfield 48-74; C-in-c of Newbourn 49-50; R 50-74; RD of Colneys 62-72; Hon Can of St E 65-74; Can (Emer) from 74; Perm to Offic Dio St E from 74. *Whitehall Cottage, Waldringfield, Woodbridge, Suff.*

WALLER, William John. b 38. Bp's Coll Cheshunt 66. **d** 68 Bedford for St Alb. **p** 69 Hertford for Cant for St Alb. C of St Hugh Lewsey Luton 68-73; All SS Oxhey 73-75; Henllys w Bettws 75-77. *Caer Bryn, Monnow Way, Newport, Gwent, NPT 6DB* (Newport 852367)

WALLER-WILKINSON, Richard Noel. b 27. Roch Th Coll 62. **d** 64 **p** 65 Newc T. C of St Jas Benwell Newc T 64-66; CF 66-72; V of St Elisabeth Harraby Carl 72-75; P-in-c of Castle Carrock w Cumrew and Croglin 75-79; Cumwhitton 75-79; R of Stowell Mem Ch Salford 79-81; V of Monton, Eccles Dio Man from 81. *Vicarage, Brackley Road, Monton, Eccles, Manchester, M30 9LG.* (061-789 2420)

WALLINGTON, Christopher Archer. b 16. Wadh Coll Ox BA (3rd cl Mod Hist) 39, MA 44. Westcott Ho Cam 39. **d** 41 Bp Duppuy for Worc **p** 42 Worc. C of St Jas Gt Dudley 41-43; Ch Ch w St Andr Malvern 43-45; St Jas Paddington 45-49; V of Frimley Green 49-52; C of St Jo Evang Meads Eastbourne 52-55; CF 55-58; V of St Steph Bexhill 58-82; Hon C of Bengeo Dio St Alb from 82. *19 Cowper Crescent, Bengeo, Hertford, Herts, SG14 3DZ.* (0992 54018)

WALLINGTON, Richard Archer. b 02. OBE 56. Wadh Coll Ox BA 29, MA 33. Ripon Hall Ox 60. **d** 61 **p** 62 Ex. C of Buckland Filleigh 61-63; R of Langtree Dio Ex from 63; RD of Torrington 77-81. *Langtree Rectory, Torrington, Devon.* (Langtree 273)

WALLIS, Canon John. b 13. Pemb Coll Ox BA (2nd cl Th) 36, MA 40. Wells Th Coll 36. **d** 37 Wakef **p** 38 Pontefract for Wakef. C of Airedale w Fryston 37-39; Birstall 39-47; V of Heckmondwike 47-69; Hartshead 69-79; RD of Birstall 59-79; Hon Can of Wakef from 65. *21 Westfields Road, Mirfield, W Yorks, WF14 9PW.*

WALLIS, John Anthony. b 36. St Pet Coll Ox BA (3rd cl Th) 60, MA 64. Clifton Th Coll 60. **d** 62 **p** 63 Blackb. C of St Mark Layton Blackpool 62-65; St Geo Leeds 65-69; Miss OMF in Korea 69-74; Nat Sec Overseas Miss Fellowship in Scotld 75-78; Home Dir Overseas Miss Fellowship from 78. *Belmont, The Vine, Sevenoaks, Kent, TN13 2TZ.*

WALLIS, Canon John Charles. b 12. DSC 44. Hatf Coll Dur BA and LTh 38, MA 51. St Bonif Coll Warm 34. **d** 39 **p** 40 Sarum. C of H Trin Trowbridge 39-41; Chap RNVR 41-46; V of Allington 46-48; Chap of Univ Coll and of Hatf Coll Dur 48-57; R of Bloxworth w Winterborne Anderson Zelstone and Tomson 57-61; Wareham w Arne (and E Holme from 76) 61-79; RD of Purbeck 66-73; Can and Preb of Sarum Cathl 66-79; Can (Emer) from 80; C-in-c of E Stoke w E Holme 67-71; E Holme 75-76. *Beechcroft, King's Road, Blandford, Dorset, DT11 7NN.*

WALLIS, Raymond Christopher. b 38. Sarum Th Coll 63. **d** 66 **p** 67 Bradf. C of Allerton 66-68; Langley Marish 68-69; Caister-on-Sea 69-73; C-in-c of E w W Bradenham 73--80; R of Upwell St Pet Dio Ely from 80; Outwell Dio Ely from 80. *Upwell Rectory, Wisbech, Cambs, PE14 9AB.* (Upwell 2213)

WALLIS, Roderick Vaughan. b 37. Univ of Leic BA 79. Univ of Warwick MA 80. Lich Th Coll 64. **d** 66 **p** 67 Ox. C of Cookham 66-70; Daventry 70-72; Team V of Em Northn 72-76; Hon C of St Matt Northn Dio Pet from 76. *28 Lingswood Park, Northampton, NN3 4TA.* (0604 401578)

WALLIS, Roger Charles Theodore. b 13. Peterho Cam BA 36, MA 54. Wells Th Coll 36. **d** 38 **p** 39 B & W. C of Wellington w W Buckland 38-39; CF (R of O) 39-45; CF 45-59; V of Hambridge w Earnshill (w Ile Brewers from 68) 59-79; Ile Brewers 61-68; Bp's Chap for Ordin Tr 63-71; Exam Chap to Bp of B & W 66-75; RD of Ilminster 72-78; Preb of Wells Cathl 74-77. *Byams, Fitzhead, Taunton, Somt.*

WALLIS, Roland Seabon. b 17. MBE 44. BSc (Lon) 38. Univ of Ex BSc *ad eund* 57. St Aug Coll Cant 75. **d** 77 **p** 78 Cant. C of Whitstable Dio Cant from 77. *22 Mickleburgh Avenue, Herne Bay, Kent, CT6 6HA.*

WALLIS, Canon William. b 10. Trin Coll Ox BA (2nd cl Mod Hist) 32, 2nd cl Th 33, MA 36. Cudd Coll 33. **d** 34 **p** 35 York. C of Saltburn-by-the-Sea 34-38; N Ormesby (in c of St Thos) 38-39; PC of Healaugh w Wighill 39-47; Chap to HM Pris Askham Grange 47; V of Pickering 47-75; Proc Conv York 51-75; RD of Pickering 52-67; Exam Chap to Abp of York from 53; Can and Preb of York Minster from 61. *Newbald House, The Rise, Thornton-le-Dale, Pickering, N Yorks.* (Thornton Dale 621)

WALLS, Archie. St Jo Coll Dur LTh 22. St Aid Coll. **d** 22 **p** 23 Carl. C of St Mark Barrow-F 23-26; All SS Chilvers Coton 26-27; V of Longford Warws 27-34; Sandal Magna w Newmillerdam 34-49; Helme 49-58; Gildersome 58-62; Hon C of St Chad City and Dio Tor from 63. *76 Doncaster Avenue, Toronto 369, Ont , Canada.*

WALLS, Gordon Richard. b 50. Univ of Windsor BA 75. **d** and **p** 77 Ont. L to Offic Dio Ont from 77. *Society of St John the Evangelist, Box 660, Bracebridge, Ont, Canada.*

WALLS, Michael Peter. b 38. Univ of Capetn BA 57. Dipl Th (Lon) 61. Wells Th Coll 59. **d** 61 **p** 62 Blackb. C of St Barn Morecambe 61-64; St Paul w St Mark Birm 64-66; Industr Chap Dio Birm 64-74; V of Temple Balsall 66-74; master

Lady Katherine Leveson's Hosp Temple Balsall 66-74; Chap Wroxall Abbey Sch Warwick 72-74; V of Kings Heath 74-76; Asst Master Bierton Comprehensive Sch Yardley and Hon C of Small Heath 76-78; Chap of Oakham Sch from 78. *79 Station Road, Oakham, Leics, LE15 6QT.* (0572 55716)

WALLS, Canon Raymond William. b 10. AKC 35. **d** 35 **p** 36 Roch. C of St Andr Bromley 35-38; St Jo Div Selsdon 38-42; c-in-c St Andr Bromley 42-45; C of St Pet Aylesford 45-46; R of Eriswell 46-52; Glemsford 52-59; C-in-c of Somerton 54-59; R of Ufford 59-77; Chap St Audry's Ment Hosp Melton 59-77; Ed *The Church in Suffolk* 61-74; Hon Can of St E from 65; Perm to Offic Dio Cant from 77. *69 Whitstable Road, Canterbury, Kent.* (Cant 65816)

WALLS, Roland Charles. b 17. Late Scho of CCC Cam 1st cl Th Trip pt i 47, BA (1st cl Th Trip pt ii) and Sen Scholefield Pri 48, MA 52. Kelham Th Coll 34. **d** 40 **p** 41 Ripon. C of St Jas Manston 40-43; St Cecilia Parson Cross Sheff 43-45; Perm to Offic Dio Ely 45-48; Fell of CCC Cam 48-62; Chap 52-55; Dean of Chap 55-58; Lect in Th Kelham Th Coll 48-51; Dom Chap to Bp of Ely 51-52; Exam Chap to Bp of Sarum 55-58; to Bp of Lich 58-61; to Bp of Sheff 58-62; to Bp of Edin from 63; Hon Chap to Bp of Derby 55-59; Commiss Accra 56-73; Select Pr Univ of Cam 56; Univ of Ox 77; Can (Res) of Sheff Cathl 58-62; Hon C-in-c of Rosslyn Chap 62-69; Lect in Div Univ of Edin 63-77; M Commun of Transfig from 65. *23 Manse Road, Roslin, Midlothian.*

WALLWORK, Harold. b 16. St Jo Coll Dur LTh and BA 41, MA 44. Oak Hill Th Coll 37. **d** 41 **p** 42 Blackb. C of St Thos Blackpool 41-44; C-in-c of Gt Houghton 44-46; Chap and Tutor Tyndale Hall Bris 46-48; C-in-c of St Thos Lanc 48-51; V 51-58; R of Ch Ch Addington Durban 58-62; Grendon Underwood w Edgcott 62-65; Richmond (Natal) 65-70; Bispham Dio Blackb from 71. *Bispham Rectory, Blackpool, Lancs.* (Blackpool 51886)

WALMISLEY, Andrew John. b 55. Univ of Ex BA 75. Ridley Hall Cam 76. **d** 78 Lon **p** 79 Kens for Lon. C of St Mary The Boltons Kens 78-81; in Amer Ch. *815 Portola Road, Portola Valley, CA94205, USA.*

WALMSLEY, Alexander David. b 07. **p** 29 Ches. C of St Paul Seacombe 28-30; St Paul Southport 30-31; Standish 31-34; 30, Dipl Th 34, MA 35. Blackb Hall Ox 33. **d** 34 **p** 35 Bradf. C of Cathl Ch Bradf 34-38; Cheltm 38-39; Battersea (in c of G and C Coll Miss) 39-43; Chap RNVR 43-46; V of Ch Ch U Armley 46-51; Adderbury w Milton 51-64; Chap to St Mary's Hosp Armley 46-51; R of Whitchurch Oxon 64-74; *1 College Yard, Gloucester, GL1 2PL.* (Gloucester 412040)

WALMSLEY, George Bernard. b 07. Univ of Leeds BA (3rd cl Cl) 29. Coll of Resurr Mirfield 25. **d** 31 **p** 32 Ban. C of Llandysilio 31-33; Llandudno 33-39; V of Beddgelert 39-46; Pentraeth w Llanddyfnan 46-51; C-in-c of St Mich AA Conv Distr S Yardley 51-55; V of All S Witton 55-59; Meerbrook 59-72; C-in-c of Quarnford 65-72. *46 Parker Street, Leek Staffs, ST13 6LB.*

WALMSLEY, John Francis. b 14. Late Scho of St Pet Hall Ox 2nd cl Cl Mods 35, BA (3rd cl Th) 37, MA 47. Wycl Hall Ox 37. **d** 38 **p** 39 Liv. C of Ravenhead 38-41; Asst Chap Mersey Miss to Seamen 41-43; Chap RNVR 43-46; C of St Nich Blundellsands (in c of St Steph Hightown) 46-48; V of St Barn Mossley Hill 48-53; Chap RN 53-70; R of Elsted w Didling and Treyford 71-79. *34 Bury Road, Alverstoke, Gosport, Hants.* (Gosport 82428)

WALMSLEY, John William. b 37. Univ of Hull BA 71, MA 73, PhD 81. Wycl Hall Ox 71. **d** 72 **p** 73 York. C of St Jas Clifton York 72-74; St Steph Acomb York 74-76; P-in-c of Shipton w Overton 76-81; Newton-on-Ouse 76-81; V of St Thos w St Maurice City and Dio York from 81. *157 Haxby Road, York, YO3 7JL* (York 52228)

WALPOLE, Geoffrey Everard. Univ of Cant BSc 60. Vic Univ of Wel MSc 61. Virginia Th Sem BD 64. **d** 64 Bp McKenzie for Wel **p** 65 Wel. Hon C of Porirua Dio Wel 64-69 and 71-76; Perm to Offic Dio Polyn and Lect Univ of S Pacific Suva 69-71; V of Porirua 76-81; Perm to Offic Dio Wel from 81. *37 Awatea Street, Porirua, NZ.* (74-331)

WALSER, Ven David. b 23. St Edm Hall Ox BA 2nd cl Mod Hist 48, Dipl Th 49, MA 53. St Steph Ho Ox 48. **d** 50 **p** 51 Bris. C of St Greg Horfield 50-54; Vice-Prin St Steph Ho Ox and LPr Dio Ox 54-60; Asst Chap Ex Coll Ox 56-57; Jun Chap Mert Coll Ox 57-60; Min Can of Ely Cathl and Chap K Sch 61-70; 61-71; Perm to Offic Dio Ely 61-71; V of Linton 71-81; R of Bartlow 73-81; St Botolph Cam Dio Ely from 81; RD of Linton 76-81; Archd of Ely from 81. *St Botolph's Rectory, Summerfield, Cambridge, CB3 9HE.* (Cam 350864)

WALSER, Emil Jonathan. b 16. St Jo Coll Dur LTh 38 BA 39, MA 43. Oak Hill Th Coll 35. **d** 39 Willesden for Lon **p** 40 Lon. C of St Mary Magd Holloway 39-42; St Lawr Pudsey 42-46; R of St Edm Whalley Range 46-52; V of Mackworth 52-65; C-in-c of Kirk Langley 57-59; R 59-65; PC (V from 68) of Baslow 65-82; RD of Bakewell and Eyam 78-81. *1 Yokecliffe Crescent, Wirksworth, Nr Derby, DE4 4ER.* (Wirksworth 2972)

WALSH, Bertram William Nicholas. b 21. TCD BA (2nd cl Mod in Celtic Lang) 44, Div Test (2nd cl) 46. **d** 46 **p** 47 Dub. C of St Pet w St Matthias Dub 46-47; St Jas Dub 47-49; Min Can of St Patr Cathl Dub 47-49; Res Pr of St Fin Barre's Cathl Cork 49-52; C of St Bart Dub 52-54; Cler v of Ch Ch Cathl Dub 54-58; Asst Master K Hosp Sch Dub 58-60; Chap St Columba's Coll Rathfarnham from 60. *130 Grange Road, Rathfarnham, Dublin 16, Irish Republic.* (Dublin 900229)

WALSH, Brian Neville. b 16. Univ of Stellenbosch BSc 48. **d** 73 Capetn. C of Kalk Bay 73-76; Grassy Pk 77-78; Lotus River 78-79; Steenberg Dio Capetn from 79. *7 Hopkirk Way, Glencairn, CP, S Africa.* (86-1297)

WALSH, David Albert. St Chad's Coll Regina LTh 52. **d** 52 **p** 53 Qu'App. I of Hazenmore 52-55; Nokomis 55-58; C of Guelph 58-61; R of St Matt Hamilton 61-66; Good Shepherd St Catharines 66-70. *9626 Melville Drive, Windsor, Ont., Canada.*

WALSH, Dennis Edwin. K Coll NS BA 67. **d** 68 NS **p** 69 Bp Arnold for NS. R of Port Morien 68-69; Lockeport 70-73; on leave. *6148 Cedar Street, Halifax, NS, Canada.* (429-3430)

WALSH, Ven Geoffrey David Jeremy. b 29. Pemb Coll Cam 2nd cl Econ Trip pt i 51, BA (2nd cl Econ Trip pt ii) 53, MA 58. Linc Th Coll 53. **d** 55 **p** 56 Lon. C of Ch Ch Southgate 55-58; SCM Sec Cam Univ and C of St Mary Gt Cam 58-61; V of St Matt Moorfields Bris 61-66; R of Marlborough 66-76; Can and Preb Sarum Cathl 73-76; Archd of Ipswich from 76; R of Elmsett W Aldham 76-80; M Gen Syn from 80. *99 Valley Road, Ipswich, IP1 4NF*

WALSH, James Hamer. d 54 **p** 55 Sask. I of Medstead 54-55; Leask 55-58; R of Matheson 58-63; Chap RCAF 63-75; I of Southn 75-80; Tilbury and Comber Dio Hur from 80. *17 Forrest Street, Tilbury, Ont, Canada.*

WALSH, John Alan. b 37. Chich Th Coll 63. **d** 66 Warrington for Liv **p** 67 Liv. C of St Anne Wigan 66-69; Newport w Longford 69-73; V of Rangemore Dio Lich from 73; Dunstall Dio Lich from 73; P-in-c of Tatenhill Dio Lich from 77. *Rangemore Vicarage, Burton-on-Trent, Staffs.* (Barton-under-Needwood 2509)

WALSH, John Quentin Evelyn. b 03. Trin Hall Cam BA 29, MA 33. Linc Th Coll 29. **d** 30 **p** 32 Ches. C of St Mich Macclesfield 30-36; St Chad Over 36-37; Witton (otherwise Northwich) 37-41; V of St John Doddington 41-70; L to Offic Dio ches from 70. *Copper Beech, Wybunbury Lane, Walgherton, Nantwich, Ches.* (Crewe 841430)

WALSH, Kirby. b 41. Mem Univ Newfld BA 67, LTh 69, MA 70. **d** 69 **p** 70 Newfld. C of Channel 69-72; I of Seal Cove 72-76; on leave 76-77; Chap Publ Inst and Reg Coll Corner Brook from 77. *160 East Valley Road, Corner Brook, Newfoundland, Canada.*

WALSH, Preb Lionel Ernest. b 10. Late Exhib of Hatf Coll Dur BA 31. Bps' Coll Cheshunt 31. **d** 33 Taunton for B & W **p** 34 B & W. C of Yeovil (in c of Preston Plucknett 38-40) 33-40; St Jo Bapt Weston-s-Mare 40-42; V of Cheddar 42-52; Martock 52-57; Yeovil w Preston Plucknett and Kingston Pitney 57-65; PC of Yeovil Marsh 57-65; Preb of Wells Cathl from 63; R of Ditcheat 65-75. *Abbey Close, Ditcheat, Shepton Mallet, Somt.* (Ditcheat 314)

WALSH, Martin Percival. Montr Dioc Th Coll LTh 67. **d** 65 Ont. C of St Thos Belleville 65-67; I of Sharbot Lake 67-74; Penit Chap Dio Ont 74-78; Ft Pitt w Onion Lake Dio Sask from 79. *Box 83, Frenchman Butte, Sask, Canada.*

WALSH, Norman. b 01. St Chad's Coll Dur. **d** 68 **p** 69 Dur. C of Dalton-le-Dale 68-73; Perm to Offic Dio Dur from 73. *Sherburn Hospital, Sherburn House, Durham, DH1 2SE.*

WALSH, Richard Edward. K Coll Halifax NS LTh 61. **d** and **p** 61 Fred. I of Gordon w Lorne 61-68; R of Rosette 68-74; Newport Dio NS from 74. *PO Box 13, Newport, NS, Canada.* (757-2396)

WALSH, Robert George. b 39. St Francis Coll Brisb ACT ThL (2nd cl) 66. **d** 66 **p** 67 Brisb. C of Maryborough 66-69; St Paul Ipswich 69-70; V of Pialba Dio Brisb 70-72; R of Hervey Bay 72-75; Kingaroy Dio Brisb from 75. *Rectory, Alford Street, Kingaroy, Queensland, Australia 4610.* (72 1071)

WALSH, Thomas Laurence. BNC Ox BA and MA 38. Ripon Hall Ox 38. **d** 39 **p** 40 Blackb. C of All SS Blackpool 39-44; St Andr Cleveleys 44-45; V of Ribby w Wrea 45-60; Staveley-in-Cartmel 60-76; Finsthwaite 60-74; L to Offic Dio Carl from 76. *Tarn Potts, Newby Bridge, Ulverston, Cumb, LA12 8AW.*

WALSH, Canon William Arthur. b 12. St Jo Coll Dur BA 34, MA 41, Dipl Th 41. **d** 35 **p** 36 York. C of St Andr Drypool 35-38; St Barn Linthorpe 38-41; Chap RAFVR 42-44; V of Ch Ch Dartford 44-77; Hon Can of Roch Cathl 71-77; Can (Emer) from 77; Perm to Offic Dio Roch from 77. *33 Correnden Road, Tonbridge, Kent.*

WALSH, William Eric. Pemb Coll Ox BA 36, MA 40.

Ripon Hall, Ox 37. **d** 40 **p** 41 Sheff. C of St Polycarp Malin Bridge 40-43; H Trin Morecambe 43-48; V of Knuzden 48-57; Garstang 57-63; Milnthorpe 63-78. *Address temp unknown.*

WALSH, William Leonard. Moore Coll Syd ThL 64. **d** 64 **p** 65 Syd. C of Liv 64-65; St John Darlinghurst Syd 66-67; C-in-c of Padstow 67-70; R of Carlton Dio Syd from 70. *27 Cameron Street, Bexley, NSW, Australia 2207.* (587-3979)

WALSHE, Brian. b 28. K Coll Lon and Warm AKC (2nd cl) 49. **d** 54 **p** 55 Portsm. C of St Pet Southsea 54-57; St Jo Bapt Rudmore Portsea 57-58; Warden Wel Coll Miss Walworth 58-62; PC of SS Aug Chesterfield 62-68; V of Langley Marish 68-76; St Alb Mart Northn Dio Pet from 76. *Vicarage, Broadmead Avenue, Northampton, NN3 2RA.* (Northn 44928)

WALTER, Canon Arthur Reginald. b 13. Keble Coll Ox BA 34, MA 38. St Mich Coll Llan 35. **d** 36 Swan B **p** 37 Mon. C of Llandrindod w Cefnllys 36-37; St Mary Mon 37-40; CF (EC) 40-46; Hon CF 46; Chap Ch of Epiph Port Said 46-54; R of Scarning 54-60; C-in-c of Wendling 56-60; R of Swanton Morley w Worthing 60-78; RD of Brisley and Elmham 69-77; Hon Can of Nor 75-78; Can (Emer) from 78; Perm to Offic Dio Nor 78-80; Actg Chap H Trin Madeira Dio Gibr in Eur from 80. *Holy Trinity, Rua do Quebra Costas 20, Funchal, Madeira.*

WALTER, Donald Alex. b 34. Ripon Hall Ox 57. **d** 60 **p** 61 Lon. C of St Steph W Ealing 60-63; R of Lucea, Ja 63-80; V of H Trin Twickenham Dio Lon from 81. *1 Vicarage Road, Twickenham Green, Middx.* (01-898 1168)

WALTER, Ian Edward. b 47. Univ of Edin MA 69. Keble Coll Ox BA 71, MA 78. Cudd Coll 71. **d** 73 **p** 74 Glas. C of Greenock 73-76; Angl Chap to Studs and C of St Mary's Cathl Glas 76-79; R of St Barn Paisley Dio Glas from 79. *St Barnabas' Rectory, Alice Street, Paisley, Renfrewshire, PA2 6DR.* (041-889 6498)

WALTER, John Allen. b 19. Univ of Lon BSc 48. FCA 56. S Dioc Min Tr Scheme 80. **d** 81 Sarum (NSM). C of Okeford Fitzpaine, Ibberton w Belchalwell & Woolland Dio Sarum from 81. *Formentor, Castle Lane, Okeford Fitzpaine, Blandford Forum, Dorset, DT11 0RJ.*

WALTER, Kenneth Ronald. b 22. Univ of Lon BA 52. Oak Hill Th Coll 47. **d** 52 **p** 53 Chelmsf. C of St Luke Walthamstow 52-54; Org Sec CPAS SE Distr 54-59; Cl Asst Sec Ch S 59-64; R of Gt Holland Dio Chelmsf from 64; RD of St Osyth from 74. *Great Holland Rectory, Frinton-on-Sea, Essex, CO13 0JS.* (Frinton 4424)

WALTER, Michael. b 36. K Coll Lon and Warm AKC 62. **d** 63 **p** 64 York. C of St John Middlesbrough 63-65; Sherborne 65-68; St Francis Bournemouth 68-69; Prec of Newc T Cathl 69-71; St Marg Dur 72-74; P-in-c of Deaf Hill w Langdale 74-77; V of Newington w Dairycoates Dio York from 77. *Newington Vicarage, St George's Road, Hull, HU3 3SP.* (Hull 23875)

WALTER, Noel. b 41. St D Coll Lamp Dipl Th 66. **d** 66 **p** 67 S'wark. C of Ascen Mitcham 66-71; Caterham 71-74; V of St Mary Welling Dio S'wark from 74. *St Mary's Vicarage, Sandringham Drive, Welling, Kent, DA16 3QU.* (01-856 0684)

WALTER, Robin. b 37. Univ Coll Dur BA (2nd cl French) 63. Linacre Coll Ox BA (3rd cl Th) 65, MA 69. St Steph Ho Ox 63. **d** 66 **p** 68 S'wark. C of St John (f St Chrys w St Jude) Peckham 66-69; Chap Univ of Lon 69-70; C of St Marg (in c of St John nevilles Cross) Durham 70-74; R of Burnmoor 74-79. *79 Harmire Road, Barnard Castle, C Durham, DL12 8DL.* (Teesdale 31741)

WALTER, William James. b 26. Em Coll Sktn. **d** 54 **p** 55 Sask. I of Turtleford 54-57; Birch Hills 57-59; Chap R Canad Navy 59-65; C of Bourne Surrey 65-67; Chap RN from 67. *c/o Ministry of Defence, Lacon House, Theobalds Road, WC1X 8RY.*

WALTERS, Andrew Farrar. b 42. Acp 67. **d** 81 Heref (NSM). Warden S Mich Coll Tenbury Wells from 81. *St Michael's College, Tenbury Wells, Worcs, WR15 8PH.*

WALTERS, Charles. b 27. Em Coll Sktn 64. **d** 66 Yukon **p** 67 Athab. C of Whitehorse 66-67; I of Slave Lake 67-72; Colinton 72-80; Squamish Dio New Westmr from 80. *Box 236, Garibaldi Highlands, BC, Canada.*

WALTERS, Christopher John Linley. b 24. St Pet Hall Ox BA 47, MA 49. Linc Th Coll 48. **d** 50 **p** 51 Roch. C of Ch Ch Dartford 50-53; Oswestry 53-56; V of The Lodge (Weston Rhyn) 56-61; St Paul Newc L 61-70; V of Pattingham, Dio Lich from 70; P-in-c of Patshull Dio Lich from 77. *Pattingham Vicarage, Wolverhampton, Staffs.* (Pattingham 700257)

WALTERS, David Michael Trenham.. b 46. St D Lamp Dipl Th 69. Bp Burgess Hall Lamp. **d** 69 Swan B. C of Killay 69-72; CF from 72. *c/o Ministry of Defence, Lansdowne House, Berkeley Square, W1X 6AA.*

WALTERS, Canon David Miles Ivor. b 12. Qu Coll Cam, BA 34, MA 38. Wells Th Coll 34. **d** 35 **p** 36 Chich. C of Bognor Regis 35-38; Chap St Steph Coll Delhi 38-40; C of Brighton 40-41; Chap RNVR 41-46; V of Kingston w Iford 46-49; St Nich Brighton 49-55; Rottingdean 55-74; Chap of Roedean Sch 55-65; Butlin's Ocean Hotel 55-72; Surr 55-78; RD of Kemp Town 66-76; Can and Preb of Chich Cathl 72-80; Can (Emer) from 80; R of Ovingdean w Rottingdean and Woodingdean 74-78. *8 Elmstead Gardens, West Wittering, Chichester, W Sussex, PO20 8NG.* (W Wittering 3644)

WALTERS, David Trevor. b 37. Late Scho of Ex Coll Ox BA 58, MA 62. St Steph Ho Ox 62. **d** 64 Bp T M Hughes for Llan **p** 65 Llan. C of St Mary Virg Cardiff 64-69; Min Can of Brecon Cathl and C of Brecon w Battle 69-73; V of Llanddew w Talachddu 73-78; Cefn Coed w Nantddu Dio Swan B from 78; R of Vaynor w Capel Taffechan Dio Swan B from 80. *Cefn Coed Vicarage, Merthyr Tydfil, Mid-Glam.* (0685-74253)

WALTERS, Donald Roderick. b 33. Late Exhib of Wadh Coll Ox BA 55, MA 59. Wells Th Coll 60. **d** 61 **p** 62 Bris. C of St Mary Redcliffe w Temple Bedminster 61-65; Tewkesbury 65-71; R of Abenhall, w Mitcheldean 71-79; RD of N Forest 78-79; Dir of Ministerial Tr Dio Glouc from 79; P-in-c of Maisemore Dio Glouc from 79; Prin Glouc Sch for Min from 79. *Maisemore Vicarage, Gloucester, GL2 8EY.* (Glouc 20864)

WALTERS, Canon Douglas Lewis. b 20. Univ of Wales BA 41. St Mich Coll Llan 41. **d** 43 **p** 44 St D. C of Milford Haven 43-48; Llanelly 48-52; R of Llangwm 52-58; V of Kidwelly Dio St D from 58; RD of Kidwelly from 77; Can of St D from 78. *Vicarage, Kidwelly, Dyfed.* (Kidwelly 802925)

WALTERS, Preb Egerton Edward Farrar. b 04. Qu Coll Cam BA 25, MA 29. Cudd Coll 27. **d** 27 **p** 28 Worc. Asst Master Wells Ho Malvern Wells 26-30; C of Gt Malvern 27-30; Chap and Ho Master Ellesmere Coll 30-36; Asst Master and Chap of Epsom Coll and LPr Dio Guildf 36-38; V of Newnham-on-Severn 38-41; Chan V of Lich Cathl 41-43; Dean's Vicar of Lich Cath 43-45; Hd Master of Cathl Sch 41-56; Hon Chap to Bp of Lich 46-56; Preb of Sandiacre in Lich Cathl 51-68; Preb (Emer) from 68; V of Shrewsbury 56-68; L to Offic Dio Swan B from 68. *Tyrgoes, Cwmcamlais, Brecon, Powys.* (Sennybridge 530)

WALTERS, Canon Francis Raymond. b 24. Ball Coll Ox BA 49, MA 54. Wycl Hall Ox 51. **d** 53 **p** 54 Derby. C of Boulton 53-56; Succr St Phil Cathl Ch Birm 56-58; Lect Qu Coll Birm 56-64; C of Harborne 58-64; V of St Nich Leic 64-73; Chap to Univ of Leic 64-73; R of Appleby Magna 73-77; P-in-c of Swithland Dio Leic from 77; Dioc Educn Sec Dio Leic from 77; Hon Can of Leic Cathl from 77. *Swithland Rectory, Loughborough, Leics.* (Woodhouse Eaves 890357)

WALTERS, George Thomas. b 1888. Late Hebr Scho and Pri of St D Coll Lamp BA (2nd cl Th) 14. **d** 14 **p** 15 St D. C of Cardigan 14-16; Clydach 16-24; V of St Luke Cwmbwrla 24-42; Bagillt 42-60; L to Offic Dio Wakef from 62. *66 Huddersfield Road, Barnsley, Yorks.* (Barnsley 5326)

WALTERS, Gibbon Muru. b 20. **d** 79 **p** 80 Auckld. C of Ahipara Parengarenga Peria Dio Auckld from 79. *Ahipara, Northland, NZ.*

WALTERS, Godfrey Norman. St Paul's Coll Grahmstn LTh (S Afr) 40. **d** 40 **p** 41 Grahmstn. C of St Phil w St Jas Port Eliz 40-44; L to Offic St Geo Cathl Capetn 44-46; R of Groot Drakenstein 46-48; St John Parow 48-50; P-in-c of St Marg Parow 50-53; R of Durbanville 53-48; Camp's Bay 58-69; St Anne Maitland Dio Capetn from 69. *St Anne's Rectory, Coronation Road, Maitland, CP, S Africa.* (511866)

WALTERS, Henry Llewellyn. b 19. St D Coll Lamp BA 41, LTh 43, BD 64. **d** 43 **p** 44 St D. C of Pembroke Dock 43-51; C-in-c of Castlemartin w Warren 51-56; R of Walton W w Talbenny (w Haroldston W from 60) 56-72; V of Cwmamman Dio St D from 73. *Cwmamman Vicarage, Garnant, Ammanford, Dyfed.* (0269-822107)

WALTERS, John Eurof Thomas. St D Coll Lamp BA 46. **d** 47 St D for Llan **p** 48 Llan. C of Pentyrch 47-48; Neath w Llantwit 48-52; Cheddleton 52-54; V of Woore 54-58; Burntwood Dio Lich from 58; Chap St Matt Hosp Burntwood from 58. *Burntwood Vicarage, Walsall, Staffs.* (Burntwood 266)

WALTERS, John Morgan. b 09. **d** 34 **p** 35 Waik. P-in-c of St Andr Ohura 34-35; V 35-37; Actg C of Haydon 39; L Bardfield 39-40; C of Ch Ch Radlett 40-42; Actg C-in-c of St Jas Watford 42-43; V of Dean w Shelton 43-48; Hexton 48-52; R of Higham Gobion 48-52; PC of High Wych 52-69; V 69-74; RD of Bp's Stortford 63-67; Perm to Offic Dio St E 75-81. *5 Cannonsfield, Bury St Edmunds, Suff.* (Bury St Edmunds 61010)

WALTERS, John Philip Hewitt. b 50. Coll of Resurr Mirfield 72. **d** 73 **p** 74 Swan B. C of Llanguicke (Pontardawe) 73-76; Brecon w Battle 76-79; Min Can of Brecon Cathl 76-79; V of Merthyr Cynog w Duffryn Honddu Dio Swan B from 79; Garthbrengy w Llandefaelog-Fach and Llanfihangel Fechan Dio Swan B from 79. *Lower Chapel Vicarage, Powys.*

WALTERS, John Reynell. St Jo Coll Morpeth ThL 65. **d** 64 **p** 65 Syd. C of Hornsby 64-67; Chap Mowll Mem and Nuffield Villages 67-72; C of E Retirement Villages Castle Hill Dio Syd from 72. *49 Burdett Street, Waitara, NSW, Australia 2077.* (41-1486)

WALTERS, John Rufus. b 15. Late Welsh Ch Scho of Univ of Wales BA (2nd cl Lat) 37. St Mich Coll Llan 37. **d** 38 Swan B for Llan **p** 39 Llan. C of Llanwonno w Ynysybwl 38-42; St Tyfaelog Pontlottyn 42-46; Caerau w Ely 46-52; V of Llanwonno 52-61; Llanbradach 61-70. *301 Eastfield Road, Peterborough.*

WALTERS, Leslie Ernest Ward. b 27. Wadh Coll Ox BA 51, MA 55. Ridley Hall Cam. **d** 57 **p** 58 Heref. C of St Pet Heref 57-59; Morden 59-61; V of Felbridge 61-68; Im w St Anselm Streatham 68-81; Hon Chap to Bp of S'wark 67-80; V of Cotmanhay and Shipley Dio Derby from 81. *Vicarage, Cotmanhay, Ilkeston, Derbys, DE7 8QL.* (Ilkeston 325670)

WALTERS, Michael William. b 39. Univ of Dur BSc 61. Clifton Th Coll 61. **d** 63 **p** 64 Guildf. C of H Trin Aldershot 63-66; Ch Ch U Armley 66-69; NE Area Sec CPAS and L to Offic Dio York 69-75; V of Hyde Dio Ches from 75; M Gen Syn from 80. *St George's Vicarage, Hyde, SK14 1DP.* (061-368 2400)

WALTERS, Nicholas Humphrey. b 45. K Coll Lon and Warm BD and AKC 67. **d** 68 **p** 69 Guildf. C of All SS Weston 68-71; Hon C of St Mary Virg Ewell 71-77; Chap and Lect NE Surrey Coll of Tech 71-77; Warden and Dir of Stud Moor Park Coll Farnham 77-80; Tutor Univ of Surrey from 80. *University of Surrey, Dept of Adult Education, Guildford, Surrey.* (Guildf 71281 ext 877)

WALTERS, Peter. b 27. Univ of Leeds BSc 48. Univ of Wales (Abth) MSc 52. Ripon Coll Cudd 78. **d** 79 **p** 80 Bris. C of Kingswood 79-81; R of Stanton St Quinton, Hullavington, Grittleton w Norton & Leigh Delamere Dio Bris from 81. *Stanton St Quinton Rectory, Chippenham, Wilts, SN14 6DE.* (Hullavington 230)

WALTERS, Canon Rhys Derrick Chamberlain. b 32. Univ of Lon BSc 55. Ripon Hall Ox. **d** 57 **p** 58 Swan B. C of Manselton Swansea 57-58; St Mary Swansea 58-62; Chap Univ Coll Swansea 58-62; PC of Totley 62-67; V of Boulton Derby 67-74; Dioc Missr Dio Sarum from 74; P-in-c of Burcombe 74-78; Can and Preb of Sarum Cathl 77-78; Res Can from 78; Treas from 79. *23 The Close, Salisbury, Wilts, SP1 2EH.* (Salisbury 22172)

WALTERS, Richard Patrick Courtney. Qu Coll St Jo Newfld 48. **d** 52 **p** 53 Newfld. C of St Mich AA St John's 52-54; R of Notre Dame 54-56; C of Grand Falls 56-58; R of Bonavista 59-64; Deer Lake 64-70; I of Botwood 70-72; Lewisporte Dio Newfld (Centr Newfld from 76) from 72. *Rectory, Lewisporte, Newfoundland, Canada.* (709-535-6361)

WALTERS, Ronald. b 06. Univ of Wales BSc (1st cl Phys) 26. St Mich Coll Llan 29. **d** 30 **p** 31 Llan. C of Mountain Ash 30-32; Penmaen 32-33; C-in-c of Six Bells 34-35; C of Blaina 35-41; St Andr Newport 41-44; R of Llanwenarth Citra 44-57; V of Beaufort 57-74; RD of Blaenau Gwent 71-74; L to Offic Dio Mon from 79. *3 St Stephen's Close, Caerwent, Gwent.*

WALTERS, Thomas. MBE 44. St Aid Coll 32. **d** 34 **p** 35 Blackb. C of St Mich Blackb 34-36; Chap HM Pris Wormwood Scrubs 36-37; Wakef 37-38; Chap Calicut w Cannamore 38-39; CF (Ind) 39-46; Men in Disp 41 (twice) 46 (thrice); Hon CF 46; Chap All SS Trimulgherry 46-47; R of W Lynn 48-50; Walsoken 50-70; RD of Lynn Marshland 57-68; Surr 59-70. *Jersey House, Bishop's Avenue, Finchley, N2 0BE.*

WALTERS, Thomas. b 24. St Deiniol's Libr Hawarden. **d** 79 **p** 80 Man. C of Bardsley Dio Man from 79. *49 Fir Tree Avenue, Oldham, Lancs, OL8 2QS.*

WALTERS, Thomas Hubert. b 16. Univ of Wales BA 39. St Mich Coll Llan 39. **d** 40 **p** 41 Mon. C of New Tredegar 40-46; Cler Org Sec C of E Children's S for S Wales 46-49; Asst Chap Miss to Seamen Glas 49; Port of Lon 49-51; Chap Miss to Seamen Newport Mon 51-57; Durban 57-61; Area Sec Miss to Seamen Portsm 61-64; V of Ch Ch Blacklands Hastings 64-81; St Andr Hastings 66-81. *23 Hughenden Place, Hastings, Sussex.*

WALTERS, Trevor Howard. b 49. Sarum Wells Th Coll 75. **d** 78 Sarum for Calg **p** 79 Calg. C of St Steph Calg 78-81; Chap Univ of Calg from 81. *2012-32nd Avenue SW, Calgary, Alta, Canada.*

WALTERS, Ven Walter. St Aid Th Coll Bal ACT ThL (1st cl) 16. Th Scho 22. **d** 16 **p** 17 Bal. C of Murrayville 16-17; P-in-c 17-28; R of Scottsdale 28-33; Bothwell Tas 33-47; Exam Chap to Bp of Tas 34-62; Can of St D Cathl Hobart 45-62; R of Latrobe 47-62; Archd of Darwin 49-62; Archd (Emer) from 62. *9 Young Street, East Devonport, Tasmania.*

WALTERS, Canon William Edward Felix. b 10. St D Coll Lamp BA 33. **d** 35 **p** 36 St A. C of Mold 35-40; CF (EC) 40-46; R of Barcheston 46-65; R of Cherington w Sutton-under-Brailes and Stourton 46-65; RD of Shipston-on-Stour 52-65; R of Hampton Lucy w Charlecote 65-75; Hon Can of Cov 62-75; Can (Emer) from 76. *Ash Grove, Charlecote, Warwick.*

WALTON, Edward Gibson. b 09. Wells Th Coll 54. **d** 55 **p** 56 Ex. C of Berry-Pomeroy 55-56; Withycombe Raleigh 56-59; V of Harberton 59-63; V of Harbertonford 59-63; C of Mortlake (in c of All SS) 63--71; V of Ch Ch Hendon 71-81. *28 Marlborough Street, Brighton, Sussex.* (Brighton 26881)

WALTON, Canon Geoffrey Elmer. b 34. Univ of Dur BA 59. Univ of Birm Dipl Th 61. Qu Coll Birm 59. **d** 61 **p** 62 Southw. C of Warsop w Sookholme 61-65; V of Norwell 65-69; Recruitment Sec ACCM 69-75; LPr Dio Chelmsf 70-75; V of H Trin Weymouth Dio Sarum from 75; Surr from 78; RD of Weymouth from 79; Can Non-res of Sarum Cathl from 81. *Vicarage, Longfield Road, Weymouth, Dorset, DT4 8RQ.* (Weymouth 786507)

WALTON, Harry. b 09. St D Coll Lamp BA 32. **d** 32 **p** 33 Blackb. C of St Osw Knuzden 32-35; St Matt Preston 35-39; St Cuthb Darwen 39-40; Offg C-in-c of Ch Ch Colne 40-44; V of Knuzden 44-48; C of St Annes-on-the-Sea (in c of St Marg) 48-55; V of St Matt Preston 55-63; Garstang 63-68; St Jude Blackb 68-72. *1 Broadway, Leyland, Preston, PR5 2EH.* (Leyland 34518)

WALTON, John Henry. ACT ThL 55. Ridley Coll Melb. **d** 56 **p** 57 Melb. C of Coburg 56 59; Min of Altona 59-62; P-in-c of Kens 62-67; I of Mitcham 67-78; Nunawading Dio Melb from 78. *67 Springvale Road, Nunawading, Vic, Australia 3131.* (878 7562)

WALTON, John James. b 1894. G and C Coll Cam BA (Wrang) 22, MA 26. Univ of Lon BSc (3rd cl Math) 22. **d** and **p** 33 Birm. C of St Mary Handsworth 33-42; Hd Master Handsworth Gr Sch from 33; LPr Dio Birm 42-46; Publ Pr from 46. *97 Cobbold Road, Felixstowe, Suffolk.*

WALTON, John Sidney. b 1899. Linc Th Coll 22. **d** 24 **p** 25 Linc. C of Gainsborough 24-29; Skegness 29-31; V of Weston St Mary w Weston Hill Lincs 31-33; R of Wilsford (w Kelby from 51) 33-53; Chap RAFVR 42-46; V of Hatherden w Tangley 53-60. *31 River Way, Christchurch, Dorset.* (Christchurch 484448)

WALTON, John Victor. b 45. Univ of Lon BSc 67. Linc Th Coll 79. **d** 81 St Alb. C of Mary Shephall Stevenage Dio St Alb from 81. *125 Collenswood Road, Shephall, Stevenage, Herts, SG2 9HB.* (Stevenage 65714)

WALTON, John William. d 50 **p** 51 Nel. V of Cobden 50-54; Nae Nae 54-59; Mangaweka 59-64; Titahi Bay 64-72; Shannon 72-76; Perm to Offic Dio Nel from 76. *18 Blythell Street, Blenheim, NZ.* (4376)

WALTON, Patrick Spencer Murray. b 21. Ripon Hall Ox. **d** 57 **p** 58 Portsm. C of Bedhampton 57-60; PC of Bream 60-66; H Ap Charlton Kings (V from 68) 66-81; R of U and Lower Slaughter w Eyford and Naunton Dio Glouc from 81. *Rectory, Lower Slaughter, Cheltenham, Glos, GL54 2HY.* (Bourton-on-the-Water 20401)

WALTON, Philip William. b 28. Univ of Dur BSc (Agr) 52. Tyndale Hall Bris 54. **d** 56 Lon **p** 58 Liv. C of St Jas Clerkenwell 56-57; St Paul St Alb 57-59; St Mark Haydock 58-60; V of St Mary Magd Wiggenhall 60-66; Sec CCCS 66-69; Chap Maisons Laffitte (N and C Eur) 69-74; V of Worthing Dio Chich from 74. *Vicarage, Shakespeare Road, BN11 4AS.* (Worthing 35379

WALTON, Reginald Arthur. b 40. St Jo Coll Nottm 80. **d** 81 Southw. C of St Mark Woodthorpe Nottm Dio Southw from 81. *22 Barden Road, Woodthorpe, Nottingham.*

WALTON, Wilfrid James. b 14. St Jo Coll Dur BA and Van Mildert Scho 39, MA 51. **d** 39 **p** 40 Lich. C of St Matt Tipton 39-42; Bloxwich 42-45; C-in-c of St Mark Walsall 45-47; Chap Western Aberdare Kenya 47-52; V of Bloxwich 52-60; R of Newport w Longford 60-61; Asst Master Aston Comprehensive Sch Sheff 61-79; L to Offic Dio Sheff from 68. *25 Main Avenue, Totley, Sheffield.* (Sheffield 367183)

WALUGUNGA, Daudi. d 64 **p** 65 Mbale. P Dio Mbale 64-73. *PO Box 984, Mbale, Uganda.*

WALUSIMBI, Charles William. b 25. **d** 77 Nam. d Dio Nam. *Namagabi Church of Uganda, PO Box 18024, Kayunga, Uganda.*

WALUSIMBI, George Asafu. Bp Tucker Coll Mukono. **d** 50 **p** 51 Ugan. P Dio Ugan 50-61; Dio Nam from 61. *PO Box 862, Jinja, Uganda.*

WALUSIMBI, John Kryptoni. d and **p** 43 Ugan. P Dio Ugan 43-60; Dio W Bugan from 60; Treas from 68. *Church of Uganda, Kako, PO Box 242, Masaka, Uganda.*

WALWO, Canon Erizefani. Bp Tucker Coll Mukono. **d** 56 Ugan **p** 58 Bp Balya for Ugan. P Dio Ugan 56-61; Dio Nam from 61; Can of Nam from 78. *Anglican Church, Nakasongola, PO, Uganda.*

WALYAWULA, Wilson. Bp Tucker Coll Mukono. **d** 64 **p**

65 Mbale. P Dio Mbale. *Church of Uganda, Bukikayi, Uganda.*

WAMALA, Ven Erisa Kaggwa. Bp Tucker Coll Mukono. **d** 54 **p** 57 Ugan. P Dio Ugan 57-60; Dio Nam 61-63; Dio W Bugan from 63; Hon Can of W Bugan 63-69; Dioc Sec and Exam Chap to Bp of W Bugan from 70; Archd of W Bugan from 73. *PO Box 242, Masaka, Uganda.*

WAMALA, Frederick. b 50. Ridley Coll Melb 74. **d** 77 Melb for Nam. C of St Hilary Kew Dio Melb from 77. *c/o St Hilary's Vicarage, John Street, Kew, Vic, Australia 3101.*

WAMALA, Canon Keziron i. **d** 42 **p** 44 Ugan. P Dio Ugan 42-60; Dio W Bugan from 60; Can of W Bugan from 69. *CMS, PO Bukuya, Mityana, Uganda.*

WAMALA, Yokana. Bp Tucker Coll Mukono. **d** 56 Ugan **p** 58 Bp Balya for Ugan. P Dio Ugan 56-60; Dio W Bugan from 60. *Kasaka, PO Kanoni, Mpigi, Uganda.*

WAMATHAGA, Kuria. **d** and **p** 69 Nai. P Dio Nai. *PO Box 48803, Nairobi, Kenya.*

WAMBI, Fibyano. **d** 48 **p** 50 U Nile. P Dio U Nile 48-61; Dio Mbale 61-80. *Nabumali, Box 984, Mbale, Uganda.*

WAMBOGA, Solomon. **d** 64 **p** 65 Mbale. P Dio Mbale. *PO Box 297, Mbale, Uganda.*

WAMONO, Ernest. **d** 59 Momb **p** 62 Maseno. P Dio Momb 59-61; Dio Maseno 61-69; Dio Maseno N from 70. *Butonge, PO Box 80, Bungoma, Kenya.*

WAMPAMBA, Canon Nekemiya. Bp Tucker Mem Coll Ugan. **d** 36 **p** 38 Ugan. P Dio Ugan 36-61; Dio Nam 61-74; Can of Nam 62-74. *PO Box 3652, Kampala, Uganda.*

WAMUKOYA, Nashon. b 41. **d** 74 **p** 75 Maseno N. P Dio Maseno N. *PO Box 109, Mumias, Kenya.*

WANALO, Ven Jackson. St Paul's Th Coll Limuru. **d** 63 **p** 64 Maseno. P Dio Maseno 63-67; Dio Nak 67-68; Dio Maseno N from 76; CF (E Afr) 68-76; Archd of Butere from 76; Exam Chap to Bp of Maseno N from 76. *PO Box 62, Maseno, Kenya.*

WANCKEL, Athol Charles. St Paul's Coll Grahmstn 58. **d** 60 **p** 61 St John's. P Dio St John's 60-67; Dio Johann from 67. *Box 933, Carletonville, Johannesburg, S Africa.*

WANDA, John. Buwalasi Th Coll 60. **d** and **p** 66 Mbale. P Dio Mbale 66-78; Dio Nak from 78. *Box 18, Kapsabet, Kenya.*

WANDABWA, Benjamin. St Paul's Th Coll Limuru 61. **d** 62 **p** 64 Maseno. P Dio Maseno 62-70; Dio Maseno N 70-76; Dio E Newfld from 76. *c/o 1 Westerland Road, St John's, Newfoundland, Canada.*

WANDERA, Canon Enos. Maseno Bible Sch. **d** 62 **p** 65 Maseno. P Dio Maseno 62-69; Dio Maseno N from 70; Hon Can of Maseno N from 72. *Box 124, Maseno, Kenya.*

WANDMAKER, Frederick. St Jo Coll Morpeth ACT ThL 63. **d** 66 **p** 67 Gippsld. C of St Paul's NSW, Australia 2000. (264-1021) 69-72; Asst Sec ABM in NSW 72-74; Sec from 74; Perm to Offic Dios Newc, Graft, Syd and C & Goulb from 72. *Australian Board of Missions, 91 Bathurst Street, Sydney, NSW, Australia 2000.* (264-1021)

WANDSWORTH, Archdeacon of. *See* Coombs, Ven Peter Bertram.

WANEKAYA, Yosek. St Paul's Dioc Div Sch Limuru 50. **d** 52 **p** 54 Momb. P Dio Momb 52-57; CF (East Afr) 57-61; P Dio Maseno from 61. *PO Box 11, Mumias, Kenya.*

WANG, Francis. b 16. **d** 73 **p** 74 Sing (APM). P Dio Sing. *5 Heng Mui Keng Terrace, Singapore 5.*

WANGARATTA, Lord Bishop of. *See* Thomas, Right Rev Maxwell McNee.

WANGOLE, Lewis. St Cypr Coll Lindi 71. **d** 73 **p** 75 Zanz T. P Dio Zanz T. *Box 6, Kihurio, Tanzania.*

WANGOYA, W Sange. b 50. St Phil Coll Kongwa 72. **d** 74 Vic Nyan **p** 74 Abp Sepeku for Vic Nyan. P Dio Vic Nyan 74-77; and from 81. *St Paul's Church, Kirumba. PO Box 278, Mwanza, Tanzania.*

WANGUBO, Stanley William. **d** 48 **p** 50 U Nile. P Dio U Nile 48-61; Dio Mbale from 61. *Namunsi, PO Mbale, Uganda.*

✠ **WANI, Most Rev Silvano Goi.** **d** 42 **p** 44 U Nile. P Dio U Nile 42-58; CF (E Afr) 44-46; Hon Can of U Nile 58-61; Dioc Sec Dio N Ugan 61-64; Cons Asst Bp of N Ugan in St Paul's Cathl Kampala 7 June 64 by Abp of Ugan; Bps of Mbale; Soroti; W Bugan; N Ugan; Ankole-K; and Ruw; Asst Bp on Nig Delta; Bp Balya; and Bp of Bukoba (Swedish Ch); Elected Bp of N Ugan 64; Trld to M & W Nile 69; to Kamp (Abp and Metrop of Prov of Ugan; w Rwanda B and Boga-Z to 80) 77; Prov Dean of Ugan, Rwanda B and Boga-Z 74-77. *P O Box 14123, Kampala, Uganda.* (Kampala 46177)

WANIALA, Canon Asanasiyo. Buwalasi Th Coll 49. **d** 50 U Nile **p** 53 Bp Tomusange for U Nile. P Dio U Nile 51-61; Dio Mbale from 61; Hon Can of Mbale from 63; Archd of Bugisu and Sebei 67-78. *PO Box 297, Mbale, Uganda.*

WANIKO, Titus Lakpini Kofo. Im Coll Ibad 57. **d** 58 **p** 59 N Nig. P Dio N Nig 58-80; Can of N Nig 69-80. *PA Kaita, Lokoja, Nigeria.*

WANJIE, Lukas Macharia. b 50. St Paul's Coll Limuru 72. **d** 75 Mt Kenya S **p** 76 Bp Ngaruiya for Mt Kenya S. P Dio Mt Kenya S 75-77; on leave 77-79; C of Mill End and Heronsgate w West Hyde 79-81. *Address temp unknown.*

WANKLING, Frank Ernest. b 19. Oak Hill Th Coll 53. **d** 55 Guildf **p** 56 Bp Hawkes for Cant. C of Em Stoughton Guildf 55-58; V of St Mich AA Blackheath Pk 58-67; PC of Penn Street w Holmer Green 67-68; V 68-75; Warden Mabledon Home Southborough 75-77; R of Norton Fitzwarren 77-80; Abbas and Templecombe w Horsington Dio B & W from 80. *Rectory, Church Hill, Templecombe, Somt, BA8 0HG.* (Templecombe 70302)

WANN, Denis Francis. TCD BA 55. **d** 56 **p** 57 Down. C of St Donard Belf 56-58; P-in-c of Lwande 59-64; Kilombero 64-67; Moro 67-72; Hon Can of Moro 72; C of Shankill (Lurgan) 72-73; R of Port Kembla 73-78; Albion Pk Dio Syd from 78. *Rectory, Tongarra Road, Albion Park, NSW, Australia 2527.* (042-56 2103)

WANOA, Pineaha. St Jo Coll Auckld 74. **d** 75 **p** 76 Wai. C of Turanga Park Dio Wai from 75. *5 Haldane Street, Gisborne, NZ.*

WANSEY, John. b 07. Selw Coll Cam BA 30, MA 34. Westcott Ho Cam 31. **d** 31 **p** 32 S'wark. C of St Pet Brockley 31-35; St Mark Bexhill 35-37; St Matt Hull 37-38; V of Appleton-le-Street w Amotherby 38-49; R of Witchampton 49-61; R of Long Crichel w Moor Crichel 49-61; V of W Lavington 61-78; Chap K Edw VII Hosp Midhurst 61-77. *93 Westgate, Chichester, PO19 3HB.*

WANSEY, Joseph Christopher. b 10. Late Exhib of Selw Coll Cam 2nd cl Cl Trip pt i 31, BA (3rd cl Geog Trip pt i) 32, 2nd cl Th Trip pt i 33, MA 36. Westcott Ho Cam 33. **d** 34 **p** 35 Chelmsf. C of Walthamstow 34-36; CMS Miss at Sapporo 37-38; Kushiro 39-40; Freetown 40-41; Chap to Bp of Sier L 40; Warden Seamen's Hostel Freetown 41; R of Flixton 41-45; Woodford 45-64; Surr 46-75; RD of Wanstead and Woodford 49-53; Proc Conv Chelmsf 51-75; V of Roydon 64-75. *6 High Street, West Wickham, Cambs, CB1 6RY.* (0220-29818)

WANSEY, Canon Paul Raymond. b 06. MC 44. Selw Coll Cam 2nd cl Th Trip pt i 27, BA (2nd cl Th Trip pt ii) 28, MA 32. Westcott Ho Cam. **d** 29 **p** 30 S'wark. C of St Mich Wandsworth Common 29-31; Chap at Villars Switzerland 31-32; C of Godstone 32-36; Streatham 36-39; CF (R of O) 39-45 (Men in Disp 40 and 43); V of St Mich E Wickham 45-51; R of Limpsfield (w Titsey from 56) 51-68; C-in-c of Titsey 54-56; Hon Can of S'wark 62-68; Can (Emer) from 68; RD of Godstone 63-66; R of Woodbridge 68-74. *3 Warren Hill Road, Woodbridge, Suffolk,* (Woodbridge 7807)

WANSEY, Canon Peter Nottidge. b 08. MC 43. Selw Coll Cam BA 31, MA 35. Westcott Ho Cam 31. **d** 32 **p** 33 S'wark. C of Putney 32-35; Chap and Tutor St Jo Coll York 36-40; CF (EC) 40-45; (Men in Disp 45); Dir of Youth Work Dio York and Asst Chap to Abp of York 46-49; CF (TA) 53-58; CF (TA R of O) 58-63; V of Eston w Normanby 49-55; Darlington 55-74; RD of Darlington 56-73; Surr 56-81; Hon Can of Dur 58-81; Can (Emer) from 81; V of Coniscliffe 74-81. *4 Lawn Road, Guildford, Surrey, GU2 5DE.* (Guildford 75775)

WANZALA, Richard. Maseno Bible Sch 69. **d** 69 Maseno. d Dio Maseno N from 69. *c/o PO Box 1, Maseno, Kenya.*

WAPAU, Adea. St Paul's Coll Thursday I. **d** 51 **p** 55 Carp. C of Torres Strait Miss 51-56; Miss Mabuiag I 56-60; Boigu I 60-66; Yam I 66-70; All S Cathl Thursday I 71-74; P-in-c of Moa I Dio Carp 74-79; C from 79. *St Paul's Mission, PO Box 79, Thursday Island, Queensland, Australia 4875.*

WARAKI, Jesse Muchemi. b 29. **d** 74 Mt Kenya **p** 76 Bp Ngaruiya for Mt Kenya S. P Dio Mt Kenya 74-75; Mt Kenya S from 75. *Box 23031, Lower Kabete, Kenya.*

WARBURTON, Andrew James. b 44. Oak Hill Th Coll 64. **d** 69 Bp Daly for Cov **p** 70 Cov. C of New Milverton 69-72; St Matt Fulham 72-76; Chesham (in c of Em Ch) 76-80; Team V of Gt Chesham Dio Ox from 80. *14a Manor Way, Chesham, Bucks.* (Chesham 784372)

WARBURTON, Canon Denis William. Ridley Coll Melb ACT ThL 51. **d** 52 **p** 53 Tas. C of St Paul Launceston 52-53; Ulverstone 53-55; Missr Tarraleah 55-60; P-in-c of Minnipa Miss 60-63; R of Scottsdale 63-66; H Trin Hobart 66-72; Dir of Relig Educn Dio Tas 68-75; Overseas Dept Dio Tas 72-75; Dept of Miss Dio Tas from 75; Can of Tas from 79. *125 Macquarie Street, Hobart, Tasmania 7000.* (002-23 7668)

WARBURTON, John Bryce. b 33. St Aid Coll 64. **d** 66 Burnley for Blackb **p** 67 Blackb. C of Padiham 66-69; Burnley 69-70; V of Tideswell 70-81; Bollington Dio Ches from 81. *Bollington Vicarage, Macclesfield, Chesh.* (Bollington 73162)

WARBURTON, Piers Eliot de Dutton. b 30. Univ of Dur BA 65. Cranmer Hall Dur 61. **d** 65 Warrington for Liv **p** 66 Liv. C of Grassendale 65-68; Pembroke Berm 68-71; R of

Sherborne St John 71-76; V of Yateley Dio Win from 76. *Yateley Vicarage, Camberley, Surrey, GU17 7LR.* (Yateley 873133)

WARBURTON, Canon Robert Tinsley. b 23. MBE (Mil) 66. TD 69. Jes Coll Cam BA 47, MA 52. Oak Hill Th Coll 47. **d** 47 **p** 48 St E. C of St Marg Ipswich 47-50; R of Dallinghoo 50-54; C-in-c of Playford w Culpho 52-54; Asst Sec St E Dioc Bd of Finance 50-54; V of Attenborough w Bramcote and Chilwell 54-67; Mansfield Dio Southw from 67; CF (TA) 55-67; CF (TAVR) from 67; Dioc Insp of Schs Dio Southw from 56; RD of Beeston 60-67; Mansfield from 67; Surr from 62; C-in-c of Teversal 68-72; Hon Can of Southw from 72. *Vicarage, Lindhurst Lane, Mansfield, Notts.* (Mansfield 21600)

WARBURTON, Sidney Burroughs. St Aid Coll 29. **d** 30 Liv **p** 31 Warrington for Liv. C of Parr 30-34; C of St Anne Sale 34-37; V 37-57; V of Woodford Ches 57-71; Perm to Offic Dio Ches from 71. *51 Stanneylands Road, Wilmslow, Cheshire.*

WARBURTON, Walter George. b 16. Bede Coll Dur BA 40, Dipl Th 42, MA 43. **d** 41 Blackb **p** 42 Burnley for Blackb. C of St Mark Witton 41-45; Ch Ch Accrington 45-46; V of St Barn Bolton 46-52; Stonefold 52-60; Gt Marsden 60-81. *145 Halifax Road, Nelson, Lancs, BB9 0EL.* (Nelson 697589)

WARBY, John Alfred. St Francis Coll Brisb. **d** 60 **p** 62 Rockptn. C of St Paul Rockptn 60-64; R of Callide Valley 64-66; St Barn N Rockptn 66-75; Dioc Chap Dio Rockptn from 75. *Box 37, North Rockhampton, Queensland, Australia 4701.* (079-28 4583)

WARCHUS, Michael Edward George. b 37. Roch Th Coll 65. **d** 68 Colchester for Chelmsf **p** 69 Chelmsf. C of Buckhurst Hill 68-71; Stainton-in-Cleveland (in c of St Marg Brookfield) 71-76; V of Carlton and Drax Dio York from 76. *Drax Vicarage, Selby, N Yorks.* (0757 618313)

WARCUP, Warner. b 1891. Univ of Lon BA (2nd cl Phil) 25, MA 29. Whittlesford Th Coll 38. **d** 38 **p** 39 S'wark. C of St Geo Mart S'wark 38-40; C-in-c of St Hilda Crofton Pk 40-43; C of H Trin Greenwich 43-45; V of Borrowdale 45-49; Marchwood 49-59; C-in-c of St Mark Hanwell 59-69. *98 Shakespeare Road, W7.* (01-567 8528)

WARD, Alan William. b 56. Trin Coll Bris 80. **d** 81 Ches. C of New Ferry Dio Ches from 81. *152 New Ferry Road, New Ferry, Wirral, Merseyside, L62 1DZ.*

WARD, Albert George. b 27. K Coll Lon and Warm BD and AKC 54. **d** 55 **p** 56 Wakef. C of Birstall 55-57; Gt Berkhamsted 57-60; V of St Columba Corby 60-66; R of Walgrave w Hannington and Wold 66-69; Usworth 69-78; St Simon S Shields Dio Dur from 78. *Vicarage, Wenlock Road, Simonside, South Shields, NE34 9AL.* (S Shields 553164)

WARD, Allan Edward Neville. b 11. Kelham Th Coll 29. **d** 35 **p** 36 York. C of St John Middlesbrough 35-37; Perm to Offic at Middlewich 37-38; C of Holmfirth 38-42; Kempston (in c of Ch of Transfig) 42-47; CF 47-67; V of Shalfleet 67-73; Thorley 67-73; R of Chale 73-77 and 78-80; P-in-c 77-78; Niton 77-80. *2 Fairy Hill, Seaview, I of W, PO34 5DG.* (Seaview 2474)

WARD, Anthony Colin. **d** 79 **p** 80 Mashon. P Dio Mashon. *c/o Anglican Diocesan Offices, PO Box UA7, Salisbury, Zimbabwe.*

WARD, Ven Arthur Frederick. b 12. Armstrong Coll Dur BA 33. Ridley Hall Cam 33. **d** 35 **p** 36 Newc T. C of St Mich Byker (in c of St Mart 37-40) Newc T 35-40; R of Ch Ch Harpurhey 40-44; V of Nelson-in-Marsden 44-55; Ch Ch Paignton 55-62; R of Shirwell w Loxhore 62-70; Archd of Barnstaple 62-70; Can Res of Ex Cathl 70-81; Prec 72-81; Archd of Ex 70-81; Archd (Emer) from 81. *Melrose, Christow, Exeter, Devon, EX6 7LY.*

WARD, Arthur John. b 32. St Aid Coll BS (Lon) 57. **d** 57 **p** 58 Sheff. C of Ecclesfield 57-60; Fulwood Sheff 60-63; Tutor St Aid Coll 63-66; L to Offic Dio Ches 64-66; R of St Lawr Denton 66-74; Tr Sec CMS Selly Oak 64-74; CMS Lon from 74. *Church Missionary Society, 157 Waterloo Road, SE1 8UU.* (01-928 8681)

WARD, Bruce Tilton. b 42. Univ of NB BA 64. St Jo Coll Winnipeg MDiv 77. **d** 76 **p** 77 Rupld. C of St Chad Winnipeg 76-79; R of Manitou Area Dio Rupld from 79. *Box 508, Winnipeg, Manit, R0G 1G0, Canada.*

WARD, Calvin. b 34. Univ of Wales BA (1st cl French) 57. Fitzw Ho Cam BA (2nd cl Th) 63, MA 67. Westcott Ho Cam 61. **d** 64 **p** 65 Birm. C of St Mich Handsworth 64-66; St Mary and St John Shaw Hill Alum Rock 66-69; V of Windhill 69-76; Esholt 76-81; Oakworth Dio Bradf from 81. *Vicarage, Sunhurst Drive, Oakworth, Keighley, W Yorks BD22 7RG.* (Haworth 43386)

WARD, Canon Charles Leslie. b 16. Lich Th Coll 36. **d** 39 **p** 40 Sheff. C of Parkgate 39-40; Rossington 40-42; Taunton 42-45; Actg Succr of Blackb Cathl 45-47; Bp's Chap for Youth 45-48; L to Offic Dio Blackb 45-48; V of St Mich AA Ashton-on-Ribble 48-51; Chap RAF 51; V of St Pet Cheltm 51-60; Northleach and Eastington w Hampnett Stowell and Yanworth 60-64; Surr from 72; V of H Trin Hendford Yeovil 64-67; Minehead 67-76; Can and Preb of Wells Cathl from 74; V of Kewstoke w Wick St Lawr 76-80; Treas of Wells Cathl from 78. *23 Vicar's Close, Wells, Somt.* (Wells 72360)

WARD, Christopher John William. b 36. Qu Coll Birm 68. **d** 69 **p** 70 Lich. C of Wednesbury 69-73; CF from 73. *c/o Ministry of Defence, Bagshot Park, Bagshot, Surrey.*

WARD, David Conisbee. b 33. St Jo Coll Cam BA 54, MA 59. **d** 80 **p** 81 S'wark (NSM). C of St Matt Surbiton Dio S'wark from 80. *5 St Matthew's Avenue, Surbiton, Surrey.*

WARD, David Robert. b 51. Oak Hill Coll 74. **d** 77 **p** 78 Wakef. C of Kirkheaton 77-81; V of Earlsheaton Dio Wakef from 81. *Earlsheaton Vicarage, Dewsbury, W Yorks, WF12 8AH.* (Dewsbury 461490)

WARD, David Towle Greenfield. b 22. Ch Coll Cam BA 47, MA 49. Linc Th Coll 47. **d** 49 **p** 50 Nor. C of St Barn Heigham 49-53; Diss 53-55; V of Gayton 55-64; Potter Heigham 64-77; PC of Repps w Bastwick 64-68; V 68-77; R of Ditchingham w Pirnough Dio Nor from 77; Hedenham Dio Nor from 77; Broome Dio Nor from 77. *Ditchingham Rectory, Bungay, Suff.* (Bungay 2716)

WARD, Edward. b 08. Wycl Hall Ox 54. **d** 54 **p** 55 Liv. Asst Chap Mersey Miss to Seamen 54-56; SPCK Port Chap from 56; C-in-c of St Gabr Conv Distr Huyton Quarry 56-59; V 59-67; Lydiate 67-75; Chap Whiston Hosp 56-67; C of St John Birkdale 75-78; Perm to Offic Dio Liv from 79. *7 Lord Street West, Southport, PR8 2DH.* (Southport 37130)

WARD, Ven Edwin James Greenfield. b 19. MVO 63. Ch Coll Cam BA 46, MA 48. Ridley Hall Cam 46. **d** 48 **p** 49 Nor. C of E Dereham w Hoe and Dillington 48-50; V of N Elmham 50-55; Chap to Watts Naval Sch N Elmham 50-54; C-in-c of Billingford 52-55; Chap R Chap Windsor Gt Park 55-67; Chap to HM the Queen from 55; R of W Stafford w Frome Billet Dio Sarum from 67; Can and Preb of Sarum Cathl from 67; Archd of Sherborne from 67. *West Stafford Rectory, Dorchester, Dorset.* (Dorchester 64637)

WARD, Ernleigh Hilbert. b 09. Bp's Coll Calc 39. **d** 41 Bp Tarafdar for Calc **p** 42 Nagp. Asst Chap Ch Ch Jubbulpore 41-43; Chap Bandikui 43-48; C of Frogmore (in c of St Luke Bricket Wood) 48-50; Wanstead 50-54; V of Gt Wakering 54-60; C-in-c of Foulness 55-56 and 57-58; R of E (w W from 61 and L Warley from 72) Horndon 60-77; Perm to Offic Dio Chelmsf from 77. *29 Wash Road, Hutton, Essex.*

WARD, Frank Neal. b 16. E Anglican Min Tr Course 78. **d** 80 **p** 81 Nor (APM). Hon C of Kelling w Salthouse Dio Nor from 80; Weybourne w U Sheringham Dio Nor from 80. *Newlands, Sharrington, Melton Constable, Norf.*

WARD, Geoffrey. Cranmer Hall Dur 77. **d** 79 **p** 80 Ripon. C of Garforth 79-81; V of Holmfield Dio Wakef from 81. *Ramsden House, Beechwood Road, Holmfield, Halifax, HX2 9AR.* (Halifax 244586)

WARD, Geoffrey Edward. b 30. Linc Th Coll 62. **d** 64 **p** 65 Pet. C of Oundle 64-68; Weston Favell 68-70; Team V 70-72; R of Cottingham w Middleton and E Carlton Dio Pet from 72. *Cottingham Rectory, Market Harborough, Leics, LE16 8XG.* (Rockingham 771277)

WARD, Geoffrey James. Moore Th Coll Syd ACT ThL 53. **d** and **p** 54 Syd. C of St John Parramatta 54-56; R of St Mary's 56-58; Perm to Offic Dio Melb from 58; L to Offic Dio Syd 63-73. *Sandy Creek Road, Riddell's Creek, Vic, Australia 3431.* (054-28 5365)

WARD, George Henry. b 08. Univ of Sheff BA 29, MA 30. Ridley Hall Cam 36. **d** 37 **p** 38 Sheff. C of Wath-upon-Dearne 37-39; Goole 39-44; V of Rawcliffe 44-49; Owston 49-56; C-in-c of Moss 51-56; V of Greasborough 56-67; Worsbrough 67-73; Perm to Offic Dio Sheff from 73. *Address temp unknown.*

WARD, Harry Wellington. b 46. Ch Div Sch of the Pacific Calif MDiv 78. Codr Coll Barb 74. **d** 77 Calif **p** 78 Nass. C of St Paul Long Is 77-80; Prin St Jo Coll Nass from 80. *Box N-4858, Nassau, Bahamas, W Indies.*

WARD, Herbert. b 1900. Kelham Th Coll 21. **d** 26 **p** 27 Cov. C of St Thos Cov 26-29; Helmsley 29-33; V of Huttons Ambo 33-38; Osmotherley 38-45; Leake Yorks 45-55; V of Over and Nether Silton w Kepwick 45-55; Gt Ayton w Easby (and Newton-in-Cleveland from 57) 55-67; C-in-c of Newton-in-Cleveland 55-57. *198 Windy Hill Lane, Marske-by-the-Sea, Redcar, Cleveland.* (Redcar 471347)

WARD, Herbert. b 1897. Edin Th Coll 50. **d** and **p** 51 Aber. C Dio Aber and Ork 51-52; R of Kirkwall 52-54; P-in-C of Stromness 52-54; Asst Chap HM Pris Wandsworth 54-55; Chap HM Pris Camp Hill 55; Dartmoor 55-56; C of St Martin-in-the-Fields Westmr 56-57; St Matt Bethnal Green 58-59; Chap Westmr Hosp 59-60; C of Calne 61-62; All SS Portsea 62-63; Chap at Taormina 63-65; Hon Chap Br Embassy Rabat 66-70; Perm to Offic Dio Chich from 70. *11a Guildford Street, Brighton, BN1 3LS.*

WARD, Jack. Tyndale Hall Bris. **d** 57 Lich **p** 58 Stafford for Lich. C of Bucknall 57-60; Tettenhall Wood 60-61; V of

Mow Cop 61-79. *9 Wentworth Drive, Rookery, Stoke-on-Trent, ST9 9QB.*

WARD, John Raymond. b 31. St Jo Coll Dur BA 54, Dipl Th 56. **d** 56 **p** 57 Ripon. C of Leeds 56-60; Seacroft (in c of St Richard) 60-63; V of Kirkstall 63-75; Bramhope Dio Ripon from 75. *26 Leeds Road, Bramhope, Leeds, LS16 9BQ.* (Arthington 842543)

WARD, John Stephen Keith. b 38. Univ of Wales (Cardiff) BA (Phil) 62. Linacre Coll Ox BLitt 68. Westcott Ho Cam 72. **d** 72 Lon **p** 73 Edmonton for Lon. Hon C of Hampstead 72-75; Fell and Dean of Trin Hall Cam from 75. *Trinity Hall, Cambridge.*

WARD, John Stewart. b 43. St Jo Coll Dur BA 66. Ripon Coll Cudd 77. **d** 79 **p** 80 Ripon. C of Ch Ch High Harrogate Dio Ripon from 79. *11a Church Square, Harrogate, N Yorks, HG1 4SP.*

WARD, Keith Raymond. b 37. Univ of Dur BSc 60. Chich Th Coll 63. **d** 65 **p** 66 Newc T. C of St Luke Wallsend 65-68; Wooler (in c of Doddington 68-74; and Ilderton 70-74) 68-74; V of Dinnington 74-81; Bedlington Dio Newc T from 81. *Vicarage, Church Lane, Bedlington, NE22 5ER.*

WARD, Kenneth Arthur. b 22. St D Coll Lamp BA 50. Chich Th Coll 50. **d** 52 **p** 53 Pet. C of St Barn Wellingborough 52-55; Stevenage (in c of H Trin) 55-58; R of Daventry (w Norton 73-79) Dio Pet from 58; Surr from 64; RD of Daventry 68-76. *Rectory, Daventry, Northants.* (Daventry 2638)

WARD, Leslie Alan James. b 38. K Coll Lon and Warm AKC 61. **d** 62 **p** 63 Nor. C of St Anne Earlham 62-65; Gt Yarmouth (in c of St Paul) 65-70; R of Burgh Castle Dio Nor from 70; Belton Dio Nor from 70. *Belton Rectory, Great Yarmouth, Norf.* (Great Yarmouth 780210)

WARD, Louis Arthur. Ripon Hall Ox 72. **d** 73 **p** 74 Bris. C of Corsham 73-76; Chap Qu Eliz Hosp Bris 76-78; Bp's Chap for the Arts 76-80; V of Bitton 78-80; Perm to Offic Dio Bris from 80. *31 Apsley Road, Clifton, Bristol, BS8 2SN.*

WARD, Malcolm Warner. St Barn Coll Adel 45. ACT ThL 47. **d** 47 **p** 48 Perth. C of Cottesloe 47-49; R of Quairading 49-54; Chap St Geo Coll Perth 54-55; R of Meckering 55-57; York Dio Perth from 57. *Rectory, York, W Australia 6302.* (York 81)

WARD, Michael Anthony. b 42. Sarum Th Coll 67. **d** 70 **p** 71 Sarum. C of Bridport 70-74; Team V of Swanborough 74-77; P-in-c of Shalbourne and Ham 77-79; Chute w Chute Forest 77-79; Team R of Wexcombe Dio Sarum from 79. *Shalbourne Vicarage, Marlborough, Wilts, SN8 3HQ.* (Marlborough 570421)

WARD, Michael Reginald. b 31. BNC Ox BA (2nd cl Jurispr) 54, MA 58. Tyndale Hall, Bris 54. **d** 56 **p** 57 Lon. C of St Mary Ealing 56-59; Morden 59-61; Midl and E Anglia Area Sec CCCS 61-66; L to Offic Dio Pet 62-64; Dio Cov 65-66; V of St Jo Evang (w St Andr Chelsea from 73) 66-76; P-in-c of St Andr Chelsea 72-73; Hawkesbury w Hawkesbury Upton 76-80; Hillesley Alderley & Trensham 79-80; Bibury w Winson and Barnsley Dio Glouc from 80. *Vicarage, Bibury, Cirencester, Glos.* (Bibury 387)

WARD, Peter Garnet. b 28. GRSM 51. Ridley Hall Cam. **d** 61 **p** 62 Liv. C of Maghull 61-64; Chap and Asst Master Kenya High Sch 64-73; Perm to Offic Dio Chich 74-75 and from 77; P-in-c of Coleman's Hatch 75-77. *St Michael's, Parrock Lane, Hartfield, E Sussex, TN7 4AS.* (Hartfield 338)

WARD, Philip Paul Ben. b 35. Univ of Tor BA 61. ALCD 66. **d** 66 **p** 67 Ox. C of Chenies 66-68; Ardsley 68-70; Finham 70-73; V of Terrington St Clem 73-81; R of Dalhousie Dio Fred from 81. *Box 2050 Dalhousie, NB, Canada E0K 1B0.* (506-684 2150)

WARD, Philip Percival Ford. b 33. City Univ Lon BSc 61. Wells Th Coll 67. **d** 69 Bris **p** 70 Malmesbury for Bris. C of All SS Clifton w St Mary Virg Tyndall's Pk 69-72; P-in-c of St Osw Bedminster Down 72-76; V 76-77; V of St Jo Div Fishponds Dio Bris from 77; P-in-c of All SS Fishponds 77-80. *St John's Vicarage, Fishponds, Bristol, BS16 3NW.* (Bristol 654130)

WARD, Richard. b 09. St Aug Coll Cant 63. **d** 64 Lon **p** 65 Willesden for Lon. C of L Stanmore 64-69; V of Hoar Cross 69-78; P-in-c of Newborough w Needwood 76-78. *Rose Cott, Hoar Cross, Burton-on-Trent, Staffs, DE13 8RA.* (Hoar Cross 215)

WARD, Robert Arthur Philip. Qu Coll Birm 77. **d** 79 **p** 80 Birm. C of St Paul Balsall Heath Dio Birm from 79. *c/o St Paul's Vicarage, Trafalgar Road, Moseley, Birmingham B13 8BJ.*

WARD, Robert Charles Irwin. b 48. Univ of Leic LLB 70. St Jo Coll Dur 78 **d** 80 **p** 81 Newc T. C of St Mich Byker City and Dio Newc T from 80. *St Michael's Church, Byker, Newcastle-on-Tyne.*

WARD, Robert Grant. Univ of W Ont BA 62. Hur Coll BTh 64. **d** 64 Hur for Moos **p** 65 Moos. C of Moose Factory 64-67; R of Fort Albany 67-69; I of Walpole I 70-75; Tilbury Dio Hur from 75. *17 Forrest Street, Tilbury, Ont., Canada.* (519-682 1335)

WARD, Canon Ronald Arthur. Univ of Lon BD 34, BA 37, MA 47, PhD 49. **d** and **p** 49 Roch. C of Ch Ch Tunbridge Wells and Tutor of Lon Coll of Div 49-51; Prof of NT Wycl Coll Tor 52-63; Actg C of Messiah Ch Tor 52-60; Exam Chap to Bp of Tor 55-63; to Bp of Fred from 69; Commiss Ja 59-63; Hon C of St John York Mills Tor 60-63; R of Kirby Cane Norf 63-67; R of Ellingham 63-67; St John Stone St John 67-74; Commiss Nel from 64; Can of Ch Ch Cathl Fred 71-74; Hon Can from 74. *58 Union Street, St Stephen, NB, Canada.*

WARD, Stanley Gordon. b 21. Qu Coll Cam BA 43, MA 47. E Midl Jt Ordin Tr Scheme 76. **d** 79 Sherwood for Southw **p** 80 Southw. Hon C of Wollaton Dio Southw from 79. *7 Wollaton Vale, Wollaton, Nottingham.*

WARD, Stephen Philip. b 49. Univ of Sheff BA 72. St Steph Ho Ox 77. **d** 79 **p** 80 Leic. C of Narborough 70-80; St Thos Brentwood Dio Chelmsf from 81. *29 St Thomas Road, Brentwood, Essex.* (Brentwood 225688)

WARD, Thomas Peter. St Aug Coll Kumasi. **d** and **p** 31 Accra. P Dio Accra; P-in-c of Bodi 44-49; Larteh 49-54; Winneba 54-57; Saltpond 57-60; Dundwa 60-72; Hon Can of Accra 61-72; Can of Kum 73-77; P-in-c of St Paul Obuasi 73-77. *c/o Christ Church, Cape Coast, Ghana.*

WARD, Timothy William. b 49. Open Univ BA 74. St Deiniol's Libr Hawarden 78. **d** 79 Birm **p** 80 Aston for Birm. C of St Mary Handsworth Dio Birm from 79. *63 Lechlade Road, Great Barr, Birmingham, B43 5ND.*

WARD, Trevor Michael. b 53. AKC 75. St Aug Coll Cant 75. **d** 76 **p** 77 York. C of Northallerton w Kirby Sigston 76-78; Kirkleatham 79-81; Marton-in-Cleveland (in c of Easterside) Dio York from 81. *7 Easterside Road, Middlesbrough, TS4 3QB.* (Middlesbrough 316144)

WARD, Walter Bryan. St Paul's Coll Univ of Syd BA 28. ACT ThL 29. Th Scho 42. **d** 30 **p** 31 N Queensld. Asst Master All S Sch Charters Towers 28-32; M of Bush Bro of St Barn 30-33; C of Mackay 33-36; R of Ingham 37-41; Chap RAAF 41-46; Warden of St Osw Hostel Brisb 46-47; R of Cleveland 47-51; RD of Brisb S from 50; R of St Mary Kangaroo Point Brisb 51-57; Commiss in Austr for N Queensld 53-57 and from 67; R of St Luke Toowoomba 57-66; St Thos Toowong Brisb 66-75; Hon Can of Brisb 58-63; Archd of the Downs 63-68; Brisb 68-75; Hon Miss Chap Dio Brisb from 75. *10 Ramon Street, Kenmore, Queensland, Australia 4069.* (378-5499)

WARD, William. Wycl Hall Ox 63. **d** 64 **p** 65 York. C of Helmsley 64-66; v Cho and Bursar of York Minster 66-68; LPr Dio York 67-68; V of Stillington w Marton-in-the-Forest Moxby and Farlington 68-73; Langtoft w Cottam Foxholes and Butterwick 73-78; Perm to Offic Dio York from 79. *3 Huby Road, Sutton-on-Forest, York.*

WARD, William Edward. b 48. AKC 71. St Aug Coll Cant 71. **d** 72 **p** 73 Heref. C of St Martin Heref 72-77; Team V of Blakenhall Heath Dio Lich from 77. *78 Chestnut Road, Forest Estate, Leamore, Walsall, WS3 1AP.* (Walsall 407768)

WARD, William Francis. b 35. Ely Th Coll 61. **d** 64 **p** 65 Newc T. C of St Anthony Byker Newc T 64-67; St Marg Newlands Glas 67-69; R of Ascen Mosspark Glas 69-74; Chap RN 74-78; R of Arbroath Dio Brech from 78. *St Mary's Rectory, Springfield Terrace, Arbroath, Angus.* (Arbroath 73392)

WARD-ANDREWS, Canon Lewes. b 12. Kelham Th Coll 29. M SSM 36. **d** 36 **p** 37 Liv. C of St Nich Liv 36-40; St John Bedminster 40-46; Ho of SSM Kelham 46-58; L to Offic Dio Southw 46-60; C-in-c of St Geo w St Jo Bapt Nottm Dio Southw from 60; Hon Can of Southw from 66. *4 Ayton Close, Nottingham, NG2 1HF.* (Nottm 864881)

WARD-BODDINGTON, Canon Douglas. b 20. SOC 69. **d** 72 **p** 73 S'wark. C of Ch Ch S'wark 72-77; Chap St Vincent's Algarve Portugal 77-80; VG Dio Gibr in Eur from 80; Can of Gibr Cathl from 80; Perm to Offic Dio Lon from 81. *2 Hammersmith Terrace, W6 9TS.* (01-748 1330)

WARD-HILL, Thomas Haydn. b 1900. Late Scho and Exhib of Qu Coll Ox BA (2nd cl Math) 21, MA 25. **d** 32 **p** 33 St D. Asst Master Llandovery Coll 21-48; Hon C of Llandingat 32-39; Publ Pr Dio St D 39-48; V of Stoke St Milburgh w Heath 48-51; PC of Hopton Cangeford 48-51; Seq of Cold Weston 48-51; Chap and Asst Master Dulwich Coll 51-61; Publ Pr Dio S'wark 52-61; R of Knockin w Maesbrook 61-66; Asst Master and Chap Oswestry Sch 66-73; L to Offic Dio Lich from 69. *Orchard Croft, Queen's Road, Oswestry, Salop.* (Oswestry 3870)

WARDALE, Robert Christopher. b 46. Univ of Newc T BA 69. Coll of the Resurr Mirfield 77. **d** 79 **p** 80 Dur. C of St Mary Cockerton Dio Dur from 79. *St Mary's Vicarage, Cockerton, Darlington, Co Durham, DL3 9EX.* (0325 63705)

WARDEN, Ven John Hubert. Univ of Witwatersrand BMus 60. St Paul's Coll Grahmstn. **d** 63 **p** 64 Grahmstn. C of

St Barn Port Eliz 63-64; St Sav E Lon 64-66; R of Sabie w Lydenburg 66-69; Rustenburg 70-72; Sunnyside 72-80; Archd of Pret from 77; Dir Ecumen Research Unit Dio Pret from 80. *PO Box 17128, Groenkloof, Pretoria, S Africa.*

WARDLE, Edward Christian. b13. **d** 62 **p** 63 Ripon. C of Farnley 62-64; Wortley 64-66; R of Llanwyddelan w Manafon 66-80; P-in-c of Stottesdon Dio Heref from 80. *Stottesdon Vicarage, Cleobury Mortimer, Kidderminster, Worcs.*

WARDLE, John Alan. Jes Coll Cam BA 29, MA 34. Coll of Resurr Mirfield 30. **d** 32 **p** 33 Wakef. C of St Pet Barnsley 32-35; St Giles Reading 35-36; St Thos Huddersfield 37-45; L to Offic Dio Wakef 47-49; P-in-c of H Cross Miss Orlando Johann 49-55; Miss P at St Aug Miss Penhalonga Dio Mashon (Dio Mutare from 81) from 56. *St Augustine's Mission, Penhalonga, Zimbabwe.*

WARDLE, John Alexander. b 30. TD 73. BA (Lon) 59. Univ of Man MA 81. Oak Hill Th Coll. **d** 57 **p** 58 Blackb. C of St Mark Blackpool 57-60; St Jo Div Tunbridge Wells 60-62; V of St Luke Maidstone 62-69; Hartford 69-79; CF (TAVR) 67-73; R of Barton Seagrave w Warkton Dio Pet from 79. *Barton, Seagrave Rectory, Kettering, Northants, NN15 6SR* (Kettering 513629)

WARDLE, John Argyle. b 47. St Jo Coll Dur BA 71, Dipl Th 72. Cranmer Hall Dur 68. **d** 73 **p** 74 Southw. C of Mansfield 73-77; Chap St Felix Sch Southwold from 77. *30 The Drive, Reydon, Southwold, Suff.*

WARDLE-HARPUR, Canon Charles Noel. b 03. St Edm Hall Ox BA (3rd cl Hist) 25, MA 29. Wycl Hall Ox 26. **d** 26 **p** 27 Chelmsf. C of Barking 26-30; St Mary Prittlewell (in c of St Luke) 30-31; Min of St Luke's Distr Prittlewell 31-37; R of Lambourne w Abridge 37-39; V of St Mary Virg Loughton 39-42; C-in-c of Ch Ch Attercliffe St Bart Carbrook and St Alb Darnall Sheff 42-46; V of St Nich w St Clem Roch 46-49; H Trin S Shore Blackpool 49-58; Surr from 47; Proc Conv Blackb 55-58; V of Stockton-on-Tees (w St Jas Ap from 60) 58-72; RD of Stockton from 59; Hon Can of Dur 59-72; Can (Emer) from 72; Proc Conv Dur 59-72. *19 Elm Crescent, Charlbury, Oxford.*

WARDLE-HARPUR, James. b 31. St Jo Coll Dur BA 55. Wells Th Coll 55. **d** 56 **p** 57 Sheff. C of St Cecilia Parson Cross Sheff 56-59; Maltby 59-61; V of St Jude Hexthorpe Doncaster 61-64; USPG Miss at Pattoki 64-68; R of Vic Pk Man 68-75; V of Foxton w Gumley and Laughton (and Lubenham from 79) Dio Leic from 75. *Foxton Vicarage, Market Harborough, Leics.* (East Langton 245)

WARDMAN, Ven John Lindow. St Barn Coll Adel ACT ThL 48. **d** and **p** 48 Adel. C of Unley 48-49; R of Toodyay 49-51; Miss Dio New Guinea 51-62; R of Mt Hawthorn 62-72; Commiss Polyn 62-70; R of St Mary S Perth from 72; Can of Perth from 73; Archd of Perth 77-78 and from 80; Swan 77-80. *Rectory, Ridge Street, South Perth, W Australia 6151.* (367 1243)

WARDROBE, Bevan. b 26. Hatf Coll Dur BA 53. Cudd Coll 53. **d** 54 **p** 55 Lon. C of Southgate 54-59; PV of Lich Cathl and Asst Master Cathl Sch 59-67; Subchanter 63-67; Hd Master of Song Sch and V Cho of York Minster from 67; L to Offic Dio York from 67. *2a Minster Court, York, YO1 2JD.* (York 22976)

WARDROP, David John. b 34. ALCD (1st cl) 59. **d** 59 **p** 60 Lon. C of All SS Harrow Weald 59-62; Chap RNR from 61; V of St Aid Ernesettle Plymouth 62-64; Broad Clyst w Westwood 64-67; Bp's Chap for Ecumen Relations 64-67; Asst Gen Sec ICF 67-76; P-in-c of Pertenhall w Swineshead 76-80; R of Wymington w Podington Dio St Alb from 80. *Rectory, Wymington, Rushden, Northants, NN10 9LL.* (Rushden 57800)

WARDROP, George Davidson. **d** 74 Melb **p** 75 Brisb. C of St Mary Magd Adel 74; M Bush Bro of St Paul Brisb 74-77; R of Otway Dio Bal from 78. *St Aidan's Rectory, Apollo Bay, Vic, Australia 3233.* (052-37 6615)

WARDROP, James Young Inglis. b 12. Univ of Glas MA 32. **d** 35 **p** 36 Glas. C of St Columba Clydebank 35-37; P-in-c of H Trin Riddrie Glas 37-39; C of St Mary's Cathl Glas 39-41; R of St John Girvan 41-44; CF (EC) 44-47; Perm to Offic Dio Glas 47-48; P-in-c of St Barn Dennistoun City and Dio Glas from 48. *c/o Hillcrest, 27 Westercraigs, Glasgow, G31 2HY.*

WARDS, Allan Ross. b 41. Univ of Vic Wel BA 63, Massey Univ Palmerston N MA 80. St Jo Coll Auckld LTh 77. **d** 77 **p** 78 Wel. C of All SS Palmerston N 77-79; Kapiti 79-81; V of St John Wainuiomata Dio Wel from 81. *Vicarage, 117 Main Road, Wainuiomata, NZ.*

WARDS, Lawrence Charles. Univ of Cant BA 62. NZ Bd of Th Stud LTh 64. Ch Ch Coll 61. **d** 64 **p** 65 Ch Ch. C of Timaru 64-67; Fendalton 67-68; V of Kumara 68-72; Akaroa 72-78; Linc Dio Ch Ch from 78. *St Stephen's Vicarage, Lincoln, NZ.*

WARE, Alfred Henry Michael. b 09. St Steph Ho Ox 45. **d** 47 **p** 48 Ox. C of SS Mary and John Ox 47-51; Taplow 51-53; Burnham 53-56; V of All SS Boyne Hill Maidenhead Dio Ox from 56; Surr 57-67. *All Saints' Vicarage, Boyne Hill, Maidenhead, Berks.* (Maidenhead 21933)

WARE, Austin Neville. b 14. St D Coll Lamp BA 37. St Mich Coll Llan 37. **d** 39 Ban for Llan **p** 41 Llan. C of St Mary Seven Sisters 39-42; St Andr Drypool Hull 42-44; St Geo Leeds 44-45; Em Loughborough 45-47; R of Elton 47-55; V of Winster 49-55; St Barn Hull 55-58; R of W and E Heslerton (w Knapton from 75) 58-79; V of Knapton 58-75; C-in-c of Yedingham 75-79. *Craigsmoor, Trearddur Bay, Anglesey, Gwyn.*

WARE, Colin Leslie George. St Francis Coll Brisb ACT ThL 45. **d** 46 Melb **p** 47 Brisb. C of St John Foots Cray 46-47; Miss Chap Dio Brisb 47-50; R of Mossman 50-55; Booval 55-60; Newtown 60-65; Chap Gladesville Ment Hosp and L to Offic Dio Syd 65-69; C-in-c of Villawood 70-73; R of Wilcannia 73-74; V of Pine Rivers 74-76; Pine Rivers N 76-78; Perm to Offic Dio Brisb 78-80; P-in-c of Norman Pk Dio Brisb from 80. *Box 97, Morningside, Queensld, Australia 4170.*

WARE, John Franklin Jones. b 07. Univ of Wales BA (3rd cl Hist) 30. Keble Coll Ox 3rd cl Th 32, BA 33, Ma 36. **d** 32 **p** 33 Ban. C of Llanfachreth w Llanynghenedl and Llanfiguel (in c of Valley) 32-35; Risca 35-40; CF (EC) 40-46; V of Penmaen 46-48; R of Chailey 48-65; V of St Phil Hove 65-79. *10 Evelyn Terrace, Fairfield Park, Bath, BA1 6EX.*

WARE, Canon John Lawrence. b 37. Univ of Nottm BA (2nd cl Th) 59. Ridley Hall Cam 62. **d** 62 Bp Gerard for Sheff **p** 63 Sheff. C of Attercliffe w Carbrook Sheff 62-66; Ranmoor 66-68; R of Liddington 68-74; Social and Industr Adv to Bp of Bris from 74; P-in-c of St Thos Mart Bris 74-79; Hon Can of Bris from 76; V of Kingswood Dio Bris from 79. *Kingswood Vicarage, Bristol, BS15 4AD.* (Kingswood 673627)

WARE, Leonard Melville. **d** 62 **p** 63 Tor. C Scarborough, St Geo and of H Trin Oshawa 62-63; P-in-c of H Trin Oshawa 63-64; P-in-c of St Pet Oshawa 63-66; R of Grafton 66-79; R of Colborne 66-79; St Geo Scarborough City and Dio Tor from 79. *3765 St Clair Avenue East, Scarborough, Toronto, Ont, Canada.*

WARE, Stephen John. b 55. St D Coll Lamp BA 76. Ripon Coll Cudd 77. **d** 79 Bp McKie for Cov **p** 80 Cov. C of Lighthorne w Chesterton & Moreton Morrell w Newbold Pacey Dio Cov from 79. *1 Compton Road, Lighthorne Heath, Leamington Spa, CV33 9TL.* (Kineton 640818)

WAREHAM, Alfred Berkley. Mem Univ of Newfld Qu Coll Newfld 54. **d** 59 **p** 60 Newfld. C of Bay St Geo 59-60; Grand Falls 60-64; R of Meadows 64-69; L to Offic Dio Newfld from 71. *60 Amherst Heights, St John's, Newfoundland, Canada.*

WAREING, Stephen Richard. b 1896. Selw Coll Cam BA 23, MA 26. St Paul's Coll Burgh 15. **d** 21 **p** 22 Linc. C of Caistor w Holton-le-Moor and Clixby 21-24; Langley Mill 24-26; Min Can of Cathl Ch Hamilton NZ 26-28; Dom Chap to Bp of Waik 27-28; Exam Chap 28-34; V of Putararu 28-29; V of Te Awamutu and Chap Waikeria Reform and Tokanui Mental Hosp 29-36; C of Hagley 37-40; R of Pedmore 40-68. *c/o Barclays Bank, 81 High Street, Stourbridge, Worcs.*

WARIF, John Michael. **d** 71 **p** 72 Papua. P Dio Papua. *Movi PMB, via Goroka, Papua New Guinea.*

WARING, Cecil Clarke. **d** 58 **p** 59 Bal. Hon C of Warrnambool Dio Bal from 59. *216 Koroit Street, Warrnambool, Vic., Australia 3280.* (055-62 7496)

WARING, James Henry. **d** 50 **p** 52 Hur. R of St Steph and St Andr Sarnia 51-54; Glencoe 54-56; R of Burford 56-61; Wallaceburg 61-71; St John Sarnia 71-77. *250 Mary Street, Waterloo, Ont., Canada.*

WARING, John Valentine. b 29. **d** 67 **p** 68 St A. C of Bistre 67-71; St Thos Blackpool 71-72; R of Levenshulme Dio Man from 72. *20 Windsor Road, Levenshulme, Manchester, M19 2EB.* (061-224 8525)

WARING, Wilfrid Harold. b 11. TD 46. Late Exhib of Jes Coll Cam 2nd cl Cl Trip pt i 32, BA (2nd cl Th Trip pt i) 33, MA 37. Ripon Hall Ox 33. **d** 34 **p** 35 Worc. C of St Thos Dudley 34-39; CF (TA R of O) from 39; CF (EC) 39-46; Hon CF 46; Chap of Rishworth Sch and Perm to Offic Dio Wakef 47-65; Chap Hulme Gr Sch Oldham and L to Offic Dio Man 65-67; V of Saddleworth 67-77. *8a Kirkby Road, Ripon, N Yorks, HG4 2ET.* (Ripon 5880)

WARKE, Ven Robert Alexander. b 30. TCD BA 52, BD 60. U Th Sem NY 59. **d** 53 **p** 54 Down. C of Newtownards 53-56; St Cath w St Victor Dub 56-58; Rathfarnham 58-64; Min Can of St Patr Cathl Dub 59-64; Ch of Ireland Press Officer in Dub 63-71; I of Dunlavin w Hollywood U 64-67; Drumcondra w N Strand and St Barn 67-71; Zion Ch Rathgar City and Dio Dub from 71; RD of Taney 77-80; Archd of Dub from 80. *18 Bushy Park Road, Rathgar, Dublin 6, Irish Republic.* (Dublin 972865)

WARLAND, Cyril John. b 21. St Cath S Ox BA (3rd cl Th) 43, MA 56. Cudd Coll. **d** 44 **p** 45 Bradf. C of St Wilfred Lidget

Green 44-46; Goldthorpe 47-56; R of Tavy St Mary Dio Ex from 56; RD of Tavistock from 77; P-in-c of Walkhampton Dio Ex from 80. *Tavy St Mary Rectory, Tavistock, Devon, PL19 9PP.* (Mary Tavy 210)

WARLAND, Peter William. b 35. K Coll Lon and Warm 56. **d** 60 **p** 61 Liv. C of Pemberton 60-64; Warrington (in c of St John) 64-66; V of All SS Farnworth 66-71; Chap RN from 71. *c/o Ministry of Defence, Lacon House, Theobalds Road, WC1X 8RY.*

WARMAN, Canon Cyril Aidan Oswald. b 08. Pemb Coll Ox 3rd cl Math Mods 28, BA (2nd cl Th) 30, MA 35. Ridley Hall Cam 30. **d** 31 S'wark **p** 32 Man for S'wark. C of Battersea 31-33; Rugby (in c of St Pet) 33-37; V of Shepshed 37-46; Manningham 46-52; Normanton 52-66; Kellington w Whitley 66-74; RD of Wakef 59-66; Hon Can of Wakef 62-74; Can (Emer) from 74. *34 St Oswald Road, Bridlington, N Humberside, YO16 5SD.* (Bridlington 73436)

WARMAN, Ven Francis Frederic Guy. b 04. Worc Coll Ox BA (3rd cl Th) 26, MA 30. Ridley Hall Cam 26. **d** 27 Cov **p** 28 Chelmsf for Cov. C of St Nich Radford Cov 27-30; Chilvers Coton 30-32; V of St Jas Selby 32-36; PC of Beeston 36-43; V of St Marg w Ch Ch Ward End 43-46; RD of E Birm 44-46; V of Aston-juxta-Birm 46-65; Proc Conv Birm 45-75; Hon Can of Birm Cathl 48-65; Surr from 45-65; RD of Aston 64-65; Can Res of Birm and Archd of Aston 65-77; Archd (Emer) from 77; Perm to Offic Dio Chich from 77. *76 Winterbourne Close, Lewes, Sussex.* (Lewes 2440)

WARMAN, John Richard. b 37. Late Exhib of Pemb Coll Ox 2nd cl Cl Mods 59, BA (2nd cl Th) 61. Ridley Hall Cam 61. **d** 63 Warrington for Liv **p** 64 Liv. C of Huyton 63-67; Asst Chap Univ of Liv 67-68; Bp's Univ Chap 68-74; P-in-c of Holbrook 74-80; L Eaton 74-80; R of Sawley Dio Derby from 80. *Sawley Rectory, Long Eaton, Nottingham, NG10 3AB.* (06-076 4900)

WARMOLL, Reginald Harry. Late Scho of St Cath Coll Cam 1st cl Geog Trip pt i 38, BA (1st cl Geog Trip pt ii) 39, MA 43. Coll of Resurr Mirfield 40. **d** 42 Grimsby for Linc **p** 43 Linc. C of Grantham 42-46; Chap and Asst Master Shoreham Gr Sch 46-47; Lect Newland Park Tr Coll and L to Offic Dio Ox 47-52, Chap and Lect St Jo Tr Coll York 52-58; Tutor St Monica's Coll and Chap Mampong Conv 58-61 and from 70; Adisadel Coll Accra 61-70; L to Offic Dio Accra 62-73; Dio Kum from 73; Hon Can of Kum from 74. *PO Box 17, Mampong, Ashanti, Ghana.*

WARNE, John Norman. b 20. Univ of Nottm LLB 55. Qu Coll Birm. **d** 58 Birm **p** 59 Aston for Birm. [f Barrister] C of Acocks Green 58-61; V of Madingley 61-64; Asst Dir of Educn Dio Ely 61-64; Dir and Sec of Relig Educn Sarum 64-70; Can and Preb of Sarum Cathl 67-80; V of St Aldhelm Branksome 70-80; Blackheath Dio Birm from 80. *Address temp unknown.*

WARNER, Alan Winston. b 51. Univ of Lon BSc 73. Coll of Resurr Mirfield 73. **d** 76 **p** 77 Lich. C of St Anne Willenhall 76-78; Berkswich w Walton 78-81; V of St Greg Gt Wednesfield Dio Lich from 81. *Vicarage, Blackhalve Lane, Wednesfield, Staffs.* (Wolverhampton 731677)

WARNER, Andrew Compton. b 35. Fitzw Ho Cam BA 58, MA 62. Westcott Ho Cam 59. **d** 60 Bp Dale for Cant **p** 61 Guildf. C of Addlestone 60-64; C-in-c of Ash Vale Conv Distr 64-71; V of Hinchley Wood 71-80; R of Gt Bookham Dio Guildf from 80. *Rectory, Church Road, Gt Bookham, Leatherhead, Surrey.* (Bookham 52404)

WARNER, Clifford Chorley. b 38. E Midl Jt Ordin Tr Scheme Nottm 76. **d** 79 Repton for Derby **p** 80 Derby (APM). C of Swanwick w Pentrich Dio Derby from 79. *17 Amber Heights, Ripley, Derby, DE5 3SP.*

WARNER, Cyril Robert. b 04. Linc Th Coll 33. **d** 35 Bedford for St Alb **p** 36 St Alb. C of Hitchin 35-39; Chap Cheltm Coll 39-42; Chap RNVR 42-47; R of Beaconsfield 47-69; Surr 54-69; RD of Burnham 61-69; V of The Lee 69-74; C-in-c of Hawridge w Cholesbury 73-74. *Bay Cottage, Stone Drive, Colwall, Malvern, Worcs.* (Colwall 40284)

WARNER, David. b 40. K Coll Lon and Warm AKC 63. **d** 64 **p** 65 Wakef. C of Castleford 64-68; Warden of Hollowford Tr and Conf Centr Sheff 68-72; R of Wombwell Dio Sheff from 72. *Wombwell Rectory, Barnsley, S Yorks.* (Barnsley 752166)

WARNER, David Brooke. Univ of Melb B Com 49. ACT ThL 50. **d** 51 **p** 52 Melb. C of S Yarra 51-53; Newton Heath 53-55; Southgate 55; Min of Eltham 56-60; Ringwood 60-66; I of Burwood 66-72; Exam Chap to Abp of Melb 71-74; I of All SS St Kilda E 73-75; Perm to Offic Dio Melb 75-77; P-in-c of Kooyong Dio Melb from 77. *59 Guildford Road, Surrey Hills, Vic, Australia 3127.* (83-2237)

WARNER, David Leonard John. b 24. Kelham Th Coll 47. **d** 51 **p** 52 Lon. C of St Mich AA Mill Hill 51-54; St Sav Pimlico 54-56; R of Rustenburg 56-64; P-in-c of Rustenburg W Miss Distr 61-64; R of St Wilfrid Hillcrest Pret 64-68; V of Epiph Bournemouth 68-77; Whitchurch w Tufton and Litchfield Dio Win from 77; RD of Whitchurch from 79. *Vicarage, Whitchurch, Hants, RG28 7AS.* (Whitchurch 2535)

WARNER, Dennis Vernon. b 46. Univ of Lon BA (Cl) 68, BD 71. St Aug Coll Cant 71. **d** 72 **p** 73 Lich. C of W Bromwich 72-75; Uttoxeter w Bramshall 75-78; Asst at Lich Dioc Office and L to Offic Dio Lich from 79. *33 Dovecliffe Crescent, Stretton, Burton-on-Trent, Staffs, DE13 0JH.*

WARNER, George Francis. b 36. Trin Coll Ox BA (2nd cl Lit Hum) 60, MA 64. Qu Coll Cam BA (2nd cl Th Trip pt ii) 63. Westcott Ho Cam 61. **d** 63 Bp Warner for Birm **p** 64 Birm. C of St Geo Birm 63-66; Maidstone 66-69; Chap Wellington Coll Crowthorne 69-78; R of Caludon Team Min Dio Cov from 78. *Stoke Rectory, Walsgrave Road, Coventry, CV2 4BG.* (Cov 457681)

WARNER, Henry Homan. b 17. **d** 44 Down for Derry **p** 45 Derry. C of St Aug Derry 44-47; Kidlington 47; St Mary Newry 47-50; I of Langfield 50-55; C of St Bart Dub 55-57; I 57-64; Asst Chap Miss to Seamen 65-66; P-in-c of St Jo Evang Sandymount 68-80. *c/o 18 Trimleston Drive, Booterstown, Co Dublin, Irish Republic.* (Dublin 692704)

WARNER, Jacob Reginald. Hur Coll Dipl Th 69. **d** 69 **p** 70 Hur. I of Thamesford w Lakeside 69-74; Hanover Dio Hur from 74. *187 8th Street, Hanover, Ont., Canada.* (519-364 3525)

WARNER, James Morley. b 32. SOC 66. **d** 69 Willesden for Lon **p** 70 Lon. C of K Chas Mart S Mymms 69-72; St Steph Bush Hill Pk Lon 72-75; V of St Jo Evang, Hendon Dio Lon from 75. *Vicarage, Vicarage Road, NW4 3PX.* (01-202 8606)

WARNER, Canon John Raymond. Univ of Adel BA (2nd cl Hist) 58. St Jo Coll Morpeth ACT ThL 60. **d** 61 **p** 62 Adel. C of Mt Gambier 61-63; P-in-c of Woodville Gdns Miss Distr 63-64; Whylla W 64-68; R of Port Linc 68-74; Warrnambool Dio Bal from 74; Hon Can of Bal 75-76; Can from 76. *Rectory, Warrnambool, Vic., Australia 3280.* (055-62 2175)

✠ **WARNER, Right Rev Kenneth Charles Harman.** b 1891. DSO 19. Trin Coll Ox BA (2nd cl Jurispr) 12, MA 21. Univ of Edin DD (*hon causa*) 50. Cudd Coll 23. **d** 23 **p** 24 Cant. C of St Geo Ramsgate 23-27; Chap RAF Manston 27-28; Egypt 28-31; Palestine 31-32; Cranwell 33; Provost, Can and R of St Mary's Cathl Glas 33-38; Select Pr Univ of Cam 39; Univ of Ox 51-52; Archd of Linc and Can Linc Cathl 38-46; Cons Ld Bp of Edin in St Mary's Cathl Edin 22 Jan 47 by Bp of Glas (Primus); Bps of St Andr; Arg Is; Moray; Aber; and Brech; Bp Suffr of Grimsby; and Bp Van der Oord (Old Catholic Bp of Haarlem); res 61; Commiss St John's 56-67; Asst Bp in Dio of Cant from 62. *Perry Wood House, Sheldwich, Faversham, Kent.* (Selling 263)

WARNER, Michael John William. b 41. Sarum Th Coll 68. **d** 71 **p** 72 Ex. C of Plympton 71-75; V of St Goran w Caerhays 75-78; Newport 78-79; Bp's Tawton 78-79. *40 Godolphin Road, Longrock, Penzance, Cornw, TR20 8JP.*

WARNER, Nigel Bruce. b 51. St Jo Coll Cam BA 72, MA 76. Wycl Hall Ox 75. **d** 77 **p** 78 St Alb. C of St Mary Luton 77-80; Prec of Dur Cathl from 80. *8 The College, Durham, DH1 3EQ.* (Durham 64733)

WARNER, Robert William. b 32. TCD Wall Bibl Scho BA (1st cl Or Lang Mod) 54, Div Test (1st cl) 56, MA and BD 65. **d** 56 **p** 57 Man. C of St Martin's Conv Distr Royal Oak Wythenshawe 56-60; R of St Steph w St Mark Hulme Man 60-66; Droylsden 66-76; Stand Dio Man from 76. *Stand Rectory, Whitefield, Manchester, M25 7NE.* (061-766 2619)

WARNER, Samuel John. b 10. TCD BA 34, MA 50. **d** 34 **p** 36 Arm. C of St Mark Portadown 34-39; I of St Edm Dunmanway 39-43; R of Heynestown 43-47; Ballymore 47-64; Hon V Cho of Arm Cathl 57-64; I of Laghey 64-79; RD of Tirhugh 68-79; Boylath 70-79; Can of Raph 72-79. *Coolkelure, Laghey, Co Donegal, Irish Republic.*

WARNER, Thomas Edward. b 06. TCD 1st cl Ment and Mor Phil 26 and 27, Weir and Ryan Pris 27, BA and 1st cl Div Test 28, BD 32, MA and BLitt 39, MLitt 60. Univ of Lon BD (2nd cl) 49, PhD 54. **d** and **p** 30 Lim. C of Rathkeale w Nantenan 30-33; Asst Master St Paul's Sch Darjeeling 33-34; R of Corbally 34-36; Chap Pannal Ash Coll 36-37; C of Gt w L Driffield 37-40; Chap RAF 41-61; Men in Disp 42 and 45; Chap Wycl Coll Stonehouse 61-75. *West End, Pearcroft Road, Stonehouse, Glos, GL10 2JZ.* (Stonehouse 2065)

WARNER, Canon William James Munro. Univ of Queensld MA 61. Cudd Coll 61. **d** 63 **p** 64 Lon. C of Poplar 63-67; St Matt Sherwood Brisb 67-68; Chap St Jo Coll St Lucia Brisb 68-70; R of Surfers Paradise 71-74; St Thos Toowong City and Dio Brisb from 75; Exam Chap to Abp of Brisb from 78; Can of Brisb from 81. *67 High Street, Toowong, Queensland, Australia 4066.* (370 1655)

WARNES, Brian Leslie. Kelham Th Coll. **d** 67 **p** 68 Man. C of Tonge Moor 67-71; Asst Chap Univ of Natal 71-81; C of St Paul's Durban Dio Natal from 81. *54 John Geekie Road, Glenmore 4001, Durban, S Africa.*

WARNES, Frank William. b 18. Bps' Coll Cheshunt 61. **d** 62 **p** 63 Guildf. C of Godalming 62-65; St Mary Is of Scilly 65-68; V of Roxton w Gt Barford 68-74; St Gulval Dio Truro from 74. *Gulval Vicarage, Penzance, Cornw.* (Penzance 2699)

WARNES, Warren Hugh. b 23. St Barn Coll Adel ACT ThL 49. **d** and **p** 50 Adel. C of Ch Ch N Adel 50-51; Miss Chap at Pinnaroo 51-55; C of Narracoorte 55-57; P-in-c of Tailem Bend Miss 57-58; C of Northolt 58-60 and (in c of St Hugh) 62-64; R of Tatiara 60-62; V of King's Heath 64-71; R of Rockingham w Caldecott 71-73; V of Gretton w Rockingham and Caldecott Dio Pet from 73. *Vicarage, Gretton, Corby, Northants, NN17 3BU.* (Rockingham 770237)

WARNICA, William Howard. Univ of Tor BA 59. Wycl Coll Tor LTh 62, BTh 63. **d** 62 **p** 63 Tor. C of Medonte 62-64; St Geo-on-the-Hill Tor 64-66; I of Bradf 66-73; St Columba City and Dio Tor from 73. *2723 St Clair Avenue East, Toronto, Ont., Canada.* (416-755 0301)

WARNOCK, Ralph Ernest. b 46. Univ of Sask BEducn 73. Em & Chad's Coll Sktn MDiv 80. **d** and **p** 80 Qu'App. C of Big Country Dio Qu'App from 80. *Box 164, Kerrobert, Sask, Canada, S0L 1R0.*

WARR, Ven Arthur Edward. St Jo Coll Morpeth ACT ThL 27. **d** 27 **p** 28 Graft. C of Casino 27-30; R of Bowraville 30-34; U Hastings 34-38; S Graft 38-42; Kempsey 42-49; Archd of Kempsey 46-47; Clarence 47-49; South 65-69; Archd (Emer) from 69; Sub-Dean of Ch Ch Cathl Graft 46-49; Dean and R 49-65; R of Port MacQuarie 65-69. *9 Owen Street, Port Macquarie, NSW, Australia.*

WARREN, Very Rev Alan Christopher. b 32. Late Chor Exhib of CCC Cam 2nd cl Th Trip pt i 54, BA 56, MA 60. Ridley Hall Cam 56. **d** 57 Dover for Cant **p** 58 Cant. C of St Paul Cliftonville 57-59; St Andr Plymouth 59-62; Chap Kelly Coll Tavistock 62-64; V of H Ap Leic 64-72; Dioc Missr Cov 72-78; Hon Can of Cov from 72; M Gen Syn Cov 77-78; Provost and V of St Martin's Cathl City and Dio Leic from 78; M Gen Syn from 80. *Provost's House, St Martins East, Leicester, LE1 5FX.* (Leic 25294)

✠ **WARREN, Right Rev Alwyn Keith.** MC 45. CMG 67. Magd Coll Ox BA (Nat Sc Chem) 22, MA 26. Cudd Coll 24. **d** 25 **p** 26 Cant. C of Ashford Kent 25-29; V of Ross and S Westland 29-31; Waimate 31-34; Merivale 34-40; Archd of Ch Ch 37-44; Dean 40-51; VG 40-44 and 46-51; Chap NZEF 44-45; Commiss Centr Tang from 52; Cons Ld Bp of Ch Ch in Ch Ch Cathl 1 Nov 51 by Bp of Dun; Bps of Auckld; Nel; Wel; Wai; Waik; and Aotearoa; res 66; Sub-Prelate O of St John of Jer from 61. *193 Memorial Avenue, Christchurch 5, NZ.* (585-636)

✠ **WARREN, Right Rev Cecil Allan.** Univ of Syd BA 51. Late Lucas-Tooth Scho of Qu Coll Ox BA (2nd cl Th) 56, MA 59. ACT ThL 52. **d** 50 **p** 51 C and Goulb. C-in-c of Adaminaby 50-51; P-in-c 51-53; Perm to Offic Dio Ox 53-55; C of St Mary Virg Ox 55-57; St Jo Bapt Canberra 57-60; R of St Phil Canberra 60-63; Org Sec Ch S and Dir of Forward in Faith Movement Dio C & Goulb 63-65; Can of C & Goulb 63-65; Dioc Comm Dio C & Goulb from 63; Exam Chap to Bp of C & Goulb 64-71; Cons Asst Bp of C & Goulb in St Andr Cathl Syd 21 Sept 65 by Abp of Syd; Bps of C & Goulb; Bath; Graft; and Newc; Apptd Bp of C & Goulb 72. *Jamieson House, Constitution Avenue, Reid, Canberra, ACT, Australia 2601.* (062-48 0811)

WARREN, Christopher Bruce. TCD BA 58, MA 61. **d** 62 **p** 63 Cash. C of Waterford 62-64; R of Askeaton w Shanagolden and Loughil 64-66; Kilcolman 66-73; R of St Werburgh Dub 73-74; Kilrossanty Dio Lism from 74. *Rectory, Stradbally, Co Waterford, Irish Republic.*

WARREN, Clifford Frederick. b 32. St D Coll Lamp BA 53, St Mich Coll Llan 54. **d** 56 Llan **p** 57 Mon for Wales. C of Whitchurch 56-68; Perm to Offic Dio Llan 68-70; C of Llanedeyrn 70-76; R of Machen Dio Mon from 76. *Rectory, Machen, Newport, Gwent, NP1 8SA.* (Machen 440321)

WARREN, David Clinton. b 53. Univ of Waterloo Ont BRE 76, BA 78. Wycl Coll Tor MDiv 80. **d** 80 **p** 81 Bp Read for Tor. C of Ch Ch Scarborough Dio Tor from 80. *155 Markham Road, Scarborough, Ont, Canada, M1J 2H8.*

WARREN, Desmond Benjamin Moore. b 22. TCD BA 44, MA 49. Bps' Coll Cheshunt 46. **d** 48 **p** 49 Chelmsf. C of Moulsham 48-52; St Mary Virg at Walls Colchester 52-55; V of Elmstead 55-63; R of Sandy 63-78; P-in-c of Westmill 78-79; Gt Munden 78-79; R of Westmill w Gt Munden Dio St Alb from 79. *Westmill Rectory, Buntingford, Herts, SG9 9LL.* (Royston 71389)

WARREN, Ernest Bruce. b 24. Univ of Lon BD 54. K Coll Lon and Warm AKC 54. **d** 54 Bp Wellington for Truro **p** 55 Truro. C of St Austell 54-58; Hitchin 58-62; PC of Talland w Polperro 62-67; C-in-c of Lansallos 62-64; R 64-67; V of Lostwithiel 67-77; Perranzabuloe w Perranporth Dio Truro from 77. *Perranzabuloe Vicarage, Penhallow, Truro, TR4 9LR.* (Perranporth 3245)

WARREN, Canon Frederick Noel. b 30. TCD BA 52, MA 58, BD 66. QUB PhD 72. **d** 53 **p** 54 Connor. C of St Matt Belf 53-56; St Geo Belf 56-59; I of St Paul Castlewellan 59-65; Clonallon w Warrenpoint 65-69; Newcastle Dio Drom from 69; Dom Chap to Bp of Down 70-73; Exam Chap to Bp of Down from 73; Can of St Anne's Cathl Belf 73-76; Can and Preb of St Patr Cathl Dub from 76. *Rectory, Newcastle, Co Down, BT33 0HD, N Ireland.* (Newcastle 2439)

WARREN, Geoffrey Richard. b 44. Qu Coll Birm 68. **d** 69 **p** 70 St Alb. C of Waltham Cross 69-73; Radlett 73-78; Tring Dio St Alb 78-80; Team V from 80. *Rectory, Aldbury, Tring, Herts, HP23 5RS.* (Aldbury Common 244)

WARREN, Preb Henry Fiennes. b 21. Keble Coll Ox BA 42, MA 47. Cudd Coll 42. **d** 48 **p** 49 B & W. C of Weston-super-Mare 48-53; R of Exford 53-75; RD of Wiveliscombe 65-73; Proc Conv B & W from 69; Preb of Wells Cathl from 73; R of W Monkton Dio B & W from 75. *West Monkton Rectory, Taunton, Somt.* (W Monkton 412226)

WARREN, John Edwin. St Barn Th Coll Adel 66. **d** 69 **p** 70 Adel. C of St Cuthb Prospect 69-71; P-in-c of Warradale w Darlington 71-77; R of Glenuga Dio Adel from 77. *76 Sydney Street, Glenuga, S Australia 5064.* (79-6201)

WARREN, John Herbert Edwin. b 02. St Steph Ho Ox 27. **d** 30 **p** 31 Lon. C of St Mary Magd Paddington 30-34; Perm to Offic at St Matt Westmr 34-37; C of St Aug S Kens 37-42; V of St Pet and St Paul Teddington 42-47; St Paul Grove Pk Chiswick 47-66; Perm to Offic Dio Ex from 66. *18 Laura Grove, Paignton, Devon.* (Paignton 50675)

WARREN, Kenneth John. b 20. Univ of Leeds BA 49. Roch Th Coll 59. **d** 61 **p** 62 Ex. C of St D w St Mich AA Ex 61-63; Paignton 63-68; Wavertree 68-73; Brixham 73-76; P-in-c of Whitestone w Oldridge 76-81; R of Lapford Dio Ex from 81; Nymet Rowland w Coldridge Dio Ex from 81. *49 Highfield, Lapford, Crediton, Devon.* (Lapford 321)

WARREN, Malcolm Clive. b 46. St D Univ Coll Lamp Dipl Th 74. Bp Burgess Th Hall Lamp 71. **d** 74 **p** 75 Mon. C of St Andr Lliswerry Newport 74-78; Risca 78-79; V of St Hilary Greenway Dio Mon from 79. *Vicarage, Menai Way, Trowbridge, Cardiff.* (Cardiff 793460)

WARREN, Martin Moutray. Magd Coll Ox BA 55, Dipl Th 56, MA 59. Westcott Ho Cam 57. **d** 58 **p** 59 Ch Ch. C of Timaru 58-60; St Pet Riccarton 60-63; V of Geraldine 63-68; Hornby Dio Ch Ch from 68. *452 Main South Road, Christchurch 4, NZ.* (497-311)

WARREN, Michael John. Kelham Th Coll 59. **d** 64 Hulme for Man **p** 65 Man. C of St Chris Withington 64-67; Worsley w Ellenbrook 67-69; Witney 69-72; V of S w New Hinksey 72-80. *c/o New Hinksey Vicarage, Oxford, OX1 4RD.* (Ox 44254)

WARREN, Michael Meade King. b 18. Lich Th Coll 38. **d** 42 **p** 43 Taunton for B & W. C of Wellington w W Buckland 42-46; M of Bush Bro of St Barn Dio N Queensld 46-51 and 55-58; V of Sampford Arundel Somt 51-55; Chap St Barn Sch Ravenshoe Queensld 56-58; R of Huish Champflower w Clatworthy 59-61; Alyth w Meigle 61-69; R of Blairgrowrie 68-69; Mooi River 69-72; Witham Friary w Marston Bigot Dio B & W from 72. *Witham Friary Rectory, Frome, Somt.* (Upton Noble 340)

WARREN, Norman Leonard. b 34. CCC Cam BA (2nd cl Mus Trip pt i) 58, MA 62. Ridley Hall Cam 58. **d** 60 **p** 61 Cov. C of Bedworth 60-63; V of St Paul Leamington 63-77; M Gen Syn Dio Cov 75-77; R of Morden Dio S'wark from 77. *Rectory, London Road, Morden, Surrey.* (01-648 3920)

WARREN, Paul Kenneth. b 41. Selw Coll Cam BA (2nd cl Th) 63, MA 67. Cudd Coll 64. **d** 67 Carl for Blackb **p** 68 Blackb. C of Lanc 67-70; Chap Univ of Lanc 70-78; Prin Grizedale Coll Univ of Lanc 75-78; V of Langho Dio Blackb from 78; M Gen Syn from 80. *St Leonard's Vicarage, Billington, Blackburn, Lancs, BB6 9NA* (Whalley 2246)

WARREN, Peter. b 40. FCA 64. Oak Hill Coll 77. **d** 79 **p** 80 Lich. C of St Giles Newc L Dio Lich from 79. *3 Westlands Avenue, Newcastle-under-Lyme, Staffs, ST5 2PU.* (0782 623677)

WARREN, Robert. b 54, TCD Div Test 76, BA 78, MA 81. Div Hostel Dub 73. **d** 78 **p** 79 Lim. C of St Mich Lim 78-81; R of Adare Dio Lim from 81; Youth Adv Dio Lim from 79. *Rectory, Adare, Co Limerick, Irish Republic.* (061 94227)

WARREN, Robert Irving. Univ of BC BA 58. Angl Th Coll BC LTh 61. **d** 61 **p** 63 Caled. C of Burns Lake Miss 61-66; on leave 66-69; V of Hazelton 69-75; I of St Barn City and Dio New Westmr from 75. *1002 Fifth Avenue, New Westminster, BC, V3M 1Y5, Canada.*

WARREN, Canon Robert Peter Resker. b 39. Jes Coll Cam BA 63. ALCD 65. **d** 65 **p** 66 Man. C of Rusholme 65-68; Bushbury (in c of St Jas Fordhouses) 68-71; V of St Thos Crookes City and Dio Sheff from 71; M Gen Syn Dio Sheff from 75; RD of Hallam from 78; Hon Can of Sheff from 82.

18 Hallam Gate Road, Sheffield S10 5BT. (Sheffield 660743)

WARREN, Samuel Richard Alan. Moore Th Coll Syd ACT ThL 52. **d** 52 **p** 53 Syd. C of Marrickville 52-54; CMS Miss at Groote Eylandt 54-59; C-in-c of St Paul Oatley 59-64; Miss at Asuncion Paraguay 64-68; R of St Pet Flores Buenos Aires 69-76; Perm to Offic Dio Syd 76-77. *Address temp unknown.*

WARREN, Thomas. d 65 Bp Coadj for Newfld **p** 66 Newfld. C of Flower's Cove 65-67; Corner Brook 67-69; R of Belleoram 69-72; C of Channel 72-76; I of Brooklyn Dio Centr Newfld from 76. *Box 71, Lethbridge, Bonavista Bay, Newfoundland, Canada.*

WARRI, Bishop of. *See* Dafiewhare, Right Rev John Onyaene.

WARRI, Dean of. *See* Bovi, Very Rev Alfred Wodeha.

WARRIA, Langley. b 06. **d** 70 **p** 73 Carp. C of Yorke Island 70-72; P-in-c of Coconut Island 73-74; Hon C Yorke Island Dio Carp from 74. *Box 79, Thursday Island 4875, Queensland, Australia.*

WARRIA, Napoleon. d 73 **p** 75 Carp. C of Yorke Island 73-78; P-in-c of Warraber I Dio Carp from 78. *c/o PO Box 79, Thursday Island, Qld, Australia 4875.*

WARRINER, Leonard. b 15. **d** 79 Ox **p** 80 Buckingham for Ox (APM). C of Chalfont St Pet Dio Ox from 79. *Briar Rose, Winkers Lane, Chalfont St Peter, Bucks, SL9 0AJ.*

WARRINGTON, Lord Bishop Suffragan of. *See* Henshall, Right Rev Michael.

WARRINGTON, Archdeacon of. *See* Woodhouse, Ven Charles David Stewart.

WARRINGTON, Clement Egbert. b 10. Univ of Dur LTh 35. Lon Coll of Div 31. **d** 34 **p** 35 Portsm. C of St John Portsea 34-37; Chap RAF Halton 38; Iraq 38-39; P-in-c of Ascen Mosspark Glas 39-44; R of Ashwicken w Leziate 44-47; V of St Clem Spotland Dio Man from 47; Surr from 48. *Spotland Vicarage, Rochdale, Lancs.* (Rochdale 48972)

WARRINGTON, Canon George Garnett. b 10. TCD BA 37, MA 47. **d** 37 **p** 38 Kilm. C of Kinawley and H Trin 37-42; Chap RAFVR 42-46; I of Rossinver (w Finner from 75) Dio Kilm from 46; Bp's C of Finner 51-75; Can of Kilm 71-80; Can and Preb of St Patr Cathl Dub from 80. *Rectory, Bundoran, Co Donegal, Irish Republic.* (Bundoran 07241294)

WARRINGTON, Gwynfa Lewis Jones. b 44. St D Coll Lamp 64. **d** 67 **p** 68 Swan B. C of Gorseinon 67-70; Pemb Dk 70-74; V of Rhosmarket (or Rosemarket) w Freystrop 74-78; R of Llangwm 78-80; V of Ystradfellte w Pontneathvaughan Dio Swan B from 80. *Ystradfellte Vicarage, Aberdare, Mid Glam.* (Glynneath 720405)

WARRINGTON, William Leslie. b 03. Chich Th Coll 26. **d** 28 **p** 29 Sheff. C of St Mich AA Northfield Rotherham 28-31; Balby 31-34; All SS Leamington 34-35; P-in-c of Luderitz and Keetmanshoop SW Afr 35-38; C of St Pet Rushden 39-41; R of St John Wednesbury 41-52; V of Salt 52-68. *223 Weston Road, Stafford.* (Stafford 42184)

WARUI, Rowland. St Paul's Th Coll Limuru 64. **d** 67 **p** 68 Mt Kenya. P Dio Mt Kenya 67-74; Dio Mt Kenya E from 75. *Box 189 Embu, Kenya.*

WARWICK, Lord Bishop Suffragan of. *See* Arnold, Right Rev Keith Appleby.

WARWICK, Archdeacon of. *See* Taylor, Ven Edward.

WARWICK, Gordon Melvin. b 31. N Ordin Course 79. **d** 80 **p** 81 Wakef (APM). C of Darrington w Wentbridge Dio Wakef from 80. *14 Hillcroft Close, Darrington, Nr Pontefract, W Yorks, WS8 3BD.*

WARWICK, John Michael. Fitzw Ho Cam BA 58, MA 62. Ely Th Coll 58. **d** 60 **p** 61 Pet. C of Towcester w Easton Neston 60-63; Leighton Buzzard 63-64; Boston 64-66; C-in-c of Sutterton 66-72; V 72-74; Long Sutton Dio Linc from 74. *Vicarage, Long Sutton, Spalding, Lincs.* (Holbeach 362033)

WASDELL, David. b 42. Univ of Dur BSc 64. BD (Lon) 68. Clifton Th Coll 65. **d** 69 **p** 70 Chich. C of H Trin Eastbourne 69-71; St Mary Becontree 72-77; Dir Urban Ch Project and Publ Pr Dios Chelmsf and Lon 77-81. *115 Poplar High Street, E14 0AE.*

WASEY, Alfred. b 1892. St Cath Coll Cam BA 17. **d** 19 **p** 20 Man. C of St Aug Pendlebury 19-21; Bothal (in c of Hebburn) 21-29; Stockton Heath 29-32; R of Stowell Mem Ch Salford 32-44; V of All SS Elton Bury 44-53; Calderbrook 53-60; Marston Chesh 60-64. *59 Statham Avenue, Lymm, Chesh.* (Lymm 4265)

WASHINGTON, Patrick Leonard. b 44. Univ of Nottm BSc 66. St Steph Ho Ox 65. **d** 68 and **p** 69 Guildf. C of Fleet 68-71; Farnham 71-74; Team V of Staveley and Barrow Hill Dio Derby from 74. *191 Middlecroft Road, Staveley, Chesterfield, S43 3NQ.* (Chesterfield 72724)

WASHINGTON, Simon. H Cross Coll Rang. **d** 59 **p** 60 Rang. P Dio Rang 59-70; Dio Mand from 70. *St Luke's Church, Indaw, Burma.*

WASIF, Aziz. St Geo Th Coll Jer 61. **d** 62 Jer for Egypt. d Dio Egypt. *All Saints' Cathedral, Cairo, Egypt.* (71702)

WASIU, Jerry. d 73 Carp. C of Bamaga Dio Carp from 73. *c/o PO Box 79, Thursday Island, Qld, Australia 4875.*

WASONGO, Paul. b 39. **d** 71 **p** 73 Maseno S. P Dio Maseno S. *Box 380, Kisumu, Kenya.*

WASSALL, Keith Leonard. b 45. Chich Th Coll 68. **d** 71 **p** 72 Lich. C of Upper Gornal 71-74; Codsall 74-75; St Mark Shelton 75-76; P-in-c 76-77; Team V of H Evang Hanley 77-79; C of Pembroke Berm 79-81; V of St Pet Rickerscote Dio Lich from 81. *106 Rickerscote Road, Rickerscote, Stafford, ST17 4HB.* (Stafford 52878)

WASSON, Canon Everett Lawrence. Univ of Tor BA 22. Wycl Coll Tor BD 28. Columb Univ MA 32. **d** 23 **p** 24 Tor. C of Ch of Messiah Tor 23-31; C of Transfig Tor 33-36; R 36-56; Can of Tor from 56; Hon C of Ch of Ascen Tor 61-63. *16 Crescent Drive, Palo Alto, California, USA.*

WASTELL, Eric Morse. b 33. Univ of Wales Dipl Th 62. St Mich Coll Llan 59. **d** 62 **p** 63 Swan B. C of Oystermouth 62-65; St John's Cathl Antig 65-66; R of St Mary Antig 66-73; Dioc Regr Antig 69-74; Hon Can of Antig 71-74; Exam Chap to Bp of Antig 71-74; R of St Paul Antig 73-74; V of St Gabr Swansea Dio Swan B from 74. *St Gabriel's Vicarage, Swansea, W Glam.* (Swansea 464011)

WASTIE, David Vernon. b 37. Chich Th Coll 80. **d** 81 Win. C of Bitterne Park Dio Win from 81. *24 Lacon House, Bitterne Park, Southampton, SO4 4JA.*

WASWA, Canon Kezekiya. CMS Tr Coll Buwalasi 38. **d** 39 **p** 41 U Nile. P Dio U Nile 39-61; Dio Mbale 61-69; Hon Can of U Nile 58-61; Mbale from 61. *PO Box 984, Mbale, Uganda.*

WATAWA, Alusutaluko. b 27. **d** and **p** 74 Mbale. P Dio Mbale. *Buginyanya, Box 512, Mbale, Uganda.*

WATCHORN, Brian. b 39. Em Coll Cam 1st cl Th Trip pt i 59, BA (2nd cl Th Trip pt ii) 61, MA 65. Ex Coll Ox BA (by incorp) 62. Ripon Hall Ox 61. **d** 63 Hulme for Man **p** 64 Man. C of Bolton-le-Moors 63-65; Lect 65-66; Chap G and C Coll Cam 66-74; V of St Geo Chesterton Dio Ely from 75. *St George's Vicarage, Chesterfield Road, Cambridge, CB4 1LN.* (Cam 67374)

WATERER, Anthony Tatham. b 14. ARCA Royal Exhib 38. Cudd Coll 45. **d** 47 **p** 48 Chich. C of Arundel w Stoke and Tortington 47-48; Henfield 48-50; V of Farnham w Scotton 50-73; Asst Chap to Scotton Banks Sanat 50-51; R of Staveley w Copgrove 53-72; Rawreth w Rettendon Dio Chelmsf from 73; Perm to Offic Dio Win 72. *Rawreth Rectory, Wickford, Essex, SS11 8SH.* (Wickford 66766)

WATERFORD, Archdeacon of. *See* Armstrong, Ven Arthur Patrick.

WATERFORD, Bishop of. *See* Cashel.

WATERFORD, Dean of. *See* Mayne, Very Rev John Andrew Brian.

WATERHOUSE, Albert Edward. b 01. K Coll Lon and Warm. **d** and **p** 56 Roch. C of Frindsbury 56-60; V of Birling 60-71; C-in-c of Ryarsh 69-71; Perm to Offic Dio Chich from 72. *Half Acre, Northiam, Rye, E Sussex, TN31 6QL.* (Rye 3216)

WATERHOUSE, Eric Thomas Benjamin. b 24. Dipl Th (Lon) 60. Qu Coll Birm 50. **d** 51 **p** 52 Lich. C of St Pet Wolverhampton 51-56; Lower Gornal 56-57; V of St Mark Walsall 57-60; R of Kington w Dormston 60-64; St Clem Worc 64-77; P-in-c of Abberton and Bishampton w Throckmorton (and Naunton Beauchamp from 79) Dio Worc 77-80; R from 80. *Bishampton Rectory, Pershore, WR10 2LT.* (Bishampton 648)

WATERHOUSE, Peter. b 46. Univ of Leeds Dipl Th 68. Linc Th Coll 68. **d** 70 Jarrow for Dur **p** 71 Dur. C of Consett 70-73; Heworth 73-76; V of St Chad Stockton-on-Tees Dio Dur from 76. *St Chad's Vicarage, Ragpath Lane, Stockton-on-Tees, Cleve.* (Stockton 64737)

WATERHOUSE, Robert George. d 80 **p** 81 N Queensld. C of H Trin Mackay Dio N Queensld from 80. *c/o PO Box 234, Mackay, Qld, Australia 4740.*

WATERMAN, Albert Thomas. b 33. Roch Th Coll 61. **d** 64 **p** 65 Roch. C of St Alb Dartford 64-67; V of St Jo Evang Ilkeston 67-75; St Francis Mackworth 75-79; St Alb Dartford Dio Roch from 79. *51 Watling Street, Dartford, Kent, DA1 1RW.* (Dartford 24052)

WATERMAN, Anthony Michael Charles. Selw Coll Cam BA 54, MA 58. Austr Nat Univ PhD 68. St Jo Coll Winnipeg BTh 62. **d** 62 **p** 63 Rupld. Prof of Econ St Jo Coll Winnipeg 62-64 and from 67; Research Scho Austr Nat Univ 64-67; Hon C of St Aid Winnipeg 68-71; on leave 71-72; Hon C of St Thos Winnipeg 72-74. *171 Brock Street, Winnipeg, Manit, Canada.*

WATERMAN, James Robert. ACT ThL 32. **d** 33 **p** 34 Melb. C of St Paul Geelong 33-34; St John Toorak 35-36; C of St John Heidelberg and Asst Chap Austin Hosp 36-38; Chap RAF (Austr) 36-38; V of Manangatong 38-39; C of St Mary Caulfield 39-40; Min of Belmont 40-41; Chap AIF 41-50; Min of Mount Duneed w Torquay 50-54; V of Sandringham 54-61; Ocean Grove 61-68; All SS Malvern 68-72; Perm to Offic Dio Melb from 73. *3 Humble Street, Barwon Heads, Vic, Australia 3227.* (54-2693)

✠ **WATERMAN, Right Rev Robert Harold.** Bp's Univ Lennox BA 14, BD 33, DD 40. **d** 20 **p** 21 Ott. C of Bearbrook 20-21; R 21-27; R of Pembroke 27-33; Smith's Falls 33-37; Ch Ch Cathl Hamilton 37-48; Dean of Niag 38-48; Cons Bp Coadj of NS in All SS Cathl Halifax NS 27 Jan 48 by Abps of Queb and NS; Bps of Montr; Fred; Newfld; Ott; Alg; and Maine; Apptd Ld Bp of NS 51; res 63. *40 Vaudry Street, Apt 6, Lennoxville, PQ, Canada.*

WATERS, Arthur Brian. b 34. St Deiniol's Libr Hawarden 71. **d** 73 **p** 74 Mon. C of Bedwellty 73-76; P-in-c of All SS Newport Mon 76-80; V 80-81; V of Mynyddislwyn Dio Mon from 81. *Vicarage, Pontllanfraith, Blackwood, Gwent.* (Blackwood 224240)

WATERS, Charles Eric. b 14. Late Exhib of Hatf Coll Dur LTh 37, BA 38. St Aug Coll Cant 34. **d** 38 **p** 39 Dur. C of St Cuthb Bensham 38-41; Whitburn 41-46; V of Witton-le-Wear 46-55; PC of E Grafton 55-62; V of Tidcombe w Fosbury 55-62; R of Bromham 62-79; C-in-c of Chittoe 72-73; V 73-79. *Flat B, 4 Queens Road, Tunbridge Wells, Kent.*

WATERS, Charles Theodore Newton. b 27. K Coll Cam BA 48, MA 51. Ridley Hall Cam 49. **d** 51 **p** 52 Chelmsf. C of St Mary Becontree 51-53; L to Offic St Andr Catford 61-62; C of St Jo Bapt Southend Lewisham 62-63; Clapham 63-66; Morden 66-68. *26 Chichester Road, Park Hill, Croydon, CR0 5NP.*

WATERS, Gordon Keith. b 31. Linc Th Coll 69. **d** 71 Repton for Derby **p** 72 Derby. C of Ripley Dio Derby 71-74; C-in-c of Marlpool 74-80; Team V of Whorlton Dio Newc T 80-81; Team R from 81. *Whorlton Rectory, Westerhope, Newcastle-on-Tyne, NE5 1NN.* (Newc T 869648)

WATERS, John Michael. b 30. Qu Coll Cam 3rd cl Math Trip pt i 51, BA (2nd cl Th Trip pt ii) 53. Ridley Hall Cam 53. **d** 55 **p** 56 Liv. C of Ch Ch Southport 55-57; Farnworth 57-62; V of H Trin Blackb 63-70; Chap to Birm Cathl 70-74; Sec Birm Coun of Chr Chs 70-77; Bp's Chap for Ecumen Action 74-77; V of Hednesford Dio Lich from 77; RD of Rugeley from 78. *Vicarage, Hednesford, Staffs.* (Hednesford 2635)

WATERS, Nicholas Marshall Stephenson. b 35. Selw Coll Cam BA 59, MA 63. Wells Th Coll 59. **d** 61 **p** 62 Chich. C of Eastbourne 61-64; Asst Chap Ardingly Coll Dio Chich from 64. *6 Standgrove, Ardingly, Haywards Heath, Sussex, RH17 6SF.* (Ardingly 892256)

WATERS, Ross Desmond. Univ of Qld BD 74. St Francis Coll Brisb. **d** 75 **p** 76 Brisb. C of St Luke Toowoomba 75-78; Chap St Jo Coll Brisb from 79. *St John's College, St Lucia, Brisbane, Australia 4067.* (371 1798)

WATERS, Stephen Percy. **d** 55 **p** 56 C & Goulb. C of Young 55-57; P-in-c of Barmedman 57-62; R of Cobargo 62-64; Murrumburrah 65-73; Perm to Offic Dio C & Goulb from 73. *159 Neill Street, Murrumburrah, NSW, Australia.*

WATERSON, Harold. b 03. Tyndale Hall Bris 42. **d** 42 **p** 44 Blackb. C of The Sav Blackb 42-46; V of St Andr Bradf 46-51; Withnell 51-58; St Pet U Holloway 58-72; L to Offic Dio Cant from 72. *9 Ashurst Road, Maidstone, Kent, ME14 5PZ.*

WATERSON, John Hayden Lionel. King's Coll Cam 3rd cl Nat Sc Trip pt i 34, BA (2nd cl Mor Sc Trip pt ii) 35, MA 39. Cudd Coll 35. **d** 36 **p** 37 Derby. C of Staveley 36-39; All SS Cathl Wakef 39-43; Min Can and C of Ripon Cathl and Chap of St Mary Magd Hosp Ripon 43-49; R of Stoke D'Abernon Dio Guildf from 49; St Antholin Lect at St Bart Gt Smithfield Lon 57-62. *Rectory, Stoke D'Abernon, Cobham, Surrey, KT11 3PU.* (Cobham 2502)

WATERSON, Raymond Arthur. b 25. Wells Th Coll 69. **d** 70 **p** 71 Glouc. C of Wotton St Mary Without 70-74; Cirencester 74-79; P-in-c of Falfield w Rockptn Dio Glouc from 79. *Falfield Vicarage, Wotton-under-Edge, Glos.* (Falfield 236)

WATERSTONE, Canon Albert Thomas. b 23. TCD BA (1st cl Mod) 45, Div Test (1st cl) 46. BD 67. **d** 46 **p** 47 Oss. C and Dean's V of Kilkenny Cathl 46-50; C-in-c of Borris-in-Ossory w Aghaboe 50-51; I 52-54; Fiddown w Kilmacow 54-64; RD of Durrow 56-64; R of Tullamore (w Tyrellspass from 73) w Lynally and Rahan Dio Meath from 64; Dir of Ordinands Meath and Kildare from 78; Can of Meath from 81. *St Catherine's Rectory, Tullamore, Co Offaly, Irish Republic.* (Tullamore 21367)

WATERSTREET, John Donald. b 34. Trin Hall Cam BA 58, MA 62. Lich Th Coll 58. **d** 60 Birm **p** 61 Aston for Birm. C of Blackheath 60-64; Aston-juxta-Birm 64-67; R of Sheldon 67-77; RD of Coleshill 75-77; V of Selly Oak Dio Birm from 77. *Selly Oak Vicarage, Bristol Road, Birmingham, B29 6ND.* (021-472 0250)

WATHERSTON, Peter David. b 42. Univ of Lon BSc 69. FCA 76. Ridley Hall Cam 75. **d** 77 Stepney for Lon **p** 78 Lon. C of St Andr Isl Dio Lon from 77-82; Chap Mayflower Family Centre Canning Town from 82. *3 Cooper Street, E16 1QU.* (01-476 9895)

WATKEYS, Glyn Goring. b 11. St D Coll Lamp BA 35. **d** 35 **p** 36 Llan. C of Gellygaer 35-39; Llanblethian w Cowbridge 39-48; V of Trealaw 48-58; Gabalfa 58-73. *61 Rhydelig Avenue, Heath, Cardiff, S Glam.* (Cardiff 63193)

WATKIN, Stephen Roy. b 23. Worc Ordin Coll 66. **d** 68 **p** 69 Ches. C of Sutton 68-72; V of Aston-by-Sutton 73-76; P-in-c of Hulme Walfield 76-77; V 77-80; P-in-c of Eaton 76-77; V 77-80; P-in-c of Ipstones Dio Lich from 80; Onecote w Bradnop Dio Lich from 80. *Ipstones Vicarage, Stoke-on-Trent, Staffs, ST10 2LF.* (Ipstones 313)

WATKINS, Alfred Felix Macirone. b 20. Glouc Th Course 70. **d** 72 **p** 73 Glouc. C of Yate 72-75; V of Parkend Dio Glouc from 75. *Parkend Vicarage, Lydney, Glos, GL15 4HL.* (Dean 562284)

WATKINS, Anthony John. b 42. St D Coll Lamp BA (2nd cl Hist) 64. St Steph Ho Ox 64. **d** 66 **p** 67 S'wark. C of St Jo Evang E Dulwich 66-71; Tewkesbury 71-75; Prec and Chap Chor of Ches Cathl 75-81; L to Offic Dio Ches 75-81; V of Brixworth w Holcot Dio Pet from 81. *Brixworth Vicarage, Northampton, NN6 9DF.* (Northn 880286)

WATKINS, David. b 54. Moore Th Coll Syd BTh. **d** 81 Syd. C of St Andr Cronulla Dio Syd from 81. *Souter House, 57 Kingsway, Cronulla, NSW, Australia 2230.*

WATKINS, Edward George. Moore Th Coll Syd ACT ThL 59. **d** 60 **p** 61 Adel. C of Unley 60-62; P-in-c of Franklin Harbour Miss 62-67; R of Wingecarribee w Robertson 67-69; R of Norwood 69-75; Strathgordon 75-76; Lakes Entrance 76-80; Belgrave Dio Melb from 80. *Vicarage, Main Road, Belgrave, Vic, Australia 3160.*

WATKINS, Gordon Derek. b 29. **d** 53 Lon for Col Bp **p** 54 Graft. C of Grafton 53-56; Bundaberg 56-57; St Luke Toowoomba 57-58; V of Texas 58-60; P-in-c of Millmerran 60-61; C of St Wilfrid Harrogate 61-63; V of Upton Pk 63-67; R of Gt & L Bentley 67-73; R of Gt Canfield 73-78; Pastoral Sec Dio Lon from 78. *21 The Drummonds, Hartland Road, Epping, Essex.*

WATKINS, Herbert Ernest. b 22. Clifton Th Coll 39. Oak Hill Th Coll 43. **d** 46 **p** 47 Bradf. C of St Paul Buttershaw 46-48; Rodbourne-Cheney 48-49; Lenton 49-52; V of Ch Ch U Armley 52-58; Rodbourne Cheney 58-73; Tockwith 73-77; Bilton-in-Ainsty 73-77; Hurdsfield Dio Ches from 77. *Hurdsfield Vicarage, Macclesfield, Chesh.* (Macclesfield 24587)

WATKINS, John. Qu Coll Newfld. **d** 30 **p** 31 Newfld. C of Harbour Buffett 30-31; I 31-43; R of Hermitage 43-70; Can of Newfld 63-70. *Milltown, Bay D'Espoire, Milltown, Newfoundland, Canada.*

WATKINS, John Burton. St Jo Coll Auckld LTh 64. **d** 57 **p** 58 Waik. C of New Plymouth 57-59; V of Kawhia 59-60; Mangakino 60-62; Pio Pio 62-64; Te Kuiti 64-67; R of Black River Ja 67-73; Lacovia 67-73; on leave 73-76; Hon C of St Andr Epsom Auckld 76-77; V of Kaitaia 77-80; St Marg Hillsborough Dio Auckld from 80. *102 Hillsborough Road, Mount Roskill, Auckland, NZ.* (659-604)

WATKINS, Laurence Neville. St Jo Coll Auckld LTh 35. **d** 27 Nel **p** 28 Ripon. C of Ch Ch Nel NZ 27; Leeds 27-29; Asst Chap St Jo Cathl Hong Kong 29-32; V of Hororata 32-36; Mangaweka 36-38; Wadestown w Northland 38-48; Hawera 48-52; Asst Miss Wel City Miss 52-54; Hosp Chap Wel 54-64; Chap to Bp of Wel 63-64; C of St Andr w St Luke Grimsby 64-65; C-in-c of St Marg Conv Distr Ilford 65-66; C of Karori 66-67; P-in-c of Clevedon 67-68; C of Takapuna 68-71; Birkenhead 72-73; P-in-c of Karori 73; Perm to Offic Dio Wel from 74. *4 Hinau Street, Eastbourne, NZ.* (Eastbourne 7566)

WATKINS, Michael Morris. b 32. Univ of Leeds MRCS, LRCP, (Lon) 60. St Jo Coll Nottm 77. **d** and **p** 81 Barking for Chelmsf. C of St Andr Hornchurch Dio Chelmsf from 81. *85 Kenilworth Gardens, Hornchurch, Essex, RM12 4SG.*

WATKINS, Paul Llewellyn. Univ of Dur MA 73. Moore Th Coll Syd ACT ThL 64. BD (Lon) 64. **d** 64 **p** 65 Newc. C of Mereweather 64-66; on leave 66-68; C of Hamilton 69-71; R of Cessnock 71-72; Williamtn 72-80; Mayfield Dio Newc from 80. *Rectory, Durham Street, Mayfield, NSW, Australia 2304.* (68 1620)

WATKINS, Peter Gordon. b 34. St Pet Coll Ox BA 57, MA 61. Wycl Hall Ox 58. **d** 59 Stafford for Lich **p** 60 Lich. C of St Geo Wolverhampton 59-60; St Chad Burton-on-Trent 60-61; St Jas Piccadilly 61-63; in Amer Ch 63-65; V of St Matt Ealing Common Dio Lon from 66. *7 North Common Road, W5.* (01-567 3820)

WATKINS, Robert Henry. b 30. New Coll Ox BA 54, MA 60. Westcott Ho Cam 59. **d** 60 **p** 61 Newc T. C of H Cross Fenham Newc T 60-63; Morpeth 63-67; V of Delaval 67-80; Lanercost w Kirkambeck and Walton Dio Carl from 80;

Warden of Readers Dio Newc T 78-80. *Lanercost Priory, Brampton, Cumb.* (Brampton 2478)

WATKINS, Thomas George. b 02. ALCD 32. **d** 32 **p** 33 Blackb. C of Em Preston 32-34; H Trin Burnley 34-37; Penwortham 37-40; R of Hoole 40-68; Surr 62-68. *5 Ashford Crescent, Barton, Preston, Lancs, PR3 5JU.* (Broughton 862850)

WATKINS, Thomas George David. b 03. St Paul's Coll Burgh 22. **d** 27 **p** 28 Pet. C of St Mich AA Northn 27-34; R of Twywell 34-45; CF (R of O) 39-45; Hon CF 45; V of Townstal w St Sav Dartmouth 45-57; V of Paddock Wood 57-59; Yelverton 59-67; Stoke Gabriel 67-69; L to Offic Dio Ex from 69. *15 Asheldon House, Asheldon Road, Wellswood, Torquay, Devon.* (Torquay 22422)

WATKINS, Walter. St Deiniol's Libr Hawarden 80. **d** 81 Birkenhead for Ches. C of Lache or Saltney Dio Ches from 81. *20 Park Road West, Curzon Park, Chester, CH4 8BG.*

WATKINS, William Hywel. St D Coll Lamp BA (3rd cl Mod Hist) 58. Wycl Hall Ox 58. **d** 61 **p** 62 St D. C of Llanelly 61-68; V of Llwynhendy 68-78; Slebech w Uzmaston Dio St D from 78. *Uzmaston Vicarage, Haverfordwest, Dyfed.* (Haverfordwest 2325)

WATKINS-JONES, Arthur Basil. b 24. Sarum Th Coll 67. **d** 69 Sherborne for Sarum **p** 70 Sarum. C of Broadstone 69-73; C-in-c of Winterbourne Stickland and Turnworth w Winterbourne Houghton 73-76; R (w Winterbourne Whitechurch and Winterbourne Clenston) 76-78; P-in-c of H Angels Lilliput Poole Dio Sarum from 78. *Holy Angels Vicarage, Lilliput, Poole, Dorset.* (Canford Cliffs 708567)

WATKINS-WRIGHT, Richard Kenneth David. b 39. Westcott Ho Cam 66. **d** 70 Bp McKie for Cov **p** 71 Cov. C of Bilton Rugby 70-74; Asst Chap St Geo Hosp Lon 74-75; Chap Oakwood Hosp Maidstone 76-78; V of Gt w L Gransden Dio Ely from 79. *Great Gransden Vicarage, Sandy, Beds, SG19 3AF.* (07677-227)

WATLING, Arthur Edward. b 28. St Chad's Coll Dur BA (2nd cl Psychol) 57. Linc Th Coll 57. **d** 59 **p** 60 York. C of St Cuthb Middlesbroough 59-61; Whitby 61-64; V of Eastwood Dio Sheff from 64. *St Stephen's Vicarage, Doncaster Road, Rotherham, S Yorks, S65 2BL.* (Rotherham 77615)

WATMOUGH, Hubert Gordon. b 1897. Mert Coll Ox BA (2nd cl Mod Hist) 22. Wells Th Coll 33. **d** 33 Liv **p** 34 Warrington for Liv. C of St Marg Walton-on-the-Hill 33-36; St Mary Liscard 36-38; Gt Yarmouth 38-42; R of Newbiggin 42-46; Newbiggin w Milburn 46-49; V of Sutton St Nich (or Lutton) 49-53; Chap HM Pris Stafford 53-58; R of Wold Newton w Hawerby and Beesby 58-62; Perm to Offic Dio Liv from 63. *Melton Grange Rest Home, 47 Cambridge Road, Southport, Merseyside, PR9 9PR.*

WATNEY, Douglas Percy. Univ of BC BA 25. Angl Th Coll BC LTh 27, BD 33, DD 48. Selw Coll Cam BA (2nd cl Th Trip pt ii) 31, MA 45. Wells Th Coll 31. **d** 27 **p** 29 New Westmr. C of St Mary Kerrisdale BC 27-29; Lect Angl Th Coll E Vancouver 31-37; Prof 37-54; Libr 38-54; Exam Chap to Bp of Koot 37-46; to Bp of New Westmr 47-70; Chap RCN 44-46; Can of New Westmr 51-60; I of St Anselm Vancouver 53-60; Miss Archd of New Westmr 60-66; Vancouver 66-70; Dep Prolocutor Gen Synod of Canada 62-65; Prolocutor 65-67; Hon Archd and L to Offic New Westmr 70-72. *1670 Western Parkway, Vancouver 8, BC, Canada.*

WATSON, Alan. b 34. Univ of Lon LLB 58. Linc Th Coll 58. **d** 60 Maidstone for Cant **p** 61 Cant. C of All SS Spring Pk 60-63; Sheerness 63-68; R of Allington (w St Pet from 74) Maidstone Dio Cant from 68; C-in-c of St Pet Maidstone 73-74. *35 Poplar Grove, Maidstone, Kent, ME16 0DE* (Maidstone 58704)

WATSON, Alan. b 41. K Coll Lon and Warm AKC 64. **d** 65 **p** 66 Dur. C of St Ignatius Bp Wearmouth 65-68; St Cecilia Parson Cross 68-70; W Harton 70-72; Team V 72-74; R of Our Lady of Mercy and St Thos of Cant Gorton Dio Man from 74. *Clergy House, Balmain Avenue, Gorton, Manchester, M18 7PF.* (061-223 0421)

WATSON, Alan William Martin. b 03. OBE 46. Keble Coll Ox BA (2nd cl Mod Hist) 25. Sarum Th Coll **d** 31 **p** 32 Sarum. C of Gillingham 31-33; Chap RN 34-58; Hon Chap to HM the Queen 56-58; R of Spexhall w Wissett 58-69. *Martin Cottage, Levington, Ipswich, Suff, IP10 0NA.*

WATSON, Andrew. b 35. St Paul's Coll Grahmstn 60. **d** 62 **p** 63 Capetn. C of Plumstead 62-65; Namaqualand 65-66; Sea Point 66-68; R of Worcester w Touws River 68-73; C of St Sav Croydon 73-74; St Laur in I of Thanet 74-76; St Sav Claremont 76-78; R of Robertson 78-81; Dundee Dio Natal from 81. *Box 285, Dundee, Natal, S Africa.*

WATSON, Basil Alderson. b 16. OBE 65. Selw Coll Cam 2nd cl Hist Trip pt i BA 38, (2nd cl Th Trip pt i 39), MA 44. Westcott Ho Cam 39. **d** 40 Ely **p** 41 Bp Price for Ely. C of H Trin Cam 40-41; Sugley (in c of Denton) 41-44; Sec Newc T Dioc Youth Coun 43-44; Chap RNVR 44-47; RN 46-70; Chap and Tutor RN Coll Greenwich 52-55; V of St Lawr Jewry City and Dio Lon from 70; RD of City 76-78. *St Lawrence Jewry Next Guildhall, EC2V 5AA.* (01-600 9478)

WATSON, Canon Cecil Henry Barrett. b 14. Jes Coll Ox BA 35, MA 39. Bps' Coll Cheshunt 35. **d** 37 **p** 38 Southw. C of St Giles W Bridgford (in c of All Hallows Lady Bay) 37-48; R of Ordsall 48-58; RD of Retford 53-58; R and V of Gedling Dio Southw from 58; RD of Gedling from 58; Surr from 60; Hon Can of Southw from 61; P-in-c of Netherfield 69-78. *Gedling Rectory, Nottingham.* (Nottingham 248174)

WATSON, Cyril Coleridge. Montr Dioc Th Coll 48. Sir Geo Williams Univ Montr BA 52. **d** 50 **p** 51 Montr. C of St Matt Montr 50-51; I of N Clarendon 51-54; C (Col Cl Act) of Darnall 54-55; Wombwell 55-56; Perm to Offic at Lady Marg Walworth 56-57; I of Cobden 57-63; Kars w Osgoode 63-67; Renfrew 67-73; Good Shepherd Cornw 73-79; St Marg City and Dio Ott from 79. *30 Bedford Crescent, Ottawa, Ont, Canada.* (613-746 8641)

WATSON, Canon David Christopher Knight. b 33. St Jo Coll Cam BA 57, MA 61. Ridley Hall Cam. **d** 59 Roch **p** 60 Tonbridge for Cant. C of St Mark Gillingham 59-62; H Sepulchre Cam 62-65; Heworth York 65-73; R of St Michle-Belfrey City and Dio York 73-82; Can Prov of York Minster from 81. *86 East Parade, York, YO3 7YH.* (York 24190)

WATSON, Canon Derek Richard. b 38. Selw Coll Cam BA 61, MA 65. Cudd Coll 62. **d** 64 **p** 65 S'wark. C of All SS New Eltham 64-66; Chap Ch Coll Cam 66-70; Dom Chap to Bp of S'wark 70-73; V of St Mark Surbiton 73-77; C-in-c of St Andr Surbiton 75-77; V of St Andr and St Mark Surbiton 77-78; Can Res and Treas of S'wark Cathl from 78; Dir of Ordinands and Post Ordin Tr Dio S'wark from 78. *97a Knatchbull Road, SE5.* (01-737 1061)

WATSON, Preb Donald Wace. b 17. Qu Coll Cam BA 39, MA 43. Lich Th Coll 39. **d** 41 **p** 42 Lich. C of St Andr W Bromwich 41-43; Fenton 43-47; C-in-c of Birches Head Conv Distr 47-48; V of St Steph Smethwick 48-51; Kingstone w Gratwich 51-55; Kinver Dio Lich from 55; Preb of Lich Cathl from 78. *Kinver Vicarage, Stourbridge, W Midl.* (Kinver 2556)

WATSON, Douglas John Muirhead. b 29. Keble Coll Ox BA 52, MA 56. Ely Th Coll 58. **d** 60 Maidstone for Cant **p** 61 Cant. C of St Pet and St Paul Charlton Dover 60-62; St Pet-in-Thanet 62-66; V of St Francis of Assisi W Wickham 66-72; Headcorn Dio Cant from 72. *Vicarage, Headcorn, Kent.* (Headcorn 890342)

WATSON, Edward John. b 48. Churchill Coll Cam BA 70, MA 74. Chich Th Coll 79. **d** 81 Warrington for Liv. C of Our Lady & St Nich w St Anne City and Dio Liv from 81. *Liverpool Parish Church, Old Churchyard, Liverpool, L2 8TZ.* (051-236 5287)

WATSON, Canon Edward Vincent Cornelius. b 14. TCD BA 39, MA 61. **d** and **p** 40 Lim. C-in-c of Seirkieran and of Aghancon and Kilcoleman 43-47; I of Killermogh w Durrow 47-51; Monasterevan 51-61; Rathmines Dio Dub from 61; Can of Ch Ch Cathl Dub from 80. *Rectory, Purser Gardens, Rathmines, Dublin 6, Irish Republic.* (Dublin 971797)

WATSON, Frederick. b 1897. Univ of Lon BA (2nd cl Engl) 21. St Aug Coll Cant. **d** 27 Cant for Col Bp **p** 28 Tinn for Madr. Miss Dio Madr 27-46; Lect Bp Heber Coll Trichinopoly 27-34; Prin (Bp Heber Sch) 34-46; C of Rickmansworth 47-48; R of Hockliffe 48-72; V of Chalgrave 48-72. *121 High Street, Chard, Somt.*

WATSON, George. b 11. New Coll Ox BA (3rd cl Physics) 32, 4th cl Th 34, MA 43. St Steph Ho Ox 32. **d** 34 **p** 35 Glas. C of H Trin Paisley 34-39; St Mark Swindon 39-41; St Luke Kingston-on-Thames 41-42; V of Cwmcarn 42-47; L to Offic in St Bede's Ch for Deaf and Dumb Clapham 47-51; LPr Dio Chelmsf 51-65; Chap to Deaf and Dumb 51-65; V of St Alb Mart Westcliff-on-Sea 65-76. *22 Wordsworth Road, Salisbury, Wilts, SP1 3BH.* (Salisbury 6833)

WATSON, Graeme Campbell Hubert. b 35. Ch Ch Ox 3rd cl Cl Mods 56, BA (2nd cl Lit Hum) 58, 2nd cl Th 59, MA 61. Coll of Resurr Mirfield 59. **d** 61 Arg Is for Edin **p** 62 Edin. C of St Mary's Cathl Edin 61-63; C of St John Carrington 63-67; Tutor St Cypr Th Coll Lindi, Tanzania 67-69; Sub-Warden Angl Th Coll Dar-S 69-74; P-in-c of St Alb Dar-S 74-77; C-in-c of Kingston St Mary 77-80; V (w Broomfield) 80-81; Broomfield 77-80; R of Kingston St Mary w Broomfield and Cheddon Fitzpaine Dio B & W from 81. *Kingston St Mary Vicarage, Taunton, Somt.* (Kingston St Mary 257)

WATSON, Hartley Roger. b 40. K Coll Lon and Warm. **d** 64 **p** 65 Lon. C of St Mark Noel Pk Wood Green 64-67; St Mary Magd Munster Square St Pancras 67-68; St Jo Div Vartry Road Tottenham 68-70; Chap RAF 70-76; R of St Breoke Wadebridge Dio Truro from 76. *Rectory, Trevanion Road, Wadebridge, Cornw, PL27 7NZ.* (Wadebridge 2501)

WATSON, Henry Stanley. b 36. **d** 72 **p** 74 Stepney for Lon. C of St Jas the L Bethnal Green 72-75; St Mark Vic Pk Dio Lon from 76. *1 St Mark's Gate, Old Ford, E9 5HT.*

WATSON, Ian Arthur. b 29. Late Exhib of Ex Coll Ox BA 50, MA 54. Chich Th Coll 57. **d** 59 Ox **p** 61 Ex. Asst Master Bloxham Sch 59-60; Asst Chap All H Sch Rousdon and L to Offic Dio Ex 60-66; Chap Ashbury Coll Ott 66-68; Hd Master Edin Ho Sch New Milton 68-73; Perm to Offic Dio Win 70-73; Hd Master Ex Cathl Sch 73-79; Heathmount Sch from 80; Asst PV Ex Cathl from 73. *c/o Heath Mount School, Woodhall Park, Hertford.* (0920 830230)

WATSON, Ian Leslie Stewart. b 50. Wycl Hall Ox 79. **d** 81 Ex. C of St Andr Plymouth Dio Ex from 81. *3 Saint Paul's Street, Stonehouse, Plymouth, Devon.* (0752 25640)

WATSON, Ian William. b 15. Oak Hill Th Coll 37. **d** 40 **p** 41 Lon. C of All SS Isl 40-42; St Luke Kilburn 42-44; St Luke Ramsgate 44-45; St Jas W Teignmouth 45-49 Berry Pomeroy w Bridgetown 49-53; R of Halwell w Morleigh 53-61; Milton Abbot w Dunterton 61-81. *3 Aspen Close, Bishopsmead, Tavistock, Devon, PL19 9LN.* (Tavistock 4746)

WATSON, Jeffrey John Seagrief. b 39. Late Scho of Em Coll Cam BA 61, MA 65. Clifton Th Coll 62. **d** 65 **p** 66 Roch. C of Ch Ch Beckenham 65-69; St Jude Southsea 69-71; V of Ch Ch Win 71-81; Exam Chap to Bp of Win from 76; V of Bitterne Dio Win from 81. *Vicarage, Bitterne, Southampton.* (Southn 446488)

WATSON, Jerome Douglas. b 17. TCD BA (3rd cl Mod Lang) 49, MA 58. **d** 53 **p** 54 Connor. C of Whiterock Belf 53-57; Enniskillen 57-58; Woodhouse 58-64; C-in-c of Armitage Bridge 64-70; L to Offic Dio Wakef from 70. *5 St Joseph's Mount, Pontefract, W Yorks.*

WATSON, John. b 16. Oak Hill Th Coll 76. **d** 78 Chelmsf **p** 79 Colchester for Chelmsf. C of Lexden Dio Chelmsf from 78. *19 Acland Avenue, Lexden, Colchester, Essex, CO3 3RS.* (Colchester 79950)

WATSON, John. Univ of Leeds MA 41. Coll of Resurr Mirfield 41. **d** 42 B & W **p** 43 Taunton for B & W. C of St Jo Bapt Eastover Bridgwater 42-43; H Trin Leamington Spa 43-47; V of St Paul Warwick 47-55; Hon C of St Matt Bayswater Dio Lon from 59. *8 Prince Edward Mansions, Hereford Road, W2.* (01-229 0633)

WATSON, John. b 34. K Coll Lon and Warm AKC 59. **d** 60 **p** 61 Dur. C of St Pet Stockton-on-Tees 60-64; H Trin Darlington 64-66; V of Swalwell 66-68; Perm to Offic Dio Dur 68-69; Dio Leic 69-74; Dio Man 74-76. *9 Briarfield, Egerton, Bolton, Lancs, BL7 9TX.* (Bolton 591481)

WATSON, John Davidson. b 25. Kelham Th Coll. **d** 58 **p** 59 Ex. C of St Marychurch 58-61; Brixham 61-70; V of Treverbyn 70-73; St Jude S Shields 73-78; Rekendyke Dio Dur from 78. *Vicarage, St Jude's Terrace, South Shields, T & W, NE33 5PB.* (S Shields 552338)

WATSON, John Derrick. b 35. K Coll Lon 56. Edin Th Coll 60. **d** 61 **p** 62 Lon. C of St Etheldreda Fulham 61-64; Stevenage (in c of H Trin) 64-71; V 71-74; V of St Luke Leagrave Dio St Alb from 74; RD of Luton from 80. *St Luke's Vicarage, High Street, Leagrave, Luton, Beds.* (Luton 52737)

WATSON, John Francis Wentworth. b 28. St Jo Coll Nottm LTh 59. **d** 59 **p** 60 Guildf. C of Egham 59-62; C-in-c of St Paul's Conv Distr Howell Hill Ewell 62-66; R of Ashtead 66-72; V of Plymouth Dio Ex from 72; Surr from 74; M Gen Syn Dio Ex from 75. *St Andrew's Vicarage, Bainbridge Avenue, Hartley, Plymouth, Devon.* (Plymouth 772139)

WATSON, John Harold. b 39. Open Univ MA 74. ACT PhD 81. Westcott Ho Cam 65. **d** 67 **p** 68 Cant. C of St Martin w St Paul Cant 67-69; CF 69-76; R of Esperance 76-77; Chap Guildf Gr Sch Perth 77-79; Chap R Russell Sch Croydon 79-80; Warden of Lee Abbey Internat Students Club Dio Lon from 81. *26/27 Courtfield Gardens, SW5 0PQ.* (01-373 7286)

WATSON, John Henry. **d** 41 **p** 43 Alg. C of Haileybury w Cobalt 41-43; R 43-46; I of Cobalt 46-47; Espanola 47-50; Gravenhurst 50-56; R of Noranda 56-65; Miss at Rouyn 60-65; I of Bala 68-80; Archd of Muskoka 76-80. *Box 598, Gravenhurst, Ont, Canada.*

WATSON, John Lionel. b 39. G and C Coll Cam BA 61, MA 65. Ridley Hall Cam 62. **d** 64 Warrington for Liv **p** 65 Liv. C of St Philemon w St Silas Toxt Pk 64-69; Morden (in c of St Geo) 69-73; St Phil Cam 73-74; Chap Elstree Sch Woolhampton 74-77; V of Woolhampton w Midgham (and Beenham Valence from 81) Dio Ox from 77. *Rectory, New Road Hill, Midgham, Reading, RG7 5RY.* (Woolhampton 2264)

WATSON, John Robertson Thomas. b 27. Div Hostel Dub 68. **d** 70 **p** 71 Connor. C of St Steph Belf 71-73; Swanlinbar w Templeport Dio Kilm from 73. *c/o Rectory, Swanlinbar, Co Cavan, Irish Republic.*

WATSON, Laurence Leslie. b 31. Keble Coll Ox BA 55, MA 59. Ely Th Coll. **d** 57 **p** 58 Birm. C of Solihull 57-60; Digswell 60-62; V of St Steph Smethwick 62-67; Billesley Common Dio Birm from 67. *29 Beauchamp Road, Billesley, Birmingham 13.* (021-444 1737)

WATSON, Leonard Alexander David. b 37. Univ of Man BSc 59. Coll of Resurr Mirfield 62. **d** 64 **p** 65 Sheff. C of Rawmarsh 64-68; Empangeni 69-74; Team V of E Runcorn w Halton 74-78; Sanderstead Dio S'wark from 78. *67 Hyde Road, Sanderstead, Surrey, CR2 9NS.* (01-657 6805)

WATSON, Canon Leslie. b 09. Armstrong Coll Dur BA 34, MA 38, MLitt 49. STh (Lambeth) 78. Ripon Hall Ox 34. **d** 36 **p** 37 Newc T. C of H Sav Tynemouth 36-40; St Andr Corbridge 40; Chap RAFVR 40-46; Chap of Stagshaw (in c of Halton) 46-49; V of St Pet Monkseaton 49-56; Haltwhistle 56-74; RD of Hexham 69-71; Hon Can of Newc 70-76; Can (Emer) from 76. C-in-c of Lambley 72-74. *22 Seaton Crescent, Monkseaton, Whitley Bay, NE25 8DG.* (Whitley Bay 525713)

WATSON, Lionel George. b 09. Lich Th Coll 52. **d** 54 B & W **p** 55 Taunton for B & W. C of St Jo Evang Weston 54-59; R of Donyatt w Horton (w Broadway and Ashill from 75) 59-79. *c/o Broadway Rectory, Ilminster, Somt.* (Ilminster 2559)

WATSON, Michael Henry. b 44. Vic Univ of Wel NZ BA 65, MA 66. Wycl Hall Ox 75. **d** 77 **p** 78 Roch. C of Farnborough 77-81; Chap Vic Univ of Wel from 81. *8 Kelburn Parade, Kelburn, Wellington, NZ.* (739-208)

WATSON, Peter Robert. Univ of Syd BEcon 60. Moore Th Coll Syd ACT ThL (2nd cl) 61. **d** 61 Bp Kerle for Syd **p** 62 Syd. C of Chatswood 61-63; C-in-c of Seven Hills w Lalor Pk 63-74; Can of St Jo Provisional Cathl Parramatta 69-74; R of Miranda Dio Syd from 74. *Rectory, Jackson Avenue, Miranda, NSW, Australia 2228.* (524-8369)

✠ **WATSON, Right Rev Richard Charles Challinor.** b 23. Late Scho of New Coll Ox BA (2nd cl Engl) and MA 48, Liddon Stud and 2nd cl Th 49. Westcott Ho Cam 50. **d** 51 **p** 52 Chelmsf. C of Stratford 51-53; Tutor Wycl Hall Ox 53-54; Chap 54-57; L to Offic Dio Ox 55-61; Exam Chap to Bp of Roch 55-61; to Bp of Chelmsf 62-70; Chap Wadh Coll Ox 57-62; Chap and V Temporal of Hornchurch 62-70; Cons Ld Bp Suffr of Burnley in Liv Cathl 7 April 70 by Abp of York; Bps of Blackb; Ches; Liv; Roch; Sheff; and others; Hon Can of Blackb from 70; R of Burnley 70-77; Suffr Bp in Conv from 80. *Palace House, Burnley, Lancs.*

WATSON, Canon Richard John Sutton. b 38. K Coll Lon and Warm AKC 62. **d** 63 **p** 64 Carl. C of St Jas Barrow-F 63-65; Maryport 65-68; V of Clifton-in-Workington 68-71; V of St Jo Bapt Upperby City and Dio Carl from 71; RD of Carl from 79; Hon Can of Carl Cathl from 81. *Upperby Vicarage, Carlisle, Cumb.* (Carlisle 23380)

WATSON, Richard Rydill. b 47. Sarum & Wells Th Coll 74. **d** 77 **p** 78 York. C of Cayton w Eastfield 77-81. *Address temp unknown.*

WATSON, Robert Bewley. b 34. Univ of Bris BA 59. Clifton Th Coll 56. **d** 61 **p** 62 Ches. C of Bebington 61-65; St Jo Bapt Woking (in c of H Trin Knaphill) 65-68; V of Knaphill Dio Guildf from 68. *Trinity House, Chobham Road, Knaphill, Woking, Surrey GU21 2SY.* (Brookwood 3489)

WATSON, Robert Bruce Scoular Jameson. Univ of Dur LTh 32. Keble Coll Ox BA 43, MA 47. Lich Th Coll 29. **d** 31 Bp de Salis for B & W **p** 32 B & W. C of Minehead 31-37; Hurstpierpoint 37-40; Perm to Offic Dio Ox 40-43; Actg C of St Helen Abingdon 42-44; C 44-45; Chislehurst 45-52; Harpenden 52-56; V of Bayford 56-75; Perm to Offic Dio Chelmsf from 75; Dio St Alb from 75; Dio Lon from 75. *83 Overstone Road Harpenden, AL5 5PL.* (Harpenden 61651)

WATSON, Robert Leslie. b 01. Wells Th Coll 24. **d** 25 **p** 26 B & W. C of All SS Weston Bath 25-28; Burnham 28-33; All H Barking Lon 34-37; Chap Toc H Lon 33-37; S Austr 37-39; York 39-42; Aden 42-44; Calc 44-46; Chap Civ Orph Asyls and Perambur Dio Madr 47-48; Ch of S India 48-57; V of Churt 57-64; R of Withycombe w Rodhuish 64-68; Perm to Offic Dio Glouc from 68; B & W from 74. *9 The Lerburne, Wedmore, Somt, BS28 4ED.*

WATSON, Roger Brian. b 45. Cranmer Hall Dur 67. **d** 70 **p** 71 Blackb. C of St John Sandylands Heysham 70-74; Wallingford 74-77; Winchmore Hill Dio Lon from 77. *58 Church Hill, Winchmore Hill, N21 1JA.* (01-882 3298)

WATSON, Ronald Marwood. b 25. Roch Th Coll 68. **d** 70 **p** 71 Ripon. C of Horsforth 70-71; All SS Leeds 71-73; Baildon (in c of St Jas) 73-75; R of Stowell Mem Ch Salford 75-77; C of Tonge Moor (in c of St Aid) Dio Man from 77. *392 Crompton Way, Bolton, Lancs.*

WATSON, Stuart James. b 50. Univ of W Ont BA 72. Trin Coll Tor MDiv 77. **d** 77 Niag **p** 78 Bp Clarke for Niag. C of Grace Ch Milton 77-80; I of Bay Ridges Dio Tor from 80. *906 St Martin's Drive, Pickering, Ont, Canada L1W 1M9.*

WATSON, Terence David. b 38. Jes Coll Ox BA 61, MA 67. Chich Th Coll 73. **d** 74 **p** 75 Lewes for Chich. C of All SS Sidley 74-78; Woodham Dio Guildf from 78. *158 St Michael's Road, Sheerwater, Woking, Surrey, GU21 5QA.* (Byfleet 41680)

WATSON, Thomas Anthony. b 23. Chich Th Coll 50. **d** 52 **p** 53 Ex. C of Ashburton 52-54; Bideford 54-57; V of Bp's Nympton 57-59; R of Rose Ash 57-59; Asst P Lusaka 59-62; R of Broken Hill 62-65; V of St Francis Honicknowle Devonport 65-72; R of Silverton Dio Ex from 72; Butterleigh Dio Ex from 72. *Silverton Rectory, Exeter, Devon.* (Ex 860350)

WATSON, Thomas Heys. b 16. Clifton Th Coll 36. **d** 40 **p** 41 Newc T. C of St Mich Byker Newc T 40-42; All SS Blackb 42-46; V of St Paul Accrington 46-53; R of Whittington-in-Lonsdale 53-61; V of Whittle-le-Woods 61-75; R of Hesketh w Becconsall 75-80. *c/o Hesketh Rectory, Hesketh Bank, Preston, Lancs, PR4 6SQ.* (Hesketh Bank 2345)

WATSON, Timothy Patrick. b 38. ALCD 66. **d** 66 **p** 67 Lon. C of Em Northwood 66-70; Team V of High Wycombe 70-76; Gen Sec CCCS 76-82; R of All SS Weston Bath w N Stoke Dio B & W from 82. *Weston Vicarage, Bath, Avon.* (Bath 21159)

WATSON, Vernon Owen. Univ of Dur LTh 38. Oak Hill Th Coll 35. **d** 38 Lon **p** 39 Willesden for Lon. C of St Pet Islington 38-42; St Barn Mitcham 42-45; Warlingham w Chelsham 45-51; Writtle 51-52; C of St Jas w St Phil Islington 53-56; St Steph Hounslow 56-62; Perm to Offic Dio Lon from 62; Dio Ox from 63. *Flat 2, 14 Spey Road, Reading, Berks.*

WATSON, William. b 36. Ripon Hall Ox 64. **d** 66 Bp McKie for Cov **p** 67 Cov [f in CA] C of H Trin Leamington 66-69; V of Salford Priors 69-74; Malin Bridge 74-79; Chap R Shrewsbury Hosp Copthorne from 79. *6 Knowsley Drive, Bicton Heath, Shrewsbury, SY3 8BQ.* (Shrewsbury 68620)

WATSON, William Henry Dunbar. d 58 Hur **p** 60 Ont. C of St Jas Lon 58-60; R of Elizabethtn 60-63; C of St Cuthb Tor 63-66. *c/o 71 Bronson Avenue, Ottawa, Ont, Canada.*

WATSON, William Lysander Rowan. b 26. TCD Pri BA (1st cl Hist Mod) 47, Div Test 49, MA 50. Clare Coll Cam MA (by Incorp) 52. St Pet Hall Ox MA (by Incorp) 57. **d** 49 **p** 50 Dub. C of Chapelizod and Kilmainham Dub 49-51; Tutor Ridley Hall Cam 51-55; Chap 55-57; St Pet Coll Ox from 57; Fell and Tutor from 59; Dean of Degrees 67-76; Sen Tutor 77-81; C of St Pet-le-Bailey Ox 58-61; Lect in Th Univ of Ox from 60; Exam Chap to Bp of Derby from 70. *St Peter's College, Oxford.* (Oxford 48436)

WATSON PEGMAN, John Basil. b 24. **d** 58 **p** 59 Ripon. C of Far Headingley 58-61; V of Hovingham 61-64; R of Slingsby 61-64; Guisborough w Commondale 64-68; Chap Miss to Seamen Rotterdam 68-69; Port of Lon 69-73; Sen Chap 73-74; Regional Dir E Engl from 74; Publ Pr Dio Chelmsf 69-74; L to Offic Dio Linc from 74; Perm to Offic Dios Ely, St E, Southw, Pet, Leic and Nor from 74. *159 Manthorpe Road, Grantham, Lincs, NG31 8DH.* (Grantham 3056)

WATSON WILLIAMS, Richard Hamilton Patrick. b 31. SS Coll Cam BA 57, MA 62. St Aug Coll Cant. **d** 59 Guildf **p** 60 Bp Dale for Cant. C of Dorking 59-63; Portsea (in c of St Faith) 63-66; V of Culgaith 66-71; V of Kirkland 66-71; Wigton 71-79; Warden Man Dioc Conf Ho and P-in-c of Crawshawbooth Dio Man from 79. *St John's Vicarage, Conference House, Burnley Road, Rossendale, Lancs,)*

WATT, Very Rev Alfred Ian. b 34. Edin Th Coll. **d** 60 **p** 61 Brech. C of St Paul's Cathl Dundee 60-63; Prec 63-66; R of Arbroath 66-69; Provost of St Ninian's Cathl Perth from 69. *47 Balhousie Street, Perth, PH1 5HJ.* (Perth 26874)

WATT, Allan Donald Gale. St Paul's Coll Grahmstn. **d** 71 **p** 73 Pret. C of Nelspruit 71-72; R of Lyttelton Dio Pret from 75. *PO Box 14338, Verwoerdburg 0140, Pretoria, S Africa.* (62-9502)

WATT, Brian Val. Moore Th Coll Syd 62. ACT ThL (2nd cl) 63. **d** 63 **p** 64 Syd. C of Miranda 63-64; Sylvania Heights 64-65- R of Lithgow 65-69; C-in-c of Forestville Provisional Distr 69-70; R 71-77; St Pet E Lindfield 77-80; Prec St Andr Cathl Dio Syd from 81. *22 Gladstone Parade, Lindfield, NSW, Australia 2070.* (269-0642)

WATT, James. b 1891. **d** 18 Carl **p** 19 Barrow-F for Carl. C of Ch Ch Whitehaven 18-21; Hesket-in-the-Forest 21-25; Broughton Moor (in c of St Columba) 25-27; R of Kirklinton w Hethersgill 27-62; Surr 27-62. *Kirklinton Park House, Kirklinton, Carlisle, Cumb.* (Kirklinton 211)

WATT, William McMillin. St Aid Coll 31. **d** 34 **p** 35 Liv. C of St John Ainsdale 34-37; Roby 37-41; V of All SS Princes Pk 41-55; Long Crendon 61-70; C-in-c of Oving w Pitchcott 70-74; N Marston w Granborough 70-74. *21 Abbot Ridge, Long Crendon, Bucks.*

WATT, William Montgomery. b 09. Univ of Edin MA (1st cl Cl) 30, Ferguson Scho 31, PhD 44. Late Exhib of Ball Coll Ox BA (2nd cl Lit Hum) 32, BLitt and MA 36. Univ of Aber Hon DD 66. Cudd Coll 38. **d** 39 Willesden for Lon **p** 40 Lon. C of St Mary the Boltons S Kens 39-41; Old St Paul Edin 41-43; Chap Dio Jer 43-46; Exam Chap to Bp in Jer 46; Lect Univ of Edin 46-53; Reader 53-64; Prof of Arabic and Islamic Stud 64-79; Hon C of Old St Paul Edin 46-59; St Columba Edin 59-62; Dalkeith Dio Edin from 80; Lasswade Dio Edin from 80. *The Neuk, Dalkeith, Midlothian, EH22 1JT.* (031-663 3197)

WATT, William Stephen. d 64 Bp Snell for Tor **p** 67 Tor. C of Highland Creek 64-67; All SS Kingsway 67-70; R of H Trin Guildwood Tor 70-74; St Paul Runnymede Tor 74-79. *85 Coe Hill Drive, Toronto, Ont, Canada.*

WATT-WYNESS, Gordon. b 25. St Jo Coll Dur 70. **d** 72 Hull for York **p** 73 York. C of Scarborough 72-76; R of Rossington Dio Sheff from 76. *Rossington Rectory, Doncaster, Yorks.* (Doncaster 867597)

WATTERSON, William Howard. b 16. Univ of Dur LTh 39, BA 47, MA 58. St Aid Coll 36. **d** 39 **p** 40 Wakef. C of St Andr Wakef 39-41; Seacombe Wallasey 41-43; Chap RAFVR 43-46; Perm to Offic Dio Dur 46-47; Asst Master Qu Eliz Gr Sch Ashbourne 48-53; Waterloo Gr Sch Liv 53-72; Perm to Offic Dio Ches from 53; Dio Liv 53-69; Dio Ox from 72; L to Offic Dio Liv from 70; Asst Master Aylesbury High Sch 72-77. *166 Ingram Avenue, Bedgrove, Aylesbury, Bucks, HP21 7DH.*

WATTHEY, Arthur Edward. b 20. St Cath Coll Cam BA 45, MA 48. St Aug Coll Cant 73. **d** 73 **p** 74 Leic (APM). C of St Cuthb Gt Glen 73-76; Prin Guthlaxton Coll 70-81; Hon C of Carlton Curlieu w Ilston-on-the-Hill and Shangton w Burton Overy 76-81; Perm to Offic Dio Leic from 81. *c/o 2 The Chase, Great Glen, Leicester, LE8 0EQ.*

✠ **WATTON, Right Rev James Augustus.** Univ of W Ont BA 37, DD (*jure dig*) 55. Hur Coll Ont LTh 38. **d** 38 **p** 39 Hur. C of Hur Coll Chap Lon 38; Lucknow w Dungannon Port Albert and Ripley 38-39; Merlin w Ouvry and Erieau 39-41; I of Wyoming w Camlachie and Wanstead 41-44; R of Geraldton 44-47; Kirkland Lake 47-54; Timmins 54-57; Can of Moos 45-47; Dean 55-57; R of St John Port Hope 57-58; St Mich AA Tor 58-63; Cons Ld Bp of Moos in St Matt Cathl Timmins 1 May 63 by Abp of Alg; Bp of Ott; Bp Coadj of Tor; and Bps Suffr of Moos; Tor; and Hur; res 80; Elected Metrop of Prov of Ont 74; res 79. *Southampton, Ont, N0H 1L0, Canada.*

WATTON, Robert Newman Kingsley. b 45. Qu Coll Birm 72. **d** 74 **p** 75 Truro. C of St Madron w Morvah 74-78; P-in-c of Lostwithiel Dio Truro from 78; Lanivet and of Lanhydrock Dio Truro from 81; Adv in Relig Educn Dio Truro 78-81. *Vicarage, North Street, Lostwithiel, Cornw, PL22 0EF.* (Bodmin 872394)

WATTS, Anthony John. b 30. K Coll Lon and Warm AKC 59. **d** 60 **p** 61 Dur. C of Whitburn 60-63; Croxdale 63-65; V of St Pet Warrington 65-70; V of Peel 70-78; C-in-c of St Mark Bury 78-81; V of Ch Ch Davyhulme Dio Man from 81. *14 Welbeck Avenue, Davyhulme, Manchester, M31 1GJ.* (061-748 2018)

WATTS, Canon Arthur James. b 08. Late Scho of Hatf Coll Dur BA (Hons) and Maltby Exhib 30, MA 47. **d** 32 **p** 33 Ex. Chap and Asst Master All H Sch Honiton 32-34; C of St Jas w St Anne 34-36; Sidmouth (in c of St Francis of Assisi) 36-40; V of Townstal and Chap of Dartmouth 40-45; V of Watlington 45-51; Surr from 41; R of Harpsden w Bolney 51-77; Gen Dioc Insp of Educn Dio Ox 45-56; Dir 56-65; Chap Henley War Mem Hosp from 53; Hon Can of Ch Ch Ox from 59; Proc Conv Ox 63-77; RD of Henley 64-73; L to Offic Dio Ox from 77. *Juniper Cottage, Harpsden, Henley-on-Thames, Oxon, RG9 4HL.* (Henley 5343)

WATTS, Charles George. b 08. ALCD 37. **d** 37 **p** 38 Chelmsf. C of Walthamstow 37-40; C-in-c of H Trin Springfield 40-43; Org Chelmsf Dioc Coun for Youth 43-47; Chap HM Pris Wormwood Scrubs 47-55; V of St Jo Evang w St Mary U Edmon 55-60; R of Limehouse 60-75; Perm to Offic Dio Swan B from 75. *Crwys Villa, Irfon Terrace, Llanwrtyd Wells, Powys.* (05913-463)

WATTS, Clement William. Ridley Coll Melb ACT ThL 67. **d** 68 **p** 69 Melb. C of Ch Ch Berwick 68-70; St Jo Blackburn 70-71; V of St Luke Springvale N 71-75; Emerald 75-80. *c/o Vicarage, Church Street, Emerald, Vic, Australia 3782.*

WATTS, Canon Frank Walter. K Coll Lon and Warm AKC 53. **d** 54 **p** 55 Llan. C of Llandough w Leckwith 54-56; Llanishen 56-59; Marlow 59-60; V of Black Bourton w Carterton 60-63; C-in-c of Brize Norton (w Carterton from 63) 61-63; V 63-69; R of Boyup Brook 69-71; Midl Junction 71-77; Kalgoorlie-Boulder Dio Perth from 78; Hon Can of Perth from 78. *Box 439, Kalgoorlie, W Australia 6430.* (21 2329)

WATTS, Frederick Elmore. Univ of Melb BA 11, MA 13. ACT 11. Trin Coll Tor BD 21. **d** 11 **p** 12 Melb. C of St Steph Richmond Vic 11-14; Min of Hastings Vic 14-21; R of St Paul Port Pirie 21-25; Hd of St Paul's Bro 16-25; Miss to Seamen Chap at Genoa and Savona and Chap of Turin 25-26; Miss to Seamen Chap Kobe 26-40; Newc 40-41; Freetown (W Afr) 41-44; Fremantle 44-46; R of Kelmscott-Armadale 47-51; Perm to Offic Dio Perth 51-59; P-in-c of Kellerberrin 59-61;

Chap Forrest River Miss 62-63; C of E Claremont 63-64; Norseman 65. *c/o Church Office, Cathedral Avenue, Perth, W Australia.*

WATTS, Geoffrey Frederick. b 46. Chich Th Coll 70. **d** 73 Crediton for Ex **p** 74 Ex. C of Barton 73-75; St Jas Ex 76-79; Team V of Littleham w Exmouth Dio Ex from 79. *4 Rolle Road, Exmouth, EX8 2AB.* (Exmouth 72328)

WATTS, George Reginald. b 15. Or Coll Ox BA (2nd cl Mod Hist) 37, MA 43. **d** 57 **p** 58 Truro. Hd Master Gonvena Ho Sch and C of St Minver 57-71; Forrabury w Minster and Trevalga 71-73; R of St Mellion w Pillaton Dio Truro from 73. *Rectory, St Mellion, Cornw.* (St Dominic 50329)

WATTS, Gordon Sidney Stewart. b 40. **d** 66 **p** 67 Connor. C of St Steph Belf 66-69; CF from 69. *Ministry of Defence, Bagshot Park, Bagshot,* (021-291539)

WATTS, Harold Thomas. b 1897. Wycl Hall Ox. **d** 26 **p** 27 Ox. C of Faringdon 26-29; Ch Ch w St Andr Malvern 29-31; V of Bredwardine w Brobury 31-49; R of Sutton St Nich w St Mich 49-55; C-in-c of Blakemere 39-49; RD of Weobley 43-49; Weston 52-55; Perm to Offic Dio Ox from 55. *Beech Trees, Alben Road, Binfield, Berks.*

WATTS, Treas Horace Gordon. b 20. TCD BA 42, MA 52. **d** 43 **p** 44 Lim. C of Tralee and Dioc C of Ardf and Agh 43-46; I of St Edm Dunmanway 46-51; Drimoleague w Caheragh 51-56; R of Fanlobbus (or Dunmanway) (w Drinagh from 59) 56-76; St Edm Fanlobbus 56-76; Preb of Cork Cathl from 67; Cloyne Cathl 67-68; Treas from 68; I of Douglas Dio Cork from 76. *Rectory, Douglas, Co Cork, Irish Republic.* (021-291539)

WATTS, Ian Harold. b 15. St Pet Coll Ox BA (1st cl Geog) 39, MA 47. **d** 65 N Nig. Sen Lect and Hon Chap Ahmadu Bello Univ Zaria Nig 65-68; Chap Uppingham Sch 68-73; Asst Master Holmfirth Sch 73-74; Batley Gr Sch 74-79; Hon C of Mirfield 73-79; Asst Chap H Trin Cannes Dio Gibr (Gibr in Eur from 80) from 79. *1 Rue Général, Ferrié, Cannes, France.* (93-385461)

WATTS, Jack Cecil Arthur. **d** and **p** 43 Perth. R of Carl 43-47; Mundaring 47-52; Wembley 52-75; Hon Can of St Geo Cathl Perth 64-75; Perm to Offic Dio Perth from 75. *St John's Cottage, Deanmore Road, Karrinyup, W Australia 6018.* (41-6605)

WATTS, James. b 24. St Aug Coll Cant 57. **d** 57 Dover for Cant **p** 58 Cant. C of Willesborough 57-61; R of Smarden 61-70; V of St Nich-at-Wade w Sarre 70-74; C-in-c of Chislet w Hoath 71-74; V of St Jas Westgate-on-Sea Dio Cant from 74. *Vicarage, Orchard Gardens, Westbrook, Margate, Kent.* (Thanet 32073)

WATTS, Canon John Douglas Edward. Univ of BC Angl Th Coll BC LTh 63. **d** and **p** 63 Koot. I of Michel 63-67; C of Terrace 67-69; Whitehorse 69-73; I of Old Crow 73-76; Carmacks and Pelly 76-79; Haines Junction Dio Yukon from 79; Can of Yukon from 80. *Box 5321, Haines Junction, Yukon, Canada.*

WATTS, John Harry. b 24. St Aid Coll 57. **d** 59 **p** 60 Derby. C of Fairfield and of King Sterndale 59-61; Wirksworth 61-65; V of S Wingfield Dio Derby from 65; P-in-c of Wessington Dio Derby from 77. *South Wingfield Vicarage, Alfreton, Derby, DE5 7LJ.* (Alfreton 832484.)

WATTS, Canon John Henry Holman. Univ of BC BA 37. Angl Th Coll BC LTh 38. **d** and **p** 38 New Westmr. C of Gibson's Landing w Robert's Creek and Sechelt 38; I 38-39; M of Bro of Good Shepherd Milestone 41-45; I of Redcliff 45-48; Sub-Warden St Chad's Coll Regina and I of St Mich Regina 48-53; R of Maple Creek 54-57; Rosetown 57-64; Hon Can of Regina Cathl 59-77; Can (Emer) from 77; Exam Chap to Bp of Qu'App 63-74; I of Estevan 64-71; St Mich w St Luke Moose Jaw 70-77; Hon C of St John Moose Jaw Dio Qu'App from 77. *269 Iroquois Street West, Moose Jaw, Sask, Canada.*

WATTS, Kenneth Francis. b 17. St Francis Coll Brisb ACT ThL 39. **d** 40 **p** 41 Brisb. C of St Aug Hamilton 40-45; C-in-c of St Anne Nanango 45-46; V of Gin Gin 47-48; L to Offic Dio Brisb 48-49; C of St Pet Southport 49-51; V of All SS Booval 51-55; Perm to Offic (Col Cl Act) as C of Maidstone 55-58; R of Elmstone w Preston-next-Wingham 58-63; R of Stourmouth 59-63; V of Cheriton Street 63-78; All S Cheriton w Newington 78-80; Katikati Dio Waik from 80. *c/o Box 125, Katikati, NZ.*

WATTS, Kenneth Robert. b 53. Univ of Manit BSc 75. St Jo Coll Winnipeg MDiv 78. **d** 78 **p** 79 Athab. C of All SS Fort McMurray 78-81; I of Em Sexsmith Dio Athab from 81. *PO Box 354, Sexsmith, Alta, Canada, T0H 3C0.*

WATTS, Canon Louis Mitchell. Univ of Sask BA 31. Em Coll Sktn LTh 31, DD (*hon causa*) 62. **d** 30 **p** 31 Sask. C of H Trin Sktn 30-31; Perdue w Kinley and Leney 31-33; I of Wilkie 34-35; C of St Geo Cathl Kingston 35-41; I of Wainwright 41-42; St Faith (w St Mich 47-51) Edmon 42-57; Kenora 57-70; Can of Keew 57-59; Dean 59-70; Hon Can of Keew from 70. *21 Roberts Crescent, Brampton, Ont, Canada.*

WATTS, Michael. b 32. St Cath S Ox 3rd cl Th BA 57, MA 61. St Steph Ho Ox 57. **d** 58 **p** 59 Ox. C of St Mich Ox 58-60; Chap New Coll Ox 60-72; Chap Ch Ch Ox 60-81; Prec 64-81; C of St Mary Magd Ox 63-73; R of Sulhamstead-Abbots w Ufton Nervet Dio Ox from 81. *Ufton Nervet Rectory, Reading, Berks.* (Burghfield Common 2328)

WATTS, Paul George. b 43. Univ of Nottm BA (2nd cl Th) 67. Wells Th Coll 67. **d** 69 **p** 70 Sherwood for Southw. C of Sherwood 69-74; Chap Trent Poly Nottm 74-79; Publ Pr Dio Southw 74-80; V of All SS Nottm Dio Southw from 80. *All Saints' Vicarage, Nottingham, NG7 4DP.* (Nottm 704197)

WATTS, Peter Alan Witney. b 37. Univ of Dur BA (2nd cl Pol and Econ) 59. Univ of Birm Dipl Th 61. Qu Coll Birm 59. **d** 61 Aston for Birm **p** 62 Birm. C of Hamstead 61-65; Ward End 65-66; V of Ch Ch Ward End Birm 66-73; St Chad Sutton Coldfield Dio Birm from 73. *Vicarage, Hollyfield Road, Sutton Coldfield, W Midl, B75 7SN.* (021-329 2995)

WATTS, Peter Francis. b 48. Univ of Wales (Cardiff) Dipl Th 71. St Mich Th Coll Llan 67. **d** 71 **p** 72 Swan B. C of St Mary Swansea 71-74; Newton-Nottage 74-77; V of Hirwaun 77-81; P-in-c of Menheniot Dio Truro from 81. *Vicarage, Menheniot, Liskeard, Cornw, PL14 3SU* (Liskeard 42195)

WATTS, Ronald. b 21. St D Coll Lamp BA 47. **d** 48 **p** 49 Llan. C of Merthyr Tydfil 48-50; Ystradyfodwg 50-52; Chap RAF 52-58; R of Kiklhampton (w Morwenstow from 72) Dio Truro from 58; C-in-c of Morwenstow 63-72. *Kilkhampton Rectory, Bude, Cornw.* (Kilkhampton 314)

WATTS, Wilfred Richard James. b 11. St Mich Coll Llan. **d** 66 Glouc **p** 66 Tewkesbury for Glouc. C of Coleford w Staunton 66-69; V of Viney Hill Dio Glouc from 69. *Viney Hill Vicarage, Lydney, Glos.* (Blakeney 253)

WATTS, William George Duncan. b 12. Kelham Th Coll 32. **d** 38 **p** 39 Bris. C of St Jo Bapt Bedminster 38-42; LPr Dio Bloemf 42-53; V of Welkom 53-59; C of Teyateyaneng 59-60; St Aid Leeds 60-62; V of S Elmsall 62-70; R of Benefield 70-80; L to Offic Dio Pet from 80. *5 Lime Avenue, Oundle, Peterborough.*

WATTS-JONES, William Vyvyan Francis Kynaston. b 22. Em Coll Cam BA 43, MA 47. Ridley Hall Cam 47. **d** 49 **p** 50 Sheff. C of Ch Ch Fulwood Sheff 49-52; Plymouth 52-54; V of All SS Darlaston 54-60; Bilton 60-70; Asst Master St Pet Colleg Ch Sch Wolverhampton 72-74; R of St Thos Brampton Dio Derby from 74. *408 Chatsworth Road, Chesterfield, Derbys, S40 3BG.* (Chesterfield 32717)

WAUGH, Nigel John William. b 56. TCD Div Test 76, BA 78, MA 81. Div Hostel Dub 73. **d** 79 **p** 80 Connor. C of Ballymena 79-82; Ballyholme Dio Down from 82. *4 Kilmaine Avenue, Bangor, Co Down, N Ireland.*

WAWERU, David Njoroge. St Paul's Th Coll Limuru. **d** and **p** 68 Nak. P Dio Nak 68-73. *PO Box 244, Nakuru, Kenya.*

WAWERU, John Mwangi. St Phil Coll Kongwa. **d** and **p** 70 Nai. C of All SS Cathl Nai 70-72; V of Kithangathini 72-76; P-in-c of H Trin and St Luke City and Dio Nai from 77. *Box 50878, Nairobi, Kenya.*

WAWERU, Joseph. b 41. St Paul's Coll Limuru. **d** 72 **p** 74 Mt Kenya. P Dio Mt Kenya 72-75; Dio Mt Kenya S from 75. *Box 214, Thika, Kenya.*

WAXHAM, Derek Frank. b 33. Oak Hill Th Coll 76. **d** 79 Stepney for Lon **p** 80 Lon. C of St Paul w St Steph Old Ford Bow Dio Lon from 79. *39 Hewlett Road, Bow, E3.*

WAY, Albert James. St D Coll Lamp BA 61, Dipl Th 63. **d** 63 **p** 64 Llan. C of Neath w Llantwit 63-68; St John Watford 68; R of Clayhidon 68-76; V of Llanbadoc w Llanllowell Dio Mon from 76. *Rectory, Llanllowell, Usk, NP5 1LJ.* (Usk 2346)

WAY, Andrew Lindsay. b 43. Linc Th Coll 76. **d** 78 Chelmsf **p** 79 Bradwell for Chelmsf. C of Shenfield Dio Chelmsf from 78. *93 Oliver Road, Shenfield, Brentwood, Essex.*

WAY, Anthony Hilton. b 21. Chich Th Coll 57. **d** 59 Lewes for Chich **p** 60 Chich. C of St Paul w St Bart Chich 59-61; Hangleton 61-63; PC of Horam 63-70; V of Ditchling 70-77; Asst Dioc Sec Dio Chich from 77; Chap to Dioc Ch Ho Chich from 79. *17 First Avenue, Worthing, W Sussex, BN14 9NJ.* (Worthing 37454)

WAY, Clive Alexander. Moore Th Coll Syd 62. ACT ThL (2nd cl) 63. **d** 63 **p** 64 Syd. C of St John Parramatta 63-65; Beecroft 65-66; C-in-c of Sefton and Chester Hill Provisional Distr 66-68; R of Erskineville 68-72; Chap Homes of Peace Dio Syd from 72. *120 Ray Road, Epping, NSW, Australia 2121.*

WAY, Francis. **d** and **p** 48 Sing. C of Malacca and Prin St D Chinese Sch Malacca 48-55; St Pet Sing 59; Chap Sing Angl High Sch from 59; L to Offic Dio Sing 63-69. *c/o St Peter's, Singapore 6.*

WAY, John Chudleigh. b 1899. RMC Sandhurst 17. Wycl Hall, Ox 30. **d** 32 **p** 33 Chelmsf. C of St Paul Clacton 32-35;

Croydon 35-39; V of Kingsley w Oakhanger 39-43; Winkleigh 43-56; RD of Chulmleigh 55-56; R of Broughton Gifford w Gt Chalfield 56-64; V of Chirton w Marden and Patney 64-70. *Little Melands, Oakway, Chesham Bois, Bucks, HP6 5PQ* (Amersham 3214)

WAY, Canon John William. St Jo Coll Winnipeg. **d** 47 **p** 48 Calg. C of Okotoks 47; V of Carbon 48-51; Brooks 51-54; R of Chilliwack 54-62; St Barn Calg 62-72; St Barn Medicine Hat 72-77; Innisfail Dio Calg from 77; Hon Can of Calg from 73. *Box 126, Innisfail, Alta, Canada.* (227-3075)

WAY, Lawrence William. b 32. St Mich AA Th Coll Llan 77. **d** 79 **p** 80 Llan. C of Merthyr Dyfan Dio Llan from 79. *2 Highfield Road, Colcot, Barry, S Glam.* (Barry 745601)

WAY, Michael David. b 57. AKC and BD 78. St Steph Ho Ox 79. **d** 80 Ex. C of Bideford 80-81; Hon C of Wembley Pk Dio Lon from 81; Asst Master St Aug Sch Kilburn from 81. *150 Wembley Hill Road, Wembley, Middx.* (01-904 3558)

WAY, Paul David. b 31. Jes Coll Cam BA 55, MA 59. Coun for Nat Acad Awards BEducn 79. Ridley Hall Cam. **d** 57 **p** 58 Chelmsf. C of Barking 57-60; Goring 60-63; R of W Blatchington 63-75; Perm to Offic Dio S'wark from 75. *27 Riefield Road, Eltham, SE9 2QD.*

WAY, Wilbur George. Univ of Tor BA 63. Trin Coll Tor STB 66. **d** and **p** 66 Bp Greenwood for Carib. C of N Kamloops 66-67; I of Quesnel 67-73; R of Revelstoke Dio Koot from 73. *St Peter's Rectory, Revelstoke, BC, Canada.* (837-3275)

✠ **WAY, Right Rev Wilfrid Lewis Mark.** b 05. Late Cl Scho of Trin Coll Cam 1st cl Cl Trip pt i 25, BA (2nd cl Cl Trip pt ii) 27, MA 35. Westcott Ho Cam 27. **d** 28 **p** 29 Liv. C of St Faith Gt Crosby 28-34; St Bart Brighton 34-37; UMCA Miss at Zanz I 37; C of Korogwe 37-38; P-in-c of Zanz 38-40; Msalabani 40-44; Mkuzi 44-45; Kideleko 48-51; Warden of Kalole Th Coll Dio Zanz 51-52; Cons Ld Bp of Masasi in Westmr Abbey 18 Oct 52 by Abp of Cant; Bps of Chich; Nyasa; Glas; and Zanz; Bp Suffr of Kens; and Bp Vernon; res 59; R of Averham w Kelham 60-71; Asst Bp of Southw 60-71. *Rose Cottage, Redhills Lane, Durham City.*

WAY, Winfrid Hilary. Lich Th Coll. **d** 32 **p** 34 Lich. C of Newport w Longford 32-35; Heath Town 35-40; Actg C-in-c of Tettenhall 40-41; Chap RAFVR 41-46; V of Silverdale 46-54; Stonehouse 54-67; Chap Standish Ho Hosp 56-67; RD of Stonehouse 63-67; R of Stow-on-the-Wold Dio Glouc from 67. *Rectory, Stow-on-the-Wold, Glos, GL54 1AA.* (Stow 30607)

WAYE, Munden. d 66 **p** 67 Newfld. C of Trinity E 66-67; I of Cartwright 67-72; R of Buchans 72-76; Badger's Quay Dio Newfld from 77. *Box 119, Badger's Quay, Newfoundland, Canada.* (709-536 2485)

WAYE, Richard John. b 48. McGill Univ Montr BTh 78. Montr Dioc Th Coll STM 79. **d** 80 **p** 81 Ont. C-in-c of Tamworth Ont 80; C of St Thos Belleville 80-81; on leave. *c/o 71 Bronson Avenue, Ottawa, Ont, Canada.*

WAYNE, Kenneth Hammond. b 31. Bps' Coll Cheshunt 58. **d** 61 **p** 62 Leic. C of St Hugh's Conv Distr Eyres Monsell Leic 61-62; Em Loughborough 62-65; V of Breedon-on-the-Hill w Isley Walton 65-73; St Phil City and Dio Leic from 73; C-in-c of Staunton Harold 65-73. *Vicarage, St Philip's Road, Leicester, LE5 5TR.* (Leic 736204)

WAYTE, Alleyn Robert. b 33. Trin Coll Ox BA 56, MA 60. Westcott Ho Cam 60. **d** 61 Shrewsbury for Lich **p** 62 Stafford for Lich. C of Cannock 61-66; C-in-c of Dawley Magna 66-75; V of Stretton w Claymills Dio Lich from 75. *Stretton Vicarage, Burton-on-Trent, Staffs, De13 0HD,* (Burton-T 65141)

WAYTE, Christopher John. b 28. Univ of Lon BSc (Eng) 54. Wells Th Coll 54. **d** 56 Dover for Cant **p** 57 Cant. C of St Martin Maidstone 56-60; W Wickham 60-61; Birchington 61-64; Min of St Nich Conv Distr Buckland Valley Dover 64-68; R of Biddenden 68-80; P-in-c of Boughton Monchelsea Dio Cant from 80. *Boughton Monchelsea Vicarage, Maidstone, Kent, ME17 4BU.* (Maidstone 43321)

WEALE, Colin Alexander. b 26. St D Coll Lamp BA 49. STh (Lambeth) 81. Sarum Th Coll 49. **d** 51 **p** 52 Swan B. C of St Mary Swansea 51-55; Min Can of Brecon Cathl and C of St Mary Brecon 55-59; V of Llanbister w Llanbadarn-Fynydd and Llananno 59-61; R of H Trin (w Ch Ch from 69) Bengeo Dio St Alb from 61. *Bengeo Rectory, Hertford, SG14 3BS.* (Hertford 54537)

WEANGA BWAYA, George William. Bp Usher-Wilson Coll Buwalasi. **d** 64 Mbale. d Dio Mbale. *Church of Uganda, Makuya, Mbale, Uganda.*

WEARE, Edward Albert. Em Coll Sktn 55. **d** 58 **p** 59 Keew. C of Red Lake 58-60; I of Claresholm w Nanton 60-71; Hon Can of Calg 70-79; Chap Univ of Calg 71-78; R of St Andr Calg 73-74; Dom Chap to Bp of Calg 74-79; Perm to Offic Dio BC 80-81; Dir of Temple Pastures and Evang Min Dio Ott from 81. *c/o 71 Bronson Avenue, Ottawa, K1R 6G6, Canada.*

WEARE, Oswald William. b 07. **d** 43 **p** 44 Lich. C of Rushall 43-45; C-in-c of Ascen Conv Distr (Friar Pk) West Bromwich 45-48; C of Woodhouse 48-49; St Jude Manningham and C-in-c of St Mich AA Bradf 49-52; Chap of Philanthr S Farm Sch Redhill 52-54; R of Lyndon w Manton and Martinsthorpe 54-58; V of Gretton 58-66; Hambleton w Egelton 66-70; Stillington 70-76. *24 Roseberry Road, Hartlepool, Cleve.* (Hartlepool 64695)

WEARE, Sydney Vincent. Linc Coll Ox BA 48, MA 52. Univ of W Austr MA (*ad eund*) 57. Westcott Ho Cam 48. **d** 50 **p** 51 Lon. [f Solicitor] C of St Steph St John's Wood 50-55; CF (TA) 54-55; Sub-Warden and Chap St Geo Coll Univ of W Austr 55-59; Actg Warden 56; Tutor in Hist 55-59; L to Offic Dio Perth 55-59; Lect Woolaston Th Coll 57; Dom and Exam Chap to Abp of Melb 59-62; V of Aston Rowant w Crowell 62-66; R of St Mary S Perth 66-72; Exam Chap to Abp of Perth 67-75; P-in-c of Cottesloe 72-75; Assoc R of Northam 75-76; Nedlands 76-77; R of Rosalie-Shenton Pk 77-79; P-in-c of Lolworth 80-81; Conington 80-81. *42 Rosalie Street, Shenton Park, W Australia 6008.*

WEARING, Ian. SS Coll Cam BA 61, MA 65. Linc Th Coll 62. **d** 64 **p** 65 Derby. C of Chesterfield 64-68; St Ambrose Chorlton-on-Medlock and Asst Chap Univ of Man 68-69. *Bland's Cottage, Howgill, Sedbergh, Yorks.*

WEARMOUTH, Paul Frederick. b 37. Wells Th Coll 60. **d** 62 Man **p** 63 Hulme for Man. C of Ch Ch Bradford 62; St Thos Bedford Leigh 63-66; Prestbury 66-67; Ho Master Castleview Sch Hylton Castle from 71. *66 Solar House, Sunderland, SR1 3EQ.*

WEARNE, Mervyn Spencer. d 61 **p** 62 Armid. C of Narrabri 61-64; V of Mungindi 64-67; Manilla 67-69; Walgett 69-74; Perm to Offic Dio Bath from 75. *Cuttabunda, Goodooga, NSW, Australia 2838.*

WEARNE, Michael John. b 34. St Paul's Coll Grahmstn 76. **d** 78 **p** 79 Natal. C of St Martin Durban N Dio Natal from 78. *9 Regent Place, Durban North 4051, S Africa.*

WEARS, Robert. b 15. St Aid Coll 49. **d** 52 **p** 53 Dur. C of Stranton 52-55; V of Merrington 55-62; Ferryhill 62-80. *11 Cleveland Avenue, High Thirkley Park, Shildon, Co Durham, Dl2 2ND.*

WEATHERHEAD, Thomas Leslie. b 14. Hatf Coll Dur BA and LTh 37. St Aug Coll Cant 32. **d** 37 **p** 38 Ripon. C of H Spirit Beeston Hill 37-40; Wensley (in c of Leyburn) 40-42; Chap RAFVR 42-47; C of Halton 47-48; PC of New Mills 48-59; Surr 49-65; R of Staveley 59-65; Dean and R of Ch Ch Cathl Nassau 65-72; R of Felmingham 72-79; C-in-c of Suffield Dio Nor 72-74; R 74-79; C-in-c of Colby w Banningham and Tuttington 72-74; R 74-79; RD of Tunstead 76-79; Surr 78-79. *The Garth, West Burton, N Yorks, Dl8 4JS.*

WEATHERLEY, Stuart Matthew. b 36. ACT ThL 71. **d** 73 **p** 74 Wang. C of Shepparton 73-75; Wodonga 75-76; Maryborough 76-78; V of Pine Rivers N 78-80; R of Gatton Dio Brisb from 80. *68 Railway Street, Gatton, Queensland, Australia 4343.* (62 1006)

WEAVER, Canon Allan James. b 04. Lon Coll of Div 37. **d** 39 **p** 40 S'wark. [f Lay Miss] C of St Jude S'wark 39-41; Org Sec CMS Dios Dur and Newc T 41-43; V of St Jude S'wark 43; C-in-c of Ch Ch S'wark 43-48; R 48-67; C-in-c of St Paul S'wark 43-48; RD of S'wark and Newington 60-65; Hon Can of S'wark 63-67; Can (Emer) from 67; V of Clodock w Longtown Craswall and Llanveynoe 67-70. *2 Sunny Bank, Hilperton Road, Trowbridge, Wilts, BA14 7JE.*

WEAVER, Canon Cedric. b 12. Univ of Lon AKC 34, BD 44. **d** 35 **p** 36 Sheff. C of Kimberworth 35-38; C-in-c of Whinney Hill Conv Distr 38-45; V of Thorne 45-61; Surr 45-77; V of St Aid Doncaster 61-77; Warden Sheff Dioc Readers from 73; Hon Can of Sheff 73-77; Can (Emer) from 77; Perm to Offic Dios Sheff and Linc from 78. *Ulverton, Upperthorpe Road, Westwoodside, Doncaster, S Yorks DN9 2AQ* (Haxey 752373)

WEAVER, David Anthony. b 43. Hatf Coll Dur BSc (2nd cl Chem) 65. Lich Th Coll 68. **d** 71 **p** 72 Lich. C of Walsall Wood 71-75; Much Wenlock w Bourton 75-76; P-in-c of Fort Chimo 76-79; V of Mow Cop Dio Lich from 79. *Mow Cop Vicarage, Stoke-on-Trent, Staffs.* (S-o-T 515077)

WEAVER, Ven Douglas Charles. NZ Bd of Th Stud LTh 64. **d** 63 Bp McKenzie for Wel **p** 64 Wel. C of Ch Ch Wanganui 63-67; V of Waverley-Waitotara 67-71; Waiwhetu Dio Wel 71-75; Dir Chr Educn and Stewardship Dio Wel 75-78; V of Pahiatua Dio Wel from 78; Archd of Wairarapa from 80. *18 Albert Street, Pahiatua, NZ.* (7434)

WEAVER, Frank Joseph. St Aid Coll. **d** 46 **p** 47 Man. C of Eccles 46-51; V of Cadishead 51-70. *20 Woodgarth Lane, Worsley, Manchester, M28 4PS.* (061-794 3682)

WEAVER, George Edward. b 1900. **d** 53 **p** 54 Bp Stuart for Worc. C of St Geo Kidderminster 53-55; V of St Paul Tipton 55-57; Dilhorne 57-64; R of Drayton Bassett 64-71; C-in-c of

St Mary St Giles and All SS Conv Distr Canwell 64-71. *26 Priory Road, Old Swinford, Stourbridge, W Midl, DY8 2HG.* (Stourbridge 6888)

WEAVER, Gilbert Kneel. b 1895. St Steph Ho Ox 55. **d** 56 **p** 57 Ex. C of Bideford 56-58; V of Upottery 58-65. *Cleve, Upottery, Honiton, Devon.* (Honiton 239)

WEAVER, Canon John. Ex Coll Ox 3rd cl Mods 50, BA 51, 2nd cl Lit Hum 52, 2nd cl Th 54, MA 55. St Steph Ho Ox 52. **d** 55 **p** 56 Ex. C of St D Ex 55-58; Clydesdale 58-59; P-in-c of St Mark's Miss 59-65; Clydesdale w Umzimkulu 65-81; Hon Can of St John's 74-77 and from 81; Archd of E Griqualand 77-81; R of Springvale Dio Natal from 81. *PO Box 504, Ixopo 4630, S Africa.*

WEAVER, Kenneth Schofield. b 34 [f in CA]. **d** 77 **p** 78 Tor. C of Ch of the Resurr Tor 77-80; on leave. *777 Coxwell Avenue, Toronto, Canada, M4C 3C6.*

WEAVER, Michael Howard. b 39. Chich Th Coll 63. **d** 66 **p** 67 Worc. C of St Jo Bapt Kidderminster 66-69; Chap St Jo Bapt Cathl Belize 69-71; Team V of Droitwich 71-76; V of Arundel w S Stoke and Tortington Dio Chich from 76; Chap HM Pris Ford from 77. *Vicarage, Maltravers Street, Arundel, W Sussex.* (Arundel 882573)

WEAVER, Owen. Univ of Syd 49. PhC (NSW) 52. PhC MPS (GB) 53. Moore Th Coll Syd 57. ACT ThL (2nd cl) 58, Th Scho 66. **d** 58 Syd **p** 58 Bp Hilliard for Syd. C of Merrylands 58-59; Nowra 59-61; R of Port Hedland 61; C of St Clem Mosman 62-63; Chap at Norf I 63-65; C-in-c of Hillview 65-70. *3 Lions Avenue, Lurnea, NSW 2170, Australia.*

WEAVER, Paul Blake. b 48. Univ of Syd BA 69. ACT ThL 75. BD (Lon) 76. Moore Th Coll Syd 76. **d** 77 Syd. C of St Alb Epping 77-81; R of Botany-Mascot Dio Syd from 81. *6 Walker Avenue, Mascot, NSW, Australia 2020.* (667-1940)

WEAVER, Roy. b 38. Oak Hill Th Coll 63. **d** 66 Bp McKie for Cov **p** 67 Cov. C of Bedworth 66-69; Knutsford w Toft 69-72; All H Miss Ch Cheadle 72-74; R of Talke Dio Lich from 74. *Talke Rectory, Crown Bank, Stoke-on-Trent, Staffs, ST7 1PU.* (Kidsgrove 2348)

WEAVER, Canon Thomas James. b 04. **d** 53 **p** 54 Down. C of Maralin 53-55; St Geo and St Mich Stamford 55-56; R of St Steph Chorlton-on-Medlock 56-60; V of Ch Ch Kens W Derby 60-74; RD of Toxteth from 72; P-in-c of St Cypr Edge Hill Liv 74-75; V (w Ch Ch Toxteth) 75-77; Hon Can of Liv Cathl from 77. *24 Wirral View, Connah's Quay, Deeside, Clwyd, CH5 4TE.*

WEAVER, William. b 40. Univ of Man BA (Th) 63, BD 65. **d** 74 **p** 75 Ripon. Lect Leeds Univ from 67. *5 Hollin Drive, Leeds, LS16 5NE.* (Leeds 752096)

WEBB, Canon Albert. b 22. K Coll Lon AKC 49. St Bonif Coll Warm 49. **d** 50 **p** 51 Southw. C of Warsop w Sookholme 50-52; V of Cleeve Prior 52-59; H Innoc Kidderminster 59-66; Evesham Dio Worc from 66; Surr from 68; RD of Evesham 73-79; Hon Can of Worc from 75. *Vicarage, Croft Road, Evesham, Worcs, WR11 4NE.* (0386-6219)

WEBB, Alexander Harvey. b 07. [f Sol]. Linc Th Coll 36. **d** 38 **p** 39 Chelmsf. C of St Barn L Ilford 38-40; C-in-c of Stanford le Hope 40-41; Min of St Nich Conv Distr Elm Park w S Hornchurch 41-44; C of St Pet-in-Thanet (in c of St Andr Reading Street) 44-48; V of Laughton w Wildsworth 48-52; R of Sudbrooke w Scothern 52-59; V of Reepham 59-69; RD of E Lawres 61-64; Lawres 67-69; C of Holbeach 69-71; Perm to Offic Dio Lich from 71. *Flat 5, Abbeyfields House, Vyrnwy Place, Oswestry, Salop.* (Owestry 62564)

WEBB, Anthony John. b 24. Sarum Wells Th Coll 79. **d** 81 Taunton for B & W. C of Yeovil Dio B & W from 81. *9 Derwent Gardens, Yeovil, Somerset, BA21 5LJ.*

WEBB, Arthur George. b 11. K Coll Lon 33. **d** 38 Lon **p** 39 Willesden for Lon. C of St Paul Canonbury 38-41; Luton 41-46; V of All SS Haggerston 46-52; St Ethelburga St Leonards-on-Sea 52-60; Chapel Royal Brighton 60-77; Chap R Sussex County Hosp Brighton 64-77; Sidlesham 77-80; Perm to Offic Dio Lich from 80. *62 Wissage Road, Lichfield, Staffs, WS13 6SW.* (Lich 22562)

WEBB, Arthur Robert. b 33. LCP 67. Wells Th Coll 69. **d** & **p** 70 Lon. C of West Drayton 70-72; Min Can of St E from 72; Hd Master St Jas Cathl Middle Sch from 72; L to Offic Dio St E from 72; Succr of St E Cathl from 81. *3 Crown Street, Bury St Edmunds, Suff, IP33 1QX.* (Bury St E 3866)

WEBB, Charles John. b 1900. Roch Th Coll. **d** 60 **p** 61 S'wark. C of St Sav w St Matt Ruskin Pk 60-73; Perm to Offic Dio Chich from 73. *14a Grand Parade, St Leonards-on-Sea, TN37 6DN.* (Hastings 428106)

WEBB, Cyril George. b 19. Roch Th Coll 64. **d** 66 **p** 67 Bp Cornwall for Win. C of St Andr Bournemouth 66-71; V of Micheldever (and E Stratton w Woodmancote and Popham from 73) 71-79; C-in-c of E Stratton w Woodmancote and Popham 71-73; V of Bubwith w Ellerton and Aughton Dio York from 79. *Bubwith Vicarage, Selby, N Yorks.* (Bubwith 242)

WEBB, Daniel Edward. Univ of W Ont BA 63. Hur Coll BTh 66. **d** 66 **p** 67 Hur. C of Galt 66-69; R of Ch of Epiph Lon 69-72; Ch of Good Shepherd Woodstock 72-77; Paris Dio Hur from 77. *162 Grand River Street North, Paris, Ont., Canada.* (519-442 4334)

WEBB, David Basil. b 30. Ch Coll Cam BA 54, MA 58. Ripon Hall Ox 54. **d** 55 **p** 56 S'wark. C of Wimbledon 55-57; Chap Em Coll Cam 57-60; PC of Langley Mill 60-64; R of Farnborough Kent 64-73; Dunstable (Team R from 78) Dio St Alb from 73; RD of Dunstable from 81. *8 Furness Avenue, LU6 3BN.* (Dunstable 64467)

WEBB, Douglas. AKC (2nd cl) 40. Univ of Lon BD (1st cl) 40. Qu Coll Birm 40. **d** 41 **p** 42 Glouc. C of St Mark Glouc 41-43; U Beeding and Bramber w Botolphs 43-45; Shoreham 45-48; Wallasey 48-50; C and Sacr of Blackb Cathl 50-52; V of St Jas L Darwen 52-59; Wilburton Dio Ely from 59. *Wilburton Vicarage, Ely, Cambs.* (Haddenham 271)

WEBB, Eric Roland. b 1895. LRCP (Lon) 19. St George's Windsor. **d** 51 **p** 53 Ex. C of Heavitree 51-52; Whipton 52-55; C-in-c of Spreyton 55-56; V of Culgaith 56-66; V of Kirkland 56-66; L to Offic Dio Carl from 66. *81 Greengate, Levens, Kendal, LA8 8NF.* (Sedgwick 60745)

WEBB, George Cresswell Naesmyth. *See* Naesmyth of Posso, George Cresswell Naesmyth.

WEBB, George Humfrey Mackay. b 18. Worc Ordin Coll 66. **d** 68 Huntingdon for Ely **p** 69 Ely. C of Stow-Bardolph w Wimbotsham 68-72; C-in-c of (R & V from 73) of Hockwold w Wilton Dio Ely from 72; C-in-c (R from 73) of Weeting Dio Ely from 72. *Hockwold Rectory, Thetford, Norf.* (Feltwell 271)

WEBB, Graham James. b 31. **d** 75 **p** 76 Mon (APM). C of Griffithstown Dio Mon from 75. *2 Heol Teilo, New Inn, Pontypool, Gwent, NP4 5RP.*

WEBB, Graeme John. b 46. Univ of Vic NZ MA 68. St Jo Coll Auckld. **d** 78 **p** 79 Wel. C of Feilding 78-81; V of Taihape Dio Wel from 81. *Box 260, Taihape, NZ.*

WEBB, Harold William. b 37. Univ of Dur BA 59. St Steph Ho Ox. **d** 61 **p** 62 S'wark. C of St Nich Plumstead Kent 61-65; De Aar Kimb K 65; R of Prieska 65-68; Vryburg 68-70; Sacr of Wakef Cathl 71-72; V of Lane End Dio Ox from 72. *Lane End Vicarage, High Wycombe, HP14 3EX.* (High Wycombe 881913)

WEBB, Canon Ivo Frederick Fiennes. b 06. St Edm Hall, Ox BA 26, MA 31. Wells Th Coll 27. **d** 29 Bp Wood for Newc T **p** 30 Newc T. C of St Pet Wallsend 29-35; V of Seaton Hirst 35-48; Surr 40-76; R of Attleborough 48-76; Proc Conv Nor 50-69; RD of Rockland 66-70; Thetford and Rockland 70-76; Hon Can of Nor 70-76; Can (Emer) from 76; Perm to Offic Dio Truro from 76. *1 Summerfields, Saltash, Cornw, PL12 4AB.* (Saltash 6621)

WEBB, Canon Jack Raymond Conran. b 19. St Edm Hall Ox BA (3rd cl Mod Hist) 41. Cudd Coll 41. **d** 43 **p** 44 S'wark. C of St Cath Hatcham 43-47; Roehampton 47-50; Wimbledon (in c of St Mark) 50-53; V of St Pet Battersea 53-57; St Aug Croydon 57-65; Ch Ch S Ashford 65-72; V of St Francis W Wickham Dio Cant from 72; M Gen Syn Cant 72-80; Hon Can of Cant Cathl from 79. *2 Tae Grove, West Wichkam, Kent, BR4 9JS.* (01-777 6010)

WEBB, James Rowland. b 33. Roch Th Coll. **d** 67 **p** 68 Ex. C of Tavistock 67-70; Chap RN from 70. *c/o Ministry of Defence, Lacon House, Theobalds Road, WC1X 8RY.*

WEBB, John Christopher Richard. b 38. ACA 63. Wycl Hall Ox 64. **d** 67 Lon **p** 68 Willesden for Lon. C of Mill Hill 67-71; CF from 71. *Silverdale, Whalley Lane, Uplyme, Lyme Regis, Dorset.*

WEBB, John Stirling. b 46. Moore Coll Syd ThL 71. **d** 73 Syd **p** 73 Bp Robinson for Syd. C of Glenbrook 73-75; Asst Missr Dept of Evang 76-77; Min of St Martin Georges Hall Dio Syd from 77. *176 Birdwood Road, Georges Hall, NSW, Australia 2198.* (727 6258)

WEBB, Michael John. b 49. Linc Coll Ox BA (Th) 70, MA 74. Linc Th Coll 70. **d** 72 **p** 73 St Alb. C of Tring 72-75; Chipping Barnet (w Arkley from 78) 75-81; Team V of Cullercoats Dio Newc T from 82. *St Hilda's Vicarage, Preston Gate, Marden, North Shields, NE30 3UH.* (0632-576595

WEBB, Neville Edwin. b 33. BA (Lon) 60. Oak Hill Th Coll 55. **d** 60 **p** 61 Win. C of Shirley 60-62; Portsdown 62-65; Chap Aysgarth Sch Bedale 65-70; Temple Grove Sch 70-75; Denstone Prep Sch from 75. *Denstone Prep School, Smallwood Manor, Uttoxeter, Staffs, ST14 8NS.* (Uttoxeter 2014)

WEBB, Nicholas David Jon. b 38. Univ of Dur BA (2nd cl Cl) 61. Coll of the Resurr Mirfield 61. **d** 63 **p** 64 Wakef. C of Royston 63-66; Prec of Wakef Cathl 66-70; R of Thornhill Dio Wakef from 70; V of Lower Whitley Dio Wakef from 73. *Rectory, Frank Lane, Thornhill, Dewsbury, W Yorks WF12 0JW.* (Dewsbury 465064)

WEBB, Peter Henry. b 55. Univ of Nottm BA 77. St Steph Ho Ox 77. **d** 79 **p** 80 Chich. C of St Jas L Lancing 79-82;

Eastbourne (in c of St Pet Hydneye) Dio Chich from 82. *St Peter's Parsonage, The Hydneye, Hampden Park, Eastbourne, E Sussex.* (Eastbourne 54392)

WEBB, Richard Lacey. b 09. ALCD 30. **d** 32 Taunton for B & W **p** 33 B & W. C of Keynsham 32-35; R of Gt Wacton w L Wacton 36-41; V of Castleacre w Newton by Castleacre 41-49; Dioc Inspector of Schs 42-49; R of Garboldisham 49-66; Blo-Norton 49-66; RD of Rockland 63-66; V of St Alb Lakenham 66-77. *32 Ipswich Road, Norwich, NR4 6QR.* (Norwich 51348)

WEBB, Walter Herbert. **d** 22 **p** 24 Grahmstn. C of Queenstown CGH 22-26; C of St Thos Durban 26-28; P-in-c of Congella 28-33; V of St Mary Greyville Durban 33-46; CF (S Afr) 40-46; V of Stanger 46-51; C of St Thos Durban 51-52; R of Springfontein 53-56; Ficksburg and Dir of St Luke's Miss 56-61; C of St Marg Bloemf 60-61; St Marg Witbank 61-64; Germiston 64-65; R of St Phil w St Mark Port Eliz 65-66; Molteno 66-69; Steynsburg 66-69; L to Offic Dio Natal 69-70; Actg R of Umzinto 70-72. *4 Ocean View Road, Winklespruit, Natal, S Africa.*

WEBB, William John. b 43. Cudd Coll 68. **d** 71 **p** 72 Pet. C of Weston Favell Dio 71-73; Newport w Longford 74-77; Berkswich w Walton 77-79; P-in-c of Stonnall Dio Lich from 79; Wall Dio Lich from 79. *Stonnall Vicarage, Walsall, WMidl.* (Brownhills 2293)

WEBB, William Perceval. b 02. ALCD 32. **d** 32 **p** 33 Chelmsf. C of Walthamstow 32-35; Chap of Wrekin Coll 35-37; CF (TA) from 35; CF (EC) 39-42; Hon CF 42; V of St Mary Birkenhead 37-38; Hoylake 38-47; R of Barcombe 47-70; Perm to Offic Dio Chich from 70. *Tall Trees, Church Road, Buxted, Uckfield, Sussex.*

WEBBER, Eric Michael. AKC (2nd cl) 43, Sambrooke Exhib 42, Plumptre Pri 42 Bicknell Pri 43. Univ of Lon BD 54. ATh (S Afr) 54. **d** 43 **p** 44 S'wark. C of H Spirit Clapham 43-47; Wimbledon (in c of St Mark) 47-50; LPr Dio Zulu 50-51; R of Eshowe 51-56; Lapworth 56-58; R of Baddesley-Clinton 56-58; R and Dean of St D Cathl Hobart 59-71; Chap St Mich Colleg Sch Hobart from 59; Exam Chap to Bp of Tas 62-71; Commiss Polyn 62-68; Sen Lect Relig Educn Hobart Dio Tas from 71. *23 Delta Avenue, Taroona, Tasmania 7006.* (002-27 8378)

WEBBER, Harry Gill. b 09. AKC 41. **d** 41 **p** 42 S'wark. C of All SS S Wimbledon 41-44; LPr Dio Ox 44-48; C of Good Shepherd Conv Distr Ford Estate Bp Wearmouth 48-51; Min 51-52; PV and Sacr Linc Cathl 52-55; Succr 55-57; Hon PV from 57; V of Friskney 57-65; Dioc Insp of Schs Dio Linc 60-62; R of Claxby w Normanby-le-Wold 65-69; Nettleton 65-69; S Kelsey 65-69; N Owersby w Thornton-le-Moor 65-69; Stainton-le-Vale w Kirmond-le-Mire 65-69; Chap St John's Hosp Bracebridge Heath 69-74; Perm to Offic Dio Linc from 77. *124 Highgate, Cleethorpes, DN35 8NU.*

WEBBER, John Arthur. b 45. Keble Coll Ox BA 67, Dipl Th 68, MA 71. Cudd Coll 70. **d** 71 **p** 72 Llan. C of All SS Penarth 71-74; USPG Miss Dacca from 75. *c/o USPG, 15 Tufton Street, SW1 3QQ.*

WEBBER, Kenneth George. b 22. Sarum Wells Th Coll 75. **d** 78 Sarum **p** 79 Bp D J Wilson for Sarum (NSM). Hon C of Kinson Dio Sarum from 78. *20 Wicket Road, Bournemouth, BH10 5LT.*

WEBBER, Lionel Frank. b 35. St Mich Coll Llan 59. **d** 60 Hulme for Man **p** 61 Man. C of the Sav Bolton-le-Moors 60-63; Aberavon 63-65; R of Stowell Mem Ch Salford 65-69; V of H Trin Aberavon 69-74; Team V of Stantonbury 74-76; R of Basildon (and Nevendon from 78) Dio Chelmsf from 76; RD of Basildon from 79. *Rectory, Town Centre, Basildon, Essex, SS14 1DX.* (Basildon 22455)

WEBBER, Michael Champneys Wilfred. b 48. Univ of Man BA 71, MA (Th) 78. Cudd Coll 73. **d** 75 **p** 76 S'wark. C of Caterham 75-79; Kidbrooke (in c of St Nich) Dio S'wark 79-82; Team V from 82. *66a Whetstone Road, SE3 8PZ.* (01-856 6317)

WEBBER, Peter Cecil. b 21. ALCD 55. **d** 55 **p** 56 S'wark. C of St Luke Wimbledon Pk 55-58; V of St Jo Bapt Beckenham 58-67; St Jo Bapt Folkestone Dio Cant from 67; Chap Beckenham Maternity Hosp 58-67; RD of Elham from 80. *4 Cornwallis Avenue, Folkestone, Kent.* (Folkestone 53732)

WEBBER, Reginald. b 21. Bp's Coll Calc. **d** and **p** 65 Nagp. P Dio Nagp 65-68; C of St Mark w St Bart Dalston 69-70; H Trin Southall 70-73. *Address temp unknown.*

WEBER, Douglas John Craig. b 20. Ex Coll Ox 2nd cl Mods 40, BA and MA 46, 2nd cl Lit Hum 47. Sarum Th Coll. **d** 49 **p** 50 Portsm. C of St Mark Portsea 49-52; Alverstoke 52-55; V of Hook w Warsash Dio Portsm from 55. *112 Osborne Road, Warsash, Southampton, SO3 6GH.* (Locksheath 2324)

WEBSTER, Very Rev Alan Brunskill. b 18. Qu Coll Ox BA (2nd cl Mod Hist) 39, Liddon Stud 40, 2nd cl Th 41, MA 43, BD 54. Westcott Ho Cam 41. **d** 42 **p** 43 Sheff. C of Attercliffe w Carbrook and St Alb Darnall Sheff 42-44; Arbourthorne 44-46; Chap and Libr of Westcott Ho Cam 46-48; Vice-Prin 48-53; V of Barnard Castle 53-59; RD of Barnard Castle 54-59; Warden of Linc Th Coll 59-70; Can and Preb of Linc Cathl 64-70; Dean of Nor 70-78; M Gen Syn from 70; Ch Comm from 73; Dean of St Paul's Cathl Lon from 78. *9 Amen Court, EC4M 7BU.* (01-236 2827)

WEBSTER, David Edward. b 39. Edin Th Coll 62. **d** 64 Warrington for Liv **p** 65 Liv. C of Maghull 64-69; R of St Mary Wavertree 69-76; Team V of Greystoke 76-81; R of Lowton Dio Liv from 81. *Rectory, Slag Lane, Lowton, Warrington, Gtr Man, WA3 2ED* (0942-728434)

WEBSTER, David Robert. b 32. Selw Coll Cam BA (3rd cl th) 56, MA 60. Linc Th Coll 56. **d** 58 **p** 59 Dur. C of Billingham 58-61; Doncaster 61-64; Chap Doncaster R Infirm 61-64; V of Lumley 64-76; Belmont Dio Dur from 76. *Belmont Vicarage, Durham, DH1 2QW.* (Durham 61545)

WEBSTER, Dennis Eric. b 39. Fitzw Ho Cam 2nd cl Engl Trip pt i 59, BA (2nd cl Engl Trip pt ii) 60, MA 64. Linacre Coll Ox MA 70. Wycl Hall Ox 62. **d** 65 Cant **p** 66 Dover for Cant. C of Ch Ch Herne Bay 65-68; Tulse Hill 68-69; Missr in Kenya 70-75; Chap Pierrepont Sch Frensham from 75. *24 Longdown Road, Lower Bourne, Farnham, Surrey, GU10 3JC.*

WEBSTER, Derek Herbert. b 34. Univ of Hull BA 55. BD (Lon) 55. Univ of Leic MEducn 68, PhD 73. Linc Th Coll 76. **d** 76 Linc **p** 77 Grimsby for Linc (NSM) Lect Univ of Hull and C of Cleethorpes Dio Linc from 76. *25 Clee Road, Cleethorpes, S Humberside, DN35 8AD.*

WEBSTER, Canon Douglas. b 20. St Pet Coll Ox BA (2nd cl Th) 42, MA 46. Wycl Coll Tor Hon DD 67. Wycl Hall Ox 42. **d** 43 **p** 44 Liv. C of St Helens 43-46 (in c of St Andr 44-46); Ch Ch Crouch End 46-47; Tutor at Lon Coll of Div 47-53; L to Offic Dios S'wark and Lon 48-63; Dio Ox 63-66; Home Educn Sec CMS 53-61; Commiss U Nile 58-61; Theologian Missr CMS 61-65; Commiss Mbale from 61; Soroti from 63; Polyn 69-78; Exam Chap to Bp of Chelmsf from 62; Hon Can of Chelmsf 63-69; Chavasse Lect in World Miss Wycl Hall Ox 63-65; Prof of Miss Selly Oak Colls Birm 66-69; Can Res of St Paul's Cathl Lon from 69; Prec 69-82; Chan from 82; Commiss Niger from 75; Sub-Chap O of St John of Jer 77-81; Chap from 81. *1 Amen Court, EC4M 7BU.* (01-248 1817)

WEBSTER, Geoffrey William. b 36. St Alb Ministerial Tr Scheme 77. **d** 80 St Alb **p** 81 Hertf for St Alb. C of Harlington Dio St Alb from 80. *74 Brian Road, Harlington, Nr Dunstable, Beds.* (Toddington 2915)

WEBSTER, Preb George Raymond Munthe. b 07. Peterho Cam BA 28, MA 32. Cudd Coll 29. **d** 30 **p** 31 Ox. C of St Mary Virg (in c of St Sav from 35) Reading 30-42; V of Sunningdale 42-60; Surr from 46; V of H Trin Heref 60-75; RD of Heref City 70-75; Pastoral care of Bishopstone, Kenchester and Bridge Sollars Dio Heref from 73; Preb of Heref Cathl from 73. *Three Trees, Court Farm Lane, Tillington, Hereford.* (Hereford 760800)

WEBSTER, Glyn Hamilton. b 51. St Jo Coll Dur 74. **d** 77 **p** 78 York. C of All SS Huntingdon York 77-81; V of St Luke City and Dio York from 81. *70 Burton Stone Lane, York, YO3 6BZ.* (York 54232)

WEBSTER, James Harold. Em Coll Sktn 32, Hon DD 65. **d** 27 Yukon for M'Kenz R **p** 30 M'Kenz R. Miss at Bernard Harbour 27-28; Coppermine River 28-32; Miss at Shingle Point 33-34; Coppermine 34-52; Hon Can of Arctic 39-52; Archd of Aklavik 52-58; I of All SS Cathl Aklavik 52-58; Delaware 58-63; R of Walkerton 63-65; Blenheim 65-73. *Box 271, Ridgetown, Ont., Canada.*

WEBSTER, John Christopher. b 50. Univ of Newc T BA 73. Univ of Nottm Dipl Th 79. St Jo Coll Nottm 78. **d** 81 Dur. C of Gateshead Fell Dio Dur from 81. *14 Church Road, Gateshead, Tyne & Wear, NE9 5RD.*

WEBSTER, John Maurice. b 34. Sarum Wells Th Coll 73. **d** 76 **p** 77 Win. C of Hythe Dio Win from 76. *Avery Lodge, Long Lane, Marchwood, Southampton, Hants.*

WEBSTER, Kaye Anthony. ACT ThDip 70. **d** 65 **p** 66 Melb. C of Surrey Hills 65-68; Dept of Evangelism and Ex 68-71; I of Highett 71-81; R of Hagley w Westbury Dio Tas from 81. *St Mary's Rectory, Hagley, Tasmania 7257.* (003 92 2273)

WEBSTER, Martin Duncan. b 52. Univ of Nottm BSc 74, Dipl Th 76. Linc Th Coll 75. **d** 78 Chelmsf **p** 79 Bradwell for Chelmsf. C of Thundersley 78-81; Canvey I (in c of St Kath) Dio Chelmsf 81-82; Team V from 82. *5 Waterdene Mews, Canvey Island, Essex.* (Canvey 682586)

WEBSTER, Martyn Richard. b 54. St Chad's Coll Dur BA 76. St Steph Ho Ox 76. **d** 78 **p** 79 Worc. C of St Martin w St Pet Worc 78-81; Swindon New Town Dio Bris from 81. *135 County Road, Swindon, Wilts, SN1 2EB.* (0793-36679)

WEBSTER, Michael. b 21. Jes Coll Cam BA (2nd cl Hist Trip pt ii) 45, MA 47. Westcott Ho Cam 45. **d** 47 **p** 48 Cov. C of H Trin Leamington 47-50; Rugby (in c of St Geo) 50-53; V of Desborough 53-57; C-in-c of Rushton 55-57; V of Selly Oak 57-77; R of Lapworth Dio Birm from 77; Baddesley

Clinton Dio Birm from 77. *Lapworth Rectory, Solihull, W Midl, B94 5NX.* (Lapworth 2098)

WEBSTER, Peter. b 26. Cranmer Hall Dur 68. **d** 70 Bp Gerard for Sheff **p** 71 Sheff. C of Tickhill w Stainton 70-72; Conisborough 72-73; V of Walkley Sheff 73-77; Rawcliffe Dio Sheff from 77; Surr from 80. *Rawcliffe Vicarage, Goole, Humb.* (Goole 83298)

WEBSTER, Robert Leslie. Univ of Manit BA 67. Trin Coll Tor MDiv 72. **d** and **p** 72 Koot. on leave 72-73; I of Shuswap Lakes 74-78; C of All SS Winnipeg Dio Rupld from 78. *222 Furby Street, Winnipeg, Manit, Canada.*

WEDDERBURN, John Alroy. b 07. St Aid Coll 46. **d** 47 **p** 48 Blackb. C of Adlington 47-51; V of St Jo Div Coppull 51-54; Hornby w Claughton 54-72. *Beckermet Cottage, Ambleside Road, Windermere, Cumbria.*

WEDDERSPOON, Canon Alexander Gillan. b 31. Jes Coll Ox BA 54, MA 61. BD (Lon) 62. Cudd Coll. **d** 61 **p** 62 S'wark. C of Kingston T 61-63; Lect in Relig Educn Univ of Lon 63-66; Educn Adv C of E Sch Coun from 66; L to Offic Dio Lon 63-70; Can Res of Win Cathl from 70; Vice Dean from 80; Exam Chap to Bp of Win from 76. *5 The Close, Winchester, Hants.* (Winchester 64923)

WEDGWOOD, Preb Charles Mervyn. b 16. Selw Coll Cam 2nd cl Hist Trip pt i 37, BA (2nd cl Archaeol and Anthrop Trip) 38, MA 46. Wycl Hall Ox 38. **d** 40 Bp Willis for Leic **p** 41 Leic. C of Melton Mowbray 40-46; Chap RAFVR 42-46; V of Copt Oak 46-50; Kirby Muxloe 50-54; Chap to Towle Recovery Homes Woodhouse Eaves 46-50; RD of Sparkenhoe iii 53-54; V of Claughton w Grange 54-56; Keynsham w Qu Charlton 56-67; R of Burnett 56-67; Chap Keynsham Hosp 56-67; Wellington Hosps 67-72; Surr from 62; Preb of Wells Cathl from 63; V of Wellington w W Buckland (w Nynehead from 68) 67-72; C-in-c of Nynehead 67-68; V of Combe Downe (w Monkton Combe from 73 and S Stoke from 81) 72-81; RD of Bath 76-81. *12 Bailbrook Lane, Lower Swainswick, Bath, Avon, BA1 7AH.* (Bath 313866)

WEDGWOOD, George Peter. b 26. Univ of Dur BA 51, Dipl Th (w distinc) 52, MA 56. **d** 52 **p** 53 Carl. C of St Mark Barrow-F 52-54; Chap and Asst Master Sedbergh Sch 54-57; PC of St Cuthb Dur 57-63; Chap and Master Dur Hich Sch 58-63; Chap and Sen Lect in Div St Kath Coll Liv 63-69; Prin Lect from 69; Hd of Div Liv Inst of Higher Educn from 76. *St Katherine's College, Stand Park Road, Liverpool, L16 9JD.*

WEDGWOOD, Keith. b 20. Hertf Coll Ox Squire and Meeke Scho 40, BA (3rd cl Th) 42, MA 46. Wycl Hall Ox 42. **d** 43 **p** 44 Worc. C of Hartlebury 43-46; St Martin w Whittington Worc 46-49; Succr of All SS Cathl Derby 49-52; V Cho of Sarum Cathl 52-68; Succr 55-68; Publ Pr Dio Sarum 53-68; Surr 56-68; Asst Master Sarum Cathl Sch 52-68; R of Coverdale w Hillsboro Canada 68-72; C-in-c of Osmington w Poxwell 72-77; V of The Iwernes and Sutton Waldron Dio Sarum from 77; Fontwell Magna Dio Sarum from 81. *Iwerne Minster Vicarage, Blandford, Dorset, DT11 8NF.* (0747-8181129)

WEDGWOOD, Peter John. b 20. Worc Ordin Coll. **d** 66 **p** 67 Worc. C of Claines Dio Worc from 66; Hon Chap Alice Ottley Sch Worc from 73. *28 Cornmeadow Lane, Claines, Worcester, WR3 7NY.* (Worc 53730)

WEDMORE, John Foreshew. b 10. Ball Coll Ox BA and MA 37. Westcott Ho Cam 37. **d** 38 **p** 39 Birm. C of St Francis Bournville 38-44; Richmond 44-46; St Mich E Wickham 46-49; V of Ch Ascen Blackheath 49-68; Clevedon 68-76; Perm to Offic Dio Bris from 76. *71 Kingsdown Parade, Bristol, BS6 5UG.* (Bristol 425666)

WEEGAR, Donald Fraser. Bp's Univ Lennox BA 24, LST 26. **d** 26 **p** 27 Ott. C of Smith's Falls 26-28; I of Russell 28-35; Min of St Pet Merivale Ott 35-42; R of Clayton 42-47; Carleton Place 47-59; I of Iroquois 59-67. *PO Box 1766, Carleton Place, Ottowa 14, Canada.*

✠ **WEEKES, Right Rev Ambrose Walter Marcus.** b 19. CB 70. Plumtre Pri and AKC 41, Barry Pri 42. Linc Th Coll 41. **d** 42 **p** 43 Roch. C of St Luke New Brompton 42-44; Chap RNVR 44-46; RN 46-72; Chap of the Fleet and Archd for the RN 69-72; Hon Chap to HM the Queen from 69; Can of Gibr 71-73; Chap at Tangier 72-73; Dean of Gibr 73-77; Cons Asst Bp of Gibr in Chap of RN Coll Greenwich 25 July 77 by Bp of Lon; Bps of Roch, Chich, Fulham & Gibr, St Hel and Cyprus; and Bps Armstrong, Isherwood, Capper, Cabral and Swift; Apptd Bp Suffr of Dio Gibr in Eur 80; Dean of H Trin Cathl Brussels from 81. *5a Gregory Place, W8 4NG.* (01-937 2796)

WEEKES, David John. Magd Coll Cam BA 59, MA 68. K Coll Aber MTh 73. Clifton Th Coll 62. **d** 64 **p** 65 Ches. C of Cheadle 64-68; Chap Ntare Sch Mbarara 69-73; Fettes Coll Edin from 74. *Arniston House, Fettes College, Edinburgh, EH4 1QU.* (332-6301)

WEEKS, Canon Frank Ernest Walter. b 01. Linc Th Coll 44. **d** 45 **p** 46 Lon. C of St Cypr Clarence Gate 45-49; Loughton (in c of St Nich) 49; R of St Pet Peebles 51-63; P-in-c of St Andr Innerleithen 51-58; Dioc Chap Dio St Andr 63-69; R of Auchterarder 69-73; R of Muthill 69-73; Can of St Ninian's Cathl Perth 71-73; Hon Can from 74. *53 Oakbank Road, Perth, PH1 1HG.*

WEEKS, John Huguenin. b 28. TCD BA 53, MA 61. Sarum Th Coll 61. **d** 63 **p** 64 Lon. C of Hillingdon 63-69; V of St Faith Brentford 69-74; St Matt Yiewsley Dio Lon from 74. *93 High Street, Yiewsley, West Drayton, Middx.* (W Drayton 42093)

WEEKS, Jonathan Everton. b 41. Codr Coll Barb 74. **d** 76 **p** 77 Windw Is. Chap to Bp of Windw Is 76-79; P-in-c of St John Grenada Dio Windw Is from 79. *St John's Rectory, St John's, Grenada, W Indies.*

WEGOYE, Canon Yona. Buwalasi Th Coll 49. **d** 51 U Nile **p** 53 Bp Tomusange for U Nile. P Dio U Nile 51-61; Dio Mbale from 61; Hon Can of Mbale from 63; Tutor Buwalasi Th Coll 65-67. *PO Box 473, Mbale, Uganda.*

WEHREN, Niklaus. b 28. Open Univ BA 79. Cranmer Hall Dur. **d** 65 Blackb **p** 66 Lanc for Blackb. C of Ch Ch Blackpool 65-67; Watford 67-73; V of Stagsden Dio St Alb from 73. *Stagsden Vicarage, Bedford, MK43 8SQ.* (Oakley 3232)

WEIGALL, Anthony FitzRoy. b 12. Ch Ch Ox BA 34, MA 38. Westcott Ho Cam 34. **d** 36 **p** 37 Guildf. C of Dorking 36-39; CF (R of O) from 39; R of Brandon Ferry w Wangford 45-47; V of Rushmere St Andr 47-56; R of Barming 56-77; Perm to Offic Dio Ely from 79. *10 Hawthorne Road, Stapleford, Cambridge, CB2 5DU.*

WEIGHT, Norman Crossley. b 15. St D Coll Lamp BA 37. St Mich Coll Llan 39. **d** 39 Mon **p** 40 Llan for Mon. C of Llanhilleth 39-42; Rumney Mon 42-47; C-in-c of Llanddewi Fach w Llandegveth 47-53; R of St Mark Cheetham Hill Man 53-60; V of Shore Dio Man from 60. *Shore Vicarage, Littleborough, Lancs.* (Littleborough 78356)

WEIL, Canon Ernest James. b 13. Sarum Th Coll 50. **d** and **p** 53 Southw. C of St Jo Evang Carrington 53-56; V of St Bart Nottm 56-62; St Cypr Sneinton 62-68; Bawtry w Austerfield 68-74; V of Mission 68-74; Surr from 62; RD of Bawtry 68-74; Hon Can of Southw 73-78; Can (Emer) from 78; R of Epperstone 74-78; Gonalston 74-78; P-in-c of Oxton 74-78. *48 Springfield Road, Southwell, Notts, NG25 0BT.*

WEINSTOCK, Haim Zebulun. St Aid Coll 57. **d** 58 **p** 59 York. C of Marfleet 58-61; R of Sigglesthorne 61-68; Preston-in-Holderness 68-79; R of Sproatley 68-79. *c/o Preston Rectory, Hull, HU12 8TB.* (Hull 898375)

WEIR, John Michael Vavasour. b 48. AKC and BD 72. St Aug Coll Cant 72. **d** 73 **p** 74 St Alb. C of Hatfield Hyde 73-77; St Mich AA Watford 77-80; Asst Chap of St Edm Oslo 80-81; V of St Pet w St Thos Bethnal Green Dio Lon from 81. *Vicarage, St Peter's Avenue, E2 7AE.* (01-739 2717)

WEISS, Ivan Daniel. Univ of Natal BA Kelham Th Coll 54. **d** 58 **p** 59 Bloemf. C of St Marg Bloemf 58-60; Douglas Missr 60-61; Springfontein 61-62; V of Welkom 62-70; Can of Bloemf 68-70; Chap Rhodes Univ 71-74; C of St Mich and St Geo Cathl Ch Grahmstn 71-74; Sen Chap to Abp of Capetn 74-81; R of Green Point Dio Capetn from 80. *41 Cheviot Place, Green Point 8001, CP, S Africa.* (44-3847)

WEKANDA, Kusai. Bp Tucker Coll Mukono 63. **d** 64 **p** 65 Mbale. P Dio Mbale. *Church of Uganda, Kigunga, Uganda.*

WEKIYA, Silas. Bp Tucker Coll Mukono. **d** 59 Ugan **p** 61 Nam. P Dio Ugan 59-61; Dio Nam from 61. *c/o PO Box 4013, Bugembe, Uganda.*

WELANDER, Canon David Charles St Vincent. b 25. Univ of Lon 47. ALCD 47, BD 47. **d** 48 **p** 49 Nor. C of H Trin Heigham 48-51; Tutor Oak Hill Th Coll 51-52; Chap and Tutor Lon Coll of Div and L to Offic Dio LOn 52-56; PC of Iver 56-63; V of Ch Ch Cheltm 63-75; M Gen Syn from 71; RD of Cheltm 73-75; Can Res of Glouc from 75. *6 College Green, Gloucester, GL1 2LX.* (Gloucester 21954)

WELBOURN, David Anthony. b 41. K Coll Lon and Warm BD (2nd cl) and AKC 63. **d** 64 **p** 65 Dur. C of St Chad Stockton-on-Tees 64-67; S Westoe and Industr Chap Dio Dur 69-74; Industr Chap to Sunderland Chs 74-80; Industr Missr Dio Nor from 80. *6 Wroxham Road, Sprowston, Norwich, NR7 8TZ.* (Nor 401599)

WELBOURN, Frederick Burkewood. b 12. Em Coll Cam BA 34, MA 38. Trin Coll Cam Stanton Stud 37. Westcott Ho Cam 36. **d** 38 **p** 39 Ely. Chap of G and C Coll Cam 38-41; Trin Hall Cam 40-43; Gen Sec Schs SCM and LPr Dio Lon 43-46; Chap and Tutor Makerere Coll Kampala 46-55; Warden Mitchell Hall Makerere Univ Coll Kampala 55-64; Sen Lect 63-64; Exam Chap to Bp of Ugan 54-59; to Bp of Nam 60-64; Prin Dunford Coll 64-65; Lect Univ of Bris 66-78; L to Offic Dio Bris from 69. *44 Church Road, Winterbourn Down, Bristol BS17 1BX.*

WELBY, Peter Edlin Brown. b 34. Open Univ BA 75. St Jo

Coll Dur 75. **d** 77 **p** 78 Dur. C of Bp Auckld 77-79; S Westoe 79-81; V of Tudhoe Dio Dur from 81. *21 York Villas, Tudhoe, Spennymoor, Co Durham, DL16 6LP* (Spennymoor 3147)

WELCH, Charles. b 04. St Aid Coll 61. **d** 62 **p** 63 York. C of St Barn Linthorpe 62-66; R of Foston w Flaxton 66-76. *Ataraxia, Thornton-le-Clay, York.*

WELCH, Derek. Keble Coll Ox BA 51, MA 57. Coll of Resurr Mirfield 51. **d** 53 **p** 54 York. C of St Jo Middlesbrough 53-58; Oswaldtwistle 58-59; V of St Andr Accrington 59-65; Salesbury 66-72; St Annes-on-Sea Dio Blackb from 73. *Vicarage, St Annes-on-Sea, Lancs.* (St Annes-on-Sea 722725)

WELCH, Ernest John. b 08. Worc Ordin Coll 58. **d** 60 **p** 61 Ex. C of Torrington 60-62; Tamerton Foliot 62-64; R of Halwill w Beaworthy 64-73; Publ Pr Dio Truro 73-78. *31 Glenfield Place, Hodge Lea, Milton Keynes, Bucks, MK12 6JH.*

WELCH, Francis Hughan. b 16. BD (Lon) 67. SOC 67. **d** 70 **p** 71 St Alb. L to Offic St Pet St Alb 70-71; C of St Steph St Alb 71-75; C-in-c 75-80; Chap St Alb City Hosp 80-81; C of St Pet City and Dio St Alb from 81. *2 Pondwicks Close, St Albans, Herts, AL1 1DG.* (St Alb 57247)

WELCH, Frederick George. b 23. St Cath Coll Cam BA 44, MA 48. BD (Lon) 59. St Aug Coll Cant 63. **d** 74 Mt Kenya **p** 76 Bp Ngaruiya for Mt Kenya S. P Dio Mt Kenya 74; Mt Kenya S from 75. *Alliance High School, Box 7, Kikuyu, Kenya.* (Kikuku 2195)

WELCH, Grant Keith. b 40. K Coll Lon and Warm AKC 63. **d** 64 **p** 65 Southw. C of Nottm 64-68; V of Cinderhill 68-73; R of Weston Favell Dio Pet from 73; Master of St John's Hosp Weston Favell from 73; Surr from 76. *Weston Favell Rectory, Northampton.* (Northampton 43162)

WELCH, Harold. b 1887. **d** 28 **p** 29 Nagp. BCMS Miss at Sagor 28-34 and 35; CF (Ind) 42-46; Hon CF 46; Can of Nagp 48-51; PC of St George Gt Yarmouth 51-56; R of Sharrington 56-62; C-in-c of Hunworth w Stody 56-62; R of Easton w Letheringham 62-66; L to Offic Dio St E 66-74; Perm to Offic Dio Ches from 75. *3 Wynnstanley House, Northwich Road, Knutsford, Chesh.*

WELCH, Harold Gerald. b 16. St Cath S Ox BA 3rd cl Phil Pol and Econ 48, MA 53. Wycl Hall Ox 48. **d** 50 **p** 51 St E. C of St Jo Bapt Ipswich 50-53; V of Offton w Willisham and Nettlestead 53-58; St Paul Lozells 58-65; Austrey Dio Birm from 66; Warton Dio Birm from 66. *Vicarage, Austrey, Atherstone, Warws, CV9 3EB.*

WELCH, Ivor Thomas Ronald. b 29. Coll of Ven Bede Dur BA 53. Trin Coll Bris 79. **d** 81 Pet. C of Desborough Dio Pet from 81. *5 Cromwell Close, Desborough, Kettering, Northants, NN14 2PJ.* (Kettering 761809)

WELCH, Ven Malcolm Cranstoun. Ch Ch Coll. **d** and **p** 61 Wel. C of St Pet Wel 61-64; Chap Well Hosp 64-69; V of Greymouth 69-76; All SS City and Dio Nel from 76; Archd of Mawhera 75-76; Nel from 76. *30 Vanguard Street, Nelson, NZ.* (84-383)

WELCH, Michael Robin. b 33. MBE 81. St Chad's Coll Dur BSc 55. Wells Th Coll 57. **d** 59 **p** 60 Dur. C of St Hilda S Shields 59-63; CF (R of O) from 61; Warden and Tr Officer Newc T Dioc Youth Tr Centre 63-68; Social and Industr Adv Dio Portsm from 68; V of All SS Portsea w St Jo Bapt Rudmore Dio Portsm from 72. *All Saints Vicarage, Commercial Road, Portsmouth, Hants.* (Portsmouth 20983)

WELCH, Canon Sidney. St Jo Coll Morpeth 57. **d** 59 **p** 60 Graft. C of Lismore 59-61; V of Wyan w Rappville 61-63; R of Bellingen 63-69; Port Macquarie Dio Graft from 70; Can of Graft from 71. *Rectory, Port Macquarie, NSW 2444, Australia.* (065 831031)

WELCH, Stephan John. b 50. Univ of Hull BA 74. Univ of Birm Dipl Th 76. Qu Coll Birm 74. **d** 77 **p** 78 St Alb. C of Waltham Cross 77-80; V of Reculver Dio Cant from 80. *Reculver Vicarage, Bishopstone Lane, Herne Bay, Kent, CT6 6RA.* (Herne Bay 5154)

✠ **WELCH, Right Rev William Neville.** b 06. Keble Coll Ox BA 27, MA 32. Wycl Hall Ox 27. **d** 29 **p** 30 Worc. C of Kidderminster 29-32; St Mich St Alb 32-34; Org Sec Miss to Seamen for E Distr 34-39; L to Offic Dio Chelmsf 33-39; Perm to Offic Dios Ely, Nor and St E 33-39; V of Grays Thurrock 39-43; Gt Ilford 43-53; Gt Burstead 53-56; Surr from 43; RD of Barking 46-53; Proc Conv Chelmsf 47-51; Hon Can of Chelmsf 51-53; Archd of Southend 53-72; Cons Ld Bp Suffr of Bradwell in S'wark Cathl 25 April 68 by Abp of Cant; Bps of Chelmsf; Roch; Cov; Chich; and Sarum; Bps Suffr of Grimsby; Colchester; Barking; Aston; Dover; and Buckingham; and Bp McKie; res 73. *112 Earlham Road, Norwich, Norf, NR2 3HE.*

WELCHMAN, Richard Neville de Beaufort. b 11. St Pet Hall Ox BA (2nd cl Engl Lang and Lit) 33, Dipl Th (w distinc) 34, MA 37. Wycl Hall Ox 33. **d** 34 **p** 35 Ex. C of St Andr Plymouth 34-40; CF (EC) 40-45; CF (TA) from 48; PC of Yelverton 45-54; R of Lifton 54-62; Kelly w Bradstone 59-62; RD of Tavistock 56-61; V of Pinhoe 62-76; Publ Pr Dio Ex from 77. *Flat 5, Culver, Longdown, Exeter, Devon.*

WELCHMAN, Roger de Beaufort. b 08. Qu Coll Cam BA (2nd cl Th Trip pt i) 30, MA 34. Wycl Hall Ox 30. **d** 31 **p** 32 Ex. C of St Andr (in c of St Cath from 35) Plymouth 31-39; PC of St Matthias Plymouth 39-55; Chap RAFVR 41-45; Surr 49-55; R of Corfe Castle 55-73. *Larksgate, Townsend Mead, Corfe Castle, Wareham, Dorset, BH20 5EU.* (Corfe Castle 480334)

WELDON, Francis John. St Paul's Coll Grahmstn 61. **d** 64 **p** 65 Grahmstn. C of St Cuthb Port Eliz 64-68; P-in-c of All SS Port Eliz 68-70; Adelaide and Bedford 70-78; R of St Jo Bapt Ft Beaufort 75-76; St Jas Graaff Reinet Dio Geo from 78. *35 Somerset Street, Graaff Reinet, CP, S Africa.*

WELDON, William Ernest. b 41. TCD BA 62, MA 66. **d** 64 **p** 65 Connor. Miss of Trin Coll Miss Belf 64-67; C of Carmoney 67-71; Chap RN from 71. *c/o Ministry of Defence, Lacon House, Theobalds Road, WC1X 8RY.*

WELFORD, Alan Traviss. Late Scho of St Jo Coll Cam 1st cl Nat Sc Trip pt i 34, BA 35 3rd cl Th Trip pt i 36, 1st cl Mor Sc Trip pt ii 37, MA 39, ScD 64. **d** 37 **p** 38 Roch. C of Crayford 37-38; Chap St Jo Coll Cam 38-45; Jun Bursar 40-45; Fell and Tutor from 56; Select Pr Univ of Cam 43; LPr Dio Ely 45; Princeton Univ USA 45-46; Lect in Experimental Psychology Univ of Cam 47-68; Prof of Psychology Univ of Adel 68-79; Perm to Offic Dio Adel 68-79. *c/o 86 Mackinnon Parade, N Adelaide, S Australia 5006.*

WELHAM, Clive Richard. b 54. **d** 80 **p** 81 S'wark. C of Bellingham Dio S'wark from 80. *51 Dunfield Road, SE6.*

WELLARD, Colin Herbert. St Jo Coll Morpeth ACT ThL 59, Th Scho 66. **d** 58 **p** 59 Armid. C of Armid 58-60; P-in-c of Collarenebri 60-64; Boggabilla 64-68; V of Bundarra Dio Armid from 68. *Vicarage, Bundarra, NSW, Australia 2359.* (Bundarra 21)

WELLER, John Beresford. b 15. Tyndale Hall Bris 39. Univ of Lon BD 52. **d** 42 Lewes for Chich **p** 43 Chich. C of H Trin Worthing 42-44; V of Hemingford Grey 44-49; Em Ch Wimbledon 49-54; H Trin Heigham 54-60; Harlow 60-77; Chap Hillingdon Hosp 60-75; Bp Herbert Ho Nor 60; Harlow Coll 61-65; Surr 61-80; RD of Harlow 73-80; V of Hatfield Broad Oak and Bush End 77-80; Hon C of Duffield Dio Derby from 81. *19 Milford Road, Duffield, Derby.*

WELLER, John Christopher. b 25. St Pet Hall Ox BA 49 (2nd cl Phil Pol and Econ) 50, MA 52. Univ of Nottm BD 57. Qu Coll Birm 50. **d** 51 **p** 52 Southw. C of All SS Nottm 51-54; St Jas Conv Distr Porchester Nottm 54-58; R of Highlands 58-64; Exam Chap to Bp of Mashon 62-64; Warden St John's Sem Lusaka 64-71; Min of St Anne's Eccles Distr West Heath 71-81; Exam Chap to Bp of Birm from 71; Warden and Chap Resthaven Home Dio Glouc from 81. *Resthaven, Pitchcombe, Nr Stroud, Glos, GL6 6LS.* (0452-812682)

WELLER, Richard Morton. b 33. Selw Coll Cam BA 57, MA 61. Wells Th Coll 61. **d** 63 Bp McKie for Cov **p** 64 Cov. C of Stockingford 63-66; Pontefract 66-68; C-in-c of St Jas Conv Distr Stockton-on-Tees 68-74; V of E Ardsley Dio Wakef from 74. *Vicarage, East Ardsley, Wakefield, W Yorks, WF3 2LJ.* (Wakefield 822184)

WELLER, Ronald Howden. Wycl Hall Ox. **d** 60 **p** 61 Birm. C of Edgbaston 60-63; V of Broxbourne 63-70; Hon Can and V of St Andr Cathl Sing 70-74; L to Offic Dio Dun from 74. *Box 108, Wakatipu, Otago, NZ.*

WELLER, William John France. MBE (Mil) 58. Ridley Hall Cam 60. **d** 61 **p** 62 Ex. C of St Aug Plymouth 61-63; Ringwood 63-65; R of Stratfieldsaye (w Hartley Wespall 74) 65-75; C-in-c of Hartley Wespall w Stratfield Turgis 65-74; RD of Odiham 69-74; P-in-c of Southwick w Boarhunt 75-78; Perm to Offic Dio Ex from 78. *1 Kerri House, The Square, N Tawton, Devon.*

WELLING, Anthony Wyndham. b 29. Ely Th Coll 55. **d** 58 Ches. C of St Paul Coppenhall Crewe 58-60. *Broadway Barn, High Street, Ripley, Surrey.* (0483 225384)

WELLINGS, Preb Horace Henry. Fitzw Hall Cam BA 19, MA 23. **d** 19 Man for Carl **p** 20 Carl. C of St Jas Carl 19-24; St Geo Birm 24-27; V of St Paul W Brixton 27-34; St Geo Newc L 34-63; Preb of Pipa Parva in Lich Cathl 59-65; Preb (Emer) from 65; Surr 57-65; R of Ightfield w Calverhall 63-65. *6 The Bungalows, Terry's Cross, Woodmancote, Henfield, Sussex.* (Henfield 493487)

WELLINGTON, Lord Bishop of. *See* Norman, Right Rev Edward Kinsella.

WELLINGTON, Assistant Bishops of. *See* Wiggins, Right Rev Maxwell Lester; and Rosevear, Right Rev William James Watson.

WELLINGTON, Dean of. *See* Thomas, Very Rev James.

WELLINGTON, Canon Douglas Arthur. St Francis Coll Brisb ACT ThL 48. **d** 48 **p** 49 N Queensld. C of St John Cairns 48-51; Miss P at Simanggang 52-54; Saratok 54-56; Mirani 56-60; R of Ingham 61-67; St Pet Townsville 67-79; Can of N

Queensld from 72; Perm to Offic Dio Syd from 79. *50 Tulip Street, Greystanes, NSW, Australia 2145.*

WELLINGTON, James Frederick. b 51. Univ of Leic LLB 72. Fitzw Coll Cam BA 76. Ridley Hall Cam 74. **d** 77 Edmon for Lon **p** 78 Lon. C of John Keble Ch Mill Hill 77-80; St Mich Wood Green Dio Lon from 80. *24 Berwick Road, N22 5QB.* (01-888 7532)

WELLINGTON, Wilfrid Lloyd. Rhodes Univ Grahmstn BA 36. St Paul's Coll Grahmstn LTh 38. **d** 38 **p** 39 Johann. C of St Mary's Cathl Johann 38-42; R of Nigel 42-43; CF (S Afr) 42-46; C of Germiston 46-47; R of Roodepoort 47-49; V of Newcastle 49-52; St Cypr Durban 52-60; Estcourt 60-68; Archd of Ladysmith 60-68; Dean and R of St Sav Cathl Pmbg 68-76; Perm to Offic Dio Natal from 79. *Chapter Close, Taunton Road, Pietermaritzburg, Natal, S Africa.*

WELLMAN, Jack Dover. St Cath S Ox BA (3rd cl Th) 47, MA 52. Ripon Hall Ox 45. **d** 47 **p** 48 Roch. C of Ch Ch Dartford 47-49; St Marg Lee 49-51; St Mich Chester Square 51-53; Chap RAF 53-55; V of Em Hampstead Dio Lon from 56. *Emmanuel Vicarage, Lyncroft Gardens, NW6 1JU* (01-435 1911)

WELLOCK, Peter Noel. Univ of Melb BA 56, B Educn 60. ACT ThL (1st cl) 62. Murdoch Univ W Austr PhD 77. **d** 59 **p** 60 St Arn. C of Mildura 59-62; L to Offic Dio Syd 63-64; Tutor St Jo Bapt Th Coll Suva 64-65; C of H Trin Cathl Suva 64-66; V of Laucala Bay Suva 66-68; Perm to Offic Dio Polyn 69-70; Exam Chap to Bp of Polyn 71-72; Dioc Educn Officer Polyn 70-72; Dir Coun for Chr Educn Dio Perth 73-78; Curriculum Officer Educn Dept W Austr from 78; Perm to Offic Dio Perth from 78. *40 Napier Street, Cottesloe, W Australia 6011.* (384 2353)

WELLS, Archdeacon of. *See* Haynes, Ven Peter.

WELLS, Bishop of. *See* Bath and Wells

WELLS, Dean of. *See* Mitchell, Very Rev Patrick Reynolds.

WELLS, Andrew Stuart. b 48. St Jo Coll Dur BA 71, Dipl Th 73. **d** 74 Hulme for Man **p** 75 Middleton for Man. C of Walmsley 74-77; H Family Failsworth 77-79; R of Openshaw Dio Man from 79. *30 Ornsay Walk, Openshaw Village, Manchester, M11 2JA.* (061-231 4365)

WELLS, Antony Ernest. b 36. Oak Hill Th Coll 58. **d** 61 **p** 62 Lon. C of St Jas L Bethnal Green 61-64; Miss SAMS Asuncion Paraguay 64-69; V of St Athanasius Kirkdale 69-73; Miss SAMS Argent 73-75; V of Warfield 75-81; St Jo Div Fairfield City and Dio Liv from 81. *St John's Vicarage, Lockerby Road, Liverpool, L7 0HG.* (051-263 4001)

WELLS, Anthony Martin Giffard. b 42. St Jo Coll Nottm 72. **d** 74 **p** 75 Roch. C of Ch Ch Orpington 74-78; P-in-c of Odell Dio St Alb from 78; Pavenham Dio St Alb from 78; RD of Sharbrook from 81. *Odell Rectory, Church Lane, Odell, Bedford, MK43 7AA.* (Bedford 720234)

WELLS, Bryan Arthur. b 47. Univ of Lon BMus 72. Coll of the Resurr Mirfield 77. **d** 79 Bradwell for Chelmsf. C of St Marg Leigh 79-80. *c/o 38 Fleming Avenue, Leigh-on-Sea, Essex, SS9 3AW.*

WELLS, Canon Charles. b 07. Late Exhib of Ch Coll Cam 2nd cl Mod Lang Trip 26, BA (2nd cl Engl Trip) 28, MA 32. Westcott Ho Cam 28. **d** 30 Bradf **p** 31 York for Bradf. C of St Osw Chapel Green L Horton 30-32; Guiseley 33-34; H Trin S Shore (in c of St Mary) Blackpool 34-38; V of Habergham 38-44; All SS w St Pet R Stamford 44-54; St Bart Hyde Win 55-73; RD of Win 62-71; Hon Can of Win 70-73; Can (Emer) from 73. *Pines, Clewers Hill, Waltham Chase, Southampton.*

WELLS, Christopher Paul. b 49. Univ of Wales (Cardiff) Dipl Th 77. St Mich Aa Coll Llan 74 **d** 77 **p** 78 St A. C of Flint 77-80. *c/o 273 Chester Road, Flint, Clwyd, CH6 5SE.* (Flint 2086)

WELLS, Colin Durant. b 20. Univ of Lon BSc 43. St Deiniol's Libr Hawarden 76. **d** 78 Ban **p** 80 Ches. C of Llanidan 78; Perm to Offic Dio Ches from 80. *Key House Farm, Smith Lane, Mobberley, Knutsford, Cheshire, WA16 6JY.*

WELLS, David Henry Nugent. b 20. Late Scho of St Chad's Coll Dur 39, BA (1st cl Cl) 42, MA 46, Dipl Th (w distinc) 47. **d** 47 **p** 48 Lich. C of St Paul Wednesbury 47-48; Rugeley 48-50; Hanley 50-53; R of Leigh Staffs 53-57; Ashley 57-64; V of Hales 57-64; Alrewas w Fradley 64-73; V of Wichnor 64-73; R of Upton Magna 73-81; V of Withington 73-81; V of Uffington, Upton Magna and Withington Dio Lich from 81. *Upton Magna Rectory, Shrewsbury, Salop, SY4 4TZ.* (Upton Magna 283)

WELLS, Donald Edwin Leonard. St Chad's Coll Regina. **d** 56 **p** 58 Qu'App. I of Major 56-58; Mortlach 58-61; I of Ogema 63-66; Rocanville 66-70; R of Biggar 70-76; Oxbow 76-80; Raymore Dio Qu'App from 80. *Box 333, Raymore, Sask, Canada.*

WELLS, Canon Edward Arthur. b 23. Oak Hill Th Coll. **d** 57 **p** 58 Lich. C of Heath Town 57-60; R of Mettingham w Ilketshall St John 60-62; Sproughton (w Burstall from 63) from 62; V of St Nich Ipswich 74-80; Hon Can of St E Cathl from 79; Chap Ipswich Hosp from 80. *1 Crescent Road, Ipswich, Suff.* (0473-54046)

WELLS, Eric George. b 09. Wycl Hall Ox 42. Univ Lon Dipl in Th 44. **d** and **p** 43 Roch. C of St Jas Tunbridge Wells 43-46; V of All S Eastbourne 46-57; S w N Bersted 57-79; RD of Bognor 61-77; Perm Offic Dio Chich from 78. *12 Princess Avenue, Bognor Regis, Sussex, PO21 2QT.* (0243-863337)

WELLS, Ernest Stanley. Univ of W Ont BA 44. Hur Coll LTh 44. **d** 42 **p** 44 Hur. C of Pelee I 42-44; Merlin 44; Ailsa Craig Brinsley and McGillivray 44-47; St Mark Windsor 47-51; R of Petrolia 51-54; Strathroy 54-62; Leamington 62-72; St Paul and St Steph Stratford 72-81; Can of Hur 69-81. *192 Cobourg Street, Stratford, Ont, Canada.*

WELLS, Fred Elliott. d and **p** 50 River. C of Broken Hill 50-54; R of Riverton 54-59; P-in-c of Somerton Pk 59-66; Warradale w Darlington 66-68; Parkside 68-76. *7 St Anne's Place, Parkside, S Australia 5063.* (08-71 3254)

WELLS, George Reginald. b 11. K Coll Cam 3rd cl Cl Trip pt i 31, BA (2nd cl Th Trip pt i) 33. Cudd Coll 33. **d** 34 **p** 35 Wakef. C of Penistone 34-37; Chap St Paul's Sch Darjeeling 38-45; Miss Dio Nagp 46-58; Archd of Nagp 57-61; P-in-c of All SS Cathl Nagp 58-61; V of Hagbourne 61-74; P-in-c of Gt Coxwell w Coleshill 74-80; Buscot 74-80; Eaton Hastings 74-80. *8 Greystone Avenue, Dumfries, Scotland.*

WELLS, Jeremy Stephen. b 47. Univ of Nottm BA 69. Chich Th Coll 72. **d** 73 **p** 74 Birm. C of St Mich AA S Yardley 73-76; St Marychurch, Torquay 76-78; C-in-c of H Trin Bridgwater Dio B & W from 78. *Holy Trinity Vicarage, Hamp Street, Bridgwater, Somt.* (Bridgwater 2610)

WELLS, John. b 11. Kelham Th Coll 29. **d** 34 **p** 35 Bradf. C of St Luke Eccleshill 34-37; St Benedict Ardwick 37-41; C-in-c of Horton Bank Top Conv Distr 41-51; R of St Gabr Hulme Man 51-57; M Bro of St Barn (N Queensld) 57-60; Min of Mary Kathleen 57-60; Chap of N Staffs R Infirm and City Gen Hosp Stoke-on-Trent 62-76; Perm to Offic Dio Southw from 76. *4 Upton Field, Southwell, Notts, NG25 0QA.* (Southwell 812310)

WELLS, John Michael. b 35. Late Exhib of Mert Coll Ox BA 58, MA 61. Westcott Ho Cam 60. **d** 62 **p** 63 Chelmsf. C of Hornchurch 62-64; St Marg Barking 64-66; H Trin Hermon Hill Wanstead 66-69; V of St Nich Elm Pk Hornchurch 69-76; R of Wakes Colne w Chappel 76-79; Hon Chap of Chelmsf Cathl 79-81; Project Officer to Cathl Centre Chelmsf 79-81; CMS Area Sec Dios Chelmsf and Ely from 81; Perm to Offic Dio Ely from 81. *Arlington, Links Drive, Chelmsford, CM2 9AW.*

WELLS, (David) John Rowse. Kelham Th Coll 53. M SSM 57. **d** 57 **p** 58 Southw. LPr Dio Southw 57-59; L to Offic Dio Adel 59-65; Tutor St Mich Th Coll Crafers 63-65; Asst P at Teyateyaneng 65-67; R of Mantsonyane 67-72; Miss at All SS Modderpoort 72-76. *St Augustine's Priory, Modderpoort, OFS, S Africa.* (Modderpoort 1)

WELLS, Mark Wynne-Eyton. b 20. Peterho Cam BA 48, MA 54. Westcott Ho Cam 48. **d** 50 **p** 51 Chich. C of Heene 50-53; Sullington 53-57; R of Slinfold Dio Chich 57-59; C of Umtali 59-62; V of Stoke-by-Nayland Dio St E from 62; V of Levenheath Dio St E from 63; RD of Hadleigh 71-76. *Vicarage, Stoke-by-Nayland, Colchester, Essex, CO6 4QH.* (Nayland 262248)

WELLS, Norman Charles. b 18. Keble Coll Ox BA (2nd cl Th) 40, MA 44. St Steph Ho Ox 40. **d** 42 **p** 43 Lon. C of St Alb Teddington 42-46; St Aug Kens 46-52; V of St Pet Fulham 52-62; St Marg-on-Thames 62-73; Highbridge Dio B & W from 73; RD of Burnham from 76; Exam Chap to Bp of B & W from 76. *Vicarage, Highbridge, Somt.* (Burnham-on-Sea 783671)

WELLS, Oswald Bertie. b 18. Linc Th Coll M SSF 56. **d** 48 **p** 49 Man. C of Leigh Lancs 48-51; C-in-c of St Phil and St Jas Plaistow 57-59; Fr Guardian SSF 59-66; C of Loughton Dio Chelmsf from 81. *2 Baldwins Hill, Loughton, Essex.* (01-508 4602)

WELLS, Canon Rex Albert. b 10. Ex Coll Ox BA 33, MA 36. Ripon Hall Ox 32. **d** 34 **p** 35 St Alb. C of Luton 34-37; V Cho of Sarum Cathl 37-44; Publ Pr Dio Sarum 38-44; V of St Aldhelm Branksome 44-51; Iwerne Minster w Sutton Waldron 51-75; The Iwernes and Sutton Waldron 75-77; Hon Chap to Bp of Sarum from 62; RD of Sturminster Newton 64-72; Blackmore Vale 73-77; Can and Preb of Sarum Cathl 72-77; Can (Emer) from 77; Warden Coll of St Barn Lingfield from 77; Publ Pr Dio S'wark from 77. *College of St Barnabas, Blackberry Lane, Lingfield, Surrey, RH7 6NJ.* (Dorman's Park 366)

WELLS, Richard John. b 46. St Mich Coll Llan Dipl Th 70. Cudd Coll 70. **d** 71 York **p** 72 Hull for York. C of St Alb Hull 71-75; Addlestone 75-80; V of Weston, Surrey Dio Guildf from 80. *1 Chestnut Avenue, Esher, Surrey.* (01-398 1849)

WELLS, Robert Crosby. b 28. St Jo Coll Dur BA 52. **d** 54

Lanc for Blackb **p** 55 Blackb. C of H Trin S Shore Blackpool 54-59; C-in-c of St Chris Conv Distr Lea Lancs 59-69; V of Ribby w Wrea Dio Blackb from 69. *Wrea Green Vicarage, Ribby Road, Preston, Lancs, PR4 2NA.* (Kirkham 683587)

WELLS, Roderick John. b 36. Univ of Dur BA (2nd cl Th) 63. Cudd Coll 63. **d** 65 **p** 66 S'wark. C of St Mary Lambeth 65-68; C-in-c 68-71; R of Skegness (w Winthorpe from 77) 71-78; P-in-c of Winthorpe 77; R of Gt and L Coates w Bradley Dio Linc from 78. *28 Great Coates Road, Grimsby, Humb.* (Grimsby 54878)

WELLS, Ronald Charles. b 20. AKC 50. St Bonif Coll Warm. **d** 51 **p** 52 Chelmsf. C of Prittlewell 51-56; Min of St Aid Eccles Distr Leigh-on-Sea 56-65; R of All SS Springfield 65-80; V of St Pet Prittlewell Dio Chelmsf from 80. *Vicarage, Eastbourne Grove, Westcliff-on-Sea, Essex, SS0 0QF.* (0702 49545)

WELLS, Stephen Glossop. b 22. CCC Ox BA 48, MA 48. Westcott Ho Cam 48. **d** 50 **p** 51 Lon. C of All SS Poplar 50-56; R of Saltford (w Corston and Newton St Loe from 80) Dio B & W from 56; C-in-c of Corston w Newton St Loe 76-80; RD of Chew Magna from 80. *Saltford Rectory, Bristol.* (Saltford 2275)

WELLS, Victor Edwin. b 25. Wycl Hall Ox 64. **d** 64 **p** 65 Sheff. C of Kimberworth 64-66; V of Fishlake 66-73; St Hilda Shiregreen Sheff 73-77; C-in-c of Sykehouse 66-73. *47 Firth Park Avenue, Sheffield, S5 6HF.* (Sheff 386308)

WELLS, Canon William Alan John. St Francis Coll Brisb ACT ThL 51. **d** 52 **p** 53 Brisb. C of Charleville 52-53; Bundaberg 53-54; St Francis Nundah Brisb 54-57; Chap of Southport Sch 57-61; St Hilda's Sch Whitby 62-63; St Mich Coll Belize 64-68; P-in-c of All SS Belize 64-68; Hd Master of St Matt Sch Nass 68-70; C of St Silas Pentonville Islington 71-72; R of St Patr Grenada Windw Is 72-73; St Patr Saint Vinc 73-75; Can of St Jo Bapt Cathl Bel from 77; Exam Chap to Bp of Bel from 77; P-in-c of Ecumen Centre Belmopan Dio Bel from 77; VG Dio Bel from 78. *Rectory, Belmopan, Belize, Central America.* (08-2208)

WELLS, William David Sandford. b 41. Or Coll Ox BA (Th) 64, MA 66. Ridley Hall Cam 63. **d** 65 **p** 66 Worc. C of Gt Malvern 65-70; V of Crowle Dio Worc from 70; P-in-c of Himbleton w Huddington Dio Worc from 78. *Vicarage, Crowle, Worcs, WR7 4AT.* (Upton Snodsbury 617)

WELLS, Wilfred Modupeh Emmanuel. Fourah Bay Coll 59. **d** 62 **p** 63 Sier L. P Dio Sier L. *St Michael's Vicarage, Waterloo, Sierra Leone.*

WELLWOOD, Michael Frederick. b 46. Univ of W Ont BA 69. Hur Coll Lon MDiv 72. **d** 72 **p** 73 Hur. I of Florence, Aughrim & Bothwell 72-76; CF (Canad) from 76. *Chaplain's Office, CFB Chilo, Manit., Canada.*

WELSBY, Canon Paul Antony. b 20. Univ Coll Dur BA (2nd cl Mod Hist) 42, MA 45. Long Reading Pr 41, PhD (Sheff) 58. Linc Th Coll 42. **d** 44 Dover for Cant **p** 45 Cant. C of Boxley 44-47; St Mary-le-Tower Ipswich 47-52; R of Copdock w Washbrook (and Belstead from 58) 52-66; RD of Samford 64-66; Proc Conv St E 64-70; Exam Chap to Bp of Roch from 66; Can Res of Roch Cathl from 66; Dir of Post Ordin Tr Dio Roch from 66; M Gen Syn 70-80; Vice-Pres of Dioc Syn 73-80; Prolocutor of Cant Conv 73-80; Chap to HM the Queen from 80. *Southgate, The Precinct, Rochester, Kent, ME1 1TH.* (Medway 45722)

WELSFORD, Alan. Univ of Dur BA 57. St Steph Ho Ox 57. **d** 59 Knaresborough for York **p** 60 Ripon. C of St Aid Leeds 59-61. *Address temp unknown.*

WELSH, Angus Alexander. b 30. Trin Coll Cam BA (2nd cl Mod and Med Lang Trip) 54, MA 59. St Jo Coll Dur Dipl Th 56. **d** 56 **p** 57 Newc T. C of Jesmond Newc T 56-60; St Jas and St Basil Newc T 60-62; V of Bacup 62-68; Chap Tristan Da Cunha 68-71; R of St Phil St Vincent 72-78; Heysham Dio Blackb from 78. *Rectory, Main Street, Heysham, Lancs, LA3 2RN.* (Heysham 51422)

WELSH, Donald Vivian. b 21. Univ of Liv BA 41. Linc Coll Ox BA 48, MA 52. Ely Th Coll 49. **d** 51 **p** 52 Liv. C of St Jo Bapt w St Thos Toxt Pk 51-52; Walton-on-the-Hill 52-54; Chap RN 54-58; Chap City of Lon Freemen's Sch 58-59; Woking Gr Sch and Chaworth St Jas Sch CSMV 59-65; Ranelagh Sch Bracknell from 65; Perm to Offic Dio Ox from 65. *13 Batty's Barn Close, Wokingham, Berks.*

WELSH, Gerald. b 17. **d** 78 Glas. Hon C of Ardrossan Dio Glas from 78. *29 Sannox Drive, Saltcoats, Ayr, KA21 6JD.*

WELSH, John Raynham. b 39. K Coll Lon and Warm AKC 65. **d** 66 **p** 67 Lon. C of St Pet and St Paul Harlington 66-67; Hampton 67-71; Chap W Middx Hosp 71-78; Hon C of All SS Isleworth 71-79. *33 Lyndhurst Avenue, Sunbury-on-Thames, TW16 6QZ.*

WELSH, Maxwell Wilfred. b 29. Bp's Coll Calc 55. **d** 58 **p** 59 Madras. In Ch of S India 58-62; Chap Kharagpur Calc 62-65; V of St Thos Calc 65-70; Byculla Bom 70-72; C of Cannock 73-76; Team V of Wednesfield 76-78; V of Milton Dio Lich from 79. *Vicarage, Baddeley Green Lane, Milton, Staffs.* (Stoke-on-Trent 534062)

WELSH, Philip Peter. b 48. Keble Coll Ox BA (2nd cl Engl) 69, MA 73. Selw Coll Cam 2nd cl Th Trip pt ii BA 72. Westcott Ho Cam 71. **d** 73 **p** 74 S'wark. C of W Dulwich 73-76; St Andr Surbiton 76-79; Lect St Steph Coll Delhi 79-81; V of Malden Dio S'wark from 81. *Old Malden Vicarage, Church Road, Worcester Park, Surrey.* (01-330 2118)

WELSH, Robert Leslie. b 32. Univ of Sheff BA 54. St Jo Coll Dur Dipl Th 58. **d** 58 **p** 59 Dur. C of S Westoe 58-62; Darlington (in c of St Columba) 62-66; CF (TA) 64-67; V of E Rainton Dio Dur from 66; PC of W Rainton Dio Dur 66-67; R from 67. *Rectory, West Rainton, Houghton-le-Spring, T & W, DH4 6PA*

WELTON, Canon Erik Godfrey. Kelham Th Coll. **d** 31 **p** 32 Bloemf. Miss (SSM) at Modderpoort 31-33; C of Cathl Ch Bloemf 33-34; R of Wepener 34-35; C of St Cypr Cathl Ch Kimb 35-37; R of St Alb Kimb w St Edw Kenilworth 37-40; CF (S Afr) 40-43; L to Offic Dio Kimb K 43-47; Warden Bp's Hostel Kimb 43-47; R of Middleburg 47-55; K Wm's Town 55-65; Can of Grahmstn 59-70 and 74-76; Hon Can from 76; R of St Sav E Lon grahmstn 65-74; Archd of E Lon 70-74; P-in-c of Gonubie Dio Grahmstn from 75. *23 8th Avenue, Gonubie, CP, S Africa.* (137)

WELTON, Leslie John Francis. b 04. Late Pri and Research Stud of Univ of Liv BA 29, MA 31, PhD 35. Egerton Hall Man 35. **d** 38 **p** 39 Liv. C of St Jas Wigan 38-39; St Andr Clubmoor 39-40; St Cath Abercromby Square Liv 40-41; V of St Mary Edge Hill 41-50; Allensmore 50-54; St Jas Glouc 54-60; R of Rickinghall Inferior w Rickinghall Superior 60-73; C-in-c of Hinderclay 60-73; L to Offic Dio Nor 73-75; P-in-c of Marsham 75-78; Burgh Next Aylsham 75-78; Perm to Offic Dio Nor from 78. *14 Nelson Road, Sheringham, Norf, NR26 8BU.* (Sheringham 823130)

WEMIDA, Caleb George Osedayo. Im Coll Ibad 59. **d** 61 **p** 62 Ondo-B. P Dio Ondo. *St Stephen's Vicarage, Iju-Akure, Nigeria.*

WEMYSS, Gary. b 52. St Jo Coll Dur 79. **d** 80 **p** 81 Blackb. C of St Jas City and Dio Blackb from 80. *30 Conway Avenue, Blackburn, BB1 8EZ.*

WENDELBORN, Robert Mark. b 35. St Jo Coll Auckld 70. **d** 71 **p** 72 Waik. C of St Pet Cathl Hamilton 71-73; V of Waitara Dio Waik from 74. *PO Box 18, Waitara, NZ.* (Waitara 8811)

WENHAM, John Terence. b 31. G & C Coll Cam BA 57, MA 60. Ely Th Coll 58. **d** 60 **p** 61 Ex. C of St Marychurch 60-63; Hatfield Hyde 63-65; C-in-c of Woburn Dio St Alb 65-66; V 66-71; C-in-c of Battlesden w Pottesgrove 65-66; R 66-71; R of Welwyn (w Ayot St Pet from 75) Dio St Alb from 71; RD of Hatfield from 75. *6 Hobbs Hill, Welwyn, Herts.* (Welwyn 4150)

WENHAM, John William. b 13. Pemb Coll Cam 3rd cl Math Trip pt i 33, 3rd cl Geog Trip pt i 34, BA 35, 2nd cl Th Trip pt i 36, MA 39. Univ of Lon BD 43. **d** 38 Lon **p** 39 Willesden for Lon. Tutor Lon Coll of Div 38-41; C of St Matt Cam 41-43; Chap RAFVR 43-47; C of Ch Ch Cockfosters (in c of St Paul Hadley Wood) 47-48; V of St Nich Dur 48-53; Vice-Prin Tyndale Hall Bris 53-67; Tutor 67-69; Lect in NT Greek Univ of Bris 67-69; Publ Pr Dio Bris 53-70; Proc Conv Bris 65-70; Warden Latimer Ho Ox 70-73; L to Offic Dio Ox 70-73; C of Cottisford and Hardwick 73-75; Perm to Offic Dio Sarum from 75. *55 Bainton Road, Oxford, OX2 7AG.* (Oxford 58820)

WENHAM, Ronald Walter. Wycl Coll Tor LTh 41. **d** and **p** 36 Niag for Arctic. Miss at Fort Chimo 36-41; R of Mount Forest Riverstown and Farewell Ont 42-48; I of Dorch 48-51; Hespeler 51-56; St Steph Brantford 56-64 R of Clinton 64-69; I of Wiarton 69-71. *Box 306, Wiarton, Ont, Canada.*

WENT, John Stewart. b 44. CCC Cam BA 66, 1st cl Th Trip pt 11 and Jun Scholefield Pri 67. Oak Hill Th Coll 67. **d** 69 Lon **p** 70 Willesden for Lon. C of Em Northwood 69-75; V of H Trin Margate Dio Cant from 75. *Vicarage, Northdown Way, Margate, Kent, CT9 3QU* (Thanet 24037)

WENTZELL, Fernald William. K Coll NS BA 60, LTh 62. **d** 61 **p** 62 Bp W W Davis for NS. R of Canso 62-64. *c/o Synod Office, 5732 College Street, Halifax, NS, Canada.*

WEPUKHULU, Yokana. b 22. **d** and **p** 74 Mbale. P Dio Mbale. *Box Butiri, Mbale, Uganda.*

WERAGA, Erisafati Matovu. **d** 41 **p** 43 Centr Tang. C of Rubungo 41-46; Kigoma 46-48; Gihwahuru 48-57; Kasulu 57-63. *Box 4350, Kampala, Uganda.*

WERE, Dishan Jackson. Bp Usher-Wilson Coll Buwalasi. **d** 64 **p** 65 Mbale. P Dio Mbale 64-72; Dio Bukedi from 72; Dioc Sec from 76. *Box 170, Tororo, Uganda.*

WERE, Isiraeri. Bp Tucker Coll Mukono 63. **d** 64 **p** 65 Mbale. P Dio Mbale 64-72; Dio Bukedi from 72. *Bulumbi, PO Box 1062, Busia, Uganda.*

WERE, John Owen. OBE 68. Univ of Adel BA 33. St Jo

Coll Morpeth 35. ACT ThL 36. Lucas Tooth Scho 37. Ch Ch Ox BA (3rd cl Th) 39, MA 43. **d** 36 **p** 37 River. C of St Pet Broken Hill 37; Perm to Offic Dios Cant, Ox and Lon 37-40; R of Narrandera 40-44; Chap RAN 44-62; Sen Chap and Archd 62-67; I of Gisborne 67-77; Perm to Offic Dio Melb from 77. *1 Frederick Street, Red Hill, Vic, Australia 3937.*

WERE, Sitefano. Bp Tucker Coll Mukono 54. **d** 57 **p** 59 U Nile. P Dio U Nile 57-61; Dio Mbale 61-72; Dio Bukedi from 72. *Church of Uganda, Masaba, Uganda.*

WERE, Wycliffe. d 65 **p** 66 Maseno. P Dio Maseno 65-69; Dio Maseno N from 70. *PO Box 266, Butere, Kenya.*

WERE, Zefaniya Barasa. Bp Tucker Coll Mukono. **d** 62 **p** 63 Mbale. P Dio Mbale 62-72; Dio Bukedi from 72; Archd of Tororo 75-81. *Box 170, Tororo, Uganda.*

WERE-MBAALE, Charles George William. Bp Usher-Wilson Coll Buwalasi. **d** 64 Mbale. d Dio Mbale. *Katerema, PO Box 211, Tororo, Uganda.*

WERNER, David Robert Edmund. b 33. Clifton Th Coll 61. **d** 63 **p** 64 St A. C of Holywell 63-68; Llanrhos 68-70; Perm to Offic Dio Ex 70-71; R of Tedburn St Mary Dio Ex from 71; RD of Kenn from 80. *Rectory, Tedburn St Mary, Exeter, Devon.* (Tedbury St Mary 253)

WERNER, Donald Kilgour. b 39. Univ of Wales BA (2nd cl Phil and Hist) 61. Linacre Ho Ox BA (2nd cl Th) 64, MA 67. Wycl Hall Ox 61. **d** 64 **p** 65 St A. C of Wrexham 64-69; Chap Brasted Place Coll 69-73; Hon C of St Paul Ap Clifton 73-76; Chap Univ of Bris 73-76; Univ of Keele 77-79; P-in-c of Keele 77-79; Dir of Evang and C of St Mich-le-Belfrey City and Dio York from 79. *St Cuthberts Centre, Peasholme Green, York.*

WERRELL, Ralph Sidney. b 29. Tyndale Hall, Bris 54. **d** 56 **p** 57 Lich. C of Penn Fields 56-60; St Sav w St Matt Denmark Hill 60-61; R of Danby Wiske w Yafforth 61-65; C-in-c of Hutton Bonville 61-65; R of Combs 65-75; V of Ch Ch Bootle 75-80; R of Scole w Billingford, Brockdish, Thorpe Abbots and Thorpe Parva Dio Nor from 80; P-in-c of Brockdish w Thorpe Abbots 80. *Scole Rectory, Diss, Norf.* (Scole 250)

WERWATH, Wolfgang Albert Richard Kurt. b 22. Ripon Hall Ox 54. **d** 56 **p** 57 Man. C of All SS Hamer Rochdale 56-58; St Agnes N Reddish 58-59; V of St Luke Chadderton 59-67; PC of Whitfield 67-68; V 68-75; Bretby w Newton Solney Dio Derby from 75. *Vicarage, St Mary's Close, Newton Solney, Burton-on-Trent, Staffs.* (Burton-on-Trent 703728)

WESLEY, Charles Boyd. b 43. Westcott Ho Cam 76. **d** 79 **p** 80 St E. C of Haverhill Dio St E from 79. *12 Feltwell Place, Haverhill, Suffolk, CB9 0AN.*

WESLEY, John. d 57 Bp Clarke for Moos **p** 60 Moos. I of Albany 57-60; Rupert's Ho 60-77; Kashechewan Dio Moos from 78. *Kashechewan, via Moosonee, Ont, Canada.*

✠ **WESONGA, Right Rev Akisoferi.** Buwalasi Dioc Th Coll. **d** 54 **p** 56 U Nile. P Dio U Nile 54-61; Dio Mbale 61-62; Dean of St Andr Cathl Mbale 63-69; Dioc Sec 65-66; Hon Can of Mbale from 69; Prov Sec Ugan, Rwanda B and Boga-Z 72-80; Cons Ld Bp of Mbale in St Andr Cathl Mbale 25 Jan 81 by Abp of Uganda; Bps of Bukedi, Soroti, Mityana, N Maseno, Nam and Busoga. *PO Box 473, Mbale, Uganda.*

WESSELS, Ven Henry Douglas. St Paul's Coll Grahmstn Dipl Th 68. **d** 67 **p** 68 Bloemf. C of Kroonstad 68-71; St Matthias Welkom Dio Bloemf 71-74; R from 74; Archd of Kroonstad from 80. *PO Box 231, Welkom, OFS, S Africa.* (017-23497)

WESSON, John Graham. b 38. St Pet Coll Ox BA (Chem) 62, MA 68. Dipl Th 63. Clifton Th Coll 63. **d** 65 Warrington for Liv **p** 66 Liv. C of Ch Ch Southport 65-68; St Ebbe Ox 68-71; Chap Polytechnic of Centr Lon 71-76; Chap of St Thos City and Dio Edin from 76. *16 Belgrave Road, Edinburgh, EH12 6NF.* (031-334 1309)

WEST, Arthur. b 20. Linc Th Coll. **d** 60 **p** 61 York. C of Cottingham 60-64; V of Ruswarp w Sneaton 64-68; Nether w U Poppleton Dio York from 68; RD of Ainsty from 77. *15 Nether Way, Upper Poppleton, York, YO2 6JQ.* (York 794744)

WEST, Bernard Kenneth. b 31. Linc Th Coll. **d** 67 Barking for Chelmsf **p** 68 Chelmsf. C of E Ham 67-71; Gt Bookham 71-73; R of Esperance 73-76; C of Dalkeith 76-79; Perm to Offic Dio Perth 79-80; P-in-c of Carine Dio Perth from 80. *43 Glengarry Drive, Duncraig, W Australia 6023.* (448-1421)

WEST, Clive. Dipl Th (Lon) 68. Qu Univ Belf BD 75. TCD **d** 64 **p** 65 Connor. C of Ch Ch Cathl Lisburn 64-68; Asst Master Lisnagarvey Secondary Sch Lisburn 68-70; C of All SS Belf 70-75; R of Mullabrack w Kilchuney Dio Arm from 76. *Mullabrack Rectory, Whitesides Hill, Portadown, Co Armagh, N Ireland.*

WEST, David Albert. Moore Th Coll Syd 64. ACT ThL 67. **d** 67 **p** 68 Syd. C of Beecroft 67-70; Penrith 71; R of Naremburn 72-76; P-in-c of Churchill 76-80; S Queanbeyan Dio C & Goulb from 80. *89 Cooma Street, Queanbeyan. NSW, Australia 2620.*

WEST, David Marshall. b 48. St Jo Coll Dur BA 70. Qu Coll Birm Dipl Th 72. **d** 73 **p** 74 Birm. C of Wylde Green 73-75; St Paul Wokingham 76-79; V of Hurst Dio Ox from 79. *Hurst Vicarage, Reading, Berks.* (Hurst 17)

WEST, Derek Elvin. b 47. Univ of Hull BA 69. Westcott Ho Cam 71. **d** 73 **p** 74 Barking for Chelmsf. C of St Pet Walthamstow 73-77; Chingford 77-80; Team V of W Slough Dio Ox from 80. *298 Stoke Poges Lane, Slough, SL1 3LL.* (Slough 39062)

WEST, Donald Henry. d and **p** 56 Niag. C of Ancaster 56-58; R of Elora w Drayton 58-61; Acton 61-65; H Trin Hamilton 65-70. *1391 Cahill Drive, Ottawa 6, Ont., Canada.*

WEST, Eric Edward. b 32. Univ of Leeds BA 60. Bps' Coll Cheshunt 63. **d** 64 **p** 65 St Alb. C of Biscot Dio St alb 64-71; V from 71. *161 Bishopscote Road, Luton, Beds, LU3 1PD.*

✠ **WEST, Right Rev Francis Horner.** b 09. Late Exihib of Magd Coll Cam BA 31, 2nd cl Hist 30, 2nd cl Th Trip 32, MA 35. Ridley Hall Cam 31. **d** 33 **p** 34 Ripon. C of St Agnes Burmantofts Leeds 33-36; H Trin Cam 36; Tutor and Chap Ridley Hall Cam 36-38; V of St Andr Starbeck 38-42; CF (R of O) 39-46; Dir of Service Ordination Cands 46-47; Archd of Newark 47-62; V of Upton 46-51; V of E Retford 51-54; RD of Retford 51-53; Select Pr Univ of Cam 62; Cons Ld Bp Suffr of Taunton in Westmr Abbey 2 Feb 62 by Abp of Cant; Bps of Lon; B & W; Worc; Heref; Leic; and Portsm; Bp Suffr of Penrith; and Bps Gelsthorpe, D J Wilson, F M E Jackson and W L M Way, and others; res 77; R of Dinder 62-71; Preb of Wells Cathl 62-77; Warden of Readers Dio B & W 70-77; Chap to Retired Clergy Archd of Wilts and Hon Asst Bp of Bris from 78. *11 Castle Street, Aldbourne, Marlborough, Wilts.* (Marlborough 40630)

WEST, George Edward. b 08. Roch Th Coll 62. **d** 63 **p** 64 Derby. C of Ripley Derbys 63-66; V of Barrow-on-Trent w Twyford 66-74. *41 Poplar Road, Gt Wyrley, Staffs, WS6 6HD.*

WEST, Gerald Eric. b 18. **d** 80 **p** 81 Ches. C of Bramhall Dio Ches from 80. *255 Bramhall Moor Lane, Hazel Grove, Stockport, Cheshire, SK7 5JL.*

WEST, Harold Reginald. b 15. Univ Dur BA 43, MA 46. Coll of Resurr Mirfield. **d** 45 **p** 46 Newc T. C of H Trin North Shields 45-48; Sugley 48-55; V of Cresswell 55-61; St Luke City and Dio Newc T from 61. *6 Claremont Terrace, Newcastle upon Tyne 2.* (Newc T 23341)

WEST, Henry Cyrano. b 28. K Coll Lon and Warm. **d** 51 **p** 52 Leic. C of St Pet Braunstone Leic 51-53; St Anne Wandsworth 53-55; Raynes Pk 55-58; CF 58-63; V of Sculcoates 63-71; C-in-c of St Jude w St Steph Hull 67-71; Publ Pr Dio Cov 71-75; Dio Man from 75; Sec Cov Coun of Social Service 71-75; Gtr Man Coun for Vol Service from 75. *21 Alkrington Green, Middleton, Manchester, M24 1ED.* (061-643 4410)

WEST, James. b 15. Univ Coll Southn 39. Univ of Lon BA 39, BD 44. Sarum Th Coll 39. **d** 40 **p** 41 Bris. C of St Mich AA Windmill Hill 40-43; St Mary Southn 43-44; Chilvers Coton 44-45; V of Ryton-on-Dunsmore 45-56; C-in-c of Bubbenhall 49-54; V of Pilton w Ashford 56-81; Surr 74-81. *10 Park Place, Wadebridge, Cornw, PL27 7EA.* (Wadebridge 3945)

WEST, John Henry. St Jo Coll Morpeth. ACT ThL 61. **d** 60 **p** 61 Newc. C of Maitland 60-66; P-in-c of Swansea Newc 66-70; R of Denman 70-79; Mt Vincent Dio Newc from 79. *Rectory, Barton Street, Kurri Kurri, NSW, Australia 2327.* (37 1061)

WEST, John Herbert. b 1900. Univ of Leeds BA 23, MA 45. Univ of Lon BD 25, Westcott Ho Cam 43. **d** 43 Bradf **p** 43 Bp Mounsey for Bradf. C of St Marg Thornbury 43-44; Bingley 44-45; V of Burton-in-Lonsdale 45-56; R of Sutton w Duckmanton 56-65; V of Littlebury 65-74. *15 The Orchard, Newton, Swansea.* (Swansea 66166)

WEST, Leonard Ernest. b 10. ALCD (1st cl) 38 (LTh from 74). **d** 38 Bedford for St Alb **p** 39 St Alb. C of Ch Ch Watford 38-42; V of Mold Green 42-49; R of L Thurlow w L Bradley 49-54; Surr from 48; C-in-c of Gt Bradley 52-54; R (w L Bradley) 54-61; Stradishall w Denston 61-64; RD of Clare 61-64; V of St Andr Watford 64-75; Perm to Offic Dios St A and Lich from 76. *11 Oldcastle Avenue, Guilsfield, Welshpool, Powys.* (Welshpool 2415)

WEST, Canon Michael Brian. b 39. Univ of Bris BSc (2nd cl Physics) 60. Linc Th Coll. **d** 66 **p** 67 St Alb. C of Hatfield 66-69; Industr Chap Herts and Beds Industr Miss and L to Offic Dio St Alb 69-81; Hon Can of St Alb 78-81; Sheff from 81; Sen Industr Chap Dio Sheff from 81. *21 Endcliffe Rise Road, Sheffield, S11 8RU.* (Sheff 661921)

WEST, Michael Frederick. b 50. Trin Coll Ox BA 72, MA 76. Westcott Ho Cam 72. **d** 74 **p** 75 Lich. C of Wolverhampton 74-78; Hanley (in c of St Luke Wellington) Dio Lich

78-79; Team V from 79. *33 Wellington Street, Hanley, Stoke-on-Trent, Staffs. S-on-T 29100)*

WEST, Michael Oakley. b 31. Wells Th Coll 62. **d** 63 **p** 64 Bris. C of Swindon 63-66; Chap at Tripoli 66-68; R of Lydiard Millicent w Lydiard-Tregoz 68-75; V of Breage w Germoe Dio Truro from 75. *Breage Vicarage, Helston, Cornwall.* (Helston 3449)

WEST, Peter Harcourt. b 29. Oak Hill Th Coll 56. Dipl Th (Lon) 59. **d** 59 **p** 60 Ely. C of Histon 59-60; Hampreston 60-61; Braintree 61-63. *Westgates, Witham Road, Black Notley, Braintree, Essex.* (Braintree 23048)

WEST, Philip William. b 48. Magd Coll Ox BA 70, MA 78. Univ of Nottm BA (Th) 74. St Jo Coll Nottm 72. **d** 75 **p** 76 Pet. C of Rushden 75-79; Pitsmoor w Ellesmere Dio Sheff from 79. *13 Ella Road, Sheffield, S4 7EE.*

WEST, Reginald George. b 14. ACA 39. FCA 57. Worc Ordin Coll. **d** 68 **p** 69 Pet. C of Oundle w Ashton 68-73; V of Weedon Lois w Plumpton and Moreton Pinkney 73-79. *57 Greenacres Way, Newport, Shropshire, TF10 9PH.*

WEST, Reginald Roy. b 28. St Deiniol's Libr Hawarden 74. **d** 74 **p** 75 Mon. C of Abergavenny 74-77; V of St Jas Tredegar Dio Mon from 77. *St Jame's Vicarage, Poplar Road, Tredegar, Gwent, NP2 4LH.* (Tredegar 2510)

WEST, Richard Wilfrid Anthony. b 20. Magd Coll Cam BA 41, MA 45. Wells Th Coll 41. **d** 43 Guildf **p** 44 Bp Golding-Bird for Guildf. C of St Martin Dorking 43-47; Leatherhead 47-49; V of Brockham Green Dio S'wark from 50; P-in-c of Betchworth dio S'wark from 81. *St Michaels Vicarage, Betchworth, Surrey.* (Betchworth 2102)

WEST, Canon Ronald Cameron. b 06. AKC 33. **d** 33 **p** 34 Birm. C of St Paul Blackheath Staffs 33-36; Yardley Wood 36-38; Banbury (in c of St Hugh Easington) 38-39; V of Wroxton w Balscote 39-50; Enstone 50-55; Hon Ed Ox Dioc Year Book 54-76; PC of Freeland 55-68; V 68-80; Dioc Insp of Schs Ox 57-72; Hon Chap to Bp of Ox from 65; RD of Woodstock 76-80; Hon Can of Ch Ch Ox 79-80; Can (Emer) from 80. *12 Treassowe Road, Penzance, Cornw, TR18 2AU.* (Penzance 66612)

WEST, Sidney George. Univ of Sask BA 36. Em Coll Sktn LTh 36. **d** 36 Sask for Athab **p** 36 Athab. Miss at Fort McMurray 36-37; I of High Prairie 37-40; L to Offic Dio Calg 40-42; Itin P Dio Edmon 42-43; Chap CAOS 43-46; Perm to Offic Dio Tor 47-52; R of Ch of Good Shepherd Mt Dennis Tor 52-63; Publ Inst Chap Tor 63-73; Hon C of St Matt Islington Tor 64-73; R of Dunbarton 73-78. *313 Preston Parkway, Cambridge, N3H 4Z4, Canada.*

WEST, Thomas. b 13. Worc Ordin Coll 63. **d** 64 **p** 65 Linc. C of St Nich w St John Newport Linc 64-68; V of Torksey 68-75; Marton 68-75; Old Leake 75-80. *6 Ravendale, Barton on Humber, S Humb, DN18 6AR.*

WESTALL, Nigel Everard Hawksley. b 1900. Late Sedgwick Exhib of Qu Coll Cam BA 23, MA 58. Cudd Coll 23. **d** 27 **p** 28 Lon. Asst Chap Deaf and Dumb Assoc W Lon Distr 27-29; Chap in c Clapham distr 29-33; All SS Ch for Deaf and Dumb W Ham 33-37; R Assoc for Deaf and Dumb Dio Lon (in c of St John of Beverley Finsbury Pk) 37-40; V of Caundle Stourton w Caundle Purse 40-46; C of St Luke Skerton 46-49; Waltham Abbey w St Thos Upshire (in c of Upshire) 49-56; V of Horndon-on-the-Hill 56-67. *Address temp unknown.*

WESTALL, Robert Cyril. b 07. Late Th Exhib of St Chad's Coll Dur BA (3rd cl Th) and Jenkyn's Scho 28, Declamation Pri 29. **d** 30 **p** 31 Ox. C of Aylesbury 30-32; St Mary Penzance 32-34; Carshalton (in c of Good Shepherd) 34-36; All SS Brighton 36-38; Perm to Offic at St Sav Eastbourne 38-39; R of Edburton 39-45; Chardstock all SS 45-58; V of Chardstock St Andr 52-58; R of Pontesbury (1st and 2nd portions) 58-66; Dodbrooke 66-76; RD of Pontesbury 60-66; of Woodleigh 70-76; Publ Pr Dio Ex from 77. *Pynes House, Cheriton Fitzpaine, Crediton, Devon.* (Cheriton Fitzpaine 505)

WESTBERG, Daniel Arnold. b 49. Dartmouth Coll New Hampshire USA BA 71. Univ of Tor MA 72. Wycl Coll Tor MDiv 78. **d** 78 **p** 79 Tor. C of Ch of Messiah Tor 78-80; I of Cannington Dio Tor from 80. *Box 29, Cannington, Ont, Canada.*

WESTBROOK, Colin David. b 36. Or Coll Ox BA (2nd cl Mod Lang) 59, Dipl Th 60, MA 64. St Steph Ho Ox 59. **d** 61 **p** 62 Llan. C of St Martin Roath 61-66; Roath 66-74; V of Llanfihangel Llantarnam 74-79; St John Bapt Newport Dio Mon from 79. *St John's Vicarage, Oakfield Road, Newport, Gwent, NP7 4LP.* (Newport 65581)

WESTBROOK, George. b 03. Wycl Coll Tor LTh 30. **d** 29 **p** 30 Tor. C of St Phil Weston 29-30; Milton NS 30-32; St Barn Isl 32-35; St Phil and St Jas Ilfracombe 35-37; L to Offic in St Mark Walthamstow 37-40; R of Holton w Bratton St Maur 40-45; V of All SS Clapham Park 45-53; R of Palgrave 53-63. Drinkstone 63-69; R of Tostock 63-69. *18 Post Mill Close, Ipswich, IP4 2RF.*

WESTBROOK, Richard Henry. b 09. **d** 67 bp T G S Smith for Leic **p** 68 Leic. C of L Bowden 67-70; R of Carlton Curlieu w Ilston-on-the-Hill and Shangton (w Burton Overy from 76) 70-81; C-in-c of Burton Overy 74-76; Perm to Offic Dios Leic and Pet from 81. *12 Main Street, Seaton, Oakham, Leicester.* (Morcott 627)

WEST BUGANDA, Lord Bishop of. *See* Senyonjo, Right Rev Christopher Disani.

WESTCOTT, Cuthbert Philip Brooke. b 09. Magd Coll Ox BA (4th cl Mod Lang) 32, MA 36. Westcott Ho Cam 36. **d** 36 **p** 37 Pet. C of Kingsthorpe 36-39; Pershore w Pinvin and Wick 39-41; Chap RAFVR 41-47; Chap to Harborne Colleg Sch 47-48; Asst Chap St John's Sch Leatherhead and L to Offic Dio Guildf 48-50; Chap at Dibrugarh 50-53; Jorhat 53-54; St Paul's Sch Darjeeling 54-56; Chap at Milan 62-65; Bordighira and San Remo 71-74; Palermo 75-77; Actg Chap St Jean de Luz Biarritz and Pau 77-80; Perm to Offic Dio Birm from 80. *37 Gillhurst Road, Harborne, Birmingham, B17 8PD.*

WESTCOTT, Donald Ralph. b 27. Univ of Bris BA 51. Ridley Hall Cam 51. **d** 53 **p** 54 York. C of Marfleet 53-56; St Jo Bapt New Windsor 56-57; R of St Thos Ardwick Man 57-63; CF (TA) 58-60; V of Benchill 63-70; R of Islip Dio Ox from 70; R of Noke Dio Ox from 70; C-in-c of Woodeaton Dio Ox from 70. *Islip Rectory, Oxford.* (Kidlington 2163)

WESTCOTT, Gerald Francis. b 09. Jes Coll Ox BA 31, 1st cl Nat Sc and BSc 32, Dipl Th 33, MA 35. Wycl Hall Ox 32. **d** 33 **p** 34 Roch. C of St Jo Evang Penge 33-35; St Luke Ramsgate 35-39; I of Old Ch Calc 39-46; Area Sec CMS for Dios York and Ripon 46-58; V of Thornton 58-62; CMS Sec Midl Region and Area Sec Dios Birm and Cov 62-74. *47 Almsford Oval, Harrogate, N Yorks, HG2 8EJ.*

WESTERN, Canon Robert Geoffrey. b 37. Univ of Man BSc (2nd cl Metallurgy) 60. Univ of Birm Dipl Th 62. Qu Coll Birm 60. **d** 62 **p** 63 Bradf. C of Sedbergh 62-65; PV of Linc Cathl and Asst Master Cathl Sch 65-73; Hd Master from 74; L to Offic Dio Linc from 65; Can and Preb of Linc Cathl from 74. *8 Eastgate, Lincoln.* (Lincoln 28489)

WESTFALL, Robert John. St Chad's Coll Regina. **d** 64 **p** 65 Qu'App. I of Borderland 64-66; Oyen 66-68; R of Shaunavon 68-74; Outlook 74-79; St Barn Moose Jaw Dio Qu'App from 79. *552 Hochelaga Street East, Moose Jaw, Sask, Canada.*

WESTGARTH, Frederic Cecil. b 1893. Mert Coll Ox BA 19, MA 26. Wells Th Coll 19. **d** 20 **p** 22 Newc T. C of St Paul Cullercoats 20-22; St Andr Newc T 22-24; Bamburgh 24-25; St Pet Wallsend 25-29; Min of Lynemouth Distr Ch Woodhorn 29-36; V of St Osw-in-Lee w Bingfield and Wall 36-52; R of Thorneyburn w Greystead 52-69. *High Fold, Graham Street, Penrith, Cumb, CA11 9LB.* (Penrith 4403)

WESTGATE, Alvin Roy. b 47. Univ of Windsor Ont BA 72. Atlantic Sch of Th Halifax NS MDiv 75. **d** 75 **p** 76 Fred. C of Hammond River Dio Fred from 75. *5 Millar Apts, Fairvale, Kings Co, NB, Canada.*

WEST HAM, Archdeacon of. *See* Dawes, Ven Peter Spencer.

WESTIN, Canon Harald Malcolm Douglas. Montr Dioc Th Coll. **d** and **p** 56 Montr. R of Ormstown 56-58; I of Mascouche 58-62; R of Stony Hill 62-66; McAdam 66-70; Amherst 70-74; St Pet Cathl Charlottetown Dio NS from 74; Can from 79. *21 Fitzroy Street, Charlottetown, PEI, Canada.* (894-8058)

WEST INDIES, Metropolitan of Province of. *See* Woodroffe, Most Rev George Cuthbert Manning.

WESTLAKE, Michael Paul. b 34. Ex Coll Ox BA (2nd cl Th) 56, MA 64. Wells Th Coll 59. **d** 61 **p** 62 Bris. C of Southmead 61-67; V of St Thos w St Anne Eastville City and Dio Bris from 67; P-in-c of St Mark Easton City and Dio Bris from 79. *St Thomas's Vicarage, Eastville, Bristol 5.* (Bristol 518329)

WESTLAKE, Peter Alan Grant. b 19. CMG 72. MC 43. CCC Ox MA 48. Univ of Wales (Bangor) BD 81. **d** 81 Ban. C of LLandegfan w Beaumaris Dio Ban from 81. *53 Church Street, Beaumaris, Gwynedd.*

WESTLEY, Stuart. b 24. Late Scho of Em Coll Cam 2nd cl Math Trip pt i, 43, BA 48, 2nd cl Th Trip pt i 49, MA 53. Wells Th Coll 49. **d** 50 **p** 51 Man. C of St Marg Prestwich 50-53; Tonge w Alkrington 53-55; Min of St Ambrose Oldham 55-58; Asst Master Arnold Schs Blackpool 58-66; Bramhall Gr Sch 66-70; L to Offic Dio Blackb 58-78; Dio Ches 67-70; Asst Chap Denstone Coll Uttoxeter 70-73; Chap Ermysted's Gr Sch Skipton from 73; Hon C of St Mich Blackpool 75-77; Perm to Offic Dio Bradf 77-78; L to Offic from 78. *2 Side Gate Lane, Lothersdale, Keighley, W Yorks, BD20 8EU.* (Cross Hills 35646)

WESTLEY, William Arthur. St Aid Coll 50. **d** 52 Ches **p** 54 Wakef. C of Prenton 52-53; Hemsworth 54-57; V of Otane 57-60. *Otane, Hawke's Bay NZ.*

WESTMACOTT, Francis Eric. b 03. Sarum Th Coll 34. **d** 36 **p** 37 Wakef. C of Lightcliffe 36-38; Dom and Dioc Chap to Bp of Wakef 38-42; V of Hepworth 42-47; R of Harkstead (w Erwarton from 49) 47-60; Barsham w Shipmeadow Dio St E 60-74; P-in-c 75-80. *c/o The Old Forge, Ringsfield, Beccles, Suff.* (Beccles 712162)

WESTMACOTT, Preb Ian Field. b 19. Wells Th Coll 59. **d** 60 **p** 61 B & W. C of Weston-s-Mare 60-63; V of Long Ashton Dio B & W from 63; RD of Portishead from 72; Preb of Wells Cathl from 77. *Long Ashton Vicarage, Bristol.* (Long Ashton 3109)

WEST MALAYSIA, Lord Bishop of. *See* Koh, Right Rev Roland.

WESTMAN, Linton George. Bp's Univ Lennox LST 59. **d** and **p** 59 Queb. Miss at Fitch Bay 59-63; I of Danville 63-73; Gen Sec and Planning Officer Dio Queb 73-75; R of Bury Dio Queb from 75. *RR1, Sawyerville, PQ, Canada.*

WESTMINSTER, Archdeacon of. *See* Rt Rev E G Knapp-Fisher.

WESTMINSTER, Dean of. *See* Carpenter, Very Rev Edward Frederick.

WESTMORELAND, Joseph. b.02. Linc Th Coll 25. **d** 28 **p** 29 Linc. C of St Mary and St Jas Grimsby (in c of St Hugh from 30) 28-31; Dunstable 31-33; V of Horbling 33-39; PC of St Aug Grimsby 39-59; Chap of Holyrood 59-62; V of Sherborne w Windrush 62-70. *The Mead House, Sherborne, Cheltenham, Glos, GL54 3DR.* (Windrush 239)

WESTMORLAND and FURNESS, Archdeacon of. *See* Attwell, Ven Arthur Henry.

WESTMUCKETT, John Spencer. b 30. Univ of Lon BA 54. Oak Hill Th Coll. **d** 55 **p** 56 S'wark. C of H Trin Sydenham 55-57; CF from 57. *c/o Williams & Glyns Bank Ltd., Whitehall, SW1.*

WESTNEY, Michael Edward William. b 29. Lich Th Coll 64. **d** 65 Ox **p** 66 Buckingham for Ox. C of Hughenden 65-68; Banbury (in c of St Hugh Easington) 68-71; Team V of Trunch 71-78; V of St Matt Reading Dio Ox from 78. *St Matthew's Vicarage, Southcote Lane, Reading, Berks, RG3 3AX.* (Reading 53755)

WESTON, Arnold. b 50. Rhodes Univ Grahmstn BA 73. St Jo Coll Nottm 73. 58-59; P-in-c 59-61; V of Warragul 61-62; Poowong and Loch 62-66; R of Maffra 66-76; Dom Chap to Bp of Gippsld 73-81; Hon Can of St Paul's Cathl Sale 74-81; R of Bairnsdale 76-81; St Paul Westmeadows Dio Melb from 81. *Vicarage, Raleigh Street, Westmeadows, Vic, Australia 3047.*

WESTON, Christopher James. b 20. G and C Coll Cam BA 46, MA 49. Ridley Hall Cam 47. **d** 49 **p** 50 Lon. C of Neasden w Kingsbury 49-53; Asst Chap St Andr Sch Sing 53-55; Chap Cheltm Coll 56-63; V of Clifton Rotherham 63-70; P-in-c of St Nich Stevenage Dio St Alb 70-71; V from 71. *2a North Road, Stevenage, Herts, SG1 4AT.* (Stevenage 54355)

WESTON, David Wilfrid Valentine. b 37. M OSB 60. **d** 67 **p** 68 Ox. L to Offic Dio Ox from 67; Prior OSB Nashdom Abbey 71-74; Abbot from 74. *Nashdom Abbey, Burnham, Bucks, SL1 8NL.* (Burnham 3176)

WESTON, Douglas Neil. b 51. Jes Coll Ox BA 73, MA 78. Ridley Hall Cam 74. **d** 76 Willesden for Lon **p** 77 Lon. C of St Mary Ealing 76-80; P-in-c of Dean w Yelden, Melchbourne and Shelton Dio St Alb from 80; Pertenhall w Swineshead Dio St Alb from 80. *Vicarage, Upper Dean, Huntingdon, PE18 0ND* (Riseley 531)

WESTON, Ven frank Valentine. b 35. Qu Coll Ox BA (2nd cl Th) 60, MA 64. Lich Th Coll 60. **d** 61 **p** 62 Man. C of Atherton 61-65; Chap Coll of Ascen Selly Oak Birm 65-69; Prin 69-76; Edin Th Coll 76-82; Can of Edin 76-82; Archd of Ox from 82. *Archdeacon's Lodging, Christ Church, Oxford.* (Ox 43847)

WESTON, Frederick Victor Henry. b 41. Qu Coll Cam BA 63, MA 67. St D Coll Lamp LTh 65. **d** 65 **p** 66 Llan. C of St Paul Grangetown 65-67; Cymmer w Abercregan 67-69; St Mary Haverhill 69-74; R of Gt w L Whelnetham 74-79. *c/o Whelnetham Rectory, Bury St Edmunds, Suff.* (Sicklesmere 332)

WESTON, Harold John. b 24. Worc Ordin Coll 65. **d** 67 **p** 68 Pet. C of St Mich AA Northn 67-71; St Jo Bapt Pet 71-74; R of Peakirk w Glinton Dio Pet from 75. *Glinton Rectory, Peterborough, PE6 7JR.* (Pet 252265)

WESTON, Ivan John. b 45. Chich Th Coll 71. **d** 74 **p** 75 Chelmsf. C of St Mary Magd Harlow 74-77; Chap RAF from 77. *c/o Ministry of Defence, Adastral House, Theobalds Road, WC1X 8RU.*

WESTON, James Donald. b 05. Univ of Dur LTh 31. St Aid Coll 27. **d** 31 **p** 32 Ches. C of St Paul Portwood 31-33; St John Egremont 33-35; St Jo Bapt Moordown Bournemouth 35-37; St Thos Stockport and Chap Stockport Inst 37-43; SPG Area Sec Dios Win 43-64; Sarum 43-46 and 59-64; Portsm 43-64; Chic 50-64; Bris 56-64; USPG Area Sec Dio Sarum 65-75; Perm to Offic Dios Portsm 43-64; Chic 50-64; Sarum 59-64; Bris 59-64; L to Offic Dios Win 43-64; Sarum 65-75; Chap to R Nat Sanat Bournemouth 50-52. *9 New Road, Colden Common, Nr Winchester, Hants, SO21 1RU* (0962 713503)

WESTON, John Ogilvy. b 30. St Pet Coll Ox BA 66, MA 70. Linc Th Coll 71. **d** 71 **p** 72 Leic. Hon C of Long Clawson 71-75; Lect Nottm Coll of Educn 66-75; Trent Poly from 75; Perm to Offic Dios Leic and Southw from 76. *West End House, Long Clawson, Melton Mowbray, LE14 4PE.* (Melt Mowbray 822586)

WESTON, Canon Keith Aitken Astley. b 26. Trin Hall Cam BA 51, MA 55. Ridley Hall Cam 51. **d** 53 **p** 54 B & W. C of Ch Ch Weston-super-Mare 53-56; St Mark Cheltm 56-59; PC of Ch Ch Clevedon 59-64; R of St Ebbe w St Pet-le-Bailey City and Dio Ox from 64; RD of Ox 71-76; Exam Chap to Bp of Nor from 72; M Gen Syn Ox from 75; Hon Can of Ch Ch Cathl Ox from 81. *St Ebbe's Rectory, Pennyfarthing Place, Oxford, OX1 1QE.* (Oxford 48154)

WESTON, Ralph Edward Norman. b 30. Worc Ordin Coll 67. **d** 69 **p** 70 Birm. C of Harborne 69-71; CF 71-75; Chap Oswestry Sch from 75. *The School, Oswestry, Salop.*

WESTON, Stephen. b 48. St Steph Ho Ox 74. **d** 77 Bp Garrett for Leic **p** 78 Leic. C of Wigston Magna 77-82; Corringham Dio Chelmsf from 82. *St John's Church House, Corringham, Essex.*

WESTON, Stephen John Astley. b 55. Univ of Aston in Birm BSc 77. Ridley Hall Cam 78. **d** 81 Reading for Ox. C of St Mary Chesham Dio Ox from 81. *31 Chapman's Crescent, Chesham, Bucks.* (0494 786686)

WESTON, William Edward. St Jo Coll Morpeth ThL 43. **d** and **p** 44 Newc. Asst C of Mount Vincent w Kurri Kurri 44-45; Singleton 45-48; P-in-c of Clarence Town 49; L to Offic Dio Cant 50-51; R of Adamstown 51-58; Queanbeyan 59-66; Dee Why w Brookvale 66-79; Gordon Dio Syd from 79; Ed of S Churchman 60-64. *745 Pacific Highway, NSW, Australia 2072.* (498-2596)

WESTROPP, Canon Ralph Michael Lanyon. b 07. New Coll Ox BA 29, MA 42. Westcott Ho Cam 42. **d** 43 **p** 44 Lon. C of St Jo Bapt Greenhill 43-46; V of Sudbury Middx 46-52; Cookham 52-61; Commiss Zulu from 58; Capetn 59-65; V of St Mary Windermere 61-70; V of Natland 70-75; RD of kendal 70-75; Commiss Swaz from 70; Hon Can of Carl 72-75; Can (Emer) from 75. *Inglewood House, Kirkby Lonsdale, Carnforth, Lancs, LA6 2DH.* (0468 71409)

WESTRUP, Canon George Allan. b 02. Late Scho of Ch Coll Cam 1st Cl Mod Lang Trip pt i BA (2nd cl Mod Lang Trip pt ii) 24, MA 30. Westcott Ho Cam 30. **d** 31 **p** 32 S'wark. C of All SS S Lambeth 31-34; Warlingham w Chelsham 34-36; V of St Mich AA S'wark 36-41; St Jo Div Merton 41-51; R of Buckland (Surrey) 51-59; Charlwood 59-72; Hon Can of S'wark 71-72; Can (Emer) from 72; Perm to Offic Dio Ex 79-81; Dio B & W from 72. *The Haven, Ellicombe, Minehead, Somerset, TA24 6TR.* (Minehead 5014)

WESTRUP, Wilfrid Allan. b 08. Late Scho of Ch Coll Cam BA 30, MA 34. Westcott Ho Cam 30. **d** 32 **p** 33 S'wark. C of St Mich E Wickham 32-34; St Hilda Crofton Pk 34-39; V of Hazelwell 39-52; Chap of Cranbrook Sch 52-64; Asst Lect Hastings Coll of Further Educn 64-73. *Sharon, Hartley Hill, Cranbrook, Kent, Tn17 3QD.* (Cranbrook 712595)

WESTWELL, George Leslie Cedric. b 31. Lich Th Coll. **d** 61 **p** 63 Ripon. C of Rothwell 61-63; St Bart Armley 63-66; St Martin Maidstone 66-68; R of Otham 68-72; V of St Martin Maidstone 72-77; Bethersden w High Halden 77-79; R of Lichborough w Maidford and Farthingstone 79-80; Perm to Offic Dios Chich and Cant from 80. *196 Harley Shute Road, St Leonards-on-Sea, E Sussex, TN38 9JH.* (Hastings 426864)

WESTWOOD, Jack Wallace Galer. b 09. Late Scho and Pri of St D Coll Lamp BA (2nd cl Hist) 30. St Mich Coll Llan 31. **d** 32 **p** 33 Llan. C of Gellygaer 32-38; Llangynwyd 38-40; C-in-c St Marg Crynant 40-44; Org Sec CMS in Dios Ches Ban and St A 44-51; Area Sec Dios Ex and Truro 51-54; C-in-c of Bedford Chap Ex 54-57; V of Eynsham 57-76. *28 Montagu Road, Botley, Oxford.*

WESTWOOD, John Richard. b 55. Clare Coll Cam BA 77 (2nd cl Th), MA 81. Ripon Coll Cudd 77. **d** 79 **p** 80 Pet. C of Oakham w Hambleton and Egleton Dio Pet from 79; Braunston w Brooke Dio Pet from 81. *2 Chiltern Close, Oakham, Leics.* (Oakham 55366)

WESTWOOD, Peter. b 38. K Coll Lon and Warm AKC 64. Open Univ BA 76. **d** 65 **p** 66 York. C of St Steph Acomb York 65-68; Chap HM Borstal Onley 68-73; HM Pris Leic 73-77; Maidstone 77-81; HM Pris Dur from 81; L to Offic Dio Leic 74-77. *HM Prison, Old Eluet, Durham.* (Durham 62621)

WESTWOOD, Thomas George Hedley. **d** 66 **p** 67 Melb. C of St Jas Dandenong 66; Nobel Pk 66-70; St Geo Reservoir 70-71; Perm to Offic Dio Melb from 71. *Box 20, Beechworth, Vic., Australia 3747.*

✠ **WESTWOOD, Right Rev William John.** b 25. Late

Exhib of Em Coll Cam BA (2nd cl Th Trip pt i) 50, MA 55. Westcott Ho Cam 50. **d** 52 **p** 53 York. C of Hull 52-57; R of Lowestoft 57-65; RD of Lothingland 59-65; V of St Pet Mancroft Nor 65-75; RD of Nor 66-71; Hon Can of Nor from 68; M Gen Syn 70-75; and from 77; Ch Comm 73-78; Cons Ld Bp Suffr of Edmonton in St Paul's Cathl 24 June 75 by Abp of Cant; Bps of Lon, Nor, Chelmsf, Birm, Derby and Lich; Bps Suffr of Stepney, Kens, Willesden, Fulham & Gibr, Colchester, Bradwell, Shrewsbury, Warrington and Dudley; and others; Chairman C of E Information C'tte from 79. *6 Gower Street, WC1E 6DP.* (01-636 5572)

WETELAU, John Ashwin. Bp Patteson Th Centre Kohimarama 68. **d** 70 melan. d Dio Melan 70-73; Dio Polyn 74; Chap Selwyn Coll Guadalcanal and L to Offic Dio Centr Melan 75-78; P-in-c of Santo Bush Dio New Hebr (Vanuatu from 80) from 78. *Bengie, Santo, Vanuatu.*

WETHERALL, Cecil Edward. b 29. St Jo Coll Dur 49. **d** 56 **p** 57 St E. C of St Aug Ipswich 56-59; R of Hitcham (w Finborough Parva from 79) Dio St E from 59; P-in-c of Brettenham 61-63; Kettlebaston Dio St E from 71; Finborough Parva 75-79. *Hitcham Rectory, Ipswich, Suff, IP7 7NF.* (Bildeston 740350)

WETHERALL, Canon Theodore Sumner. b 10. Late Exhib of Or Coll Ox 1st cl Cl Mods 31, BA (2nd cl Lit Hum) 33, MA and Liddon Stud 36. Cudd Coll 36. **d** 37 Bp Mounsey for Bradf **p** 38 Bradf. C of St Jo Evang Greengates 37-39; LPr Dio Ox and Chap Fell and Lect of CCC Ox 39-47; Chap to Bp of Derby in Univ of Ox 39-47; Select Pr Univ of Ox 45-47; Exam Chap to Bp of Ox 46-47; Dur 48-65; Bradf 48-55; Prin of St Chad's Coll Dur 48-65; L to Offic Dio Dur 48-65; Hon Can of Dur 58-65; V of St Edw Barnsley 65-69; Huddersfield 69-76; RD of Huddersfield 69-76; Exam Chap to Bp of Wakef 69-76; Hon Can of Wakef 70-76; Can (Emer) from 76; Perm to Offic Dio Derby from 76. *2 Lomas Cottages, Litton, Tideswell, Buxton, Derbys.* (Tideswell 871042)

WETHERELL, Evan William. Univ of Queensld BA (2nd cl Ment and Mor Phil) 36, MA 47. St Francis's Coll Brisb. **d** 41 **p** 44 Brisb. Chap C of E Gr Sch Brisb 41-51; Vice Prin 45-51; R of St Andr S Brisb 51-60; Dean and V of St Pet Cathl Armid 60-69; I of Ch Ch S Yarra Dio Melb from 70. *677 Punt Road, South Yarra, Vic, Australia 3141.* (03-26 3573)

WETHERELL, Philip Anthony. b 45. AKC 72. St Aug Coll Cant 72. **d** 73 **p** 74 Barking for Chelmsf. C of St Sav Walthamstow 73-75; Tutor and Chap to Bp of Damar at Namibia Internat Peace Centre Sutton Courtenay 75-76; C of St Mary Knighton 76-80; Team V of Southn (City Centre) Dio Win from 80. *12 The Avenue, Southamton, SO1 2SQ.* (Southn 34080)

WETMORE, Stuart Andrew. b 50. State Univ of NY BA 76. Atlantic Sch of Th Halifax 77. **d** 78 Bp Wetmore (NY) for NS for Arctic **p** 79 Arctic. C of Gt Whale River Dio Arctic 78-80; I from 80. *St Edmund's Mission, Great Whale River, Quebec, Canada, J0M 1G0.*

WETTERSTROM, Jon Thomas. b 42. **d** 78 Bp Spence for Auckld **p** 79 Auckld. Hon C of Takapuna 78-79; Whangarei Dio Auckld from 79. *Box 5098, Whangarei, Northland, NZ.*

WEVUGIRA, Semeoni. d 37 **p** 39 Ugan. P Dio Ugan 37-61; Dio Nam 61-71; Dio W Bugan 71-77; Dio Mityana 77-80. *PO Box 242, Masaka, Uganda.*

WEX, Jeremy John. b 50. Rhodes Univ Grahmstn BA 73. St Jo Coll Nottm 73. **d** 75 **p** 76 Capetn. C of St Jo Wynberg 75-78; Hosp Chap Capetn from 79. *6 Pillans Road, Rosebank 7700, CP, S Africa.* (66-6033)

WEYIKAMA-KHATONDI, Alfred. Bp Usher-Wilson Coll Buwalasi. **d** 64 Mbale. d Dio Mbale. *Church of Uganda, PO Bududa, Mbale, Uganda.*

WEYMAN, John Derek Henry. b 31. Wells Th Coll 69. **d** 70 **p** 71 Guildf. C of Headley 70-76; V of Westcott Dio Guildf from 76. *Westcott Vicarage, Dorking, Surrey.* (Dorking 885309)

WEYMONT, Martin Eric. b 48. St Jo Coll Dur BA 69, MA 74. Westcott Ho Cam 71. **d** 73 **p** 74 Birm. C of Blackheath 73-76; Hon C of St Anselm Belmont 76-79; P-in-c of W Twyford Dio Lon from 79. *48 Brentmead Gardens, NW10.* (01-965 4437)

WHALE, Jeffery Walter George. b 33. Univ of Lon BSc (2nd cl Phys) 60. Cudd Coll 60. **d** 62 Bp McKie for Cov **p** 63 Cov. C of Rugby 62-68; P Missr of St Geo Conv Distr Britwell Farnham Royal 68-77; P-in-c of Datchet 77-78; R of Riverside Dio Ox from 78. *Datchet Vicarage, Slough, Berks, SL3 9JW.* (Slough 41777)

WHALE, Noel Raymond. b 41. St Steph Ho Ox. 67. **d** 70 **p** 71 Ox for Melb. C of Amersham 70-73; All SS Geelong 73-76; P-in-c of Altona Dio Melb from 76. *7 Bent Street, Altona, Vic, Australia 3018.* (398 1005)

WHALE, Peter Richard. b 49. Down Coll Cam BA 74, MA 78. Univ of Auckld MA 72. Univ of Otago BD 78. St Jo Coll Auckld 75. **d** 77 Bp Spence for Auckld **p** 78 Auckld. C of Takapuna 77-81; Asst Chap K Coll Auckld from 81. *46 Golf Avenue, Otahuhu, Auckland, NZ.*

WHALER, Herbert Riggall. St Andr Coll Pampisford 47. **d** 49 **p** 50 Linc. C of Horncastle 49-51; R of Bucknall Dio Linc from 51; R of Horsington w Stixwould Dio Linc from 51; C-in-c of Kirkby-on-Bain Dio Linc 59-61; R from 61; C-in-c of Roughton w Haltham Dio Linc 59-61; R from 61; R of Thornton w Martin Dio Linc from 61; C-in-c of Scrivelsby w Dalderby Dio Linc 63-66; R from 66; C-in-c of Thimbleby Dio Linc from 80. *Stixwould Vicarage, The Cottage, Stixwould, Lincoln.* (Woodhall Spa 52064)

WHALES, Jeremy Michael. STh (Lambeth) 72. Wycl Hall Ox 59. **d** 61 **p** 62 S'wark. C of Ch Ch Wimbledon 61-64; Asst Chap and Lect St Paul's Coll Cheltm 64-73; Chap and Sen lect from 73. *5 Robert Burns Avenue, Cheltenham, Glos.*

WHALLEY, Anthony Allen. b 41. Linc Th Coll 77. **d** 79 Reading for Ox. **p** 80 Ox. C of Upton-cum-Chalvey Slough Dio Ox from 79. *3 Burlington Avenue, Slough, Berks, SL1 2JY.* (Slough 73495)

WHALLEY, Edward Penston. b 02. SS Coll Cam BA 24, MA 28. Linc Th Coll 34. **d** 35 **p** 36 Chich. C of Selsey 35-38; Knebworth 38-44; R of Homersfield w St Cross S Elmham 44-66; Lydgate w Ousden 66-72; Perm to Offic Dio St E from 73; L to Offic Dio Nor 73-80. *College of St Barnabas, Blackberry Lane, Lingfield, Surrey, RH7 6NJ.*

WHALLEY, Edward Ryder Watson. G and C Coll Cam BA 54, MA 59. Westcott Ho Cam 55. **d** 57 **p** 58 Blackb. C of Ashton-on-Ribble 57-60; Chap Magd Coll Cam 60-63; C of Arnold 63-67. *471 Footscray Road, SE9.*

WHALLEY, Michael Thomas. b 30. K Coll Lon and Warm AKC 55. **d** 56 **p** 57 Southw. C of All SS Nottm 56-58; New Clifton Conv Distr 58-60; Mansfield 60; V of St Faith N Wilford 60-66; Asst Chap HM Pris Man 66-67; Chap HM Borstal Dover 67-69; Asst Gov HM Pris Linc 69-73; Pris Service Coll 73-75; LPr Dio Linc 70-75; Chap HM Pris Aylesbury 75-79; C of Aylesbury Dio Ox from 79. *4 Cubb Field, Hartwell Estate, Aylesbury, Bucks.* (Aylesbury 25008)

WHALLEY, Ramsdale. b 13. Lich Th Coll 40. **d** 43 Tewkesbury for Glouc **p** 44 Glouc. C of St Laur Stroud 43-45; Broadstairs 45-48; St Barn Hove and Chap Hove Gen Hosp 48-50; P-in-c of St Serf Shettleston Glas 50-53; V of Treslothan 53-61; Chap Barncoose Hosp Redruth 53-61; V of Froyle 61-66; R of H Trin Win 66-77. *9 Fairview Drive, Colkirk, Fakenham, Norf.* (Fakenham 3410)

WHARTON, Christopher Joseph. b 33. Keble Coll Ox BA 57, MA 61. **d** 79 St Alb **p** 80 Bedford for St Alb (APM). C of St Nich Harpenden Dio St Alb from 79. *97 Overstone Road, Harpenden, Herts.* (Harpenden 61164)

WHARTON, James Thomas. b 09. Late Scho of Em Coll Cam BA 31, MA 36. **d** 69 **p** 70 Bris. Hon C of Henleaze 69-72; C-in-c of Abbots Leigh 72-74. *14 Lewmond Avenue, Wells, Somt, BA5 2TS.*

WHARTON, John Martin. b 44. Van Mildert Coll Dur BA (2nd cl Soc) 69. Linacre Coll Ox BA (3rd cl Th) 71, MA 76. Ripon Hall Ox 69. **d** 72 **p** 73 Birm. C of St Pet Birm 72-75; St Jo Bapt Croydon 75-77; Dir Pastoral Stud Ripon Coll Cudd from 77; C of Cuddesdon Dio Ox from 79. *2 College Field, Cuddesdon, Oxford, OX9 9HL.* (Wheatley 4356)

WHARTON, Thomas Anthony. b 21. Bps' Coll Cheshunt, 49. **d** 52 **p** Southw. C of Beeston 52-56; Ambleside 56-58; V of Northowram 58-65; Chipping Norton Dio Ox from 65. *Vicarage, Chipping Norton, Oxon.* (Chipping Norton 2688)

WHATELEY, David. b 44. Ripon Hall Ox 71. **d** 73 Bp McKie for Cov **p** 74 Cov. C of Chilvers Coton w Astley 73-76; Chap Miss to Seamen Bangkok 76-78; Fremantle 78-79; Bunb from 79. *Flying Angel Club, Bunbury, W Australia 6230.* (21-2370)

WHATLEY, Preb Henry Lawson. b 16. Worc Coll Ox BA (3rd cl Th) 38. Wells Th Coll 38. **d** 39 **p** 40 Worc. C of All SS Bromsgrove 39-43; CF (EC) 44-47; R of Aston Ingham 45-63; R of The Lea 47-63; Colwall w U Colwall Dio Heref from 63; Preb of Heref Cathl from 76. *Colwall Rectory, Malvern, Worcs.* (Colwall 40330)

WHATLEY, Lionel Frederick. b 50. Univ of Port Eliz Dipl Educn 75. St Paul's Coll Grahmstn Dipl Th 79. **d** 79 **p** 80 Port Eliz. C of St Kath Uitenhage Dio Port Eliz from 79. *28 Aalwyn Drive, Fairbridge Heights, Uitenhage 6230, S Africa.*

WHATMORE, Terence James Brian. b 38. St Mich Coll Llan 64. **d** 66 **p** 67 Roch. C of St Jo Bapt Sevenoaks 66-70; St Julian Newport Mon 70-72; V of St Benedict Bordesley 72-81; Chap of St Mark Florence Dio Gibr in Eur from 81. *16-18 via Maggio, Florence, Italy.* (294764)

WHATMOUGH, Kenneth Douglas. Trin Coll Tor MA 34. **d** 34 **p** 35 Tor. C of St Pet Cobourg 34-36; St Jas Cathl Tor 36-37; R of Perrytown 37-40; Birch Cliff 40-48; Aurora 48-52; Lorne Pk 52-71; Hon C of St Geo-on-the-Hill City and Dio Tor from 70. *997 Porcupine Avenue, Port Credit, Ont, Canada.*

WHATMOUGH, Michael Anthony. b 50. Univ of Ex BA

72. Edin Th Coll BD 81. **d** 81 Edin. C of St Hilda and of St Fillan City and Dio Edin from 81. *1a Oxgangs Avenue, Edinburgh, EH13 9JA.*

WHATUIRA, William. b 29. **d** 77 Aotearoa for Wai. C of Wairoa Mohaka Past Dio Wai from 77. *Ruataniwha Road, North Clyde, PO Wairoa, NZ.*

WHAWELL, Arthur Michael. b 38. Sarum Wells Th Coll 74. **d** 76 **p** 77 York. C of Cottingham 76-79; P-in-c of Bessingby Dio York from 79; Carnaby Dio York from 79. *Bessingby Vicarage, West Hill, Bridlington, N Humb.* (Bridlington 70399)

WHEALE, Alan Leon. b 43. AKC 69. Bp Collins Mem Pri Ch Hist 69. St Aug Coll Cant 69. **d** 70 **p** 71 Lich. C of Tamworth 70-73; Cheddleton 73-75; V of Garrett's Green 75-78; Perry Beeches Dio Birm from 78. *313 Beeches Road, Birmingham, B42 2QR.*

WHEALE, Gerald Arnold. b 32. St Jo Coll Dur BA 56. Univ of Man MEducn 74, PhD 79. Ridley Hall Cam 56. **d** 58 **p** 59 Man. C of Tonge w Alkrington 58-60; Chap and Tutor Ijebu-ode Gr Sch Lagos 60-62; R of St Jas (w St Clement from 73) Moss Side Dio Man from 62. *68 Dudley Road, Whalley Range, Manchester, M16 8DE.* (061-226 1684)

WHEAT, Charles Donald Edmund. b 37. Univ of Nottm BA (2nd cl Th) 70, Marsden Pri 70. Univ of Sheff MA 76. Kelham Th Coll 57. **d** 62 Bp Gerard for York **p** 63 Sheff. C of St Paul Arbourthorne Sheff 62-67; L to Offic Dio Southw from 67; Dio Sheff from 73; SSM from 69; Chap and Lect St Martin's Coll of Educn Lanc 70-73; Prior SSM Priory Sheff 73-75; C of St John Ranmoor 75-77; Asst Chap Univ of Sheff 75-77; Chap 77-80; Prov of SSM in Engl 81-82; Dir SSM from 82; L to Offio Dio Blackb from 81. *St Paul's Priory, Quernmore Park, Lancaster, LA2 9HN.*

WHEAT, Christopher Henry. Late Exhib of Keble Coll Ox BA (3rd cl Th) 29, MA 36. Cudd Coll 32. **d** 33 **p** 34 Carl. C of St Geo Mart Barrow-F 33-36; Cathl Ch Bloemf 36-39; Chap of St Andr Sch Bloemf 37-39; R of Jagersfontein w Fauresmith and Koffiefontein 39-45; Ficksburg 45-51; Kroonstad 51-62; Archd of Kroonstad 51-65; Goldfields 65-69; V of Virginia 62-69; Dean and R of St Mark's Cathl Geo 69-72; Hon Can of Bloemf 71-75; C of St Geo Knysna 72-75. *7 Protea Street, Paradise Estate, Knysna, CP, S Africa.* (Knysna 119)

WHEATLEY, Very Rev Arthur. b 31. Coates Hall Th Coll Edin 68. **d** and **p** 70 Brech. C of St Salvador 70-71; C-in-c of St Ninian Dundee 71-76; R of H Trin Elgin w Lossiemouth 76-80; Can of St Andr Cathl Inverness 78-80; Provost from 80. *15 Ardross Street, Inverness, IV3 5NS.* (0463 33535)

WHEATLEY, Colin William. b 24. Trin Coll Cam BA 50, MA 61. Sarum Th Coll 50. **d** 53 **p** 54 Win. C of Ch Ch Portswood Southn 53-56; Lymington 56-59; P-in-c of St Pet Stornoway w Eorropaidh 59-63; V of Rowlestone w Llancillo 63-66; V of Walterstone 63-66; R of Kentchurch w Llangua 63-66; St Kiaran Campbeltown 66-70; Botley Dio Portsm from 70. *Botley Rectory, Southampton.* (Botley 2518)

WHEATLEY, Ernest Henry. **d** 49 **p** 50 Graft. C of Port Macquarie 49-50; V of Burringbar w U Tweed 50-52; U Clarence 52-53; R of Centr Macleay w Smithtown 53-55; State Sec ABM for W Austr 55-58; L to Offic Dio Syd 58-59; R of Islington 59-72; Belmont 72-81; Perm to Offic Dio Newc from 81. *22 Brook Street, Arcadia Vale, NSW, Australia 2283.*

WHEATLEY, James. b 40. Linc Th Coll 66. **d** 68 **p** 69 Newc T. C of Morpeth 68-72; St Pet Cowgate Newc T 72-74; St Paul Cullercoats 74-76; V of St Bede Newsham Blyth Dio Newc T from 76. *St Bede's Vicarage, Newsham, Blyth, Northumb, NE24 4AS.* (Blyth 2391)

WHEATLEY, John. b 14. **d** 77 **p** 78 Newc T (APM). C of Sleekburn Dio Newc T from 77. *20 Cypress Gardens, Blyth, Northumb, NE24 2LP.*

WHEATLEY, Maurice Samuel. b 13. K Coll Lon 32, AKC (1st cl) 36. Chich Th Coll 36. **d** 37 **p** 38 Chelmsf. C of Coggeshall w Markshall 37-39; SPG Miss Dio Madag 39-49; CF (S Afr) 40-46; Prin St Paul's Coll Ambat 47-49; SPG Area Sec Dios Derby Leic and Southw 50-54; Youth and Educn Sec 54-60; Men Cands Sec 60-64; USPG 65-72; Appt and Tr Sec 68-72; Publ Pr Dio S'wark 61-72; Commiss N Queensld 62-78; Hon Can of N Queensld 68-78; R of Pembroke, Berm 72-80; Area Sec USPG Dio Sarum from 80. *30 Barnes Close, Sturminster Newton, Dorset.* (0258-73066)

WHEATLEY, Paul Charles. b 38. Univ of Dur BA 61. Linc Th Coll 61. **d** 63 **p** 64 Bris. C of Bishopston 63-68; Youth Chap Bris 68-73; V of St Paul's Covingham Swindon 73-77; R of Dorcan Swindon 77-79; Ross-on-Wye 79-82; P-in-c of Brampton Abbotts 79-82; RD of Ross and Archenfield from 79; Team R of Ross-on-Wye w Brampton Abbotts, Bridstow and Peterstow Dio Heref from 82. *Rectory, Ross-on-Wye, Herefs.* (Ross-on-Wye 2175)

WHEATLEY, Peter John. b 33. St Barn Coll Adel ACT ThL 69. **d** 69 **p** 70 Adel. C of Toorak Gardens 69-70; P-in-c of Findon Seaton Pk 71-73; R of St Paul Port Adel 73-77; Grange Dio Adel from 77. *7 Charles Sturt Avenue, Grange, S Australia 5022.* (356 8119)

WHEATLEY, Peter William. b 47. Qu Coll Ox BA 69, MA 73. Pemb Coll Cam 2nd cl Th Trip pt ii BA 71, MA 75. Ripon Hall Ox 72. **d** 73 **p** 74 Kens for Lon. C of Fulham 73-78; M Gen Syn from 75; V of H Cross w St Jude and St Pet, St Pancras 78-82; St Jas W Hampstead Dio Lon from 82; P-in-c of All S Loudoun Road Hampstead Dio Lon from 82. *1 St James' House, Sherriff Road, NW6.* (01-624 5434)

WHEATON, Christopher. b 49. St John's Coll Nottm BTh, LTh 80. **d** 80 **p** 81 S'wark. C of St Jas Hatcham Dio S'wark from 80. *St Michael's Community Centre, Desmond Street, New Cross, SE14 6JF.* (01-692 0921)

WHEATON, Canon David Harry. b 30. Late Exhib of St Jo Coll Ox BA 53, MA 56. BD (Lon) 55. Oak Hill Th Coll 58. **d** 59 **p** 60 Lon. C of Cockfosters 59-62; Tutor Oak Hill Coll 59-62; R of Ludgershall Bucks 62-66; V of St Paul Onslow Square Kens 66-71; Prin of Oak Hill Coll from 71; Perm to Offic Dio St Alb from 72; L to Offic Dio Lon from 73; Hon Can of St Alb Cathl from 76. *Oak Hill Theological College, Chase Side, Southgate, N14.* (01-449 0467)

WHEATON, Ralph Ernest. b 32. St Jo Coll Dur BA (2nd cl Hist) 54, Dipl Th 58. Cranmer Hall Dur. **d** 58 **p** 59 Leic. C of Evington 58-63; V of Bardon Hill 63-71; Whitwick 71-81; RD of Akeley S 79-81; V of Blyth w Barnby Moor Dio Southw from 81. *Blyth Vicarage, Worksop, Notts.* (Blyth 229)

WHEBLE, Eric Clement. b 23. SOC 68. **d** 71 **p** 72 Cant. C of H Trin Selhurst Croydon 71-78; St Sav Croydon 78-80; St Osw Norbury 80-81; Team V of Selsdon Dio Cant from 81. *St Francis Vicarage, Tedder Road, Selsdon, S Croydon, Surrey.* (01-657 7864)

✠ **WHEELDON, Right Rev Philip William.** b 13. OBE 46. Down Coll Cam BA 35, MA 42. Westcott Ho Cam 35. **d** 37 **p** 38 Guildf. C of Farnham 37-40; CF (EC) 39-46; Hon CF from 46; Dom Chap to Abp of York 46-49; LPr Dio York 46-49; Hon Chap to Abp of York 50-54; Gen Sec CACTM 49-54; Preb of Wedmore ii in Wells Cathl 52-54; Cons Ld Bp Suffr of Whitby in York Minster 30 Nov 54 by Abp of York; Bps of Sheff; B & W; Ripon; Wakef; and Blackb; Bps Suffr of Hull; Selby; Jarrow; Kens; Stockport; and Pontefract; and Bp Gerrard; Trld to Kimb K 61; res 65; re-apptd 68; res 76; Asst Bp of Worc 66-68; in Dio Wakef from 77; Commiss Kimb K 66-68. *Westgate Close, Clifton, Brighouse, W Yorks, HD6 4HJ.* (Brighouse 715414)

WHEELDON, Thomas Frederick Ronald. St Chad's Coll Dur 43. **d** 45 **p** 46 Dur. C of St Paul W Hartlepool 45-47; S Moor 47-48; St Jas Gateshead (in c of H Trin) 49-52; R of Redmarshall 52-75; Elton 54-75. *11 Lilac Close, Carlton, Stockton-on-Tees.*

WHEELDON, Walter Thomas. MBE 80. Moore Th Coll Syd 53. **d** 54 **p** 56 Gippsld. I of Boolarra 54-57; Bruthen 57-60; Chap RAN and L to Offic Dio Syd 60-80; Perm to Offic Dio Gippsld 79-80; C of H Trin Berrima Dio Syd from 80. *14 Waite Street, Moss Vale, NSW, Australia 2577.*

WHEELDON, William Dennis. b 25. Univ of Leeds, BA (2nd cl Phil) 51. Coll of Resurr Mirfield 52. **d** 54 Wakef **p** 56 Arg Is for Wakef. M CR 55-76; Sub-Warden Hostel of Resurr Leeds 56-59; Tutor Codr Coll Barb 59-63; Vice-Prin 63-66; Prin Coll of Resurr Mirfield 66-75; Exam Chap to Bp of Wakef 69-76. *89 New Mills Road, Birch Vale, Nr Stockport, SK12 5BX.*

WHEELER, Alexandria Charles. b 36. **d** 73 **p** 74 Kimb K (APM). L to Offic Dio Kimb K 73-75; P-in-c of Ritchie Dio Kimb K from 75. *9a Schmidtsdrift Road, Kimberley, CP, S Africa.* (Kimberley 28212)

WHEELER, Alexander Quintin Henry. b 51. BA (Lon) 73. St Jo Coll Nottm 74. **d** 77 Bp McKie for Cov **p** 78 Cov. C of St Jo Evang Kenilworth 77-80; Madeley Dio Heref from 80. *1 Spencer Drive, Sutton Hill, Telford, TR7 4JY.*

WHEELER, Anthony William. b 28. **d** 76 **p** 77 Bris (APM). Hon C of Shirehampton Dio Bris from 76. *76 Kingsweston Avenue, Shirehampton, Bristol, BS11 0AL.* (Avonmouth 822261)

WHEELER, Desmond Reginald Sessel. b 18. Rhodes Univ BA 49. St Paul's Coll Grahmstn LTh 51. **d** 50 **p** 51 Johann. C of St Mary Rosettenville Johann 50-51; St Alb Ferreira's Town Johann 51-52; R of Piet Retief 52-53; C (Col Cl Act) of Reading 54-56; St Aug Queen's Gate Kens 56-58; Chap at Brussels 58-59; R of Zeal Monachorum 60-63; R of Bondleigh w Brushford 60-63; V of St Jo Evang Sutton-on-Plym 63-70; V of Bps Teignton Dio Ex from 70. *Bishop's Teignton Vicarage, Teignmouth, Devon, TQ14 9RH.* (Teignmouth 5247)

WHEELER, Eric William. b 17. GOC 73. **d** and **p** 76 Glouc. C of St Paul City and Dio Glouc from 76. *24 Bloomfield Road, Gloucester, GL1 5BL.* (0452-411161)

WHEELER, Frank George Michael. b 10. Univ of Reading BA (1st cl French) 33. Linc Th Coll 68. **d** 69 Southw **p** 70 Sherwood for Southw. C of St Pet w St Jas Nottm 69-73; Perm to Offic Dio Southw from 73. *11 Walsingham Road, Woodthorpe, Nottingham, NG5 4NU.*

WHEELER, Frederick William. Lon Coll of Div 1898. **d** 01 **p** 03 Lon. C of H Trin Lincoln's Inn Fields Lon 01-04; Baildon Yorks 04-08; Em Sheff 08-11; Kamloops BC 14-16; TCF 16-19; Miss at Main Line 25-30; Sorrento 30-47; L to Offic Dio Koot 47-54 and 56-69; Dio BC from 54. *214 Russell Street, Victoria, BC, Canada.*

WHEELER, George William Byars. Univ of Tor BA 45, MA 48. Wycl Coll Tor LTh 50. **d** 49 **p** 50 Tor. I of Highland Creek 49-60; R of St Crispin Tor 60-65; Assoc Ed *Canad Churchman* 65-67; C of St Nich Birch Cliff Tor 69-81. *62 Chine Drive, Scarborough, M1M 2K7, Ont, Canada.*

WHEELER, Canon Gordon Ledwell. b 10. Univ of Dur LTh 33. Lich Th Coll 29. **d** 33 **p** 34 Man. C of St Pet Bury 33-36; Chap Miss to Seamen Port of Man, Org Sec for NW Distr and LPr Dios St A, Ban, Ches, Man, Blackb and Carl 36-41; V of Thornton-le-Fylde 41-75; Can of Blackb 66-75; Can (Emer) from 75. *51a Preston Old Road, Marton, Blackpool, FY3 9PR.* (Blackpool 692416)

WHEELER, Graham John. b 39. Univ of Wales Dipl Th 66, BD 78. St Mich Coll Llan 63. **d** 66 **p** 67 Llan. C of St Martin roath 66-71; Cadoxton-Juxta-Barry 71-75; Perm to Offic Dio Llan 75-79; C of Highcliffe w Hinton Admiral Dio Win from 79. *250 Lymington Road, Highcliffe, Christchurh, Dorset, BH23 5ET.*

WHEELER, Henry Gilbert Reginald. b 07. **d** 66 **p** 69 Ex. C of Countess Wear 66-81; Publ Pr Dio Ex from 81. *23 Lucas Avenue, Exeter, Devon, EX4 6LZ.* (Exeter 73827)

WHEELER, James Albert. b 49. Sarum Wells Th Coll 74. **d** 76 **p** 77 Roch. C of All SS Orpington 76-79; St Pet w St Marg Roch 79-81; St John Bexley Dio Roch from 81. *71 Penhill Road, Bexley, Kent.* (01-303 4582)

WHEELER, John David. b 31. Selw Coll Cam BA 54, MA 58. Ely Th Coll 54. **d** 56 **p** 57 S'wark. C of Old Charlton 56-60; Northolt (in c of St Jos) 61-63; V of Bush Hill Pk 64-71; St Pet Ealing Dio Lon 71-74; St Paul (and St Clem from 79) Truro 74-80; Commiss Damar (Namibia from 80) from 70; P-in-c of St Sav Hammersmith Dio Lon from 80. *St Saviour's Vicarage, Cobbold Road, W12.* (01-743 4769)

WHEELER, John David William. Sarum Th Coll 60. **d** 62 Blackb **p** 63 Burnley for Blackb. C of Thornton-le-Fylde 62-64; Area Sec Miss to Seamen Lon 64-66; C of Kirstead w Langhale and Brooke 67-70; Chap Miss to Seamen Vic Dks Lon 70-72. *Address temp unknown.*

WHEELER, John Gordon. b 22. St Francis Coll Brisb 70. **d** 74 **p** 75 Wang. C of H Trin Benalla 74-77; Swan Hill Dio Bend from 77. *7 Standen Street, Swan Hill, Vic, Australia 3585.*

WHEELER, Julian Aldous. b 48. Univ of Nottm BTh 74. Kelham Th Coll 70. **d** 75 **p** 76 Ex. C of Bideford 75-79; Asst Master Bideford Commun Coll from 79. *1 Southholme Terrace, Bideford, Devon, EX39 4BX.* (023-72 3948)

WHEELER, Keith. Wollaston Coll W Austr 65. **d** 67 **p** 68 Perth. C of Belmont 67-69; Actg Youth Officer Dio Perth 69-70; C of St Matt Glenroy 71-72; Scarborough 72-73; R of Kununurra 73-77; Wyalkatchem Dio Perth from 77. *Rectory, Honour Avenue, Wyalkatchem, W Australia 6485.* (81 1052)

WHEELER, Malcolm John Stuart. K Coll Lon. **d** 39 Waik **p** 45 Ripon. C of St Paul Okato 39-40; Ch Ch Harrogate 40-46; Hawera 46-48; V of Foxton w Shannon 48-51; Pahiatua 51-61; Awapuni 61-69; Hawera 69-78; Silverstream 78-80; Perm to Offic Dio Wel from 80. *12 Kew Grove, Paraparaumu, NZ.*

WHEELER, Raymond Norman. Moore Th Coll Syd 57. **d** 58 Syd **p** 59 Bp Hilliard for Syd. C-in-c of Jannali-Como w Oyster Bay 58-59; W Kembla 59-61; R of Ashbury 61-71; C-in-c of N Bexley Provisional Distr 71-75; L to Offic Dio Syd 76-78; R of St Pet Burwood E Dio Syd from 78. *80 Acton Street, Croydon, NSW, Australia 2132.* (745-2704)

WHEELER, Richard Anthony. b 23. St Chad's Coll Dur BA 46, MA 48, Dipl Th (w distinc) 48. **d** 48 **p** 49 Lich. C of St Mary Kingswinford 48-52; St Agnes w St Pancras Toxt Pk 52-54; V of Up Holland 54-64; R of H Trin Dorchester w Frome Whitfield 64-73; Team V of Dorchester Dio Sarum from 73. *6 Albert Road, Dorchester, Dorset.* (Dorchester 62803)

WHEELER, Richard Roy. b 44. K Coll Lon BD 72. St Aug Coll Cant 72. **d** 74 Kingston for S'wark **p** 74 S'wark. C of St Matt Brixton Dio S'wark from 74. *1 St Matthew's Road, Brixton, SW2 1ND.* (01-733 4912)

WHEELER, Robert Frank. St Chad's Coll Regina. **d** 48 **p** 49 Qu'App. C of Wawota 48-49; V 49-52; R of Weyburn 52-53; I of Old Crow 53-57; Watson Lake 57-60; Telegraph Creek 60-75; Hon C of Ch Ch Cathl Whitehorse 75-76. *c/o Whitehorse General Hospital, Whitehorse, Yukon, Canada.*

WHEELER, Robert James. Mich Coll Crafers 63. **d** 67 Syd for Brisb **p** 68 Brisb. C of St Clem Stafford 68-70; V of All SS Mitchell 71-73; P-in-c of Geelong N w Norlane Melb 73-76; I 76-78; C of St Jas King Street City and Dio Syd from 78. *52 Iandra Street, Concord West, NSW, Australia 2138.* (232-3592)

WHEELER, Robert William. b 10. Oak Hill Coll. **d** 77 **p** 78 Bp Bradwell for Chelmsf. Hon C of Hockley Dio Chelmsf from 77. *275 Main Road, Hawkwell, Hockley, Essex. SS5 4NR.* (0702-202524)

WHEELER, Stephen. Tyndale Hall, Bris 26. **d** 28 **p** 29 Nagp. Miss at Saugor 28-33; Chap (ACS) Indore 33-37; Jubbulpore 37-38; R of Cusop 38-46; CF (TA-R of O) from 39; V of Walshaw 46-50; Min of St Paul's Chap Jersey 50-53; R of Meavy w Sheepstor 53-59; V of Stokenham w Sherford and Beesands 59-67; L to Offic Dio Ex from 68. *9 Clampitt Road, Ipplepen, Newton Abbot, Devon, TQ12 5RJ.* (Ipplepen 812659)

WHEELER, Vere Stewart Manton. b 10. St Chad's Coll Dur 46. **d** 49 Tewkesbury for Glouc **p** 50 Glouc. C of Stroud 49-52; Stow-on-the-Wold w Broadwell 52-55; R of Rendcomb 55-58; P-in-c of St Gabr Rang 59-66; C of All SS Glouc 67-79. *6-8 Whitfield Street, Gloucester, GL1 1NA* (Gloucester 24790)

WHEELER, William Thomas. Moore Th Coll Syd 62. ACT ThL 63. **d** 63 **p** 64 Syd. C of Beecroft 63-64; Castle Hill 64-65; Kiama 65-66; Chap RAAF from 66; L to Offic Dio Perth 68-74; Perm to Offic Dio Adel 74-79; Dio Brisb from 79. *RAAF Base, Amberley, Queensland, Australia 4305.*

WHEELER, William Thomas Pope. b 1900. Chich Th Coll 40. **d** and **p** 42 Blackb. C of St Cuthb Lytham 42-43; Bp's Youth Chap Dio Blackb 43-44; L to Offic as C-in-c of St Pet and St Paul Shelford 44-46; R of Colwick 46-50; V of Oxton 50-52 New Basford 52-64; Hunwick 64-65; St Pet Mountsorrel 65-67; L to Offic Dio Liv 68-69; Pet and Ely 69-72; Leic 72-74; Southw 74-79. *8 Arnold's Lane, Whittlesey, Peterborough, Northants.*

WHEELOCK, Canon John Richard. b 18. TCD BA (2nd cl Mod) 41, Div Test (1st cl) 42, MA 51. **d** 42 **p** 43 Kilm. C of Drumgoon and Ashfield 42-44; I of Clongish 44-51; Swanlinbar w Templeport 51-56; Annagh Dio Kilm from 56; RD of S Kilm 64-77; RD of E Kilm 71-77; Can of Kilm Cathl from 72; C-in-c of Cloverhill Dio Kilm from 74. *Rectory, Belturbet, Co Cavan, Irish Republic.* (Belturbet 42)

WHEELWRIGHT, Michael Harvey. b 39. Bps' Coll Cheshunt 64. **d** 67 **p** 68 Leic. C of Glen Parva w S Wigston 67-70; Evington 70-74; V of St Eliz Nether Hall 74-79; Chap Prudhoe Hosp Northumb from 79. *61 Dene Road, Wylam, Northumb.*

WHELAN, John Bernard. b 17. Univ of Dur LTh 41. Oak Hill Th Coll 38. **d** 47 **p** 48 Carl. C of Ambleside w Rydal 47-50; St Luke Barrow F Dio Carl 50-54; SPG Miss in Korea 54-66; Dioc Dir of Relig Educn 62-66; Perm to Offic Dio Man 67-68; C of Bury 68-71; Asst Chap Crumpsall Hosp Man 71-73; Chap N Man Gen Hosp Man from 73. *6 Holland Road, Crumpsall, Manchester 8.* (061-740 9860)

WHELAN, Peter Warwick Armstrong. b 34. Univ of Southn BTh 80. Open Univ BA 80. Sarum Th Coll 69. **d** 71 Sherborne for Sarum **p** 72 Bp McInnes for Sarum. C of St Mark Sarum 71-73; Solihull (in c of St Helen) 73-77; V of Shirley Dio Birm 77-82; Team R from 82. *Vicarage, Bishopton Close, Shirley, Solihull, B90 4AH.* (021-744 3123)

WHELAN, Weldon Deverell. St Jo Coll Auckld. **d** 41 **p** 42 Waik. C of St Pet Cathl Hamilton 41-42 and 44-45; CF (NZ) 42-44; P-in-c of Huntly 45; Inglewood 46; St Marg Te Kauwhata 46-48- V 48-50; Taumaruniu 50-52; Ohura 52-54; Waihi 54-60; W New Plymouth 60-68; Raglan 68-80; Can of Waik 62-80; Perm to Offic Dio Waik from 80. *34 Gillies Avenue, Hamilton, NZ.* (55-337)

WHENT, Canon Leonard George. **d** and **p** 40 Bunb. C of Albany 40-41; Actg R of Pinjarra 41-42; R 42-52; Chap AIF 44-46; Chap of Fairbridge Farm Sch Pinjarra 52-56; R of Donnybrook 56-60; Northn 60-61; Cranbrook 61-67; Can of Bunb 61-67; Hon Can from 67; L to Offic Dio Perth from 67. *37 Waverley Road, Coolbellup, W Australia 6163.* (37 3571)

WHEREAT, Canon Leslie Sidney. **d** 48 **p** 50 N Queensld. C of Ayr 48-51; M of Bush Bro Cloncurry 52-57; C of Stoke-on-Trent 58-59; Tewkesbury 59-63; R of Gordonvale 63-81; N Mackay Dio N Queensld from 81; Can of N Queensld from 69. *Box 107, North Mackay, N Queensland, Australia.*

WHETTEM, John Curtiss. b 27. Peterho Cam BA 50, MA 55. Wycl Hall Ox 50. **d** 52 Malmesbury for Bris **p** 53 Bris. C of Ch Ch Clifton 52-55; All SS Wandsworth 55-58; V of Soundwell 58-63; Dioc Youth Chap Bris 63-68; Bp's Cathl Chap Bris 64-68; V of N Mundham w Hunston 68-80; C-in-c of Merston 75-80; Team R of Swanborough Dio Sarum from

80. *Manningford Bruce Rectory, Pewsey, Wilts, SN9 6JW.* (Upavon 308)

WHETTER, Michael Arnold. b 30. Univ of Bris BA (2nd cl Hist) 51. Wells Th Coll 53. **d** 55 Tewkesbury for Glouc **p** 56 Glouc. C of Dursley 55-58; Coppenhall 58-61; R of H Trin Ches 61-71; V of St Alb Stockport Dio Ches from 71. *Vicarage, Offerton Lane, Stockport, Chesh, SK2 5AG.* (061-480 3773)

WHIBLEY, Roderick Marden. St Paul's Coll Grahmstn. **d** 68 **p** 69 Grahmstn. C of St Alb Vincent 68-72; Ch Ch E Lon Grahmtn 72-75. *116 Main Road, Amalinda, East London, CP, S Africa.*

WHIFFEN, William Timothy. b 25. SS Coll Cam 1st cl Math Trip pt i, 48, BA (Sen Opt Math Trip pt ii) 50, MA 54. Linc Th Coll. **d** 52 **p** 53 Liv. C of St Mich AA Wigan 52-56; Ch Ch Galle Face Colom 57; in Ch of S Ind 57-69; V of Clay Cross 69-74; Sec USPG (Overseas Div) from 74; Team R of Woughton Dio Ox from 79; M Gen Syn from 80. *Rectory, Woughton Park, Milton Keynes, MK6 3AU.* (Milton Keynes 670070)

WHIGHT, Jack Cyril. Univ of Brisb BA 39. Ridley Coll Melb. **d** 40 **p** 41 Goulb. C of Cootamundra 40-41; Young 41-44; R of Tarcutta 44-47; Asst Master Trin Gr Sch Melb 47-56; LPr Dio Melb 56-61; Perm to Offic Dio Brisb 61-79. *c/o 169 Dornoch Terrace, Highgate Hill, Queensland, Australia 4101.* (44 4692)

WHILD, Canon James Edward. Univ of Bris BA 52. Tyndale Hall Bris 48. **d** 53 Stafford for Cant **p** 54 Lich. C of Wel w Eyton 53-56; Asst Chap Miss to Seamen Rotterdam 56; Syd 56-58; R of Chatswood 58-64; St Mark Darling Point City and Dio Syd from 64; Exam Chap to Abp of Syd from 71; Hon Can of Syd 73-77; Can from 77. *53 Darling Point Road, Darling Point, NSW, Australia 2027.* (328 1125)

WHINNEY, Ven Michael Humphrey Dickens. b 30. Pemb Coll Cam 2nd cl Hist Trip pt i 54, BA 55, 2nd cl Th Trip pt ii 56, MA 59. Ridley Hall Cam 55. **d** 57 **p** 58 Chelmsf. C of Rainham 57-60; Hd of Cam Univ Miss Bermondsey 60-67; L to Offic Dio S'wark 61-67; V of St Jas w Ch Ch Bermondsey 67-73; Archd of S'wark from 73; Bp Suffr Desig of Aston. *17 Stradella Road, Herne Hill, SE24* (01-274 6767)

WHINTON, William Francis Ivan. b 35. N Ordin Course 77. **d** 80 Ches **p** 81 Stockport for Ches. C of Stockport Dio Ches from 80. *12 Alsfeld Way, New Mills, Stockport, Cheshire, SK12 3DD.*

WHIPP, Canon Cecil Wallis. b 1898. AKC (1st cl) 23. **d** 23 **p** 24 S'wark. C of St Barn Sutton 23-27; Succr of Leic Cathl 27-32; V of Cosby 32-38; St Aug Newfoundpool Leic 38-43; St Jas Gtr Leic 43-59; Hon Can of Leic 56-58; Can (Emer) from 59; V of Stoke-sub-Hambdon 58-67; L to Offic Dio B & W from 67. *2 Mill Close, East Coker, Yeovil, Somt.* (W Coker 2834)

WHITAKER, David Arthur Edward. New Coll Ox BA 50, MA 55. Wells Th Coll 51. **d** 53 **p** 54 Southw. C of W Bridgford 53-56; CF 56-58; V of New Clifton 58-63; R of St John Maseru 63-69; Feniton 69-76; R of Buckerell 69-76; P-in-c of Tiverton Dio Ex 76-78; R from 78. *St Peter's Rectory, Tiverton, Devon.* (Tiverton 2265)

WHITAKER, Canon Edward Charles. b 16. St Edm Hall Ox BA (2nd cl Th) 38, MA 68. BD (Lambeth) 81. Lich Th Coll 38. **d** 39 **p** 40 Carl. C of St Matt Barrow-F 39-42; St John Workington 42-45; R of Nether Denton 45-49; V of Culgaith 49-56; V of Kirkland 49-56; Kirkby Ireleth 56-73; Plumpton Wall 73-81; Hon Can of Carl 69-81; Can (Emer) from 81; Exam Chap to Bp of Carl 75-81; P-in-c of Lazonby 76-79. *Chestnut Cottage, Beokside, Kirkby-in-Furness, Cumb, LA17 7TG.*

WHITBY, Lord Bishop Suffragan of. *See* Barker, Right Rev Clifford Conder.

WHITCOMBE, Guy Rowland. b 09. OBE 55. New Coll Ox BA 31, MA 35. Cudd Coll 35. **d** 35 **p** 36 Lon. C of St Andr Undershaft w St Mary Axe Lon 35-37; St John Hampstead 37-39; CF (EC) 39-45; CF 45-61; V of Harrow 61-74; Perm to Offic Dio St E from 74; Dio Nor from 75. *Ridge House, Rickinhall Superior, Suff.* (Botesdale 227)

WHITCOMBE, Michael George Stanley. b 34. Keble Coll Ox BA 58, MA 62. Wycl Hall Ox Dipl Th 59. **d** 60 **p** 61 Cov. C of St Nich Nuneaton 60-63; Chap of All SS Sch Jess Sabah 63-67; V of St Paul Warw 67-68; Asst Master St Paul's Coll Hong Kong 68-69; Chap Dioc Boys' Sch Hong Kong 69-72; L to Offic Dio Hong 68-72; V of Lightcliffe 72-79; R of St Columba Largs 79-81; St Francis Ipswich Dio St E from 81. *190 Hawthorn Drive, Ipswich, IP2 0QQ* (Ipswich 52791)

WHITCOMBE, Stanley Edward Cuthbert. b 07. K Coll Lon. **d** and **p** 42 Glouc. C of St Jas Glouc 42-45; V of Upleadon 45-47; Gorsley w Clifford's Mesne 47-54; R of Shipton Oliffe w Shipton Sollars 54-56; C of Stratford-on-Avon (in c of St Jas Gt) 56-59; R of Brinklow 59-65; R of Harborough Magna 60-61; Chap St Mary's Hosp Harborough Magna 60-61; R of Bourton-on-Dunsmore w Frankton 65-72; Perm to Offic Dio Cov 72-73; Perm to Offic Dio Wakef 73-79; Glas & Gall 79-81; Wakef from 81. *10 Cricketers Close, Ackworth, Pontefract, W Yorks, WF7 7PW.*

WHITCROFT, Graham Frederick. b 42. Oak Hill Th Coll 64. **d** 66 **p** 67 Nor. C of Cromer 66-69; Attercliffe 69-72; V of St John's Kimberworth Pk Dio Sheff from 72. *21 Birks Road, Kimberworth Park, Rotherham, S Yorks.* (Rotherham 552268)

WHITCROFT, Thomas Henry. b 30. Univ of the S Tenn BA 52. Univ of Pittsburgh MSW 73. Gen Th Sem NY STB 59. **d** 59 Washington **p** 59 Bp Street for Chicago. In Amer Ch 59-77; V and Hon Can of Ch Ch Cathl Dio Montr from 77. *1444 Union Avenue, Montreal, Quebec, H3A 2B8, Canada.* (514-845 6211)

WHITE, Alan. b 18. Univ of Man BSc (1st cl Math) 39. MSc 40. St Cath S Ox BA (2nd cl Th) 42, MA 46. Univ of Leeds MEducn 52. Ripon Hall Ox 40. **d** 42 **p** 43 Leic. C of St Marg Leic 42-45; Chap and Asst Master Leeds Gr Sch 45-56; LPr Dio Ripon 45-56; Asst Master Bromsgrove Sch 56-72; Chap from 72; LPr Dio Worc from 56. *25 Leadbetter Drive, Bromsgrove, Worcs, B61 7JG.* (Bromsgrove 77955)

WHITE, Alan. b 43. Univ of Ex BA (2nd cl French) 65. Chich Th Coll 65. **d** 68 **p** 69 Lon. C of St Matt U Clapton 68-72; Southgate 72-76; P-in-c of St Pet-le-Poer Muswell Hill Dio Lon 76-79; V from 79. *163 Colney Hatch Lane, N10 1HA.* (01-883 1526)

WHITE, Basil Rowntree. b 14. BA (2nd cl Engl) Lon 36. **d** 62 Stafford for Lich **p** 63 Shrewsbury for Lich. Hd Master St Pet C of E High Sch and Hon C of Stoke-on-Trent 62-75; Perm to Offic Dio Ripon 75-81; P-in-c of Fornham St Martin and Timworth Dio St E from 81. *Rectory, Old Hall Lane, Fornham St Martin, Bury St Edmunds, Suff.* (Bury St Edmunds 4182)

WHITE, Brian Thomas. b 47. St Barn Coll Belair 77. **d** and **p** 80 River. C of Griffith Dio River from 80. *Flat 5, 90/92 Binya Street, Griffith, NSW, Australia 2680.*

WHITE, Bruce Edward. Univ of Auckld BA 65. St Jo Coll Auckld LTh 67. **d** 67 **p** 68 Wai. C of Rotorua 67-74; V of Hikurangi Maori Past 74-78; Mt Maunganui Dio Wai from 78. *Box 5022, Mount Maunganui, NZ.*

WHITE, Charles William Langston. b 13. Lon Coll Div 52. **d** 54 **p** 55 S'wark. C of Im w St Anselm Streatham 54-57; V of St Sav Guildf 57-68; R of St Leonards-on-Sea 68-76; L to Offic Dio Jer from 76. *PO Box 19462, Jerusalem, Israel.*

WHITE, Christopher Norman Hessler. b 32. TD 76. St Cath Coll Cam BA 56, MA 60. Cudd Coll. **d** 59 **p** 60 Birm. C of Solihull 59-62; St Aid Leeds 62-65; CF (TA) 64-67; CF (TAVR) from 67; V of Aysgarth 65-74; R of Richmond Yorks (w Hudswell from 76) Dio Ripon from 74; RD of Richmond 75-80; C-in-c of Hudswell 76. *Rectory, Richmond, N Yorks, DL10 7AQ.* (Richmond 3398)

WHITE, Clarence Herbert. Em Coll Sktn BA and LTh 46, BD 49. **d** 46 **p** 48 Sktn. Miss at Lanigan and Kildrum 46-48; Watson and Le Roy 48-50; R of St Mark Sktn 50-53; Chap RCAF 53-60 and from 63; P-in-c of Mossbank 61-62. *RCAF, Trenton, Astra, Ont, Canada.*

WHITE, Clarence John. ACT ThL 60. Univ of Queensld BA 71. St Francis Coll Brisb. **d** 60 **p** 62 Brisb. C of Lutwyche 60-61; H Trin Fortitude Valley 61-62; St Matt Groveley Brisb 62-65; V of St Martin Tara 65-68; R of Rosewood 68-70; Perm to Offic Dio Brisb from 70; Asst Chap C of E Gr Sch E Brisb from 72. *30 Oaklands Parade, E Brisbane, Queensland, Australia 4169.* (391 6160)

WHITE, Clement. b 25. AKC 50. St Bonif Coll Warm 50. **d** 51 **p** 52 Newc T. C of All SS Gosforth 51-54; St Andr Newc T 54-56; Seaton Hirst 56-59; V of St Jo Evang Percy Tynemouth 59-69; St Pet Monkseaton Dio Newc T from 69. *Vicarage, Elmwood Road, Monkseaton, Whitley Bay, Northumb NE25 8EX.* (Whitley Bay 521991)

WHITE, Crispin Michael. b 42. Bps' Coll Cheshunt, 62. **d** 65 **p** 66 Lon. C of St Paul's Harrow 65-67; St Mich AA Mill Hill 67-68; I of St Clem Miss (E) Labrador 68-71; W Reg Padre Toc H 71-75; Mid-E Reg Padre Toc H from 75. *68 Thorpe Park Road, Peterborough, Cambs, PE3 6LJ.*

WHITE, Cyril Norman. b 03. ALCD 26. **d** 30 **p** 31 Ox. C of H Trin Walton Bucks 30-36; R of Ellesborough 36-76; Chap to Stoke Mandeville Hosp 46-75; Perm to Offic Dio Ox from 76. *The Corner Cottage, Wooburn, High Wycombe, Bucks.*

WHITE, Dale St John. Rhodes Univ St Paul's Coll Grahmstn. **d** 57 **p** 58 Johann. C of St Pet Krugersdorp 57-60; St Alb Miss Johann 60-65; L to Offic Dio Johann from 65. *PO Box 81, Roodepoort, Transvaal, S Africa.* (011-763 2650)

WHITE, David Hamilton. Oak Hill Th Coll 63. **d** 63 **p** 64 Syd. C of St Mich Wollongong 63-65; Bondi 66; Kensington 66-69; C-in-c of S Coogee 69-73; R of Milton Dio Syd from 73. *12 Charles Street, Milton, NSW, Australia 2538.* (044-55 1495)

WHITE, David John. b 26. Univ of Leeds BA 53. Coll of Resurr Mirfield 53. **d** 55 **p** 56 Chich. C of Brighton 55-58; St

Jas Wednesbury 58-60; St Jo Evang Taunton (in c of St Mich Galmington) 60-61; R of Morton 61-62; in RC Church 62-73; rec back into Angl Commun by Bp of Lewes for Bp of Chich; Perm to Offic Dio Nor from 73; Lect Whitelands Coll Putney 72-75; R of Tregony w St Cuby and Cornelly 75-79; Castle Bromwich Dio Birm from 78. *Rectory, Rectory Lane, Castle Bromwich, Birmingham, B36 9DH.* (021-747 2281)

WHITE, David John. b 44. Chich Th Coll 71. **d** 73 Warrington for Liv **p** 74 Liv. C of Hindley 73-77; Orford 77-79; P-in-c of Good Shepherd Bishop Wearmouth Dio Dur 79-81; V from 81. *Good Shepherd Vicarage, Forest Road, Sunderland, SR4 0DX.* (Sunderland 56870)

WHITE, Derek James. Univ of Birm BA (2nd cl Th) 56. Chich Th Coll 56. **d** 58 **p** 59 Chich. C of Moulsecoomb w Stanmer and Falmer 58-61; Asst Chap Ardingly Coll 61-63; Chap 63-72; C of Glynde w Firle and Beddingham 72-73; V of U Beeding Dio Chich from 73; R of Bramber w Botolphs Dio Chich from 73. *Beeding Parsonage, Steyning, W Sussex.* (Steyning 813130)

WHITE, Dudley William. d 59 **p** 60 Swan B. C of Sketty 59-66; R of New Radnor w Llanfihangel Nantmelan 66-70; V of Penyfai 70-77; St Jude Swansea Dio Swan B from 77. *St Jude's Vicarage, Swansea, W Glam.*

WHITE, Edwin Charles. BD Lon 64. Moore Th Coll Syd ACT ThL 64. **d** 64 **p** 65 Syd. C of Eastwood 64-67; Kangaroo Valley 67-68; P-in-c of Menindee 68-72; R of Kambalda 72-74; C of Marrickville 74; Perm to Offic Dio Syd 75-77; C of Punchbowl 77; C-in-c of Provisional Par of Putney 78-80; R of St Andr Riverwood Dio Syd from 80. *9 Littleton Street, Riverwood, NSW, Australia 2210.* (53-7624)

WHITE, Egbert Douglas. b 06. Keble Coll Ox BA 28, MA 32. Wycl Hall Ox 28. **d** 34 **p** 35 B & W. C of St Paul Weston-S-Mare 34-36; C-in-c of Locking 40-42; C of Kewstoke w Milton 44-49; V of Mudford Dio B & W from 49; R of Chilton Cantelo w Ashington Dio B & W from 67. *St Mary's Vicarage, Mudford, Yeovil, Somt.* (Marston Magna 381)

WHITE, Ernest Stanley. b 13. St Chad's Coll Dur BA 35, MA and Dipl Th 38. **d** 36 **p** 37 Blackb. C of St Steph Burnley 36-40; C-in-c 40-46; Ashbourne w Mapleton 46-49; V of St Bart Ewood Blackb 49-59; St Mich AA Ashton-on-Ribble 59-78. *12 Howick Cross Lane, Penwortham, Preston, Lancs, PR1 0NR.*

WHITE, Francis. b 49. Univ of Wales (Cardiff) BSc (Econ) 70. Univ of Nottm Dipl Th 78. St Jo Coll Nottm 77. **d** 80 Dur **p** 81 Jarrow for Dur. C of St Nich City and Dio Dur from 80. *15 Providence Row, Durham, DH1 1RS.*

WHITE, Canon Frank. b 11. Linc Th Coll. **d** 36 **p** 37 Wakef. C of Penistone 36-39; St Paul King Cross 39-46; CF (EC) 41-46; R of High Hoyland w Clayton W 46-50; V of Liversedge 50-56; Lightcliffe Dio Wakef from 56-72; Asst RD of Halifax 61-68; Proc Conv Wakef 61-72; Hon Can of Wakef 63-72; Can (Emer) from 72; RD of Brighouse and Elland 68-72; R of Leathley w Farnley 72-79; Perm to Offic Dio Bradf from 79. *Vicarage, Hubberholme, Skipton, BD23 5JE.* (Kettlewell 215)

WHITE, Frederick Stanley. b 28. SOC 62. **d** 67 Ches **p** 68 Birkenhead for Ches. C of Eastham 67-72; Asst Chap Mersey Miss to Seamen 72-75; V of Jurby Dio S & M from 75; Chap of St Jude Andreas Dio S & M from 75; RD of Ramsey from 78; R of Andreas Dio S & M from 79. *Rectory, Village Road, Kirk Andreas, Ramsey, IM.* (062-488 419)

WHITE, Frederick William Hartland. b 22. MBE (Mil) 62. Kelham Th Coll 39. **d** 45 Dur for Newc T **p** 46 Newc T. C of St John Newc T 45-50; CF 50-74; ACG 70-74; Hon Chap to HM the Queen from 73; V of Harrow Dio Lon from 74. *St Mary's Vicarage, Church Hill, Harrow, Middx.* (01-422 2652)

WHITE, Gavin Donald. b 27. McGill Univ Montr 46. Univ of Tor BA 49. Trin Coll Tor BD 61. Gen Th Sem NY STM 68. Univ of Lon PhD 70. St Steph Ho Ox 51. **d** 53 Lon for Col Bp **p** 54 Queb. C of St Matt Queb 53-55; Chap Dew Line 56-57; Miss Knob Lake 57-58; Kideleko 59-62; Lect St Paul's U Th Coll Limuru 62-66; L to Offic Dio Zanz T 62-66; C of St Steph Rosslyn Hampstead 68-70; Lect Univ of Glas from 71; L to Offic Dios of Glasgow, Galloway from 71. *99 Mossgiel Road, Glasgow, G43 2BY.* (041-632 3151)

WHITE, Geoffrey Brian. b 54. Jes Coll Ox BA 76, MA 80. St Steph Ho Ox 76. **d** 79 **p** 80 Wakef. C of St Pet Huddersfield 79-82; Flixton Dio Man from 82. *Curates House, Church Road, Flixton, Manchester, M31 3HR.*

WHITE, Geoffrey Gordon. b 28. Selw Coll Cam BA 50, MA 54. Cudd Coll 51. **d** 53 Bris for Sarum **p** 54 Sarum. C of Bradf-on-Avon 53-56; St Jo Div Kennington 56-61; V of St Wilfrid Leeds 61-63; Chap K Coll Hosp Lon 63-66; V of Aldwick 66-76; Good Shepherd Preston Dio Chich from 76. *272 Dyke Road, Brighton, BN1 5AE.* (B'ton 552737)

WHITE, Geoffrey Howard. b 10. Kelham Th Coll 27. **d** 34 **p** 35 Leic. C of St Mich AA Belgrave 34-37; H Trin Eltham 37-39; CF 39-46; V of Loweswater (w Buttermere from 61) 45-74; C-in-c of Buttermere 49-61. *Jenkin, Loweswater, Cockermouth, Cumb.* (090-085234)

WHITE, Gordon Benjamin James. b 13. Worc Ord Coll 60. **d** 62 Tewkesbury for Glouc **p** 63 Glouc. C of Stroud 62-65; PC of Leonard Stanley Dio Glouc 65-68; V from 68; RD of Stonehouse 68-79. *Leonard Stanley Vicarage, Stonehouse, Glos.* (Stonehouse 3161)

WHITE, Gordon William. Qu Coll Newfld 56. **d** 59 **p** 60 Newfld. C of Bell I 59-64; P-in-c 64-67; I of Whitbourne 67-72; L to Offic Dio Newfld from 72. *St John's, Newfoundland, Canada.*

WHITE, Harold Kent. b 05. St Cath S Ox BA (2nd cl Th) 27, MA 37. St Steph Ho Ox 28. **d** 28 **p** 29 Mon. C of St Geo Tredegar 28-37; Libr of Pusey Ho Ox L to Offic Dio Ox and Perm to Offic Dio Mon 37-41; PC of H Spirit Beeston Hill 41-44; Chap RNVR 44-46; RN 46-60; R of Waldershare w Coldred 60-62; C-in-c of Tilmanstone 60-62; V of St Mary Aldermary Lon 62-75; Perm to Offic Dio S'wark 62-69; Chap St Geo Venice 75-76. *Dorsoduro 870, 30123 Venice, Italy.* (Venice 36068)

WHITE, Canon Hugh Vaughan. b 1889. Keble Coll Ox BA 10, MA 14. Can Scho Linc 12. **d** 13 **p** 14 Sarum. C of St Edm Sarum 13-19; V of Broad Hinton 19-66; R of Winterbourne Bassett 52-66; RD of Avebury 39-55; Can and Preb of Hurstbourne and Burbage in Sarum Cathl 50-67; Can (Emer) from 67. *Maristow Nursing Home, 16 Bourne Avenue, Salisbury, Wilts.*

WHITE, John Austin. b 42. Univ of Hull BA 64. Coll of Resurr Mirfield 64. **d** 66 **p** 67 Ripon. C of St Aid Leeds 66-69; Asst Chap Univ of Leeds 69-73; Chap N Ordin Course from 73; L to Offic Dio Man from 73. *23 Sandy Lane, Stretford, Manchester, M32 9DB.*

WHITE, John Emlyn. b 34. St Aid Coll 59. **d** 62 **p** 63 Bris. C of Cricklade w Latton and Eisey 62-63; Kingswood 63-66; Ashton-on-Ribble 66-69; V of Heyhouses (or Sabden) 69-71; Chap to Roundway Hosp and Old Pk House Devizes 71-77; K Coll and Belgrade Children Hosps Denmark Hill Dio S'wark from 77. *14 Sunset Road, SE5 8EA.* (01-737 4132)

WHITE, John Francis. b 47. Qu Coll Cam 2nd cl Cl Trip pt i 68, BA (3rd cl Cl Trip pt ii) 69, MA 73. Cudd Coll 72. **d** 72 **p** 73 Wakef. Sacr of Wakef Cathl 72-73; Prec 73-76; V of Thurlstone Dio Wakef from 76; P-in-c of Hoylandswaine Dio Wakef from 81. *Thurlstone Vicarage, Sheffield, S30 6QS.* (Barnsley 763170)

WHITE, John Gordon. b 20. AKC (1st cl) 48. **d** 49 **p** 50 Ripon. C of Halton 49-51; Goring 51-56; C-in-c of St Giles Conv Distr Shoreham and Chap Shoreham Hosp Dio Chich from 56. *15 The Drive, Shoreham-by-Sea, Sussex, BN4 5GA.* (Shoreham 3715)

WHITE, John Neville. b 41. Univ of Edin MA 63. Cranmer Hall Dur Dipl Th 65. **d** 65 Dur **p** 66 Jarrow for Dur. C of Sedgefield 65-68; St Mich Stoke 68-72; V of St Cuthb Wrose City and Dio Brad from 72. *71 Wrose Road, Bradford, Yorks, BD2 1LN.* (Bradford 611631)

WHITE, Jonathan Roger. b 36. Univ of Lon BSc (Eng) 61. Cudd Coll 63. **d** 65 Hulme for Man **p** 66 Man. C of Swinton 65-67; Prestwich 67-70; R of Stowell Mem Ch Salford 70-74; P in Swan Group of Pars 74-77; P-in-c of Monks Risborough Dio Ox from 77; Gt Kimble w L Kimble Dio Ox from 77. *Monks Risborough Rectory, Aylesbury, Bucks HP17 9JE.* (Princes R'Bro' 3162)

WHITE, Canon Joseph George. d 61 **p** 62 Ches. C of Frodsham 61-65; V of Rainow w Saltersford 65-72; C-in-c of Macclesfield Forest 66-72; Team V of Ches 72-75; Dioc Dir of Educn Ches from 74; L to Offic Dio Ches 75-79; Hon Can of Ches Cathl from 79; P-in-c of Capenhurst Dio Ches from 79. *33 Abbots Grange, Liverpool Road, Chester, CH2 1AJ.* (Chester 381766)

WHITE, Julian Edward Llewellyn. b 53. St D Coll Lamp BA 79. Bp Burgess Th Coll 73. **d** 79 **p** 80 Mon. C of St Mark Newport Dio Mon from 79. *5 Stamford Court, Allt-yr-yn, Barrack Hill, Newport, Gwent.*

WHITE, Keith. b 54. Liv Poly BA 78. Wycl Hall Ox 78. **d** 81 Edin. C of St Thos City and Dio Edin from 81. *81 Glasgow Road, Edinburgh, EH12 8LJ.*

WHITE, Kenneth Charles. b 26. Tyndale Hall Bris 48. **d** 54 U Nile **p** 56 Momb. Chap Lotome Sch Karamoja 54-55; P Dio Momb 55-57; C of Morden 57-60; V of Ramsey St Mary w Pondsbridge 60-66; Ch Ch Leyton 66-81; Totland Bay Dio Portsm from 81. *Christ Church Vicarage, Totland Bay, Freshwater, IW.* (098-383 2031)

WHITE, Kenneth Charles. b 15. TD 51, 1st Clasp 58. FCIS 70. St Deiniol's Libr Hawarden 76. **d** 77 **p** 78 Ches. Hon C of Upton 77-79; R of Warburton Dio Ches from 79. *Rectory, Bent Lane, Warburton, Lymm, Chesh.* (Lymm 3163)

WHITE, Louis. K Coll Halifax NS. **d** 46 **p** 48 NS. R of Ship Harbour 48-52; Antigonish 52-54; Blue Rocks and La Havre 54-61; Bridgetown 61-68; Woodside Dio NS from 68. *343 Pleasant Street, Dartmouth, NS, Canada.* (463-1206)

WHITE, Malcolm Robert. b 46. Univ of Man BSc 68. St Jo Coll Dur 74. **d** 77 **p** 78 York. C of St Barn Linthorpe Middlesbrough 77-81; Sutton-in-Holderness w Wawne Dio York from 81. *19 Church Street, Sutton-on-Hull, Hull, HU7 4TL.* (Hull 711814)

WHITE, Martin. b 50. St Jo Coll dur BA 72, Dipl Th 73. Cranmer Hall Dur 72. **d** 74 **p** 75 Derby. C of Ripley 74-78; Normanton-by-Derby 78-80; V of Sinfin Dio Derby from 80. *St Stephen's House, Sinfin Lane, Sinfin, Derby, DE2 9GP.* (Derby 760186)

WHITE, Noel Louis. TCD BA 45. Div Test (1st cl) 46. MA 58. **d** 46 **p** 47 Down. C of St Patr Ballymacarett 46-50; Chap Govt Secondary Sch Rumbek 50-54; CMS Miss at Yambio 54-59 Mundri 59-60; R of St Silas Belf 62-74; Asst Gen Sec CMS Ireland 74-78. *136 Sydenham Avenue, Belfast, BT4 2DU, N Ireland.* (Belfast 654271)

WHITE, Canon Norman Frederick Hooton. b 1897. Westcott Ho Cam 45. **d** 45 **p** 46 Southw. C of St Mary Bulwell 45-50; V of Misterton (w W Stockwith from 57) 50-59; C-in-c of W Stockwith 55-57; Bawtry w Austerfield 59-68; V of Misson 60-68; RD of Bawtry 59-68; Surr from 60; Hon Can of Southw 66-73; Can (Emer) from 73; L to Offic Dio Southw from 68. *33 Elm Close, Mapperley Road, Nottingham, NG3 5AH.*

WHITE, Patrick George Hilliard. b 42. Univ of Tor BA 69. Wycl Coll Tor MDiv 77. **d** 77 Bp Read for Tor **p** 78 Tor. C of St Matt Islington Tor 77-79; I of Oak Ridges Dio Tor from 79. *Yonge Street, Oak Ridges, Ont, Canada, L0G 1P0.*

WHITE, Peter Francis. b 27. St Edm Hall Ox BA 51, MA 55. Ridley Hall Cam 51. **d** 53 **p** 54 York. C of Drypool 53-56; V of St Edm Dartford 56-62; CF 62-78; R of Barming Dio Roch from 78. *Barming Rectory, Maidstone, Kent.* (Maidstone 26263)

WHITE, Peter John. b 23. Hertf Coll Ox BA 45, MA 49. Wycl Hall Ox 45. **d** 47 **p** 48 Bradf. C of St Steph Bowling Bradf 47-49; St Mary Magd Torquay 49-52; PC of St Boniface Devonport 52-59; V of Mancetter 59-62; CMS Area Sec for Dios Glouc Worc and Heref 62-69; V of Chipping Campden (w Ebrington from 75) Dio Glouc from 69; C-in-c of Ebrington 69-75; RD of Campden from 73. *Vicarage, Chipping Campden, Glos, GL55 6HU.* (Evesham 840671)

WHITE, Peter John. b 26. St Aid Coll 57. **d** 60 **p** 61 Liv. C of St Gabr Toxt Pk 60-62; Huyton 62-63; V of Thornham 63-68; C of Keighley 68-71; Newington w Dairycoates 71-75; Frodingham 75-80; R of Mareham-le-Fen and Revesby and Moorhouses w Wilksby, Moorby and Claxby Pluckacre Dio Linc from 80. *Mareham-le-Fen Rectory, Boston, Lincs, PE22 7QU.* (M-le-Fen 502)

WHITE, Peter Julian William. b 46. Univ of Melb BA 75. Trin Coll Melb 75. **d** 76 **p** 77 Wang. C of Shepparton 76-78; P-in-c of Merlynston Dio Melb from 79. *Vicarage, Glyndon Avenue, Merlynston, Vic, Australia 3058.* (350 4819)

WHITE, Peter Murchie Finch. Univ of Leeds BA (2nd cl Engl) 63. Coll of Resurr Mirfield 64. **d** 66 SW Tang. C of Milo Dio SW Tang from 66. *Milo Njombe, Tanzania.*

WHITE, Phillip George. b 33. St D Coll Lamp BA 54. St Mich Coll Llan 54. **d** 56 Llan **p** 57 Mon for Wales. C of Tongwynlais 56-58; Mountain Ash 58-60; Aberavon 60-62; CMS Area Sec Middx 62-64; V of Treherbert w Tynewydd and Ynysefeio 64-77; P-in-c of Treorchy 75-76; V of Pyle w Kenfig Dio Llan from 77. *Vicarage, Pyle Road, Pyle, Bridgend, Mid-Glam.* (Kenfig Hill 740500)

WHITE, Canon Raymond. Chich Th Coll 28. **d** 31 **p** 32 Chich. C of St Jo Evang Brighton 31-34; Chap S Afr Ch Rly Miss Pret 34-38; V of Fairwarp 38-47; CF (EC) 40-45; S Afr Ch Rly Miss Grahmstn 47-50; Dio Pret 50-57; Hd of S Afr Ch Rly Miss 51-57; Hon Can of Pret 52-57; Hd of Rhod and Nyasa Rly Miss 57-60; R of Lomagundi 60-67; P-in-c of Hatfield 67-76; Hon Can of Mashon from 76. *c/o Box UA7, Salisbury, Zimbabwe.*

WHITE, Raynor James. NZ Bd of Th Stud LTh 65. Coll Ho Ch Ch. **d** 59 Wel **p** 60 Bp Rich for Wel. C of Fielding 59-60; Levin 60-64; V of Foxton 64-71; Miramar 71-74; C of Paraparamu 74-76. *c/o Box 5450, Frankton, Hamilton, NZ.*

WHITE, Canon Richard. b 18. Sarum Th Coll 46. **d** 49 **p** 50 York. C of Redcar 49-52; St Martin Scarborough 52-54; V of St Chad York 54-59; Marske-in-Cleveland Dio York from 59; Can and Preb of York Minster from 78. *Marske-by-the-Sea Vicarage, Redcar, Cleve, TS11 7BN.* (Redcar 482896)

WHITE, Richard Allen. b 25. Open Univ BA 78. Sarim Wells Th Coll 78. **d** 81 Win. C of Bursledon Dio Win from 81. *11 Quay Haven, Lower Shanwick, Southampton.*

WHITE, Richard Clement. b 01. Ex Coll Ox BA (2nd cl Mod Hist) 26, MA 31. **d** 27 **p** 28 Cov. C of Rugby (in c of St Pet 27-28) 27-29; Perm to Offic Dios Lon and Ex 29-30; Lect and Tutor St Luke's Coll Ex Asst Master Ex Sch and C of Heavitree 30-31; Warden of Stephenson Hall Lect Univ of Sheff LPr Dio Sheff and Exam Chap to Bp of Sheff 31-33; Prin K Alfred's (Dioc Tr) Coll Win 33-46; Perm to Offic Dio St D 41-46; V of Hardingstone 46-51; R of Gt w L Packington 51-54. *6 St Barnabas House, Newland, Malvern, Worcs.*

WHITE, Robert Boyd. TCD Sizar 02, Scho 04, BA (Mod Cl Sen Mod Mod Lit) and Ferrar Mem Pri 06, MA 13. **d** 11 **p** 12 Arm. C of Killyman 11-16; Tartaraghan 16-21; C-in-c of Newtownhamilton (and Belleek from 53) 21-54; RD of Creggan 51-54; Exam Chap to Abp of Arm 52-65. *Redcliff Hotel, Seacliff Road, Bangor, Co Down, N Ireland.*

WHITE, Robert Bruce. b 42. Sarum Wells Th Coll 71. **d** 73 **p** 74 Barking for Chelmsf. C of St Barn Woodford 73-75; C-in-c of Sutton w Shopland 75-78; P-in-c 78-79; R of Southend-on-Sea Dio Chelmsf from 79; P-in-c of Westcliff-on-Sea Dio Chelmsf from 80. *Rectory, Honiton Road, Southend-on-Sea, SS1 2RY.*

WHITE, Robin Edward Bantry. b 47. TCD BA (Mod) 70, Div Test 72, BD 79. **d** 72 **p** 73 Dub. C of Zion Ch Rathgar Dub 72-76; Taney 76-79; Min Can of St Patr Cathl Dub 76-79; I of Abbeystrewry U Dio Ross from 79. *Rectory, Skibbereen, Co Cork, Irish Republic.* (028-21234)

WHITE, Roger Charles. b 37. St Alb Ministerial Tr Scheme 77. **d** 80 St Alb **p** 81 Hertf for St Alb. C of Wilshamstead and Houghton Conquest Dio St Alb from 80. *9 Moss Lane, Elstow, Beds, MK42 9YT.*

WHITE, Roger David. b 37. Univ of Wales Dipl Th 66. St Mich Coll Llan 63. **d** 66 **p** 67 Llan. C of Mountain Ash 66-71; Port Talbot 71-74; V of Caer Rhun w Llangelynnin Dio Ban from 74. *Caerhun Vicarage, Ty'n-y-Groes, Conwy, Gwyn, LL32 8UG.* (Ty'n-y-Groes 250)

WHITE, Roger Ian Scott. b 41. Univ of Leeds BA (2nd cl Gen) 62. Coll of Resurr Mirfield 62. **d** 64 **p** 65 Glouc. C of Wotton-under-Edge 64-69; Asst Master Lawrence Sheriff Sch Rugby 71-80; C of Rugby 73-80. *Hans Ehrenberg-Gymnasium, Bielefeld, W Germany.*

WHITE, Roger John. Eden Th Sem USA BD 65. Kelham Th Coll 60. **d** 66 Ripon **p** 67 Knaresborough for Ripon. C of Manston 66-69. *1200 Ranworth, Godfrey, Illinois 62035, USA.*

WHITE, Roy Sidney. b 34. Sarum Th Coll 62. **d** 65 **p** 66 Cant. C of Selsdon 65-68; Ranmoor (in c of St Columba Crosspool) 68-72; V of St Andr Croydon 72-78; Dir Abp Coggan Tr and Service Centre Dio Cant from 78. *70 Pollards Hill North, Norbury, SW16 4NY.* (01-679 4908)

WHITE, Sidney. St Francis Coll Brisb 62. **d** 63 Bp Hudson for Brisb **p** 63 Brisb. C of St Luke Toowoomba 63-65; Maryborough 65-67; V of Gin Gin 67-70; Perm to Offic Dio Bris from 70. *89 Bazaar Street, Maryborough, Queensland, Australia 4650.*

WHITE, Thomas Arthur. b 11. Univ of Wales BA 38. St Mich Coll Llan 39. **d** 39 **p** 40 Llan. C of St Sav Roath 39-42; All SS Gainsborough 42; St Dunstan Bedminster 42-50; V of St Jude w St Matthias Bris 50-80; CF (TA) 64-80. *26 Park Place, Upper Eastville, Bristol, BS5 8RG.*

WHITE, Trevor John. b 37. St Pet Coll Ox BA 61, MA 65. Wycl Hall Ox. **d** 63 **p** 64 Lich. C of Walsall 63-67; V of Greasborough 67-73; Chap Nat Nautical Sch Portishead from 73. *The Chaplain's House, Nautical School, Portishead, Bristol.* (Portishead 843589)

WHITE, Vernon Philip. b 53. Clare Coll Cam BA 75, MA 79. Or Coll Ox MLitt 80. Wycl Hall Ox Dipl Th 76. **d** 77 Ox **p** 78 Reading for Ox. Tutor Wycl Hall Ox from 77. *Wycliffe Hall, Banbury Road, Oxford, OX2 6PW.*

WHITE, William Henry. b 10. **d** 39 **p** 40 Argent. Miss (S Amer MS) Chaco Miss 39-49; of Walcot 49-50; Alvechurch 50-54; R of Ombersley w Doverdale 54-77. *Sinton Lodge, Ombersley, Worcs, WR9 0ET.*

WHITE-THOMSON, Very Rev Ian Hugh. b 04. Late Exhib of BNC Ox BA (3rd cl Mod Hist) 27, MA 37. Univ of Kent Hon DCL 71. Cudd Coll 28. **d** 29 **p** 30 Cant. C of Ashford Kent 29-34; R of St Martin w St Paul Cant 34-39; Res Chap to Abp of Cant 39-47; Six-Pr Cant Cathl 40-50; V of Folkestone 47-55; RD of Elham 47-55; Chap to HM the King 47-52; to HM the Queen 52-63; Hon Can of Cant 50-55; Proc Conv Cant 51-55; Archd of Northumb and Can Res of Newc T and Exam Chap to Bp of Newc T 55-63; Dean of Cant 63-76; Dean (Emer) from 76. *Camphill, Harville Road, Wye, Ashford, Kent.* (Wye 812210)

WHITECHURCH, William. b 04. AKC 33. Wadh Coll Ox MA 52, BM, BCh 52. Westcott Ho Cam. **d** 34 **p** 35 Dur. C of St Marg Dur 34-37. *Teign Royd, Teignmouth, Devon, TQ14 9BX.*

WHITEFIELD, Geoffrey George. b 27. Em Coll Cam BA 50, MA 55. Wycl Hall Ox 58. **d** 59 Dunwich for St E **p** 60 St E. C of St Mary Bury St Edms 59-63; V of Old Newton w Stowupland 63-81; Chap of Gipping 67-81; RD of Stowmarket 77-81; R of Lydgate w Ousden and Cowlinge Dio St E from 81. *Lydgate Rectory, Newmarket, Suff.*

WHITEHEAD, Barry. b 30. Or Coll Ox BA 53, MA 62. St Steph Ho Ox 53. **d** 55 **p** 56 Liv. C of St Dunstan Edge Hill 55-58; Upholland 58-61; Industr Chap Kirkby 61-68; Wigan

Dio Liv from 68; CF (TA) 64-67; CF (TAVR) 67-78; V of Aspull Dio Liv from 77. *Vicarage, Bolton Road, Aspull, Wigan, Lancs, WN2 1PR.* (Wigan 331236)

WHITEHEAD, Brian. b 36. SOC 74. **d** 75 Cant **p** 77 Croydon for Cant. C of St Aug Croydon 75-78; St Mary Torquay 78-80; V of St Mark Ford, Devonport Dio Ex from 80. *ST Mark's Vicarage, Cambridge Road, Ford, Plymouth, PL2 1PU.* (Plymouth 558135)

WHITEHEAD, Burton Jones. b 30. St D Coll Lamp BA 56. **d** 57 **p** 58 Mon. C of St Andr Newport 57-59; Chap St Woolos Cathl Newport 59-62; V of Crumlin 62-64; Asst Chap HM Pris Pentonville 64-66; Chap HM Pris Gartree 66-70; L to Offic 66-70; R of Didcot 70-79. *c/o Rectory, Didcot, Oxon.* (Didcot 813244)

WHITEHEAD, Christopher Martin Field. b 36. ALCD 62. **d** 62 **p** 63 Man. C of St Clem Higher Openshaw 62-63; St Pet Halliwell 64-66; V of Owlerton Sheff 66-75; Hunmanby w Muston Dio York from 75. *6 Northgate, Hunmanby, Filey, N Yorks, YO14 0NT.* (0723 890294)

WHITEHEAD, Denys Gordon. Pemb Coll Ox BA (Phil Pol and Econ) 52, MA 55. Linc Th Coll. **d** 52 **p** 53 Sheff. C of St Swith Sheff 52-54; Rawmarsh 54-57; C of St Ambrose Chorlton-on-Medlock 57-60; Sec SCM Man 57-60; N and S Rhod and Nyasa 62-64; Zam 64-66; Asst P at Kitwe 60-61; L to Offic Dio N Rhod 62-64; Dio Zam 64-68; Hon Chap of St Mary Magd Woodlands Lusaka Dio Zam 68-70; Dio Lusaka from 71. *PO Box 8200, Lusaka, Zambia.*

WHITEHEAD, Derek. b 27. St Jo Coll Cam BA 50, MA 55. BD (1st cl) Lon 60. Univ of Lanc PhD 73. Wells Th Coll 55. **d** 56 **p** 57 Man. C of Ascen Lower Broughton Salford 56-59; Asst Master Lich Gr Sch 59-63; Chap Highgate Sch 63-65; Div Lect Poulton Coll (Preston Poly from 75) 65-79; Dir of Educn Dio Chich from 79. *Maresfield Rectory, Uckfield, E Sussex, TN22 2HB.* (0825-3817)

WHITEHEAD, Frederick Keith. K Coll Lon and Warm BD and AKC 58. **d** 59 Blackb **p** 60 Lanc for York. C of H Trin S Shore Blackpool 59-63; Whitfield 63-66; L to Offic Dio Derby from 66. *Steepways, Simmondley New Road, Glossop, Derby.* (Glossop 2717)

WHITEHEAD, Geoffrey Arnold. b 31. Oak Hill Th Coll 53. **p** 57 Chelmsf. C of St Mary Becontree 56-59; St Mark Cheltm (in c of St Aid) 59-62; R of Ashwellthorpe w Wreningham 62-69; Postwick 69-73; Chap St Andr Hosp Thorpe 69-73; Chap Horton Hosp Epsom Dio Guildf from 73. *Horton House, Horton Hospital, Epsom, Surrey, KT19 8PZ.* (Epsom 29696)

WHITEHEAD, Gordon James. b 42. Clifton Th Coll 66. **d** 73 Chelmsf for Chile **p** 74 Chile. Dom Chap to Bp of Chile from 73. *Iglesia Anglicana, Casilla 566, Valparaiso, Chile.*

WHITEHEAD, John Stanley. b 38. Jes Coll Cam 3rd cl Hist Trip pt i 61, BA (2nd cl Th Trip pt ii) 63, MA 67. Westcott Ho Cam 63. **d** 64 **p** 65 Wakef. C of Batley 64-67; St Mark Mitcham 67-70; All SS Frindsbury 70-72; Team V of Strood 72-75; R of Halstead Dio Roch from 75. *Halstead Rectory, Sevenoaks, Kent.* (Knockholt 32133)

WHITEHEAD, Matthew Alexander. b 44. Univ of Leeds BA 65. Univ of Birm Dipl Th 68, MA 75. Qu Coll Birm. **d** 69 **p** 70 Bradf. C of Bingley 69-72; Keele 72-74; Asst Chap Univ of Keele 72-74; V of Escomb 74-80; Witton-Pk 74-80; Dom Chap to Bp of Dur from 74; V of Birtley Dio Dur from 80. *Vicarage, Birtley, Chester-le-Street, Co Durham.* (Birtley 402115)

WHITEHEAD, Michael Hutton. b 33. St Chad's Coll Dur 54. **d** 58 **p** 59 Dur. C of St Columba Southwick Dur 58-64; V of St Ignatius Hendon Bp Wearmouth Dio Dur 64-70; R 70-81; P-in-c of H Trin Sunderland 67-81; R of Hendon and Sunderland Dio Dur from 81. *Clergy House, Bramwell Road, Hendon, Sunderland, SR2 8BY.*

WHITEHEAD, Philip. b 34. Kelham Th Coll 55. **d** 59 **p** 60 Newc T. C of Sugley 59-62; St Paul Alnwick 62-63; St Gabr Heaton Newc T 63-66; All SS Gosforth (in c of Ascen Kenton) 66-67; V of Kenton 67-75; Spittal Dio Newc T from 75; P-in-c of Scremerston Dio Newc T from 81. *Spittal Vicarage, Berwick-upon-Tweed, Northumb.* (Berwick 7342)

WHITEHEAD, Robin Lawson. b 53. Univ of Bris BA 76. St Steph Ho Ox 77. **d** 80 **p** 81 St Alb. C of Cheshunt Dio St Alb from 80. *c/o St Mary's Vicarage, Churchgate, Cheshunt, Herts.*

WHITEHEAD, Roger Milton. b 25. Pemb Coll Ox BA 50, MA 54. Ely Th Coll 50. **d** 52 **p** 53 Dur. C of Ch Ch Gateshead 52-55; K Lynn 55-56; C-in-c of Conv Distr of H Trin Clifton Estate Nottm 56-59; V 59-61; R of Elston w Elston Chap 61-64; V of E Stoke w Syerston 61-64; St John Oakfield Ryde 64-72; Albrighton 72-80; R of Euston w Barnham and Fakenham Dio St E from 80. *Barnham Rectory, Thetford, Norf.* (Elveden 287)

WHITEHEAD, Walter Charles. **d** 46 **p** 48 Bend. C of All SS Cathl Bend 46-49; P-in-c of St John Bend 49-52; V 52-53; R of Daylesford 53-56; Lang Lang 56-57; Elmore 57-61; P-in-c of Buninyong 61-63; Ballan w Gordon and Bungaree 63-67; V 67-75; Perm to Offic Dio Bal from 75. *5 Pleasant Street South, Ballarat, Vic, Australia 3350.*

WHITEHOUSE, David. **d** 66 **p** 67 Sing. Miss S Perak Miss Distr 66-67; Telok Anson 67-71; R of Mulmur 71-73; St Pet Tor 73-75; Trin Queb 75-80; Dom Chap to Bp of Queb 78-80; I of Ch of the Resurr City and Dio Tor from 80. *1100 Woodbine Avenue, Toronto, Ont, Canada.*

WHITEHOUSE, Canon Isaac. b 1900. K Coll Lon 28. **d** 30 **p** 31 Chelmsf. C of H Trin Halstead 30-33; All SS Woodford Wells 33-36; V of St Paul E Ham 36-41; Coopersale 41-46; R of Buckhurst Hill 46-64; Dioc Missr 43-47; Surr 47-64; Hon Can of Chelmsf 52-64; Can (Emer) from 64; RD of Chigwell 59-64. *3 Greenbanks, 23 Chadwick Road, Westcliff-on-Sea, Essex, SS0 8LS.* (0702-354827)

WHITEHOUSE, John Stanley. Univ of Tor BA 50. Wycl Coll Tor LTh 53. **d** 52 Bp GA Wells for Rupld **p** 53 Bran for Rupld. C of St Geo Winnipeg 52-56; I of Selkirk 56-60; R of St Andr Winnipeg 60-66; Bell's Corners 66-71; Ch of Resurr Tor 71-80; St Sav Tor 80-81; Woodbridge Dio Tor from 81. *802 Islington Avenue, Woodbridge, Ont, Canada.*

WHITEHOUSE, Maurice Edward. Perry Hall Melb. **d** 66 **p** 67 St Arn. C of Mildura 66-68; V of Manangatang (w Nyah 70) 68-72; Ouyen 72-74; I of Montmorency 74-78; Perm to Offic Dio Melb from 78. *St John's Park, Mooroolbark, Vic, Australia 3138.*

WHITEHOUSE, Stuart Wellesley. b 1893. Ex Coll Ox BA 21, MA 26. Univ of Lon BD 51. **d** 45 **p** 46 Liv. Hd Master Alsop High Sch Liv 39-53; C of St Columba Anfield 45-51; Liv 51-53; St Sav Eastbourne 53-55; V of Wookey 55-58; Perm to Offic Dio Chich 58-75; Dio St E 76-79; Dio Portsm from 79. *Laconia, Old Park Road, St Lawrence, IW, PO38 1XU.* (Ventnor 852953)

WHITELAM, John. b 20. Kelham Th Coll 36. **d** 43 **p** 44 Wakef. C of Brighouse 43-45; St Paul w St Mark Deptford 46-54; V of St Agnes Kennington Pk Dio S'wark from 54. *37 St Agnes Place, SE11 4BB.* (01-735 3860)

WHITELEY, Alan. b 42. Lich Th Coll 68. **d** 71 **p** 72 Sheff. C of Wales 71-73; Team V of Frecheville w Hackenthorpe 75-79; V of Malin Bridge Dio Sheff from 79. *253 Loxley Road, Sheffield, S6 4TG.* (Sheff 343450)

WHITELEY, Alec George Richard. b 06. Worc Ordin Coll 63. **d** 65 **p** 66 Worc. C of Belbroughton w Fairfield 65-70; R of Gt w L Witley and Hillhampton 70-77. *14 Aston Close, Kempsey, Worcester.*

WHITELEY, Denys Edward Hugh. b 14. Late Scho of Pemb Coll Ox 1st cl Cl Mods 35, BA (2nd cl Lit Hum) 37, 1st cl Th 38, Ellerton Pri 39. Ripon Hall Ox 38. **d** 39 **p** 40 Ex. C of Woodbury 39-42; Erdington 42-45; Sec SCM for Birm 45-47; L to Offic Dio Birm 45-47; Dio Ox from 48; Chap Fell and Tutor at Jes Coll Ox 47-75; Vice-Prin 66-70; Lect in Th Univ of Ox 50-75; Sen Research Fell 75-82; Exam Chap to Bp of Sarum 54-63; Select Pr Univ of Ox 64-65. *18 Clover Close, Cotswold Road, Cumnor Hill, Oxford, OX2 9JH.* (Ox 862100)

WHITELEY, Donal Royston. b 27. Qu Coll Birm 54. **d** 57 Birm **p** 58 Aston for Birm. C of Handsworth 57-60; St Mary Kingswinford (in c of Wall Heath) 60-63; R of Norton Canes 63-71; V of Wetley Rocks Dio Lich from 71. *Wetley Rocks Vicarage, Stoke-on-Trent, Staffs, ST9 0AP.* (Wetley Rocks 550251)

WHITELEY, Edward John. b 29. K Coll Cam 2nd cl Hist Trip pt i 52, 2nd cl Th Trip pt iii BA 54, MA 57. Westcott Ho Cam 54. **d** 55 Whitby for York **p** 65 York. C of South Bank 55-58; Asst Chap Marlb Coll 58-61; Chap 62-65 Asst Sec Adult C'tte C of E Bd of Educn 65-67; PC of St Aid Billingham 67-70; R of Billingham Team Min 70-72; Chap Stockton and Billingham Tech Coll 71-72; Bp Wordsworth Sch Sarum 72. *2 Church Cottage, Steeple Langford, Salisbury.* (Stapleford 452)

WHITELEY, Robert. b 36. Univ of Dur BA (2nd cl Th) 67. Cranmer Hall Dur 62. **d** 67 **p** 68 Cant. C of All SS w St Phil Maidstone 67-70; Asst Chap K Sch Roch 70-71; Chap from 71. *77 Valley View Road, Rochester, Kent.*

WHITELEY, Canon Robert Louis. b 28. Univ of Leeds BA 48. Coll of Resurr Mirfield. **d** 52 **p** 53 Man. C of Hollinwood 52-55; R of St Mary Virg Belize 56-61; V of St Mary Virg Illingworth Halifax 61-68; St Mich Arch Wakef 68-75; Res Can of Wakef 75-80; Hon Can from 80; V of Almondbury Dio Wakef from 80; RD of Almondbury from 81. *Almondbury Vicarage, Huddersfield, W Yorks, HD5 8XE.* (Huddersfield 21753)

WHITEMAN, Cedric Henry. b 28. Lich Th Coll 59. **d** 61 **p** 62 Pet. C of Abington 61-64; V of St Andr Kettering 64-79; RD of Kettering 73-79; Rotherham from 79; Can of Pet Cathl 77-79; V of Rotherham Dio Sheff from 79. *25 Moorgate, Rotherham, S Yorks, S60 2AD.* (Rotherham 64341)

WHITEMAN, Rodney David Carter. b 40. Ely Th Coll 61. **d** 64 **p** 65 Birm. C of King's Heath 64-70; V of St Steph Rednal

70-79; Erdington Dio Birm from 79; RD of Aston from 81. *Vicarage, Church Road, Erdington, Birmingham, B24 9AX.* (021-373 0884)

WHITEMAN, Vernon. b 04. **d** 27 **p** 28 Nottm (RC). Rec into Angl Commun 41; L to Offic (Col Cl Act) 43; Coll of Resurr Mirfield 43-44; C of St Pet W Harrow 44; C-in-c of St Andr Limpsfield Chart 44-46; C of St Jas Colchester (in c of St Anne) 46-47; St Mich Wood Green 47; Minehead 47-50; R of Dowlish Wake 50-56; PC of Kingstone 50-56; Clandown 56-62; V of St Pet and St Paul Enfield Lock 62-74; Perm to Offic Dios St E and Chelmsf from 75. *Well-come Cottage, Wiggens Green, Helions Bumpstead, Haverhill, Suff.* (Steeple Bumpstead 596)

WHITESIDE, John Robert. b 01. **d** 67 **p** 68 Man. Hon C of Hope Dio Man from 67. *9 Oxford Road, Salford, Manchester, M6 8LW.*

WHITESIDE, Leonard Albert. Sarum Th Coll 47. **d** 50 **p** 51 Ripon. C of All S Leeds 50-54; V of Clifford 54-60; St Mark Anlaby Dio York from 60. *1055 Anlaby Road, Hull, Yorks.* (Hull 51977)

WHITESIDE, Leslie William Hamilton. b 08. Wycl Hall Ox 32. **d** 34 **p** 35 Ox. C of St John Reading 34-39; Abbey Ch Bath 39-42; Bp's Chap for Youth in Dio Liv 42-44; Chap RNVR 44-47; R of Teston 47-55; Lullingstone 55-58; St Edm K Lombard Street Lon 58-81. *Gabriels hill, Pilgrims Way, Kemsing, Kent.*

WHITESIDE, Canon Peter George. b 30. St Cath Coll Cam BA (2nd cl Hist Trip pt ii) 55, MA 59. Cudd Coll 55. **d** 57 **p** 58 Lon. C of St Steph Roch Row 57-61; Asst Chap and Master Clifton Coll Bris. 61-63; Sen Chap and Master 63-70; L to Offic Dio Bris 62-70; Hd Master Linc Cathl Sch 70-73; L to Offic Dio Linc 71-73; Can and Preb of Linc Cathl 72-73; Can (Emer) from 73; Prin Wadhurst C of E Gr Sch Melb from 74. *Wadhurst Grammar School, Domain Street, South Yarra, Vic, Australia 3141.* (03-26 2824)

WHITFIELD, Canon Benjamin Owen. b 17. Univ of Sask BA 43. Em Coll Sktn LTh (w distinc) 43, BD 53. **d** 43 **p** 44 Bran. R of Hamiota 43-46; P-in-c of Shoal Lake 45-46; R of Birtle 46-51; St Geo Bran 51-54; St Matt Bran and Hon Can of Bran 54-60; Dean of Bran 57-60; V of Willoughton 60-62; R of Blyborough 60-62; Clee 62-70; V of Gainsborough 70-81; Can and Preb of Linc from 70; RD of Corringham 72-78; V of St Paul Morton 76-81; Wrawby Dio Linc from 81; Melton Ross Dio Linc from 81. *Wrawby Vicarage, Brigg, Humb.* (Brigg 2064)

WHITFIELD, Charles. b 25. St Pet Hall Ox BA 49, MA 53. Ridley Hall Cam 49. **d** 51 **p** 52 Sheff. C of Ecclesfield 51-54; Grassendale 54-56; C of Neasden w Kingsbury 56-58; St Martin-in-the-Fields Westmr 58-59; V of H Trin Bromley Common 59-68; Egg Buckland Dio Ex from 68; Chap The Lennard Hosps 59-68. *Egg Buckland Vicarage, Plymouth, Devon.* (Plymouth 701399)

WHITFIELD, George Joshua Newbold. b 09. Univ of Lon MA 35. AKC 30. Bps' Coll Cheshunt. **d** 62 **p** 63 Lon. Hon C of Hampton 62-74; Gen Sec Gen Syn Bd of Educn 69-74; L to Offic Dio Ex from 78; Chairman Dioc Educn C'tte from 81. *31 Foxholes Hill, Exmouth, EX8 2DQ.*

WHITFIELD, George Oakley. b 17. St Jo Coll Dur 43. **d** 45 **p** 46 Dur. C of St Pet Harton 45-48; Winlaton (in c of Rowlands Gill) 48-50; R of Hemingby (w Baumber, Gt Sturton, Edlington, Wispington, Hatton, Sotby and Ashby W from 81) Dio Linc from 50; V of Baumber w Sturton Magna 51-81; C-in-c of Hatton w Sotby 58-60; R 60-81; RD of Wraggoe 62-64. *Hemingby Rectory, Horncastle, Lincs.* (Baumber 260)

WHITFIELD, Kenneth. b 18. Lich Th Coll 54. **d** 56 **p** 57 Lich. C of St Werburgh Burslem 56-58; P-in-c of St Mary Virg Tunstall 58-59; Area Sec UMCA and L to Offic Dio Ex 60-64; Perm to Offic Dios B & W; Bris; Sarum; and Truro 60-64; V of St Marg Leeds 64-73; Chap St Pet Conv Horbury from 73. *1 Greengates, Tithe Barn Street, Horbury, Wakefield, WF4 6LJ.* (0924 270197)

WHITFIELD, Thomas Garnett. **d** 63 Bp Snell for Tor **p** 64 Tor. C of St Chad Tor 63-65; P-in-c of Bramalea 65-72; I of Malton 65-67; R of Ch Ch Mimico Tor 72-80; Bradford Dio Tor from 80. *62 Church Street, Bradford, Ont, Canada.*

WHITFIELD, Trevor. b 48. Univ of Lon BSc 71. Fitzw Coll Cam BA 78. Ridley Hall Cam 76. **d** 79 **p** 80 S'wark. C of SS Pet & Paul Battersea Dio S'wark from 79. *31 Plough Road, Battersea, SW11 2DE.*

WHITFORD, Austen Ernest Lever. b 1896. Late Scho and Exhib of St D Coll Lamp BA (3rd cl Nat Sc) 23. **d** 24 **p** 25 Man. C of St Matt L Lever 24-28; St Thos Bedford-in-Leigh 28-30; V of St Jo Evang Leigh Lancs 30-36; R of Stathern 36-39; V of Lockington w Hemington 39-42; Asst Master Denstone Coll Prep Sch 42-45; Chigwell Sch 45-57; Ld Weymouth Sch Warm 57-60; C of Forest Row 60-61; V of St Aid Burton-on-Trent 61-67. *Address temp unknown.*

WHITFORD, Bernard Arnold. b 1893. Univ of Dur LTh 16. St Aid Coll 14. **d** 16 **p** 17 Man. C of St Jas Heywood 16-18; St Geo Kidderminster 18-21; St Jas Gorton 21-23; St Marg Prestwich 23-29; I of Roundthorn 29-33; V 33-37; V of St Mary Edmon 37-45; Heybridge (w Langford from 48) 45-56; RD of Maldon 53-56; V of Earls Colne 56-60; Manuden w Berden 60-72. *c/o Mrs S Casson, 13 Ash Grove, Haywards Heath, Sussex.* (Haywards Heath 55240)

WHITFORD, Ven Edward Neville. Rhodes Univ BA 64. St Paul's Coll Grahmstn 64. **d** 65 **p** 66 Grahmstn. C of St Kath Uitenhage 65-66; St Mich AA Queenstown 66-70; R of Humansdorp 70-80; Can of Port Eliz 78-80; Archd of Uitenhage from 80; P-in-c of St Francis Xavier City and Dio Port Eliz from 80. *PO Box 10028, Linton Grange, Port Elizabeth, CP, S Africa.*

WHITFORD, Canon James William. Trin Coll Tor STh 59. **d** 55 **p** 56 Keew. I of Ignace 55-58; Keew 58-63; Pine Falls Dio Keew from 63; Hon Can of Keew from 70. *c/o General Delivery, Pine Falls, Manit., Canada.* (204-367 8347)

WHITHAM, Allan Victor. Moore Coll Syd ThL 65. **d** 65 Syd **p** 66 Bp Loane for Syd. C of Cronulla 65-67; Min of Whalan 67-72; C-in-c of St Jas Mt Druitt Dio Syd 72-80; R from 80. *40 Halinda Street, Whalan, NSW, Australia 2770.* (625-9374)

WHITING, Arthur. K Coll Lon and Warm 54. **d** 55 **p** 56 Win. C of Andover 55-58; V of St Jude Shirley Warren 58-78; Chap Southn Gen and Children's Hosps 59-73; SW Hosp 75-78; Perm to Offic Dios Sarum and Win from 78. *10 Paget Close, Colehill, Wimborne Minster, Dorset, BH21 2SW.* (Wimborne 884948)

WHITING, Brian Arthur Arnold. b 22. TD 65. St Cath Coll Ox BA 49, MA 54. Wells Th Coll. **d** and **p** 64 B & W. CF (TA) 53-65; SCF (TA) 65-67; CF (TAVR) 67-69; C of Crewkerne 64-65; V of N Petherton (w Northmoor Green from 75) Dio B & W from 65; Bp's Chap 77-79. *Dower House, North Petherton, Bridgwater, Somt, TA6 6SE.* (0278-662429)

WHITING, Frances Joan. b 21. Univ of Manit BComm 43, MA 54. **d** 75 **p** 78 Rupld. Hon C of St Chad Winnipeg Dio Rupld from 75. *500 Stradbrook Avenue, Apt 507, Winnipeg, Manitoba, Canada, R3L 0K1.*

WHITING, Leslie John. b 27. **d** 61 **p** 62 S'wark. C of St Clem E Dulwich 61-64; Parkstone w Branksea I 64-69; L Coates (in c of Willows Estate) 69-70; C of St Matt Willesden Dio Lon 70-74; V from 74. *St Matthew's Vicarage, St Mary's Road, NW10.* (01-965 3748)

WHITING, Owen. b 06. Fitzw Ho Cam 3rd cl Econ Trip pt i 35, BA (3rd cl Th Trip pt i) 37, MA 41. Linc Th Coll 37. **d** 38 **p** 39 Pet. C of St Jo Bapt Pet 38-42; Chap of Denstone Coll 42-48; Qu Th Coll Birm 48-51; LPr Dio Birm 48-51; R of St Phil Hulme and of St Jo Bapt Hulme and of H Trin Hulme Man and of All SS Chorlton-on-Medlock 51-58; PV of Truro Cathl 58-61; Chap Truro Cathl Sch 58-61; LPr Dio Truro 58-61; V of St Sav (w St Pet from 71) Eastbourne 62-76. *College of St Barnabas, Blackberry Lane, Lingfield, Surrey, RH7 6NJ.*

WHITING, Thomas Edward. Moore Th Coll Syd 32. Univ of Syd BA 33, MA 35, ACT ThL 34, Th Scho 45. **d** 33 Bp Wylde for Bath **p** 34 Bath. Asst Chap All SS Coll Bath 33-36; C of Cowra 36-37; Perm to Offic Dio Goulb 37; C of Canberra 37-44; R of Binda 44-50; Bega 50-65; Can of St Sav Cathl Goulb 59-76; R of Boorowa 67-76; Perm to Offic Dio C & Goulb from 77. *126 Sydney Road, Kelso, NSW, Australia 2795.*

WHITLA, William John. Univ of Tor BA 57, MA 61. Trin Coll Tor 58, STB 61. Mert Coll Ox DPhil 68. **d** 61 **p** 62 Tor. C of Ch Ch Cathl Fred 61-63; Gen Sec SCM NB 61-63; C of St Thos Tor 63-65; Lect in Humanities and Engl York Univ Tor 63-64; Asst Prof 64-65; Assoc Prof 68-77; Prof from 77; Hon C of St Jude Tor 68-72; H Trin City and Dio Tor from 73. *76 Evans Avenue, Toronto, Ont, Canada.*

WHITLEY, Charles Francis. Late Pri TCD BA (2nd cl Or Lang Mod) 42, Div Test (1st cl) 43, Wall Bibl Scho 44, MA and BD 45, PhD 49. **d** 43 **p** 44 Arm. C of Dundalk 43-45; Zion Ch Rathgar Dub 45-49; Tutor in Th at St Jo Coll Dur and OT Lect Univ of Dur 49-52; V of St Barn Bolton 52-53; Lect in Hebr and OT at Univ Coll of N Wales 53-67; Sen Lect from 67. *Elmbank, Llandegfan, Anglesey, Gwyn.* (Glyn Garth 384)

WHITLEY, Eric Keir. b 47. Univ of Salford BSc 68. Trin Coll Bris 77. **d** 79 **p** 80 Southw. C of St Ann w Em Nottm Dio Southw from 79. *22 Palmerston Gardens, Shelton Street, Nottingham. NG3 1NH.* (Nottm 56921)

WHITLEY, John Duncan Rooke. b 29. Trin Coll Cam BA 51, MA 55. Coll of Resurr Mirfield 52. **d** 54 **p** 55 Newc T. C of Ashington 54-59; Chiswick 59-61; V of Ware 61-71; Can Missr of Edin 71-74; Dioc Insp of Ch Schs Dio Edin 72-74; L to Offic Dio Edin from 74. *3 Marchmont Street, Edinburgh, EH9 1EJ.* (031-229 2331)

WHITLEY, John William. b 46. TCD BA 68. St Jo Coll Dur BA 71. Cranmer Hall Dur 68. **d** 71 **p** 72 Connor. C of St

Mary Magd Belfast 71-73; St Cleopas Toxteth City and Dio Liv 73-78; P-in-c from 78. *23 Bilston Road, A'gburth, Liverpool, L17 6AS.* (051-427 2734)

WHITLOCK, George William. b 07. AKC 34. **d** 34 **p** 35 Lon. C of H Innoc Kingsbury 34-36; Pr of Ludlow 36-40; CF 40-56; V of Methwold 56-61; Diddington Dio Ely from 61; Southoe w Hail Weston Dio Ely from 61; C-in-c of L Paxton Dio Ely 68-77; V from 77. *Diddington Vicarage, Huntingdon, PE18 9XU.* (Huntingdon 810215)

WHITLOCK, James Frederick. b 44. Ch Coll Cam Ba 75, MA 78. Westcott Ho Cam 73. **d** 76 St Germans for Truro **p** 77 Truro. C of Newquay 76-79; P-in-c of St Mawgan w St Ervan and St Eval 79-81; R 81; Dioc Dir of Ordinands Dio Truro and Dom Chap to Bp of Truro from 82. *Stable Flat, Trelissick, Truro, Cornw.* (Devoran 865211)

WHITLOW, Very Rev Brian William. St Edm Hall Ox BA (2nd cl Engl Lit) 36, Dipl Th 37. Bp's Univ Lennox MEducn 52. Gen Synod BD (1st cl) 61. Angl Th Coll BC Hon DD 67. Westcott Ho Cam 37. **d** 38 Ripon **p** 39 Knaresborough for Ripon. C of St Aid Leeds 38-41; Chap RAFVR 41-46; Chap Bp's Coll Sch Lennox 46-52; P-in-c Wakeham w York 52-55; Dean and R of Ch Ch Cathl Vic Dio BC 55-80; Dean (Emer) from 80; Perm to Offic Dio BC from 80. *912 Vancouver Street, Victoria, BC, Canada.* (604-383 3616)

WHITMORE, Edward James. b 36. BD (Lon) 66. Tyndale Hall Bris 65. **d** 68 **p** 69 Centr Tang. Tutor St Phil Th Coll Kongwa 68-72; L to Offic Dio Centr Tang 72-76; Dio Blackb from 77; Asst Master Hutton Gr Sch Preston from 76. *23 Priory Crescent, Penwortham, Preston, Lancs.* (Preston 746522)

WHITMORE, Gordon Eugene John. b 24. K Coll Lon 47 and Warm 57. **d** 58 **p** 59 Truro. C of Redruth 58-60; V of Tywardreath w Tregaminion 60-64; V of St Sampson 63-64; Prin of Croft Sch Stratford-on-Avon 64-77. *c/o The Croft School, Stratford-on-Avon, Warws.* (Stratford-on-Avon 2351)

WHITNALL, (Dominic) Robert Edward. b 14. Magd Coll Ox BA (3rd cl Th) 37. Cudd Coll 37. M CR 47. **d** 38 **p** 39 Derby. C of Staveley 38-44; Miss P at Sophiatown Johann 47-59; P-in-c 59-61; Rosettenville 61-66. *House of the Resurrection, Mirfield, Yorks, WF14 0BN.* (Mirfield 493318)

WHITNEY, Philip Charles. Qu Univ Ont BA 57. Wycl Coll Tor BTh 60. **d** 60 **p** 61 Tor. C of Transfig Tor 60-62; V of Clinton 62-66; U Fraser 66-69; I of Langley 70-75; on leave. *Box 2278, Salmon Arm, BC, Canada.*

WHITNEY, Russell Lee. b 45. Cornell Univ NY BA 57, MA 59. Univ of Tor PhD 69. **d** 79 Fred. C of Johnston Dio Fred from 79. *Kierstead Farm, R.R. 2, Apohaqui, NB, Canada, E0G 1A0.*

✠ **WHITSEY, Right Rev Hubert Victor.** b 16. St Edm Hall Ox BA (2nd cl Phil Pol and Econ) 48, MA 53. Westcott Ho Cam 48. **d** 49 **p** 50 Blackb. C of Chorley 49-51; PC of Farington 51-55; St Thos Halliwell 55-60; CF (R of O) from 53; C-in-c of St Aid Conv Distr Langley 60-64; V of All SS and Marts Langley 64-68; Hon Can of Man 63-68; Can (Emer) from 68; Proc Conv Man 65-67; V of Downham 68-71; Cons Ld Bp Suffr of Hertf in St Albans Cathl 1 Nov 71 by Abp of Cant; Bps of Blackb; Roch; St Alb; and Chelmsf; Bps Suffr of Willesden and Bedford; Trld to Ches 74; res 81. *Hill Top, Twiston, Clitheroe, Lancs, BB7 4DB.* (Gisburn 668)

WHITTA, Rex Alfred Rought. b 28. Univ of Birm Dipl Th 63. QU Coll Birm 61. **d** 63 **p** 64 York. C of St Aug Newland (in c of St Cuthb) 63-66; V of Elloughton and Brough (w Brantingham from 68) 66-74; C-in-c of Brantingham 66-68; R of Redcar w Kirkleatham 74-78; V of Redcar Dio York from 78. *St Peter's Vicarage, Aske Road, Redcar, Cleveland, TS10 2BP.* (0642-484700)

WHITTAKER, Arthur. b 30. Oak Hill Th Coll. **d** 60 Lanc for York **p** 61 Blackb. C of Bispham 60-64; V of St Cypr Edge Hill 64-73; CMS Area Sec Dios Ban, St A, Ches and S & M 73-74; C of Maghull 74; V of Bilsborrow Dio Blackb from 74. *Bilsborrow Vicarage, Preston, Lancs, PR3 0RL.* (Brock 40269)

WHITTAKER, Arthur George. b 14. **d** 60 **p** 61 Leic. C of Ibstock 60-62; St Phil Leic 62-63; V of Hadfield 63-72; Friday Bridge Dio Ely from 72; Coldham 72-81. *27 Moseley Crescent, Cashes Green, Stroud, Glos.*

WHITTAKER, Brian Lawrence. b 39. Clifton Th Coll 63. **d** 66 **p** 67 St E. C of Whitton 66-69; Normanton 69-74; P-in-c of Ch Ch Dukinfield 74-77; H Trin (and Ch Ch from 77) Stalybridge Dio Ches 74-77; V from 77. *Vicarage, Hough Hill Road, Stalybridge, Chesh, SK15 2HB.* (061-338 2030)

WHITTAKER, George Brian. Univ of Lon BD 36. ALCD 36. **d** 36 **p** 37 Ely. C of St Matt Cam 36-40; Transfig Newington Hull 40-42; LPr (in c of St Jas Porchester) Dio Southw 42-45; R of Southoe w Hail Weston V 45-51; R and V of Dry Drayton 51-62; R of Hardwicke 51-62; C-in-c of Childerley 51-62; RD of Bourn 55-62; R of Roche 62-72; C-in-c of Withiel 62-63; R 63-72; V of Lelant 72-78. *12 Church Place, St Ives, Cornw, TR26 1LU.* (St Ives 6509)

WHITTAKER, Henry Allan. b 06. **d** 74 **p** 76 Fred. C of Restigouche 75-79. *c/o Anglican Rectory, Glen Levit, Restigouche, NB, Canada.*

WHITTAKER, Ivan Harrison. b 08. Westcott Ho Cam 44. **d** 46 **p** 47 Lon. C of St Paul Bow Common 46-53; V of St Mich Mark Street Shoreditch 53-60; Chap St Mary's Conv Lon 60-63; Shrine of Our Lady of Walsingham 63-65; St Mich Sch Otford 65-73; Perm to Offic Dio Chich from 74. *1 Griffiths Avenue, North Lancing, Sussex, BN15 0HJ.* (Lancing 63250)

WHITTAKER, James Rawstron. b 14. Worc Coll Ox BA 38, MA 46. Wells Th Coll 38. **d** 40 **p** 41 York. C of St Mary Bishophill Sen w St Clem York 40-43; Hornsea w Bewholme 43-47; R of Neen Sollars w Milson 47-55; V of Annscroft 55-70; R of Pontesbury 3rd portion 55-70; PC of Longden 55-70; V of Amleley 70-81; C-in-c of Kinnersley 74-81. *142 Eign street, Hereford, HR3 0AP.* (Hereford 68961)

WHITTAKER, John. b 09. Late Bp Jenkyns Scho of St Jo Coll Dur BA 35, MA and Dipl Th 38. **d** 36 **p** 37 Blackb. C of St Jo Div Blackb 36-38; St John Silverdale 38-39; St Thos Blackb 39-40; C-in-c 40-45; V of Coppull 45-74. *9 Birkacre Brow, Coppull, Chorley, Lancs.* (Coppull 791993)

WHITTAKER, Canon John. b 20. Ch Coll Cam BA 47, MA 49. Ridley Hall Cam 46. **d** 48 **p** 49 Man. C of Astley Bridge 48-51; St Paul Kersal 51-53; R of St Agnes Birch-in-Rusholme 53-66; V of St Jas New Bury Farnworth 66-75; Hon Can of Man Cathl from 71; R of Middleton Dio Man from 75. *Rectory, Mellalieu Street, Middleton, Manchester, M24 3DN.* (061-643 2693)

WHITTAKER, John. b 27. Oak Hill Th Coll 53. **d** 55 **p** 56 Blackb. C of St Thos Blackpool 55-57; St Helens 58-60; V of Hensingham 60-67; Skelmersdale 67-77; Chap W Cumb Hosp 60-67; V of Faringdon w L Coxwell Dio Ox from 77; RD of Vale of White Horse from 80. *Vicarage, Faringdon, Oxon, SN7 8AB.* (Faringdon 20154)

WHITTAKER, Kenneth. b 48. K Coll Lon BA (Hist) 69. Jes Coll Cam 3rd cl Th Trip Pt ii 71, BA 72, MA 74. Westcott Ho Cam 70. **d** 72 **p** 73 Man. C of Middleton 72-76; Asst Master Cheadle Hulme Sch from 78. *1 Glossop Road, Hayfield, Derbys, SK12 5NG.* (New Mills 46703)

WHITTAKER, Peter Harold. b 39. K Coll Lon and Warm AKC 62. **d** 63 Warrington for Liv **p** 64 Liv. C of Walton-on-the-Hill 63-67; Ross-on-Wye 67-70; R of St Mary Magd Bridgnorth 70-78; P-in-c of Oldbury 70-78; RD of Bridgnorth 78-81; Team R of Bridgnorth 78-81; Preb of Heref Cathl 80-81; V of Leighton Buzzard w Egginton, Hockliffe and Billington Dio St Alb from 81. *Vicarage, Leighton Buzzard, Beds, LU7 7AB.* (0525-373217)

WHITTAKER, William Joseph. b 04. TCD BA 33, Div Test 35, MA 48. **d** 36 **p** 37 Down. C of Willowfield 36-38; St Patr Ballymena 38-42; C-in-c of Timahoe 42-44; I of Hacketstown w Clonmore 44-45; C of Ballymacarrett 45-47; I of Killinchy Kilmood and Tullynakill 47-50; R of St Columba Knock Belf 50-76; Can of St Anne's Cathl Belf 64-74; Can and Preb of St Patr Cathl Dub 74-76. *23 Barton Drive, Rathfarnham, Dublin 14, Irish Republic.* (Dublin 960308)

WHITTALL, John Duncan. b 44. Bps' Univ Lennox BA 65. Trin Coll Tor. **d** and **p** 69 Montr. C of St Barn, St Lambert 69-72; I of St Steph, St Hubert 72-74; St Bart Hamilton 74-80; Dean of Men Trin Coll Tor and Chap St Mich Oakville from 80. *Trinity College, Hoskin Avenue, Toronto, Ont, Canada.* (416-978 2522)

WHITTAM, Canon Kenneth Michael. b 26. Ball Coll Ox BA 50, MA 54. Cudd Coll 50. **d** 52 **p** 53 Blackb. C of Adlington 52-55; St Thos St Annes-on-Sea 55-58; R of Halton w Aughton 58-62; Colne 62-66; Chap and Asst Master Highgate Sch 66-75; L to Offic Dio Lon 66-75; V of Shotwick Dio Ches from 75; Res Can of Ches from 75; Can Missr Dio Ches from 75. *Vicarage, Shotwick, Chester, CH1 6HX.* (Saughall 880576)

WHITTAM, Vivian Owen. b 10. Univ of Rang BA 31. Univ of Serampore BD 36. Bp's Coll Calc 33. **d** 36 **p** 37 Rang. Asst Chap Cathl Ch Rang 36-40 and P-in-c of Tamwe Miss 38-40; Chap at St Matt Moulmein 40-42; Lashio 42; Bhusaval 42-43; Bilaspur 43-45; Saugor 45-46; Insein 46-48; C of St Pet Harrow 48-50; C-in-c of St Mich Cricklewood 50-51; V 51-59; Ch Ch W Green Tottenham 59-75; Commiss Rang 63-71; Hon C of St Andr Southgate Dio Lon from 75. *36 Chandos Court, The Green, Southgate, N14 7AA.* (01-886 5014)

WHITTEN, Francis Delight. b 52. Trin Coll Tor 75. **d** 77 **p** 78 E Newfld. C of Heart's Delight 77-78; R 78-80; C of Carleton Place 80; Pembroke Dio Ott from 80. *Pembroke, Ont, Canada.*

WHITTEN, Leonard. Mem Univ Newfld BA 62. **d** and **p** 62 Newfld. I of Labrador 62-68; Gander Bay 68-73; Corner

Brook E Dio Newfld (W Newfld from 76) from 73. *2 Clarence Street, Corner Brook, Newfoundland, Canada.* (709-634-3059)

WHITTER, Frank Cedric. b 06. St Bonif Coll Warm 27. Univ of Dur LTh 33. **d** 33 Bp Palmer for Glouc **p** 34 Glouc. C of St Barn Tuffley 33-36; UMCA Miss Masasi 36-38; C of Marlborough 38-40; St Jas Cowley 40-42; Marlborough 42-46; V of Lytchett Minster 46-53; PC of Wool w E Burton (and Coombe Keynes from 60) 53-71. *Southridge Cottage, Mutton Hall Hill, Heathfield, E Sussex, TN21 8NE.*

WHITTINGHAM, Keith Robert. b 49. Brock Univ Ont BA 72. Trin Coll Tor MDiv 76. **d** 76 Bp Clarke for Niag **p** 77 Niag. C of St Mary Hamilton 76-78; St Chris Burlington 78-81; R of Jordan Dio Niag from 81. *Box 12, Jordan, Ont, Canada.* (416-562 4347)

WHITTINGHAM, Ronald Norman. b 43. Linc Coll Ox 2nd cl Cl Mods 63, BA (2nd cl Th) 65, MA 68. Coll of Resurr Mirfield 65. **d** 67 **p** 68 Lich. C of Horninglow 67-69; Market Drayton 69-70; Uttoxeter 71-75; P-in-c of St Paul Burton-on-Trent 75-80; V of Shareshill Dio Lich from 80. *Vicarage, Church Road, Shareshill, Wolverhampton, Staffs WV10 7LA.* (Cheslyn Hay 414521)

WHITTINGTON, David John. b 45. Qu Coll Ox BA (1st cl Mus) and Liddon Stud 67, 2nd cl Th 69, MA 71. Coll of Resurr Mirfield 69. **d** 71 Mon **p** 72 Ox. Chap St Woolos Cathl Newport 71-72, Chap Qu Coll Ox 72-76; C of St Mary Virg Ox 72-76; V of Stockton-on-Tees (w St Jo Bapt from 78) Dio Dur from 76. *92 Oxbridge Lane, Stockton, Cleveland.* (Stockton 65619)

WHITTINGTON, Frederick Charles. Em Coll Sktn. **d** 34 **p** 35 Bran. C of Miniota 34-35; I of Bethany 35-38; R of St Mary Virg Bran 38-47; Chap CASF 41-45; I of Loughboro 47-50; Chap to Kingston Penit 50-63; I of Leeds Rear 63-69. *395 Pine Street, Gananoque, Ont, Canada.* (613-382 3990)

WHITTLE, Alan. b 29. K Coll Lon and Warm AKC and BD 52. **d** 53 **p** 54 B & W. C of Combe Down 53-55; Twiverton 55-57; R of Denmark 57-60; Collie 60-62; Exam Chap to Bp of Bunb 60-63; R of Katanning 62-64; St Mary S Perth 64-66; Aston Rowant w Crowell 66-68; Publ Pr Dio S'wark 69-72; Asst Master Henry Thornton Sch Clapham Common 68-72; V of Ch Ch Mitcham Dio S'wark from 72. *Christ Church Vicarage, Collier's Wood, SW19 2NY.* (01-542 5125)

WHITTLE, Fred. Keble Coll Ox BA (2nd cl Jurispr) 40, MA 44. Cudd Coll 40. **d** 41 **p** 42 Pet. C of St Matt Northn 41-47; St Pet W Molesey 47-49; Isham 49-51; V of Warmington 51-58; R of Orlingbury w Pytchley 58-71; Gt w L Addington Dio Pet from 71. *Great Addington Rectory, Kettering, Northants.* (Cranford 257)

WHITTLES, Ven James Edward. Em Coll Sktn 27. **d** 31 **p** 32 Sask. C of Denholm Sask 31-32; Miss at Sunset Prairie 32-36; Burn's Lake 36-41; Chap CASF 41-46; R of All SS Vancouver 46-55; Synod Sec 55-71; Archd of Athab 57-71; R of Faust 70-71; V of N Thompson River 71-80; Dioc Treas and Dom Chap to Bp of Carib 75-76; Archd of Carib 75-80; Archd (Emer) from 80. *RR2, Gibsons, BC, Canada.*

WHITTOCK, Michael Graham. b 47. Univ of Hull BA (Hist) 69. Fitzw Ho Cam BA (2nd cl Th Trip pt ii) 71. U Th Sem Richmond Va USA 72. **d** 72 Warrington for Liv **p** 73 Liv. C of St Chad Kirkby 72-76; St Mary Prescot (in c of St Paul) 76-79; R of Methley w Mickletown Dio Ripon from 79. *Rectory, Churchside, Methley, Leeds.* (Castleford 515278)

WHITTON, Alan. Lon Coll of Div 60. **d** 63 Chelmsf for Cant for Col Bp **p** 64 Arctic. Miss at Baker Lake 63-72; R of Canora w Kamsack 72-78; Winona Dio Niag from 78. *Box 363, Winona, Ont, Canada.* (416-643 2180)

WHITTON, Norman. b 17. Edin Th Coll. **d** 67 **p** 68 Carl. C of Egremont 67-70; V of Brough w Stainmore 70-76; P-in-c of St Elisabeth Harraby Carl 76-80. *c/o St Elisabeth's Vicarage, Harraby, Carlisle, CA1 3QA.* (Carlisle 26440)

WHITTON, Robert Archibald. b 17. Univ of Edin MA 37. Edin Th Coll 38. **d** 40 **p** 41 Glas. C of H Trin Ayr 40-44; R of St Mary Stromness 44-45; St Olaf Kirkwall (w St Mary Stromness) 45-51; Archd of Orkney 47-51; R of St Mich Helensburgh 51-59; Perm to Offic Dio Edin 59; Chap Fettes Coll Edin 59-60. *36 Bryce Road, Currie, Midlothian.*

WHITTY, Harold George. b 41. TCD BA 64, Div Test 65, MA 67. **d** 65 **p** 66 Down. C of Willowfield 65-68; Ch Ch Cathl Lisburn 68-71; Dom Chap to Bp of Connor 70-71; Asst Dir of Exhibs CMJ from 71; C of Cockfosters 72-75; Team V of Exe Valley Group Dio Ex from 75. *Withleigh Vicarage, Tiverton, Devon.* (Tiverton 254004)

WHITWELL, John Peter. b 36. Qu Coll Birm 62. **d** 65 **p** 66 Lon. C of Stepney 65-68; Chingford 68-71; V of St Sav Walthamstow 71-78; P-in-c of L Ilford Dio Chelmsf from 78. *Little Ilford Rectory, Manor Park, E12 6HA.* (01-478 2182)

WHITWELL, Martin Corbett. b 32. Pemb Coll Ox BA (3rd cl Mod Hist) 55, MA 59. Clifton Th Coll 55. **d** 57 **p** 58 Lich. C of St Jude Wolverhampton 57-60; Aldridge 60-66; Asst Master Chetwynd Ho Sch Streetly 66-67; Chap Sandbach Co Secondary Sch 68-74; C of Chipping Camden 70-71; Perm to Offic Dio Chich 74-75; Dio Bris 75-76; C of St Cath Tranmere 76-80; V of L Leigh w Nether (or Lower) Whitley Dio Ches from 80. *Whitley Vicarage, Warrington, Lancs, WA4 4EN.* (Norcott Brook 339)

WHITWORTH, Alan. b 24. Univ of Nottm Dipl Educn 66. ACP 66. St Deiniol's Libr Hawarden 80. **d** 80 **p** 81 Ches (APM). C of Capesthorne w Siddington & Marton 80-81; P-in-c of Eaton and Hulme Walfield Dio Ches from 81. *St Michael's Vicarage, Hulme Walfield, Congleton, Chesh.*

WHITWORTH, Duncan. b 47. AKC BD 69. St Aug Coll Cant 69. **d** 70 Hulme for York **p** 71 Man. C of Tonge Moor 70-73; St Jo Evang U Norwood 73-78; Asst Chaplain at St Geo Madrid Dio Gibr (Gibr in Eur from 80) from 78. *c/o British Embassy, Madrid, Spain.*

WHITWORTH, Edward Stanley. b 12. St Barn Coll Adel 77. **d** 78 Adel. C of St Matt Kens 78-79; Burnside Dio Adel from 79. *80 Lambert Road, Royston Park, S Australia 5070.* (42 2940)

WHITWORTH, Eric Watkinson. b 06. Univ Coll Dur 25. Lich Th Coll 28. **d** 30 **p** 32 Lich. C of Whitchurch 30-32; V of Woodlands St Mary 32-64; V of Eastbury 44-64; V of E Garston 58-64; R of Hook Norton w Swerford and Showell 64-68; V of Chiselhampton w Stadhampton 68-74; R of Drayton St Leon 68-74. *4 High Street, Tisbury, Salisbury, Wilts, SP3 6PS.* (0747-870710)

WHITWORTH, Patrick John. b 51. Ch Ch Ox BA 72, MA 76. Univ of Dur MA 78. St Jo Coll Dur Dipl Th 75. **d** 76 **p** 77 York. C of Mich-le-Belfrey 76-79; H Trin Brompton w St Paul Onslow Sq Dio Lon from 79. *4a Neville Street, SW7.*

WHITWORTH-HARRISON, Bernard. St Cath Coll Ox 30, BA 36. MA 38. **d** 34 **p** 36 Ox. C of Chilton 34-49; Kingsbury (in c of Hurley and Wood End) 49-52; V of Crondall 52-58; Cornish Hall End 58-62; R of Langham 62-74; Perm to Offic Dio Ely from 76. *Crossways, Brinkley Road, Dullingham, Newmarket, CB8 9UW.* (Stetchworth 354)

WHIU, Wiremu Te Koroho. **d** 78 Bp Spence for Auckld **p** 79 Auckld. Hon C of Waimate N Maori Past Dio Auckld from 78. *Ohaewai Road, Kaikohe, NZ.*

WHONSBON-ASTON, Ven Charles William. OBE 72. ACT ThL 27. Moore Th Coll Syd 27. **d** 27 **p** 28 Syd. C of St D Syd 28-29; Ch Ch St Lawrence Syd 29-31; V of Levuka 31-34; P-in-c of Mukawa 34-39; V of Viti Levu W 39-43; Apia W Samoa 43-58; Archd of Fiji 58-63; Polyn 63-67; Archd (Emer) from 67; V of Levuka 58-63; Dep VG Polyn 64-67; L to Offic Dio Polyn 67-68; Hon Can of Suva 68-73; Can 73-74; Perm to Offic Dio Syd from 75. *43 Farrer-Brown Court, Nuffield Village, Castle Hill, NSW, Australia 2154.* (634-2404)

WHYBRAY, Roger Norman. b 23. Keble Coll Ox 1st cl sc Mod Lang 42, BA (2nd cl Th) 44, MA 48, DPhil 62, BD 81, DD 81. Linc Th Coll 44; Liddon Stud 45-46. **d** 46 Southn for Win **p** 47 Win. C of St Mich Basingstoke 46-48; Fell and Tutor in OT at Gen Th Sem New York 48-50; Lect at Qu Coll Birm 51-52; C of St Pet Harborne 51-52; Miss SPG and Prof of OT at Centr Th Coll Tokyo 52-65; Kennicott Hebr Fell Univ of Ox 60-62; Lect in Th Univ of Hull from 65; Reader from 69; Prof of Hebr and OT Stud from 78; L to Offic Dio York from 65. *4 Chestnut Avenue, Hessle, N Humb, HU13 0RH.*

WHYE, Canon Alexander George. b 01. Keble Coll Ox BA 23, MA 27. St Aug Coll Cant 23. **d** 25 Bp Shaw for Ox **p** 26 Ox. C of Olney 25-29; Cowley Ox 29-39; V 39-59; Surr 41-72; RD of Cowley 57-59; V of S w New Hinksey 59-72; Hon Can of Ch Ch Ox 62-79; Can (Emer) from 79. *25 Banbury Road, Kidlington, Oxford, OX5 1AQ.* (Kidlington 5071)

WHYHAM, Anthony Bertram Jarvis. **d** 48 **p** 49 Alg. I of St Brice N Bay 48-56; Azilda 56-59; Onaping 59-60; Epiph Sudbury 60-67; Sturgeon Falls Dio Alg from 67. *Box 489, Sturgeon Falls, Ont, Canada.*

WHYMAN, Oliver. b 27. LCP 57. **d** 63 **p** 64 S'wark. C of Ch Ch Streatham 63-68; L to Offic Dio S'wark from 68. *37 Jubilee Court, London Road, Thornton Heath, Surrey, CR4 6JL.*

WHYNTIE, Howard William. b 24. Cudd Coll 55. **d** 56 Dover for Cant **p** 57 Cant. C of Bearsted 56-59; Margate 59-61; R of Beeston w Ashmanhaugh and Hoveton 61-66; V of Tunstead w Sco Ruston 61-66; R of Wells-next-the-Sea 66-71; P-in-c of Holkham w Egmere and Waterden 66-71; Rd of Burnham and Walsingham 70-71; L to Offic Dio Nor from 74. *22 Pakefield Road, Lowestoft, Suff, NR33 0HS.* (Lowestoft 67157)

WHYTE, Athenry John. St Jo Coll Melb ACT ThL 12. **d** 12 **p** 13 Melb. C of St Jas Melb 12-13; Actg R of Leopold 13; C of St Phil Collingwood 13-15; Min of Warburton 15-16; C of H Trin Kew 18-20 and 26-27; Min of Croydon 20-24 and 27-29; P-in-c of St Matt Cheltenham 29-37; I of St Paul Frankston 37-50; St Cath Caulfield 50-58; Perm to Offic Dio

Melb from 58. *18 Clarence Street, Elsternwick, Vic, Australia 3185.*

WHYTE, Duncan Macmillan. b 25. St Jo Coll Dur BA 50. St Cath S Ox BA (2nd cl Th) 51, MA 57. Wycl Hall Ox 49. **d** 51 **p** 53 Liv. C of Garston 51-56; St Leonards-on-Sea 56-59; V of St Simon Southsea 59-67; Gen Sec Lon City Miss from 67; Hon C of St Jo Evang Blackheath Dio S'wark from 68. *192 Charlton Road, SE7.* (01-856 7306)

WHYTE, Henry Lewis. b 38. ALCD 70 (LTh from 74). **d** 70 **p** 71 Chich. C of St Mary Crawley 70-74; V of St Jas w Ch Ch Bermondsey Dio S'wark from 74. *St James's Vicarage, Thurland Road, SE16 4AA.* (01-237 3010)

WHYTE, Canon Herbert Blayney. b 21. TCD BA 43, MA 53. **d** 44 **p** 45 Dub. C of Crumlin 44-47; Succr of St Patr Cathl Dub 47-50; Bp's V and Libr of St Canice's Cathl Kilk and Regr Dios Oss Ferns and Leigh 50-58; Dom Chap to Bp of Oss 50-58; Dioc Sec Dio Oss 55-68; RD of Fiddown and of Offerlane 55-58; Preb of Mayne in St Canice's Cathl Kilk 56-58; I of Maryborough 58-68; Crumlin Dio Dub from 68; Cler V of Ch Ch Cathl Dub from 68; Can of Ch Ch Cathl Dub from 80. *118 Kimmage Road West, Dublin 12, Irish Republic.* (Dublin 505878)

WHYTE, (Hadrian) John Richard Slessor. St Paul's Coll Grahmstn LTh 51, MCR 61. **d** 51 **p** 52 Johann. C of Maraisburg 51-53; St Alb Miss Johann 53-55; P-in-c 55-56; C of St Mary's Cathl Salisbury S Rhod 56-59; L to Offic Dio Wakef 60-62; Perm to Offic Dio Llan 62-69; Chap St Martin's Sch Johann and L to Offic Dio Johann 69-76, R of Mazoe Valley Dio Mashon from 76. *Box 186, Bindura, Zimbabwe.*

WHYTE, Malcolm Dorrance. b 29. Univ of Man BA (Th) 50, BD 53. Wycl Hall Ox 57. **d** 57 **p** 58 Roch. C of Roch 57-60; V of Ravenhead 60-67; Em Southport Dio Liv from 67; RD of N Meols from 79. *12 Allerton Road, Southport, Lancs.* (Southport 2743)

WHYTE, Canon Robert Angus. b 12. Wycl Hall Ox. **d** 43 **p** 44 Roch. C of St Jas Gravesend 43-47; Bp Hannington Ch Hove (in c of H Cross) 47-54; V of St Luke Tunbridge Wells Dio Roch from 54; Hon Can of Roch from 78. *158 Upper Grosvenor Road, Tunbridge Wells, Kent.* (Tunbridge Wells 21374)

WHYTE, Robert Euan. b 44. St Pet Coll Ox BA (2nd cl Th) 67. Cudd Coll 67. **d** 69 **p** 70 S'wark. C of Ch of Ascen Blackheath 69-73; Hither Green 73-75; Hon C of Heston 75-77; Rusthall Dio Roch from 77. *6 Ashley Gardens, Rusthall, Tunbridge Wells, Kent, TN4 8TY.* (Tunbridge Wells 21357)

WHYTE, Thomas Arthur. b 15. Univ of Man BA (Th) 48. Wycl Hall Ox 56, **d** 56 Liv **p** 57 Warrington for Liv. C of Ormskirk 56-59; V of Hunts Cross 59-71; Roby Dio Liv from 71. *11 Church Road, Roby, Liverpool, L36 9TL.* (051-489 1438)

WHYTE, Canon William Thomas. Montr Dioc Th Coll. **d** 67 **p** 68 Montr. C of St Jas Ap Montr 67-69; R of Grace Ch City and Dio Montr from 69; Hon Can of Montr from 77. *531 Pilon Street, La Salle, Quebec, Canada, H8P 3M1.* (514-366 8554)

WHYTEHEAD, Mary Jessica. b 54. Univ of Manit BA 75. Trin Coll Tor MDiv 78. **d** 78 **p** 79 Rupld. C of St Luke Winnipeg 78-80. *c/o 130 Nassau St N, Winnipeg, Manit, Canada, R3L 0J5.*

WIBBERLEY, Anthony Norman. b 36. AKC and BSc (Special) 58. Sarum Wells Th Coll 76. **d** 79 **p** 80 Ex. C of Tavistock Dio Ex from 79. *30 Glanville Road, Tavistock, Devon, Pl19 0ED.*

WICKENS, John Philip. b 33. Open Univ BA 76. K Coll Lon and warm 57. **d** 61 **p** 62 S'wark, C of Hatcham Pk b 33. K Coll Lon and Warm 57. **d** 61 **p** 62 S'wark. C of Hatcham Pk 61-64; In Amer Ch 64-66; Tutor Richmond Fellowship from 66; C of Ch Ch Sutton Dio S'wark from 68. *8 Orchard Road, Sutton, Surrey.*

WICKENS, Raymond Percy. b 1894. St Chad's Coll Dur BA 23, Dipl Th 23. Chich Th Coll 23. **d** 23 **p** 24 Southw. C of Hucknall Torkard 23-33; V of E Markham w W Drayton 33-42; All SS New Clipstone 42-50; R of Monksilver w Elworthy 50-59; C-in-c of Barrington 59-61. *12 Blounts Court, Potterne, Devizes, Wilts.*

WICKENS, Ronald Hughie. Trin Coll Tor STB 62. **d** 62 **p** 63 Niag. C of St Thos St Catherine's 62-63; I of Kinistino 63-66; C of Nanaimo 66-68; R of St Richard Vanc 68-74; St Marg Vanc 74-80; on leave. *3888 Dumfries Street, Vancouver, BC, Canada.*

WICKERSON, Peter Evans. b 45. Hur Coll Ont BA 66, MDiv 73. **d** 73 Hur. I of Port Lambton, Courtright & Sombra 73-74; Chap Cant Coll Univ of Windsor Ont from 74. *Canterbury College, Windsor, Ont., Canada.*

WICKERT, David Jack. b 42. K Coll Lon and Warm AKC 65. **d** 66 **p** 67 S'wark. C of E Wickham 66-71; V of St Andr Wimbledon 71-76; St Jo Evang Waterloo Rd Lambeth Dio S'wark from 76; St Andr Lambeth Dio S'wark from 76. *Vicarage, Secker Street, SE1 8UF.* (01-928 4470)

✠ **WICKHAM, Right Rev Edward Ralph.** Univ of Lon BD 37. Univ of Salford Hon D Litt 73; St Steph Ho Ox 38. **d** 38 **p** 39 Newc T. C of Ch Ch Shieldfield 38-41; Chap R Ordnance Factory Swynnerton 41-44; C-in-C of Swynnerton 43-44; Dioc Missr to Industry Dio Sheff 44-59; Hon Chap to Bp of Sheff 50-59; Can Res of Sheff 51-59; Univ of Sheff Sir H Stephenson Fell 55-57; Cons Ld Bp Suffr of Middleton in York Minster 30 Nov 59 by Abp of York; Bps of Dur; Sheff; and Man; Bps Suffr of Selby; Whitby; Burnley; and Hull; and Bps Gerard and Graham; res 82; Select Pr Univ of cam 62; Pro-Chan Univ of Salford from 75; Chairman of Idustr C'tte Gen Syn Working Party on U Shop Agreements 76 and the Future of Work 79. Asst Bp in Dio Man from 82. *12 Westminster Road, Eccles, Manchester.* (061-789 3144)

WICKHAM, John Brooks. St Jo Coll Auckld LTh (1st cl) 65. **d** 65 **p** 66 Wai. C of St Jo Cathl Napier 65-68; V of Tolaga Bay 68-73; St Aug Napier 73-78; Can of Wai 76-78; V of St Mark Remuera 78-80; Min Educator Dio Wai from 80. *21 Cameron Road, Napier, NZ.* (56954)

WICKHAM, Lionel Ralph. b 32. St Cath Coll Cam 2nd cl Th Trip pt i 55, BA 57, 2nd cl Th Trip pt iii and Burney Pri 59, MA 61. Westcott Ho Cam 57. **d** 59 Bp Dunlop for Linc **p** 60 Linc. C of Boston 59-61; Tutor Cudd Coll 61-63; V of Cross Stone 63-67; Lect in Th Univ of Southn 67-78; Sen Lect from 78; L to Offic Dio Win 68-81; V of Honley w Brockholes Dio Wakef from 81. *Honley Vicarage, Huddersfield, Yorks.* (Huddersfield 61178)

WICKHAM, Norman George. b 25. Kelham Th Coll 46. **d** 51 **p** 52 Leic. C of Syston 51-54; Min of St Gabr Eccles Distr Leic 54-57; R of Wingerworth 57-69; Team V of St Jo Evang Edin 69-79; Vice-Provost and Can of St Mary's Cathl Edin 74-79; R of Ch Ch Morningside City and Dio Edin from 79. *4 Morningside Road, Edinburgh, E10 4DD.* (031-229 6556)

WICKHAM, Robert George. b 05. Late Exhib of Hertf Coll Ox BA (2nd cl Mod Hist) 27, 2nd cl Th 29, MA 31. Wycl Hall, Ox 27. **d** 29 **p** 30 Sarum. Asst Chap Marlb Coll 29-37; Hd Master Twyford Sch Win 37-63; Chap from 37. *Primrose Cottage, Exton, Southampton, SO3 1NW.*

WICKING, Canon David Henry. ACT ThL 43. **d** 41 **p** 42 Gippsld. C of Rosedale 41-42; Leongatha 42-43; V of Bruthen 43-45; Chap RAAF 45-46; R of Delegate 46-51; Lang Lang 51-52; Corowa 52-68; Hon Can of St Paul's Pro-Cathl Hay 63-68; Can (Emer) from 68. *9 Airlie Street, Corowa, NSW, Australia 2646.*

WICKS, Henry George. b 11. AKC 40. **d** 40 S'wark **p** 41 Glouc. C of H Trin S'wark 40; St Jas Glouc 40-42; Barnwood 42-45; V of Cainscross (w Selsley from 75) 45-76; Chap Cashes Green Hosp 58-76; Perm to Offic Dio Ex from 77. *6 Broadmead, Woodbury, Exeter, Devon, EX5 1HR.* (Woodbury 32043)

✠ **WICKS, Right Rev Ralph Edwin.** OBE 82. ACT ThL 43. **d** 44 **p** 45 Brisb. C of H Trin Fortitude Valley 44-47; St Jas Toowoomba 47-49; R of Goondiwindi 49-54; H Trin Fortitude Valley Brisb 54-63; St Jas Toowoomba 63-72; Hon Can of Brisb 58-73; Archd of the Downs 72-73; W Area from 73; Home Miss Sec Brisb 72-73; Cons Asst Bp of Brisb in St Jo Evang Cathl Brisb 25 July 73 by Abp of Brisb; Bps of Carp, N Queensld, Rockptn, Graft and Wang; and others; Res Can of St John's Cathl Brisb from 77; Admin St John's Cathl Brisb from 81. *211 Taringa Parade, Taringa, Queensland, Australia 4068.* (378 5604)

WIDDAS, Preb John Anderson. b 38. Kelham Th Coll 58. **d** 63 **p** 64 Lich. C of Short Heath 63-66; Tamworth 66-69; V of Chesterton 69-74; R of St Chad City and Dio Lich from 74; Surr from 75; RD of Lich from 77; Preb of Lich Cathl from 80; P-in-c of Fairwell (or Farewell) and of Gentleshaw 80-82. *St Chad's Rectory, The Windings, Lichfield, Staffs.* (Lich 22254)

WIDDECOMBE, Charles Donald. b 14. Univ of Lon BD 38. **d** 48 **p** 49 Ox. [f Baptist Min] CF (EC) 41-46; Hon CF 46; C of Upton w Chalvey 48-53; Littleham w Exmouth 53-59; V of Yetminster w Ryme Intrinseca Dio Sarum from 59. *Yetminster Vicarage, Sherborne, Dorset, DT9 6LG.* (Yetminster 872237)

WIDDECOMBE, Malcolm Murray. b 37. Tyndale Hall Bris 57. **d** 62 **p** 63 Bris. C of H Trin Bris 62-65; St Luke w Ch Ch Bris 65-67; C-in-c of St Phil and St Jacob w Em City and Dio Bris 67-74; V from 74; RD of Bristol City from 79. *7 Kings Drive, Bishopton, Bristol, BS7 8JW.* (Bristol 43169)

WIDDESS, Chan Arthur Geoffrey. b 20. Late Scho Ch Coll Cam 1st cl Cl Trip pt i 41. BA 42, 1st cl Th Trip pt i, 43, MA 46. Ridley Hall, Cam 42. **d** 45 **p** 46 Liv. C of St Helens 45-47; Sch of Or Stud and CMS Tr Coll 47-48; Lect Centr Th Coll Shanghai 49-50; Asst Master St Steph Boys' Coll Stanley Hong Kong 50-51; Prof of OT United Th Coll Bangalore 51-52; Tutor St John's Coll Dur 52-55; Vice-Prin 55-56; Lect in Th Univ of Dur 52-56; Exam Chap to Bp of Leic 53-78; V of St Nich Leic and Chap for Angl Studs Leic Univ 56-63; Hon Can of Leic 61-63; Prin of St Aid Coll 63-70; Lect in OT Stud Univ of Man 67-69; V of Huntington 70-76; Exam Chap to Abp of York from 70; Can Res and Treas of York Minster 76-81; Preb of York Minster from 76; Can Res and Chan from 81. *10 Precentor's Court, York, YO1 2EJ.* (York 20877)

WIDDESS, Peter Henry. b 53. Jes Coll Cam BA 74. Ripon Coll Cudd 75. **d** 77 **p** 78 Dur. C of H Trin Darlington 77-79; The Resurr Man 79-82; L to Offic Dio Gibr in Eur from 82. *Pfarrhus, 7841 Malsburg-Marzell 2, West Germany.*

WIDDICOMBE, Alexander Charles Ernest. Jes Coll Cam 2nd cl Engl Trip pt i 31, BA (2nd cl Mod and Med Lang Trip pt ii) 32, MA 36. Wells Th Coll 33. **d** 34 **p** 35 Ches. C of St Pet Rock Ferry 34-35; Audlem 35-36; Min Can and Libr of Ely Cathl and Asst Master Cathl Choir Sch 36-39; Sub-Warden St Jo Coll Umtata 39-43; C of St Andr Lusikisiki 43-45; Asst Ed Sec SPG 45-46; R of Maclear w Ugie 46-50; C of St Mich Queenstown 50-51; R of Nelspruit 51-56; Primrose 56-59; Flempton w Hengrave and Lackford 59-62; Min of St Geo Eccles Distr Bury St Edms 62-66; Surr 63-71; R of Chedburgh w Depden and Rede 66-71; Sundays River Valley 72-75; St Francis Port Eliz 75-79; P-in-c of St John Bathurst Dio Grahmstn from 79. *Box 45, Bathurst 6166, CP, S Africa.*

WIDDICOMBE, Peter John. b 52. Univ of Manit BA 74. Univ of Ox MPhil 77. Wycl Coll Tor MDiv 81. **d** 81 Tor. C of St Luke City and Dio Tor from 81. *904 Coxwell Avenue, Toronto, Ont, Canada, M4C 3G3.*

WIDDOWS, David Charles Rowland. b 52. Hertf Coll Ox BA 75, MA 79. Univ of Nottm BA 77. St Jo Coll Nottm. **d** 79 **p** 80 Man. C of Blackley Dio Man from 79. *101 Broomhall Road, Higher Blackley, Manchester, M9 3PA.* (061-740 6774)

WIDDOWS, Edward John. b 45. Lon Coll of Div 66. **d** 70 **p** 71 Warrington for Liv. C of Formby 70-72; C of Uckfield, of Isfield and of Horsted Parva 72-73; Babbacombe 73-76; V of St Sithney 76-78; RD of Kerrier 77-78; V of Bude Haven Dio Truro from 78. *8 Falcon Terrace, Bude, Cornwall, EX23 8LJ.* (Bude 2318)

WIDDOWS, John Christopher. b 46. Trin Coll Cam BA 69, MA 72. Cudd Coll 69. **d** 71 **p** 72 Dur. C of East Herrington 71-76; Team V of Chelmsley Wood 77-80; V of St Hilda Halifax Dio Wakef from 80. *St Hilda's Vicarage, Halifax, Yorks, HX1 4HE.* (Halifax 54448)

WIDDOWSON, Charles Leonard. ALCD (1st cl) 62. **d** 62 **p** 63 Southw. C of Radcliffe-on-Trent 62-66; V of Ch Ch Newark-on-Trent 66-69; C-in-c of Fairy Meadow 69-70; R 71-78; Perm to Offic Dio Melb from 78. *241 Tooronga Road, Glen Iris, Vic, Australia 3146.*

WIEBE, John. Univ of Manit BMin 79. St Jo Coll Winnipeg. **d** 79 **p** 80 Bran. C of Kelwood, McCreary, Kinosota, Bluff Creek & Reedy Creek Dio Bran from 79. *Kelwood, Manitoba, Canada, R0J 0Y0.*

WIEBE, Terrance Robert. b 51. Richmond Coll BA 76. Wycl Coll Tor MDiv 79. **d** and **p** 79 Sask. C of Leask Dio Sask from 79. *Box 433, Leask, Saskatchewan, Canada, S0J 1M0.*

WIEDEMANN, William George. **d** 37 **p** 38 Melan. Miss at Sag Sag 37-41; R of Kilmore 41-46; Nagambie 46-58; Seymour 58-60; Can of Wang 58-67; Dir of Promotion Dio Wang 60-62; R of Murchison w Rushworth 62-66; Rutherglen 66-71; Archd of Wang 67-71; Perm to Offic Dio Melb from 71. *BSL Settlement, Carrum Downs, Vic, Australia 3200.*

WIELAND, Norman Charles. b 24. K Coll Lon and Warm AKC 49. **d** 50 **p** 51 Man. C of Ch Ch Moss Side 50-53; St Anne Longsight Royton 53-54; Portland 54-57; Chap HM Borstal Inst Portland 54-57; R of Ch Ch Moss Side 57-76; RD of Hulme 62-73. *39 Church Lane, Prestwich, Manchester, M25 5AN.*

WIGAN, Canon Bernard John. b 18. St Edm Hall Ox BA (3rd cl Th) 40, MA 44. Cudd Coll 40. **d** 42 **p** 43 Ox. C of St Barn Ox 42-44; St Phil and St Jas Ox 44-45; R of Woodeaton 45-47; Standlake 47-49; Yelford 48-49; V of E Malling 49-57; R of L Berkhamsted 57-59; V of Markbeech 59-65; Exam Chap to Bp of Roch from 63; L to Offic Dio Roch 65-68; Hon Can of Roch from 68. *119 Western Road, Hurstpierpoint, W Sussex, BN6 9SY.*

WIGBY, Robert Allan. Univ of Tor BA 48. Wycl Coll Tor LTh 50. **d** 50 **p** 51 Tor. I of St Luke Mulmur 50-53; Coldwater 53-54; Markham 54-68; R of St Eliz Queensway Tor 68-75; Brighton Dio Tor from 75. *Box 57, Brighton, Ont., Canada.* (613-475 2000)

WIGFIELD, Thomas Henry Paul. b 26. Edin Th Coll 46. **d** 49 **p** 50 Dur. C of Seaham Harbour 49-52; St Marg Dur 52-54; PC of Fatfield 54-63; Asst Dir Chs' Television Centre 63-79; Hd of Services Found for Chr Communication from 79. *Hillside, Merry Hill Road, Bushey, Herts, WD2 1DR.* (01-950 4426)

WIGGEN, Richard Martin. b 42. Open Univ BA 78. Qu Coll Birm 64. **d** 67 Pontefract for Wakef **p** 68 Wakef. C of Penistone w Midhope 67-70; Leeds 70-73; Asst Youth Chap Dio Glouc 73-76; Youth Officer Dio Liv 76-80; V of Kirkstall Dio Ripon from 80. *Kirkstall Vicarage, Leeds, LS5 3HD.* (Leeds 781007)

WIGGETT, Harry Alfred. b 37. Univ of S Africa BA. Bp Gray Th Coll Capetn LTh 64. **d** 63 **p** 64 Capetn. C of St Jas Sea Point 63-66; Pinelands 66-69; R of Hoetjes Bay 69-72; R of Ceres 72-81; Bergvliet Dio Capetn from 81. *45 Glen Alpine Way, Bergvliet 7800, CP, S Africa.* (72-8892)

WIGGINS, Gordon Vaughan. Moore Th Coll Syd ACT ThL 59. **d** 60 Graft. C of Tweed Heads 60-62; Actg Prin Andrew Kerr Mem Home and Perm to Offic Dio Melb 62-66; Hon C of St Mary Magd St Mary's Dio Syd from 69. *22 Knox Street, St Mary's, NSW, Australia 2750.* (623-6207)

WIGGINS, Karl Patrick. b 38. ARICS 64. BD (Lon) 72. Trin Coll Bris 71. **d** 72 **p** 73 Roch. C of Hildenborough 72-76; Hon C of St Barn Reading Dio Ox from 76. *21 Talfourd Avenue, Earley, Reading.* (Reading 81718)

WIGGINS, Leslie James. Moore Th Coll Syd ACT ThL 52. **d** and **p** 53 Syd. C of Haberfield 53-54; C-in-c of Mascot 55-57; R of Greenwich 58-63; NSW Sec Bush Ch Aid S 64-66; Asst Federal Sec 66-68; L to Offic Dio Syd 64-68; C-in-c of Chester Hill Provisional Distr 68-70; Sen Res Master and Chap Trin Gr Sch Kew Dio Melb 71-76; Dir C of E Boys S and L to Offic Dio Melb from 76. *8 Westmore Drive, Heathmont, Vic, Australia 3135.*

✠ **WIGGINS, Right Rev Maxwell Lester.** Univ of NZ BA 37. NZ Bd of Th Stud LTh 38. Coll Ho Ch Ch. **d** 38 **p** 39 Ch Ch. C of Merivale 38-41; V of Oxford 41-44; Miss at Berega 45-46; Mvumi 46-47; Hd Master Alliance Secondary Sch Dodoma 48-53; Dean of Dodoma Cathl 49-53; Can of Centr Tang 53-59; Exam Chap to Bp 53-63; Prin St Phil Th Kongwa 54-57; Miss at Bukoba 57-59; Archd of S Vic Nyan 56-59; Cons Asst Bp in Centr Tang (Bp of S Vic Nyan) in Cathl of H Spirit Dodoma 11 June 59 by Bp of Centr Tang; Bps of Zanz; and Ugan; and Bps Omari and Olang; Apptd Bp of Vic Nyan 63; res 76; Asst Bp of Wel from 76; VG from 76. *18a Hill Street, Wellington, NZ.* (728-732)

WIGGINS, Sydney Arthur. b 02. St Aug Coll Cant. **d** 62 **p** 63 Lon. C of Southgate 62-67; V of Broad Hinton 67-75; R of Winterbourne Bassett 67-75. *Broadford, Church Walk, Bishop's Cannings, Devizes, Wilts SN10 2LE.*

WIGGINTON, Canon Peter Walpole. b 20. Edin Th Coll 40. Univ of Dur LTh 44. **d** 43 **p** 44 Derby. C of St Jas Derby 43-46; Brimington 46; Gedling 46-49; PV of Southw Minster 49-52; V of Rolleston w Fiskerton and Morton 52-56; R of E Keal Dio Linc from 56; R of W Keal Dio Linc from 56; RD of Bolingbroke from 66; Can and Preb of Linc Cathl from 77. *West Keal Rectory, Spilsby, Lincs, PE23 4BJ.* (Spilsby 53534)

WIGGS, Robert James. b 50. Pemb Coll Cam BA 72. Qu Coll Birm 78. **d** 80 **p** 81 Chelmsf. C of St John Stratford Dio Chelmsf from 80. *58 Caernarvon Road, Stratford, E15.*

WIGHT, ISLE OF, Archdeacon of. *See* Carpenter, Ven Frederick Charles.

WIGHT, John Geoffrey. Univ of Melb BA (2nd cl Gen) 54. St Jo Coll Morpeth ACT ThL (2nd cl) 56. **d** 57 **p** 58 Melb. C of St Andr Brighton 57-59; Ch Ch Geelong 59-60; V of Newport 60-64; Min of Bennettswood 64-71; I of St Jas Syndal 71-81; St Mary S Camberwell Dio Melb from 81. *Vicarage, Bowen Street, Camberwell, Vic, Australia 3124.*

WIGHTMAN, William David. b 39. Univ of Birm BA (2nd cl Th) 61. Wells Th Coll 61. **d** 63 **p** 64 Sheff. C of Rotherham 63-67; Castlechurch 67-70; V of St Aid Buttershaw 70-76; Cullingworth Dio Bradf from 76. *Cullingworth Vicarage, Bradford, W Yorks.* (Cullingworth 272434)

WIGLEY, Harry Maxwell. b 38. Oak Hill Th Coll 61. **d** 64 **p** 65 Ches. C of Overchurch (or Upton) 64-67; Ch Ch Chadderton 67; Gateacre 67-69; V of St Jo Evang Gt Horton City and Dio Bradf from 69. *19 Dracup Road, Bradford, W Yorks, BD7 4HA.* (Bradford 571565)

WIGMORE, Canon Verschoyle Dudley. Wycl Coll Tor Univ of Tor LTh 41. **d** 41 **p** 42 Tor. C of Chap of Mess Tor 41-43; I of Alliston and W Essa 43-48; R of Calvary Ch Tor 48-55; St Olave City and Dio Tor from 55; Dioc Sec of Synod Dio Tor from 75; Can of Tor from 77. *8 Mossom Place, Toronto, Ont., Canada.* (416-769 5686)

WIGMORE, William Brodie. Univ of W Ont BA 55. Hur Coll LTh 53. **d** 53 **p** 54 Hur. R of Woodhouse 54-56; Ch Ch Lon 56-66; H Trin Kitchener 66-72; Dom Chap to Bp of Hur 60-70; R of Old St Paul Woodstock Dio Hur from 72. *222 Victoria Street North, Woodstock, Ont., Canada.* (519-537 3912)

WIGNALL, Paul Graham. b 49. Univ of Lanc BA 72. Qu Coll Cam BA 74, MA 78. Westcott Ho Cam 72. **d** 74 Ely **p** 75 Huntingdon for Ely. C of Good Shepherd Chesterton 74-76;

Prec of Dur Cathl 76-80; Tutor and Chap Ripon Coll Cudd from 80; P-in-c of Aston Rowant and Crowell Dio Ox from 81. *Ripon College, Cuddesdon, Oxford, OX9 9EX.* (Wheatley 4595)

WIGRAM, Andrew Oswald. BD (Lon) 64. Bps' Coll Cheshunt 61. **d** 64 **p** 65 York. C of Marton-in-Cleveland 64-69; Sch Chap Dio Momb 69-77; Exam Chap to Bp of Nai from 77; Warden Trin Coll Nai from 77. *Box 72430, Nairobi, Kenya.*

WIGRAM, Canon Sir Clifford Woolmore, Bt. b 11. Trin Coll Cam 2nd cl Hist Trip 31, BA (2nd cl Th Trip) 32, MA 36. Ely Th Coll 33. **d** 34 **p** 35 Lon. C of St Anne Brondesbury 34-37; Chap Ely Th Coll 37-40; L to Offic Dio Ely 38-40 Perm to Offic Dio Ox 40; C of Long Ashton 40-42; St Jo Bapt Holland Rd Kens 42-45; V of Marston St Lawr w Warkworth (w Thenford from 75) Dio Pet from 45; C-in-c of Thenford 72-75; Can (Non-res) of Pet from 73. *Vicarage, Marston St Lawrence, Banbury, Oxon, OX17 2DA.* (Banbury 710300)

WIGRAM, Marcus Walter. b 17. G and C Coll BA 38. Glouc Th Course 70. **d** 72 Ches **p** 73 Stockport for Ches. C of Bromborough 72-76; V of Lindow 76-78; Pott-Shrigley Dio Ches from 78. *Pott-Shrigley Vicarage, Macclesfield, SK10 5RS.* (Bollington 73316)

WIGRAM, Oswald Thomas Edward. b 05. Wycl Hall Ox 36. [f CMS Miss] **d** 37 Lon for Col Bp **p** 40 Momb. CMS Miss Dio Momb from 37; Weithaga 37-43; Kabete 43-46; Embu 47-49; Chap of Uasin Gishu and RD of Nzoia 49-53; Prin of Christian Leadership Centre Embu 55-57; V of Fordcombe 57-62; P-in-c of Holne 63-70; Perm to Offic Dio Ex from 70. *Highlands Park, Chudleigh, Newton Abbot, Devon, TQ13 0JZ.* (Chudleigh 852331)

WIGSTON, Kenneth Edmund. b 28. Lich Th Coll 55. **d** 58 **p** 59 Sheff. C of St Andr Sharrow 58-61; Kidlington 61-68; R of Airdrie 68-78; Gartcosh 68-78; St Osw King's Park City and Dio Glas from 78. *1 King's Park Avenue, Glasgow, G44 4UW.* (041-632 1852)

WIHAPI, Pataana. St John's Coll Auckld. **d** 74 Wai. C of Taupo Dio Wai from 74. *77 Kaimanawa Street, Taupo, NZ.*

WIHAPI, Wiremu Kepa. b 23. **d** 77 Aotearoa for Wai **p** 78 Wai. Hon C of Te Puke Past Dio Wai from 77. *PO Box 102, Waitangi, Te Puke, NZ.*

WIIG, Brian. b 46. Univ of Alta BA 70. Em & St Chad Coll Sktn LTh 74. **d** and **p** 74 Bran. I of Devon Miss The Pas 74-80; Teslin Dio Yukon from 80. *St Philip's Church, Teslin, Yukon Territory, Canada YOA 1BO.*

WIKELEY, John Roger Ian. b 41. K Coll Lon and Warm AKC 64. **d** 65 Warrington for Liv **p** 66 Liv. C of H Trin Southport 65-69; Padgate (in c of Woolston) Dio Liv 69-71; Team V 71-73; R from 73. *Rectory, Padgate, Warrington, Ches, WA2 0PD.* (Padgate 821555)

WILBOURNE, David Jeffrey. b 55. Jes Coll Cam BA 78. Westcott Ho Cam 79. **d** 81 York. C of Stainton-in-Cleveland Dio York from 81. *11 Pennyman Way, Stainton, Middlesborough, Cleve, TS8 9BL.* (Middlesborough 591551)

WILBOURNE, Geoffrey Owen. b 29. Lich Th Coll 60. **d** 62 **p** 63 York. C of Marfleet 62-65; V of Ellerton Priory w Aughton and E Cottingwith 65-70; Team V of Scalby w Ravenscar 70-73; V of St Nich Hull 73-76; Keyingham Dio York from 76. *Keyingham Vicarage, Hull, N Humb.* (Keyingham 2175)

WILCOCK, Christopher John. b 45. TCD BA 68, MA 72. Div Hostel Dub 75. **d** 77 **p** 78 Down. C of Holywood Dio Down from 77. *20 Princess Gardens, Holywood, Co Down, N Ireland.*

WILCOCK, Michael Jarvis. b 32. Univ of Dur BA 54. Tyndale Hall Bris 60. **d** 62 **p** 63 Liv. C of Ch Ch Southport 62-65; All S Langham Place St Marylebone 65-69; V of St Faith Maidstone 69-77; Dir of Pastoral Studies Trin Coll Bris from 77; Publ Pr Dio Bris from 77. *Trinity College, Stoke Hill, Bristol, BS9 1JP.* (0272-34021)

WILCOCKSON, Stephen Anthony. b 51. Univ of Nottm BA 73. Univ of Ox BA (Th) 75, MA 81. Wycl Hall Ox 73. **d** 76 **p** 77 Bradf. C of St Lawr Pudsey 76-78; Wandsworth 78-81; V of Rock Ferry Dio Ches from 81. *Vicarage, St Peter's Road, Rock Ferry, Birkenhead, L42 1PY.* (051-645 1622)

WILCOX, Anthony Gordon. b 41. ALCD 67. **d** 67 **p** 68 Glouc. C of Ch Ch Cheltm 67-72; Beccles 72-74; team V 74-81; V of All SS Ipswich Dio St E from 81. *264 Norwich Road, Ipswich, Suff, IP1 4BT.* (Ipswich 52975)

WILCOX, Canon Arthur Whitman. Univ of Manit St Jo Coll Winnipeg BA 42, LTh 47. **d** 47 **p** 48 Bran. C of Ch Ch Melita 47-49; R of Minnedosa 49-52; St Andr Winnipeg 52-61; St Paul Edmon 61-71; Can of Edmon 67-71; R of St Martin City and Dio Calg from 71; Hon Can of Calg from 78. *3315-35th Street SW, Calgary, Alta, Canada.* (249-1553)

WILCOX, Brian Howard. b 46. Westcott Ho Cam 71. **d** 73 **p** 74 Pet. C of Kettering 73-78; V of Eye Dio Pet from 78. *Eye Vicarage, Peterborough, PE6 7ON.* (Pet 222334)

WILCOX, David. b 35. Roch Th Coll 66. **d** 68 **p** 69 S'wark. C of Newington 68-73; Mottingham (in c of St Alb) 73-77; V of Ch Ch Shooter's Hill Dio S'wark from 77. *Christ Church Vicarage, Shooter's Hill, SE18.* (01-856 5858)

WILCOX, Canon David Peter. b 30. St Jo Coll Ox BA (2nd cl Th) 52 MA 56. Linc Th Coll 52. **d** 54 **p** 55 S'wark. C of St Helier Morden 54-56; St Mary Virg Ox 56-59; Publ Pr Dio Linc 59-63; Tutor Linc Th Coll 59-60; Chap 60-61; Sub-Warden 61-63; in Ch of S India 64-70; V of Gt Gransden and R of L Gransden 70-72; Res Can of Derby 72-77; Can (Emer) from 77; Exam Chap to Bp of Derby 72-77; Surr 72-77; M Gen Syn 73-77; Prin Ripon Coll Cudd from 77; P-in-c of Cuddesdon Dio Ox from 77. *Ripon College, Cuddesdon, Oxford, OX9 9EX.* (Wheatley 4427)

WILCOX, Frank Charles. **d** 55 **p** 57 Bal. P-in-c of Edenhope 56-60; V of Mortlake 60-61; P-in-c of Natimuk 61-68; R 68-71; Kaniva 71-75; Perm to Offic Dio Bal from 75. *6 Dundas Street, Edenhope, Vic, Australia 3318.*

WILCOX, Graham James. b 43. Qu Coll Ox BA (2nd cl Mod Hist) 64, MA 75. Ridley Hall Cam 64. **d** 66 **p** 67 Birm. C of St Aug Edgbaston 66-69; Sheldon 69-72; Asst Chap Wrekin Coll Wellington, Salop 72-74; C of Asterby Group 74-77; R of Asterby w Goulceby 77-81; Donington-on-Bain 77-81; Scamblesby w Calkwell 77-81; Gayton-le-Wold w Biscathorpe 77-81; Stenigot 77-81; Benniworth w Market Stainton and Ranby 77-81; R of Asterby Group Dio Linc from 81. *The Parsonage, Donington-on-Bain, Louth, Lincs, LN11 9TL.* (Stenigot 286)

WILCOX, Hugh Edwin. b 37. St Edm Hall Ox BA (3rd cl Th) 62, MA 66. St Steph Ho Ox 62. **d** 64 Chelmsf **p** 65 Colchester for Chelmsf. C of St Jas Colchester 64-66; SCM Sec and Hon C of St Paul Ap Clifton 66-68; Sec Internat Affairs Divn Br Coun of Chs (w Conf of Br Miss Societies) from 68; Asst Gen Sec BCC 74-76; Publ Pr Dio S'wark 69-76; V of Ware Dio St Alb from 76. *31 Thunder Court, Ware, Herts, SG12 0PT.* (Ware 4817)

WILCOX, Jeffry Reed. b 40. K Coll Lon and Warm AKC 65, BA 78. **d** 66 **p** 67 Dur. C of St Paul Ryhope 66-69; Cockerton 69-71; P-in-c of St Luke Pallion Bp Wearmouth Dio Dur from 71. *St Luke's Vicarage, Pallion, Sunderland, T & W, SR4 6SF.* (Sunderland 56554)

WILCOX, Joe. b 21. Lich Th Coll. ACT ThL 62. **d** 62 Stafford for Lich **p** 63 Shrewsbury for Lich. C of Tamworth 62-66; Tettenhall Wood 66-67; V of St Luke Leek 67-75; P-in-c of Ellington 75-80; Grafham 75-80; Spaldwick w Barham and Woolley 75-80; Easton 75-80; R of Holywell w Needingworth Dio Ely from 80. *Holywell Rectory, St Ives, Huntingdon, Cambs, PE17 3QT.* (St Ives 63348)

WILCOX, John Bower. b 28. K Coll Lon and Warm AKC 55. **d** 58 **p** 59 Liv. C of Orford 58-60; St Mary W Derby 60-63; R of Aisthorpe w Scampton and W Thorpe 63-74; Brattleby 64-74; Industr Chap to Bp of Linc 63-74; Chap Teesside Industr Miss Dios Dur and York from 74. *21 Forth Road, Redcar, Cleve, TS10 1PN.* (Redcar 484393)

WILCOX, Poihakena. b 27. **d** 79 **p** 80 Wai. Hon C of Ruatoki-Whakatane Dio Wai from 79. *Awakeri Hot Springs, R.D. 2, Whakatane, NZ.*

WILCOX, Raymond Trevor. b 22. St D Coll Lamp BA 47. **d** 48 **p** 49 Mon. C of Llanfrechfa 48-50; Griffithstown 50-52; St Paul Walsall 52-54; CF 54-57; C-in-c of Bentley Conv Distr Walsall 57-58; V 58-78; P-in-c of Colton Dio Lich from 78; Blithfield Dio Lich from 78. *Colton Rectory, Rugeley, Staffs, WS15 3JW.* (Rugeley 2333)

WILCOX-JONES, Owen McInnis. b 1895. St D Coll Lamp BA 15. **d** 19 **p** 20 Ban for St A. C of Llansilin 19-21; Llanhilleth 21-22; Holywell 22-25; Llangwm (in c of Dinmael) 25-28; V of Trofarth 28-37; R of Llanelidan 37-48; V of Pool Quay w Arddleen 48-66; L to Offic Dios Lich and St Asaph from 66. *24 Grey Friars, Oswestry, Salop.* (Oswestry 4134)

WILD, Edwin Arnold. b 13. Peterho Cam 2nd cl Hist Trip pt i 34, BA (3rd cl Th Trip pt i) 35. MA 44. Wells Th Coll 36. **d** 37 **p** 38 Pet. C of Abington 37-40; CF (EC) 40-46; C of St Jo Bapt Pet 46-48; CF 48-62; Men in Disp (Korea) 52; R of Barton-le-Cley 62-70; Higham Gobion 62-70; V of Ash w West Marsh 70-77. *12 The Suttons, Camber, Rye, Sussex.* (Camber 497)

✠ **WILD, Right Rev Eric.** b 14. Keble Coll Ox BA (3rd cl Th) 37, MA 45. **d** 37 **p** 38 Liv. C of St Ann Stanley 37-40; St Jas Haydock 40-42; Chap RNVR 42-46; V of St Geo Wigan 46-52; Hindley 52-59; Surr from 52; Dir of Relig Educn Pet 59-62; R of Cranford w Grafton Underwood 59-62; Can of Pet 61-62; Can (Emer) from 62; Gen Sec NS 62-67; Sec C of E Schs Coun 62-67; R of Milton 67-72; Archd of Berks 67-72; Cons Ld Bp Suffr of Reading in Ch Ch Cathl Ox 13 July 72 by Abp of Cant; Bps of Lon; Chich; Pet; Ches; Linc; Portsm;

Derby; St Alb; Ox; Blackb; and others; res 82. *2 Spleen Place, Spleen, Newbury, Berks.*

WILD, George Walter. b 11. Linc Th Coll 68. **d** 69 **p** 70 Derby. C of Boulton 69-72; P-in-c of Loscoe 72-77; Hon C of Cotmanhay Dio Derby from 77. *43 Archer Street, Ilkeston, Derbys, DE7 8JX.* (Ilkeston 301535)

WILD, Very Rev John Herbert Severn. b 04. Late Scho of BNC Ox 1st cl Cl Mods 25, BA (3rd cl Lit Hum) 27, 2nd cl Th 28, MA 30. Univ of Dur Hon DD 58. Westcott Ho Cam 28. **d** 29 Bp Wood for Newc T **p** 30 Newc T. C of St Aid Newc T 29-33; Chap, Fell and Tutor of Univ Coll Ox 33-45; Master and Chap 45-51; Hon Fell from 51; L to Offic Dio Ox 33-51; Exam Chap to Bp of Lich 33-51; to Bp of Guildf 36-51; to Bp of Blackb 37-48; to Bp of Heref 49-51; to Bp of Pet 50-51; Commiss Colom 38-47; Select Pr Univ of Ox 48-49; Dean of Dur 51-73; Dean (Emer) from 73; Ch Comm 58-73; Chap O of St John of Jer from 67; L to Offic Dio B & W from 73. *Deacon's House, Rapps, Ilminster, Somt, TA19 9LG.* (Ilminster 3398)

WILD, Canon Patrick. b 06. Ex Coll Ox BA (3rd cl Mod Hist) 28, Dipl Th 29, MA 33. Westcott Ho Cam 29. **d** 30 **p** 31 Newc T. C of Tynemouth (in c of St Andr Preston from 32) 30-35; St Jo Evang Smith Sq Westmr 35-38; C and PV of Southw Minster 38-39; CF (R of O) 39-46; V of Theydon Bois 46-76; RD of Chigwell 64-76; Hon Can of Chelmsf Cathl from 75. *Moorway House, Moor Road, Breadsall, Derby.*

WILD, Peter John. b 55. Univ of Leeds BA 77. Qu Coll Birm 77. **d** 80 Ripon **p** 81 Knaresborough for Ripon. C of H Trin Rothwell Dio Ripon from 80. *86 Pasture View Road, Rothwell, Leeds, LS26 0XE.* (Leeds 824717)

WILD, Robert Cyril Edwin. McGill Univ Montr BA 49. Huron Th Coll LTh 54. **d** 53 **p** 54 Hur. C of Trin Ch St Thomas 53; I of Glanworth 53-59; Sec Treas and Trav Miss Dio Sktn 59-64; Hon Can of Sktn 61-69; Chap Univ of Sask 64-70; R of St Francis Caulfield W Vancouver 70-80; St Patr Miss City and Dio Edmon from 81. *1048 Knottwood Road, Edmonton, Alta, T6K 3R4, Canada.*

WILD, Robert David Fergusson. b 10. MBE (Mil) 46. MC 45. TD 50. Late Exhib of Ex Coll Ox 3rd cl Cl Mods 31, BA (3rd cl Th) 33, MA 36. Westcott Ho Cam 34. **d** 35 **p** 36 Win. C of Eastleigh 35-36; Dom Chap to Bp of Win and Joint Sec Youth Movement Dio Win 36-37; L to Offic Dio Win 37; Asst Master Eton Coll 37-68; Chap 49-69; CF (TA) 39-50; Select Pr Univ of Cam 52; Perm to Offic Dio Ox 66-70; C-in-c of Staplegrove 70-71; Bicknoller 73. *The Railway House, Stogumber, Taunton, Somt.* (Stogumber 414)

WILD, Roger Bedingham Barratt. b 40. ALCD 64. **d** 65 **p** 66 Bradf. C of St Pet Shipley 65-68; Pudsey 68-71; P-in-c of St Jas Rawthorpe Huddersfield 71-73; V 73-78; H Trin City and Dio Ripon from 78. *Holy Trinity Vicarage, College Road, Ripon, Yorks, HG4 2AE.* (Ripon 5865)

WILD, Roger Longson. b 13. K Coll Lon and Warm 55. **d** 57 **p** 58 S'wark. C of St Mark Woodcote 57-59; Godstone (in c of St Steph S Godstone) 59-63; V of St Paul Kingston Hill 63-74; R of Easton w Martyr Worthy Dio Win from 74. *Easton Rectory, Winchester, Hants, SO21 1EG.* (Itchen Abbas 291)

WILD, William Stanley. b 12. TD 47. Worc Coll Ox BA (3rd cl Th) 36, MA 45. Ripon Hall Ox 35. **d** 36 **p** 37 Ex. C of Braunton 36-39; Chap Achimota Sch 46-63; L to Offic Dio Accra 62-64; Asst Master Belmont Sch Holmbury 64-66; Headfort Sch Kells 68-77; Perm to Offic Dio Ex from 78. *Pixies Hill, Holne, Newton Abbot, S Devon.*

WILDE, David Wilson. b 37. BD (Lon) 62. ALCD 61. **d** 62 **p** 63 Wakef. C of Kirkheaton 62-66; Attenborough w Bramcote 66-72; Bestwood Park (in c of St Mark and Rise Pk) Dio Southw from 72. *Rectory, Bestwood Village, Nottingham.* (Nottm 278386)

WILDE, Thomas Harold. b 05. St Aid Coll 33. **d** 36 **p** 37 Man. C of Ch Ch Denton 36-40; Ch Ch Walmsley 40-43; R of St Jo Evang Cheetham 43-48; V of Hey 48-58; R of St Matt Crumpsall 58-68; V of Warmington 68-76; RD of Oundle 72-76. *29 New Road, Oundle, Peterborough, PE8 4LB.*

WILDEY, Ian Edward. b 51. St Chad's Coll Dur BA 72. Coll of Resurr Mirfield 72. **d** 74 **p** 75 Wakef. C of St Mich Arch Wakef 74-77; St Mary Barnsley 77-81; V of Ravensthorpe Dio Wakef from 81. *Vicarage, Church Street, Ravensthorpe, Dewsbury, Yorks.* (Dewsbury 465959)

WILDING, David. b 43. K Coll Lon and Warm BD and AKC 67. **d** 68 Wakef **p** 69 Pontefract for Wakef. C of Thornhill 68-70; Halifax 70-72; V of Scholes 72-79; Lightcliffe Dio Wakef from 79. *Lightcliffe Vicarage, Halifax, W Yorks.* (Halifax 202424)

WILDING, Joseph. b 14. Edin Th Coll 50. **d** 52 **p** 53 Glas. C of Dumbarton (in c of St Mungo Alexandria from 53) 52-56; R of St Mungo Alexandria Dio Glas 56-80; P-in-c from 80. *St Mungo's Rectory, Queen Street, Alexandria, Dunbartons.* (Alexandria 2633)

WILDING, Canon Thomas Davidson. Univ of W Ont BA 58. Hur Coll LTh 60. **d** 60 Hur for Tor **p** 61 Tor. C of St Jo Bapt Norway 60-63; P-in-c of St Sav Pro-Cathl Nelson 63-64; I of Castlegar 64-68; R of Boort 68-70; Penticton 70-73; Ch Ch Chatham 73-81; Can of Hur from 77; Exam Chap to Bp of Hur from 78; R of St Bart Sarnia Dio Hur from 81. *722 Cathcart Boulevard, Sarnia, Ont, Canada N7V 2N5.*

WILDRIDGE, Peter. b 24. St D Coll Lamp BA 51. **d** 52 **p** 53 St D. C of St Issell 52-55; Highgate 55-56; St Giles-in-the-Fields 56-60; V of St Pet Isl 60-80. *Address temp unknown.*

WILDS, Anthony Ronald. b 43. Univ of Dur BA 64. Bps' Coll Cheshunt 64. **d** 66 Buckingham for Ox **p** 67 Ox. C of Newport Pagnell 66-72; P-in-c of Chipili Zam 72-75; V of Chandler's Ford Dio Win from 75. *Vicarage, Hursley Road, Chandler's Ford, Eastleigh, SO5 2FT.* (Chandler's Ford 2597)

WILES, Canon Maurice Frank. b 23. Ch Coll Cam BA (2nd cl Mor Sc Trip pt i) 47, 1st cl Th Trip pt i 49, MA 52. Ridley Hall Cam 48. **d** 50 **p** 51 Ches. C of St Geo Stockport 50-52; Chap of Ridley Hall Cam 52-55; Lect in NT Univ Coll Ibad 55-59; in Div Univ of Cam 59-67; Dean of Clare Coll Cam 59-67; Exam Chap to Abp of Cant 59-63; to Bp of Roch 63-67; Prof of Christian Doctrine K Coll Lon 67-70; Regius Prof of Div Univ of Ox and Can of Ch Ch Ox from 70. *Christ Church, Oxford.*

WILES, Thomas Cyril. b 17. **d** 66 Bp Horstead for Leic **p** 67 Leic. C of St Andr Aylestone Leic 66-71; V of Fleckney (w Saddington 71-74) 71-81. *101 Rosemead Drive, Oadby, Leics, LE2 5PP.*

WILKENS, Canon William Frederic. Univ of NZ BCom 62. NZ Bd of Th Stud LTh 49. **d** and **p** 49 Nel. C-in-c of Suburban N 49-50; C of All SS Nel 50-52; V of Reefton 52-56; Sec and Regr Dio Nel from 56; Dom Chap to Bp of Nel from 56; Can of Nel from 70. *25 Richmond Avenue, Nelson, NZ.* (84-711)

WILKES, Canon Eric. b 22. Univ of Dur BA 51. St Steph Ho Ox. **d** 53 Stafford for Cant **p** 54 Lich. C of All SS Shrewsbury 53-55; St Aid Leeds 55-58; Cowley St John (in c of St Alb) Ox 58-63; V of St Marg Toxt Pk 63-71; St Marg and All H Orford Dio Liv from 71; M Gen Syn 75-80; Can of Liv Cathl from 76. *Orford Vicarage, Orford Green, Warrington, Chesh.* (Warrington 31937)

WILKES, John Comyn Vaughan. b 02. Trin Coll Ox BA 25, MA 37. Coll of Resurr Mirfield. **d** and **p** 46 Ox. Warden of Radley Coll 37-54; V of Hunslet (w Stourton from 56) 54-58; Gt Marlow 58-65; R of Preston Bissett 65-67; V of Barton Hartshorne w Chetwode 65-67; R of Gt w L Kimble 67-72. *The Old Stables, Burghill, Hereford.*

WILKES, Keith Reid. b 30. Pemb Coll Cam BA 53, MA 58. Univ of Bris MA 71. Linc Th Coll. **d** 55 **p** 56 St Alb. C of Welwyn Garden City 55-59; Publ Pr Dio Birm 59-64; Sec SCM Univ of Birm 59-64; Chap St Francis Hall Birm 59-64; Coll of St Matthias Bris 64-70; R of Ch Ch w St Ewen (w All SS from 73) Bris 70-80; Dir Educn Dio Bris from 70; Bp's Cathl Chap Dio Bris 70-74; Can of Bris 74-80; L to Offic Dio Lich from 80. *The Mount, St John's Hill, Ellesmere, Salop, SY12 0EY.* (Ellesmere 2466)

WILKES, Robert Anthony. b 48. Trin Coll Ox BA 70, MA 73. Wycl Hall Ox 71. **d** 74 Warrington for Liv **p** 75 Liv. C of Netherton Dio Liv 74-77; V from 77; Chap to Bp of Liv from 81. *50 Score Lane, Liverpool, L16 5EB.* (051-722 9543)

WILKES, Russell Oliver. MC 43. Em Coll Sktn LTh 30. Wycl Coll Tor. **d** 30 **p** 31 Keew. C-in-c of Reddit 30-32; I of Emerson 32-35; Rainy River w Stratton and Barwick 35-40; Chap CASF 40-60; R of Oak Bay 60-67; L to Offic Dio BC from 67. *3950 Larchwood Drive, Victoria, BC, Canada.*

WILKES, Thomas Clement Broadbery. b 14. Univ of Lon BA 37. Chich Th Coll 37. **d** 38 Grimsby for Linc **p** 39 Linc. C of St Jo Evang Spitalgate Grantham 38-41; Hessle 41-44; C-in-c of St Luke Scarborough 44-51; V of St Hilda York 51-56; Sen Chap Millfield Sch 56-62; R of Street 56-62; V of Yatton 62-69; R of Stambridge 69-79. *31 Radford Court, Billericay, Essex.*

WILKIE, Alan James. b 17. Chich Th Coll 39. **d** 42 **p** 43 Lich. C of St Paul Wednesbury 42-44; Porthill 44-52; Stoke-on-Trent 52-54; Chap Gen Hosp Stoke-on-Trent 52-54; L to Offic Dio Guildf 54-65; Dio Nor 66-68; Hd Master Badingham Coll Leatherhead 54-65; Wymondham 65-68; V of Lindale-in-Cartmel (w Field Broughton from 71) Dio Carl from 69; C-in-c of Field Broughton 71. *Lindale Vicarage, Grange-over-Sands, Cumb.* (Grange-over-Sands 2864)

WILKIN, Edward Lenton. **d** 54 **p** 55 New Westmr. C of St John N Vancouver 54-57; I of St Edw Richmond 57-62; Sardis 62-71; Fraser-Cheam Team Min 71-77; Langley Team Min Dio New Westmr from 77. *4598 Saddlehorn Crescent, Aldergrove, BC, Canada.*

WILKINS, Charles Edward. b 1889. St Chad's Coll Regina, 15. **d** 18 **p** 19 Qu'App. C of White Bear 18-19; R of Fleming 19-24; Melita w Pierson 24-27; I of Moorefield 27-30; C of Melksham 30-34; V of H Trin Frome 34-59; Chap

Selwood Hosp Frome 59-69; C of Lullington and Orchardleigh 61-69. *6 Rocky Park Avenue, Pomphlett, Plymstock, Plymouth, Devon, PL9 7DY.*

WILKINS, Ven Charles Frederick. Univ of W Ont BA 53. Hur Coll LTh 55. **d** 54 Hur for Calg **p** 55 Calg. C of St Steph Calg 54-55; R of Mirror 55-58; Olds 58-63; St Steph W Vanc 63-70; Archd of Vanc from 70. *692 Burrard Street, Vancouver, BC, V6C 2L1, Canada.*

WILKINS, George Percy. St Jo Coll Ox BA 38, MA 44. Cudd Coll 38. **d** 39 **p** 40 Chelmsf. C of St Mich AA Walthamstow 39-43; Cowley St John Ox 43-45; Bladon w Woodstock 45-46; R of Hanborough 46-55; Ascot Heath 55-62; V of St Steph Bournemouth 62-69; Asst Chap HM Pris Wormwood Scrubs 69-70; Chap HM Pris Lewes 70-74; HM Pris Grendon Underwood 74-78; HM Pris Dorch from 78; Chap to Retired Clergy in Archd of Dorset from 78. *32 Lockeridge Close, Blandford Forum, Dorset, DT11 7TT.* (0258 54145)

WILKINS, Harold George Oakley. St Chad's Coll Dur BA and Jenkyns Scho 35, Dipl Th (w distinc) 36. **d** 36 **p** 37 Bris. C of Avonmouth 36-38; UMCA Miss Dio Masasi 38-63; Warden of Tunduru Th Coll 48-59; Chap and Bursar St Jos Coll Chidya 59-61; C of St Mich AA Watford 63-65; Tattenham Corner and Burgh Heath 65-69; All SS W Dulwich 69-72; V of St Jo Div Balham 72-81. *13 Harberson Road, Balham, SW12 9QW.* (01-675 2623)

WILKINS, Peter. St Jo Coll Ox BA (3rd cl Hist) 33, MA 37. St Steph Ho Ox 55. **d** 56 Bp Hawkes for Cant **p** 57 Guildf. C of Aldershot 56-58; V of Cassington w Worton 58-78. *Manor Farmhouse, Bloxham, Oxon, OX15 4NB.*

WILKINS, Ralph Herbert. b 29. BD (Lon) 61. St Aug Coll Cant 72. **d** 73 Dorking for Guildf **p** 74 Guildf. C of Ch Ch Epsom 73-76; Haslemere 76-79; P-in-c of Market Lavington w Easterton Dio Sarum from 79. *Market Lavington Vicarage, Devizes, Wilts, SN10 4DT.* (Lavington 3309)

WILKINS, Roderic John. b 15. Selw Coll Cam 3rd cl Econ Trip pt i 36, BA (3rd cl Th Trip pt i) 38, MA 42. Qu Coll Birm 38. **d** 39 **p** 40 Birm. C of All SS K Heath 39-43; St Steph Leic 43-45; V of St Bart Allen's Cross 45-71; Chap Hollymoor Ment Hosp Birm from 50; R of Wishaw Dio Birm from 71; V of Middleton Dio Birm from 71. *Wishaw Rectory, Sutton Coldfield, W Midl, B76 9QB.* (Curdworth 70331)

WILKINSON, Canon Alan Bassindale. b 31. St Cath Coll Cam BA (1st cl Engl Trip pt ii) 54, MA 58, PhD 59. Coll of Resurr Mirfield. **d** 59 **p** 60 Lon. C of St Aug Kilburn 59-61; Chap St Cath Coll Cam and L to Offic Dio Ely 61-67; Hulsean Pr Univ of Cam 67; PC of Barrow Gurney 67-70; Asst Chap and Lect St Matthias Coll Fishponds 67-70; Prin Chich Th Coll 70-74; Can and Preb of Chich Cathl 70-74; Can (Emer) from 74; Dir of Aux Min Tr Dio St Alb and Warden of Verulam House 74-75; Lect Crewe and Alsager Coll of Higher Educn 75-78; Dir of Tr Dio Ripon from 78. *5 Adel Park Croft, Leeds, LS16 8HT.* (Leeds 674221)

WILKINSON, Canon Bernard Ernest. Selw Coll Dun NZ Bd of Th Stud LTh 66. **d** 65 **p** 66 Dun. C of Caversham 65-68; V of U Clutha 68-76; Oamaru Dio Dun from 76; Hon Can of Dun from 80. *1 Wharfe Street, Oamaru, NZ.* (71-677)

WILKINSON, Charles Frederick. Univ of Lon BA 49. Edin Th Coll 49. **d** 51 **p** 52 Brech. C of St Mary Magd Dundee 51-52; Chap St Ninian's Cathl Perth 52-53; Prec 53-55; V of St Alb Smethwick 55-64; R of Cottenham 64-75; V of St Jo Evang Cam Dio Ely from 75. *9 Luard Road, Cambridge.* (Cambridge 47451)

WILKINSON, David Edward Paul. b 36. Univ of Wales BSc (2nd cl Civil Eng) 57. St Mich Coll Llan 57. **d** 59 **p** 60 Swan B. C of St Mary Brecon 59-60; Min Can of Brecon Cathl 60-66; R of Llanelwedd w Llanfaredd and Cwmbach-Llechryd 66-72; V of Tycoch 72-74; Asst Master Churchmead Sch Datchet from 75; Perm to Offic Dio Ox from 80. *43 Mornington Avenue, Wokingham, Berks, RG11 4UE.* (Evesley 734363)

WILKINSON, David George. d and **p** 55 Moos. I of Swastika 55-56; Malarctic 56-58; Timmins 58-60; Kirkland Lake 60-64; Schumacher 64-65; Archd of Timmins 65-70; Dioc Sec and Treas Dio Moos 65-70. *11 Dorfman Avenue, Virginiatown, Ont., Canada.*

WILKINSON, David James. b 45. Wycl Hall Ox 68. **d** 69 **p** 70 Swan B. C of St Thos Swansea w Kilvey 69-73; Clydach 73-76; R of Llanbadarn-Fawr w Llandegley and Llanfihangel Rhydithon 76-81; V of St Nich-on-the-Hill Swansea Dio Swan B from 81. *58a Dyfed Avenue, Townhill, Swansea, W Glam.* (Swansea 54272)

WILKINSON, Canon David Reginald. b 16. St Edm Hall Ox BA (3rd cl Th) 38. MA 48. Wells Th Coll 38. **d** 39 **p** 40 Swan B. C of St Mary Swansea 39-42; Oystermouth 42-47; C of Great Barr (in c of St Chad Pheesey) 47-49; R of Llanwrthwl w Elan Valley 49-56; V of St D Brecon 56-69; St Barn Swansea Dio Swan B from 69; Hon Can of Brecon Cathl 74-76; Can from 76. *57 Sketty Road, Swansea, W Glam, SA2 0EN.* (Swansea 56601)

WILKINSON, Edwin. b 29. Oak Hill Th Coll 53. **d** 56 **p** 57 Blackb. C of Ch Ch Blackb 56-58; St Mark Cheltm 58-61; V of St Geo Tiverton 61-66; Rye Harbour w Camber 66-73; Camber w E Guldeford 73-79; Westfield Dio Chich from 79. *Vicarage, Westfield, Hastings, TN35 4SD.* (Hastings 751029)

WILKINSON, Francis William. b 10. St Chad's Coll Dur Gisborne Scho 29, Lightfoot Scho and BA (2nd cl Cl) 31, 1st cl Th 33, MA 34. **d** 33 **p** 34 Liv. C of All SS Southport 33-35; St Cath Liv 35-40; V of H Spirit Knotty Ash 40-71; Asst Master Blue Coat Sch Liv from 71. *69 Kenmare Road, Liverpool, L15 3HQ.*

WILKINSON, Frank Dodgson. Univ Coll Dur BA 07. **d** 08 **p** 09 Lon. C of All SS Harlesden 08-11; St Steph Selly Hill 11-14; The Quinton (in c of St Kath Warley) 14-16; Cromer 16-17; TCF 17-21; Hon CF 21; C of Whalley 21-23; I of Ch Ch Galle Face Ceylon 23-24; C of St Paul Canonbury Lon 25; V of St Matt Islington Lon 25-48; R of Daylesford 48-69; C-in-c of Cornwell 48-69. *Address temp unknown.*

WILKINSON, George Unsworth. b 11. St Jo Coll Dur Bp Robertson Div Pri 40. BA (*Aegr*) 41. **d** 41 **p** 42 Man. C of St Pet Blackley 41-43; C-in-c of St Geo Mossley 43-45; R of St Geo Abbey Hey 45-52; CF 52-55; C of St Andr Coulsdon 55-59; V of Stoke H Cross w Dunston 59-81. *Address temp unknown.*

WILKINSON, Glynn Frederick Evan. b 37. Em Coll Sktn LTh 65. **d** 62 **p** 64 Athab. I of Lac La Biche 62-65; R of Fairview 65-69; C of Beccles 69-72; V of Edensor 72-80; R of Barwick-in-Elmet Dio Ripon from 80. *Barwick-in-Elmet Rectory, Leeds, Yorks.* (Leeds 812218)

WILKINSON, Ven Hubert Seed. b 1897. Late Exhib of St Jo Coll Dur BA (2nd cl Mod Hist and Engl Lit) 23, Capel Cure Pri 24, MA 26. **d** 25 **p** 26 Man. C of Colne Lancs 25-29; R of Harpurhey 29-36; CF (TA) 32-36; Chester-le-Street and Offg Chap Chester-le-Street Inst and Cottage Homes 36-40; RD of Chester-le-Street 37-40; V of Allerton 40-47; PC of Winster 47-48; V of Ambleside w Rydal 48-51; Grassendale 51-68; Can Dioc of Liv 45-47; and 51-68; Can Res 68-70; Hon Can of Carl 47-51; Archd of Westmorland 47-51; of Liv 51-70; Archd (Emer) from 71; Exam Chap to Bp of Liv 45-47 and 55-70; Dir of Relig Educn Dio Carl 47-51; Commiss U Nile 47-61; Mbale 61-66. *Hammer Cottage, Warborough, Oxon, OX9 8DJ.* (Warborough 8558)

WILKINSON, James Noel Batthews. b 30. TCD BA (2nd cl Mod) 53, Div Test (1st cl) 55, MA and BD 65. **d** 55 Dub for Down **p** 56 Down. C of Dundonald 55-57; Shankill Lurgan 57-62; R of Harrington Cumb 62-66; C of Antrim 66-70; I of Im Ardoyne 70-79; Min Can of St Anne's Cathl Belf from 72; RD of Mid-Belfast 78-79; I of Derryvolgie Dio Connor from 79. *53 Kennedy Drive, Lisburn, Co Antrim, BT27 4JA,*

WILKINSON, Canon John Barry. St John's Coll Auckld LTh 57. **d** 57 **p** 58 Dun. C of Anderson's Bay 57-62; V of Tapanui 62-67; Milton 67-74; Waitaki-N Oamaru 74-80; Chap Dun Hosps and Hon Can of Dun from 80. *12 Scotland Street, Dunedin, NZ.* (773-234)

WILKINSON, John David. b 36. K Coll Lon and Warm AKC 59. **d** 60 **p** 61 Man. C of Woodhouse Pk Conv Distr 60-63; Morley w Churwell 63-65; V of Roberttown 65-75; Battyeford Dio Wakef from 75. *Battyeford Vicarage, Mirfield, W Yorks, WF14 9QT.* (Mirfield 493277)

WILKINSON, Canon John Donald. b 29. Late Exhib of Mert Coll Ox 2nd cl Cl Mods 51, BA (2nd cl Lit Hum) 53, 3rd cl Th 54, MA 56. Gen Th Sem NY Hon STD 73. Cudd Coll 54. **d** 56 **p** 57 Lon. C of St Dunstan and All SS Stepney 56-59; Tutor Ely Th Coll 60; St Geo Coll Jer 61-63; Ed Sec SPG 63-64; USPG 65-69; Dean of Stud St Geo Coll Jer 69-75; Can Res of Bethany in St Geo Colleg Ch Jer 73-75; Can (Emer) from 80; Bp's Dir of Clergy Tr Dio Lon 75-79; P-in-c of H Trin Kens Gore w All SS Ennismore Gardens 75-78; Hon C of St Mary Abbots Kens 78-79; Commiss Jer 78-79; Dir Br Sch of Archaeol Jer from 79. *Box 19283, Jerusalem.* (02-282901)

WILKINSON, John Lawrence. b 43. Ch Coll Cam BA 65, MA 69. Qu Coll Birm Dipl Th 68. Gen Th Sem NY STB 69. **d** 69 **p** 70 Leic. C of Braunstone 69-71; Hodge Hill 71-74; C-in-c of St Jas Aston Dio Birm from 74. *215 Albert Road, Aston, Birmingham, B6 5NA.* (021-327 3451)

WILKINSON, John Stoddart. b 47. St D Coll Lamp Dipl Th 70. **d** 70 **p** 71 Carl. C of St Pet Kells Whitehaven 70-72; St Geo w St Luke Barrow-F 72-73; Perm to Offic Dio Mon from 79. *18 Saint Mary Street, Bedwas, Gwent.*

WILKINSON, Joseph Henry. b 09. K Coll Lon. **d** 44 **p** 45 Glouc. C of Stroud 44-49; Camberley w Yorkstown 49; Chap Kingham Hill Sch 49-77. *Two Ways, Churchill, Oxford, OX7 6ND.* (Kingham 583)

WILKINSON, Keith Howard. b 48. Univ of Hull BA 70. Westcott Ho Cam 74. **d** 76 **p** 77 Pet. C of St Jude Pet 76-79;

Chap Eton Coll from 79. *Eton College, Windsor, Berks, SL4 6DL.*

WILKINSON, Kenneth Samuel. b 31. TCD BA and Div Test (2nd cl) 60. **d** 60 **p** 61 Dub. C of St Paul w St Michan Dub 60-63; Ch Ch Leeson Pk Dub 63-67; Min Can St Patr Cathl Dub 62-67; R of Killegney 67-70; Enniscorthy Dio Ferns from 70. *Rectory, Enniscorthy, Co Wexford, Irish Republic.*

WILKINSON, Lewis. b 14. Ripon Hall Ox 60. **d** 61 Bp McKie for Cov **p** 62 Cov. C of St Nich Warw 61-63; P-in-c of All SS Malabar Hill Bom 63-67; V of Malacca 68-70; V of Kelantan w Tregganu 71-72; Chap Malaysian Th Coll 73-74; C of Lindley 75-78; Almondbury 78-81. *Flat C, Old Vicarage, Seaton, Devon.*

WILKINSON, Maurice Pickard. Univ of Manit BA 41, MA 50. Wycl Coll Tor LTh 48. **d** 48 **p** 51 Rupld. C of St Matt Winnipeg 48-50; Exec Sec Coun for Social Service Dio Tor 50-53; C of St Geo Tor 54-55; R of St Wilfrid Tor 55-61; Gen Sec Dept of Christian Social Service 61-68; Can of Tor 65-75; Assoc Sec Canad Coun of Chs 68-75; R of Parry Sound 75-78. *7 Avenue Road, Parry Sound, Ont., Canada.*

WILKINSON, Michael Alan. b 27. Selw Coll Cam BA (2nd cl Geog Trip pts i & ii) 51. Westcott Ho Cam 52. **d** 53 Bris **p** 54 Malmesbury for Bris. C of Swindon 53-57; St Barn Knowle 57-59; Eltham (in c of St Francis Horn Pk) 59-65; of St Bart Sydenham from 65; Asst Master Lady Marg Sch Parsons Green 69-77; Perm to Offic Dio Ex from 77. *11 Plymbridge Road, Plympton St Mary, Plymouth, Devon.*

WILKINSON, Michael John. b 44. St Mich Coll Llan 73. **d** 75 Lon **p** 76 Willesden for Lon. C of St Andr Roxbourne Harrow 75-78; The Resurr Brighton 78-81; V of Waterhouses Dio Dur from 81. *21 The Wynds Esh Winning, Co Durham, DH7 9DT* (Esh Winning 76273)

WILKINSON, Norman Ellis. b 10. Peterho Cam BA 31 (2nd cl Nat Sc Trip) MA 35. Sarum Th Coll 32. **d** 33 **p** 34 Ox. C of Banbury 33-39; Chap and Asst Master of Cranleigh Sch 39-49; C-in-c of Tresco w Bryher Conv Distr Scilly Is 49-51; Min Can of Worc Cathl and Asst Master K Sch Worc 51-59; V of Broadhempston w Woodland 59-75; Perm to Offic Dio Ex 75-78; Dio Sarum from 78. *Manor Farmhouse, Walditch, Bridport, Dorset.* (Bridport 56025)

WILKINSON, Paul. b 51. Sarum Wells Th Coll 75. **d** 78 **p** 79 Bradf. C of Allerton 78-81; Baildon Dio Bradf from 81. *7 Parkmount Avenue, Baildon, Shipley, Yorks, BD17 6DS.*

WILKINSON, Peter Francis. b 20. Cudd Coll 63. **d** 65 **p** 66 Guildf. C of Chobham w Valley End 65-68; V of Yalding (w Collier Street from 72) Dio Roch from 68. *Yalding Vicarage, Maidstone, Kent.* (Maidstone 814782)

WILKINSON, Peter Frederick Francis. Univ of Tor BA 48, MA 50. Wycl Coll Tor 48. **d** 50 **p** 51 Tor. C of St Paul Bloor Street Tor 50-52; I of St Andr Hamilton 52-56; in Amer Ch 57-60; Lect Cant Coll Windsor 62-63; Univ of Windsor Ont 63-67; Asst Prof from 67; L to Offic Dio BC from 70. *1233 Kildare Road, Windsor, Ont, Canada.*

WILKINSON, Peter Howarth. b 32. St Pet Hall Ox BA (3rd cl Engl Lang and Lit) 54, MA 58. Ridley Hall Cam 56. **d** 58 **p** 59 Ches. C of Cheadle 58-62; V of Nettlebed 62-68; Hon C of Cheadle Dio Ches from 69. *20 Barcheston Road, Cheadle, Chesh.* (061-428 7699)

WILKINSON, Canon Raymond Stewart. b 19. AKC 42. Bps' Coll Cheshunt 42. **d** 43 **p** 44 St Alb. C of All SS Croxley Green 43-46; Min of St Osw Croxley Green Conv Distr 46-50; V of Abbots Langley 50-61; R of Woodchurch 61-71; Surr from 65; Proc Conv 66-71; R of Solihull Dio Birm 71-79; Team R from 79; Hon Can of Birm from 76. *Rectory, Church Hill Road, Solihull, W Midl, B91 3RQ.* (021-705 0069)

WILKINSON, Chan Robert Matthew. b 21. TCD BA 46, Div Test 47. **d** 47 **p** 48 Lim. C of St Laur w St John and H Trin Lim 47-49; St Mark Armagh 49-51; I of Mullavilly 51-55; Derryloran 55-73; Preb of Arm Cathl 67-73; Treas 73-75; Chan from 75; R of Ballymore Dio Arm from 73. *Rectory, Tandragee, Portadown, Co Armagh, N Ireland.* (Tandragee 840234)

WILKINSON, Roger. b 46. Univ of Lon BA 68, AKC 72. St Aug Coll Cant 72. **d** 73 Willesden for Lon **p** 74 Lon. C of L Stanmore 73-76; Asst Chap St Geo's Hosp Lon 76-78; Chap Hounslow Health Distr from 78. *Chaplain's Office, West Middlesex Hospital, Isleworth, Middx, TW7 6AF.* (01-560 2121)

WILKINSON, Roy Geoffrey. b 42. Sarum Th Coll 67. **d** 70 **p** 71 Edmonton for Lon. C of Belsize Pk Hampstead 70-73; Heston 73-75; Hythe 75-79; P-in-c of St Luke Woodside Croydon Dio Cant from 79. *Woodside Vicarage, Portland Road, SE25 4RA.* (01-654 1225)

WILKINSON, Simon Evelyn. b 49. Univ of Nottm BA 74. Cudd Coll 74. **d** 76 **p** 77 S'wark. C of Cheam 76-78; Warlingham (in c of St Chris) Dio S'wark from 78. *St Christopher's Parsonage, Chelsham Road, Warlingham, Surrey.* (Warlingham 4494)

WILKINSON, Thomas. b 1897. Bp Anstey Th Coll Trinid 27. **d** 28 **p** 29 Trinid. C of Cathl Ch Port of Spain Trinid 28-29; P-in-c St Agnes Port of Spain 29-32; C-in-c of All SS and St Andr Worc 32; V of Bishampton 32-64; C-in-c of Abberton w Flyford Flavell 43-62; R of Abberton w Bishampton 62-64; L to Offic Dios Worc and Cov from 64; Glouc from 71. *St Agnes, Coach Drive, Fladbury, Pershore, Worcs.* (Evesham 860656)

WILKINSON, Ven Thomas Arnold. Wycl Coll Tor 41. **d** 41 **p** 42 Tor. I of N Essa 41-44; P-in-c of All SS Kingsway Miss 44-45; All SS Kingsway Parish Dio Tor from 45; Can of St Jas Cathl Tor 62-64; Archd of Etobicoke from 64. *20 Kings Lynn Road, Toronto 18, Ont., Canada.* (416-233 1125)

✠ **WILKINSON, Right Rev Thomas Wilfrid.** Em Coll Sktn DD (*hon causa*) 67. **d** 29 Athab for Sask **p** 30 Sask. C of Hudson Bay Junction 29-30; I of Macklin 30-32; R of Tisdale 32-45; RD of Melfort 37-40; Hon Can of St Alb Cathl Prince Albert 39-50; Chap RCAF 41-45; R of Shellbrook 45-48; Melfort 48-50; R of Dauphin and P-in-c of Fork River 50-57; Hon Can of Bran 53-57; Actg Regr and Sec Dio Bran 57-65; Archd of Dauphin 57-60; Bran 60-65; Exam Chap to Bp of Bran 60-69; Dean and R of St Matt Cathl Bran 65-69; Cons Ld Bp of Bran at Winnipeg 24 June 69 by Abp of Rupld (Primate); Bps of Athab; and Qu'App; res 75. *402-1124 Esquimalt Road, Victoria, BC, Canada.*

WILKINSON, Walter Edward Robert. b 38. St Andr Univ MA (2nd cl Hist) 60. BD (Lon) 63. ALCD (1st cl) 63. **d** 63 **p** 64 Ox. C of High Wycombe (in c of St Pet Micklefield from 67) 63-70; PV, Sacr and Succr of Roch Cathl 70-74; P-in-c of Asby w Ormside 74-80; R of Cherry Burton Dio York from 80. *Rectory, Cherry Burton, Beverley, N Humb.* (Leconfield 50293)

WILKINSON, Wilfred Badger. b 21. K Coll Lon and Warm BD (2nd cl) 50, AKC (1st cl) 50. **d** 50 **p** 51 St Alb. C of Luton 50-53; Gt Berkhamsted 53-57; C-in-c of Wm Temple Conv Distr Woodhouse Pk Man 57-63; Min 63-65; R of Clifton w Glapton (Team R from 71) Dio Southw from 65. *St Mary's Rectory, Village Road, Clifton, Nottingham, NG11 8NE.* (Nottingham 211856)

WILKINSON, Canon Wilfrid Edward. St Paul's Coll Grahmstn. **d** 26 **p** 28 Johann. C of Cathl Ch Johann 26-29; R of Kens Johann 29-34; Witbank 34-44; St Mary Rosettenville 44-45; Parkhurst 55-58; Can of Johann 53-65; Addl Can from 65; R of Belgravia Johann 58-62; L to Offic Dio Johann 62-63 and 67-76; C of Vereeniging 63-67. *105 King's Court, 6 King George Street, Johannesburg, Transvaal, S Africa.* (23-9413)

WILKINSON, William David George. b 1897. Late Scho of Jes Coll Ox 2nd cl Cl Mods 18, BA (3rd cl Lit Hum) 20, MA 23. **d** 20 Swansea for St D **p** 21 St D. C of Pembroke Dock 20-25; Chief Missr Dio Swan B and SS Org in Archd of Brecon 25-33; R of Crickhowell 33-35; V of Landore 35-39; Oystermouth 39-54; Can of Builth in Brecon Cathl 48-54; V of St D Brecon w Llanilltyd 54-56; Archd of Brecon 55-69. *14 Orchard Gardens, Ithon Road, Llandridod Wells, Powys.* (Llandrindod Wells 2360)

WILKS, Alfred Leonard. b 01. Univ of Lon BSc 27. Sarum Th Coll 36. M SSJE 43. **d** 37 **p** 38 Ox. C of Cowley 37-40; L to Offic Dio Ox 44-58; Dio Capetn 58; C of St Cuthb Tsolo 58-60; St Cypr Miss Langa CP 60-64; L to Offic Dio Ox from 65. *228 Iffley Road, Oxford. OX4 1SE.* (Oxford 48116)

WILKS, Basil Worsley. b 18. Ripon Hall Ox 61. **d** 62 **p** 63 Guildf. C of Leatherhead 62-64; Chap Shiplake Coll Henley-on-Thames 64-81; L to Offic Dio Ox 64-66; Perm to Offic Dio Ox from 64. *1 Dobson's Cottages, Fawley, Henley-on-Thames, Oxon.* (Henley 3474)

WILKS, Eric Percival. b 32. Wells Th Coll 67. **d** 68 **p** 69 Worc. C of Fladbury w Throckmorton, Wyre Piddle and Moor 68-69; Perm to Offic Dio Worc from 69. *4 Catherine Cottages, Torton, Hartlebury, Kidderminster.*

WILKS, Ernest Howard. b 26. Oak Hill Th Coll 64. **d** 66 **p** 67 Ox. C of St Paul Slough 66-69; R of Gressenhall w Longham and Bittering Parva 69-77; CMS Area Sec Dios Nor and St E from 77; Perm to Offic Dio St E from 77. *Greenacres, Townhouse Road, Costessy, Norwich, NR8 5BX.* (Norwich 742908)

WILKS, Henry Charles. b 17. Univ of Lon BSc (Econ) 2nd cl 50. **d** 62 Cant. C of Boxley 62-63. *21 Valley Road, Billercay, Essex, CM11 2BS.* (Billericay 3259)

WILKS, Leslie Ronald. b 10. Oak Hill Th Coll 67. **d** 68 **p** 69 Lon. C of St Sav w St Paul Holloway 68-72; R of Easton w Letheringham 72-79; P-in-c of Polstead Dio St E from 79. *St Mary's Church, Polstead, Colchester, Essex.* (Nayland 262235)

WILLANS, William. Univ of Glas 1891. Qu Coll Belf 1893. RUI BA 1899. **d** 02 **p** 03 Ripon. C of Girlington Yorks 02-07; St Jas Carl 07-09; Baildon 09-11; St Geo Leeds 11-14; Centr Org Sec ICM for Dub and Gen L Dio Dub 14-16; I of Templeport 16-20; Carmangay 20-22; R of St John Glencoe Ont 22-25; in Amer Ch 25-29; C-in-c of Lack 29-32; Magheracross 32-50. *Rockmount, Upper Galwally Road, Belfast, N Ireland.*

WILLARD, Canon James Stanley. b 08. St Cath S Ox 3rd cl Mod Hist 30, BA 31, 2nd cl Th 32, MA 34. St Steph H Ox 30. **d** 32 **p** 33 Chelmsf. C of St Marg Leigh-on-Sea 32-41; V of St Cedd Canning Town 41-49; St Marg Leytonstone (w St Columba from 53) 49-61; C-in-c of St Columba Wanstead Slip 51-53; Surr from 50; Chap to Bp of Barking 59-70; Proc Conv Chelmsf 59-65; RD of Leyton 60-61; Barstable 61-69; V of Brentwood 61-71; Hon Can of Chelmsf 65-76; Can (Emer) from 76; Chap to Bp of Chelmsf 71-76; V of Arkesden w Wicken Bonhunt 71-75. *73 Slade Road, Holland-on-Sea, Essex, CO15 5EH.* (Clacton 812635)

WILLARD, John Fordham. b 38. K Coll Lon and Warm BD and AKC 62. **d** 63 **p** 64 S'wark. C of Ascen Balham Hill 63-67; St Francis Leigh Pk 67-73; C-in-c of St Clare Leigh Pk 73-75; R of Bp's Waltham Dio Portsm from 75; P-in-c of Upham Dio Portsm 78-79; R from 79. *Bishop's Waltham Rectory, Southampton, SO3 1EE.* (Bp's Waltham 2618)

WILLARD, William Harvey. b 51. York Univ Tor BSc 74. Nashotah Ho Wisc MDiv 79. **d** and **p** 79 Ont. C of Cathl Ch of St Geo Kingston Ont 79-81; on leave. *23 East Airy Street, Norristown, PA 19401, USA.*

WILLCOCK, Albert. b 13. St D Coll Lamp BA 41. **d** 41 **p** 42 Man. C of St Anne Longsight Royton 41-44; Tonge w Alkrington Middleton 44-47; Melton Mowbray 47-49; V of Waterfoot 49-53; Long Clawson (w Hose from 61) 53-74; R of Stonton Wyville w Glooston and Slawston and Cranoe 74-78; Perm to Offic Dios Leic and Linc from 78. *19 Teesdale Road, Grantham, Lincs, NG31 8ES.* (Grantham 73774)

WILLCOCK, Donald Thomas. b 07. Chich Th Coll 52. **d** 54 **p** 55 Chelmsf. C of Saffron Walden 54-57; V of Gt Totham 57-81. *7 Hawkes Road, Coggeshall, Colchester, Essex, CO6 1QP.*

WILLCOCK, Richard William. b 39. Hertf Coll Ox BA (2nd cl Mod Hist) 62, Liddon Stud 62, 2nd cl Th 64, MA 66. Ripon Hall Ox 62. **d** 64 **p** 65 Man. C of Ashton L 64-68; Dom Chap to Bp of Man and L to Offic 68-72; V of St Geo (w St Barn from 73) Charlestown Salford 72-75; Chap of Casterton Sch Kirkby Lonsdale 75-80; V of Bamford Dio Man from 80. *St Michael's Vicarage, Bury and Rochdale Old Road, Heywood, OL10 4AT.* (Heywood 69610)

WILLCOX, Frederick John. b 29. Kelham Th Coll 49. **d** 54 Stockport for Ches **p** 55 Ches. C of St Paul Tranmere 54-56; Publ Pr Dio Southw 57-61; Miss P of St Patr Miss Bloemf 62-65; Dir 65-70; C-in-c of St Andr w St Osmund Derby 70-73; V 73-80; St Andr Netherton, Dudley Dio Worc from 80. *Netherton Vicarage, Highbridge Road, Dudley W Midl, DY2 0HT.* (Dudley 53118)

WILLCOX, Richard John Michael. b 39. Univ of Birm BSc 62, PhD 67. Qu Coll Birm 78. **d** 80 **p** 81 Birm. C of Boldmere Dio Birm from 80. *46 Redacre Road, Boldmere, Sutton Coldfield, Birmingham, B73 5EA.*

WILLCOX, Sydney Harold. b 36. St D Coll Lamp BA 58. St Mich Coll Llan. **d** 60 **p** 61 Ban. C of Pwllheli 60-62; Llandegfan w Beaumaris 62-65; R of Llanenddwyn w Llanddwywe 65-70; Dolgellau w Llanfachraeth and Brithdir w Bryncoedifor 70-76; R of Ridgeway Dio Sarum from 76; RD of Marlborough from 81. *Chiseldon Vicarage, Swindon, Wilts.* (Swindon 740369)

WILLESDEN, Lord Bishop Suffragan of. *See* Thompson, Right Rev Geoffrey Hewlett.

WILLETT, Allen Gardiner. b 20. Univ of Bris BA (Th) 51. Univ of Lon BD 54. Clifton Th Coll 47. **d** 54 **p** 55 Man. C of Rawtenstall 54-57; Tutor St Paul's Coll Awka 57-58; Clifton Th Coll 58-60; C of Wallington 60-62; Tutor All Nations Miss Coll Taplow 62-63; V of St Luke w St Silas Bedminster 63-68; Galleywood Dio Chelmsf from 68. *Galleywood Vicarage, Beehive Lane, Chelmsford, Essex, CM2 8RN.* (Chelmsford 353922)

WILLETT, Frank Edwin. b 45. Dipl Th (Lon) 68. Kelham Th Coll 64. **d** 68 **p** 69 Shrewsbury for Lich. C of H Trin Oswestry 68-71; Bilston 71-75; P-in-c of Mufulira 75-78; Chingola 78-80; V of Stoney Middleton and Curbar Dio Derby from 80. *Curbar Vicarage, Sheffield, S30 1YF.* (0433 30387)

WILLETT, Geoffrey Thomas. b 38. Univ of Dur BA (2nd cl Mod Hist) 59, Dipl Th 61. Cranmer Hall Dur 59. **d** 62 Warrington for Liv **p** 63 Liv. C of St Paul Widnes 62-65; St Jo Bapt Harborne 65-68; V of St Andr w St Mary Wakef 68-75; H Trin Hinckley Dio Leic from 75. *Holy Trinity Vicarage, Hinckley, Leics, LE10 0AJ.* (Hinckley 635711)

WILLETT, John Ivon. b 40. Ch Ch Ox BA and Ellerton Pri 63, MA 65. Chich Th Coll 61. **d** 63 **p** 64 Leic. C of St Andr Leic 63-66; St Alb Mart Bordesley 66-72; Prec of Pet Cathl from 72. *Precentor's Lodging, Minster Precincts, Peterborough, PE1 1XX.* (Peterborough 43389)

WILLETT, Joseph Alfred. K Coll NS BA 35. **d** 37 **p** 38 NS. C of Ship Harbour 37-42; Melford 42-43; I of Eastern Passage 43-50; C of Ch Ch Dartmouth 50-52; R of Granville 52-53; Londonderry 53-54; Chap to K Coll Sch Windsor 54-72; R of Ship Harbour Dio NS from 72. *RR1, Lake Charlotte, NS, Canada.* (9 R 21)

WILLETT, Walter Robert Garfield. b 15. St Aid Coll 46. **d** 48 **p** 49 Sheff. C of Ecclesfield 48-50; CMS Miss Nigeria 50-60; Dioc Youth Org for Dios Niger, Nig Delta and Ow 52-60; V of Walton Breck 60-80. *286 Crookesmoor Road, Sheffield, S10 1BE.* (0742 669193)

WILLETTS, Alfred. b 15. **d** 62 **p** 63 Llan. C of Canton 62-65; V of Avan Vale 65-67; R of St Phil w St Mark Man 67-75; St Andr (Ch of The Apostles from 76) City and Dio Man from 75. *Rectory, Ridgway Street, Manchester, M10 7FY.* (061-205 1742)

WILLEY, Stanley Robson. **d** 55 **p** 56 C & Goulb. C of Canberra 55-56; I of Lake Bath 56-58; R of Crookwell 58-66; Tumut 66-75; Field Officer ABM in NSW 75-78; State Sec from 78; Perm to Offic Dio Syd from 75. *95 Bathurst Street, Sydney, NSW, Australia 2000.* (264-1021)

WILLFORD, Frank. b 17. St D Coll Lamp BA 39. Westcott Ho Cam 39. **d** 43 Tewkesbury for Glouc **p** 44 Glouc. C of Cirencester 43-46; St Lawr Ch Stretton 46-50; R of Burford 2nd portion w Whitton Greete and Hope Bagot 50-55; V of Taumarunui 56-59; R of Eardisley w Bollingham (w Willersley from 64) 59-81; RD of Weobley 70-72; C-in-c of Whitney w Winforton 70-81. *The Flat, Garnons, Byford, Nr Hereford.*

WILLIAMS, Albert. b 04. St Jo Coll Dur BA 30. **d** 30 Liv **p** 31 Warrington for Liv. C of St Leon Bootle 30-32; Farnworth 32-38; V of St Mark Preston 38-51; Surr from 40; V of Bamber Bridge 51-73. *Swiss Cottage, Nell Lane, Wigan Road, Leyland, PR5 2TB.* (Leyland 32584)

WILLIAMS, Albert Charles. Hur Coll. **d** 50 Hur for Moos **p** 51 Moos. Miss at Rupert's House 50-52; I of Foleyet 52-54; I of Combermere 56-59; R of Old Harbour Ja 59-60; Hearst 60-67. *Box 767, Walkerton, Ont, Canada.*

WILLIAMS, Canon Albert James. St Jo Coll Manit BD 10. **d** 11 Rupld **p** 12 Honan. C of St Matt Winnipeg 11-12; M SCC Miss at Kweiteh 12-28; Prin Dioc Middle Sch Kweiteh 19-28; V of Princeton 28-30; St Anne Steveston w Alb Bridghouse Lulu I 30-42; St Mary Virg S Hill S Vancouver Dio New Westmr from 42; Can of New Westmr from 53. *208 Robertson Street, Victoria, BC, Canada.*

WILLIAMS, Aled Jones. b 56. Univ Coll of N Wales (Bangor) BA 77. Univ Coll Cardiff Dipl Th 79. St Mich Coll Llan 77. **d** 79 **p** 80 Ban. C of Conway w Gyffin Dio Ban from 79. *27 Bangor Road, Conway, Gwynedd.* (Conway 6658)

WILLIAMS, Aled Wyn. b 47. Univ of Wales (Abth) BA 69, Powis Exhib. St Mich Coll Llan 69. **d** 71 **p** 72 St D. C of Llanelli 71-73; C-in-c of Capel Colman w Llanfihangel-Penbedw and Clydau w Penrhydd and Castellan Dio St D 73-74; V from 74; R of Whitechurch w Llanfair Nant-Gwyn Dio St D from 77. *Capel Colman Vicarage, Boncath, Dyfed.* (Boncath 458)

WILLIAMS, Alexander Ernest. b 14. Fitzw Ho Cam BA 35, MA 46. Ho of the Resurr Mirfield 79. **d** 79 **p** 80 S'wark. Hon C of Good Shepherd Carshalton Dio S'wark from 79. *88 Grosvenor Avenue, Carshalton, Surrey.*

WILLIAMS, Alfred Donald. b 26. St Aid Coll 57. **d** 59 **p** 60 Southw. C of Ordsall 59-62; V of St Mary Ladybrook Mansfield 62-70; C-in-c of Ch Ch Newark-on-Trent 70-71; R of Gotham Dio Southw from 71; C-in-c of W Leake w Ratcliffe-on-Soar and Kingston-on-Soar 72-81. *Gotham Rectory, Nottingham.* (Nottm 830608)

WILLIAMS, Alfred George. b 21. St D Coll Lamp BA (2nd cl Th) 42. **d** 46 **p** 47 St A. C of Ruabon 46-49; Lache-cum-Saltney 49-52; V of Millbrook Chesh 52-54; Aston-by-Sutton 54-64; Rock Ferry 64-77; Lache-cum-Saltney Ferry Dio Ches from 77. *5 Cliveden Road, Chester, CH4 8DR.* (0244-671702)

WILLIAMS, Allen Philpin. b 10. St D Coll Lamp BA 32. St Mich Coll Llan. **d** 34 **p** 35 St D. C of Llandyssul 34-37; Ch Ch Llanelly 37-40; C-in-c of Talley 40-48; V of Llanfairar-y-Bryn 48-58; Manordeilo (w Taliaris from 70) 58-78. *Manordeilo Vicarage, Llandeilo, Dyfed.* (Llandeilo 2296)

WILLIAMS, Andrew Gibson. b 31. Univ of Edin MA 57. Edin Th Coll 56. **d** 59 **p** 60 Wakef. C of Todmorden 59-61; Clitheroe 61-63; V of St Jas Burnley 63-65; CF (TA) 64-65; CF 65-71; R of Winterslow Dio Sarum from 71. *Rectory, Winterslow, Salisbury, Wilts.* (Winterslow 862231)

WILLIAMS, Andrew Joseph. b 55. Univ of Nottm BTh 81. St Jo Coll Nottm 77. **d** 81 Chich. C of Hollington Dio Chich from 81. *158 Old Church Road, St Leonards-on-Sea, E Sussex, TN38 9HD.*

WILLIAMS, Anthony Bensley. St Barn Coll Adel 46. ACT ThL 50. **d** and **p** 50 Adel. C of St Pet Glenelg 50-51; Miss Chap at Kilburn w Prospect N 51-54; C-in-c of Balaklava 54-57; R of Minlaton 57-63; Willunga 63-68; P-in-c of Edwardstown w Ascot Pk 68-70; R 70-75; Chap Rept Hosp Daw Pk Dio Adel from 75. *1 Lynton Avenue, Millswood, S Australia 5034.* (08-272 2037)

WILLIAMS, Anthony Francis. b 21. Trin Coll Ox BA 49, MA 53. Coll of Resurr Mirfield 49. **d** 51 **p** 52 Ex. C of Paignton 51-54; H Trin Cov 54-60; V of All SS Cov 60-67; Lindridge 67-77; Surr 65-67; P-in-c of Bluntisham w Earith Dio Ely from 77; R from 79. *Rectory, Bluntisham, Huntingdon, Cambs, PE17 3LN.* (Ramsey 841473)

WILLIAMS, Anthony Riley. b 36. Univ of Wales BA 60. Chich Th Coll 57. **d** 59 **p** 60 Ban. C of Llandinorwic 59-61; Llandegfan w Beaumaris 61-64; R of Ludchurch w Templeton 64-72; V of Lamphey w Hodgeston Dio St D from 72; RD of Castle Martin from 75. *Lamphey Vicarage, Pembroke, Dyfed.*

WILLIAMS, Arthur Edward. Moore Th Coll Syd ACT ThL 53. **d** and **p** 54 Syd. C of St Phil Syd 54-55; P-in-c of Minnipa Miss 56-60; Mt Magnet 60-62; NSW Sec Bush Ch Aid 63-64; Asst Federal Sec 64-66; R of Cammeray 66-74; W Ryde Dio Syd from 74. *14 Bellevue Avenue, West Ryde, NSW, Australia 2114.* (85-1926)

WILLIAMS, Arthur Edwin. b 33. Univ of Leeds BA 57. Coll of Resurr Mirfield. **d** 59 **p** 60 Lich. C of Wednesfield 59-62; Codsall 62-65; V of St Chad Coseley 65-73; R of Kingswinford 73-81; RD of Himley from 77; Team R of Wordsley Dio Lich from 81. *Rectory, Dunsley Drive, Wordsley, Stourbridge, Worcs.* (Kingswinford 3101)

WILLIAMS, Arthur James Daniel. Bro O of St John from 81. b 24. St D Coll Lamp BA 49. St Mich Coll Llan 49. **d** 51 **p** 52 Llan. C of Pontlottyn 51-54; Caerphilly 54-60; Dioc Youth Sec 56-62; Youth Chap 62-67; V of Gilfach Goch 60-66; Llantwit Fardre Dio Llan from 66; Surr from 72; Bro O of St John from 81. *Llantwit Fardre Vicarage, Church Village, Pontypridd, Mid-Glam, CF38 1EP.* (Newtown Llantwit 2538)

WILLIAMS, Arthur Vernon. b 14. Univ of Wales BA (2nd cl Hist) 36. Lich Th Coll 36. **d** 38 **p** 39 St A. C of Mostyn 38-41; Holywell Flint 41-45; Wrexham 45-53; V of St Geo Everton 53-58; St Pet Warrington 58-62; St Timothy Crookes Sheff 62-75; R of Thurnscoe Dio Sheff from 75. *Thurnscoe Rectory, Rotherham, S Yorks, S63 0SU.* (Rotherham 893186)

WILLIAMS, Austen. *See* Williams, Sidney Austen.

WILLIAMS, Barrie. b 33. Em Coll Cam 2nd cl Hist Trip pt i 53, BA (1st cl Hist Trip pt ii) 54, MA 58. Univ of Bris MLitt 71. STh (Lambeth) 75. Ripon Hall Ox 62. **d** 63 **p** 64 Blackb. C of Penwortham 63-65; St Martin Sarum 65-77; Chap St Edw K and Mart Cam Dio Ely from 77; Asst Chap Trin Hall Cam from 77. *Trinity Hall, Cambridge, CB2 1TJ.*

WILLIAMS, Canon Basil Hosking. Univ of NZ BA and LTh 37. **d** 37 **p** 38 Ch Ch. C of Rangiora 37-40; Sumner 41; L to Offic Dio Syd 42-54; Gen Sec CSSM in NSW 47-54; R of Five Dock 54-60; Wollongong 60-76; Exam Chap to Abp of Syd 59-70; Hon Can of Syd 63-66 and from 77; Can 66-77; Can of St Mich Provisional Cathl Wollongong 69-76; L to Offic Dio Syd from 76. *2 Belvidere Avenue, Blackheath, NSW, Australia 2785.* (047-87 8095)

WILLIAMS, Benjamin Clive. BD (Lon) 59. Westcott Ho Cam 59. **d** 61 **p** 62 Man. C of St Mark Bury 61-63; Christchurch (in c of St Mary Somerford) 63-66; R of Denton w S Heighton and Tarring Neville 66-74; C-in-c of Clapham w Patching 74-81; V of Ticehurst and Flimwell Dio Chich from 81. *Ticehurst Vicarage, Wadhurst, E Sussex, TN5 7AB.* (Ticehurst 200316)

WILLIAMS, Benjamin Frederick. b 31. St Paul's Coll Grahmstn 78. **d** 78 **p** 79 Capetn. P-in-c of Ravensmead Dio Capetn from 78. *14 Bestenbier Avenue, Elsies River, CP, S Africa 7460.*

WILLIAMS, Bernard Rhys. b 08. Selw Coll Cam BA 30, MA 34. Wycl Hall Ox 30. **d** 32 **p** 33 Cant. C of Willesborough 32-35; Yalding 35-38; Chap (Ind) (Eccles Est) Barielly 38-40; Hon CF 46; V of Ospringe 44-55; Goudhurst 55-68; V of Credenhill w Brinsop, Mansel Lacy, Yazor and Wormesley 68-73. *Goudhurst, Worton, Devizes, Wilts.*

WILLIAMS, Brian Luke. b 54. AKC 75. St Steph Ho Ox 76. **d** 77 **p** 78 Pet. C of St Mary Virg Kettering 77-80; St Gabr Fulbrook Walsall Dio Lich from 80. *51 Maple Drive, Yew Tree Estate Walsall, Staffs.* (Walsall 612340)

WILLIAMS, Brian Washington. Univ of Witwatersrand BA 45. St Paul's Coll Grahmstn. **d** 47 **p** 48 Johann. C of St Mary Rosettenville 47-50; R of Zeerust 50-54; Vanderbijl Pk 54-59; Roodepoort 59-63; Boksburg 63-73; Parkview Dio Johann from 73. *44 Tyrone Avenue, Parkview, Johannesburg, Transvaal, S Africa.* (011-41 2660)

WILLIAMS, Canon Brinley John. MBE 68. Univ of Wales 25. **d** 35 **p** 36 Wel. Chap Miss to Seamen Wel NZ 35-49; Port Adel 49-55; Halifax 73-75; Hon Can of NS from 59. *6344 Jubilee Road, Halifax, NS, Canada.* (429-1838)

WILLIAMS, Cecil Augustus Baldwin. b 09. TCD BA (Resp) 31, Bp Forster (2nd) Toplady Mem and Bibl Gr Pri (2nd cl) 31, (1st) 32, William Brooke Exhib 31, Div Test (1st cl) 32, MA 39. **d** 32 **p** 33 Down. C of St Mary Magd Belf 32-36; BCMS Kapoeta Sudan 36-39; I of Schull 40-49; Sec Ch of Ireland Jews' S 49-54; I of St Luke Dub 54-71; Part-time Sec BCMS 56-63; I of Crinken Bray 71-81. *3 St John's Close, Coleraine Road, Portstewart, Co Derry, N Ireland.*

WILLIAMS, Cecil Peter. b 41. TCD BA 63, MA 67. BD (Lon) 67. Univ of Bris MLitt 77. Clifton Th Coll 64. **d** 67 Warrington for Liv **p** 68 Liv. C of Maghull 67-70; Tutor Clifton Th Coll Bris 70-72; L to Offic Dio Bris from 70; Tutor and Libr Trin Coll Bris from 72. *26 Stoke Hill, Stoke Bishop, Bristol, BS9 1JW.* (Bristol 684493)

WILLIAMS, Canon Charles. b 1889. St Edm Hall Ox 2nd cl Math Mods 15, BA 17, 2nd cl Th 21, MA 20. **d** 20 **p** 21 Carl. C of St Jas Barrow-F 20-23; Dalton-F 23-26; V of St Mary Walney I 26-48; Beetham 48-61; Chap to HM Pris Bela River 52-61; RD of Kirkby Lonsdale 57-61; Hon Can of Carl 57-61; Can (Emer) from 61; L to Offic Dio Carl 61-68. *Calle Brasil 7, Ciudad Jardin, Las Palmas, Canary Islands.*

WILLIAMS, Charles Henry. b 11. Dorch Miss Coll 38. **d** 40 **p** 41 Newc T. C of H Trin Berwick-on-Tweed 40-44; UMCA Miss P Fiwila 44-45; Msoro 45-47; CF 47-50; C of Alnwick 50-52; V of Gosforth N 52-60; Hunslet w Stourton 60-69; Kirk Hammerton 69-74; V of Nun Monkton 69-74. *63 Wedderburn Avenue, Harrogate, N Yorks.* (Harrogate 883900)

WILLIAMS, Christopher Glynn. b 35. Univ of Capetn BSc 56. Wycl Coll Tor 77. **d** and **p** 80 Capetn. C of St Thos Rondebosch Dio Capetn from 80. *61 Campground Road, Rondebosch, CP, S Africa 7700.*

WILLIAMS, Clifford Phillips. b 11. St Jo Coll Ox BA 34, MA 38. St Mich Coll Llan 34. **d** 35 **p** 36 St A. C of Shotton 35-48; CF (EC) 40-46; V of Rossett 48-73; R of Worthenbury w Tallarn Green 73-77. *Jassamine Cottage, Threapwood, Malpas, Chesh.*

WILLIAMS, Canon Clifford Rex. b 06. **d** 43 **p** 44 Trinid. C of St Jos Trinid 43-45; Prov Sec to Abp of W Indies 43-45; C of St Mich AA Stonebridge Pk 45-46; St Gluvias w Penryn 46-48; V of St Giles-in-the-Heath w Virginstow 48-59; St Luke Camberwell 59-66; Herne Hill 66-78; Dioc Insp of Schs Dio S'wark from 62; Hon Can of S'wark Cathl 77-78; Can (Emer) from 78; Perm to Offic Dio Chich from 78. *13 Marine Parade, Seaford, Sussex, BN25 2PL.* (Seaford 895699)

WILLIAMS, Clifford Smith. b 48. Univ of N Wales (Bangor) BD 79. St Deiniol's Libr Hawarden 78. **d** 80 **p** 81 Ban. C of Caernarvon Dio Ban from 80. *30 Dinorwic Street, Caernarvon, Gwyn.*

WILLIAMS, Colin Henry. b 52. Pemb Coll Ox BA 73, MA 78. St Steph Ho Ox BA (Th) 80. **d** 81 Warrington for Liv. C of St Paul Stoneycroft City and Dio Liv from 81. *c/o St Paul's Vicarage, Carlton Lane, Liverpool, L13 6QS.*

WILLIAMS, Creswell. b 13. Univ of Wales BA 36. St D Coll Lamp 36. **d** 38 Llan **p** 39 Swan B for Llan. C of Ystradyfodwg 38-42; CF (EC) 42-46; Abercynon 46-49; CF 49-67; V of Eglwysfach w Llangynfelyn 67-78; L to Offic Dio Ban from 78. *4 Londonderry Terrace, Machynlleth, Powys.* (Machynlleth 2349)

WILLIAMS, Cyril. b 06. Univ of Wales BA 34. St Mich Coll Llan 34. **d** 35 **p** 36 St A. C of Mostyn 35-38; Llangollen 38-46; V of Llandrillo-yn-Edeyrnion 46-51; Tremeirchion 51-61; R of Denbigh 61-77; Surr from 64. *Bryniog, Nant-y-Patrick, St Asaph, Clwyd.*

WILLIAMS, Cyril Bertram. b 12. Keble Coll Ox 3rd cl Cl Mods 33, BA (2nd cl Th) 35, MA 47. Bps' Coll Cheshunt 35. **d** 36 **p** 37 Win. C of H Sav Bitterne 36-47; R of Weyhill w Penton Mewsey 47-65; V of Lapley w Wheaton Aston 65-74; Horton Leek Dio Lich from 74; C-in-c of Rushton Spencer Dio Lich from 74. *Horton Vicarage, Leek, Staffs, ST13 8PH.* (Rudyard 245)

WILLIAMS, Cyril Edward. b 23. TD 64. ACP 68. St Deiniol's Libr Hawarden 74. **d** 77 **p** 77 St A (APM). C of Brymbo w Bwlchgwyn Dio St A from 77. *Tegfan, Fronheulog Hill, Bwlchgwyn, Wrexham, Clwyd.*

WILLIAMS, David. b 1886. St D Coll Lamp LDiv 13. St Mich Th Coll Llan 14. **d** 15 **p** 16 Llan. C of St John Penydarren 15-17; Llanelly 17-19; Cwmbach 20-25; Actg Chap Co Mental Hosp Winwick 25-28; C of Cockfield 28-30; Drayton (in c of Hellesdon) 30-34; V of Glascombe w Rhulen 34-44; Llanbister (w Llanbadarn-Fynydd and Llanano from 55) 44-58. *Afan Cottage, Llangammarch Wells, Powys.* (Llangammarch 276)

WILLIAMS, David. b 11. Univ of Wales BA 57. St Mich Coll Llan 51. **d** 53 **p** 54 St D. C of Abernant w Conwyl Elfed 53-59; V of Trelechar-Bettws w Abernant 59-64; Pencarreg 64-70; Llandygwydd (w Cenarth and Cilrhedyn from 71) 70-77. *Bargates, Ynyslas, Borth, Dyfed.*

WILLIAMS, David. **d** 66 **p** 67 Glouc. C of Parkend Dio Glouc from 66. *Nook, Parkend Road, Bream, Glos.*

WILLIAMS, David. b 43. ACA 65. AKC and BD 69. St Aug Coll Cant 69. **d** 70 **p** 71 Hulme for York. C of Walkden 70-72; Deane 72-75; V of St Cath Horwich 75-81. *c/o St Catherine's Vicarage, Horwich, Bolton, BL6 5QT.* (Horwich 67162)

WILLIAMS, David Albert. b 15. St D Coll Lamp BA (2nd cl Hist) 35. St Mich Coll Llan 36. **d** 38 Ban **p** 39 Bp Wentworth-Sheilds for Ban. C of Glanadda w Penrhosgarnedd 38-40; Llanbadarn Fawr 40-49; Chap RAF 49-58; Asst Master King's Rise Boys' Sch Birm and Perm to Offic Dio Birm 58-59; Ho Master Bourne Sch Kuala Lumpur and Perm to Offic Dio Sing 59-61; Asst Master City of Cov Boarding Sch Cleobury Mortimer from 61; Perm to Offic Dio Heref 61-69; L to Offic 69-80; Perm to Offic Dio St D from 81. *c/o Barclays Bank Ltd, Llandovery, Dyfed, SA20 0AH.*

WILLIAMS, David Denoon. b 37. K Coll Lon and Warm AKC 62. **d** 63 **p** 64 Chelmsf. C of Brentwood 63-69; C-in-c of St John Bury St Edms Dio St E 69-70; V from 70. *37 Well Street, Bury St Edmunds, Suff.* (Bury St Edmunds 4335)

WILLIAMS, David Francis. b 1899. Univ of Wales BA 23. St Mich Coll Llan 32. **d** 34 **p** 35 St D. C of Llanwnda w Manorowen 34-36; Monkton 36-40; R of Rudbaxton 40-68; RD of Dungleddy 55-68. *Treforfan, Penslade, Fishguard, Dyfed.*

WILLIAMS, David Gerald Powell. b 35. Dipl Th (Wales) 62. St Mich Coll Llan 59. **d** 62 **p** 63 Llan. C of Canton 62-65; Field Tr Officer Prov Youth Coun 63-65; Prov Youth Chap and Perm to Offic Dio Llan 65-70; V of Treharris 70-75; R of Flemingston and Gileston w St Hilary 75-78; Warden of Ordins Dio Llan 77-80; Dir of Pastoral Stud and Chap St Mich Coll Llan 78-80; Sub Warden 79-80; Prov Dir of Relig Educn and Dir Ch in Wales Publications from 80. *68 Westbourne Road, Penarth, S Glam, CF6 2EX.* (Penarth 708234)

WILLIAMS, David Gordon. b 43. Selw Coll Cam BA 65, MA 69. Oak Hill Th Coll 66. **d** 68 **p** 69 Cant. C of St Luke Maidstone 68-71; St Matt Rugby 71-73; P-in-c of Budbrooke w Hampton-on-the-Hill 73-74; V 74-81; Lenton Dio Southw from 81. *Holy Trnity Vicarage, Church Street, Lenton, Nottingham, NG7 2FF.* (Nottm 787469)

WILLIAMS, David Grange Townley. Univ of S Afr BSc 47. **d** 65 Bp Snell for Tor **p** 66 Tor. C of St Hilda Fairbank Tor 65-67; I of Cannington 67-80; St Giles Barrie Dio Tor from 80. *95 Cook Street, Barrie, Ont., Canada.*

WILLIAMS, David Griffith. St D Coll Lamp BA 57. St Mich Coll Llan 57. **d** 59 **p** 60. C of Kidwelly 59-63; Haverfordwest 63-64; V of Rhosmarket (or Rosemarket) w Freystrop 64-73; R of Begelly Dio St D from 73. *Begelly Rectory, Kilgetty, Dyfed.* (Saundersfoot 2348)

WILLIAMS, David Gwynfor. b 20. Univ of Wales BA 66. St Mich Coll Llan 66. **d** 67 **p** 68 Ban. C of Portmadoc 67-70; Llanbeblig w Caernarvon 70-71; R of Llanrug Dio Ban from 71. *Llanrug Rectory, Caernarvon, LL55 4AL.* (Caernarvon 3470)

WILLIAMS, David Henry. b 33. Trin Coll Cam BA 56, MA 60, PhD 77. St D Coll Lamp. **d** 69 **p** 70 Mon. C of Monmouth 69-70; Chap St Woolos Cathl and Royal Gwent Hosp 70-71; P-in-c of Six Bells 71-76; Crumlin 79-80; Chap at Tripoli and Benghazi 76-79; R of Llanddewi Skirrid and Llanvetherine and Llangattock Lingoed and Llanfair Cilgoed Dio Mon from 80. *Llanddewi Skirrid Rectory, Abergavenny, Gwent, NP7 8AG.* (Abergav 6928)

WILLIAMS, Canon David Humphrey. b 23. Em Coll Cam BA (2nd cl Th Trip pt ii) 49, MA 54. St Steph Ho Ox 49. **d** 51 **p** 52 Southw. C of Daybrook 51-55; C-in-c of St Jo Bapt Conv Distr Bilborough 55-62; V 62-63; Hucknall Torkard (R from 71) Dio Southw from 63; Surr from 65; RD of Bulwell Dio Southw from 70; C-in-c of Bestwood Park 71-78; Hon Can of Southw Cathl from 75. *Rectory, Hucknall, Nottingham.* (Nottm 632033)

WILLIAMS, David James. b 42. Chich Th Coll 67. **d** 70 **p** 71 Cant. C of St Bart Dover 70-74; Dorking 74-77; H Trin w St Mary Guildf 77-78; P-in-c of St Paul E Molesey Dio Guildf from 78. *St Paul's Vicarage, East Molesey, Surrey, KT8 9DU.* (01-979 1580)

WILLIAMS, David John. b 43. Wadh Coll Ox BA 64. St Jo Coll Nottm 73. **d** 75 **p** 76 Lich. C of St Giles Newc L 75-78; P-in-c of Oulton Dio Lich from 79. *Oulton Vicarage, Stone, Staffs, ST15 8UB.* (Stone 3307)

WILLIAMS, David John. Univ of Melb BA 58, MA 64, PhD 68. Ridley Coll Melb ACT ThL 59. **d** 60 **p** 61 Melb. C of N Carlton 60-63; V 64-65; Tutor Ridley Coll Melb 60-65; Registrar and Tutor 65-73; Sen Tutor from 73; Perm to Offic 65-69; C of Richmond 70-73; P-in-c of N Carlton Dio Melb from 74. *170 The Avenue, Parkville, Vic, Australia 3052.* (03-387 2675)

WILLIAMS, David John. b 38. K Coll Lon and Warm AKC 62. **d** 63 **p** 64 Man. C of St Luke Benchill 63-66; St Jas Heywood 66-69; V of Leesfield 69-73; Chap Tr Ship Arethusa 73-74; Team V of Southend-on-Sea 74-80; V of Horndon-on-the-Hill Dio Chelmsf from 80. *Vicarage, Orsett Road, Horndon-on-the-Hill, Stanford-le-Hope, Essex, SS17 8NS.* (S-le-Hope 3806)

WILLIAMS, David John. b 30. Open Univ BA 79. St D Coll Lamp 64. **d** 66 St A **p** 67 Swan B for St A. C of Mold 66-69; Llanrhos 69-71; R of Llanbedr Dyffryn Clwyd w Llangynhafal Dio St A from 71; P-in-c of Llanychan Dio St A from 77. *Rectory, Llanbedr DC, Ruthin, Clwyd.* (Ruthin 2966)

WILLIAMS, David John Mihangel. b 17. OBE 74. St D Coll Lamp BA 41. **d** 44 **p** 45 Ban. C of Llangelynin 44-47; P-in-c of St Cynon Fairbourne 47-53; R of Llansadwrn (w Llanddona and Llaniestyn from 55) Dio Ban from 53; RD of Tindaethwy from 78. *Llansadwrn Rectory, Menai Bridge, Anglesey, Gwyn.* (Menai Bridge 712237)

WILLIAMS, David Kenneth. St Jo Coll Morpeth ACT ThL 49. **d** 55 **p** 56 N Queensld. C of Mt Isa 55-59; Ch Ch St Laur Syd 59-65; R of N Balmain Dio Syd from 65; Commiss Korea from 67. *New Rectory, Park Lane, Blunham, Bedford.* (Biggleswade 40298)

WILLIAMS, David Kenneth. b 21. SOC 75. **d** 78 **p** 79 St Alb. C of St Mary Rickmansworth 78-81; R of Blunham w Tempsford and L Barford Dio St Alb from 81. *Blunham Rectory, Bedford.* (Biggleswade 40298)

WILLIAMS, David Leslie. b 35. ALCD 63. **d** 63 Roch **p** 64 Ox. C of Ch Ch Bexleyheath 63-64; Faringdon 64-66; Shortlands 73-74; Dir Ch of Ugan Lit and Radio Centre 67-73; Publisher Pacific Conf of Chs Educn Programme Fiji 74-76; V of H Trin Bromley Common Dio Roch from 77. *Vicarage, Church Lane, Bromley, Kent, BR2 8LB.* (01-462 1280)

WILLIAMS, David Michael Rochfort. b 40. Dipl Th (Wales) 65. St Mich Coll Llan 62. **d** 65 Swan B for St D **p** 66 St D. C of Pembroke Dk 65-68; C-in-c of Walwyn's Castle w Robeston W 68-70; R 70-71; Industr Chap Dio Mon 71-74; V of Blaenavon w Capel Newydd 74-77; Industr Chap Dio St A from 77; L to Offic Dio St A 77-81; V of Whitford Dio St A from 81. *Whitford Vicarage, Holywell, Clwyd, CH8 9AJ.* (Mostyn 489)

WILLIAMS, David Roger. b 49. St D Coll Lamp Dipl Th 73. Bp Burgess Hall Lamp 70. **d** 73 **p** 74 Swan B. C of Llansamlet 73-76; Oystermouth 76-79; R of Aberedw w Llandilo-Graban and Llanbaddarn-y-Garreg 79-81; Crickadarn w Gwenddwr and Alltmawr 79-81; V of Brynmawr Dio Swan B from 81. *Vicarage, Dumfries Place, Brynmawr, Gwent.* (Brynmawr 310405)

WILLIAMS, David Terence. b 32. St D Coll Lamp BA 57. St Steph Ho Ox 57. **d** 59 **p** 60 Swan B. C of All SS Oystermouth 59-61; Hon C of St Silas Pentonville Islington Dio Lon from 73. *12 Legion Close, Offord Road, Islington, N1.*

WILLIAMS, Denis Ivor. Univ of Capetn BA 50. Nashotah Ho USA BD 64. **d** 64 **p** 65 Capetn. C of Simonstown 64-66; Namaqualand 66-68; L to Offic Dio Johann 68-70. *P O Box 10319, Johannesburg, CP, S Africa.*

WILLIAMS, Derek. b 27. Univ of Man BSc 49. St Deiniol's Libr Hawarden 76. **d** 78 **p** 79 St A (APM). C of Abergele Dio St A from 78. *48 Eldon Drive, Abergele, Clwyd, LL22 7DA.*

WILLIAMS, Derek Howard. Univ of Leeds BSc 49. Coll of Resurr Mirfield 49. M CR 57. **d** 51 **p** 52 Brech. C of St Salvador Dundee 51-54; L to Offic Dio Wakef 56; C of Sekhukhuniland Miss Distr 57-60; St Aug Miss Penhalonga Dio Mashon (Dio Mutare from 81) from 62. *St Augustine's, Penhalonga, Zimbabwe.*

WILLIAMS, Derek Lawrence. b 45. Dipl Th (Lon) 68. Tyndale Hall Bris 65. **d** 69 **p** 70 Cant. C of St Mary Bredin Cant 69-71; Gen Sec Inter-Coll Chr Fellowship 71-76; Perm to Offic Dio St Alb from 73; Dio Ox from 75. *38 Brookside Walk, Leighton Buzzard, Beds.*

WILLIAMS, Canon Desmond John Francis. ACT ThL (1st cl) 50. Univ of Queensld BA 57. **d** 49 **p** 50 Brisb. C of St Francis Nundah Brisb 49-50; Ch Ch Bundaberg 50-54; V of Mary Valley 54-57; R of Crow's Nest 57-59; St Mich AA New Farm Brisb 59-68; Lect St Francis Coll Milton 60; Vice-Prin 68-71; R of St Mark Albion City and Dio Brisb from 71; Hon Can of Brisb 73-74; Can Res from 74. *Rectory, Bellevue Terrace, Clayfield, Queensland, Australia 4011.* (262 3762)

WILLIAMS, Dewi Prys Wynne. b 14. St D Coll Lamp BA 43. **d** 43 **p** 44 St A. C of Llawry-Bettws and Bettws Gwerfil Goch 43-48; Bistre 48-52; V of Pennant w Hirnant 52-59; R of Llandysilio w Penhros 59-65; V of Connah's Quay 65-71; R of Caerwys 71-80. *9 Cae Delyn Caerwys, Mold, Clwyd, CH7 5BY.* (Caerwys 720)

WILLIAMS, Donald David Rees. St D Coll Lamp 37. **d** 43 **p** 44 Blackb. C of St Jo Evang Darwen 43-44; St Cuthb Darwen 44-46; Eglwysilan 46-49; R of St Bride's w Marloes 49-77. *6 New Road, Haverfordwest, Dyfed, SA61 1TS.*

WILLIAMS, Donald James. **d** 58 **p** 59 Nel. C-in-c of Granity 58-60; V 60-62; Amuri 62-67; BFBS Area Sec and

Perm to Offic Dio Ch Ch 67-70; Reg Sec Bible S in NZ 70-78; V of Akaroa Dio Ch Ch from 78. *St Peter's Vicarage, Akaroa, NZ.* (Akaroa 51)

WILLIAMS, Donald Peebles. Sarum Th Coll 12. **d** 13 **p** 14 Ex. C of Dawlish 13-16; Lightcliffe 16-17; E Teignmouth 17-20; V of Salcombe Regis 20-23; C of Ch Ch Portswood (or Highfield) 24-27 and 28-30; Highweek 27-28; Alverstoke (in c of St Faith) 30-35; V of Lake 35-48; Surr 39-48; RD of E Wight 43-48; Perm to Offic Dio Portsm 48-52; R of St Lawrence IW 52-58; Perm to Offic Dios Portsm and Chich 58-61; L to Offic Dio Auckld 61-79; Perm to Offic from 80. *201 Lichfield Big, Selwyn Village, Target Street, Auckland, NZ.*

WILLIAMS, Earle Frederick. b 32. Ch Ch Coll LTh 61. Univ of Ox BA (Th) 72. **d** 59 Wel **p** 60 Bp Rich for Wel. C of Palmerston N 59-62; Marton 62-64; I of St Phil Collingwood 64-70; C of St Mary Virg Ox 70-71; V of Titahi Bay 72-76; Chap Wel Hosps from 76. *134 Upoko Road, Wellington 3, NZ.* (862-727)

WILLIAMS, Edgar Osborne. b 1895. St Cath S Ox BA (3rd cl Th) 18, MA 21. **d** 19 St D **p** 20 Swansea for St D. C of Llanwnda w Manor-Owen 19-24; St Paul Sketty 24-29; V of St Jude w St Aid Manningham 29-52; CF (TA-R of O) 39-45; R of Nash w Thornton and Beachampton 52-56; V of The Lee 56-66; L to Offic Dio Mon 66-69; Perm to Offic Dio Ox 69-72. *Address temp unknown.*

WILLIAMS, Canon Edward Bryan. b 36. St D Coll Lamp BA 58. St Mich Coll Llan 58. **d** 60 **p** 61 St A. C of Rhyl 60-68; Dioc Youth Chap Dio St A 66-78; V of Dyserth 68-77; R of Denbigh Dio St A from 77; Hon Can of St A Cathl from 81. *Rectory, Denbigh, Clwyd.* (Denbigh 2970)

WILLIAMS, Edward Ffoulkes. b 34. Chich Th Coll 71. **d** 73 **p** 74 Worc. C of St Geo Kidderminster 73-78; Team V of St Barn w Ch Ch City and Dio Worc from 78. *Christ Church Vicarage, Tolladine Road, Worcester, WR4 9AU.* (Worcester 29924)

WILLIAMS, Edward Heaton. b 18. St Aid Coll 56. **d** 58 **p** 59 Ches. C of Timperley 58-62; V of St Pet Macclesfield 62-66; R of Wistaston 66-81; Sec Ches Dioc Miss Bd 63-67; Bd of Miss and Unity 67-69; V of St Nich Burton Dio Ches from 81. *Burton Vicarage, S Wirral, L64 5TJ.* (051-336 4070)

WILLIAMS, Elfed Owain. b 24. Univ of Newc T Dipl Adv Educn Studies 74. St Deiniol's Libr Hawarden 79. **d** 81 Bp Gill for Newc T. C of St John Whorlton Dio Newc T from 81. *Gallowhill Hall School, Whalton, Morpeth, Northumberland, NE61 3TU.*

WILLIAMS, Canon Emlyn. b 07. Jes Coll Ox BA 29, MA 32. Bp Wilson Th Coll IM 38. **d** 39 **p** 40 S & M. C of St Geo Douglas 39-40; Chap RNVR 40-46; RN 46-71; C of St Paul's Cathl Mahé Seychelles 71-73; Hon Chap of H Spirit Ardchattan Dio Arg Is from 73; Hon Can of St John's Cathl Oban from 80. *Parsonage, Ardchattan, N Connel, Argyll.*

WILLIAMS, Eric Rees. b 30. St Deiniol's Hawarden 70. **d** 72 **p** 73 St D. C of Llanelly 72-75; C-in-c of Tregaron Dio St D 75-76; V from 76. *Vicarage, Tregaron, Dyfed.* (Tregaron 280)

WILLIAMS, Eric Richard. St D Coll Lamp BA 54. **d** 56 **p** 57 Ban. C of Llanbeblig w Caernarvon 56-62; V of Dolwyddelan 62-77; Penrhyndeudraeth w Llanfrothen Dio Ban from 77. *Vicarage, Penrhyndeudraeth, Gwyn, LL48 6LG.* (076-674 324)

WILLIAMS, Ernest William Kingsley. b 22. FLCM 51. Open Univ BA 74. Wells Th Coll 63. **d** 63 **p** 64 Ex. Asst Master Okehampton Gr Sch from 54; Hon C of Okehampton 63-78; Team V of Lydford (in c of Bridestowe and Sourton) Dio Ex from 78. *St Bridget's House, Bridestowe, Okehampton, Devon, EX20 4ER.* (Bridestowe 287)

WILLIAMS, Everard. b 18. St Aid Coll 56. **d** 58 **p** 59 Ches. C of Mottram 58-62; V of Dunham-on-the-Hill 62-73; Tilton-on-the-Hill and Halstead w Lowesby and Cold Newton Dio Leic from 74. *Tilton Vicarage, Leicester.* (Tilton 244)

WILLIAMS, Frederick John. b 11. Oak Hill Coll 71. **d** 74 Roch **p** 75 Tonbridge for Roch (APM). C of Bexley 74-76; Shirwell 76-77; Heanton Punchardon 77-78; Hon C of S Molton Dio Ex from 78. *Dawn Glow, Deans Park, South Molton, Devon.* (South Molton 3491)

WILLIAMS, Frederick Joseph. b 09. SS Coll Cam BA 32, MA 36. Westcott Ho Cam 51. **d** 52 Birm **p** 53 Bp Linton for Birm. Chap K Edw Sch Birm 52-72; C of Selly Oak 52-62; Harborne 62-65; Hon C of Moseley 66-72; V of Barnt Green 72-79. *Address temp unknown.*

WILLIAMS, Frederick Vivian. b 08. St Andr Coll Pampisford 47. **d** 48 **p** 49 Lon. C of St Sav Paddington 48-54; R of Stanford w Postling 54-60; V of St Martin Croydon 60-73. *1 St Augustine's Close, Bexhill, E Sussex.* (Bexhill 221370)

WILLIAMS, Canon Geoffrey Ainsworth. b 16. Late Found Scho of Univ Coll Dur BA (2nd cl Th) 38, MA 41. **d** 39 **p** 40 Man. C of St Mary Bury 39-49; V of Habergham 49-65; Surr 50-65; RD of Burnley 61-65; Can Res of Blackb from 65; Warden of Whalley Abbey from 77. *22 Buncer Lane, Blackburn, Lancs.* (Blackburn 56706)

WILLIAMS, Canon Geoffrey Harold. Trin Coll Melb BA 37, MA 39, Hey Sharpe Prize 39. Univ of Queensld B Educn 58. ACT ThL (1st cl) 39. **d** 40 **p** 41 Melb. C of H Trin Coburg 40-42; V of Byron Bay 42-48; R of Mid-Clarence 48-49; Macksville 49-52; Chap C of E Gr Sch E Brisb from 52; Exam Chap to Bp of Graft 46-52; to Abp of Brisb from 69; Can Res of Brisb from 69. *34 Oaklands Parade, East Brisbane, Queensland, Australia 4169.* (391 5720)

WILLIAMS, George Harold. b 20. Univ of Lon BSc 49. **d** 67 **p** 68 Bris. C of Bishopsworth 67-70; V of Ch Ch Weston-s-Mare Dio B & W from 70. *18 Montpelier, Weston-super-Mare, Avon, BS23 2RH.* (Weston-s-Mare 24376)

WILLIAMS, Geoffrey Thomas. b 35. Ox Th Course (NSM) 77. **d** 80 Ox. C of St Bart Earley, Reading Dio Ox from 80. *14 Eastern Avenue, Reading, RG1 5RY.* (0734 661325)

WILLIAMS, George Maxwell Frazer. b 42. TCD BA 65, MA 69. Cudd Coll 65. **d** 67 **p** 68 Bradf. C of St Jas Bolton w St Chrys 67-70; St Chad Shrewsbury 70-73; V of Shawbury 73-79; C-in-c of Moreton Corbet 73-79; V of Short Heath Dio Lich from 79. *Short Heath Vicarage, Willenhall, W Midl, WV12 5PT.* (Bloxwich 76416)

WILLIAMS, George Melvin. b 24. Worc Ordn Coll 64. **d** 66 **p** 67 Win. C of Holdenhurst 66-70; V of Yateley 70-75; St Leon and St Ives Ringwood Dio Win from 75. *107 Woolsbridge Road, Ashley Heath, Nr Ringwood, Hants.* (Ringwood 3406)

WILLIAMS, George Nathaniel Osho. **d** 43 **p** 45 Sier L. P Dio Sier L. *Parsonage, Wilberforce, Sierra Leone.*

WILLIAMS, Glyn. b 54. AKC and BD 77. Ripon Coll Cudd 77. **d** 78 **p** 79 Ches. C of St Mich Coppenhall Crewe 78-81; St Alb Mart Northn Dio Pet from 81. *12 Oulton Rise, Northampton.* (Northn 43427)

WILLIAMS, Glyn Alun. b 17. St D Coll Lamp BA 40. **d** 41 **p** 42 St D. C of Gorslas 41-46; Llangyfelach w Morriston 46-48; Llansadwrn w Llanwrda and Capel Dewi Sant 48-50; V of Llandyssilio-Gogo 50-57; Llangendeirne 57-71; Pencarreg w Llancrwys 71-73. *11 Tirwaun, Pwll, Llanelli, Dyfed.*

WILLIAMS, Gordon. b 16. Univ of Wales Clifton Th Coll 54. **d** 55 **p** 56 Lich. C of Bucknall w Bagnall 55-58; V of St Paul W Bromwich 58-62; R of Swepstone w Snarestone 62-80. *3 Fleetwood Gardens, Market Harborough, Leics.*

WILLIAMS, Graham Ivor. Jes Coll Ox BA (2nd cl Th) 48, MA 48. Cudd Coll 48. **d** 49 **p** 50 Swan B. C of St Mary Swansea 49-53; Edgbaston 53-55; R of Nutfield Dio S'wark from 55. *Nutfield Rectory, Redhill, Surrey.* (Nutfield Ridge 2286)

WILLIAMS, Graham John. b 49. Univ of Wales (Bangor) Dipl Th 71. St Steph Ho Ox 71. **d** 72 **p** 73 Llan. C of St Jo Bapt Cardiff 72-76; Ascen Berwick Hills, Middlesbrough 76-78; V of Dormanstown Dio York from 78. *All Saints' Vicarage, South Avenue, Dormanstown, Redcar, Cleveland.* (Redcar 478334)

WILLIAMS, Graham Parry. b 46. St D Coll Lamp Dipl Th 70. Bp Burgess Th Hall Lamp 67. **d** 70 **p** 71 Mon. C of Ebbw Vale 70-73; Trevethin 73-74; V of Nantyglo 74-76; Chap RN from 76. *c/o Ministry of Defence, Lacon House, Theobald's Road, WC1X 8RY.*

WILLIAMS, Gwilym Elfred. St D Coll Lamp BA (2nd cl Welsh) 53. St Mich Coll Llan 53. **d** 56 Ban **p** 57 Wales. C of Llandudno 56-59; Aberdare 59-63; All SS Penarth 63-65; R of Eglwysilan 65-70; Mountain Ash 70-81; Llanblethian w Cowbridge, Llandough and St Mary Ch Dio Llan from 81. *Llanblethian Vicarage, Cowbridge, S Glam* (Cowbridge 2302)

WILLIAMS, Gwilym Kenneth. b 12. Univ of Wales BA 34. St Mich Coll Llan 34. **d** 35 **p** 36 St D. C of Llansadwrn w Llanwrda 35-38; Llandingat 38-42; C-in-c of Henllan Amgoed w Llangan 42-44; R of Brechfa (w Abergorlech from 52 and Llanfihangel Rhosycorn from 59) 44-60; Borth 60-80; RD of Llanbadarn Fawr 71-80; Can of St D Cathl 75-80. *3 Clos-y-Drindod, Aberystwth, Dyfed.* (Abth 615756)

✠ **WILLIAMS, Most Rev Gwilym Owen.** b 13. Jes Coll Ox BA (1st cl Engl) 33, 1st cl Th 35, MA 37. DD (Lambeth) 57. St Steph Ho Ox 36. **d** 37 **p** 38 St A. C of Denbigh 37-40; Reader in Th St D Coll Lamp 40; Chap 40-45; Warden of Ch Hostel Ban, Warden of Ordinands Dios St A and Ban; Exam Chap to Bp of Ban, and Lect in Th Univ Coll of N Wales 45-48; Chap and Tutor St Mary's Coll Ban 45-47; Can of Ban Cathl 47-48; Warden and Hd Master Llandovery Coll 48-57; LPr Dio St D 48-56; L to Offic Dio Ban 50-56; Cons Ld Bp of Ban in Llan Cathl 1 May 57 by Abp of Wales; Bps of Mon; St A; Swan B; St D; and Worc; Sub-Prelate O of St John of Jer from 65; Elected Abp of Prov of Wales 71. *Ty'r Esgob, Bangor, Gwyn, LL57 2SS.* (Bangor 2895)

WILLIAMS, Very Rev Harold Claude Noel. b 14. Hatf Coll Dur BA 37, LTh 37. Univ of S Afr MA 49. Valparaiso Univ USA Hon LLD 67. St Bonif Coll Warm 34. **d** 38 Southn for Win **p** 39 Win. C of Weeke 38-41; Chap of St Matt Coll 41-42; Asst Miss at St Matt Grahmstn 42-43; Warden 43-50; V of St Bart Hyde Win 50-54; Hon Sec Win Dioc Miss Coun 51-55; Surr from 53; R of St Mary Southn 54-58; V and Provost of St Mich Cathl Cov 58-81; Provost (Emer) from 81; Proc Conv Cov 58. *96 Stoney Road, Coventry, CV3 6HY.* (Cov 502561)

WILLIAMS, Chan Harold Edgar. b 17. St D Coll Lamp BA 40. AKC 42. **d** 42 **p** 43 Chelmsf. C of St Jo Bapt Leytonstone 42-45; St Mary Barnes 45-46; Chap RNVR 46-48; C of St Jude Swansea 48-51; Chap RN 51-55; Dir of Ordinands Dio Swan B 55-79; R of Llansantffraed and Llanhamlach 55-61; V of Hay 61-67; Brynmawr 67-76; Exam Chap to Bp of Swan B 65-67; Dioc Sch Insp from 67; Can of Brecon Cathl 72-79; Chan from 79; Sec of Ch in Wales Prov Selection Bd for Ordinands 74-78; V of Newton St Pet Dio Swan B from 76. *Vicarage, Newton, Swansea, W Glam.*

WILLIAMS, Harold James. Univ of NZ (Cant Coll) 23. Selw Th Coll 27. **d** 28 **p** 29 Dun. C of Oamaru 21-31; V of Waihi 31-33; C of St Pet Cathl Hamilton 42-46; P-in-c of H Trin Forest Gate 46-47; V 47-50; L to Offic Dio Waik 50-57. *PO Box 11, Paihia, North Auckland, NZ.*

WILLIAMS, Harry Abbott. b 19. Late Scho of Trin Coll Cam BA (1st Cl Th Trip) 41, MA 45. Cudd Coll 41. **d** 43 **p** 44 Lon. C of St Barn Pimlico 43-45; All SS Marg Street 45-48; Chap and Tutor of Westcott Ho Cam 48-51; Exam Chap to Bp of Lon 48-69; to Bp of St Alb 51-69; L to Offic Dio Ely 48-69; Fell and Lect Trin Coll Cam 51-69; Dean of Chap and Tutor 58-69. Select Pr Univ of Cam 50, 58 and 75; Hulsean Pr 62 and 75; Ox 74; L to Offic Dio Wakef from 80. *House of the Resurrection, Mirfield, W Yorks.*

WILLIAMS, Harry Clement. b 1879. Ex Coll Ox BA (4th Cl Th) 02, MA 06. Leeds Cl Scho 02. **d** 04 **p** 05 Lon. C of St Paul Haggerston 04-07; Asst Sec E Lon Ch Fund 07-17; Miss Chap to Bp of Islington 07-20; Sec E Lon Ch Fund 17-20; V of St Martin W Acton 20-38; R and V of Eastchurch 38-53; R of Warden 38-53. *8 St Stephen's Green, Canterbury, Kent.*

WILLIAMS, Ven Harry Craven. b 09. MBE (Mil) 46. Univ of Wales BA (2nd cl Phil) 32. St Mich Coll Llan 32. **d** 33 **p** 34 Swan B. C of St Mary Swansea 33-39; CF (R of O) 39-46; V of St Jude Swansea 46-50; Surr from 47; V of Sketty 50-58; Swansea 58-77; Can of Melineth in Brecon Cathl 58-63; RD of Swansea 63-69; Prec of Brecon Cathl 63-69; Archd of Gower 69-79; Archd (Emer) from 79; Can Res of Brecon Cathl 77-79 Actg Dean 78-79. *6 Knoll Avenue, Uplands, Swansea, SA2 0PS.* (Swansea 59142)

WILLIAMS, Henry Gordon. b 33. St Aid Coll 57. **d** 60 **p** 61 Man. C of St Mary Radcliffe 60-63; R of Northn Austr 63-70; Dampier w Mt Tom Price 71-72; Perm to Offic Dio NW Austr from 73. *29 Rosewood Place, Wickham, W Australia 6720.*

WILLIAMS, Ven Henry Leslie. b 19. St D Coll Lamp BA 41. St Mich Coll Llan 41. **d** 43 **p** 44 Ban. C of Aberdovey 43-45; St Mary Ban 45-48; Chap HMS Conway 48-49; C of St Mary-without-the-Walls Ches 49-53; V of Barnston Dio Ches from 53; CF (TA) from 54; RD of Wirral in 67-75; Hon Can of Ches from 72; Archd of Ches from 75; M Gen Syn from 78. *Vicarage, Barnston, Mer.* (051-648 1776)

WILLIAMS, Herbert Brian. b 18. BNC Ox BA 39, MA 48. Linc Th Coll 80. **d** 81 Linc (NSM). C of Asterby Dio Linc from 81. *Mill House, Goulceby, Louth, Lincs, LN11 9UB.*

WILLIAMS, Canon Howard. b 08. Univ of Wales BA 29, 1st cl Phil 30, MA 32. St Jo Coll Cam 36. mLitt 45. Powis Exhib and St Steph Ho Ox 30. **d** 31 **p** 32 St D. C of St Mich Abth 31-36; Perm to Offic Dio Ely 36-38; Dios St E St Alb Pet and Chelmsf 37-38; V of Llannon 38-49; Dioc Insp of Schs St D 40-50; Lect Univ of Wales 49-50; V of Bettws w Ammanford 49-57; Surr 40-75; V of Llanelly 57-75; Chap Llanelly Hosps 57-75; 4th Cursal Can of St D from 60; Treas 73-75; Exam Chap to Bp of St D from 60. *Castle Green, Llansawel, Llandeilo, Dyfed, SA19 7JH.* (Talley 350)

WILLIAMS, Howard Graham Anthony. b 04. M OSB 48. **d** 52 **p** 53 Ox. Perm to Offic Dio Ox from 52. *Nashdom Abbey, Burnham, Slough, SL1 8NL.*

WILLIAMS, Howard Kently. Univ Th Coll of WI Ja. **d** 73 **p** 75 Ja. C of Montego Bay 73-77; P-in-c of St Thos Grand Turk Dio Nass from 81. *Box 24, Grand Turk, Turks and Caicos Islands, W Indies.*

WILLIAMS, Canon Hugh. b 27. ACP 48. K Coll Lon and Warm AKC 53. **d** 54 Warrington for Liv **p** 55 Liv. C of St Chad Kirkby (in c of St Martin Southdene from 55) 54-57; St John Blackpool 57-58; V of Foulridge 58-65; H Trin Darwen 65-74; C-in-c of Hoddlesden 65-74; St Jo Evang Darwen 68-74; St Geo Darwen 69-74; Team R of St Pet Darwen w Hoddlesden 74-77; RD of Darwen 75-77; M Gen Syn Dio Blackb from 75; R of Burnley Dio Blackb from 77; Hon Can of Blackb from 78; RD of Burnley from 78; Vice Chairman Dioc Bd for Miss and Unity 78-80; Chairman from 80. *Rectory, Pasturegate, Burnley, Lancs.* (Burnley 39490)

WILLIAMS, Hugh Bowen. **d** 70 **p** 71 Mashon. P Dio Mashon from 71. *37 Cornwall Road, Avondale, Salisbury, Rhodesia.*

WILLIAMS, Hugh Llewelyn. b 09. St D Coll Lamp BA 32. **d** 32 **p** 33 Ban. C of Glanogwen 32-35; Criccieth 35-37; Llanfachraeth w Llanynghendl and Llandfugael 37-42; R of Llanfihangel-y-Traethau w Llandecwyn 42-45; Llandwrog 45-50; C of Wilmslow 50-51; V of St Jas Sutton Chesh 51-57; Stockton Heath 57-63; Ch Ch Alsager 63-73; Perm to offic Dio Ches from 74. *1 Laureston Avenue, Crewe, Chesh, CW1 1HU.*

WILLIAMS, Hugh Martin. b 45. AKC 73. St Aug Coll Cant 74. **d** 74 Lon **p** 75 Kens for Lon. C of Heston 74-78; Chap City Univ from 78. *City University, Northampton Square, EC1V 0HB.* (01-250 0207)

WILLIAMS, Hugh Wynford. b 16. St D Coll Lamp BA 38. Selw Coll Cam BA 40, MA 44. St Mich Coll Llan 40. **d** 41 **p** 42 Wakef. C of Kirkburton 41-43; Skipton 43-44; Perm to Offic Dio Bradf 44-51; Dio Pet 51-73; Chap Oundle Sch 54-73; R of Tichmarsh Dio Pet from 73; P-in-c of Clopton Dio Pet from 77. *Tichmarsh Rectory, Kettering, Northants.*

WILLIAMS, Ian Geoffrey. b 50. AKC and BD 71. St Jo Coll Nottm 72. **d** 74 **p** 75 Birm. C of St Jo Bapt Harborne 74-76; in Amer Ch 76-77; C of Hazlemere (in c of Good Shepherd) Dio Ox 77-80; Team V from 80. *Church House, Georges Hill, Widmer End, High Wycombe, Bucks.* (0494-713848)

WILLIAMS, Ian Withers. b 43. Linc Th Coll 68. **d** 69 **p** 70 Birm. C of Ch Ch Burney Lane 69-72; Cleobury Mortimer w Hopton Wafers 72-75; V of Knowbury 75-79; P-in-c of Coreley 75-79; V of Ch Ch City and Dio Lich from 79. *Christ Church Vicarage, Lichfield, Staffs, WS13 8AL.* (Lich 24431)

WILLIAMS, Ieuan Merchant. b 13. St D Coll Lamp BA 36. **d** 39 **p** 40 Sheff. C of Ardsley 39-42; Wombwell (in c of St Geo) 42-48; R of N and S Wheatley w W Burton 48-55; W Leake w Kingston-on-Soar and Ratcliffe-on-Soar 55-59; V of Burton Joyce w Bulcote 59-71; R of Brightwell Baldwin and Cuxham w Easington 71-80; C-in-c of Ewelme and Britwell Salome 76-80. *4 The Cloister, Ewelme, Oxon.*

WILLIAMS, Ifan. b 24. St D Coll Lamp. **d** 56 **p** 57 Ban. C of Llangefni w Tregaian 56-60; V of Llanfacraeth Merions 60-67; C-in-c of Bryncoedifor 65-67; R of Ffestiniog w Blaenau Ffestiniog Dio Ban from 67; Rd of Ardudwy from 80. *Rectory, Blaenau Festiniog, Gwyn.* (Blaenau F 382)

WILLIAMS, Jack. b 26. Univ of Wales (Ban) BSc 50. St Mich Coll Llan 50. **d** 52 **p** 53 St A. C of Buckley 52-55; Llanrhos 55-59; V of Bettisfield w Bronington 59; C of Ripponden 61-65; Asst Master Rishworth Sch 61-65; Chap 65-68; Hd Master from 68. *Rishworth School, Halifax, Yorks.* (Ripponden 3277)

WILLIAMS, Jacob. Codr Coll Barb 55. **d** 59 **p** 60 Gambia. P Dio Gambia from 59; Exam Chap to Bp of Gambia 66-77. *PO Box 404, Banjul, Gambia.*

WILLIAMS, James Basil. b 08. Worc Ordin Coll 54. **d** 56 **p** 57 Lich. C of Gnosall 56-59; W Bromwich 59-60; V of Adbaston 60-64; Forsbrook 64-69; Croxton w Broughton 69-73; Surr from 67. *The Firs, Adbaston, Eccleshall, Stafford, ST20 0RA.* (Adbaston 289)

WILLIAMS, James Einon. b 18. St D Coll Lamp BA 39. St Mary's Univ NS B Educn 63. **d** 46 St D **p** 47 Swan B for St D. C of Kidwelly 46-48; All SS Cathl Edmon 48-50; R of Fort Sask 50-52; Chap RCN 52-70; V of Llanarth w Llanina and Mydroilin Dio St D from 73. *Vicarage, Llanarth, Dyfed.* (Llanarth 509)

WILLIAMS, John. St D Coll Lamp LDiv 10. St Mich Coll Llan. **d** 12 **p** 13 St D. C of Nevern w Bayvil and Cilgwyn 12-14; St John Cwmbach-Llechryd 14-16; Llanguicke 17-22; V of Llandelov w Llanrheithan 22-36; Penbryn 36-62. *107 Dairy House Road, Derby.*

WILLIAMS, Canon John. b 31. K Coll Lon and Warm AKC 56. **d** 57 **p** 58 Dur. C of Cockerton 57-60; St Geo Camberwell 60-62; St Chad Roseworth Stockton-on-Tees (in c of St Jas) 62-65; PC 65-68; R of Longnewton 68-75; Dioc Social Responsibility Officer for Chs Dio Dur from 68; Hon Can of Dur Cathl from 80. *39 Darlington Road, Hartburn, Stockton-on-Tees, Cleveland, TS18 5EJ.* (Stockton 582241)

WILLIAMS, John Beattie. b 42. Univ of Wales BA (3rd cl Mod Lang) 66. Cudd Coll 67. **d** 69 **p** 69 S'wark. C of St Helier 69-70; H Trin Yeovil 70-76; C-in-c of Ebbesbourne Wake w Fifield Bavant and Alvediston 76-78; Chap to the Deaf Dio Sarum 76-78; Chap and Welfare Officer Miss to the Deaf Dio B & W from 78; Publ Pr Dio Bris from 80. *25 Lynfield Park, Weston, Bath, BA1 4ER.* (Bath 311901)

WILLIAMS, Ven John Charles. b 12. St D Coll Lamp BA (3rd Cl Hist) 34. Univ Coll Ox 34. Qu Coll Birm 36. **d** 37 **p** 38

Birm. C of Ch Ch Summerfield 37-39; Halesowen (in c of Hasbury) 39-43; V of St Luke Reddal Hill 43-48; Redditch 48-59; Surr 51-70; R of Halesowen w Hasbury and Lapal 59-70; V of Dodderhill 70-75; RD of Bromsgrove 58-59; Hon Can of Worc 65-75; Can Res 75-80; Can (Emer) from 80; Archd of Dudley 68-75; Worc 75-80; Archd (Emer) from 80; Exam Chap to Bp of Worc 69-80; Dioc Dir of Ordinands 75-79; M Gen Syn and Centr Bd of Finance 75-80. *Old Vicarage, Norton, Evesham, Worcs.*

WILLIAMS, Ven John Christopher Richard. Univ of Man BA 58. Cranmer Hall Dur. **d** 60 Middleton for Arctic **p** 62 Arctic. Miss at Sugluk 60-70; Cape Dorset 72-75; Baker Lake Arctic from 75; Hon Can of Arctic 72-75; Archd of The Keewatin Dio Arctic from 75; I of Yellowknife Dio Arctic from 78. *Box 276, Yellowknife, NWT, Canada.*

WILLIAMS, John David. b 43. St Jo Coll Dur BA 70. Univ of Wales MEducn 77. Cranmer Hall Dur 67. **d** 76 **p** 77 St D (APM). C of St Pet Carmarthen Dio St D from 76. *Pennant, Nantgaredig, Carmarthen, Dyfed, SA32 7NY.* (Nantgaredig 530)

WILLIAMS, John Edward. Univ of Wales (Abth) Dipl Th 55. St Deiniol's Libr Hawarden 76. **d** 76 **p** 77 Swan B. C of Llansamlet 76-78; R of Aberffraw w Llangwyfan Dio Ban from 78. *Aberffraw Rectory, Anglesey, Gwynedd.* (Bodorgan 318)

WILLIAMS, Canon John Edwin. Woll Coll W Austr. **d** 61 **p** 62 Perth. C of Mt Lawley 61-66; R of Manning 66-67; Wongan Hills 67-71; Wagin 71-74; Williams 74-76; Katanning Dio Bunb from 76; Hon Can of Bunb from 76. *Rectory, Box 60, Katanning, W Australia 6317.* (098-21 1986)

WILLIAMS, John Elwyn Askew. b 09. St Jo Coll Cam BA 32, MA 36. Ridley Hall Cam 32. **d** 34 **p** 35 Roch. C of St Marg Roch 34-37; Lenton 37-40; CF (EC) 40-46; C-in-c of Eakring 46-47; R 47-55; V of Winkburn 47-55; Sutton-on-the-Forest 55-61; Whitchurch 61-81; Oving w Pitchcott 74-76; P Missr 76-81; Hardwicke w Weedon 76-81; N Marston 76-81; Quainton 76-81. *Bramleys, Chalkshire Road, Butlers Cross, Aylesbury, Bucks.*

WILLIAMS, John Francis Meyler. b 34. St Jo Coll Cam BA 56, MA 60. Sarum Wells Th Coll 79. **d** 81 St E. C of Hadleigh w Layham & Shelley Dio St E from 81. *5 Brett Avenue, Hadleigh, Ipswich, Suffolk, IP7 6AH.*

WILLIAMS, Canon John Francis Oliver. b 15. TCD BA 40, MA 43. **d** 40 **p** 41 Down. C of Shankill (Lurgan) 40-42; Oldcastle 42-44; C-in-c of Clonfadforan w Castletown 44-46; R of Athboy Kildalkey and Girley 46-54; Sec of Ch of I Jews' Soc 54-56; R of St Matt Irishtown Dub 56-73; Dalkey Dio Dub from 73; RD of St Mark Dio Dub from 69; Can of Ch Ch Cathl Dub from 81. *Rectory, Church Road, Dalkey, Co Dublin, Irish Republic.* (Dublin 803369)

WILLIAMS, John Frederick. b 07. Univ of Wales BA (Engl) 28. St Mich Coll Llan 28. **d** 30 **p** 31 Ban. C of St John Portmadoc 30-33; Aberdare 33-37; V of St John Miskin 37-53; Skewen 53-62; R of Neath w Llantwit 62-69; Can of Fairwell in Llan Cathl 63-67; Prec 67-69; RD of Neath 67-69; Archd of Llan 69-71; Dean and V of Llan w Llanilterne 71-77; Perm to Offic Dio Llan from 78. *3a Park Road, Barry, S Glam.*

WILLIAMS, John Frederick Arthur. b 26. BSc (Lon) 50. Univ of Southn PhD 53. Ridley Hall Cam 63. **d** 65 **p** 66 Ely. C of H Sepulchre Cam 65-66; C-in-c of St Mark Cam 66-67; V of Ch Ch Portswood (or Highfield) Southn Dio Win from 67. *36 Brookvale Road, Southampton.* (Southn 554277)

WILLIAMS, John Gilbert. b 36. St Aid Coll 64. **d** 67 **p** 68 Ches. C of St Jo Bapt Bollington 67-69; Oxton 69-72; P-in-c of Castle Frome 72-76; Bp's Frome 72-76; Acton Beauchamp and Evesbatch 72-76; R of Kingsland Dio Heref from 76; P-in-c of Eardisland Dio Heref from 77. *Kingsland Rectory, Leominster, Herefs, HR6 9QW.* (Kingsland 255)

WILLIAMS, John Glyn. b 18. BA (Lon) 47. St Mich Coll Llan 46. **d** 49 **p** 50 Llan. C of Aberdare (in c of Cwmbach 53-59) 49-59; Cler Org Sec CECS in S Wales from 59; Perm to Offic Dios St D, Mon and Swan B from 59; L to Offic Dio Llan from 59. *40 Parkfields Road, Bridgend, Mid-Glam, CF31 4BJ.* (0656-4110)

WILLIAMS, John Gordon. b 06. Univ of Lon BA (1st cl Engl) 27, Ridley Hall Cam 30. **d** 32 **p** 33 S'wark. C of St Luke Bermondsey 32-34; H Trin Rotherhithe 34-40; Asst to Relig Dir BBC 40-50; L to Offic Dio Lon 48-53; Field Sec Nat S and of C of E Sch Coun and L to Offic Dio St Alb 50-53; V of St Columba Anfield 53-57; Chap and Educn Officer SPCK 57-72; Perm to Offic Dio Lon 62-72; Hon Min Can Ripon Cathl 72. *28 Borrage Lane, Ripon, Yorks.* (Ripon 3352)

WILLIAMS, John Heard. b 35. Univ of Bris BA (3rd cl Th) 58. Clifton Th Coll 59. **d** 59 **p** 60 Roch. C of Ch Ch Tunbridge Wells 59-65; V of St Sav Forest Gate (w St Matt West Ham from 75) Dio Chelmsf 65-76; R from 76; C-in-c of St Matt W Ham 72-75; M Gen Syn from 80. *4a Sidney Road, E7 0EF.* (01-534 6109)

WILLIAMS, John Henry. b 06. St D Coll Lamp BA 27, BD 36. Univ of Liv MA 40. St Steph Ho Ox 28. **d** 29 **p** 30 Ban. C of Holyhead 29-36; Gen Sec of S of St D 32-39; Bp's Messenger Dio Ban and Hon Chap to Bp of Ban 36-43; Sec Dioc Bd of Miss Dio Ban 36-46; R of Llanberis 43-55; V of Llanbeblig w Caernarvon 55-70; Can and Preb of Llanfair in Ban Cathl 52-65; Chan 65-70. *Awelon, Dyffryn Ardudwy, Gwyn.*

WILLIAMS, John Henry Hopkins. **d** 37 **p** 38 Swan B for Llan. C of Pentyrch 37-40; St Elis Becontree 40-42; Chap RAFVR 42-46; V of Gt Burstead 46-53; Chap RAF 53-56; V of Ch Ch Walcot 56-67; R of Kingsdon w Podymore Milton 67-78; Babcary 67-76; C-in-c of Yeovilton 67-78. *The Cottage, New Street, Somerton, Somt.*

WILLIAMS, John Herbert. b 19. St D Coll Lamp BA (2nd cl Engl) 41. Sarum Th Coll 41. **d** 43 **p** 44 Mon. C of Blaenavon 43-46; Llanishen 46-48; Bassaleg 48-51; Asst Chap HM Pris Man 51-52; Chap Holloway 52-57; Birm 57-64; Wormwood Scrubs 64-70; SE Reg and HM Remand Centre Latchmere House 71-74; ACG HM Pris Dept from 74; P-in-ord to HM the Queen from 80. *Portland House, Stag Place, SW1E 5BX.*

WILLIAMS, John James. b 08. Qu Coll Cam BA 31, MA 35. Ely Th Coll 31. **d** 32 Kens for Lon **p** 33 Lon. C of St Pet Harrow 32-35; St Jude Hampstead Garden Suburb 35-36; St Jas W Hampstead 36-38; Abingdon 38-44; V of Speen 44-50; Lathbury 50-62; V of Newport Pagnell 50-62; Surr from 52; R of St Paul Wokingham 62-73; C-in-c of S w N Moreton 73-77; Perm to Offic Dio Ox from 77. *4 Essex Place, Lambourn, Newbury, Berks, RG16 6QF.*

WILLIAMS, Canon John James. b 20. TD 61 (w clasp 67). Linc Coll Ox BA 42, MA 46. St Mich Coll Llan 42. **d** 44 **p** 45 St A. C of Rhosymedre 44-47; Flint 47-50; Eglwys Rhos 50-53; CF (TA) 49-62; SCF (TA) 62-67; CF (TAVR) 67-68; V of Whixall 53-57; Prees 57-64; Powyke w Callow End Dio Worc from 64; Hon Can of Worc from 77. *Powick Vicarage, Worcester.* (Worcester 830270)

WILLIAMS, John Noel. Univ of Leeds BA 48, M CR 59. Coll of Resurr Mirfield 48. **d** 50 **p** 51 S'wark. C of Camberwell 50-56; L to Offic Dio Wakef 59-60; Dio Johann 60-62; Dio Grahmstn 63-64; Dio Matab 65-78; R of Shabani Dio Matab from 78. *Box 81, Shabani, Zimbabwe.* (Shabani 2582)

WILLIAMS, John Peter. Univ of Tor BA 75. Wycl Coll Tor MDiv 78. **d** 78 **p** 79 Tor. C of St Geo Oshawa 78-80; Assoc P of Barrie Dio Tor from 80. *Collier Street, Barrie, Ont, Canada.*

WILLIAMS, John Peter Philip. b 49. Univ of Wales (Bangor) Dipl Th 71. Chich Th Coll 71. **d** 72 **p** 73 St A. C of Abergele 72-77; R of Henllan and Llanefydd Dio St A from 77. *Henllan Rectory, Denbigh, Clwyd, LL16 5BB.* (074571-2628)

WILLIAMS, John Richard. b 48. Rhodes Univ BA 68. AKC and BD 72. St Aug Coll Cant 72. **d** 73 **p** 74 Grahmstn. C of St Alb E Lon Grahmstn 73-74; K William's Tn 74-76; P-in-c of Alice 75-76; C of St Mary Addington Cant 77-80; of Minster-in-Sheppey Dio Cant from 80. *St Peter's House, St Peter's Close, Halfway, Sheppey, Kent, ME12 3DD.* (0795-662399)

WILLIAMS, John Roger. b 31. Univ of Bris BA 55. BD (Lon) 57. Tyndale Hall, Bris. **d** 57 **p** 58 Lon. C of H Trin Islington 57-60; Trav Sec Inter-Varsity Fellowship 60-64; V of Selly Hill 64-74; C-in-c of Chilwell w Inham Nook Dio Southw 74-75; V from 75. *Christ Church Vicarage, College Road, Beeston, Nottingham, NG9 4AS.* (Nottm 222809)

WILLIAMS, John Roger. b 37. Lich Th Coll 60. **d** 63 **p** 64 Lich. C of Wem 63-66; Wolverhampton 66-69; R of Pudleston w Whyle and Hatfield 69-74; C-in-c of Stoke Prior and of Humber 69-74; Docklow 69-74; V of Fenton 74-81; P-in-c of Shipston-on-Stour w Tidmington Dio Cov from 81; Honington w Idlicote Dio Cov from 81. *Rectory, Glen Close, Shipston-on-Stour, Warws.* (Shipston-on-Stour 62661)

WILLIAMS, John Strettle. b 44. N Ordin Course 77. **d** 80 **p** 81 Liv (APM). C of Stoneycroft Dio Liv and Chap Centr Liv Coll from 80. *28 Brook Street, Whiston, Prescot, Mer, L35 5AP.* (051-426 9598)

WILLIAMS, John Trefor. b 23. Worc Ordin Coll 65. **d** 67 **p** 68 Ex. C of Paignton 67-72; V of Winkleigh 72-80; P-in-c of Ashreigney 73-79; R 79-80; P-in-c of Brushford 75-79; V 79-80; R of Broadwood Kelly 79-80; P-in-c of Berrynarbor 80-81; Combe Martin Dio Ex 80-81; R (w Berrynarbor) from 81. *Rectory, Combe Martin, Ilfracombe, Devon.* (Combe Martin 3203)

WILLIAMS, John Worthington. Univ of Melb BA 66. Univ of Man PhD 73. Ridley Coll Melb ACT ThL 58. **d** 59 **p** 60 Melb. C of Caulfield 59-61; Brighton 61-62; St Mark Forest Hill 62-66; Perm to Offic Dio Melb 67-68; in Amer Ch 68-71; C of Cheadle, Chesh 72-73; Lect Ridley Coll Melb 74; R Melb Inst of Tech 74-78; Perm to Offic Dio Melb 75-78; I of St John Blackb Dio Melb from 78. *Vicarage, Queen Street, Blackburn, Vic, Australia 3130.* (878 8536)

WILLIAMS, Jon Standish. Univ of NZ BA 55. Univ of Otago BD 63, LTh 63. St Jo Coll Auckld 63. **d** 63 **p** 64 Waik. C of Claudelands 63-65; Stratford 65-67; P-in-c of Chartwell 67-68; V 68-71; Okato 71-73; Stratford 73-80; Raglan Dio Waik from 80. *Vicarage, Bow Street, Raglan, NZ.*

WILLIAMS, Keith Graham. b 38. ARICS 62. Univ of Reading MSc 70. Univ of Dur Dipl Th 77. St Jo Coll Dur 75. **d** 77 Pontefract for Wakef **p** 78 Wakef. C of Almondbury 77-81. *Address temp unknown.*

WILLIAMS, Kelvin George John. b 36. ALCD 62. **d** 62 **p** 63 B & W. C of Bath Abbey 62-65; Chap R Nat Hosp Bath 64-65; CF (TA) 64-65; CF 65-68; C of Clevedon 68-70; V of Ston Easton w Farrington Gurney 70-74; Bradford, Oake, Hillfarrance and Heathfield 74-76; CF (TAVR) from 70. *41 Stoke Road, Taunton, TA1 3EH.*

WILLIAMS, Kenneth Edward Chilton. b 15. AKC 2nd cl 37. Univ of Lon 34. Wells Th Coll 37. **d** 38 Tewkesbury for Glouc **p** 39 Glouc. C of Stroud 38-43; V 43-50; Surr 48-52; Min of St Paul's Conv Distr Parkeston 50-57; Chap Harwich Hosp 54-57; V of Walton-le-Soken 57-82. *49 Shepherds Mead, Dilton Marsh, Westbury, Wilts.*

WILLIAMS, Kenneth Hooper. St D Coll Lamp BA 49, LTh 51. **d** 53 St D **p** 54 Llan for St D. C of Pembroke Dk 53-56; Burry Port w Pwll 56-58; CF from 58. *c/o Glyn Mills & Co, Whitehall, S W 1.*

WILLIAMS, Kenneth Truman. **d** 75 **p** 77 Sktn. L to Offic Dio Sktn 75-80; Dio Edmon from 80. *3108-115 Street, Edmonton, Alta, Canada.*

WILLIAMS, Ven Leslie Arthur. 09. Down Coll Cam 2nd cl Hist Trip pt i 39, BA (3rd cl Th Trip pt ii) 40, MA 45. Clifton Th Coll 34. **d** 34 **p** 35 Bris. C of H Trin Bris 34-37; Perm to Offic at St Andr Gt Cam 37-40; C of Chippenham (in c of St Pet Lowden) 40-42; Chap RAFVR 42-46; C of Stoke Bishop 46-47; V of Corsham 47-53; Bishopston 53-60; Hon Chap to Bp of Bris 50-64; Exam Chap 67-79; Hon Can of Bris from 58; V of Stoke Bishop 60-67; RD of Clifton 66-77; Archd of Bris 67-79; (Emer) from 79; Surr 67-79. *18 Reedley Road, Westbury on Trym, Bristol, BS9 3ST.* (Bristol 628239)

WILLIAMS, Leslie Cecil. b 26. St D Coll Lamp BA 49. St Mich Coll Llan 49. **d** 51 **p** 52 Mon. C of Bedwas 51-53; Abergavenny 53-56; St Woolos Newport 56-57; R of Llanwern w Bishton 57-62; Chap Severalls Hosp Colchester from 62. *The Hollies, Nayland Road, Colchester, Essex, CO4 5EG.* (Colchester 74392)

WILLIAMS, Llewelyn Owen. St Pet Hall Ox 28. Clifton Th Coll 35. **d** 38 **p** 39 Ex. C of Ch Ch Ellacombe Torquay 38-40; Chap RAFVR 40-45; C of Batcombe w Upton Noble and of N w S Brewham 51-67; R of Bawdrip 67-68. *The Farm, Harewood End, Hereford.*

WILLIAMS, Lloyd. b 43. Oak Hill Th Coll 71. **d** 74 **p** 75 Bradf. C of Laisterdyke 74-77; Hoole 77-80; V of Rawthorpe Huddersfield Dio Wakef from 80. *Vicarage, Rawthorpe Lane, Dalton, Huddersfield, HD5 9PB.* (Huddersfield 28045)

WILLIAMS, Lloyd Lancelot James. Ch Ch Coll Ch Ch 66. **d** 67 Ch Ch **p** 68 Bp Warren for Ch Ch. C of Shirley 67-71; Riccarton St Pet 70-72; V of Southbridge 72-76; Wainuiomata Dio Wel from 76. *40 Wainuiomata Road, Wainuiomata, NZ.* (8204)

WILLIAMS, Mapson Thomas Denton. Moore Coll Syd ThL 55. **d** and **p** 49 Syd. C of Penshurst w Peakhurst 49; C-in-c of Herne Bay 49-52; Peakhurst and of Lugarno 52-63; R of Bulli 63-74; C-in-c of Shellharbour Dio Syd 74-76; R from 76. *12 Towns Street, Shellharbour, NSW, Australia 2529.* (Woll 951420)

WILLIAMS, Mark Naylor. b 28. CCC Cam BA 52. MA 56. Ripon Hall Ox 58. **d** 59 **p** 60 Ox. Asst Master Abingdon Sch 53-65; C of Dorchester Oxon 59-65; R of Gt Braxted 65-70; R of L Braxted 65-70; R of St Mark E Kilbride 70-74; St Jas Gt Norton Dio Sheff from 74. *Norton Rectory, Sheffield, Yorks.* (Sheff 745066)

WILLIAMS, Martin Inffeld. b 37. SS Coll Cam BA 62. Chich Th Coll 62. **d** 64 **p** 65 Lon. C of Gt Greenford (in c of St Edw Perivale 67-70) 64-70; Tutor at Chich Th Coll 70-75; Vice-Prin 75-77; V of St German Roath Dio Llan from 77. *St German's Clergy House, Metal Street, Roath, Cardiff.* (Cardiff 494488)

WILLIAMS, Maxwell Faraday. Univ of Wales BSc 31. St Mich Coll Llan 31. **d** 32 **p** 33 Llan. C of Treherbert 32-34; New Tredegar (in c of St Paul Abertysswg) 34-39; St Matt U Clapton 39-42; Swaffham Prior 42-47; Chap Reach and Perse Boys' Sch Cam from 42; R of Cheveley Dio Ely from 54; Hon CF (TA) from 59; C-in-c of Kirtling 68-74; Ashley w Silverley Dio Ely from 74; RD of Cheveley 69-76. *Cheveley Rectory, Newmarket, Suff.* (Newmarket 730372)

WILLIAMS, Maxwell Holman Bentley. b 24. Univ of Reading BA (2nd cl Pol Econ) 50. Cudd Coll 56. **d** 58 **p** 59 Sarum. C of Melksham 58-62; V of Erlestoke w E Coulston 62-66; Chap HM Detention Centre Erlestoke 62-67; C-in-c of Erlestoke 66-67; V 67; C-in-c of Gt Cheverell 66-67; R 67; R of Bemerton (w Fugglestone 67-72) 67-75. *1a East Street, Fortuneswell, Portland, Dorset, DT5 1NF.* (Portland 821731)

WILLIAMS, Canon Meredith. b 19. Univ of Wales BA 40. St Mich Coll Llan 40. **d** 42 **p** 43 Swan B. C of St Cath w H Trin Gorseinon 42-47; Llandefeilog 47-48; V of Llanfihangel Rhosycorn 48-54; C of Walton-on-Trent w Rosliston and Coton-in-the-Elms 54-56; V of Baddesley Ensor Dio Birm from 56; RD of Polesworth from 65; Hon Can of Birm from 73; Surr from 78. *Baddesley Ensor Vicarage, Atherstone, Warws, CV9 2BY.* (Atherstone 2149)

WILLIAMS, Mervyn Rees. b 28. Univ of Wales (Swansea) BA (French) 49. St Deiniol's Libr Hawarden 68. **d** 72 **p** 73 St A (APM). C of Llangollen Dio St A from 72. *12 Wern Road, Llangollen, Clwyd.* (0978-860369)

WILLIAMS, Michael John. b 31. St Edm Hall Ox BA (3rd cl Th) 53, MA 57. Wells Th Coll 53. **d** 55 **p** 56 Lon. C of St Mich Wood Green 55-59; St Aldhelm Bedminster 59-62; Witney 62-65; Thatcham 66-70; Perm to Offic Dio Ex 70-81; C of Rainhill Dio Liv from 81. *26 Calder Drive, Rainhill, Mer, L35 0NW.* (051-426 3853)

WILLIAMS, Michael Joseph. b 42. St Jo Coll Dur BA 68. Cranmer Hall Dur 64. **d** 70 Warrington for Liv **p** 71 Liv. C of St Philemon Toxteth Pk 70-75; Team V (w St Gabr) 75-78; Dir of Pastoral Stud St Jo Coll Dur from 78. *St John's College, Durham.*

WILLIAMS, Michael Robert John. b 41. Cranmer Hall Dur 67. **d** 70 **p** 71 Man. C of Middleton 70-73; C-in-c of St Mark's Conv Distr Blackley 73-79; V of St Mark White Moss, Blackley Dio Man from 79. *70 Booth Hall Road, Blackley, Manchester, M9 2BL.* (061-740 7558)

WILLIAMS, Canon Milton Wallace. St Jo Coll Morpeth NSW ACT ThL 30. **d** 31 Armid for Newc **p** 31 Newc. C of St Pet Hamilton 31-34; Singleton 34-36; R of Bullahdelah 36-39; P-in-c of Terrigal 39-41; R 41-43; New Lambton 43-47; E Maitland 47-64; Singleton 64-76; Can of Newc 58-76; Can (Emer) from 77; Commiss Polyn 62-70; Perm to Offic Dio Newc from 76. *90 Hillcrest Street, Terrigal, NSW, Australia 2260.*

WILLIAMS, Norman Francis Lionel. St Aid Coll 37. **d** 40 **p** 41 Wakef. C of Brownhill 40-43; St Phil Litherland 43-47; C-in-c of St Geo Conv Distr Huyton 47-51; V 51-52; St Mary Ince-in-Makerfield 52-57; St Andr Livesey Blackb 57-62; St Ambrose Widnes 62-78. *8 Wellfield, Widnes, Chesh, WA8 9LJ.* (051-420 7314)

WILLIAMS, Norman Henry. b 17. Univ of Bris BA (Th) 43. Qu Coll Birm 77. **d** 77 Bp McKie for Cov **p** 78 Cov (APM). C of Cathl Ch of St Mich City and Dio Cov from 77. *63 Daventry Road, Cheylesmore, Coventry, CV3 5DH.* (Cov 502448)

WILLIAMS, Ogwen Lloyd. Univ of Wales BA 42. St Mich Coll Llan 42. **d** 44 **p** 45 St A. C of Mostyn 44-47; Colwyn 47-50; Connah's Quay 50-56; V of Llanfair-Dyffryn-Clwyd 56-65; Bistre 65-80; Llanarmon-Dyffryn-Ceiriog w Llansantffraid-Glyn-Ceiriog and Pontfadog Dio St A from 80. *Glyn Ceiriog Vicarage, Llangollen, Clwyd.* (Glyn Ceiriog 245)

WILLIAMS, Oscar Dudley. b 19. **d** 81 Fred (APM). Perm to Offic Dio Fred from 81. *495 Regent Street, Fredericton, NB, Canada, E3B 3X6.*

WILLIAMS, Owen David. b 38. SOC 72. **d** 75 **p** 76 S'wark. C of Tatsfield 75-80; All SS Maidstone Dio Cant from 80. *63 College Road, Maidstone, Kent.* (Maidstone 53919)

WILLIAMS, Peris Llewelyn. b 39. St D Coll Lamp BA 59. Qu Coll Birm 59. **d** 62 **p** 63 Ches. C of Upton 62-65; Davenham 65-68; St Andr Grange Runcorn 68-73; Team V of E Runcorn w Halton 73-74; V of Backford 74-80; Witton Dio Ches from 80; Dioc Youth Officer Ches 74-80. *61 Church Road, Northwich, Chesh, CW9 5PB.* (Northwich 2943)

WILLIAMS, Peter David. b 32. Univ of Lon BSc (1st cl Engl) and AKC 56, PhD 62, BD 70. Clifton Th Coll 59. **d** 64 Warrington for Liv **p** 65 Liv. C of St Phil Southport 64-68; Chap Duncan Ho Sch Moffat 70-74; Crawfordton Ho Sch Moniaive 74-75; Starehe Sch Nai from 76. *PO Box 30178, Nairobi, Kenya.*

WILLIAMS, Peter Gregory. b 52. Austr Nat Univ Canberra BA 76, BTh 79. St Jo Coll Morpeth 76. **d** and **p** 79 C & Goulb. C of St Sav Cathl Goulb 79-81; C of St John Wodonga Dio Wang from 81. *25 Tourmaline Drive, Wodonga, Vic, Australia 3690.*

WILLIAMS, Peter John. b 55. Univ of Southn BTh 80. Chich Th Coll 76. **d** 80 **p** 81 Mon. C of Chepstow Dio Mon from 80. *St Christopher's House, Bulwark Road, Bulwark, Chepstow, Gwent, NP6 5JW.*

WILLIAMS, Peter Hurrell. b 34. Keble Coll Ox 3rd cl Cl Mods 56, BA (3rd cl Lit Hum) 58, MA 61. Tyndale Hall Bris 62. **d** 64 Aston for Birm **p** 65 Birm. C of Sparkbrook 64-67; St Pet Rushden 67-70; V of Clapham Pk 70-78; R of Stanford-le-Hope w Mucking Dio Chelmsf from 78. *Rectory, Stanford-le-Hope, Essex.* (03756-2271)

WILLIAMS, Peter Llewellyn. b 46. ACT ThL 73. Ridley Coll Melb 73. **d** 74 **p** 75 Melb. C of Hawthorn 74-76; Toorak 76; Brighton 76-79; R of Maitland Dio Willoch from 79. *Rectory, Alice Street, Maitland, S Australia 5573.* (322425)

WILLIAMS, Peter Ottrey. b 47. Univ of Cant NZ BA 68, MA 70. Univ of Leeds BA (Th) 72. Coll of Resurr Mirfield 70. **d** 73 Dorchester for Ch Ch **p** 73 Ch Ch. C of Avonside 73-74; Timaru 74-78; Chap Univ of Cant Ch Ch 75-78; V of Glenmark-Waikari Dio Ch Ch from 78. *Vicarage, Waikari, NZ.* (Waikari 37)

WILLIAMS, Peter Rodney. Chich Th Coll 60. **d** 62 **p** 63 Chich. C of Seaford w Sutton 62-65; C-in-c of Wivelsfield 65-72; V of St Jo Evang Meads, Eastbourne Dio Chich from 72. *St John's Vicarage, Meads, Eastbourne, Sussex.* (Eastbourne 21105)

WILLIAMS, Philip Charles. St Jo Coll Auckld LTh 40. **d** 34 **p** 35 Melan. Hd of Vureas Sch Melan 34-41; C of St Mich AA Ch Ch 41-42; V of Wakatipu 42-47; Tuapeka 47-56; Waikouaiti 56-60; Gore 60-70; Green I 70-76; Perm to Offic Dios Dun and Ch Ch from 76. *55 Arnold Street, Sumner, Christchurch 6, NZ.*

WILLIAMS, Philip James. b 52. St Chad's Coll Dur BA 73. Coll of Resurr Mirfield 74. **d** 76 **p** 77 Lich. C of Stoke-upon-Trent Dio Lich 76-80; Team V and Chap N Staffs Poly from 80. *Polytechnic Chaplaincy, Seaford Street, Shelton, Stoke-on-Trent, ST4 2ET.* (Stoke/Trent 48456)

WILLIAMS, Philip Morgan. St D Coll Lamp BA 12. Jes Coll Ox BA (4th cl Th) 14, MA 19. St Mich Coll Llan 15. **d** 15 Ches **p** 16 Bp Mercer for Ches. C of St Jo Bapt Crewe 15-17; St Pet Gt Worc 19-22; All SS Bromsgrove 22-24; V of Thorner 24-59. *Address temp unknown.*

WILLIAMS, Pryce Owen. b 08. Worc Ordin Coll. **d** 63 **p** 64 Roch. C of Lamorbey 63-65; V of Childerditch w L Warley 65-69; R of Latchingdon w Mundon (w N Fambridge from 72) 69-73. *2 Bryn Estyn, Leeswood, Mold, Clwyd.*

WILLIAMS, Pythias Joseph Bartholomew. St Aug Coll Cant 58. **d** 59 **p** 60 Sier L. C of St Geo Cathl Sier L 59-60; H Trin Freetown 60-61; V of St John Freetown 61-64; Regent 64-67; Gen Sec Dio Sier L from 67; C of St Geo Cathl Freetown Dio Sier L from 67. *32 Easton Street, Freetown, Sierra Leone.*

WILLIAMS, Ramsay Thomas Patrick. b 45. St Barn Coll Adel 70. **d** and **p** 73 Bal. L to Offic Dio Bal 73-74; C of Horsham 74-77; S Bal 77; R of Balmoral 77-81; S Bal Dio Bal from 81. *Holy Trinity Rectory, Yarrowee Street, Sebastopol, Vic, Australia 3356.*

WILLIAMS, Ray. b 23. St Aid Coll 56. **d** 58 **p** 59 Birm [f CMS Lay Missr] C of Sparkhill 58-60; CMS Area Sec for Dios St Alb and Chelmsf 60-65; V of Shenstone 65-73; P-in-c of St Chris Redwoodtown, Blenheim 73-78; V of Wakefield and Motupiko Dio Nel from 78; P-in-c of Murchison Dio Nel from 79. *Vicarage, Edward Street, Wakefield, NZ.* (Nel 28134)

WILLIAMS, Raymond Howel. b 27. St Jo Coll Cam 3rd cl Engl Trip pt i 46, BA (2nd cl Geog Trip pt i) 49, MA 51. Ball Coll Ox BLitt 63. **d** 73 Repton for Derby **p** 74 Liv. C of St Pet Derby 73-75; Cockfosters 75-81; V of K Chas Mart S Mymms Dio St Alb from 81. *40 Dugdale Hill Lane, Potters Bar, Herts, EN6 2DW.* (Potters Bar 54219)

WILLIAMS, Ven Reginald Ottrey. Univ of NZ BA 39. **d** 40 **p** 41 Ch Ch. C of Addington 40-42; P-in-c of Ross w S Westland 42-45; Linwood 45-49; V of Hokitika 49-52; Lincoln 52-55; Opawa 55-64; Hon Can of Ch Ch 62-68; V of Papanui 64-76; Archd of Rangiora and Westland from 68; V of Rakaia Dio Ch Ch from 76. *Vicarage, Rakaia, Canterbury, NZ.* (Rakaia 32)

WILLIAMS, Richard Elmsley. b 51. Univ of New Engl Austr BRuralSc 74. Univ of Lon MSc 76. Fitzw Coll Cam BA 79. Ridley Hall Cam 79. **d** 80 Kens for Lon **p** 81 Lon. C of St Steph E Twickenham Dio Lon from 80. *17 Sandycombe Road, E Twickenham, Middx, TW1 2LU.*

WILLIAMS, Richard Elwyn. b 57. Univ of Hull BA (Th) 79. Coll of the Resurr Mirfield 79. **d** 81 Ches. C of St Geo Altrincham Dio Ches from 81. *18 Hawarden Road, Altrincham, WA14 1NG.* (061 928 5897)

WILLIAMS, Canon Richard Glyndwr. b 18. St D Coll Lamp BA 39, BD 50. **d** 41 **p** 42 St D. C of Kidwelly 41-46; Llandudno 46-52; R of Trefiw w Llanrhychwyn 52-55; V of Llandinorwic 55-62; Warden Ch Hostel Ban 62-70; Exam Chap to Bp of Ban 63-70; Can and Prec of Ban Cathl from 68; R of Llanbeblig w Caernarfon (w Betws Garmon and Waenfawr from 71) 70-81; V of Llandysilio (Menai Bridge) Dio Ban from 81. *Vicarage, Menai Bridge, Anglesey, LL59 5DR.* (Menai Bridge 712426)

WILLIAMS, Richard Henry Lowe. b 31. Univ of Liv BA (2nd cl Engl) 52. K Coll NS BD (2nd cl) 64. Ridley Hall, Cam 54. **d** 56 **p** 57 York. C of St Andr w St Pet Drypool 56-59; Ch Fred 59-64; V of St Athanasius Kirkdale 64-68; R of Much Woolton 68-79; Croft w Southworth Dio Liv from 79; Dioc Communications Officer from 79. *Christ Church Rectory, Lady Lane, Croft, Warrington, Lancs, WA3 7AU.* (Culcheth 2294)

WILLIAMS, Richard John. b 39. St Jo Coll Auckld 69. **d** 71 **p** 73 Dun. C of St John Invercargill 71-76; V of Milton-tuapeka 76-79; Maniototo 79-81; C of St Matt City and Dio Dun from 81. *33 Carnarvon Street, Dunedin, NZ.* (30-521)

WILLIAMS, Richard Pierce. b 09. Univ of Wales BSc 31. St Mich Coll Llan 32. **d** 35 Bp Wentworth Shields for Ban for St A **p** 36 St A. C of Minera 35-37; Llanfaes w Penmon w Llangoed and Llanfihangel-din-Sylwy 37-45; R of Dolbenmaen w Llanfihangel-y-Pennant 45-55; V of Caerhun (w Llangelynin from 59) 55-62; Betws-yn-Rhos 62-73. *Arfryn, Llewelyn Avenue, Glan Conwy, Clwyd.* (Glan Conwy 464)

WILLIAMS, Canon Richard William. b 16. TCD Reid Sizar 34, BA (1st cl Ment and Mor Sc Mod) Mod Pri and Wray Pri 38, Robt King Mem Pri 39, MA and BD 46. **d** 39 Bp Kennedy for Down **p** 40 Down. C of St Donard Belf 39-43; Bangor Abbey 43-47; Sec of SCM in Schs in Ireland 47-49; I of Finvoy w Rasharkin 49-57; R of St Paul Belf 57-70; Exam Chap to Bp of Connor from 62; R of St Mark Ballysillan Belf Dio Connor from 70; Can and Preb of St Patr Cathl Dub from 73. *St Mark's Rectory, 119 Ligoniol Road, Belfast, BT14 8DN.*

WILLIAMS, Robert. b 20. Univ of Wales BA 43. St Mich Coll Llan. **d** 45 Llan for Ban **p** 46 Ban. C of Holyhead 45-55; R of Llangwnnadl w Penllech and Bryncroes Dio Ban from 55; RD of Lleyn from 76. *Llangwnnadl Rectory, Pwllheli, Gwyn, LL53 8NL.* (Tudweiliog 249)

WILLIAMS, Robert. b 07. **d** 70 Ban. Hon C of Glanadda w Penrhosgarnedd 70-77; Perm to Offic Dio Ban from 77. *38 Belmont Avenue, Bangor, Gwynedd, LL57 2NT.* (Bangor 4683)

WILLIAMS, Robert David. Late Exhib of St D Coll Lamp BA 32. **d** 33 **p** 34 Ban. C of Llandinorwic 33-38; Meyllterne (in c of Bryncroes) 38-42; R of Llanddona w Llanicstyn 42-48; V of Llanerchymedd w Rhodogeidio and Gwredog 48-57; Dolwyddelan 57-62; Llandysilio 62-75. *31 Parc Henblas, Llanfairfechan, Gwynedd.*

WILLIAMS, Robert Edward. b 17. Univ of Wales 42. St Mich Coll Llan 45. **d** 47 **p** 48 Ban. C of Llangeinwen w Llangaffo and Llanfair yn y Cwmmwd 47-52; Machynlleth w Llanwrin 52-55; V of Llanwnda w Llanfaglan Dio Ban from 55. *Llanwnda Vicarage, Caernarvon, Gwyn, LL54 7YL.* (Llanwnda 830543)

WILLIAMS, Robert Edward. b 50. Univ of Wales (Bangor) Dipl Th 71, (Cardiff) BD 74. St Mich AA Llan 72. **d** 74 **p** 75 St A. C of Flint 74-77; Asst Chap Sandbach Sch 79-80; Chap from 80. *151 Ruskin Road, Grewe, Chesh.*

WILLIAMS, Robert Edward. b 42. Univ of Ex BA (2nd cl Th) 63. Lich Th Coll. **d** 65 **p** 66 Lich. C of St Paul Wednesbury 65-67; Whitchurch 67-69; P-in-c of Whixall 69-72; P-in-c of Edstaston 69-72; CF from 72. *c/o Ministry of Defence, Bagshot Park, Bagshot, Surrey.*

WILLIAMS, Robert Ellis Greenleaf. b 12. St D Coll Lamp BA (3rd cl Engl) 34. Lich Th Coll 34. **d** 36 **p** 37 Ox. C of S Banbury Oxon 36-39; R of Wongan Hills 39-44; Qu Pk 44-48; Bayswater 48-54 (All in W Austr) Croydon w Clopton 54-58; V of Tadlow w E Hatley 54-58; V of Hatley St Geo 54-58; St Ambrose Oldham 58-66; St Aid Sudden Rochdale 66-75; Team V of H Trin Weston-super-Mare 75-78; P-in-c of All S Castleton Heywood 78-80. *36 Moor Park Avenue, Castleton, Rochdale, Lancs, OL11 3JG.* (0706-356582)

WILLIAMS, Robert George Dibdin. b 20. St Mich Coll Llan 56. **d** 58 **p** 59 St A. C of Welshpool 58-63; R of Nannerch (w Cilcain from 68) 63-75; V of Gwersyllt Dio St A from 75. *Gwersyllt Vicarage, Wrexham, Clwyd.* (Wrexham 756391)

WILLIAMS, Robert Gwynne. b 15. St D Coll Lamp BA 38. **d** 41 **p** 42 St D. C of Tenby 41-51; V of Goodrich w Marstow and Welsh Bicknor 51-81. *c/o Goodrich Vicarage, Ross-on-Wye, Herefs.* (Symonds Yat 890285)

WILLIAMS, Robert Hugh Mansfield. b 17. Selw Coll Cam BA 41, MA 44. Edin Th Coll 41. **d** 44 **p** 45 Edin. C of St Mark Portobello 44-48; St Jo Evang E Dulwich 48-54; V of Harston w Hauxton 54-60; PC of St Jo Div Gainsborough 60-65; V of St Greg Gt Cant 65-74; Sibertswold w Coldred Dio Cant from 74. *Shepherdswell Vicarage, Dover, Kent.* (Shepherdswell 830245)

WILLIAMS, Robert John. b 51. Univ Coll of N Wales (Bangor) BEducn 73. Univ Coll Cardiff BD 76. St Mich AA Llan 73. **d** 76 **p** 77 Swan B. C of Swansea 76-78; Chap Univ Coll Swansea from 78. *University Anglican Chaplaincy, House of the Good Shepherd, Eastmoor, Clyne Common, Swansea SA3 3JA.*

WILLIAMS, Robert John. b 23. **d** 81 St D. C of Newcastle Emlyn w Llandyfriog and Troedyraur Dio St D from 81. *58 Derwen Gardens, Newcastle Emlyn, Dyfed.*

WILLIAMS, Robert Loxton. b 09. ALCD 31. **d** 32 **p** 34 Lich. C of St Matt Tipton 32-35; Heworth and St Mary Castlegate w St Mich Spurriergate York 35-38; C-in-c of St Geo Conv Distr Marfleet 38-46; V of Whitwick St Geo w Swannington 46-57; R of Aspenden w Layston and Buntingford 57-64; C of Elmdon w Bickenhill 64-68; Belper 68-74; Perm to Offic Dio Derby from 74. *24 Ashes Avenue, Hulland Ward, Derby, DE6 3FT.* (Ashbourne 70727)

WILLIAMS, Robert Wilfrid Callard. b 16. St D Coll Lamp BA (2nd cl Cl) 37. Chich Th Coll 37. **d** 39 **p** 40 St D. C of Fishguard w Llanstinan 39-41; Bettws w Ammanford 41-48; V of Slebech 48-57; Letterston 57-63; Manorbier Dio St D from 63. *Vicarage, Manorbier, Tenby, Dyfed.* (Manorbier 247)

WILLIAMS, Roger Anthony. b 54. St D Coll Lamp BA 76. Qu Coll Birm 76. **d** 78 **p** 79 St D. C of Llanelli Dio St D from 78. *36 James Street, Llanelli, Dyfed, Wales.*

WILLIAMS, Roger Arthur. b 15. St Pet Hall Ox BA (3rd cl Th) 37, MA 45. Wycl Hall Ox 37. **d** 38 **p** 39 Truro. C of St Budock 38-40; Kenwyn 40-42; CF (EC) 42-46; CF (R of O) 50-70; Succr of Truro Cathl 46-47; V of St Budock 47-53; Kenwyn 53-58; RD of Carnmarth S 52-53; Cobham 66-76; R of Hartley 58-76; Chap Bromley Coll Kent from 76. *c/o The College, Bromley, Kent, BR1 1PE.* (01-460 4712)

WILLIAMS, Roger Grant. b 43. Oak Hill Coll Lon 68. **d** 73 Bp Bryant for Perth **p** 73 Perth. C of Mt Lawley 73-75; Inglewood 75-78; L to Offic Dio Melb from 79. *34 Scott Grove, Caulfield South, Vic, Australia 3162.* (578 2537)

WILLIAMS, Roger Stewart. b 54. Qu Coll Cam 75, MA 79. Wycl Hall Ox 76. **d** 79 **p** 80 Birm. C of St Paul Hamstead Dio Birm from 79. *87 Birmingham Road, Great Barr, Birmingham, B43 6NU.* (021-357 3969)

WILLIAMS, Ronald Hywell. St D Coll Lamp BA 62. **d** 63 **p** 64 Ban. C of Machynlleth 63-66; Barmouth 66-69; Hawarden 69-73; V of Llansantfraid-Glan-Conway w Eglwysbach 73-76; Rhosllanerchrugog Dio St A from 77. *Rhos Vicarage, Johnstown, Clwyd.* (Rhos 840065)

WILLIAMS, Ronald John Chantler. b 38. Univ of Adel BA 63. Univ of Bris MSc 74. St Jo Coll Morpeth ACT ThL 59. **d** 63 **p** 64 Adel. C of Toorak Gardens 63-64; L to Offic Dio Syd 65. Dom Chap to Bp of Polyn 66-67; Exam Chap 67-69; Asst P of Labasa 67-69; V 69-71; Perm to Offic Dio Bris 72-74; Dean and V of Suva Cathl 75-79; Exam Chap to Bp of Polyn 75-79; R of Campbelltown Dio Adel from 79. *640 Lower North East Road, Campbelltown, S Australia 5074.* (337 2993)

WILLIAMS, Canon Rowan Douglas. b 50. Ch Coll Cam BA 71, MA 75. Wadham Coll Ox DPhil 75. Coll of Resurr Mirfield 75. **d** 77 Huntingdon for Ely **p** 78 Ely. Tutor Westcott Ho Cam 77-80; Rep of Internat Angl Th and Doctrinal Comm from 80; Can Th of Leic Cathl from 81; Lect Univ of Cam and Hon C of St Geo Chesterton Dio Ely from 80. *39 St Kilda Avenue, Cambridge, CB4 2PN.*

WILLIAMS, Roy. Ely Th Coll 58. Dipl Th (Lon) 60. **d** 60 **p** 61 Southw. C of Daybrook 60-63; V of St Jo Bapt Bilborough 63-73; Arnold Dio Southw from 73. *Arnold Vicarage, Nottingham, NG5 8HJ.* (Nottingham 262946)

WILLIAMS, Royce. b 35. Univ of Leeds BA (1st cl Lat) 56. St Steph Ho Ox 58. **d** 60 **p** 61 Man. C of St Benedct Ardwick 60-62; St Thos Bedford Leigh 62-64; V of St Pet Blackb 64-68; Asst Master VIth Form Coll Preston 68-75; Chap W R Tuson Coll Preston 75-78; L to Offic Dio Blackb 68-78; V of St Cath Burnley Dio Blackb from 78; P-in-c of St Alb Burnley Dio Blackb 78-81; V (w St Paul) from 81. *St Catherine's Vicarage, Todmorden Road, Burnley, Lancs, BB11 3ER.* (Burnley 23351)

WILLIAMS, Samuel Glanffrwd. Univ of Wales BA (2nd cl Engl) 23. Wycl Hall Ox 65. **d** 65 Dorch for Ox **p** 65 Ox. C of Chipping Norton w Over Norton 65-66; C-in-c of Akeley w Leckhampstead 66-72. *Fenton House, Banbury Road, Chipping Norton, Oxon.*

WILLIAMS, Preb Sidney Austen. b 12. CVO 79. St Cath Coll Cam 3rd cl Engl Trip pt i 35, BA (2nd cl Anthrop Trip) 36, MA 56. Westcott Ho Cam 36. **d** 37 **p** 38 Lon. C of St Paul Harringay 37-40; Chap Toc H 40-48; C of All H Barking-by-the-Tower 45-46; Perm to Offic at St Martin-in-the-Fileds Lon 46-48; C 49-50; V of St Alb Westbury Pk Clifton 51-56; St Martin-in-the-Fields Trafalgar Square Dio Lon from 56; Chap to HM the Queen from 61; Preb of St Paul's Cathl Lon from 73. *5 St Martin's Place, WC2N 4JJ.* (01-930 1862)

WILLIAMS, Canon Simeon Dixon. Fourah Bay Coll 46. **d** 48 **p** 50 Sier L. Miss Dio Sier L 48; C of H Trin Freetown 48-50; Glouc 50-52; V of Lunsar 52-57 and 59-66; C of Attercliffe Yorks 57-59; V of Wel Sier L 66-74; St Patr Kissy Dio Sier L from 74; Can of Sier L from 75. *Box 579, Freetown, Sierra Leone.* (Freetown 23644)

WILLIAMS, Stephen. b 49. Univ of NSW BA 73. Fitzw Coll Cam BA 77. Ridley Hall Cam 75. **d** 78 Kamp **p** 79 Kens for Lon. Tutor Bp Tucker Th Coll Mukono 78; C of H Trin Brompton Rd Kens Dio Lon from 79. *St Paul's Flat, Onslow Square, SW7.*

WILLIAMS, Stephen Geoffrey. b 54. Univ of Nottm BTh 79. St Jo Coll Nottm LTh 79. **d** 79 **p** 80 Liv. C of St Paul Skelmersdale 79-81; St Mathias Burley Dio Ripon from 81. *33 Stanmore Crescent, Burley, Leeds, LS4 2RY.* (Leeds 781920)

WILLIAMS, Stephen Heath. b 51. Melb Coll of Div LTh 75. **d** 74 **p** 75 C & Goulb. C of St Paul Canberra 74-76; C of St Francis Leigh Park 76-78; R of Bribbaree 78-80; Holbrook Dio C & Goulb from 80. *St Paul's Rectory, Young Street, Holbrook, NSW, Australia 2644.*

WILLIAMS, Stephen James. b 52. Univ of Lon BSc 73. Ridley Hall Cam 73. **d** 78 Chelmsf **p** 79 Barking for Chelmsf. C of Waltham Abbey Dio Chelmsf from 78. *5a Greenyard, Waltham Abbey, Essex, EN9 1RD.*

WILLIAMS, Stephen Reginald. b 52. St Mich Ho Crafers 72. **d** 74 **p** 75 N Queensld. C of All SS Ayr 74-80; Ch Ch St Laur City and Dio Syd from 80. *507 Pitt Street, Sydney, NSW, Australia 200.*

WILLIAMS, Terence. b 36. Univ of Wales (Abth) BSc 57. Univ of Wales (Cardiff) MA 67. Univ of Aston Birm PhD 71. Glouc Ordin Course 78. **d** 81 Tewkesbury for Glouc **p** 81 Glouc (NSM). C of Deerhurst w Apperley and Forthampton w Chaceley Dio Glouc from 81. *Bryony, Prince Crescent, Corse, Staunton, Gloucester, GL19 3RF.*

WILLIAMS, Thomas Alun. b 08. Late Scho and Exhib of St D Coll Lamp BA (3rd cl Engl) 28, BD 37. St Mich Coll Llan 29. **d** 31 Ban for Llan **p** 32 Llan. C of Cadoxton-juxta-Neath 31-35; Cadoxton-juxta-Barry 35-36; Neath w Llantwit 36-41; V of Eglwys-Oen-Duw 41-44; R of Ilston w Pennard 44-51; V of Pool 51-54; Holt 54-55; St Andr Starbeck 55-68; Surr 65-68; V of Hay 68-70; V of Witton E 70-73; L to Offic Dio Llan from 73. *36 Baron Road, Penarth, S Glam.*

WILLIAMS, Thomas Avery. b 16. St D Coll Lamp BA 40. **d** 46 **p** 47 Swan B. C of Llanelly 46-52; Llansamlet 52-54; R of Maesmynis w Llanddewi'r Cwm and Llangynog 54-62; Llanelly Dio Swan B from 62. *Llanelly Rectory, Gilwern, Abergavenny, Gwent.* (Gilwern 830280)

WILLIAMS, Thomas Brian. St Jo Coll Ox BA 37, MA 44. Cudd Coll 39. **d** 40 **p** 41 Man. C of St Mary Leigh 40-43; Ascen Vic Dks 43-46; Asst Chap and Master St Edw Sch Ox 46-57; L to Offic Dio Ox 46-57; Dio Chelmsf 46-49; C of St Mary Abbots Kens 57-59; Chap and Asst Master Shrewsbury Sch 59-60; Lancing Coll 60-61; KS Cant 61-66; L to Offic Dio Cant 61-66; V of Hough-on-the-Hill Dio Linc from 66; R of Hougham w Marston Dio Linc from 67. *Hough-on-the-Hill Vicarage, Grantham, Lincs.* (Honington 269)

WILLIAMS, Thomas Bruce. b 41. Oak Hill Coll 74. **d** 76 **p** 77 Truro. C of Liskeard w St Keyne and St Pinnock 76-79; Min of Bush Ch Aid S Paraburdoo 79-80; C of W Pilbara Dio NW Austr from 80. *Box 1, Dampier, W Australia 6713.*

WILLIAMS, Canon Thomas Gerald. b 14. Ex Coll Ox 32, Jun Stud 33, BA (2nd cl Mod Hist) 35, MA 39. Chich Th Coll 35. **d** 37 **p** 38 Cant. C of Teynham 37-44; All SS Whitstable 44-49; V of Sturry 49-56; C-in-c of Fordwich 49-52; P-in-c of Sevington 56-79; R of Willesborough (w Hinxhill 62-79) 56-80; C-in-c of Hinxhill 59-62; Chap Willesborough Hosp 56-80; Hon Can of Cant 73-81; Can (Emer) from 81. *2 Heathfield Court, Heathfield Road, Ashford, Kent, TN24 8QD.* (Ashford 39328)

WILLIAMS, Thomas Glaslyn. b 08. Univ of Wales BA 45. St Aid Coll. **d** 40 **p** 41 Ban. C of Festiniog w Maentwrog 40-43; Llanidan w Llanddaniel Fab and Llanedwen 43-48; V of Pentir w Glasinfryn 48-62; R of Llangristiolus w Cerrig Ceinwen and Trewalchmai Dio Ban 62-69. *Ael-y-Bryn Valley, Holyhead, LL65 3EL.* (Valley 724)

WILLIAMS, Thomas Henry. b 1893. Univ of Birm BA 21. Handsworth Coll Lich Th Coll 23. **d** 23 **p** 24 Win. C of Ch Ch Gosport 23-26; Asst Chap Br Embassy Ch Paris 26-34; Chap at Lille and Croix 34-40; CF 40-54; SCF 50-54; Hon CF from 54. *Marylands Home, 43 Shrubend Road, Colchester, Essex.*

WILLIAMS, Canon Thomas John. St Francis Coll Brisb 59. **d** 61 **p** 62 N Queensld. C of St Jas Cathl Townsville 61-66; Gulliver Townsville 66-67; R of Mareeba 67-72; N Mackay Dio N Queensld from 72; Can of N Queensld from 74. *Rectory, North Mackay, Queensland, Australia.* (079-575380)

WILLIAMS, Thomas Trevor. Univ of Wales BA 35, St Mich Coll Llan 35. **d** 36 **p** 38 Llan. C of Llantwit Fardre 36-41; CF (EC) 41-47; Hon CF from 47; C of All S Harlesden 47-48; Org Sec for CCCS 48-51; V of St John Crossens 51-72. *The Club House, Watling Street, Bletchley, Bucks.*

WILLIAMS, Tom David. b 19. St D Coll Lamp BA 41. St Mich Coll Llan 41. **d** 43 St A For Ban **p** 45 Ban. C of Llanbeblig 43-47; Aberdovey 47-49; Llanengan w Llangian 49; Llandegai 49-53; R of Llangybi w Llanarmon 53-60; V of Llanidloes 60-75; C-in-c (V from 72) of Llangurig 66-75; RD of Arwystli 73-75; R of Criccieth w Treflys Dio Ban from 75. *Rectory, Criccieth, Gwynedd.* (Criccieth 2662)

WILLIAMS, Trefor Clough. St Mich Coll Llan. **d** 54 St A for Ban **p** 55 Ban. C of Llandudno 54-57; W Kirby 57-59; Chap Columbia Coast Miss New Westmr 59-62; R of Campbell River 62-70; I 74-77; Cortes I 66-70; R of Quathiaski Cove 67-70; St Martin-in-the-Fields Vic 70-77; on leave 77-80; C of St John Vic and Chap Vanc I Correction Centre BC from 80. *1611 Quadra Street, Victoria, BC, Canada.*

WILLIAMS, Trevor Russell. b 48. TCD BA 71. Univ of Nottm BA 73. St Jo Coll Nottm 71. **d** 74 **p** 75 Ox. C of Maidenhead 74-77; Chap QUB from 78. *12 Cloreen Park, Belfast, N Ireland.*

WILLIAMS, Trevor Stanley Morlais. b 38. Jes Coll Ox BA 63. Fitzw Coll Cam BA 67. Univ of E Afr MA 67. Westcott Ho Cam 65. **d** 67 **p** 68 Bris. Asst Chap Univ of Bris 67-70; C of St Paul Clifton 67-70; Chap and Fell of Trin Coll Ox from 70. *c/o Trinity College, Oxford.*

WILLIAMS, Vernon Davidson. b 28. **d** 75 Bunb. C of Bridgetown 75-77; Perm to Offic Dio Perth from 77. *15 Cunningham Street, Merredin, W Australia 6415.*

WILLIAMS, Vincent Handley. b 24. St Deiniol's Libr Hawarden 76. **d** 78 **p** 79 Ches. C of Barrow 78-.81; Dodleston Dio Ches from 81. *25 Manor Drive, Great Boughton, Chester, CH3 5QN.* (0344-41258)

WILLIAMS, Canon Walter George Herbert. b 19. TCD BA 40, MA 51, Div Test (1st cl) 41. **d** 42 **p** 43 Arm. C of Derryloran 42-44; Armagh 44-50; R of Caledon (w Brantry from 56) 50-61; Donaghmore w Donaghmore U Dio Arm from 61; RD of Aghaloo from 65; Can of Arm from 79. *Rectory, Castlecaulfield, Dungannon, Co Tyrone, N Ireland.* (Donaghmore 214)

WILLIAMS, Canon Walter Haydn. b 31. St D Coll Lamp BA (1st cl Hist) 53. Selw Coll Cam BA (2nd cl Th Trip pt ii) 55, MA 60. St Mich Coll Llan 55. **d** 56 **p** 57 St A. C of Denbigh 56-58; V Cho of St A Cathl 58-61; R of Llanfyllin 61-68; V of Northop 68-73; Mold Dio St A from 73; Exam Chap to Bp of St A from 71; Cursal Can of St A Cathl from 76; RD of Mold from 79; Prec of St A Cathl from 81. *Vicarage, Mold, Clwyd, CH7 1BW.* (Mold 2960)

WILLIAMS, Walter Stephen. b 52. Brock Univ Ont BA 75. Wycl Coll Tor 76. **d** 78 **p** 79 Fred. C of Bright Dio Fred 78-79; I from 79. *Zealand Station, NB, Canada, E0H 1X0.*

WILLIAMS, Watkin. St D Coll Lamp BA 43. St Mich Coll Llan. **d** 44 **p** 45 Ban. C of Llangeinwen w Llangaffo and Llanfair yn y Cwmmwd 44-47; Llangefni w Tregaian 47-53; R of Heneglwys w Trewalchmai 53-62; Ffestiniog w Maentwrog 62-67. *c/o Dinas Bran School, Llangollen, Clwyd.*

WILLIAMS, William Alfred. b 12. Univ of Wales BA (2nd cl Engl) 33. Jes Coll Ox BA 35, MA 39. St Mich Coll Llan 35. **d** 36 **p** 37 St A. C of Bistre 36-40; CF (EC) 40-46; V of Westwood 46-58; RD of Kenilworth 57-58; R of Ordsall 58-75; C-in-c of St Helen Grove 62-75; Perm to Offic Dio Southw from 76. *35 Cow Lane, Bramcote, Beeston, Nottingham, NG9 3DJ.*

WILLIAMS, William Arwyn. b 15. Univ of Wales (Abth) BA 37. Clifton Th Coll 38. **d** 40 **p** 41 Chelmsf. C of Good Shepherd Collier Row 40-42; CF (EC) 42-48; CF 48-72; SCF 52-60; DACG 60-65; ACG 65-72; Hon Chap to HM the Queen from 69; Chap Sarum Group Hosps from 72. *Lansdowne House, Manor Road, Salisbury, Wilts.* (Salisbury 4925)

WILLIAMS, Canon William Cynwyd Christopher. b 13. St D Coll Lamp BA 33. St Mich Coll Llan 34. **d** 36 **p** 37 Swan B. C of Clydach 36-39; L to Offic Dio Swan B from 39; Org Sec CMS for Dios Llan Mon Swan B and St D 44-53; V of Llandilo Talybont 53-75; Can of Brecon Cathl from 71; RD of Swansea 72-77; RD of Llwchwr 77-81; V of Penllergaer 75-81; Can Treas of Brecon Cathl 78-81; *32 Whitland Close, Penlan, Swansea, W Glam, SA5 7JS.*

WILLIAMS, Canon William David Conwyl. b 09. MBE 43. OBE 52. St D Coll Lamp BA 32. **d** 32 Malmesbury for Bris **p** 33 Bris. C of St Sav Woolcott Pk Redland Bris 32-35; CF 35-60; Hon Chap to HM the Queen 57-60; CF (R of O) 60-69; R of Devizes 60-77; Surr from 60; RD of Devizes 73-77; Can and Preb of Sarum Cathl from 74; Master of St Nich Hosp Salisbury from 77. *The Master's House, St Nicholas' Hospital, Salisbury, Wilts, SP1 2SW.* (0722-6874)

WILLIAMS, William Harvey Neil. St Chad's Coll Regina. **d** and **p** 55 Niag. C of Niag Falls 55-61; I of Harriston 61-63; Falmouth 63-65; Arichat 65-67; L to Offic Dio Niag 77-78; Hon C of Ascen Hamilton Dio Niag from 78. *57 Forest Avenue, Hamilton, Ont., Canada.* (416-528 2237)

WILLIAMS, William John. b 23. Fitzw Ho Cam BA 50, MA 55, Wycl Hall Ox 54. **d** 54 **p** 55 Leic. C of H Trin Hinckley 54-56; R of Bruntingthorpe 56-59; CF 59-69; V of Cholsey 69-73. *48 Newton Close, Langley, Slough, Berks, SL3 8DD.*

WILLIAMS, William John. Fitzw Ho Cam BA 50, MA 55. Wycl Hall, Ox 54. **d** 54 **p** 55 Leic. C of H Trin Hinckley 54-56; R of Bruntingthorpe 56-59; CF 59-69; V of Cholsey 69-73. *Address temp unknown.*

WILLIAMS, William Morgan. St D Coll Lamp BA 35. **d** 36 **p** 37 St A. C of Llangollen 36-40; LPr Dio Heref (in c of Hanwood) 40-44; C of St Osw Oswestry 44-48; V of Kinnerley w Melverley 48-61; Baschurch 61-75; L to Offic Dio Lich from 75. *8 Rosehill Close, Whittington, Oswestry, Shropshire, SY11 4DY.*

WILLIAMS-HUNTER, Ian Roy. b 44. Trin Coll Bris 71. **d** 73 **p** 74 S'wark. C of H Trin Redhill 73-75; C of Deane 76-79; R of Hartshorne Dio Derby from 79. *74 Woodville Road, Hartshorne, Burton-on-Trent, Staffs, DE11 7ET.* (B-o-T 217866)

WILLIAMS-JONES, Griffith. b 13. Edin Th Coll 41. **d** 43 **p** 44 Glas. C of St Marg Newlands 43-47; St Mich Llanrug (in c of St Gabr Cwm-y-Glo) 47-49; Llanddaniel w Llanedwen and Llanidan 49-50; Ripley (in c of St John) 50-52; PC of Langley Mill 52-60; V of King's Bromley 60-77. *3 Beech Avenue, Manor Road, Kings Bromley, Burton-on-Trent, Staffs, DE13 7HP.* (Yoxall 472338)

WILLIAMSON, Alfred Michael. b 28. Kelham Th Coll 53. **d** 58 **p** 59 Southw. C of St Geo Nottm 58-64; V of St Geo Mart Truro 64-73; V of St Agnes Dio Truro from 73. *Vicarage, St Agnes, Cornw, TR5 0SE.* (St Agnes 2328)

WILLIAMSON, Ven Alfred Norman. **d** 09 **p** 10 Bath. C of Forbes 09-10; All SS Cathl Bath 10-11; P-in-c of Geurie 11-12; Asst Min of St Thos Balmain W 12-13; C of Singleton 13-14; R of Wallsend w Plattsburgh 14-18; R of Stockton 18-26; Dom Chap to Bp of Newc 33-62; R of St John Newc 26-38; Org Sec Dio Newc 37-39; Hon Can of Newc Cathl 38-43 and 58-62; Can 43-58; R of Glouc 39-41; Stanton Chap Dio Newc 41-43 and 50-62; R of E Maitland 43-47; Commiss in Austr to Bp of Polyn 43-62; Archd of Maitland 49-51; Newc 51-62; Archd (Emer) from 62; Perm to Offic Dio Newc from 69. *c/o Diocesan Registry, Newcastle, NSW 2300, Australia.*

WILLIAMSON, Anthony William. b 33. OBE 77. Trin Coll Ox BA 56, MA 60. Cudd Coll 56. **d** 60 **p** 61 Ox. Hon C of Cowley Dio Ox from 60. *33 The Grates, Cowley, Oxford, OX4 3LJ.* (Oxford 777827)

WILLIAMSON, Claude Charles Horace. K Coll Lon. **d** 24 **p** 25 abp Butt. Rec into Angl Commun 6 July 39. Perm to Offic at St Leon Shoreditch 39-40; Actg C of St Mary Kenton 40-41; St Thos Regent Street 41-42; Perm to Offic Dio Lon 42-43; C of St Jo Evang Hammersmith 43-44; Perm to Offic Dio Lon 44-46 and from 50; Hon C of St Alphege S'wark 64-71. *Address temp unknown.*

WILLIAMSON, Edward McDonald. b 42. TCD 67. **d** 69 Lim **p** 70 Killaloe. C of St Mary's Cathl Lim 69-70; CF 70-73; C of St Mary w St Paul Penzance 73-75; V of Mullion 75-81; L to Offic Dio Truro from 81. *Hazelmere, The Commons, Mullion, Cornwall TR12 7HZ.* (Mullion 240865)

WILLIAMSON, Canon Frank. b 1898. Univ of Tor BA 25, BD 30. **d** 31 **p** 32 Man. C of Bury 31-36; V of St Andr Ramsbottom 36-56; RD of Bury 50-56; Eccles 56-67; Hon Can of Man 51-70; Can (Emer) from 70; V of Eccles 56-70. *5 Birchfield Drive, Boothstown, Worsley, Manchester.* (061-790 6453)

WILLIAMSON, George Alexander. b 08. Lon Coll of Div 29. **d** 32 **p** 33 Lon. C of St Mary W Kens 32-34; St Steph Clapham Pk 34-36; CIM Miss at Tahsien 36-38; Liangshan Tienkiang 39-51; Supt of Overseas Miss Fell in N Malaya 52-67; Hong Kong 68-73; L to Offic Dio Carl from 73. *11 Templand Park, Allithwaite, Grange-over-Sands, Lancs.*

WILLIAMSON, John. b 07. MBE 74. LCP 42. **d** 60 **p** 61 Momb. P Dio Momb 60-64; Dio Nai 64-66; Chap at Ch Ch Amsterdam 66-74; Perm to Offic Dio Sheff 78-79; Dio Roch from 79. *15 Bromley College, London Road, Bromley, Kent, BR1 1PE.* (01-460 6317)

WILLIAMSON, John Hawthorn. Univ of NZ MA 50. St Jo Coll Auckld LTh 54. **d** 55 **p** 56 Auckld. C of Otahuhu 55-57; V of Kaitaia 57-62; Dom Chap to Bp of Auckld 62-63; Exam Chap 62-66; Dir of Ordin Tr 62-64; V of New Lynn 63-67; Seatown-Strathmore 67-71; Chap Ch Ch Coll Ch Ch 71-72; Executive Officer Chr Educn Dio Ch Ch 72-79; Exam Chap to Bp of Ch Ch 75-79; Chap Cathl Gr Sch Ch Ch 76-79; Hon Can of Ch Ch 77-79; Dir Angl Chr Tr Centre Dio Popondota from 79. *Anglican Training Centre, Popondota, Papua New Guinea.*

WILLIAMSON, John Mark. b 43. Univ of Birm BA (2nd cl Phil and Th) 65. Univ of Wales (Cardiff) Dame Olive Wheeler Prize 71, MEducn 75. St D Coll Lamp LTh 67. **d** 67 B & W **p** 68 Bp D J Wilson for B & W. C of Shepton Mallet 67-70; Hon C of Dinder 70-71; Asst Master and Chap Clifton Coll Bris 71-75; Adv Teacher County of Avon from 76; Lect All SS Bris 76-78; Bp's Cathl Chap 77-78; Gen Educn Insp Northants Educn Dept from 78; Perm to Offic Dio Pet from 78. *Education Department, Northampton House, Northampton, NN1 2HX.* (Northampton 34833)

WILLIAMSON, Joseph. b 1895. MBE 75. St Aug Coll Cant 21. **d** 25 **p** 26 Lon. C of St Mich and St Geo Fulwell

25-26; St Jas Norlands Kens 26-28; Cathl Ch Grahmstn 28-32; R of Fenny Drayton 32-34; Shimplingthorne (or Shimpling) w Alpheton 34-49; CF (EC) 40-46; Hon CF 46; R of L Dunham 49-52; V of Sporle w Gt and L Palgrave 49-52; St Paul Dock St w St Mark Whitechapel 52-62; Chap Sailors' Home and Red Ensign Club 54-62. *29, Marine Drive West, West Wittering, Chichester, Sussex.* (West Wittering 2214)

WILLIAMSON, Michael John. b 39. ALCD (2nd cl) 63. **d** 64 Middleton for Man **p** 65 Man. C of Pennington 64-67; St Clem Higher Openshaw 67-69; C-in-c of St Jerome w St Silas Ardwick 69-72; Min of St Hugh Conv Distr Holts 72-77; R of Droylsden Dio Man from 77. *St Mary's Rectory, Dunkirk Street, Droylsden, Manchester, M35 7FB.* (061-370 1569)

WILLIAMSON, Paul Nicholas. b 55. Univ of Otago BTh 79. St Jo Coll Auckld 80. **d** 80 **p** 81 Dun. C of Andersons Bay Dio Dun from 80. *60 Silverton Street, Andersons Bay, Dunedin, NZ.*

WILLIAMSON, Paul Stewart. b 48. AKC and BD 71. St Aug Coll Cant 71. **d** 72 **p** 73 S'wark. C of Deptford 72-76; Hon C of Kennington 76-77; C of H Trin w St Mary Hoxton Dio Lon from 78. *Holy Redeemer Clergy House, Exmouth Market, EC1R 4QE.*

WILLIAMSON, Peter Barry Martin. b 21. Wycl Hall Ox 61. **d** 62 **p** 63 Chelmsf. C of Billericay 62-68; V of Bentley Common 68-77; St John L Thurrock Dio Chelmsf from 77. *St John's Vicarage, Victoria Avenue, Little Thurrock, Grays, RM16 2RP.* (Grays Thurrock 72101)

WILLIAMSON, Raymond Keith. Univ of Syd BA 64. Univ of Newc MA 74. St Jo Coll Morpeth. ACT ThL (2nd cl) 65. **d** 65 **p** 66 Newc. C of New Lambton 65-69; Adamstown 70; Res Tutor St Jo Coll Morpeth 70-76; Lect 76-80; P-in-c of Morpeth Dio Newc 79-80; R from 80. *Rectory, Tank Street, Morpeth, NSW, Australia 2321.* (33-6218)

WILLIAMSON, Reginald. b 13. Roch Th Coll 66. **d** 67 Ex **p** 68 Plymouth for Ex. C of Em Plymouth 67-70; V of Soulby w Crosby Garrett 70-72; Warcop w Musgrave (and Soulby w Crosby-Garrett from 74) 72-78. *75a Virginia Street, Southport, Lancs.* (Southport 41527)

WILLIAMSON, Robert John. b 55. K Coll Lon BA 77. Coll of Ressur Mirfield 78. **d** 79 Liv **p** 80 Warrington for Liv. C of Kirkby Dio Liv from 79. *89a Park Brow Drive, Kirkby, Liverpool, L32 8TF.*

WILLIAMSON, Ven Robert Kerr. b 32. Oak Hill Th Coll 61. **d** 63 **p** 64 Chich. C of Crowborough 63-66; V of Hyson Green 66-72; St Ann w Em Nottm 72-76; Bramcote 76-79; Archd of Nottm from 78. *16 Woodthorpe Avenue, Woodthorpe, Nottingham, NG5 4FD.* (Nottm 267349)

WILLIAMSON, Thomas George. b 33. K Coll Lon and Warm AKC 57. **d** 58 Derby **p** 59 Bp Sinker for Derby. C of Winshill 58-61; N and S Hykeham 61-64; R of Leasingham w Roxholme 64-80; R of Brauncewell w Dunsby 64-78; P-in-c of Cranwell 78-80; V of Billinghay w Walcot and Dogdyke Dio Linc from 80. *Billinghay Vicarage, Lincoln.* (0526 860243)

WILLIE, Andrew Robert. b 43. Univ of Bris BA 65. Fitzw Coll Cam BA (Th) 73, MA 77. Ridley Hall Cam 71. **d** 74 **p** 75 Mon. C of St Woolos Cathl Ch Newport 74-79; V of Newbridge Dio Mon from 79. *St Paul's Vicarage, Newbridge, Gwent, NP1 4FW.* (Newbridge 243297)

WILLIE, Ernest Peter. Em Coll Sktn. **d** 67 **p** 68 New Westmr. C of St Mark Vancouver 67-69; I of Hatzic 69-72; Consultant in Human Rights Angl Ch of Canada from 72. *600 Jarvis Street, Toronto, Ont., Canada.*

WILLIMENT, Paul. b 47. Univ of Leeds BSc 68. St Steph Ho Ox 70. **d** 73 **p** 74 Bradf. C of Guiseley 73-77; St Mary Virg Northn 77-80; Tutor Ho of Epiph Kuching from 80. *Box 347, Kuching, Sarawak.*

WILLINGHAM, Robert John MacLeod. b 46. St Jo Coll Winnipeg BA 77. **d** 76 **p** 77 Rupld. C of Ch Ch Selkirk 76-78; Manitou Area 78-79; Mapleton Area Dio Rupld from 79. *Box 5, Gp 354, Selkirk, Manit, Canada.*

WILLINGTON, Lloyd Stanley. Univ of Adel BA 50. St Mich Th Coll Crafers ACT ThL 54. **d** 53 **p** 54 Adel. C of St Mary Magd Adel 54-55; Brighton 55-56; P-in-c of Millicent 56-60; Prin St Thos Sch Kuch 60-68; Can of Kuch 63-68; Chap Geelong Gr Sch Corio 68-72; Geo Brown High Sch Rabaul and L to Offic Dio Papua 72-76; HdMaster Hagen High Sch and Hon C of Mt Hagen Dio Aipo from 77. *Box 380, Mount Hagen, Papua New Guinea.*

WILLINK, Simon Wakefield. Magd Coll Cam BA 52, MA 56. Cudd Coll 52. **d** 54 Bp Barkway for Cant **p** 55 Glouc. C of Thornbury 54-58; Tetbury w Beverston 58-60; R of Siddington w Preston 60-64; C of St Mich Kelburn Wel 65; V of Takapau 65-70; L to Offic Dio Wai 70-80; Dio Glouc from 81. *Grays, Sheepscombe, Stroud, Glos.* (Painswick 812067)

WILLIS, Andrew Lyn. b 48. St D Coll Lamp BA 73. Bp Burgess Hall Lamp 73. **d** 74 **p** 75 Swan B. C of Swansea (in c of St Jas from 76) 74-81; V of Clyro w Bettws and Llowes and All AA Glasbury Dio Swan B from 81. *St Peter's Vicarage, Glasbury, Hereford.* (Glasbury 657)

WILLIS, Anthony John. b 38. St D Coll Lamp BA 62. Univ of Birm Dipl Th 64. Qu Coll Birm 62. **d** 64 **p** 65 Worc. C of St Jo Bapt Kidderminster 64-68; Dunstable 68-72; V of 72-79; R of Salwarpe w Hindlip and Martin Hussingtree Dio Worc from 79. *Rectory, Salwarpe, Droitwich, WR9 0AH.* (Droitwich 778757)

WILLIS, Arthur. b 08. **d** 63 **p** 64 Win. Bro OSP Dio Win from 63. *Alton Abbey, Alton, Hants.* (0420 62145)

WILLIS, Arthur Thomas. b 28. ACCS (ACIS from 70) 52. Wycl Hall Ox 61. **d** 62 **p** 63 Birm. C of Aston 62-66; Min of St Anne's Eccles Distr West Heath 66-71; V of Shuttington w Amington 71-79; H Redeemer Acomb City and Dio York from 79. *108 Boroughbridge Road, York.* (York 798593)

WILLIS, Christopher Charles Billopp. b 32. Bps' Coll Cheshunt, 57. **d** 59 **p** 60 Lon. C of St Alb Golders Green 59-61; St Alb Harrow 61-64; V of Shaw w Whitley 64-69; L to Offic Dio Ex 69-70; Industr Training Officer 69-77; Hon C of Swimbridge 70-77; Chap W Buckland Sch Barnstaple from 77. *Yeoland House, Swimbridge, Barnstaple, Devon.* (Swimbridge 309)

WILLIS, Christopher Rawdon. St Jo Coll Ox BA (3rd cl Mod Hist) 35, MA 40. Wells Th Coll 36. **d** and **p** 37 Ox. C of Caversham 37-39; Res Dom Chap to Marq Camden 39-44; R of Winterbourne 44-48; Publ Pr Dio Bris 49-61. *Netherton Ridges, Combe-in-Teignhead, Newton Abbot, Devon.* (Shaldon 3325)

WILLIS, David George. b 45. Oakhill Coll BA 79. **d** 79 **p** 80 S'wark. C of Wallington Dio S'wark from 79. *14 Harcourt Field, Wallington, Surrey.*

WILLIS, Donald. b 09. Oak Hill Th Coll. **d** 57 **p** 58 S'wark. C of H Trin w St Paul Greenwich 57-59; Barnes 59-61; V of Rangemore 61-64; V of Dunstall 61-64; St Silas Lozells 64-70; C of Farnborough (in c of St Nich) 70-74; Perm to Offic Dio Roch from 74; Hon C of Green Street Green Dio Roch from 74; Asst Chap Bromley Hosp 77-81. *Flat 22, Bromley College, London Road, Bromley, Kent, BR1 1PE.* (01-290 1289)

WILLIS, Canon Emmanuel. Qu Coll Newfld. **d** 47 **p** 48 Newfld. C of Battle Harbour 47-48; I 48-51; C of Channel 51-52; R of Rose Blanche 52-55; Smith's Sound 55-59; Spaniard's Bay 59-70; Foxtrap 70-78; Brigus-Salmon Cove Dio E Newfld from 78; Can of E Newfld from 81. *South River, Conception Bay, Newfoundland, Canada.*

WILLIS, Eric Mackay. Bp's Hostel Linc 11. **d** 13 **p** 15 Br Columb. Chap of Univ Sch and C of St Luke Cedar Hill Vic BC 13-15; C of St Mark Lower Easton Bris 15-19; TCF 17-19; C of Chippenham 19-22; R of Shaunavon 22-23; C of Cobble Hill w Shawnigan Lake and Chap Shawnigan Lake Sch 27-33; V of St Sav Vic W 33-36; Cobble Hill w Shawnigan Lake 36-52; Chap of Shawnigan Lake Sch 52-55. *680 Ker Avenue, Victoria, BC, Canada.*

WILLIS, Ven Frederick Andrew Graves. b 13. TCD BA 37, MA 41. Westcott Ho Cam 37. **d** 37 **p** 38 Ches. C of St Nich Wallasey 37-40; Leigh w Wells 40-43; I of Dunleckney (Bagenalstown) w Nurney and Clonmulsh (w Lorum from 50 and Clonagoose from 60) 43-62; RD of Leigh 55-59; Assoc Ed Ch of Ireland Gazette 55-59; Ed 59-75; Preb of Tullamagimma in Leigh Cathl 57-62; Chan 62-78; Preb of Aghour in Kilk Cathl 57-70; Chan 70-78; Can of St Patr Cathl Dub from 59; Exam Chap to Bp of Oss 62-67; I of Urglin w Staplestown 62-77; RD of Baltinglass from 62; Archd of Oss and Leigh from 76; I of Carlow w Urglin and Staplestown Dio Leigh from 77. *Urglin Glebe, Carlow, Irish Republic.* (0503 31326)

WILLIS, Geoffrey Grimshaw. b 14. Univ of Man BA (2nd cl Lat) 35, MA 39. Univ of Nottm PhD 51, DD 69. Lich Th Coll 35. **d** 37 **p** 38 Derby. C of Cotmanhay and Shipley 37-45; C-in-c of New Mills 45-46; C-in-c of St Edm Conv Distr Allenton Derby 46-49; PC of Allenton 49; Proc Conv Derby 45-59; Ox 59-69; Lect Derby Tr Coll 46-47; PC of Fernilee 49-58; Asst Synod Sec Conv of Cant 53-69; Sec C of E Liturgical Comm 55-65; Ed Chronicle of Conv 57-69; V of Wing 58-69; R of St Mich AA Grove 58-69; Lect Cudd Coll 62-68; L to Offic Dio Ox from 70. *21 Old High Street, Headington, Oxford, OX3 9HP.* (Oxford 65212)

WILLIS, Preb George Arnold. b 16. Univ of Liv BVSc 46. Ely Th Coll 52. **d** 53 St E **p** 53 Dunwich for Cant. C of St Matt Ipswich 53-55; R of Brantham 55-60; PC of St Steph Cheltm 60-64; Dioc Missr Dio Ex 64-77; R of St Martin, St Steph, St Lawr w All H and St Paul Ex 64-74; Dep PV of Ex Cathl 64-73; Proc in Conv 70-80; Preb of Ex Cathl 73-81; Preb (Emer) from 81; Team V of Ex Centre Dio Ex 74-78; R 78-81. *23 Yewstock Crescent, Chippenham, Wilts, SN15 1QS.* (Chippenham 2396)

WILLIS, Lambert Russell. Wycl Coll Tor LTh 49. **d** 48 **p** 49 Alg. I of Sundridge 49-54; Churchill 54-65; R of St Patr Winnipeg 65-71; Archd of York 59-65; I of St Andrews

Winnipeg 71-72; St Patr Winnipeg 72-73; Dawson Creek 73-80; Grandview Dio Bran from 80. *Grandview, Manit, Canada.*

WILLIS, Canon Norman Steward. b 1894. Pemb Coll Ox BA and MA 20. Wycl Hall Ox 20. **d** 20 **p** 21 Bris. C of Malmesbury w Westport 20-23; St Paul Swindon Wilts 23-27; V of Purton 27-74; Chap Northview Hosp Purton 27-74; RD of Cricklade 42-61; Hon Can of Bris 46-76; Can (Emer) from 76. *Cheriton, North Road, Leigh Woods, Bristol.* (Bristol 733473)

WILLIS, Peter Ambrose Duncan. b 34. Lich Th Coll 58. **d** 59 Roch **p** 60 Tonbridge for Cant. C of St Jo Bapt C-in-c of Sevenoaks 59-63; R of Pembroke Tobago 63-68; C-in-c of Diptford Dio Ex 68-69; R from 69; N Huish w Avonwick Dio Ex 68-69; R from 69. *Rectory, Diptford, Totnes, Devon, TQ9 7NY.* (054882-392)

WILLIS, Robert. Em Coll Sktn LTh (Hons) 26. **d** 26 **p** 27 Sask. C-in-c of Lashburn 26-27; I 27-29; R of Wilkie 29-33; St Geo Sktn 33-35; N Battleford 35-49; RD of Battleford 36-49; Hon Can of St Geo Cathl Sktn 43-49; R of St Mark Vic 49-68; Chap to Bp of BC 62-70. *1530 Belcher Avenue, Victoria, BC, Canada.*

WILLIS, Robert Andrew. b 47. Univ of Warwick BA (2nd cl Hist & Pol) 68. Worc Coll Ox Dipl Th 71. Cudd Coll 70. **d** 72 **p** 73 Lich. C of St Chad Shrewsbury 72-75; Perm to Offic Dio Sarum from 75; V Cho of Sarum Cathl 75-77; R of Tisbury w Swallowcliffe, Ansty and Chilmark Dio Sarum from 77. *Tisbury Rectory, Park Road, Salisbury, Wilts, SP3 6LF.* (Tisbury 312)

WILLIS, Canon Selwyn Thomas. McGill Univ BA 33. Montr Th Coll. **d** 36 **p** 37 Montr. C of Ch Ch Cathl Montr 36-39; St Geo 39-41; Miss at Fort St John 41-44; CF (Canad) 45-47; R of Rawdon 47-54; Grace Ch Montr 54-62; I of St Marg City and Dio Montr 62-71; Hon Can of Montr 66-75; Can (Emer) from 75; R of Standbridge E 71-75. *Lakeshore Road, RR1, Lacolle, PQ, Canada.* (514-246 3619)

WILLIS, Thomas Charles. b 30. Bps' Coll Cheshunt 55. **d** 58 **p** 59 York. C of St Mark Anlaby 58-61; St Martin Middlesbrough 61-63; V of St Paul w Ch Ch (and St Silas from 69) Sculcoates 63-80; C-in-c of St Silas Sculcoates 67-69; V of H Trin Bridlington and Sewerby w Marton Dio York from 80. *Sewerby Vicarage, Cloverley Road, Bridlington, N Humb, YO16 5TX.* (Bridlington 75725)

WILLIS, Wallace George Herbert. Down Coll Cam 2nd cl Hist Trip pt i, 38, BA (3rd cl Th Trip pt i) 40, MA 43. Ridley Hall, Cam 39. **d** 41 **p** 42 Derby. C of Ripley 41-46; St Geo Leeds (in c of St Jas) 46-48; C-in-c of Tresco w Bryher Conv Distr Scilly Is 48-49; CF 49-69; C of Ulverstone 69-70; R 70-76. *7/22 Seaview Road, West Beach, S Australia 5024.*

WILLISTON, Canon Edward Perley. b 06. **d** 63 **p** 64 Athab. I of Sexsmith 63-67; Spirit River 67-70; R of Grand Prairie 70-74; Hon Can of St Jas Cathl Peace River 70-77; Can (Emer) from 79; I of Sexsmith 74-77; L to Offic Dio Athab from 77. *Box 354, Sexsmith, Alta., TOH 3CO, Canada.* (568-3613)

WILLISTON, Philip Norman. Bp's Univ Lennox BA 62, LST 63. **d** 63 **p** 64 Fred. I of Restigouche 63-65; Addington 65-69; R of St Mary St John 69-79; Chatham Dio Fred from 79. *21 Winslow Street, Chatham, NB, Canada.*

WILLMER, Canon Alan Charles. b 20. Lich Th Coll 40. **d** 44 Lon **p** 45 Stepney for Lon. C of St Mark Bush Hill Pk 44-47; Petworth 48-55; R of N Chapel w Ebernoe Dio Chich from 55; Can and Preb of Chich Cathl from 81. *North Chapel Rectory, Petworth, Sussex.* (North Chapel 256)

WILLMER, Derek Franklin. b 37. Wells Th Coll 67. **d** 69 **p** 70 Ches. C of All SS Cheadle Hulme 69-72; C of Ches Team Parish 72-75; Team V from 75. *Christ Church Vicarage, Gloucester Street, Chester, CH1 3HR.* (0244-380625)

WILLMINGTON, Canon John Henry William. AKC 37. St Steph Ho Ox 35. **d** 37 **p** 38 Roch. C of All SS Perry Street Northfleet 37-38; St Sav Folkestone 38-43; C-in-c 43-44; C of St Mary Walmer 44-49; V of St Steph Norbury 49-59; Bearsted 59-63; PC of Selsdon 63-68; V 68-79; Six Pr in Cant Cathl 67-74; Hon Can of Cant 74-79; Can (Emer) from 79. *22 Barrow Green Road, Oxted, Surrey, RH8 6NL.*

WILLMINGTON, John Martin Vanderlure. b 45. St D Coll Lamp BA 69. St Steph Ho Ox 69. **d** 71 Kens **p** 72 Kens for Lon. C of SS Pet and Paul Teddington 71-75; St Mary Abbots Kens (in c of St Geo Campden Hill) Dio Lon from 75. *25 Campden Hill Square, W8 7JY.* (01-727 9486)

WILLMONT, Anthony Vernon. b 35. Lich Th Coll 62. **d** 63 **p** 64 Birm. C of Yardley 63-65; H Trin Smethwick 65-68; V of Ropley w W Tisted 68-77; St Aug of Hippo Ipswich Dio St E from 77. *St Augustine's Vicarage, Bucklesham Road, Ipswich, IP3 8TJ.* (Ipswich 78654)

WILLMOT, Philip Boulton. b 15. St Pet Hall Ox BA (2nd cl Mod Hist) 36, MA 41. Westcott Ho 38. **d** 38 Southn for Win **p** 39 Win. C of St Winfrid Testwood 38-42; C-in-c of St Francis Cowley 42-43; Chap Magd Coll Ox 43-50; C of St Pet Wolvercote 46-50; Chap and Asst Master of Win Coll 50-77; L to Offic Dio Win from 60; Chap St John and St Mary Magd Hosps Win from 79. *34 Hatherley Road, Winchester, Hants, SO22 6RT.* (Winchester 2360)

WILLMOT, Richard Dyott. b 08. Lich Th Coll 30. **d** 32 **p** 33 Pet. C of St Paul Northn 32-34; H Trin Eltham 34-36; All SS w St Mark Binfield 36-39; Stanford-in-the-Vale 39-42; St Mary Virg Ewell 42-45; St Paul Addlestone 44-48; Thorpe St Andr 48-50; St Andr Hillingdon 51-53; St Andr Boscombe Hants 53-57; Epsom 57-60; All SS Battersea Pk 60-62; Perm to Offic Dio Ox 62-67; Dio Chich from 67. *15 Barry Walk, Xaverian College Estate, North Drive, Brighton, BN2 2HP.*

WILLMOTT, Oliver Leonard. b 10. Kelham Th Coll 31. Univ of Lon Dipl Th 41. **d** 38 **p** 39 Ex. C of Totnes 38-41; CF (EC) 41-46; Hon CF 47; V of Loders Dio Sarum from 47; R of Askerswell Dio Sarum from 52. *Loders Vicarage, Bridport, Dorset.*

WILLMOTT, Robert Owen Noel. b 41. Lich Th Coll 65. **d** 68 S'wark **p** 69 Bp Boys for S'wark. C of St Geo Perry Hill 68-71; Denham 71-76; P-in-c of Tingewick w Water-Stratford and Radclive w Chackmore 76-77; R of Tingewick w Water Stratford, Radclive and Chackmore Dio Ox from 77. *Tingewick Rectory, Buckingham.* (Finmere 273)

WILLMOTT, Trevor. b 50. St Pet Coll Ox BA 71. Fitzw Coll Cam Dipl Th 73. Westcott Ho Cam 72. **d** 74 Bedford for St Alb **p** 75 St Alb. C of Norton 74-77; Asst Chap of Oslo 77-79; Chap Ch Ch Naples Dio Gibr (Gibr in Eur from 80) from 79. *Via San Pasquala a Chiaia, 15b, Naples, Italy.* (411482)

WILLOCHRA, Lord Bishop of. *See* Rosier, Right Rev Stanley Bruce.

WILLOUGHBY, Bernard Digby. b 1896. Bps' Coll Cheshunt 39. **d** 42 **p** 43 Southw. C of St Mary Magd Hucknall 42-44; Gedling 44-45; R of Cossington 45-47; I of Knappagh 47-50; R of Ballinrobe Kilcommon and Ballyovie 50-73; Cong 62-73; Can and Preb of Tuam Cathl 63-73; Provost of Tuam 70-73; *Maneys, Lettergesh, Renvyle, Co Galway, Irish Republic.*

WILLOUGHBY, David Albert. b 31. St Jo Coll Dur BA 53, Dipl Th 57. **d** 57 **p** 58 Bradf. C of St Pet Shipley 57-61; Barnoldswick w Bracewell 61-62; R of St Chad Moston 62-72; V of Marown 72-80; Dioc Stewardship Adv Dio S & M from 76; Sec S & M Dioc Syn from 77; V of St Geo and St Barn w All SS Douglas Dio S & M from 80; RD of Douglas from 80. *St George's Vicarage, Devonshire Road, Douglas, IM.* (Douglas 5430)

WILLOUGHBY, Ven George Charles. b 20. TCD BA 43, Div Test (2nd cl) 44, MA 46. **d** 44 **p** 45 Derry. C of Conwall 44-47; Derry Cathl 47-51; I of Convoy 51-59; RD of Raph 57-59; All SS Clooney Dio Derry from 59; RD of Londonderry 62-69; Dir of Ords Dio Derry 62-72; Can of Derry from 69; Dioc Sec 75; Archd from 79. *All Saints' Rectory, Limavady Road, Waterside, Londonderry, BT47 1JD.* (Londondery 44306)

WILLOUGHBY, James Stanton. d and **p** 51 Dun. C of All SS Dun 51; V of Maniototo 51-56; Takapau 56-65; Ahuriri 65-72; Mahora 72-78; Perm to Offic Dio Wai from 78. *54 Battery Road, Napier, NZ.*

✠**WILLOUGHBY, Right Rev Noel Vincent.** b 26. Late Scho and Pri of TCD BA (1st cl Mod) 48, MA 52. **d** 50 **p** 51 Arm. C of Drumglass 50-53; St Cath Dub 53-55; Bray 55-59; I of Delgany 59-69; Glenageary 69-80; Hon Sec Gen Syn 75-80; Can Treas of St Patrick's Cathl Dub 77-80; Archd of Dub 78-80; Cons Ld Bp of Cash, Waterf, Lism, Oss, Ferns and Leigh in Ch Ch Cathl Dub 25 April 80 by Abp of Dub; Bps of Meath, Cork, Tuam, Derry and Clogh; and Bps Simms, Buchanan, Perdue and Herd, *The Palace, Kilkenny, Co Kilkenny, Irish Republic.* (Kilkenny 21560)

WILLOWS, Michael John. b 35. Sarum Wells Th Coll 70. **d** 72 **p** 73 Worc. C of Pershore 72-75; P-in-c of Astley 75-81; Hallow Dio Worc from 81. *Hallow Vicarage, Worcester.* (Worc 640348)

WILLOWS, Warrick Alastair. Dipl Th (S Afr) 68. St Paul's Coll Grahmstn 64. **d** and **p** 68 Matab. C of Gwelo 68-71; R of Northend 71-75; Gwelo 75-81; Archd of the Midlands 79-81; V of Hamilton Dio Bal from 81. *Rectory, Hamilton, Vic, Australia 3300.*

WILLS, David Ernest. b 37. St Jo Coll Cam 3rd cl Engl Trip pt i 57, BA 58, 3rd cl Th Trip pt ii 59, MA 62. Ridley Hall Cam 58. **d** 60 **p** 61 Cov. C of St Jo Evang Kenilworth 60-63; Em Northwood 63-66; PC of St Geo Huyton 66-69; V 69-73; Littleover Dio Derby from 73. *Vicarage, Church Street, Littleover, Derby, DE3 6GF.* (Derby 767802)

WILLS, David Stuart Ralph. b 36. Chich Th Coll 64. **d** 66 **p** 67 Truro. C of Bodmin 66-70; V of Bude Haven 70-78; Team V of Banbury Dio Ox from 78. *St Paul's House, Bretch Hill, Banbury, Oxon, OX16 0LR.* (Banbury 4003)

WILLS, Herbert Ashton Peter. b 24. St Edm Hall Ox BA

46, MA 50. Qu Coll Birm 60. **d** 60 **p** 61 Sheff. C of Stocksbridge 60-63; Chap of Repton Sch 64-69; Coll of St Matthias Bris 69-78; Asst Chap Univ of Sheff 78-80; Chap from 80. *Earnshaw Hall, Endcliffe Crescent, Broomhill, Sheffield, S10 3EG.*

WILLS, Ian Leslie. b 49. Wycl Hall Ox 77. **d** 80 **p** 81 Bris. C of St Mary Henbury 80; Gtr Corsham Dio Bris from 80. *7b Lypiatt Road, Corsham, Wilts, SN13 9JB.*

WILLS, Jack. Ridley Coll Melb ACT ThL 52. **d** and **p** 53 Bal. C of Horsham 53-55; V of Dimboola 55-57; I of N Brighton 57-65; Min of Greythorn 65-70; I of Queenscliff 70-76; Perm to Offic Dio Melb from 76. *St Paul's Court, Frankston, Vic, Australia 3199.*

WILLS, John Trevethan. b 21. Em Coll Cam BA 48, MA 52. **d** 50 **p** 51 Carl. C of Cockermouth 50-54; Chap Maryhull Hosp 54-59; Asst Master Torryburn Secondary Sch 60-61; Bell-Baxter High Sch from 62. *28 Rattray Street, Monifieth, Dundee, Angus.*

WILLS, Kenneth Charles Austen. b 21. Cudd Coll 68. **d** 70 **p** 71 Portsm. C of Petersfield w Sheet 70-73; R of W Meon w Warnford Dio Portsm from 73. *West Meon Rectory, Petersfield, Hants, GU32 1LR.* (073-086 226)

WILLS, Morley. b 35. **d** 80 **p** 81 Truro (NSM) C of St Enoder Dio Truro from 80. *21 Harrison Terrace, Truro, Cornwall.* (Truro 74741)

WILLS, Ronald Herbert. Sarum Th Coll 48. **d** 49 **p** 51 Portsm. C of St Jas Milton Portsm 49-57; Leigh-on-Sea 57-60; Ch Ch Isle of Dogs 60-61; Perivale 61-64; V of St Thos Acton Vale 64-73. *c/o St Thomas's Vicarage, Bromyard Avenue, W3.* (01-743 6701)

WILLS, Thomas Leslie. St Jo Coll Morpeth ACT ThL 63. **d** 62 **p** 63 C & Goulb. C of Young 62-67; Good Shepherd Curtin Canberra 67-69; R of Koorawatha 69-73; Tumbarumba 73-76; Boorowa 76-81; S Monaro Dio C & Goulb from 81. *Box 36, Bombala, NSW, Australia 2553.*

WILLSON, Frederick James. b 02. Dorch Miss Coll 31. **d** 34 **p** 36 S'wark. C of St Mildred Burnt Ash Hill Lee 34-36; St Luke W Norwood 36-40; V of Ch Ch Rotherhithe 40-50; CF (EC) 41-45; C-in-c of St Crispin Bermondsey 45-50; V of St Crispin w Ch Ch Bermondsey 50-51; Farndon 51-58; R of Thorpe-by-Newark 51-58; V of Stoke Ferry w Wretton 58-63; Whitington 58-63; Bawburgh 63-73; L Melton (and Gt Melton w Marlingford and Bawburgh from 73) 63-75; Gt Melton 72-73; R of Colney 72-75; C-in-c of Marlingford 71-73. *Holmfield, Flordon Road, Newton Flotman, Norwich, NR15 1QX.*

WILLSON, Prince Hycy. Fourah Bay Coll Univ of Dur BA 18, MA 21. **d** 24 **p** 25 Sier L. Asst Master Gr Sch Freetown 24-27; Tutor Fourah Bay Coll 27-36; Actg Prin 36-37; Exam Chap to Bp of Sier L 36-47; Prin CMS Gt Sch Freetown 37-47. Can of St Geo Cathl Freetown 45-47; Prin Iju-Odo Gr Sch from 54. *Manuwa Memorial Grammar School, Iju-Odo, Nigeria.*

WILLSON, Robert John. b 39. Univ of Syd BA 61. **d** and **p** 74 C & Goulb. C of Wagga Wagga 74-76; R of Berridale 76-79; St Phil O'Connor Dio C & Goulb from 79. *Box 22, O'Connor, ACT, Australia 2601.*

WILMAN, Leslie Alan. b 37. Selw Coll Cam 2nd cl Th Trip pt i, 59, BA (2nd cl Th Trip pt ii) 61, MA 65. Ridley Hall, Cam. **d** 63 **p** 64 Bradf. C of Skipton-in-Craven 63-67; Guiseley 67-69; V of Morton 69-79; C of Bingley 77-79; R of Swanton Morley w Worthing Dio Nor from 79; P-in-c of Hoe Dio Nor from 80; Beetley w E Bilney Dio Nor from 79. *Rectory, Beetley, East Dereham, Norfolk, NR20 4AB.* (Dereham 860328)

WILMER, John Watts. b 26. Lich Th Coll 56. **d** 58 **p** 59 Lich. C of Ch Ch Wolverhampton 58-60; Fenton 60-63; V of Dresden 63-76; Team V of Sutton-in-Holderness w Warne 76-80; R of Bp Wilton w Full Sutton and Kirby Underdale & Bugthorpe Dio York from 80. *Vicarage, Bishop Wilton, York, YO4 1RZ.* (Bp Wilton 230)

WILMOT, Canon Edward Franklin Slaney. Keble Coll Ox BA (3rd cl Mod Lang) 29, MA 36. Ely Th Coll 29. **d** 30 **p** 31 Cov. C of Wyken 30-34; Northfield 34-39; V of St Matt Smethwick 39-48; Kingsbury w Dosthill Hurley and Woodend 48-52; Hay Mill 52-64; Tanworth-in-Arden 64-78; Hon Can Birm Cathl 72-78; Can (Emer) from 78. *31 Beauchamp Avenue, Leamington Spa, Warws.*

WILMOT, Jonathan Anthony de Burgh. b 48. Univ of Nottm BTh 74. St Jo Coll Nottm 69. **d** 74 **p** 75 Ely. C of St Martin Cam 74-77; Asst Chap of St Mich Paris Dio (Gibr in Eur from 80) Lon (N and C Eur) from 77. *5 rue d'Aguesseau, Paris 8e, France.* (073-09-00)

WILMOT, Canon Laurence Frank. MC 44. St Jo Coll Manit BA and LTh 31, BD 48, MA 63, DD 68. Trin Coll Tor Hon DD 58. **d** 31 **p** 32 Bran. R of Pilot Mound 32-35; Swan River 35-39; RD 35-46; Miss P Swan River Valley 39-42; CF (Canad) 42-46; P-in-c of St Barn Winnipeg 45-46; Sec Gen Bd of Relig Educn 46-49; R of St Mary Magd St Vital 49-50; Warden St Jo Coll Winnipeg 50-61; Hon Can of Rupld from 50; Exam Chap to Abp of Rupld 53-62; Visiting Fell St Aug Coll Cant 63-64; Sub-Warden 64-67; Chap Whitby Psychiatric Hosp 69-72; Dir of Field Educn Rupld 72-74; Hon C of St Paul Winnipeg Dio Rupld from 81. *119 University Crescent, Winnipeg, Manit., Canada.*

WILMOT, Lawrence Graham. b 43. Univ of the Witwatersrand BComm 69. St Paul's Coll Grahmstn Dipl Th 80. **d** 80 Port Eliz. C of St Hugh Newton Park Dio Port Eliz from 80. *PO Box 7050, Newton Park, Port Elizabeth 6055, S Africa.*

WILMOT, Stuart Leslie. b 42. Oak Hill Th Coll 64. **d** 68 Stepney for Lon **p** 69 Lon. C of Spitalfields 68-71; Islington 71-74; V of St Paul Brixton 74-81; R of Mursley w Swanbourne and L Horwood Dio Ox from 81. *Mursley Rectory, Milton Keynes, Bucks, MK17 0RT.* (Mursley 369)

WILMOT, Thomas. b 50. St Jo Coll Morpeth ACT ThDip 76. **d** and **p** 77 Perth. C of H Cross Cathl Geraldton 77-79; Assoc P Spearwood-Willagee Dio Perth from 79. *77 Archibald Street, Willagee, W Australia 6156.* (337 1977)

WILMSHURST, Canon Julius John. b 07. Sarum Th Coll 38. **d** 38 Sarum **p** 40 Truro. C of Bridport 38-40; St Budock 40-43; St Paul Thornton Hth 43-47; V of St Paul Maidstone 47-63; R of Lydd 63-77; RD of S Lympne 65-75; Hon Can of Cant 68-79; Can (Emer) from 79. *19 Stanbury Crescent, Folkestone, Kent, CT19 6PB.* (Folkestone 51176)

WILMUT, Ronald William. b 09. Ripon Hall Ox. **d** 61 Aston for Birm **p** 62 Birm. C of Sutton Coldfield 61-63; V of Birchfield 63-78. *2 St Alphege Close, Solihull, W Midl, B91 3RQ.*

WILSHIRE, Robert Vidal. Univ of Queensld B Econ 61. St Francis Coll Bris 60. **d** 61 **p** 62 Brisb. C of St Nich Sandgate Brisb 61-64; Chap Southport Sch Queensld 64-66. *c/o Diocesan Secretary, Church House, 417 Ann Street, Brisbane, Queensland, Australia.*

WILSMORE, Richard Frank. b 16. Univ of New Engl Armidale BA 65. **d** 78 Graft. Hon C of Coffs Harbour Dio Graft from 78. *23 Tindara Drive, Sawtell, NSW, Australia 2452.*

WILSON, Canon Aidan William. b 10. Univ Coll Ox BA 35, MA 39. Wells Th Coll 38. **d** 39 **p** 40 Newc T. C of All SS Gosforth 39-43; Prec of St Nich Cathl Newc T 43-46; Dioc Insp of Schs 44-49; V of Sugley 46-52; Monkseaton 52-60; Berwick-on-Tweed 60-63; RD of Norham 60-63; Morpeth 63-76; Proc Conv Newc T 61-73; R of Morpeth 63-77; Hon Can of Newc T from 69. *1 Croft Place, Alnwick, Northumb.*

WILSON, Alan Thomas Lawrence. b 55. St Jo Coll Cam BA 77, MA 81. Wycl Hall Ox 77. **d** 79 Reading for Ox **p** 80 Ox. HOn C of Eynsham Dio Ox 79-80; C from 81. *Vicarage, Mill Street, Eynsham, Oxford, OX8 1JX.* (OX 881323)

WILSON, Canon Alfred Michael Sykes. b 32. Jes Coll Cam 2nd cl Hist Trip pt i 54, BA (3rd cl Th Trip pt ii) 56, MA 61. Ridley Hall Cam 56. **d** 58 **p** 59 Sheff. C of Fulwood Sheff 58-63; V of St Jo Evang Gt Horton Bradf 63-69; R of Rushden (St Mary w St Pet from 77) and Newton Bromswold Dio Pet from 69; RD of Higham from 75; C-in-c of St Pet Rushden 75-77; Can of Pet from 77. *Rectory, Rushden, Northants, NN10 0HA.* (Rushden 2554)

WILSON, Allen. b 22. TCD BA 44, BD 50. **d** 45 **p** 46 Dub. C of St Michan and St Paul Dub 45-51; St Mary Dub and Chap Dub Hosp 51-56; I of Gt Connell (w Carnalway and Kilcullen from 60) 56-64; Santry and Glasnevin 64-73; R of Rathfarnham Dio Dub from 73. *Rathfarnham Rectory, Terenure, Dublin 6, Irish Republic.*

WILSON, Amos Jeremiah Yatty Cole. Fourah Bay Coll BA 42, MAe 46. **d** 43 **p** 45 Sier L. P Dio Sier L 43-50; 53-56 and from 63; C of St Luke Hammersmith 50-52; C (Col Cl Act) of St Anne Holloway 52-53; C of St Pet Paddington 56-59; St Mary Bow 60-63. *Christ Church Parsonage, Padembe Road, Freetown, Sierra Leone.* (Freetown 22270)

WILSON, Canon Andrew. b 20. Late Scho of St Chad's Coll Dur BA (2nd cl Mod Hist) 41, Dipl Th 43, MA 44. **d** 43 **p** 44 Newc T. C of St Cuthb Newc T 43-45; St John Wallsend 45-48; P-in-c of St John Backworth 48-55; V of Horton 55-58; R of Ballachulish 58-64; Can Res Newc T from 64; Dir of Ordin Dio Newc T from 64; Exam Chap to Bp of Newc T from 69. *1 Mitchell Avenue, Newcastle upon Tyne.* (Newcastle upon Tyne 812075)

WILSON, Andrew Alan. b 47. Univ of Nottm BA (2nd cl Th) 68. St Steph Ho Ox 68. **d** 71 **p** 72 S'wark. C of St Paul Furzedown Streatham 71-75; Team V of Catford Southend and Downham 75-80; V of St Jas Malden Dio S'wark from 80. *7 Bodley Road, New Malden, Surrey, KT3 5QD.* (01-942 1860)

WILSON, Arthur. b 20. Worc Ordin Coll 62. **d** 64 **p** 65 Wakef. C of Elmsall S 64-67; V of St Andr Huddersfield 67-71; Altofts 71-78; Staincross Dio Wakef from 78. *Staincross Vicarage, Barnsley, S Yorks.* (Barnsley 382261)

WILSON, Arthur Guy Ross. b 28. St Aid Coll 58. **d** 59 Bp

Stannard for Roch **p** 60 Tonbridge for Cant. C of Bexley 59-63; Gravesend 63-66; Belvedere (in c of St Andr Bostall Heath) 66-70; V of St Matthias Preston Brighton 70-77; St Clem City and Dio Bradf from 77. *Vicarage, Barkerend Road, Bradford, BD3 8QX.* (Bradford 22881)

WILSON, Arthur Maurice Plumpton. b 1897. St Jo Coll Ox BA 21, MA 28. Westcott Ho Cam 27. **d** 28 Malmesbury for Bris **p** 29 Bris. C of St Mary Redcliffe 28-30; V of Kingswood Bris 30-35; Sea Mills 35-48; Kirkham 48-55; Northleach w Hampnett 55-60; RD of Northleach 59-60; Mansfield 60-67; V of Mansfield 60-67; Surr 60-67; C-in-c of Heyshott 67-71. *Croft End, Oak Close, Parklands, Chichester, Sussex.*

WILSON, Arthur Neville. b 43. Univ of Lon BSc (Eng) 65. Linacre Coll Ox BA 70. MA 74. St Steph Ho Ox 68. **d** 71 **p** 72 Kens for Lon. C of St Aug Whitton 71-73; Chiswick 73-76; St Mary Virg and of St Jas Littlehampton 76-81; All SS Wick 76-81; V of Whitworth Dio Man from 81. *Whitworth Vicarage, The Square, Whitworth, Rochdale, Lancs, OL12 8PY.* (Whitworth 3586)

WILSON, Bernard Hall Coombs. b 06. Armstrong Coll Dur BA (3rd cl French) 29. Ripon Hall Ox 31. **d** 32 **p** 33 Roch. C of Erith 32-35; St Martin Birm 35-37; V of St Sav Birm 37-40; Chap RAFVR 40-45; Chap Iraq Petroleum Co and L to Offic Dio Jer 46-60; Sen Chap at Kirkuk 50-60; Hon Can of Jer 51-60; V of St Bees 60-71; Chap St Bees Sch 67-71; Perm to Offic Dio Ex from 71. *37 Townlands, Willand, Cullompton, Devon, EX15 2RR.*

WILSON, Bernard Martin. b 40. St Jo Coll Cam 2nd cl Th Trip pt i 61, BA (3rd cl Th Trip pt ii) 63, MA 68. Ripon Hall Ox 72. **d** 73 Bp McKie for Cov **p** 74 Cov. C of Bilton 73-77; Dioc Development Officer Dio Birm 78-81. *223 Selly Oak Road, Kings Norton, Birmingham, B30 1HR.* (021-458 6254)

WILSON, Bertram Arthur Cuthbert David. b 11. Univ of Lon BA (3rd cl Hist) 35. AKC 37. **d** 37 **p** 38 Chelmsf. C of St Geo Becontree 37-40; St Mary Plaistow 40-44; C-in-c of St Sav Westcliff-on-Sea 44-45; St Pet Prittlewell 45-46; V of St Paul Westcliff-on-Sea 46-56; R of L Thurrock 56-66; V of Cricksea w Althorne 66-71; R of St Mary Magd Colchester 71-76; Perm to Offic Dio St Alb from 77. *8 Manor Road, Sandy, Beds.* (Sandy 80834)

WILSON, Billy. St Jo Bapt Th Coll Suva **d** 67 Polyn **p** 68 Bp Halapua for Polyn. C of H Trin Cathl Suva 68; Wailoku and Matata 68-69; Viti Levu W 69-71; P-in-c of Wailoku and Matata 71-74. *PO Box 3744, Samabula, Fiji.*

WILSON, Bruce Winston. Moore Th Coll Syd ACT ThL 65. BD (Lon) 65. **d** 65 **p** 66 Syd. C of Beverley Hills 65-67; St Mark Darling Point 68-69; Chap Univ of NSW 70-74; R of Paddington Dio Syd from 75. *The Fiveways, Glenmore Road, Paddington, NSW, Australia 2021.* (357-6356)

WILSON, Canon Bryce Clement. Moore Th Coll Syd ACT ThL 52. **d** and **p** 54 Syd. C of Liv 54-55; C-in-c of Villawood 55-57; Yagoona 57-59; R of Nowra 59-64; Bexley 64-68; Gymea w Gymea Bay 68-75; Blacktown Dio Syd from 75; Can of St John's Prov Cathl Parramatta from 80. *15 West Street, Blacktown, NSW, Australia 2148.* (622-1621)

WILSON, Cecil Henry. b 40. TCD 67. **d** 69 **p** 70 Down. C of St Jo Evang Lurgan 69-72; Min Can Drom Cathl 72-75; Youth Sec CMS Ireland 75-80; N Reg Sec from 80. *20 Knockbreda Road, Belfast, BT6 0JA. N Ireland.* (Belfast 644011)

WILSON, Canon Cecil Moffat. b 26. TCD BA 51. **d** 52 **p** 53 Kilm. C of Urney 52-54; I of Templeharry 56-59; Cloughjordan 59-64; Mountmellick 64-76; Can of Kild Cathl from 72; Treas 73-75; Archd 75-76; R of Raheny w Coolock Dio Dub from 76. *403 Howth Road, Dublin 5, Irish Republic.*

WILSON, Charles Donald. Late Scho of McGill Univ Montr BEng 55. Wycl Coll Tor BTh 60. **d** 59 **p** 60 Tor. C of Etoluioke 59; St Anne Tor 59-60; St Geo Oshawa 60-63; St Timothy Tor 63-64; I of Medonte 64-65; on leave 66-73; R of Roche's Point Dio Tor from 74. *Rectory, Roche's Point, Ont., Canada.* (416-476 3491)

WILSON, Charles Gordon. b 18. St Jo Coll Dur BA (Hons) 44, MA 47. Westcott Ho Cam 44. **d** 44 **p** 45 Sheff. C of St Geo w St Steph Sheff 44-47; Mexborough 47-50; V of St Sav Gt Moor Stockport 50-58; St Jo Bapt Crewe Dio Ches from 58. *14 Dane Bank Avenue, Crewe, Chesh, CW2 8AA.* (Crewe 68835)

WILSON, Charles Michael. b 39. Magd Coll Ox BA 63, MA 66. N-E Ordin Course 76. **d** 79 **p** 80 Dur (APM). C of St Jas Darlington Dio Dur from 79. *29 Prestcott Street, Darlington, DL1 2ND.*

WILSON, Charles Roy. b 30. St Aid Coll 56. **d** 59 Warrington for Liv **p** 60 Liv. C of St Paul Kirkdale 59-62; St Mark St Helens 62-66; V of St Matt Wolverhampton 66-74; Ripley Dio Derby from 74. *Vicarage, Mount Pleasant, Ripley, Derby, DE5 3DX.* (Ripley 43179)

WILSON, Christopher Richard Maclean. St Cath Coll Cam BA 57, MA 61. Episc Th Sch Cam USA STB 60. Clifton Th Coll 59. **d** 60 **p** 61 S'wark. C of Morden 60-62; Asst Chap Med Coll of Virginia 64-65; R of Merlin 65-67; Publ Inst Chap Dio Tor from 67. *97 Florence Avenue, Willowdale, Ont, Canada.*

WILSON, Colin Myles. b 40. St Aid Coll 64. **d** 66 **p** 67 Ches. C of Frodsham 66-68; Heald Green 68-70; St Chad Kirkby 70-72; St Andr Tower Hill Kirkby 72-73; CF from 73. *Ministry of Defence, Bagshot Park, Bagshot, Surrey, GU19 5PL.*

WILSON, Cyril Godfrey. b 09. TCD BA 31. **d** 32 **p** 33 Arm. V Cho of Arm Cathl and C of Arm 32-36; C-in-c of Caheragh 36-42; I of Tubbercurry w Kilmactigue 42-45; Castlemagner w Ballyclough 45-49; Castlemartyr, Killeagh and Dungourney 49-52; Chap RAF 52-55; Bp's C Dio Cork 56-66; I of St Edm Dunmanway 56-66; R of Mevagh w Milford (and Glenalla from 67) 66-79; RD of Kilmacrennan W 68-78; Can of Raph Cathl 76-79. *c/o Rectory, Carrigart, Co Donegal, Irish Republic.* (Carrigart 25)

WILSON, David Brian. b 47. QUB BA 68. TCD Div Test 71. **d** 71 **p** 72 Down. C of Ballyholme 71-74; Ch Ch Guildf 74-78; I of Arvagh and Carrigallen w Gowna and Columbkille 78-81; Clogherny Dio Arm from 81. *96 Church Road, Beragh, Co Tyrone, N Ireland.* (Beragh 219)

WILSON, David Gordon. b 40. Univ of Man BSc (2nd cl Botany) 61. Clare Coll Cam BA (2nd cl Th Trip pt ii) 63, MA 68. Ridley Hall Cam. **d** 65 **p** 66 S'wark. C of St Barn Clapham Common 65-69; St Paul Onslow Square Kens 69-73; V of H Ap City and Dio Leic from 73; M Gen Syn from 80. *281 Fosse Road South, Leicester, LE3 1AE.* (Leicester 824336)

WILSON, David Mark. b 53. Univ of Lon BSc 75. Wycl Hall Ox BA (Th) 77. **d** 78 Chelmsf **p** 79 Barking for Chelmsf. C of Good Shepherd Collier Row Romford 78-81; St Andr Cheadle Hulme Dio Ches from 81. *198 Bruntwood Lane, Cheadle Hulme, Cheshire, SK8 6BE.* (061-485 1154)

WILSON, David Merritt. b 26. SOC 61. **d** 64 **p** 65 S'wark. C of St Paul Brixton 64-69; Publ Pr Dio S'wark from 69. *18 Calais Street, SE5.* (01-274 5707)

WILSON, Derek Hamilton Aitken. b 21. St Edm Hall Ox BA 48, MA 58. Sarum Th Coll 58. **d** 60 **p** 61 Sarum. C of St Mark Sarum 60-63; V of Topsham 63-77; RD of Aylesbeare 76-77; R of Wolsingham w Thornley 77-80; P-in-c of Childe Okeford Manston, Hammoon & Hanford Diuo Sarum from 80. *Childe Okeford Rectory, Blandford, Dorset.* (Childe Okeford 547)

WILSON, Derick. b 33. Oak Hill Th Coll 69. **d** 71 **p** 72 Down. C of Shankill Lurgan 71-74; Willowfield 74-75; R of Knocknamuckley Dio Drom from 75. *Knocknamuckley Rectory, Portadown, Co Armagh, Bt63 5SL., N Ireland.* (Gilford 831227)

WILSON, Dominick Patrick Sarsfield. TCD BA (Sen Mod) 20, Th Exhib (2nd) 22, BD 32. **d** 22 **p** 23 Down. C of St Mary Belf 22-24; Dundalk 24-26; I of Durrus 27-31; C of Clonmel (Queenstown) 26-27 and 31-33; I of Ballydehob 33-39; Kilgariffe 39-57; RD of Collimore and Collibeg 46-72; Archd of Ross 50-72; R of Drimoleague w Caheragh 57-72. *46 Ardmahon Estate, Douglas, Cork, Irish Republic.*

WILSON, Donald Albert. b 30. Cranmer Hall Dur 68. **d** 70 **p** 71 Bradf. C of Menston-in-Wharfedale w Woodhead 70-73; St Geo and St Barn w All SS Douglas 73-75; V of Kirk Lonan 75-80; Dioc Dir of Educn 76-80. *c/o Lonan Vicarage, Laxey, IM.* (Laxey 480)

WILSON, Donald Jesse. Moore Th Coll Syd ACT ThL 59. Melb Coll of Div 62. **d** 58 **p** 59 Nel. C of All SS Nel 58-62; V of Granity 62-63; C of St Clem Mosman 64; R of St Chad Cremorne 64-73; Dural Dio Syd from 73. *Old Northern Road, Dural, NSW, Australia 2158.* (651-1119)

WILSON, Donald Keith. b 42. Moore Coll Syd ACT ThL 69. **d** 70 **p** 71 Syd. C of Darlinghurst 70-72; St Geo Engadine 72-75; R of S Cant 75-78; w Bush Ch Aid S from 78. *Box 68, Newman, W Australia 6753.* (091-75 1350)

WILSON, Donna Jeanne. b 52. McGill Univ Montr BTh 77, STM 78. Montr Dioc Th Coll 76. **d** 79 **p** 80 Montr. C of Ch Ch Cathl City and Dio Montr from 79. *3655 Ste. Famille, Route 80, Montreal, Que, Canada, H2X 2L5.*

WILSON, Douglas John. b 45. St Barn Coll Adel 70. **d** and **p** 73 Bal. C of Colac 73-77; R of Edenhope 77-79; I of Lilydale Dio Melb from 79. *81 Castella Street, Lilydale, Vic, Australia 3140.* (735 1671)

WILSON, Edward Raynold. b 01. St Aug Coll Cant 57. **d** 58 B & W **p** 60 Bp Stuart for Worc. C of Weston-s-Mare 58-59; St Barn Worc 59-61; R of Litton 61-75; R of Hinton Blewett 61-75. *Virginia House, Silver Street, Lyme Regis, dorset, DT7 3HS.*

WILSON, Eric Walter Montague. b 15. Launde Abbey Leic. **d** 62 **p** 63 Leic. C of Braunstone 62-66; R of Thurlaston 66-73; V of St Steph N Evington 73-77; Perm to Offic Dio Cant from 79. *Flat 12, 146 Minnis Road, Birchington, Kent.* (Thanet 43402)

WILSON, Francis. b 34. ACP 67. Cudd Coll 71. **d** 73 **p** 74 Newc T. C of St Francis High Heaton Newc T 73-79; V of St

John Wallsend Dio Newc T from 79. *St John's Vicarage, Station Road, Wallsend-on-Tyne, Northumb.* (Wallsend 623944)

WILSON, Frank. b 32. **d** 78 **p** 79 Edmon. I of Vermilion Dio Edmon from 79. *Box 931, Vermilion, Alta, Canada, T0B 4M0.* (403-853 5201)

WILSON, Frank. b 32. **d** 78 **p** 79 Edmon. I of St Sav Vermilion Dio Edmon from 78. *Box 93, Vermilion, Alberta, Canada.*

WILSON, Frank Cecil. b 03. **d** 65 **p** 66 Southw. C of Gedling 65-68; V of N Clifton 68-75; C-in-c of Besthorpe and Girton 68-75; Perm to Offic Dio Southw from 75. *Colanroy, Church Lane, Collingham, Newark, Notts.*

WILSON, Frederick James Davis. Brisb Th Coll ACT ThL 37. **d** and **p** 38 Brisb. C of St Francis Nundah Brisb 38-42; St Thos Beaudesert 42-43; V of Caboolture 43-47; M of Bro of St Paul Dio Brisb 47-52; R of St Paul Manly 53-79. *c/o St Paul's Rectory, Ernest Street, Manly, Queensland, Australia 4179.* (396 2746)

WILSON, Frederick John. b 25. BSc (Eng) (Lon) 45. Oak Hill Th Coll 68. **d** 70 **p** 71 S'wark. C of Wandsworth 70-75; P-in-c of Garsdon w Lea and Cleverton Dio Bris from 75; Charlton w Brokenborough Dio Bris from 80. *Rectory, Lea, Malmesbury, Wilts, SN16 9PG.* (Malmesbury 3861)

✠ **WILSON, Right Rev Godfrey Edward Armstrong.** Univ of NZ BA 48. Linc Th Coll 51. **d** 54 **p** 55 Sheff. C of St Geo w St Steph Sheff 54-58; Masterton 58-59; V of Aramoho 59-62; St Pet Wel 62-78; Min Officer Dio Wai 78-80; VG Dio Auckld from 80; Cons Asst Bp of Auckld in Cathl Ch of H Trin Auckld 12 April 80 by Abp of NZ; Bps of Nel, Ch Ch, Auckld, Wel, Dun, Wai and Aotearoa; and Bps Wiggins, Spence and Monteith. *50 Clark Road, Papakura, NZ.*

WILSON, Gordon Noel. St Jo Coll Morpeth. **d** and **p** 62 Bath. C of Bath 62-64; P-in-c of Cobar 64-68; Bro Good Shepherd Brewarrina 69-70; R of Geurie 70-75; L to Offic Dio River 75-81; Perm to Offic Dio C & Goulb from 81. *Bimbimbie Village, Merimbula, NSW, Australia 2548.*

WILSON, Harold. b 29. St Jo Coll Ox BA 53, MA 57. Ridley Hall Cam 57. **d** 59 **p** 60 Cov. C of St Mary Leamington 59-61; Walsgrave-on-Sowe (in c of Potters Green) 61-64; V of Potters Green 64-67; Chap at Barcelona 67-73; V of Bursledon Dio Win from 73; RD of Eastleigh from 75. *Vicarage, School Road, Bursledon, Southampton.* (Bursledon 2821)

WILSON, Harold Marcus. St Jo Coll Dur BA (2nd cl Th) 55, Dipl Th 57. **d** 57 **p** 58 Blackb. C of Adlington 57-60; Chap miss to Seamen Basra 60-63; Kobe 63-67; S Sheilds and L to Offic Dio Dur 67-81; P-in-c of Crowfield w Stonham Aspal and Mickfield Dio St E from 81. *Rectory, The Street, Stonham Aspal, Stowmarket, Suff, IP14 6AQ.* (Stonham 409)

WILSON, Herbert Reginald. Late Scho and Exhib of St Chad's Coll Dur BA (2nd cl Th) 22, MA 25. St Steph Ho Ox 25. **d** 26 **p** 27 Wakef. C of St John Carlinghow 26-28; St Barn Ox 28-33; Chap Magd Coll Ox 29-33; V Cho and Chamberlain of York Minster and L to Offic Dio York 33-41; Jt Ed *York Journal of Conv* 37-43; Ed 43-62; Press Sec York Ho of Conv 37-43; Synodal Sec 43-67; Treas 47-67; Proc Conv Wakef 45-50; Dioc Insp Schs Dio Wakef 41-50; V of Birchencliffe 47-50; Hooton Pagnell 50-67; RD of Wath 62-67; Hon Can of Sheff 65-67; Chap at Marseilles w Aix-en-Provence Toulon and Hyeres 67-72; Hon Chap at Toulon from 72. *Campagne Le Jonquet, Chemin du Jonquet, 83200 Toulon, France.*

WILSON, Very Rev ian George MacQueen. b 20. Edin Th Coll 47. **d** 50 **p** 51 Glas. C of St Marg Newlands 50-52; P-in-c of St Gabr Glas 52-57; R of Ch Ch Dalbeattie 57-61; St John Baillieston 61-64; St Paul Rothesay 64-75; Can of St John's Cathl Oban from 73; P-in-c of St Pet Stornoway 75-78; Syn Clk Dio Arg Is 77-79; R of Ballachulish Dio Arg Is from 78; Glencoe Dio Arg Is from 78; Dean of Arg Is from 79. *Rectory, Glencoe, Argyll.* (Ballachulish 335)

WILSON, Iorwerth Thomas. St D Coll Lamp BA 33. **d** 35 Bp Wentworth Shields for Ban for St A **p** 36 St A. C of Minera 35-39; Odiham 39-42; Eling 42-43; R of Nettleton 43-47; V of Fotherby w Brackenborough Utterby and L Grimsby 47-54; R of Ch Lawton 54-64; PC of H Trin Northwich 64-72. *Pilgrims Way, Abbey Road, Pontrhydfendigaid, Ystrad Meurig, Dyfed.*

WILSON, Irvin. b 34. Univ of Dur BA 58, Dipl Th 60. Cranmer Hall Dur 58. **d** 60 **p** 61 Bradf. C of Bingley 60-64; Manningham 64-66; C-in-c 66-68; V 68-73; Thornton Dio Bradf from 74. *Thornton Vicarage, Bradford, Yorks.* (Thornton 3200)

WILSON, Preb James Francis. b 07. Bp Wilson Coll IM 32. **d** 34 **p** 36 Lich. C of St Chad Burton-on-Trent 34-39; V of St Thos Stafford 39-40; Stretton w Wetmoor 40-50; Wootton 50-55; St Chad Burton-on-Trent 55-56; R of Turvey 56-59; Porlock (w Stoke Pero from 73) 59-77; Stoke Pero 59-73; Surr 66-77; RD of Dunster 68-73; Exmoor 73-75; Preb of Wells Cathl 76-77; Preb (Emer) from 78. *Woodbine Cottage, Cross, Axbridge, Somt.*

WILSON, James Lewis. b 39. TCD BA 62, MA 65, BD 71, Div Test 74. **d** 74 **p** 75 Clogh. C of Enniskillen 74-76; St Matt Shankill Belf 76-79; I of Killeshandra w Killegar 79-81; Derrylane 79-81; Loughgilly w Clare Dio Armagh from 81. *124 Gosford Road, Loughgilly, Armagh, BT60 2DE.* (Glenanne 265)

WILSON, James Robert. b 36. **d** 66 **p** 67 Connor. C of Ballywillan (Portrush) 67-73; V of Drummaul Dio Connor from 73; R of Duneane & Ballyscullion Dio Connor from 79. *Vicarage, Randalstown, Co Antrim, BT41 3LA, N Ireland.* (Randalstown 72561)

WILSON, Canon John Cecil Julius. LTh (NZ) 42. **d** 40 Ch Ch for Wai **p** 41 Auckld for Wai. C of St John Napier 40-43; V of Whakatane 43-49; Taradale 49-55; Havelock N Dio Wai 55-70; CF (NZ) 46-47; Hon Can of St John's Cathl Napier 58-61; Can 61-77; Can (Emer) from 77; V of Otane 70-77; Perm to Offic Dio Wai from 77. *94 Te Mata Road, Havelock North, NZ.*

WILSON, Canon John Christopher Heathcote. b 13. Qu Coll Ox BA 39, MA 41. Cudd Coll 40. **d** 41 **p** 42 Bradf. C of St Wilfrid Lidget Green 41-44; Skipton 44-47; CF 47-50; V of St Nich Hull 50-59; Kirk Ella Dio York from 59; Surr from 62; Area Dean in Hull RD 72-79; Can and Preb of York Minster from 79. *Kirk Ella Vicarage, Hull, Yorks, HU10 7TG.* (0482 653040)

WILSON, John Clifford. b 32. K Coll Lon and Warm AKC 56. **d** 57 **p** 58 Birm. C of Bordesley 57-59; King's Norton Dio Birm 59-61; V of L Aden and Chap Somaliland 61-63; V of Lydbrook 64-67; Team V with St Mary Bow w Bromley 69-73; P-in-c of St Pet Mile End w St Benet Stepney 73-80; P-in-c of Long Marton w Dufton and Milburn Dio Carl 80-81; R from 81. *Rectory, Long Marton, Appleby, Cumb.* (Kirkby Thore 269)

WILSON, John Frederick. b 33. Qu Coll Birm 58. **d** 61 **p** 62 Dur. C of Jarrow 61-65; All SS Monk Wearmouth 65-68; P-in-c All SS Belize 68-69; R of St Paul Corozal 69-71; V of Resurr Scunthorpe Dio Linc from 71. *Vicarage, Mirfield Road, Scunthorpe, Lincs.* (Scunthorpe 2196)

WILSON, John Gordon. Univ of Otago BMedSc 72, MB, ChB 73, BD 77. St Jo Coll Auckld. **d** 76 **p** 77 Dun. C of St John Invercargil 76-78; V of Riverton Dio Dun from 78. *10 Dallas Street, Riverton, Southland, NZ.*

WILSON, Canon John Hamilton. b 29. St Chad's Coll Dur BA 53. Sarum Th Coll 53. **d** 55 **p** 56 Win. C of Westend 55-59; Fishponds 59-64; V of St Francis Ashton Gate Bedminster 64-73; RD of Bedminster 68-73; Surr from 68; R of Horfield Dio Bris from 73; Hon Can of Bris from 77. *Horfield Rectory, Bristol, BS7 8ST.*

WILSON, John Henderson Foulis. Univ of St Andr MA (2nd cl Hist) 35. Edin Th Coll 36. **d** 39 **p** 40 Glas. C of Ch Ch Glas 39-41; CF (EC) 41-46; Vice-Prin Test Coll Cumbrae 46-48; Chap Edin Th Coll 48-51; R of St Andr Dunmore w St Mary Grangemouth 51-54; St Pet Fraserburgh 54-63; Exam Chap to Bp of Aber 54-63; R of Columba Crieff 63-73; P-in-c of Elie 73-78; Pittenweem 73-78. *1 Garry Place, Comrie, Perthshire.* (Comrie 8146)

WILSON, Canon John Hewitt. b 24. CB 77. TCD BA 46, Div Test (1st cl) 47, MA 61. **d** 47 **p** 48 Dub. C of St Geo Dub 47-50; Chap RAF 50-80; Cranwell 50-53; Aden 53-55; Wittering 55-57; Cottesmore 57-58; Germany 59-61; Staff Chap Air Ministry 61-63; Cranwell 63-66; Asst Chap-in-Chief FEAF 66-69; Strike Commd 69-73; Hon Chap to HM the Queen 73-80; Chap-in-Chief and Archd 73-80; Can and Preb of Linc Cathl 74-80; Can (Emer) from 80; V of The Heyfords w Rousham and Somerton Dio Ox from 81. *Glencree, Philcote Street, Deddington, Oxford, OX5 4TB.* (Deddington 38903)

WILSON, John Lake. b 34. Linc Th Coll 74. **d** 76 **p** 77 Lynn for Nor. C of King's Lynn 76-80; V of Narborough w Narford Dio Nor from 80; R of Pentney w W Bilney Dio Nor from 80. *Narborough Vicarage, King's Lynn, Norf.* (Narborough 337322)

WILSON, John Michael. b 16. Univ of Lon MB BS 42, MRCP and MD 48. **d** 53 **p** 56 Man. C of Leigh Lancs 53-57; Chap Guild of Health 58-62; C of St Martin-in-the-Fields Westmr 58-63; Lect 63-67; L to Offic Dio Birm from 67; Research Fell Univ of Birm 67-71; Lect 71-78; Sen Lect from 78. *4 Eastern Road, Selly Park, Birmingham, B29 7JP.*

WILSON, John Robert Mersa. b 41. St Jo Coll Auckld LTh 71. **d** 69 **p** 70 Auckld. C of Pukekohe 69-72; E Coast Bays 72; V of N Wairoa Dio Auckld 73-80; Hon C from 80. *c/o Box 378, Dargaville, NZ.*

WILSON, John Stafford. b 21. Tyndale Hall Bris 49. **d** 51 **p** 52 Nor. C of St Cath Mile Cross Dio Nor 51-53; BCMS Miss at Casablanca 53-57; Demnat 57-68; V of Packington w Normanton-le-Heath 68-72; St Geo Worthing Dio Chich from 72. *20 Seldon Road, Worthing, Sussex.* (Worthing 203309)

WILSON, John Walter. b 25. Univ of Dur BA 67, MSc 74. Cranmer Hall Dur 64. **d** 67 **p** 68 Dur. C of St Helen Bp Auckland 67-69; V of S Hetton 69-75; Lect Sunderland Poly from 75. *7 Holmlands Park South, Sunderland.*

WILSON, John Warwick. Ridley Coll Melb ACT ThL (2nd cl) 62, Th Scho 64. BD (2nd cl) Lon 66. **d** and **p** 64 Armid. C of H Trin Oakleigh 64; Narrabri 64-67; P-in-c of Tingha 67-68; on leave 69-72; C of St Hilary Kew 73-77; Lect Ridley Coll Melb and L to Offic Dio Melb from 73. *c/o Ridley College, Parkville, Vic, Australia 3052.* (03-380 1090)

WILSON, Joseph William Sidney. b 23. St Aid Coll 62. **d** 64 Warrington for Liv **p** 65 Liv. C of Gt Sankey 64-66; Chap Miss to Seamen Rotterdam 67-68; C of St John Birkdale 68-71; V of Eppleton 71-78; Riccall Dio York from 78. *Vicarage, Riccall, York, YO4 6PN.* (Riccall 326)

WILSON, Keith. b 38. Chich Th Coll 60. **d** 63 **p** 64 Lich. C of St Francis Friar Pk W Bromwich 63-66; Kirkley 66-70; R of Newton Flotman w Swainsthorpe 70-75; Acle Dio Nor from 75; Fishley Dio Nor from 77; RD of Blofield from 80. *Rectory, Norwich Road, Acle, Norwich, NR13 3BU.* (Great Yarmouth 750393)

WILSON, Keith Dawes. Moore Th Coll Syd. **d** and **p** 54 C & Goulb. C of Yass 54; R of Cobargo 54-59; Bombala 59-68; Junee 68-72; C of St John Canberra Dio C & Goulb from 72; Chap R Canberra Hosp from 80. *3 Amaroo Street, Reid, ACT, Australia 2601.* (062-49 1994)

WILSON, Keith James. Wollaston Th Coll W Austr ACT ThL 61. **d** 61 **p** 62 Perth. C of Scarborough 61-65; on leave 66-67; Dioc Youth Worker Perth 67-68; Min of Nallamara Balga 69-71; R of Balga 71-76; Perm to Offic Dio Perth from 77. *40 Gratwick Way, Koondoola, W Australia 6064.* (342 6404)

WILSON, Kenneth Daniel. *See* Anand, Kenneth Daniel Wilson.

WILSON, Leonard Cyril. b 07. St Paul's Miss Coll Burgh 28. **d** 33 York for Col **p** 34 Trinid. Chap of Publ Insts Port of Spain and C of St Paul San Fernando 33-34; V of Pembroke 34-38; St Clem Naparima 38-41; R of St Geo Tortola 41-45; St Geo St Kitts 45-49; C of St Greg Gt Northgate Cant 49-52; C-in-c Brockdish w Thorpe Abbotts 52-54; V of St Mary Thetford 54-58; RD of Thetford 57-58; PC of Calow 58-59; C of St Luke Derby 59-61; C-in-c of Burbage w Harpur Hill 61-63; C 63-73; L to Offic Dio Newc T from 73. *Castle Vale House, Berwick-upon-Tweed, Northumb.* (0289-7146)

WILSON, Canon Leslie Rule. b 09. Edin Th Coll 29. **d** 33 St Andr **p** 34 Edin. C of St Marg Leven w St Andr Denbeath 33-34; Old St Paul Edin 34-36; R of St Andr Fort William (w Nether Lochaber and Portree from 38) 36-42; Synod Clk Dio Arg Is and Can of Arg Is and Cumbrae 40-42; Perm to Offic Dio Dur 45; Toc H Chap India and SEAC 45-46; V of Malacca 46-53; Kuching Cathl 53-55; Provost and Can of St Thos Cathl Kuching 55-59; Perm to Offic Dio Dur 59-60; R of Geraldton W Austr 60-62; Dean and R of H Cross Cathl Geraldton 62-66; Hon Can from 66; Sub-Dean and R of All SS Cathl Thursday I 66-67; Archd of Carp 66-67; Commiss NW Austr from 66; R of Winterbourne Stickland w Turnworth 67-69; Winterbourne Houghton 67-69; V of Holmside 69-74; Perm to Offic Dio Dur 74-80; Dio Truro from 78. *Holmside, Orchard Way, Goldsithney, Penzance, Cornwall, TR20 9EY.*

WILSON, Malcolm Howard Wood. b 24. Univ of W Ont BA 59. Hur Coll Lon Ont MDiv 76. **d** 79 Bp Robinson for Hur. R of Chatsworth Dio Hur from 79. *Box 87, Chatsworth, Ont, Canada, N0H 1G0.*

WILSON, Malcolm Richard Milburn. b 30. Edin Th Coll 57. **d** 59 **p** 60 Glas. C of St Aug Dumbarton 59-61; Miss P of Chanda Nagp 62-63; C of H Trin Dunfermline 63-65; R of Newport-on-Tay w Tayport 65-70; R of St Jo Evang Baillieston w St Serf Shettleston 70-74; All SS Bearsden w St Andr Milngavie Dio Glas from 74. *Rectory, Roman Road, Bearsden, Glasgow, G61 2SQ.* (041-942 0386)

WILSON, Mark Anthony John. b 56. TCD BA 80. Div Hostel Dub 75. **d** 80 **p** 81 Dub. C of Rathfarnham Dio Dub from 80. *183 Carriglea, Firhouse, Templeogue, Dublin 16, Irish Republic.*

WILSON, Mark John Crichton. b 46. Clare Coll Cam BA 67, MA 70. Ridley Hall Cam 67. **d** 69 **p** 70 St Alb. C of Luton and E Hyde 69-72; Ashtead 72-77; Chap Epsom Coll and L to Offic Dio Guildf 77-81; V of Ch Ch Epsom Dio Guildf from 81. *Vicarage, Christ Church Road, Epsom, Surrey, KT19 8NE.* (Epsom 20302)

WILSON, Maurice James Fraser. b 06. Wells Th Coll 55. **d** 56 **p** 57 Ches. C of Bowdon 56-59; V of Hartford 59-69; P-in-c of Tilston w Shocklach 70-71; R 71-74. *Lovel Hollow, Church Road, Baschurch, Salop.*

WILSON, Mervyn Raynold Alwyn. b 33. Qu Coll Cam BA (2nd cl Hist Trip pts i and ii) 57, MA 61. Ripon Hall Ox **d** 59 **p** 60 Birm. C of Rubery 59-62; King's Norton 62-63; PC of St Bernard Hamstead 63-69; R of Bermondsey 69-78; Bulwick and Blatherwycke w Harringworth and Laxton Dio Pet from 78. *Bulwick Rectory, Corby, Northants, NN17 3DY.* (Bulwick 249)

WILSON, Mervyn Robert. b 22. Univ of Bris BA 51. BD (Lon) 58. Tyndale Hall Bris 48. **d** 52 **p** 53 Down. C of Ballymacarrett 52-56; Donaghcloney 56-59; Newtownards 59-61; R of Ballyphilip w Ardquin 61-70; St Patr Newry Dio Drom from 70; RD of Kilbroney and Newry and Mourne from 77. *1 Arthur Street, Newry, Co Down, BT34 1HR, N Ireland.* (Newry 2227)

WILSON, Michael. b 13. Trin Coll Cam BA 35, MA 39. Westcott Ho Cam 37. **d** 38 **p** 39 Win. C of Eastleigh 38-41; CF (EC) 41-46; V of St Mary Bourne 45-52; R of Ndola 52-61; Kingsland 61-65; Luanshya 66-68; C of St Mary w St Clem Bournemouth 68-73; V of Appleshaw 73-78; Novice Counsellor 3rd O SSF 73-81. *26a Quarry Road, Winchester, Hants. SO23 8JG.* (Winchester 60172)

WILSON, Michael. b 44. Univ of Liv BA 66, Fitzw Coll Cam BA (3rd cl Th pt ii) 68. MA 73. Westcott Ho Cam. **d** 69 Southw **p** 70 Sherwood for Southw. C of Worksop 69-71; Gt Malvern 71-75; V of St Anne City and Dio Leic from 75; Regr of the Leic Dioc Assoc of Readers from 78; M Gen Syn from 80. *76 Letchworth Road, Leicester, LE3 6FH.* (Leic 858452)

WILSON, Nigel John Buller. b 42. Univ of Leeds BA 74. Coll of the Resurr Mirfield 74. **d** 75 **p** 76 Pontefract for Wakef. C of Penistone 75-77; Odiham w Long Sutton and S Warnborough 77-79; P-in-c of Burstwick w Thorngumbald 79-81; Gilling E Dio York from 81. *Rectory, Gilling East, York, YO6 4JH.* (Ampleforth 254)

WILSON, Paul Thomas Wardley. b 43. AKC 67. St Aug Coll Cant. **d** 70 **p** 71 Willesden for Lon. C of Tokyngton 70-74; Social Commun Worker Dio Roch 74-81. *Address temp unknown.*

WILSON, Peter Dudley. St Paul's Coll Grahmstn 59. **d** 61 **p** 62 Capetn. C of Sea Point 61-65; P-in-c of St Helena Bay 65-67; R of Malmesbury 67-73; Archd and R of Cradock 74-78; R of Krugersdorp Dio Johann from 78. *Box 505, Krugersdorp 1740, Johannesburg, S Africa.*

WILSON, Peter Hamilton Thomas. ACT ThL 59. **d** and **p** 58 Wang. C of Shepparton 57-60; R of Cobram 60-63; Industr Chap Dio Melb from 63. *1 Little Street, Werribee, Vic. 3030, Australia.*

WILSON, Peter John. b 43. Linc Th Coll 68. **d** 71 Man **p** 72 Hulme for Man. C of Stretford 71-73; Rugby 74-79; P-in-c of St Paul Accrington 79-81. *c/o Vicarage, Barnfield Street, Accrington, Lancs.* (Accrington 33199)

WILSON, Peter McLay. b 43. Univ of Adel BEcon 74. Trin Coll Melb BD 78. **d** 77 Melb **p** 77 Bal for Melb. C of Warrnambool 77-78; R of Willaura 78-79; Broadford 79-81; P-in-c of St Jas Lavington Dio C & Goulb from 81. *Box 155, Lavington, NSW, Australia 2641.*

WILSON, Peter Sheppard. b 39. TCD BA 61, Div Test 62. **d** 62 **p** 63 Derry. C of Killowen 62-68; St Columba Portadown 68-70; I of Convoy w Monellan and Donaghmore 70-78; P-in-c of Castletown Dio S & M 78; V from 78. *Vicarage, Castletown, IM.* (82 3509)

WILSON, Quentin Harcourt. b 45. AKC 68. FTCL 75. K Coll Lon BD 76. St Aug Coll Cant 69. **d** 70 **p** 71 Lon. C of Ch Ch w St Jo and St Luke Poplar 70-72; St Jas Muswell Hill 72-77; Sacr and Succr of Ex Cathl 77-81; Min Can of St Geo Chap Windsor from 81. *24 The Cloisters, Windsor Castle, Berks.* (Windsor 66444)

WILSON, Raymond Arthur Harvey. Univ of Melb BA 63. Trin Coll Melb 63. **d** 65 **p** 66 Melb. C of Footscray 65-67; St Pet Melb 67-69; Min of Kilsyth, Montrose and Moorodbark 69-73; I of Bulleen 73-78; C of Angl Inner City Min (in c of St Phil Collingwood and N Richmond) Dio Melb from 78. *144 Hoddle Street, Abbotsford, Vic, Australia 3067.* (419 4215)

WILSON, Richard Rennison. b 38. **d** 65 **p** 66 Arm. C of Derryloran 65-68; in Amer Ch 68-69; C of Stormont Belf 69-70; I of Rathdowney 70-77; Baltinglass w Ballynure, Stratford-on-Slaney and Rathvilly Dio Leigh from 77. *The Rectory, Baltinglass, Co Wicklow, Irish Republic.*

WILSON, Robert Brian. b 29. K Coll Lon and Warm AKC 55. **d** 56 **p** 57 Ripon. C of Wortley 56-60; Chap Allerton 60-63; V of St Pet w St Cuthb Hunslet Moor 63-70; Bilton 70-80; Gt w L Ouseburn w Marton w Grafton Dio Ripon from 80. *Great Ouseburn Vicarage, York, YO5 9RQ.* (Green Hammerton 30546)

WILSON, Robert Malcolm. b 35. Univ of St Andr Fife MA 59. ALCD (2nd cl) 62. **d** 62 **p** 63 S'wark. C of Wallington 62-66; St Nich Durham 66-70; V of St Pet Colchester, Dio Chelmsf from 70. *St Peter's Vicarage, Colchester, Essex.*

WILSON, Robert Michael. b 33. Linc Th Coll 73. **d** 75 **p** 76 Pontefract for Wakef. C of Knottingley 75-78; P-in-c of St Luke Cleckheaton Dio Wakef from 78; Cleckheaton, Whitechapel Dio Wakef from 81. *62 Whitcliffe Road, Cleckheaton, W Yorks.*

WILSON, Robert Robinson. b 09. St Aid Coll 43. **d** 43 Ballingarry 45 Wakef. C of All S Halifax 43; Woodhouse 44-47; V of All S Bolton 47-50; Earls Heaton 50-57; Platt Bridge 57-68; R of Full Sutton w Skirpenbeck 68-75; Perm to Offic Dio Carl from 76. *14 Kirkstead Road, Belle Vue, Carlisle, CA2 7RD.* (Carl 20231)

WILSON, Robert Stoker. b 39. Univ of Dur BSc 62. Oak Hill Th Coll 62. **d** 64 **p** 65 Newc T. C of St Paul Elswick Newc T 64-68; Kirkheaton 68-70; Sen Youth Worker and Chap Shrewsbury Ho Liv 70-73; Dioc Youth Chap Dio Dur 73-77; P-in-c of St Steph S Shields Dio Dur 73-78; R from 78; P-in-c of St Aid S Shields Dio Dur from 81. *45 Lawe Road, South Shields, NE33 2EN.* (South Shields 561831)

✠ **WILSON, Right Rev Roger Plumpton.** b 05. KCVO 74. Late Scho of Keble Coll Ox 1st cl Cl Mods 26, BA (2nd cl Lit Hum) 28, MA 34. DD (Lambeth) 49. Westcott Ho Cam 35. **d** 35 Liv **p** 36 Warrington for Liv. C of St Paul Prince's Pk 35-38; St Jo Evang Westmr 38-39; V of H Trin S Shore Blackpool 39-44; Radcliffe-on-Trent 44-49; Archd of Nottm 44-49; V of Shelford 46-49; Surr 47-49; Select Pr Univ of Ox 54-55; Cons Ld Bp of Wakef in York Minster 25 Apl 49 by Abp of York; Bps of Southw; Ripon; Newc T; and Heref; Bps Suffr of Penrith; and Willesden; and Bps Gerard, Hardy, Weller, and Mounsey; Trld to Chich 58; res 74; Clk of the Closet 63-74. *Kingsett, Wrington, Bristol, BS18 7NH.*

WILSON, Canon Ronald. b 11. St Aid Coll. **d** 51 **p** 52 Southw. C of Lenton 51-53; St Anne Worksop 53-55; C-in-c of St Barn Conv Distr Lenton Abbey 55-58; V 58-63; Pinchbeck 63-78; RD of Elloc W from 70; Can and Preb of Linc Cathl 72-78; Can (Emer) from 78. *65 West End Road, Wyberton, Boston, Lincs.* (Boston 68993)

WILSON, Canon Spencer William. b 08. AKC 35. **d** 35 **p** 36 Liv. C of Ormskirk (in c of Lathom Pk) 35-38; Walton-on-the-Hill (in c of St Aid) 38-42; V of St Jas Haydock Dio Liv from 42; Surr from 48; Hon Can of Liv Cathl from 71. *169 Church Road, Haydock, St Helen's, Merseyside, WA11 0NJ.* (Ashton-in-Makerfield 727956)

WILSON, Stanley. b 24. TCD BA 45, MA 50. **d** 46 **p** 47 Connor. C of St Bart Belf 46-50; St Polycarp Finaghy 50-54; Seapatrick 54-55; I of Ballymascanlon 55-60; R of Woodschapel 60-63; Industr Chap Dio Worc 63-65; C-in-c of St Paul Worc 65-67; Chap Worc Hosps 67-77; V of The Guitings w Cutsdean and Farmcote Dio Glouc from 77. *Vicarage, Temple Guiting, Cheltenham, Glos, GL54 5RP.* (Guiting Power 268)

WILSON, Stephen Charles. b 51. Univ of Newc T BA 73. Em Coll Cam BA (Th) 78. Westcott Ho Cam 77. **d** 79 Kens for Lon **p** 80 Lon. C of All SS Fulham Dio Lon from 79. *73 Parkview Court, SW6.* (01-731 1609)

WILSON, Stuart Michael. b 47. Univ of Surrey BSc 71. St Steph Ho Ox BA 73, MA 78. **d** 74 Lon **p** 75 Edmon for Lon. C of St Paul Tottenham 74-78; C-in-c of S Kenton Conv Distr Dio Lon from 78. *1 Rydal Gardens, Wembley, Middx, HA9 8SA.* (01-904 9745)

WILSON, Sydney John. b 19. Wells Th Coll 63. **d** 64 Guildf for Ox **p** 64 Ox. C of Windsor 64-67; V of Basildon Berks 67-74; C-in-c of Ashampstead 67-70; V of St Bart Hyde Win 74-81. *103 Kings Road, Fleet, Hants, GU13 9AR.*

WILSON, Thomas Hargreaves. Bp's Univ Lennox BA 59. Wells Th Coll 59. **d** 61 **p** 62 Ott. C of Pembroke 61-62; St Martin Ott 62-65; V of Wakefield w Lascelles Dio Ott from 65. *PO Box 39, Wakefield, PQ, Canada.* (1-819-459-2905)

WILSON, Thomas Irven. b 30. TCD BA 51, Div Test 52, MA 58. **d** 53 Kilm for Connor **p** 54 Connor. C of Ballymena 53-56; Chap RAF from 57; Hon Chap to HM the Queen from 80. *c/o Ministry of Defence, Adastral House, WC1X 8RU.*

WILSON, Canon Thomas Roderick. b 26. St Pet Hall Ox BA 50, MA 55. Sarum Th Coll 50. **d** 52 **p** 53 Blackb. C of Morecambe 52-56; Altham w Clayton-le-Moors 56-58; V of H Trin Habergham Eaves Burnley 58-78; RD of Burnley 70-78; Hon Can of Blackb from 75; V of St Chris Bare Morecambe 78-81; P-in-c of St Jas and of St Paul Accrington Dio Blackb from 81. *Vicarage, Barnfield Street, Accrington, BB5 2AQ.* (Accrington 33199)

WILSON, Victor Isaac. b 23. St Deiniol's Libr Hawarden 69. **d** 71 **p** 72 Ches. C of Davenham 71-75; V of Latchford 75-80; Stalybridge Dio Ches from 80. *St Paul's Vicarage, Stalybridge, Gtr Man.* (061-338 2514)

WILSON, Walter. b 33. **d** 60 **p** 61 Sheff. C of St Swith Sheff 60-64; Chap Industr Miss Dio Sheff 64-66; C of Attercliffe w Carbrook Sheff 66-69; R of Swallow w Cabourn 69-72; Dioc Youth Officer, Dio Heref 72-77; Chap of Ipswich Sch from 77. *37 Henley Road, Ipswich, Suff.* (Ipswich 55561)

WILSON, Walter George. b 1893. Coll of Resurr Mirfield 19. **d** 22 **p** 23 Man. C of St Pet Fleetwood 22-24; St Thos Dudley 24-26; Bideford 26-31; Sidmouth (in c of St Francis of Assisi) 31-36; V of Colyton 36-64; L to Offic Dio Win 64-76. *The Chantry, Hereford Road, Monmouth, Gwent, NP5 3PA.*

WILSON, William Bell. b 04. AKC 28. **d** 27 **p** 28 Newc T. C of St Mary Virg Newc T 27-29; Banstead w Burgh Heath (in c of Nork) 30-32; St Barbara Cov 32-34; Min of Distr of St Geo City and Dio Cov 34-39; V 39-71; Chap RAFVR 41-45; Perm to Offic Dio Cov from 71. *2 St James Close, Alveston, Stratford-on-Avon.*

WILSON, William Gerard. b 42. St Chad's Coll Dur BA 65, Dipl Th 67. **d** 67 **p** 68 Man. C of Hollinwood 67-71; V of St Jas Oldham 71-79; R of Birch-in-Rusholme w Fallowfield Dio Man from 79. *197 Old Hall Lane, Manchester, M14 6HJ.* (06-224 1310)

✠ **WILSON, Right Rev William Gilbert.** b 18. TCD BA 39, Div Test and Aramaic and Syriac Pri 40, MA and BD 44, PhD 49. **d** 41 Down **p** 42 Bp Hind for Down. C of St Mary Magd Belf 41-44; Bangor 44-47; I of Armoy w Loughguile 47-76; Preb of St Sav Cathl Connor 64-76; Dean of Connor 76-81; R of Ch Ch Cathl Lisburn 76-81; Cons Ld Bp of Kilm, Elph and Ard in St Anne's Cathl Belf 21 Sept 81 by Abps of Arm and Dub; Bps of Meath, Connor, Tuam, Down, Cash, Clog, Derry and Lim; and others. *See House, Kilmore, Cavan, Irish Republic.* (Cavan 31336)

WILSON, William Hubert. b 08. Late Cho Exhib of Clare Coll Cam 3rd cl Hist Trip pt i 29, BA (2nd cl Th Trip pt i) 31, MA 34. Westcott Ho Cam 31. **d** 32 **p** 33 Birm. C of St Mary Handsworth 32-35; St Luke Chelsea 35-39; V of H Trin Southall 39-47; St Mark Hamilton Terrace 47-64; R of Ch Stretton 64-72; Chap at Tel Aviv 72-76. *Kilronaig, Wester Carie, Rannoch Station, Perthshire, PH17 2QJ.*

WILTON, Albert Edward. b 10. **d** 67 **p** 68 Mashon. Hon C St Eliz Salisbury 67-68; St Paul's Coll Grahmstn 69; C of All SS Plumstead 70-72; R of Worcester Capetn 72-75; Devil's Peak 75-77; Perm to Offic Dio St E from 77. *8 Jermyns Road, Reydon, Southwold, Suff.*

WILTON, Harry Owens. b 22. St Aid Coll 43. **d** 46 **p** 47 Liv. C of St Cyp Edge Hill 46-49; H Trin Hull 49-51; Area Sec CCCS NW Engl 51-53; V of All S Southport 53-56. *23 Beacon Drive, West Kirby, Wirral, Mer, L48 7EB.* (051-625 6533)

WILTSE, Joseph August Jean Paul Milton. Univ of Leeds BA (2nd cl Phil and Engl Lit) 64. Coll of Resurr Mirfield 64. **d** 66 Wakef **p** 67 Pontefract for Wakef. C of Airedale w Fryston 66-70; C of St John Burns Lake 71-73; on leave 74-76 and from 78; C of Golden 76-77. *PO Box 1440, Fernie, BC, Canada.*

WILTSHIRE, Archdeacon of. *See* Smith, Ven Brian John.

WILTSHIRE, Albert. b 19. Qu Coll Birm 49. **d** 51 **p** 52 Dur. C of St Jo Bapt Stockton-on-Tees 51-55; Bran (in c of St Agatha Bran Colliery) 55-57; PC of Ven Bede Monk Wearmouth 57-59; V of Carlinghow 59-63; Woodhorn w Newbiggin 63-71; Chatton w Chillingham 71-75; Chap of O of H Paraclete Whitby 75-77; P-in-c of Felton 77-80; V of Cornhill w Carham Dio Newc T from 80; Branxton Dio Newc T from 81. *Vicarage, Cornhill-on-Tweed, Northumb, TD12 4EQ.* (Coldstream 2105)

WILTSHIRE, John Herbert Arthur. b 27. SOC 63. **d** 66 **p** 67 S'wark. C of Good Shepherd w St Pet Lee 66-70; Min of Em Conv Distr W Dulwich 69-79; R of Coulsdon Dio S'wark from 79. *232 Coulsdon Road, Coulsdon, Surrey.* (Downland 52152)

WILTSHIRE, Canon Percy. St Jo Coll Auckld **d** 25 Auckld **p** 30 Wel. C of Stratford 26; All SS Palmerston N 27-32; V of Mangatainoka-Pongaroa 32-39; Hunterville 39-44; Pahautanui 44-50; Khandallah Wel 50-58; Can of Wel 52-69; V of Martinborough 58-60; Chap Wanganui Hosp 60-69; Can (Emer) from 70. *Selwyn Village, Point Chevalier, Auckland, NZ.* (861-233)

WILTSHIRE, Richard George. b 31. **d** 78 Bp Ndwandwe for Johann **p** 79 Johann (NSM). P-in-c of St Anne Stilfontein Dio Johann from 78. *PO Box 383, Stilfontein, S Africa 2550.*

✠ **WIMBUSH, Right Rev Richard Knyvet.** b 09. Or Coll Ox 2nd cl Cl Mods 30, BA (1st cl Th) 32, MA 35. Cudd Coll 32. **d** 34 **p** 35 Ox. Chap of Cudd Coll 34-37; C of Pocklington 37-39; St Wilfrid Harrogate 39-42; R of Melsonby 42-48; Prin Edin Th Coll 48-63; Can of St Mary's Cathl Edin 48-63; Exam Chap to Bp of Edin 49-62; Cons Bp of Argyll and The Isles in Edin Cathl 25 Jan 63 by Bp of Glas (Primus); Bps of Moray; St Andr; Aber; Brech and Edin; Bp Suffr of Aston; and Bp Graham; Select Pr Ox Univ 71; Elected Primus of Episc Ch in Scotld 74; res 77; Asst Bp in Dio York from 77; P-in-c of Etton w Dalton Holme Dio York from 77. *Etton Rectory, Beverley, N Humb, HU17 7PQ.* (Dalton Holme 684)

WIMBUSH, Timothy. b 44. St Steph Ho Ox. **d** 68 Bp Sinker for Birm **p** 69 Birm. C of Hob's Moat 68-71; W

Wycombe 71-76; R of Epwell w Sibford, Swalcliffe and Tadmarton Dio Ox from 76. *Rectory, Sibford Gower, Banbury, OX15 5RW.* (Swalcliffe 555)

WIMMER, Michael John. Univ of Natal BA 64. Coll of Resurr Mirfield 65. **d** 67 S'wark for Johann **p** 68 Johann. C of Johann Cathl 67-70; R of Bloemhof Dio Johann from 71; R of St Barn Lichtenburg w Zeerust 71-73; Vereeniging Dio Johann from 74; P-in-c of Vanderbijl Pk Dio Johann from 78. *Box 3167, Three Rivers, Johannesburg, S Africa.*

WIMSHURST, Michael Alexander. b 33. St Jo Coll Ox BA 58. Westcott Ho Cam 59. **d** 60 **p** 61 S'wark. C of Lewisham 60-65; Cathl Ch of Redemption New Delhi 66-67; Ajmer Delhi 67-70; V of St Pet (w St Paul from 73) Battersea Dio S'wark from 71. *21 Plough Road, SW11.* (01-228 8027)

WINBOLT LEWIS, Martin John. b 46. Fitzw Coll Cam BA 69, MA 72. St Jo Coll Nottm LTh 75. **d** 75 Stepney for Lon **p** 76 Lon. C of Highbury 75-78; St Nich Nottm 79-81; R of Carlton-Colville w Mutford w Rushmere Dio Nor from 81. *Rectory, Waters Avenue, Carlton-Colville, Lowestoft, Suff.* (Lowestoft 65217)

WINCH, Victor Edward. b 17. Selw Coll Cam BA 47, MA 52. Assoc Inst Bankers 41. Ridley Hall Cam. **d** 48 **p** 49 Chelmsf. C of Gt Baddow 48-50; Org Sec CPAS for SW Area 50-54; V of St Mary-in-Castle Hastings 54-69; V of Em Hastings 54-69; Kirdford w Plaistow Dio Chich from 69; Chap Buchanan Hosp 59-69. *Kirdford Vicarage, Billinghurst, Sussex.* (Kirdford 210)

WINCHESTER, Lord Bishop of. *See* Taylor, Right Rev John Vernon.

WINCHESTER, Assistant Bishop in Diocese of. *See* Dehqani-Tafti, Right Rev Hassan Barnaba.

WINCHESTER, Archdeacon of. *See* Cartwright, Ven Edward David.

WINCHESTER, Dean of. *See* Stancliffe, Very Rev Michael Staffurth.

WINCHESTER, George Flett. St Chad's Coll Regina. **d** 60 **p** 61 Edmon. Chap St Greg Miss Kitscoty 60-63; C of St Pet Lutton Place Edin 63-64; V of Westlock 64-67; Westaskiwin Dio Edmon from 67. *5105 46th Avenue, Westaskiwin, Alta., Canada.* (403-352 5672)

WINCHESTER, John. b 1899. K Coll Lon 29. **d** 32 **p** 33 Lich. C of St Lawr Darlaston 32-36; V of Longdon-on-Tern 36-46; R of Rodington 37-46; St Pet Oldham Road w St Jas L Man 46-50; Tibberton 50-68; R of Kynnersley 55-68; Perm to Offic Dio Sarum from 68. *123 Dorchester Road, Poole, Dorset, BH15 3RY.* (Parkstone 745096)

WINCHESTER, Paul. b 44. St Pet Coll Ox BA (2nd cl Th) 66, MA 70. Ridley Hall Cam 67. **d** 69 **p** 70 Lich. C of Heath Town 69-72; Perm to Offic Dio Sarum from 73; Asst Master Broadstone Middle Sch from 73. *123 Dorchester Road, Poole, Dorset, BH15 3RY.*

WINCOTT, Stanley Cyrus. b 18. K Coll Lon AKC 49. St Bonif Coll Warm 49. **d** 49 **p** 50 Win. C of St Jo Bapt Moordown Bournemouth 49-53; N Stoneham w Bassett 53-58; V of St Mary Extra (Pear Tree) 58-80. *30 Milbury Crescent, Bitterne, Southampton.*

WINDEBANK, Clive Leonard. b 41. Late Exhib of New Coll Ox BA 62. **d** 78 **p** 79 Cyprus. P Dio Cyprus. *16th Street North, Ahmadi, Kuwait.*

WINDER, John William. SS Coll Cam BA 37, MA 41. Ridley Hall Cam 37. **d** 39 **p** 40 Wakef. C of H Trin Huddersfield 39-43; Sowerby Bridge w Norland 43-48; V of Stainland 48-53; St Paul Manningham 53-66; R of Bolton-by-Bowland 66-81. *2 Croft Rise, Menston, Ilkley, W Yorks, LS29 6LU.*

WINDER, Canon Robert George. St Jo Coll Morpeth. **d** 50 **p** 51 Bath. C of Brewarrina 50-52; Taree 52-53; Singleton 54; Waratah 54-55; P-in-c of Wallsend W 55-59; C of Ascen Mitcham 59-60; R of Denman 61-70; Raymond Terrace Dio Newc from 70; Can of Ch Ch Cathl Newc from 79. *Rectory, Sturgeon Street, Raymond Terrace, NSW, Australia 2324.* (87-2027)

WINDERBANK, Frank. b 34. Open Univ BA 80. Sarum Th Coll 61. **d** 63 Wakef **p** 64 Pontefract for Wakef. C of Lindley 63-66; Staveley 66-70; Publ Pr Dio Southw 70-78; Org Sec CECS Dios Derby, Linc and Southw 70-78; Gtr Lon from 78; Publ Pr Dio Lon 78-81; Dio S'wark from 81. *135a Sheen Lane, East Sheen, SW14 8AE.* (01-878 0673)

WINDLE, Christopher Rodney. b 45. St D Coll Lamp BA 66. Qu Coll Birm Dipl Th 68. **d** 70 **p** 71 Ches. C of Lache w Saltney Ferry 70-73; Stockton Heath 73-76; P-in-c of St Barn Conv Distr Bredbury Dio Ches from 76. *St Barnabas Vicarage, Osborne Street, Lower Bredbury, Stockport, SK6 2DA.* (061-494 1191)

WINDMILL, Roy Stanley. b 17. Sarum Th Coll. **d** 54 B & W **p** 55 Taunton for B & W. C of Wells 54-58; R of Honiley w Wroxall 58-64; Ed Cov Dioc Leaflet from 59; V of Meriden 64-66; C of H Trin Cov 66-70; C-in-c of Kineton 70-75; Combroke w Compton Verney 70-75; C of Wraxall (in c of St Bart Failand) 75-78; C-in-c of Holton Somt 78-82. *c/o Holton Rectory, Wincanton, Somt.* (Wincanton 32163)

WINDROSS, Andrew. b 49. Univ of Wales (Bangor) BA 71. Cudd Coll 71. **d** 74 **p** 75 Wakef. C of St Jo Bapt Wakef 74-78; Team V of Bow Dio Lon from 78. *All Hallows Rectory, Devons Road, E3.*

WINDSOR, Dean of. *See* Mann, Right Rev Michael Ashley.

WINDSOR, Graham. b 38. G & C Coll Cam BA 57, MA 64, PhD 67. BD (Lon) 60. Trin Coll Bris 79. **d** 79 Chelmsf **p** 80 Barking for Chelmsf. C of Rainham Dio Chelmsf from 79. *68 Askwith Road, Rainham, Essex.* (Rainham 51902)

WINDWARD ISLANDS, Lord Bishop of the. *See* Woodroffe, Most Rev George Cuthbert Manning.

WINDWARD ISLANDS, Dean of the. (Vacant)

WINFIELD, David John. b 48. Univ of Cant NZ BA 72. St Jo Coll Auckld LTh 73. **d** 73 **p** 74 Ch Ch. C of Ashburton 73-75; Timaru 75-78; P-in-c of Avonhead Dio Ch Ch from 77; V of Amberley Dio Ch Ch from 78. *Vicarage, Amberley, NZ.* (Amberley 33)

WINGATE, David Hugh. Qu Coll Cam BA 48, MA 53. Qu Coll Birm 47. **d** 49 **p** 50 Cov. C of Wyken 49-52; V of Wolston 52-56; All SS Cov 56-60; R of Patterdale 60-66; Chap Leeds United Hosps 66-71; Garlands, Cumberland and Westmorland Hosp Carl from 71; V of Cotehill w Cumwhinton Dio Carl from 72. *Cotehill Vicarage, Armathwaite, Carlisle, Cumb, CA4 9TB.* (Wetherall 60323)

WINGFIELD, Eric John. b 16. Univ of Queensld BA 51. ACT ThL 43. St Francis Coll Brisb. **d** and **p** 44 Brisb. C of St Jas Toowoomba 44-45; H Trin Fortitude Valley 45-49; Chap Mitchell River Miss 49-53; Regr and Sec Dio Carp 53-55; LPr Dio Brisb 55-57; Perm to Offic at St Matt Westmr 57-58; R of Wadingham w Snitterby 59-77; V of Cowbit (w St Jas Moulton and Weston w Weston Hills from 78) 77-81; P-in-c of St Jas Moulton 77-78; Weston w Weston Hills 78. *1a Fallowfield, Luton, Beds, LU3 1UL.*

WINGFIELD, Ven John William. b 15. St Aid Coll 46. **d** 47 **p** 48 Truro. C of Madron w Morvah 47-50; R of Perranuthnoe 50-59; V of St Budock 59-67; St Goran w Caerhays 67-70; Sec Truro Dioc Conf 61-70; RD of St Carnmarth 65-67; R of Redruth 70-73; Hon Can of Truro 70-81 Can (Emer) from 81; Sec Truro Dioc Syn 70-80; V of St Clem 73-79; M Gen Syn Truro 77-80; Archd of Bodmin 79-81; Archd (Emer) from 81. *16 Lanyon Road, Playing Place, Truro, Cornw, TR3 6HF.*

WINGFIELD-DIGBY, Andrew Richard. b 50. Keble Coll Ox BA 72. Wycl Hall Ox 74. **d** 77 Lon **p** 78 Edmon for Lon. C of Cockfosters (in c of Hadley Wood from 81) Dio Lon from 77. *32 Crescent East, Hadley Wood, Herts.* (01-449 2572)

WINGFIELD DIGBY, Very Rev Richard Shuttleworth. b 11. Ch Coll Cam 2nd cl Econ Trip pt i 33, BA (2nd cl Th Trip pt i) 35, MA 39. Westcott Ho Cam 35. **d** 36 **p** 37 Cov. C of St Andr Rugby 36-46; CF (EC) 40-45; V of All SS Newmarket 46-53; R of Bury 53-66; Surr 57-66; RD of Bury 62-66; Hon Can of Man 65-66; Can (Emer) from 66; Dean of Pet 66-80; Dean (Emer) from 80. *Byways, Higher Holton, Nr Wincanton, Somt, BA9 8AP.* (Wincanton 32137)

WINGFIELD-DIGBY, Canon Stephen Basil. b 10. MBE 45. Men in Disp 44. Ch Ch Ox BA (Hist) 32, Dipl Th 33, MA 36. Wycl Hall Ox 33. **d** 36 **p** 37 Sarum. C of St Paul Fisherton Anger 36-38; C-in-c of St Geo Conv Distr Oakdale 38-46; Min 46-47; CF (EC) 40-45; V of Sherborne w Castleton and Lillington 47-68; Chap Sherborne Sch for Girls 47-68; Surr 48-68; RD of Sherborne 54-68; Can of Sarum Cathl 55-68; Can Res 68-79; Can (Emer) from 79; Treas 71-78; Archd of Sarum 68-79; Archd (Emer) from 79. *77 Banks Road, Sandbanks, Poole, Dorset.* (Canford Cliffs 709079)

WINIATA, Huia Hapia. b 26. St Jo Coll Auckld. **d** 76 Wel **p** 77 Aotearoa for Wel. C of Rangitikei-Manawatu Maori Distr Dio Wel from 76. *Mason Durie Memorial Hostel, Pembroke Street, Palmerston North, NZ.*

WINIATA, Wihapi Te Kanohimohoao. b 35. **d** 77 Aotearoa for Wai. C of Ohinemutu Past Dio Wai from 77. *PO Box 1162, Rotorua, NZ.*

WINKS, Paul David. b 45. Univ of Ex BA 67. Cudd Coll 68. **d** 70 **p** 71 Lich. C of Rickerscote, Stafford 70-73; Chap RAF 73-75; C of Yate 76-77; Team V of Westerleigh in Yate New Town Dio Bris from 77. *Vicarage, Shorthill Road, Westerleigh, Bristol, BS17 4QQ.* (Chipping Sodbury 312152)

WINLO, Ronald. b 14. AKC 41. Open Univ BA 74. **d** 41 **p** 42 Guildf. C of St Paul The Hythe Egham 41-44; CF (EC) 44-48; Hon CF 48; R of Que Que S Rhod 48-52; C of Ditcheat Somt 53-54; V of Paulton 54-61; R of Bayswater W Austr 61-65; V of Kirkby Malzeard w Dallowgill 66-81. *27 Ripley Drive, Harrogate, N Yorks, HG1 3JD.* (0423 69242)

WIN MAUNG, John. H Cross Coll Rang. **d** 59 **p** 60 Rang. P Dio Rang. *St Lukes Church, Dawwa, Burma.*

WINNARD, Jack. b 30. Oak Hill Coll 79. **d** 81 Warrington for Liv. C of Skelmersdale Dio Liv from 81. *6 Wilcove, Skelmersdale, Lancs, NN8 8NF.*

WINNETT, Canon Arthur Robert. b 10. Univ of Lon BA 30, BD 31, 1st cl Study of Relig 33, PhD 53, DD 76. K Coll Lon 31. **d** 33 **p** 34 S'wark. C of Morden and Lect Lon Coll of Div 33-35; Publ Pr Dio Dur 35-38; Tutor St Jo Coll Dur 35-38; Libr 36-38; Chap St Hild's Coll Dur 36-38; C of Caterham 38-42; Perm to Offic at Send 39-42; V of Cuddington 42-50; Rowledge 50-59; Exam Chap to Bp of Guildf from 47; V of Grayshott 59-70; Hon Can of Guildf 61-75; Can (Emer) from 75; R of Ockham w Hatchford 70-75; Perm to Offic Dio Win from 75. *54 Orchards Way, Highfield, Southampton, SO2 1RE.* (Southampton 558795)

WINSALL-HALL, Warwick Guy Campbell. b 38. St Barn Th Coll Adel ACT ThDip 80. **d** 81 Adel. C of St Phil Broadview Dio Adel from 81. *12 Meredith Street, Broadview, S Australia 5083.*

WINSLOW, Lawrence Harold. b 40. Sir Geo Wm's Univ Montr BComm 61. Wycl Coll Tor MDiv 77. **d** 77 **p** 78 Alg. C of Thunder Bay 77-80; I of Marathon Dio Alg from 80. *Box 87, Manitouwadge, Ont, Canada.*

WINSOR-CUNDELL, William. b 1900. Lich Th Coll 22. **d** 25 **p** 26 Sheff. C of Attercliffe 25-27; Towcester w Easton Neston 27-30; Banbury (in c of Neithrop) 30-36; V of Shipton-under-Wychwood 36-78; PC of Milton-under-Wychwood 55-68; V 68-78. *31 Maugersbury Park, Stow-on-the-Wold, Glos.*

WINSTANLEY, Alan Leslie. b 49. Univ of Nottm BTh, ALCD 72. St Jo Coll Nottm 68. **d** 72 **p** 73 Blackb. C of St Andr Livesey 72-75; Gt Sankey 75-78; V of Penketh 78-81; w SAMS from 81. *c/o Allen Gardiner House, Pembury Road, Tunbridge Wells, Kent, TN2 3QU.*

WINSTANLEY, Canon Cyril Henry. b 04. Univ of Liv BA 26, MA 30. Ridley Hall Cam 30. **d** 32 **p** 33 Liv. C of St Sav Everton 32-34; St Cypr Edge Hill 34-36; V of St Matt Bootle 36-41; Ch Ch (Bp Chavasse Mem Ch) Norris Green 41-72; RD of W Derby 61-71; Can Dioc of Liv 66-72; Can (Emer) from 73. *49 Menlove Gardens West, Liverpool, L18 2ET.* (051-722 9177)

WINSTANLEY, John Graham. b 47. K Coll Lon 67. St Aug Cant 70. **d** 71 **p** 72 S'wark. C of Wimbledon Pk 71-75; Chap Univ of Salford and L to Offic Dio Man 75-79; R of St Paul Kersal, Salford Dio Man from 79. *123 Nevile Road, Salford, M7 0PP.* (061-792 6212)

WINSTON, Jeremy Hugh. b 54. Univ of Wales BEducn 76. Univ of Ox BA 78. St Steph ho Ox 76. **d** 79 **p** 80 Mon. C of Bassaleg Dio Mon from 79. *99 The Uplands, Rogerstone, Newport, Gwent, NP1 9FE.*

WINSTONE, Peter John. b 30. Jes Coll Ox BA 52, MA 56. Ridley Hall Cam 53. **d** 55 **p** 56 Win. C of H Sav Bitterne 55-58; Keighley 58-60; PC of St Sav Fairweather Green 60-66; V 66-67; Clapham w Keasden Dio Bradf from 67. *Clapham Vicarage, Lancaster.* (Clapham 240)

WINT, Vecas Emanuel. d 76 Ja (APM). C of Mandeville Dio Ja from 76. *16 Greenvale Road, Mandeville PO., Jamaica, W Indies.*

✠ **WINTER, Right Rev Allen Ernest.** Moorehouse Scho Univ of Melb BA (1st cl Cl Phil) and Bromby Pri in Bibl Gr 26, Stewart Pri in Div 27, MA 28. ACT ThL (1st cl) 27, ThD (*jur dig*) 51. Lucas-Tooth Scho 29. Univ Coll Ox BA (3rd cl Th) 32 MA 51. **d** 27 **p** 28 Melb. C of S Yarra 27-29; C of St Jas Ivanhoe 32-35; Min of Sunshine 35-39; I of St Luke Brighton 39-48; Chap AIF 42-46; I of Ch Ch Essendon 48-49; Can and R of All SS Cathl Bath 49-51; Cons Ld Bp of St Arn in St Paul's Cathl Melb 29 June 51 by Abp of Melb; Bps of Bal; Gippsld; Bend; and Wang; Bp of Geelong (Bp Coadj of Melb); and Bps Hart and James; res 73; Chap St Jo Coll Morpeth and Perm to Offic Dio Newc 74; Dio Melb from 74. *11 Bella Vista Road, Caulfield, Vic, Australia 3161.*

WINTER, Anthony Cathcart. b 28. Ridley Hall, Cam 54. **d** 56 Warrington for Liv **p** 57 Liv. C of St D Childwall 56-58; Hackney 58-63; V of All SS Newmarket 63-74; L to Offic Dio St E from 74; Perm to Offic Dio Lon 78-81; C of St Andr-by-the-Wardrobe City and Dio Lon from 81. *St Andrew's House, St Andrew's Hill, EC4V 5DE.* (01-248 7546)

WINTER, Bruce William. b 39. Univ of Queensld BA 73. Moore Coll Syd ACT ThL 68, Th Scho 70. **d** 69 **p** 70 Brisb. C of St James Toowoomba 69-72; Coorparoo 72-73; P-in-c of St Geo Sing 73; V 74-78; Lect Moore Th Coll Syd from 78. *28 Taleeban Road, Tambourine Bay, NSW, Australia 2066.*

WINTER, Charles James. Univ of Syd BA 56. Moore Th Coll Syd ACT ThL (1st cl) 53. **d** 57 **p** 58 Melb. C of St Thos Essendon 57-59; P-in-c of Orroroo 59-61; Leigh Creek 61-63; Chap at Mentone Gr Sch Dio Melb from 63. *105 Caroline Street, S Yarra, Vic, Australia 3141.* (550 4211)

WINTER, Dennis Graham St Leger. Univ of Lon BSc (with AKC) 54. BD (2nd cl) Lon 62. Tyndale Hall Bris 59. **d** 61 **p** 62 Ex. C of St Pancras Pennycross Plymouth 61-64; St Faith Virg and Mart Maidstone 64-66; V of Paddock Wood Dio Roch from 66. *Vicarage, Paddock Wood, Kent.* (Paddock Wood 3917)

WINTER, Ernest Philip. b 18. Univ of Bris BA 49. St Cath S Ox BLitt 54, MA 56. Worc Ord Coll 57. **d** 58 Worc **p** 59 Bp Stuart for Worc. C of St Barn Worc 58-61; V of Reddal Hill 61-79; P-in-c of U Arley Dio Worc from 79; Wribbenhall Dio Worc from 81. *Upper Arley Vicarage, Bewdley, Worcs.* (Arley 300)

WINTER, Henry David. Sarum Th Coll 51. **d** 53 **p** 54 Man. C of St Jas Hope Salford 53-55; St Luke Heywood 55-58; R of St Mich Hulme 58-63; V of St Paul Colchester Dio Chelmsf from 63. *141 North Station Road, Colchester, Essex.* (Colchester 78383)

WINTER, Jonathan Gay. b 37. K Coll Lon and Warm AKC 64. **d** 65 **p** 66 S'wark. C of All SS W Dulwich 65-69; Asst Master Kidbrooke Sch 69-77; Norwood Sch from 77. *160 Turney Road, SE21.* (01-274 3060)

WINTER, Norman Gladwyn. b 50. Late Scho Ch Ch Ox BA 72, BA (Th) 74, MA 76. Wycl Hall Ox 72. **d** 76 **p** 77 Liv. C of St Mich Huyton 76-80; M Skelmersdale Ecumen Centre Dio Liv from 80. *214 Egerton, Tanhouse, Skelmersdale, Lancs, WN8 6AF.* (Skelmersdale 23610)

WINTER, Raymond McMahon. b 23. Selw Coll Cam BA 52, MA 60. Wycl Hall Ox. **d** 61 **p** 62 Nor. C of Gaywood 61-64; C-in-c of Horstead Dio Nor from 64; Bp's Youth Chap Dio Nor 64-71; Chap Loretto School Midlothian 71-74; P-in-c of Latchingdon w Mundon and N Fambridge 74-75; Riddlesworth w Gasthorpe and Knettishall Dio Nor from 75; Brettenham w Rushford and Shadwell Dio Nor from 75; Garboldisham Dio Nor from 77; Blo-Norton Dio Nor from 77. *Riddlesworth Rectory, Diss, Norf.* (Garboldisham 245)

WINTER, Thomas Andrew. Wadh Coll Ox BA 51, MA 63. Ely Th Coll 51. **d** 53 Stafford for Cant **p** 54 Lich. C of Horninglow 53-56; Capetn Cathl 56-60; Chap City Pris 59-60; P-in-c of Milnerton 60-69; R of Sea Point Dio Capetn from 69. *St James Rectory, Sea Point, CP, S Africa.* (441826)

WINTER, Walter Charles Milton. b 1893. Late Sizar of Em Coll Cam Stewart of Rannoch Scho 13, BA (3rd cl Cl Trip) 15, MA 20. Ridley Hall Cam 15. **d** 16 **p** 17 Man. C of Bolton 16-18; Luton 18-23; CF Aldershot 23-24; Catterick 24-25; V of St Jo Bapt Ipswich and Chap Ipswich Municipal Infirm 25-38; V of Ch Ch Clifton 38-51; Ch Ch Win 51-65. *223 Havant Road, Drayton, Portsmouth.*

WINTER, William. b 21. **d** and **p** 74 Keew. C of Kingfisher Lake Dio Keew from 74. *St Matthew's Church, Kingfisher Lake, via Central Patricia, Ont., Canada.*

WINTERBOTHAM, Anthony James Marshall. b 27. Magd Coll Cam BA 51, MA 55, Wells Th Coll. **d** 57 **p** 58 Portsm. C of Portsea 57-63; Asst Chap Wel Coll Crowthorne 63-67; Chap Portsm Gr Sch from 67; Hon Chap Portsm Cathl from 67. *4 Poynings Place, St Nicholas Street, Portsmouth, Hants, PO1 2PB.* (Portsmouth 825068)

WINTERBOTTOM, Ian Edmund. b 42. Univ of St Andr MA 66. Univ of Nottm Dipl Th 68. Linc Th Coll 66. **d** 68 **p** 69 Blackb. C of St Steph Blackb 68-71; Wingerworth 71-73; P-in-c of Brimington Dio Derby 73-77; R from 77. *Brimington Rectory, Chesterfield, Derbys, S43 1JG.* (Chesterfield 73103)

WINTERBOURNE, George. b 20. SOC 64. **d** 67 **p** 68 Guildf. C of Cove w S Hawley 67-71; Perm to Offic Dio Guildf 72; Hon C of Aldershot 73-78; Perm to Offic Dio B & W from 79. *41 Park Road Congresbury, Bristol, BS19 5HJ.* (Yatton 838344)

WINTERBURN, Ieuan Thomas. Univ of Wales BA 37. Univ of S Afr BA (Soc) 48. St Bonif Coll Warm 37. **d** 39 **p** 40 St D. C of Llanelly 39-44; St Cypr Cathl Kimb 44-45; R of De Aar w Britstown and Richmond 45-50; C of St Mary's Cathl Johann 50-52; Chap HM Pris Johann 50-52; P-in-c of Clairwood w Bluff 52-54; V of Durban S 54-55; Bluff 55-59; C of Cheam (in c of St Alb) 59-60; V of St Sav Denmark Pk 60-64; Sub-Dean of St Paul's Cathl Mahé 64-66; Dean 66-68; Archd of Seychelles 64-68; R of St Andr Standerton w Evander 70-72; Chap St Steph Coll Balla Balla 72-76; C of Bulawayo Cathl 76-78; R of St Marg of Scotld Northend Bulawayo 78-81; Borth Dio St D from 81; Eglwysfach w Llancyn-Felyn Dio St D from 81. *Vicarage, Borth, Dyfed.* (Borth 458)

WINTERBURN, Maurice. b 14. Oak Hill Th Coll 61. **d** 62 **p** 63 Lon. C of St Jas L Bethnal Green 62-65; Ealing 65-68; V of Stambermill 68-79; P-in-c of Lye 74-79. *36 Whittingham Road, Halesowen, W Midl, B63 3TF.* (021-550 04 34)

WINTERS, Cyril Alfred John. b 04. ALCD 38. **d** 37 **p** 38 Chelmsf. C of St Sav Forest Gate 37-39; Publ Pr Dio St Alb 39-40; Actg C of St Neots 40-41; Chap and Asst Master Kimbolton Sch 41-43; V of Stow w Quy 43-46; R of Horseheath 46-51; Bartlow 46-51; C of Wensley w Leyburn (in c of Leyburn) 51-53; Ecclesall-Bierlow Sheff 53-56; St Jas Islington 56-58; V of St Mark Bolton 58-62; Barlaston 62-66; C-in-c of Dilhorne 66-69. *Dulverton Hall, St Martin's Square, Scarborough, Yorks.*

WINTERS, Canon James Alvin. McGill Univ Montr BA 48. Trin Coll Tor BD 51. **d** 51 **p** 52 Ott. C of St Barn Ott 51-55; I of Vanleek Hill 55-60; Hosp Chap Ott 60-67; R of St Aid Ott 67-78; St Barn City and Dio Ott from 78; Hon Can of Ott from 73; Exam Chap to Bp of Ott from 78. *70 James Street, Ottowa, Ont, Canada.*

WINTERS, Canon Robert Hunter. b 23. Moore Th Coll Syd 42. ACT ThL (2nd cl) 44. **d** 48 Bath **p** 52 Chich. C of All SS Cathl Bath 48-49; Parkes Dio Bath 49; Asst Master Harewood Sch Bexhill 50-51; C of St Thos Ap Hove 51-54; St Patr Hove 54-56; Finchley 56-61; V of St Sav Eltham Dio S'wark from 61; Commiss Polyn from 67; Hon Can of Polyn from 78. *98 Middle Park Avenue, SE9.* (01-850 6829)

WINTERSGILL, Allan Vernon. b 19. St Jo Coll Dur BA 49. Ely Th Coll 49. **d** 50 **p** 51 Lon. C of St Luke Old Street 50-52; St Paul S Harrow 52-55; Ilkeston (in C of St Bart Hallam Fields) 55-57; V of St Barn 57-70; V of St Jas Northn 70-81; Staverton w Helidon and Catesby Dio Pet from 81. *Staverton Vicarage, Daventry, Northants, NN11 6JJ.* (Daventry 2466)

WINTERTON, Graeme James. b 39. Div Coll Melb LTh 63. ACT ThL 71. **d** 71 **p** 72 Melb. C of Kew 71-72; P-in-c of Doveton 72-74; I of Preston E 74-79; Parkdale Dio Melb from 79. *62 Robert Street, Parkdale, Vic, Australia 3195.* (90 2881)

WINTLE, Anthony Robert. b 44. Dipl Th (Wales) 68. St Mich Coll Llan 65. **d** 68 Bp T M Hughes for Llan **p** 69 Llan. C of All SS Llan N 68-70; Baglan 70-75; V of Treharris Dio Llan from 75. *Vicarage, Treharris, Mid Glam, CF46 5AB.* (Treharris 410280)

WINTON, Don. St Barn Coll Adel ACT ThL 41. **d** 41 **p** 42 Adel. C of St Paul Port Adel 41-45; P-in-c of Mt Pleasant (w Mannum Miss) 45-51. *32 Broadbent Terrace, Whyalla, S Australia.*

WINTON, Leonard Edward. d 46 **p** 47 Bath. C-in-c of Wyalong 46-47; R 47-53; Cumnock 53-60; Kandos 60-66; C of Burwood Dio Syd from 67; L to Offic Dio Syd from 65. *14 Moore Street, Campbelltown, NSW, Australia 2560.* (046-25 5163)

WINTON, Stanley Wootton. b 30. Sarum Wells Th Coll 70. **d** 72 **p** 73 Ches. C of St Jas w St Bede Birkenhead 72-75; V 75-79; R of Ellesmere Port Dio Ches from 79. *Rectory, Vale Road, Ellesmere Port, Cheshire.* (051-355 2516)

WINTON, Willie Alfred. b 12. TD 50. MBE 63. Late Welsh Ch Scho and Pri of St D Coll Lamp BA (1st cl Hist) 33. Jes Coll Ox BA (2nd cl Hist) 35, MA 39. St Mich Coll Llan 35. **d** 36 **p** 37 Llan. C of St Jo Bapt Cardiff 36-39; CF (TA) 39-45 and 46-63; Men in Disp 46; C-in-c of All SS Cardiff 46-49; Chap HM Pris Cardiff 46-49; R of Canton 49-66; V of Whitchurch 66-81; Can of Fairwell in Llan Cathl 67-81. *52a Bishops Road, Whitchurch, Cardiff, CF4 1LW.* (691730)

WINWARD, Stuart James. b 36. Lich Th Coll 65. **d** 68 **p** 69 Blackb. C of Lytham 68-71; Padiham 71-73; V of Musbury Dio Blackb from 73. *St Thomas's Vicarage, Musbury, Helmshore, Rossendale, BB4 4JA.* (Rossendale 213302)

WIPPELL, David Stanley. b 46. Univ of Queensld BSc 67. Selw Coll Cam BA 77. Westcott Ho Cam 76. **d** 78 Buckingham for Ox **p** 79 Dorchester for Ox. C of St Mich Summertown Dio Ox from 78; Asst Chap St Edw Sch from 78; Chap St Hugh Coll Ox from 80. *St Edward's School, Woodstock Road, Oxford.*

WISBECH, Archdeacon of. *See* Patterson, Ven William James.

WISDOM, Walter Charles. TCD BA 32, Downes Oratory Pr 33, Div Test 33, MA 37. **d** 33 **p** 34 Down. C of St Mary Belfast 33-34; CMS Miss Dio Fukien 34-39; V of Rakaia 39-42; Temuka 42-46; Sumner 46-51; Glenmark 51-62; Hon Can of Ch Ch 59-62; L to Offic Dio Ch Ch from 62. *86 Bishop Street, Christchurch, NZ.*

WISE, David Reginald. b 46. Univ of Glas BSc 68. QUB PhD 74. Edin Th Coll 72. **d** 74 Aber **p** 75 Glas. Chap of St Andr Cathl Aber 74-75; C of H Trin Ayr 75-78; R of Airdrie 78-81; P-in-c of Gartcosh 78-81; St Nich Leic 81-82; Sen Angl Chap Univ of Leic from 81; Team V of H Spirit City and Dio Leic from 82. *27 Knighton Road, Leicester, LE2 3HL.* (Leic 707643)

WISE, Geoffrey John. b 23. Qu Coll Birm. **d** 63 **p** 64 Mashon. C of Avondale 63-64; Highlands 64-66; R of Belvedere 66-70; C of Highlands Salisbury 70-74; R of Fort Vic 74-76; Cottesmore w Barrow 76-79; P-in-c of Ashwell w Burley 76-79; R of Cottesmore and Barrow w Ashwell and Burley Dio Pet from 79. *Cottesmore Rectory, Oakham, Leics, LE15 7DJ.* (Oakham 812202)

WISE, John Warren. Moore Th Coll Syd ACT ThL 65. **d** 66 Bp Loane For Syd **p** 67 Syd. C of Wollongong 66-67; Mascot 68-69; Min of Whalan 69-71; R of S Canterbury 71-74; CF (Austr) from 74. *Box 52, Mil PO, Bandiana, Vic., Australia 3694.*

WISE, Very Rev Randolph George. b 25. VRD 64. Qu Coll Ox BA (2nd cl Th) 49, MA 55. Linc Th Coll 49. **d** 51 **p** 52 S'wark. C of Lady Marg Walworth 51-53; Stocksbridge 53-55; V of Lady Marg Walworth (w St Mary Magd from 56) 55-60; Stocksbridge 60-66; Industr Chap to Bp of Lon 66-76; V of St Botolph without Aldersgate Lon 72-76; R of Notting Hill Dio Lon from 76; M Gen Syn Lon 80-81; Dean of Pet from 81. *Deanery, Peterborough, PE1 1XS.* (Peterborough 62780)

WISEMAN, David John. b 51. BD (Lon) 80. Cranmer Hall Dur 77. **d** 80 **p** 81 Lich. C of Bilston Dio Lich from 80. *10 Broad Street, Bilston, W Midl, WV14 0BP.*

WISEMAN, John Mervin. Sir Geo Williams Univ Montr BA 56. Trin Coll Tor LTh 59. **d** 59 **p** 60 Tor. C of St Mich AA Tor 59-63; R of Roche's Point 63-66; St Sav Tor 66-77; St Pet City and Dio Tor from 77. *190 Carlton Street, Toronto, Ont., Canada.* (416-924 1891)

WISHART, Michael Leslie. b 45. Univ of Wales (Cardiff) Dipl Th 73. St Mich AA Coll Llan 70. **d** 73 **p** 74 Swan B. C of Llangyfelach 73-76; Chap RN 76-80; V of Beguildy and Heyope Dio Swan B from 80. *Vicarage, Beguildy, Knighton, Powys, LD7 1YE.* (Beguildy 252)

WISKEN, Brian Leonard. b 34. Univ of Dur BA 58. Linc Th Coll 58. **d** 60 **p** 61 Dur. C of All SS Lobley Hill Gateshead 60-63; All H Ipswich 63-65; Min of All SS Conv Distr Scunthorpe 65-69; V 69-71; R of Panton w Wragby 71-75; V of Langton-by-Wragby 71-75; Cleethorpes Dio Linc from 75-77; R from 77. *42 Queen's Parade, Cleethorpes, Humb, DN35 0DG.* (Cleethorpes 63234)

WISKEN, Robert Daniel. d and **p** 60 Rockptn. [f in CA] C of S Barn N Rockptn 60; V of St Matt N Rockptn 61-63; R of Winton 63-65; Luddington w Hemington and Thurning 65-69; C-in-c of Clopton 66-69; V of All SS Ipswich 69-73; Sompting 73-78; Cler Org Sec SW Area CECS 78-80; Publ Pr Dio Win 80; R of Edmundbyers w Muggleswick Dio Dur from 80. *Edmundbyers Rectory, Consett, Co Durham, DH8 9NG.* (0207-55634)

WISKER, George Richard. b 35. SOC 69. **d** 72 **p** 73 Cant. C of Ch Ch Croydon 72-76; St Erkenwald Barking Dio Chelmsf 76-77; P-in-c from 77. *St Erkenwald's Vicarage, Levett Road, Barking, Essex.* (01-594 2271)

WISSLER, Kenneth John. b 46. Univ of Delaware BA 68. Univ Kings Coll 69. **d** 70 NS. I of Blandford 71-75; Shelburne Dio NS from 76. *Box 196, NS, Canada.*

WISWELL, Douglas Morgan. b 1893. K Coll NS BA 14, MA 19, Hon DCL 69. Late Rhodes Scho of Ch Ch Ox BA 21, Dipl Th 22, MA 25. Leeds Cl Scho 22. **d** 22 **p** 23 Ripon. C of Leeds 22-25; Ch Ch Cathl Montr 25-30; V of St Pet Morley w Churwell All SS 31-46; Pembury 46-63. *Woodlands House, Camden Park, Tunbridge Wells, Kent, TN2 5AA.* (Tunbridge Wells 26976)

WITBOOI, Benjamin Cornelius. b 52. Univ of W Cape BA 73. **d** 75 **p** 76 Capetn. C of Steenberg 75-76; Resurr Bonteheuwel 76-78; P-in-c of Kraaifontein Dio Capetn from 78. *Rectory, Fourth Avenue, Kraaifontein, CP, S Africa.* (32-4648)

WITBROCK, John Anthony. Univ of NZ BA 58, MA 59. Coll Ho Ch Ch 57. **d** 60 Dun for Ch Ch **p** 62 Ch Ch. C of St Alb Ch Ch 60-62; Avonside 62-65; V of Lyttelton Dio Ch Ch from 65. *17 Winchester Street, Lyttelton , NZ.*

WITCHELL, David William. b 47. Univ of Nottm BTh 75. St Jo Coll Nottm LTh 75. **d** 75 **p** 76 Pet. C of St Mary Virg Northn 75-78; Oakham w Hambleton and Egleton 78-81; V of Weedon Bec w Everdon Dio Pet from 82. *Vicarage, Weedon, Northants, NN7 4PL.* (Weedon 40359)

WITCHER, Graham Frank. b 38. Lon Bible Coll Northwood BD 61. Regent's Pk Coll Ox MA 68. New Coll Edin PhD 74. **d** 75 **p** 76 Calg. Chap Deerholme Sch Red Deer 75-78; I of Okotoks Dio Calg from 78. *Box 398, Okotoks, Alta, Canada.* (683-4261)

WITCOMB, Canon Cyril Albert. b 14. Mert Coll Ox BA 38, MA 43. Westcott Ho Cam 39. **d** 40 **p** 41 Sarum. C of Melksham 40-43; Chap RNVR 43-46; PC of St Jas Southbroom 46-54; Hon Chap to Bp of Sarum 54-61; V of Melksham 54-61; Surr 54-61; RD of Bradf-on-Avon 56-61; Can and Preb of Alton Australis in Sarum Cathl 60-61; V of St Piran Jos N Nig 61-63; R Wilton w Netherhampton 63-70; RD of Wilton 64-68; Can and Preb of Sarum Cathl from 65; V of Calne w Blackland 70-76; Surr 70-81; RD of Avebury 72-73; Calne 73-76; V of Woodford Valley 76-81. *G Park Lane, Salisbury, SP1 3NP.* (0722-331982)

WITCOMB, Frederick George. b 01. St D Univ Coll Lamp LDiv 27, BD 33. **d** 27 St D for Llan **p** 28 Mon for Llan. C of Penyfai 27-29; Beddington 29-35; L to Offic in C of Ch Ch Salfords 35-40; V of St Luke Eltham 40-48; St Marg Streatham Hill 48-57; RD of Streatham 54-57; V of Stow-Bardolph w Wimbotsham 57-62; R of St Leon Bridgetown Barb 62-66; L to Offic Dio St D from 66. *31 Hamilton Terrace, Milford Haven, Dyfed.* (06462-2932)

WITCOMB, William Richard. b 03. Univ Coll Dur LTh 28. St Aug Coll Cant 23. **d** 27 **p** 28 Linc. C of Frodingham 27-28; St Cypr w St Chad Hay Mill 28-31; PC of St Basil Deritend 31-37; V of Em Sparkbrook 37-45; R of Saxelby w Grimston and Shoby 45-50; C of Wynberg Cp 50-51; R of Sharnford w Wigston Parva 51-57; V of Ravensthorpe w Teeton and Coton 57-60; St Andr Northn 60-65; Ab-Kettleby w Wartnaby and Holwell 65-76; Perm to Offic Dio Pet from 76. *22 Glebelands, Spratton, Northampton, NN6 8JB.*

WITCOMBE, Michael David. b 53. St D Coll Lamp BA 76. Qu Coll Birm 76. **d** 78 Bp Reece for Llan **p** 79 Llan. C of Neath w Llantwit 78-80; Whitchurch Dio Llan from 80. *10 Keynsham Road, Whitchurch, Cardiff, CF4 1TS.*

WITHAM, Charles Frederick. b 1897. St D Coll Lamp 45. **d** 47 **p** 48 Cov. C of Long Compton 47-51; V of Badby w Newnham 51-70; L to Offic Dio Southw from 70. *The White House, Goverton, Bleasby, Nottingham, NG14 7FN.*

WITHAM, Edward Peter. b 48. Univ of W Austr BA 70. Trin Coll Melb BD 74. **d** and **p** 75 Perth. Actg Chap Hale Sch 76; C of Applecross 77-78; Chap Ch Ch Gr Sch Perth from 78. *Christ Church Grammar School, Claremont, W Australia 6010.* (384 2395)

WITHERIDGE, John Stephen. b 53. Univ of Kent at Cant BA 76. Ch Coll Cam BA 78. Ridley Hall Cam 78. **d** 79 **p** 80 St Alb. C of Luton Beds 79-82; Asst Chap Marlborough Coll from 82. *Marlborough College, Wilts, SN8 1PA.*

WITHERS, Alexander John. St Jo Coll Morpeth ACT ThL 33. **d** 33 **p** 34 Graft. C of Casino 33-34; P-in-c of Grevillea 34-36; Liston 36-37; P-in-c of Lowanna 37-38; V of N Graft 38-42; Chap AIF 42-45; R of Bowraville 46-48; Youth Sec ABM in NSW 48-49; R of Narrandera 49-69; Perm to Offic Dio River from 69. *PO Box 393, Narrandera, NSW, Australia 2700.* (069-59 1101)

WITHERS, David Clarence. St Mich Coll Crafers 60. **d** 65 **p** 66 Adel. C of Edwardstown 65-67; Elizabeth 67-69; P-in-c of Northfield 69-75; R of Gawler 75-78; L to Offic Dio Adel from 78. *28 Battams Road, Marden, S Australia 5070.* (42 7761)

WITHERS, James Arthur. St Jo Coll Auckld 66. **d** 68 Auckld. C of Takapuna 68-73; V of Tuakau 73-77; Par Distr of Birkdale-Beachhaven 77-80; All SS Ponsonby City and Dio Auckld from 80. *1a Ponsonby Terrace, Auckland, NZ.* (761-304)

WITHERS, Michael. b 41. TCD BA 66. Univ of Edin BD 70. U Th Sem NY STM 71. **d** 71 **p** 73 Down. C of Seagoe 71-77; Seapatrick 77-80; R of St Chris Belf Dio Down from 80. *3 Clonallon Gardens, Belfast, BT4 2BY.* (Belf 653592)

WITHERS-LANCASHIRE, Leonard Walter Hicks. b 08. Kelham Th Coll 27. **d** 32 **p** 33 Cant. C of Westbere 32-34; St Mich AA Beckenham 34-38; All SS Brighton 38-40; Chap of All H Ditchingham 40-43; C of St Edm Forest Gate 43-44; St Andr Coulsdon (in c of St Francis) 44-46; R of Fillingham 46-54; V of Ingham w Cammeringham 48-54; St Jo Div Gainsborough 54-59; C of Stanwell 59; W Wycombe 62-69; Gedling 69-76; Netherfield 69-76; Perm to Offic Dio Chich from 77. *19a Bridge Road, Worthing, W Sussex.* (Worthing 208830)

WITHERS GREEN, Timothy. b 30. K Coll Lon and Warm 51. **d** 55 **p** 56 Lon. C of Greenhill 55-58; St Helier (in c of Bp Andrewes Ch) 58-61; V of Belmont 61-79; Commiss Carp 61-66; CF (TAVR) from 71; R of Hexham Dio Newc T from 79. *Rectory, Hexham, Northumb, NE46 3EW.* (Hexham 2031)

WITHEY, Michael John. b 45. Open Univ BA 80. Oak Hill Th Coll 71. **d** 74 **p** 75 St Alb. C of St Paul St Alb 74-76; St Francis Luton 76-80; V of Woodside w E Hyde Dio St Alb from 80. *Woodside Vicarage, Luton, Beds.* (Luton 25401)

WITHINGTON, Charles Fraser. Ridley Coll Melb ThL 43. **d** 44 **p** 45 Melb. C of All SS St Kilda 44-45; V of Craojingolong 45-48; I of Leopold 48-52; V of Kingsville w Spotswood 52-55; Asst Chap Geelong C of E Gr Sch Corio 55-59; V of Ch Ch Hawthorn 59-63; Chap Trin C of E Gr Sch Kew 63-66; V of St Mary S Camberwell 66-76; C of Portland 77-79; Perm to Offic Dio Bal from 79. *127 Ballarat Road, Creswick, Vic, Australia 3363.*

WITHINGTON, George Kenneth. b 37. Univ of Birm BA 59. Wells Th Coll 59. **d** 61 **p** 62 Bris. C of Hartcliffe 61-65; V of St Jo Bapt Park Swindon 65-73; Cricklade w Latton w Eisey Dio Bris from 73. *Cricklade Vicarage, Swindon, Wilts.* (Swindon 750300)

WITHINGTON, Harold. St Andr Coll Whittlesford. **d** 42 **p** 43 Lich. C of St Matt Tipton 42-45; St Bart Wednesbury 45-47; R of Biddulph Moor 47-51; V of Ch of Ven Bede Gateshead 51-61; R of Ebchester 61-70. *Address temp unknown.*

WITHINGTON, Keith. b 32. St D Coll Lamp BA 55. Qu Coll Birm. **d** 57 **p** 58 Birm. C of Bournville Dio Birm 57-61; V from 61; RD of Moseley from 81. *61 Linden Road, Birmingham 30.* (021-472 1209)

WITHY, John Daniel Forster. b 38. ALCD 64. **d** 64 **p** 65 Connor. C of St Aid Belf 64-68; Dir of Chr Conference Centre Sion Mills from 68. *120 Melmont Road, Strabane, Co Tyrone, N Ireland.* (Sion Mills 205)

WITHYCOMBE, Robert Stanley Morse. Univ of Syd BA (2nd cl Hist) 61. BD (2nd cl) Lon 63. Moore Th Coll Syd ACT ThL (1st cl) 63. **d** 63 **p** 64 Syd. Lect Moore Th Coll Syd 63-65; Hon C of E Willoughby 63-65; St Barn Cam 65-67; Gen Sec Inter-Varsity Fellowship (NZ) 68-72; L to Offic Dio Wel 68-72; Lect and Dean of Studs Moore Th Coll Syd 72-76; Warden St Mark's Libr and Inst of Th Canberra from 76. *Box 67, Canberra, ACT, Australia 2600.*

✠ **WITT, Right Rev Howell Arthur John.** Univ of Leeds BA 42. Coll of Resurr Mirfield 42. **d** 44 **p** 45 Mon. C of Usk w Glascoed Chap and Monkswood w Gwehelog 44-48; St Geo Camberwell 48-49; Chap of Exper Rocket Range Woomera 49-54; R of St Mary Magd Adel 54-57; P-in-c of S Elizabeth 57-65; Cons Ld Bp of NW Austr in Cathl of H Cross Geraldton 30 Nov 65 by Abp of Perth; Bps of Kalg; and Bunb; and Bps Frewer, Riley, and Macdonald; Trld to Bath 81. *Bishopscourt, Bathurst, NSW, Australia 2795.* (063-31 1175)

WITTEN, Robert Eric. b 44. Ridley Coll Melb 72. **d** 73 **p** 74 Armid. C of St John Tamworth 73-76; V of Mungindi 76-80; Boggabilla Dio Armid from 81. *Vicarage, Boggabilla, NSW, Australia 2409.*

WITTENBACH, Canon Henry August. b 1900. Univ of Melb BA 24. ACT ThL (1st cl) 22. **d** 23 **p** 24 Melb. C of St Mark Fitzroy Melb 23-24; CMS Miss at Canton 25-27; Hd Master H Trin Coll Canton 28-30; Warden of St Andr Hostel and Lect U Th Coll Canton 30-33; Asst P Kwang Shiu District 33-38; Supt Refugee Relief Work Chung Shan 38-40; V of St Andr Kowloon 41-45; Can (Emer) of St John's Cathl Hong Kong from 41; East Asia Sec CMS 47-58; Men Candidates' Sec 51-58; Asia Sec 58-61; Sec CMS 61-65; C of Enfield 56-65; H Trin w All SS Kens 65-70; Asst Dir Coll of Prs 65-70; C of Enfield Dio Lon from 72. *19 Hillside Crescent, Enfield, Middx, EN2 0HP.* (01-363 5613)

WITTEY, William Francis George. b 05. AKC 31. **d** 31 **p** 32 Chelmsf. C of St Barn W Silvertown 31-34; Min of St Jo Div Distr Becontree 34-35; V 35-44; Perm to Offic Dios Chelmsf and Ex from 45; C of St Mary Church w Shiphay 46-52; V of St Barn Carl 52-63; Torpenhow 63-72; Perm to Offic Dio Carl from 72. *Martindale Cottage, Ayside, Grange over Sands, Cumb.* (Newby Bridge 31215)

WITTON-DAVIES, Canon Carlyle. b 13. Late Exhib of Univ of Wales BA (1st cl Hebr) 34. Ex Coll Ox BA (2nd cl Th) 37, Jun Hall-Houghton Septuagint Pri 38, Sen 39, MA 40. Cudd Coll 36. **d** 37 **p** 38 St A. C of Buckley 37-40; Sub-Warden of St Mich Coll Llan and L to Offic Dio Llan 40-44; Exam Chap to Bp of Mon 40-44; to Bp in Jer 45-49; to Bp of St D 50-56; to Bp of Ox from 65; Missr St Geo Coll Ch Jer 44-49; Can of Jer 47-49; Dean and Prec of St D Cathl 49-56; Surr from 51; Chap O of St John Jer from 53; Archd of Ox 56-82; Can of Ch Ch Ox from 56; Sub-Dean of Ch Ch Cathl Ox from 72. *c/o Christ Church, Oxford.*

WITTS, Cyril Charles. b 14. Sarum Th Coll 47. **d** 49 **p** 50 Lon. C of St Anselm Hatch End 49-53; V of St Steph U Holloway 53-59; R of Elton 59-67; R of Water Newton 61-67; R of Stibbington 61-67; V of St Mary Magd Enfield 67-78; Chap Commun of St Denys Warm 78-81; Asst Chap Conv SS of Bethany Boscombe from 81. *18 Southlea Avenue, Southbourne, Bournemouth, Dorset, BH6 3AB.* (0202 431633)

WITTS-HEWINSON, Very Rev William Edwin. Linc Th Coll 42. **d** 42 **p** 43 Worc. C of St Jo Bapt Kidderminster 42-44; St Barn Rainbow Hill Worc 44-47; Miss Dio Lebom 47-48; C of Beaufort W 48-52; V of St Paul Geo 52-68; C of St Mark's Cathl Geo 69-70; R of H Trin Belvidere 70-72; St Jas Graaff Reinet 72-78; Archd of Karoo 72-78; St Mark's from 78; Dean and R of St Mark's Cathl City and Dio Geo from 78. *Deanery, Church Street, George, CP, S Africa.* (George 2313)

WITTSTOCK, Barry Ian. b 54. St Paul's Coll Grahmstn 77. **d** 78 **p** 79 Grahmstn. C of St Mark E Lon Dio Grahmstn from 79. *St Mark's Church, Church Lane, East London 5247, CP, S Africa.*

WITTY, Ven Robert John. Coll Ho Ch Ch. **d** 39 **p** 40 Ch Ch. C of Lyttelton 39-42; P-in-c of Te Ngawi 42-43; C of Avonside 43; V of Lyttelton w Lyttelton W and Governor's Bay 43-46; Lyttelton 46-59; Chap Miss to Seamen Banks Peninsula 43-46; V of New Brighton 59-64; St Luke Ch Ch 64-78; Hon Can of Ch Ch 59-69; Archd of Ch Ch from 71; Dep VG 74-76; VG from 76; Commiss Polyn from 77; P Asst to Bp of Ch Ch from 78. *79 Bassett Street, Christchurch 6, NZ.* (859-508)

WIXON, Jack. b 44. Lich Th Coll 68. **d** 71 **p** 72 Blackb. C of Adlington 71-74; St Annes-on-Sea 74-76; V of St Jas Chorley Dio Blackb from 76. *St James's Vicarage, Chorley, Lancs.* (Chorley 63153)

WODEMAN, Cyril Peter Guy. b 28. Qu Coll Cam 2nd cl Cl Trip pt i 50, BA (2nd cl Cl Trip pt ii) 51, MA 55. Cranmer Hall Dur 72. **d** 73 **p** 74 Blackb. C of Penwortham 73-77; V of St Steph Burnley Dio Blackb from 77. *St Stephen's Vicarage, Todmorden Road, Burnley, Lancs, BB11 3ER.* (Burnley 24733)

WODERO, Gibson. Buwalasi Th Coll 62. **d** 64 **p** 65 Mbale. P Dio Mbale. *PO Box 297, Mbale, Uganda.*

WODI, Herbert. b 32. St Paul's Coll Awka. **d** 74 **p** 76 Nig Delta. P Dio Nig Delta. *Box 32, Elele, Nigeria.*

WOELLER, Ven David John. Univ of Manit BA 47. Trin Coll Tor LTh 52. **d** 51 **p** 52 Edmon. C of St Geo Tor 51-52; I of Marwayne 52-53; C of St Thos Hamilton 54-56; R of Orangeville 56-61; Dir Relig Educn Dio Montr 61-64; Personnel Dir Miss Dept Angl Ch in Canada 65-69; Hon C of St Mich AA Tor 69-74; Archd Without Territorial Jurisd Dio Hur from 75. *Box 308, London, Ont., Canada.* (519-434 6893)

WOGALE, Alban. **d** 77 **p** 79 New Hebr. P Dio New Hebr 77-80; Dio Vanuatu from 80. *Mota, Banks Island, Vanuatu.*

WOGU, Jonah Achinihu. b 31. **d** 75 **p** 76 Aba. P Dio Aba. *St Thomas's Parsonage, Ukpakiri, via Aba, Nigeria.*

WOKE, Alexander Ghinda Enyinda. Trin Coll Umuahia 58, **d** 60 Nig Delta. d Dio Nig Delta. *St Paul's Parsonage, Opobo Town, Nigeria.*

WOKOMA, Atkinson Mbrenagogo. **d** 27 **p** 29 Niger. CMS P Dio Niger 27-52; Dio Nig Delta 52-60. *Wokomas' Polo, Buguma, via Degamo, Nigeria.*

WOKSEN, Barnabas. Patteson Th Centre Kohimarama. **d** 72 Melan. d Dio Melan 72-75; Dio New Hebr from 75. *Ureparapara, Banks Islands, New Hebrides.*

WOLF, James Garnett. b 47. Simon Fraser Univ BC BA 73. Vanc Sch of Th MDiv 75. **d** and **p** 75 New Westmr. C of St Jo Evang N Vanc 75-77; P Assoc of St Paul Winnipeg 77-79; R of Ch Ch Winnipeg Dio Rupld from 79. *1735 Croydon Avenue, Winnipeg, Manit, Canada.*

WOLFE, Charles Uriah. b 06. **d** 70 **p** 73 Ja (APM). P Dio Ja. *6 Cedar Gardens Road, Box 195, Mandeville, Jamaica, WI.*

WOLFE, Desmond Alfred. St Paul's Coll Grahmstn 32. **d** 36 **p** 37 Capetn. C of H Redeemer Sea Point 36-39; Claremont 39-44; St John's Hostel Capetn 44-46; R of Worc 46-52; Maitland 52-57; H Trin Paarl 57-62; St Matt Claremont 62-80; Perm to Offic Dio Capetn from 80. *4 Mortimer Road, Wynberg 7800, CP, S Africa.* (77-6014)

WOLFE, Kenneth Wesley. b 19. QUB MB 42. Linc Th Coll. **d** 57 Oss **p** 61 B & W. C of Dunleckney (Bagenalstown) 57-58; Portishead 60-63; St Aldhelm Branksome 68-76; Rugby (in c of St Pet) 76-80; Hon C of St Alb Northn Dio Pet from 80. *40 Greenfield Avenue, Northampton, NN3 2AF.* (Northn 406369)

WOLFE, Canon Michael Matheson. b 29. Pemb Coll Ox BA 49, MA 53. Cudd Coll 51. **d** 53 **p** 54 Bris. C of St Matt Moorfields Bris 53-57; P-in-c of Gordon Chap Fochabers 57-58; Asst Ho Master Aberlour Orph 57-58; Sub-Warden 58-59; V of St Paul Southport 59-65; Up Holland Dio Liv 65-73; R from 73; M Gen Syn Liv from 75; RD of Ormskirk from 78; Hon Can of Liv from 78; Surr from 78. *Up Holland Rectory, Skelmersdale, Lancs, WN8 0EW.* (Up Holland 622936)

WOLFENDEN, Peter Graham. b 40. St Pet Coll Ox BA (Th) 63, MA 66. Linc Th Coll 62. **d** 64 Blackb **p** 65 Burnley for Blackb. C of Adlington 64-66; Asst Master Barton Peveril Gr Sch 66-69; Chap Bp Wordsworth Sch Sarum 69-72; Asst Master Cramlington High Sch 75-78; Hon C of Ponteland Dio Newc T from 75; Hd Master Coates Middle Sch Ponteland from 78. *23 Richmond Way, Ponteland, Newcastle upon Tyne.* (Ponteland 25404)

WOLFERSTAN, John. **d** and **p** 60 New Westmr. I of Deep Cove 62-65; Hatzic 65-71; P-in-c of Richmond St Edward 71-74; Perm to Offic Dio BC 74. *3885 Rumble Road, Saltair, RR2, Ladysmith, BC, Canada.*

WOLFF, Ven Charles Edward Fabian. Dioc Th Coll Montr LTh 33. **d** 34 **p** 35 Edmon. C-in-c of St Mary Vegreville 34-35; I 35-37; I of Barrhead 37-41; Sedgewick 41-42; Chap CASF 42-46; R of St Steph Edmon 46-63; Can of Edmon 50-60; Exam Chap to Bp of Edmon 54-63; Archd of Edmon 60-63; Archd (Emer) from 63; R of St Luke Cedar Hill 63-77; Perm to Offic Dio BC from 77. *3416 Veteran Street, Victoria, BC, Canada.* (592-9634)

WOLFF, Curt Heinz. St Paul's Coll Grahmstn LTh 66. **d** 64 **p** 65 Capetn. C of Somerset W 64-67; R of Ceres Dio Capetn from 67. *Rectory, Ceres, CP, S Africa.*

WOLING, Canon Yafesi. Buwalasi Th Coll 54. **d** 56 **p** 59 U Nile. P Dio U Nile 56-61; Dio Mbale 61-72; Dio Bukedi from 72; Hon Can of Mbale 71-72; Can of Bukedi from 72. *Church of Uganda, Agule, Box 4017, Pallisa, Uganda.*

WOLSEY, Canon Ronald George. Clifton Th Coll and St Aid Coll. **d** 43 **p** 44 Bris. C of St Phil and St Jacob w Em Bris 43-44; St Mich Highworth w Sevenhampton and Inglesham 44-47; Clifton 47-50; V of Stratton St Marg 50-60; Marshfield w Cold Ashton 60-66; St Andr w St Bart Bris 66-76; RD of Horfield 73-76; R and V of Wroughton 76-80; Hon Can of Bris Cathl from 77. *8 Clarendon Drive, Wootton Bassett, Wilts.* (Wootton Bassett 702201)

WOLSTENCROFT, Alan. b 37. Cudd Coll. **d** 69 Hulme for Man **p** 70 Man. C of St Thos Halliwell 69-71; Stand 71-73; V of St Martin Wythenshawe 73-80; RD of Withington from 78; V of Brooklands Dio Man from 80. *186 Brooklands Road, Sale, M33 3PB.* (061-973 5947)

WOLSTENHOLME, Reginald Arthur. b 1896. Wells Th Coll. **d** 63 **p** 64 B & W. C of Frome Selwood 63-74. *3 Heath Drive, Frome, Somt.* (Frome 63136)

WOLSTENHULME, Arthur James. b 20. Univ of Leeds BA (2nd cl Cl) 42. Coll of Resurr Mirfield 42. **d** 44 **p** 46 Man. C of St Aug Tonge Moor 44-45; Hollinwood 45-48; Palfrey 48-52; V of St Pet Cov 52-56; New Bilton 56-66; Kingsthorpe Dio Pet from 66; R (w St D Northn from 73). *Kingsthorpe Rectory, Green End, Northampton, NN2 6RD.* (Northampton 714286)

WOLTERS, Very Rev Conrad Clifton. b 09. St Jo Coll Dur LTh 32, BA 33, MA 36. ALCD (1st cl) 32. **d** 33 **p** 34 S'wark. C of Ch Ch Gipsy Hill 33-37; Ch Ch Beckenham 37-41; V of St Luke Wimbledon Park 41-49; R of Sanderstead 49-59; Can Res of Newc T Cathl 59-62; Provost and V of Newc T Cathl 62-76; Provost (Emer) from 76; Exam Chap to Bp of Newc T 59-76; Chap S of St Marg E Grinstead from 76. *The Cottage, St Margaret's Convent, E Grinstead, Sussex, RH19 3LD.* (E Grinstead 22406)

WOLVERHAMPTON, Bishop Suffragan of. *See* Rogerson, Right Rev Barry.

WOMERSLEY, Walter John. K Coll Lon and Warm AKC 52. **d** 53 **p** 54 Linc. C of St Pet-at-Gowts Linc 53-59; Chap of Whitestone Sch Bulawayo 59-70; Uplands Sch Transvaal from 77; R of White River 70-77; L to Offic Dio Pret from 77. *PO Box 244, White River, Transvaal, S Africa.*

WON, Jonathan Songho. b 38. Univ of Yonsei Seoul 62. Episc Th Sch Cam Massachusetts 67. **d** 70 Bp D J Campbell for Taejon **p** 71 Taejon. P Dio Taejon; Dioc Sec and Dom Chap to Bp of Taejon from 76. *Box 22, Taejon 300, Korea.*

WONG, Daniel Tak-Wing. b 45. Chinese Univ of Hong Kong BSocSc 67, MDiv 75. Chung Chi Coll. **d** 75 **p** 77 Hong. C of St Mary's Ch Hong Dio Hong from 75. *2a Tai Hank Road, Causeway Bay, Hong Kong.*

WONG, Fook Ping. U Th Coll Canton. **d** 23 **p** 26 Hong. P Dio Hong; Dio Sing 28-32; V Dio Hong 32-55; Dio S China from 55. *Christchurch, Shekki, Chungshan, Kwangting, China.*

WONG, James Yui Kok. Univ of Syd BA 63. Trin Th Coll Sing BTh 66. Fuller Th Coll Pasadena Calif MA 72. **d** 66 **p** 67 Sing. P Dio Sing; Exam Chap to Bp of Sing from 73; Chap St Andr Jun Coll Sing from 79. *St Andrew's Junior College, Malan Road, Singapore 0410.*

WONG, Stephen. b 40. **d** and **p** 78 Sabah. P Dio Sabah 78-80; Dio Kuch from 80. *St Faith's Church, Kenyalang, Kuching, Malaysia.*

WONG, Stephen Nai-Lon. Yen Ching Univ Peiping BA 32. Ming Hwa Coll Hong 51. **d** 53 **p** 55 Hong. Hd Master Kei Yan Sch Hong 53-63; Hon C of St Steph Chap Stanley Hong 53-55; St Mary Hong 55-62; Actg V of St Jas Hong 62-63; C of Melb Cathl 63-67; Chap of Chinese Miss and Asst Chap Miss to Seamen in Melb 63-67; Perm to Offic Dio Melb from 67. *10 Waratah Street, Oakleigh, Vic, Australia 3167.* (57-5601)

WONNACOTT, Charles Edward. b 14. Wycl Hall Ox 62. **d** 63 **p** 64 Blackb. C of St Paul Blackpool 63-66; Ringwood (in c of St Paul Bisterne) 66-68; All SS Sidley, Bexhill 70-73; P-in-c and Seq of Peasmarsh 73-76; R (w Beckley) 76-81; Perm to Offic Dio Win from 81. *3 Cedar Avenue, St Leonard's, Ringwood, Hants.* (Hampreston 5457)

WOO, John William. Univ of Melb BComm 62. ACT ThL (2nd cl) 65. Ridley Coll Melb 63. **d** 69 Sabah. C of Tawau Sabah 69-70; Negri Sembilan 70-72; Perm to Offic Dio Melb 72-76; Dio Syd from 77. *31 Kuppa Toad, Ryde, NSW, Australia 2112.*

WOOD, Alexander. b 09. St Chad's Coll Regina. **d** 34; **p** 35 Qu'App. C of Windthorst 34-35; I 35-37; I of Togo 37-38; C of St Paul Regina 38; I of Oxbow 38-45; C of St Cuthb Colinton w St Mungo Balerno 45-48; P-in-c of St Ebba Eyemouth 48-55; R of Ringmore w Kingston 55-77; Publ Pr Dio Ex from 77. *2 West Park Wood, Staverton, Totnes, Devon.* (Staverton 626)

WOOD, Allan Thomas Joseph. ACT ThL 68. Ridley Coll Melb 65. **d** 69 Melb. C of Surrey Hills Dio Melb 69-71; St John Blackburn 71-72; P-in-c of St Mark Reservoir W 72-73; C of Booval 73-75; R of St Andr S Brisb Dio Brisb from 75. *160 Vulture Street, South Brisbane, Australia 4101.* (44 3808)

WOOD, Anthony James. b 38. Kelham Th Coll 58. **d** 63 **p** 64 Lich. C of St Alkmund w Harlescott Shrewsbury 63; Harlescott 63-66; Porthill 66-70; C-in-c of Priors Lee 70-76; V of Barton-under-Needwood Dio Lich from 76. *Vicarage, Barton-under-Needwood, Burton-on-Trent, Staffs, DE13 8HU.* (Barton 2359)

WOOD, Anthony Robert. St Jo Coll Morpeth 64. ACT ThL 65. **d** 65 **p** 66 C & Goulb. C of Temora 65-69; Good Shepherd Curtin Canberra 69-70; Killara 70-73; R of Bankstown Dio Syd from 73. *461 Chapel Road, Bankstown, NSW, Australia 2200.* (70-1883)

WOOD, Anthony Roger. b 45. St Mich Th Coll Crafers ThL 72. ACT ThSchol 74. **d** 72 **p** 73 Murray. C of Ch Ch Mt Gambier 72-76; R of Mannum w Mt Pleasant 76-80; L to Offic Dio Adel from 80. *St Barnabas' College, Belair, S Australia 5052.*

WOOD, Ven Arnold. b 18. Clifton Th Coll 63. **d** 65 **p** 66 Wakef. C of Kirkheaton 65-67; V of Ch Ch Mt Pellon 67-73; Pelynt 73-81; R of Lanreath 73-81; RD of W Wivelshire 76-81; Archd of Cornw from 81. *Petherton, Kenwyn Road, Truro, Cornw, TR1 3SH.* (Truro 2866)

WOOD, Arthur Edward. b 02. St Steph Ho Ox 51. **d** 53 Ox **p** 54 Reading for Cant. C of St Paul Ox 53-55; Clewer (in c of St Agnes Spital) 55-59; V of St Paul Ox 59-64; Chap St Mary's Conv w St Jos Hosp Chiswick 64-66; C-in-c of St Francis's Conv Distr Hammerfield Boxmoor 66-75; Perm to Offic Dio St Alb from 75. *1 Hanover Green, St John's Road, Hemel Hempstead, Herts, HP1 1QH.* (Hemel Hempstead 42666)

WOOD, Barry John Burns. Univ of Witwatersrand BA 67. St Paul's Coll Grahmstn 66. **d** 68 Bp Carter for Johann **p** 69 Johann. C of Randfontein 68-70; P-in-c of Regent Hill 70-72; R of Robertsham 72-76; Belville Dio Capetn from 76. *43 Teddington Street, Belville, CP, S Africa.* (97-1558)

WOOD, Canon Blake Gregory Moncrieff. Univ of Tor BA 35. Univ Coll Ox BA (2nd cl Th) 48, MA 53. St Jo Coll Manit DD 68. Wycl Coll Tor LTh 39. **d** 39 **p** 40 Tor. C of Ch Ch Tor 39-44; Chap CASF 44-46; C of H Trin Brompton 46-48; R of Ch of Comforter Tor 48-52; Dean of Resid and Asst Prof at St Jo Coll Winnipeg 52-61; Prof 61-78; Dean of Div 62-78; Can of Rupld 68-80; Hon Can from 80; Hon C of St Aid Winnipeg 71-77. *271 Montrose Street, Winnipeg, Manit, Canada.*

WOOD, Brian Frederick. b 31. Univ of Leeds BA 52. Coll of Resurr Mirfield. **d** 57 Liv **p** 58 Warrington for Liv. C of St Anne Wigan 57-60; Elland 60-63; V of Carlinghow Batley 63-73; Drighlington Dio Wakef from 73. *Drighlington Vicarage, Bradford, Yorks, BD11 1LS.* (Drighlington 852402)

WOOD, Canon Charles Joseph. b 1891. **d** and **p** 54 Glas. C of St Mary's Cathl Glas and Hosp Chap 54-62; P-in-c of Eyemouth 62-66; I of Arran Dio Arg Is from 67; Hon Can of cumbrae from 78. *Sandbraes House, Whiting Bay, Isle of Arran, KA27 8RE.* (Whiting Bay 312)

WOOD, Charles Laver. b 24. Wells Th Coll 66. **d** 68 Bp McKie for Cov **p** 69 Cov. C of St Mich Stoke 68-71; V of Ramsey w L Oakley Dio Chelmsf from 71. *Ramsey Vicarage, Harwich, Essex.* (Ramsey 291)

WOOD, Christopher. b 44. Rhodes Univ of S Afr BA. St Bede's Coll 79. **d** 80 St John's. d Dio St John's. *PO Box 25, Umtata, Transkei.*

WOOD, Very Rev Clyde Maurice. **d** and **p** 65 Melb. C of St John Bentleigh 65-66; St Paul Ringwood 66-67; Dept of Evang and Ex 67-70; C-in-c of Armadale and Hawksburn 70-74; R and Can Res of Darwin Cathl Dio N Terr 74-78; Dean and R from 78. *PO Box 181, Darwin, NT, Australia 5794.* (089-81 9099)

WOOD, Colin George William. St Jo Coll Dur BA **d** 33 **p** 34 Liv. C of St Mary Gt Sankey 33-36; Halsall 36-39; CF (EC) 39-45; C of Warrington 45-47; V of St Mary Waterloo 47-53; R of Cheddington 53-62; V of Mentmore 53-62; Ed *Braille Th Times* from 58; RD of Ivinghoe 61-63; V of Streatley 62-74; Chap at St John Angl Ch Menton 75-77; Perm to Offic Dio Sarum from 80. *2 Ashley Court, Knightsdale Road, Weymouth, Dorset.*

WOOD, Cyril Edgar Baldwin. St Jo Coll Morpeth ACT ThL (2nd cl) 47. **d** 47 **p** 48 Bath. M Bro of Good Shepherd 47-53; C of Bourke 48; P-in-c of Brewarinna 49-51; R of Bourke 52; C of Ch Ch St Lawr Syd 53-56; Sec ABM Vic 57-61; C of St Paul's Cathl Melb 57-61; R of Honiara 61-65; Can of Melan 62-65; Commiss Melan 65-74; Centr Melan from 76; V of Noble Pk 65-69; Broadmeadows 69-70; St Phil Mt Waverley 70-81; St Chad Chelsea Dio Melb from 81. *10 Thames Promenade, Chelsea, Vic, Australia 3196.*

WOOD, David Abell. b 25. Qu Coll Cam BA 50, MA 54. Wells Th Coll 50. **d** 50 Bp J J Willis for Truro **p** 51 Truro. C of Bodmin 50-52; Industr Chap Dio Lich 52-55; C-in-c of St Geo Wolverhampton 55-56; V and P Warden of St Geo Ho Wolverhampton 56-67; Perm to Offic Dio Heref 67-70; Warden of Communicare Team Min Killingworth Dio Newc T from 70. *77 Angus Close, Killingworth Township, Newcastle upon Tyne.* (Newcastle 681497)

WOOD, David Arthur. b 30. Univ Man BA 51, Dipl Soc Admin 55. Lich Th Coll 59. **d** 61 **p** 62 Man. C of Ch Ch Ashton L 61-64; All SS Elton Bury (in c of St Francis) 64-68; Youth Chap Dio Newc T 68-72; V of Cramlington Dio Newc T 72-73; R from 73. *Rectory, Cramlington, Northumberland, NE23 6QF.* (Cramlington 712259)

WOOD, David Graeme. b 53. Univ of Melb BA 75. Trin Coll Melb BD 78. **d** 78 **p** 79 Melb. C of All SS Geelong 78-80; St Matt Cheltenham Dio Melb from 80. *1/15-17 Cameron Street, Cheltenham, Vic, Australia 3192.*

WOOD, Edward Berryman. b 33. Ely Th Coll. **d** 57 **p** 58 Guildf. C of Aldershot 57-60; Worplesdon (in c of St Alb) 60-62; V of Littleport 62-64; St Jo Div Balham 64-71; Hon Chap to Bp of S'wark 67-81; V of All SS New Eltham Dio S'wark from 71. *Vicarage, Bercta Road, SE9 3TZ.* (01-850 9894)

WOOD, Edward Francis. b 28. Chich Th Coll 56. **d** 58 **p** 59 Newc T. C of St Francis High Heaton Newc T 58-62; St Phil Newc T 62-64; Delaval (in c of New Hartley) 64-67; C-in-c of St Mark's Conv Distr Shiremoor 67-68; V 68-78; Dioc Adv on Broadcasting and C of St Geo Jesmond City and Dio Newc T from 78. *8 Hartside Gardens, Newcastle upon Tyne, NE2 2JR.* (0632-812523)

WOOD, Eric Basil. b 25. St Edm Hall Ox BA and MA 50. Cudd Coll 50. **d** 51 **p** 52 St Alb. C of Cheshunt 51-54; St Pancras 54-57; Leatherhead 57-62; V of Mapledurham 62-68; C-in-c of Drayton 68-72; V 72-81; P-in-c of Buckland and of Littleworth and of Pusey Dio Ox from 81. *Buckland Vicarage, Faringdon, Oxon, SN7 8QN.* (Buckland 618)

WOOD, Eric Stanley. b 16. AKC 40. **d** 40 **p** 41 Liv. C of St Bridget Wavertree 40-42; St Pet Aintree (in c of St Giles) 42-43; Sutton Liv 43-48; Prescot 48-50; V of Banks 50-55; R of Newton-in-Makerfield 55-64; Lowton 64-81. *5 Eastwood Road, Burtonwood, Warrington, Chesh.*

WOOD, Ernest Charles Anthony. b 06. RM Acad Woolwich 25. Wycl Hall Ox 52. **d** 53 **p** 54 Roch. C of St Pet w St Marg Roch 53-55; C-in-c of Nurstead w Ifield 55-60; R 60-78; Perm to Offic Dio Roch from 78. *14 Maryland Drive, Barming, Maidstone, Kent, ME16 9EW.*

WOOD, Francis Gilbert. b 10. Bp Wilson Coll IM 31. **d** 34 **p** 35 Lon. C of St Mary Stratford Bow 34-37; Gt Berkhamsted 37-40; CF 40-60; Caribbean Area 46-49; SCF Bovington Camp 49-52; Hong Kong 52-55; Ches Area and Staff Chap W Commd 55-58; SCF 58-59; Bulford 59-60; R of Pulham St Mary Magd 60-68; RD of Redenhall 65-68; R of Ditchingham w Pirnough 68-77; Hedenham 68-77; C-in-c of Broome 68-74; R 74-77; RD of Depwade 74-76. *Address temp unknown.*

WOOD, Frederick Harry. b 29. BD (Lon) 58. Tyndale Hall Bris 55. **d** 59 Blackb **p** 60 Lanc for York. C of Ch Ch Blackb 59-62; Newburn (in c of Throckley) 62-64; PC of Ven Bede Gateshead 64-69; V of S Cave and Ellerker (w Broomfleet from 76) 69-81; Irlam Dio Man from 81. *Vicarage, Vicarage Road, Irlam, Manchester, M30 6WA.* (061-775 2461)

WOOD, Frederick Leonard. b 19. BEM (Mil) 59. Worc Ordin Coll. **d** 64 **p** 65 Ex. C of St Paul Preston Paignton 64-68; V of Chas w St Matthias Plymouth 68-81. *9 Belfield Rise, Marldon, Paignton, Devon, TQ3 1NX.*

WOOD, Geoffrey. b 33. Tyndale Hall Bris 56. **d** 61 **p** 62 Ches. C of Higher Tranmere 61-64; Newburn w Throckley 64-68; R of Gt Smeaton w Appleton Wiske (and Birkby and Danby Wiske w Hutton Bonville from 79) Dio Ripon from 69; C-in-c of Birkby 73-79; Danby Wiske w Hutton Bonville 76-79. *Great Smeaton Rectory, Northallerton, Yorks.* (Great Smeaton 205)

WOOD, George Albert. b 22. St Paul's Coll Grahmstn 52. **d** 54 **p** 55 Pret. C of Hillcrest 54-57; W Suburbs Pret 57-60; Cheam (in c of St Osw) 60-63; R of Eshowe 63-69; Can of Zulu 68-73; Dean of St Mich AA Cathl Eshowe 70-73; R of Ch K Port Eliz 74-77; Area Secr USPG Dio Chich from 78. *50 Wivelsfield, Haywards Heath, RH16 4EW.* (Haywards Hth 54531)

WOOD, George John Edmund. b 09. Roch Th Coll 69. **d** 70 **p** 71 Cant. C of St Jude Thornton Heath 70-72; St Mary of Nazareth W Wickham 72-76; Perm to Offic Dios Cant and Chich from 77. *91 Cross Road, Southwick, Brighton, BN4 4HH.* (Brighton 591755)

WOOD, George Robert. b 26. Em Coll Cam BA 52. Oak Hill Th Coll 52. **d** 53 **p** 54 Carl. C of St Jas Denton-Holme Carl 53-56; V of St Matt Cam 56-60; NW Area Sec CPAS 60-61; R of Watermillock Carl 61-74; V of Holme Eden

74-76; Chap Lindley Lodge Masham 76-78; Prec of H Trin Hull 78-80; V of Chipping Dio Blackb from 80; P-in-c of Whitewell Dio Blackb from 80. *Vicarage, Chipping, Lancs, PR3 2QH.* (Chipping 252)

WOOD, Gerald Richard. b 12. Nor Ordin Course 73. **d** 75 Nor **p** 76 Lynn for Nor. Hon C of Thornage 75-77; Weybourne w U Sheringham 77-80; Kelling w Salthouse 77-80; Blakeney Dio Nor from 80. *The Croft, Saxlingham-by-Holt, Norfolk, NR25 7LB.*

WOOD, Gordon Cooper. b 20. St Pet Hall Ox BA 43, MA 46. Wycl Hall Ox. **d** 44 **p** 45 Ripon. C of Ch Ch Armley Leeds 44-46; CF 46-49; V of St Clem Sheepscar Leeds 49-65; Roundhay Dio Ripon from 65. *St John's Vicarage, Oakwood Grove, Leeds, LS8 2PA.* (Leeds 658583)

WOOD, Gordon Edward. b 12. Ely Th Coll 63. **d** 64 **p** 65 Ely. C of H Trin w St Mary Ely 64-66; R of Houghton Ely 66-74; R of Wyton Ely 66-74; V of Billingborough 74-80; Sempringham w Pointon w Birthorpe 74-80; Horbling 74-80. *2 Rose Cottage, Needingworth Road, St Ives, Huntingdon, Cambs.*

WOOD, Harold George. b 08. Univ of Lon BD 34. Lon Coll of Div 31. **d** 34 **p** 35 Bris. C of Swindon 34-37; H Trin Kingswood (in c of Ascen Mount Hill) 37-42; V of St Barn Ashley Road Bris 42-47; St Paul Bedminster 47-55; R of Stapleton 55-70; V of Bitton 70-74; Hon C of St Barn Sutton Dio S'wark from 75. *79 Warwick Road, Sutton, Surrey.* (01-642 3253)

WOOD, Jack Frederick. b 15. **d** 75 **p** 76 Matab. P Dio Matab 75-80; C of Estcourt Dio Natal from 80. *Box 123 Estcourt, Natal, S Africa.*

WOOD, James. b 09. St Jo Coll Morpeth ACT ThL 39. **d** 39 **p** 40 Bath. M of Bro of Good Shepherd 39-45; R of Tottenham 41-42; Brewarrina 42-45; Vice-Prin of Bro Good Shepherd 43-45; C of Old Basford 45-47; R of Ingoldmells w Addlethorpe 47-59; RD of Candleshoe 52-74; PC of Skirbeck Quarter 59-69; V 69-74. *St Nicholas House, Normanton, Grantham, Lincs.* (Honington 567)

WOOD, John. b 37. **d** 77 **p** 79 Edin (APM). C of Haddington Dio Edin from 77. *7 Herdmanflatt, Haddington, E Lothian.*

WOOD, John Anthony Scriven. b 48. Univ of Leeds BSc 70. St Jo Coll Nottm 76. **d** 79 Stafford for Lich **p** 80 Lich. C of St Mich AA Colwich and of St Steph Gt Haywood Dio Lich from 79. *13 Earlsway, Great Haywood, Stafford, ST18 0RP.*

WOOD, John Arthur. b 23. Roch Th Coll 68. **d** 70 **p** 71 Ripon. C of St Jas Wetherby 70-71; C-in-c of Arbourthorne Sheff 71-75; Team V of Arbourthorne in Manor Team Ministry (Sheff Manor from 76) 75-81; R of Rodney Stoke w Draycott Dio B & W from 81. *Vicarage, Vicarage Lane, Draycott, Cheddar, BS27 3SH.* (Cheddar 742315)

WOOD, John Norman. b 19. Univ of Man St Andr Coll Pampisford. **d** 45 **p** 46 Lich. C of Bushbury 45-47; Hednesford 47-50; V of Tottenhill w Wormegay 50-53; R of Gt w L Snoring 53-63; C-in-c of Hindringham 59-63; V of St Mark Bolton 63-71; V of St Luke Chadderton 71-80; Lumb-in-Rossendale Dio Man from 80. *Vicarage, 894 Burnley Road East, Lumb-in-Rossendale, BB4 9PQ.* (Rossendale 227020)

WOOD, John Samuel. b 47. Lanchester Coll of Tech Cov BSc 69. Westcott Ho Cam 72. **d** 81 St E (NSM). C of Haverhill Dio St E from 81. *38 Galley Road, Hundon, Sudbury, Suffolk, CO10 8SA.*

WOOD, Keith. b 49. St Steph Ho Ox 76. **d** 78 **p** 79 Chich. C of Bognor 78-81; Hangleton Dio Chich from 81. *378 Old Shoreham Road, Hove, Sussex, BN3 7GJ.* (Brighton 418812)

WOOD, Keith Ernest. b 33. Qu Coll Ox BA 55, BCL 56, Dipl Th 57, MA 70. Wycl Hall Ox 56. **d** 58 **p** 59 Chelmsf. C of Barking 58-61; Min of St Andr Eccles Distr Basildon 61-70; V of Brampton Bierlow Dio Sheff from 70. *Brampton Vicarage, Christchurch Road, Wath-on-Dearne, Rotherham, Yorks, S63 6NW.* (Rotherham 873210)

WOOD, Kenneth. b 22. MBE 55. CEng. Linc Th Coll 63. **d** 65 Hulme for Man **p** 65 Man. C of Newton Heath 65-67; Littleham w Exmouth 67-69; V of St Bonif Devonport 70-74; R of Cheriton Bp 74-78; V of L Hulton Dio Man from 78. *St John's Vicarage, Walkden, Manchester, M28 5RN.* (061-790 2338)

WOOD, Laurence Henry. Kelham Th Coll 47. **d** 52 **p** 53 Wakef. C of Ravensthorpe 52-55; Almondbury 55-58; V of Linthwaite 58-64; R of Bonsall 64-70; V of Cromford 64-70; Longwood 70-76; Liversedge Dio Wakef from 76. *Vicarage, Knowler Hill, Liversedge, W Yorks, WF15 6LJ.* (Heckmondwike 402414)

WOOD, Margaret Patricia. b 34. St Jo Coll Auckld LTh 75, STh 77. **d** 76 **p** 78 Ch Ch. C of Avonhead 76-79; Chap and Prin Bp Julius Hall Dio Ch Ch from 79. *90 Waimairi Road, Christchurch 4, NZ.* (487-782)

✠ **WOOD, Right Rev Maurice Arthur Ponsonby.** b 16. Qu Coll Cam BA 38, MA 42. DSC 44. Ridley Hall Cam 40. **d** 40 **p** 41 Lon. C of St Paul Portman Square 40-43; Chap RNVR 43-46; R of St Ebbe Ox 47-52; V of Islington 52-61; RD of Islington 52-61; Proc Conv Lon 55-71; Commiss Syd 61-71; Prin Oak Hill Th Coll 61-71; Exam Chap to Bp of Nor 62-71; Preb of Holborn in St Paul's Cathl Lon 69-71; Cons Ld Bp of Norwich in St Paul's Cathl Lon 29 Sept 71 by Abp of Cant; Bps of Lon; Win; Chich; Ches; Linc; St E; Leic; Heref; Ely; Bang; Bris; Chelmsf; Roch; Chile; Derby; St Alb; Ox; and others. Chap RNR from 71. *The Bishop's House, Norwich, NR3 1SB.* (Nor 29001)

WOOD, Nicholas Martin. b 51. AKC 74. St Aug Coll Cant 74. **d** 75 **p** 76 Chelmsf. C of E Ham w Upton Pk 75-78; St Luke Leyton 78-81; V of St Aug Rish Green Romford Dio Chelmsf from 81. *St Augustine's Vicarage, Birkbeck Road, Rush Green, Romford, Essex.*

WOOD, Nowell Wakeley. b 07. FRICS 46. Ripon Hall, Ox 63. **d** 64 **p** 65 Roch. C of Shortlands 64-67; R of Halstead 67-75. *3 Broadwater Down, Tunbridge Wells, Kent.*

WOOD, Peter Palmer. b 36. Univ of Nottm BA (2nd cl Geog) 58. Bps' Coll Cheshunt 58. **d** 60 **p** 61 Chich. C of Aldrington 60-64; St Matthias Preston Sussex 64-67; St Anne Lewes 67-70; The Quinton 70-72; V of Kirkby-Wharfe w Ulleskelf Dio York from 72. *Kirkby Wharfe Vicarage, Tadcaster, N Yorks.* (Tadcaster 833379)

WOOD, Peter Thomas. b 31. Clifton Th Coll 57. **d** 60 **p** 61 Chelmsf. C of Woodford Wells 60-63; SAMS Dio Chile 63-72; Hd Master St Paul's Vina del Mar 63-68; R of St Pet Vina del Mar 68-72; V of Ch Ch Clevedon 72-81; Chap St Brandon's Sch Clevedon 72-81. *c/o Christ Church Vicarage, Clevedon, Avon.* (Clevedon 873391)

WOOD, Philip Hervey. b 42. Sarum Wells Th Coll 73. **d** 74 **p** 75 Cov. C of H Trin Cov 74-75; Finham 75-77; St Mary Magd Wandsworth Common 78-81; R of Ewhurst Dio Chich from 81; Bodiam Dio Chich from 81. *Ewhurst Rectory, Robertsbridge, E Sussex, TN32 5TB.* (Staplecross 268)

WOOD, Philip Hindley. b 07. St Pet Hall Ox BA and Dipl Th 39, MA 44. Wycl Hall Ox 39. **d** 40 **p** 41 Liv. C of St Cath Wigan 40-42; Ch Ch Surbiton Hill 42-47; V of Ch Ch Croydon 47-58; Org Sec CPASW Midl Distr and L to Offic Dio Birm 58-63; V of St Jo Evang Carl 63-72. *35 Castle Head Close, Ambleside Road, Keswick, Cumb.*

WOOD, Philip James. b 48. Univ of Bris BSc 69. Oak Hill Coll 71. **d** 74 Lon **p** 75 Stepney for Lon. C of Isl 74-77; Stapenhill 77-80; V of St Luke Walthamstow Dio Chelmsf from 80. *St Luke's Vicarage, Greenleaf Road, E17 6QQ.* (01-520 2885)

WOOD, Randolph Scott. **d** 58 NS for Sktn **p** 59 Sktn. I of Watson 58-62; I of Pathlow 59-62; R of St Matt Sktn 62-65; CF (Canad) from 65. *Canadian Forces Base, Calgary, Alta., Canada.* (242 1161)

WOOD, Raymond John Lee. b 28. ACII 55. Linc Th Coll 66. **d** 68 Ox **p** 69 Buckingham for Ox. C of Beaconsfield (in c of St Thos Holtspur from 70) 68-72; Offg CF 70-72; V of Wath-upon-Dearne w Adwick-upon-Dearne 72-77; Surr 72-77; R of St Tudy w Michaelstow Dio Truro from 77. *St Tudy Rectory, Nr Bodmin, Cornw, PL30 3NH.* (0208-850374)

WOOD, Reginald John. b 16. Worc Ordin Coll 61. **d** 63 **p** 64 B & W. C of St Jo Bapt Weston-s-Mare 63-65; Radstock 65-68; R of Seavington w Lopen 68-80. *c/o Seavington Rectory, Ilminster, Somt.* (South Petherton 40762)

WOOD, Canon Reginald Kingsley. b 02. St Aid Coll 39. **d** 39 **p** 40 Sheff. C of Stocksbridge 39-41; St Mary Doncaster (in c of St Aid) 41-45; V of Bolsterstone w Deepcar 45-49; St Phil w St Anne Sheff 49-56; Thorpe-Salvin 56-59; R of Bradfield 60-67; Tankersley 67-70; Hon Can of Sheff 65-70; Can (Emer) from 71; Perm to Offic Dio Sheff from 70. *1 Cherrytree Close, Sheffield, S Yorks, S11 9AF.* (Sheffield 584756)

✠ **WOOD, Right Rev Richard James.** b 20. Wells Th Coll 51. **d** 52 **p** 53 Sarum. C of Calne 52-55; St Mark's Cathl Geo 55-58; R of Beaufort W w Vic W 58-62; St Andr Riversdale 62-65; Chap S Afr Defence Force 65-68; P-in-c of Fort Beaufort and of Adelaide w Bedford 69-70; Keetmanshoop 70-73; Cons Ld Bp Suffr of Damar in St Alb Cathl Ch Pret 19 June 73 by Abp of Capetn; Bps of Lebom, Kimb K, Swaz, Pret, Johann, Natal and Bloemf; and Bp J Carter; res 77; Asst Bp of Damar 77; Executive Sec Afr Bureau 76-77; Chap Hull Coll of Higher Educn 77-79; V of St Mary Virg Lowgate Hull 77-79; Asst Bp in Dio York 79; L to Offic Dio Dar-S from 79. *Box 25017, Ilala, Dar-es-Salaam, Tanzania.*

WOOD, Richard Olivier Ronald. b 19. TCD BA 42, MA 51. **d** 43 **p** 44 Down. C of St Bart Belfast 43-45; CF (EC) 45-47; Men in Disp 49; CF 47-74; V of Kemble w Poole Keynes (w Somerford Keynes and Sharncote) 74-81. *Pencrug Gwynfe, Llangadog, Dyfed, SA19 9RP.* (055 04686)

WOOD, Robert James. b 17. Univ of Lon BA 49. Roch Th Coll. **d** 60 **p** 61 Lon. C of Ch Ch Crouch End 60-62; Gt Stanmore 62-65; C-in-c of H Innoc Hornsey Dio Lon 65-68;

V from 68. *Holy Innocents' Vicarage, Tottenham Lane, N8 7EL.* (01-340 1930)

WOOD, Robert Thomas James Kirkman. b 26. Trin Coll Cam BA 47, MA 50. Qu Coll Birm 48. **d** 50 **p** 51 Birm. C of Yardley 50-53; Faversham 53-56; CF 56-59; R of St Mary-in-the-Marsh 59-61; R of Newchurch 59-61; CF from 61; ACG from 74; Hon Chap to HM the Queen 78-81. *Little Saxtons, Appledore, Ashford, Kent.*

WOOD, Roger Graham. b 49. Chich Th Coll 74. **d** 76 **p** 77 Bradf. C of H Trin Skipton 76-79; Youth Chap Dio Bradf from 79. *34 Hope Hill View, Cottingley, Nr Bingley, W Yorks, BD16 1RJ.*

WOOD, Roger William. b 43. Univ of Leeds BA (2nd cl Engl) 65, MA 67. Fitzw Coll Cam BA (2nd cl Th Trip pt ii) 69, MA 75. Westcott Ho Cam 67. **d** 70 **p** 71 St Alb. C of Bp's Stortford 70-74; Sundon w Streatley 74-80; V of Streatley Dio St Alb from 80. *228 Barton Road, Warden Hill, Luton.* (Luton 591499)

✠ **WOOD, Right Rev Roland Arthur.** Bp's Univ Lennox BA 56, LST 58. DD. **d** 58 Ott for Rupld **p** 58 Rupld. C of St Matt Winnipeg 58-60; R of Selkirk 60-64; C of St Jo Evang Cathl Sktn 64-67; R of Yorkton 67-71; Dean and R of St Jo Evang Cathl Sktn 71-82; Cons Ld Bp of Sktn in St Jo Evang Cathl Sktn 16 Dec 81 by Abp of Prov of Rupld and Abp Scott (Primate); Bps of Edmon, Bran, Calg, Qu'App, Sask and Rupld; and others. *1104 Elliott Street, Saskatoon, Sask, Canada.*

WOOD, Roland Clifford. b 04. Lon Coll of Div 24. **d** 28 **p** 29 Chich. C of Eastbourne 28-30; Arundel w Tortington 30-32; in Amer Ch 32-33; C of St Barn Hove 33-34; Waldron 34-39; PC of H Trin Brighton 39-41; R of Pett 41-53; Perm to Offic Dio Chich 53; C-in-c of Clymping 55-61; Sen Chap HM Pris Ford 60-69; Cler Regr Dio Chich from 70. *38 Parkside Avenue, Littlehampton, Sussex.* (Littlehampton 3845)

WOOD, Ronald Ernest. b 49. Sarum Wells Th Coll 79. **d** 81 Taunton for B & W. C of St Jo Bapt Weston-s-Mare Dio B & W from 81. *St John's House, Upper Church Road, Weston-s-Mare, Avon, BS23 2HX.*

WOOD, Ronald Henry. Ridley Coll Melb 63. **d** 63 **p** 64 Bend. C of All SS Cathl Bend 63-66; R of Malmsbury 66-69; C of St Paul Bend 75-76; R of Inglewood Dio Bend from 77. *St Augustine's Rectory, Sullivan Street, Inglewood, Vic, Australia 3517.*

WOOD, Ronald Herbert. St Columb's Hall Wang 66. **d** 68 Carp **p** 69 N Queensld. C of Mt Isa Dio N Queensld 68-73; R of Sarina Dio N Queensld from 73. *Rectory, Sarina, Queensland, Australia.* (Sarina 97)

WOOD, Roy Lewis. Rhodes Univ Grahmstn BA 50, LLB 52. Ball Coll Ox BCL 55. LTh (S Afr) 58. St Paul's Coll Grahmstn 57. **d** 58 **p** 59 Natal. C of St Sav Cathl Pietermaritzburg 58-61; V of Karkloof 61-65; R of St Martin Durban N 65-72. *Naramata, BC, Canada.*

WOOD, Canon Shirley Arthur Ralph. Univ of Tor BA 36. Wycl Coll Tor Hon DD 58. Wycl Coll Tor. **d** 36 **p** 37 Tor. C of St Alb Tor 36-38; I of Kinmount 39-41; Lakefield 41-45; R of Thornhill 45-56; R of St Jo Evang Cathl Sktn 56-62; Can Res of Sktn 56-58; Dean 58-62; R of St Wilfrid Tor 63-74; Can of Tor from 72. *9 Northwood Crescent, Belleville, Ont., Canada.*

WOOD, Sidney Gordon. Roch Th Coll 62. **d** 63 **p** 64 S'wark. C of Kingston T 63-65; Stokenchurch w Cadmore-End 65-66; R of Heyford Warren w Lower Heyford and Rousham 66-69; V of Coleford Somt 69-71; St Edm Chingford 71-76; P-in-c of St Luke Gt Ilford 76-79. *c/o St Luke's Vicarage, Ilford, Essex.* (01-478 1104)

WOOD, Stanley Ernest. Selw Coll Dun LTh 38. **d** 37 **p** 38 Dun. C of St Paul's Cathl Dun 37-38; Gore 38-42; V of Waimea Plains Par Distr 42-48; Balcutha 48-55; Taieri-Green Is 55-60; Taieri 60-71; Winton w Otautau 71-79; Chap Cherry Farm Hosp Dio Dun from 80. *30 Carlyle Road, Mosgiel, NZ.* (4045)

✠ **WOOD, Right Rev Stanley Mark.** b 19. Univ of Wales BA (2nd cl Gr and Latin) 40. Coll of Resurr Mirfield 40. **d** 42 **p** 43 Llan. C of St Mary Virg Cardiff 42-45; Sophiatown Miss Distr 45-46; R of Bloemhof and P-in-c of Bloemhof Miss Distr 46-50; P-in-c of St Cypr Miss Johann 50-55; R of Marandellas 55-65; Can of Mashon 61-65; Dean and R of Salisbury Rhod 65-71; Cons Ld Bp of Matab in Cathl Ch of St Mary and All SS Salisbury Rhod 3 Jan 71 by Bp of Malawi; Abp of Capetn; Bps of Mashon; Zam; Swaz; and Bp Suffr of Malawi; res 77; Asst Bp of Heref 77-81; Apptd Bp Suffr of Ludlow 81; Preb of Heref Cathl from 77. *The Palace, Gateway, Hereford, HR4 9BL.* (0432-53863)

WOOD, Thomas. b 19. Late Scho of Univ of Leeds BA (1st cl Engl) 41, BD 45, MA (w distinc) 47. Coll of Resurr Mirfield 41. **d** 43 **p** 44 Southw. C of St Anne Worksop 43-47; Mansfield 47-52; PC of Seascale 52-57; D J James Prof of Pastoral Th at St D Univ Coll Lamp from 57; Dep Prin 71-77; Hd of Dept of Th from 77; Select Pr Univ of Cam 61. *St David's University College, Lampeter, Dyfed.* (Lampeter 422351)

WOOD, Thomas Elwyn. b 13. Coll of the Resurr Mirfield 77. **d** 77 **p** 78 Bradf. C of Linton-in-Craven Dio Bradf from 77. *Garregwen, High Bank, Threshfield, Skipton, Yorks.*

WOOD, Thomas Henry. b 36. St D Coll Lamp 58. **d** 60 **p** 61 Mon. C of Pontnewynydd 60-61; All SS Middlesbrough 65-69; Fleetwood (in c of St D) 69-74; V of Ferndale 74-78. *c/o Vicarage, Ferndale, Rhondda, Mid Glam.* (Ferndale 730366)

WOOD, Preb Thomas Patrick Scarborough. Trin Coll Dub BA 41, BD 54. **d** 42 **p** 43 Dub. C of Portarlington w Ballykean and Cloneyhurke 42-44; St Geo Dub 44-46; C-in-c of Ballysumaghan 46-49; I of Rathaspick w Rusagh and Streete 49-56; Calry Dio Elph from 56; Dom Chap to Bp of Kilm from 57; Preb of Elph Cathl from 67; RD of S Elph 67-75. *Calry Rectory, Sligo, Irish Republic.* (Sligo 2656)

WOOD, Canon Wilfred Denniston. b 36. Dipl Th (Lambeth) 62. Codr Coll Barb 57. **d** 61 Barb for Lon **p** 62 Lon. C of St Steph (w St Thos from 64) Hammersmith 62-74; Bp's Chap for Commun Relns Dio Lon 67-74; V of Catford Dio S'wark from 74; Hon Can of S'wark Cathl from 77; RD of E Lewisham from 77. *31 Bromley Road, SE6 2TS.* (01-698 2871)

WOOD, William. b 03. St Jo Coll Morpeth ACT ThL 31. **d** 31 **p** 32 Bath. M of Bush Bro Dubbo 31-37; L to Offic (Col Cl Act) at All SS Fulham 37-38; C of St Steph Brighton 38-39; Perm to Offic Dio Sarum 39-41; and 45-69; Dio Lon from 47; S'wark 47-75; C-in-c of Devizes 41-45; Missr and Chairman Lon Healing Miss 49-68; Chap and Trustee from 68. *55 Kingsway, Banbury, Oxon, OX16 9NX.* (Banbury 3623)

WOOD, William Alfred. b 16. FCIS 63. Qu Coll Birm 73. **d** 74 **p** 75 Birm (APM). Hon C of Sutton Coldfield Dio Birm from 74. *1 Vaughton Drive, Sutton Coldfield, W Midl, B75 6AQ.* (021-378 4061)

WOOD, William Geoffrey. St Cath S Ox BA (*sc* Engl Lit) 21, MA 30. **d** 26 **p** 27 Ox. Asst Master K Alfred's Sch Wantage and L to Offic Dio Ox 26-29; Asst Master CAthl Sch and Dep Min Can of Bris Cathl 29-60; Perm to Offic Dio St Alb from 61. *20 Oakwood Road, Bricket Wood, St Albans, Herts, AL2 3PX.* (Garston 72837)

WOOD, William George. b 31. Oak Hill Th Coll 61. **d** 63 **p** 64 Guildf. C of St Jo Bapt Woking 63-69; V of All SS Camberwell Dio S'wark from 69. *Vicarage, Blenheim Grove, SE15.* (01-639 3052)

WOODALL, Hugh Gregory. b 11. Keble Coll Ox BA (3rd cl Th) 33, MA 37. Cudd Coll 33. **d** 34 **p** 35 Chich. C of Horsham 34-37; Cathl Ch Guildf (in c of St Luke) 37-40; Actg C of Hurstpierpoint 40-41; CF (EC) 41-46; Men in Disp 46; C-in-c of Hampden Pk Conv Distr Willingdon 46-52; V of Firle w Beddingham 52-55; Boston Spa 55-80; Chap Askham Grange Pris York 58-65; RD of Tadcaster 72-78. *Kirklea, Gracious Street, Huby, York, YO16 1HR.* (0347-810705)

WOODALL, Reginald Homer. Univ of Wales Dipl Th 59. St Mich Coll Llan 59. **d** 61 **p** 62 St A. C of Newtown 61-65; Rhosddu 65-66; Hawarden 66-70; CF 70-74; C of St Jude Thornton Heath (in c of St Aid) 74-77; Team V of Cannock 77-79; Basildon Dio Chelmsf from 79. *82 Worthing Road, Laindon, Basildon, SS15 6JU.*

WOODALL, Ronald Selkirk. b 09. Univ of Man BA (2nd cl Engl Lang and Lit) 30. St Jo Coll Dur Dipl Th 32. **d** 32 **p** 33 Dur. C of St Andr w St Anne Bp Auckld 32-34; Winlaton (in c of Rowlands Gill) 34-37; V of E Rainton 37-43; Longton 43-60; Asst Master Qu Eliz Gr Sch Blackb 60-66; L to Offic Dio Blackb 60-66; Dio Carl 63-66; V of Thornthwaite w Braithwaite 66-74; L to Offic Dio Carl from 74. *Winsele, Lonsties, Keswick, Cumb, CA12 4TD.*

WOODBRIDGE, David Charles. Moore Th Coll Syd ACT ThL (2nd cl) 62. **d** 62 **p** 63 Syd. C of Bowral 62-63; Chap Roper River Miss 64-65; C of Albion Pk 65-66; Forest Hill 66-67; Chap Roper River Miss 67-69; Groote Eylandt Miss 70-79; R of Port Kembla Dio Syd from 79. *111 Military Road, Port Kembla, NSW, Australia 2505.* (042-741028)

WOODBRIDGE, Denis John. Univ of Melb BA (1st cl Cl) 56. Cudd Coll. **d** 59 Ox for Cant for Melb **p** 60 Melb. C of Geelong 59-60; Pascoe Vale 61-62; Asst Chap C of E Gr Sch Melb 62-72; Chap from 74; Miss Dio Papua 72-74. *c/o MCEGS, Domain Road, South Yarra, Vic., Australia 3141.*

WOODBRIDGE, Trevor Geoffrey. BSc (2nd cl Eng) Lon 52. ALCD 57. **d** 58 **p** 59 Win. C of Bitterne 58-61; Ilkeston (in c of St Bart Hallam Fields) 61-65; CMS Area Sec Dios Ex and Truro from 65; Reg Sec SW Engl from 70; L to Offic Dio Ex and Perm to Offic Dio Truro 66-81; Team V of Clyst Valley Team Min Dio Ex from 82. *Vicarage, Rockbeare, Exeter, EX5 2EG.* (Whimple 822569)

WOODBURN, Henry. **d** 26 **p** 27 Graft. C of Kyogle 26-27; M of Bush Bro of Our Sav Copmanhurst 27-28; V of Burringbar 28-31; Coraki 31-32; Perm to Offic (Col Cl Act) 34;

C of Padiham 34-36; Gt Yarmouth 36-46; CF (R of O) 39-48; R of Winterton w E Somerton 46-47; Bowraville 48-52; Ballina 52-55; R of St Francis Nundah Brisb 55-67; L to Offic Dio Brisb 67-72; Perm to Offic Dio Melb from 72. *23 Tulip Grove, Cheltenham, Vic, Australia 3192.* (93-6383)

WOODBURN, William John. b 19. St Aug Coll Cant 61. **d** 62 **p** 63 B & W. C of Bathwick 62-65; V of Brompton Regis w Withiel Florey 65-70; H Trin Bridgwater 70-78; C of Midsomer Norton Dio B & W from 78. *2 Hill View, Chilcomptol Road, Midsomer Norton, Bath, Avon.* (M Norton 418096)

WOODCOCK, John Charles. Kelham Th Coll 52. **d** 56 Southw for Bloemf **p** 57 Bloemf. C of Modderpoort 56-58; Welkom 58-62; Teyateyaneng Miss 62-69; Masite 69-71; St Jas Maseru 71-76; St Aug Modderpoort Dio Bloemf from 76. *St Augustine's Priory, Modderpoort, OFS, S Africa.*

WOODCOCK, Leonard. b 08. AKC 40. Univ of Lon BD 40. **d** 40 **p** 41 Chelmsf. C of St Paul E Ham 40-43; CF (EC) 43-46; Hon CF from 46; R of Quendon w Rickling 47-52; Thundersley 52-75; Surr 58-75; RD of Wickford 65-73. *73 Nelson Road, Leigh-on-Sea, Essex, SS9 3HX.*

WOODD, Basil John. b 07. Jes Coll Cam 3rd cl Hist Trip 30, BA (3rd cl Th Trip pt i) 31, MA 35. Westcott Ho Cam 31. **d** 32 **p** 33 Guildf. C of Gt Bookham 32-34; Banstead 34-37; St Aug Bournemouth 37-40; V of Swavesey 40-46; Clapton w Thurning 46-48; R of Etton w Helpston 48-59; Gt Gonerby 59-68. *College of St Barnabas, Blackberry Lane, Lingfield, Surrey, RH7 6NJ.*

WOODD, Canon Frederick Hampden Basil. b 06. Late Exhib of Jes Coll Cam BA and Lady Kay Scho 28, MA 32. Westcott Ho Cam 28. **d** 29 Roch **p** 30 Bp King for Roch. C of Tonbridge 29-32; CMS Miss 32-47; P-in-c of Ch of Resurr Osaka 35-40; Chap Trin Coll Kandy 41-45; I of St Paul Kandy 45-47; V of St Andr Boscombe 48-71; Surr from 51; RD of Bournemouth 60-67; Hon Can of Win 62-71; Can (Emer) from 71. *122 Alresford Road, Winchester, Hants.* (Winchester 3332)

WOODD, John Keene. b 18. **d** 76 **p** 77 Waik. Hon C of Te Awamutu Dio Waik from 76. *56 Te Rahu Road, Te Awamutu, New Zealand.*

WOODERSON, Michael George. b 39. Univ of Southn BA (2nd cl French) 61. BD (3rd cl) Lon 69. Lon Coll of Div 66. **d** 69 Kingston T for S'wark **p** 70 S'wark. C of Morden 69-73; Aldridge (in c of St Thos Coppy Hall from 76) 73-81; V of Chasetown Dio Lich from 81. *Vicarage, High Street, Chasetown, Walsall, Staffs, WS7 8XG.* (Burntwood 6276)

WOODERSON, Timothy George Arthur. b 39. St Chad's Coll Dur BA 61, Dipl Th 63. **d** 63 **p** 64 Portsm. C of St Mary Hayling I 63-66; Miss P Dio N Guinea 66-70; C of Rowner 71-77; R of Bermondsey Dio S'wark from 78. *193 Bermondsey Street, SE1 3UW.* (01-407 5273)

WOODFIELD, Robert Ronald. b 13. Ch Coll Cam 2nd cl Cl Trip pt i 34, BA 35, 2nd cl Th Trip pt i 36, MA 49. Ridley Hall Cam 35. **d** 37 **p** 38 Blackb. C of H Trin Morecambe 37-39; Habergham 39-42; High Wycombe 42-43; Chap Watts Naval Tr Sch N Elmham 43-48; C of Faringdon 48-49; Newbury 50-53; R of Shaw w Donnington 53-71; Leadenham (w Welbourn to 73) 71-78; Welbourn 73-78. *Crossroads, High Toynton, Horncastle, Lincs, LN9 6NR.*

WOODFIELD, Ven Samuel Percy. Selw Coll Cam BA 15, MA 19. **d** 15 **p** 16 St Alb. C of St Mary Hitchin 15-19; Hd Master Norton Sch Letchworth 17-19; C of Sawbridgeworth 19-21; Vice-Prin Dioc Tr Coll Pietersburg 22-24; Prin 24-38; Exam Chap to Bp of Pret 22-56; Hon Can of St Alb Cathl Pret 32-59 and from 65; Can 59-64; P-in-c of Native Miss Distr and Coloured and Ind Work Pret and Chap Westfort Leper Inst 38-54; Archd of Pret Native Miss Distr 45-55; W Transvaal 55-59; E and W Transvaal 59-60; Barberton 60-63; Archd (Emer) from 64; Prin Dioc Tr Coll Pietersburg 54-59; R of Waterval Boven 59-67. *Irene Homes, Irene, Transvaal, S Africa.* (6-5116)

WOODFORD, Andrew Roy. b 12. Sarum Th Coll 61. **d** 62 **p** 63 Sarum. C of Pewsey 62-65; V of Burbage 65-71; R of Charleton w Buckland-Tout-Saints 71-79; Perm to Offic Dio Ex from 80. *Schiehallion, School Lane, Thorverton, Nr Exeter, Devon.*

WOODFORD, Frank. b 14. **d** 53 Cov **p** 54 Linc. C of St Mich Stoke Cov 53-54; Flixborough w Burton-on-Stather 54-57; R of Kettlethorpe w Laughterton 57-68; V of Newton-on-Trent 57-68; Billinghay w Walcot and Dogdyke 68-79. *13 Flintham Close, Metheringham, Lincoln.*

WOODFORD, Harry. b 11. AKC 35. **d** 35 **p** 36 Sheff. C of Rawmarsh 35-38; Ch Stretton 38-48; CF (RAChD) 42-46; PC of St Mary Virg Shipley 48-62; V of Southbourne 62-76; R of W Thorney 62-76; C of Littlehampton 76-77; Compton, The Mardens, Racton, Lordington and Stoughton Dio Chich from 77. *Vicarage, Stoughton, Chichester, PO18 9JJ.* (Compton 327)

WOODGATE, Douglas Digby. b 09. Univ of Bris BA (3rd cl French) 32. Wells Th Coll 33. **d** 34 **p** 35 S'wark. C of Lewisham 34-36; St Mich AA Notting Hill 36-42; Bilborough w Strelley 42-45; V of Elkesley w Bothamsall 45-80. *4 Elm Tree Court, Potter Street, Worksop, Notts.*

WOODGATE, Michael James. b 35. Univ of Dur BA 60. St Steph Ho Ox 60. **d** 62 **p** 63 S'wark. C of St Pet Streatham Dio S'wark 62-69; V from 69; Surr from 78; RD of Streatham from 78. *10 Valley Road, SW16 2XN.* (01-769 2922)

WOODGER, John McRae. b 36. Tyndale Hall Bris 60. **d** 63 **p** 64 Heref. C of St Pet Heref 63-66; Macclesfield 66-69; V of Llangarron w Llangrove 69-74; P-in-c of Garway 70-74; R of Ch Stretton Dio Heref from 74. *Rectory, Church Stretton, Shropshire.* (Ch Stretton 722585)

WOODGER, John Page. b 30. St Aid Coll 56. Dipl Th (Lon) 58. **d** 59 **p** 60 Sheff. C of Kimberworth 59-62; Goole 62-63; V of Balne w Pollington 63-70; Chap HM Borstal Inst Pollington 62-70; C of Halesowen w Hasbury and Lapal 70-74; V of Cookley 74-81; Team V of Droitwich Dio Worc from 81. *29 Old Coach Road, Droitwich, Worc, WR9 8BB.* (0905 772229)

WOODGER, Richard William. b 50. Sarum Wells Th Coll 76. **d** 79 **p** 80 Guildf. C of Chessington 79-82; Frimley Dio Guildf from 82; Frimley Green Dio Guildf from 82. *20 Winterbourne Walk, Paddock Hill, Frimley, Surrey.*

WOODHALL, Michael Leslie. b 36. AIB 67. Linc Th Coll 72. **d** 74 **p** 75 Dur. C of St Hilda w St Thos S Shields 74-76; Barnard Castle (in c of Startforth) 76-78, P-in-c of St Mary Virg w St Pet Conv Distr Bp Wearmouth 78-80; V of St Cypr w St Jas Leeds Dio Ripon from 80. *Vicarage, Coldcotes Avenue, Leeds, LS9 6ND.* (Leeds 493746)

WOODHALL, Canon Norman John. b 10. Late Acad Clk of Magd Coll Ox BA 35, MA 39. Ripon Hall Ox 34. **d** 35 **p** 36 Birm. C of St Mich Boldmere 35-40; CF (EC) 40-45; Hon CF from 45; CF (TA) 57-67; CF (TAVR) 67-75; R of Gate Burton 45-51; PC of Knaith 45-51; R of Lea 48-51; Chelsfield 51-58; V of Basingstoke 58-69; Hamble 69-75; Surr 59-69; RD of Basingstoke 59-69; Hon Can of Win 64-75; Can (Emer) from 75. *Abbeymead Cottage, School Lane, Hamble, Southampton, SO3 5JD.* (Hamble 2198)

WOODHALL, Peter. b 32. Edin Th Coll 57. **d** 60 Penrith for Carl **p** 61 Carl. C of St Barn Carl 60-63; Hon Chap at St Paul's Estoril 63-65; Chap RN 66-82; Team R of Scilly Is Dio Truro from 82. *Chaplaincy, St Mary's, Isles of Scilly, TR21 0NA.* (Scillonia 22421)

WOODHAM, Richard Medley Swift. b 43. SOC 71. **d** 73 **p** 74 Roch. C of St Aid Gravesend 73-75; Chessington 75-78; R of Horstead Dio Nor from 78; Warden Horstead Conf Ho from 78; Dioc Youth Officer & Bp's Chap for York from 78. *Horstead Rectory, Norwich, NR12 7EP.* (Norwich 737215)

WOODHAMS, Brian Watson. b 11. St Jo Coll Dur BA 36. Oak Hill Th Coll 32. **d** 36 **p** 37 Lon. C of St Mary Magd Holloway 36-39; St Jas L Bethnal Green 39-41; Ch Ch New Malden w Coombe 41-43; V of St Mark Victoria Park Lon 43-44; St Jas L Bethnal Green 44-50; St Jude Mapperley Nottm 50-66; Chap Mapperley Ment Hosp 50-66; Proc Conv Southw from 55; Hon Can of Southw 60-65; Archd of Newark 65-80; V of Farndon 66-71; R of Thorpe-by-Newark 66-71; C-in-c of Staunton w Flawborough 68-71; R 71-80; C-in-c of Kilvington 68-71; R 71-80; M Gen Syn 78-79. *2 Lunn Lane, S Collingham, Newark, Notts, NG23 7LP.*

WOODHAMS, George Douglas. Univ of Tor BA 56. McGill Univ Montr BD 59. Selw Coll Cam BA 61, MA 66. Montr Dioc Th Coll. **d** 59 Bp W W Davis for NS **p** 60 NS. C of St Kath Uitenhage 62-63; Chap Morija Tr Coll Les 63-66; Asst Master Chogoria High Sch Kenya 66-68; Hd Master from 68. *Chogoria High School, PO Chogoria, Kenya.*

WOODHART, Norman. ACT ThL 51. Moore Th Coll Syd 41. **d** 42 **p** 43 Syd. C of St Steph the Mart Penrith 42; St Pet Hornsby 42; C-in-c of The Oaks and Burragorang 43-44 and 48-52; CMS Miss Roper River 44-47: Chap Norf I 52-54; P-in-c of Lithgow 54; R of Glenmore Road 55-75; L to Offic Dio Syd from 75. *23 Vernon Avenue, Eastlakes, NSW, Australia 2018.* (667-2740)

WOODHEAD, Alan Howard. b 37. Open Univ BA 73. St Aid Coll 62. **d** 65 **p** 66 Ripon. C of Kirkstall 65-68; Marfleet 68-71; V of Barmby Moor w Fangfoss 71-81. *c/o Barmby Moor Vicarage, York.* (Pocklington 2657)

WOODHEAD, Christopher Godfrey. b 26. Pemb Coll Cam BA (3rd cl Th Trip pt i) 50, MA 55. Ely Th Coll 50. **d** 52 **p** 53 Wakef C of Barnsley 52-54; St Mich AA Mill Hill 54-58; Sandridge 58-66; R of Earl Stonham 66-72; V of Hoo St Werburgh Dio Roch from 72. *Hoo St Werburgh Vicarage, Rochester, Kent.* (Medway 250291)

WOODHEAD, Canon Henry Hamilton. b 22. TCD BA 45. **d** 47 **p** 48 Down. C of Seagoe 47-50; I of Donagh and Cloncha w Clonmany 50-57; Badoney 57-65; Dioc Adv on Chr Stewardship Dio Derry from 60; R of Killowen Dio Derry from 65; RD of Limavady from 75; Can of St Columb Cathl Derry from 81. *St John's Rectory, Coleraine, Co Derry, N Ireland.* (Coleraine 2629)

WOODHEAD-KEITH-DIXON, James Addison. b 25. St Aid Coll 44. **d** 48 **p** 49 Carl. C of Upperby 48-50; Dalton-in-Furness 50-52; V of Blawith w Lowick 52-59; Lorton 59-80; Chap of Puerto de la Cruz Teneriff Dio Gibr from 80. *All Saints Church, Taoro Park, Puerto de la Cruz, Teneriff.* (371638)

WOODHOUSE, Ven Andrew Henry. b 23. DSC 45. Qu Coll Ox BA 48, MA 49. Linc Th Coll 48. **d** 50 **p** 51 Lon. C of All SS Poplar 50-56; V of W Drayton 56-70; RD of Hillingdon 67-70; R of Wistanstow Dio Heref from 70; P-in-c of Acton-Scott 70-73; Archd of Ludlow from 70. *Wistanstow Rectory, Craven Arms, Salop, SY7 8DG.* (Craven Arms 3244)

WOODHOUSE, Ven Charles David Stewart. b 35. Kelham Th Coll 55. **d** 59 **p** 60 Ripon. C of Halton 59-63; Youth Chap at Kirkby 63-66; C of Pembroke Berm 66-69; Asst Gen Sec CEMS 69-70; Gen 70-76; P-in-c of Ideford w Luton & Ashcombe 76; R 76-81; Dom Chap to Bp of Ex 76-81; V of St Pet Hindley Dio Liv from 81; Archd of Warrington from 81. *St Peter's Vicarage, Wigan Road, Hindley, Wigan, Lancs, WN2 3DF.* (Wigan 55505)

WOODHOUSE, Claude. Ridley Coll Melb 27. **d** 27 **p** 32 Gippsld. C of Warragul 27-28; C-in-c of Alberton Par Distr 28-32; V of Omeo 32-35; Drouin w Bunyip and Nar-nar-goon 35-43; RD of Warrigul 39-43; I of St Mark Fitzroy 43-47; Ch Ch St Kilda 47-71; Perm to Offic Dio Melb from 71. *98 Railway Parade, Seaford, Vic, Australia 3198.* (786-1734)

WOODHOUSE, Canon David. Selw Coll Cam 2nd cl Th Trip pt i 58, BA (2nd cl Th Trip pt ii) 60, MA 64. St Steph Ho Ox 60. **d** 62 **p** 63 Linc. C of Boston 62-64; St Gabr w All SS Pimlico 64-66; Chap Woodbridge Sch 66-73; V of Heap Bridge 73-75; Dir Educn Dio Wakef from 75; Can Res of Wakef from 75. *Education Office, Church House, 1 South Parade, Wakefield, WF1 1LP.*

WOODHOUSE, David Edwin. b 45. BSc (Lon) 68. Cudd Coll 68. **d** 71 **p** 72 S'wark. C of St Jo Evang E Dulwich 71-74; L to Offic Dio S'wark 74-77; Perm to Offic Dio Bris 77-79; Publ Pr from 79. *Vicarage, Morris Street, Swindon, Wilts, SN2 2HT.* (Swindon 22741)

WOODHOUSE, David Maurice. b 40. BA (Lon) 62. Clifton Th Coll 63. **d** 65 **p** 66 Lich. C of All SS Wel 65-69; Meole-Brace 69-71; V of Colwich Dio Lich from 71; P-in-c of Gt Haywood Dio Lich from 78. *Colwich Vicarage, Little Haywood, Stafford, ST18 0TS.* (0889-881262)

WOODHOUSE, Hugh Frederic. b 12. TCD 3rd cl Cl 31, 2nd cl Ment and Mor Sc 31, 1st cl Engl Lit 32, Sen Exhib and Dunbar Ingram Mem Pri 32, BA (1st cl Hist and Pol Sc) Mod and Scho 34, Carson Bibl Pri Downes Oratory Pri (2nd) Eccles Hist Pri and Abp King Pri (1st) 35, Div Test (1st cl), Robert King Mem Pri and Moncrieff Cox Mem Pri 36, Th Exhib (1st) and BD 37, DD 52, MA 67. **d** 37 **p** 38 Down. C of St Donard Belf 37-39; Bangor 40-44; I of Aghalee 44-46; Newtownards 46-51; Exam Chap to Bp of Down 51; Prof of Eccles Hist at Wycl Coll Tor 51-54; Prin and Prof of Eccles Hist Angl Th Coll Vancouver 54-59; Commiss Capetn 58-64; Prof of Dogmatic Th Univ of K Coll Halifax 59-63; Regius Prof of Div Univ of Dub from 63; Fell of TCD from 74. *25 Eaton Brae, Dublin 14, Irish Republic.*

WOODHOUSE, James. b 29. Univ of Lon BA (2nd cl Geog) 52. Lich Th Coll. **d** 61 **p** 62 York. C of Whitby 61-64; Pocklington w Yapham-cum-Meltonby and Owsthorpe w Kilnwick Percy 64-66; C-in-c of Roos w Tunstall-in-Holderness 66-69; R 69-72; C-in-c of Garton-in-Holderness w Grimston and Hilston 66-69; V 69-72; V of Nunthorpe-in-Cleveland Dio York from 72. *Nunthorpe Vicarage, Middlesbrough, Cleve, TS7 0PD.* (Middlesbrough 316570)

WOODHOUSE, John William. Univ of NSW BSc 69. Moore Coll Syd ACT ThL 74. BD (Lon) 75. **d** and **p** 76 Syd. C of St Barn Broadway Syd 76-79; Perm to Offic Dio Ches from 79. *2 Gatley Road, Cheadle, Chesh, SK8 1PY.*

WOODHOUSE, Canon Keith Ian. b 33. K Coll Lon and Warm 54. **d** 58 **p** 59 Dur. C of St Chad Roseworth Stockton-on-Tees Cov Distr 58-61; St Aid Man 61-64; V of Peterlee Dio Dur from 64; RD of Easington from 72; Hon Can of Dur Cathl from 79. *Vicarage, Manor Way, Peterlee, Co Durham.* (Peterlee 862630)

WOODHOUSE, Patrick Henry Forbes. b 47. Ch Ch Ox BA 69. ALCD 71. St Jo Coll Nottm 69. **d** 72 **p** 73 Birm. C of St Martin Birm 72-74; Whitchurch 75-76; Harpenden (in c of St Mary Kinsbourne Green) 76-80; Miss in Dar-S 80-81; P-in-c of Dean Dio Carl from 81; Officer for Social Responsibility Dio Carl from 81. *Dean Rectory, Workington, Cumb, CA14 4TH.* (Lamplugh 332)

WOODHOUSE, Ven Samuel Mostyn Forbes. b 12. Ch Ch Ox BA 34, MA 42. Wells Th Coll 35. **d** 36 **p** 37 Blackb. C of Lanc 36-39; CF 39-45; V of H Trin S Shore Blackpool 45-49; Surr from 45; V of Leominster 49-56; RD of Leominster 56; R of St Steph (w St Nich St Leon and All SS from 59) Bris 57-67; Commiss Melb from 62; Can Res of St Paul's Cathl Lon 67-78 Can (Emer) from 78; Archd of Lon 67-78; Archd (Emer) from 78; Perm to Offic Dio B & W from 79. *Under Copse Cottage, Redhill, Wrington, Bristol, BS18 7SH.* (0934-862711)

WOODHOUSE, William Henry. b 12. SS Coll Cam BA 36, MA 40. Chich Th Coll 36. **d** 38 **p** 39 Lon. C of All S St Marg-on-Thames 38-47; Chap RNVR 40-47; R of Southery 47-51; V of Wisbech St Mary 51-61; RD of Wisbech 57-61; R of Yate 61-74; C-in-c of Dodington w Wapley and Codrington 67-71; R of N Cerney (w Bagendon from 74) Dio Glouc from 74; RD of Cirencester from 77. *2 Burford Road, Cirencester, Glos, GL7 1AF.* (0285 68938)

WOODLAND, Robert Alan. b 29. Bps' Coll Cheshunt 59. **d** 61 **p** 62 St Alb. C of Cheshunt 61-66; V of All SS Oxhey 66-76; Hainault 76-81; V of Bicknoller w Crowcombe & Sampford Brett Dio B & W from 81. *Vicarage, Bicknoller, Somerset.*

WOODLEY, David James. b 38. K Coll Lon and Warm BD and AKC 61. **d** 62 **p** 63 Chich. C of Lancing 62-64; St Pet St Alb 64-67; Chap All SS Sch Kota Kinabalu 67-70; P-in-c of Tuaran 69-70; Perm to Offic Dio Linc 71-72; V of Westoning w Tingrith 72-77; Asst Chap HM Pris Wormwood Scrubs 77-79; Chap HM Pris Cardiff from 79. *c/o HM Prison, Cardiff.*

WOODLEY, John Francis. b 34. Jes Coll Ox BA (2nd cl Th) 56, MA 60. Bps' Coll Cheshunt 58. **d** 60 **p** 61 Chelmsf. C of Forest Gate 60-63; St Thos Hanwell 63-65; St Mary Osterley Isleworth 65-69; V of W Twyford 69-78; Yaxley Dio Ely from 78. *Vicarage, Church Street, Yaxley, Peterborough, Cambs PE7 3LH.* (Pet 240339)

WOODLEY, John Francis Chapman. b 33. St D Coll Lamp BA 58. Edin Th Coll 58. **d** 60 **p** 61 Edin. C of All SS Edin 60-65; Chap St Andr Cathl Aber 65-67; Prec 67-71; R of St Osw King's Pk Glas 71-77; P-in-c of H Name Cumbernauld Dio Glas from 77. *Rectory, Fleming Road, Cumbernauld, Glasgow, G67 1LJ.* (Cumbernauld 21599)

WOODLEY, Canon Ronald John. b 25. Bps' Coll Cheshunt 50. **d** 53 **p** 54 York. C of St Martin Middlesbrough 53-58; Whitby 58-61; C-in-c of Ascen Conv Distr Berwick Hills Middlesbrough Dio York 61-66; V 66-71; R of Stokesley Dio York from 71; RD of Stokesley from 77; Can & Preb of York from 82. *Stokesley Rectory, Middlesbrough, Cleve, TS9 5AP.* (Stokesley 710405)

WOODLIFFE, Leslie Jestyn Lewis. b 35. St Mich Coll Llandaff 76. **d** 78 **p** 79 St D. C of Henfynyw w Aberaeron & Llanddewi Aberarth 78-80; V of Llangeler Dio St D from 80. *Vicarage, Llangeler, Llandysul, Dyfed.* (Velindre 370449)

WOODMAN, Oliver Nigel. b 47. Sarum Th Coll 67. **d** 70 Lon (NSM). C of Stepney 70-71; Ovingdean w Rottingdean and Woodingdean Dio Chich from 80. *6 Cowley Drive, Woodingdean, Brighton, E Sussex, BN2 6WA.*

WOODMAN, Peter Wilfred. b 36. St D Coll Lamp BA (2nd cl Hist) 58. Wycl Hall Ox 58. **d** 60 **p** 61 Mon. C of New Tredegar 60-61; St Paul Newport 61-64; Llanfrechfa 64-66; Dioc Messenger Dio Mon 66-67; V of Llantillio-Pertholey w Bettws 67-74; Bassaleg Dio Mon from 74. *Bassaleg Vicarage, Newport, NP1 9NF.* (Rhiwderin 3258)

WOODROFFE, Alexander Noel Lake. Moore Th Coll Syd. **d** 42 Nel. C of Nel Cathl 42-44; Hd Master Harewood Sch Bexhill from 48. *The Clock House, St Leonards-on-Sea, Sussex.*

✠ **WOODROFFE, Most Rev George Cuthbert Manning.** b 18. KBE 80 (CBE 73). Codr Coll Barb BA 45, LTh 45, MA 47. **d** 44 **p** 45 Windw Is. C of St Geo Cathl St Vincent 44-47; V of St Simon 47-49; R of St Andr Barb 49-56; St Jos Barb 56-62; St John Barb 62-67; St Geo Cathl Kingstown 67-69; Cons Ld Bp of Windw Is in St Geo Cathl Kingstown St Vinc 29 Sept 69 by Abp of WI; Bps of Barb; and Trinid; Bps Suffr of Stabroek; and Trinid; and Bp Piggott; Elected Abp and Metrop of WI 80. *Bishop's House, PO Box 128, Kingstown, St Vincent, W Indies.* (809-45 61895)

WOODROFFE, Ian Gordon. b 46. Edin Th Coll 69. **d** 72 Ely **p** 73 Huntingdon for Ely. C of Soham 72-75; P-in-c of Swaffham Bulbeck and Youth Officer Dio Ely 75-80; V of St Jas Cam Dio Ely from 80. *St James's Vicarage, Wulfstan Way, Cambridge, CB1* (0223-246419)

WOODROW, Brian Ernest. b 34. Univ of Sask BA 67. Trin Coll Tor STB 70. **d** 69 **p** 70 Qu'App. C of Big Country 70-71; Willow Creek Pastoral Distr 71-74; I of Oxbow 75-76; Hosp Chap Regina and Hon C of All SS Regina 77-80; Hosp Chap Dio Sktn from 80. *1701 Jackson Avenue, Saskatoon, Sask, Canada.*

WOODROW, Harold James. Univ of Lon BSc 32. Coll of Resurr Mirfield 47. M CR 50. **d** 49 **p** 50 Wakef. L to Offic Dio Wakef 50-52; C of St Aug Miss Penhalonga 52-69; L to Offic Dio Johann 72-75; and from 78; C of St Mary and All SS

Cathl Salisbury 75-78. *Box 49027, Rosettenville, Johannesburg, S Africa.*

WOODROW, Norman Wilson. b 21. TCD BA 44, MA 50, Div Test 46. **d** 46 **p** 47 Down. C of St John Newcastle Co Down 46-50; St Jo Bapt Leytonstone 50-54; R of Pitsea 54-63; C of Newtownards 63-64; V of Saintfield Dio Down from 64; RD of Killinchy from 78. *Vicarage, Saintfield, Co Down, N Ireland.* (Saintfield 510286)

WOODROW, Ronald Frederick. St Columb's Hall Wang 60. **d** 62 **p** 64 Wang. C of Milawa 62-64; Corowa 64-66; R of Bright 66-69; Chiltern 69-74; Ingham 74-76; Nagambie Dio Wang from 76. *Rectory, High Street, Nagambie, Vic, Australia 3608.*

WOODROW, Walter Eric. St Columb's Hall Wang 30. **d** 30 **p** 31 Wang. C of Seymour 30-32; Perm to Offic Dio Wang 32-33; C of Albury 33-34; Junee 34-35; P-in-c of Springsure 35-36; C of Winton 37-38; St Mark Warwick 38-43; V of St Pet Millmerran 43-48; Laidley 48-55; St D Allora 55-74; Perm to Offic Dio Brisb from 74. *St David's Rectory, Allora, Queensland 4362, Australia.*

WOODS, Alan Geoffrey. b 42. Sarum Th Coll. **d** 70 Malmesbury for Bris **p** 71 Bris. C of St Francis Ashton Gate, Bedminster 70-73; Dioc Youth Chap Swindon and Warden Legge Ho Wroughton Bris 73-76; P-in-c of Neston 76-79; Team V of Gtr Corsham 79-81; V of Charminster Dio Sarum from 81. *Charminster Vicarage, Dorchester, Dorset, DT2 9QF.* (Dorchester 62477)

WOODS, Albert. b 12. St Paul's Coll Burgh. St Chad's Coll Regina LTh 47. **d** 41 **p** 42 Qu'App. C of Heward and Radville 41-43; I of Nokomis w Govan 43-44; R of Arcola 44-45; Oxbow 46; C of St Paul's Pro-Cathl Regina and Lect St Chad's Th Coll 46-49; I of St Geo Thorndale w Grace Ch Nissouri 49-50; C of Huyton (in c of St Gabr) 50-51; V of St Andr Litherland 51-56; Chap Whiston Co Hosp 50-51; CF (TA) from 50; V of St Barn Rainbow Hill Worc 56-61; C-in-c of Ch Ch Tolladine Worc 58-61; V of Elmley Castle w Netherton and Bricklehampton 61-63; Dioc Adviser on Christian Stewardship Dio Worc 58-63; Dir 63-66; V of Gt and L Hampton 66-71; U w Nether Swell 71-78. *Address temp unknown.*

WOODS, Charles William. b 31. Lich Th Coll. **d** 58 **p** 59 Lich. C of Hednesford (in c of St Mich Rawnsley from 60) 58-62; V of Wilnecote 62-67; Basford 67-76; Chasetown 76-81; P-in-c of Donington Dio Lich from 81. *Donington Rectory, Albrighton, Wolverhampton, Staffs.* (Albrighton 2279)

WOODS, Christopher Guy Alistair. b 35. Univ of Dur BA 60. Clifton Th Coll 60. **d** 62 **p** 63 Chelmsf. C of Rainham 62-65; St Thos Edin 65-69; Sec Spanish and Portuguese Ch Aid Society 69-79; C of Willesborough (in c of Ch Ch) 74-80; V of Bapchild w Tonge Dio Cant from 80; Murston Dio Cant from 80. *Bapchild Vicarage, Sittingbourne, Kent.* (Sittingbourne 72929)

WOODS, Christopher Samuel. b 43. Qu Coll Birm 75. **d** 76 Warrington for Liv **p** 77 Liv. C of All SS Childwall 76-79; V of Parr Mount Dio Liv from 79. *Vicarage, Traverse Street, Parr Mount, St Helens, Mer.* (St Helens 22778)

WOODS, David Arthur. Univ of Bris BA 52. Tyndale Hall Bris. **d** 53 **p** 54 Truro. C of Camborne 53-56; Ch Ch Bromley 56-58; V of H Trin Tewkesbury 58-66; Stapleford 66-70; Surr 69-70; V of Fowey Dio Truro from 70; RD of St Austell from 80. *Vicarage, Fowey, Cornw.* (Fowey 3535)

WOODS, David Winston. b 39. K Coll Lon and Warm BD and AKC 62. **d** 63 **p** 64 Carl. C of St Luke Barrow-F 63-65; St John Workington 65-67; V of Appleby 67-71; Scunthorpe 71-76; R of Mablethorpe w Stane (w Trusthorpe from 78) Dio Linc from 76; P-in-c of Trusthorpe 76-78. *Rectory, Sutton Road, Trusthorpe, Mablethorpe, Lincs, LN12 2PH.* (Mablethorpe 2296)

WOODS, Edward Christopher John. b 44. NUI BA 67. TCD 66. **d** 67 **p** 68 Arm. C of Drumglass Dio Arm 67-70; Ballysillan 70-73; R of Kilcolman 73-78; RD of Killarney 75-78; R of Portarlington Dio Kild from 78; Chan of Kild Cathl from 81. *Rectory, Portarlington, Co Laoise, Irish Republic.* (Portlaoise 23144)

WOODS, Eric John. b 51. Magd Coll Ox BA 72, MA 77. Trin Coll Cam BA (Th) 77. Westcott Ho Cam 75. **d** 78 **p** 79 Bris. C of St Mary Redcliffe w Temple Bedminster 78-81; Asst Chap Univ of Bris from 81; Hon C of St Paul Clifton Dio Bris from 80. *13 Elgin Park, Redland, Bristol, BS6 6RU.* (Bris 736720)

✠ **WOODS, Most Rev Frank.** KBE 72. Late Exhib of Trin Coll Cam 2nd cl Hist Trip pt i 28, BA (2nd cl Th Trip pt i) 30, MA 33. DD (Lambeth) 57. Westcott Ho Cam 30. **d** 31 **p** 32 Portsm. C of St Mary Portsea 31-33; Chap Trin Coll Cam and Exam Chap to Bp of Bris 33-36; Vice-Prin Wells Th Coll 36-45; CF (R of O) 39-45; V of Huddersfield 45-52; RD of Huddersfield 45-52; Hon Can of Wakef and Proc Conv Wakef 47-52; Chap to HM the King 51-52; to HM the Queen 52; Cons Ld Bp Suffr of Middleton in York Minster 2 Feb 52 by Abp of York; Bps of Dur; Lich; Sheff; Newc T; Ripon; Man; and Wakef; Bps Suffr of Whitby; Selby; Penrith; Hulme; Warrington; Pontefract; Burnley; and Stockport; and Bps Gerard, Weller, Hubbard and Wilson; Can Res of Man Cathl 52-57; Trld to Melb 57; Elected Primate of Austr 71; res 77. *2 Hughes Street, Balwyn, Vic, Australia 3103.*

WOODS, Frederick James. b 45. Univ of Southn BA 66, MPhil 74. Fitzwm Coll Cam BA (Th) 76, MA 79. Ridley Hall Cam 74. **d** 77 Bp McKie for Cov **p** 78 Cov. C of H Trin Stratford-on-Avon 77-81; V of Ch Ch Warm Dio Sarum from 81. *Vicarage, Avon Road, Warminster, Wilts, BA12 9PR.* (Warm 21229)

WOODS, Geoffrey Edward. b 49. BD (Lon) 70. Trin Coll Bris 71. **d** 73 **p** 74 S'wark. C of Gipsy Hill 73-77; Uphill 77-79; R of Swainswick w Langridge and Woolley Dio B & W from 79. *Rectory, Upper Swainswick, Bath, BA1 8BX.* (Bath 859220)

WOODS, Howard Charles. b 04. Trin Coll Ox BA 26, MA 30. Westcott Ho Cam 32. **d** 33 **p** 34 Ox. C of Windsor (in c of All SS from 35) 33-36; Perm to Offic at St D (in c of St Mich AA) Ex 36-37; Min Can of Worc Cathl and L to Offic Dio Worc 37-39; Chap of Worc R Infirm 37-39; R of St Martin w Whittington Chap Worc 39-47; Garsington 47-58; RD of Cuddesdon 54-58; Woodstock 61-64; R of Bladon w Woodstock 58-64; Stratton Audley w Godington 64-71. *Flat 19, Manormead, Tilford Road, Hindhead, Surrey.* (Hindhead 5608)

WOODS, Ven James Christopher. Episc Th Sch Cam Mass STB 64. **d** and **p** 64 Roch (USA). in Amer Ch 64-75; I of St Pet Winnipeg 76-78; R of Ch Ch Selkirk Dio Rupld from 78; Archd of Selkirk from 78. *220 Sophia Street, Selkirk, Manit, Canada.*

WOODS, John Mawhinney. b 19. Edin Th Coll 55. **d** 58 **p** 59 St Andr. C of Kirkcaldy 58-60; R of Walpole St Pet 60-75; Provost of St Andr Cathl Inverness 75-80; V of The Suttons w Tydd Dio Linc from 80. *Sutton St James Vicarage, Spalding, Lincs.*

WOODS, John William Ashburnham. b 22. Univ of Reading BSc 50. N-W Ordin Course 73. **d** 71 N Zam **p** 74 Sheff. C of Kitwe 71-72; Goole 73-75; R of Firbeck w Letwell Dio Sheff from 75; V of Woodsetts Dio Sheff from 75; Bp's Adv Dio Sheff from 80. *Rectory, Letwell, Worksop, Notts.* (Worksop 730346)

WOODS, Joseph Richard Vernon. b 31. Cudd Coll 58. **d** 60 **p** 61 Newc T. [f Solicitor] C of St Gabr Heaton Newc T 60-63; R of Naparima Trinid 63-67; Chap Long Grove Hosp Epsom 68-76; C-in-c of St Francis Ewell Dio Guildf 76-79; V from 79. *61 Ruxley Lane, Ewell, Surrey.* (01-393 5616)

WOODS, Michael Spencer. b 44. K Coll Lon and Warm BD and AKC 66. **d** 67 Nor **p** 68 Thetford for Nor. C of St Francis's Conv Distr Heartsease Sprowston 67-70; P-in-c of Betong 70-74; V in Hempnall Group 74-77; Team V of Hempnall 77-79; Team V of Halesworth Dio St E from 79. *Spexhall Rectory, Halesworth, Suff.*

WOODS, Norman Harman. b 35. K Coll Lon and Warm BD and AKC 62. **d** 63 **p** 64 Lon. C of Poplar 63-68; C-in-c of St Alb W Leigh Conv Distr Havant 68-76; V of St Leon Hythe Dio Cant from 76. *Vicarage, Hythe, Kent.* (Hythe 66217)

WOODS, Philip Raymond. K Coll Lon and Warm AKC 66. **d** 68 **p** 69 Linc. C of Grantham Dio Linc 68-72; Team V 72-73; C of H Trin Northwood 73-76; Gt Greenford (in c of St Edw, Perivale Pk) Dio Lon from 76. *The Presbytery, Medway Drive, Greenford, Middx, UB6 8LN.* (01-997 4953)

✠ **WOODS, Right Rev Robert Wylmer.** b 14. KCVO 71. Trin Coll Cam 3rd cl Engl Trip pt i 35, BA (3rd cl Th Trip pt i) 37, MA 40. Westcott Ho Cam 37. **d** 38 Lon **p** 39 St Alb. C of St Edm K Lombard Street 38-39; Hoddesdon 39-42; CF (EC) 42-46; Exam Chap to Bp of Leic 46-51; V of S Wigston w Glen Parva 46-51; Archd of Sing and V of St Andr Cathl Sing 51-58; Exam Chap to Bp of Sing 51-56; Archd of Sheff 58-62; R of Tankersley 58-62; Commiss Wel 60-72; Sing 61-70; Dean of Windsor 62-71; Dom Chap to HM the Queen 62-71; Cons Ld Bp of Worc in St Paul's Cathl 20 Feb 71 by Abp of Cant; Bps of Lon; Pet; Linc; Leic; Heref; Glouc; Bris; Roch; and Derby; Bps Suffr of Buckingham; Fulham; Horsham; Kingston T; Kens; Warrington; and Willesden; and Bps Allenby, Carpenter, Sansbury, Vockler and Baines; res 81; Prelate to Most Distinguished O of St Mich and St Geo from 71. *Torsend House, Tirley, Glos, GL19 4EU.*

WOODS, Ronald Palin. b 16. Bps' Coll Cheshunt 48. **d** 49 **p** 50 Linc. C of St Mary and St Jas Grimsby 49-54; V of Ingham w Cammeringham and R of Fillingham 54-59; C of Shangani Reserve 59-61; P-in-c of Bembesi 61-63; Asst P of Que Que 63-64; R of Diego Martin 65-70; V of Balsall Heath 70-72; Miss Rhod Rly Miss 72-73; C of St Cuthb Gwelo

73-75; V of Wankie 75-76; C of Spalding 77-78; V of Wrangle 78-81; All SS Grimsby Dio Linc from 81. *All Saints Vicarage, Hainton Avenue, Grimsby, Lincs.* (Grimsby 2122)

WOODS, Ven Samuel Edward. b 10. Trin Coll Cam 3rd cl Hist Trip pt i 31, BA (3rd cl Th Trip pt i) 34, MA 37. Westcott Ho Cam 35. **d** 36 Cant for Ch Ch **p** 37 Ch Ch. SCM Chap Dio Ch Ch 36-41; Asst Chap of Ch Coll Ch Ch 38-39; Prec of Cathl Ch Ch Ch 39-41; V of Ross 41-42; Chap RNZAF 42-46; V of H Trin Southport 46-50; R of Bp's Hatfield 50-55; Surr 50-52; Commiss Ch Ch 52-55; V of Sydenham NZ 55-59; Archd of Rangiora and Westland 55-59; and 63-68; Timaru 68-71; Sumner 59-63; Hosps Chap 59-60; V of Merivale 60-68; Timaru 68-71; Chap Barnsley Hall Hosp Bromsgrove 72-73; P-in-c of Rakaia 73-74; V of Mayfield w Mt Somers 73-74; Archd of Akaroa and Ashburton 74-77; Archd (Emer) from 77. *The Cottage, Port Levy, Purau Bay, Christchurch, NZ.*

WOODS, Theodore Frank Spreull. b 37. Trin Coll Cam (2nd cl Nat Sc Trip pt i) 58. Wells Th Coll 60. **d** 62 **p** 63 Leic. C of St Luke's Conv Distr Stocking Farm Leic 62-67; Actg Prin St Aid Coll Dogura 67-69; Chap Balob Tr Coll Lae 69-71; L to Offic Dio Papua 72-77; V of St Jo Bapt Knighton Leic 77-80; Chap C of E Gr Sch Brisb from 80. *23 Barker Street, E Brisbane, Australia 4169.* (391 8501)

WOODS, Thomas. b 1895. Trin Coll Cam 3rd cl Hist Trip pt i 20, BA (3rd cl Hist Trip pt ii) 21, MA 33. Ripon Hall Ox 21. **d** 22 **p** 23 Dur. C of St Aid S Shields 22-24; All SS New Shildon 24-27; S Westoe 27-29; V of St Hilda Millfield Sunderland 29-36; Kellington w Whitley 36-42; Blyth w Runskill and Barnby 42-53; Bottisham 53-65; Surr 62-65; Perm to Offic Dio Ox 66-72; Dio Ely from 72. *Manormead Nursing Home, Tilford Road, Hindhead, Surrey.*

WOODS, William David. Univ of Sask BA 64. Em Coll Sktn LTh 63. **d** 62 Carib **p** 65 Sktn. d Dio Carib 62-65; I of St Mark Sktn 65-67; R of Atikokan 71-74. *1168 East 12th Avenue, Vancouver, BC, Canada.*

WOODSFORD, Andrew Norman. b 43. Univ of Nottm BA 65. Ridley Hall Cam 65. **d** 67 **p** 68 Southw. C of Radcliffe-on-Trent 67-70; C-in-c of St Mary Ladybrook Mansfield 70-73; Barton-in-Fabis 73-80; Thrumpton 73-80; R of Gamston w Eaton & W Drayton Dio Southw from 81. *Gamston Rectory, Retford, Notts, DN22 0QB.* (Gamston 706)

WOODWARD, Anthony John. b 50. Univ of Salford BSc 78. Univ of Nottm Dipl Th 79. St Jo Coll Nottm. **d** 81 Man. C of Deane Dio Man from 81. *281 Deane Church Lane, Bolton, BL3 5QE.*

WOODWARD, Arthur Robert Harry. b 28. **d** 76 **p** 77 Mashon. P Dio Mashon. *c/o Box UA7, Salisbury, Zimbabwe.*

WOODWARD, Dalton Laurence. **d** 56 **p** 57 Ont. I of Roslin 56-59; Powassan Dio Alg from 59. *Box 218, Powassan, Ont., Canada.* (705-729-5470)

WOODWARD, Geoffrey Wallace. b 23. St Jo Coll Cam BA 47, MA 50. Westcott Ho Cam 47. **d** 49 **p** 50 York. C of St Jo Middlesbrough 49-52; Rugeley 52-54; Edgmond 54-55; V of Whorlton 55-59; St Thos Middlesbrough 59-65; Nunthorpe-in-Cleveland 65-72; St Martin Scarborough 72-79; Goathland Dio York from 79. *Goathland Vicarage, Whitby, N Yorks, YO22 5AN.* (0947 86227)

WOODWARD, Preb Herbert Vivian. b 10. Univ of Leeds, BSc (2nd cl Physics) 31. Coll of Resurr Mirfield, 31. **d** 33 **p** 34 Lich. C of Good Shepherd W Bromwich 33-35; Horninglow 35-42; Offg C-in-c of Meir 42-46; V 46-60; St Martin Rough Hills Wolverhampton 60-69; St Jo Bapt Stafford 69-80; Preb of Lich Cathl 73-80; Preb (Emer) from 80. *60 Croydon Drive, Penkridge, Staffs, ST19 5DW.*

WOODWARD, Canon Horace James. b 22. K Coll Lon and Warm AKC 49. **d** 50 **p** 51 Portsm. C of St Mary Portsea 50-56; V of St Mich Wandsworth Common 56-62; N Sheen 62-67; St Matt Redhill 67-74; V of Warlingham w Chelsham and Farleigh Dio S'wark from 74; Hon Can of S'wark Cathl from 79. *Vicarage, Warlingham, Surrey.* (Upper Warlingham 4125)

WOODWARD, John Clive. b 35. St D Coll Lamp BA 56. St Jo Coll Dur 56. **d** 58 **p** 59 Mon. C of Risca 58-63; Chepstow 63-66; Chap St Lawr Hosp Chepstow 63-66; V of Ynysddu 66-74; Christchurch Dio Mon from 74. *Christchurch Vicarage, Newport, Gwent.* (Caerleon 420701)

WOODWARD, Maurice George. b 29. Selw Coll Cam BA 56, MA 58. Wells Th Coll 56. **d** 58 Southw **p** 59 Bp Gelsthorpe for Southw. C of Gedling 58-61; Succr of Leic Cathl 61-64; Chap Leic R Infirm 62-64; V of Barrow-upon-Soar 64-77; CF (R of O) from 63; Hon Chap Leic Cathl 64-77; V of Clare w Poslingford Dio St E from 77. *Clare Vicarage, Sudbury, Suff, CO10 8NY.* (Clare 277209)

WOODWARD, Canon Peter Cavell. b 36. St Cath Coll Cam 2nd cl Cl Trip pt i 57, BA (2nd cl Th Trip pt ia) 58, MA 62. Bps' Coll Cheshunt. **d** 60 **p** 61 Chelmsf. C of St Anne Chingford 60-63; USPG Miss Dio Madag 63-69; Dio Tam 69-75; V of Weedon Bec (w Everdon from 76) 75-81; C-in-c of Everdon 75-76; RD of Daventry 79-81; Can (Non-res) of Pet Cathl from 81; V of Brackley Dio Pet from 81. *Vicarage, Brackley, Northants.* (Brackley 702767)

WOODWARD, Raymond Albert. Univ of Syd BA 51. Moore Th Coll Syd ACT ThL 47. **d** 47 **p** 48 Syd. C of St Barn Broadway Syd 47-49; H Trin Kingsford 49-51; C-in-c of S Granville Provisional Distr 51-52; C of St Phil and St Jas Ilfracombe 53-54; Parkstone 54; Asst Master Heath Brow Sch Hemel Hempstead 54-56; Perm to Offic Dio St Alb 54-56; Dio Momb 58-61; Dio Maseno 61-62; Asst Master Illawarra Gr Sch Wollongong 63-79; Chap 64-79; L to Offic Dio Syd 64-79; R of Hurtsville Dio Syd from 79. *2 The Avenue, Hurtsville, NSW, Australia 2200.* (57-1482)

WOODWARD, Reginald Charles Huphnill. b 19. Univ of Lon BA (2nd cl Engl) 41. Wells Th Coll. **d** 43 **p** 44 Linc. C of St Giles Linc 43-46; Chap and Succr of St Mary's Cathl Edin 46-47; Hd Master St Mary's Cathl Choir Sch 47-53; Succr of St Mary's Cathl Edin 47-51; Asst Master KS Grantham 53-70; Hd of Lower Sch 74-79; LPr Dio Linc 53-79. *104 Harrowby Road, Grantham, Lincs.*

WOODWARD, Richard Tharby. b 39. Univ of Man BA (2nd cl Mod Hist) 60. Chich Th Coll 60. **d** 62 Southw **p** 63 Bp Gelsthorpe for Southw. C of St Mark Mansfield 62-65; Chap Liddon Ho 65-69; Min of St Mich Conv Distr Beaconsfield 69-76; Team V of Beaconsfield Dio Ox from 76. *St Michael's Parsonage, Beaconsfield, Bucks, HP9 2BN.* (Beaconsfield 3464)

WOODWARD, Canon Stanley Carr. b 03. Ex Coll Ox 2nd cl Cl Mods 24, BA (1st cl Th) 26, MA 30. Wycl Hall Ox 26. **d** 27 **p** 29 Lich. C of Cheadle 27-30; CMS Miss Nishinomiya 30-31; Dio Tokyo 31-32; Fukuoka 32-34; Prof of Centr Th Coll Tokyo and Exam Chap to Bps of Tokyo S Tokyo and Hok 36-40; L to Offic Dio Ja 41-42; V of St Mark Pet 42-49; Dioc Chap to Bp of Pet 43-50; R of Uppingham w Ayston 49-66; Cosgrove 66-72; RD of Uppingham (f Rutland iii) 50-61; Preston 67-72; C-in-c of Wardley w Belton 51-57; Surr 53-72; Exam Chap to Bp of Pet 54-72; Proc Conv Pet 55-64; Can (non-res) of Pet 56-72; Can (Emer) from 73; L to Offic Dios Pet and Ely from 72. *16 Lucks Lane, Buckden, Huntingdon, PE18 9TF.* (Huntingdon 810843)

WOODWARD-COURT, John Blunden. b 13. Ripon Hall Ox 52. **d** 53 **p** 54 Cov. C of Nuneaton 53-55; V of Snitterfield w Bearley 55-74; P-in-c of Barton-on-the-Heath Dio Cov from 74; Wolford w Burmington Dio Cov 74-76; V from 76; P-in-c of Cherington w Stourton Dio Cov 75-76; R from 76; P-in-c of Barcheston Dio Cov 75-76; R from 76. *Great Wolford Vicarage, Shipston-on-Stour, Warws.* (Barton-on-the-Heath 361)

WOODWARDS, David George. b 36. BD (Lon) 62. K Coll Lon MTh 73. Oak Hill Th Coll 62. **d** 64 **p** 65 York. C of H Trin Heworth York 64-66; Tutor and Chap St Pet Coll Kaduna 67-71; V of Edwardstone and R of Groton Dio St E from 72; P-in-c of L Waldingfield Dio St E from 81; RD of Sudbury from 81. *Groton House, Groton, Suff, CO6 5EH.* (Boxford 210197)

WOODWELL, Ven Francis Robert. St Jo Coll Morpeth ACT ThL 51. **d** 50 **p** 51 C & Goulb. C of Albury 50-53; R of Thuddungra 53-57; Dioc Commiss C & Goulb 57-59; R of Cooma 59-63; All SS Canberra 63-66; Bega 66-74; Archd of Monoro S Coast 73-74; Goulb 74-81; SW from 81; R of Tumut Dio C & Goulb from 81. *Box 182 Tumut, NSW, Australia 2720.*

WOODWORTH, Gerald Mark David. b 39. TCD BA (2nd cl Ment and Mor Sc Mod) 62, Div Test (2nd cl) 64, MA 69. **d** 64 **p** 65 Dub. C of Zio Ch Rathgar 64-67; Min Can of St Patr Cathl Dub 65-67; C of Kilkenny 67-70; V Cho St Canice's Cathl Kilk 67-70; Dioc Regr and Libr Oss 67-70; I of Bandon U (w Rathclaren from 76) Innishannon U Dio Cork from 79; Exam Chap to Bp of Cork from 78; RD of Cork Mid-W from 79. *Rectory, Bandon, Cork, Irish Republic.* (Bandon 41259)

WOOKEY, Stephen Mark. b 54. Em Coll Cam BA 76, MA 80. Wycl Hall Ox 77. **d** 80 Edmon for Lon **p** 81 Lon. C of Cockfosters Dio Lon from 80. *2 Chalk Lane, Cockfosters, Barnet, Herts, EN4 9JQ.* (01-449 4042)

WOOLCOCK, Alfred. S Th (Canada) 40. **d** 33 **p** 34 NS. C of River John NS 33-35; R of Port Morien NS 35-38; C of Tardebigge (in c of Webheath) 38-39; V of Catshill 39-47; CF (EC) 42-46; I of Englehart 47-49; R of Port Dalhousie 49-55; Can Commiss for Ind Work Dio Sask 55-60; Archd of Sask 56-60; I of St Mark Oshawa 61-75. *RR2 Port Perry, Ont, Canada.*

WOOLCOCK, Byron William. Montr Dioc Th Coll 60. **d** 65 Montr for Yukon **p** 66 Yukon. R of Dawson 65-67; R of Rawdon 69-71; I of Birch Hills 71-72; on leave 72-78; I of Churchill Falls Joint Min Dio E Newfld from 78. *Churchill Falls, Labrador, Newfld, Canada.*

WOOLCOCK, John. b 47. Sarum Wells Th Coll 70. **d** 72

p 73 Carl. C of St Pet Kells 72-76; St Matt Barrow-in-Furness 76-78; R of Distington Dio Carl from 78. *Rectory, Church Road, Distington, Workington, Cumb, CA14 5TE.* (Harrington 830384)

WOOLCOTT, Bruce Alan. Moore Th Coll Syd ACT ThL 56. **d** 57 Syd **p** 59 Bp Hilliard for Syd. C of Corrimal 57-58; Parramatta 58-61; Merrylands 61-62; R of Hedland w Roebourne 62-64; C-in-c of Figtree Provisional Distr 64-68; R of Emu Plains w Castlereagh 68-72; C-in-c of Provisional Par Belfield 73-77; R of Sutton Forest Dio Syd from 77. *Rectory, Church Street, Bundanoon, NSW, Australia 2578.* (Bundanoon 19)

WOOLCOTT, Herbert Denis. b 12. Univ of Dur LTh 37, BD (Lon) 53. Oak Hill Th Coll 34. **d** 37 **p** 38 S'wark. C of H Trin Richmond 37-39; St Andr L Cam 39-41; Chap RAF 41-47; R of Woodchester 47-56; V of Eastwood 56-77; Perm to Offic Dio Glouc 79-81; Dio Chelmsf from 81. *3 Mountain Ash Close, Leigh-on-Sea, Essex, SS9 4SY.*

WOOLDRIDGE, Derek Robert. b 33. Univ of Nottm BA (2nd cl Econ Hist) 57. Oak Hill Th Coll. **d** 59 **p** 60 Derby. C of H Trin Chesterfield 59-63; H Trin Heworth 63-70; R of St Paul City and Dio York from 70. *100 Acomb Road, York, YO2 4ER.* (York 792304)

WOOLDRIDGE, John Bellamy. b 27. Tyndale Hall, Bris 54. **d** 56 **p** 57 Ches. C of Norbury 56-58; Bramcote 58-60; V of Eccleston 60-66; NW Area Sec CPAS 66-68; C-in-c of Knutsford 68-71; V (w Toft) 71-79; Gt Clacton Dio Chelmsf from 79. *Great Clacton Vicarage, Clacton-on-Sea, Essex, CO15 4AR.* (Clacton-on-Sea 23435)

WOOLDRIDGE, Simon Lee. b 50. Canberra Coll of Min BTh 79. **d** 78 **p** 79 C & Goulb. C of Wagga Wagga 78-80; R of Tarcutta Dio C & Goulb from 81. *St Mark's Rectory, PO Box 1, Tarcutta, NSW, Australia 2652.*

WOOLF, William John. b 05. **d** 53 **p** 54 Worc. C of Bromsgrove 53-55; Pershore 55-58; V of N Somercotes 58-73; R of S Somercotes 59-73. *Pear Tree Cottage, Chapel Lane, Manby, Louth, Lincs LN11 8HQ.* (S Cockerington 550)

WOOLFENDEN, Dennis George. b 12. Univ of Leeds BSc (2nd cl Gas Eng) 35. Cranmer Hall Dur. **d** 68 Colchester for Chelmsf **p** 69 Chelmsf. C of Barking 68-72; R of Wakes Colne w Chappel 72-76; V of St Nich Elm Pk Hornchurch 76-80. *2 Dunstan Close, Chichester, W Sussex, PO19 4NZ.*

WOOLFENDEN, Thomas. Ely Th Coll 45. **d** 47 **p** 48 Pet. C of All SS Wellingborough 47-50; Malvern Link 50-51; V of Podington w Farndish 51-63; Geddington (w Newton-in-the-Willows to 73) (and Weekley from 73) Dio Pet from 63. *Geddington Vicarage, Kettering, Northants.* (Kettering 742200)

WOOLHOUSE, Kenneth. b 38. BNC Ox BA (2nd cl Th) 61, MA 65. Cudd Coll 61. **d** 64 **p** 65 Linc. C of Old Brumby 64-67; Chap of Cov Cathl 68-75; P-in-c of St Mich and St Geo Conv Distr White City Hammersmith 75-81; Birdham w Itchenor W Dio Chich from 81. *Birdham Rectory, Crooked Lane, Chichester, W Sussex, PO20 7HB.* (Birdham 512442)

WOOLHOUSE, Thomas Edgar. b 06. Lich Th Coll. **d** 66 Shrewsbury for Lich **p** 67 Stafford for Lich. C of Oswestry 66-71; V of Weston Lullingfield 71-77; R of Hordley 71-77; Hon C of St Andr Shifnal Dio Lich from 78. *3 Innage Croft, Idsall Green, Shifnal, Salop.* (Telford 461159)

✠ **WOOLLCOMBE, Right Rev Kenneth John.** b 24. Late Exhib and Casberd Scho of St Jo Coll Ox 2nd cl Th 48, BA 49, MA 53, Ellerton Pri 51, Hon Fell 71. Univ of the S Sewanee STD (*hon causa*) 63. Trin Coll Hartford Conn Hon DD 75. Westcott Ho Cam 49. **d** 51 **p** 52 Linc. C of St Jas Grimsby 51-53; Fell Chap and Lect of St Jo Coll Ox and L to Offic Dio Ox 53-60; Tutor 56-60; Exam Chap to Bps of Worc and Wakef 57-60; to Bp of Ox 58-60; Prof of Dogmatic Th Gen Th Sem Ny 60-63; Prin Edin Th Coll 63-71; Can of Edin 63-71; Cons Ld Bp of Ox in Westmr Abbey 16 March 71 by Abp of Cant; Bps of Lon; Win; Chich; Glas (primus); Edin; Nor; Pet; Linc; Moray; Heref; Glouc; Brech; Arg Is; Guildf; Portsm; Sarum; St Alb; St Andr; and others; res 78; Asst Bp in Dio Lon 78-81; Can Res of St Paul's Cathl Lon from 81. *5 Amen Court, EC4M 7BU.*

WOOLLER, Herbert. b 22. Worc Ordin Coll 62. **d** 64 **p** 65 Wakef. C of St Andr Wakef 64-68; V of Sharlston 68-78; Lundwood Dio Wakef from 78. *Lundwood Vicarage, Barnsley, S Yorks.* (Barnsley 203194)

WOOLLEY, Alfred Russell. b 1899. Wadham Coll Ox BA (2nd cl Hist) 22, MA 25. Trin Coll Cam MA (by incorp) 29. Westcott Ho Cam **d** 60 **p** 61 Ox. L to Offic Dio Ox 60-62; R of Gestingthorpe 62-67; St Lawr IW 67-74; Perm to Offic Dio St E from 74; Dio Chelmsf from 76. *Gestingthorpe Hall, Halstead, Essex, CO9 3BB.* (Hedingham 60638)

WOOLLEY, Canon Christopher Andrew Lempriere. b 15. Ch Ch Ox BA 37, MA 70. Ely Th Coll 37. **d** 39 **p** 40 Lon. C of St Aug Kilburn 39-46; Miss at Liuli 46-52; Prin of St Paul's Tr Coll Liuli 52-55; P-in-c of Milo 55-62; Archd of Njombe 58-62; Can of H Cross Cathl Liuli Dio SW Tang 59-70; Hon Can from 70; P-in-c of Mbeya 62-70; V of Horley w Hornton Dio Ox from 70; C-in-c of Hanwell Dio Ox from 70. *Horley Vicarage, Banbury, Oxon.* (Wroxton St Mary 381)

WOOLLEY, Cyril George. **d** 70 **p** 71 Lon. M SSJE 60; L to Offic Dio Leic from 80. *St John's House, 2 Woodland Avenue, Leicester, LE2 3HG.*

WOOLLEY, Edward Ross. Wycl Coll Tor BA 52. **d** 53 **p** 54 Tor. I of Minden 53-60; R of Bradf Tor 60-66; Birch Cliff Tor 66-73; Ch K City and Dio Tor from 73. *475 Rathburn Road, Islington, Toronto, Ont, Canada.* (416-621 3630)

WOOLLEY, Francis Bertram Hopkinson. b 43. Sarum Wells Th Coll 75. **d** 78 **p** 79 Worc. C of Halesowen 78-81; Team V of Droitwich Dio Worc from 81. *Vicar's House, 61 Drovers Way, Droitwich, Worcs, WR9 9DA.*

WOOLLEY, James Cayford. b 46. Univ of Tor BA 68. Wycl Coll Tor BTh 71. **d** 71 **p** 72 Tor. C of Eglinton 71-75; R of Stayner and Wasaga Beach 75-81; St Thos A Becket City and Dio Tor from 81. *3535 South Common Court, Mississauga, Ont, Canada.*

WOOLLEY, John Alexander. **d** 63 Warrington for Liv **p** 64 Liv. C of St Mich Garston 63-65; Gt Crosby (in c of All SS) 65-71; R of Croft w Southworth 71-75; Chap Ryhope Hosps Sunderland from 75. *6 Brookside Gardens, Sunderland, T & W.* (Sunderland 51854)

WOOLLEY, William Burrell. b 17. Kelham Th Coll 34. **d** 40 **p** 41 Liv. C of St Paul Stanley 40-44; Actg C of St Alphege Solihull 44-45; C of All SS Shrewsbury 45-48; St Steph the Mart Liv 48-50; Chap Radium Inst Liv 48-50; V of Smallthorne 50-59; St Paul Burton-on-Trent 59-75; P-in-c of Church Eaton Dio Lich from 75; Bradeley Dio Lich from 75; P-in-c of Moreton (and Church Eaton from 78) Dio Lich from 76. *Church Eaton Rectory, Stafford, ST20 0AG.* (Stafford 823091)

WOOLMER, John Shirley Thursby. b 42. Wadh Coll Ox Ba 63, MA 69. St Jo Coll Bramcote 70. **d** 71 **p** 72 Win. Asst Master Win Coll 63-75; Asst Chap 72-75; C of St Aldate City and Dio Ox from 75. *60 Abingdon Road, Oxford, OX1 4PE.*

WOOLNER, Canon Douglas Kenneth. b 19. Univ of Lon 47. Chich Th Coll 51. **d** 52 **p** 53 St E. C of All H Ipswich 52-56; R of Claydon w Barham 56-71; V of St Bart Ipswich Dio St E from 71; Hon Can of St E from 77. *Vicarage, Newton Road, Ipswich, Suff.* (Ipswich 77441)

WOOLSEY, Ven Gary Frederick. Univ of W Ont BA 64. Hur Coll BTh 66. **d** and **p** 67 Keew. L to Offic Dio Keew 67-68; I of Trout Lake 68-72; Norway Ho 72-76; Churchill 76-80; Archd of Keew 72-74 and from 80; York 76-80; Archd (Emer) from 74; Exam Chap to Bp of Keew from 80. *Box 118, Kenora, Ont, P9N 3X1, Canada.* (807-468 7011)

WOOLSTENHOLMES, Cyril Esmond. b 16. Bede Coll Dur BA 37. Dipl Th 38. MA 41. **d** 39 **p** 40 Dur. C of Leadgate 39-44; St Cuthb Darlington (in c All SS of Blackwell) 44-46; St Paul W Hartlepool (in c of Ch Ch) 46-50; L to Offic Dio Dur 47-50; V of Tudhoe Grange 50-67; R of Shadforth Dio Dur from 67. *Shadforth Rectory, Durham, DH6 1LF.* (Durham 720223)

WOOLVEN, Ronald. b 36. Oak Hill Th Coll 60. **d** 63 **p** 64 Chelmsf. C of Ch of Good Shepherd Romford 63-68; Widford Chelmsf 68-73; P-in-c of Barling Magna w L Wakering Dio Chelmsf from 73. *Little Wakering Vicarage, Southend-on-Sea, Essex.* (Southend-on-Sea 219200)

WOOLWICH, Lord Bishop Suffragan of. *See* Marshall, Right Rev Michael Eric.

WOOSTER, Patrick Charles Francis. b 38. Qu Coll Birm 63. **d** 65 Malmesbury for Bris **p** 66 Bris. C of Chippenham w Tytherton Lucas 65-70; Cockington w Chelston 70-72; V of Stone w Woodford (and Hill from 73) Dio Glouc from 72; C-in-c of Hill 72-73. *Stone Vicarage, Berkeley, Glos.* (Falfield 260277)

WOOTTEN, Canon Donald Thomas Frederick. Em Coll Sktn 57. **d** 60 **p** 61 Athab. I of Spirit River 60-63; Fort McPherson Dio Arctic 63-66; Dio Athab 66-70; Dio Mack 71-73; R of Macklin 73-74; N Battleford Dio Sktn from 74; Hon Can of Sktn from 80. *1601-99th Street, N Battleford, Sask, Canada.*

WOOTTON, Frank Jeremy. b 20. Trin Coll Ox BA 42, MA 45. Cudd Coll 46. **d** 47 **p** 48 S'wark. C of St Jo Div Kennington 47-51; Tideswell 51-54; Chaddesdon (in c of St Phil) 54-56; V of Scarcliffe 56-63; Denford w Ringstead 64-70; Woolfardisworthy w Buck Mills 70-71; Perm to Offic Dio Ox from 71; Perm to Offic Dio Derby 72-76; C of King Sterndale 73-74; Perm to Offic Dio Pet from 75. *c/o St Alban's Vicarage, Broadmead Avenue, Northampton, NN3 2RA.* (Northn 407074)

WOOTTON, Canon Richard William Frederick. b 14. MBE 46. CCC Ox 1st cl Cl Mods 34, 1st cl Lit Hum 36, BA 36, MA 39, Dipl Th (w distinc) 47. Wycl Hall Ox 46. **d** 47 Lon **p** 48 Lah. P-in-c of Gojra Miss 48-51; Prin St Jo Div Sch Narowal 52-53; Tutor Gujranwala Th Sem 53-61; Hon Can of Lah from 58; Prin CA Tr Coll 61-66; Asst Translations Sec BFBS 66-69; Dep Sec 69-70; Sec 70-73; Lect of St Jo Bapt Knighton 73-80; Chap for Commun Relns Dio Leic 74-80; L to Offic Dio Sarum from 81. *Dolphin Cottage, Giddy Lake, Wimborne, BH21 2QT.* (0202 882077)

WOPYET, Britton. d 78 New Hebr **p** 80 Vanuatu. P Dio New Hebr 78-80; Dio Vanuatu from 80. *Motolava, Banks Group, Vanuatu.*

WORBOYS, Charles William. b 19. Oak Hill Th Coll 61. **d** 62 **p** 63 Lich. C of Bucknall w Bagnall 62-65; V of W Thurrock w Purfleet 65-71; Shalford Essex 71-75; Warden Holbeck and Bethel Trust from 75; L to Offic Dio St E from 76. *Mirembe, Coddenham, Ipswich, Suff.*

WORCESTER, Lord Bishop of. *See* Goodrich, Right Rev Philip Harold Ernest.

WORCESTER, Assistant Bishop of. *See* Allenby, Right Rev David Howard Nicholas.

WORCESTER, Archdeacon of. *See* Coleman, Ven Peter Everard.

WORCESTER, Dean of. *See* Baker, Very Rev Thomas George Adames.

WORDEN, Gordon Henry. b 46. Qu Univ Ont BA 68. Huron Coll BTh 71. **d** and **p** 71 Ott. C of St Smith's Falls 71-73; I of Mattawa 73-76; Stafford 76-79; St Lawr E Dio Ott from 79. *207 First Street East, Cornwall, Ont, Canada.* (613-933 3973)

WORDSWORTH, Allan. b 05. Univ of Dur BA 38, Dipl Th 40, MA 41. Wells Th Coll 39. **d** and **p** 40 Blackb. C of St Annes-on-the-Sea 40-45; V of St Bede Nelson-in-Marsden 45-52; E Coatham 52-72. *24b Sir William Turner's Court, Kirkleatham, Cleve.*

WORDSWORTH, Jeremy Nathaniel. b 30. Clare Coll Cam BA 54, MA 58. Ridley Hall, Cam 54. **d** 56 **p** 57 Chelmsf. C of Gt Baddow 56-59; Chap Felsted Sch 59-63; Sherborne Sch 63-71; PV and Succr of S'wark Cathl 71-73; C-in-c of Stone 73-75; Warden of Readers Dio Worc from 73; V of St Andr Malvern Dio Worc from 76. *St Andrew's Vicarage, Longridge Road, Malvern, Worcs.* (Malvern 3912)

WORDSWORTH, Paul. b 42. Univ of Birm BA (3rd cl Th) 64. Wells Th Coll 64. **d** 66 **p** 67 York. C of Anlaby 66-71; Marfleet 71-72; Team V 72-77; V of Sowerby Dio York from 77; C-in-c of Sessay Dio York from 77. *Sowerby Vicarage, Thirsk, Yorks.* (0845-23546)

WOREK, Nicholson. Bp Patteson Th Centre Kohimarama 70. **d** 77 **p** 79 New Hebr. P Dio New Hebr 77-80; Dio Vanuatu from 80. *Vetuboso, Vanualava, Vanuatu.*

WORFOLK, James Joseph. Wycl Coll Tor STh 55. **d** 62 Bp Snell for Tor. C of St Eliz Tor 62-69; St Rich City and Dio Tor from 69. *27 Robin Hood Road, Islington, Ont, Canada.*

WORGAN, Maurice William. b 40. Ely Th Coll 62. **d** 65 Cant **p** 66 Dover for Cant. C of Cranbrook 65-69; St Martin Maidstone 69-72; R of Lyminge w Paddlesworth (and Stanford w Postling from 73) Dio Cant from 72; C-in-c of Stanford w Postling 72-73. *Lyminge Rectory, Folkestone, Kent.* (Lyminge 862432)

WORLEY, John Melville. **d** 64 Ondo. d Dio Ondo 64-70. *c/o Bishopscourt, PO Box 25, Ondo, Nigeria.*

WORLEY, William. b 37. St Jo Coll Dur 69. **d** 72 Bp Skelton for Dur **p** 73 Dur. C of Consett 72-76; V of Seaton Carew Dio Dur from 76; CF (TA) from 77. *Seaton Carew Vicarage, Hartlepool, Cleveland.* (Hartlepool 62463)

WORMALD, Louis Percival. b 03. Univ of Leeds BSc (3rd cl Zoology) 23. **d** 43 **p** 44 St E. C of Thornham Magna w Parva 43-45; St Barn Hove 45-46; St Alkmund Shrewsbury 46-47; St Edm Mansfield Woodhouse 47; Blyth (in c of Langold) 47-49; C-in-c of Linstead w Chediston 49-57; V 57-59; Assington 59-68; Perm to Offic Dio Chelmsf from 68. *55 Blenheim Road, Clacton-on-Sea, Essex, CO15 1DN.* (0255 35106)

WORMALD, Roy Henry. b 42. Chich Th Coll 64. **d** 67 Barking for Chelmsf **p** 68 Chelmsf. C of St Mich AA Walthamstow 67-69; St Thos and St Jo Bapt Cov 69-72; St Mich Wood Green 72-77; P-in-c of St Mellitus Hanwell Dio Lon 77-81; V (w St Mark) from 81. *Vicarage, Church Road, W7.* (01-567 6535)

WORRELL, Theodore Wainwright Clarke. St Pet Coll Ja. **d** 65 Kingston for Ja **p** 66 Ja. C of Stony Hill 65-66; Cross Roads 66-68; R of Port Maria 68-78. *c/o Rectory, Port Maria, Jamaica, W Indies.* (099-42217)

WORSDALL, John Robin. b 33. Univ of Dur BA 57. Linc Th Coll 62. **d** 63 Linc **p** 64 Bp Dunlop for Linc. C of St Jo Evang Grantham 63-66; Folkingham 66-68; V of New Bolingbroke w Carrington 68-74; C-in-c of Langrick 70-74; P-in-c of N Somercotes 74-81; S Somercotes 74-81; Stickney Dio Linc from 81. *Vicarage, Spilsby Road, New Leake, Boston, PE22 8JT.* (New Leake 485)

WORSDELL, William Charles. b 35. K Coll Lon and Warm AKC 59. **d** 60 **p** 61 Glouc. C of St Aldate Glouc 60-66; PC of St Barn Devonport 66-68; V 68-72; R of Uplyme 72-77; Withington and Compton Abdale w Haselton Dio Glouc from 77. *Withington Rectory, Cheltenham, Glos, GL54 4BG.* (Withington 242)

WORSFOLD, John. Keble Coll Ox BA (3rd cl Engl) and MA 50. Cudd Coll 50. **d** 51 **p** 52 S'wark. C of H Spirit Clapham 51-62; Richmond 62-63; St Geo Shirley 63-80; St Sav Croydon Dio Cant from 80. *96 Lodge Road, Croydon, CR0 2PF.* (01-684 2526)

WORSLEY, Very Rev Godfrey Stuart Harling. b 06. ALCD 28. **d** 29 Cant **p** 31 Croydon for Cant. C of St Paul Thornton Heath 29-30; Croydon 30-33; CF 33-43; SCF 43-49; DACG 49-54; R of Kingsland 54-60; RD of Leominster 56-60; Preb of Cublington in Heref Cathl 59-60; Proc Conv Heref 59-60; Dean of Gibr 60-69; Dean (Emer) from 69; R of Pen-Selwood 69-79. *Arrow Cottage, Eardisland, Nr Leominster, Herefs.* (Pembridge 241)

WORSLEY, James Duncan. b 14. Univ of Dur LTh 40. Tyndale Hall Bris 37. **d** 40 **p** 41 Man. C of St Clem Broughton 40-41; St Pet Halliwell 41-43; Bucknall w Bagnall 43-47; V of Biddulph 47-54; Chap Biddulph Grange Orthopaedic Hosp 50-54; V of St Thos Launceston 54-61; Ullenhall w Aspley 61-72; Hunningham 72-79; Wappenbury w Weston-under-Wetherley 72-79; Chap Weston-under-Wetherley Hosp 72-79. *24 Banneson Road, St Mary's Fields, Nether Stowey, Bridgwater, Somt.* (Nether Stowey 732169)

WORSLEY, Richard John. b 52. Qu Coll Cam BA 74, MA 78. Qu Coll Birm Dipl Th 79. **d** 80 **p** 81 Cov. C of Styvechale Dio Cov from 80. *55 Watercall Avenue, Styvechale, Coventry.*

WORSLEY, Ronald Freeman. b 23. **d** 61 **p** 62 Ches. C of St Phil Chorley 61-64; Timperley 64-68; V of Waverton 68-75; St Steph Congleton 75-82; Eastham Dio Chesh from 82. *Vicarage, Ferry Road, Eastham, Wirral, Mer.* (051-327 2182)

WORSTEAD, Eric Henry. b 14. BD (1st cl) Lon 44, BA 46, MTh 54. **d** and **p** 64 Niger. P Dio Niger 64-66; Hon C of St Thos Southborough 67-72; Dep Prin Whitelands Coll of Educn 67-72; P-in-c of High Hurst Wood 73-78. *Flat 2, Waterside, Crowborough Hill, Crowborough, Sussex.* (Crowborough 2126)

WORT, Ernest Winstone. b 13. SOC 66. **d** 68 **p** 69 Chich. C of Aldwick 68-72; V of Mendham w Metfield and Withersdale 72-77; C of Haverhill 77-79; Hon C Aldwick Dio Chich from 79. *5 St Johns Close, Bognor Regis, PO21 5RX.* (823156)

WORTH, Douglas Albert Victor. b 09. St Cath Coll Cam 2nd cl Hist Trip pt i 31, BA (2nd cl Th Trip pt i) 32, MA 47. Wells Th Coll 32. **d** 33 Ripon **p** 34 Knaresborough for Ripon. C of Em Leeds 33-35; St Jo Evang Smith Square Westmr 35-38; Chap Toc H 38-39; C of St Jo Evang Smith Square Westmr 39-42; All SS Hove 42-43; Bp's Chap for Youth Dio Chich 43-47; Chap and Lect Coll of St Mark and St John Chelsea 47-66; Prin Lect 67-71; Perm to Offic Dio Glouc from 71; Lect Glouc Sch for Min from 76. *Rose Cottage, Chalford Hill, Stroud, Glos.* (Brimbscombe 2572)

WORTH, Frederick Stuart. b 30. Oak Hill Th Coll 60. **d** 62 **p** 63 Ex. C of Okehampton (w Inwardleigh 63) 62-68; R of St Nich w H Trin Dunkeswell 68-78; C-in-c of Luppitt 69-72; Upottery 72-76; V of Sheldon 73-78; Ed Ex Dioc Directory from 76; RD of Honiton from 77; R of Uplyme Dio Ex from 78; P-in-c of Combe Pyne w Rousdon Dio Ex from 82. *Uplyme Rectory, Lyme Regis, Dorset, DT7 3TX.* (Lyme Regis 3256)

WORTHEN, Peter Frederick. b 38. Oak Hill Th Coll 71. **d** 71 Bp Russell for Roch **p** 72 Roch. C of Tonbridge 71-75; P-in-c of High Halstow w Hoo St Mary (and All H from 76) Dio Roch 75-76; R from 76. *Rectory, High Halstow, Rochester, Kent, ME3 8SA.* (Medway 250637)

WORTHING, George Herbert Murray. b 01. Univ of Wales BSc 23. St Mich Coll Llan 28. **d** 29 **p** 30 Swan B. C of Llangyfelach w Morriston 29-37; R of Whitton w Pilleth and Bleddfa 37-43; V of Manselton 43-45; R of Llansantffraed-juxta-Usk (w Llanddetty and Glyncollwng 45-53) 45-56; Llanbedr-Ystradyw w Patricio 56-60; Rockptn 60-66; PC of Falfield 60-66; R of Newington Bagpath w Kingscote and Ozleworth 66-70; Perm to Offic Dio Glouc from 70. *Church Cottage, Nympsfield, Stonehouse, Glos, GL10 3UH.*

WORTHINGTON, Bruce William. b 44. St Francis Coll Brisb ACT ThL 69. **d** 68 **p** 69 Rockptn. C of St Luke Wandal 68-72; Pk Avenue Rockptn 72-73; S Gladstone 73-74; R of Barcaldine 74-77; Clermont Dio Rockptn from 77. *Rectory, Clermont, Queensland, Australia 4721.*

WORTHINGTON, George. b 35. K Coll Lon and Warm AKC 60. **d** 61 **p** 62 Dur. C of St Pet Stockton-on-Tees 61-65; Poulton-le-Fylde 65-67; V of Trawden 67-76; P-in-c of Arkholme Dio Blackb 76-78; V (w Gressingham and Whittington) from 78; P-in-c of Gressingham 76-78; Whittington 77-78. *Arkholme Vicarage, Carnforth, Lancs, LA6 1AX.* (Hornby 21359)

WORTHINGTON, John Clare. b 17. St Jo Coll Cam BA

39, MA 46. Westcott Ho Cam 39 and 46. **d** 48 **p** 49 Sheff. C of Rotherham 48-51; CF 51-65; V of Ellingham w Harbridge (and Ibsley from 82) Dio Win from 65; RD of Christchurch 79-82. *Ellingham Vicarage, Ringwood, Hants, BH24 3PJ.* (Ringwood 3723)

WORTLEY, John Trevor. Univ of Dur BA 57, MA 60. PhD (Lon) 69. Edin Th Coll. **d** 59 **p** 60 Wakef. C of St Jo Evang Huddersfield 59-64; Chap and Dean of Res St Jo Coll Winnipeg 64-66; Hon C of St Mary Bryanston Square St Marylebone 66-69; Asst Prof of Hist Univ of Manit 69-71; P-in-c of Grace Ch Winnipeg 71-76; Hon C of St Mich AA Winnipeg 76-77; All SS Winnipeg Dio Rupld from 77. *225 Hill Street, Winnipeg, Manit, Canada.*

WORTON, Norman. Univ of Lon 34. ALCD 38. **d** 38 **p** 39 Cant. C of Ch Ch Croydon 38-41; CMS Miss Dio U Nile 41-47; C of Durrington 47-49; Horsham (in c of St Mark) 49-53; R of Westbourne 53-59; V of Forest Side and PC of Stansted 57-59; V of St Phil Hove 59-65; L to Offic Dio Syd from 65. *33 Medusa Street, Mosman, NSW, Australia 2088.* (969-5587)

WORWOOD, Canon Frank Edward. b 11. ALCD 34. **d** 34 Taunton for B & W **p** 35 Bp de Salis for B & W. C of St Mark Lyncombe Bath 34-39; V of St Geo Battersea w St Jas Nine Elms 39-48; Portsdown 48-61; R of W Bridgford 61-81; RD of W Bingham 61-81; Surr 65-81; Hon Can of Southw 72-81; Can (Emer) from 81. *1 Eastwood Road, Radcliffe-on-Trent, Notts.* (06073 5647)

WOTHERSPOON, David Colin. b 36. Portsm Coll of Tech CEng, M IMechE 65. St Jo Coll Dur 76. **d** 78 Blackb **p** 79 Lanc for Blackb. C of St Gabr Blackb 78-81; V of Witton Dio Blackb from 81. *Witton Vicarage, Buncer Lane, Blackburn, Lancs.* (Blackburn 676615)

WOTTI, Canon Christopher. Buwalasi Th Coll 57. **d** 59 **p** 60 U Nile. P Dio U Nile 59-61; Dio Mbale from 61; Hon Can of Mbale from 69. *PO Box 473, Mbale, Uganda.*

WOTTON, David Ashley. Chich Th Coll 71. **d** 74 **p** 75 Cant. C of Allington 74-77; Ham Dio S'wark from 77. *99 Barnfield Avenue, Kingston-upon-Thames, Surrey.* (01-549 8296)

WOTTON, Roy Arthur Wilcox. Univ of Syd BA 47. Moore Th Coll Syd 36. ACT ThL 37. **d** 38 **p** 39 Syd. C of St Mary Waverley 38-39; Manly 39-46; Chap AIF 42-46; R of St Mary Concord N 46-51; Gordon 51-79; L to Offic Dio Newc 79-80; Dio Syd from 80. *4 Currawong Street, Blue Bay, NSW, Australia 2261.*

WOTWALI, Yekoyada. Bp Tucker Coll Mukono. **d** 64 **p** 65 Mbale. P Dio Mbale. *PO Bugobero, Mbale, Uganda.*

WOULDHAM, Ralph Douglas Astley. b 19. Univ of Leeds BA 48. Coll of Resurr Mirfield 48. **d** 50 **p** 51 Ripon. C of St Wilfrid Halton 50-53; Perm to Offic Dio Newc T 53-56; V of Bolam 56-62; R of Usworth 62-69; V of Cleadon 69-79; Lowick w Kyloe Dio Newc T from 79. *1 Main Street, Lowick, Berwick-on-Tweed, TD15 2UD.* (Berwick-on-Tweed 88229)

WRAGG, Alwyn Lumley. b 10. Univ of Sheff BA 32, MA 33. OBE 62. St Steph Ho Ox 32. **d** 34 Derby **p** 35 Bp Crick for Derby. C of Bolsover 34-38; Chap RN 38-65; Hon Chap to HM the Queen 63-65; Publ Pr Dio S'wark 65-71; Perm to Offic Dio Guildf from 71. *16 Hipley Court, Warren Road, Guildford, Surrey, GU1 2HT.* (Guildford 77857)

WRAGG, John Gordon. b 17. Univ of Sheff BA 39. ALCD 41. **d** 41 **p** 42 Newc T. C of St Marg Scotswood 41-43; Menston w Woodhead 43-46; Umhlatuzana 46-49; Ashbourne w Mapleton 49-53; V of Rosherville 53-56; Mooi River 56-58; Durban S 58-62; V of Spittal 62-75; R of Wark Dio Newc T from 75; P-in-c of Birtley Dio Newc T 75-77; V from 77. *Wark Rectory, Hexham, Northumb.* (Wark 30223)

WRAGG, Peter Robert. b 46. Univ of Lon BSc 68, Sarum Wells Th Coll 71. **d** 74 **p** 75 Kens for Lon. C of Feltham 74-79; Team V of Hackney Dio Lon from 79. *59a Kenninghall Road, E5 8BS.* (01-985 1804)

WRAIGHT, John Radford. b 38. St Chad's Coll Dur BA 62, Dipl Th 64. **d** 64. **p** 65 Dur. C of Shildon 64-67; Newton Aycliffe 67-70; St John and St Herbert (in c of St Herbert) Darlington 70-75; P-in-c (Ecumen Team) of Livingston Edin 75-80; Team V of H Trin and St Barn City and Dio Carl from 80. *Holy Trinity Vicarage, Wigton Road, Carlisle, CA2 7BB.* (Carl 26284)

WRAITH, Canon Lawrence Victor. b 08. Egerton Hall Man 28. **d** 32 **p** 33 Man. C of St Mark Heyside 32-35; St Anne Longsight 35-37; Lydney w Aylburton 37-39; V of Coleford w Staunton R 39-48; R of Yate 48-61; Hon Chap to Bp of Glouc 46-75; Surr from 52; R of Hempsted 61-75; Hon Can of Glouc from 64; Hon Sec Glouc Dioc Conf 62-70. *38a Boxbush Road, Coleford, Glos, GL16 8DN.* (Dean 32818)

WRAKE, John. b 28. Clifton Th Coll 56. **d** 59 **p** 60 Chelmsf. C of Gt Baddow 59-62; CF 62-66; V of Tilton-on-the-Hill and Halstead w Lowesby and Cold Newton Dio Leic 66-73; R of Maresfield 73-79. *c/o Maresfield Rectory, Uckfield, Sussex.* (Uckfield 3817)

WRANGHAM-HARDY, Canon John Francis. MBE (Mil) 57. TD 50. Univ of Leeds BA (2nd cl Geog) 32. Wells Th Coll 34. **d** 35 **p** 36 Ripon. C of Ch Ch Harrogate 35-38; Harewood (in c of E Keswick) 38-47; CF (TA) 39-65; R of Addingham 47-53; Guiseley 53-67; Surr 53-67; Exam Chap to Bp of Bradf 54-57; Hon Can of Bradf 59-67; Can (Emer) from 67; Asst Chap O of St John of Jer from 60; DACGN 60-65; Hon Chap to HM the Queen 62-64 and from 67; R of Green's Norton w Bradden Dio Pet from 67; RD of Towcester from 69; Chap to Ld Mayor Lon 74-75; Sub-Chap O St Jo of Jer from 80. *Green's Norton Rectory, Towcester, Northants, NN12 8BL.* (Towcester 50279)

WRANKMORE, Bernard Arthur. Bp Gray Coll Zonnebloem. **d** 60 **p** 61 Capetn. C of Retreat 60-62; Chap Miss to Seamen City and Dio Capetn from 62. *The Missions to Seamen, Alfred Street, Cape Town, CP, S Africa.* (453100)

WRAPSON, Donald. b 36. St Aid Coll 61. **d** 65 **p** 66 Man. C of St Sav Bacup 65-69; St Matt Wolverhampton 69-72; Normanton-by-Derby 72-78; V of Dordon w Freasley Dio Birm from 78. *Dordon Vicarage, Tamworth, Staffs, B78 1TE.* (Tamworth 892294)

WRATTEN, Martyn Stephen. b 34. K Coll Lon and Warm AKC 58. **d** 59 **p** 60 S'wark. C of Wandsworth Common 59-62; Putney (in c of All SS) 62-65; Pembury 65-70; R of Stone 70-76; Chap Joyce Green Hosp 70-73; Stone Ho Hosp 73-76; Netherne Hosp Coulsdon from 76; C-in-c of St Luke Conv Distr Netherne, Merstham Dio S'wark from 76. *Chaplaincy, Netherne Hospital, Coulsdon, Surrey, CR3 1NQ.* (Downland 56700)

WRAY, Bertie. b 1899. St Mich Coll Llan 56. **d** 57 **p** 58 Mon. C of Chepstow w St Arvans and Penterry 57-59; R of Llansoy w Llanfihangel-tor-y-Mynydd and Llangunnog 59-70; L to Offic Dio Mon from 70. *Leacot, Coleford Road, Tutshill, Chepstow, Gwent.*

WRAY, Christopher. b 48. Univ of Hull BA 70. New Coll Ox Dipl Th 73. Cudd Coll Ox 70. **d** 73 Wakef **p** 74 Pontefract for Wakef. C of Brighouse 73-76; Almondbury 76-78; Tong w Holme Wood 78-80; V of Ingleton w Chapel-le-Dale Dio Bradf from 80. *Ingleton Vicarage, Carnforth, Lancs.* (Ingleton 41440)

WRAY, Karl. b 51. Coll of Resurr Mirfield 75. **d** 78 **p** 79 Man. C of St Phil w St Steph Salford Dio Man from 78. *115 Canon Hussey Court, George Street, Salford, M3 5JB.* (061-834 0889)

WRAY, Kenneth Martin. b 43. Linc Th Coll 72. **d** 75 **p** 76 Bradf. C of Shipley 75-79; V of New Edlington Dio Sheff from 79. *Vicarage, Broomhouse Lane, Edlington, Doncaster, Yorks.* (Rotherham 863148)

WRAY, Kenneth Norman. Moore Th Coll Syd. **d** and **p** 53 Syd. C of St Phil Eastwood 53-54; R of Merrylands 54-57; C-in-c of Belfield 57-64; E Lindfield 64-72; R 72-77; L to Offic Dio Syd from 77. *74 Duntroon Avenue, East Roseville, NSW, Australia 2069.* (407-1070)

WRAY, Laurence Willy. b 1896. Wycl Hall Ox 30. **d** 30 **p** 31 Leic. C of Donisthorpe 30-32; V of Whitwick St Geo w Swannington 32-45; Belton 45-69; CF 38-51. *4 Orchard Close, Lea, Ross-on-Wye, Herefs.*

WRAY, Llewellyn Frank. b 49. St Barn Coll Adel 70. **d** 73 **p** 74 Adel. C of Unley 73-75; P-in-c of Kangaroo I 75-79; R of Angaston Dio Adel from 79. *12 Schilling Street, Angaston, S Australia 5353.* (085-4 2087)

WRAYFORD, Geoffrey John. b 38. Ex Coll Ox BA (3rd cl Th) 61, MA 65. Linc Th Coll 61. **d** 63 **p** 64 Glouc. C of Cirencester w Watermoor 63-69; Chap (and V from 70) Chelmsf Cathl 69-74; V of Canvey I 74-76; Team R 76-80; P-in-c of Woodlands Dio B & W from 80; St Jo Bapt Frome Dio B & W from 80; Ch Ch Frome Dio B & W from 80. *St John's Vicarage, Frome, Somt, BA11 1PU.* (0373-62325)

WREN, Arthur. b 10. Worc Ordin Coll 65. **d** 66 Penrith for Carl **p** 67 Carl. C of Stanwix 66-70; R of Sebergham w Welton 70-75; L to Offic Dio Carl 75-76; Perm to Offic from 77. *c/o Walton Vicarage, Brampton, Cumbria, CA8 2DH.*

WREN, Christopher John. b 54. Univ of Dur BEducn 76. St Steph Ho Ox 77. **d** 79 **p** 80 Dur. C of St Pet Stockton-on-Tees Dio Dur from 79. *70 Tunstall Road, Hartburn, Stockton-on-Tees, Cleve, TS18 5LT.*

WREN, John Aubrey. b 46. St Chad's Coll Dur BA (Th) 69. Cudd Coll 72. **d** 74 Ox **p** 75 Reading for Ox. C of Fenny Stratford 74-77; Team V of the Resurr Brighton Dio Chich from 77. *St Luke's Vicarage, Queen's Park Terrace, Brighton, BN2 2YA.* (Brighton 603946)

WRENN, Peter Henry. b 34. Univ of Lon BA (3rd cl Engl) 56. Qu Coll Birm 58. **d** 60 **p** 61 Derby. C of Dronfield 60-64; Hessle 64-65; PC of Loscoe 65-68; V 68-70; Asst Chap Solihull Sch 71-77; Chap from 77. *63 Shakespeare Drive, Shirley, Solihull, W Midl.* (021-744 3941)

WREXHAM, Archdeacon of. *See* Foster, Ven Raymond Samuel.

WRIGHT, Alan James. b 38. Chich Th Coll 63. **d** 66 Warrington for Liv **p** 67 Liv. C of St Dunstan Edge Hill 66-69; St Geo and St Jas Manzini 69-71; C-in-c of Seaforth 71-76; V of All SS Taunton Dio B & W from 76. *All Saints Vicarage, Taunton, Somt, TA1 2DE.*

WRIGHT, Albert Trevor. b 1900. TD 55. St Jo Coll Dur LTh and BA 25, MA 28. Lon Coll of Div **d** 25 **p** 26 Man. C of St Jas Higher Broughton 25-29; St Paul Kersal 29; V of St Anne Clifton Lancs 29-35; St Jas Heywood 35-45; CF (TA) from 35; CF (EC) 39-44; V of Keynsham (w Qu Charlton from 55) 45-55; PC of Qu Charlton 46-55; C-in-c of Burnett 52-55; V of Berrow 55-64; Kenn 64-67; C-in-c of Kingston Seymour 66-67. *60 Stoddens Road, Burnham-on-Sea, Somt, TA8 2DA.*

WRIGHT, Alexander McIver. Ridley Coll Melb 41. ACT ThL 49. **d** 42 **p** 44 Bend. C of Laanecoorie 42; Raywood 42-43; Daylesford 43-44; I of Mooroopna 44-45; Chap RAAF 45; R of Cohuna 46-58; Dioc Regr Dio Bend 58-70; V of Golden Square 58-70; I of Footscray 70-80; Perm to Offic Dio Melb from 80. *25 Clarke Street, Portarlington, Vic, Australia 3223.*

WRIGHT, Alfred John. b 22. Wycl Hall Ox 66. **d** 66 Buckingham for Ox **p** 67 Ox. C of St Jo Evang Newbury 66-71; V of E Challow (w W Challow to 77) Dio Ox from 71; Chap Commun of St Mary Virg Wantage from 75. *East Challow Vicarage, Wantage, Oxon, OX12 9RP.* (Wantage 3083)

WRIGHT, Alfred Samuel. Univ of Lon BSc (3rd cl Botany) 21, MSc 49. Westcott Ho Cam 54. **d** 55 **p** 56 St Alb. C of Gt Berkhamsted and Asst Master Berkhamsted Sch 55-56; C-in-c of Westoning and C-in-c of Tingrith 56-57; V of Westoning w Tingrith 57-69. *49 Spensley Road, Westoning, Bedford.*

WRIGHT, Anthony Robert. b 49. Lanchester Poly Cov BA 70. St Steph Ho Ox 70. **d** 73 Buckingham for Ox **p** 74 Ox. C of St Mich AA Amersham-on-the-Hill 73-76; St Giles Reading 76-78; P-in-c of Prestwood Dio Ox from 78. *Prestwood Vicarage, Great Missenden, Bucks.* (Gt Missenden 2130)

WRIGHT, Antony John. b 31. **d** 79 **p** 80 Truro (APM). C of St Breoke Dio Truro from 79. *Gazebo, Tinner's Way, New Polzeath, Wadebridge, Cornwall, PL27 6UE.* (Trebetherick 3565)

WRIGHT, Canon Aubrey Kenneth William. AKC 43, BD 43, BA (2nd cl) 44. Linc Th Coll 43. **d** 44 Dover for Cant **p** 45 Croydon for Cant. C of H Trin Selhurst 44-47; Addington (in c of Spring Pk) 47-49; Min of All SS Conv Distr Spring Pk Croydon 49-57; V 57-58; Cheriton Street 58-63; R of W Wickham 63-72; RD of Croydon 66-72; Hon Can of Cant from 72; V of Ashford 72-81; RD of E Charing 72-81; R of Barham w Bishopsbourne and Kingston Dio Cant from 81. *Rectory, Barham, Canterbury, Kent, CT4 6PA.* (Barham 340)

WRIGHT, Canon Barry Owen. b 38. SOC 66. **d** 69 **p** 70 S'wark. C of Ascen Plumstead 69-74; Hon C of St Mary Welling Dio S'wark from 74; Hon Can of S'wark Cathl from 79. *73 Woodbrook Road, SE2 0PB.* (01-854 4509)

WRIGHT, Benjamin. ACT ThL 66. Wollaston Coll W Austr 62. **d** 64 **p** 65 Perth. C of Applecross 64-67; P-in-c of Narembeen 67-69; R 69-71; Moora 71-76; Alice Springs 76-80; Hon Can of Darwin Cathl 78-80; R of Scarborough Dio Perth from 80. *154 Northstead Street, Scarborough, W Australia 6019.* (341-3861)

WRIGHT, Bernard Holmes. b 12. **d** 64 **p** 65 Leic. C of St Barn Leic 64-69; V of H Trin Loughborough Dio Leic from 69. *Holy Trinity Vicarage, Loughborough, Leics.* (Loughborough 212466)

WRIGHT, Canon Brian Garnett O'Brien. St Pet Coll Ja 44. St Aug Coll Cant 59. **d** 46 **p** 47 Ja. C of Montego Bay 46-47; R of Buff Bay 48-51; Annotto Bay 49-51; Vaughansfield and H Trin Montego Bay 51-53; Vere 53-63; Liguanea Dio Ja from 63; Can of Ja from 76. *18 Worthington, Kingston 5, Jamaica, W Indies.* (092-70651)

WRIGHT, Cecil Leonard. St Jo Coll Auckld 49. **d** 51 **p** 52 Auckld. C of St Aid Remuera Auckld 51-53; P-in-c of Bay of Islands 53-54; V of Hokianga 54-58; Arch Hill 58-60; Bombay 60-71; Orewa 71-78; Hon C of Birkdale-Beachaven 79-80. *605 Glenfield Road, Auckland 10, NZ.*

WRIGHT, Charles Frederick Peter. b 16. Late Scho of Qu Coll Ox 2nd cl Cl Mods 37, BA (2nd cl Lit Hum) 39, 2nd cl Th 40, MA 42. Westcott Ho Cam. **d** 41 **p** 42 Sheff. C of Stocksbridge 41-43; Goole 43-47; Ecclesall 47-50; R of Brown Candover w Swarraton and Northington 50-54; V of Long Sutton 54-61; Welton St Mary 61-69; Lect Linc Th Coll 61-63; L to Offic Dio Linc from 69. *The Hermitage, Snelland, Lincoln, LN3 5AA.* (067-35 325)

WRIGHT, Charles George Lloyd. Angl Th Coll BC LTh 65. **d** 65 **p** 66 New Westmr. C of St Sav Vancouver 65-66; St Jas Vancouver Dio New Westmr from 66. *303 East Cordova Street, Vancouver 4, BC, Canada.*

WRIGHT, Charles Low. b 08. Keble Coll Ox BA 30. Ely Th Coll 30. **d** 31 **p** 32 Roch. C of St Luke New Brompton 31-37; St Mary Ch 37-41; PC of St Jas L Plymouth 41-43; C-in-c of St Martin's Conv Distr Barton Torquay 43-56; V of St Mary Magd Barnstaple 56-73; Perm to Offic Dio Ches from 78. *46 Shakespeare Drive, Cheadle, Chesh.*

WRIGHT, Charles Miers. b 12. St Pet Hall, OX BA 34, MA 38. Wycl Hall, Ox 34. **d** 36 **p** 37 Ex. C of Charles Plymouth 36-41; Stoke Damerel 41-44; V of Froxfield 44-48; R of Long Bredy w L Bredy 48-53; C-in-c of Puncknowle w Swyre 48-53; V of Leaton 53-63; V of Preston-Gobalds 53-63; R of Nymet Rowland w Coleridge 63-68; Burton Overy 68-73. *Brock Park, Chagford, Devon.*

WRIGHT, Charles Piachaud. b 05. Ball Coll Ox BA 27, BSc 28, MA 35. Linc Th Coll 48. **d** 49 **p** 50 Lon. C of St Mary Abbots Kens 49-54; V of St Mary Virg Isleworth 54-56; V of St Barn Kens 56-60; Miss Dio Lebom 60-66; L to Offic Dio Win 67-71; V of Lyddington w Stoke Dry and Seaton 71-78; Commiss Lebom from 71. *12 St Swithun Street, Winchester, Hants.*

WRIGHT, Christopher Joseph Herbert. b 47. St Cath Coll Cam BA 69, MA 73, PhD 77. Ridley Hall Cam 75. **d** 77 **p** 78 Roch. C of Tonbridge 77-81; w BCMS N India from 81. *c/o Bible Churchmen's Missionary Soc, 251 Lewisham Way, SE4 1XF.*

WRIGHT, Christopher Nigel. b 39. Magd Coll Cam 58. Kelham Th Coll 60. **d** 65 **p** 66 Ches. C of Ellesmere Port 65-69; Latchford 69-72; Gt Budworth 72-75; St Andr Wigan 75-77; V of New Springs Wigan 77-81; St Aid Bamber Bridge Dio Blackb from 81. *St Aidan's Vicarage, Longshaw Street, Bamber Bridge, Preston, Lancs.* (0772 35317)

WRIGHT, Clarence Samuel. Bp's Univ Lennox LST 34. **d** 34 Niag for Koot **p** 35 Blackb. C of St Pet Accrington 34-35; St Jo Evang Caterham Valley 35-37; I of Oyama 37-41; serving w CASF 41-45; Dio Tor 47-49; I of Bancroft 49-50; Aldershot 50-73. *Apt 1106, 5170 Lakeshore Road East, Ont., Canada.*

WRIGHT, Canon Clifford Nelson. b 35. K Coll Lon and Warm BD and AKC 59. **d** 60 **p** 61 St Alb. C of Stevenage 60-67; V of St Luke Camberwell 67-80; RD of Camberwell 75-80; Hon Can of S'wark Cathl 79-80; Can (Emer) from 80; Team R of Basingstoke Dio Win from 81. *Rectory, Church Street, Basingstoke, Hants, RG21 1QT.* (Basingstoke 26654)

WRIGHT, Colin George. b 39. St Jo Coll Auckld. **d** 70 **p** 71 Dun. C of St Paul's Cathl City and Dio Dun from 70; Chap Dun and Wakari Hosps 73-80; on leave. *9 Michie Street, Dunedin, NZ.* (Dunedin 69-467)

WRIGHT, Colin Trevor. b 33. Em Coll Sktn LTh 61. **d** 61 Edmon for Keew **p** 62 Keew. C of St Alb Pro-Cathl Kenora 61-63; Chap St Greg Miss Kitscoty 63-68; P-in-c of St Chad Edmon 68-70; I of St Mich AA Edmon 70-72; V of Birchwood 72-77; R of Swan River Dio Bran from 77. *Box 729, Swan River, Manit., Canada.*

WRIGHT, David Evan Cross. b 35. K Coll Lon and Warm BD (2nd cl) and AKC 64. **d** 65 **p** 66 Newc T. C of Morpeth 65-69; St Jas Benwell Newc T 69-70; Bushey 70-74; V of High Wych 74-77; R (w Gilston and Eastwick) 77-80; V of St Mary Marshalswick City and Dio St Alb from 80. *St Mary's Vicarage, Sherwood Avenue, Marshalswick, Herts.* (St Alban 51544)

WRIGHT, David Hanson. b 14. Hertf Coll Ox BA 36, MA 46. **d** 61 **p** 62 Man. C of Westhoughton 62-67; St Matt w St Barn Bolton 75-77; New Bury 77-78; Hon C of St Phil Bolton Dio Man from 79. *8 Moorside Avenue, Bolton, Lancs, BL1 6BE.* (Bolton 40121)

WRIGHT, David Henry. b 23. Keble Coll Ox BA 49. St Steph Ho Ox 52. **d** 54 **p** 55 Lon. C of St Silas Pentonville 54-57; V of St Clem Barnsbury 57-66; St Anne Wandsworth 66-73; R of Dunkeld w Birnam Dio St Andr from 73; P-in-c of St Columba Stanley 73-75; R of St Andr Strathtay (w St Marg Aberfeldy to 80) Dio St Andr from 75. *Rectory, Birnam, Dunkeld, Perthshire, PH8 0BL.* (Dunkeld 329)

WRIGHT, Derek Anthony. b 35. ACP 66. N-E Ordin Course 80. **d** 81 Dur. C of Bp Auckland Dio Dur from 81. *15 Warkworth Avenue, Bishop Auckland, Co Durham, DL14 6LU.*

WRIGHT, Eber Edward. b 1894. Lon Coll of Div 19. **d** 19

Chelmsf **p** 20 Llan. C of St Pet Upton Cross Forest Gate 19-20; St Paul Newport 20-23; St John Weston Bath 23-28; St Paul Carlton-in-the-Willows (in c of St Mich Porchester) 28-30; R of Burgh Castle 30-33; Strumpshaw w Bradeston 33-44; CF (EC) 40-41; V of St Mary Magd Albrighton 44-63; Surr 47-63. *32 Dudley Walk, Goldthorn Park, Wolverhampton, Staffs.*

WRIGHT, Canon Edgar Francis. b 14. Linc Th Coll 42. **d** 44 **p** 45 Linc. C of Grantham 44-51; V of Deeping St Nich 51-55; All SS w St Pet Stamford 55-79; Vice-Dean of Stamford 58-79; Surr 59-79; Can and Preb of Linc Cathl 62-79; Can (Emer) from 79; R of St Jo Bapt Stamford 72-79. *10 Rutland Terrace, Stamford, Lincs, PE9 2QD.* (Stamford 55718)

WRIGHT, Edward. b 1894. Lon Coll of Div 20. **d** 23 **p** 24 Bradf. C of St Mary Eastwood 23-26; Middleton 26-28; V of St Cleopas Toxt Pk 28-34; St Thos Preston 34-42; Ch Ch Mountsorrel 42-47; PC of Boulton 47-50; R of St Pet Thetford 50-52; PC of Brassington 52-55; R of Norton-in-Hales 55-60; L to Offic Dio Derby 60-63; Dio Bradf 64-75. *9 Flower Garth, Harrogate Road, Bradford, W Yorks, BD10 0QB.*

WRIGHT, Edward Denzil Chetwood. b 07. Magd Coll Ox BA 29, MA 32. Wells Th Coll 31. **d** 32 **p** 33 Wakef. C of Castleford 32-34; Felkirk (in c of Brierley) 34-38; V of Penistone w Midhope 38-42; Chap RNVR 42-46; Surr 39-42; V of Seamer w Cayton and E Ayton 46-62; Willoughton 62-72; R of Blyborough 62-72; Heapham 67-72; V of Corringham w Springthorpe 67-72; RD of Aslackhoe 63-64; Corringham 69-72. *The Yews, Brattleby, Lincoln, LN1 2SQ.*

WRIGHT, Edward Leslie. b 03. Cranmer Hall Dur 63. **d** 64 **p** 65 Chelmsf. C of Barkingside 64-65; St Chad Chadwell Heath 65-68; Basildon, Berks 68-70; C-in-c of Aldworth and of Ashamptead 70-74. *1 Church Lane, Ashampstead, Reading, RG8 8SL.*

WRIGHT, Edward Michael. b 37. St Cath S Ox BA 61, MA 65, Dipl Th 63. Cudd Coll 62. **d** 64 **p** 65 Lon. C of St Andr Willesden Green 64-68; Chap St Anne's Sch Nass 68-71; V of St Steph Lewisham 71-80; St Barn w St Paul City and Dio Ox from 80; Commiss Nass from 72. *Vicarage, St Barnabas Street, Oxford, OX2 6BG.* (Oxford 57530)

WRIGHT, Eric James. b 38. Univ of Syd LLB 59. **d** 74 **p** 78 C & Goulb. Hon C of Good Shepherd Curtin Dio C & Goulb from 74. *12 Pope Street, Hughes, ACT, Australia 2605.* (062-81 1608)

WRIGHT, Eric William. b 09. Wycl Hall Ox 70. **d** 70 **p** 71 York. C of Danby w Castleton Dio York from 70. *Westerdale Vicarage, Whitby, Yorks, YO21 2DT.* (Castleton 547)

WRIGHT, Evan Gilbert. b 03. Late Scho of St D Coll Lamp BA 31, BD 42. Univ of Liv MA 48. **d** 31 **p** 32 Ban. C of Llangefni w Tregaian 31-39; R of Llanfihangel Ysceifiog w Llanffinnan 39-45; V of Glanadda w Penrhosgarnedd 45-66; Sec Ban Dioc Conf 54-62; Prec and Can of Ban 55-57; Treas 57-62; Archd of Ban 62-73. *Maestirion, Caerhun, Bangor, Gwynedd.* (Bangor 52105)

WRIGHT, Francis Wilfred. St Jo Coll Auckld. **d** 61 **p** 62 Auckld. C of Whangarei Auckld 61-64; St Luke Mt Albert Auckld 64-66; L to Offic Dio Polyn 67-68; V of Waimate N 68-71; Birkenhead 71-77; Hon C of Devonport Dio Auckld from 77; Perm to Offic Dio Auckld from 78. *32 Merani Street, Belmont, Auckland 9, NZ.*

WRIGHT, Frank Robert Harris. **d** 49 **p** 50 NZ. C of Sydenham 49-52; V of Ross w S Westland 52-55; Rakaia 55-60; Ashburton 60-64; Amberley 64-73. *Leithfield, NZ.*

WRIGHT, Canon Frank Sidney. b 22. St Pet Hall Ox BA 45, 2nd cl Mod Hist 47, MA 47. Westcott Ho Cam 47. **d** 49 **p** 50 Dur. C of St Mich AA Bp Wearmouth 49-53; Barnard Castle 53-55; R of St Matt Stretford 55-66; Proc Conv Man 63-70; Can Res of Man 66-74; Sub-Dean 72-74; Can from 74; Tutor Univ of Man from 74. *184 Withington Road, Manchester, M16 8WA.* (061-881 1229)

WRIGHT, Frederick John. b 15. AKC 42. **d** 42 Stafford for Lich **p** 43 Lich. C of Brierley Hill 42-45; St John Walsall 45-49; V of Good Shepherd W Bromwich 49-54; R of Headless Cross 54-67; Romsley 67-80. *255 Birmingham Road, Bromsgrove, Worcs, B61 0EP.* (Bromsgrove 79521)

WRIGHT, Frederick John. b 21. **d** 70 **p** 71 Glouc. C of Ch Ch Glouc 70-73; Wotton-under-Edge 73-76; R of Woolstone w Gotherington and Oxenton Dio Glouc from 76; P-in-c of Kemerton Dio Glouc from 80. *Rectory, Malleson Road, Gotherington, Cheltenham, GL52 4EX.* (Bishop's Cleeve 2921)

WRIGHT, George Edward. b 13. Univ of Sheff MSc 36, MB, BCh 38, MD 70. **d** 55 **p** 56 Truro. Hon C of All SS Falmouth 55-68; Penwerris 68-74; Falmouth Dio Truro from 74. *60 Park Road, Falmouth, Cornw.* (Falmouth 312835)

WRIGHT, George Frederick. b 12. Kelham Th Coll 30. **d** 36 **p** 37 Lon. C of St Matthias Bethnal Green 36-38; Chiswick 38-43; St Alb Holborn 43-45; Perm to Offic Dio Lon 45-48; C of St Jas Gt Bethnal Green 48-52; V of St Clem w St Barn and St Matt Finsbury 52-62; E Markham w Askham 62-77; Perm to Offic Dio Southw from 77. *Rutland House, Low Street, Collingham, Newark, NG23 7NL.* (Newark 892876)

WRIGHT, Gerald Grattan. b 32. Delaware State Coll USA BSc 72. Ripon Hall Ox 73. **d** 76 **p** 77 Reading for Ox. C of St Pet Wolvercote City and Dio Ox from 76. *28 Davenant Road, Oxford, OX2 8BX.* (Oxford 52617)

WRIGHT, Graham. b 50. Oak Hill Coll 73. **d** 76 **p** 77 Pet. C of St Giles Northampton 76-79; The Resurr City and Dio Man from 79. *7 Derrett Close, Beswick, Manchester, M11 3SH.*

WRIGHT, Horace Edward. b 12. AKC 36. **d** 36 **p** 37 Chelmsf. C of Hornchurch 36-42; Wanstead 42-47; C-in-c of St Barn Hadleigh 47-56; Min 56-58; V 58-60; C of St Mark Marylebone 61-62; Leamington (in c of St Alb Mart) 62-65; V of Brailes w Winderton 65-78; Sutton-under-Brailes 76-78; RD of Shipston 68-78; Perm to Offic Dio St E from 78. *19 Henniker Road, Debenham, Stowmarket, Suff.* (Debenham 530)

WRIGHT, Canon Ignatius Clarence. St Pet Coll Ja. **d** 59 Ja **p** 61 Kingston for Ja. C of St Paul L Lon Ja 59-60; R 60-71; Vere Dio Ja from 71; Can of Ja from 76. *Rectory, Alley PO, Vere, Jamaica, W Indies.* (098-63238)

WRIGHT, James Charles. St Chad's Coll Regina LTh 52. **d** 52 **p** 53 Qu'App. C of St Geo Moose Jaw 52-53; I of Ituna and Bangor 53-54; Wadena 54-58; in Amer Ch 58-63; I of Broadview 63-65; Stoughton 65-68; Ridgeway 68-73; H Trin Hamilton Dio Niag from 73; Dom Chap to Bp of Niag 75-80. *c/o 9 Clarendon Avenue, Hamilton, Ont., Canada.* (416-388 2190)

WRIGHT, James Robert Murrell. Univ of Sask BEducn 59, BA 61. Em Coll Sktn LTh 64. **d** 60 **p** 61 Sktn. I of Battleford 60-65; L to Offic Dio Bran from 70. *McKay Indian Residential School, Dauphin, Manit, Canada.*

WRIGHT, John. b 49. Univ of Nottm BTh 73. Kelham Th Coll 69. **d** 73 **p** 74 Lich. C of St Mich Tividale 73-77. *c/o 8 Pennington House, Brades Rise, Brades Village, Oldbury, Warley, W Midl.*

WRIGHT, John Alastair. b 30. Cranmer Hall Dur. **d** 64 **p** 65 Blackb. C of Thornton-le-Fylde 64-67; Asst Chap Miss to Seamen Liv 67-68; Chap Walvis Bay 68-70; South Shields 70-72; L to Offic Dio Dur 71-72; V of St Luke Darlington 72-78; Commun Chap Darlington from 78. *8 Trinity Road, Darlington, Co Durham, DL3 7AS.* (Darlington 62714)

WRIGHT, John Douglas. b 42. Univ of Birm BSc 64. St Steph Ho Ox. **d** 69 **p** 70 Roch. C of St Mary Virg Swanley 69-74; Stockwell Green 74-79; V of St Jo Evang Leigh Dio Man from 79. *Vicarage, Gordon Street, Leigh, Lancs.* (Leigh 672868)

WRIGHT, Preb John Godwin. b 09. AKC 35. **d** 35 **p** 36 B & W. C of Chard 35-39; Twerton-on-Avon 39-42; R of N w S Barrow 42-51; PC of Lovington 42-51; PC of St Thos Wells 51-68; V (w Horrington 70-74) 68-74; Preb of Wells Cathl from 71. *24 Broderip, Cossington, Bridgwater, Somt, TA7 8LB.* (Chilton Polden 722671)

WRIGHT, John Gordon. b 27. St D Coll Lamp Phillips Scho 49, Sen Scho 50, BA (2nd cl Th) 50. Univ of Birm MA 51. **d** 52 Lich **p** 53 Stafford for Cant. C of St Mary and All SS Palfrey Walsall 52-54; St Giles Cam 55-57; Chap and Asst Master St Olave and St Sav Sch Orpington 57-73 and from 74; Perm to Offic at Gt Ilford 57-60 and 63-65; Hon C of Limpsfield w Titsey 60-62; Chap St Mary's Hosp Ilford 65-68; Hon C of Crayford 68-76; Chap St Olave's and St Saviour's Sch Orpington from 68. *3 Kingsmead Court, 123 London Road, Bromley, Kent.* (01-464 4029)

WRIGHT, John Harold. Univ of Dur BA 58. Ely Th Coll 58. **d** 61 **p** 62 Linc. C of Boston 61-64; Willesborough 64-68; R of Eastwell w Boughton Aluph 68-75; V of Westwell 68-75; Rolvenden Dio Cant from 75. *Rolvenden Vicarage, Cranbrook, Kent.* (Rolvenden 235)

WRIGHT, Canon John Richard Martin. b 12. Late Scho of St Jo Coll Dur BA (1st cl Hist) and Lightfoot Scho 34, Thompson Hist Pri 35, MA 37. **d** 35 **p** 36 S'wark. C of St Paul-at-Hook 35-38; Ch Ch Purley 38-41; Bury St Edms Cathl 41-45; R of Bradfield St Geo w Rushbrook 45-53; Barrow 53-76; V of St Mary Denham 53-76; RD of Thingoe 70-76; Hon Can of St E Cathl 74-76; Can (Emer) from 76; R of Edmundbyers w Muggleswick 76-80. *c/o Edmundbyers Rectory, Consett, Co Durham, DH8 9NQ.* (Edmundbyers 55634)

WRIGHT, Canon John Stafford. b 05. Late Scho of SS Coll Cam 2nd cl Cl Trip pt i 26, BA (2nd cl Th Trip pt i) 27, MA 31. Tyndale Hall Bris 27. **d** 28 **p** 29 Sarum. C of St Mary Weymouth 28-30; Lect and Tutor Tyndale Hall Clifton Bris 32-37; Vice-Prin 30-32; and 37-45; Prin 51-69; Sen Tutor Oak Hill Coll Southgate 45-51; Hon Can of Bris 67-69; Can (Emer) from 69. *6 Kensington Place, Bristol, BS8 3AH.* (0272-738143)

WRIGHT, John van Nostrand. b 42. Univ of W Ont BA 65. McGill Univ BD 69. Montr Dioc Th Coll LTh 69. **d** and **p** 69 Montr. C of St Jas Ap Montr 69-72; Ch Ch Guildf 72-74; Chap Trin Coll Sch Port Hope Tor 74-76; Prec of Ch Ch Cathl Montr 76-78; R of Pointe Claire 78-80; St Jas Ap City and Dio Montr from 80. *1439 Ste Catherine Street West, Montreal, PQ, Canada.* (514-849 7577)

WRIGHT, Canon Joseph de Pencier. Qu Univ Kingston. Bp's Coll Lennox LST 39. **d** 39 **p** 40 Tor. C of St Mary Virg Tor 39-41; St Clem Tor 41-44; Chap RCAF 44-46; R of St John Bowmanville 46-49; Barrie 49-54; St Cuthb Leaside Tor 54; Can of Tor from 64; P-in-c of King Dio Tor from 77. *266 Patricia Boulevard, King City, Ont, Canada.*

WRIGHT, Joseph James. b 16. AKC 39. Univ of Lon BD 39. Ely Th Coll 39. **d** 39 **p** 40 Lon. C of St Andr Bethnal Green 39-46; Prittlewell 46-49; Min of St Steph Conv Distr Prittlewell 49-50; V of Em Forest Gate (w St Pet Upton Cross from 62) Dio Chelmsf from 50; C-in-c of St Pet Upton Cross 60-62. *2b Margery Park Road, Forest Gate, E7.* (01-534 6329)

WRIGHT, Canon Kenneth William. b 13. Coll of Resurr Mirfield 37. **d** 39 Willesden for Lon **p** 40 Lon. C of H Redeem w St Phil Clerkenwell 39-42; St Pet Acton Green 42-45; All SS Boyne Hill (in c of St Paul Maidenhead) 45-50; PC of St Mary Stony Stratford 50-57; V of Fenny Stratford (w Water Eaton from 74) 57-75; R 75-79; C-in-c of L Brickhill 57-58; RD of Bletchley 63-70; Milton Keynes 70-72; C-in-c of Simpson 69-72; Hon Can of Ch Ch Ox 70-79; Can (Emer) from 79. *15 Station Road, Collingham, Newark, Notts, NG23 7RA.*

WRIGHT, Canon Kenyon Edward. b 32. Univ of Glas MA 53. Fitzw Coll Cam BA 55. Serampore Coll MTh 61. Wesley Ho Cam 53. Methodist Min 57-71; unified into Ch of N India by Bp of Calc 71; Publ Pr Dio Cov 72-74; Dir of Internat Ministry Cov Cathl 72-81; Can Res of Cov Cathl 74-81; Can (Emer) from 81; Gen Sec of Scot Chs Council & Warden of Scot Chs Ho Dunblane from 81. *Scottish Churches House, Dunblane, Perthshire.*

WRIGHT, Leonard John. b 24. Sarum Wells Th Coll 77. **d** 80 Sarum **p** 81 Sherborne for Sarum. C of Gillingham Dio Sarum from 80. *18 Sandilands Close, E Stour, Nr Gillingham, Dorset.*

WRIGHT, Leslie Frank. b 08. Coll of Resurr Mirfield 71. **d** 71 **p** 72 Pet. C of St Alb Mart Northn 71-78; L to Offic Dio Lich 78-81; Dio Ex from 81. *65 Pellew Way, Teignmouth, Devon.*

WRIGHT, Leslie Vandernoll. Trin Hall Cam BA (2nd cl Hist Trip pt i) 49, MA 54. Ridley Hall Cam 49. **d** 51 **p** 52 Guildf. C of H Trin Aldershot 51-53; H Trin Cambridge 53-57; V of St Nich Marston Ox 57-59; Stowe 61-65; Asst Chap Stowe Sch 61-65; Hd Master St Mich Prep Sch Five Oaks Jersey 65-66; Perm to Offic Dio Chich 66-68; Chap of Vevey 68-73; Hd Master St Geo Girls Sch Clarens, Montreux from 73. *St George's Girls School, Clarens, Montreux, Switzerland.*

WRIGHT, Martin Neave. b 37. K Coll Lon and Warm AKC (1st cl) 61. **d** 62 **p** 63 Pet. C of St Columba Corby 62-65; Industr Chap to Bp of Pet 65-71; Dean of Port Harcourt Christian Coun Project Nigeria 71-75; V of Port Harcourt 71-75; Exam Chap to Bp of Nig Delta 72-75; P-in-c of Honiley Dio Cov from 75; Wroxall Dio Cov from 75; Bp of Cov Chap for Industry from 75. *Honiley Rectory, Kenilworth, CV8 1NP.* (Haseley Knob 267)

WRIGHT, Michael. b 30. St Chad's Coll Dur BA (2nd cl Th) 55, Dipl Th 56. **d** 56 Grimsby for Cant **p** 57 Linc. C of St Aid New Cleethorpes 56-59; Skegness (in c of St Clem) 59-62; PC of St Mich Louth 62-68; V 68-73; R of Stewton 62-73; St Pet Warmsworth Dio Sheff from 73; Warden of Readers from 81. *Warmsworth Rectory, Warmsworth Road, Doncaster, S Yorks, DN4 0TW.* (Doncaster 853324)

WRIGHT, Michael Christopher. b 44. Univ of Leeds BA 65. Univ of Bradf MSc 75. Wells Th Coll. **d** 67 **p** 68 York. C of Dormanstown 67-69; L to Offic Dio Linc from 70; Dio Sheff from 73; Hon C of Crowle Dio Linc from 81. *17 Eastoft Road, Crowle, Scunthorpe, DN17 4LP.*

WRIGHT, Michael John. b 38. Chich Th Coll 59. **d** 62 Tewkesbury for Cant **p** 63 Glouc. C of Yate 62-65; Kirkbymoorside w Gillamoor (w Bransdale and Farndale from 72) 65-68; V 68-73; V of Bransdale w Farndale 68-72; Communications Officer Dio York 72-74; V of Ormesby 74-80; M of Abp's Coun on Evang 74-76; P-in-c of St Cuthb Middlesbrough Dio York from 81. *20 Tavistock Street, Middlesbrough, Cleve, TS5 6AX.* (0642 816247)

WRIGHT, Michael Matthew. b 32. St Edm Hall Ox BA (3rd cl Th) 55, MA 59. Wells Th Coll. **d** 57 **p** 58 Ox. C of High Wycombe 57-60; Tilehurst 60-62; CF from 62. *c/o Ministry of Defence, Bagshot Park, Bagshot, Surrey.*

WRIGHT, Nicholas Thomas. b 48. Ex Coll Ox BA 71, MA 75. Wycl Hall Ox 71. **d** 75 **p** 76 Ox. Research Fell (and Chap from 76) Mert Coll Ox 75-78; Fell and Chap Down Coll Cam 78-81; Asst Prof McGill Univ Montr from 81. *3420 University Street, Montreal, PQ, Canada.*

WRIGHT, Nigel Gordon McIver. **d** 80 **p** 81 Melb. C of St Chris Bentleigh 80-81; St Matt Glenroy Dio Melb from 81. *9 Hilda Street, Glenroy, Vic, Australia 3046.*

WRIGHT, Paul. b 54. AKC and BD 78. Ripon Coll Cudd 78. **d** 79 **p** 80 Roch. C of St Geo Beckenham Dio Roch from 79. *31 Clifford House, Calverley Close, Beckenham, Kent, BR3 1UH.*

WRIGHT, Peter. b 35. K Coll Lon and Warm AKC 61. **d** 62 Bp Gerard for York **p** 63 Sheff. C of Goole 62-67; V of Norton Woodseats Sheff 67-80; R of Aston w Aughton Dio Sheff from 80. *Aston Rectory, Worksop Road, Sheffield, Yorks, S31 0EB.* (Sheff 872272)

WRIGHT, Peter Gordon. St Aid Coll 55. **d** 57 **p** 58 Southw. C of Mansfield Woodhouse 57-61; V of Coddington w Barnby-in-the-Willows Dio Southw from 61. *Coddington Vicarage, Newark, Notts.* (Newark 3084)

WRIGHT, Peter Raymond. b 33. K Coll Lon and Warm AKC 56. **d** 59 **p** 60 Glouc. C of Berkeley 59-61; Cirencester 61-65; R of King's Stanley 65-79; V of St Osw Coney Hill City and Dio Glouc from 79. *St Oswald's Vicarage, Coney Hill, Gloucester, GL4 7LX.* (Gloucester 23618)

WRIGHT, Peter Reginald. b 34. Univ of Dur BA 60. Linc Th Coll 60. **d** 62 **p** 63 Chelmsf. C of L Ilford 62-65; St Aid Billingham 65-68; Team V 70-71; R 71-76; L to Offic Dio Dur 68-70; Chap Portsm Poly from 76. *c/o 30 Manners Road, Southsea, Hants.*

WRIGHT, Peter Westrope. b 24. Kelham Th Coll. **d** 48 Lon **p** 49 Stepney for Lon. C of St Barn Pimlico 48-50; All SS Sidley Bexhill 50-59; R of E Blatchington 59-73; C-in-c of St Mich Lewes 73-75; Team V Lewes Dio Chich from 75. *St Michael's Rectory, Lewes, Sussex.* (Lewes 4723)

WRIGHT, Philip. b 32. G and C Coll Cam BA 53, MA 57. Wells Th Coll. **d** 57 **p** 58 Dur. C of Barnard Castle 57-60; Heworth 60-64; PC of Tow Law 64-70; V of Tanfield 70-78; Ch Ch Gateshead Dio Dur from 78. *Christ Church Vicarage, Bewick Road, Gateshead, T & W, NE8 4DR.* (Gateshead 771840)

WRIGHT, Philip Arthur. b 08. MBE 54. St Andr Coll Whittlesford 36. **d** 38 **p** 39 Liv. C of St Mary Bootle 38-40; Saffron Walden 40-44; CF (EC) 44-45; CF (TA) 45-74; V of Littlebury 45-54; Chap Saffron Walden U 46-54; V of Woodford Bridge 54-65; Roxwell 65-78; Surr 61-78. *Queen Anne Cottage, Greensted, Ongar, Essex.* (Ongar 363901)

WRIGHT, Philip Nelson. St Jo Coll Auckld LTh 39. **d** 39 **p** 40 Auckld. C of St Barn Mt Eden Auckld 39-42; CF (NZ) 42-44; V of Paparoa 44-51; Fairlie 51-54; St Luke Ch Ch 54-64; Kaiapoi 64-68; Otaio w Blue Cliffs 68-75; C of Merivale Dio Ch Ch from 74; Chap St Geo Hosp Ch Ch from 75. *144 Merivale Lane, Christchurch 1, NZ.* (558-658)

WRIGHT, Phillip. b 35. St Aid Coll 59. **d** 61 Sheff **p** 62 Bp Gerard for York. C of Goldthorpe 61-65; V of St Jude Hexthorpe Doncaster 65-71; All SS Kettering Dio Pet from 71. *80 Pollard Street, Kettering, Northants.*

WRIGHT, Reginald Noel. Trin Coll Tor STh 49. **d** 48 **p** 49 Calg. C of Hanna 48-50; R 50-53; St Mark Calg 53-56; St John Moose Jaw 56-67; L to Offic Dio Qu'App 67-77. *130 Angus Crescent, Regina, Sask, Canada.* (306-522 4969)

WRIGHT, Canon Robert Benjamin de Blois. Bp's Univ Lennox LST 48. **d** 47 Niag for Alg **p** 48 Alg. C of St Paul Fort William 47-49; I of Thessalon 49-51; R of Neworo 51-55; Picton 55-64; Ch Ch Belleville Dio Ont from 64; Can of St Geo Cathl Kingston from 62; Exam Chap to Bp of Ont from 76. *44 Everett Street, Belleville, Ont, Canada.* (613-968 7717)

WRIGHT, Robert Charles. b 31. Roch Th Coll 65. **d** 67 **p** 68 Ripon. C of Manston 67-70; Moor Allerton 70-74; P-in-c of Terrington St John (w Tilney St Lawr from 76) 74-79; Walpole St Andr 74-75; Tilney Dio Ely 79-80; V from 80; Terrington St John Dio Ely from 80; Tilney St Lawr Dio Ely from 80. *Vicarage, Church Road, Terrington St John, Wisbech, Cambs, PE14 7SA.*

WRIGHT, Canon Robert Doogan. b 24. TCD BA 46. **d** 47 **p** 48 Connor. C of Carnmoney 47-49; St Jas Belf 49-51; St Matt Belfast (in c of St Columba Highfield) 51-53; C-in-c of Whiterock 53-57; I of Magheragall 57-64; R of St Mark Ballysillan 64-70; I of Carrickfergus Dio Connor from 70; Preb of Connor from 79. *Rectory, North Road, Carrickfergus, Co Antrim, N Ireland.* (Carrickfergus 63244)

WRIGHT, Robert Sheraton Gillard. b 50. Carleton Coll Ott BA 72. Wilfrid Laurier Univ Ont MA 78. Huron Coll Lon Ont MDiv 75. **d** 80 Ont. C of N Augusta Kitley Dio Ont from 80. *Anglican Rectory, Frankville, Ont, Canada, K0E 1H0.* (613-275 1058)

WRIGHT, Ven Royston Clifford. b 22. Univ of Wales BA 42. St Steph Ho Ox 43. **d** 45 **p** 46 Mon. C of Bedwas 45-47; St Jo Bapt Newport 47-49; Walton (in c of Miss of Good Shepherd) 49-51; Chap RNVR Mersey 50-51; RN 51-68; V of Blaenavon w Capel Newydd 68-74; RD of Pontypool 73-74;

R of Ebbw Vale 74-77; Can of Mon 74-77; Surr from 76; Archd of Mon 77; Newport from 77. *16 Stow Park Crescent, Newport, Gwent, NPT 4HD.* (Newport 64919)

WRIGHT, Samuel John. b 18. St D Coll Lamp BA 50. **d** 52 **p** 53 St A. C of Rhosddu 52-55; Sutton St Geo 55-58; V of St Pet (w St Matt from 69) Birkenhead 58-74; C-in-c of St Matt Birkenhead 67-69; Chap St Cath Hosp Birkenhead from 64; C-in-c of St Mary w St Paul Birkenhead 69-74; St Jo Evang Birkenhead 71-74; R of Birkenhead Priory 74-75; V of Marbury Dio Ches from 75. *Marbury Vicarage, Whitchurch, Salop.* (Whitchurch 3758)

WRIGHT, Simon Christopher. b 44. K Coll Lon and Warm AKC 67. **d** 68 Southn for Win **p** 69 Win. C of Bitterne Pk 68-72; Kirkby 72-74; V of St Anne Wigan 74-79; Dioc Dir of Ordinands and Dom Chap to Abp of York from 79. *Bishopthorpe, York, YO2 1QE.* (York 707021)

WRIGHT, Thomas Frederick. Hur Coll Ont LTh 22. **d** 22 **p** 23 Hur. I of Merlin 22-23; C of All SS Windsor 23-25; St Luke Yarmouth Heights 25-26 (all in Ont); in Amer Ch 26-35; Perm to Offic (Col Cl Act) at St Aug Bexhill 35-40; C-in-c of St Richard Conv Distr Three Bridges 40-44; Chap RAF 44-54; I of Wembley 54-56; Canmore 56-67. *Lang Road, RR1, Ganges, Salt Spring Island, BC, Canada.*

WRIGHT, Thomas Stephen. b 31. Fitzw Ho Cam BA 54, MA 58. Bps' Coll Cheshunt 56. **d** 57 **p** 58 St Alb. C of Bp's Stortford 57-62; St Jas Cathl Bury St Edm 62-64; R of Hartest w Boxted Dio St E from 64; Hon Chap to Bp of St E from 66; Hon Min Can of St E Cathl from 67; RD of Sudbury from 70; C-in-c of Somerton Dio St E from 71. *Hartest Rectory, Bury St Edmunds, Suff, IP29 4DH.* (Hartest 259)

WRIGHT, Timothy John. b 41. K Coll Lon and Warm AKC and BD (2nd cl) 63. **d** 64 **p** 65 Ox. C of Highfield Ox 64-68; Asst Chap Worksop Coll 68-71; Chap Malvern Coll 71-77; Ho Master and Asst Chap from 77. *1 The College, Malvern, Worcs.*

WRIGHT, Tom. Ch Coll Hobart. **d** 39 **p** 40 Kalg. C of Leonora 39-40; R 40-44; Norseman 44-52; Beverley 52-56; St Hilda Perth 57-71; Rosalie 71-77; Perm to Offic Dio Perth from 77. *13 Eaton Court, 38 Scarborough Beach Road, N Perth, W Australia 6006.* (444-5916)

WRIGHT, Trevor John. Univ of Otago BSc 63, BD 66. Univ of Man PhD 73. **d** 65 Bp McKenzie for Wel **p** 66 Wel. C of All SS Palmerston N 65-69; Gisborne 69; Perm to Offic Dio Man 69-73; Tutor Macquarie Univ Syd 73-76; Lect St Jo Coll Morpeth from 77; Vice Warden from 81. *St John's College, Morpeth, NSW, Australia 2321.*

WRIGHT, William Easton. b 20. Linc Th Coll 52. **d** 53 **p** 54 Ex. C of Petrockstowe w Petersmarland 53-56; R of Farway w Northleigh and Southleigh 56-69; Offwell w Widworthy (w Cotleigh, Farway, Northleigh and Southleigh from 72) Dio Ex from 69; C-in-c of Cotleigh 69-72; RD of Honiton 65-68. *Offwell Rectory, Honiton, Devon, EX14 9SB.* (Wilmington 480)

WRIGHT, William Edwin. St Jo Coll Morpeth ACT ThL 56. **d** and **p** 57 C & Goulb. C of St Paul Canberra 57; Adaminaby 58-59; R 59-61; Boorowa 61-67; R of Marulan 69-73; Gundagai Dio C & Goulb from 73. *Rectory, Gundagai, NSW, Australia.* (069-44 1063)

WRIGHT, William Henry Laurence. b 11. Em Coll Cam BA 35, MA 45. **d** 37 **p** 38 Bris. C of Ch Ch Clifton 37-38; Bishopston 38-40; Chap RAFVR 40-46; P-in-c of Gretna and Langholm 46; Chap Loretto Sch Musselburgh 47-71; R of Campbeltown 71-79. *West Manse House, Kilcrennan, Argyll.*

WRIGHT, Canon William Hutchinson. b 27. St Jo Coll Dur BA 50. **d** 55 **p** 56 Sheff. C of Kimberworth and Asst Industr Missr Dio Sheff 55-59; Industr Missr Dio Dur 59-81; L to Offic Dio Dur from 59; Hon Can of Dur from 72. *109 Bishopton Road, Stockton-on-Tees, Teesside.* (Stockton 68817)

✠ **WRIGHT, Most Rev William Lockridge.** Trin Coll Tor LTh 27, DD (*jure dig*) 41. DCL (Lennox) 53. Wycl Coll Tor DD 56. Montr Dioc Coll DD 57. Huron Coll DD 57. Laurentian Univ Ont Hon LLD 64. **d** 26 **p** 27 Ont. C of St Geo Tor 26-28; I of Tweed 28-32; C of Ch Ch Cathl Hamilton 32-36; R of St Geo Tor 36-40; St Luke Pro-Cathl Sault Ste Marie 40-44; Dean of Alg 40-44; Cons Ld Bp of Alg in Sault Ste Marie Cathl 30 May 44 by Abp of Hur; Bps of Moos; Niag; Ott; Ont; and Michigan; Bp Suffr of Tor; and Abp de Pencier: Elected Metrop of Prov of Ont 55; res 74. *Box 637, Sault Ste Marie, Ont., Canada.* (705-256-2560)

WRIGHT, Ven William Richmond. Bp's Coll Lennox. **d** 43 **p** 44 Ott. C of Ch Ch Cathl Ott 43-45; I of Petawawa 45-50; C of St John Ott 50-52; I of Ellwood Leitrim and Hawthorn Ott 52-62; Pembroke 62-70; St Richard Ott 70-79; Archd of Lanark 67-70; Dom Chap to Bp of Ott from 71; Can of Ott 71-73; Archd of Ott W 73-79; New Edin and Govt Relns from 79; Exam Chap to Bp of Ott from 79; I of St Bart City and Dio Ott from 79. *125 MacKay Street, Ottawa, K1M 2B4, Ont, Canada.*

WRIGHTON, George Richard. b 11. Wells Th Coll 66. **d** and **p** 67 Sarum. C of Westbury 67-68; C-in-c of Ebbesbourne Wake w Fifield Bavant and Alvediston 68-70; V 70-72; V of Winterbourne Zelstone w Thomson, Anderson and Kingston 72-75. *Westbourne Cottage, Selworthy Green, Minehead, Somt.*

WRIGHTSON, Bertram Pilcher. Univ of Melb BA 49 MA 50. BD (Lon) 59. Ridley Coll Melb ACT ThL (2nd cl) 45. **d** 46 Melb for Bunb **p** 47 Bunb. C of H Trin Coburg 46-48; Melb Dioc Centre 48-50; R of Harvey 50-57; C of Denmark 57; Boyup Brook 57-58; P-in-c of Williams 58-60; Chap of Groote Eylandt 60-64; C of Northam 64-67 and 71-72; R of Kellerberrin 67-71; C of Northam 71-72; P-in-c of Murchison 73; Chap St Geo Hosp Mt Lawley 74-75; R of Exmouth 75-76; Perm to Offic Dio Perth from 77; Dio Bunb from 78. *136 Valentine Road, Binningup, Bunbury, W Australia 6230.* (097-201085)

WRIGLEY, Canon Philip Arthur. b 07. Late Exhib of St Jo Coll Dur LTh 33, BA 34. St Aid Coll 29. **d** 34 **p** 35 Man. C of St John Farnworth 34-39; V of St Gabr Middleton Junction 39-49; R of St Aid Man 49-54; V of Farnworth 54-69; Hon Can of Man 64-69; Can (Emer) from 69; RD of Farnworth 66-69; Proc Conv Man 66-69; R of Stoke Bliss w Kyre Wyard 69-72; C of All SS Worc 72-76; Middleton 76-80. *1 Highwell Avenue, Bromyard, Herefs, HR7 4EL.* (Bromyard 83725)

WRIGLEY, William Vickers. b 10. K Coll Cam 3rd cl Hist Trip pt i 31, BA (3rd cl Th Trip pt i) 32, MA 36. Wells Th Coll. **d** 33 **p** 35 Leic. C of St Mary Hinckley 33-35; Newport w Longford 35-37; Queenstown 38-46; CF (S Afr) 40-45; R of Barkly E w Dordrecht and Indwe 46-48; Walmer 48-52; C of Northallerton 52-53; R of Hawnby w Old Byland 53-57; V of Hutton Buscel 57-70; Wykeham 57-70; Old Malton 70-75; C of Rillington (in c of Thorpe Bassett) Dio York from 76; Actg RD of Buckrose 77-80. *Beech House, Low Moorgate, Rillington, N Yorks, YO17 8JW.* (Rillington 513)

WROTH, Malcolm Gregory. b 46. Univ of W Austr BA 74. Trin Coll Melb BD 76. **d** 77 **p** 78 Perth. On leave 77-78; C of Mosman Pk 78-80; R of Kellerberrin-Tammin Dio Perth from 80. *3 Sewell Street, Kellerberrin, W Australia 6410.* (090-45 4184)

WU, Samuel. Philippine Christian Colls BA 53. Gen Th Sem NY STB 55. **d** 54 **p** 55 Philippines [f in Amer Ch] V of Ch of Good Shepherd Kowloon Dio Hong from 65. *Church of the Good Shepherd, Kianghsi Street, Kowloon, Hong Kong.* (3-658437)

WU, Theodore Sheng-te. Yenchung Univ Peking 33. **d** 41 **p** 42 Hong. Asst Master Dioc Boys' Sch and LPr Dio Hong 42-78. *100 True Light Bldg, 20/F Flat F, Third Street, Sai Ying Poon, Hong Kong.*

WYATT, Alfred Henry. b 04. Univ of Lon Dipl Th 32. AKC (2nd cl) 33. **d** 33 **p** 34 Roch. C of Ch Ch Dartford 33-35; Ramsey St Mary (in c of Pondsbridge) 35-36; St John March 36-39; V of St Mary Whittlesey w Angle Bridge 39-48; R of Exton 48-50; Org Sec Midl Distr SPCK from 50; C of Radcliffe-on-Trent 51-56; Chap Saxondale Hosp 51-56; C of Beeston 56-58; V of Flintham w Kneeton 58-73; RD of Binham 68-73. *13 Horsegate, Whittlesey, Peterborough, PE1 1JP.*

WYATT, Colin. b 27. Ex Coll Ox BA 54, MA 55. BD (2nd cl) Lon 62. Tyndale Hall Bris. **d** 63 Bp Gelsthorpe for Southw for Sarum **p** 64 Sarum. C of Radipole 63-66; Southborough 66-67; V of Tetsworth 67-72; P-in-c of Adwell w S Weston 68-72; Lect at Bible Training Inst Glas 72-74; R of Hurworth 74-79; C-in-c of Dinsdale w Sockburn 74-76; R 76-79; R of Sadberge Dio Dur from 79. *Rectory, Sadberge, Darlington, Co Durham, DL2 1RP.* (Dinsdale 332269)

WYATT, David Stanley Chadwick. b 36. Fitzw Ho Cam BA 59, MA 71. Ely Th Coll 59. **d** 61 **p** 62 Man. C of Rochdale 61-63; Dom Chap to Bp of Man 63-68; R of St Paul w Ch Ch Salford Dio Man from 68; Exam Chap to Bp of Man 72-76. *St Paul's Church House, Ellor Street, Salford, M6 5AN.* (061-736 8868)

WYATT, Canon George Murray. Hur Coll LTh 48. **d** 47 **p** 48 Hur. C of St Jas Stratford 47-48; R of Blyth 48-50; St Alb Pro-Cathl Kenora 50-56; Sec Keew Synod 51-53; Can of Keew 55-56; R of All SS Niag Falls 56-62; Grace Ch St Cath 62-73; Stoney Creek Dio Niag from 73; Hon Can of Niag from 70. *Rectory, Stoney Creek, Ont., Canada.* (416-662 1412)

WYATT, Norman Dick. b 01. St Aid Coll 35. **d** 36 **p** 37 Glas. C of H Trin Paisley 36-40; St Ninian Pollokshields (in c of St Mark Kinning Pk) Glas 40-45; C-in-c of St Mark Kinning Pk Glas 45-46; P-in-c of St Gabr Govan 46-51; R of St Jas Springburn Glas 51-56; R of St Pet Peterhead 56-64; Ch Ch Dalbeattie 64-70. *24 Gordon Crescent, Newton Mearns, Glasgow.* (041-639 4201)

WYATT, Peter John. b 38. Kelham Th Coll 58. **d** 64

Southn for Win **p** 65 Win. C of Stoneham N w Bassett 64-68; Brixham 68-69; R of Dominica 69-75; Kabwe and N Midl 76-78; P-in-c of Ettington 78-79; Butlers Marston w Pillerton Hersey and Pillerton Priors 79; V of Butlers Marston and The Pillertons w Ettington Dio Cov from 79. *Ettington Vicarage, Stratford-on-Avon, Warws.* (Ettington 225)

WYATT, Royston Dennis. b 36. FRICS 67. Sarum Wells Th Coll 74. **d** 77 Sarum **p** 78 Sherborne for Sarum. (NSM). C of Canford Magna Dio Sarum from 77. *64 Floral Farm, Canford Magna, Wimborne, Dorset.*

WYBREW, Canon Hugh Malcolm. b 34. Qu Coll Ox BA (2nd cl Th) 58, MA 62. Linc Th Coll 59. **d** 60 **p** 61 S'wark. C of St Jo Evang E Dulwich 60-64; Tutor St Steph Ho Ox 65-66; Chap 66-71; Chap at Bucharest, Sofia and Belgrade 71-73; V of Pinner Dio Lon from 73; Commiss Gibr 78-80; Gibr in Eur from 80; Hon Can of Gibr from 78; M Gen Syn Lon from 80. *Vicarage, Church Lane, Pinner, Middx, HA5 3AA.* (01-866 3869)

WYER, Keith George. b 45. AKC and BD 71. St Aug Coll Cant 71. **d** 72 **p** 73 Birm. C of Moseley 72-76; Chap (RNR) 73-77; C of Walsall 76-77; Min (in c of St Martin's) 77-79; Perm to Offic Dio Bris from 80; Chap Colston's Sch & RNR Bris from 80. *2 Fry's Close, Stapleton, Bristol, BS16 1AS.* (Bris 651697)

WYERS, George Harry. b 1893. Keble Coll Ox BA (*sc* Th) 21, MA 24. Univ of Lon BA 24, 2nd cl Med and Mod Lang 30. Cudd Coll 21. **d** 21 **p** 22 Ox. C of H Trin Ox 21-23; Marston Oxon 23-25; Chap and Lect St Paul's Coll Cheltm 25-53; R of Bradenham 53-55; C of Chalfont St Pet 56-57. *Picton Lodge, Marsham Way, Gerrard's Cross, Bucks.*

WYLAM, Canon Arthur Reginald Batchelor. b 07. Late Scho of Or Coll Ox BA (3rd cl Mod Hist) 28, MA 35. Cudd Coll 28. **d** 30 **p** 31 Glouc. C of Hampnett w Stowell and Northleach 30-34; St Jo Bapt Pet 34-36; V of Mundham w Seething 36-43; R of Haddiscoe w Toft Monks 43-53; Witton w Brundall and Bradeston 53-63; Gt w L Snoring 63-73; Hon Can of Nor 70-73; Hon Can (Emer) from 73. *The Old Rectory, North Barsham, Walsingham, Norf.* (Walsingham 226)

WYLAM, John. b 43. K Coll Lon and Warm AKC 66. **d** 67 **p** 68 Derby. C of St Bart Derby 67-70; M SSF 70-73; Seaton Hirst (in c of St Andr) 74-77; V of St Silas Byker City and Dio Newc T from 77. *196 Heaton Park Road, Newcastle upon Tyne, NE6 5AP.* (Newc T 655353)

WYLD, Peter Houldsworth. b 20. Magd Coll Ox BA and MA 53. Cudd Coll 53. **d** 55 **p** 56 Lich. C of Stafford 55-60; St Geo Luanshya 60-61; R 61-65; w USPG 66-71; Gen Editor 71-74; Dir C of E Enquiry Centre 74-78; C of Hatfield 78-79; R of Appleton Dio Ox from 79. *Appleton Rectory, Abingdon, Oxon.* (Cumnor 2458)

WYLLIE, James Alistair. b 48. Univ of Natal BA 69. St Chad's Coll Dur 73. **d** 73 **p** 74 Natal. C of St Alphege Pmbg 73-81; R of Northlands Dio Natal from 81. *6 Blackwood Place, Northlands, Natal, S Africa.*

WYMAN, Arthur Howard. b 23. Kelham Th Coll 46. **d** 50 **p** 51 Heref. C of St Mary Magd Bridgnorth 50-52; St Geo Southall 52-58; C-in-c of Uxbridge Moor 58-71; V of St Pet Harrow 71-80; R of Belton w Osgathorpe Dio Leic from 80. *Rectory, Belton, Loughborough, Leics, LE12 9UN.* (Coalville 222266)

WYNBURNE, John Paterson Barry. b 48. St Jo Coll Dur BA 70. Wycl Coll Tor MDiv 72. Ridley Hall Cam 72. **d** 73 Willesden for Lon **p** 74 Lon. C of Gt Stanmore 73-76; Chap of Ch of Resurr Bucharest w Sofia 76-77; C of St Mart Dorking 78-80; V of Send Dio Guildf from 80. *Send Vicarage, Woking, Surrey.* (Guildford 222193)

WYNBURNE, Victor Barry. b 06. MBE 49. TCD BA 33, MA 37. Wycl Coll Tor 24. **d** 33 **p** 34 Glouc. C of St Jas Glouc 33-36; Asst Chap of St John's Pro-Cathl Buenos Aires and Chap of Flores 36-39; C of St Jas Bermondsey 39-40; Gt Yarmouth 40-43; R of Winfarthing 43-46; Archd of Seychelles and Sub-Dean of St Paul's Cathl Mahé 47-50; R of Woodchurch Kent 50-58; Chap at The Hague Holland 58-68; R of Ickenham 68-77; Perm to Offic Dio Ex from 77. *7 River View Close, Colyton, Devon, EX13 6PX.* (Colyton 52906)

WYNDHAM, John Hebden. Moore Th Coll Syd ACT ThL 60. **d** 61 Syd **p** 61 Bp Kerle for Syd. C of Ryde 61; St Paul (in c of St Mich) Syd 62; Ceduna 63-64; Miss Chap Minnipa Miss 63-64; P-in-c of Tarcoola 64-66; R of Norseman 66-67; CF (Austr) 67-69; C-in-c of Northmead 69-72; R of Milton 72-73; L to Offic Dio Syd 74 and 77; C of Darlinghurst 75-76; C-in-c of Belfield Dio Syd from 77. *72 Burwood Road, Belfield, NSW, Australia.* (642-1705)

WYNES, Michael John. b 33. K Coll Lon and Warm AKC 57. **d** 58 **p** 59 St Alb. C of Gt Berkhamsted 58-62; St Matt St Leonards-on-Sea 62-65; Wilton 65-68; R of Berkley w Rodden 68-77; V of Westbury-sub-Mendip w Easton Dio B & W from 77; Priddy Dio B & W from 77. *Westbury-sub-Mendip Vicarage, Wells, Somt.* (Priddy 293)

WYNGARD, Ernest Clive. b 30. Univ of Leeds BA 52. Coll of Resurr Mirfield 52. **d** 54 **p** 55 Dur. C of Bp Wearmouth 54-59; Winlaton (in c of High Spen) 59-61; PC of Castleside 61-67; V of Beamish 67-80; RD of Lanchester 74-80; V of St Giles City and Dio Dur from 80. *St Giles Vicarage, Gilesgate, Durham.* (Durham 64241)

WYNN, Baden Charles. b 34. Moore Coll Syd 72. **d** 74 **p** 75 Armid. V of Baradine 74-77; C of St Pet Cathl Armid 77-81. *c/o 417 Ann Street, Brisbane, Australia.*

WYNN, Ernest Brian. Moore Th Coll Syd ACT ThL 60. **d** 61 Syd **p** 61 Bp Kerle for Syd. C of Narrabeen 61-64; P-in-c of St Mark's Provisional Distr Sylvania 64-68; C-in-c of Matraville 68-72; Ermington w Rydalmere Dio Syd 72-74; R from 74. *471 Kissing Point Road, Ermington, NSW, Australia.* (85-6477)

WYNN-EVANS, James Naylor. b 34. Magd Coll Ox BA 55. Linc Th Coll. **d** 59 **p** 60 Sheff. C of Goole 59-62; Hatfield 62-63; Chap HM Borstal Hatfield 62-67; C-in-c of Dunscroft 63-67; C of St Columba Edin 67-69; R of St Marg City and Dio Edin from 69; Chap to Bp of Edin 67-75; P-in-c of St Phil City and Dio Edin from 76. *1 Gayfield Place, Edinburgh, EH7 4AB.* (031-556 1566)

WYNNE, Alan John. b 46. Mansfield Coll Ox BA (Th) 71, MA 75. St Steph Ho Ox 68. **d** 71 **p** 72 St Alb. C of St Pet Watford 71-74; Chap Liddon Ho Lon 74-75; Chap and Asst Master Abp Tenison's Gr Sch Kennington Lon from 75. *Archbishop Tenison's School, Kennington, SE11.* (01-735 6437)

WYNNE, Canon Edward. St D Coll Lamp BA 37. **d** 39 **p** 40 St A. C of Brymbo 39-42; Welshpool 42-47; Lect of Bolton 47-49; V of Chatburn 49-54; V of St Gabr Blackb 54-81; RD of Blackb 70-79; Hon Can of Blackb from 77. *c/o 641 Whalley New Road, Blackburn, Lancs.* (Blackburn 48430)

WYNNE, Geoffrey. b 41. K Coll Lon and Warm BD and AKC 64. BSc (Lon) 75. **d** 66 **p** 67 Lich. C of Wolverhampton 66-70; Chap Wolverhampton Poly from 70; Dir of Ords Dio Lich from 76. *1 Compton Park, Wolverhampton, WV3 9DU.* (Wolverhampton 712051)

WYNNE, James Arthur Hill. b 13. **d** 47 **p** 48 Clogh. C of Kilmore Drumsnatt and Tydavnet 47-50; St Hilda Darlington 50-52; V of St Oswin S Shields 52-67; Coundon Dio Dur from 67. *Coundon Vicarage, Collingwood Street, Bishop Auckland, Co Durham, DL14 8LG.* (Bp Auckld 603312)

WYNNE, Reginald Noel. Bp's Coll Calc 52. **d** 55 Bp Hollis **p** 56 Bp Sarjant. Ch of S India 56-62; V of St Steph Bandra Bom 62-66; Regr Bom 63-66; P-in-c of Hillcrest 67-68; Keith 68-72; Asst Chap Pulteney Gr Sch Dio Adel from 73. *5 Chardonnay Crescent, Wynn Vale, S Australia 5127.*

WYNNE, Preb Richard William Maurice. b 19. TCD BA 44, Div Test 44, MA 68. **d** 44 **p** 45 Dub. C of Clontarf 44-49; Rathmines 49-52; I of Delgany 52-58; Monkstown 58-78; Preb of St Patr Cathl Dub from 76; V of St Ann City and Dio Dub from 78; St Steph City and Dio Dub from 78. *17 St Mary's Road, Ballsbridge, Dublin 4, Irish Republic.* (Dublin 600852)

WYNNE, Ronald Charles. Selw Coll Cam BA 38, 2nd cl Th Trip pt i 39, MA 42. Bp's Coll Calc. **d** 42 **p** 43 Colom. C of St Steph Trincomalee 42-43; P-in-c 43-45; C of Basingstoke (in c of All SS) 46-50; All SS Fleet 50-56; V of Lockerley w E Dean 56-60; C of St Geo Cathl Kingstown 61-62; R 62-67; C of St Carantoc's Miss Francistown 68-70; Miss at Etsha, Botswana from 70. *Box 130, Maun, Botswana.*

WYNNE, Thomas Francis. b 10. St Deiniol's Libr Hawarden 72. **d** 73 **p** 74 St A (APM). C of Llanrhos 73-80. *Falcon House, Roumania Drive, Craig-y-Don, Llandudno, Gwyn.*

WYNNE, Trevor. b 35. St Mich AA Coll Llan 72. **d** 74 **p** 75 Llan. C of Llangynwyd 74-77; V of Trealaw Dio Llan from 77. *Vicarage, Trealaw, Rhondda, CF40 2UF.* (Tonypandy 2147)

WYNNE-GREEN, Roy Rowland. Chich Th Coll 67. **d** 70 Lanc for Blackb **p** 71 Blackb. C of Fleetwood (in c of St Nich) 70-73; Centr Torquay 73-75; Chap of SW Hosp and Asst Chap St Thos Hosp Lon from 75. *c/o St Thomas' Hospital, SE1.* (01-928 9292)

WYNNE-JONES, Dyfed. b 56. Univ of Cardiff DTh 79. Coll of St Mich AA Llan 77. **d** 79 **p** 80 Ban. C of Porthmadog Dio Ban from 79. *2 Marine Terrace, Porthmadog, Gwyn, LL49 9BL.*

WYNNE-JONES, Nicholas Winder. b 45. Late Exhib of Jes Coll Ox BA 67, MA 72. Selw Coll Cam 70. **d** 72 Lon **p** 73 Kens for Lon. C of All S Langham Place 72-75; Chap Stowe Sch from 75. *Stowe School, Buckingham.*

WYNNE-OWEN, Canon David. b 1899. St Chad's Coll Dur BA 21, Dipl Th 22. **d** 22 **p** 23 Lich. C of Wem 22-31; Edgemond 31-35; Stoke-on-Trent 35-37; R of St John Wednesbury 37-41; C of Wybunbury 41-46; Chap Commun of Jes of Nazareth Westcote 46-47; M SSF from 47; Novice Master SSF 54-57; Min 57-67; Min Gen 67-70; Can and Preb of Sarum 66-70; Can (Emer) from 70; Min in Amer Prov of SSF from 70. *Little Portion Friary, Mount Sinai, New York 11766, USA.*

WYSS, Francis. b 32. Open Univ BA 72. Wells Th Coll 68. **d** 59 Dar-S (RC) **p** 60 Gwelo (RC). Rec into Angl Commun by Bp of Matab 69. C of St Steph w St Thos Shepherd's Bush 70; C-in-c of St Mich and St Geo Conv Distr White City Hammersmith 71-72; Stirchley 72-74. *Blumenstrasse-34, CH-4900 Langenthal, Switzerland.* (063-2206 91)

X

XABA, Canon Ephraim. Isandhlwana Th Coll. **d** 31 **p** 33 Zulu. C of Mafitleng 31-36; Vryheid 36-47; Dir of Inhlwathi Miss 47-52; Mahashini 52-61; Can of Pro-Cathl Vryheid 43-62; Can (Emer) from 62. *519 Inhlwathi Private Bag, PO Nongoma, Zululand.*

XABA, Misael. St Bede's Coll Umtata. **d** 67 **p** 69 Zulu. C of St D Vryheid 67-70; P-in-c of All SS Vumanhlamvu Miss 70-73; Mahashini Miss Dio Zulu from 74. *PB 526, Nongoma, Zululand.*

XULU, Canon Edmund Mzonjani Thokozani. St Pet Coll Alice 62. **d** 64 **p** 65 Zulu. P Dio Zulu; Can of Zulu from 79. *Box 67, Nongoma, Zululand.*

XUNDU, Mcebisi Osman. St Bede's Coll Umtata 57. **d** 59 **p** 60 St John's. P Dio St John's 59-77. *PO St Cuthbert's, Transkei, S Africa.*

Y

YACOMENI, Peter Frederick. b 34. Worc Coll Ox BA 58, MA 61. Wycl Hall Ox 58. **d** 60 **p** 61 S'wark. C of New Malden w Coombe 60-64; St Jas L Bethnal Green 64-68; V of St Luke w Ch Ch Bris 68-75; Bishopsworth Dio Bris from 75. *Bishopworth Vicarage, Fernsteed Road, Bristol, BS13 8HE.* (Bris 642734)

YALLOP, John. b 47. Oakhill Coll BA (Th) 79. **d** 79 **p** 80 Sheff. C of Brinsworth Dio Sheff from 79. *25 Kynance Crescent, Brinsworth, Rotherham, S Yorks, S60 5EW.*

YAMBIO, Lord Bishop of. *See* Dotiro, Right Rev Yeremaya Kufuta.

YANDELL, Canon Owen James. b 20. Trin Hall Cam BA (2nd cl Hist Trip pts i and ii) 42, MA 46. Wycl Hall Ox 42. **d** 44 **p** 45 Portsm. C of Farlington 44-47; Bath Abbey 47-50; V of Langley Birm 50-57; Stoneycroft 57-67; St John Birkdale 67-73; Sec Dioc Bd of Educn Liv and Dir of Educn Dio Liv from 73; R of Sefton Dio Liv from 73; Can of Liv Cathl from 76; Surr from 73. *Rectory, Glebe End, Sefton, Merseyside, L29 6YB* (051-531 7021)

YANNY, Gebrail. b 49. **d** 77 Egypt. d Dio Egypt. *c/o Box 1427, Cairo, Egypt.*

YAP, Foh Yu. d 79 **p** 80 Sabah. P Dio Sabah. *PO Box 17, Sandakan, Sabah, Malaysia.*

YAPP, Kenneth Gordon. BD (Lon) 63. Moore Th Coll Syd ACT ThL 63. **d** 63 **p** 64 Syd. C of Dapto 63-65; CMS Miss Far East 67-74; V of All SS Jakarta 74-80. *c/o 93 Bathurst Street, Sydney, Australia 2000.*

YARKER, Canon Francis Bospidnick. b 12. Univ of Lon BD (2nd cl) 38. ALCD 38. **d** 38 Cant **p** 39 Ex. C of Ch Ch Folkestone 38-39; St Andr Plymouth 39-42; L to Offic in St Chris Conv Distr Crownhill Plymouth 41-42; in St Mark Conv Distr Watford 42-45; V of All SS Luton 45-55; Chap Luton and Dunstable Hosp 47-53; V of St Francis of Assisi W Wickham 55-66; St Laur in I of Thanet w Manston 66-77; Hon Can of Cant Cathl 76-79; Can (Emer) from 79. *5 Sea View Terrace, Rye, Sussex.* (Rye 3744)

YARNOLD, Grenville Dennis. b 09. Mert Coll Ox BA (2nd cl Nat Sc) and Scott Scho 31, MA and DPhil 35. Linc Th Coll 42. **d** 42 **p** 43 Southw C of St Pet w St Jas Nottm 42-44; Beeston 44-49; Chap Linc Dioc Tr Coll 49-51; LPr Dio Linc 50-51; V of Malden 51-56; Warden of St Deiniol's Libr Hawarden and L to Offic Dio St A 56-62; V of Llanwddyn Dio St A 62-73; RD of Llanfyllin 69-73; Exam Chap to Bp of St A 71-77; Preb and Sacrist of St A Cathl from 71; Res Can St A Cathl 74-77; Can (Emer) from 78. *13 Ffordd Siarl, St Asaph, Clwyd, LL17 0PT.* (St Asaph 582024)

YARROW, David Alexander. b 35. Jes Coll Cam BA 58, MA 62. Univ of NB PhD 73. Montr Dioc Th Coll 74. **d** 75 **p** 76 Fred. C of Trin St John 75-78; I of Chomedy-Bordeaux Dio Montr from 78. *733 Bruno Street, Chomedy, Ville de Laval, PQ, Canada.* (514-681 5127)

YARROW, John Noel. b 1894. Univ of Leeds BA 19. Coll of Resurr Mirfield, 12. **d** 21 **p** 22 Wakef. C of Ravensthorpe 21-27; Heckmondwike (in c of St Sav) 27-30; V of Kinsley 30-41; S Elmsall 41-61; Hon Can of Wakef 61-62; Perm to Offic Dio Win from 62. *Flat 3, 5 St Winifred's Road, Bournemouth, Dorset. BH2 6NY.* (Bournemouth 25322)

YATES, Albert Leslie. b 02. St Andr Coll Pampisford. **d** 49 **p** 50 Lich. C of Stone 49-52; Stoke-on-Trent 52-56; V of St Mary and All SS Palfrey Walsall 56-61; Tong 61-70; Perm to Offic Dio Lich from 71; York from 78. *Address temp unknown.*

YATES, Andrew Martin. b 55. St Chad's Coll Dur BA (Th) 77. Linc Th Coll 78. **d** 80 **p** 81 Sheff. C of St Marg and St Thos Brightside City and Dio Sheff from 80. *85 Beacon Road, Brightside, Sheffield, S9 1AB.* (Sheff 615017)

YATES, Anthony Hugh. b 39. Univ of Wales BA 62. Wycl Hall Ox 62. **d** 65 **p** 66 Man. C of St Crispin Withington 65-68; St Cecilia Parson Cross Sheff 68-73; V of St Thos Middlesbrough Dio York from 73. *St Thomas's Clergy House, Longlands Road, Middlesbrough, Cleve. TS3 9DH.* (0642 244908)

YATES, Arthur Stanley. BD (Lon) 43, BA (Lon) 45 Univ of Leeds, PhD 49. Ripon Hall, Ox. **d** 61 **p** 62 Chelmsf. [f Methodist Min] C of Gidea Pk 61-63; Lect in Div Coll of St Mark and St John Chelsea 63-74; Sen Lect Relig Stud Plymouth from 74; Publ Pr Dio Ex from 74. *1 Langton Road, Harrowbeer Lane, Yelverton, Devon.* (Yelverton 3897)

YATES, Byron Brockton. Trin Coll Tor BA 66, STB 69. **d** and **p** 69 Tor. C of Cobourg 69-72; R of Belmont 72-81; Bowmanville Dio Tor from 81. *124 Queen Street, Bowmanville, Ont, Canada.*

YATES, Colin George. b 13. Bp Wilson Th Coll IM 35. **d** 38 **p** 39 Blackb. C of Ashton-on-Ribble 38-43; CF (EC) 43-46; V of Ch Ch Preston 48-55; C-in-c of Torrisholme Conv Distr Dio Blackb 55-59; Min 59-69; V of Torrisholme 69-79. *114 Woodplumpton Road, Fulwood, Preston, Lancs.*

YATES, David. d 70 **p** 73 Mashon. P Dio Mashon. *The Rectory, Crowhill Road, PO Borrowdale, Salisbury, Rhodesia.*

YATES, Eric Henry. b 16. Late Exhib Univ of Dur St Chad's Coll Dur BA (2nd cl Th) 38, MA 41. **d** 39 **p** 40 Dur. C of Horden 39-41; Malvern Link 41-44; St Jo Bapt Kidderminster 44-46; Min Can of Ely Cathl 46-48; Libr Ely Cathl 46-53; Sacr 47-48; L to Offic Dio Ely 46-48; V of Witchford w Wentworth 48-53; Chap Cho of Ches Cathl, Asst Master Cathl Choir Sch and LPr Dio Ches 53-61; Asst Master Dover Gr Sch 61-70; L to Offic Dio Cant 61-76; Chap St Steph Coll Broadstairs 71-74; Asst Master 74-76; C-in-c of Batcombe w Upton Noble 76-82; S w N Brewham 76-82. *24 Dunvegan Close, New North Road, Exeter, Devon, EX4 4AF.* (Exeter 56543)

YATES, Ernest Jordan Halley. b 10. **d** 79 **p** 80 Grahmstn (APM). C of St Martin Gonubie Dio Grahmstn from 79. *9 Smith Street, Gonubie 5256, CP, S Africa.*

YATES, Gavin Harrison. Univ of Cant BA 60. Ch Ch Coll LTh 64. **d** 61 **p** 62 Wel. C of St Paul's Cathl Ch Wel 61-65; Asst Dir Christian Educn Coun Dio Wel 65-67; V of Westport 67-70; Dean and V of Ch Ch Cathl Nel 70-81; Exam Chap to Bp of Nel 71-81; V of St Mark Remuera Dio Auckld from 81. *1a St Mark's Road, Remuera, Auckland 5, NZ.*

YATES, Howard. b 22. N-W Ordin Course 73. **d** 76 **p** 77 Liv. C of Newchurch Dio Liv from 76. *2 Chatsworth Avenue, Culcheth, Warrington, WA3 4LB.* (Culcheth 2226)

YATES, James Ainsworth. b 21. Bps' Coll Cheshunt 56. **d** 58 **p** 59 St Alb. C of Dunstable 58-60; V of Shillington 60-79; R of Gravenhurst L 62-72; V of Gravenhurst U (w Gravenhurst L from 72) 62-79; RD of Shefford 69-79; V of Sandon, Wallington and Rushden w Clothall Dio St Alb from 79. *Sandon Vicarage, Payne End, Buntingford, Herts, SG9 0QU.* (Kelshall 256)

✠ **YATES, Right Rev John.** b 25. Late Scho of Jes Coll Cam BA 49, MA 52. Linc Th Coll 49. **d** 51 **p** 52 Lon. C of Ch Ch Southgate 51-54; Tutor Linc Th Coll and LPr Dio Linc 54-59; Chap 56-59; V of Bottesford w Ashby 59-65; Surr from 60; Exam Chap to Bp of Linc from 61; to Bp of Lich from 67; Prin Lich Th Coll 66-72; L to Offic Dio Lich 66-72; Preb of Lich Cathl 71-72; Cons Ld Bp Suffr of Whitby in Beverley Minster 25 Jan 72 by Abp of York; Bps of Dur, Ripon, Carl, Southw, Bris, Lich and Linc; Bps Suffr of Jarrow, Hull, Grimsby and Shrewsbury; and others; Trld to Glouc 75. *Bishopscourt, Pitt Street, Gloucester, GL1 2BQ.* (Gloucester 24598)

YATES, John Dennis. b 28. Wells Th Coll. **d** 57 **p** 58 Man. C of All SS Elton Bury 57-60; Cannock (in c of St John Heath

Hayes) 60-62; R of St John Moston 62-73; V of St Pet Bury 73-76; R of St Mary Stoke Ipswich Dio St E from 76; P-in-c of Wherstead Dio St E from 76. *8 Belstead Road, Ipswich, Suff.* (Ipswich 51895)

YATES, John Edmund. b 09. Univ of Man Jun Bp Lee Pri 35, Wellington Scho 36, BD (w distinc) and Research Scho in Th 37, MA 39, DD 63. Egerton Hall Man 36. **d** 37 **p** 38 Man. C of All SS Stand 37-40; St Jas. Birch-in-Rusholme 40-42; V of St Mich AA Lawton Moor 42-48; Chap of Baguley Sanat 44-48; Lect in Th UCNW Ban 48-51; L to Offic Dio Ban 49-62; Lect in Bibl Hist Univ of Sheff 51-52; Chap RAF 52-62; R of Cossington Dio Leic from 62. *Cossington Rectory, Leicester.* (Sileby 2208)

YATES, John Martin Coucher. b 35. Qu Coll Cam BA 59, MA 63. Ridley Hall Cam 59. **d** 61 **p** 62 Man. C of Middleton Lancs 61-64; Lect U Th Coll Hong Kong 64-66; L to Offic Dio Hong 66-68; V of Haselbury Plucknett w N Perrott 68-79; C-in-c of Misterton 73-79; Mells w Kilmersdon, Elm, Whatley, Vobster Babington & Chantry Dio B & W from 79. *Rectory, Mells, Frome, BA11 3PT.* (0373 812320)

YATES, Keith Leonard. b 36. K Coll Lon BD AKC 61. Univ of Nottm MPhil 79. Wells Th Coll. **d** 69 **p** 70 St Alb. C of Ch Ch Luton 69-73; Hon C of St Andrew Luton 73-76; L to Offic Dio Linc 76; R of Grimoldby w Manby 76-80; V of Cockerington N w S and Alvingham 76-80; Yarburgh 76-80; P-in-c of Gt w L Carlton 77-80; Lect Sarum Wells Th Coll from 80. *19 The Close, Salisbury, Wilts, SP1 2EE.* (Salisbury 434856)

YATES, Kenneth. b 44. Kelham Th Coll 65. **d** 70 Knaresborough for Ripon **p** 71 Ripon. C of Leeds 70-74; Worksop Priory 74-75; Publ Pr Dio Southw from 75; Hon C of Bawtry 75-78; Cantley Dio Sheff from 81. *15 Kirkhill Close, Armthorpe, Doncaster, DN3 3SW.* (Doncaster 831980)

YATES, Michael John Whitworth. b 39. Selw Coll Cam 2nd cl Th Trip pt i 60, BA (3rd cl Th Trip pt ii) 62. Oak Hill Th Coll 62. **d** 64 **p** 65 Nor. C of St Luke New Catton 64-68; V in Lowestoft Group (C-in-c of St Jo Evang Lowestoft) 68-74; Perm to Offic Dio Bradf from 75. *5 Belle Hill, Giggleswick, Settle, BD24 0BA.*

YATES, Michael Peter. b 47. Univ of Leeds Emsley Scho 67, BA (2nd cl Th) 69, MA (with Distinc) 70. Coll of Resurr Mirfield 69. **d** 71 **p** 72 Ches. C of St Andr Crewe 71-76; V of Wheelock 76-79; Chap Rainhill Hosp Prescot from 79. *Rainhill Hospital, Prescot, Merseyside, L35 4PQ.* (051-426 6511)

YATES, Peter Francis. b 47. Univ of Sheff BA 69. Univ of Nottm Dipl Th 71. Kelham Th Coll 69. **d** 74 Doncaster for Sheff **p** 75 Sheff. C of Mexborough 74-78; St Jo Bapt Sevenoaks 78-81. *The Monastery, Crawley Down, Sevenoaks, Kent.*

YATES, Thomas Roy Fairclough. b 26. St Deiniol's Libr Hawarden 77. **d** 79 **p** 80 Ches. C of Thornton Hough 79-80; Bromborough 80-82; Hamworthy Dio Sarum from 82. *56 Keyworth Road, Turlin Moor, Hamworthy, Poole, Dorset.*

YATES, Timothy Edward. b 35. Magd Coll Cam 2nd cl Hist Trip pt i 57, BA (2nd cl Th Trip pt ii) 59, MA 62. Univ of Uppsala DTh 78. Ridley Hall Cam 58. **d** 60 Tonbridge for Cant **p** 61 Roch. C of Tonbridge 60-63; Tutor St John's Coll Dur from 63; L to Offic Dio Dur from 63; Hon Stud Chap St Nich Dur 63-70; Warden of Cranmer Hall Dur 71-79; P-in-c of Darley Dio Derby from 79. *Rectory, Hall Rise, The Parkway, Darley Dale, Matlock, Derbys.* (Darley Dale 4866)

YATES, Timothy Michael. b 52. Rhodes Univ Grahmstn BSocSc 75. Univ of Nottm Dipl Th 78. **d** 80 Capetn. C of St Steph Pinelands Dio Capetn from 80. *26 North Way, Pinelands 7405, Cape Town, S Africa.* (53-1773)

YATES, William Herbert. b 35. Univ of Man BA 59. Chich Th Coll 60. **d** 61 Lanc for Blackb **p** 62 Blackb. C of St Steph Blackpool 61-65; St Jo Evang Wednesbury 65-69; V of Porthill 69-78; R of Norton-le-Moors Dio Lich from 78. *Norton-le-Moors Rectory, Stoke-on-Trent, Staffs, ST6 8BZ* (Stoke-on-Trent 534622)

YATES-ROUND, Joseph Laurence John. b 25. SOC 73. **d** 76 **p** 77 Roch (APM). C of St Pet Tonbridge Dio Roch from 76. *91e London Road, Tonbridge, Kent.*

YAW THAT, Del Salai. H Cross Th Coll Kokine 48. **d** 50 **p** 51 Rang. P Dio Rang 50-77. *c/o St Mark's Church, Prome, Burma.*

YAXLEY, Canon Robert William. b 05. Univ of Birm BSc (2nd cl Chem) 25. ARIC 27. Ripon Hall Ox 29. **d** 31 **p** 32 Birm. C of St Mich Boldmere 31-35; V of St Silas Lozells 35-39; Cradley 39-51; St Anne Moseley 51-75; Hon Can of Birm from 65. *Flat 24, 20 Moor Green Lane, Moseley, Birmingham B13 8ND.* (021-449 8647)

YEANDLE-HIGNELL, John Wilfred. b 07. K Coll Lon. St Cath S Ox BA and MA 46. **d** 30 **p** 31 Glouc. C of St Jo Evang Cinderford (in c of St Mich AA Soudley) 30-33; Broadwell 33; R of U Slaughter w Eyford 33-39; Berry Narbor 39-42; CF (EC) from 40; R of Wytham 42-50; PC of Binsey 42-50. *The Bungalow, Marshall Road, Cowley, Oxford.* (Oxford 78865)

YEARSLEY, John Symons. b 01. Univ of Liv BA 27, MA 33. Ripon Hall Ox 56. **d** 56 **p** 57 Birm. C of Yardley 56-57; C-in-c of Shustoke 57-60; V of St Jas Aston 60-74; Perm to Offic Dio Birm from 75. *62 Arden Road, Acocks Green, Birmingham 27.*

YEBOAH, Canon Edmund. Cudd Coll. **d** 54 **p** 55 Accra. P Dio Accra; Hon Can of Accra 73-75; Can from 75; Exam Chap to Bp of Accra from 75. *Trinity College, Box 48, Legon, Ghana.* (Accra 76541)

YEBUAH, Canon Jacob Kwanina. d and **p** 32 Accra. P Dio Accra 32-72; Dio Kum from 73; Can of Kum from 74. *PO Box 33, Nkawie, Ashanti, Ghana.*

YEEND, Walter Archibald John. b 12. AKC 40. **d** 40 **p** 41 Guildf. C of W Molesey 40-42; C-in-c of All SS Leatherhead 42-43; St Matt Westmr 43-45; V of W Molesey Dio Guildf from 45. *Vicarage, West Molesey, Surrey.* (01-979 2805)

YEO, Chin Chye. Trin Th Coll sing 59. **d** 62 **p** 63 Sing. P Dio Sing. *1a Hamilton Road, Singapore 8.*

YEO, Delmont Arthur. Wycl Coll Tor. **d** 43 Tor **p** 63 NS. I of Port Hill 63-69; I of Liscomb 69-74. *Sherbrooke, NS, Canada.* (522-2664)

YEO, George Henry. b 13. MBE 46. TCD 64. **d** 65 Raph **p** 66 Derry. C-in-c of Clonleigh w Donaghmore 65-68; R of Taughboyne 68-72; C of Royston 72-75; P-in-c of St Marg New Galloway Dio Gall from 75. *St Margaret's Rectory, New Galloway, Castle Douglas, Kircudbrights.* (New Galloway 235)

YEO, Lester John. b 55. Ex Coll Ox BA 77, MA 81. Coll of the Ressur Mirfield 78. **d** 80 **p** 81 Ex. C of Plymstock Dio Ex from 80. *7 Rockville Park, Plymstock, Plymouth, PL9 7DG.*

YEOMAN, David. b 44. Univ of Wales Dipl Th 69. St Mich Coll Llan 66. **d** 70 **p** 71 Bp T M Hughes for Llan. C of St Jo Bapt Cardiff 70-72; Caerphilly 72-76; V of Ystrad Rhondda 76-81. *c/o Vicarage, Ystrad Rhondda, Mid Glam.* (Tonypandy 434426)

YEOMAN, Douglas. b 35. ACII 35. **d** 77 **p** 78 Edin (APM). C of St Martin City and Dio Edin from 77; Wester Hailes Dio Edin from 81. *6 Craiglockhart Crescent, Edinburgh, EH14 1EY*

YEOMANS, Ernest Harold. b 07. K Coll NS STh 44. **d** and **p** 39 NS. C of Neil's Harbour 39-42; P-in-c from 39; R of New Waterford 42-46; C of Blakenall Heath 46-50; V of Ancaster 50-57; Honington 50-57; R of Eakring 57-61; V of Winkburn 57-61; St Aug Leic 61-75; L to Offic Dio Leic from 75. *16 Woodlands Drive, Groby, Leicester, LE6 0BQ.* (Leic 879164)

YEOMANS, Herbert Thomas. b 07. Late Scho of Selw Coll Cam 2nd cl Hist Trip pt i 28, BA (2nd cl Hist Trip pt ii) 29, MA 43. Linc Th Coll 29. **d** 32 **p** 33 Southw. C of Bulwell 32-35; Gt Yarmouth 35-37; St Pet Mancroft Nor 37-38; V of W Pinchbeck 38-45; Chap RAFVR 40-45; V of Morton-by-Gainsbrorough 45-48; St Mary-below-Hill w St Benedict Linc 48-52; Brixham (w Churston Ferrers 52-53) 52-56; All SS Lower Brixham 52-56; All SS w St Mary Brixham 56-62; Long Buckby w Brington 62-65; Chitterne 65-69; Bremhill w Foxham 69-81. *Daracombe, The Clays, Market Lavington, Wilts.*

YEOMANS, Robert John. b 44. K Coll Lon and Warm AKC 66. **d** 67 **p** 68 Heref. C of Pontesbury 67-70; Asst Youth Officer Dio St Alb 70-72; Project Officer Gen Syn Bd of Educn St Alb 73-77; V of Ch of Ch and St John w St Luke, Isle of Dogs, Dio Lon from 77. *Vicarage, Manchester Road, Isle of Dogs, E14 9BN.* (01-987 1915)

YEOMANS, Thomas Henry. b 14. **d** 60 **p** 61 Wakef [f in CA] C of Penistone 60-62; V of Helme 62-71; V of St Mich Wincle (w Wildboar Clough from 73) 71-79. *Vicarage Cottage, Crewe Greeen, Crewe, Chesh.*

YEOW, Swee Hong. b 14. **d** 73 **p** 74 Sing (APM). P Dio Sing. *St Andrew's Cathedral, Singapore 6.*

YERBURGH, David Savile. b 34. Magd Coll Cam BA 57, MA 61. Wells Th Coll 57. **d** 59 **p** 60 Glouc. C of Cirencester 59-63; Bitterne Pk 63-67; V of St Jo Evang Churchdown 67-74; Charlton Kings Dio Glouc from 74; RD of Glouc N 73-74. *63 Church Street, Charlton, Kings, Cheltenham, Glos, GL53 8AT.* (Cheltenham 580067)

YERBURGH, Peter Charles. b 31. Magd Coll Cam BA 53, MA 57. Wells Th Coll 53. **d** 55 **p** 56 Sarum. C of St Jas Southbroom 55-58; Chap Cathl Sch Wells 58-71; Durlston Court Sch from 71. *Durlston Court School, Barton-on-Sea, Hants.* (New Milton 615882)

YERBURGH, Ven Richard Eustre Marryat. ED 58. Univ of BC BA 28, MA 31. **d** 32 **p** 33 BC. C of St Mary Oak Bay 32-35; I of Creston 36-37; Colwood w Langford 37-40; RCASC 40-46; I of Enderby 46-48; V of Osoyoos Oliver 48-51; Chaplaincy Service CAOS 51-52; R of Fernie 52-56; Michel 53-56; Can of Koot 54-62; R of Kimberley 56-62; C of St Pet Prince Rupert 62-63; Ocean Falls 63-66; Vanderhoof 66-73; Archd of Caled 70-73; Archd (Emer) from 73; L to

Offic Dio Koot from 73. *Box 503, Oliver, BC, Canada.*

YEROKUN, Amos. b 34. **d** 76 **p** 77 Ilesha. P Dio Ilesha. *Christ Church, Erin-Ilesha, Nigeria.*

YE SHAW, Very Rev. H Cross Coll **d** 59 **p** 60 Rang. P Dio Rang 60-70; Dio Pa-an from 70; Dean of St Pet Cathl Pa-an from 74. *St Peter's Cathedral, Bishop's Kone, Pa-an, Burma.*

YEULETT, George Eric. b 04. Qu Coll Cam BA 27, MA 30. Bps' Coll Cheshunt 27. **d** 28 **p** 29 Lon. C of St Mich Sutton Court Chiswick 28-31; St Steph Paddington 31-36; LDHM of St Pet Conv Distr Grange Pk 36-42; V 42-44; St Steph Paddington (w St Luke from 52) 44-53; C-in-c of St Luke Tavistock Rd Paddington 44-52; V of St Martin W Acton 53-71; Perm to Offic Dio Chich from 76. *2 Poole Farm Court, South Road, Hailsham, Sussex.* (Hailsham 842452)

YEUNG, Peter Ka-Lim. Internat Chr Univ Tokyo BA 69. Trin Coll Tor MDiv 74. **d** and **p** 74 Niag. C of St Geo Guelph 74-75; Ancaster 75-77; Dir Miss to Seamen Hamilton 77-78; CF (Canad) from 78. *Canadian Forces Base, Penhold, Alta, Canada.*

YEUNG, Robert Yu Kwong. b 24. Vanc Sch of Th 66. **d** 69 New Westmr. d Dio New Westmr 69-80; Chap Miss to Seamen Vanc from 80. *4419 West 14th Avenue, Vancouver 8, BC, Canada.*

YIN, Canon Roy Henry Bowyer. K Coll Cam 2nd cl Math Trip pt i 30, BA (2nd cl Hist Trip pt ii) 32, MA 36. Cudd Coll 32. **d** 33 Bp Price for Ely **p** 34 Linc. C of St Giles w St Pet Cam and Chap K Coll Cam 33-37; Chap Hurstpierpoint Coll 37-46; St Thos Coll Colom 46-62; Lect Univ of Malaya and L to Offic Dio Sing 64-69; V of St Hilda's Ch Katong 70-75; Synod Sec Dio Sing 72-75; L to Offic Dio Sing from 75; Hon Can of Sing from 80. *114a Newton Road, Singapore 11.* (Sing 2525108)

YIP, Francis Sai-san. Union Th Coll Hong Kong 55. **d** 55 **p** 57 Hong. P-in-c of H Carpenter Kowloon 55-63; V of Good Shepherd Kowloon 63-65; P-in-c of H Carpenter Kowloon Dio Hong from 65; Commiss Jess 67-69; Sabah from 69. *1 Dyer Avenue, Kowloon, Hong Kong.* (3-620301)

YIP, Paul King Hei. b 29. Montr Dioc Th Coll LTh 65. **d** 63 **p** 64 Hong. P-in-c of La Salle Miss Montr 64; C of St Mary Hong 65; R of Olds 68-71; St Mark Calg 71-77; Squamish 78-80; St Mary Virg City and Dio New Westmr from 80. *121 East Columbia Street, New Westminster, BC, Canada.*

YIP, Canon Tung Shan. b 14. **d** 74 **p** 75 Sing. P Dio Sing 74-81; Hon Can of Sing 78-81; Can (Emer) from 81. *4 Queen Astrid Park, Singapore 10.*

YIP, Yat Heng. Union Th Coll Hong Kong 38. **d** 43 **p** 43 Hong. P Pakhoi 43-47; V of Tsintsuen 47-51; Tsang-Hsing 51-59; P-in-c Kam Tin 59-66; L to Offic Dio Hong from 66. *c/o Bishop's House, Hong Kong.*

YISA, Canon James Aliu. Im Coll Ibad 61. **d** 63 **p** 64 N Nig. P Dio N Nig 63-80; Dio Kaduna from 80; Can of Kaduna from 80. *Box 14, Bida, Nigeria.*

YOANE, Benjamina Ruate. Bp Gwynne Coll Mundri 61. **d** 64 Bp Dotiro for Sudan **p** 66 Sudan. P Dio Sudan 64-76; Dio Yambio from 76. *ECS, Nzara, Equatoria Province, Sudan.*

YOLOYE, Daniel Agbefidiya. Melville Hall Ibad 34. **d** 35 **p** 37 Lagos. P Dio Lagos 35-52; Dio Ibad 52-65. *c/o St Matthew's Vicarage, Ijebu-Ujesha, Via Ilesha, Nigeria.*

YONA, Daniel. b 38. St Phil Coll Kongwa 73. **d** and **p** 74 Vic Nyan. P Dio Vic Nyan. *Box 3015, Malya, Tanzania.*

YONG, Chen Fah. b 42. Moore Coll Syd 73. **d** and **p** 74 Sabah. P Dio Sabah; Exam Chap to Bp of Sabah from 81. *Box 69, Kota Kinabalu, Sabah, Malaysia.* (Kota Kinabalu 52084)

YONG, Ven Ping Chung. Mem Univ Newfld BA 68. **d** 69 Newfld for Sabah **p** 70 Sabah. P Dio Sabah; Archd of Sabah from 77. *PO Box 17, Sandakan, Sabah, Malaysia.*

YORK, Lord Archbishop of, Primate of England, and Metropolitan. *See* Blanch, Most Rev and Right Hon Stuart Yarworth.

YORK, Assistant Bishops in Diocese of. *See* Cockin, Right Rev George Eyles Irwin; Wimbush, Right Rev Richard Knyvet; and Holderness, Right Rev George Edward.

YORK, Archdeacon of. *See* Stanbridge, Ven Leslie Cyril.

YORK, Dean of. *See* Jasper, Very Rev Ronald Claud Dudley.

YORK, Humphrey Bowmar. b 28. St Chad's Coll Dur BA 54. **d** 55 **p** 56 Dur. C of Beamish 55-57; Tettenhall Regis 57-62; R of Lanreath 62-67; C-in-c of Pelynt w Lansallos 62-63; V of Pelynt 63-67; P-in-c of Luxulyan 67-74; Lanlivery (and Luxulyan from 74) Dio Truro from 67; RD of Bodmin from 76. *Luxulyan Vicarage, Bodmin, Cornw.* (St Austell 850880)

YORK, Reginald Frank. b 15. Sarum Th Coll 67. **d** 68 **p** 69 Sarum. C of St Mark Sarum 68-71; R of Childe Okeford and Manston w Hammoon (and Hanford from 73) 71-80; Chap Old Manor Hosp Sarum from 80. *39 Fowler's Road, Salisbury, Wilts, SP1 2QP.*

YORKE, Alexander Sawyerr. Im Coll Ibad 67. **d** 69 **p** 77 Gambia. P Dio Gambia. *Anglican Mission, Upper River Division, Basse, Gambia.*

YORKE, John Andrew. b 47. Cranmer Hall Dur 70. **d** 73 **p** 74 Stepney for Lon. C of Ch Ch w All SS Spitalfields 73-78; R of Tuktoyaktuk Dio Arctic from 78. *PO Box 238, Tuktoyaktuk, NWT X0E 1C0, Canada.*

YORKE, Canon Leslie Henry. Univ of Dur LTh 34. St Aug Coll Cant 33. **d** 33 **p** 34 Pet C of Abington 33-36; Chap Middx Hosp 36-39; V of St Mich Cricklewood 39-41; St Mich AA Mill Hill 41-48; R of Tillington 48-56; Petworth 50-56; Seq of Egdean 50-56; Rd of Petworth 54-56; R of Aldrington 56-58; V of Haywards Heath 58-62; Christchurch w Mudeford 62-76; Hon Can of Win Cathl 70-76; Can (Emer) from 76; RD of Christchurch 71-74. *Address temp unknown.*

YORKE, Canon Michael Leslie. b 39. Magd Coll Cam Law Trip pt i 61, BA Th Trip pt ia) 62, MA 66. Cudd Coll 62. **d** 64 **p** 65 Cant. C of Croydon 64-68; C and Succr of St Mary Virg Cathl Chelmsf 68-69; Chap and Prec 69-73; Dep Dir Research & Tr Chelmsf Cathl Centre 72-74; C-in-c of Ashdon w Hadstock 74-76; R 76-78; Can Res of Chelmsf Cathl from 78. *115 Rainsford Avenue, Chelmsford, Essex, CM1 2PF.* (Chelmsf 67773)

YORKSTONE, Peter. b 48. Univ of Tech Loughborough BTech 72. Oak Hill Coll 79. **d** 81 Blackb. C of St Thos Blackpool Dio Blackb from 81. *14 Mather Street, Layton, Blackpool, Lancs, FY3 8RA.*

YOUELL, Canon George. b 10. Univ of Keele MA 69. St Steph Ho Ox 33. **d** 33 Ches **p** 34 Wakef for Ches. C of St Jo Bapt Ches 33-37; Cler Dir ICF for NW Area 37-39; CF 39-46; R of Ightfield w Calverhall 47-52; V of Leek 52-61; RD of Leek 52-56; Commiss Lagos 48-60; Archd of Stoke-on-Trent 56-70; Chap Univ of Keele 61-68; Hon Can of Lich 67-70; V of Horton 68-70; Can Res of Ely Cathl 70-81; Vice-Dean 73-81. *Stranton Cottage, Wattisfield Road, Walsham le Willows, Bury St Edmunds, Suffolk.*

YOUENS, Ven John Ross. b 14. CB 70. OBE 59. MC 45. Kelham Th Coll 31. **d** 39 **p** 40 Southw. C of Warsop w Sookholm 39-40; CF (EC) 40-45; CF 45-74; Hon Chap to HM the Queen 63-69; Chap from 69; Chap-Gen to the Forces 66-74; Archd (Emer) from 74; Perm to Offic Dio Guildf from 75. *Bulfigs, Hook Heath Road, Woking, Surrey, GU22 0QE.*

YOULD, Guy Martin. b 37. Keble Coll Ox BA (2nd cl Mod Hist) 61, Dipl Th 62, MA 65, BD 68. STh (Lambeth) 75. Univ of Hull PhD 80. St Steph Ho Ox 61. **d** 63 **p** 64 York. C of St John Middlesbrough 63-65; Perm to Offic Dio Ox 65-68; L to Offic from 68; Chap Magd Coll Ox 66-68; Asst Chap Radley Coll Abingdon 68-71; L to Offic Dio Nor 71; C of W Kirby 71-74; Chap Loretto Sch Musselburgh and L to Offic Dio Edin 74; V of Liscard 74-78; Sub-Warden St Barn Th Coll Belair Adel 78-80; C of St Leon & St Jude Doncaster 80-81; V of Brodsworth w Hooton Pagnell, Frickley, Clayton and Marr Dio Sheff from 81. *Brodsworth Vicarage, Doncaster, S Yorks, DN5 7XH.* (Doncaster 722613)

YOULL, Cyril Thomas. b 26. Qu Coll Birm 73. **d** 75 Bp Parker for Cov **p** 76 Bp mcKie for Cov (APM). C of H Trin Leamington 75-78; Hon C of St Cuthb Leaside City and Dio Tor from 78. *1867 Bay View Avenue, Toronto, Ont, Canada, M4G 3E4.*

YOUMATOFF, George. Trin Coll Tor STh 55. **d** 55 **p** 56 Edmon. I of Hardistry 55-58; CF (Canad) 58-71; I of Bayfield 71-76; St John Brantford 76-77. *Box 116, Bayfield, Ont., Canada.*

YOUNG, Canon Allan Edward Norton. Hur Coll. **d** 55 **p** 56 Hur. I of St D Windsor 55-58; St Barn Lon 58-63; Tillsonburg 63-69; All SS Lon Dio Hur from 69; Can of Hur from 80. *135 Inkerman Street, London, Ont 41, Canada.* (519-439 4611)

YOUNG, Allan Keith. Univ of Tor BA 58 BSW 59. Trin Coll Tor STB 62. **d** 62 Tor **p** 63 Caled for Tor. C of St Bart Tor 62-66; Prince Rupert 66-70; I of Kitimat Dio Caled from 70. *1739 Gyrfalion Street, Kitimat, BC, Canada.* (604-632 2369)

YOUNG, Andrew Harold Urquhart. b 49. Univ of Tas BA 72. St Jo Coll Morpeth BTh 78. **d** 79 **p** 80 Tas. C of Devonport 79-80; P-in-c of George Tn Dio Tas from 80. *Rectory, Anne Street, George Town, Tasmania 7253.*

YOUNG, Andrew John. b 50. St Jo Coll Dur BA 73. Westcott Ho Cam 73. **d** 75 Tewkesbury for Glouc. C of Nailsworth 75-76. *17 Stone Lane, Yeovil, Somt.*

YOUNG, Bernard Dwight Orson. b 47. Codr Coll Barb 66. **d** 70 Barb for Guy **p** 71 Guy. C of Port Mourant 71-72; R of Suddie w Queenstown 72-75. *Address temp unknown.*

YOUNG, Brian Thomas. b 42. Linc Th Coll 67. **d** 70 Bp Ramsbotham for Newc T **p** 71 Newc T. C of Monkseaton 70-73; Berwick-on-Tweed 73-77; P-in-c of Gt Broughton Dio Carl 77-80; V (w Broughton Moor) from 80. *Vicarage, Great Broughton, Cockermouth, Cumb, CA13 0YL.* (0900 825317)

YOUNG, Canon Cecil Edwyn. b 13. Dorch Miss Coll 31. **d** 36 **p** 37 Lon. C of St Pet Lon Dks 36-41; St Mich AA N Kens (in c of St Francis) 41-44; R of Broughton 44-47; Ripton Regis 44-47; V of St Silas Pentonville 47-53; R of Stepney 53-64; RD of Stepney 56-64; Commiss Trinid 57-62; Capetn 58-64; Damar 61-70; N Queensld from 66; New Guinea 69-70; Papua 71-72; Preb of St Paul's Cathl Lon 59-64; R of Our Lady and St Nich Liv 64-73; RD of Liv 64-73; Can Dio Liv 66-74; Chap to HM the Queen from 72; Qu Chap of the Savoy from 73; Hon Can of N Queensld from 74. *Queen's Chapel of the Savoy, Savoy Hill, WC2R 0DA.* (01-836 7221)

YOUNG, Charles John. b 24. G I Mech E 50. Qu Coll Birm 52. **d** 55 Bp Stuart for Cant **p** 56 Worc. C of St Thos Dudley 55-58; Beeston 58-61; V of All H W Bridgford 61-66; R of Kirkby-in-Ashfield 66-75; V of Balderton Dio Southw from 75. *Vicarage, Main Street, Balderton, Newark, Notts NG24 3NN.* (0636-704811)

YOUNG, Christopher Terence. b 53. Univ of Capetn BA 76. Univ of S Africa BTh 80. St Bede's Th Coll Umtata 79. **d** 80 **p** 81 Capetn. C of St Sav Claremont Dio Capetn from 80. *8 Bowwood Road, Claremont, Cape, S Africa 7700.*

YOUNG, Clive. b 48. St Jo Coll Dur BA 70. Ridley Hall Cam 70. **d** 72 **p** 73 Willesden for Lon. C of St Cath Neasden 72-75; Hammersmith 75-79; P-in-c of St Paul w St Steph Old Ford, Bow Dio Lon from 79. *St Paul's Vicarage, St Stephen's Road, Bow, E3.* (01-980 9020)

YOUNG, Daniel George Harding. b 52. New & Westmr Colls Ox BA 76. Cranmer Hall Dur 77. **d** 80 **p** 81 Lich. C of Bushbury Dio Lich from 80. *27 Morrison Avenue, Bushbury, Wolverhampton, WV10 9TZ.*

YOUNG, David. b 37. S Th (Lambeth) 79. Linc Th Coll 64. **d** 67 Pontefract for Wakef **p** 68 Wakef. C of Crofton 67-68; Heckmondwike 68-71; V of Stainland 71-76; R of Patrington w Winestead 76-80; Chap St John's Hosp Linc from 80; Lawn Hosp Linc from 81. *The Hollies, Dunston, Lincoln.* (Metheringham 20465)

YOUNG, David Charles. b 44. Oriel Coll Ox BA 66, MA 70. SOC 74. **d** 77 **p** 78 Birm. C of St Pet Harborne 77-81; P-in-c of St Germain Edgbaston Dio Birm from 81. *180 Portland Road, Birmingham, B16 9TD.* (021-429 3431)

YOUNG, David John. b 43. Univ of Nottm BA (1st cl Engl) 64. Coll of Resurr Mirfield 64. **d** 66 Sherwood for Southw **p** 67 Southw. C of Warsop w Sookholme 66-68; Harworth w Bircotes 68-71; C-in-c of Hackenthorpe 71-73; Team V of Frecheville and Hackenthorpe 73-75; V of St Phil Chaddesden Dio Derby from 75. *St Philip's Vicarage, Taddington Road, Chaddesden, Derby, DE2 4JU.* (Derby 673428)

✠ **YOUNG, Right Rev David Nigel de Lorentz.** b 31. Ball Coll Ox BA (1st cl Math) 54, MA 58. Wycl Hall Ox 57. **d** 59 **p** 60 Liv. C of All H Allerton 59-62; St Mark Hamilton Terrace St John's Wood 62-63; CMS 63-67; Dir of Buddhist Stud Lanka Th Coll Ceylon 65-67; Lect Univ of Man 67-70; Perm to Offic Dios Ches and Man 67-70; V of Burwell 70-75; Gt w L and Steeple Gidding 75-76; Hon Can of Ely 75-77; Archd of Huntingdon 75-77; R of Hemingford Abbots 76-77; Cons Ld Bp of Ripon in York Minster 21 Sept 77 by Abp of York; Bps of Dur, Blackb, Wakef, Newc T, Bradf, Sheff, Southw and Man; Bps Suffr of Huntingdon, Hull, Doncaster, Whitby, Hulme, Sherwood, Lanc, Birkenhead, Knaresborough, Selby, Burnley, Stockport and Jarrow; and others. *Bishop Mount, Ripon, N Yorks, HG4 5DP.* (Ripon 2045)

YOUNG, Derek John. b 42. Bp Burgess Hall Lamp 70. **d** 73 **p** 74 Mon. C of Griffithstown 73-76; Ebbw Vale 76-77; V of Penmaen Dio Mon from 77; Crumlin Dio Mon from 81. *Vicarage, Central Avenue, Oakdale, Blackwood, Gwent NP2 0JS.* (Blackwood 223043)

YOUNG, Desmond Terence. b 17. TCD BA 40, MA 43, Div Test 41. **d** 41 **p** 42 Derby. C of Hadfield 41-44; Derby 44-47; CF 47-55; I of Fertagh 55-62; Inistioge w The Rower 62-74; C-in-c of Thomastown 62-74; RD of Kells 65-74; C of St Edm Roundhay 74-77; V of Epiph Gipton Leeds Dio Ripon from 77. *154 Amberton Road, Leeds, LS9 6SP.* (Leeds 658707)

YOUNG, Donald. b 13. OBE 66. Chich Th Coll 32. **d** 36 **p** 37 Southw. C of St John Carrington 36-40; Prec of Wakef Cathl 40-44; Chap RNVR 44-45; RN 45-68; V of All SS Falmouth 69-70; Altarnon w Bolventor 70-76; RD of Trigg Major 72-75; Perm to Offic Dio Truro from 76; Dio Ex from 79. *Rutland, Widemouth Bay, Bude, Cornw, EX23 0AD.* (028-885484)

YOUNG, Donald Arthur. b 44. Atlantic Sch of Th Halifax 75. **d** and **p** 77 Centr Newfld. C of Buchans Dio Centr Newfld from 77. *Anglican Rectory, Buchans, Newfoundland, Canada.*

YOUNG, Frederick Charles. b 32. TCD BA (2nd cl Ment and Moral Sc Mod) 56, Downes Liturgy Pri (2nd) 57, Div Test 58, MA 59, MLitt 63. **d** 58 **p** 59 Dub. C of St Mary Donnybrook 58-63; Taney 63-66; I of St Jas Bray 66-70; Commiss Gambia 69-74; R of Dalkey 70-73; Hd of RE Dept Langley Pk Sch for Boys Beckenham from 73; P-in-c of All SS w St Marg U Norwood Dio Cant from 81. *51 Chevening Road, Upper Norwood, SE19 3TD.* (01-653 4379)

YOUNG, Frederick Fraser. b 21. **d** 77 **p** 78 Brisb. Perm to Offic Dio Brisb 77-79; C of St Luke Toowoomba 80-81; P-in-c of Dirranbandi Dio Brisb from 81. *Box 57, Dirranbandi, Queensland, Australia 4392.*

YOUNG, Frederick John. Down Coll Cam BA 34, MA 38. Ely Th Coll 34. **d** 35 **p** 36 S'wark. C of Ascen Lavender Hill 35-41; V of St Mich AA and Chap Br Hosp for Mothers and Babies Woolwich 41-74; Surr from 73; Perm to Offic Dio S'wark from 74. *1 Isla Road, SE18 3AA.* (01-854 8339)

YOUNG, Canon Geoffrey Maxwell. b 12. Ch Coll Cam BA 34, 2nd cl Th Trip pt i 35, MA 38. Westcott Ho Cam 34. **d** 35 **p** 36 Bradf. C of St Wilfrid Lidget Green 35-38; St Osw Guiseley 38-45; CF (EC) 40-45; V of St Marg Thornbury 45-49; Farningham 49-57; Chap Parkwood Hosp Swanley 50-57; V of Kemsing 57-66; C-in-c of Woodlands 66; V of W Malling w Offham 66-81; C-in-c of Leybourne 72-76; Hon Can of Roch 73-81; Can (Emer) from 81. *c/o 138 High Street, West Malling, Kent.* (W Malling 842245)

YOUNG, George Alfred. b 17. Em Coll Sktn BA 46, LTh 47, BD 58. **d** 46 **p** 47 Sask. I of Fort Pitt 46-50; R of Bourlamaque 50-54; RCAF Chap 53-54; R of S Porcupine 54-58; Archd of Moos 55-60; Exam Chap to Bp of Moos 56-59; R of Carleton Place 59-64; H trin Guildwood Tor 64-70; I of Richvale 70-72; R of Inuvik 73-75; I of Slave Lake Dio Athab from 75. *Box 115, Slave Lake, Alta, T0G 2A0, Canada.* (403-849 3628)

YOUNG, Canon George Victor. Wycl Coll Tor. **d** 55 **p** 56 Tor. I of Westmount 55-59; R of St Anne Tor 59-81; Can of Tor from 72. *651 Dufferin Street, Toronto, Ont, Canada.*

YOUNG, George William. b 31. ALCD 55 (LTh from 74). **d** 56 Warrington for Liv **p** 57 Liv. C of Em Everton 56-58; St Pet Halliwell 58-61; V of Newburn w Throckley 61-67; PC of Tyler's Green 67-69; V 69-80; Area Sec SAMS for W of Engl from 80; Perm to Offic Dio Ex from 80; L to Offic Dio Ox from 80. *5 Beech Tree Road, Holmer Green, High Wycombe, Bucks, HP15 6UZ.*

YOUNG, Henry Lawrence. TCD MA 46. **d** 47 **p** 48 Connor. C of Ballywillan 47-49; Cavan 49-50; I of Derryheen 50-51; CF 51-60; I of Laghey 60-64; R of Gt Casterton w Pickworth Tickencote and L Casterton 64-70; L to Offic Dio Moray 71-78; Dio St Andr from 78. *50 Firbank Road, Letham, Perth, Scotland.*

YOUNG, Ivan Richard. b 1899. CCC Cam 19. Univ of Dur LTh 22. Chich Th Coll 20. **d** 22 **p** 23 Lon. C of St Andr w St Mich Enfield 22-24; Harpenden 25-30; Perm to Offic at Golder's Green 30-31; C of All H Tottenham 31-33; Chipping Barnet 33-37; V of Kensworth 37-81. *Plantation Cottage, Wiggington, Nr Tring, Herts.* (Tring 5384)

YOUNG, James Leversedge. Univ of NZ MA 58. Bp's Univ Lennox. LST 60. **d** 59 **p** 60 Queb. P-in-c of Magdalen Is 59-64; St Clem Miss Harrington Harbour 64-68; Mutton Bay 68-71; Field Officer Dept of Chr Educn Melb 71-73; Perm to Offic Dios Melb and Wang 74-80; Dio Tas from 80. *20 Swanston Street, New Town, Tasmania 7008.*

YOUNG, Jeremy Michael. b 54. Ch Coll Cam BA 76, MA 80. Coll of Ressur Mirfield 78. **d** 80 **p** 81 Dur. C of Spennymoor w Whitworth Dio Dur from 80. *82 Hawthorn Road, Middlestone Moor, Spennymoor, Co Durham, DL16 7EW.*

YOUNG, John David. b 37. BD (Lon) 65. Univ of Sussex MA (Educn) 77. Clifton Th Coll 62. **d** 65 **p** 66 Ex. C of St Jude Plymouth 65-68; Asst Master Northgate Gr Sch for Boys Ipswich and L to Offic Dio St E 68-71; Chap and Lect (Sen from 73) Bp Otter Coll of Educn Chich 71-81; W Sussex Inst of Higher Educn 77-81; Chap Coll of Ripon & York St John from 81. *The College, Lord Mayor's Walk, York, YO3 7EX.* (York 56771)

YOUNG, John Frederick (Jonathan). b 25. St D Coll Lamp BA 51. St Mich Coll Llan 51. MSSJE 62-71. **d** 53 **p** 54 Llan. C of St Martin w St Cypr Roath 53-59; L to Offic Dio Ox from 59; Bp's Chap for Commun Relns Dio Birm from 72. *51 Beaudesert Road, Handsworth, Birmingham 20.* (021-554 5137)

YOUNG, John Kenneth. b 14. Late Scho of Clare Coll Cam 1st cl Math Trip pt i, 33, Found Exhib 34, BA (2nd cl Th Trip pt i) 35, MA 39. Cudd Coll 35. **d** 37 **p** 38 Dur. C of St Jas W Hartlepool 37-38; Medomsley 38-43; V of Wismar w Demerara River 43-48; Dean of Georgetn Guy 48-57; PC of Harton 57-66; V of Eastgate 66-73; P-in-c of Rookhope 72-73; V of Forcett and Stanwick w Aldbrough Dio Ripon from 73. *Stanwick Vicarage, Aldbrough St John, Richmond, N Yorks, DL11 7RS.* (Piercebridge 278)

YOUNG, John Kenneth. Edin Th Coll 62. **d** 64 **p** 65 Newc T. C of All SS Gosforth 64-67; St Gabr Heaton Newc T 67-69; R of Bowers Gifford (w N Benfleet from 72) 69-75; P-in-c of Kirkwhelpington 75-79; Kirkheaton 75-79; V of Kirkwhelpington w Kirkharle, Kirkheaton and Cambo Dio

Newc T from 79. *Kirkwhelpington Vicarage, Newcastle-upon-Tyne, NE19 2RT.* (Otterburn 40260)

YOUNG, John Robert. b 43. St Mich Th Coll 63. **d** 68 N Terr for Melb **p** 69 Melb. C of Darwin 68-70; Murrumbeena 70-72; St Luke Stocking Farm Leic 72-74; P-in-c of Burwood E 74; St Mark Reservoir W 75-78; I of Montmorency Dio Melb from 78. *6 Price Avenue, Montmorency, Vic, Australia 3094.* (435-3483)

YOUNG, John Strang Walker. b 55. Magd Coll Ox MA 80. St Steph Ho Ox 77. **d** 80 **p** 81 Nor. C of St Marg w St Nich King's Lynn Dio Nor from 80. *121 Loke Road, King's Lynn, Norfolk, PE30 2BG.* (K Lynn 5162)

YOUNG, John William. Qu Coll Newfld. **d** 37 **p** 38 Newfld. C-in-c of Salvage 37-38; R of Rose Blanche 38-42; I of Herring Neck 42-47; R of Canso w Queensport 47-56; St Alb Syd Dio NS from 56. *Box 21, Pier Postal Station, Sydney, NS, Canada.* (564-4333)

YOUNG, Jonathan Priestland. b 44. K Coll Lon and Warm AKC 68. **d** 69 **p** 70 S'wark. C of Clapham 69-73; St Mark Mitcham 73-74; V of Godmanchester Dio Ely from 74. *Godmanchester Vicarage, Huntingdon, PE18 8AQ.* (0480-53354)

YOUNG, Leonard John. Worc Ordin Coll 59. **d** and **p** 61 Birm. C of Erdington 61-64; V of St Paul W Smethwick 64-68; St Pet Worc 68-72; C-in-c of Wichenford 72-75. *1 Church Lane, Saxilby, Lincoln.*

YOUNG, Leslie Clement. b 03. Westcott Ho Cam 52. **d** 53 **p** 54 S'wark. C of St Olave Mitcham 53-56; Min Conv Distr of St Phil Reigate 56-58; V of St Paul Westleigh 58-61; St John Terrington 61-64; Thorney Abbey w Wrydecroft Knarr Fen and Willow Hall 64-74; Perm to Offic Dio Ely from 76. *11 Woburn Drive, Thorney, Peterborough.*

YOUNG, Malcolm Ryswinn. b 36. Ch Coll Cam BA 60, MA 64. ALCD 63 (LTh from 74). **d** 63 **p** 64 Guildf. C of Egham 63-67; L to Offic Dio Guildf 67-71; Dio Roch from 71; Asst Chap (and Asst Master from 77) King's Sch Roch from 71. *Paddock House, King Edward Road, Rochester, ME1 1UB.* (Medway 49663)

YOUNG, Martin Edward. b 20. Or Coll Ox BA 41, MA 45. Cudd Coll Ox 41. **d** 43 **p** 44 Ox. C of Newbury 43-45; Wymondham 45-49; Gt Berkhamsted 49-51; V of Littlemore 51-64; R of Wootton w Quinton (and Preston Deanery from 72) 64-78; V of Welford w Sibbertoft Dio Pet from 78. *Welford Vicarage, Northampton, NN6 7HS.* (064-581252)

YOUNG, Noel. b 26. St Aid Coll. **d** 56 Warrington for Liv **p** 57 Liv. C of Garston 56-59; St Paul Oldham 59-61; R of Goldhanger w L Totham 61-65; Min of St Aid Eccles Distr Leigh-on-Sea 65-69; V of St Aid Leigh-on-Sea 69-72; R of Kilnasoolagh U 73-78; Tullow w Shillelagh, Aghold & Mullinacuff Dio Leigh from 79. *Rectory, Tullow, Co Carlow, Irish Republic.* (0503 51481)

YOUNG, Paul Goodwin. b 07. Late Scho of Em Coll Cam 1st cl Cl Trip pt i 28, BA (2nd cl Cl Trip pt ii) 30, MA 38. Coll of Resurr Mirfield 30. **d** 32 **p** 33 Derby. C of New Mills 32-35; St Hilda Leeds 35-39; Sub-Warden of St Paul's Coll Grahmstn 39-40; Chap St Andr Coll Grahmstn and P-in-c of St Bart Grahmstn 40-43; P-in-c of St Alb Vincent 43-48; C of St Steph Worc 48-49; R of Astley 49-59; Redmarley D'Abitot 59-74; Perm to Offic Dio Ex from 74. *8 Shepherd's Meadow, Beaford, Winkleigh, Devon.*

YOUNG, Ven Peter Claude. b 16. Ex Coll Ox BA (2nd cl Th) 38, BLitt 40, MA 42, MLitt 80. Wycl Hall Ox 38. **d** 40 **p** 41 Ex. C of Ottery St Mary 40-44; Stoke Damerel (in c of St Bart's Miss Ch) 44-47; R of Highweek w Abbotsbury 47-59; PC of Em Plymouth 59-65; Preb of Ex Cathl 62-65; Archd of Cornw and Can Res of Truro 65-81; Archd & Can (Emer) from 81; Exam Chap to Bp of Truro 65-81. *31 Princes Road, Tivoli, Cheltenham, Glos.*

YOUNG, Peter John. Pemb Coll Cam BA 49. Ridley Hall Cam 49. **d** 51 **p** 52 Ches. C of Cheadle 51-54; Miss CIM from 54. *St Gabriel's Mission, Jalan Itan, Kuala Lumpur, Malaysia.*

YOUNG, Philip Anderson. b 53. St Jo Coll Dur BA 75. Fitzw Coll Cam BA (Th) 77. Ridley Hall Cam 72. **d** 78 **p** 79 S'wark. C of Surbiton 78-80. *Monument Cottage, Norwich Road, N Walsham, Norfolk, NR28 0JA.*

YOUNG, Canon Raymond Grant. b 11 **d** 43 **p** 44 Liv. C of Ince-in-Makerfield 43-45; Pemberton 46; Chap to Deaf and Dumb Assoc Dios Win and Portsm 46-59; Perm to Offic Dio Portsm 48-59; V of Marchwood 59-70; Chap to the Deaf Dios Win and Portsm from 70; Hon Can of Win 77-81; Can (Emer) from 81. *66 Chalvington Road, Chandlers Ford, Eastleigh, Hants, SO5 3DF.* (Chandlers Ford 61519)

YOUNG, Roger Alan. b 50. Qu Univ Kingston Ont BA 72. Trin Coll Tor MDiv 75. **d** and **p** 75 Ott. C of St Matt Ott 75-77; R of Clayton Dio Ott from 77. *Rectory, Clayton, Ont, Canada.* (613-256 2233)

YOUNG, Roger Alan. b 46. Sarum Wells Th Coll 74. **d** 77 Portsm. C of Petersfield 77-78; Crofton Hants 78-81. *c/o 30 Vian Close, Bridgemary, Gosport, Hants, PO13 0TX.*

YOUNG, Roger de Mowbray. b 1889. Linc Coll Ox BA (3rd cl Mod Hist) 12, MA 29. Wells Th Coll **d** 26 **p** 27 York. C of Hornsea w Goxhill 26-28; St John Newland Hull 28-33; E Grinstead 33-37; V of U Beeding 38-51; R of Bramber w Botolph's 38-51; Perm to Offic Dio Chich 58-68. *225 Harley Shute Road, St Leonards-on-Sea, E Sussex, TN38 9JJ.*

YOUNG, Roger Edward. b 40. Univ of Dur BSc (2nd cl) 62. Cudd Coll 64. **d** 66 **p** 67 Llan. C of Eglwysilan 66-68; Llanishen w Lisvane 68-74; C-in-c of St Luke's Conv Distr Rhydyfelin 74-78; R of Ystradyfodwg Dio Llan from 78. *St David's Rectory, Ton Pentre, Rhondda, Mid Glam, CF41 7AX.* (Tonypandy 434201)

YOUNG, Canon Stanley. St Jo Coll Dur BA 36. Ely Th Coll 36. **d** 37 **p** 38 S'wark. C of St Luke Camberwell 37-40; Min Can of Carl 40-45; Warden St Anne's Ch Ho Soho 45-48; C of St Mary Bourne Street Pimlico 48-50; L to Offic at Pemb Coll Cam Miss 50-53; V of Aldermaston (w Wasing from 57) 53-69; RD of Bradfield 63-68; V of Long Crendon (w Chearsley and Nether Winchendon from 80) Dio Ox from 70; P-in-c of Chearsley w Nether Winchendon 77-80; Can (Non-res) of Ch Ch Cathl Ox from 81. *Long Crendon Vicarage, Aylesbury, Bucks.* (Long Crendon 208363)

YOUNG, Stanley Edward William. MA (Lambeth) 60. Linc Th Coll 27. **d** 31 **p** 32 Lich. C of H Cross Shrewsbury 31-42; Chap Prestfelde Sch 42-49; Hd Master 49 61; L to Offic Dio Lich 57-61; Chap at Lugano and Amer Sch in Switzerland Lugano 61-63; Lausanne and Le Rosey Sch Lausanne 63-65; Lugano 65-77. *6911 Carabbia, Lugano, Switzerland.* (091-541410)

YOUNG, Stephen. b 33. St Edm Hall Ox MA 61. St Jo Coll Nottm 75. **d** 77 **p** 78 Portsm. C of Crofton 77-81; Rainham Dio Chelmsf from 81. *34 Warwick Road, Rainham, RM13 9XU.* (Rainham 55810)

YOUNG, Stephen Edward. b 52. AKC and BD 73. St Aug Coll Cant 74. **d** 75 Warrington for Liv **p** 76 Liv. C of Walton-on-the-Hill Dio Liv from 75. *Rectory, Walton Village, Liverpool, L4 6TJ.* (051-525 3130)

YOUNG, Stuart McLaren. St Jo Coll Morpeth ThL 66. **d** 65 **p** 66 Melb. C of St John E Malvern 65-66; Boxhill 66-69; I of Balaclava 69-73; St Alb W Coburg Dio Melb from 73. *127 Gordon Street, West Coburg, Vic, Australia 3058.* (03-36 1767)

YOUNG, Thomas. b 1894. Trin Coll Cam BA 19, MA 22. Wells Th Coll 19. **d** 20 **p** 21 Cant. C of St Geo Ramsgate 20-23; Aysgarth 23-25; R of Middleham 25-36; V of Rudby-in-Cleveland w Middleton 36-42; CF (TA-R of O) 39-44; Hon CF 44; V of Trumpington 44-55; RD of Barton 51-55; V of Witherslack 55-64; RD of Cartmel 60-64. *Ellon, Broad Oak, Sturminster Newton, Dorset.* (Sturminster Newton 72495)

YOUNG, Vivian Alan. b 01. Keble Coll Ox BA 23. Ely Th Coll 23. M SSJE 35. **d** 24 Ripon **p** 25 Knaresborough for Ripon. C of St Hilda Leeds 24-33; Perm to Offic Dio Ox 33-35; C of St Cuthb Tsolo 35-51 and 54-62; St Cypr Native Miss Capetn 51-54; P-in-c of St Cypr Langa Capetn 62-65; Can of Capetn 63-65; L to Offic Dio Ox 65-81; Commiss Damar 70-75; Perm to Offic Dio Lon from 81. *St Edward's House, 22 Great College Street, SW1P 3QA.*

YOUNG, Walter Howlett. b 08. Clifton Th Coll 72. **d** 34 B & W **p** 35 Bp de Salis for B & W. C of St Sav Bath 34-37; Abbey Ch Bath 37-38; R of Hinton Blewett 38-43; Chap RNVR 43-46; Chap HM Pris Leyhill Glouc 46-50; C of Wraxall w Failand 50-67; V of Compton Dando 67-73; R of Chelwood 67-73. *Stone Edge Cottage, Stone Edge Batch, Tickenham, Clevedon, Somt BS21 6SE.* (Nailsea 2944)

YOUNG, William Maurice. b 32. St Jo Coll Nottm 80. **d** 81 Lich. C of H Spirit Harlescott Dio Lich from 81. *14 Maple Drive, Heath Farm, Shrewsbury, SY1 3SE.* (0743 50907)

YOUNGE, Charles William. b 04. St Aid Coll. **d** 31 **p** 32 Wakef. C of St Geo Barnsley 31-33; Long Benton 33-36; St John Mansfield 36-39; C-in-c of St Aug Bull Farm Conv Distr Mansfield 39-47; V of St Jo Div Bulwell 47-72; Perm to Offic Dio Southw from 73. *11 Maplebeck Road, Arnold, Notts.* (Nottingham 262695)

YOUNGE, George Wilfred. b 1899. Hatf Coll Dur LTh 24. Lich Th Coll 21. **d** 25 **p** 26 Man. C of St Sav Preston Lancs 25-27; CF Woolwich 27-28; Aldershot 28-29; Plymouth 29-32; Gibr 32-37; Hilsea 37-38; Bovington 38-40; Active Service 40-45; Aldershot 45-49; R of Kirk Deighton 49-71. *Flat 1, 35 Rutland Drive, Harrogate, Yorks.*

YOUNGER, Jeremy Andrew. b 46. Univ of Nottm BA (2nd cl Th) 68. Univ of Bris MA 71. Wells Th Coll 68. **d** 70 **p** 71 Win. C of Basingstoke 70-74; Harpenden 74-77; Dir of Communications & Chap Sarum & Wells Th Coll 77-81; V of All SS w St Jo Evang Clifton Dio Bris from 81. *All Saints Vicarage, Clifton, Bristol, BS8 3ED.* (Bristol 736779)

YOUNGMAN, Donald Arthur. b 10. AKC (2nd cl) 37. **d** 37

p 38 Chelmsf. C of St Jo Bapt Tilbury Dk 37-39; C-in-c of St Patr Barking 39-43; Chap RAFVR 43-47; C of Almondbury (in c of St Mich) 47-48; Min of St Luke's Conv Distr Prittlewell 48-51; Chap RAF 51-57; R of St Mich w All SS Long Stanton 57-69; C-in-c of Rampton 69-74. *4 Church Close, Hunstanton, Norf, PE36 6BE.*

YOUNGMAN, Frank Arthur. b 05. Magd Coll Cam 2nd cl Cl Trip pt i 26, BA (3rd cl Hist Trip pt ii) 27, MA 31. Westcott Ho Cam 35. **d** 35 **p** 36 Dur. C of St Cuthb Dur 35-38; Chap Dur Sch 35-45; Asst Master and L to Offic Dio Dur 38-53; C of St Cuthb Darlington (in c of Blackwell) 53-56; V of H Trin Stockton-on-Tees 56-59; Steeple Ashton w Semington 59-66; RD of Bradf (Dio Sarum) 61-66; R of Studland 66-72. *Brook Cottage, Wass, Coxwold, York, YO6 4BH.*

YOUNGMAN, William Allen. **d** 52 **p** 53 Qu'App. I of Wawota 52-54; Kisbey 54-56; Assiniboia 56-60; I of Sorrento 60-61; St Andr Burnaby 61-68; Perm to Offic Dio BC from 71. *840 Waddington Road, Nanaimo, BC, Canada.*

YOUNGSON, David Thoms. b 38. Cudd Coll 71. **d** 73 **p** 74 Dur. C of Norton 73-76; St Paul Hartlepool 76-79; P-in-c of St Jo Bapt Stockton-on-Tees Dio Dur from 79. *St John's Vicarage, Durham Road, Stockton, TS19 0DZ.* (Stockton 64119)

YOUSSEF, Michael. **d** 75 Syd **p** 75 Bp Short for Syd. C of Caringbah 75-76; on leave. *12 Combara Avenue, Caringbah, NSW, Australia 2229.*

YSABEL, Lord Bishop of. *See* Pogo, Right Rev Ellison Leslie.

YU, Patrick Tin-Sik. b 50. McMaster Univ Hamilton Ont BA 74. Wycl Coll Tor MDiv 81. **d** 81 Tor. C of Epiph Scarborough Dio Tor from 81. *700 Kennedy Road, Scarborough, Ont, Canada, M1K 2B5.*

YUE, David. b 37. Union Th Coll Hong Kong 66. **d** 69 **p** 71 Hong. C of St Paul Hong 69-72; L to Offic Dio Hong from 72; Hd Master Yat Sau Sch Hong from 76. *Yat Sau Primary School, Hong Kong.* (3-273006)

YUEN, Martin Phau Hong. b 19. Univ of Auckld BCom 62. **d** and **p** 74 Sabah. P Dio Sabah. *St James' Church, Box 12, Kudat, Sabah, Malaysia.* (Kudat 285)

✠ **YUGUSUK, Right Rev Benjamina Wani.** Bp Gwynne Coll Mundri 51. **d** 53 **p** 55 Sudan. P Dio Sudan from 55; Hon Can of Sudan 67-71; Archd of Bari from 71; Exam Chap to Bp in Sudan from 71; Cons Asst Bp in Sudan 24 Jan 71 in All SS Cathl Khartoum by Abp in Jer; Bps of Sudan; Iran; Jordan; Mt Kenya; and Asst Bp in Jer; Apptd Bp of Rumbek 76. *c/o St Barnabas' Cathedral, Rumbek, Lakes Province, Sudan.*

YUILL, Allan Clyde Hamilton. Moore Th Coll Syd 48. ACT ThL 49. **d** and **p** 49 Syd. C of St Steph Willoughby 49-51; St Kevin Dublin 51-52; C-in-c of Berowra w Asquith 53-54; C of Wollongong 54; Chap Sec to Abp of Syd from 54-60; C of St Andr Cathl Syd 56-60; Chatswood 60-61; Hon Chap to Abp of Syd 60-71; Chap from 71; R of H Trin Millers Point Syd 61-73; L to Offic Dio Syd 73-74; C of St Thos City and Dio Syd from 74; Commiss Parag from 76. *34 McLaren Street, N Sydney, Australia 2060.* (929-2432)

YUKON, Lord Bishop of. *See* Ferris, Right Rev Ronald Curry.

YULE, John David. b 49. G and C Cam BA 70, MA 74, Phd 76. Westcott Ho Cam 79. **d** 81 Ely. C of Cherry Hinton Dio Ely from 81. *4 Chelwood Road, Cambridge, CB1 4LK.*

YUN, Gabriel Kyong Sun. St Mich Sem Oryudong. **d** 68 **p** 70 Taejon. P Dio Taejon 68-74; Dio Pusan from 74. *Anglican Church, Dae Chong Dong, 2-18, Chung-Ku, Pusan 600, Korea.* (42-5846)

YUN, Paul Hwan. St Mich Sem Oryudong. **d** 66 **p** 67 Taejon. P Dio Taejon. *PO Box 19, Ch'onju 310, Korea.*

YUSEPH, Samuel Alilu. Im Coll Ibad 58. **d** 60 **p** 61 Lagos. P Dio Lagos. *St Peters, Faji, Lagos, Nigeria.*

Z

ZABANEH, Bishara Ibrahin Nicola. **d** 79 **p** 80 Jer. P Dio Jer. *Irbid, Jordan.*

ZACHAU, Eric. b 31. K Coll Lon and Warm 57. **d** 58 **p** 59 Dur. C of Bp Wearmouth 58-62; Ryhope 62-63; V of Beadnell 63-69; Earsdon w Backworth 69-81; Bamburgh and Lucker Dio Newc T from 81. *Vicarage, Bamburgh, Northumberland.* (066-84295)

ZAGALYA, Yeka Safati. Bp Tucker Coll Mukono. **d** 42 **p** 43 Ugan. P Dio Ugan 42-61; Dio Nam 61-67. *c/o Kiyunga, Box 4533, Bulopi, Uganda.*

ZAIR, Richard George. b 52. Univ of Newc T BSc 74. St Jo Coll Dur 79. **d** 80 **p** 81 Bris. C of Bishopsworth Dio Bris from 80. *30 Brookdale Road, Headly Park, Bishopsworth, Bristol, BS13 7PZ*

ZAKARIASY, Florent. St Paul's Coll Ambat. **d** 50 **p** 52 Madag. P Dio Madag 50-69; Dio Tam from 69. *Mananjary, Madagascar.*

ZAKE, Nasanaeri. Bp Tucker Mem Coll Mukono. **d** 22 **p** 24 Ugan. P Dio Ugan 22-73; Dio Nam from 73. *PO Box 15075, Kampala, Uganda.*

ZAMBESI, Michael. St Jo Coll Lusaka. **d** 53 **p** 54 Mashon. P Dio Mashon 53-81; Dio Mutare from 81. *Rectory, Sakubva, Zimbabwe.*

ZAMBIA, CENTRAL, Bishop of. *See* Taylor, Right Rev Robert Selby.

ZAMBIA, NORTHERN, Bishop of. *See* Mabula, Right Rev Joseph.

ZAM'MIMBA, Effet. **d** 74 **p** 75 Mashon. P Dio Mashon. *6071 Tafara, PO Mabvuku, Salisbury, Zimbabwe.*

ZAMORA, Juan. **d** 78 Bp Skinner for Chile. d Dio Chile. *Casilla 561, Vina del Mar, Chile.*

ZANTSI, Bachelor. **d** 54 **p** 59 St Jo Kaffr. Miss O of Ethiopia Dio St John's 54-67; Dio Grahmstn 67-72; Dio Port Eliz from 72. *Box 129, Somerset East, CP, S Africa.*

ZANZIBAR AND TANGA, Lord Bishop of. *See* Ramadhani, Right Rev John Acland.

ZANZIBAR AND TANGA, Assistant Bishop in. *See* Lukindo, Right Rev Yohana.

ZARIBUGIRE, Very Rev Aburaimu. Bp Tucker Coll Mukono 60. **d** 61 **p** 63 Ankole-K. P Dio Ankole-K 61-67; Dio Kig from 67; Dean of Kig Cathl from 70; Archd of Kig from 74. *Box 1200, Mpalo, Kigezi, Uganda.*

ZASS-OGILVIE, Ian David. b 38. K Coll Lon and Warm AKC 65. ARICS 72, FRICS 80. **d** 66 **p** 67 Dur. C of Washington 66-70; Social and Industr Adv to Bp of Dur for N Dur 70-73; L to Offic Dio Newc T 73-75; V of St Jo Evang Percy Tynemouth 75-78; Hon C of St Mary Bryanston Square St Marylebone 78-81; V of St Jo Evang Bromley Dio Roch from 81. *St John's Vicarage, Orchard Road, Bromley, Kent, BR1 2PR.* (01-460 1844)

ZAU LAI, **d** 69 Rang **p** 71 Mand. P Dio Rang 69-70; Dio Mand from 70. *Sumprubum, Burma.*

ZAU KRIM, John. **d** 59 **p** 60 Rang. P Dio Rang 65-70; Dio Mand from 70. *Namti, Myitkyina District, Burma.*

ZEAL, Stanley Allan. b 33. Univ of Leeds BA 55. Coll of REsurr Mirfield. **d** 57 **p** 58 S'wark. C of Perry Hill 57-61; Cobham (in c of St John) 61-64; R of Ash w Ash Vale 64-69; V of Aldershot Dio Guildf from 69. *Vicarage, Aldershot, Hants.* (Aldershot 20108)

ZHENJE, Titus. b 46. **d** 72 **p** 73 Matab. C of Sizinda 72-75; Mkoba Dio Matab 75-78; P-in-c 78-80; C of Roath 80-81, P-in-c of Mkoba Dio Matab from 81. *St Philip's Rectory, Stand 1298, Village 13, Mkobo, Gwelo, Zimbabwe.*

ZIBI, Mbuto Nditini. St Bede's Coll Umtata 62. **d** 63 **p** 65 St John's. P Dio St Johns. *PO Holy Cross, Transkei, S Africa.*

ZIGODE, Peter Charles Gideon Mqulusi. b 29. **d** 76 **p** 78 Zulu. C of Mvunyane Dio Zulu from 76. *Mhlungwane Store, Private Bag 1326, Vryheid 3100, Zululand, S Africa.*

ZIKURIKIRA, Ven Nomani. b 26. **d** and **p** 73 Rwa. P Dio Rwa 73-75; Dio Kiga from 75; Archd Dio Kiga from 79. *BP 18, Gatsibo, Rwanda.*

ZIMBA, Alford. b 25. **d** 71 **p** 72 S Malawi. P Dio S Malawi 71-73 and from 75; Dio Lake Malawi 73-74. *PO Kasupe, Malawi.*

ZIMBE, Batolomayo. **d** 52 **p** 55 Ugan. P Dio Ugan 52-60; Dio W Bugan 60-68; Dio Nam from 68. *Box 1701, Busunju, Uganda.*

ZIMMERMAN, John Charles Augustus. NZ Bd of Th Stud LTh 29. **d** 29 **p** 30 Wai. C of St Aug Napier 29-32; Ashburton 32-33; All SS Palmerston N 33-34; Perm to Offic at St Alphege Hendon 34-35; St Benedict Ardwick 35-37; P-in-c of Ohura 37; V of Huntley 37-43; Fitzroy 43-47. Perm to Offic at Ch Ch Wanganui 50-52; Dio Wai 52-55. *141 Panama Road, Otahuhu, Auckland 6, NZ.*

ZIMMERMAN, John Keith. b 48. Univ of Tor BA 76. Trin Coll Tor MDiv 79. **d** and **p** 79 Qu'App. C of Big Country 79-80; Pipestone Dio Qu'App from 80. *Box 456, Wolesley, Sask, Canada.*

ZIMMERMAN, John Walter Richard. b 41. St Jo Coll Auckld 69. **d** 71 **p** 72 Auckld. C of Devonport Auckld 71-72; Papatoetoe 72-75; St Andr Epsom Auckld 75-76; V of St John Campbells Bay Dio Auckld from 76; Exam Chap to Bp of Auckld from 81. *27 Sunrise Avenue, Auckland 10, NZ.* (478-7944)

ZIMMERMAN, Canon William John. Univ of Tor BA 34. Wycl Coll Tor LTh 36. **d** 36 Tor for Sktn **p** 37 Sktn. Miss of

Radisson 36-38; I of Radisson Borden and Halcyonia 38-40; Chatsworth w Desborough and Holland Township 40-42; Kerwood w Adelaide and Warwick 42-45; Prin of Mohawk Inst Brantford 45-75; Can of Hur 58-75; Can (Emer) from 75. *Box 394, Brantford, Ont, Canada.*

ZINDO, Daniel Manaseh. b 44. Bp Tucker Coll Mukono 73. **d** 72 **p** 74 Bp Dotiro for Sudan. P Dio Sudan 72-76; Dio Yambio from 76. *ECS, Yambio, Sudan.*

ZINGANI, Canon Michael Joab. **d** 45 **p** 49 Nyasa. P Dio Nyasa 45-64; Dio Malawi 64-70; Hon Can of Lake Malawi from 72. *Tandwe Village, Box 34, Ntchisi, Malawi.*

ZIQU, McDonald Mfanelo. St Bede's Coll Umtata 65. **d** 66 **p** 67 St John's. P Dio St John's. *PO St Mark's 4328, Transkei, S Africa.* (St Mark's 5)

ZONDI, Arnold. St Bede's Coll Umtata 64. **d** 65 Bp Cullen for Zulu **p** 66 Zulu. P Dio Zulu 65-74. *St Mathias Church, PO Utrecht, Natal, S Africa.*

ZULL, Aaron Beatty. Westmont Coll Santa Barbara Calif BA 67. Univ of Tor MA 73. Wycl Coll Tor MDiv 75. **d** 75 Bp Read for Tor **p** 76 Tor. C of St Geo Oshawa 75-77; I of Oak Ridges 77-80. *c/o RR1, Richmond Hill, Ont, Canada.*

✠ **ZULU, Right Rev Alphaeus Hamilton.** Univ of S Africa BA 39, LTh 40. Univ of Natal Hon PhD 75. **d** 40 **p** 42 Natal. C of St Faith's Miss Durban 40-52; P-in-c 52-60; Hon Can of Natal 57-61; Cons Asst Bp of St John's in St Geo Cathl Capetn 27 Nov 61 by Abp of Capetn; Bps of Grahmstn; Kimb K; Natal; St John's Bloemf; Zulu; Maur; Fond du Lac (USA); Long I (USA); and Bps Bayne and Cullen; Trld to Zulu 66; res 75. Perm to Offic Dio Natal from 76. *PO Box 177, Edendale 4505, Natal, S Africa.*

ZULU, Azaria. b 31. **d** 76 Zulu. C of Mahlabathini Dio Zulu from 76. *Private Bag 39, Mahlabathini 3865, Zululand.*

ZULU, Clement Mbuyiselwa. b 46. St Pet Coll Natal 77. **d** 79 **p** 80 Natal. C of Ekuvukeni Kwa-Mashu Dio Natal from 79. *c/o PO Box 40035, Red Hill 4071, S Africa.*

✠ **ZULU, Right Rev Lawrence Bekisisa.** Selw Coll Cam BA 65, MA 69. St Pet Coll Rosettenville 58. **d** 60 **p** 61 Zulu. P Dio Zulu 61-70; L to Offic Dio Grahmstn 70-75; Can of Grahmstn 73-75; Dir of Relig Educn Grahmstn 73-75; Cons Ld Bp of Zulu in Cathl of St Mich and St Geo Grahmstn 16 Nov 75 by Abp of Capetn; Bps of Swaz, St John's, Bloemf, Johann, Port Eliz, Natal, Lebom, Kimb K, St Hel and Grahmstn; and others. *Box 147, Eshowe, Zululand.* (Eshowe 147)

ZULULAND, Lord Bishop of. *See* Zulu, Right Rev Lawrence Bekisisa.

ZUNGU, David Bhekumuzi. b 35. **d** 76 **p** 78 Zulu. C of Kwa Mbusi Ukristu Eshowe Dio Zulu from 76. *PO Box 276, Eshowe 3815, Zululand.*

ZWALF, Willem Anthony Louis. b 46. AKC 68. St Aug Coll Cant 70. **d** 71 **p** 72 Kens for Lon. C of St Etheldreda w St Clem Fulham 71-74; Chap The City Univ Lon 74-78; V of Coalbrookdale (w Ironbridge and L Wenlock from 79) Dio Heref from 78; P-in-c of Ironbridge 78-79; L Wenlock 78-79. *Vicarage, Coalbrookdale, Telford, Salop, TF8 7NR.* (Iron bridge 3309)

APPENDIX

The following are the names and records of Clergymen whose addresses the Editor has been unable to obtain, and with whom, therefore, he could not communicate. Every effort has been made to trace their present whereabouts, but without success.

Owing to the pressure of space it has been found necessary to delete all Clergy whose names have appeared in this section of several issues of Crockford.

ABDY, Charles Leslie. b 1897. Linc Th Coll 29. **d** 31 **p** 32 S'wark. C of St Sav Denmark Pk 31-33; M of Coll of St Sav Carshalton 33-35; Publ Pr Dio S'wark 34-35; Org Sec Bp of S'wark's Youth Coun 33-37; C of Ascen Balham Hill 35-37; Caterham 37-41; V of St Jas Malden 41-53; R of St Mawgan w St Martin-in-Meneage 53-56; St Levan 56-61.

AINSLEY, John Alwyn. b 32. St D Coll Lamp BA 53. St Mich Coll Llan 53. **d** 55 **p** 56 Llan. C of Merthyr Tydfil 55-57; Roath 57-62; V of Sandbach Heath 62-64; Dioc Youth Chap Dio Pet 64-69; Leadership Tr Officer C of E Youth Coun 69-71; Sec for Youth Work C of E Bd of Educn 71-72; Dir of Lay Tr and Commun Service for Dio Worc 72-78.

AKHURST, Philip. b 34. Keble Coll Ox BA 58. ALCD 62. **d** 61 **p** 62 S'wark. C of All SS Shooter's Hill Plumstead 61-63; W Thurrock w Purfleet 63-67.

ANDREWS, Thomas George Desmond. TCD **d** 63 Down **p** 64 Tuam for Down. C of Ballymacarrett 63-66; Ballynafeigh 66-70; I of Scarva 70-75.

ARMSTRONG, Arthur Patrick. b 1898. TCD BA 20, Div Test (2nd cl) 22, MA 42. **d** 22 Clogh **p** 23 Down for Arm. C of Enniskillen 22-23; Miss (DUM) at Hazaribagh 23-27; C of St Pet and St Audoen Dub 28-29; Chap and Regr Kirwan Ho Dub 29-42; I of Cahir w Clogheen U 42-68; RD of Cahir 45-67; Lism Cahir 55-68; Preb of Kilrosanty and Treas of Lism Cathl 56-60; Preb of St Patr and Treas of Waterf Cathl 56-60; Prec 58-60; Preb of Rossduff and Chan of Waterf Cathl 60-68; Preb of Dysart and Chan of Lism Cathl 60-68; Archd of Waterf and Lism 61-68.

ARMSTRONG, John James. b 15. Trin Coll Dub BA 38, Div Test 40, MA 42. **d** 40 **p** 41 Down. C of St Patr Ballymacarrett 40-46; Neasden w Kingsbury 46-49; Chap and Engl Master Trin Coll Kandy 49-52; P-in-c of Kandy Distr Chaplaincy; C of St Marylebone 52-55; Hd of Trin Coll Miss Belf 55-58; Chap Miss to Seamen Port Sudan 58-60; Dunkirk and N France 60-63; C of Derriaghy 63-73; Hd of S Ch Miss Ballymacarrett 73-75; C of Seagoe 75-78.

ASKEY, Thomas Cyril. b 29. Univ of Sheff BSc 50. N-W Ordin Course 70. **d** 73 Stockport for Ches **p** 74 Ches. C of Gawsworth 73-76; V of Alvanley 76-78.

ASPINWALL, Herbert Victor. Univ Coll Dur LTh 10. BA 11, MA 15, St Aid Coll. **d** 12 **p** 13 Sarum. C of H Trin Trowbridge 12-15; St Pet Hale Chesh 15-18 and 22-26; St Geo Stockport 18-22; V of St Mark Dukinfield 26-33; Barnston 33-53.

ATKINSON, Donald. Magd Coll Cam 1st cl Hist Trip pt i 53, BA (2nd cl Hist Trip pt ii) 54, MA 57. Chich Th Coll. **d** 56 Bp Hawkes for Cant **p** 57 Guildf. C of Dorking 56-58; St Andr Uxbridge 59-60; Hd Master Friern Barnet Gr Sch 60-78.

BAKER, Harry Stephen. b 20. St Jo Coll Nottm 71. **d** 70 **p** 71 Argent. P Dio Argent 71-75.

BAKER, William George. St Cath S Ox BA 37, MA 42. **d** 38 Sheff **p** 42 Wakef. C of Swinton Dio Sheff 38-42; Mt Pelon 42-45; Sutton-in-Ashfield 45-47; Kirkburton 47-51; Kingsbury (in c of Dosthill) 51-53; V of Moreton Staffs 53-76.

BANYARD, Douglas Edward. b 21. SOC 69. **d** 71 **p** 72 Cant. C of Selsdon 71-77.

BARKER, George Thomas. b 1893. Selw Coll Cam BA 14, MA 38. Ely Th Coll 15. **d** 16 Stafford for Lich **p** 17 Lich. C of St Andr Walsall 16-26; St Nich Linc 26-28; V of Orby 28-49; Wingrave 49-69; Chap Mt Tabor Conv 49-64; Chap HM Borstal Aylesbury 50-52; Perm to Offic Dio Ox 70-78; Dio Ripon 71-78.

BARKER, Lewis Edward. **d** 35 **p** 36 Sheff. C of All SS Sheff 35-37; Herne Bay 37-39; V of Scopwick w Kirkby Green 39-46; Min of Conv Distr of Good Shepherd Little Coates 46-47; R of Hemingby 47-50; C of Horncastle 48-49; V of Scamblesby w Calkwell 49-50; CF 50-52; C of Fringford 60; R of Warkleigh w Slatterleigh and Chittlehamholt 60-62; Clophill 62-69.

BARRETT, Wilfred. b 19. Univ of Dur BA 46, MA 49. Wycl Hall Ox 55 and 56. **d** 57 **p** 58 Roch. C of St Paul Northumb Heath and Asst Master Erith Gr Sch 57-60; V of Wilmington 60-72.

BARTON, Dale. Selw Coll Cam 3rd cl Nat Sc Trip pt ia 69, BA (3rd cl Th Trip pt iii) 71, MA 75. Linc Th Coll 71. **d** 73 **p** 74 Newc T. C of All SS Gosforth 73-78.

BATCHELOR, Kenneth Burder. b 01. Fitzw Hall Cam BA 22 MA 39. St Mich Th Coll Llan 32. **d** 34 Warrington for Liv **p** 35 Liv. C of St Paul Southport 34-36; Asst Chap Hurstpierpoint Coll 36-38; C of St Jas w St John Bris 38-40; St Barn Knowle 40-43; Actg C of Gt Somerford 43-45; R of Cold Ashton 45-47; C of Downend 47-49; V of Elberton 49-56; C-in-c of Littleton-on-Severn 49-54; R (w Elberton from 56) 54-61; PC of Holt Wilts 61-67.

BEACOCK, Nicholas Julian. b 41. Univ of Dur BA (3rd cl Th) 62. Linc Th Coll 63. **d** 65 Barking for Chelmsf **p** 66 Chelmsf. C of St Barn L Ilford 65-70; Homeless Projects Officer Chr Action 70-78.

BELCHER, John Malcolm. b 32. Roch Th Coll 62. **d** 65 **p** 66 Ripon. C of Richmond 65-68; V of Startforth 68-72.

BELL, Alan. b 29. Linc Th Coll 64. **d** and **p** 65 Linc. C of Spilsby w Hundleby 65-67; V of Burgh-on-Bain 67-76; Kelsten w Calcethorpe and E Wykeham 67-75; R of Ludford Magna w Ludford Parva 67-75; Missr in Alford Group 76; Org Sec CECS 76-78.

BELL, Ronald. ALCD (2nd cl) 63. **d** 63 Warrington for Liv **p** 64 Liv. C of St Paul Kirkdale 63-66; St Luke Wimbledon 66-67; Asst Sec Internat S for Evang of Jews 67-78.

BENNETT, Arthur. Ripon Hall Ox 55. **d** 56 **p** 57 Man. C of Crumpsall 56-58; V of Leesfield 58-62; Saul w Frethern and Framilode 62-67; R of Shipton Moyne 67-71.

BICKLEY, Maurice Lincoln. b 21. Dipl Th (Lon) 44. **d** 49 **p** 50 Bris. C of Fishponds 49-54; V of St Thos Ap Eastville Bris 54-62; Ascen Crownhill Devonport 62-73.

BILLAM, John. St Aid Coll 63. **d** 66 Shrewsbury for Lich **p** 67 Stafford for Lich. C of Ch Ch, Wellington 66-70.

BLOFELD, Robert James. b 10. Men in Disp 45. MBE 68. Worc Coll Ox 3rd cl Cl Mods 31, BA (2nd cl Phil, Pol and Econ) 33, Dipl in Th 34, MA 36. Wycl Hall Ox 33. **d** 34 Warrington for Liv **p** 35 Liv. C of Ch Ch Ince-in-Makerfield 34-36; St Sav Everton 36-37; St Helen's 37-40; CF (EC) 40-46; Hon CF 46.

BOLTON, George Edward. b 01. Bps' Coll Cheshunt. **d** 63 **p** 64 Blackb. C of All SS Blackpool 63-65; H Trin Darwen 65-70; St Leon Balderstone 70-73.

BOLTON, John Donald. b 40. Edin Th Coll 61. **d** 65 **p** 66 Edin. C of Rosslyn Chap 65-67; C-in-c of St Barn Cathl Miss Edin 67-73.

BOSLEY, Raymond Arnold Christopher. b 03. Bp Wilson Th Coll IM. **d** 31 **p** 34 York. C of St Mary Bridlington 31-33; St Barn Hull 33-35; Penwortham 35-36; R of St Bart Salford 36-42; Elwick Hall (w Hart from 53) 42-56; C-in-c of Hart 45-53; V of Monkhesleden 57-61; PC (V from 69) of St Edm Gateshead 61-72; Perm to Offic Dio Dur 72-77.

BOSTON, James Terrell. b 47. Amer Univ Washington BA 68. Ripon Coll Cudd 76. **d** 76 Ox for Oregon USA. L to Offic Dio Ox 76-77; in Amer Ch.

BOWKER, Moses Edward. Wycl Hall Ox. **d** 61 **p** 67 Blackb. C of Oswaldtwistle 61-67; L to Offic Dio Blackb from 67.

BOXER, Ronald Malcolm Gordon. Edin Th Coll. **d** 59 **p** 60 Aber. Chap to St Andr Cathl Aber 59-62; Prec 62-63; C of St Clem Aber 63-64; St Marg Aber 64-69.

BOYD, Roland Philip. b 46. AKC 75. St Aug Coll Cant 75. **d** 76 **p** 77 Glouc. C of Dursley 76-77.

BREAKEY, Richard Digby Lloyd. Trin Coll Dub Daunt Exhib and 1st cl Phil 29, BA (Mod) and Downes Exhib 30. **d** 32 **p** 33 Clogh. C of Fivemiletown and Aghalurcher 32-34;

Tydavnet 34-35; All SS Blenheim Grove Camberwell 35; All SS Hertford 35-36; Harlow 36-40; R of Farnham 40-45; CF (EC) 40-42; V of Finstock 45-54; R of Aston Rowant w Crowell 54-62; C-in-c of Beech Hill 62-63.

BRINKER, Rudolph. St Aid Coll 34. Univ of Liv MA 42. Univ of Man PhD 44. **d** 34 Fulham for Roch **p** 36 Fulham for Lon. Chap CMJ Warsaw 34-36; Lwow 36-39; Liv Distr 39-45; Lect in Hebrew and Ancient Semetic Lang 44-45; Perm to Offic Dio Guildf 47-54.

BROOKE, Peter Miles. Oak Hill Th Coll 61. **d** 64 **p** 65 Roch. C of St Jo Evang Penge 64-66; I of Belmont 66-68; Swan River Bran 68-71; C of Iver 71-72; V of Gt and L Badminton w Acton Turville 72-74.

BRYANT, David Henderson. b 37. K Coll Lon and Warm BD and AKC 60. **d** 61 **p** 62 Sarum. C of H Trin Trowbridge 61-63; Ewell 63-67; V of Leiston w Sizewell 67-73; Chap RN 73-74; C of Northam 74-75; P-in-c of Clavering w Langley and Arkesden 75-77.

BRYCE, Alfred Walter. b 10. Trin Coll Dub BA 43, MA 54. **d** 45 **p** 46 Cashel. C of Thurles 45-48; C-in-c of Dungarvan 48-50; R of Dungarvan w Ringaroonah 50-55; CF 55-60; R of Ballynascreen 60-62; I of Banagher 62-72.

BUCKLE, Wilson Barmby. b 07. Qu Coll Birm 58. **d** 59 **p** 60 Sheff. C of Wombell 59-61; C-in-c of Dunscroft Conv Distr 61-63; V of Whitgift w Adlingfleet 63-69; Thorpe-Salvin 69-74.

BURLEY, John James Reginald. b 17. Worc Ordin Coll 64. **d** 66 **p** 67 Wakef. C of Gomersal 66-67; St Jo Bapt-in-Bedwardine Worc 67-70; V of Catshill 70-74; R of Redmarley D'Abitot 74-76.

BUTCHER, David. Kelham Th Coll 16. **d** 23 **p** 24 Man. C of St Pet Swinton 23-30; V of Oakenrod 30-72.

BUTTERWORTH, Roderick. b 35. K Coll Lon and Warm 58. **d** 59 **p** 60 Wakef. C of Castleford 59-63; V of St Geo Sowerby 63-67; V of St Mary Sowerby 67; Mytholmroyd 68-75.

CALVERT, John Stephen. Univ of Lon BSc (Econ) 53. Wycl Coll Tor BTh 61. **d** 61 **p** 62 Sask. C of Pelican Narrows Lac La Ronge 61-63; St John Preston (in c of Ch Ch) 63-70.

CAREY, Alan Lawrence. b 29. K Coll Lon and Warm AKC 53. **d** 54 **p** 55 Cov. C of St Nich Radford Cov 54-57; Burnham Bucks 57-65; C-in-c of St Andr Conv Distr Cippenham Burnham 65-77.

CARMAN, Percival. b 01. St Cath S Ox BA 30, MA 36. St Steph Ho Ox 30. **d** 31 Warrington for Liv **p** 32 Liv. C of St Paul Southport 31-34; Pontesbury (1st and 2nd portions) 34-36; Walton-on-the-Hill (in c of Good Shepherd) 36-39; V of St Mary Waterloo 39-47; Gt Sankey 47-63; Banks 63-68.

CASDAGLI, Emmanuel Theodore. b 04. Wycl Hall Ox 54. **d** 54 **p** 55 Roch. C of Sundridge 54-55; V of Dunton Green 55-59; R of Owermoigne w Warmwell 59-64; Chap Dorset Co Hosp 64-66; Odstock Hosp 66-70; Odstock & Newbridge Hosps & Sarum Gen Infirm 70-72.

CHARLTON, Wilfred Joseph. St Bonif Coll Warm 25. **d** 28 Lich for Madag **p** 29 Capetn. Miss at Tananarive and Warden of Boys' Hostel Madag 28-29; C of St Mary Ilford 32-33; St Mary Woodstock 29-32 and 33-34; R of St Anne Maitland 34-38: V of Sundon w Streatley 39-43; Lidlington 43-46; Husborne Crawley 47-49; R of Cottered w Broadfield and Throcking 49-54; Chetton w Glazeley and Deuzhill 54-60.

CHERRY, David. Roch Th Coll 59. **d** 61 **p** 62 Ripon. C of Seacroft 61-67; R of Bamford-in-the-Peak 67-75.

CLARK, Michael David. b 45. Jes Coll Ox BA 67, MA 72. Trin Coll Bris 72. **d** 72 **p** 73 Ches. C of Cheadle 72-77; SAMS Miss 77-78.

CLARK, Robert Henry. b 32. Oak Hill Th Coll 61. **d** 64 Warrington for Liv **p** 65 Liv. C of St Mark, Haydock 64-67; Higher Tranmere 67-75; V of Platt Bridge Dio Liv 75-78.

CLAYDON, Evan. b 1898. Qu Coll Cam BA 21, MA 25. Ridley Hall Cam 21. **d** 22 **p** 23 B & W. C of Walcot St Swithin 22-25; LPr Dio Chelmsf 25-26; CMS Miss Dera Ismail Khan 26-28; Chap (Eccles Est) at Peshawar 28 and 32-33; Risalpur 28-31; Kohat 29; Abbottabad 33-34; Nowshera 34; Quetta 34-35; Multan 36-40; Simla 40 and 42-44; CF (Ind) 41-42; Ambala 42-43; Pindi 44-45; Hon CF 46; Can of Lah Cathl 47; Ferozepur 46; Abbottabad 46-47; R of Dittisham 48-53; V of St Olave Woodberry Down 53-56; R of Morningthorpe w Fritton 56-63; RD of Depwade 57-58.

COLEBROOK, Christopher John. b 36. Univ of Lon BA (2nd cl Cl) 60, BD 69. St D Coll Lamp 60. **d** 62 Mon for Swan B **p** 63 Swan B. C of Llandilo-Talybont 62-66; Llansamlet 66-71; V of Nantmel (and St Harmon w Llanwrthwl 71-76) Dio Swan B 71-78.

COLEBROOK, Peter Acland. b 29. Edin Th Coll 52. **d** 55 Edin for St Andr **p** 56 St Andr. C of Rosyth 55-56; Lochgelly 56-59; Northfield 59-62; St Mary Bideford 62-66; Asst Master Evercreech Sch 66-72; Duchy Manor Sch Mere Wilts from 72; Perm to Offic Dio B & W 72-78.

COLLIER, John. b 13. St Jo Coll Dur BA 49. **d** 50 **p** 51 Blackb. C of Clayton-le-Moors 50-55; V of Wray (w Tatham Fells from 56) 55-58; St Phil Griffin Blackb 58-66.

COLLINS, Barry Douglas. b 47. Kelham Th Coll 66. **d** 70 **p** 71 Man. C of Peel Green 70-73; St Phil w St Steph Salford 73-75; R of H Trin Blackley 75-79.

COLLIS, Thomas William. b 1894. Qu Coll Birm 31. **d** 33 **p** 34 Wakef. C of St Aug Halifax 33-35; PV of Wells Cathl 35-37; Cler Org Sec NE Distr and L to Offic Dio Dur 37-38; V of Salton 38-45; C-in-c of Hovingham 42-45; V of Kilburn 45-49; Perm to Offic Dio Glouc 49-50; Dio Nor from 56; V of Bushley 50-54; R of Stock Gaylard w Lydlinch 55-56.

COLLMAN, Morris Gilbert. Qu Coll Birm 68. **d** 69 Ex. C of St Thos, Ex 69-78.

COLMAN, Jeremy Crackanthorp. b 41. Linc Th Coll 68. **d** 71 Lich. C of St Edw Leek 71.

COOKE, Samuel. b 17. Tyndale Hall Bris. **d** 49 **p** 50 Rang. P Dio Rang 49-55; Chap RAF 55-58; PC of Ch Ch Macclesfield 58-62; H Trin Scarborough 62-76.

CORFMAT, Percy Thomas Walter. b 14. K Coll Lon AKC 47. **d** 47 **p** 48 Guildf. Chap to Deaf and Dumb Dio Guildf 47-50; L to Offic at St Francis Ch for Deaf and Dumb Redhill 48-50; Chap E Lon Distr Deaf and Dumb 50-53; L to Offic at All SS Ch for Deaf and Dumb W Ham 50-53; Chap to Deaf and Dumb Dio St Alb 53-63; Dio Cant 63-72; Chap Miss for Deaf and L to Offic Dio Leic 72-73; Chap Coun for Deaf Dio Ox 73-78.

COWX, Tom. b 03. Ridley Coll Melb ACT ThL 28. **d** 28 **p** 29 Bp Stephen for Melb. C of St Geo Malvern Vic 28-29; Perm to Offic (Col Cl Act) at St Mary Cottingham 30-35; C of Guisborough 35-37; V of Rosedale 37-47; CF (TA-R of O) from 40; V of St Paul Middlesbrough 47-53; N Cave w N and S Cliffe 53-69; R of Hotham 55-69; Perm to Offic Dio York from 69.

CRANKSHAW, Frederick Francis Le Brun. St Aid Coll 36. **d** 38 Ripon **p** 39 Knaresborough for Ripon. C of St Edm Roundhay 38-40; Chap RAFVR 40-46; V of Bolton-on-Swale 46-78; RD of Richmond West 55-78; Proc Conv Ripon 64-78.

CRAWFORD, Maurice Victor. TCD BA 42, MA 48. **d** 43 Bp Hind for Down **p** 44 Down. C of Trin Coll Miss Belfast 43-46; Lenton 46-47; Attenborough w Bramcote 47-48; CF 48-54; Hon CF 54; R of Gt Hanwood 54-57; V of Marcham w Garford 57-60; C of St Geo Dub 61-64; Cler V of Ch Ch Cathl Dub 64-69; Asst Teacher Sch Kells 70-75.

CREEARS, Francis. b 1900. AKC 37. **d** 37 Lich **p** 38 Stafford for Lich. C of Wolverhampton 37-40; CF (EC) 40-45; C-in-c of Oxley Conv Distr 46-52; Min 52-53; V of Coseley 53-56; R of Church Kirk 56-70; L to Offic Dio Blackb 70-78.

CULLUM, John Donald. b 34. BD (Lon) 66. Ripon Hall Ox 63. **d** 66 **p** 67 Bris. C of Southmead 66-69; Perm to Offic Dio Bris 69-78.

CYAFUBIRE, Alfred. b 46. Bp Tucker Coll Mukono 67. **d** 71 **p** 72 Rwanda. P Dio Rwanda 71-72.

D'AGUIAR, Lawrence. Codr Coll Barb. **d** 56 **p** 57 Barb. C of St Jos w St Aid Barb 57-58; St Matthias w St Lawr Barb 58-60; Scarborough 60-65; C-in-c of Hutton Cranswick w Skerne 65-67; C of Northallerton w Kirby Sigston 67-69.

DAKIN, James Benjamin. SS Coll Cam 2nd cl Hist Trip pt i 32, BA 33, MA 37. Westcott Ho Cam 33. **d** 34 **p** 35 Man. C of Bury Lancs 34-37; Chap Toc H W Lon Area 37-40; BEf 40; LPr Dio Lon from 38; Chap Toc H for S Region 41-44; Asst Gen Sec C of E Council on Foreign Rel 44-45; C-in-c of St Pet Cornhill 45-46; Tutor at Dorchester Coll 46-48; Sec Br Coun of Chs Foreign Workers and Refugees Comm 48-50; Consult Sec World Coun of Ch Reconstr Dept 48-50; Adviser Orthodox Ch Affairs World Coun of Ch (Inter-Ch Aid Dept) and Dir Relig Affairs US Zone Germany 50-53.

DALE, Peter Ernest. b 41. St Pet Coll Ox BA 62, MA 68. Univ of Sussex DPhil 65t. BD (2nd cl) Lon 68. Tyndale Hall Bris 65. **d** 68 Ely **p** 69 Huntingdon for Ely. C of St Paul Cam 68-71; Bletchley w Water Eaton 71-78.

DAVENPORT, George Parry. Late Scho and Exhib of St D Coll Lamp BA (2nd cl Engl) 37. Sarum Th Coll 37. **d** 39 **p** 40 Swan B. C of Builth and Alltmawr 39; St Mary Brecon 39-41; Aberdare 41-47; Chap and Master at Chigwell Sch 47-76.

DAVIDSON, John. Edin Th Coll 62. **d** 66 **p** 67 Glas. C of Helensburgh 66-69; Kirkby (in c of St Mark, Northwood) 70-73.

DAVIES, Bernard. St D Coll Lamp BA (2nd cl Phil) 49. **d** 51 **p** 52 Mon. C of New Tredegar 51-53; Gellygaer 53-54; PC of Deeping St Nich 56-58; R of St Mary Beswick Man 58-63; V of Stand Lane 63-66.

DAVIES, Charles. b 1889. **d** 28 **p** 29 Man. C of St Luke Cheetham 28-31; St Jo Bapt Hulme 31-36; V of Rainow w Saltersford 36-50; Barnton 50-53; R of Byley w Lees 53-58;

Perm to Offic Dio Ches 58-78.

DAVIES, David Alcuin. Selw Coll Cam 3rd cl Cl Trip pt i 36, BA (3rd cl Cl Trip pt ii) 37. Ripon Hall Ox 37. **d** 39 **p** 40 Mon. C of Ebbw Vale 39-45; St Mary Gateshead 45-56; Perm to Offic Dio Dur 56-66.

DAVIES, David Scourfield. b 13. Univ of Wales BA 36. Univ of Leeds MA 50. St Mich Coll Llan 42. **d** 43 **p** 44 Mon. C of Rhymney 43-47; Brighouse 47-49; V of Upperthong 49-53; R of Lockwood 53-71; V of Kirkburton 71-76; Surr 71-78.

DAVIES, Graham Dudley. St D Coll Lamp BA 52, LTh 54. **d** 54 **p** 56 Llan. C of Aberdare w Cwmbach 54-60; Perm to Offic Dio Birm 60-76.

DAVIES, John Benson Evan. St Mich Coll Llan 24. **d** 26 **p** 27 Ban. C of Llangoed 26-27; Festiniog w Maentwrog 27-37; V of Corris 37-52; Edern w Nevin 52-55; Surr from 54; V of St Padarn's Welsh Ch Isl 55-74; St D Welsh Ch Ch Paddington 63-64.

DAVIES, John Thomas David. Jes Coll Ox BA 20. Wells Th Coll 22. **d** 26 **p** 28 Llan. C of St John Canton Cardiff 26-28; Perm to Offic at Port Talbot 28-29; C of W Teignmouth 29-31; Perm to Offic at St Jo Evang w St Anselm Clifton 32; C of Ch Ch Sutton Surrey 33-34; Westmr Cler Bureau 34-38; Perm to Offic at St John Wembley 38-40; All SS U Tooting 41; St John Ladbroke Grove 42-43; St Jude Kens 43-45; Perm to Offic Dio Lon 45-51; C of Bexley 51-53.

de BOARD, Robert. Selw Coll Camb BA 59, MA 63. Chich Th Coll 59. **d** 61 **p** 62 Wakef. C of Huddersfield 61-66; Industr Chap Wakef 63-66.

DELAP, William Alexander. Angl Th Coll BC 29. **d** 32 **p** 34 Caled. Miss of Telegraph Creek 32-33; Supt Prince Rupt Coast Miss 33-37; C of Ardamine 37-38; I of Mulrankin 38-62; Can of Clone and Crosspatrick in Ferns Cathl 56-62.

DeSILVA, Gamage Samuel. **d** 54 **p** 55 Kurun. P Dio Kurun 54-74; C of H Trin Cookridge Adel Ripon 74-78.

DEVONSHIRE, Roger George. K Coll Lon and Warm AKC 62. **d** 63 **p** 64 S'wark. C of Rotherhithe 63-67; Kingston Hill 67-71; Chap RN 71-75.

DICK, Daniel Thomas. b 1895. Ch Coll Cam BA 19, MA 24. **d** 19 **p** 20 Dur. C of St Paul Darlington 19-23; Stranton (in c of St Matt) 23-25; Min of Annfield Plain 25-29; V 29-33; V of Gorleston 33-42; Beverley Minster 42-47; Cromer 47-60; Surr 33-60.

DIXON, Thomas. Univ Coll Dur BA 33. **d** 34 **p** 35 Sheff. C of St Mary Sheff 34-36; Org Dir ICF for NE Area 37-39; V of Shildon 39-48; Chap CCG Frankfurt 48-50; Chap at Zurich 50-55; RD of Switzerland 54-55; R of Dinnington 55; V of St Swith Sheff 55-59; St Mich Harrow Weald 59-67; St Martin w St Andr Kentish town St Pancras 67-78.

DOWIE, Donald Campbell. Univ of Leeds BA (2nd cl Lat) 58. Coll of Resurr Mirfield 58. **d** 60 Lon **p** 61 Kens for Lon. C of St Andr Kingsbury 60-63; Chap Bloxham Sch 64-75.

DOWNING, John Derek Hall. Qu Coll Ox BA (2nd cl Th) 62, MA 68. Univ of Lon. MSc 68. Coll of Resurr Mirfield 61. **d** 63 **p** 64 Lon. C of St Steph Hammersmith 63-65; Stepney 65-68; Hon C 68-69.

EBBIT, Robert David. b 22. Trin Coll Dub BA 44, MA 56. **d** 45 **p** 46 Connor. C of St Mich Belf 45-47; CF from 47; DACG 65.

EDWARDS, Walter Harry. b 12. **d** 60 **p** 61 Leic. C of Kibworth Beauchamp 60-63; R of Bodham 63-69; V of E w W Beckham 63-69; R of Dunkeld w Birnam 69-73.

ELLIOTT, Charles Middleton. b 39. Late Scho of Linc Coll Ox BA 60, DPhil 63. Linc Th Coll 62. **d** 64 **p** 65 Southw. C of Wilford 64-65; H Cross Cathl Lusaka 65-69; w World Coun of Chs 69-72; Sen Research Fell Univ of E Anglia 72-74; Sen Lect 74-78; Hon Min Can Nor Cathl 74-78.

ELLISON, John Rowland. Univ of Dur LTh 35. Bp Wilson Th Coll IM 32. **d** 35 **p** 36 Liv. C of H Trin Walton Breck 35-38; St Paul Widnes 38-41; C-in-c of St Jas Conv Distr Eccleston Park 41-47; V of All SS Newton-le-Willows 47-50; St Paul Widnes 50-54; PC of H Trin Ripon 54-59; V of St Nich Wallasey 59-78.

ELU, Daniel. St Paul's Th Coll Moa I. **d** 69 **p** 70 Carp. C of Moa I 69-70.

EMERY, David John. b 37. Univ of Dur BA (3rd cl Psychology) 59. Chich Th Coll 63. **d** 65 Warrington for Liv & 66 Liv. C of Up Holland 65-68; St Faith Gt Crosby 68-70; V of St Barn Warrington 70-73.

ENGLISH, Philip Trevor. b 37. Univ of Dur BSc 60, Dipl Th 62. Cranmer Hall, Dur. **d** 62 **p** 63 Birm. C of Hall Green 62-66; Chap St John's Cathl Hong Kong 66-67; of Dorridge 67-72.

EVANS, Gwilym Albert. St Mich Coll Llan 26. **d** 27 **p** 28 Llan. C of Cadoxton-juxta-Neath 27-28; Kingsbury (in c of Hurley and Woodend) Warws 28-33; Heanor (in c of All SS Marlpool) 33-35; V of Horsley 35-44; PC of Swanwick 44-49; R of Town Barningham (or Barningham-Winter) 49-50; Barningham Northwood w Matlask 49-50; PC of Ticknal 50-56; R of Gillingham Norf 56-63; Gt w L Poringland and Howe 63-67; Perm to Offic Dio Nor 68-75.

EVANS, John David Vincent. Lich Th Coll. **d** 68 **p** 70 Pet. C of Kingsthorpe 68-69; Corby 69-72; L to Offic Dio Pet (in RD of Rutland) 72-74.

EVISON, Charles Henry. b 08. St Andr Coll Pampisford 48. **d** 49 **p** 50 Linc. C of All SS Gainsborough 49-51; C-in-c 51-52; R of Lea and PC of Kanith 52-57; Linc Dioc Insp of Schs 55-70; V of Goxhill 57-64; R of Binbrook 64-74; Swinhope w Thorganby 64-74.

EXON, Roland Henry Charles. St Cath S Ox BA 33, MA 37. Cudd Coll 51. **d** 52 **p** 53 Chich. C of Good Shepherd Preston Brighton 52-53; Chap Heritage Craft Schs Chailey 53-54; Ardingly Coll 54-57; Asst Master Carn Brea School Bromley 57-60; C of St Luke Reigate (in c of St Pet Doversgreen) 60-64; Odiham (in c of S Warnborough) 64; Chap and Asst Master Embley Pk Sch Romsey 65-75.

FINCH, Charles Edward Oscar. b 1889. Late Rustat Scho of Jes Coll Cam, Lady Kay Scho 09, Gatford Scho and BA 11, MA 16. Cl Tr Sch Cam 11. **d** 12 **p** 13 Cant. C of St Pet Croydon 12-16; SPG Miss at Nandyal 17-27; C of St Pet-in-Thanet (in c of St Andr) 27-31; V of Swavesey 31-34; R of King's Stanley 34-46; Gissing 46-59.

FISCHER, John Hugo. b 38. St Paul'S Coll Grahmstn 70. **d** 71 **p** 72 Capetn. C of Wynberg 71-74; Clanwilliam 74-75.

FISH, Frederic John. b 1894. St Edm Hall Ox BA (2nd cl Mod Hist) 23, MA 49. MC 16. Bp's Coll Cheshunt. **d** 25 **p** 26 Lon. C of St Pet Hornsey 25-27; St Benet Fink Tottenham 27-29; Perm to Offic at All SS Highgate 29-30; Chap (Eccles Est) Lah Cathl 30-33; Quetta 33-34; Multan 35-36; New Delhi 37-38; Simla 36-37 and 38; Ferozepore 30 and 38; Jullundur 39-44; Dalhousie 44; Lah Cathl 44-45; Rawalpindi 45-46; Murree 46; Hon CF 47; CF 47-49; Perm to Offic at St Jude-on-the-Hill Hampstead 49; at St Andr Hove 49-51; C of St Brelade (in c of St Aubin) Jersey 51-56; V of All SS Jersey 56-67.

FORREST, Frank. St Aid Coll 40. **d** 40 **p** 41 Lich. C of Chesterton 40-42; Hanley w Hope 42-45; Tamworth (in c of Hopwas) 45-47; R of Sawley 47-54; V of Chesterton 54-61; Barton-under-Needwood 61-63; Shareshill 63-68.

FRANCIS, Philip Harwood. St Cath Coll Cam 3rd cl Math Trip pt i 21, BA (3rd cl Math Trip pt ii) 22, MA 26. Chich Th Coll 34. **d** 35 **p** 36 S'wark. C of St Luke W Norwood 35-37; Knutsford 37-38; V of Marthall 38-57; Stoughton 57-77; R of Racton w Lordington 57-77.

FREEMAN, Shirley Beckett. b 14. Ch Coll Cam 2nd cl Hist Trip pt i 35, BA and Exhib 36, 2nd cl Th Trip pt i 37, MA 40. Ridley Hall, Cam 36. **d** 38 Tewkesbury for Glouc **p** 39 Glouc. C of St Mary w St Matt Cheltm 38-40; R of Bromsberrow 40-47; V of Gt w L Dalby 47-52; R of Landford w Plaitford 52-65; Long w L Bredy 65-75; Compton Valence 65-75.

FREEMAN, Walter Leonard. b 1895. AKC 22. Sarum Th Coll 23. **d** 24 **p** 25 York. C of Holme-on-Spalding Moor 24-28; St Mary Beverley 28-32; St Pet Bournemouth (in c of St Swithun from 35) 32-36; Margate (in c of St Aug) 36-38; V of Brixworth 38-51; Hardingstone 51-68.

FRICKER, Alfred Spartan. ALCD 27. **d** 28 **p** 29 Llan. C of Caerau w Ely 28-31; Llanishen w Lisvane 31-35; C-in-c of St Cath Conv Distr Caerphilly 35-52; V of St Matt Luton 52-60; R of Meppershall 60-71; R of U w Lower Stondon 60-71.

FRIZZELLE, David St Clair Alfred. Kelham Th Coll 36. **d** 41 **p** 42 York. C of Sutton-in-Holderness 41-43; St Barn Linthorp (in c of St Jas Middlesbrough 43-45; Chap RAF-VR 45-48; RAF 48-72.

GARDINER, Brian John. b 31. Chich Th Coll. **d** 60 **p** 61 St Alb. C of Leighton Buzzard 60-63; Haywards Heath 63-64; St Jo Evang Brighton 64-66; V of Scaynes Hill 66-71; C of Caversham (in c of St Andr) 73-77.

GAUGE, Barrie Victor. b 41. Late Exhib and Scho of St D Coll Lamp BA (2nd cl Th) 62. Selw Coll Cam BA (2nd cl Th Trip pt iii) 64, MA 74. **d** 65 **p** 66 St A. C of Newtown w Llanllwchaiarn and Aberhafesp 65-68; Prestatyn 68-73; R of Bodfari 73-76.

GEARY, Benjamin Handley. VC 15. Keble Coll Ox BA 14, MA 18. Wycl Hall Ox 19. **d** 21 **p** 22 Chelmsf. C of W Ham 21-23; CF Portsm 23-27; Aldershot 27.

GEORGE, Wilfrid. b 1894. St Aid Coll 29. **d** 31 **p** 32 Liv. C of St Jo Evang Knotty Ash 31-33; Lezayre (in c of Sulby) 33-36; V of Marown 36-46; Jurby 46-66; Chap of St Jude Andreas 56-66; L to Offic Dio S & M 67-74.

GERRARD, Patrick Maynard. CCC Cam BA 60. Linc Th Coll 63. **d** 65 **p** 66 Newc T. C of Cramlington 65-68; Old Brumby (in c of Westcliffe) 68-72.

GIBSON, Guy Grant. b 47. Ch Ch Ox BA (Nat Sc) 69,

MA 73. Univ of Nottm MTh 72. Lon Coll Div 69. **d** 71 **p** 73 Roch. C of St Paul Beckenham 72-74.

GILL, Stanley. Clifton Th Coll 37. **d** 39 **p** 40 Newc T. C of St Marg Scotswood 39-40; CF (EC) 40-46; Hon CF from 46; C of Woodhorn w Newbiggin 46-49; Hornsea w Goxhill 49-50; V of Chatton (w Chillingham from 55) 50-60; Alston w Garrigill Nenthead and Kirkhaugh 60-67; Cornhill w Carham 67-74; Surr 61-74; Branxton 71-74.

GILMORE, Charles James Frederick. MBE 45. St Jo Coll Ox BA 31, MA 35. Wycl Hall Ox 31. **d** 32 **p** 33 Guildf. C of Stoke-next-Guildf 32-34; St Luke Battersea 34-36; Chap RAF 36-49; Asst Chap-in-Chief Air Ministry 46-49; Admin Sec Chs' Coun for Health & Healing 69-75.

GODFREY, William Basil. b 1892. Keble Coll Ox BA 15, MA 20. **d** 15 Heref **p** 17 Llan for Heref. C of Hope w Shelve 15-17; Roath 17-34; R of Llanthewy-Vach w Llandegveth 34-37; Llanfair Kilgeddin w Llanfihangel Gobion (and Llangattock-juxta-Usk from 52) 37-69; L to Offic Dio Mon 70-78.

GOODE, Alfred Edward. St Jo Coll Dur BA 20. **d** 20 **p** 21 S & M. C of St Geo Douglas 20-23; Ashton-on-Ribble 23-30; V of St Mich AA Ashton-on-Ribble 30-48; Lund 48-56.

GOULD, Frank. b 24. K Coll Lon and Warm AKC 51. **d** 52 **p** 53 S'wark. C of St Jo Evang E Dulwich 52-55; Roehampton 55-57; C-in-c of St Jo Div Earlsfield 57-60; V 60-64; St Andr Catford 64-73.

GRAHAM, John Galbraith. Late Scho of K Coll Cam BA 43, 3rd cl Th Trip pt i 46, MA 46. Ely The Coll 46. **d** 48 **p** 49 S'wark. C of St Jo Evang E Dulwich 48-49; Chap St Chad's Coll Dur 49-52; C of Aldershot 52-55; Min of St Mich Conv Distr Beaconsfield 55-62; Chap to Reading Univ 62-72; C of St Pet Eaton Square w Ch Ch Broadway 72-74; R of Houghton w Wyton 74-79.

GRAINGER, Walter Noel Chatterton. b 03. Qu Coll Birm 27. K Coll Lon 29. **d** 30 **p** 31 Lon. C of St Barn Homerton 30-33; St Mich Golders Green 33-39; CF (TA) 39-45; V of St Phil Tottenham 45-51; St Mich Golders Green 51-60; K Chas Mart S Mymms 60-67; Okewood 67-78.

GRANT, Alfred Edmund. b 36. Sarum Th Coll 68. · 70 **p** 71 Malmesbury for Bris. C of Penhill 70-78.

GRIFFITH, Peter. b 51. St Mich AA Llan 74. **d** 77 St A. C of Denbigh 77-78.

GRIFFITHS, Frederick Griffith. AKC 36. **d** 36 **p** 37 Roch. C of Frindsbury 36-38; Durrington 38-39; St John Southend Lewisham 39-44; Feltham 44-47; LDHM of St Aug Whitton 47-49; C of Helmsley w Sproxton Carlton and Rievaulx (in c of Pockley) 49-50; V of Carlton Miniott w Sand-Hutton 50-54; R of Merredin W Austr 54-56; C of St Pet Burnley 56-58; V of St Paul Burnley 58-61; R of Bolton Abbey w Barden 61-78.

GRIFFITHS, Robert Fred. b 20. St Aid Coll 47. **d** 50 **p** 51 Worc. C of Redditch 50-52; Hartlebury 52-55; St Nich w St Pet Droitwich 55-58; St Barn Worc 58-61; R of Astley 61-69; C-in-c of St Richard's Conv Distr Fairfield 69-78.

HABGOOD, Stephen Roy. b 52. Univ Coll Cardiff Dipl Th 77. St Mich AA Coll Llan 75. **d** 77 Llan **p** 78 Bp Reece for Llan. C of Whitchurch 77-81.

HADLEY, John Spencer Fairfax. b 47. Ch Ch Coll Ox BA 70, MA 73. Univ of Leeds BA (Th) 72. Coll of Resurr Mirfield 70. **d** 73 Stepney for Lon. **p** 74 Lon. C of Stoke Newington 73-78.

HAINES, Charles Loftus. b 1888. Trin Coll Dub BAS 10, Div Test (2nd cl) 11, MA 27. **d** 12 Cashel for Waterf **p** 13 Cashel. C of Clonegam Guilcagh and Mothel 12-14; W Wycombe 14-16; Dromod 16-22; TCF 18-19; Dioc C of Ardf and Arghadoe 22-24; R of Dromod and Kilcrohane 24-59; Can of Kilpeacon in Lim Cathl 40-44; Treas of St Mary's Cathl Lim 44-47; Chan 47-59; RD of Killarney 44-59; Dean of Ardf and Agh 47-59.

HALL, James Thompson. b 22. St Chad's Coll Dur BA 45, Dipl Th 47, MA 48. **d** 47 Burnley for Blackb **p** 48 Blackb. C of Clitheroe 47-50; H Trin S Shore Blackpool 50-53; PC of St Geo Over Darwen 53-57; V of Grindleton 57-61; L to Offic Dio Bradf 61-78.

HALL, John Redvers. Univ of Dur BA 59, Dipl Th 62. **d** 61 **p** 62 Leic. C of Lutterworth w Cotesbach 61-63; Em Loughborough 63-66; L to Offic Dio Leic 66-70; Lect at Loughborough Tech Coll 66-70; Lanc and Morecambe Coll of Further Educn from 70; L to Offic Dio Blackb from 70; C of Wharton (in c of St Mary Borwick) 70-71.

HALL, Peter. Univ of Dur BA (2nd cl Th) 54. **d** 56 York **p** 73 Newc T. C of St Barn Linthorpe, Middlesbrough 56; Asst Master Friends' Sch Gt Ayton 58-60; Pontefract High Sch 60-65; Darlington High Sch 65-68; Humbersknott Sch 68-73; C of Monkseaton 73.

HANCOCK, Michael. b 26. Ex Coll Ox BA 50, MA 54. Sarum Th Coll 50. **d** 52 **p** 53 Ex. C of Bideford 52-56; S Molton 56-59; Withycombe Raleigh w Exmouth 59-61; V of Culmstock 61-75; V of Sheldon 69-72.

HARPER, Robert. b 08. Lon Coll Div 46. **d** 46 St D for E Szech **p** 47 E Szech. Miss Dio E Szech 46-51; Asst Chap Old Miss Ch Calc 52-53; Chap 53-55; P-in-c Telok Anson 55-58; V of Lower Perak 58-69; R of St Florence w Redberth 70-78.

HARRIS, Reginald Walter Norwood. b 03. Kelham Th Coll 25. **d** 30 **p** 31 Chelmsf. C of Wanstead 30-32; St Martin Knowle 32-33; St Geo St Kitts 33-35; R of St Mary Antig 35-37; C of All SS Ascot 37-78; R of St Pet Kitts BWI 38-49; V of Gt and L Hampton 49-66; Temple Guiting w Cutsdean 66-72.

HARRISON, Edward Albert Samuel. b 01. AKC 28. **d** 29 Glouc **p** 35 Lon. C of St John Coleford 29; St Mark Vic Pk 35-36; Perm to Offic at S Hackney 36-37; C of St Leon Shoreditch 37-39; Chap of Centr Home Whipps Cross Hosp and Forest Ho Leytonstone 39-60; C of St Cedd Becontree 54-56; V 56-58; C of Clee w Cleethorpes 60-63; PC of New Clee 63-68.

HART, Eric. Bp's Univ Lennox. **d** 26 **p** 28 Queb. Asst Miss magd Is Miss 26-27; Miss at Shigawake w Hopetown 27-28; Peninsula 28-30; C of St Andr Clifton 30-34; V of Hilderstone 34-40; St Jas Hull 40-53; V of St Luke Hull 40-53; Skipsea w Ulrome 53-55; R of Middle w E Claydon 55-59.

HATHAWAY, John George. Wycl Coll Tor. **d** 11 Tor for Calg **p** 12 Calg. Miss at Strathmore 11-14; Rimbey 14-18; Carmangay 18-20; H Trin Bordesley 20-25; C of St John Sparkhill 25-31; PC of St Edm Tyseley 31-36; V of St Matt Duddeston 36-40; PC of Settle 40-51.

HAWES, Godfrey Marcus. b 34. St Pet Hall, Ox BA (3rd cl Th) 57, MA 61. Wycl Hall, Ox 57. **d** 59 Sheff **p** 60 Bp Gerard for Sheff. C of Darfield 59-60; Ecclesfield 60-65; R of Hesketh w Becconsall 65-74.

HAWKES, Lawrence Earl. Univ of Tor BA 34. Wycl Coll Tor. **d** 36 **p** 37 Fred. Miss at Aberdeen w Brighton 36-43; R of Andover 43-52; Tweed and N Addington Ont 52-64; Fort McMurray 64-67; I of Smith's Sound 67-68; Seal Cove 68-70; Churchill Falls 70-71; R of Madawaska 71-74; Miss at Ft Smith 74-75.

HAYDOCK, Canon William. Bp Wilson Th Coll IM 26. Univ Coll Nottm 31. **d** 28 **p** 29 Liv. C of Aughton 28-31; Org Sec CMJ N Midl Distr Publ Pr Dio Southw and Perm to Offic Dio Pet 31-35; R of Saxelbye w Grimston and Shoby 35-37; Cler Deputn Sec Dr Barnado's Homes Dios Chesh Blackb Man and Liv 37-40; CF (EC) 40-45; Hon CF 45-48; CF (TA) from 48; V of St Mich Blundellsands 45-67; Can of Liv; Can (Emer) from 67; Dom Chap to Bp of S & M 67-69.

HEATLIE, James Welsh. b 09. Univ of Edin MA 30. **d** 32 **p** 33 Glas. C of H Trin Paisley 32-35; Falkirk (in c of St Mary Grangemouth) 35-36; H Trin Motherwell (in c of St Marg Mossend) 36-39; Ch Ch Glas 39-41; H Trin Dunfermline (w St Finnian Lochgelly) 41-43; P-in-c opf St Andr Gartcosh 43-50; R of Laurencekirk 50-53; Cruden 53-57; P-in-c of Cambuslang w Newton 57-62; Chap HM Pris Pentonville 62-63; HM Borstal Inst Feltham 63-65; V of St Pet Stockport 65-78.

HENDERSON, William Desmond. b 27. TCD BA and Div Test 56, MA 64. **d** 56 **p** 57 Arm. C of Derryloran (Cookstown) 56-59; Conwall 59-62; R of Killoughter 62-64; Kilrush 64-66; Tubbercurry w Kilmactigue 66-75.

HERON, Ian Crawford. b 16. Magd Coll Cam BA 37, MA 53. Wells Th Coll 53. **d** 55 **p** 56 Glouc. C of Tetbury w Beverston 55-57; R of Taynton 57-61; R of Tibberton 57-61; Stow-on-Wold 61-67.

HOLDEN, John Worrall. b 44. K Coll Lon AKC 67. St Aug Coll Cant 69. **d** 70 **p** Repton for Derby. C of St Bart Derby 70-72; Publ Pr Dio Derby 72-74; C of St Helier Morden 74-77.

HOLT, Samuel. **d** 53 **p** 54 Bradf. C of St Mary Magd Manningham 53-55; C-in-c of St Jas Conv Distr Woodhall 55-59; V 59-66; Marsden 66-71; Liversedge 71-76.

HOMAN, Cyril James. TCD BA and Div Test 08, MA 38. Ridley Hall Cam 08. **d** 09 **p** 10 Derry. C of Conwall 09-14; I of Kilteevogue 14-21; Raph w Reymochy 21-59; Can of Raph 22-38; Archd of Raph 38-57; Exam Chap to Bp of Derry 38-59; Dean of Raph 57-59.

HORSEY, Maurice Alfred. b 30. SOC 61. **d** 64 **p** 65 St Alb. C of All SS Oxhey 64-67; Coulsdon 67-71; V of St Sav Denmark Pk 71-77.

HOWELL, John Lamb. St D Coll Lamp BA 03. **d** 04 **p** 06 Llan. C of All SS Crindau Newport 04-08; St Mark Eldon 08-10; St Jo Evang Worksop 10-12; St Jude Eldon Sheff 12-13; All SS Elton Bury 13-16; All SS Stretford 16-18; St Cath Pontypridd 18-19; C-in-c of Pwllgwaun Conv Distr 19-23; V 23-30; V of King's Pyon w Birley 30-45; R of Aston Botterell 45-55.

HOWLAND, Antony Arthur. b 09. Chich Th Coll 31. **d** 35 **p** 36 Assam. Asst Chap Dio Assam 35-38; Chap at Tezpur

38; Dibrugarh 38-46; In Amer Ch 47-52; Chittagong 52-63; Menton 63-65.

HUGHES, Philip Dunkley. b 26. BD (Lon) 59. Univ of Birm MB, ChB 66. **d** 75 * 76 Worc. C of Kidderminster 75-78.

HURST, Alaric Desmond St John. Late Scho of New Coll Ox BA 49, MA 57. Wells Th Coll 48. **d** 51 Wakef **p** 53 Ripon. C of H Trin Huddersfield 51-52; St Geo Leeds 52-54; C-in-c of Conv Distr of Wigmore w Hempstead 54-55; C of Gravesend 55-57; St Edm Dartford 57-58; St Steph Walbrook Lon 58-59; V of St Paul Pudsey 59-63; Writtle 63-69.

IRONS, Richard John Graham. K Coll Cam BA 60, MA 64. Cudd Coll 61. **d** 63 **p** 64 Lon. C of St Mary Bryanston Square St Marylebone 63-67.

IZARD, Robin Thomas. Qu Coll Birm 61. **d** 62 **p** 63 Chich. C of Battle 62-65; Bognor 65-67; P-in-c of St Mark Nai 67-73.

JACQUES, Joe Francis. Clifton Th Coll. **d** 48 **p** 49 Pet. C of Duston 48-50; Uppingham w Ayston 50-54; Ripley 58-60; PC of Hayfield 60-72.

JAMES, Michael John. b 29. Ho of Resurr Mirfield. **d** 59 **p** 60 Carl. C of St Mary Windermere 59-61; H Trin Carl 61-63; C-in-c of St Luke's Conv Distr Morton Carl 63-67; V of Lambley w Knaresdale 67-72.

JAMES, Richard Lindsay. b 39. Kelham Th Coll 61. **d** 66 Ripon **p** 67 Knaresborough for Ripon. C of Seacroft 66-78.

JEGEDE, Zacchaeus Oluwafemi. Im Coll Ibad 57. **d** 59 Ondo-B **p** 60 Bp Awosika for Ondo-B. P Dio Ondo-B 59-62; Ondo 62-67; Perm to Offic Dio Man 68-78.

JENKINS, John Thomas. Down Coll Cam BA 19, MA 22. **d** 32 **p** 33 St A. C of Colwyn Bay 32-34; V of Capel Garmon 34-45; Connah's Quay 45-53; Llanstephan 53-64; Llanybri w Llandilo Abercowin 57-64.

JENNINGS, John. Trin Coll Dub BA 11, Div Test (2nd cl) 12, BD 37. **d** 12 **p** 13 Kilm. C of Killesher 12-15; All SS Clooney 15-18; Bradley Staffs 18-19; Kilnamanagh 19-24; I of Inishmagrath w Dowra 24-32; Kildallon (w Newtowngore and Corrawallen from 56) 32-64; Can of Kilm and RD of Kildallon 56-64; Exam Chap to Bp of Kilm 58-64.

JIRASINGHE, George Charles Galloway. b 15. **d** 34 **p** 37 Colom. C of Baddegama Miss 34-38; St Mich & AA Polwatte Colom 38-45; Supt Miss Baddegama Miss 45-49; I of St Steph Negombo; St Steph Marawala; St Phil Kurana; Negombo Miss 49-56; Ch of Ascen Bandarawela; Haputale & Diyatalawa; Ch Ch Dehiwala 64-74; C of St Nich Plumstead 74-78.

JOHN, Cynan Arlandwr. b 1890. K Coll Lon and Warm. **d** 50 **p** 51 S'wark. C of H Trin U Tooting 51-52; St Mark Kennington 52-53; H Trin S'wark 53-57; R of Coates 57-59; Hon C of All SS Tooting Graveney 59-63; St Helier Surrey 60-62; St Aug U Tooting 62-65; St Olave Mitcham 66-68; Perm to Offic Dios Lon and S'wark 69-74; Chap The Nat Hosps Lon from 70.

JOHNSTON, Arthur Walter. b 29. Sarum Th Coll 54. **d** 57 **p** 58 Sheff. C of Wombwell 57-59; Conisborough 59-62; Yeovil 62-66; R of Swainswick (w Langridge from 69) 66-73; R of Langridge 66-69.

JOHNSTONE, James Alexander Maxwell. b 1890. Egerton Hall, Man. **d** 28 **p** 29 Man. C of St John Farnworth 28-30; Perm to Offic at Cheddleton 30-33; L to Offic Dio Lich 33-34; C of Skelmersdale 34-36; V of Barnby-on-Don 36-37; Satterthwaite 37-46; Crosscrake 46-56; Rampside 56-62; V of Dendron 56-62.

JONES, Albert John. Univ of Wales, BA 36. St Mich Coll Llan 38. **d** 38 **p** 40 St D. C of Cwmamman 38-44; C-in-c of Llangynog 44-45; V of Trelech-ar-Bettws 45-47; Llangynog (w Llangain from 65) 47-78.

JONES, Bransby Albert Hussey. b 1893. Wadh Coll Ox BA and MA 20. Can Sch Linc 19. **d** 20 Ban for St A **p** 21 St A. C of Mold 20-23; Gresford 23-28; Brighton 28-31; V of St Andr Portslade 31-35; Moulsecoomb 35-48; Bosham 48-63.

JONES, Thomas Charles. b 1896. St D Coll Lamp BA 25. **d** 25 **p** 26 St D. C of Cwmamman 25-28; Llandefeilog w Cwmffrwd 28-33; V of Llanddeiniol 33-37; Llangennech 37-45; Llanfihangel-Abercowin 45-63; Surr 43-63; RD of St Clears 60-63.

JOSLIN, Peter. b 39. ALCD 65. **d** 64 **p** 65 Ox. C of Didcot 64-66; St Paul w St Mary Camberley 66; R of Elstead 73-75.

KEE, Robert. TCD BA 15. Div Test 16, MA 22. **d** 14 **p** 16 Down. C of St Nich Belf 14-19; St Luke Belf 19-20; Ch Ch Belf 20-22; St Paul Hendon Bp Wearmouth 22-25; St Thos Blackb 25-26; R of St Bart Salford 26-36; V of Mosley Common 36-62.

KERR, Francis Vincent Quartus. Univ of Dur LTh 16. **d** 16 **p** 17 Dur. C of St Mary W Rainton 16-18; R of Kilfinaghty (w Kilsiely and Clonlea from 23) 18-32; Ashby-by-Partney 32-33; C of Rathkeale w Nantenan 33-34; C-in-c of Ballinaclough w Templederry 35; I of Castleisland w Ballycushlane 35-39; R of S Otterington 39-44; I of Newcastle w Rathronan 44-52.

KERR, Robert Joseph. b 1899. TCD BA 32, MA 38. **d** 30 **p** 31 Dub. C of St Geo Dub 30-33; I of Derryvullan N 33-38; V of St Michan w St Paul Dub 38-44; St Geo Dub 44-71; Prof of Past Th Univ of Dub 48-56; RD of St Mark 51-69; Can of Ch Ch Cathl Dub 55-71.

KERRIDGE, Donald George. b 32. Bp's Coll Cheshunt, 61. **d** 62 **p** 63 Ripon. C of Manston 62-66; Hawksworth Wood 66-71; C-in-c of St Paul Darlington 71-72; Asst Chap Brentwood Sch Essex 72-75.

KERSHAW, Savile. Chich Th Coll. **d** 64 **p** 65 Wakef. C of Staincliffe 64-66; Saltley 66-68; Small Heath 68-78.

KIFF, Garfield James. b 1886. St Mich Coll Llan 26. **d** 27 **p** 28 Llan. C of Pontlottyn 27-29; Distr Sec and Lect RTS for NL Distr and Pr Dio Man 29-31; V of Calderbrook 31-34; Good Shepherd Rochdale 34-57; LPr Dio Ban 57-78.

KING, Canon Herbert Ernest. St Jo Coll Perth ACT ThL 10. Univ of W Austr BA 27. **d** 10 **p** 11 Perth. C-in-c of Northn 10-19; C of Midland Junction 19-21; R of Queen's Pk 21-22; Guildf 22-30; Cottesloe St Luke 30-34; RD of Cottesloe Distr 33-34; Sec SPG for Ireland 35-42; R of Caston 42-69; V of Griston 46-69; RD of Breckles 48-50 and 54-59; Hon Can of Nor 53-69; Can (Emer) 70-78.

KIRBY, Bernard William Alexander. b 39. Keble Coll Ox BA 62. Coll of Resurr Mirfield 62. **d** 65 **p** 72 S'wark. Hon C of St Phil w St Bart Battersea 72-76, Perm to Offic Dio S'wark 76-78.

KIRKWOOD, Michael Robert Russell. b 20. Ripon Hall Ox 58. **d** 60 **p** 61 Bris. C of Ch Ch Hengrove 60-63; Asst to Bp's Social and Industr Adv Bris 63-73; Bp's Cathl Chap 64-67; Dioc Chap Dio St Andr from 73.

KYBIRD, Paul. b 49. Selw Coll Cam BA 72. Qu Coll Birm 72. **d** 74 **p** 75 Leic. C of Em Ch Loughborough 74-77.

LAWREY, Leslie John. Em Coll Cam BA 45, MA 49. Ridley Hall, Cam 45. **d** 47 **p** 48 Warrington for Liv. C of Ch Ch Southport 47-50; Morden 50-53; Inter-Sch Chr Fellowship 53-63; Perm to Offic Dio Win 60-68; Dio Sarum 69-70; Dio Ex from 71.

LEE, William Dunsmore. Late Wansborough Sch of Hatf Coll Dur BA 36, MA 49. Univ of Lon BD 46. **d** 36 **p** 37 Newc T. C of Sleekburn 36-39; Cambois (in c of St Andr) 39-41; Morpeth 41-44; PC of Nenthead 44-49; V of Whitley St Helen 49-75.

LESSONS, Martin Victor. b 48. K Coll Lon BA (Hist) 69. Jes Coll Cam BA (Th) 72. Westcott Ho Cam 71. **d** 73 Nor. C of St Pet Mancroft Nor 73-75.

LEWIS, Francis Chad. AKC 39. **d** 39 **p** 40 Worc. C of St Aug Holly Hall Dudley 39-42; CF 42-67.

LIDDLE, Gladstone Wilfred. b 48. St Chad's Coll Dur BA (Th) 69. St Steph Ho Ox 71. **d** 73 **p** 74 St Alb. C of Hockerhill 73-78.

LILLINGSTON, Henry Gough. b 06. Selw Coll Cam BA 29. MA 33. Ridley Hall, Cam 29. **d** 31 **p** 32 Nor. C of St Marg w St Nich King's Lynn 31-34; E Dereham w Hoe and Dillington 34-36; R of Catfield 36-41; CF (EC) 41-46; R of Gt Bircham w Bircham Newton and Bircham Tofts 46-50; Marsham and of Burgh-next-Aylsham 50-59; Smallburgh w Barton Turf 59-61; V of Dilham 60-61; Champ and Sen Master Burebank Sch 62-67; Asst Master Cawston Coll 67-71.

LIPP, Alistair. b 1896. Edin Th Coll 24. Univ of Dur LTh 26. **d** 26 **p** 27 Glas. C of St Geo Maryhill Glas 26-29; C-in-c of Ascen Mosspark Glas 29-39.

LITTLEJOHN, Theodore Harold. Roch Th Coll 62. **d** 64 **p** 65 Ex. C of Tamerton Foliot 64-65; Crediton 65-69; V of St Bridget Wavertree 69-72; C of Honiton 73-76; C-in-c of St Aug Plymouth 76-77.

LITTLER, Malcolm Kenneth. b 34. St D Coll Lamp BA (2nd cl Hist) 55. **d** 57 **p** 58 St D. C of Llanelli 57-60; Llandeilo Fawr 60-61; R of Punchestown 61-64; Lampeter Velfrey 64-68; V of Llanwnda w Manorowen and Goodwick 68-74; Llanfynydd 74-78.

LOCK, David Stephen. b 28. **d** 63 **p** 64 S'wark. C of H Redeemer Streatham Vale 63-66; Hatcham Dio S'wark 66-74.

LONG, Samuel Godfrey. b 04. Coll of Resurr Mirfield 45. **d** 47 **p** 48 York. C of Hornsea 47-50; St Aug Haggerston Lon 50-51; Chap S Afr Ch Rly Miss Dio S Rhod 51-52; Dio Kimb K 52-53; Perm to Offic Dio Lon 53-54; Dio St E 54-55; R of L w Gt Glemham 55-62; L to Offic Dio St E 62-75.

LONGWORTH, Clifford Jack. b 39. Lich Th Coll 67. **d** 70 **p** 71 Lich. C of St Chad Coseley 70-74.

LOOKER, Stanley George. Lich Th Coll 64. **d** 65 **p** 66 Lich. C of Rugeley 65-67; Carshalton Dio S'wark 67-71; Cramlington 71-74.

LOUGHTON, Michael. b 34. K Coll Lon and Warm BD

and AKC 58. **d** 59 **p** 60 Chelmsf. C of Chingford 59-62; St Eliz Eastbourne 62-65; R of St Jo Bapt-sub-Castro Lewes 65-74.

LOWERS, Alfred John Stephen Mortimer. b 01. Univ of Dur LTh 32. ALCD 32. **d** 32 **p** 33 S'wark. C of St Paul Brixton 32-35; Greenwich 35-37; St Giles (in c of St Barn) Colchester 37-39; Corsham 40-47; R of Foxley (in c of Norton) 47; Westerleigh 47-72.

LUMGAIR, David. b 06. CBE (Mil) 59. AIB 27. FCCS (FCIS from 70) 60. Sarum Th Coll 61. **d** 62 63 Edin. Chap and Sacr of St Mary's Cathl Edin 62-64; V of Shotwick 64-67; Dom Chap to Bp of Ches 64-67; R of Ballaugh 67-70; V of Santan 70-72; Sec Dioc Syn S & M 70-72; Hon Chap RM U 73; Chap St Vincent Chap Edin 75-77.

LYON, John Richard George. b 21. Em Coll Cam BA (3rd cl Hist) 43, MA 54. Linc Th Coll 44. **d** 45 Stepney for Lon **p** 46 Lon. C of All SS Poplar 45-49; St Cypr Cathl Kimberley 49-52; Commiss Geo 52-56; PV and Succr of S'wark Cathl 52-54; V of St Pet Loughborough 54-56; Prin Kilworthy Ho Tavistock 62-71; Perm to Offic Dio Ex 64-68; L to Offic 68-71; V of Bickleigh W 71-77.

McCANDLESS, John Hamilton Moore. b 24. TCD 61. **d** 63 **p** 64 Connor. C of St Matt Shankill Belf 63-66; I of Termonmaguirke 66-69; C of Jordanstown 69-70; I of Ballinderry 70-74.

McKENNA, Terence. TCD BA (2nd cl Semitic Langs Mod) 66, MA 69. St Pet Coll Ox BA (3rd cl Th) 68. Wycl Hall Ox 68. **d** 68 **p** 69 Cork. C of H Trin Cork 68-70; I of Rathcormack 70-72; Abbeystrewry 72-74.

McNAIR, William Henry. Univ of Lon BA 41. Cudd Coll 55. **d** 55 Blackb **p** 56 Lanc for Blackb. Asst Master Rossall Sch 55-58; L to Offic Dio Melb 58; V of Curry Rivel w Weston 59-62; C of Bath Abbey 62; L to Offic Dio Derby 62-64; Perm to Offic Dio Adel 64-70.

MAGUIRE, Michael Timothy Gale. b 34. Wycl Hall Ox 58. Dipl Educn (w distinc) 61. **d** 61 **p** 62 Win. C of Southn 61-63; Bp's Youth Chap Dio Win 63-67; Asst Sec C of E Coun Social Aid 67-69.

MAIN, David. Univ of Man BA (1st cl Semitic Lang) 40. St Jo Coll Ox BA (2nd cl Or Lang) 48, MA 53. Cudd Coll 40. **d** 41 **p** 42 Blackb. C of St Jo Evang Blackb 41-42; CF 42-46; Perm to Offic Dio Ox 46-48; SPCK Miss and Chap at Maadi 48-52; Chap of St Mich AA Heliopolis 52-57; R of Bracon Ash w Hethel 57-75.

MAJOR, Carl Reginald. Mem Univ of Newfld BA and LTH 59. Qu Th Coll Newfld 53. **d** 58 **p** 59 Newfld. R of Bay L'Argent 58-59; Battle Harbour 59-61 and 63-64; P-in-c of Milden 61-63; I of Happy Valley 64-68; St Steph Antig 68-72; Whitbourne 72-73; R of All SS Port of Spain 73-77.

MASON, Leslie Donald. OBE 55. St Jo Coll Dur BA 38, Dipl Th 39, MA 41. **d** 39 **p** 40 Dur. C of Seaham w Seaham Harbour 39-40; Chester-le-Street 40-42; C-in-c of St Luke w Hartlepool 42-44; Thorpe Thewles 44; LPr Dio Lagos 45-47; Asst Master Igbobi Coll Lagos 45-47; Prin Ch Sch Ado-Ekito 48-66; Hon Can of Ondo 60-66.

MASSEY, Richard Standring. b 20. **d** 52 **p** Cov. C of Finham 52-55; Ottery St Mary 55-57; Dartmouth 57-60; St Jas Teignmouth 60-63; Tor Mohun 64-69; St Jo Evang Torquay 69-73; Centr Torquay 73-74.

MAUGHAN, Herbert Hamilton. Keble Coll OX BA 05, MA 15. **d** 07 Colchester for St Alb **p** 08 St Alb. C of St Sav Hitchin 07-09; St Cuthb Philbeach Gardens 09-10; St Mich Brighton 10-12; Asst Chap Ellesmere Coll 14-16; LDHM of N Hillingdon 30-31.

MAURICE, Kenneth. b 07. St D Coll Lamp BA 34. **d** 33 Taunton for B & W. C of Wembdon 33-35; Dawlish 35-36; Sidmouth 36-39; R of Buckerell 39; Perm to Offic at Dawlish 42-45; C 45-46; Clevedon 46-47; Chap at Lausanne 47-48; Estoril 48-49; Perm to Offic at Minehead Somt 49; Dio Heref 50-51; at Kewstoke Weston-super-Mare 51-57; R of Cruwys Morchard 57-68.

MERCER, Geoffrey Hamish. Selw Coll Cam BA 13, MA 20. Leeds Cl Scho 13. **d** 14 **p** 15 Wakef. C of St Mary Barnsley 14-17; Lightcliffe 17-18; Served in Army 18-19; C of H Spirit Leeds 19-20; Dom Chap to Bp of Maur 20-22; Warden of St Paul's Th Coll Maur and Chap of Rose Hill w Beau Bassin 20-24; Perm to Offic Dio Ripon 24-25; SPG Deputn 24-25; C of St Chad Far Headingley 25-28; V of Pool 28-38; PC of Oulton 38-59; Chap of Oulton Hall Mental Hosp 50-59.

MICHELL, Charles Henry. Univ of Manit LLB 21. Clifton Th Coll 32. **d** 35 **p** 37 S'wark. C of All SS Blenheim Grove Camberwell 35-39; Cromer 39-42; Chap RAF 42-45; C or Orilla Tor 45-48; R of King 48-57; Oak Ridges Tor 57-62; C-in-c of Uxbridge 63-65; Perm to Offic Dio Sarum 66-67; R of Oborne w Poynington 67-78.

MILNE, John Barrett. b 08. GM 41. Ho of Resurr Mirfield. **d** 57 **p** 58 Chich. C of Petworth 57-58; St Mary Virg E Grinstead 58-62; Chap Sch of St Helen and St Kath Abingdon 63-64; R of Ovingdean 64-73.

MISKIN, Christopher Richard. b 22. **d** 69 Mashon. Chap Springvale Sch Marandellas 70-73.

MOKOTSO, Solomon Lesole. St Pet Coll Alice, LTh 67. **d** 66 **p** 67 Bloemf. P Dio Bloemf 67-77; Perm to Offic Dio Birm 77-78.

MOLL, David Henry. b 27 St Chad's Coll Dur 49. **d** 54 **p** 55 Newc T. V of St Pet Wallsend 54-57; Wymondham Norf 57-61; R of Yaxham 61-67; R of Welborne 61-67; Poringland w Howe 67-75; C-in-c of Framingham Earl 70-75.

MOODY, Colin John. b 36. Chich Th Coll 61. **d** 63 **p** Chich. C of Hove 63-69; St Barn Dulwich 69-70; Perm to Offic Dio Bris 70-71; Dio Chich 71-78.

MORETON, Ernest Gilbert. b 04. St Aid Coll 31. **d** 33 **p** 34 York. C of Heworth 33-35; Selby Abbey 35-36; V of St Jas Scarborough 36-48; CF (TA - R of O) 39-41; CF (EC) 41-45; V of St Alb Hull 48-58; r of Terrington 58-63; R of Dalby w Whenby 58-63; Scawton w Cold Kirby 63-65; C-in-c of Old Byland 63-65.

MORGAN, Robert Frederick. b 15. Ch Coll Cam 2nd cl Hist Trip pt i 36, BA (2nd cl Th Trip pt i) 38, MA 41. Ridley Hall Cam 37. **d** 39 **p** 40 Cov. C of H Trim Leamington 39-43; CF (EC) 43-46; C of St Mich Stoke Cov 47-49; V of Hartshill 49-59; R of Holbrood w Stutton 59-70; V of Ven Bede Gateshead 70-72; Team V of Gateshead (in c of Ven Bede) 73-75; V of Ickleton 75-78.

MORGAN, Owen. St D Coll Lamp BA 39. **d** 40 **p** St A. C of Corwen 40-42; Minera w Coedporth 42-44; Llangyfelach w Morriston 44-52; R of Llanvillo w Llandefaelog-Tre'r-Graig 52-59; V of Cefn Coed w Nantddu 59-78.

MORGAN-SMITH, Bernard George. St Chad's Coll Dur BA 29, Dipl Th 30, MA 32. Ely Th Coll 30. **d** 31 **p** 32 S'wark. C of St Jude Peckham 31-34; St John Walham Green 34-40; St Jo Diov Earlsfield 40-41; V of Pawlett 41-46; St Aid Bris 46-75; Perm to Offic Dio Bris 75-78.

MORRELL, William David. Univ Of Otago BA 63. NZ Bd of Th Stud LTh 66. St Jo Coll Auckld. **d** 66 **p** 68 Dun. C of Roslyn 66-71; Asst Chap Ch Ch Hosp 72-77.

MORRIS, Joseph Herbert. b 1897. Worc Ordin Coll 53. **d** 53 Worc **p** 54 Bp C E Stuart for Worc. C of St Martin w Whittington Chap Worc 53-55; V of Eldersfield 55-66.

MORRIS, Kenneth Owen. b 12. Univ of Wales BA (2nd cl Phil) 34. St Mich Coll Llan 35. **d** 37 **p** 38 St A. C of Rhosymedre (in c from 39) 37-46; CF (TA - R of O) from 39; CF (EC) 40-46; V of Raveningham w Norton Subcourse 46-54; Hales w Heckingham 48-54; R of Benington (w Aston from 59) 54-60; C-in-c of Aston 54-59; L to Offic Dio Chelmsf 60-67; Dio St Alb 60-78.

MULLER, Vernon. Univ of Natal BA 61. St Chad's Coll Dur Dipl Th 64. **d** 64 Chelmsf **p** 65 Natal. C of St Martin Durban N 64-68: R of Queensburgh 68-76.

MULLINS, Malcolm David. b 42. St Edm Hall Ox BA (2nd cl Th) 63. St Steph Ho Ox 63. **d** 65 Warrington for Liv **p** 66 Liv. C of Kirkby 65-69; H Redeemer (in c of Good Shepherd Blackfen) Lamorbey 69-75; Solihull (in c of St Cath) 75-78.

MUNNS, (Philip) Peter Lomas. BA (2nd cl Hist) Lon 62. Kelham Th Coll 48. M SMM 60. **d** 52 **p** 53 Bloemf. Miss at Modderpoort Miss 52-56; Kroonstadt Miss 56-58; LPr Dio Southw 58-62; Warden St Aug Miss Modderpoort 62-63.

MURPHY, John Llewellyn. St D Coll Lamp BA 37. **d** 38 Sheff. C of Kirk Sandal 37-40; St Jas Doncaster 40-45; C-in-c of Whinney Hill Conv Distr 45-47; R of Adwick-le-Street 47-54; V of Firbeck w Letwell 54-68; Loversall 68-75.

NDUMBU, Joel Mbithi Gideon. b 30. Clare Coll Cam Dipl Th 68, BA 73. Ridley Hall Cam 67. **d** 68 Huntingdon for Ely **p** 69 Ely. C of Chesterton 68-71; Cherry Hinton 73-75.

NEVILLE, George. Ch Coll Cam BA (2nd cl Th Trip) 22, MA 26. Wycl Hall, Ox 22. **d** 23 **p** 24 Liv. C of St Paul Southport 23-25; St Steph (in c of St Matt) Rashcliffe 25-29; Chap of Luxor Egypt 29-30; Perm to Offic at St Chrys Everton Liv 30-31; LPr Dio Carl 34-35 and 45-67.

NEWHOOK, Cleophas James. Mem Univ of Newfld BA 65. Keble Coll Ox BA 67. Qu Th Coll Newfld 65. **d** 67 **p** 68 S'wark for Newfld. C of St Mich AA S Beddington 67-73.

NEWMAN, William Herbert White. Univ of Dur LTh 22. Chich Th Coll. **d** 23 Southn for Win **p** 25 Win. C of St Barn Southn 23-27; Lyminster 27-31; St Steph Buckland Portsea 31-33; Caversham (in c of St Barn Emmer Green) 33-36; V of Horton w Studley 36-46; R of St Martin Martinhoe w St Pet Trentishoe 46-52; C of Portchester 53-57; Wymering 57-60; Waterlooville 60-62.

NEY, Hans Dieter. b 36. Ridley Hall Cam 69. **d** 72 **p** 73 Dur. C of Usworth 72-78.

NICHOLAS, William Ronald. b 06. St D Coll Lamp BA 28. Wells Th Coll 28. **d** 29 **p** 31 St D. C of H Trin Aberystwyth 29-31; Tenby w Gumfreston 31-36; R of St Lawr w Ford 36-42; V of Lamphey w Hodgeston 42-53;

Johnston w Steynton 53-74.

NICHOLS, Derek Edward. b 33. Univ of Lon BD 58. Chich Th Coll 72. **d** 72 **p** 73 Portsm. C of Hayling S 73-75; V of Locks Heath 75; Perm to Offic Dio Lind 75-78.

NOBBS, Edward Frank Leslie. b 35. Keble Coll Ox BA 59, MA 63. Ely Th coll 59. **d** 61 **p** Ex. C of St Gabr Plymouth 61-64; Gt Marlow (in c of St Mary Marlow Bottom) 65-69; Asst Master Charters Sch Sunnningdale and Perm to Offic Dio Ox 69-72; Pindar Sch Eastfield, Scarborough and Perm to Offic Dio York 72-78.

NOBLE, Bruce Harvey. b 37. Univ of Queensld BA 61. Qu Coll Ox BA (2nd cl Th) 69. St Francis Coll Brisb ACT ThL (2nd cl) 63. **d** 63 Bp Hudson for Brisb **p** 63 Brisb. C of Annunc Camp Hill Brisb 63-65; Bundaberg 65-66; St Matt Sherwood Brisb 66-67; C-in-c of St Geo Preston 69-72; H Trin Cov 72-78.

NORMAN, Harry. b 13. St Barn Coll Adel 33. ACT ThL 38. **d** 38 **p** 39 Adel. C of Ch Ch Adelk 38-40; Chap AIF 40-46 (Men in Disp 45); LPr Dio Adel 40-46; Cf 46-57; Commiss Bunb from 52-78.

NOTLEY, Dennis Arthur. b 02. Clifton Th Coll 38. **d** 40 **p** 41 Lich. C of Cobridge 40-43; St Bride Old Trafford 43-45; V of St Paul Brixton 45-52; R of Ipsley 52-64; V of Grimley w Holt 66-73; C of Steeton 74-75.

NYE, Harold Eustace Bertram. Univ Coll Dub (NUI) BA 12. **d** 14 **p** 15 Nor. C of st Phil Heigham 14-16; Matlock 16-18, Romford 18-20; Perm to Offic Dio Chelmsf 20-23; R of Scampton (W Aisthorpe and W Thorpe V from 35) 23-47.

O HARBOURN, Edward Gordon Lawrence. b 34. St D Coll Lamp BA 59. **d** 60 **p** 61 Mon. C of St Andr Newport 60-65; V of Six Bells 65-70; Chap of St Margaret's C of E High Sch Aigburth Liv 70-73; C of St Mary w St Columb Liscard 73-78.

OATES, Alexander John. b 38. Clifton Th Coll 63. **d** 67 **p** 68 S'wark. C of St Sav Brixton Hill 67-68; Westcombe Pk 68-71; Stechford 71-74; R of Greenhithe 74-77.

OATES, Thomas Nichols. b 45. Harvard Univ BA 71. Jes Coll Cam 76. **d** 76 W Mass **p** 77 Lon. In Amer Ch 76-77; C of St Helen Bishopsgate Lon 77-78.

OLADIPO, Emmanuel Olugboyega. Im Coll Ibad 64. **d** 67 **p** 68 Ibad. P Dio Ibad 67-73; C of Eaglescliffe 73-75.

OLIVER, James Aldridge Ivan. St Cath Coll Can BA 48, MA 53. Coll of Resurr Mirfield, 48. **d** 50 **p** 51 Lon. C of St Barn Northolt 50-52; St Barn Pimlico 56-59; C-in-c of Resurr Conv Distr Berkley Scunthorpe 59-69; C of St Andr w St Luke Grimsby 70-74.

ORME, John Theodore Warrington. AKC 39. **d** 39 Willesden for Lon **p** 40 Lon. C of St Paul Finchley 39-41; St Paul Harringay 41-43; Master Denmead Sch 43-44; The Mall and Rutland Ho Sch 44-45; Perm to Offic Dio Lon 44-45; Chap Hove Coll Hove 45-47; Asst Master Beaumont Ho Sch Rickmansworth 48-52; Perm to Offic Dio St Alb 49-52; Dio Lon 68-70; Dio Ox 70-71.

OSWELL, Charles Medcalf. Sarum Th Coll 22. Univ of Dur LTh 24. **d** 24 **p** 25 Man. C of St Luke Heywood 24-26; Almondbury 26-32; V of Ryhill 32-44; Winterbourne St Martin 44-49; Chap to HM Pris Dorchester 47-49; V of N Cave w N and S Cliffe 49-52; Cold Aston w Notgrove 52-53; Birchencliffe 53-55; Farnley Tyas 55-77; Chap Storthes Hall Hosp 55-57.

OWEN, Roy Meredith. b 21. Univ of Wales, BA 43. St Mich Coll Llan 43. **d** 45 **p** 46 Llan. C of St Martin Roath 45-47; Penarth w Lavernock 47-51; Merthyr Dyfan w E Barry 51-56; V of Llangeinor 56-62; V of Poltyclun w Talygarn 62-78.

PAIN, John Holland. b 04. Wadh Coll Ox BA (3rd cl Engl Lit) 25, 2nd cl Th 27, MA 32. Wycl Hall, Ox 27. **d** 27 **p** 28 Liv. C of St Helens 27-30; V of Ch Ch Ince-in-Makerfield 30-35; St Sav Everton 35-38; Gerrards Cross 38-51; Ranmoor 51-59; RD of Hallam 57-59; V of Framfield 59-69; Perm to Offic Dio Chich 69-78.

PARFIT, Eric George. St Jo Coll Cam BA 32, MA 36. Ridley Hall Cam 32. **d** 36 **p** 37 Lon. C of St Mary Bryanston Square 36-40.

PARKIN, Terence Derek. b 36. Lich Th Coll 64. **d** 66 **p** 67 Lich. C of St Chad Lich 66-70; Penn 70-72; V of St Aid Shobnall Burton-on-Trent 72-77.

PARRY, Edward Morris. Late Butler Scho of St D Coll Lamp BA (2nd cl Engl) 38. Ripon Hall, Ox. **d** 39 **p** 40 Liv. C of Em Fazakerley 39-41; Chap RAFVR 41-47; RAF 47-69.

PATERSON, Stuart Maxwell. b 37. Lich Th Coll 58. **d** 60 **p** 61 Derby. C of Ilkeston 60-64; PC of Somercotes 64-70; R of Wingerworth 70-73; M Gen Syn 70-73.

PATTEN, Michael Frederick. b 37. Lon Coll of Div 62. **d** 65 Barking for Chelmsf **p** 66 Chelmsf. C of Leyton 65-69; St Luke w Ch Ch Bris 69-70.

PEACOCK, Leslie Vernon. b 1893. Sarum Th Coll 38. **d** and **p** 39 Chich. C of W Grinstead w Partridge Green 39-41; Chap RAFVR 41-46; V of Selmeston w Alciston 46-53; PC of Chideock 53-59.

PERCY, Henry Cooper. b 1880. Headingley Coll Leeds 01. **d** 10 **p** 11 Dur. [f Wesleyan Min] C of St Jas W Hartlepool 10-12; Whickham 12-13; Pannal 14-16; Keighley 16-19; Pershore 19-20; Ch Ch Cockermouth 21-23; Ayr (in c of St John's Miss) 23-26; Tiverton 26-29; Crediton 29-34; V of Bampton Aston w Shifford 34-35.

PHILLIPS, Arthur Harry. AKC 34. St Stephen Ho Ox. **d** 34 **p** 35 Lon. C of St Jas Norlands 34-37; Palmers Green 37-40; Min of H Redeemer Conv Distr S Greenford 40-41; CF 41-44; C of St Mary L Cam 67-73.

PICKARD, Ronald William. ALCD 39. **d** 39 **p** 40 York. C of St Andr Drypool 39-41; Chap RNVR 41-46; RN 46-51; Min of Ch Ch Maracaibo and Chap at Maracaibo Oilfields Venezuela 51-62; Chap at Lima Peru Dio Argent 62-63; Dio Chile 63-69; Hon Can of St Andr Cathl Santiago 65-69.

PIKE, Sidney Gilbert Bassett. Late Scho of Em Coll Cam BA 06, MA 19. Ridley Hall Cam 07. **d** 07 **p** 08 Glouc. Chap Cheltm Coll 07-09; C of Shortlands 09-11; Org Sec S Amer MS for SW Distr 11-15; V of Chirstow 15-25; Farcet 25-28; R of Wambrook 28-34; V of Abbot's Kerswell 34-44; R of Belstone w Sticklepath 44-57; L to Offic Dio Ex 57-73.

PIKE, William Prenter. b 41. TCD BA 63, Div Test 64. Va Th Sem USA BD 68. **d** 64 **p** 65 Dub. C of St Mary Crumlin 64-67; on leave 67-69; Monkstown 69-72; R of Tralee 72-75; Dingle 72-75; Ballymacelligott 72-75; in Amer Ch from 75.

PITT, William Philip Basil. OBE 77. Mert Coll Ox BA 30, MA 33. Wells Th Coll 30. **d** 31 Bris **p** 32 Malmesbury for Bris. C of Horfield 31-35; W Southbourne (in c of St Chris) 35-40; CF (EC) 40-47; Men in Disp 46; Hon CF from 47; Chap Wellingborough Sch 47-67; Ho Master 51-66; Chap at Tripoli 68-70; Tunis 70-71; Kyrenia 71-76.

POTTER, Phillip. b 45. Univ of Reading BA (3rd cl Hist) 67. Chich Th Coll 67. **d** 70 **p** 71 Kens for Lon. C of St Jo Evang Notting Hill 70-71.

PRESTON, Arthur. b 08. Univ of Glas MA 28. St Andr Univ Berry Scho and BD 31. Linc Th Coll. **d** 43 **p** 44 Dur. C of Houghton-le-Spring 43-49; V of Wheatley Hill 49-55; Ch Ch Gateshead 55-70; Chap Bensham Gen and Fountain View Hosps from 55; RD of Gateshead 66-69; Surr 66-78; R of Allendale 70-78.

PRICE, Alun Huw. b 47. St D Coll Lamp Dipl Th 70. **d** 70 **p** St D. C of St D Carmarthen 70-73; V of Bettws Evan w Brongwyn 73-77.

PULLEN, James Stephen. b 43. Univ of Lon BSc (2nd cl Math) 64. Linacre Coll Ox BA (2nd cl Th) 68. St Steph Ho Ox 66. **d** 68 **p** 69 Man. C of Chorlton-cum-Hardy 68-72; St Leon and St Jude (in c of St Luke Scawthorpe) Doncaster 72-73; Chap St Olave's Gr Sch Orpington 73-75; Haileybury Coll Hertford 75-78.

RAWSON, Christopher Wilfrid. Linc Th Coll 13. **d** 20 **p** 23 Newc T. C of St Mary Blyth (in c of St John's Miss Cowpen Quay 24) 20-24; St John Newc T 24-26; V of Doddington 26-28.

REES, Philip William Watkins. b 11. St D Coll Lamp BA 33. St Steph Ho Ox 33. **d** 34 **p** 35 Swan B. C of Llanguicke w Pontardawe 34-38; St Jude Swansea 38-46; V of Llanfihangel Fechan w Dyffryn Honddu 46-53; St Mark Swansea 53-78.

RHODES, Clifford Oswald. b 11. St Pet Hall Ox BA (2nd cl Phil Pol and Econ) 34, MA 38. Wycl Hall Ox 38. **d** 38 **p** 39 Man. C of St Luke Benchill 38-40; CF (EC) 40-45; LPr Dio S'wark 46-58; Ed *The Record* 46-49; *C of E Newspaper* 49-59; Hon Chap of St Bride Fleet Street Lon 52-54; C of St Marg Lothbury Lon 54-58; Dir and Sec of Modern Churchmen's U 54-60; R of Somerton 58-79; P-in-c of Heyford Warren w Lower Heyford and Rousham 76-79; R of The Heyfords w Rousham and Somerton 79-81.

RICHARDS, David Powell. St Mich Coll Llan 33. **d** 34 Lon for Col Bp **p** 35 Willoch. M of Bush Bro Quorn 34-38; C of Ogley Hay w Brownhills 38-42; Gt Barr 42-43; V of St Marg w Michaelchurch Eckley and Newton 43-63; R of Abbeydorr 63-78; R of Bacton 63-78.

RICHARDS, Norman Frank. Univ of Wales BA (2nd cl Hist) 47. Univ of Lon PhD 55. Ripon Hall Ox 61. **d** 62 **p** 63 Derby. C of Newbold w Dunston 62-63; Hd Master Newbold C of E Primary Sch 59-63; Faversham C of E Junior Sch 64-68; C of Faversham 64-68; Admin Asst Loughborough Univ from 68.

RICHARDSON, Harold. b 22. Worc Ordin Coll 62. **d** 64 Penrith for Carl **p** Carl. C of St Barn Carl 64-66; V of Rockliffe W Cargo 66-74.

RISDON-BROWN, Samuel. b 1887. **d** 35 **p** 36 Cant. C of Seasalter 35-38; V of Sturry 38-41; R of Biddenden 48-54; Corton-Denham w Sandford Orcas 54-72.

ROBERTSON-LUXFORD, James Odiarne. Ch Ch Ox BA 05, MA 25. AKC 26. Bps' Coll Cheshunt. **d** 26 Kens for

Lon **p** 27 Lon. C of St Barn Kens 26-29; St Aug Fulham 30-34; Perm Offic at Ch Ch Tottenham 34-39; Dio Chich 39-40; C-in-c of Wilden and Ravensden 41-45; R of L Staughton 45-49; Perm to Offic Dio St Alb 49-52; Publ Pr 52-60.

ROBINSON, John Godfrey. b 27. K Coll Cam BA 49, MA 53. Wells Th Coll 51. **d** 53 **p** 54 York. C of St Columba Scarborough 53-57; Milo 57-62; P-in-c 62-63; Educn Sec Dio SW Tang 63-64; Lit Sec 64; V of Stainton-in-Cleveland 65-69; C of St Jas Clacton-on-Sea 70-72; Dioc Chap Dio Birm 72-76.

ROBINSON, Richard Hugh. b 35. St Jo Coll Cam 3rd cl Econ Trip pt i 56, BA (3rd cl Or Stud Trip pt i) 58, MA 62. Ridley Hall Cam 58. **d** 60 Ches. C of St Andr Cheadle Hulme 60-61; Hon C of Alvanler w Manley 62-64; Perm to Offic Dio York from 64.

ROGERS, William Walton. Univ of Dur LTh 09, BA 16, MA 23. CM Coll Isl 06. **d** 09 Lon for Col Bp **p** 10 Vic CMS Miss Dio Hong 09-10; Canton 10-11; Tutor St Paul's Coll Hong Kong 11-12; Prin of H Trin Coll Canton 13-23; Lect U Th Coll Canton 23-26; V of St Andr Kowloon 27-34; St Paul Leamington 34-47; Surr from 47; V of Ansley 47-51; Perm to Offic Dio Birm 51-64.

ROQUES, Antoine William Wanklyn. b 39. Clare Coll Cam 2nd cl Cl Trip pt i, 60, BA (2nd cl Th Trip pt ii) 62. Cudd Coll 62. **d** 64 **p** 65 Ox. C of Banbury w Neithrop 64-67; Perm to Offic Dio Ox 67-68.

ROWE, Kenneth Waller. b 17. **d** 66 Ripon **p** 67 Knaresborough for Ripon. C of Potternewton 66-68; V of Kirkby Ravensworth w Dalton 68-76.

ROWLANDS, Arthur. b 1893. ALCD 30. **d** 30 **p** 31 Lon. C of St Mary Hornsey Rise 30-33; Org Sec CPAS for SW Distr & Publ Pr Dio Bris 33-36; V of St Bart Bris 36-50; St Mich AA Claughton 50-57; R of Holton w Bratton St Maurice 57-61; V of St Ann Warrington 61-64; St Marg w Michaelchurch Eckley and Newton 64-70.

RUDD, Colin Richard. b 41. K Coll Lon and Warm AKC 64. **d** 65 **p** 66 Win. C of N Stoneham w Bassett 65-70; R of Rotherwick 70-74; Hook w Greywell 70-78.

RUDD, Dennis Hillyer Chadd. b 10. AKC 36. **d** 36 **p** 37 York. C of N Ormesby 36-37; All SS Middlesbrough 37-38; Perm to Offic at St Pet Limehouse 38-39; C of Eye and Braiseworth 39-41; Sutton Surrey 41-43; Easington w Skeffling and Kilnsea Welwick and Holmpton 43-45; P-in-c of St Columb Bathgate 45-47; V of Thrimby w Gt Strickland 47-54; PC of St Mark S Shields 54-59; V of Deaf Hill w Langdale 59-73; Perm to Offic Dio Dur 73-78.

RUMNEY, Ralph. **d** 30 **p** 31 Dur. C of Bp Wearmouth 30-33; V of St Jude Newc T 33-37; St Mark Sidall 37-54; R of Langley 54-56; V of Alverthorpe 56-62.

RUSSELL, Joseph George. b 1900. TCD BA (Jun Mods) 22, MA 32. **d** 23 **p** 25 Cash. C of H Trin Cathl Waterf 24-28; Cler V Cho and C of St Mary's Cathl Lim 28-34; I of Shinrone w Ettagh 34-41; R of Kilmocomogue 41-48; I of St Luke (w St Ann Shandon) Cork 48-55; RD of Lower Ormond 40-41; Glansalney W and Bere 46-55; Can of Brigown in Cloyne Cathl 51-55; Can of St Mich in St Fin Barre's Cathl Cork 51-55; Treas of St Colman's Cathl Cloyne and Can of Cahirlag in St Fin Barre's Cathl Cork 55; RD of Kinalea Citra 50-55; R of Ousby w Melmergy 57-64; V of Eaton Leics 64-67.

SANDERS, Henry William Evan. LCD 58. **d** 62 **p** 64 Southw. C of St Ann Nottm 62-65; St Pet and St Paul Dagenham 65-67; W Thurrock w Purfleet 67-73; W Ham 73-78.

SARGENT, John Philip Hugh. b 34. Or Coll Ox BA (4th cl Th) 55, MA 63. Chich Th Coll. **d** 57 **p** 58 Heref. C of Kington 57-59; St Mary Magd Bridgnorth 59-63; Leighton Buzzard 63-64; V of Stonebroom 64-73; Chap Southn Gen Hosp 74-78.

SAUNDERS, George William. b 03. ALCD 36. **d** 36 **p** 37 Lon. C of St D Islington 36-40; St Paul Kingston Hill 40-43; Warlingham w Chelsham 43-45; V of H Trin Kilburn 45-50; St Barn Bethnal Green 50-60; V of St Jas W Ealing 60-77.

SAVAGE, Frederick John. b 1896. Clifton Th Coll 50. **d** 51 **p** 52 Leic. C of H Trin Hinckley 51-54; V of Arnesby w Shearsby 54-57; St Jas Pentonville 57-64; Perm to Offic Dios Lon and Ox 65-78.

SAWBRIDGE, Thomas. Lich Th Coll 32. **d** 34 **p** 35 Lich. C of Newport 35; Perm to Offic at Ch Ch Wellington 35-57; C of Coseley 38-40; L to Office Dio Lich 40-48; V of Calton Dio Lich 48-50; R of Luderitzbught w Keetmanshoop and Orangemouth Damara 60.

SCANTLEBURY, James Stanley. b 48. St Jo Coll Dur BA (Th) 69. Westcott Ho 70. **d** 72 **p** 73 Carl. C of St Jo Bapt Upperby Carl 72-75; H Trin w St Mary Guildf 75-77.

SCOTT, James. TCD BA 37, Div Test (2nd Cl) 38, MA 44. **d** 38 **p** 39 Wor. C of Old Hill 38-41; St Paul Lozells 41-44; Dioc Chap (in c of Pype Hayes) 44-47; C of Aston Juxta Birm 47-48; V of St Jas Halifax (w St Mary Virg from 53) 48-77;Chap Halifax R Infirm 49-53.

SEMPLE, Mervyn George. b 08. TCD BA 32, MA 54. **d** 32 **p** 33 Oss. C of Maryborough 32-35; R of Timahoe w Timogue and Luggacurren 35-40; C of St cath and St Victor Dub 40-41; CF 41-54; C of Shirley Surrey 54-55; R of St Mary-in-the-Marsh 55-58; R of Newchurch 55-58; V of Dunkirk 58-73.

SEYMOUR, Canon Percy Wilson. TCD BA 11, MA 18. **d** 11 **p** 12 Worc. C of St John Dudley 11-14; St Mark Mansfield 14-19; Glossop 19-20; Hawarden (in c of St francis Sandycroft) 21-26; v of St Pet Vauxhall 26-66; Hon Can of S'wark 64-66; Can (Emer) 66-78.

SHAND, John. Univ of Aber MA 27. Edin Th Coll 32. **d** 34 **p** 35 Edin. C of St Martin Edin (in c of St Salvador's Miss Stenhouse) 34-41; L to Offic Dio Ox 43-44; Chap of St Andr Home Joppa and C of Old St Paul 44-55; Offg P-in-c of Monymusk w Kemnay 45-56; P-in-c of St Ninian Comely Bank 46-49; Sub-Warden of St Jo Coll Umtata 49-50; Warden 50-54; Dir of Relig Educn Dio Johann 54-56; C of Tsolo 56-59; R of Buckie 69-71.

SHANNON, Norman William. Oak Hill Th Coll 64. **d** 66 Ches. C of St Andr Cheadle Hulme 66-67.

SHARPE, Victor Clifford. Ridley Hall, Cam 46. **d** 46 **p** 47 Nor. C of Sheringham 46-49; V of Honingham w E Tuddenham 49-57; Ormesby w Scratby 57-66; R of Garboldisham 66-75; Blo-Norton 66-75.

SHAW, Job Maxwell Joseph Charles Matthew. b 1894. Selw Coll Cam 3rd cl Hist Trip pt i, 22, BA (3rd cl Hist Trip pt ii) 23, MA 26. Westcott Ho Cam 23. **d** 24 **p** 25 Wakef. C of St Aug Halifax 24-26; C-in-c of Airedale Conv Distr Castleford 26-29; R of Whitwood Mere 29-35; V of Tickhill 35-38; R of Rossington 38-61; Surr 35-64; Ed Sheff Dioc Year Book 39-42; Asst RD of Doncaster 44-51; V of Felixkirk w Boltby 61-64; C-in-c of Kirkby Knowle w Cowesby 61-64; C-in-c of Gt Linford w Willen and Gt w L Woolstone 64-67. Kelham Th Coll 36. Univ of Lon BA (3rd cl Phil) 49. CCC Cam BA (2nd cl Mor Sc Trip pt ii) 51. M SSM 43. **d** 43 **p** 44 Sheff. C of Parson Cross Sheff 43-48; L to Offic Dio Southw 48-60; Perm to Offic Dio Ely 49-51; Chap and Tutor Kelham Th Coll 51-60; Tutor St Mich Th Coll Crafers 60-63; Sub Prior 63-65; L to Offic Dio Adel 60-65; Chap Univ of Lanc 65-74.

SHEPPARD, Ian Arthur Lough. b 33. Sarum Wells Th Coll 71. **d** 74 Tewkesbury for Glouc **p** 75 Tewkesbury for Cant for Glouc. C of Bp's Cleeve w Southam 74-78.

SHORT, Kenneth Richard MacDonald. b 36. Dickinson Coll Penn BA 57. Colgate Roch Div Sch NY BD 60. Univ of Roch MA 70. Univ of Ox DPhil 72. **d** 75 Reading for Ox **p** 75 Ox- C of Steeple Aston 75-78.

SHUCKSMITH, John Barry. b 37. Dipl Th (Lon) 68. Oak Hill Th Coll 64. **d** 68 S'wark **p** 69 Stepney for S'wark. C of Tooting Graveney 68-71.

SIDDLE, Thomas. b 03. Lon Coll of Div 44. **d** 46 **p** 47 Man. C of St Paul Halliwell 46-48; Chadderton 48; Chadderton 48; V of St Mary Hawkshaw Lane 49-73.

SILLERY, William. b 1894. Em Coll Sktn 25. Bp's Coll Prince Albert 29. MRST 23. **d** 30 **p** 33 Sask. C of Kinistino 30-32; Lindsay 32-34; P-in-c of St Geo and St Cath Prince Albert 34-36; C of Eglingham 37-38; V of All SS Duddo 38-44; CF (R of O) from 39; R of St Adamnan Duror 44-45; C of St John Dumfries 46-47; P-in-c of Greyfriars Kirkcudbright 47-48; C of Ch Ch Woking (in c of St Paul Maybury) 48-51; V of St D Holloway 51-53; R of Gunhouse w Burringham 53-56; Fiskerton 56-58.

SIMPSON, Robert. b 1900. Late Scho of Univ of Man BSc 23. Buckle Research Scho 26, MSc 28. New Coll Ox DPhil 31. TCD MA 59. FCP 42. Egerton Hall Man 24. **d** 24 **p** 25 Man. C of St Clem Ordsall Salford 24-26; Asst Master Cranleigh Sch 28-33; Chap Prin Lawr Mem R Mil Sch Lovedale India 33-37; Hd Master Ashburton Sch 37-38; Perm to Offic Dio St E 38-39; R of Mellis 39-44; Lect Achimota College Gold Coast 43-50; Prin Wolmers Sch Kingston Ja 51-53; Perm to Offic Dios Ox and York from 53.

SISSONS, Gordon. b 34. ACP 58. Roch Th Coll 68. **d** 70 **p** 71 Warrington for Liv. C of H Trin Formby 71-75.

SPARKES, Richard Graham Brabant. b 21. St Jo Coll Ox BA 42, MA 47. Westcott Ho Cam 54. **d** 55 **p** 56 Wakef. C of St Paul Morley 55-57; St Wilfrid Halton 57-59; Leeds 59-62; V of St Paul Hook 62-69; Oulton 69-75.

SPEAR, Canon Edward Norman. b 1898. Wadh Coll Ox BA (3rd cl Mod Hist) 21, 2nd cl Th 23, MA 25. Wycl Hall Ox 21. **d** 23 **p** 24 Lon. C of St Luke Hackney 23-25; Actg Vice-Prin Wycl Hall Ox 25-26; CMS Miss Dio Trav 26-30; V of Grinton and Marrick 30-32; St Agnes Burmantofts 32-34; CMS Miss Dio Dorn 34-48; Tutor Dioc Div Sch and Regr Dio Dorn 35-38; Miss at Khammamett 38-40; CMS Sec Dio Dorn 40-48; Archd of Kistna 40-48; V of Ch Ch Cheltm 49-52; RD of Cheltm 51-52; Can Miss of Glouc

52-57; Exam Chap to Bp of Glouc 52-57; Proc Conv Glouc 55-59; V of Ch Ch Glouc City 57-61; Dunster 65-68; Hon Can of Glouc Cathl 58-61; Can (Emer) from 61; R of Wootton Courtenay 61-68; R of Luccombe 61-68; C of Porlock 68-71.

SPELLMAN, John. Wells Th Coll 61. **d** 63 **p** 64 S'wark. C of St Jo Evang E Dulwich 63-65; St Phil and St Mark Camberwell 65-68; St Leon Streatham 68-71.

STANLEY, Charles Geoffrey Nason. b 1884. TCD BA 06. **d** 07 **p** 08 Cash. C of Drumcannon 07-14; Cappoquin w Chap of Villierstown 14-16; I of Kilrosanty w Rossmire 16-34; Dean of Lism 34-60; R of Lism (w Cappoquin from 56) 34-60; RD of Waterford 57-60.

STANNARD, Harold Frederick David. b 12. AKC 37. **d** 37 **p** 38 Truro. C of St Columb Major 37-43; Chap RAFVR 43-46; R of Dowsby w Dunsby 46-48; W Quantoxhead 48-77.

STEELE, Arthur Henry Macdonald. Selw Coll Cam BA 36. Linc Th Coll 38. **d** 38 **p** 39 Linc. C of Scunthorpe 38-39; St Faith Linc 39-46; Chap RAFVR 43-46; V of Gosberton Clough 46-49; C of St Luke w Norwood 49-57; R of St Aug w St Mary Coslany Nor 57-69; Chap HM Pris Nor 58-69; V in Dereham Group (C-in-c of Hockering and of N Tuddenham) 69-72.

STEER, Martin Leslie Martin Leslie. b 41. Univ of Dur BA 65. Oak Hill Th Coll 65. **d** 67 Barking for Chelmsf **p** 68 Chelmsf. C of Rayleigh 67-70; CF 70-77. b 41. Univ of Dur BA 65. Oak Hill Th Coll 65. **d** 67 Barking for Chelmsf **p** 68 Chelmsf. C of Rayleigh 67-70; CF 70-77.

STEVENS, Albert. Sarum Th Coll 36. **d** 38 **p** 39 Bris. C of St Steph Southmead 38-40; Kingswood 40-43; St Mary Fishponds 43-45; Surr from 45; R of Chew Stoke 45-54; Rd of Chew Magna 51-62; R of Ubley 54-62; R of Compton Martin 54-62; R of Compton Martin 54-62; W Coker 62-66; V of Brent 66-74; L to Offic Dio B & W 74-78.

STEVENSON, Leslie. b 06. Late Exhib of St Jo Coll Ox BA (2nd cl Th) 28. Ely Th Coll. **d** 29 **p** 30 Chelmsf. C of St Steph Upton Pk 29-31; All H S'wark 31-35; St Andr Battersea 35-36; Perm to Offic as C-in-c of St Chrys Peckham 36-37; Asst Sec Actors' Ch U 37-38; LPr Dio Lon 38; V of St Mary Lambeth 38-45; Ch Ch Clapham 45-54; R of Winterbourne 54-70; R of Luckington w Alderton 70-71.

STEWART, Maxwell Neville Gabriel. Hertf Coll Ox BA (2nd cl Engl) 58, MA 62. Dipl Th 59. Univ of Essex, MA 69. Wycl Hall, Ox 58. **d** 60 **p** 61 Birm. C of St Matt Perry Beeches 60-62; Chap Rosenberg Coll St Gallen 62-64; Asst Lect NE Essex Coll of Tech 64-67; Lect from 67.

STONE, Jeffrey Peter. Lich Th Coll 58. **d** 61 **p** 62 Southw. C of Newark-on-Trent 61-65; V of St Mich AA Sutton-in-Ashfield 65-69; C-in-c of Daybrook 69-72.

SUMMERS, Frederic Walter. b 16. Jes Coll Ox BA (3rd cl Th) 48, MA 53. Linc Th Coll. **d** 50 **p** 51 S'wark. C of Lambeth 50-54; V of St Jo Evang Kingston 54-70; C-in-c of Stourton Caundle w Caundle Purse 73-75.

SWARBRIGG, David Cecil. b 42. TCD BA 64, MA 67. **d** 65 **p** 66 Connor. C of Ch Ch Lisburn 65-67; Thames Ditton 72-78.

SWINN, Peter William. b 37. Clifton Th Coll 63. **d** 66 **p** 67 S'wark. C of H Redeemer Streatham Vale 66-69; St Jude Mapperley 69-71; C-in-c of St Anne Nottm 69-71; Normanton-on-Trent 71-77; Marnham 71-77.

TACKLEY, Frederick James. b 05. St Edm Hall Ox BA 33, MA 46. St Andr Whittlesford 34. **d** 35 **p** 36 Dur. C of St Mary Gateshead 35-39; C-in-c of All SS Conv Distr Lobley Hill Gateshead 39-46; V of St Aid S Shields 46-56; Monk Sherborne w Pamber 56-68; R of Edmundbyers w Muggleswick 68-75.

TAIT, Thomas William. b 07. Late Exhib of St Cath S Ox BA 30, MA 33. Clifton Th Coll 40. Edin Th Coll 42. **d** 43 Edin for Moray **p** 44 Moray. C of H Trin Elgin 43-44; H Trin Bordesley 44-46; Selly Oak 46-49; Kingsbury (in c of Dosthill) 49-50; V of Quarnford 50-53; R of Hevingham 53-56; R of Brampton 53-56; V of Bordesley 56-59; R of Fitz 59-64; Chap of L Berwick 59-64; R of Ch Lawton 64-67.

TARBET, Michael. Keble Coll Ox BA 34, MA 55. Wells Th Coll 34. **d** 35 **p** 36 Lon. C of H Trin Wealdstone 35-38; Lyme Regis 38-40; RAFVR 40-46; L to Offic Dio Chich 50-51; Dio Guildf 51-61; Perm to Offic Dio Ox 61-71.

TAYLOR, Donald Alastair. St Paul's Coll Maur. **d** and **p** 65 St Alb (for Col). C of St Mary Virg Ware 65-66; Miss at Mahoe 67-69; L to Offic Dio Ox 72-75; Dio Chelmsf 76-78; Commiss Sey 73-75.

TAYLOR, Marcus Iles. Ely Th Coll 48. **d** 49 **p** 50 Cant. C of Bearsted 49-53; V of Appledore w Kennardington 53-56; Cookham Dean 56-71.

TAYLOR, William Thomas. b 02. St Barn Coll Adel 29. ACT ThL 32. **d** 32 **p** 33 Adel. C of St Aug Unley 32-34; P-in-c of Wanigela 35-38; Boianai 38-41; C of S Yorke Penin Miss 41-42; P-in-c 42-44; Chap AIF 44-46; R of S Yorke Penin 46-47; Kapunda 47-49; Warden of St Francis Semaphore 49-50; R of Grange S Austr 50-54; Gt w L Saxham 55-59; Gimingham 59-65; R of Trimingham 59-65; Chap E Mundesley Hosp 59-65; R of Stradishall w Denston 65-72; L to Offic Dio St E 72-78.

THOMAS, Evan Tudor. b 11. St Mich Coll Llan 49. **d** 51 **p** 53 Ban. C of Llanfairfechan 51-53; Llandyssul w Capel Dewi 53-55; St Issells 55-59; V of Morfil w Pontfaen and Llanychllwydog (w Puncheston w L Newcastle and Castlebythe from 73) 59-78.

THOMAS, Owen Edgar. St D Coll Lamp BA 21. **d** 24 Ban for St A **p** 25 St A. C of Rhosddu 24-27; Pont Blyddyn 27-35; Bistre 35-36; V of Bettisfield 36-48; R of Uggeshall w Sotherton 48-57; V of St Pet and St Paul Wangford w Henham 50-57; RD of N Dunwich 50-57; Surr 50-64; V of Gt Ashfield w Badwell Ash 57-64.

THOMPSON, James Norman Leslie. b 17. Univ of Lon BSc (2nd cl Chem) 41. Linc Th Coll 47. **d** 49 **p** 50 Leic. C of Glen Parva w S Wigston 49-52; Lect and Chap at Loughborough Coll 52-75.

THORNTON, Kenneth William. b 10. Hatf Coll Dur LTh 53. Edin Th Coll 33. **d** 36 **p** 37 Brech. C of St Paul's Cathl Dundee 36-40; H Trin Cov 40-43; C-in-c of St Pet Abbeydale Sheff 43-44; C of Attercliffe 44-45; R of Todwick 45-53; V of Wingfield w Syleham 53-62; R of Monks Eleigh w Chelsworth 62-75.

TIDSWELL, Norman. b 09. Univ of NZ Bp's Coll Cheshunt. **d** 46 **p** 47 Waik. C of St Pet Cathl Hamilton 46-48; P-in-c of St John Whangamomona 48-51; C of St Geo Ovenden Halifax 51-56; V of Birchencliffe 56-78.

TOON, John Samuel. b 30. Bp's Coll Cheshunt 65. **d** 65 **p** 66 Southw. C of Newark-on-Trent 65-67; Clewer 67-70; R of Fort Vermilion 70; Osgathorpe 70-72; I of Big River Sask 73-76; C of Maidstone 76-77.

TOPLEY, Thomas. St Aid Coll 07. **d** 09 **p** 11 Down. C of St Aid Belf 09-11; St Mary Belf 11-13; I of Ardclinis 13-16; R of Ballintoy 16-21; I of Ramoan 21-54; Surr 21-54; Chap Dalriada Distr Hosp 21-54.

TOWNEND, Arthur Osmond. Univ of Dur BA 1898, MA 10. **d** 1900 **p** 01 Dur. C of Tudhoe 1900 Ch Ch Accrington 03-04; Kegworth w Isley Walton 04-14; V of Lullington 14-33; L to Offic Dio Leic 33-46.

TUCKWELL, Ronald Lewis. St Barn Coll Adel ACT ThL (2nd cl) 66. **d** 66 Adel. C of Mt Gambier 66-67; Hon C of Loxton 70-71.

TURNER, Bernard Henry. K Coll Lon BA (3rd cl Lat) 50. Ripon Hall Ox 60. **d** and **p** 61 St E. C of Shotley 61-63; Chap and Sen Cl Master Shirley Ho Schg Watford 63-64; R of Gt Horwood 64-65; Perm to Offic Dio Ely 66-78.

TURNER, Herbert. b 1890. Late Scho of QUB BSc (1st cl) 14. Trin. Coll Dub Abp King, Bp Forster, Downes Div, Eccles Hist and Hebr Pris 22, Div Test (1st cl) and BA 23. MRCS (Engl), LRCP (Lon) 43. **d** 23 **p** 24 Dub. C of Ch ch Lesson Pk Dub 23-26; Min Can of St Patr Cathl Dub 24-26; Hd of Trin Coll Miss Belf 26-30; C-in-c of St simon Belf 30-31; CMS Miss at Patpara 31-35; Perm to Offic Dio Lon 44-48 and 50-52; Dio S'wark 43-48 and 50-52; LDHM of Ch Ch Harlington 52-58.

TURNER, John Arthur. St Jo Coll Dur BA 37, Dipl Th 38, Dur MA 40. **d** 38 **p** Man. C of St Mich AA Peel Green 38-40; All SS Elton 40-43; V of St Jas Burnley 43-46; Chap at Nakuru and Distr 46-50; Chap Nairobi Sch 51-52; R of Long Stanton w Easthope 53-56; Chasetown 56-76; Perm to Offic Dio Lich 76-78.

TURNS, Keith Leslie. b 37. Univ of Dur BA 69. Univ of Birm Dipl Th 71. **d** 71 Dur **p** 74 Bp Skelton for Dur. Hon C of S Mich & St Hilda Bp Wearmouth 71-73; L to Offic Dio Dur 73-78.

TURVEY, James Hilton. b 1900. **d** 53 **p** 54 Sask. I of Star City 53-56; Prince Albert E 56-63; Dom Chap to Bp of Sask 60-63; V of All SS Blackb 63-68.

TYLER, Brian Sidney. b 32. Chich Th Coll. **d** 64 **p** 65 Chich. C of St Mich AA Brighton 64-69; C-in-c and Seq of St Pet w St Mary Southwick 69-76; Perm to Offic Dio Chich 77-78.

VANDERSTOCK, Alan. b 31. Univ of Dur Van Mildert Exhib BA 57. Dipl Th (w distinc) 59. Cranmer Hall Dur 57. **d** 59 **p** 60 Man. C of St Paul Kersal Salford 59-63; C-in-c of St Aid Conv Distr Kersal Salford 63-67; LPr Dio Cant from 67.

VERITY, George Beresford. b 1887. Univ Coll Dur LTh 13. Ja Ch Th Coll. **d** 12 WI **p** 13 Bp Farrar for WI. C of All SS Kingston 12-13; Tutor of Th Coll Cross Roads 14-19; C of Halfway Tree 15-20; Hd Master Dioc Coll Mandeville 20-22; R of Montpelier 22-28; (all in Ja); C of Coberley and Colesbourne 28-37; R of Cowley (w Coberley and Colesbourne from 37) 31-41; V of St Helen N Kens 41-46.

VINCENT, Peter Sidney Percy. b 23. K Coll Lon and

Warm AKC 54. **d** 55 **p** 56 Lon. C of Stonebridge 55-57; St Pancras 57-59; St Sav Luton (in c of St Mich and St Geo Farley Hill) 59-64; V of St Jo Div Rastrick 64-71; Gawber 71-77; C of Forest Row 77-78.

WADE-STUBBS (formerly STUBBS), Edward Pomery Flood George Hedley. St Jo Coll Dur LTh 39, BA 40. Tyndale Hall Bris 36. **d** 40 **p** 41 Lich. C of St John Burslem 40-42; St Jas Handsworth 42-44; Hawkhurst 44-46; St Mark (in c of St Barn) Cheltm 51-53; R of Gt Witcombe w Bentham 53-62; Markdale Ont 62-63; Sutton Veny 63-66; V of Norton Bavant 63-66; C of Patchway 67-70. b 30. **d** 73 Capetn. C of Fish Hoek 73-77.

WALKER, John Fort. Keble Coll Ox BA 36, MA 41. Linc Th Coll 36. **d** 37 **p** 38 Pet. C of All SS w St Kath Northn 37-42; C-in-c of Good Shepherd Conv Distr Ford Estate Sunderland 42-47; PC of St Columba Southwick 47-53; Cockerton 53-60; Proc Conv Dur 57-61; R of St Martin (w Whittington 60-62) 60-70.

WALMSLEY, Gilbert Clayton. b 05. Univ of Dur LTh 27. St Jo Coll Dur BA 28, MA 31. St Aid Coll 24. **d** 28 **p** 29 Ches. Claf St Paul Seacombe 28-30; St Paul Southport 30-31 Standish 31-34; St Geo Chorley 34-36; St Paul Balckb 36-37; V of Haslingden Grane 37-47; R of St Clem Broughton Salford 47-56; Perm to Offic Dios Liv and Man 56-57; C of St Jas Heywood 57-60; St Mich AA Wigan 60-63; Sale 63-66; St Pet Paddington 66-67; Perm to Offic Dio Liv 68-78.

WATCHAM, Horace Leonard. St Columb Hall Wang 26. ACT ThL 28. **d** 28 **p** 29 Wang. C of Murchison 28-29; Numurkah 29-31; (both in Vic) Perm to Offic (Col Cl Act) at Bolton Percy 32-33; St John Newland 33-34; C 34-35; P-in-c of Bulwer w Himeville and Underberg 37-38.

WATKINS, Alfred John. St D Coll Lamp BA 31. **d** 31 Bris **p** 32 Malmesbury for Bris. C of St Jo Div Fishponds 31-33; St Mich AA Watford 33-36; St Paul Swindon 36-37; St Etheldreda Fulham 37-38; Ruislip 38-39; CF (TA) 39-44; Hon CF 44; R of Tempsford 45-47; V of St Jas Watford 47-53; Wilshamstead 53-55; Gt w L Driffield 55-68; Chap E Riding Gen Hosp 55-63; Surr 56-68; Perm to Offic Dio B & W 68-78.

WEBB, Rex Alexander Francis. ACT ThL 65. Ely Th Coll 56. **d** 58 **p** 59 Win. C of Millbrook 58-60; M Bro of Good Shepherd Dubbo 60-63; Vic-Prin 65; C of Bourke 61-62; P-in-c of Brewarrina 62-63; Tennant Creek 63-67; P-in-c of Katherine 68-73; Winton 73-74.

WEIR, Peter. b 1892. OBE 18. Wadh Coll Ox BA and MA 18. Bp Wilson Th Coll IM 32. **d** 33 **p** 34 S and M. C of St Thos Douglas 33-35; St Anne Aigburth 35-37; V of Ch Ch Heaton 37-48; Ickleton w Hinxton 48-55; Lezayre 55-57; R of Hamerton 57-63; V of Winwick 57-63; RD of Leightonstone 63; Perm to Offic Dio Ely 63-69.

WELLS, Clement John Lethbridge. b 1891. St Jo Coll Ox BA BM ChB 21, MA 46. Wycl Hall Ox. **d** 64 **p** 65 Ox. L to Offic Dio Ox 64-68; C-in-c of Over w Nether Worton 68-78.

WENSLEY, John Ettery. b 29. K Coll Lon and Warm AKC 53. **d** 54 **p** 55 Man. C of Atherton 54-57; St Pancras 57-60; St Mary Portsea 60-61; All SS Portsea 61-62; St Pet Battersea 68-69.

WHATMORE, Michael John. b 30. Univ of Bris BA (2nd cl Gen) 51. St Cath S Ox BA (3rd cl Th) 53, MA 57. Wycl Hall, Ox 56. **d** 56 **p** 58 Roch. C of Bexley 56-57; Keston 57-59; St Mark Bromley 59-61; Distr Sec BFBS 61-64; R of Stanningley 64-67; V of Speke 67-71; Asst Master Barton Peveril Gr Sch Eastleigh, Southn 71-78.

WHITE, Howard Christopher Graham. b 43. Univ of Leeds BA (2nd cl Engl and Hist) 65. Coll of Resurr Mirfield 67. **d** 67 Lon **p** 68 Willesden for Lon. C of Friern Barnet 67-71; C-in-c of Uxbridge Moor 71-73; Asst Chap RADD from 73; Hon C of Corringham 74-78.

WHITE, John Bernard Valentine. b 07. TCD BA 30, MA 37. **d** 30 **p** 31 Oss. C and Dean's V of St Canice's Cathl Kilk 30-32; I of Kilmanagh w Callan 32-33; CF 34-54; Chap at Lobitos Peru 54-58; Ecuador 54-58; Dioc C Dio Cork 58-65; Chap Miss to Seamen Cork 58-65.

WHITTINGHAM, Albert Edward. St D Coll Lamp BA 31. **d** 30 **p** 32 Ches. C of St Mark Dukinfield 30-36; V of Henbury 36-45; CF (EC) 40-45; Chap of Birm United Hosp 45-47; R of Longnewton 47-66; C of Acton-Burnell w Pitchford 70-73.

WHITTLE, Glen Charles. b 36. Univ of Montana BA (Hist) 58. Linc Th Coll 69. **d** 71 **p** 72 Linc. C of Ruckland (in S Ormsby Group) 72-75.

WHITTON, Eric. b 33. ALCD 59. **d** 60 **p** 61 S'wark. C of Mortlake w E Sheen 60-64; St Matt Surbiton 64-66; Youth Tr Chap Dio Lon 66-72; Youth Work Officer Gen Syn Bd of Educn 72-74; Trg Officer 74-78.

WHITTON, Paul Nicholas. b 45. St Chad Coll Dur BA 67. Edin Th Coll 68. **d** 70 Carl C of St Barn Carl 70-78.

WIBROW, Horatio Mace. b 1891. Westcott Ho Cam 45. **d** 45 **p** 46 Nor. C of Drayton w Hellesdon 45-48; C-in-c of St Paul's Conv Distr Hellesdon 48-49; V of Halvergate w Tunstall 49-54; Bintry w Themelthorpe 54-57; Woodbastwick w Panxworth 57-63; Perm to Offic Dio Nor 63-78.

WILKINSON, Sydney. b 24. Wycl Coll Tor. **d** 56 **p** 57 Arctic. Miss at Gt Whale River 56-60; I of Nor 60-61; Miss at Pangnirtung 61-64; R of Peterhead 64-69.

WILLCOCK, Brian Bartley. b 34. St Aid Coll 59. **d** 60 **p** 61 Man. C of Heywood 60-62; Droylsden 62-64; Bexleyheath 64-65; St Thos Heaton Norris 65-66; V of St Mark Chadderton 66-73.

WILLIAMS, Brynmor. Late Scho of St D Coll Lamp BA (1st cl Th) and Th Pri 33. Univ of Lon BD (2nd cl) 40, MTh 42. **d** 33 **p** 34 Swan B. C of Clydach 33-40; V of Llanganten w Llanynis 40-48; Lect Univ of Wales 43-48; V of Llansamlet 48-75; Surr 49-75; Exam Chap to Bp of Swan B 58-75; Lect Univ coll of Swansea 60-75.

WILLIAMS, David. b 33. Ch Coll Cam 3rd cl Cert Eng Stud pt i 55, BA 9pt ii 56), MA 60. Cranfield Inst of Tech DCAe 63 (converted to MSc 72). Sarum Wells Th Coll 71. **d** 73 **p** 74 Ex. C of St Jas Ex 73-75; Publ pr Dio Ex 75-78.

WILLIAMS, Norman. b 09. Univ of Wales BSc 34. St Mich Coll Llan 36. **d** 36 **p** 37 Mon. C of St Jas Tredegar 36-42; L to Offic at All SS Miss Ch for Deaf and Dumb W Ham 42-48; Chap to Deaf and Dumb Dio Chich 48-55; Chap RAF 55-64; R of Checkendon 64-73.

WILLIAMS, Richard Edward. b 02. St Bonif Coll Warm 37. **d** 39 **p** 40 St D. C of Milford Haven 39-44; Chap All SS Santos w Miss to Seamen Santos 44-47; Org Sec Miss to Seamen Prov of Wales and Heref 47-48; LPr Dio St D 48; R of Herbrandston 48-55; V of St Martin Haverfordwest 55-73; V of Lambston 60-73; Can of Caerfarchell in St D Cathl 65-73.

WILLIAMS, William David Brynmor. b 48. Univ of Wales (Swansea) Dipl Th 71. St D Coll Lamp 71. **d** 72 **p** 73 Swan B. C of Killay 72-74; Wokingham 74-75; CF 75-78.

WILSON, Robert. b 14. St Cath S Ox BA (2nd cl Engl Lang and Lit) 36, MA 40. Linc Th Coll 37. **d** 38 **p** 39 York. C of Selby Abbey 38-40; Epsom 40-41; St Thos Bp Wearmouth (in c of St Pet) 42-44; V of Dormanstown 44-48; Dean's V and Sec of Friends of Lich Cathl 48-54; Perm to Offic Dio Lich 48-54; V of Everton w Mattersey 54-48; Chap and Asst Master Mattersey Hall Sch 54-58; Poundswick Gr Sch Man 58-62; Lect Man Coll of Educn 62-63; Sen Lect 63-66; Prin Lect 66-67.

WILSON, William Twamley. TCD Div Test 19, BA 19, MA 23. **d** 19 **p** 21 Oss. C of Maryborough 20-23; Seagoe 23-25; Birr 25-27; I of Balllngarry w Lockeen 27-35; Brinny w Templemartin 35-52; Kilnagross w Kilmalooda 52-59; Can of Timoleague in Ross Cathl 57-60; Desertmore in Cork Cathl 57-60; Prec of Ross Cathl 59-64; I of Kilgariffe 59-68; Chan of St Fin Barre Cathl Cork 64-68.

WINGATE, Andrew David Carlile. b 44. Worc Coll Ox BA (1st cl Lit Hum 66) BPhil 68, MA 71. Linc Th Coll 70. **d** 72 **p** 73 Worc. C of Halesowen 72-78.

WINSOR, James Michael. b 47. Lake Forest Coll Ill BA 69. Cudd Coll 69. **d** 72 Ox **p** 73 Buckingham for Ox. C of St Andr Headington Ox 72-75.

WOOD, Eric Stanley. b 21. Edin Th Coll 49. **d** 52 **p** 53 S'wark. C of St Pet Walworth 52-55; Odendaalsrus 55-56; R 56-60; Virginia Bloemf 60-62; C of St Pet St Helier (in c of Bp Andrewes Ch) 62-63; H Trin w St Mary Ely 47-67; Hanley 68-72; C-in-c of St Mark Shelton 72-74; C-in-c of Etruria 72-75.

WOOD, Jack Barrington. St Aug Coll Cant 57. **d** 57 **p** 58 Southw. C of Basford 57-60; Chap Miss to Seamen S Shields 60-62; Sing 62-65; L to Offic Dio Dur 61-62; Dio Sing 62-65; V of Bradpole 65-74.

WRAY, William Richard Spalding. b 1897. Fitzw Hall Cam BA 23, MA 26. Ridley Hall Cam 24. **d** 24 **p** 25 Ely. C of St Mary Ely 24-29; St Aug Wisbech 29-33; St Pet (in c of St Swith) Bournemouth 33-35; Perm to Offic at St Jo Bapt (in c of St Aug) Margate 35-36; C of Bridlington 36-39; V of Ravenscar w Stainton Dale 39-46; PC of Gateforth w Hambleton 46-53; V of Collingham 53-69; L to Offic Dio Ripon 69-78.

WRIGHT, James Eric. b 1889. CCC Cam BA 10, MA 27. **d** 13 **p** 14 Lon. C of St Andr Whitehall Pk 13-15; Chap at St Mary Cairo and Chap to Bp in Jer 16-18; Dom Chap to Bp in Jer and Miss at Jer 18-23; R of Lillingstone-Dayrell w Lillingstone Lovell 23-27; V of All H Leeds 27-31; St Luke Harrogate 31-48; Hawkley (w Priors Dean from 49) 48-54.

YORKE, Edward Frederick. b 06. G and C Coll Cam BA 28, MA 32. Tyndale Hall Bris 28. **d** 31 Bris **p** 32 Malmesbury for Bris. C of St Matt Kingsdown Bris 31-32; Cheltm 32-34; Ch Ch Beckenham 34-36; V of St Luke Prestonville 36-40; St Pet Tunbridge Wells 40-42; St Luke W Hampstead 42-50; Home Sec CMJ 50-66; Perm to Offic Dio Lon 50-66; R of Denver 66-70; Perm to Offic Dio St Alb 70-78.

INDEX OF PARISHES—ENGLISH

D indicates Diocese and Rural Deanery number P indicates Patron
I indicates Incumbent (and Assistant Curate[s])

SPECIAL NOTES

Under Section 86 of the Pastoral Measure 1968 all Districts (other than Conventional Districts) became Parishes and under Section 87 all Perpetual Curates became Vicars.

In the following Index, as in the Biographies of the Clergymen concerned, the style 'Curate-in-charge' is invariably used for those who are temporarily placed in charge of a Parish to perform the duties of the Incumbent.

The first Parish to appear under the name of a place containing more than one Parish is indicated, in a Clergyman's Biography, by the place name alone. Subsequent parishes are referred to both by the Dedication of the Parish Church and the place name.

ABBAS and TEMPLE COMBE (St Mary Virg) w Horsington (St Jo Bapt), *Somt*. R. **D** B & W 5 *See* Temple Combe.

ABBERLEY (St Mary Virg), *Worcs*. R. **D** Worc 12 **P** *Bp* **I** H R BEVAN.

ABBERTON (St Andr) w Lagenhoe (St Mary), *Essex*. R. **D** Chelmsf 21 **P** *Bp and Lord Chan* alt **I** R A S L CHATTERJI DE MASSEY.

ABBERTON (St Edburga), Naunton Beauchamp (St Bart Ap) and Bishampton (St Jas) w Throckmorton, *Worcs*. R. **D** Worc **P** *Ld Chan and Bp (alt)* **I** E T B WATERHOUSE.

ABBESS RODING (St Edm) w Beauchamp Roding, *Essex*. R. **D** Chelmsf 23 **P** *Sir H G Maryon-Wilson Bt and Bp* **I** E W C EXELL.

ABBEYDALE (St Jo Evang), V. **D** Sheff 2 *See* Sheffield.

ABBEYDALE (St Pet), V. **D** Sheff 2 *See* Sheffield.

ABBEY DORE (H Trin and St Mary), *Herefs*. R. **D** Heref *See* Ewyas Harold.

ABBEY HEY (St Geo), *Gtr Man*.. **D** Man 1 *See* Gorton.

ABBEY WOOD (St Mich AA). **D** S'wark 17 *See* Plumstead.

ABBOTTS ANN (St Mary) and Upper Clatford w Goodworth Clatford, *Hants*. R. **D** Win **P** *Bp and T P de Paravicini Esq* **I** A R GRAHAM.

ABBOT'S BICKINGTON, *Devon*.. **D** Ex *See* Milton Damerel.

ABBOTS BROMLEY (St Nich), *Staffs*. V. **D** Lich 4 **P** *Bp and D and C of Lich* alt **I** R M VAUGHAN.

ABBOTSBURY (St Nich) w Portesham and Langton Herring, *Dorset*. V. **D** Sarum 6 **P** *Lady Teresa Agnew and Bp (Alt)* **I** H J K JACQUES.

ABBOTSHAM (St Hel), *Devon*. V. **D** Ex 17 **P** *Miss M E Sealy* **I** H G JONES *p-in-c*.

ABBOT'S KERSWELL (BVM), *Devon*. V. **D** Ex 11 **P** *Ld Chan* **I** L GREENSIDES.

ABBOTS LANGLEY (St Lawr), *Herts*. V. **D** St Alb 13 **P** *Bp* **I** B K ANDREWS, D P SCRACE *c*.

ABBOTS-LEIGH (H Trin) w Leigh Woods (St Mary Virg), *Avon*. V. **D** Bris 5 **P** *Bp* **I** L J JONES.

ABBOTSLEY (St Marg of Antioch VM), *Cambs*. V. **D** Ely 13 **P** *Ball Coll Ox* **I** D R SORFLEET.

ABBOTS MORTON (St Pet), *Worcs*. R. **D** Worc 1 *See* Church Lench.

ABBOTS RIPTON (St Andr) w Wood Walton, *Cambs*. R. **D** Ely 10 **P** *Lord de Ramsey* **I** (Vacant).

ABDON (St Marg) w Clee St Margaret, *Salop*. R. **D** Heref 12 **P** *Bp* **I** S C MORRIS P-IN-C OF ABDON, A G SEABROOK P-IN-C OF CLEE ST MARG.

ABENHALL (St Mich) w Mitcheldean (St Mich AA), *Glouc*. R. **D** Glouc 6 **P** *Dioc Bd of Patr* **I** K R KING.

ABERDEEN PARK (St Sav). **D** Lon 6 *See* Highbury.

ABERFORD (St Ricarius or Recarius) w Saxton and Towton, *W Yorks*. V. **D** York 9 **P** *Abp and Or Coll Ox* **I** B W HARRIS.

ABINGDON (St Helen w Ch Ch, St Nich and St Mich) w Shippon (St Mary Magd), *Oxon*. V. **D** Ox 11 **P** *Bp* **I** D MANSHIP, D H RUDDY *chap*, D J ALLPORT *c*, G N MAUGHAN *c*.

ABINGER (St Jas) w Coldharbour (Ch Ch), *Surrey*. R. **D** Guildf 6 **P** *C J A Evelyn Esq and CPS* alt **I** A M CARDALE.

ABINGTON (St Pet and St Paul), *Northants*. R. **D** Pet 5 **P** *Bp* **I** F E PICKARD, D C ROBINSON *c*.

(St Alb Mart) V. **D** Pet *See* Northampton.

ABINGTON, GREAT (St Mary), *Cambs*. V w Abington, Little (St Mary Virg), *Cambs*. V. **D** Ely 4 **P** *Mart Mem Trust* **I** R J BLAKEWAY-PHILLIPS *p-in-c*.

ABINGTON-PIGOTTS, *Cambs*.. **D** Ely 8 *See* Litlington.

AB-KETTLEBY (St Jas) w Wartnaby and Holwell, *Leics*. V. **D** Leic 4 **P** *V of Rothley 1 turn Bp 2 turns* **I** (Vacant).

AB LENCH, *Worcs*.. **D** Worc 1 *See* Church Lench.

ABRAM (St Jo Evang), *Gtr Man*. V. **D** Liv 12 **P** *R of Wigan* **I** R CRANKSHAW.

ABRIDGE (H Trin), *Essex*.. **D** Chelmsf 2 *See* Lambourne.

ABSON (St Jas Gt), *Avon*.. **D** Bris 4 *See* Pucklechurch.

ABTHORPE (St Jo Bapt) w Slapton, *Northants*.. **D** Pet 2 **P** *Trustees and T L Langton-Lockton (Alt)* **I** A F B ROGERS *p-in-c*.

ABY (All SS), *Lincs*.. **D** Linc 12 *See* Belleau.

ACASTER-MALBIS (H Trin), *N Yorks*. V. **D** York 2 **P** *Mrs F E Slamczynski, R A G & J R Raimes* **I** M W ESCRITT.

ACASTER SELBY, *N Yorks*.. **D** York *See* Appleton Roebuck.

ACCRINGTON (St Jas), *Lancs*. V. **D** Blackb 1 **P** *Hulme Trustees* **I** T R WILSON *p-in-c*.

(St Andr) V. **D** Blackb 1 **P** *V of Accrington* **I** G M C JONES *p-in-c*.

(Ch Ch) V. **D** Blackb 1 **P** *Trustees* **I** G STOREY.

(St Jo Evang) V. **D** Blackb 1 **P** *V of Accrington* **I** D E CROOK.

(St Mary Magd) V. **D** Blackb 1 **P** *V of Accrington* **I** M S HART.

(St Pet) V. **D** Blackb 1 **P** *V of Accrington* **I** T A G BILL *p-in-c*.

(St Paul) V. **D** Blackb 1 **P** *V of Ch Ch Accrington* **I** T R WILSON *p-in-c*.

(St Jo Bapt Baxenden) V. **D** Blackb 1 **P** *Bp* **I** B E HARDING.

ACHURCH (St Jo Bapt), *Northants*. R. **D** Pet *See* Aldwincle.

ACKLAM, EAST (St Jo Bapt) w Leavening, *N Yorks*. R. **D** York 3 *See* Burythorpe.

ACKLAM, WEST (St Mary), *Cleve*. V. **D** York 22 **P** *Trustees* **I** D P BODYCOMBE, W SAVAGE *hon c*.

ACKLINGTON (St Jo Div), *Northumb*. V. **D** Newc T 7 **P** *Bp and Trustees* **I** A D DUNCAN.

ACKWORTH (St Cuthb w All SS), *W Yorks*. R. **D** Wakef 11 **P** *Chan of Duchy of Lanc* **I** A P COURTLEY.

ACLE (St Edm K and Mart), *Norf*. R. **D** Nor 1 **P** *Bp* **I** K WILSON.

ACOCK'S GREEN (St Mary Virg), *W Midl*. V. **D** Birm 13 **P** *Trustees* **I** C J EVANS.

ACOL, *Kent*.. **D** Cant 9 *See* Birchington.

ACOMB (St Steph), *N Yorks*. V. **D** York 1 *See* York.

ACONBURY, *Herefs*. V. **D** Heref *See* Dewchurch.

ACRISE (St Martin), *Kent*. R. **D** Cant 6 **P** *Abp* **I** J B E CHITTENDEN.

ACTON (St Mary) w Worleston (St Osw), *Chesh*. V. **D** Ches 15 **P** *R C Roundell Esq & Bp* **I** D A MARTIN.

ACTON (St Mary), *Gtr Lon*. R. **D** Lon 5 **P** *Bp* **I** M R PARSONS.

EAST (St Dunstan w St Thos) V. **D** Lon **P** *Bp* **I** W J MORGAN.

GREEN (St Alb Mart) V. **D** Lon 5 **P** *Bp* **I** H B BARRY.

(St Pet) V. **D** Lon 5 **P** *Bp* **I** M F GODDARD *p-in-c*, A C LEE *c*.

(St Sav) [for Deaf and Dumb], Old Oak Road. **D** Lon 5 **P** *RADD* **I** (Vacant).

NORTH (St Gabr), V. **D** Lon 5 **P** *Bp* **I** E J ALCOCK.

SOUTH (All SS), V. **D** Lon 5 **P** *Bp* **I** H B BARRY *c-in-c*.

VALE (St Thos),. **D** Lon *See* East Acton.

WEST (St Martin), V. **D** Lon 5 **P** *Bp* **I** J S BODDINGTON.

ACTON (All SS) w G and L Waldingfield (St Lawr), *Suff*. V. **D** St E 12 **P** *Bp 2 turns, Miss M F J N Majendie 1 turn* **I** T P DUFFY, D G WOODWARDS P-IN-C OF L WALDINGFIELD.

ACTON-BEAUCHAMP (St Giles) w Evesbatch (St Andr) and Stanford Bishop, *Worcs*. R. **D** Heref 2 **P** *Bp and Mart Mem Trust* **I** D W GOULD P-IN-C OF STANFORD BP, P A GUIVER P-IN-C OF ACTON BEAUCHAMP W EVESBATCH.

ACTON BURNELL (St Mary) w Pitchford (St Mich), *Salop*. R. **D** Heref 11 **P** *Rev E W Serjeantson 2 turns, Exors of Sir Charles Grant 1 turn* **I** C J W C HATCLIFFE *p-in-c*, V G CLARK *c*.

ACTON-ROUND, *Salop*. V. **D** Heref 9 **P** *Univ of Cam* **I** (Vacant).

ACTON-SCOTT (St Marg), *Salop*. R. **D** Heref 11 **P** *Dioc Bd of Patr* **I** H D G JENKYNS *p-in-c*.
ACTON TRUSSELL (St Jas Gt) w Bednall (All SS), *Staffs*. V. **D** Lich 3 **P** *Hulme's Trustees* **I** R CHEADLE *p-in-c*.
ACTON TURVILLE, *Avon*. V. **D** Glouc 8 *See* Badminton.
ADBASTON (St Mich AA) *Staffs*. V. **D** Lich 15 **P** *Bp* **I** W E FOSTER *p-in-c*.
ADBOLTON, *Notts*.. **D** Southw *See* Holme Pierrepont.
ADDERBURY (St Mary Virg) w Milton (St Jo Evang), *Oxon*. V. **D** Ox 6 **P** *New Coll Ox* **I** J P VYVYAN.
ADDERLEY (St Pet), *Salop*. R. **D** Lich 23 **P** *Lt-Col J V Corbet* **I** D M MORRIS.
ADDINGHAM (St Pet), *W Yorks*. R. **D** Bradf 5 **P** *Trustees* **I** D A A SHAW, I J PRICE *c*.
ADDINGHAM (St Mich AA) w Gamblesby (St Jo Evang), *Cumb*. V. **D** Carl 6 **P** *D and C of Carl* **I** R J GLOVER *p-in-c*.
ADDINGTON (St Mary BV), *Surrey*. V. **D** Cant 16 **P** *Abp of Cant* **I** C J MORGAN-JONES, G FELLOWS *c*.
ADDINGTON (St Mary Virg), *Bucks*. R. **D** Ox 25 **P** *Dioc Bd of Patr* **I** A P A BARNES.
ADDINGTON (St Marg) w Trottiscliffe (St Pet and St Paul), *Kent*. R. **D** Roch 6 **P** *Bp* **I** H J M BURY *c-in-c*.
ADDINGTON, GREAT (All SS) w Addington, Little (St Mary Virg), V *Northants*. R. **D** Pet 9 **P** *Bp* **I** F WHITTLE.
ADDINGTON, NEW (St Edw K and Confessor), *Surrey*. V. **D** Cant 16 **P** *Abp* **I** C M S SNOW.
ADDISCOMBE (St Mary Magd), *Surrey*. V. **D** Cant 16 **P** *Trustees* **I** P B PRICE, J G MILLER *c*.
(St Mildred), V. **D** Cant 16 **P** *Abp* **I** G D S GALILEE.
ADDLESTONE (St Paul), *Surrey*. V. **D** Guildf 7 **P** *Bp* **I** M J FARRANT, R P CALDER *c*, G F GILCHRIST *c*.
ADDLETHORPE, *Lincs*.. **D** Linc 8 *See* Ingoldmells.
ADEL (St Jo Bapt), *W Yorks*. R. **D** Ripon 5 **P** *Trustees* **I** D F THOMPSON.
(H Trin Cookridge), V. **D** Ripon 5 **P** *R of Adel* **I** C ISBISTER.
ADFORTON (St Andr), Herefs. **D** Heref *See* Leintwardine.
ADISHAM (H Innoc), *Kent*. R. **D** Cant 1 **P** *Abp* **I** P V R PENNANT *p-in-c*.
ADLESTROP (St Mary Magd), *Glos*.. **D** Glouc 16 *See* Oddington.
ADLINGFLEET (All SS), *Humb*. V. **D** Sheff 9 *See* Whitgift.
ADLINGTON (St Paul), *Lancs*. V. **D** Blackb 4 **P** *Bp* **I** R A ANDREW.
ADMARSH-IN-BLEASDALE (St Eadnor) w Calder Vale, *Lancs*. V. **D** Blackb 10 **P** *Bp and V of Lancaster* alt **I** A R LINTON *p-in-c*.
ADSTOCK, *Bucks*.. **D** Ox *See* Padbury.
ADSTONE, *Northants*.. **D** Pet *See* Blakesley.
ADWELL (St Mary), *Oxon*.. **D** Ox 1 *See* Weston, South.
ADWICK-LE-STREET (St Lawr), *S Yorks*. R. **D** Sheff 8 **P** *Capt J R R Fullerton* **I** S L RAYNER.
ADWICK-UPON-DEARNE (St Jo Bapt), *S Yorks*. V. **D** Sheff 10 *See* Wath-on-Dearne.
AFFPUDDLE (St Lawr) w Toners Puddle or Turnerspuddle *Dorset*.. **D** Sarum *See* Bere Regis.
AIGBURTH (St Anne), *Mer*. V. **D** Liv 2 **P** *Trustees* **I** J C ANDERS.
AIKTON (St Andr), *Cumb*. R. **D** Carl 3 **P** *MMT and Earl of Lonsdale* alt **I** R S BARNETT.
AILBY, *Lincs*.. **D** Linc 8 *See* Alford.
AINDERBY STEEPLE (St Helen) w Yafforth (All SS) and Scruton (St Rhadegunda), *N Yorks*. V. **D** Ripon **P** *Bp* **I** P B CARTER.
AINSDALE (St John), *Mer*. V. **D** Liv 8 **P** *Bp and Archd of Liv and R of Walton* **I** J E MORRIS, I H BLYDE *c*.
AINSTABLE (St Mich AA), *Cumb*. V. **D** Carl 6 *See* Kirkoswald.
AINSWORTH (Ch Ch) or Cockeymoor, *Gtr Man*. V. **D** Man 16 **P** *Bp* **I** K P BULLOCK.
AINTREE (St Pet), *Mer*. V. **D** Liv 5 **P** *R of Sephton* **I** W ARMSTRONG.
(St Giles) V. **D** Liv 5 **P** *Bp* **I** D K KING.
AIREDALE (H Cross) w Fryston, *W Yorks*. V. **D** Wakef 11 **P** *Bp* **I** P J SWEETING.
AIRMYN (St D), *Humb*. V. **D** Sheff 9 *See* Hook.
AISHOLT, *Somt*. V. **D** B & W 17 **P** *MMT* **I** A R MOSS *c-in-c*.
AISLABY (St Marg) and Ruswarp, *N Yorks*. V. **D** York 27 **P** *Abp* **I** J E D CAVE *p-in-c*.
AISTHORPE (St Pet) w Scampton (St Jo Bapt) and Thorpe le Fallows (St Mary Magd) w Brattleby (St Cuthb), *Lincs*. R. **D** Linc 3 **P** *Dioc Bd of Patr and Rev E D C Wright* **I** C M H FRERE.
AKELEY (St Jas), *Bucks*.. **D** Ox *See* Buckingham N.
AKENHAM, *Suff*.. **D** St E 4 *See* Whitton.
ALBANY STREET (Ch Ch), *Lon*.. **D** Lon 26 *See* St Pancras.
ALBERBURY (St Mich AA) w Cardeston (St Mich), *Salop*. V. **D** Heref 13 **P** *Bp and Sir M Leighton Bt (alt)* **I** R SHARP.
ALBOURNE (St Bart) w Sayers Common and Twineham, *W Sussex*. R. **D** Chich 14 **P** *Bp 2 turns, Ex Coll Ox 1 turn* **I** J S HASTWELL.
ALBRIGHTON (St Mary Magd), *Salop*. V. **D** Lich 25 **P** *Ch Hosp and Haberdashers' Co* alt **I** R B BALKWILL *p-in-c*.
ALBRIGHTON (St Jo Bapt), *Salop*. V. **D** Lich 26 *See* Battlefield.
ALBURGH (All SS), *Norf*. R. **D** Nor *See* Earsham.
ALBURY (St Pet and St Paul) w St Martha, *Surrey*. R. **D** Guildf 2 **P** *Albury Estate Trustees* **I** S ORME.
ALBURY w Tiddington (St Helen), *Oxon*. R. **D** Ox 5 *See* Haseley, Great.
ALBURY (St Mary),*Herts*. V. **D** St Alb 4 *See* Braughing.
ALBY (St Ethelbert) w Thwaite (All SS), *Norf*. R. **D** Nor 3 **P** *Ld Walpole and Bp* alt **I** D A POPE *p-in-c*.
ALCESTER (St Nich) w Arrow (H Trin), Oversley, and Weethley (St Jas), *Warws*. R. **D** Cov 7 **P** *Marq of Hertf* **I** A J STALLY.
ALCISTON, *E Sussex*. V. **D** Chich *See* Selmeston.
ALCOMBE (St Mich Arch), *Somt*. V. **D** B & W 21 **P** *Bp* **I** A F MILLS.
ALCONBURY (St Pet and St Paul) w Weston, *Cambs*. V. **D** Ely 10 **P** *D and C of Westmr* **I** B E CLOSE *p-in-c*.
ALDBOROUGH (St Mary) w Thurgarton and Gunton w Hanworth and Bessingham, *Norf*. R. **D** Nor **P** *Bp, E C Lilly Esq and the Hon L E Harbord* **I** (Vacant).
ALDBOROUGH (St Andr) w Dunsforth and Boroughbridge (St Jas) and Roecliffe, *N Yorks*. V. **D** Ripon 3 **P** *D and C of York and Bp* alt **I** R NOYES.
ALDBOROUGH HATCH (St Pet), *Essex*. V. **D** Chelmsf 7 **P** *Crown* **I** W A C BARNES.
ALDBOURNE (St Mich), *Wilts*.. **D** Sarum 26 *See* Whitton.
ALDBROUGH (St Paul), *N Yorks*.. **D** Ripon 1 *See* Stanwick.
ALDBROUGH and Mappleton w Goxhill and Withernwick, *Humb*. V. **D** York 14 **P** *Ld Chan 1st turn, Abp 2nd turn, Archd of E Riding 3rd turn* **I** K G SKIPPER.
ALDBURY (St Jo Bapt), *Herts*. R. **D** St Alb *See* Tring.
ALDEBURGH (St Pet and St Paul) w Hazlewood, *Suff*. V. **D** St E 19 **P** *Mrs C J Vernon Wentworth* **I** W D HUTCHINSON.
ALDEBY (St Mary Virg) w Wheatacre (All SS) and Burgh St Peter (St Mary Virg), *Norf*.. **D** Nor 14 *See* Raveningham.
ALDENHAM (St Jo Bapt), *Herts*. V. **D** St Alb 1 **P** *Ld Aldenham* **I** G R S RITSON *p-in-c*.
ALDERBURY (St Mary Virg), *Wilts*. V. **D** Sarum 17 **P** *Bp* **I** C Y POOLEY, G F H MITCHELL *c*.
ALDERFORD (St Jo Bapt) w Attlebridge (St Andr) and Swannington (St Marg), *Norf*. R. **D** Nor 6 **P** *D and C of Nor and Bp* alt **I** A J HAWES.
ALDERHOLT (St Jas Gt and St Clem), *Dorset*. V. **D** Sarum 11 **P** *Dioc Bd of Patr* **I** J A HENSON.
ALDERLEY (St Mary, formerly St Lawr), *Chesh*. R. **D** Ches 12 **P** *Trustees* **I** W GARLICK.
ALDERLEY (St Kenelm) w Hillesley (St Giles), *Glos*. R. **D** Glouc *See* Kingswood.
ALDERLEY EDGE (St Phil), *Chesh*.. **D** Ches 13 *See* Chorley, St Philip.
ALDERMASTON (St Mary) w Wasing (St Nich) and Brimpton (St Pet), *Berks*. V. **D** Ox 12 **P** *Dioc Bd of Patr, Sir W Mount, Bt, and Worc Coll Ox.* **I** R B MILLER.
ALDERMINSTER (St Mary and H Cross), *Worcs*. V. **D** Cov 9 **P** *S for Maint of Faith* **I** J E BLUCK *p-in-c*.
ALDERNEY (St Anne), V. **D** Win 13 **P** *Crown* **I** E J BENNETT.
ALDERSBROOK (St Gabr), *Essex*. V. **D** Chelmsf 7 **P** *R of Wanstead* **I** D C L MAY.
ALDERSHOT (St Mich Arch), *Hants*. V. **D** Guildf 1 **P** *Bp* **I** S A ZEAL, J W BRANSON *c*.
(H Trin), V. **D** Guildf 1 **P** *CPAS* **I** C MANCHESTER.
(St Aug), V. **D** Guildf 1 **P** *Bp* **I** B D GOLDSMITH.
(St Geo Conv Distr Badshot Lea). **D** Guildf 1 **P** *Bp* **I** T M JOHNS *p-in-c*.
ALDERTON, *Wilts*.. **D** Bris *See* Luckington.
ALDERTON (St Marg) w Gt Washbourne (st Mary), *Glos*. R. **D** Glouc 18 **P** *Bp 2 turns Dioc Bd of Patr 1 turn* **I** J G EDELSTON.
ALDERTON (St Marg), *Northants*. R. **D** Pet 2 *See* Stoke Bruerne.

ALDERTON (St Andr) w Ramsholt and Bawdsey (St Mary Virg), *Suff.* R. **D** St E 7 **P** *Bp 1 turn, Exors of G L Archer 2 turns* **I** G W W VINCENT.
ALDFORD (St Jo Bapt), *Chesh.* R. **D** Ches 5 *See* Bruera.
ALDHAM (St Marg), *Essex.* R. **D** Chelmsf 22 **P** *Mart Mem Trust* **I** P H ADAMS, S G HUCKLE *c.*
ALDHAM Suff. R **D** St E 3 *See* Elmsett.
ALDINGBOURNE (St Mary), *W Sussex.* V. **D** Chich 1 **P** *Bp* **I** (Vacant).
ALDINGHAM (St Cuthb) and Dendron and Rampside, *Cumb.* R. **D** Carl 15 **P** *Crown and V of Dalton (alt)* **I** A GASKELL.
ALDINGTON (St Martin) w Bonnington and Bilsington, *Kent.* R. **D** Cant 12 **P** *Abp* **I** J W DILNOT.
ALDRIDGE (St Mary Virg), *W Midl.* R. **D** Lich 9 **P** *Mart Mem Trust* **I** J D DELIGHT, M J BUTT *c,* D J BUTTERFIELD *c,* R D H BURSELL *hon c.*
ALDRINGHAM (St Andr) w Thorpe (St Pet), *Suff.* V. **D** St E 19 **P** *CPS* **I** C F COWLEY.
ALDRINGTON (St Leon), *W Sussex.* R. **D** Chich 13 **P** *Bp* **I** (Vacant).
ALDSWORTH, *Glos.* V. **D** Glouc 15 *See* Sherborne.
ALDWARK (St Steph), *N Yorks..* **D** York 5 *See* Alne.
ALDWICK (St Richard), *W Sussex.* V. **D** Chich 1 **P** *Bp* **I** N J M A F COCHRANE, E W WORT *hon c.*
ALDWINCLE (St Pet) and (All SS) w Thorpe Achurch (St Jo Bapt) and Pilton (All SS) w Wadenhoe (St Mich AA) and Stoke Doyle (St Rumbold), *Northants.* R. **D** Pet 11 **P** *S of Merchant Venturers of Bris 2 turns, C G Capron 1 turn, G Ward Hunt 1 turn.* **I** W S SHIRE.
ALDWORTH (St Mary) w Ashampstead, *Berks.* V. **D** Ox 12 **P** *S Jo Coll Cam and Simeon Trustees* **I** S EDMONDS.
ALEXANDRA PARK (St Sav), V. **D** Lon 23 *See* Wood Green, St Saviour.
ALEXTON **D** Leic 5 *See* Allexton.
ALFINGTON (St Jas and St Anne), *Devon.* V. **D** Ex 7 **P** *Ld Coleridge* **I** P J MCGEE.
ALFOLD (St Nich) and Loxwood (St Jo Bapt), *Surrey and W Sussex.* R. **D** Guildf 2 **P** *CPAS and Bp* **I** D K INNES.
ALFORD (All SS) w Hornblotton (St Pet), *Somt..* **D** B & W 4 *See* Six Pilgrims.
ALFORD (St Wilf) w Rigsby (St Jas) and Ailby, *Lincs.* V. **D** Linc 8 **P** *Bp* **I** G I GEORGE-JONES, M F J BRADLEY *missr.*
ALFRETON (St Martin), *Derbys.* V. **D** Derby 1 **P** *Bp* **I** A HEATON.
ALFRICK (St Mary Magd) w Lulsley (St Giles) and Suckley (St Jo Bapt) and Leigh and Bransford, *Worcs.* V. **D** Worc 2 **P** *Crown and Bp (alt)* **I** R HANSON.
ALFRISTON (St Andr) w Lullington, *E Sussex.* V. **D** Chich 15 **P** *Ld Chan* **I** H F DANIELS.
ALGARKIRK Lincs. R **D** Linc 21 *See* Fosdyke.
ALKBOROUGH, or AUKBOROUGH (St Jo Bapt) w Whitton (St Jo Bapt), West Halton and Winteringham *Humb.* V. **D** Linc 4 **P** *Em Coll Cam and Bp* **I** G L TOWELL.
ALKERTON, *Oxon..* **D** Ox *See* Shennington.
ALKHAM (St Anthony) w Capel-le-Ferne (St Mary) and Hougham-by-Dover (St Lawr), *Kent.* V. **D** Cant 5 **P** *Abp* **I** J D KING.
ALKMONTON (St John) w Yeaveley (H Trin), *Derbys.* V. **D** Derby 14 **P** *Bp and V of Shirley* **I** D F P DAWE.
ALKRINGTON, *Gtr Man..* **D** Man *See* Tonge.
ALL CANNINGS (All SS) w Etchilhampton (St Andr), *Wilts..* **D** Sarum *See* Bishop's Cannings.
ALL HALLOWS, Barking-by-the-Tower. **D** Lon 1 *See* London.
ALLEN, WEST (Ch Ch), *Northumb..* **D** Newc T 4 *See* Allendale.
ALLENDALE (St Cuthb w St Pet) w Whitfield (H Trin), *Northumb.* R. **D** Newc T **P** *Visc Allendale and J C Blackett-Ord Esq (alt)* **I** R J BOND.
ALLEN'S CROSS (St Bart), *Worcs.* V. **D** Birm 4 **P** *Bp* **I** W A S PARKER.
ALLENSMORE (St Andr), *Herefs.* V. **D** Heref 1 **P** *Crown* **I** S W E JONES.
ALLENTON and Shelton Lock (St Edm), *Derbys.* V. **D** Derby 15 **P** *Bp* **I** J B DICKINSON.
ALLER (St Andr), *Somt.* R. **D** B & W 10 *See* Langport.
ALLERSTON (St John), *N Yorks.* V. **D** York 24 *See* Ebberston.
ALLERTHORPE (St Botolph), *Humb.* V. **D** York 7 *See* Thornton.
ALLERTON or CHAPEL ALLERTON, *Somt..* **D** B & W 1 *See* Mark.
ALLERTON (St Pet), *W Yorks.* V. **D** Bradf 1 **P** *Bp* **I** P M HAWKINS, J C BLAKE *c,* A HOLLIDAY *hon c.*
ALLERTON (All H), *Mer.* V. **D** Liv 2 **P** *Col J D Bibby* **I** K AYAD *c,* J I DAVIES *c,* R A JEAVONS *c.*
ALLERTON-BYWATER (St Mary L), *N Yorks.* V. **D** Ripon 7 **P** *V of Kippax* **I** E H HOWES.
ALLESLEY (All SS), *W Midl..* **D** Cov 2 **P** *J R L Thomson-Bree Esq* **I** A E BURN.
ALLESLEY PK (St Chris), *W Midl.* V. **D** Cov 3 **P** *Bp* **I** D C ROBINSON.
ALLESTREE (St Edm), *Derbys.* V. **D** Derby 12 **P** *Bp* **I** A T REDMAN, W ILLINGWORTH *c,* J LYNN *c.*
(St Nich) V. **D** Derby 12 **P** *Bp* **I** G K G GRIFFITH, J L H RICE *c.*
ALLEXTON (St Pet), Leics.. **D** Leic *See* Hallaton.
ALLHALLOWS (All H), *Cumb.* V. **D** Carl 11 **P** *Bp* **I** D V SCOTT.
ALLINGTON (St Nich) w Maidstone (St Pet), *Kent.* R. **D** Cant 15 **P** *Abp* **I** A WATSON, T W BROADBENT *c.*
ALLINGTON (St Swith), *Dorset.* V. **D** Sarum *See* Bridport.
ALLINGTON (St Jo Bapt) w Boscombe (St Andr), *Wilts.* R. **D** Sarum 17 *See* Bourne Valley.
ALLINGTON, EAST (St Andr), *Devon.* R. **D** Ex 14 **P** *Bp* **I** C C ROBINS *p-in-c.*
ALLINGTON, WEST (H Trin) w East (St Jas) and Sedgbrook (St Lawr), *Lincs.* R. **D** Linc 19 **P** *Ld Chan* **I** J M ASHLEY.
ALLITHWAITE (St Mary), *Cumb.* V. **D** Carl 14 **P** *Bp* **I** P F W FROST.
ALLONBY (Ch Ch) w West Newton (St Matt), *Cumb.* V. **D** Carl 11 **P** *V of Bromfield and Bp* alt **I** B T TUFFIELD *p-in-c.*
ALMELEY (St Mary), *Herefs.* V. **D** Heref 5 **P** *Bp* **I** (Vacant).
ALMER, *Dorset..* **D** Sarum *See* Morden.
ALMODINGTON, *W Sussex..* **D** Chich 3 *See* Earnley.
ALMONDBURY (All H), *W Yorks.* V. **D** Wakef 5 **P** *Dioc Bd of Patr* **I** R L WHITELEY, C W DIXON *c,* R J LINDSAY *c.*
ALMONDSBURY (St Mary Virg), *Avon.* V. **D** Bris 6 **P** *Bp* **I** B G CARNE, H P KINGDON *hon c.*
ALNE (St Mary) w Aldwark (St Steph), *N Yorks.* V. **D** York 5 **P** *CPAS and Mart Mem Trust* alt **I** W R HENDERSON.
ALNHAM, *Northumb..* **D** Newc T *See* Alwinton.
ALNMOUTH (St Jo Bapt), *Northumb.* V. **D** Newc T 7 *See* Lesbury.
ALNWICK (St Mich AA and St Paul), w Edlingham and Bolton, *Northumb.* V. **D** Newc T 7 **P** *Duke of Northumb* **I** J H CHICKEN, H H BAKER *c.*
ALPERTON (St Jas), *Gtr Lon.* V. **D** Lon 18 **P** *Trustees* **I** J B ROOT, A G FOUTS *c.*
ALPHAMSTONE w Lamarsh (H Innoc) and Pebmarsh (St Jo Bapt), *Essex.* R. **D** Chelmsf 18 **P** *Ld Chan and Earl of Verulam* alt **I** S S V HOUGH.
ALPHETON, *Suff..* **D** St E *See* Shimplingthorne.
ALPHINGTON (St Mich AA), *Devon.* R. **D** Ex 3 **P** *Dioc Bd of Patr* **I** O B EATON.
ALRESFORD, *Essex.* R. **D** Chelmsf 28 **P** *Hulme Trustees* **I** E S BRITT *p-in-c.*
ALRESFORD, NEW (St Jo Bapt) w Ovington (St Pet) and Itchen Stoke, *Hants.* R. **D** Win 6 **P** *Bp* **I** G E BEECHEY.
ALRESFORD, OLD (St Mary Virg) and Bighton, *Hants.* R. **D** Win **P** *Bp* **I** M SAUNDERS.
ALREWAS (All SS) w Fradley (St Steph), *Staffs.* V. **D** Lich 2 **P** *Bp* **I** J E COLSTON.
ALSAGER (St Mary Magd), *Chesh.* V. **D** Ches 11 **P** *Bp* **I** A OWENS.
(Ch Ch), V. **D** Ches 11 **P** *Bp* **I** H R TATE.
ALSAGERS BANK (St John), *Staffs.* V. **D** Lich 17 **P** *Bp* **I** L HAMLETT.
ALSOP-EN-LE-DALE (St Mich AA), *Derbys.* V. **D** Derby 8 *See* Parwich.
ALSTON (St Aug) w Garrigill (St Jo Evang), Nenthead (St John) and Kirkhaugh (St Paraclete), *Cumb.* V. **D** Newc T 4 **P** *Bp* **I** (Vacant).
ALSTONFIELD (St Pet), *Staffs.* V. **D** Lich 13 **P** *C Harpur Crewe Esq* **I** J W HAMPTON *p-in-c.*
ALTARNON (St Nonna) w Bolventor *Cornw..* **D** Truro 11 *See* North Hill.
ALTCAR (St Mich and AA), *Mer.* V. **D** Liv 8 **P** *Bp* **I** J E SMITH.
ALTHAM (St Jas) w Clayton-le-Moors (All SS), *Lancs.* V. **D** Blackb 1 **P** *Exors of Wm Hallam and Trustees* **I** E ANGUS, S J R HARTLEY *c.*
ALTHORNE (St Andr), *Essex..* **D** Chelmsf 13 *See* Cricksea.
ALTHORPE (St Osw) w Keadby, *Humb.* R. **D** Linc 1 **P** *Crown* **I** (Vacant).
ALTOFTS (St Mary Magd), *W Yorks.* V. **D** Wakef 13 **P** *Meynell Ingram Trustees* **I** S K L VICK.
ALTON (St Pet), *Staffs.* V. **D** Lich 14 **P** *Dioc Bd of Patr* **I** W H GOLDSTRAW.

ALTON (St Lawr), *Hants.* V. **D** Win 1 **P** *D and C of Win* **I** R F S EKE, J R EVANS *c.*
(All SS), V. **D** Win 1 **P** *Bp* **I** M C SURMAN *p-in-c.*
ALTON BARNES (St Mary Virg) w Alton Priors (All SS) and Stanton St Bernard (All SS), *Wilts.* R. **D** Sarum 27 *See* Swanborough.
ALTON PANCRAS, *Dorset.* V. **D** Sarum 5 *See* Piddletrenthide.
ALTRINCHAM (St Geo), *Gtr Man.* V. **D** Ches 10 **P** *V of Bowdon* **I** R K FAULKNER, R E WILLIAMS *c,* E HENSHALL *hon c.*
(St Jo Evang), V. **D** Ches 10 **P** *Bp* **I** W J MOXON.
ALVANLEY (St Jo Evang), *Chesh.* V. **D** Ches 3 **P** *Bp* **I** M J FENTON.
ALVASTON (St Mich AA), *Derbys.* V. **D** Derby 15 **P** *PCC* **I** P G C BECK *p-in-c.*
ALVECHURCH (St Lawr), *Worcs.* R. **D** Worc 7 **P** *Bp* **I** L R AITKEN.
ALVEDISTON (St Mary), *Wilts.* V. **D** Sarum 19 *See* Ebbesbourne Wake.
ALVELEY (St Mary Virg), *Salop.* V. **D** Heref 9 **P** *P de M H Thompson Esq* **I** W C MASSEY.
ALVERDISCOTT, OR ALSCOTT, *Devon.* R. **D** Ex 20 *See* Newton Tracey.
ALVERSTOKE (St Mary), *Hants.* R. **D** Portsm 1 **P** *Bp* **I** W E REES, E W L DAVIES *c,* W H PRICE *c.*
ALVERTHORPE (St Paul), *W Yorks.* V. **D** Wakef 12 **P** *Bp* **I** E GEE.
ALVESCOT (St Pet) w Black Bourton (St Mary) Shilton, Westwell and Holwell, *Oxon.* R. **D** Ox **P** *Mrs P Allen 1st turn, D and C of Ox 2nd and 5th turns, J Heyworth Esq 3rd turn and Mrs A Bulley 4th turn* **I** (Vacant).
ALVESTON (St Helen), *Avon.* V. **D** Bris 6 **P** *D and C of Bris* **I** C D SUTCH *p-in-c.*
ALVESTON (St Jas), *Warws.* V. **D** Cov 8 **P** *R of Hampton Lucy* **I** R A NOISE.
ALVINGHAM (St Adelwold) w Cockerington N (St Mary), and Cockerington S (St Leon), *Lincs.* V. **D** Linc *See* Mid Marsh Group.
ALVINGTON (St Andr), *Glos..* **D** Glouc 7 *See* Woolaston.
ALVINGTON WEST (All SS), *Devon.* V. **D** Ex 14 **P** *D and C of Sarum* **I** K E JACKSON *p-in-c.*
ALWALTON (St Andr), *Cambs.* R. **D** Ely 14 **P** *Earl Fitzwilliam* **I** (Vacant).
ALWINGTON (St Andr), *Devon.* R. **D** Ex 17 *See* Parkham.
ALWINTON (St Mich AA) w Holystone, Kidland and Alnham (St Mich), *Northumb.* V. **D** Newc T 7 **P** *Ld Chan and Duke of Northumb* **I** R B S BURSTON.
AMBASTON, *Derbys..* **D** Derby 15 *See* Elvaston.
AMBERGATE (St Anne), V. **D** Derby 12 **P** *The Johnson Family* **I** T E JONES *p-in-c.*
AMBERLEY (St Mich) w Stoke, North, *W Sussex.* V. **D** Chich 7 **P** *Bp* **I** N J C GREENFIELD *p-in-c.*
AMBERLEY (H Trin), *Glos.* R. **D** Glouc 9 **P** *Dioc Bd of Patr* **I** C D J G BURSLEM.
AMBERLEY (Dedic unknown), *Herefs..* **D** Heref 4 *See* Marden.
AMBLE (St Cuthb), *Northumb.* V. **D** Newc T 7 **P** *Bp* **I** A SIMPSON.
AMBLECOTE (H Trin), *W Midl.* V. **D** Worc 11 **P** *Bp* **I** P TONGUE.
AMBLESIDE (St Mary Virg and St Anne) w Brathay (H Trin), *Cumb.* V. **D** Carl 14 **P** *Dioc Bd of Patr* **I** K J COVE.
AMBROSDEN (St Mary) w Merton and Piddington, *Oxon..* **D** Ox 2 **P** *Trustees of F A W Page-Turner Esq, Ex Coll Ox and PCC* **I** R W MAPPLEBECKPALMER (FORMERLY PALMER).
AMCOTTS (St Thos la Becket) w Luddington and Garthorpe, *Humb.* R. **D** Linc 1 **P** *Crown* **I** (Vacant).
AMERSHAM (St Mary) w Coleshill (All SS), *Bucks.* R. **D** Ox 20 **P** *Capt T Tyrwhitt Drake* **I** A CAMPBELL.
(St Mich AA Amersham-on-the-Hill). **D** Ox 20 **P** *Bp* **I** G B GRIFFITHS, P R BINNS *c,* J C H LEE *c.*
AMESBURY (St Mary and St Melorus), *Wilts.* V. **D** Sarum 18 **P** *D and C of Windsor* **I** P R LEWIS.
AMINGTON (St Editha), *Staffs..* **D** Birm 10 *See* Shuttington.
AMOTHERBY (St Helen) w Appleton-le-Street (All SS) and Barton-le-Street (St Mich AA), *N Yorks.* V. **D** York 21 **P** *Abp and Meynell Ch Trust* **I** (Vacant).
AMPFIELD (St Mark), *Hants.* V. **D** Win 10 **P** *Univ of Ox* **I** J G HOBBS *p-in-c.*
AMPLEFORTH (St Hilda) w Oswaldkirk (St Osw), *N Yorks.* R. **D** York 20 **P** *Abp and Exors of Ld Feversham* alt **I** P CAUWOOD.
AMPNEY (St Pet) w (St Mary) w Ampney Crucis, Harnhill and Driffield, *Glos.* R. **D** Glouc 13 **P** *Maj P H G Bengough* **I** P G C JEFFRIES.
AMPORT ST MARY (St Mary) and Grateley (St Leon) and Monxton (St Mary Virg) and Quarley, *Hants.* V. **D** Win 2 **P** *D & C of Chich, The de Paravicini family, The R Found of St Katherine in Ratcliffe and Bp* **I** M J GRYLLS.
AMPTHILL (St Andr) w Millbrook (St Mich AA) and Steppingley, *Beds.* R. **D** St Alb 15 **P** *Ld Chan* **I** L G STURMAN.
AMPTON (St Pet and St Paul) w Little Livermere (St Pet), *Suff.* R. **D** St E *See* Ingham.
AMWELL, GREAT (St Jo Bapt) w St Margaret, *Herts.* V. **D** St Alb 8 **P** *Bp and Haileybury and Imperial Service Coll* **I** C E C WALKER.
AMWELL, LITTLE (H Trin), *Herts.* V. **D** St Alb 8 **P** *CPS* **I** J V BUDD.
ANCASTER (St Martin), *Lincs.* V. **D** Linc 23 **P** *Bp* **I** L G BLANCHARD.
ANCOATS Gtr Man. **D** Man 1 *See* Manchester.
ANCROFT (St Anne) w Scremerston (St Pet), *Northumb.* V. **D** Newc T 11 **P** *Bp* **I** P WHITEHEAD P-IN-C OF SCREMERSTON.
ANDERBY (St Andr) w Cumberworth (St Helen), *Lincs.* R. **D** Linc 8 **P** *Magd Coll Cam* **I** R FIELDEN.
ANDOVER (St Mary Virg) w Foxcott, *Hants.* V. **D** Win 2 **P** *Win Coll* **I** P J CHANDLER.
(St Mich AA), V. **D** Win 2 **P** *Bp* **I** J R COLEBROOK, D F KING *hon c.*
ANDOVERSFORD, *Glos..* **D** Glouc 15 *See* Dowdeswell.
ANERLEY (H Trin), *Surrey.* V. **D** Roch *See* Penge.
ANFIELD (St Simon and St Jude), *Mer.* V. **D** Liv 5 **P** *Trustees* **I** M DEAN *p-in-c.*
(St Columba), V. **D** Liv 5 **P** *Bp* **I** P B CAVANAGH, L W C FEATHAM *c,* D R THOMAS *c.*
(St Marg), V. **D** Liv 6 **P** *Bp* **I** B R ELSDON.
ANGELL TOWN (St Jo Evang), *Surrey..* **D** S'wark 3 *See* Brixton Hill.
ANGERSLEIGH (St Mich AA), *Somt..* **D** B&W 23a *See* Trull.
ANGMERING (St Marg) w Ham and Bargham V, *W Sussex.* R. **D** Chich 1 **P** *J F L Somerset Esq* **I** J E C NICHOLL.
ANLABY (St Pet), *Humb.* V. **D** York 17 **P** *Trustees* **I** T R J DICKENS.
(St Mark), V. **D** York 17 **P** *Abp* **I** L A WHITESIDE.
ANMER (St Mary Virg), *Norf.* R. **D** Nor *See* Dersingham.
ANNESLEY (Our Lady and All SS), *Notts.* V. **D** Southw 12 **P** *Maj R Chaworth-Musters* **I** A S G HART.
ANNFIELD PLAIN (St Aid), *Durham.* V. **D** Dur *See* Collierley.
ANNSCROFT Salop. **D** Heref 13 *See* Longden.
ANSFORD (St Andr), or Almsford, *Somt.* R. **D** B&W 4 *See* Castle Cary.
ANSLEY (St Lawr), *Warws.* V. **D** Cov 5 **P** *CPS* **I** T M GOULDSTONE *p-in-c.*
ANSLOW (H Trin), *Staffs.* V. **D** Lich **P** *MMT* **I** M D BIRT.
ANSTEY (St Mary), *Leics.* R. **D** Leic 17 **P** *R of Thurcaston* **I** J B SEATON.
ANSTEY (St Geo), *Herts.* R. **D** St Alb *See* Hormead, Great.
ANSTEY, WEST (St Petrock), w Anstey, East (St Mich), *Devon..* **D** Ex 19 *See* Oakmoor.
ANSTON (St Jas Ap), *Lancs.* V. **D** Sheff 5 **P** *Bp* **I** D G MANNING *c.*
ANSTY (St Jas), V w Shilton (St Andr), *Warws.* V. **D** Cov 5 **P** *Ld Chan* **I** K R HAGAN *p-in-c.*
ANSTY Wilts. **D** Sarum 19 *See* Swallowcliffe.
ANTINGHAM (St Mary) w Thorpe Market, *Norf..* **D** Nor 5 *See* Trunch.
ANTINGHAM (St Marg), *Norf..* **D** Nor *See* Walsham, North.
ANTONY w Sheviock, *Cornw.* R. **D** Truro **P** *Col Sir J G Carew Pole Bt* **I** G HARPER.
ANTROBUS (St Mark), *Chesh.* V. **D** Ches 4 *See* Appleton Thorn.
ANWICK (St Edith), *Lincs.* V. **D** Linc 22 **P** *Bp* **I** (Vacant).
APETHORPE (St Leon) w Woodnewton, *Northants.* V. **D** Pet 11 **P** *Ld Brassey* **I** B W TURNER.
APLEY (St Andr), *Lincs.* V. **D** Linc 3 *See* Stainfield.
APPERLEY, *Glos..* **D** Glouc 10 *See* Deerhurst.
APPLEBY (St Lawr), *Cumb.* V. **D** Carl 1 **P** *D and C of Carl and Bp alt* **I** R W GRAYSON.
APPLEBY MAGNA (St Mich), *Leics* and *Derbys.* R. **D** Leic 12 **P** *Dioc Bd of Patr* **I** C G S COX.
APPLEBY (St Bart), *Humb.* V. **D** Linc 4 **P** *Trustees of Ld St Oswald* **I** R J G PARKER.
APPLEDORE (St Pet and St Paul) w Stone-in-Oxney (St Mary Virg) and Ebony w Kenardington, *Kent.* V. **D** Cant 13 **P** *Abp* **I** A N B TOWSE.

APPLEDORE (St Mary), *Devon.* V. **D** Ex 17 *See* Northam.
APPLEFORD (St Pet and St Paul), *Oxon..* **D** Ox 11 *See* Sutton Courtenay.
APPLESHAW and Kimpton (SS Pet & Paul) and Thruxton (SS Pet & Paul) and Fyfield (St Nich), *Hants.* V. **D** Win **P** *Bp, D and C of Win, R J Routh Esq and M H Routh Esq* **I** I J TOMLINSON.
APPLETON, *Norf.* V. **D** Nor 23 *See* Sandringham.
APPLETON (St Laur), *Oxon.* R. **D** Ox 11 **P** *Magd Coll Ox* **I** P H WYLD.
APPLETON-LE-MOORS (Ch Ch), *N Yorks.* V. **D** York *See* Lastingham.
APPLETON-LE-STREET, *N Yorks.* V. **D** York 21 *See* Amotherby.
APPLETON-ROEBUCK (All SS) w Acaster Selby (St Jo Evang), *N Yorks.* V. **D** York 2 **P** *Abp* **I** H E HUTCHINSON *p-in-c.*
APPLETON THORN (St Cross) and Antrobus, *Chesh..* **D** Ches 4 **P** *V of Gt Budworth and Bp* alt. **I** B M BENNETT.
APPLETON WISKE (St Mary), *N Yorks..* **D** Ripon 1 *See* Great Smeaton.
APPLETREE, *Northants.* R. **D** Pet *See* Boddington.
APPLEY BRIDGE (All SS Conv Distr), *Lancs..* **D** Blackb 4 **P** *Bp* **I** C J STEVENSON *c-in-c.*
APSLEY END (St Mary), *Herts.* V. **D** St Alb *See* Chambersbury.
(St Benedict, Bennetts End Conv Distr). **D** St Alb 3 **P** *Bp* **I** (Vacant).
APULDRAM (St Mary Virg), *W Sussex.* V. **D** Chich 3 **P** *D and C of Chich* **I** R C RATCLIFF *p-in-c,* A E KEMP *hon c.*
ARBORFIELD (St Bart) w Barkham (St Jas), *Berks.* R. **D** Ox 16 **P** *Dioc Bd of Patr* **I** I H BULL.
ARDELEY, or YARDLEY (St Lawr), *Herts.* V. **D** St Alb 5 **P** *D and C of St Paul's* **I** M P THOMAS.
ARDINGLY (St Pet), *W Sussex.* R. **D** Chich 11 **P** *Mart Mem Trust* **I** D F PERRYMAN.
ARDINGTON, *Oxon..* **D** Ox 19 *See* Wantage Downs.
ARDLEIGH (St Mary Virg), *Essex.* V. **D** Chelmsf 22 **P** *Ld Chan* **I** R A DONCASTER.
ARDLEY (St Mary or St Thos) w Fewcot (All SS), *Oxon.* R. **D** Ox *See* Fritwell.
ARDSLEY (Ch Ch), *S Yorks.* V. **D** Sheff 10 **P** *R of Darfield* **I** D R JUPE, R D BALDOCK *c.*
ARDSLEY, EAST (St Mich AA) w (St Gabr), *W Yorks.* V. **D** Wakef 12 **P** *E C S J G Brudenell Esq* **I** R M WELLER.
ARDSLEY, WEST (St Mary), *W Yorks..* **D** Wakef 10 *See* Woodkirk.
ARDWICK, *Gtr Man..* **D** Man 1 *See* Manchester.
ARELEY-KING's (St Bart), *Worcs.* R. **D** Worc 12 **P** *R of Martley* **I** G E COOKE.
ARKENDALE (St Bart), *N Yorks.* V. **D** Ripon 4 **P** *V of Knaresborough* **I** P FAIRBURN.
ARKENGARTHDALE (St Mary), *N Yorks.* V. **D** Ripon 1 *See* Grinton.
ARKESDEN (St Mary Virg), *Essex..* **D** Chelmsf *See* Clavering.
ARKHOLME w Gressingham (St John) and Whittington-in-Lonsdale, *Lancs* V. **D** Blackb 13 **P** *D and C of Ch Ch Ox, V of Lancaster and V of Melling (in turn)* **I** G WORTHINGTON.
ARKLEY (St Pet), *Herts.* V. **D** St Alb 2 *See* Barnet, Chipping.
ARKSEY (All SS), *S Yorks.* V. **D** Sheff 8 **P** *Dioc Bd of Patr* **I** G O CUMMINGS.
ARLECDON (St Mich), *Cumb.* V. **D** Carl 12 *See* Frizington.
ARLESEY (St Pet) w Astwick (St Guthlac), *Beds.* V. **D** St Alb 22 **P** *Dioc Bd of Patr* **I** J F W ANDRE.
ARLEY (St Wilfrid), *Warws.* R. **D** Cov 5 **P** *C H F Ransom and N W H Sylvester Esq* **I** G L HUMPHRIES *p-in-c.*
ARLEY, UPPER (St Pet), *Worcs.* V. **D** Worc 10 **P** *Bp* **I** E P WINTER *p-in-c.*
ARLINGHAM (St Mary Virg), *Glos.* V. **D** Glouc 9 **P** *Dioc Bd of Patr* **I** D J BICK *p-in-c.*
ARLINGTON (St Pancras), *E Sussex.* V. **D** Chich 15 **P** *Bp of Lon* **I** J R P ASHBY.
ARLINGTON, *Devon..* **D** Ex 18 *See* Kentisbury.
ARMATHWAITE, *Cumb..* **D** Carl 6 *See* Hesket-in-the-Forest.
ARMINGHALL (St Mary Virg), *Norf.* V. **D** Nor 10 **P** *D and C of Nor* **I** H R CRESSWELL.
ARMITAGE (St Jo Bapt), *Staffs.* R. **D** Lich 4 **P** *Bp* **I** D R H THOMAS.
ARMITAGE BRIDGE (St Paul), *W Yorks.* V. **D** Wakef 5 **P** *V of Almondbury and Dioc Bd of Patr* **I** (Vacant).
ARMLEY (St Bart) w New Wortley (St Mary of Bethany w Armley Hall (H Trin), *W Yorks.* V. **D** Ripon 8 **P** *Bp, Dioc Bd of Patr and Hyndman Trustees* **I** R G N PLANT, K P ATHERLEY *c.*
UPPER (Ch Ch), V. **D** Ripon 8 **P** *CPS* **I** S ALLEN, G C TURNER *c.*
ARMTHORPE (St Leon and St Mary), *S Yorks.* R. **D** Sheff 8 **P** *Bp* **I** J R PEEK.
ARNCLIFFE (St Osw) w Halton Gill, *N Yorks.* V. **D** Bradf 10 **P** *Trustees* **I** M B SLAUGHTER *p-in-c.*
ARNE (St Nich), *Dorset..* **D** Sarum 9 *See* Wareham.
ARNESBY (St Pet) w Shearsby *Leics.* V. **D** Leic 13 **P** *Bp* **I** S V CARTWRIGHT *p-in-c,* D M WILSON *c.*
ARNOLD (St Mary), *Notts.* V. **D** Southw 13 **P** *Bp* **I** R WILLIAMS, L E D CLARK *c.*
ARNSIDE (St Jas), *Cumb.* V. **D** Carl 17 **P** *V of Beetham* **I** W A BATEY *p-in-c,* H R NAUNTON *hon c.*
ARRETON (St Geo), *Isle of Wight.* V. **D** Portsm 6 **P** *Trustees* **I** F J CHASE *p-in-c.*
ARRINGTON (St Nich), *Cambs.* V. **D** Ely 8 **P** *Bp and Dioc Bd of Patr (alt)* **I** J H THOMSON.
ARROW, *Warws..* **D** Cov 7 *See* Alcester.
ARTHINGTON (St Pet), *W Yorks.* V. **D** Ripon 4 *See* Pool.
ARTHINGWORTH (St Andr) w Kelmarsh (St Denys) and Harrington (St Pet and St Paul), *Northants.* R. **D** Pet 6 **P** *Bp 2 turns, Col C G Lancaster 1 turn* **I** (Vacant).
ARTHURET (St Mich AA), *Cumb.* R. **D** Carl 2 **P** *Col Sir Fergus Graham Bt* **I** P N S PHILLIPS.
ARUNDEL (St Nich) w South Stoke (St Leon) and Tortington (St Mary Magd), *W Sussex.* V. **D** Chich 1 **P** *Bp 2 turns, Duke of Norf 1 turn* **I** M H WEAVER.
ASBY (St Pet) w Ormside (St Jas), *Cumb.* R. **D** Carl 1 **P** *Bp* **I** R W GRAYSON, D A SOUTHWARD *c.*
ASCOT HEATH (All SS), *Berks.* R. **D** Ox 11a **P** *Bp* **I** C HEWETSON, T D RAWDON-MOGG *c.*
ASCOT, SOUTH (All S), *Berks.* V. **D** Ox 11a **P** *Bp* **I** D S JONES, A T SCOTT *c.*
ASCOTT-UNDER-WYCHWOOD (H Trin), *Oxon.* V. **D** Ox 3 **P** *Bp* **I** P G SMITH.
ASFORDBY (All SS), *Leics.* R. **D** Leic 4 **P** *Dioc Bd of Patr* **I** R T H PEARSE.
ASGARBY (St Andr), *Lincs..* **D** Linc 22 *See* Kirkby-Laythorpe.
ASGARBY (St Swithin), *Lincs.* V. **D** Linc 7 *See* Hagworthingham.
ASH (Ch Ch), *Salop.* V. **D** Lich 27 **P** *R of Whitchurch* **I** E A COOKE *p-in-c.*
ASH (St Pet), *Surrey.* R. **D** Guildf 1 **P** *Warden and Fell of Win Coll* **I** H F JACKSON, N D BIDEN *c.*
ASH (St Nich) w Westmarsh (H Trin), *Kent.* V. **D** Cant 1 **P** *Abp* **I** C C BARLOW.
ASH VALE (St Mary), *Surrey.* V. **D** Guildf 1 **P** *Bp* **I** H G MEIRION-JONES.
ASH (St Pet and St Paul) w Ridley (St Pet), *Kent.* R. **D** Roch 1 **P** *A C M B Scott Esq* **I** D F SPRINGTHORPE.
ASH-BOCKING (All SS), *Suff.* V. **D** St E 1 *See* Swilland.
ASH-IN-MARTOCK (H Trin), *Somt.* V. **D** B & W 11 *See* Martock.
ASH PRIORS (H Trin), *Somt.* V. **D** B & W 22 **P** *Mart Mem Trust* **I** (Vacant).
ASHAMPSTEAD (St Clem Romanus), *Berks.* V. **D** Ox 12 *See* Aldworth.
ASHBOURNE (St Osw) w Mapleton (St Mary), *Derbys.* V. **D** Derby 8 **P** *Bp* **I** D H SANSUM.
(St Jo Bapt). **D** Derby 8 **P** *Wright Trustees* **I** D H SANSUM *min.*
ASHBRITTLE (St Jo Bapt) w Bathealton (St Bart) w Stawley and Kittisford (St Nich), *Somt.* R. **D** B & W 22 **P** *G and C Coll Cam 5 turns, Bp and J Quicke* **I** J D FOWLER *c-in-c.*
ASHBURNHAM (St Jas), V w Penhurst *E Sussex.* R. **D** Chich 17 **P** *Ashburnham Chr Trust* **I** J D BICKERSTETH, L C STEAD *c.*
ASHBURTON (St Andr) w Buckland-in-the-Moor, *Devon.* V. **D** Ex 11 **P** *D and C of Ex* **I** J T CHARNLEY.
ASHBURY (St Mary Virg), *Devon..* **D** Ex *See* Northlew.
ASHBURY (BVM), V w Compton Beauchamp (St Swithin), Knighton and Longcot w Fernham, *Berks.* V. **D** Ox 17 **P** *Ld Chan* **I** D R BURDEN.
ASHBY (St Pet) w Fenby and Brigsley (St Helen), *Humb.* R. **D** Linc 10 **P** *Ld Chan* **I** D N SAMUEL.
ASHBY (St Paul), *Humb..* **D** Linc 4 *See* Bottesford.
ASHBY (St Edm) w Oby, Thurne, and Clippesby (St Pet), *Norf.* R. **D** Nor *See* Rollesby.
ASHBY (St Mary), R w Thurton (St Ethlebert) w Claxton and Carleton, *Norf.* R (*See Bramerton Group*).. **D** Nor 10 **P** *Mart Mem Trust and Bp* **I** (Vacant).
ASHBY (St Mary Virg), *Suff..* **D** Nor 15 *See* Somerleyton.
ASHBY-BY-PARTNEY (St Helen), *Lincs..* **D** Linc 7 *See* Partney.

ASHBY-DE-LA-LAUNDE (St Hybald), *Lincs.* V. D Linc 22 P *Dioc Bd of Patr* I (Vacant).
ASHBY-DE-LA-ZOUCH (St Helen), *Leics.* V. D Leic 12 P *D A G Shields Esq* I J E BOWERS.
(H Trin), V.. D Leic 12 P *V of Ashby-de-la-Zouch* I L A DUTTON.
ASHBY-FOLVILLE (St Mary) w Twyford (St Andr) and Thorpe Satchville (St Mich AA), *Leics.* V. D Leic 8 P *Dioc Bd of Patr* I S G SHEPPARD.
ASHBY MAGNA, *Leics.*. D Leic *See* Willoughby Waterleys.
ASHBY PARVA (St Pet), *Leics.*. D Leic *See* Leire.
ASHBY PUERORUM (St Andr), *Lincs.*. D Linc 11 *See* Fulletby.
ASHBY ST LEDGERS, *Northants.*. D Pet *See* Welton.
ASHBY, WEST (All SS), *Lincs.* V. D Linc *See* Hemingby.
ASHCHURCH (St Nich), *Glos.* R. D Glouc 10 P *Lady Cayley* I K R CORLESS.
ASHCOMBE (St Nectan), *Devon.* R. D Ex 6 *See* Ideford.
ASHCOTT (All SS), *Somt.* R. D B & W 7 *See* Shapwick.
ASHDON (All SS) w Hadstock, *Essex.* R. D Chelmsf 27 P *Ld Chan and E H Vestey Esq (alt)* I C C RICHES.
ASHE (H Trin and St Andr) w Deane (All SS), *Hants.* R. D Win 5 *See* Waltham, North.
ASHELDHAM (St Laur), *Essex.* R. D Chelmsf 13 *See* Dengie.
ASHEN, *Essex.* R. D Chelmsf 18 *See* Ridgewell.
ASHENDON (St Mary), *Bucks.* V. D Ox 21 *See* Wotton Underwood.
ASHFIELD, *Suff.* V. D St E *See* Earl Soham.
ASHFIELD, GREAT (All SS) w Badwell Ash (St Mary) and Hunston (St Mich), *Suff.* R. D St E 9 P *Dioc Bd of Patr 1 turn, Bp 2 turns* I C LEFFLER.
ASHFORD (St Mary Virg), *Kent.* V. D Cant 10 P *Abp* I J M A ROBERTS *c.*
SOUTH (Ch Ch), V. D Cant 10 P *Abp* I R G E GAZZARD, J E OWEN *c.*
ASHFORD (H Trin) w Sheldon (St Mich AA), *Derbys.* V. D Derby 9 P *V of Bakewell* I G R PHIZACKERLEY *p-in-c.*
ASHFORD (St Pet), *Devon.* R. D Ex 15 *See* Pilton.
ASHFORD (St Matt), *Lon.*. D Lon 13 P *Ld Chan* I B E HODGES.
(St Hilda), V. D Lon 13 P *Bp* I S J BLOOD.
ASHFORD BOWDLER, *Salop.* V. D Heref 12 *See* Ashford Carbonell.
ASHFORD CARBONELL (St Mary) w Ashford Bowdler (St Andrew), *Salop.* V. D Heref 12 P *Bp of Birm* I D B HEWLETT.
ASHILL (BVM) w Broadway (St Aldhelm and St Eadburga), *Somt.* R. D B & W 20 *See* Donyatt.
ASHILL (St Nich) w Saham-Toney, *Norf.* R. D Nor P *Bp and New Coll Ox (alt)* I A F MELLOWS.
ASHINGDON (St Andr) w S Fambridge (All SS), *Essex.* R. D Chelmsf 16 P *CCC Cam* I S HANKEY.
ASHINGTON (St Vinc), *Somt.*. D B & W 12 *See* Chilton Cantelo.
ASHINGTON (St Pet and St Paul) w Buncton (All SS), Wiston and Washington, *W Sussex.* R. D Chich 7 P *Maj J Goring and Bp (alt)* I J M WALKER.
ASHINGTON (H Sepulchre), *Northumb.* V. D Newc T 10 P *Bp* I J H G BUNKER.
ASHLEWORTH (St Andr and St Bart), *Glos.* R. D Glouc 2 *See* Hasfield.
ASHLEY, *Glos.*. D Bris *See* Crudwell.
ASHLEY (St Eliz), *Chesh.* V. D Ches 10 P *Bp* I A E HARRIS.
ASHLEY (St Mary), R w Silverley, V *Cambs.*. D Ely 4 P *Mrs D A Bowlby and Dioc Bd of Patr (alt)* I M F WILLIAMS *c-in-c.*
ASHLEY (St Jo Bapt), *Staffs.* R. D Lich 15 P *Meynell Trust* I A V ALBUTT.
ASHLEY (St Mary Virg) w Weston-by-Welland and Sutton Bassett, *Northants.* R. D Pet 10 P *Bp and E C Danby Esq* alt I H B PRUEN.
ASHLEY, *Hants.* R. D Win 10 *See* Somborne, King's.
ASHLEY GREEN (St Jo Evang), *Bucks.* V. D Ox *See* Chesham, Great.
ASHMANHAUGH (St Swithin), *Norf.* V. D Nor 8 *See* Beeston.
ASHMANSWORTH (St Jas) w Crux Easton R *Hants.* V. D Win 5 *See* Highclere.
ASHMORE (St Nich), *Dorset.* R. D Sarum 13 P *R Sturge Esq* I J A P STANDEN MCDOUGAL.
ASHOVER (All SS), *Derbys.* R. D Derby 3 P *Exors of Rev J B Nodder* I P G NORMAN.
ASHOW (The Assumption of Our Lady), *Warws.*. D Cov 4 *See* Stoneleigh.
ASHPERTON (St Bart). *Herefs.*. D Heref 6 *See* Stretton Grandison.
ASHPRINGTON (St D), Cornworthy and Dittisham (St Geo) *Devon,* R. D Ex 13 P *Bp of Exeter* I J D HAMILTON.
ASHREIGNEY (St Jas), *Devon.* R. D Ex 16 P *Dioc Bd of Patr* I A J MACKERACHER.
ASHTEAD (St Giles) w (St Geo), *Surrey.* R. D Guildf 10 P *Bp* I R G ASKEW, F J ASHE *c,* P C SYKES *c.*
ASHTON (St Jo Bapt) w Trusham (St Mich AA), *Devon.* R. D Ex 6 *See* Christow.
ASHTON (St Mich AA) w Hartwell (St Jo Bapt), *Northants.* R. D Pet 2 P *Ld Chan* I M G T WALKEY.
ASHTON (St Mary Magd), *Northants.* V. D Pet 11 *See* Oundle.
ASHTON GATE (St Francis of Assisi), *Avon.*. D Bris 1 *See* Bedminster.
ASHTON GIFFORD (Boyton, Sherrington, Codford St Pet and St Mary and Upton Lovell), *Wilts.* R. D Sarum P *Dioc Bd of Patr 1st turn, Ld Chan 2nd turn, Pemb Coll Ox 3rd turn* I J H TIPPING.
ASHTON-HAYES (St Jo Evang), *Chesh.* V. D Ches 2 P *Keble Coll Ox* I J D MILLER.
ASHTON-IN-MAKERFIELD (H Trin), *Gtr Man.* R. D Liv 12 P *Earl of Derby* I D R ABBOTT.
(St Thos Ap) w (St Luke Miss), V. D Liv 12 P *R of Ashton-in-Makerfield* I F FINNEY.
ASHTON KEYNES (H Cross), V w Leigh, *Wilts.* R. D Bris 11 P *Bp* I N J MONK.
ASHTON-ON-MERSEY (St Martin), *Gtr Man.* R. D Ches 10 P *S for Maint of Faith* I (Vacant).
(St Mary Magd), V. D Ches 10 P *Trustees* I J M INNES, K HODSON *c.*
ASHTON-ON-RIBBLE (St Andr), *Lancs.* V. D Blackb 12 P *Trustees* I D J LEYLAND.
(St Mich AA) V. D Blackb 12 P *Bp* I D L SEARS.
ASHTON-UNDER-HILL (St Barbara), *Worcs.*. D Glouc 10 *See* Beckford.
ASHTON-UNDER-LYNE (St Mich AA), *Gtr Man.* R. D Man 2 P *Trustees of late Earl of Stamford* I A E RADCLIFFE, J M PRESTON *c,* S C TATTON-BROWN *c.*
(Ch Ch), V. D Man 2 P *Crown and Bp* alt I E D BLANCHARD, P K TOWNLEY *c.*
(H Trin), V. D Man 2 P *Trustees* I (Vacant).
(St Jas Ap), V. D Man 2 P *Trustees* I D SHARPLES.
(St Pet) V. D Man 2 P *R of Ashton L* I J R CLATWORTHY.
ASHTON, WEST (St John), *Wilts.* V. D Sarum 24 P *Mart Mem Trust* I (Vacant).
ASHURST (St Jas Greater), *W Sussex.* R. D Chich 7 P *Dioc Bd of Patr* I C R BOFF.
ASHURST (St Martin), *Kent.*. D Roch *See* Speldhurst.
ASHWATER (St Pet ad Vincula) and Halwill w Beaworthy, *Devon.* R. D Ex 9 P *Ld Chan and Maj L J Melhuish* alt I E K P INCE.
ASHWELL w Burley, *Leics.* R. D Pet 12 *See* Cottesmore.
ASHWELL (St Mary Virg), *Herts.* R. D St Alb 5 P *Bp* I J S H MULLETT.
ASHWELLTHORPE (All SS) *Norf.* R. D Nor 13 *See* Wreningham.
ASHWICK (St Jas) w Oakhill (All SS) and Binegar (H Trin), *Somerset.* R. D B & W 6 P *Bp* I (Vacant).
ASHWICKEN (All SS) w Leziate, *Norf.* R. D Nor 25 P *Bp* I (Vacant).
ASHWORTH (St Jas), *Gtr Man.* V. D Man 17 *See* Norden.
ASKAM (St Pet), *Cumb.*. D Carl 15 *See* Ireleth.
ASKERN (St Pet), *S Yorks.* V. D Sheff 8 P *Bp* I P H NOBLE.
ASKERSWELL (St Mich), *Dorset.* R. D Sarum 2 P *Bp* I O L WILLMOTT.
ASKHAM (St Columba), *Cumb.* V. D Carl 1 *See* Lowther.
ASKHAM, *Notts.*. D Southw *See* East Markham.
ASKHAM BRYAN (St Nich) w Askham Richard (St Mary), *N Yorks.* V. D York 2 P *Trustees of Rev G N Ward and Exors of Major Wailes-Fairburn (alt)* I J E MARTIN.
ASKRIGG (St Osw) w Stalling Busk, *N Yorks.* V. D Ripon 2 P *V of Aysgarth* I (Vacant).
ASLACKBY (St Jas) w Kirkby Underwood (St Mary and All SS), *Lincs.* V. D Linc 13 P *Earl of Ancaster 1 turn, St Jo Coll Dur 2 turns* I K T STREET.
ASLACTON (St Mich), *Norf.* V. D Nor 11 *See* Moulton Great.
ASLOCKTON (St Thos), *Notts.*. D Southw 9 *See* Whatton-in-the-Vale.
ASPALL (St Mary of Grace), *Suff.* V. D St E *See* Debenham.
ASPATRIA (St Kentigern) w Hayton (St Jas L), *Cumb.* V. D Carl 11 P *Bp* I G G DOUGLAS.
ASPENDEN (St Mary) w Layston (St Bart) and Buntingford, *Herts.* R. D St Alb 5 P *Mart Mem Trust and CPAS* alt I J MOORE.

ASPLEY, *Warws.*. **D** Cov 7 *See* Ullenhall.
ASPLEY (St Marg), *Notts.* V. **D** Southw 14 **P** *Trustees* **I** R W LOCKHART, P TOWNER *c.*
ASPLEY GUISE (St Botolph) w Husborne Crawley and Ridgmont, *Beds.* R. **D** St Alb **P** *Bp 1st and 4th turns, Ld Chan 2nd turn and Trustees of Duke of Bedford's Estates 3rd turn* **I** R W HUBAND.
ASPULL (St Eliz of Hungary), *Gtr Man.* V. **D** Liv 12 **P** *Trustees* **I** B WHITEHEAD.
(St Jo Bapt).. **D** Liv 12 *See* Haigh.
ASSINGTON (St Edm K & Mart), *Suff.* V. **D** St E 12 **P** *Bp* **I** J K COTTON *p-in-c.*
ASTBURY (St Mary) w Smallwood (St Jo Bapt), *Chesh.* R. **D** Ches 11 **P** *Sir R J Baker-Wilbraham Bt & R of Astbury* **I** A D DEAN.
ASTERBY GROUP (Goulceby, Donnington-on-Bain, Scamblesby w Chalkwell, Gayton-le-Wold, Biscathorpe, Stenigot, Benniworth, Market Stainton and Rainby), *Lincs.* R. **D** Linc 11 **P** *Dioc Bd of Patr, Mrs Hutchinson Higgins, J Heneage Esq, F Smith Esq and J R Fox Esq* **I** G J WILCOX, H B WILLIAMS *c.*
ASTHALL (St Nich) and Swinbrook w Widford *Oxon.* V. **D** Ox 9 **P** *Bp and Capt D Mackinnon* **I** J T M HINE.
ASTLEY (St Mary Virg), *Warws.* V. **D** Cov 5 *See* Chilvers Coton.
ASTLEY (St Mary), *Salop.* V. **D** Lich 27 **P** *Govs of Shrewsbury Sch* **I** D D PRICE.
ASTLEY (St Steph), *Gtr Man.* V. **D** Man 6 **P** *V of Leigh* **I** J T FINNEY.
ASTLEY (St Pet), *Worcs.* R. **D** Worc 12 **P** *Guild of All S* **I** J G BARNISH *p-in-c.*
ASTLEY ABBOTS (St Calixtus), *Salop.* R. **D** Heref 9 *See* Bridgnorth.
ASTLEY BRIDGE (St Paul), *Gtr Man.* V. **D** Man 19 **P** *Crown and Bp* alt **I** J M BACON.
ASTON (St Jas), *W Midl.* V. **D** Birm 7 **P** *V of Aston* **I** J L WILKINSON *c-in-c,* J AUSTEN *c,* A J R GANDON *c.*
ASTON, *Salop.*. **D** Lich 29 *See* Uppington.
ASTON (BVM) w Benington (St Pet), *Herts.* R. **D** St Alb 12 **P** *Ld Chan and Ripon Cl Coll Corp* alt **I** N F BONE.
ASTON-ABBOTS (St Jas Gt) w Cublington (St Nich), *Bucks.* V. **D** Ox 27 *See* Wingrave.
ASTON w Aughton (All SS), *S Yorks.* R. **D** Sheff 5 **P** *Bp* **I** P WRIGHT, C G G EVERETT *c.*
ASTON BOTTERELL w Wheathill and Loughton, *Salop.* R. **D** Heref 9 **P** *Bp and Mrs Nesbitt* **I** M A J HARDING *p-in-c.*
ASTON w Burston, *Staffs.* V. **D** Lich 19 **P** *Trustees* **I** (Vacant).
ASTON-BY-SUTTON (St Pet), *Chesh.* V. **D** Ches 3 **P** *B H Talbot Esq* **I** A H CLARE.
ASTON CANTLOW (St Jo Bapt) and Wilmcote (St Andr) w Billesley, *Warws.* V. **D** Cov 7 **P** *S for Maint of Faith* **I** N J TAYLOR.
ASTON CLINTON (St Mich AA), Bucklands (All SS) and Drayton Beauchamp (St Mary), *Bucks.* R. **D** Ox 30 **P** *Jes Coll Ox* **I** T A LEWIS.
ASTON (St Giles), *Herefs.*. **D** Heref *See* Downton.
ASTON EYRE, *Salop.*. **D** Heref 9 *See* Morville.
ASTON FLAMVILLE, *Leics.*. **D** Leic 16 *See* Burbage.
ASTON-INGHAM, *Herefs.*. **D** Heref *See* Linton.
ASTON-JUXTA (St Pet and St Paul), *W Midl.* V. **D** Birm 7 **P** *Aston Trustees* **I** J HOLDEN.
ASTON-LE-WALLS Northants. R **D** Pet 1 *See* Chipping Warden.
ASTON, LITTLE (St Pet), *Staffs.*. V. **D** Lich 2 **P** *Trustees of late Hon E S Parker-Jervis* **I** R J OLIVER.
ASTON MAGNA (St Jo Evang), *Worcs.*. **D** Glouc *See* Blockley.
ASTON, NORTH (St Mary Virg), *Oxon.*. **D** Ox *See* Steeple Aston.
ASTON-ON-TRENT (All SS) w Weston-on-Trent (St Mary Virg), *Derbys.* R. **D** Derby 15 **P** *Trustees and Bp* **I** J TRANTER.
ASTON ROWANT (St Pet and St Paul) w Crowell (Nativ of St Mary Virg), *Oxon.* R. **D** Ox 1 **P** *Bp and W H Wykeham Musgrave Esq* **I** P G WIGNALL *p-in-c.*
ASTON-SANDFORD (St Mich AA), *Bucks.* R. **D** Ox 21 **P** *Peache Trustees* **I** R H FAULKNER.
ASTON-SOMERVILLE (St Mary), *Worcs.* R. **D** Glouc 18 *See* Childswyckham.
ASTON-SUB-EDGE, *Glos.*. **D** Glouc 12 *See* Weston-sub-Edge.
ASTON-TIRROLD (St Mich) w Aston Upthorpe, *Oxon.* R. **D** Ox *See* Moreton, North.
ASTWICK (St Guthlac). *Beds.*. **D** St Alb *See* Arlesey.
ASTWOOD (St Pet) w Hardmead, *Bucks.* V and R. **D** Ox 28 *See* Crawley, North.
ASTWOOD BANK (St Matthias and St Geo), *Worcs.* V. **D** Worc 7 **P** *Dioc Bd of Patr* **I** I C COOPER *p-in-c.*
ASWARBY (St Denis), w Swarby (BVM and All SS), *Lincs.*. **D** Linc *See* Lafford, S.
ASWARDBY (St Helen) w Sausthorpe (St Andr), *Lincs.* R. **D** Linc 7 **P** *Dioc Bd of Patr* **I** J S THOROLD.
ATCHAM (St Eata), *Salop.* V. **D** Lich 26 **P** *R F L Burton Esq* **I** G S LLOYD.
ATHELHAMPTON, *Dorset.*. **D** Sarum *See* Puddletown.
ATHELINGTON, *Suff.*. **D** St E 17 *See* Stradbroke.
ATHERINGTON (St Mary) w High Bickington (St Mary), *Devon.* R. **D** Ex 16 **P** *Marl Coll and D and C of Ex* **I** C P BARRETT.
ATHERSLEY (St Helen) and NEW LODGE, *S Yorks.* V. **D** Wakef 8 **P** *Bp* **I** J S HALL.
ATHERSTONE (St Mary), *Warws.* V. **D** Cov 5 **P** *V of Mancetter* **I** J H TYERS.
ATHERSTONE-ON-STOUR (St Mary Virg), *Warws.*. **D** Cov 8 *See* Preston-on-Stour.
ATHERTON (St Jo Bapt), *Gtr Man.* V. **D** Man 6 **P** *Ld Lilford* **I** W R HARTLEY, D I ROSS *c,* S D RUDKIN *c.*
ATLOW (St Phil and St Jas), *Derbys.* R. **D** Derby 8 *See* Hulland.
ATTENBOROUGH (St Mary) w Toton (st Pet), *Notts.* V. **D** Southw 8 **P** *CPAS* **I** F T BEECH, J CORRIE *c,* J E GOLDINGAY *hon c.*
ATTERBY, *Lincs.* **D** Linc 3 *See* Bishop Norton.
ATTERCLIFFE (Ch Ch), *S Yorks.* R. **D** Sheff 1 *See* Sheffield.
ATTERTON, *Leics.*. **D** Leic 16 *See* Witherley.
ATTINGTON, *Oxon.*. **D** Ox *See* Tetsworth.
ATTLEBOROUGH (H Trin), *Warws.* V. **D** Cov 5 **P** *V of Nuneaton* **I** R HIGGINBOTTOM.
ATTLEBOROUGH MAJOR AND MINOR (Assump BVM) w Besthorpe, *Norf.* R. **D** Nor **P** *C R Mirfield and Mrs S P J Scully* **I** (Vacant).
ATTLEBRIDGE (St Andr), *Norf.*. **D** Nor 6 *See* Alderford.
ATWICK (St Pet or St Laur), *Humb.*. **D** York 14 *See* Hornsea.
ATWORTH (St Mich AA), V *Wilts.*. **D** Sarum 24 **P** *D and C of Bris and V of Melksham* alt **I** G E GRIFFITHS.
AUBOURN (St Pet) w Haddington, *Lincs.* V. **D** Linc 18 **P** *Capt H N Nevile, Ld Middleton, CCC Ox and Bp* **I** P BYRON-DAVIES.
AUDENSHAW (St Steph), *Gtr Man.* V. **D** Man 2 **P** *Bp and Crown* alt **I** S H TOMLINE.
(St Hilda) V. **D** Man 2 **P** *Bp and Crown* alt **I** B BASON.
AUDLEM (St Jas Gt) w Burleydam (St Mich and St Mary BV), *Chesh.* V. **D** Ches 15 **P** *Bp* **I** D ROSTRON.
AUDLEY (St Jas), *Staffs.* V. **D** Lich 17 **P** *Ch S Trust* **I** (Vacant).
AUGHTON (St Sav), *Lancs.*. **D** Blackb 13 *See* Halton.
AUGHTON (St Mich), *Lancs.* R. **D** Liv 9 **P** *Bp* **I** M J SMOUT.
(Ch Ch), V. **D** Liv 9 **P** *R of Aughton* **I** E BRAMHALL, C L BRAY *c.*
AUGHTON (All SS), *S Yorks.*. **D** Sheff *See* Aston.
AUGHTON (All H or All S), *Humb.* V. **D** York 10 *See* Ellerton Priory.
AUKBOROUGH, *Humb.*. **D** Linc 4 *See* Alkborough.
AULT (or Hault) Hucknall (St Jo Bapt), *Derbys.* V. **D** Derby 2 **P** *Duke of Devonshire* **I** C M G BRINKWORTH.
AUNBY (St Thos-à-Becket), *Lincs.*. **D** Linc 14 *See* Careby.
AUNSBY (St Thos of Cant) w Dembleby (St Lucia), *Lincs.*. **D** Linc *See* Lafford, S.
AUST, *Avon.*. **D** Bris 6 *See* Olveston.
AUSTERFIELD (St Helena), *S Yorks.*. **D** Southw 1 *See* Bawtry.
AUSTREY (St Nich), *Warws.* V. **D** Birm 10 **P** *Ld Chan* **I** H G WELCH.
AUSTWICK (Ch of the Epiph), *N Yorks.* V. **D** Bradf 7 **P** *V of Clapham* **I** J DALBY *p-in-c.*
AUTHORPE (St Marg) w Tothill, *Lincs.* R. **D** Linc *See* Withern.
AVEBURY (St Jas) w Winterbourne Monkton (St Mary Magd) and Berwick Bassett, *Wilts.* V. **D** Sarum 26 *See* Kennet, Upper.
AVELEY (St Mich), *Essex.* V. **D** Chelmsf 15 **P** *Bp* **I** J M PRESTON, D C JESSETT *c.*
AVENING w Cherington, *Glos.* R. **D** Glouc 17 **P** *D and C of Glouc 2 turns, E M M Tarlton Esq 1 turn* **I** R E GLEED.
AVERHAM (St Mich) w Kelham (St Wilfrid), *Notts.* R. **D** Southw 3 **P** *Fidelity Trust* **I** (Vacant).
AVETON GIFFORD (St Andr), *Devon.* R. **D** Ex 14 **P** *Bp* **I** W G HOWELLS.
AVINGTON, *Berks.* R. **D** Ox 14 *See* Kintbury.

AVINGTON (St Mary), *Hants.* R. **D** Win 6 *See* Itchen Abbas.
AVON DASSETT (St Jo Bapt) Compton, Farnborough and Fenny Compton, *Warws.* R. **D** Cov 8 **P** *Trustees of R H A Holbech, CCC Ox and Bp (alt)* **I** J T RANDALL.
AVONMOUTH (St Andr), *Avon.* V. **D** Bris 6 **P** *Bp* **I** C N BAILEY.
AVONWICK CHAPEL, *Devon.* **D** Ex 13 *See* Huish, North.
AWBRIDGE (All SS) w Sherfield English *Hants.* V. **D** Win 10 **P** *Bp and CPAS* **I** A R CROAD.
AWLISCOMBE (St Mich AA), *Devon.* R. **D** Ex **P** *Bp* **I** S H HAMILTON.
AWRE (St Andr) w Blakeney (All SS), *Glos.* V. **D** Glouc 6 **P** *Haberdashers' Co* **I** G A SATTERLY.
AWSWORTH (St Pet) w Cossall (St Cath), *Notts.* V. **D** Southw 8 **P** *Bp* **I** D A ROBERTS.
AXBRIDGE (St Jo Bapt) w Shipham and Rowberrow, *Somt.* R. **D** B & W 1 **P** *D and C of Wells and Bp* alt. **I** J SMITH.
AXFORD, *Wilts.*. **D** Sarum 26 *See* Whitton.
AXMINSTER (St Mary), *Devon.* V. **D** Ex 5 **P** *Bp* **I** A RICHMOND *c.*
AXMOUTH (St Mich) w Musbury, *Devon.* V. **D** Ex 5 **P** *CPAS and D and C of Ex* **I** B J R GERRY.
AYCLIFFE (St Andr), *Dur.* V. **D** Dur 12a **P** *D and C of Dur* **I** M W TIPPER.
AYLBURTON, *Glos.*. **D** Glouc 7 *See* Lydney.
AYLESBEARE, *Devon.*. **D** Ex 1 *See* Clyst St Geo.
AYLESBURY (St Mary w St Jo Evang), *Bucks.* V. **D** Ox 21 **P** *Bp* **I** S L HUCKLE *c*, C C G SHAW *c*, M T WHALLEY *c*.
(H Trin), V. **D** Ox 21 **P** *CPS* **I** D S BREWIN, F Y C HUNG *c.*
AYLESBY (St Lawr), *Humb.* V. **D** Linc 10 **P** *H Spilman Esq* **I** R W J HOGGETT.
AYLESFORD (St Pet), *Kent.* V. **D** Roch 6 **P** *D and C of Roch* **I** A E HEATHCOTE.
AYLESHAM, *Kent.* V. **D** Cant 1 **P** *Abp* **I** S D RILEY.
AYLESTONE, *Leics.*. **D** Leic *See* Leicester.
AYLMERTON (St Jo Bapt) w Runton (H Trin), *Norf.* R. **D** Nor 5 **P** *Bp* **I** J H BLOOM.
AYLSHAM (St Mich), *Norf.* V. **D** Nor 3 **P** *D and C of Cant* **I** J W M VYSE, N J A PUMPHREY *c.*
AYLTON (Dedic unknown) w Pixley (St Andr), Munsley and Putley, *Herefs.* R. **D** Heref *See* Tarrington.
AYMESTREY (St Jo Bapt and St Alkmund) w Leinthall Earles (St Andr), *Herefs.* V. **D** Heref 7 **P** *Ld Chan* **I** (Vacant).
AYNHO (St Mich) w Newbottle and Charlton, *Northants.* R. **D** Pet 1 **P** *Miss E A J Cartwright and Earl of Birkenhead (alt)* **I** (Vacant).
AYOT ST PETER Herts. R **D** St Alb 7 *See* Welwyn (St Mary).
AYOT ST LAWRENCE, *Herts.* R. **D** St Alb 14 *See* Kimpton.
AYRES QUAY (St Steph), *T & W.*. **D** Dur 8 *See* Bishop Wearmouth.
AYSGARTH (St Andr) and Bolton w Redmire, *N Yorks.* V. **D** Ripon 2 **P** *Trin Coll Cam and R of Wensley (alt)* **I** M E BROWN.
AYSTON, *Leics.* R. **D** Pet *See* Uppingham.
AYTHORPE RODING (St Mary), *Essex.* R. **D** Chelmsf 23 *See* Leaden Roding.
AYTON, EAST (St Jo Bapt), *N Yorks.*. **D** York *See* Seamer.
AYTON, GREAT (Ch Ch) w Easby and Newton in Cleveland (St Osw), *N Yorks.* V. **D** York 25 **P** *Abp* **I** A J G ELLERY.

BABBACOMBE (All SS), *Devon.* V. **D** Ex 10 **P** *V of St Marychurch, Torquay* **I** M F GLARE.
BABCARY (H Cross), *Somt.*. **D** B & W 4 *See* Six Pilgrims.
BABINGLEY, *Norf.*. **D** Nor *See* Wolferton.
BABINGTON, *Somt.*. **D** B & W *See* Mells.
BABRAHAM (St Pet), *Cambs.* V. **D** Ely 7 **P** *Col Sir R Adeane* **I** (Vacant).
BABWORTH (All SS), *Notts.* R. **D** Southw 5 **P** *Sir J H I Whitaker Bt* **I** E F JESSUP.
BACKFORD (St Osw K and Mart), *Chesh.* V. **D** Ches 9 **P** *Bp* **I** D R BUCKLEY.
BACKWELL (St Andr), *Avon.* R. **D** B & W 16 **P** *Dioc Bd of Patr* **I** R M A CLARK.
BACKWORTH (St John), *T & W.* V. **D** Newc T *See* Earsdon.
BACONSTHORPE (St Mary Virg) w Plumstead (St Mich), *Norf.* R. **D** Nor *See* Barningham.
BACTON (St Faith), *Herefs.* R. **D** Heref *See* Ewyas Harold.
BACTON (St Mary Virg) w Wyverstone (St Geo), *Suff.* R. **D** St E 6 **P** *Rev S Priston and Ld Chan* **I** C J DOWNER P-IN-C OF COTTON.
BACTON (St Andr), w Edingthorpe (All SS) w Witton and Ridlington, *Norf.* V. **D** Nor **P** *Bp, Earl of Kimberley and Duchy of Lanc* **I** G R W BURTON.
BACUP (St Jo Evang), *Lancs.* V. **D** Man 18 **P** *Hulme Trustees* **I** M HOLT.
(Ch Ch), V. **D** Man 18 **P** *Trustees* **I** R HARRIS.
(St Sav), V. **D** Man 18 **P** *Ch S Trust* **I** D H KINGHAM.
BADBY (St Mary) w Newnham (St Mich AA), *Northants.* V. **D** Pet 15 **P** *Bp* **I** R W DOOLEY.
BADDESLEY-CLINTON (St Mich), *W Midl.* R. **D** Birm 11 **P** *T W Ferrers-Walker Esq* **I** M WEBSTER.
BADDESLEY ENSOR (St Nich), *Warws.* V. **D** Birm 10 **P** *PCC* **I** M WILLIAMS.
BADDESLEY, N (St Jo Bapt), *Hants.* V. **D** Win 10 *See* Chilworth.
BADDESLEY, S (St Mary), *Hants.* V. **D** Win 9 *See* Boldre, East.
BADDILEY (St Mich), *Chesh.* R. **D** Ches 15 *See* Wrenbury.
BADDOW, GREAT (St Mary Virg), *Essex.* V. **D** Chelmsf 12 **P** *CPAS* **I** R A LENS VAN RIJN *c*, P C NICHOLSON *c*, C M SPERRING *c*.
BADDOW, LITTLE (St Mary Virg), *Essex.* R. **D** Chelmsf 12 **P** *Bp* **I** R E TURNER.
BADGER (St Giles), *Salop.* R. **D** Lich 25 **P** *Or Coll Ox and Ld Chan* alt **I** J R P BAGGALEY.
BADGEWORTH (H Trin) w Shurdington (St Paul), *Glos.* V. **D** Glouc 11 **P** *Bp* **I** J B HUNNISETT.
BADGWORTH (St Congar) w Biddisham (St Jo Bapt), *Somt.* R. **D** B & W 2 *See* Weare.
BADINGHAM (St Jo Bapt) w Bruisyard (St Pet) and Cransford (St Pet), *Suff.* R. **D** St E 18 **P** *Dioc Bd of Patr 5 turns, Hon G N Rous 1 turn* **I** P H T HARTLEY P-IN-C OF BADINGHAM W BRUISYARD.
BADLESMERE w Leaveland, *Kent.* R. **D** Cant 7 **P** *Earl Sondes* **I** E A MARSH.
BADLEY (St Mary), *Suff.* V. **D** St E 1 *See* Needham Market.
BADMINTON (St Mich AA) w L Badminton and Acton Turville, *Avon.* V. **D** Glouc 8 **P** *Duke of Beaufort* **I** T T GIBSON.
BADSEY (St Jas) w Aldington, *Worcs.* V. **D** Worc 1 **P** *Ch Ch Ox* **I** P D MITCHELL.
BADSHOT LEA (St Geo), *Surrey.*. **D** Guildf 3 *See* Aldershot.
BADSWORTH (St Mary Virg), *W Yorks.* R. **D** Wakef 11 **P** *Earl of Derby* **I** R H TAYLOR.
BADWELL ASH, *Suff.* **D** St E *See* Ashfield, Great.
BAG ENDERBY (St Marg), *Lincs.*. **D** Linc 7 *See* Somersby.
BAGBOROUGH, WEST (St Pancras), *Somt.* R. **D** B & W *See* Bishop's Lydeard.
BAGBY (St Mary), *N Yorks.* R. **D** York 26 *See* Thirkleby.
BAGENDON (St Marg), *Glos.* R. **D** Glouc 13 *See* Cerney, North.
BAGINTON (St Jo Bapt), *Warws.* R. **D** Cov *See* Stoneleigh.
BAGNALL (St Chad), *Staffs.*. **D** Lich 16 *See* Bucknall.
BAGSHOT (St Anne), *Surrey.* V. **D** Guildf 5a **P** *Ld Chan* **I** H J SMITH.
BAGSHOT, *Berks.*. **D** Sarum *See* Shalbourne.
BAGTHORPE (St Mary), *Norf.* R. **D** Nor *See* Syderstone.
BAGULEY or BROOKLANDS (St Jo Div), *Gtr Man.* V. **D** Man 10 *See* Brooklands.
BAGWORTH (H Rood), *Leic.* V. **D** Leic 17 *See* Thornton.
BAILDON (St Jo Evang), *W Yorks.* V. **D** Bradf 1 **P** *Trustees* **I** B GRAINGER, I T RODLEY *c*, P WILKINSON *c*, G R JONES *hon c*.
BAINTON (St Mary), *Cambs.* R. **D** Pet 13 *See* Barnack.
BAINTON (St Andr), *Humb.* R. **D** York 13 **P** *St Jo Coll Ox* **I** R W HOWE *p-in-c*.
BAKEWELL (All SS) w Over Haddon (St Ann), *Derbys.* V. **D** Derby 9 **P** *D and C of Lich* **I** E R URQUHART.
BALBY (St Jo Div), *S Yorks.* V. **D** Sheff 8 **P** *Bp* **I** H LIDDLE.
BALCOMBE (St Mary), *W Sussex.* R. **D** Chich 11 **P** *Rev P B Secretan* **I** H ELLSLEY.
BALDERSBY (St Jas), *N Yorks.*. **D** York 26 *See* Thirsk.
BALDERSTONE (St Leon), *Lancs.* V. **D** Blackb 2 **P** *V of Blackb* **I** C W D CARROLL.
BALDERSTONE (St Mary), *Gtr Man.*. **D** Man 17 *See* Rochdale.

BALDERTON (St Giles), *Notts*. V. **D** Southw 3 **P** *Ld Chan* **I** C J YOUNG.
BALDHU (St Mich AA), *Cornw*. V. **D** Truro 6 **P** *Visc Falmouth* **I** R J REDRUP *p-in-c*.
BALDOCK (St Mary Virg) w Bygrave (St Marg) *Herts*. R. **D** St Alb 12 **P** *Bp and Marq of Salisbury (alt)* **I** J D ATKINSON.
BALE or BATHLEY, *Norf*.. **D** Nor *See* Gunthorpe.
BALHAM (St Mary Virg), *Surrey*. V. **D** S'wark 7a **P** *Bp* **I** J W PAUL.
(St Jo Div), V. **D** S'wark 7a **P** *Keble Coll Ox* **I** (Vacant).
BALHAM HILL (Ch of Ascen), *Surrey*. V. **D** S'wark 7a **P** *Bp* **I** M P N JEWITT.
BALKING (St Nich), *Oxon*.. **D** Ox 17 *See* Uffington.
BALKWELL (St Pet), *T & W*. V. **D** Newc T 6 *See* Tynemouth.
BALLINGDON, *Suff*.. **D** St E 15 *See* Sudbury.
BALLINGHAM (St Dubricius), *Herefs*. R. **D** Heref 4 *See* Dewchurch, Little.
BALL'S POND (St Paul), *Lon*. V. **D** Lon 6 *See* Islington.
BALNE, *Humb*. V. **D** Sheff 9 *See* Pollington.
BALSALL COMMON (St Pet), *W Midl*. V. **D** Birm 11 **P** *Bp* **I** J R MORGAN.
BALSALL HEATH (St Paul), *W Midl*. V. **D** Birm 5 **P** *Bp* **I** J L COOPER, R A P WARD *c*.
(St Barn), V. **D** Birm 5 **P** *Bp* **I** L D P BOYD *p-in-c*.
BALSCOTE, *Oxon*.. **D** Ox *See* Wroxton.
BALSHAM (H Trin), *Cambs*. R. **D** Ely 4 **P** *Gov of Charterhouse* **I** H A POTTS.
BALTONSBOROUGH (St Dunstan) w Butleigh (St Leon), *Somt*. V. **D** B & W 7 **P** *Bp* **I** C. J. HUDSON C-IN-C OF W BRADLEY & LOTTISHAM *p-in-c*.
BAMBER BRIDGE (St Sav), *Lancs*. V. **D** Blackb 6 **P** *V of Blackburn* **I** W T BARNES.
(St Aid), V. **D** Blackb 6 **P** *Bp* **I** C N WRIGHT.
BAMBURGH (St Aid) and Lucker, *Northumb*. V. **D** Newc T 8 **P** *Ld Armstrong 2 turns Trustees 1 turn* **I** E ZACHAU.
BAMFORD (St Mich AA), *Gtr Man*. V. **D** Man 17 **P** *Bp* **I** R W WILLCOCK.
BAMFORD-IN-THE-PEAK (St Jo Bapt), *Derbys*. R. **D** Derby 9 **P** *H G Barnes Esq* **I** D N HOWELL-EVERSON.
BAMPTON (St Patr) w Mardale (H Trin), *Cumb*. V. **D** Carl 1 **P** *Earl of Lonsdale* **I** J BERRY *p-in-c*.
BAMPTON (St Mich AA), *Devon*. V. **D** Ex 8 **P** *Dioc Bd of Patr* **I** D M CLARRIDGE.
BAMPTON w Clanfield (Bampton Proper (St Mary Virg), Bampton Aston (St Jas Gt), Bampton Lew (H Trin), Clanfield (St Steph), Shifford (St Mary)), *Oxon*. V. **D** Ox 9 **P** *Bp, Dioc Bd of Patr, St Jo Coll Ox, D and C of Ox and B Babington-Smith Esq* **I** A C G SCOTT.
BANBURY (St Mary) Grimsbury (St Leon), *Oxon*. R. **D** Ox 6 **P** *Bp* **I** I W H BEACHAM, R J CHARD *team v*, D S R WILLS *team v*.
BANHAM (BVM), *Norf*.. **D** Nor 18 *See* Quidenham.
BANKFOOT (St Matt), *W Yorks*. V. **D** Bradf 2 **P** *Bp* **I** J R POOLE.
BANKS (St Steph), *Lancs*. V. **D** Liv 8 **P** *R of N Meols* **I** L R THOMAS.
BANNINGHAM, *Norf*.. **D** Nor *See* Colby.
BANSTEAD (All SS), *Surrey*. V. **D** Guildf 9 **P** *Bp* **I** T NEW, A J KEEP *c*, A P HUTCHISON *hon c*.
BANWELL (St Andr), *Avon*. V. **D** B & W 3 **P** *D and C of Bris* **I** J A JUDGE.
BAPCHILD (St Laur) w Tonge, *Kent*. V. **D** Cant **P** *Abp and L Doubleday Esq* **I** C G A WOODS.
BARBON (St Bart) w Middleton (H Ghost), *Cumb*.. **D** Carl *See* Kirkby Lonsdale.
BARBOURNE (St Steph), *Worcs*.. **D** Worc 6 *See* Worcester.
BARBY (St Mary) w Onley, *Northants*. R. **D** Pet 3 **P** *Bp* **I** V M SCOTT.
BARCHESTON (St Martin), *Warws*. R. **D** Cov 9 **P** *Bp* **I** J B WOODWARD-COURT.
BARCOMBE (St Mary and St Bart), *E Sussex*. R. **D** Chich 15 **P** *Ld Chan* **I** T FLETCHER.
BARDFIELD, GREAT (St Mary Virg) w Bardfield, Little (St Kath), *Essex, V*. **D** Chelmsf 23 **P** *Ch U Trustees* **I** N C CLIFT.
BARDNEY (St Lawr, St Jo Div Southrey, St Andr Stainfield, St Andr Apley, All SS Gautry St Andr Minting and St Marg Waddingworth), *Lincs). R*. **D** Linc **P** *Bp 2 turns, Dioc Bd of Patr 1 turn and St Jo Coll Cam 1 turn* **I** (Vacant).
BARDON HILL (St Pet), *Leics*.. **D** Leic 11 *See* Coalville.
BARDSEA (H Trin), *Cumb*. V. **D** Carl 15 **P** *Miss D M La Touche and Resident Landowners* alt **I** B DAWSON.
BARDSEY (All H) w East Keswick (St Mary Magd), *W Yorks*. V. **D** Ripon 4 **P** *Hon Mrs M A M Lane Fox* **I** W T SNELSON.
BARDSLEY (H Trin), *Gtr Man*. V. **D** Man 15 **P** *Hulme Trustees* **I** F G SIMPKIN, T WALTERS *c*.
BARDWELL (St Pet and St Paul), *Suff*.. **D** St E 9 *See* Ixworth.
BARE (St Chris), *Lancs*. V. **D** Blackb 8 *See* Morecambe.
BARFORD (St Pet) w Wasperton (St Jo Bapt) and Sherbourne, *Warws*. R. **D** Cov 8 **P** *Maj J M Mills, R of Hampton-Lucy and CMT Smith-Ryland Esq* **I** F M GRIFFITH.
BARFORD, *Norf*.. **D** Nor *See* Wramplingham.
BARFORD, GREAT (All SS), *Beds*. V. **D** St Alb 17 *See* Roxton.
BARFORD, LITTLE (St Denys), *Beds*.. **D** St Alb *See* Tempsford.
BARFORD ST MARTIN (St Martin), Dinton, Baverstock, Compton Chamberlayne and Burcombe (The Nadder Group), *Wilts*. R. **D** Sarum **P** *All S Coll Ox, A K MacKenzie-Charrington, Bp and Prior of St John's Hosp Wilton* **I** H J TREASURE.
BARFORD ST MICHAEL w Barford St John, *Oxon*. V. **D** Ox *See* Deddington.
BARFREYSTONE (St Nich), *Kent*.. **D** Cant 1 *See* Nonington.
BARGHAM, *W Sussex*. V. **D** Chich 1 *See* Angmering.
BARHAM (St Jo Bapt) w Bishopsbourne and Kingston, *Kent*. V. **D** Cant 1 **P** *Abp* **I** A K W WRIGHT.
BARHAM (St Giles), *Cambs*.. **D** Ely 11 *See* Spaldwick.
BARHAM (St Mary Virg) w Claydon, *Suff*. R. **D** St E 1 *See* Claydon.
BARHOLME (St Martin) w Stow (St Jo Bapt), *Lincs*. V. **D** Linc 13 **P** *Bp* **I** G C SMITH.
BARKBY (St Mary), *Leics*. V. **D** Leic 9 **P** *A J P Pochin Esq* **I** H ADKINS.
BARKESTONE (St Pet and St Paul) w Plungar (St Helen), *Leics*. V and Redmile (St Pet). **D** Leic 3 **P** *Crown* **I** (Vacant).
BARKHAM (St Jas) , *Berks*. R. **D** Ox 16 *See* Arborfield.
BARKING (St Marg w St Paul and St Patr) w Creeksmouth and Fisher Street, *Essex*. R. **D** Chelmsf 1 **P** *All S Coll Ox and Bp* **I** P A BLAIR, A G PURSER *team v*, E W RUSSELL *team v*, G DARVILL *c*.
(St Erkenwald), V. **D** Chelmsf 1 **P** *Bp* **I** G R WISKER *p-in-c*.
BARKING-BY-THE-TOWER (All H). **D** Lon 1 *See* London.
BARKING (St Mary) w Darmsden (St Andr) and Great Bricett (St Mary and St Lawr) *Suff*. R. **D** St E *See* Ringshall.
BARKING-ROAD (H Trin), *Essex*.. **D** Chelmsf 5 *See* Canning Town (St Matthias).
BARKINGSIDE (H Trin), *Essex*. V. **D** Chelmsf 7 **P** *V of Ilford* **I** C REEVES.
(St Cedd's Conv Distr). **D** Chelmsf 7 **P** *Bp* **I** H TREBLE *min*.
(St Francis of Assisi), V. **D** Chelmsf 7 **P** *Bp* **I** J A ALLARD.
(St Geo) V. **D** Chelmsf 7 **P** *Bp* **I** R W MARRIOTT.
(St Laur), V. **D** Chelmsf 7 **P** *Bp* **I** C J TRAVERS.
BARKISLAND (Ch Ch) w West Scammonden (St Bart), *W Yorks*. V. **D** Wakef 2 **P** *V of Halifax* **I** J R FLACK, G FISHER *c*.
BARKSTON, *N Yorks*.. **D** York *See* Sherburn-in-Elmet.
BARKSTON (St Nich) w Syston (St Mary), V *Lincs*.. **D** Linc 23 **P** *Sir Anthony Thorold Bt* **I** R BERRY.
BARKWAY (St Mary Magd) w Reed (St Mary) and Buckland (St Andr), *Herts*. V. **D** St Alb 5 **P** *Dioc Bd of Patr* **I** R L MACQUEEN, D H BUXTON *hon c*.
BARKWITH GROUP, (E Barkwith (St Mary Virg), w W Barkwith (All SS), Hainton w Sixhills, E Torrington w W Torrington and S Willingham), *Lincs*. R. **D** Linc 5 **P** *D and C of Lincoln, J N Heneage, K Coll Lon and Dioc Bd of Patr (in turn)* **I** A C SIMPSON.
BARLASTON (St Jo Bapt), *Staffs*. V. **D** Lich 19 **P** *Countess of Sutherland* **I** G L SIMPSON.
BARLAVINGTON (St Mary), *W Sussex*. R. **D** Chich 6 **P** *Exors of J S Courtauld Esq* **I** R G JOHNSON *p-in-c*.
BARLBOROUGH (St Jas), *Derbys*. R. **D** Derby 2 **P** *S R Sitwell Esq* **I** G E BENCE.
BARLBY (All SS), *Humb*. V. **D** York 6 **P** *V of Hemingbrough* **I** R L BROWN.
BARLESTONE (St Giles), *Leics*. V. **D** Leic 15 **P** *Bp* **I** P WAKEFIELD.
BARLEY (St Marg), *Herts*. R. **D** St Alb 5 **P** *Crown* **I** R L MACQUEEN.
BARLEYTHORPE, *Leics*.. **D** Pet 22 *See* Langham.
BARLING (All SS) w Wakering (St Mary Virg), *Essex*. V. **D** Chelmsf 16 **P** *D and C of St Paul's and Bp* alt **I** R WOOLVEN *p-in-c*.

BARLINGS (St Edw K and Mart, St Hugh, St Jo Bapt and Sudbrooke (St Edw), *Lincs.* V. **D** Linc 3 **P** *Dioc Bd of Patr 1st and 2nd turns, Earl of Scarborough 3rd turn.* **I** K JARDIN.
BARLOW, *N Yorks.*. **D** York 8 *See* Brayton.
BARLOW, GT (St Lawr), *Derbys.* V. **D** Derby 3 **P** *R of Stavely* **I** N P HOLMES *p-in-c.*
BARLOW MOOR (Em Ch), *Gtr Man.*. **D** Man 10 *See* Didsbury.
BARMBY-MARSH (St Helen), *Humb.* V. **D** York *See* Howden, The.
BARMBY MOOR (St Cath) w Fangfoss (St Martin), *Humb.* V. **D** York 7 **P** *Abp* **I** J D WALKER P-IN-C ALLERTHORPE *p-in-c.*
BARMER, *Norf.*. **D** Nor 1 *See* Syderstone.
BARMING (St Marg), *Kent.* R. **D** Roch 6 **P** *Ld Chan* **I** P F WHITE.
BARMING HEATH (St Andr), *Kent.*. **D** Cant 14 *See* Maidstone.
BARMSTON (All SS), w Fraisthrope (St Edm), *Humb.* R. **D** York *See* Skipsea.
BARNACK (St Jo Bapt) w Ufford (St Andr) and Bainton (St Mary), *Cambs.* R. **D** Pet 13 **P** *Bp and St Jo Coll Cam* alt **I** C MAYHEW.
BARNACRE (All SS), *Lancs.* V. **D** Blackb 10 **P** *Maj Shepherd Cross* **I** M SUTCLIFFE.
BARNARD CASTLE (St Mary Virg), *Durham.* V. **D** Dur 10 **P** *Trin Coll Cam* **I** (Vacant).
BARNARDISTON, *Suff.* R. **D** St E 8 **P** *Miss A Hallam* **I** (Vacant).
BARNBURGH (St Pet) w Melton-on-the-Hill, *S Yorks.* R. **D** Sheff 10 **P** *Ld Chan 2 turns, Bp 1 turn* **I** (Vacant).
BARNBY (St Jo Bapt), *Suff.* R. **D** Nor 15 *See* N Cove.
BARNBY-IN-THE-WILLOWS (All SS), *Notts.* V. **D** Southw 3 *See* Coddington.
BARNBY MOOR (St Jas), *Notts.*. **D** Southw 7 *See* Blyth.
BARNBY-ON-DUN (St Pet w St Paul), *S Yorks.* V. **D** Sheff 8 **P** *Bp* **I** T W HARRIS P-IN-C OF FENWICK.
BARNEHURST (St Martin), *Kent.* V. **D** Roch 15 **P** *Bp* **I** A E SPEERS.
BARNES (St Mary Virg), *Surrey.* R. **D** S'wark 13 **P** *D and C of St Paul's* **I** J W D SIMONSON.
(St Mich AA), V. **D** S'wark 13 **P** *D and C of St Paul's* **I** A F TREADWELL, J S KINGSNORTH *hon c.*
(H Trin) V. **D** S'wark 13 **P** *R of Barnes* **I** C HEARD, C W CALCOTT-JAMES *c.*
BARNET, CHIPPING (St Jo Bapt) w Arkley (St Pet), *Herts.* R. **D** St Alb 2 **P** *Crown* **I** A G K ESDAILE, R LEGG *c*, G F STRATTON *c.*
EAST (St Mary Virg), *Herts.* R. **D** St Alb 2 **P** *Crown* **I** H E STEED.
(H Trin Lyonsdown), V. **D** St Alb 2 **P** *CPS* **I** R A POTTER.
MYMMS (Ch Ch), V. **D** Lon 16 **P** *CPS* **I** (Vacant).
NEW (St Jas), V. **D** St Alb 2 **P** *CPS* **I** M G H LACKEY, B PENN *c.*
VALE (St Mark), V. **D** St Alb 2 **P** *Bp* **I** S J KNOWERS *p-in-c.*
BARNET, FRIERN (St Jas Gt), *Gtr Lon.* R. **D** Lon 16 **P** *D and C of St Paul's* **I** V A STOCK, W S CROFT *c.*
(All SS), V. **D** Lon 16 **P** *Bp* **I** A V BENJAMIN.
(St Pet-le-Poer). **D** Lon 23 *See* Muswell Hill.
BARNETBY-LE-WOLD (St Mary and St Barn), *Humb.* V. **D** Linc 6 **P** *Bp* **I** (Vacant).
BARNETBY, NEW *Humb.*. **D** Linc 6 *See* Melton Ross.
BARNEY (St Mary), w Thursford, *Norf.* V. **D** Nor 24 **P** *Lord Hastings* **I** G H PATTINSON.
BARNHAM (St Mary) and Eastergate (St Geo), *W Sussex.* V. **D** Chich 1 **P** *Bp and D and C of Chich* **I** T L G PACKER.
BARNHAM, *Suff.*. **D** St E 9 *See* Euston.
BARNHAM BROOM (St Pet and St Paul) w Bixton, Kimberley and Carleton Forehoe (St Mary), Little Brandon, Coston w Runhall, Garveston w Thuxton, Hardingham, Wramplingham w Barford, *Norf.* R. **D** Nor 12 **P** *Patr Bd* **I** D R RYE, P J STEPHENS *team v.*
BARNINGHAM (St Mich AA) w Hutton Magna and Wycliffe, *N Yorks.* R. **D** Ripon 1 **P** *Bp and V of Gilling* **I** (Vacant).
BARNINGHAM (St Andr), *Suff.*. **D** St E 9 *See* Hopton-by-Thetford.
BARNINGHAM, LITTLE (St Andr), *Norf.* R. **D** Nor 3 *See* Wickmere w Wolterton.
BARNINGHAM (St Mary Virg) w Matlaske (St Pet) and Baconsthorpe, Plumstead and Hempstead, *Norf.* R. **D** Nor **P** *Sir C E Mott-Radclyffe, D and C of Nor, CPAS and Duchy of Lanc* **I** S F HOOPER.
BARNOLDBY-LE-BECK (St Helena), *Humb.* R. **D** Linc 10 **P** *Ld Chan* **I** W J A NUNNERLEY.
BARNOLDSWICK (H Trin w St Mary-le-Gill) and Bracewell (St Mich), *Lancs.* V. **D** Bradf 10 **P** *Bp* **I** J S LONG, M J BAMFORTH *c.*
BARNSBURY (St D w St Clem), *Lon.* V. **D** Lon 3 **P** *Bp* **I** P H ALLEN.
(St Andr), V. **D** Lon 3 **P** *V of H Trin Islington and CPS* **I** (Vacant).
BARNSLEY (St Mary Virg), *Glos.* R. **D** Glouc 14 *See* Bibury.
BARNSLEY (St Mary Virg), *S Yorks.* R. **D** Wakef 8 **P** *Bp* **I** J C K BRUMPTON, W P B CARLIN *c*, S COOPER *c.*
(St Edw the Confessor), V. **D** Wakef 8 **P** *Bp* **I** T H BONE.
(St Geo), V. **D** Wakef 8 **P** *Bp* **I** J E DAINTY.
(St Jo Bapt and St Pet), V. **D** Wakef 8 **P** *Bp* **I** R A B MACE.
BARNSTAPLE (St Pet w H Trin and St Mary Magd) w Goodleigh (St Gregory) and Landkey, *Devon.* R. **D** Ex 15 **P** *Dioc Bd of Patr* **I** S L LEACH, M PRATT *team v*, M R SELMAN *team v*, W H BARTON *c*, D B COOK *c.*
(St Paul, Sticklepath), V. **D** Ex 15 **P** *Bp* **I** (Vacant).
BARNSTON (Dedic unknown), *Essex.* R. **D** Chelmsf 23 **P** *CPAS* **I** A M PARRY.
BARNSTON (Ch Ch), *Mer.* V. **D** Ches 8 **P** *Bp* **I** H L WILLIAMS, R RAWLINSON *c.*
BARNT GREEN (St Andr), *Worcs.* V. **D** Birm *See* Cofton-Hackett.
BARNTON (Ch Ch), *Chesh.* V. **D** Ches 4 **P** *Bp* **I** P M GREENSLADE.
BARNWELL, *Cambs.*. **D** Ely 3 *See* Cambridge, St Andrew L.
BARNWELL (St Andr) w (All SS) w Thurning and Luddington, *Northants.* R. **D** Pet 11 **P** *MMT and R K Measures Esq* **I** P E BUSTIN.
BARNWOOD (St Lawr), *Glos.* V. **D** Glouc 1 **P** *D and C of Glouc* **I** M O SEACOME.
BARRINGTON (St Mary Virg), *Somt.*. **D** B & W *See* Shepton Beauchamp.
BARRINGTON (All SS), *Cambs.* V. **D** Ely 8 **P** *Trin Coll Cam* **I** M W BAKER *p-in-c.*
BARRINGTON, GREAT (St Mary Virg) w Barrington, Little (St Pet), *Glos.* V. **D** Glouc 15 *See* Sherborne.
BARROW (St Bart), *Chesh.* R. **D** Ches 2 **P** *D Okell Esq* **I** J C CLARKE.
BARROW (St Giles), *Salop.*. **D** Heref 14 *See* Willey.
BARROW Leics. R **D** Pet 22 *See* Cottesmore.
BARROW (All SS), *Suff.* R. **D** St E 13 **P** *St Jo Coll Cam 3 turns, Bp 1 turn* **I** J W BRIDGEN.
BARROW-GURNEY (St Mary Virg and St Edm K and Mart), *Avon.* V. **D** B & W 16 **P** *Maj M A Gibbs* **I** P R W TOMLINSON.
BARROW HILL (St Andr), *Derbys.* V. **D** Derby 2 *See* Staveley.
BARROW-IN-FURNESS (St Geo Mart w St Luke and St Perran's, Roose), *Cumb.* R. **D** Carl 15 **P** *Bp* **I** C GILLHESPEY, N S GOSSWINN *team v*, J F AMBROSE *c.*
(St Aid), V. **D** Carl 15 **P** *Bp* **I** G G BROWN.
(St Jas Gt), V. **D** Carl 15 **P** *Dioc Bd of Patr* **I** D R KING.
(St Jo Evang), V. **D** Carl 15 **P** *Dioc Bd of Patr* **I** E NOTMAN.
(St Mary Virg). **D** Carl 15 *See* Walney, Isle of.
(St Mark). **D** Carl 15 **P** *Bp* **I** W L HALLING, G I SALKELD *c.*
(St Matt), V. **D** Carl 15 **P** *Bp* **I** S DOUBTFIRE, P L F ALLSOP *c.*
(St Mich). **D** Carl 15 *See* Rampside.
(St Paul, Newbarns w Hawcoat), V. **D** Carl 15 **P** *Simeon Trustees* **I** F A DEAN.
BARROW, NORTH (St Nich) w Barrow South (St Pet), *Somt.*. **D** B & W 4 *See* Six Pilgrims.
BARROW-ON-HUMBER (H Trin) w New Holland (Ch Ch), *Humb.* V. **D** Linc 6 **P** *Ld Chan* **I** R T SHAW.
BARROW-UPON-SOAR (H Trin), *Leics.* V. **D** Leic 10 **P** *St Jo Coll Cam* **I** (Vacant).
BARROW-ON-TRENT (St Wilfrid) w Twyford (St Andr), *Derbys.* V. **D** Derby 15 **P** *Hdmaster and Sen Masters of Repton Sch* **I** H T LINDLEY C-IN-C OF SWARKESTONE *c-in-c.*
BARROWBY (All SS), *Lincs.* R. **D** Linc 19 **P** *Duke of Devonshire* **I** E R HARRIS.
BARROWDEN (St Pet) w Wakerley (St Jo Bapt) w S Luffenham, *Leics.* R. **D** Pet 13 **P** *Marq of Ex and Ball Coll Ox (alt)* **I** J F CULROSS.
BARROWFORD (St Thos), *Lancs.* V. **D** Blackb 6a **P** *Dioc Bd of Finance* **I** J W HARTLEY.
BARSBY, *Leics.* V. **D** Leic 8 *See* Ashby Folville.
BARSHAM (H Trin) w Shipmeadow, *Suff.* R. **D** St E *See* Ringsfield.
BARSHAM, EAST (All SS) w Barsham, North (All SS) and Barsham, West (Assump of BVM), *Norf.* V. **D** Nor 21 **P** *Capt J D A Keith* **I** C G COLVEN *p-in-c.*
BARSTON (St Swith), *W Midl.* V. **D** Birm 11 **P** *Trustees* **I** (Vacant).
BARTESTREE (St Jas), *Herefs.*. **D** Heref 4 *See* Lugwardine.

(St Mark, Battersea Rise), V. **D** S'wark 1 **P** *V of Battersea* **I** K J BALE.
(St Mary-le-Park), V. **D** S'wark 1 **P** *Earl Spencer , Bp, and V of Battersea* **I** D W GRIGGS *c*.
(St Paul), V. **D** S'wark 1 *See* St Pet.
(St Pet w St Paul), V. **D** S'wark 1 **P** *V of Battersea* **I** M A WIMSHURST, T WHITFIELD *c*.
(St Phil w St Bart), V. **D** S'wark 1 **P** *Bp* **I** C E BLANKENSHIP.
(St Sav, Battersea Park), V. **D** S'wark 1 **P** *CPS* **I** A J TOMBLING.
See also WANDSWORTH COMMON..
BATTISFORD, *Suff.* V. **D** St E *See* Ringshall.
BATTLE (St Mary), *E Sussex*. Dean and V. **D** Chich 17 **P** *Trustees* **I** R A BIRD, G E DIAMOND *hon c*.
BATTLEFIELD (St Mary Magd) w Albrighton (St Jo Bapt), *Salop.* V. **D** Lich 26 **P** *J F Sparrow Esq* **I** M W TURNER *p-in-c*.
BATTLESDEN (St Pet) w Pottesgrove (St Mary Virg), *Beds.*. **D** St Alb *See* Woburn.
BATTYEFORD (Ch the King) w Knowle (St Pet), *W Yorks.* V. **D** Wakef 10 **P** *V of Mirfield* **I** J D WILKINSON.
BAUGHURST (St Steph) w Ramsdell (Ch Ch) and Wolverton w Ewhurst and Hannington, *Hants.* R. **D** Win 3 **P** *Bp, Duke of Wellington and Ld Chan* **I** J E FRANKS.
BAULKING (St Nich), *Oxon.* V. **D** Ox 17 *See* Uffington.
BAUMBER (St Swithin) w Great Sturton (All SS), *Lincs.* V. **D** Linc *See* Hemingby.
BAUNTON (St Mary Magd), *Glos.*. **D** Glouc 13 *See* Stratton.
BAUNTON (H Trin), *Dorset.*. **D** Sarum 2 *See* Bothenhampton.
BAVERSTOCK (St Editha), *Wilts.* R. **D** Sarum *See* Barford St Martin.
BAWBURGH (St Mary and St Walstan), *Norf.* V. **D** Nor 13 *See* Melton, Little.
BAWDESWELL (All SS) w Foxley (St Thos), *Norf.* R. **D** Nor 6 **P** *Bp* **I** R K BROOKES *p-in-c*.
BAWDRIP (St Mich AA), *Somt.* R. **D** B & W 17 **P** *Bp* **I** J F RIGG.
BAWDSEY (St Mary Virg), *Suff.* V. **D** St E 7 *See* Alderton.
BAWSEY, *Norf.*. **D** Nor *See* Gaywood.
BAWTRY (St Nich) w Austerfeld (St Helen) *S Yorks.* V. **D** Southw 1 **P** *Bp* **I** G W J SPRINGETT.
BAXENDEN (St Jo Bapt), *Lancs.*. **D** Blackb 1 *See* Accrington.
BAXTERLEY (no Dedic) *Warws.* R. **D** Birm 10 **P** *Ld Chan and Sir W F S Dugdale Bt* alt **I** (Vacant).
BAYDON (St Nich), *Wilts.*. **D** Sarum 26 *See* Whitton.
BAYFIELD (St Marg), *Norf.* R. **D** Nor 24 *See* Letheringsett.
BAYFORD, *Somt.*. **D** B & W 5 *See* Cucklington.
BAYFORD (St Mary), *Herts.* V. **D** St Alb 8 *See* Berkhamsted, Little.
BAYLHAM (St Pet), *Suff.* R. **D** St E 1 *See* Blakenham, Great.
BAYSTON HILL (Ch Ch), *Salop*, V. **D** Lich 26 **P** *V of St Julian, Shrewsbury* **I** J H FIELDSEND, M H TUPPER *hon c*.
BAYSWATER. **D** Lon *See* Paddington.
BAYTON (St Bart), *Worcs.*. **D** Worc 12 *See* Mamble.
BEACHAMPTON (St Mary Virg), *Bucks.* R. **D** Ox 23 *See* Nash.
BEACHAMWELL (St Mary w St John and All SS) w Shingham *Norf.* R. **D** Ely 17 **P** *Bp and Exors of Mrs P Villiers-Stuart* alt **I** (Vacant).
BEACHLEY (St Jo Evang), *Gwent.* V. **D** Glouc 7 *See* Tidenham.
BEACONSFIELD (St Mary w All SS, St Mich AA New Beaconsfield and St Thos Holtspur), *Bucks.* R. **D** Ox 20 **P** *Dioc Bd of Patr* **I** M M FITZWILLIAMS, C EVERETT-ALLEN *team v*, R T WOODWARD *team v*, I A TERRY *c*.
BEADNELL (St Ebba), *Northumb.* V. **D** Newc T 8 **P** *V of Bamburgh* **I** W WADDLE.
BEAFORD w Roborough (St Pet) and St Giles-in-the-Wood, *Devon.* R. **D** Ex 20 **P** *MMT of E Trust, Ld Chan and Misses Barnard in turn* **I** W E SMYTH.
BEALINGS, GREAT (St Mary), w Bealings, Little (All SS), *Suff.* R. **D** St E 7 *See* Playford.
BEAMINSTER AREA (Beaminster, Broadwindsor w Burstock, Seaborough, Melplash w Mapperton, South Perrott w Mosterton, Chedington Toller Popcorum w Hooke, Netherbury w Solway-Ash and Stoke Abbott), *Dorset.* R. **D** Sarum **P** *Bp and Sir R P Williams Bt* **I** T M F BILES, J M STOW *team v*.
BEAMISH (St Andr), *Durham.* V. **D** Dur 7 **P** *Bp* **I** B MOSS.
BEARDEN (St Nich), *Essex.* V. **D** Chelmsf 26 *See* Berden.
BEARLEY (St Mary Virg), *Warws.* V. **D** Cov 9 *See* Snitterfield.
BEARPARK (St Edm Mart), *Durham.* V. **D** Dur 2 **P** *D and C of Dur* **I** A D PARKES *p-in-c*.
BEARSTED (H Cross), *Kent.* V. **D** Cant 15 **P** *Abp* **I** A S DUKE P-IN-C OF THURNHAM, F J GREEN *hon c*.
BEARWOOD (St Mary Virg), *W Midl.* V. **D** Birm 5 *See* Smethwick.
BEARWOOD (St Cath), *Berks.* R. **D** Ox 16 **P** *Bp* **I** I R DOWSE.
BEAUCHAMP RODING, *Essex.*. **D** Chelmsf 23 *See* Abbess Roding.
BEAUDESERT (St Nich) w Henley-in-Arden (St Jo Bapt) and Ullenhall, *Warws.* R. **D** Cov 7 **P** *MMT, Bp and High Bailiff of Henley-in-Arden* **I** P H BENNETT.
BEAULIEU (BV and Child) and Exbury (St Kath), *Hants.* V. **D** Win 9 **P** *Ld Montague of Beaulieu* **I** K G DAVIS.
BEAUMONT, *Cumb.*. **D** Carl 3 *See* Kirkandrews-on-Eden.
BEAUMONT (St Leon) w Moze, *Essex.* R. **D** Chelmsf *See* Tendring.
BEAUWORTH (St Jas), *Hants.*. **D** Win 6 *See* Cheriton.
BEAUXFIELD or WHITFIELD (St Pet) w Guston (St Martin), *Kent.*. **D** Cant 5 *See* Whitfield.
BEAWORTHY (St Alb), *Devon.* R. **D** Ex *See* Halwill.
BEBINGTON (St Andr), *Mer.* R. **D** Ches 8 **P** *Ch S Trust* **I** G M TURNER, D W HOSKIN *c*, N L ROBINSON *c*.
BEBINGTON, HIGHER (Ch Ch), *Mer.* V. **D** Ches 8 **P** *Can C R Troughton* **I** L R RIDLEY.
BECCLES (St Mich AA), *Suff.* R. **D** St E 14 **P** *Dioc Bd of Patr* **I** M D SUTTON, J B GIRDWOOD *team v*.
BECCONSALL, *Lancs.*. **D** Blackb 6 *See* Hesketh.
BECK ROW (St John) w Kenny Hill, *Suff.*. **D** St E *See* Barton-Mills.
BECKBURY, *Salop.* R. **D** Lich 25 **P** *Ld Chan* **I** J R P BAGGALEY.
BECKENHAM (St Geo), *Kent.* R. **D** Roch 11 **P** *Bp* **I** J D SAVILLE, P WRIGHT *c*.
(Ch Ch), V. **D** Roch 11 **P** *Ch Trust Fund Trust* **I** A P BAKER, A N KNIGHTS JOHNSON *c*.
(H Trin Penge-lane), V. **D** Roch 11 **P** *Bp* **I** P E LONGBOTTOM.
(St Barn), V. **D** Roch 11 **P** *Keble Coll* **I** E E TURNER.
(St Jas Elmers End), V. **D** Roch 11 **P** *Bp* **I** K W BRASSELL, C J GARLAND *c*, D F PRESTON *c*.
(St Jo Bapt), V. **D** Roch 11 **P** *Trustees and Bp* **I** J C PORTHOUSE, R M DE VIAL *c*, A J EDWARDS *c*.
(St Mich AA) w (St Aug), V. **D** Roch 11 **P** *S for Maint Faith and Bp* **I** D C GOODERHAM.
(St Paul), V. **D** Roch 11 **P** *Bp* **I** J FROST.
BECKERING, *Lincs.*. **D** Linc 23 *See* Lissington.
BECKERMET or CALDERBRIDGE (St Bridget) w Ponsonby, *Cumb.* V. **D** Carl 12 *See* Beckermet St John.
BECKERMET (St John and St Bridget) w Ponsonby, *Cumb.* V. **D** Carl 12 **P** *Trustees* **I** G A CROSSLEY.
BECKFORD (St Jo Bapt) w Ashton-under-Hill (St Barbara), *Worcs.* V. **D** Glouc 10 **P** *CPAS* **I** H G PHILLIPS *p-in-c*.
BECKHAM, W (St Helen w All SS), *Norf.* V. **D** Nor 24 **P** *D and C of Nor* **I** H BRANDWOOD *p-in-c*, E S C COGGINS *hon c*.
BECKINGHAM (All SS), w Fenton, *Lincs.* R. **D** Linc 23 **P** *Bp 2 turns, Revs J R H and H C Thorold 1 turn* **I** A W STEEDMAN.
BECKINGHAM (All SS) w Walkeringham (St Mary Magd), *Notts.* V. **D** Southw 1 **P** *Ld Chan and Bp* alt **I** R B FEARN.
BECKINGTON (St Greg) w Standerwick Berkley, Rodden, Lullington and Orchardleigh, *Wilts.* R. **D** B & W 16a **P** *Bp 3 turns, Ch S Trust 1 turn and A Duckworth Esq 1 turn* **I** W T H B DAVIES.
BECKLEY (All SS) and Peasmarsh (St Pet and St Paul), *E Sussex.* R. **D** Chich 22 **P** *Univ Coll Ox and SS Coll Cam (alt)* **I** C F HOPKINS.
BECKLEY (The Assump of St Mary Virg), *Oxon.* V. **D** Ox 5 **P** *Exors of Mrs W Cooke* **I** A G A DE VERE.
BECKTON MISSION (St Mich), *Essex.*. **D** Chelmsf 1 *See* Ham, East.
BECKWITHSHAW (St Mich AA), *N Yorks.* V. **D** Ripon *See* Pannal.
BECONTREE (St Thos), *Essex.* V. **D** Chelmsf 1 **P** *Bp of Lon* **I** M SILVERSIDES *p-in-c*.
(St Alb), V. **D** Chelmsf 1 **P** *Trustees* **I** D S AINGE *p-in-c*.
(St Cedd), V. **D** Chelmsf 1 **P** *Bp* **I** R C JONES *p-in-c*.
(St Elisabeth), V. **D** Chelmsf 1 **P** *Bp* **I** P A LETFORD *p-in-c*.
(St Geo), V. **D** Chelmsf 1 **P** *Bp* **I** P A EVANS *c-in-c*.
(St Jo Div) V. **D** Chelmsf 1 **P** *Bp* **I** SIR J W C ROLL.
(St Mary), V. **D** Chelmsf 1 **P** *CPAS* **I** A KEMP, B G KYRIACOU *c*.

(St Pet), V. **D** Chelmsf 1 **P** *Bp* **I** J V FISHER *c-in-c.*
BEDALE (St Greg), *N Yorks.* R. **D** Ripon 2 **P** *Sir Henry Beresford-Peirse Bt* **I** F W A LEDGARD, H K DEWIS *c,* J E GREER *c.*
BEDDINGHAM (St Andr), *E Sussex..* **D** Chich 15 *See* Firle.
BEDDINGTON (St Mary Virg), *Surrey.* R. **D** S'wark 8 **P** *K Bond Esq* **I** D A RICHARDSON.
NORTH (All SS), V. **D** S'wark 8 **P** *Bp* **I** M J P DYMOCK, D WALFORD *hon c.*
SOUTH (St Mich AA), V. **D** S'wark 8 **P** *Bp* **I** J M DEAN.
BEDFIELD (St Nich) w Monk Soham, *Suff.* R. **D** St E *See* Worlingworth.
BEDFONT (St Mary Virg), *Gtr Lon.* V. **D** Lon 10 **P** *Ld Chan* **I** K N BOWLER, I C DAVIES *c.*
BEDFORD (All SS), V. **D** St Alb 16 **P** *Bp* **I** T D DESERT.
(Ch Ch), V. **D** St Alb 16 **P** *Bp* **I** D HUMPHRIES, H R BALFOUR *c,* A CLITHEROW *hon c.*
(St Andr), V. **D** St Alb 16 **P** *Ld Chan* **I** J A L HULBERT, J POOLE *c,* A R THREADGILL *c.*
(St Jo Bapt and St Leon), R. **D** St Alb 16 **P** *MMT* **I** T V E OVERTON.
(St Martin, Bishop of Tours), V. **D** St Alb 16 **P** *Bp* **I** V S CHALLEN.
(St Mich AA), V. **D** St Alb 16 **P** *Bp* **I** A B J COBB.
(St Paul), V. **D** St Alb 16 **P** *Bp* **I** N G COULTON.
(St Pet de Merton w St Cuthb), R. **D** St Alb **P** *Ld Chan* **I** D D FRICKER.
BEDFORD (St Thos), *Gtr Man..* **D** Man 6 *See* Leigh.
BEDFORD PARK (St Mich AA).. **D** Lon 10 *See* Chiswick.
BEDGROVE, (H Spirit), *Bucks.* V. **D** Ox 21 **P** *Dioc Bd of Patr* **I** R B HOWELL.
BEDHAMPTON (St Thos), *Hants.* R. **D** Portsm 3 **P** *Bp* **I** M J KETLEY *c.*
See also LEIGH PARK..
BEDINGFIELD (St Mary) and Thorndon w Rishangles, *Suff.* R. **D** St E 16 **P** *MMT 3 turns, Bp 1 turn* **I** J W LARTER P-IN-C OF BEDINGFIELD, A RIDGE P-IN-C OF THORNDON W RISHANGLES.
BEDINGHAM (St Andr), *Norf..* **D** Nor *See* Woodton.
BEDLINGTON (St Cuthb), *Northumb.* V. **D** Newc T 1 **P** *D and C of Dur* **I** K R WARD.
BEDMINSTER (St Aldhelm, St Dunstan, St Francis Ashton Gate, St Paul), *Avon.* R. **D** Bris 1 **P** *Bp* **I** A H G JONES, M L TAYLOR *team v,* R S EYRE *c,* J F HOUSE *hon c.*
(St Mich AA Windmill Hill), V. **D** Bris 1 **P** *Bp* **I** P L CHAMBERS, R J SALTER *c.*
(St Mary Virg Redcliffe w Temple or H Cross and St Jo Bapt), *Avon.* V. **D** Bris 1 **P** *Bp* **I** K J CLARK, H R L BONSEY *c,* P N CLARK *c,* G G STIMPSON *hon c.*
(St Osw Bedminster Down), V. **D** Bris 1 **P** *Bp* **I** M W SEARLE.
BEDNALL (All SS), *Staffs..* **D** Lich 3 *See* Acton Trussell.
BEDSTONE (St Mary) w Hopton Castle, *Salop.* R. **D** Heref 10 *See* Clungunford.
BEDWORTH (All SS), *Warws.* R. **D** Cov 5 **P** *Mart Mem and C of E Trusts* **I** P D HOWARD *c,* R A SLATER *c.*
BEDWYN MAGNA (St Mary), *Wilts.* V. **D** Sarum 27 **P** *Bp* **I** (Vacant).
BEDWYN PARVA (St Mich), *Wilts.* V. **D** Sarum 27 **P** *Bp* **I** (Vacant).
BEEBY (All SS), *Leics.* R. **D** Leic 8 **P** *Beeby Ch S Trust* **I** D L PRISTON.
BEECH HILL (St Mary Virg), *Berks.* V. **D** Ox 15 *See* Grazeley.
BEECHINGSTOKE (St Steph), *Wilts.* R. **D** Sarum 27 *See* Woodborough.
BEEDING, LOWER (H Trin w St Jo Evang), *W Sussex.* V. **D** Chich 4 **P** *Bp* **I** W T ARMSTRONG.
BEEDING, UPPER (St Pet), *W Sussex.* V. **D** Chich 7 **P** *Bp* **I** D J WHITE.
BEEDON (St Nich), *Berks.* V. **D** Ox 14 **P** *Bp* **I** C A SELMAN.
BEEFORD (St Leon) w Lissett (St Jas of Compostella) and Dunnington (St Nich), *Humb.* R. **D** York 14 **P** *Abp* **I** J R NEWTON, J N CHARTERS *c.*
BEELEY (St Anne) w Edensor (St Pet), *Derbys.* V. **D** Derby 9 **P** *Duke of Devonshire* **I** R A BEDDOES *p-in-c.*
BEELSBY (St Andr), *Humb.* R. **D** Linc 10 **P** *Bp* **I** D N SAMUEL.
BEENHAM-VALENCE (St Mary), *Berks.* V. **D** Ox *See* Woolhampton.
BEER (St Mich), *Devon.* V. **D** Ex 5 **P** *Ld Clinton* **I** R O H EPPINGSTONE.
BEERCROCOMBE (St Jas), *Somt.* R. **D** B & W 23a *See* Hatch-Beauchamp.
BEER-HACKETT (St Mich) w Thornford, *Dorset.* R. **D** Sarum 7 *See* Thornford.
BEESBY, *Lincs.* **D** Linc 10 *See* Wold Newton.
BEESBY-IN-THE-MARSH (St Andr), *Lincs.* R. **D** Linc 8 *See* Saleby.
BEESTON (St Andr), *Norf.* R. **D** Nor 4 **P** *D and C of Nor* **I** D J TUCK.
BEESTON (St Lawr) w Ashmanhaugh (St Swithin), *Norf.* R. **D** Nor **P** *Sir R Preston 2 turns, Bp 1 turn* **I** W BLATHWAYT *p-in-c.*
BEESTON (St Mary Virg), *W Yorks.* V. **D** Ripon 8 **P** *V of Leeds* **I** J M OLIVER, M P BERESFORD-PEIRSE *c.*
HILL (Ch of H Spirit), V. **D** Ripon 8 **P** *V of Leeds* **I** P S PAINE.
BEESTON (St Jo Bapt), *Notts.* V. **D** Southw 8 **P** *Duke of Devonshire* **I** J A JOHNSON, A M LUCKCUCK *c,* G J PIGOTT *c.*
BEESTON-NEXT-MILEHAM (St Mary), *Norf.* R. **D** Nor 20 **P** *Ch S Patr Bd* **I** D J MUNT.
BEESTON REGIS (All SS), *Norf.* R. **D** Nor 5 **P** *Duchy of Lanc* **I** A R HAYWARD.
BEETHAM (St Mich AA), *Cumb.* V. **D** Carl 17 **P** *Bp* **I** (Vacant).
BEETLEY (St Mary) w E Bilney (St Mary Magd), *Norf..* **D** Nor **P** *V Wells Esq* **I** L A WILMAN *p-in-c.*
BEGBROKE, *Oxon.* R. **D** Ox 10 **P** *BNC Ox 1 turn , Trustees, 3 turns* **I** E G A W PAGE-TURNER *p-in-c,* D C PARKER *c.*
BEIGHTON (St Mary), *S Yorks.* V. **D** Sheff 1 **P** *Bp* **I** A G LIVESLEY.
BEIGHTON (All SS) w Moulton, *Norf.* R. **D** Nor 1 **P** *Bp* **I** J T H BRITTON *p-in-c.*
BEKESBOURNE (St Pet), *Kent.* V. **D** Cant 1 *See* Patrixbourne.
BELAUGH (St Pet), *Norf.* R. **D** Nor *See* Wroxham.
BELBROUGHTON (H Trin) w Fairfield (St Mark), *Worcs.* R. **D** Worc 11 **P** *St Jo Coll Ox* **I** (Vacant).
BELCHALWELL, *Dorset..* **D** Sarum 13 *See* Okeford-Fitzpaine.
BELCHAMP ST PAUL (St Andr), *Essex.* V. **D** Chelmsf 18 **P** *D and C of Windsor* **I** E POWELL.
BELCHAMP-OTTEN (All SS) w Belchamp Walter (St Mary) and Bulmer (St Andr), *Essex.* R. **D** Chelmsf 18 **P** *Dioc Bd of Patr 1 turn, S P St C Raymond Esq 2 turns* **I** R T HOWARD.
BELCHAMP WALTER (St Mary), *Essex.* **D** Chelmsf 18 *See* Belchamp Otten.
BELCHFORD (St Pet and St Paul), *Lincs.* R. **D** Linc 11 **P** *Ld Chan* **I** (Vacant).
BELFIELD (St Ann), *Gtr Man.* V. **D** Man 17 **P** *Bp* **I** C R M POYNTING.
BELFORD (St Mary), *Northumb.* V. **D** NewcT 8 **P** *Trustees* **I** T HUSBAND.
BELGRAVE, *Leics..* **D** Leic 1 *See* Leicester.
BELHUS PARK (All SS Eccles Distr), *Essex..* **D** Chelmsf 15 **P** *Bp* **I** A J MAY.
BELLE ISLE (St John and St Barn), *W Yorks..* **D** Ripon 8 **P** *Bp* **I** A F W WALLACE.
BELLE VUE (St Cath), *W Yorks.* v. **D** Wakef 7 *See* Sandal Magna.
BELLEAU (St Jo Bapt) w Claythorpe, Aby (All SS), and Greenfield, *Lincs.* R. **D** Linc *See* Withern.
BELLERBY (St Jo Evang), *N Yorks.* V. **D** Ripon 2 *See* Leyburn.
BELLINGHAM (St Dunstan), *Kent.* V. **D** S'wark 20 **P** *Bp* **I** G C MASON, C R WELHAM *c,* R B CRANE *hon c.*
BELLINGHAM-OTTERBURN GROUP (Bellingham, Thorneyburn, Greystead, Corsenside, Falstone, Otterburn, Elsdon, Horsley and Byrness), *Northumb.* R. **D** Newc T **P** *Bp* **I** A G CHARLES, W M GOLIGHTLY *team v,* P A G D PRIDHAM *team v,* G I M STRONG *team v.*
BELMONT (St Mary Magd), *Durham.* V. **D** Dur 2 **P** *Crown* **I** D R WEBSTER.
BELMONT (St Pet), *Lancs.* V. **D** Man 19 **P** *V of Bolton* **I** A PARKER.
BELMONT (St Anselm), *Gtr Lon.* V. **D** Lon 24 **P** *Bp* **I** M B TINGLE.
BELMONT (St Jo Bapt), *Surrey.* V. **D** S'wark 8 **P** *R of Cheam* **I** E J S PLAXTON, A G DUCKETT *hon c.*
BELPER (St Pet w St Jo Bapt), *Derbys.* V. **D** Derby 12 **P** *V of Duffield* **I** R H ELDRIDGE *p-in-c,* G F SMALL *c.*
(Ch Ch and Milford), V. **D** Derby 12 **P** *Bp* **I** G O MARSHALL *p-in-c.*
BELSTEAD, *Suff..* **D** St E *See* Copdock.
BELSTONE (St Mary) w Sticklepath Chap, *Devon.* R. **D** Ex *See* Tawton, South.
BELTINGHAM (St Cuthb) w Henshaw (All H), *Northumb.* V. **D** NewcT 4 **P** *V of Haltwhistle* **I** J E LINTON.
BELTON (St Jo Bapt) and Osgathorpe (St Mary), *Leic.* V. **D** Leic 11 **P** *Bp* **I** A H WYMAN.

BELTON (St Pet and St Paul), *Humb*. R. **D** Linc 23 **P** *Ld Brownlow* **I** R BERRY.
BELTON (All SS), *Suff*. R. **D** Nor 2 **P** *Bp* **I** L A J WARD.
BELTON (St Pet), *Leics*. V. **D** Pet 12 *See* Wardley.
BELTON-IN-I OF AXHOLME (All SS), *Lincs*. V. **D** Linc 1 **P** *Exors of R F Cooper-Collinson* **I** A L ADAMS.
BELVEDERE (All SS), *Kent*. V. **D** Roch 15 **P** *Dioc Bd of Patr* **I** C D ELLIOTT, R J MIDDLEWICK *c*.
(St Aug), V. **D** Roch 15 **P** *Bp* **I** K R CHEESEMAN.
BEMBRIDGE (H Trin), *Isle of Wight*. V. **D** Portsm 6 **P** *V of Brading* **I** D C CLARKE.
BEMERTON (St Jo Evang and St Mich AA), *Wilts*. R. **D** Sarum 16 **P** *Crown 2 turns, Bp 1 turn* **I** P C MAGEE, E TRAVERSE *team v*, R G GOODSHIP *c*, G R KAY *c*.
BEMPTON (St Mich), *Humb*. V. **D** York 12 **P** *Admin of J B Harrison-Broadley Esq* **I** R G HIRST *p-in-c*.
BEN RHYDDING (St Jo Evang), *W Yorks*. V. **D** Bradf 5 **P** *V of Ilkley* **I** M A SAVAGE.
BENACRE (St Mich), *Suff*. R. **D** St E *See* Covehithe.
BENCHILL (St Luke), *Gtr Man*. V. **D** Man 10 **P** *Bp* **I** D O FORSHAW, K J MASSEY *c*.
BENEFIELD (St Mary), *Northants*. R. **D** Pet 11 **P** *Major D Watts-Russell* **I** D W J TWEDDLE *p-in-c*.
BENENDEN (St Geo) and (St Marg), *Kent*. V. **D** Cant 11 **P** *Abp* **I** C F SMITH *p-in-c*.
BENFIELDSIDE (St Cuthb), *Durham*. V. **D** Dur 7 **P** *Bp* **I** E I ROBERTSON.
BENFLEET, NORTH (All SS), *Essex*. R. **D** Chelmsf 10 *See* Bowers Gifford.
BENFLEET, SOUTH, *Essex*. V. **D** Chelmsf 13 **P** *D and C of Westmr* **I** A G BANKS.
BENGEO (H Trin) w (Ch Ch) and Tonwell (St Leon), *Herts*. R. **D** St Alb 8 **P** *T Abel Smith Esq* **I** C A WEALE, C A WALLINGTON *hon c*.
BENGEWORTH (St Pet), *Worcs*. V. **D** Worc 1 **P** *Bp* **I** B W E BANKS.
BENHALL Suff. R **D** St E *See* Sternfield.
BENHILTON (All SS), *Surrey*. V. **D** S'wark 8 **P** *Bp* **I** W G HARRIS-EVANS, G W HOLMES *c*.
BENINGTON (All SS), *Lincs*. R. **D** Linc 20 **P** *Ld Chan* **I** (Vacant).
BENINGTON (St Pet), *Herts*.. **D** St Alb *See* Aston.
BENNINGTON, LONG (St Swith) w Foston (St Pet), *Lincs*. V. **D** Linc 19 **P** *Duchy of Lanc* **I** R AMIS.
BENNIWORTH (St Julian) w Market Stainton, V and Ranby (St German), *Lincs*. R. **D** Linc *See* Asterby Group.
BENSHAM T & W. **D** Dur 4 *See* Gateshead.
BENSON (or Bensington) (St Helen), *Oxon* . V. **D** Ox 5 **P** *Ch Ch Ox* **I** A E BARTON.
BENTHALL (St Bart), *Salop*. V. **D** Heref 14 *See* Broseley.
BENTHAM (St Jo Bapt), *Lancs*. R. **D** Bradf 7 **P** *Bp* **I** J BRADBERRY.
(St Marg), V. **D** Bradf 7 **P** *Bp* **I** N J A KINSELLA.
BENTHAM (St Pet), *Glos*.. **D** Glouc 2 *See* Witcombe, Great.
BENTLEY (St Mary) and Binsted (H Cross), *Hants*. R. **D** Win **P** *D and C of Win and Archd of Surrey* **I** G C G TRASLER *p-in-c*.
BENTLEY, *W Midl*.. **D** Lich 9 *See* Walsall.
BENTLEY (St Mary) w Tattingstone (St Mary BV), *Suff*. V. **D** St E 5 **P** *Bp and Dioc Bd of Patr* **I** E B ARMSON.
BENTLEY (St Pet), *S Yorks*.. **D** Sheff 8 **P** *Bp* **I** D J POMERY.
BENTLEY COMMON (St Paul), *Essex*. V. **D** Chelmsf 9 **P** *Bp* **I** C CHARLTON *p-in-c*.
BENTLEY, GREAT (St Mary Virg), *Essex*. R. **D** Chelmsf 28 **P** *Bp* **I** C D BOULTON *p-in-c*.
BENTLEY, NEW (St Phil and St jas), *S Yorks*.. **D** Sheff 8 **P** *Bp* **I** (Vacant).
BENTON, LONG (St Bart), *T & W*. V. **D** Newc T 5a **P** *Ball Coll Ox* **I** R W GOUNDRY, H PRIESTNER *c*.
(St Mary Magd), V. **D** Newc T 5a **P** *Ball Coll Ox* **I** B A MCKAY.
BENTWORTH (St Mary) and Shalden (St Pet and St Paul) and Lasham (St Mary), *Hants*. R Paul) and Lasham (St Mary), *Hants*. R. **D** Win 1 **P** *Mrs M Cazalet, G S Baker Esq and J L Jervoise Esq* **I** (Vacant).
BENWELL, *T & W*.. **D** Newc T 5b *See* Newcastle upon Tyne.
BENWICK (St Mary Virg), *Cambs*. R. **D** Ely 19 **P** *Mrs F Hurliman and Bp (in turn)* **I** J C HARRINGTON.
BEOLEY (St Leon), *Worcs*. V. **D** Worc 7 **P** *Trustees* **I** J E COOK *p-in-c*, J W PEARSON *c*.
BEPTON (St Mary), *W Sussex*. R. **D** Chich 5 *See* Cocking.
BERDEN (St Nich), *Essex*. V. **D** Chelmsf 26 *See* Manuden.
BERECHURCH (St Marg w St Mich), *Essex*.. **D** Chelmsf 21 **P** *Bp* **I** C J A HARVEY.
BERE-FERRERS (St Andr) w Bere-Alston (H Trin), *Devon*. R. **D** Ex 22 **P** *Dioc Bd of Patr* **I** J H HEATH.
BERE REGIS (St Jo Bapt) and Affpuddle w Turners Puddle, *Dorset*. V. **D** Sarum 10 **P** *Ball Coll Ox 2 turns, Bp 1 turn* **I** D W SHAW.
BERGH APTON (St Pet w St Paul) w Yelverton (St Mary Virg), *Norf*. R. **D** Nor 14 **P** *J H G Thursby Esq and Ld Chan* alt **I** (Vacant).
BERGHOLT, EAST (St Mary Virg), *Suff*. R. **D** St E 5 **P** *Em Coll Cam* **I** P CRAWFORD.
BERGHOLT, WEST, *Essex*. R. **D** Chelmsf 22 **P** *Bp* **I** D R E COOK.
BERINSFIELD (St Mary and St Berin), *Oxon*.. **D** Ox 5 *See* Dorchester.
BERKELEY (St Mary Virg) w Wick, Breadstone and Newport, *Glos*. V. **D** Glouc 5 **P** *Exors of Ld Berkeley* **I** N R LIFTON, J L JUDD *c*.
BERKHAMSTED, *Herts*.. **D** St Alb 3 *See* Northchurch.
BERKHAMSTED, GREAT (St Pet) w (All SS), *Herts*. R. **D** St Alb 3 **P** *Ld Brownlow* **I** H R DAVIS, R J METIVIER *c*, B G SAUNDERS *c*.
BERKHAMSTED, LITTLE (St Andr) w Bayford, Essendon and Ponsbourne, *Herts*. R. **D** St Alb 8 **P** *Marq of Salisbury 2 turns, Bp 1 turn, CPAS 1 turn* **I** J ANDREWS, J H B COTTON *c*.
BERKLEY (St Mary Virg) w Rodden, *Somt*. R. **D** B & W 16a *See* Beckington.
BERKSWELL (St Jo Bapt), *W Midl*. R. **D** Cov 4 **P** *Trustees* **I** G P W DINGLE.
BERKSWICH, or BASWICH (H Trin), w Walton (St Thos), *Staffs*. V. **D** Lich **P** *Bp* **I** M N GRIFFIN.
BERMONDSEY (St Mary Magd w St Olave, St John and St Luke), *Surrey*. R. **D** S'wark 2 **P** *CPS Ld Chan and Bp* **I** T G A WOODERSON, J E SMITH *c*.
(St Anne), V. **D** S'wark 2 **P** *Trustees* **I** (Vacant).
(St Crispin w Ch Ch), V. **D** S'wark 2 **P** *Hyndman Trustees* **I** P GRAY.
(St Jas w Ch Ch Parker's Row), V. **D** S'wark 2 **P** *Crown, Bp, and R of Bermondsey* **I** H L WHYTE, G R P ASHENDEN *c*.
SOUTH (St Aug of Hippo), V. **D** S'wark 2 **P** *Bp* **I** P E H GOLDING.
(St Bart), V. **D** S'wark 2 **P** *Bp* **I** G E NEELY.
BERNERS RODING, *Essex*.. **D** Chelmsf 11 *See* Ld Chan.
BERRICK SALOME (St Helen), *Oxon*.. **D** Ox 5 *See* Chalgrove.
BERRINGTON (All SS) w Betton Strange, *Salop*. R. **D** Heref 11 **P** *Dioc Bd of Patr* **I** D E HOWARD *p-in-c*.
BERROW (BVM) and Breane (St Bridget), *Somt*. R. **D** B & W 2 **P** *Archd of Wells* **I** W S J KEMM.
BERROW (St Faith) w Pendock (Dedic unknown) and Eldersfield, *Worcs*. V. **D** Worc 5 **P** *Bp 2 turns, D and C of Worc 1 turn* **I** N J DAVIS.
BERRYNARBOR (St Pet), *Devon*. R. **D** Ex *See* Combe Martin.
BERRY POMEROY (St Mary), *Devon*.. **D** Ex *See* Broadhempston.
BERSTED, SOUTH (St Mary Magd) w Bersted, North (H Cross), *W Sussex*. V. **D** Chich 1 **P** *Abp of Cant* **I** H G PRUEN, G A TOOLEY *c*.
BERWICK (St Mich AA) w Selmeston and Alciston, *E Sussex*. R. **D** Chich 15 **P** *Mrs M J Newson and D and C of Chich (alt)* **I** V W HOUSE.
BERWICK (St Jas), *Wilts*. V. **D** Sarum 21 *See* Stapleford.
(St Jo Bapt), *Wilts*. R. **D** Sarum 19 **P** *Dioc Bd of Patr* **I** A STOTT.
BERWICK BASSETT, *Wilts*.. **D** Sarum 26 *See* Avebury.
BERWICK ST LEONARD, *Wilts*.. **D** Sarum 19 *See* Fonthill-Bp.
BERWICK, LITTLE, *Salop*. Chap. **D** Lich 26 **P** *Mrs R Angell-James* **I** (Vacant).
BERWICK-ON-TWEED (H Trin), *Northumb*. V. **D** Newc T 11 **P** *Bp* **I** J K NEWSOME *c*.
(St Mary), V. **D** Newc T 11 **P** *D and C of Dur* **I** (Vacant).
BESFORD (St Pet), *Worcs*.. **D** Worc 3 *See* Defford.
BESSELSLEIGH (St Lawr) w Dry Sandford (St Helen) and Cothill, *Oxon*. R. **D** Ox 11 **P** *Trustees 2 turns, Bp 1 turn* **I** J S REYNOLDS.
BESSINGBY (St Magnus), *Humb*. V. **D** York 12 **P** *Reps of G Wright Esq* **I** A M WHAWELL *p-in-c*.
BESSINGHAM (St Mary), *Norf*.. **D** Nor *See* Aldborough.
BESTHORPE (All SS), *Norf*. V. **D** Nor *See* Attleborough.
BESTHORPE (H Trin), *Notts*.. **D** Southw 3 *See* Scarle, South.
BESTWOOD (St Matt), *Notts*. V. **D** Southw 12 **P** *Bp* **I** J E M K NEALE.

BILLINGBOROUGH (St Andr), *Lincs*. V. **D** Linc 13 **P** *Crown* **I** H J THEODOSIUS.
BILLINGE (St Aid), *mer*. V. **D** Liv 12 **P** *R of Wigan* **I** D LYON.
BILLINGFORD (St Pet), *Norf.*. **D** Nor 20 *See* Elmham, North.
BILLINGFORD (St Leon), *Norf.* R. **D** Nor 17 *See* Scole.
BILLINGHAM (St Cuthb), *Cleve*. V. **D** Dur 14 **P** *D and C of Dur* **I** R CORKER.
(St Aid), V. **D** Dur 14 **P** *Dioc Bd of Patr* **I** P T HIRST, M G BISHOP *team v*, J D MILLER *team v*.
BILLINGHAY (St Mich) w Walcot (St Osw) and Dogdyke, *Lincs*. V. **D** Linc 22 **P** *Earl Fitzwilliam* **I** T G WILLIAMSON.
BILLINGSHURST (St Mary), *W Sussex*. V. **D** Chich 4 **P** *Bp* **I** D E E TANSILL, J P HURD *c*.
BILLINGSLEY (St Mary) w Sidbury (H Trin), *Salop*. R. **D** Heref 9 **P** *Bp* **I** R E F DORE.
BILLINGTON (St Mich AA), *Beds*. R. **D** St Alb *See* Leighton-Buzzard.
BILLOCKBY, *Norf.*. **D** Nor 2 *See* Rollesby.
BILNEY, EAST, *Norf.* R. **D** Nor 20 *See* Beetley.
BILNEY, WEST, *Norf.*. **D** Nor *See* Pentney.
BILSBORROW (St Hilda), *Lancs*. V. **D** Blackb 10 **P** *V of St Michael's-on-Wyre* **I** A WHITTAKER.
BILSBY (H Trin) w Farlesthorpe (St Andr), *Lincs*. V. **D** Linc 8 **P** *Bp and G A Fletcher Esq* alt **I** G I GEORGE-JONES.
BILSDALE (St Hilda), *N Yorks*. V. **D** York *See* Ingleby Greenhow.
BILSDALE or BILSDALE MIDCABLE (St Jo Div), *N Yorks*. V. **D** York *See* Upper Ryedale.
BILSINGTON (St Pet and St Paul), *Kent*.. **D** Cant 12 *See* Bonnington.
BILSTHORPE (St Marg), *Notts*. R. **D** Southw 15 **P** *Dioc Bd of Patr* **I** W G CALTHROP-OWEN.
BILSTON (St Leon w St Mary and St Chad), *W Midl*, R. **D** Lich **P** *Dioc Bd of Patr* **I** P J CHAPMAN, M GODFREY *team v*, J A GUTTRIDGE *team v*, D J WISEMAN *c*.
BILTON (St Mark), *Warws*. R. **D** Cov 6 **P** *N Assheton Esq* **I** D K CALLARD, A J HOBSON *c*.
BILTON (St Jo Evang), *N Yorks*. V. **D** Ripon 4 **P** *Bp* **I** D W TORDOFF.
BILTON (St Helen) w Bickerton, *N Yorks*.. **D** York 2 *See* Tockwith.
BILTON-IN-HOLDERNESS (St Magd or St Pet), *N Yorks*. V. **D** York 15 **P** *Abp* **I** R HUNTER.
BILTON, NEW (St Osw K and Mart), *Warws*. V. **D** Cov 6 **P** *Dioc Trustees* **I** M BARNSLEY.
BINBROOK (St Mary w St Gabr), *Lincs*. R. **D** Linc 10 **P** *Ld Chan* **I** R J CROOKES.
BINCOMBE (H Trin) w Broadwey (St Nich) Upwey and Buckland-Ripers *Dorset*. R. **D** Sarum 6 **P** *G and C Coll Cam 2 turns, M B F Frampton 1 turn and Bp 1 turn* **I** A S B FREER.
BINDERTON (St Andr), *W Sussex*.. **D** Chich 8 *See* Dean, West.
BINEGAR (H Trin), *Somt*. R. **D** B & W 6 *See* Ashwick.
BINFIELD (All SS w St Mark), *Berks*. R. **D** Ox 11a **P** *Ld Chan* **I** G M NEWMAN *c*.
BINGFIELD (St Mary), *Northumb*. V. **D** Newc T 4 *See* St Oswald-in-Lee.
BINGHAM (All SS), *Notts*. R. **D** Southw 9 **P** *Crown* **I** (Vacant).
BINGLEY (All SS), *W Yorks*. R. **D** Bradf **P** *Bp* **I** M W BULL, R C WALLACE *team v*, P J BRINDLE *hon c*.
(H Trin), V. **D** Bradf 1 **P** *Bp* **I** J A HOLFORD.
(St Sav Harden) w (St Matt Wilsden), V. **D** Bradf 11 **P** *Bp, V of Bradf Archd of Bradf and V of Bingley* **I** (Vacant).
BINHAM (St Mary), *Norf.* V. **D** Nor 24 *See* Hindringham.
BINLEY (St Bart) w Coombe Fields, *W Midl*. V. **D** Cov 1 **P** *Bp* **I** E W JONES, D T PETTIFOR *c*.
BINSEY Oxon. V **D** Ox *See* Oxford, St Frideswide.
BINSTEAD (H Cross), *Isle of Wight*. R. **D** Portsm 6 **P** *Bp* **I** VEN F C CARPENTER P-IN-C.
BINSTED (St Mary), *W Sussex*.. **D** Chich *See* Walberton.
BINSTED (H Cross), *Hants*.. **D** Win *See* Bentley.
BINTON (St Pet), *Warws*. R. **D** Cov 7 *See* Temple Grafton.
BINTRY (or Bintree) (St Swith) w Themelthorpe (St Andr), *Norf.* R. **D** Nor 6 *See* Twyford.
BIRCH, GREAT (St Agnes), w Little Birch and Layer Breton (St Mary Virg), *Essex*. R. **D** Chelmsf 21 **P** *Bp 2 turns Trustees of J G Round 1 turn* **I** G ARMSTRONG.
BIRCH, MUCH (St Mary w St Thos à Becket) w Birch, Little (St Mary), Dewchurch, Much (St D), Llanwarne and Llandinabo, *Herefs*. R. **D** Heref 4 **P** *W A Twiston Davies Esq 1st turn, Bp 2nd, 4th and 5th turns, Ld Chan 3rd turn*. **I** P G NEWBY, F MORLEY *c*.
BIRCH-IN-HOPWOOD (St Mary), *Gtr Man*. V. **D** Man 17 **P** *R of Middleton* **I** E GREENHALGH.
BIRCH-IN-RUSHOLME (St Jas) w Fallowfield (H Innoc), *Gtr Man*. R. **D** Man 5 **P** *Bp* **I** W G WILSON, N D HAWLEY *c*.
(St Agnes), R. **D** Man 4 **P** *Bp* **I** H W MAYOR.
BIRCHAM, GREAT (St Mary Virg) w Bircham Newton (All SS) and Bircham Tofts (St Andr), *Norf.* R. **D** Nor 23 **P** *Miss A C Henderson, J A Henderson Esq, and Mrs H U Bateman (jointly) and HM The Queen* alt **I** R J HAMMOND *p-in-c*.
BIRCHANGER (St Mary Virg), *Essex*. R. **D** Chelmsf 26 **P** *New Coll Ox* **I** T G EVANS-PUGHE.
BIRCHENCLIFFE (St Phil Ap), *W Yorks*. V. **D** Wakef 4 **P** *V of Lindley* **I** A GRIFFITHS.
BIRCHES HEAD (St Matt), *Staffs*.. **D** Lich *See* Hanley, H Evang.
BIRCHFIELD (H Trin) w Witton, *W Midl*. V. **D** Birm 3 **P** *Bp* **I** B THORLEY.
BIRCHINGTON (All SS) w Acol (St Mildred), *Kent*. V. **D** Cant 9 **P** *Abp* **I** W A D COLLINS.
BIRCHOVER (or Rowtor) (Ch of Jes), *Derbys*.. **D** Derby 9 *See* Stanton-in-Peak.
BIRCHWOOD (St Luke), *Lincs*. V. **D** Linc 15 **P** *Bp* **I** T R STOKES.
BIRCLE (St Jo Bapt), *Lancs*.. **D** Man 12 *See* Birtle.
BIRDBROOK (St Aug of Cant) w Sturmer (St Mary), *Essex*. R. **D** Chelmsf 18 *See* Ridgewell.
BIRDHAM (St Jas) w Itchenor W (St Nich), *W Sussex*. R. **D** Chich 3 **P** *Bp* **I** K WOOLHOUSE *p-in-c*.
BIRDINGBURY or BIRBURY (St Leon), *Warws*. R. **D** Cov *See* Leamington Hastings.
BIRDSALL, *N Yorks*.. **D** York 3 *See* Langton.
BIRKBY, *W Yorks*.. **D** Wakef 4 *See* Huddersfield.
BIRKBY N Yorks. R **D** Ripon 1 *See* Great Smeaton.
BIRKDALE (St Pet), *Mer*. V. **D** Liv 8 **P** *Trustees* **I** A DAWSON.
(St Jas), V. **D** Liv 8 **P** *Trustees* **I** D D ROBERTS.
(St John), V. **D** Liv 8 **P** *Trustees* **I** J W C HARDING, M BUCKLEY *c*.
BIRKENHEAD (St Mary w St Paul), *Chesh*. V. **D** Ches 1 **P** *Simeon Trustees* **I** (Vacant).
BIRKENHEAD (St Jas w St Bede), *Merseyside*. V. **D** Ches 1 **P** *Trustees* **I** C G DICKENSON, J A HESKETH *c*.
(St Winifred Welsh Ch), I. **D** Ches 1 **P** *Bp* **I** D T P EVANS *c-in-c*.
See also CLAUGHTON.
BIRKENHEAD PRIORY (St Anne, St Mark, St Pet w St Matt), *Merseyside*. R. **D** Ches 1 **P** *Dioc Bd of Patr* **I** G V M ROBINSON, C F PICKSTONE *c*, B E STATHAM *c*, A SYKES *c*.
BIRKENSHAW (St Paul) w Hunsworth, *W Yorks*. V. **D** Wakef 9 **P** *V of Birstall* **I** C D E CLARKE.
BIRKIN (St Mary) w Haddlesey (St Jo Bapt), *N Yorks*. R. **D** York 8 **P** *Simeon Trustees* **I** A G GREENHOUGH.
BIRLEY (St Pet), *Herefs*. V. **D** Heref 7 *See* King's Pyon.
BIRLING (All SS), *Kent*. V. **D** Roch 6 *See* Ryarsh.
LOWER (Ch Ch), V. **D** Roch 1 *See* Snodland.
BIRLINGHAM (St Jas the Great), *Worcs*.. **D** Worc 3 *See* Pershore.
BIRMINGHAM (St Martin) w Deritend (St John w St Basil), *W Midl*. R. **D** Birm 1 **P** *Trustees* **I** A P HALL, C L ALLEN *c*, K G GALE *c*, J S LAWRENCE *c*, R C MACFARLANE *hon c*.
(All SS), R. **D** Birm 1 *See* Bp Latimer Ch.
(Bp Latimer Ch w All SS and St Chrys), V. **D** Birm 1 **P** *Trustees* **I** R F BASHFORD.
(Ch Ch Summerfield), V. **D** Birm 2 **P** *R of Birm* **I** J B KNIGHT, H K SYMES-THOMPSON *c*.
(St Bonif), V. **D** Birm 2 **P** *Bp* **I** C A G KERR.
(St Chrys), V. **D** Birm 1 *See* Bp Latimer Ch.
(St Edm Tyseley), V. **D** Birm 8 **P** *Crown* **I** C P COPELAND.
(St Geo), R. **D** Birm 1 **P** *Trustees* **I** E C RUDDOCK, D J COLLYER *hon c*.
(St Jo Evang Ladywood), V. **D** Birm 1 **P** *R of Birm* **I** N S POWER.
(St Jude), V. **D** Birm 1 **P** *Crown and Bp* alt **I** (Vacant).
(St Luke w St Thos and Immanuel), V. **D** Birm 1 **P** *Trustees* **I** J D PHILPOTT, B J NASH *c*.
(St Paul), V. **D** Birm 1 **P** *Trustees* **I** R S O STEVENS.
(St Pet), V. **D** Birm 1 **P** *Bp* **I** R BENNETT *p-in-c*, H R M OAKLEY *c*.
(St Phil Cathl Ch), R. **D** Birm 1 **P** *Bp* **I** D R MACINNES *min*.
See also ASTON, BORDESLEY, CASTLE BROMWICH, DERITEND, DUDDESTON, EDGBASTON, ERDINGTON, KING'S HEATH, LOZELLS, NECHELLS, SALTLEY, SMALL HEATH, SPARKBROOK, WARD END, AND WATER ORTON..

(St Andr Livesey), V. **D** Blackb 5 **P** *Trustees* **I** B ROBINSON.
(St Barn) V. **D** Blackb 2 **P** *Bp* **I** H H DANIEL *p-in-c.*
(St Bart Ewood), V. **D** Blackb 5 **P** *Bp* **I** (Vacant).
(St Gabr), V. **D** Blackb 2 **P** *Bp* **I** A SIDDALL.
(St Jas) V. **D** Blackb 2 **P** *Bp* **I** R BRAITHWAITE, G WEMYSS *c.*
(St Luke w St Phil), V. **D** Blackb 2 **P** *Bp* **I** B T JONES.
(St Mich AA w St Jo Evang and H Trin), V. **D** Blackb 2 **P** *V of Blackb* **I** C J SHIPLEY, S P BALLARD *c.*
(St Pet w All SS), V. **D** Blackb 2 **P** *V of Blackb* **I** (Vacant).
(St Silas), V. **D** Blackb 2 **P** *Five Trustees* **I** T J F HEIGHWAY.
(St Steph), V. **D** Blackb 2 **P** *Five Trustees* **I** J W DIXON, A C TAYLOR *c.*
(St Thos w St Jude), V. **D** Blackb 2 **P** *Bp and Trustees (Alt)* **I** R MASHEDER.
BLACKDOWN (H Trin), *Dorset.*. **D** Sarum 4 *See* Broadwindsor.
BLACKFORD (St Jo Bapt) *Cumb.* V. **D** Carl 2 *See* Rockliffe.
BLACKFORD (St Mich), *Somt.* R. **D** B & W 4 *See* Compton Pauncefoot.
BLACKFORD (H Trin), *Somt.*. **D** B & W *See* Wedmore.
BLACKFORDBY (St Marg), *Leics.* V. **D** Leic 12 **P** *Bp* **I** A D MACEWAN.
BLACKHALL (St Andr), *Durham.* V. **D** Dur 3 **P** *Bp* **I** C V COLE.
BLACKHEATH (St Paul), *W Midl.* V. **D** Birm 6 **P** *Bp* **I** J N WARNE, W R GOING *c.*
BLACKHEATH (All SS), *Kent.* V. **D** S'wark 20 **P** *V of Lewisham* **I** R E PARSONS *hon c.*
(St Jo Evang), V. **D** S'wark 17 **P** *CPAS* **I** M R KELSEY, D M WHYTE *hon c.*
(The Ascen), V. **D** S'wark 20 **P** *V of Lewisham* **I** E R NEWNHAM *c.*
PARK (St Mich AA) V. **D** S'wark 17 **P** *John Cator Esq* **I** D H F SHIRESS, A SCOTT *c.*
BLACKHEATH (St Martin) w Chilworth (St Thos), *Surrey.* V. **D** Guildf 5 **P** *Bp* **I** GIBBONS *p-in-c.*
BLACKHILL (St Aid), *Durham.* V. **D** Dur 7 **P** *Bp* **I** T M RHODES.
BLACKLAND (St Pet), *Dorset.*. **D** Sarum *See* Calne.
BLACKLEY (St Andr), *Gtr Man.* R. **D** Man 7 **P** *Bp* **I** D J ERRIDGE, D C R WIDDOWS *c.*
(St Mark, White Moss), V. **D** Man **P** *D and C of Man* **I** M R J WILLIAMS.
(St Paul), R. **D** Man 7 **P** *Crown and Bp* alt **I** T S R CHOW.
(St Pet), R. **D** Man 7 **P** *D and C of Man* **I** L S J R AITKEN.
(H Trin) R. **D** Man 7 **P** *Crown and Bp* alt **I** N M E CLAPP.
BLACKMANSTONE, *Kent.*. **D** Cant 13 *See* Dymchurch.
BLACKMOOR (St Matt), *Hants.* V. **D** Portsm 4 **P** *Earl of Selborne* **I** R J INKPEN, J O CHERRILL *c.*
BLACKMORE (St Lawr) and Stondon Massey, *Essex.* V. **D** Chelmsf 6 **P** *Bp* **I** M H KNOTT.
BLACKPOOL (St Jo Evang), *Lancs.* V. **D** Blackb 8 **P** *Trustees* **I** R IMPEY, R W E AWRE *c*, R NICHOLSON *c.*
(Ch Ch w All SS), V. **D** Blackb 8 **P** *Bp and Trustees* **I** P GASCOIGNE.
(H Cross, South Shore, Eccles Distr). **D** Blackb 8 **P** *Bp* **I** W N DAWSON.
(H Trin South Shore), V. **D** Blackb 8 **P** *H de Vere Clifton Esq* **I** S J FINCH, A PARKINSON *c.*
(St Mark, Layton), V. **D** Blackb 8 **P** *CPAS* **I** J J PAISLEY.
(St Mary's Eccles Distr). **D** Blackb 8 **P** *Bp* **I** I HOLLIN.
(St Mich AA), V. **D** Blackb 8 **P** *Bp* **I** W B GORNALL.
(St Nich Marton Moss), V. **D** Blackb **P** *Bp* **I** J F LEONARD.
(St Paul), V. **D** Blackb 8 **P** *Trustees* **I** D I G DAVIES.
(St Pet), V. **D** Blackb 8 **P** *Trustees* **I** C HOOLE.
(St Steph), V. **D** Blackb 8 **P** *Trustees* **I** A D AINSLEY, J M DIXON *c*, G G FIELD *c*, M J HARMAN *c*, E K SILLIS *c*, D B FOSS *hon c.*
(St Thos), V. **D** Blackb 8 **P** *CPAS* **I** J A SLATER, P YORKSTONE *c.*
(St Wilfrid, Mereside), V. **D** Blackb 8 **P** *Bp* **I** J S MCDONALD.
BLACKROD (St Cath), *Gtr Man.* V. **D** Man 13 **P** *V of Bolton* **I** P F DAVEY.
BLACKTOFT (H Trin), *Cumb.* V. **D** York 16 *See* Laxton.
BLACK TORRINGTON (St Mary) Bradford and Thornbury, *Devon.* R. **D** Ex 9 **P** *Dioc Bd of Patr 2 turns, Trustees 1 turn* **I** G L MATTHEWS *p-in-c.*
BLACKWALL **D** Lon 7 *See* Poplar.
BLACKWATER, *Hants.*. **D** Guildf 1 *See* Hawley.
BLACKWELL (St Werburgh), *Derbys.* V. **D** Derby 1 **P** *Bp* **I** H STOPPARD.
BLADON, *Oxon.*. **D** Ox 10 *See* Woodstock.
BLAGDON (St Andr) w Charterhouse-on-Mendip (St Hugh), *Somt.* V. **D** B & W **P** *Sir John Wills Bt* **I** E P NEEP.
BLAISDON (St Mich) *Glos.* R. **D** Glouc 6 *See* Westbury-on-Severn.
BLAKEDOWN (St Jas Gt), *Worcs.*. **D** Worc 10 *See* Churchill-in-Halfshire.
BLAKEMERE (St Leon), *Herefs.*. **D** Heref *See* Moccas.
BLAKENALL HEATH (Ch Ch), *W Midl.* R. **D** Lich 9 **P** *Patr Bd* **I** D A SMITH, R H W ARGUILE *team v*, W E WARD *team v*, R A SWALLOW *c.*
BLAKENEY (All SS), *Glos.* V. **D** Glouc 6 *See* Awre.
BLAKENEY w Little Langham, *Norf.* R (*in Blakeney Group - See Bishop's Langham and Stiffkey*).. **D** Nor 24 **P** *Brig Sir R H Anstruther-Gough-Calthorpe* **I** D P MAURICE, G R WOOD *hon c.*
BLAKENHAM, GREAT (St Mary) w Blakenham, Little w Baylham (St Pet) and Nettlestead, *Suff.* R. **D** St E 1 **P** *Bp 2 turns, Mart Mem Trust 1 turn* **I** R S EXCELL.
BLAKESLEY (St Mary) w Adstone, *Northants.* V. **D** Pet 2 **P** *Hertf Coll Ox and Sons of the Clergy Corp* alt. **I** A J MILLYARD.
BLANCHLAND (St Mary Virg Abbey Ch) w Hunstanworth, *Northumb.* V. **D** Newc T 3 **P** *Ld Crewe Trustees 1 turn, W Parlour Esq 2 turns* **I** P C ROBSON *p-in-c.*
BLANDFORD-FORUM (St Pet and St Paul) and Langton Long w Blandford St Mary, *Dorset.* R. **D** Sarum 10 **P** *Bp 3 turns, Worc Coll Ox 1 turn* **I** R A BABINGTON, V FLETCHER *hon c.*
BLANDFORD ST MARY (St Mary), *Dorset.* R. **D** Sarum 10 *See* Blandford Forum.
BLANKNEY (St Osw), *Lincs.* R. **D** Linc 18 **P** *Bp* **I** (Vacant).
BLASTON (St Giles w St Mich), *Leics.*. **D** Leic 5 *See* Medbourne.
BLATCHINGTON, EAST (St Pet), *E Sussex.* R. **D** Chich **P** *Bp* **I** E C ANDREWS.
BLATCHINGTON, WEST (St Pet), *E Sussex.* R. **D** Chich 13 **P** *Bp* **I** T W THOMAS.
BLATHERWYCKE w Laxton (All SS), *Northants.*. **D** Pet 13 *See* Bulwick.
BLAWITH (St Jo Bapt) w Lowick (St Luke), *Cumb.* V. **D** Carl 15 **P** *J H Mather Esq and Mart Mem Trust* alt **I** J T HOCKING.
BLAXHALL w Stratford (St Andr) and Farnham, *Suff.* R. **D** St E 19 *See* Glemham.
BLAYDON-ON-TYNE, *T & W.*. **D** Dur 1 *See* Stella.
BLEADON (St Pet and St Paul), *Somt.* R. **D** B & W 3 **P** *Guild of All S* **I** D W SCHOLER *p-in-c.*
BLEAN (St Cosmos and St Damian), *Kent.* V. **D** Cant 3 **P** *Master of Eastbridge Hosp* **I** R R MAXWELL.
BLEASBY (St Mary Virg) w Halloughton (St Jas), *Notts.* V. **D** Southw 15 **P** *Ld Chan* **I** B HILL *c-in-c.*
BLEASDALE (St Eadnor), *Lancs.*. **D** Blackb 7 *See* Admarsh-in-Bleasdale.
BLETCHINGLEY, *Surrey.*. **D** S'wark *See* Bletchingley.
BLEDINGTON (St Leon), *Glos.*. **D** Glouc *See* Westcote.
BLEDLOW (H Trin) w Saunderton and Horsenden (St Mich AA), *Bucks.* R. **D** Ox 21 **P** *Ld Carrington* **I** T H D EDWARDS.
BLEDLOW RIDGE (St Paul), *Bucks.*. **D** Ox 32 *See* Wycombe, W..
BLENDWORTH (H Trin) w Chalton (St Mich) and Idsworth (St Hubert), *Hants.* R. **D** Portsm 3 **P** *L S White Esq* **I** (Vacant).
BLETCHINGDON (St Giles), *Oxon.* R. **D** Ox 2 **P** *Qu Coll Ox* **I** (Vacant).
BLETCHINGLEY, or Blechingley, (St Mary Virg), *Surrey.* R. **D** S'wark 10 **P** *Em Coll Cam* **I** J B M FREDERICK.
BLETCHLEY (St Mary), *Bucks.* R. **D** Ox 26 **P** *M Bennit Esq* **I** I J PUSEY *p-in-c*, M C STANTON-SARINGER *c.*
NORTH (Conv Dist).. **D** Ox 26 **P** *Bp* **I** R C THORP *missr.*
BLETSOE Beds. R **D** St Alb 21 *See* Riseley.
BLEWBURY (St Mich AA), *Berks.* V. **D** Ox 18 **P** *Bp* **I** H J PICKLES.
BLICKLING (St Andr) w Ingworth (St Laur), *Norf.* R (*See Cawston Group*).. **D** Nor 3 **P** *Bp* **I** R R DOMMETT *p-in-c.*
BLIDWORTH (St Mary of the Purification and St Lawr), *Notts.* V. **D** Southw 2 **P** *Ld Chan* **I** C SAWYER.
BLINDLEY HEATH (St Jo Evang), *Surrey.* V. **D** S'wark 10 **P** *R of Godstone* **I** H G C CLARKE.
BLISLAND (St Protus and St Hyacinth) w St Breward, *Cornw.* R. **D** Truro 8 **P** *SMT and D and C of Truro* alt **I** C R SARGISSON *p-in-c.*
BLISWORTH (St Jo Bapt), *Northants.* R. **D** Pet 2 **P** *Mart Mem Trust* **I** H BUNKER.
BLITHFIELD (St Leon), *Staffs.* R. **D** Lich 4 **P** *Ld Bagot* **I** R T WILCOX *p-in-c.*
BLOCKLEY (St Pet and St Paul) w Aston Magna (St Jo Evang), *Glos.* V. **D** Glouc 12 **P** *Ld Dulverton and V of Bromsgrove* alt **I** M W NORTHALL.
BLOFIELD (St Andr) w Hemblington (All SS), *Norf.* R. **D** Nor 1 **P** *G and C Coll Cam* **I** A G BAKER.

BONGATE or APPLEBY (St Mich), *Cumb.*. **D** Carl 1 *See* Appleby.
BONINGALE (St Chad), *Salop.* V. **D** Lich 25 **P** *Mart Mem Trust* **I** W J TURNER.
BONNINGTON (St Rumwold) w Bilsington (St Pet and St Paul), *Kent.* R. **D** Cant *See* Aldington.
BONSALL (St Jas Ap), *Derbys.* R. **D** Derby 17 **P** *Bp* **I** H J LOWNDS.
BOOKHAM, GREAT (St Nich), *Surrey.* R. **D** Guildf 10 **P** *Bp* **I** A C WARNER, N CORNELL *c.*
BOOKHAM, LITTLE, *Surrey.*. **D** Guildf *See* Effingham.
BOOSBECK w Moorsholm (St Aid), *Cleve.* V. **D** York 19 **P** *Abp* **I** K A SWINSON.
BOOTHBY GRAFFOE (St Andr), *Lincs.*. **D** Linc *See* Graffoe.
BOOTHBY-PAGNELL (St Andr), *Lincs.* R. **D** Linc *See* Ingoldsby.
BOOTLE (St Mich AA), Corney (St Jo Bapt), Whicham and Whitbeck, *Cumb.* R. **D** Carl 12 **P** *Earl of Lonsdale* **I** I F BLACK.
BOOTLE (Ch Ch), *Mer.* V. **D** Liv 1 **P** *Bp* **I** R W E MILLINGTON.
(St Leon), V. **D** Liv 1 **P** *Trustees* **I** (Vacant).
(St Matt), V. **D** Liv 1 **P** *Bp* **I** R W STEPHENS, G E GREENWOOD *c.*
(SS Mary w Paul), V. **D** Liv 1 **P** *Bp and Trustees* **I** A HETHERINGTON.
BOOTON (St Mich AA) w Brandiston (St Nich), *Norf.* R. **D** Nor 6 **P** *F P Elwin's Exors and Dioc Bd of Patr (alt)* **I** F G COATES *c-in-c.*
BORASTON, *Salop.*. **D** Heref 12 *See* Burford.
BORDEN (St Pet and St Paul), *Kent.* V. **D** Cant 14 **P** *S for the Maint of Faith* **I** J R DAVIS.
BORDESLEY (St Andr), *W Midl.* V. **D** Birm 8 **P** *Bp and Trustees* alt **I** J HIGGINS.
(St Alb Mart w St Patr), V. **D** Birm 8 **P** *Keble Coll Ox* **I** D H HUTT, B M DUTSON *c.*
(St Benedict), V. **D** Birm 13 **P** *Keble Coll Ox* **I** S J PIMLOTT, D P BAZEN *hon c.*
(St Osw of Worc), V. **D** Birm 8 **P** *Bp and Trustees* alt **I** (Vacant).
(St Patr), V. **D** Birm 8 *See* St Alb.
BORDESLEY GREEN (St Paul), *W Midl.* V. **D** Birm 13 **P** *Crown* **I** (Vacant).
BOREHAM (St Andr), *Essex.* V. **D** Chelmsf 12 **P** *Bp* **I** W J T SMITH.
BOREHAM, *Wilts.*. **D** Sarum *See* Bishopstrow.
BOREHAM WOOD (All SS and St Mich and AA), *Herts.* R. **D** St Alb 1 **P** *Bp* **I** M J CROW, N J ELDER *team v,* K B JONES *team v,* T P LEWIS *team v.*
BORLEY, *Essex.* R. **D** Chelmsf 18 *See* Foxearth.
BOROUGH FEN, *Cambs.* V. **D** Pet 18 *See* Newborough.
BOROUGH GREEN (Good Shepherd), *Kent.* V. **D** Roch 8 **P** *Bp* **I** J G K BATSON.
BOROUGHBRIDGE (St Mich), *Somt.* V. **D** B & W 19 *See* Burrowbridge.
BOROUGHBRIDGE (St Jas) w Roecliffe (St Mary Virg), *N Yorks.* V. **D** Ripon 3 *See* Aldborough.
BORROWDALE w Grange, *Cumb.* V. **D** Carl 10 **P** *V of Crosthwaite* **I** R C JOHNS *p-in-c.*
BORSTAL, *Kent.*. **D** Roch *See* Rochester.
BOSBURY (H Trin), *Herefs.* V. **D** Heref 6 **P** *Bp* **I** M H CROSS *p-in-c.*
BOSCASTLE **D** Truro 12 *See* Davidstow.
BOSCOMBE, *Dorset.*. **D** Win 7 *See* Bournemouth.
BOSCOMBE (St Andr), *Wilts.* R. **D** Sarum 17 *See* Bournemouth.
BOSHAM (H Trin), *W Sussex.* V. **D** Chich 8 **P** *Bp* **I** W D MARSDEN-JONES.
BOSLEY (St Mary Virg) w N Rode (St Mich), *Chesh.* V. **D** Ches 13 **P** *V of Prestbury and Bp* **I** F N KEEN.
BOSSALL (St Botolph) w Buttercrambe (St John) and Howsham (St Jo Evang) *N Yorks.*. **D** York 4 *See* Sand Hutton.
BOSSINGTON (St Jas), *Hants.*. **D** Win 10 *See* Broughton.
BOSTON (St Botolph w St Jas), *Lincs.* V. **D** Linc 20 **P** *Bp* **I** T COLLINS, R J ANNIS *lect,* K A ALMOND *c,* J D DUCKETT *c.*
BOSTON SPA (St Mary Virg), *W Yorks.* V. **D** York 9 **P** *Ch Ch Ox* **I** R M C SEED.
BOTESDALE (St Mary), *Suff.*. **D** St E 16 *See* Redgrave.
BOTHAL (St Andr), *Northumb.* R. **D** Newc T 10 **P** *Duke of Northumberland* **I** J A PYLE.
BOTHAMSALL, *Notts.*. **D** Southw *See* Elkesley.
BOTHENHAMPTON, or BAUNTON (H Trin) w Walditch (St Mary w Ch Ch), *Dorset.* V. **D** Sarum *See* Bridport.
BOTLEY (All SS), *Hants.* R. **D** Portsm 2 **P** *Bp* **I** C W WHEATLEY.
BOTLEYS w Lyne (H Trin), *Surrey.* V. **D** Guildf 7 **P** *Bp and Mrs R Parker* alt. **I** RT REV ST J S PIKE.
BOTOLPHS (St Botolph), *W Sussex.*. **D** Chich 7 *See* Bramber.
BOTTESFORD (St Mary Virg) w Muston (St Jo Bapt), *Leics.* R. **D** Leic 3 **P** *Duke of Rutland* **I** W N METCALFE.
BOTTESFORD (St Pet Ap) w Ashby (St Paul), *Humb.* R. **D** Linc 4 **P** *Bp and others* **I** W R HURDMAN, D BUTTERWORTH *team v,* R H JENNINGS *team v,* M A SEELEY *c.*
BOTTISHAM (H Trin), *Cambs.* V. **D** Ely 6 **P** *Trin Coll Cam* **I** F T DUFTON *p-in-c.*
BOTUS FLEMING (St Mary), *Cornw.* R. **D** Truro 9 *See* Landrake.
BOUGHTON (All SS), *Norf.*. **D** Ely 16 *See* Fincham.
BOUGHTON (St Jo Bapt), *Cambs.* R. **D** Pet 5 **P** *Bp* **I** G G CARNELL.
BOUGHTON (St Matt), *Notts.* V. **D** Southw 6 **P** *Ld Chan* **I** C D HIBBERT.
BOUGHTON ALUPH, *Kent.*. **D** Cant 10 *See* Eastwell.
BOUGHTON-MALHERBE (St Nich), *Kent.* R. **D** Cant 15 *See* Lenham.
BOUGHTON-MONCHELSEA (St Pet), *Kent.* V. **D** Cant 15 **P** *Abp* **I** C J WAYTE *p-in-c.*
BOUGHTON-UNDER-BLEAN (St Pet St Paul and St Barn) w Dunkirk (Ch Ch), *Kent.* V. **D** Cant 7 **P** *Abp* **I** P D SALES.
BOULDON (All SS), *Salop.*. **D** Heref *See* Diddlebury.
BOULGE (St Mich AA), *Suff.* R. **D** St E 7 *See* Bredfield.
BOULTHAM (St Helen), *Lincs.* R. **D** Linc 15 **P** *Dioc Patr C'tte* **I** V I DALBY, M W ELFRED *c.*
BOULTON (St Mary Virg), *Derbys.* V. **D** Derby 15 **P** *Miss G M Robotham* **I** J W ALLUM *c-in-c.*
BOUNDS GREEN (St Gabr), *Lon.* V. **D** Lon 22 *See* Edmonton.
BOURN (St Helen and St Mary), *Cambs.* V. **D** Ely 1 **P** *Ch Coll Cam* **I** M H HILLS.
BOURNBROOK (St Wulstan), *W Midl.*. **D** Birm 5 *See* Selly Oak.
BOURNE (St Pet and St Paul), *Lincs.* V. **D** Linc 13 **P** *Dioc Bd of Patr* **I** G J LANHAM.
BOURNE, THE, (St Thos), *Surrey.* V. **D** Guildf 3 **P** *Archd of Surrey* **I** C W HERBERT, G A HODGE *c.*
BOURNE END, *Herts.* V. **D** St Alb 3 *See* Sunnyside.
BOURNE END (St Mark), *Bucks.* V. **D** Ox 32 *See* Hedsor.
BOURNE VALLEY (Allington w Boscombe, Cholderton, Newton Tony, Idmiston w Porton, Winterbourne Earls, Dauntsey, Winterbourne Gunner), *Wilts.* R. **D** Sarum 17 **P** *Dioc Bd of Patr* **I** J HARVEY, D G G DAVIES *team v.*
BOURNEMOUTH (St Pet w St Swith, H Trin and St Steph), *Dorset.* R. **D** Win 7 **P** *Patr Bd* **I** D H R JONES, J D CORBETT *team v,* R SMITH *team v,* E H P NORTON *hon c.*
(All SS West Southbourne), V. **D** Win 7 **P** *V of Christchurch* **I** B G APPS, W R NESBITT *c.*
(Ch Ch Conv Dist Westbourne). **D** Win 7 **P** *Trustees* **I** J A MOTYER *min.*
(Ch of Epiph Muscliff), V. **D** Win 7 **P** *Bp* **I** W A SWAIN, D G KINGSLAND *c.*
(St Alb), V. **D** Win 7 **P** *Bp* **I** B D GROVE *p-in-c.*
(St Ambrose), V. **D** Win 7 **P** *Bp* **I** J G SCOTT.
(St Andr), V. **D** Win 7 **P** *Trustees* **I** A G HARBIDGE.
(St Andr Boscombe), V. **D** Win 7 **P** *Bp* **I** D HASLAM, P A MACCARTY *c.*
(St Aug), V. **D** Win 7 **P** *Bp* **I** (Vacant).
(St Clem Boscombe), V w (St Mary Virg), V. **D** Win 7 **P** *Dioc Bd of Finance* **I** W A ARIES, M E GALLOWAY *c.*
(St Francis of Assisi), V. **D** Win 7 **P** *Commun of the Resurr Mirfield* **I** D PEEL.
(St Jas Pokesdown), V. **D** Win 7 **P** *Bp* **I** R J H TEARE.
(St Jo Bapt Moordown), V. **D** Win 7 **P** *Bp* **I** R L BOWLES.
(St Jo Evang Surrey Road), V. **D** Win 7 **P** *Bp* **I** J A GUILLE *p-in-c.*
(St Jo Evang Boscombe), V. **D** Win 7 **P** *Peache Trustees* **I** (Vacant).
(St Kath Southbourne), V. **D** Win 7 **P** *Trustees* **I** R B JONES, W R NESBITT *c.*
(St Luke, Winton), V. **D** Win 7 **P** *Bp* **I** J G PEARSON.
(St Mary Virg), V. **D** Win 7 *See* St Clem.
(St Mich AA), V. **D** Win 7 **P** *Bp and R Ives* alt **I** D D MOOR.
(St Paul), V. **D** Win 7 **P** *Ch S Trust* **I** G E WALLACE.
(St Chris Southbourne) V. **D** Win 7 **P** *Bp* **I** F H VEAR, W R NESBITT *c.*
BOURNES, THE, *Kent.*. **D** Cant 1 *See* Bekesbourne, Bishopsbourne, and Patrixbourne.
BOURNVILLE (St Francis), *W Midl.* V. **D** Birm 5 **P** *Bp* **I** K WITHINGTON.
BOURTON, *Salop.* V. **D** Heref 11 *See* Much Wenlock.
BOURTON (St Jas), *Wilts.*. **D** Ox *See* Shrivenham.

BOURTON (St Geo), *Dorset*. V. **D** Sarum 22 *See* Upper Stour.
BOURTON, GREAT, *Oxon*.. **D** Ox 6 *See* Cropredy.
BOURTON-ON-DUNSMORE (St Pet) w Frankton (St Nich) and Stretton-on-Dunsmore w Princethorpe, *Warws*. R. **D** Cov 6 **P** *Bp 2 turns, Simeon Trustees 1 turn and Mrs J H Shaw-Fox 1 turn* **I** G W BROUGH.
BOURTON-ON-THE-HILL (St Lawr), *Glos*. R. **D** Glouc 16 **P** *Ld Dulverton* **I** S T LAMBERT *p-in-c*.
BOURTON-ON-THE-WATER (St Lawr) w Clapton (St Jas), *Glos*. R. **D** Glouc 16 **P** *Wadh Coll Ox* **I** C H PICKTHORN.
BOVENEY, *Bucks*.. **D** Ox 24 *See* Eton.
BOVERIDGE, *Dorset*.. **D** Sarum 11 *See* Cranborne.
BOVEY, NORTH (St Jo Bapt), *Devon*.. **D** Ex *See* Moretonhampstead.
BOVEY TRACEY (St Pet and St Paul and St Thos of Cant), *Devon*. V. **D** Ex 11 **P** *Crown* **I** K M C MELROSE.
(St Jo Evang), V. **D** Ex 11 **P** *Guild of All S* **I** J A PEASE.
BOVINGDON (St Lawr), *Herts*. V. **D** St Alb 3 **P** *Ch S Trust* **I** D R CROAD.
BOVINGER (St Germain), *Essex*.. **D** Chelmsf 6 *See* Bobbingworth.
BOW (St Mary) w Bromley St Leonard (St Mary Virg w St Andr), *Lon*. R. **D** Lon 4 **P** *Bp* **I** F R BENTLEY, N P HENDERSON *team v*, A WINDROSS *team v*.
(St Mark, Victoria Park), V. **D** Lon 4 **P** *MMT* **I** G S KENDALL *c*, J T PAGE *c*, H S WATSON *c*.
(St Paul, Old Ford w St Steph N Bow), V. **D** Lon 4 **P** *Hyndman Trustees* **I** C YOUNG *p-in-c*, D F WAXHAM *c*, C D HEWITT *hon c*.
BOW (Nymet Tracey) w Broad Nymet, *Devon*. R. **D** Ex 2 **P** *Dioc Bd of Patr* **I** B H GALE.
BOW COMMON (St Paul w St Luke, Burdett Road), *Lon*. V. **D** Lon 4 **P** *Bp* **I** R G KIRKBY, J G ROWE *c*.
BOWDEN, GREAT (St Pet and St Paul), w Welham, *Leics*. V. **D** Leic 5 **P** *Bp* **I** (Vacant).
BOWDEN HILL (St Anne), *Wilts*. V. **D** Bris 7 *See* Lacock.
BOWDEN, LITTLE (St Nich), *Leics*. R. **D** Leic 5 **P** *Bp* **I** J E PEERS.
(St Hugh), V. **D** Leic 5 **P** *Bp* **I** B L STAFFORD, L N KING *hon c*.
BOWDON (St Mary Virg), *Gtr Man*. V. **D** Ches 10 **P** *Bp* **I** M H RIDGWAY.
BOWERCHALKE (Most H Trin), *Wilts*. V. **D** Sarum 19 *See* Broadchalke.
BOWERS GIFFORD (St Marg) w N Benfleet, *Essex*. R. **D** Chelmsf 10 **P** *Brig R Bryers and Em Coll* **I** R P M BROOKE *p-in-c*.
BOWES (St Giles) w Startforth, *Dur*. V. **D** Ripon **P** *Earl of Lonsdale and Lord of the Manor* **I** C D'AGUIAR.
BOWES PARK (St Mich at Bowes), *Lon*. V. **D** Lon 21 **P** *Bp* **I** (Vacant).
BOWLING (St Jo Evang), *W Yorks*. V. **D** Bradf 2 **P** *V of Bradf* **I** R J H FRY, M A TAYLOR *c*.
(St Steph), V. **D** Bradf 2 **P** *CPAS* **I** N L JACKSON.
BOWNESS-ON-SOLWAY (St Mich), *Cumb*. R. **D** Carl 3 **P** *Earl of Lonsdale* **I** R BRIGHT.
BOWTHORPE (Conv Distr), *Norf*.. **D** Nor 13 **P** *Bp* **I** R J SIMPSON *min*.
BOX (St Thos à Becket) w Hazlebury, R, *Wilts*. V. **D** Bris 9 **P** *Bp* **I** T R S SMITH.
BOX HILL (St Andr), *Surrey*.. **D** Guildf 9 *See* Headley.
BOXFORD (St Andr) w Stockcross (St Jo Evang) and Speen (St Mary), *Berks*. R. **D** Ox 14 **P** *Bp* **I** D. CRAWLEY P-IN-C OF SPEEN, N C SANDS.
BOXFORD (St Mary Virg) w Hadleigh Hamlet, *Suff*. R. **D** St E 12 **P** *Ld Chan* **I** A W HARRISON.
BOXGROVE (St Mary and St Blaise), *W Sussex*. V. **D** Chich 3 **P** *Duke of Richmond and Gordon* **I** B J MARSHALL.
BOXLEY (St Mary Virg and All SS), *Kent*. V. **D** Cant 15 **P** *Abp* **I** M L COOPER P-IN-C OF DETLING.
BOXMOOR (St Jo Evang), *Herts*. V. **D** St Alb 3 **P** *Bp* **I** A J S FREEMAN, R E MERRY *c*.
(St Francis's Conv Distr Hammerfield). **D** St Alb 3 **P** *Bp* **I** (Vacant).
BOXTED (St Pet) w Langham, *Essex*. V. **D** Chelmsf 22 **P** *Duchy of Lanc and Bp (alt)* **I** D LANCASHIRE.
BOXTED (H Trin), *Suff*.. **D** St E *See* Hartest.
BOXWELL (St Mary) w Leighterton (St Andr), Didmarton w Oldbury-on-the-Hill and Sopworth, *Glos*. R. **D** Glouc 17 **P** *J F R Huntley Esq and Duke of Beaufort* alt **I** R F ROTHERY.
BOXWORTH (St Pet), *Cambs*. R. **D** Ely 1 **P** *G E P Thornhill Esq* **I** H A MOSEDALE.
BOYLESTONE (St Jo Bapt), *Derbys*.. **D** Derby 14 *See* Church Broughton.
BOYNE HILL, *Berks*.. **D** Ox *See* Maidenhead.
BOYNTON, *Humb*. V. **D** York 12 *See* Rudston.
BOYTON (St Andr) w Capel St Andr (St Andr) and Hollesley, *Suff*. R. **D** St E 7 **P** *Trustees* **I** J M GATES.
BOYTON, *Cornw*. V. **D** Truro 11 *See* North Tamerton.
BOYTON w Sherrington (St Mich AA), *Wilts*. R. **D** Sarum *See* Ashton Gifford.
BOZEAT (St Mary) w Easton Maudit (St Pet and St Paul), *Northants*. V. **D** Pet 7 **P** *Bp and Marq of Northn* alt **I** N E PALMER.
BRABOURNE (St Mary BV) w Smeeth (St Mary), *Kent*. V. **D** Cant 12 **P** *Abp* **I** J M STEPHENS.
BRACEBOROUGH (St Marg) w Wilsthorpe, *Lincs*. R. **D** Linc *See* Baston.
BRACEBRIDGE (All SS), *Lincs*. V. **D** Linc 15 **P** *Mrs B M Ellison-Lendrum* **I** A P BETTS.
BRACEBRIDGE HEATH (St Jo Evang), *Lincs*. V. **D** Linc 15 **P** *Bp* **I** W J HAWTHORNE *c*.
BRACEBY (St Marg), *Lincs*.. **D** Linc 14 *See* Sapperton.
BRACEWELL (St Mich), *Lancs*. V. **D** Bradf 10 *See* Barnoldswick.
BRACKENBOROUGH, *Lincs*.. **D** Linc 12 *See* Fotherby.
BRACKENFIELD (H Trin), *Derbys*. V. **D** Derby 1 *See* Wessington.
BRACKLEY (St Pet w St Jas) and (St John and St Jas), *Northants*. V. **D** Pet 1 **P** *Bp* **I** P C WOODWARD.
BRACKNELL (H Trin), *Berks*. V. **D** Ox 11a **P** *Bp* **I** A SMITHSON, J G W DICKIE *c*, P NEWTON *c*.
BRACON ASH (St Nich) w Hethel, *Norf*. R. **D** Nor 13 *See* Wreningham.
BRADBOURNE (All SS) w Brassington (St Jas) *Derbys*. V. **D** Derby 17 **P** *Duke of Devonshire and Bp* **I** J D LYTLE.
BRADDEN, *Northants*.. **D** Pet 2 *See* Green's Norton.
BRADELEY (All SS), *Staffs*. V. **D** Lich **P** *Bp* **I** W B WOOLLEY *p-in-c*.
BRADENHAM (St Botolph), *Bucks*.. **D** Ox 32 *See* Wycombe, W.
BRADENHAM, EAST (St Mary) w Bradenham West (St Andr), *Norf*. R. **D** Nor *See* Shipdham.
BRADENSTOKE, *Wilts*. V. **D** Sarum 25 *See* Lyneham.
BRADESTON (St Mich), *Norf*.. **D** Nor 1 *See* Witton.
BRADFIELD (St Lawr), *Essex*. V. **D** Chelmsf 25 **P** *Bp* **I** (Vacant).
BRADFIELD (St Andr) w Buckhold (H Trin) and Southend (St Pet), *Berks*. R. **D** Ox 12 **P** *Ch S Trust* **I** S T LANE.
BRADFIELD (St Nich), *S Yorks*. R. **D** Sheff 7 **P** *V of Ecclesfield* **I** E G PERRENS.
BRADFIELD-COMBUST, *Suff*. R. **D** St E 13 *See* Stanningfield.
BRADFIELD ST CLARE (St Clare), *Suff*. R. **D** St E *See* Bradfield St George.
BRADFIELD ST GEORGE (St Geo) w Bradfield St Clare and Felsham w Gedding, *Suff*, R. **D** St E **P** *Bp 1st turn, St Jo Coll Cam 2nd turn, Marquis of Bris 3rd turn and J G Aldous Esq 4th turn* **I** J HOBBS.
BRADFIELD (St Giles), *Norf*.. **D** Nor 5 *See* Trunch.
BRADFORD (St Giles) w Oake, Hillfarrance and Heathfield, *Somt*. R. **D** B & W 22 **P** *Bp and M V Spurway Esq* **I** N KENT.
BRADFORD (St Pet Cathl Ch), *W Yorks*. V. **D** Bradf 3 **P** *Simeon Trustees* **I** VERY REV B D JACKSON, A C S J WALKER *c*.
(All SS Little Horton), V. **D** Bradf 2 **P** *Trustees* **I** L E AUSTIN.
(St Aug Undercliffe), V. **D** Bradf 3 **P** *V of Bradf* **I** (Vacant).
(St Jas Bolton w St Chrys), V. **D** Bradf 3 **P** *Bp* **I** D SUTCLIFFE, D J TOMPSETT *c*.
(St Clem Barkerend), V. **D** Bradf 3 **P** *Bp 2 turns Trustees 1 turn* **I** A G R WILSON.
(St Columba, Horton w St Andr Listerhills), V. **D** Bradf 2 **P** *Bp* **I** C I JUDD.
(St Cuthb Wrose), V. **D** Bradf 3 **P** *Crown* **I** J N WHITE.
(St Jo Evang Great Horton), V. **D** Bradf 2 **P** *V of Bradf* **I** H M WIGLEY, K G CROCKER *c*, L J SLOW *hon c*.
(St Mich AA). **D** Bradf 1 *See* Manningham.
(St Osw Little Horton), V. **D** Bradf 2 **P** *Bp* **I** P A ANDREWS. *See also* BOWLING, LIDGET GREEN AND MANNINGHAM..
BRADFORD, *Devon*. R. **D** Ex 9 *See* Black Torrington.
BRADFORD (Ch Ch), *Gtr Man*.. **D** Man *See* Manchester (St Aidan).
(St Paul), R. **D** Man 1 *See* Clayton.
BRADFORD ABBAS (St Mary) w Clifton Maybank, *Dorset*. V. **D** Sarum 7 **P** *Win Coll* **I** R J MENTERN *c-in-c*.
BRADFORD-ON-AVON (H Trin), *Wilts*. V. **D** Sarum 24 **P** *D and C of Sarum* **I** W A MATTHEWS, P J STONE *c*.
(Ch Ch), V. **D** Sarum 24 **P** *V of H Trin Bradford-on-Avon* **I** J R SARGANT.

BRADFORD PEVERELL (The Assump of BVM), Stratton (St Mary), Frampton (St Mary) and Sydling St Nicholas (St Nich), *Dorset*. R. **D** Sarum 5 **P** *Win Coll and Bp (Alt)* **I** K J SCOTT.
BRADING (St Mary) w Yaverland (St Jo Bapt), *Isle of Wight*. V. **D** Portsm 6 **P** *Trin Coll Cam and Commdr P V Monck* **I** E S HAYDEN.
BRADLEY (All SS), *Derbys*. R. **D** Derbys 8 *See* Hulland.
BRADLEY (All SS), *Hants*. R. **D** Win 6 *See* Preston Candover.
BRADLEY (St Geo), *Humb*.. **D** Linc 9 *See* Coates, Little.
BRADLEY (St Jo Bapt), *Worcs*. R. **D** Worc 2 *See* Feckenham.
BRADLEY (St Martin), *Staffs*. V. **D** Lich 12 **P** *Trustees* **I** F J T BRUMWELL.
BRADLEY W Yorks. **D** Bradf 11 *See* Cononley.
BRADLEY (St Thos), *N Yorks*. V. **D** Wakef 4 **P** *Bp* **I** N BUSSEY, A J TURNER *c*, A E DIXON *hon c*.
BRADLEY, GREAT (BVM), *Suff*. R. **D** St E 8 **P** *R A Vestey Esq* **I** L J FRANCIS P-IN-C OF L WRATTING *p-in-c*.
BRADLEY-LE-MOORS (St Leon), *Staffs*. V. **D** Lich 14 **P** *Earl of Shrewsbury and Talbot* **I** W H GOLDSTRAW.
BRADLEY, NORTH (St Nich) w Southwick (St Thos) *Wilts*. V. **D** Sarum 24 **P** *Win Coll* **I** (Vacant).
BRADLEY, WEST (Dedic unknown), *Somt*. V. **D** B & W 9 *See* Pennard, West.
BRADMORE, *Notts*.. **D** Southw *See* Bunny.
BRADNINCH (St Disen), *Devon*. V. **D** Ex 4 **P** *D and C of Windsor* **I** K P EVANS.
BRADNOP Staffs. **D** Lich 16 *See* Onecote.
BRADOC (BVM) , *Cornw*.. **D** Truro 13 *See* Boconnoc.
BRADON, S and N, *Somt*. R. **D** B & W 20 *See* Puckington.
BRADPOLE (H Trin), *Dorset*. V. **D** Sarum *See* Bridport.
BRADSHAW (St Maxentius), *Gtr Man*. V. **D** Man 19 **P** *V of Bolton* **I** W G THOMPSON.
BRADSHAW, *W Yorks*.. **D** Wakef 1 *See* Halifax.
BRADSTONE, *Devon*. R. **D** Ex 22 *See* Kelly.
BRADWELL (St Barn), *Derbys*. V. **D** Derby 9 **P** *D and C of Lich* **I** A K GREENHOUGH.
BRADWELL (St Nich), *Suff*, R. **D** Nor 2 **P** *Bp* **I** A J LIDDON.
BRADWELL (St Laur), *Bucks*. V. **D** Ox 26 *See* Stantonbury.
BRADWELL (St Pet and St Paul), w Kencot (St Geo) and Kelmscot (St Geo), *Oxon*. V. **D** Ox *See* Filkins.
BRADWELL-JUXTA-COGGESHALL (H Trin), *Essex*. R. **D** Chelmsf 19 *See* Stisted.
BRADWELL-JUXTA-MARE (St Thos Ap), *Essex*. R. **D** Chelmsf 13 **P** *Bp* **I** J A P BOOTH.
BRADWELL, NEW (St Jas), *Bucks*. V. **D** Ox 26 *See* Stantonbury.
BRADWORTHY (St Jo Bapt), *Devon*. V. **D** Ex 9 **P** *Crown* **I** P SUTTON.
BRAFFERTON (St Aug or St Pet) w Pilmoor and Myton-on-Swale (St Mary), *N Yorks*. V. **D** York 5 **P** *Execs of Sir E C Milnes-Coates Bt* **I** J D HARRIS-DOUGLAS.
BRAFIELD-ON-GREEN (St Laur), *Northants*. V. **D** Pet 4 *See* Houghton, Little.
BRAILES (St Geo) w Winderton, *Warws*. V. **D** Cov 9 **P** *Provost and Chapter of Cov* **I** N J MORGAN.
BRAILSFORD (All SS) w Shirley (St Mich), *Derbys*. R. **D** Derbys 8 **P** *Earl Ferrers* **I** P J BOWLES.
BRAINTREE (St Mich Arch), *Essex*. V. **D** Chelmsf 19 **P** *Ch Trust Fund* **I** B DAVIES.
BRAISEWORTH, *Suff*.. **D** St E *See* Eye.
BRAISHFIELD (All SS), *Hants*. V. **D** Win 10 *See* Farley Chamberlayne.
BRAITHWAITE, *Cumb*.. **D** Carl *See* Thornthwaite.
BRAITHWELL (All H or St Jas), *S Yorks*. R. **D** Sheff 6 **P** *Earl Fitzwilliam* **I** E P ECCLES.
BRAMBER (St Nich) w Botolphs (St Botolph), V *W Sussex*. R. **D** Chich 7 **P** *Bp* **I** D J WHITE.
BRAMCOTE (St Mich), *Notts*. V. **D** Southw 8 **P** *CPAS* **I** J G HUMPHREYS, D H BOWLER *c*.
BRAMDEAN (St Simon and St Jude), *Hants*. R. **D** Win 6 *See* Hinton Ampner.
BRAMERTON (St Pet), w Surlingham (St Mary w St Sav), *Norf*. R (*in Bramerton Group - See also Ashby, Framingham, Rockland, Bergh Apton*).. **D** Nor 14 **P** *Maj C Fellowes 2 turns, Bp 1 turn* **I** M S STEDMAN, R J BAWTREE *team v*, C W T CHALCRAFT *team v*.
BRAMFIELD (St Andr) w Stapleford (St Mary Virg) and Waterford, *Herts*. R. **D** St Alb 8 **P** *T Abel Smith Esq and Grocers' Company (alt)* **I** H D KENNEDY.
BRAMFIELD (St Andr) w Walpole (St Mary Virg), *Suff*. V. **D** St E 15 *See* Wenhaston.
BRAMFORD (St Mary) w *Suff*. V. **D** St E 1 **P** *D and C of Cant* **I** R G CHRISTIAN.
BRAMHALL (St Mich AA), *Gtr Man*. V. **D** Ches 16 **P** *Trustees* **I** R H HACK, E R MOORE *c*, J N ROSKILLY *c*, G E WEST *c*.
BRAMHAM (All SS), *W Yorks*. V. **D** York 9 **P** *Hon M A M Lane Fox* **I** J R D SHAW.
BRAMHOPE (St Giles), *W Yorks*. V. **D** Ripon 5 **P** *Trustees* **I** J R WARD.
BRAMLEY (H Trin) and Grafham, *Surrey*. V. **D** Guildf 2 **P** *Ld Chan* **I** J G EDWARDS.
BRAMLEY (St Pet), *W Yorks*. V. **D** Ripon 8 **P** *V of Leeds* **I** G M STONESTREET, J S LEE *c*, R J PEARSON *c*.
BRAMLEY (St Francis) and Ravenfield (St Jas), *S Yorks*. V. **D** Sheff 7 **P** *Bp* **I** R J HARRIS.
BRAMLEY (St Jas or All SS), *Hants*. V. **D** Win 3 **P** *Qu Coll Ox* **I** R S COSSINS.
BRAMPFORD-SPEKE (St Pet), w Cowley (St Anthony), *Devon*. V. **D** Ex 2 **P** *Ld Chan* **I** G LINDEN.
BRAMPTON (St Martin), *Cumb*. V. **D** Carl 2 **P** *C H Roberts Esq* **I** A W PENN.
BRAMPTON, OLD (St Pet and St Paul) V and Loundsley Green, *Derbys*. R. **D** Derby 3 **P** *Bp* **I** M T FERMER, J D J GOODMAN *team v*.
(St Thos Ap and Mart), R. **D** Derby 3 **P** *Bp* **I** W V F K WATTS-JONES, K M D SCOTT *hon c*.
LOWER (St Mark's), V. **D** Derby 3 **P** *Bp* **I** W M FELL.
BRAMPTON (St Mary Magd), *Cambs*. R. **D** Ely 10 **P** *Bp* **I** W M DEBNEY.
BRAMPTON (St Pet), *Norf*. R. **D** Nor 3 **P** *Bp* **I** C B MORGAN.
BRAMPTON (St Pet), *Suff*. R. **D** St E 15 *See* Westhall.
BRAMPTON-ABBOTTS (St Mich AA), *Herefs*. R. **D** Heref *See* Ross-on-Wye.
BRAMPTON ASH (St Mary) w Dingley (All SS) and Braybrooke (All SS), *Northants*. R. **D** Pet 8 **P** *Earl Spencer 2 turns, M J J S Nicolson Esq 1 turn*. **I** A R TWYFORD.
BRAMPTON BIERLOW (Ch Ch), *S Yorks*. V. **D** Sheff 10 **P** *V of Wath-on-Dearne* **I** K E WOOD, D J COX *c*.
BRAMPTON BRYAN (St Barn), *Herefs*.. **D** Heref 12 *See* Wigmore Abbey.
BRAMPTON CHURCH (St Botolph) w Chapel Brampton and Harlestone, *Northants*. R.. **D** Pet 6 **P** *Earl Spencer and CCC Ox* **I** D D F SMITH.
BRAMSHALL (St Lawr), *Staffs*. R. **D** Lich 20 *See* Uttoxeter.
BRAMSHAW (St Pet), *Hants*. and *Wilts*. V. **D** Sarum 17 **P** *D and C of Sarum* **I** H CHANT *p-in-c*.
BRAMSHOTT (St Mary) w Liphook, *Hants*. R. **D** Portsm 4 **P** *Qu Coll Ox* **I** R A EWBANK.
BRANCASTER (St Mary Virg) w Burnham Deepdale and Titchwell, *Norf). R.* **D** Nor **P** *H S N Adams Esq and Bp* **I** H M A CRAWSHAW.
BRANCEPETH (St Brandon), *Durham*. R. **D** Dur 2 **P** *Bp* **I** A D CHESTERS.
BRANDESBURTON (St Mary), *Humb*. R. **D** York 14 **P** *St Jo Coll Cam* **I** T GILL.
BRANDESTON w Kettleburgh (St Andr), *Suff*. V. **D** St E 18 **P** *Michael Round-Turner Esq 2 turns, C Astin Esq 1 turn* **I** K W A ROBERTS *p-in-c*.
BRANDISTON (St Nich), *Nor*.. **D** Nor *See* Booton.
BRANDON (St Jo Evang) w (St Agatha) and Brandon Colliery, *Durham*. V. **D** Dur 2 **P** *R of Brancepeth* **I** R J STRETTON, J W GEEN *c*.
BRANDON-FERRY (St Pet) w Wangford (St Denys), Santon Downham (St Mary Virg) and Santon (All SS), *Suff*. R. **D** St E 11 **P** *S G Brown Esq and Miss S Crocker 2 turns, Ld Chan 1 turn, Bp 1 turn* **I** R CROWTHER, H L J SHARMAN *c*.
BRANDON, LITTLE *Norf*.. **D** Nor 12 *See* Barnham Broom.
BRANDSBY (All SS), *N Yorks*. R. **D** York 5 *See* Crayke.
BRANDWOOD (St Bede), *W Midl*. V. **D** Birm 4 **P** *Bp* **I** R F JENKINS.
BRANKSEA I (St Mary), *Dorset*. V. **D** Sarum 14 *See* Parkstone.
BRANKSOME (All SS), *Dorset*. V. **D** Sarum 14 **P** *Mart Mem Trust* **I** J R J KERRUISH.
(St Aldhelm, Branksome Park), V. **D** Sarum 14 **P** *Bp* **I** R L RAIKES *p-in-c*.
(St Clem), V. **D** Sarum 14 **P** *MMT* **I** M G BOULTER, P D STEVENS *c*.
See also PARKSTONE.
BRANSCOMBE Devon. V **D** Ex 7 *See* Sidmouth.
BRANSDALE (St Nich) w Farndale (St Mary), *N Yorks*. V. **D** York 20 *See* Kirkbymoorside.
BRANSFORD (St Jo Bapt), *Worcs*.. **D** Worc 4 *See* Leigh.

BRANSGORE (St Mary), *Hants*. V. **D** Win 8 **P** *P W Jesson Esq* **I** P C ELKINS.
BRANSTON (All SS), *Lincs*. R. **D** Linc 18 **P** *Govs of Stowe Sch* **I** B A STALLEY.
BRANSTON-BY-BELVOIR (St Guthlac), *Leics*. R. **D** Leic 2 *See* Croxton-Kerrial.
BRANSTON (St Sav), *Staffs*. V. **D** Lich **P** *Simeon Trustees* **I** D B SIMMONDS.
BRANT BROUGHTON (St Helen) w Stragglethorpe (St Mich), *Lincs*. R. **D** Linc 23 **P** *Exors of Sir R V Sutton Bt* **I** R CLARK.
BRANTHAM (St Mich AA) w Stutton (St Pet), *Suff*. R. **D** St E 5 **P** *Bp and Em Coll Cam (alt)* **I** A L HAIG.
BRANTINGHAM, *Humb*. V. **D** York 16 *See* Elloughton.
BRANXTON (St Paul), *Northumb*. V. **D** Newc T 11 **P** *D and C of Dur* **I** A WILTSHIRE.
BRASSINGTON, *Derbys*.. **D** Derby *See* Bradbourne.
BRASTED (St Martin), *Kent*. R. **D** Roch 7 **P** *Abp of Cant* **I** J H B TALBOT.
BRATHAY (H Trin), *Cumb*. V. **D** Carl 14 *See* Ambleside.
BRATOFT (St Pet and St Paul) w Irby-in-Marsh (All SS), *Lincs*. R. **D** Linc 8 **P** *Bp* **I** R H IRESON.
BRATTLEBY Lincs. R **D** Linc 3 *See* Aisthorpe.
BRATTON (St Jas Gt), *Wilts*. V. **D** Sarum 22 **P** *V of Westbury* **I** J P R SAUNT.
BRATTON CLOVELLY (St Mary Virg) w Germansweek, *Devon*. R. **D** Ex **P** *Bp* **I** H A GREAVES.
BRATTON ST MAUR, *Somt*. V. **D** B & W 5 *See* Pitcombe.
BRATTON FLEMING (St Pet), *Devon*. R. **D** Ex 18 **P** *G and C Coll Cam* **I** J H HORNBY *p-in-c*.
BRAUGHING (St Mary) w Little Hadham, Albury, Furneux Pelham and Stocking Pelham, *Herts*. V. **D** St Alb **P** *Bp of Lon 1st turn, Maj-Gen E H Goulburn 2nd turn and Bp 3rd turn* **I** T D L LLOYD, E E JOURDAIN *c*.
BRAUNCEWELL (All SS), w Dunsby, *Lincs*. R. **D** Linc 22 *See* Leasingham.
BRAUNSTON, *Northants*. R. **D** Pet 3 **P** *Jes Coll Ox* **I** M W HUNNYBUN.
BRAUNSTON (All SS) w Brooke (St Pet), *Leics*. V. **D** Pet 12 **P** *D and C of Linc* **I** A A HORSLEY, J R WESTWOOD *c*.
BRAUNSTONE, *Leics*.. **D** Leic 17 *See* Leicester.
BRAUNTON (St Brannock) w Saunton (St Anne) and Knowle, *Devon*. V. **D** Ex 15 **P** *Bp* **I** R P REEVE, G MORGAN *hon c*.
BRAXTED, GREAT (All SS), *Essex*. R. **D** Chelmsf 29 **P** *CCC Cam* **I** J A BURLEY.
BRAXTED, LITTLE (St Nich), *Essex*. R. **D** Chelmsf 29 **P** *Commdr P Du Cane* **I** J A BURLEY.
BRAY (St Mich) w Braywood, *Berks*. V. **D** Ox 13 **P** *Bp* **I** N HOWELLS, W I BARBOUR *c*.
BRAYBROOKE (All SS), *Northants*.. **D** Pet 8 *See* Brampton Ash.
BRAYESWORTH (St Mary), *Suff*.. **D** St E *See* Braiseworth.
BRAYTON (St Wilfrid) w Barlow, *N Yorks*. R. **D** York 8 **P** *Abp* **I** R ROGERS, D G RICHARDSON *team v*, J A ROBERTSON *team v*.
BREADSALL (All SS), *Derbys*. R. **D** Derby 13 **P** *Personal Representative of the late Mrs F C J H Jenny* **I** P A CROWE.
BREAGE (St Breaca) w Germoe (St Germoe), *Cornw*. V. **D** Truro 4 **P** *HM the Queen* **I** M O WEST.
BREAM (St Jas Ap and Mart), *Glos*. V. **D** Glouc 7 **P** *Bp* **I** J P W REES.
BREAMORE (St Mary), *Hants*. V. **D** Win 8 **P** *Sir W Hulse Bt* **I** M DUPLOCK.
BREANE (St Bridget), *Somt*.. **D** B & W 2 *See* Berrow.
BREARTON (St Jo Bapt), *N Yorks*.. **D** Ripon 4 *See* Nidd.
BREASTON (St Mich) w Wilne (St Chad) and Draycott, *Derbys*. R. **D** Derby 13 **P** *Bp* **I** W A PEMBERTON.
BRECCLES (St Marg), *Norf*. V. **D** Nor 19 *See* Stow-Bedon.
BREDBURY (St Mark), *Gtr Man*. V. **D** Ches 16 **P** *Bp* **I** P A CAMPBELL.
(St Barn Conv Distr). **D** Ches 16 **P** *Bp* **I** C R WINDLE *p-in-c*.
BREDE (St Geo) w Udimore (St Mary), *E Sussex*. R. **D** Chich 22 **P** *Mrs P H Crook and Exors of A K Holmes* **I** P H N HARVEY.
BREDENBURY (St Andr) w Grendon Bishop and Wacton, *Herefs*. R. **D** Heref 2 **P** *V of Bromyard and H H Barneby Esq* alt **I** J ADAMS *p-in-c*.
BREDFIELD (St Andr) w Boulge (St Mich AA), *Suff*. R. **D** St E 7 **P** *Ld Chan 2 turns, Dr W F Evans and Maj Gen C M F White 1 turn* **I** E PEARSON *c-in-c*.
BREDGAR (St Jo Bapt) w Bicknor (St Jas) and Hucking (St Mary), *Kent*. V. **D** Cant 14 **P** *Abp* **I** J M SHORROCK.
BREDHURST (St Pet), *Kent*.. **D** Roch 2 *See* Gillingham, South.
BREDICOT, *Worcs*. R. **D** Worc 8 *See* Tibberton.
BREDON (St Giles) w Bredon's Norton, *Worcs*. R. **D** Worc 3 **P** *Bp* **I** C J RIDOUT.
BREDWARDINE (St Andr) w Brobury (St Mary Magd), *Herefs*. V. **D** Heref 1 **P** *MMT* **I** J C DE LA T DAVIES P-IN-C OF MOCCAS *p-in-c*.
BREDY, LONG (St Pet) w Little (St Mich AA), *Dorset*. R. **D** Sarum *See* Bride Valley.
BREEDON-ON-THE-HILL (St Mary and St Hardulph) w Isley Walton (All SS) and Worthington (St Matt) w Newbold and Griffy Dam, *Leics*. V. **D** Leic 12 **P** *D A G Shields Esq and Ch Coll Cam (alt)* **I** D V OSBORNE.
BREIGHTMET (St Jas), *Gtr Man*.. **D** Man 19 **P** *Bp and Crown* alt **I** J H SMITH.
BREINTON (St Mich), *Herefs*. V. **D** Heref 4 **P** *Bp* **I** W B HAYNES.
BREMHILL (St Martin) w Foxham (St Jo Bapt), *Wilts*. V. **D** Sarum 25 **P** *Bp* **I** (Vacant).
BREMILHAM, *Wilts*. V. **D** Bris 9 *See* Foxley.
BRENCHLEY (All SS), *Kent*. V. **D** Roch 10 **P** *D and C of Cant* **I** J D MEACHAM.
BRENDON (St Brendan), *Devon*. R. **D** Ex 18 *See* Lynton.
BRENT, EAST (BVM) w Lympsham, *Somt*. R. **D** B & W 2 **P** *Bp and Rev F J Evans* **I** (Vacant).
BRENT-ELEIGH (St Mary) w Milden or Milding (St Pet), *Suff*. R. **D** St E 10 *See* Monks Eleigh.
BRENT-KNOLL (St Mich), *Somt*. V. **D** B & W 2 **P** *Archd of Wells* **I** (Vacant).
BRENT PELHAM (St Mary), w Meesden (St Mary), *Herts*. V. **D** St Alb *See* Hormead, Great.
BRENT, SOUTH (St Petroc), *Devon*. V. **D** Ex 13 **P** *Bp* **I** D J M NIBLETT.
BRENT TOR w N Brentor Chap, *Devon*.. **D** Ex 22 *See* Lydford.
BRENTFORD (St Paul w St Lawr and St Geo M), *Gtr Lon*. V. **D** Lon 10 **P** *Bp* **I** A A COURT.
(St Faith), V. **D** Lon 10 **P** *Bp* **I** J S BOWDEN *hon c*.
BRENTINGBY, *Leics*.. **D** Leic *See* Melton Mowbray.
BRENTS (St Jo Evang) w Davington (St Mary Magd), Oare (St Pet) and Luddenham (St Mary Virg), *Kent*. V. **D** Cant 7 **P** *Abp and Ld Chan* alt **I** M J A ANDERSON.
BRENTWOOD (St Thos of Cant), *Essex*. V. **D** Chelmsf 9 **P** *Dioc Bd of Patr* **I** F E TESTER, S P WARD *c*.
(St Geo Mart). **D** Worc 1 **P** *Dioc Bd of Patr* **I** D A C STRANACK.
BRENZETT, *Kent*. V. **D** Cant 13 *See* Brookland.
BRERETON (St Mich AA), *Staffs*. V. **D** Lich 4 **P** *V of Rugeley* **I** J F SMART.
BRERETON w Swettenham, *Chesh*. R. **D** Ches 11 **P** *Dioc Bd of Patr & MMT* **I** J P MARTIN.
BRESSINGHAM (St Jo Bapt) w North and South Lopham and Fersfield *Norf*. R. **D** Nor 17 **P** *Mart Mem Trust, St Jo Coll Cam and R D A Woode Esq* **I** R H SMITH.
BRETBY (St Wystan) w Newton Solney (St Mary Virg), *Derbys*. V. **D** Derby 16 **P** *Bp and P W Ratcliff Esq* **I** W A R K WERWATH.
BRETFORTON Worcs. V **D** Worc *See* Offenham.
BRETHERTON (St Jo Bapt), *Lancs*. R. **D** Blackb 4 **P** *R of Croston* **I** (Vacant).
BRETTENHAM (BVM), *Suff*. R. **D** St E 10 *See* Thorpe Morieux.
BRETTENHAM (St Andr) w Rushford (St John) and Shadwell, *Norf*. R. **D** Nor 18 **P** *Exors of John Musker Esq* **I** R M M WINTER *p-in-c*.
BRETTON (H Spirit) *Cambs*.. **D** Pet *See* Peterborough.
BREWHAM, NORTH AND SOUTH (St Jo Bapt), *Somt*. V. **D** B & W 5 **P** *Bp* **I** (Vacant).
BREWOOD (St Mary Virg and St Chad). *Staffs*. V. **D** Lich 3 **P** *Bp* **I** R SCHOTTELVIG.
BRICETT, GREAT (St Mary and St Lawr), *Suff*.. **D** ST E 1 *See* Barking.
BRICKET WOOD (St Luke), *Herts*. V. **D** St Alb **P** *CPAS Trust* **I** N P J BELL.
BRICKHILL, BOW (All SS), *Bucks*. R. **D** Ox 27 *See* Brickhill.
BRICKHILL, GREAT (St Mary Virg) w Little (St Mary Magd) and Bow Brickhill, [Bucks]. R. **D** Ox 27 **P** *Sir P D P Duncombe Bt, Bp and Rev R C Morrell* **I** (Vacant).
BRICKLEHAMPTON (St Mich AA), *Worcs*.. **D** Worc 3 *See* Elmley Castle.
BRIDE VALLEY (Burton Bradstock and Chilcombe, Shipton Gorge, Litton Cheney, Long w Little Bredy and Puncknowle w Swyre), *Dorset*. R. **D** Sarum **P** *Bp, Sir R P Williams Bt and G A Pitt-Rivers Esq* **I** T SALISBURY, H G SMITH *team v*.
BRIDEKIRK (St Bridget), *Cumb*. V. **D** Carl 10 **P** *Trustees* **I** P C KNAPPER.

BRIDESTOWE (St Bridget), *Devon.* R. D Ex 22 *See* Lydford.
BRIDFORD (St Thos à Becket), *Devon.* R. D Ex 6 *See* Christow.
BRIDGE (St Pet), *Kent.*. D Cant 1 *See* Patrixbourne.
BRIDGE SOLLARS (St Andr), *Herefs.* V. D Heref 4 *See* Kenchester.
BRIDGERULE (St Bridget), *Devon.* V. D Ex *See* Pyworthy.
BRIDGETOWN (St Jo), *Devon.*. D Ex 13 *See* Totnes.
BRIDGFORD, WEST (St Giles), *Notts.* R. D Southw 11 P *Waddington Trustees* I P N HUMPHREYS, NEWCOMBE *c,* A LINNING *hon c.*
(All Hallows, Lady Bay) V. D Southw 11 P *Bp* I E P BAILEY.
BRIDGHAM (St Mary) w Roudham, *Norf.* R. D Nor 18 P *Ld Chan 4 turns, Mrs Percy Musker 1 turn* I H R ELLIOT.
BRIDGNORTH (St Mary Magd w St Leon), Tasley (St Pet and St Paul) Astley Abbotts and Oldbury, *Salop.* R. D Heref 9 P *Maj Gen E H Goulburn, Wrekin Coll Wellington, Dioc Bd of Patr and Ld Chan* I P C MASON *team v,* D T MERRY *team v,* R S PAYNE *c,* W A D BAKER *hon c.*
BRIDGWATER (St Mary) w Chilton Trinity (H Trin), *Somt.* V. D B & W 17 P *Ld Chan* I E R AYERST.
(H Trin), V. D B & W 17 P *Bp* I J S WELLS *c-in-c.*
(St Francis), V. D B & W 17 P *Bp* I (Vacant).
(St Jo Bapt Eastover) and Chedzoy (St Mary Virg), R. D B & W 17 P *Bp* I B A NEWTON *c-in-c.*
BRIDLINGTON (St Mary), *Humb.* R. D York 12 P *Simeon Trustees* I J J NOLAN, J R BOOTH *c.*
(H Trin) and Sewerby w Marton, V. D York 12 P *Abp* I T C WILLIS.
(Ch Ch), V. D York 12 P *R of Bridlington* I J G COUPER.
(Em Ch), V. D York 12 P *Trustees* I J L BADGER.
BRIDPORT (Allington, Bothenhampton w Walditch and Bradpole), *Dorset.* R. D Sarum P *Bp and J C F Gundry Esq* I H E MONTAGUE-YOUENS, G A G LOUGHLIN *team v,* D G SMITH *team v.*
BRIDSTOW (St Bridget) w Peterstow (St Pet), *Herefs.* V. D Heref *See* Ross-on-Wye.
BRIERCLIFFE (St Jas), *Lancs.* V. D Blackb 3 P *Hulme Trustees* I P H HALLAM, D CLEGG *c.*
BRIERFIELD (St Luke), *Lancs.* V. D Blackb 6a P *Bp* I K BARRETT.
BRIERLEY, *S Yorks.*. D Wakef 8 *See* Felkirk.
BRIERLEY HILL (St Mich), *W Midl.* R. D Lich 1 P *R of Kingswinford* I D N AUSTERBERRY.
BRIGG (or Glanford Bridge) (St Jo Evang), *Humb.* V. D Linc 6 P *Bp* I R A COCHRANE.
BRIGHAM (St Bridget), *Cumb.* V. D Carl 10 P *Earl of Lonsdale* I I RENWICK *p-in-c.*
BRIGHOUSE (St Martin) w (St Jas), *W Yorks.* B. D Wakef 2 P *Bp* I R I J MATTHEWS, P J BEVAN *c.*
BRIGHSTONE (St Mary Virg) and Brooke w Mottistone, *Isle of Wight,* R. D Portsm 7 P *Bp and D and C of St Paul's Cathl* I S C PALMER.
BRIGHTLING (St Thos of Cant) w Dallington (St Giles), *E Sussex.* R. D Chich 18 P *Maj M Grissell and Bp (alt)* I V R D HELLABY.
BRIGHTLINGSEA (All SS w St Jas), *Essex.* V. D Chelmsf 28 P *Ld Chan* I M R C SWINDLEHURST.
BRIGHTON (St Pet Par Ch) w Chap Royal and St Jo Evang, *E Sussex.* V. D Chich 10 P *Bp* I D TURNER, C R BURROWS *c,* W R PRATT *c.*
(Ch Ch), V. D Chich 10 P *V of Brighton* I P CLARK *p-in-c.*
(H Trin), V. D Chich 10 P *V of Brighton* I (Vacant).
(St Anne), V. D Chich 14a P *V of Brighton* I B J LOVATT.
(St Aug). D Chich 10 *See* Preston.
(St Bart), V. D Chich 10 P *Wagner Trustees* I J M HOLDROYD.
(St Geo Mart), V. D Chich 10 P *CPS* I B J LOVATT *p-in-c.*
(St Mark, w St Matt, Kemp Town), V. D Chich 14a P *Bp V of Brighton, 3 others and Trustees* alt I P W EARDLEY.
(St Mary Virg) w (St Jas) V. D Chich 14a P *Bp, V of Brighton and 3 others* I F J BACON.
(St Mich AA) w (All SS), V. D Chich 10 P *V of Brighton* I B HOPPER, G D HEWETSON *c.*
(St Nich of Myra), V. D Chich 10 P *Bp* I R H ECKERSLEY.
(St Paul), V. D Chich 10 P *Wagner Trustees* I J MILBURN, J N BALDRY *c.*
(The Annunc of St Mary Virg), V. D Chich 10 P *Wagner Trustees* I R BULLIVANT, M S PORTEOUS *c.*
The Resurrection (St Alb Preston, St Luke, St Martin, St Sav Preston, St Wilfrid), *Sussex.* R. D Chich 10 P *Dioc Bd of Patr* I B L BRANDIE, R S CRITTALL *team v,* J A WREN *team v,* R J CASWELL *c,* J F HALE *c.*
See also MOULSECOOMB, PATCHAM, PRESTON AND WHITEHAWK.
BRIGHTSIDE, *S Yorks.*. D Sheff *See* Sheffield.
BRIGHTWALTON (All SS) w Catmore, Leckhampstead Chaddleworth and Fawley, *Berks.* R. D Ox 14 P *P L Wroughton Esq, Bp and D and C of Westmr* I R B H GREAVES.
BRIGHTWELL (St Agatha) w Sotwell, (St Jas), *Oxon.* R. D Ox 18 P *Bp* I R G HAYNE.
BRIGHTWELL, *Suff.*. D St E *See* Martlesham.
BRIGHTWELL BALDWIN (St Bart), *Oxon.* R. D Ox 1 P *F D Wright Esq* I M R TALBOT *p-in-c.*
BRIGMERSTON, *Wilts.*. D Sarum 18 *See* Figheldean.
BRIGNALL (St Mary), *Dur.* R. D Ripon 1 *See* Rokeby.
BRIGSLEY (St Helen), *Humb.* R. D Linc 10 *See* Ashby.
BRIGSTOCK (St Andr) w Stanion (St Pet), *Northants.* V. D Pet 10 P *Bp* I L E VINER.
BRILL (All SS), Boarstall (St Jas), Chilton (St Mary) and Dorton, *Bucks.* V. D Ox 21 P *Sir J Aubrey-Fletcher and Gore-Langton* I P R BUGG.
BRILLEY (St Mary Virg), w Michaelchurch (St Mich AA), *Herefs.* R. D Heref 5 P *Bp of Birm* I (Vacant).
BRIMFIELD (St Mich), *Herefs.* R. D Heref 7 P *Bp* I J T V JONES.
BRIMINGTON (St Mich), *Derbys.* R. D Derby 2 P *V of Chesterfield* I I E WINTERBOTTOM.
BRIMPSFIELD (St Mich) w Elkstone (St Jo Evang) and Syde (St Mary), *Glos.* R. D Glouc 13 P *Bp, Mrs G M Price and Dioc Bd of Patr* in turn I P NEWING.
BRIMPTON, *Berks.*. D Ox *See* Aldermaston.
BRIMSCOMBE (H Trin), *Glos.* V. D Glouc *See* Woodchester.
BRINDLE (St Jas), *Lancs.* R. D Blackb 4 P *Trustees* I (Vacant).
BRINGHURST (St Nich) w Great Easton (St Andr) and Drayton [Leics]. V. D Leic 5 P *D and C of Pet* I J C HUGHES.
BRINGTON (All SS) w Moleworth (St Pet) and Old Weston (St Swithin), *Cambs.* R. D Ely 11 P *Bp of Ches 1 turn, Bp of Ely 2 turns* I G L NORTH.
BRINGTON (St Mary w St John), *Cambs* w Whilton and Norton, *Northants.* R. D Pet P *Dioc Bd of Patr and The Earl Spencer (alt)* I N V KNIBBS.
BRININHAM (St Maurice), *Norf.* V. D Nor 24 P *Trustees* I M F C TAYLOR.
BRINKBURN (St Oswin), *T & W.*. D Dur 6 *See* South Shields.
BRINKBURN, *Northumb.*. D Newc T *See* Framlingham, Long.
BRINKHILL (St Phil), *Lincs.* R. D Linc 7 *See* Harrington.
BRINKLEY (BVM), *Cambs.* R. D Ely 4 *See* Burrough Green.
BRINKLOW (St Jo Bapt), *Warws.* R. D Cov 6 P *Ld Chan* I (Vacant).
BRINKSWAY (St Aug), *Gtr Man.*. D Ches 16 *See* Stockport.
BRINKWORTH (St Mich) w Dauntsey, *Wilts.* R. D Bris 11 P *Bp* I C L SUTCH.
BRINNINGTON (St Luke) w Portwood (St Paul), *Gtr Man.* V. D Ches 16 P *Bp* I E SAMBROOK.
BRINSLEY (St Jas Gt) w Underwood (St Mich AA), *Notts.* V. D Southw 12 P *Bp* I (Vacant).
BRINSOP (St Geo), *Herefs.* V. D Heref 4 *See* Credenhill.
BRINSWORTH (St Geo) w Catcliffe (St Mary), *S Yorks.* V. D Sheff 6 P *Bp* I G HARPER, J YALLOP *c.*
BRINTON (St Andr), *Norf.*. D Nor 24 *See* Thornage.
BRISLEY (St Bart), *Norf.* R. D Nor 20 P *Ch Coll Cam* I A W SAWYER *p-in-c.*
BRISLINGTON (St Luke), *Avon.* V. D Bris 2 P *Bp* I P R LEVERTON *p-in-c,* C M J TURNER *c.*
(St Anne), V. D Bris 2 P *Bp* I T E SIMPER *p-in-c.*
(St Chris), V. D Bris 2 P *Simeon Trustees* I A G MILLICAN.
(St Cuthb), V. D Bris 2 P *Bp* I R G CLIFTON *p-in-c.*
BRISTOL (All H, Easton), *Avon.* V. D Bris 3 P *R of St Steph* I (Vacant).
(Ch Ch w St Ewen and All SS), R. D Bris 3 P *Mrs A M Cole and P W Hart Esq* I (Vacant).
(H Cross, Inns Court), V. D Bris 2 P *Bris Ch Trustees* I R J BURBRIDGE *p-in-c.*
(H Trin w St Gabr and St Lawr, Easton), V. D Bris 3 P *Bris Trustees* I V R BARRON.
(St Agnes) and (St Simon Ap), w (St Werburgh) R. D Bris 3 P *Bp and Ld Chan* Alt I J K KIMBER, L MASTERS *team v,* C S SMITH *hon c.*
(St Andr) w (St Bart), V. D Bris 4 P *Bp* I J C BURNETT.
(St Anne w St Thos Eastville), V. D Bris 7 P *Bp* I M P WESTLAKE, M G TUCKER *hon c.*

(St Aug L Coll Green w St Geo Brandon Hill), V. D Bris 3 P *D and C of Bris* I (Vacant).

(St Jas) w (St Pet), V. D Bris 3 P *Bris Trustees* I (Vacant).

(St Jo Bapt) w (St Mary-le-Port), R. D Bris 3 P *Trustees* I (Vacant).

(St Jude w St Matthias-on-Weir), V. D Bris 3 P *Bp* I (Vacant).

(St Luke) w (Ch Ch), V. D Bris 3 P *V of St Phil* I R H TREBY *p-in-c*.

(St Mark, Lower Easton), V. D Bris 3 P *Bp* I M P WESTLAKE *p-in-c*.

(St Matt Kingsdown), V. D Bris 4 P *Trustees* I R V BRAZIER *p-in-c*, A C HORNE *c*.

(St Mich Two Mile Hill). D Bris 5 *See* Two Mile Hill.

(St Mich-on-the-Mount Without), R. D Bris 3 P *Bris Trustees* I L L BURN *p-in-c*.

(St Nath Cotham w St Kath Bishopston), V. D Bris 4 P *Bp* I R V BRAZIER.

(St Paul w St Barn), V. D Bris 3 P *Bris Trustees* I J K KIMBER *p-in-c*, C M G NESBITT *hon c*.

(St Phil and St Jacob w Em Ch), V. D Bris 3 P *Bris Trustees* I M M WIDDECOMBE.

(St Steph) w (St Nich) and (St Leon), R. D Bris 3 P *Ld Chan and D and C of Bris* I C F PILKINGTON, N J KIRBY *hon c*.

EAST (St Aid, St Ambrose, St Geo, St Leon Redfield, St Matt Moorfields), R. D Bris 8 P *Patr Bd* I D G MITCHELL, B W JONES *team v*, T J MCCABE *team v*, H C CROOKS *c*, R M PARTRIDGE *c*.

See also BEDMINSTER, KNOWLE, AND CLIFTON..

BRISTON (All SS), *Norf*.. D Nor *See* Burgh Parva.

BRITFORD (St Pet), *Wilts*. V. D Sarum 17 P *D and C of Sarum* I E F W KNIGHT *c-in-c*.

BRITWELL-SALOME (St Nich), w Britwell-Prior, *Oxon*. R. D Ox 1 P *Marq of Lansdowne* I (Vacant).

BRIXHAM (All SS w St Mary Virg) w Churston Ferrers, *Devon*. V. D Ex 10 P *Crown* I D V COSSAR, P G HARRISON *c*.

BRIXTON (St Mary), *Devon*. V. D Ex 21 P *D and C of Windsor* I D S MADDOCKS.

BRIXTON (St Matt), *Surrey*. V. D S'wark 3 P *Abp* I R W H NIND, G G MOORGAS *c*, R R WHEELER *c*, D L MOORE *hon c*.

(Ch Ch Brixton Road), V. D S'wark 4 P *CPAS* I C PINDER *p-in-c*.

(St Paul), V. D S'wark 3 P *Trustees* I (Vacant).

EAST (St Jude), V. D S'wark 3 P *Trustees* I (Vacant).

BRIXTON HILL (St Sav), *Surrey*. V. D S'wark 3 P *Ch S and others* I (Vacant).

ANGELL TOWN (St Jo Evang), V. D S'wark 3 P *Bp* I M S ARMITAGE, D J EVANS *c*.

BRIXTON DEVERILL (St Mich), *Wilts*. R. D Sarum 22 *See* Deverills.

BRIXWORTH (All SS) w Holcot, *Northants*. V. D Pet 6 P *Bp* I A J WATKINS.

BRIZE NORTON (St Britius), *Oxon*. V. D Ox *See* Minster-Lovell.

BROAD TOWN, *Wilts*.. D Sarum 25 *See* Clyffe Pypard.

BROADBOTTOM (St Mary Magd), *Gtr Man*.. D Ches 15 *See* Mottram-in-Longdendale.

BROADCHALKE (All SS) w Bowerchalke (Most Holy Trin), *Wilts*. V (*in Chalke Valley Group - see Bishopstone*). D Sarum 19 P *K Coll Cam* I A STOTT.

BROAD CLYST (St Jo Bapt) w Westwood (St Paul), *Devon*. V. D Ex 1 P *Sir R Acland Bt* I M C BOYES.

BROADFIELD, *Herts*.. D St Alb 5 *See* Cottered.

BROADHEATH (St Alb), *Gtr Man*. V. D Ches 10 P *Bp* I M W MALLETT.

BROADHEATH (Ch Ch), *Worcs*. V. D Worc 2 P *Bp* I (Vacant).

BROADHEMBURY (St Andr Ap and Mart) w Payhembury (St Mary), *Devon*. V. D Ex 7 P *Ex Coll Ox and Walter Drewe Esq* I K J POWELL *hon c*.

BROADHEMPSTON, Woodland (St Jo Bapt), Berry Pomeroy and Littlehempston, *Devon*. V. D Ex 13 P *Duke of Somt and Bp 1 turn, Crown 1 turn* I R H BAKER.

BROAD HINTON (St Pet-ad-Vincula), *Wilts*. V. D Sarum 26 *See* Kennet, Upper.

BROADMAYNE (St Martin) and West Knighton (St Pet) w Owermoigne (St Mich AA) w Warmwell (H Trin), *Dorset*. R. D Sarum 5 P *Maj G A Mc Cree one turn, Sir R P N Williams, Bt one turn, MMT 2 turns* I R T HUGHES.

BROADOAK (St Paul), *Dorset*.. D Sarum 2 *See* Symondsbury.

BROADSTAIRS (H Trin), *Kent*. R. D Cant 9 P *V of St Pet-in-I of Thanet* I E J POWE.

BROADSTONE (St Jo Bapt), *Dorset*. V. D Sarum 14 P *Bp* I S J T BUFFREY *p-in-c*, P J GREWCOCK *c*.

BROADWAS, *Worcs*.. D Worc *See* Knightwick.

BROADWATER (St Mary), *W Sussex*. R. D Chich 9 P *Mart Mem Trust* I W C L FILBY, D C MARSHALL *c*, D L PARKER *c*.

BROADWATER DOWN (St Mark), *E Sussex*. V. D Chich 20 P *Bp* I P J BURCH.

BROADWATERS (St Oswald-in-Usmere), *Worcs*.. D Worc *See* Kidderminster.

BROADWAY, *Somt*.. D B & W 20 *See* Ashill.

BROADWAY (St Mich AA) *Worcs*. V. D Worc 1 P *Peache Trustees* I W K BLACKBURN.

BROADWELL (St Paul), *Glos*. R. D Glouc 16 P *Dioc Bd of Patr* I (Vacant).

BROADWEY (St Nich), *Dorset*.. D Sarum 6 *See* Bincombe.

BROADWINDSOR (St Jo Bapt) w Burstock (St Andr), Blackdown (H Trin), and Drimpton (St Mary), and Seaborough, *Dorset*. R. D Sarum *See* Beaminster Area.

BROADWOOD KELLY, *Devon*. R. D Ex 16 P *Dioc Bd of Patr* I A J MACKERACHER.

BROADWOODWIDGER (St Nich), *Devon*. V. D Ex 22 P *Bp, M W Kelly Esq and Countess de Wolovey* I A W H DICK *p-in-c*.

BROBURY (St Mary Magd), *Herefs*.. D Heref 1 *See* Bredwardine.

BROCKDISH (St Pet and St Paul) w Thorpe Abbots, *Norf*. R. D Nor 17 *See* Scole.

BROCKENHURST (St Nich), *Hants*. V. D Win 9 P *E Morant Esq* I D P BREWSTER, L C BABER *c*.

BROCKHALL (St Pet and St Paul), *Northants*. R. D Pet 3 *See* Dodford.

BROCKHAM GREEN (Ch Ch), *Surrey*. V. D S'wark 12 P *Maj-Gen E H Goulburn* I R W A WEST.

BROCKHAMPTON (All SS) w Farley, *Herefs*. V. D Heref P *D and C of Heref* I R V HOWARD JONES.

BROCKHOLES (St Geo), *W Yorks*.. D Wakef 5 *See* Honley.

BROCKLESBY (All SS), R w Limber Magna (St Pet) V *Lincs*.. D Linc 6 P *Earl of Yarborough* I S PHILLIPS.

BROCKLEY (St Nich), *Avon*. R. D B & W 16 *See* Chelvey.

BROCKLEY (St Andr), *Suff*. R. D St E 13 *See* Whepstead.

BROCKLEY (St Cypr), *Kent*.. D S'wark *See* Crofton Park.

(St Pet), V. D S'wark 19 P *Bp* I G D GRAHAM.

BROCKLEY HILL (St Sav), *Surrey*. V. D S'wark 18 P *V of Ch Ch Forest Hill* I J W TIPPING.

BROCKMOOR (St John), *W Midl*. V. D Lich 1 P *Bp and Crown* alt I R BILLS *p-in-c*.

BROCKWORTH (St Geo), *Glos*. V. D Glouc 2 P *Dioc Bd of Patr* I P H NAYLOR.

BRODSWORTH (St Mich) w Hooton Pagnell, Frickley, Clayton and Marr, *S Yorks*. V. D Sheff 10 P *Bp, Maj W Warde-Aldam, Mrs B Warde-Norbury and Mrs S Grant-Dalton* I G M YOULD.

BROKENBOROUGH (St Jo Bapt), *Wilts*.. D Bris 9 *See* Charlton.

BROKERSWOOD (All SS), *Wilts*. V. D Sarum 24 *See* Dilton Marsh.

BROMBOROUGH (St Barn), *Mer*. R. D Ches 9 P *D and C of Ches* I N P CHRISTENSEN, I A F LEGERTON *c*.

BROME (St Mich), *Norf*.. D Nor *See* Broome.

BROME (St Mary) w Oakley (St Nich) and Thrandeston w Stuston, *Suff*. R. D St E 16 P *Dioc Bd of Patr and MMT* alt I J F B JOWITT.

BROMESWELL, *Suff*. R. D St E 7 *See* Eyke.

BROMFIELD (St Mungo) w Waverton, *Cumb*. V. D Carl 3 P *Bp* I (Vacant).

BROMFIELD (St Mary Virg), *Salop*. V. D Heref 12 P *Earl of Plymouth* I G ELLIOTT.

BROMHAM (St Nich) w Chittoe and Sandy Lane, *Wilts*. R. D Sarum P *Dioc Bd of Patr and S Spicer Esq* I R G BROWN.

BROMHAM (St Owen) w Oakley (St Mary), *Beds*. V. D St Alb 19 P *Bp* I D C KING.

BROMLEY (St Pet and St Paul), *Kent*. V. D Roch 12 P *Bp* I D H BARTLEET, T J MERCER *c*, J W THACKER *c*.

(H Trin Bromley Common), V. D Roch 12 P *Crown* I D L WILLIAMS.

(St Andr), V. D Roch 12 P *Bp* I G R O'LOUGHLIN, I A L LITTLE *hon c*.

(St Aug, Bromley Common), V. D Roch 12 P *Bp* I B J ASH.

(St Jo Evang), V. D Roch 12 P *Bp* I I D ZASS-OGILVIE.

(St Luke, Bromley Common), V. D Roch 12 P *Bp* I R D SMITH.

(Ch Ch Bromley Park), V. D Roch 12 P *CPAS* I H W J HARLAND, J BEANEY *c*.

(St Mark), V. D Roch 12 P *V of Bromley* I E HOLLAND, C J STONE *c*.

BROMLEY ST LEONARD (St Mary Virg w St Andr). V. **D** Lon 4 *See* Bow.
(All H Devons Road), R. **D** Lon 4 **P** *Grocers' Co* **I** F R BENTLEY.
(St Frideswide). **D** Lon 4 *See* Poplar.
(St Gabr South Bromley), V. **D** Lon 4 *See* Poplar.
(St Mich AA), V. **D** Lon 4 *See* Poplar.
BROMLEY, GREAT w Little (St Mary Virg), *Essex*. R. **D** Chelmsf 25 **P** *C R Mirfield and Wadh Coll Ox* **I** D H T PICTON.
BROMPTON (H Trin). V. **D** Lon 15 *See* Kensington.
BROMPTON (St Thos) w Deighton, *N Yorks*. V. **D** York 23 **P** *D and C of Dur* **I** (Vacant).
BROMPTON (All SS) w Snainton (St Steph), *N Yorks*. V. **D** York 24 **P** *Abp* **I** C C FORSTER.
BROMPTON-RALPH (St Mary Virg), *Somt*. R. **D** B & W 18 *See* Monksilver.
BROMPTON-REGIS (St Mary Virg) w Withiel Florey, Upton (St Jas) and Skilgate (St Jo Bapt), *Somt*. R. **D** B & W 21 **P** *Em Coll Cam, Keble Coll Ox and Bp* **I** (Vacant).
BROMPTON-ON-SWALE (St Paul), *N Yorks*.. **D** Ripon 1 *See* Easby.
BROMSBERROW (St Mary), *Glos*. R. **D** Glouc *See* Redmarley D'Abitot.
BROMSGROVE (St Jo Bapt), *Worcs*. V. **D** Worc 7 **P** *D and C of Worc* **I** F J MUSHEN *p-in-c*, A ROBERTS *c*.
(All SS), V. **D** Worc 7 **P** *V of Bromsgrove* **I** B GILBERT *c-in-c*.
BROMSHALL (St Lawr), *Staffs*. R. **D** Lich 20 *See* Bramshall.
BROMYARD (St Pet), *Herefs*. V. **D** Heref 2 **P** *Bp* **I** D W GOULD.
BRONDESBURY (Ch Ch w St Lawr), *Gtr Lon*. R. **D** Lon 18 **P** *Ld Chan* **I** S P H STUBBS.
(St Anne) w (H Trin), Kilburn, V. **D** Lon 18 **P** *Bp and CPS* alt **I** C R GOWER *p-in-c*.
(St Lawr), V. **D** Lon 18 *See* Brondesbury.
BROOK, *Kent*.. **D** Cant 2 *See* Wye.
BROOKE (St Pet), *Norf*.. **D** Nor *See* Kirstead.
BROOKE (St Pet), *Leics*. V. **D** Pet 22 *See* Braunston.
BROOKE (St Mary Virg) w Mottistone, *Isle of Wight*. R. **D** Portsm 7 *See* Brighstone.
BROOKEND, *Glos*.. **D** Glouc 5 *See* Sharpness.
BROOKFIELD (St Anne), *also* (St Mary).. **D** Lon 26 *See* St Pancras.
BROOKLAND (St Aug) w Fairfield and Ivychurch w Old Romney and Midley and Brenzett w Snargate and Snave, *Kent*. V. **D** Cant 13 **P** *Abp* **I** L P FORD P-IN-C OF OLD ROMNEY.
BROOKLANDS or Baguley (St Jo Div), *Gtr Man*. V. **D** Man 10 **P** *Bp and Dr T P Nevell* **I** A WOLSTENCROFT, J READER *c*.
BROOKSBY (St Mich AA), *Leics*.. **D** Leic *See* Hoby.
BROOKTHORPE (St Swith) w Whaddon (St Marg) and Harescombe (St Jo Bapt), *Glos*. V. **D** Glouc 4 **P** *D and C of Glouc, R W Neeld Esq and Bp* alt **I** G N BIRD, T B GRETTON *p-in-c*.
BROOKWOOD, *Surrey*.. **D** Guildf *See* Woking.
BROOM LEYS (St D), *Leics*. V. **D** Leic 11 **P** *Bp* **I** J B BARNES.
BROOME (St Mich), *Norf*. R. **D** Nor 11 **P** *Brig W G Carr* **I** D T G WARD.
BROOME (St Pet), *Worcs*. R. **D** Worc 11 **P** *H Bourne Esq* **I** W R ILIFFE.
BROOMFIELD Somt. V **D** B & W *See* Kingston St Mary.
BROOMFIELD (St Marg), *Kent*.. **D** Cant 15 *See* Leeds.
BROOMFIELD (St Mary), *Essex*. V. **D** Chelmsf 12 **P** *Bp* **I** A A MACKENZIE.
BROOMFLEET (St Mary Virg) w Faxfleet, *Humb*.. **D** York *See* Cave, South.
BROOMHALL (St Mark), *S Yorks*.. **D** Sheff 4 *See* Sheffield.
BROSELEY (All SS), w Benthall, *Salop*. R. **D** Heref 14 **P** *Ld Forester* **I** W W LUCAS.
BROTHERTOFT (St Gilbert) *Lincs*. V. **D** Linc 21 **P** *Bp* **I** W ANNAKIN.
BROTHERTON (St Edw the Confessor), *N Yorks*. V. **D** Wakef 11 **P** *D and C of York* **I** C G H KASSELL.
BROTTON PARVA (St Marg), *Cleve*. R. **D** York 19 **P** *Abp* **I** E SMITS.
BROUGH, *Humb*.. **D** York 16 *See* Elloughton.
BROUGH (St Mich) w Stainmore (St Mary and St Steph), *Cumb*. V. **D** Carl 1 **P** *Bp and Col G W A Tufton*, alt **I** S E ABLEWHITE.
BROUGHAM Cumb. **D** Carl *See* Clifton.
BROUGHTON (St Jo Bapt), *Lancs*. V. **D** Blackb 12 **P** *Trustees* **I** W G ARMSTRONG, E AMBROSE *c*.
BROUGHTON and DUDDON (St Mary Magd), *Cumb*. V. **D** Carl 15 **P** *V of Millom and Ch Patr Trust (alt)* **I** G C ANTHONY.
BROUGHTON (All SS) w Oldhurst (St Pet) and Woodhurst (St Jo Bapt), *Cambs*. R. **D** Ely 12 **P** *Bp* **I** (Vacant).
BROUGHTON (St Pet), *Staffs*.. **D** Lich 15 *See* Croxton.
BROUGHTON (St Mary), *Salop*. V. **D** Lich 27 **P** *R Thompson Esq* **I** C P COLLIS SMITH.
BROUGHTON (St Mary), *Humb*. R. **D** Linc 6 **P** *Mart Mem Trust* **I** E A STRICKLAND.
BROUGHTON (St Osw or All SS) Marton and Thornton, *N Yorks*. R. **D** Bradf 10 **P** *Ch Ch Ox and Trustees* **I** D C MCCOULL.
BROUGHTON, *Lancs*.. **D** Man 8 *See* Salford.
BROUGHTON (St Lawr) w Milton Keynes (All SS), *Bucks*. R. **D** Ox 26 **P** *Dioc Bd of Patr* **I** N J COTTON *p-in-c*.
BROUGHTON (St Andr), *Northants*. R. **D** Pet 8 **P** *Bp* **I** J L LESLIE.
BROUGHTON (St Mary) w Bossington (St Jas) and Mottisfont, *Hants*. R. **D** Win 10 **P** *J Dent Esq and M Dent Esq* **I** D R HOWE.
BROUGHTON w Newington, North (St Mary Virg), *Oxon*. R. **D** Ox 6 **P** *Ld Saye and Sele* **I** D BISHOP *p-in-c*.
BROUGHTON ASTLEY (St Mary), *Leics*. R. **D** Leic 13 **P** *Fidelity Trust* **I** P E HANCOCK.
BROUGHTON-GIFFORD (St Mary Virg) w Gt Chalfield (All SS), *Wilts*. R. **D** Sarum 24 **P** *Mrs M E Floyd 1 turn, Ld Chan 2 turns, D and C of Bris 3 turns* **I** R E DUNNINGS.
BROUGHTON, GREAT (Ch Ch), w Broughton Moor, *Cumb*. V. **D** Carl **P** *Bp* **I** B T YOUNG.
BROUGHTON-HACKETT, *Worcs*.. **D** Worc *See* Upton Snodsbury.
BROUGHTON, HIGHER, *Gtr Man*.. **D** Man 8 *See* Salford.
BROUGHTON MOOR (St Columba), *Cumb*.. **D** Carl *See* Broughton, Great.
BROUGHTON, NETHER (St Mary Virg), *Leics*. R. **D** Leic 4 *See* Dalby, Old.
BROUGHTON-POGIS (St Pet) w Filkins (St Pet), V *Oxon*. R. **D** Ox *See* Filkins.
BROUGHTON SULNEY (St Luke), *Notts*. R. **D** Southw *See* Hickling.
BROWN and Chilton Candover (St Pet), *Hants*.. **D** Win *See* Candover Valley.
BROWN EDGE (St Anne), *Staffs*. V. **D** Lich 16 **P** *Bp* **I** A W MOSELEY.
BROWNHILL (St Sav), *W Yorks*. V. **D** Wakef 10 **P** *V of Batley* **I** J H CATLEY.
BROWNHILLS, *W Midl*.. **D** Lich 2 *See* Ogley Hay.
BROWNSOVER (St Mich AA), *Warws*.. **D** Cov 6 *See* Clifton-on-Dunsmore.
BROWNSTONE, *Devon*.. **D** Ex *See* Modbury.
BROWNSWOOD PARK (St Jo Evang), *Lon*. V. **D** Lon 2 **P** *Corp of City of Lon* **I** T G SUMMERS.
BROXBOURNE (St Aug) w Wormley (St Laur), *Herts*. V. **D** St Alb 6 **P** *Peache Trustees and Bp* **I** D MOWBRAY, A C TAYLOR *c*.
BROXHOLME (All SS), *Lincs*. R. **D** Linc 2 **P** *Dioc Bd of Patr* **I** E R COOK.
BROXTED (St Mary) w Chickney (St Mary) and Tilty (St Mary Virg) and Little Easton, *Essex*. R. **D** Chelmsf 23 **P** *Mrs F Spurrier 2 turns J L Crammer-Byng Esq 1 turn* **I** J M FILBY.
BROXTOWE (St Martha's Eccles Distr), *Notts*.. **D** Southw 8 **P** *Bp* **I** R CATCHPOLE.
BRUERA (St Mary Virg) w Alford (St Jo Bapt), *Chesh*. V. **D** Ches 5 **P** *D and C of Ches* **I** A J H SCOTT.
BRUISYARD, *Suff*.. **D** St E *See* Badingham.
BRUMBY, OLD (St Hugh), *Lincs*. R. **D** Linc 4 **P** *Bp* **I** A DUTFIELD, P W ABRAHAMS *team v*, E L RENNARD *c*.
BRUNDALL (St Lawr), *Norf*.. **D** Nor *See* Witton.
BRUNDISH, *Suff*.. **D** St E *See* Wilby.
BRUNDON, *Suff*.. **D** St E 15 *See* Sudbury.
BRUNSTEAD (St Pet), *Norf*.. **D** Nor *See* Stalham.
BRUNSWICK (Ch Ch & St Sav), *Gtr Man*. R. **D** Man 5 **P** *Bp* **I** M L GOODER, A P HOBSON *c*.
BRUNTCLIFFE (St Andr), *W Yorks*. V. **D** Wakef 9 **P** *Vs of Morley and Batley* alt **I** P HUMPLEBY.
BRUNTINGTHORPE (St Mary), *Leics*. R. **D** Leic *See* Kimcote.
BRUSHFORD, *Somt*.. **D** B & W 21 *See* Dulverton.
BRUSHFORD (St Mary Virg), *Devon*. V. **D** Ex 16 **P** *D and C of Ex* **I** A J MACKERACHER.
BRUTON (St Mary Virg) w Wyke (H Trin) and Redlynch (St Pet) and Lamyatt (St Mary and St Jo Evang), *Somt*. R. **D** B & W 5 **P** *Bp and Copleston Trustees* **I** P J BLAKE.

BRYANSTON, *Dorset*.. **D** Sarum 10 *See* Durweston.
BRYANSTON SQUARE (St Mary).. **D** Lon 25 *See* St Marylebone.
BRYANSTON STREET (Ch of Annunc).. **D** Lon 25 *See* St Marylebone.
BRYMPTON D'EVERCY (St Andr), *Somt*. R. **D** B & W 11 **P** *C E B Clive-Ponsonby-Fane Esq* **I** A C DEAN.
BRYN (St Pet), *Gtr Man*. V. **D** Liv 12 **P** *Bp* **I** P MORRIS.
BUBBENHALL (St Giles), *Warws*.. **D** Cov 6 *See* Ryton-on-Dunsmore.
BUBWITH (All SS) w Ellerton and Aughton, *Humb*. V. **D** York 10 **P** *Abp, Ld Chan and D and C of York* **I** C G WEBB.
BUCKBY, LONG (St Lawr) w Watford (St Pet and St Paul), *Northants*. V. **D** Pet 6 **P** *Ld Chan and Bp* alt. **I** F M L PARKER.
BUCKDEN (St Mary), *Cambs*. V. **D** Ely 13 **P** *Bp* **I** (Vacant).
BUCKENHAM w Hassingham (St Mary) and Strumpshaw (St Pet), *Norf*. R. **D** Nor 1 **P** *Bp and Mart Mem Trust* alt **I** A E BRANSBY.
BUCKENHAM, NEW (St Martin), *Norf*. V. **D** Nor *See* Quidenham.
BUCKENHAM, OLD (All SS), *Norf*.. **D** Nor 18 *See* Quidenham.
BUCKENHAM PARVA, *Norf*. V. **D** Nor 18 *See* Tofts, West.
BUCKERELL (St Mary and St Giles), *Devon*. R. **D** Ex 7 **P** *D and C of Ex* **I** R K R COATH.
BUCKFASTLEIGH (H Trin) w Dean Prior (St Geo Mart), *Devon*. V. **D** Ex 13 **P** *Rev H Mylcreest 2 turns, Ld Churston 1 turn* **I** R C STEELE-PERKINS.
BUCKHOLD (H Trin w St Simon and St Jude), *Berks*.. **D** Ox 12 *See* Bradfield.
BUCKHORN-WESTON, *Dorset*.. **D** Sarum *See* Kington Magna.
BUCKHURST HILL (St Jo Bapt), *Essex*. R. **D** Chelmsf 2 **P** *Bp* **I** J G HUNTER, K E JONES *team v*, D J GILCHRIST *c*, W G BOYD *hon c*.
BUCKINGHAM (St Pet and St Paul), *Bucks*. V. **D** Ox 23 **P** *Bp* **I** J W BELL, K J DAVIES *c*.
BUCKINGHAM, NORTH (Akeley, Leckhampstead, Lillingstone Dayrell w Lovell, Lillingstone Lovell, Maids Moreton w Foscott), *Bucks*. r. **D** Ox 23 **P** *Ch Society Trust, R Gilbert Esq, D J Williams Esq and D J Robarts Esq* in turn **I** D M TINSLEY.
BUCKLAND, *Kent*.. **D** Cant 7 *See* Teynham.
BUCKLAND (St Mich) w Laverton, *Glos*. R. **D** Glouc 18 **P** *Exors of C T Scott* **I** M BLAND.
BUCKLAND (St Mary Virg), *Berks*. V. **D** Ox 17 **P** *Dioc Bd of Patr* **I** E B WOOD *p-in-c*.
BUCKLAND Bucks. V **D** Ox 30 *See* Aston Clinton.
BUCKLAND (St Andr), *Herts*. R. **D** St Alb 5 *See* Barkway w Reed.
BUCKLAND (St Mary Virg), *Surrey*. R. **D** S'wark 12 **P** *All S Coll Ox* **I** W J MONTAGUE.
BUCKLAND-BREWER (St Mary and St Benedict), *Devon*. V. **D** Ex 17 *See* Parkham.
BUCKLAND-DINHAM (St Mich AA), *Somt*. V. **D** B & W 16a **P** *Bp* **I** (Vacant).
BUCKLAND, EAST (St Mich), *Devon*.. **D** Ex 19 *See* Filleigh.
BUCKLAND FILLEIGH (St Mary and H Trin), *Devon*. R. **D** Ex 20 *See* Shebbear.
BUCKLAND-IN-DOVER (St Andr) and Buckland Valley (St Nich), *Kent*. R. **D** Cant 4 **P** *Abp* **I** L G TYZACK, D L CAWLEY *c*, J HEWES *c*.
BUCKLAND-IN-THE-MOOR, *Devon*.. **D** Ex 11 *See* Ashburton.
BUCKLAND-MONACHORUM (St Andr), *Devon*. V. **D** Ex 22 **P** *Bp* **I** C C HUGHES.
BUCKLAND NEWTON (Holyrood), *Dorset*. V. **D** Sarum 7 **P** *Col L L Yeatman* **I** D HOPLEY.
BUCKLAND-RIPERS (St Nich), *Dorset*. R. **D** Sarum *See* Bincombe.
BUCKLAND ST MARY (St Mary Virg), *Somt*. R. **D** B & W 20 **P** *Dioc Bd of Patr* **I** L J HEMMONS *p-in-c*.
BUCKLAND-TOUT-SAINTS (St Pet), *Devon*.. **D** Ex 14 *See* Charleton.
BUCKLAND VALLEY (St Nich) *Kent*.. **D** Cant 4 *See* Buckland-in-Dover.
BUCKLAND, WEST, *Somt*.. **D** B & W 22 *See* Wellington.
BUCKLAND, WEST (St Pet), *Devon*. R. **D** Ex 18 *See* Swimbridge.
BUCKLEBURY (St Mary) w Marlston (St Mary), *Berks*. V. **D** Ox 14 **P** *G E H Palmer Esq* **I** A D R HOLMES, B TAYLOR *hon c*.
BUCKLESHAM (St Mary) and Foxhall *Suff*.. **D** St E 2 *See* Nacton.
BUCKMINSTER (St Jo Bapt) w Sewstern (H Trin), Sproxton (St Bart) and Coston *St Andr), Leics*. V. **D** Leic 4 **P** *Sir H Tollemache* **I** E SMITH.
BUCKNALL (St Marg of Antioch V and M), *Lincs*. R. **D** Linc 11 **P** *Bp* **I** H R WHALER.
BUCKNALL (St Mary Virg) w Bagnall (St Chad), *Staffs*. R. **D** Lich 18 **P** *Bp, A D Owen Esq and Lady E K G Owen* **I** G BOTTOMLEY, R GRIFFITHS *team v*, C N THOMAS *team v*, R H LYNE *c*.
BUCKNELL Oxon. R **D** Ox 2 *See* Bicester.
BUCKNELL (St Mary), w Buckton, Llanfair-Waterdine and Stowe, *Salop*. V. **D** Heref 10 **P** *Earl of Powis, J C Rogers Esq and Grocers' Co* **I** B A GILL.
BUCKS MILLS (St Anne), *Devon*. V. **D** Ex 17 *See* Woolfardisworthy.
BUCKTHORPE (St Andr), *Humb*.. **D** York *See* Bugthorpe.
BUCKWORTH, *Cambs*. R. **D** Ely 10 **P** *Bp* **I** B E CLOSE *p-in-c*.
BUDBROOKE (St Mich), w Hampton-on-the-Hill, *Warws*. V. **D** Cov 4 **P** *MMT* **I** T J JOHNSON.
BUDOCK **D** Truro 3 *See* St Budock.
BUDE HAVEN (St Mich), *Cornw*. V. **D** Truro 10 **P** *PCC* **I** E J WIDDOWS.
BUDLEIGH, EAST (All SS), *Devon*. V. **D** Ex 1 *See* Bicton.
BUDLEIGH SALTERTON (St Pet), *Devon*. V. **D** Ex 1 **P** *Clinton Devon Estates Co* **I** D CHEVERTON.
BUDWORTH, LITTLE (St Pet), *Chesh*. V. **D** Ches 6 *See* Whitegate.
BUGBROOKE or BUCHEBROC (St Mich AA or St Mary), *Northants*. R. **D** Pet 3 **P** *Exors of Rev E W Harrison* **I** T R PARTRIDGE.
BUGLAWTON (St Jo Evang), *Chesh*. V. **D** Ches 11 **P** *R of Astbury* **I** J K MOWLL.
BUGTHORPE (St Andr), *Humb*. V. **D** York 7 *See* Kirby Underdale.
BUILDWAS (H Trin) and Leighton w Eaton Constantine and Wroxeter, *Salop*. V. **D** Lich 29 **P** *Bp, Ld Barnard and Mart Mem and C of E Trusts* **I** T W B FOX.
BULCOTE (H Trin), *Notts*.. **D** Southw 13 *See* Burton Joyce.
BULFORD (St Leon), *Wilts*. V. **D** Sarum 18 **P** *Sec of State for Defence* **I** M H DAWKINS *p-in-c*.
BULKINGTON (St Jas), *Warws*. V. **D** Cov 5 **P** *Ld Chan* **I** W D C SCOTT, A A GRAY *c*, D H ROBINSON *c*.
BULKINGTON (Ch Ch), *Wilts*.. **D** Sarum 23 *See* Seend.
BULKWORTHY, *Devon*.. **D** Ex 9 *See* Milton Damerel.
BULLEY (St Mich AA), *Glos*.. **D** Glouc 6 *See* Churcham.
BULLINGHOPE, UPPER (St Pet) w Bullinghope Lower, and Grafton, *Herefs*. V. **D** Heref 3 **P** *Bp* **I** J F BAULCH.
BULLINGTON, *Lincs*.. **D** Linc 3 *See* Rand.
BULLINGTON (St Mich AA), *Hants*.. **D** Win *See* Barton Stacey.
BULMER, *Essex*.. **D** Chelmsf 18 *See* Belchamp Otten.
BULMER (St Martin) w Welburn (St Jo Evang) and Castle Howard, *N Yorks*. R. **D** York 4 **P** *G A Howard Esq* **I** R S P MARRS.
BULPHAN (St Mary Virg), *Essex*. R. **D** Chelmsf 15 **P** *Mrs H Larner* **I** H V CROSSLEY *p-in-c*.
BULWELL (St Mary Virg), *Notts*. R. **D** Southw 12 **P** *Bp* **I** W S BEASLEY, R W BRECKLES *c*.
(St Jo Div), V. **D** Southw 12 **P** *Bp* **I** J P FEWKES.
BULWICK (St Nich) and Blatherwycke w Harringworth (St Jo Bapt), and Laxton (All SS), *Northants*. R. **D** Pet 13 **P** *G T G Conant, 3 turns, F & A George Ltd 1 turn* **I** M R A WILSON.
BUNBURY (St Boniface), *Chesh*. V. **D** Ches 5 **P** *Haberdashers' Co* **I** T S ATKINS.
BUNCTON (All SS), *W Sussex*.. **D** Chich 7 *See* Ashington.
BUNGALOW TOWN (Good Shepherd), (W Sussex].. **D** Chich 9 *See* Lancing.
BUNGAY (St Mary w H Trin), *Suff*. V. **D** St E 14 **P** *Dioc Bd of Patr* **I** F W FULLER, J B DAVIS *c*.
BUNNY (St Mary Virg) w Bradmore, *Notts*. V. **D** Southw 10 **P** *Lady Shrigley-Ball* **I** C E JONES.
BUNTINGFORD, *Herts*.. **D** St Alb *See* Aspenden.
BUNWELL (St Mich AA) w Carleton Rode and Tibenham, *Norf*. R. **D** Nor **P** *Bp and Dioc Bd of Patr (alt)* **I** (Vacant).
BURBAGE (St Cath) w Aston Flamville (St Pet), *Leics*. R. **D** Leic 16 **P** *Ball Coll Ox* **I** W GRIMWOOD.
BURBAGE (All SS), *Wilts*. V. **D** Sarum *See* Wexcombe.
BURBAGE (Ch Ch) w Harpur Hill (St Jas), *Derbys*. V. **D** Derby 10 *See* Buxton.

BURCOMBE (St Jo Bapt), *Wilts.* V. **D** Sarum *See* Barford St Martin.
BURCOTE, *Oxon..* **D** Ox 5 *See* Clifton Hampden.
BURES (St Mary Virg), *Suff.* V. **D** St E 12 **P** *Dioc Bd of Patr* **I** C D G PATTERSON.
BURFORD (St Jo Bapt) w Fulbrook (St Jas) and Taynton (St Jo Evang), *Oxon.* V. **D** Ox 9 **P** *Bp (3 turns) C T R Wingfield Esq (1 turn)* **I** G H PARSONS.
BURFORD, 1st Portion (Dedic unknown), Nash (St Jo Bapt) and Boraston, *Salop.* R. **D** Heref 12 **P** *Dioc Bd of Patr* **I** G H M THOMPSON *team v.*
2nd Portion, Whitton (St Mary Virg), w Greete (St Jas) and Hope Bagot (St Jo Bapt), *Herefs.* R. **D** Heref 12 **P** *Dioc Bd of Patr* **I** G H M THOMPSON *team v.*
3rd Portion, Burford (St Mary) w L Hereford, *Salop.* R. **D** Heref 12 **P** *Dioc Bd of Patr and Bp of Birm* **I** G H M THOMPSON *team v.*
BURGATE (St Mary Virg), *Suff.* R. **D** St E 16 **P** *Bp* **I** R M KNOTT *p-in-c.*
BURGESS HILL (St Jo Evang), *W Sussex.* V. **D** Chich 14 **P** *R of Clayton w Keymer* **I** A R TREEN, M J LEWIS *c,* D H THORNLEY *c.*
(St Andr), V. **D** Chich 14 **P** *Bp* **I** A D MCKEMEY.
BURGH-LE-MARSH (St Pet and St Paul), *Lincs.* V. **D** Linc 8 **P** *Bp* **I** R H IRESON.
BURGH (St Marg and St Mary Virg), *Norf.* R. **D** Nor 2 *See* Rollesby.
BURGH ST PETER (St Mary Virg) or Wheatacre Burgh, *Norf..* **D** Nor *See* Aldeby.
BURGH (St Andr), *Suff.* R. **D** St E 19 *See* Grundisburgh.
BURGH-BY-SANDS (St Mich), w Kirkbampton (St Pet), *Cumb.* V. **D** Carl 3 **P** *Dioc Bd of Patr* **I** J STRONG.
BURGH CASTLE (St Pet and St Paul), *Suff.* R. **D** Nor 2 **P** *Ld Chan* **I** L A J WARD.
BURGH HEATH, *Surrey..* **D** Guildf 9 *See* Tattenham Corner.
BURGH-NEXT-AYLSHAM (St Mary Virg), *Norf.* R. **D** Nor 3 **P** *Miss M K Grix* **I** A B BOAR *p-in-c.*
BURGH-ON-BAIN (St Helen), *Lincs.* V. **D** Linc 12 **P** *Reps of Late Sir John Fox* **I** (Vacant).
BURGH PARVA (St Mary) w Briston (All SS), *Norf.* R. **D** Nor 24 **P** *Bp* **I** H J BLACKER.
BURGHCLERE (The Ascen w All SS) w Newtown (St Mary and St Jo Bapt) and Ecchinswell w Sydmonton *Hants.* R. **D** Win **P** *Earl of Carnarvon* **I** A JARDINE, J R REPATH *c.*
BURGHFIELD (St Mary Virg), *Berks.* R. **D** Ox 12 **P** *Earl of Shrewsbury* **I** J W R MORRISON.
BURGHILL (St Mary), *Herefs.* V. **D** Heref 4 **P** *Dioc Bd of Patr* **I** P W LIND-JACKSON.
BURGHWALLIS (St Helen), R w Skelbrooke (All H or St Mich AA), *S Yorks.* V. **D** Sheff 8 **P** *Maj G Anne and Univ of Cam 2 turns, Bp 1 turn* **I** S K REYNOLDS *p-in-c.*
BURHAM and Wouldham (All SS), *Kent.* R. **D** Roch **P** *Bp and Ld Chan (alt)* **I** (Vacant).
BURITON (St Mary), *Hants.* R. **D** Portsm 4 **P** *Bp* **I** R H GRANGER *p-in-c.*
BURLESCOMBE (St Mary), *Devon.* V. **D** Ex 4 *See* Sampford-Peverell.
BURLESTON, *Dorset..* **D** Sarum 5 *See* Puddletown.
BURLEY (H Cross), *Leics..* **D** Pet *See* Cottesmore.
BURLEY (St Mathias), *W Yorks.* V. **D** Ripon 5 **P** *Trustees* **I** W H COOKE, E J TOWNSON *c,* S G WILLIAMS *c.*
BURLEYDAM (St Mich and St Mary BV), *Ches.* V. **D** Ches 15 *See* Audlem.
BURLEY-IN-WHARFEDALE (St Mary BV), *W Yorks.* V. **D** Bradf 5 **P** *Bp* **I** D B ALDRED.
BURLEY VILLE (St Jo Bapt), *Hants.* V. **D** Win 8 **P** *V of Ringwood* **I** W F SHAIL.
BURLINGHAM (St Edm w St Andr and St Pet) w Lingwood (St Pet), *Norf.* R. **D** Nor 1 **P** *Ch S Trust* **I** G W GLEW.
BURMANTOFTS (St Steph w St Agnes), *W Yorks.* V. **D** Ripon 6 **P** *Trustees* **I** J C BURCH.
BURMARSH Kent. R **D** Cant 13 *See* Dymchurch.
BURMINGTON (St Barn and St Nich), *Warws..* **D** Cov 9 *See* Wolford.
BURNAGE (St Marg), *Gtr Man.* R. **D** Man 4 **P** *Bp* **I** (Vacant).
(St Nich), R. **D** Man 10 **P** *Trustees* **I** B W BARKER.
BURNBY (St Giles), *Humb.* R. **D** York 10 **P** *Nat Westminster Bank Ltd* **I** J S SELLER.
BURNESIDE (St Osw), *Cumb.* V. **D** Carl 17 **P** *Trustees* **I** D J DUNCANSON.
BURNESTON (St Lambert), *N Yorks.* V. **D** Ripon 2 *See* Kirklington.
BURNEY LANE (Ch Ch), *W Midl.* V. **D** Birm 13 *See* Ward End.
BURNHAM, *Essex.* V. **D** Chelmsf 13 **P** *N D Beckett Esq and Walsingham Coll Trust Assoc* **I** R P CASEBOW.
BURNHAM (St Pet), *Bucks.* V. **D** Ox 24 **P** *Eton Coll* **I** D G THOMAS *p-in-c,* J G CRUICKSHANK *c.*
(St Andr Cippenham). **D** Ox 24 *See* Slough, West.
BURNHAM-DEEPDALE (St Mary), *Norf.* R. **D** Nor *See* Brancaster.
BURNHAM-ON-SEA (St Andr), *Somt.* V. **D** B & W 2 **P** *D and C of Wells* **I** R C DEAN, J C ANDREWS *c,* E F W AWRE *hon c,* A BROMHAM *hon c.*
BURNHAM-SUTTON w Burnham Ulph, Burnham Westgate, and Burnham-Norton, *Norf.* R. **D** Nor 21 **P** *Ld Chan and Ch Coll Cam* **I** C J ISAACSON.
BURNHAM THORPE (All SS) w Burnham Overy, *Norf.* R. **D** Nor 21 **P** *Dioc Bd of Patr and Ld Chan* **I** C J ISAACSON.
BURNLEY (St Pet), *Lancs.* R. **D** Blackb 3 **P** *Bp* **I** H WILLIAMS, A BROWN *c.*
(All SS Habergham), V. **D** Blackb 3 **P** *Bp* **I** J K BROCKBANK, A S DEAN *c.*
(H Trin Habergham Eaves), V. **D** Blackb 3 **P** *Hulme Trustees* **I** B H PITHERS *p-in-c,* M M BIRCHALL *c,* P A SMITH *c.*
(St Alb w St Paul), V. **D** Blackb 3 **P** *Bp* **I** R WILLIAMS, M C F KING *c.*
(St Andr) w (St Marg), V. **D** Blackb 3 **P** *Bp and R of St Pet Burnley* alt **I** B ROBINSON, B TONGE *c.*
(St Cath), V. **D** Blackb 3 **P** *R of Burnley* **I** R WILLIAMS, M C F KING *c.*
(St Cuthb), V. **D** Blackb 3 **P** *R of Burnley* **I** J L SUTCLIFFE.
(St Jas), V. **D** Blackb 3 **P** *Crown* **I** J K RUSSON.
(St Jo Bapt Gannow), V. **D** Blackb 3 **P** *R of Burnley* **I** J K BROCKBANK *p-in-c.*
(St Marg), V. **D** Blackb 3 *See* Burnley.
(St Mark), V. **D** Blackb 3 **P** *Bp* **I** A C TAYLOR.
(St Matt Ap Habergham Eaves), V. **D** Blackb 3 **P** *R of Burnley* **I** B H PITHERS, P A SMITH *c.*
(St Steph), V. **D** Blackb 3 **P** *R of Burnley* **I** C P G WODEMAN.
BURNMOOR (St Barn), *N Yorks.* R. **D** Dur 5 **P** *Earl of Dur* **I** B C JOHNSON.
BURNOPFIELD (St Jas Ap and Mart), *Durham.* V. **D** Dur 7 **P** *Bp* **I** (Vacant).
BURNSALL (St Wilfrid), *N Yorks.* R. **D** Bradf 10 **P** *Trustees* **I** P E BUSH *p-in-c.*
BURNT HOUSE LANE (Conv Distr) *Devon..* **D** Ex 3 *See* Exeter.
BURNT YATES N Yorks. **D** Ripon 3 *See* Ripley.
BURNTWOOD (Ch Ch), *Staffs.* V. **D** Lich 2 **P** *V of St Mary, Lich* **I** J E T WALTERS.
BURPHAM (St Mary), *W Sussex.* V. **D** Chich 1 **P** *D and C of Chich* **I** H P SCHNEIDER.
BURPHAM (St Luke), *Surrey.* V. **D** Guildf 5 **P** *Bp* **I** M C HUGHES.
BURRINGHAM (St Jo Bapt), *Humb..* **D** Linc 4 *See* Gunhouse.
BURRINGTON (H Trin) and Churchill (St Jo Bapt), *Avon.* V. **D** B & W 3 **P** *D & C of Bris and Dioc Bd of Finance* **I** E J GREEN.
BURRINGTON (H Trin), *Devon.* V. **D** Ex 16 **P** *Dioc Bd of Patr* **I** C P BARRETT.
BURRINGTON, *Herefs..* **D** Heref *See* Downton.
BURROUGH GREEN (St Aug), w Brinkley (BVM) and Carlton (St Pet), *Cambs.* R. **D** Ely 4 **P** *Exors of C Binney, St Jo Coll Cam and R A Vestey in turn* **I** (Vacant).
BURROUGH-ON-THE-HILL (BVM), *Leics.* R. **D** Leic 8 *See* Somerby.
BURROWBRIDGE (St Mich), *Somt.* V. **D** B & W 23 *See* Stoke St Gregory.
BURSCOUGH BRIDGE (St Jo Bapt), *Lancs.* V. **D** Liv 9 **P** *V of Ormskirk* **I** P H MILLER, P K BARBER *c.*
BURSLEDON (St Leon), *Hants.* V. **D** Win 15 **P** *Bp* **I** H WILSON, D LITTLEFAIR *c,* R A WHITE *c.*
BURSLEM (St Jo Bapt), *Staffs.* R. **D** Lich 17a **P** *Mart Mem Trust* **I** P L C SMITH.
(St Paul), V. **D** Lich 17a **P** *Bp* **I** C CRUMPTON.
(St Werburgh), V. **D** Lich 17a **P** *Bp* **I** F DAVIES.
BURSTALL (St Mary), *Suff.* V. **D** St E *See* Sproughton.
BURSTEAD, GREAT, *Essex.* R. **D** Chelmsf 10 **P** *Bp* **I** P D ELVY.
BURSTEAD, LITTLE (St Mary), *Essex..* **D** Chelmsf *See* Billericay.
BURSTOCK (St Andr), *Dorset..* **D** Sarum 4 *See* Broadwindsor.
BURSTON, *Staffs..* **D** Lich 19 *See* Aston.
BURSTON (St Mary Virg) *Norf.* R. **D** Nor *See* Winfarthing.

BURSTOW (St Bart), *Surrey*. R. **D** S'wark 12 **P** *Ld Chan* **I** (Vacant).
BURSTWICK (All SS) w Thorngumbald (St Mary), *Humb*. V. **D** York 15 **P** *Abp* **I** (Vacant).
BURTLE (St Phil and St Jas), *Somt*. V. **D** B & W 7 **P** *Bp* **I** H L BAXTER *c-in-c*.
BURTON (St Jas), *Cumb*. V. **D** Carl 17 **P** *Simeon Trustees* **I** M W GARNER *c-in-c*.
BURTON (St Nich), *Chesh*. V. **D** Ches 9 **P** *St John's Hosp Lich Trustees* **I** E H WILLIAMS.
BURTON w COATES, *W Sussex*. R. **D** Chich 6 **P** *Miss J B Courtauld* **I** R G JOHNSON *p-in-c*.
BURTON (St Luke) w Sopley (St Mich AA), *Hants*. V. **D** Win 8 **P** *Bp and D and C of Cant* alt **I** A SESSFORD.
BURTON ABBOTS or Black Bourton (St Mary), *Oxon*.. **D** Ox *See* Black Bourton.
BURTON AGNES (St Martin) w Harpham (St Jo of Beverley), *Humb*. R. **D** York **P** *Ld Chan* **I** D S HAWKINS.
BURTON BRADSTOCK (St Mary) and Chilcombe, *Dorset*. R. **D** Sarum *See* Bride Valley.
BURTON-BY-LINCOLN (St Vinc), *Lincs*. R. **D** Linc 3 **P** *Ld Monson* **I** E R COOK *p-in-c*.
BURTON DASSETT, or DASSETT MAGNA (All SS), *Warws*. V. **D** Cov 8 **P** *Bp* **I** A L FERMOR.
BURTON EAST, *Dorset*.. **D** Sarum 9 *See* Wool.
BURTON-FLEMING or N Burton (St Cuthb), w Fordon (St Jas), *Humb*. V. **D** York 12 **P** *Mart Mem Trust* **I** W B JOHNSTON *c-in-c*.
BURTON-HASTINGS, *Warws*. V. **D** Cov 5 *See* Wolvey.
BURTON-IN-LONSDALE (All SS), *N Yorks*. V. **D** Bradf 7 *See* Thornton-in-Lonsdale.
BURTON JOYCE (St Helen) w Bulcote (H Trin), *Notts*. V. **D** Southw 13 **P** *Mart Mem Trust* **I** D W JOHNSON.
BURTON-LATIMER (St Mary Virg), *Northants*. R. **D** Pet 8 **P** *Bp* **I** W E PITT.
BURTON-LE-COGGLES (St Thos à Becket), *Lincs*. V. **D** Linc *See* Ingoldsby.
BURTON LEONARD N Yorks. **D** Ripon 3 *See* Bishop Monkton.
BURTON, LONG (St Jas Gt), *Dorset*. V. **D** Sarum 7 **P** *Bp* **I** D HOPLEY.
BURTON-ON-STATHER (St Andr) w Normanby, Thealby and part of Coleby, and Flixborough (All SS), *Humb*. V and R. **D** Linc 4 **P** *Sir R A B Sheffield, Bt*. **I** P B HEARN.
BURTON-ON-TRENT (St Modwen) w (H Trin), *Staffs*. V. **D** Lich **P** *Bp* **I** (Vacant).
(All SS w Ch Ch), V. **D** Lich **P** *CPAS* **I** J G BLACKETT.
(St Aid Shobnall), V. **D** Lich **P** *Bp* **I** H PERRINS.
(St Chad), V. **D** Lich **P** *Bp* **I** P SMITH.
(St Paul w St Marg), V. **D** Lich **P** *Lord Burton* **I** F W OSBORN *c*.
BURTON OVERY, *Leics*. R. **D** Leic 6 *See* Carlton Curlieu.
BURTON PEDWARDINE (St Andr w St Mary and St Nich), *Lincs*. R. **D** Lich *See* Heckington.
BURTON PIDSEA (St Pet, formerly St Pet and St Paul) w Humbleton (St Pet and St Paul) and Elsternwick (St Laur), *Humb*. V. **D** York 15 **P** *D and C of York and Ld Chan* alt **I** (Vacant).
BURTONWOOD (St Mich AA), *Chesh*. V. **D** Liv 11 **P** *R of Warrington* **I** R S NAYLOR *p-in-c*.
BURWARDSLEY (St Jo Div), *Chesh*. V. **D** Ches 5 *See* Harthill.
BURWARTON (St Laur) w Cleobury, North (SS Peter and Paul), *Salop*. R. **D** Heref 9 **P** *Visc Boyne* **I** M A J HARDING *p-in-c*.
BURWASH (St Bart), *E Sussex*. R. **D** Chich 18 **P** *BNC Ox* **I** R P B DURRANT.
BURWASH WEALD (St Phil), *E Sussex*. V. **D** Chich 18 **P** *Bp* **I** I P HUNTER.
BURWELL (St Mich), *Lincs*.. **D** Linc 12 *See* Muckton.
BURWELL (St Mary B Virg) w St Andr Chap. *Cambs*. V. **D** Ely 3 **P** *Mrs D A Bowlby* **I** I R SECRETT.
BURY (St Jo Evang) w Houghton (St Nich), *W Sussex*. V. **D** Chich 6 **P** *Pemb Coll Ox* **I** D TICEHURST *p-in-c*.
BURY (H Cross), *Cambs*. R. **D** Ely 12 **P** *Bp* **I** P R CUTTING.
BURY (St Mary Virg), *Lancs*. R. **D** Man 12 **P** *Earl of Derby* **I** J R SMITH.
(All SS Elton), V. **D** Man 12 **P** *R of Bury* **I** J I MCFIE, L D LARCOMBE *c*, C M S RANDALL *c*.
(H Trin), V. **D** Man 12 **P** *R of Bury* **I** K LIVESEY *p-in-c*.
(St Jas Woolfold), V. **D** Man 12 **P** *R of Bury* **I** (Vacant).
(St John), V. **D** Man 12 **P** *R of Bury* **I** H G THOMAS.
(St Mark), V. **D** Man 12 **P** *R of Bury* **I** (Vacant).
(St Paul), V. **D** Man 12 **P** *Trustees* **I** A BORSBEY.
(St Pet), V. **D** Man 12 **P** *R of Bury* **I** I J FOX.
(St Steph Elton), V. **D** Man 12 **P** *V of All SS Bury* **I** D H BRACEY.
(Ch K), V. **D** Man 12 **P** *R of Bury* **I** J ARCUS *c-in-c*, P J BEDDINGTON *c*.
BURY, NEW *Gtr Man*.. **D** Man 14 *See* Farnworth.
BURY ST EDMUNDS (St Mary and St Pet), *Suff*. V. **D** St E 13 **P** *Hyndman Trustees* **I** M J WALKER, I H BARHAM *hon c*.
(All SS), V. **D** St E 13 **P** *Bp* **I** H TRODDEN.
(St Geo), V. **D** St E 13 **P** *Bp* **I** D C LOWE, R G CLARKE *c*.
(St Jas Cathl), V. **D** St E 13 **P** *Bp* **I** VERY REV R FURNELL.
(St Jo Evang), V. **D** St E 13 **P** *Bp* **I** D D WILLIAMS *c-in-c*.
BURYTHORPE (All SS) Acklam (St Jo Bapt) and Leavening (St Bedes) w Westow (St Mary), *N Yorks*. R. **D** York 3 **P** *Abp* **I** P J W BLACKBURN.
BUSBRIDGE (St Jo Bapt), *Surrey*. R. **D** Guildf 4 **P** *Dioc Bd of Patr* **I** H I GORDON-CUMMING.
BUSCOT (St Mary Virg), *Oxon*. R. **D** Ox *See* Coxwell, Great.
BUSH END (St Jo Evang), *Essex*.. **D** Chelmsf 3 *See* Hatfield Broad Oak.
BUSH HILL PARK (St Mark), *Gtr Lon*. V. **D** Lon 21 **P** *Bp* **I** D G BROOKER.
(St Steph), V. **D** Lon 21 **P** *V of Edmon* **I** G P BROWN, R W M BOWDER *c*, D M DEWEY *hon c*.
BUSHBURY (St Mary), *W Midl*. R. **D** Lich 12 **P** *Patr Bd* **I** J F MOCKFORD, C R JOHNSON *team v*, R W TAYLOR *team v*, G A F GRIFFIN *c*, D G H YOUNG *c*.
BUSHEY (St Jas and St Paul), *Herts*. R. **D** St Alb 1 **P** *Bp* **I** P B MORGAN, P R STEARN *c*.
BUSHEY HEATH (St Pet), *Herts*. V. **D** St Alb 1 **P** *Bp* **I** G B AUSTIN.
BUSHLEY (St Pet), *Worcs*. V. **D** Worc 5 *See* Longdon.
BUSLINGTHORPE (St Mich), *Lincs*.. **D** Linc 5 *See* Faldingworth.
BUSSAGE (St Mich AA), *Glos*. V. **D** Glouc 4 **P** *Bp* **I** S R STEVENS.
BUTCOMBE (St Mich AA). *Avon*. R. **D** B & W 3 *See* Wrington.
BUTLEIGH (St Leon), *Somt*. V. **D** B & W 7 *See* Baltonsborough.
BUTLERS MARSTON (St Pet and St Paul) and the Pillertons w Ettington, *Warws*. V. **D** Cov **P** *D and C of Ch Ch Ox 1st turn, Bp, Mrs E Brownlow, Miss M L Shirley, Maj J Shirley and Mrs J Shirley 2nd turn and Mrs M Howell 3rd turn* **I** P J WYATT.
BUTLEY. **D** St E *See* Chillesford.
BUTTERCRAMBE (St John), *N Yorks*. V. **D** York 4 *See* Bossall.
BUTTERLEIGH, *Devon*. R. **D** Ex 4 **P** *Bp* **I** T A WATSON.
BUTTERMERE (St Jas), *Cumb*. V. **D** Carl 10 *See* Loweswater.
BUTTERMERE, *Wilts*.. **D** Sarum *See* Shalbourne.
BUTTERSHAW (St Paul), *W Yorks*. V. **D** Bradf 2 **P** *Bp* **I** J BEARDSMORE.
(St Aid), V. **D** Bradf 4 **P** *Bp* **I** A N FROSTICK.
BUTTERTON (St Bart), *Staffs*. V. **D** Lich 13 **P** *V of Mayfield* **I** J W HAMPTON *p-in-c*.
BUTTERTON, *Staffs*.. **D** Lich *See* Newcastle-under-Lyme.
BUTTERWICK, *Lincs*.. **D** Linc 20 *See* Freiston.
BUTTERWICK, *N Yorks*.. **D** York 13 *See* Langtoft.
BUTTERWICK, EAST (St Andr), *Lincs*.. **D** Linc 4 *See* Messingham.
BUTTERWICK, WEST (St Mary Virg), *Humb*. V. **D** Linc 1 **P** *V of Owston Ferry* **I** A J RHODES.
BUTTSBURY (St Mary), *Essex*.. **D** Chelmsf 9 *See* Ingatestone.
BUXHALL (St Mary) w Shelland (K Chas Mart), *Suff*. R. **D** St E 6 **P** *Trin Hall Cam* **I** C N KENDALL.
BUXLOW, *Suff*.. **D** St E 25 *See* Knodishall.
BUXTED (St Marg Queen), *E Sussex*. R. **D** Chich 16 **P** *Abp* **I** K W JONES.
(St Mary), V. **D** Chich 16 **P** *Wagner Trustees* **I** P R F SANDERSON *p-in-c*.
BUXTON (St Jo Bapt w St Anne, St Jas Gt and St Mary Virg) w Burbage and King Sterndale, *Derbys*. R. **D** Derby 10 **P** *Dioc Bd of Patr* **I** J OLDHAM, M A L DAVID *team v*, E W FISHER *team v*, C M ROBERTS *team v*, L E GILCHRIST *c*, R E COOPER *hon c*.
(Trin Chap), V. **D** Derby 10 **P** *Five Trustees* **I** M HANDFORD *min*.
BUXTON (St Andr) w Oxnead (St Mary Magd), *Norf*. V. **D** Nor 3 **P** *Bp* **I** F R K HARE.
BUXWORTH (St Jas), *Derbys*.. **D** Derby 5 *See* Chinley.
BYERS GREEN (St Pet) w Newfield, *Durham*. R. **D** Dur 9 **P** *Bp* **I** G W R HARPER *p-in-c*.

BYFIELD (H Cross) w Boddington (St Jo Bapt), *Northants*. R. **D** Pet 1 **P** *Em Coll Cam and CCC Ox* **I** W P K KENTIGERN-FOX.
BYFLEET (St Mary Virg), *Surrey*. R. **D** Guildf 11 **P** *Ld Chan* **I** J M STEVENETTE.
WEST (St Jo Bapt), V. **D** Guildf 11 **P** *Bp* **I** J A M JENKINS.
BYFORD (St Jo Bapt), *Herefs*. R. **D** Heref 4 *See* Letton.
BYGRAVE (St Marg), *Herts*. R. **D** St Alb 12 *See* Baldock.
BYKER, *Northumb*.. **D** Newc T 5a *See* Newcastle upon Tyne.
BYLAUGH, *Norf*.. **D** Nor *See* Elsing.
BYLEY (St Jo Evang) w Lees, *Chesh*. R. **D** Ches 6 **P** *V of Middlewich* **I** E W COX.
BYRNESS, *Northumb*. R. **D** Newc T 2 *See* Horsley.
BYTHAM, CASTLE (St Jas), *Lincs*. V. **D** Linc *See* Castle Bytham.
BYTHAM PARVA (St Medard), *Lincs*. R. **D** Linc **I** G S HOAR.
BYTHORN (St Laur), *Cambs*.. **D** Ely 11 *See* Keyston.
BYTON (St Mary), *Herefs*. R. **D** Heref 5 *See* Staunton-on-Arrow.
BYWELL (St Pet), *Northumb*. V. **D** Newc T 3 **P** *Archd of Northumb* **I** L ROBINSON, L H CROSS *hon c*.

CABOURN (St Nich), *Lincs*. V. **D** Linc 5 *See* Swallow.
CADBURY (St Mich AA), *Devon*. V. **D** Ex 2 **P** *D and C of Ex and Bp* alt **I** (Vacant).
CADBURY, NORTH (St Mich), *Somt*. R. **D** B & W 4 *See* Camelot.
CADBURY, SOUTH (St Thos à Becket), *Somt*. R. **D** B & W 4 *See* Camelot.
CADDINGTON (All SS), *Beds*. V. **D** St Alb 20 **P** *D and C of St Paul's* **I** A J D SMITH.
CADEBY, *Lincs*.. **D** Linc 12 *See* Ormsby, North.
CADEBY, *S Yorks*. R. **D** Sheff 8 *See* Sprotborough.
CADEBY w Sutton Cheney, *Leics*. R. **D** Leic 15 **P** *Cadeby Hall Farm Ltd 2 turns Admin of late Mrs E Talbot 1 turn* **I** E R BOSTON.
CADELEIGH (St Bart), *Devon*. R. **D** Ex 8 *See* Washfield.
CADISHEAD (St Mary), *Gtr Man*. V. **D** Man 3 **P** *Bp* **I** A J BOOTH.
CADMORE-END (St Mary-le-Moor), *Oxon*. V. **D** Ox 32 *See* Stokenchurch.
CADNEY (All SS) w Howsham, and Newstead, *Humb*. V. **D** Linc 6 **P** *Bp* **I** A J KERSWILL *p-in-c*.
CAENBY (St Nich), *Lincs*.. **D** Linc 3 *See* Owmby.
CAERHAYES, *Cornw*.. **D** Truro *See* St Gorran.
CAINSCROSS or Ebley (St Matt) w Selsley, *Glos*. V. **D** Glouc 9 **P** *Sir J Marling Bt and Bp* **I** I E BURBERY, C A JEFFERIES *c*, R G STURMAN *c*.
CAISTER (H Trin), *Norf*. R. **D** Nor 2 **P** *Mrs M F Bell* **I** D J ROLAND-SHRUBB, T F DRURY *hon c*.
CAISTOR (St Pet and St Paul) and Clixby (All H), *Lincs*. V. **D** Linc 5 **P** *Bp* **I** D SAUNDERS.
CAISTOR (St Edm K and Mart) w Markshall or Marketshall, *Norf*. R. **D** Nor 14 **P** *Mrs E H Hawkins* **I** H R CRESSWELL.
CALBOURNE (All SS) w Newtown (H Spirit) and Porchfield, *Isle of Wight*. R. **D** Portsm 7 **P** *Bp* **I** (Vacant).
CALCEBY, *Lincs*.. **D** Linc 7 *See* Ormsby, South.
CALCETHORPE (St Faith), *Lincs*.. **D** Linc 12 *See* Kelstern.
CALCOT (St Birinus), *Berks*. V. **D** Ox **P** *St Magd Coll Ox* **I** P C FAULKNER.
CALDBECK (St Mungo or Kentigern), Castle Sowerby (St Kentigern) and Sebergham, (St Mary), *Cumb*. R. **D** Carl 3 **P** *Bp and D and C (alt)* **I** C G REID.
CALDECOT, *Norf*.. **D** Nor *See* Oxburgh.
CALDECOTE (St Theobald and St Chad), *Warws*.. **D** Cov 5 *See* Weddington.
CALDECOTE (St Mich AA), *Cambs*.. **D** Ely 1 *See* Toft.
CALDECOTE (St Mary Magd), *Cambs*.. **D** Ely 14 *See* Stilton.
CALDECOTE (St Jo Bapt), *Northants*.. **D** Pet *See* Chelveston.
CALDECOTE (St Jo Evang), *Leics*. V. **D** Pet 10 *See* Gretton.
CALDECOTE (All SS), *Beds*. V. **D** St Alb 17 **P** *Grocers' Co* **I** A E N BLISS.
CALDER VALE (St Jo Evang), *Lancs*. V. **D** Blackb 10 *See* Admarsh-in-Bleasdale.
CALDERBRIDGE (St Bridget), *Cumb*.. **D** Carl *See* Beckermet (St Bridget).
CALDERBROOK (St Jas), *Gtr Man*. V. **D** Man 17 **P** *Bp* **I** D R SUTTON.
CALDMORE (St Mich AA), *W Midl*.. **D** Lich 9 *See* Walsall.
CALDWELL (St Giles), *Derbys*.. **D** Derby 16 *See* Stapenhill.
CALEDONIAN ROAD **D** Lon 6 *See* Islington.
CALIFORNIA (St John), *Berks*. V. **D** Ox 16 **P** *Dioc Bd of Patr* **I** K G HUMPHREYS.
CALKE (St Giles), *Derbys*.. **D** Derby 15 *See* Ticknall.
CALKWELL, *Lincs*.. **D** Linc 11 *See* Scamblesby.
CALLINGTON (St Mary Virg) w South Hill (St Sampson) *Cornw*. R. **D** Truro 9 **P** *PCC* **I** N S FOX.
CALLOW (St Mary), *Herefs*. V. **D** Heref 3 *See* Dewsall.
CALNE (St Mary Virg w H Trin) w Blackland (St Pet), *Wilts*. V. **D** Sarum 25 **P** *Bp* **I** J L REYNOLDS, G O MADDOX *c*, E C POGMORE *c*.
CALOW (St Pet), *Derbys*. V. **D** Derby 3 **P** *V of Chesterfield* **I** R A BRADBURY *p-in-c*.
CALSTOCK (St Andr), *Cornw*. R. **D** Truro 9 **P** *Duke of Cornw* **I** G W RUMING.
CALSTONE-WELLINGTON (St Mary Virg) w Blackland (St Pet), *Wilts*. R. **D** Sarum 25 *See* Oldbury.
CALTHORPE (St Marg), *Norf*. V. **D** Nor 3 *See* Erpingham.
CALTON (St Mary), *Staffs*. V. **D** Lich 13 **P** *Bp* **I** W R D ALEXANDER *p-in-c*.
CALUDON TEAM MINISTRY, (Stoke St Michael w St Catherine, St Mary Magd Wyken, Holy Cross Belgrave Sq), *W Midl*. R. **D** Cov 1 **P** *Bp and Ld Chan* **I** G F WARNER, C A BRADSHAW *team v*, M R MORGAN *team v*, J E SADLER *team v*, R P PAUL *c*.
CALVERHALL or Corra (H Trin), *Salop*. V. **D** Lich 27 *See* Ightfield.
CALVERLEIGH (St Mary Virg), *Devon*. R. **D** Ex 8 *See* Washfield.
CALVERLEY (St Wilfrid), *W Yorks*. V. **D** Bradf 3 **P** *Bp* **I** G G LANE.
CALVERTON (All SS), *Bucks*. V. **D** Ox 23 **P** *Dioc Bd of Patr* **I** C H J C NORTHAM.
CALVERTON (St Wilfrid), *Notts*. V. **D** Southw 15 **P** *Bp* **I** T O HOYLE.
CAM (St Geo) w Stinchcombe (St Cypr), *Glos*. V. **D** Glouc 5 **P** *Bp* **I** J N K HARRIS.
LOWER (St Bart), V. **D** Glouc 5 **P** *Bp* **I** A J MINCHIN, G G C MINORS *c*.
CAMBER and East Guldeford (St Mary), *E Sussex*. V. **D** Chich *See* Rye.
CAMBERLEY w Yorktown (St Mich), *Surrey*. V. **D** Guildf 5a **P** *Bp* **I** F A E CHADWICK, L MILLS *c*.
(St Paul), V. **D** Guildf 5a **P** *Bp* **I** R S CROSSLEY, C C NEAL *c*.
CAMBERWELL (St Giles), *Surrey*. V. **D** S'wark 15 **P** *Bp* **I** R W G BOMFORD, L S A MARSH *c*.
(All SS Blenheim Grove), V. **D** S'wark 15 **P** *CPAS* **I** W G WOOD.
(Ch Ch), V. **D** S'wark 15 **P** *Trustees* **I** E B DAVIS.
(St Geo of England w Trin Coll Miss), V. **D** S'wark 15 **P** *Bp* **I** P ADAMS.
(St Jas Ap Knatchbull Road), V. **D** S'wark *See* Kennington.
(St Luke, Peckham), V. **D** S'wark 15 **P** *Bp* **I** G S DERRIMAN.
(St Mich AA w All S and Em Ch), *Wyndham Road*. V. **D** S'wark 5 **P** *Trustees* **I** I M HUBBARD *c*, H MORGAN *c*.
(St Phil w St Mark), V. **D** S'wark 15 **P** *Crown* **I** (Vacant).
CAMBO (H Trin), *Northumb*. V. **D** Newc T *See* Kirkwhelpington.
CAMBOIS (St Pet), *Northumb*. V. **D** Newc T 1 **P** *Provst and Chapter of Newc T* **I** C SCOTT *p-in-c*.
CAMBORNE (St Martin and St Meriadoc), *Cornw*. R. **D** Truro 2 **P** *Ch S* **I** A B E BROWN, G E BOTTOMLEY *hon c*, A J HANCOCK *hon c*.
CAMBRIDGE (H Sepulchre w All SS), *Cambs*. V. **D** Ely 2 **P** *PCC* **I** C M RUSTON, R M COMBES *c*.
(H Trin), *Cambs*. V. **D** Ely 2 **P** *Peache Trustees* **I** R M REES, A S TREASURE *c*.
(St Andr Gt), V. **D** Ely 2 **P** *D and C of Ely* **I** (Vacant).
(St Andr L) (or Barnwell), V. **D** Ely 2 **P** *Trustees* **I** M L DIAMOND *c-in-c*, J E FITZGERALD *c*.
(St Barn), V. **D** Ely 2 **P** *V of St Paul, Cam* **I** A D LENNON *p-in-c*, C M BUTT *c*, H P HUTCHISON *c*.
(St Benedict), V. **D** Ely 2 **P** *CCC Cam* **I** M J M COOMBE.
(St Botolph), R. **D** Ely 2 **P** *Qu Coll Cam* **I** D WALSER.
(St Clem), V. **D** Ely 2 **P** *Jes Coll Cam* **I** (Vacant).
(St Edw K and Mart). **D** (Extra Dioc) **P** *Trin Hall Cam* **I** B WILLIAMS *chap*.
(St Giles w St Pet), V. **D** Ely 2 **P** *Bp* **I** (Vacant).
(St Jas), V. **D** Ely 2 **P** *Bp* **I** I G WOODROFFE, E W HUTCHISON *hon c*.
(St Jo Evang), V. **D** Ely 2 **P** *Bp* **I** C F WILKINSON, A P C SMITH *c*.
(St Mark), V. **D** Ely 2 **P** *Dioc Bd of Patr* **I** W H LOVELESS.

(St Martin), V. D Ely 2 P *V of St Paul's Cam* I P PHENNA, P D GARDNER *c*, R LONGFOOT *c*.
(St Mary Gt w St Mich AA), V. D Ely 2 P *Trin Coll Cam* I M C O MAYNE, K MAUDSLEY *c*, D RAYNER *c*.
(St Mary L), V. D Ely 2 P *Master and Fellows of Peterho Cam* I J OWEN.
(St Matt w St Jas) V. D Ely 2 P *V of St Andr L Cam* I S SIMS.
(St Paul), V. D Ely 2 P *Ch Trust Fund* I M R W FARRER, R W MORGAN *c*.
(St Phil), V. D Ely 2 P *Ch Trust Fund Trust* I (Vacant).
CAMDEN TOWN (All SS).. D Lon 26 *See* St Pancras.
CAME (St Pet), *Dorset*. R. D Sarum 5 *See* Winterbourne Came.
CAMEL, WEST (All SS), *Somt*. R. D B & W *See* Camel, Queen.
CAMEL, QUEEN (St Barn) w Marston Magna, W Camel, Rimpton and Corton Denham, *Somt*. V. D B & W P *Bp and Dioc Bd of Patr, D and C of Bris and Bp of Lon* I P G CLARKE *c*.
CAMELEY (St Jas and St Barn Temple Cloud), *Avon*. R. D B & W 15 *See* Clutton.
CAMELFORD, *Cornw*.. D Truro 12 *See* Lanteglos.
CAMELOT (Compton Pauncefoot, Blackford, Maperton, N Cadbury, N Cheriton, S Cadbury and Yarlington), *Somt*. R. D B & W 4 P *Dioc Bd of Patr* I (Vacant).
CAMELSDALE (St Paul), *Surrey*. V. D Chich 5 P *Crown* I M J HOY.
CAMERTON (St Pet) w Seaton (St Paul), *Cumb*. V. D Carl 11 P *D and C of Carl* I I H BOWMAN.
CAMERTON (St Pet) w Dunkerton, Foxcote and Shoscombe, *Avon*. R. D B & W P *Bp* I R E S BENNETT.
CAMMERINGHAM (St Mich), *Lincs*. V. D Linc 3 *See* Ingham.
CAMPDEN HILL (St Geo), *Lon*.. D Lon 11 *See* Kensington.
CAMP HILL (St Mary and St John) w Galley Common, *Warws*. V. D Cov 5 P *Bp* I S D SNEATH.
CAMPSALL (St Mary Magd), *S Yorks*. V. D Sheff 8 P *Bp* I T B CLARK.
CAMPSEA ASHE (St Jo Bapt) w Marlesford (St Andr), *Suff*. R. D St E 16 P *Crown and J S Shreiber Esq* alt I E W ROLT.
CAMPTON (All SS), *Beds*. R. D St Alb 22 P *Sir D Osborn Bt* I R F DAY.
CANDLESBY (St Benedict) w Scremby (St Pet and St Paul), *Lincs*.. D Linc 7 *See* Partney.
CANDOVER VALLEY, The, (Brown and Chilton Candover, Northington and Swarraton Preston Candover w Nutley and Bradley), *Hants*. R. D D and C of Win and Ld Ashburton I K V BATT.
CANEWDON (St Nich) w Paglesham (St Pet), *Essex*. V. D Chelmsf 16 P *D and C of Westmr and Hyndman Trustees* alt I N J KELLY.
CANFIELD, GREAT (St Mary), *Essex*. R. D Chelmsf 23 P *Mrs G Maryon-Wilson* I P H F DUNCAN *p-in-c*.
CANFIELD, LITTLE, *Essex*.. D Chelmsf 23 *See* Takeley.
CANFORD CLIFFS, *Dorset*.. D Sarum 14 *See* Parkstone.
CANFORD MAGNA, *Dorset*. V. D Sarum 11 P *Canford Sch Ltd* I I K W SAVILE, J A MUMFORD *c*, R D WYATT *c*, R DODGSON *hon c*.
CANLEY (St Steph), *Warws*.. D Cov 3 P *Bp* I D I BRUCE.
CANNINGTON (St Mary Virg), *Somt*. V. D B & W 17 P *Bp* I M H STAGG *c-in-c*.
CANNING TOWN (St Matthias w H Trin Barking Road and St Gabr), *Essex*. V. D Chelmsf 5 P *Bp* I R I BRIGGS *c-in-c*.
(St Cedd), V. D Chelmsf 5 P *Bp* I D J MASON.
(Dockland Settlement and Malvern Coll Miss), V. D Chelmsf 5 P *Trustees* I (Vacant).
CANNOCK (St Luke) w Chadsmoor (St Aid), *Staffs*. R. D Lich 4 P *D and C of Lich* I J K LINFORD, J C OAKES *team v*, W D PUGH *team v*, R C GILBERT *c*, W K ROWELL *c*, M C RUTTER *c*.
CANONBURY D Lon 6 *See* Islington.
CANON FROME (St Jas), *Herefs*. V. D Heref 6 *See* Stretton Grandison.
CANON-PYON (St Lawr) w King's Pyon (St Mary) and Birley (St Pet), *Herefs*. V. D Heref 7 P *Bp and D and C of Heref* I W N TAVERNOR.
CANTELOFF, *Norf*.. D Nor *See* Hethersett.
CANTERBURY (St Dunstan w H Cross), V. D Cant 3 P *Abp* I H O ALBIN, C S MATTHEWS *hon c*.
(All SS), V. D Cant 3 P *Abp* I D MATTHIAE.
(St Mary Bredin), V. D Cant 3 P *Simeon Trustees* I J C MEEK.
(St Martin w St Paul), R. D Cant 3 P *Abp* I R G HUMPHRISS, M J HIGGS *c*.
(St Pet and St Alphege w St Marg and St Mildred w St Mary de Castro), *Kent*. R. D Cant 3 P *Abp, Ld Chan, D and C of Cant in turn* I C C G TUFTON.
(St Steph Hackington), R. D Cant 3 P *Archd of Cant* I A E PEARCE.
CANTLEY (St Marg) w Limpenhoe (St Botolph K) V and Southwood (St Edm), *Norf*. V. D Nor *See* Reedham.
CANTLEY (St Wilfred), *S Yorks*. V. D Sheff 8 P *Guild of All S* I D N GIBBS, R H DAVIES *c*, T R EDGAR *c*, K YATES *hon c*.
CANVEY ISLAND (St Anne) *Essex*. R. D Chelmsf 13 P *Bp* I T J STEVENS, J E COOPER *team v*, M D WEBSTER *team v*.
CANWELL (St Mary St Giles and All SS Conv Distr). D Lich 2 P *Bp* I K P HALLETT *p-in-c*, W G MCNAMEE *c*.
CANWICK (All SS), *Lincs*. V. D Linc 18 P *Mercers' Co* I D PINK *p-in-c*.
CAPEL (St Jo Bapt), *Surrey*. V. D Guildf 6 P *Ld Chan* I T P NICHOLSON *p-in-c*.
CAPEL (St Thos of Cant), *Kent*. V. D Roch *See* Tudeley.
CAPEL St Andr (St Andr), *Suff*.. D St E 7 *See* Boyton.
CAPEL LE FERNE, *Kent*.. D Cant 5 *See* Alkham.
CAPEL ST MARY (St Mary Virg) w Little Wenham, *Suff*. R. D St E 5 P *S for Maint of Faith* I D W W PEARCE.
CAPENHURST (H Trin), *Chesh*. R. D Ches 9 P *Bp* I J G WHITE *p-in-c*.
CAPESTHORNE (H Trin) w Siddington (All SS) and Marton (St Jas), *Chesh*. V. D Ches 13 P *Lt-Col W Bromley-Davenport* I A S DOUGLAS.
CARBIS BAY (All SS), *Cornw*. V. D Truro 5 P *Bp* I W F BUNYAN.
CARBROOK (St Bart), *S Yorks*.. D Sheff 1 *See* Sheffield.
CARBROOKE (St Pet and St Paul) w Ovington, Woodrising and Scoulton, *Norf*. V. D Nor 19 P *Univ of Cam, S for Maint of Faith and Earl of Verulam (alt)* I P E JEFFORD *p-in-c*, H A R EDGELL P-IN-C OF WOODRISING AND SCOULTON.
CARBURTON, *Notts*.. D Southw 7 *See* Worksop.
CAR-COLSTON (St Mary) w Screveton (St Wilfrid), *Notts*. V. D Southw 9 P *Lt-Col T M Blagg* I A CHAPPELL.
CARDESTON, *Salop*.. D Heref *See* Alberbury.
CARDINGTON (St Jas), *Salop*. V. D Heref 11 P *Rt Hon Sir F Corfield Q.C.* I M BROMFIELD.
CARDINGTON (St Mary), *Beds*. V. D St Alb 19 P *S Whitbread Esq* I P A TUBBS.
CARDYNHAM (St Mewbred), *Cornw*. R. D Truro 8 P *Dioc Bd of Patr and R M Coode Esq* alt I M B KENNAWAY.
CAREBY (St Steph) w Holywell (St Wilfrid) and Aunby (St Thos à Becket), *Lincs*. R. D Linc P *Hon Mrs A I Fane* I G S HOAR.
CARGO, *Cumb*.. D Carl 3 *See* Rockliffe.
CARHAM, *Northumb*.. D Newc T *See* Cornhill.
CARHAMPTON (St Jo Bapt), *Somt*. V. D B & W 21 P *Bp* I (Vacant).
CARHARRACK, *Cornw*.. D Truro *See* St Gwennap.
CARISBROOKE (St Mary), *Isle of Wight*. V. D Portsm 7 P *Qu Coll Ox* I M S COOPER.
(St Nich-in-Castro), V. D Portsm 7 P *Queen's Coll Ox* I M S COOPER.
(St Jo Bapt), V. D Portsm 7 P *Ch Patr Trust* I C C JENKIN.
CARLBY (St Steph), *Lincs*. R. D Linc 13 P *Marq of Ex* I (Vacant).
CARLETON (St Pet), *Norf*.. D Nor *See* Ashby.
CARLETON (St Mich), *N Yorks*. V. D Wakef 11 P *V of Pontefract* I C H JENNO.
CARLETON (St Mary Virg) and Lothersdale (Ch Ch), *W Yorks*. R. D Bradf 10 P *Ch Ch Ox* I G D RHODES.
CARLETON EAST (St Mary w St Pet), *Norf*. R. D Nor 13 P *Bp* I P MCFADYEN.
CARLETON, FOREHOE, *Norf*. R. D Nor 12 *See* Barnham Broom.
CARLETON-IN-CRAVEN (St Mary Virg), *W Yorks*. R. D Bradf 10 *See* Carleton.
CARLETON-RODE (All SS), *Norf*. R. D Nor 11 *See* Bunwell.
CARLIN HOW w Skinningrove, *Cleve*. V. D York 19 P *Abp* I J W THEOBALD *c-in-c*.
CARLINGHOW (St Jo Evang), *W Yorks*. V. D Wakef 10 P *V of Batley and V of Brownhill* alt I D C TURNBULL.
CARLISLE (H Trin and St Barn), *Cumb*. R. D Carl 3 P *Bp and D and C of Carl* I T H M SAMPSON, J K GREG *team v*, J R WRAIGHT *team v*.
(St Aid w Ch Ch and St Andr, Botcherby), V. D Carl 3 P *Bp* I R D BAXTER.
(St Cuthb w St Mary), V. D Carl 3 P *Bp and D and C of Carl* I D T I JENKINS.
(St Elisabeth, Harraby), V. D Carl 3 P *Bp* I M COMBER.

(St Herbert Currock w St Steph), V. **D** Carl 3 **P** *Crown and Bp* alt **I** J E BELL.
(St Jas Denton-Holme), V. **D** Carl 3 **P** *Trustees* **I** J D RUSHTON, D T OSMAN *c*.
(St Jo Evang), V. **D** Carl 3 **P** *CPAS* **I** P J BYE, R J CREW *c*, C MCCORMACK *c*.
(St Jo Bapt Upperby), V. **D** Carl 3 **P** *D and C of Carl* **I** R J S WATSON, A MITCHELL *c*.
(St Luke's, Morton), V. **D** Carl 3 **P** *Bp* **I** P E MANN.
CARLTON (St Pet), *Cambs*. R. **D** Ely 4 *See* Burrough Green.
CARLTON (St Andr), *Leics*. R. **D** Leic 15 *See* Nailstone.
CARLTON (St Jo Bapt), *Notts*. V. **D** Southw 13 **P** *Bp* **I** T SHORT.
CARLTON (St Pet), *Suff*.. **D** St E 19 *See* Kelsale.
CARLTON (St Jo Evang), *W Yorks*. V. **D** Wakef 8 **P** *Dioc Bd of Patr* **I** P SCHOLFIELD *c-in-c*.
CARLTON (St Aid), *N Yorks*.. **D** York *See* Helmsley.
CARLTON (St Mary Virg) and Drax, *S Yorks*.. **D** York 8 **P** *Abp and Ch Trust Fund Trustees* **I** (Vacant).
CARLTON CASTLE (H Cross), *Lincs*. R. **D** Linc 40 *See* Reston.
CARLTON (St Mary) w Chellington (St Nich), *Beds*. R. **D** St E 21 *See* Harrold.
CARLTON-COLVILLE (St Pet) w Mutford (St Andr) w Rushmere (St Mich AA), *Suff*. R. **D** Nor 15 **P** *Simeon Trustees* **I** M J WINBOLT LEWIS.
CARLTON CURLIEU (St Mary), Ilston-on-the-Hill (St Mich AA) and Shangton (St Nich) w Burton Overy, *Leics*. R. **D** Leic **P** *MMT 1st turn, Rev J H N Llewelyn 2nd turn and Sir G C J Palmer, Bt 3rd turn* **I** (Vacant).
CARLTON, EAST (St Pet), *Northants*. R. **D** Pet 10 *See* Cottingham.
CARLTON, GREAT (St Jo Bapt) w Carlton, Little (St Edith), *Lincs*. R. **D** Linc *See* Mid Marsh Group.
CARLTON-IN-CLEVELAND (St Botolph), *Cleve*.. **D** York *See* Whorlton.
CARLTON-IN-LINDRICK (St Jo Evang), *Notts*. R. **D** Southw 7 **P** *Ld Chan* **I** J C A LAMBERT.
CARLTON-IN-THE-WILLOWS (St Paul), *Notts*. R. **D** Southw 13 **P** *MMT* **I** W W HARRISON.
CARLTON-LE-MOORLAND (St Mary) w Stapleford (All SS), *Lincs*. V. **D** Linc 18 **P** *Ld Middleton, Capt H N Nevile, CCC Ox and Bp* **I** P BYRON-DAVIES.
CARLTON MINIOTT (St Laur), *N Yorks*.. **D** York 26 *See* Thirsk.
CARLTON, NORTH (no Dedic) w South (St Jo Bapt), *Lincs*. V. **D** Linc 3 **P** *Ld Monson* **I** D SCOTT *p-in-c*.
CARLTON-ON-TRENT (St Mary), *Notts*. V. **D** Southw 4 **P** *Bp* **I** D G HATTER.
CARLTON-SCROOP (St Nich) w Normanton (St Nich), *Lincs*. R. **D** Linc *See* Caythorpe.
CARNABY, *Humb*. V. **D** York 12 **P** *Abp* **I** A M WHAWELL *p-in-c*.
CARNFORTH (Ch Ch), *Lancs*. V. **D** Blackb 13 **P** *Bp* **I** R P PRICE.
CARNMENELLIS (H Trin), *Cornw*.. **D** Truro 2 *See* Redruth.
CARR MILL (St David, *Mer*. V. **D** Liv 10 **P** *Bp and V of St Mark, St Helens*. **I** K M KENT.
CARRINGTON (St Geo), *Gtr Man*.. **D** Ches 10 *See* Partington.
CARRINGTON (St Paul) w Frithville, *Lincs*. V. **D** Linc 20 *See* Bolingbroke, New.
CARRINGTON (St Jo Evang), *Notts*. V. **D** Southw 14 **P** *Bp* **I** G MALTBY, D GILL *c*.
CARRSHIELD or WEST ALLEN, *Northumb*. V. **D** Newc T 4 *See* Allendale.
CARSHALTON (All SS), *Surrey*. R. **D** S'wark 8 **P** *Bp* **I** L C EDWARDS, L A BREWSTER *hon c*.
(Good Shepherd), V. **D** S'wark 8 **P** *Bp* **I** G H JEFF, A E WILLIAMS *hon c*.
CARSINGTON, *Derbys*.. **D** Derby *See* Wirksworth.
CARTERTON (St Jo Evang), *Oxon*.. **D** Ox 9 **P** *Ch Ch Ox* **I** M F LOVELESS.
CARTMEL (Priory Ch of St Mary and St Mich), *Cumb*. V. **D** Carl 14 **P** *H Cavendish Esq* **I** D M STIFF.
CARTMEL FELL (St Anthony), *Cumb*. V. **D** Carl 17 **P** *Bp and Trustees* Alt **I** K PARTINGTON.
CASSINGTON (St Pet), *Oxon*. V. **D** Ox *See* Freeland.
CASSOP (St Paul) w Quarrington, *Durham*. V. **D** Dur 12a **P** *Bp* **I** J R STRINGER.
CASTERTON (H Trin). **D** Carl *See* Kirkby Lonsdale.
CASTERTON, GREAT (St Pet and St Paul), w Pickworth (St Mary), Tickencote (St Pet) and Casterton, Little (All SS), *Leics*. R. **D** Pet 13 **P** *Marq of Ex 2 turns, J E L P Wingfield Esq 1 turn, Ld Chesham 1 turn* **I** W W PAGE.
CASTLE ACRE (St Jas) w Newton (St Mary's), *Norf*. V. **D** Nor 20 **P** *Bp 1 turn, Earl of Leic 2 turns* **I** R NAZER.
CASTLE ASHBY (St Mary Magd), *Northants*. R. **D** Pet 7 *See* Grendon.
CASTLE BROMWICH (St Mary and St Marg), *W Midl*. R. **D** Birm 9 **P** *Earl of Bradf* **I** D J WHITE.
(St Clem), V. **D** Birm 9 **P** *Bp* **I** W J SILLITOE, D COLE *c*, N C FOSTER *c*.
CASTLE BYTHAM (St Jas), *Lincs*. V. **D** Linc **P** *D and C of Linc, Bp, Ld Chan and Hon Mrs A I Fane in turn* **I** G S HOAR.
CASTLE CAMPS (All SS), *Cambs*. R. **D** Ely 4 **P** *Bp and Gov of Charterho (alt)* **I** H S FINKENSTAEDT.
CASTLE CARROCK (St Pet) w Cumrew (St Mary) and Croglin (St Jo Bapt), *Cumb*. R. **D** Carl 2 **P** *D and C of Carl* **I** K P O'DONOHUE.
CASTLE CARY (All SS) w Ansford (St Andr), or Almsford, *Somt*. V. **D** B & W 4 **P** *Bp* **I** D N BOX, R E HEBDITCH *c*.
CASTLE CHURCH (St Mary Virg), *Staffs*. V. **D** Lich **P** *Bp* **I** R H SARGENT, S A HOLLOWAY *c*.
CASTLE COMBE (St Andr), *Wilts*. R. **D** Bris 9 **P** *Bp and Win Coll* alt **I** M W DITTMER, J E B MARSH *c*.
CASTLE DONINGTON (St Edw), *Leics*. V. **D** Leic 10 **P** *Trustees of Ld Gretton* **I** R N EVERETT.
CASTLE-EATON (St Mary Virg), *Wilts*. R. **D** Glouc *See* Meysey-Hampton.
CASTLE EDEN (St Jas Ap and Mart), R w Monkhesleden (St John w St Mary), *Durham*. V. **D** Dur 3 **P** *Bp* **I** F LUMSDEN.
CASTLE FROME (St Mich AA) w Frome Hill (St Matt), *Herefs*. R. **D** Heref 6 **P** *Mrs N Roberts* **I** P A GUIVER P-IN-C OF CASTLE FROME.
CASTLE HALL (H Trin), *Gtr Man*.. **D** Ches 14 *See* Stalybridge.
CASTLE HEDINGHAM (St Nich), *Essex*. V. **D** Chelmsf 24 **P** *5 Trustees incl Miss M Majendie* **I** R H D SMITH *p-in-c*.
CASTLE HOWARD, *N Yorks*.. **D** York 4 *See* Bulmer.
CASTLE RISING (St Lawr), *Norf*. R (*See Sandringham Group*).. **D** Nor 23 **P** *Lt Col H R Howard* **I** (Vacant).
CASTLE SOWERBY, *Cumb*.. **D** Carl *See* Caldbeck.
CASTLE TOWN (St Thos), *Staffs*.. **D** Lich 5 *See* Stafford.
CASTLE VALE (St Cuthb), *W Midl*. V. **D** Birm 12 **P** *Bp* **I** C P BURTON.
CASTLEFORD (All SS) w Wheldale, *W Yorks*. R. **D** Wakef 11 **P** *Duchy of Lanc* **I** S FELL.
(St Mich), V. **D** Wakef 11 **P** *Bp* **I** E I CHETWYND.
CASTLEMORTON (St Greg), Hollybush (All SS) and Birtsmorton, *Worcs*. R. **D** Worc 5 **P** *Bp, D and C of Westmr, and Trustees of late F B Bradley-Birt Esq* **I** P T B B LUTTON.
CASTLESIDE (St Jo Evang), *Durham*. V. **D** Dur 7 **P** *Bp* **I** R L FERGUSON.
CASTLETHORPE (St Simon and St Jude), *Bucks*.. **D** Ox 28 *See* Hanslope.
CASTLETON (St Edm), *Derbys*. V. **D** Derby *See* Hope.
CASTLETON, *Dorset*. V. **D** Sarum 7 *See* Sherborne.
CASTLETON MOOR (St Martin), *Gtr Man*. V. **D** Man 17 **P** *Bp* **I** F J JONES.
CASTLETOWN (St Marg of Scotld), *T & W*. V. **D** Dur 8 **P** *Bp* **I** P F D SPARGO.
CASTON (H Cross) w Griston, Merton and Thompson, *Norf*. R. **D** Nor **P** *Bp and Ld Walsingham* **I** J COOKE.
CASTOR (St Kyneburgha) w Sutton and Upton, *Cambs*. R. **D** Pet 14 **P** *Bp 2 turns Cdr J Hopkinson 1 turn* **I** (Vacant).
CATCLIFFE (St Mary), *S Yorks*. **D** Sheff 6 *See* Brinsworth.
CATCOTT (St Pet), *Somt*. v. **D** B & W 7 **P** *Bp* **I** F L R GRAHAM *c-in-c*.
CATERHAM (St Lawr [not used] and St Mary Virg), *Surrey*. R. **D** S'wark 9 **P** *Bp* **I** D FRAYNE.
CATERHAM VALLEY (St Jo Evang), *Surrey*. V. **D** S'wark 9 **P** *Bp* **I** I KITTERINGHAM, B D PRATT *c*.
CATESBY (St Mary), *Northants*. V. **D** Pet 3 *See* Staverton.
CATFIELD (All SS), *Norf*. R. **D** Nor 9 **P** *Bp* **I** J A ROBERTS *p-in-c*.
CATFORD (St Laur), *Kent*. V. **D** S'wark 20 **P** *Bp* **I** W D WOOD, B BOOTH *c*.
(St Andr), V. **D** S'wark 20 **P** *Bp* **I** R B JORDAN, J R HILTON *hon c*.
(St John, Southend) and Downham, R. **D** S'wark 20 **P** *Bp* **I** C R LANSDALE, P D HENDRY *team v*, R E HORTON *team v*, J B NAYLOR *team v*, E G R ASTILL *c*, E C G BAILEY *c*, C H RAZZALL *c*, N N KIRKUP *hon c*.
CATHERINGTON (All SS) w Clanfield (St Jas), *Hants*. V. **D** Portsm 3 **P** *Bp* **I** R W KILVERT, D R DIVALL *c*.
CATHERSTON-LEWESTON (St Mary), *Dorset*. R. **D** Sarum 2 *See* Charmouth.

CHESTER-LE-STREET (St Mary and St Cuthb), *Durham.* R. D Dur 1 P *St Jo Coll Dur* I I D BUNTING, R F BIANCHI *c.*
CHESTERTON (St Andr), *Cambs.* V. D Ely 2 P *Trin Coll Cam* I J T CARRE, J C POLKINGHORNE *c.*
(St Geo), V. D Ely 2 P *Bp* I B WATCHORN, R D WILLIAMS *hon c.*
(St Luke w St Aug), V. D Ely 2 P *Bp* I P H TAMPLIN *c.*
(Good Shepherd), V. D Ely 2 P *Bp* I M E H SUTER, B J W CAVE-BROWNE-CAVE *c.*
CHESTERTON Warws. V D Cov 8 *See* Lighthorne.
CHESTERTON (H Trin), *Staffs.* V. D Lich 17 P *Crown* I V T OXFORD.
CHESTERTON (St Mich) w Haddon (St Mary), *Cambs.* R. D Ely 14 P *Mrs H R Horne and C E Horne Esq* I (Vacant).
CHESTERTON, Great (St Mary) w Middleton Stoney and Wendlebury, *Oxon.* V. D Ox 2 P *New Coll, Ch Ch Ox and Bp (alt)* I D H B THOMAS.
CHESWARDINE (St Swith), *Salop.* V. D Lich 23 P *Archd of Salop and E N Hall Esq* alt I R B MORRIS.
CHETTISHAM (St Mich AA), *Cambs.*. D Ely 15 P *D and C of Ely* I N MUNT.
CHETTLE (St Mary), *Dorset.* R. D Sarum 10 P *Exors of Mrs E M Bourke* I J A P STANDEN MCDOUGAL.
CHETTON (St Giles) w Deuxhil and Glazeley (St Bart), *Salop.* R. D Heref 9 P *Lancing Coll Sussex* I R E F DORE.
CHETWODE (St Nich and St Mary), *Bucks.*. D Ox 25 *See* Swan.
CHETWYND (St Mich AA), *Salop.* R. D Lich *See* Newport.
CHEVELEY (St Mary and the H Host of Heaven), *Cambs.* R. D Ely 4 P *Mrs D A Bowlby and Dioc Bd of Patr (alt)* I M F WILLIAMS.
CHEVENING (St Botolph), *Kent.* R. D Roch 7 P *Abp* I M G HEWETT.
CHEVERELL, LITTLE (St Pet), *Wilts.* R. D Sarum 23 P *Bp* I (Vacant).
CHEVERELL MAGNA (St Pet), *Wilts.* R. D Sarum 23 *See* Erlestoke.
CHEVINGTON (St Jo Div), *Northumb.* V. D Newc T 7 P *Bp* I T W RICHARDSON.
CHEVINGTON (All SS) w Hargrave and Whepstead w Brockley, *Suff.* R. D St E 13 P *Guild of All S 2 turns, Dioc Bd of Patr 1 Turn, Bp 2 turns.* I C C KEVILL-DAVIES.
CHEVITHORNE (St Thos), *Devon.*. D Ex 8 *See* Washfield.
CHEW MAGNA (St Andr) w Dundry (St Nich), *Avon.* V. D B & W 15 P *Mrs D H F Luxmoore-Ball* I J S BARKER, F J TANNER *hon c.*
CHEW-STOKE (St Andr) w Nempnett-Thrubwell (St Mary Virg), *Avon.* R. D B & W 15 P *Bp and S for Maint of Faith* I B W HOWARTH.
CHEWTON MENDIP (St Mary Magd) w Ston Easton and Litton, *Somt.* V. D B & W 6 P *Earl Waldegrave* I J D A STEVENS.
CHICHELEY (St Lawr), *Bucks.* V. D Ox 28 *See* Sherington.
CHICHESTER (St Paul and St Pet Gt), *W Sussex.* V. D Chich 3 P *D and C of Chich* I D S WALFORD *c.*
(St Pancras w St John), R. D Chich 3 P *Trustees* I M GRIFFITHS.
(St Wilfrid Conv Distr Parklands). D Chich 3 P *Bp* I A J C FREEMAN *p-in-c.*
CHICKENLEY HEATH (St Mary Virg), *W Yorks.*. D Wakef 10 *See* Gawthorpe.
CHICKERELL, WEST w Fleet (H Trin), *Dorset.* R. D Sarum 6 P *Bp* I O J NEWNHAM.
CHICKLADE (All SS), *Wilts.* R. D Sarum 19 *See* Hindon.
CHICKNEY (St Mary), *Essex.* R. D Chelmsf 23 *See* Broxted.
CHIDDINGFOLD, *Surrey.* R. D Guildf 4 P *Ld Chan* I J G NICHOLLS.
CHIDDINGLY, *E Sussex.* V. D Chich 18 P *Knole Trustees* I H S ROBINSON.
CHIDDINGSTONE (St Mary Virg) w Chiddingstone Causeway (St Luke), *Kent.* R. D Roch 9 P *Abp and Bp of Roch* I J F BOYCE.
CHIDEOCK St Giles), *Dorset.* V. D Sarum 2 P *Bp* I P G BLOOMFIELD *p-in-c.*
CHIDHAM (St Mary), *W Sussex.* V. D Chich 8 P *Bp* I N J SMITH.
CHIEVELEY (St Mary Virg) w Winterbourne (St Jas) and Oare (St Bart), *Berks.* V. D Ox 14 P *Archd of Berks* I C T SCOTT-DEMPSTER.
CHIGNALS, THE, (Chignall Smealey and Chignell St James) w Mashbury, *Essex.* R. D Chelmsf 12 P *CPAS 2 turns, Bp 1 turn* I W T HUXLEY.
CHIGWELL (St Mary), *Essex.* R. D Chelmsf 2 P *Bp* I H R DIBBENS, R J FREEMAN *team v,* J G JARMAN *c.*
CHIGWELL ROW (All SS), *Essex.* R. D Chelmsf 2 P *Crown* I S B N COOPER.
CHILBOLTON (St Mary L) w Wherwell (St Pet and H Cross), *Hants.* R. D Win 2 P *Bp and Marjorie, Countess of Brecknock* I C M HUBBARD.
CHILCOMB, *Hants.*. D Win *See* Winchester (All SS).
CHILCOMBE, *Dorset.* R. D Sarum *See* Burton Bradstock.
CHILCOMPTON (St Jo Bapt) w Downside and Stratton-on-the-Fosse, *Somt.* V. D B & W 16b P *MMT, Bp and V of Midsomer Norton* I C F PENN.
CHILCOTE, *Leics.*. D Lich 6 *See* Clifton Camville.
CHILDE OKEFORD (St Nich) and Manston (St Nich) w Hammoon (St Mary) and Hanford (St Mich AA), *Dorset.* V. D Sarum 13 P *Dioc Bd of Patr* I D H A WILSON *p-in-c.*
CHILDERDITCH (All SS and St Faith) *Essex.*. D Chelmsf 9 *See* Warley, Gt.
CHILDERLEY, *Cambs.*. D Ely 1 *See* Toft.
CHILDREY (St Mary), *Oxon.*. D Ox 19 *See* Ridgeway.
CHILDS ERCALL (St Mich AA), *Salop.* V. D Lich 23 P *Sir J V Corbet Bt* I (Vacant).
CHILD's HILL (All SS), *Gtr Lon.* V. D Lon 17 P *Bp* I J P WAINWRIGHT.
CHILDSWYCKHAM (St Mary Virg) w Aston Somerville, *Worcs.* V. D Glouc 18 P *Bp and Dioc Bd of Patr (Alt)* I A M LEE.
CHILDWALL (All SS), *Mer.* V. D Liv 2 P *Bp* I F A O D DAWSON *c.*
(St D), V.. D Liv 2 P *Bp* I J W O'RYAN.
CHILFROME (H Trin), *Dorset.* R. D Sarum 5 *See* Cattistock.
CHILHAM (St Mary), *Kent.* V. D Cant 2 P *Visc Massarene and Ferrard* I F J E EVANS.
CHILLENDEN (All SS), *Kent.* R. D Cant 1 *See* Goodnestone next Wingham.
CHILLESFORD (St Pet) w Butley, *Suff.* R. D St E 7 *See* Orford.
CHILLINGHAM (St Pet), *Northumb.* V. D Newc T *See* Chatton.
CHILLINGTON, *Somt.*. D B & W *See* Cudworth.
CHILMARK (St Marg of Antioch), *Wilts.*. D Sarum 19 *See* Tisbury.
CHILTHORNE DOMER (St Mary Virg), *Somt.* R. D B & W 11 *See* Tintinhull.
CHILTINGTON, EAST, *E Sussex.* R. D Chich 15 *See* Plumpton.
WEST (St Mary), *E Sussex.* R. D Chich 7 P *Bp* I K A LUCAS.
CHILTON (St Aid), *Durham.* V. D Dur 12a P *Bp* I M S SNOWBALL.
CHILTON (All SS), *Oxon.*. D Ox 18 *See* Harwell.
CHILTON (St Mary) w Dorton, *Bucks.*. D Ox 21 *See* Brill.
CHILTON (St Mary), *Suff.* R. D St E *See* Sudbury.
CHILTON CANDOVER (St Nich), *Hants.*. D Win 6 *See* Brown Candover.
CHILTON-CANTELO (St Jas Gt) w Ashington (St Vinc) *Somt.* R. D B & W 12 P *Dioc Bd of Patr* I E D WHITE.
CHILTON-FOLIAT (St Mary), *Wilts.*. D Sarum 26 *See* Whitton.
CHILTON-MOOR (St Andr Ap), *T & W.* V. D Dur 5 P *Bp* I W H REED.
CHILTON-SUPER-POLDEN (St Edw Mart) w Edington (St Geo), *Somt.* V. D B & W 7 P *Bp* I F L R GRAHAM *c-in-c.*
CHILTON TRINITY (H Trin), *Somt.*. D B & W 17 *See* Bridgwater.
CHILVERS-COTON (All SS) w Astley (St Mary Virg), *Warws.* V. D Cov 5 P *F H M Fitzroy Newdegate Esq* I D R SPILLER, F J CURTIS *c.*
CHILWELL (Ch Ch) w Inham Nook (St Barn), *Notts.* V. D Southw 8 P *CPAS* I J R WILLIAMS, T D ATKINS *c,* K H TURNER *c.*
CHILWORTH (St Thos), *Surrey.*. D Guildf 5 *See* Blackheath.
CHILWORTH (St Denys) w N Baddesley, *Hants.* V. D Win 10 P *Mrs P M A T Chamberlayne MacDonald* I M S MILLIKEN.
CHINGFORD (St Pet and St Paul w All SS and St Francis), *Essex.* R. D Chelmsf 8 P *J H B Heathcote Esq* I P T C MASHEDER *c,* D I MILNES *c.*
SOUTH (St Edm), V. D Chelmsf 8 P *Bp* I E C FORD.
(St Anne), V. D Chelmsf 8 P *Bp* I J A L HARRISSON, L C ACKLAM *c,* E C NORTON *hon c.*
CHINLEY w Buxworth (St Jas), *Derbys.* V. D Derby 5 P *Bp* I T R MARTIN.
CHINNOCK, EAST (St Mary), *Somt.* R. D B & W *See* Hardington-Mandeville.

CHINNOCK, MIDDLE (St Marg) w West Chinnock (St Mary Virg), *Somt.*. D B & W 11 *See* Norton-sub-Hamdon.
CHINNOR (St Andr) w Emmington and Sydenham, *Oxon.* R. D Ox 1 P *W H Wykeham-Musgrave Esq, Dioc Bd of Patr and Peache Trustees* I R W HORNER.
CHIPPENHAM (St Marg), *Cambs.* V. D Ely 3 P *Exors of Col G P Tharp* I D J KIGHTLEY *c-in-c.*
CHIPPENHAM (St Andr), V w Tytherton Lucas (St Nich), R *Wilts.*. D Bris 9 P *D and C of Ch Ch Ox* I J E ALLEN *p-in-c.*
(St Paul) w Hardenhuish (St Nich) and Langley Burrell (St Pet) and Kington St Michael, R. D Bris P *Bp, Miss P M Christian and Dr R E Scott* I D N COPELAND, J E G OSWALD *team v.*
(St Pet Lowdon), V. D Bris 9 P *Bp* I P S HUGHES, B H BOLLEN *hon c.*
CHIPPERFIELD (St Paul), *Herts.* V. D St Alb 10 P *Trustees* I C R BLAMIRE-BROWN.
CHIPPING (St Bart), *Lancs.* V. D Blackb 12 P *Bp* I G R WOOD.
CHIPPING BARNET (St Jo Bapt), *Herts.*. D St Alb 2 *See* Barnet, Chipping.
CHIPPING CAMPDEN (St Jas) w Ebrington, *Glos.* V. D Glouc 12 P *Earl of Harrowby 2 turns, Peache Trustees 1 turn* I P J WHITE.
CHIPPING NORTON (St Mary Virg) w Over Norton, *Oxon.* V. D Ox 3 P *D and C of Glouc* I T A WHARTON.
CHIPPING ONGAR (St Martin of Tours), *Essex.* R. D Chelmsf 6 P *Guild of All S* I J P VAUGHAN-JONES, B J OLIVER *c*, E H ROBERTS *hon c.*
CHIPPING SODBURY (St Jo Bapt) w Old Sodbury (St Jo Bapt), *Avon.* V. D Glouc 8 P *D & C of Worc* I B M P FINCH.
CHIPPING WARDEN (St Pet and St Paul) w Edgcote and Aston-le-Walls (St Leon), *Northants.* R. D Pet 1 P *Bp 1st turn, Mrs Bowlby 2nd turn, R Courage 3rd turn* I A P CLARK.
CHIPSTABLE (All SS) w Raddington (St Mich) and Huish Champflower w Clathworthy, *Somt.* R. D B & W 22 P *Bp 2 turns Maj T F Trollope-Bellew 1 turn* I M J BALCHIN *c-in-c.*
CHIPSTEAD (St Marg), *Surrey.* R. D S'wark 12 P *Abp of Cant* I J C BLAIR-FISH.
CHIRBURY (St Mich AA), *Salop.* V. D Heref 13 P *Sir David Wakeman Bt* I K J F BRADBURY.
CHIRTON, *Wilts.*. D Sarum 23 *See* Cherrington.
CHISELBOROUGH (St Pet and St Paul), *Somt.* R. D B & W 11 *See* Norton-sub-Hamdon.
CHISELDON (H Cross) w Draycot-Foliat, *Wilts.* V. D Sarum 26 *See* Ridgeway.
CHISHALL, LITTLE, *Cambs.*. D Chelmsf 27 *See* Heydon.
CHISHILL, GREAT (St Swith), *Cambs.* V. D Chelmsf 27 P *Ch Soc Trust* I (Vacant).
CHISLEHAMPTON, *Oxon.*. D Ox *See* Stadhampton.
CHISLEHURST (St Nich w St John), *Kent.* R. D Roch 12 P *Bp* I J C ALLEN.
(Ch Ch), V. D Roch 12 P *CPAS* I R W COTTON, A F ARNOTT *hon c.*
WEST (Ch of the Annunc), V. D Roch 12 P *Keble Coll Ox* I D V REED, G HOLDSTOCK *c*, A SHACKLETON *c.*
CHISLET (St Mary Virg) w Hoath (H Cross), *Kent.* V. D Cant 4 *See* St Nicholas-at-Wade.
CHISWICK (St Nich) w (St Mary Magd), *Gtr Lon.* V. D Lon 10 P *D and C of St Paul's* I P A TUFT, P BUTLER *c*, J W CHARLES *c.*
(Ch Ch Turnham Green), V. D Lon 10 P *Bp* I D T JARVIS.
(St Mich), Sutton Court, V. D Lon 10 P *V of St Martin-in-the-Fields* I M F BARNEY.
(St Mich AA Bedford Park), V. D Lon 10 P *Bp* I M H CHAMPNEYS.
(St Paul, Grove Park), V. D Lon 10 P *V of Chiswick* I A M GRIME.
CHITHURST, *W Sussex.*. D Chich *See* Trotton.
CHITTERNE (All SS w St Mary), *Wilts.* V. D Sarum 21 *See* Tilshead.
CHITTLEHAMHOLT (St John), *Devon.* V. D Ex 19 *See* Warkleigh.
CHITTLEHAMPTON (St Hieritha), *Devon.* V. D Ex 19 P *Ld Clinton* I J H B ANDREWS.
CHITTOE (St Mary Virg), *Wilts.* V. D Sarum *See* Bromham.
CHITTS HILL (St Cuthb).. D Lon 27 *See* Wood Green.
CHIVELSTONE (St Sylvester), *Devon.*. D Ex 14 *See* Portlemouth, East.
CHIVESFIELD, *Herts.*. D St Alb 12 *See* Graveley.
CHOBHAM (St Lawr) w Valley End (St Sav), *Surrey.* V. D Guildf 5a P *Commdr H W Acworth, RN and Bp (alt)* I T C G THORNTON.
See also WEST END..
CHOLDERTON (St Nich), *Wilts.* R. D Sarum 17 *See* Bourne Valley.
CHOLESBURY (St Laur), *Bucks.* V. D Ox 30 *See* Hawridge.
CHOLLERTON (St Giles) w Thockrington (St Aidan), *Northumb.* V. D Newc T 2 P *Mrs Enderby* I J W NAYLOR *p-in-c.*
CHOLSEY (St Mary), *Oxon.* V. D Ox 18 P *Ld Chan* I (Vacant).
CHOPPINGTON (St Paul), *Northumb.* V. D Newc T 1 P *D and C of Newc T* I R G FORD.
CHOPWELL (St John), *T & W.* V. D Dur 4a P *Bp* I T E SIMPSON.
CHORLEY (St Laur), *Lancs.* R. D Blackb 4 P *Bp* I E V JONES, J C HARDY *hon c.*
(All SS), V. D Blackb 4 P *Bp* I R C PULLEN.
(St Geo), V. D Blackb 4 P *R of Chorley* I T VAUGHAN.
(St Jas), V. D Blackb 4 P *R of Chorley* I J WIXON.
(St Pet), V. D Blackb 4 P *R of Chorley* I C BERRYMAN, S CRABTREE *c.*
CHORLEY (St Phil), *Chesh.* V. D Ches 12 P *Trustees* I F H B LEESE.
CHORLEYWOOD (Ch Ch), *Herts.* V. D St Alb 10 P *CPAS* I D J SAVILLE, L N CAVAN *c.*
(St Andr), V. D St Alb 10 P *Bp* I RT REV G E D PYTCHES, B J KISSELL *c.*
CHORLTON-CUM-HARDY (St Clem Bp of Rome w St Clem Chap of Ease), *Gtr Man.* R. D Man 5 P *D and C of Man* I D BONSER, M S NORTHCOTT *c*, R CORTEEN *hon c.*
(St Werburgh), R. D Man 5 P *Crown and Bp* alt I R J BIRCHETT, J W BLAIR *c.*
CHORLTON-ON-MEDLOCK (St Ambrose), *Gtr Man.* R. D Man 5 *See* St Ambrose, Manchester.
CHRISHALL (H Trin), *Essex.* V. D Chelmsf 27 P *Bp* I W H A COOPER *p-in-c.*
CHRISTCHURCH (H Trin) w Mudeford (All SS), *Dorset.* V. D Win 8 P *Bp* I B TREVOR-MORGAN, S E HOGBEN *c*, G J MARCER *c.*
CHRISTIAN MALFORD (All SS) w Sutton Benger (All SS) and Tytherton Kellaways (St Giles), *Wilts.* R. D Bris 9 P *Bp D & C of Sarum and L W Neeld Esq* I HON F A R RICHARDS.
CHRISTLETON (St Jas), *Chesh.* R. D Ches 2 P *H C L Garnett Esq* I C D MACK.
CHRISTON (St Mary Virg), *Avon.* R. D B & W 1 *See* Loxton.
CHRISTOW w Bridford (St Thos à Becket) and Ashton (St Jo Bapt) w Trusham (St Mich AA), *Devon.* R. D Ex 6 P *Visc Exmouth, MMT, Sir J Carew-Pole Bt and S for Maint of Faith* I W S PEARS.
CHUDLEIGH (St Mary and St Martin), *Devon.* V. D Ex 11 P *MMT* I C T PIDSLEY.
CHUDLEIGH-KNIGHTON (St Paul) w Heathfield (St Cath), *Devon.* V. D Ex 11 P *Dioc Bd of Patr* I J M LUCAS.
CHULMLEIGH (St Mary Magd), *Devon.* R. D Ex 16 P *MMT* I V J R RICHARDS.
CHURCH, or CHURCH KIRK (St Jas), *Lancs.* R. D Blackb 1 P *Hulme Trustees* I L SEED.
CHURCH ASTON (St Andr), *Salop.* R. D Lich 21 P *R of Edgmond* I J MARSHALL.
CHURCH BROUGHTON (St Mich AA) w Boylestone and Sutton on the Hill (St Mich), *Derbys.* R. D Derby 14 P *R A Mallender Esq 1 turn Miss C M Auden 1 turn Exors of R H R Buckston 2 turns and Worc Coll Ox 2 turns* I D H BUCKLEY P-IN-C OF TRUSLEY.
CHURCHDOWN (St Bart), *Glos.* V. D Glouc 2 P *D and C of Bris* I R G D SLUMAN.
(St Jo Evang), V. D Glouc 2 P *Bp* I E F GILES, J O'BRIEN *hon c.*
CHURCH EATON (St Editha), *Staffs.*. D Lich *See* Moreton.
CHURCH GRESLEY (St Geo and St Mary) w Linton (Ch Ch), *Derbys.* V. D Derby 16 P *Simeon Trustees* I C M SHAW.
CHURCH HONEYBOURNE, *Worcs.*. D Glouc *See* Honeybourne, Church.
CHURCH HULME (St Luke), *Chesh.*. D Ches 11 *See* Holmes Chapel.
CHURCH-KNOWLE (St Pet) w Kimmeridge (no Dedic), *Dorset.* R. D Sarum 9 *See* Steeple.
CHURCH LAWFORD (St Pet) w King's Newnham (St Laur), *Warws.* R. D Cov *See* Wolston.
CHURCH LAWTON (All SS), *Chesh.*. D Ches 12 *See* Lawton, Church.

CHURCH LENCH (All SS) w Ab Lench, Abbots Morton and Rous Lench (St Pet), *Worcs*. R. **D** Worc 1 **P** *Bp* **I** A K SWANN.
CHURCH MINSHULL (St Bart) w Leighton and Minshull Vernon (St Pet), *Chesh*. V. **D** Ches 15 **P** *Bp* **I** P E GAINS.
CHURCH OAKLEY (St Leon), *Hants*.. **D** Win 3 *See* Oakley, Church.
CHURCH PREEN, *Salop*.. **D** Heref 11 *See* Hughley.
CHURCH STRETTON (St Lawr), *Salop*. R. **D** Heref 11 **P** *CPS* **I** J M R WOODGER.
CHURCHAM (St Andr) w Bulley (St Mich AA) and Minsterworth *Glos*. V. **D** Glouc 6 **P** *Bp and D and C of Glouc* **I** G P JENKINS.
CHURCHILL (St Jo Bapt), *Avon*.. **D** B & W 3 *See* Burrington.
CHURCHILL (All SS), *Oxon*. R. **D** Ox 3 *See* Sarsden.
CHURCHILL-IN-HALFSHIRE (St Jas Gt) w Blakedown (St Jas Gt), *Worcs*. R. **D** Worc 10 **P** *Visc Cobham* **I** J GLOVER *p-in-c*.
CHURCHILL-IN-OSWALDSLOW (St Mich), *Worcs*. R. **D** Worc 3 *See* White Ladies Aston.
CHURCHOVER (H Trin) w Willey (St Leon), *Warws*. R. **D** Cov 6 **P** *Bp* **I** E A MORRIS *p-in-c*.
CHURCHSTANTON (St Pet and St Paul), *Devon* w Otterford (St Leon) *Somt*. R. **D** B & W 23a **P** *Bp and Mrs F E Hampson* **I** L J HEMMONS.
CHURCHSTOKE (St Nich) w Hyssington (St Etheldreda) and Sarn, (H Trin) *Powys*. V. **D** Heref 10 **P** *Earl of Powis 2 turns, Crown 1 turn* **I** W T BRYAN.
CHURCHSTOW (St Mary Virg) w Kingsbridge (St Edm K and Mart), *Devon*. V. **D** Ex 14 **P** *Bp* **I** (Vacant).
CHURCHTOWN (St Helen), *Lancs*.. **D** Blackb 7 *See* Garstang.
CHURSTON FERRERS (St Mary Virg) w Galmpton Chapel, *Devon*.. **D** Ex *See* Brixham.
CHURT (St Jo Evang), *Surrey*. V. **D** Guildf 3 **P** *Archd of Surrey* **I** G S PARKINSON.
CHUTE (St Nich) w Chute Forest (St Mary), V, *Wilts* and *Dorset*. V. **D** Sarum *See* Wexcombe.
CHYNGTON **D** Chich 15 *See* Seaford.
CINDERFORD (St Jo Evang), *Glos*. V. **D** Glouc 7 **P** *Crown* **I** C MYNETT, E A BLADON *hon c*.
(St Steph), V. **D** Glouc 7 **P** *CPS* **I** A D FRASER.
CINDERHILL (Ch Ch), *W Midl*. V. **D** Southw 14 **P** *Bp* **I** R H TEBBS *c*.
CIRENCESTER (St Jo Bapt) w Watermoor (H Trin), *Glos*. V. **D** Glouc 13 **P** *Bp* **I** J A LEWIS, J E BECK *c*, A C BERRY *c*, P F GREEN *c*, H G E MOSS *c*.
CITY ROAD (St Clem and St Matt).. **D** Lon 2 *See* Finsbury.
CLACTON, GREAT (St Jo Bapt), *Essex*. V. **D** Chelmsf 28 **P** *CPS* **I** J B WOOLDRIDGE, P A GREENHALGH *c*.
CLACTON, LITTLE (St Jas), *Essex*. V. **D** Chelmsf *See* Weeley.
CLACTON-ON-SEA (St Paul), *Essex*. V. **D** Chelmsf 28 **P** *CPS* **I** A F RICHARDS, D W HART *hon c*.
(St Jas), V. **D** Chelmsf 28 **P** *Bp* **I** J D JAMES, A D BARNES *c*.
CLAINES, *Worcs*.. **D** Worc 6 *See* Worcester.
CLANDON, EAST (St Thos of Cant), *Surrey*. R. **D** Guildf 5 **P** *Bp and Earl of Onslow* alt **I** (Vacant).
CLANDON, WEST (St Pet and St Paul), *Surrey*. R. **D** Guildf 5 **P** *Bp and Earl of Onslow* alt **I** (Vacant).
CLANDOWN (H Trin), *Avon*. V. **D** B & W 16b **P** *V of Midsomer Norton* **I** P G COBB.
CLANFIELD, *Oxon*. V. **D** Ox 9 *See* Bampton Aston.
CLANFIELD, *Hants*.. **D** Portsm *See* Catherington.
CLANNABOROUGH (St Petrock), *Devon*.. **D** Ex 2 *See* Down.
CLAPHAM (St Jas) w Keasden (St Matt), *N Yorks*. V. **D** Bradf 7 **P** *Bp* **I** P J WINSTONE.
CLAPHAM (St Mary Virg) w Patching (St Jo Div), *W Sussex*.. **D** Chich 9 **P** *Abp and A P F C Somerset Esq* **I** (Vacant).
CLAPHAM (St Thos of Cant), *Beds*. V. **D** St Alb 19 **P** *MMT* **I** G G CANSDALE.
CLAPHAM (H Trin w St Pet and St Paul), *Clapham Old Town Team Ministry*. **D** S'wark 3 **P** *Bp and Dioc Bd of Patr* **I** D JACKSON, D S GATLIFFE *team v*, P G ATKINSON *c*, R M ELLERY *c*, C T CAVANAGH *hon c*, H J N FULLERTON *hon c*.
(Ch Ch) and (St Jo Evang), V. **D** S'wark 3 **P** *Bp* **I** D S GATLIFFE *p-in-c*.
(H Spirit), V. **D** S'wark 3 **P** *Bp* **I** P J E MACAN *p-in-c*, E W MASON *c*.
CLAPHAM COMMON (St Barn). **D** S'wark 1 *See* Battersea.
CLAPHAM OLD TOWN TEAM MINISTRY **D** S'wark *See* Clapham.
CLAPHAM PARK (All SS), V. **D** S'wark 3 **P** *CPAS* **I** R J GROVES.
(St Jas), V. **D** S'wark 3 **P** *CPAS* **I** V A SHEEN.
(St Steph), V. **D** S'wark 6 **P** *Trustees* **I** (Vacant).
CLAPTON, *Cambs*.. **D** Ely 9 *See* Croydon.
CLAPTON (St Jas), *Glos*.. **D** Glouc 16 *See* Bourton-on-the-Water.
CLAPTON (St Jas Gt) w (Ch Ch), *Lon*. V. **D** Lon 2 **P** *R of Hackney* **I** (Vacant).
(All SS), V. **D** Lon 2 **P** *R of Hackney* **I** (Vacant).
(All S Clapton Park), V. **D** Lon 2 **P** *Trustees* **I** J F D PEARCE, S J W COX *c*.
(St Matt Upper Clapton), V. **D** Lon 2 **P** *D and C of Cant* **I** G FEATHERSTONE.
(St Thos Ap Clapton Common), V. **D** Lon 2 **P** *R of Hackney* **I** G FEATHERSTONE, K EVANS *c*.
CLAPTON or CLOPTON (St Pet), *Northants*.. **D** Pet *See* Clopton.
CLAPTON-IN-GORDANO (St Mich), *Avon*. R. **D** B & W 16 *See* Easton-in-Gordano.
CLARBOROUGH (St Jo Bapt) w Hayton (St Pet), *Notts*. V. **D** Southw 5 **P** *Bp* **I** (Vacant).
CLARE (St Pet and St Paul) w Poslingford (St Mary), *Suff*. V. **D** St E 8 **P** *Duchy of Lanc and Dioc Bd of Patr* **I** M G WOODWARD.
CLAREMONT (H Angels), *Gtr Man*. V. **D** Man 8 *See* Pendleton.
CLATFORD, UPPER (All SS) w Goodworth Clatford (St Pet), *Hants*. R. **D** Win *See* Abbotts Ann.
CLATWORTHY, *Somt*.. **D** B & W 22 *See* Huish Champflower.
CLAUGHTON (St Chad), *Lancs*.. **D** Blackb 13 *See* Hornby.
CLAUGHTON w Grange (Ch Ch & St Mich), *Mer* V. **D** Ches 1 **P** *Bp* **I** J M G DAVIES.
CLAVERDON (St Mich AA), w Preston Bagot, *Warws*. V. **D** Cov 7 **P** *Bp and Mrs F W P Ryland* alt **I** (Vacant).
CLAVERING (St Mary and St Clem) w Langley (St Jo Evang) and Arkesden, *Essex*. V. **D** Chelmsf 26 **P** *Govs of Ch Hosp and Keble Coll Ox* **I** M J ATKINSON.
CLAVERLEY (All SS), *Salop*. V. **D** Heref 9 **P** *Bp* **I** C J RABY.
CLAVERTON (St Mary Virg), *Avon*. R. **D** B & W 13 **P** *R L D Skrine Esq* **I** D W HARVEY.
CLAWSON, LONG (St Remigius), w Hose (St Mich), *Leics*. V. **D** Leic 4 **P** *Dioc Bd of Patr and Bp* alt **I** J S SAVIGE *p-in-c*.
CLAWTON (St Leon), *Devon*. R. **D** Ex 9 **P** *Bp* **I** (Vacant).
CLAXBY (St Andr), *Lincs*.. **D** Linc 8 *See* Willoughby.
CLAXBY (St Mary) w Normanby-le-Wold, *Lincs*. R. **D** Linc *See* Walesby.
CLAXBY PLUCKACRE Lincs. **D** Linc 11 *See* Mareham-le-Fen.
CLAXTON w Carleton (St Pet), *Norf*. V. **D** Nor 14 *See* Ashby w Thurton.
CLAY COTON (St Andr), *Northants*. R. **D** Pet 6 *See* Yelvertoft.
CLAY CROSS (St Bart), *Derbys*. V. **D** Derby 3 **P** *V of N Wingfield* **I** G H J DUNNING.
CLAY HILL. **D** Lon 20 *See* Enfield.
CLAYBROOKE (St Pet) w Wibtoft (Assump of Our Lady) And Frolesworth, *Leics*. V. **D** Leic **P** *Crown and Archd of Loughborough* **I** S A HADDELSEY.
CLAYDON (St Jas) w Mollington (All SS), *Oxon*. V. **D** Ox 6 **P** *Bp* **I** F DUKE *c-in-c*.
CLAYDON w Barham (St Mary Virg), *Suff*. R. **D** St E 1 **P** *H V Carter Esq and T Drury Esq (alt)* **I** B A TOLL.
CLAYDONS, The (All SS Middle Claydon, E Claydon St Mary, Steeple Claydon St Mich AA), *Bucks*. R. **D** Ox 25 **P** *Sir R B Verney* **I** R F HANNAY.
CLAYGATE (H Trin), *Surrey*. V. **D** Guildf 8 **P** *CPS* **I** R K HYATT.
CLAYHANGER, *Devon*. R. **D** Ex 8 **P** *R L Williams Esq* **I** D M CLARRIDGE.
CLAYHIDON (St Andr), *Devon*. R. **D** Ex 4 *See* Hemyock.
CLAYPOLE, (N and S Claypole, Westborough, Dry Doddington and Stubton), *Lincs*. R. **D** Linc 23 **P** *Dioc Bd of Patr* **I** P R M CORSER.
CLAYTHORPE, *Lincs*.. **D** Linc 12 *See* Belleau.
CLAYTON (St Jo Bapt), *W Yorks*. V. **D** Bradf 2 **P** *V of Bradf* **I** C P HUTCHINSON, R J LEWIS-NICHOLSON *c*.
CLAYTON (St Jo Bapt) w Keymer (St Cosmas and St Damian), *W Sussex*. R. **D** Chich 14 **P** *BNC Ox* **I** R L CLARKE, M C E BOOTES *c*, A G G RICHARDS *hon c*.
CLAYTON (St Jas), *Staffs*. V. **D** Lich 17 **P** *Bp* **I** R K LEGG.

CLAYTON (St Cross) w Bradford (St Paul), *Gtr Man.* R. **D** Man 1 **P** *Bp* **I** K BUTTERWORTH.
CLAYTON, *S Yorks.* V. **D** Sheff 10 *See* Frickley.
CLAYTON WEST w High Hoyland (All SS), *S Yorks.* R. **D** Wakef 7 **P** *Bp* **I** S J THORNTON.
CLAYTON-LE-MOORS (All SS), *Lancs.* V. **D** Blackb 1 *See* Altham.
CLAYWORTH (St Pet w St Nich), *Notts.* R. **D** Southw 1 *See* Everton w Mattersey.
CLEADON (All SS), *T & W.* V. **D** Dur 6 **P** *R of Whitburn* **I** A M BARTLETT.
CLEADON PARK (St Mark w St Cuthb), *T & W.* V. **D** Dur 6 **P** *Bp* **I** J MAUGHAN.
CLEARWELL (St Pet), *Glos.* V. **D** Glouc 7 **P** *Bp* **I** D J F ADDISON *p-in-c.*
CLEASBY (St Pet), *N Yorks.* V. **D** Ripon 1 *See* Manfield.
CLEATOR (St Leon), *Cumb.* V. **D** Carl 12 *See* Cleator Moor.
CLEATOR MOOR (St Jo Evang) w Cleator (St Leon), *Cumb.* V. **D** Carl 12 **P** *Bp* **I** K B B TOPPING.
CLECKHEATON (Whitechapel), *W Yorks.* V. **D** Wakef 9 **P** *Sir M Wilson Bt* **I** R M WILSON *p-in-c.*
(St Jo Evang), V. **D** Wakef 9 **P** *V of Birstall* **I** M G INMAN.
(St Luke Evang), V. **D** Wakef 9 **P** *Bp* **I** R M WILSON *p-in-c.*
CLEE (H Trin and St Mary), *Humb.* R. **D** Linc 9 **P** *Bp* **I** R S R PATSTON.
NEW (St Jo Evang and St Steph), *Humb.* V. **D** Linc 9 **P** *Bp* **I** J W ELLIS *c-in-c*, J ELLIS *c.*
CLEE ST MARGARET, *Salop.* V. **D** Heref 12 *See* Abdon.
CLEETHORPES (St Pet) and (St Aid), *Humb.* R. **D** Linc 9 **P** *Bp* **I** B L WISKEN, J DUNN *team v*, R D JAMES *team v*, D H WEBSTER *c.*
CLEETON (St Mary) w Silvington (St Mich), *Salop.* V. **D** Heref 9 **P** *Bp and Mrs Hamilton* alt **I** R HEYWOOD-WADDINGTON *c-in-c.*
CLEEVE (H Trin) w Chelvey and Brockley, *Avon.* V. **D** B & W 16 **P** *V of Yatton and Bp* **I** P A G ETTERLEY.
CLEEVE, OLD (St Andr) w Leighland and Treborough, *Somt.* R. **D** B & W 21 **P** *Selw Coll Cam 2 turns, G Wolseley Esq 1 turn* **I** C H TOWNSHEND.
CLEEVE PRIOR (St Andr) and The Littletons, (S w N and Middle Littleton), *Worcs.* V. **D** Worc 1 **P** *D and C of Worc and D and C of Ox* **I** D R EVANS.
CLEHONGER (All SS), *Herefs.* V. **D** Heref 1 **P** *Bp* **I** A J MORTIMER *p-in-c.*
CLENCHWARTON (St Marg), *Norf.* R. **D** Ely 18 **P** *Bp* **I** I W SMITH, C J RODEN *c.*
CLENT (St Leon), *Worcs.* V. **D** Worc 11 **P** *Ld Chan* **I** R E N STREVENS.
CLEOBURY MORTIMER (St Mary Virg) w Hopton Wafers (St Mich AA), *Salop.* V. **D** Heref 12 **P** *Keble Coll Ox and Maj P R E Woodward* **I** R A HORSFIELD P-IN-C OF DODDINGTON, A E GRIFFITHS *c*, S J F MAXFIELD *c.*
CLEOBURY, N, *Salop.* R. **D** Heref 9 *See* Burwarton.
CLERKENWELL (St Jas w St Jo Bapt and St Pet), *Lon.* V. **D** Lon 3 **P** *PCC and CPS* **I** J M B ROBERTS.
(H Redeemer) w (St Phil), V. **D** Lon 3 **P** *Trustees* **I** P LAISTER.
(St Mark, Myddelton Square), V. **D** Lon 3 **P** *Corp of Lon* **I** A H APPS, D E CLAYDEN.
CLEVEDON (St Andr), *Avon.* V. **D** B & W 16 **P** *Ld Chan* **I** J W PRICE, R D TURNER *c.*
(Ch Ch), V. **D** B & W 16 **P** *Simeon Trustees* **I** J M DRUCE *hon c.*
EAST (All SS), V. **D** B & W 16 **P** *S for Maint of Faith* **I** W R T MARRIOTT.
SOUTH (St Jo Evang), V. **D** B & W 16 **P** *S for Maint of Faith* **I** D P RUNDLE.
CLEVELEYS (St Andr), *Lancs.* V. **D** Blackb 8 **P** *Trustees* **I** J B SELVEY.
CLEVERTON, *Wilts.* R. **D** Bris *See* Garsdon.
CLEWER (St Andr), *Berks.* R. **D** Ox 13 **P** *Prov and Fells of Eton Coll* **I** D SHAW, F T BONHAM *c.*
(All SS Conv Distr Dedworth). **D** Ox 13 **P** *Bp* **I** J A STONE *missr.*
(St Steph), V. **D** Ox 13 **P** *S for Maint of Faith* **I** J N SCOTT.
CLEY-NEXT-THE-SEA (St Marg) w Wiveton (St Mary Virg), *Norf.* R. **D** Nor 24 **P** *Keble Coll Ox* **I** D P MAURICE, J A RIVERS *hon c.*
CLIBURN, *Cumb.*. **D** Carl *See* Clifton.
CLIDDESDEN (St Leon), *Hants.* R. **D** Win 3 **P** *Earl of Portsm* **I** R J A PERRETT-JONES.
CLIFFE-AT-HOO (St Helen) w Cooling, *Kent.* R. **D** Roch 5 **P** *D and C of Roch* **I** D J MACROW.
CLIFFORD (St Mary), *Herefs.* V. **D** Heref 1 **P** *J M S W Trumper Esq* **I** W R KING *p-in-c.*
CLIFFORD (St Luke), *W Yorks.* V. **D** York 9 **P** *Hon M A M Lane-Fox* **I** (Vacant).
CLIFFORD CHAMBERS, *Warw.* R. **D** Glouc 12 *See* Welford.
CLIFFORD'S MESNE (St Pet), *Glos.*. **D** Glouc 6 *See* Gorsley.
CLIFTON (St Andr w St Jas Chap), *Avon.* V. **D** Bris 3 **I** (Vacant).
(All SS w St Jo Evang), V. **D** Bris 5 **P** *Bp* **I** J A YOUNGER, D C MACDONALD *c.*
(Ch Ch), V. **D** Bris 5 **P** *Simeon Trustees* **I** P M BERG.
(H Trin Hotwells w St Pet Clifton Wood and St Andr L), V. **D** Bris 5 **P** *Simeon Trustees* **I** J J R COLLINGWOOD.
(St Alb, Westbury Pk), V. **D** Bris 5 **P** *Bp* **I** J S SMITH, B J PULLAN *c.*
(St Paul Ap), V. **D** Bris 5 **P** *Bp* **I** M W MATTHEWS *p-in-c*, E J WOODS *hon c.*
CLIFTON (St Cuthb), Brougham and Cliburn (St Cuthb), *Cumb.* R. **D** Carl 6 **P** *Earl of Lonsdale and Lt Col G W A Tufton* **I** T W H RUTHERFORD.
CLIFTON (H Trin), *Derbys.* V. **D** Derby 8 **P** *J R G Stanton, L A Clowes and V of Ashbourne* in turn **I** N DAUGHTRY.
CLIFTON (St Anne), *Gtr Man.* V. **D** Man 3 **P** *Bp* **I** W J GASH.
CLIFTON, *Oxon.*. **D** Ox *See* Deddington.
CLIFTON (All SS), *Beds.* R. **D** St Alb 22 **P** *Bp* **I** D A IRELAND.
CLIFTON (St Mary Virg, St Francis and H Trin) w Glapton, *Notts.* R. **D** Southw 11 **I** W B WILKINSON, F E BALDWICK *team v*, J S M HARDING *c.*
CLIFTON (St Jo Evang), *W Yorks.* V. **D** Wakef 2 **P** *Bp* **I** J A RICHARDSON.
CLIFTON (St Jas), *S Yorks.* V. **D** York 1 *See* York.
CLIFTON (St Jas), *S Yorks.* V. **D** Sheff 6 **P** *Bp* **I** V A VOUT.
CLIFTON CAMVILLE (St Andr) w Chilcote (St Matt) and Statfold (All SS), *Staffs.* R. **D** Lich 6 **P** *Major R Reed* **I** A C SOLOMON.
CLIFTON GREEN (St Thos), *Gtr Man.* V. **D** Man 3 **P** *Bp* **I** (Vacant).
CLIFTON HAMPDEN (St Mich AA) w Burcot, *Oxon.*. **D** Ox 5 *See* Dorchester.
CLIFTON-IN-WORKINGTON (St Luke), V *Cumb.*. **D** Carl 11 **P** *R of Workington* **I** J W HAYWOOD.
CLIFTON MAYBANK, *Dorset.*. **D** Sarum 7 *See* Bradford Abbas.
CLIFTON, NORTH and South (St Geo Mart), *Notts.* V. **D** Southw *See* Harby.
CLIFTON-ON-DUNSMORE (St Mary Virg) w Brownsover (St Mich AA) and Newton, *Warws.* V. **D** Cov 6 **P** *A M Boughton Leigh Esq* **I** W G JARVIS, G P EVANS *c.*
CLIFTON-ON-TEME (St Kenelm), Lower Sapey and the Shelsleys, *Worcs.* V. **D** Worc 2 **P** *Bp and A F Evans* **I** P J B HOBSON, R A DENNISTON *c*, L J BIRCH *hon c.*
CLIFTON-REYNES (St Mary Virg) w Emberton, Newton Blossomville (St Nich) and Tyringham w Filgrave, *Bucks.* R. **D** Ox 28 **P** *M E Farrer Esq, D E Sutthery Esq and G E C Konig Esq* **I** (Vacant).
CLIFTONVILLE, *Kent.*. **D** Cant 8 *See* Margate.
CLIPPESBY, *Norf.*. **D** Nor *See* Ashby.
CLIPSHAM (St Mary), *Leics.* R. **D** Pet 12 *See* Greetham.
CLIPSTON (All SS) w Naseby (All SS) and Haselbech (St Mich), *Northants.* R. **D** Pet 6 **P** *Ch Coll Cam 1st turn, Dioc Bd of Patr 2nd turn, Miss D K Smee 3rd turn* **I** (Vacant).
CLIPSTONE, NEW (All SS), *Notts.* V. **D** Southw 2 **P** *Bp* **I** G S CHEETHAM.
CLITHEROE (St Mary Magd), *Lancs.* V. **D** Blackb 7 **P** *R Peel Esq* **I** J C HUDSON.
(St Jas), R. **D** Blackb 7 **P** *Trustees* **I** (Vacant).
(St Paul, Low Moor), V. **D** Blackb 7 **P** *Bp* **I** (Vacant).
CLIVE (All SS) w Grinshill (All SS), *Salop.* V. **D** Lich 27 **P** *D R Thompson Esq* **I** (Vacant).
CLIVE VALE (All S), *E Sussex.* V. **D** Chich *See* Hastings.
CLIVIGER (St Jo Evang), *Lancs.*. **D** Blackb 3 *See* Holme.
CLIXBY (All H), *Lincs.*. **D** Linc 5 *See* Caistor.
CLODOCK (St Clydog) w Longtown (St Pet), Llanveynoe (St Beuno and St Pet), Craswall (St Mary), St Margaret's, Michaelchurch Escley and Newton, *Herefs.* V. **D** Heref 1 **P** *MMT, Dio Bd of Patr and Mrs C M Hunter* **I** F E RODGERS.
CLOFORD (St Mary Virg), *Somt.* V. **D** B & W 16a *See* Wanstrow.
CLOPHILL (St Mary), *Beds.* R. **D** St Alb 22 **P** *Ball Coll Ox* **I** P J SWINDELLS.
CLOPTON (St Mary), *Suff.* R. **D** St E 7 **P** *Bp* **I** F ROWELL.
CLOPTON (St Pet), *Northants.* R. **D** Pet 11 **P** *Exors of F G Mitchell* **I** H W WILLIAMS *p-in-c.*

CLOSWORTH (All SS), *Somt.*. **D** B & W 12 *See* Yeovil.
CLOTHALL (St Mary Virg), *Herts.* R. **D** St Alb 12 *See* Baldock.
CLOUGHTON (St Mary Virg), *N Yorks.* V. **D** York 18 **P** *V of Scalby* **I** J W KENNEDY.
CLOVELLY (All SS) *Devon.* R. **D** Ex 17 **P** *Hon Mrs B C Asquith* **I** D A BATES.
CLOWNE (St Jo Bapt), *Derbys.* R. **D** Derby 2 **P** *Ld Chan* **I** L R R HARRIS.
CLUBMOOR (St Andr), *Lancs.* V. **D** Liv 6 **P** *Bp* **I** D ROBINSON, M E GREENWOOD *c.*
CLUN (St Geo) w Chapel Lawn (St Mary), Bettws-y-Crwyn and Newcastle, *Salop.* V. **D** Heref 10 **P** *Earl of Powis* **I** E F BUCKLEY.
CLUNBURY (St Swith) w Clunton (St Mary), *Salop.* V. **D** Heref 10 *See* Clungunford.
CLUNGUNFORD (St Cuthb) w Clunbury, Clunton, Bedstone and Hopton Castle, *Salop.* R. **D** Heref 10 **P** *J S E Roche Esq, Earl of Powis, MSC Brown Esq and Sir H Ripley Bt* **I** R H BASTEN.
CLUTTON (St Aug) w Cameley and Temple Cloud, *Avon.* R. **D** B & W 15 **P** *Earl of Warwick 2 turns, J P Hippisley 1 turn* **I** A R HAWKINS.
CLYFFE PYPARD (St Pet), Tockenham (St Giles) and Broad Town (Ch Ch), *Wilts.* V. **D** Sarum 25 **P** *Mrs Wilson and Ld Chan* Alt **I** J E A HOPKINS.
CLYMPING (St Mary), *W Sussex.* V. **D** Chich 1 **P** *Ld Chan* **I** P H D GOODERHAM *p-in-c.*
CLYST HYDON (St Andr), *Devon.* R. **D** Ex *See* Plymtree.
CLYST ST GEO (St Geo) Aylesbeare, Clyst Honiton, Clyst St Mary, Farringdon, Rockbeare, Sowton and Woodbury Salterton (Clyst Valley Team Min), *Devon.* R. **D** Ex 1 **P** *Clyst Valley Patr Bd* **I** D H LARGE, W W JACOBSON *team v*, T G WOODBRIDGE *team v.*
CLYST ST LAWR, *Devon.* R. **D** Ex *See* Plymtree.
COALBROOKDALE (H Trin), Ironbridge and Little Wenlock, *Salop.* V. **D** Heref 14 **P** *Bp, Ld Forester, V of Much Wenlock and V of Madeley* **I** W A L ZWALF, D HARRIS *c.*
COALEY (St Bart), *Glos.* V. **D** Glouc 5 **P** *Bp* **I** D J BICK.
COALPIT HEATH (St Sav), *Avon.* V. **D** Bris 7 **P** *Bp* **I** B RAVEN *p-in-c.*
COALVILLE (Ch Ch) and Bardon Hill (St Pet) *Leics.* V. **D** Leic 11 **P** *Simeon Trustees and V of Hugglescote and V of Hugglescote* **I** R A HINTON, W J PEAL *c.*
COATES, *W Sussex.*. **D** Chich 6 *See* Burton.
COATES (H Trin), *Cambs.* R. **D** Ely 19 **P** *Ld Chan* **I** J BIDDER.
COATES (St Matt), Rodmarton and Sapperton w Frampton Mansell, *Glos.* R. **D** Glouc 13 **P** *Guild of All S, Earl of Bathurst and Bp* **I** R A BOWDEN, J F GREGORY *hon c.*
COATES (St Edith), *Lincs.* V. **D** Linc 2 **P** *Bp* **I** J M SPURRELL *p-in-c.*
COATES, LITTLE (St Mich) and Great (St Nich) w Bradley (St Geo), *Humb.* R. **D** Linc 9 **P** *Patr Bd* **I** R J WELLS, M D LILES *team v*, B K NEWTON *team v*, P G LEWIS *c.*
COATES, NORTH (St Nich), *Humb.* R. **D** Linc 12 **P** *Duchy of Lanc* **I** P PARKINSON.
COATHAM, EAST (Ch Ch), *Cleve.* V. **D** York 19 **P** *Trustees* **I** R W SMITH.
COBERLEY (St Giles) w Cowley, *Glos.* R. **D** Glouc 13 **P** *Ld Chan and Exors of Col Elwes* alt **I** S I PULFORD.
COBHAM (St Andr), V *Surrey.* V. **D** Guildf 10 **P** *C H C Combe Esq* **I** J D SMITH.
COBHAM (St Mary Magd) w Luddesdown, *Kent.* V. **D** Roch 1 **P** *Earl of Darnley and CPAS* alt **I** P M THOMSON.
COBRIDGE (Ch Ch), *Staffs.*. **D** Lich *See* Hanley, H Evang.
COCKAYNE-HATLEY (St Jo Bapt), *Beds.*. **D** St Alb 17 *See* Potton.
COCKERHAM (St Mich) w Winmarleigh (St Luke), *Lancs.* V. **D** Blackb 11 **P** *Bp and Trustees* alt **I** R N HAMBLIN.
COCKERINGTON, NORTH (St Mary) and South (St Leon), *Lincs.* V. **D** Linc 12 *See* Alvingham.
COCKERMOUTH (All SS) w (Ch Ch) w Embleton and Wythop, *Cumb.* R. **D** Carl 10 **P** *Patr Bd* **I** J L R CRAWLEY, C S FULLER *team v.*
COCKERTON (St Mary), *Durham.* V. **D** Dur 11 **P** *Bp* **I** M P KENT, D H FROST *c*, R C WARDALE *c.*
COCKEYMOOR (Ch Ch), *Gtr Man.*. **D** Man 12 *See* Ainsworth.
COCKFIELD (St Mary), *Durham.* R. **D** Dur 10 **P** *Bp* **I** L J PAUL.
COCKFIELD (St Pet), *Suff.* R. **D** St E 10 **P** *St Jo Coll Cam* **I** C T CATTON.
COCKFOSTERS (Ch Ch), *Gtr Lon.* V. **D** Lon 21 **P** *Ch Trust Fund Trust* **I** D E D CHURCHMAN, M R GREENFIELD *c*, A R WINGFIELD DIGBY *c*, A R WINGFIELDDIGBY *c*, S M WOOKEY *c.*
COCKING w Bepton (St Mary) and W Lavington, *W Sussex.* R. **D** Chich **P** *Ld Chan and Cowdray Trust (alt)* **I** A D CHARLTON.
COCKINGTON (St Geo and St Mary) w Chelston (St Matt), *Devon.* V. **D** Ex 10 **P** *Bp* **I** J C DONALDSON, J GREEN *c.*
COCKLEY-CLEY (All SS) w Gooderstone (St Geo), *Norf.* R (*See Hilborough Group*).. **D** Nor 19 **P** *Bp* **I** (Vacant).
COCKSHUTT (St Simon and St Jude), *Salop.* V. **D** Lich 22 *See* Petton.
COCKTHORPE, *Norf.*. **D** Nor 24 *See* Stiffkey.
CODDENHAM (St Mary Virg) w Gosbeck (St Mary) and Hemingstone w Henley, *Suff.* R. **D** St E 1 **P** *Pem Coll Cam, D and C of Nor and Ld de Saumarez* in turn **I** R S OWENS.
CODDINGTON, *Chesh.*. **D** Ches 5 *See* Farndon.
CODDINGTON (All SS), *Heref.* R. **D** Heref 6 **P** *Bp* **I** M H CROSS *p-in-c.*
CODDINGTON (All SS) w Barnby in the Willows (All SS), *Notts.* V. **D** Southw 3 **P** *Bp* **I** P G WRIGHT.
CODFORD (St Mary Virg) w (St Pet) and Upton Lovell (St Aug) *Wilts.* R. **D** Sarum *See* Ashton Gifford.
CODICOTE (St Giles), *Herts.* V. **D** St Alb 7 **P** *Abp* **I** (Vacant).
CODNOR (St Jas), *Derbys.* V. **D** Derby 6 **P** *Crown* **I** N HILL.
CODRINGTON, *Avon.*. **D** Bris *See* Yate New Town.
CODSALL (St Nich), *Staffs.* V. **D** Lich 3 **P** *Ld Wrottesley* **I** G SMITH, C R GOUGH *c.*
COFFINSWELL, *Devon.*. **D** Ex 10 *See* Haccombe.
COFTON (St Mary) w Starcross, *Devon.* V. **D** Ex 6 **P** *Earl of Devon, D & C of Sarum and Ex* **I** D E CAVAGHAN.
COFTON-HACKETT (St Mich AA) w Barnt Green, *Worcs.* V. **D** Birm **P** *Bp* **I** I AVEYARD *p-in-c.*
COGENHOE (St Pet), *Northants.* R. **D** Pet 4 **P** *Dioc Bd of Patr* **I** J M OULESS.
COGGES (St Mary), *Oxon.* V. **D** Ox 9 **P** *Trustees* **I** R A LEAVER *c-in-c.*
COGGESHALL (St Pet-ad-Vincula), Gt and Little, w Markshall (St Marg), *Essex.* R and V. **D** Chelmsf 21 **P** *S for Maint of Faith 1 turn, Bp 2 turns* **I** D M BEETON.
COKER, EAST (St Mich AA) w Sutton Bingham (All SS), *Somt.* V. **D** B & W 12 **P** *D and C of Ex* **I** D J HUNT *p-in-c.*
COKER, WEST (St Martin of Tours), *Somt.* R. **D** B & W 10 **P** *Dioc Bd of Patr* **I** M K RAIKES *p-in-c.*
COLAN, *Cornw.*. **D** Truro 7 *See* St Colan.
COLATON RALEIGH (St Jo Bapt), *Devon.* V. **D** Ex *See* Otterton.
COLBURY (Ch Ch), *Hants.* V. **D** Win 9 **P** *P C V Barker-Mill Esq* **I** N BOAKES.
COLBY (St Giles) w Banningham (St Botolph) and Tuttington (St Pet and St Paul), *Norf.* R. **D** Nor 8 **P** *Bp 2 turns, D C Barber Esq 1 turn* **I** W M C BESTELINK.
COLCHESTER (St Anne), V. **D** Chelmsf 21 **P** *Bp* **I** T V HODDER.
(St Barn), V. **D** Chelmsf 21 **P** *Bp* **I** (Vacant).
(St Botolph w H Trin and St Giles), V and R. **D** Chelmsf 21 **P** *Bp* **I** P G EVANS.
(Ch Ch w St Mary Virg), R.. **D** Chelmsf 21 **P** *Bp* **I** C J ELLIOTT, J MARVELL *c.*
(St Jas Gtr w All SS St Nich and St Runwald), R. **D** Chelmsf 21 **P** *Bp* **I** T THOMPSON, I C MORTER *c*, P S LANSLEY *hon c.*
(St John), V. **D** Chelmsf 21 **P** *Archd of Colchester* **I** B W NICHOLSON.
(St Leon) and (St Mary Magd) and (St Steph), R. **D** Chelmsf 21 **P** *Patr Bd 2 turns, Ld Chan 1 turn* **I** B J RUDDOCK.
(St Mich AA Myland), R. **D** Chelmsf 21 **P** *Ball Coll Ox* **I** J F BLORE.
(St Paul), V. **D** Chelmsf 21 **P** *Bp* **I** H D WINTER.
(St Pet), V. **D** Chelmsf 21 **P** *Simeon Trustees* **I** R M WILSON. **I** B C SNAITH *team v.*
COLD ASH (St Mark Evang w St Bart), *Berks.* V. **D** Ox *See* Hermitage.
COLD ASHBY, *Northants.* V. **D** Pet 6 *See* Guilsborough.
COLD ASHTON (H Trin), *Avon.* R. **D** Bris 8 *See* Marshfield.
COLD ASTON (St Andr) w Notgrove (St Bart) and Turkdean (All SS), *Glos.* V. **D** Glouc 15 **P** *Ld Chan and Bp* **I** J W HUGHES.
COLD BRAYFIELD, *Bucks.*. **D** Ox *See* Lavendon.
COLD HARBOUR (Ch Ch), *Surrey.* V. **D** Guildf 6 *See* Abinger.

COLD HIGHAM (St Luke), *Northants.* R. **D** Pet 2 *See* Pattishall.

COLD KIRBY (St Mich), *N Yorks.* R. **D** York 20 *See* Scawton.

COLD NEWTON, *Leics.* V. **D** Leic 8 *See* Tilton-on-the-Hill.

COLD NORTON (St Steph) w Stow Maries (St Mary and St Marg), *Essex.* R. **D** Chelmsf 14 **P** *Bp and Govs of Charterho Sch* alt **I** S E PETERS *p-in-c.*

COLD OVERTON (St Jo Bapt), *Leics.* R. **D** Leic 8 *See* Knossington.

COLD SALPERTON (All SS), *Glos..* **D** Glouc 15 *See* Dowdeswell.

COLD WALTHAM (St Giles), *W Sussex.* V. **D** Chich 7 **P** *D and C of Chich* **I** H E S NEWBOLD *p-in-c.*

COLD WESTON (St Mary), *Salop.* R. **D** Heref 12 **P** *Dioc Bd of Patr* **I** A G SEABROOK P-IN-C OF STOKE ST MILBURGH *p-in-c.*

COLDEN COMMON (H Trin), *Hants.* V. **D** Win 15 **P** *V of Twyford* **I** M C DAUBUZ.

COLDEN PARVA, *Humb..* **D** York *See* Aldborough.

COLDHAM (St Etheldreda), *Cambs.* V. **D** Ely 20 **P** *Bp* **I** (Vacant).

COLDRED (St Pancras), *Kent..* **D** Cant 5 *See* Sibertswold.

COLDRIDGE, *Devon..* **D** Ex *See* Nymet Rowland.

COLEBROOKE (St Andr), *Devon.* R. **D** Ex 2 **P** *D and C of Ex* **I** B H GALES.

COLEBY, *Humb..* **D** Linc 4 *See* Burton-on-Stather.

COLEBY (All SS), *Lincs.* V. **D** Linc 18 **P** *Or Coll Ox* **I** F W NAIRN *c-in-c.*

COLEFORD (St Jo Evang) w Staunton (All SS), *Glos.* V and R. **D** Glouc 7 **P** *Bp* **I** C J H WAGSTAFF, M J D IRVING *c,* P A NASH *c,* P W SMITH *c.*

(Ch Ch, Forest of Dean), *Glos.* V. **D** Glouc 7 *See* Dean Forest.

COLEFORD (H Trin) w Holcombe (St Andr), *Somt.* V. **D** B & W 16b **P** *V of Kilmersdon and Bp* **I** A COLEMAN.

COLEHILL (St Mich AA), *Dorset.* V. **D** Sarum 11 **P** *Govs of Wimborne Minster* **I** M D JEFFREY.

COLEMAN'S HATCH (H Trin), *E Sussex..* **D** Chich 20 *See* Hartfield.

COLEMERE, *Salop..* **D** Lich 22 *See* Lyneal.

COLE-ORTON (St Mary Virg), *Leics..* **D** Leic 11 *See* Whitwick St Geo.

COLERNE (St Jo Bapt), *Wilts.* V. **D** Bris 9 **P** *New Coll Ox* **I** R C H SAUNDERS *p-in-c.*

COLESBOURNE (St Jas Ap and M), *Glos.* R. **D** Glouc 13 **P** *H W G Elwes Esq* **I** S I PULFORD *p-in-c.*

COLESHILL (All SS), *Oxon.* V. **D** Ox 17 *See* Coxwell, Gt.

COLESHILL (St Pet and St Paul), *Warws.* V. **D** Birm 9 **P** *S Wingfield Digby Esq MP 3 turns Ld Leigh 1 turn* **I** J F CAPPER, A E CORBETT *hon c.*

COLESHILL (All SS), *Bucks..* **D** Ox 20 *See* Amersham.

COLEY (St John), *W Yorks.* V. **D** Wakef 2 **P** *V of Halifax* **I** K H SHARPE.

COLEGATE (St Sav), *W Sussex.* V. **D** Chich 4 **P** *Mrs E C Calvert* **I** P H ADDENBROOKE *c-in-c.*

COLINDALE. **D** Lon *See* Hendon.

COLKIRK (St Mary) w Oxwick (All SS) Whissonsett and Horningtoft, *Norf.* R. **D** Nor 20 **P** *C S P D Lane Esq and Dioc Bd of Patr* alt **I** A W SAWYER.

COLLATON (St Mary Virg), *Devon.* V. **D** Ex 10 **P** *Bp* **I** (Vacant).

(St Jo Bapt), V. **D** Ex 10 **P** *Bp* **I** D A PINCHES.

COLLIER ROW, *Essex.* V. **D** Chelmsf 4 *See* Romford.

COLLIER STREET (St Marg), *Kent.* V. **D** Roch 6 *See* Yalding.

COLLIERLEY (St Thos) w Annfield Plain, *Durham.* V. **D** Dur **P** *Bp and Crown* **I** M J SMITH.

COLLINGBOURNES, THE (Collingbourne Kingston St Mary w Collingbourne Ducis) and Everleigh, *Wilts.* V. **D** Sarum *See* Wexcombe.

COLLINGHAM (St Osw) w Harewood, *W Yorks.* V. **D** Ripon 4 **P** *G H H Wheler Esq Earl of Harewood and Dioc Bd of Patr* **I** B M OVEREND.

COLLINGHAM, NORTH (All SS) w Collingham, South (St Jo Bapt), *Notts.* V. **D** Southw 3 **P** *D and C of Pet and Ld Chan* alt **I** R J STEVENS.

COLLINGTON (St Mary Virg), *Herefs.* R. **D** Heref 2 *See* Edvin Ralph.

COLLINGTREE (St Columba) w Courteenhall (St Pet and St Paul) and Milton Malsor, *Northants.* R. **D** Pet **P** *Maj-Gen Sir H Wake Bt 1st turn, G P Walker 2nd turn and Hyndman Bounty Trust 3rd turn* **I** R V P CUMMINGS.

COLLYHURST, *Gtr Man..* **D** Man 1 & 4 *See* Manchester.

COLLYWESTON (St Andr) w Duddington and Tixover, *Northants.* R. **D** Pet 13 **P** *Bp and Ld Chan (alt)* **I** J W AUBREY.

COLMER or COLMORE (St Pet-ad-Vincula), *Hants..* **D** Win 1 *See* Tisted, East.

COLMWORTH, *Beds..* **D** St Alb *See* Wilden.

COLN-ROGERS (St Andr) w Coln St Denys (St Jas Gt), *Glos.* R. **D** Glouc 15 *See* Chedworth.

COLN ST ALDWYN (Decollation of St Jo Bapt), Hatherop, Quenington, Eastleach and Southrop *Glos.* V. **D** Glouc **P** *Earl of St Aldwyn, D and C Glouc, St T Bazley Bt and Wadh Coll Ox* **I** D L COWMEADOW.

COLN ST DENYS (St Jas Gt) *Glos.* R. **D** Glouc 15 *See* Coln Rogers.

COLNBROOK (St Thos), *Bucks..* **D** Ox 24 *See* Riverside.

COLNE (St Helen), *Cambs..* **D** Ely 12 *See* Somersham.

COLNE (St Bart), *Lancs.* R. **D** Blackb 6a **P** *Hulme Trustees* **I** N D HAWTHORNE, P F BARNES *c.*

(Ch Ch), V. **D** Blackb 6a **P** *Hulme Trustees* **I** J C PRIESTLEY.

(H Trin), V. **D** Blackb 6a **P** *Bp* **I** D LOWE.

COLNE-ENGAINE (St Andr), *Essex.* R. **D** Chelmsf 24 **P** *Govs of Ch Hosp* **I** A R BENNETT.

COLNEY (St Pet), *Herts.* V. **D** St Alb 1 **P** *Reps of late Countess of Caledon and Trustees* **I** M T BEER.

COLNEY (St Andr), *Norf.* R. **D** Nor 13 **P** *Trustees and Exors of E H Barclay* alt **I** (Vacant).

COLNEY HEATH (St Mark), *Herts.* V. **D** St Alb 7 **P** *Can A Bennett and 2 other trustees* **I** D R VENESS, A D T GORTON *c.*

COLSTERWORTH (St Jo Bapt), *Lincs.* R. **D** Linc 14 **P** *Bp* **I** (Vacant).

COLSTON-BASSETT (St Jo Div), *Notts.* V. **D** Southw 10 **P** *Ld Chan* **I** C B PERKINS *p-in-c.*

COLTISHALL (St Jo Bapt) w Gt Hautbois, *Norf.* R. **D** Nor 3 **P** *D and C of Nor* **I** L J LEE.

COLTON (H Trin), w Satterthwaite (All SS) and Rusland (St Paul), *Cumb.* V. **D** Carl 14 **P** *Certain Landowners* **I** F C HAMBREY.

COLTON (St Andr), *Norf.* R. **D** Nor *See* Easton.

COLTON (BVM), *Staffs.* R. **D** Lich 4 **P** *Bp 2 turns, S M Duke Esq 1 turn* **I** R T WILCOX *p-in-c.*

COLTON, *N Yorks..* **D** York *See* Bolton Percy.

COLWALL (St Jas Gt), *Herefs.* R. **D** Heref 6 **P** *Bp* **I** H L WHATLEY.

COLWICH (St Mich AA), *Staffs.* V. **D** Lich 4 **P** *Bp* **I** D M WOODHOUSE, P G F CANNELL *c,* J A S WOOD *c.*

COLWICK (St Jo Bapt), *Notts.* R. **D** Southw 13 **P** *Trustees* **I** R J SMITH.

COLYTON (St Andr), *Devon.* V. **D** Ex 5 **P** *D and C of Ex* **I** H H RANN.

COMBE (St Swith), *Berks.* V. **D** Ox 14 *See* Inkpen.

COMBE-ABBAS (or Temple Combe) (St Mary Virg), *Somt.* R. **D** B & W 5 *See* Abbas.

COMBE DOWN (H Trin) w Monkton Combe and South Stoke, *Avon.* V. **D** B & W 13 **P** *R of Bath, Trustees and W H G Samler* **I** R R B PLOWMAN *c,* S T B FORBES ADAM *hon c.*

COMBE-FLOREY (St Pet and St Paul), *Somt.* R. **D** B & W 22 *See* Lydeard.

COMBE-HAY (Dedic unknown), *Avon.* R. **D** B & W 13 **P** *CPAS* **I** (Vacant).

COMBE-IN-TEIGNHEAD Devon. R **D** Ex 11 *See* Stoke-in-Teignhead.

COMBE-LONGA (St Lawr Mart), *Oxon.* V. **D** Ox 10 **P** *Linc Coll Ox* **I** G H P THOMPSON.

COMBE MARTIN (St Pet) and Berrynarbor *Devon.* R. **D** Ex 18 **P** *Bp* **I** J T WILLIAMS.

COMBE PYNE (St Mary Virg) w Rousdon (St Pancras), *Devon.* R. **D** Ex 5 **P** *All H Educl Found* **I** F S WORTH *p-in-c.*

COMBE RALEIGH (St Nich), *Devon.* R. **D** Ex 5 *See* Honiton.

COMBE ST NICHOLAS (St Nich) w Wambrook, *Somt.* V. **D** B & W 19 **P** *Bp and Lt-Col R Eames* **I** (Vacant).

COMBERTON (St Mary Virg), *Cambs.* V. **D** Ely 1 **P** *Jes Coll Cam* **I** R STEPHENSON.

COMBERTON, GREAT (St Mich), w Comberton, Little (St Pet), *Worcs.* R. **D** Worc 3 *See* Elmley Castle.

COMBROKE (St Mary Virg and St Marg) w Compton Verney, *Warws.* R. **D** Cov 8 **P** *Bp* **I** R MIGHALL.

COMBS (St Mary), *Suff.* R. **D** St E 6 **P** *Bp* **I** E R CROUCHMAN.

COMBWICH, *Somt..* **D** B & W 18 *See* Otterhampton.

COMPSTALL (St Paul), *Gtr Man..* **D** Ches 16 *See* Werneth.

COMPTON (St Mary), The Mardens (St Pet), Stoughton (St Mary) Lordington and Racton (Dedic unknown), *W Sussex.* V. **D** Chich **P** *Bp of Lon 1 turn, Bp of Chich 2 turns* **I** J L W ROBINSON, H WOODFORD *c.*

COMPTON (St Nich), *Surrey.* R. **D** Guildf 5 **P** *Maj Jas M Molyneux* **I** N P NICHOLSON *p-in-c.*

COMPTON (All SS) w Shawford, *Hants*. R. **D** Win 12 **P** *Bp* **I** N J OVENDEN.
COMPTON-ABBAS (St Mary Virg), *Dorset*. R. **D** Sarum 19 *See* Shaston.
COMPTON ABBAS, or WEST COMPTON (St Mich), w Wynford Eagle (St Laur) and Toller Fratrum (St Basil), *Dorset*. R. **D** Sarum *See* Maiden Newton.
COMPTON ABDALE (St Osw), *Glos*.. **D** Glouc 15 *See* Withington.
COMPTON BASSETT (St Swith), *Wilts*. R. **D** Sarum 25 **P** *Crown* **I** (Vacant).
COMPTON-BEAUCHAMP, *Oxon*.. **D** Ox *See* Ashbury.
COMPTON BISHOP (St Andr) w Loxton and Christon, *Somt*. V. **D** B & W **P** *Bp* **I** G MILLIER C-IN-C OF COMPTON BISHOP.
COMPTON-CHAMBERLAYNE (St Mich), *Wilts*.. **D** Sarum *See* Barford St Martin.
COMPTON DANDO (St Mary Virg) and Chelwood, *Avon*. V. **D** B & W 15 *See* Publow.
COMPTON-DUNDON (St Andr), *Somt*. V. **D** B & W *See* Somerton.
COMPTON GIFFORD (Em Ch), *Devon*. V. **D** Ex 23 *See* Plymouth.
COMPTON GREENFIELD (All SS), *Avon*. R. **D** Bris 6 **P** *Bp* **I** J H R ORBELL.
COMPTON, LITTLE (St Denys) w Chastleton, Cornwell, Little Rollright and Salford, *Warws* and *Oxon*. V. **D** Ox **P** *Ch Ch Ox, Dioc Bd of Patr and Bp* **I** J RECORD.
COMPTON, LONG (St Pet and St Paul), *Warws*. V. **D** Cov 9 **P** *Bp* **I** E J RAINSBERRY.
COMPTON-MARTIN (St Mich AA) w Ubley (St Bart) *Avon*. R. **D** B & W 15 **P** *Bp* **I** (Vacant).
COMPTON, OVER (St Mich), and Compton, Nether (St Nich), Trent (St Andr) and Sandford Orcas, *Dorset*. R. **D** Sarum *See* Queen Thorne.
COMPTON PARVA (St Mary and St Nich) w E Ilsley, *Berks*. V. **D** Ox 14 **P** *Bp* **I** J B LEWIS.
COMPTON PAUNCEFOOT (St Mary Virg) w Blackford (St Mich), *Somt*. R. **D** B & W 4 *See* Camelot.
COMPTON-VALENCE (St Thos of Cant), *Dorset*. R. **D** Sarum 5 *See* Winterbournes.
COMPTON VERNEY, *Warws*.. **D** Cov 8 *See* Combroke.
COMPTON WYNYATES, *Warws*.. **D** Cov 9 *See* Tysoe.
CONDICOTE (St Nich), *Glos*. R. **D** Glouc 16 *See* Longborough.
CONDOVER (SS Andr and Mary), *Salop*. V. **D** Heref 11 **P** *Bp* **I** C J W CHATCLIFFE *p-in-c*.
CONEY WESTON (St Mary Virg), *Suff*.. **D** St E 9 *See* Hopton-by-Thetford.
CONGERSTONE (St Mary Virg), *Leics*. V. **D** Leic 15 **P** *Dioc Bd of Patr* **I** E R BOSTON *p-in-c*.
CONGHAM (St Andr), *Norf*.. **D** Nor *See* Grimston.
CONGLETON (St Pet), *Chesh*. V. **D** Ches 11 **P** *Simeon Trustees* **I** (Vacant).
(St Jas), V. **D** Ches 11 **P** *Bp* **I** D A BOYD.
(St Steph), V. **D** Ches 11 **P** *Bp* **I** (Vacant).
(St Mich North Rode). **D** Ches *See* North Rode.
CONGRESBURY (St Andr) w Puxton and Hewish St Ann, *Avon*. V. **D** B & W 3 **P** *MMT* **I** J SIMMONDS.
CONINGSBY (St Mich AA) w Tattershall, *Lincs*. R. **D** Linc **P** *Dioc Bd of Patr 1st turn, Earl of Ancaster 2nd turn* **I** M E PERCIVAL.
CONINGTON, *Cambs*.. **D** Ely 14 *See* Holme.
CONINGTON, *Cambs*.. **D** Ely 5 *See* Fen Drayton.
CONISBROUGH (St Pet), *S Yorks*.. **D** Sheff 8 **P** *Bp* **I** I S CHISHOLM, D M GILKES *c*.
CONISCLIFFE (St Edwin), *Durham*. V. **D** Dur 11 **P** *Bp of Dur* **I** J S HANNON.
CONISHOLME (St Pet), *Lincs*.. **D** Linc 12 *See* Grainthorpe.
CONISTON, CHURCH (St Andr), *Cumb*. V. **D** Carl 15 **P** *Peache Trustees* **I** M C RIDYARD *p-in-c*.
CONISTON, COLD (St Pet), *N Yorks*. V. **D** Bradf 6 **P** *Trustee* **I** C F TREVOR *p-in-c*.
CONISTONE (St Mary), *N Yorks*.. **D** Bradf 10 *See* Kettlewell.
CONONLEY (St Jo Evang) w Bradley, *N Yorks*. V. **D** Bradf 11 **P** *Bp* **I** S R MCDOUGALL.
CONSETT (Ch Ch), *Durham*. V. **D** Dur 7 **P** *Bp* **I** J J E SAMPSON, R SHAW *c*.
CONSTABLE LEE (St Paul), *Lancs*. V. **D** Man 18 **P** *CPAS* **I** P HEYWOOD, J E BOADEN *hon c*.
CONSTANTINE **D** Truro 4 *See* St Constantine.
COOKBURY, *Devon*.. **D** Ex *See* Holsworthy.
COOKHAM (H Trin), *Berks*. V. **D** Ox 13 **P** *Maj D M Rogers* **I** W J GROVER.
COOKHAM-DEAN (St Jo Bapt), *Berks*. V. **D** Ox 13 **P** *V of Cookham* **I** J F W V COPPING.
COOKHILL (St Paul), *Worcs*.. **D** Worc 1 *See* Inkberrow.
COOKLEY (St Mich), *Suff*.. **D** St E 16 *See* Huntingfield.
COOKLEY (St Pet), *Worcs*. V. **D** Worc 10 **P** *Bp* **I** R W CIRCUS *p-in-c*.
COOKRIDGE (H Trin), *W Yorks*. V. **D** Ripon 5 *See* Adel.
COOLING, *Kent*.. **D** Roch *See* Cliffe-at-Hoo.
COOMBE, *Surrey*.. **D** S'wark *See* Malden, New.
COOMBE BISSETT (St Mich AA) w Homington (St Mary Virg), *Wilts*. V. **D** Sarum 19 **P** *Bp and D and C* alt **I** P F CHAPMAN.
COOMBE-KEYNES, *Dorset*. V. **D** Sarum 9 *See* Wool.
COOMBES (Dedic unknown), *W Sussex*. R. **D** Chich 9 *See* Lancing.
COOPERSALE (St Alb), *Essex*. V. **D** Chelmsf 2 **P** *Bp* **I** R J HARDING.
COPDOCK (St Pet) w Washbrook (St Mary) and Belstead (St Mary), *Suff*. R. **D** St E 7 **P** *Joan B Harris and Dioc Bd of Patr (alt)* **I** J G L COLLYER *p-in-c*.
COPFORD w Easthorpe (St Mary Virg), *Essex*. R. **D** Chelmsf 21 **P** *Ld Chan and Duchy of Lanc* **I** L J MIDDLETON.
COPGROVE (St Mich AA), *N Yorks*. R. **D** Ripon 4 *See* Farnham.
COPLE (All SS) w Willington (St Lawr), *Beds*. V. **D** St Alb 17 **P** *Ch Ch Ox* **I** C P HUITSON.
COPLEY (St Steph), *W Yorks*. V. **D** Wakef 1 **P** *V of Halifax* **I** A J POOLMAN.
COPMANFORD, *Cambs*.. **D** Ely 14 *See* Upton.
COPMANTHORPE (St Giles), *N Yorks*. V. **D** York 2 **P** *V of St Mary Bishophill Junior, York* **I** J C STONEHOUSE.
COPNOR (St Alb), *Hants*. V. **D** Portsm 5 **P** *Bp* **I** J H CATLIN.
(St Cuthb), V. **D** Portsm 5 **P** *Bp* **I** C R ABBOTT, R HERBERT *c*.
COPP or GT ECCLESTON (St Anne), *Lancs*. V. **D** Blackb 10 **P** *V of St Mich-on-Wyre* **I** P W LEAKEY.
COPPENHALL, *Chesh*.. **D** Ches 15 *See* Crewe.
COPPENHALL (St Lawr), *Staffs*. V. **D** Lich 3 *See* Dunston.
COPPULL (Dedic unknown), *Lancs*. V. **D** Blackb 4 **P** *R of Standish* **I** A C G RAWE.
(St Jo Div), V. **D** Blackb 4 **P** *R of Standish* **I** R G GREENALL.
COPSTON MAGNA (St Jo Bapt), *Warws*.. **D** Cov 5 *See* Withybrook.
COPTHORNE (St Jo Evang), *Surrey & W Sussex*. V. **D** Chich 12 **P** *Mrs B H Locker-Lampson* **I** F W BUTLER.
COPT OAK Leics. V **D** Leic *See* Oaks-in-Charnwood.
COPYTHORNE (St Mary), *Hants*.. **D** Win 9 *See* Eling, North.
CORBRIDGE (St Andr) w Halton, *Northumb*. V. **D** Newc T 3 **P** *D and C of Carl* **I** G B CHADWICK, H H HUNTER *c*.
CORBY (St Jo Bapt w Epiph), *Northants*. R. **D** Pet 10 **P** *G Brudenell Esq* **I** R D HOWE, P A TABERNACLE *c*.
(St Columba), V. **D** Pet 10 **P** *Bp* **I** M W M SAUNDERS, K P FITZGIBBON *c*.
(St Pet and St Andr) w Great (St Mich) and Little Oakley, R. **D** Pet 10 **P** *Bp, Boughton Estates Ltd and H W Guinness Esq* **I** R G KNIGHT, M R COPSON *team v*, D J T MILLER *team v*.
(Danesholme Conv Distr). **D** Pet 10 **P** *Bp* **I** (Vacant).
CORBY GLEN (St Jo Evang) w Irnham (St Andr), Swayfield and Swinstead and Creeton (St Pet) w Counthorpe, *Lincs*. V. **D** Linc **P** *Ld Chan 2 turns, Reps of late Sir W B Jones Bt 1 turn* **I** M J DOWN.
CORELEY (St Pet) w Doddington (St Jo Bapt), *Salop*. R. **D** Heref 12 **P** *Dioc Bd of Patr and Maj P R E Woodward* **I** A C GOULD P-IN-C OF CORELEY, R A HORSFIELD P-IN-C OF DODDINGTON.
CORFE (St Nich), *Somt*. V. **D** B & W 23a *See* Pitminster.
CORFE CASTLE (St Edw Mart) (in St Aldhelm Group), *Dorset*. R. **D** Sarum 9 **P** *H J R Bankes Esq* **I** G S M SQUAREY.
CORFE-MULLEN (St Hubert), *Dorset*. R. **D** Sarum 11 **P** *Bp* **I** M R LAMBERT.
CORHAMPTON (Dedic unknown), *Hants*.. **D** Portsm *See* Meonstoke.
CORLEY (St Mary), *Warws*. R. **D** Cov 5 **P** *Ch S Trust* **I** J F LAW *p-in-c*.
CORNARD MAGNA (St Andr), *Suff*. V. **D** St E 12 **P** *Bp* **I** H E CATCHPOLE.
CORNARD PARVA (All SS), *Suff*. R. **D** St E 12 **P** *Bp and Dioc Bd of Patr* alt **I** J K COTTON *p-in-c*.
CORNELLY, ST., *Cornw*.. **D** Truro 6 *See* Tregony.
CORNEY, *Cumb*.. **D** Carl *See* Bootle.
CORNFORTH (H Trin), *Durham*. V. **D** Dur 12a **P** *Bp* **I** S P FLETCHER.

COVENTRY EAST (St Anne and All SS, St Pet and St Barn), *W Midl.* R. **D** Cov 1 **P** *Dioc Bd of Patr* **I** J H GARTON, A W MORGAN *team v,* P R SPENCER *team v,* D G THOMAS *team v,* M P COONEY *c,* J R TYSOE *c.*
COVERHAM w Horsehouse, *N Yorks.* V. **D** Ripon *See* Middleham.
COVINGTON (All SS), *Cambs.* R. **D** Ely 11 **P** *Earl Fitzwilliam* **I** F ANDREW.
COWARNE, LITTLE *Herefs..* **D** Heref *See* Pencombe.
COWBIT (St Mary) w Moulton (St Jas) and Weston, *Lincs.* V. **D** Linc 17 **P** *Ld Chan 1st turn, Dioc Bd of Patr 2nd turn, V of Moulton 3rd turn* **I** (Vacant).
COWDEN (St Mary Magd), *Kent.* w Hammerwood (St Steph) *E Sussex* R. **D** Chich **P** *Ch S Trust* **I** J G SHELDON.
COWES, EAST (St Jas) w Whippingham (St Mildred), R *Isle of Wight.* V. **D** Portsm 7 **P** *Ld Chan* **I** W J SCOTT.
COWES, WEST (H Trin), *Isle of Wight.* V. **D** Portsm 7 **P** *CPAS* **I** R F PARKER.
(St Faith's). **D** Portsm 7 **P** *Bp* **I** R W PIKE.
(St Mary), V. **D** Portsm 7 **P** *V of Carisbrooke* **I** J V BEAN, D BILLOWES *c,* J S COLE *c.*
COWESBY (St Mich AA), *N Yorks.* R. **D** York 26 **P** *Abp* **I** D W B MCCULLOCH *p-in-c.*
COWFOLD (St Pet), *W Sussex.* V. **D** Chich 14 **P** *Bp of Lon* **I** B BRENTON.
COWGILL (St Jo Evang), *Cumb.* V. **D** Bradf 7 *See* Dent.
COWICK, EAST w West (H Trin), *Humb.* V. **D** Sheff 9 **P** *Bp* **I** H G SALISBURY *p-in-c.*
COWLAM (St Andr or St Mary), *Humb.* R. **D** York 13 *See* Sledmere.
COWLEIGH (St Pet), *Worcs..* **D** Worc 6 *See* Malvern Link.
COWLEY (St Anthony), *Devon..* **D** Ex 2 *See* Brampford-Speke.
COWLEY, *Glos.* R. **D** Glouc 13 *See* Coberley.
COWLEY (St Laur), *Gtr Lon.* R. **D** Lon 9 **P** *Bp* **I** N A CHALK.
COWLEY, *Oxon..* **D** Ox *See* Oxford.
COWLING (H Trin), *N Yorks.* V. **D** Bradf 11 **P** *Bp* **I** R D CARTER.
COWLINGE (St Marg), *Suff.* R. **D** St E 8 *See* Lydgate.
COWPEN, *Northumb..* **D** Newc T *See* Horton.
COWPLAIN (St Wilfrid), *Hants.* V. **D** Portsm 3 **P** *Bp* **I** A C J EASTWOOD, P F B FISKE *c.*
COWTONS, The (St Mary N and St Mary S), *N Yorks.* V. **D** Ripon **P** *V of Gilling, Abp and Dioc Bd of Patr* in turn **I** P W RUSHTON *p-in-c.*
COXHEATH, *Kent..* **D** Roch *See* Farleigh, East.
COXHOE (St Mary), *Durham.* V. **D** Dur 12a **P** *Bp* **I** I S PELTON.
COXLEY (Ch Ch), *Somt..* **D** B & W 6 *See* Wells.
COXWELL, GREAT (St Giles) w Coleshill, Buscot and Eaton Hastings, *Oxon.* V. **D** Ox **P** *Bp and Ld Faringdon* **I** R C SWANBOROUGH.
COXWELL, LITTLE (St Mary), *Oxon..* **D** Ox 17 *See* Faringdon.
COXWOLD (St Mich) and Husthwaite (St Nich), *N Yorks.* V. **D** York 5 **P** *Abp* **I** J THOM.
CRADLEY (St Jas Ap and Mart), *Herefs.* R. **D** Heref 6 **P** *Bp* **I** (Vacant).
CRADLEY (St Pet), *W Midl.* V. **D** Worc 9 **P** *R of Halesowen* **I** D ROGERS.
CRADLEY HEATH (St Luke), *W Midl..* **D** Worc 9 *See* Reddal Hill.
CRAGG VALE (St Jo Bapt-in-the-Wilderness), *W Yorks.* V. **D** Wakef 3 **P** *V of Halifax* **I** B A SMITH *p-in-c.*
CRAGHEAD (St Thos), *Durham.* V. **D** Dur 7 **P** *HM the Queen* **I** (Vacant).
CRAKEHALL (St Gregory) w Langthorne *N Yorks..* **D** Ripon 2 **P** *Sir Henry de la Poer Beresford-Peirse Bt* **I** (Vacant).
CRAMBE (St Mich) and Huttons Ambo (St Marg), *N Yorks.* V. **D** York *See* Whitwell.
CRAMLINGTON (St Nich), *Northumb.* R. **D** Newc T 1 **P** *Bp* **I** D A WOOD, P R SANDFORD *team v.*
CRANBORNE (St Mary and St Bart) w Boveridge, Edmondsham, Wimborne and Woodlands, *Dorset.* R. **D** Sarum **P** *Marq of Salisbury, Earl of Shaftesbury and C M Medlycott Esq* **I** R P PRANCE.
CRANBOURNE (St Pet), *Berks.* V. **D** Ox 11a **P** *Bp* **I** R CROUCH *p-in-c.*
CRANBROOK (St Dunstan), *Kent.* V. **D** Cant 11 **P** *Abp* **I** G A LUCKETT.
CRANFIELD (St Pet and St Paul), *Beds.* R. **D** St Alb 19 **P** *MMT* **I** D H HUNT.
CRANFORD (St Dunstan), *Gtr Lon.* R. **D** Lon 10 **P** *Exors of Earl of Berkeley* **I** S J S BEEBEE, T W STEVENS *c.*
(H Angels), LDHM. **D** Lon 10 **P** *Bp* **I** S J S BEEBEE *c-in-c.*
CRANFORD (St Jo Bapt and St Andr) w Grafton Underwood (St Jas), *Northants.* R. **D** Pet 8 **P** *Maj Sir F Robinson Bt and Boughton Estates* alt **I** (Vacant).
CRANHAM (All SS), *Essex.* R. **D** Chelmsf 4 **P** *St Jo Coll Ox* **I** K D ARCHER.
PARK (St Luke), V. **D** Chelmsf 4 **P** *Bp* **I** N J H REEVES, H KOPSCH *c.*
CRANHAM (St Jas Gt), *Glos.* R. **D** Glouc 4 *See* Miserden.
CRANLEIGH (St Nich), *Surrey.* R. **D** Guildf 2 **P** *C A Chadwych-Healey Esq* **I** J ROUNDHILL, A N PEARMAIN *c.*
CRANLEY GARDENS (St Pet),. **D** Lon 15 *See* Kensington.
CRANMORE, EAST (St Jas) and West (St Bart), *Somt..* **D** B & W 6 *See* Doulting.
CRANOE, *Leics..* **D** Leic *See* Stonton Wyville.
CRANSFORD (St Pet), *Suff..* **D** St E *See* Badingham.
CRANSLEY, *Northants..* **D** Pet *See* Loddington.
CRANTOCK (St Carantoc), *Cornw.* V. **D** Truro 7 *See* St Crantoc.
CRANWELL (St Andr), *Lincs.* V. **D** Linc 22 **P** *Dioc Bd of Patr* **I** M J FEIT.
CRANWICH (St Mary), *Norf.* R. **D** Nor 19 **P** *CPAS* **I** J V ANDREWS.
CRANWORTH (St Mary Virg) w Letton and Southbergh (St Andr), *Norf.* R. **D** Nor 12 **P** *MMT* **I** A G N DAYNES *p-in-c.*
CRASWALL, *Herefs..* **D** Heref *See* Clodock.
CRATFIELD (St Mary) w Heveningham (St Marg) and Ubbeston (St Pet) w Huntingfield and Cookley, *Suff.* R. **D** St E 15 **P** *Simeon Trustees and Hon Mrs S Peel (alt)* **I** K C FRANCIS.
CRATHORNE (All SS), *N Yorks.* R. **D** York 25 **P** *Ld Crathorne* **I** D C KING *p-in-c.*
CRAWLEY (St Mary) w Littleton (St Cath), *Hants.* R. **D** Win 12 **P** *Dioc Bd of Patr* **I** R L B JOHNSON.
CRAWLEY (St Pet), *Oxon..* **D** Ox 9 *See* Hailey.
CRAWLEY (St Jo Bapt), *W Sussex.* R. **D** Chich 12 **P** *Bp* **I** B H V BROWN, B L HACKSHALL *team v,* E A PASSINGHAM *team v,* I D F MOSS *c.*
(St Mary, Southgate), R. **D** Chich **P** *Bp and CPAS* **I** A F HAWKER, H G PEARSON *team v.*
(Broadfield Conv Distr). **D** Chich **I** A J B KEITH.
CRAWLEY DOWN (All SS), *W Sussex.* V. **D** Chich 12 **P** *R of Worth* **I** R M SWEET-ESCOTT.
CRAWLEY, NORTH (St Firmin), w Astwood (St Pet) and Hardmead, *Bucks.* R. **D** Ox 28 *See* Sherington.
CRAWSHAWBOOTH (St Jo Evang), *Lancs.* V. **D** Man 18 **P** *Trustees* **I** R H P WATSON WILLIAMS *p-in-c.*
CRAY (St Mary w St Paulinus), *Kent.* V. **D** Roch 16 **P** *Bp* **I** R OSBORNE.
(St Barn), V. **D** Roch 16 **P** *CPAS* **I** D A S BOYES, M A HARRIS *c.*
CRAY, FOOTS (All SS), *Kent.* R. **D** Roch 13 **P** *Ld Chan* **I** P J HINCHEY.
CRAY, NORTH (St Jas), *Kent.* R. **D** Roch 13 **P** *Bp* **I** P H ROLTON.
CRAYFORD or EARDE (St Paulinus), *Kent.* R. **D** Roch 15 **P** *Bp* **I** D G E CARPENTER, G D BROSTER *c.*
CRAYKE (St Cuthb), w Brandsby (All SS) and Yearsley, *N Yorks..* **D** York 5 **P** *Crown and Abp* alt **I** (Vacant).
CREACOMBE Devon. **D** Ex 19 *See* Witheridge.
CREAKE, NORTH (St Mary), *Norf.* R. **D** Nor 21 **P** *Bp and Earl Spencer* alt **I** (Vacant).
CREAKE, SOUTH (St Mary Virg), *Norf.* V. **D** Nor 21 **P** *Guild of All S* **I** (Vacant).
CREATON, GREAT (St Mich AA), *Northants.* R. **D** Pet 6 *See* Cottesbrooke.
CREATON, LITTLE, *Northants.* V. **D** Pet 6 *See* Spratton.
CREDENHILL (St Mary) w Brinsop (St Geo) Mansel Lacy (St Mich), Yazor (St Mary Virg) and Wormesley (St Mary), *Herefs.* R. **D** Heref 4 **P** *T G H Ecroyd Esq, Bp, and Maj D J C Davenport (Two Turns)* **I** G O FARRAN.
CREDITON (H Cross), *Devon.* V. **D** Ex 2 **P** *Crediton Govs* **I** B DUNCAN, N H FREATHY *c.*
CREECH (St Mich), *Somt.* V. **D** B & W 23 **P** *MMT* **I** K J JONES.
CREED, *Cornw..* **D** Truro 6 *See* Grampound.
CREETING (St Mary), *Suff.* R. **D** St E 1 **P** *Dioc Bd of Patr* **I** P DAVISON *c-in-c.*
(St Pet). R. **D** St E 1 *See* Earl Stonham.
CREETON w Counthorpe, *Lincs.* R. **D** Linc *See* Corby Glen.
CRENDON, LONG (St Mary) w Chearsley and Nether Winchendon, *Bucks.* V. **D** Ox **P** *Bp and R V Spencer-Bernard* **I** S YOUNG.
CRESLOW, *Bucks..* **D** Ox 27 *See* Whitchurch.
CRESSAGE (Ch Ch) w Sheinton (St Pet and St Paul), *Salop.* V. **D** Heref *See* Wenlock.

CRESSING (All SS), *Essex*. V. **D** Chelmsf *See* Notley, White.
CRESSINGHAM, GREAT (St Mich) w Cressingham Little (St Andr) and Threxton, *Norf*. R (*See Hilborough Group*). **D** Nor 19 **P** *Sir Richard Prince-Smith Bt and Bp* **I** (Vacant).
CRESSWELL (St Bart), *Northumb*.. **D** Newc T 10 **P** *Bp* **I** (Vacant).
CRESWELL, *Staffs*. R. **D** Lich 5 *See* Seighford.
CRESWELL (St Mary Magd), *Derbys*.. **D** Derby 2 *See* Elmton.
CRETINGHAM (St Pet), *Suff*. V. **D** St E 18 *See* Earl Soham.
CREWE or MONKS COPPENHALL (Ch Ch), *Chesh*. V. **D** Ches 15 **P** *Bp* **I** W C W FOSS.
(St Andr), V. **D** Ches 15 **P** *Bp* **I** J S GAISFORD.
(St Barn), V. **D** Ches 15 **P** *Bp* **I** R D POWELL.
(St Jo Bapt), V. **D** Ches 15 **P** *Bp* **I** C G WILSON.
(St Mich Coppenhall), R. **D** Ches 15 **P** *Bp* **I** D C KELLY, R P ELLIOTT *c*.
(All SS and St Paul, Coppenhall), V. **D** Ches 15 **P** *Bp* **I** A LITTON, J W MUSTHER *c*.
(St Pet), V. **D** Ches 15 **P** *Bp* **I** (Vacant).
CREWE GREEN (St Mich AA), *Chesh*. V. **D** Ches 15 **P** *Trustees* **I** (Vacant).
CREWKERNE (St Bart w Ch Ch) w Wayford (St Mich), *Somt*. R. **D** B & W 19 **P** *Ld Chan* **I** P B CURTIS.
CRICH (St Mary), *Derbys*. V. **D** Derby 1 **P** *Trustees* **I** G K BATHIE.
CRICHEL, LONG (St Mary Virg), w Crichel, Moor (St Mary Virg), *Dorset*. R. **D** Sarum 11 *See* Witchampton.
CRICK (St Marg), *Northants*. R. **D** Pet 6 **P** *St Jo Coll Ox* **I** J SPILMAN.
CRICKET, *Somt*.. **D** B & W *See* Winsham.
CRICKET-MALHERBIE (St Mary Magd), *Somt*. R. **D** B & W 19 *See* Knowle St Giles.
CRICKLADE (St Mary w St Sampson) w Latton (St Jo Bapt) and Eisey (St Mary Virg), *Wilts*. R. **D** Bris 10 **P** *D and C of Bris* **I** G K WITHINGTON.
CRICKLEWOOD (St Pet), *Gtr Lon*. V. **D** Lon 17 **P** *Bp* **I** D COLEMAN, R M TAYLOR *c*.
(Little St Pet Conv Distr). **D** Lon 17 **P** *Bp* **I** (Vacant).
(St Gabr), V. **D** Lon 18 *See* Willesden.
(St Mich), V. **D** Lon 18 **P** *Bp* **I** I G MUIR *c-in-c*.
CRICKSEA or Creeksea (All SS) w Althorne (St Andr) and Latchingdon w North Fambridge, *Essex*. V. **D** Chelmsf **P** *Abp of Cant 1st turn, Ld Chan 2nd turn and Bp 3rd turn* **I** V C CASTLE, D I GORDON *hon c*, V R HARROD *hon c*, C W J HODGETTS *hon c*.
CRIFTINS-BY-ELLESMERE (St Matt Evang), *Salop*. V. **D** Lich 22 **P** *Bp and V of Ellesmere* **I** J H GREEN.
CRIMPLESHAM w Stradsett, *Norf*. V. **D** Ely 17 **P** *Bp* **I** G H GAUNT *p-in-c*.
CRINGLEFORD (St Pet), *Norf*. V. **D** Nor 13 **P** *Great Hosp Trustees* **I** J F CROFT *c*.
CROCKEN HILL (All S), *Kent*. V. **D** Roch 1a **P** *Bp* **I** S C HEMMING CLARK.
CROCKER HILL, *Hants*.. **D** Portsm 1 *See* Fareham.
CROCKHAM HILL (H Trin), *Kent*. V. **D** Roch 9 **P** *J St A Warde Esq* **I** R J MASON *p-in-c*.
CROFT (St Mich AA) w Yarpole (St Leon), *Herefs*. R. **D** Heref 7 *See* Eye.
CROFT w Southworth (Ch Ch), *Chesh*. R. **D** Liv 11 **P** *Earl of Derby* **I** R H L WILLIAMS, R BUSHELL *c*.
CROFT (St Mich AA) and Huncote, *Leics*. R. **D** Leic 13 **P** *Bp and Soc for Maint of Faith* **I** G F COOPER *p-in-c*.
CROFT (All SS), *Lincs*. V. **D** Linc 8 **P** *J D E Barnard Esq and E C Barnard Esq* **I** D C BAKER *p-in-c*.
CROFT (St Pet), *N Yorks*. R. **D** Ripon 1 **P** *Crown* **I** (Vacant).
CROFTON (H Rood), *Hants*. V. **D** Portsm 1 **P** *Bp* **I** J M MAYBURY, R A FORSE *c*, P L SIBLEY *c*.
CROFTON (All SS) w New Crofton, *W Yorks*. R. **D** Wakef 13 **P** *Duchy of Lanc* **I** M W ROBERTS.
CROFTON (St Paul), *Kent*. V. **D** Roch 16 **P** *V of Orpington* **I** C J REED.
CROFTON PARK (St Hilda) w Brockley (St Cypr), *Kent*. V. **D** S'wark 18 **P** *V of Lewisham* **I** (Vacant).
CROGLIN (St Jo Bapt), *Cumb*. R. **D** Carl *See* Castle Carrock.
CROMER (St Pet and St Paul), *Norf*. V. **D** Nor 5 **P** *CPAS* **I** D J OSBORNE, J W STUBENBORD *c*.
CROMFORD (St Mary) w (St Mark), *Derbys*. V. **D** Derby 17 **P** *Dioc Bd of Patr* **I** H J LOWNDS.
CROMHALL (St Andr) w Tortworth, *Avon*. R. **D** Glouc 8 **P** *Or Coll Ox and Earl of Ducie* **I** W F BURLTON, D W PARKER *hon c*.
CROMPTON (H Trin), *Gtr Man*.. **D** Man 15 *See* Shaw.
CROMPTON, EAST (St Jas), *Gtr Man*. V. **D** Man 15 **P** *Bp* **I** R W BAILEY.
CROMPTON, HIGH (St Mary), *Gtr Man*. V. **D** Man 15 **P** *Bp* **I** L BROOKHOUSE.
CROMWELL (St Giles), *Notts*. R. **D** Southw 4 **P** *S for Maint of Faith* **I** C K BUCK *p-in-c*.
CRONDALL (All SS) and Ewshot (St Mary), *Hants*. V. **D** Guildf 3 **P** *Bp* **I** A J F VOAKE.
CROOK (St Cath), *Durham*. R. **D** Dur 13 **P** *R of Brancepeth* **I** R I SMITH.
CROOK (St Cath), *Cumb*. V. **D** Carl 17 **P** *V of Kendal* **I** R G FORWARD.
CROOKES, *S Yorks*.. **D** Sheff 4 *See* Sheffield.
CROOKHAM (Ch Ch), *Hants*. V. **D** Guildf 1 **P** *V of Crondall* **I** F J M EVANS, R A MILLER *c*.
CROOME D'ABITOT, *Worcs*.. **D** Worc 5 *See* Severn Stoke.
CROOME, HILL, *Worcs*. R. **D** Worc 5 *See* Earl's Croome.
CROPREDY (St Mary Virg) w Gt Bourton (All SS) and Wardington, *Oxon*. V. **D** Ox **P** *Bp* **I** J D M TURNER, R A UPTON *c*.
CROPSTON, *Leics*. R. **D** Leic 17 *See* Thurcaston.
CROPTHORNE (St Mich AA) w Charlton (St Jo Evang), *Worcs*. V. **D** Worc 3 **P** *D and C of Worc 2 turns, Bp 1 turn* **I** F P BROWN.
CROPTON (St Gregory), *N Yorks*. V. **D** York 24 *See* Middleton.
CROPWELL BISHOP (St Giles), *Notts*. V. **D** Southw 9 **P** *Ld Chan* **I** C B PERKINS *p-in-c*.
CROPWELL BUTLER (St Pet), *Notts*.. **D** Southw 9 *See* Tythby.
CROSBY (St Geo), *Humb*. V. **D** Linc 4 **P** *Lt-Col E C R Sheffield* **I** (Vacant).
CROSBY-GARRETT (St Andr), *Cumb*. R. **D** Carl 1 *See* Soulby.
CROSBY-ON-EDEN (St Jo Evang), *Cumb*. V. **D** Carl 2 *See* Irthington.
CROSBY RAVENSWORTH (St Lawr), *Cumb*. V. **D** Carl 1 **P** *Dioc Bd of Patr* **I** D A SOUTHWARD.
CROSCOMBE (St Mary Virg) w Dinder (St Mich AA), *Somt*. R. **D** B & W *See* Pilton.
CROSLAND MOOR (St Barn), *W Yorks*. V. **D** Wakef 6 **P** *Bp of Wakef* **I** D I WALKER.
CROSLAND, SOUTH (H Trin), *W Yorks*. V. **D** Wakef 6 **P** *V of Almondbury* **I** W N ELLIOTT.
CROSS-CANONBY (St Jo Evang), *Cumb*. V. **D** Carl 11 **P** *D and C of Carl* **I** B T TUFFIELD.
CROSS GREEN **D** Ripon 7 *See* Leeds.
CROSSCRAKE (St Thos), *Cumb*. V. **D** Carl 17 **P** *V of Heversham* **I** D HAMPSON.
CROSSENS (St John), *Mer*. V. **D** Liv 8 **P** *Trustees* **I** R D BAKER.
CROSS HEATH (St Mich AA), *Staffs*. V. **D** Lich 17 **P** *Bp* **I** A J DAVIES.
CROSS ROADS (St Jas) w Lees, *W Yorks*. V. **D** Bradf 11 **P** *Bp* **I** P K LEE.
CROSS STONE (St Paul), *S Yorks*. V. **D** Wakef 3 **P** *V of Halifax* **I** J R TARR.
CROSTHWAITE (St Mary Virg), *Cumb*. V. **D** Carl 17 **P** *Dioc Bd of Patr* **I** K PARTINGTON.
CROSTHWAITE (St Kentigern), *Cumb*. V. **D** Carl 10 **P** *Bp* **I** D J FOSTER *hon c*.
CROSTON (St Mich), *Lancs*. R. **D** Blackb 4 **P** *Can R A Rawstorne* **I** F B BRUCE.
CROSTWICK (St Pet), *Norf*. V. **D** Nor 4 *See* Spixworth.
CROSTWIGHT, *Norf*.. **D** Nor *See* Honing.
CROUCH END (Ch Ch).. **D** Lon *See* Hornsey.
CROUGHTON (All SS) w Evenley (St Geo), *Northants*. R. **D** Pet 1 **P** *Bp and Magd Coll Ox (alt)* **I** G J GREEN.
CROWAN, ST (St Crewenna w St Jas) w Godolphin, *Cornw*. V. **D** Truro **P** *Bp and Sir J Molesworth Bt* **I** (Vacant).
CROWBOROUGH (All SS), *E Sussex*.. **D** Chich 20 **P** *Ld Chan* **I** P J F M LENON, G P HERBERT *c*.
CROWCOMBE (H Ghost), *Somt*.. **D** B & W 18 *See* Bicknoller.
CROWELL (Nativ of St Mary Virg), *Oxon*.. **D** Ox *See* Aston Rowant.
CROWFIELD w Stonham Aspal (St Mary and St Lambert) and Mickfield, *Suff*. V. **D** St E 1 **P** *Hon J V B Saumarez and Bp* **I** H M WILSON *p-in-c*.
CROWHURST (St Geo), *Surrey*. V. **D** S'wark 10 **P** *Bp* **I** N L G HILL, D J ABEL *c*.
CROWHURST (St Geo), *E Sussex*. R. **D** Chich 17 *See* Catsfield.
CROWLAND (St Mary w St Guthlac and St Bart), *Lincs*. R. **D** Linc 17 *See* Croyland.
CROWLE (St Osw), *Humb*. V. **D** Linc 1 **P** *Bp* **I** M J BOUGHTON, M C WRIGHT *hon c*.

CROWLE (St Jo Bapt), *Worcs.* V. **D** Worc 8 **P** *Can J R Bamber* **I** W D S WELLS.
CROWMARSH GIFFORD and Newnham Murren, *Oxon.*. **D** Ox *See* Wallingford.
CROWN EAST and Rushwick (St Thos), *Worcs.*. **D** Worc 2 **P** *Bp* **I** (Vacant).
CROWN HILL (Ascen), *Devon.*. **D** Ex 23 *See* Plymouth.
CROWNTHORPE, *Norf.*. **D** Nor 13 *See* Wicklewood.
CROWTHORNE (St Jo Bapt), *Berks.* V. **D** Ox 16 **P** *Bp* **I** P R L HALE, C J H PARSONS *c.*
CROWTON (Ch Ch), *Chesh.* V. **D** Ches 6 **P** *V of Weaverham* **I** A E OATES.
CROXALL (St Jo Bapt) w Oakley, *Derbys.* R and V. **D** Derby 16 *See* Walton-on-Trent.
CROXBY (All SS), *Lincs.*. **D** Linc 5 *See* Thoresway.
CROXDALE (St Bart), *Durham.* R. **D** Dur 2 **P** *D and C of Dur* **I** H J H STEVINSON *p-in-c.*
CROXDEN (St Giles) w Hollington, *Staffs.* V. **D** Lich 20 **P** *Bp* **I** A S TOWLSON *p-in-c.*
CROXLEY GREEN (All SS), *Herts.* V. **D** St Alb 10 **P** *V of Rickmansworth* **I** M C KING.
(St Osw), V. **D** St Alb 10 **P** *Bp* **I** D MORGAN.
CROXTON (St Jas) and Eltisley, *Cambs.* R. **D** Ely 1 **P** *Lady Fox* **I** W STOTT *p-in-c.*
CROXTON (St Jo Evang), *Humb.* R. **D** Linc 6 **P** *Ld Chan* **I** (Vacant).
CROXTON, *Norf.*. **D** Nor 21 *See* Fulmodeston.
CROXTON (All SS), *Norf.* V. **D** Nor 18 **P** *Bp* **I** D W PRICE.
CROXTON (St Paul) w Broughton (St Pet), *Staffs.*. **D** Lich 15 **P** *Bp and J Hall Esq* alt **I** W E FOSTER *p-in-c.*
CROXTON-KERRIAL (St Jo Bapt) and Knipton w Harston and Branston-by-Belvoir, *Leics.* V. **D** Leic 3 **P** *Duke of Rutland* **I** R I HANLON.
CROXTON, SOUTH *Leics.*. **D** Leic 8 *See* Gaddesby.
CROYDON (St Jo Bapt w St Geo), *Surrey.* V. **D** Cant 16 **P** *Abp* **I** C A C HILL, J B G ANDERSON *c*, J P C REED *c.*
(All SS Spring Park), V. **D** Cant 16 **P** *Abp* **I** D A TASSELL, B REED *c.*
(Ch Ch Broad Green), V. **D** Cant 16 **P** *Simeon Trustees* **I** C D FORD, J W DAVIES *c.*
(Em), V. **D** Cant 16 **P** *Trustees* **I** G W KUHRT *p-in-c*, J M TALBOT *hon c.*
(St Andr), V. **D** Cant 16 **P** *Trustees* **I** D J TAYLOR.
(St Aug), V. **D** Cant 16 **P** *Abp* **I** D B TONKINSON.
(St Luke, Woodside), V. **D** Cant 16 **P** *V of St Jas Croydon* **I** R G WILKINSON *p-in-c.*
(St Martin, Croydon Common), V. **D** Cant 16 **P** *Abp* **I** B M BRANCHE.
(St Matt), V. **D** Cant 16 **P** *V of Croydon* **I** R TAYLOR *p-in-c.*
(St Mich AA w St Jas), V. **D** Cant 16 **P** *Five Lay Trustees* **I** N GODWIN, N S CLARK *c.*
(St Pet), V. **D** Cant 16 **P** *V of Croydon* **I** R J M GROSVENOR.
(St Sav), V. **D** Cant 16 **P** *Abp* **I** F R HAZELL, R G H BROWN *c*, D J MCKAVANAGH *c*, J WORSFOLD *c.*
CROYDON w Clapton, *Cambs.* R (*See Shingay Group*). **D** Ely 8 **P** *Bp and Dioc Bd of Patr (alt)* **I** J H THOMSON.
CROYLAND or CROWLAND (St Mary w St Guthlac and St Bart), *Lincs.* R. **D** Linc 17 **P** *Earl of Normanton* **I** S SWIFT.
CRUCKTON (St Thos), *Salop.*. **D** Heref 17 *See* Pontesbury.
CRUDWELL (All SS) w Ashley (St Jas Ap and Mart), *Wilts.* R. **D** Bris 11 **P** *Duchy of Lanc and Reps of the late W A Sole* alt **I** W K THOMAS P-IN-C OF OAKSEY *p-in-c.*
CRUMPSALL (St Matt w St Mary), *Gtr Man.* R. **D** Man 7 **P** *Bp* **I** H F K CHEALL.
LOWER (St Thos), R. **D** Man 7 **P** *Bp* **I** A E DAVIES.
CRUNDALE (St Mary) w Godmersham (St Laur), *Kent.* R. **D** Cant 2 **P** *Abp* **I** D WALKER.
CRUWYS-MORCHARD (H Cross), *Devon.*. **D** Ex 8 *See* Washfield.
CRUX-EASTON (St Mich AA), *Hants.* R. **D** Win 5 *See* Highclere.
CUBBINGTON (St Mary), *Warws.* V. **D** Cov 11 **P** *Bp* **I** K LINDOP.
CUBERT, ST, *Cornw.* V. **D** Truro 7 *See* St Cubert.
CUBLEY (St Andr) w Marston Montgomery (St Giles), *Derbys.* R. **D** Derby 8 **P** *Bp* **I** D F P DAWE.
CUBLINGTON (St Nich), *Bucks.* R. **D** Ox 27 *See* Aston-Abbotts.
CUBY, ST, *Cornw.*. **D** Truro 6 *See* Tregony.
CUCKFIELD (H Trin), *W Sussex.* V. **D** Chich 11 **P** *Bp* **I** E H A HAYDEN, G A EVANS *c.*
CUCKLINGTON (St Lawr) w Stoke Trister (St Andr) and Bayford, *Somt.* R. **D** B & W *See* Charlton Musgrove.
CUDDESDON (All SS), *Oxon.* V. **D** Ox 5 **P** *Bp* **I** D P WILCOX *p-in-c*, J M WHARTON *c.*
CUDDINGTON (St Nich), *Bucks.*. **D** Ox *See* Haddenham.
CUDDINGTON (St Mary Virg), *Surrey.* V. **D** Guildf 9 **P** *Bp* **I** B L PREECE, M J HARVEY *c.*
CUDHAM (St Pet and St Paul) and Downe, *Kent.* V. **D** Roch 16 **P** *Bp and Ch S Trust* **I** I R A LEAKEY.
CUDWORTH (St Mich) w Chillington (St Jas), *Somt.* V. **D** B & W 19 **P** *Bp* **I** W M HISLOP.
CUDWORTH (St Jo Bapt), *S Yorks.* V. **D** Wakef 8 **P** *Bp* **I** P F KEELING.
CULBONE (St Culbone), *Somt.* R. **D** B & W 21 *See* Oare.
CULFORD (St Mary) w West Stow (St Mary) and Wordwell (All SS), *Suff.* R. **D** St E 13 **P** *Bp* **I** L R PIZZEY.
CULGAITH (All SS), *Cumb.* V. **D** Carl 6 *See* Edenhall.
CULHAM (St Paul), *Oxon.*. **D** Ox 5 *See* Dorchester.
CULLERCOATS (St Paul), or Whitley Bay, *T & W.* V. **D** Newc T 6 **P** *Trustees* **I** P V RENDELL, P BAYES *c*, D F TITTLEY *c.*
(St Geo, St Aid Billy Mill and St Hilda Marden), R. **D** Newc T 6 **P** *Trustees* **I** G F REVETT, P J DENNIS *team v*, M J WEBB *team v*, F T HOLT *c*, R A MACEY *hon c.*
CULLINGWORTH (St Jo Evang), *W Yorks.* V. **D** Bradf 11 **P** *Bp* **I** W D WIGHTMAN.
CULLOMPTON (St Andr), *Devon.* V. **D** Ex 4 **P** *CPAS 5 turns, Exors of W Wyndham and CPAs (1 turn)* **I** J V MAPSON, R G BILLINGHURST *c.*
CULM DAVEY (St Mary), *Devon.*. **D** Ex 4 *See* Hemyock.
CULMINGTON (All SS) w Onibury, *Salop.* R. **D** Heref 12 **P** *Lady Jewel Magnus Allcroft* **I** G ELLIOTT.
CULMSTOCK (All SS), *Devon.* R. **D** Ex 4 *See* Hemyock.
CULPHO (St Botolph), *Suff.* V. **D** St E 19 *See* Playford.
CULVERTHORPE (St Bart), *Lincs.*. **D** Linc 19 *See* Heydour.
CULWORTH (St Mary Virg) w Sulgrave (St Jas L) and Thorpe Mandeville (St Jo Bapt), *Northants.* R. **D** Pet 1 **P** *CPS 1st turn, Dioc Bd of Patr 2nd turn, D L P Humfrey 3rd turn* **I** S BROWN.
CUMBERWORTH (St Helen), *Lincs.*. **D** Linc 8 *See* Anderby.
CUMBERWORTH (St Nich) w Denby Dale, *W Yorks.* R. **D** Wakef 7 **P** *Bp* **I** N S FOX.
CUMDIVOCK, *Cumb.*. **D** Carl *See* Dalston.
CUMNOR (St Mich), *Oxon.* V. **D** Ox 11 **P** *St Pet Coll Ox* **I** N D DURAND.
CUMREW (St Mary), *Cumb.* V. **D** Carl 2 *See* Castle Carrock.
CUMWHINTON, *Cumb.*. **D** Carl 2 *See* Cotehill.
CUMWHITTON, *Cumb.* V. **D** Carl 2 **P** *D and C of Carl* **I** (Vacant).
CUNDALL (St Mary and All SS) w Norton-le-Clay (St Jo Evang), *N Yorks.* V. **D** Ripon 3 **P** *Maj A J R Collins* **I** P F STIRK, J W VALENTINE *c.*
CURBAR, *Derbys.*. **D** Derby *See* Stoney Middleton.
CURDRIDGE (St Pet), *Hants.* V. **D** Portsm 2 **P** *D and C of Win* **I** L G SHOTLANDER.
CURDWORTH (St Nich and St Pet-ad-Vincula), *Warws.* R. **D** Birm 12 **P** *Bp 2 turns, Lord Norton and Capt Wakefield 1 turn each* **I** G M COLLINS.
CURLAND, *Somt.*. **D** B & W *See* Staple Fitzpaine.
CURRIDGE, *Berks.*. **D** Ox 14 *See* Hermitage.
CURROCK, *Cumb.*. **D** Carl *See* Carlisle.
CURRY-MALLET (St Jas), *Somt.* R. **D** B & W 20 **P** *Duchy of Cornwall* **I** R BEEVERS.
CURRY RIVEL (St Andr) w Fivehead and Swell, *Somt.* V. **D** B & W **P** *D and C of Bris 1 turn and P G H Speke 2 turns* **I** J L SIMPSON *p-in-c.*
CURY, St w St Gunwalloe, *Cornw.*. **D** Truro 4 *See* St Cury.
CUSOP (St Mary), *Herefs.* R. **D** Heref 1 **P** *CPAS* **I** W R KING *p-in-c.*
CUSTOM HOUSE (St Matt). **D** Chelmsf 9 *See* Victoria Docks.
CUTCOMBE (St Jo Evang) w Luxborough (St Mary Virg), *Somt.*. **D** B & W *See* Exton.
CUTSDEAN, *Glos.*. **D** Glouc 16 *See* Temple Gutting.
CUXHAM (H Rood) w Easington (St Pet), *Oxon.* R. **D** Ox 1 **P** *Mert Coll Ox* **I** M R TALBOT *p-in-c.*
CUXTON (St Mich AA) and Halling, *Kent.* R. **D** Roch 5 **P** *Bp and D and C of Roch* **I** A T VOUSDEN.
CUXWOLD (St Nich), *Lincs.* R. **D** Linc 5 *See* Rothwell.

DACRE (St Andr), *Cumb.* V. **D** Carl 6 **P** *Trustees* **I** K H SMITH.
DACRE (H Trin) w Hartwith, *N Yorks.* V. **D** Ripon 3 **P** *Bp, D and C of Ripon, V of Masham and Mrs K A Dunbar* **I** R G PLACE.

DADLINGTON (St Jas Gt), *Leics.* V. **D** Leic 16 *See* Stoke Golding.
DAGENHAM (St Pet and St Paul), *Essex.* V. **D** Chelmsf 1 **P** *Ch Soc Trust* **I** D J LEE *c.*
(St Martin), V. **D** Chelmsf 1 **P** *Bp* **I** G W J NUNN.
DAGLINGWORTH (H Rood) w Duntisbourne Rouse (St Mich) and Duntisbourne Abbots (St Pet), and Winstone (St Bart), *Glos.* R. **D** Glouc 13 **P** *Ld Chan (1st turn), Dioc Bd of Patr (2nd turn) and CCC Ox (3rd turn)* **I** E HISCOX.
DAGNALL, *Bucks.*. **D** St Alb 18 *See* Edlesborough.
DAIRYCOATES (St Mary and St Pet), *Humb.* V. **D** York 17 *See* Newington.
DAISY HILL (St Jas), *Gtr Man.* V. **D** Man 18 **P** *Bp* **I** W J TWIDELL.
DALBURY (All SS) w Long Lane (Ch Ch) and Trusley (All SS), *Derbys.* R. **D** Derby 14 **P** *V of Sutton-on-the-Hill and Mrs F H Coke-Steel* **I** J O DRACKLEY *p-in-c,* D H BUCKLEY P-IN-C OF TRUSLEY.
DALBY (St Lawr), *Lincs.* V. **D** Linc 7 *See* Partney.
DALBY (St Pet) w Whenby (St Martin), *N Yorks.* R. **D** York 21 **P** *Abp* **I** W BESWICK.
DALBY-ON-THE-WOLDS (St Jo Bapt), *Leics.* V. **D** Leic 4 *See* Dalby, Old.
DALBY, GT (St Swith), w Dalby, L (St Jas), *Leics.* V. **D** Leic 8 **P** *Coutts & Co* **I** G L SLATER.
DALBY, OLD (St Jo Bapt) w Nether Broughton (St Mary Virg), *Leics.* V. **D** Leic 4 **P** *Bp* **I** C J R DAYBELL.
DALDERBY, *Lincs.*. **D** Linc 11 *See* Scrivelsby.
DALE ABBEY (All SS), *Derbys.*. **D** Derby 13 *See* Stanton-by-Dale.
DALHAM (St Mary), *Suff.* R. **D** St E 11 *See* Gazeley.
DALLAGH GILL (or Dallowgill) (St Pet), *N Yorks.* V. **D** Ripon 3 *See* Kirkby Malzeard.
DALLINGHOO (St Marg) w Pettistree (St Pet) and Lowdham (no dedic), *Suff.* R. **D** St E 18 **P** *Ld Chan and Trustees* alt **I** E PEARSON.
DALLINGTON, *Northants.*. **D** Pet *See* Northampton.
DALLINGTON (St Giles), *E Sussex.* R. **D** Chich *See* Brightling.
DALSTON w Cumdivock (St Mich AA w St Jo Evang), *Cumb.* V. **D** Carl 3 **P** *Bp* **I** W KELLY.
DALSTON (H Trin w St Phil), *Lon.* V. **D** Lon 2 **P** *Bp* **I** M B SHREWSBURY, A W TUFFIN *c.*
(St Mark w St Bart), V. **D** Lon 2 **P** *CPS* **I** D H PATEMAN.
DALTON (St Jas), *N Yorks.*. **D** Ripon 1 *See* Kirkby Ravensworth.
DALTON, *N Yorks.* V. **D** York 26 *See* Topcliffe.
DALTON (St Mich AA), *Lancs.* V. **D** Liv 9 **P** *Bp* **I** (Vacant).
DALTON (H Trin), *S Yorks.* V. **D** Sheff 6 **P** *Bp* **I** W A BUTT.
DALTON-IN-FURNESS (St Mary), *Cumb.* V. **D** Carl 15 **P** *Bp* **I** T PARK, C P ARNESEN *c.*
DALTON-LE-DALE (H Trin w St Andr), *Durham.* V and R. **D** Dur 3 **P** *D and C of Dur* **I** E B PATEMAN.
DALTON HOLME, *Humb.*. **D** York *See* Etton.
DALWOOD (St Pet), *Devon.*. **D** Ex 5 *See* Stockland.
DAMERHAM (St Geo) w Martin (All SS), *Wilts.* V. **D** Sarum 19 **P** *Hyndman Trustees and V of Damerham* **I** R M W POWELL *p-in-c.*
DANBURY (St Jo Bapt), *Essex.* R. **D** Chelmsf 12 **P** *Ld Fitzwalter* **I** D F STAVELEY *c.*
DANBY (St Hilda) w Castleton and Fryup *N Yorks.* V. **D** York 27 **P** *Visc Downe* **I** D ADAM, E W WRIGHT *c.*
DANBY WISKE w Hutton Bonville, *N Yorks.*. **D** Ripon *See* Great Smeaton.
DANEHILL (All SS), *E Sussex.* V. **D** Chich 16 **P** *Ch S Trust* **I** D C MARKHAM *p-in-c.*
DANESHOLME CONV DISTR, *Northants.*. **D** Pet *See* Corby.
DARENTH (St Marg), *Kent.* V. **D** Roch 1a **P** *D and C of Roch* **I** D G THOMAS.
DARESBURY (All SS), *Chesh.* V. **D** Ches 4 **P** *Trustees of P G Greenall Esq* **I** S BECKETT.
DARFIELD (All SS), (Consolidated Medieties), *S Yorks.* R. **D** Sheff 10 **P** *Trustees* **I** J I BATTY.
DARLASTON (St Lawr), *Staffs.* R. **D** Lich 10 **P** *Simeon Trustees and Bp* **I** S C RAWLING.
(All SS), V. **D** Lich 10 **P** *Simeon Trustees* **I** C J HAYWARD *p-in-c.*
DARLEY (Ch Ch), *N Yorks.*. **D** Ripon 3 *See* Thornthwaite.
DARLEY (St Helen), w South Darley (St Mary BV), *Derbys.* R. **D** Derby 17 **P** *Bp and R of Darley Dale* **I** K E SERVANTE P-IN-C SOUTH DARLEY, T E YATES P-IN-C DARLEY.
DARLEY ABBEY (St Matt), *Derbys.* V. **D** Derby **P** *Dioc Bd of Patr* **I** J H BLADES.
DARLINGSCOTT, *Warws.*. **D** Cov 9 *See* Tredington.
DARLINGTON (St Cuthb), *Durham.* V. **D** Dur 11 **P** *Ld Barnard* **I** D J BELL *c.*
(H Trin), V. **D** Dur 11 **P** *Archd of Dur* **I** H LEE, R D LEAMING *c,* J C PUDDEFOOT *c.*
(St Hilda w St Columba) Conv Distr. **D** Dur 11 **I** (Vacant).
(St Jas), V. **D** Dur 11 **P** *Crown* **I** D G SMITH, C M WILSON *c.*
(St Jo Evang) w (St Herbert), V. **D** Dur 11 **P** *Crown* **I** A D MIDDLETON.
(St Mark w St Paul), V. **D** Dur 11 **P** *Bp and St John's Coll Dur* **I** S M C SANDHAM, I D GOMERSALL *c.*
(St Matt and St Luke), V. **D** Dur 11 **P** *Bp* **I** M H PERRY.
DARLTON (St Giles), *Notts.*. **D** Southw 6 *See* Dunham-on-Trent.
DARMSDEN, *Suff.*. **D** St E *See* Barking.
DARNALL (H Trin), *S Yorks.* V. **D** Sheff *See* Sheffield.
DARRINGTON (All H or St Luke and All SS) w Wentbridge (St Jo Evang), *W Yorks.* V. **D** Wakef 11 **P** *Bp* **I** L R DALTON, G M WARWICK *c.*
DARSHAM (All SS), *Suff.* V. **D** St E 19 **P** *Earl of Stradbroke* **I** I C ROBINSON.
DARTFORD (H Trin), *Kent.* V. **D** Roch 1a **P** *Bp* **I** R B GRIFFIN, R WALLACE *c.*
(Ch Ch), V. **D** Roch 1a **P** *V of Dartford* **I** M P P HOWARD, A POMFRET *hon c.*
(St Alb), V. **D** Roch 1a **P** *V of Dartford* **I** A T WATERMAN, J C ANSELL *c.*
(St Edm K and Mart), V. **D** Roch 1a **P** *Bp* **I** B R INGRAM.
DARTINGTON (St Mary w St Barn), *Devon.* R. **D** Ex 13 **P** *Bp* **I** J G BISHOP.
DARTMOUTH (St Sav and St Petrox w St Barn) w (St Clem) Townstal, *Devon.* V. **D** Ex 13 **P** *Trustees of Sir J Seale Bt and Dioc Bd of Patr* **I** I J BUTLER.
DARTON (All SS), *S Yorks.* V. **D** Wakef 8 **P** *Bp* **I** S MCCARRAHER.
DARWEN, LOWER (St Jas), *Lancs.* V. **D** Blackb 5 **P** *V of Blackb* **I** A SOWERBUTTS.
DARWEN (St Pet) w Hoddlesden (St Paul), *Lancs.* R. **D** Blackb 5 **P** *Dioc Bd of Patr* **I** P H DEARDEN, J STEWART *team v.*
(St Barn), V. **D** Blackb 5 **P** *Bp* **I** B DUNN.
(St Cuthb), V. **D** Blackb 5 **P** *Bp* **I** W FIELDING.
(St Jas), V. **D** Blackb 5 **P** *V of Blackb* **I** (Vacant).
DATCHET (St Mary Virg), *Berks.*. **D** Ox 24 *See* Riverside.
DATCHWORTH (All SS) w Tewin (St Pet), *Herts.* R. **D** St Alb 12 **P** *Bp* **I** P R BETTS, J H HORNER *hon c.*
DAUBHILL (St Geo Mart), *Gtr Man.* V. **D** Man 11 *See* Bolton-le-Moors.
DAUNTSEY (St Jas Gt), *Wilts.* R. **D** Bris *See* Brinkworth.
DAVENHAM (St Wilfrid), *Chesh.* R. **D** Ches 6 **P** *Bp* **I** T S MCCANN, M B W PEMBERTON *c.*
DAVENTRY (H Cross w St Jas), *Northants.* R. **D** Pet **P** *Dioc Bd of Patr* **I** K A WARD.
DAVIDSTOW (St D) w Boscastle and Forrabury, Minster, Trevalga, St Juliot, Lesnewth, Otterham, *Cornw.* R. **D** Truro 12 **P** *Duchy of Cornwall 1 turn, Dioc Bd of Patr 2 turns* **I** (Vacant).
DAVINGTON (St Mary Magd), *Kent.*. **D** Cant 7 *See* Brents.
DAVYHULME (St Mary Virg), *Gtr Man.* V. **D** Man 9 **P** *Bp* **I** J M SINCLAIR, C H ELLIS *c,* H RIGBY *c.*
(Ch Ch), V. **D** Man 9 **P** *Bp* **I** A J WATTS.
DAW GREEN (St Jo Bapt), *W Yorks.*. **D** Wakef 5 *See* Dewsbury.
DAWDON (St Hilda and St Helen), *Durham.* V. **D** Dur 3 **P** *Bp* **I** H T RUSHFORD.
DAWLEY (St Jerome). V. **D** Lon 18 *See* Hillingdon.
DAWLISH (St Greg), *Devon.* V. **D** Ex **P** *D and C of Ex* **I** J R C TAYLOR, J H HAMMOND *c,* D W MATTOCK *c.*
DAYBROOK (St Paul), *Notts.* V. **D** Southw 14 **P** *Bp* **I** D R MOORE.
DAYLESFORD (St Pet), *Glos.*. **D** Ox 3 *See* Kingham.
DEAL (St Leon) w Sholden, *Kent.* R. **D** Cant 8 **P** *Abp* **I** R A V MARCHAND.
(St Andr), R. **D** Cant 8 **P** *Abp* **I** L L LANCASTER.
(St Geo Mart), V. **D** Cant 8 **P** *Abp* **I** E F SMITH.
DEAN (St Osw), *Cumb.* R. **D** Carl 10 **P** *A R and J H Sherwen* **I** P H F WOODHOUSE *p-in-c.*
DEAN (All H) w Yelden (St Mary), Melchbourne and Shelton, *Beds.* V. **D** St Alb 21 **P** *Dioc Bd of Patr and MMT* **I** D N WESTON *p-in-c.*
DEAN, EAST, *Hants.*. **D** Win 10 *See* Lockerley.
DEAN, East (All SS), *W Sussex.* V. **D** Chich 8 **P** *Bp* **I** D M REEVE.
DEAN, EAST (St Simon and St Jude) w Friston and Jevington (St Mary), *E Sussex.* V. **D** Chich 19 **P** *D and C of Chich 2 turns, Duke of Devonshire 1 turn* **I** A H H HARBOTTLE, G ARONSOHN *hon c.*

DEAN FOREST, Christ Church w English Bicknor, *Glos.* V. **D** Glouc 7 **P** *Crown 3 turns, S for Maint Faith 1 turn* **I** J R SPENCER.
DEAN PRIOR (St Geo Mart), *Devon.* V. **D** Ex 13 *See* Buckfastleigh.
DEAN, WEST, w Binderton (St Andr), *W Sussex.* V. **D** Chich 8 **P** *D and C of Chich* **I** D M REEVE.
DEAN, WEST (All SS), *E Sussex.* R. **D** Chich *See* Litlington.
DEAN, WEST (St Mary), w Grimstead, East (H Trin), *Wilts.* R. **D** Sarum 17 **P** *Bp* **I** D M HART.
DEANE (All SS), *Hants.* R. **D** Win 5 *See* Waltham, North.
DEANE (St Mary), *Gtr Man.* R. **D** Man **P** *Bp and Simeon Trustees* **I** R B JACKSON, S E BROOK *team v,* A J WOODWARD *c.*
DEANSHANGER (H Trin), *Northants.* R. **D** Pet 2 *See* Passenham.
DEARHAM, *Cumb.* V. **D** Carl 11 **P** *Bp* **I** D C BICKERSTETH *p-in-c.*
DEARNLEY (St Andr), *Gtr Man.* V. **D** Man 17 **P** *Bp* **I** D FINNEY.
DEBACH, *Suff..* **D** St E *See* Charsfield.
DEBDEN (St Mary Virg and All SS) and Wimbish (All SS) w Thunderley, *Essex.* R. **D** Chelmsf 27 **P** *Bp* **I** R W REED.
DE BEAUVOIR TOWN (St Pet).. **D** Lon *See* Hackney, West.
DEBENHAM (St Mary Magd) w Aspall and Kenton, *Suff.* V. **D** St E 18 **P** *Ld Henniker 2 turns Bp 1 turn* **I** (Vacant).
DEDDINGTON (St Pet and St Paul) w Barford (St Mich and St John), Clifton and Hempton (St Jo Evang), *Oxon.* V. **D** Ox 6 **P** *D and C of Windsor and Bp* **I** R HANNAH.
DEDHAM (St Mary Virg), *Essex.* V. **D** Chelmsf 22 **P** *Duchy of Lanc and Lectureship Trustees* alt **I** R J RICHARDS.
DEDWORTH GREEN (All SS), *Berks..* **D** Ox 13 *See* Clewer.
DEENE, *Northants..* **D** Pet *See* Weldon.
DEEPING (St Jas), *Lincs.* V. **D** Linc 13 **P** *Marq of Ex* **I** (Vacant).
DEEPING ST NICH (St Nich) and Tongue End, *Lincs.* V. **D** Linc 17 **P** *Bp* **I** (Vacant).
DEEPING GATE, *Cambs.* V. **D** Pet 19 *See* Maxey.
DEEPING, WEST (St Andr), *Lincs.* R. **D** Linc 13 **P** *Ld Chan* **I** G C SMITH.
DEEPLISH (St Luke), *Gtr Man..* **D** Man 17 *See* Rochdale.
DEERHURST (H Trin or St Mary) and Apperley w Forthampton and Chaceley, *Glos.* V. **D** Glouc 10 **P** *Bp, G J Yorke Esq and V of Longdon* **I** D C FIELD, T WILLIAMS *c.*
DEFFORD (St Jas) w Besford (St Pet), *Worcs.* V. **D** Worc 3 **P** *D and C of Westmr* **I** R H HOWES.
DEIGHTON, *N Yorks..* **D** York 23 *See* Brompton.
DELAMERE (St Pet), *Chesh.* R. **D** Ches 6 **P** *Crown* **I** B D A SPURRY.
DELAVAL (Our Lady) w Seaton Sluice (St Paul) and New Hartley (St Mich), *Northumb.* V. **D** Newc T 1 **P** *Ld Hastings* **I** M F FENWICK, J R PRINGLE *c.*
DELAVAL, NEW, *Northumb..* **D** Newc T *See* Horton.
DEMBLEBY (St Lucia), *Lincs..* **D** Linc 22 *See* Aunsby.
DENABY MAIN (All SS), *S Yorks.* V. **D** Sheff 8 **P** *Bp* **I** R C DAVIES.
DENBURY (St Mary Virg), *Devon.* R. **D** Ex *See* Ogwell.
DENBY (St Mary Virg), *Derbys.* V. **D** Derby **P** *Exors of Capt P J B Drury-Lowe* **I** R T SHORTHOUSE *p-in-c.*
DENBY (St Jo Evang), *W Yorks.* V. **D** Wakef 7 **P** *V of Penistone* **I** N A MOORE.
DENBY GRANGE, *W Yorks..* **D** Wakef 7 *See* Flockton.
DENCHWORTH (St Jas), *Oxon.* V. **D** Ox 19 **P** *Worc Coll Ox* **I** (Vacant).
DENDRON (St Matt), *Cumb..* **D** Carl 15 *See* Aldingham.
DENFORD (H Trin), *Berks.* V. **D** Ox 14 *See* Hungerford.
DENFORD (H Trin) w Ringstead (Nativ BVM), *Northants.* V. **D** Pet 9 **P** *Col N V Stopford Sackville* **I** B M QUENNELL.
DENGIE (St Jas) w Asheldam (St Laur), *Essex.* R. **D** Chelmsf 13 **P** *St Jo Coll Cam 2 turns, Bp 1 turn* **I** S G BROWN.
DENHAM (St Mary), *Bucks.* R. **D** Ox 20 **P** *L B R Way Esq* **I** P CRICK.
DENHAM (St Jo Bapt), *Suff..* **D** St E *See* Hoxne.
DENHAM (St Mary), *Suff.* V. **D** St E 13 **P** *Bp* **I** J W BRIDGEN, I S HOLDSWORTH *c.*
DENHOLME GATE (St Paul), *W Yorks.* V. **D** Bradf 11 **P** *Bp* **I** J N ROWE.
DENMARK HILL (St Matt), *Surrey..* **D** S'wark *See* Lambeth (St Sav).
DENMEAD (All SS), *Hants.* V. **D** Portsm 3 **P** *Ld Chan* **I** J R HERKLOTS, E K W SKEET *c.*
DENNINGTON (St Mary), *Suff.* R. **D** St E 18 **P** *Dioc Bd of Patr* **I** P H T HARTLEY P-IN-C OF BADINGHAM W BRUISYARD *p-in-c.*
DENSHAW (Ch Ch), *Gtr Man.* V. **D** Man 15 **P** *Bp* **I** S L CLAYTON.
DENSTON or DENARDISTON (St Nich), *Suff.* V. **D** St E 8 *See* Stradishall.
DENSTONE (All SS) w Ellastone and Stanton, *Staffs.* V. **D** Lich 20 **P** *Lt-Col Sir W Bromley-Davenport and Bp* **I** T E RASTALL.
DENT (St Andr) w Cowgill (St Jo Evang), *Cumb.* V. **D** Bradf 7 **P** *Sidesmen of Dent and Bp* alt **I** R M ROBINSON.
DENTON (St Mary) w Ingleton (St Jo Evang), *Durham.* V. **D** Dur 11 **P** *V of Staindrop 2 turns, V of Gainford 1 turn.* **I** N B BURT.
DENTON (St Mary Magd) w Wootton (St Martin) and Swingfield (St Pet), *Kent.* R. **D** Cant 6 **P** *Abp* **I** R J C LLOYD *hon c.*
DENTON (St Lawr), *Gtr Man.* R. **D** Man 2 **P** *Earl of Wilton* **I** (Vacant).
(Ch Ch), R. **D** Man 2 **P** *Crown and Bp* alt **I** J K TUTTON.
DENTON (St Andr), *Lincs.* R. **D** Linc *See* Harlaxton.
DENTON (St Mary Virg), *Norf.* R. **D** Nor *See* Earsham.
DENTON (St Marg), *Northants.* V. **D** Pet 4 **P** *Marq of Northn* **I** J C DAVIES.
DENTON (St Leon) w S Heighton and Tarring Neville, *E Sussex.* R. **D** Chich 15 **P** *Lt-Commdr T T Brandreth, RN and MMT (alt)* **I** A F STONE.
DENTON (St Helen), *W Yorks.* V. **D** Bradf 5 *See* Weston.
DENTON (All SS), *Cambs..* **D** Ely 15 *See* Stilton.
DENTON-HOLME, *Cumb..* **D** Carl 3 *See* Carlisle (St Jas).
DENTON, OVER, *Cumb..* **D** Carl 2 *See* Gilsland.
DENVER (St Mary), *Norf.* R. **D** Ely 17 **P** *G and C Coll Cam* **I** L F B CUMINGS.
DEOPHAM (St Andr) w Hackford (St Mary Virg), *Norf..* **D** Nor *See* Wicklewood.
DEPDEN (St Mary Virg), *Suff.* R. **D** St E 13 *See* Chedburgh.
DEPTFORD (St Andr), *T & W..* **D** Dur 8 *See* Bishop Wearmouth.
DEPTFORD (St Paul), R w (St Mark, V), *Kent..* **D** S'wark 19 **P** *Bp* **I** D J DIAMOND, H D POTTER *c,* K N COCKING *hon c.*
(St John), V. **D** S'wark 19 **P** *Trustees* **I** (Vacant).
(St Luke and St Nich), V. **D** S'wark 19 **P** *MMT, C of E Patr Trust, Peache Trustees and CPAS* **I** W G CORNECK, D J ISON *c.*
DERBY (St Werburgh), *Derbys.* V. **D** Derby **P** *Simeon Trustees* **I** (Vacant).
(All SS Cathl), V. **D** Derby **P** *Bp* **I** VERY REV B H LEWERS, C A THROWER *c.*
(St Alkmund w St Aid), V. **D** Derby **P** *Simeon Trustees* **I** H W R BYWATER, U H PEART *hon c.*
(St Andr w St Osmund), V. **D** Derby 11 **P** *Bp* **I** M J THISTLEWOOD.
(St Anne), V. **D** Derby **P** *Bp* **I** G W BURNINGHAM.
(St Aug), V. **D** Derby 11 **P** *V of St Chad, Derby* **I** G H NUTTALL.
(St Barn), V. **D** Derby **P** *Bp* **I** G D KENDREW, J S CRAWSHAW *c.*
(St Bart), V. **D** Derby 11 **P** *Bp* **I** A G MESSOM.
(St Chad), V. **D** Derby 11 **P** *CPAS* **I** K R UPTON.
(St Jas Gt), V. **D** Derby 11 **P** *Bp* **I** P J C MONTGOMERY.
(St Jo Evang), V. **D** Derby **P** *Bp* **I** G W BURNINGHAM.
(St Luke), V. **D** Derby **P** *Bp* **I** P D PETERKEN, J M HIPKINS *c,* A W MCDOWALL *c.*
(St Mark), V. **D** Derby **P** *Bp* **I** K J PEARCE.
(St Paul), V. **D** Derby **P** *Bp* **I** (Vacant).
(St Pet and Ch Ch w H Trin), V. **D** Derby 11 **P** *CPAS* **I** P J G COTTINGHAM.
(St Thos Ap), V. **D** Derby 11 **P** *Bp* **I** D B CONSTABLE, J T ARCHER *c.*
DEREHAM, EAST (St Nich), *Norf.* V. **D** Nor 12 **P** *Ld Chan* **I** H A TAIT, M S KIVETT *c.*
DEREHAM, WEST (St Andr), *Norf..* **D** Ely 16 *See* Fincham.
DERITEND (St John w St Basil), *W Midl.* V. **D** Birm 1 *See* Birmingham.
DERRINGHAM BANK, *Humb..* **D** York *See* Hull.
DERRINGTON (St Matt), *Staffs.* V. **D** Lich 5 *See* Seighford.
DERRY HILL (Ch Ch), *Wilts.* V. **D** Sarum 25 **P** *V of Calne* **I** (Vacant).

DERSINGHAM w Anmer and Shernborne, *Norf.* V. **D** Nor **P** *Bp 1st turn, H M the Queen 2nd turn* **I** H G POLLOCK.

DESBOROUGH (St Giles), *Northants.* V. **D** Pet 8 **P** *Bp* **I** A R TWYFORD, I T R WELCH *c.*

DESFORD (St Martin), *Leics.* R. **D** Leic 17 **P** *Ld Chan* **I** (Vacant).

DETHICK (St Jo Bapt) w Lea and Holloway (Ch Ch), *Derbys.* V. **D** Derby 17 **P** *PCC* **I** J B HURST.

DETLING (St Martin), *Kent.* V. **D** Cant 14 *See* Thurnham.

DEUXHILL, *Salop.*. **D** Heref 9 *See* Chetton.

DEVERILLS, THE, (Brixton Deverill, Kingston-Deverill, Monkton Deverill, Longbridge-Deverill, Hill-Deverill and Crockerton), *Wilts.* R. **D** Sarum 22 **P** *Dioc Bd of Patr 3 turns, Bp 1 turn* **I** (Vacant).

DEVIZES (St John w BVM), *Wilts.* R. **D** Sarum 23 **P** *Ld Chan* **I** C BRYANT.

(St Pet), V. **D** Sarum 23 **P** *Bp* **I** J A CROFT.

DEVONPORT (St Aubyn), *Devon.* V. **D** Ex 23 **P** *Dioc Bd of Patr and Crown* alt **I** (Vacant).

(St Barn), V. **D** Ex 23 **P** *R of Stoke Damerel* **I** J E SUMMERS.

(St Bart), V. **D** Ex 23 **P** *Bp* **I** A R LEIGH.

(St Boniface), V. **D** Ex 23 **P** *Bp* **I** D C PEMBERTON.

(St Budeaux), V. **D** Ex 23 **P** *V of St Andr Plymouth* **I** M D D JONES.

(St Francis, Honicknowle), V. **D** Ex 23 **P** *Ld Chan* **I** I C R CALDWELL, J E G ASHMAN *c.*

(St Mark, Ford), V. **D** Ex 23 **P** *Trustees* **I** B WHITEHEAD.

(St Mich), V. **D** Ex 23 **P** *R of Stoke Damerel* **I** (Vacant).

(St Phil Weston Mill), V. **D** Ex 23 **P** *Bp* **I** (Vacant).

(St Thos, N Keyham), V. **D** Ex 23 **P** *Bp* **I** J M B SMETHURST.

STOKE DAMEREL (St Andr w St Luke), R. **D** Ex 23 **P** *Trustees of Ld St Levan* **I** G D CRYER, A P HARVEY *c.*

DEVORAN (St Jo Evang), *Cornw.* V. **D** Truro 6 **P** *Bp* **I** R M CATLING.

DEWCHURCH, LITTLE (St D) w Aconbury, Ballingham (St Dubricius), and Bolstone, *Herefs.* V. **D** Heref 4 **P** *D and C of Heref and Bp* alt **I** J F BAULCH *p-in-c.*

DEWCHURCH, MUCH, *Herefs.* V. **D** Heref 4 *See* Birch, Much.

DEWLISH (All SS), *Dorset.*. **D** Sarum 5 *See* Milborne St Andrew.

DEWSALL (St Mich) w Callow (St Mary), *Herefs.* R. **D** Heref 3 **P** *D and C of Heref* **I** J F BAULCH.

DEWSBURY (All SS), *W Yorks.* V. **D** Wakef 10 **P** *Bp* **I** R T G SHARP, R W CRESSEY *c.*

(St Mark), V. **D** Wakef 10 **P** *Bp* **I** C P JOHNSON *p-in-c.*

(St Matt West Town w St Jo Bapt Daw Green), V. **D** Wakef 10 **P** *Bp and V of Dewsbury* alt **I** (Vacant).

DEWSBURY MOOR (St Jo Evang), *W Yorks.* V. **D** Wakef 10 **P** *V of Dewsbury* **I** J H SPRINGBETT.

DEXTHORPE, *Lincs.*. **D** Linc 30 *See* Ulceby.

DIBDEN (All SS), *Hants.* R. **D** Win 9 **P** *Mart Mem and C of E Trusts* **I** C R MILES.

DICKER, UPPER *E Sussex.* V. **D** Chich 18 *See* Hellingly.

DICKLEBURGH (All SS) w Langmere, Thelveton Frenze (St Andr) and Shimpling, *Norf.* R. **D** Nor 17 **P** *Bp, Trin Coll Cam, Ld Chan and Lady Mann* **I** S J O SPIKIN P-IN-C OF RUSHALL.

DIDBROOK, w Stanway (St Pet) and Hailes, *Glos.* V. **D** Glouc **P** *Earl of Wemyss and March* **I** J D LAWTON *c.*

DIDCOT (All SS), *Oxon.* R. **D** Ox 18 **P** *BNC Ox* **I** N C WADSWORTH, G W SIMPSON *c.*

(St Pet), V. **D** Ox 18 **P** *Bp* **I** E G CLEMENTS *c,* D J HOPKINSON *c.*

DIDDINGTON (St Laur), *Cambs.* V. **D** Ely 13 **P** *G E P Thornhill Esq* **I** G W WHITLOCK.

DIDDLEBURY or Delbury (St Pet) w Bouldon (All SS) and Munslow (St Mich), *Salop.* R. **D** Heref 12 **P** *D and C of Heref and R M W Powell (alt)* **I** S C MORRIS.

DIDLING (St Andr), *W Sussex.*. **D** Chich 5 *See* Elsted.

DIDLINGTON, *Norf.* (*See Hilborough Group*). **D** Nor 19 **P** *CPAS* **I** (Vacant).

DIDMARTON, *Glos.* R. **D** Glouc 17 *See* Boxwell.

DIDSBURY (St Jas and Em), *Gtr Man.* R. **D** Man **P** *Bp and CPS* **I** D M HALLATT, N J W BARKER *team v,* R H V PAYNE *c.*

WEST (Ch Ch), R. **D** Man 10 **P** *Trustees* **I** N GRIFFITHS.

DIGBY, *Lincs.*. **D** Linc 22 *See* Bloxholme.

DIGSWELL (St Jo Evang), *Herts.* R. **D** St Alb 7 **P** *S for Maint of Faith* **I** J D THOMPSON, G R JAMES *c,* J R ROGERS *c.*

(Panshanger Conv Distr). **D** St Alb 7 **P** *Bp* **I** C S PRICE *min.*

DILHAM, *Norf.* V. **D** Nor 8 *See* Smallburgh.

DILHORNE (All SS), *Staffs.* V. **D** Lich 14 **P** *D and C of Lich* **I** R E F DOW *p-in-c.*

DILTON (St Mary), *Wilts.*. **D** Sarum 22 *See* Westbury.

DILTON MARSH (H Trin) w Brokerswood (All SS), *Wilts.* V. **D** Sarum 22 **P** *Bp* **I** R J RAY *p-in-c.*

DILWYN (St Mary Virg) w Stretford, *Herefs.* V. **D** Heref 7 **P** *Bp* **I** P D REES *p-in-c.*

DINDER (St Mich AA), *Somt.*. **D** B & W 6 *See* Croscombe.

DINES GREEN (St Mich), *Worcs.* V. **D** Worc 2 **P** *Bp* **I** C F GREEN *p-in-c.*

DINGLEY (All SS), *Northants.* R. **D** Pet 8 *See* Brampton Ash.

DINNINGTON (St Matt), *Northumb.* V. **D** Newc T 5 **P** *Bp* **I** J T SPENCE.

DINNINGTON (St Leon), *S Yorks.* R. **D** Sheff 5 **P** *M C M Althorpe Esq* **I** B C ASHLEY.

DINNINGTON (St Nich), *Somt.* R. **D** B & W *See* Hinton St George.

DINSDALE (St Jo Bapt) w Sockburn (All SS), V *Durham.* R. **D** Dur 11 **P** *D and C of Dur, Govs of Sherburn Hosp and Ch S Trust* **I** R R A GRAHAM.

DINTING VALE (H Trin), *Derbys.* V. **D** Derby 5 **P** *Bp* **I** G R PERCY *p-in-c.*

DINTON (St Pet and St Paul), *Bucks.*. **D** Ox 21 *See* Stone.

DINTON (St Mary), *Wilts.*. **D** Sarum *See* Barford St Martin.

DIPTFORD (St Mary), *Devon.* R. **D** Ex 13 **P** *Bp* **I** P A D WILLIS.

DIPTON (St Jo Evang), *Durham.* V. **D** Dur 7 **P** *Bp* **I** L STOKES.

DISCOYD (St Mich), *Herefs.*. **D** Heref 5 *See* Presteigne.

DISEWORTH (St Mich AA), *Leics.*. **D** Leic *See* Whatton, Long.

DISHFORTH (Ch Ch), *N Yorks.* V. **D** York 26 *See* Topcliffe.

DISHLEY, *Leics.* V. **D** Leic 10 *See* Thorpe Acre.

DISLEY (St Mary the Virg), *Chesh.* V. **D** Ches 16 **P** *Ld Newton* **I** P H SHAW.

DISS (St Mary Virg), *Norf.* R. **D** Nor 17 **P** *Bp* **I** G C JAMES, R N MYERSCOUGH *hon c.*

DISTINGTON (The H Spirit), *Cumb.* R. **D** Carl 11 **P** *Earl of Lonsdale* **I** J WOOLCOCK.

DITCHEAT (St Mary Magd) w E Pennard and Pylle, *Somt.* R. **D** B & W 6 **P** *Rev D S Salter and Bp* **I** D M OWEN.

DITCHFORD, *Warws.*. **D** Cov 9 *See* Stretton-on-Fosse.

DITCHINGHAM (St Mary Virg) w Pirnough (All H), *Norf.* R. **D** Nor 1 **P** *Bp* **I** D T G WARD.

DITCHLING (St Marg), *E Sussex.* V. **D** Chich 14 **P** *Bp* **I** K C JEFFERY.

DITTERIDGE (St Chris), *Wilts.* R. **D** Bris 9 **P** *A W Northey Esq* **I** G C C SPENCER *p-in-c.*

DITTISHAM (St Geo), *Devon.* **D** Ex 13 *See* Ashprington.

DITTON (St Pet), *Kent.* R. **D** Roch 6 **P** *Trustees* **I** J C GARDINER.

DITTON (St Mich), *Chesh.* V. **D** Liv 7 **P** *Trustees* **I** W E L BROAD, R GIBBARD *team v.*

DITTON PRIORS (St Jo Bapt), *Salop.* V. **D** Heref 9 **P** *Bp* **I** M A J HARDING.

DIXON GREEN (St Thos), *Gtr Man.*. **D** Man 14 *See* Farnworth.

DIXTON (St Pet) w Wyesham (St Jas), *Gwent.* V. **D** Heref 8 **P** *Dioc Bd of Patr* **I** B E D W PHILLIPS.

DOBCROSS (H Trin) w Scouthead (St paul), *Gtr Man.* V. **D** Man 15 **P** *Bp* **I** C W M BARLOW.

DOCKENFIELD, *Surrey.*. **D** Guildf 3 *See* Frensham.

DOCKING (St Mary Virg), *Norf.* V. **D** Nor 23 **P** *Bp* **I** R J HAMMOND.

DOCKLOW (St Bart), *Herefs.* V. **D** Heref 7 *See* Pudleston.

DODBROOKE (St Thos of Cant), *Devon.* R. **D** Ex 14 **P** *Bp* **I** C C ROBINS *p-in-c.*

DODDENHAM (St Andr), *Worcs.*. **D** Worc 2 *See* Knightwick.

DODDERHILL (St Aug of Cant), *Worcs.* V. **D** Worc 8 **P** *Bp* **I** C R CAMPLING *p-in-c.*

DODDINGHURST (All SS), *Essex.* R. **D** Chelmsf 9 **P** *Bp* **I** I S PARKER.

DODDINGTON (St Jo Bapt) w Wychling (St Marg), *Kent.* V. **D** Cant 7 **P** *Archd of Cant* **I** T W HILL.

DODDINGTON (St John), *Chesh.* V. **D** Ches 15 **P** *Sir Evelyn Delves-Broughton Bt* **I** D M COLLINS.

DODDINGTON (St Mary), *Cambs.* R. **D** Ely 19 **P** *Lady Glover-Hurlimann* **I** J C HARRINGTON.

DODDINGTON (St Jo Bapt), *Salop.* V. **D** Heref 12 *See* Coreley.

DODDINGTON (St Pet) w Whisby, *Lincs.*. **D** Linc 18 *See* Skellingthorpe.

DODDINGTON (St Mary and St Mich), *Northumb.* V. **D** Newc T 8 *See* Wooler.

DODDINGTON, GREAT (St Nich), *Northants.* V. **D** Pet 7 **P** *Ld Chan* **I** M B SEGAL.
DODDISCOMBSLEIGH (St Mich), *Devon.* R. **D** Ex 6 *See* Dunsford.
DODFORD (H Trin and St Mary), *Worcs.* V. **D** Worc 7 **P** *Bp* **I** (Vacant).
DODFORD (St Mary Virg) w Brockhall (St Pet and St Paul), R *Northants.* V. **D** Pet 3 *See* Flore.
DODINGTON (St Mary) w Wapley and Codrington, *Avon.*. **D** Bris *See* Yate New Town.
DODINGTON, *Salop.* **D** Lich 28 *See* Whitchurch.
DODINGTON (All SS), *Somt.* R. **D** B & W 18 *See* Holford.
DODLESTON (St Mary), *Chesh* w Kinnerton, Higher (All SS), *Chesh.* R. **D** Ches 2 **P** *D and C of Ches* **I** O W LLOYD, V H WILLIAMS *c.*
DODWORTH (St Jo Bapt), *S Yorks.* V. **D** Wakef 8 **P** *V of Silkstone* **I** E L S DERRY.
DOGDYKE, *Lincs.*. **D** Linc 11 *See* Billinghay.
DOGMERSFIELD, *Hants.* R. **D** Win 4 *See* Winchfield.
DOGSTHORPE, *Cambs.* R. **D** Pet 14 *See* Peterborough (All Saints').
DOLLIS HILL (St Paul).. **D** Lon 28 *See* Oxgate.
DOLPHINHOLME (St Mark) w Quernmore (St Pet), *Lancs.* V. **D** Blackb 11 **P** *Bp and V of Lanc* alt. **I** L J HAKES.
DOLTON, *Devon.* R. **D** Ex 20 **P** *Ch Assoc Trust* **I** G B BELL.
DONCASTER (St Geo) w St Andr Chap *S Yorks.* V. **D** Sheff 8 **P** *Bp* **I** G LAWN, N H TAYLOR *c.*
(Ch Ch w St Jo Evang), V. **D** Sheff 8 **P** *S for Maint of Faith* **I** E R GASKILL, W CHARLTON *c.*
(St Aid Wheatley Hills), V. **D** Sheff 8 **P** *Bp* **I** R H ELLIS.
(St Jas), V. **D** Sheff 8 **P** *Bp* **I** P HALLETT.
(St Jude, Hexthorpe), V. **D** Sheff 8 **P** *Hyndman Trustees* **I** J R HUMPHREYS.
(St Leon and St Jude), V. **D** Sheff 8 **P** *Crown* **I** D C DARLEY, A J BEHRENS *c*, S P COKER *c.*
(St Mary, Wheatley), V. **D** Sheff 8 **P** *Hyndman Trustees* **I** J R SMITH.
(St Pet Warmsworth), R. **D** Sheff 8 **P** *Mrs M Pearse* **I** M WRIGHT, R W F HOWELL *c.*
(Cantley Estate Conv Distr). **D** Sheff 8 **P** *Bp* **I** N J PAY *c-in-c.*
(West Bessacarr Conv Distr). **D** Sheff 8 **P** *Bp* **I** J M OSGERBY *p-in-c.*
DONHEADS (St Andr and St Mary Virg w Charlton), *Wilts.* R. **D** Sarum **P** *Dioc Bd of Patr and New Coll Ox* **I** H M DEANE-HALL.
DONINGTON, *Leics.* V. **D** Leic 11 *See* Hugglescote.
DONINGTON (St Mary and H Rood), *Lincs.* V and R. **D** Linc 21 **P** *Simeon Trustees* **I** J P PATRICK.
DONINGTON (St Cuthb) w Boscobel, *Salop.* R. **D** Lich 25 **P** *MMT* **I** C W WOODS.
DONINGTON-ON-BAIN (St Andr), *Lincs.* R. **D** Linc *See* Asterby Group.
DONISTHORPE (St Jo Evang and St Hilda Moira) w Stretton-en-le-Field (St Mich), *Leics*, V. **D** Leic 12 **P** *Ch S Trust 1 turn, Bp 3 turns* **I** G W PUNSHON.
DONNINGTON, *Berks.*. **D** Ox 14 *See* Shaw.
DONNINGTON (St Mary), *Herefs.* R. **D** Glouc 6 *See* Dymock.
DONNINGTON (St Geo), w H Trin Chap *W Sussex.* V. **D** Chich 3 **P** *Ld Chan* **I** A R HARCUS *p-in-c.*
DONNINGTON WOOD (St Matt), *Salop.* V. **D** Lich 27 **P** *Bp* **I** H J PASCOE, J H K NORTON *c.*
DONYATT (St Mary Virg), w Horton, Broadway and Ashill, *Somt.* R. **D** B & W 20 **P** *Bp and W P Palmer Esq* **I** J F SERTIN.
DONYLAND, EAST (St Lawr), *Essex.* R. **D** Chelmsf 21 **P** *A E Havens Esq* **I** C COOK.
DORCHESTER (All SS and St Pet) w Frome Whitfield, Fordington and W Fordington, *Dorset.* R. **D** Sarum 5 **P** *Dioc Bd of Patr 3 turns, Ld Chan 1 turn* **I** J J HAMILTON-BROWN, P S MACPHERSON *team v*, R A WHEELER *team v*, A A ROBERTS *c.*
DORCHESTER (St Pet and St Paul) w Berinsfield, Stadhampton w Chiselhampton, Clifton Hampden, Culham, Drayton St Leonard and Newington, Marsh Baldon, Toot Baldon and Nuneham, *Oxon.* R. **D** Ox 5 **P** *Bp* **I** R M NICHOLS, G G B CANNING *team v*, P L DEWEY *team v*, A R MOORE *team v*, M J WALKER *c.*
DORDON (St Leon) w Freazley, *Warws.* V. **D** Birm 10 **P** *V of Polesworth* **I** D WRAPSON.
DORE (Ch Ch), *S Yorks.* V. **D** Sheff 2 **P** *Earl Fitzwilliam* **I** L C LOWTHER.
DORKING (St Martin), V w Ranmore (St Barn), R *Surrey.*. **D** Guildf 6 **P** *Bp* **I** J A SILK.
(St Paul), V. **D** Guildf 6 **P** *Ch Par Trust* **I** (Vacant).
DORMANSLAND (St Jo Evang), *Surrey.* V. **D** S'wark 10 **P** *Bp* **I** N T MOFFATT.
DORMANSTOWN (All SS), *Cleve.* V. **D** York 19 **P** *Abp* **I** G J WILLIAMS.
DORMINGTON (St Pet) w Mordiford (H Rood), R, *Herefs.* V. **D** Heref 4 **P** *A T Foley Esq and Maj R T Hereford* alt **I** W I O MCDONALD *c-in-c.*
DORMSTON (St Nich), *Worcs.*. **D** Worc 3 *See* Kington.
DORNEY (St Jas), *Bucks.*. **D** Ox 24 *See* Riverside.
DORRIDGE (St Phil), *W Midl.* V. **D** Birm 11 **P** *Bp* **I** M B SANDERS.
DORRINGTON (St Jas), *Lincs.* V. **D** Linc 22 **P** *Dioc Bd of Patr* **I** S JACKSON.
DORRINGTON (St Edw K and Conf), *Salop.* V. **D** Heref 11 **P** *Mrs Jasper More* **I** (Vacant).
DORSINGTON (St Pet), *Warws.* R. **D** Glouc 12 *See* Pebworth.
DORSTONE (St Faith VM), *Herefs.* R. **D** Heref 1 **P** *T F Powell Esq* **I** J C DE LA T DAVIES *p-in-c.*
DORTON, *Bucks.*. **D** Ox 21 *See* Chilton.
DOSTHILL (St Paul) w Wood End (St Mich), *Staffs.* V. **D** Birm 10 **P** *Bp* **I** A D BINNIE.
DOUGLAS (Ch Ch), *Lancs.* V. **D** Blackb 4 **P** *Bp* **I** R PROBART, D R E JACKSON *c.*
DOULTING (St Aldhelm) w Downhead (All SS), and W Cranmore (St Bart), *Somt.* V. **D** B & W 6 *See* Shepton Mallet.
DOVECOT (H Spirit), *Mer.* V. **D** Liv 6 **P** *Bp* **I** N CARTER.
DOVER (St Mary Virg), *Kent.* V. **D** Cant 5 **P** *Abp, Ld Warden and Ld Lieut of Kent* **I** E M HUGHES.
(St Martin of Tours), V. **D** Cant 5 **P** *CPAS* **I** B J DUCKETT.
(St Nich Buckland Valley). **D** Cant 5 *See* Buckland-in-Dover.
(St Pet and St Paul, Charlton), R. **D** Cant 5 **P** *Keble Coll Ox* **I** P G JONES.
DOVERCOURT (All SS w St Aug), *Essex.* V. **D** Chelmsf 25 **P** *Bp* **I** W G STINSON *c-in-c*, J J J BARRETT *c.*
DOVERDALE (St Mary), *Worcs.* R. **D** Worc 2 *See* Ombersley.
DOVERIDGE (St Cuthb), *Derbys.* V. **D** Derby 14 **P** *Duke of Devonshire* **I** T F BEEDELL.
DOWBIGGIN, *Cumb.*. **D** Bradf 7 *See* Cautley.
DOWDESWELL (St Mich) and Andoversford w The Shiptons and Cold Salperton, *Glos.* R. **D** Glouc 15 **P** *MMT and C of E Trust and Mrs E M Fieldhouse* **I** G A J HUTTON.
DOWLAND, *Devon.*. **D** Ex *See* Iddesleigh.
DOWLES (no ch), *Salop.* R. **D** Worc 10 *See* Ribbesford.
DOWLISH WAKE (St Andr) w Dowlish, West, Chaffcombe, Knowle St Giles, Cricket Malherbie and Kingstone, *Somt.* R. **D** B & W 19 **P** *P G H Speke Esq, Dioc Bd of Finance, Bp and D and C of Wells (in turn)* **I** R B BAGOTT.
DOWN-AMPNEY (All SS) w Poulton (St Mich AA), *Glos.* V. **D** Glouc 14 **P** *Ch Ch Ox and Bp* alt **I** R H NESHAM.
DOWN-HATHERLEY (St Mary and Corpus Christi) w Twigworth (St Matt), *Glos.* V. **D** Glouc 2 **P** *Ld Chan* **I** T BERESFORD-DAVIES.
DOWN St Mary (St Mary Virg) w Clannaborough (St Petrock), *Devon.*. **D** Ex 2 *See* Woolfardisworthy, East.
DOWN STREET (Ch Ch).. **D** Lon 19 *See* Westminster.
DOWNE (St Mary Magd), *Kent.* V. **D** Roch 16 *See* Cudham.
DOWNE, WEST, *Devon.* R. **D** Ex 15 *See* Ilfracombe.
DOWNEND (Ch Ch), *Avon.* V. **D** Bris 7 **P** *Peache Trustees* **I** A O JOYCE, R J CARLTON *c*, L P R MEERING *c*, P J ROBERTS *c*, D J ROBERTSON *c*, J P HICKINBOTHAM *hon c.*
DOWNHAM (St Marg) w South Hanningfield (St Pet), *Essex.* R. **D** Chelmsf 11 **P** *Bp* **I** M F PETTITT.
DOWNHAM (St Leon), *Lancs.* V. **D** Blackb 7 **P** *Ld Clitheroe* **I** F E CHARD.
DOWNHAM (St Mark). **D** S'wark 18 *See* Catford.
DOWNHAM, LITTLE (St Leon) w Pymoor (H Trin), *Cambs.* R. **D** Ely 15 **P** *Bp* **I** J K HODDER.
DOWNHAM MARKET (St Edm K) w Bexwell (St Mary Virg), *Norf.* R. **D** Ely 17 **P** *Bp* **I** B H COOPER.
DOWNHEAD (All SS), *Somt.*. **D** B & W 6 *See* Doulting.
DOWNHOLME (St Mich AA), *N Yorks.*. **D** Ripon 1 *See* Grinton.
DOWNLEY (St Jas), *Bucks.*. **D** Ox 32 *See* Wycombe, High.
DOWNSIDE (Ch Ch), *Somt.* V. **D** B & W *See* Chilcompton.
DOWNTON (St Lawr), *Wilts.* V. **D** Sarum 17 **P** *Win Coll* **I** D J LETCHER.
DOWNTON-ON-THE-ROCK (St Giles) w Burrington (St Geo), Aston (St Giles), and Elton (BVM), *Salop.* R. **D** Heref 12 *See* Wigmore Abbey.

DUNKESWELL (St Nich) w Dunkeswell Abbey (H Trin), *Devon.* V. **D** Ex 5 **P** *MMT* **I** N J WALL P-IN-C OF LUPPITT.
DUNKIRK (Ch Ch), *Kent.* V. **D** Cant 7 *See* Boughton-under-Blean.
DUNMOW, GREAT (St Mary), *Essex.* V. **D** Chelmsf 23 **P** *Ld Chan* **I** J MATTHEWS, P J STREET *hon c.*
DUNMOW, LITTLE (St Mary), *Essex.* V. **D** Chelmsf 23 **P** *CPAS* **I** A M PARRY.
DUNNINGTON (St Nich), *Humb.* R. **D** York **P** *Abp* **I** S R STANLEY.
DUNNINGTON (St Nich), *N Yorks..* **D** York 14 *See* Beeford.
DUNSBY (All SS), *Lincs.* R. **D** Linc 13 *See* Dowsby.
DUNSBY, *Lincs..* **D** Linc 11 *See* Brauncewell.
DUNSCROFT (Ch Ch) *S Yorks.* V. **D** Sheff 8 **P** *Bp* **I** I HARLAND *c-in-c,* P M DAWES *c.*
DUNSDEN (All SS), *Oxon..* **D** Ox *See* Shiplake.
DUNSFOLD (St Mary and All SS), *Surrey.* R. **D** Guildf 2 **P** *Ld Chan* **I** R J SANDERS.
DUNSFORD (St Mary) w Doddiscombsleigh (St Mich), *Devon.* V. **D** Ex 6 **P** *Exors of Lt-Col F E A Fulford* **I** E G PATTISON.
DUNSFORTH, *N Yorks..* **D** Ripon 3 *See* Aldborough.
DUNSTABLE (St Pet), *Beds.* R. **D** St Alb 18 **P** *Bp* **I** D B WEBB, M R ABBOTT *team v,* B L DRIVER *team v,* J A JOHNSON *team v.*
DUNSTALL (St Mary), *Staffs.* V. **D** Lich **P** *Lt-Col Sir R J Hardy Bt* **I** J A WALSH.
DUNSTER (St Geo), *Somt.* V. **D** B & W 21 **P** *Lt Col G W F Luttrell* **I** C D ALDERSON.
DUNS TEW (St Mary Magd), *Oxon..* **D** Ox *See* Westcote Barton.
DUNSTON (St Nich w Ch Ch), *T & W.* V. **D** Dur 4a **P** *Bp* **I** G D HERON.
DUNSTON (St Pet), *Lincs.* V. **D** Linc 18 *See* Nocton.
DUNSTON (St Remigius), *Norf.* V. **D** Nor 14 *See* Stoke-Holy-Cross.
DUNSTON (St Leon) w Coppenhall (St Lawr), *Staffs.* V. **D** Lich 3 **P** *G E P Thorneycroft Esq* **I** R CHEADLE *p-in-c.*
DUNTERTON (St Constantine), *Devon.* R. **D** Ex 22 *See* Milton Abbot.
DUNTISBOURNE ABBOTS (St Pet), *Glos.* R. **D** Glouc 13 *See* Daglingworth.
DUNTISBOURNE ROUS (St Mich), *Glos.* R. **D** Glouc 13 *See* Daglingworth.
DUNTON (St Mary Magd) w Wrestlingworth (St Pet) and Eyeworth (All SS), *Beds.* V. **D** St Alb 17 **P** *Ld Chan and Dioc Bd of Patr (alt)* **I** W J BERRY.
DUNTON (St Martin), *Bucks.* R. **D** Ox 25 *See* Hoggeston.
DUNTON, *Norf..* **D** Nor *See* Sculthorpe.
DUNTON BASSETT (All SS), *Leics.* V. **D** Leic *See* Leire.
DUNTON GREEN (St Jo Div), *Kent.* V. **D** Roch 7 *See* Riverhead.
DUNTON-WAYLETT (St Mary), *Essex..* **D** Chelmsf 10 *See* Basildon.
DUNWICH (St Jas), *Suff.* V. **D** St E 19 *See* Westleton.
DURHAM (St Osw K and Mart w St Mary-le-Bow, R and St Mary L, R), *Durham.* V. **D** Dur 2 **P** *D and C of Dur* **I** B J H DE LA MARE, D JASPER *c.*
(All SS Newton Hall), V. **D** Dur **P** *D and C of Dur* **I** D LOMAS *p-in-c,* F J L DEWAR *hon c.*
(St Cuthb), V. **D** Dur 2 **P** *D and C of Dur* **I** J N GREAVES, H E S LITTLE *c.*
(St Giles), V. **D** Dur 2 **P** *D and C of Dur* **I** E C WYNGARD.
(St Marg of Antioch), R. **D** Dur 2 **P** *D and C of Dur* **I** S C DAVIS, C S ROGERSON *c,* J C SHULER *c.*
(St Nich), V. **D** Dur 2 **P** *CPAS* **I** F WHITE *c.*
DURLEIGH, *Somt.* V. **D** B & W 17 **P** *Ld Chan* **I** E R AYERST.
DURLEY (Holy Cross), *Hants.* R. **D** Portsm **P** *Bp* **I** L G SHOTLANDER.
DURRINGTON (St Symphorian), *W Sussex.* V. **D** Chich 9 **P** *Bp* **I** (Vacant).
DURRINGTON (All SS), *Wilts.* V. **D** Sarum 18 **P** *D and C of Win* **I** (Vacant).
DURSLEY (St Jas Gt) w Woodmancote (St Mark), *Glos.* R. **D** Glouc 5 **P** *Bp* **I** E J HOSKIN.
DURSTON (St Jo Bapt), *Somt..* **D** B & W *See* Newton, North.
DURWESTON (St Nich) and Bryanston, *Dorset.* V. **D** Sarum 10 **I** P M JENKINS *p-in-c.*
DUSTON (St Luke), *Northants.* V. **D** Pet 4 **P** *Bp* **I** P GARLICK, B LEE *c.*
DUXFORD (St Pet), *Cambs.* V. **D** Ely 7 **P** *Bp* **I** R A BIRT *p-in-c,* K C OVERTON *c.*
DYER'S HILL (St Luke or Sale Mem Ch), *S Yorks..* **D** Sheff 1 *See* Sheffield.
DYMCHURCH (St Pet and St Paul) w Burmarsh (All SS) and Newchurch (St Pet and St Paul), *Kent.* R. **D** Cant 13 **P** *Abp* **I** (Vacant).
DYMOCK (St Mary BV), *Glos* w Donnington (St Mary), *Herefs* and Kempley, *Glos.* R. **D** Glouc 6 **P** *Can J E Gethyn-Jones, Earl Beauchamp and M Hellyer Esq (in turn)* **I** R J LEGG *p-in-c.*
DYNDOR (St Andr), *Herefs.* R. **D** Heref 4 *See* Holme Lacy.
DYRHAM (St Pet), *Avon..* **D** Bris 7 *See* Pucklechurch.

EAGLE (All SS), *Lincs.* V. **D** Linc 18 *See* Swinderby.
EAGLESCLIFFE, *Cleve..* **D** Dur *See* Egglescliffe.
EAKRING (St Andr), *Notts.* R. **D** Southw 15 **P** *Dioc Bd of Patr* **I** W G CALTHROP-OWEN.
EALING (St Mary), *Gtr Lon.* V. **D** Lon 5 **P** *Bp* **I** M J SAWARD, J E SHARPE *c,* C J SKILTON *c.*
(Christ the Sav), V. **D** Lon 5 **P** *Bp* **I** J K BRIGHAM *c.*
(St Barn), V. **D** Lon 5 **P** *Bp* **I** R F SWAN.
(St Paul, W Ealing), V. **D** Lon 5 **P** *Bp* **I** D S MARCH.
(St Pet Mount Park), V. **D** Lon 5 **P** *Bp* **I** R HAYES, A C BALL *c.*
(St Steph, W Ealing), V. **D** Lon 5 **P** *D and C of St Paul's* **I** R F SWAN, W H ROBERTS *c.*
(St Matt, Ealing Common), V. **D** Lon 5 **P** *Bp* **I** P G WATKINS.
(St Jas, Ealing Dean), V. **D** Lon 5 **P** *Bp* **I** S F DAKIN *p-in-c.*
(St John, W Ealing), V. **D** Lon 5 **P** *Bp* **I** S F DAKIN, J W FULTON *c,* A WALLACE *c,* G B HEWITT *hon c.*
(All SS), V. **D** Lon 5 **I** R F BUNCE.
EARBY (All SS), *Lancs.* V. **D** Bradf 10 **P** *Bp* **I** R A C GREENLAND.
EARDISLAND (St Mary Virg), *Herefs.* V. **D** Heref 7 **P** *Bp of Birm* **I** J G WILLIAMS *p-in-c.*
EARDISLEY (St Mary Magd) w Bollingham (St Silas) and Willersley (St Mary Magd), *Herefs.* R. **D** Heref 5 **P** *Bp and D and C of Ch Ch Ox* alt **I** (Vacant).
EARITH (St Mary Virg), *Cambs..* **D** Ely 13 *See* Bluntisham.
EARL SHILTON (St Simon and St Jude), w Elmesthorpe (St Mary), *Leics.* V. **D** Leic 16 **P** *Bp* **I** A E TAYLOR.
EARL SOHAM (St Mary) w Cretingham (St Pet) and Ashfield, *Suff.* R. **D** St E 18 **P** *Ld Henniker, Wadh Coll Ox and Ld Chan* **I** P S ROBINSON.
EARL STERNDALE (St Mich AA) w Monyash (St Leon), *Derbys.* V. **D** Derby 10 **P** *V of Hartington and V of Bakewell* **I** J F HILDAGE.
EARL STONHAM w Stonham Parva (St Mary Virg) and Creeting (St Pet), *Suff.* R. **D** St E 1 **P** *Pemb Coll Cam, Dioc Bd of Patr and Exors of Miss J E P Hickman (in turn)* **I** B E H BAKER *p-in-c.*
EARLESTOWN (St Jo Bapt), *Mer.* V. **D** Liv 11 **P** *R of Newton-in-Makerfield* **I** J M BURGESS.
EARLEY (St Pet), *Berks.* V. **D** Ox 15 **P** *Dioc Bd of Patr* **I** W D S LARK, A R LONG *c,* D M MATHESON *hon c.*
(St Bart), V. **D** Ox 15 **P** *Bp* **I** M C BRUNSDEN, G T WILLIAMS *c.*
(St Nicolas), V. **D** Ox 15 **P** *Dioc Bd of Patr* **I** R BROWN.
EARLHAM (St Mary) *Norf.* V. **D** Nor 4a **P** *Trustees* **I** B A SHERSBY.
(St Anne), V. **D** Nor 4a **P** *Bp* **I** R G DARRAH.
EARLS BARTON (All SS), *Northants.* V. **D** Pet 7 **P** *Dioc Bd of Patr* **I** M R H BAKER.
EARLS COLNE (St Andr), *Essex.* V. **D** Chelmsf 24 **P** *Dioc Bd of Patr* **I** A S J HOLDEN.
EARL'S COURT. **D** Lon 15 *See* Kensington.
EARL'S CROOME (St Nich) w Hill Croome (St Mary) and Strensham (St Jo Bapt), *Worcs..* **D** Worc **P** *Trustees of Rev G Le Strange Amphlett 2 turns, Bp 1 turn* **I** N B HOLT.
EARLSDON (St Barbara), *Warws..* **D** Cov 2 *See* Coventry.
EARLSFIELD (St Andr), *Surrey.* V. **D** S'wark 7 **P** *Bp* **I** R H MONK.
(St Jo Div), V. **D** S'wark 7 **P** *Bp* **I** S M BURDETT *p-in-c.*
EARLSHEATON (St Pet), *W Yorks.* V. **D** Wakef 10 **P** *V of Dewsbury* **I** D R WARD.
EARNLEY w E Wittering and Almodington *W Sussex.* R. **D** Chich 3 **P** *Bp 1st and 3rd turns, Bp of Lon 2nd turn* **I** P I CARMICHAEL.
EARNSHILL (Sin), *Somt..* **D** B & W 20 *See* Hambridge.
EARSDON (St Alb) w Backworth (St John), *T & W.* V. **D** Newc T 6 **P** *Bp* **I** (Vacant).
EARSHAM (All SS) w Alburgh (All SS) and Denton (St Mary Virg), *Norf.* R. **D** Nor **P** *Abp of Cant, Maj J W Meade and St Jo Coll Cam* **I** D J NAPLEY.
EARTHAM (St Marg), *W Sussex.* V. **D** Chich 1 *See* Slindon.

EASBY, *N Yorks*.. D York *See* Ayton, Great.

EASBY (St Agatha) w Brompton-on-Swale (St Paul), *N Yorks*. V. D Ripon 1 P *Bp* I J A STEGGALL.

EASEBOURNE (St Mary), *W Sussex*. V. D Chich 5 P *Cowdray Trust Ltd* I D B EVANS.

EASINGTON (St Mary Virg), *Durham*. R. D Dur 3 P *Bp* I E G LONG.

COLLIERY (Ascen), V. D Dur 3 P *Bp* I A W HODGSON.

EASINGTON (St Pet), *Oxon*.. D Ox 1 *See* Cuxham.

EASINGTON (All SS) w Liverton (St Martin), *Cleve*. R. D York 19 P *Ld Chan* I D R J PENNEY.

EASINGTON (All SS) w Skeffling (St Helen) and Kilnsea (St Helen), *Humb*. V. D York 15 P *Ld Chan* I L D CHRISTIE.

EASINGWOLD (St Jo Bapt and All SS) w Raskelfe (St Mary), *N Yorks*. V. D York 5 P *Abp* I D M PORTER.

EAST BRIDGFORD (St Pet), *Notts*. R. D Southw 9 P *Magd Coll Ox* I A HAYDOCK P-IN-C OF KNEETON.

EAST CROMPTON, *Gtr Man*.. D Man *See* Crompton, East.

EAST DOWN, *Devon*.. D Ex 18 *See* Kentisbury.

EAST DRAYTON (St Pet) w Stokeham (St Pet), *Notts*. R. D Southw 6 P *D and C of York* I M G H B TUDOR *p-in-c*.

EAST FARNWORTH and Kearsley (St John w All SS and St Pet Farnworth and Prestolee), *Gtr Man*. R. D Man 14 P *Bp* I [illegible], H G PAUL *team v*, H G SMITH *team v*, R LADDS *hon c*.

EAST GOSCOTE (St Hilda), *Leics*. V. D Leic 9 P *Archd of Leic* I D F BREWIN.

EAST HAM, *Essex*.. D Chelmsf 5 *See* Ham, East.

EAST HARDWICK (St Steph), *W Yorks*. V. D Wakef 11 P *Cawood Trustees* I C H JENNO.

EAST HARSLEY (St Osw), *N Yorks*. V. D York 23 *See* Osmotherley.

EAST MARKHAM (St Jo Bapt) w Askham (St Nich), *Notts*. R. D Southw 6 P *S for Maint of Faith* I M G H B TUDOR.

EAST MEON (All SS), *Hants*. V. D Portsm 4 P *Ld Chan* I R J B SMITH.

EAST STOKE (St Osw), *Notts*.. D Southw 3 *See* Stoke, East.

EAST STRATTON, *Hants*.. D Win *See* Woodmancote.

EAST THORPE, *W Yorks*.. D Wakef 10 *See* Mirfield.

EASTBOURNE (St Mary Virg), *E Sussex*. V. D Chich 19 P *Bp* I C H G BESS, Q M RONCHETTI *c*, M R STARR *c*, P H WEBB *c*.

(All SS), V. D Chich 19 P *Trustees* I G T RIDEOUT, C M JOHNSTON *c*.

(All S), V. D Chich 19 P *Ch S* I A T HINDLEY.

(Ch Ch), V. D Chich 19 P *V of Eastbourne* I L G HALLAM.

(H Trin), V. D Chich 19 P *V of Eastbourne* I R M BRETTELL, R TULLY *c*, G H STEVENS *hon c*.

(St Andr), V. D Chich 19 P *Bp* I R W COTTON.

(St Elisabeth), V. D Chich 19 P *Bp* I B H KING.

(St Jo Evang Meads), V. D Chich 19 P *Trustees* I P R WILLIAMS, H G BAWTREE-WILLIAMS *c*, B H JEFFORD *c*.

(St Mich AA), V. D Chich 19 P *V of Eastbourne* I D C COULING.

(St Phil), V. D Chich 19 P *Bp* I C TOLWORTHY.

(St Richard), V. D Chich 19 P *Bp* I R E BUTLER.

(St Sav) w (St Pet), V. D Chich 19 P *Keble Coll Ox* I D W ALLEN, P W SHEPHERD *c*, H B JOHNSON *hon c*.

EASTBRIDGE, *Kent*.. D Cant *See* Dymchurch.

EASTBURN, *W Yorks*.. D Bradf 11 *See* Steeton.

EASTBURY (St Jas Gt) w Eastgarston (All SS), *Berks*. V. D Ox 14 P *Bp and Ch Ch Ox* I M C CLARKE.

EASTBY, *N Yorks*.. D Bradf 10 *See* Embsay.

EASTCHURCH (All SS) w Leysdown (St Clem) and Harty (St Thos Ap), *Kent*. R & V. D Cant 14 P *Keble Coll Ox and Abp* alt I P E BLAGDON-GAMLEN.

EASTCOTE (St Lawr), *Gtr Lon*. V. D Lon 9 P *Bp* I D M H HAYES, M A NARUSAWA *c*.

EASTER, HIGH (St Mary Virg) w Margaret Roding, *Essex*. V. D Chelmsf 23 P *Bp of Lon and Trustees* alt I G F BARTLAM.

EASTERGATE W Sussex. R D Chich 1 *See* Barnham.

EASTERN GREEN (St Andr), *W Midl*. V. D Cov 3 P *R of Allesley* I D D J TOOBY.

EASTERTON (St Barn), *Wilts*. V. D Sarum 23 *See* Market Lavington.

EASTGARSTON (All SS), Berks.. D Ox *See* Eastbury.

EASTGATE (All SS), *Durham*. V. D Dur 13 P *Bp* I A J BEALING *c-in-c*.

EASTHAM (St Mary BV), *Mer*. V. D Ches 9 P *D and C of Ches* I R F WORSLEY.

EASTHAM (St Pet and St Paul), w Rochford (St Mich), *Worcs*. R. D Worc *See* Teme Valley, South.

EASTHAMPSTEAD (St Mich AA and St Mary Magd), *Berks*. R. D Ox 11a P *Ch Ch Ox* I L G TYLER, J M P HEDGES *team v*, A J DORBER *c*.

EASTHOPE, *Salop*.. D Heref *See* Long Stanton.

EASTINGTON (St Mich AA) w Frocester (St Pet w St Andr), *Glos*. R. D Glouc 9 P *Dioc Bd of Patr, Lady Cooper and Lady Wills* I N E L BAKER.

EASTLEACH (St Andr, St Mich and St Mart) and Southrop, *Glos*. V. D Glouc *See* Coln St Aldwyn.

EASTLEIGH (Ch of the Resurr), *Hants*. V. D Win 15 P *Bp* I B N HARLEY, M W STEPHENSON *c*.

EASTLING (St Mary), *Kent*. R. D Cant 7 P *MMT* I I C HAWKINS.

EASTNEY (St Marg w St Columba), *Hants*. V. D Portsm 5 P *Bp* I P L LAW.

EASTNOR (St Jo Bapt), *Herefs*. R. D Heref *See* Ledbury.

EASTOFT (St Bart), *Humb*.. D Sheff *See* Whitgift.

EASTON, *Avon*.. D Bris *See* Bristol.

EASTON (St Mary) w Martyr Worthy (St Swith), *Hants*. R. D Win P *Ld Chan and Bp* I R L WILD.

EASTON (St Pet), *Cambs*. V. D Ely 11 P *Bp* I M A JENNER *p-in-c*.

EASTON, *Lincs*.. D Linc 2 *See* Stoke, North w South.

EASTON (St Pet) w Colton and Marlingford, *Norf*. V. D Nor P *Ld Chan, Archd of Norf and Lady Evans-Lombe* I R M BURT.

EASTON (St Paul), *Somt*. V. D B & W 1 *See* Westbury-sub-Mendip.

EASTON (All SS) w Letheringham, *Suff*. R. D St E 18 P *MMT* I G J J MCDONALD *p-in-c*.

EASTON, GREAT (St John and St Giles), *Essex*. R. D Chelmsf 23 P *Mart Mem and C of E Trusts* I J MATTHEWS *c-in-c*.

EASTON, GREAT (St Andr), *Leics*. V. D Leic 5 *See* Bringhurst.

EASTON-GREY, *Wilts*.. D Bris *See* Sherston Magna.

EASTON-IN-GORDANO (St Geo) w Portbury (St Mary Virg) and Clapton-in-Gordano (St Mich), *Avon*. R. D B & W 16 P *Bp and Ox Trust of Churches* I R F D KINSEY *p-in-c*, W R T MARRIOTT C-IN-C OF CLAPTON-IN-GORDANO.

EASTON, LITTLE, *Essex*. R. D Chelmsf 23 *See* Broxted.

EASTON-MAUDIT (St Pet and St Paul), *Northants*. V. D Pet 7 *See* Bozeat.

EASTON NESTON, *Northants*. V. D Pet *See* Towcester.

EASTON-ON-THE-HILL, *Northants*. R. D Pet 13 P *Marq of Ex* I A J H FRANCIS.

EASTON-ROYAL (H Trin), *Wilts*.. D Sarum 27 *See* Milton Lilbourne.

EASTOVER, *Somt*.. D B & W *See* Bridgwater.

EASTRINGTON, *Humb*. V. D York *See* Howden, The.

EASTROP (St Mary), *Hants*. R. D Win 3 P *CPAS* I D A ROSS.

EASTRY (St Mary BV), *Kent*. V. D Cant 8 P *Abp* I (Vacant).

EASTVILLE (St Paul) and New Leake (St Jude) w Midville (St Pet), *Lincs*. V. D Linc 7 P *Bp* I (Vacant).

EASTVILLE (St Anne), *Glos*.. D Bris *See* Bristol.

EASTWELL w Boughton Aluph (All SS), *Kent*. R. D Cant 10 P *Abp* I J F GLEADALL P-IN-C OF BOUGHTON ALUPH.

EASTWELL (St Mich), *Leics*. R. D Leic 3 P *Ld Chan* I A E H CLAYTON *p-in-c*.

EASTWICK, *Herts*.. D St Alb *See* Gilston.

EASTWOOD (St Laur and All SS), *Essex*. V. D Chelmsf 13 P *Ld Chan* I M A BALLARD.

(St D), V. D Chelmsf 13 P *Bp* I F A OSWIN.

EASTWOOD (St Mary), *Notts*. R. D Southw 12 P *J H Plumtre Esq* I D G GOODMAN, J A K GUEST *c*.

EASTWOOD (St Steph), *W Yorks*. V. D Sheff 6 P *Bp* I A E WATLING.

EASTWORTH (All SS), *Surrey*.. D Guildf 7 *See* Chertsey.

EATON (Ch Ch) and Hulme Walfield, *Chesh*. V. D Ches 11 P *Lt-Col R H Antrobus and R of Astbury* I A WHITWORTH *p-in-c*.

EATON (St Denys), *Leics*. V. D Leic 3 P *Ld Chan* I A E H CLAYTON *p-in-c*.

EATON (St Andr w Ch Ch), *Norf*. V. D Nor 4a P *D and C of Nor* I R J HANMER, S R BOXALL *c*, J E LITTLEWOOD *c*, P G RUTHERFORD *c*.

EATON (All SS), *Notts*.. D Southw 5 *See* Gamston.

EATON BISHOP (St Mich AA), *Herefs*. R. D Heref 1 P *Bp* I A J MORTIMER *p-in-c*.

EATON BRAY (St Mary Virg) w Edlesborough, *Beds*. V. D St Alb 18 P *Dioc Bd of Patr* I B P MOORE.

EATON-CONSTANTINE (St Mary), *Salop*. R. D Lich *See* Leighton-under-the-Wrekin.

EATON-HASTINGS (St Mich AA), *Oxon*. R. D Ox *See* Coxwell, Great.

EATON SOCON (St Mary), *Cambs*. V. D St Alb 17 P *Mrs E Hurst* I P A W COTTON.

EATON SQUARE (St Pet).. **D** Lon 19 *See* Westminster.
EATON-UNDER-HEYWOOD (St Edith), *Salop..* **D** Heref 11 *See* Hope Bowdler.
EBBERSTON (St Mary Virg) w Allerston (St John), *N Yorks.* V. **D** York 24 **P** *Abp* **I** (Vacant).
EBBESBOURNE WAKE (St Jo Bapt) w Fifield Bavant (St Martin) and Alvediston (St Mary), *Wilts.* V (*in Chalke Valley Group - see Bishopston*). **D** Sarum 19 **P** *Bp 2 turns, V of Broadchalke 1 turn* **I** A STOTT.
EBCHESTER (St Ebba), *T & W.* R. **D** Dur 7 **P** *Bp* **I** D E HILBORNE.
EBERNOE (H Trin), *W Sussex.* V. **D** Chich 6 *See* North Chapel.
EBONY, *Kent..* **D** Cant 12 *See* Stone-in-Oxney.
EBRINGTON (St Eadburgha), *Glos.* V. **D** Glouc 12 *See* Chipping Camden.
ECCHINSWELL (St Lawr) w Sydmonton (St Mary), *Hants.* V. **D** Win *See* Burghclere.
ECCLES (St Mary Virg) w St Andr, *Gtr Man.* R. **D** Man 3 **P** *Bp and A Cooper Esq* **I** M ARUNDEL, D J BRIERLEY *team v.*
(St Paul, Monton), V. **D** Man 5 **P** *V of St Andr Eccles* **I** R N WALLER-WILKINSON.
ECCLES (St Mary Virg), *Norf.* R. **D** Nor 18 *See* Quidenham.
ECCLES-NEXT-THE-SEA (St Mary), *Norf.* R. **D** Nor 9 *See* Hempstead.
ECCLESALL (All SS), *S Yorks..* **D** Sheff 2 *See* Sheffield.
ECCLESFIELD (St Mary Virg), *S Yorks.* V. **D** Sheff 3 **P** *PCC* **I** D C JAMES.
(St Paul Wordsworth Ave), V. **D** Sheff 3 **P** *Bp* **I** R W PALMER.
ECCLESHALL (H Trin) w Slindon (St Chad), *Staffs.* V. **D** Lich 15 **P** *Bp* **I** R F JACKSON.
ECCLESHILL (St Luke), *W Yorks.* V. **D** Bradf 3 **P** *V of Bradf* **I** D H SHREEVE, C W HUMPHRIES *c.*
ECCLESTON (St Mary BV) and Pulford (St Mary Virg), *Chesh.* R. **D** Ches 2 **P** *Duke of Westmr* **I** L R SKIPPER.
ECCLESTON (St Mary), *Lancs.* R. **D** Blackb 4 **P** *Dioc Bd of Patr* **I** P G ASPDEN.
ECCLESTON (Ch Ch), *Mer.* V. **D** Liv 10 **P** *Trustees* **I** J HAMILTON, N E D S SCHIBILD *c.*
(St Thos), V. **D** Liv 10 **P** *Col L C King Wilkinson* **I** R G GARNER, R LEATHERBARROW *c.*
(St Luke), V. **D** Liv 10 **P** *Trustees* **I** E HOPKINS.
(St Matt), Thatto Heath, V. **D** Liv 10 **P** *Bp* **I** J H RICHARDS.
ECCLESTON, GREAT, *Lancs..* **D** Blackb 7 *See* Copp.
ECCLESTON PARK (St Jas), *Mer.* V. **D** Liv 10 **P** *Bp* **I** A K GOODE.
ECKINGTON (St Pet and St Paul) w Renishaw (St Matt) Handley and Ridgeway, *Derbys.* R. **D** Derby 2 **P** *Crown* **I** R P FISHER, A W HUNKIN *c.*
ECKINGTON (H Trin), *Worcs.* V. **D** Worc 3 **P** *D and C of Westmr* **I** R H HOWES.
ECTON (St Mary Magd), *Northants.* R. **D** Pet **P** *Crown* **I** F M A PAYNE.
EDALE (H and Undivided Trin), *Derbys.* V. **D** Derby 9 **P** *Local Landowners* **I** A MURRAY-LESLIE *p-in-c.*
EDBURTON (St Andr), *W Sussex.* R. **D** Chich 14 **P** *Abp of Cant* **I** (Vacant).
EDDINGTON (St Sav), *Wilts..* **D** Ox 14 *See* Hungerford.
EDENBRIDGE (St Pet and St Paul), *Kent.* V. **D** Roch 9 **P** *Bp* **I** R J MASON, R AMES-LEWIS *c*, G H ANDREW *c.*
EDENFIELD, *Lancs.* V. **D** Man 12 **P** *R of Bury* **I** C D DOUGLAS.
EDENHALL (St Cuthb) w Langwathby (St Pet) and Culgaith (All SS), *Cumb.* V. **D** Carl 6 **P** *D and C of Carl* **I** R J GLOVER *p-in-c.*
EDENHAM (St Mich AA), *Lincs.* V. **D** Linc 13 **P** *Earl of Ancaster* **I** B W LOWCOCK.
EDENSOR (St Pet), *Derbys.* V. **D** Derby 9 *See* Beeley.
EDENSOR (St Paul), *Staffs.* V. **D** Lich 18 **P** *Crown* **I** (Vacant).
EDENTHORPE **D** Sheff 8 *See* Kirk Sandall.
EDGBASTON (St Bart), *W Midl.* V. **D** Birm 2 **P** *Brig Sir R Anstruther-Gough-Calthorpe Bt* **I** E D COOMBES.
(St Aug of Hippo), V. **D** Birm 2 **P** *Bp* **I** J M LUCAS.
(St Geo), V. **D** Birm 2 **P** *Brig Sir R Anstruther-Gough-Calthorpe Bt* **I** D J W BRADLEY.
(St Germain), V. **D** Birm 2 **P** *Trustees* **I** D C YOUNG *p-in-c.*
(St Mary and St Ambrose), V. **D** Birm 2 **P** *Bp and Brig Sir R Anstruther-Gough-Calthorpe Bt jointly* **I** A N GRAHAM.
EDGCOTE, *Northants.* R. **D** Pet 1 *See* Chipping Warden.
EDGCOTT (St Mich), *Bucks.* R. **D** Ox 25 *See* Grendon Underwood.
EDGE, THE (St Jo Bapt) w Pitchcombe, *Glos.* R. **D** Glouc 4 **P** *Bp* **I** G N BIRD.
EDGEFIELD (St Pet and St Paul), *Norf.* R. **D** Nor 24 **P** *S for Maint of Faith* **I** S S GREGORY, R M HARPER *c*, P W E CURRIE *hon c.*
EDGE HILL (St Cath), *Mer.* V. **D** Liv 4 **P** *Trustees* **I** (Vacant).
(St Dunstan), V. **D** Liv 4 **P** *Earle Trustees* **I** R J HUTCHINSON, D BENSON *c.*
(St Mary), V. **D** Liv 4 **P** *Bp* **I** A GODSON.
(St Nath Windsor), V. **D** Liv 4 **P** *Trustees* **I** N BLACK *p-in-c.*
(St Steph Mart). **D** Liv *See* Liverpool.
EDGESIDE (St Anne), *Lancs.* V. **D** Man 18 **P** *Trustees* **I** G R LOXHAM.
EDGEWORTH, *Glos.* R. **D** Glouc 4 *See* Miserden.
EDGMOND (St Pet), *Salop.* R. **D** Lich 21 **P** *Exors of G W Corbet Esq* **I** N J CHARRINGTON, J ALFORD *c.*
EDGTON (St Mich), *Salop..* **D** Heref *See* Hopesay.
EDGWARE (St Marg), *Gtr Lon.* R. **D** Lon 17 **P** *MMT and C of E Trust* **I** G D A BENNET, P H JORDAN *c*, S F KIMBER *c*, C SPIVEY *c.*
EDINGALE (H Trin), *Staffs.* V. **D** Lich 6 **P** *Bp* **I** (Vacant).
EDINGLEY (St Giles) w Halam (St Mich), *Notts.* V. **D** Southw 15 **P** *Bp* **I** J M IRVINE *p-in-c.*
EDINGTHORPE (All SS), *Norf.* R. **D** Nor 8 *See* Bacton.
EDINGTON (St Geo), *Somt..* **D** B & W 7 *See* Chilton-Super-Polden.
EDINGTON (St Mary, St Kath and All SS) w Imber (St Giles), *Wilts.* V. **D** Sarum 23 **P** *Bp* **I** (Vacant).
EDITH WESTON (St Mary) w Normanton w N Luffenham and Lyndon w Manton, *Leics.* R. **D** Pet 12 **P** *Earl of Ancaster, Sir J Conant Bt and Em Coll Cam (in turn)* **I** P T MILLER.
EDLASTON (St Jas), *Derbys.* R. **D** Derby 8 *See* Osmaston-by-Ashbourne.
EDLESBOROUGH w Dagnall, *Bucks.* V. **D** St Alb 18 *See* Eaton Bray.
EDLINGHAM (St Jo Bapt) w Bolton, *Northumb.* V. **D** Newc T 7 *See* Alnwick.
EDLINGTON (St Helen) w Wispington, *Lincs.* V. **D** Linc *See* Hemingby.
EDLINGTON, NEW (St Jo Bapt), *S Yorks.* V. **D** Sheff 8 **P** *Bp* **I** K M WRAY.
EDMONDSHAM (St Nich), *Dorset.* R. **D** Sarum *See* Cranborne.
EDMONDTHORPE (St Mich), *Leics.* R. **D** Leic 4 *See* Wymondham.
EDMONTON (All SS), *Gtr Lon.* V. **D** Lon 21 **P** *D and C of St Paul's* **I** B W OAKLEY, E V REES *c*, J M STRIDE *c.*
(St Aldhelm), V. **D** Lon 21 **P** *V of Edmonton* **I** A V COLDERWOOD.
(St Alphege), V. **D** Lon 21 **P** *Bp* **I** L A MILLINS.
(St Gabr Bounds Green), V. **D** Lon 22 **P** *Bp* **I** R H GIBBS *hon c.*
UPPER (St Jas), V. **D** Lon 21 **P** *D and C of St Paul's* **I** (Vacant).
(St Mary) w (St Jo Evang), V. **D** Lon 21 **P** *Bp and D and C of St Paul's alt* **I** D W GOUGH, J S ALDIS *hon c.*
LOWER (St Mich), V. **D** Lon 21 **P** *D and C of St Paul's* **I** B W OAKLEY *p-in-c.*
(St Pet Ap w St Mart),. **D** Lon 21 **P** *Bp* **I** R J JONES *p-in-c.* *See also* BUSH HILL PARK..
EDMUNDBYERS (St Edmund) w Muggleswick, *Durham.* R. **D** Dur 13 **P** *D and C of Dur* **I** R D WISKEN.
EDSTASTON (St Mary Virg), *Salop.* V. **D** Lich 27 **P** *R of Wem* **I** J MACDONALD.
EDSTON, GREAT (St Mich), *N Yorks.* V. **D** York *See* Normanby.
EDVIN LOACH, *Worcs..* **D** Heref 2 *See* Tedstone Delamere.
EDVIN RALPH (St Mich) w Collington (St Mary Virg) and Thornbury (St Anne), *Herefs.* R. **D** Heref 2 **P** *Dioc Bd of Patr* **I** J ADAMS *p-in-c.*
EDWALTON (H Rood), *Notts.* V. **D** Southw 10 **P** *Exors of Lt-Col J N Chaworth Musters* **I** E W SHEERAN.
EDWARDSTONE (St Mary Virg) w Groton (St Bart), *Suff.* V and R. **D** St E 12 **P** *Dioc Bd of Patr* **I** D G WOODWARDS P-IN-C OF L WALDINGFIELD.
EDWINSTOWE (St Mary), *Notts.* V. **D** Southw 7 **P** *Trustees of Earl Manvers* **I** J FORD.
EFFINGHAM (St Laur) w L Bookham, *Surrey.* V. **D** Guildf 10 **P** *Keble Coll Ox* **I** C M SCOTT.
EGDEAN (St Bart), *W Sussex.* R. **D** Chich 6 **P** *Bp* **I** J H GREENE.
EGERTON (St Jas), *Kent.* V. **D** Cant 9 *See* Charing Heath.
EGG BUCKLAND (St Edw), *Devon.* V. **D** Ex 23 **P** *Ld Chan* **I** C WHITFIELD.
EGGESFORD (All SS), *Devon.* R. **D** Ex 16 **P** *Earl of Portsm* **I** V J R RICHARDS *p-in-c.*
EGGINGTON, *Beds.* V. **D** St Alb *See* Leighton-Buzzard.

EGGINTON (St Wilfrid), *Derbys.* R. D Derby 14 *See* Etwall.
EGGLESCLIFFE (St Jo Bapt), *Cleve.* R. D Dur 14 P *Bp* I C PURVIS, M P SAUNDERS *c.*
EGGLESTONE (H Trin), *Durham.* V. D Dur 10 P *Crown* I (Vacant).
EGGLETON, *Herefs..* D Heref 6 *See* Stretton Grandison.
EGHAM (St Jo Bapt), *Surrey.* V. D Guildf 7 P *Ch S Trust* I J R HARGREAVES, J A CHEESEMAN *c.*
(St Paul, The Hythe), V. D Guildf 7 P *Bp* I A N KELLY.
EGLETON, *Leics.* V. D Pet 12 *See* Hambleton.
EGLINGHAM (St Maurice), *Northumb.* V. D Newc T 8 P *Bp* I (Vacant).
EGLOSHAYLE (St Conan), *Cornw.* V. D Truro 8 P *Bp* I (Vacant).
EGLOSKERRY (St Kyriacus, or Coriantus, and St Petroc), *Cornw.* V. D Truro 11 P *Bp 2 turns, Duchy of Cornw 1 turn* I R W P HOWLETT.
EGMANTON (St Mary), *Notts.* V. D Southw 6 P *S for Maint of Faith* I I CLARK.
EGMERE, *Norf..* D Nor *See* Holkham.
EGREMONT, *Mer..* D Ches 7 *See* Wallasey.
EGREMONT (St Mary w St John) and Haile, *Cumb.* R. D Carl 12 P *Bp, Lord Egremont and Earl of Lonsdale* I E R CHAPMAN, G W H HARTLEY *team v,* R A MOATT *c.*
EGTON (St Mary Virg) w Newland, *Cumb.* V. D Carl 15 P *Trustees* I R D GREENWOOD.
EGTON (St Hilda) w Grosmont (St Matt), *N Yorks.* V. D York 27 P *Abp* I C E FOX.
EIGHTON BANKS (St Thos), *T & W.* V. D Dur 4 P *Bp* I (Vacant).
EISEY (St Mary Virg), *Glos..* D Bris 8 *See* Cricklade.
ELBERTON, *Avon..* D Bris *See* Littleton-on-Severn.
ELBURTON, *Devon..* D Ex 21 P *CPAS* I K H S COOMBE.
ELDERSFIELD (St Jo Bapt), *Worcs.* V. D Worc 5 *See* Berrow.
ELDON (St Mark), *Durham.* V. D Dur 9 P *Crown* I D C HANNAM.
ELFORD (St Pet), *Staffs.* R. D Lich 6 P *Bp* I P B GRAHAM.
ELHAM (St Mary Virg), *Kent.* V. D Cant 6 P *Abp and Mert Coll Ox* I T PITT *p-in-c,* R J C LLOYD *hon c.*
ELING (St Mary), *Hants.* R. D Win 9 *See* Totton.
ELING, NORTH, or COPYTHORNE (St Mary), *Hants.* V. D Win 9 P *Bp of Liv* I (Vacant).
ELKESLEY (St Giles) w Bothamsall (St Pet), *Notts.* V. D Southw 5 P *S for Maint of Faith* I R W H MILLER.
ELKSTONE w Syde, *Glos..* D Glouc 13 *See* Brimpsfield.
ELKSTONE (St Jo Bapt), *Staffs..* D Lich 13 *See* Warslow.
ELLACOMBE (Ch Ch), *Devon..* D Ex 10 *See* Torquay.
ELLAND (St Mary Virg w St Mich AA and All SS), *W Yorks.* R. D Wakef 2 P *V of Halifax* I J C GORE, J A BOOTH *c.*
ELLASTONE (St Pet) and Stanton, *Staffs.* V. D Lich *See* Denstone.
ELLEL (St John), *Lancs.* V. D Blackb 11 P *V of Cockerham* I W GUY.
ELLENHALL (St Mary) w Ronton or Ranton, *Staffs.* V. D Lich 15 P *Earl of Lichfield* I J D ANDREWS P-IN-C OF ELLENHALL, J S COOKE C-IN-C OF RANTON.
ELLERBURNE (St Hilda), *N Yorks.* V. D York 24 *See* Thornton Dale.
ELLERKER (All SS), *Humb..* D York *See* Cave South.
ELLERTON PRIORY (St Mary) w Aughton (All H or All S), *Humb.* V. D York 10 *See* Bubwith.
ELLESBOROUGH (St Pet and St Paul), *Bucks.* R. D Ox 30 P *Chequers Trustees* I P D F HORNER *c-in-c.*
ELLESMERE (BVM), *Salop.* V. D Lich 22 P *Ld Brownlow* I N A FENN.
ELLESMERE PORT (Ch Ch) w Stoak (St Lawr), *Chesh.* R. D Ches 9 P *Bp* I S W WINTON, A E ATKINSON *team v,* H J HUTTON *team v,* A D BRADDOCK *c.*
ELLINGHAM (All SS and St Mary), w Harbridge and Ibsley, *Hants.* V. D Win 8 P *Earl of Normanton* I J C WORTHINGTON.
ELLINGHAM (St Mary) w Kirby Cane (All SS), *Norf.* R. D Nor *See* Gillingham.
ELLINGHAM (St Maurice) w S Charlton (St Jas Ap) *Northumb.* V. D Newc T 8 P *D and C of Dur and Duke of Northumberland* I (Vacant).
ELLINGHAM, LITTLE (St Pet), w Ellingham, Great (St Jas), *Norf.* R. D Nor 18 P *Bp* I D H ELTON.
ELLINGTON (All SS), *Cambs.* V. D Ely 11 P *Peterho Cam* I M A JENNER *p-in-c.*
ELLISFIELD (St Martin) w Farleigh Wallop (St Andr) and Dummer (All S), *Hants.* R. D Win 3 P *Dioc Bd of Patr* I T F KIME.
ELLISTOWN (St Chris), *Leics.* V. D Leic 11 P *Bp* I J E SCOTT.
ELLOUGH (All SS) w Weston, and Henstead, *Suff.* R. D St E 14 *See* Sotterley.
ELLOUGHTON (St Mary Virg) and Brough w Brantingham, *Humb.* V. D York 16 P *Abp and D and C of Dur* jointly I M ANKER.
ELM (All SS), *Cambs.* V. D Ely 20 P *Bp* I (Vacant).
ELM (St Mary), *Somt.* R. D B & W 16a *See* Mells.
ELM PARK (St Nich), *Essex..* D Chelmsf *See* Hornchurch.
ELMBRIDGE (St Mary) w Rushock (St Mich AA), R *Worcs.* V. D Worc 8 *See* Elmley Lovett.
ELMDON (St Nich) w Wenden Lofts and Strethall, *Essex.* R. D Chelmsf 27 P *MMT and Dioc Bd of Patr* I J D R RAWLINGS.
ELMDON (St Nich) w Bickenhill (St Pet), *W Midl.* R. D Birm 11 *See* Bickenhill.
ELMERS END, *Kent..* D Roch *See* Beckenham.
ELMHAM, NORTH (BVM) w Billingford (St Pet), *Norf.* V. D Nor 20 P *Bp and Earl of Leic* alt I A D DERISLEY.
ELMHAM, SOUTH (St Jas w All SS and St Mich), *Suff..* D St E *See* Rumburgh.
(St Cross). D St E 14 *See* Homersfield.
(St Marg w St Pet). D St E *See* Flixton.
ELMLEY CASTLE (St Mary) w Netherton and Bricklehampton (St Mich AA) and Comberton, Great (St Mich), w Comberton, Little (St Pet), *Worcs.* V. D Worc 3 P *Bp* I J A DALE *p-in-c.*
ELMLEY LOVETT (St Mich) w Hampton Lovett and Elmbridge (St Mary) w Rushock, *Worcs.* R. D Worc 8 P *Ch Coll Cam and Bp (alt)* I N H ATTY.
ELMORE (St Jo Bapt) w Longney, *Glos..* D Glouc 9 P *Archd of Glouc and Ld Chan* I L S BRUCE *p-in-c.*
ELMSALL, NORTH, *W Yorks..* D Wakef 11 *See* South Kirkby.
ELMSALL, SOUTH (St Mary Virg), *W Yorks..* D Wakef 11 P *Bp* I D M RIPPINGALE.
ELMSETT (St Pet) w Aldham (St Mary), *Suff.* R. D St E 3 P *Bp and Mart Mem and C of E Trust* I H G HARRISON P-IN-C OF KERSEY *p-in-c.*
ELMSTEAD (St Ann and St Laur), *Essex.* V. D Chelmsf 25 P *Jes Coll Cam* I M C S BEVER *p-in-c.*
ELMSTED, (St Jas Gt), w Hastingleigh (St Mary Virg), *Kent.* V. D Cant 2 P *Abp* I D WALKER.
ELMSTHORPE (St Mary), *Leics.* R. D Leic 16 *See* Earl Shilton.
ELMSTONE HARDWICKE (St Mary Magd), *Glos.* V. D Glouc 11 *See* Swindon.
ELMSTONE (Dedic unknown) w Preston-next-Wingham (St Mildred) and Stourmouth, *Kent.* V. D Cant 1 P *Ld Fitzwalter and D and C of Cant (alt)* I D W J SAMPSON.
ELMSWELL (St John), *Suff.* R. D St E 10 P *MMT* I J A C PERROTT.
ELMTON (St Pet) w Creswell (St Mary Magd), *Derbys.* V. D Derby 2 P *Bp* I (Vacant).
ELSDON (St Cuthb), *Northumb.* R. D Newc T 2 *See* Otterburn.
ELSECAR (H Trin), *S Yorks.* V. D Sheff 7 P *Earl Fitzwilliam* I A HALLIDIE SMITH.
ELSENHAM, *Essex.* V. D Chelmsf 26 P *Bp* I B R GREEN.
ELSFIELD (St Thos of Cant), *Oxon.* V. D Ox 5 P *Ch Ch Ox* I A G A DE VERE.
ELSHAM (All SS), *Humb.* V. D Linc 6 P *Bp* I D G TUCKER.
ELSING (St Mary Virg) w Bylaugh (St Mary), *Norf.* R. D Nor 6 P *Dioc Bd of Patr and Vice-Adm Sir E Evans-Lombe, RN* alt I P P K ROBIN.
ELSON (St Thos), *Hants.* V. D Portsm 1 P *Dioc Bd of Patr* I K W JACKSON.
ELSTEAD (St Jas), *Surrey.* R. D Guildf 4 P *Archd of Surrey* I J T MCDOWALL.
ELSTED (St Paul) w Didling (St Andr) and Treyford (St Pet), *W Sussex.* R. D Chich 5 P *Bp* I R M KENNARD *hon c.*
ELSTERNWICK, *Humb..* D York *See* Humbleton.
ELSTON (All SS), *Notts.* R. D Southw 3 P *Mrs Vivian Kindersley* I G A FIRTH.
ELSTOW (St Mary and St Helen), *Beds.* V. D St Alb 19 P *S Whitbread Esq* I M J M NORTON, D G PRESTON *hon c.*
ELSTREE (St Nich), *Herts.* R. D St Alb 1 P *Ld Chan* I W J ELLIOTT.
ELSWICK, *Northumb..* D Newc T 5b *See* Newcastle upon Tyne.
ELSWORTH (H Trin) w Knapwell, *Cambs.* R. D Ely 1 P *Bp 4 turns, Crown 1 turn* I H A MOSEDALE.
ELTHAM (St Jo Bapt), *Kent.* V. D S'wark 17 P *Dioc Bd of Patr* I P V L JOHNSTONE, E W M KELLY *c.*
(H Trin), V. D S'wark 17 P *Bp* I C LOWSON, N E DAVIES *hon c.*

(St Barn Well Hall), V. D S'wark 17 P *Bp* I J E NEAL *p-in-c*.
(St Luke, Well Hall), V. D S'wark 17 P *Bp* I M A HART.
(St Pet Lee), V. D S'wark 17 P *Bp* I (Vacant).
(St Sav), V. D S'wark 17 P *Bp* I R H WINTERS.
NEW (All SS), V. D S'wark 17 P *Bp* I E B WOOD, M C JOHNSON *c*, M J KINGSTON *c*.
ELTISLEY (St Pandionia and St Jo Bapt), *Cambs.*. D Ely 1 *See* Croxton.
ELTON (All SS), *Derbys*. R. D Derby 17 P *PCC* I K E SERVANTE P-IN-C SOUTH DARLEY *p-in-c*.
ELTON, *Herefs*.. D Heref *See* Downton.
ELTON, *Cleve*. R. D Dur 14 P *St Chad's Coll Dur* I (Vacant).
ELTON (All SS), *Cambs*. R. D Ely 14 P *Sir Richard Proby Bt* I P O POOLEY.
ELTON, *Gtr Man*.. D Man *See* Bury.
ELTON-ON-THE-HILL (St Mich AA), *Notts*. R. D Southw 9 *See* Granby.
ELVASTON (St Bart) w Thurlaston and Ambaston, *Derbys*. V. D Derby 15 *See* Shardlow.
ELVEDEN or ELDEN (St Andr and St Patr), *Suff*. R. D St E 11 P *Earl of Iveagh* I K S DOBSON.
ELVETHAM, *Hants*. R. D Win 4 *See* Hartley Wintney.
ELVINGTON (H Trin) w Sutton-on-Derwent (St Mich AA) and East Cottingwith, *Humb*. R. D York 6 P *Mrs M B E Darlington and Visc St Vincent (alt)* I R A HALL, D W GOODWIN *hon c*.
ELWICK HALL (St Pet), *Cleve*. R. D Dur 12 *See* Hart.
ELWORTH (St Pet) w Warmingham (St Leon), *Chesh*. V. D Ches 11 P *V of Sandbach, Q H Crewe, J C Crewe* I I O JONES.
ELY (H Trin w St Mary and St Pet w St Etheldreda), *Cambs*. V. D Ely 15 P *D and C of Ely* I N MUNT, D J DALES *c*, A G F VILLER *c*.
EMBERTON (All SS) w Tyringham (St Pet) and Filgrave, *Bucks*. R. D Ox 28 *See* Clifton Reynes.
EMBLETON (or Emildon) (H Trin) w Craster and Newton and Rennington w Rock, *Northumb*. V. D Newc T 7 P *Mert Coll Ox* I C TURNBULL.
EMBLETON (St Cuthb) w Wythop (St Marg), *Cumb*.. D Carl *See* Cockermouth.
EMBSAY (St Mary virg), w Eastby, *N Yorks*. V. D Bradf 10 P *R of Skipton* I R R BARRETT.
EMERY DOWN (Ch Ch), *Hants*. V. D Win 9 *See* Lyndhurst.
EMLEY (St Mich), *W Yorks*. R. D Wakef 7 P *Ld Savile* I E O ROBERTS.
EMMINGTON (St Nich), *Oxon*. R. D Ox 1 *See* Chinnor.
EMNETH (St Edm K and Mart), *Norf*. V. D Ely 20 P *Bp* I J R SANSOM *p-in-c*.
EMPINGHAM (St Pet), *Leics*. R. D Pet 12 P *Bp* I RT REV J P BURROUGH.
EMPSHOTT, *Hants*.. D Portsm *See* Greatham.
EMSCOTE (All SS), *Warws*.. D Cov 11 *See* Warwick.
EMSWORTH (St Jas), *Hants*. R. D Portsm 3 *See* Warblington.
ENBORNE w Hamstead Marshall, *Berks*. R. D Ox *See* Woodhay, West.
ENDERBY w Lubbesthorpe (St Jo Bapt), *Leics*. V. D Leic 13 P *Exors of G B Drummond* I G F GILL.
ENDON (St Luke) w Stanley, *Staffs*. V. D Lich 16 P *V of Leek* I A J ALBAN.
ENFIELD (St Andr), *Gtr Lon*. V. D Lon 21 P *Trin Coll Cam* I P B MORGAN, P J HARBORD *c*, H A WITTENBACH *c*, T B MURRAY *hon c*.
(Jesus Ch Forty-Hill), V. D Lon 21 P *V of Enfield* I (Vacant).
(St Geo), V. D Lon 21 P *Bp* I A C J ROGERS.
(St Jas Enfield Highway), V. D Lon 21 P *V of Enfield* I T P CHALLIS, J RYELAND *c*.
(St Jo Bapt Clay Hill), V. D Lon 21 P *V of Enfield* I (Vacant).
(St Luke, Clay Hill), V. D Lon 21 P *Bp* I M A SHEARMAN.
(St Mary Magd), V. D Lon 21 P *Bp* I J A SAMPFORD, C S SCOTT *c*.
(St Matt Ponders End), V. D Lon 21 P *V of Enfield* I E C CARDALE, W J LOWRY *c*.
(St Mich AA), V. D Lon 21 P *V of Enfield* I R J BROWN, D M DEWEY *hon c*.
(St Pet and St Paul, Enfield Lock), V. D Lon 21 P *Bp* I F J SHEPHERD, D H GOODBURN *c*.
(St Giles Conv Distr). D Lon 21 I (Vacant).
See also BUSH HILL PARK..
ENFORD (All SS), *Wilts*. V. D Sarum 18 *See* Netheravon.
ENGLEFIELD (St Mark), *Berks*.. D Ox 12 *See* Theale.
ENGLEFIELD GREEN (St Jude), *Surrey*. V. D Guildf 7 P *Bp* I R E FALKNER.
ENGLISHCOMBE, or INGLESCOMBE (St Pet), *Avon*.. D B & W *See* Bath (St Barn, Twerton Hill).
ENHAM ALAMEIN (St Geo), *Hants*.. D Win 2 *See* Smannell.
ENMORE (St Mich) w Goathurst (St Edw K and Mart), *Somt*.. D B & W *See* Spaxton.
ENMORE GREEN, *Dorset*. R. D Sarum 13 *See* Shaston.
ENNERDALE (St Mary), *Cumb*. V. D Carl 12 *See* Lamplugh.
ENNISMORE GARDENS (All SS). D Lon 19 *See* Westminster.
ENSBURY (St Thos), *Dorset*. V. D Sarum 14 P *Bp* I J G B MORGAN.
ENSTONE (St Kenelm) w Heythrop (St Nich), *Oxon*. V. D Ox 3 P *Bp* I N D J CARNE.
ENVILLE (St Mary BV), *Staffs*. R. D Lich 7 P *Mrs E Bissell* I A A COLLINS *p-in-c*.
EPPERSTONE (H Cross), *Notts*. R. D Southw 13 P *Bp and Commdr M B P Franklin* I J E O CHANDLER.
EPPING (St Jo Bapt), *Essex*. V. D Chelmsf 2 P *Dioc Bd of Patr* I A J ABBEY.
EPPING UPLAND (All SS), *Essex*. V. D Chelmsf 2 P *Exors of Miss Marter and Bp* I C F J BARD *p-in-c*.
EPPLETON (All SS), *T & W*. V. D Dur 5 P *Crown* I J J STEPHENSON.
EPSOM (St Martin and St John), *Surrey*. V. D Guildf 9 P *Bp* I A G SHRIVES, P S KNIGHT *c*, M C PRESTON *c*, M D RANKEN *c*.
(Ch Ch), V. D Guildf 9 P *Bp* I M J C WILSON, W H MCLEES *c*.
(St Barn), V. D Guildf 9 P *Bp* I M F H GODWIN, J B APPLETON *c*.
EPWELL (St Anne) w Sibford Swalcliffe and Tadmarton, *Oxon*. V. D Ox 6 P *Worc Coll Ox (1 turn) New Coll Ox (2 turns)* I T WIMBUSH, N W RICHARDS *c*.
EPWORTH (St Andr), *Humb*. R. D Linc 1 P *Crown* I A MAKEL.
ERDINGTON (St Barn), *W Midl*. V. D Birm 7 P *Aston Trustees* I R D C WHITEMAN, J P SHEEHY *c*.
(All SS Gravelly Hill), V. D Birm 7 P *Bp* I B M DODDS, H SMITH *c*.
(St Chad), V. D Birm 7 P *Bp* I L A GREEN.
(St Mary, Pype Hayes), V. D Birm 7 P *Trustees* I P J GILL.
ERGHAM, *Humb*.. D York *See* Grindale.
ERIDGE GREEN (H Trin), *E Sussex*. V. D Chich 20 *See* Frant.
ERISWELL (St Pet), *Suff*. R. D St E 13 P *Earl of Iveagh* I K S DOBSON.
ERITH (St Jo Bapt), *Kent*. V. D Roch 15 P *Bp* I R C BUNYAN.
(Ch Ch), V. D Roch 15 P *Bp* I G S TYERS, N JACKSON *c*.
(St Paul, Northumberland Heath), V. D Roch 15 P *CPAS* I J R BALCH, I H MURRAY *c*.
ERLESTOKE (H Sav) w Cheverell Magna (St Pet), *Wilts*. V. D Sarum 23 P *Trustees* I (Vacant).
ERMINGTON (St Pet and St Paul), *Devon*. V. D Ex 21 P *Crown and Bp* alt I R T COX.
ERPINGHAM (St Mary) w Calthorpe (St Marg), *Norf*. R. D Nor 3 P *Bp, CPAS and Gt Hosp Nor in turn* I D A POPE *p-in-c*.
ERWARTON (St Mary), *Suff*.. D St E *See* Shotley.
ERYHOLME (St Mary), *N Yorks*. V. D Ripon 1 P *V of Gilling* I (Vacant).
ESCOMB (St Jo Evang), *Durham*. V. D Dur 9 P *Bp* I N M J W BEDDOW.
ESCOT (St Phil and St Jas), *Devon*. V. D Ex 7 P *Sir J Kennaway Bt* I O R TENNANT.
ESCRICK (St Helen) and Stillingfleet w Naburn, *N Yorks*. R. D York P *Hon Mrs I C Forbes-Adam, D and C of York and Abp* I G D HARRIS.
ESH (St Mich AA) w Langley Park (All SS), *Durham*. V. D Dur 7 P *Crown* I P M HOOD.
ESHER (Ch Ch), *Surrey*. R. D Guildf 8 P *Wadh Coll Ox* I D E BENTLEY, C R F COHEN *c*, E W BUGDEN *hon c*.
ESHOLT (St Paul), *W Yorks*. V. D Bradf 5 P *Lt Col R E Crompton, MBE* I (Vacant).
ESKDALE (St Cath) Irton, Muncaster and Waberthwaite, *Cumb*. V. D Carl 12 P *Bp, Sir G W Pennington-Ramsden, Bt, and Five Trustees* I R H GURNEY.
ESKDALESIDE or SLEIGHTS (St Jo Evang) w Ugglebarnby (All SS) and Sneaton, *N Yorks*. V. D York 27 P *Abp* I M D A DYKES.
ESSENDINE (St Mary Virg), *Leics*. V. D Pet 13 *See* Ryhall.
ESSENDON (St Mary Virg), *Herts*. R. D St Alb 8 *See* Berkhamsted, Little.
ESSINGTON (St Jo Evang), *Staffs*. V. D Lich 12 P *Bp & Simeon Trustees* I (Vacant).

FACCOMBE (St Barn), *Hants*. R. D Win 2 *See* Hurstbourne Tarrant.
FACEBY (St Mary Magd), *N Yorks*.. D York *See* Whorlton.
FACIT (St Jo Evang), *Lancs*. V. D Man 17 P *Bp* I A J HOWELL.
FAILAND, *Avon*.. D B & W *See* Wraxall.
FAILSWORTH (St Jo Evang), *Gtr Man*. R. D Man 15 P *Crown and Bp* alt I J D QUANCE.
(H Trin), R. D Man 15 P *Crown and Bp* alt I W P EVANS.
(H Family), R. D Man 15 P *Bp* I R COOKE.
FAIRBURN, *N Yorks*.. D York *See* Ledsham.
FAIRFIELD, *Cumb*.. D Liv *See* Liverpool.
FAIRFIELD (St Pet), *Derbys*. V. D Derby 10 P *Six Trustees* I R S CANEY.
FAIRFIELD, *E Sussex*.. D Cant *See* Brookland.
FAIRFIELD, *Humb*.. D Linc 9 *See* Scartho.
FAIRFIELD (St Mark), *Worcs*.. D Worc 11 *See* Belbroughton.
FAIRFIELD (St Richard's Conv Distr), *Worc*.. D Worc 1 P *Bp* I (Vacant).
FAIRFORD (St Mary Virg), *Glos*. V. D Glouc 14 P *D and C of Glouc* I D M BELL-RICHARDS.
FAIRHAVEN (St Paul), *Lancs*. V. D Blackb 9 P *H T de Vere Clifton Esq* I J GREEN.
FAIRLIGHT (St Andr), *E Sussex*. V. D Chich 22 P *MMT* I R F GIBSON.
FAIR OAK (St Thos), *Hants*. V. D Win 15 P *Bp* I K M BELL.
FAIRSTEAD (St Mary) w Terling (All SS), V *Essex*. R. D Chelmsf 29 P *Ld Rayleigh* I A J LANGTON-DURHAM (FORMERLY DURHAM).
FAIRWARP (Ch Ch), *E Sussex*. V. D Chich 16 P *Bp* I J A COTTON.
FAIRWEATHER GREEN (St Sav), *Yorks*. V. D Bradf 1 P *Bp* I P AINSWORTH.
FAIRWELL or FAREWELL (St Bart), *Staffs*. V. D Lich 2 P *MMT* I W E HASSALL.
FAKENHAM (St Pet and St Paul) *Norf*. R. D Nor 21 P *Trin Coll Cam* I H F BUCKINGHAM, R J DIXON *hon c*.
FAKENHAM, GREAT and LITTLE, *Suff*.. D St E *See* Euston.
FALCONHURST (St Leon), *Kent*. R. D Cant 12 P *E Wood Esq* I (Vacant).
FALDINGWORTH (All SS), w Buslingthorpe (St Mich), *Lincs*. R. D Linc 5 P *Dioc Bd of Patr 3 turns, Govs of Charterho 2 turns* I A G D SHEARWOOD *c-in-c*.
FALFIELD (St Geo) w Rockhampton (St Osw), *Avon*. V. D Glouc 8 P *Archd of Glouc and others 1st, 2nd and 4th turns, Rev J F W Leigh and others 3rd turn* I R A WATERSON *p-in-c*.
FALINGE (St Edm), *Gtr Man*.. D Man 17 *See* Rochdale.
FALKENHAM (St Ethelbert), *Suff*. V. D St E 2 *See* Kirton.
FALKINGHAM, *Lincs*.. D Linc *See* Folkingham.
FALLOWFIELD Gtr Man. R D Man 5 *See* Birch-in-Rusholme.
FALMER, *E Sussex*.. D Chich *See* Stanmer.
FALMOUTH (K Chas Mart), *Cornw*. R. D Truro 3 P *Bp* I W J P BOYD, G E WRIGHT *hon c*.
(All SS), V. D Truro 3 P *Bp* I A E A MURRAY-STONE.
FALSTONE, *Northumb*. R. D Newc T *See* Bellingham-Otterburn.
FAMBRIDGE, NORTH, *Essex*.. D Chelmsf *See* Latchingdon.
FAMBRIDGE, SOUTH (All SS), *Essex*. R. D Chelmsf 16 *See* Ashingdon.
FANGFOSS, *Humb*.. D York *See* Barmby Moor.
FAR COTTON, *Northants*.. D Pet 7 *See* Northampton (St Mary).
FAR FOREST (H Trin), *Worcs*. V. D Worc 10 *See* Rock.
FAR HEADINGLEY, *W Yorks*.. D Ripon 10 *See* Headingley, Far.
FARCET (St Mary), *Cambs*.. D Ely *See* Stanground.
FAREHAM (St Pet and St Paul) w Funtley and Crocker Hill, *Hants*. V. D Portsm 1 P *Bp* I L F CHADD, A GORDON *c*.
(H Trin w St Columba), R. D Portsm 1 P *Bp* I B L H CARPENTER, B A SAUNDERS *team v*, K I UPHILL *team v*, H J DIMMER *c*, E T JONES *c*.
(St Jo Evang), V. D Portsm 1 P *CPAS* I J M C COLBOURN.
FARFORTH, *Lincs*.. D Linc 7 *See* Ruckland.
FARINGDON (All SS) w Coxwell, Little (St Mary), *Oxon*. V. D Ox 17 P *Simeon Trustees* I J WHITTAKER.
FARINGDON (or Farringdon) (All SS), *Hants*.. D Win 1 *See* Chawton.
FARINGDON, LITTLE (Dedic unknown), *Oxon*. V. D Ox 9 *See* Langford.
FARINGTON (St Paul), *Lancs*. V. D Blackb 6 P *V of Penwortham* I R A MOORE.
FARLAM (St Thos of Cant) and Nether Denton *Cumb*. V. D Carl 2 P *Bp* I C JONES.
FARLEIGH-HUNGERFORD (St Leon) w Tellisford (All SS), *Somt*. R. D B & W 16a *See* Rode Major.
FARLEIGH, *Surrey*.. D S'wark *See* Warlingham.
FARLEIGH, EAST (St Mary) and Coxheath, *Kent*. V. D Roch 6 P *Ld Chan* I C J CALEY.
FARLEIGH WALLOP (St Andr), *Hants*. R. D Win 3 *See* Ellisfield.
FARLEIGH, WEST (All SS), *Kent*. V. D Roch 6 *See* Teston.
FARLESTHORPE (St Andr), *Lincs*. V. D Linc 8 *See* Bilsby.
FARLEY-CHAMBERLAYNE (St John) w Braishfield, V *Hants*. R. D Win *See* Michelmersh.
FARLEY (All SS) w Pitton (St Pet), *Wilts*. V. D Sarum 17 P *Trustees* I D M HART *p-in-c*.
FARLEY HILL, *Beds*.. D St Alb *See* Luton.
FARLINGTON (St Andr), *Hants*. R. D Portsm 3 P *Dr A Leatherdale and Mrs Brooks* I J R PILKINGTON.
FARLINGTON, *N Yorks*.. D York *See* Stillington.
FARLOW (St Giles), *Salop*. V. D Heref 9 P *Bp* I (Vacant).
FARMBOROUGH (All SS) w Priston (St Luke), *Avon*. R. D B & W 13 P *MMT and W Vaughan-Jenkins Esq* I R F H HINE.
FARMCOTE (St Faith), *Glos*. V. D Glouc 16 *See* Guiting Power.
FARMINGTON (St Pet), *Glos*. R. D Glouc 15 *See* Northleach.
FARNBOROUGH (All SS) w Ilsley, West (All SS), *Berks*.. D Ox *See* Wantage Downs.
FARNBOROUGH (Par Ch dedic unknown), *Hants*. R. D Guildf 1 P *CPAS* I P M RENOUF, G R W HALL *c*, J H LANGSTAFF *c*.
SOUTH (St Mark), V. D Guildf 1 P *Bp* I P H GATES.
FARNBOROUGH (St Giles the Abbot), *Kent*. R. D Roch 16 P *Em Coll Cam* I J P DRUCE, M G GRIBBLE *c*, G W JOHNSON *c*.
FARNBOROUGH (St Botolph), *Warws*.. D Cov 8 *See* Avon Dassett.
FARNCOMBE (St Jo Evang), *Surrey*. R. D Guildf 4 P *Bp* I D W HEDGES, B M LLEWELLYN *c*.
FARNDALE (St Nich also St Mary), *N Yorks*.. D York 20 *See* Kirkbymoorside.
FARNDISH, *Beds*.. D St Alb *See* Podington.
FARNDON (St Chad) and Coddington (St Mary), *Chesh*. V. D Ches 5 P *Duke of Westmr and D and C of Ches* I E BRIERLEY.
FARNDON (St Pet), *Notts*. V. D Southw 3 P *Ld Chan* I R BEARDALL.
FARNDON, EAST (St Jo Bapt), *Northants*. R. D Pet 6 *See* Oxenden.
FARNHAM, *Dorset*.. D Sarum *See* Tollard Royal.
FARNHAM (St Mary Virg), *Essex*. R. D Chelmsf 26 P *Lt-Col W D Gosling* I B W OTTAWAY *p-in-c*.
FARNHAM, *Suff*. V. D St E 19 *See* Blaxhall.
FARNHAM (St Andr), *Surrey*. R and V. D Guildf 3 P *Bp* I D C GRAY, M S KING *c*, P G PHILLIPS *c*.
FARNHAM (St Osw) w Scotton (St Thos Ap) and Staveley (All SS) and Copgrove (St Mich AA), *N Yorks*. V. D Ripon 4 P *Bp, Dioc Bd of Patr, MMT and Maj A J R Collins* I C C PEAKE.
FARNHAM-ROYAL (St Mary) w Hedgerley, *Bucks*. R. D Ox 24 P *Bp and Eton Coll* I T M STEEL, S F BEDWELL *c*, P R WADSWORTH *c*.
(St Mich Conv Distr). D Ox 24 *See* Slough, West.
(St Geo Britwell). D Ox 24 *See* Slough, West.
FARNINGHAM (St Pet and St Paul), *Kent*. R. D Roch 1a *See* Eynsford.
FARNLEY (St Mich AA), *N Yorks*. R. D Ripon 8 P *Bp* I (Vacant).
FARNLEY, *W Yorks*. V. D Bradf 5 *See* Leathley.
FARNLEY TYAS (St Lucius), *W Yorks*. V. D Wakef 5 P *Bp* I (Vacant).
FARNSFIELD (St Mich), *Notts*. V. D Southw 15 P *Bp* I G D MILLS.
FARNWORTH (St Luke formerly St Wilfrid), *Chesh*. V. D Liv 7 P *V of Prescot* I D POSTLES.
FARNWORTH (St John), *Gtr Man*. V. D Man 14 *See* East Farnworth.
(All SS), V. D Man 14 *See* East Farnworth.
(St Jas w St Geo New Bury), V. D Man 14 P *Bp* I W B ANDERSON, D R JONES *c*.
(St Pet), V. D Man *See* East Farnworth.
(St Steph Kearsley Moor), V. D Man 14 P *V of St John, Farnworth* I K F WAINWRIGHT.

(St Thos Dixon-Green), V. D Man 14 P *Bp* I H W ROBERTS.
FARRINGDON (St Pet), *Dorset*.. D Sarum 13 *See* Orchard East.
FARRINGDON (St Petrock and St Barn) *Devon*.. D Ex 1 *See* Clyst St Geo.
FARRINGDON (or Faringdon) (All SS), *Hants*.. D Win 1 *See* Chawton.
FARRINGTON GURNEY (St Jo Bapt), *Avon*. V. D B & W 16b P *Bp* I (Vacant).
FARSLEY (St Jo Evang), *W Yorks*. V. D Bradf 3 P *V of Calverley* I D BRIGGS.
FARTHINGHOE (St Mich) w Hinton-in-the-Hedges and Steane, *Northants*. R. D Pet 1 P *Ld Chan and Bp* I M BERRY.
FARTHINGSTONE (St Mary Virg), *Northants*.. D Pet 3 *See* Lichborough.
FARWAY (St Mich AA) w Northleigh (St Giles) and Southleigh (St Lawr), *Devon*.. D Ex 5 *See* Offwell.
FATFIELD (St Geo), *T & W*. V. D Dur 1 P *Earl of Dur* I A G RICHARDS.
FAULKBOURNE (St German), *Essex*. R. D Chelmsf 29 *See* Notley, White.
FAULS (H Em), *Salop*. V. D Lich 27 P *Bp* I W A HUMPHREYS.
FAVERSHAM (St Mary of Charity), *Kent*. V. D Cant 7 P *D and C of Cant* I G R D MANLEY.
FAWKENHURST (St Leon), *Kent*.. D Cant 12 *See* Falconhurst.
FAWKHAM (St Mary Virg), *Kent*. R. D Roch 1 P *D and C of Roch* I A C FORD.
FAWLER, *Oxon*.. D Ox *See* Finstock.
FAWLEY (St Mary Virg), *Berks*. V. D Ox 19 *See* Brightwalton.
FAWLEY (St Mary Virg), *Bucks*. R. D Ox *See* Hambleden Valley.
FAWLEY (All SS), *Hants*. R. D Win 9 P *Bp* I C R RICH, N C VENNING *c*.
FAWLEY, *Herefs*.. D Heref *See* Brockhampton.
FAWSLEY (St Mary), *Northants*. V. D Pet 3 *See* Charwelton.
FAXFLEET, *Humb*.. D York 16 *See* Broomfleet.
FAXTON (St Dewy's), *Northants*. R. D Pet 6 *See* Lamport.
FAZAKERLEY (Em Ch w St Geo Sparrow Hall and St Paul), *Mer*. V. D Liv 5 P *Dioc Bd of Patr* I A V DOUGLAS *team v*, M I STOCKLEY *team v*. *See also* WALTON-ON-THE-HILL..
FAZELEY (St Paul), *Staffs*. V. D Lich 6 P *Bp* I K P HALLETT.
FEATHERSTON, SOUTH, *W Yorks*.. D Wakef 11 *See* Purston.
FEATHERSTONE (All SS), *W Yorks*. V. D Wakef 11 P *Ch Ch Ox* I E CHEETHAM.
FECKENHAM (St Jo Bapt) w Bradley (St Jo Bapt), *Worcs*. R. D Worc 8 P *Bp* I H S BILL.
FEERING (All SS), *Essex*. V. D Chelmsf 21 P *Bp* I A R MOODY.
FELBRIDGE (St Jo Div), *Surrey*. V. D S'wark 10 P *Dioc Bd of Patr* I S G BOWEN.
FELBRIGG w Metton (St Andr) and Sustead (St Pet and St Paul), *Norf*. R. D Nor *See* Roughton.
FELIXKIRK (St Felix) w Boltby (H Trin), *N Yorks*. V. D York 26 P *Abp* I W C SLADE.
FELIXSTOWE (St Pet and St Paul) w (St Andr), *Suff*. V. D St E 2 P *Ch Trust Fund Trust* I M H BATEMAN.
(St Jo Bapt), V. D St E 2 P *Bp* I K FRANCIS, C J N GATES *hon c*.
FELKIRK (St Pet) w Brierley, *W Yorks*. V. D Wakef 8 P *Bp* I J COWPERTHWAITE.
FELLING (Ch Ch), *T & W*. V. D Dur 4 P *CPAS* I (Vacant).
FELMERSHAM (St Mary) *Beds*. V. D St Alb 21 P *Bp* I (Vacant).
FELMINGHAM, (St Andr), *Norf*. R. D Nor 8 P *Bp* I W M C BESTELINK.
FELPHAM (St Mary), V w Middleton (St Nich), *W Sussex*. R. D Chich 1 P *D and C of Chich* I J H GROWNS, I E MORRISON *c*.
FELSHAM (St Pet) w Gedding, *Suff*. R. D St E *See* Bradfield St George.
FELSTED (H Cross), *Essex*. V. D Chelmsf 19 P *CPAS* I L J VICK.
FELTHAM (St Dunstan) *Gtr Lon*. V. D Lon 10 P *Bp* I C L SENTANCE, A H BURLTON *c*, M J COLLETT *c*.
FELTHORPE (St Marg), *Norf*. R. D Nor *See* Drayton.
FELTON (St Mich Arch) and Preston Wynne, *Herefs*.. D Heref *See* Bodenham.
FELTON (St Mich AA), *Northumb*. V. D Newc T 7 P *Bp* I D J SMITH.
FELTON COMMON or FELTON WINFORD (St Cath), *Avon*. V. D B & W 15 P *Mrs D Pullman* I R E HICKES.
FELTWELL (St Mary), *Norf*. R. D Ely 16 P *Bp* I S W DAVIES.
FEN-DITTON (St Mary Virg), *Cambs*. R. D Ely 6 P *Bp* I L A MARSH.
FEN-DRAYTON (St Mary) w Conington, *Cambs*. V. D Ely 5 P *Crown and Ch Coll Cam* I H BAMBER *p-in-c*.
FEN-OTTERY, *Devon*.. D Ex *See* Tipton.
FENBY, *Humb*.. D Linc 10 *See* Ashby.
FENCE-IN-PENDLE (St Anne), *Lancs*. V. D Blackb 6a P *Ld Chan* I R A HALE.
FENHAM (H Cross), *Northumb*. V. D Newc T 5 P *Bp* I W A GOFTON, M A CUMING *c*, A FEATHERSTONE *c*.
FENISCLIFFE (St Francis), *Lancs*. V. D Blackb 5 P *Bp* I R NICHOLSON.
FENISCOWLES (Immanuel), *Lancs*. V. D Blackb 5 P *V of Blackb* I A E BLAND.
FENITON (St Andr), *Devon*. R. D Ex 7 P *G W L Courtenay Esq* I R K R COATH.
FENNY BENTLEY (St Edw K and Mart) w Thorpe (St Leon) and Tissington (St Mary), *Derbys*. R. D Derby 8 P *Bp and A Cowdry Esq* I C H READ, D H SANSUM P-IN-C OF THORPE.
FENNY COMPTON (St Pet and St Clare), *Warws*.. D Cov 8 *See* Avon Dassett.
FENNY DRAYTON (St Mich AA), *Leics*. R. D Leic 16 *See* Higham-on-the-Hill.
FENNY STRATFORD (St Martin) and Water Eaton (St Frideswide), *Bucks*. R. D Ox 26 P *Bp* I P M HICKLEY, D G EVERETT *team v*.
FENSTANTON (St Pet and St Paul), *Cambs*. V. D Ely 10 P *Bp* I W N C GIRARD, D W VALENTINE *hon c*.
FENTON, *Lincs*.. D Linc 23 *See* Beckingham.
FENTON (Ch Ch w St Mich AA), *Staffs*. V. D Lich 18 P *R of Stoke-on-Trent* I A D COX *c*.
FENWICK, *S Yorks*.. D Sheff 8 *See* Moss.
FEOCK D Truro 6 *See* St Feock.
FERNHAM, *Oxon*.. D Ox *See* Longcot.
FERNHURST (St Marg), *W Sussex*. V. D Chich 5 P *Cowdray Trust Ltd* I C J HANKINS.
FERNILEE (H Trin), *Derbys*. V. D Ches 16 *See* Taxal.
FERRIBY, NORTH (All SS), *Humb*. V. D York 17 P *V of H Trin Hull* I D J BULMAN, M A LOWE *c*.
FERRIBY, SOUTH (St Nich), *Humb*. R. D Linc 6 P *Bp* I I H TINKLER.
FERRING (St Andr), *W Sussex*. V. D Chich 9 P *D and C of Chich* I R D T PATERSON.
FERRY, EAST, *Lincs*.. D Linc 4 *See* Scotter.
FERRY FRYSTON (St Andr), *W Yorks*. V. D Wakef 11 P *D and C of York* I E D ALLISON.
FERRYHILL (St Luke Evang w St Osw St Columb St Aid and St Cuthb), *Durham*. V. D Dur 12a P *D and C of Dur* I P A BALDWIN.
FERSFIELD (St Andr), *Norf*. R (*See Winfarthing Group*).. D Nor *See* Bressingham.
FETCHAM (St Mary), *Surrey*. R. D Guildf 10 P *Bp* I D W BRYANT.
FEWCOT (All SS), *Oxon*. V. D Ox 2 *See* Ardley.
FEWSTON w Blubberhouses (St Mich and St Andr), *N Yorks*. V. D Bradf 5 P *Bp* I K FAWCETT.
FIDDINGTON (St Martin), *Somt*.. D B & W 18 *See* Stoke Courcy.
FIELD BROUGHTON (St Pet), *Cumb*. V. D Carl 14 *See* Lindale-in-Cartmel.
FIELD-DALLING (St Andr) w Saxlingham (St Marg), *Norf*. V. D Nor 24 P *Bp and Keble Coll Ox* alt I W M BROWN *p-in-c*.
FIFEHEAD MAGDALEN Dorset. V D Sarum 13 *See* Gillingham.
FIFEHEAD-NEVILLE (All SS), W Fifehead St Quintin, *Dorset*. R. D Sarum 13 *See* Hazelbury-Bryan.
FIFIELD (St Jo Bapt) w Idbury (St Nich), *Oxon*. R. D Ox *See* Shipton-under-Wychwood.
FIFIELD BAVANT (St Martin), *Wilts*. R. D Sarum 19 *See* Ebbesbourne Wake.
FIGHELDEAN (St Mich AA) w Milston and Brigmerston, *Wilts*. V. D Sarum 18 P *Bp and Sec of State for Defence* alt I M H DAWKINS *p-in-c*.
FILBY (All SS) w Thrigby w Mautby (St Pet and St Paul) w Stokesby, Herringby and Runham, *Norf*. R. D Nor P *Bp, I F M Lucas Esq, R T Daniel Esq, Archd of Nor and Miss Z K Daniel* I M HALL.
FILEY (St Osw K and Mart w St John), *N Yorks*. V. D York 18 P *PCC* I W F H CURTIS.
FILGRAVE (St Pet), *Bucks*. R. D Ox 28 *See* Emberton.

FILKINS (St Pet) w Bradwell, Broughton, Kelmscott and Kencot, *Oxon*. V. **D** Ox 9 **P** *Bp, Ch S Trust, F R Goodenough Esq and S K H Goodenough Esq* **I** A J BURDON.
FILLEIGH (St Paul) w East Buckland (St Mich), *Devon*.. **D** Ex *See* South Molton.
FILLINGHAM Lincs. R **D** Linc 3 *See* Ingham.
FILLONGLEY (St Mary and All SS), *Warws*. V. **D** Cov 5 **P** *Bp* **I** J F LAW *p-in-c*.
FILTON or FYLTON (St Pet), *Avon*. R. **D** Bris 4 **P** *Bp* **I** J M HENTON, J F JENKINS *c*.
FIMBER (St Mary Virg), *Humb*. V. **D** York 13 *See* Fridaythorpe.
FINBOROUGH MAGNA (St Andr) w Onehouse and Harleston, *Suff*. V. **D** St E 6 **P** *Bp* **I** H WAKE.
FINBOROUGH PARVA (St Mary), *Suff*. V. **D** St E *See* Hitcham.
FINCHAM (St Martin w St Mich) w Boughton West Dereham and Wereham Marham Shouldham and Shouldham Thorpe, *Norf*. R. **D** Ely 17 **P** *Bp* **I** E BATY, J D SMITH *c*.
FINCHAMPSTEAD (St Jas), *Berks*. R. **D** Ox 16 **P** *Dioc Bd of Patr* **I** D T CROSSLEY.
FINCHINGFIELD w Cornish Hall End (St Jo Evang), *Essex*. V. **D** Chelmsf 19 **P** *D G Ryder Esq and Bp* **I** P H JONES.
FINCHLEY (St Mary), *Gtr Lon*. R. **D** Lon 16 **P** *Bp* **I** P L BROCK, C W M AITKEN *c*, P M FLYNN *c*, S D HAINES *c*, D W A STRIDE *hon c*.
(All SS), V. **D** Lon 16 **P** *Bp* **I** T CUNNINGHAM-BURLEY, K D MOULE *c*.
(Ch Ch), V. **D** Lon 16 **P** *CPS* **I** P N L PYTCHES, E P J FOSTER *c*.
(H Trin), V. **D** Lon 16 **P** *Bp* **I** L B HILL, R H JORDAN *c*.
(St Barn Woodside Park), V. **D** Lon 16 **P** *CPS* **I** J S H COLES, D W C ROBINSON *c*.
(St Luke), V. **D** Lon 16 **P** *CPS* **I** F SEARS.
(St Paul, Long Lane), V. **D** Lon 16 **P** *Simeon Trustees* **I** F SEARS *c-in-c*.
FINDERN (All SS), *Derbys*. V. **D** Derby 16 **P** *Bp* **I** L N HEDGES.
FINDON (St Jo Bapt), *W Sussex*. V. **D** Chich 9 **P** *Bp* **I** E R GILLIES.
FINEDON (St Mary Virg), *Northants*. V. **D** Pet 9 **P** *Bp* **I** J P BEAUMONT.
FINGEST (St Bart), *Bucks*. V. **D** Ox *See* Hambleden Valley.
FINGHALL, *N Yorks*. R. **D** Ripon *See* Spennithorne.
FINGRINGHOE (St Andr), *Essex*. V. **D** Chelmsf 21 **P** *Bp* **I** R J HANDSCOMBE.
FINHAM (St Martin-in-the-fields), *W Midl*. V. **D** Cov 3 **P** *Bp* **I** P W SIMPSON, B R ROBERTS *c*.
FINMERE (St Mich) w Mixbury (All SS), *Oxon*. R. **D** Ox 2 **P** *Trustees 2 turns, Bp 1 turn* **I** A HICHENS *p-in-c*.
FINNINGHAM (St Bart) w Westhorpe (St Marg), *Suff*. R. **D** St E 6 **P** *Dioc Bd of Patr and Ch U* alt **I** H L MILES.
FINNINGLEY (H Trin and St Osw), *Notts*. R. **D** Southw 1 **P** *Dioc Bd of Patr* **I** P J POWLESLAND.
FINSBURY (St Clem) w (St Barn) City Road and (St Matt) King Square, *Lon*. V. **D** Lon 3 **P** *D and C of St Paul's* **I** J M SHIER.
See also CLERKENWELL, ST LUKE, AND SHOREDITCH..
FINSBURY PARK (St Thos), *Lon*. V. **D** Lon 3 **P** *Abp of Cant* **I** D H HUMPHREY.
FINSTALL (St Godwald), *Worcs*. V. **D** Worc 7 **P** *V of Stoke Prior* **I** D T TONGE *p-in-c*.
FINSTHWAITE (St Pet), *Cumb*.. **D** Carl *See* Leven Valley.
FINSTOCK (H Trin) w Fawler, *Oxon*. V. **D** Ox 3 **P** *V of Charlbury* **I** J C S NIAS.
FIRBANK (St Jo Evang) w Howgill (H Trin) and Killington (All SS), *Cumb*. V. **D** Bradf 7 **P** *V of Sedbergh and Ld Chan (alt)* **I** B W LEVICK.
FIRBECK (St Pet) w Letwell (St Pet), *S Yorks*. R. **D** Sheff 5 **P** *Bp* **I** J W A WOODS.
FIRLE, WEST (St Pet), w Beddingham (St Andr), *E Sussex*. V. **D** Chich 15 *See* Glynde.
FIRSBY (St Andr) w Great Steeping, R (All SS), *Lincs*. V. **D** Linc 7 **P** *Mrs J M Fox-Robinson* **I** J S THOROLD.
FIRSBY (St Jas), *Lincs*. R. **D** Linc 3 *See* Spridlington.
FIRTREE (St Mary Virg), *Durham*. V. **D** Dur 9 *See* Witton-le-Wear.
FIRVALE, *S Yorks*.. **D** Sheff *See* Sheffield.
FISHBOURNE, NEW (St Pet and St Mary), *W Sussex*. R. **D** Chich 3 **P** *Ld Chan* **I** G R C FOLLIS.
FISHERTON ANGER (St Paul), *Wilts*. R. **D** Sarum 16 *See* Salisbury.
FISHERTON-DELAMERE (St Nich), *Wilts*. V. **D** Sarum 21 *See* Wylye.
FISHLAKE (St Cuthb), *S Yorks*. V. **D** Sheff 9 **P** *D and C of Durham* **I** F BICKERTON.
FISHLEY (St Mary), *Norf*. V. **D** Nor 1 **P** *Bp* **I** K WILSON.
FISHPOND, *Dorset*.. **D** Sarum *See* Hawkchurch.
FISHPONDS (St Mary), *Avon*. R. **D** Bris 4 **P** *Bp* **I** B P BARNES, C F MOSELEY *hon c*.
(All SS), V. **D** Bris 7 **P** *Bp* **I** D J KETTLE *p-in-c*, K R BROWN *c*.
(St Jo Div), V. **D** Bris 7 **P** *Bp* **I** P P F WARD, K R BROWN *c*, G S PARFITT *c*.
FISHTOFT (St Guthlac), *Lincs*. R. **D** Linc 20 **P** *Dioc Bd of Patr* **I** G B WAGHORN.
FISKERTON (St Clem) w Reepham, *Lincs*. R. **D** Linc **P** *Mercers' Co D and C of Pet* **I** J C STEVENSON.
FISKERTON, *Notts*.. **D** Southw 15 *See* Rolleston.
FITTLETON (All SS), *Wilts*. R. **D** Sarum 18 *See* Netheravon.
FITTLEWORTH (St Mary), *W Sussex*. R. **D** Chich 6 **P** *D and C of Chich* **I** K HYDE-DUNN *p-in-c*.
FITZ (St Pet and St Paul), *Salop*.. **D** Lich 26 *See* Montford.
FITZHEAD (St Jas), *Somt*. R. **D** B & W *See* Milverton.
FIVEHEAD (St Martin) w Swell (St Cath), *Somt*. V. **D** B & W *See* Curry Rivel.
FLACKWELL HEATH **D** Ox 32 *See* Marlow, Little.
FLADBURY (St Jo Bapt) w Wyre Piddle and Moor (St Thos), *Worcs*. R. **D** Worc 3 **P** *Bp* **I** J O C CHAMPION, J H PARFITT *c*.
FLAMBOROUGH (St Osw), *Humb*. V. **D** York 12 **P** *Abp* **I** R G HIRST *p-in-c*.
FLAMSTEAD (St Leon), *Herts*. V. **D** St Alb 14 **P** *Univ Coll Ox* **I** P F BRADSHAW, D J KERR *c*, G H KING *c*.
FLAUNDEN (St Mary Magd), *Herts*.. **D** Ox 20 *See* Latimer.
FLAWBOROUGH (St Pet), *Notts*.. **D** Southw *See* Staunton.
FLAX-BOURTON (St Mich AA), *Avon*. R. **D** B & W 16 **P** *Ld Wraxall* **I** P R W TOMLINSON.
FLAXLEY (St Mary Virg), *Glos*. V. **D** Glouc 6 *See* Westbury-on-Severn.
FLAXTON (St Laur), *N Yorks*. R. **D** York 4 *See* Foston.
FLECKNEY (St Nich), *Leics*. V. **D** Leic 6 **P** *Bp* **I** B R GLOVER.
FLECKNOE (St Mark), *Worcs*.. **D** Cov 6 *See* Grandborough.
FLEDBOROUGH (St Gregory), *Notts*. R. **D** Southw 6 **P** *Dioc Bd of Patr* **I** J BROWN.
FLEET (All SS), *Hants*. V. **D** Guildf 1 **P** *Bp* **I** J P GRUNDY, L T ATHERTON *c*.
FLEET (H Trin), *Dorset*. V. **D** Sarum 6 *See* Chickerell.
FLEET (St Mary Magd), *Lincs*. R. **D** Linc 16 **P** *Dioc Bd of Patr* **I** (Vacant).
FLEET-MARSTON (St Mary Virg), *Bucks*. R. **D** Ox 29 *See* Waddesdon.
FLEETWOOD (St Pet), *Lancs*. V. **D** Blackb 9 **P** *Meynell Trustees* **I** G T S SOUTHGATE, W I CROMBIE *c*.
FLEMPTON (St Cath) w Hengrave and Lackford (St Lawr), *Suff*. R. **D** St E 13 **P** *Bp 1 turn, Mrs. V Gough and R W Gough Esq 1 turn* **I** L R PIZZEY *p-in-c*.
FLETCHAMSTEAD (St Jas), *W Midl*. V. **D** Cov 3 **P** *Bp* **I** N D BEAMER, R D BENNETT *c*.
FLETCHING (St Andr and St Mary Virg), *E Sussex*. V. **D** Chich 16 **P** *Abp* **I** J F ELSON.
FLETTON (St Marg), *Cambs*. R. **D** Ely 14 **P** *Earl Fitzwilliam* **I** K S S JAMAL.
FLIMBY (St Nich), *Cumb*. V. **D** Carl 11 **P** *Bp* **I** W F R BATSON.
FLIMWELL E Sussex. V **D** Chich 20 *See* Ticehurst.
FLINTHAM (St Aug of Cant) w Kneeton (St Helen), *Notts*. R. **D** Southw 9 **P** *C J Neal Esq and M T Hildyard Esq* **I** A CHAPPELL *p-in-c*, A HAYDOCK P-IN-C OF KNEETON.
FLITCHAM (BVM), *Norf*. V (*See Sandringham Group*). **D** Nor 23 **P** *HM the Queen* **I** (Vacant).
FLITTON (St Jo Bapt), *Beds*.. **D** St Alb *See* Pulloxhill.
FLITWICK (St Pet and St Paul w St Andr), *Beds*. V. **D** St Alb 15 **P** *Dioc Bd of Patr* **I** R O HUBBARD.
FLIXBOROUGH (All SS), *Humb*. R. **D** Linc 4 *See* Burton-on-Stather.
FLIXTON, *Suff*.. **D** Nor *See* Blundeston.
FLIXTON (St Mary) w Homersfield, S Elmham (St Marg, St Pet and St Cross), *Suff*. R. **D** St E 14 **P** *Maj-Gen Sir A H S Adair Bt 2 turns, Bp 1 turn 2 turns, Bp 1 turn* **I** P A SKOULDING.
FLIXTON (St Mich), *Gtr Man*. R. **D** Man 9 **P** *Bp* **I** T E KENNAUGH, N R LITHERLAND *c*, G B WHITE *c*.
(St John), V. **D** Man 9 **I** J A DEY, J HURST *c*.

FLOCKTON (St Jas Gt) w Denby Grange, *W Yorks.* V. D Wakef 7 P *Carter Trustees* I A CROW.
FLOOKBURGH (St Jo Bapt), *Cumb.* V. D Carl 14 P *H Cavendish Esq* I J H CAM.
FLORDON (St Mich AA), *Norf.* R. D Nor 13 P *Mrs I D Gilham and Ch Coll Cam* alt I (Vacant).
FLORE (All SS) w Dodford and Brockhall, *Northants.* V. D Pet 3 P *Ch Ch Ox and Bp (alt)* I J W LATHAM.
FLOWTON (St Mary), *Suff.* R. D St E 1 *See* Somersham.
FLUSHING (St Pet), *Cornw.*. D Truro 3 *See* Mylor.
FLYFORD FLAVEL Worcs. R D Worc *See* Upton Snodsbury.
FOBBING (St Mich), *Essex.* R. D Chelmsf 15 P *Crown* I G BARTLETT *p-in-c.*
FOLESHILL (St Laur), *W Midl.* V. D Cov 2 P *Ld Chan* I M CAMPLING.
(St Paul), V. D Cov 2 P *V of Foleshill* I A J CANNING, R E SPITTLE *c.*
FOLEY PARK (H Innoc), *Worcs.*. D worc 12 *See* Kidderminster.
FOLKE (St Laur) w N Wootton, Haydon and Caundle Purse, *Dorset.*. D Sarum 7 P *D and C of Sarum 2 turns, Maj K S D Wingfield-Digby 2 turns, Mrs C B Ireland-Smith 1 turn* I D J HILLIER *p-in-c.*
FOLKESTONE (St Mary and St Eanswythe w St Mich AA), *Kent.* V. D Cant 6 P *Abp* I P G L COLE, C L RICHARDSON *c.*
(H Trin w Ch Ch), V. D Cant 6 P *Abp* I R O STROUD, J M GLEDHILL *c.*
(St Jo Bapt) V. D Cant 6 P *CPAS* I P C WEBBER, I J FERGUSON *c.*
(St Pet), V. D Cant 6 P *Trustees* I H F CAPENER.
(St Sav), I. D Cant 6 P *Abp* I N J C PIGOTT *c*, T R SMITH *c.*
FOLKESWORTH (St Helen) w Morborne (All SS), *Cambs.* R. D Ely 15 P *Bp and Ld Chan (alt)* I H BUTLER *p-in-c.*
FOLKINGHAM (St Andr), w Laughton, *Lincs.*. D Linc *See* Lafford, S.
FOLKINGTON (St Pet), *E Sussex.* R. D Chich 15 P *Mrs Gwynne-Longland* I J R P ASHBY.
FOLKTON (St Jo Evang), *N Yorks.*. D York 18 *See* Willerby.
FOLLIFOOT (St Joseph and St Jas), *N Yorks.*. D Ripon 4 *See* Spofforth.
FONTHILL-BISHOP (ALL SS) w Berwick St Leonard, *Wilts.* R. D Sarum 19 P *Bp* I J ELLIS.
FONTHILL-GIFFORD (H Trin), *Wilts.* R. D Sarum 19 P *Exors of M Shaw-Stewart* I J ELLIS.
FONTMELL MAGNA (St Andr), *Dorset.* R. D Sarum 13 P *Ld Wolverton* I K WEDGWOOD.
FOOTS CRAY (All SS), *Kent.* R. D Roch 13 *See* Cray, Foots.
(St Andr Eccles Distr). D Roch 13 *See* Sidcup.
FORCETT (St Cuthb) and Stanwick w Aldbrough, *N Yorks.* V. D Ripon 1 P *Dioc Bd of Patr* I J K YOUNG.
FORD (St Mark), *Devon.*. D Ex 23 *See* Devonport.
FORD, *Herefs.*. D Heref 7 *See* Stoke Prior.
FORD (St Mich AA), w Etal (St Mary Virg), *Northumb.* R. D Newc T 11 P *Ld Joicey* I R M GILL *c-in-c.*
FORD (St Mich AA), *Salop.* V. D Heref 13 P *Bp* I R SHARP.
FORD (St Andr), *W Sussex.* R. D Chich 1 *See* Yapton.
FORD END (St Jo Evang), *Essex.* V. D Chelmsf *See* Waltham, Great.
FORD ESTATE (Good Shepherd Eccles Distr), *T & W.*. D Dur 8 *See* Bishop Wearmouth.
FORD, OLD.. D Lon *See* Bow.
FORDCOMBE (St Pet), *Kent.*. D Roch *See* Penshurst.
FORDHAM (St Pet and St Mary Magd), *Cambs.* V. D Ely 3 P *Jes Coll Cam* I J D A LINN.
FORDHAM (St Mary), *Norf.* V. D Ely 17 P *D and C of Nor* I T H W SWAN *p-in-c.*
FORDHAM (All SS), *Essex.* R. D Chelmsf 22 P *Balliol Coll Ox and Trinitarian Bible S* alt I A G SMITH.
FORDINGBRIDGE (St Mary Virg), *Hants.* V. D Win 8 P *K Coll Cam* I R S GURR.
FORDINGTON, *Lincs.*. D Linc 8 *See* Ulceby.
FORDINGTON (St Geo), *Dorset.* R. D Sarum 5 *See* Dorchester.
WEST (St Mary), R. D Sarum 5 *See* Dorchester.
FORDLEY, *Suff.*. D St E 19 *See* Middleton.
FORDON (St Jas), *Humb.*. D York *See* Burton Fleming.
FORDWICH (St Mary Virg), *Kent.* R. D Cant 3 *See* Sturry.
FOREBRIDGE (St Paul), *Staffs.* V. D Lich 5 P *V of Castlechurch* I J J N QUIN.
FOREMARK (St Sav), *Derbys.* V. D Derby 16 P *Messrs Coutts & Co* I (Vacant).
FOREST, *Chesh.*. D Ches 13 *See* Rainow.
FOREST and FRITH (St Jas L) w Harwood (St Jude), *Durham.* V. D Dur 10 P *Ld Barnard* I H G PROCTOR.
FOREST GATE (Em) w Upton Cross (St Pet), *Essex.* V. D Chelmsf 5 P *Bp* I J J WRIGHT, A L JAGGARD *c.*
(All SS), V. D Chelmsf 5 P *Bp* I G P LAW.
(St Edm K and Mart), V. D Chelmsf 5 P *Bp* I P S ANDERSON *p-in-c.*
(St Jas),. D Chelmsf 5 *See* Stratford.
(St Mark), V. D Chelmsf 5 P *CPS* I M W WALLACE.
(St Sav) w (St Matt, West Ham), R. D Chelmsf 5 P *Dioc Bd of Patr* I J H WILLIAMS, R LOVE *team v.*
FOREST HILL (Ch Ch), *Kent.* V. D S'wark 18 P *Earl of Dartmouth* I J W HIND, J F FORD *c*, N J M KAVANAGH *c.*
(St Paul), V. D S'wark 18 P *Bp and V of Ch Ch Forest Hill* alt I J W HIND *p-in-c.*
(St Sav), V. D S'wark 18 *See* Brockley Hill.
FOREST HILL (St Nich) w Shotover, *Oxon.* V. D Ox *See* Wheatley.
FOREST ROW (H Trin), *W Sussex.* V. D Chich 12 P *V of E Grinstead* I J M TARRANT.
FOREST SIDE (Ch Ch) w Stansted (St Paul), *W Sussex.* V. D Chich 8 P *Rt Hon Earl of Bessborough* I P M BADEN.
FOREST TOWN (St Alb), *Notts.* V. D Southw 2 P *Bp* I I E GIBBS.
FORMBY (St Pet), *Mer.* V. D Liv 8 P *R of Walton* I J K EASTELL, M J HAMMOND *c*, K L MILLER *c.*
(H Trin), V. D Liv 8 P *Trustees* I C A QUINE, P D TAYLOR *c.*
(St Luke), V. D Liv 8 P *Bp* I T A MOON.
FORNCETT ST MARY w Forncett St Peter (St Pet and St Paul), *Norf.* R. D Nor 11 P *St Jo Coll Cam* I (Vacant).
FORNHAM ALL SS (All SS), *Suff.* R. D St E 13 P *Bp* I W G PECK.
(St Martin w St Genevieve) and Timworth (St Andr), *Suff.* R. D St E 17 P *Capt J D Macae and Bp* alt I B R WHITE *p-in-c.*
FORRABURY (St Symphorian) w Minster (St Methiana), and Trevalga (St Petrock), *Cornw.* R. D Truro *See* Davidstow.
FORSBROOK (St Pet), *Staffs.* V. D Lich 14 P *Bp* I R F GARDNER.
FORTHAMPTON (St Mary Virg) w Chaceley (St Jo Bapt), *Glos.* V. D Glouc *See* Deerhurst.
FORTON (All SS), *Staffs.* R. D Lich 15 P *D and C of Lich* I M S TYLER-WHITTLE *p-in-c.*
FORTON (St Jo Evang), *Hants.* V. D Portsm 1 P *Dioc Bd of Patr* I R DICKSON *c.*
FOSBURY (Ch Ch), *Wilts.* V. D Sarum 27 *See* Tidcombe.
FOSCOTT (St Leon), *Bucks.* R. D Ox 23 *See* Maids Moreton.
FOSDYKE (All SS), w Algarkirk (SS Pet and Paul), *Lincs.* V. D Linc 21 P *Dioc Bd of Patr* I (Vacant).
FOSTON (St Bart), *Leics.* R. D Leic 13 *See* Countesthorpe.
FOSTON (St Pet), *Lincs.*. D Linc 19 *See* Bennington.
FOSTON (All SS) w Flaxton (St Laur), *N Yorks.* R. D York *See* Whitwell.
FOSTON-ON-THE-WOLDS (St Andr), *Humb.* V. D York 13 P *Abp* I J R NEWTON.
FOTHERBY (St Mary) (Brackenboro, Utterby, Little Grimsby, Ludborough, Ormsby North, Wyham, Cadeby, Covenham and Fulstow), *Lincs.* R. D Linc 12 P *Ld Chan 1st turn, Dioc Bd of Patr and MM Sleight Esq 2nd turn and Bp 3rd turn* I D N LAMBERT.
FOTHERINGAY, *Northants.*. D Pet *See* Tansor.
FOULDEN, *Suff.*. D Nor *See* Oxburgh.
FOULNESS (St Mary Virg), *Essex.* R. D Chelmsf 11 *See* Wakering, Great.
FOULRIDGE (St Mich AA), *Lancs.* V. D Blackb 6a P *Bp* I K PALMER.
FOULSHAM (H Innoc), *Norf.* R. D Nor 6 P *Lady Hastings* I J M S PICKERING *p-in-c.*
FOUNTAINS (St Cuthb and St Osw, St Lawr, St Mich), *N Yorks.* R. D Ripon 3 P *D and C of Ripon* I (Vacant).
FOUR ELMS (St Paul), *Kent*, V. D Roch 9 P *Bp* I D CHAPMAN *p-in-c.*
FOUR MARKS (Good Shepherd), *Hants.*. D Win 6 P *Bp* I J R PALMER.
FOUR OAKS (All SS), *W Midl.* V. D Birm 12 P *Bp* I (Vacant).
FOVANT (St Geo), Sutton Mandeville (All SS) and Teffont-Evias w Teffont Magna, *Wilts.* R. D Sarum P *Reformation Ch Trust and Bp* I K C COOPER.
FOWEY, *Cornw.* V. D Truro 1 P *Ch S Trust* I D A WOODS.
FOWLMERE (St Mary Virg), *Cambs.* R. D Ely 8 P *Bp* I M C DONALD.
FOWNHOPE (St Mary), *Herefs.* V. D Heref P *D and C of Heref* I R V HOWARD JONES.
FOXCOTE or FORSCOTE (St Jas Less) w Shoscombe, *Somt.* R. D B & W *See* Camerton.

FOXCOTT, *Hants*.. **D** Win 2 *See* Andover.
FOXEARTH (St Pet and St Paul) w Pentlow (St Geo and St Greg), Liston and Borley, *Essex*. R. **D** Chelmsf 18 **P** *Miss Bull, Miss Yelloby, H E Foster Esq and C R Dew Esq in turn* **I** E F L BROWN.
FOXHALL, *Suff*.. **D** St E 2 *See* Nacton.
FOXHAM (St Jo Bapt), *Wilts*.. **D** Sarum 25 *See* Bremhill.
FOXHOLES, *N Yorks*.. **D** York 13 *See* Langtoft.
FOXLEY, *Norf*.. **D** Nor *See* Bawdeswell.
FOXLEY (Dedic unknown) w Bremilham, *Wilts* R and V. **D** Bris 11 **P** *Rt Hon Ld Lilford* **I** B TAYLOR.
FOXT (St Mark Evang) w Whiston (St Mildred), *Staffs*. V. **D** Lich 14 **P** *Successors of the late Maj R J Beech and Mrs C I Townley* alt **I** J B HARROP P-IN-C OF COTTON.
FOXTON (St Lawr), *Cambs*. V. **D** Ely 8 **P** *Bp* **I** R P BURN *p-in-c*.
FOXTON (St Andr) w Gumley (St Helen) and Laughton and Lubenham (All SS), R *Leics*. V. **D** Leic **P** *Bp 1st turn, R T Paget 2nd turn, D and C of Linc 3rd turn* **I** J WARDLE-HARPUR.
FOY, *Herefs*.. **D** Heref *See* Sellack.
FRADLEY (St Steph), *Staffs*.. **D** Lich 2 *See* Alrewas.
FRADSWELL, *Staffs*. R. **D** Lich 5 *See* Gayton.
FRAISTHORPE (St Edm), *Humb*.. **D** York 12 *See* Barmston.
FRAMFIELD (St Thos à Becket of Cant), *E Sussex*. V. **D** Chich 16 **P** *Mrs Haire* **I** J B CROSS.
FRAMILODE (St Pet), *Glos*. R. **D** Glouc 3 *See* Saul.
FRAMINGHAM EARL (St Andr), *Norf*. R. **D** Nor 14 **P** *J D Alston Esq* **I** R B HEMS.
FRAMINGHAM-PIGOT (St Andr), *Norf*. R (*See Bramerton Group*). **D** Nor 14 **P** *Bp* **I** (Vacant).
FRAMLINGHAM (St Mich) w Saxtead (All SS), *Suff*. R. **D** St E 18 **P** *Pemb Coll Cam* **I** D J PITCHER.
FRAMLINGTON, LONG (St Mary Virg), w Brinkburn, *Northumb*. V. **D** Newc T 7 **P** *Bp* **I** J P H CLARK.
FRAMPTON (St Mary), *Dorset*.. **D** Sarum 5 *See* Bradford Peverell.
FRAMPTON (St Mary Virg), *Lincs*. V. **D** Linc 21 **P** *Trustees* **I** J K HORNE.
FRAMPTON-COTTERELL (St Pet and St Paul), *Avon*. R. **D** Bris 7 **P** *S for Maint of Faith* **I** J M CLUTTERBUCK.
FRAMPTON MANSELL, *Glos*. R. **D** Glouc 13 *See* Sapperton.
FRAMPTON-ON-SEVERN (St Mary Virg) w Whitminster, *Glos*. V. **D** Glouc 9 **P** *Bp and Lt Col P H G Bengough* alt **I** D J BICK *p-in-c*, R P CHIDLAW *c*.
FRAMSDEN (St Mary), *Suff*. V. **D** St E 18 *See* Pettaugh.
FRANCE LYNCH (St Jo Bapt), *Glos*. V. **D** Glouc 4 **P** *V of Bisley* **I** T P HEARN.
FRANKBY (St Jo Div) w Greasby (St Nich), *Mer*. V. **D** Ches 8 **P** *D and C of Ches* **I** K P LEE.
FRANKLEY (St Leon), *Worcs*. R. **D** Birm 4 **P** *Bp* **I** M T DENNY.
FRANKTON (St Nich), *Warws*.. **D** Cov 6 *See* Bourton-on-Dunsmore.
FRANKTON, WELSH (St Andr), *Salop*.. **D** Lich 24 *See* Welsh Frankton.
FRANKWELL, *Powys*.. **D** Lich 26 *See* Shrewsbury (St George).
FRANSHAM, GT (All SS), W Fransham, Little (St Mary Virg), *Norf*. R. **D** Nor 20 **P** *Magd Coll Cam 2 turns, Hertf Coll Ox 1 turn, Ch S Trust 2 turns, Dioc Bd of Patr 2 turns* **I** B R A COLE.
FRANT (St Alb) w Eridge (H Trin), *E Sussex*. R. **D** Chich 20 **P** *Bp and Marq of Abergavenny* **I** P N HAMILTON.
FRATING (Dedic unknown) w Thorington (St Mary Magd), R *Essex*.. **D** Chelmsf 28 **P** *St Jo Coll Cam* **I** F J GRIGGS *p-in-c*.
FRECHEVILLE (St Cypr) w Hackenthorpe (Ch Ch), *S Yorks*. R. **D** Sheff 1 **P** *Dioc Bd of Patr* **I** J K MOORE, C L NORWOOD *team v*, M R H BELLAMY *c*.
FRECKENHAM (St Andr) w Worlington (All SS), *Suff*. R. **D** St E *See* Barton-Mills.
FRECKLETON (H Trin), *Lancs*. V. **D** Blackb 9 **P** *Bp* **I** T F UNSWORTH.
FREEFOLK, *Hants*.. **D** Win 5 *See* Overton.
FREEHAY (St Chad), *Staffs*. V. **D** Lich 14 **P** *R of Cheadle* **I** J D STARKEY P-IN-C OF OAKAMOOR.
FREELAND (St Mary Virg) and Cassington, *Oxon*. V. **D** Ox 10 **P** *D and C of Ch Ch Ox and SSJE* **I** P H RYE.
FREEMANTLE (Ch Ch), *Hants*. R. **D** Win 11 **P** *Bp* **I** M N FULLAGAR.
FREETHORPE (All SS) w Wickhampton, *Norf*. V. **D** Nor 1 **P** *Ch S Trust and Exors of Mrs Hamor* alt **I** J T H BRITTON *p-in-c*.
FREISTON (St Jas) w Butterwick (St Andr), *Lincs*. V. **D** Linc 20 **P** *Bp* **I** B R GRELLIER.
FREMINGTON (St Pet), *Devon*. V. **D** Ex 15 **P** *MMT* **I** D C KNIGHT.
FRENCHAY (St Jo Bapt), *Avon*. R. **D** Bris 7 **P** *St Jo Coll Ox* **I** R J THOMAS *p-in-c*.
FRENSHAM (St Mary), *Surrey*. V. **D** Guildf 3 **P** *Ld Chan* **I** N W ALEXANDER.
FRESHFORD (St Pet), *Somt* w Limpley Stoke (St Mary) and Hinton Charterhouse, *Avon*. R. **D** B & W 13 **P** *Simeon Trustees and R of Norton St Philip* **I** A G PAGE.
FRESHWATER (All SS), *Isle of Wight*. R. **D** Portsm 7 **P** *St Jo Coll Cam* **I** D E HENLEY.
FRESSINGFIELD (St Pet and St Paul) w Weybread (St Andr) and Wingfield, *Suff*. R. **D** St E **P** *Bp, Em Coll Cam and Ch S Trust in turn* **I** T B POWNALL *p-in-c*.
FRESTON (St Pet) w Woolverstone, *Suff*.. **D** St E 5 *See* Holbrook.
FRETHERNE (St Mary Virg), *Glos*. R. **D** Glouc 3 *See* Saul.
FRETTENHAM (St Swith) w Stanninghall, *Norf*. R. **D** Nor 4 **P** *Ch S* **I** (Vacant).
FRIAR-MERE (St Thos), *Gtr Man*. V. **D** Man 15 **P** *Bp* **I** N J FEIST.
FRICKLEY (All SS) w Clayton, *S Yorks*.. **D** Sheff *See* Brodsworth.
FRIDAY BRIDGE (St Mark), *Cambs*. V. **D** Ely 20 **P** *Bp* **I** (Vacant).
FRIDAYTHORPE (St Jas) or Tang w Fimber and Thixendale (St Mary Virg), *Humb*. V. **D** York 13 **P** *Abp* **I** (Vacant).
FRIERN BARNET. **D** Lon 24 *See* Barnet.
FRIESTHORPE (St Pet), *Lincs*. R. **D** Linc 5 *See* Wickenby.
FRIETH (St Jo Evang), *Bucks*.. **D** Ox 32 *See* Hambleden.
FRIEZLAND (Ch Ch), *Gtr Man*. V. **D** Man 15 **P** *Trustees* **I** D W HIRST.
FRILSHAM (St Frideswide), *Berks*. R. **D** Ox 12 *See* Yattendon.
FRIMLEY (St Pet w St Francis), *Surrey*. R. **D** Guildf 5a **P** *R of Ash* **I** J ROSE-CASEMORE, P W C HOLT *c*, R W WOODGER *c*.
FRIMLEY GREEN (St Andr), *Surrey*. V. **D** Guildf 5a **P** *Bp* **I** B K BESSANT, R W WOODGER *c*.
FRINDSBURY (All SS) w Upnor (St Phil and St Jas), *Kent*. V. **D** Roch **P** *Bp* **I** D NOBLE.
FRING (All SS), *Nor*. V. **D** Nor 23 **P** *D and C of Nor* **I** D A PORTER *p-in-c*.
FRINGFORD (St Mich) w Hethe (St Edm and St Geo) and Newton Purcell (St Mich) w Shelswell *Oxon*. R. **D** Ox 2 **P** *Ld Chan and Exors of J F Dewar-Harrison (alt)* **I** A HICHENS *p-in-c*.
FRINSTED (St Dunstan) w Wormshill (St Giles) and Milstead (St Mary and H Cross), *Kent*. R. **D** Cant 14 **P** *R Leigh Pemberton Esq, Mrs McCandlish, M Nightingale Esq and Exors of Mrs C S Black* **I** J M SHORROCK.
FRINTON-ON-SEA (St Mary), *Essex*. R. **D** Chelmsf 28 **P** *CPAS* **I** L V ROWE.
FRISBY-ON-THE-WREAKE (St Thos of Cant) w Kirby Bellars (St Pet), *Leics*. V. **D** Leic 4 **P** *Bp 1st and 3rd turns, Exors of Miss R M Byron 2nd turn* **I** (Vacant).
FRISKNEY (All SS), *Lincs*. V. **D** Linc 8 **P** *Bp* **I** C S RUSHFORTH.
FRISTON (St Mary Virg), *E Sussex*.. **D** Chich *See* Dean, East.
FRISTON, *Suff*. V. **D** St E **P** *Mrs A C Vernon-Wentworth* **I** (Vacant).
FRITH (St Jas L), *Durham*.. **D** Dur *See* Forest.
FRITHELSTOCK (St Mary and St Gregory), *Devon*. V. **D** Ex *See* Torrington, Great.
FRITHVILLE, *Lincs*. V. **D** Linc 20 *See* Sibsey.
FRITTENDEN (St Mary), *Kent*.. **D** Cant 11 *See* Sissinghurst.
FRITTON (St Cath), *Norf*.. **D** Nor *See* Morningthorpe.
FRITTON (St Edm), *Suff*. R. **D** Nor 15 **P** *Mrs H M Cubitt* **I** R M BURLTON *c-in-c*.
FRITWELL (St Olave) w Souldern and Ardley w Fewcot, *Oxon*. V. **D** Ox 2 **P** *Wadh Coll Ox and St Jo Coll Cam* **I** G A DE BURGH-THOMAS.
FRIZINGHALL (St Marg), *W Yorks*. V. **D** Bradf 1 **P** *Bp* **I** (Vacant).
FRIZINGTON (St Paul) and Arlecdon, *Cumb*. V. **D** Carl 12 **P** *Bp* **I** N S DIXON.
FROCESTER, *Glos*.. **D** Glouc *See* Eastington.
FRODESLEY (St Mark), *Salop*. R. **D** Heref 11 **P** *Trustees of late S J Northam Esq* **I** C J W C HATCLIFFE *p-in-c*.
FRODINGHAM (St Lawr), *Humb*. V. **D** Linc 4 **P** *Ld St Oswald* **I** E B GREATHEAD, M DUNFORD *c*, N A THORNLEY *c*.
FRODINGHAM, NORTH (St Elgin), *Humb*. V. **D** York 13 **P** *Ch S Trust* **I** J R NEWTON.

GATESHEAD (St Mary Virg w H Trin and Ven Bede), *T & W*. R. **D** Dur 4 **P** *Bp and Crown* alt **I** J D HODGSON, T J TROTTER *team v*, T L JAMIESON *c*.
(All SS Lobley Hill), V. **D** Dur 4a **P** *Bp* **I** G B KIRKUP.
(Ch Ch), V. **D** Dur 4 **P** *Bp* **I** P WRIGHT.
(St Geo), V. **D** Dur 4 **P** *Trustees* **I** E M T UNDERHILL.
(St Helen, Low Fell), V. **D** Dur 4 **P** *Bp* **I** A H TRORY.
(St Jas), R. **D** Dur 4 **P** *Bp* **I** (Vacant).
(St Cuthb w St Paul Bensham), V. **D** Dur 4 **P** *Bp* **I** (Vacant).
(St Chad, Bensham), V. **D** Dur 4 **P** *Bp* **I** J THOMPSON.
GATESHEAD FELL (St Jo Evang), *T & W*. R. **D** Dur 4 **P** *Bp* **I** W J TAYLOR, J C WEBSTER *c*.
GATLEY (St Jas Ap), *Gtr Man*. V. **D** Ches 16 **P** *R of St Thos Stockport* **I** R E READ, A COOK *c*.
GATTEN (St Paul Ap), *Isle of Wight*. **D** Portsm 6 *See* Shanklin.
GATTON, *Surrey*.. **D** S'wark *See* Merstham.
GAULBY or GALBY (St Pet) w King's Norton or Norton-by-Galby (St Jo Bapt) and L Stretton (St Jo Bapt or St Clem), *Leics*. R. **D** Leic 6 **P** *Ch S Trust* **I** (Vacant).
GAUTBY (All SS) w Waddingworth (St Marg), *Lincs*.. **D** Linc 11 *See* Bardney.
GAWBER (St Thos), *S Yorks*. V. **D** Wakef 8 **P** *V of Darton* **I** C KELLETT.
GAWCOTT (H Trin) w Hillesden (All SS), *Bucks*.. **D** Ox 23 *See* Lenborough.
GAWSWORTH (St Jas), *Chesh*. R. **D** Ches 13 **P** *T Richards Esq* **I** R SIMPSON.
GAWTHORPE and CHICKENLEY HEATH (St Mary Virg), *W Yorks*. V. **D** Wakef 10 **P** *Bp* **I** R J BRADNUM.
GAYDON (St Giles) w Chadshunt (All SS), *Warws*. V. **D** Cov 8 **P** *Bp* **I** A L FERMOR.
GAYHURST w Ravenstone (All SS), Stoke Goldington (St Pet) and Weston Underwood (St Laur), *Bucks*. R. **D** Ox 28 **P** *Ld Hesketh and Bp* **I** A K PRING.
GAYTON (St Nich), *Norf*. V. **D** Nor 25 **P** *Bp* **I** J P GRANT.
GAYTON (St Mary) w Tiffield (St Jo Bapt), *Northants*. R. **D** Pet 2 **P** *SS Coll Cam and Bp* alt **I** D A W BROWN.
GAYTON (St Pet), w Fradswell, *Staffs*. V. **D** Lich **P** *Earl of Harrowby and Bp* alt **I** J E H POWELL.
GAYTON-LE-MARSH (St Geo Mart), *Lincs*. R. **D** Linc *See* Withern.
GAYTON-LE-WOLD (St Pet) w Biscathorpe (St Helen), *Lincs*. R. **D** Linc *See* Asterby Group.
GAYTON-THORPE (St Mary Virg) w East Walton (St Mary Virg), *Norf*. R. **D** Nor 25 **P** *Capt H Birkbeck* **I** J P GRANT *p-in-c*.
GAYWOOD (St Faith) w Bawsey and Mintlyn, *Norf*. R. **D** Nor 25 **P** *Bp* **I** D W A RIDER, M C GRAY *c*.
GAZELEY (All SS) w Dalham (St Mary) and Moulton, *Suff*. V. **D** St E 11 **P** *Maj the Hon J P Philipps, Ch Coll Cam, Bp (in turn)* **I** A M R PLATT.
GEDDING (St Mary Virg), *Suff*. R. **D** St E 10 *See* Felsham.
GEDDINGTON (St Mary Magd) w Weekley (St Mary Virg), *Northants*. V. **D** Pet 8 **P** *Boughton Estates* **I** T WOOLFENDEN.
GEDLING (All H), *Notts*. R. **D** Southw 13 **P** *Dioc Bd of Patr* **I** C H B WATSON.
GEDNEY (St Mary Magd), *Lincs*. V. **D** Linc 16 **P** *Crown* **I** (Vacant).
(Ch Ch Drove End), V. **D** Linc 16 *See* Lutton.
GEDNEY HILL (H Trin), *Lincs*. V. **D** Linc 16 **P** *Bp* **I** O G FOLKARD *c-in-c*.
GEE CROSS (H Trin), *Gtr Man*. V. **D** Ches 14 **P** *V of Werneth* **I** G D OSGOOD.
GELDESTON (St Mich AA) w Stockton (St Mich AA), *Norf*. R. **D** Nor 14 *See* Gillingham.
GELSTON, *Lincs*.. **D** Linc 14 *See* Hough-on-the-Hill.
GENTLESHAW (Ch Ch), *Staffs*. V. **D** Lich 2 **P** *MMT* **I** W E HASSALL.
GEORGEHAM (St Geo), *Devon*. R. **D** Ex 15 **P** *MMT* **I** B J B CARR.
GERMANSWEEK, *Devon*. V. **D** Ex 12 *See* Bratton Clovelly.
GERMOE, ST, *Cornw*.. **D** Truro *See* Breage.
GERRANS **D** Truro 6 *See* St Gerrans.
GERRARD'S CROSS (St Jas), *Bucks*. V. **D** Ox 20 **P** *Simeon Trustees* **I** J G HARRISON.
GESTINGTHORPE, R *Essex*.. **D** Chelmsf 18 *See* Maplestead, Gt.
GIDDING, GREAT (St Mich), w Gidding, Little (St Jo Evang) and Gidding, Steeple (St Andr), *Cambs*. V. **D** Ely 11 **P** *Ld Chan, Earl Fitz-William and W Dennis Esq in turn* **I** (Vacant).
GIDEA PARK (St Mich AA), *Essex*. V. **D** Chelmsf 4 **P** *Bp* **I** F LEECH.
GIDLEIGH (H Trin) w Throwleigh, *Devon*. R. **D** Ex *See* Chagford.
GIGGLESWICK (St Alkelda), *N Yorks*. V. **D** Bradf 6 **P** *Trustees* **I** J H RICHARDSON.
GILCRUX, *Cumb*.. **D** Carl *See* Plumbland.
GILDERSOME (St Pet), *W Yorks*. V. **D** Wakef 9 **P** *V of Batley* **I** D BARRACLOUGH.
GILLAMOOR, *N Yorks*.. **D** York 20 *See* Kirby Moorside.
GILLCAR (St Silas), *S Yorks*.. **D** Sheff 2 *See* Sheffield.
GILLING (St Agatha) and Kirkby Ravensworth w Dalton, *N Yorks*. V. **D** Ripon 1 **P** *Bp and Mrs M W Ringrose-Wharton* **I** J R W SILLER P-IN-C OF MELSONBY, T H BULLEN *c*.
GILLING, EAST (The H Cross), *N Yorks*. R. **D** York 20 **P** *Trin Coll Cam* **I** N J B WILSON *p-in-c*.
GILLINGHAM (St Mary Magd) w Upberry, *Kent*. V. **D** Roch 2 **P** *Dioc Bd of Finance* **I** R THOMSON.
(H Trin Twydall) V. **D** Roch 2 **P** *Bp* **I** P C ABSOLON.
(St Aug Rock Avenue), V. **D** Roch 2 **P** *Bp* **I** S P GRAY.
(St Barn), V. **D** Roch 2 **P** *Bp* **I** D A LOW, R W CADE *hon c*.
(St Luke), V. **D** Roch 2 **P** *Bp* **I** B LAMB.
(St Mark), V. **D** Roch 2 **P** *Hyndman Trustees* **I** T C COLLETT-WHITE, P J S PERKIN *c*.
GILLINGHAM (St Mary Virg Gillingham, St Simon and St Jude Milton, St Mary Magd Fifehead Magdalen, All SS, Kington Magna St Jo Bapt, Buckhorn Weston), The Stours (Ch Ch E Stour, St Mary W Stour, St Mich AA Stour Provost, and St Andr Todber), *Dorset*. R. **D** Sarum **P** *Bp* **I** J MCNEISH, F F HICKS *team v*, R C MOORSOM *team v*, L J WRIGHT *c*.
GILLINGHAM (St Mary w All SS) w Gelderston (St Mich AA) and Stockton (St Mich AA) w Ellingham and Kirby Cane, *Norf*. R. **D** Nor **P** *Bp, MMT and Ld Chan* **I** R H BLANKLEY.
GILLINGHAM, SOUTH (St Pet and St Matt w All SS), *Kent*. V. **D** Roch 2 **P** *Bp* **I** P A BIRD, R J A HAMER *c*, J KING *c*, J P KIRBY *c*.
GILMORTON (All SS) w Peatling Parva (St Andr), *Leics*. R. **D** Leic 14 **P** *Bp and Guild of All S* **I** N C W BROOKS.
GILSLAND (St Mary Magd), *Cumb*. R. **D** Carl **P** *Bp* **I** A W PENN *p-in-c*.
GILSTON (St Mary) w Eastwick, *Herts*.. **D** St Alb 4 *See* High Wych.
GIMINGHAM (All SS), *Norf*.. **D** Nor 5 *See* Trunch.
GIPPING (Chap), *Suff*.. **D** St E 6 **P** *Trustees* **I** (Vacant).
GIPSY HILL (Ch Ch), *Surrey*. V. **D** S'wark 6 **P** *CPAS* **I** C E G TENNANT, P J MUNBY *c*.
GIPTON THE EPIPHANY W Yorks. V **D** Ripon 6 *See* Leeds.
GIRLINGTON (St Phil), *W Yorks*. V. **D** Bradf 1 **P** *Simeon Trustees* **I** A D GREENHILL.
GIRTON (St Andr), *Cambs*. R. **D** Ely 5 **P** *Ld Chan* **I** A H LEIGHTON.
GIRTON, *Notts*. V. **D** Southw *See* Scarle, South.
GISBURN (St Mary), *Lancs*. V. **D** Bradf 6 **P** *Bp* **I** S A SELBY.
GISLEHAM, *Suff*. **D** Nor 15 *See* Kessingland.
GISLINGHAM (St Mary), *Suff*. R. **D** St E 16 **P** *MMT* **I** L TRENDER *p-in-c*.
GISSING (St Mary Virg), *Norf*. R. **D** Nor *See* Winfarthing.
GITTISHAM (St Mich), *Devon*. R. **D** Ex 5 *See* Honiton.
GIVENDALE, GREAT (St Ethelburga), *Humb*.. **D** York *See* Millington.
GLADSTONE PARK (St Francis of Assisi), *Gtr Lon*. V. **D** Lon 18 **P** *Bp* **I** D J IRWIN, R F BUSHAU *c*, R T COOK *c*.
GLAISDALE (St Thos), *N Yorks*. V. **D** York 27 **P** *Abp* **I** W K HALL.
GLANDFORD, *Norf*.. **D** Nor *See* Letheringsett.
GLANFORD BRIDGE, *Humb*.. **D** Linc *See* Brigg.
GLAPTHORNE (St Leon), *Northants*. V. **D** Pet *See* Southwick.
GLAPTON, *Notts*.. **D** Southw 11 *See* Clifton.
GLASCOTE, *Staffs*.. **D** Lich 6 *See* Tamworth.
GLASS HOUGHTON (St Paul), *W Yorks*. V. **D** Wakef 11 **P** *Bp* **I** J VICKERMAN.
GLASSON (Ch Ch), *Lancs*. V. **D** Blackb 11 **P** *Bp* **I** A K BISBROWN.
GLASTON (St Andr) w Bisbrooke (St Jo Bapt), *Leics*.. **D** Pet *See* Morcott.
GLASTONBURY (St Jo Bapt) w Godney (H Trin), *Somt*. V. **D** B & W 7 **P** *Bp* **I** A.G. CLARKSON C-IN-C OF W PENNARD, W M MARSHALL *c*.
(St Benedict), V. **D** B & W 7 **P** *Bp* **I** (Vacant).
GLATTON (St Nich), *Cambs*. R. **D** Ely 14 **P** *Bp, Crown and J Heathcote Esq in turn* **I** G J SHARPE.
GLAZEBURY (All SS), *Lancs*. V. **D** Liv 11 **P** *Earl of Derby* **I** R H WAGSTAFF.

GLAZELEY (St Bart), Salop.. D Heref 9 See Chetton.
GLEADLESS (Ch Ch and St Pet Basegreen), S Yorks. R. D Sheff 1 P Dioc Bd of Patr I D T THOMAS, A G ANDERSON team v, S D HOLDAWAY c.
GLEADLESS VALLEY, W Yorks. R. D Sheff 1 P Dioc Bd of Patr I D E PEET, D R HERBERT team v.
GLEMHAM, GREAT and Little, Blaxhall, Stratford St Andr and Farnham, Suff. R. D St E 19 P Earl of Guildf, Lady Blanche Cobbold and Dioc Bd of Patr (alt) I R JOBLING.
GLEMSFORD (St Mary Virg), Suff. R. D St E 12 P Bp I C M LAWSON.
GLENDON, Northants. R. D Pet 8 See Rushton.
GLENFIELD (St Pet), Leics. R. D Leic 17 P Bp I P F TAMBLING.
GLEN MAGNA (St Cuthb) w Stretton Magna (St Giles), Leics. V. D Leic 6 P Bp I (Vacant).
GLEN PARVA (St Thos Ap) w S Wigston, Leics. V. D Leic 6 P Bp I G RICHERBY, P G HOLMES hon c.
GLENTHAM (St Pet), Lincs. V. D Linc 3 See Owmby.
GLENTWORTH (St Mich), Lincs. V. D Linc 2 P Earl of Scarborough I T P O PECK.
GLINTON, Cambs. D Pet 14 See Peakirk.
GLODWICK, Gtr Man.. D Man 15 See Oldham.
GLOOSTON (St Jo Bapt), Leics. R. D Leic 3 See Stonton Wyville.
GLOSSOP (All SS), Derbys. V. D Derby 5 P Archd of Chesterfield and Trustees I P H HEATH.
GLOUCESTER (St Aldgate, Finlay Road), Glos. V. D Glouc 1 P Bp I R H KENT, N C M SALTER c.
(All SS), V. D Glouc P Bp I D J GREENMAN p-in-c, H J HUMPHRIES c.
(Mariners' Ch). D Glouc 1 I T B GRETTON chap.
(St Cath), V. D Glouc 1 P Bp I R J LLEWELYN.
(St Jas), V. D Glouc 1 P Bp I W DONALD c.
(St Steph formerly St Luke L), V. D Glouc 1 P Bp I J W HURRELL.
(St Mark Kingsholm), V. D Glouc 1 P Bp I D R LYON.
(St Mary de Crypt w Ch Ch), R. D Glouc 1 P Bp and Ld Chan I D M PATON, J F LEAVER hon c.
(St Mary de Lode w St Nich), V. D Glouc 1 P D and C of Glouc and Bp I S J RIGGS.
(St Paul), V. D Glouc 1 P Bp I P M G BARNARD, R A O J HAYWARD c, E W WHEELER c.
(St Barn Tuffley), V. D Glouc 1 P Bp I (Vacant).
(St Geo Lower Tuffley), V. D Glouc 1 P Bp I H S RINGROSE, G BAISLEY c, T R C OVERTHROW c.
(St Osw Coney Hill). D Glouc 1 P Crown I P R WRIGHT.
GLYMPTON (St Mary), Oxon. R. D Ox 10 P E W Towler Esq I R J MULRENAN p-in-c.
GLYNDE (St Mary Virg) w W Firle (St Pet) and Beddingham (St Andr), E Sussex. V. D Chich 15 P D and C of Windsor and Bp alt I M T MORGAN p-in-c.
GNOSALL (St Lawr), Staffs. V. D Lich 15 P Bp I M J POPE, W J BLAKEMAN c.
GOADBY, Leics. V. D Leic 5 See Billesdon.
GOADBY MARWOOD (St Denys), Leics.. D Leic See Scalford.
GOATHILL (St Pet), Dor.. D B & W 12 See Milborne Port.
GOATHLAND (BVM), N Yorks. V. D York 27 P Abp I G W WOODWARD.
GOATHURST, Somt.. D B & W See Enmore.
GOBOWEN, Salop.. D Lich 24 See Hengoed.
GODALMING (St Pet and St Paul), Surrey. V. D Guildf 4 P Bp I M C BROWN.
GODINGTON (H Trin), Oxon. R. D Ox 2 See Stratton Audley.
GODLEY (St Jo Bapt) w Newton Green, Gtr Man. V. D Ches 14 P R of Cheadle I G L COOKSON.
GODMANCHESTER (St Mary Virg), Cambs. V. D Ely 10 P D and C of Westmr I J P YOUNG.
GODMANSTONE (H Trin), Dorset. R. D Sarum 5 See Cerne Abbas.
GODMERSHAM, Kent.. D Cant See Crundale.
GODNEY (H Trin), Somt.. D B & W See Glastonbury.
GODOLPHIN (St Jo Bapt), Cornw. V. D Truro See Crowan.
GODSHILL (All SS), Isle of Wight. V. D Portsm 6 P Guild of All S I T P J HEWITT.
(St Alb Conv Distr). D Portsm 6 P V of Godshill I (Vacant).
GODSTONE (St Nich), Surrey. R. D S'wark 10 P C G Hoare Esq I C STUDDERT-KENNEDY, L D HARMAN c.
GODWICK, Nor.. D Nor See Tittleshall.
GOFF'S OAK (St Jas), Herts.. D St Alb 6 See Cheshunt.
GOLANT, Cornw.. D Truro See St Sampson.
GOLBORNE (St Thos), Gtr Man. R. D Liv 11 P Earl of Derby I H CUNLIFFE.
GOLCAR (St Jo Evang), W Yorks. V. D Wakef 6 P V of Huddersfield I A R B ROBINSON.
GOLDENHILL (St Jo Evang), Staffs. V. D Lich 17a P Bp I D C F TUDOR.
GOLDER'S GREEN (St Alb and St Mich), Gtr Lon. V. D Lon P Bp I R Y BALDRY.
GOLDHANGER (St Pet) w Little Totham (All SS), Essex. R. D Chelmsf 14 P HB Gardner Esq I R G BROMBY p-in-c.
GOLDINGTON (St Mary Virg), Beds. V. D St Alb 16 P Bp I K M L H BANTING, R D BRANSON c, A J DAVIS c, J K DIXON c.
(N Brickhill, Bedford Conv Distr). D St Alb 16 P Bp I J A S PAYNE COOK min.
GOLDSBOROUGH (St Mary), N Yorks. R. D Ripon 4 P Earl of Harewood I P FAIRBURN.
GOLDSWORTH PARK, Surrey. V. D Guildf P Bp I A W A KNOWLES.
GOLDTHORPE (St John and St Mary Magd) w Hickleton, S Yorks. V. D Sheff 10 P Commun Resurr Mirfield 2 turns, Visc Halifax 1 turn I J F COOKE c, T A PARKINSON c.
GOLTHO Lincs. V D Linc 3 See Rand.
GOMERSAL (St Mary Virg), W Yorks. V. D Wakef 9 P Bp I M F CLEVERLEY.
GOMSHALL, Surrey.. D Guildf 2 See Shere.
GONALSTON (St Lawr), Notts. R. D Southw 13 P Commdr M B P Franklin and Bp I J E O CHANDLER.
GONERBY, GREAT (St Sebastian), Lincs. R. D Linc 19 P V of Grantham I F H CHALK.
GOOD EASTER (St Andr), Essex. V. D Chelmsf 23 P D and C of St Paul's I (Vacant).
GOODERSTONE (St Geo), Norf. V. D Nor 19 See Cockley Cley.
GOODLEIGH (St Gregory), Devon. R. D Ex 15 See Barnstaple.
GOODMANHAM (All H), Humb. R. D York 10 P Abp I M EXLEY.
GOODMAYES (All SS), Essex. V. D Chelmsf 7 P Hyndman Trustees I R C MATTHEWS.
(St Paul), V. D Chelmsf 7 P Bp I G S RICHARDSON.
GOODNESTONE (H Cross) w Chillenden (All SS), and Knowlton (St Clem), Kent. V. D Cant 1 P Abp I P V R PENNANT p-in-c.
GOODNESTONE (St Bart) w Graveney (All SS), Kent. V. D Cant 7 See Preston-next-Faversham.
GOODRICH (St Giles Abbot and Confess) w Marstow (St Matt) and Welsh Bicknor (St Marg), Herefs. V. D Heref 8 P Bp I (Vacant).
GOODRINGTON (St Geo Conv Distr), Devon.. D Ex 10 See Paignton.
GOODSHAW (St Mary and All SS), Lancs. V. D Man 18 P Hulme Trustees I R E MALLINSON p-in-c.
GOODWORTH-CLATFORD, Hants.. D Win See Clatford, Upper.
GOOLE (St Jo Evang) and Old Goole (St Mary), Humb. V. D Sheff 9 P Bp I T E LEACH, C GUILLOTEAU c.
GOOSE GREEN (St Paul), Gtr Man. V. D Liv 12 P Bp I P W PLUNKETT.
GOOSEY (All SS), Oxon.. D Ox 17 See Stanford-in-the-Vale.
GOOSNARGH (St Mary Virg), W Whittingham, Lancs. V. D Blackb 10 P Bp I J SHAW.
GOOSTREY (St Luke), Chesh. V. D Ches 11 P V of Sandbach I C H HUGGILL.
GOREFIELD (St Paul), Cambs. V. D Ely 20 P Bp I J TOFTS.
GORING (St Mary), W Sussex. V. D Chich 9 P Bp I P H E BENNETT, K J TUFFEL c.
(Conv Distr of Maybridge, St Richard).. P Bp I C G F KIRKHAM p-in-c.
GORING (St Thos of Cant), Oxon. V. D Ox 7 P Ch Ch Ox I S T HOLMES, B W BARRETT hon c.
GORLESTON (St Andr), Norf. V. D Nor 2 P Ch Trust Fund Trust I C C COOPER, J J QUINN c, A FROGGATT hon c.
(St Mary Magd), V. D Nor P Bp and Ch Trust I B W TOMLINSON.
GORNAL, LOWER (St Jas), W Midl. V. D Lich 1 P Bp I M JEAVONS.
GORNAL, UPPER (St Pet), W Midl. V. D Lich 1 P V of Sedgley I N S READE, J MOUNTFORD c.
GORSLEY (Ch Ch) w Clifford's Mesne (St Pet), Glos. V. D Glouc 6 P R of Newent 2 turns, V of Linton 1 turn I I L DAVIES p-in-c.
GORTON (St Jas), Gtr Man. R. D Man 1 P D and C of Man I C G BEESON.

(Our Lady of Mercy and St Thos of Cant), R. D Man 1 P *Bp and Trustees* I A WATSON.
(St Geo Abbey Hey), R. D Man 1 P *Bp and HM the Queen* I T P F KENNY.
(Em), R. D Man 1 P *Bp* I J A CARR.
(St Phil), R. D Man 1 P *Crown and Bp* alt I (Vacant).
GOSBECK (St Mary), *Suff.* R. D St E 1 *See* Coddenham.
GOSBERTON (St Pet and St Paul), *Lincs.* V. D Linc 17 P *D and C of Linc* I (Vacant).
GOSBERTON CLOUGH (St Gilbert and St Hugh) and Quadring, *Lincs.* V. D Linc P *Bp* I E T CHAPMAN.
GOSFIELD, *Essex.* V. D Chelmsf 24 P *Exors of Commdr J A Lowe* I P C FORD.
GOSFORTH (St Mary) w Nether Wasdale and Wasdale Head, *Cumb.* R. D Carl 12 P *Bp, Earl of Lonsdale, V of St Bees and Dioc Bd of Finance Ltd* I F BOWYER.
GOSFORTH (St Nich), *T & W.* V. D Newc T 5 P *Bp* I P W H RUDGE.
(All SS), V. D Newc T 5 P *Bp* I J R LITTLE, C C ROWLAND *c*, J P SMITH *c*.
NORTH (St Columba), *T & W.* V. D Newc T 5 P *S for Maint of Faith* I P ELLIOTT.
GOSPEL LANE (St Mich), *W Midl.* V. D Birm 11 P *Bp* I C J ALDRIDGE.
GOSPEL OAK (St Martin), *Lon..* D Lon 26 *See* St Pancras.
GOSPORT (H Trin), *Hants.* V. D Portsm 1 P *Dioc Bd of Patr* I J R CAPPER.
(Ch Ch), V. D Portsm 1 P *Bp* I D G JAMES.
(St Matt Conv Distr Bridgemary). D Portsm 1 P *Bp* I K J PARFITT *p-in-c*.
GOSSOPS GREEN (St Alb), *W Sussex..* D Chich *See* Ifield.
GOTHAM (St Lawr), *Notts.* R. D Southw 11 P *Bp* I A D WILLIAMS.
GOTHERINGTON, *Glos..* D Glouc 10 *See* Woolstone.
GOUDHURST (St Mary Virg), *Kent.* V. D Cant 11 P *Abp* I R C CAMPBELL-SMITH.
GOUGH SQUARE (H Trin).. D Lon 1 *See* London (St Bride).
GOULCEBY (All SS), *Lincs..* D Linc 11 *See* Asterby.
GOXHILL (All SS), *Humb.* V. D Linc 6 P *Ld Chan* I R D GWYNNE *p-in-c*.
GOXHILL D York 14 *See* Aldbrough.
GRADE, ST (St Grade), *Cornw.* R. D Truro 4 *See* St Grade.
GRAFFHAM (St Giles) w Woolavington (St Pet), *W Sussex.* R. D Chich 6 P *Bp* I D F GRANT.
GRAFFOE (St Andr Boothby Graffoe, St Pet Navenby, All SS Wellingore; Skinnard and St Jo Bapt Temple Bruer). *Lincs.* R. D Linc P *J C M Fullerton Esq, Ch Coll Cam, D and C of Linc and Visc Chaplin* I D A HUGHES.
GRAFHAM (All SS), *Cambs.* R. D Ely 11 P *Bp* I M A JENNER *p-in-c*.
GRAFHAM (St Andr), *Surrey.* V. D Guildf *See* Bramley.
GRAFTON, *Herefs..* D Heref 3 *See* Bullinghope, Upper.
GRAFTON, EAST (St Nich) w Tidcombe (St Mich) and Fosbury (Ch Ch), *Wilts.* V. D Sarum *See* Wexcombe.
GRAFTON-FLYFORD Worcs. R D Worc *See* Upton Snodsbury.
GRAFTON REGIS (St Mary), *Northants.* R. D Pet *See* Stoke Bruerne.
GRAFTON UNDERWOOD (St Jas Ap), *Northants.* R. D Pet *See* Cranford.
GRAINSBY (St Nich), *Lincs.* R. D Linc 10 P *Reps of Late C L E Haigh Esq* I G L BIERLEY.
GRAINTHORPE (St Clem) w Conisholme (St Pet), *Lincs.* V. D Linc 12 P *Magd Coll Cam and Bp* alt I P PARKINSON.
GRAMPOUND w CREED, *Cornw..* D Truro 6 *See* Probus.
GRANBOROUGH (St Jo Bapt), *Bucks.* V. D Ox 25 *See* Marston, North.
GRANBY (All SS) w Elton-on-the-Hill, *Notts.* V. D Southw 9 P *Bp* I C B PERKINS *p-in-c*.
GRANDBOROUGH (St Pet) w Willoughby and Flecknoe, *Warws.* V. D Cov 6 P *Mrs Seabroke, Bp and Wolfhamcote Farms Ltd* I D W PHARAOH *p-in-c*.
GRANGE DE LINGS, *Lincs..* D Linc 3 *See* Dunholme.
GRANGE-IN-BORROWDALE (H Trin), *Cumb..* D Carl 10 *See* Borrowdale.
GRANGE-OVER-SANDS (St Paul), *Cumb.* V. D Carl 14 P *Bp* I M H G FOX.
GRANGE PARK (St Pet), *Gtr Lon.* V. D Lon 21 P *Bp* I H J PITCHFORD.
GRANGETOWN (St Aid), *T & W.* V. D Dur 8 P *V of Ryhope* I T L MATTHEWS.
GRANGETOWN (St Hilda of Whitby), *Cleve.* V. D York 22 P *Abp* I C P HORTON.
GRANSDEN, GREAT (St Bart), w Gransden, Little (St Pet and St Paul), *Cambs.* V and R. D Ely 13 P *Clare Coll Cam* I R K D WATKINS-WRIGHT.
GRANTCHESTER (St Andr and St Mary), *Cambs.* V. D Ely 7 P *CCC Cam* I N T BREWSTER.
GRANTHAM (St Wulfram w St Jo Evang Spitalgate) w Manthorpe (St Jo Evang), Harrowby (Ascen), Earlesfield (Epiph) and Londonthorpe (St Jo Bapt), *Lincs.* R. D Linc 19 P *Bp* I R A HOWE, T A BRIGHTON *team v*, N D L DE KEYSER *team v*, S R HAWORTH *team v*, S SALTER *team v*, J M THOMPSON *team v*, M J BUNCE *c*.
(St Anne), V. D Linc 19 P *Bp* I N H COLLARD.
(St Jo Evang Spitalgate), V. D Linc 19 *See* Grantham.
GRAPPENHALL (St Wilfrid), *Chesh.* R. D Ches 4 P *Trustees of P G Greenall Esq* I L J FORSTER.
GRASBY (All SS) w Owmby w Searby (St Nich), *Lincs.* V. D Linc 5 P *Ld Tennyson and D & C of Linc* I D SAUNDERS *p-in-c*.
GRASMERE (St Osw), *Cumb.* R. D Carl 14 P *Qu Coll Ox* I R J W BEVAN.
GRASSENDALE (St Mary Virg), *Mer.* V. D Liv 2 P *Trustees* I V F E ROGERS.
GRASSLOT (St Andr), *Cumb..* D Carl 11 *See* Netherton.
GRATELEY (St Leon) w Quarley, *Hants..* D Win 2 *See* Amport.
GRATWICH (St Mary), *Staffs..* D Lich 20 *See* Kingstone.
GRAVELEY (St Botolph) w Papworth St Agnes and Yelling (H Cross) and Toseland (St Mich), *Cambs.* R. D Ely 1 P *Jesus Coll Cam, St J H Sperling Esq and Ld Chan (in turn)* I M W BISHOP.
GRAVELEY (St Mary) w Chivesfield, *Herts.* R. D St Alb *See* Wymondley, Great.
GRAVELLY HILL (All SS), *W Midl..* D Birm 7 *See* Erdington.
GRAVENEY (All SS), *Kent..* D Cant 6 *See* Preston-next-Faversham.
GRAVENHURST, UPPER (St Giles) w Lower, *Beds.* V. D St Alb 22 P *Bp* I R P W LANHAM.
GRAVESEND (St Jas w St Geo) w (H Trin) Milton-next-Gravesend, *Kent.* R. D Roch 3 P *Bp* I R C L PILGRIM.
(H Family w St Marg Ifield), R. D Roch 3 P *Bp and Maj R W Edmeades* I J R BARTLETT.
(St Aid), V. D Roch 3 P *Bp* I B PEARSON.
(St Mary), V. D Roch 3 P *R of Gravesend* I H A ATHERTON, O T LALL *hon c*.
GRAYINGHAM (St Radegunda), *Lincs.* R. D Linc 6 P *Bp* I M B KIDDLE.
GRAYRIGG (St Jo Evang), *Cumb.* V. D Carl 17 P *V of Kendal* I R D MURRAY *p-in-c*.
GRAYS (St Pet and St Paul), *Essex.* V. D Chelmsf 15 P *Bp* I P A NEWMAN *team v*, D J L AGASSIZ *p-in-c*, S J TUDGEY *c*.
(All SS), V. D Chelmsf 15 P *Bp* I D J L AGASSIZ *p-in-c*.
GRAYSHOTT (St Luke), *Surrey* and *Hants.* V. D Guildf 3 P *Bp* I S G RICHARDS.
GRAYSWOOD (All SS), *Surrey.* V. D Guildf 4 P *Bp* I G J CURTIS *c-in-c*.
GRAZELEY (H Trin) w Beech Hill (St Mary Virg), *Berks.* V. D Ox 15 P *Bp* I J R HART *c*.
GREASBROUGH (St Mary), *S Yorks.* V. D Sheff 6 P *Earl Fitzwilliam* I W F HOWE, C R OXLEY *c*.
GREASBY (St Nich), *Mer..* D Ches 8 *See* Frankby.
GREASLEY (St Mary), *Notts.* V. D Southw 12 P *Bp* I P G WALKER.
GREAT ALNE (St Mary Magd), *Warws..* D Cov 9 *See* Kinwarton.
GREAT BARR (St Marg), *W Midl.* V. D Lich 9 P *Exors of Lady Bateman and Scott* I J S REANEY.
(St Chad's Pheasey). D Lich 9 *See* Pheasey.
GREAT BUDWORTH (St Mary and All SS), *Chesh.* V. D Ches 4 P *D and C of Ch Ch Ox* I J T ANNET.
GREAT CROSBY (St Luke), *Mer.* V. D Liv 1 P *R of Sefton* I R J LEE, J PARR *c*.
(St Faith), V. D Liv 1 P *St Chad's Hall, Dur* I P GOODRICH, A W J MAGNESS *c*, D A SMITH *c*.
GREATHAM, *W Sussex.* R. D Chich 7 *See* Parham.
GREATHAM (St Jo Bapt), *Cleve.* V. D Dur 12 P *Master of Greatham Hosp* I D E F OGDEN.
GREATHAM (St Jo Bapt) w Empshott (H Rood), *Hants.* R. D Portsm 4 P *Mrs Luttrell West* I P S DUFFETT *p-in-c*.
GREATHAM HOSPITAL (St Mary and St Cuthb), *Cleve..* D Dur 12 P *Bp* I D E F OGDEN *master*.
GREAT HAYWOOD (St Steph), *Staffs.* V. D Lich 4 P *Earl of Lich and Trustees* I D M WOODHOUSE *p-in-c*, J A S WOOD *c*.
GREAT SMEATON (All H or St Elvy), R w Appleton-Wiske (St Mary) and Birkby (St Pet) and Danby Wiske w Hutton Bonville (St Laur), *N Yorks.* V.

(St Mich du Valle), R. D Win 13 P *Crown* I P SIMPSON.
(H Trin), V. D Win 13 P *Trustees* I P C DELIGHT.
(St Andr), R. D Win 13 P *Crown* I F M DRAKE *c.*
(St Jo Evang), V. D Win 13 P *Trustees* I M J HANCOCK.
(Ste Marguerite de la Forêt), R. D Win 13 P *Crown* I J R A SHAW.
(Ste Marie du Castel), R. D Win 13 P *Crown* I R G NELSON.
(St Martin), R. D Win 13 P *Crown* I F M TRICKEY.
(St Matt Cobo), V. D Win 13 P *R of Ste Marie du Castel* I C V COLMAN.
(St Pierre du Bois), R. D Win 13 P *Crown* I (Vacant).
(St Phil de Torteval), R. D Win 13 P *Crown* I K C CADMAN.
(St Sampson), R. D Win 13 P *Crown* I (Vacant).
(St Sav), R. D Win 13 P *Crown* I F COOPER.
(St Steph), V. D Win 13 P *R of St Peter Port* I M C MILLARD, H S RIDGE *hon c.*

GUESTLING (St Lawr) and Pett (St Mary and St Pet), *E Sussex*. R. D Chich 22 P *Dioc Bd of Patr and Bp (alt)* I J H READ.

GUESTWICK (St Pet), *Norf.* V. D Nor 6 P *Mrs M E E Long* I J M S PICKERING *p-in-c.*

GUILDEN MORDEN (St Mary), *Cambs.* V (*See Shingay Group*). D Ely 8 P *Jes Coll Cam* I (Vacant).

GUILDEN-SUTTON (St Jo Bapt), *Chesh.* V. D Ches 2 *See* Plemstall.

GUILDFORD (H Trin w St Mary), *Surrey*. R. D Guildf 5 P *Bp* I R C A CAREY, C J ELSON *c,* J V M GORDON CLARK *c,* C D SEMPER *hon c.*
(All SS Onslow Village). D Guildf 5 P *Bp* I W M POWELL, J K MOORE *hon c.*
(Ch Ch). D Guildf 5 P *Simeon Trustees* I M B G PAIN, N C TURTON *c.*
(Em Stoughton), V. D Guildf 5 P *Simeon Trustees* I J F SALTER, J N HAMILTON *c.*
(St Francis, Westborough), R. D Guildf P *Bp* I R A LINDLEY, G M HOLDAWAY *team v,* A W C LOCKHART *team v.*
(St Nicolas), R. D Guildf 5 P *Bp* I B TAYLOR, R M SANDERS *c.*
(St Pet Stoke Hill). D Guildf 5 P *Bp* I D V LEWIS.
(St Sav) w Stoke-next-Guildford (St Jo Evang), R. D Guildf 5 P *Simeon Trustees* I J C SKINNER, D M CASTLETON *c,* M J H ROUND *c.*

GUILSBOROUGH (St Etheldreda) w Hollowell (St Jas) and Cold Ashby, *Northants.* V. D Pet 6 P *Mrs G S Collier 2 turns Bp 1 turn* I W G GIBBS.

GUISBOROUGH (St Nich w St Pet-in-Commondale), *Cleve.* R. D York 19 P *Abp* I R S GIBSON, P R A R HOARE *c.*

GUISELEY (St Osw), *W Yorks.* R. D Bradf 5 P *Trustees* I J R JOHN, J C BARNES *c,* C DODD *hon c.*

GUIST, *Norf.*. D Nor *See* Twyford.

GUITING POWER or LOWER (St Mich AA) w Farmcote (St Faith), *Glos.* V. D Glouc 16 *See* Guitings, The.

GUITINGS, THE, Cutsdean and Farmcote, *Glos.* V. D Glouc 16 P *E R Cochrane Esq and Ch Ch Ox (alt)* I S WILSON.

GULDEFORD, EAST (St Mary), *E Sussex*.. D Chich 22 *See* Camber.

GULVAL, ST (St Gulval), *Cornw.* V. D Truro 5 *See* St Gulval.

GUMLEY (St Helen), *Leics.* R. D Leic 5 *See* Foxton.

GUNBY (St Nich), *Lincs.*. D Linc 14 *See* Stainby.

GUNBY (St Pet), *Humb.*. D Linc 8 *See* Welton-Le-Marsh.

GUNHOUSE or GUNNESS (St Barn) w Burringham (St Jo Bapt), *Humb.* R. D Linc 4 P *Bp of Lon* I D F BUTTON.

GUNNERSBURY (St Jas), *Gtr Lon.* V. D Lon 10 P *V of St Geo Brentford* I J C HIBBERD.

GUNNESS, *Humb.*. D Linc *See* Gunhouse.

GUNTHORPE (St Mary) w Bale (All SS), *Norf.* R. D Nor 24 P *Exors of Capt M E B Sparke* I P G FLATHER, F J P SMITH *hon c.*

GUNTHORPE, *Leics.* V. D Pet 12 *See* Lyndon.

GUNTON w Hanworth (St Bart), *Norf.* R. D Nor *See* Aldborough.

GUNTON (St Pet), *Suff.* R. D Nor 15 P *CPAS* I A B DINES.

GUNWALLOW, ST *Cornw.*. D Truro *See* Cury St.

GURNARD (All SS Conv Distr), *Isle of Wight*.. D Portsm 7 P *Bp* I J V BEAN *p-in-c,* J S COLE *c.*

GUSSAGE (St Andr), *Dorset*.. D Sarum *See* Pentridge.

GUSSAGE (St Mich AA w All SS), *Dorset.* R. D Sarum 10 P *Archd of Dorset and Bp* I J A P STANDEN MCDOUGAL.

GUSTON (St Martin), *Kent.* R. D Cant 5 *See* Whitfield.

GUYHIRN (St Mary Magd) w Ring's End, *Cambs.* V. D Ely 20 P *Bp* I R M C NURSE *p-in-c.*

GWINEAR, *Cornw.*. D Truro 5 *See* St Gwinear.

HABBERLEY (St Mary), *Salop.* R. D Heref 13 P *Dr J H Chitty* I (Vacant).

HABERGHAM, *Lancs.*. D Blackb 3 *See* Burnley.

HABROUGH (St Marg), *Humb.* V. D Linc 10 P *Dioc Bd of Patr* I S R KENYON.

HACCOMBE (St Blase) w Coffinswell (St Bart), *Devon.* R. D Ex 10 P *R V Carew Esq* I (Vacant).

HACCONBY, *Lincs.*. D Linc 13 *See* Morton.

HACEBY, *Lincs.*. D Linc 22 *See* Newton.

HACHESTON (All SS), *Suff.*. D St E 18 *See* Parham.

HACKENTHORPE (Ch Ch), *S Yorks.*. D Sheff 1 *See* Frecheville.

HACKFORD (St Mary Virg), *Norf.*. D Nor 13 *See* Deopham.

HACKFORD, *Norf.*. D Nor *See* Reepham.

HACKINGTON (St Steph), *Kent.*. D Cant 3 *See* Canterbury (St Stephen).

HACKLETON, *Northants.* V. D Pet 4 *See* Horton.

HACKNESS (St Mary also St Hilda) w Harwood Dale, *N Yorks.* V. D York 18 P *Ld Derwent* I J W KENNEDY *p-in-c.*

HACKNEY (St Jo Bapt), *Lon.* R. D Lon 2 P *Ld Amherst* I D RHODES, G W GARNER *team v,* P R WRAGG *team v,* A J HOOPER *c,* N R J FUNNELL *hon c.*
(St Luke), V. D Lon 2 P *Trustees of St Olave, Hart Street* I B SNELLING.
SOUTH (St John of Jer w Ch Ch), R. D Lon 2 P *Ld Amherst* I E H JONES.
(St Mary Virg of Eton w St Aug of Cant Hackney Wick), V. D Lon 2 P *Trustees Eton Miss* I P A A WALKER, A P R KYRIAKIDES *hon c.*
(St Mich AA London Fields), V. D Lon 2 P *R of Hackney* I R F ATKINS.
WEST (St Barn), R. D Lon 2 P *Bp* I F A PRESTON, P M G P G DE FORTIS *c.*
(St Pet De Beauvoir Town), V. D Lon 2 P *H A Benyon Esq* I J S BAGGLEY.

HACKTHORN (St Mich), V w Cold Hanworth, *Lincs.* R. D Linc 3 P *Mrs B K Eley* I D SCOTT.

HADDENHAM (H and Undivided Trin), *Cambs.* V. D Ely 15 P *Archd of Ely* I B PETTY *p-in-c.*

HADDENHAM (St Mary Virg) w Cuddington and Kingsey, *Bucks.* V. D Ox 21 P *D and C of Roch* I J E R POLLARD, J W S FIELDGATE *c,* P MCEACHRAN *hon c.*

HADDINGTON, *Lincs.*. D Linc 6 *See* Aubourn.

HADDISCOE (St Mary) w Toft Monks (St Marg), *Norf.*. D Nor 14 *See* Raveningham.

HADDLESEY (St Jo Bapt), *N Yorks.*. D York *See* Birkin.

HADDON, *Cambs.*. D Ely 14 *See* Chesterton.

HADDON, EAST (St Mary Virg), *Northants.* V. D Pet 6 *See* Ravensthorpe.

HADDON, WEST (All SS) w Winwick (St Mich AA), *Northants.* V. D Pet 6 P *Miss Bannerman and Bp* alt I A F RIDLEY.

HADFIELD (St Andr), *Derbys.* V. D Derby 5 P *Bp* I D W BAILEY.

HADHAM, LITTLE (St Cecilia), *Herts.* R. D St Alb *See* Braughing.

HADHAM, MUCH (St Andr), w Perry Green (St Thos), *Herts.* R. D St Alb 4 P *Bp of Lon* I M A MCADAM, C M COCKIN *hon c.*

HADLEIGH (St Jas L), *Essex.* R. D Chelmsf 13 P *Dr P W M Copeman* I A J MORLEY.
(St Barn), V. D Chelmsf 13 P *Bp* I J G AMBROSE.

HADLEIGH (St Mary Virg w Layham (St Andr) and Shelley (All SS), *Suff.* R. D St E 3 P *Abp of Cant and St Jo Coll Cam* alt I J R BETTON, J F M WILLIAMS *c.*

HADLEY (H Trin), *Salop.* V. D Lich 27 P *Bp and others* I J R TYE.

HADLOW (St Mary), *Kent.* V. D Roch 9 P *Miss I King* I G LANE, E F P BRYANT *c.*

HADLOW DOWN (St Mark), *E Sussex.* V. D Chich 16 P *Bp* I P R F SANDERSON *p-in-c.*

HADNALL (St Mary Magd), *Salop.* V. D Lich 27 P *R B Thompson* I D D PRICE.

HADSTOCK (St Botolph), *Essex.* R. D Chelmsf 27 *See* Ashdon.

HADZOR (St Jo Bapt) w Oddingley (St Jas) and Tibberton w Bredicot, *Worcs.* V. D Worc 8 P *J F Bennett Esq 1 turn, D and C of Worc 2 turns, R J G Berkeley Esq 1 turn* I D J HEWITT.

HAGBOURNE, EAST w West (St Andr), *Oxon.* V. D Ox 18 P *Bp* I F T STARBUCK.

HAGGERSTON (St Chad) *Lon.* V. D Lon 2 P *Crown* I D F SHARPE.
(All SS Haggerston Road), V. D Lon 2 P *Ld Chan* I M H ROSS *p-in-c.*
(St Paul, Broke Road), V. D Lon 2 P *Bp* I (Vacant).

HAGLEY (St Jo Bapt), *Worcs*. R. **D** Worc 11 **P** *Visc Cobham* **I** J G DAVIES, M J BEAVER *c*.
HAGNABY (St Andr), *Lincs*. V. **D** Linc *See* Bolingbroke.
HAGNABY (St Thos Mart), *Lincs*.. **D** Linc 8 *See* Hannah.
HAGWORTHINGHAM (H Trin) w Asgarby (St Swith), V and Lusby (St Pet), *Lincs*. R. **D** Linc *See* Bolingbroke.
HAIGH (St D) and Aspull (St Jo Bapt), *Gtr Man*. V. **D** Liv 12 **P** *R of Wigan* **I** E ROWLANDS.
HAIL WESTON, *Cambs*.. **D** Ely 13 *See* Southoe.
HAILE (Dedic unknown), *Cumb*. V. **D** Carl *See* Egremont.
HAILES, *Glos*.. **D** Glouc 18 *See* Didbrook.
HAILEY (St John) w Crawley (St Pet), *Oxon*. V. **D** Ox 9 **P** *Bp* **I** R E MEREDITH *p-in-c*.
HAILSHAM (St Mary), *E Sussex*. V. **D** Chich 19 **P** *Ch S Trust* **I** R G H PORTHOUSE.
HAINAULT (St Paul), *Essex*. V. **D** Chelmsf 7 **P** *Bp* **I** (Vacant).
HAINTON (St Mary) w Sixhills (All SS), *Lincs*.. **D** Linc 5 *See* Barkwith Group.
HAINWORTH, *W Yorks*. V. **D** Bradf 11 *See* Ingrow.
HALAM (St Mich), *Notts*. V. **D** Southw 15 *See* Edingley.
HALBERTON (St Andr), *Devon*. V. **D** Ex 4 **P** *D and C of Bris* **I** C A TESTER.
HALE (St Pet), *Gtr Man*. V. **D** Ches 10 **P** *V of Bowdon* **I** D ASHWORTH.
HALE (St Jo Evang), *Surrey*. V. **D** Guildf 3 **P** *Bp* **I** M H SELLORS.
HALE (St Mary), *Chesh*. V. **D** Liv 7 **P** *P Fleetwood-Hesketh, Rev D Tinne, P F Pierce Esq, Mrs V Belcher, M I Blackburne Esq* **I** D L SCOTT.
HALE (St Mary) w Charford, South, *Hants*. V. **D** Win 8 **P** *Maj T V B Booth Jones* **I** W D LEWIN.
HALE END, *Essex*.. **D** Chelmsf *See* Walthamstow.
HALE MAGNA and PARVA (St Jo Bapt), *Lincs*. R. **D** Linc 22 *See* Helpringham.
HALES (St Mary), *Staffs*. V. **D** Lich 23 **P** *E N Hall Esq and Archd of Salop* alt **I** R B MORRIS.
HALES (St Marg) w Heckingham (St Greg), *Norf*.. **D** Nor 14 *See* Raveningham.
HALESOWEN (St Jo Bapt) w Hasbury (St Marg) and Lapal (St Pet), *W Midl*. R. **D** Worc **P** *Bp and Visc Cobham* **I** C L V ATKINSON, P M J GINEVER *team v*, H J OSBORNE *team v*, A N JEVONS *c*.
HALESWORTH w Linstead, Chediston, Holton (St Pet), Blyford, Spexhall and Wissett, *Suff*. R. **D** St E **P** *Ld Chan, Dioc Bd of Patr and Col J Day* **I** G W ARRAND, J F SERJEANT *team v*, M S WOODS *team v*.
HALEWOOD (St Nich), *Mer*. R. **D** Liv 7 **P** *Bp* **I** O V EVA, P R JEFFERY *c*, C R TYRRELL *c*, C CRITCHLEY *hon c*.
(St Mary), V. **D** Liv 7 **P** *Bp* **I** (Vacant).
HALFORD (St Mary), *Warws*. R. **D** Cov 9 **P** *Bp* **I** J E BLUCK *p-in-c*.
HALFORD, *Salop*.. **D** Heref *See* Sibdon Carwood.
HALIFAX (St Jo Bapt), *W Yorks*. V. **D** Wakef 1 **P** *Crown* **I** R J HARRIES, R JONES *c*.
(All SS Salterhebble) V. **D** Wakef 1 **P** *Trustees* **I** S FORBES.
(All S Haley Hill). **D** Wakef **P** *Trustees* **I** G B THOMAS.
(H and Undivided Trin).. V. **D** Wakef 1 **P** *V of Halifax* **I** J M GRIFFITHS *p-in-c*.
(H Nativ Mixenden), V. **D** Wakef 1 **P** *Bp* **I** C G N DEY.
(St Aug), V. **D** Wakef 1 **P** *Trustees* **I** D C ELLIS.
(St Geo Mart Ovenden), V. **D** Wakef 1 **P** *V of Halifax* **I** C P EDMONDSON.
(St Hilda), V. **D** Wakef 1 **P** *Bp* **I** J C WIDDOWS.
(St Jas w St Mary Virg), V. **D** Wakef 1 **P** *V of Halifax* **I** J M GRIFFITHS *p-in-c*.
(St Jo Evang Warley), V. **D** Wakef 1 **P** *V of Halifax* **I** F CARLESS, J S BRADBERRY *hon c*.
(St Jude, Salterhebble), V. **D** Wakef 1 **P** *Trustees* **I** M J WALKER.
(St Mary Virg Illingworth), V. **D** Wakef 1 **P** *V of Halifax* **I** (Vacant).
(St Thos Ap Charlestown), V. **D** Wakef 1 **P** *V of Halifax* **I** L GREENWOOD.
(St John, Bradshaw), V. **D** Wakef 1 **P** *Bp* **I** M SQUIRES.
(St Paul, King Cross), V. **D** Wakef 1 **P** *Bp* **I** (Vacant).
(St Mark, Siddal), V. **D** Wakef 1 **P** *Ch Trust Fund* **I** P J JEFFERY.
HALL GREEN (Ascen). *W Midl*. V. **D** Birm 11 **P** *Bp* **I** F GOUGE, E N L FRANCE *c*, E E MOLE *hon c*.
(St Pet), V. **D** Birm 5 **P** *Bp* **I** R BROOKSTEIN, A J G NEWMAN *c*.
HALLAM FIELDS (St Bart), *Derbys*.. **D** Derby 13 *See* Ilkeston.
HALLATON (St Mich AA) w Horninghold and Allexton, *Leics*. R. **D** Leic 5 **P** *Dioc Bd of Patr, Bp and Mrs E M A B Bewicke (alt)* **I** (Vacant).
HALLEN, *Avon*.. **D** Bris *See* Henbury.
HALLING (St Jo Bapt w St Lawr), *Kent*.. **D** Roch 5 *See* Cuxton.
HALLINGBURY, GREAT (St Giles), *Essex*. R. **D** Chelmsf 3 **P** *Bp* **I** H W J SILKSTONE.
HALLINGBURY, LITTLE (St Mary Virg), *Essex*. R. **D** Chelmsf 3 **P** *Govs of Charterho* **I** A W D RITSON.
HALLINGTON (St Laur), *Lincs*.. **D** Linc 12 *See* Raithby.
HALLIWELL (St Paul), *Gtr Man*. V. **D** Man 11 **P** *Ch S Trust* **I** D J BRACEWELL.
(St Pet), V. **D** Man 11 **P** *Ch S Trust* **I** R F OLDFIELD, R A MACHIN *c*, M SMITH *c*.
(St Luke Evang), V. **D** Man 11 **P** *Trustees* **I** S T REID.
(St Marg). **D** Man 11 **P** *Trustees* **I** D HAZLEHURST.
(St Thos), V. **D** Man 11 **P** *Trustees* **I** W BALDWIN.
HALLOUGHTON (St Jas), *Notts*.. **D** Southw *See* Bleasby.
HALLOW (St Phil and St Jas), *Worcs*. V. **D** Worc 2 **P** *Bp* **I** M J WILLOWS *p-in-c*.
HALLWOOD (St Mark), *Chesh*. V. **D** Ches **P** *Dioc Bd of Patr* **I** R W DENT.
HALSALL (St Cuthb), *Lancs*. R. **D** Liv 9 **P** *Maj D Blundell* **I** W H BULLOUGH.
HALSE (St Jas), *Somt*. R. **D** B & W *See* Milverton.
HALSETOWN (St Jo Evang), *Cornw*. V. **D** Truro 5 **P** *D and C of Truro* **I** J H HARPER.
HALSHAM (All SS), *Humb*. R. **D** York 15 **P** *Hon P M Shipton* **I** W BERRIMAN *p-in-c*.
HALSTEAD (St Andr w H Trin) w Greenstead Green, *Essex*. V. **D** Chelmsf **P** *Bp* **I** R P ANGWIN, S CARTER *c*, L M HIPKINS *c*, R F TOBIN *c*.
HALSTEAD, *Leics*. R. **D** Leic 8 *See* Tilton on the Hill.
HALSTEAD (St Marg), *Kent*. R. **D** Roch 7 **P** *D and C of Roch* **I** J S WHITEHEAD.
HALSTOCK (St Mary), *Dorset*. V and R. **D** Sarum *See* Melbury.
HALSTOW, HIGH (St Marg) w All Hallows and Hoo St Mary, *Kent*. R. **D** Roch 5 **P** *MMT and Ch S Trust* **I** P F WORTHEN.
HALSTOW, LOWER (St Marg), *Kent*. V. **D** Cant 14 *See* Upchurch.
HALTHAM (St Benedict), *Lincs*.. **D** Linc 11 *See* Roughton.
HALTON (St Wilfrid) w Aughton (St Sav), *Lancs*. R. **D** Blackb 13 **P** *R T Sanderson Esq* **I** J C HOUGHTON.
HALTON (St Mary), *Chesh*. V. **D** Ches **P** *Bp* **I** R V JAMES.
HALTON, *E Sussex*.. **D** Chich *See* Hastings.
HALTON (St Mich AA), *Bucks*. R. **D** Ox 30 **P** *Dioc Bd of Patr* **I** A F MEYNELL *p-in-c*.
HALTON (St Wilfrid), *N Yorks*. V. **D** Ripon 7 **P** *Bp* **I** R P GREENWOOD, P E NIXON *c*.
HALTON, EAST (St Pet), *Humb*. V. **D** Linc 10 **P** *Dioc Bd of Patr* **I** S R KENYON.
HALTON GILL, *N Yorks*.. **D** Bradf *See* Arncliffe.
HALTON-HOLGATE (St Andr), *Lincs*. R. **D** Linc 7 **P** *Bp* **I** J S THOROLD.
HALTON, WEST (St Etheldreda), *Humb*. R. **D** Linc *See* Alkborough.
HALTWHISTLE (H Cross), *Northumb*. V. **D** Newc T 4 **P** *Bp* **I** R B COOK.
HALVERGATE (St Pet and St Paul) w Tunstall, *Norf*. V. **D** Nor 1 **P** *Bp* **I** J T H BRITTON *p-in-c*.
HALWELL (St Leon) w Moreleigh (All SS), R *Devon*. V. **D** Ex 13 **P** *D and C of Ex 1 turn, Bp 2 turns* **I** R J K LAW.
HALWILL (St Pet and St Jas) w Beaworthy (St Alb), *Devon*. R. **D** Ex 9 *See* Ashwater.
HAM (St Geo Mart), *Kent*.. **D** Cant 7 *See* Northbourne.
HAM, *Wilts*.. **D** Sarum *See* Shalbourne.
HAM (St Andr), *Surrey*. V. **D** S'wark 11 **P** *K Coll Cam* **I** J A RUSSELL, D A WOTTON *c*.
(St Richard), V. **D** S'wark 11 **P** *Bp* **I** D F MOODY, B J LEE *c*.
HAM, *W Sussex*.. **D** Chich 1 *See* Angmering.
HAM, HIGH (St Andr), *Somt*. R. **D** B & W 10 *See* Langport.
LOW (Chap). **D** B & W 10 *See* Langport.
HAM, EAST (St Mary Magd w St Bart) w Upton Pk (St Alb), *Essex*. R. **D** Chelmsf 5 **P** *Patr Bd* **I** S R LOWE, J M FELLOWS *team v*, C L OWENS *team v*, C W SHELDRAKE *c*.
(St Geo and St Ethelbert), V. **D** Chelmsf 5 **P** *Bp* **I** B J LLOYD.
(St Paul), V. **D** Chelmsf 5 **P** *CPS* **I** B T LYONS.
HAM, WEST (All SS), *Essex*. V. **D** Chelmsf 5 **P** *Crown* **I** R T K GRIFFIN, N O TOOLEY *c*.
(St Matt).. **D** Chelmsf 5 *See* Forest Gate (St Sav).
See also CANNING TOWN, FOREST GATE, PLAISTOW, STRATFORD, UPTON CROSS, AND VICTORIA DOCKS..
HAMBLE (St Andr), *Hants*. V. **D** Win 15 **P** *Win Coll* **I** R E P SEROCOLD.
HAMBLEDEN (St Mary) w Frieth (St Jo Evang) and Skirmett (All SS), *Bucks*. R. **D** Ox *See* Hambledon Valley.

HAMBLEDEN VALLEY (Hambleden, Fawley, Fingest, Medmenham and Turville), *Bucks*. R. **D** Ox **P** *Bp, Visc Hambleden and Miss M F Mackenzie* **I** K R JOYCE, G D BALLARD *c*, E R M HENDERSON *c*.
HAMBLEDON (St Pet), *Surrey*. R. **D** Guildf 4 **P** *MMT* **I** D J THOMPSON.
HAMBLEDON (St Pet and St Paul), *Hants*. V. **D** Portsm 2 **P** *Ld Chan* **I** C V HERBERT.
HAMBLETON (St Mary Virg), *Lancs*. V. **D** Blackb 10 **P** *V of Kirkham* **I** E SWINNERTON.
HAMBLETON (St Andr) w Egleton, *Leics*. V. **D** Pet 12 *See* Oakham.
HAMBLETON w Gateforth *N Yorks*. V. **D** York **P** *Abp* **I** N TEWKESBURY.
HAMBRIDGE (St Jas L) w Earnshill (Sin) and Ile Brewers (All SS), *Somt*. V. **D** B & W *See* Ilton.
HAMER (All SS), *Gtr Man*.. **D** Man 17 *See* Rochdale.
HAMERINGHAM (All SS) w Scrafield (St Mich) and Winceby (St Marg), *Lincs*. R. **D** Linc 11 **P** *Dioc Bd of Patr* **I** A A EDE.
HAMERTON (All SS), *Cambs*. R. **D** Ely 11 **P** *G R Petherick Esq* **I** (Vacant).
HAMMERSMITH (St Paul), *Lon*. V. **D** Lon 7 **P** *Bp* **I** R A M THACKER, J G W OLIVER *c*.
(H Innoc), V. **D** Lon 7 **P** *Bp* **I** J A MCATEER.
(St Kath Westway), V. **D** Lon 7 **P** *Bp* **I** J G ELLIS.
(St Jo Evang), V. **D** Lon 7 **P** *V of Hammersmith* **I** J G CANNING, A H MEAD *c*.
(St Luke, Uxbridge Rd), V. **D** Lon 7 **P** *Bp* **I** M J MACDONALD *p-in-c*.
(St Mary, Stamford Brook),. **D** Lon 7 **P** *CPAS* **I** F P SPRACKLING.
(St Matt Sinclair Rd W Kensington), V. **D** Lon 7 **P** *Trustees* **I** I G FALCONER.
(St Pet), V. **D** Lon 7 **P** *Bp* **I** R G B FOXCROFT.
(St Sav), V. **D** Lon 7 **P** *Bp* **I** J D WHEELER *p-in-c*.
(St Simon), V. **D** Lon 7 **P** *Simeon Trustees* **I** M I TUNGAY.
(St Steph Uxbridge Rd) w (St Thos Ap), V. **D** Lon 7 **P** *Bp* **I** J H ASBRIDGE, J COOPER *c*.
WHITE CITY ESTATE (St Mich and St Geo Conv Distr). **D** Lon 7 **P** *Bp* **I** M J HAYES *p-in-c*.
HAMMERWICH (St Jo Bapt), *Staffs*. V. **D** Lich 2 **P** *Trustees* **I** J A FIELDING-FOX.
HAMMERWOOD (St Steph) w Holtye (St Pet), *E Sussex*. V. **D** Chich *See* Cowden.
HAMMOON or HAM MOHUN (St Paul), *Dorset*.. **D** Sarum 13 *See* Childe Okeford.
HAMNISH, *Herefs*.. **D** Heref *See* Kimbolton.
HAMPDEN, GREAT (St Mary Magd), w Hampden, Little, *Bucks*. R. **D** Ox 30 **P** *Exors of Earl of Buckingham* **I** P A J HILL.
HAMPDEN PARK (St Mary), *E Sussex*. V. **D** Chich 19 **P** *Bp* **I** D G NEWMAN.
(St Pet Conv Distr, Hydneye). **D** Chich 19 **P** *Bp* **I** (Vacant).
HAMPNETT (St Matt), *Glos*.. **D** Glouc *See* Northleach.
HAMPRESTON (All SS), *Dorset*. R. **D** Sarum 11 **P** *MMT* **I** C J BLISSARD-BARNES, R H O HILL *c*, W J SALMON *c*.
HAMPSTEAD (St John), *Gtr Lon*. V. **D** Lon 19 **P** *Dioc Bd of Patr* **I** G M DOWELL, M A JOHNSON *c*.
(All S Loudoun Rd), V. **D** Lon 19 **P** *Bp* **I** P W WHEATLEY *p-in-c*.
(Ch Ch), V. **D** Lon 19 **P** *Trustees* **I** C J F SCOTT.
(Em Ch), V. **D** Lon 19 **P** *Trustees* **I** J D WELLMAN.
(St Cuthb), V. **D** Lon 19 **P** *Ch Trust Fund Trust* **I** R MORGAN.
(St Jas, West End Lane), V. **D** Lon 19 **P** *Trustees* **I** P W WHEATLEY, D H T LEE *c*, T C RICHARDSON *c*.
(St John, Downshire Hill), Propr Chap. **D** Lon 19 **P** *Trustees* **I** R SMITH *min*.
(St Jude on the Hill, Garden Suburb), V. **D** Lon 17 **P** *Bp* **I** J M PORTEUS.
(St Luke), V. **D** Lon 19 **P** *Trustees* **I** P A E REES.
(St Mary Virg Primrose Hill) w (St Paul, Avenue Road) (No Ch), V. **D** Lon 19 **P** *Trustees* **I** R P H BUCK, J G HESKINS *c*, F W STEPHENS *c*.
(St Mary, Priory Rd), V. **D** Lon 19 **P** *CPS* **I** (Vacant).
(St Pet), V. **D** Lon 19 **P** *D and C of Westmr* **I** D E BARNES, S R KIRBY *c*.
(St Sav Eton Rd), V. **D** Lon 19 **P** *V of Hampstead* **I** J C NEIL-SMITH.
(St Steph w All H), V. **D** Lon 19 **P** *Dioc Bd of Patr and D and C of Cant* **I** R A W COOGAN.
(H Trin Finchley Rd), V. **D** Lon 19 **P** *Trustees* **I** E J SMITH.
HAMPSTEAD-MARSHALL, *Berks*.. **D** Ox 14 *See* Enborne.
HAMPSTEAD-NORREYS (St Mary) w Langley, *Berks*. V. **D** Ox 14 *See* Hermitage.
HAMPSTEAD RD (St Jas).. **D** Lon 26 *See* St Pancras.
HAMPSTHWAITE (St Thos à Becket), *N Yorks*. V. **D** Ripon 4 **P** *Sir Cecil Aykroyd Bt* **I** J F WALKER.
HAMPTON (St Mary), *Gtr Lon*. V. **D** Lon 8 **P** *Ld Chan* **I** J A ROGERS.
(All SS), V. **D** Lon 8 **P** *Ld Chan* **I** D R BONNER *c*, M M NATHANAEL *c*.
(St Jas Hampton Hill), V. **D** Lon 8 **P** *V of Hampton* **I** J N CHUBB.
(St Jo Bapt Hampton Wick), V. **D** Lon 8 **P** *Ld Chan* **I** G L CARNES.
HAMPTON, GREAT and LITTLE (St Andr), *Worcs*. V. **D** Worc 1 **P** *Ch Ch Ox* **I** R E MEYER.
HAMPTON-IN-ARDEN (St Mary and St Bart), *W Midl*. V. **D** Birm 11 **P** *Guild of All S* **I** H K SLY, W J JENNINGS *hon c*.
HAMPTON BISHOP (St Andr), *Herefs*. R. **D** Heref 4 **P** *Bp* **I** J C B HALL-MATTHEWS *p-in-c*, M F JEFFERY *c*.
HAMPTON GAY (St Giles), *Oxon*. V. **D** Ox 10 **P** *Exors of Mrs Barry* **I** E G A W PAGE-TURNER *p-in-c*, D C PARKER *c*.
HAMPTON LOVETT (St Mary and All SS), *Worcs*. R. **D** Worc 8 *See* Elmley Lovett.
HAMPTON LUCY w Charlecote (St Leon) and Loxley (St Nich), *Warws*. R. **D** Cov 8 **P** *Sir E J W H Cameron-Ramsay-Fairfax-Lucy 1st, 3rd and 4th turns, Col A M H Gregory-Hood 2nd turn* **I** J H CORKE.
HAMPTON POYLE (St Mary Virg), *Oxon*. R. **D** Ox 2 **P** *Ex Coll Ox* **I** M P PULESTON.
HAMSEY (St Pet) w Offham (St Pet), *E Sussex*. R. **D** Chich 15 **P** *Exors of Sir H Shiffner Bt* **I** R G NEWHAM *c-in-c*.
HAMSEY GREEN (St Antony), *Surrey*.. **D** S'wark 9 *See* Sanderstead.
HAMSTALL-RIDWARE (St Mich AA), *Staffs*. R. **D** Lich 4 **P** *Ld Leigh 2 turns, Bp 1 turn* **I** R E P DAVIES.
HAMSTEAD (St Paul, *W Midl*. V. **D** Birm 3 **P** *Bp* **I** J W MASDING, A BALL *c*, R S WILLIAMS *c*.
(St Bernard), V. **D** Birm 3 **P** *Bp* **I** J R BARNETT.
HAMSTEELS (St Jo Bapt), *T & W*. V. **D** Dur 7 **P** *Crown* **I** P M HOOD.
HAMSTERLEY (St Jas), *Dur*. V. **D** Dur 9 **P** *Bp* **I** C BRENNEN *p-in-c*.
HAMWORTHY (St Mich), *Dorset*. R. **D** Sarum 14 **P** *MMT* **I** B C ALDIS, T R F YATES *c*.
HANBOROUGH (St Pet and St Paul), *Oxon*. R. **D** Ox 10 **P** *St Jo Coll Ox* **I** H D L THOMAS.
HANBURY (St Werburgh), *Staffs*. V. **D** Lich **P** *Bp* **I** F POWELL *c-in-c*.
HANBURY (St Mary Virg), *Worcs*. R. **D** Worc 8 **P** *Bp* **I** C H ROBINSON *p-in-c*.
HANBY, *Lincs*.. **D** Linc 2 *See* Ingoldsby.
HANDCROSS, *W Sussex*.. **D** Chich 11 *See* Slaugham.
HANDFORTH (St Chad), *Chesh*. V. **D** Ches 16 **P** *R of Cheadle* **I** S P ISHERWOOD, P H SMITH *c*.
HANDLEY (All SS), *Chesh*.. **D** Ches *See* Tattenhall.
HANDLEY, *Dorset*.. **D** Sarum *See* Pentridge.
HANDSWORTH (St Mary), *W Midl*. R. **D** Birm 3 **P** *Bp* **I** J C H TOMPKINS, T W WARD *c*.
(St Andr), V. **D** Birm 3 **P** *Bp* **I** J A HERVE *p-in-c*, W G GOLBOURNE *c*.
(St Mich), V. **D** Birm 3 **P** *Bp* **I** E PRICE.
(St Jas), V. **D** Birm 3 **P** *Bp* **I** J N HACKETT, D K CHANDA *c*, H S EDWARDS *c*.
(St Jo Evang). **D** Birm 3 *See* Perry Barr.
(St Pet), V. **D** Birm 3 **P** *Bp* **I** J P FAULDS.
HANDSWORTH (St Mary), *S Yorks*. R. **D** Sheff 1 **P** *Dioc Bd of Patr* **I** B E LENG.
HANDSWORTH-WOODHOUSE (St Jas), *S Yorks*. V. **D** Sheff 1 **P** *Bp* **I** R J BUCKLEY.
HANFORD (St Matthias), *Staffs*. V. **D** Lich 19 **P** *Bp* **I** E H FINNEMORE.
HANFORD (St Mich AA), *Dorset*. V. **D** Sarum 13 *See* Childe Okeford.
HANGER HILL (Ascen), *Gtr Lon*. V. **D** Lon 5 **P** *Bp* **I** I R HENDERSON, P W HOWLDEN *hon c*, H ROM *hon c*.
HANGING HEATON (St Paul), *W Yorks*. V. **D** Wakef 10 **P** *V of Dewsbury* **I** N A CARTER, B A GEESON *hon c*.
HANGLETON (St Helen w St Richard), *E Sussex*. V. **D** Chich 13 **P** *Bp* **I** T J INMAN, K WOOD *c*.
HANHAM (Ch Ch) w Hanham Abbots (St Geo), *Avon*. V. **D** Bris 8 **P** *Bp* **I** K F DIMOLINE.
HANKERTON (H Cross), *Wilts*. V. **D** Bris *See* Charlton.
HANLEY, H Evang, w Hope, (St Luke Wellington, St Matt Birches Head, H Trin Northwood, Ch Ch Cobridge and St Mark Shelton), *Staffs*. R. **D** Lich 17a **P** *Bp* **I** G M K MORGAN, C R GOODLEY *team v*, R V HEADING *team v*, L H SKINNER *team v*, M F WEST *team v*.
(All SS), V. **D** Lich *See* Stoke-upon-Trent.
(St Jude), V. **D** Lich *See* Stoke-upon-Trent.

HANLEY CASTLE (St Mary Virg), Hanley Swan (St Gabr) and Welland (St Jas), *Worcs*. V. D Worc 5 P *Ld Chan and Sir B Lechmere Bt in turn* I (Vacant).
HANLEY WILLIAM (All SS) w Hanley Child (St Mich AA), *Worcs*. R. D Worc 12 *See* Stoke Bliss.
HANNAH (St Andr), R and Hagnaby (St Thos Mart), R w Markby (St Pet), *Lincs*. V. D Linc 8 P *Bp and B B Smyth Esq* alt I G I GEORGE-JONES.
HANNEY, WEST (St Jas Gt), w Hanney, East, *Oxon*. V. D Ox 19 P *Bp* I D A PEARCE.
HANNINGFIELD, EAST (All SS), *Essex*. R. D Chelmsf 12 P *Trustees* I A D OST.
WEST (St Mary and St Edw), R *Essex*. R. D Chelmsf 17 P *Dioc Bd of Patr* I H H DAVIS.
HANNINGTON, *Wilts*.. D Bris *See* Highworth.
HANNINGTON, *Northants*. R. D Pet 6 *See* Walgrave.
HANNINGTON, *Hants*. R. D Win *See* Wolverton.
HANOVER SQUARE (St Geo).. D Lon 19 *See* Westminster.
HANSLOPE (St Jas Gt) w Castlethorpe (St Simon and St Jude), *Bucks*. V. D Ox 28 P *Bp* I C M G BEAKE.
HANWELL (St Mary), *Gtr Lon*. R. D Lon 6 P *Bp* I F T SECOMBE.
(St Mellitus w St Mark), V. D Lon 6 P *Bp* I R H WORMALD.
(St Thos Ap), V. D Lon 6 P *Crown* I D A CATON.
(St Chris Cuckoo Estate), V. D Lon 6 P *Bp* I W WALKER.
HANWELL (St Pet), *Oxon*. R. D Ox 6 P *Ld Buckhurst* I C A L WOOLLEY *c-in-c*.
HANWOOD, GREAT (St Thos), *Salop*. R. D Heref 13 P *Col H de Grey-Warter* I S P BURTWELL.
HANWORTH (St Geo), *Gtr Lon*. R. D Lon 10 P *Lee Abbey Council* I R L HOLLANDS *c*.
(All SS), V. D Lon 10 P *Bp* I J A FLETCHER.
(St Richard of Chich), V. D Lon 10 P *Bp* I K C EMMETT.
HANWORTH (St Bart), *Norf*. R. D Nor 5 *See* Gunton.
HANWORTH, COLD, *Lincs*.. D Linc 3 *See* Hackthorn.
HAPPISBURGH (St Mary Virg) w Walcot (All SS), *Norf*. V. D Nor 9 P *Bp* I D F COOMBES.
HAPTON (St Marg Conv Distr), *Lancs*.. D Blackb 3 P *Bp* I (Vacant).
HAPTON, *Norf*.. D Nor *See* Wreningham.
HARBERTON (St Andr) w HARBERTONFORD (St Pet), *Devon*. V. D Ex 13 P *D and C of Ex* I J SHEPHEARD-WALWYN *p-in-c*.
HARBERTONFORD (St Pet), *Devon*.. D Ex 13 *See* Harberton.
HARBLEDOWN (St Mich), *Kent*. R. D Cant 3 P *Abp* I C MUNT.
HARBORNE (St Pet), *W Midl*. V. D Birm 2 P *Bp* I M J R COUNSELL, L E SPICER *c*.
(St Faith w St Laur), V. D Birm 2 P *Bp* I J A ROSSINGTON.
(St Jo Bapt), V. D Birm 2 P *Ch S Trust* I T O WALKER, A PEMBERTON *c*, K L SHILL *c*.
HARBORNE, NORTH (H Trin), *W Midl*.. D Birm 5 *See* Smethwick.
HARBOROUGH MAGNA (All SS), *Warws*. R. D Cov 6 P *A H C W Boughton-Leigh Esq* I (Vacant).
HARBRIDGE, *Hants*.. D Win *See* Ellingham.
HARBURY (All SS), *Warws*. V. D Cov 10 P *Bp* I F R MACKLEY.
HARBY (St Mary Virg) w Stathern, *Leics*. R. D Leic 3 P *Peterhouse Cam and Duke of Rutland (alt)* I J S SAVIGE.
HARBY w Swinethorpe (All SS) and Thorney w Wigsley, Broadholme and N and S Clifton, *Notts*. V. D Southw P *Bp and Ld Chan (alt)* I M W BRIGGS.
HARDEN (St Sav), *W Yorks*.. D Bradf 11 *See* Bingley.
HARDENHUISH, *Wilts*. R. D Bris *See* Chippenham, St Paul.
HARDHAM (St Botolph), *W Sussex*. R. D Chich 7 P *Sir B W de S Barttelot Bt* I F G KERR-DINEEN.
HARDINGHAM (St Geo), *Norf*.. D Nor 12 *See* Barnham Broom.
HARDINGSTONE (St Edm) and Horton and Piddington, *Northants*. V. D Pet 4 P *Bp* I B MCCLELLAN.
HARDINGTON (BVM), *Somt*.. D B & W 16a *See* Hemington.
HARDINGTON-MANDEVILLE (St Mary Virg) w East Chinnock and Pendomer (St Roch), *Somt*. R. D B & W 11 P *MMT* I D C F FARRINGTON.
HARDLEY (St Marg), *Norf*.. D Nor *See* Chedgrave.
HARDMEAD (Assump of BVM), *Bucks*. R. D Ox 28 *See* Astwood.
HARDRAW w Lunds, *N Yorks*. V. D Ripon 2 P *Exors of R Fawcett Esq, S H Willan Esq and V of Aysgarth in turn* I C C R MERIVALE.
HARDRES, LOWER (St Mary), w Nackington (St Mary), *Kent*. R. D Cant 2 *See* Petham.
HARDRES, UPPER (St Pet and St Paul), w Stelling (St Mary), *Kent*. R. D Cant 2 P *Lady J Trower* I W H J BURT *p-in-c*.
HARDWICK, *Norf*. D Nor *See* Runcton, North.
HARDWICK (St Mary), *Oxon*.. D Ox 9 *See* Ducklington.
HARDWICK (St Marg), *Norf*.. D Nor *See* Shelton.
HARDWICK (St Mary) w Tusmore, *Oxon*. R. D Ox 2 P *Hon Mrs G M R Collins* I H J F EDGINGTON *c-in-c*.
HARDWICK (St Mary), *Cambs*. R. D Ely 1 P *Bp* I J S BEER.
HARDWICKE (St Nich), *Glos*.. D Glouc 9 P *Bp* I G J B STICKLAND.
HARDWICKE (H Trin), *Herefs*. V. D Heref 1 P *T F Powell Esq* I W R KING *p-in-c*.
HARDWICKE, *Bucks*. R. D Ox *See* Schorne.
HARDWYCKE (St Leon), *Northants*. R. D Pet 7 P *Mrs Lacon* I R F COTTINGHAM.
HAREBY (St Pet and St Paul), *Lincs*.. D Linc 7 *See* Bolingbroke.
HAREFIELD (St Mary Virg), *Gtr Lon*. V. D Lon 9 P *Hon Mrs Fitzroy Newdegate* I D G A CONNOR, J D CORNISH *c*.
HARESCOMBE (St Jo Bapt), *Glos*. R. D Glouc 3 *See* Brookthorpe.
HARESFIELD (St Pet), *Glos*. R. D Glouc 3 *See* Standish.
HAREWOOD, *W Yorks*.. D Ripon 4 *See* Collingham.
HARFORD (St Petroc), *Devon*. R. D Ex 21 P *Felsted Sch* I D W OBEE *c-in-c*.
HARGHAM, *Norf*.. D Nor 18 *See* Wilby.
HARGRAVE (St Pet), *Chesh*. V. D Ches 5 P *Bp* I K HARRIS.
HARGRAVE (All SS), *Northants*. R. D Pet 9 *See* Stanwick.
HARGRAVE, *Suff*.. D St E *See* Chevington.
HARKSTEAD (St Mary), *Suff*. R. D St E 5 *See* Chelmondiston.
HARLASTON (St Matt), *Staffs*. R. D Lich 6 P *Bp* I (Vacant).
HARLAXTON (Wyville, Hungerton, Denton and Stroxton), *Lincs*. R. D Linc 14 P *Bp, Sir B Welby Bt, D and C of Linc and Dioc Bd of Patr* I A C SWINDELL.
HARLESCOTT (H Spirit), *Salop*. V. D Lich 26 P *Bp* I C P BURKETT *c*, D W G UFFINDELL *c*, W M YOUNG *c*.
HARLESDEN. D Lon *See* Willesden.
HARLESTON (St Jo Bapt), *Norf*.. D Nor 17 *See* Redenhall.
HARLESTON (St Aug), *Suff*. R. D St E 6 *See* Onehouse.
HARLESTONE (St Andr), *Northants*. R. D Pet *See* Brampton Ch.
HARLEY (St Mary) w Kenley (St Jo Bapt), *Salop*. R. D Heref *See* Wenlock.
HARLEY WOOD (All SS), *W Yorks*. V. D Wakef 3 *See* Todmorden.
HARLING, EAST w West (St Pet and St Paul), *Norf*. R. D Nor 18 P *Mrs B H Garnham Williams 2 turns, Lady Nugent 1 turn* I H R ELLIOT.
HARLINGTON (St Pet and St Paul), *Gtr Lon*. R. D Lon 9 P *Bp* I D R JENKINS, P C NICHOLSON *hon c*.
(Ch Ch Miss). D Lon 9 P *Bp* I R N MCCANN *p-in-c*.
HARLINGTON (St Mary Virg), *Beds*. V. D St Alb 18 P *Bp* I G W WEBSTER *c*.
HARLOW (St Mary Virg w St Jo Bapt), *Essex*. V. D Chelmsf 3 P *Simeon Trustees and Bp alt* I R F H HOWARTH, S P SPRINGETT *c*.
(St Mary Magd), V. D Chelmsf 3 P *V of Harlow* I R W GREENLAND, T MASLEN *c*.
NEW TOWN (St Paul) w L Parndon (St Mary), R. D Chelmsf 3 P *Patr Bd* I D M KNIGHT.
HARLOW GREEN (St Ninian Conv Distr), *T & W*.. D Dur 4 P *Bp* I S ROBBINS *p-in-c*.
HARLOW-HILL (All SS), *N Yorks*.. D Ripon 4 *See* Harrogate, Low.
HARLTON (Assump of the BVM), *Cambs*. R. D Ely 7 P *Jes Coll Cam* I K G TAYLOR *p-in-c*.
HARMONDSWORTH (St Mary), *Gtr Lon*. V. D Lon 9 P *Exors of Rev H M S Taylor* I R K HAMMERTON.
HARMSTON (All SS), *Lincs*. V. D Linc 18 P *Dioc Bd of Patr* I F W NAIRN *c-in-c*.
HARNHAM (All SS) w (St Geo), *Wilts*. V. D Sarum 16 P *V of Britford 2 turns, Bp 1 turn* I J C TOWNSEND, I H S STRATTON *c*.
HARNHILL w Driffield, *Glos*. R. D Glouc 13 *See* Ampney.
HAROLD HILL (St Paul's), *Essex*.. D Chelmsf *See* Romford.
HAROLD WOOD, *Essex*.. D Chelmsf 4 *See* Hornchurch.
HAROME (St Sav) w Stonegrave, Nunnington and Pockley, *N Yorks*. V. D York 20 P *Abp, Archd of Cleveland and V of Helmsley (jtly) 1 turn, Crown 1 turn, Abp 1 turn* I J B BATEMAN.
HARPENDEN (St Nich), *Herts*. R. D St Alb 14 P *Ld Chan* I J R A LLEWELLIN, D ELLIOTT *c*, D G MIHILL *c*,

C J WHARTON *c.*
(St Jo Bapt), V. **D** St Alb 14 **P** *Dioc Bd of Patr* **I** G A J MARTIN.
HARPFORD (St Greg), *Devon.* V. **D** Ex 7 *See* Newton Poppleford.
HARPHAM (St John of Beverley), *Humb.*. **D** York 12 *See* Burton Agnes.
HARPLEY (St Lawr), *Norf.* R. **D** Nor 20 **P** *Exors of Miss A C Beck* **I** (Vacant).
HARPOLE (All SS), *Northants.* R. **D** Pet 3 **P** *Earl Fitzwilliam* **I** C F JOHNSON.
HARPSDEN (St Marg) w Bolney, *Oxon.* R. **D** Ox 7 **P** *All S Coll Ox* **I** M R PRITCHARD *p-in-c.*
HARPSWELL (St Chad), *Lincs.*. **D** Linc 2 *See* Hemswell.
HARPTREE, EAST (St Laur) w Harptree West (St Mary Virg) and Hinton Blewett, *Avon.* R and V. **D** B & W 15 **P** *Duchy of Cornw* **I** V C HATHERLEY.
HARPURHEY (Ch Ch), *Gtr Man.* R. **D** Man 7 **P** *Trustees* **I** T R HINDLEY.
(St Steph), R. **D** Man 7 **P** *Crown and Bp* alt **I** T R HINDLEY.
HARRIETSHAM (St Jo Bapt), *Kent.* R. **D** Cant 15 **P** *All S Coll Ox* **I** A J H SALMON.
HARRINGAY (St Paul), *Lon.* V. **D** Lon 22 **P** *Bp* **I** J F SEELEY, J A TAYLOR *hon c.*
HARRINGTON (St Mary), *Cumb.* R. **D** Carl 11 **P** *E S C Curwen Esq* **I** P H DAVIDGE.
HARRINGTON (St Mary) w Brinkhill (St Phil), *Lincs.* R. **D** Linc 7 **P** *Sir T C W Ingilby Bt* **I** P E FLUCK *c-in-c.*
HARRINGTON, *Northants.*. **D** Pet *See* Arthingworth.
HARRINGWORTH, *Northants.*. **D** Pet 13 *See* Bulwick.
HARROGATE, HIGH (Ch Ch), *N Yorks.* V. **D** Ripon 4 **P** *Bp* **I** R T W MCDERMID, J S WARD *c.*
(St Mark), V. **D** Ripon 4 **P** *Peache Trustees* **I** S J A TURNER.
(St Wilfrid and St Luke), V. **D** Ripon **P** *Bp* **I** H GARSIDE, T DEVAMANIKKAM *c.*
(St Pet) V. **D** Ripon 4 **P** *CPS* **I** A N B SUGDEN, W J HIRST *hon c,* F W LISTER *hon c.*
LOW (St Mary) w Harlow Hill (All SS), *N Yorks.* V. **D** Ripon 4 **P** *Peache Trustees* **I** A BODY.
HARROLD (St Pet or All SS) w Carlton (St Pet) and Chellington (St Nich), *Beds.* V. **D** St Alb 21 **P** *Ball Coll Ox 2 Turns, Bp 1 turn* **I** D R THURBURN-HUELIN.
HARROW (St Mary), *Gtr Lon.* V. **D** Lon 24 **P** *Trustees* **I** F W H WHITE.
(Ch Ch Roxeth), V. **D** Lon 24 **P** *CPS* **I** E S SHIRRAS.
(St Jo Bapt Greenhill), V. **D** Lon 24 **P** *Bp Archd of Northolt and V of Harrow* **I** R L RAMSDEN *c.*
NORTH (St Alb), V. **D** Lon 24 **P** *Bp* **I** D G J CADDY, P J EDGE *c,* H C SMITH *c.*
(St Pet), V. **D** Lon 24 **P** *Bp* **I** (Vacant).
SOUTH (St Paul), V. **D** Lon 24 **P** *R of St Bride, Fleet St* **I** R J PIKE.
(St Andr), V. **D** Lon 24 **P** *Bp* **I** (Vacant).
HARROW GREEN (H Trin and St Aug of Hippo), *Essex.* V. **D** Chelmsf 8 **P** *Bp* **I** P R HANSON.
HARROW ROAD. **D** Lon 16 *See* Paddington and Kensal Green.
HARROW WEALD (All SS), *Gtr Lon.* V. **D** Lon 24 **P** *Trustees* **I** I K CHISHOLM, W S M SIMONSON *hon c.*
HARROW WEALD and WEALDSTONE (St Mich AA), *Gtr Lon.*. **D** Lon 24 **P** *Bp* **I** B T LLOYD *p-in-c,* A M ANSELL *c,* F C SIMPKINS *c.*
HARROWDEN, GREAT (All SS), w Little (St Mary Virg) and Orlingbury (St Mary), *Northants.* V. **D** Pet 7 **P** *Earl Fitzwilliam and Bp* alt **I** G J JOHNSON.
HARSTON (All SS) w Hauxton, *Cambs.* V. **D** Ely 7 **P** *Bp 2 turns, D and C 1 turn* **I** M T ALLEN.
HARSTON (St Mich AA), *Leics.* R. **D** Leic 2 *See* Knipton.
HARSWELL, *Humb.*. **D** York *See* Seaton Ross.
HART (St Mary Magd) w Elwick Hall (St Pet), *Cleve.* V. **D** Dur 12 **P** *Bp of Dur & Bp of Man (alt)* **I** G A HOWE.
HARTBURN (St Andr) w Meldon (St Jo Evang), *Northumb.* V. **D** Newc T 10 **P** *Ld Chan* **I** A F DONNELLY.
HARTCLIFFE (St Andr), *Avon.* V. **D** Bris 1 **P** *Bp* **I** G D TEAGUE *c.*
HARTEST w Boxted (All SS), *Suff.* R. **D** St E 12 **P** *Crown* **I** T S WRIGHT.
HARTFIELD (St Mary) w Coleman's Hatch (H Trin), *E Sussex.* R. **D** Chich 20 **P** *Earl de la Warr and Bp and Bp* **I** P D S BLAKE.
HARTFORD (St Jo Bapt), *Ches.* V. **D** Ches 6 **P** *Mrs I H Wilson, Mrs R H Emmett, and Mrs J M Wearne* **I** M P MARSHALL, M D HOLLINGWORTH *c.*
HARTFORD (All SS), *Cambs.* V. **D** Ely 10 **P** *Bp* **I** R JEFFREE.
HARTHILL (All SS) w Burwardsley (St Jo Div), *Chesh.* V. **D** Ches 5 **P** *Bp and G R Barbour Esq* **I** F MAWSON *p-in-c.*
HARTHILL (All H), *S Yorks.* R. **D** Sheff 5 **P** *Bp* **I** W A STRATFORD.
HARTING (St Mary and St Gabr), *W Sussex.* R. **D** Chich 5 **P** *Bp* **I** K L MASTERS.
HARTINGTON (St Giles) and Biggin (St Thos), *Derbys.* V. **D** Derby 10 **P** *Duke of Devonshire* **I** A D GIBSON.
HARTLAND (St Nectan) w Welcombe (St Nectan), *Devon.* V. **D** Ex 17 **P** *Bp* **I** L M COULSON.
HARTLEBURY (St Jas Gt w Bishop's Wood (St Jo Evang), *Worcs.* R. **D** Worc 12 **P** *Bp* **I** A H B MCCLATCHEY.
HARTLEPOOL (St Hilda w St Andr), *Cleve.* R. **D** Dur 12 **P** *Bp* **I** W BENTLEY.
(H Trin), V. **D** Dur 12 **P** *Bp* **I** M O C JOY.
HARTLEPOOL, WEST (Ch Ch), *Cleve.*. **D** Dur 12 *See* Stranton.
(All SS), V. **D** Dur 12 *See* Stranton.
(St Aid w St Columba), V. **D** Dur 12 **P** *Bp* **I** R V CHADWICK, R A CHAPMAN *c.*
(St Jas Conv Distr Owton Manor). **D** Dur 12 **I** J M LANGFORD *p-in-c.*
(St Luke), V. **D** Dur 12 **P** *Bp* **I** P TOWNSEND, R L VERNON *c.*
(St Paul), V. **D** Dur 12 **P** *Bp* **I** J R BULLOCK, K FLETCHER *c.*
(St Osw), V. **D** Dur 12 **P** *Bp* **I** J C G POLLOCK *c.*
HARTLEY (All SS), *Kent.* R. **D** Roch 1 **P** *Miss I King* **I** P H D A LOCK.
HARTLEY-MAUDITT, *Hants.* R. **D** Win 1 *See* Worldham, East.
HARTLEY, NEW (St Mich), *Northumb.*. **D** Newc T 1 *See* Delaval.
HARTLEY WESPALL (St Mary BV) w Stratfield Turgis, *Hants.* R. **D** Win 4 *See* Stratfieldsaye.
HARTLEY WINTNEY (St Jo Evang), Elvetham, Winchfield and Dogmersfield, *Hants.* V. **D** Win 4 **P** *Bp and Sir R Anstruther-Gough-Calthorpe Bt* **I** J W EARP, J D ALDERMAN *c.*
HARTLIP (St Mich AA) w Stockbury (St Mary Magd), *Kent.* V. **D** Cant 14 **P** *Abp* **I** M J CHANDLER.
HARTON (St Pet), *T & W.* V. **D** Dur 6 **P** *D and C of Dur* **I** G G DEWHURST, A DRIVER *c,* B HAILS *c.*
HARTON, WEST, or HARTON COLLIERY (All SS), *T & W.* V. **D** Dur 6 **P** *D and C of Dur & Bp* **I** T HART, P S RAMSDEN *c.*
HARTPURY (St Mary Virg) w Corse (St Marg) and Staunton (St Jas), *Glos.* V. **D** Glouc 2 **P** *Bp 2 turns, Mrs F M Hayes 1 turn* **I** J G EVANS *c.*
HARTSHEAD (St Pet), *W Yorks.* V. **D** Wakef 9 **P** *V of Dewsbury* **I** E SIMPSON.
HARTSHILL (H Trin), *Warws.* V. **D** Cov 5 **P** *V of Mancetter* **I** D J SMITH.
HARTSHILL (H Trin), *Staffs.* V. **D** Lich 18 **P** *Bp* **I** J W SPRAY.
HARTSHORNE (St Pet), *Derbys.* R. **D** Derby 16 **P** *MMT* **I** I R WILLIAMS-HUNTER.
HARTWELL (St Jo Bapt), *Northants.* V. **D** Pet 2 *See* Ashton.
HARTWITH (St Jude Ap) *N Yorks.* V. **D** Ripon 3 *See* Dacre.
HARTY (St Thos Ap), *Kent.*. **D** Cant 13 *See* Leysdown.
HARVINGTON (St Jas Gt) and Norton (St Egwin) and Lenchwick, *Worcs.* R. **D** Worc 1 **P** *D and C of Worc* **I** C R S EVE.
HARWELL (St Matt) w Chilton (All SS), *Oxon.* V. **D** Ox 18 **P** *CPAS and Dioc Bd of Patr* **I** N A RUSSELL.
HARWICH (St Nich), *Essex.* V. **D** Chelmsf 25 **P** *Bp* **I** W S DODD.
HARWOOD (St Jude), *Durham.*. **D** Dur 10 *See* Forest.
HARWOOD (Ch Ch), *Gtr Man.* V. **D** Man 19 **P** *Trustees* **I** A J DOBB, J R BROCKLEHURST *c.*
HARWOOD DALE, *N Yorks.*. **D** York *See* Hackness.
HARWOOD, GREAT (St Bart), *Lancs.* V. **D** Blackb 7 **P** *V of Blackb* **I** J R HASLAM.
(St John). **D** Blackb 7 **P** *Trustees* **I** H DUNKINSON *c.*
HARWORTH (All SS) w Bircotes (Ch Ch), *Notts.* V. **D** Southw 1 **P** *Sir J H I Whitaker Bt* **I** (Vacant).
HASCOMBE (St Pet), *Surrey.* R. **D** Guildf 4 **P** *S for Maint of Faith* **I** R C D MACKENNA *p-in-c.*
HASELBECH Northants. R **D** Pet *See* Clipston.
HASELBURY-PLUCKNETT (St Mich AA) w Misterton and N Perrott (St Martin), *Somt.* V. **D** B & W 11 **P** *Ld Chan 2 turns, Bp 2 turns and H W F Hoskyns 1 turn* **I** R G PENMAN.
HASELEY (St Mary), *Warws.* R. **D** Cov 4 *See* Hatton.
HASELEY, GREAT (St Pet) w Albury (St Helen), Tiddington and Waterstock *Oxon.*. **D** Ox 5 **P** *D and C of Windsor* **I** A R METHUEN *p-in-c.*
HASELOR (St Mary and All SS), *Warws.*. **D** Cov 7 *See* Kinwarton.

HASELTON (St Andr), Glos.. D Glouc 15 See Withington.
HASFIELD (St Mary) w Tirley and Ashleworth (St Andr and St Bart), V Glos. R. D Glouc 2 P Mrs M Brooksbank, Ld Chan and Bp in turn I P M DACK.
HASKETON (St Andr), Suff. R. D St E 7 P Bp I (Vacant).
HASLAND (St Paul), Derbys. R. D Derby 3 P V of Chesterfield I H R O ANDERSON.
HASLEMERE (St Bart and St Chris), Surrey. R. D Guildf 4 P Ld Chan I R N MORTON, J W SMITH c.
HASLINGDEN (St Jas Gt) w Haslingden Grane (St Steph), Lancs. V. D Blackb 1 P Hulme Trustees and Bp alt I (Vacant).
(St Pet). D Blackb 1 See Laneside.
HASLINGFIELD, Cambs. V. D Ely 7 P Dioc Bd of Patr I K G TAYLOR p-in-c.
HASLINGTON (St Matt), Chesh. V. D Ches 15 P Bp I D W SMITH.
HASSINGHAM (St Mary), Norf.. D Nor 1 See Buckenham.
HASTINGLEIGH (St Mary Virg), Kent. R. D Cant 2 See Elmsted.
HASTINGS (St Clem w All SS), E Sussex. R. D Chich 21 P Bp I F R CUMBERLEGE.
(All S Clive Vale), V. D Chich 21 P R of Upper St Leonards I B TRILL.
(Ch Ch Blacklands), V. D Chich 21 P Ch Patr Trust and Bp alt I T S STRATFORD.
(Em Ch and St Mary-in-the-Castle), V. D Chich 21 P Trustees and Hyndman Trustees alt I R S BROOKS.
(H Trin), V. D Chich 21 P Bp I D J TAYLOR.
(St Andr), V. D Chich 21 P Bp I T S STRATFORD.
(St Mary Magd). D Chich 21 See St Leonards.
HASWELL (St Paul), Durham. V. D Dur 3 P Bp I W H SPARKS.
HATCH, WEST (St Andr), Somt. V. D B & W 23a P D and C of Wells I R BEEVERS.
HATCH-BEAUCHAMP (St Jo Bapt) w Beercrocombe , Somt. R. D B & W 23a P Trustees I R BEEVERS.
HATCH END (St Anselm), Gtr Lon. V. D Lon 24 P Bp I C PEARCE.
(St Geo Headstone), V. D Lon 24 P Bp I P HEMINGWAY.
HATCHAM (St Jas w St Geo and St Mich), Kent. V. D S'wark 19 P CPS I M J J PAGET-WILKES, C WHEATON c.
(St Cath), V. D S'wark 19 P Haberdashers' Co I C R B BIRD, G C BEAUCHAMP c, G H GREEN c.
HATCHAM PARK (All SS), Surrey and Kent. V. D S'wark 19 P Trustees 2 turns, Haberdashers' Co 1 turn I O J BEAMENT.
HATCHFORD (St Matt and All SS), Surrey. V. D Guildf 10 See Ockham.
HATCLIFFE (St Mary), Humb.. D Linc 10 See Ravendale, East.
HATFIELD (St Leon), Herefs. V. D Heref 7 See Pudleston.
HATFIELD (St Lawr), S Yorks. V. D Sheff 8 P Capt A B Coventry, R N I J W SWEED.
HATFIELD or BISHOP'S HATFIELD (St Etheldreda), Herts. R. D St Alb 7 P Marq of Salisbury I W C D TODD, G MORGAN c, A P MOTTRAM c, M OSBALDESTON c.
HATFIELD BROAD OAK or HATFIELD REGIS (St Mary Virg) and Bush End, Essex. V. D Chelmsf 3 P Bp I W H CORREY.
HATFIELD HEATH (H Trin), Essex. V. D Chelmsf 3 P V of Hatfield, Broad Oak I W E DICKINSON.
HATFIELD HYDE (St Mary Magd), Herts. V. D St Alb 7 P Marq of Salisbury I R W DRAY, P G BANHAM c.
HATFIELD PEVEREL (St Andr) w Ulting (All SS), Essex. V. D Chelmsf 29 P Bp I R E TOZER.
HATFORD (H Trin), Oxon. R. D Ox 17 See Stanford-in-the-Vale.
HATHERDEN (Ch Ch) w Tangley (St Thos) and Weyhill and Penton Mewsey, Hants. V. D Win 2 P Bp and Qu Coll Ox I J M DRY.
HATHERLEIGH, Devon. V. D Ex 12 P Daily Prayer U Trust I C N HILLYER.
HATHERN (St Pet and St Paul), Leics. R. D Leic 10 P Bp I S SAMUEL p-in-c.
HATHEROP (St Nich), Glos. R. D Glouc See Coln St Aldwyn.
HATHERSAGE (St Mich), Derbys. V. D Derby 9 P Duke of Devonshire I M F H HULBERT p-in-c.
HATHERTON (St Sav), Staffs. V V. D Lich 3 P Ld Hatherton I J K LINFORD.
HATLEY COCKAYNE (St Jo Bapt), Beds. R. D St Alb 14 See Potton.
HATLEY, EAST (St Denis), Cambs. R. D Ely See Gamlingay.
HATLEY ST GEORGE (St Geo), Cambs. R. D Ely See Gamlingay.
HATTERSLEY (St Barn Ap and Mart), Gtr Man. V. D Ches 14 P Bp I J E W BOWERS, N A ASHTON c, M C LOSACK c.
HATTON (H Trin) w Haseley (St Mary), and Rowington (St Lawr) w Lowsonford, Warws V. D Cov 4 P Bp I M D B LONG.
HATTON (St Steph) w Sotby (St Pet), Lincs. R. D Linc See Hemingby.
HAUGH (St Leon), Lincs. V. D Linc 7 P Mert Coll Ox I P E FLUCK c-in-c.
HAUGHAM (All SS), Lincs. V. D Linc 12 See Tathwell.
HAUGHLEY (St Mary) w Wetherden (St Mary), Suff. V. D St E 6 P Bp and Ld Chan alt I D R SUTCH.
HAUGHTON (St Giles), Staffs. R. D Lich P Preb T F Royds I J S COOKE C-IN-C OF RANTON.
HAUGHTON (St Anne), Gtr Man. R. D Man 2 P Heirs of J W Sidebotham Esq I M ASHWORTH.
(St Mary Virg), R. D Man 2 P Bp I C J C FRITH, A PORTER c.
HAUGHTON-LE-SKERNE, Durham. R. D Dur 11 P Bp I A F LAZONBY, W M MACNAUGHTON c, S J ROBINSON c.
HAULT HUCKNALL (St Jo Bapt), Derbys.. D Derby 3 See Ault Hucknall.
HAUTBOIS, GREAT, Norf.. D Nor See Coltishall.
HAUTBOIS, LITTLE, Norf.. D Nor See Lammas.
HAUXTON (St Edm), Cambs. V. D Ely 7 See Harston.
HAUXWELL (St Osw), N Yorks.. D Ripon See Spennithorne.
HAVANT (St Faith), Hants. R. D Portsm 3 P Bp I D F BROWN.
(St Alb West Leigh Conv Distr). D Portsm 3 I A N STAMP p-in-c.
HAVENSTREET (St Pet), Isle of Wight. V. D Portsm 6 See Swanmore.
HAVERHILL (St Mary Virg), Suff. V. D St E 8 P Bp I C B WESLEY c, J S WOOD c.
HAVERING-ATTE-BOWER (St Jo Evang), Essex. V. D Chelmsf 4 P CPAS I R A GRINSTED.
HAVERINGLAND, Norf. V. D Nor I (Vacant).
HAVERSHAM (St Mary) w Linford, Little (St Leon), Bucks. R. D Ox 28 P CPAS I D LUNN p-in-c.
HAVERTHWAITE (St Anne) and Finsthwaite, Cumb.. D Carl See Leven Valley.
HAWCOAT, Cumb.. D Carl 3 See Barrow-in-Furness.
HAWERBY, Humb.. D Linc 10 See Wold Newton.
HAWES (St Marg), N Yorks. V. D Ripon 2 P V of Aysgarth I C C R MERIVALE.
HAWKCHURCH (St Jo Bapt) w Fishpond, Bettiscombe and Marshwood w Pilsdon, Devon. R. D Sarum 2 P Keble Coll Ox, M A Pinney Esq and Bp in turn I J AFFLECK p-in-c.
HAWKE, MT, Cornw.. D Truro See Mithian.
HAWKEDON D St E 8 See Chedburgh.
HAWKESBURY (St Mary) w Hawkesbury Upton (St Andr), Avon. V. D Gloue 8 P Mrs Dreyfus I T T GIBSON p-in-c.
HAWKHURST (St Lawr w All SS), Kent. V. D Cant 11 P Ch Ch Ox I W A LEAH.
HAWKINGE (St Mich), Kent. R. D Cant 6 P Abp I J B E CHITTENDEN.
HAWKLEY (St Pet and St Paul) w Priors Dean, Hants. V. D Portsm 4 P Bp I B F FORSTER p-in-c.
HAWKRIDGE (St Giles) w Withypool (St Andr), Somt. R. D B & W 21 P Miss D J M Etherington I J A ATKIN c.
HAWKSHAW LANE (St Mary), Gtr Man. V. D Man 12 P C F Whowell Esq I E A RUEHORN.
HAWKSHEAD (St Mich) and Low Wray (St Marg) w Sawrey, Cumb. V. D Carl 14 P Bp I (Vacant).
HAWKSWORTH (St Mary Virg and All SS) w Scarrington (St John of Beverley), Notts. R. D Southw 9 P D and C of Linc and MMT alt I S F RISING.
HAWKSWORTH WOOD (St Mary), w Moor Grange (St Andr), W Yorks. V. D Ripon 5 P Trustees of Leeds Vicarage I J H NICHOLL, K A PAYNE c.
HAWKWELL (St Mary), Essex. R. D Chelmsf 16 P CPAS I A R HIGTON, J R TAYLOR c.
HAWLEY, S Hants.. D Guildf 1 See Cove.
HAWLEY (H Trin) w Blackwater, Hants. V. D Guildf 1 P Keble Coll Ox and Bp I I M HANCOCK, A P PINCHIN c.
HAWLING, Glos.. D Glouc See Sevenhampton.
HAWNBY (All SS) w Old Byland, N Yorks. R. D York See Upper Ryedale.

HAWORTH (St Mich AA), *W Yorks.* R. **D** Bradf 11 **P** *V of Bradf and Haworth Ch Lands Trust* I B F ASHDOWN.
HAWRIDGE (St Mary) w Cholesbury (St Laur), *Bucks.* R. **D** Ox 30 **P** *Bp 2 turns, Neale's Trustees 1 turn* I A PAICE *p-in-c.*
HAWSKER (All SS) w Stainsacre, *N Yorks.* V. **D** York *See* Fylingdales.
HAWSTEAD (All SS) w Nowton (St Pet) and Stanningfield w Bradfield Combust, *Suff.* R. **D** St E 13 **P** *O R Oakes, Esq 2 turns, Marquis of Bris 1 turn, Bp 1 turn* I J B CHALKLEN, H M FORD *c.*
HAWTHORN (St Mich), *Durham.* R. **D** Dur 3 **P** *I Pemberton Esq* I J W BEATTIE.
HAWTON (All SS), *Notts.* R. **D** Southw *See* Newark.
HAXBY (St Mary) w Wigginton (St Mary), *N Yorks.* R. **D** York 1 **P** *Abp and Ld Chan* alt I B W MAGUIRE, R A STONE *team v.*
HAXEY (St Nich), *Humb.* V. **D** Linc 1 **P** *Ld Chan* I P W DADD.
HAY MILLS (St Cypr), *W Midl.* V. **D** Birm 13 **P** *Bp* I C S SIMS, C A LEES *c.*
HAYDOCK (St Jas Gt), *Mer.* V. **D** Liv 10 **P** *R of Ashton-in-Makerfield* I S W WILSON, J R HOWARTH *hon c.*
(St Mark), V. **D** Liv 10 **P** *Trustees* I M M H JONES.
HAYDON, *Dorset..* **D** Sarum 7 *See* Folke.
HAYDON BRIDGE (St Cuthb), *Northumb.* V. **D** Newc T 4 **P** *Bp* I A C BENIAMS.
HAYES (St Mary Virg), *Gtr Lon.* R. **D** Lon 9 **P** *Keble Coll Ox* I R C JENNINGS, B E S GODFREY *hon c.*
(St Anselm), V. **D** Lon 9 **P** *Bp* I M J COLCLOUGH *p-in-c.*
(St Edm Conv Distr Yeading). **D** Lon 9 I N A TAYLOR *c-in-c.*
(St Nich Conv Distr). **D** Lon 9 I L V GIDDENS *p-in-c.*
HAYES (St Mary Virg), *Kent.* R. **D** Roch 12 **P** *D and C of Roch* I P G H THOMAS.
HAYFIELD (St Matt), *Derbys.* V. **D** Derby 5 **P** *Resident Freeholders* I R J CASTLE.
HAYLING (St Mary, Hayling S), *Hants.* V. **D** Portsm 3 **P** *Dioc Bd of Patr* I N G O'CONNOR, M B BEEVOR *c.*
(St Pet Conv Distr, Hayling N). **D** Portsm 3 **P** *Bp* I H W COOPER *c-in-c.*
HAYNES (St Mary), *Beds.* V. **D** St alb 22 **P** *Sir Danvers Osborn Bt* I E A QUIN.
HAYNFORD (All SS) w Stratton Strawless (St Marg), *Norf.* R. **D** Nor 3 **P** *Bp* I H M W PALMER.
HAYTON (St Jas L), *Cumb.* R. **D** Carl 11 *See* Aspatria.
HAYTON (St Mary Magd) w Talkin, *Cumb.* V. **D** Carl 2 **P** *D and C of Carl* I I S VAUGHAN.
HAYTON (St Martin) *Humb. Yorks..* **D** York *See* Shipton Thorpe.
HAYTON, *Notts..* **D** Southw *See* Clarborough.
HAYWARDS HEATH (St Wilfrid), *W Sussex.* R. **D** Chich 11 **P** *Bp* I F J BERNARDI, G BOND *team v,* D G HOLLANDS *team v,* K A BRADSHAW *c,* J S LOXTON *c.*
(St Richard), V. **D** Chich 11 **P** *Bp* I P J EDWARDS, M A EGGERT *hon c.*
HAZELBURY-BRYAN (St Mary and St Jas) w Stoke Wake, Fifehead Neville (All SS) and Mappowder (St Pet & St Paul), *Dorset.* R. **D** Sarum 13 **P** *Duke of Northumb 5 turns, F O Kent Esq 1 turn & Bp 2 turns* I P G HOOPER.
HAZELBURY-PLUCKNETT (St Mich AA), *Somt..* **D** B & W 11 *See* Haselbury-Plucknett.
HAZELEIGH (St Nich), *Essex.* R. **D** Chelmsf 14 *See* Woodham Mortimer.
HAZELWELL (St Mary Magd), *W Midl.* V. **D** Birm 5 **P** *Bp* I A C PRIESTLEY.
HAZELWOOD (St Jo Evang), *Derbys.* V. **D** Derby 12 **P** *Bp* I J F B GOODWIN.
HAZLEBURY, *Wilts.* R. **D** Bris 7 *See* Box.
HAZLEMERE (H Trin), *Bucks.* V. **D** Ox 32 **P** *Peache Trustees* I W J OLHAUSEN, I G WILLIAMS *team v.*
HAZLEWOOD, *Suff..* **D** St E 19 *See* Aldeburgh.
HEACHAM, *Norf.* V. **D** Nor 23 **P** *Bp* I R P POTT.
HEADBOURNE WORTHY (St Swith) and King's Worthy (St Mary), *Hants.* R. **D** Win 12 **P** *Master of Univ Coll Ox and Ld Northbrook* I M J F LYNN, D JAMES *c.*
HEADCORN (St Pet and St Paul), *Kent.* V. **D** Cant 15 **P** *Abp* I D J M WATSON.
HEADINGLEY (St Mich AA), *W Yorks.* V. **D** Ripon 5 **P** *V of Leeds* I O A CONWAY.
HEADINGLEY, FAR (St Chad), *W Yorks.* V. **D** Ripon 5 **P** *Ld Grimthorpe* I S R BAXTER *c.*
HEADINGTON, *Oxon..* **D** Ox *See* Oxford.
HEADINGTON QUARRY, *Oxon..* **D** Ox *See* Oxford.
HEADLESS CROSS (St Luke), *Worcs.* R. **D** Worc *See* The Ridge, Redditch.
HEADLEY (All SS), *Hants.* R. **D** Guildf 3 **P** *Qu Coll Ox* I D L H HEAD, P C OWEN *team v,* P H C DICKENS *c.*
HEADLEY (St Mary) w Box Hill (St Andr), *Surrey.* R. **D** Guildf 9 **P** *Bp* I R D ROBINSON.
HEADLEY (St Pet), *Hants..* **D** Win 5 *See* Kingsclere Woodlands.
HEADON (St Pet) w Upton, *Notts.* R. **D** Southw 6 **P** *G Harcourt-Vernon Esq* I M G H B TUDOR *p-in-c.*
HEADSTONE (St Geo).. **D** Lon 22 *See* Hatch End.
HEAGE (St Luke), *Derbys.* R. **D** Derby 12 **P** *V of Duffield* I (Vacant).
HEALAUGH (St Helen and St Jo Bapt) w Wighill (All SS) and Bilbrough, *N Yorks.* V. **D** York 2 **P** *Abp* I (Vacant).
HEALD GREEN (St Cath), *Gtr Man.* V. **D** Ches 16 **P** *Bp* I D C GARNETT, D J DERBYSHIRE *c.*
HEALEY (Ch Ch), *Lancs..* **D** Man *See* Rochdale.
HEALEY (St Jo Evang), *Northumb.* V. **D** Newc T 3 **P** *V of Bywell St Pet* I R W B MASSINGBERD-MUNDY *c-in-c.*
HEALEY (St Paul), *N Yorks.* V. **D** Ripon 3 *See* Masham.
HEALING (St Pet and St Paul), *Humb.* R. **D** Linc 10 **P** *Bp* I J W ABBOTT.
HEANOR (St Lawr w St Mary, Langley), *Derbys.* V. **D** Derby 6 **P** *Trustees* I R N MCMULLEN *p-in-c.*
(All SS Marlpool). **D** Derby 6 **P** *V of Heanor* I B S ALLEN.
HEANTON-PUNCHARDON (St Aug) w Marwood, *Devon.* R. **D** Ex **P** *CPAS 3 turns, St Jo Coll Cam 1 turn* I R M C BEAK, W G BENSON *c,* R W CRANSTON *c.*
HEAP BRIDGE (St Geo), *Gtr Man..* **D** Man 12 *See* Heywood.
HEAPEY (St Barn), *Lancs.* V. **D** Blackb 4 **P** *V of Leyland* I A E LUCAS.
HEAPHAM (All SS) *Lincs..* **D** Linc 2 *See* Corringham.
HEARTSEASE (St Francis), *Norf..* **D** Nor 4 *See* Norwich.
HEATH (All SS), *Derbys.* V. **D** Derby 3 **P** *Duke of Devonshire* I D N GOUGH.
HEATH, *Salop..* **D** Heref *See* Stoke St Milburgh.
HEATH (St Leon) w Reach, *Beds.* V. **D** St Alb 18 **P** *V of Leighton Buzzard* I W E BARROW.
HEATH TOWN (H Trin), *W Midl.* V. **D** Lich 12 **P** *CPAS* I J E MEDCALF.
HEATHER (St Jo Bapt), *Leics.* R. **D** Leic 11 *See* Ibstock.
HEATHERLANDS (St Jo Evang), *Dorset..* **D** Sarum *See* Parkstone.
HEATHERYCLEUGH (St Thos), *Durham.* V. **D** Dur 13 **P** *Bp* I C SMITH.
HEATHFIELD, *Somt..* **D** B & W 22 *See* Bradford.
HEATHFIELD (All SS), *E Sussex.* V. **D** Chich 18 **P** *Bp* I F W TOZER.
(St Richard), V. **D** Chich 18 **P** *Bp* I D G CLUER.
HEATON (St Barn), *W Yorks.* V. **D** Bradf 1 **P** *Trustees* I C B HOLLIS.
(St Martin), V. **D** Bradf 1 **P** *Bp* I P G ROGERS.
HEATON (Ch Ch), *Lancs.* V. **D** Man 11 **P** *Rev K M Bishop* I R E H JOHNSON, D A HILES *c.*
HEATON (St Gabr), *Northumb..* **D** Newc T 5 *See* Newcastle upon Tyne.
HEATON MERSEY (St Jo Bapt), *Gtr Man.* R. **D** Man 4 **P** *Bp* I B W NEWTH.
HEATON MOOR (St Paul), *Gtr Man.* R. **D** Man 4 **P** *Trustees* I E N TAYLOR.
HEATON NORRIS (Ch w All SS), *Gtr Man.* R. **D** Man 4 **P** *Bp* I R J GILPIN.
(St Thos), *Lancs.* R. **D** Man 4 **P** *D and C of Man* I R J ALDERSON.
HEATON REDDISH (St Mary Virg), *Gtr Man.* R. **D** Man 4 **P** *Trustees* I M F JONES.
HEAVITREE, *Devon..* **D** Ex 3 *See* Exeter.
HEBBURN (St Cuthb), *T & W.* V. **D** Dur 6 **P** *R of Jarrow* I H J DOBBIN.
(St Jo Evang), V. **D** Dur 6 **P** *Bp* I J M HANCOCK, R K HOPPER *c.*
(St Osw), V. **D** Dur 6 **P** *Crown* I (Vacant).
HEBRON (St Cuthb), *Northumb..* **D** Newc T 10 *See* Longhirst.
HEBDEN (St Pet), *N Yorks..* **D** Bradf 10 *See* Linton.
HEBDEN BRIDGE (St Jas Gt w St John), *W Yorks.* V. **D** Wakef 3 **P** *V of Halifax* I J E DURNFORD.
HECK, *S Yorks..* **D** Sheff *See* Hensall.
HECKFIELD (St Mich) w Mattingley and Rotherwick, *Hants.* V. **D** Win 4 **P** *New Coll Ox 2 turns, V of Heckfield 1 turn* I P P S BROWNLESS.
HECKINGHAM (St Greg), *Norf..* **D** Nor 14 *See* Hales.
HECKINGTON (St Andr) w Howell (St Osw) and Burton Pedwardine, R *Lincs.* V. **D** Linc **P** *Bp 2 turns, Rev A C Foottit 1 turn* I J A DAY.
HECKMONDWIKE (St Jas), *W Yorks.* V. **D** Wakef 9 **P** *V of Birstall* I K C GRAIN, J K BUTTERWORTH *c.*
HEDDINGTON (St Andr), *Wilts.* R. **D** Sarum 25 *See* Oldbury.

HEDDON-ON-THE-WALL (St Andr), *Northumb.* V. **D** Newc T 3 **P** *Ld Chan* **I** J P SENIOR.
HEDENHAM (St Pet), *Norf.* R. **D** Nor 11 **P** *Brig-Gen W G Carr* **I** D T G WARD.
HEDGE END (St Jo Evang), *Hants.* V. **D** Win 15 **P** *Bp* **I** M S UNDERHILL.
HEDGEFIELD (St Hilda), *Durham.* V. **D** Dur 4a **P** *Bp* **I** (Vacant).
HEDGERLEY (St Mary Virg), *Bucks.* R. **D** Ox *See* Farnham-Royal.
HEDNESFORD (St Pet), *Staffs.* V. **D** Lich 4 **P** *Bp* **I** J M WATERS, J H MARTIN *c.*
HEDON (St Aug) w Paull (St Andr and St Mary), *Humb.* V. **D** York 15 **P** *Abp* **I** W H MCLAREN.
HEDSOR (St Nich) and Bourne End (St Mark), *Bucks.* V. **D** Ox 32 **P** *Bp* **I** H HARTLEY.
HEDWORTH (St Nich), *T & W.* V. **D** Dur 6 **P** *Crown* **I** P W H EASTMAN, R M BECK *c.*
HEELEY (Ch Ch), *S Yorks.*. **D** Sheff 1 *See* Sheffield.
HEENE (St Botolph), *W Sussex.* R. **D** Chich 9 **P** *D and C of Chich* **I** J H MONEY.
HEIGHAM (St Barn w St Bart), *Norf.* V. **D** Nor 4a **P** *Bp* **I** M P BIRD, C SIMMONDS *c.*
(Most H Trin), R. **D** Nor 4a **P** *Ch Trust Fund* **I** G F BRIDGER, K S SWITHINBANK *c.*
(St Thos), V. **D** Nor 4a **P** *Bp* **I** W IVES.
HEIGHINGTON (St Mich) w Bolam, *Durham.* V. **D** Dur 11 **P** *D and C of Dur* **I** H W JACKSON.
HEIGHINGTON, *Lincs.*. **D** Linc 18 *See* Washingborough.
HEIGHTINGTON (St Giles), *Worcs.*. **D** Worc 10 *See* Rock.
HEIGHTON, SOUTH, *E Sussex.*. **D** Chich *See* Denton.
HELHOUGHTON w Raynham St Martin, *Norf.* R. **D** Nor 20 **P** *Marq Townshend* **I** (Vacant).
HELIDON (St Jo Bapt), *Northants.* V. **D** Pet 3 *See* Staverton.
HELIONS BUMPSTEAD, *Essex.*. **D** Chelmsf *See* Steeple Bumpstead.
HELLAND (St Helena), *Cornw.* R. **D** Truro 8 **P** *MMT* **I** M B KENNAWAY *p-in-c.*
HELLESDON (St Mary), *Norf.* V. **D** Nor 4 **P** *Bp* **I** D M HOARE, A D PARSONS *c.*
HELLIFIELD (St Aid), *N Yorks.* V. **D** Bradf 6 **P** *Ch Ch Ox* **I** G WALKER.
HELLINGLY (St Pet and St Paul) and U Dicker (H Trin), *E Sussex.* V. **D** Chich 18 **P** *Abp of Cant and Bp* **I** F J FOX-WILSON *p-in-c.*
HELLINGTON, *Norf.*. **D** Nor *See* Rockland.
HELMDON (St Mary Magd) w Stuchbury and Radstone (St Laur), *Northants.* R. **D** Pet 1 **P** *Univ of Ox and Mert Coll Ox* alt **I** R F CALDWELL.
HELME (Ch Ch), *W Yorks.* V. **D** Wakef 6 **P** *Bp* **I** D TURNER *p-in-c.*
HELMINGHAM (St Mary) w Framsden and Pettaugh w Winston, *Suff.* R. **D** St E 18 **P** *Ld Tollemache, Ld Chan and MMT (alt)* **I** A CALDWELL.
HELMSLEY (All SS) w Sproxton (St Chad), Carlton (St Aid), and Rievaulx, *N Yorks.* V. **D** York 20 **P** *Exors of Earl of Feversham* **I** D G C M SENIOR.
HELMSLEY, GATE, and HELMSLEY, UPPER, *N Yorks.* R. **D** York 4 *See* Sand Hutton.
HELPERTHORPE (St Pet), *N Yorks.* V. **D** York 3 *See* Weaverthorpe.
HELPRINGHAM (St Andr) w Hale Magna and Parva Scredington and Swaton w Spanby, *Lincs.* V. **D** Linc 22 **P** *Ld Chan 1st and 4th turns, D and C of Linc 2nd turn and Dioc Bd of Patr 3rd turn* **I** B G HARRIS.
HELPSTON (St Botolph), *Cambs.* R. **D** Pet 14 *See* Etton.
HELSBY (St Paul) and Dunham-on-the-Hill (St Luke), *Chesh.* V. **D** Ches 3 **P** *Bp* **I** R W HOWARD.
HELSINGTON (St Jo Div), *Cumb.* V. **D** Carl 17 **P** *V of Kendal* **I** A F J LOFTHOUSE.
HELSTON (St Mich w All SS), *Cornw.* V. **D** Truro 4 **P** *Qu Coll Ox* **I** H PENTREATH.
HEMBLINGTON (All SS), *Norf.* V. **D** Nor 1 *See* Blofield.
HEMEL HEMPSTEAD (St Mary, St Barn Adeyfield, St Pet Gadebridge, St Paul Highfield, St Alb Warners End), *Herts.* R. **D** St Alb 3 **P** *Ld Chan* **I** R W H KINGSTON, J H BARRALL *team v,* S A BEAKE *team v,* D L GAMBLE *team v,* G L JONES *team v,* A NAYLOR-SMITH *team v,* P G SMITH *team v,* W B CARPENTER *hon c.*
HEMINGBROUGH (BVM), *N Yorks.* V. **D** York 6 **P** *Abp* **I** J F TAYLOR.
HEMINGBY (Baumber, Great Sturton, Edlington, Wispington, Hatton, Sotby and Ashby West), *Lincs.* R. **D** Linc 11 **P** *Bp 2 turns, Ld Chan 2 turns and Dioc Bd of Patr 1 turn* **I** G O WHITFIELD.
HEMINGFORD ABBOTS (St Marg), *Cambs.* R. **D** Ely 10 **P** *Ld Hemingford* **I** R K SLEDGE.
HEMINGFORD GREY (St Jas), *Cambs.* V. **D** Ely 10 **P** *Mrs G A Scott* **I** K A VORLEY.
HEMINGSTONE (St Greg) w Henley (St Pet), *Suff.* V. **D** St E 1 *See* Coddenham.
HEMINGTON, *Leics.*. **D** Leic *See* Lockington.
HEMINGTON (BVM) w Hardington (BVM), *Somt.*. **D** B & W 16a *See* Norton St Philip.
HEMINGTON, *Northants.*. **D** Pet *See* Polebrooke.
HEMLEY (All SS), *Suff.* R. **D** St E 2 *See* Waldringfield.
HEMPNALL [Hempnall (St Marg), Fritton w Morningthorpe w Shelton and Hardwick, Topcroft, Woodston w Bedingham], *Norf.* R. **D** Nor 11 **P** *Patr Bd* **I** J D M SMITH, S R NAIRN *team v.*
HEMPSTEAD (St Andr), *Essex.*. **D** Chelmsf *See* Radwinter.
HEMPSTEAD (St Andr) w Lessingham (All SS) and Eccles-next-the-Sea (St Mary), *Norf.* R. **D** Nor 9 **P** *K Coll Cam 3 turns, Vice-Adm Sir C E Evans Lombe 1 turn* **I** D F COOMBES *p-in-c.*
HEMPSTEAD (All SS), *Norf.* V. **D** Nor *See* Barningham.
HEMPSTED (St Swith), *Glos.* R. **D** Glouc 1 **P** *Bp* **I** D F MATTHEWS.
HEMPSTON, LITTLE, or HEMPSTON-ARUNDEL (St Jo Bapt), *Devon.*. **D** Ex *See* Littlehempston.
HEMPTON (H Trin) w Pudding Norton, *Norf.* V. **D** Nor 21 **P** *Crown* **I** (Vacant).
HEMPTON, *Oxon.*. **D** Ox *See* Deddington.
HEMSBY (St Mary), *Norf.* V. **D** Nor 2 **P** *Maj R A Ferrier* **I** R D PAGE.
HEMSWELL (All SS) w Harpswell (St Chad), *Lincs.* V. **D** Linc 2 **P** *MMT 2 turns, Ch Soc 1 turn* **I** T P O PECK.
HEMSWORTH (St Helen), *W Yorks.* R. **D** Wakef 11 **P** *Mrs M Pearse* **I** C W JACKSON.
(Abp Holgate's Hosp). **D** Wakef 11 **I** E L FACEY *master.*
HEMYOCK w Culm Davey (St Mary) Clayhidon (St Andr) and Culmstock (All SS), *Devon.* R. **D** Ex 4 **P** *Dioc Bd of Patr* **I** A C B GROSSE.
HENBURY (St Thos), *Chesh.* V. **D** Ches 13 **P** *Bp* **I** D H EVANS.
HENBURY (St Mary Virg) w Hallen (St Jo Div), *Avon.* V. **D** Bris 6 **P** *Ld Middleton 1 turn, Bp 3 turns* **I** H B TROTTER, R D HINDLEY *c.*
HENDFORD (H Trin), *Somt.*. **D** B & W 12 *See* Yeovil.
HENDON (St Ignatius) and Sunderland (H Trin), *T & W.* V. **D** Dur **P** *Bp and R of Bishop Wearmouth (alt)* **I** M H WHITEHEAD, P J IGO *c,* M H M STAPLEFORD *c.*
HENDON (St Mary), *Gtr Lon.* V. **D** Lon 17 **P** *Bp* **I** J BORRILL, A H COOKE *c,* A A DANKS *c.*
(Ch Ch), V. **D** Lon 17 **P** *Bp* **I** (Vacant).
(St Jo Evang),. **D** Lon 17 **P** *Bp* **I** J M WARNER, J C WALKER *c.*
(St Alphage), V. **D** Lon 17 **P** *Bp* **I** H D MOORE, B DAGNALL *c,* A D MAYES *c.*
COLINDALE (St Matthias), V. **D** Lon 17 **P** *Bp* **I** D J BARNETT.
HENDRED, EAST (St Aug) w West (Holy Trin), *Oxon.*. **D** Ox *See* Wantage Downs.
HENFIELD (St Pet) w Shermanbury (St Giles) and Woodmancote (St Pet), *W sussex.* V. **D** Chich 14 **P** *Bp* **I** T M TYLER, D G MILLER *c.*
HENGOED (St Barn) w Gobowen, *Salop.* V. **D** Lich 24 **P** *R of Selattyn* **I** J M ALLEN.
HENGRAVE, *Suff.*. **D** St E 13 *See* Flempton.
HENGROVE (Ch Ch), *Avon.*. **D** Bris 2 **P** *Bp and Simeon Trustees* **I** J B PARSONS *p-in-c.*
HENHAM (St Mary Virg), *Essex.* V. **D** Chelmsf 26 **P** *Ch S Trust* **I** B R GREEN.
HENHAM, *Suff.*. **D** St E *See* Wangford.
HENLEAZE (St Pet), *Avon.* V. **D** Bris 5 **P** *Bp* **I** P J COUSINS, R W DENT *c.*
HENLEY (St Pet), *Suff.* V. **D** St E 1 *See* Hemingstone.
HENLEY-IN-ARDEN (St Jo Bapt), *Warws.*. **D** Cov 7 *See* Beaudesert.
HENLEY-ON-THAMES (St Mary Virg), *Oxon.* R. **D** Ox 7 **P** *Bp* **I** A PYBURN.
See also ROTHERFIELD GREYS.
HENLOW (St Mary), *Beds.* V. **D** St Alb 22 **P** *Ld Chan* **I** A W NEWALL.
HENNOCK (St Mary), *Devon.* V. **D** Ex 11 **P** *MMT* **I** A G LOUGH.
HENNY, GREAT and Henny, Little w Middleton (St Mary) and Wickham St Paul w Twinstead, *Essex.* R. **D** Chelmsf 18 **P** *Earl of Verulam, Bp, D and C of Lon and Ld Chan (alt)* **I** B A CAREW.
HENSALL (St Paul) w Heck (St Jo Bapt), *S Yorks.* V. **D** Sheff 9 **P** *Bp* **I** E A JONES.
HENSHAW, *Northumb.*. **D** Newc T *See* Beltingham.

HENSINGHAM (St Jo Evang), *Cumb*. V. **D** Carl 12 **P** *Earl of Lonsdale* **I** W KELLY, J G RILEY *c*.
HENSTEAD, *Suff*.. **D** St E *See* Ellough.
HENSTRIDGE (St Nich) and Charlton Horethorne w Stowell, *Somt*. V. **D** B & W **P** *K S D Wingfield-Digby Esq 1st turn, Bp 2nd and 3rd turns* **I** J H SWINGLER.
HENTLAND (St Dubricius) w Hoarwithy (St Cath), *Herefs*. V. **D** Heref 8 **P** *D and C of Heref* **I** (Vacant).
HENTON (Ch Ch), *Somt*. V. **D** B & W 1 *See* Wookey.
HEPTONSTALL (St Thos Ap), *W Yorks*. V. **D** Wakef 3 **P** *V of Halifax* **I** P N CALVERT.
HEPWORTH (St Pet), *Suff*. R. **D** St E 9 **P** *K Coll Cam* **I** (Vacant).
HEPWORTH (H Trin), *W Yorks*. V. **D** Wakef 7 **P** *V of Kirkburton* **I** J D M JONES.
Hereford (All SS w St Barn), *Herefs*. V. **D** Heref 3 **P** *D and C of Windsor* **I** H D BROAD, A HART *c*.
(H Trin), V. **D** Heref 3 **P** *Bp* **I** D W DALE.
(St Jo Bapt), V. **D** Heref 3 **P** *D and C of Heref* **I** N S RATHBONE.
(St Martin), V. **D** Heref 3 **P** *Bp* **I** J F BAULCH, S A EVASON *c*, R C GREEN *c*, J B SMITH *c*, G B TALBOT *c*.
(St Nich), R. **D** Heref 3 **P** *Ld Chan* **I** N COLLINGS.
(St Pet w St Owen and St Jas), V. **D** Heref 3 **P** *Simeon Trustees* **I** G FLEMING *c*, J A STEVENS *c*.
HEREFORD, LITTLE (St Mary Magd), *Salop*. R. **D** Heref 12 *See* Burford.
HERMITAGE (H Trin) and Curridge w Hampstead Norreys Cold Ash and Yattendon w Frilsham, [Berks]. R. **D** Ox 14 **P** *Bp, G E H Palmer Esq and Dioc Bd of Patr* **I** D N SWAIN, R J GODFREY *team v*.
HERMITAGE (St Mary), *Dorset*.. **D** Sarum 7 *See* Hilfield.
HERMON HILL (H Trin), *Essex*.. **D** Chelmsf 8 *See* Woodford, S.
HERNE (St Martin), *Kent*. V. **D** Cant 4 **P** *Abp* **I** D J BRETHERTON, P J CABLE *c*, I J LOVETT *c*, R G MACKENZIE *c*.
HERNE BAY (Ch Ch) w (St Jo Evang), *Kent*. V. **D** Cant 4 **P** *Simeon Trustees* **I** A A W DAWKINS, R W HARRIS *c*.
(St Bart), V. **D** Cant 4 **P** *Abp* **I** H J L STEPHENS.
HERNE HILL (St Paul), *Surrey*. V. **D** S'wark 16 **P** *Bp* **I** G R BENNETT.
HERNE HILL ROAD (St Sav), *Kent*. V. **D** S'wark 16 *See* Lambeth.
HERNHILL (St Mich), *Kent*. V. **D** Cant 7 **P** *Abp* **I** R C HOULDSWORTH.
HERODSFOOT (All SS), *Cornw*.. **D** Truro *See* Duloe.
HERRIARD (St Mary) w Winslade, *Hants*.. **D** Win *See* Upton Grey.
HERRINGBY, *Norf*.. **D** Nor *See* Stokesby.
HERRINGFLEET (St Marg), *Suff*.. **D** Nor 15 **P** *Ld Somerleyton* **I** E C BROOKS *c-in-c*.
HERRINGSWELL, *Suff*. R. **D** St E 11 **P** *Exors of Capt LL S Davies 1 turn, Ld Chan 2 turns* **I** T H LAWRENCE *p-in-c*.
HERRINGTHORPE (St Cuthb), *S Yorks*. V. **D** Sheff 6 **P** *Bp* **I** D E REEVES.
HERRINGTON (St Aid) w (St Cuthb), *T & W*. V. **D** Dur 5 **P** *Bp* **I** E VARLEY.
EAST. **D** Dur 8 *See* Sunderland.
HERSHAM (St Pet), *Surrey*. V. **D** Guildf 8 **P** *Bp* **I** (Vacant).
HERSTMONCEUX (All SS), *E Sussex*. R. **D** Chich 18 **P** *Very Rev J H S Wild* **I** W A HAWKINS.
HERSTON (St Mark), *Dorset*.. **D** Sarum 9 *See* Swanage.
HERTFORD (All SS w St John), *Herts*. V. **D** St Alb 8 **P** *Marq of Townshend and Ld Chan alt* **I** R HAW, G D BOOKER *hon c*, P W RICKETTS *hon c*.
(St Andr w St Nich and St Mary), R. **D** St Alb 8 **P** *Duchy of Lanc* **I** D S DORMOR, T W GLADWIN *c*.
HERTINGFORDBURY (St Mary w St John), *Herts*. R. **D** St Alb 8 **P** *Duchy of Lanc* **I** E CARSON, W E ELVES *c*.
HESKET-IN-THE-FOREST (St Mary) w Calthwaite and Armathwaite (Ch and St Mary) *Cumb*. V. **D** Carl 6 **P** *D and C of Carl and E P Ecroyd Esq* **I** E J BEWES.
HESKETH (All SS) w Becconsall, *Lancs*. R. **D** Blackb 6 **P** *Trustees* **I** K DAGGER.
HESLERTON, WEST (All SS), and Heslerton, East (St Andr) w Knapton and Yedingham, *N Yorks*. R. **D** York *See* Sherburn.
HESLINGTON (St Paul), *N Yorks*. R. **D** York 6 **P** *Abp* **I** F G HUNTER.
HESSAY N Yorks. **D** York 2 *See* Rufforth.
HESSENFORD (St Anne), *Cornw*. V. **D** Truro 9 **P** *V of St Germans* **I** J D FERGUSON.
HESSETT (St Ethelbert K and Mart of Kent), *Suff*. R. **D** St E 10 *See* Beyton.
HESSLE (All SS), *Humb*. V. **D** York 17 **P** *Ld Chan* **I** E R BARNES, P A W JONES *c*, A SUTHERLAND *c*, D A WALKER *c*.
HESTON (St Leon), *Gtr Lon*. V. **D** Lon 10 **P** *Bp* **I** T J L MAIDMENT, G MOFFAT *c*.
HESWALL (St Pet), *Mer*. R. **D** Ches 8 **P** *Lt-Col W B Davenport* **I** R E MORRIS, R MOUGHTIN *c*.
HETHE (St Edm and St Geo), *Oxon*. R. **D** Ox 2 *See* Fringford.
HETHEL (All SS), *Norf*.. **D** Nor *See* Bracon Ash.
HETHERSETT (St Remigius) w Canteloff, *Norf*. R. **D** Nor 13 **P** *G and C Coll Cam* **I** M B SEXTON, D SHAKESPEARE *c*.
HETHERSGILL, *Cumb*.. **D** Carl *See* Kirklinton.
HETTON-LE-HOLE (St Nich), *T & W*. R. **D** Dur 5 **P** *Bp* **I** G LYNN.
HETTON, SOUTH (H Trin), *Durham*. V. **D** Dur 3 **P** *Bp* **I** G A BLACKWELL.
HEVENINGHAM, *Suff*.. **D** St E *See* Cratfield.
HEVER (St Pet) w Markbeech (H Trin), *Kent*. R. **D** Roch 9 **P** *Bp and T G Talbot* **I** D CHAPMAN.
HEVERSHAM (St Mary), *Cumb*. V. **D** Carl 17 **P** *Trin Coll Cam* **I** J C HANCOCK.
HEVINGHAM (St Mary Virg and St Botolph), *Norf*. R. **D** Nor 3 **P** *Sir T Beevor* **I** C B MORGAN.
HEWELSFIELD (St Mary Magd), *Glos*. V. **D** Glouc 7 *See* St Briavels.
HEWISH ST ANN (St Ann), *Avon*. V. **D** B & W 3 *See* Congresbury.
HEWORTH (St Mary), *T & W*. V. **D** Dur 4 **P** *Bp* **I** R J KNELL, A J CLARKE *c*.
(St Alb), V. **D** Dur 4 **P** *V of St Mary, Heworth* **I** M L MALLESON.
(St Andr Leam Lane), V. **D** Dur **P** *Bp* **I** T R LEE *c*.
HEWORTH (H Trin), *N Yorks*.. **D** York 1 *See* York.
HEXHAM (St Andr Abbey Ch), *Northumb*. R. **D** Newc T 4 **P** *Mercers' Co and Visc Allendale alt* **I** T WITHERS GREEN, R A BAILY *c*.
HEXHAMSHIRE (St Helen), *Northumb*.. **D** Newc T 4 *See* Whitley.
HEXTHORPE (St Jude), *S Yorks*. V. **D** Sheff 8 *See* Doncaster.
HEXTON (St Faith), *Herts*. V. **D** St Alb *See* Barton-le-Cley.
HEY or LEES (St Jo Bapt), *Lancs*. V. **D** Man 15 **P** *R of Ashton L* **I** J B KELLY.
HEYBRIDGE (St Andr) w Langford (St Giles), *Essex*. V. **D** Chelmsf 14 **P** *D and C of St Paul's and Lt Col R G G Byron alt* **I** K B ROBINSON *p-in-c*.
HEYDON (H Trin) w Little Chishall (St Nich), *Cambs*. R. **D** Chelmsf 27 **P** *R J Harvey Esq* **I** (Vacant).
HEYDON (St Pet and St Paul) w Irmingland, *Norf*. R (*See Cawston Group*).. **D** Nor 3 **P** *Pemb Coll Cam* **I** F G COATES.
HEYDOUR (St Mich AA) w Culverthorpe (St Bart) and Welby (St Bart), *Lincs*. V. **D** Linc *See* Wilsford.
HEYFORD (St Pet and St Paul) w Stowe Nine Churches (St Mich w St Jas), *Northants*. R. **D** Pet **P** *Rev J L Crawley and Dioc Bd of Patr* **I** J T SHORT.
THE HEYFORDS (Heyford Warren and Lower Heyford) w Rousham (St Leon and St Jas) and Somerton (St Jas), *Oxon*. R. **D** Ox **P** *New Coll Ox 1st turn, T Cottrell-Dormer Esq 2nd turn, CCC Ox 3rd turn, P W G Barnes Esq 4th turn* **I** H WILSON.
HEYHOUSES or SABDEN (St Nich), *Lancs*. V. **D** Blackb 5 **P** *G P le G Starkie Esq* **I** C D MCWILLIAM.
HEYHOUSES-ON-THE-SEA, *Lancs*.. **D** Blackb *See* St Annes-on-the-Sea.
HEYSHAM (St Pet), *Lancs*. R. **D** Blackb 11 **P** *C Fletcher-Twemlow Esq* **I** A A WELSH.
(St John, Sandylands), V. **D** Blackb 11 **P** *Bp* **I** R H SMART.
HEYSHOTT (St Jas), *W Sussex*. R. **D** Chich 5 **P** *Bp* **I** C BOXLEY *p-in-c*.
HEYSIDE (St Mark), *Gtr Man*. V. **D** Man 15 **P** *Trustees* **I** T N HOWARD.
HEYTESBURY (St Pet and St Paul) and Sutton Veny w Tytherington (St Jas), Knook (St Marg) and Norton Bavant, *Wilts*. V. **D** Sarum 22 **P** *Bp* **I** P R ENGLISH.
HEYTHROP (St Nich), *Oxon*. R. **D** Ox 3 *See* Enstone.
HEYWOOD (St Luke), *Gtr Man*. V. **D** Man 17 **P** *R of Bury* **I** A SHACKLETON.
(St Jas), V. **D** Man 17 **P** *Bp* **I** D K PRYCE, K M TOMLIN *c*.
(St Marg) V. **D** Man 17 **P** *Bp* **I** P K HARRISON.
(All S Castleton), V. **D** Man 17 **P** *Bp* **I** J KIRKWOOD *p-in-c*.

HEYWOOD (H Trin), *Wilts*. V. **D** Sarum 24 **P** *CPAS* **I** (Vacant).
HIBALDSTOW (St Hibald), *Humb*. V. **D** Linc 6 **P** *Bp* **I** J M S KING.
HICKLETON (St Wilfrid or St Dennis), *S Yorks*.. **D** Sheff 10 *See* Goldthorpe.
HICKLING (St Mary), *Norf*. V. **D** Nor 9 **P** *Maj J M Mills* **I** (Vacant).
HICKLING (St Luke) w Kinoulton (St Luke) and Broughton Sulney, *Notts*. R. **D** Southw **P** *Bp, Crown and Qu Coll Cam in turn* **I** (Vacant).
HIGH BEECH (H Innoc) w Upshire (St Thos), *Essex*. V. **D** Chelmsf 2 **P** *Bp* **I** P HAWORTH *p-in-c*.
HIGH BICKINGTON, *Devon*.. **D** Ex 16 *See* Atherington.
HIGH BRAY (All SS) w Charles (St Jo Bapt), *Devon*.. **D** Ex *See* South Molton.
HIGH CROMPTON (St Mary), *Gtr Man*.. **D** Man 14 *See* Crompton, High.
HIGH CROSS (St Jo Evang), *Herts*. V. **D** St Alb 8 **P** *Dioc Bd of Patr* **I** H J SHARMAN.
HIGH ERCALL (St Mich AA), *Salop*. V. **D** Lich 29 **P** *Ld Barnard* **I** H L PHAIR.
HIGH HALDEN (St Mary Virg), *Kent*.. **D** Cant 11 *See* Bethersden.
HIGH LANE (St Thos), *Chesh*. V. **D** Ches 16 **P** *R of Stockport* **I** J SUTTON.
HIGH LEIGH or LEGH (St Jo Evang), *Chesh*. V. **D** Ches *See* Tabley, Over.
HIGH OFFLEY (St Mary Virg) w Knightley (Ch Ch), *Staffs*. V. **D** Lich 15 **P** *Bp* **I** R HARRISON.
HIGH RODING (All SS), *Essex*.. **D** Chelmsf 23 *See* Leaden Roding.
HIGH STOY (Hilfield, Hermitage, Leigh w Chetnole and Batcombe), *Dorset*. R. **D** Sarum 7 **P** *Bp* **I** D A K GREENE *c-in-c*.
HIGH WYCH (St Jas Gt) and Gilston w Eastwick, *Herts*. R. **D** St Alb 4 **P** *V of Sawbridgeworth 2 turns, Trustees of A S Bowlby 1 turn* **I** P C RUMSEY.
HIGH WYCOMBE, *Bucks*.. **D** Ox 32 *See* Wycombe, High.
HIGHAM (St Mary) w Merston (St John), *Kent*. V. **D** Roch 5 **P** *St Jo Coll Cam* **I** B SHACKLETON, M H CLARKE *hon c*.
HIGHAM (St Mary), *Suff*. V. **D** St E 3 **P** *Bp* **I** C L ROWE *c-in-c*.
HIGHAM (St Steph) w Kentford, R *Suff*. V. **D** St E 11 *See* Kentford.
HIGHAM-FERRERS (St Mary) w Chelveston (St Jo Bapt), *Northants*. V. **D** Pet 9 **P** *Earl Fitzwilliam and Bp* alt **I** R W DAVISON, M J L PERROTT *c*.
HIGHAM-GOBION (St Marg), *Beds*. R. **D** St Alb *See* Barton-le-Cley.
HIGHAM-ON-THE-HILL (St Pet) w Fenny Drayton, *Leics*. R. **D** Leic 16 **P** *Provost and C of Leic* **I** R E REYNOLDS.
HIGHAMPTON (H Cross), *Devon*. R. **D** Ex 20 *See* Shebbear.
HIGHAMS PARK, *Essex*.. **D** Chelmsf *See* Walthamstow.
HIGHBRIDGE (St Jo Evang), *Somt*. V. **D** B & W 2 **P** *Bp* **I** N C WELLS.
HIGHBROOK (All SS) and W Hoathly, *W Sussex*. V. **D** Chich 11 **P** *Ld Chan* **I** M E G ALLEN.
HIGHBURY (Ch Ch) w St Jo Evang Highbury Vale and St Sav Aberdeen Park, *Lon*. V. **D** Lon 3 **P** *Trustees* **I** C J E LEFROY, R E HANCOCK *c*.
(St Aug), V. **D** Lon 3 **P** *Trustees* **I** A H MUST.
(St Jo Evang Highbury Vale). **D** Lon 3 *See* Highbury.
(St Sav Aberdeen Park). **D** Lon 3 *See* Highbury.
HIGHCLERE (St Mich AA) w Ashmansworth (St Jas) and Crux Easton, *Hants*. R. **D** Win 5 **P** *Earl of Carnarvon* **I** P J W RAINE.
HIGHCLIFFE (St Mark) w Hinton Admiral (St Mich AA), *Hants*. V. **D** Win 8 **P** *Bp and Sir G Meyrick Bt* Alt **I** J N SEAFORD, G J WHEELER *c*.
HIGHFIELD (St Matt), *Gtr Man*. V. **D** Liv 12 **P** *Trustees* **I** W BYNON, G THOMAS *c*.
HIGHFIELD, *Oxon*.. **D** Ox *See* Oxford.
HIGHFIELD (or Ch Ch Portswood), *Hants*. V. **D** Win 11 *See* Southampton.
HIGHGATE (St Mich), *Lon*. V. **D** Lon 23 **P** *Bp* **I** J J FIELDING, D W C MOSSMAN *c*.
(All SS), V. **D** Lon 23 **P** *Bp* **I** J S BOWDEN *hon c*.
(St Aug of Cant), V. **D** Lon 23 **P** *Bp* **I** R BENCE.
HIGHGATE HILL. **D** Lon *See* Holloway, Upper.
HIGHLEY, (St Mary), *Salop*. V. **D** Heref 9 **P** *MMT* **I** J BRITTAIN.
HIGHMORE (St Paul), *Oxon*. V. **D** Ox 7 *See* Nettlebed.
HIGHNAM (H Innoc) w Lassington (St Osw) and Rudford (St Mary Virg), *Glos*. R. **D** Glouc 6 **P** *D and C of Glouc and Trustees* **I** P J GREEN *p-in-c*.
HIGHTERS HEATH (Immanuel), *W Midl*. V. **D** Birm 5 **P** *Bp* **I** D E MCCORMACK, P R BROWN *c*, H SNAPE *c*.
HIGHTOWN (St Barn), *W Yorks*. V. **D** Wakef 9 **P** *Bp* **I** R S STOKES.
HIGHTOWN (St Steph), *Mer*. V. **D** Liv 1 **P** *Bp* **I** E N JENKINS.
HIGHWAY (St Pet), *Wilts*.. **D** Sarum 25 *See* Hilmarton.
HIGHWEEK (All SS) w Abbotsbury (St Mary Virg) and Teigngrace (St Pet and St Paul), *Devon*. R. **D** Ex 11 **P** *Bp* **I** C R KNOTT.
HIGHWOOD (St Paul), *Essex*. V. **D** Chelmsf *See* Writtle.
HIGHWORTH (St Mich) w Sevenhampton (St Jas), and Hannington (St Jo Bapt), *Wilts* and Inglesham (St Jo Bapt), *Glos*. V. **D** Bris 10 **P** *Bp 4 turns, Mrs C B Fry 1 turn* **I** B R PHILLIPS, A F ANDREWS *c*, T S MAGSON *c*.
HILBOROUGH (All SS) w Bodney (St Mary), *Norf*. R (*in Hilborough Group - See also Cockley-Cley, Cressingham, Oxburgh, Didlington*).. **D** Nor 19 **P** *Maj J C T Mills* **I** D A ABRAHAM, J S GORDON *hon c*.
HILDENBOROUGH (St Jo Evang), *Kent*. V. **D** Roch 9 **P** *V of Tonbridge* **I** D R CORFE, S G STEPHENSON *c*.
HILDERSHAM (H Trin), *Cambs*. R. **D** Ely 4 **P** *Trustees* **I** R J BLAKEWAY-PHILLIPS *p-in-c*.
HILDERSTONE (Ch Ch), *Staffs*. V. **D** Lich 19 **P** *D Candy Esq* **I** H MYERS *p-in-c*.
HILFIELD (St Nich) w Hermitage (St Mary), *Dorset*.. **D** Sarum 7 *See* High Stoy.
HILGAY (All SS w St Mark), *Norf*. R. **D** Ely 17 **P** *Hertf Coll Ox* **I** T H W SWAN *p-in-c*.
HILL (St Jas), *Warws*. V. **D** Birm 12 **P** *Bp* **I** K PUNSHON.
HILL (St Mich), *Avon*. V. **D** Glouc 5 *See* Stone.
HILL DEVERILL (Assump BVM), *Wilts*. V. **D** Sarum 22 *See* Deverills.
HILLESDEN (All SS), *Bucks*. V. **D** Ox 23 *See* Gawcott.
HILLESLEY (St Giles), *Avon*. V. **D** Glouc 8 *See* Alderley.
HILLFARRANCE (H Cross), *Somt*.. **D** B & W 22 *See* Oake.
HILLHAMPTON, *Worcs*.. **D** Worc 12 *See* Witley, Great.
HILLINGDON (St Jo Bapt), *Gtr Lon*. V. **D** Lon 9 **P** *Bp* **I** M BELHAM, M H GABRIEL *c*.
(St Andr), V. **D** Lon 9 *See* Uxbridge.
(St Jerome, Dawley), V. **D** Lon 9 **P** *Hyndman Trustees* **I** N A MANNING.
(All SS), V. **D** Lon 9 **P** *Bp* **I** R A PHILLIPS, A A HORSMAN *c*.
HILLINGTON (St Mary Virg), *Norf*. R (*See Sandringham Group*).. **D** Nor 23 **P** *Hon G F ff Dawnay* **I** (Vacant).
HILLMORTON (St Jo Bapt), *Warws*. V. **D** Cov 6 **P** *Bp and R of Rugby* **I** R S STAUNTON.
HILLOCK (St Andr), *Gtr Man*.. **D** Man 19 **P** *Bp and R of Stand* **I** D L PETERS.
HILLSBOROUGH (Ch Ch) and Wadsley Bridge, *S Yorks*. V. **D** Sheff 4 **P** *CPS* **I** C SMITH.
HILMARTON (St Laur) w Highway (St Pet), *Wilts*. V. **D** Sarum 25 **P** *Crown* **I** G H JONES *p-in-c*.
HILPERTON (St Mich AA) w Whaddon, *Wilts*. R. **D** Sarum 24 **P** *Visc Long* **I** P H BELL *p-in-c*.
HILSEA, *Hants*.. **D** Portsm *See* Portsea (St Mark).
HILSTON, *Humb*.. **D** York 15 *See* Garton-in-Holderness.
HILTON, *Cumb*.. **D** Carl 1 *See* Appleby.
HILTON (St Mary Magd), *Cambs*. V. **D** Ely 10 **P** *Bp* **I** W N C GIRARD.
HILTON-BY-CLEVELAND (St Pet), *Cleve*. V. **D** York 25 **P** *H A Shaw Esq* **I** (Vacant).
HILTON (All SS) w Melcombe Horsey (St Andr), and Cheselbourne (St Martin), *Dorset*. V. **D** Sarum 10 *See* Milton Abbas.
HIMBLETON (St Mary Magd) w Huddington (St Jas), *Worcs*. V. **D** Worc 8 **P** *D and C of Worc* **I** W D S WELLS *p-in-c*.
HIMLEY (St Mich AA), *Staffs*. R. **D** Lich **P** *Earl of Dudley* **I** R D PAYNE.
HINCHLEY WOOD (St Chis), *Surrey*. V. **D** Guildf 8 **P** *Bp* **I** A R ARNOLD.
HINCKLEY (Ch of the Assump of St Mary Virg), *Leics*. V. **D** Leic 16 **P** *Bp* **I** E W PLATT.
(H Trin), V. **D** Leic 16 **P** *Dioc Bd of Patr* **I** G T WILLETT, M E THOMAS *c*.
HINDERCLAY (St Mary Virg) w Wattisfield (St Marg), *Suff*. R. **D** St E 9 **P** *J Holt Wilson Esq and MMT* alt **I** J A E RUTHERFORD P-IN-C OF HINDERCLAY.
HINDERWELL (St Hilda) w Roxby (St Nich), *N Yorks*. R. **D** York 27 **P** *Abp* **I** D J DERMOTT, D R SAMWAYS *hon c*.
HINDHEAD (St Alb), *Surrey*. V. **D** Guildf 3 **P** *Archd of Surrey* **I** J N E BUNDOCK.
HINDLEY (All SS), *Gtr Man*. V. **D** Liv 12 **P** *R of Wigan* **I** B C CLARK.
(St Pet), V. **D** Liv 12 **P** *St Pet Coll Ox* **I** C D S WOODHOUSE.

HINDLEY GREEN (St Jo Evang), *Gtr Man.* V. **D** Liv 12 **P** *Bp* **I** D G CLAWSON.
HINDLIP (St Jas Gt) w Martin Hussingtree (St Mich AA) *Worcs.* R. **D** Worc *See* Salwarpe.
HINDOLVESTON (St Geo Mart), *Norf.* V. **D** Nor 6 **P** *D and C of Nor* **I** J M S PICKERING *p-in-c.*
HINDON (St Jo Bapt) w Chicklade (All SS) and Pertwood (St Pet), *Wilts..* **D** Sarum 19 *See* Knoyle, East.
HINDRINGHAM (St Martin) and Binham (St Mary), *Norf.* R. **D** Nor 24 **P** *D and C of Nor and Bp (alt)* **I** G F FARNWORTH.
HINDSFORD (St Anne), *Gtr Man.* V. **D** Man 6 **P** *Bp* **I** (Vacant).
HINGHAM (St Andr), *Norf.* R. **D** Nor 12 **P** *Trustees* **I** H A R EDGELL.
HINKSEY, NORTH (St Laur), *Oxon.* V. **D** Ox 8 **P** *Bp* **I** J E CRISP, S F MORRIS *c.*
HINKSEY, SOUTH (St Lawr w St Jo Evang New Hinksey), *Oxon.* V. **D** Ox 8 **P** *Bp* **I** E J C DAVIS.
HINSTOCK (St Osw) and Sambrook, *Salop.* R. **D** Lich 21 **P** *Bp and R of Edgmond* **I** D B SKELDING.
HINTLESHAM (St Nic) w Chattisham (All SS and St Marg), *Suff.* R. **D** St E 3 **P** *St Chad's Coll Dur 3 turns, Bp 1 turn* **I** S PETTITT *p-in-c.*
HINTON ADMIRAL (St Mich AA), *Hants..* **D** Win 8 *See* Highcliffe.
HINTON AMPNER (All SS) w Bramdean (St Simon and St Jude) and Kilmeston (St Andr), *Hants.* R. **D** Win 6 **P** *D and C of Win and Crown* alt **I** D C HANCOCK.
HINTON-BLEWETT (St Marg), *Avon.* R. **D** B & W 15 *See* Harptree, E.
HINTON CHARTERHOUSE (St Jo Bapt), *Avon..* **D** B & W *See* Freshford.
HINTON-IN-THE-HEDGES (H Trin) w Steane (St Pet), *Northants..* **D** Pet 1 *See* Farthinghoe.
HINTON-MARTEL (St Jo Evang), *Dorset.* R. **D** Sarum 11 **P** *Earl of Shaftesbury* **I** W H BARNARD.
HINTON-ON-THE-GREEN (St Pet), *Worcs.* R. **D** Worc 1 *See* Sedgebarrow.
HINTON PARVA, *Wilts..* **D** Bris *See* Bishopstone.
HINTON PARVA or STANBRIDGE, *Dorset.* R. **D** Sarum *See* Witchampton.
HINTON ST GEORGE (St Geo) w Dinnington (St Nich), *Somt.* R. **D** B & W *See* Merriott.
HINTON ST MARY (St Pet), *Dorset.* V. **D** Sarum 13 *See* Sturminster Newton.
HINTON WALDRIST (St Marg), *Oxon.* R. **D** Ox 17 *See* Longworth.
HINTS (St Bart), *Staffs.* V. **D** Lich 2 **P** *Trustees* **I** K P HALLETT *p-in-c,* M D GLENN *c,* W G MCNAMEE *c.*
HINXHILL (St Mary), *Kent.* R. **D** Cant 10 *See* Willesborough.
HINXTON (BVM and St Jo Evang), *Cambs.* V. **D** Ely 7 **P** *Jes Coll Cam* **I** R A BIRT *p-in-c.*
HINXWORTH (St Nich) w Newnham (St Vincent) and Radwell (All SS), *Herts.* R. **D** St Alb 5 **P** *Bp 3 turns, W A Farr Esq 1 turn, R Smyth Esq 1 turn* **I** V L NORTH P-IN-C OF RADWELL, F W J PICKARD P-IN-C OF HINXWORTH W NEWNHAM.
HIPSWELL (St Jo Evang), *N Yorks.* V. **D** Ripon 1 **P** *Bp* **I** R MANN.
HISTON (St Andr w St Etheldreda), *Cambs.* V. **D** Ely 5 **P** *MMT* **I** A B TURTON.
HITCHAM (St Mary), *Bucks.* R. **D** Ox 24 **P** *Eton Coll* **I** P S JUDD *team v,* D G THOMAS *p-in-c.*
HITCHAM (All SS) w Finborough Parva, *Suff.* R. **D** St E **P** *Bp and Pemb Coll Ox (alt)* **I** C E WETHERALL.
HITCHIN (St Mary w H Sav), *Herts.* R. **D** St Alb 9 **P** *Patr Bd* **I** K N JENNINGS, J D BARNARD *team v,* D J COCKERELL *team v,* N N STEADMAN *team v,* R S ANDREWS *c,* T J G NEWCOMBE *c,* R VICKERS *c.*
HITHER GREEN (St Swith), *Kent.* V. **D** S'wark 20 **P** *V of Lewisham* **I** (Vacant).
HITTISLEIGH (St Andr), *Devon.* R. **D** Ex 12 **P** *Bp and B Drew Esq* alt **I** C J L NAPIER.
HIXON (St Pet), *Staffs.* V. **D** Lich 4 **P** *Bp* **I** A LITTLE *c-in-c.*
HOAR CROSS (Ch of the H Angels), *Staffs.* V. **D** Lich **P** *Meynell Ch Trustees* **I** J HOWE *p-in-c.*
HOARWITHY, *Herefs.* V. **D** Heref 8 *See* Hentland.
HOATH, *Kent..* **D** Cant *See* Chislet.
HOATHLY, EAST (Dedic unknown), *E Sussex.* R. **D** Chich 16 **P** *Bp* **I** A C GINNO *c-in-c.*
HOATHLY, WEST (St Marg), *E Sussex.* V. **D** Chich 11 *See* Highbrook.
HOB'S MOAT (St Mary), *W Midl.* V. **D** Birm 11 **P** *Bp* **I** P H ROE, M H JACKSON *c.*
HOBY (All SS) cum Rotherby (All SS) with Brooksby and Ragdale, *Leics.* R. **D** Leic 9 **P** *Dioc Bd of Patr* **I** R H CHATHAM.
HOCKERILL (All SS), *Herts.* V. **D** St Alb 4 **P** *Bp of Lon* **I** G L EDWARDS, A I JOHNSON *c,* A I JOHNSTON *c,* D M ROGERS *c.*
HOCKERING (St Mich), *Norf.* R. **D** Nor 12 **P** *J V Berney Esq* **I** (Vacant).
HOCKERTON (St Nich), *Notts.* R. **D** Southw 15 *See* Kirklington.
HOCKHAM, GREAT (H Trin) w Little Hockham, Wretham and Illington, *Norf.* V. **D** Nor 18 **P** *Sutton Hosp (2 turns), Exors of T V Lowe Esq (1 turn) and G W Nurse Esq (1 turn)* **I** (Vacant).
HOCKINGTON (St Andr), *Cambs.* V. **D** Ely 7 *See* Oakington.
HOCKLEY (St Pet), *Essex.* V. **D** Chelmsf 16 **P** *Wadh Coll Ox* **I** R W WHEELER *hon c.*
HOCKLEY HEATH, *W Midl..* **D** Birm 10 *See* Packwood.
HOCKLIFFE (St Nich), *Beds.* R. **D** St Alb *See* Leighton-Buzzard.
HOCKWOLD (St Pet) w Wilton (St Jas), *Norf.* R. **D** Ely 16 **P** *G and C Coll Cam* **I** G H M WEBB.
HOCKWORTHY, *Devon.* V. **D** Ex 4 *See* Holcombe Rogus.
HODDESDON (St Paul), *Herts.* V. **D** St Alb 6 **P** *Peache Trustees* **I** P J GANDON, F A RICE *hon c.*
HODDLESDEN (St Paul), *Lancs.* V. **D** Blackb 5 *See* Darwen.
HODGE HILL (St Phil and St Jas), *W Midl.* R. **D** Birm 9 **P** *Bp* **I** M C DODD, J V MARCH *team v,* A P GREENFIELD *c.*
HODNET (St Luke) with Weston-under-Redcastle, V and Peplow, *Salop.* R. **D** Lich 23 **P** *Brig A W G Heber-Percy* **I** N R TORRINGTON.
HOE, *Norf..* **D** Nor 20 **P** *Ld Chan* **I** L A WILMAN *p-in-c.*
HOGGESTON (H Cross) w Dunton, *Bucks.* R. **D** Ox *See* Schorne.
HOGHTON (H Trin), *Lancs.* V. **D** Blackb 6 **P** *V of Leyland* **I** J GARDINER.
HOGNASTON (St Bart), *Derbys..* **D** Derby 8 *See* Hulland.
HOGSTHORPE (St Mary), *Lincs.* V. **D** Linc 8 **P** *Bp* **I** A E R EMERSON *p-in-c.*
HOLBEACH (All SS), *Lincs.* V. **D** Linc 16 **P** *Bp* **I** C R EVANS, I JACKSON *c,* R S PIMPERTON *c.*
HOLBEACH BANK (St Martin), *Lincs..* **D** Linc 16 *See* Lutton.
HOLBEACH FEN (St Jo Bapt), *Lincs.* V. **D** Linc 16 **P** *Bp* **I** L H N CARTER.
HOLBEACH HURN (St Luke), *Lincs.* V. **D** Linc 16 **P** *V of Holbeach* **I** (Vacant).
HOLBEACH MARSH (St Mark Evang w St Matt Ap and Evang), *Lincs.* V. **D** Linc 16 **P** *V of Holbeach* **I** (Vacant).
HOLBECK (St Luke Evang, Beeston Hill), *N Yorks.* V. **D** Ripon 8 **P** *Bp, Meynell Church Trust and V of Leeds* **I** J R HOLMES.
HOLBECK (St Winifred), *Notts..* **D** Southw *See* Norton Cuckney.
HOLBETON (All SS), *Devon.* V. **D** Ex 21 **P** *Crown* **I** K W KNIGHT.
HOLBORN (St Alb Mart, Brooke Street w St Pet, Saffron Hill), *Lon.* V. **D** Lon 20 **P** *D and C of St Paul's* **I** J B GASKELL, D N C HOULDING *c.*
(St Geo Mart, Queen Square and H Trin w St Bart, Gray's Inn Road), R. **D** Lon 20 **P** *Ch S Trust* **I** (Vacant).
HOLBROOK (All SS) w Freston (St Pet) and Woolverstone (St Mich AA), *Suff.* R. **D** St E 5 **P** *Bp* **I** J BROOKS.
HOLBROOK (St Mich), *Derbys.* V. **D** Derby 12 **P** *Sir Gilbert Inglefield* **I** P LYNE *p-in-c.*
HOLBROOKS (St Luke), *W Midl.* V. **D** Cov 2 **P** *Bp* **I** H HUGHES, K J HOOPER *c.*
HOLCOMBE (St Andr), *Somt.* R. **D** B & W 16b *See* Coleford.
HOLCOMBE (Em), *Gtr Man.* R. **D** Man 12 **P** *R of Bury* **I** R M F HAIGH, D R TILSTON *c.*
HOLCOMBE-BURNELL (St Jo Bapt), *Devon.* V. **D** Ex 6 **P** *Bp* **I** N J DAVEY.
HOLCOMBE ROGUS (All SS) w Hockworthy, *Devon.* V. **D** Ex 4 *See* Sampford-peverell.
HOLCOT (St Mary and All SS), *Northants..* **D** Pet 6 *See* Brixworth.
HOLDENBY (All SS), *Northants.* R. **D** Pet 6 *See* Ravensthorpe.
HOLDENHURST (St Jo Evang) w Throop, *Dorset.* V. **D** Win 7 **P** *Bp* **I** K G BACHELL.
(St Barn Conv Distr Queen's Park). **D** Win 7 **P** *Bp* **I** (Vacant).
HOLDFAST, *Worcs..* **D** Worc 5 *See* Queenhill.
HOLDGATE (H Trin) w Tugford (St Cath), *Salop.* R. **D** Heref 12 **P** *Bp* **I** S C MORRIS P-IN-C OF ABDON *p-in-c.*

HOLFORD (St Mary Virg) w Dodington (All SS), *Somt.* R. **D** B & W 18 *See* Quantoxhead.

HOLKHAM (St Withiburga) w Egmere (St Edm) and Waterden (All SS), *Norf.* R (*See Wells Group*). **D** Nor 21 **P** *Earl of Leicester* **I** D J CHAPMAN *p-in-c.*

HOLLACOMBE (St Petroc), *Devon.* R. **D** Ex 9 *See* Holsworthy.

HOLLAND FEN (All SS) w Amber Hill (St Jo Bapt) and Chap Hill (H Trin), *Lincs.* V. **D** Linc 21 **P** *R of Algarkirk* **I** (Vacant).

HOLLAND, GREAT (All SS), *Essex.* R. **D** Chelmsf 28 **P** *CPAS* **I** K R WALTER.

HOLLAND, NEW (Ch Ch), *Humb.*. **D** Linc 6 *See* Barrow-on-Humber.

HOLLAND-ON-SEA (St Bart), *Essex.* V. **D** Chelmsf **P** *CPS* **I** A I PAGET.

HOLLESLEY (All SS), *Suff.* R. **D** St E 7 *See* Boyton.

HOLLINFARE (St Helen), *Ches.* V. **D** Liv 11 **P** *R of Warrington* **I** C E B HOLBROOK.

HOLLINGBOURNE (All SS), *Kent.* V. **D** Cant 15 **P** *Abp* **I** A C BELL *p-in-c.*

HOLLINGTON (St Leon), *E Sussex.* R. **D** Chich 21 **P** *Exors of M St A Vaughan Esq* **I** J A A FLETCHER, A J WILLIAMS *c.*

(St Jo Evang), V. **D** Chich 21 **P** *CPS* **I** R H G JOHNSTON, E M HAVELL *c.*

HOLLINGTON, *Staffs.*. **D** Lich 20 *See* Croxden.

HOLLINGWORTH (St Mary), *Gtr Man.* V. **D** Ches 14 **P** *Trustees* **I** E PRATT.

HOLLINWOOD (St Marg), *Gtr Man.* V. **D** Man 15 **P** *R of Prestwich* **I** A GEORGE.

HOLLOWAY (Ch Ch), *Derbys.*. **D** Derby *See* Dethick.

HOLLOWAY (Em w St Barn Hornsey Road), *Lon.* V. **D** Lon 3 **P** *CPAS* **I** P W DEARNLEY *p-in-c,* P A BROADBENT *c.*

(St Geo Tufnell Park), V. **D** Lon 3 **P** *Trustees* **I** D I LISTER.

(St Mark w St Anne, Tollington Pk), V. **D** Lon 3 **P** *V of St John, Upper Holloway* **I** F M TRETHEWEY *c.*

(St Mary Magd w St Jas), V. **D** Lon 3 **P** *V of Islington* **I** (Vacant).

(St Sav w St Paul, Hanley Road), V. **D** Lon 3 **P** *CPAS* **I** W F NORTON.

UPPER (St Pet w St John), V. **D** Lon 3 **P** *Trustees* **I** D E SPRATLEY.

(All SS), V. **D** Lon 3 **P** *CPAS* **I** (Vacant).

(St Steph), V. **D** Lon 3 **P** *Bp* **I** P J TRENDALL *p-in-c.*

(St Andr Whitehall Park), V. **D** Lon 3 **P** *Trustees* **I** D J CURRY.

(St Luke), V. **D** Lon 3 **P** *Trustees* **I** T J PIGREM.

See also ISLINGTON..

HOLLOWELL (St Jas), *Northants.* V. **D** Pet 6 *See* Guilsborough.

HOLLY HALL (St Aug Bp of Hippo), *Worcs.*. **D** Worc 19 *See* Dudley.

HOLLYBUSH w Birtsmorton, *Herefs.* V. **D** Worc 5 *See* Castle Morton.

HOLLYM (St Nich, formerly St Cath) w Welwick (St Mary) and Holmpton (St Nich), *Humb.* V. **D** York 15 **P** *Abp and Ld Chan* alt **I** A C HODGE *p-in-c.*

HOLMBRIDGE (St D), *W Yorks.* V. **D** Wakef 5 **P** *V of Almondbury* **I** E R BELL.

HOLMBURY (St Mary), *Surrey.* R. **D** Guildf *See* Wotton.

HOLME (H Trin), *Cumb.* V. **D** Carl 17 **P** *V of Burton-in-Kendal* **I** P C BATTERSBY *p-in-c.*

HOLME (St Giles) w Conington, *Cambs.* V. **D** Ely 14 **P** *Crown and J H B Heathcote Esq (alt)* **I** G J SHARPE.

HOLME-BY-NEWARK (St Giles), *Notts.*. **D** Southw 3 *See* Langford.

HOLME CULTRAM (St Mary), *Cumb.* V. **D** Carl 3 **P** *Univ of Ox* **I** J K TOWERS.

(St Cuthb), V. **D** Carl 11 **P** *V of Holme Cultram* **I** D G BLAKE.

HOLME, EAST (St Jo Evang), *Dorset.* V. **D** Sarum 9 *See* Wareham.

HOLME EDEN (St Paul), *Cumb.* V. **D** Carl 2 **P** *Dioc Bd of Patr* **I** J S CASSON.

HOLME-HALE (St Andr), *Norf.* R. **D** Nor 19 *See* Necton.

HOLME-IN-CLIVIGER (St Jo Evang), *Lancs.* V. **D** Blackb 3 **P** *Mrs P Creed* **I** L W SAVAGE.

HOLME-LACY (St Cuthb) w Dyndor (St Andr), *Herefs.*. **D** Heref 4 **P** *Bp and Worc Coll Ox* **I** J F BAULCH *p-in-c,* A R OSBORNE *c.*

HOLME-NEXT-RUNCTON, *Norf.*. **D** Ely *See* Runcton, South.

HOLME-NEXT-THE-SEA (St Mary Virg), *Norf.* V. **D** Nor *See* Hunstanton St Mary.

HOLME-PIERREPONT (St Edm) w Adbolton, *Notts.* R. **D** Southw 9 **P** *Dioc Bd of Patr* **I** G N PEARCE *c-in-c.*

HOLME-ON-SPALDING MOOR (All SS), *Humb.* V. **D** York 10 **P** *St Jo Coll Cam* **I** N STRONG.

HOLMER (St Bart) w Huntington, *Herefs.* V. **D** Heref 3 **P** *D and C of Heref* **I** J C DALE.

HOLMER GREEN (Ch Ch), *Bucks.* V. **D** Ox 20 *See* Penn Street.

HOLMES CHAPEL or CHURCH HULME (St Luke), *Chesh.* V. **D** Ches 11 **P** *V of Sandbach* **I** W E P TYSON.

HOLMESFIELD (St Swith), *Derbys.* V. **D** Derby 3 **P** *K Tudor* **I** A RIVERS.

HOLMFIELD (St Andr), *W Yorks.* V. **D** Wakef 1 **P** *Bp* **I** G WARD.

HOLMFIRTH (H Trin) w Thongsbridge (H Trin), *W Yorks.* V. **D** Wakef 5 **P** *V of Kirkburton* **I** J M SAUSBY.

HOLMPTON (St Nich), *Humb.* R. **D** York 15 *See* Hollym.

HOLMSIDE (St Jo Evang), *Durham.* V. **D** Dur 7 **P** *Crown* **I** (Vacant).

HOLMWOOD (St Mary Magd), *Surrey.* V. **D** Guildf 6 **P** *Bp* **I** W D LANG.

NORTH (St Jo Evang), V. **D** Guildf 6 **P** *Bp* **I** I C S FENTON, W LITTLEWOOD *hon c.*

HOLNE (St Mary Virg), *Devon.* V. **D** Ex 13 **P** *Dioc Bd of Patr* **I** P G HARRISON *p-in-c.*

HOLNEST (The Assump), *Dorset.*. **D** Sarum *See* Wootton Glanville.

HOLSWORTHY (St Pet and St Paul) w Hollacombe and Cookbury, *Devon.* R. **D** Ex 9 **P** *Dioc Bd of Patr* **I** R M REYNOLDS.

HOLT (St Mary), *Leics.* R. **D** Leic 5 *See* Medbourne.

HOLT (St Andr), *Norf.* R. **D** Nor 24 **P** *St Jo Coll Cam* **I** S S GREGORY, R M HARPER *c,* P W E CURRIE *hon c.*

HOLT (St Jas Gt), *Dorset.* V. **D** Sarum *See* Wimborne Minster.

HOLT (St Kath), *Wilts.* V. **D** Sarum 24 **P** *D and C of Bris 3 turns, Mrs M E Floyd 1 turn, Ld Chan 2 turns* **I** R E DUNNINGS.

HOLT (St Martin), *Worcs.* R. **D** Worc 2 *See* Grimley.

HOLTBY, *N Yorks.* R. **D** York 4 *See* Stockton-on-the-Forest.

HOLTON (St Nich), *Somt.* R. **D** B & W 4 **P** *MMT* **I** (Vacant).

HOLTON (St Bart) w Waterperry (St Mary Virg), *Oxon.* R. **D** Ox 5 **P** *Dioc Bd of Patr* **I** D M W ROBINSON.

HOLTON (St Pet), w Blyford (All SS), V *Suff.* R. **D** St E *See* Halesworth.

HOLTON ST MARY (St Mary) w Great Wenham (St Jo Evang), *Suff.* R. **D** St E 3 **P** *Bp and Sir Charles Rowley Bt* alt **I** W S HERRINGTON *p-in-c.*

HOLTON-LE-BECKERING, *Lincs.*. **D** Linc 5 *See* Lissington.

HOLTON-LE-CLAY (St Pet), *Linc.* V. **D** Linc 10 **P** *Ld Chan* **I** T R SHEPHERD.

HOLTON-LE-MOOR (St Luke), *Lincs.*. **D** Linc 5 *See* Kelsey, South.

HOLTS (St Hugh Conv Distr), *Gtr Man.*. **D** Man 15 **P** *Bp* **I** N RICHARDSON *c-in-c.*

HOLTSPUR, *Bucks.*. **D** Ox 20 *See* Beaconsfield.

HOLTYE, *E Sussex.*. **D** Chich *See* Hammerwood.

HOLWELL, *Leics.* V. **D** Leic 4 *See* Ab-Kettleby.

HOLWELL, *Oxon.*. **D** Ox *See* Westwell.

HOLWELL, (St Pet), *Herts.* R. **D** St Alb *See* Ickleford.

HOLWELL (St Laur), *Dorset.*. **D** Sarum 7 *See* Caundles, The.

HOLYBOURNE (H Rood) w Neatham, *Hants.* V. **D** Win 1 **P** *D and C of Win* **I** G F DOWDEN *p-in-c.*

HOLY ISLAND (St Mary), *Northumb.* V. **D** Newc T 11 **P** *Bp* **I** D A BILL.

HOLYSTONE, *Northumb.*. **D** Newc T *See* Alwinton.

HOLYWELL (St Jo Bapt) w Needingworth, *Cambs.* R. **D** Ely 12 **P** *Bp* **I** J WILCOX.

HOLYWELL (St Wilfrid), *Lincs.*. **D** Linc 14 *See* Careby.

HOLYWELL, *Northumb.*. **D** Newc T *See* Seghill.

HOMERSFIELD (St Mary) w St Cross, South Elmham (St Geo), *Suff.*. **D** St E 14 *See* Flixton.

HOMERTON (St Barn w St Paul), *Lon.* V. **D** Lon 2 **P** *Bp and Grocers' Co* **I** J F D PEARCE, T B JONES *c,* A SIMPSON *c.*

HOMINGTON (St Mary Virg), *Wilts.*. **D** Sarum 19 *See* Coombe Bissett.

HONEYBOURNE, CHURCH (St Ecgwin), w Cow Honeybourne, *Worcs.* V. **D** Glouc 12 **P** *Bp* **I** L POWELL.

HONEYCHURCH, *Devon.*. **D** Ex *See* Sampford Courtenay.

HONICKOWLE (St Francis), *Devon.* V. **D** Ex 23 *See* Devonport.

HONILEY (St Jo Bapt), *Warws.* R. **D** Cov 4 **P** *Maj J C Wade* **I** M N WRIGHT.

HONING (St Pet and St Paul) w Crostwight, *Norf.* R. **D** Nor *See* Smallburg.

HONINGHAM (St Andr) w East Tuddenham (All SS), *Norf.* V. **D** Nor 12 **P** *Dioc Bd of Patr* **I** (Vacant).
HONINGTON (All SS) w Idlicote (St Jas Greater), *Warws.* V. **D** Cov 9 **P** *Bp* **I** (Vacant).
HONINGTON, or HUNNINGTON (St Wilfred), *Lincs.* V. **D** Linc 23 **P** *Sir H T Tollemache Bt* **I** R BERRY.
HONINGTON (All SS) w Sapiston and Troston, *Suff.* R. **D** St E 9 **P** *Ld Chan 2 turns, Duke of Grafton 1 turn* **I** P M OLIVER *p-in-c.*
HONITON (St Paul) and (St Mich Arch) w Gittisham (St Mich) and Combe Raleigh (St Nich), *Devon.* R. **D** Ex **P** *Dioc Bd of Patr, Earl of Devon and Reps of Late A A Marker* **I** J W I TREVELYAN, P L C PRICE *hon c.*
HOOK-NORTON (St Pet) w Great Rollright, Swerford & Wigginton *Oxon.* R. **D** Ox **P** *Bp, Dioc Bd of Patr & Jes Coll Ox* **I** (Vacant).
HONLEY (St Mary Virg) w Brockholes (St Geo), *W Yorks.* V. **D** Wakef 5 **P** *V of Almondbury* **I** L R WICKHAM.
HONOR OAK PARK (St Aug), V. **D** S'wark 18 **P** *Bp* **I** J M L L BOGLE.
HONYNGHAM (St Marg), *Warws.*. **D** Cov *See* Hunningham.
HOO ALL HALLOWS, *Kent.* V. **D** Roch 5 *See* Halstow, High.
(St Mary Virg). **D** Roch *See* Halstow, High.
(St Werburgh), V. **D** Roch 5 **P** *D and C of Roch* **I** C G WOODHEAD.
HOO, *Suff.*. **D** St E *See* Monewden.
HOOE (St Osw), *E Sussex.* V. **D** Chich 17 **P** *St Edm Hall 1 turn, D and C of Cant 2 turns* **I** L HARDAKER.
HOOE (St Jo Evang), *Devon.* V. **D** Ex 21 **P** *Keble Coll Ox* **I** A B ROBINSON.
HOOK (St Mary) w Warsash, *Hants.* V. **D** Portsm 1 **P** *Bp* **I** D J C WEBER.
HOOK (St Mary Virg) w Airmyn (St D), *S Yorks.* V. **D** Sheff 9 **P** *Bp and Ch Soc Trust* **I** C W ANTHONY.
HOOK (St Paul), *Surrey.* V. **D** S'wark 11 **P** *Crown* **I** W MULLENGER *c.*
HOOK w Greywell, *Hants.* R. **D** Win 4 **P** *Bp* **I** B G RICHARDS *p-in-c.*
HOOK-NORTON (St Pet) w Swerford (St Mary) and Wigginton (St Giles), *Oxon.* R. **D** Ox 3 **P** *Bp, Dioc Bd of Patr and Jes Coll Ox* in turn **I** G M HOOPER.
HOOKE, *Dorset.*. **D** Sarum *See* Toller, Great.
HOOLE (St Mich), *Lancs.* R. **D** Blackb 6 **P** *Reps of Rev E C Dunne* **I** W F SPALDING.
HOOLE (All SS), *Chesh.* V. **D** Ches 2 **P** *Simeon Trustees* **I** A B MARTIN, C E GALE *c*, K I HOBBS *c.*
HOOTON (St Paul), *Chesh.* V. **D** Ches 9 **P** *Trustees* **I** R W CAMPBELL.
HOOTON PAGNELL (All SS), *S Yorks.*. **D** Sheff *See* Brodsworth.
HOOTON ROBERTS (St Jo Bapt), *S Yorks.* R. **D** Sheff 7 **P** *Earl Fitzwilliam* **I** G GREENWOOD.
HOPE, *Kent.*. **D** Cant *See* Romney, New.
HOPE (St Pet) and Castleton, *Derbys.* V. **D** Derby **P** *Bp and D and C of Lich* **I** M F COLLIER.
HOPE (H Trin) w Shelve, *Salop.* R. **D** Heref 13 **P** *New Coll Ox 3 turns, J More Esq 1 turn* **I** N D MINSHALL.
HOPE (H Trin), *Staffs.*. **D** Lich 18 *See* Hanley.
HOPE (St Jas), *Gtr Man.*. **D** Man 8 *See* Salford.
HOPE-BAGOT (St Jo Bapt), *Salop.* R. **D** Heref 12 *See* Burford (2nd portion).
HOPE-BOWDLER (St Andr) w Eaton-under-Heywood (St Edith), *Salop.* R. **D** Heref 11 **P** *Dioc Bd of Patr and Maj H Sandford* **I** M BROMFIELD.
HOPE-MANSEL (St Mich), *Herefs.* R. **D** Heref *See* Weston-under-Penyard.
HOPE-UNDER-DINMORE (St Mary Virg), *Herefs.* V. **D** Heref *See* Bodenham.
HOPESAY (St Mary) w Edgton (St Mich), *Salop.* R. **D** Heref 10 **P** *Earl of Powis 2 turns, H Sandford Esq 1 turn* **I** V IRWIN *p-in-c.*
HOPTON (St Marg) w Corton, *Suff.* V. **D** Nor **P** *Ld Chan and D and C of Nor* **I** C R CHAPMAN.
HOPTON-BY-THETFORD (All SS) w Market Weston and Barningham (St Andr) w Coney Weston (St Mary Virg), *Suff.* R. **D** St E 9 **P** *Bp* **I** M T RANYARD.
HOPTON CANGEFORD, *Salop.* V. **D** Heref 12 **P** *Miss M F Rouse-Boughton* **I** A G SEABROOK P-IN-C OF STOKE ST MILBURGH *p-in-c.*
HOPTON CASTLE (St Edw), *Salop.*. **D** Heref *See* Bedstone.
HOPTON, UPPER (St Jo Evang), *W Yorks.* v. **D** Wakef 10 **P** *V of Mirfield* **I** I W HARRISON *p-in-c.*
HOPTON-WAFERS (St Mich AA), *Salop.* R. **D** Heref 12 *See* Cleobury Mortimer.
HOPWOOD (St Jo Evang), *Gtr Man.* V. **D** Man 17 **P** *R of Bury* **I** J A JONES.
HORAM (Ch Ch), *E Sussex.* V. **D** Chich 18 **P** *Bp* **I** P H AMOS.
HORBLING (St Andr), *Lincs.* V. **D** Linc 13 **P** *Bp* **I** H J THEODOSIUS.
HORBURY (St Pet) w Horbury Bridge, *W Yorks.* V. **D** Wakef 12 **P** *Provost of Wakefield* **I** O J AISBITT.
HORBURY JUNCTION (St Mary Virg), *W Yorks.* V. **D** Wakef 12 **P** *Dioc Bd of Patr* **I** S G D PARKINSON.
HORDEN (St Mary), *Cleve.* V. **D** Dur 3 **P** *Bp* **I** A BOWSER, K A MITCHELL *c.*
HORDLE (All SS), *Hants.* V. **D** Win 9 **P** *Bp* **I** M G ANDERSON, J G SMITH *c*, P S PLUNKETT *hon c.*
HORDLEY Salop. R **D** Lich 22 *See* Petton.
HORFIELD (H Trin w St Andr and St Edm), *Avon.* R. **D** Bris 4 **P** *Bp* **I** J H WILSON, P H DENYER *c*, C W GONIN *hon c.*
(St Greg), V. **D** Bris 4 **P** *Bp* **I** J A MORLEY-BUNKER.
HORHAM, *Suff.* R. **D** St E 17 *See* Stradbroke.
HORKESLEY, GREAT (All SS), *Essex.* R. **D** Chelmsf 22 **P** *Ball Coll Ox* **I** P PRICE.
HORKESLEY, LITTLE (St Pet and St Paul), *Essex.* V. **D** Chelmsf 22 **P** *W Otter-Barry Esq* **I** P M DAVIS.
HORKSTOW (St Maurice), *Humb.* V. **D** Linc 6 **P** *Dioc Bd of Patr* **I** I H TINKLER.
HORLEY (St Etheldreda) w Hornton (St Jo Bapt), *Oxon.* V. **D** Ox 6 **P** *Ld Chan* **I** C A L WOOLLEY.
HORLEY (St Bart), *Surrey.* V. **D** S'wark 12 **P** *Christ's Hosp* **I** S H MASLEN, D O ISHERWOOD *c*, O E KILLINGBACK *c.*
HORMEAD, GREAT (St Nich) w Little Hormead (St Mary), Anstey and Brent Pelham w Meesden, *Herts.* V. **D** St Alb **P** *St Jo Coll Cam 1st turn, Ch Coll Cam 2nd turn and Bp 3rd turn* **I** F L MORRIS, J H S SPREAD *c.*
HORNBLOTTON (St Pet), *Somt.* R. **D** B & W 4 *See* Alford.
HORNBY (St Marg) w Claughton, R *Lancs.* V. **D** Blackb 13 **P** *E J Battersby Esq and Dioc Bd of Patr* alt **I** H KELLETT.
HORNBY (St Mary), *N Yorks.* V. **D** Ripon 2 **P** *D and C of York* **I** (Vacant).
HORNCASTLE (St Mary w H Trin) w Low Toynton, *Lincs.* V. **D** Linc 11 **P** *Bp 2 turns, Earl of Ancaster 1 turn* **I** G A NEALE.
HORNCHURCH (St Andr), *Essex.* Chap and V. **D** Chelmsf 4 **P** *New Coll Ox* **I** A C H PEATFIELD, M M WATKINS *c.*
(All SS Ardleigh Green), V. **D** Chelmsf 4 **P** *Bp* **I** E L JONES.
(H Cross), V. **D** Chelmsf 4 **P** *Bp and New Coll Ox* **I** R B N HAYCRAFT.
(St Nich Elm Park), V. **D** Chelmsf 4 **P** *Bp* **I** D S MILLER.
(St Pet Harold Wood), V. **D** Chelmsf 4 **P** *New Coll Ox* **I** O M THOMSON, R BACKHOUSE *c*, G J HUTCHISON *c*, K MOULDER *c.*
SOUTH (St John and St Matt), V. **D** Chelmsf 4 **P** *MMT* **I** R F DAVIS *c-in-c*, M E PORTER *c.*
HORNDON, EAST (All SS) w West (St Nich) and Warley, Little (St Pet), *Essex.* R. **D** Chelmsf 9 **P** *Bp and Brentwood Sch* **I** P J BOULTON-LEA.
HORNDON-ON-THE-HILL (St Pet and St Paul), *Essex.* V. **D** Chelmsf 15 **P** *D and C of St Paul's* **I** D J WILLIAMS.
HORNE (St Mary Virg), *Surrey.* R. **D** S'wark 10 **P** *Bp* **I** J R HARVEY.
HORNING (St Benedict), *Norf.* V. **D** Nor 8 **P** *Bp* **I** W BLATHWAYT.
HORNINGHOLD (St Pet), *Leics.*. **D** Leic 5 *See* Hallaton.
HORNINGLOW (St Jo Div), *Staffs.* V. **D** Lich **P** *Trustees* **I** P J JEFFERIES, C J P DRAYCOTT *c.*
HORNINGSEA (St Pet), *Cambs.* V. **D** Ely 6 **P** *St Jo Coll Cam* **I** P R SMYTHE.
HORNINGSHAM (St Jo Bapt), *Wilts.* V. **D** Sarum 22 **P** *Bp* **I** A T JOHNSON *p-in-c.*
HORNINGSHEATH or HORRINGER, GT (St Leon) and Horringer, L w Ickworth (St Mary), *Suff.* R. **D** St E 13 **P** *Marchioness of Bris* **I** (Vacant).
HORNINGTOFT, *Norf.*. **D** Nor *See* Whissonsett.
HORNSEA (St Nich) w Atwick (St Pet or St Laur), *Humb.* V. **D** York 14 **P** *Ld Chan* **I** E J GUNN.
HORNSEY (St Mary), *Lon.* R. **D** Lon 23 **P** *Bp* **I** G B SEABROOK *p-in-c.*
(H Innoc Tottenham Lane), V. **D** Lon 23 **P** *Bp* **I** R J WOOD.
(St Geo), V. **D** Lon 23 **P** *Bp* **I** G B SEABROOK, E NICOL *c*, J A TAYLOR *hon c.*
(St Luke), V. **D** Lon 23 **P** *Bp* **I** B KINGSMILL-LUNN *p-in-c.*
(Ch Ch Crouch End), V. **D** Lon 23 **P** *Bp* **I** D H HUBBARD, R J GINN *c*, H L M SOWDON *hon c.*
See also HARRINGAY, MUSWELL HILL, AND STROUD GREEN..
HORNSEY RISE (St Mary), *Lon.* V. **D** Lon 3 **P** *Trustees* **I** P J TRENDALL.
HORNSEY ROAD (Em). **D** Lon 3 *See* Holloway.

HORNTON, *Oxon.*. D Ox *See* Horley.
HORRABRIDGE (St Jo Bapt), *Devon.* V. D Ex 22 *See* Sampford Spiney.
HORRINGER (St Leon), *Suff.*. D St E 13 *See* Horningsheath.
HORRINGTON, *Somt.* V. D B & W 6 *See* Wells.
HORSEHEATH (All SS), *Cambs.* R. D Ely 4 P *Govs of Charterho and Bp (alt)* I V C RYDER *p-in-c,* H W NESLING *hon c.*
HORSEHOUSE, *N Yorks.*. D Ripon 2 *See* Coverham.
HORSELL (St Mary Virg), *Surrey.* V. D Guildf 11 P *Bp* I C J FOWLES, B ASHLEY *c,* C EDMONDS *c.*
HORSENDEN (St Mich AA), *Bucks.*. D Ox 21 *See* Bledlow.
HORSEY (All SS), *Norf.* R. D Nor 9 P *Bp* I L O HARRIS *p-in-c.*
HORSFORD (All SS), *Norf.* V. D Nor 7 P *Bp* I J B BOSTON.
HORSFORTH (St Marg), *W Yorks.* V. D Ripon 5 P *Hon Mrs G Fraser* I J R SWAIN, P MOORHOUSE *c.*
HORSHAM (St Mary w St Mark, H Trin and St John), *W Sussex.* V. D Chich 4 P *Abp of Cant* I T J S THOMAS, R C COLES *c,* W E JERVIS *c,* A A JONES *c,* J L REEVES *c.*
HORSHAM ST FAITH (St Andr and St Marg), *Norf.* V. D Nor 4 P *Bp* I J B BOSTON.
HORSINGTON (St Jo Bapt), *Somt.* R. D B & W 5 *See* Abbas.
HORSINGTON (All SS), w Stixwould (St Pet), *Lincs.* R. D Linc 11 P *Dioc Bd of Patr* I H R WHALER.
HORSLEY (St Clem), *Derbys.* V. D Derby P *Bp* I D HUGHES *p-in-c.*
HORSLEY (St Martin) and Newington Bagpath w Kingscote, [Glos]. V. D Glouc 17 P *Bp 2 turns, Dioc Bd of Patr 1 turn* I L J HENDRY.
HORSLEY (H Trin) w Byrness, *Northumb.* V. D Newc T 2 *See* Otterburn.
HORSLEY, EAST (St Martin), *Surrey.* R. D Guildf 10 P *D and C of Cant* I E B HUBAND.
HORSLEY, WEST (St Mary), *Surrey.* R. D Guildf 10 P *Mrs K L Weston* I H W FORDER.
HORSLEY WOODHOUSE (St Susanna), *Derbys.* V. D Derby P *Bp* I E J GEORGE.
HORSMONDEN (St Marg), *Kent.* R. D Roch 10 P *Bp* I M G M SMITH.
HORSPATH (St Giles), *Oxon.* V. D Ox 5 P *Dioc Bd of Patr* I C J BUTLER *p-in-c.*
HORSTEAD (All SS), *Norf.* R. D Nor 5 P *K Coll Cam* I R M S WOODHAM.
HORSTED-KEYNES (St Giles), *E Sussex.* E. D Chich 11 P *Bp* I A G GLEDHILL.
HORSTED PARVA (St Mich AA), *E Sussex.* R. D Chich 16 P *Rev S P Hayllar* I C J PETERS, C G STABLES *hon c.*
HORTON (St Jas Elder) w Sodbury, *Avon.* R. D Glouc 8 P *CPAS and Duke of Beaufort* I K V ENSOR.
HORTON (St Mich), V *Staffs.*. D Lich 16 P *Bp* I C B WILLIAMS.
HORTON (St Mary Virg) w New Delaval and Cowpen *Northumb.* V. D Newc T 1 P *V of Woodhorn* I A F JAMES.
HORTON (St Barn) w Studley, *Oxon.* V. D Ox 5 P *V of Beckley* I A G A DE VERE *c-in-c.*
HORTON (St Mich), *Berks.*. D Ox 24 *See* Riverside.
HORTON (St Mary Magd) or Hackleton w Piddington, *Northants.* V. D Pet *See* Hardingstone.
HORTON (St Wolfrida) w Chalbury, *Dorset.* V. D Sarum P *Earl of Shaftesbury* I (Vacant).
HORTON, GT and L, *W Yorks.*. D Bradf 2 *See* Bradford.
HORTON-IN-RIBBLESDALE (St Osw), *N Yorks.* V. D Bradf 6 P *Bp* I G K S J POTTER *p-in-c.*
HORTON-KIRBY (St Mary), *Kent.* V. D Roch 1a P *Bp* I L E LAKER.
HORWICH (H Trin), *Gtr Man.* V. D Man 13 P *V of Deane* I D W GATENBY, S GREENHALGH *c.*
(St Cath), V. D Man 13 P *Five Trustees* I (Vacant).
HORWOOD Devon. R D Ex 20 *See* Newton Tracey.
HORWOOD, GREAT (St Jas), *Bucks.* R. D Ox 25 P *New Coll Ox* I (Vacant).
HORWOOD, LITTLE (St Nich), *Bucks.* V. D Ox 25 *See* Swanbourne.
HOSE (St Mich), *Leics.* V. D Leic 4 *See* Clawson, Long.
HOTHAM (St Osw), *Humb.* R. D York 16 P *Ld Chan* I P N HAYWARD.
HOTHFIELD (St Marg), *Kent.* R. D Cant 10 P *G W A Tufton Esq* I J F GLEADALL P-IN-C OF BOUGHTON ALUPH *p-in-c.*
HOTON (St Leon), *Leics.* V. D Leic 10 *See* Prestwold.
HOUGH-ON-THE-HILL (All SS) w Brandon and Gelston, *Lincs.* V. D Linc 23 P *Ld Brownlow* I T B WILLIAMS.
HOUGHAM-BY-DOVER (St Lawr), *Kent.* V. D Cant 5 *See* Alkham.
HOUGHAM (All SS) w Marston (St Mary), *Lincs.* R. D Linc 23 P *Revs J R H and H C Thorold* I T B WILLIAMS.
HOUGHTON (St Bart), or Tosside, *N Yorks.*. D Bradf *See* Tosside.
HOUGHTON (St Jo Evang), *Cumb.* V. D Carl 3 P *Trustees* I J MCALLEN, D M FOWLER *c.*
HOUGHTON (St Nich), *W Sussex.*. D Chich 6 *See* Bury.
HOUGHTON (St Mary) w Wyton, *Cambs.* R. D Ely 10 P *Bp* I D D BILLINGS.
HOUGHTON (All SS), *Hants.*. D Win *See* Stockbridge.
HOUGHTON CONQUEST (All SS), *Beds.* R. D St Alb *See* Wilshamstead.
HOUGHTON, GREAT (St Mary), *Northants.* R. D Pet 4 P *Magd Coll Ox* I F A GORSUCH.
HOUGHTON-IN-THE-DALE, *Norf.*. D Nor *See* Walsingham.
HOUGHTON-LE-SPRING (St Mich AA), *T & W.* R. D Dur 5 P *Bp* I P G C BRETT, M JACKSON *c.*
HOUGHTON, LITTLE (St Mary BV), w Brafield-on-Green (St Laur), *Northants.* V. D Pet 4 P *Miss Smyth and C V Davidge Esq* I O H OWEN.
HOUGHTON, NEW (Ch Ch), *Derbys.*. D Derby 2 *See* Pleasley.
HOUGHTON-NEXT-HARPLEY (St Martin), *Norf.* V. D Nor 21 P *Marq of Cholmondeley* I (Vacant).
HOUGHTON-ON-THE-HILL (St Cath) w Keyham (All SS), *Leics.* R. D Leic 8 P *Bp* I G P DAVIDSON.
HOUGHTON-ON-THE-HILL (St Mary), *Norf.*. D Nor 19 *See* Pickenham, North.
HOUGHTON REGIS (All SS), *Beds.* V. D St Alb 18 P *Dioc Bd of Patr* I G M NEAL, G E W BUCKLER *c,* K N P R RASMUSSEN *c.*
(St Thos Ap Conv Distr Parkside). D St Alb 18 P *Bp* I (Vacant).
HOUND (St Edw the Confessor w St Mary) w Netley Abbey, *Hants.* V. D Win 15 P *Win Coll* I E S SKETCHLEY.
HOUNSLOW (H Trin), *Gtr Lon.* V. D Lon 10 P *Bp* I J H BARTER, G A BARBER *c,* J W GARRATT *c,* N LAWRENCE *c.*
(St Paul, Hounslow Heath), V. D Lon 10 P *Bp* I D K GRAY.
(St Steph), V. D Lon 10 P *Bp* I G N HEATH.
(Good Shepherd Conv Distr). D Lon 10 P *Bp* I A BARRETT *p-in-c.*
HOUNSLOW, E (St Mary Virg), V. D Lon 10 *See* Isleworth.
HOVE (All SS), *E Sussex.* V. D Chich 13 P *Bp* I H GLAISYER, R A STIDOLPH *c,* K G SWABY *c.*
(Bp Hannington Mem Ch w H Cross), V. D Chich 13 P *Trustees* I M B LEA, P T W DAVIES *c.*
(H Trin Conv Distr). D Chich 13 P *Bp* I H F HULBERT *p-in-c.*
(St Andr Waterloo Street), V. D Chich 13 P *V of Hove* I (Vacant).
(St Andr), V. D Chich 13 P *V of Hove* I G R WALKER.
(St Barn and St Agnes) V. D Chich 13 P *Bp and V of Hove (alt)* I S D HORSEY.
(St Jo Bapt), V. D Chich 13 P *V of Hove* I D G SMITH *p-in-c.*
(St Patr), V. D Chich 13 P *Bp* I P CLARK *p-in-c,* T M S MORLEY *c.*
(St Phil), V. D Chich 13 P *Bp* I S W J BARTON.
(St Thos Ap), V. D Chich 13 P *Bp* I D RANKIN.
HOVERINGHAM (St Mich), *Notts.*. D Southw 15 *See* Thurgarton.
HOVETON (St John and St Pet), *Norf.*. D Nor *See* Wroxham.
HOVINGHAM (All SS), *N Yorks.* V. D York 21 P *Sir M Worsley, Bt* I P H S CRAWFORD *p-in-c.*
HOW CAPLE (St Andr w St Mary) w Sollers Hope (St Mich), *Herefs.* R. D Heref 8 P *Bp* I J A P HOSKYNS P-IN-C OF K CAPLE *p-in-c.*
HOWDEN, THE (Barmby-Marsh, Eastrington, Howden, Laxton, Blacktoft, Newport and Wressle), *Humb.* R. D York P *Abp 4 turns Ld Chan 1 turn* I B KEETON, R M HAINES *team v,* P P OCKFORD *team v,* G W H ARMSTRONG *c,* G M I SMETHURST *hon c.*
HOWDON PANNS, *T & W.*. D Newc T *See* Willington Team Parish.
HOWE (St Mary), *Norf.*. D Nor *See* Poringland.
HOWE BRIDGE (St Mich AA), *Gtr Man.* V. D Man 6 P *Trustees* I R I MCCALLA.
HOWELL (St Osw), *Lincs.* R. D Linc 22 *See* Heckington.

HOWGILL (H Trin), *Lancs.* V. **D** Bradf 7 *See* Firbank.
HOWICK (St Mich), *Northumb.* R. **D** Newc T 7 *See* Longhoughton.
HOWSHAM, *Humb..* **D** Linc 6 *See* Cadney.
HOWSHAM, *N Yorks..* **D** York *See* Bossall.
HOXNE (St Pet and St Paul) w Denham (St Jo Bapt), and Syleham (St Mary), *Suff.* V. **D** St E **P** *Bp and Dioc Bd of Patr (alt)* **I** J W DRAPER.
HOXTON (St Jo Bapt w Ch Ch), *Lon.* V. **D** Lon 2 **P** *Archd of Lon and Haberdashers' Co* **I** A W ROBINSON, D S LAKE *c.*
(H Trin w St Mary), V. **D** Lon 2 **P** *Bp* **I** P S WILLIAMSON *c.*
(St Anne w St Columba Kingsland Road), V. **D** Lon 2 **P** *Crown* **I** A N SYMONDSON *p-in-c.*
HOYLAKE (H Trin), *Mer.* V. **D** Ches 8 **P** *Bp* **I** J RICHARDS.
HOYLAND, HIGH (All SS), *S Yorks..* **D** Wakef 7 *See* Clayton West.
HOYLAND, NETHER (St Pet), *S Yorks.* V. **D** Sheff 7 **P** *Earl Fitzwilliam* **I** W CLARK.
(St Andr), V. **D** Sheff 7 **P** *R of Tankersley* **I** A G HURST.
HOYLANDSWAINE (St Jo Evang), *S Yorks.* V. **D** Wakef 8 **P** *Simon W Fraser Esq* **I** J F WHITE *p-in-c.*
HUBBERHOLME (St Mich AA), *N Yorks.* V. **D** Bradf *See* Kettlewell.
HUCCLECOTE (St Phil and St Jas), *Glos.* V. **D** Glouc 1 **P** *Bp* **I** G S R COX, G R MARTIN *c*, P J THOMAS *c.*
HUCKINGE (St Mary), *Kent.* V. **D** Cant 14 *See* Bredgar.
HUCKNALL TORKARD (St Mary Magd and St Jo Evang w St Pet and St Paul), *Notts.* R. **D** Southw 12 **P** *Bp* **I** D H WILLIAMS, H W GODFREY *team v*, G HERRETT *team v*, E ASHBY *c.*
HUCKNALL-UNDER-HUTHWAITE (All SS), *Notts.* V. **D** Southw 2 *See* Huthwaite.
HUDDERSFIELD (St Pet) w (St Paul), *W Yorks.* V. **D** Wakef 4 **P** *Dioc Bd of Patr* **I** I C KNOX.
(H Trin), V. **D** Wakef 4 **P** *Simeon Trustees* **I** J V DEARDEN.
(St Cuthb, Birkby), V. **D** Wakef 4 **P** *Bp* **I** M F B HARDY.
(St Jas Rawthorpe). **D** Wakef 5 **P** *Dioc Bd of Patr* **I** L WILLIAMS.
(St John Evang),. **D** Wakef 4 **P** *Dioc Bd of Patr* **I** J A CRABB, C STERRY *c*, P J STONIER *c.*
(St Thos Ap), V. **D** Wakef 4 **P** *Dioc Bd of Patr* **I** R H BUTTOLPH.
HUDDINGTON (St Jas), *Worcs..* **D** Worc *See* Himbleton.
HUDSWELL (St Mich AA), *N Yorks..* **D** Ripon 1 *See* Richmond.
HUGGATE, *Humb..* **D** York *See* Warter.
HUGGLESCOTE (St Jo Bapt) w Donington, *Leics.* V. **D** Leic 11 **P** *Bp* **I** B W KERBY.
HUGHENDEN (St Mich AA), *Bucks.* V. **D** Ox 32 **P** *Dioc Bd of Patr* **I** P BULLOCK-FLINT.
HUGHLEY (St Jo Bapt) w Church Preen (St Jo Bapt), *Salop.* R. **D** Heref *See* Wenlock.
HUGILL or INGS (St Anne), *Cumb.* V. **D** Carl 17 **P** *V of Kendal* **I** I D H ROBINS *p-in-c.*
HUISH (St Jas L), *Devon.* R. **D** Ex 20 *See* Merton.
HUISH (St Nich) w Oare (H Trin), *Wilts.* R. **D** Sarum 27 *See* Wilcot.
HUISH CHAMPFLOWER (St Pet), w Clatworthy (St Mary Virg), *Somt.* R. **D** B & W 22 *See* Chipstable.
HUISH EPISCOPI (St Mary Virg) w Pitney (St Jo Bapt), *Somt.* R. **D** B & W 10 *See* Langport.
HUISH, NORTH w Avonwick, *Devon.* R. **D** Ex 13 **P** *D R Buchanan-Allen Esq* **I** P A D WILLIS, C E G JONES *c.*
HUISH, SOUTH, *Devon.* R. **D** Ex 14 *See* Malborough.
HULCOTE (St Nich) w Salford (St Mary), *Beds.* R. **D** St Alb 19 **P** *Dioc Bd of Patr* **I** D H HUNT *p-in-c.*
HULCOTT (All SS), *Bucks.* R. **D** Ox 21 *See* Bierton.
HULL (Most H and Undivided Trin), *Humb.* V. **D** York 17 **P** *Trustees* **I** G B BRIDGMAN, R G SHARPE *c*, M BATES *hon c.*
(St Alb) V. **D** York 17 **P** *Abp* **I** D J BAKER, D B EMMOTT *c.*
(Ch of Ascen Derringham Bank), V. **D** York 17 **P** *Crown and Abp* alt **I** (Vacant).
(St Cuthb), V. **D** York 17 **P** *Abp* **I** (Vacant).
(St John, Newland), V. **D** York 17 **P** *Abp* **I** M H VERNON, P J MOTT *c.*
(St Mary Virg Lowgate), V. **D** York 17 **P** *Abp* **I** R EVELEIGH *p-in-c.*
(St Mary, Sculcoates), V. **D** York 17 **P** *V of St Steph, Sculcoates, Hull* **I** J E TINSLEY, J G LEEMAN *c*, J C THEWLIS *hon c.*
(St Martin), V. **D** York 17 **P** *Abp* **I** K G BEAKE.
(St Matt w St Barn), V. **D** York 17 **P** *V of H Trin Hull* **I** J A BAGSHAWE.
(St Mich AA), V. **D** York 17 **P** *Abp* **I** J B KNOS.
(St Nich Chap), V. **D** York 17 **P** *Abp* **I** M P PICKERING.
(St Steph, Sculcoates), V. **D** York 17 **P** *Ld Chan 2 turns, Abp and V of Hull 1 turn, Abp 1 turn* **I** F A C S BOWN *p-in-c.*
See also DRYPOOL, MARFLEET, NEWINGTON, AND SCULCOATES..
HULLAND (Ch Ch) w Atlow (St Phil and St Jas) and Bradley (All SS) and Hoonaston, *Derbys.* R. **D** Derby 8 **P** *Bp, D and C of Lich, Trustees and Sir I P A Munro Walker-Okeover Bt (in turn)* **I** G D BENNETT.
HULLAVINGTON (St Mary Magd), *Wilts..* **D** Bris *See* Stanton St Quintin.
HULME, *Gtr Man..* **D** Man 5 *See* Manchester.
HULME, CHURCH, or HOLMES CHAPEL (St Luke), *Chesh..* **D** Ches 12 *See* Holmes Chapel.
HULME WALFIELD (St Mich), *Chesh.* V. **D** Ches *See* Eaton.
HUMBER (St Mary Virg), *Herefs.* R. **D** Heref *See* Stoke Prior.
HUMBERSTON (St Pet), *Humb.* V. **D** Linc 10 **P** *Bp* **I** H T OAKES.
HUMBERSTONE, *Leics..* **D** Leic 1 *See* Leicester.
HUMBLEDON (St Mary Virg w St Pet Conv Distr), *T & W..* **D** Dur 8 *See* Bishop Wearmouth.
HUMBLETON (St Pet and St Paul or St Pet) w Elsternwicke (St Laur), *Humb.* V. **D** York 15 *See* Burton Pidsea.
HUMBY, GREAT, *Lincs..* **D** Linc 14 *See* Somerby.
HUMBY, LITTLE *Lincs..* **D** Linc 14 *See* Ropsley.
HUMSHAUGH (St Pet), *Northumb.* V. **D** Newc T 2 **P** *Bp* **I** S V PRINS.
HUNCOAT (St Aug), *Lancs.* V. **D** Blackb 1 **P** *Bp* **I** J G REEVES.
HUNCOTE (St Jas Greater), *Leics..* **D** Leic 13 *See* Croft.
HUNDLEBY (St Mary), *Lincs.* V. **D** Linc 7 *See* Spilsby.
HUNDON (All SS), *Suff.* V. **D** St E 8 **P** *Jes Coll Cam* **I** (Vacant).
HUNGARTON (St Jo Bapt), *Leics.* V. **D** Leic 8 **P** *Sir Anthony Nutting Bt* **I** R MALSBURY.
HUNGERFORD (St Lawr) w Denford (H Trin) and Eddington (St Sav), *Berks* and *Wilts.* V. **D** Ox 14 **P** *D and C of Windsor* **I** R J KINGSBURY.
HUNGERTON, *Lincs..* **D** Linc 14 *See* Harlaxton.
HUNMANBY (All SS) w Muston (All SS), *N Yorks.* V. **D** York 18 **P** *MMT* **I** C M F WHITEHEAD.
HUNNINGHAM (St Marg), *Warws.* V. **D** Cov 10 **P** *Ld Chan* **I** D R JACKSON.
HUNSDON (St Dunstan?) w Widford and Wareside, *Herts.* R. **D** St Alb **P** *Dioc Bd of Patr* **I** R MEREDITH.
HUNSINGORE (St Jo Bapt), *N Yorks.* V. **D** Ripon 3 *See* Kirk-Hammerton.
HUNSLET (St Mary Virg), *W Yorks.* V. **D** Ripon 8 **P** *Bp* 2 turns *and V of Leeds* 1 turn **I** (Vacant).
(St Pet w St Cuthb), V. **D** Ripon 8 **P** *Bp* **I** T G MUNRO.
HUNSTANTON ST MARY (St Mary Virg) w Ringstead Parva Holme-next-the-Sea and Thornham, *Norf.* V. **D** Nor 23 **P** *H le Strange Esq and Bp (alt)* **I** P I ALLTON, J S HUNT *hon c.*
(St Edm), V. **D** Nor 23 **P** *H Le Strange Esq* **I** J HELEY.
HUNSTANWORTH (St Jas), *Durham..* **D** Newc T *See* Blanchland.
HUNSTON (St Leodegar), *W Sussex..* **D** Chich 3 *See* Mundham.
HUNSTON, *Suff..* **D** St E *See* Ashfield, Great.
HUNSWORTH, *W Yorks..* **D** Wakef 9 *See* Birkenshaw.
HUNTINGDON (All SS w St Jo Bapt and St Jo Evang), *Cambs.* R. **D** Ely 10 **P** *Bp* **I** M S MACDONALD.
(St Barn), V. **D** Ely 10 **P** *Bp* **I** (Vacant).
(St Mary) V w (St Benedict), R. **D** Ely 10 **P** *Ld Chan* **I** M S MACDONALD.
HUNTINGFIELD (St Mary) w Cookley (St Mich), *Suff..* **D** St E *See* Cratfield.
HUNTINGTON (All SS), *N Yorks.* V. **D** York 1 *See* York.
HUNTINGTON (St Mary Magd), *Herefs..* **D** Heref *See* Holmer.
HUNTINGTON (St Thos), *Herefs..* **D** Heref *See* Kington.
HUNTLEY (St Jo Bapt) w May Hill *Glos.* R. **D** Glouc 6 **P** *Bp* **I** G N CRAGO *p-in-c.*
HUNTON (St John), *N Yorks.* V. **D** Ripon 2 *See* Patrick Brompton.
HUNTON, *Kent..* **D** Roch 6 *See* Linton.
HUNTON (St Jas), *Hants..* **D** Win *See* Stoke Charity.
HUNTS CROSS (St Hilda), *Mer.* V. **D** Liv 7 **P** *Bp* **I** W L M STOREY, J C LYNN *c.*
HUNTSHAM (All SS), *Devon.* R. **D** Ex 8 **P** *Bp* **I** D M CLARRIDGE.
HUNTSHAW Devon. R **D** Ex 20 *See* Newton Tracey.
HUNTSPILL (St Pet and All H) and E Huntspill (All SS), *Somt.* R. **D** B & W 2 **P** *Ball Coll Ox* **I** A J M VIRGIN.

HUNWICK (St Paul), *Durham*. V. **D** Dur 9 **P** *V of Auckland* **I** G G GRAHAM.
HUNWORTH W Stody, *Norf.* R. **D** Nor 24 *See* Thornage.
HURDSFIELD (H Trin), *Chesh.* V. **D** Ches 13 **P** *Hyndman Trustees* **I** H E WATKINS.
HURLEY (St Mary Virg), *Berks.* V. **D** Ox 13 **P** *Dioc Bd of Patr* **I** D W CHISHOLM.
HURSLEY (All SS) w Pitt (Ch of the Good Shepherd), *Hants.* V. **D** Win 12 **P** *D E H Wilkie Cooper Esq* **I** G K BROWN.
HURST (St Leon), *Kent.* R. **D** Cant 12 *See* Fawkenhurst.
HURST (St Jo Evang), *Gtr Man.* V. **D** Man 2 **P** *Crown and Bp* alt **I** J F PETTY.
HURST (St Nich), *Berks.* V. **D** Ox 16 **P** *Bp* **I** D M WEST.
HURST GREEN (St Jo Evang), *Lancs.* V. **D** Bradf 6 **P** *V of Mitton* **I** B M CAVE.
HURST GREEN (H Trin), *E Sussex.* V. **D** Chich 18 **P** *Bp* **I** A N OLIVER.
HURST GREEN (St John), *Surrey.* V. **D** S'wark 10 **P** *Bp* **I** G F R RUSSELL.
HURSTBOURNE-PRIORS (St Andr), *Hants..* **D** Win *See* Longparish.
HURSTBOURNE TARRANT (St Pet) and Faccombe (St Barn) w Vernham Dean and Linkenholt *Hants.* V. **D** Win **P** *Bp* **I** I D GARDNER.
HURSTMONCEUX, *E Sussex..* **D** Chich *See* Herstmonceux.
HURSTPIERPOINT (H Trin w St Geo), *W Sussex.* R. **D** Chich 14 **P** *David Campion Esq* **I** M C JUDGE.
HURSTWOOD, HIGH (H Trin), *E Sussex.* V. **D** Chich 16 **P** *Abp* **I** K W JONES *p-in-c*, S M DAVIDSON *c.*
HURWORTH (All SS), *Durham.* R. **D** Dur 11 **P** *Ch S Trust, D and C of Dur and Govs of Sherburn Hosp* **I** R R A GRAHAM.
HUSBANDS BOSWORTH w Mowsley (St Nich) and Knaptoft and Theddingworth (All SS), *Leics.* R. **D** Leic **P** *Dioc Bd of Patr 1st and 2nd turns, Bp 3rd turn* **I** T R FISHER.
HUSBORNE CRAWLEY (St Mary Magd) w Ridgmont (All SS), *Beds..* **D** St Alb *See* Aspley Guise.
HUSTHWAITE *N Yorks.* V. **D** York 5 *See* Coxwold.
HUTHWAITE (All SS), *Notts.* V. **D** Southw 2 **P** *V of Sutton in Ashfield* **I** T G OLIVER.
HUTTOFT (St Marg of Antioch), *Lincs.* V. **D** Linc 8 **P** *Bp* **I** R FIELDEN *p-in-c.*
HUTTON (St Mary Virg), *Avon.* R. **D** B & W 3 **P** *Dioc Bd of Finance* **I** (Vacant).
HUTTON (All SS), *Essex.* R. **D** Chelmsf 9 **P** *D and C of St Paul's* **I** R ORTON.
HUTTON BONVILLE N Yorks. V **D** Ripon 1 *See* Great Smeaton.
HUTTON-BUSCEL (St Matt), *N Yorks.* V. **D** York 24 *See* Wykeham.
HUTTON CRANSWICK (St Pet formerly St Andr) w Skerne (St Leon), *N Yorks.* V. **D** York 13 **P** *Abp* **I** L R W JARVIS.
HUTTON MAGNA (St Mary) w Wycliffe (St Mary), R *Dur.* V. **D** Ripon 1 *See* Barningham.
HUTTON-IN-THE-FOREST (St Jas), *Cumb..* **D** Carl 6 *See* Skelton.
HUTTON, OLD (St Jo Bapt), w New Hutton (St Steph), *Cumb.* V. **D** Carl 17 **P** *V of Kendal* **I** R D MURRAY.
HUTTON ROOF w Lupton, *Cumb..* **D** Carl *See* Kirkby Lonsdale.
HUTTONS AMBO (St Marg), *N Yorks.* V. **D** York 21 *See* Crambe.
HUXHAM, *Devon..* **D** Ex 2 *See* Poltimore.
HUYTON (St Mich AA), *Mer.* V. **D** Liv 10 **P** *Earl of Derby* **I** J A STANLEY, A A ROSS *c*, I SIMPSON *c.*
(St Geo), V. **D** Liv 10 **P** *Bp* **I** D G TOWLER, W F BAZELY *c.*
QUARRY (St Gabr), V. **D** Liv 10 **P** *V of Huyton* **I** G E TURNER, K W HITCH *c.*
HYDE (St Geo), *Gtr Man.* V. **D** Ches 14 **P** *R of Stockport* **I** M W WALTERS, R D PETERS *c.*
(St Thos Ap w St Andr), V. **D** Ches 14 **P** *Bp* **I** J D ADEY.
HYDE (H Ascen), *Hants.* V. **D** Win 8 **P** *Keble Coll Ox* **I** P G CANE.
HYDE (St Bart), *Hants.* V. **D** Win 12 *See* Winchester.
HYDE, EAST (H Trin), *Beds.* V. **D** St Alb 20 *See* Woodside.
HYDE, WEST (St Thos of Cant), *Herts..* **D** St Alb 10 *See* Rickmansworth.
HYKEHAM, NORTH (All SS), w Hykeham, South (St Mich AA), *Lincs.* V, R. **D** Linc 18 **P** *Bp and Ld Chan* **I** A E BENNETT, J A C BELL *c.*
HYLTON, *T & W..* **D** Dur 8 *See* Bishop Wearmouth.
HYSON GREEN, *Notts..* **D** Southw *See* Nottingham.
HYSSINGTON, *Powys..* **D** Heref *See* Churchstoke.
HYTHE (St Leon), *Kent.* V. **D** Cant 6 **P** *R of Saltwood* **I** N H WOODS, L J W COX *c*, R S LADDS *c.*
HYTHE (St Jo Bapt), *Hants.* V. **D** Win 9 **P** *Bp* **I** P F MURPHY, J M WEBSTER *c.*
HYTHE, WEST *Kent..* **D** Cant 11 *See* Lympne.

IBBERTON (St Eustace), *Dorset.* R. **D** Sarum 13 *See* Okeford-Fitzpaine.
IBSLEY (St Martin), *Hants..* **D** Win *See* Ellingham.
IBSTOCK (St Denys) w Heather (St Jo Bapt), *Leics.* R. **D** Leic 11 **P** *Bp and MMT* **I** D M BUXTON.
IBSTONE (St Nich) *Bucks.* (*See Hambleden Valley Group*). **D** Ox *See* Stokenchurch.
ICKBURGH (St Pet) w Langford (St Andr), *Norf.* R. **D** Nor 19 **P** *Ld Amherst* **I** J V ANDREWS.
ICKENHAM (St Giles), *Gtr Lon.* R. **D** Lon 9 **P** *Eton Coll* **I** P M H KELLY.
ICKFORD Bucks and Oxon. **D** Ox 21 **P** *Bp* **I** R H COLLIER *c-in-c.*
ICKHAM (St Jo Evang) w Wickhambreaux and Stodmarsh, *Kent.* R. **D** Cant 1 **P** *Abp, Ch Trust Fund Trust and Archd of Cant* **I** J A P TYLER.
ICKLEFORD (St Kath) w Holwell, *Herts.* R. **D** St Alb **P** *Dioc Bd of Patr* **I** R I OAKLEY.
ICKLESHAM (St Nich), *E Sussex.* V. **D** Chich 22 **P** *Ld Chan* **I** (Vacant).
ICKLETON (St Mary Magd), *Cambs.* V. **D** Ely 7 **P** *Ld Chan* **I** R A BIRT *p-in-c.*
ICKLINGHAM (St Jas w All SS), *Suff.* R. **D** St E 11 **P** *Earl of Iveagh* **I** K S DOBSON.
ICKWORTH (St Mary), *Suff..* **D** St E 11 *See* Horningsheath.
ICOMB (St Mary), *Glos.* R. **D** Glouc 16 *See* Westcote.
IDBURY (St Nich), *Oxon..* **D** Ox 3 *See* Fifield.
IDDESLEIGH (St Jas) w Dowland, *Devon.* R. **D** Ex 20 **P** *Bp* **I** G B BELL.
IDE (St Ida), *Devon.* V. **D** Ex 6 *See* Dunchideock.
IDE HILL (St Mary Virg), *Kent..* **D** Roch 7 *See* Sundridge.
IDEFORD (St Mary Virg), Luton and Ashcombe, *Devon.* R. **D** Ex 11 **P** *Bp, Soc for Maint of Faith and V of Bp's Teignton* **I** S M BEAUMONT.
IDEN E Sussex. R **D** Chich 22 *See* Rye.
IDLE (H Trin), *W Yorks.* V. **D** Bradf 3 **P** *V of Calverley* **I** G E JONES, A A GLOVER *hon c.*
IDLICOTE (St Jas Gt), *Warws.* R. **D** Cov 9 *See* Honington.
IDMISTON (All SS), *Wilts.* V. **D** Sarum 17 *See* Bourne Valley.
IDRIDGEHAY (St Jas), *Derbys.* V. **D** Derby 17 **P** *D and C of Lich* **I** J H FLINT *c.*
IDSWORTH, *Hants..* **D** Portsm *See* Blendworth.
IFFLEY (St Mary Virg), *Oxon.* V. **D** Ox 4 *See* Oxford.
IFIELD (St Marg) w Langley Green (St Leon) and Gossops Green (St Alb), *W Sussex.* R. **D** Chich 12 **P** *Bp* **I** J A TIBBS, M J BRIDGER *team v*, R J TINNISWOOD *team v*, K A MCRAE *c.*
IFIELD, *Kent..* **D** Roch *See* Gravesend.
IFORD (St Nich), *E Sussex..* **D** Chich 15 *See* Kingston.
IFORD (St Sav), *Dor.* V. **D** Win 7 **P** *Bp* **I** D E C JARDINE.
IGHTFIELD (St Jo Bapt) w Calverhall (or Corra) (H Trin), *Salop.* R. **D** Lich 27 **P** *T C Heywood-Lonsdale Esq* **I** E A COOKE.
IGHTHAM (St Pet), *Kent.* R. **D** Roch 8 **P** *Sir John Winnifrith* **I** D J SILCOCK.
IKEN Suff. R **D** St E *See* Orford.
ILAM (H Cross) w Blore-Ray (St Bart) and Okeover, *Staffs.* V. **D** Lich 13 **P** *Sir I Walker-Okeover* **I** A O L HODGSON *p-in-c.*
ILCHESTER (St Mary Virg) w Northover (St Andr), Limington, Yeovilton and Podymore, *Somt.* R. **D** B & W 10 **P** *Bp of Lon 7 turns, Bp of B & W 1 turn and Wadham Coll Ox 1 turn* **I** D J RICHARDS.
ILDERTON (St Mich), *Northumb.* R. **D** Newc T 8 *See* Wooler.
ILE ABBOTS (St Mary Virg), *Somt.* V. **D** B & W *See* Ilton.
ILE BREWERS (All SS), *Somt.* V. **D** B & W 20 *See* Hambridge.
ILFORD, GREAT (St Clem), *Essex.* V. **D** Chelmsf 7 **P** *All S Coll Ox* **I** (Vacant).
(St Alb), V. **D** Chelmsf 7 **P** *Bp* **I** J R SLATER.
(St Andr Bp Jacob Mem Ch), V. **D** Chelmsf 7 **P** *Bp* **I** J C RIDDELSDELL.
(St Jo Evang Seven Kings), V. **D** Chelmsf 7 **P** *Bp* **I** S J TYLER.
(St Luke), V. **D** Chelmsf 7 **P** *Bp* **I** K A L HINDS.

(St Marg Conv Distr). D Chelmsf 7 P *Bp* I G A MUMFORD *min.*
(St Mary Virg), V. D Chelmsf 7 P *V of Ilford* I J B BARNES, A S ALLEN *c.*
ILFORD, LITTLE (St Mich AA w St Mary Virg CE), *Essex*. R. D Chelmsf 5 P *Hertf Coll Ox* I J P WHITWELL *p-in-c*, M OAKES *c.*
(St Barn), V. D Chelmsf 5 P *Bp* I B J ARSCOTT *p-in-c.*
ILFRACOMBE (H Trin), Lee (St Matt), West Down, Woolacombe (St Sabinus) and Bittadon (St Pet), *Devon*. R. D Ex 15 P *Bp* I A S CHANDLER, M J HOMEWOOD *team v*, J M KIRKPATRICK *team v.*
(St Phil and St Jas), V. D Ex 15 P *Ch Trust* I A D EDWARDS *p-in-c.*
ILKESTON (St Mary Virg), *Derbys*.. D Derby 13 P *Bp* I A C ROBERTSON, W F P ENOCH *c.*
(H Trin), V. D Derby 13 P *Bp* I A C ROBERTSON *p-in-c.*
(St Jo Evang), V. D Derby 13 P *V of St Mary, Ilkeston* I C J W LEE.
ILKETSHALLS, THE (St Andr, St Lawr, St Marg and St Jo Bapt), *Suff*.. D St E *See* Rumburgh.
ILKETSHALL ST JOHN, *Suff*.. D St E *See* Mettingham.
ILKLEY (All SS), *W Yorks*. v. D Bradf 5 P *Hyndman Trustees* I R CLELAND.
(St Marg), V. D Bradf 5 P *Community of the Resurr* I R S FILE, G L BUCKLEY *hon c.*
ILLINGTON, *Norf*.. D Nor *See* Hockham.
ILLINGWORTH (St Mary Virg), *W Yorks*.. D Wakef 1 *See* Halifax.
ILLOGAN w Trevenson and Portreath, *Cornw*. R. D Truro 2 P *Ch S Trust* I A S REYNOLDS *hon c.*
ILMER (St Pet), *Bucks*.. D Ox 21 *See* Princes Risborough.
ILMINGTON (St Mary) w Stretton-on-Fosse (St Pet) and Ditchford, *Warws*. R. D Cov 9 P *MMT* I A G BURGESS.
ILMINSTER (St Mary Virg) w Whitelackington (St Mary Virg), *Somt*. V. D B & W 20 P *Bp* I W D JONES.
ILSHAM (St Matthias), *Devon*.. D Ex 10 *See* Torquay.
ILSINGTON (St Mich), *Devon*. V. D Ex 11 P *D and C of Windsor* I D W REYNOLDS.
ILSLEY, EAST (St Mary), *Berks*. R. D Ox 14 *See* Compton Parva.
ILSLEY, WEST, *Berks*.. D Ox *See* Farnborough.
ILSTON-ON-THE-HILL, *Leics*.. D Leic *See* Carlton Curleu.
ILTON (St Pet) w Hambridge, Earnshill, Ile Brewers and Ile Abbots, *Somt*. V. D B & W P *Bp 4 turns, D and C of Bris 1 turn* I C D R BOOTS.
IMBER (St Giles), *Wilts*. V. D Sarum 23 *See* Edington.
IMMINGHAM (St Andr), *Humb*. V. D Linc 10 P *Dioc Bd of Patr* I H W P HALL, D BEVERLEY *c.*
IMPINGTON (St Andr), *Cambs*. V. D Ely 5 P *Archd of Ely* I (Vacant).
INCE (St Jas), *Chesh*.. D Ches 3 *See* Thornton-in-the-Moors.
INCE-IN-MAKERFIELD (Ch Ch), *Gtr Man*. V. D Liv 12 P *Simeon Trustees* I (Vacant).
(St Mary), V. D Liv 12 P *Simeon Trustees* I R CAPPER.
INCHBROOK, *Glos*.. D Glouc 9 *See* Nailsworth.
INGATESTONE (St Edm and St Mary) w Buttsbury (St Mary), *Essex*. R. D Chelmsf 9 P *Bp* I E F HUDSON.
INGESTRE (St Mary) w Tixall, *Staffs*.. D Lich P *Earl of Shrewsbury* I E G H TOWNSHEND *p-in-c.*
INGHAM (St Bart) w Ampton and Great and Little Livermere *Suff*. R. D St E P *Bp 3 turns, D J Turner Esq 1 turn* I R H NORBURN.
INGHAM (All SS) w Cammeringham (St Mich) w Fillingham (St Andr), *Lincs*. V. D Linc 3 P *Bp and Ball Coll Ox* I C M H FRERE.
INGHAM (H Trin) w Sutton, *Norf*. R. D Nor 9 P *Bp* I J A ROBERTS *p-in-c.*
INGLEBY, *Lincs*.. D Linc 2 *See* Saxilby.
INGLEBY ARNCLIFFE (All SS), *N Yorks*.. D York 23 *See* Osmotherley.
INGLEBY GREENHOW (St Andr) w Bilsdale Priory, *N Yorks*. V. D York 25 P *Abp, Ld De L'Isle and Ld Feversham* I C KETTLE.
INGLESCOMBE (St Pet) or Englishcombe, *Avon*. V. D B & W 16 *See* Englishcombe.
INGLESHAM (St Jo Bapt), *Wilts*. V. D Bris 8 *See* Highworth.
INGLETON (St Mary Virg) w Chapel-le-Dale or Ingleton Fells, *N Yorks*. V. D Bradf 7 P *Bp* I C WRAY.
INGLETON (St Jo Evang), *Durham*.. D Dur 11 *See* Denton.
INGOL (St Marg), *Lancs*.. D Blackb 12 P *Bp* I J EATOCK.
INGOLDISTHORPE (St Mich), *Norf*. R. D Nor 23 P *Bp* I D A PORTER *p-in-c.*
INGOLDMELLS (St Pet w St Paul) w Addlethorpe (St Nich), *Lincs*. R. D Linc 8 P *Wadh Coll Ox and Ld Chan alt* I (Vacant).
INGOLDSBY (St Bart) w Lavington (or Lenton), Osgodby, Keisby, Hanby, Bassingthorpe, Westby, Bitchfield, Burton-le-Coggles and Boothby Pagnell, *Lincs*. R. D Linc P *Ch Coll Cam, Sir H T Tollemache, D and C of Linc, Bp and Dioc Bd of Patr in turn* I K MORLEY.
INGRAM (St Mich), *Northumb*. R. D Newc T 8 *See* Wooler.
INGRAVE (St Nich) w Great Warley and Childerditch, *Essex*. R. D Chelmsf 9 P *CPS, Hon G C D Jeffreys and MMT* I S E MARSDEN *p-in-c*, E BARRETT *c.*
INGROW (St Jo Evang) w Hainworth, *W Yorks*. V. D Bradf 11 P *Bp* I H B S CARTWRIGHT.
INGS, *Cumb*.. D Carl *See* Hugill.
INGWORTH, *Norf*.. D Nor *See* Blickling.
INHAM NOOK (St Barn), *Notts*.. D Southw 8 *See* Chilwell.
INKBERROW (St Pet) w Cookhill (St Paul) and Kington w Dormston, *Worcs*. V. D Worc 1 P *Bp* I L L GUEST.
INKPEN (St Mich) and Combe (St Swith), *Berks*. R. D Ox *See* Woodhay, West.
INSKIP (St Pet), *Lancs*. V. D Blackb 10 P *V of St Michael's-on-Wyre* I E GREENHALGH.
INSTOW (St Jo Bapt), *Devon*. R. D Ex 17 P *Trustees* I J C SPEAR.
INTAKE (All SS), *S Yorks*. V. D Sheff 8 P *Bp* I T M PAGE, J N COBB *c*, J S B CROSSLEY *hon c.*
INTWOOD w Keswick Norf. R D Nor 13 P *Miss Unthank* I P MCFADYEN.
INWARDLEIGH, *Devon*. R. D Ex 12 *See* Okehampton.
INWORTH (All SS), *Essex*. R. D Chelmsf 29 *See* Messing.
IPING, *W Sussex*.. D Chich *See* Stedham.
IPING MARSH (The Good Shepherd), *W Sussex*.. D Chich 5 *See* Lynch.
IPPLEPEN (St Andr) w Torbyran, R *Devon*. V. D Ex 10 P *D and C of Windsor* I F BUFFETT.
IPPOLYTS, ST, *Herts*.. D St Alb 7 *See* St Ippolyts.
IPSDEN, *Oxon*.. D Ox *See* Stoke, North.
IPSLEY (St Pet), *Worcs*. R. D Worc 7 P *MMT* I R M ADAMS, P J M FLUCK *team v*, D J R RITCHIE *team v*, J W DAVEY *c*, S FOSTER *c.*
IPSTONES (St Leon), *Staffs*. V. D Lich 16 P *Bp* I S R WATKIN *p-in-c.*
IPSWICH (All H), *Suff*. V. D St E 4 P *Bp* I R F PALLANT, R A E KENT *c.*
(All SS), V. D St E 4 P *Bp* I A G WILCOX.
(St Andr), V. D St E 4 P *Bp* I D M PINE.
(St Aug of Hippo), V. D St E 4 P *Bp* I A V WILLMONT.
(St Bart Rose Hill). D St E 4 P *Bp* I D K WOOLNER, P M HAMLET *c.*
(St Clem) w (H Trin), R. D St E 4 P *CPS* I F G BURNINGHAM.
(St Francis), R. D St E 4 P *Bp* I M G S WHITCOMBE, A E ALLARDICE *team v.*
(St Helen), R. D St E 4 P *CPS* I A B LEIGHTON *c-in-c.*
(St Jo Bapt), V. D St E 4 P *Simeon Trustees* I J C CASSELTON, G I HOUSE *c*, J S MCINTYRE *c.*
(St Marg), V. D St E 4 P *Simeon Trustees* I C P GANE, G S GREEN *c*, A B LEIGHTON *c.*
(St Mary at Elms), V. D St E 4 P *PCC* I J H M DIXON *c-in-c.*
(St Mary Stoke), R. D St E 4 P *Bp* I J D YATES, S GILL *team v.*
(St Mary-le-Tower w St Lawr and St Steph), V. D St E 4 P *Bp 2 turns Ch Patr Trust 1 turn* I (Vacant).
(St Matt), R. D St E 4 P *Ld Chan* I D S MEIKLE, D CUTTS *c.*
(St Mich), V. D St E 4 P *Simeon Trustees* I G W J ORAM *p-in-c.*
(St Nich), V. D St E 4 P *PCC* I (Vacant).
(St Mary at Quay), V. D St E 4 P *Bp* I (Vacant).
(St Thos), V. D St E 4 P *Bp* I G W SILLIS.
IRBY-IN-THE-MARSH (All SS), *Lincs*. V. D Linc 8 *See* Bratoft.
IRCHESTER (St Kath), *Northants*. V. D Pet 9 P *Bp* I R SCHOFIELD.
IREBY (St Jas) w Uldale, *Cumb*. V. D Carl 10 *See* Bolton.
IRELAND WOOD (St Paul), *W Yorks*. V. D Ripon 5 P *R of Adel* I (Vacant).
IRELETH w Askam (St Pet), *Cumb*. V. D Carl 15 P *V of Dalton-in-Furness* I D SANDERSON.
IRLAM (St Jo Bapt), *Gtr Man*. V. D Man 3 P *Trustees* I F H WOOD.
IRMINGLAND, *Norf*.. D Nor *See* Heydon.
IRNHAM (St Andr) w Corby Glen (St Jo Evang), *Lincs*. R. D Linc *See* Corby Glen.
IRON-ACTON (St Jas L), *Avon*. R. D Bris 7 P *Ch Ch Ox* I A F WAKER.

IRONBRIDGE (St Luke), *Salop*. R. **D** Heref 14 *See* Coalbrookdale.
IRONVILLE (Ch Ch), *Derbys*. V. **D** Derby 6 **P** *Wright Trustees* **I** P F TAYLOR.
IRSTEAD (St Mich), *Norf*.. **D** Nor *See* Neatishead.
IRTHINGTON (St Kentigern) and Crosby-on-Eden, *Cumb*. V. **D** Carl 2 **P** *Bp* **I** D RIDGWAY.
IRTHLINGBOROUGH (All SS) w (St Pet), *Northants*. R. **D** Pet 9 **P** *Earl Fitzwilliam* **I** J W B PHILLIPS.
IRTON (St Paul), *Cumb*.. **D** Carl 12 *See* Eskdale.
ISEL (St Mich AA) w Setmurthy, *Cumb*. V. **D** Carl 10 *See* Bassenthwaite.
ISFIELD (St Marg), *E Sussex*. R. **D** Chich 16 **P** *Abp* **I** C J PETERS, C G STABLES *hon c*.
ISHAM (St Pet) w Pytchley (All SS), *Northants*. R. **D** Pet 8 **P** *Bp* **I** P R GATENBY.
ISLE ABBOTS, *Somt*.. **D** B & W 22 *See* Ile Abbots.
ISLE BREWERS, *Somt*.. **D** B & W *See* Hambridge.
ISLE OF DOGS. **D** Lon 7 *See* Poplar.
ISLE OF GRAIN (St Jas) w Stoke (St Pet and St Paul), *Kent*. V. **D** Roch 5 **P** *Dioc Bd of Patr* **I** A E NORRIS.
ISLE OF MAN **D** S & M *See* Man, Isle of.
ISLEHAM (St Andr), *Cambs*. V. **D** Ely 3 **P** *Ld Chan* **I** D J KIGHTLEY *c-in-c*.
ISLEWORTH (All SS), *Gtr Lon*. V. **D** Lon 10 **P** *D and C of Windsor* **I** J D R HAYWARD.
(St Francis), V. **D** Lon 10 **P** *Bp* **I** G R SMITH *p-in-c*.
(St Jo Bapt), V. **D** Lon 10 **P** *V of Isleworth* **I** B L COTTRELL, E DOWSE *hon c*.
(St Mary, Spring Grove, Osterley), V. **D** Lon 10 **P** *CPS* **I** J J CONGDON.
(St Mary Virg), V. **D** Lon 10 **P** *Bp* **I** G J PHILLIPS.
ISLEY-WALTON (All SS), *Leics*. R. **D** Leic 12 *See* Breedon-on-the-Hill.
ISLINGTON, *Norf*.. **D** Ely 18 *See* Wiggenhall.
ISLINGTON (St Mary Virg), *Lon*. V. **D** Lon 3 **P** *Trustees* **I** G L CLAYDON, J T HENDERSON *c*, D SINGH *c*, D C M FLETCHER *hon c*, R M VINCE *hon c*.
(St Andr w H Trin and All SS Barnsbury), V. **D** Lon 3 **P** *Trustees* **I** R G CLARKE, C M S R THOMAS *c*, M W THOMPSON *c*.
(St Jas Ap w St Phil), V. **D** Lon 3 **P** *Clothworkers' Co* **I** W G MARLOW *p-in-c*.
(St Jude, Mildmay Park), V. **D** Lon 3 **P** *Trustees* **I** J RISBY, F W BRIDGER *c*, C W ELLISON *hon c*.
(St Padarn Welsh Ch), I. **D** Lon 3 **P** *Bp* **I** (Vacant).
(St Paul, Ball's Pond, Canonbury), V. **D** Lon 3 **P** *Trustees* **I** J RISBY *p-in-c*.
(St Pet), V. **D** Lon 3 **P** *V of Islington* **I** W G MARLOW *p-in-c*.
(St Silas w All SS and St Jas Pentonville). V. **D** Lon 3 **P** *Bp* **I** A T J SALTER, D F PAULEY *c*, D T WILLIAMS *hon c*.
(St Steph w St Bart and St Matt, Canonbury Rd), V. **D** Lon 3 **P** *V of Islington* **I** O J THOMAS.
ISLIP, *Oxon*. R. **D** Ox 2 **P** *D and C of Westmr* **I** D R WESTCOTT.
ISLIP (St Nich), *Northants*. R. **D** Pet 9 **P** *L G Stopford Sackville Esq* **I** C P M JONES *p-in-c*.
ISTEAD RISE, *Kent*. V. **D** Roch 3 **P** *Bp* **I** (Vacant).
ITCHEN-ABBAS (St Jo Bapt) w Avington (St Mary), *Hants*. R. **D** Win 6 **P** *Bp* **I** R MCLEOD.
ITCHEN-STOKE, *Hants*.. **D** Win 6 *See* Ovington.
ITCHINGFIELD (St Nich), *W Sussex*. R. **D** Chich 4 **P** *Bp* **I** J W MARTIN.
ITCHINGTON, LONG (H Trin), V w Bascote, *Warws*.. **D** Cov 10 **P** *Bp* **I** F L MARRIOTT.
ITTERINGHAM (St Mary), *Norf*. R. **D** Nor 3 *See* Wickmere.
IVEGILL (Ch ch), *Cumb*. V. **D** Carl 6 *See* Skelton.
IVER (St Pet), *Bucks*. V. **D** Ox 24 **P** *Trustees* **I** T E F COULSON.
IVER HEATH (St Marg), *Bucks*. R. **D** Ox 24 **P** *Bp and two Trustees* **I** M J PEEL.
IVINGHOE (St Mary Virg) w Pitstone or Pightlesthorne (St Mary) and Slapton (H Cross), *Bucks*. V. **D** Ox 27 **P** *Bp and Ch Ch Ox* **I** W J MEAD.
IVINGTON (St John) w Monkland (All SS), *Herefs*. V. **D** Heref 7 **P** *V of Leominster and D and C of Windsor* **I** J F CLINGO.
IVYBRIDGE (St Jo Evang), *Devon*. V. **D** Ex 21 **P** *Bp* **I** D W OBEE, P T W SABINE *c*.
IVYCHURCH Kent. R **D** Cant 13 *See* Brookland.
IWADE (All SS), *Kent*. V. **D** Cant 13 *See* Bobbing.
IWERNES, THE (Iwerne Courtney St Mary and Iwerne Stepleton, Iwerne Minster St Mary and Sutton Waldron St Bart), *Dorset*. V. **D** Sarum 10 **P** *D and C of Windsor, G Pitt-Rivers Esq, Bp and Dioc Bd of Patr (in turn)* **I** K WEDGWOOD.
IXWORTH (St Mary Virg) w Ixworth Thorpe (All SS) and Bardwell, *Suff*. V. **D** St E 9 **P** *St John Coll Ox, Dioc Bd of Patr and Bp (alt)* **I** P M OLIVER.

JACKFIELD (St Mary Virg), *Salop*. R. **D** Heref 14 **P** *Bp* **I** W W LUCAS *p-in-c*.
JACOBSTOW (St Jas) w Warbstow and Treneglos, *Cornw*. R. **D** Truro 10 **P** *Earl of St Germans and Bp* **I** V D LAURENCE.
JACOBSTOWE, *Devon*. R. **D** Ex *See* Exbourne.
JARROW (St Paul), St Pet, St Mark, St Jo Bapt and St Andr Chap), *T & W*. R. **D** Dur 6 **P** *Bp* **I** G C CAREY *team v*, J CLASPER *team v*, P G H HISCOCK *team v*, K LUMSDON *team v*, D R D MARTINEAU *team v*, J H PICKEN *c*.
(Ch Ch Grange), R. **D** Dur 6 **P** *Ld Northbourne* **I** E S BAIRD, G H LAWES *c*.
(St Pet), V. **D** Dur 6 **P** *Bp* **I** (Vacant).
JARVIS BROOK (St Mich AA), *E Sussex*. V. **D** Chich 20 **P** *Bp* **I** D N JENKINS.
JERSEY (St Helier), R. **D** Win 14 **P** *Crown* **I** T A GOSS.
(All SS), V. **D** Win 14 **P** *R of St Helier* **I** J H SPRUYT.
GOURAY (St Martin), V. **D** Win 14 **P** *Crown and Bp* alt **I** (Vacant).
GROUVILLE (St Martin), R. **D** Win 14 **P** *Crown* **I** L W HIBBS.
(H Trin), R. **D** Win 14 **P** *Crown* **I** A KEOGH.
(St Andr), V. **D** Win 14 **P** *Dean of Jersey* **I** D J SPRINGHAM.
(St Brelade w St Aubin Distr Ch), R. **D** Win 14 **P** *Crown* **I** M A HALLIWELL, A T G M HAMPTON *team v*.
(St Clem), R. **D** Win 14 **P** *Crown* **I** C P HARRISON, C K THACKER *c*.
(St Jas), V. **D** Win 14 **P** *Bp* **I** J N HOLLIS.
(St Jo Bapt), R. **D** Win 14 **P** *Crown* **I** P G K MANTON.
(St Lawr Mart), R. **D** Win 14 **P** *Crown* **I** C L L BINDER.
(St Luke), V. **D** Win 14 **P** *Bp and Crown* alt **I** J N HOLLIS.
(St Mark Evang), V. **D** Win 14 **P** *Bp* **I** W N HALL.
(St Martin), R. **D** Win 14 **P** *Crown* **I** L J TURNER, J D DODD *hon c*.
(St Mary Virg), R. **D** Win 14 **P** *Crown* **I** M V HARRISON.
(St Matt Millbrook), V. **D** Win 14 **P** *Crown* **I** C L L BINDER.
(St Ouen w St Geo), R. **D** Win 14 **P** *Crown* **I** D A J GURNEY.
(St Paul). **D** Win 14 **P** *Trustees* **I** M A FIELD *min*.
(St Pet), R. **D** Win 14 **P** *Crown* **I** B J GILES.
(St Sav), R. **D** Win 14 **P** *Crown* **I** B W COLEMAN.
(St Simon), V. **D** Win 14 **P** *Bp and Crown* alt **I** J H SPRUYT *c-in-c*.
JESMOND, *T & W*.. **D** Newc T 5 *See* Newcastle upon Tyne.
JEVINGTON (St Andr), *E Sussex*.. **D** Chich 19 *See* Dean, East.

KEA, ST (All H), *Cornw*. V. **D** Truro 6 *See* St Kea.
KEADBY, *Humb*.. **D** Linc 1 *See* Althorpe.
KEAL, EAST (St Helen), *Lincs*. R. **D** Linc 7 **P** *Dioc Bd of Patr* **I** P W WIGGINTON.
KEAL, WEST (St Helen), *Lincs*. R. **D** Linc 7 **P** *Exors of Lt Col Sir W Cracroft-Amcotts* **I** P W WIGGINTON.
KEARSLEY MOOR, *Gtr Man*.. **D** Man *See* Farnworth.
KEASDEN (St Matt), *N Yorks*.. **D** Bradf 7 *See* Clapham.
KEDINGTON or KETTON, *Suff*. R. **D** St E 8 **P** *Walsingham Coll Trust Assoc* **I** W H O MASON.
KEDLESTON (All SS), *Derbys*. R. **D** Derby 12 **P** *Exors of Ld Scarsdale* **I** G A CHESTERMAN.
KEELBY (St Bart), *Lincs*. V. **D** Linc 10 **P** *Dioc Bd of Patr* **I** R W J HOGGETT.
KEELE (St Jo Bapt), *Staffs*. V. **D** Lich 17 **P** *Howard Sneyd* **I** M R H TURNER *p-in-c*, E C GRESHAM *c*.
KEEVIL (St Leon), *Wilts*. V. **D** Sarum 24 **P** *D and C of Win* **I** D BURDEN.
KEGWORTH (St Andr), *Leics*. R. **D** Leic 10 **P** *Ch Coll Cam* **I** W D M STURDY.
KEIGHLEY (St Andr) w (St Pet) and Lawkholme, *W Yorks*. R. **D** Bradf 11 **P** *Bp* **I** R B GREGORY, J RICHARDSON *c*.
(All SS), V. **D** Bradf **P** *Bp and Incumbent of Keighley* **I** D M K LAWSON.
KEINTON MANDEVILLE (St Mary Magd) w Lydford-on-Fosse, W and E, *Somt*. R. **D** B & W 4 **P** *Ch S, J H Cordle Esq and Dr O W Holmes (1 turn), Lt Col W A Whitehead (2 turns), Bp (1 turn)* **I** J PAINTER.
KEISBY, *Lincs*.. **D** Linc 2 *See* Ingoldsby.
KELBROOK (St Mary), *Lancs*. V. **D** Bradf 10 **P** *Bp* **I** A D PROCTER *p-in-c*.
KELBY, *Lincs*.. **D** Linc 23 *See* Wilsford.
KELHAM (St Wilfrid), *Notts*.. **D** Southw 3 *See* Averham.

KELLING (St Mary) w Salthouse (St Nich), *Norf.* R. D Nor 24 P *Bp of Nor, Bp of Liv and Ld Walpole (in turn)* I H OLDALE, F N WARD *hon c.*
KELLINGTON (St Edm) w Whitley (All SS), *N Yorks.* V. D Wakef 11 P *Dioc Bd of Patr* I W R HOGAN.
KELLOE (St Helen), *Durham.* V. D Dur 12a P *Bp* I R V STAPLETON *p-in-c.*
KELLS, *Cumb..* D Carl 12 *See* Whitehaven.
KELLY (St Mary Virg) w Bradstone, *Devon.* R. D Ex 22 P *M W Kelly Esq, Bp and Countess de Wolovey* I A W H DICK *p-in-c.*
KELMARSH, *Northants..* D Pet *See* Arthingworth.
KELMSCOTT (St Geo), *Oxon..* D Ox 9 *See* Bradwell.
KELSALE (St Mary) w Carlton (St Pet), *Suff.* R. D St E 19 P *Dioc Bd of Patr* I P J BURGOYNE *p-in-c.*
KELSALL (St Phil), *Chesh.* V. D Ches 2 P *V of Tarvin* I R SELWOOD.
KELSEY, NORTH (St Nich), *Lincs.* V. D Linc 6 P *Bp* I A J KERSWILL *p-in-c.*
KELSEY, SOUTH (St Mary) w (St Nich) w Holton-le-Moor, *Lincs.* R. D Linc 5 P *Bp* I F RODGERS.
KELSHALL (St Faith), *Herts.* R. D St Alb 5 P *Ld Chan* I J G E STONE *p-in-c.*
KELSTERN (St Faith) w Calcethorpe (St Faith) and Wykeham, East, *Lincs.* V. D Linc 12 P *Dioc Bd of Patr 3 turns, M M Sleight Esq 1 turn* I R J CROOKES *p-in-c.*
KELSTON (St Nich), *Avon.* R. D B & W *See* Bath.
KELVEDON (St Mary Virg), *Essex.* V. D Chelmsf 29 P *Bp* I D J D THORNTON, A E PAYTON *hon c.*
KELVEDON HATCH (St Nich), *Essex.* R. D Chelmsf 9 P *Bp* I G B KEMP.
KEMBERTON (St Andr), w Sutton Maddock (St Mary Virg) and Stockton, *Salop.* R. D Lich 25 P *MMT and C Goulburn Esq* I A E MELLY.
KEMBLE (All SS), Poole Keynes, Somerford Keynes and Sharncote, *Glos.* V. D Glouc 13 P *Dioc Bd of Patr, Duchy of Lanc and Miss R E Phillips (in turn)* I K A BRISTOW.
KEMERTON (St Nich), *Worcs.* R. D Glouc 10 P *Dioc Bd of Patr* I F J WRIGHT *p-in-c.*
KEMPLEY (St Mary), *Glos..* D Glouc *See* Dymock.
KEMPSEY (St Mary Virg) and Severn Stoke w Croome D'Abitot, *Worcs.* V. D Worc 5 P *D and C of Worc and Croome Estate Trustees* I R C TOOGOOD.
KEMPSEY, NORTON (St Jas Gt), *Worcs.* V. D Worc 8 *See* Norton.
KEMPSFORD (St Mary Virg), w Whelford (St Ann), *Glos.* V. D Glouc 14 P *Bp* I S J LUGG.
KEMPSTON (St Paul), *Norf.* V. D Nor 20 *See* Litcham.
KEMPSTON (All SS), *Beds.* V. D St Alb 16 P *Bp* I K C HABERMEHL.
(Ch of Transfig), V. D St Alb 16 P *Bp* I D V DRAPER, I W ARTHUR *c.*
KEMSING (St Mary Virg) w Woodlands, *Kent.* V. D Roch 8 P *Dioc Bd of Patr* I K P T DANIELS.
KENARDINGTON (St Mary), *Kent.* V. D Cant 13 *See* Appledore.
KENCHESTER (St Mich) w Bridge Sollars (St Andr), *Herefs.* R. D Heref 4 P *Ld Chan* I (Vacant).
KENCOT (St Geo), *Oxon..* D Ox *See* Bradwell (St Pet and St Paul).
KENDAL (H Trin w All H), *Cumb.* V. D Carl 17 P *Master and Fells of Trin Coll Cam* I J HODGKINSON.
(St Geo), V. D Carl 17 P *V of Kendal* I J BRUCE.
(St Thos), V. D Carl 17 P *CPAS Trustees* I R G FORWARD, A THORP *c.*
KENDERCHURCH (St Mary), *Herefs.* V. D Heref *See* Ewyas Harold.
KENILWORTH (St Nich), *Warws.* V. D Cov 4 P *Ld Chan* I F S BULL, J C MERRETT *c.*
(St Jo Evang), V. D Cov 4 P *Simeon Trustees* I D D GRITTEN, D J PHIPPS *c.*
KENINGHAM, *Norf..* D Nor *See* Mulbarton.
KENLEY (St Jo Bapt), *Salop.* R. D Heref 11 *See* Harley.
KENLEY (All SS), *Surrey.* V. D S'wark 9 P *Abp of Cant* I M VONBERG.
KENN (St Andr), *Devon.* R. D Ex *See* Exminster.
KENN or KEN (St Jo Evang) w Kingston Seymour (All SS), *Avon.* V. D B & W *See* Yatton Moor.
KENNERLEIGH, *Devon..* D Ex *See* Woolfardisworthy, East.
KENNET, EAST, *Wilts..* D Sarum *See* Overton.
KENNET, UPPER (Avebury w Winterbourne Monkton and Berwick Bassett, Broad Hinton, Overton and Fyfield w E Kennet and Winterbourne Bassett), *Wilts.* R. D Sarum 26 P *Bp* I G R J FORCE-JONES, B A TIGWELL *team v.*
KENNETT (St Nich), *Cambs.* R. D Ely 3 P *Mrs M De Pache* I J D A LINN.
KENNINGHALL (St Mary), *Norf..* D Nor 18 *See* Quidenham.
KENNINGTON (St Mary), *Kent.* V. D Cant 10 P *Abp* I D HERYET.
KENNINGTON (St Swith), *Oxon.* V. D Ox 11 P *Bp* I J M LOVELAND.
KENNINGTON (St Jo Div w St Jas Ap), *Surrey.* V. D S'wark 4 P *Bp and Cuddesdon Th Coll* I L DENNEN, W G EAST *c*, N P GODFREY *c.*
(St Mark) V. D S'wark 4 P *Abp of Cant* I T N RIVETT-CARNAC, B FERNYHOUGH *c.*
(St Mich AA). D S'wark 15 *See* Camberwell.
PARK (St Agnes), V. D S'wark 5 P *Trustees* I J WHITELAM.
SOUTH. D S'wark *See* Lambeth.
KENNINGTON CROSS (St Anselm), *Surrey.* R. D S'wark 4 *See* Lambeth North.
KENSAL GREEN (St Jo Evang), *Lon.* V. D Lon 14 P *Bp* I R D BEAL.
KENSAL RISE (St Martin, Dean Vaughan Mem), *Lon.* V. D Lon 18 P *Bp* I J E TOWNSEND.
KENSAL TOWN (St Thos) w St Andr and St Phil, *Lon.* V. D Lon 11 P *Hyndman Trustees* I F E GILL *p-in-c.*
KENSINGTON (Ch Ch), *Mer..* D Liv 4 *See* West Derby.
KENSINGTON (St Mary Abbots w St Geo Campden Hill), *Lon.* V. D Lon 11 P *Bp* I I L ROBSON, R F MCLAREN *c*, M J THOMPSON *c*, J M V WILLMINGTON *c.*
(All SS w St Columb, Notting Hill), V. D Lon 11 *See* Notting Hill.
(H Trin, Brompton w St Paul, Onslow Square) V. D Lon 12 P *Bp and Marts Mem Trust* I J T C B COLLINS, J D IRVINE *c*, J A K MILLAR *c*, P J WHITWORTH *c*, S WILLIAMS *c.*
(H Trin, Prince Consort Road w All SS, S Kens), V. D Lon 15 P *D and C of Westmr Abbey* I H A H MOORE *p-in-c*, M S ISRAEL *c.*
(St Aug, Queen's Gate), V. D Lon 11 P *Keble Coll Ox* I K V HEWITT, T L H TWENTYMAN *c.*
(St Barn, Addison Road), V. D Lon 11 P *V of Kens* I P W SEMPLE.
(St Clem and St Mark, Notting Hill), V. D Lon 11 *See* Notting Hill.
(St Cuthb, Philbeach Gardens w St Matthias, Warwick Road), V. D Lon 12 P *Trustees* I J VINE.
(St Helen w H Trin, Latimer Road), V. D Lon 11 P *Bp* I R E ADFIELD.
(St Jas, Norlands), V. D Lon 11 P *Bp* I F T C BYRON, J W CHARLES *c.*
(St Jo Bapt, Holland Road), V. D Lon 11 P *Trustees* I (Vacant).
(St Jo, Ladbroke Grove, Notting Hill), V. D Lon 11 *See* Notting Hill.
(St Jude, Courtfield Gardens), V. D Lon 12 P *Lady Magnus Allcroft* I D J T RYMER.
(St Luke, Redcliffe Square), V. D Lon 12 P *CPS* I C J G BARTON.
(St Mary, The Boltons), V. D Lon 12 P *V of Brompton* I G DAVIES, J BROWNING *c.*
(St Mich AA, Ladbroke Grove w Ch ch, Notting Hill), V. D Lon 11 P *S for Maint of Faith* I A B ANDREWS, G H CHIPLIN *c.*
(St Pet, Kens Pk Rd, Notting Hill), V. D Lon 11 P *Bp* I P R MYLES *p-in-c.*
(St Phil, Earl's Court Road), V. D Lon 11 P *Bp* I J G DULFER.
(St Steph, Gloucester Road), V. D Lon 11 P *Guild of All S* I H A H MOORE, D PRIEST *c.*
WEST. D Lon 7 *See* Fulham (St Andr) and Hammersmith (St Matt).
KENSWORTH (St Mary), *Beds.* V. D St Alb 18 P *D and C of St Paul's* I (Vacant).
KENTCHURCH (BVM), *Herefs.* w Llangua (St Jas), *Gwent.* R. D Heref *See* Ewyas Harold.
KENTFORD (St Mary) w Higham Green (St Steph), *Cambs.* V. D St E 11 P *Trin Hall Cam and T D Barclay Esq* alt I T H LAWRENCE.
KENTISBEARE (St Mary) w Blackborough, *Devon.* R. D Ex 4 P *CPAS and Exors of W Wyndham (1 turn) CPAS (5 turns)* I J V MAPSON, J L GOODALL *c.*
KENTISBURY (St Thos), Trentishoe (St Pet), East Downe (St Jo Bapt) and Arlington (St Jas), *Devon.* R. D Ex 18 P *Bp* I H G AYRE.
KENTISH TOWN D Lon 26 *See* St Pancras.
KENTMERE (St Cuthb), *Cumb.* V. D Carl 17 *See* Staveley.
KENTON (All SS) w Mamhead (St Thos Ap) and Powderham, *Devon.* V. D Ex 6 P *D and C of Sarum, S for Maint of Faith and Earl of Devon* I J F PARKINSON, W T COWLAN *hon c*, R D DEASY *hon c.*

KENTON (St Mary Virg), *Lon.*. D Lon 24 **P** *Bp* **I** P JERMYN, R P ANDREW *c*, C G BACK *c*.
SOUTH (Annunc Conv Distr). D Lon 18 **P** *Bp* **I** S M WILSON *c-in-c*.
KENTON (Ch of Ascen), *Northumb.* V. D Newc T 5 **P** *Bp* **I** J DEWAR.
KENTON (All SS), *Suff.* V. D St E *See* Debenham.
KENWYN (St Cuby) w Tregavethan, *Cornw.* V. D Truro 6 **P** *Bp* **I** M S BYROM.
KERDISTON, *Norf.*. D Nor *See* Reepham.
KERESLEY (St Thos) w Coundon, *W Midl.* V. D Cov 2 **P** *Bp* **I** J PANTING, C F MEEHAN *c*.
KERSAL MOOR (St Paul), *Gtr Man.*. D Man 8 *See* Salford.
KERSEY (St Mary), w Lindsey, *Suff.* V. D St E 3 **P** *Bp* **I** R J DEDMAN P-IN-C OF LINDSEY, H G HARRISON P-IN-C OF KERSEY.
KESGRAVE, *Suff.* V. D St E 4 **P** *Bp* **I** D R W HARES.
KESSINGLAND (St Edm) w Gisleham, *Suff.* R. D Nor 15 **P** *Bp* **I** B S T MORGAN.
KESTON (no Dedic), *Kent.* R. D Roch 12 **P** *D and C of Roch* **I** G F HYDER.
KESWICK (St Jo Evang), *Cumb.* V. D Carl 10 **P** *Trustees* **I** V M S ELLIS.
KESWICK (All SS), *Norf.*. D Nor *See* Intwood.
KESWICK, EAST (St Mary Magd), *W Yorks.*. D Ripon 4 *See* Bardsey.
KETLEY (St Mary Virg), *Salop.* V. D Lich 27 **P** *Bp* **I** (Vacant).
KETSBY, *Lincs.*. D Linc 7 *See* Ormsby.
KETTERING (St Pet and St Paul), *Northants.* R. D Pet 8 **P** *L M M Saunders Watson Esq* **I** F PEARCE, S H M GODFREY *c*, J M LOVEDAY *c*.
(All SS), V. D Pet 8 **P** *Trustees* **I** P WRIGHT.
(St Andr), V. D Pet 8 **P** *Bp* **I** P A JEPPS.
(St Mary Virg), V. D Pet 8 **P** *S for Maint of Faith* **I** H S HODGETTS.
KETTERINGHAM (St Pet), *Norf.* V. D Nor 13 **P** *Dioc Bd of Patr* **I** M B SEXTON.
KETTLEBASTON (St Mary Virg), *Suff.* R. D St E 10 **P** *Guild of All S* **I** C E WETHERALL *p-in-c*.
KETTLEBURGH Suff. D St E *See* Brandeston.
KETTLESHULME, *Chesh.*. D Ches *See* Taxal.
KETTLESTONE (All SS), *Norf.* R. D Nor 21 **P** *Rev E M Reynolds* **I** (Vacant).
KETTLETHORPE (St Pet and St Paul), *Lincs.* R. D Linc 2 **P** *Dioc Bd of Patr* **I** L SALT.
KETTLEWELL (St Mary) w Conistone (St Mary) and Hubberholme, *N Yorks.* V. D Bradf **P** *Bp, V of Arncliffe and Exors of Late J Perfect* **I** (Vacant).
KETTON (St Mary Virg), *Leics.* V. D Pet 13 **P** *Bp* **I** R H PRIESTNALL.
KEW (St Anne), *Surrey.* V. D S'wark 13 **P** *Crown* **I** P MCCRORY.
KEWSTOKE (St Paul) w Wick St Lawrence (St Lawr), *Avon.* V. D B & W 3 **P** *Ld Chan* **I** B STRANGE.
KEXBY, *Lincs.*. D Linc 2 *See* Heapham.
KEXBY (St Paul) w Wilberfoss (St Jo Bapt), *N Yorks.* V. D York 7 **P** *Visc De Vesci and Lord Leconfield's Trustees (alt)* **I** A N DAWKINS *p-in-c*.
KEYHAM, *Devon.*. D Ex *See* Devonport.
KEYHAM, *Leics.*. D Leic *See* Houghton-on-the-Hill.
KEYINGHAM (St Nich), *Humb.* V. D York 15 **P** *Abp* **I** G O WILBOURNE.
KEYMER (St Cosmas and Damian), *W Sussex.*. D Chich 14 *See* Clayton.
KEYNSHAM (St Jo Bapt, St Marg, St Mich), *Avon.* R. D B & W 15 **P** *Dioc Bd of Patr* **I** G G BRADSHAW, S H BAYNES *c*, C M RICHARDS *hon c*.
KEYSOE (St Mary) w Bolnhurst (St Dunstan) and L Staughton (All SS), *Beds.* V. D St Alb 21 **P** *Bp 2 turns, CCC Ox 1 turn* **I** J C LAIRD.
KEYSTON (St Jo Bapt), W Bythorn (St Laur), *Cambs.* R. D Ely 11 **P** *Earl Fitzwilliam 2 turns, Bp 1 turn* **I** H M PEARCE *p-in-c*.
KEYWORTH (St Mary Virg), *Notts.* R. D Southw 10 **P** *Bp* **I** J L OTTEY.
KIBWORTH-BEAUCHAMP (St Wilfrid) w Kibworth Harcourt, *Leics.* R. D Leic 6 **P** *Mert Coll Ox* **I** F W DAWSON.
KIDBROOKE (St Jas), *Kent.* R. D S'wark 17 **P** *Bp and Trustees* **I** R A VOGT, M C W WEBBER *team v*, L T E EDEN *c*, R M F SIMONS *c*, K F SITCH *c*, H F E COLLIS *hon c*, M KITCHEN *hon c*.
KIDDERMINSTER (St Mary and All SS) w Trimpley (H Trin) and Franche (St Barn and St Jas), *Worcs.* V. D Worc 10 **P** *Bp* **I** I M GRIGGS, I R S WALKER *team v*, H HODGKINSON *c*, E B PRUEN *c*.
(H Innoc Foley Park), V. D Worc 10 **P** *Dioc Bd of Patr* **I** M A J GOODE *p-in-c*, R G JONES *c*.
(St Geo), V. D Worc 10 **P** *V of Kidderminster* **I** J R ILSON, B G HINTON *c*, A J MOWATE *hon c*.
(St Jo Bapt), V. D Worc 10 **P** *V of Kidderminster* **I** F D HILLEBRAND.
(St Osw, Broadwaters), V. D Worc **P** *Bp* **I** (Vacant).
KIDDINGTON (St Nich), *Oxon.* R. D Ox 10 **P** *Bp* **I** J BIDDLESTONE *p-in-c*.
KIDLAND, *Northumb.*. D Newc T *See* Alwinton.
KIDLINGTON (St Mary Virg), *Oxon.* R. D Ox 8 **P** *Patr Bd* **I** M P PULESTON, N R MARTIN *c*.
KIDMORE END (St Jo Bapt), *Oxon.* V. D Ox 7 **P** *Bp* **I** J M SMITH.
KIDSGROVE (St Thos), *Staffs.* V. D Lich 17 **P** *MMT* **I** C M DAY, P M CARTER *c*.
KILBURN. D Lon *See* Hampstead, Willesden, and Paddington.
KILBURN, WEST (St Luke Evang w St Simon and St Jude, Kensal Green), V. D Lon 14 **P** *CPAS* **I** A F L COLSON, M C CRADDUCK *c*.
KILBURN, *N Yorks.*. D York *See* Thirkleby.
KILBY (St Mary Magd), *Leics.* V. D Leic 6 **P** *Hon Ann Brooks* **I** (Vacant).
KILDALE (St Cuthb), *N Yorks.* R. D York 25 **P** *Mrs C M Sutcliffe* **I** C KETTLE *p-in-c*.
KILDWICK (St Andr), *W Yorks.* V. D Bradf 11 **P** *Ch Ch Ox* **I** I F N BUSBY.
KILHAM (All SS) and Lowthorpe w Ruston Parva, *Humb.* V. D York **P** *Ld Chan and C T Legard Esq* **I** D S HAWKINS *p-in-c*.
KILKHAMPTON (St Jas Gtr) w Morwenstow (St Jo Bapt), [Cornw]. R. D Truro 10 **P** *P J Thynne Esq and Bp* **I** R WATTS.
KILLAMARSH (St Giles), *Derbys.* R. D Derby 2 **P** *Crown* **I** C HILTON.
KILLINGHALL (St Thos Ap), *N Yorks.* V. D Ripon 4 **P** *Sir T C W Ingilby Bt* **I** J F WALKER *c-in-c*.
KILLINGHOLME (St Denis), *Humb.* V. D Linc 10 **P** *Dioc Bd of Patr* **I** S R KENYON.
KILLINGTON (All SS), *Cumb.*. D Bradf 7 *See* Firbank.
KILLINGWORTH (St Jo Evang), *Northumb.* V. D Newc T 1 **P** *V of Long Benton* **I** M S JONES *p-in-c*, F W BARTLEY *c*.
KILMERSDON (St Pet and St Paul), *Somt.* V. D B & W 16a **P** *Mells* **I** (Vacant).
KILMESTON (St Andr), *Hants.*. D Win 6 *See* Hinton-Ampner.
KILMINGTON (St Mary Virg), *Wilts.* R. D B & W 5 **P** *Bp* **I** D A MUNRO.
KILMINGTON (St Giles) w Shute (St Mich), *Devon.* V. D Ex 5 **P** *D and C of Ex and Bp* Alt. **I** D J R MOSELEY.
KILNDOWN (Ch Ch), *Kent.* V. D Cant 11 **P** *Crown* **I** T W P JOHNSON.
KILNHURST (St Thos), *S Yorks.* V. D Sheff 10 **P** *Ld Chan* **I** P S TURNER.
KILNSEA (St Helen), *Humb.*. D York 15 *See* Easington.
KILNWICK, *Humb.* V. D York *See* Watton.
KILNWICK PERCY, *Humb.* V. D York 7 *See* Pocklington.
KILPECK (St Mary and St D), *Herefs.* V. D Heref 1 **P** *Ld Chan* **I** M M L EDGE *p-in-c*.
KILSBY (St Faith), *Northants.* V. D Pet 3 **P** *Bp* **I** V M SCOTT.
KILTON (St Nich) w Lilstock (St Andr), *Somt.* V. D B & W 18 *See* Kilve.
KILVE (St Mary Virg) w Stringston, Kilton and Lilstock, *Somt.* R. D B & W 18 *See* Quantoxhead.
KILVERSTONE (St Andr), *Norf.* R. D Nor 18 **P** *Ch Patr Trust* **I** D W PRICE.
KILVINGTON (St Mary), *Notts.* R. D Southw 3 **P** *E G Staunton Esq* **I** (Vacant).
KILVINGTON, SOUTH (St Wilfrid), *N Yorks.* R. D York 26 *See* Thirsk.
KILWORTH, SOUTH (St Nich) w North (St Andr), *Leics.* R. D Leic 14 **P** *Trustees of Col H D Belgrave and Crown* **I** S W DOGGETT.
KIMBERLEY (H Trin), *Notts.* R. D Southw 8 **P** *Bp* **I** E L BANKS.
KIMBERLEY, *Norf.*. D Nor *See* Barnham Broom.
KIMBERWORTH (St Thos), *S Yorks.* V. D Sheff 6 **P** *Dioc Bd of Patr* **I** H W HALFORD.
(St John's), V. D Sheff 6 **P** *Bp* **I** G F WHITCROFT.
KIMBLE, GREAT (St Nich), W Little Kimble (All SS), *Bucks.* R. D Ox 21 **P** *Exors of Earl of Buckingham* **I** J R WHITE *p-in-c*.
KIMBLESWORTH (St Phil and St Jas), *Durham.* V. D Dur 2 **P** *Crown* **I** G L PATTISON *p-in-c*.

KIMBOLTON (St Andr), *Cambs.* V. **D** Ely 11 **P** *Duke of Man and Four Trustees* **I** (Vacant).
KIMBOLTON (St Jas) w Middleton-on-the-Hill (St Mary Virg) and Hamnish (St Dubricius w All SS), *Herefs.* V. **D** Heref 7 **P** *Bp* **I** A TALBOT-PONSONBY.
KIMCOTE (All SS) w Walton and Bruntingthorpe, *Leics.* R. **D** Leic 14 **P** *MMT and Bp* **I** N TOON *p-in-c.*
KIMMERIDGE (no Dedic), *Dorset.* V. **D** Sarum 9 *See* Church Knowle.
KIMPTON (St Pet and St Paul) w Ayot St Lawr, *Herts.* V and R. **D** St Alb 14 **P** *Bp* **I** P G LIDDELL *p-in-c,* L S PULLAN *hon c.*
KIMPTON, *Hants.* R. **D** Win 2 *See* Appleshaw.
KINETON (St Pet), *Warws.* V. **D** Cov 8 **P** *Ld Willoughby de Broke* **I** R MIGHALL.
KING CROSS (St Paul), *W Yorks.* V. **D** Wakef 1 *See* Halifax, St Paul.
KING SQUARE. **D** Lon *See* Finsbury.
KING STERNDALE (Ch Ch), *Derbys.* V. **D** Derby 10 *See* Buxton.
KINGERBY (St Pet), *Lincs.* V. **D** Linc *See* Kirkby.
KINGHAM (St Andr) w Churchill, Daylesford (St Pet) and Sarsden, *Oxon and Glos.* R. **D** Ox **P** *Ch S Trust and Ld Wyfold* **I** N J BENNETT.
KING'S BROMLEY (All SS), *Staffs.* V. **D** Lich 2 **P** *D and C of Lich* **I** (Vacant).
KING'S CAPLE (St Jo Bapt), *Herefs.*. **D** Heref *See* Sellack.
KING'S CLIFFE (All SS or St Jas), *Northants.* R. **D** Pet 13 **P** *Bp* **I** P J M BRYAN.
KING'S HEATH (All SS), *W Midl.* v. **D** Birm 5 **P** *V of Moseley* **I** J F DUNCAN, I M R MICHAEL *c.*
KING'S HEATH (St Aug), *Northants.* V. **D** Pet 4 **P** *Bp* **I** B LEATHERLAND.
KING'S KERSWELL (St Mary), *Devon.* V. **D** Ex 10 **P** *V of St Marychurch* **I** A R JAMES.
KING'S LANGLEY (All SS), *Herts.* V. **D** St Alb 3 **P** *Abp of Cant* **I** M J DUVALL *c.*
KING'S LYNN (St Marg w St Nich), *Norf.* R. **D** Nor 25 **P** *D and C of Nor* **I** G W F LANG, S COX *c*, J S W YOUNG *c.*
(All SS w St Mich AA), R. **D** Nor 25 **P** *Bp* **I** W G BRIDGE.
(St Jo Evang), V. **D** Nor 25 **P** *Bp* **I** P M RYLEY.
(St Pet), R. **D** Nor 25 **P** *Dioc Bd of Patr* **I** A D KINGCOME.
KING'S NORTON (St Nicolas), *W Midl.* R. **D** Birm 4 **P** *Patr Bd* **I** W B NORMAN, D C L EVE *team v,* P G HUZZEY *team v.*
KING'S NORTON, or NORTON BY GALBY (St Jo Bapt) w L Stretton (St Jo Bapt or St Clem), *Leics.* V. **D** Leic 6 *See* Gaulby.
KING'S PYON (St Mary) w Birley (St Pet), *Herefs.* V. **D** Heref 7 *See* Canon Pyon.
KING'S RIPTON (St Pet), *Cambs.* R. **D** Ely 10 **P** *Ld de Ramsey* **I** (Vacant).
KING'S SOMBORNE (St Pet and St Paul) w L Somborne, *Hants.* V. **D** Win 10 *See* Somborne.
KING'S STANLEY (St Geo), *Glos.* R. **D** Glouc 9 **P** *Jes Coll Cam* **I** R P MUNN *p-in-c.*
KING'S SUTTON (St Pet and St Paul), *Northants.* V. **D** Pet 1 **P** *S for Maint of Faith* **I** B M OMAN.
KING'S TEIGNTON (St Mich), *Devon.* V. **D** Ex 11 **P** *Bp* **I** P H SYMONS.
KING'S WALDEN (St Mary), *Herts.* V. **D** St Alb 9 **P** *Sir T Pilkington* **I** K G MARTIN.
KING'S WORTHY (St Mary), *Hants.* R. **D** Win 12 *See* Headbourne Worthy.
KINGSBRIDGE (St Edm K and Mart), *Devon.*. **D** Ex 14 *See* Churchstow.
KINGSBURY (H Innoc), *Gtr Lon.* V. **D** Lon 18 **P** *D and C of St Paul's* **I** A W PORTER.
(St Andr), V. **D** Lon 18 **P** *Crown* **I** D P MANN, G F JENKINS *c.*
KINGSBURY (St Pet and St Paul) w Hurley (Ch of Resurr), *Warws.* V. **D** Birm 10 **P** *Bp* **I** P J PRIVETT.
KINGSBURY EPISCOPI (St Martin) w E Lambrook, *Somt.* V. **D** B & W 20 **P** *Bp 2 turns, D and C of Wells 1 turn* **I** K W PUDDY.
KINGSCLERE (St Mary), *Hants.* V. **D** Win 5 **P** *Bp* **I** R R LEGG.
KINGSCLERE-WOODLANDS (St Paul) w Headley (St Pet), *Hants.* V. **D** Win 5 **P** *V of Kingsclere* **I** R D C RABBETTS.
KINGSCOTE (St Jo Bapt), *Glos.* V. **D** Glouc 17 *See* Horsley.
KINGSDON, *Somt.*. **D** B & W 10 *See* Charlton Adam.
KINGSDOWN (St Jo Evang), *Kent.* V. **D** Cant *See* Ringwould.
KINGSDOWN (St Cath), *Kent.*. **D** Cant *See* Lynsted.
KINGSDOWN (St Edm) w Mappiscombe, *Kent.* R. **D** Roch 8 **P** *D and C of Roch* **I** K F GRIFFIN.
KINGSEY (St Nich), *Oxon.*. **D** Ox *See* Haddenham.
KINGSHOLM (St Mark), *Glos.*. **D** Glouc 1 *See* Gloucester.
KINGSHURST (St Barn), *W Midl.* V. **D** Birm 9 **P** *Bp* **I** M GARLAND.
KINGSLAND (St Mich), *Herefs.* R. **D** Heref 7 **P** *Dioc Bd of Patr* **I** J G WILLIAMS.
KINGSLEY (St Jo Evang), *Chesh.* V. **D** Ches 3 **P** *V of Frodsham* **I** G H SANSOME.
KINGSLEY (St Werburgh), *Staffs.* R. **D** Lich 14 **P** *Mrs Beech* **I** T V EDWARDS.
KINGSLEY (All SS) w Oakhanger (St Mary Magd), *Hants.* V. **D** Win 1 *See* Worldham, East.
KINGSNORTH (St Mich) w Shadoxhurst (St Pet and St Paul), *Kent.* R. **D** Cant 10 **P** *Abp* **I** W E M LENNOX.
KINGSNYMPTON (St Jas Ap), *Devon.*. **D** Ex *See* South Molton.
KINGSTANDING (St Luke), *W Midl.* V. **D** Birm 3 **P** *Bp* **I** M S JOHNSON.
(St Mark), V. **D** Birm 3 **P** *Bp* **I** A D BUIK.
KINGSTHORPE (St Jo Bapt, St D and St Mark), *Northants.* R. **D** Pet **P** *Dioc Bd of Patr* **I** A J WOLSTENHULME, M A CRAGGS *team v,* R R ROBINSON *team v.*
KINGSTON ST MARY (St Mary Virg) w Broomfield (All SS) and Cheddon Fitzpaine (St Mary Virg), *Somt.* V. **D** B & W **P** *D and C of Bris 1st turn, Bp 2nd turn* **I** G C H WATSON.
KINGSTON (St Giles), *Kent.* R. **D** Cant 1 *See* Bishopsbourne.
KINGSTON (St Pancras) w Iford (St Nich) and Rodmell, *W Sussex.* V. **D** Chich 15 **P** *Bp* **I** G H PATON.
KINGSTON, *W Sussex.* V. **D** Chich 1 *See* Preston, East.
KINGSTON (All SS and St Andr), *Cambs.* R. **D** Ely 1 **P** *Bp* **I** M H HILLS.
KINGSTON, *Devon.*. **D** Ex *See* Ringmore.
KINGSTON (St Jas), *Isle of Wight.* R. **D** Portsm 7 *See* Shorwell.
KINGSTON (St Jas) (in St Aldhelm Group), *Dorset,* V. **D** Sarum 9 **P** *Lt Col H E Scott* **I** H J LLOYD.
KINGSTON BAGPUIZE (St Jo Bapt), *Oxon.* R. **D** Ox 11 *See* Fyfield.
KINGSTON BUCI or Kingston-by-Sea (St Julian), *W Sussex.* R. **D** Chich 13 **P** *Ld Egremont* **I** K GRACE *p-in-c.*
KINGSTON-DEVERILL (St Mary) w Monkton Deverill (Alfred, King of the West Saxons), *Wilts.* R. **D** Sarum 22 *See* Deverills.
KINGSTON HILL (St Paul), *Surrey.* V. **D** S'wark 11 **P** *Dioc Bd of Patr* **I** D S MARKWELL *hon c.*
KINGSTON LACY (St Steph) w Shapwick (St Bart), *Dorset.* V. **D** Sarum 11 **P** *R H J Bankes Esq* **I** (Vacant).
KINGSTON LISLE (St Jo Bapt), *Oxon.*. **D** Ox 19 *See* Sparsholt.
KINGSTON-ON-SOAR (St Wilfrid), V. **D** Southw 11 *See* Leake, West.
KINGSTON-PITNEY, *Somt.*. **D** B & W *See* Yeovil.
KINGSTON SEYMOUR (All SS), *Avon.*. **D** B & W 16 *See* Kenn.
KINGSTON-UPON-HULL, *Humb.*. **D** York 17 *See* Hull and Sculcoate.
KINGSTON-UPON-THAMES (All SS w St Jo Evang), *Surrey.* V. **D** S'wark 11 **P** *K Coll Cam and Trustees (alt)* **I** J T MARTIN, P EVANS *c.*
(St Luke w Good Shepherd), V. **D** S'wark 11 **P** *Bp* **I** C W B VICKERY, M J F MANNALL *hon c.*
KINGSTON VALE (St Jo Bapt), *Surrey.* V. **D** S'wark 11 **P** *Bp* **I** R M EDWARDS.
KINGSTONE (St John and All SS), *Somt.*. **D** B & W *See* Dowlish Wake.
KINGSTONE (St Mich AA), *Herefs.* V. **D** Heref 1 **P** *Bp* **I** A J MORTIMER.
KINGSTONE (St Jo Bapt) w Gratwich (St Mary), *Staffs.* V. **D** Lich 20 **P** *Bp* **I** P GLEDHILL *p-in-c.*
KINGSWAY. **D** Lon *See* St Giles-in-the-Fields.
KINGSWEAR (St Thos of Cant), *Devon.* V. **D** Ex 10 **P** *Crown* **I** J GOULD.
KINGSWINFORD (St Mary), *W Midl.* V. **D** Lich 1 **P** *Dioc Bd of Patr* **I** F N LEWIS, M R CRUMPTON *min,* A A LONG *c.*
KINGSWOOD (H Trin w Ch of Ascen), *Avon.* V. **D** Bris 8 **P** *Bp* **I** J L WARE.
KINGSWOOD (St Mary Virg) w Alderley and Hillesley, *Glos.* R. **D** Glouc 5 **P** *Bp, Dioc Bd of Patr and R M G S Hale Esq* **I** D L PARKINSON *p-in-c.*
KINGSWOOD (St Andr), *Surrey.* V. **D** S'wark 12 **P** *Bp and Trustees* **I** S EVANS.

KINGTON (St Mary) w Huntington (St Thos), *Herefs.* V and R. D Heref 5 P *D and C of Heref* I G O ASSON, K J M GEWEN *c*, J H ROOSE-EVANS *c*.

KINGTON (St Jas) w Dormston (St Nich), *Worcs.* R. D Worc 3 *See* Inkberrow.

KINGTON LANGLEY (St Pet), *Wilts.*. D Bris 9 *See* Langley Fitzurse.

KINGTON MAGNA w Buckhorn Weston *Dorset.* R. D Sarum 13 *See* Gillingham.

KINGTON ST MICHAEL, *Wilts.* V. D Bris *See* Chippenham, St Paul.

KINGTON, WEST (St Mary Virg), *Wilts.* R. D Bris 9 P *Bp* I M W DITTMER.

KINGWESTON (All SS), *Somt.* R. D B & W 4 *See* Barton St David.

KINLET (St Jo Bapt), *Salop.* V. D Heref 12 *See* Neen Savage.

KINNERLEY (St Mary) w Melverley (St Pet), *Salop.* V. D Lich 24 P *Bp and Earl of Bradf* alt. I G G HODSON.

KINNERSLEY (St Jas) w Norton Canon (St Nich), *Heref.* R. D Heref 5 P *D and C of Heref* I S C SNEYD P-IN-C OF NORTON CANON.

KINNERTON (St Mary Virg), *Powys.* V. D Heref 5 *See* Radnor, Old.

KINNERTON, HIGHER (All SS), *Clwyd.*. D Ches 2 *See* Dodleston.

KINOULTON (St Luke), *Notts.* V. D Southw *See* Hickling.

KINSHAM (All SS), *Herefs.* V. D Heref 5 *See* Staunton-on-Arrow.

KINSLEY (The Ascen), *W Yorks.* V. D Wakef 11 P *Bp* I E H FISKE *c-in-c*.

KINSON (St Andr), *Hants.* R. D Sarum 14 P *MMT* I J R MOORE, M J ARCHER *c*, K G WEBBER *hon c*.

KINTBURY (St Mary Virg) w Avington, *Berks.* V. D Ox 14 P *Dioc Bd of Patr and Bp (alt)* I A G MILLARD.

KINVER (St Pet?), *Staffs.* V. D Lich 7 P *Dioc Bd of Patr* I D W WATSON.

KINWARTON (St Mary Virg) w Great Alne (St Mary Magd) and Haselor (St Mary and All SS), *Warws.* R. D Cov 7 P *Bp* I F WAIN.

KIPPAX (St Mary Virg and St Mich) w Gt Preston (St Aid), *W Yorks.* V. D Ripon 7 P *Bp* I T KEDDIE.

KIPPINGTON (St Mary), *Kent.* V. D Roch 7 P *Dioc Bd of Patr* I J B LOWE.

KIRBY BEDON (St Andr w St Mary) w Bixley (St Wandregesilus) and Whitlingham, *Norf.* R. D Nor 14 P *BNC Ox 2 turns, Bp 1 turn* I I J BAILEY *p-in-c*.

KIRBY BELLARS (St Pet), *Leics.* V. D Leic 4 *See* Frisby-on-the-Wreake.

KIRBY CANE (All SS), *Norf.*. D Nor 14 *See* Ellingham.

KIRBY-GRINDALYTHE (St Andr), *Humb.*. D York 3 *See* Weaverthorpe.

KIRBY-IN-CLEVELAND (St Aug), *Cleve.* V. D York 25 P *Abp* I S C NICHOLLS.

KIRBY-LE-SOKEN (St Mich), *Essex.* R. D Chelmsf 28 P *Bp* I P GARNER.

KIRBY-MISPERTON (St Lawr) w Barugh, Habton and Ryton, *N Yorks.* R. D York 24 P *Exors of Earl of Feversham* I N N JONES *p-in-c*.

KIRBY MUXLOE (St Bart), *Leics.* R. D Leic 17 P *Bp* I J C SEYMOUR.

KIRBY-ON-THE-MOOR (or Kirby Hill), *N Yorks.* V. D Ripon 3 P *Bp* I P F STIRK.

KIRBY SIGSTON, *N Yorks.*. D York *See* Northallerton.

KIRBY UNDERDALE (All SS) w Bugthorpe (St Andr), *Humb.* R. D York *See* Bishop Wilton.

KIRDFORD (St Jo Bapt) w Plaistow (H Trin), *W Sussex.* V. D Chich 6 P *Ld Egremont* I V E WINCH.

KIRK BRAMWITH (St Mary), *S Yorks.* R. D Sheff 8 P *Duchy of Lanc* I T W HARRIS P-IN-C OF FENWICK *p-in-c*.

KIRK-DEIGHTON (All SS), *N Yorks.* R. D Ripon 4 *See* Spofforth.

KIRK ELLA (St Andr), *Humb.* V. D York 17 P *Exors of Miss M Foord* I J C H WILSON.

KIRK-FENTON, *N Yorks.* V. D York 9 P *Abp* I G Y GAINES *c-in-c*.

KIRK-HALLAM (All SS), *Derbys.* V. D Derby 13 P *Bp* I H D PROUT.

KIRK-HAMMERTON (St Jo Bapt) w Nun Monkton and Hunsingore, *N Yorks.* V. D Ripon 3 P *Col R Stanyforth's Exors, Dioc Bd of Patr, J H Dent Esq and Bp* I W J M C PATERSON.

KIRK-IRETON (H Trin), *Derbys.* R. D Derby 17 P *Bp* I J H FLINT *c*.

KIRK LANGLEY (St Mich), *Derbys.* R. D Derby 12 P *G Meynell Esq* I H A DANE *p-in-c*, E DIXON *c*.

KIRK-LEVINGTON (St Martin), *Cleve.* V. D York 25 P *Abp* I D MOORE.

KIRK SANDALL (St Osw) and Edenthorpe, *S Yorks.* R. D Sheff 8 P *Crown* I P J GARRATT.

KIRK SMEATON (St Mary) w L Smeaton, *N Yorks.* R. D Wakef 11 P *Earl Fitzwilliam* I E L THACKER *p-in-c*.

KIRKANDREWS-ON-EDEN (St Mary) w Beaumont and Grinsdale (St Kentigern), *Cumb.* R. D Carl 3 P *Earl of Lonsdale* I G N DOBSON *p-in-c*.

KIRKANDREWS-ON-ESK (St Andr), *Cumb.* R. D Carl 2 *See* Nicholforest.

KIRKBAMPTON, *Cumb.*. D Carl *See* Burgh-by-Sands.

KIRKBRIDE (St Bridget) w Newton Arlosh (St Jo Evang), *Cumb.* R. D Carl 3 P *Earl of Lonsdale and V of Holme Cultram* alt I P EVANS.

KIRKBURN (St Mary), *Humb.* V. D York 13 P *Ld Chan* I W E COWLING.

KIRKBURTON (All H), *W Yorks.* V. D Wakef 7 P *Bp* I H C E BOX.

KIRKBY (St Pet) w Kingerby, *Lincs.* D Linc P *Bp and M F Young Esq (alt)* I (Vacant).

KIRKBY (St Chad) w Southdene (St Martin), *Mer.* R. D Liv 5 P *Patr Bd* I T A GIBSON, P H BURMAN *team v*, M J GILLINGHAM *team v*, D R LESLIE *team v*, M F BARTLETT *c*.

(St Mark, Northwood), *Lancs.* V. D Liv 5 P *Dioc Bd of Patr* I M C BOYLING *team v*, J A GARNETT *c*.

KIRKBY, EAST (St Nich), w Miningsby, *Lincs.* V. D Linc *See* Bolingbroke.

KIRKBY-FLEETHAM w Fencote, *N Yorks.* V. D Ripon 2 P *Bp* I K MCLEOD.

KIRKBY GREEN, *Lincs.*. D Linc 18 *See* Scopwick.

KIRKBY-IN-ASHFIELD (St Wilfred), *Notts.* R. D Southw 2 P *Duke of Portland* I I G COLLINS.

(St Thos), V. D Southw 2 P *Bp* I F CROWTHER.

KIRKBY-IN-CLEVELAND, *Cleve.*. D York *See* Kirby-in-Cleveland.

KIRKBY-IN-MALHAMDALE (St Mich), *N Yorks.* V. D Bradf 6 P *Provost and Chapter of Bradf Cathl* I C F TREVOR.

KIRKBY IRELETH (St Cuthb), *Cumb.* V. D Carl 15 P *D and C of York* I J B PARKER.

KIRKBY KNOWLE (St Wilfrid), *N Yorks.* R. D York 26 P *Abp* I W C SLADE.

KIRKBY LAYTHORPE (St Denys) w Asgarby (St Andr), *Lincs.* R. D Linc 22 P *Marq of Bris* I R J ABRAHAM.

KIRKBY LONSDALE (St Mary Virg and St John), Hutton Roof w Lupton, Casterton, Barbon w Middleton, and Mansergh, *Cumb.* R. D Carl 17 P *Kirkby Lonsdale Bd of Patr* I W G BETTRIDGE, W TURNER *team v*.

KIRKBY MALLORY (All SS), *Leics.* R. D Leic 13 *See* Thurlaston.

KIRKBY MALZEARD (St Andr) w Dallagh Gill (or Dallowgill St Pet), *N Yorks.* V. D Ripon 3 P *V of Masham* I (Vacant).

KIRKBYMOORSIDE (All SS) w Gillamoor, Bransdale (St Nich) and Farndale (St Mary), *N Yorks.* V. D York 20 P *Exors of Earl of Feversham* I L P CLARE.

KIRKBY-ON-BAIN (St Mary) w Tumby, *Lincs.* R. D Linc 11 P *Ld Chan* I H R WHALER.

KIRKBY OVERBLOW (North Rigton and Weeton), *N Yorks.* r. D Ripon 4 P *Bp* I B A TUNSTALL.

KIRKBY RAVENSWORTH (St Pet and St Felix) w Dalton (St Jas), *N Yorks.* V. D Ripon 1 *See* Gilling.

KIRKBY-SIGSTON, *N Yorks.*. D York *See* Northallerton.

KIRKBY-STEPHEN (St Steph) w Mallerstang, *Cumb.* V. D Carl 1 P *Earl of Lonsdale 2 turns, Col G W A Tufton 1 turn* I W F GREETHAM.

KIRKBY-THORE (St Mich) w Temple Sowerby (St Jas) and Newbiggin, *Cumb.* R. D Carl 1 P *Col G W A Tufton 3 turns, M T Hill 1 turn* I D F WALKER.

KIRKBY UNDERWOOD (St Mary and All SS), *Lincs.*. D Linc 13 *See* Aslackby.

KIRKBY-WHARFE (St Jo Bapt) w Ulleskelf, *N Yorks.* V. D York 9 P *A A Warburton Esq and H A Bromet Esq* I P P WOOD.

KIRKBY-WISKE (St Jo Bapt) w Maunby (St Mich AA), *N Yorks.* R. D Ripon 2 P *Duke of Northumb* I N ASHBY.

KIRKBY WOODHOUSE (St Jo Evang), *Notts.* V. D Southw 2 P *Bp* I S A LOWE.

KIRKCAMBECK, *Cumb.*. D Carl 2 *See* Lanercost.

KIRKDALE (St Mary and St Athanasius), *Mer.* V. D Liv 3 P *Simeon Trustees* I W A BRETHERTON.

(St Lawr), V. D Liv 3 P *CPAS* I G D BUCKLAND. *See also* LIVERPOOL..

KIRKDALE (St Greg) w Nawton (St Hilda), *N Yorks.* V. D York 20 P *Univ of Ox* I D HARROP.

KIRKHAM (St Mich), *Lancs.* V. D Blackb 9 P *D and C of Ch Ch Ox* I R A NELSON, F HARRISON *hon c*.

KIRKHARLE (St Wilfred), *Northumb.* V. **D** Newc T *See* Kirkwhelpington.
KIRKHAUGH, *Northumb..* **D** Newc T *See* Alston.
KIRKHEATON (St Bart), *Northumb.* R. **D** Newc T *See* Kirkwhelpington.
KIRKHEATON (St Jo Bapt) w (St Bart Grange Moor), *W Yorks.* R. **D** Wakef 5 **P** *Ch Trust Fund* **I** RT REV P B HARRIS, P G HARDING *c*, P E IRWIN-CLARK *c*.
KIRKHOLT (St Thos), *Gtr Man.* V. **D** Man 17 **P** *Bp* **I** (Vacant).
KIRKLAND (St Lawr), *Cumb.* V. **D** Carl 6 **P** *D and C of Carl* **I** V D CLARKE *p-in-c*.
KIRKLEATHAM (St Cuthb) and (St Hilda), *Cleve.* R. **D** York 19 **P** *Abp* **I** C LINGARD.
KIRKLEY w Lowestoft (St Jo Evang), *Suff.* R. **D** Nor 15 *See* Lowestoft.
KIRKLINGTON (St Mich) w Burneston and Wath, *N Yorks.* R. **D** Ripon 2 **P** *Capt Prior-Wandesforde, Mrs Anderson, Ch S Trust and Dioc Bd of Patr* **I** R P THOMAS.
KIRKLINGTON (St Swith) w Hockerton (St Nich), *Notts.* V. **D** Southw 15 **P** *Bp* **I** G D MILLS *p-in-c*.
KIRKLINTON (St Cuthb) w Hethersgill (St Mary) and Scaleby (All SS), *Cumb.* R. **D** Carl 2 **P** *Trustees* **I** C H COWPER.
KIRKMANSHULME (St Cypr), *Gtr Man..* **D** Man 4 *See* Longsight.
KIRKNEWTON (St Greg), *Northumb.* V. **D** Newc T 8 *See* Wooler.
KIRKOSWALD (St Osw), Renwick (All SS) and Ainstable, *Cumb.* V. **D** Carl 6 **P** *Bp and E P Ecroyd Esq* **I** J M ALLEN.
KIRKSTALL (St Steph), *W Yorks.* V. **D** Ripon 5 **P** *Trustees of Leeds Parish Ch* **I** R M WIGGEN.
KIRKSTEAD (St Leon), *Lincs..* **D** Linc 11 *See* Woodhall Spa.
KIRKTHORPE (St Pet), *W Yorks.* V. **D** Wakef 7 *See* Warmfield.
KIRKWHELPINGTON (St Bart) w Kirkharle, Kirkheaton and Cambo, *Northumb.* V. **D** Newc T **P** *Ld Chan, J Palmer-Anderson Esq and Bp* **I** J K YOUNG.
KIRMINGTON (St Helen), *Humb.* V. **D** Linc 6 **P** *Earl of Yarborough* **I** S PHILLIPS.
KIRMOND-LE-MIRE (St Martin), *Lincs..* **D** Linc 5 *See* Stainton-le-Vale.
KIRSTEAD (St Marg) w Langhale and Brooke (St Pet), *Norf.* R. **D** Nor 11 **P** *Ld Chan and G and C Coll Cam* alt **I** H L DAVIES.
KIRTLING, *Cambs.* V. **D** Ely 4 **P** *Mrs D A Bowlby and Countess of Ellesmere (alt)* **I** A V DAVIS.
KIRTLINGTON (St Mary Virg), *Oxon.* V. **D** Ox 2 **P** *St Jo Coll Ox* **I** R G BENNETT.
KIRTON (H Trin), *Notts.* R. **D** Southw 6 **P** *S for Maint of Faith* **I** I CLARK.
KIRTON (St Mary) w Falkenham (St Ethelbert), *Suff.* R. **D** St E 2 **P** *Ld Chan* **I** B T THOMPSON, S R HAROLD *c*.
KIRTON HOLME, *Lincs..* **D** Linc 21 *See* Brothertoft.
KIRTON-IN-HOLLAND (St Pet and St Paul), *Lincs.* V. **D** Linc 21 **P** *Mercers' Co* **I** P R HODGSON, J F UDY *c*.
KIRTON-IN-LINDSEY (St Andr), *Humb.* V. **D** Linc 6 **P** *Bp* **I** M B KIDDLE.
KISLINGBURY (St Luke) w Rothersthorpe (St Pet and St Paul), *Northants.* R. **D** Pet 3 **P** *Bp 2 turns, Dioc Bd of Patr 1 turn* **I** D G SAINT.
KITT GREEN, *Gtr Man..* **D** Liv *See* Pemberton.
KITTISFORD, *Somt..* **D** B & W 22 *See* Bathealton.
KNAITH (St Mary), *Lincs.* V. **D** Linc 2 **P** *Lt-Col J W E Sandars* **I** H J KNIGHT.
KNAPHILL (H Trin), *Surrey.* V. **D** Guildf 11 **P** *V of St Jo Bapt Woking* **I** R B WATSON.
KNAPTOFT, *Leics.* R. **D** Leic 5 *See* Mowsley.
KNAPTON, *Norf..* **D** Nor *See* Paston.
KNAPTON N Yorks. V **D** York 3 *See* Heslerton, W.
KNAPWELL (All SS), *Cambs..* **D** Ely 1 *See* Elsworth.
KNARESBOROUGH (St Jo Bapt and H Trin). *N Yorks.* V. **D** Ripon **P** *Bp* **I** N G L R MCDERMID, N S BROADBENT *c*, R T COOPER *c*, P L DUNBAR *c*, C W BICKERSTETH *hon c*.
KNARESDALE, *Northumb..* **D** Newc T 4 **P** *Ld Chan* **I** (Vacant).
KNEBWORTH (St Mary), *Herts.* R. **D** St Alb 12 **P** *Trustees* **I** R M JAMES, J TAPLIN *c*.
KNEESALL (St Bart), *Notts.* V. **D** Southw 4 **P** *Dioc Bd of Patr* **I** B JAMES *p-in-c*.
KNEETON (St Helen), *Notts.* V. **D** Southw 9 *See* Flintham.
KNETTISHALL (All SS), *Norf..* **D** Nor 18 *See* Riddlesworth.
KNIGHTLEY (Ch Ch), *Staffs..* **D** Lich 15 *See* High Offley.
KNIGHTON, *Leics..* **D** Leic 1 *See* Leicester.
KNIGHTON-ON-TEME (St Mich), *Worcs.* V. **D** Worc 12 **P** *V of Lindridge* **I** P C AUDSLEY.
KNIGHTON, WEST (St Pet), *Dorset..* **D** Sarum *See* Broadmayne.
KNIGHTSBRIDGE,. **D** Lon *See* Westminster.
KNIGHT'S ENHAM (St Mich AA), *Hants.* R. **D** Win 2 **P** *Bp* **I** A D PICTON *p-in-c*.
KNIGHTWICK (St Mary) w Doddenham (St Andr), Broadwas (St Mary Magd) and Cotheridge (St Leon), *Worcs.* R. **D** Worc 2 **P** *D and C of Worc* **I** D C SALT.
KNILL (St Mich), *Herefs.* R. **D** Heref 5 **P** *Sir J Walsham Bt* **I** (Vacant).
KNIPTON (All SS), w Harston (St Mich AA), *Leics.* R. **D** Leic 3 *See* Croxton-Kerrial.
KNIVETON (St Mich AA), *Derbys..* **D** Derby **P** *Bp* **I** (Vacant).
KNOCKHOLT (St Kath), *Kent.* R. **D** Roch 7 **P** *D and C of Roch* **I** J H NEWMAN.
KNOCKIN (St Mary) w Maesbrook (St Jo Evang), *Salop.* R. **D** Lich 24 **P** *Earl of Bradf* **I** G G HODSON *p-in-c*.
KNODISHALL (St Lawr) w Buxlow, *Suff.* R. **D** St E 19 **P** *Ch S Trust* **I** (Vacant).
KNOOK (St Marg), *Wilts..* **D** Sarum 22 *See* Heytesbury.
KNOSSINGTON (St Pet) w Cold Overton, *Leics.* R. **D** Leic 8 **P** *MMT* **I** A T GREEN *p-in-c*.
KNOTTING (St Marg) w Souldrop (All SS), *Beds.* R. **D** St Alb 21 **P** *Bp* **I** H D JONES *p-in-c*.
KNOTTINGLEY (St Botolph) w Knottingley, East (Ch Ch), *W Yorks.* V. **D** Wakef 11 **P** *Bp and V of Pontefract* alt **I** W T HICKS, S P KELLY *c*.
KNOTTY ASH (St Jo Evang), *Mer.* V. **D** Liv 6 **P** *R of West Derby* **I** H B SIVITER.
KNOWBURY (St Paul), *Salop.* V. **D** Heref 12 **P** *Bp* **I** A C GOULD P-IN-C OF CORELEY.
KNOWL HILL (St Pet) w Littlewick (St Jo Evang), *Berks.* V. **D** Ox 13 **P** *Bp and Trustees* alt **I** P H ELSTON.
KNOWLE (St Giles) w Cricket Malherbie (St Mary Magd), *Somt..* **D** B & W *See* Dowlish Wake.
KNOWLE (St Jo Bapt St Lawr and St Anne), *W Midl.* V. **D** Birm 11 **P** *H G Everitt Esq* **I** J V F RUSHER, R W L MOBERLY *c*.
KNOWLE (H Nativ w St Martin), *Avon.* R. **D** Bris 2 **P** *Bp* **I** J O BRADLEY, R G MINSON *team v*.
(St Barn), V. **D** Bris 2 **P** *Bp* **I** H FARLIE *c-in-c*.
KNOWLTON (St Clem), *Kent.* R. **D** Cant 1 *See* Goodnestone next Wingham.
KNOWSLEY (St Mary Virg), *Mer.* V. **D** Liv 6 **P** *Earl of Derby* **I** S M MUNNS, J T LEIGHTON *hon c*.
KNOWSTONE (St Pet), *Devon..* **D** Ex 19 *See* Oakmoor.
KNOYLE, EAST, or BISHOP or GREAT (St Mary), Hindon w Chicklade and Pertwood, *Wilts.* R. **D** Sarum 19 **P** *Bp and Ld Chan (alt)* **I** L W DAFFURN *c-in-c*.
KNOYLE, WEST, or LITTLE or ODIERN (Dedic unknown), *Wilts..* **D** Sarum *See* Mere.
KNUTSFORD (St Jo Bapt) w Toft, *Chesh.* V. **D** Ches 12 **P** *Lds of the Manor, Bp and Mrs L L M Brown* **I** W M D PERSSON, R J KIRKLAND *c*.
(St Cross), V. **D** Ches 12 **P** *Mrs I A Legh* **I** T ETHERIDGE.
KNUTTON (St Mary), *Staffs.* V. **D** Lich 17 **P** *Sir Alexander Stanier* **I** P G HOUGH.
KNUZDEN (St Osw), *Lancs.* V. **D** Blackb 2 **P** *Bp* **I** (Vacant).
KNYPERSLEY (St Jo Evang), *Staffs.* V. **D** Lich 16 **P** *CPAS* **I** S ORME.
KYLOE (St Nich), *Northumb.* V. **D** Newc T *See* Lowick.
KYME, SOUTH (St Mary and All SS), w Kyme, North (St Luke), *Lincs.* V. **D** Linc 22 **P** *Dioc Bd of Patr* **I** (Vacant).
KYNNERSLEY (St Chad), *Salop.* R. **D** Lich 21 *See* Tibberton.
KYRE-WYARD (St Mary), *Worcs.* R. **D** Worc 12 *See* Stoke Bliss.

LACEBY (St Marg) w Irby-upon-Humber, *Humb.* R. **D** Linc 10 **P** *Ridley Hall, Cam and Ld Yarborough* **I** J E BASSETT.
LACEY-GREEN (St Jo Evang), *Bucks.* V. **D** Ox 21 **P** *R of Princes Risborough* **I** (Vacant).
LACHE, or SALTNEY (St Mark) w Saltney Ferry, *Chesh.* V. **D** Chesh 2 **P** *Bp* **I** A G WILLIAMS, W WATKINS *c*.
LACKFORD, *Suff..* **D** St E *See* Flempton.
LACOCK (St Cyriac) w Bowden Hill (St Anne), *Wilts.* V. **D** Bris 9 **P** *A M Burnett-Brown Esq 2 turns, Lady Hollenden 1 turn* **I** R V LENTON.
LADBROKE (All SS) w Radbourne, *Warws.* R. **D** Cov 10 **P** *Maj J W Chandos-Pole* **I** (Vacant).

LANGLEY (St Mich AA w H Trin), *W Midl*. V. **D** Birm 6 **P** *Crown* **I** F E GILES.
(St John), V. **D** Birm 6 **P** *Bp* **I** R T ETHERIDGE.
LANGLEY BURRELL (St Pet), *Wilts*. R. **D** Bris *See* Chippenham, St Paul.
LANGLEY FITZURSE (St Pet), *Wilts*. V. **D** Bris 7 **P** *Bp* **I** D G GARDNER.
LANGLEY GREEN (St Leon), *W Sussex*.. **D** Chich *See* Ifield.
LANGLEY-MARISH (St Mary Virg), *Berks*. R. **D** Ox 24 **P** *Patr Bd* **I** J M PEIRCE, A C DIBDEN *team v*, G W FARMER *team v*, R C HINGLEY *team v*.
LANGLEY MILL (St Andr w St Jo Aldecar), *Derbys*. V. **D** Derby 6 **P** *V of Heanor* **I** A J BAILEY.
LANGLEY-PARK (All SS), *Durham*.. **D** Dur 7 *See* Esh.
LANGLEYBURY (St Paul), *Herts*. V. **D** St Alb 13 **P** *E H Loyd Esq* **I** G A DREW.
LANGMERE (no church), *Norf*.. **D** Nor 17 *See* Dickleburgh.
LANGOLD (St Luke), *Notts*. V. **D** Southw 7 **P** *Bp* **I** N C TIMBERLAKE.
LANGPORT (All SS) w Huish Episcopi, Pitney, Aller, High w Low Ham, Drayton and Muchelney, *Somt*. R. **D** B & W 10 **P** *Bp, Archd of Wells, D and C of Bris and Worc Coll Ox* **I** A E N MOLESWORTH, R C P TERRELL *team v*.
LANGRICK (St Marg of Scotld) w Wildmore (St Pet), *Lincs*. V. **D** Linc 21 *See* Brothertoft.
LANGRIDGE (St Mary Magd), *Avon*.. **D** B & W 13 *See* Swainswick.
LANGRISH (St Jo Evang), *Hants*. V. **D** Portsm 4 **P** *Ld Chan* **I** R J B SMITH.
LANGTHORNE (St Mary Magd), *N Yorks*.. **D** Ripon 2 *See* Crakehall.
LANGTOFT (St Mich AA), *Lincs*. V. **D** Linc *See* Baston.
LANGTOFT (St Pet) w Foxholes (St Mary), Butterwick (St Nich) and Cottam (H Trin), *N Yorks*. V. **D** York 13 **P** *Abp and Keble Coll Ox* **I** J R MEERES.
LANGTON (St Andr Ap) w Birdsall (St Mary), *N Yorks*. R. **D** York 3 **P** *Ld Chan and Ld Middleton* alt **I** H D PIKE *p-in-c*.
LANGTON-BY-HORNCASTLE (St Marg) w Old Woodhall, *Lincs*. R. **D** Linc 11 **P** *Bp* **I** (Vacant).
LANGTON-BY-PARTNEY (St Pet and St Paul) w Sutterby (St Jo Bapt), *Lincs*. R. **D** Linc 7 **P** *J C P Langton Esq* **I** (Vacant).
LANGTON-BY-WRAGBY (St Giles), *Lincs*. V. **D** Linc 11 **P** *Dioc Bd of Patr, MMT and Bp* **I** P M LACY.
LANGTON CHURCH (St Pet) w Tur Langton and Thorpe Langton, *Leics*. R. **D** Leic 5 **P** *Bp* **I** T H JONES.
LANGTON GREEN (All SS), *Kent*. V. **D** Roch 10 **P** *R of Speldhurst* **I** C K CHANNER.
LANGTON-HERRING (St Pet), *Dorset*.. **D** Sarum 6 *See* Portesham.
LANGTON LONG (All SS) *Dorset*. R. **D** Sarum 10 *See* Blandford-Forum.
LANGTON MATRAVERS (St Geo) (in St Aldhelm Group), *Dorset*. R. **D** Sarum 9 **P** *Bp* **I** J R STEWART.
LANGTON-ON-SWALE (St Wilfrid), *N Yorks*. R. **D** Ripon 2 **P** *D and C of York* **I** K MCLEOD.
LANGTREE (Dedic unknown), *Devon*. R. **D** Ex 20 **P** *Ld Clinton* **I** R A WALLINGTON.
LANGTREE (Checkendon, Stoke-Row and Woodcote), *Oxon*. R. **D** Ox **P** *Bp, Univ Coll Ox and St Jo Coll Cam* **I** D T W SALT.
LANGWATHBY, *Cumb*.. **D** Carl *See* Edenhall.
LANGWITH, UPPER (or Langwith Bassett) (H Cross) w Whaley Thorns, *Derbys*. R. **D** Derby **P** *Bp and Duke of Devonshire* **I** G R BEVAN.
LANGWORTH (St Hugh), *Lincs*.. **D** Linc 3 *See* Barlings.
LANHYDROCK (St Hyderock), *Cornw*. V. **D** Truro 8 **P** *Bp* **I** R N K WATTON *p-in-c*, H C T OLIVEY *c*.
LANIVET (Dedic unknown) w Nanstallon (St Steph), *Cornw*. R. **D** Truro 8 **P** *Dioc Bd of Patr* **I** R N K WATTON *p-in-c*, H C T OLIVEY *c*.
LANLIVERY and Luxulyan, *Cornw*. V. **D** Truro 8 **P** *Dioc Bd of Patr 2 turns Bp 1 turn Archd of Bodmin 1 turn* **I** H B YORK *p-in-c*.
LANNARTH or LANNER (Ch Ch), *Cornw*. V. **D** Truro *See* Redruth.
LANREATH (St Marnarck), *Cornw*. R. **D** Truro 13 **P** *Commdr J B Kitson, R N and Capt M F Buller* alt **I** B J FREETH *p-in-c*.
LANSALLOS (St Ildierna), *Cornw*. R. **D** Truro 13 **P** *Dioc Bd of Patr and Mr W G Mills* alt **I** J K P S ROBERTSHAW *p-in-c*.
LANTEGLOS-BY-CAMELFORD (St Julitta w St Thos) w St Adwena, *Cornw*. R. **D** Truro 12 **P** *Duchy of Cornw* **I** D S MANDER.
LANTEGLOS-BY-FOWEY (St Wyllow), *Cornw*. V. **D** Truro 13 **P** *D and C of Truro* **I** I H MORRIS *p-in-c*.
LAPFORD (St Thos of Cant), *Devon*. V. **D** Ex 16 **P** *Bp* **I** K J WARREN.
LAPLEY (All SS) w Wheaton Aston (St Mary), *Staffs*. V. **D** Lich 3 **P** *Keble Coll Ox* **I** A R ROAKE.
LAPWORTH (St Mary Virg), *Warws*. R. **D** Birm 11 **P** *Mert Coll Ox and T W Ferrers-Walker Esq* **I** M WEBSTER.
LARKFIELD (H Trin), *Kent*. V. **D** Roch 6 **P** *Dioc Bd of Patr* **I** R J R LEA, A J POWELL *c*.
LARLING, *Norf*.. **D** Nor *See* Shropham.
LASBOROUGH (St Mary), *Glos*. R. **D** Glouc 17 *See* Weston-Birt.
LASHAM (St Mary), *Hants*.. **D** Win *See* Bentworth.
LASSINGTON (St Osw), *Glos*. R. **D** Glouc 6 *See* Highnam.
LASTINGHAM (St Mary formerly St Pet) w Appleton-le-Moors, *N Yorks*. V. **D** York 20 **P** *Abp* **I** F J A HEWITT.
LATCH (St Mark), *Ches*.. **D** Ches 2 *See* Lache.
LATCHFORD (Ch Ch), *Chesh*. V. **D** Ches 4 **P** *R of Grappenhall* **I** A SHAW.
(St Jas Greater), V. **D** Ches 4 **P** *R of Grappenhall* **I** G J HARDMAN *c*, C M KEMP *c*.
LATCHINGDON (Ch Ch) and North Fambridge (H Trin), *Essex*. R. **D** Chelmsf *See* Cricksea.
LATHBURY, *Bucks*. R. **D** Ox 28 *See* Newport Pagnell.
LATIMER (St Mary Magd) w Flaunden (St Mary Magd), V *Bucks*. R. **D** Ox 20 **P** *Ld Chesham* **I** D M RYLE *c-in-c*.
LATTON (St Mary Virg), *Essex*. V. **D** Chelmsf 3 **P** *Trustees of J L M Arkwright Esq* **I** J A PRATT, C W W HOWARD *c*.
LATTON, *Wilts*.. **D** Bris *See* Cricklade.
LAUGHTON (All SS) w Ripe and Chalvington, *E Sussex*. R. **D** Chich 15 **P** *Earl of Chich, Hertf Coll Ox and BNC Ox (in turn)* **I** R M FINCH *p-in-c*.
LAUGHTON (St Luke), *Leics*. R. **D** Leic 5 *See* Foxton.
LAUGHTON, *Lincs*.. **D** Linc *See* Folkingham.
LAUGHTON (All SS), V w Wildsworth (St Jo Bapt), *Lincs*.. **D** Linc 2 **P** *Meynell Ch Trustees* **I** J R HOPCRAFT *p-in-c*.
LAUGHTON-EN-LE-MORTHEN (All SS) w Thorpe (St Jo Bapt), *S Yorks*. V. **D** Sheff 5 **P** *Bp* **I** J L JONES.
LAUNCELLS (St Swith), *Cornw*.. **D** Truro 10 *See* Marhamchurch.
LAUNCESTON (St Mary Magd), *Cornw*. V. **D** Truro 11 **P** *Bp* **I** W G R K STEER.
(St Steph). **D** Truro 11 *See* St Stephen's-by-Launceston.
(St Thos Ap), V. **D** Truro 11 *See* St Stephens-by-Launceston.
LAUNTON Oxon. R **D** Ox 2 *See* Bicester.
LAVANT, EAST (St Mary), R w Lavant, Mid (St Nich), *W Sussex*. R. **D** Chich 3 **P** *Duke of Richmond and Gordon* **I** K W CATCHPOLE.
LAVENDER HILL (The Ascen), *Surrey*. V. **D** S'wark 1 **P** *Keble Coll Ox* **I** J H CUTHBERT, T B HUDSON *hon c*.
LAVENDON (St Mich), w Cold Brayfield (St Mary), *Bucks*. R. **D** Ox 28 **P** *Exors of Mrs W R Soames* **I** D P CIANCHI *p-in-c*.
LAVENHAM (St Pet and St Paul), *Suff*. R. **D** St E 10 **P** *G and C Coll Cam* **I** H CRICHTON.
LAVER, HIGH (All SS) w Magdalen Laver (St Mary Magd) and Little Laver, *Essex*. R. **D** Chelmsf 6 **P** *Bp* **I** E W COLEMAN *p-in-c*.
LAVER, LITTLE (St Mary Virg), *Essex*. R. **D** Chelmsf 6 *See* Laver, High.
LAVERSTOCK (St Andr), *Wilts*. V. **D** Sarum 16 **P** *D and C of Sarum* **I** W G BULL.
LAVERSTOKE, *Hants*.. **D** Win 5 *See* Overton.
LAVERTON (BVM), *Somt*.. **D** B & W 16a *See* Norton St Philip.
LAVERTON, *Glos*.. **D** Glouc 18 *See* Buckland.
LAVINGTON (or Lenton) (St Pet), *Lincs*. **D** Linc *See* Ingoldsby.
LAVINGTON, BISHOP'S or WEST (All SS), *Wilts*. V. **D** Sarum 23 **P** *Bp* **I** M OSBORN *p-in-c*.
LAVINGTON, WEST (St Mary Magd), *W Sussex*.. **D** Chich *See* Cocking.
LAVINGTON MARKET, *Wilts*.. **D** Sarum *See* Market Lavington.
LAWFORD (St Mary), *Essex*. R. **D** Chelmsf 25 **P** *St Jo Coll Cam* **I** (Vacant).
LAWFORD, LONG, *Warws*.. **D** Cov 8 *See* Newbold-on-Avon.
LAWHITTON (St Mich), *Cornw*. R. **D** Truro 11 **P** *Bp* **I** J E COX *p-in-c*.
LAWKHOLME (H Trin), *W Yorks*. V. **D** Bradf 11 *See* Keighley.

LAWRENCE WESTON (St Pet), *Avon*. V. **D** Bris 6 **P** *Bp* **I** S R P SPILSBURY, B R ARMAN *c*.

LAWSHALL (All SS), *Suff*. R V Sinecure. **D** St E 10 **P** *Lord de Saumarez* **I** J D CUTHBERTSON *p-in-c*.

LAWTON or CHURCH LAWTON (All SS), *Chesh*. R. **D** Ches 11 **P** *R G Lawton Esq* **I** R SUTTON.

LAWTON MOOR (St Mich AA), *Gtr Man*. V. **D** Man 10 **P** *Bp* **I** M GRAHAM.

LAXFIELD (All SS), *Suff*. V. **D** St E 17 **P** *Simeon Trustees* **I** R A MARCHANT.

LAXTON, *Northants*.. **D** Pet 13 *See* Bulwick.

LAXTON or LEXINGTON (St Mich), *Notts*. V. **D** Southw 4 **P** *Dioc Bd of Patr* **I** R PALIN *p-in-c*.

LAXTON (St Pet) w Blacktoft (H Trin), *Humb*. V. **D** York *See* Howden, The.

LAYER-BRETON, *Essex*.. **D** Chelmsf *See* Birch, Great.

LAYER-DE-LA-HAYE, *Essex*. V. **D** Chelmsf 21 **P** *Bp* **I** E J SIBSON.

LAYER-MARNEY (St Mary Virg), *Essex*. R. **D** Chelmsf 21 **P** *Maj and Mrs Charrington* **I** G ARMSTRONG.

LAYHAM (St Andr) w Shelley (All SS), *Suff*. R. **D** St E 3 *See* Hadleigh.

LAYSTON, *Herts*.. **D** St Alb *See* Aspenden.

LAYTON (St Mark), *Lancs*. V. **D** Blackb 6 *See* Blackpool . **I** J B MYNORS .

LAZONBY (St Nich), *Cumb*. R. **D** Carl *See* Salkeld, Great.

LEA (St Chris), *Lancs*. V. **D** Blackb **P** *Bp* **I** K J PHILLIPS.

LEA, *Derbys*.. **D** Derby 17 *See* Dethick.

LEA (St Giles), *Wilts*. R. **D** Bris *See* Garsdon.

LEA (St Helen), *Lincs*. R. **D** Linc 2 **P** *Dioc Bd of Patr* **I** H J KNIGHT.

LEA, THE (St Jo Bapt), *Herefs*. R. **D** Heref *See* Weston-under-Penyard.

LEA HALL (St Richard), *Worcs*. V. **D** Birm 13 **P** *Bp* **I** A C GRIFFITHS.

LEA MARSTON (St Jo Bapt), *Warws*. V. **D** Birm 9 *See* Nether Whitacre.

LEADEN RODING w Aythorpe Roding (St Mary) and High Roding (All SS), *Essex*. R. **D** Chelmsf 23 **P** *Ld Chan Bp, and Ch S* **I** J H MAYOH.

LEADENHAM (St Swith) w Welbourn (St Chad), *Lincs*. R. **D** Linc 23 **P** *Lt-Col W Reeve and Hyndham Trustees* **I** (Vacant).

LEADGATE (St Ives), *Durham*. V. **D** Dur 7 **P** *Bp* **I** R ATTLEY.

LEAFIELD (St Mich AA), *Oxon*. V. **D** Ox 3 **P** *Bp* **I** P G SMITH.

LEAGRAVE, *Beds*.. **D** St Alb *See* Luton.

LEAKE (St Mary Virg) w Ch Ch *Lincs*. V. **D** Linc *See* Old Leake.

LEAKE (St Mary) w Over (St Mary) and Nether Silton (All SS) and Kepwick, *N Yorks*. V. **D** York **P** *Abp* **I** D W B MCCULLOCH.

LEAKE, EAST (St Mary Virg), *Notts*. R. **D** Southw 11 **P** *Bp* **I** D W S JAMES, J B PLUMPTRE *c*.

LEAKE, WEST (St Helena) w Ratcliffe-on-Soar (H Trin) and Kingston-on-Soar (St Wilfrid), *Notts*. R. **D** Southw 11 **P** *Ld Belper* **I** (Vacant).

LEAMINGTON HASTINGS (All SS) and Birdingbury, *Warws*. V. **D** Cov 6 **P** *Bp and Mrs Lodder (alt)* **I** G T HUGHES *p-in-c*.

LEAMINGTON PRIORS (All SS w St Alb Mart), *Warws*. V. **D** Cov 11 **P** *Bp* **I** I D CAMPBELL, M A MORRIS *c*, S MANN *hon c*.

(H Trin), V. **D** Cov 11 **P** *Bp* **I** M W MANSBRIDGE.

(St Jo Bapt), V. **D** Cov 11 **P** *Bp* **I** W H POULTNEY *c*.

(St Mark). **D** Cov 11 *See* Milverton, New (St Mark).

(St Mary), V. **D** Cov 11 **P** *CPS* **I** R J CLARKE.

(St Paul). **D** Cov 11 **P** *CPS* **I** A J M DOW.

LEASINGHAM (St Andr), *Lincs*. R. **D** Linc 22 **P** *Dioc Bd of Patr 1st turn, Marquess of Bris 2nd turn* **I** M J FEIT.

LEATHERHEAD (St Mary and St Nich w All SS), *Surrey*. V. **D** Guildf 10 **P** *D and C of Roch* **I** A D MORRIS, G NAZER *c*.

LEATHLEY (St Osw) w Farnley, *N Yorks*. R. **D** Bradf 5 **P** *Bp 3 turns, Maj Horton-Fawkes 1 turn* **I** (Vacant).

LEATON (H Trin) w Preston Gobalds, *Salop*. V. **D** Lich 27 **P** *Mrs C J Thompson* **I** M W TURNER.

LEAVELAND, *Kent*. R. **D** Cant 6 *See* Badlesmere.

LEAVENHEATH (St Matt), *Suff*. V. **D** St E 3 *See* Stoke-by-Nayland.

LEAVENING, *N Yorks*.. **D** York 3 *See* Burythorpe.

LEAVESDEN (All SS), *Herts*. V. **D** St alb 13 **P** *Bp* **I** M L LESITER, J E COTTER *c*, J W S NEWCOME *c*.

LECHLADE (St Lawr), *Glos*. V. **D** Glouc 14 **P** *Em Coll Cam* **I** M J PAGE.

LECK (St Pet), *Lancs*. V. **D** Blackb 13 **P** *Ld Kay-Shuttleworth* **I** J F FOSTER *p-in-c*.

LECKFORD, *Hants*.. **D** Win *See* Longstock.

LECKHAMPSTEAD (St Jas Ap), *Berks*. V. **D** Ox 14 *See* Brightwalton.

LECKHAMPSTEAD (St Mary Virg), *Bucks*. R. **D** Ox 23 *See* Buckingham N.

LECKHAMPTON (St Pet and St Paul), *Glos*. R. **D** Glouc 11 **P** *Bp* **I** G R H SMITH.

(St Phil and St Jas) w Cheltenham (St Jas), V. **D** Glouc 11 **P** *Bp* **I** D C NYE, A M LYNETT *c*.

LECONFIELD, *Humb*.. **D** York 11 *See* Lockington.

LEDBURY (St Mich AA) w Eastnor *Herefs*. R. **D** Heref 6 **P** *Bp and Hon Mrs Hervey-Bathurst* **I** C M OLDROYD.

LEDSHAM (All SS) w Fairburn (St Jas), *W Yorks*. V. **D** York 8 **P** *G H Wheler Esq* **I** D G COUPER.

LEE (St Matt), *Devon*. V. **D** Ex 15 *See* Ilfracombe.

LEE (St Marg), *Kent*. R. **D** S'wark 20 **P** *Ld Chan* **I** R C B BUTLER.

(Ch of Good Shepherd w St Pet), V. **D** S'wark 20 **P** *R of Lee* **I** O N EVERSON.

(St Aug Grove Park), V. **D** S'wark 20 **P** *Bp* **I** S C INGHAM *c*.

(St Mildred), V. **D** S'wark 20 **P** *Bp* **I** R S J SANGER.

LEE, *Hants*.. **D** Win 10 *See* Romsey.

LEE, THE (St Jo Bapt), *Bucks*. V. **D** Ox 30 **P** *Bp* **I** A PAICE *p-in-c*.

LEE BROCKHURST (St Pet), *Salop*. V. **D** Lich 27 **P** *Ld Barnard* **I** N MACGREGOR.

LEE-ON-THE-SOLENT (St Faith), *Hants*. V. **D** Portsm 1 **P** *Bp* **I** M S KENNING.

LEEBOTWOOD (St Mary) w Longnor (St Mary), *Salop*. V. **D** Heref 11 **P** *Dioc Bd of Patr* **I** (Vacant).

LEEDS (St Pet) w Quarry Hill and Sheepscar (St Thos w St Luke), *W Yorks*. V. **D** Ripon 6 **P** *Trustees* **I** H E CRICHLOW *chap*, K H STAPLETON *lect*.

(All H w St Simon) w Wrangthorn, V. **D** Ripon 5 **P** *Bp and Dioc Bd of Patr* **I** J B LANGDON.

(All SS w St Hilda and St Sav Cross Green, Richmond Hill), V. **D** Ripon 7 **P** *Bp* **I** A C BETTS, S W JONES *c*.

(All S Hook Mem w Ch of the H Name), V. **D** Ripon 5 **P** *V of Leeds* **I** A E SANDERS, R W ASPDEN *c*.

(Em Ch), V. **D** Ripon 5 **P** *Trustees* **I** A H OVERELL *c-in-c*.

(St Aid Bp Woodford Mem Ch), V. **D** Ripon 6 **P** *V of Leeds* **I** P O SANDERSON, J P GUTTERIDGE *c*, A P KAUNHOVEN *c*.

(St Cypr w St Jas), V. **D** Ripon 6 **P** *Bp* **I** M L WOODHALL.

(St Geo), V. **D** Ripon 5 **P** *Simeon Trustees and Bp* **I** M H BOTTING, P D G HOOPER *c*.

(St Marg), V. **D** Ripon 5 **P** *Trustees* **I** (Vacant).

(St Matt Little London), V. **D** Ripon 6 **P** *Simeon Trustees* **I** (Vacant).

(St Phil Osmondthorpe), V. **D** Ripon 7 **P** *Bp* **I** G R GREEN.

(St Wilfrid), V. **D** Ripon 6 **P** *Bp* **I** D BOOTH.

(Ch of Epiph Bp Burroughs Mem Gipton), V. **D** Ripon 6 **P** *Bp* **I** D T YOUNG.

(H Trin), V. **D** Ripon 6 **P** *Trustees* **I** A S GRIGGS.

(Ven Bede, Wyther), V. **D** Ripon 8 **P** *Bp* **I** C W MALPASS.

LEEDS (St Nich) w Broomfield (St Marg), *Kent*. V. **D** Cant 15 **P** *Abp* **I** A C BELL *p-in-c*.

LEEK (St Edw the Confessor w All SS and St Luke), *Staffs*. R. **D** Lich **P** *Bp* **I** J Y CROWE, G L HANCOX *team v*, D ORMSTON *team v*, D J PALMER *c*.

LEEK WOOTTON (All SS), *Warws*. V. **D** Cov 4 **P** *Ld Leigh* **I** C NETTLESHIP.

LEEMING (St Jo Bapt), *N Yorks*. V. **D** Ripon 2 **P** *V of Burneston* **I** N E DAVIES.

LEES, *Chesh*.. **D** Ches *See* Byley.

LEES (St Jo Bapt), *Gtr Man*.. **D** Man 15 *See* Hey.

LEES W Yorks. **D** Bradf 11 *See* Cross Roads.

LEESFIELD (St Thos Ap), *Gtr Man*. V. **D** Man 15 **P** *Crown and Bp* **I** A T P HARRISON.

LEGBOURNE (Little Cawthorpe, Muckton, Burwell and Walmsgate), *Lincs*. V. **D** Linc 12 **P** *Bp 2 turns, Viscount Chaplin 1 turn and Trustees 1 turn* **I** J F DOWMAN.

LEGHS, GREAT (St Mary), *Essex*.. **D** Chelmsf 11 *See* Leighs, Great.

LEGHS, LITTLE (St Jo Evang), *Essex*.. **D** Chelmsf 11 *See* Leighs, Little.

LEGSBY (St Thos), *Lincs*. V. **D** Linc 5 **P** *Bp* **I** A V SEARLE-BARNES.

LEICESTER (St Martin's Cathl Ch), *Leics*. V. **D** Leic 1 **P** *Bp* **I** VERY REV A C WARREN.

(All SS), V. **D** Leic 2 **P** *Bp* **I** (Vacant).

(All S), V. **D** Leic 2 **P** *Bp* **I** (Vacant).

(Ch Ch, Thurnby Lodge), V. **D** Leic 1 **P** *Bp* **I** E J C LOSEBY.

(Conv Distr of St Theodore of Cant Rushey Mead). **D** Leic 1 **P** *Bp* **I** J J LEONARD *p-in-c*.

(H Ap), V. **D** Leic 2 **P** *Trustees and Prin of Ridley Hall*

Cam **I** D G WILSON, N A BARKER *c*, A HETHERINGTON *c*, J B MYNORS *hon c*.
(H Trin and St Jo Div), V. **D** Leic 2 **P** *Peache Trustees* **I** J R KEELEY, P A H SIMMONDS *c*, F R ENTWISTLE *hon c*.
(Martyrs), V. **D** Leic 2 **P** *Bp and Prin of Ridley Hall Cam* **I** R N T MOORE *c-in-c*.
(St Aidan, New Parks), V. **D** Leic 2 **P** *Bp* **I** B R GLOVER.
(St Alb), V. **D** Leic 1 **P** *Bp* **I** K F MIDDLETON *p-in-c*.
(St Andr), V. **D** Leic *See* H Spirit **I** B BADGE.
(St Andr, Aylestone), R. **D** Leic 2 **P** *Bp* **I** S A JACKSON, J W MOTT *c*.
(St Anne), V. **D** Leic 2 **P** *Bp* **I** M WILSON.
(St Aug of Cant, Newfoundpool), V. **D** Leic 2 **P** *Bp* **I** P W J FOLKS.
(St Barn, New Humberstone), V. **D** Leic 1 **P** *Bp* **I** N H JIGNASU *p-in-c*.
(Par Distr of BEAUMONT LEYS). **D** Leic 2 **I** T S BYRON *min*.
(St Chad), V. **D** Leic 1 **P** *Bp* **I** J A SWAINE, K M DEAN-JONES *c*, R P TICKLE *c*.
(St Chris), V. **D** Leic 2 **P** *Bp* **I** N J POCOCK, N R BRALESFORD *c*.
(St Denys, Evington), V. **D** Leic 1 **P** *Bp* **I** C FINCH, P STREET *c*.
(St Eliz, Nether Hall), V. **D** Leic 1 **P** *Dioc Bd of Patr* **I** D V TREANOR *p-in-c*.
(St Gabr), V. **D** Leic 1 **P** *Bp* **I** R B HUNT.
(St Hugh, Eyres Monsell), V. **D** Leic 2 **P** *Bp* **I** J K MCCOLLOUGH, J M BROWN *c*.
(St Jas, Aylestone Park), V. **D** Leic 2 **P** *Bp* **I** G RICHARDSON.
(St Jas Greater), V. **D** Leic 2 **P** *Bp* **I** D N HOLE.
(St Jo Bapt, Knighton), V. **D** Leic 2 **P** *Bp* **I** P G P FARRELL.
(St Luke, Stocking Farm), V. **D** Leic 1 **P** *Bp* **I** P D A COLLINS, B D S FAIRBANK *c*.
(St Marg of Antioch), V. **D** Leic 2 **P** *Bp* **I** O S BENNETT.
(St Mary, Humberstone), V. **D** Leic 2 **P** *Dioc Bd of Patr* **I** D V TREANOR, M L DICKINSON *c*.
(St Mark), V. **D** Leic 1 **P** *Bp* **I** G HURST *p-in-c*.
(St Mary de Castro), V. **D** Leic 2 **P** *Bp* **I** (Vacant).
(St Mary Magd w St Guthlac, Knighton), V. **D** Leic 2 **P** *Bp* **I** H T P EVANS, K F CULVERWELL *c*, M J PENNY *c*.
(St Matt w St Geo), V. **D** Leic 1 **P** *Bp* **I** K F MIDDLETON, N J BURTON *c*.
(St Mich AA, Belgrave), V. **D** Leic 1 **P** *Bp* **I** K F MIDDLETON *p-in-c*.
(St Mich AA, Knighton), V. **D** Leic 2 **P** *Bp* **I** D C SAWYER.
(St Nich), V. **D** Leic 2 *See* H Spirit.
(St Paul), V. **D** Leic 2 **P** *Bp* **I** G W H SEALY.
(St Pet w St Hilda), V. **D** Leic 1 **P** *Bp* **I** (Vacant).
(St Pet, Belgrave), V. **D** Leic 1 **P** *Bp* **I** E K L QUINE, G H JEFFS *hon c*.
(St Pet, Braunstone), R. **D** Leic 17 **P** *Bp* **I** K NEWBON, R C ASHLEY *team v*.
(St Phil), V. **D** Leic 1 **P** *Trustees* **I** K H WAYNE, J H BELL *c*.
(St Sav), V. **D** Leic 1 **P** *Bp* **I** J M ANDERSON.
(St Steph, N Evington), V. **D** Leic 1 **P** *Bp* **I** I S C RICHARDS *p-in-c*.
LEIGH Wilts. **D** Bris *See* Ashton Keynes.
LEIGH (St Clem), *Essex*. R. **D** Chelmsf 13 **P** *Bp* **I** R C SMITH, S F FOSTER *c*.
(St Marg), V. **D** Chelmsf 13 **P** *Bp* **I** E C F STROUD, R A J BUCKINGHAM *c*.
(St Jas), V. **D** Chelmsf 13 **P** *Bp* **I** A CROSS.
(St Aid), V. **D** Chelmsf 13 **P** *Bp* **I** D F A SUTHERLAND.
LEIGH (All SS), *Staffs*. R. **D** Lich 20 **P** *Bp* **I** K R THACKER.
LEIGH (St Mary Virg), *Gtr Man*. V. **D** Man 6 **P** *Ld Lilford* **I** D A MUSTON, J J MARSDEN *c*.
(St Thos Bedford-Leigh), V. **D** Man 6 **P** *V of Leigh* **I** R H MARSHALL *c*.
(St Jo Evang), V. **D** Man 6 **P** *Crown and Bp* alt **I** J D WRIGHT.
(St Pet Westleigh), V. **D** Man 6 **P** *Bp Chan of Dio and V of Leigh* **I** D T N PARRY.
(St Paul, Westleigh), V. **D** Man 6 **P** *V of Leigh* **I** T D HARGREAVES-STEAD.
LEIGH (St Mary), *Kent*. V. **D** Roch 9 **P** *Trustees* **I** G C M MILES.
LEIGH (St Bart), *Surrey*. V. **D** S'wark 12 **P** *J Charrington Esq* **I** G C CUTCHER.
LEIGH (St Andr) w Batcombe and Chetnole (St Pet), *Dorset*.. **D** Sarum 7 *See* High Stoy.
LEIGH (St Edburga) w Bransford (St Jo Bapt), *Worcs*.. **D** Worc *See* Alfrick.
LEIGH DELAMERE (St Marg), *Wilts*.. **D** Bris *See* Stanton St Quintin.
LEIGH, HIGH (St Jo Evang), *Chesh*.. **D** Ches 12 *See* High Leigh.
LEIGH, LITTLE (St Mich AA), w Nether Whitley (St Luke), *Chesh*. V. **D** Ches **P** *V of Gt Budworth and Trustees of P G Greenall Esq* **I** M C WHITWELL.
LEIGH-ON-MENDIP (St Giles) w Stoke St Mich, *Somt*. V. **D** B & W 16a **P** *Miss A K S Lambton and V of Doulting* **I** (Vacant).
LEIGH PARK (St Francis), *Hants*. V. **D** Portsm 3 **P** *Bp* **I** P S G ROYLE, K P BIDGOOD *c*.
(St Clare Conv Distr). **D** Portsm 3 **P** *Bp* **I** (Vacant).
LEIGH, THE (St Cath), *Glos*. V. **D** Glouc 2 *See* Norton, Glos.
LEIGH WOODS (St Mary Virg), *Avon*. V. **D** Bris *See* Abbots Leigh.
LEIGHLAND, *Somt*.. **D** B & W 21 *See* Cleeve, Old.
LEIGHS, GREAT (St Mary), *Essex*. R. **D** Chelmsf 16 **P** *Linc Coll Ox* **I** S J BRYANT.
LEIGHS, LITTLE (St Jo Evang), *Essex*. R. **D** Chelmsf 16 **P** *Reformation Ch Trust* **I** S J BRYANT *c-in-c*.
LEIGHTERTON (St Andr), *Glos*. R. **D** Glouc 17 *See* Boxwell.
LEIGHTON (H Trin), *Powys*.. **D** Heref 13 *See* Trelystan.
LEIGHTON w Minshull Vernon (St Pet), *Chesh*.. **D** Ches 15 *See* Church Minshull.
LEIGHTON-BROMSWOLD (St Mary Virg), *Cambs*. V. **D** Ely 11 **P** *Bp* **I** G L NORTH.
LEIGHTON-BUZZARD (All SS w St Andr) w Egginton, Hockliffe and Billington, *Beds*. V. **D** St Alb 18 **P** *Bp* **I** P H WHITTAKER, P G BERRETT *c*, K ROBINSON *c*.
LEIGHTON-UNDER-THE-WREKIN (St Mary) w Eaton Constantine and Wroxeter, *Salop*. V. **D** Lich *See* Buildwas.
LEINTHALL EARLES (St Andr), *Herefs*.. **D** Heref *See* Aymestrey.
LEINTHALL STARKES (St Mary Magd), *Herefs*.. **D** Heref *See* Wigmore.
LEINTWARDINE (St Mary Magd) w Adforton (St Andr), *Herefs*.. **D** Heref 12 *See* Wigmore Abbey.
LEIRE (St Pet) w Ashby Perva and Dunton Bassett, *Leics*.. **D** Leic **P** *Balliol Coll Ox and Archd of Loughborough* **I** K H BILNEY.
LEISTON (St Marg) w Sizewell (St Nich), *Suff*. V. **D** St E 19 **P** *Haberdashers' Co* **I** J W DREW.
LELANT, ST UNY (St Uni), *Cornw*. V. **D** Truro 5 **P** *Bp* **I** (Vacant).
LEMINGTON, *Glos*. R. **D** Glouc 16 *See* Todenham.
LEMSFORD (St John), *Herts*. V. **D** St Alb 7 **P** *Lady Brocket* **I** R S INGAMELLS.
LENBOROUGH (Gawcott, Hillesden, Padbury and Adstock), *Bucks*. V. **D** Ox 23 **P** *Ch Ch Ox, Ld Chan and Univ of Cam (in turn)* **I** A F T NEWELL.
LENCHWICK, *Worcs*.. **D** Worc 3 *See* Norton.
LENHAM (St Mary) w Boughton-Malherbe (St Nich), *Kent*. V. **D** Cant 15 **P** *Visc Chilston and Ld Cornwallis* **I** R A SHEEKEY.
LENTON (St Pet), *Lincs*. V. **D** Linc 14 *See* Lavington.
LENTON (Sacred and Undivided Trin w Priory Ch of St Anthony), *Notts*. V. **D** Southw 14 **P** *CPAS* **I** D G WILLIAMS.
(St Barn Lenton Abbey), V. **D** Southw 14 **P** *CPAS* **I** H M KITCHEN *p-in-c*.
LEOMINSTER (St Pet and St Paul), *Herefs*. V. **D** Heref 7 **P** *Bp* **I** M W HOOPER, R NORTH *c*.
LEONARD STANLEY (St Swith), *Glos*. V. **D** Glouc 9 **P** *Mrs Hollings and Mrs Fisher* **I** G B J WHITE.
LEPPINGTON, *N Yorks*.. **D** York 7 *See* Scrayingham.
LEPTON (St Jo Evang), *W Yorks*. V. **D** Wakef 7 **P** *R of Kirkheaton* **I** D P LITTLE.
LESBURY (St Mary) w Alnmouth, *Northumb*. V. **D** Newc T 7 **P** *Newc T Dioc Soc* **I** J B RUTHERFORD.
LESNEWTH (St Mich), *Cornw*.. **D** Truro *See* Davidstow.
LESSINGHAM (All SS), *Norf*.. **D** Nor 9 *See* Hempstead.
LETCHWORTH (St Mich), *Herts*. R. **D** St Alb 9 **P** *Guild of All S* **I** R G DINNIS, N P MORRELL *c*.
(St Paul) w Willian, V. **D** St Alb 9 **P** *Bp* **I** P J PAVEY, N P MORRELL *c*.
LETCOMBE-REGIS (St Andr) w Letcombe-Basset, *Oxon*.. **D** Ox 19 *See* Ridgeway.
LETHERINGHAM, *Suff*.. **D** St E *See* Easton.
LETHERINGSETT (St Andr) w Bayfield (St Marg) w Glandford (St Martin), *Norf*. R. **D** Nor 24 **P** *Keble Coll Ox* **I** D P MAURICE.
LETTON (St Jo Bapt) w Staunton-on-Wye (St Mary Virg), Byford (St Jo Bapt), Mansel Gamage (St Giles), and Monnington-on-Wye (St Mary), *Herefs*. R. **D** Heref 5 **P** *Exors of Mrs Dew 1 turn, D and C of Ch Ch Ox 3 turns,*

Sir R Cotterell Bt 2 turns, Reps of Col Chester Master 1 turn I S C SNEYD P-IN-C OF NORTON CANON p-in-c.
LETTON, Norf.. D Nor See Cranworth.
LETWELL (St Pet), S Yorks. V. D Sheff 5 See Firbeck.
LEUSDEN (St Jo Bapt), Devon. V. D Ex See Widecombe-in-the-Moor.
LEVEN (H Trin) w Catwick (St Mich), Humb. R. D York P Simeon Trustees and Exors of Sir H M Strickland-Constable, Bt. (alt) I P E R HALL.
LEVEN VALLEY, (Haverthwaite St Anne, Finsthwaite St Pet, Staveley-in-Cartmell St Mary), Cumb. V. D Carl 14 P Bp, V of Colton and Mrs C M Chaplin I D R O GRANT.
LEVENS (St Jo Evang), Cumb. V. D Carl 17 P Trustees I A F J LOFTHOUSE.
LEVENSHULME (St Pet), Gtr Man. R. D Man 4 P Trustees I J V WARING, N SWAINSON c.
(St Andr), R. D Man 4 P Crown and Bp alt I J L CLEGG.
(St Mark) R. D Man 4 P Crown and Bp alt I G ARMSTEAD.
LEVER BRIDGE (St Steph and All Marts), Gtr Man. V. D Man 11 P Crown and Bp alt I D M DUNN.
LEVER, GREAT (St Simon and St Jude), Gtr Man.. D Man 11 See Bolton-le-Moors.
LEVER, GREAT (St Mich) w (St Bart), Gtr Man. R. D Man 14 P Bp and Trustees I J C MELLING.
LEVER, LITTLE (St Matt), Gtr Man. V. D Man 14 P V of Bolton I C H TELFORD, I C ANTHONY hon c.
LEVERINGTON (St Leon), Cambs. R. D Ely 20 P Bp I P H N COLLINS.
LEVERSTOCK GREEN (H Trin), Herts. V. D St Alb See Chambersbury.
LEVERTON (St Helena), Lincs. R. D Linc 20 P Ld Chan I A J F SHARP.
LEVERTON, NORTH (St Martin) and South Leverton (All SS), Notts. V. D Southw 5 P Bp I R AKERMAN.
LEVINGTON (St Pet), Suff.. D St E 2 See Nacton.
LEVISHAM (St Jo Bapt) w Lockton (St Andr), N Yorks. R. D York 24 P Abp I (Vacant).
LEW-TRENCHARD (St Pet) w Thrushelton (St Geo), Devon. R. D Ex See Marystowe.
LEWANNICK (St Martin), Cornw. V. D Truro 11 See North Hill.
LEWCOMBE, Dorset.. D Sarum 4 See Chelborough, East.
LEWES (All SS, St Anne, St Mich and St Thos), E Sussex. R. D Chich 15 P Ld Chan 3 turns, Patr Bd 1 turn I J G P HABGOOD, P W WRIGHT team v, D BASTIDE c, G LINNEGAR c.
(St Jo Bapt-sub-Castro), R. D Chich 15 P Bp I R M BELL.
(St Jo Bapt Southover), R. D Chich 15 P CPAS I P J J MARKBY.
LEWISHAM (St Mary Virg), Kent. V. D S'wark 20 P Earl of Dartmouth I D GARLICK, E G R ASTILL c, P W TIERNAN c.
(St Steph), V. D S'wark 20 P Keble Coll Ox I G KIRK, F D GARDOM hon c.
LEWKNOR (St Marg), Oxon. V. D Ox See Tetsworth.
LEWSEY, Beds. V. D St Alb See Luton.
LEXDEN (St Leon), Essex. R. D Chelmsf 21 P D P Papillon Esq I P A MARSHALL, H HEATH c, J WATSON c.
LEXHAM, EAST (St Andr), w Lexham, West (St Nich), Norf. R. D Nor 20 See Litcham.
LEYBOURNE (St Pet and St Paul), Kent. R. D Roch 6 P Sir D Hawley Bt I R J R LEA p-in-c, A J POWELL c, J POWELL c.
LEYBURN (St Matt) w Bellerby (St Jo Evang), N Yorks. V. D Ripon 2 P Ld Bolton and Mrs M Scragg alt I D F JOHNSON, A S BROWN c.
LEYLAND (St Andr), Lancs. V. D Blackb 6 P Trustees I K BROADHURST, K LOGAN c.
(St Ambrose), V. D Blackb 6 P V of Leyland I A F RANSON.
(St Jas Ap), V. D Blackb 6 P Sir Henry Farington Bt I R HOLLINGHURST.
LEYSDOWN (St Clem) w Harty (St Thos Ap), Kent. V. D Cant 13 See East Church.
LEYSTERS (St Andr), Herefs. V. D Heref 7 See Bockleton.
LEYTON (St Mary Virg w St Edw), Essex. V. D Chelmsf 8 P Simeon Trustees I N J F BINGHAM, P A O'GORMAN c.
(All SS), V. D Chelmsf 8 P V of Leyton I D S LOCK.
(Ch Ch), V. D Chelmsf 8 P Church Trust Fund Trust I (Vacant).
(Em), V. D Chelmsf 8 P Bp I (Vacant).
(St Cath). D Chelmsf 8 P V of Leyton I J M V DRUMMOND.
(St Luke, Temple Mills), V. D Chelmsf 8 P Bp I (Vacant).
(St Paul), V. D Chelmsf 8 P V of Leyton I P G KING.
LEYTONSTONE (St Jo Bapt), Essex. V. D Chelmsf 8 P Bp I C T EDMONDSON.
(St Andr), V. D Chelmsf 8 P Bp I D MOTTERSHEAD.
(St Marg) w Wanstead Slip (St Columba), V. D Chelmsf 8 P Bp I R N ROWE.
LEZANT (St Briochus), Cornw. R. D Truro 11 P Bp I J E COX p-in-c.
LEZIATE (All SS), Norf. R. D Nor 25 See Ashwicken.
LICHBOROUGH (St Martin) w Maidford (St Pet and St Paul) and Farthingstone (St Mary Virg), Northants. R. D Pet 2 P Bp, Capt R Grant-Renwick and Melan Miss (alt) I J A ELLIS.
LICHFIELD (St Chad), Staffs. R. D Lich P D and C of Lich I J A WIDDAS, B HARRIS c, A F POPPLEWELL c, P J RAINSFORD c.
(Ch Ch), V. D Lich 2 P Bp I I W WILLIAMS, I C CONWAY hon c.
(St John's Hosp). D Lich 2 P Bp I H I CLUTTERBUCK master.
(St Mich w St Mary), R. D Lich P D & C of Lich I C M SAVAGE, J PATTEN c.
LICKEY, THE (H Trin) w Blackwell (St Cath), Worcs. V. D Birm 4 P V of Bromsgrove I P D CHIPPENDALE, R W E SPENCER c.
LIDDINGTON, Wilts.. D Bris 8 See Lyddington.
LIDGET GREEN (St Wilfrid), W Yorks. V. D Bradf 2 P Bp I D J NUDDS, L F CRAWLEY c.
LIDLINGTON (St Marg), Beds. V. D St Alb See Marston Morteyne.
LIFTON (St Mary), Devon. R. D Ex 22 P Countess de Wolovey, Bp and M W Kelly Esq I A W H DICK p-in-c.
LIGHTBOWNE (St Luke), Gtr Man. R. D Man 7 P D and C of Man I A J L LEWIS.
LIGHTCLIFFE (St Matt), W Yorks. V. D Wakef 2 P V of Halifax I D WILDING.
LIGHTHORNE (St Laur) w Chesterton (St Giles) and Moreton Morrell (H Cross) w Newbold Pacey (St Geo Mart), Warws. R. D Cov 8 P Ld Willoughby de Broke 2 turns, Col J Little 1 turn, Qu Coll Ox 1 turn I T L F MANDER, S J WARE c.
LIGHTWATER (All SS), Surrey. V. D Guildf 5a P Bp and Ld Chan (alt) I A R KENNEDY.
LILBOURNE (All SS), Northants. V. D Pet 6 See Yelvertoft.
LILLESHALL (St Mich AA), Salop. V. D Lich 21 P Bp I G K SMITH.
LILLEY, Herts.. D St Alb See Offley.
LILLINGSTONE-DAYRELL (St Nich, Bp of Myra) w Lovell (St Nich), Bucks. R. D Ox 23 See Buckingham N.
LILLINGSTONE LOVELL (Assumption BVM), Bucks.. D Ox 23 See Buckingham N.
LILLINGTON (St Martin), Dorset. R. D Sarum 7 See Sherborne.
LILLINGTON (St Mary Magd), Warws. V. D Cov 11 P Bp I D J PHILLPOT, P G EDWARDS c.
LILLIPUT (H Angels), Dorset.. D Sarum 14 P Bp I A B WATKINS-JONES p-in-c, J D BARNES c.
LILSTOCK, Somt.. D B & W See Kilton.
LIMBER MAGNA (St Pet), Lincs. V. D Linc 6 See Brocklesby.
LIMBURY (St Aug), Beds. V. D St Alb 20 P Bp I J M SCHOFIELD.
LIMEHOUSE (St Anne w St Pet), Lon. R. D Lon 4 P BNC Ox I C M IDLE.
LIMINGTON (St Mary Virg), Somt. R. D B & W 10 See Ilchester.
LIMPENHOE, Norf.. D Nor See Cantley.
LIMPLEY STOKE (St Mary), Avon.. D B & W 13 See Freshford.
LIMPSFIELD (St Pet w St Andr), w Titsey Surrey. R. D S'wark 10 P R Leveson-Gower I J N HIGGINS, B C CASTLE c, T G LEARY c, B C C COMPTON hon c.
LINBY (St Mich) w Papplewick (St Jas), Notts. R. D Southw 12 P C W Chadburn Esq I P M GOLDTHORPE p-in-c.
LINCOLN (All SS), V. D Linc 15 P Bp I (Vacant).
(St Botolph w St Kath and All SS), V. D Linc 15 P Bp I P C HAWKER.
(St Faith w St Martin), V. D Linc 15 P Bp I D L STEVENS, D G KENNEDY c.
(St Giles), V. D Linc 15 P Bp I E B BARLOW.
(St Jo Bapt Ermine), V. D Linc 15 P Bp I J C ALLEN.
(St Mary le Wigford w St Mark), V. D Linc 15 P Bp I M A M ST JOHN-CHANNELL p-in-c.
(St Nich) w (St John) Newport, V. D Linc 15 P Bp and D and C of Linc alt I P CLARKE, S GOLDSMITH c.
(St Pet-at-Gowts w St Andr), V. D Linc 15 P Bp I D J BAKER.
(St Swith), V. D Linc 15 P Bp I J W DENNIS.
MINSTER (St Mich-on-the-Mount, St Mary Magd w St Paul, St Pet-in-Eastgate w St Marg), R. D Linc 15 P Archd of Linc, D and C of Linc and Bp (in turn)

I J B BAYLEY, D E SMITH *c*.
LINDAL-IN-FURNESS (St Pet) w Marton, *Cumb*. V. D Carl 15 P *Trustees* I D R JACKSON.
LINDALE-IN-CARTMEL (St Paul) w Field Broughton (St Pet), *Cumb*. V. D Carl 14 P *Bp and Dioc Bd of Patr* I A J WILKIE.
LINDFIELD (All SS), *W Sussex*. V. D Chich 11 P *Ch S Trust* I H B S MORLEY.
LINDLEY (St Steph) w Quarmby, *W Yorks*. V. D Wakef 4 P *V of Huddersfield* I S COATHAM.
LINDOW (St Jo Evang), *Chesh*. V. D Ches 12 P *Bp* I J TABERN.
LINDRIDGE (St Lawr), *Worcs*. V. D Worc 12 P *D and C of Worc* I P C AUDSLEY.
LINDSELL (St Mary Virg), *Essex*. V. D Chelmsf 23 *See* Stebbing.
LINDSEY, *Suff*. V. D St E 3 *See* Kersey.
LINFORD, GREAT (St Andr), *Bucks*. R. D Ox 26 *See* Stantonbury.
LINFORD, LITTLE (St Leon), *Bucks*. V. D Ox 28 *See* Haversham.
LINGEN (St Mich AA), *Herefs*. V. D Heref 5 P *Bp* I R A PERRY *p-in-c*.
LINGFIELD (St Pet and St Paul), *Surrey*. V. D S'wark 10 P *Bp* I A B RAMSAY, F KENDALL *hon c*.
LINGWOOD (St Pet), *Norf*.. D Nor *See* Burlingham.
LINKENHOLT (St Pet), *Hants*. R. D Win 2 *See* Vernham Dean.
LINKINHORNE (St Melori), *Cornw*. V. D Truro 13 P *Rev R Hitchens* I M B GEACH.
LINLEY (St Leon) w Willey and Barrow, *Salop*. R. D Heref 14 P *Ld Forester* I W W LUCAS *p-in-c*.
LINSLADE (St Barn w St Mary), *Bucks*. V. D Ox 27 P *Bp* I R G M RUSSELL.
LINSTEAD (St Marg of Antioch) w Chediston and Halesworth (St Mary), *Suff*. R. D St E *See* Halesworth.
LINTHORPE, *Cleve*.. D York 22 *See* Middlesbrough.
LINTHWAITE (Ch Ch), *W Yorks*. V. D Wakef 6 P *V of Almondbury* I C H COON.
LINTON (St Mary Virg), *Cambs*. V. D Ely 4 P *Bp* I E J COTGROVE, M W B O'LOUGHLIN *c*.
LINTON (Ch Ch), *Derby*. V. D Derby 16 *See* Church Gresley.
LINTON (St Mary Virg) w Upton Bishop (St Jo Bapt) and Aston-Ingham, *Herefs*. R. D Heref P *St Jo Coll Ox, Col E D L Whatley and D and C of Heref in turn* I D A TIPPER.
LINTON (St Nich) w Hunton (St Mary), *Kent*. R. D Roch 6 P *Abp of Cant and Ld Cornwallis* I D G SHERRIFF.
LINTON-IN-CRAVEN (St Mich) w Hebden (St Pet), *N Yorks*. R. D Bradf 10 P *D and C of Ripon* I G KNIGHT, T E WOOD *c*.
LINWOOD (St Cornelius), *Lincs*. R. D Linc 5 P *MMT* I A V SEARLE-BARNES.
LIPHOOK, *Hants*.. D Portsm 4 *See* Bramshott.
LISCARD (St Mary w St Columba), *Mer*. V. D Ches 7 P *Bp* I L H MAYES, J E NICE *c*.
(St Thos), V. D Ches *See* Wallasey.
LISKEARD (St Martin) w St Keyne (St Kayna) and St Pinnock, *Cornw*. V. D Truro 13 P *Patr Trust* I D H P DAVEY, S COFFIN *c*, W J F COX *c*.
LISS (St Pet and St Mary Virg), *Hants*.. D Portsm *See* Lyss.
LISSETT (St Jas of Compostella), *Humb*. R. D York 14 *See* Beeford.
LISSINGTON (St Jo Bapt) w Holton-le-Beckering (All SS), *Lincs*. V. D Linc 5 P *Dioc Bd of Patr and D and C of York* alt I A G D SHEARWOOD.
LISSON GROVE (St Paul).. D Lon 25 *See* St Marylebone.
LISTON, *Essex*. R. D Chelmsf 18 *See* Foxearth.
LITCHAM (All SS) w Kempston (St Paul) and E and W Lexham, *Norf*. R. D Nor 22 P *Bp 2 turns Exors of H Olesen 1 turn W R B Foster Esq 2 turns* I D J MUNT.
LITCHFIELD (St Jas L), *Hants*. R. D Win 5 *See* Whitchurch w Tufton.
LITHERLAND or ORRELL HEY (St Phil), *Mer*. V. D Liv 1 P *Five Trustees* I G D TAYLOR, S D BESSANT *c*.
(St Andr), V. D Liv 1 P *Bp* I (Vacant).
(St John and St Jas), V. D Liv 1 P *CPAS* I D V ROUCH.
(St Paul, Hatton Hill). D Liv 1 P *Bp* I J M COURTIE.
LITLINGTON (St Kath) w Abington Pigotts (St Mich AA), *Cambs*. V (*See Shingay Group*). D Ely 8 P *M D de Courcy-Ireland Esq and Bp (alt)* I (Vacant).
LITLINGTON w West Dean, *E Sussex*. R. D Chich 15 P *R C Brown Esq and Duke of Devonshire* I (Vacant).
LITTLE DRAYTON (Ch Ch), *Salop*. V. D Lich 23 P *V of Market Drayton* I J O DAVIES.
LITTLE EATON (St Paul), *Derbys*. V. D Derby 12 P *V of St Alkmund, Derby* I P LYNE *p-in-c*.
LITTLE HEATH (Ch Ch), *Herts*. V. D St Alb P *CPS* I J SCHILD.
LITTLE HEMPSTON (St Jo Bapt), *Devon*.. D Ex 13 *See* Hempston, Little.
LITTLE HULTON (St Jo Bapt), *Gtr Man*. V. D Man 14 P *Bp* I K WOOD.
LITTLE TORRINGTON (St Giles), *Devon*.. D Ex 20 *See* Torrington, Little.
LITTLEBOROUGH (H Trin), *Gtr Man*. V. D Man 17 P *V of Rochdale* I J B PETTIFER.
LITTLEBOROUGH, *Notts*. V. D Southw 5 *See* Sturton-le-Steeple.
LITTLEBOURNE (St Vinc Spanish D and Mart), *Kent*. V. D Cant 1 P *D and C of Cant* I D B STEVEN.
LITTLEBURY (H Trin), *Essex*.. D Chelmsf 27 *See* Saffron Walden.
LITTLEDEAN (St Ethelbert), *Glos*. R. D Glouc 7 P *CPS* I M BRAMLEY-MOORE *p-in-c*.
LITTLEHAM (St Swith), *Devon*. R. D Ex 17 P *Trustees* I P V SIMPSON *p-in-c*.
LITTLEHAM (St Marg w St Andr) -cum- Exmouth (H Trin w St Andr and St Sav), *Devon*. R. D Ex 1 P *D and C of Ex* I R T URWIN, F A R MINAY *team v*, G F WATTS *team v*, K H SHAFEE *c*, M VINCER *c*.
LITTLEHAMPTON (St Mary Virg), *W Sussex*. V. D Chich 1 P *Bp* I D W HEWITT, L R D RYDER *c*.
(St Jas), V. D Chich 1 P *Bp* I D W HEWITT *p-in-c*, L R D RYDER *c*.
LITTLEHEMPSTON (St Jo Bapt), *Devon*.. D Ex *See* Broadhempston.
LITTLEMORE (St Nich), *Oxon*. V. D Ox 4 P *Or Coll Ox* I D G NICHOLLS *p-in-c*.
LITTLEOVER (St Pet), *Derbys*. V. D Derby 11 P *PCC* I D E WILLS, R T B RODGERS *c*, A R VIGARS *c*.
LITTLEPORT (St Geo) w Little Ouse (St John) and Littleport (St Matt), *Norf* and *Cambs*. V. D Ely 15 P *Bp* I J H MARTIN *p-in-c*, R H ROLLETT *c*.
LITTLETHORPE (St Mich AA), *N Yorks*.. D Ripon 3 *See* Ripon.
LITTLETON (St Cath), *Hants*. R. D Win 12 *See* Crawley.
LITTLETON (St Mary Magd), *Gtr Lon*. R. D Lon 13 P *Mrs C Harrison* I R J B DAKIN *c-in-c*.
LITTLETON-DREW (All SS), *Wilts*.. D Bris *See* Nettleton.
LITTLETON, HIGH (H Trin), *Somt*. V. D B & W 15 P *Hyndman Trustees* I M G PROSSER.
LITTLETON-ON-SEVERN (St Mary de Malmesbury) w Elberton (St John), *Avon*. R. D Bris 6 P *Bp* I M A PAICE *p-in-c*.
LITTLETON, SOUTH (St Mich), w North (St Nich) and Middle, *Worcs*.. D Worc 1 *See* Cleeve Prior.
LITTLETON, WEST, *Avon*.. D Bris 8 *See* Tormarton.
LITTLEWICK (St Jo Evang), *Berks*. V. D Ox 13 *See* Knowl Hill.
LITTLEWORTH (H Ascen), *Oxon*. V. D Ox 17 P *Or Coll Ox* I E B WOOD *p-in-c*.
LITTON (St Mary Virg), *Somt*.. D B & W *See* Chewton Mendip.
LITTON CHENEY (St Mary), *Dorset*. R. D Sarum *See* Bride Valley.
LIVERMERE, GREAT (St Pet), *Suff*. R. D St E *See* Ingham.
LIVERMERE, LITTLE, *Suff*.. D St E *See* Ampton.
LIVERPOOL (Our Lady and St Nich w St Anne), *Mer*. R. D Liv 3 P *Sir W Gladstone* I D C GRAY, R J ROGERS *c*, E J WATSON *c*, R T NELSON *hon c*.
(All S Springwood), V. D Liv 2 P *Crown* I G G AMEY, R R EARNSHAW *c*.
(St Anne, Stanley), V. D Liv 6 P *R of W Derby* I A L TAYLOR, P M FREEMAN *c*.
(St Bride) w (St Sav), V. D Liv 3 P *Trustees* I R E DICKINSON *team v*.
(St Jo Div Fairfield) V. D Liv 6 P *Trustees* I A E WELLS.
(St Jude Cantril Farm). D Liv 6 I N J EDWARDS, S F BOULD *c*.
(St Mich Upper Pitt Street), V. D Liv 3 P *Hyndman Trustees* I A SCAIFE *team v*.
(St Paul, Stoneycroft), V. D Liv 6 P *St Chad's Coll Dur* I B J FORSTER, C H WILLIAMS *c*.
(St Phil w St D), V. D Liv 6 P *Bp* I H H FORRESTER.
(St Steph Mart Edgehill w St Cath Abercromby Square), V. D Liv 3 P *St Chad's Coll Dur* I D H MCKITTRICK, E W PUGH *hon c*.
(St Frideswyde Thornton), V. D Liv 1 P *Bp* I C RENWICK.
See also WEST DERBY, EDGE HILL, EVERTON, KIRKDALE, MOSSLEY HILL, TOXTETH, TOXTETH PARK, AND WALTON-ON-THE-HILL..

LIVERSEDGE (Ch Ch), *W Yorks.* V. **D** Wakef 9 **P** *V of Birstall* **I** L H WOOD.
LIVERTON (St Martin, formerly St Mich), *Cleve.* V. **D** York 19 *See* Easington.
LIVESEY (St Andr), *Lancs..* **D** Blackb 2 *See* Blackburn.
LLANCILLO, *Herefs..* **D** Heref *See* Rowlestone.
LLANDINABO, *Herefs..* **D** Heref 4 *See* Birch, Much.
LLANFAIR-WATERDINE (St Mary), *Radnors* w Stowe (St Mich), *Salop..* **D** Heref 10 *See* Bucknell.
LLANGARRON (St Deinst) w Llangrove (or Longrove) (Ch Ch), *Herefs.* V. **D** Heref 8 **P** *D and C of Heref and Dioc Bd of Patr* **I** T F HORSINGTON *p-in-c.*
LLANGUA, *Gwent..* **D** Heref *See* Kentchurch.
LLANROTHAL (St Jo Bapt), *Herefs.* R. **D** Heref 8 *See* Welsh Newton.
LLANVEYNOE, *Herefs..* **D** Heref *See* Clodock.
LLANWARNE, *Herefs..* **D** heref 4 *See* Birch, Much.
LLANYBLODWEL (St Mich), *Salop.* V. **D** Lich 24 **P** *Bp* **I** H E BRISCOE.
LLANYMYNECH (St Agatha), *Salop.* R. **D** Lich 24 **P** *Bp* **I** T VILLIERS.
LOAD ST MARY or LONG LOAD (Ch Ch), *Somt.* V. **D** B & W 10 *See* Sutton, Long.
LOCKERLEY (St Jo Evang) and East Dean w Tytherley, East (St Pet) and West (St Pet), *Hants.* V. **D** Win 10 **P** *H Dalgety Esq 2 turns Dioc Bd of Patr 1 turn* **I** J L H PAGE, L C COLLIER *c.*
LOCKING (St Aug), *Avon.* V. **D** B & W 3 **P** *MMT* **I** J H MARDON.
LOCKINGE, (All SS), w Lockinge, West, *Oxon..* **D** Ox 19 *See* Wantage Downs.
LOCKINGTON (St Nich) w Hemington, *Leics.* V. **D** Leic 10 **P** *Exors of J Curzon Esq* **I** R N EVERETT *p-in-c.*
LOCKINGTON (St Mary Virg) and Lund (All SS) and Scorborough (St Leon) w Leconfield (St Cath), *Humb.* R. **D** York 11 **P** *Abp* **I** (Vacant).
LOCKLEAZE (St Mary Magd w St Francis), *Avon.* V. **D** Bris 4 **P** *Bp* **I** T D BARR.
LOCKS HEATH (St Jo Bapt), *Hants.* V. **D** Portsm 1 **P** *Bp* **I** N CHATFIELD, M J SHEFFIELD *c.*
LOCKTON, *N Yorks..* **D** York 24 *See* Levisham.
LOCKWOOD (Em Ch), *W Yorks.* R. **D** Wakef 5 **P** *V of Almondbury* **I** N L BRADBURY *c.*
LODDINGTON (St Mich AA), *Leics.* V. **D** Leic 8 **P** *Bp* **I** A T GREEN *c-in-c.*
LODDINGTON (St Leon w St Andr) w Cransley (St Andr), *Northants.* R. **D** Pet 8 **P** *Ld Chan and Bp* alt **I** (Vacant).
LODDISWELL, *Devon..* **D** Ex *See* Woodleigh.
LODDON (H Trin) w Sisland, *Norf.* V. **D** Nor 14 **P** *Bp 3 turns, E B G Gilbert Esq 1 turn* **I** P E GREEN.
LODE (St Jas), *Cambs.* V. **D** Ely 6 **P** *Bp* **I** M MAKOWER *c-in-c.*
LODERS (St Mary Magd), *Dorset.* V. **D** Sarum 2 **P** *Mrs P M G Laskey and Ld Chan* alt **I** O L WILLMOTT.
LODGE, THE, or WESTON RHYN (St John), *Salop.* V. **D** Lich 24 **P** *Bp* **I** J DURNELL.
LODSWORTH (St Pet), *W Sussex.* V. **D** Chich *See* Lurgashall.
LOFTHOUSE (Ch Ch), *N Yorks.* V. **D** Ripon 7 *See* Rothwell.
LOFTUS-IN-CLEVELAND (St Leon), *Cleve.* R. **D** York 19 **P** *Ld Chan* **I** J W THEOBALD.
LOIS-WEEDON (St Mary Virg and St Pet), *Northants.* V. **D** Pet 2 *See* Weedon Lois.
LOLWORTH (All SS), *Cambs.* R. **D** Ely 5 **P** *S for Maint of Faith* **I** J H JONES *p-in-c.*
LONDESBOROUGH (All SS), *Humb.* R. **D** York 10 **P** *Dr R F Ashwin* **I** J S SELLER.
LONDON, CITY OF:.
GUILD CHURCHES.
(All H Lon Wall). **D** Lon 1 **P** *Ld Chan* **I** A J TANNER *p-in-c,* M J BEECH *c.*
(St Andr Holborn). **D** Lon 1 **P** *Bp* **I** R E D SHARPLEY, K W BREED *c.*
(St Benet, Welsh Ch). **D** Lon 1 **P** *Bp* **I** T J THOMAS.
(St Botolph-without-Aldersgate). **D** Lon 1 **P** *Bp* **I** P S BURNETT *c.*
(St Dunstan-in-the-West). **D** Lon 1 **P** *Abp of Cant* **I** A T J SALTER *p-in-c.*
(St Ethelburga within Bishopsgate). **D** Lon 1 **P** *Bp* **I** A J TANNER *p-in-c.*
(St Kath Cree). **D** Lon 1 **P** *Bp* **I** (Vacant).
(St Lawr Jewry). **D** Lon 1 **P** *City Corp* **I** B A WATSON, R S O'BRIEN *c.*
(St Marg Pattens). **D** Lon 1 **P** *L Chan* **I** G HUELIN.
(St Martin Ludgate). **D** Lon 1 **P** *D and C of St Paul's* **I** P J E LILLINGSTON.
(St Mary Abchurch). **D** Lon 1 **P** *CCC Cam* **I** E G MOORE.
(St Mary Aldermary). **D** Lon 1 **P** *Ld Chan and HM the Queen* **I** H RILEY *c-in-c.*
(St Mary Woolnoth). **D** Lon 1 **P** *HM the Queen* **I** G C HARDING.
(St Mich Paternoster Royal). **D** Lon 1 **P** *(Missions to Seamen Chapel)* **I** W J D DOWN *chap.*
(St Nich Cole Abbey). **D** Lon 1 **P** *Abp of Cant* **I** (Vacant).
PARISH CHURCHES.
(All H, Barking-by-the-Tower [Toc H Ch] w St Dunstan-in-the-East), V. **D** Lon 1 **P** *Abp of Cant* **I** P DELANEY.
(St Andr-by-the-Wardrobe w St Anne, Blackfriars), R. **D** Lon 1 **P** *PCC 1 turn, Mercers' Co 2 turns, Eton Coll 1 turn* **I** F P COLEMAN, A C WINTER *c.*
(St Andr Undershaft w St Mary Axe), R. **D** Lon 1 *See* St Helen, Bishopsgate.
(St Bart L in St Bart's Hosp), V. **D** Lon 1 **P** *St Bart's Hosp* **I** R H ARNOLD.
(St Bart Gt, Smithfield), R. **D** Lon 1 **P** *D and C of Westmr* **I** A W S BROWN.
(St Botolph-without-Bishopsgate), R. **D** Lon 1 **P** *D and C of St Paul's* **I** A J TANNER, C C HARRISON *hon c.*
(St Botolph, Aldgate w H Trin Minories), V. **D** Lon 1 **P** *Bp* **I** M A JOHNSON, G H STEVENS *hon c.*
(St Bride, Fleet Street w Bridewell and H Trin, Gough Square), R. **D** Lon 1 **P** *D and C of Westmr* **I** D D L MORGAN, W D BOULTON *c,* J M H MORRIS *hon c.*
(St Clem, Eastcheap w St Martin, Orgar), R. **D** Lon 1 **P** *D and C of St Paul's* **I** H FEARN.
(St Edm K w St Nich, Acons; All H, Lombard Street; St Benet, Gracechurch; St Leon, Eastcheap and St Dionis, Backchurch), R. **D** Lon 1 **P** *Abp, D and C of Cant; and Bp of Lon* **I** H R G COOKE *p-in-c.*
(St Giles, Cripplegate w St Bart, Moor Lane; St Alphage, London Wall; St Luke, Old Street; St Mary, Charterhouse and St Paul, Clerkenwell), R. **D** Lon 1 **P** *D and C of St Paul's* **I** E L B C ROGERS, F M ANDERTON *c.*
(St Helen, Bishopsgate w St Andr Undershaft and St Martin Outwich and St Mary Axe), R. **D** Lon 1 **P** *Merchant Taylors' Co* **I** R C LUCAS, J K SPENCE *c.*
(St Jas, Garlickhithe w St Mich, Queenhithe and H Trin-the-Less, Garlick Hill), R. **D** Lon 1 **P** *D and C of St Paul's* **I** D W C MOSSMAN.
(St Magnus Mart w St Marg, New Fish Street and St Mich, Crooked Lane), R. **D** Lon 1 **P** *Dioc Bd of Patr* **I** A J C B GILL.
(St Marg Lothbury w St Steph, Coleman Street; St Chris-le-Stocks; St Bart-by-the-Exchange; St Olave, Old Jewry; St Martin, Pomeroy; St Mildred, Poultry and St Mary, Colechurch), R. **D** Lon 1 **P** *Simeon Trustees* **I** H J SMITH.
(St Mary-at-Hill w St Andr Hubbard; St Geo, Botolph Lane and St Botolph, Billingsgate), R. **D** Lon 1 **P** *Ball Coll Ox 2 turns, PCC 1 turn, Abp of Cant 1 turn* **I** B A C KIRK-DUNCAN.
(St Mary-le-Bow w St Pancras, Soper Lane; All H, Honey Lane; All H, Bread Street; St Jo Evang, Watling Street; St Aug w St Faith; St Mildred, Bread Street and St Marg Moyses), R. **D** Lon 1 **P** *Grocers' Co 1 turn, Abp 2 turns* **I** G E HUDSON.
(St Mich Cornhill w St Pet-le-Poer and St Benet Fink), R. **D** Lon 1 **P** *Drapers' Co* **I** J E SCOTT *p-in-c.*
(St Olave, Hart Street and All H, Staining w St Cath, Coleman), R. **D** Lon 1 **P** *Trustees* **I** L E M CLAXTON.
(St Pet-on-Cornhill), R. **D** Lon 1 **P** *City Corp* **I** A J N COOK, J H L CROSS *c.*
(St Sepulchre, Holborn Viaduct w Ch Ch, Greyfriars and St Leon, Foster Lane), R. **D** Lon 1 **P** *St Jo Coll Ox* **I** A W S BROWN.
(St Steph, Walbrook w St Swith, London Stone; St Benet, Sherehog; St Mary, Bothaw and St Laur, Pountney), R. **D** Lon 1 **P** *Grocers' Co and Magd Coll Cam* **I** E C VARAH, J G C ELDRID *c.*
(St Vedast, Foster Lane w St Mich-le-Querne; St Matt, Friday Street; St Pet Cheap; St Alb, Wood Street; St Olave, Silver Street; St Mich, Wood Street; St Mary, Staining; St Anne and St Agnes, Gresham Street; and St John Zachary), R. **D** Lon 1 **P** *D and C of St Paul's* **I** G A FFRENCH-BEYTAGH, G A REDDINGTON *c.*
See also CHARTERHOUSE, FINSBURY, HOLBORN, AND SPITALFIELDS..
LONDON DOCKS (St Pet w St John, Wapping), R. **D** Lon 4 **P** *Bp* **I** M J FOIZEY.
LONDON FIELDS (St Mich AA),. **D** Lon 2 *See* Hackney, South.
LONDONDERRY (St Mark), *W Midl.* V. **D** Birm 6 **P** *Bp* **I** F B SALTER.
LONDONTHORPE (St Jo Bapt), *Lincs..* **D** Linc 19 *See* Grantham.

LONG ASHTON (All SS), *Avon*. V. **D** B & W 16 **P** *Bp* **I** I F WESTMACOTT.
LONG CROSS (Ch Ch), *Surrey*. V. **D** Guildf 7 **P** *Bp* **I** RT REV ST J S PIKE.
LONG DITTON (St Mary), *Surrey*. R. **D** S'wark 11 **P** *Bp* **I** C W PRITCHARD.
LONG EATON (St Lawr w St Jas), *Derbys*. V. **D** Derby 13 **P** *Bp* **I** G M KNOX.
(St John), V. **D** Derby 13 **P** *Bp* **I** S COCKBURN.
LONG LANE (Ch Ch), *Derbys*. V. **D** Derby 14 *See* Dalbury.
LONG LOAD (Ch Ch) *Somt*.. **D** B & W 10 *See* Load St Mary.
LONG MARTON (St Marg and St Jas) w Dufton and Milburn, *Cumb*. R. **D** Carl 1 **P** *Col G W A Tufton* **I** J C WILSON.
LONG NEWNTON (H Trin), *Glos*.. **D** Bris *See* Newnton, Long.
LONG PRESTON (St Mary Virg), *N Yorks*. V. **D** Bradf 6 **P** *D and C of Ch Ch Ox* **I** J G HOYLAND *p-in-c*.
LONG SLEDDALE (St Mary), *Cumb*.. **D** Carl 11 *See* Sleddale, Long.
LONG STANTON (All SS), *Cambs*. R. **D** Ely 5 **P** *Magd Coll Cam and Bp* alt **I** (Vacant).
LONG STANTON (St Mich AA) w Easthope (St Pet), *Salop*. V. **D** Heref *See* Wenlock.
LONGBOROUGH, Sezincote, Condicote (St Nich) and the Swell, *Glos*. V. **D** Glouc 16 **P** *Ld Leigh, Susanna Peake, Rosina Ethel Davies and D and C of Ch Ch Ox (in turn)* **I** E B HYDE.
LONGBRIDGE (St Jo Bapt), *W Midl*. V. **D** Birm 4 **P** *Bp* **I** L J OAKES.
LONGBRIDGE-DEVERILL (St Pet and St Paul w Assump BVM), and Hill Deverill, *Wilts*. V. **D** Sarum 22 *See* Deverills.
LONGCOT (St Mary Virg) w Fernham (St John), *Oxon*.. **D** Ox *See* Ashbury.
LONGDEN (St Ruthen) and Annscroft (Ch Ch), *Salop*. R. **D** Heref 13 **P** *Bp* **I** C O HURFORD.
LONGDON (St Jas Gt), *Staffs*. V. **D** Lich 2 **P** *Mart Mem and C of E Trusts* **I** R A ELLIS *p-in-c*.
LONGDON (St Mary), Bushley (St Pet) and Queenhill (St Nich) w Holdfast, *Worcs*. V. **D** Worc 5 **P** *Bp, D and C of Westmr and S for Maint of Faith* **I** L DAVIES.
LONGDON-ON-TERN (St Bart), *Salop*. V. **D** Lich 29 **P** *MMT and Bp* alt **I** W S FROST.
LONGFIELD (St Mary Magd), *Kent*. R. **D** Roch 1 **P** *Ld Chan* **I** J R CHALLICE.
LONGFLEET (St Mary), *Dorset*. V. **D** Sarum 14 **P** *MMT* **I** K G W PRIOR, T J G LOW *c*.
LONGFORD (St Chad), *Derbys*. R. **D** Derby 14 **P** *Bp* **I** J O DRACKLEY *p-in-c*.
LONGFORD, *Salop*.. **D** Lich *See* Newport.
LONGFORD (St Thos), *W Midl*. V. **D** Cov 2 **P** *Bp* **I** A E DARBY.
LONGFRAMLINGTON **D** Newc T *See* Framlington, Long.
LONGGROVE, *Herefs*.. **D** Heref *See* Llangarron.
LONGHAM (St Andr w St Pet) w Bittering Parva (St Pet w St Paul), R *Norf*. V. **D** Nor *See* Gressenhall.
LONGHIRST (St Jo Evang) w Hebron (St Cuthb), *Northumb*. V. **D** Newc T 10 **P** *Bp* **I** R T FLEMING.
LONGHOPE (All SS), *Glos*. R. **D** Glouc 6 **P** *Ch S Trust* **I** G M PENFOLD.
LONGHORSLEY (St Helen), *Northumb*. V. **D** Newc T 10 **P** *Ld Chan* **I** R G RHODES *p-in-c*.
LONGHOUGHTON (St Pet and St Paul) w Howick (St Mich), *Northumb*. V. **D** Newc T 7 **P** *Duke of Northumb and Bp* alt **I** J W SHEWAN.
LONGLEVENS, *Glos*.. **D** Glouc *See* Wotton (St Mary Without).
LONGNEWTON (St Mary) w Elton, *Cleve*. R. **D** Dur 14 **P** *St Chad's Coll Dur and Bp (alt)* **I** N C JONES.
LONGNEY, *Glos*. V. **D** Glouc 3 *See* Elmore.
LONGNOR, *Salop*.. **D** Heref *See* Leebotwood.
LONGNOR (St Bart), *Staffs*. V. **D** Lich 13 **P** *V of Alstonfield* **I** A C F NICOLL.
LONGPARISH or MIDDLETON (St Nich) w Hurstbourne Priors (St Andr), *Hants*. V. **D** Win *See* Barton Stacey.
LONGRIDGE (St Lawr) w (St Paul), *Lancs*. V. **D** Blackb 12 **P** *Hulme Trustees* **I** E P A FURNESS.
LONGSDON (St Chad), *Staffs*. V. **D** Lich 16 **P** *Bp* **I** B H PEEL.
LONGSIGHT (St Jo Evang) w Kirkmanshulme (St Cypr), *Gtr Man*. R. **D** Man 4 **P** *Trustees* **I** N W DAWSON.
(St Luke), R. **D** Man 1 **P** *Trustees* **I** H ACKERLEY. *See also* ROYTON..
LONGSLEDDALE, *Cumb*.. **D** Carl *See* Skelsmergh.
LONGSTOCK (St Mary) w Leckford (St Nich), *Hants*. V. **D** Win 10 **P** *St Jo Coll Ox* **I** J F O BOWN *p-in-c*.
LONGSTONE (St Giles), *Derbys*. V. **D** Derby 9 **P** *V of Bakewell* **I** B J EVERETT *p-in-c*.
LONGSTOWE (St Mary), *Cambs*. R. **D** Ely 1 **P** *Selw Coll Cam* **I** J M PLUMLEY *p-in-c*.
LONGTHORPE (St Botolph), *Cambs*. V. **D** Pet 14 **P** *Earl Fitzwilliam* **I** M W R COVINGTON.
LONGTON (St Andr), *Lancs*. V. **D** Blackb 6 **P** *Canon R G Rawstorne* **I** (Vacant).
LONGTON (St Jas L and St Jo Bapt), *Staffs*. R. **D** Lich 18 **P** *Bp* **I** N BURGESS *c*.
(St Mary and St Chad), V. **D** Lich 18 **P** *Bp* **I** R H PRENTIS.
LONGTON, NEW (All SS), *Lancs*. V. **D** Blackb 6 **P** *Bp* **I** R I MCMASTER.
LONGTOWN (St Pet), *Herefs*.. **D** Heref *See* Clodock.
LONGWOOD (St Mark) w Outland (St Mary), *W Yorks*. V. **D** Wakef 6 **P** *V of Huddersfield* **I** D R DRAKE-BROCKMAN.
LONGWORTH (St Mary) w Hinton Waldrist (St Marg), *Oxon*. R. **D** Ox 17 *See* Cherbury.
LOOE, EAST (St Mary) w Looe, West (St Nich), *Cornw*. V. **D** Truro 13 **P** *Bp* **I** (Vacant).
LOOSE (All SS), *Kent*. V. **D** Cant 15 **P** *Abp* **I** G A PARLETT.
LOPEN (All SS), *Somt*. V. **D** B & W *See* Merriott.
LOPHAM, NORTH (St Nich), W Lopham, South (St Andr), *Norf*. R (*See Winfarthing Group*).. **D** Nor *See* Bressingham.
LOPPINGTON (St Mich), *Salop*. V. **D** Lich 27 **P** *Bp* **I** T W BOULCOTT.
LORDINGTON, *W Sussex*.. **D** Chich *See* Racton.
LORRIMORE SQUARE (St Paul). **D** S'wark *See* Newington.
LORTON (St Cuthb) and Loweswater w Buttermere, *Cumb*. V. **D** Carl 10 **P** *Bp and Earl of Lonsdale* **I** D A EDWARDS.
LOSCOE (St Luke), *Derbys*. V. **D** Derby 6 **P** *Bp* **I** L H HILL *c*.
LOSTOCK (Conv Distr), *Gtr Man*.. **D** Man 13 *See* Bolton.
LOSTOCK GRALAM (St Jo Evang), *Chesh*. V. **D** Ches 6 **P** *V of Witton* **I** C J REES.
LOSTOCK HALL, *Lancs*.. **D** Blackb 6 *See* Preston.
LOSTWITHIEL (St Bart), *Cornw*. V. **D** Truro 8 **P** *D and C of Truro* **I** R N K WATTON *p-in-c*, H C T OLIVEY *c*.
LOTHERSDALE (Ch Ch), *N Yorks*. V. **D** Bradf 10 *See* Carleton.
LOTHERTON, *W Yorks*.. **D** York *See* Aberford.
LOTTISHAM (St Mary Virg), *Somt*.. **D** B & W 7 *See* Pennard, West.
LOUDWATER, *Bucks*. V. **D** Ox 32 **P** *MMT* **I** (Vacant).
LOUGHBOROUGH (All SS), *Leics*. R. **D** Leic 10 **P** *Em Coll Cam* **I** L G E HANCOCK.
(Em Ch), R. **D** Leic 10 **P** *Em Coll Cam* **I** M T H BANKS, C J D GREENE *c*.
(Good Shepherd), V. **D** Leic 10 **P** *Bp* **I** R SKEPPER.
(H Trin), V. **D** Leic 10 **P** *Bp* **I** B H WRIGHT.
(St Pet), V. **D** Leic 10 **P** *Bp* **I** D PATERSON.
LOUGHTON (All SS), *Bucks*. R. **D** Ox 26 **P** *Dioc Bd of Patr* **I** R A HARROW *p-in-c*.
LOUGHTON (St Jo Bapt w St Nich), *Essex*. R. **D** Chelmsf 2 **P** *Lt-Commdr J Maitland, RN* **I** G R HOLLEY, M M CAMP *c*, O B WELLS *c*.
(St Mary Virg) w (St Mich AA), R. **D** Chelmsf 2 **P** *Dioc Bd of Patr* **I** J F PRICE, A C BRYER *team v*, P HAWORTH *c*.
LOUGHTON, *Salop*.. **D** Heref *See* Aston Botterell.
LOUND (St Jo Bapt), *Suff*. R. **D** Nor 15 *See* Blundeston.
LOUNDSLEY GREEN, *Derbys*.. **D** Derby 3 *See* Brampton, Old.
LOUTH (St Jas, St Martin, H Trin, St Mich AA, St Marg, St Andr, St Helen and All SS), *Lincs*. R. **D** Linc 12 **P** *Dioc Bd of Patr* **I** D W OWEN, R P HOLLINGSHURST *team v*, J W TRAVERS *team v*, F A TAYLOR *c*.
LOVERSALL (St Kath), *S Yorks*, V. **D** Sheff 8 *See* Wadworth.
LOVINGTON (St Thos à Becket), *Somt*.. **D** B & W 4 *See* Six Pilgrims.
LOW FELL (St Helen), *T & W*.. **D** Dur 4 *See* Gateshead (St Helen).
LOW MOOR (St Paul), *Lancs*.. **D** Blackb 7 *See* Clitheroe.
LOW MOOR (St Mark), *W Yorks*. V. **D** Bradf 2 **P** *Bp* **I** J W JERVIS.
(H Trin), V. **D** Bradf 2 **P** *V of Bradf* **I** D F BROWN.
LOW TEAM, *T & W*.. **D** Dur 4 *See* Gateshead (St Paul).
LOW WRAY (St Marg), *Cumb*.. **D** Carl 14 *See* Hawkshead.
LOWDEN (St Pet), *Wilts*.. **D** Bris 7 *See* Chippenham.
LOWDHAM, *Suff*.. **D** St E *See* Dalinghoo.

LOWDHAM (St Mary) w Gunthorpe (St Jo Bapt) and Caythorpe (St Aid), *Notts*. V. **D** Southw 13 **P** *Bp* **I** B A HOPKINSON.
LOWER GORNAL (St Jas), *Staffs*.. **D** Lich 1 *See* Gornal, Lower.
LOWER PEOVER (St Osw), *Chesh*.. **D** Ches 12 *See* Peover, Lower.
LOWESBY, *Leics*.. **D** Leic *See* Tilton-on-the-Hill.
LOWESTOFT (St Marg) and Kirkley (St Pet), *Suff*. R. **D** Nor 15 **P** *Dioc Bd of Patr* **I** A GLENDINING, W G ANNESLEY *team v*, A A G OLD *team v*, A W OVERY *hon c*.
(Ch Ch), V. **D** Nor 15 **P** *CPAS* **I** P R PAYN.
(St Jo Evang), V. **D** Nor 15 *See* Kirkley.
LOWESWATER (St Bart) w Buttermere (St Jas), *Cumb*. V. **D** Carl 10 *See* Lorton.
LOWFIELD HEATH, *Surrey*.. **D** Chich *See* Crawley.
LOWICK (St Luke), *Cumb*. V. **D** Carl 15 *See* Blawith.
LOWICK (St Jo Bapt) w Kyloe (St Nich), *Northumb*. V. **D** Newc T 11 **P** *D and C of Dur* **I** R D A WOULDHAM.
LOWICK (St Pet) w Sudborough (All SS) and Slipton (St Jo Bapt), *Northants*. R. **D** Pet 9 **P** *L G Stopford Sackville Esq and Bp* alt **I** C P M JONES.
LOWTHER (St Mich) w Askham (St Columba), V *Cumb*. R. **D** Carl 1 **P** *Earl of Lonsdale* **I** W N S HALL.
LOWTHORPE (St Martin) w Ruston Parva (St Nich), *Humb*. V. **D** York *See* Kilham.
LOWTON (St Luke), *Gtr Man*. R. **D** Liv 11 **P** *Earl of Derby* **I** D E WEBSTER.
LOWTON ST MARY (St Mary), *Gtr Man*. V. **D** Liv 11 **P** *Bp* **I** R A LALLY.
LOXBEARE (Dedic unknown), *Devon*. R. **D** Ex 8 *See* Washfield.
LOXHORE (St Mich AA), *Devon*. R. **D** Ex 18 *See* Shirwell.
LOXLEY Warws. V **D** Cov 8 *See* Hampton Lucy.
LOXTON (St Andr) w Christon (St Mary Virg) *Avon*. R. **D** B & W *See* Compton Bishop.
LOXWOOD (St Jo Bapt), *W Sussex*.. **D** Guildf 2 *See* Alfold.
LOYS WEEDON (St Mary Virg and St Pet), *Northants*. V. **D** Pet 2 *See* Lois-Weedon.
LOZELLS (St Paul), *W Midl*. V. **D** Birm 7 **P** *Aston Trustees* **I** (Vacant).
(St Silas), V. **D** Birm 7 **P** *Aston Trustees* **I** (Vacant).
LUBBESTHORPE (St Jo Bapt), *Leics*. V. **D** Leic 13 *See* Enderby.
LUBENHAM Leics. V **D** Leic *See* Foxton.
LUCCOMBE (St Mary Virg), *Somt*. R. **D** B & W 21 **P** *Bp* **I** S W SMERDON *p-in-c*.
LUCKER (St Hilda), *Northumb*. V. **D** Newc T 8 *See* Bamburgh.
LUCKINGTON (St Mary) w Alderton (St Giles), *Wilts*. R. **D** Bris 11 **P** *Archd of Swindon and Bp* alt **I** W H THOMSON-GLOVER *c-in-c*.
LUCTON, *Herefs*. V. **D** Heref 7 *See* Eye.
LUDBOROUGH (St Mary), *Lincs*. R. **D** Linc *See* Fotherby.
LUDDENDEN (St Mary) w Luddendenfoot, *W Yorks*. V. **D** Wakef 3 **P** *Bp and V of Halifax* **I** G SMITH.
LUDDENDENFOOT (St Mary Virg), *W Yorks*. V. **D** Wakef 3 *See* Luddenden.
LUDDENHAM (St Mary Virg), *Kent*. R. **D** Cant 6 *See* Oare.
LUDDESDOWN, *Kent*.. **D** Roch *See* Cobham.
LUDDINGTON (All SS), *Warws*.. **D** Cov 8 *See* Stratford-on-Avon.
LUDDINGTON (St Osw) w Garthorpe (St Mary Chap), *Humb*. V. **D** Linc 1 *See* Amcotts.
LUDDINGTON (St Marg) *Northants*. R. **D** Pet 11 *See* Barnwell.
LUDFORD (St Giles), *Salop*. V. **D** Heref 12 **P** *Exors of H E Whitaker* **I** (Vacant).
LUDFORD MAGNA (St Mary) w Ludford Parva *Lincs*. R. **D** Linc 12 **P** *Dioc Bd of Patr* **I** (Vacant).
LUDGERSHALL (St Mary) w Wotton Underwood (All SS) and Ashendon, *Bucks*. R. **D** Ox 21 **P** *Bp and CPAS* **I** C S JEE.
LUDERSHALL and Faberstown (St Jas), *Wilts*. R. **D** Sarum **P** *Dioc Bd of Patr* **I** P D CHESTERS.
LUDGVAN (St Ludgvan), *Cornw*. R. **D** Truro 5 *See* St Ludgvan.
LUDHAM (St Cath), *Norf*. V. **D** Nor 9 **P** *Bp* **I** (Vacant).
LUDLOW (St Laur w St John and St Leon), *Salop*. R. **D** Heref 12 **P** *Earl of Plymouth* **I** W J R MORRISON.
LUFFENHAM, NORTH (St Jo Bapt), *Leics*.. **D** Pet *See* Edith Weston.
LUFFENHAM, SOUTH, *Leics*. **D** Pet *See* Barrowden.
LUFFINCOTT Devon. R **D** Ex 9 *See* Tetcott.
LUFTON (St Pet and St Paul), *Somt*. R. **D** B & W 11 **P** *Bp* **I** A C DEAN.
LUGWARDINE (St Pet) w Bartestree (St Jas) and Weston-Beggard (St Jo Bapt), *Herefs*. V. **D** Heref 4 **P** *D and C of Heref* **I** S C PARSONS.
LULLINGSTONE (St Botolph), *Kent*. R. **D** Roch 8 *See* Eynsford.
LULLINGTON (All SS), *Derbys*. V. **D** Derby 16 **P** *Bp* **I** W F BATES.
LULLINGTON (All SS), *Somt*.. **D** B & W 16a *See* Beckington.
LULLINGTON, *E Sussex*.. **D** Chich *See* Alfriston.
LULSLEY (St Giles), *Worcs*.. **D** Worc *See* Alfrick.
LULWORTH, WEST (H Trin) w East Lulworth (St Andr), *Dorset*. V. **D** Sarum *See* Lulworths, The.
LULWORTHS, THE (H Trin w St Andr) w Winfrith Newburgh and Chaldon, *Dorset*. R. **D** Sarum **P** *Bp 3 turns, Sir J W Weld 1 turn* **I** E FARROW.
LUMB (St Mich), *Lancs*. V. **D** Man 18 **P** *Crown and Bp* alt **I** J N WOOD.
LUMLEY (Ch Ch), *Durham*. V. **D** Dur 1 **P** *Bp* **I** L G BARRON.
LUND (St Jo Evang), *Lancs*. V. **D** Blackb 9 **P** *D and C of Ch Ch Ox* **I** M S MALKINSON.
LUND (All SS), *Humb*.. **D** York 11 *See* Lockington.
LUNDS, *N Yorks*. V. **D** Ripon 2 *See* Hardraw.
LUNDWOOD (St Mary Magd), *S Yorks*. V. **D** Wakef 8 **P** *Bp* **I** H WOOLLER.
LUNDY ISLAND (St Helen), *Devon*. R. **D** Ex 17 **P** *Bp* **I** A D EDWARDS *p-in-c*.
LUPPITT (St Mary), *Devon*. V. **D** Ex 5 *See* Upottery.
LUPSET (St Geo), V. **D** Wakef 12 **P** *Bp* **I** R G A FERGUSON, H GALLAGHER *c*.
LUPTON **D** Carl *See* Hutton Roof.
LURGASHALL (St Lawr) w Lodsworth and Selham, *W Sussex*. R. **D** Chich 6 **P** *Ld Egremont and Cowdray Trust Ltd* **I** N G MAY.
LUSBY (St Pet), *Lincs*. R. **D** Linc 7 *See* Hagworthingham.
LUSTLEIGH (St Jo Bapt), *Devon*, R. **D** Ex 11 **P** *Bp* **I** E W F DEACON.
LUTON, *Devon*.. **D** Ex 6 *See* Ideford.
LUTON (Ch Ch), *Kent*. R. **D** Roch 4 **P** *R of Chatham* **I** B R F ROCHE, I G PRIOR *c*.
LUTON (St Mary), *Beds*. V. **D** St Alb 20 **P** *Peache Trustees* **I** D J BANFIELD, D B FOSTER *c*, E H LURKINGS *hon c*.
(All SS w St Pet), V. **D** St Alb 20 **P** *Bp* **I** J ORME, P A NEED *c*, R J PARSONS *c*.
(H Cross Conv Distr Marsh Farm). **D** St Alb 20 **P** *Bp* **I** F B NICHOLS *min*.
(St Andr), V. **D** St Alb 20 **P** *Bp* **I** J R BROWN.
(St Anne), V. **D** St Alb 19 **P** *Bp, V of St Mary, Luton and Peache Trustees* **I** D H GUMMER.
(St Francis), V. **D** St Alb 20 **P** *Bp, V of Luton and Peache Trustees (Jt)* **I** D C CASSON, R J RYAN *c*.
(St Matt), V. **D** St Alb 20 **P** *CPS* **I** W G SEAL.
(St Jo Bapt Farley Hill), V. **D** St Alb 20 **P** *Bp* **I** J V PAYTON.
(St Luke, Leagrave) V. **D** St Alb 20 **P** *Bp* **I** J D WATSON.
(St Paul) V. **D** St Alb 20 **P** *Peache Trustees* **I** P J MILLAM.
(St Sav), V. **D** St Alb 20 **P** *Bp* **I** G S NORTHCOTT.
(St Hugh, Lewsey), V. **D** St Alb 20 **P** *Bp* **I** N H LAMB *c*, J REASON *c*.
LUTTERWORTH (St Mary) w Cotesbach (St Mary), *Leics*. R. **D** Leic 14 **P** *Ld Chan* **I** P J CASSWELL.
LUTTON or Sutton (St Nich) w Gedney Drove End and Holbeach Bank, *Lincs*. V. **D** Linc 16 **P** *V of Long Sutton* **I** D R HILL V OF LUTTON AND GEDNEY DROVE END.
LUTTON, *Northants*.. **D** Pet *See* Polebrooke.
LUTTONS AMBO (St Mary Virg), *N Yorks*. V. **D** York 3 *See* Weaverthorpe.
LUXBOROUGH (St Mary Virg), *Somt*.. **D** B & W 21 *See* Cutcombe.
LUXULYAN (St Cyric and St Julitta), *Cornw*. V. **D** Truro 8 *See* Lanlivery.
LYDBROOK (H Jesus), *Glos*. V. **D** Glouc 7 **P** *Bp* **I** D C S BOWLER.
LYDBURY NORTH (St Mich AA), *Salop*. V. **D** Heref 10 **P** *Earl of Powis* **I** V IRWIN.
LYDD (All SS), *Kent*. R. **D** Cant 13 **P** *Abp* **I** G P CHIDGEY.
LYDDEN (St Mary Virg), *Kent*.. **D** Cant *See* Temple Ewell.
LYDDINGTON, or LIDDINGTON, w Wanborough (All SS), *Wilts*. R. **D** Bris 10 **P** *Bp 1 turn, Ld Chan 2 turns* **I** A G THOMAS.
LYDDINGTON (St Andr) w Stoke Dry (St Andr) and Seaton (All H), *Leics*. V. **D** Pet 12 **P** *Bp, Marq of Ex and R E M Elborne Esq* **I** A J GOUGH.
LYDE, *Herefs*.. **D** Heref 10 *See* Pipe.

LYDEARD (St Lawr) w Combe Florey (St Pet and St Paul) and Tolland (St Jo Bapt), *Somt*. R. **D** B & W 23 **P** *Ld Chan 2 turns, R O Hancock Esq 1 turn* **I** F V HODGE.
LYDFORD (St Petrock) w Bridestowe (St Bridget) and Sourton (St Thos of Cant) and Brent Tor (St Mich) w North Brentor Chapel (Ch Ch) *Devon*. R. **D** Ex 22 **P** *Bp and Duchy of Cornwall* alt **I** E W K WILLIAMS *team v*, R D ORMSBY *c*.
LYDFORD-ON-FOSSE, WEST (St Pet) w EAST (St Mary Virg) *Somt*.. **D** B & W *See* Keinton Mandeville.
LYDGATE (St Anne), *Gtr Man*. V. **D** Man 15 **P** *Bp* **I** C C W AIRNE, E OGDEN *hon c*.
LYDGATE (St Mary) w Ousden (St Pet) and Cowlinge (St Marg), *Suff*. R. **D** St E 11 **P** *Dioc Bd of Patr and R A Vestey Esq (alt)* **I** G G WHITEFIELD.
LYDHAM (H Trin), *Salop*.. **D** Heref 10 *See* More.
LYDIARD MILLICENT (All SS) w Lydiard Tregoz (St Mary), *Wilts*. R. **D** Bris 10 **P** *Pemb Coll Ox and Bp* alt **I** D J E ATTWOOD *c*.
LYDIATE (St Thos), *Mer*. V. **D** Liv 9 **P** *R of Halsall* **I** B J GERRARD.
LYDLINCH (St Thos à Becket), *Dorset*. R. **D** Sarum 13 *See* Stock Gaylar.
LYDNEY (St Mary) w Aylburton, *Glos*. V. **D** Glouc 7 **P** *Ld Chan* **I** M J LEEFIELD, H K COWLEY *c*, R HUMPHRIS *c*.
LYE, THE (Ch Ch) and Stambermill (St Mark), *W Midl*. V. **D** Worc **P** *Bp and CPAS (alt)* **I** G D COOPER.
LYFORD (St Mary) w Charney-Bassett (St Pet), *Oxon*. V. **D** Ox 17 *See* Cherbury.
LYGHE (St Mary), *Kent*. V. **D** Roch *See* Leigh.
LYME REGIS (St Mich Arch), *Dorset*. V. **D** Sarum 2 **P** *Bp* **I** M J DELL.
LYMINGE (St Mary and St Eadburg) w Paddlesworth (St Osw) and Stanford w Postling, *Kent*. R. **D** Cant 6 **P** *Abp* **I** M W WORGAN.
LYMINGTON (St Thos Ap), *Hants*. V. **D** Win 9 **P** *Bp* **I** E J C HASELDEN, W ROBSON *c*.
LYMINSTER (St Mary Magd), *W Sussex*. V. **D** Chich 1 **P** *Eton Coll on nom of BNC Ox* **I** D L SATTERFORD.
LYMM (St Mary Virg), *Chesh*. R. **D** Ches 4 **P** *Bp* **I** G L DAVIES.
LYMPNE (St Steph) w West Hythe, *Kent*. V. **D** Cant 12 **P** *Abp* **I** J W NEILSON.
LYMPSHAM (St Chris), *Somt*. R. **D** B & W 2 *See* Brent, East.
LYMPSTONE (Nativ of BVM), *Devon*. R. **D** Ex 1 **P** *S for Maint of Faith* **I** J M PEGG.
LYNCH or LINCH (St Luke) w Iping Marsh, *W Sussex*. V. **D** Chich 5 **P** *Cowdray Trust Ltd and Dickinson Trust Ltd* **I** R G PIGGOTT.
LYNCHMERE (St Pet), *W Sussex*. V. **D** Chich 5 **P** *Dioc Bd of Patr* **I** R G H HORNE.
LYNCOMBE (St Mark Evang) w (St Bart), *Somt*.. **D** B & W 13 *See* Bath (St Bart).
SOUTH (St Luke),. **D** B & W 13 *See* Bath (St Luke).
LYNDHURST (St Mich AA) w Emery Down (Ch Ch), *Hants*. V. **D** Win 9 **P** *P J P Green Esq and Bp* alt **I** H W J M LLOYD.
LYNDON (St Martin) w Manton (St Mary Virg), Martinsthorpe and Gunthorpe, *Leics*.. **D** Pet *See* Edith Weston.
LYNE (H Trin), *Surrey*.. **D** Guildf 7 *See* Botleys.
LYNEAL (St Jo Evang) w Colemere, *Salop*. V. **D** Lich 22 **P** *Ld Brownlow* **I** (Vacant).
LYNEHAM w Bradenstoke (St Mary Virg), *Wilts*. V. **D** Sarum 25 **P** *Crown* **I** (Vacant).
LYNEMOUTH (St Aidan), *Northumb*. V. **D** Newc T 10 **P** *Bp* **I** (Vacant).
LYNESACK (St Jo Evang), *Durham*. V. **D** Dur 10 **P** *Bp* **I** R D BUTT.
LYNFORD (St Leon), *Norf*.. **D** Nor 19 *See* Mundford.
LYNG (St Bart), *Somt*. V. **D** B & W 23 *See* Stoke St Gregory.
LYNG (St Marg) w Sparham (St Mary Virg), *Norf*. R. **D** Nor 6 **P** *Vice-Adm Sir E Evans-Lombe, RN and Dioc Bd of Patr* alt **I** P P K ROBIN.
LYNMOUTH (St Jo Bapt), *Devon*. R. **D** Ex 18 *See* Lynton.
LYNSTED (St Pet and St Paul) w Kingsdown (St Cath), *Kent*. V. **D** Cant 7 **P** *Archd of Cant* **I** W H G HILL.
LYNTON (St Mary Virg) w Brendon (St Brendan) Countisbury (St Jo Evang) and Lynmouth (St Jo Bapt) Barbrook Parracombe (Ch Ch) and Martinhoe (St Martin), *Devon*. R. **D** Ex 18 **P** *Dioc Bd of Patr* **I** L H MORRISON *team v*, K E NEWELL *c*.
LYONS (St Mich AA), *T & W*. R. **D** Dur 5 **P** *Crown* **I** J B HUNT.
LYONSDOWN (H Trin), *Herts*.. **D** St Alb *See* Barnet.
LYONSHALL (St Mich AA) w Titley (St Pet), *Herefs*. V. **D** Heref 5 **P** *Bp of Birm 2 turns CPS 1 turn* **I** D R LOWE *p-in-c*.
LYSS (St Pet and St Mary Virg), *Hants*. R. **D** Portsm 4 **P** *Bp* **I** N BARNETT.
LYTCHETT MATRAVERS (St Mary Virg), *Dorset*. R. **D** Sarum 14 **P** *Dioc Bd of Patr* **I** J W F HAMBLEN *p-in-c*.
LYTCHETT-MINSTER, *Dorset*. V. **D** Sarum 14 **P** *Bp* **I** A J CARTER.
LYTHAM (St Cuthb), *Lancs*. V. **D** Blackb 9 **P** *Dioc Bd of Patr* **I** D S D SHELLEY *hon c*.
(St Jo Div), V. **D** Blackb 9 **P** *H T de Vere Clifton Esq* **I** C J CARLISLE.
LYTHE (St Osw), *N Yorks*. V. **D** York 27 **P** *Abp* **I** P C FERGUSON.

MABE (St Laudus), *Cornw*.. **D** Truro *See* St Mabe.
MABLETHORPE (St Mary) w Stane (All SS) and Trusthorpe (St Pet), *Lincs*. R. **D** Linc 8 **P** *Bp of Lon 2 turns, Bp of Linc 1 turn* **I** D W WOODS, W D W BAKER *c*, R W PARKER *c*, C S OWST *hon c*.
MACCLESFIELD (All SS now called St Mich), *Chesh*. V. **D** Ches 13 **P** *Simeon Trustees* **I** M F GEAR, R J AVERY *c*, J E COYNE *c*, T D HERBERT *c*.
(Ch Ch), V. **D** Ches 13 **P** *CPAS* **I** (Vacant).
(Ch of Resurr, Upton Priory). **D** Ches 13 **P** *Bp* **I** D J SAMBELL.
(St Jo Evang), V. **D** Ches 13 **P** *Bp* **I** C B G AP IVOR.
(St Paul), V. **D** Ches 13 **P** *Bp* **I** K M BURGHALL.
(St Pet), V. **D** Ches 13 **P** *Bp* **I** C H L CLAY.
MACKWORTH (All SS), *Derbys*. V. **D** Derby 12 **P** *G S Clark-Maxwell Esq* **I** H A DANE *p-in-c*, E DIXON *c*.
(St Francis), V. **D** Derby **P** *Bp* **I** E G CULL.
MADDINGTON, *Wilts*.. **D** Sarum *See* Shrewton.
MADEHURST (St Mary Magd), *W Sussex*. V. **D** Chich 1 **P** *Bp* **I** J R M COSSAR.
MADELEY (Aqueduct Ch St Mich), *Salop*. V. **D** Heref 14 **P** *CPAS* **I** V J PRICE, A Q H WHEELER *c*.
MADELEY (All SS formerly St Leon), *Staffs*. V. **D** Lich 17 **P** *C Crewe Esq and Q Crewe Esq* **I** J POTTS.
MADINGLEY (St Mary Magd), *Cambs*. V. **D** Ely 5 **P** *Bp* **I** (Vacant).
MADLEY (Nativ St Mary Virg), w Tyberton (St Mary), *Herefs*. V. **D** Heref 1 **P** *D and C of Heref* **I** W L PATERSON.
MADRESFIELD (St Mary Virg), *Worcs*. R. **D** Worc *See* Newland.
MADRON, *Cornw*.. **D** Truro *See* St Madron.
MAER (St Pet), *Staffs*. V. **D** Lich 15 **P** *Exors of Miss J Harrison* **I** J D D PORTER *p-in-c*.
MAESBROOK (St Jo Evang), *Salop*.. **D** Lich 24 *See* Knockin.
MAGDALEN-LAVER (St Mary Magd), *Essex*.. **D** Chelmsf 6 *See* Laver, High.
MAGHULL (St Andr), *Mer*. R. **D** Liv 9 **P** *Bp, Archd of Warrington and R of Halsall* **I** I L DAVIS, C D BENGE *team v*, G A PERERA *team v*, W H TULLOCH *hon c*.
MAIDA HILL. **D** Lon *See* St Marylebone.
MAIDEN BRADLEY (All SS), *Wilts* . V. **D** Sarum 22 *See* Mere.
MAIDEN NEWTON and VALLEYS (Frome Vauchurch, Compton Abbas, Wynford Eagle, Toller Fratrum), *Dorset*. R. **D** Sarum 5 **P** *Lady T Agnew, G C Wyndham Esq, Ld Wynford, Sir R P Williams and Bp* **I** I L JOHNSON.
MAIDENHEAD (St Andr w St Mary Magd), *Berks*. V. **D** Ox 13 **P** *Trustees* **I** F M TRUMBLE *c*.
(All SS, Boyne Hill), V. **D** Ox 13 **P** *Bp* **I** A H M WARE.
(Good Shepherd Cox Green), V. **D** Ox 13 **P** *Bp* **I** D J CAWTE.
(St Luke), V. **D** Ox 13 **P** *Bp* **I** R A CHEEK *c*.
(St Pet, Furze Platt), V. **D** Ox 13 **P** *Bp* **I** F S EBBITT, J S HODGE *c*.
MAIDENWELL (St Pet), *Lincs*.. **D** Linc 36 *See* Ruckland.
MAIDFORD (St Pet and St Paul), *Northants*. R. **D** Pet 2 *See* Lichborough.
MAIDS MORETON (St Edm) w Foscott (St Leon), *Bucks*. R. **D** Ox 23 *See* Buckingham N.
MAIDSTONE (All SS w St Phil) and Tovil (St Steph), *Kent*. V. **D** Cant 15 **P** *Abp* **I** P A NAYLOR, R D BAXENDALE *c*, A H NORMAN *c*.
(St Andr), Barming Heath, V. **D** Cant 15 **P** *Abp and Crown* alt **I** J P LEFROY.
(St Faith Virg and Mart), V. **D** Cant 15 **P** *Abp* **I** K E O JAMIESON *p-in-c*.
(St Luke Evang), V. **D** Cant 15 **P** *Trustees* **I** C SAMPSON, G DAVIS *c*.
(St Martin), V. **D** Cant 15 **P** *Abp* **I** G H SIDAWAY, P BOWERS *c*, R DIXON *c*.

MANNINGFORD BRUCE (St Pet) w Manningford Abbas, *Wilts.* R. **D** Sarum 27 *See* Swanborough.
MANNINGHAM (St Luke), *W Yorks.* V. **D** Bradf 1 **P** *CPS* **I** R CHESTERFIELD *p-in-c.*
(St Chad), V. **D** Bradf 1 **P** *Keble Coll Ox* **I** S R CROWE.
(St Mary Magd) w (St Mich AA), V. **D** Bradf 1 **P** *C R Mirfield* **I** K D PENFOLD *p-in-c*, S R B HUMPHREYS *c*, D M D S POLLARD *c.*
(St Paul w St Jude), V. **D** Bradf 1 **P** *Trustees* **I** J C HALSALL *p-in-c.*
MANNINGTON (St Mary), *Norf..* **D** Nor 3 *See* Itteringham.
MANNINGTREE (St Mich AA), *Essex.* V. **D** Chelmsf 25 *See* Mistley.
Manor Park **D** Chelmsf *See* Ilford, Little.
MANOR PARK (St Jo Bapt) Conv Distr. **D** Ox 24 *See* Stoke Poges.
MANSEL GAMAGE (St Giles), *Herefs.* V. **D** Heref 4 *See* Letton.
MANSEL LACY (St Mich) w Yazor (St Mary Virg), *Herefs.* V. **D** Heref 4 *See* Credenhill.
MANSFIELD (St Pet and St Paul), *Notts.* V. **D** Southw 2 **P** *Bp* **I** R T WARBURTON, D L HARPER *c*, W B IRVINE *c*, J PULMAN *c.*
(St Aug), V. **D** Southw 2 **P** *Bp* **I** J W R HILLIARD.
(St Barn Pleasley Hill), V. **D** Southw 2 **P** *Bp* **I** R G SKINNER.
(St Jo Evang), V. **D** Southw 2 **P** *Bp* **I** J R RICE-OXLEY.
(St Lawr), V. **D** Southw 2 **P** *Bp* **I** P HANCOCK.
(St Mark), V. **D** Southw 2 **P** *Bp* **I** P R ALLIN, S J HADLEY *c.*
(St Mary, Ladybrook), V. **D** Southw 2 **P** *Bp* **I** G E HOLLOWAY.
MANSFIELD WOODHOUSE (St Edm K and Mart), *Notts.* V. **D** Southw 2 **P** *Bp* **I** D DAVIES.
MANSTON (St Jas), *W Yorks.* V. **D** Ripon 7 **P** *R of Barwick-in-Elmet* **I** D R WALKER, P A SUMMERS *c.*
MANSTON (St Nich) *Dorset..* **D** Sarum 13 *See* Childe Okeford.
MANTHORPE (St Jo Evang), *Lincs.* V. **D** Linc 6 *See* Grantham.
MANTON (St Hibald), *Humb.* R. **D** Linc 6 **P** *Bp* **I** M B KIDDLE.
MANTON (St Mary Virg), *Leics..* **D** Pet *See* Lyndon.
MANUDEN (St Mary) w Berden, *Essex.* V. **D** Chelmsf 26 **P** *Exors of Mrs Penny and govs of Ch Hosp* alt **I** P R MASTERTON *p-in-c.*
MAPERTON (St Pet and St Paul), *Somt.* R. **D** B & W 4 *See* Camelot.
MAPLEBECK (St Radegund), *Notts.* V. **D** Southw 15 **P** *Earl Fitzwilliam* **I** W G CALTHROP-OWEN *p-in-c.*
MAPLEDURHAM, *Oxon..* **D** Ox 7 *See* Caversham.
MAPLEDURWELL (St Mary), *Hants.* V. **D** Win 4 *See* Newnham.
MAPLESTEAD, GREAT (St Giles) and Little (St Jo Bapt) w Gestingthorpe, *Essex.* V. **D** Chelmsf 18 **P** *Knights of Hosp of St John of Jer and Ch Adopt Soc* **I** K F BELBEN.
MAPLETON (St Mary), *Derbys..* **D** Derby 8 *See* Ashbourne.
MAPPERLEY (H Trin), *Derbys.* V. **D** Derby 13 *See* West Hallam.
MAPPERLEY (St Jude), *Notts..* **D** Southw 14 *See* Nottingham.
MAPPERTON w Melplash (Ch Ch), *Dorset.* R. **D** Sarum *See* Beaminster Area.
MAPPISCOMBE, *Kent..* **D** Roch *See* Kingsdown.
MAPPLETON, *Humb.* V. **D** York 14 *See* Aldbrough.
MAPPOWDER (St Pet and St Paul), *Dorset.* R. **D** Sarum 13 *See* Hazelbury-Bryan.
MARAZION (All SS w St Mich), *Cornw.* V. **D** Truro 5 **P** *V of St Hilary* **I** J D CURSON *p-in-c.*
MARBURY (St Mich), *Chesh.* V. **D** Ches 5 **P** *Bp* **I** S J WRIGHT.
MARCH (St Wendreda), *Cambs.* R. **D** Ely 19 **P** *MMT* **I** R H SALMON.
(St John), R. **D** Ely 19 **P** *Bp* **I** G D CORDY.
(St Mary w St Mary Magd), R. **D** Ely 19 **P** *Bp* **I** M K BROADHEAD.
(St Pet), R. **D** Ely 19 **P** *Bp* **I** M K BROADHEAD.
MARCHAM (All SS) w Garford (St Luke), *Oxon.* V. **D** Ox 11 **P** *D and C of Ch Ch Ox* **I** H CLEGG.
MARCHINGTON (St Pet) w Marchington Woodlands (St John), *Staffs.* V. **D** Lich 20 **P** *V of Hanbury* **I** O G EDE.
MARCHWOOD (St Jo Ap), *Hants.* R. **D** Win 9 **P** *Bp* **I** P BRADFORD.
MARCLE, LITTLE (St Mich AA), *Herefs.* R. **D** Heref 6 **P** *Bp* **I** (Vacant).
MARDALE (H Trin), *Cumb.* V. **D** Carl 1 *See* Bampton.
MARDEN (St Mary Virg) w Amberley and Wisteston, *Herefs.* V. **D** Heref 4 **P** *D and C of Heref* **I** L G MOSS.
MARDEN (St Mich AA), *Kent.* V. **D** Cant 11 **P** *Abp* **I** A C M HARGREAVES.
MARDEN (All SS), *Wilts.* V. **D** Sarum 23 *See* Chirton.
MARDEN, EAST w North, *W Sussex.* R. **D** Chich 8 *See* Compton.
MARDEN, UP (St Mich), *W Sussex..* **D** Chich 8 *See* Compton.
MAREHAM-LE-FEN (St Helen) and Revesby (St Lawr) and Moorhouses (St Lawr) w Wilksby (All SS), Moorby (All SS) and Claxby Pluckacre, *Lincs.* R. **D** Linc 11 **P** *Bp and Mrs A D Lee (alt)* **I** P J WHITE.
MAREHAM-ON-THE-HILL (All SS), *Lincs.* V. **D** Linc 11 **P** *Bp* **I** A A EDE.
MARESFIELD (St Bart), *E Sussex.* R. **D** Chich 16 **P** *Ch Trust Fund Trust* **I** G W R BERRY.
MARFLEET (St Giles), *Humb.* R. **D** York 17 **P** *Dioc Bd of Patr* **I** P J ANDERSON *team v*, R E CHESTERTON *team v*, P J RIVETT *team v.*
MARGARET MARSH (St Marg), *Dorset..* **D** Sarum 13 *See* Orchard, East.
MARGARET RODING, *Essex..* **D** Chelmsf 23 *See* High Easter.
MARGARET STREET (All SS).. **D** Lon 25 *See* St Marylebone.
MARGARETTING (St Marg), *Essex.* V. **D** Chelmsf *See* Fryerning.
MARGATE (St Jo Bapt), *Kent.* V. **D** Cant 9 **P** *Abp* **I** N BALDOCK, E E J FRANKLIN *c*, L P SMITH *c.*
(All SS Westbrook), V. **D** Cant 9 **P** *Abp* **I** L F TABOR.
(H Trin), V. **D** Cant 9 **P** *CPS* **I** J S WENT, C E N DAVIS *c.*
(St Paul, Cliftonville), V. **D** Cant 9 **P** *Trustees* **I** D A LUGG.
MARHAM (H Trin), *Norf..* **D** Ely 17 *See* Fincham.
MARHAMCHURCH (Sancta Marvenne) w Launcells (St Swith), [Cornw]. R. **D** Truro 10 **P** *Trustees* **I** K W NOAKES.
MARHOLM (St Mary Virg), *Cambs.* R. **D** Pet 14 **P** *Earl Fitzwilliam* **I** J S BELL *p-in-c.*
MARIANSLEIGH (St Marina or St Mary), *Devon..* **D** Ex 19 *See* Oakmoor.
MARISTOW, *Devon..* **D** Ex *See* Marystowe.
MARK (H Cross) w Allerton, *Somt.* V. **D** B & W 2 **P** *Bp and D and C of Wells* **I** A K KNIGHT.
MARK CROSS, *E Sussex..* **D** Chich 20 *See* Rotherfield.
MARKBEECH (H Trin), *Kent.* V. **D** Roch 9 *See* Hever.
MARKBY (St Pet), *Lincs..* **D** Linc 8 *See* Hannah.
MARKET BOSWORTH (St Pet) w Shenton (St Jo Evang), *Leics.* R. **D** Leic 15 **P** *Dioc Bd of Patr* **I** N ROBINSON.
MARKET DEEPING (St Guthlac), *Lincs.* R. **D** Linc 13 **P** *Ld Chan* **I** D E DAVIES.
MARKET DRAYTON (St Mary), *Salop.* V. **D** Linc 23 **P** *Lt-Col Sir J V Corbet* **I** D M MORRIS.
MARKET HARBOROUGH (St Dionysius), *Leics.* V. **D** Leic 5 **P** *Bp* **I** N C CROWE, K P ASHBY *c.* *See also* BOWDEN, GREAT AND LITTLE.
MARKET LAVINGTON (St Mary of the Assump) w Easterton (St Barn), *Wilts.* V. **D** Sarum 23 **P** *Bp and D and C of Ch Ch Ox* alt **I** R H WILKINS *p-in-c.*
MARKET OVERTON Leics. R **D** Pet *See* Teigh.
MARKET RASEN (St Thos), *Lincs.* V. **D** Linc 5 **P** *Ld Chan* **I** A V SEARLE-BARNES.
MARKET STAINTON (St Mich Arch), *Lincs.* V. **D** Linc 11 *See* Benniworth.
MARKET WEIGHTON (All SS), *humb.* V. **D** York 10 **P** *Abp* **I** M EXLEY.
MARKET WESTON (St Mary Virg), *Suff.* R. **D** St E 9 *See* Hopton.
MARKFIELD (St Mich) w Stanton-under-Bardon (St Mary and All SS), *Leics.* R. **D** Leic 17 **P** *Mart Mem and C of E Trusts* **I** E J HART.
MARKHAM CLINTON (All SS) w Bevercotes (No Church), *Notts.* V. **D** Southw *See* Tuxford.
MARKINGTON (St Mich) w S Stainley (St Wilfred) and Bishop Thornton (St Jo Bapt), *N Yorks.* V. **D** Ripon 3 **P** *Bp (1st turn), D and C of Ripon (2nd turn) and Trustees (3rd turn)* **I** S D ASKEW.
MARKS GATE (St Mark), *Essex..* **D** Chelmsf 1 *See* Chadwell Heath.
MARKS TEY (St Andr), *Essex.* R. **D** Chelmsf 22 **P** *Bp* **I** P H ADAMS, S G HUCKLE *c.*
MARKSBURY (St Pet), *Avon.* R. **D** B & W 13 **P** *Dioc Bd of Patr* **I** (Vacant).
MARKSHALL (St Marg), *Essex..* **D** Chelmsf *See* Coggeshall.
MARKSHALL, *Norf..* **D** Nor 14 *See* Caistor.
MARKYATE (St Jo Bapt), *Herts.* V. **D** St Alb 14 **P** *Bp* **I** L E OGLESBY.
MARLBOROUGH (St Pet and St Paul Aps w St Mary Virg) and Preshute, *Wilts.* R. **D** Sarum 26 **P** *Bp* **I** W S DOWN, C G FOX *team v*, M F D CRIPPS *c.*

MARLBROOK TEAM MINISTRY **D** B & W *See* Bath.
MARLDON (St Jo Bapt), *Devon.* V. **D** Ex 10 **P** *Bp* **I** D J PROTHERO.
MARLESFORD, *Suff..* **D** St E *See* Campsea Ashe.
MARLEY HILL (St Cuthb), *T & W.* V. **D** Dur 4a **P** *Crown* **I** A GALES.
MARLINGFORD (Assump of BVM), *Norf.* R. **D** Nor *See* Easton.
MARLOW, GREAT (All SS) *Bucks.* V. **D** Ox 32 **P** *Bp* **I** S R DAY, R SAUNDERS *c.*
MARLOW, LITTLE (St Jo Bapt) w Flackwell Heath (Ch Ch), *Bucks.* V. **D** Ox 32 **P** *Dioc Bd of Patr* **I** E J HART, J CRAWFORD *c.*
MARLPOOL (All SS), *Derbys..* **D** Derby 6 *See* Heanor.
MARLSTON (St Mary), *Berks..* **D** Ox 14 *See* Bucklebury.
MARNHAM (St Wilfrid), *Notts.* V. **D** Southw 4 **P** *Bp* **I** D G HATTER.
MARNHULL (St Greg), *Dorset.* R. **D** Sarum 13 **P** *Dioc Bd of Finance* **I** J C PRIESTMAN.
MARPLE (All SS), *Gtr Man.* V. **D** Ches 16 **P** *R of Stockport* **I** J R CLAYDON, D M MOORE *c.*
LOW (St Martin), V. **D** Ches 16 **P** *Keble Coll Ox* **I** J MACKEY.
MARR (St Helen), *S Yorks..* **D** Sheff *See* Brodsworth.
MARSDEN (St Bart), *W Yorks.* V. **D** Wakef 6 **P** *V of Almondbury* **I** G HIGGINS.
MARSDEN, GREAT (St Jo Evang), *Lancs.* V. **D** Blackb 6a **P** *Crown* **I** (Vacant).
MARSDEN, LITTLE (St Paul), *Lancs.* V. **D** Blackb 6a **P** *Bp* **I** J W LEE.
MARSH BALDON (St Pet) and Toot Baldon (St Laur) w Nuneham Courtenay *Oxon.* R. **D** Ox *See* Dorchester.
MARSH CHAPEL (St Mary), *Lincs.* V. **D** Linc 12 **P** *Trustees* **I** P PARKINSON.
MARSH-GIBBON (St Mary Virg), *Bucks..* **D** Ox 25 *See* Swan.
MARSHAM (All SS), *Norf.* R. **D** Nor 3 **P** *Bp* **I** A B BOAR *p-in-c.*
MARSHFIELD (St Mary Virg) w Cold Ashton (H Trin), *Avon.* V. **D** Bris 8 **P** *New Coll Ox* **I** (Vacant).
MARSHLAND (St Jas), *Norf.* V. **D** Ely 18 **P** *Bp* **I** C N BALES.
MARSHWOOD (St Mary), *Dorset..* **D** Sarum 4 *See* Bettiscombe.
MARSKE (St Edm), *N Yorks..* **D** Ripon 1 *See* Grinton.
MARSKE-IN-CLEVELAND (St Germain and St Mark), *Cleve.* V. **D** York 19 **P** *Trustees* **I** R WHITE, J H DAVIS *c.*
NEW, V. **D** York **P** *Abp* **I** A HUGHES.
MARSTON (St Mary), *Leics.* R. **D** Leic 16 *See* Barwell.
MARSTON (St Mary), *Lincs..* **D** Linc 23 *See* Hougham.
MARSTON, *Oxon..* **D** Ox *See* Oxford.
MARSTON ST LAWRENCE w Warkworth (St Mary) and Thenford (St Marg Virg), *Northants.* V. **D** Pet 1 **P** *Miss M Blencowe and Ld Chan* **I** S C W B WIGRAM.
MARSTON BIGOT (St Leon), *Somt..* **D** B & W 16a *See* Witham Friary.
MARSTON GREEN (St Leon), *W Midl.* V. **D** Birm 9 **P** *Trustees* **I** R P HEAPS, R E MARTIN *c.*
MARSTON, LONG (All SS) and Wilstone (St Cross), *Herts.* V. **D** St Alb 3 *See* Puttenham.
MARSTON, LONG (All SS), *N Yorks.* R. **D** York 2 **P** *C York Esq* **I** J A RENDALL.
MARSTON MAGNA (BVM), w Rimpton, *Somt.* R. **D** B & W 12 *See* Camel, Queen.
MARSTON MEYSEY (St Jas), *Wilts.* V. **D** Glouc 14 *See* Meysey Hampton.
MARSTON MONTGOMERY (St Giles), *Derbys..* **D** Derby *See* Cubley.
MARSTON MORTEYNE (St Mary Virg) w Lidlington (St Marg), *Beds.* R. **D** St Alb **P** *St Jo Coll Cam and Bp (alt)* **I** J GREENWAY.
MARSTON, NORTH (St Mary) w Granborough (St Jo Bapt), *Bucks.* V. **D** Ox *See* Schorne.
MARSTON-ON-DOVE (St Mary) w Scropton (St Paul), *Derbys.* V. **D** Derby 14 **P** *Exors of J M Spurrier* **I** B FREER.
MARSTON-SICCA (St Jas Gt), *Warws..* **D** Glouc *See* Quinton.
MARSTON, SOUTH (St Mary Magd) w Stanton Fitzwarren (St Leon), R *Wilts..* **D** Bris 10 *See* Stratton St Marg.
MARSTON STANNETT, *Herefs..* **D** Heref *See* Pencombe.
MARSTON TRUSSELL (St Nich), *Northants.* R. **D** Pet 6 *See* Oxenden.
MARSTOW, *Herefs..* **D** Heref *See* Goodrich.
MARSWORTH (All SS), *Bucks..* **D** Ox *See* Cheddington.
MARTHALL (All SS) w Over Peover *Chesh.* V. **D** Ches 12 **P** *Dioc Bd of Patr* **I** D M LOWE.
MARTHAM (St Mary), *Norf.* V. **D** Nor 2 **P** *D and C of Nor* **I** E A CUNNINGTON.
MARTIN (H Trin) w Martin Dales (St Hugh), *Lincs.* V. **D** Linc 18 **P** *Bp* **I** J L M LE MARCHAND *p-in-c.*
MARTIN (St Mich), *Lincs..* **D** Linc 11 *See* Thornton.
MARTIN Wilts. V **D** Sarum 19 *See* Damerham.
MARTIN HUSSINGTREE (St Mich AA), *Worcs.* R. **D** Worc 6 *See* Hindlip.
MARTINDALE (St Pet), *Cumb.* V. **D** Carl 6 **P** *W H Parkin Esq* **I** D A REED *p-in-c.*
MARTINHOE (St Martin), *Devon.* R. **D** Ex 18 *See* Lynton.
MARTLESHAM (St Mary Virg) w Brightwell (St Jo Bapt), *Suff.* R. **D** St E 2 **P** *Bp* **I** B D LILLISTONE.
MARTLEY (St Pet) and Wichenford, *Worcs.* R. **D** Worc **P** *D and C of Worc and Dioc Bd of Patr (alt)* **I** A T BARTLETT *p-in-c.*
MARTOCK (All SS) w Ash (H Trin), *Somt.* V. **D** B & W 11 **P** *Bp* **I** P N H CONEY.
MARTON (St Paul), *Lancs.* V. **D** Blackb 8 **P** *V of Poulton-le-Fylde* **I** J CAYTON, A C RUSSELL *c,* M HAIGH *hon c.*
MARTON, *Cumb..* **D** Carl 15 *See* Lindal.
MARTON, *Humb..* **D** York 12 *See* Sewerby.
MARTON (St Jas), *Chesh..* **D** Ches 13 *See* Capesthorne.
MARTON (St Esprit), *Warws.* V. **D** Cov 10 **P** *Bp* **I** (Vacant).
MARTON (St Marg), *Lincs.* V. **D** Linc 2 **P** *Bp* **I** L SALT.
MARTON (Ch Ch) w Grafton (All SS), *N Yorks.* V. **D** Ripon 3 *See* Ouseburn, Gt.
MARTON-IN-CHIRBURY (St Mark), *Salop.* V. **D** Heref 13 **P** *V of Chirbury* **I** K J F BRADBURY.
MARTON-IN-CLEVELAND (St Cuthb), *N Yorks.* V. **D** York 22 **P** *Abp* **I** R M FIRTH, T M WARD *c.*
MARTON-IN-CRAVEN (St Pet) w Thornton-in-Craven (St Mary), *N Yorks.* R. **D** Bradf 10 *See* Broughton.
MARTON-IN-THE-FOREST, *N Yorks..* **D** York *See* Stillington.
MARTYR-WORTHY, *Hants..* **D** Win *See* Easton.
MARWOOD (St Mich AA), *Devon.* R. **D** Ex 15 *See* Heanton-Punchardon.
MARY CHURCH (St Mary), *Devon.* V. **D** Ex 10 *See* St Mary Church.
MARY TAVY, *Devon..* **D** Ex 22 *See* Tavy St Mary.
MARYLEBONE. **D** Lon 25 *See* St Marylebone.
MARYPORT (St Mary Virg) w (Ch Ch), *Cumb.* V. **D** Carl 11 **P** *Trustees* **I** (Vacant).
MARYSTOWE (St Mary Virg) w Coryton (St Andr) and Stowford w Lew-Trenchard w Thrushelton, *Devon.* V. **D** Ex **P** *T Newman Esq 1st turn Mrs A M Baring-Gould 2nd turn, P L Donkin Esq 3rd turn and R H Woollocombe Esq 4th turn* **I** (Vacant).
MASBROUGH (St Paul w St John), *S Yorks.* V. **D** Sheff 7 *See* Ferham Pk, Rotherham.
MASHAM (St Mary Virg) and Healey, *N Yorks.* V. **D** Ripon 3 **P** *Trin Coll Cam* **I** F LINDARS.
MASHBURY (no Dedic), *Essex..* **D** Chelmsf 12 *See* Chignals, The.
MASSINGHAM, GREAT (St Mary), *Norf.* R. **D** Nor 20 **P** *Bp* **I** (Vacant).
MASSINGHAM, LITTLE (St Andr), *Norf.* R. **D** Nor 20 **P** *J L Brereton Esq* **I** (Vacant).
MATCHING (St Mary Virg), *Essex.* V. **D** Chelmsf 3 **P** *Felstead Charity Trust* **I** W A HOWARTH.
MATFEN (H Trin w All SS), *Northumb.* V. **D** Newc T 3 *See* Stamfordham.
MATFIELD (St Luke), *Kent.* V. **D** Roch 10 **P** *V of Brenchley* **I** B E E MARSHALL *p-in-c.*
MATHON (St Jo Bapt), *Herefs.* V. **D** Heref 6 **P** *D and C of Westmr* **I** (Vacant).
MATLASKE, *Norf..* **D** Nor *See* Barningham, North.
MATLOCK (St Giles w St Jo Bapt), *Derbys.* R. **D** Derby 17 **P** *Bp and V of Crich* **I** J F STATHAM *p-in-c.*
MATLOCK BANK (All SS), *Derbys.* V. **D** Derby 17 **P** *Bp* **I** B J COLEMAN *p-in-c,* K J ORFORD *hon c.*
MATLOCK BATH (H Trin), *Derbys.* V. **D** Derby 17 **P** *Trustees* **I** H COLLARD.
MATSON (St Kath), *Glos.* R. **D** Glouc 1 **P** *D and C of Glouc* **I** B C E COKER, J A B PADDOCK *c.*
MATTERDALE (Dedic unknown), *Cumb..* **D** Carl 6 *See* Greystoke.
MATTERSEY (All SS), *Notts.* V. **D** Southw 1 *See* Everton.
MATTINGLEY (Dedic unknown), *Hants.* V. **D** Win 4 *See* Heckfield.
MATTISHALL (All SS) w Mattishall Burgh (St Pet), *Norf.* V. **D** Nor 12 **P** *G and C Coll Cam* **I** P H MOSS *c-in-c.*
MAULDEN (St Mary), *Beds.* R. **D** St Alb 15 **P** *Bp* **I** D LEWTHWAITE.

MAUNBY, *N Yorks*.. **D** Ripon 2 *See* Kirkby Wiske.
MAUTBY (St Pet and St Paul), *Norf.* R. **D** Nor 2 *See* Filby.
MAVESYN RIDWARE (St Nich), *Staffs*. R. **D** Lich 4 **P** *Bp* **I** R E P DAVIES.
MAVIS ENDERBY (St Mich), *Lincs*. R. **D** Lich *See* Bolingbroke.
MAWDESLEY (St Pet) w Bispham, *Lancs*. R. **D** Blackb 4 **P** *R of Croston* **I** G E STEPHENS.
MAWGAN, ST, *Cornw*.. **D** Truro *See* St Mawgan.
MAWNAN (St Maunanus and St Steph), *Cornw*. R. **D** Truro 3 **P** *J P Rogers Esq and O F Price Esq* **I** J RUSCOE.
MAWNEYS (St Jo Div), *Essex*. V. **D** Chelmsf 2 *See* Romford.
MAXEY (St Pet) w Northborough (St Andr), *Cambs*. V. **D** Pet 14 **P** *D and C of Pet* **I** A SHEASBY.
MAXSTOKE (St Mich AA), *W Midl*. V. **D** Birm 9 **P** *Ld Leigh 1 turn S Wingfield Digby Esq 3 turns* **I** J F CAPPER.
MAYBUSH (St Pet), *Hants*. V. **D** Win 11 **P** *Bp* **I** R G DISS, C R SMITH *c*.
MAYFAIR (Ch Ch).. **D** Lon 19 *See* Westminster.
MAYFIELD (St Dunstan), *E Sussex*. V. **D** Chich 18 **P** *Keble Coll Ox* **I** V J ALLARD *c*.
MAYFIELD (St Jo Bapt), *Staffs*. V. **D** Lich 20 **P** *Ch S Trust* **I** D T M K SERVICE.
MAYLAND (St Barn), *Essex*. V. **D** Chelmsf 13 **P** *Bp* **I** L BLANEY *c-in-c*.
MEANWOOD (H Trin), *W Yorks*. V. **D** Ripon 5 **P** *Bp* **I** J S DODD.
MEARE (BVM and All SS), *Somt*. V. **D** B & W 7 **P** *Bp* **I** A.G. CLARKSON C-IN-C OF W PENNARD *c-in-c*.
MEARS ASHBY (All SS), *Northants*. V. **D** Pet 7 **P** *Bracegirdle Trustees* **I** R F COTTINGHAM.
MEASHAM (St Lawr) w Willesley (St Thos), *Leics*. V. **D** Leic 12 **P** *CPAS* **I** (Vacant).
MEAVY (St Pet), R w Sheepstor (Dedic unknown), V *Devon*.. **D** Ex 22 **P** *Ld Chan and Ld Roborough* **I** R H CHITTENDEN.
MEDBOURNE (St Giles) w Holt (St Mary) and Stockerston w Blaston, *Leics*. R. **D** Leic 5 **P** *Archd of Leic 1 turn, St Jo Coll Cam 2 turns* **I** R T MATHEWS.
MEDMENHAM (St Pet), *Bucks*. V. **D** Ox *See* Hambledon Valley.
MEDOMSLEY (St Mary Magd), *Durham*. V. **D** Dur 7 **P** *Bp* **I** R D FRASER.
MEDSTEAD (St Andr) w Wield (St Jas), V *Hants*. R. **D** Win 1 **P** *Ld Chan* **I** G K MATTHEW.
MEERBROOK (St Matt), *Staffs*. V. **D** Lich 16 **P** *V of Leek* **I** (Vacant).
MEESDEN (St Mary), *Herts*. V. **D** St Alb 5 *See* Brent Pelham.
MEETH, *Devon*.. **D** Ex *See* Merton.
MEIR (H Trin), *Staffs*. V. **D** Lich 14 **P** *Bp* **I** T J HARVEY, P M COLLINS *c*.
MEIR HEATH (St Francis) *Staffs*. V. **D** Lich 18 **P** *Bp* **I** J W PAWSON.
MELBECKS (H Trin), *N Yorks*. V. **D** Ripon 1 *See* Muker.
MELBOURN (All SS), *Cambs*. V. **D** Ely 8 **P** *D and C of Ely* **I** J K GREASLEY.
MELBOURNE (St Mich and St Mary), *Derbys*. V. **D** Derby 15 **P** *Bp* **I** F ROSS.
MELBOURNE, *Humb*. V. **D** York 7 *See* Thornton.
MELBURY (Cattistock w Chilfrome, Rampisham, Wraxall, Corscombe, Evershot, Frome St Quintin, Melbury Bubb, Melbury Osmond, Melbury Sampford, Halstock and East and West Chelborough), *Dorset*. R. **D** Sarum **P** *Bp, Lady J T Agnew, D A Block Esq, St Jo Coll Cam and Dioc Bd of Patr* **I** R J S BURN, D BANYARD *team v*, D G N MURCH *team v*.
MELBURY ABBAS (St Thos), *Dorset*. R. **D** Sarum *See* Shaston.
MELBURY BUBB (St Mary Virg), *Dorset*.. **D** Sarum *See* Melbury.
MELBURY OSMUND (St Osmund) w Melbury Sampford (St Mary), *Dorset*. R. **D** Sarum *See* Melbury.
MELCHBOURNE (St Mary Magd), *Beds*. V. **D** St Alb *See* Yelden.
MELCOMBE HORSEY (St Andr), *Dorset*. R. **D** Sarum 10 *See* Hilton.
MELCOMBE REGIS, *Dorset*.. **D** Sarum *See* Radipole.
MELDON (St Jo Evang), *Northumb*. R. **D** Newc T 10 *See* Hartburn.
MELDRETH (H Trin), *Cambs*. V. **D** Ely 8 **P** *D and C of Ely* **I** J K GREASLEY.
MELFORD, LONG (H Trin), *Suff*. R. **D** St E 12 **P** *Bp* **I** C J SANSBURY.
MELKSHAM (St Mich AA w St Andr and St Barn), *Wilts*. R. **D** Sarum 24 **P** *Dioc Bd of Patr* **I** K F M C FISHER, S E W GUY *team v*, S F TREEBY *team v*.
MELLING (St Wilfrid) w Tatham (St Jas L), *Lancs*. V. **D** Blackb 13 **P** *Exors of Rev H Rennington and Churchwardens* alt **I** W H C FAWCETT.
MELLING (St Thos), *Mer*. V. **D** Liv 9 **P** *R of Halsall* **I** M E PLUNKETT.
MELLIS (St Mary Virg), *Suff*. R. **D** St E 16 **P** *Bp* **I** L TRENDER *p-in-c*.
MELLOR (St Mary), *Lancs*. V. **D** Blackb 2 **P** *V of Blackb* **I** D J HOWSON.
MELLOR (St Thos), *Gtr Man*. V. **D** Derbys 5 **P** *Bp* **I** R M PHILLIPS.
MELLS (St Andr) w Kilmersdon, Babington, Elm (St Mary) Vobster (St Edm), Whatley (St Geo) and Chantry, *Somt*. R. **D** B & W 16a **P** *Miss A K S Lambton 2 turns, Ld Hylton 1 turn* **I** J M C YATES *c-in-c*.
MELMERBY, *Cumb*.. **D** Carl *See* Ousby.
MELPLASH (Ch Ch), *Dorset*. V. **D** Sarum 4 *See* Mapperton.
MELSONBY (St Jas Gt) *N Yorks*.. **D** Ripon 1 *See* Middleton Tyas.
MELTHAM (St Bart), *W Yorks*. V. **D** Wakef 6 **P** *V of Almondbury* **I** P SPIVEY.
MELTHAM MILLS (St Jas Ap), *W Yorks*. V. **D** Wakef 6 **P** *Simeon Trustees* **I** D TURNER.
MELTON (St Andr), *Suff*. R. **D** St E 7 **P** *D and C of Ely* **I** M L H BOYNS.
MELTON, *Humb*. V. **D** York 17 *See* Welton.
MELTON CONSTABLE (St Pet) w Swanton Novers, *Norf*. R. **D** Nor 24 **P** *Lady Hastings* **I** M F C TAYLOR.
MELTON, GREAT (All SS and St Mary), *Norf*. R. **D** Nor 13 *See* Melton, Little.
MELTON, HIGH, or MELTON-ON-THE-HILL (All H or St Jas), *S Yorks*.. **D** Sheff 10 *See* Barnburgh.
MELTON, LITTLE (All SS) and Great w Bawburgh, *Norf*. V. **D** Nor **P** *Em Coll Cam 1 turn, Trustees of Vice-Adm Sir E M Evans-Lombe 2 turns, D and C of Nor 1 turn* **I** R A LOVELESS.
MELTON MOWBRAY (St Mary) w Thorpe Arnold (St Mary Virg), *Leics*. V. **D** Leic 4 **P** *Peache Trustees* **I** D E B LAW, D W A KING *team v*, C P DOBBIN *c*.
MELTON ROSS (Ascen) w New Barnetby, *Humb*. V. **D** Linc 6 **P** *Earl of Yarborough* **I** B O WHITFIELD.
MELTONBY (St Jas), *Humb*. V. **D** York *See* Pocklington.
MELVERLEY (St Pet), *Salop*. R. **D** Lich 24 *See* Kinnerley.
MEMBURY (St Jo Bapt), *Devon*. V. **D** Ex 5 *See* Yarcombe.
MENDHAM (All SS) w Metfield (St Jo Bapt) and Withersdale, *Suff*. V. **D** St E 17 **P** *Bp 1 turn, S for Maint of Faith 2 turns, Em Coll 1 turn* **I** R S SMITH.
MENDLESHAM (St Mary), *Suff*. V. **D** St E 6 **P** *S for Maint of Faith* **I** P T GRAY.
MENHENIOT (St Lalluwy) w Merrymeet, *Cornw*. V. **D** Truro 13 **P** *Ex Coll Ox* **I** P F WATTS *p-in-c*.
MENSTON-IN-WHARFEDALE (St Jo Div) w Woodhead, *W Yorks*. V. **D** Bradf 5 **P** *Bp* **I** J M HECKINGBOTTOM.
MENTMORE (St Mary Virg), *Bucks*. V. **D** Ox 27 *See* Cheddington.
MEOLE BRACE (H Trin), *Salop*. V. **D** Lich 26 **P** *Mrs D M Bather* **I** P C RUFFLE.
MEOLS, GREAT (St Jo Bapt), *Mer*. V. **D** Ches 8 **P** *Bp* **I** L A THOMPSON.
MEONSTOKE (St Andr) w Corhampton and Exton (St Pet and St Paul), *Hants*. R. **D** Portsm 2 **P** *Bp* **I** J W BEAUMONT.
MEOPHAM (St Jo Bapt) w Nurstead (St Mildred), *Kent*. V. **D** Roch 1 **P** *D and C of Roch and Maj R W Edmeades* **I** D M P GILES.
MEPAL, *Cambs*.. **D** Ely 15 *See* Witcham.
MEPPERSHALL (St Mary Virg), *Beds*. R. **D** St Alb 22 **P** *St Jo Coll Cam* **I** G H WALLER.
MERE (St Mich Archangel) w W Knoyle and Maiden Bradley, *Wilts*. V. **D** Sarum 22 **P** *Bp* **I** W H V ELLIOTT.
MERESIDE (St Wilfrid), *Lancs*.. **D** Blackb 11 *See* Blackpool.
MEREVALE (St Mary Virg), *Warws*. V. **D** Birm 10 **P** *Sir W Dugdale Bt* **I** (Vacant).
MEREWORTH (St Lawr) w W Peckham (St Dunstan), *Kent*. R. **D** Roch 6 **P** *Visc Falmouth and D and C of Roch* **I** A E RAMSBOTTOM.
MERIDEN (St Lawr), *W Midl*. R. **D** Cov 4 **P** *Provost and Chapter of Cov* **I** M J LEATON.
MERRINGTON (St Jo Evang), *Durham*. V. **D** Dur 9 **P** *D and C of Dur* **I** B K RUSSELL *p-in-c*.
MERRIOTT (All SS) w Hinton, Dunnington and Lopen, *Somt*. V. **D** B & W **P** *D and C of Bris 2 turns Bp 1 turn* **I** J C KING.

MERROW (St Jo Div), *Surrey*. R. **D** Guildf 5 **P** *Earl of Onslow* **I** R ROE.
MERSEA, EAST (St Edm K and Mart), *Essex*. R. **D** Chelmsf 21 *See* Mersea West.
MERSEA, WEST (St Pet and St Paul) w Mersea, East (St Edm K and Mart), *Essex*. V. **D** Chelmsf 21 **P** *Bp* **I** J A G SWALLOW.
MERSHAM (St Jo Bapt), *Kent*. R. **D** Cant 12 **P** *Abp* **I** J H WAITE *p-in-c*.
MERSTHAM (St Cath) w Gatton (St Andr), *Surrey*. R. **D** S'wark 12 **P** *Abp* **I** P E DUVAL, C A CROFTS *c*.
(St Luke's Conv Distr Netherne). **D** S'wark 12 **I** M S WRATTEN *c-in-c*.
MERSTHAM, SOUTH (All SS), *Surrey*. V. **D** S'wark 12 **P** *Bp* **I** B L HAMMOND.
MERSTON (St Giles), *W Sussex*. R. **D** Chich *See* Oving.
MERSTON or MARESTON, *Kent*.. **D** Roch *See* Higham.
MERTHER, *Cornw*.. **D** Truro *See* Lamorran.
MERTON (All SS) w Meeth (St Mich AA) and Huish (St Jas L), *Devon*. R. **D** Ex 20 *See* Petrockstowe.
MERTON (St Pet), *Norf*.. **D** Nor 19 *See* Caston.
MERTON (St Swith Bp of Win), *Oxon*.. **D** Ox *See* Ambrosden.
MERTON (St Mary Virg), *Surrey*. V. **D** S'wark 14 **P** *Bp* **I** P G SOUTHWELL-SANDER, N H THOMPSON *c*, G J BENTLEY *hon c*.
(St Jas), V. **D** S'wark 14 **P** *V of Merton and Miss M Corfield* **I** M A J OADES, G R BERRIDGE *c*.
(St Jo Div), V. **D** S'wark 14 **P** *V of Merton and Miss M Corfield* **I** T J HAZELGROVE.
MESHAW Devon. R **D** Ex 19 *See* Witheridge.
MESSING (All SS) w Inworth, *Essex*. V. **D** Chelmsf 29 **P** *Dioc Bd of Patr and Lady Acland* alt **I** M H CLARKE.
MESSINGHAM (H Trin) w East Butterwick (St Andr), *Humb*. V. **D** Linc 4 **P** *Bp* **I** E A BACON.
METFIELD (St Jo Bapt) w Withersdale, *Suff*. V. **D** St E 17 *See* Mendham.
METHERINGHAM (St Wilfrid), *Lincs*. V. **D** Linc 18 **P** *Marchioness of Bris* **I** D W BATES.
METHLEY (St Osw) w Mickletown, *W Yorks*. R. **D** Ripon 7 **P** *Bp (3 turns) and Duchy of Lanc (1 turn)* **I** M G WHITTOCK.
METHWOLD (St Geo), *Norf*. V. **D** Ely 16 **P** *Ld Chan* **I** J B ROWSELL.
METTINGHAM (All SS), *Suff*. R. **D** St E *See* Ringsfield.
METTON (St Andr), *Nor*.. **D** Nor 5 *See* Felbrigg.
MEVAGISSEY (St Pet), *Cornw*. V. **D** Truro 1 **P** *Bp* **I** (Vacant).
MEXBOROUGH (St Jo Bapt), *S Yorks*. V. **D** Sheff 10 **P** *Archd of York* **I** D STAPLES.
MEYSEY-HAMPTON (St Mary) w Marston Meysey (St Jas) and Castle Eaton, *Wilts*. R. **D** Glouc 14 **P** *Ch S Trust* **I** H BUSK *p-in-c*.
MICHAELCHURCH (St Mich), *Herefs*.. **D** Heref 8 *See* Tretire.
MICHAELCHURCH (St Mich AA), *Herefs*. R. **D** Heref 5 *See* Brilley.
MICHAELCHURCH ESKLEY (St Mich AA), *Herefs*.. **D** Heref 1 *See* St Margaret's.
MICHAELSTOW, *Cornw*.. **D** Truro *See* St Teath.
MICHELDEVER (St Mary) and E Stratton (All SS) w Woodmancote (St Jas) and Popham (St Cath), *Hants*. V. **D** Win 12 **P** *Ld Northbrook 3 turns, Bp 2 turns* **I** J B NEW.
MICHELMERSH (St Mary) w Timsbury and Farley-Chamberlayne w Braishfield, *Hants*. R. **D** Win 10 **P** *Bp and Woodham Trustees* **I** D B KINGTON.
MICKFIELD, *Suff*.. **D** St E 1 *See* Crowfield.
MICKLEFIELD (St Mary Virg), *N Yorks*. V. **D** York 8 **P** *Abp* **I** (Vacant).
MICKLEHAM (St Mich), *Surrey*. R. **D** Guildf 6 **P** *Govs of St John's Sch Leatherhead* **I** P R INCE.
MICKLEHURST (All SS), *Gtr Man*. V. **D** Ches 14 **P** *Bp* **I** D BOOTH.
MICKLEOVER (All SS), *Derbys*. V. **D** Derby 14 **P** *MMT* **I** B S W CROCKETT.
(St John), V. **D** Derby 11 **P** *Bp* **I** D MILNER.
MICKLETON (St Lawr), *Glos*. V. **D** Glouc 12 **P** *Ld Chan* **I** J C HUNTRISS *p-in-c*.
MICKLETOWN, *W Yorks*.. **D** Ripon 7 *See* Methley.
MICKLEY (St Geo), *Northumb*. V. **D** Newc T 3 **P** *Bp* **I** J E SYMONS.
MICKLEY (St Jo Evang), *N Yorks*. V. **D** Ripon 3 **P** *V of Masham* **I** G T JONES.
MIDDLEHAM (St Alkelda and St Mary) and Coverham w Horsehouse, *N Yorks*. R. **D** Ripon 2 **P** *Bp and Mrs E J Anne Craven Smith-Milnes* **I** D GUEST.
MIDDLESBROUGH (All SS), *Cleve*. V. **D** York 22 **P** *Abp* **I** J W GODDARD, P B P PREIST *c*.
(St Aid w St Alb Mart), V. **D** York 22 **P** *Abp* **I** P B P PREIST *c*.
(St Chad), V. **D** York 22 **P** *Abp* **I** H CLARK.
(St Columba w St Paul), V. **D** York 22 **P** *Abp* **I** E APPLEYARD *p-in-c*.
(St Cuthb), V. **D** York 22 **P** *Abp* **I** M J WRIGHT *p-in-c*, S D HARROP *c*.
(St Jo Evang), V. **D** York 22 **P** *Abp* **I** J K ELSTONE.
(St Martin of Tours, Linthorpe), V. **D** York 22 **P** *Abp* **I** R BENTINCK, S D HARROP *c*.
(St Osw), V. **D** York 22 **P** *Abp* **I** S FOX *p-in-c*.
(St Barn Linthorpe), V. **D** York 22 **P** *Abp* **I** I D REID, C C MARNHAM *c*.
(St Thos), V. **D** York 22 **P** *Abp* **I** A H YATES, D PERCY *c*.
(Ascen Berwick Hills), V. **D** York 22 **P** *Abp* **I** J F MASSHEDAR *c*.
MIDDLESMOOR w Ramsgill, *N Yorks*.. **D** Ripon 3 *See* Nidderdale, Upper.
MIDDLESTOWN (St Luke) w Netherton (St Andr), *W Yorks*. V. **D** Wakef 12 **P** *R of Thornhill* **I** D H PRIOR.
MIDDLETON (St Jo Bapt), *Warws*. V. **D** Birm 12 **P** *Bp* **I** R J WILKINS.
MIDDLETON, *Cumb*.. **D** Carl *See* Barbon.
MIDDLETON (All SS), *Essex*. R. **D** Chelmsf 18 *See* Henny, Great.
MIDDLETON (St Nich), *W Sussex*.. **D** Chich *See* Felpham.
MIDDLETON-S-GEORGE (St Laur), *Cleve*. R. **D** Dur 11 **P** *Bp* **I** M Q KING.
MIDDLETON (St Mary Virg), *Herefs*.. **D** Heref *See* Kimbolton.
MIDDLETON, *Salop*. V. **D** Heref 12 *See* Bitterley.
MIDDLETON (St Leon), *Gtr Man*. R. **D** Man 17 **P** *Trustees* **I** J WHITTAKER, R K TITFORD *c*, M NELSON *hon c*.
MIDDLETON (St Mary Virg) w East Winch, *Norf*. V. **D** Nor 25 **P** *Sir O Lancaster and Bp (alt)* **I** A E GREEN.
MIDDLETON, *Northants*. R. **D** Pet 20 *See* Cottingham.
MIDDLETON (St Mary Virg), *N Yorks*. V. **D** Ripon 8 **P** *V of Rothwell* **I** W D JONES.
(St Cross), V. **D** Ripon 8 **P** *Dioc Bd of Patr* **I** T N STUBBS.
MIDDLETON (St Nich), *Hants*.. **D** Win 4 *See* Longparish.
MIDDLETON (St Cuthb), *N Yorks*. V. **D** York 25 *See* Rudby-in-Cleveland.
MIDDLETON (St Andr) w Cropton (St Greg), *N Yorks*. V. **D** York 24 **P** *Abp* **I** N BUTCHER *p-in-c*.
MIDDLETON (H Trin) w Fordley, *Suff*. R. **D** St E 19 **P** *CPS* **I** C RALPH.
MIDDLETON-BY-WIRKSWORTH (H Trin), *Derbys*. V. **D** Derby 17 **P** *V of Wirksworth* **I** G BUSBY.
MIDDLETON-BY-YOULGREAVE (St Mich AA), *Derbys*.. **D** Derby 9 *See* Youlgreave.
MIDDLETON CHENEY (All SS), w Chacombe or Chalcombe, V *Northants*. R. **D** Pet 1 **P** *BNC Ox 2 turns, Bp 1 turn* **I** M B MORETON.
MIDDLETON-IN-CHIRBURY (H Trin), *Salop*. V. **D** Heref 13 **P** *V of Chirbury* **I** N D MINSHALL.
MIDDLETON-IN-TEESDALE (St Mary Virg), *Durham*. R. **D** Dur 10 **P** *Crown* **I** (Vacant).
MIDDLETON JUNCTION (St Gabr), *Gtr Man*. V. **D** Man 17 **P** *Bp* **I** I B COOK.
MIDDLETON-ON-THE-WOLDS (St Andr), *Humb*. R. **D** York 13 **P** *Mrs D E Winter* **I** R W HOWE *p-in-c*.
MIDDLETON-SCRIVEN (St Jo Bapt), *Salop*. R. **D** Heref 9 **P** *Bp* **I** R E F DORE.
MIDDLETON STONEY (All SS), *Oxon*.. **D** Ox 2 *See* Chesterton, Gt.
MIDDLETON-TYAS (St Mich) and Melsonby, *N Yorks*. V. **D** Ripon 1 **P** *Univ Coll Ox and Bp* **I** J R W SILLER P-IN-C OF MELSONBY.
MIDDLEWICH (St Mich AA) *Chesh*. V. **D** Ches 6 **P** *Bp* **I** (Vacant).
MIDDLEZOY (H Cross) and Othery and Moorlinch w Stawell and Sutton Mallett, *Somt*. V. **D** B & W 7 **P** *Bp of Worc 1st turn, Bp of B & W 2nd and 3rd turns* **I** J TINSLEY.
MIDGHAM, *berks*.. **D** Ox 12 *See* Woolhampton.
MIDHURST (St Mary Magd and St Denis), *W Sussex*. V. **D** Chich 5 **P** *Cowdray Trust* **I** A PULLIN.
MIDLEY, *Kent*. R (no church). **D** Cant 13 *See* Brookland.
MID MARSH GROUP (Alvingham, Yarburgh, North Cockerington, Carlton, Grimoldby and Manby), *Lincs*. R. **D** Linc **P** *Rear Admiral G Penrose 1st turn, Bp 2nd turn, D and C of Linc 3rd turn and Baron Deramore 4th turn* **I** R D BUCKMAN.
MIDSOMER NORTON (St Jo Bapt), *Avon*. V. **D** B & W 16b **P** *Ch Ch Ox* **I** P G COBB, W J WOODBURN *c*.

MIDVILLE, *Lincs.*. **D** Linc 7 *See* Eastville.
MILBER (St Luke), *Devon.* V. **D** Ex 11 **P** *Bp* **I** J F BOARDMAN.
MILBORNE PORT (St Jo Evang) w Goathill (St Pet), *Somt.* V. **D** B & W 12 **P** *Trustees 1 turn Sir Christopher Medlycott, Bt (2 turns)* **I** G R SHRIMPTON.
MILBORNE ST ANDREW (St Andr) w Dewlish (All SS), *Dorset.* V. **D** Sarum 5 **P** *Rev J L Baillie* **I** P H MATTHEWS *p-in-c.*
MILBURN, *Cumb.*. **D** Carl 1 *See* Long Marton.
MILCOMBE, *Oxon.*. **D** Ox *See* Bloxham.
MILDEN or MILDING (St Pet), *Suff.*. **D** St E 10 *See* Brent Eleigh.
MILDENHALL (St Mary) w Red Lodge, *Suff.* R. **D** St E *See* Barton-Mills.
MILDENHALL (St Jo Bapt), *Wilts.* R. **D** Sarum 26 **P** *Miss P E G Courtman* **I** (Vacant).
MILDMAY PARK (St Jude), V. **D** Lon 6 *See* Islington.
MILE CROSS (St Cath), *Norf.*. **D** Nor 4 *See* Norwich.
MILE END. **D** Lon 8 *See* Stepney and Spitalfields.
MILEHAM, *Norf.* R. **D** Nor 20 **P** *Bp* **I** D J MUNT.
MILES PLATTING, *Gtr Man.*. **D** Man 1 *See* Manchester.
MILFORD (H Trin), *Derbys.* V. **D** Derby 12 *See* Ch Ch Belper.
MILFORD (St Jo Evang), *Surrey.* V. **D** Guildf 4 **P** *V of Witley* **I** J S HARRIS.
MILFORD (All SS), *Hants.* V. **D** Win 9 **P** *Bp* **I** C G PAYNE.
MILL END, *Herts.*. **D** St Alb *See* Rickmansworth.
MILL HILL (St Paul), *Gtr Lon.* V. **D** Lon 17 **P** *Bp* **I** J R HARROLD.
(St Mich AA), V. **D** Lon 17 **P** *Bp* **I** L F RICE *hon c.*
(John Keble Ch), V. **D** Lon 17 **P** *Bp* **I** O R OSMOND.
MILLAND (St Luke), *W Sussex.* V. **D** Chich 5 **P** *Bp* **I** W P RENNISON.
MILLBROOK (St Mich AA), *Beds.*. **D** St Alb *See* Ampthill.
MILLBROOK (H Trin w St Nich), *Hants.* R. **D** Win 11 **P** *Bp* **I** R N H HOLYHEAD *p-in-c.*
MILLBROOK (St Jas), *Gtr Man.* V. **D** Ches 14 **P** *Bp and Trustees* **I** J E HOLLINS.
MILLBROOK (All SS), *Cornw.* V. **D** Truro *See* St John.
MILLFIELD, *T & W.*. **D** Dur 8 *See* Bishop Wearmouth.
MILLHOUSES (St Osw), *S Yorks.*. **D** Sheff 2 *See* Sheffield.
MILLINGTON w Great Givendale (St Ethelburga), *Humb.* V. **D** York 7 **P** *Abp* **I** (Vacant).
MILLOM (H Trin w Ch Ch Kirksanton, and The Hill Chap), *Cumb.* V. **D** Carl 15 **P** *Bp* **I** J HOGARTH.
(St Geo mart w Haverigg St Luke, *Cumb.* V. **D** Carl 15 **P** *Five Trustees* **I** E H ISAAC.
MILLWALL (St Luke).. **D** Lon 7 *See* Poplar.
MILNROW (St Jas), *Gtr Man.* V. **D** Man 17 **P** *V of Rochdale* **I** M R EDWARDS.
MILNSBRIDGE (St Luke), *W Yorks.* V. **D** Wakef 6 **P** *V of Almondbury* **I** (Vacant).
MILNTHORPE (St Thos), *Cumb.* V. **D** Carl 17 **P** *V of Heversham* **I** J D KELLY.
MILSON, *Salop.*. **D** Heref *See* Neen Sollars.
MILSTEAD (St Mary and the H Cross), *Kent.*. **D** Cant 13 *See* Frinsted.
MILSTON, *Wilts.* R. **D** Sarum 18 *See* Figheldean.
MILTON (SS Peter w Jude), *Somt.* V. **D** B & W 3 **P** *Ld Chan* **I** C D TAYLOR.
MILTON (St Jo Bapt), *Kent.*. **D** Cant 3 *See* Thanington.
MILTON (All SS), *Cambs.* R. **D** Ely 6 **P** *K Coll Cam* **I** F J KILNER *p-in-c.*
MILTON (St Phil and St Jas), *Staffs.* V. **D** Lich 16 **P** *Bp* **I** M W WELSH.
MILTON, *Oxon.*. **D** Ox *See* Adderbury.
MILTON (St Blaise), *Oxon.*. **D** Ox 11 *See* Steventon.
MILTON (St Jas Gt), *Hants.* V. **D** Portsm 5 **P** *V of Portsea* **I** C R GEORGE, B G HIGGINS *c*, M E C JOYCE *c*, M N S DUNCAN *hon c.*
MILTON (St Simon and St Jude), *Dorset.*. **D** Sarum 13 *See* Gillingham.
MILTON (St Mary Magd), *Dorset.* R. **D** Win 8 **P** *V of Milford* **I** S A OUTHWAITE, J M STARR *c.*
MILTON ABBAS or ABBEY (St Jas Gt), Hilton w Cheselbourne and Melcombe Horsey, *Dorset.* R. **D** Sarum 10 **P** *Bp 3 turns, G A L F Pitt-Rivers Esq 1 turn* **I** S M ROYLE.
MILTON-ABBOT (St Aegidius) w Dunterton (St Constantine), *Devon.* R. **D** Ex 22 **P** *Duke of Bedford* **I** G A SMITH *c.*
MILTON-BRYAN, *Beds.*. **D** St Alb *See* Eversholt.
MILTON CLEVEDON (St Jas Ap), *Somt.* V. **D** B & W 5 *See* Evercreech.
MILTON-DAMEREL w Newton St Petrock, Abbots Bickington, and Bulkworthy, *Devon.* R. **D** Ex 9 **P** *Mrs Palmer, F B Hobbs Esq, and Bp* **I** G E CHIPPINGTON.
MILTON-ERNEST (All SS), *Beds.* V. **D** St Alb 21 **P** *Maj H B Turnor* **I** D J REES.
MILTON, GREAT (St Mary Virg), *Oxon.* V. **D** Ox 5 **P** *Bp* **I** E P BAKER.
MILTON-KEYNES (All SS), *Bucks.* R. **D** Ox 26 *See* Broughton.
(Ch The Cornerstone), V. **D** Ox **P** *Bp* **I** R H BAKER.
MILTON-LILBOURNE (St Pet) w Easton Royal (H Trin), *Wilts.* V. **D** Sarum 27 **P** *Wadh Coll Ox 2 turns, Bp 1 turn* **I** J A CRACE.
MILTON, LITTLE (St Jas) w Ascott, *Oxon.* V. **D** Ox 5 **P** *Bp* **I** (Vacant).
MILTON MALSOR (H Cross), *Northants.* R. **D** Pet *See* Collingtree.
MILTON-NEXT-GRAVESEND (St Pet and St Paul), *Kent.* R. **D** Roch 3 **P** *Bp* **I** H P W DAY, D HITCHCOCK *c.*
(Ch Ch), V. **D** Roch 3 **P** *Bp* **I** C R LEVEY, J S KING *hon c.* *See also* GRAVESEND..
MILTON REGIS-NEXT-SITTINGBOURNE (H Trin), *Kent.* V. **D** Cant 14 **P** *D and C of Cant* **I** W DRURY.
MILTON, SOUTH (All SS), *Devon.* V. **D** Ex 14 **P** *D and C of Sarum* **I** A W J DELVE *p-in-c.*
MILTON-UNDER-WYCHWOOD (St Simon and St Jude) w Bruern and Lyneham, *Oxon.* V. **D** Ox *See* Shipton-under-Wychwood.
MILTON, WEST, *Dorset.*. **D** Sarum *See* Powerstock.
MILVERTON (St Mich AA) w Halse and Fitzhead, *Somt.* V. **D** B & W 22 **P** *Archd of Taunton 4 turns, Bp and V of Wiveliscombe 1 turn* **I** J B LUMBY *p-in-c.*
MILVERTON, NEW (St Mark w Ch Ch), *Warws.* V. **D** Cov 15 **P** *CPAS* **I** B C RUFF.
MILVERTON, OLD (St Jas), *Warws.* V. **D** Cov 11 **P** *M Heber-Percy Esq* **I** (Vacant).
MILWICH (All SS), *Staffs.* V. **D** Lich **P** *H A Dive Esq* **I** K J FOSTER.
MINCHINHAMPTON (H Trin), *Glos.* R. **D** Glouc 9 **P** *Bp* **I** M G P VOOGHT, J K CRICHTON *hon c.*
MINEHEAD (St Mich and St Andr), *Somt.* V. **D** B & W 21 **P** *Exors of G F Luttrell Esq* **I** C H SARALIS, M D THAYER *c.*
MINETY (St Leon) w Oaksey (All SS), *Wilts.* V. **D** Bris 11 **P** *Bp and Archd of Wilts* alt **I** W K THOMAS P-IN-C OF OAKSEY.
MININGSBY, *Lincs.*. **D** Linc 7 *See* Kirkby, East.
MINLEY (St Andr), *Hants.* V. **D** Guildf 1 **P** *Bp and Keble Coll Ox* **I** I M HANCOCK.
MINSTEAD (All SS), *Hants.* R. **D** Win 9 **P** *P J P Green Esq* **I** (Vacant).
MINSTER (St Merthiana), *Cornw.* R. **D** Truro 12 *See* Davidstow.
MINSTER-IN-SHEPPEY (St Mary and St Sexburga), *Kent.* V. **D** Cant 14 **P** *CPS 2 turns, Abp 1 turn* **I** B R HARRIS, J R WILLIAMS *c.*
MINSTER-IN-THANET (St Mary) w Monkton, *Kent.* V. **D** Cant 9 **P** *Abp* **I** G BEDFORD.
MINSTER-LOVELL (St Kenelm) and Brize Norton, *Oxon.* V. **D** Ox 9 **P** *Eton Coll and Ch Ch Ox* **I** D C FROST.
MINSTERLEY (H Trin), *Salop.* V. **D** Heref 13 **P** *Dioc Bd of Patr* **I** (Vacant).
MINSTERWORTH (St Pet), *Glos.* V. **D** Glouc *See* Churcham.
MINTERNE MAGNA (St Andr), *Dorset.* R. **D** Sarum 5 *See* Cerne Abbas.
MINTING (St Andr), *Lincs.* R. **D** Linc *See* Bardney.
MINTLYN, *Norf.*. **D** Nor 25 *See* Gaywood.
MIREHOUSE (St Andr), *Cumb.* V. **D** Carl *See* Whitehaven.
MIRFIELD (St Mary Virg) w Northorpe (St Luke), *W Yorks.* V. **D** Wakef 10 **P** *Bp* **I** J MELLORS, A HEZEL *c*, H W SMITH *hon c.*
(St Paul, Eastthorpe), V. **D** Wakef 10 **P** *V of Mirfield* **I** (Vacant).
MISERDEN (St Andr) w Edgeworth and Cranham, *Glos.* R. **D** Glouc 4 **P** *Mrs Huntley Sinclair and Q T P M Riley Esq* **I** J A HARPER.
MISSENDEN, GREAT (St Pet and St Paul), *Bucks.* V. **D** Ox 30 **P** *Bp* **I** D RYDINGS *p-in-c.*
MISSENDEN, LITTLE (St Jo Bapt), *Bucks.* V. **D** Ox 30 **P** *Earl Howe* **I** F F C ROBERTS.
MISSON (St Jo Bapt or All SS), *Notts.* V. **D** Southw 1 **P** *Bp* **I** G W J SPRINGETT.
MISTERTON (St Leon) w Walcote, *Leics.* R. **D** Leic 14 **P** *E B B Richards Esq* **I** C R TENNANT *p-in-c.*
MISTERTON (St Leon), *Somt.* V. **D** B & W *See* Haselbury-Plucknett.

MORETON BAGOTT (H Trin), *Worcs.* R. **D** Cov 7 *See* Oldberrow.
MORETON-CORBET (St Bart), *Salop.* R. **D** Lich 27 **P** *Lt-Col Sir J Corbet Bt* **I** C J BRADLEY.
MORETONHAMPSTEAD (St Andr), North Bovey and Manaton, Bovey and Manaton, *Devon.* R. **D** Ex 11 **P** *Bp 3 turns, Dioc Bd of Patr 1 turn* **I** R D PEEK.
MORETON-IN-THE-MARSH (St D), *Glos.* R. **D** Glouc 16 *See* Batsford.
MORETON JEFFRIES, *Herefs.*. **D** Heref 2 *See* Stoke Lacy.
MORETON MORRELL w Newbold Pacey, *Warws.*. **D** Cov 8 *See* Lighthorne.
MORETON, NORTH (All SS), w Moreton, South (St Jo Bapt) Aston Tirrold and Aston Upthorne, *Oxon.* R. **D** Ox **P** *Magd Coll Ox and Archd of Berks* alt **I** A F OTTER.
MORETON-ON-LUGG (St Andr) w Pipe and Lyde (St Pet), *Herefs.* R. **D** Heref 4 *See* Wellington.
MORETON PINKNEY, *Northants.*. **D** Pet *See* Weedon Lois.
MORETON-SAYE (St Marg of Antioch), *Salop.* R. **D** Lich 23 **P** *Brig A W G Heber-Percy* **I** J H BIGBY.
MORETON VALENCE (St Steph), *Glos.* V. **D** Glouc 3 *See* Standish.
MORGAN'S VALE (St Birinus), *Wilts.* V. **D** Sarum 17 *See* Redlynch.
MORLAND (St Laur) w Thrimby and Great Strickland, *Cumb.* V. **D** Carl 1 **P** *D and C of Carl* **I** G W MARKHAM.
MORLEY (St Matt), *Derbys.* R. **D** Derby 13 **P** *Bp* **I** A T REDMAN *p-in-c.*
MORLEY (St Botolph w St Pet), *Norf.* R. **D** Nor 13 **P** *D and C of Nor* **I** J W TANBURN.
MORLEY (St Pet) w Churwell (All SS), *W Yorks.* V. **D** Wakef 9 **P** *Bp* **I** S M HIND, A S MACPHERSON *c.*
(St Andr), V. **D** Wakef 9 *See* Bruntcliffe.
(St Paul), V. **D** Wakef 9 **P** *Vs of Batley and Morley* alt **I** H T ANNEAR.
MORNINGTHROPE (St Jo Bapt) w Fritton (St Cath), *Norf.*. **D** Nor *See* Hempnall.
MORPETH (St Mary Virg, St Jas, St Aidan and St Luke), *Northumb.* R. **D** Newc T 10 **P** *Bp* **I** G F BATESON, T AMBROSE *c*, J A FERGUSON *c*, P LISTER *c*, B L G PETFIELD *c*.
MORRIS GREEN (St Bede), *Gtr Man.*. **D** Man 11 *See* Bolton.
MORSTON, *Norf.*. **D** Nor 24 *See* Stiffkey.
MORTEHOE (St Mary Magd), *Devon.* V. **D** Ex 15 **P** *D and C of Ex* **I** H K KINGDON.
MORTIMER. **D** Ox *See* Stratfield-Mortimer.
MORTIMER WEST END (St Sav) w Padworth (St Jo Bapt), *Hants.* V. **D** Ox 12 **P** *Benyon Trust and Ld Chan (alt)* **I** N GILMORE.
MORTIMER, WOODHAM (St Marg), *Essex.* R. **D** Chelmsf 14 *See* Woodham Mortimer.
MORTLAKE (St Mary Virg) w East Sheen (Ch Ch and All SS), *Surrey.* R. **D** S'wark 13 **P** *Patr Bd* **I** I P M CUNDY, P D MAURICE *team v*, J R BINNS *c*, D C BOUTFLOWER *c*, V J FILER *c*.
MORTOMLEY (St Sav), *S Yorks.* V. **D** Sheff 7 **P** *Bp* **I** G C THOMAS.
MORTON (St Luke), *W Yorks.* V. **D** Bradf 11 **P** *Bp* **I** D H HINTON.
MORTON (H Cross), *Derbys.* R. **D** Derby 1 **P** *St Jo Coll Cam and Bp (alt)* **I** L N CHILDS.
MORTON (St Phil and St Jas), *Salop.* V. **D** Lich 24 **P** *Ld Chan* **I** T VILLIERS.
MORTON (St Jo Bapt) w Hacconby (St Andr), *Lincs.* V. **D** Linc 13 **P** *Bp* **I** M E ADIE.
MORTON (St Denis), *Notts.*. **D** Southw 15 *See* Rolleston.
MORTON (St Paul), *Lincs.* V. **D** Linc 2 **P** *Bp* **I** D F BOUTLE.
MORTON-ON-THE-HILL (St Marg), *Norf.*. **D** Nor *See* Weston Longville.
MORVAH, *Cornw.*. **D** Truro 5 *See* St Madron.
MORVAL (St Wenna), *Cornw.* V. **D** Truro 13 **P** *Ld Chan* **I** D H P DAVEY *p-in-c.*
MORVILLE (St Greg Gt) w Aston Eyre, *Salop.* V. **D** Heref 9 **P** *Univ of Cam* **I** (Vacant).
MORWENSTOW (St Jo Bapt), *Cornw.*. **D** Truro 10 *See* Kilkhampton.
MOSBROUGH (St Mark), *S Yorks.* V. **D** Sheff 1 **P** *Bp* **I** D CARNELLEY.
MOSELEY (St Mary), *W Midl.* V. **D** Birm 5 **P** *Bp* **I** R J MORRIS *c*, R W GRIMLEY *hon c*, J G HASLAM *hon c*.
(St Agnes), V. **D** Birm 5 **P** *V of Moseley* **I** S BECK, H A AYKROYD *c*, C E C CHITTENDEN *hon c*.
(St Anne), V. **D** Birm 5 **P** *V of Moseley* **I** L C BROTHERTON.
MOSLEY COMMON (St John), *Gtr Man.* V. **D** Man 6 **P** *Bp* **I** J G BELL.
MOSS w Fenwick (St John), *S Yorks.* V. **D** Sheff 8 **P** *Bp* **I** T W HARRIS P-IN-C OF FENWICK.
MOSS SIDE (Ch Ch), *Lancs.* R. **D** Man 5 **P** *Bp* **I** H OGDEN.
(St Jas w St Clem Greenheys), R. **D** Man 5 **P** *Bp* **I** G A WHEALE.
MOSSER (St Phil), *Cumb.* V. **D** Carl 10 **P** *Bp* **I** T R B HODGSON.
MOSSLEY (H Trin), *Chesh.* V. **D** Ches 11 **P** *R of Astbury* **I** G C W MATTHEWS.
MOSSLEY (St Geo), *Gtr Man.* V. **D** Man 2 **P** *R of Ashton L* **I** A ATHERTON.
MOSSLEY HILL (St Matt and St Jas), *Mer.* V. **D** Liv 2 **P** *Trustees* **I** K J RILEY, P R FORSTER *c*.
(St Barn), V. **D** Liv 2 **P** *Bp* **I** W H HARRINGTON.
MOSTERTON, *Dorset.*. **D** Sarum 4 *See* Perrott, South.
MOSTON (St Mary), *Gtr Man.* R. **D** Man 7 **P** *D and C of Man* **I** D J LOW.
(St Chad), R. **D** Man 7 **P** *Bp* **I** G G ROXBY.
(St John), R. **D** Man 7 **P** *Bp* **I** R E V EVANS.
MOTCOMBE (St Mary), *Dorset.* R. **D** Sarum 13 *See* Shaston.
MOTSPUR PARK **D** S'wark *See* Raynes Park.
MOTTINGHAM (St Andr), *Kent.* R. **D** S'wark 17 **P** *Bp* **I** C M BYERS, M F MAGEE *c*.
(St Edw), V. **D** S'wark 17 **P** *Bp* **I** (Vacant).
MOTTISFONT, *Hants.*. **D** Win *See* Broughton.
MOTTISTONE (St Pet and St Paul), *Isle of Wight.* R. **D** Portsm 7 *See* Brooke.
MOTTRAM-IN-LONGDENDALE (St Mich) w Broadbottom (St Mary Magd) and Woodhead (St Jas), *Gtr Man.* V. **D** Ches 14 **P** *Bp* **I** J R PRICE.
MOULSECOOMB (St Andr), *W Sussex.* R. **D** Chich 10 **P** *Bp* **I** B S HAYLLAR, B M CROWTHER-ALWYN *team v*, W E M HARRIS *team v*.
MOULSFORD (St Jo Bapt), *Oxon.* V. **D** Ox 18 **P** *Bp* **I** A IRVING, A L THOMAS *p-in-c.*
MOULSHAM, *Essex.*. **D** Chelmsf *See* Chelmsford.
MOULSOE (St Mary of the Assump), *Bucks.* R. **D** Ox 28 **P** *Ld Carrington* **I** D M EVANS.
MOULTON (St Steph Mart), *Chesh.* V. **D** Ches 6 **P** *R of Davenham* **I** J CORRADINE.
MOULTON (All SS), *Lincs.* V. **D** Linc 17 **P** *Dioc Bd of Patr* **I** N HULME.
(St Jas Ap and Mart), V. **D** Linc 17 *See* Cowbit.
MOULTON, *Norf.*. **D** Nor 1 *See* Beighton.
MOULTON (St Pet and St Paul), *Northants.* V. **D** Pet 5 **P** *Ch S Trust* **I** V H J GILLETT.
MOULTON (St Pet), *Suff.* R. **D** St E 11 *See* Gazeley.
MOULTON, Gt and L (St Mich) w Aslacton (St Mich), *Norf.* R. **D** Nor 11 **P** *Bp* **I** J R LAW.
MOUNT BURES (St John), *Essex.* R. **D** Chelmsf 22 **P** *Crown and Rev A C F Davies* **I** A C COX *c-in-c.*
MOUNT HAWKE, *Cornw.*. **D** Truro *See* Mithian.
MOUNT PELLON (Ch Ch), *W Yorks.* V. **D** Wakef 1 **P** *Bp* **I** A J FOSTER, H MAKIN *c*.
MOUNT THEYDON, *Essex.*. **D** Chelmsf *See* Stapleford Tawney.
MOUNTFIELD (All SS), *E Sussex.* V. **D** Chich 17 **P** *Exors of Lt-Commdr H S Egerton RN* **I** H SPRIGGS.
MOUNTFITCHET, STANSTED, *Essex.*. **D** Chelmsf *See* Stansted Mountfitchet.
MOUNTNESSING (St Giles), *Essex.* V. **D** Chelmsf 9 **P** *Bp* **I** I S PARKER.
MOUNTSORREL (Ch Ch), *Leics.* V. **D** Leic 10 **P** *CPAS* **I** G F J CRATE.
(St Pet), *Leics.* V. **D** Leic 10 **P** *Bp* **I** T R BELL.
MOW COP (St Luke), *Chesh.*. **D** Ches 12 *See* Odd Rode.
MOW COP (St Thos), *Staffs.* V. **D** Lich 17a **P** *Crown* **I** D A WEAVER.
MOWSLEY (St Nich) w Laughton (St Luke) and Knaptoft, *Leics.* R. **D** Leic 5 *See* Husbands Bosworth.
MOXBY, *N Yorks.*. **D** York *See* Stillington.
MOXLEY (All SS), *W Midl.* V. **D** Lich 10 **P** *Crown* **I** D R HARTLAND.
MOZE, *Essex.*. **D** Chelmsf 28 *See* Beaumont.
MUCH COWARNE, *Herefs.*. **D** Heref *See* Stoke Lacy.
MUCH MARCLE (St Bart) w Yatton, *Herefs.* V. **D** Heref 6 **P** *R E Money-Kyrle Esq* **I** G F HOLLEY.
MUCH WENLOCK (H Trin) w Bourton (H Trin), *Salop.*. **D** Heref *See* Wenlock.
MUCH WOOLTON (St Pet), *Mer.* R. **D** Liv 2 **P** *Bp* **I** J V ROBERTS, P C CATON *c*, C P COTTEE *c*, V J WALKER *hon c*.
MUCHELNEY (St Pet and St Paul), *Somt.* V. **D** B & W 10 *See* Langport.
MUCKING (St Jo Bapt), *Essex.* V. **D** Chelmsf 15 *See* Stanford-le-Hope.

NEENTON (All SS), *Salop*. R. **D** Heref 9 **P** *Capt W M Lowry-Corry* **I** M A J HARDING.
NELSON-IN-MARSDEN (St Mary Virg), *Lancs*. V. **D** Blackb 6a **P** *Trustees* **I** C A KELLY.
(St Phil), V. **D** Blackb 6a **P** *Bp* **I** A HOLME.
(St Bede). **D** Blackb 6a **P** *Bp* **I** (Vacant).
NEMPNETT-THRUBWELL (St Mary Virg), *Avon*. R. **D** B & W 15 *See* Chew-Stoke.
NENTHEAD, *Cumb*.. **D** Newc T *See* Alston.
NESS, GREAT (St Andr) w Ness, Little (St Martin), *Salop*. V. **D** Lich 22 **P** *Ld Chan 2 turns, Guild of All S 1 turn* **I** A HULSE.
NESTON (St Phil and St Jas), *Wilts*. V. **D** Bris 9 *See* Corsham, Greater.
NESTON (St Mary and St Helen), *Chesh*. V. **D** Ches 9 **P** *D and C of Ches* **I** A V SHUFFLEBOTHAM, W B FAULL *c*, S F HAMILL-STEWART *c*, R HAMILTON *c*.
NETHER DENTON (St Cuthb), *Cumb*.. **D** Carl *See* Farlam.
NETHER HALL (St Eliz), *Leics*. V. **D** Leic 1 *See* Leic.
NETHER HOYLAND, *S Yorks*.. **D** Sheff *See* Hoyland, Nether.
NETHER PEOVER (St Osw), *Chesh*.. **D** Ches 13 *See* Peover, Nether.
NETHER STOWEY (St Mary Virg) w Over Stowey (St Pet and St Paul), *Somt*. V. **D** B & W 18 **P** *D and C of Windsor and MMT* alt **I** R L PARKER.
NETHER WALLOP, *Hants*.. **D** Win *See* Over Wallop.
NETHER WHITACRE (St Giles) w Lea Marston (St Jo Bapt), *Warws*. R. **D** Birm 9 **P** *Bp* **I** E J A CLARKE.
NETHERAVON (All SS) w Fittleton (All SS) and Enford (All SS), *Wilts*. V. **D** Sarum 18 **P** *Bp 2 turns, Govs of Ch Hosp 1 turn* **I** J E JACKSON.
NETHERBURY (St Mary) w Solway-Ash (H Trin), *Dorset*. V. **D** Sarum *See* Beaminster Area.
NETHEREXE, *Devon*.. **D** Ex 2 *See* Rewe.
NETHERFIELD (St Jo Bapt), *E Sussex*. V. **D** Chich 17 **P** *Bp* **I** H SPRIGGS.
NETHERFIELD (St Geo), *Notts*. V. **D** Southw 13 **P** *Dioc Bd of Patr* **I** R J SMITH.
NETHERHAMPTON, *Wilts*.. **D** Sarum *See* Wilton.
NETHERLEY (Ch Ch), *Mer*. V. **D** Liv 7 **P** *Bp* **I** C D HENDRICKSE, D BAILEY *c*.
NETHERNE (St Luke Conv Distr), *Surrey*.. **D** S'wark 12 *See* Merstham.
NETHERTHONG (All SS), *W Yorks*. V. **D** Wakef 5 **P** *V of Almondbury* **I** J N CAPSTICK.
NETHERTHORPE, *S Yorks*.. **D** Sheff *See* Sheffield.
NETHERTON (St Andr), *W Yorks*.. **D** Wakef 7 *See* Middlestown.
NETHERTON, *Worcs*.. **D** Worc 9 *See* Elmley Castle.
NETHERTON (St Andr), *W Midl*.. **D** Worc 9 *See* Dudley.
NETHERTON (All S) w Grasslot (St Andr), *Cumb*. V. **D** Carl 11 **P** *Bp* **I** E MANN, P M P BERESFORD *c*.
NETHERTON (St Osw), *Mer*. V. **D** Liv 1 **P** *Bp* **I** R A WILKES, D W FLEWKER *c*.
NETHERWITTON (St Giles), *Northumb*. V. **D** Newc T 10 **P** *V of Hartburn* **I** A F DONNELLY.
NETLEY ABBEY, *Hants*.. **D** Win 15 *See* Hound.
NETLEY MARSH (St Matt), *Hants*. V. **D** Win 9 *See* Totton.
NETTESWELL, *Essex*. R. **D** Chelmsf 3 *See* Tye Green.
NETTLEBED (St Bart) w Bix, Pishill and Highmore, *Oxon*. V. **D** Ox 7 **P** *Earl of Macclesfield, Dioc Bd of Patr and CPS* **I** B ANDREW.
NETTLECOMBE (St Mary Virg), *Somt*. R. **D** B & W 18 *See* Monksilver.
NETTLEDEN (St Laur) w Potten End (H Trin), *Herts*. V. **D** St Alb 3 **P** *Bp* **I** A L JONES.
NETTLEHAM (All SS), *Lincs*. V. **D** Linc 3 **P** *Bp* **I** (Vacant).
NETTLESTEAD (St Mary Virg), *Kent*. R. **D** Roch 6 *See* Peckham, East.
NETTLESTEAD, *Suff*.. **D** St E *See* Blakenham, Great.
NETTLETON (St Mary) w Littleton Drew (All SS), *Wilts*. R. **D** Bris 9 **P** *Archd of Swindon and Bp* **I** G H M N SHELFORD *p-in-c*.
NETTLETON (St Jo Bapt), *Lincs*. R. **D** Linc 5 **P** *Dioc Bd of Patr* **I** H CLAREY *p-in-c*.
NEVENDON (St Pet), *Essex*. R. **D** Chelmsf 10 *See* Basildon.
NEW BRIGHTON, *Mer*.. **D** Ches *See* Wallasey.
NEW BURY, *Gtr Man*.. **D** Man *See* Farnworth.
NEW FERRY (St Mark Evang), *Mer*. V. **D** Ches 8 **P** *R of Bebington* **I** A E BACKHOUSE, W P BENN *c*, P A L MADDOCK *c*, A W WARD *c*.
NEW HAW (All SS), *Surrey*. V. **D** Guildf 7 **P** *Bp* **I** R P ROBINS.
NEW LEAKE (St Jude), *Lincs*.. **D** Linc 7 *See* Eastville.
NEW MILL (Ch Ch) w (St Mary Hill End), *W Yorks*. V. **D** Wakef 7 **P** *V of Kirkburton* **I** R L WAINWRIGHT.
NEW MILLS (St Geo) w (St Jas L), *Derbys*. V. **D** Derby 5 **P** *V of Glossop* **I** A BATSLEER.
NEW SOUTHGATE (St Paul).. **D** Lon 24 *See* Southgate, New.
NEW SPRINGS, *Gtr Man*.. **D** Liv *See* Wigan.
NEW TOWN (H Trin), *Herts*.. **D** St Alb 4 *See* Bishop's Stortford.
NEWALL GREEN (St Francis), *Gtr Man*. V. **D** Man 10 **P** *Bp* **I** R R USHER *p-in-c*.
NEWARK (St Mary Magd, St Leon and Ch Ch) w Hawton, Cotham and Shelton, *Notts*. R. **D** Southw **P** *Bp and Crown* **I** G M M M THOMSON, M R F MACLACHLAN *team v*, W H THACKRAY *team v*, R P WALFORD *team v*, G M BOULT *c*.
NEWBALD, NORTH, *Humb*. V. **D** York 16 **P** *Abp* **I** J WALKER.
NEWBALL, *Lincs*.. **D** Linc 24 *See* Stainton-by-Langworth.
NEWBARNS (St Paul), *Cumb*.. **D** Carl 16 *See* Barrow-in-Furness.
NEWBIGGIN (St Edm), *Cumb*. R. **D** Carl 1a *See* Kirkby-Thore.
NEWBIGGIN (St Bart), *Northumb*.. **D** Newc T 10 *See* Woodhorn.
NEWBIGGIN-ON-LUNE Cumb. **D** Carl 1 *See* Orton.
NEWBOLD, *Leics*.. **D** Leic *See* Worthington.
NEWBOLD (St Pet), *Gtr Man*.. **D** Man 17 *See* Rochdale.
NEWBOLD (St Jo Evang) w Dunston, *Derbys*. R. **D** Derby 3 **P** *V of Chesterfield* **I** R J ROSS, C DUNKLEY *c*, J E HUNT *c*, R A JUPP *c*, P S RHODES *c*.
NEWBOLD DE VERDUN (St Jas), *Leics*. R. **D** Leic 15 **P** *Trin Coll Ox* **I** C J HALL.
NEWBOLD-ON-AVON (St Botolph) w Lawford, Long, *Warws*. V. **D** Cov 6 **P** *H A F W Boughton-Leigh Esq* **I** J D E SMITH.
NEWBOLD-ON-STOUR (St D), *Warws*.. **D** Cov 9 *See* Tredington.
NEWBOLD PACEY, *Warws*. **D** Cov 8 *See* Moreton Morrell.
NEWBOROUGH (All SS) w Needwood (Ch Ch), *Staffs*. V. **D** Lich **P** *Dioc Bd of Patr and V of Hanbury (alt)* **I** (Vacant).
NEWBOROUGH (St Bart) w Borough Fen, *Cambs*. V. **D** Pet 14 **P** *Crown* **I** C MACKENZIE-LOWE.
NEWBOTTLE (St Matt), *T & W*. V. **D** Dur 5 **P** *Bp* **I** R F SKINNER.
NEWBOTTLE (St Jas) w Charlton, *Northants*. V. **D** Pet 1 *See* Aynho.
NEWBOURN (St Mary), *Suff*. R. **D** St E 2 *See* Waldringfield.
NEWBROUGH (St Pet), *Northumb*.. **D** Newc T 4 *See* Warden.
NEWBURGH (Ch Ch), *Lancs*. V. **D** Liv 9 **P** *Earl of Derby* **I** G JENNINGS.
NEWBURN (St Mich AA w St Mary Virg and H Trin) w Throckley, *Northumb*. V. **D** Newc T 5b **P** *MMT* **I** G G HOWARTH.
NEWBURY (St Nich), w (St Jo Evang), Speenhamland (St Mary Virg) and (St Geo Wash Common), *Berks*. R. **D** Ox 14 **P** *Bp* **I** W R D CAPSTICK, G E BENNETT *team v*, D. CRAWLEY P-IN-C OF SPEEN *team v*, P S V NASH-WILLIAMS *team v*, P A DALLAWAY *c*.
(St Jo Evang), R. **D** Ox 14 **P** *Bp* **I** (Vacant).
NEWBY, *N Yorks*.. **D** Ripon 7 *See* Skelton.
NEWBY, *N Yorks*.. **D** York 18 *See* Scarborough.
NEWCASTLE (St Jo Div), *Salop*.. **D** Heref *See* Bettws-y-Crwyn.
NEWCASTLE-UNDER-LYME (St Giles) w Butterton (St Thos), *Staffs*. R. **D** Lich 17 **P** *Simeon Trustees* **I** J A LEDWARD, T HOUGHTON *c*, P WARREN *c*.
(St Geo), V. **D** Lich 17 **P** *R of Newc L* **I** G F JONES *c-in-c*.
(St Paul), V. **D** Lich 17 **P** *Trustees* **I** M D HARDING.
NEWCASTLE UPON TYNE (St Nich Cathl Ch), *T & W*. V. **D** Newc T 5 **P** *Bp* **I** VERY REV C G H SPAFFORD.
(St Andr), V. **D** Newc T 5 **P** *V of Newc T* **I** G SMITH *p-in-c*.
(St Ann), V. **D** Newc T *See* Ch Ch.
(St Aug of Hippo, Elswick, w St Monica), V. **D** Newc T 5b **P** *Bp* **I** J M DUCKETT.
(St Jas and St Basil), V. **D** Newc T 5b **P** *Bp* **I** J M TRUMAN.
(St Jo Bapt), V. **D** Newc T 5 **P** *V of Newc T* **I** J R DUDLEY.
(Ch Ch Shieldfield w St Ann), V. **D** Newc T 5 **P** *Bp* **I** T EMMETT.
(Clayton Mem Ch Jesmond), V. **D** Newc T 5 **P** *Trustees* **I** D R J HOLLOWAY, P D HARDINGHAM *c*, A F MUNDEN *c*.
(H Spirit, Denton), V. **D** Newc T 5b **P** *Bp* **I** B BENISON.

(H Trin War Mem Ch Jesmond), V. **D** Newc T 5 **P** *Trustees* **I** M C LIPPIATT, A JACKSON *hon c.*
(St Aid Benwell), V. **D** Newc T 5b **P** *Bp* **I** (Vacant).
(St Anthony, Byker), V. **D** Newc T 5a **P** *Bp* **I** D B GODSELL, P BROWN *c,* B SKELTON *c.*
(St Barn w St Jude), V. **D** Newc T 5 **P** *V of Jesmond and CPAS* **I** R W BURROWS.
(St Francis, High Heaton), V. **D** Newc T 5a **P** *Bp* **I** W J HATCHLEY.
(St Gabr Heaton), V. **D** Newc T 5a **P** *Bp* **I** C M F UNWIN, N J THISTLETHWAITE *c.*
(St Geo Jesmond), V. **D** Newc T 5 **P** *Bp* **I** M J MIDDLETON, G W RILEY *c,* E F WOOD *c.*
(St Hilda, Jesmond), V. **D** Newc T 5 **P** *Bp* **I** R CHAPMAN.
(St Jas Benwell), V. **D** Newc T 5b **P** *Bp* **I** M N F HAIG, R K BRYANT *c.*
(St Luke Evang), V. **D** Newc T 5 **P** *Bp* **I** H R WEST.
(St Marg Scotswood), V. **D** Newc T 5b **P** *Bp* **I** (Vacant).
(St Mark), V. **D** Newc T 5a **P** *Ch Trust Fund Trust* **I** H D OWEN.
(St Martin Byker), V.. **D** Newc T 5a **P** *Bp* **I** A P DAVIES.
(St Matt Ap Evang and Mart w St Mary Virg), V. **D** Newc T 5b **P** *Bp* **I** H W WALKER.
(St Mich w St Lawr Byker), V. **D** Newc T 5a **P** *Bp* **I** R C I WARD *c.*
(St Osw Eccles Distr Walker Gate). **D** Newc T 5a **P** *Bp* **I** S A CHETWYND *min.*
(St Paul, Elswick), V. **D** Newc T 5b **P** *Trustees* **I** B E SEAMAN, A S ADAMSON *c.*
(St Pet Cowgate), V. **D** Newc T 5b **P** *Bp* **I** P ADAMSON, S S DYSON *hon c.*
(St Phil), V. **D** Newc T 5b **P** *Bp* **I** F R DEXTER.
(St Silas Byker), V. **D** Newc T 5a **P** *Bp* **I** J WYLAM.
(St Steph Low Elswick), V. **D** Newc T 5b **P** *Church S* **I** G R CURRY.
(St Thos Mart Chap). **D** Newc T 5 **P** *St Mary Magd Trust* **I** I HARKER *master,* S B PATTISON *hon c.*
(The Epiph), R. **D** Newc T **P** *Bp* **I** R D TAYLOR, C P ANDREWS *team v,* M OXBROW *team v.*
NEWCHAPEL (St Jas), *Staffs.* V. **D** Lich 17a **P** *CPAS* **I** E J ABLETT.
NEWCHURCH Kent. R **D** Cant 13 *See* Dymchurch.
NEWCHURCH (Dedic unknown), *Chesh.* R. **D** Liv 11 **P** *Earl of Derby* **I** D A PANKHURST, H YATES *c.*
NEWCHURCH (St Nich w St Jo), *Lancs.* R. **D** Man 18 **P** *Bp and V of Whalley* alt **I** A T TOOMBS, J CAWTHORNE *hon c.*
NEWCHURCH (All SS), *Isle of Wight,* V. **D** Portsm 6 **P** *Bp* **I** (Vacant).
NEWCHURCH-IN-PENDLE (St Mary), *Lancs.* V. **D** Blackb 6a **P** *Hulme Trustees* **I** J P RICHARDSON.
NEWDIGATE (St Pet), *Surrey.* R. **D** Guildf 6 **P** *Ld Chan* **I** D PARKER.
NEWENDEN, *Kent..* **D** Cant 10 *See* Sandhurst.
NEWENT (St Mary), *Glos.* R. **D** Glouc 6 **P** *Bp* **I** I W MARCHANT, A MATTHEWS *c.*
NEWFOUNDPOOL (St Aug of Cant), *Leics..* **D** Leic 1 *See* Leicester.
NEWHALL (St Jo Evang), V. **D** Derby 16 **P** *Bp* **I** K W FRYER.
NEWHAVEN (St Mich AA and Ch Ch), *E Sussex.* R. **D** Chich 15 **P** *CPS* **I** R A STEDMAN.
NEWHEY (St Thos), *Gtr Man.* V. **D** Man 17 **P** *Bp* **I** J HENDERSON.
NEWICK (St Mary), *E Sussex.* R. **D** Chich 16 **P** *Ch S* **I** J P BAKER.
NEWINGTON (St Mary Virg) w Bobbing and Iwade, *Kent.* V. **D** Cant 14 **P** *Abp and Archd of Maidstone jt* **I** M J CHANDLER.
NEWINGTON (St Giles), *Oxon..* **D** Ox 5 *See* Dorchester.
NEWINGTON (St Mary Virg w St Gabr), *Surrey.* R. **D** S'wark 5 **P** *Bp* **I** D E W M WALKER.
(All SS Surrey Square). **D** S'wark *See* Walworth (All SS).
(St Matt), V. **D** S'wark 5 *See* H Trin S'wark.
(St Paul, Lorrimore Square), V. **D** S'wark 5 **P** *Bp* **I** G D SHAW.
NEWINGTON (St Jo Bapt) w Dairycoates (St Mary and St Pet), *Humb.* V. **D** York 17 **P** *Abp* **I** M WALTER.
(Transfig), V. **D** York 17 **P** *Abp* **I** (Vacant).
NEWINGTON BAGPATH, *Glos..* **D** Glouc 17 *See* Horsley.
NEWINGTON-NEXT-HYTHE, *Kent..* **D** Cant *See* Cheriton.
NEWINGTON, NORTH, *Oxon..* **D** Ox *See* Broughton.
NEWINGTON, SOUTH (St Pet-ad-Vincula), *Oxon.* V. **D** Ox *See* Bloxham.
NEWLAND (All SS) w Redbrook (St Sav), *Glos.* V. **D** Glouc 7 **P** *Bp* **I** D J F ADDISON *p-in-c.*
NEWLAND (St Leon), Guarlford and Madresfield, *Worcs.* R. **D** Worc 4 **P** *Countess Beauchamp and Beauchamp Trustees* **I** D H MARTIN.
NEWLAND, *N Yorks..* **D** York *See* Hull.
NEWLANDS, *Cumb.* V. **D** Carl 10 *See* Thornthwaite.
NEWLYN, EAST (St Newlina), *Cornw.* V. **D** Truro 7 **P** *Bp* **I** P B DENNY.
NEWLYN (St Pet w St Andr), *Cornw.* V. **D** Truro 5 **P** *Bp* **I** G M ELMORE.
NEWMARKET (St Mary) w (St Agnes) Exning, *Suff.* R. **D** St E 11 **P** *Dioc Bd of Patr and Bp* **I** R J HAWKINS.
(All SS), V. **D** St E 11 **P** *Bp* **I** J A HATHAWAY.
NEWNHAM (St Pet and St Paul), *Kent.* V. **D** Cant 7 **P** *Exors of Sir J Croft Bt and Abp* **I** (Vacant).
NEWNHAM (St Mich AA), *Northants.* V. **D** Pet 3 *See* Badby.
NEWNHAM (St Nich) w Nately Scures, Mapledurwell, and Up Nately, *Hants.* R. **D** Win 4 **P** *Qu Coll Ox and Lady Malmesbury (alt)* **I** B COWELL *p-in-c.*
NEWNHAM (St Vincent) w Radwell (All SS) *Herts.* V. **D** St Alb 5 *See* Hinxworth.
NEWNHAM, KING'S, *Warws..* **D** Cov *See* Church Lawford.
NEWNHAM MURREN, *Oxon..* **D** Ox 18 *See* Wallingford.
NEWNHAM-ON-SEVERN (St Pet), *Glos.* V. **D** Glouc 6 **P** *Bp* **I** G A SATTERLY *p-in-c.*
NEWNTON, LONG (H Trin) , *Glos.* R. **D** Bris 11 **P** *Capt T Sotheron-Escourt* **I** E J L TIPPETT *p-in-c.*
NEWNTON, NORTH (St Jas), *Wilts..* **D** Sarum *See* Swanborough.
NEWPORT (St Mary Virg), *Essex.* V. **D** Chelmsf 26 **P** *Bp* **I** R N HUMPHRIES.
NEWPORT (St Jo Bapt), *Devon.* V. **D** Ex 15 **P** *Bp* **I** A T H JONES.
NEWPORT (St Thos Ap), *Isle of Wight.* V. **D** Portsm 7 **P** *Bp* **I** J F BUCKETT.
NEWPORT (St Steph), *N Yorks.* V. **D** York *See* Howden, The.
NEWPORT (St Nich) w Longford (St Mary) and Chetwynd, *Salop.* R. **D** Lich 21 **P** *Bp and Mrs Burton Borough* **I** R T HIBBERT.
NEWPORT PAGNELL (St Pet and St Paul) w Lathbury, [Bucks]. V. **D** Ox **P** *Bp and Ch Ch Ox* **I** D R P HAYES, M D COOKE *c,* R MAYNARD *c.*
NEWQUAY (St Mich), *Cornw.* V. **D** Truro 7 **P** *Bp* **I** J D SHEPHERD.
NEWSHAM, *Northumb..* **D** Newc T *See* Blyth.
NEWSOME (St Jo Evang), *W Yorks.* V. **D** Wakef 5 **P** *R of Lockwood* **I** (Vacant).
NEWSTEAD, *Humb..* **D** Linc 6 *See* Cadney.
NEWSTEAD ABBEY and COLLIERY, *Notts.* V. **D** Southw 12 **P** *Newstead Colliery* **I** (Vacant).
NEWSTEAD (St Mary Virg), *Notts.* V. **D** Southw 12 **I** (Vacant).
NEWTIMBER (St Jo Evang), w Pyecombe, *W Sussex.* R. **D** Chich 14 **P** *Ld Chan and Bp* alt **I** G JEFFERY *p-in-c.*
NEWTON (St Marg), *Cambs.* V. **D** Ely 7 *See* Shelford, Little.
NEWTON (St Jo Bapt), *Herefs..* **D** Heref *See* St Margaret's.
NEWTON, *Warws...* **D** Cov 6 *See* Clifton-on-Dunsmore.
NEWTON (St Botolph) w Haceby, *Lincs..* **D** Linc *See* Lafford, S.
NEWTON (All SS), *Suff.* R. **D** St E 12 **P** *Peterho Cam* **I** J K COTTON *p-in-c.*
NEWTON ABBOT CHAP (St Leon w St Paul), *Devon..* **D** Ex *See* Wolborough.
NEWTON ARLOSH, *Cumb..* **D** Carl *See* Kirkbride.
NEWTON AYCLIFFE (St Clare), *Durham..* **D** Dur 12a **P** *Bp* **I** G G GIBSON, J R SCORER *c,* J T SKINNER *c.*
NEWTON BLOSSOMVILLE, *Bucks..* **D** Ox *See* Clifton-Reynes.
NEWTON-BROMSWOLD (St Pet), *Northants.* R. **D** Pet 9 *See* Rushden.
NEWTON-BY-CASTLEACRE, *Norf.* V. **D** Nor *See* Castle Acre.
NEWTON-BY-TOFT (St Mich), *Lincs..* **D** Linc 5 *See* Toft.
NEWTON-FERRERS (H Cross) w Revelstoke (St Pet), *Devon.* R. **D** Ex 21 **P** *Bp and Exors of John Yonge Esq* **I** R P FAIRBROTHER.
NEWTON-FLOTMAN w Swainsthorpe, *Norf.* R. **D** Nor 13 **P** *Bp* **I** (Vacant).
NEWTON FLOWERY FIELD (St Steph), *Gtr Man.* V. **D** Ches 14 **P** *Bp* **I** N TOPPING.
NEWTON GREEN, *Gtr Man..* **D** Ches 15 *See* Godley.
NEWTON HALL, *Durham.* V. **D** Dur *See* Durham.

NEWTON HALL (St Jas), *Northumb.* V. **D** Newc T 3 **P** *Trustees* **I** (Vacant).
NEWTON HARCOURT (St Luke), *Leics.* V. **D** Leic 6 *See* Wistow.
NEWTON HEATH (All SS), *Gtr Man.* R. **D** Man 4 **P** *D and C of Man* **I** W S BRISON, A HIRST *c.*
(St Mark). **D** Man 1 *See* Manchester (St Phil).
(St Wilfrid and St Anne), R. **D** Man 7 **P** *Crown* **I** I R SHACKLETON *p-in-c,* W P EVANS *c.*
NEWTON-IN-CLEVELAND, *N Yorks..* **D** York *See* Ayton, Great.
NEWTON-IN-MAKERFIELD (Em Ch), *Mer.* R. **D** Liv 11 **P** *Earl of Derby* **I** A R DAWSON.
(St Pet), V. **D** Liv 11 **P** *Ld Newton* **I** N MEREDITH.
(All SS). **D** Liv 11 **P** *Bp* **I** C F HOPE.
NEWTON-IN-MOTTRAM (St Mary), *Gtr Man.* V. **D** Ches 14 **P** *V of Mottram* **I** P W DILL.
NEWTON-IN-THE-ISLE, *Cambs.* R. **D** Ely 20 **P** *Bp* **I** J TOFTS.
NEWTON KYME (St Andr), *N Yorks.* R. **D** York 9 **P** *Newton Kyme Estate Ltd* **I** D R BRANDON *c-in-c.*
NEWTON-LE-WILLOWS, *Mer..* **D** Liv 11 *See* Newton-in-Makerfield.
NEWTON LONGVILLE (St Faith) w Stoke Hammond, Whaddon and Tattenhoe, *Bucks.* R. **D** Ox 27 **P** *New Coll Ox, Univ of Cam and Exors of Lt-Col W Selby Lowndes* **I** W R B CHOWN.
NEWTON, NORTH (St Pet) w St Michaelchurch, Thurloxton and Durston, *Somt.* R. **D** B & W 17 **P** *Bp 3 turns, Sir B Slade Bt 1 turn* **I** G COOKE.
NEWTON, OLD (St Mary) w Stowupland (H Trin), *Suff.* V. **D** St E 6 **P** *CPS and Dioc Bd of Patr* **I** (Vacant).
NEWTON-ON-OUSE (St Mary, formerly All SS), *N Yorks.* V. **D** York 5 **P** *Abp* **I** (Vacant).
NEWTON-ON-RAWCLIFFE (St John), *N Yorks.* V. **D** York 24 **P** *Abp* **I** (Vacant).
NEWTON-ON-TRENT (St Pet), *Lincs.* V. **D** Linc 2 **P** *Dioc Bd of Patr* **I** L SALT.
NEWTON POPPLEFORD (St Luke) w Harpford (St Greg), *Devon.* V. **D** Ex 7 **P** *V of Aylesbeare and Dioc Bd of Patr* alt **I** R G MERWOOD.
NEWTON PURCELL (St Mich) w Shelswell (St Ebba), *Oxon.* R. **D** Ox 2 *See* Fringford.
NEWTON REGIS (St Mary) w Seckington (All SS), *Warws.* R. **D** Birm 10 **P** *Miss Inge-Innes-Lillingston and Dioc Trustees (alt)* **I** J T SAMMONS.
NEWTON-REIGNY (St Jo Bapt), *Cumb.* R. **D** Carl *See* Penrith.
NEWTON ST CYRES (St Cyr and St Juletta), *Devon.* V. **D** Ex 2 **P** *Dioc Bd of Patr* **I** J G M SCOTT.
NEWTON ST LOE (H Trin), *Avon.* R. **D** B & W 15 *See* Corston.
NEWTON ST PETROCK, *Devon..* **D** Ex *See* Milton Damerel.
NEWTON SOLNEY (St Mary Virg), *Derbys.* V. **D** Derby 16 *See* Bretby.
NEWTON, SOUTH (St Andr), *Wilts.* V. **D** Sarum 21 **P** *Earl of Pembroke* **I** E R BROADBENT *p-in-c.*
NEWTON-TONY (St Andr), *Wilts.* R. **D** Sarum 17 *See* Bourne Valley.
NEWTON TRACEY, Alverdiscott (All SS), Huntshaw (St Mary Magd), Yarnscombe (St Andr) and Horwood (St Mich), *Devon.* R. **D** Ex 20 **P** *Bp 1st turn, ld Chan 2nd turn, Ld Clinton 3rd turn* **I** B M TINSLEY.
NEWTON VALENCE (St Mary) w Selborne (St Mary) and East Tisted w Colmer, *Hants.* V. **D** Win **P** *Bp and Earl of Selborne and Sir J B Scott* **I** J D CURTIS.
NEWTON, WEST, *Norf.* R. **D** Nor 23 *See* Sandringham.
NEWTOWN (K Chas Mart), *Staffs..* **D** Lich *See* Loppington.
NEWTOWN (K Chas Mart), *Salop.* V. **D** Lich 27 **P** *R of Wem* **I** T W BOULCOTT.
NEWTOWN, *Gtr Man..* **D** Liv *See* Pemberton.
NEWTOWN (H Spirit) w Porchfield, *Isle of Wight.* V. **D** Portsm 7 *See* Calbourne.
NEWTOWN (H Trin), *Hants.* V. **D** Portsm 2 *See* Soberton.
NEWTOWN (St Jo Bapt), *W Yorks..* **D** Ripon 10 *See* Leeds.
NEWTOWN (St Mary and St Jo Bapt), *Hants..* **D** Win 5 *See* Burghclere.
NEWTOWN LINFORD (All SS), *Leics.* V. **D** Leic 17 **P** *Ld Deramore* **I** W H G FLETCHER.
NIBLEY, NORTH (St Martin) w The Ridge, *Glos..* **D** Glouc 5 *See* Wotton-under-Edge.
NICHOLFOREST (St Nich) and Kirkandrews-on-Esk, *Cumb.* V. **D** Carl 2 **P** *Col Sir F Graham, Bt* **I** W B MITCHELL.
NIDD, or NYDD (St Marg and St Paul) w Brearton (St Jo Bapt), *N Yorks.* V. **D** Ripon 4 **P** *Visc Mountgarret and V of Knaresborough* alt **I** W DILLAM P-IN-C OF NIDD, C W ODLING-SMEE P-IN-C OF BREARTON.
NIDDERDALE, UPPER (St Chad Middlesmoor, St Mary Virgin Ramsgill, St Cuthb Pateley Bridge and St Mary Greenhow Hill), *N Yorks.* V. **D** Ripon 3 **P** *D & C of Ripon and V of Masham and Healey* **I** M D EMMEL, S E ARCHER *c.*
NINEBANKS (St Mark) *Northumb..* **D** Newc T 4 *See* Allendale.
NINFIELD (St Mary), *E Sussex.* R. **D** Chich 17 **P** *D and C of Cant 2 turns St Edm Hall 1 turn* **I** L HARDAKER.
NITON (St Jo Bapt), *Isle of Wight.* R. **D** Portsm 6 **P** *Qu Coll Ox* **I** T E LOUDEN.
NOCTON (All SS) w Dunston (St Pet), *Lincs.* V. **D** Linc 18 **P** *British Field Products Ltd* **I** R RODGER.
NOEL PARK (St Mark).. **D** Lon 22 *See* Wood Green.
NOKE (St Giles), *Oxon.* R. **D** Ox 2 **P** *D and C of Westmr* **I** D R WESTCOTT.
NO-MAN'S HEATH (St Mary Virg), *Leics.* V. **D** Lich 6 **P** *Bp* **I** J T SAMMONS *c-in-c.*
NONINGTON (St Mary Virg) w Barfreystone (St Nich), *Kent.* V. **D** Cant 1 **P** *Abp and St Jo Coll Ox* alt **I** E L W BELL *p-in-c.*
NORBITON (St Pet), *Surrey.* V. **D** S'wark 11 **P** *V of Kingston-T* **I** A H MASON.
NORBURY (St Steph), *Surrey.* V. **D** Cant 16 **P** *Abp* **I** M A COLLIS, V H PERRY *hon c.*
(St Osw), V. **D** Cant 16 **P** *Abp* **I** P A THOMPSON.
(St Phil), V. **D** Cant 16 **P** *Abp* **I** W J LOVEGROVE, P MARTIN *c.*
NORBURY (St Thos), *Chesh.* V. **D** Ches 16 **P** *Ld Newton* **I** C A BARTON, C H POVALL *c.*
NORBURY (St Mary Virg) w Snelston (St Pet), *Derbys.* R. **D** Derby 8 **P** *J R G Stanton, L A Clowes and V of Ashbourne (in turn)* **I** N DAUGHTRY.
NORBURY (All SS), *Salop..* **D** Heref 10 *See* Myndtown.
NORBURY (St Pet), *Staffs.* R. **D** Lich 15 **P** *D and C of Lich* **I** M S TYLER-WHITTLE *p-in-c.*
NORDELPH (H Trin), *Norf.* V. **D** Ely 17 **P** *C E Townley Esq* **I** P G HUTTON *p-in-c.*
NORDEN (St Paul) w Ashworth (St Jas), *Gtr Man.* V. **D** Man 17 **P** *Bp* **I** K N PROCTOR.
NORHAM (St Cuthb) w Duddo (All SS), *Northumb.* V. **D** Newc T 11 **P** *Provost and C of Newc and D and C of Dur* alt **I** R THOMPSON.
NORHILL (St Mary Virg), *Beds..* **D** St Alb 14 *See* Northill.
NORK PARK (St Paul), *Surrey.* V. **D** Guildf 9 **P** *H M the Queen* **I** P E NAYLOR.
NORLAND (St Luke), *W Yorks.* V. **D** Wakef 1 *See* Sowerby Bridge.
NORLANDS (St Jas). **D** Lon 15 *See* Kensington.
NORLEY (St Jo Evang), *Chesh.* V. **D** Ches 3 **P** *Bp* **I** W M DAVIES.
NORMACOT (H Evangelists), *Staffs.* V. **D** Lich 18 **P** *Dioc Bd of Patr* **I** C LANTSBERY.
NORMANBY (St Helen), *Cleve.* V. **D** York 22 *See* Eston.
NORMANBY (St Andr) w Edston, Gt (St Mich) and Salton, *N Yorks.* R. **D** York **P** *Abp and St John's Coll Cam* alt **I** D A BAKER.
NORMANBY, *Lincs..* **D** Linc 4 *See* Burton-on-Stather.
NORMANBY (St Pet), nr Lincoln, *Lincs..* **D** Linc 3 *See* Owmby.
NORMANBY-LE-WOLD (St Pet), *Lincs..* **D** Linc 5 *See* Claxby.
NORMANTON (St Nich), *Lincs..* **D** Linc 23 *See* Carlton Scroop.
NORMANTON Leics. R **D** Pet 12 *See* Edith-Weston.
NORMANTON (All SS), *W Yorks.* V. **D** Wakef 13 **P** *Trin Coll Cam* **I** D M HUGHES, M BEAUFORT-JONES *c,* J A BRADSHAW *c.*
NORMANTON-BY-DERBY (St Giles), *Derbys.* V. **D** Derby 11 **P** *CPAS* **I** R B BLOWERS, R JOYCE *c,* G K KNOTT *c.*
NORMANTON, SOUTH (St Mich), *Derbys.* R. **D** Derby 1 **P** *MMT* **I** R TAYLOR.
NORMANTON-LE-HEATH, *Leics.* R. **D** Leic 12 *See* Packington.
NORMANTON-ON-SOAR (St Jas Gt), *Notts.* R. **D** Southw 11 **P** *Bp* **I** A CLARKE *p-in-c.*
NORMANTON-ON-TRENT (St Matt), *Notts.* V. **D** Southw 4 **P** *Bp* **I** D G HATTER.
NORRIS BANK (St Martin), *Gtr Man.* R. **D** Man 4 **P** *Crown and Bp* alt **I** W G DAVIS.
NORRIS GREEN (St Chris), *Mer.* V. **D** Liv 6 **P** *Bp* **I** W M TODD, W B MAKIN *hon c.*

(Ch Ch Bp Chavasse Mem Ch), V. **D** Liv 6 **P** *Bp* **I** J W BANNER.
NORTH AUDLEY STREET. **D** Lon *See* Westminster.
NORTH BUCKINGHAM See Buckingham, North]. **I** (Vacant).
NORTH CAVE (All SS) w N and S Cliffe (St John), *Humb.* V. **D** York 16 **P** *P Carver* **I** P N HAYWARD.
NORTH CHAPEL (St Mich AA) w Ebernoe, V *W Sussex.* R. **D** Chich 6 **P** *Ld Egremont* **I** A C WILLMER.
NORTH COLLINGHAM (All SS), *Notts.*. **D** Southw 3 *See* Collingham, North.
NORTH COVE (St Botolph) w Barnby, *Suff.* R. **D** Nor 15 **I** R STEVENS *p-in-c.*
NORTH CURRY (St Pet and St Paul), *Somt.* V. **D** B & W 23 **P** *D and C of Wells* **I** M D LEWIS.
NORTH DALTON (All SS), *Humb.* V. **D** York 13 **P** *Abp* **I** R W HOWE *p-in-c.*
NORTH GRIMSTON (St Nich) and Wharram *N Yorks.*. **D** York 3 *See* Settrington.
NORTH HILL w Altarnon (St Nonna), Bolventor and Lewannick (St Martin), *Cornw.* R. **D** Truro 11 **P** *Dioc Bd of Patr 2 turns, Ld Chan 1 turn* **I** P H FRYER, R A D V THORN *team v.*
NORTH LEIGH, *Oxon.* V. **D** Ox 10 **P** *Ld Chan* **I** (Vacant).
NORTH LEVERTON, *Notts.*. **D** Southw *See* Leverton, North.
NORTH MEOLS (St Cuthb), *Mer.* R. **D** Liv 8 **P** *Col R F Hesketh* **I** W H PICK.
NORTH MUSKHAM (St Wilfrid), *Notts.*. **D** Southw 4 *See* Muskham, North.
NORTH NEWTON (St Pet), *Somt.* V. **D** B & W *See* Newton, North.
NORTH RODE, *Chesh.*. **D** Ches 13 *See* Bosley.
NORTH SHIELDS, *T & W.*. **D** Newc T 6 *See* Tynemouth.
NORTH TAMERTON, *Devon.* V. **D** Truro 11 *See* Tamerton, North.
NORTH WEALD **D** Chelmsf 10 *See* Weald.
NORTH WHEATLEY, *Notts.*. **D** Southw *See* Wheatley, North.
NORTH WINGFIELD, *Derbys.*. **D** Derby *See* Wingfield, North.
NORTHALL, *Gtr Lon.*. **D** Lon *See* Northolt.
NORTHALLERTON (All SS) w Kirby Sigston (St Laur) and Romanby (St Jas), *N Yorks.* V. **D** York 23 **P** *D and C of Dur* **I** J CASTLEDINE, G R WALKER *c.*
NORTHAM (St Marg) w Westward Ho! (H Trin) and Appledore, *Devon.* R. **D** Ex 17 **P** *D and C of Windsor* **I** D N CHANCE, K FELTHAM *team v.*
NORTHAM (St Aug of Cant), *Hants.*. **D** Win 11 *See* Southampton.
NORTHAMPTON (All SS w St Kath), *Northants.* V. **D** Pet 5 **P** *Bp* **I** V C R MALAN, T J HIGGINS *c.*
(Ch Ch). **D** Pet 5 **P** *Bp* **I** S B H DELVES-BROUGHTON.
(Em), R. **D** Pet 5 **P** *Dioc Bd of Patr* **I** M J M GLOVER, N C BEATTIE *team v,* J A HAWKINS *team v,* R V WALLIS *hon c.*
(H Sepulchre w St Andr and St Lawr), V. **D** Pet 5 **P** *Bp* **I** H A L T TIBBS, W A SIMONS *c.*
(H Trin), V. **D** Pet 5 **P** *Bp* **I** M R MILES.
(St Alb Mart), V. **D** Pet 5 **P** *Bp* **I** B WALSHE, G WILLIAMS *c,* K W WOLFE *hon c.*
(St D).. **D** Pet 5 *See* Kingsthorpe.
(St Giles), V. **D** Pet 5 **P** *Simeon Trustees* **I** P A M GOMPERTZ, R J P BARRIBAL *c.*
(St Jas), V. **D** Pet 4 **P** *Bp* **I** J C ROYDS.
(St Matt), V. **D** Pet 5 **P** *Dioc Bd of Patr* **I** J I MORTON.
(St Mary, Dallington), V. **D** Pet 4 **P** *Earl Spencer* **I** A E PANTON.
(St Mary Virg), V. **D** Pet 4 **P** *Bp* **I** G I BURGON, H M BOWRON *c.*
(St Mich AA w St Edm K and M), V. **D** Pet 5 **P** *Bp* **I** R THICKNESSE.
(St Paul), V. **D** Pet 5 **P** *Bp* **I** I C HUNT.
(St Pet), R. **D** Pet 5 **P** *R Foundation of St Kath* **I** B R MARSH, J W A FAVELL *c.*
NORTHAMPTON ST BENEDICT, *Northants.* V. **D** Pet 4 **P** *Bp* **I** W B BEER.
NORTHAW (St Thos à Becket), *Herts.* V. **D** St Alb 6 **P** *Maj and Mrs F R Dore* **I** J C SYKES.
NORTHBOROUGH, *Cambs.*. **D** Pet *See* Maxey.
NORTHBOURNE (St Aug) and Tilmanstone (St Andr) w Betteshanger (St Mary Virg) and Ham (St Geo Mart), *Kent.* R. **D** Cant 8 **P** *Abp, Ld Northbourne and Northbourne Court, Deal (alt)* **I** J C BROOKS.
NORTHCHURCH (St Mary), *Herts.* R. **D** St Alb 3 **P** *Duchy of Cornw* **I** J T TABOR.
NORTHENDEN (St Wilfrid), *Gtr Man.* R. **D** Man 10 **P** *Bp* **I** G S FORSTER.
(Wm Temple Conv Distr). **D** Man 5 *See* Woodhouse Park.
NORTHFIELD (St Laur), *W Midl.* R. **D** Birm 4 **P** *Keble Coll Ox* **I** T M THOMPSON, B J H LAMB *c,* P W NOKES *c,* P B CLIFF *hon c,* D C MERCHANT *hon c.*
NORTHFIELD (St Mich AA), *Humb.* V. **D** Sheff 7 *See* Ferham Pk, Rotherham.
NORTHFLEET (St Botolph), *Kent.* V. **D** Roch 3 **P** *Crown* **I** D M P BEATER.
(All SS Perry Street), V. **D** Roch 3 **P** *Bp* **I** A R GORDON.
NORTHIAM (St Mary), *E Sussex.* R. **D** Chich 22 **P** *MMT* **I** H A SMITH.
NORTHILL or NORHILL (St Mary Virg) w Moggerhanger, *Beds.* R. **D** St Alb 17 **P** *Bp and Grocers' Co* **I** T H GIRLING.
NORTHINGTON and Swarraton (St Jo Evang), *hants.*. **D** Win *See* Candover Valley.
NORTHLEACH (St Pet and St Paul) and Eastington w Hampnett (St Matt) and Farmington (St Pet), *Glos.* V. **D** Glouc 15 **P** *Bp* **I** J P BROWN *p-in-c.*
NORTHLEIGH (St Giles), *Devon.* R. **D** Ex 5 *See* Farway.
NORTHLEW (St Thos of Cant) w Ashbury, *Devon.* R. **D** Ex **P** *Crown* **I** H A GREAVES.
NORTHMOOR (St Denys), *Oxon.*. **D** Ox 9 *See* Windrush, Lower.
NORTHMOOR GREEN (St Pet and St John), *Somt.* V. **D** B & W 17 *See* Petherton, North.
NORTHOLT or NORTHALL (St Mary), *Gtr Lon.* R. **D** Lon 6 **P** *BNC Ox* **I** J V STEWART, M L NICHOLAS *c,* P V A ADKINS *hon c.*
(St Jos the Worker), V. **D** Lon 6 **P** *Dioc Bd of Patr* **I** M J MARKEY.
(St Barn Northolt Pk), V. **D** Lon 6 **P** *Bp* **I** J RHODES-WRIGLEY, A W D GABB-JONES *c.*
NORTHORPE (St Jo Bapt), *Lincs.*. **D** Linc 4 *See* Scotton.
NORTHOVER (St Andr), *Somt.* R and V. **D** B & W *See* Ilchester.
NORTHOWRAM (St Matt), *W Yorks.* V. **D** Wakef 2 **P** *Bp* **I** J W MUIR.
NORTHREPPS (St Mary Virg), *Norf.* R. **D** Nor 5 **P** *Duchy of Lanc* **I** D L AINSWORTH.
NORTHUMBERLAND HEATH, *Kent.*. **D** Roch *See* Erith.
NORTHWICH (St Helen), *Chesh.*. **D** Ches 6 *See* Witton.
(St Luke and H Trin), V. **D** Ches 6 **P** *Bp* **I** D F REAGON.
NORTHWOLD (St Andr), *Norf.* R. **D** Ely 16 **P** *Bp* **I** (Vacant).
NORTHWOOD (H Trin), *Staffs.*. **D** Lich *See* Hanley, H Evang.
NORTHWOOD (H Trin), *Gtr Lon.* V. **D** Lon 24 **P** *Trustees* **I** R M D DE BRISAY, W H E BEALE *hon c.*
(Em), V. **D** Lon 24 **P** *Trustees* **I** R T BEWES, I R BENTLEY *c,* A D ROSE *c.*
NORTHWOOD, *Isle of Wight.* R. **D** Portsm 7 **P** *Bp* **I** R F PARKER.
NORTHWOOD, *Liv.*. **D** Liv 5 *See* Kirkby.
NORTHWOOD HILLS (St Edm). **D** Lon 24 *See* Pinner.
NORTON (All SS), *Wilts.*. **D** Bris *See* Stanton St Quintin.
NORTON, *Kent.* R. **D** Cant 7 **P** *Ld Chan* **I** W H G HILL.
NORTON (St Berteline and St Chris), *Chesh.* V. **D** Ches **P** *Dioc Bd of Patr* **I** R MCGREEVY.
NORTON (St Jas Gt), *S Yorks.* R. **D** Sheff 2 **P** *C C C Cam* **I** M N WILLIAMS, S P BAILEY *c.*
NORTON (St Mary Virg), *Cleve.* V. **D** Dur 14 **P** *Bp* **I** M S SIMMONS.
(St Mich AA), V. **D** Dur 14 **P** *V of Norton* **I** W M BREWIN.
NORTON (St Mary Virg) w The Leigh (St Cath) and Evington, *Avon.* V. **D** Glouc 2 **P** *D and C of Bris and Ld Chan* **I** (Vacant).
NORTON (All SS), *Northants.*. **D** Pet *See* Brington.
NORTON (St Geo), *Herts.* V. **D** St Alb 9 **P** *Bp* **I** D R GRAEBE, D A HALL *c.*
NORTON w Tostock Suff. **R D** St E 9 *See* Pakenham.
NORTON (St Egwin) and Lenchwick, *Worcs.* V. **D** Worc 1 *See* Harvington.
NORTON (St Mich AA), *Worcs.* V. **D** Worc 11 **P** *Bp* **I** F J MUSHEN.
NORTON-JUXTA-MALTON (St Pet), *N Yorks.* V. **D** York 3 **P** *Abp* **I** D B COOPER.
NORTON-BAVANT (All SS), *Wilts.* V. **D** Sarum 22 *See* Heytesbury.
NORTON-BY-TWYCROSS, *Leics.*. **D** Leic *See* Orton-on-the-Hill.
NORTON CANES (St Jas), *Staffs.* R. **D** Lich 4 **P** *Bp* **I** M J NEWMAN.
NORTON-CANON (St Nich), *Herefs.*. **D** Heref *See* Kinnersley.
NORTON-CUCKNEY (St Mary) w Holbeck (St Winifred), *Notts.* V. **D** Southw 7 **P** *Duke of Portland* **I** P H F STURDY.

NORTON DISNEY (St Pet), *Lincs.*. **D** Linc 18 *See* Thurlby.
NORTON, EAST (All SS), *Leics.* V. **D** Leic 8 *See* Tugby.
NORTON FITZWARREN (All SS), *Somt.* R. **D** B & W 23 **P** *MMT* **I** A S GRAESSER.
NORTON-IN-HALES (St Chad w Em), *Salop.* R. **D** Lich 23 **P** *CPAS* **I** (Vacant).
NORTON KEMPSEY (St Jas Gt) w Whittington (St Phil and St Jas), *Worcs.* V. **D** Worc *See* Worcester, St Martin.
NORTON-LE-CLAY (St Jo Evang), *N Yorks.* V. **D** Ripon 3 *See* Cundall.
NORTON-LE-MOORS (St Bart), *Staffs.* R. **D** Lich 16 **P** *Ld Norton* **I** W H YATES.
NORTON LEES, *S Yorks.*. **D** Sheff *See* Sheffield.
NORTON LINDSEY (H Trin), *Warws.*. **D** Cr 9 *See* Wolverton.
NORTON-MALREWARD (H Trin), *Avon.* R. **D** B & W 15 **P** *Bp* **I** B W HOWARTH.
NORTON-MANDEVILLE (All SS), *Essex.*. **D** Chelmsf 6 *See* Ongar, High.
NORTON ST PHILIP (St Phil and St Jas) w Hemington, Hardington and Laverton, *Somt.* V. **D** B & W 16a **P** *J B Owen-Jones Esq and Bp (alt)* **I** G H GILLESPIE.
NORTON SUBCOURSE (St Mary), *Norf.*. **D** Nor 14 *See* Raveningham.
NORTON-SUB-HAMDON (St Mary Virg), w W Chinnock, Chiselborough (St Pet and St Paul) and Middle Chinnock, *Somt.* R. **D** B & W 11 **P** *Bp* **I** A P NICHOLS.
NORTON WOODSEATS (St Chad), *S Yorks.* V. **D** Sheff 2 *See* Sheffield.
NORWELL (St Lawr), *Notts.* V. **D** Southw 4 **P** *Bp* **I** B JAMES.
NORWICH (Ch Ch New Catton), *Norf.* V. **D** Nor 4 **P** *R of St Clem Nor* **I** J F MCGINLEY.
(St Andr), V. **D** Nor 4b **P** *PCC* **I** (Vacant).
(St Aug w St Mary Virg-at-Coslany), R. **D** Nor 4b **P** *D and C of Nor and Bp* alt **I** L A HUBBARD *p-in-c.*
(St Cath, Mile Cross), V. **D** Nor 4 **P** *Major W F Batt and others* **I** D M SALWAY, W A HOWARD *c.*
(St Francis Heartsease), V. **D** Nor 4b **P** *Bp* **I** A D MCGREGOR.
(St Geo Tombland w St Simon and St Jude), V. **D** Nor 4b **P** *Bp* **I** J H FERLEY *c-in-c.*
(St Giles w St Benedict), V. **D** Nor 4b **P** *Bp and ld Chan (alt)* **I** F H W MILLETT.
(St Helen), V. **D** Nor 4b **P** *Nor Gt Hosp Trust* **I** C N LAVENDER *c-in-c.*
(St Jo Bapt Maddermarket), R. **D** Nor 4b **P** *New Coll Ox* **I** C H PALFREY.
(St Mary-in-the-Marsh), V. **D** Nor 4b **P** *D and C of Nor* **I** RT REV C. K. SANSBURY *c-in-c.*
(St Mary Magd w St Jas Gt), V. **D** Nor 4b **P** *D and C of Nor* **I** M J MENIN.
(St Pet Mancroft), V. **D** Nor 4b **P** *PCC* **I** D M SHARP, J A AVES *c*, D H CLARK *hon c*, R J M COLLIER *hon c.*
Parmentergate Team Ministry St John de Sepulchre w St Julian and St Etheldreda), R. **D** Nor **P** *Patr Bd* **I** M S MCLEAN, B F SHORT *team v.*
(St Steph), V. **D** Nor 4b **P** *D and C of Nor* **I** J O'BYRNE *c-in-c.*
OVER-THE-WATER (St Geo, Colegate), *Norf.* R. **D** Nor 4b **P** *D and C of Nor* **I** L A HUBBARD *p-in-c.*
NORWOOD (St Mary Virg), *Gtr Lon.* R. **D** Lon 6 **P** *S for Maint of Faith* **I** N T POLLOCK.
NORWOOD (St Leon), *S Yorks.*. **D** Sheff 3 *See* Sheffield.
NORWOOD, SOUTH (St Mark w St Geo), *Surrey.* V. **D** Cant 16 **P** *Abp* **I** P E THROWER.
(H Innoc), V. **D** Cant 16 **P** *Abp* **I** R D NEWMAN.
(St Alb Mart), V. **D** Cant 16 **P** *Abp* **I** J A P HOLDSWORTH.
NORWOOD, UPPER (All SS w St Marg), V. **D** Cant 16 **P** *V of Croydon* **I** F C YOUNG *p-in-c*, J F ANDREWS *hon c.*
(St Jo Evang), V. **D** Cant 16 **P** *Abp* **I** L G CRASKE.
NORWOOD, WEST (St Luke), *Surrey.* V. **D** S'wark 6 **P** *Abp* **I** W J N DURANT *c.*
NOTGROVE (St Bart), *Glos.* R. **D** Glouc 15 *See* Cold Aston.
NOTLEY, BLACK (St Pet and St Paul), *Essex.* R. **D** Chelmsf 19 **P** *St Jo Coll Cam* **I** G A POTTER.
NOTLEY, WHITE (St Etheldreda) w Faulkbourne (St German) and Cressing, *Essex.* V. **D** Chelmsf 29 **P** *Bp, V of Witham and Lt Col J O Parker* **I** E R LITTLER.
NOTTING HILL (St John, St Clem and St Mark, All SS w St Columb), *Lon.* R. **D** Lon 11 **P** *Dioc Bd of Patr* **I** J K BROWNSELL *team v*, D W RANDALL *team v*, W H BAYNES *c*, G M EVANS *c*, P D KING *c.*
NOTTINGHAM (St Mary Virg and St Cath w St Luke), *Notts.* V. **D** Southw 14 **P** *Bp* **I** M J JACKSON.
(All SS), V. **D** Southw 14 **P** *Trustees* **I** P G WATTS, J WALKER *c.*
(St Andr), V. **D** Southw 14 **P** *Trustees* **I** R G LACEY.
(St Ann w Em), V. **D** Southw 14 **P** *Trustees* **I** J P NEILL, E WHITLEY *c.*
(St Geo w St Jo Bapt), V. **D** Southw 14 **P** *Bp* **I** L WARD-ANDREWS *c-in-c.*
(St Jas Porchester), V. **D** Southw 13 **P** *Bp* **I** D C BIGNELL *c.*
(St Jude, Mapperley), V. **D** Southw 14 **P** *CPAS* **I** H I L RUSSELL, C J CULLWICK *c.*
(St Mark, Woodthorpe), V. **D** Southw 13 **P** *Bp* **I** D J BARTLETT, R A WALTON *c.*
(St Matthias). **D** Southw 14 *See* Sneinton.
(St Nich), R. **D** Southw 14 **P** *CPAS* **I** D J HUGGETT.
(St Paul, Hyson Green), V. **D** Southw 14 **P** *CPAS* **I** C J HALL, J H TOVEY *c.*
(St Pet w St Jas), R. **D** Southw 14 **P** *Bp* **I** M C GOLDSMITH, J S DUNNING *c.*
(St Sav), V. **D** Southw 14 **P** *CPAS* **I** R G HOYE.
(St Steph Hyson Green), V. **D** Southw 14 **P** *CPAS* **I** W V BECKETT.
See also CARLTON AND SNEINTON.
NOWTON (St Pet), *Suff.* R. **D** St E 10 *See* Hawstead.
NUFFIELD (H Trin), *Oxon.* R. **D** Ox 7 **P** *MMT* **I** (Vacant).
NUN-MONKTON, *N Yorks.* V. **D** Ripon 3 *See* Kirk-Hammerton.
NUNBURNHOLME (St Jas), *Humb.* R. **D** York 10 **P** *Abp* **I** J S SELLER.
NUNEATON (St Nich), *Warws.* V. **D** Cov 5 **P** *Crown* **I** G J HARDWICK.
(St Mary Virg), V. **D** Cov 5 **P** *V of Nuneaton* **I** J D MOORE.
NUNEHAM COURTENAY, *Oxon.*. **D** Ox 5 *See* Marsh Baldon.
NUNHEAD (St Antony) *Surrey.* V. **D** S'wark 15 **P** *Bp* **I** R SCREECH, W C SMITH *c.*
(St Silas), V. **D** S'wark 15 **P** *Bp* **I** (Vacant).
NUNKEELING (St Helen or St Mary Magd), *Humb.* V. **D** York 14 *See* Sigglesthorne.
NUNNEY (All SS) w Wanstrow and Cloford, *Somt.* R. **D** B & W 16a **P** *S for Maint of Faith and C N Clarke Esq* **I** J G PESCOD *p-in-c.*
NUNNINGTON (All SS and St Jas), *N Yorks.* R. **D** York 20 *See* Stonegrave.
NUNTHORPE-IN-CLEVELAND (St Mary Virg), *Cleve.* V. **D** York 25 **P** *Abp* **I** J WOODHOUSE.
NUNTON, *Wilts.*. **D** Sarum 17 *See* Odstock.
NURSLING (St Boniface) w Rownhams (St Jo Div), *Hants.* R. **D** Win 10 **P** *Bp* **I** D H BOURNON.
NURSTEAD Kent. R **D** Roch 3 *See* Meopham.
NUTBOURNE, *W Sussex.*. **D** Chich 7 *See* Pulborough.
NUTFIELD (St Pet and St Paul), *Surrey.* R. **D** S'wark 12 **P** *Jes Coll Ox* **I** G I WILLIAMS.
LOWER (Ch Ch), V. **D** S'wark 12 **P** *CPS* **I** (Vacant).
NUTHALL, or NUTTALL (St Patr), *Notts.* R. **D** Southw 8 **P** *Bp* **I** J J STAFFORD.
NUTHURST (St Andr), *W Sussex.* R. **D** Chich 4 **P** *Bp of Lon* **I** C H SELLARS.
NUTHURST, *Warws.*. **D** Birm *See* Packwood.
NUTLEY (St Jas L), *E Sussex.* V. **D** Chich 16 **P** *R of Maresfield* **I** G W R BERRY.
NUTLEY, *Hants.*. **D** Win *See* Preston Candover.
NYDD, *N Yorks.*. **D** Ripon *See* Nidd.
NYMET ROWLAND (St Bart) w Coldridge (St Matt), *Devon.* R. **D** Ex 16 **P** *Bp* **I** K J WARREN.
NYMET ST GEORGE (St Geo), *Devon.* R. **D** Ex *See* South Molton.
NYMET TRACEY, *Devon.*. **D** Ex *See* Bow.
NYMPSFIELD (St Bart), *Glos.* R. **D** Glouc 9 *See* Uley.
NYNEHEAD (All SS), *Somt.* V. **D** B & W 22 *See* Wellington and Distr.

OADBY (St Pet), *Leics.* V. **D** Leic 6 **P** *Leic Racecourse Holdings Ltd* **I** R J TONKIN, W BROWN *c.*
OAKAMOOR (H Trin) w Cotton, *Staffs.* V. **D** Lich 14 **P** *R of Cheadle* **I** J B HARROP P-IN-C OF COTTON, J D STARKEY P-IN-C OF OAKAMOOR.
OAKDALE (St Geo), *Dorset.* R. **D** Sarum 14 **P** *Bp* **I** G MUXLOW, F J MILVERTON *team v.*
OAKE (St Bart), *Somt.*. **D** B & W 22 *See* Bradford.
OAKENGATES (H Trin), *Salop.* V. **D** Lich 27 **P** *Bp* **I** (Vacant).
OAKENROD (St Geo w St Alb), *Gtr Man.*. **D** Man 17 **P** *Bp* **I** P L SCOTT.
OAKENSHAW (St Andr) w Woodlands, *W Yorks.* V. **D** Bradf 2 **P** *Bp* **I** P T TAYLOR.
OAKFIELD (St John), *Isle of Wight.*. **D** Portsm 6 *See* Ryde.
OAKFORD (St Pet), *Devon.* R. **D** Ex 8 *See* Washfield.

OAKHAM (All SS) w Hambleton and Egleton, *Leics*. V. **D** Pet 12 **P** *E R Hanbury Esq and D & C of Linc (alt)* **I** A A HORSLEY, J R WESTWOOD *c*.
OAKHANGER, *Hants*.. **D** Win *See* Kingsley.
OAKHILL, *Somt*.. **D** B & W *See* Ashwick.
OAKINGTON or HOCKINGTON (St Andr), *Cambs*. V. **D** Ely 5 **P** *Qu Coll Cam* **I** J C ALEXANDER.
OAKLEY, *Derbys*.. **D** Derby 16 *See* Croxall.
OAKLEY, *Bucks*.. **D** Ox 21 **P** *Bp* **I** (Vacant).
OAKLEY, *Beds*.. **D** St Alb *See* Bromham.
OAKLEY, *Suff*.. **D** St E *See* Brome.
OAKLEY, CHURCH (St Leon) w Wootton (St Lawr), *Hants*. R. **D** Win 3 **P** *Qu Coll Ox and D and C of Win* **I** J C LITTON.
OAKLEY, GREAT (St Mich) w Little Oakley, *Northants*. V. **D** Pet 10 *See* Corby.
OAKLEY, GREAT (All SS), *Essex*. R. **D** Chelmsf 25 **P** *St Jo Coll Cam* **I** F W BURGESS.
OAKLEY, LITTLE (St Mary), *Essex*. R. **D** Chelmsf 25 *See* Ramsey.
OAKMOOR TEAM MINISTRY (Bishopsnympton, Rose Ash, Mariansleigh, Molland, Knowstone, E and W Anstey), *Devon*. R. **D** Ex 19 **P** *Dioc Bd of Patr* **I** C S TULL, B J BREWER *team v*, J LLOYD *team v*.
OAKRIDGE (St Bart), *Glos*. V. **D** Glouc 4 *See* Bisley.
OAKS-IN-CHARNWOOD (St Jas Ap) and Copt Oak (St Pet), *Leics*. V. **D** Leic **P** *Dioc Bd of Patr* **I** G A PADDOCK, G H MALLORY *c*.
OAKSEY (All SS), *Wilts*. R. **D** Bris *See* Minety.
OAKWOOD (St Jo Bapt), *Surrey*. V. **D** Guildf *See* Okewood.
OAKWOOD (St Thos), *Gtr Lon*. V. **D** Lon 21 **P** *Bp* **I** J POTHEN, J H TYNDALL *c*.
OAKWORTH (Ch Ch), *W Yorks*. V. **D** Bradf 11 **P** *Bp* **I** C WARD.
OARE (St Mary Virg) w Culbone (St Culbone), *Somt*. R. **D** B & W 21 **P** *Bp* **I** L W MATHEWS *c-in-c*.
OARE (St Pet) w Luddenham (St Mary Virg) and Stone, *Kent*. V. **D** Cant 6 *See* Brents.
OARE (St Bart), *Berks*.. **D** Ox 14 *See* Chieveley.
OARE, *Wilts*.. **D** Sarum *See* Huish.
OATLANDS (St Mary), *Surrey*. V. **D** Guildf 8 **P** *Bp* **I** R W GIBBIN.
OBORNE or WOBOURNE (St Cuthb) w Poyntington, *Dorset*. R. **D** Sarum *See* Queen Thorne.
OBY, *Norf*.. **D** Nor 2 *See* Ashby.
OCCOLD (St Mich) w Redlingfield, *Suff*. R. **D** St E 16 **P** *C Champion Marshall Esq* **I** J W LARTER P-IN-C OF BEDINGFIELD *p-in-c*.
OCKBROOK (All SS), W Borrowash (St Steph), *Derbys*. V. **D** Derby 13 **P** *Maj J Pares* **I** M F LEIGH, J W DAINES *hon c*.
OCKENDON, NORTH (St Mary Magd), *Essex*. R. **D** Chelmsf 4 **P** *Bp* **I** F J HACKETT *p-in-c*.
OCKENDON, SOUTH (St Nich), *Essex*. R. **D** Chelmsf 15 **P** *Guild of All S* **I** H BLACK.
OCKER HILL, *W Midl*.. **D** Lich *See* Tipton.
OCKHAM (All SS) w Hatchford (St Matt and All SS), *Surrey*. R. **D** Guildf 10 **P** *Bp* **I** C C STILL.
OCKLEY (St Marg w St Jo Evang), *Surrey*. R. **D** Guildf 6 **P** *Bp* **I** M A R COLLINS.
OCLE PYCHARD (St Jas Gt) and Ullingswick, *Herefs*.. **D** Heref **P** *Bp* **I** D W GOULD *p-in-c*.
ODCOMBE (St Pet and St Paul), *Somt*. R. **D** B & W 11 **P** *Ch Ch Ox* **I** A C DEAN.
ODD DOWN, *Avon*.. **D** B & W 13 *See* Bath.
ODD RODE (All SS), *Chesh*. R. **D** Ches 11 **P** *R of Astbury* **I** R N W ELBOURNE.
ODDINGLEY (St Jas), *Worcs*.. **D** Worc 8 *See* Hadzor.
ODDINGTON (H Ascen) w adlestrop (St Mary Magd), *Glos*. R. **D** Glouc 16 **P** *Bp and Ld Leigh* **I** (Vacant).
ODDINGTON, *Oxon*. R. **D** Ox 2 *See* Charlton-on-Otmoor.
ODELL (All SS), *Beds*. R. **D** St Alb 21 **P** *Ld Luke of Pavenham* **I** A M G WELLS *p-in-c*.
ODIHAM (All SS) w S Warnborough (St Andr) and Long Sutton, *Hants*. V. **D** Win 4 **P** *Bp and St Jo Coll Ox* **I** A J GRACIE, K W J KELLAND *p-in-c*.
ODSTOCK (St Mary) w Nunton (St Andr) and Bodenham, *Wilts*. R. **D** Sarum 17 **P** *Earl of Radnor* **I** RT REV L A BROWN *p-in-c*.
OFFCHURCH (St Greg), *Warws*. V. **D** Cov 10 **P** *Bp* **I** M L LANGRISH *p-in-c*.
OFFENHAM (St Mary and St Milburgh and Bretforton (St Leon), *Worcs*. V. **D** Worc **P** *Bp and Ch Ch Ox* **I** W A BATES.
OFFHAM (St Mich AA), *Kent*. R. **D** Roch 6 *See* Malling, West.
OFFLEY (St Mary Magd) w Lilley (St Pet), *Herts*. V. **D** St Alb 9 **P** *G S Hughes Trustees 2 turns, St Jo Coll Cam 1 turn* **I** P FORBES.
OFFORD D'ARCY w Offord Cluny (All SS), *Cambs*. R. **D** Ely 13 **P** *Ld Chan* **I** E J PRYKE.
OFFTON (St Mary) w Willisham, *Suff*. V. **D** St E 1 *See* Somersham.
OFFWELL w Widworthy (St Cuthb), Cotleigh (St Mich) and Farway (St Mich AA) w Northleigh (St Giles) and Southleigh (St Lawr), *Devon*. R. **D** Ex 5 **P** *Dioc Bd of Patr* **I** W E WRIGHT, C L CAUDWELL *team v*.
OGBOURNE, *Wilts*.. **D** Sarum 26 *See* Ridgeway.
OGLEY HAY (St Jas) w Brownhills, *W Midl*. V. **D** Lich 2 **P** *Bp* **I** H THORNLEY, P J RICHMOND *c*.
OGWELL and Denbury, *Devon*. R. **D** Ex **P** *Bp and S for Maint of Faith* **I** D A ATKINSON.
OKEFORD, CHILDE, *Dorset*.. **D** Sarum 13 *See* Childe Okeford.
OKEFORD-FITZPAINE and Ibberton (St Eustace) w Belchalwell (St Aldhelm) and Woolland (Dedic unknown), *Dorset*. R. **D** Sarum 9 **P** *G Pitt-Rivers (3 turns) and M J Scott-Williams Esq (1 turn)* **I** M J POMEROY, J A WALTER *c*.
OKEFORD SHILLING, *Dorset*.. **D** Sarum *See* Shillingstone.
OKEHAMPTON (All SS w St Jas) w Inwardleigh, *Devon*. R. **D** Ex 12 **P** *Lt Col V W Calmady-Hamlyn and Simeon Trustees* **I** R N RAYNER, P J M K DOUGLAS *c*.
OKEWOOD (St Jo Bapt) and Forest Green (H Trin), *Surrey*. V. **D** Guildf 2 **P** *J P M H Evelyn Esq* **I** M A R COLLINS *p-in-c*.
OLD BYLAND, *N Yorks*.. **D** York *See* Hawnby.
OLD FORD. **D** Lon 7 *See* Bow.
OLD HILL (H Trin), *Worcs*. V. **D** Worc 9 **P** *Ch S Trust* **I** R G C BROWNING, G T DAINTREE *c*.
OLD LEAKE (St Mary Virg) w Wrangle, *Lincs*. V. **D** Linc **P** *Bp and Dioc Bd of Patr* **I** J A CRUST.
OLD STRATFORD (H Trin), *Northants*. R. **D** Pet 2 *See* Passenham.
OLD STREET (St Luke), R. **D** Lon 2 *See* St Luke.
OLD TRAFFORD, *Gtr Man*.. **D** Man 10 *See* Trafford, Old.
OLDBERROW w Morton Bagot, *Warw*.. **D** Cov 9 *See* Spernall.
OLDBURY (Ch Ch), *Worcs*. V. **D** Birm 6 **P** *Bp* **I** (Vacant).
OLDBURY (St Nich), *Salop*. R. **D** Heref 9 *See* Bridgnorth.
OLDBURY (Heddington, Calstone Wellington, Yatesbury, Cherhill), *Wilts*. R. **D** Sarum 25 **P** *Bp, CPAS, Marq of Lansdowne and SuLdr R E Money-Kyrle* **I** R C BUTLER, E LEWIS *c*.
OLDBURY-ON-SEVERN (St Arida), *Avon*. R. **D** Glouc 8 **P** *D and C of Ch Ch Ox* **I** N STOCKS.
OLDBURY-ON-THE-HILL, *Glos*.. **D** Glouc 17 *See* Boxwell.
OLDHAM (St Mary Virg w St Pet, H Trin Coldhurst St Andr), *Gtr Man*. R. **D** Man 15 **P** *Patr Bd* **I** S M BANNISTER, J S G COTMAN *team v*, C A POWELL *team v*, I K STUBBS *team v*, G O'NEILL *c*.
(All SS North Moor), V. **D** Man 15 **P** *Trustees* **I** A J MULLETT.
(H Trin Waterhead), V. **D** Man 15 **P** *Crown and Bp* alt **I** C E SHAW.
(St Ambrose), V. **D** Man 15 **P** *Crown and Bp* alt **I** B P H JAMES.
(St Barn), V. **D** Man 15 **P** *Crown and Bp* alt **I** J R MCMANUS.
(St Chad, Limeside), V. **D** Man 15 **P** *Bp* **I** G K TIBBO.
(St Jas), V. **D** Man 15 **P** *R of Prestwich* **I** P PLUMPTON.
(St John, Chadderton or Werneth), V. **D** Man 15 **P** *Crown and Bp* alt **I** (Vacant).
(St Mark w Ch Ch Glodwick), V. **D** Man 15 **P** *Trustees* **I** B HOLT.
(St Matt w St Aid Roundthorn), V. **D** Man 15 **P** *Bp* **I** S CARTWRIGHT.
(St Paul), V. **D** Man 15 **P** *Bp* **I** H G SUTCLIFFE.
(St Steph and All Marts Lower Moor), V. **D** Man 15 **P** *Bp* **I** T E JONES.
(St Thos Moorside), V. **D** Man 15 **P** *Trustees* **I** J H GRAY.
(St Thos Ap Werneth), V. **D** Man 15 **P** *Crown and Bp* alt **I** A J BUTTERWORTH.
OLDHURST (St Pet), *Cambs*.. **D** Ely 12 *See* Broughton.
OLDLAND (St Anne) w (All SS) Longwell Green, *Avon*. R. **D** Bris **P** *Bp* **I** J A H BOWES, A R GEORGE *team v*.
OLDRIDGE, *Devon*.. **D** Ex *See* Whitestone.
OLLERTON (St Giles) w New Ollerton (St Paulinus), *Notts*. V. **D** Southw 7 **P** *Bp* **I** C D HIBBERT, J L SMITH *c*.

OLNEY (St Pet and St Paul), *Bucks.* V. D Ox 28 P *Bp* I R W COLLINS.
OLTON (St Marg), *W Midl.* V. D Birm 11 P *Trustees* I N S DODDS, K ATKINSON *c.*
OLVESTON (St Mary BV) w Aust, *Avon.* V. D Bris 6 P *D and C of Bris* I M A PAICE *p-in-c,* N E SPENCER *hon c.*
OMBERSLEY (St Andr) w Doverdale *Worcs.* V. D Worc 8 P *Bp and Ld Sandys* alt I A H DOYLE.
ONECOTE w Bradnop, *Staffs.* V. D Lich 16 P *V of Leek* I S R WATKIN *p-in-c.*
ONEHOUSE (St Jo Bapt) w HARLESTON (St Aug), *Suff.* R. D St E 6 *See* Finborough Magna.
ONGAR, HIGH (St Mary w St Jas) w Norton Mandeville (All SS), *Essex.* R. D Chelmsf 6 P *Ch S* I D J BROOMFIELD.
ONIBURY (St Mich), *Salop..* D Heref *See* Culmington.
ONLEY, *Northants.* R. D Pet 4 *See* Barby.
ONSLOW SQUARE (St Paul), V. D Lon 15 *See* Kensington.
OPENSHAW (St Barn), *Gtr Man.* R. D Man 1 P *Trustees* I A S WELLS.
HIGHER (St Clem), R. D Man 1 P *Trustees* I B G FLUX.
ORBY (All SS), *Lincs.* V. D Linc 8 P *Bp* I R H IRESON.
ORCHARD EAST (St Thos) w Margaret Marsh (St Marg) w W Orchard (St Luke) and Farrington, *Dorset..* D Sarum 13 *See* Shaston.
ORCHARD-PORTMAN (St Mich) w Thurlbear (St Thos) and Stoke St Mary, *Somt.* R. D B & W 23a *See* Staple-Fitzpaine.
ORCHARDLEIGH (St Mary Virg), *Somt.* V. D B & W 16a *See* Beckington.
ORCHESTON (St Geo w St Mary), *Wilts.* R. D Sarum 21 *See* Tilshead.
ORCOP, *Herefs..* D Heref *See* St Weonards.
ORDSALL (All H), *Notts.* R. D Southw 5 P *Bp* I J L MARSHALL.
ORDSALL Gtr Man. D Man 8 *See* Salford.
ORE (St Helen), *Sussex.* R. D Chich 21 P *Simeon Trustees* I C A F T SPRAY.
(Ch Ch), V. D Chich 21 P *Simeon Trustees* I D J N MADDOCK.
ORFORD (St Marg and All H), *Lancs.* V. D Liv 11 P *Bp* I E WILKES, G B ATHERTON *c.*
(St Andr), V. D Liv 11 P *Bp* I J HILTON.
ORFORD (St Bart) w Sudbourne (All SS), Chillesford, Butley and Iken (St Botolph), *Suff.* R. D St E P *Clergy Orph Corp 1st turn, Bp 2nd and 3rd turns* I (Vacant).
ORGARSWICK, *Kent..* D Cant *See* Dymchurch.
ORLESTONE (St Mary) w Ruckinge (St Mary Magd) and Warehorne, *Kent.* R. D Cant 12 P *Abp and Ld Chan (alt)* I (Vacant).
ORLETON (St Geo), *Herefs.* V. D Heref 7 P *Govs of Lucton Sch* I J T V JONES.
ORLETON (St Jo Bapt), *Worcs..* D Worc 12 *See* Stanford-on-Teme.
ORLINGBURY (St Mary), *Northants.* R. D Pet 7 *See* Harrowden, Great.
ORMESBY (St Cuthb), *Cleve.* R. D York 22 P *Abp* I A BILL, J D DAGLISH *c.*
ORMESBY ST MARG w Scratby and Ormesby St Mich, *Norf.* V. D Nor 2 P *D and C of Nor* I F J CLAYTON *hon c.*
ORMESBY, NORTH (H Trin), *Cleve.* V. D York 22 P *Abp* I D H LAMBERT, P F LANGFORD *c.*
ORMSBY, NORTH, or NUN (St Helen), V w Wyham (All SS) and Cadeby, R *Lincs..* D Linc *See* Fotherby.
ORMSBY, SOUTH (St Leon), R w Ketsby, Calceby, V and Driby R *Lincs..* D Linc 7 P *H J Massingberd-Mundy Esq* I P E FLUCK.
ORMSIDE or ORMSHED (St Jas), *Cumb.* R. D Carl 1 *See* Asby.
ORMSKIRK (St Pet and St Paul), *Lancs.* V. D Liv 9 P *Earl of Derby* I K THORNTON, R E DENNIS *c,* P J MARSHALL *c.*
ORPINGTON (All SS formerly St Nich), *Kent.* V. D Roch 16 P *D and C of Roch* I R R LUNNON, R I KNIGHT *c,* J S COX *hon c,* M T SKINNER *hon c.*
(Ch Ch), V. D Roch 16 P *Trustees* I A C EAVES, D M F NEWMAN *c.*
(St Andr), V. D Roch 16 P *Bp* I J A GROVES.
ORRELL (St Luke), *Mer* V. D Liv 12 P *Bp* I S M COATES.
ORRELL HEY, *Mer..* D Liv *See* Litherland.
ORSETT (St Giles and All SS), *Essex.* R. D Chelmsf 15 P *Bp* I H V CROSSLEY.
ORSTON (St Mary) w Thoroton (St Helen), *Notts.* V. D Southw 9 P *D and C of Linc* I (Vacant).
ORTON (All SS) and Tebay w Ravenstonedale (St Osw) and Newbiggin-on-Lune (St Aid), *Cumb.* V. D Carl 1 P *Bp* I N B SCOTT *p-in-c.*
ORTON (All SS), *Northants.* V. D Pet 8 *See* Rothwell.
ORTON, GREAT (St Giles), *Cumb.* R. D Carl 3 P *MMT and Earl of Lonsdale* alt I R S BARNETT.
ORTON LONGUEVILLE (H Trin) w St Botolph Bridge, *Cambs.* R. D Ely 14 P *Cl Orph Corp* I (Vacant).
ORTON-ON-THE-HILL (St Edith of Polesworth) w Twycross (St Jas Gt) and Norton-by-Twycross (H Trin), *Leics.* V. D Leic 15 P *Ld Chan 2 turns, Earl Howe 1 turn* I K W BASTOCK.
ORTON-WATERVILLE (St Mary), *Cambs.* R. D Ely 14 P *Pemb Coll Cam* I C J GARDNER.
ORWELL (St Andr), *Cambs.* R. D Ely 8 P *Bp and Dioc Bd of Patr (alt)* I J H THOMSON.
OSBALDWICK (St Thos) w Murton, *N Yorks.* V. D York P *Abp* I C H HARRISON.
OSBASTON, *Leics.* R. D Leic 15 *See* Cadeby.
OSBOURNBY (St Pet and St Paul) w Scott Willoughby (St Andr), *Lincs..* D Linc *See* Lafford, S.
OSGATHORPE (St Mary), *Leics.* R. D Leic 11 *See* Belton.
OSGODBY, *Lincs..* D Linc 2 *See* Ingoldsby.
OSMASTON-BY-ASHBOURNE (St Martin) w Edlaston, *Derbys.* V. D Derby 8 P *Sir Ian Walker-Okeover Bt and Bp* alt I N T VINCENT *hon c.*
OSMINGTON (St Osmund) w Poxwell, *Dorset.* V. D Sarum *See* Preston.
OSMONDTHORPE (St Phil), V. D Ripon 7 *See* Leeds.
OSMOTHERLEY (St Pet) w East Harlsey (St Osw) and Inglby Arncliffe, *N Yorks.* V. D York 23 P *J B Barnard 1 turn, Ld Chan 2 turns* I C E MILLER.
OSMOTHERLEY (St Jo Evang), *N Yorks..* D Carl 15 *See* Ulverston.
OSPRINGE (St Pet and St Paul), *Kent.* V. D Cant 7 P *St Jo Coll Cam* I I C HAWKINS.
OSSETT (H and Undivided Trin), *W Yorks.* V. D Wakef 10 P *V of Dewsbury* I J R SCARTH.
OSSETT, SOUTH (Ch Ch), *W Yorks.* V. D Wakef 10 P *Bp* I K W STAGGS.
OSSINGTON (Holy Rood), *Notts.* V. D Southw 4 P *Mrs P Goedhuis* I B JAMES *p-in-c.*
OSTERLEY (St Mary Spring Grove), *Gtr Lon.* V. D Lon 14 *See* Isleworth.
OSWALDKIRK, *N Yorks..* D York *See* Ampleforth.
OSWALDTWISTLE (Im), *Lancs.* V. D Blackb 1 P *Trustees* I J BEALL.
(All SS), V. D Blackb 1 P *Bp* I O HUGHES.
(St Paul), V. D Blackb 1 P *Trustees* I M D RATCLIFFE.
OSWESTRY (St Osw), *Salop.* V. D Lich 24 P *Earl of Powis* I M HILL, D LEAK *c.*
(H Trin), V. D Lich 24 P *V of Oswestry* I J M R A REAKES-WILLIAMS.
OSYTH, ST, *Essex..* D Chelmsf *See* St Osyth.
OTFORD (St Bart), *Kent.* V. D Roch 8 P *D and C of Westmr* I F C BUNCH.
OTHAM (St Nich), *Kent.* R. D Cant 15 P *Abp* I J W HAWTHORNE.
OTHERY (St Mich), *Somt.* V. D B & W *See* Middlezoy.
OTLEY (All SS), *W Yorks.* V. D Bradf 5 P *Bp* I D M KENDRICK, D PEEL *c,* G PERCIVAL *c.*
OTLEY (St Mary), *Suff.* R. D St E 7 P *Bp* I F ROWELL.
OTTERBOURNE (St Matt), *Hants.* V. D Win 15 P *Mrs P Chamberlayne-Macdonald* I F J BIANCHI.
OTTERBURN (St Jo Evang) w Elsdon (St Cuthb), Horsley (H Trin) and Byrness, *Northumb.* V. D Newc T *See* Bellingham-Otterburn.
OTTERDEN (St Lawr), *Kent.* R. D Cant 7 *See* Stalisfield.
OTTERFORD (St Leon), *Somt.* V. D B & W 23a *See* Churchstanton.
OTTERHAM (St Denis), *Cornw..* D Truro *See* Davidstow.
OTTERHAMPTON (All SS) w Combwich (St Pet) and Stockland (St Mary Magd), *Somt.* R. D B & W 18 P *Exors of Mrs Bailey Everard and Bp* alt I J B RITCHIE.
OTTERINGTON, NORTH and South *N Yorks.* R. D York *See* Thornton-le-Street.
OTTERSHAW (Ch Ch), *Surrey.* V. D Guildf 7 P *Bp* I B COTTER.
OTTERTON (St Mich AA) and Colaton Raleigh, *Devon.* V. D Ex 1 P *Bp and Ld Clinton* I W G TURNBULL.
OTTERY (St Mary Virg, K Edw Confessor and All SS), *Devon.* V. D Ex 7 P *Bp* I P J MCGEE, G E BUSSELL *c.*
OTTRINGHAM (St Wilfrid), w Sunk Is, *Humb.* V. D York 15 P *Abp* I W BERRIMAN.
OUGHTIBRIDGE, *S Yorks.* V. D Sheff 7 P *V of Wadsley* I L E G BONIFACE.
OUGHTRINGTON (St Pet), *Chesh.* R. D Ches 10 P *Bp* I W J MCKAE.
OULTON (St Jo Evang), *Staffs.* V. D Lich 19 P *Simeon Trustees* I D J WILLIAMS *p-in-c.*

MARSTON, NEW (St Mich AA), *Oxon.* V. **D** Ox 4 **P** *Bp* **I** A G MILES.
WOLVERCOTE (St Pet) w Summertown (St Mich AA), *Oxon.* R. **D** Ox 8 **P** *Bd of Patr* **I** L B FOSDIKE, C C S NEILL *team v*, M J OTTAWAY *team v*, E A JOHNSON *c*, W L A PRYOR *c*, G G WRIGHT *c*.
OXGATE (St Paul), *Gtr Lon.*. **D** Lon *See* Neasden.
OXHEY (St Matt), *Herts.* V. **D** St Alb 13 **P** *Dioc Bd of Patr* **I** P M PALMER, D A GUNN-JOHNSON *c*.
(All SS) w Oxhey Chap, V. **D** St Alb 13 **P** *Bp* **I** (Vacant).
OXHILL (St Laur), *Warws.* R. **D** Cov 9 *See* Tysoe.
OXLEY (Ch of Epiph), *W Midl.* V. **D** Lich 12 **P** *Bp* **I** C G PREECE.
OXNEAD (St Mary Magd), *Norf.*. **D** Nor 3 *See* Buxton.
OXON, *Salop.* V. **D** Lich 26 *See* Shelton.
OXSHOTT (St Andr), *Surrey.* V. **D** Guildf 10 **P** *Bp* **I** J D GREEN.
OXTED (St Mary Virg), *Surrey.* R. **D** S'wark 10 **P** *Bp* **I** G BENNETT, J M COURTENAY *c*, F A HARDING *c*, I T RIDING *c*.
OXTON (St Sav), *Mer.* V. **D** Ches 1 **P** *J B C Robin Esq* **I** C ALSBURY *c*, D B BAMBER *c*, K A ROWLANDS *c*.
OXTON (St Pet and St Paul), *Notts.* V. **D** Southw 15 **P** *Ld Chan* **I** J E O CHANDLER *p-in-c*.
OXWICK (All SS), *Norf.*. **D** Nor 20 *See* Colkirk.
OZLEWORTH (St Nich), *Glos.*. **D** Glouc 5 *See* Wotton-under-Edge.

PACKINGTON (H Rood) and Normanton-le-Heath, *Leics.* V. **D** Leic 12 **P** *MMT and Crown* alt **I** E W KILLER.
PACKINGTON, GREAT (St Jas) w Packington, Little, *Warws.* V. **D** Cov 4 **P** *Earl of Aylesford* **I** M J LEATON.
PACKWOOD (St Giles) w Nuthurst (St Thos) and Hockley Heath, *Warws.* V. **D** Birm 11 **P** *F W Martin Esq and Bp* alt **I** H H FOX, A C R CLARKE *c*.
PADBURY (St Mary Virg) w Adstock (St Cecilia), *Bucks.*. **D** Ox 23 *See* Lenborough.
PADDINGTON (St Jas w H Trin and St Paul), *Lon.* V. **D** Lon **P** *Bp* **I** C H L DAVEY, D G S BARTON *c*, R W MACKENNA *c*.
(Em, Harrow Road), V. **D** Lon 14 **P** *Hyndman Trustees* **I** S V DURANT.
(St Aug w St John Kilburn), V. **D** Lon 14 **P** *S for Maint of Faith* **I** R J AVENT, S J MEIGH *c*.
(St D, Paddington Green *Welsh Ch*). **D** Lon 14 **P** *Bp* **I** T J THOMAS *c-in-c*.
(St Jo Evang, Hyde Park Crescent w St Mich AA), V. **D** Lon 14 **P** *Dioc Bd of Patr* **I** T J BIRCHARD, C D V RICHARDS *hon c*.
(St Mary, Paddington Green), V. **D** Lon 14 **P** *Bp* **I** A E J FOSTER.
(St Mary Magd, Woodchester Street), V. **D** Lon 14 **P** *Keble Coll Ox* **I** M J STEPHENSON.
(St Matt, St Petersburgh Place, Bayswater), V. **D** Lon 2 **P** *Lady Magnus-Allcroft* **I** R L PARSONAGE, J WATSON *hon c*.
(St Pet, Elgin Avenue), V. **D** Lon 14 **P** *Ch Patr Trust* **I** (Vacant).
(St Sav, Warwick Avenue), V. **D** Lon 14 **P** *Bp* **I** J SLATER.
(St Steph w St Luke, Westbourne Pk Rd), V. **D** Lon 14 **P** *Bp* **I** T J KNIGHTS.
See also KENSAL GREEN AND KILBURN.
PADDLESWORTH (St Osw), *Kent.*. **D** Cant 5 *See* Lyminge.
PADDOCK (All SS), *W Yorks.* V. **D** Wakef 4 **P** *V of Huddersfield* **I** C THOMSON.
PADDOCK WOOD (St Andr), *Kent.* V. **D** Roch 9 **P** *D and C of Cant* **I** D G S L WINTER, R T GREEN *c*, S R KNIGHT *hon c*.
PADGATE (Ch Ch), *Chesh.* R. **D** Liv 11 **P** *R of Warrington* **I** J R I WIKELEY, J L HIGHAM *team v*, M H MILLS *team v*, M S FINLAY *c*.
PADIHAM (St Leon) w Higham (St Jo Evang), *Lancs.* V. **D** Blackb 3 **P** *G P le G Starkie Esq* **I** W H C KINGSTON, J HODGSON *c*, B STEVENSON *c*.
PADSTOW (St Petrock), *Cornw.* V. **D** Truro 7 **P** *Trustees* **I** M A BOXALL.
PADWORTH (St Jo Bapt), *Berks.*. **D** Ox *See* Mortimer West End.
PAGE GREEN. **D** Lon *See* Tottenham.
PAGHAM (St Thos à Becket), *W Sussex.* V. **D** Chich 1 **P** *Abp* **I** J W MAYNARD.
PAGLESHAM (St Pet), *Essex.* R. **D** Chelmsf 16 *See* Canewdon.
PAIGNTON (St Jo Bapt w St Andr St Mich and St Boniface), *Devon.* V. **D** Ex 10 **P** *Dioc Bd of Patr* **I** W L ROPER, G K MAYER *c*, M J PEARSON *c*.
(Ch Ch), V. **D** Ex 10 **P** *Peache Trustees* **I** R A P GELL.
(Goodrington Conv Distr). **D** Ex 10 **P** *Bp* **I** R P THORP *c-in-c*.
(St Paul, Preston), V. **D** Ex 10 **P** *Bp* **I** D G BELING.
PAILTON (St Denys), *Warws.*. **D** Cov *See* Monks Kirby.
PAINSWICK (St Mary Virg) w Sheepscombe (St Jo Ap), *Glos.* V. **D** Glouc 4 **P** *Ld Chan* **I** G H MCKINLEY.
PAKEFIELD (All SS and St Marg), *Suff.* R. **D** Nor 15 **P** *CPS* **I** F DYSON.
PAKENHAM (BVM) w Norton (St Andr) and Tostock (St Andr), *Suff.* V. **D** St E 9 **P** *Bp and Peterho Cam* **I** G R ADDINGTON HALL.
PALFREY (St Mary and All SS), V. **D** Lich 9 *See* Walsall.
PALGRAVE (St Pet), *Suff.* R. **D** St E 16 **P** *MMT* **I** R M KNOTT *p-in-c*.
PALGRAVE, *Norf.*. **D** Nor *See* Sporle.
PALLING, *Norf.*. **D** Nor *See* Waxham.
PALLION (St Luke), *T & W.*. **D** Dur 8 *See* Bishop Wearmouth.
PALMERS GREEN (St Jo Evang), *Gtr Lon.* V. **D** Lon 21 **P** *V of Southgate* **I** B D WALKER, J T OWEN *c*, J F PECKETT *c*.
PAMBER, *Hants.*. **D** Win *See* Sherbornes, The.
PAMPISFORD (St Jo Bapt), *Cambs.* V. **D** Ely 7 **P** *Exors of C Binney* **I** (Vacant).
PANCRASWYKE (St Pancras), *Devon.*. **D** Ex 9 *See* Pyworthy.
PANFIELD (St Mary), *Essex.* R. **D** Chelmsf 19 **P** *Bp* **I** R W OSWALD.
PANGBOURNE (St Jas L), *Berks.* R. **D** Ox 12 **P** *Ch S Trust* **I** J C HUTCHINSON *p-in-c*.
PANNAL (St Robert of Knaresbro) w Beckwithshaw, *N Yorks.* V. **D** Ripon 4 **P** *Bp and Peache Trustees* **I** J T SCOTT.
PANTON (St Andr), *Lincs.*. **D** Linc 11 *See* Wragby.
PANXWORTH (All SS), *Norf.*. **D** Nor 1 *See* Ranworth.
PAPPLEWICK (St Jas), *Notts.* V. **D** Southw 12 *See* Linby.
PAPWORTH ST AGNES, *Cambs.*. **D** Ely 2 *See* Graveley.
PAPWORTH-EVERARD (St Pet), *Cambs.* R. **D** Ely 1 **P** *Dioc Bd of Patr* **I** (Vacant).
PAR (St Mary Virg), *Cornw.* V. **D** Truro 1 **P** *Crown* **I** R N STRANACK, G CHAPMAN *c*, R J M MAY *c*, D B PUGH *hon c*.
PARHAM (St Pet) w Wiggonholt and Greatham, *W Sussex.* R. **D** Chich 7 **P** *Cowdray Trust and Dickinson Trust* **I** R A MACDONALD.
PARHAM (St Mary) w Hacheston (All SS), *Suff.* V. **D** St E 18 **P** *Ch S Trust* **I** E W ROLT *c-in-c*.
PARKEND (St Paul), *Glos.* V. **D** Glouc 7 **P** *Bp* **I** A F M WATKINS, G W J BATTEN *c*, D WILLIAMS *c*.
PARKESTON (St Paul Conv Distr), *Essex.* Min. **D** Chelmsf 25 **P** *Bp* **I** L J BUFFEE *min.*
PARKFIELD (H Trin), *Gtr Man.* V. **D** Man 17 **P** *R of Middleton* **I** (Vacant).
PARKGATE (Ch Ch), *W Yorks.* V. **D** Sheff 6 *See* Rawmarsh.
PARKHAM (St Jas), Alwington (St Andr) and Buckland Brewer, *Devon.* R. **D** Ex 17 **P** *Crown 2 turns, Lt-Col E C Pine-Coffin 1 turn, Archd of Barnstaple 1 turn* **I** J E DENNETT.
PARKSTONE (St Pet and St Osmund) w Branksea I *Dorset.* V. **D** Sarum 14 **P** *Bp 2 turns Trustees 1 turn* **I** P R HUXHAM *c-in-c*, P W HOLLAND *c*, C F E ROWLEY *c*, E D CATLEY *hon c*.
(St Jo Evang Heatherlands), V. **D** Sarum 14 **P** *MMT* **I** W H ANDREW, S J ABRAM *c*, C J MURRAY *c*, T TAYLOR *c*.
(St Luke), V. **D** Sarum 14 **P** *Ch Trust Fund Trust* **I** J R BLYTH.
(Transfig, Canford Cliffs w St Nich, Sandbanks), V. **D** Sarum 14 **P** *Bp* **I** J V H REES.
PARLEY, WEST (All SS), *Dorset.* R. **D** Sarum 11 **P** *P Prideaux-Brune Esq* **I** F G RASON.
PARNDON, GREAT (St Mary), *Essex.* R. **D** Chelmsf 3 **P** *Bp* **I** D P CLACEY *c*, D A OATES *c*.
PARNDON, LITTLE , *Essex.*. **D** Chelmsf *See* Harlow, New Town.
PARR (St Pet), *Mer.* R. **D** Liv 10 **P** *Dioc Bd of Patr* **I** J BRONNERT *team v*, E LONGMAN *team v*, R J E MAJOR *c*.
PARR-MOUNT (H Trin), *Mer.* V. **D** Liv 10 **P** *V of St Helens* **I** C S WOODS.
PARRACOMBE (Ch Ch), *Devon.* R. **D** Ex 18 *See* Lynton.
PARSON CROSS (St Cecilia), *S Yorks.*. **D** Sheff 3 *See* Sheffield.
PARSON-DROVE, *Cambs.* V. **D** Ely 20 *See* Southea.
PARSON'S GREEN (St Dionis),. **D** Lon 11 *See* Fulham.
PARTINGTON (St Mary) w Carrington (St Geo), *Gtr Man.* V. **D** Ches 10 **P** *Bp* **I** I J HUTCHINGS, E H J R BIRD *c*, M J HUNTER *c*, W A PATTERSON *c*.

PARTNEY (St Nich) w Dalby (Dedic unknown), Ashby-by-Partney, Skendleby and Candlesby w Scremby, *Lincs.* R Ashby-by-Partney, Skendleby and Candlesby w Scremby, *Lincs.* R. **D** Linc 7 **P** *Earl of Ancaster, Bp, Dioc Bd of Patr and Mrs C D Bowser (in turn)* **I** G C MARTIN.
PARTRIDGE GREEN (St Mich AA), *W Sussex.*. **D** Chich 4 *See* Grinstead, West.
PARWICH (St Pet) w Alsop-en-le-Dale (St Mich AA), *Derbys.* V. **D** Derby 8 **P** *Sir John Crompton-Inglefield* **I** C H READ.
PASSENHAM (St Guthlac) w Old Stratford, Deanshanger (H Trin), and Puxley, *Northants.* R. **D** Pet 2 **P** *MMT* **I** A C BARKER.
PASTON (St Mary) w Knapton (St Pet), *Norf.* V. **D** Nor *See* Trunch.
PASTON (All SS), *Cambs.* R. **D** Pet 14 **P** *Bp* **I** G T RIMMINGTON.
PATCHAM (All SS), *W Sussex.* V. **D** Chich 15a **P** *MMT* **I** D L N GUTSELL, D R BYRNE *c.*
(Ch K), V. **D** Chich 15a **P** *Bp* **I** G SUMMERGOOD.
PATCHING (St Jo Div), *W Sussex.* R. **D** Chich 9 *See* Clapham.
PATCHWAY (St Chad), *Avon.* V. **D** Bris 4 **P** *Bp* **I** J R FLORY, A G PALMER *c.*
PATELEY BRIDGE w Greenhow Hill, *N Yorks.*. **D** Ripon 3 *See* Nidderdale, Upper.
PATNEY (St Swith), *Wilts.* R. **D** Sarum 23 *See* Cherrington or Chirton.
PATRICK BROMPTON (St Patr) w Hunton, *N Yorks.* V. **D** Ripon 2 **P** *Bp* **I** (Vacant).
PATRICROFT (Ch Ch), *Gtr Man.* V. **D** Man 3 **P** *Bp* **I** A E BURLES.
PATRINGTON (St Patr) w Winestead (St German), *Humb.* R. **D** York 15 **P** *Dioc Bd of Patr 2 turns, CPAS 1 turn* **I** A C HODGE *p-in-c.*
PATRIXBOURNE (St Mary) w Bridge (St Pet) and Bekesbourne (St Pet), *Kent.* V. **D** Cant 1 **P** *Abp* **I** R GILBERT.
PATSHULL (St Mary), *Staffs.* V. **D** Lich 7 **P** *Earl of Dartmouth* **I** C J L WALTERS *p-in-c.*
PATTERDALE (St Patr), *Cumb.* R. **D** Carl 6 **P** *Trustees* **I** S E CRAWLEY.
PATTINGHAM (St Chad), *Staffs.* V. **D** Lich 7 **P** *Bp* **I** C J L WALTERS.
PATTISHALL (H Cross) w Cold Higham (St Luke), *Northants.* V. **D** Pet 2 **P** *Bp and S for Maint of Faith* alt **I** (Vacant).
PATTISWICK (St Mary), *Essex.* R. **D** Chelmsf 19 *See* Stisted.
PAUL (St Pol de Leon), *Cornw.* V. **D** Truro 5 **P** *Ld Chan* **I** R H CADMAN.
PAULERSPURY (St Jas Ap), *Northants.* R. **D** Pet 2 **P** *New Coll Ox* **I** P TOWNSEND.
PAULL (St Andr and St Mary), *Humb.* V. **D** York 15 *See* Hedon.
PAULSGROVE (St Mich AA), *Hants.* V. **D** Portsm 3 **P** *Bp* **I** C S TREVOR.
PAULTON (H Trin), *Avon.* V. **D** B & W 16b **P** *Bp and R of Chewton Mendip (alt)* **I** (Vacant).
PAUNTLEY (St Jo Evang) w Upleadon and Oxenhall, *Glos.*. **D** Glouc *See* Redmarley D'Abitot.
PAVENHAM (St Pet), *Beds.* V. **D** St Alb 21 **P** *Ld Luke* **I** A M G WELLS *p-in-c.*
PAWLETT (St Jo Bapt), *Somt.* V. **D** B & W 17 *See* Puriton.
PAXTON, GREAT (H Trin), *Cambs.* V. **D** Ely 13 **P** *D and C of Linc* **I** E J PRYKE.
LITTLE (St Jas), V. **D** Ely 13 **P** *D and C of Linc* **I** G W WHITLOCK.
PAYHEMBURY (St Mary), *Devon.* V. **D** Ex 7 *See* Broadhembury.
PEACEHAVEN (Ascen), *E Sussex.* V. **D** Chich 15 **P** *Bp* **I** I R PHELPS.
PEAK FOREST, *Derbys.*. **D** Derby *See* Wormhill.
PEAKIRK (St Pega) w Glinton, *Cambs.* R. **D** Pet 14 **P** *D and C of Pet* **I** H J WESTON.
PEASEDOWN ST JOHN (St Jo Bapt) w Wellow, *Avon.* V. **D** B & W **P** *Bp and Maj le G G W Horton-Fawkes* **I** R H P HAZELTON.
PEASEMORE (St Barn), *Berks.* R. **D** Ox 14 **P** *Bp* **I** C A SELMAN.
PEASENHALL (St Mich), *Suff.* V. **D** St E 19 **P** *CPAS* **I** J L THICKITT.
PEASLAKE (St Mark), *Surrey.*. **D** Guildf 2 *See* Shere.
PEASMARSH (St Pet and St Paul), *E Sussex.* V. **D** Chich 22 *See* Beckley.
PEATLING, MAGNA (All SS), *Leics.* V. **D** Leic 13 *See* Willoughby-Waterleys.
PEATLING, PARVA, *Leics.*. **D** Leic *See* Gilmorton.
PEBMARSH (St Bapt), *Essex.*. **D** Chelmsf 18 *See* Alphamstone.
PEBWORTH (St Pet) *Worcs* w Dorsington (St Pet), *Warws.* R. **D** Glouc 12 **P** *Bp and Maj C T Tomes* **I** R E OWEN.
PECKHAM (St Mary Magd w St Paul), *Surrey.* V. **D** S'wark 15 **P** *CPS* **I** R V KING.
(St John w St Andr), V. **D** S'wark 15 **P** *Bp* **I** W G CAMPEN *c*, J E LANE *c.*
(St Luke). **D** S'wark *See* Camberwell.
(St Sav Denmark Park), *Surrey.* V. **D** S'wark 16 **P** *Bd of Patr* **I** (Vacant).
PECKHAM, EAST (H Trin) and Nettlestead (St Mary Virg), *Kent.* V. **D** Roch 6 **P** *D and C of Cant, Mrs M Bullock and St Pet Coll Ox* **I** E S HAVILAND.
PECKHAM, WEST, *Kent.*. **D** Roch *See* Mereworth.
PECKLETON (St Mary Magd), *Leics.* R. **D** Leic 13 *See* Thurlaston.
PEDMORE (St Pet), *Worcs.* R. **D** Worc 11 **P** *Feoffees of Old Swinford Hosp* **I** R STOCKLEY.
PEEL (St Paul), *Lancs.* R. **D** Man **P** *Bp, Archd of Rochdale and Ld Kenyon* **I** W A TAYLOR, R D BULL *team v.*
PEEL GREEN (St Mich AA) w Barton-on-Irwell (St Cath), *Gtr Man.*. **D** Man 3 **P** *Trustees* **I** A PARK.
PEEL HALL (St Rich of Chich), *Gtr Man.* V. **D** Man 10 **P** *Bp* **I** D GILBERT.
PELDON (St Mary Virg) w Gt and L Wigborough, *Essex.* R. **D** Chelmsf 21 **P** *Ch S Trust and Mrs C M Wheatley* **I** E C LENDON.
PELSALL (St Mich AA), *W Midl.* V. **D** Lich 9 **P** *Bp* **I** A G SADLER, A P BROWN *c.*
PELTON (H Trin), *Durham.* V. **D** Dur 1 **P** *R of Chester-le-Street* **I** (Vacant).
WEST (St Paul) V. **D** Dur 1 **P** *Bp* **I** D MURPHY.
PELYNT (St Nun) R *Cornw.* V. **D** Truro 13 **P** *Capt M F Buller and Commdr J B Kitson, R N* alt **I** B J FREETH *p-in-c.*
PEMBERTON (St Jo Div), *Gtr Man.* R. **D** Liv 12 **P** *R of Wigan* **I** J A SOUTHERN.
(St Francis, Kitt Green). V. **D** Liv 12 **P** *Bp of Liverpool and R of Wigan* **I** (Vacant).
(St Mark, Newtown), V. **D** Liv 12 **P** *Trustees* **I** A MARSHALL, K CLAPHAM *c.*
PEMBRIDGE (St Mary) w Moorcourt and Shobdon, *Herefs.* R. **D** Heref 5 **P** *Ld Chan, Miss R Whitehead, John R Whitehead* **I** M C BIRCHBY.
PEMBURY (St Pet), *Kent.* V. **D** Roch 10 **P** *Ch Ch Ox* **I** C HODGSON, G T CUNLIFFE *c.*
PENCOMBE (St John) w Marston Stannett and Little Cowarne, *Herefs.* R. **D** Heref 2 **P** *Esso Pension Trust Ltd* **I** J ADAMS *p-in-c.*
PENCOYD (St Dennis), *Herefs.* V. **D** Heref 8 *See* Tretire.
PENCOYS (St Andr), *Cornw.*. **D** Truro 2 *See* Redruth.
PENDEEN (St Jo Bapt), *Cornw.* V. **D** Truro 5 **P** *Bp, A P H Aitken Esq and E C Aitken Esq* **I** A ROWELL.
PENDLEBURY (Ch Ch), *Gtr Man.* V. **D** Man 3 **P** *Bp* **I** D G GRIFFIN.
(St Aug of Cant), V. **D** Man 3 **P** *Bp* **I** F E BROWN.
(St Jo Evang), V. **D** Man 8 **P** *Trustees* **I** E H WAGSTAFFE.
PENDLETON (St Thos), *Gtr Man.* V. **D** Man 8 **P** *V of Eccles and Bp* **I** T W ELLIS.
(St Ambrose), V. **D** Man 8 **P** *Trustees, J W Earle Esq and R N Birley Esq* **I** G HOWARD.
(H Angels, Claremont), V. **D** Man 8 **P** *Bp* **I** A G CAPES.
PENDLETON-IN-WHALLEY (All SS), V *Lancs.*. **D** Blackb 7 **P** *Trustees* **I** J G COLE *p-in-c.*
PENDOCK (Dedic unknown), *Worcs.* R. **D** Worc 5 *See* Berrow.
PENDOMER (St Roch), *Somt.* R. **D** B & W 11 *See* Hardington Mandeville.
PENGE (Ch Ch w H Trin), *Kent.* V. **D** Roch 11 **P** *CPAS* **I** B H STEVENS.
(St Jo Evang), V. **D** Roch 11 **P** *Simeon Trustees* **I** C J ROOKWOOD.
(St Paul), V. **D** Roch 11 **P** *Ch Patr Trustees* **I** D J SMITH.
PENHILL (St Pet), *Wilts.* V. **D** Bris 10 **P** *Bp* **I** R D MARTIN.
PENHURST, *E Sussex.*. **D** Chich *See* Ashburnham.
PENISTONE (St Jo Bapt), *S Yorks.* V. **D** Wakef 8 **P** *Bp* **I** J C NORTON, P C BELLENES *c.*
PENKETH (St Paul), *Mer.* V. **D** Liv 7 **P** *Bp* **I** P W HOCKLEY.
PENKEVIL ST MICHAEL, *Cornw.* R. **D** Truro 6 *See* St Michael, Penkevil.
PENKHULL (St Thos), *Staffs.* V. **D** Lich 18 **P** *R of Stoke-on-Trent* **I** I MAITIN.
PENKRIDGE (St Mich AA) w Stretton (St Jo Evang), *Staffs.* V. **D** Lich 3 **P** *Exors of Ld Hatherton*

I R CHEADLE, D R OSBORNE *c*, A D KEAY *hon c*.
PENN (St Bart), *Staffs*. V. **D** Lich 7 **P** *Bp* **I** G FROST, T D HAWKINGS *c*.
PENN (H Trin), *Bucks*. V. **D** Ox 20 **P** *Earl Howe* **I** O MUSPRATT.
PENN FIELDS (St Phil), *Staffs*. V. **D** Lich 7 **P** *Ch Trust Fund* **I** W H NASH, A R JACK *c*, D LUMB *c*.
PENN STREET (H Trin) w Ch Ch Holmer Green, *Bucks*. V. **D** Ox 20 **P** *Earl Howe* **I** N J STOWE.
PENNARD, EAST (All SS), w Pylle (St Tho of Cant), *Somt*. R. **D** B & W 6 *See* Ditcheat.
PENNARD, WEST (St Nich) w W Bradley (Dedic unknown) and Lottisham (St Mary Virg), *Somt*. V. **D** B & W 7 **P** *Bp* **I** A.G. CLARKSON C-IN-C OF W PENNARD , C. J. HUDSON C-IN-C OF W BRADLEY & LOTTISHAM.
PENNINGTON (St Mich AA), *Cumb*. V. **D** Carl 15 **P** *Bp* **I** D R JACKSON.
PENNINGTON (Ch Ch), *Gtr Man*. V. **D** Man 6 **P** *Simeon Trustees* **I** N WAIN, K B ASHWORTH *c*.
PENNINGTON (St Mark), *Hants*. V. **D** Win 9 **P** *V of Milford-on-Sea* **I** J D PIBWORTH.
PENNYCROSS (St Pancras w St Martin), *Devon*.. **D** Ex 23 *See* Plymouth.
PENNYWELL (St Thos Conv Distr). **D** Dur 8 *See* Bishop Wearmouth.
PENPONDS (H Trin), *Cornw*. V. **D** Truro 2 **P** *Crown* **I** R A L HESKETH.
PENRITH (St Andr w Ch Ch) w Newton Reigny and Plumpton Wall, *Cumb* R. **D** Carl **P** *Bp* **I** W A BATTY, J M S FALKNER *c*, D RIDLEY *c*.
PENRYN BOROUGH, *Cornw*.. **D** Truro 3 *See* St Gluvias.
PENSAX (St Jas Gt), *Worcs*. V. **D** Worc 12 **P** *V of Lindridge* **I** H R BEVAN *p-in-c*.
PEN-SELWOOD (St Mich), *Somt*. R. **D** B & W 5 **P** *Bp* **I** J W EVERETT.
PENSFORD (St Thos à Becket), *Avon*. V. **D** B & W 15 *See* Publow.
PENSHAW (All SS), *T & W*. R. **D** Dur **P** *Bp* **I** B MCKENZIE.
PENSHURST (St Jo Bapt) and Fordcombe, *Kent*. R. **D** Roch 10 **P** *Visc de L'Isle and Dudley, VC* **I** J C TADMAN, C G F CLARK *c*.
PENSNETT (St Mark), *W Midl*. V. **D** Lich 1 **P** *Bp* **I** (Vacant).
PENSTHORPE, *Norf*. R. **D** Nor 21 **P** *Marq Townshend and Crown* **I** (Vacant).
PENTEWAN, *Cornw*.. **D** Truro 1 *See* St Austell.
PENTLOW, *Essex*.. **D** Chelmsf *See* Foxearth.
PENTNEY (St Mary Magd) w W Bilney (St Cecilia), *Norf*. V. **D** Nor 25 **P** *Bp* **I** J L WILSON.
PENTON GRAFTON (St Mich AA), *Hants*.. **D** Win 2 *See* Weyhill.
PENTON-MEWSEY (H Trin), *Hants*. R. **D** Win 2 *See* Weyhill.
PENTONVILLE. **D** Lon 2 **D** and 6 *See* Islington.
PENTRICH, *Derbys*.. **D** Derby *See* Swanwick.
PENTRIDGE (St Rumbold) w Handley (BVM) and Gussage (St Andr), *Dorset*. R. **D** Sarum 10 **P** *D and C of Windsor and Earl of Shaftesbury* alt **I** F G CHAMBERLAIN.
PENWERRIS (St Mich AA), *Cornw*. V. **D** Truro 3 **P** *V of St Gluvias* **I** R S WALLACE.
PENWORTHAM (St Mary), *Lancs*. V. **D** Blackb 6 **P** *Can R G Rawstorne* **I** D F REES, P D TAYLOR *c*.
(St Leon), V. **D** Blackb 6 **P** *Bp* **I** D R NORTH.
PENZANCE (St Mary w S Paul), *Cornw*. V. **D** Truro 5 **P** *Bp* **I** W R NEWTON, J RIGBY *c*.
(St Jo Bapt), V. **D** Truro 5 **P** *Bp* **I** M R JUPE.
PEOPLETON (St Nich) and White Ladies Aston w Churchill and Spetchley, *Worcs*. R. **D** Worc 3 **P** *Bp and Maj RJG Berkeley (alt)* **I** W F CUMMINS.
PEOVER, Lower or Nether (St Osw), *Chesh*. V. **D** Ches 12 **P** *Univ of Man* **I** J C SLADDEN.
PEOVER, OVER (St Lawr), *Chesh*. V. **D** Ches *See* Marthall.
PEPER HAROW (St Nich), *Surrey*. R. **D** Guildf 4 **P** *Bp* **I** A RANSOME *p-in-c*.
PEPLOW, *Salop*.. **D** Lich 23 *See* Hodnet.
PERCY (St Jo Evang), *T & W*.. **D** Newc T 6 *See* Tynemouth.
PERIVALE (St Nich), *Gtr Lon*. R. **D** Lon 6 **P** *S for Maint of Faith* **I** (Vacant).
PERLETHORPE (St Jo Evang), *Notts*. V. **D** Southw 7 **P** *Trustees of Earl Manvers* **I** R S C BAILY *p-in-c*.
PERRAN-AR-WORTHAL, ST *Cornw*.. **D** Truro *See* St Stythians.
PERRANUTHNOE, ST (St Piran and St Mich), *Cornw*. R. **D** Truro 5 *See* St Hilary.
PERRANZABULOE, ST (St Piran) w Perranporth (St Mich), *Cornw*. V. **D** Truro 6 **P** *D and C of Truro* **I** E B WARREN.
PERROTT, NORTH (St Martin), *Somt*. R. **D** B & W *See* Haselbury Plucknett.
PERROTT, SOUTH (St Mary) w Mosterton and Chedington (St Jas), *Dorset*. R. **D** Sarum *See* Beaminster Area.
PERRY BARR (St Jo Evang), *W Midl*. V. **D** Birm 3 **P** *Ld Calthorpe* **I** B H PARRY, M V ROBERTS *c*.
PERRY BEECHES, *W Midl*. V. **D** Birm 3 **P** *Trustees* **I** A L WHEALE, A BARTLETT *c*.
PERRY COMMON (St Martin), *W Midl*. V. **D** Birm 7 **P** *Bp* **I** J E M BARBER.
PERRY GREEN (St Thos), *Herts*.. **D** St Alb 4 *See* Hadham, Much.
PERRY HILL (St Geo), *Kent*. V. **D** S'wark 18 **P** *Trustees* **I** A G GIBSON.
PERRY STREET, *Kent*.. **D** Roch *See* Northfleet.
PERSHORE (St Edburga) w Pinvin (St Nich), Wick and Birlingham, *Worcs*. V. **D** Worc 3 **P** *D and C of Westmr and D and C of Worc* **I** W J M COOMBS, P A ROBERTS *c*.
PERTENHALL (St Pet) w Swineshead (St Nich), *Beds*. R. **D** St Alb 21 **P** *Dioc Bd of Patr* **I** D N WESTON *p-in-c*.
PERTWOOD (St Pet), *Wilts*. R. **D** Sarum 19 *See* Hindon.
PETERBOROUGH (St Jo Bapt), *Cambs*. V. **D** Pet 14 **P** *Bp* **I** A J HOWITT, P G F LAWLEY *c*.
(St Barn), V. **D** Pet 14 **P** *Bp* **I** M D DAVIES *p-in-c*.
(All SS), V. **D** Pet 14 **P** *Bp* **I** E G ORLAND.
(Christ the Carpenter), V. **D** Pet 14 **P** *Bp* **I** J HUMPHRIES.
(St Jude), V. **D** Pet 14 **P** *Bp* **I** R S GILES, S EVANS *c*, K H WILKINSON *c*.
(St Mark), V. **D** Pet 14 **P** *Bp* **I** J K KING.
(St Mary), V. **D** Pet 14 **P** *D and C of Pet* **I** J BATES.
(St Paul), V. **D** Pet 14 **P** *Bp* **I** B SECKER.
(H Spirit, Bretton), V. **D** Pet 14 **P** *Bp* **I** J S BELL, C D ALLEN *c*.
PETERCHURCH (St Pet), *Herefs*. V. **D** Heref 1 **P** *Bp* **I** J C DE LA T DAVIES P-IN-C OF MOCCAS.
PETERLEE (St Cuthb), *Durham*. V. **D** Dur 3 **P** *Bp* **I** K I WOODHOUSE, A L BELL *c*, J E LUND *c*, N P VINE *c*.
PETERSFIELD (St Pet) w Sheet (St Mary), *Hants*. V. **D** Portsm 4 **P** *Bp* **I** R H GRANGER, J K COOMBS *c*, P E B ROBINSON *c*.
PETERSHAM (St Pet), *Surrey*. V. **D** S'wark 13 **P** *Bp* **I** R A BROWNRIGG.
PETERSMARLAND (St Pet) *Devon*. V. **D** Ex 20 *See* Petrockstowe.
PETERSTOW (St Pet), *Herefs*. R. **D** Heref 8 *See* Bridstow.
PETHAM (All SS) w Waltham and Lower Hardres w Nackington, *Kent*. R. **D** Cant 2 **P** *Abp and St Jo Coll Ox (alt)* **I** R A LOVE *p-in-c*.
PETHERICK, LITTLE or ST PETROCK MINOR (St Petrock), *Cornw*. R. **D** Truro *See* St Issey.
PETHERTON, NORTH (St Mary Virg) w Northmoor Green, *Somt*. V. **D** B & W 17 **P** *Trustees* **I** B A A WHITING, N A F TOWNEND *hon c*.
PETHERTON, SOUTH (St Pet and St Paul) w The Seavingtons, *Somt* V. **D** B & W **P** *D and C of Wells* **I** C E THOMAS, C PAXTON *hon c*.
PETHERWYN, NORTH (St Peder or Paternus), *Devon*. V. **D** Truro 11 **P** *Bp 2 turns and Duchy of Cornw 1 turn* **I** R W P HOWLETT.
PETHERWYN, SOUTH w Trewen, *Cornw*. V. **D** Truro 11 **P** *Univ of Ox* **I** J E COX *p-in-c*.
PETROCKSTOWE (St Petrock) w Petersmarland (St Pet) and Merton (All SS) w Meeth (St Mich AA) and Huish, *Devon*. R and V. **D** Ex 20 **P** *Ld Clinton 2 turns, Bp 1 turn* **I** I P GREGORY.
PETT (St Mary and St Pet), *E Sussex*.. **D** Chich 22 *See* Guestling.
PETTAUGH (St Cath) w Winston (St Andr) w Framsden (St Mary), *Suff*.. **D** St E 18 *See* Helmingham.
PETTISTREE (St Pet), *Suff*.. **D** St E 18 *See* Dallinghoo.
PETTON w Cockshutt (St Simon and St Jude) and Weston Lullingfield (H Trin) w Hordley (St Mary Virg), *Salop*. R. **D** Lich 22 **P** *Bp and CPS* **I** (Vacant).
PETTON CHAP, *Devon*. V. **D** Ex 8 **P** *V of Bampton* **I** D M CLARRIDGE.
PETTS WOOD (St Francis), *Kent*. V. **D** Roch 16 **P** *Bp* **I** H S HOROBIN.
PETWORTH (St Mary), *W Sussex*. R. **D** Chich 6 **P** *Ld Egremont* **I** J H GREENE, W W HEATH *c*.
PEVENSEY (St Nich), *E Sussex*. V. **D** Chich 19 **P** *Bp* **I** R A PUGH.
PEWSEY (St Jo Bapt), *Wilts*. R. **D** Sarum 27 **P** *Earl of Radnor* **I** J C DAY, T S FIELD *hon c*.

PHEASEY (St Chad), *W Midl.* V. **D** Lich 9 **P** *Dioc Bd of Patr* **I** C M BEAVER.
PHILLACK, ST (St Felicitas, Matron and Mart) w St Gwithian (St Gothian) and Gwinear, *Cornw.* R. **D** Truro 5 **P** *Bp and Miss A D La Touche* **I** R E F CANHAM *p-in-c.*
PHILLEIGH, ST (St Felix), *Cornw.* R. **D** Truro 6 *See* Ruan St Lanihorne.
PICCADILLY (St Jas). **D** Lon 19 *See* Westminster.
PICKENHAM, NORTH (St Andr), w Houghton-on-the-Hill (St Mary), *Norf.* R. **D** Nor 19 **P** *Ch S Trust* **I** D G W GREEN.
PICKENHAM, SOUTH (All SS), *Norf.* R. **D** Nor 19 **P** *G Moreton Esq* **I** D G W GREEN.
PICKERING (St Pet and St Paul), *N Yorks.* V. **D** York 24 **P** *Abp* **I** W H BATES.
PICKHILL (All SS), *N Yorks.* V. **D** Ripon 2 **P** *Dioc Bd of Patr* **I** N ASHBY.
PICKWELL, *Leic..* **D** Leic *See* Somerby.
PICKWORTH (St Andr) w Walcot (St Nich), *Lincs..* **D** Linc *See* Lafford, S.
PICKWORTH (St Mary), *Leics.* R. **D** Pet 13 *See* Casterton, Great.
PIDDINGHOE (St Jo Evang), *E Sussex.* V. **D** Chich 15 *See* Telscombe.
PIDDINGTON (St Nich), *Oxon..* **D** Ox *See* Ambrosden.
PIDDINGTON, *Northants.* V. **D** Pet 4 *See* Horton.
PIDDLE, NORTH *Worcs.* R. **D** Worc 3 *See* Upton Snodsbury.
PIDDLEHINTON (St Mary Virg), *Dorset.* R. **D** Sarum 5 *See* Piddletrenthide.
PIDDLETOWN (St Mary Virg), *Dorset..* **D** Sarum 8 *See* Puddletown.
PIDDLETRENTHIDE (All SS) w Plush (St Jo Bapt), Alton Pancras and Piddlehinton, *Dorset.* V. **D** Sarum 5 **P** *D and C of Sarum and Win and Eton Coll in turn* **I** D N G PARRY *c-in-c.*
PIDLEY w Fenton (All SS), *Cambs..* **D** Ely 12 *See* Somersham.
PIERCEBRIDGE (St Mary), *Durham..* **D** Dur 10 **P** *Bp* **I** J S HANNON.
PILHAM (All SS), *Lincs.* R. **D** Linc 2 *See* Blyton.
PILL (Ch Ch), *Avon.* V. **D** B & W 16 **P** *Bp* **I** R F D KINSEY.
PILLATON (St Odulph), *Cornw..* **D** Truro *See* St Mellion.
PILLERTON HERSEY w Pillerton Priors, *Warws..* **D** Cov 9 *See* Butlers Marston.
PILLING (St Jo Bapt), *Lancs.* V. **D** Blackb 10 **P** *Ld of the Manor* **I** T GREEN.
PILMOOR, *N Yorks..* **D** York *See* Brafferton.
PILNING (St Pet) w Severn Beach and Northwick, *Avon.* V. **D** Bris 6 **P** *Bp* **I** J H R ORBELL *p-in-c.*
PILSDON (St Mary), *Dorset.* R. **D** Sarum 4 *See* Bettiscombe.
PILSLEY (St Mary Virg), *Derbys.* V. **D** Derby 3 *See* Wingfield, North.
PILTON (St Jo Bapt) w Croscombe, Wootton North (St Pet) and Dinder, *Somt.* V. **D** B & W **P** *Bp and Peache Trustees* **I** N R E JACOBS.
PILTON (St Mary Virg) w Ashford (St Pet), *Devon.* V. **D** Ex 15 **P** *Ld Chan* **I** A E GEERING.
PILTON, *Leics.* R. **D** Pet 12 *See* Preston.
PILTON (All SS) w Wadenhoe (St Mich AA) and Stoke Doyle (St Rumbold), *Northants.* R. **D** Pet *See* Aldwincle.
PIMLICO **D** Lon 19 *See* Westminster.
PIMPERNE (St Pet), *Dorset.* R. **D** Sarum 10 **P** *Dioc Bd of Patr* **I** D A FARQUHARSON-ROBERTS.
PINCHBECK (St Mary), *Lincs.* V. **D** Linc 17 **P** *Mrs B S Corley* **I** J FAIRWEATHER.
PINHOE (St Mich AA), *Devon.* V. **D** Ex 1 **P** *Bp* **I** P GREEN.
PINKNEY (St Jo Bapt), *Wilts..* **D** Bris 9 *See* Sherston Magna.
PINNER (St Jo Bapt), *Gtr Lon.* V. **D** Lon 24 **P** *V of Harrow* **I** H M WYBREW, M C BRANDON *c*, G A HAMEY *c*, D F P TOUW *c*, M S NATTRASS *hon c.*
(St Edm Northwood Hills), V. **D** Lon 24 **P** *Bp* **I** R J AMES, J E IVES *c*, K E LIMBERT *c.*
PINVIN (St Nich), *Worcs..* **D** Worc 3 *See* Pershore.
PINXTON (St Helen), *Derbys.* R. **D** Derby 1 **P** *Bp* **I** W STOCKTON.
PIPE AND LYDE (St Pet), *Herefs.* V. **D** Heref 4 *See* Moreton-on-Lugg.
PIPE RIDWARE (St Jas), *Staffs.* V. **D** Lich 4 **P** *Ld Leigh 2 turns, Bp 1 turn* **I** R E P DAVIES.
PIRBRIGHT (St Mich AA), *Surrey.* V. **D** Guildf 11 **P** *Ld Chan* **I** J CUNNINGHAM.
PIRNOUGH (All H), *Norf..* **D** Nor 14 *See* Ditchingham.
PIRTON (St Mary), *Herts.* V. **D** St Alb 9 **P** *D and C of Ely* **I** D A CLENDON *c-in-c.*
PIRTON (St Pet), *Worcs.* R. **D** Worc 3 *See* Stoulton.
PISHILL (Dedic unknown), *Oxon.* V. **D** Ox 7 *See* Nettlebed.
PITCHCOMBE (Dedic unknown), *Glos..* **D** Glouc 4 *See* Edge.
PITCHCOTT (St Giles), *Bucks.* R. **D** Ox 25 *See* Oving.
PITCHFORD (St Mich), *Salop.* R. **D** Heref 11 *See* Acton Burnell.
PITCOMBE (St Leon) w Shepton Montague (St Pet) and Bratton St Maur, *Somt.* V. **D** B & W 5 **P** *Bp and MMT* **I** A C Q ATKIN *p-in-c.*
PITMINSTER (St Andr and St Mary) w Corfe (St Nich), *Somt.* V. **D** B & W 23a **P** *Dioc Bd of Finance and Maj J G Newton* alt **I** E A CROWE.
PITNEY-LORTIE (St Jo Bapt), *Somt..* **D** B & W 10 *See* Huish Episcopi.
PITNEY YEOVIL (All SS), Sin R *Somt..* **D** B & W 12 *See* Yeovil.
PITSEA (St Mich), *Essex.* R. **D** Chelmsf 10 **P** *Bp* **I** (Vacant).
PITSFORD (All SS), *Northants.* R. **D** Pet 6 **P** *Bp* **I** M HERBERT *p-in-c.*
PITSMOOR (Ch Ch) w Ellesmere, *S Yorks.* V. **D** Sheff **P** *CPS and Dioc Bd of Patr (alt)* **I** D J H SPARKES, G E HOVENDEN *c*, P W WEST *c.*
PITSTONE or PIGHTLESTHORNE (St Mary), *Bucks.* V. **D** Ox 27 *See* Ivinghoe.
PITT (Ch of the Good Shepherd), *Hants..* **D** Win 12 *See* Hursley.
PITTINGTON (St Lawr), *Durham.* V. **D** Dur 2 **P** *D and C of Dur* **I** (Vacant).
PITTON, *Wilts..* **D** Sarum 17 *See* Farley.
PIXLEY (St Andr), *Herefs.* R. **D** Heref 6 *See* Aylton.
PLAISTOW (St Mary), *Essex.* V. **D** Chelmsf 5 **P** *V of W Ham* **I** R M C PAXON *p-in-c.*
(St Phil and St Jas w St Andr), V. **D** Chelmsf 5 **P** *Bp* **I** (Vacant).
PLAISTOW (St Mary), *Kent.* V. **D** Roch 12 **P** *Bp* **I** P R HENWOOD, A A GORHAM *c.*
PLAITFORD (St Pet), *Hants.* R. **D** Sarum 17 *See* Landford.
PLATT (St Mary Virg), *Kent.* V. **D** Roch 8 **P** *Bp* **I** R V DOUGLAS.
PLATT, *Gtr Man..* **D** Man *See* Rusholme.
PLATT BRIDGE (St Nath), *Gtr Man.* V. **D** Liv 12 **P** *Bp* **I** (Vacant).
PLAXTOL (no Dedic), *Kent.* R. **D** Roch 8 **P** *Bp* **I** (Vacant).
PLAYDEN (St Mich), *E Sussex.* V. **D** Chich 22 *See* Rye.
PLAYFORD (St Mary) w Culpho (St Botolph) and Gt w Little Bealings, *Suff.* V. **D** St E 7 **P** *Ld Cranworth 1 turn, Marchioness of Bris 2 turns* **I** G F L HOLLINGSWORTH.
PLEASLEY (St Mich) w New Houghton (Ch Ch), *Derbys.* R. **D** Derby 2 **P** *H B Davie-Thornhill Esq* **I** J O GOLDSMITH *p-in-c.*
PLEASLEY HILL, *Notts..* **D** Southw *See* Mansfield.
PLEMSTALL (St Pet) w Guilden Sutton (St Jo Bapt), *Chesh.* V. **D** Ches 2 **P** *Capt P Egerton Warburton* **I** J A MALBON.
PLESHEY (H Trin), *Essex.* V. **D** Chelmsf 11 **P** *J J Tufnell Esq* **I** P A W MORRIS *p-in-c.*
PLUCKLEY (St Nich w St Mary), *Kent.* R. **D** Cant 10 **P** *Abp* **I** E N BATH *p-in-c.*
PLUMBLAND (St Cuthb) w Gilcrux (St Mary), *Cumb.* R. **D** Carl 11 **P** *Bp and Mrs F S Chance* alt **I** F L PRICE.
PLUMPTON (St Mich AA w All SS) w E Chiltington, *E Sussex.* R. **D** Chich 15 **P** *Bp* **I** D B LAUGHTON.
PLUMPTON, *Northants..* **D** Pet 2 *See* Weedon Lois.
PLUMPTON WALL (St Jo Evang), *Cumb.* V. **D** Carl *See* Penrith.
PLUMSTEAD (St Mich), *Norf.* R. **D** Nor 24 *See* Baconsthorp.
PLUMSTEAD (St Mark w St Marg), *Kent.* V. **D** S'wark 17 **P** *Bp* **I** D B A JOHNSON.
(All SS Shooter's Hill), V. **D** S'wark 17 **P** *CPAS* **I** R H SMART, A L AYRES *c.*
(Ch of the Ascen), V. **D** S'wark 17 **P** *Bp* **I** G A SAUNDERS.
(St Jo Bapt w St Jas and St Paul), V. **D** S'wark 17 **P** *Simeon Trustees and CPAS* **I** G R BARTER, B V ROGERS *c.*
(St Mich AA Abbey Wood), V. **D** S'wark 17 **P** *Bp* **I** J O ARDLEY.
(St Nich), V. **D** S'wark 17 **P** *V of Plumstead* **I** F G HARTE.
(William Temple Ch Conv Distr Abbey Wood). **D** S'wark 17 *See* Thamesmead.
PLUMSTEAD, GREAT (St Mary Virg) w Plumstead, Little (St Gervasius and St Protasius), *Norf.* V. **D** Nor 1 **P** *Bp 2 turns, D and C of Nor 1 turn* **I** H B FRANCIS *p-in-c.*

PLUMTREE (St Mary), *Notts.* R. **D** Southw 10 **P** *Dioc Bd of Finance* **I** S J OLIVER.
PLUNGAR (St Helen), *Leics.* V. **D** Leic 2 *See* Barkestone.
PLUSH (St Jo Bapt), *Dorset.*. **D** Sarum 5 *See* Piddletrenthide.
PLYMOUTH (St Andr w St Mich W Hoe) and East Stonehouse (St Geo w St Paul), *Devon.* V. **D** Ex 23 **P** *Ch Patr Trust* **I** J F W WATSON, G M COTTER *c*, A PERRIS *c*, B J H PORTER *c*, I L S WATSON *c*.
(Ascen Crownhill), V. **D** Ex 23 **P** *Bp* **I** L M MALSOM.
(Em Ch Compton Gifford), V. **D** Ex 23 **P** *V of Charles, Plymouth* **I** P S STEPHENS, L J T GARDNER *c*.
(St Aug), V. **D** Ex 23 **P** *Trustees* **I** C R CHUDLEY.
(Chas w St Matthias), V. **D** Ex 23 **P** *CPS ist, 2nd, and 3rd turns and Trustees of St Matthias advowson 4th turn* **I** (Vacant).
(St Gabr Peverell Park), V. **D** Ex 23 **P** *Bp* **I** J J STARK, L J HOWARTH *c*.
(St Jude), V. **D** Ex 23 **P** *Trustees* **I** D L LUMB, P W BECKLEY *c*.
(St Pet w All SS), V. **D** Ex 23 **P** *Keble Coll Ox* **I** S PHILPOTT, J M ROBINSON *c*.
(St Simon), V. **D** Ex 23 **P** *Trustees* **I** (Vacant).
(H Spirit, Southway), V. **D** Ex 23 **P** *Ld Chan* **I** C W H GOODWINS *p-in-c*, A F TREMLETT *c*.
(St Pancras w St Martin, Pennycross), V. **D** Ex 23 **P** *Trustees* **I** L E DENNY, A G FORMAN *c*.
(St Jo Evang Sutton-on-Plym), V. **D** Ex 23 **P** *Keble Coll Ox* **I** B R LAY.
(St Mary Virg Laira), V. **D** Ex 23 **P** *Bp* **I** A G COOKMAN.
(St Aid Ernesettle), V. **D** Ex 23 **P** *Bp* **I** R A SOUTHWOOD.
(St Jas L Ham), V. **D** Ex 23 **P** *Keble Coll Ox* **I** J F RICHARDS.
PLYMPTON (St Mary BV), *Devon.* V. **D** Ex 21 **P** *Bp* **I** F A J MATTHEWS.
(St Maurice), *Devon.* R. **D** Ex 21 **P** *D and C of Windsor* **I** G J SMITH *c*.
PLYMSTOCK (St Mary and All SS), *Devon.* V. **D** Ex 21 **P** *D and C of Windsor* **I** G SUNDERLAND, D M HUNTER *c*, L J YEO *c*.
PLYMTREE (St Jo Bapt) w Clyst Hydon and Clyst St Lawr, *Devon.* R. **D** Ex 7 **P** *Or Coll Ox, D and C of Ex and MMT* **I** O R TENNANT.
POCKLEY (St Jo Bapt), *N Yorks.*. **D** York 20 *See* Harome.
POCKLINGTON (All SS) w Yapham (St Martin), Meltonby (St Jas), Owsthorpe and Kilnwick Percy, *Humb.* V. **D** York 7 **P** *Abp* **I** (Vacant).
PODINGTON (St Mary) w Farndish (St Mich), *Beds.* V. **D** St Alb *See* Wymington.
PODYMORE-MILTON (St Pet) *Somt.* R. **D** B & W 10 *See* Ilchester.
POINTON, *Lincs.*. **D** Linc 13 *See* Sempringham.
POKESDOWN (St Jas), *Dorset.*. **D** Win 7 *See* Bournemouth.
POLEBROOKE (All SS) w Lutton (St Pet) and Hemington, *Northants.* R Pet) and Hemington, *Northants.* R. **D** Pet 11 **P** *Bp, Earl Fitzwilliam and K Measures Esq (in turn)* **I** F S MACE.
POLEGATE (St John), *E Sussex.* V. **D** Chich 19 **P** *Bp* **I** P R THOMPSON, L F GRIMWADE *c*.
POLESWORTH (St Editha) w Birchmoor, *Warws.* V. **D** Birm 10 **P** *Ld Chan* **I** D C BYFORD.
POLING (St Nich), *W Sussex.* V. **D** Chich 1 **P** *Bp* **I** D L SATTERFORD.
POLLINGTON (St Jo Bapt) w Balne *Humb.* V. **D** Sheff 9 **P** *Bp* **I** C D GEORGE.
POLPERRO, *Cornw.*. **D** Truro 13 *See* Talland.
POLSTEAD (St Mary), *Suff.* R. **D** St E 3 **P** *St Jo Coll Ox* **I** L R WILKS *p-in-c*.
POLTIMORE (St Mary Virg) w Huxham (St Mary Virg), *Devon.* R. **D** Ex 2 **P** *Bp* **I** (Vacant).
PONDERS END. **D** Lon *See* Enfield.
PONDSBRIDGE (St Thos), *Cambs.*. **D** Ely 12 *See* Ramsey St Mary.
PONSANOOTH, *Cornw.*. **D** Truro 3 *See* St Gluvias.
PONSBOURNE (St Mary Virg), *Herts.* V. **D** St Alb 8 **P** *CPAS* **I** (Vacant).
PONSONBY, *Cumb.*. **D** Carl *See* Beckermet, (St Bridget).
PONTEFRACT (St Giles), *W Yorks.* V. **D** Wakef 11 **P** *Bp* **I** E V DAVEY.
(All SS), V. **D** Wakef 11 **P** *Bp* **I** E FOWKES.
PONTELAND (St Mary Virg), *Northumb.* V. **D** Newc T 5b **P** *Mert Coll Ox* **I** P G CANNER, C G THORNE *c*, P G WOLFENDEN *hon c*.
PONTESBRIGHT, *Essex.*. **D** Chelmsf 20 *See* Wakes Colne.
PONTESBURY (St Geo) and Cruckton (St Thos), *Salop.* R 1st and 2nd Portions. **D** Heref 13 **P** *St Chad's Coll Dur* **I** D H ROBERTS.
3rd Portion w Longden.. **D** Heref 13 *See* Longden.
PONTON, GREAT (H Cross), *Lincs.* R. **D** Linc 14 **P** *Bp* **I** H BRIGGS.
PONTON, LITTLE (St Guthlac), *Lincs.* R. **D** Linc 14 **P** *Maj H B Turner* **I** H BRIGGS *p-in-c*.
POOL (St Wilfrid) w Arthington (St Pet), *W Yorks.* V. **D** Ripon 4 **P** *V of Otley and C E W Sheepshanks Esq* **I** L W KITCHEN.
POOLE (St Jas) w St Paul, *Dorset.* V. **D** Sarum 14 **P** *Ch S Trust* **I** J H POTTER.
POOLE KEYNES, *Glos.* R. **D** Glouc 13 *See* Kemble.
POOLE'S PARK (St Anne), *Lon.* V. **D** Lon 6 *See* Holloway (St Anne, Tollington Park).
POOLEY BRIDGE, *Cumb.*. **D** Carl *See* Barton.
POOLTON (St Luke), *Mer.* V. **D** Ches 8 *See* Wallasey.
POORTON, NORTH (St Mary Magd), *Dorset.* R. **D** Sarum 2 *See* Powerstock.
POPHAM (St Cath), *Hants.*. **D** Win *See* Micheldever.
POPLAR (All SS) w (St Frideswide Bromley-by-Bow) and (St Gabr and St Steph), *Lon.* R. **D** Lon 4 **P** *Patr Bd* **I** M BOURNE, P D G INGLEDEW *c*, W R LOW *c*.
(Ch of Ch and St John, Manchester Road w St Luke, Isle of Dogs), V. **D** Lon 4 **P** *Bp* **I** R J YEOMANS, T W HURCOMBE *team v*.
POPPLETON, NETHER (St Everilda) w Upper (All SS), *N Yorks.* V. **D** York 2 **P** *Abp* **I** A WEST.
PORCHESTER (St Jas), *Notts.* V. **D** Southw 13 *See* Nottingham.
PORCHFIELD, *Isle of Wight.*. **D** Portsm 7 *See* Calbourne.
PORINGLAND, GREAT (All SS) w Poringland L and Howe, *Norf.* R. **D** Nor 14 **P** *G H W Wheeler Esq and The Dominican Council* alt **I** R B HEMS.
PORLOCK (St Dubricius) w Stoke Pero (Dedic unknown), *Somt.* R. **D** B & W 21 **P** *Ld Chan* **I** E F KIRKPATRICK.
PORTBURY (St Mary Virg), *Avon* V. **D** B & W 16 *See* Easton-in-Gordano.
PORTCHESTER (St Mary), *Hants.* V. **D** Portsm 1 **P** *Mrs E S Borthwick-Norton* **I** M L S THOMAS, R J S EVENS *c*, G S VARNHAM *c*.
PORTESHAM (St Pet) w Langton Herring (St Pet), *Dorset.* V. **D** Sarum *See* Abbotsbury.
PORTFIELD (All SS), *W Sussex.* V. **D** Chich *See* Whyke.
PORTHILL (St Andr), *Staffs.* V. **D** Lich 17 *See* Wolstanton.
PORTHLEVEN (St Bart) w Sithney, *Cornw.* V. **D** Truro 4 **P** *Bp* **I** R B M HAYES.
PORTHPEAN, *Cornw.*. **D** Truro 1 *See* St Austell.
PORT ISAAC (St Pet), *Cornw.* V. **D** Truro 12 **P** *I of St Endellion* **I** P FOOT *p-in-c*.
PORTISHEAD (St Pet), *Somt.* R. **D** B & W 16 **P** *Mrs M E N Briggs* **I** N J EVA, V H JONES *c*.
PORTLAND (All SS w St Geo) w Southwell (St Andr), *Dorset.* R. **D** Sarum 6 **P** *Bp* **I** C F BROWN, E S MITCHELL *c*.
(St Jo Bapt), V. **D** Sarum 6 **P** *Hyndman Trustees* **I** M J BENNETT.
PORTLEMOUTH, EAST (St Winwalloe Onolaus), South Pool and Chivelstone, *Devon.* R. **D** Ex **P** *Ld Chan 1st and 3rd turns, Bp 2nd turn and E Roberts, Shirley Tyler and N Tyler jt 4th turn* **I** (Vacant).
PORTMAN SQUARE **D** Lon *See* St Marylebone.
PORTON, *Wilts.*. **D** Sarum *See* Bourne Valley.
PORTSDOWN (Ch Ch), *Hants.* V. **D** Portsm 3 **P** *Simeon Trustees* **I** J K HEWITT, P HANCOCK *c*, M MORGAN *c*, A H PRICE *c*, K J RANDALL *c*.
PORTSEA (St Mary and St Barn), *Hants.* V. **D** Portsm 5 **P** *Win Coll* **I** J M BROTHERTON, B R BARNES *c*, H G A JALLAND *c*, M K SPARROW *c*.
(All SS w St Jo Bapt Rudmore), V. **D** Portsm 5 **P** *V of Portsea and Bp* **I** M R WELCH.
(Ch of the Ascen), V. **D** Portsm 5 **P** *Bp* **I** M P MORGAN.
(St Geo), V. **D** Portsm 5 **P** *Bp* **I** D C DAVIES.
(St Jude, Southsea), V. **D** Portsm 5 **P** *CPAS* **I** A H M TURNER, A A BRAITHWAITE *c*, I D BROWN *c*.
(St Luke), V. **D** Portsm 5 **P** *CPS* **I** E H RIGLER.
(St Mark, North End), V. **D** Portsm 5 **P** *V of Portsea* **I** W R G SARGENT, C BEARDSLEY *c*, V J PEARCY *c*, C J SWIFT *c*.
(St Sav), V. **D** Portsm 5 **P** *Bp* **I** T KNIGHT, M C HALAHAN *hon c*.
(H Spirit, Southsea), V. **D** Portsm 5 **P** *Bp* **I** D DUNN, G K TAYLOR *c*.
(St Pet Ap Southsea), V. **D** Portsm 5 **P** *Bp* **I** K A BAILEY, T J COOPER *c*.
(St Simon, Southsea), V. **D** Portsm 5 **P** *CPS* **I** E A PRATT, A R HOWE *c*, P A LEWIS *c*.

PORTSLADE (St Nicolas), *W Sussex*. V. **D** Chich 13 **P** *Ld Sackville* **I** R H RUSHFORTH, J H KIMBERLEY *c*.
(St Pet and St Andr), V. **D** Chich 13 **P** *Bp* **I** J R LAMBETH *p-in-c*.
(Good Shepherd Conv Distr Mile Oak). **D** Chich 13 **I** E L BUNDOCK *p-in-c*.
PORTSMOUTH (St Thos à Becket Cathl Ch and St Mary), *Hants*. V. **D** Portsm 5 **P** *Bp* **I** (Vacant).
PORTSWOOD, *Hants*.. **D** Win 11 *See* Southampton.
PORTWOOD (St Paul), *Gtr Man*. V. **D** Ches 16 *See* Brinnington.
POSBURY CHAP (St Luke), *Devon*. V. **D** Ex 2 **P** *Sir John Shelley Bt* **I** B DUNCAN.
POSLINGFORD (St Mary Virg), *Suff*. V. **D** St E 8 *See* Clare.
POSTBRIDGE CHAP, *Devon*.. **D** Ex 22 *See* Princetown.
POSTLING, *Kent*.. **D** Cant 5 *See* Lyminge.
POSTWICK (All SS), *Norf*. R. **D** Nor 1 **P** *MMT and C of E Trust* **I** W C SNOOK.
POTT-SHRIGLEY (St Chris), *Chesh*. V. **D** Ches 13 **P** *MMT and C of E Trust* **I** M W WIGRAM.
POTTEN END (H Trin), V. **D** St Alb 3 *See* Nettleden.
POTTER HANWORTH (St Andr), *Lincs*. R. **D** Linc 18 **P** *Ld Chan* **I** R RODGER *c-in-c*.
POTTER HEIGHAM (St Nich), *Norf*. V. **D** Nor 9 **P** *Bp* **I** G E NICHOLSON *p-in-c*.
POTTERNE (St Mary Virg), *Wilts*. V. **D** Sarum 23 **P** *Bp* **I** K A HUGO.
POTTERNEWTON (St Martin), *N Yorks*. V. **D** Ripon 6 **P** *Trustees* **I** J D W KING, R A G SHANKS *c*.
POTTERS BAR (St Mary Virg and All SS), *Herts*. V. **D** Lon 16 **P** *Bp* **I** F W B PERKINS *hon c*.
POTTERS GREEN (St Phil), *W Midl*. V. **D** Cov 1 **P** *Ld Chan* **I** T E LONGFIELD.
POTTERS-MARSTON (St Mary), *Leics*. R. **D** Leic 16 *See* Barwell.
POTTERSPURY (St Nich) w Furtho (St Bart) and Yardley Gobion (St Leon), *Northants*. V. **D** Pet 2 **P** *Jes Coll Ox and Duke of Grafton* alt **I** G S MURRAY.
POTTESGROVE, *Beds*.. **D** St Alb *See* Battlesden.
POTTON (St Mary) w Cockayne-Hatley and Sutton, *Beds*. R. **D** St Alb 17 **P** *Ld Chan 3 turns, St Jo Coll Ox 1 turn* **I** I J STEWARDSON.
POUGHILL Devon. R **D** Ex 2 *See* Woolfardisworthy, East.
POUGHILL (St Olaf K and Mart), *Cornw*. V. **D** Truro 10 **P** *Trustees* **I** L H KEENAN.
POULNER (St Jo Bapt), *Hants*.. **D** Win 8 *See* Ringwood.
POULSHOT (St Pet), *Wilts*. R. **D** Sarum 23 **P** *Bp* **I** F M HENLY.
POULTON (St Mich AA), *Glos*. V. **D** Glouc 14 *See* Down-Ampney.
POULTON-LE-FYLDE (St Chad), *Lancs*. V. **D** Blackb 9 **P** *Dioc Bd of Patr* **I** P F GOODSON, J RADCLIFFE *c*.
POULTON-LE-SANDS (H Trin), *Lancs*.. **D** Blackb 8 *See* Morecambe.
POUND HILL (St Barn Conv Distr), *W Sussex*.. **D** Chich 12 **P** *Bp* **I** P C KEFFORD *p-in-c*.
POUNDON, *Bucks*.. **D** Ox 25 *See* Twyford.
POUNDSTOCK (St Winwaloe), *Cornw*. V. **D** Truro 10 **P** *Guild of All S* **I** J G EDWARDS *p-in-c*.
POWDERHAM (St Clem Bp and Mart), *Devon*. R. **D** Ex 6 *See* Kenton.
POWERSTOCK (St Mary Virg) w West Milton, Witherstone and N Poorton (St Mary Magd), *Dorset*. V. **D** Sarum 2 **P** *D and C of Sarum* **I** (Vacant).
POWYKE or POWICK (St Pet) w Callow End (St Jas), *Worcs*. V. **D** Worc 4 **P** *Croome Estate Trustees* **I** J J WILLIAMS.
POXWELL, *Dorset*.. **D** Sarum 6 *See* Osmington.
POYNINGS (H Trin), *W Sussex*. R. **D** Chich 14 **P** *Ld Chan* **I** (Vacant).
POYNTINGTON (All SS), *Dorset*. R. **D** Sarum 7 *See* Oborne.
POYNTON (St Geo), *Chesh*. V. **D** Ches 16 **P** *Bp* **I** R H C LEWIS, F HOLMES *c*.
PREEN, CHURCH (St Jo Bapt), *Salop*. V. **D** Heref 20 *See* Hughley.
PREES (St Chad), *Salop*. V. **D** Lich 27 **P** *Bp* **I** W A HUMPHREYS.
PREESALL (St Osw), *Lancs*. V. **D** Blackb 10 **P** *Bp* **I** R F JACKSON.
PRENTON (St Steph), *Mer*. V. **D** Ches 1 **P** *Bp* **I** L R LAWRENCE, J BENT *c*, D P BROCKBANK *c*, T JORDAN *c*, J M QUIGLEY *hon c*.
PRESCOT (St Mary Virg), *Mer*. V. **D** Liv 10 **P** *K Coll Cam* **I** J MILLS, P E BALL *c*.
PRESHUTE (St Geo), *Wilts*. V. **D** Sarum 26 *See* Marlborough.
PRESTBURY (St Pet), *Chesh*. V. **D** Ches 13 **P** *Mrs C Legh* **I** D W MOIR, V A M TRILL *c*.
PRESTBURY (St Mary), *Glos*. V. **D** Glouc 11 **P** *W Bagshot de la Bere Esq* **I** G I HAZLEWOOD, J T GUNN *c*.
PRESTEIGNE (St Andr) w Discoyd (St Mich), *Powys*. and *Herefs*. R. **D** Heref 5 **P** *Bp* **I** R A PERRY.
PRESTOLEE (H Trin), *Gtr Man*.. **D** Man 14 *See* East Farnworth.
PRESTON (St Jo Evang w Ch Ch, St Pet w St Geo, St Steph and St Sav w St Jas Ap), *Lancs*. R. **D** Blackb 12 **P** *Preston Patr Bd* **I** M J HIGGINS, C J W JACKSON *team v*, A R W RIMMER *team v*, G O SPEDDING *team v*.
(All SS), V. **D** Blackb 12 **P** *Trustees* **I** B G FELCE.
(Em Ch), V. **D** Blackb 12 **P** *V of Preston* **I** (Vacant).
(St Cuthb), V. **D** Blackb 12 **P** *Bp* **I** F W B KENNY, J F HARPER *c*.
(St Jude w St Paul), V. **D** Blackb 12 **P** *Bp* **I** P S GRIERSON.
(St Luke), V. **D** Blackb 12 **P** *Trustees* **I** (Vacant).
(St Mark), V. **D** Blackb 12 **P** *Trustees and V of Preston (alt)* **I** D L SEARS *p-in-c*.
(St Mary), V. **D** Blackb 12 **P** *Trustees* **I** E E CHAMBERLAIN.
(St Matt), V. **D** Blackb 12 **P** *Bp* **I** M TITTERINGTON.
(St Osw), V. **D** Blackb 12 **P** *Bp* **I** N K GRAY *p-in-c*.
(St Thos), V. **D** Blackb 12 **P** *Hyndman Trustees* **I** (Vacant).
(St Jas, Lostock Hall), V. **D** Blackb 6 **P** *Bp* **I** P B SAMMAN.
PRESTON (St Pet w St John), *W Sussex*. V. **D** Chich 15a **P** *Bp* **I** D E W LOCKYER, E R FIDDAMAN *c*.
(St Alb), V. **D** Chich 10 *See* Brighton.
(St Luke, Prestonville), V. **D** Chich 15a **P** *Trustees* **I** (Vacant).
(St Matthias), V. **D** Chich 15a **P** *V of Preston* **I** J G POLLOCK.
(St Sav), V. **D** Chich 10 *See* Brighton.
(St Aug of Cant), V. **D** Chich 15a **P** *Bp* **I** A TODD.
(Good Shepherd), V. **D** Chich 15a **P** *Bp* **I** G G WHITE, B M FLETCHER-JONES *hon c*.
PRESTON (St Jo Bapt), *Glos*. R. **D** Glouc 6 **P** *Bp* **I** R J LEGG *p-in-c*.
PRESTON (All SS), *Glos*. V. **D** Glouc 13 *See* Siddington.
PRESTON (St Pet and St Paul) and Ridlington (St Mary Magd and St Andr) w Wing and Pilton, *Leics*. R. **D** Pet 12 **P** *W Belgrave Esq, Earl of Ancaster and Bp* **I** P K PEIRSON.
PRESTON (St Mary), *Suff*. R. **D** St E 10 *See* Thorpe Morieux.
PRESTON (St Andr) w Sutton-Poyntz and Osmington w Poxwell, *Dorset*. R. **D** Sarum 6 **P** *Bp and J H C Lane Esq* **I** C C PERRY, N H BLISS *team v*.
PRESTON. **D** Lon *See* Wembley.
PRESTON-BAGOT, *Warws*.. **D** Cov 7 *See* Claverdon.
PRESTON-BISSETT (St Jo Bapt) and Barton Hartshorn w Chetwode, *Bucks*.. **D** Ox 25 *See* Swan.
PRESTON CANDOVER (St Mary Virg) w Nutley and Bradley (All SS), *Hants*.. **D** Win *See* Candover Valley.
PRESTON-CAPES, *Northants*.. **D** Pet *See* Charwelton.
PRESTON DEANERY (St Pet and St Paul), *Northants*. V. **D** Pet 4 *See* Wootton.
PRESTON, EAST (St Mary or All H) w Kingston, *W Sussex*. V. **D** Chich 1 **P** *D and C of Chich* **I** I J BRACKLEY.
PRESTON-GOBALDS, *Salop*.. **D** Lich 27 *See* Leaton.
PRESTON, GT (St Aid), *W Yorks*. V. **D** Ripon 7 *See* Kippax.
PRESTON-IN-HOLDERNESS (All SS) and Sproatley, *N Yorks*. R. **D** York **P** *Abp* **I** D F BAKER.
PRESTON-NEXT-FAVERSHAM (St Cath) and Goodnestone (St Bart) w Graveney (All SS), *Kent*. V. **D** Cant 7 **P** *Abp* **I** G B HUNT.
PRESTON-NEXT-WINGHAM, *Kent*.. **D** Cant 1 *See* Elmstone.
PRESTON-ON-STOUR (BVM) and Whitchurch w Atherstone-on-Stour, *Warws*. V. **D** Cov 8 **P** *Capt J W West* **I** A J RUSSELL.
PRESTON-ON-TEES (All SS), *Cleve*. V. **D** Dur 14 **P** *Bp* **I** E Z MBALI.
PRESTON-ON-WYE, *Herefs*.. **D** Heref *See* Moccas.
PRESTON-PATRICK (St Patrick), *Cumb*. V. **D** Carl 17 **P** *Bp* **I** P M SMITH.
PRESTON PLUCKNETT (St Jas), *Somt*.. **D** B & W 12 *See* Yeovil.
PRESTON WEALDMOORS (St Laur), *Salop*. R. **D** Lich 21 *See* Tibberton.
PRESTON WYNNE, *Herefs*.. **D** Heref *See* Felton.
PRESTWICH (St Mary Virg), *Gtr Man*. R. **D** Man 16 **P** *Trustees* **I** T N EVANS, R A BROADBENT *c*, B H MANNING *c*.
(St Gabr), V. **D** Man 16 **P** *Bp* **I** S C TATTON-BROWN *p-in-c*.

(St Hilda), V. **D** Man 16 **P** *Trustees* **I** (Vacant).
(St Marg Holyrood), V. **D** Man 16 **P** *R of Prestwich* **I** D N A CLEGG, G L CROOK *c.*
PRESTWOLD (St Andr) w Hoton (St Leon), *Leics.*. **D** Leic 10 *See* Wymeswold.
PRESTWOOD (H Trin), *Bucks.* V. **D** Ox 30 **P** *Exors of Mrs Disraeli* **I** A R WRIGHT *p-in-c,* P J M JUSTICE *hon c.*
PRICKWILLOW (St Pet w St Jas), *Cambs.* V. **D** Ely 15 **P** *V of H Trin and St Mary, Ely* **I** N MUNT.
PRIDDY (St Lawr), *Somt.* V. **D** B & W 1 **P** *Bp* **I** M J WYNES.
PRIMROSE HILL (St Mary Virg). **D** Lon 21 *See* Hampstead.
PRINCE CONSORT ROAD (H Trin). **D** Lon 19 *See* Kensington.
PRINCES RISBOROUGH (St Mary) w Longwick and Ilmer (St Pet), *Bucks.* R. **D** Ox 21 **P** *Crown* **I** W H JONES.
PRINCETOWN (St Mich AA) w Postbridge and Huccaby Chap, *Devon.* V. **D** Ex *See* Widecombe-in-the-Moor.
PRIORS DEAN, *Hants.*. **D** Portsm 4 *See* Hawkley.
PRIORS HARDWICK (St Mary BV) w Priors Marston and Wormleighton, *Warws.* V. **D** Cov 10 **P** *Earl Spencer* **I** C P K BARNES.
PRIORS LEE (St Pet), *Salop.* V. **D** Lich 27 **P** *V of Shifnal* **I** A M BALL.
PRIORS MARSTON (St Leon), *Warws.*. **D** Cov 10 *See* Priors Hardwick.
PRIORY CROSS GROUP, *Norf.*. **D** Ely *See* Fincham.
PRISTON (St Luke), *Avon.*. **D** B & W *See* Farmborough.
PRITTLEWELL (Annunc BVM and St Paul), *Essex.* V. **D** Chelmsf 11 **P** *Bp* **I** S T ERSKINE, R E CARLILL *c.*
(St Cedd's Eccles Distr). **D** Chelmsf 11 *See* Westcliff.
(St Luke), V. **D** Chelmsf 11 **P** *Bp* **I** M L LEESON.
(St Pet), V. **D** Chelmsf 11 **P** *Bp* **I** R C WELLS.
(St Steph), V. **D** Chelmsf 11 **P** *Bp* **I** R J STANLEY.
PRIVETT, *Hants.* V. **D** Portsm 4 *See* Froxfield.
PROBUS, ST (St Probus and St Grace), Ladock and Grampound with Creed *Cornw.* R. **D** Truro 6 **P** *Dioc Bd of Patr* **I** R L RAVENSCROFT, A K TORRY *team v.*
PRUDHOE (St Mary Magd), *Northumb.* V. **D** Newc T 3 **P** *Trustees* **I** R B HICKS, C R MURRIE *c.*
PUBLOW (All SS) w Pensford, Compton Dando and Chelwood, *Avon.* R. **D** B & W 15 **P** *Bp* **I** H B TASKER.
PUCKINGTON (St Andr) w Bradon and Stocklynch, *Somt.*. **D** B & W *See* Shepton Beauchamp.
PUCKLECHURCH (St Thos of Cant) w Abson (St Jas Gt) and Dyrham (St Pet), *Avon.* V. **D** Bris 7 **P** *D and C of Bris and J R W Blaythwayt Esq* alt **I** J D O HINTON.
PUDDING NORTON (St Marg), *Norf.* R. **D** Nor 21 *See* Hempton.
PUDDINGTON (St Thos à Becket), *Devon.* R. **D** Ex 8 *See* Woolfardisworthy, East.
PUDDLEHINTON, *Dorset.*. **D** Sarum *See* Piddlehinton.
PUDDLETOWN (St Mary Virg) w Athelhampton and Burleston and Tolpuddle, *Dorset.* V. **D** Sarum 5 **P** *Trustees of W J Brymer, D and C of Ch Ch Ox and Hon V H E Harmsworth (alt)* **I** J A MITCHELL-INNES.
PUDLESTON-CUM-WHYLE w Hatfield (St Leon), Docklow, Stoke Prior and Ford and Humber, *Herefs.* R. **D** Heref 7 **P** *Bp 2 turns V of Leominster 1 turn* **I** W P JOHNS P-IN-C OF FORD.
PUDSEY (St Lawr), *W Yorks.* V. **D** Bradf 3 **P** *V of Calverley* **I** J W WALLER, A G C SMITH *c.*
(St Paul), V. **D** Bradf 3 **P** *Bp* **I** (Vacant).
PULBOROUGH (St Mary), w Nutbourne, *W Sussex.* R. **D** Chich 7 **P** *Ld Egremont* **I** B S C A MALTIN, W J SELLERS *c.*
PULFORD (St Mary Virg), *Chesh.* R. **D** Ches 2 *See* Eccleston.
PULHAM (St Mary Magd w St Mary Virg), *Norf.* R. **D** Nor **P** *Crown* **I** G R EPPS.
PULHAM (St Thos à Becket), *Dorset.* R. **D** Sarum 7 **P** *G M Halsey Esq* **I** D HOPLEY.
PULLOXHILL (St Jas Ap) w Flitton (St Jo Bapt), *Beds.* V. **D** St Alb 15 **P** *Ball Coll Ox* **I** (Vacant).
PULVERBATCH (St Edith), *Salop.* R. **D** Heref 11 **P** *MMT* **I** C O HURFORD *p-in-c.*
PUNCKNOWLE (St Mary BV) w Swyre (H Trin), *Dorset.* R. **D** Sarum *See* Bride Valley.
PURBROOK (St Jo Bapt), *Hants.* V. **D** Portsm 3 **P** *Bp* **I** G G GEBAUER.
PURFLEET, *Essex.*. **D** Chelmsf 15 *See* Thurrock, West.
PURITON (St Mich AA) and Pawlett (St Jo Bapt), *Somt.* V. **D** B & W 17 **P** *D and C of Windsor 2 turns, Ld Chan 1 turn* **I** C C E MEREDITH.
PURLEIGH (All SS), *Essex.* R. **D** Chelmsf 14 **P** *Or Coll Ox* **I** S E PETERS *p-in-c.*
PURLEY, *Berks.* R. **D** Ox 12 **P** *Ld Chan* **I** D EVANS.
PURLEY (Ch Ch), *Surrey.* V. **D** S'wark 9 **P** *Bp* **I** J H CARROLL.
(St Barn), V. **D** S'wark 9 **P** *Bp* **I** E A NOON *c-in-c.*
(St Mark, Woodcote), V. **D** S'wark 9 **P** *Bp* **I** P M HAYNES.
(St Swith), V. **D** S'wark 9 **P** *Bp* **I** G F HARRIS *c.*
PURLWELL (St Andr), *W Yorks.* R. **D** Wakef 10 *See* Batley.
PURSTON (St Thos) w South Featherston, *W Yorks.* V. **D** Wakef 11 **P** *Bp* **I** A S RAMSDEN.
PURTON (St Mary), *Wilts.* V. **D** Bris 10 **P** *Earl of Shaftesbury and Bp* **I** R H D BLAKE.
PUSEY (All SS), *Oxon.* R. **D** Ox 17 **P** *Bp* **I** E B WOOD *p-in-c.*
PUTFORD, *Devon.*. **D** Ex 9 *See* Sutcombe.
PUTLEY, *Herefs.* R. **D** Heref 6 *See* Aylton.
PUTNEY (St Mary and All SS), *Surrey.* V. **D** S'wark 7 **P** *D and C of Worc* **I** J S FRASER, A D WAKEFIELD *c.*
(St Marg), V. **D** S'wark 7 **P** *Bp* **I** C M JONES *c.*
PUTTENHAM (St Jo Bapt) w Wanborough (St Bart), V *Surrey.* R. **D** Guildf 5 **P** *Ld Chan and Exors of T I Perkins* alt **I** A W BRANT *p-in-c.*
PUTTENHAM (St Mary) w Long Marston (All SS) and Wilstone (St Cross), *Herts.* R. **D** St Alb *See* Tring.
PUXLEY, *Northants.*. **D** Pet 2 *See* Passenham.
PUXTON (St Sav), *Avon.* V. **D** B & W 3 *See* Congresbury.
PYECOMBE, *W Sussex.* R. **D** Chich 14 *See* Newtimber.
PYLLE (St Thos of Cant), *Somt.* R. **D** B & W 6 *See* Pennard, East.
PYPE HAYES, *W Midl.*. **D** Birm *See* Erdington.
PYRFORD, *Surrey.*. **D** Guildf *See* Wisley.
PYRTON (St Mary) w Shirburn (All SS), *Oxon.* V. **D** Ox *See* Watlington.
PYTCHLEY (All SS), *Northants.* V. **D** Pet 4 *See* Isham.
PYWORTHY w Pancrasweek (St Pancras) and Bridgerule, *Devon.* R. **D** Ex 9 **P** *Dioc BD of Patr* **I** (Vacant).

QUADRING (St Marg), *Lincs.* V. **D** Linc *See* Gosberton Clough.
QUAINTON (St Mary and H Cross), *Bucks.* R. **D** Ox *See* Schorne.
QUANTOXHEAD (St Mary Virg and St Etheldreda) w Kilve, Stringston, Kilton, Lilstock and Holford w Dodington, *Somt.* R. **D** B & W 18 **P** *Lt Col G W F Luttrell, Lady Gass, Bp and Miss E P Acland-Hood* **I** W H MINSHULL.
QUARLEY (St Mich), *Hants.* R. **D** Win 2 *See* Grateley.
QUARNDON (St Paul), *Derbys.* V. **D** Derby 12 **P** *Exors of Ld Scarsdale* **I** A R MILROY.
QUARNFORD (St Paul), *Staff.* V. **D** Lich 13 **P** *C Harpur-Crewe Esq* **I** A C F NICOLL *p-in-c.*
QUARRINGTON, *Durham.*. **D** Dur *See* Cassop.
QUARRINGTON (St Botolph) w Old Sleaford (St Giles), *Lincs.* R. **D** Linc 22 **P** *Bp* **I** F H BAILEY.
QUARRY BANK (Ch Ch), *W Midl.* V. **D** Lich 1 **P** *Crown and Bp* alt **I** T G CHAPMAN.
QUATFORD (St Mary Magd), *Salop.* V. **D** Heref 9 **P** *Bp* **I** D T MERRY *p-in-c.*
QUATT MALVERN (St Andr), *Salop.* R. **D** Heref 9 **P** *Lady Labouchere* **I** W C MASSEY *p-in-c.*
QUEDGELEY (St Jas), *Glos.*. **D** Glouc 9 **P** *Bp* **I** (Vacant).
QUEEN CAMEL, *Somt.*. **D** B & W 12 *See* Camel.
QUEEN THORNE (Over and Nether Compton, Trent, Sandford Orcas, Orborne and Poyntington), *Dorset.* R. **D** Sarum **P** *Bp, J M Goodden Esq, MMT and Maj K S D Wingfield-Digby* **I** A E H RUTTER.
QUEENBOROUGH (H Trin), *Kent.* V. **D** Cant 14 **P** *Abp* **I** R N MURCH.
QUEENHILL (St Nich) w Holdfast, *Worcs.* V. **D** Worc 5 *See* Longdon.
QUEEN SQUARE (St Geo Mart), R. **D** Lon 2 *See* Holborn.
QUEENSBURY (H Trin), *W Yorks.* V. **D** Bradf 2 **P** *Bp* **I** J READ.
QUEENSBURY (All SS), *Gtr Lon.*. **D** Lon 24 **P** *Crown* **I** L D MACKENZIE.
QUENDON (Dedic unknown) w Rickling (All SS) and Wicken Bonhunt, *Essex.* R. **D** Chelmsf 26 **P** *Bp, Earl of Inchcape and Keble Coll Ox* **I** F M BEST.
QUENIBOROUGH (St Mary), *Leics.* V. **D** Leic 9 **P** *Peache Trustees* **I** (Vacant).
QUENINGTON (St Swith) w Coln St Aldwyn, V and Hatherop, R *Glos.* R. **D** Glouc *See* Coln St Aldwyn.
QUERNMORE (St Pet), *Lancs.* R. **D** Blackb 11 *See* Dolphinholme.
QUETHIOCK (St Hugh), *Cornw.*. **D** Truro 13 *See* St Ives.

RATHMELL-IN-CRAVEN (H Trin) w Wigglesworth, *N Yorks*. V. **D** Bradf 6 **P** *Bp* **I** J H RICHARDSON *p-in-c*.
RATLEY-ON-EDGEHILL, *Warws*.. **D** Cov 8 *See* Radway.
RATLINGHOPE (St Marg), *Salop*. V. **D** Heref 10 *See* Wentnor.
RATTERY (BVM), *Devon*. V. **D** Ex 13 **P** *R V Carew Esq* **I** J G BISHOP.
RATTLESDEN (St Nich), *Suff*. R. **D** St E 10 **P** *Bp* **I** D O WALL.
RAUCEBY, NORTH (St Pet) w South, *Lincs*. V. **D** Linc *See* Wilsford.
RAUGHTON HEAD Cumb. V **D** Carl 3 **P** *Dioc Bd of Patr* **I** P V FISHER *p-in-c*.
RAUNDS (St Pet), *Northants*. V. **D** Pet 9 **P** *Bp* **I** J R B CANHAM.
RAVELEY, GT and L, *Cambs*.. **D** Ely 12 *See* Upwood.
RAVENDALE, EAST (St Martin), w Ravendale, West, and Hatcliffe (St Mary), R *Humb*. V. **D** Linc 10 **P** *Trustees and Bp* alt **I** D N SAMUEL.
RAVENFIELD (St Jas), *S Yorks*.. **D** Sheff 7 *See* Bramley.
RAVENHEAD (St Jo Evang), *Mer*. V. **D** Liv 10 **P** *V of St Helens* **I** J S PARRY.
RAVENINGHAM (St Andr), Haddiscoe, Hales, Norton Subcourse, Thurlton, *Norf*. R. **D** Nor 14 **P** *Patr Bd* **I** J R P BARKER, S W PEARCE *team v*, D H HETHERINGTON *c*.
RAVENSCAR (St Hilda), *N Yorks*. V. **D** York 18 *See* Scalby.
RAVENSCOURT PARK (St Pet).. **D** Lon 12 *See* Hammersmith.
RAVENSDEN, *Beds*.. **D** St Alb *See* Wilden.
RAVENSHEAD (St Pet), *Notts*. V. **D** Southw 2 **P** *Bp* **I** A A CONN.
RAVENSTHORPE (St Sav), *W Yorks*. V. **D** Wakef 10 **P** *V of Mirfield* **I** I E WILDEY.
RAVENSTHORPE (St Denys), w E Haddon (St Mary Virg) and Holdenby (All SS), *Northants*. V. **D** Pet 6 **P** *Bp 2 turns, Crown 1 turn* **I** P F ROWE.
RAVENSTONE (St Mich), *Derbys* and *Leics*. R. **D** Leic 11 **P** *Ld Chan* **I** L BUCKROYD.
RAVENSTONE (All SS) w Weston Underwood (St Laur), *Bucks*. V. **D** Ox 28 *See* Gayhurst.
RAVENSTONEDALE Cumb. **D** Carl *See* Orton.
RAWCLIFFE (St Jas), *Humb*. V. **D** Sheff 9 **P** *V of Snaith* **I** (Vacant).
RAWDON (St Pet), *W Yorks*. V. **D** Bradf 5 **P** *Trustees* **I** S G HOARE.
RAWMARSH (St Mary) w Parkgate (Ch Ch), *S Yorks*. R. **D** Sheff 6 **P** *Ld Chan* **I** B L HOLDRIDGE, R D E BOLTON *c*.
RAWRETH (St Nich) w Rettendon (All SS), *Essex*. R. **D** Chelmsf 16 **P** *Ld Chan and Pemb Coll Cam* alt **I** A T WATERER.
RAWTENSTALL (St Mary), *Lancs*. V. **D** Man 18 **P** *CPAS* **I** P BARRATT.
RAWTHORPE, *W Yorks*.. **D** Wakef *See* Huddersfield.
RAYDON (All SS), *Suff*. R. **D** St E 3 **P** *Reformation Ch Trust* **I** W S HERRINGTON *p-in-c*.
RAYLEIGH (H Trin), *Essex*. R. **D** Chelmsf 16 **P** *MMT* **I** G W HATCH, A OATES *c*, M D W PADDISON *c*.
RAYNE (All SS), *Essex*. R. **D** Chelmsf 19 **P** *Dioc Bd of Patr* **I** M G SELLIX.
RAYNES PARK (St Sav), *Surrey*. V. **D** S'wark 14 **P** *Bp* **I** P KETTLE.
(H Cross Motspur Pk), V. **D** S'wark 14 **P** *Bp* **I** R H MCLEAN.
RAYNHAM-ST MARTIN, *Norf*. R. **D** Nor 20 *See* Helhoughton.
REACH, *Cambs*.. **D** Ely 3 *See* Swaffham Prior.
READ-IN-WHALLEY (St Jo Evang) *Lancs*. V. **D** Blackb 7 **P** *V of Whalley* **I** H A REID.
READING (Ch Ch Whitley), *Berks*. V. **D** Ox 15 **P** *Bp* **I** J DEUCHAR, J MORRISON *c*, C H C EDWARDS *hon c*.
(All SS), V. **D** Ox 15 **P** *Bp* **I** P T H JONES, D L ADAMS *c*, J W MORTIBOYS *c*, C J WALKER *c*.
(H Trin), V. **D** Ox 15 **P** *V of St Mary , Reading* **I** B D F T BRINDLEY, G C ROWLANDS *c*.
(St Agnes w St Paul), V. **D** Ox **P** *Bp* **I** J A COX.
(St Barn), R. **D** Ox 15 **P** *Bp* **I** C F BOND, K P WIGGINS *hon c*.
(St Giles w St Sav), R and V. **D** Ox 15 **P** *Bp* **I** A C BOULT, L E GOODING *c*, M D SMITH *c*.
(St Jo Evang w St Steph), V. **D** Ox 15 **P** *Simeon Trustees* **I** J G MCKECHNIE, R H BULL *c*, B H MEARDON *c*.
(St Luke), V. **D** Ox 15 **P** *V of St Giles, Reading* **I** R J PREECE.
(St Mark). **D** Ox 15 **P** *Bp* **I** J A R METHUEN, D J DAVIS *c*.
(St Mary Chap Castle Street), V. **D** Ox 15 **P** *Trustees* **I** C T M BROWNE *min*.
(St Mary Virg w St Laur), V. **D** Ox 15 **P** *Bp* **I** G D RESTALL.
(St Matt), V. **D** Ox 15 **P** *Bp* **I** M E W WESTNEY.
GREYFRIARS, V. **D** Ox 15 **P** *Trustees* **I** P N DOWNHAM.
REARSBY (St Mich), *Lincs*. R. **D** Leic 9 *See* Ratcliffe-on-the-Wreak.
REASBY, *Lincs*.. **D** Linc *See* Stainton-by-Langworth.
RECULVER (St Mary), *Kent*. V. **D** Cant 4 **P** *Abp* **I** S J WELCH.
RED POST (Bloxworth, Morden w Almer and Charborough, Winterbourne Zelstone w Tomson, Anderson and Kingston), *Dorset*. V. **D** Sarum 10 **P** *Mrs V M Chattey, H W Drax Esq and Bp (in turn)* **I** R J FORBES.
REDBOURN (St Mary), *Herts*. V. **D** St Alb 14 **P** *Earl of Verulam* **I** J G PEDLAR, R C A LESLIE *c*, A D OSBORNE *c*.
REDBOURNE, *Humb*. V. **D** Linc *See* Scawby.
REDBROOK (St Sav), *Glos*. V. **D** Glouc 7 *See* Newland.
REDCAR (St Pet), *Cleve*. V. **D** York 19 **P** *Trustees* **I** R A R WHITTA, M SPENCELEY *c*.
REDCLIFFE (St Mary Virg), *Avon*. V. **D** Bris 1 *See* Bedminster.
REDDAL HILL or CRADLEY HEATH (St Luke), *W Midl*. V. **D** Worc 9 **P** *Crown* **I** J M BRIERLEY.
REDDISH (St Elisabeth), *Gtr Man*. R. **D** Man 4 **P** *Col Sir W Houldsworth Bt* **I** G G MARSHALL, H BEMBRIDGE *c*, A J GRIST *c*.
NORTH (St Agnes), R. **D** Man 4 **P** *Crown and Bp* alt **I** K BOYCE.
REDDITCH (St Steph), *Worcs*. V. **D** Worc 7 **P** *Bp* **I** (Vacant).
THE RIDGE (Headless Cross, St Geo, Webheath and Crabb's Cross), *Worcs*. R. **D** Worc **P** *Bp* **I** S HUTCHINSON, D P LINGWOOD *team v*, C H MORGAN *team v*, F E THOMAS *team v*.
REDE (All SS), *Suff*. R. **D** St E 13 *See* Chedburgh.
REDENHALL (Assump BVM) w Wortwell and Harleston (St Jo Bapt), *Norf*. R. **D** Nor 17 **P** *Duke of Norf and Bp* **I** (Vacant).
REDGRAVE (St Botolph) w Botesdale (St Mary) and Rickinghall, *Suff*. R. **D** St E 16 **P** *P J Holt Wilson Esq* **I** D F HAYDEN.
REDHILL (Ch Ch), *Avon*.. **D** B & W *See* Wrington.
REDHILL (St Jo Bapt), *Hants*. R. **D** Portsm 3 *See* Rowlands Castle.
REDHILL (St Jo Evang), *Surrey*. V. **D** S'wark 12 **P** *Bp* **I** M J GOSS.
(St Matt), V. **D** S'wark 12 **P** *Bp* **I** R D W HAWKINS, D S C TUDOR *c*.
(H Trin Brass Mem Ch), V. **D** S'wark 12 **P** *Simeon Trustees* **I** C J E BRIDGLAND.
REDISHAM, GREAT (St Pet) w Redisham, Little, *Suff*. V. **D** St E 14 *See* Ringsfield.
REDLAND, *Avon*. V. **D** Bris 4 **P** *Ch Trust Fund Trustees* **I** J M PERRIS.
REDLINGFIELD, *Suff*.. **D** St E *See* Occold.
REDLYNCH (St Pet), *Somt*. V. **D** B & W 5 *See* Bruton.
REDLYNCH (St Mary) w Morgan's Vale (St Birinus), *Wilts*. V. **D** Sarum 17 **P** *Dioc Bd of Finance and V of Downton jointly, 1 turn, V of Downton, 2 turns* **I** R SHARPE.
REDMARLEY D'ABITOT (St Bart) and Bromsberrow w Pauntley, Upleadon and Oxenhall, *Glos*. R. **D** Glouc 6 **P** *Mrs E B Niblett and Bp* **I** W J MOXON, R W MARTIN *c*.
REDMARSHALL (St Cuthb), *Cleve*. R. **D** Dur 14 **P** *Crown* **I** T J D OLLIER.
REDMILE (St Pet), *Leics*. R. **D** Leic 3 *See* Barkestone.
REDMIRE (St Mary), *N Yorks*.. **D** Ripon 2 *See* Bolton (St Oswald).
REDNAL (St Steph Mart), *W Midl*. V. **D** Birm 4 **P** *Bp* **I** S R F DRAKELEY.
REDRUTH (St Euny w St Andr) w Lanner, Pencoys (St Andr) and Carnmenellis (H Trin), *Cornw*. R. **D** Truro 2 **P** *Dioc Bd of Patr, Bp and Mart Mem and C of E Trust* **I** H E HOSKING, M PETERS *team v*, G V BENNETTS *c*.
REED (St Mary), *Herts*.. **D** St Alb 5 *See* Barkway.
REEDHAM (St Jo Bapt) w Cantley w Limpenhoe and Southwood, *Norf*. R. **D** Nor 1 **P** *Ch S Trust 2 Turns, Lt-Col E R F Gilbert 1 Turn* **I** J F HEADLAND.
REEPHAM (St Pet and St Paul), *Lincs*. V. **D** Linc *See* Fiskerton.
REEPHAM (Nativ of St Mary Virg) w Hackford, Whitwell (St Mich AA) and Kerdiston, *Norf*. R. **D** Nor 6 **P** *Trin Coll Cam 3 turns, Ch S Trust 2 turns* **I** G DODSON *p-in-c*.
REGENT SQUARE (St Pet). **D** Lon 26 *See* St Pancras.
REGENT STREET (St Thos). **D** Lon 19 *See* Westminster.
REGENT'S PARK. **D** Lon *See* St Pancras.
REIGATE (St Mary Magd), *Surrey*. V. **D** S'wark 12 **P** *Trustees* **I** M J H FOX *c*, K W HABERSHON *hon c*.
(St Mark), V. **D** S'wark 12 **P** *Bp* **I** W G M LEWIS.
(St Luke), V. **D** S'wark 12 **P** *Bp* **I** I F M PULLENAYEGUM, R F VICKERY *c*.

RIPPLE (St Mary), *Worcs*. R. **D** Worc **P** *Bp and Trustees of Rev G le S Amphlett (alt)* **I** D L T SCOTT.

RIPPONDEN (St Bart) w Rishworth (St John), *W Yorks*. V. **D** Wakef 1 **P** *Bp* **I** J R FLACK, G FISHER *c*.

RIPTON, ABBOTS, *Cambs*.. **D** Ely 10 *See* Abbots Ripton.

RIPTON-REGIS (St Pet), *Cambs*. R. **D** Ely 13 *See* King's Ripton.

RISBY (St Bart), *Humb*.. **D** Linc 4 *See* Roxby.

RISBY (St Giles) w Great and Little Saxham and Westley, *Suff*. R. **D** St E **P** *Ld Chan, Lady Stirling and Marq of Bris* **I** H M LE FEUVRE.

RISE (All SS), *Humb*.. **D** York 14 *See* Sigglesthorne.

RISEHOLME (St Mary) and Grange-de-Lings, *Lincs*. R. **D** Linc 3 *See* Dunholme.

RISELEY (All SS) w Bletsoe (St Mary), *Beds*. V. **D** St Alb 21 **P** *MMT* **I** P PHILLIPS.

RISHANGLES (St Marg) w Thorndon (All SS), *Suff*.. **D** St E *See* Bedingfield.

RISHTON (St Pet and St Paul), *Lancs*. V. **D** Blackb 7 **P** *Trustees* **I** R MCCULLOUGH.

RISHWORTH (St John), *W Yorks*.. **D** Wakef 1 *See* Ripponden.

RISLEY (All SS), *Derby*, R. **D** Derby 13 **P** *Bp* **I** N J CLAYTON *p-in-c*.

RISSINGTONS, THE (St Jo Bapt w St Pet and St Lawr), *Glos*. R. **D** Glouc **P** *C T R Wingfield, Ld Chan and Dioc Bd of Patr* **I** J DAVEY.

RISTON, LONG (St Marg), *Humb*. V. **D** York 14 *See* Skirlaugh.

RIVENHALL (St Mary and All SS), *Essex*. R. **D** Chelmsf 29 **P** *Dioc Bd of Patr* **I** D NASH.

RIVER (St Pet and St Paul), *Kent*. R. **D** Cant 5 **P** *Abp* **I** F R SMALE.

RIVERHEAD (St Mary Virg) w Dunton Green, *Kent*. V. **D** Roch 7 **P** *R of Sevenoaks and Bp* **I** C J D WALKER, M A BROWN *c*.

RIVERSIDE (Colnbrook St Thos, Datchet St Mary Virg, Dorney St Jas, Wraysbury St Andr and Horton St Mich), *Bucks and Berks*. R. **D** Ox 24 **P** *Patr Bd* **I** J W G WHALE, J E HALL *team v*, S J NEWELL *team v*.

RIVINGTON, *Lancs*. V. **D** Man 13 **P** *PCC* **I** J JERMY *p-in-c*.

ROADE (St Mary), *Northants*. V. **D** Pet 4 **P** *Bp 2 turns, R of Ashton 1 turn* **I** C H DAVIDSON.

ROBERTTOWN (All SS), *W Yorks*. V. **D** Wakef 9 **P** *V of Birstall* **I** M J CASTERTON.

ROBOROUGH, *Devon*.. **D** Ex *See* Beaford.

ROBY (St Bart), *Mer*. V. **D** Liv 10 **P** *Earl of Derby* **I** T A WHYTE.

ROCESTER (St Mich), *Staffs*. V. **D** Lich 20 **P** *Trustees* **I** A P FOTHERGILL.

ROCHDALE (St Chad, St Pet Newbold, St Aid Sudden, Good Shepherd), *Grt Man*. R. **D** Man 17 **P** *Patr Bd* **I** L S DRAKE *team v*, P T KERR *team v*, P ROBINSON *c*.

(All SS Hamer), V. **D** Man 17 **P** *Bp* **I** B L CORDINGLEY.

(Ch Ch Healey), V. **D** Man 17 **P** *Crown and Bp (alt)* **I** (Vacant).

(St Alb), V. **D** Man 17 *See* Oakenrod.

(St Clem Spotland), V. **D** Man 17 **P** *Bp* **I** C E WARRINGTON.

(St Edm Falinge), V. **D** Man 17 **P** *Bp* **I** L C MEPSTED *c-in-c*.

(St Luke Deeplish), V. **D** Man 17 **P** *Bp* **I** (Vacant).

(St Mary, Balderstone), V. **D** Man 17 **P** *Five Trustees* **I** J V BYRNE, C H KEY *c*.

(St Mary w St Jas, Wardleworth), V. **D** Man 17 **P** *V of Rochdale* **I** (Vacant).

ROCHE (St Gonand of the Rock), *Cornw*. R. **D** Truro 1 **P** *Toc H 3 turns, Dioc Bd of Patr 1 turn* **I** N H TOOGOOD *p-in-c*.

ROCHESTER (St Pet w St Marg and St Nich w St Clem), *Kent*. V. **D** Roch 4 **P** *Bp and D and C of Roch* **I** B J JEWISS, M B PERKINS *c*, P H RENYARD *hon c*.

(St Matt Borstal), V. **D** Roch 4 **P** *V of Roch* **I** J A PEAL.

(St Justus), V. **D** Roch 4 **P** *Bp* **I** M H J DUNN.

ROCHFORD, *Essex*. R. **D** Chelmsf 16 **P** *Bp* **I** A N GODSELL.

ROCHFORD (St Mich), *Worcs*.. **D** Worc *See* Eastham.

ROCK (St Phil and St Jas), *Northumb*. V. **D** Newc T 7 *See* Rennington.

ROCK (St Pet and St Paul) w Heightington (St Giles) and Far Forest, *Worcs*. V. **D** Worc 10 **P** *V of Ribbesford w Bewdley* **I** W ELLIOTT.

ROCK FERRY (St Pet), *Mer*. V. **D** Ches 1 **P** *Bp* **I** S A WILCOCKSON.
See also TRANMERE.

ROCKBEARE (St Mary w St Andr), *Devon*.. **D** Ex 1 *See* Clyst St Geo.

ROCKBOURNE (St Andr) w Whitsbury (St Leon), *Hants*. R. **D** Win 8 **P** *W R Van Straubenzee Esq and Cdr R Purvis, RN* **I** A E H KEYES.

ROCKCLIFFE (St Mary) w Cargo and Blackford, *Cumb*. V. **D** Carl 3 **P** *D and C of Carl* **I** J S DAVIDSON.

ROCKHAMPTON (St Osw), *Avon*.. **D** Glouc 8 *See* Falfield.

ROCKINGHAM (St Leon), *Northants*.. **D** Pet 10 *See* Gretton.

ROCKLAND (St Pet w All SS and St Andr), *Norf*. R. **D** Nor 18 **P** *CCC Cam* **I** D H ELTON *p-in-c*.

ROCKLAND (St Mary) w Hellington, *Norf*. R (*See Bramerton Group*).. **D** Nor 14 **P** *Bp* **I** (Vacant).

ROCKWELL GREEN, *Somt*.. **D** B & W *See* Wellington.

RODBOROUGH (St Mary Magd), *Glos*. R. **D** Glouc 9 **P** *Bp* **I** J E FORRYAN.

RODBOURNE (H Rood), *Wilts*.. **D** Bris 9 *See* Corston.

RODBOURNE-CHENEY (St Mary), *Wilts*. V. **D** Bris 10 **P** *CPAS* **I** A D ROWLEY, P S FREAR *c*, D F MILLS *c*, W T PADGET *c*.

RODDEN (Dedic unknown), *Somt*.. **D** B & W 16a *See* Berkley.

RODE MAJOR (St Lawr) w Rode Hill (Ch Ch) and Woolverton (St Lawr) and Farleigh-Hungerford (St Leon) w Tellisford (All SS), *Somt*. R. **D** B & W 16a **P** *Bp* **I** P J RILEY.

RODHUISH, *Somt*.. **D** B & W 23 *See* Withycombe.

RODINGTON (St Geo), *Salop*. R. **D** Lich 29 **P** *Bp* **I** W S FROST.

RODMARTON (St Pet), *Glos*. R. **D** Glouc 13 *See* Coates.

RODMELL (St Pet), *E Sussex*. R. **D** Chich 15 *See* Kingston.

RODMERSHAM, *Kent*. V. **D** Cant **P** *Abp* **I** W F SHERGOLD.

RODNEY-STOKE (St Leon) w Draycott, *Somt*. R. **D** B & W 1 **P** *Bp* **I** J A WOOD, P D CORRICK *c*.

ROECLIFFE, *N Yorks*.. **D** Ripon 3 *See* Aldborough.

ROEHAMPTON (H Trin), *Surrey*. V. **D** S'wark 7 **P** *Bp* **I** D S PAINTER, R W SIMMONDS *c*, E SUTHERLAND *c*.

ROFFEY (All SS), *W Sussex*. V. **D** Chich 4 **P** *Bp* **I** A R REED, P GRAVES *c*.

ROGATE (St Bart), *W Sussex*. V. **D** Chich 5 **P** *Ld Chan* **I** (Vacant).

ROKEBY (St Mich or St Mary) w Brignall (St Mary), *Dur*. R. **D** Ripon 1 **P** *Ld Chan and Bp* alt **I** A A HARRISON *c-in-c*.

ROKER, *T & W*.. **D** Dur 8 *See* Monk Wearmouth.

ROLLESBY (St Geo) w Burgh (St Marg and St Mary Virg) w Billockby w Ashby, Oby, Thurne and Clippesby *Norf*. R. **D** Nor **P** *Bp, R J H Tacon and Dioc Bd of Patr* **I** R H ELPHICK.

ROLLESTON, *Leics*. V. **D** Leic 5 *See* Billesdon.

ROLLESTON (St Mary) , *Staffs*. R. **D** Lich **P** *MMT* **I** M D BIRT.

ROLLESTON (H Trin) w Fiskerton and Morton (St Denis), *Notts*. V. **D** Southw 15 **P** *Ld Chan* **I** N H TODD, J M BURGESS *c*.

ROLLESTONE (St Andr), *Wilts*. R. **D** Sarum 21 *See* Shrewton.

ROLLRIGHT, GREAT (St Andr), *Oxon*. R. **D** Ox *See* Hook-Norton.

ROLLRIGHT, LITTLE (St Phil), *Oxon*. R. **D** Ox 5 *See* Salford.

ROLVENDEN (St Mary Virg), *Kent*. V. **D** Cant 11 **P** *Abp* **I** J H WRIGHT.

ROMALDKIRK (St Romald) w Cotherstone (St Cuthb), *N Yorks*. R. **D** Ripon 1 **P** *Earl of Strathmore and Bp* alt **I** D D MARTIN.

ROMANBY (St Jas), *N Yorks*.. **D** York 23 *See* Northallerton.

ROMANSLEIGH, *Devon*.. **D** Ex *See* South Molton.

ROMFORD (St Edw Confessor), *Essex*. V. **D** Chelmsf 4 **P** *New Coll Ox* **I** D W M JENNINGS, D L STOKES *c*.

(Ascen Collier Row), V. **D** Chelmsf 4 **P** *Trustees* **I** G P LAUT.

(Good Shepherd Collier Row), V. **D** Chelmsf 4 **P** *Trustees* **I** J B BATTMAN.

(St Alb). **D** Chelmsf 4 **P** *Bp* **I** R E ANDERSON.

(St Andr), R. **D** Chelmsf 4 **P** *New Coll Ox* **I** D B PAUL.

(St Aug Rush Green). **D** Chelmsf 4 **P** *Bp* **I** N M WOOD.

(St Geo Harold Hill), V. **D** Chelmsf **P** *Bp* **I** R G SMITH.

(St Jas Collier Row), V. **D** Chelmsf 4 **P** *Bp* **I** L A LUNN.

(St Jo Div Mawneys), V. **D** Chelmsf 4 **P** *Bp* **I** R F TELFORD.

(St Paul's Harold Hill), V. **D** Chelmsf 4 **P** *Bp* **I** C S CARTER.

ROMNEY, NEW (St Nich) w Hope and St Mary's Bay and St Mary in the Marsh (St Mary Virg), *Kent*. V. **D** Cant 13 **P** *Abp and Ld Chan (alt)* **I** L P FORD P-IN-C OF OLD ROMNEY.

ROMNEY, OLD, *Kent*. R. **D** Cant 13 *See* Brookland.

RUDDINGTON (St Pet), *Notts.* V. **D** Southw 11 **P** *Simeon Trustees* **I** A C SHRIMPTON.
RUDFORD, *Glos.*. **D** Glouc *See* Highnam.
RUDGWICK (H Trin), *W Sussex.* V. **D** Chich 4 **P** *Bp* **I** T A B CHARLES.
RUDHAM, EAST (St Mary) w Rudham, West (St Pet) and Broomsthorpe (St John), *Norf.* V. **D** Nor 21 **P** *Marq Townsend and Marq of Cholmondeley* alt **I** (Vacant).
RUDSTON (All SS) and Boynton, *Humb.* V. **D** York 12 **P** *Abp* **I** A HORSFIELD *p-in-c.*
RUFFORD (St Mary), *Lancs.* R. **D** Blackb 6 **P** *G Starkie Esq* **I** E E S JONES.
RUFFORTH (All SS) w Moor Monkton (All SS) and Hessay, *N Yorks.* V. **D** York 2 **P** *Mart Mem and C of E Trust and Abp* alt **I** J A RENDALL.
RUGBY (St Andr), *Warws.* R. **D** Cov 6 **P** *Exors of the late Earl of Craven* **I** A A COLDWELLS, J R BOMYER *c,* M D S GREIG *c,* J D NIXON *c.*
(St Matt Evang), V. **D** Cov 6 **P** *Ch Trust Fund Trustees* **I** A E HAVARD *c,* A S MAIRS *c.*
RUGELEY (St Aug of Cant), *Staffs.* V. **D** Lich 4 **P** *D and C of Lich* **I** J EASTON, D J FAIRWEATHER *c.*
RUISHTON (St Geo) w Thorn Falcon (H Cross), *Somt.* V. **D** B & W 23a **P** *Bp and E R C Batten Esq* alt **I** T A THOMAS.
RUISLIP (St Martin), *Gtr Lon.* V. **D** Lon 9 **P** *D and C of Windsor* **I** K F TOOVEY, D M BRADSHAW *c,* J T SMITH *c.*
(St Paul, Ruislip Manor), V. **D** Lon 9 **P** *Bp* **I** (Vacant).
SOUTH (St Mary), V. **D** Lon 9 **P** *Bp* **I** B G COPUS.
RUMBOLDSWHYKE, *W Sussex.* **D** Chich *See* Whyke.
RUMBURGH (St Mich AA and St Felix) w S Elmham (All SS, St Jas and St Mich) w The Ilketshalls (St Andr, St Lawr, St Marg and St Jo Bapt), *Suff.* V. **D** St E **P** *Ld Chan 1st turn, Sir A H S Adair Bt 2nd turn, Bp 3rd turn, Duke of Norf 4th turn* **I** T V COOK.
RUNCORN (All SS), *Chesh.* V. **D** Ches 3 **P** *D and C of Ch Ch Ox* **I** D G THOMAS.
(H Trin), V. **D** Ches **P** *Bp* **I** T A MCCARTHY.
(St Andr Grange), V. **D** Ches **P** *Bp* **I** W D F VANSTONE.
(St Jo Evang Weston), V. **D** Ches 3 **P** *Bp* **I** K J PRITCHARD.
(St Mich AA), V. **D** Ches 3 **P** *Bp* **I** A GIBSON.
RUNCTON, NORTH (All SS) w Hardwick and Setchey, *Norf.* R. **D** Nor 25 **P** *W N Gurney Esq* **I** F HOUGHTBY.
RUNCTON, SOUTH (St Andr) w Holme and Wallington, *Norf.* R. **D** Ely 17 **P** *Trustees of H E Peel Esq* **I** I R LILLEY *c-in-c.*
RUNHALL, *Norf.*. **D** Nor 12 *See* Coston.
RUNHAM (St Pet) and (St Paul), *Norf.* V. **D** Nor *See* Filby.
RUNNINGTON (St Pet and St Paul), *Somt.* R. **D** B & W 22 *See* Langford Budville.
RUNTON (H Trin), *Norf.*. **D** Nor 5 *See* Aylmerton.
RUNWELL (St Mary), *Essex.* R. **D** Chelmsf *See* Wickford.
RUSCOMBE (St Jas Gt) w Twyford (St Mary Virg), *Berks.* V. **D** Ox 16 **P** *Bp* **I** A J FEARN.
RUSHALL (St Mich), *W Midl.* V. **D** Lich 9 **P** *Sir C Buchanan Bt* **I** T B SIMISTER, R M HAINES *c.*
RUSHALL, *Norf.*. **D** Nor 17 *See* Needham.
RUSHALL (St Matt), *Wilts.* R. **D** Sarum 18 *See* Upavon.
RUSHBROOKE, *Suff.* R. **D** St E 10 **P** *Marq of Bris* **I** R M RIMMER *p-in-c.*
RUSHBURY (St Pet), *Salop.* R. **D** Heref 11 **P** *Bp of Birm* **I** M BROMFIELD.
RUSHDEN (St Mary and St Pet) w Newton Bromswold (St Pet), *Northants.* R. **D** Pet 9 **P** *CPAS* **I** A M S WILSON, J E BATEMAN *c,* G A GRUBB *c,* G O STONE *c.*
RUSHDEN, *Herts.* V. **D** St Alb 5 *See* Sandon.
RUSHFORD (St John), *Norf.*. **D** Nor 18 *See* Brettenham.
RUSHMERE, *Suff.* **D** Nor 15 *See* Carlton-Colville.
RUSHMERE (St Andr), *Suff.* V. **D** St E 4 **P** *Marchioness of Bris* **I** M J TURNER.
RUSHOCK, *Worcs.*. **D** Worc *See* Elmbridge.
RUSHOLME (H Trin), *Gtr Man.* R. **D** Man 5 **P** *CPAS* **I** R J SALISBURY, E E LOBB *c,* G A POLLITT *c.*
RUSHTON (All SS) and Pipewell w Glendon and Thorpe Malsor, *Northants.* R. **D** Pet 8 **P** *Mert and Keble Colls Ox* **I** A J GARDINER.
RUSHTON SPENCER (St Laur), *Staffs.* V. **D** Lich 16 **P** *V of Leek* **I** C B WILLIAMS *c-in-c.*
RUSKIN PARK (St Sav, Herne Hill Road w St Matt), *Surrey.* V. **D** S'wark 3 **P** *Trustees of Lon Coll of Div* **I** (Vacant).
RUSKINGTON (All SS), *Lincs.* R. **D** Linc 22 **P** *Dioc Bd of Patr* **I** S JACKSON.
RUSLAND (St Paul), *Cumb.* V. **D** Carl 14 *See* Satterthwait.
RUSPER (St Mary Magd), *W Sussex.* R. **D** Chich 4 **P** *Bp* **I** M O DODD *p-in-c.*
RUSTHALL (St Paul), *Kent.* V. **D** Roch 10 **P** *R of Speldhurst* **I** N J MANTLE, C SYMES *hon c,* R E WHYTE *hon c.*
RUSTINGTON (St Pet and St Paul), *W Sussex.* V. **D** Chich 1 **P** *Bp* **I** F J S EVANS, W G S SNOW *hon c.*
RUSTON, EAST, *Norf.*. **D** Nor *See* Stalham.
RUSTON PARVA (St Nich), *Humb.* V. **D** York 12 *See* Lowthorpe.
RUSTON SCO or SOUTH RUSTON, *Norf.*. **D** Nor 8 *See* Tunstead.
RUSWARP (St Bart), *N Yorks.*. **D** York 27 *See* Aislaby.
RUYTON-XI-TOWNS (St Jo Bapt), *Salop.* V. **D** Lich 22 **P** *Bp* **I** R D BRADBURY.
RYARSH (St Martin w birling (All SS), *Kent.* V. **D** Roch 6 **P** *Bp and Miss I N King* **I** H J M BURY.
RYBURGH, GREAT (St Andr) w Little Ryburgh, Gateley, and Testerton (St Remigius), *Norf.* R. **D** Nor 21 **P** *M Tatham Esq 2 turns, Ch Coll Cam 1 turn* **I** F A HILL.
RYDAL (St Mary), *Cumb.* V. **D** Carl 14 **P** *Dioc Bd of Patr* **I** D DIXON *p-in-c.*
RYDE (All SS), *Isle of Wight.* V. **D** Portsm 6 **P** *Bp* **I** R S HAINES *hon c.*
(H Trin), V. **D** Portsm 6 **P** *Bp* **I** W T BANCE *p-in-c.*
(St Helen). **D** Portsm 6 *See* St Helens.
(St Jas), I. **D** Portsm 6 **P** *Ch S Trust* **I** D E A MARROW *min.*
(St John, Oakfield), V. **D** Portsm 6 **P** *V of St Helens, IW* **I** L FOX.
RYE, (Rye Harbour, Playden, Iden, Camber and East Guldeford), *E Sussex.* R. **D** Chich **P** *Bp, Duke of Devonshire and Lt-Commdr E C S Macpherson R N* alt **I** W D MAUNDRELL, S J G SEAMER *team v,* J BANNISTER *c.*
RYE PARK (St Cuthb), *Herts.* V. **D** St Alb 6 **P** *Dioc Bd of Patr* **I** B DAWSON.
RYHALL (St Jo Evang) w Essendine (St Mary Virg), *Rutld.* V. **D** Pet 13 **P** *Marq of Ex* **I** F C HODGKINSON.
RYHILL (St Jas), *W Yorks.* V. **D** Wakef 13 **P** *Bp* **I** (Vacant).
RYHOPE (St Paul), *T & W.* V. **D** Dur 8 **P** *Bp* **I** G W FLETCHER, P GRUNDY *c.*
RYLSTONE (St Pet), *N Yorks.* R. **D** Bradf 10 **P** *CPAS* **I** M B SLAUGHTER *p-in-c.*
RYME INTRINSECA (St Hippolytus), *Dorset.* R. **D** Sarum 7 *See* Yetminster.
RYSTON (St Mich) w Roxham, *Norf.* V. **D** Ely 17 **P** *D and C of Nor* **I** L F B CUMINGS.
RYTHER (All SS), *N Yorks.* R. **D** York 8 **P** *Ld Chan* **I** R E MESSER *p-in-c.*
RYTON (Dedic unknown), *Salop.* R. **D** Lich 25 **P** *Or Coll Ox and Ld Chan (alt)* **I** J R P BAGGALEY.
RYTON-ON-DUNSMORE (St Leon) w Bubbenhall (St Giles), *Warws.* V. **D** Cov 6 **P** *D and C of Cov 2 turns, Bp 1 turn* **I** J T SYKES.
RYTON-ON-TYNE (H Cross), *T & W.*. **D** Dur 4a **P** *Bp* **I** S TOWARD.

SABDEN (St Nich), *Lancs.*. **D** Blackb 7 *See* Heyhouses.
SACOMBE (St Cath), *Herts.* R. **D** St Alb *See* Munden, Little.
SACRISTON (St Pet), *Durham.* V. **D** Dur 2 **P** *Crown* **I** D H LAWES.
SADBERGE (St Andr), *Durham.* R. **D** Dur **P** *Bp* **I** C WYATT.
SADDINGTON (St Helen), *Leics.* R. **D** Leic 6 *See* Smeeton-Westerby.
SADDLEWORTH (St Chad), *Gtr Man.* V. **D** Man 15 **P** *Bp* **I** J SYKES.
SAFFRON HILL. **D** Lon *See* Holborn.
SAFFRON WALDEN (St Mary Virg) w Wendens Ambo (St Mary Virg) and Littlebury, *Essex.* R. **D** Chelmsf 27 **P** *Patr Bd* **I** A R H RODWELL, I G COOMBER *team v,* R G BUTLER *c,* R H ROE *c,* R A STAVELEY-WADHAM *c.*
SAHAM-TONEY (St Geo), *Norf.* R. **D** Nor *See* Ashill.
ST ADWENA, *Cornw.*. **D** Truro 12 *See* Lanteglos.
ST AGNES (St Agnes), *Cornw.* V. **D** Truro 6 **P** *D and C of Truro* **I** A M WILLIAMSON.
ST ALBANS (Abbey and Cathl Ch of St Alb), *Herts.* R. **D** St Alb 11 **P** *Bp* **I** (Vacant).
(Ch Ch), V. **D** St Alb 11 **P** *Trustees* **I** B M REES.
(H Trin, Frogmore), V. **D** St Alb 1 **P** *CPAS* **I** (Vacant).
(St Mary, Marshalswick), V. **D** St Alb 11 **P** *Bp* **I** D E C WRIGHT.
(St Mich), V. **D** St Alb 11 **P** *Earl of Verulam* **I** HON H G DICKINSON.
(St Paul), V. **D** St Alb 11 **P** *V of St Pet St Alb* **I** A H MEDFORTH, A J H DAILEY *c,* R F DONALD *c.*
(St Pet), V. **D** St Alb 11 **P** *Crown* **I** R W GILL, F H WELCH *c.*

(St Sav), V. **D** St Alb 11 **P** *Bp* **I** D D HART.
(St Steph), V. **D** St Alb 11 **P** *Lt-Col A B Waddell Dudley* **I** B H MUNRO, B G RODFORD *hon c.*
St Aldhelm Group Ministry **D** Sarum 9 *See* Corfe Castle, Steeple w Tyneham, Church Knowle and Kimmeridge, *See* Kingston; Worth Matravers; Langton Matravers.
ST ALLEN (St Alleyne), *Cornw.*. **D** Truro 6 **P** *Bp* **I** (Vacant).
ST ANNE-IN-THE-GROVE, *W Yorks.* V. **D** Wakef 1 *See* Southowram.
ST ANNES-ON-THE-SEA (St Anne), *Lancs.* V. **D** Blackb 9 **P** *H T de Vere Clifton Esq* **I** D WELCH.
(St Thos), V. **D** Blackb 9 **P** *H T de Vere Clifton Esq* **I** O G VIGEON.
(St Marg of Antioch), V. **D** Blackb 9 **P** *H T de Vere Clifton Esq* **I** H W VERITY.
ST ANNE'S PARK (St Anne), V. **D** Bris 1 *See* Brislington.
ST ANTHONY-IN-MENEAGE, *Cornw.* V. **D** Truro 4 *See* Manaccan.
ST ANTHONY-IN-ROSELAND, *Cornw.*. **D** Truro *See* St Gerrans.
ST AUDRIES (St Audrie), *Somt.*. **D** B & W 23 *See* Quantockshead, West.
ST AUSTELL (H Trin) w Porthpean and Pentewan, *Cornw.* V. **D** Truro 1 **P** *Crown* **I** J VIPOND, H R RICH *c,* A SYKES *hon c.*
ST BEES (St Mary and St Bega), *Cumb.* V. **D** Carl 12 **P** *Trustees* **I** P R BRYAN.
ST BLAZEY (St Blaise), *Cornw.* V. **D** Truro 1 **P** *Bp* **I** P HASTROP.
ST BREOCKE (St Breock), *Cornw.* R. **D** Truro 7 **P** *Bp and Dioc Bd of Patr* **I** H R WATSON, A J WRIGHT *c.*
ST BREWARD (Dedic unknown), *Cornw.*. **D** Truro 8 *See* Blisland.
ST BRIAVELS (St Mary Virg) w Hewelsfield (St Mary Magd), *Glos.* V. **D** Glouc 7 **P** *D and C of Heref* **I** (Vacant).
ST BUDEAUX, *Devon.* V. **D** Ex 23 *See* Devonport.
ST BUDOCK (St Budocus), *Cornw.* V. **D** Truro 3 **P** *Bp* **I** J T RHAM.
ST BURYAN w St Levan (St Levan) and Sennen (St Sennen), *Cornw.* R. **D** Truro 5 **P** *Duchy of Cornw* **I** M A FRIGGENS, M J ADAMS *c.*
ST CLEER, *Cornw.* V. **D** Truro 13 **P** *Ld Chan* **I** G P POWELL.
ST CLEMENT, *Cornw.* V. **D** Truro *See* Truro.
ST CLEMENT DANES, R. **D** Lon 19 *See* Westminster.
ST CLETHER, *Cornw.*. **D** Truro *See* Laneast.
ST COLAN, *Cornw.* V. **D** Truro 7 *See* St Columb Minor.
ST COLUMB MAJOR (St Columba) w St Wenn *Cornw.* R. **D** Truro 7 **P** *Bp* **I** A G COOKE.
ST COLUMB MINOR (St Columba) w Colan *Cornw.* V. **D** Truro 7 **P** *Bp* **I** J F EDWARDS, D G STAFFORD *c.*
ST CONSTANTINE (St Constantine K of Cornwall), *Cornw.* V. **D** Truro 4 **P** *D and C of Truro* **I** E H ATKINSON.
ST CORNELLY (St Cornelius), *Cornw.*. **D** Truro *See* Probus.
ST CRANTOC (St Carantoc), *Cornw.* V. **D** Truro 7 **P** *S for Maint of Faith* **I** D S J CHADWICK *p-in-c.*
ST CREED (St Andr), *Cornw.* R. **D** Truro 6 *See* Creed.
ST CUBERT, *Cornw.* V. **D** Truro 7 **P** *Dioc Bd of Patr* **I** P E TIDMARSH.
ST CUBY, *Cornw.*. **D** Truro *See* Tregony.
ST CURY w St Gunwalloe, *Cornw.* V. **D** Truro 4 **P** *J P Rogers Esq* **I** P R LONG *p-in-c.*
ST DAY (H Trin), *Cornw.* V. **D** Truro 2 **P** *D and C of Truro* **I** T M J VAN CARRAPIETT *c-in-c.*
ST DECUMAN'S (St Decuman), *Somt.* V. **D** B & W 18 **P** *Bp* **I** R M BARNETT.
ST DENNIS (St Denys), *Cornw.* R. **D** Truro 1 **P** *Bp* **I** C T COOK.
ST DEVEREUX (St David) w Wormbridge (St Pet), *Herefs.* R. **D** Heref 1 **P** *G M D Clive Esq* **I** M M L EDGE *p-in-c.*
ST DOMINIC (St Dominica), *Cornw.* R. **D** Truro 9 **P** *Duchy of Cornwall and S for Maint of Faith* alt **I** B F THOMPSON *p-in-c.*
ST ELWYN (St Elwyn), *Cornw.* V. **D** Truro 5 **P** *D and C of Truro* **I** F R HARWOOD.
ST ENDELLION (St Endellienta), *Cornw.* R. **D** Truro 12 **P** *Bp* **I** (Vacant).
ST ENODER (St Enoder), *Cornw.* R. **D** Truro 7 **P** *Bp* **I** J C PARSONS *p-in-c,* M WILLS *c.*
ST ENODOC (St Enodoc), *Cornw.*. **D** Truro 12 *See* St Minver.
ST ERME (St Hermes), *Cornw.* R. **D** Truro 6 **P** *D and C of Truro* **I** (Vacant).
ST ERNY, *Cornw.*. **D** Truro 9 *See* Landrak.
ST ERTH, *Cornw.* V. **D** Truro 5 **P** *D and C of Truro* **I** A T NEAL *p-in-c.*
ST ERVAN w St Eval, *Cornw.* R. **D** Truro 7 *See* St Mawgan-in-Pydar.
ST EWE (All SS), *Cornw.* R. **D** Truro 1 **P** *Exors of Rear-Adm Sir C J Graves Sawle Bt and Miss G Carlyon* **I** (Vacant).
ST FEOCK (St Feock), *Cornw.* V. **D** Truro 6 **P** *Bp* **I** P C ROSE.
ST GENNYS (St Genesius), *Cornw.* V. **D** Truro 10 **P** *Earl of St Germans* **I** (Vacant).
ST GEORGE (St George), *Salop.* V. **D** Lich 27 **P** *Bp* **I** W E MAIDEN.
ST GEORGE-IN-THE-EAST. **D** Lon 4 *See* Whitechapel.
ST GEORGE MARTYR, Queen Square. **D** Lon 20 *See* Holborn.
ST GEORGE, Hanover Square.. **D** Lon 15 *See* Westminster.
ST GERMANS (St Germanus), *Cornw.* V. **D** Truro 9 **P** *D and C of Windsor* **I** R E B MAYNARD.
ST GERMOE (St Germoe), *Cornw.*. **D** Truro 4 *See* Breage.
ST GERRANS w St Anthony-in-Roseland, *Cornw.* R. **D** Truro 6 **P** *Bp* **I** H C S FOWLER.
ST GILES-IN-THE-FIELDS, *Lon.* R. **D** Lon 15 **P** *bp* **I** G C TAYLOR, I M G MACKENZIE *c.*
(H Trin Kingsway w St Jo Evang Drury Lane), V. **D** Lon 15 **P** *Bp* **I** F J ARROWSMITH *p-in-c.* *See also* BLOOMSBURY.
ST GILES-IN-THE-HEATH (St Giles), *Devon.*. **D** Truro 11 *See* Werrington.
ST GILES-IN-THE-WOOD (St Giles-in-the-Wood), *Devon.* V. **D** Ex 20 *See* Beaford.
ST GLUVIAS w Ponsanooth and Penryn Borough, *Cornw.* V. **D** Truro 3 **P** *bp* **I** D H NICHOLS.
ST GORAN (St Goranus) w Caerhays (St Mich AA), *Cornw.* V. **D** Truro 1 **P** *Bp and G G Fortescue Esq (alt)* **I** F J R OTTO.
ST GRADE (St Grade), *Cornw.* R. **D** Truro 4 *See* St Ruan.
ST GULVAL (St Gulval), *Cornw.* V. **D** Truro 5 **P** *Ld Chan* **I** F W WARNES.
ST GUNWALLOE, *Cornw.*. **D** Truro 4 *See* St Cury.
ST GWENNAP (St Weneppa) w Carharrack, *Cornw.* V. **D** Truro *See* St Stythians.
ST GWINEAR (St Gwinear), *Cornw.*. **D** Truro 5 *See* Phillack.
ST GWITHIAN (St Gothian), *Cornw.*. **D** Truro 5 *See* Phillack.
ST HELENS (St Helen), *Isle of Wight.* V. **D** Portsm 6 **P** *Bp* **I** D M LOW.
ST HELENS (St Helen), *Mer.* V. **D** Liv 10 **P** *Trustees* **I** K W COATES, R BRITTON *c.*
(St Mark, Cowley Hill), V. **D** Liv 10 **P** *Trustees* **I** A P JELBART.
(H Trin). **D** Liv 10 *See* Parr Mount.
(St Thos), V. **D** Liv 10 *See* Eccleston.
(St Matt). **D** Liv 10 *See* Eccleston.
ST HELIER (St Pet), *Surrey.* V. **D** S'wark 8 **P** *Bp* **I** G P NAIRN-BRIGGS, C J BOSWELL *c,* A G BROWN *c,* P A BURROWS *c.*
ST HILARY (St Hilary of Poitiers) w Perranuthnoe, *Cornw.* V. **D** Truro **P** *D and C of Truro, Bp and R Parker Esq* **I** J D CURSON *p-in-c.*
ST ILLOGAN (St Illogan) w Trevenson and Portreath, *Cornw.* R. **D** Truro 2 *See* Illogan.
ST IPPOLYTS (St Ippolyts), *Herts.* V. **D** St Alb 9 **P** *Bp* **I** K ALLISON *p-in-c.*
ST ISSEY and Little Petherick or Petrick Minor, *Cornw*, V. **D** Truro **P** *Keble Coll Ox* **I** B W KINSMEN.
ST IVE (St Ivo w St Pensilva) w Quethiock (St Hugh), *Cornw.* R. **D** Truro 13 **P** *Bp and Crown* **I** G PERRY.
ST IVES (All SS), *Cambs.* V. **D** Ely 12 **P** *Guild of All S* **I** R O JENNINGS.
ST IVES (St Ia the Virg of Porthia), *Cornw.* V. **D** Truro 5 **P** *V of Lelant* **I** D C FREEMAN.
ST IVES, *Hants.*. **D** Win 8 *See* Ringwood.
ST JOHN w Millbrook, *Cornw.* V. **D** Truro **P** *Sir J G Carew Pole Bt and Bp.* **I** D R TILLEY.
ST JOHN-IN-THE-VALE w Wythburn, *Cumb.* V. **D** Carl 10 **P** *Bp and V of Crosthwaite* alt **I** C G DARRALL.
ST JOHN-IN-THE-WILDERNESS, *W Yorks.*. **D** Wakef *See* Cragg Vale.
ST JOHN LEE (St John of Beverley), *Northumb.* R. **D** Newc T 4 **P** *Visc Allendale* **I** L F T EDDERSHAW.
ST JOHN, Little Ouse, *Cambs.* V. **D** Ely 16 *See* Ouse, Little (St John).

ST JOHN'S CHAPEL IN WEARDALE (St Jo Bapt), *Durham*. V. **D** Dur 13 **P** *Bp* **I** C SMITH.
ST JOHN'S WOOD (St Mark Hamilton Terrace), *Lon*. V. **D** Lon 25 **P** *Crown* **I** D A R AIRD, S J A FARRER *c*.
(St John's Wood Church, formerly St John's Wood Chapel), V. **D** Lon 25 **P** *Bp* **I** T J RAPHAEL, G S BRADLEY *c*.
ST JULIOT (St Juliot), *Cornw*. R. **D** Truro **I** (Vacant).
ST JUST-IN-PENWITH (St Just), *Cornw*. V. **D** Truro 5 **P** *Ld Chan* **I** D J M L JASPER.
ST JUST-IN-ROSELAND (St Just) w St Mawes, *Cornw*. R. **D** Truro 6 **P** *A M J Galsworthy Esq* **I** P J DURNFORD P-IN-C OF PHILLEIGH.
ST KEA (All H), *Cornw*. V. **D** Truro 6 **P** *V of St Clem Truro* **I** R J REDRUP.
ST KEVERNE, *Cornw*. V. **D** Truro 4 **P** *CPAS* **I** A F MATTHEW.
ST KEW (St Jas Gt), *Cornw*. V. **D** Truro 12 **P** *Exors of Rev H D Jackson* **I** P FOOT *p-in-c*.
ST KEYNE (St Kayna), *Cornw*.. **D** Truro *See* Liskeard.
ST LADOCK (St Ladoca), *Cornw*.. **D** Truro *See* Ladock, St.
ST LAURENCE-IN-THANET (St Laur) w Manston (St Cath), *Kent*. V. **D** Cant 9 **P** *Abp* **I** P G F NORWOOD *p-in-c*, A C CHRISTIAN *c*, R JONES *c*.
ST LAWRENCE, *Essex*. R. **D** Chelmsf 13 **P** *Bp* **I** J A P BOOTH.
ST LAWRENCE (St Lawr), *Isle of Wight*. R. **D** Portsm 6 **P** *Bp* **I** A TEDMAN *p-in-c*, D N STEVENSON *c*.
ST LEONARDS (St Leon), *Bucks*. V. **D** Ox 30 **P** *Trustees* **I** A PAICE *p-in-c*.
ST LEONARDS-ON-SEA (St Leon), *E Sussex*. R. **D** Chich 21 **P** *Hyndman Trustees* **I** W B G MATHER *c*, J D MORRIS *hon c*.
(Ch Ch and St Mary Magd), R. **D** Chich 21 **P** *Bp and Trustees* **I** D G CARTER, D M JARMY *c*.
(St Matt Silverhill), R. **D** Chich 21 **P** *Simeon Trustees* **I** S P GAMESTER.
(St Pet w St Paul), V. **D** Chich 21 **P** *Bp* **I** (Vacant).
UPPER (St Jo Evang), R. **D** Chich 21 **P** *Trustees* **I** K W CLINCH.
WEST (St Ethelburga), V. **D** Chich 21 **P** *Hyndman Trustees* **I** A I SMYTH.
ST LEVAN (St Levan), *Cornw*. R. **D** Truro 5 *See* St Buryan.
ST LUDGVAN, *Cornw*. R. **D** Truro 5 **P** *Ld St Levan* **I** A PARSONS *p-in-c*.
ST LUKE, OLD STREET w St Mary, Charterhouse and St Paul, Clerkenwell, *Lon*. R. **D** Lon 1 *See* St Giles, Cripplegate.
ST MABE (St Laudus), *Cornw*. V. **D** Truro 3 **P** *Bp* **I** C J K FIRTH.
ST MABYN, *Cornw*. R. **D** Truro 8 **P** *Visc Falmouth* **I** (Vacant).
ST MADRON (St Maddern) w Morvah (St Briget of Sweden), *Cornw*. V. **D** Truro 5 **P** *Bp* **I** R G GILBERT *p-in-c*.
ST MARGARET'S-ON-THAMES (All SS), *Lon*. V. **D** Lon 10 **P** *Bp* **I** (Vacant).
ST MARGARET'S (St Marg) w Michaelchurch Escley (St Mich AA) and Newton (St Jo Bapt), *Herefs*. V. **D** Heref 1 *See* Clodock.
ST MARGARET-AT-CLIFFE (St Marg) w West Cliffe (St Pet) and East Langdon w West Langdon, *Kent*. V. **D** Cant 5 **P** *Abp* **I** S T EASTER.
ST MARK, HILGAY, *Norf*.. **D** Ely 17 *See* Hilgay.
ST MARTIN-BY-LOOE (St Martin of Tours), *Cornw*. R. **D** Truro 13 **P** *Rev W M M Picken* **I** M B E FORREST.
ST MARTIN-IN-MENEAGE (St Martin), *Cornw*.. **D** Truro 4 *See* St Mawgan.
ST MARTIN-IN-THE-FIELDS **D** Lon *See* Westminster.
ST MARTIN (St Martin), *Salop*. V. **D** Lich 24 **P** *Ld Trevor* **I** E OSMAN.
ST MARY BOURNE (St Pet) w Woodcott (St Jas), *Hants*. V. **D** Win 5 **P** *Bp* **I** S W PAKENHAM.
ST MARYCHURCH (St Mary), *Devon*. V. **D** Ex 10 **P** *D and C of Ex* **I** J H MITCHELL, R W BECK *c*, R GREGORY *hon c*, F E SHAW *hon c*.
ST MARY IN THE MARSH, *Kent*. R. **D** Cant 13 *See* Romney, New.
ST MARYLEBONE w (H Trin), *Lon*. R. **D** Lon 25 **P** *Crown* **I** C K H COOKE, R M SALENIUS *c*.
(Ch Ch and St Paul, Rossmore Road w St Mark, Old Marylebone Road and St Luke), R. **D** Lon 25 **P** *Crown* **I** W P LANG, G W CRAIG *c*.
(All S, Langham Place w St Pet, Vere Str and St Jo Evang, Charlotte Str), R. **D** Lon 25 **P** *Crown* **I** A C J CORNES *c*, R W SIMPSON *c*.
(All SS, Margaret Street), V. **D** Lon 25 **P** *Bp* **I** C J SOMERS-EDGAR *c*.
(The Annunc, Bryanston Street), V. **D** Lon 25 **P** *Bp* **I** M W BURGESS, G BRISCOE *c*.
(St Cypr, Clarence Gate), V. **D** Lon 25 **P** *Bp* **I** P R HARDING *p-in-c*.
(St Mary, Bryanston Square), R. **D** Lon 25 **P** *Crown* **I** V L T HARVEY, R D BLAKELEY *c*.
(St Mark, Old Marylebone Road w St Luke, Nutford Place), V. **D** Lon 25 *See* Ch Ch St Marylebone.
(St Paul, Portman Square), V. **D** Lon 25 **P** *CPS* **I** G H CASSIDY, R K TOWNLEY *c*.
See also ST JOHN'S WOOD.
ST MARY-LE-STRAND, R. **D** Lon 15 *See* Westminster.
ST MAWES, *Cornw*.. **D** Truro *See* St Just-in-Roseland.
ST MAWGAN (St Mawgan) w St Martin-in-Meneage (St Martin), *Cornw*. R. **D** Truro 4 **P** *Bp* **I** P R LONG *p-in-c*.
ST MAWGAN (St Mawgan and St Nich) w St Ervan and St Eval, *Cornw*. R. **D** Truro 7 **P** *D & C and Exors of Lt Col E N Willyams (alt)* **I** (Vacant).
ST MELLION (St Melanus) w Pillaton (St Odulph), *Cornw*. R. **D** Truro 9 **P** *Maj J T Coryton and D and C of Truro Cathl* alt **I** G R WATTS.
ST MERRYN (St Merryn), *Cornw*. V. **D** Truro 7 **P** *Bp* **I** J M G BOULTBEE.
ST MEVAGISSEY, *Cornw*.. **D** Truro *See* Mevagissey, St.
ST MEWAN (St Mewan), *Cornw*. R. **D** Truro 1 **P** *Lords of the Manor of Trewoon* **I** D W W BALDWIN *p-in-c*.
ST MICHAEL PENKEVIL, *Cornw*. R. **D** Truro 6 **P** *Visc Falmouth* **I** A R W GRAY.
ST MICHAEL-AT-BOWES. **D** Lon 20 *See* Bowes Park.
ST MICHAEL-CAERHAY, *Cornw*.. **D** Truro *See* Caerhays.
ST MICHAELCHURCH, *Somt*. V. **D** B & W 17 *See* Newton, North.
ST MICHAEL'S-ON-WYRE (St Mich), *Lancs*. V. **D** Blackb 10 **P** *R P Hornby Esq* **I** L DAVIES.
ST MINVER (St Menefrida) and St Michael (St Mich) w St Enodoc (St Enodoc), *Cornw*. R. **D** Truro 12 **P** *Dioc Bd of Patr* **I** A L GENT, K W BANNISTER *hon c*.
ST MYLOR (St Mylor), *Cornw*.. **D** Truro 3 *See* Mylor, St.
ST NECTAN, *Cornw*.. **D** Truro 8 *See* St Winnow.
ST NEOT (St Neot), *Cornw*. V. **D** Truro 13 **P** *S H Grylls Esq* **I** E G ALLSOPP.
ST NEOTS (St Mary), *Cambs*. V. **D** Ely 14 **P** *J C Rowley Esq* **I** B CURRY, T R HENTHORNE *hon c*.
ST NEWLYN, EAST (St Newlina), *Cornw*.. **D** Truro 7 *See* Newlyn, East St.
ST NICHOLAS, *Devon*.. **D** Ex 10 *See* Shaldon.
ST NICHOLAS-AT-WADE (St Nich) w Sarre and Chislet w Hoath, *Kent*. V. **D** Cant 4 **P** *Abp* **I** R D PLANT *c*.
ST OSWALD-IN-LEE w Bingfield (St Mary) and Wall, *Northumb*. V. **D** Newc T **P** *Bp* **I** G E SINFIELD *p-in-c*.
ST OSWALD-IN-USMERE (St Osw), *Worcs*. V. **D** Worc 12 *See* Broadwaters.
ST OSYTH (St Pet w St Paul and St Osyth) *Essex*. V. **D** Chelmsf 28 **P** *Bp* **I** P H BEARD.
ST PADARN, WELSH CHURCH. **D** Lon 6 *See* Islington.
ST PANCRAS w St Jas and Ch Ch, *Lon*. V. **D** Lon 20 **P** *D and C of St Paul's* **I** D J L BEAN, J FRANCIS *c*.
(All H, Gospel Oak),. **D** Lon 19 *See* Hampstead, St Steph.
(Ch Ch, Albany Road), V. **D** Lon 20 **P** *Bp* **I** (Vacant).
(H Cross, Cromer Street w St Jude and St Pet), V. **D** Lon 20 **P** *Bp* **I** (Vacant).
(H Trin, Clarence Way w St Barn, Kentish Town), V. **D** Lon 20 **P** *D and C of St Paul's* **I** I M SCOTT.
(St Anne, Brookfield), V. **D** Lon 20 **P** *Bp* **I** J D BECKWITH.
(St Benet and All SS, Lupton Street, Kentish Town), V. **D** Lon 20 **P** *D and C of St Paul's* **I** (Vacant).
(St Luke, Oseney Crescent w St Paul, Camden Square), V. **D** Lon 20 **P** *Crown* **I** P N CASSIDY.
(St Mark, Prince Albert Road), V. **D** Lon 19 **P** *D and C of St Paul's* **I** T P N D JONES.
(St Martin w S Andr, Vicars Road, Kentish Town), *Lon*. V. **D** Lon 20 **P** *Allcroft Trustees* **I** D A COBB *p-in-c*.
(St Mary, Brookfield), V. **D** Lon 20 **P** *Bp* **I** H S M BARKER.
(St Mary Virg, Somers Town), V. **D** Lon 20 **P** *D and C of St Paul's* **I** P DYSON, J TETLOW *c*.
(St Mary Magd, Munster Sq), V. **D** Lon 20 **P** *Bp* **I** G M HEAL, J W PARKER *hon c*.
(St Mich w All SS and St Thos, Camden Road), V. **D** Lon 20 **P** *V of St Pancras* **I** A R B PAGE.
(St Silas Mart, Prince of Wales Road, Kentish Town), V. **D** Lon 20 **P** *Bp* **I** D A COBB.
KENTISH TOWN (no Dedic), V. **D** Lon 20 **P** *V of St Pancras* **I** W G KNAPPER.
OLD ST PANCRAS, V. **D** Lon 20 **P** *D and C of St Paul's* **I** P DYSON *p-in-c*.

SAMPFORD COURTENAY w Honeychurch (St Mary), *Devon*. R. **D** Ex 12 **P** *K Coll Cam 1st and 3rd turns, Keble Coll 2nd turn, Dioc Bd of Patr 4th turn* **I** D J T BICKERTON.
SAMPFORD-PEVERELL (St Jo Bapt) w Uplowman, Holcombe Rogus w Hockworthy and Burlescombe, *Devon*. R. **D** Ex 4 **P** *Patr Bd* **I** A B NELSON, I F MARSH *team v.*
SAMPFORD-SPINEY (St Mary) w Horrabridge (St Jo Bapt), *Devon*. R. **D** Ex 22 **P** *D and C of Windsor* **I** T FREEMAN.
SANCREED (St Crida), *Cornw*. V. **D** Truro 5 **P** *D and C of Truro* **I** (Vacant).
SANCTON (All SS), *Humb*. V. **D** York 10 **P** *Abp* **I** J WALKER.
SANDAL (St Cath Belle Vue), *W Yorks*. V. **D** Wakef 13 **P** *V of Sandal* **I** R ADAIR.
SANDAL MAGNA (St Helen) w Newmillerdam, *W Yorks*. V. **D** Wakef 13 **P** *Peache Trustees* **I** R D STRAPPS.
SANDBACH (St Mary), *Chesh*. V. **D** Ches 11 **P** *Dioc Bd of Patr* **I** J B RIGBY, J R D HUGHES *c.*
SANDBACH HEATH (St Jo Evang), V. **D** Ches 11 **P** *V of Sandbach* **I** G J A MYCOCK.
SANDERSTEAD (All SS, St Edmund Riddlesdown and St Antony, Hamsey Green), *Surrey*. R. **D** S'wark 9 **P** *Dioc Bd of Patr* **I** C J F SCOTT, W C HEATLEY *team v,* L A D WATSON *team v,* G F MCPHATE *c,* K V G SMITH *c.*
(St Mary), V. **D** S'wark 9 **P** *Bp* **I** V I JULIAN.
SANDFORD (All SS). **D** B & W 3 *See* Winscombe.
SANDFORD (St Swith) w Upton Hellions (St Mary), *Devon*. R. **D** Ex 2 **P** *Govs of Crediton Ch* **I** C G EDWARDS *p-in-c.*
SANDFORD, DRY *Oxon*.. **D** Ox *See* Besselsleigh.
SANDFORD-ON-THAMES (St Andr), *Oxon*. V. **D** Ox 4 **P** *Dioc Bd of Patr* **I** D J FEHRENBACH.
SANDFORD ORCAS (St Nich), *Dorset*. R. **D** Sarum 7 *See* Compton, Over.
SANDFORD ST MARTIN (St Martin), *Oxon*.. **D** Ox *See* Westcote Barton.
SANDGATE (St Paul), *Kent*. V. **D** Cant 6 **P** *V of Folkestone* **I** E D SCHOFIELD.
SANDHURST (St Nich) w Newenden, *Kent*. R. **D** Cant 11 **P** *Abp* **I** J H G W GREEN.
SANDHURST (St Lawr), *Glos*. V. **D** Glouc 2 **P** *Bp* **I** (Vacant).
SANDHURST (St Mich AA), *Berks*. R. **D** Ox 11a **P** *Bp* **I** R E J PACKER, B L CURNEW *c.*
SANDHUTTON (St Mary) w Gate and Upper Helmsley, and Bossall w Buttercrambe *N Yorks*. V. **D** York 4 **P** *Abp 2 turns, D and C of Dur 1 turn* **I** B A BROWNBRIDGE.
(St Leon), *N Yorks*.. **D** York 26 *See* Thirsk.
SANDIACRE (St Giles), *Derbys*. R. **D** Derby 13 **P** *Ld Chan* **I** (Vacant).
SANDIWAY (St Jo Evang), *Chesh*. V. **D** Ches 6 **P** *Bp* **I** J V GRIFFITH.
SANDON (St Andr), *Essex*. R. **D** Chelmsf 12 **P** *Qu Coll Cam* **I** E H BEAVAN.
SANDON Staffs. V **D** Lich **P** *Earl of Harrowby* **I** (Vacant).
SANDON (All SS), Wallington (St Mary) and Rushden w Clothall (St Mary Virg), *Herts*. V. **D** St Alb 5 **P** *Bp 2 turns, Duchy of Lanc 1 turn, Marq of Salisbury 1 turn* **I** J A YATES.
SANDOWN (Ch Ch), *Isle of Wight*. V. **D** Portsm 6 **P** *CPS* **I** C R SLOUGH.
(St Jo Evang), V. **D** Portsm 6 **P** *Bp* **I** C R SLOUGH, W R LING *hon c.*
SANDRIDGE (St Leon), *Herts*. V. **D** St Alb 14 **P** *Earl Spencer* **I** G T H JARVIS.
SANDRINGHAM (St Mary Magd) w West Newton (St Pet and St Paul) and Appleton, *Norf*. R (*in Sandringham Group - See also Castle Rising, Flitcham, Hillington, Wolferton*).. **D** Nor 23 **P** *HM the Queen* **I** J G M W MURPHY.
SANDWICH (St Clem w St Mary the Virgin, St Pet and St Stonar), *Kent*. R. **D** Cant 8 **P** *Archd of Cant* **I** D S NAUMANN.
SANDY (St Swith w All SS), *Beds*. R. **D** St Alb 17 **P** *F L Pym Esq* **I** E E J ROWLAND.
SANDYLANDS (St John), *Lancs*.. **D** Blackb 11 *See* Heysham.
SANKEY, GREAT *Chesh*. V. **D** Liv 7 **P** *Ld Lilford* **I** G MCKIBBIN.
SANTON, *Norf*. and Santon-Downham, *Suff*.. **D** St E *See* Brandon Ferry.
SAPCOTE (All SS), *Leics*. R. **D** Leic 16 **P** *Dioc Bd of Patr* **I** D W TYLDESLEY.
SAPEY, LOWER (St Bart), *Worcs*. R. **D** Worc *See* Clifton-on-Teme.
SAPEY, UPPER (St Mich) w Wolferlow (St Andr), *Herefs*. R. **D** Heref 2 **P** *Sir F Winnington Bt and Pers Rep of T P Barneby Esq* **I** R J COLBY *p-in-c.*
SAPISTON, *Suff*.. **D** St E 9 *See* Honington.
SAPPERTON (St Kenelm) w Frampton-Mansell, *Glos*. R. **D** Glouc 13 *See* Coates.
SAPPERTON (St Nich) w Braceby (St Marg), *Lincs*. R. **D** Linc 14 **P** *Sir O Welby Bt 3 turns, Bp 1 turn* **I** W B FOSTER.
SARISBURY (St Paul) w Swanwick, *Hants*. V. **D** Portsm 1 **P** *V of Titchfield* **I** R H MOSELEY.
SARK (St Pet), V. **D** Win 13 **P** *Le Seigneur de Serq* **I** P LUND.
SARN (H Trin), *Powys*.. **D** Heref *See* Churchstoke.
SARNESFIELD, *Herefs*.. **D** Heref *See* Weobley.
SARRATT (H Cross), *Herts*. R. **D** St Alb 10 **P** *Bp* **I** A J F TOMLINSON.
SARRE, *Kent*.. **D** Cant 8 *See* St Nicholas-at-Wade.
SARSDEN (St Jas) w Churchill (All SS), *Oxon*.. **D** Ox *See* Kingham.
SARUM, *Wilts*.. **D** Sarum *See* Salisbury.
SATLEY (St Cuthb), *Durham*. V. **D** Dur 13 **P** *Crown* **I** G D NESHAM.
SATTERLEIGH (St Pet), *Devon*.. **D** Ex 19 *See* Warkleigh.
SATTERTHWAITE (All SS) w Rusland (St Paul), *Cumb*. V. **D** Carl 14 *See* Colton.
SAUGHALL, GREAT (All SS), *Chesh*. V. **D** Ches 9 **P** *Bp* **I** G ROBINSON.
SAUL (St Jas Gt) w Fretherne (St Mary Virg) and Framilode (St Pet), *Glos*. V. **D** Glouc 9 **P** *Bp, V of Standish and Sir J Darell, Bt* **I** A T GAINEY.
SAUNDBY (St Martin), *Notts*.. **D** Southw *See* Bole.
SAUNDERTON, *Bucks*. R. **D** Ox 21 *See* Bledlow.
SAUNTON, *Devon*.. **D** Ex *See* Braunton.
SAUSTHORPE (St Andr), *Lincs*.. **D** Linc 7 *See* Aswardby.
SAVERNAKE FOREST (St Kath V and Mart), *Wilts*. V. **D** Sarum 26 **P** *Bp* **I** (Vacant).
SAVILE TOWN (St Mary), *W Yorks*.. **D** Wakef 10 *See* Thornhill Lees.
SAWBRIDGEWORTH (Gt St Mary), *Herts*. V. **D** St Alb 4 **P** *Bp* **I** R H CHILD.
SAWLEY (All SS), *Derby*. R. **D** Derby 13 **P** *D and C of Lich* **I** J R WARMAN, W H HOPKINSON *c.*
SAWREY (St Pet), *Cumb*. V. **D** Carl *See* Hawkshead.
SAWSTON (St Mary Virg), *Cambs*. V. **D** Ely 7 **P** *Trustees of H Towgood Esq* **I** R L POWELL *p-in-c.*
SAWTRY (All SS), *Cambs*. R. **D** Ely 14 **P** *Duke of Devonshire and Visc Valentia* alt **I** A R TAYLOR.
SAXBY (All SS), *Lincs*. R. **D** Linc 6 **P** *R H Hope-Barton Esq* **I** I H TINKLER.
SAXBY Lincs. **D** Linc 3 *See* Spridlington.
SAXBY (St Pet) w Stapleford (St Mary Magd), Garthorpe (St Mary) and Wyfordby (St Mary Virg), *Leics*. R. **D** Leic 4 **P** *Ld Gretton and Sir H Tollemache* alt **I** (Vacant).
SAXELBYE (St Pet) w Grimston and Shoby, *Leics*. R. **D** Leic 4 **P** *K J M Wright Esq 2 turns, V of Rothley 1 turn* **I** T C H CLARE.
SAXHAM, GREAT (St Andr) w Little (St Nich) and Westley (St Mary), *Suff*.. **D** St E *See* Risby.
SAXILBY (St Botolph w St Andr) w Ingleby, *Lincs*. V. **D** Linc 2 **P** *Bp* **I** E R COOK.
SAXLINGHAM (St Marg). *Norf*. R. **D** Nor 24 *See* Field Dalling.
SAXLINGHAM-NETHERGATE (St Mary Virg) w Saxlingham-Thorpe, *Norf*. R. **D** Nor 1 **P** *Miss J Hicks* **I** J H DOBSON.
SAXMUNDHAM (St Jo Bapt), *Suff*. R. **D** St E 19 **P** *Mrs A H V Aldous* **I** H L BOREHAM.
SAXON STREET (H Trin), *Cambs*.. **D** Ely 4 *See* Wood Ditton.
SAXTEAD, *Suff*.. **D** St E *See* Framlingham.
SAXTHORPE (St Andr) w Corpusty, *Norf*. V (*See Cawston Group*).. **D** Nor 3 **P** *Pemb Coll Cam* **I** R R DOMMETT *p-in-c.*
SAXTON (All SS) w Towton, *N Yorks*.. **D** York *See* Aberford.
SAYERS COMMON (Ch Ch), *W Sussex*.. **D** Chich 14 *See* Albourne.
SCALBY (St Lawr) w Ravenscar (St Hilda), *N Yorks*. V. **D** York 18 **P** *Abp 1 turn, D and C of Nor 2nd and 3rd turns* **I** C N TUBBS.
SCALDWELL, *Northants*.. **D** Pet 6 *See* Maidwell.
SCALEBY Cumb. R **D** Carl *See* Kirklinton.
SCALFORD (St Egelwin) w Wycombe Chap and Chadwell w Goadby Marwood, *Leics*. V. **D** Leic 4 **P** *Bp* **I** J C DEVER.

SCAMBLESBY (St Martin) w Calkwell, *Lincs*. V. **D** Linc *See* Asterby Group.
SCAMMONDEN, EAST, *W Yorks*.. **D** Wakef 6 *See* Slaithwaite.
WEST. **D** Wakef 2 *See* Barkisland.
SCAMPSTON, *N Yorks*.. **D** York *See* Rillington.
SCAMPTON (St Jo Bapt), *Lincs*. R. **D** Linc 3 *See* Aisthorpe.
SCARBOROUGH (St Mary w Ch Ch and the Holy Apostles), *N Yorks*. V. **D** York 18 **P** *Abp* **I** E A CROFTON, P M S GEDGE *c*, G E JOHNSON *c*.
(All SS), V. **D** York 18 *See* St Sav.
(St Columba), V. **D** York 18 **P** *Abp* **I** D VASEY.
(St Jas) and (H Trin), V. **D** York 18 **P** *Abp and CPAS* **I** F H BLANCHARD.
(St Martin), V. **D** York 18 **P** *Trustees* **I** C J HAWTHORN, C GREENWELL *c*, G A M DALE *hon c*.
(St Sav w All SS), V. **D** York 18 **P** *Abp* **I** F MITCHELL.
(St Luke), V. **D** York 18 **P** *Abp* **I** S J SMITH.
(St Mark, Newby), V. **D** York 18 **P** *Abp* **I** J D PURDY.
SCARCLIFFE (St Leon), *Derbys*. V. **D** Derby 2 **P** *Bp* **I** (Vacant).
SCARISBRICK (St Mark), *Lancs*. V. **D** Liv 9 **P** *V of Ormskirk* **I** H SANDERSON.
SCARLE, NORTH (All SS), *Lincs*. R. **D** Linc 18 *See* Swinderby
SCARLE, SOUTH (St Helen) w Besthorpe (H Trin) w Girton and Spalford, *Notts*. V. **D** Southw 3 **P** *Ld Chan* **I** R J STEVENS C-IN-C OF SOUTH SCARLE.
SCARNING (St Pet and St Paul) w Wendling, *Norf*. R. **D** Nor 20 **P** *Trustees of Vice-Adm Sir E M Evans Lombe and Ld Chan* alt **I** H A TAIT *p-in-c*.
SCARRINGTON (St John of Beverley), *Notts*.. **D** Southw 9 *See* Hawksworth.
SCARTHO (St Giles), *Humb*. R. **D** Linc 9 **P** *Jes Coll Ox* **I** B A J PEARMAIN.
(St Matt Fairfield Conv Distr). **D** Linc 9 **I** (Vacant).
SCAWBY (St Hibald) and Redbourne, *Humb*. V. **D** Linc **P** *Lt Col R Sutton-Nelthorpe 2 turns and Duke of St Alb 1 turn* **I** M H USHER.
SCAWTON (St Mary) w Cold Kirby (St Mich), R *N Yorks*.. **D** York *See* Upper Ryedale.
SCAYNES HILL (St Aug of Cant), *E Sussex*. V. **D** Chich 11 **P** *Bp* **I** W A J GIBB.
SCHOLES (St Phil and St Jas), *W Yorks*. V. **D** Wakef 9 **P** *Bp* **I** S C JONES.
SCHORNE (Hoggeston, Dunton, N Marston, Granborough, Whitchurch, Oving, Pitchcott, Hardwicke, and Quainton), *Bucks*. R. **D** Ox **P** *Bp, Worc Coll Ox, D and C of Windsor, Sir R B Verney Bt and New Coll Ox* **I** P A LAWRENCE, D R HEMSLEY *team v*.
SCILLY, ISLES OF, ST MARY'S (St Mary Virg) w Tresco (St Nich), St Martin, St Agnes, and Bryher, *Cornw*. V. **D** Truro 6 **P** *Duke of Cornwall* **I** P WOODHALL, F B CORKE *team v*.
SCISSETT (St Aug), *W Yorks*. V. **D** Wakef 7 **P** *Exors of P G Norton Esq* **I** A PARRY.
SCOFTON w Osberton, *Notts*. V. **D** Southw 7 **P** *G M T Foljambe Esq* **I** A H BROWN *p-in-c*.
SCOLE (St Andr) w Billingford (St Leon), Brockdish, Thorpe Abbots and Thorpe Parva, *Norf*. R. **D** Nor 17 **P** *Bp, Lady Mann, MMT, Ex Coll Ox and Archd of Norf* **I** R S WERRELL.
SCOPWICK (H Cross) w Kirkby Green, *Lincs*. V. **D** Linc 18 **P** *Ld Chan and Trustees of the late Earl of Londesborough* **I** J L M LE MARCHAND.
SCORBOROUGH w Leconfield Humb. R **D** York 11 *See* Lockington.
SCOREBY **D** York 7 *See* Stamford Bridge.
SCORTON (St Pet), *Lancs*. V. **D** Blackb 10 **P** *Bp* **I** A R LINTON *p-in-c*.
SCOTBY, *Cumb*. V. **D** Carl 2 **P** *Trustees* **I** F W BOVILL.
SCOTFORTH (St Paul), *Lancs*. V. **D** Blackb 11 **P** *Trustees* **I** D G BELLINGER, A S PYE *c*.
SCOTHERN (St Germain), *Lincs*. V. **D** Linc 3 *See* Dunholme.
SCOTSWOOD (St Marg), *T & W*.. **D** Newc T 5b *See* Newcastle upon Tyne.
SCOTTER (St Pet) w East Ferry (St Mary Virg), *Lincs*. R. **D** Linc 4 **P** *Rev F J S Evans* **I** D W R BIRD.
SCOTTON (St Genewys) w Northorpe (St Jo Bapt), *Lincs*. R. **D** Linc 4 **P** *Ld Chan* **I** (Vacant).
SCOTTON (St Thos Ap), *N Yorks*.. **D** Ripon 9 *See* Farnham.
SCOTTOW (All SS), *Norf*. V. **D** Nor 8 **P** *Bp* **I** R J TUCK *p-in-c*.
SCOULTON, *Norf*. R. **D** Nor 19 *See* Woodrising.
SCOUTHEAD (St Paul), *Gtr Man*.. **D** Man 15 *See* Dobcross.
SCRAFIELD (St Mich), *Lincs*.. **D** Linc 11 *See* Hammeringham.
SCRAPTOFT (All SS), *Leics*. V. **D** Leic 8 **P** *Sir J A T Sharp KCB MC* **I** R MALSBURY.
SCRATBY, *Norf*.. **D** Nor *See* Ormesby.
SCRAYINGHAM (St Pet and St Paul or St Pet) w Leppington (in Stamford Bridge Group) *N Yorks*. R. **D** York 7 **P** *Ld Leconfield's Trustees 1st and 3rd turns, Crown 2nd turn, Ld Chan 4th turn* **I** (Vacant).
SCREDINGTON (St Andr), *Lincs*. V. **D** Linc 22 *See* Helpringham.
SCREMBY (St Pet and St Paul), *Lincs*. R. **D** Linc 7 *See* Candlesby.
SCREMERSTON, *Northumb*.. **D** Newc T *See* Ancroft.
SCREVETON (St Wilfrid), *Notts*.. **D** Southw *See* Car Colston.
SCRIVELSBY (St Benedict) w Dalderby, *Lincs*. R. **D** Linc 11 **P** *Exors of F S Dymoke Esq* **I** H R WHALER.
SCROOBY (St Wilfrid) w Ranskill, *Notts*. V. **D** Southw 5 **P** *Bp* **I** D WALKER.
SCROPTON (St Paul), *Derbys*. V. **D** Derby 14 *See* Marston-on-Dove.
SCRUTON N Yorks. **D** Ripon 2 *See* Ainderby Steeple.
SCULCOATES (St Steph), *N Yorks*.. **D** York *See* Hull.
(St Mary). **D** York *See* Hull.
(St Paul w Ch Ch and St Silas), V. **D** York **P** *Abp* **I** R LOVATT.
SCULTHORPE (St Mary and All SS) w Dunton, *Norf*. R. **D** Nor 21 **P** *Mrs Labouchere 3 turns, Ld Chan 1 turn* **I** J H L PENNOCK *p-in-c*.
SCUNTHORPE (St Jo Evang), *Humb*. V. **D** Linc 4 **P** *Ld St Oswald* **I** C I MILLER.
(All SS), V. **D** Linc 4 **P** *Bp* **I** A P JOHNSON.
(Resurr), V. **D** Linc 4 **P** *Bp* **I** J F WILSON.
SEA HOUSES Northumb. **D** Newc T 8 *See* Sunderland, North.
SEA MILLS (St Edyth), V. **D** Bris 6 **P** *Bp* **I** (Vacant).
SEABOROUGH (Dedic unknown), *Dorset*. R. **D** Sarum 4 *See* See Broadwindsor.
SEACOMBE (St Paul), *Mer*. V. **D** Ches 8 *See* Wallasey.
SEACROFT (St Jas w Ch of the Ascen), *W Yorks*. R. **D** Ripon 7 **P** *Dioc Bd of Patr* **I** D R GRICE, W R HOGG *team v*, M O SEARLE *team v*, S TURNBULL *team v*.
SEAFORD (St Leon) w Chyngton (St Luke), *E Sussex*. V. **D** Chich 15 **P** *Ld Chan* **I** M R THOMPSON, M W THOMAS *c*.
SEAFORTH, *Mer*. V. **D** Liv 1 **P** *Sir W Gladstone* **I** M C DAVIES, P G ROBERTS *c*.
SEAGRAVE (All SS) w Walton-le-Wolds (St Mary), *Leics*. R. **D** Leic 9 **P** *Dioc Bd of Finance and Jt PCC (alt)* **I** A W UNDERWOOD *c-in-c*.
SEAGRY (St Mary Virg), *Wilts*. V. **D** Bris *See* Somerford Magna.
SEAHAM (St Mary) w Seaham Harbour (St Jo Evang), *Durham*. V. **D** Dur 3 **P** *Marq of Londonderry* **I** N C HEAVISIDES.
SEAHAM, NEW (Ch Ch), *Durham*. V. **D** Dur 3 **P** *Marq of Londonderry* **I** P C HOLLAND.
SEAL (St Pet and St Paul), *Kent*. V. **D** Roch 7 **P** *Ld Sackville* **I** J S BARNARD.
(St Lawr), V. **D** Roch 7 **P** *Bp* **I** D M L LYNCH *p-in-c*.
SEALE (St Lawr), *Surrey*. R. **D** Guildf 3 **P** *Archd of Surrey* **I** (Vacant).
SEALE, NETHER (St Pet) w Over (St Matt), *Derbys*. R. **D** Derby 16 **P** *C W Worthington Esq* **I** W F BATES.
SEAMER (St Martin) w E Ayton (St Jo Bapt), *N Yorks*. V. **D** York 18 **P** *Abp* **I** C BLACKMORE.
SEAMER-IN-CLEVELAND (St Martin), *N Yorks*. V. **D** York 25 **P** *Ld Leconfield's Trustees* **I** (Vacant).
SEARBY Lincs. V **D** Linc 5 *See* Grasby.
SEASALTER (St Alphege), *Kent*. V. **D** Cant 4 **P** *D and C of Cant* **I** P N H MORETON.
SEASCALE (St Cuthb) and Drigg, *Cumb*. V. **D** Carl 12 **P** *Dioc Bd of Patr* **I** W J P GRIME.
SEATON (St Paul), *Cumb*.. **D** Carl 6 *See* Camerton.
SEATON (St Greg), *Devon*. V. **D** Ex 5 **P** *Dioc Bd of Patr* **I** C J N GEORGE.
SEATON (All H), *Leics*.]. R. **D** Pet 12 *See* Lyddington.
SEATON CAREW (H Trin), *Cleve*. V. **D** Dur 12 **P** *Bp* **I** W WORLEY.
SEATON DELAVAL (St Steph), *Northumb*.. **D** Newc T 1 *See* Seghill.
SEATON HIRST (St John), *Northumb*. V. **D** Newc T 10 **P** *Bp* **I** M NELSON, R BEST *c*, J D CHADD *c*, J SMITH *c*.
SEATON ROSS GROUP (Everingham, Harswell, Bielby, Thornton and Allerthorpe), *Humb*. R. **D** York 10 **P** *Ld Chan and Abp* **I** P S THORNTON, J D WALKER P-IN-C ALLERTHORPE.
SEATON SLUICE (St Paul), *Northumb*.. **D** Newc T 1 *See* Delaval.

SEATON, WEST (H Trin), *Cumb.* V. **D** Carl 11 **P** *Trustees* **I** M P BRION.
SEAVIEW (St Pet), *Isle of Wight.* V. **D** Portsm 6 **P** *Bp* **I** D M LOW.
SEAVINGTON (St Mich w St Mary), *Somt..* **D** B & W *See* Petherton, South.
SEBERGHAM (St Mary), *Cumb.* R. **D** Carl 3 *See* Caldbeck.
SECKINGTON (All SS), *Warws.* R. **D** Birm 9 *See* Newton Regis.
SEDBERGH (St Andr and St Greg Gt) Cautley and Garsdale, *Cumb..* **D** Bradf 7 **P** *Trin Coll Cam* **I** D A INESON, E P E LONG *c,* B W LEVICK *hon c.*
SEDGBROOK, *Lincs..* **D** Linc 19 *See* Allington, West.
SEDGEBERROW (St Mary Virg) w Hinton-on-the-Green (St Pet), *Worcs.* R. **D** Worc 1 **P** *Laslett's Trustees and D and C of Worc* alt **I** C J JOHNSTON-HUBBOLD.
SEDGEFIELD (St Edm), *Durham.* R. **D** Dur 12a **P** *Bp* **I** N R EDMONDSON.
SEDGEFORD (St Mary Virg) w Southmere, *Norf.* V. **D** Nor 23 **P** *D and C of Nor* **I** T L LIVERMORE *p-in-c.*
SEDGEHILL, *Wilts.* V. **D** Sarum 19 *See* Semley.
SEDGLEY (All SS), *W Midl.* V. **D** Lich 1 **P** *Bp* **I** B M HARRIS, A T BALL *c.*
(St Mary Virg Hurst Hill), V. **D** Lich 1 **P** *Bp and V of Sedgley* **I** I L J FROOM.
SEDLESCOMBE (St Jo Bapt) w Whatlington (St Mary Magd), *E Sussex.* R. **D** Chich 17 **P** *Ld Chan and Ld Sackville* alt **I** D A F PRINCE.
SEEND (H Cross) w Bulkington (Ch Ch), *Wilts.* V. **D** Sarum 23 **P** *D and C of Sarum 3 turns, Bp 1 turn* **I** J F LEE.
SEER GREEN (H Trin), *Bucks.* V. **D** Ox 20 **P** *Bp* **I** M OSBORNE *p-in-c.*
SEETHING (St Marg of Antioch and St Remigius), *Norf.* V. **D** Nor 14 *See* Mundham.
SEFTON (St Helen), *Mer.* R. **D** Liv **P** *Bp* **I** O J YANDELL, E J BATY *hon c.*
SEFTON PARK, *Mer.* **D** Liv *See* Toxteth Park.
SEGHILL or SIGHILL (H Trin) w Seaton Delaval (St Steph) and Holywell (St Mary), *Northumb.* V. **D** Newc T 1 **P** *Crown* **I** A MURRAY.
SEIGHFORD (St Chad) w Derrington (St Matt) and Cresswell, *Staffs.* V. **D** Lich **P** *Maj R C Eld 4 turns C F Twemlow Esq 1 turn* **I** D C FELIX.
SELATTYN (St Mary), *Salop.* R. **D** Lich 24 **P** *A Lloyd Esq* **I** C J LAWSON.
SELBORNE (St Mary), *Hants.* V. **D** Win 1 *See* Newton Valence.
SELBY (Abbey Ch of Our Lord, St Mary and St Germain), *N Yorks.* V. **D** York 8 **P** *Abp* **I** A C A SMITH, C C ELLIS *c.*
(St Jas Ap), V. **D** York 8 **P** *Simeon Trustees* **I** D BOND.
SELHAM (St Jas Ap), *W Sussex..* **D** Chich *See* Lurgashall.
SELHURST, *Surrey..* **D** Cant *See* Croydon.
SELLACK (St Tyssilio) w King's Caple (St Jo Bapt) and Foy (St Mary), *Herefs.* V. **D** Heref 8 **P** *D and C of Heref 2 turns, Brig A F L Clive 1 turn* **I** J A P HOSKYNS P-IN-C OF K CAPLE.
SELLINDGE (St Mary) w Monks Horton (St Pet) and Stowting (St Mary Virg), *Kent.* V. **D** Cant 12 **P** *Abp* **I** P GOODSELL *p-in-c.*
SELLING (St Mary Virg), *Kent.* V. **D** Cant 7 **P** *Abp* **I** J V H RUSSELL *p-in-c.*
SELLY HILL (St Steph), *Warws.* V. **D** Birm *See* Selly Park.
SELLY OAK (St Mary), *W Midl.* V. **D** Birm 2 **P** *Trustees* **I** J D WATERSTREET.
SELLY PARK (St Steph and St Wulstan), *Warws.* V. **D** Birm **P** *Trustees* **I** C R BEVINGTON, I W Y GEMMELL *c,* K J R GODSELL *hon c.*
SELMESTON (Dedic unknown) w Alciston, *E Sussex..* **D** Chich *See* Berwick.
SELSDON (St Jo Div w St Francis), *Surrey.* R. **D** Cant 16 **P** *Abp* **I** A F SIMPER, E C WHEBLE *team v.*
SELSEY (St Pet), *W Sussex..* R and V. **D** Chich 3 **P** *Bp* **I** V R CASSAM, H K MAYBURY *c.*
SELSIDE (St Thos), *N Yorks.* V. **D** Carl 17 *See* Skelsmergh.
SELSLEY (All SS), *Glos.* V. **D** Glouc 9 *See* Cainscross.
SELSTON (St Helen w St Mich AA) w Westwood (St Mary), *Notts.* V. **D** Southw 12 **P** *Wright Trustees* **I** J F JACKLIN, D C GRIEVE *c,* J ROBINSON *c.*
SELWORTHY (All SS), *Somt.* R. **D** B & W 21 **P** *Sir R Dyke Acland Bt* **I** E J MILLER *p-in-c.*
SEMER, (All SS), *Suff.* R. **D** St E 3 *See* Whatfield.
SEMINGTON (St Geo), *Wilts..* **D** Sarum 24 *See* Steeple-Ashton.
SEMLEY (St Leon) and Sedgehill, *Wilts.* R. **D** Sarum 19 **P** *Ch Ch Ox* **I** (Vacant).
SEMPRINGHAM (St Andr Abbey Ch) w Pointon (Ch Ch) and Pointon Fen (St John) w Birthorpe, *Lincs.* V. **D** Linc 13 **P** *Crown* **I** H J THEODOSIUS.
SEND (St Mary Virg), *Surrey.* V. **D** Guildf 11 **P** *Bp* **I** J P B WYNBURNE.
SENNEN (St Sennen), *Cornw.* R. **D** Truro 5 *See* St Buryan.
SENNICOTS (St Mary), *W Sussex.* Chap. **D** Chich 8 *See* Funtington.
(St Frideswyde Conv Distr Thornton). **D** Liv 1 *See* Liverpool.
SESSAY (St Cuthb), *N Yorks.* R. **D** York 26 **P** *Visc Downe* **I** P WORDSWORTH *c-in-c.*
SETMURTHY (St Barn), *Cumb.* V. **D** Carl 10 *See* Isel.
SETTLE (H Ascen), *N Yorks.* V. **D** Bradf 6 **P** *Trustees* **I** E ASHBY.
SETTRINGTON (All SS) w North Grimston and Wharram, *N Yorks.* R. **D** York 3 **P** *Ld Brownlow, Ld Middleton and Abp* **I** W F J EVERITT.
SEVEN KINGS (St Jo Evang), *Essex.* V. **D** Chelmsf 7 *See* Ilford, Great.
SEVENHAMPTON (St Jas), *Glos..* **D** Bris *See* Highworth.
SEVENHAMPTON (St Andr) w Charlton Abbots (St Martin) and Hawling (St Edw) w Whittington, *Glos.* V. **D** Glouc 15 **P** *Bp, E Bailey Esq, MM & C of E Trust and Miss S M Evans-Lawrence* **I** P B HOBBS.
SEVENOAKS (St Nich), *Kent.* R. **D** Roch 7 **P** *Trustees* **I** K F W PRIOR, D S ALLISTER *c,* P F HULLAH *c.*
(St Jo Bapt), V. **D** Roch 7 **P** *Guild of All S* **I** M P SHIELDS, R G FROST *c,* G W LOVEJOY *hon c.*
(St Luke, Kippington Conv Distr). **D** Roch 7 **P** *Bp* **I** J H M HARGREAVES *min,* J M C PARKS *hon c.*
SEVERN STOKE (St Denys) w Croome D'abitot, *Worcs.* R. **D** Worc 5 *See* Kempsey.
SEVINGTON (St Mary), *Kent.* R. **D** Cant 9 **P** *Ch S Trust* **I** J H WAITE *p-in-c.*
SEWERBY (St Jo Evang) w Marton, *Humb..* **D** York 12 *See* H Trin, Bridlington.
SEWSTERN (H Trin), *Leics.* V. **D** Leic 3 *See* Buckminster.
SEZINCOTE, *Glos..* **D** Glouc 16 *See* Longborough.
SHABBINGTON, *Bucks.* V. **D** Ox 21 **P** *Bp* **I** R H COLLIER.
SHACKERSTONE (St Pet) *Leics.* V. **D** Leic 15 *See* Nailstone.
SHACKLEFORD (St Mary), *Surrey.* R. **D** Guildf 4 **P** *Bp* **I** A RANSOME *p-in-c.*
SHACKLEWELL. **D** Lon *See* Hackney, West.
SHADFORTH (St Cuthb), *Durham.* R. **D** Dur 2 **P** *D and C of Dur* **I** C E WOOLSTENHOLMES.
SHADINGFIELD (St Jo Bapt), *Suff.* R. **D** St E 14 *See* Sotterley.
SHADOXHURST (St Pet and St Paul), *Kent.* R. **D** Cant 10 *See* Kingsnorth.
SHADWELL (St Paul w St Jas Ratcliffe), *Lon.* R. **D** Lon 4 **P** *Bp* **I** (Vacant).
SHADWELL, *Norf..* **D** Nor 18a *See* Brettenham.
SHADWELL (St Paul), *W Yorks.* V. **D** Ripon 6 **P** *V of Thorner* **I** E PICKERSGILL.
SHAFTESBURY (H Trin), *Dorset.* R. **D** Sarum 13 *See* Shaston.
(St Jas Gt), R. **D** Sarum 13 *See* Shaston.
SHAFTESBURY AVENUE (St John). **D** Lon 2 *See* Bloomsbury.
SHALBOURNE (St Mich AA) w Bagshot, Ham (All SS) and Buttermere, *Wilts..* **D** Sarum *See* Wexcombe.
SHALDEN (St Pet and St Paul), *Hants.* R. **D** Win 1 *See* Bentworth.
SHALDON (St Nich and St Pet), *Devon.* V. **D** Ex 10 **P** *S for Maint of Faith* **I** H R PHILLIPS *p-in-c.*
SHALFLEET, *Isle of Wight.* V. **D** Portsm 7 **P** *Ld Chan 3 turns Bp 1 turn* **I** J F R RYALL *p-in-c.*
SHALFORD (St Andr), *Essex..* **D** Chelmsf 19 *See* Wethersfield.
SHALFORD (St Mary Virg), *Surrey.* V. **D** Guildf 5 **P** *Ld Chan* **I** K J MORGAN.
SHALSTONE (St Edw Confessor and K) w Biddlesden, *Bucks..* **D** Ox *See* Westbury.
SHAMLEY GREEN (Ch Ch), *Surrey.* V. **D** Guildf 2 **P** *Bp* **I** C L M SCOTT.
SHANGTON (St Nich), *Leics..* **D** Leic 6 *See* Carlton Curlieu.
SHANKLIN (St Blasius), *Isle of Wight,* R. **D** Portsm 6 **P** *Bp* **I** K F A PARKINSON.
(St Paul Ap Gatten), V. **D** Portsm 6 **P** *Ch Patr Trust* **I** P G ALLEN *p-in-c.*
(St Sav-on-the-Cliff), V. **D** Portsm 6 **P** *Bp* **I** J E HAIR *p-in-c.*
SHAP (St Mich AA) w Swindale, *Cumb.* V. **D** Carl 1 **P** *Earl of Lonsdale* **I** J MELLISH.

SHAPWICK (St Mary Virg) w Ashcott (All SS), *somt.* V. **D** B & W 7 **P** *Ld Vestey* **I** H L BAXTER.
SHAPWICK (St Bart), *Dorset.* V. **D** Sarum 11 *See* Kingston Lacy.
SHARD END (All SS), *W Midl.* V. **D** Birm 9 **P** *Keble Coll Ox* **I** M G B C CADDY.
SHARDLOW (St Jas) w Gt Wilne, Elvaston (St Bart), Thurlaston and Ambaston, *Derbys.* R. **D** Derby 15 **P** *Sutton Trustees and Earl of Harrington* **I** P E HARDING *c-in-c.*
SHARESHILL (St Mary of the Assump), *Staffs.* V. **D** Lich 3 **P** *Bp* **I** R N WHITTINGHAM.
SHARLSTON (St Luke), *W Yorks.* V. **D** Wakef 13 *See* Wragby.
SHARNBROOK (St Pet), *Beds.* V. **D** St Alb 21 **P** *Bp* **I** H D JONES, D E CLAYPOLE WHITE *c.*
SHARNCOTE (All SS), *Glos.* V. **D** Glouc 13 *See* Somerford Keynes.
SHARNFORD (St Helen) w Wigston Parva (St Mary), *Leics.* R. **D** Leic 16 **P** *Ld Chan* **I** W W EVANS.
SHARPNESS w Purton (St John) and Brookend, *Glos.* V. **D** Glouc 5 **P** *Exors of Earl of Berkeley* **I** D P MINCHEW.
SHARRINGTON (All SS), *Norf.* R. **D** Nor 24 **P** *MMT* **I** P G FLATHER *p-in-c.*
SHARROW (St Andr), *S Yorks.* V. **D** Sheff 2 *See* Sheffield.
SHASTON (Compton-Abbas, Melbury Abbas, Motcombe w Enmore Green Shaftesbury and East Orchard w Margaret Marsh), *Dorset.* R. **D** Sarum 13 **P** *Dioc Bd of Patr* **I** D G C CAIGER, J A H CLEGG *team v,* E S O JACSON *team v.*
SHAUGH PRIOR (St Edw), *Devon.* V. **D** Ex 21 **P** *D and C of Windsor* **I** H R J JAMES.
SHAW or CROMPTON (H Trin), *Gtr Man.* V. **D** Man 15 **P** *R of Prestwich* **I** S W LEACH.
SHAW (St Mary) w Donnington, *Berks.* R. **D** Ox 14 **P** *Dioc Bd of Patr* **I** J H L BLICK.
SHAW (Ch Ch) w Whitley, *Wilts.* V. **D** Sarum 24 **P** *V of Melksham* **I** G E GRIFFITHS.
SHAW HILL, ALUM ROCK (St Mary and St John), *W Midl.* V. **D** Birm 13 **P** *Bp* **I** C E E STEELE.
SHAWBURY (St Mary Virg), *Salop.* V. **D** Lich 27 **P** *Lt-Col Sir J Corbet Bt* **I** C J BRADLEY.
SHAWELL (All SS), *Leics.* R. **D** Leic 14 *See* Stanford.
SHAWFORD, *Hants..* **D** Win 12 *See* Compton.
SHEARSBY, *Leics.* R. **D** Leic 13 *See* Arnesby.
SHEBBEAR (St Mich) w Buckland Filleigh, Highampton and Sheepwash, *Devon.* V. **D** Ex 20 **P** *Bp, Ld Chan and Capt P B Browne* **I** N G MEAD.
SHEDFIELD (St Jo Bapt), *Hants.* V. **D** Portsm 2 **P** *Dioc Bd of Patr* **I** G B MORRELL.
SHEEN (St Luke), *Staffs.* V. **D** Lich 13 **P** *Bp* **I** A C F NICOLL *p-in-c.*
SHEEN, EAST (Ch Ch and All SS), *Surrey..* **D** S'wark 13 *See* Mortlake.
SHEEN, NORTH (St Phil and All SS), *Surrey.* V. **D** S'wark 13 **P** *Bp* **I** R LAMONT.
SHEEPSCOMBE, *Glos.* V. **D** Glouc 4 *See* Painswick.
SHEEPSTOR (Dedic unknown), *Devon.* V. **D** Ex 22 *See* Meavy.
SHEEPWASH (St Lawr), *Devon.* V. **D** Ex 20 *See* Shebbear.
SHEEPY MAGNA w Sheepy-Parva (All SS) and Ratcliffe-Culey (All SS), *Leics.* R. **D** Leic 15 *See* Sibson.
SHEERING (St Mary Virg), *Essex.* R. **D** Chelmsf 3 **P** *Ch Ch Ox* **I** F G STEEL.
SHEERNESS (H Trin) w (St Paul), *Kent.* V. **D** Cant 14 **P** *V of Minster-in-Sheppey* **I** A B SHARPE, J D FOULKES *c,* D R PAGET *c.*
SHEET (St Mary), *Hants..* **D** Portsm 4 *See* Petersfield.
SHEFFIELD (Cathl Ch of St Pet and St Paul w St Paul and St Jude, Moorfields), *S Yorks.* V. **D** Sheff 1 **P** *Sheff Ch Burgesses and Simeon Trustees* **I** VERY REV W F CURTIS.
(St Andr Sharrow), V. **D** Sheff 2 **P** *Trustees* **I** W HUDSON, G TOLLEY *c.*
(St Aug Endcliffe), V. **D** Sheff **P** *Sheff Ch Burgesses* **I** M E CHARLES.
(St Barn and St Mary), V. **D** Sheff 2 **P** *Sheff Ch Burgesses and Provost (alt)* **I** J A SMITH, D J S MUNRO *c,* R L PAMPLIN *c.*
(St Cecilia, Parson Cross), V. **D** Sheff 3 **P** *Bp* **I** G K BOSTOCK, G ROBERTS *c.*
(St Cuthb Firvale), V. **D** Sheff 3 **P** *Sheff Ch Burgesses* **I** G V LETTS, D V A BROWN *c,* J B PEARS *hon c.*
(H Trin Millhouses), V. **D** Sheff 2 **P** *Bp* **I** D H THORPE.
(St Jo Evang Park), V. **D** Sheff 1 **P** *Sheff Ch Burgesses* **I** G V BEWLEY, M G R D SMITH *c.*
(St Leon Norwood), V. **D** Sheff 3 **P** *Bp* **I** F BALL.
(St Mark, Broomhall), V. **D** Sheff 4 **P** *Sheff Ch Burgesses* **I** J R GILES.
(St Matt), V. **D** Sheff 2 **P** *Bp* **I** A V LONGWORTH, L L GUSH *c.*
(St Silas, Gillcar), V. **D** Sheff 2 **P** *Sheff Ch Burgesses* **I** J M THOMPSON *c-in-c.*
(St Steph w St Phil and St Anne and St Bart and St Nath, Netherthorpe), R. **D** Sheff 2 **P** *Patr Bd* **I** D J FORD, H O FAULKNER *team v.*
(St Thos Crookes), V. **D** Sheff 4 **P** *CPAS* **I** R P R WARREN, J B FOOTE *c,* F J MARSH *c.*
(St Timothy Crookes), V. **D** Sheff 4 **P** *Sheff Ch Burgesses* **I** G G MACINTOSH.
ABBEYDALE (St Osw) Millhouses, V. **D** Sheff 2 **P** *Sheff Ch Burgesses* **I** E H COX, M ALFLATT *c.*
(St Pet), V. **D** Sheff 2 **P** *Sheff Ch Burgesses* **I** D R A BACON.
(St Jo Evang), V. **D** Sheff 2 **P** *Trustees* **I** T HUDSON.
ATTERCLIFFE (Ch Ch) w Carbrook (St Bart), V. **D** Sheff 1 **P** *Bp 1st and 3rd Turns, Sheff Ch Burgesses 2nd turn Provost of Sheff 4th Turn* **I** R D DE BERRY.
BRIGHTSIDE (St Thos and St Marg), V. **D** Sheff 3 **P** *Sheff Ch Burgesses and Crown (alt)* **I** G TAYLOR, A M YATES *c.*
DARNALL (H Trin), V. **D** Sheff 1 **P** *Bp* **I** R J A HASLAM.
ECCLESALL-BIERLOW (All SS), V. **D** Sheff 2 **P** *Provost of Sheff* **I** J N COLLIE, R H CADMAN *c,* M F HOLLAND *c.*
FULWOOD (Ch Ch), V. **D** Sheff 4 **P** *Trustees* **I** P H HACKING, R S BROOKS *c,* J O FORRESTER *c,* R W JACKSON *c,* J S HEPWORTH *hon c.*
HEELEY (Ch Ch), V. **D** Sheff 1 **P** *1st Ld of Treasury* **I** A F HOMER.
MANOR (St Aid w St Luke and St Swith, Arbourthorne (St Paul) and Manor Park (William Temple). **D** Sheff 1 **P** *Patr Bd* **I** I K DUFFIELD *team v,* E HUME *team v,* N P A JOWETT *team v,* W A B MCCABE *team v.*
NORTON LEES (St Paul), V. **D** Sheff 2 **P** *R of Norton* **I** M P HIRONS.
NORTON WOODSEATS (St Chad), V. **D** Sheff 2 **P** *Bp* **I** M R KEMP.
OWLERTON (St Jo Bapt), V. **D** Sheff 4 **P** *CPS* **I** D T BOTTLEY, A J MAGOWAN *c.*
RANMOOR (St Jo Evang), V. **D** Sheff 4 **P** *Trustees* **I** R M JARRATT, D G STAFFORD *c.*
SHIREGREEN (St Hilda), V. **D** Sheff 3 **P** *Bp* **I** A R LOWE.
SHIREGREEN, LOWER (St Jas and St Chris), V. **D** Sheff 3 **P** *Provost of Sheff* **I** C W LONG.
WALKLEY (St Mary), V. **D** Sheff 4 **P** *Bp* **I** A R BILLINGS.
WOODTHORPE (St Cath), V. **D** Sheff 1 **P** *Crown* **I** B A HUTTON.
SHEFFORD (St Mich AA), *Beds.* V. **D** St Alb 22 **P** *Archd of Bedford and R of Clifton* **I** R F DAY.
SHEFFORD, GREAT or WEST (St Mary) w Shefford, East or Little (H Innoc), *Berks..* **D** Ox 14 *See* Welford.
SHEINTON (St Pet and St Paul), *Salop.* R. **D** Heref 11 *See* Cressage.
SHELDON (St Giles), *W Midl.* R. **D** Birm 9 **P** *S Wingfield-Digby Esq* **I** A S J LEMON.
SHELDON (St Mich AA), *Derbys.* V. **D** Derby 9 *See* Ashford.
SHELDON (St Jas Greater), *Devon.* V. **D** Ex 5 **P** *Bp* **I** N J WALL P-IN-C OF LUPPITT.
SHELDWICH (St Jas), *Kent.* V. **D** Cant 7 **P** *D and C of Cant* **I** E A MARSH.
SHELF (St Mich AA), *W Yorks.* V. **D** Bradf 2 **P** *Bp* **I** P R THOMAS, G H COLES *hon c.*
SHELFANGER (All SS), *Norf.* R. **D** Nor 17 *See* Winfarthing.
SHELFORD (St Pet and St Paul), *Notts.* V. **D** Southw 9 **P** *Ld Chan* **I** G N PEARCE.
SHELFORD, LITTLE (All SS) w Newton, *Cambs.* R. **D** Ely 7 **P** *Bp* **I** S G TAYLOR.
SHELFORD MAGNA (St Mary Virg), *Cambs.* V. **D** Ely 7 **P** *Bp* **I** C J HERBERT.
SHELLAND, *Suff..* **D** St E *See* Buxhall.
SHELLEY (St Pet), *Essex.* R. **D** Chelmsf 6 **P** *Keble Coll Ox* **I** J P VAUGHAN-JONES.
SHELLEY, *Suff..* **D** St E *See* Layham.
SHELLEY (Em), *W Yorks.* V. **D** Wakef 7 **P** *V of Kirkburton* **I** A BEAUMONT.
SHELLINGFORD (St Faith Virg and Mart), *Oxon.* R. **D** Ox 17 **P** *Kitemore Estate Co* **I** D G PECK.
SHELLOW BOWELS, *Essex..* **D** Chelmsf 16 *See* Willingale.
SHELSLEYS, THE (All SS w St Andr), *Worcs.* R. **D** Worc *See* Clifton-on-Teme.
SHELSWELL, *Oxon.* R. **D** Ox 2 *See* Newton Purcell.
SHELTHORPE (Good Shepherd), *Leics.* V. **D** Leic *See* Loughborough.

SHELTON (St Mary), *Beds.*. **D** St Alb *See* Dean.
SHELTON (St Mark), *Staffs.*. **D** Lich *See* Hanley, H Evang.
SHELTON (St Mary and All SS), *Notts.*. **D** Southw *See* Newark.
SHELTON w Oxon (Ch Ch), *Salop.* V. **D** Lich 26 **P** *V of Shrewsbury* **I** (Vacant).
SHELTON w Hardwick (St Mary), *Norf.*. **D** Nor *See* Hempnall.
SHELVE (All SS), *Salop.*. **D** Heref *See* Hope.
SHENFIELD (St Mary Virg), *Essex.* R. **D** Chelmsf 9 **P** *R Courage Esq* **I** E C TELFORD, A L WAY *c.*
SHENINGTON (H Trin) w Alkerton (St Mich AA) and Shutford (St Martin), *Oxon.*. **D** Ox *See* Wroxton.
SHENLEY (St Mary), *Bucks.* R. **D** Ox 26 **P** *S for Maint of Faith* **I** R A HARROW *p-in-c.*
SHENLEY (St Botolph), *Herts.* R. **D** St Alb 1 **P** *Dioc Bd of Patr* **I** D B PERKINS *p-in-c.*
SHENLEY GREEN (St D), *W Midl.* V. **D** Birm 4 **P** *Bp* **I** D J PENDLETON.
SHENSTONE (St Jo Bapt), *Staffs.* V. **D** Lich 2 **P** *MM and C of E Trusts* **I** R D TOLEY, J B ASTON *hon c.*
SHENTON (St Jo Evang), *Leics.* R. **D** Leic 15 *See* Market Bosworth.
SHEPHALL (St Mary Virg), *Herts.* V. **D** St Alb *See* Stevenage.
SHEPHERD'S BUSH. **D** Lon *See* Hammersmith.
SHEPHERDSWELL (St Andr), *Kent.*. **D** Cant 4 *See* Sibertswold.
SHEPLEY (St Paul), *W Yorks.*. **D** Wakef 7 **P** *V of Kirkburton* **I** C J COLLISON *p-in-c.*
SHEPPERTON (St Nich), *Lon.* R. **D** Lon 13 **P** *Bp* **I** P W BALL, R F SOWTER *c.*
SHEPRETH (All SS), *Cambs.* V. **D** Ely 8 **P** *Bp* **I** M W BAKER *p-in-c.*
SHEPSHED (St Botolph), *Leics.* V. **D** Leic 10 **P** *Ld Crawshaw* **I** J G FROSTICK, G H RICHMOND *c.*
SHEPTON BEAUCHAMP (St Mich) w Barrington, Stocklinch, Puckington and Bradon, *Somt.* R. **D** B & W 20 **P** *C R Mirfield 4 turns, R T A Cooper Esq 1 turn* **I** R G SMITH.
SHEPTON MALLET (St Pet and St Paul) w Doulting, *Somt.* R. **D** B & W 6 **P** *Duchy of Cornw and Bp* alt **I** P B BIBBY, R W H ALLEN *c.*
SHEPTON-MONTAGUE (St Pet), *Somt.* V. **D** B & W 5 *See* Pitcombe.
SHERBORNE (St Mary Magd), Windrush (St Pet), The Barringtons and Aldsworth, *Glos.* V. **D** Glouc 15 **P** *Ld Sherborne, C T R Wingfield Esq and D and C of Ch Ch Ox (in turn)* **I** C H MCCARTER *p-in-c.*
SHERBORNE (St Mary Virg) w Castleton and Lillington (St Martin), *Dorset.* V. **D** Sarum 7 **P** *Maj K S D Wingfield-Digby* **I** F P P GODDARD, N J C LLOYD *c*, C J LUCKRAFT *c.*
SHERBORNES, THE w Pamber [Sherborne St John, (St Andr), Monk Sherborne, (All SS)], *Hants.* R. **D** Win 3 **P** *Bp and Qu Coll Ox* **I** J E G DAVIES.
SHERBOURNE (All SS), *Warws.* V. **D** Cov 8 *See* Barford.
SHERBURN (St Mary), *Durham.* V. **D** Dur 2 **P** *D and C of Dur* **I** (Vacant).
(Hosp). **D** Dur 2 **P** *Bp* **I** G B PATTISON *master.*
SHERBURN (St Hilda) and West and East Heslerton w Yedingham, *N Yorks.* V. **D** York 3 **P** *D and C of York, Crown and S L E Hastings Esq* **I** J R ARMFELT.
SHERBURN-IN-ELMET (All SS) w Barkston, *N Yorks.* V. **D** York 9 **P** *Abp* **I** D C W POST.
SHERE (St Jas) w Peaslake (St Mark) and Gomshall, *Surrey.* R. **D** Guildf 2 **P** *Mrs Bray Moffet* **I** P T SEAL, G EGERTON *c.*
SHEREFORD, *Norf.*. **D** Nor 21 *See* Toftrees.
SHERFIELD-ENGLISH (St Leon), *Hants.* R. **D** Win 10 *See* Awbridge.
SHERFIELD-ON-LODDON (St Leon), *Hants.* R. **D** Win 3 **P** *Bp* **I** J F W ANDERSON.
SHERFORD (St Martin), *Devon.*. **D** Ex 14 *See* Stokenham.
SHERIFF HUTTON (St Helen and H Cross), *N Yorks.* V. **D** York 5 **P** *Abp and Dioc Bd of Patr* alt **I** D W D LEE *p-in-c.*
SHERIFFHALES (St Mary) w Woodcote (St Pet), *Staffs.* V. **D** Lich 25 **P** *Bp* **I** N W RAYBOULD.
SHERINGHAM (St Pet), *Norf.* V. **D** Nor 5 **P** *Bp* **I** A R ASTIN.
SHERINGHAM, UPPER (All SS), *Norf.* V. **D** Nor 24 *See* Weybourne.
SHERINGTON (St Laud) w Chicheley (St Lawr) N Crawley, Astwood and Hardmead, *Bucks.* R. **D** Ox 28 **P** *Bp, Maj J G B Chester, R J Harvey Esq and MMT* in turn **I** J B CORFIELD.
SHERMANBURY (St Giles), *W Sussex.* R. **D** Chich 14 *See* Henfield.
SHERNBORNE (St Pet and St Paul), *Norf.*. **D** Nor *See* Dersingham.
SHERRINGTON (St Mich AA), *Wilts.* R. **D** Sarum 21 *See* Boyton.
SHERSTON MAGNA (H Cross) w Pinkney (St Jo Bapt) and Easton-Grey, R *Wilts.* V. **D** Bris 11 **P** *D and C of Bris* **I** W H THOMSON-GLOVER *c-in-c.*
SHERWOOD (St Martin), *Notts.* V. **D** Southw 14 **P** *Bp* **I** I GATFORD, R A SCRIVENER *c.*
SHEVINGTON (St Ann), *Gtr Man.* V. **D** Blackb 4 **P** *R of Standish* **I** G DEWHURST.
SHEVIOCK (St Mary Virg), *Cornw.*. **D** Truro *See* Anthony.
SHIELDFIELD (Ch Ch), *T & W.*. **D** Newc T 5 *See* Newcastle upon Tyne.
SHIFFORD, *Oxon.*. **D** Ox *See* Bampton-Aston.
SHIFNAL (St Andr), *Salop.* V. **D** Lich 25 **P** *J Brooke Esq* **I** W J TURNER, T E WOOLHOUSE *hon c.*
SHILBOTEL (St Jas), *Northumb.* V. **D** Newc T 7 **P** *Trustees* **I** H SCOTT.
SHILDON (St John), *Durham.* V. **D** Dur 9 **P** *Bp* **I** V G ASHWIN, I S CARTER *c.*
SHILDON, NEW (All SS), *Durham.* V. **D** Dur 9 **P** *Bp* **I** R W CROOK.
SHILLINGFORD (St Geo), *Devon.*. **D** Ex 6 *See* Dunchideock.
SHILLINGSTONE or SHILLING-OKEFORD (H Rood), *Dorset.* R. **D** Sarum 13 **P** *Bp* **I** R S FERGUSON.
SHILLINGTON (All SS), *Beds.* V. **D** St Alb 22 **P** *Bp* **I** R P W LANHAM.
SHILTON, *Oxon.* V. **D** Ox 9 *See* Alvescot.
SHILTON (St Andr), *Warws.*. **D** Cov 5 *See* Ansty.
SHIMPLING (St Geo), *Norf.* R. **D** Nor *See* Dickleburgh.
SHIMPLINGTHORNE (St Geo) w Alpheton (St Pet and St Paul), *Suff.* R. **D** St E 12 *See* Stanstead.
SHINCLIFFE (St Mary Virg), *Durham.* R. **D** Dur 2 **P** *D and C of Dur* **I** R BROWN, R D THOMSON *c.*
SHINEY ROW (St Osw), *Durham.* V. **D** Dur 5 **P** *Crown* **I** E VARLEY.
SHINFIELD (St Mary), *Berks.* V. **D** Ox 15 **P** *D and C of Heref* **I** E A ESSERY.
SHINGAY, *Cambs.*. **D** Ely 9 *See* Wendy.
SHINGHAM, *Norf.*. **D** Ely 17 *See* Beachamwell.
SHIPBOURNE (St Giles), *Kent.* V. **D** Roch 9 **P** *P V Cazalet Esq* **I** E E M EARLE.
SHIPDHAM (All SS) w East and West Bradenham, *Norf.* R. **D** Nor 12 **P** *Bp and Reps of Late Miss E Adlington* **I** F W IRWIN.
SHIPHAM (St Leon) w Rowberrow (St Mich), *Somt.* R. **D** B & W *See* Axbridge.
SHIPHAY COLLATON, *Devon.*. **D** Ex *See* Collaton (St Jo Bapt).
SHIPLAKE (St Pet and St Paul) w Dunsden (All SS), *Oxon.* V. **D** Ox 7 **P** *D and C of Windsor and Dioc Bd of Patr* **I** N G PRINT.
SHIPLEY (St Paul), *W Yorks.* V. **D** Bradf 1 **P** *Simeon Trustees* **I** J R HENSON.
(St Pet), V. **D** Bradf 1 **P** *V of Shipley* **I** J D THOMPSTONE, M P SHORT *c.*
SHIPLEY (St Mary Virg), *W Sussex.* V. **D** Chich 4 **P** *Trustees* **I** A O SILLS.
SHIPLEY (Ch Ch), *Derbys.*. **D** Derby 13 *See* Cotmanhay.
SHIPMEADOW (St Bart), *Suff.* R. **D** St E 14 *See* Barsham.
SHIPPON (St Mary Magd), *Oxon.* V. **D** Ox 11 *See* Abingdon.
SHIPSTON-ON-STOUR w Tidmington, *Warws.* R. **D** Cov 9 **P** *Jes Coll Ox 2 turns, D and C of Worc 1 turn* **I** J R WILLIAMS *p-in-c.*
SHIPTON (St Jas), *Salop.*. **D** Heref *See* Wenlock.
SHIPTON (H Evang) w Overton (St Cuthb), *N Yorks.* V. **D** York 5 **P** *Abp* **I** (Vacant).
SHIPTON-BELLINGER (St Pet), *Hants.* V. **D** Win 2 **P** *Bp* **I** G G CHAPMAN.
SHIPTON-GORGE (St Martin), *Dorset.*. **D** Sarum *See* Burton Bradstock.
SHIPTON-MOYNE (St Jo Bapt) w Westonbirt and Lasborough, *Glos.* R. **D** Glouc 17 **P** *Capt T Sotheron Estcourt and Weston Birt Sch Ltd* **I** E T PETTENGELL *p-in-c.*
SHIPTON-OLIFFE (St Osw) w Shipton-Sollars (St Mary), *Glos.* R. **D** Glouc 15 *See* Dowdeswell.
SHIPTON-ON-CHERWELL (H Cross), *Oxon.* R. **D** Ox 10 **P** *Duke of Marlborough* **I** E G A W PAGE-TURNER *p-in-c*, D C PARKER *c.*

SHIPTON-THORPE (All SS) w Hayton (St Martin), *Humb.* V. **D** York 10 **P** *Abp* **I** J S SELLER *p-in-c.*

SHIPTON-UNDER-WYCHWOOD (St Mary Virg) and Langley w Milton-under-Wychwood, Fifield and Idbury, *Oxon.* V. **D** Ox **P** *Bp* **I** G LINDLEY.

SHIRBURN (All SS) w Pyrton (St Mary), *Oxon.* V. **D** Ox 1 *See* Pyrton.

SHIREBROOK (H Trin), *Derbys.* V. **D** Derby 2 **P** *Bp* **I** T J MARSHALL.

SHIREGREEN, *S Yorks.*. **D** Sheff 3 *See* Sheffield.

SHIREHAMPTON (St Mary), *Avon.* V. **D** Bris 6 **P** *Bp* **I** F R SYMONS, A W WHEELER *hon c.*

SHIREMOOR (St Mark), *T & W.* V. **D** Newc T *See* Tynemouth.

SHIREOAKS (St Luke Evang), *Notts.* and *S Yorks.* V. **D** Southw 7 **P** *Bp* **I** G P STRETTON.

SHIRESHEAD (St Jas formerly St Paul), *Lancs.* V. **D** Blackb 11 **P** *V of Cockerham* **I** W D ROBINSON *p-in-c.*

SHIRLAND (St Leon), *Derbys.* R. **D** Derby 1 **P** *Archd of Chesterfield and Trustees* **I** V CRABTREE.

SHIRLEY (St Jas), *W Midl.* R. **D** Birm 11 **P** *R of Solihull* **I** P W A WHELAN, C J SMITH *c.*

SHIRLEY (St Jo Evang), *Surrey.* V. **D** Cant 16 **P** *Abp* **I** A H R QUINN, A C COLLIER *hon c.*

(St Geo Monk's Orchard), V. **D** Cant 16 **P** *Abp* **I** R N HARLEY.

SHIRLEY Derbys. V **D** Derby 8 *See* Brailsford.

SHIRLEY (St Jas), *Hants.* V. **D** Win 11 **P** *CPS* **I** D I GODDARD, J R CARDWELL *c*, M H SABELL *hon c.*

SHIRLEY WARREN (St Jude), *Hants.* V. **D** Win 11 **P** *Bp* **I** J M NOCKELS.

SHIRWELL (St Pet) w Loxhore (St Mich AA), *Devon.* R. **D** Ex 18 **P** *Sir John Chichester Bt and Bp* alt **I** (Vacant).

SHOBDON (St Jo Evang), *Herefs.*. **D** Heref *See* Pembridge.

SHOBNALL (St Aid), *Staffs.* V. **D** Lich 8 *See* Burton-on-Trent.

SHOBROOKE (St Swithun), *Devon.* R. **D** Ex 2 **P** *Bp* **I** B DUNCAN *p-in-c.*

SHOBY, *Leics.*. **D** Leic 4 *See* Saxelbye.

SHOCKLACH (St Edith), *Chesh.* V. **D** Ches 5 **P** *Bp* **I** G H GREENHOUGH.

SHOEBURY, NORTH (St Mary Virg), *Essex.* V. **D** Chelmsf 11 **P** *Ld Chan* **I** G H G PLASTOW *p-in-c.*

SHOEBURY, SOUTH, or SHOEBURYNESS (St Andr), *Essex.* R. **D** Chelmsf 11 **P** *Hyndman Trustees* **I** P A G RAYNER *p-in-c*, R A CARTWRIGHT *hon c.*

SHOLDEN (St Nich), *Kent.* V. **D** Cant 8 *See* Deal.

SHOLING (St Mary), *Hants.* V. **D** Win 11 **P** *Bp* **I** J E IRONSIDE, J C DENING *c.*

SHOOTER'S HILL (All SS), *Kent.* (Ch Ch), V. **D** S'wark *See* Plumstead.

(Ch Ch), V. **D** S'wark 17 **P** *Bp* **I** D WILCOX.

SHOPLAND (no church), *Essex.* V. **D** Chelmsf 16 *See* Sutton, Great.

SHORE (St Barn), *Gtr Man.* V. **D** Man 17 **P** *D and C of Man* **I** N C WEIGHT.

SHOREDITCH (St Leon w St Michael), *Lon.* V. **D** Lon 2 **P** *Bp and Archd of Lon* **I** P H RONAYNE.

SHOREHAM (St Pet and St Paul), *Kent.* V. **D** Roch 8 **P** *D and C of Westmr* **I** G S SIMPSON.

SHOREHAM BEACH (Good Shepherd), *W Sussex.* V. **D** Chich 13 **P** *Bp* **I** C BLAGG.

SHOREHAM, NEW (St Mary), *W Sussex.* V. **D** Chich 13 **P** *Bp* **I** P J NICKOLS-RAWLE *c.*

OLD (St Nich), *W Sussex.* V. **D** Chich 13 **P** *Bp* **I** M SHEPPARD, P J NICKOLS-RAWLE *c.*

(St Giles Conv Distr). **D** Chich 13 **P** *Bp* **I** J G WHITE *c-in-c*, M C LEAL *c.*

SHORNE (St Pet and St Paul), *Kent.* V. **D** Roch 3 **P** *D and C of Roch* **I** D B RUNCORN.

SHORTHAMPTON, *Oxon.*. **D** Ox *See* Charlbury.

SHORT HEATH (H Trin), *W Midl.* V. **D** Lich 12 **P** *Crown and Bp* alt **I** G M F WILLIAMS, P BROWN *c*, M A SEARS *c.*

SHORT HEATH (St Marg), *W Midl.* V. **D** Birm 7 **P** *Bp* **I** A E POWER.

SHORTLANDS (BVM), *Kent.* V. **D** Roch 11 **P** *Bp* **I** D S R REDMAN.

SHORTWOOD, *Glos.*. **D** Glouc 9 *See* Nailsworth.

SHORWELL (St Pet) w Kingston (St Jas), R *Isle of Wight.* V. **D** Portsm 7 **P** *Bp* **I** (Vacant).

SHOSCOMBE, *Avon.*. **D** B & W 16b *See* Foxcote.

SHOTESHAM (All SS w St Mary and St Botolph), *Norf.* V. **D** Nor 11 **P** *Maj C Fellowes* **I** J H DOBSON.

SHOTLEY (St John), *Northumb.* V. **D** Newc T 3 **P** *Ld Crewe's Trustees* **I** J ROSS *c-in-c.*

SHOTLEY (St Mary Virg) w Erwarton (St Mary), *Suff.*. **D** St E *See* Chelmondiston.

SHOTOVER, *Oxon.*. **D** Ox *See* Forest Hill.

SHOTTERMILL (St Steph), *Surrey.* V. **D** Guildf 4 **P** *Archd of Surrey* **I** C F TICKNER.

SHOTTERY, *Warws.*. **D** Cov 8 *See* Stratford-on-Avon.

SHOTTESBROOKE (St Jo Bapt), R w White Waltham (BVM), *Berks.* V. **D** Ox 13 **P** *J L E Smith Esq* **I** K N SENIOR.

SHOTTESWELL (St Laur), *Warws.* V. **D** Cov 8 *See* Warmington.

SHOTTISHAM (St Marg) w Sutton (All SS), *Suff.* R. **D** St E 7 **P** *Bp* **I** H D A CULLEN.

SHOTTON (St Sav), *Durham.* V. **D** Dur 3 **P** *Bp* **I** G HARRIS.

SHOTWICK (St Mich), *Chesh.* V. **D** Ches 9 **P** *D and C of Ches* **I** K M WHITTAM.

SHOULDHAM (St Mary BV), *Norf.*. **D** Ely 17 *See* Fincham.

SHOULDHAM THORPE (St Mary), *Norf.*. **D** Ely 17 *See* Fincham.

SHOWELL (St Mary), *Oxon.*. **D** Ox *See* Hook-Norton.

SHRAWARDINE (St Mary), *Salop.*. **D** Lich 26 *See* Montford.

SHRAWLEY (St Mary) and the Witleys w Hillhampton, *Worcs.* R. **D** Worc 12 **P** *Bp* **I** J G BARNISH.

SHREWSBURY (St Mary Virg w St Mich and All SS), *Salop.* V. **D** Lich 26 **P** *Bp* **I** B T MADDOX, J C G SELVINI *c.*

(H Cross, Abbey Ch), V. **D** Lich 26 **P** *Bp* **I** R J C LUMLEY, S CARTER *c.*

(H Trin w St Julian), V. **D** Lich 26 **P** *Bp and CPS* **I** P M JAMES.

(St Alkmund), V. **D** Lich 26 **P** *Bp* **I** C K BEAVAN *c-in-c.*

(St Chad), V. **D** Lich 26 **P** *Bp* **I** M POLLIT, I C BROWNE *c*, P A E CHESTER *c.*

(St Geo of Cappadocia, Frankwell), V. **D** Lich 26 **P** *V of St Chad, Shrewsbury* **I** G H JONES.

(St Giles), V. **D** Lich 26 **P** *Bp* **I** J D CUTTER, G USHER *c.*

SHREWTON (St Mary) w Maddington and Rollestone (St Andr), *Wilts.* V. **D** Sarum 21 **P** *Ld Chan* **I** S M W TRICKETT.

SHRIVENHAM (St Andr) w Watchfield (St Thos) and Bourton, *Oxon.* V. **D** Ox 17 **P** *Ld Chan* **I** J M WADE.

SHROPHAM (St Ethelbert) w Larling and Snetterton, *Norf.* V. **D** Nor 18 **P** *Maj E H C Gamier MC 2 turns, Bp 1 turn* **I** (Vacant).

SHROTON (St Mary), *Dorset.*. **D** Sarum 10 *See* Iwerne Courtney.

SHRUB END (All SS), *Essex.* V. **D** Chelmsf 21 **P** *Bp* **I** C J GOULDING.

SHUCKBURGH, LOWER (St Jo Bapt), *Warws.* V. **D** Cov 10 **P** *Sir Charles Shuckburgh Bt* **I** P L JACKSON.

SHUDY-CAMPS (St Mary), *Cambs.* V. **D** Ely 4 **P** *Bp and Gov of Charterho (alt)* **I** H S FINKENSTAEDT.

SHURDINGTON (St Paul), *Glos.* V. **D** Glouc 11 *See* Badgeworth.

SHUSTOKE, *Warws.*. **D** Birm *See* Over Whitacre.

SHUTE (St Mich), *Devon.* V. **D** Ex 5 *See* Kilmington.

SHUTFORD, *Oxon.*. **D** Ox *See* Shenington.

SHUTTINGTON (St Matt) w Amington (St Editha), *Warws.* V. **D** Birm 10 **P** *Bp* **I** J R FAGAN.

SHUTTLEWORTH (St John-in-the-Wilderness), *Gtr Man.*. **D** Man *See* Ramsbottom.

SIBBERTOFT, *Northants.*. **D** Pet *See* Welford.

SIBDON CARWOOD (St Mich AA), w Halford (St Thos), *Salop.* V. **D** Heref 11 **P** *Maj H R Holden and Bp* alt **I** J H T GRIFFIN.

SIBERTSWOLD or SHEPHERDSWELL (St Andr) w Coldred (St Pancras), *Kent.* V. **D** Cant 5 **P** *Abp* **I** R H M WILLIAMS.

SIBFORD (H Trin), *Oxon.* V. **D** Ox 6 *See* Epwell.

SIBLE HEDINGHAM, *Essex.* R. **D** Chelmsf 24 **P** *Bp* **I** B J RODWELL.

SIBSEY (St Marg) w Frithville and New Bolingbroke w Carrington, *Lincs.* V. **D** Linc **P** *Ld Chan* **I** D L LOAKE.

SIBSON (St Barn or St Botolph), *Cambs.*. **D** Ely *See* Stibbington.

SIBSON (St Botolph) w Sheepy and Ratcliffe Culey, *Leics.* R. **D** Leic 15 **P** *Pemb Coll Ox and MMT (alt)* **I** D R HAYBALL.

SIBTHORPE (St Pet), *Notts.* V. **D** Southw 3 **P** *Bp* **I** G A FIRTH.

SIBTON (St Pet), *Suff.* V. **D** St E 19 **P** *Lt-Col J A Brooke* **I** J L THICKITT *p-in-c.*

SIDBURY (St Pet and St Giles) w Sidford, *Devon.* V. **D** Ex 7 **P** *D and C of Ex* **I** J O ALLEN, A D CLARK *c*, E NORMINGTON *c.*

SIDBURY, *Salop.*. **D** Heref 9 *See* Billingsley.

SIDCUP (St Jo Evang), *Kent.* V. **D** Roch 13 **P** *D and C of Roch* **I** S L S ALLEN, I HARPER *c*, C O DARBY *hon c.*

(Ch Ch), V. **D** Roch 13 **P** *Ch Trust Fund Trust* **I** K A SHORT *hon c.*
(St Andr), V. **D** Roch 13 **P** *Bp* **I** A J HOWARD.
SIDDAL (St Mark), V. **D** Wakef 1 *See* Halifax.
SIDDINGTON (All SS), *Chesh.*. **D** Ches 14 *See* Capesthorne.
SIDDINGTON (St Mary w St Pet) w Preston (All SS), *Glos.* R. **D** Glouc 13 **P** *Ld Chan and R Chester-Master Esq* alt **I** P J SUDBURY.
SIDESTRAND (St Mich), *Norf.* R. **D** Nor 5 **P** *Bp* **I** D L AINSWORTH.
SIDLESHAM (St Mary), *W Sussex.* V. **D** Chich 3 **P** *Bp* **I** F J HAWKINS.
SIDLEY (All SS), *E Sussex.*. **D** Chich 17 *See* Bexhill-on-Sea.
SIDLOW BRIDGE (Em Ch), *Surrey.* R. **D** S'wark 12 **P** *Exors of E Brocklehurst* **I** D G N CLARK.
SIDMOUTH (St Mich w St Giles), Woolbrook (St Francis), Salcombe Regis (St Pet) and Branscombe (St Winifred), [Devon]. R. **D** Ex 7 **P** *Dioc Bd of Patr* **I** R C LOWRIE, M M COURTNEY *team v*, P C SPENCER *team v.*
(All SS), V. **D** Ex 7 **P** *CPAS* **I** E VEVERS.
SIGGLESTHORNE (St Laur) and Rise w Nunkeeling (St Helen or St Mary Magd) and Bewholme (Ch Ch) *Humb.* R. **D** York 14 **P** *Crown and Ld Chan* alt **I** J C L HAWKINS.
SIGHILL, *Northumb.*. **D** Newc T *See* Seghill.
SILCHESTER (St Mary), *Hants.* R. **D** Win 3 **P** *Duke of Wellington* **I** (Vacant).
SILEBY (St Mary), *Leics.* V. **D** Leic 9 **P** *A J P Pochin Esq* **I** R J HUNTING.
SILKSTONE (All SS), *S Yorks.* V. **D** Wakef 8 **P** *Bp* **I** D BIRCH.
SILKSWORTH (St Matt), *T & W.* V. **D** Dur 8 **P** *Bp* **I** C M HILL *c.*
SILLOTH (Ch Ch w St Paul), *Cumb.* V. **D** Carl 11 **P** *Simeon Trustees 2 turns, V of Holm Cultram 1 turn* **I** F A H TOMPKINS.
SILSDEN (St Jas Gt), *W Yorks.* V. **D** Bradf 11 **P** *Trustees* **I** J D NOWELL.
SILSOE (St Jas Gt), *Beds.* V. **D** St Alb 15 **P** *Bp* **I** B L NIXON.
SILTON (St Nich), *Dorset.* R. **D** Sarum 13 **P** *Mrs N Y Troyte-Bullock* **I** (Vacant).
SILTON, OVER (St Mary) w Silton, Nether (All SS), *N Yorks.* V. **D** York 26 *See* Leake.
SILVERDALE (St John w Old St John), *Lancs.* V. **D** Blackb 13 **P** *V of Warton* **I** J E N COLEMAN.
SILVERDALE (St Luke), *Staffs.* V. **D** Lich 17 **P** *Exors of Col Sneyd* **I** P E BOOTH.
SILVERLEY, *Cambs.*. **D** Ely 6a *See* Ashley.
SILVERSTONE (St Mich), *Northants.* V. **D** Pet 2 *See* Whittlebury.
SILVERTON (St Mary), *Devon.* R. **D** Ex 4 **P** *Bp* **I** T A WATSON.
SILVERTOWN, WEST (St Barn). **D** Chelmsf 5 *See* Woolwich, North.
SILVINGTON (St Mich), *Salop.* R. **D** Heref 9 *See* Cleeton.
SIMONBURN (St Mungo), *Northumb.* R. **D** Newc T 2 **P** *Bp* **I** J B JACKSON *p-in-c.*
SIMONSIDE, *T & W.*. **D** Dur 6 *See* South Shields (St Simon).
SIMPSON (St Thos Ap), *Bucks.* R. **D** Ox 26 *See* Woughton.
SINFIN (St Steph), *Derbys.* V. **D** Derby **P** *CPAS* **I** M WHITE, D J PHYPERS *c.*
SINFIN MOOR, *Derbys.* V. **D** Derby 11 **P** *Bp* **I** J D KILFORD *p-in-c.*
SINGLETON (St Mary), *W Sussex.* R. **D** Chich **P** *Bp* **I** D M REEVE.
SINGLETON, GREAT (St Anne), *Lancs.* V. **D** Blackb 9 **P** *Major Drumbeck* **I** J LAW.
SINNINGTON (All SS), *N Yorks.* V. **D** York 24 **P** *Simeon Trustees* **I** R W J INDER.
SISLAND (or Sizeland), *Norf.* R. **D** Nor 14 *See* Loddon.
SISSINGHURST (H Trin) w Frittenden, *Kent.* V. **D** Cant 11 **P** *CPAS* **I** I M BUTLER.
SITHNEY (St Sithney), V. **D** Truro *See* Porthleven.
SITTINGBOURNE (St Mich), *Kent.* V. **D** Cant 14 **P** *Abp* **I** F E TURNER.
(H Trin), V. **D** Cant 14 **P** *Abp* **I** F A RAPLEY *c-in-c.*
(St Mary), V. **D** Cant 14 **P** *D and C of Cant* **I** P T MACKENZIE *p-in-c.*
SIX PILGRIMS, THE (Alford w Hornblotton, Babcary, Lovington, N w S Barrow),. **D** B & W 4 **P** *Ch S, D & C of Wells, Dioc Bd of Finance and Bp (in turn)* **I** R A C SIMMONS.
SIXHILLS (All SS), *Lincs.*. **D** Linc 5 *See* Hainton.
SIZEWELL, *Suff.*. **D** St E *See* Leiston.
SKEFFINGTON, *Leics.* R. **D** Leic 8 *See* Billesdon.
SKEFFLING (St Helen), *Humb.* V. **D** York 15 *See* Easington.
SKEGBY (St Andr), *Notts.* V. **D** Southw 2 **P** *Ld Chan* **I** J OGLEY.
SKEGNESS (St Clem w St Matt) and Winthorpe (St Mary), *Lincs.* R. **D** Linc 8 **P** *Bp and Earl of Scarborough (alt)* **I** E G ADLEY.
SKELBROOKE (All H or St Mich AA), *S Yorks.* V. **D** Sheff 8 *See* Burghwallis.
SKELLINGTHORPE (St Lawr) w Doddington (St Pet), *Lincs.* V. **D** Linc 18 **P** *MMT and C of E Trust* **I** R W KAY.
SKELMANTHORPE (St Aid), *W Yorks.* V. **D** Wakef 7 **P** *Bp* **I** S D EARIS.
SKELMERSDALE (St Paul), *Lancs.* V. **D** Liv 9 **P** *V of Ormskirk* **I** G R RICHENS, J WINNARD *c.*
SKELSMERGH (St Jo Bapt) w Selside (St Thos) and Longsleddale (St Mary), *Cumb.* V. **D** Carl 17 **P** *V of Kendal and Dioc Bd of Patr* alt **I** L J PEAT.
SKELTON (St Mich) and Hutton-in-the-Forest (St Jas) w Ivegill, *Cumb.* R. **D** Carl 6 **P** *CCC Ox, D and C of Carl and Bp (in turn)* **I** R P H FRANK.
SKELTON (St Giles or All SS), *N Yorks.* R. **D** York 5 **P** *Abp* **I** (Vacant).
SKELTON (Christ the Consoler) w Newby, *N Yorks.* V. **D** Ripon 3 **P** *Mr R Compton* **I** K F LORD.
SKELTON-IN-CLEVELAND (All SS w Old All SS) w Upleatham, *Cleve.* R. **D** York **P** *Abp* **I** D L E BERRY.
SKENDLEBY (St Pet), *Lincs.*. **D** Linc 7 *See* Partney.
SKERNE, *Humb.*. **D** York *See* Hutton Cranswick.
SKERTON (St Luke), *Lancs.* V. **D** Blackb 11 **P** *Trustees* **I** (Vacant).
(St Chad), V. **D** Blackb 11 **P** *Bp* **I** B MORGAN.
SKEYTON (All SS), *Norf.* R. **D** Nor 8 *See* Swanton Abbot.
SKIDBROOKE w Saltfleet Haven, *Lincs.* V. **D** Linc 12 *See* Saltfleetby.
SKIDBY (St Mich), *Humb.* V. **D** York 17 **P** *Abp* **I** A E HILL.
SKILGATE (St Jo Bapt), *Somt.* R. **D** B & W *See* Upton.
SKILLINGTON (St Jas), *Lincs.* V. **D** Linc 14 **P** *Rev J R H and H C Thorold* **I** H BRIGGS *p-in-c.*
SKINNAND, *Lincs.* R. **D** Linc *See* Graffoe.
SKINNINGROVE, *Cleve.*. **D** York *See* Carlin How.
SKIPSEA (All SS) w Ulrome (St Andr) and Barmston w Fraisthorpe, *Humb.* V. **D** York **P** *Abp, Dr W Kane and M W Wickham-Boynton Esq* **I** (Vacant).
SKIPTON-IN-CRAVEN (H Trin), *N Yorks.* R. **D** Bradf 10 **P** *Ch Ch Ox* **I** C L MARTINEAU, S N HOBSON *c.*
(Ch Ch), V. **D** Bradf 10 **P** *R of Skipton* **I** D A CARPENTER.
SKIPTON-ON-SWALE or SKIPTON BRIDGE (St Jo Div), *N Yorks.*. **D** York 26 *See* Thirsk.
SKIPWITH (St Helen), *N Yorks.* V. **D** York 6 *See* Thorganby.
SKIRBECK (St Nich), *Lincs.* R. **D** Linc 20 **P** *Dioc Bd of Patr* **I** A F WAKELIN.
(H Trin) V. **D** Linc 20 **P** *Trustees* **I** B C OSBORNE.
SKIRBECK QUARTER (St Thos), V *Lincs.*. **D** Linc 20 **P** *Dioc Bd of Patr* **I** R H STANDLEY.
SKIRLAUGH (St Aug) w Long Riston (St Marg), *Humb.* V. **D** York 14 **P** *Abp* **I** D W PERRY.
SKIRMETT (All SS), *Bucks.*. **D** Ox 32 *See* Hambleden.
SKIRPENBECK (Dedic unknown), *Humb.* R. **D** York 7 **P** *Ld Leconfield's Trustees 1st and 3rd turns, Crown 2nd turn, Ld Chan 4th turn* **I** (Vacant).
SKIRWITH (St Jo Evang) w Ousby (St Luke) and Melmerby (St Jo Bapt), *Cumb.* V. **D** Carl 6 **P** *Dioc Bd of Patr* **I** W BURDON.
SLAD (H Trin) w Uplands (All SS), *Glos.* V. **D** Glouc 4 **P** *V of Painswick* **I** J C EADE.
SLADE GREEN (St Aug), *Kent.* V. **D** Roch 15 **P** *Bp* **I** C F JOHNSON.
SLAIDBURN (St Andr), *Lancs.* R. **D** Bradf 6 **P** *Ch S Trust* **I** G H GAZE.
SLAITHWAITE (St Jas) w East Scammonden, *W Yorks.* V. **D** Wakef 6 **P** *V of Huddersfield* **I** C R TOWNSEND.
SLALEY (St Mary Virg), *Northumb.* V. **D** Newc T 3 **P** *Bp* **I** T J ATKINS *p-in-c.*
SLAPTON (St Jas Greater), *Devon.* V. **D** Ex 14 **P** *Bp* **I** R A DURANT.
SLAPTON (H Cross), *Bucks.* R. **D** Ox 27 *See* Ivinghoe.
SLAPTON (St Botolph), *Northants.* R. **D** Pet *See* Abthorpe.
SLAUGHAM (St Mary) w Handcross, *W Sussex.* R. **D** Chich 11 **P** *Mrs E L E Warren* **I** J E POSTILL.
SLAUGHTER, UPPER w Lower (St Mary), Naunton (St Andr) and Eyford, *Glos.* R. **D** Glouc 16 **P** *F E Broome*

Witts Esq and Bp alt I P S M WALTON.
SLAUGHTERFORD (St Nich), *Wilts*.. D Bris *See* Biddestone.
SLAWSTON, *Leics*.. D Leic *See* Stonton Wyville.
SLEAFORD, NEW (St Denis), *Lincs*. V. D Linc 22 P *Bp* I H G MITCHELL, P E COPPEN *c*, H C MIDDLETON *c*.
SLEAFORD, OLD (St Giles), *Lincs*.. D Linc 22 *See* Quarrington.
SLEDDALE, LONG *Cumb*.. D Carl *See* Burnside.
SLEDMERE (St Mary) and Wetwang (St Nich) w Cowlam (St Andr), *Humb*. V. D York 13 P *Sir M T R Sykes Bt and Abp (alt)* I (Vacant).
SLEEKBURN (St John), *Northumb*. V. D Newc T 1 P *D and C of Newc T* I C SCOTT, J WHEATLEY *c*.
SLEIGHTS, *N Yorks*.. D York *See* Eskdaleside.
SLIMBRIDGE (St Jo Evang), *Glos*. R. D Glouc 5 P *Magd Coll Ox* I E C CHARLESWORTH.
SLINDON (St Mary) w Eartham, *W Sussex*. R. D Chich 1 P *Miss L J Izard and D and C of Chich* alt I J R M COSSAR *p-in-c*.
SLINFOLD (St Pet), *W Sussex*. R. D Chich 4 P *Bp* I D CHANING-PEARCE.
SLINGSBY (All SS), *N Yorks*. R. D York 21 P *Exors of Lady A F Macleod* I P H S CRAWFORD *p-in-c*.
SLIPTON (St Jo Bapt), *Northants*. V. D Pet *See* Lowick.
SLOANE STREET (H Trin). D Lon *See* Chelsea
SLOLEY (St Bart), *Norf*. R. D Nor 6 *See* Worstead.
SLOOTHBY , *Lincs*.. D Linc 8 *See* Willoughby.
SLOUGH (St Paul), *Berks*. V. D Ox 24 P *Trustees* I R H PICKERING, M A HILL *c*.
(St Mary Upton cum Chalvey), R. D Ox 24 P *Bp* I G A HENDY, A G BIGNELL *c*, R W S DAND *c*, G R HAMBORG *c*, A A WHALLEY *c*.
WEST (Britwell, Cippenham, Manor Pk and Farnham Royal S), R. D Ox 24 P *Dioc Bd of Patr* I W M HETLING, J N DAY *team v*, D C KNIGHT *team v*, D E WEST *team v*.
See also LANGLEY MARISH AND FARNHAM ROYAL..
SLYNE (St Luke) w Hest, *Lancs*. V. D Blackb 13 P *Bp* I T G MCALISTER.
SMALL HEATH (St Aid), *W Midl*. V. D Birm 8 P *Trustees* I J F P MORRISON-WELLS.
(St Greg Gt), V. D Birm 8 P *Bp* I P W HIPKIN.
SMALL HYTHE, *Kent*. V. D Cant 10 *See* Tenterden.
SMALLBRIDGE (St Jo Bapt), *Gtr Man*. V. D Man 17 P *Bp* I T G BLOFELD.
SMALLBURGH (St Pet) w Dilham and Honing w Crostwight, *Norf*. R. D Nor P *Bp, Trustees and T R Cubitt Esq* I F L THOMAS.
SMALLEY (St Jo Bapt), *Derbys*. V. D Derby 6 P *Bp* I L J JAMES.
SMALLTHORNE (St Sav), *Staffs*. V. D Lich 17a P *R of Norton-le-Moors* I R J COSSLETT.
SMALLWOOD (St Jo Bapt), *Chesh*.. D Ches 11 *See* Astbury.
SMANNELL (Ch Ch) w Enham Alamein, *Hants*. R. D Win 2 P *Bp* I T G MILWARD.
SMARDEN (St Mich), *Kent*. R. D Cant 10 P *Abp* I PHILLIPS, M J MCENERY *c*.
SMEATON, LITTLE, *N Yorks*.. D Wakef 11 *See* Kirk Smeaton.
SMEETH, *Kent*.. D Cant *See* Brabourne.
SMEETON-WESTERBY (Ch Ch) w Saddington (St Helen), *Leics*. R. D Leic 6 P *R of Kibworth Beauchamp and Bp* I F W DAWSON *p-in-c*.
SMETHCOTE (St Mich AA) w Woolstaston (St Mich AA), *Salop*. R. D Heref 11 P *Hulme Trustees and Exors of Col F A Wolryche-Whitmore* I (Vacant).
SMETHWICK (Old Ch), *W Midl*. V. D Birm 6 P *Trustees* I B A HALL.
(H Trin w St Alb), V. D Birm 6 P *Bp* I J D POTTER.
(St Matt w St Chad), V. D Birm 6 P *Bp and V of Smethwick* alt I R K DANIEL.
(St Mary Virg Bearwood), V. D Birm 6 P *V of Smethwick* I B A MCQUILLEN.
(St Steph and St Mich), V. D Birm 6 P *Bp* I R V ALLEN.
WEST (St Paul), V. D Birm 6 P *Bp* I N J NELSON.
SMISBY (St Jas), *Derbys*. V. D Derby 15 P *Bp* I R BAGNALL.
SMITHFIELD (St Bart).. D Lon 1 *See* London.
SNAILWELL (St Pet), *Cambs*. R. D Ely 3 P *Exors of Col G Tharp* I D J KIGHTLEY *c-in-c*.
SNAINTON, *N Yorks*.. D York *See* Brompton.
SNAITH (St Lawr), *Humb*. V. D Sheff 9 P *Bp* I H G SALISBURY.
SNAPE Suff. V D St E *See* Sternfield.
SNAPE CASTLE (St Mary), *N Yorks*.. D Ripon 3 *See* Well.
SNARESTON, *Leics*. R. D Leic 12 *See* Swepston.
SNARFORD (St Lawr), *Lincs*.. D Linc 5 *See* Snelland.
SNARGATE, *Kent*.. D Cant 13 *See* Brookland.
SNAVE, *Kent*.. D Cant 13 *See* Brookland.
SNEAD (St Mary Virg), *Powys*.. D Heref 10 P *Lt Col A P Sykes* I R B DAVIES *p-in-c*.
SNEATON (St Hilda), *N Yorks*. R. D York *See* Eskdaleside.
SNEINTON (St Steph) w (St Alb Mart), *Notts*. V. D Southw 14 P *Bp* I J W W TYSON.
(St Chris), V. D Southw 14 P *Trustees* I S R CARTER.
(St Cypr Carlton Hill), V. D Southw 14 P *Bp* I G C FRANCE.
(St Matthias), V. D Southw 14 P *Bp* I K L BENNETT.
SNELLAND (All SS) w Snarford (St Lawr), *Lincs*. R. D Linc 5 P *Bp and Dioc Bd of Patr* I A G D SHEARWOOD.
SNELSTON (St Pet), *Derbys*. R. D Derby 8 *See* Norbury.
SNETTERTON (All SS), *Norf*.. D Nor 18 *See* Shropham.
SNETTISHAM (St Mary Virg), *Norf*. V. D Nor 23 P *CPAS* I D A PORTER.
SNEYD (H Trin), *Staffs*. V. D Lich 17a P *Bp* I M G JOHNSON *p-in-c*.
SNEYD GREEN (St Andr), *Staffs*.. D Lich 17a P *Bp* I W B COONEY.
SNIBSTON (St Jas), *Leics*. V. D Leic 11 P *Bp* I D JENNINGS *p-in-c*.
SNITTERBY (St Nich), *Lincs*. R. D Linc 6 *See* Wadingham.
SNITTERFIELD (St Jas Gt) w Bearley (St Mary Virg), *Warws*. V. D Cov 7 P *Bp and V of Wootton Wawen* I S W M HARTLEY.
SNODLAND (All SS) w Lower Birling (Ch Ch), *Kent*. R. D Roch 1 P *Bp and CPAS* I J E TIPP.
SNOREHAM, *Essex*.. D Chelmsf 13 *See* Latchingdon.
SNORING, GREAT (St Mary) w Snoring, Little (St Andr), *Norf*. R. D Nor 21 P *St Jo Coll Cam* I P G FLATHER *p-in-c*.
SNOWSHILL (St Barn), *Glos*. R. D Glouc 18 *See* Stanton.
SOBERTON (St Pet) w New Town (H Trin), *Hants*. R. D Portsm 2 P *Bp* I A W BENNETT.
SOCKBURN (All SS), *Durham*. V. D Dur 11 *See* Dinsdale.
SODBURY, LITTLE, *Glos*.. D Glouc *See* Horton.
OLD (St Jo Bapt). D Glouc *See* Chipping Sodbury.
SOHAM (St Andr) w Barway (St Nich), *Cambs*. V. D Ely 3 P *Pemb Coll Cam* I M G F SHEARS.
SOHAM, MONK, *Suff*.. D St E *See* Bedfield.
SOHO, *Lon*.. D Lon 19 *See* Westminster.
SOLIHULL (St Alphege), *W Midl*. R. D Birm 11 P *S for Maint of Faith* I R S WILKINSON, P M ALLCOCK *team v*, J DE WIT *team v*, M C FREEMAN *team v*, M S D LEAFE *c*, J MORLEY *c*.
SOLLERS HOPE, *Herefs*. R. D Heref 8 *See* How Caple.
SOLWAY ASH (H Trin), *Dorset*.. D Sarum 4 *See* Netherbury.
SOMBORNE, KING'S (St Pet and St Paul) w Ashley, *Hants*. V. D Win 10 P *P V Barker-Mill Esq 2 turns, Miss Innes 1 turn* I (Vacant).
SOMERBY (All SS) w Burrough-on-the-Hill (St Mary Virg) and Pickwell (All SS), *Leics*. V. D Leic 8 P *Dioc Bd of Patr and Bp* alt I A L LATTIMORE.
SOMERBY (St Marg), *Lincs*.. D Linc 6 *See* Bigby.
SOMERBY (St Mary Magd) w Great Humby, *Lincs*. R. D Linc 14 P *Earl of Ancaster* I W B FOSTER.
SOMERCOTES (St Thos), *Derbys*. V. D Derby 1 P *Bp* I P DAWKES.
SOMERCOTES, NORTH (St Mary), *Lincs*. V. D Linc 12 P *Duchy of Lanc* I T J WALKER *p-in-c*.
SOMERCOTES, SOUTH (St Pet), *Lincs*. R. D Linc 12 P *Duchy of Lanc* I T J WALKER *p-in-c*.
SOMERFORD-KEYNES (All SS) w Sharncote (All SS), *Wilts*.. D Glouc *See* Kemble.
SOMERFORD MAGNA or BROAD (St Pet and St Paul) w Somerford Parva (St Jo Bapt) and Seagry (St Mary Virg) *Wilts*. R. D Bris 11 P *Bp, MMT and Ex Coll Ox* I I C MAXWELL.
SOMERLEYTON (St Mary Virg) w Ashby (St Mary Virg), *Suff*. R. D Nor 15 P *Ld Somerleyton* I E C BROOKS.
SOMERS TOWN D Lon *See* St Pancras.
SOMERSAL-HERBERT (St Pet), *Derbys*. R. D Derby 14 *See* Sudbury.
SOMERSBY (St Marg) w Bag Enderby (St Marg), *Lincs*. R. D Linc 7 P *Dioc Bd of Patr* I P E FLUCK *c-in-c*.
SOMERSHAM (St Jo Bapt) w Pidley-cum-Fenton (All SS) and Colne (St Helen), *Cambs*. R. D Ely 12 P *Bp* I A P LUDLOW.
SOMERSHAM (St Mary) w Flowton (St Mary) and Offton (St Mary) w Willisham, *Suff*. R. D St E 1 P *MMT and Bp (alt)* I J M POTTER.

SOMERTON (St Mich AA) w Compton Dundon, Charlton Adam, Charlton Mackrell and Kingsdon *Somt*. V. **D** B & W 10 **P** *Bp of Lon 1st Turn, Bp of B & W 2nd and 3rd turns* **I** A T BUDGETT, V L DALEY *c*.
SOMERTON Oxon. R **D** Ox *See* The Heyfords.
SOMERTON (St Marg), *Suff*. R. **D** St E 12 **P** *Bp* **I** T S WRIGHT *c-in-c*.
SOMERTON, EAST, *Norf*.. **D** Nor *See* Winterton.
SOMERTON, WEST (St Mary), V. **D** Nor 2 **P** *D and C of Nor* **I** E A CUNNINGTON.
SOMPTING (St Mary BV), *W Sussex*.. **D** Chich 9 **P** *O of St John of Jer* **I** R J FRIARS.
SONNING (St Andr), *Berks*. V. **D** Ox 16 **P** *Bp* **I** G S G STOKES.
SOOKHOLM (St Pet and St Paul), *Notts*.. **D** Southw 2 *See* Warsop.
SOPLEY (St Mich AA), *Hants*. V. **D** Win 8 *See* Burton.
SOPWORTH, *Wilts*. R. **D** Glouc 17 *See* Boxwell.
SOTBY (St Pet), *Lincs*.. **D** Linc 11 *See* Hatton.
SOTHERTON, *Suff*.. **D** St E *See* Uggeshall.
SOTTERLEY (St Marg) w Willingham (St Mary), Shadingfield (St Jo Bapt), Ellough (All SS), Weston (St Pet) and Henstead, *Suff*. R. **D** St E 14 **P** *Lt Col M E St J Barne, Exors of Dr F G L Barnes and Bp* **I** (Vacant).
SOTWELL, *Oxon*.. **D** Ox 18 *See* Brightwell.
SOULBURY (All SS), *Bucks*. V. **D** Ox 27 *See* Stewkley.
SOULBY (St Luke) w Crosby-Garrett (St Andr), *Cumb*. V. **D** Carl 1 *See* Warcop.
SOULDERN (St Mary Virg), *Oxon*. R. **D** Ox *See* Fritwell.
SOULDROP (All SS), *Beds*.. **D** St Alb *See* Knotting.
SOUNDWELL (St Steph), *Avon*. V. **D** Bris 8 **P** *Bp* **I** W R HARRISON, P DIXON *c*.
SOURTON (St Thos of Cant), *Devon*. V. **D** Ex 22 *See* Lydford.
SOUTH BANK (St Jo Evang), *N Yorks*. V. **D** York 22 **P** *Abp* **I** R W CALVERT.
SOUTH HILL (St Sampson), *Cornw*. R. **D** Truro 9 *See* Callington.
SOUTH KIRKBY (All SS) w Elmsall, *W Yorks*. V. **D** Wakef 11 **P** *Guild of All S* **I** E BROWN *c*.
SOUTH LEIGH (St Jas Gt), *Oxon*. V. **D** Ox 9 **P** *Bp* **I** P WALKER *c-in-c*.
SOUTH MILFORD (St Mary Virg), *N Yorks*. R. **D** York 8 **P** *Abp* **I** G MURFET *p-in-c*.
SOUTH MOLTON (Nymet St George, Filleigh, East Buckland, High Bray w Charles, Warkleigh, Satterleigh, Chittlehamholt, Kingsnympton, Romansleigh, North Molton and Twitchen), *Devon*. R. **D** Ex **P** *Dioc Bd of Patr* **I** W M RUMBALL *c*, G C W TWYMAN *c*, F J WILLIAMS *hon c*.
SOUTH MOOR (St Geo), *Durham*. V. **D** Dur 7 **P** *Bp* **I** J R TROOP.
SOUTH NORMANTON, *Derbys*.. **D** Derby *See* Normanton, South.
SOUTH POOL (St Cyriac), *Devon*. R. **D** Ex 14 *See* Portlemouth, East.
SOUTH SHIELDS (St Hilda w St Thos), *T & W*. V. **D** Dur 6 **P** *D and C of Dur* **I** A J VINCENT, E A JAY *hon c*.
(H Trin), V. **D** Dur 6 *See* Rekendyke.
(St Aid), V. **D** Dur 6 **P** *Bp* **I** R S WILSON *p-in-c*.
(St Francis), V. **D** Dur 6 *See* Rekendyke.
(St Jude), V. **D** Dur 6 *See* Rekendyke.
(St Oswin, Brinkburn), V. **D** Dur 6 **P** *Crown* **I** G F FINN.
(St Simon, Simonside), V. **D** Dur 6 **P** *Crown* **I** A G WARD.
(St Steph), R. **D** Dur 6 **P** *D and C of Dur* **I** R S WILSON.
SOUTH WEALD **D** Chelmsf 10 *See* Weald.
SOUTH WESTOE (St Mich AA), V. **D** Dur 6 **P** *Bp* **I** J D SLYFIELD.
SOUTH WINGFIELD (All SS), *Derbys*. V. **D** Derby 1 **P** *Duke of Devonshire* **I** J H WATTS P-IN-C OF WESSINGTON.
SOUTHACRE (St Geo), *Norf*. R. **D** Nor 20 **P** *H A Birkbeck Esq* **I** R NAZER.
SOUTHALL (H Trin), *Gtr Lon*. V. **D** Lon 6 **P** *CPS* **I** P B D CRICK *c-in-c*.
(St Geo), V. **D** Lon 6 **P** *D and C of St Paul's* **I** M K RUMALSHAH *p-in-c*.
(Ch the Redeemer), V. **D** Lon 6 **P** *Bp* **I** G T GRAINGER.
(Emmanuel Conv Distr). **D** Lon 6 **P** *Bp* **I** R L SMITH *min*.
SOUTHALL GREEN (St Jo Evang), *Gtr Lon*. V. **D** Lon 6 **P** *CPS* **I** D L E BRONNERT, P B D CRICK *c*, P R TURP *c*.
SOUTHAM (St Jas) w Stockton, *Warws*. R. **D** Cov 10 **P** *Crown 3 turns, New Coll Ox 1 turn* **I** T KNIGHT, A METCALFE *c*, T T RUTHERFORD *c*.
SOUTHAM, *Glos*.. **D** Glouc 10 *See* Bishop's Cleeve.
SOUTHAMPTON (City Centre) (St Mary) w (H Trin) (St Matt), (St Aug of Cant Northam), (St Pet and St Paul w All SS), and (St Mich w H Rood, St Lawr, St John and St Jas), *Hants*. R. **D** Win 11 **P** *Bp* **I** R J MILNER, H C HALL *team v*, C J OFFER *team v*, D C SELF *team v*, H J STRINGER *team v*, P A WETHERELL *team v*.
(Ch Ch Portswood or Highfield), V. **D** Win 11 **P** *Bp* **I** J F A WILLIAMS.
(Lord's Hill), V. **D** Win **P** *Bp* **I** C L ATKINS.
(St Alb), V. **D** Win 11 **P** *Bp* **I** E F CHIVERS.
(St Barn) V. **D** Win 11 **P** *Bp* **I** J A EXALL.
(St Chris Thornhill), V. **D** Win 11 **P** *Bp* **I** J R TURPIN.
(St Denys, Portswood), V. **D** Win 11 **P** *Bp* **I** J L PHEIFFER.
(St Mark), V. **D** Win 11 **P** *CPS* **I** P D COOPER *p-in-c*.
(St Mary Extra or Pear Tree), V. **D** Win 11 **P** *Bp* **I** M HARLEY.
SOUTHBERGH (St Andr), *Norf*.. **D** Nor 12 *See* Cranworth.
SOUTHBOROUGH (St Pet w Ch Ch and St Matt), *Kent*. V. **D** Roch 10 **P** *CPAS* **I** A R J WAGSTAFF, J H NODDINGS *c*, M C HOWARD *hon c*.
(St Thos), V. **D** Roch 10 **P** *Bp* **I** D COX.
SOUTHBOURNE (St Jo Evang) w West Thorney, *W Sussex*. V. **D** Chich **P** *Bp* **I** R W POIL.
SOUTHBOURNE, *Dorset*.. **D** Win 7 *See* Bournemouth.
SOUTHBROOM (St Jas Gt), V. **D** Sarum 23 **P** *D and C of Sarum* **I** K E BROWN.
SOUTHCHURCH (H Trin), *Essex*. R. **D** Chelmsf 11 **P** *Abp* **I** J H GORE.
(Ch Ch), V. **D** Chelmsf 11 **P** *Bp* **I** G F DEAR.
SOUTHDENE, *Mer*.. **D** Liv 5 *See* Kirkby.
SOUTHDOWN, *Somt*.. **D** B & W *See* Twiverton.
SOUTHEA (Em Ch) w Murrow (Corpus Christi) and Parson Drive, *Cambs*. V. **D** Ely 20 **P** *Bp* **I** R M C NURSE.
SOUTHEASE, *E Sussex*. R. **D** Chich 15 *See* Telscombe.
SOUTHEND (St John), *Kent*. V. **D** S'wark 20 *See* Catford.
SOUTHEND-ON-SEA (St Jo Bapt w St Mark, All SS w St Francis and St Erkenwald), *Essex*. R. **D** Chelmsf 11 **P** *Bp and Keble Coll Ox* **I** R B WHITE, L A A CARTER *team v*, J CLOWES *team v*.
See also LEIGH, PRITTLEWELL, SOUTHCHURCH, THORPE BAY, AND WESTCLIFF-ON-SEA
SOUTHERY (St Mary Virg), *Norf*. R. **D** Ely 17 **P** *Guild of All S* **I** T H W SWAN *p-in-c*.
SOUTHFIELDS (St Barn), *Surrey*. V. **D** S'wark 7 **P** *Bp* **I** G HEAL.
(St Mich AA), V. **D** S'wark 7 **P** *Ch Soc* **I** J V DAVIES, W MUNCEY *c*.
SOUTHFLEET (St Nich), *Kent*. R. **D** Roch 3 **P** *CPAS* **I** C D GOBLE.
(St Barn Istead Rise). V. **D** Roch 3 **P** *Bp* **I** R SMITH.
SOUTHGATE (Ch Ch), *Lon*. V. **D** Lon 21 **P** *V of Edmonton* **I** B W MOUNTFORD, N E GREEN *c*, W J PHILLIPS *hon c*.
(St Andr), V. **D** Lon 21 **P** *Bp* **I** J LAING, V O WHITTAM *hon c*.
SOUTHGATE, NEW (St Paul), *Lon*. V. **D** Lon 16 **P** *V of Southgate* **I** C G POPE.
SOUTHILL (All SS), *Beds*. V. **D** St Alb 22 **P** *S Whitbread Esq* **I** M G BOURKE.
SOUTHLEIGH (St Lawr), *Devon*. R. **D** Ex 5 *See* Farway.
SOUTHMEAD (St Steph), *Avon*. V. **D** Bris 6 **P** *Bp* **I** (Vacant).
SOUTHMERE, *Norf*.. **D** Nor 23 *See* Sedgeford.
SOUTHMINSTER (St Leon), *Essex*. V. **D** Chelmsf 13 **P** *Govs of Charterhouse* **I** M CLEEVE.
SOUTHOE (St Leon) w Hail Weston, *Cambs*. R. **D** Ely 13 **P** *Mert Coll Ox* **I** G W WHITLOCK.
SOUTHOLT, *Suff*.. **D** St E *See* Worlingworth.
SOUTHOWRAM (St Anne-in-the-Grove), *W Yorks*. V. **D** Wakef 2 **P** *V of Halifax* **I** P MILLS.
SOUTHPORT (St Cuthb), *Mer*.. **D** Liv 8 *See* North Meols.
(All SS), V. **D** Liv 8 **P** *Trustees* **I** (Vacant).
(All S), V. **D** Liv 8 **P** *V of All SS Southport* **I** E NEWBON.
(Ch Ch), V. **D** Liv 8 **P** *Trustees* **I** G C GRINHAM, C E POTTER *c*.
(Em), V. **D** Liv 8 **P** *PCC* **I** M D WHYTE.
(H Trin), V. **D** Liv 8 **P** *Trustees* **I** J F COWLING, R E SWANN *c*.
(St Luke), V. **D** Liv 8 **P** *V of H Trin Southport* **I** R J BRUNSWICK.
(St Paul), V. **D** Liv 8 **P** *Trustees* **I** D J REYNOLDS.
(St Phil), V. **D** Liv 8 **P** *V of Ch Ch Southport* **I** A R AIRD.
(St Simon and St Jude), V. **D** Liv 8 **P** *Trustees* **I** J C RIMMER.
SOUTHREPPS (St Jas), *Norf*.. **D** Nor 5 *See* Trunch.
SOUTHREY, *Lincs*.. **D** Linc 3 *See* Bardney.
SOUTHROP (St Pet), *Glos*. V. **D** Glouc 14 *See* Eastleach.
SOUTHSEA, *Hants*.. **D** Portsm 5 *See* Portsea.
SOUTH SHORE, *Lancs*.. **D** Blackb *See* Blackpool.
SOUTHTOWN (St Mary), *Nor*. V. **D** Nor 2 **P** *Bp* **I** P H ATKINS.

SOUTHWARK (Cathl Ch of St Sav and St Mary Overie), *Surrey*. R. D S'wark 5 P *Bp* I VERY REV H E FRANKHAM, A B HAWLEY *c*.
(Ch Ch), R. D S'wark 5 P *Marshall's Charity* I P B CHALLEN, D CURWEN *c*, H J NORTON *c*.
(H Trin w St Matt), R. D S'wark 5 P *Bp* I J A F GALBRAITH, M N A TORRY *c*.
(St Alphege), V. D S'wark 5 P *Trustees* I E MATHIESON.
(St Geo Mart w St Mich AA and St Steph), R. D S'wark 5 P *Corp of Lon 1 turn Ld Chan 3 turns* I C E V BOWKETT.
(St Hugh's Conv Distr Charterho Miss). D S'wark 5 P *The Charterhouse* I A B HAWLEY *c-in-c*, T B ENSOR *c*.
(St Jude w St Paul), V. D S'wark 5 P *CPS* I C E V BOWKETT *c-in-c*.
(St Mary Magd). D S'wark 5 *See* Walworth.
SOUTHWATER (H Innoc), *W Sussex*. V. D Chich 4 P *V of Horsham* I P MESSENGER.
SOUTHWELL (Cathl Ch of St Mary Virg), *Notts*. R. D Southw 15 P *Bp* I VERY REV J M IRVINE.
(H Trin), V. D Southw 15 P *CPAS* I E A C CARDWELL.
SOUTHWICK (St Mich AA), *W Sussex*. R. D Chich 13 P *Ld Chan* I F MITCHINSON, H F MCNEIGHT *hon c*.
(St Pet). D Chich *See* Portslade (St Andr).
SOUTHWICK (H Trin), *T & W*. R. D Dur 8 P *D and C of Dur* I C R MASON *c-in-c*.
(St Columba), V. D Dur 8 P *Bp* I K L STOCK, D R M SMITH *hon c*.
(St Cuthb Conv Distr). D Dur 8 P *Bp* I D A PARKER *p-in-c*.
See also BISHOP WEARMOUTH..
SOUTHWICK (St Mary Virg) w Glapthorne (St Leon), *Northants*. V. D Pet 11 P *C G Capron Esq* I D W J TWEDDLE.
SOUTHWICK (St Jas) w Boarhunt (St Nich), *Hants*. V. D Portsm 2 P *Mrs E S Borthwick Norton* I A R MOORE *p-in-c*.
SOUTHWICK (St Thos), *Wilts*.. D Sarum 24 *See* Bradley, North.
SOUTHWOLD (St Edm K and Mart), *Suff*. V. D St E 15 P *Simeon Trustees* I N S BEDFORD.
SOUTHWOOD (St Edm), *Norf*.. D Nor 1 *See* Cantley.
SOUTHWORTH (Ch Ch), *Chesh*. R. D Liv 11 *See* Croft.
SOWE, *W Midl*. V. D Cov 2 *See* Walsgrave-on-Sowe.
SOWERBY (St Pet, St Geo and St Mary), *W Yorks*. V. D Wakef 1 P *Dioc Bd of Patr* I W J GIBSON.
SOWERBY (St Osw), *N Yorks*. V. D York 26 P *Abp* I P WORDSWORTH.
SOWERBY BRIDGE (Ch Ch) w Norland (St Luke), *W Yorks*. V. D Wakef 1 P *V of Halifax* I J TOWNEND.
SOWTON (St Mich AA), *Devon*.. D Ex 1 *See* Clyst St Geo.
SPALDING (St Mary and St Nich w St Pet), *Lincs*. V. D Linc 17 P *Feoffees* I D G JAKEMAN.
(St Jo Bapt),. D Linc 17 P *Bp* I J C MOON, E J CONNOR *c*, D J OSBOURNE *c*.
(St Paul), V. D Linc 17 P *Bp and V of Spalding* I D A COWLING.
SPALDWICK (St Jas) w Barham (St Giles) and Woolley (St Mary), *Cambs*. V. D Ely 11 P *Bp* I M A JENNER *p-in-c*.
SPANBY, *Lincs*.. D Linc 13 *See* Swaton.
SPARHAM (St Mary Virg), *Norf*. R. D Nor *See* Lyng.
SPARKBROOK (Ch Ch), *W Midl*. V. D Birm 8 P *Aston Trustees* I J P RICHARDSON *p-in-c*.
(Em Ch), V. D Birm 8 P *Aston Trustees* I E F PARSONS.
(St Agatha), V. D Birm 8 P *Bp* I L D P BOYD *p-in-c*.
SPARKFORD (St Mary Magd) w Weston Bampfylde (H Cross), *Somt*. R. D B & W 4 P *Exors of the Late H E Bennett Esq and CPS* Alt I P F L CONNOR.
SPARKHILL (St Jo Evang), *W Midl*. V. D Birm 8 P *Dioc Trustees* I D H GARNER.
SPARKWELL (All SS), *Devon*. V. D Ex 21 P *D and C of Windsor* I F R HEASMAN.
SPARSHOLT (H Rood and St Mary Virg) w Kingston-Lisle (St Jo Bapt), *Oxon*.. D Ox 19 *See* Ridgeway.
SPARSHOLT (St Steph) w Lainston, (St Pet), *Hants*. V. D Win 12 P *Ld Chan* I E D CARTWRIGHT.
SPAXTON (St Marg) w Goathurst, Enmore and Charlynch (St Mary Virg), *Somt*. R. D B & W P *Bp, Ch Trust Fund and MMT* I J S BARKS *c*.
SPEEN (St Mary), *Berks*. V. D Ox 14 *See* Boxford.
SPEENHAMLAND (St Mary Virg), R. D Ox 14 *See* Newbury.
SPEETON (St Leon), *N Yorks*. V. D York 12 *See* Reighton.
SPEKE (St Aid and All SS), *Mer*. R. D Liv 7 P *Bp* I D R G LOCKYER, G AMOS *team v*.
SPELDHURST (St Mary Virg) w Groombridge (St Jo Evang) and Ashurst (St Martin), *Kent*. R. D Roch 10 P *Dioc Bd of Patr and Ld Sackville* I M P BEEK, J A TEBBOTH *c*.
SPELSBURY (All SS) w Chadlington (St Nich), *Oxon*. V. D Ox 3 P *Ch Ch Ox* I (Vacant).
SPENCER'S WOOD (St Mich AA), *Berks*. V. D Ox 15 P *Bp* I J R HART *c*.
SPENNITHORNE (St Mich AA) w Finghall and Hauxwell (St Osw), *N Yorks*. R. D Ripon P *R J Dalton Esq and M C A Wyville Esq alt* I W H PRUDOM.
SPENNYMOOR (St Paul) w Whitworth, *Durham*. V. D Dur 9 P *D and C of Dur* I R A H GREANY, J M YOUNG *c*.
SPERNALL (St Leon), Morton Bagot (H Trin) and Oldberrow (St Mary), *Warws*. R. D Cov 7 P *Mrs J M Pinney and Ld Chan* alt I F A CARROLL.
SPETCHLEY, *Worcs*. R. D Worc 3 *See* White Ladies Aston.
SPETISBURY (St Jo Bapt) w Charlton Marshall (St Mary Virg), *Dorset*. R. D Sarum 10 P *Bp* I D B PENNAL *p-in-c*.
SPEXHALL (St Pet) w Wissett (St Andr), *Suff*. R. D St E *See* Halesworth.
SPILSBY (St Jas) w Hundleby (St Mary), *Lincs*. V. D Linc 7 P *Earl of Ancaster* I J S THOROLD, G PEACE *c*.
SPITALFIELDS (Ch Ch w All SS Mile End New Town), *Lon*. R. D Lon 4 P *Mart Mem and C of E Trusts* I E G STRIDE.
SPITALGATE (St Jo Evang), *Lincs*.. D Linc 7 *See* Grantham.
SPITTAL (St Jo Evang), *Northumb*. V. D Newc T 11 P *Mercers' Co and Bp* alt I P WHITEHEAD P-IN-C OF SCREMERSTON.
SPIXWORTH w Crostwick (St Pet), *Norf*. R. D Nor 4 P *Bp and J N Longe Esq* I (Vacant).
SPOFFORTH (All SS) w Follifoot (St Jos and St Jas) and Kirk-Deighton (All SS), *N Yorks*. R. D Ripon 4 P *Bp* I T V THOMAS.
SPONDON (St Werburgh), *Derbys*. V. D Derby 13 P *Capt J A E Drury-Lowe* I T E M BARBER.
SPORLE w Great and Little Palgrave (St Mary Virg), *Norf*. V. D Nor 19 P *Dioc Bd of Patr* I B R A COLE *p-in-c*.
SPOTLAND (St Clem), *Gtr Man*.. D Man 17 *See* Rochdale.
SPRATTON (St Andr) w L Creaton, *Northants*. V. D Pet 6 P *Bp* I F P BAKER.
SPREYTON (St Mich), *Devon*. V. D Ex 12 P *Bp and B Drewe Esq* alt I C J L NAPIER.
SPRIDLINGTON (St Hilary) w Saxby (St Helen) and Firsby (St Jas), *Lincs*. R. D Linc 3 P *Maj-Gen W Hutton 2 turns, Earl of Scarborough 1 turn* I P V APPLETON *p-in-c*.
SPRING GROVE (St Mary). D Lon 14 *See* Isleworth.
SPRING PARK (All SS), V. D Cant 16 *See* Croydon.
SPRINGFIELD (All SS), *Essex*. R. D Chelmsf 12 P *Air-Com N S Paynter* I T L CARD.
(H Trin), V. D Chelmsf 12 P *Simeon Trustees* I S RITCHIE.
NORTH,. D Chelmsf P *Bp* I O F B TRELLIS.
(Conv Distr of Chelmer, East Springfield),. D Chelmsf P *Bp* I K G HOLLOWAY *min*.
SPRINGFIELD (St Chris), *W Midl*. V. D Birm 5 P *Trustees* I H A AYKROYD *c*.
SPRINGTHORPE (St Geo and St Lawr), *Lincs*. R. D Linc 2 *See* Corringham.
SPRINGWOOD, *Mer*.. D Liv *See* Liverpool.
SPROATLEY (St Swithin), *Humb*. R. D York *See* Preston-in-Holderness.
SPROTBOROUGH (St Mary Virg) w Cadeby (St Jo Evang), *S Yorks*. R. D Sheff 8 P *Ld Cromwell* I (Vacant).
SPROUGHTON (All SS) w Burstall (St Mary), *Suff*. R. D St E 5 P *Marchioness of Bris* I N CLARKE *p-in-c*.
SPROWSTON (St Mary and St Marg w St Cuthb), *Norf*. V. D Nor 7 P *D and C of Nor* I D J TUCK, I G H COHEN *c*.
SPROXTON (St Chad), *N Yorks*.. D York *See* Helmsley.
SPROXTON (St Bart). D Leic *See* Buckminster.
SQUIRRELS HEATH (All SS), *Essex*. V. D Chelmsf 4 *See* Hornchurch All SS.
STADHAMPTON (St Jo Bapt) w Chislehampton, *Oxon*.. D Ox 5 *See* Dorchester.
STAFFORD (St Mary, St Chad, St Bertelin and Ch Ch), *Staffs*. R. D Lich P *Bp and R of Stafford* I M MORETON, G BABB *team v*, C F LILEY *team v*, D J MELLOR *team v*, M J FISHER *c*, S G THORBURN *c*.
(St Jo Bapt), V. D Lich P *Bp* I E G H TOWNSHEND, C BROWN *c*.
(St Paul). D Lich *See* Forebridge.
(St Pet Rickerscote), V. D Lich P *Bp* I K L WASSALL.
(St Thos Castle Town), V. D Lich P *Hyndman Trustees* I G E O'BRIEN.

STAFFORD, WEST (St Andr), w Frome Billet, *Dorset*. R. **D** Sarum 5 **P** *Brig S Floyer-Acland* **I** E J G WARD.
STAGSDEN, *Beds*. V. **D** St Alb 19 **P** *MMT* **I** N WEHREN.
STAINBOROUGH (St Jas Chap), *W Yorks*.. **D** Wakef 8 **I** (Vacant).
STAINBURN (St Jo Evang), *N Yorks*.. **D** Ripon 4 *See* Rigton, North.
STAINBY (St Pet) w Gunby (St Nich), *Lincs*. R. **D** Linc 14 **P** *Exors of Rev W L de B Thorold* **I** M J B NUTTALL *p-in-c*.
STAINCLIFFE (Ch Ch), *W Yorks*. V. **D** Wakef 10 **P** *V of Batley* **I** J B QUARRELL.
STAINCROSS (St John), *S Yorks*. V. **D** Wakef 8 **P** *Bp* **I** A WILSON.
STAINDROP (St Mary), *Durham*. V. **D** Dur 10 **P** *Ld Barnard* **I** K LORAINE.
STAINES (St Mary BV), *Surrey*. V. **D** Lon 13 **P** *Ld Chan* **I** D S RICHARDSON *p-in-c*.
(St Pet), V. **D** Lon 13 **P** *Ld Chan and Bp* alt **I** D S RICHARDSON.
(Ch Ch). **D** Lon 13 **P** *Bp* **I** L O LINDO.
STAINFIELD (St Andr) w Apley (St Andr), *Lincs*.. **D** Linc 3 *See* Bardney.
STAINFORTH (St Pet), *N Yorks*. V. **D** Bradf 6 *See* Langcliffe.
STAINFORTH (St Mary), *S Yorks*. V. **D** Sheff 8 **P** *Bp* **I** C HORSEMAN.
STAINLAND (St Andr), *W Yorks*. V. **D** Wakef 2 **P** *V of Halifax* **I** E CRAIG.
STAINLEY, NORTH, (St Mary Virg), *N Yorks*. V. **D** Ripon 3 **P** *Bp* **I** D W EYLES *p-in-c*, G T JONES *c-in-c*.
STAINLEY, SOUTH, *N Yorks*.. **D** Ripon 3 *See* Markington.
STAINMORE, *Cumb*.. **D** Carl 1 *See* Brough.
STAINTON (St Winifrid), *S Yorks*.. **D** Sheff *See* Tickhill.
STAINTON-BY-LANGWORTH (St Jo Bapt) w Newball, Coldstead and Reasby, *Lincs*. V. **D** Linc 3 *See* Barlings.
STAINTON-IN-CLEVELAND (St Pet and St Paul), *N Yorks*. V. **D** York 25 **P** *Abp* **I** T G GRIGG, D J WILBOURNE *c*.
STAINTON-LE STREET (All SS), or Stainton, Great, *Durham*. R. **D** Dur 14 *See* Bishopton.
STAINTON-LE-VALE (St Andr), R w Kirmond-le-Mire (St Martin), *Lincs*. V. **D** Linc *See* Walesby.
STAINWITH, *Lincs*.. **D** Linc 8 *See* Woolsthorpe.
STALBRIDGE (St Mary), *Dorset*. R. **D** Sarum 13 **P** *CCC Cam* **I** F W PUGH.
STALHAM (St Mary) and East Ruston w Brunstead (St Pet), *Norf*. V. **D** Nor 9 **P** *R Neville Esq and R Ives Esq (alt)* **I** D G BLYTH.
STALISFIELD (St Mary) w Otterden (St Lawr), *Kent*. R. **D** Cant 7 *See* Throwley.
STALLINGBOROUGH (St Pet and St Paul), *Humb*. V. **D** Linc 10 **P** *Bp* **I** J W ABBOTT.
STALLING-BUSK, *N Yorks*.. **D** Ripon 2 *See* Askrigg.
STALMINE (St Jas), *Lancs*. V. **D** Blackb 10 **P** *V of Lanc* **I** (Vacant).
STALYBRIDGE (St Paul), *Gtr Man*. V. **D** Ches 14 **P** *Trustees* **I** V I WILSON.
(H Trin and Ch Ch Castle Hall), V. **D** Ches 14 **P** *Trustees and Hyndman's Trustees* **I** B L WHITTAKER, P I DENNISON *c*.
STALYBRIDGE (St Geo), *Gtr Man*. V. **D** Man 2 **P** *R of Ashton L and Ld Deramore* **I** P DENBY.
STAMBERMILL (St Mark), *Worcs*. V. **D** Worc *See* Lye, The.
STAMBOURNE (St Pet and St Thos), *Essex*. R. **D** Chelmsf 24 *See* Toppesfield.
STAMBRIDGE, *Essex*. R. **D** Chelmsf 16 **P** *Govs of Charterho 3 turns, Ld Chan 1 turn* **I** M K TAILBY *p-in-c*.
STAMFORD (All SS w St Pet and St Jo Bapt), *Lincs*. V. **D** Linc 13 **P** *Marq of Ex 1 turn, Ld Chan 1 turn* **I** J H RICHARDSON, D M BOND *hon c*.
(Ch Ch Conv Distr). **D** Linc 13 **I** D SCHOFIELD *p-in-c*.
(St Geo w St Paul), R. **D** Linc 13 **P** *Marq of Ex* **I** J ORMSTON.
(St Mary), R. **D** Linc 13 **P** *Marq of Ex* **I** D A G H DAVIES.
STAMFORD BARON (St Martin), *Northants*. V. **D** Pet 13 **P** *Marq of Ex* **I** (Vacant).
STAMFORD BRIDGE (St Jo Bapt) w Catton and Scoreby (in Stamford Bridge Group), *Humb*. R. **D** York 7 **P** *Ld Leconfield's Trustees 1st and 3rd turns, Crown 2nd turn, Ld Chan 4th turn* **I** (Vacant).
Stamford Bridge Group of Parishes **D** York 7 *See* Catton, Scrayingham, Skirpenbeck.
STAMFORD BROOK (St Mary). **D** Lon 12 *See* Hammersmith.
STAMFORD HILL **D** Lon 2 & 22 *See* Clapton and Tottenham.
STAMFORDHAM (St Mary Virg) w Matfen (H Trin w All SS), *Northumb*. V. **D** Newc T 3 **P** *Ld Chan* **I** A H M HIGGS.
STANBRIDGE (St Jo Bapt) w Tilsworth (All SS), *Beds*. V. **D** St Alb *See* Totternhoe.
STANBRIDGE or L HINTON, *Dorset*.. **D** Sarum 11 *See* Hinton Parva.
STAND (All SS), *Gtr Man*. R. **D** Man 16 **P** *Ld Wilton* **I** R W WARNER.
STANDERWICK, *Wilts*.. **D** B & W 16a *See* Beckington.
STANDISH (St Wilfred), *Lancs*. R. **D** Blackb 4 **P** *Bp* **I** B G MOORE.
STANDISH (St Nich) w Haresfield (St Pet) and Moreton Valence (St Steph), *Glos*. V. **D** Glouc 9 **P** *Bp* **I** G C BAYNTON.
STANDLAKE (St Giles), *Oxon*.. **D** Ox 9 *See* Windrush, Lower.
STANDON (St Mary), *Herts*. V. **D** St Alb 4 **P** *Ch Trust Fund* **I** J L PELLEY.
STANDON (All SS), *Staffs*. R. **D** Lich 15 **P** *Bp* **I** J H DEAKIN *p-in-c*.
STANE (All SS), *Lincs*.. **D** Linc 39 *See* Mablethorpe.
STANFIELD (St Marg), *Norf*. R. **D** Nor 20 **P** *Miss M M Davies* **I** D J MUNT.
STANFORD (All SS), *Kent*. R. **D** Cant 5 *See* Lyminge.
STANFORD (St Nich), *Northants*. w Swinford (All SS) and Catthorpe (St Thos) w Shawell (All SS), *Leics*. V. **D** Leic 14 **P** *Ld Chan and Dioc Bd of Patr* **I** L T HAYNES.
STANFORD (All SS), *Norf*. V. **D** Nor 18 **P** *Bp* **I** (Vacant).
STANFORD BISHOP, *Herefs*.. **D** Heref *See* Acton-Beauchamp.
STANFORD-DINGLEY (St Denys), *Berks*. R. **D** Ox 12 **P** *Ch S Trust* **I** W H GIRLING *c-in-c*.
STANFORD-IN-THE-VALE (St Denys) w Goosey (All SS) and Hatford (St Geo) *Oxon*. V. **D** Ox 17 **P** *D and C of Westmr and Simeon Trustees (alt)* **I** R W C JEFFERY.
STANFORD-LE-HOPE (St Marg of Antioch) w Mucking (St Jo Bapt), *Essex*. R. **D** Chelmsf 15 **P** *MMT* **I** P H WILLIAMS, C J MYHILL *c*.
STANFORD-ON-SOAR (St Jo Bapt), *Notts*. R. **D** Southw 11 **P** *Dioc Bd of Patr* **I** D W S JAMES *c-in-c*.
STANFORD-ON-TEME w Orleton (St Jo Bapt) and Stockton-on-Teme (St Andr), *Worcs*. R. **D** Worc 12 **P** *Bp* **I** P C AUDSLEY.
STANFORD RIVERS (St Marg), *Essex*. R. **D** Chelmsf 6 **P** *Duchy of Lanc* **I** D T CALLUM.
STANGROUND (St Jo Bapt) w Farcet (St Mary), *Cambs*. R. **D** Ely 14 **P** *Patr Bd* **I** J P GILDING, D J BOXALL *team v*.
STANHOE (All SS) w Barwick, *Norf*. R. **D** Nor 23 **P** *R S C Ralli Esq* **I** R H TOMLINSON *c-in-c*.
STANHOPE (St Thos), *Durham*. R. **D** Dur 13 **P** *Chan of the Duchy of Lanc* **I** S B HALLAM.
STANION (St Pet), *Northants*. V. **D** Pet 10 *See* Brigstock.
STANLEY (St Thos Ap and Mart), *Durham*. V. **D** Dur 13 **P** *Bp* **I** (Vacant).
STANLEY (St Andr), *Derbys*. V. **D** Derby 13 **P** *Bp* **I** B A H KILLICK.
STANLEY, *Staffs*.. **D** Lich 16 *See* Endon.
STANLEY (St Pet), *W Yorks*. V. **D** Wakef 12 **P** *V of Wakefield* **I** P J HICKS.
STANLEY PONTLARGE, *Glos*.. **D** Glouc 18 *See* Winchcombe.
STANMER (Dedic unknown) w Falmer (St Lawr), *W Sussex*. V. **D** Chich 10 **P** *Bp* **I** A N ROBINSON *p-in-c*.
STANMORE, GREAT (St Jo Evang), *Gtr Lon*. R. **D** Lon 24 **P** *R Bernays Esq* **I** M H V BOWLES, A J DAVEY *c*, J R HOLROYD *c*.
STANMORE, LITTLE, or WHITCHURCH (St Lawr), *Gtr Lon*. R. **D** Lon 24 **P** *Bp* **I** C J E SPENCER.
STANNINGFIELD (St Mich) w Bradfield Combust, *Suff*. R. **D** St E 10 *See* Hawstead.
STANNINGHALL, *Norf*.. **D** Nor 4 *See* Frettenham.
STANNINGLEY (St Thos), *W Yorks*. R. **D** Ripon 8 **P** *V of Leeds* **I** R W SHAW, S JARRATT *c*.
STANNINGTON (St Mary Virg), *Northumb*. V. **D** Newc T 1 **P** *Bp* **I** B G SULLIVAN.
STANNINGTON (Ch Ch), *S Yorks*. V. **D** Sheff 4 **P** *V of Ecclesfield* **I** R F NEWMAN, S MILLS *c*.
STANSFIELD (All SS), *Suff*.. **D** St E 8 **P** *Ld Chan* **I** J H M BOWER *p-in-c*.
STANSTEAD (St Jas) w Shimplingthorne and Alpheton, *Suff*. R. **D** St E 12 **P** *Ch S Trust 1 turn, Dioc Bd of Patr 2 turns* **I** J D CUTHBERTSON.
STANSTEAD-ABBOTTS (St Andr), *Herts*. V. **D** St Alb 8 **P** *Peache Trustees* **I** (Vacant).
STANSTEAD ST MARGARET (St Marg), *Herts*. V. **D** St Alb *See* Amwell, Great.
STANSTED, *W Sussex*.. **D** Chich 8 *See* Forest Side.

STANSTED (St Mary Virg), *Kent*. R. **D** Roch 8 **P** *Bp* **I** D G CLARK.

STANSTED MOUNTFITCHET (St Mary Virg w St Jo Evang), *Essex*. V. **D** Chelmsf 26 **P** *Bp* **I** B E ROSE, A J PROUD *c*.

STANTON (St Mich AA) w Snowshill (St Barn), *Glos*. R. **D** Glouc 18 **P** *Bp* **I** M BLAND.

STANTON (All SS), *Suff*. R. **D** St E 9 **P** *Crown* **I** F T HOWARD.

STANTON (St Gabr), *Dorset*.. **D** Sarum 2 *See* Whitechurch Canonicorum.

STANTON-BY-BRIDGE (St Mich) w Swarkestone (St Jas), *Derbys*. R. **D** Derby 15 **P** *C Harpur-Crewe Esq* **I** H T LINDLEY C-IN-C OF SWARKESTONE, R BAGNALL *p-in-c*.

STANTON-BY-DALE (St Mich AA) w Dale Abbey (All SS), *Derbys*. R. **D** Derby 13 **P** *Bp* **I** I E GOODING *p-in-c*, M S PARKYN *c*.

STANTON DREW (St Mary Virg), *Avon*. V. **D** B & W 15 **P** *Archd of Bath* **I** W D RUSSELL.

STANTON FITZWARREN (St Leon), *Wilts*.. **D** Bris *See* Stratton St Marg.

STANTON HARCOURT (St Mich), *Oxon*.. **D** Ox 9 *See* Windrush, Lower.

STANTON-IN-PEAK (H Trin) w Birchover or Rowtor Chap (Ch of Jesus), *Derbys*. V. **D** Derby 9 **P** *H B C Davie Thornhill Esq* **I** D V GIDLING *p-in-c*, D J PRYOR *hon c*.

STANTON-LACY (St Pet), *Salop*. V. **D** Heref 12 **P** *Earl of Plymouth* **I** G ELLIOTT.

STANTON LONG **D** Heref See Long Stanton **I** (Vacant).

STANTON-ON-HINE HEATH (St Andr), *Salop*. V. **D** Lich 27 **P** *Sir Alex Stanier Bt* **I** C J BRADLEY *p-in-c*.

STANTON-ON-THE-WOLDS (All SS), *Notts*. R. **D** Southw 10 **P** *Trustees of Sir A Bromley* **I** J L OTTEY *c-in-c*.

STANTON-ON-WYE (St Mary Virg), *Herefs*. R. **D** Heref 9 *See* Staunton-on-Wye.

STANTON PRIOR (St Lawr), *Avon*. R. **D** B & W 13 **P** *Duchy of Cornwall* **I** (Vacant).

STANTON ST BERNARD (All SS), *Wilts*. R. **D** Sarum 27 *See* Alton Barnes.

STANTON ST JOHN (St Jo Bapt), *Oxon*. R. **D** Ox *See* Wheatley.

STANTON ST QUINTIN (St Giles), Hullavington and Grittleton w Norton and Leigh Delamere, *Wilts*. R. **D** Bris 11 **P** *Bp, Eton Coll and R W Neeld Esq (in turn)* **I** P WALTERS.

STANTON-UNDER-BARDON (St Mary and All SS), *Leics*. V. **D** Leic 17 *See* Markfield.

STANTONBURY (Bradwell, Gt Linford, New Bradwell), *Bucks*. R. **D** Ox 26 **P** *R Uthwatt Esq and Dioc Bd of Patr* **I** C J V DRUMMOND, D G BOWEN *team v*, P GREEN *team v*, J D HAYWARD *team v*, B L COX *c*.

STANWAY (St Albright), *Essex*. R. **D** Chelmsf 22 **P** *Magd Coll Ox* **I** A F BELL.

STANWAY, *Glos*. V. **D** Glouc 18 *See* Didbrook.

STANWELL (St Mary BV), *Gtr Lon*. V. **D** Lon 13 **P** *Ld Chan* **I** R J MACKLIN.

STANWICK (St Jo Bapt) w Aldbrough, *N Yorks*. V. **D** Ripon 1 *See* Forcett.

STANWICK (St Lawr) w Hargrave (All SS), *Northants*. R. **D** Pet 9 **P** *Ld Chan 2 turns Exors of Sir K Murchison 1 turn* **I** J F L EAGLE.

STANWIX (St Mich AA), *Cumb*. V. **D** Carl 3 **P** *Bp* **I** L G HIGDON, C E SUTTON *c*.

STAPENHILL (St Pet) w Caldwell (St Giles), *Staffs*. V. **D** Derby 16 **P** *Ch S Trust* **I** M P MAUDSLEY, J N PEARSON *c*.

STAPLE (St Jas), *Kent*. R. **D** Cant 1 **P** *Abp* **I** E R A ALDER *p-in-c*.

STAPLE-FITZPAINE (St Pet) w Bickenhall, Orchard-Portman (St Mich), Thurlbear (St Thos) and Stoke St Mary, *Somt*. R. **D** B & W 23 **P** *Bp* **I** M S M ROBINSON *p-in-c*.

STAPLEFIELD (St Mark), *W Sussex*. V. **D** Chich 11 **P** *V of Cuckfield* **I** A E T HOBBS.

STAPLEFORD, *Lincs*.. **D** Linc 18 *See* Carlton le Moorland.

STAPLEFORD (St Andr), *Cambs*. V. **D** Ely 7 **P** *D and C of Ely* **I** C K H DAVISON.

STAPLEFORD (St Mary Magd), *Leics*. V. **D** Leic 3 *See* Saxby.

STAPLEFORD (St Mary) w Berwick (St Jas), *Wilts*. V. **D** Sarum 21 **P** *D and C of Windsor* **I** J P ADAMS.

STAPLEFORD (St Mary Virg), *Herts*. R. **D** St Alb 8 *See* Bramfield.

STAPLEFORD (St Helen), *Notts*. V. **D** Southw 8 **P** *CPAS* **I** A GRAHAM, M J BROCK *c*.

STAPLEFORD ABBOTS (St Mary), *Essex*. R. **D** Chelmsf 2 *See* Lambourne.

STAPLEFORD TAWNEY (St Mary) w Theydon Mount (St Mich), *Essex*. R. **D** Chelmsf 2 **P** *Mrs C S E Armitage* **I** J A D LEGG *p-in-c*.

STAPLEGROVE (St John), *Somt*. R. **D** B & W 23 **P** *Bp* **I** A BECK *p-in-c*.

STAPLEHURST (All SS), *Kent*. R. **D** Cant 11 **P** *St Jo Coll Cam* **I** T H VICKERY.

STAPLETON (H Trin), *Avon*. R. **D** Bris 7 **P** *Bp* **I** J N CAMPBELL.

STAPLETON (St Mary), *Cumb*.. **D** Carl 2 *See* Bewcastle.

STAPLETON (St Jo Bapt), *Salop*. R. **D** Heref 11 **P** *Rev D B Haseler* **I** (Vacant).

STAPLETON (St Martin), *Leics*. R. **D** Leic 16 *See* Barwell.

STARBECK (St Andr), *N Yorks*. V. **D** Ripon 4 **P** *V of Ch Ch Harrogate* **I** M B TAYLOR.

STARCROSS (St Paul), *Devon*. V. **D** Ex 6 *See* Cofton.

STARSTON (St Marg), *Norf*. R. **D** Nor 17 **P** *Bp* **I** T H CHILD *c-in-c*.

STARTFORTH (St Mich or H Trin), *Durham*. V. **D** Ripon *See* Bowes.

STATFOLD, *Staffs*.. **D** Lich *See* Clifton Camville.

STATHERN (St Guthlac), *Leics*.. **D** Leic *See* Harby.

STAUGHTON, GREAT, *Cambs*. V. **D** Ely 13 **P** *St Jo Coll Ox* **I** P J TAYLOR.

STAUGHTON, LITTLE, *Cambs*.. **D** St Alb *See* Keysoe.

STAUNTON (All SS), *Glos*. R. **D** Glouc 7 *See* Coleford.

STAUNTON (St Mary) w Flawborough (St Pet), *Notts*. R. **D** Southw 3 **P** *E G Staunton, Esq* **I** (Vacant).

STAUNTON (St Jas), *Glos*. R. **D** Glouc 2 *See* Hartpury.

STAUNTON HAROLD (Priv Chap), *Leics*.. **D** Leic 12 **P** *Earl Ferrers* **I** (Vacant).

STAUNTON-ON-ARROW (St Pet) w Byton (St Mary) and Kinsham (All SS), *Herefs*. R. **D** Heref 5 **P** *M King King and D L Arkwright* alt **I** M C BIRCHBY P-IN-C OF STAUNTON-ON-ARROW W BYTON, R A PERRY P-IN-C OF KINSHAM.

STAUNTON-ON-WYE (St Mary Virg), *Herefs*. R. **D** Heref 4 *See* Letton.

STAVELEY (St Jas Ap and Mart) w Kentmere (St Cuthb), *Cumb*. V. **D** Carl 17 **P** *V of Kendal* **I** S SWIDENBANK.

STAVELEY (St Jo Bapt) w Barrow Hill (St Andr), *Derbys*. R. **D** Derby 2 **P** *Duke of Devonshire and Bp and Archd of Chesterfield* **I** R J MARK, S MILLINGTON *team v*, P L WASHINGTON *team v*.

STAVELEY (All SS) w Copgrove, *N Yorks*. R. **D** Ripon 4 *See* Farnham.

STAVELEY-IN-CARTMEL (St Mary), *Cumb*.. **D** Carl *See* Leven Valley.

STAVERTON (St Paul) w Landscove (St Matt) *Devon*. V. **D** Ex 13 **P** *D and C of Ex* **I** C A CARDALE.

STAVERTON (St Cath) w Boddington (St Mary Magd), *Glos*. V. **D** Glouc 11 **P** *Bp* **I** J B T HOMFRAY.

STAVERTON (St Mary Virg) w Helidon (St Jo Bapt) and Catesby (St Mary), *Northants*. V. **D** Pet 3 **P** *Ch Ch Ox and Bp* alt **I** A V WINTERSGILL.

STAVERTON (St Paul), *Wilts*. V. **D** Sarum 24 **P** *R of Trowbridge* **I** P H BELL *p-in-c*.

STAWLEY (St Mich), *Somt*. R. **D** B & W *See* Bathealton.

STEANE (St Pet), *Northants*. R. **D** Pet *See* Hinton.

STEBBING (St Mary Virg) w Lindsell (St Mary Virg), *Essex*. V. **D** Chelmsf 23 **P** *Bp* **I** P SWINBANK.

STECHFORD (All SS), *W Midl*. V. **D** Birm 13 **P** *St Pet Coll Ox* **I** A T W REYNOLDS, A J TABRAHAM *hon c*.

STEDHAM (St Jas) w Iping (St Mary), *W Sussex*. R. **D** Chich 5 **P** *Bp 1st and 3rd turns, Ld Egremont 2nd turn* **I** O Q HAIGH *c-in-c*.

STEEP (All SS), *Hants*. V. **D** Portsm 4 **P** *Ld Chan* **I** D J SNELGAR.

STEEPING, GREAT (All SS), *Lincs*.. **D** Linc 7 *See* Firsby.

STEEPING, LITTLE (St Andr), *Lincs*. R. **D** Linc 7 **P** *Earl of Ancaster* **I** J S THOROLD.

STEEPLE (St Mich) w Tyneham, Church Knowle and Kimmeridge (in St Aldhelm Group), *Dorset*. R. **D** Sarum 9 **P** *Gen Reps of J W G Bond 1 turn Maj J Mansel 2 turns* **I** G S M SQUAREY.

STEEPLE (St Lawr), *Essex*. V. **D** Chelmsf 13 **P** *Bp and Ld Fitzwalter* alt **I** L BLANEY *c-in-c*.

STEEPLE-ASHTON (St Mary Virg) w Semington (St Geo), *Wilts*. V. **D** Sarum 24 **P** *Magd Coll Cam* **I** D BURDEN.

STEEPLE ASTON (St Pet and St Paul) w N Aston and Tackley, *Oxon*. R. **D** Ox 10 **P** *BNC Ox, St Jo Coll Ox and Col A D Taylor* **I** M G HAYTER.

STEEPLE BARTON, *Oxon*.. **D** Ox *See* Westcote Barton.

STEEPLE BUMPSTEAD (St Mary) w Helions Bumpstead, Essex. V. D Chelmsf 18 P Ld Chan I G R MANSFIELD.
STEEPLE CLAYDON (St Mich AA), Bucks.. D Ox 25 See Claydons, The.
STEEPLE GIDDING, Cambs.. D Ely See Gidding, Great.
STEEPLE LANGFORD (All SS), Wilts. R. D Sarum 21 See Wylye.
STEEPLE-MORDEN (St Pet and St Paul), Cambs. V (See Shingay Group). D Ely 8 P New Coll Ox I (Vacant).
STEEPLETON (St Mich), Dorset.. D Sarum 1 See Winterbourne Abbas.
STEEPLETON IWERNE (St Mary), Dorset. R. D Sarum 10 P Dioc Bd of Patr I (Vacant).
STEETON (St Steph) w Eastburn, W Yorks. V. D Bradf 11 P V of Kildwick I J M BEARPARK, T A ASHBY c.
STELLA (St Cuthb), T & W. R. D Dur 4a P Bp I F J B BLACKBURN.
STELLING (St Mary), Kent.. D Cant 2 See Hardres, Upper.
STENIGOT (St Nich), Lincs. R. D Linc See Asterby Group.
STEPNEY (St Dunstan and All SS w St Aug and St Phil), Lon. R. D Lon P Bp I N E MCCURRY, N R HOLTAM c, D G ROSS c.
(H Trin, Morgan Street, Mile End Old Town), V.. D Lon 4 P Bp I F R BENTLEY.
(St Mary, Cable Street), V. D Lon 4 P Bp I P C CLYNICK.
(St Pet w St Benet, Mile End Road), V. D Lon 4 P D and C of Cant I D J ADLINGTON p-in-c, R A VAUGHAN hon c. See also Bow COMMON..
STEPPINGLEY, Beds.. D St Alb See Ampthill.
STERNDALE, Derbys.. D Derby 10 See Earl Sterndale and King Sterndale.
STERNFIELD (St Mary Magd) w Benhall (St Mary) and Snape (St John), Suff. R. D St E P Mrs A H V Aldous 1st turn, Mrs A C Vernon-Wentworth 2nd turn, Mrs M A Bertin 3rd turn I J A TERRY.
STERT (St Jas), Wilts. D Sarum 23 See Urchfont.
STETCHWORTH (St Pet), Cambs. V. D Ely 4 P Duke of Sutherland I G I ARNOLD p-in-c.
STEVENAGE (St Geo), Herts. R. D St Alb 12 P Bp I R D HOYAL c.
(H Trin), V. D St Alb 12 P Bp I M D TERRETT.
(All SS) V. D St Alb 12 P Bp I S PURVIS, M J BURNS c.
(St Hugh, Chells), V. D St Alb 12 P Bp I J H GREEN.
(St Mary, Shephall), V. D St Alb 12 P Bp I N A S BURY, J A SAGE c, J V WALTON c.
(St Nich), V. D St Alb 12 P Bp I C J WESTON.
(St Pet, Broadwater), V. D St Alb 12 P Bp I T M BEAUMONT.
STEVENTON (St Mich AA) w Milton (St Blaise), Oxon. V. D Ox 11 P D and C of Westmr and Ch Ch Ox (alt) I A M G STEPHENSON, K ATKINSON c.
STEVENTON (St Nich), Hants. R. D Win 5 See Waltham, North.
STEVINGTON (St Mary Virg), Beds. V. D St Alb 21 P Bp I P N JEFFERY p-in-c, G W COWLEY hon c.
STEWKLEY (St Mich AA) w (H Trin) Soulbury and Drayton Parslow, Bucks. V. D Ox 27 P Bp, Earl of Rosebery and MMT I J P DRAKE.
STEYNING (St Andr), W Sussex. V. D Chich 7 P MMT I C R BOFF.
STIBBARD (All SS), Norf. R. D Nor 21 P Exors of Can J A Appleton I F A HILL.
STIBBINGTON (St Jo Bapt) w Sibson (St Barn or St Botolph), Cambs. R. D Ely 14 P Earl Fitzwilliam I P O POOLEY p-in-c.
STICKFORD (St Helen), Lincs. V. D Linc 7 P Ld Chan I (Vacant).
STICKLEPATH, Devon.. D Ex See Barnstaple.
STICKNEY (St Luke), Lincs. R. D Linc 7 P Dioc Bd of Patr I J R WORSDALL p-in-c.
STIFFKEY (St John w St Mary) and Cockthorpe w Morston, Bishop's Langham. Norf. R (See Blakeney Group). D Nor 24 P Dioc Bd of Patr, Bp and Sir R H Anstruther-Gough-Calthorpe, Bart, (in turn) I J R L R FAWCETT.
STIFFORD (St Mary), Essex. R. D Chelmsf 15 P Bp I C S STUDD.
STILLINGFLEET (St Helen) w Naburn (St Matt), N Yorks. V. D York See Escrick.
STILLINGTON (St Jo Div), Durham. V. D Dur See Grindon.
STILLINGTON (St Nich) and Marton w Moxby and Farlington, N Yorks. V. D York 5 P Abp I (Vacant).
STILTON (St Mary Magd) w Denton (All SS), and Caldecote (St Mary Magd), Cambs. V. D Ely 14 P Bp and Ld Chan alt I H BUTLER p-in-c.
STINCHCOMBE (St Cypr), Glos.. D Glouc 5 See Cam.
STINSFORD (St Mich), Winterbourne Came w Whitcombe and Winterbourne Monkton, Dorset. V. D Sarum 5 P Lady T J Agnew, W R Elworthy Esq and Earl of Portarlington (in turn) I J S RICHARDSON p-in-c.
STIRCHLEY (Ch of Ascen), W Midl. V. D Birm P R of King's Norton I H B MARLOW.
STISTED (All SS) w Bradwell-juxta-Coggeshall (H Trin) and Pattiswick (St Mary), Essex. R. D Chelmsf 19 P Abp of Cant, Mrs Wells Jennings and Bp I M G MUGGLETON.
STIVICHALL, W Midl. V. D Cov 4 See Styvechale.
STIXWOULD (St Pet), Lincs. V. D Linc 11 See Horsington.
STOAK, or STOKE (St Lawr), Chesh. V. D Ches 10 See Ellesmere Port.
STOCK (St Barn) w Lydlinch (St Thos à Becket), Dorset. R. D Sarum 13 P Col L L Yeatman 2nd and 5th turns, G Pitt-Rivers Esq 1st 4th and 6th turns, V of Iwerne Minster 3rd turn I (Vacant).
STOCK HARVARD (All SS), Essex. R. D Chelmsf 11 P Rev J G T Tatham I J J BUNTING, B G HALL hon c, J T HOWDEN hon c.
STOCKBRIDGE (St Pet) w Houghton (All SS), Hants. R. D Win 10 P Bp and Ld Chan I L K P SMITH.
STOCKBURY (St Mary Magd), Kent.. D Cant 13 See Hartlip.
STOCKCROSS (St Jo Evang), Berks. V. D Ox 14 See Boxford.
STOCKERSTON (St Pet), Leics. R. D Leic 5 See Medbourne.
STOCKING PELHAM (St Mary), Herts.. D St Alb 4 See Furneaux Pelham.
STOCKINGFORD (St Paul), Warws. V. D Cov 5 P V of Nuneaton I A R HOOTON.
STOCKLAND (St Mich AA) w Dalwood (St Pet), Devon. V. D Ex 5 P Dioc Bd of Patr I C S HOPE.
STOCKLAND-BRISTOL (St Mary Magd), Somt. V. D B & W 18 See Otterhampton.
STOCKLAND GREEN (St Mark), W Midl. V. D Birm 7 P Crown I A T P NEWSUM.
STOCKLEIGH-ENGLISH (St Mary Virg), Devon. R. D Ex 2 See Woolfardisworthy, East.
STOCKLEIGH-POMEROY (St Mary Virg), Devon.. D Ex 2 See Woolfardisworthy, East.
STOCKLYNCH-OTTERSAY (St Mary Virg) w Stocklynch-Magdalen (St Mary Magd), Somt. R. D B & W 20 See Puckington.
STOCKPORT (All SS now called St Mary w St Steph), Gtr Man. R. D Ches 16 P G and C Coll Cam I A M FAIRHURST, W F I WHINTON c.
(St Alb), V. D Chesh 16 P Bp I M A WHETTER.
(St Geo), V. D Ches 16 P Trustees I C D BIDDELL, K D N KENRICK c.
(St Mark, Edgeley), V. D Ches 16 P Bp I J J C NODDER.
(St Matt Edgeley), V. D Ches 16 P Bp I S J BARNES.
(St Pet), V. D Ches 16 P Ch Union I R J GILLINGS p-in-c.
(St Thos), R. D Ches 16 P I N Symonds Esq I R J GILLINGS, H B EALES c, D J JOHNSON c.
(St Aug Brinksway w Cheadle Heath), V. D Ches 16 P Bp I D A PARKER.
(St Sav Great Moor), V. D Ches 16 P Trustees I T H CLEMETSON.
STOCKSBRIDGE (St Matthias), S Yorks. V. D Sheff 7 P Bp I S G N BRINDLEY, E A N SMITH c.
STOCKTON (St Mich), Warws.. D Cov 10 See Southam.
STOCKTON (St Chad), Salop. R. D Lich See Kemberton.
STOCKTON (St Mich AA), Norf. R. D Nor 14 See Geldeston.
STOCKTON, Wilts.. D Sarum See Yarnbury.
STOCKTON HEATH (St Thos), Chesh. V. D Ches 4 P Trustees of P G Greenall Esq I A C DAVIES, C M WADDLETON c, W J S J L WALL c.
STOCKTON-ON-TEES (St Thos), Cleve. V. D Dur 14 P Bp I D J WHITTINGTON, C GWILLIAM c.
(St Chad Roseworth), V. D Dur 14 P Bp I P WATERHOUSE.
(St Jas Conv Distr). D Dur 14 P Bp I (Vacant).
(St Jo Bapt) Cleve. V. D Dur 14 P Bp I D T YOUNGSON p-in-c.
(St Mark's Conv Distr). D Dur 14 P Bp I (Vacant).
(St Paul), V. D Dur 14 P Crown I M J CARTWRIGHT.
(St Pet), V. D Dur 14 P Bp I G S PEDLEY, D E B REED c, C J WREN c.
(H Trin), V. D Dur 14 P Bp I M P CHAPPELL chap, G S PEDLEY p-in-c.
STOCKTON-ON-TEME, Worcs.. D Worc See Stanford-on-Teme.
STOCKTON-ON-THE-FOREST (H Trin) w Holtby and Warthill (St Mary), N Yorks. R. D York P Abp I C G ELLIOT-NEWMAN.

STONDON, UPPER (All SS) w Lower, *Beds.* R. **D** St Alb 22 **P** *Bp* **I** G H WALLER.
STONE (All SS) w Woodford and Hill, *Glos.* V. **D** Glouc 5 **P** *Maj R Jenner-Fust and V of Berkeley* alt **I** P C F WOOSTER.
STONE (St Mich), *Staffs.* R. **D** Lich 19 **P** *Bp* **I** (Vacant).
(Ch Ch), V. **D** Lich 19 **P** *Simeon Trustees* **I** B C REEVE.
STONE (St Jo Bapt) w Dinton and Hartwell, *Bucks.* R. **D** Ox 21 **P** *Bp and The Grocers Co* **I** D J COOKE.
STONE (St Mary), *Kent.* R. **D** Roch 1a **P** *Bp* **I** J F CLAUSEN.
STONE (BVM), *Worcs.* V. **D** Worc 10 **P** *Ld Chan* **I** D L SMITH *p-in-c.*
STONE-IN-OXNEY (St Mary Virg) w Ebony, *Kent.* V. **D** Cant 12 *See* Appledore.
STONEBRIDGE (St Mich AA). **D** Lon 18 *See* Willesden.
STONEBROOM (St Pet), *Derbys.* V. **D** Derby 1 **P** *Bp* **I** L N CHILDS.
STONEFOLD (St John), *Lancs.* V. **D** Blackb 1 **P** *V of Haslingden* **I** T A G BILL *p-in-c.*
STONEGATE (St Pet), *E Sussex.* V. **D** Chich 20 **P** *Hon Hilda Beryl Courthope and Hon Elinor Daphne Courthope* **I** M L HILL-TOUT *p-in-c.*
STONEGRAVE (H Trin) w Nunnington (All SS and St Jas), *N Yorks..* **D** York 20 *See* Harome.
STONEHAM, NORTH (St Nich), w Bassett (St Mich AA), *Hants.* R. **D** Win 15 **P** *Exors of E Willis Fleming Esq* **I** R B JONES, J H CHANNER *c,* D E HALE *hon c.*
STONEHAM, SOUTH (St Mary and St Agnes) w Swaythling, *Hants.* V. **D** Win 11 **P** *R of Southn* **I** G D FULLER.
STONEHOUSE (St Cyr), *Glos.* V. **D** Glouc 9 **P** *Crown* **I** L W FORD.
STONEHOUSE, EAST (St Geo w St Paul and St Matt), *Devon.* V. **D** Ex 23 *See* Plymouth.
STONELEIGH (St Mary) w Ashow and Baginton, *Warws.* V and R. **D** Cov 4 **P** *Ld Leigh and Lt-Col Sir W H Bromley-Davenport* **I** P H GOODERICK.
STONELEIGH (St Jo Bapt), *Surrey.* V. **D** Guildf 9 **P** *Bp* **I** C J MORGAN.
STONESBY (St Pet), *Leics.* V. **D** Leic 4 *See* Waltham-on-the-Wolds.
STONESFIELD (St Jas Gt), *Oxon.* R. **D** Ox 10 **P** *Duke of Marlborough* **I** (Vacant).
STONEY MIDDLETON (St Martin) w Curbar (All SS), *Derbys.* V. **D** Derby 9 **P** *V of Baslow* **I** F E WILLETT.
STONEY STANTON (St Mich), *Leics.* R. **D** Leic 16 **P** *Miss Disney* **I** G F COOPER *p-in-c.*
STONEYCROFT (All SS), *Mer.* V. **D** Liv 6 **P** *Bp* **I** G J T TAYLOR, J S WILLIAMS *c.*
STONHAM-ASPAL (St Mary and St Lambert), *Suff.* R. **D** St E 1 *See* Crowfield.
STONHAM PARVA (St Mary Virg), *Suff.* R. **D** St E 1 *See* Earl Stonham.
STONNALL (St Pet), *Staffs.* V. **D** Lich 2 **P** *V of Shenstone* **I** W J WEBB *p-in-c.*
STONTON WYVILLE (St Denys) w Glooston (St Jo Bapt), Slawston (All SS) and Cranoe (St Mich), *Leics.* R. **D** Leic 5 **P** *Trustees of G L T Brudenell Esq* **I** R M CHATFIELD.
STONY STRATFORD (St Giles w St Mary Virg), *Bucks.* V. **D** Ox 26 **P** *Bp* **I** C H J C NORTHAM, J RONE *c.*
STOODLEIGH (St Marg), *Devon.* R. **D** Ex 8 *See* Washfield.
STOPHAM (St Mary BV), *W Sussex.* R. **D** Chich 6 **P** *Sir B W de S Barttlelot Bt* **I** F G KERR-DINEEN.
STOPSLEY (St Thos), *Beds.* V. **D** St Alb 20 **P** *Bp* **I** F A ESTDALE.
STORRIDGE (St Jo Evang), *Herefs.* V. **D** Heref 6 **P** *R of Cradley* **I** (Vacant).
STORRINGTON (St Mary), *W Sussex.* R. **D** Chich 7 **P** *Keble Coll Ox* **I** J A NORMAN.
STOTFOLD (St Mary BV), *Beds.* V. **D** St Alb 22 **P** *Bp* **I** V L NORTH P-IN-C OF RADWELL.
STOTTESDON (St Mary), *Salop.* V. **D** Heref 9 **P** *Bp* **I** E C WARDLE *p-in-c.*
STOUGHTON W Sussex. V **D** Chich 5 *See* Compton.
STOUGHTON (Em), *Surrey..* **D** Guildf 5 *See* Guildford.
STOUGHTON (St Mary), *Leics.* V. **D** Leic 6 *See* Thurnby.
STOULTON (St Edm K and Mart) w Drakes Broughton (St Barn Ap and Mart) and Pirton (St Pet), *Worcs.* V. **D** Worc 3 **P** *Trustees of Croome Estate 1 turn, Bp 2 turns* **I** B J PALMER.
STOUR, EAST w Stour, West, *Dorset..* **D** Sarum *See* Gillingham.
STOUR PROVOST w Stour Row and Todber, *Dorset.* R. **D** Sarum *See* Gillingham.
STOURBRIDGE, *W Midl..* **D** Worc *See* Swinford, Old.
STOURMOUTH, *Kent..* **D** Cant 1 *See* Elmstone.
STOURPAINE (H Trin) *Dorset.* V. **D** Sarum 10 **P** *Dioc Bd of Patrons 2 turns, D and C of Sarum 1 turn* **I** D A FARQUHARSON-ROBERTS *p-in-c.*
STOURPORT (St Mich w All SS), *Worcs.* V. **D** Worc 12 **P** *V of Kidderminster* **I** P V FEDDEN, K M HARROLD *c.*
STOURS, THE (Stour Provost w Stour Row, Stour East, Stour West). **D** Sarum *See* Gillingham.
STOURTON, *Warws..* **D** Cov 12 *See* Cherington.
STOURTON (St Pet), *Wilts.* and *Somt.* R. **D** Sarum 22 *See* Upper Stour.
STOVEN, *Suff..* **D** St E *See* Westhall.
STOW (St Jo Bapt), *Lincs..* **D** Linc 13 *See* Barholme.
STOW (St Mary) w Sturton (St Hugh), *Lincs.* R. **D** Linc 2 **P** *Bp* **I** J M SPURRELL.
STOW w Quy (St Mary Virg), *Cambs.* V. **D** Ely 8 **P** *Bp* **I** R A MINTER.
STOW-BARDOLPH (H Trin) w Wimbotsham (St Mary Virg), *Norf.* R. **D** Ely 17 **P** *Bp* **I** P G HUTTON *p-in-c.*
STOW-BEDON (St Botolph) w Breckles (St Marg), *Norf.* R. **D** Nor 19 **P** *Bp* **I** J COOKE *p-in-c.*
STOW LONGA (St Botolph), *Cambs.* V. **D** Ely 11 **P** *Bp* **I** (Vacant).
STOW MARIES (St Mary and St Marg), *Essex..* **D** Chelmsf 13 *See* Cold Norton.
STOW-ON-THE-WOLD or STOW ST EDWARD w Broadwell (St Paul), *Glos.* R. **D** Glouc 16 **P** *Dioc Bd of Patr* **I** W H WAY.
STOW, WEST, *Suff..* **D** St E *See* Culford.
STOWE, *Salop..* **D** Heref *See* Llanfair-Waterdine.
STOWE (Assump of St Mary Virg), *Bucks.* V. **D** Ox 23 **P** *Govs of Stowe Sch* **I** M D DRURY *c-in-c.*
STOWE-BY-CHARTLEY (St Jo Bapt), *Staffs.* V. **D** Lich 20 **P** *Dioc Bd of Patr* **I** A LITTLE.
STOWE, LONG (St Mary), *Cambs.* R. **D** Ely 2 *See* Longstowe.
STOWE NINE CHURCHES, *Northants..* **D** Pet *See* Heyford.
STOWELL (St Mary Magd), *Somt.* R. **D** B & W *See* Charlton Horethorne.
STOWELL (St Leon), *Glos..* **D** Glouc 15 *See* Chedworth.
STOWEY (St Mary Virg) w Bishop's Sutton (H Trin), *Avon.* V. **D** B & W 15 **P** *Bp* **I** (Vacant).
STOWFORD (St John), *Devon.* R. **D** Ex *See* Marystowe.
STOWLANGTOFT (St Geo) w Langham, *Suff.* R. **D** St E 9 **I** C LEFFLER.
STOWMARKET (St Pet and St Mary), *Suff.* V. **D** St E 6 **P** *CPS* **I** P C MOORE, N G ROBINSON-JOICE *c,* M P SKLIROS *hon c.*
STOWTING (St Mary Virg), *Kent.* R. **D** Cant 11 *See* Sellindge.
STOWUPLAND, *Suff..* **D** St E *See* Newton, Old.
STRADBROKE (All SS) w Horham and Athelington (St Mary), *Suff.* R. **D** St E 17 **P** *Bp 4 turns, Rev J E Soden 1 turn* **I** D J STREETER.
STRADISHALL (St Marg) w Denston (St Nich), V *Suff.* R. **D** St E 8 *See* Wickhambrook.
STRADSETT, *Norf..* **D** Ely 17 *See* Crimplesham.
STRAGGLETHORPE (St Mich), *Lincs..* **D** Linc 23 *See* Brant Broughton.
STRAMSHALL (St Mich AA), *Staffs.* V. **D** Lich 20 **P** *V of Uttoxeter* **I** W H O MOSS *c-in-c.*
STRANTON (All SS) w Hartlepool, West (Ch Ch), *Cleve.* V. **D** Dur 12 **P** *St Jo Coll Dur* **I** M A JENNETT, D COOK *c,* M J M HUGHES *c,* J C B PEMBERTON *c.*
STRATFIELD-MORTIMER (St Mary Virg), *Berks.* V. **D** Ox 12 **P** *Eton Coll* **I** G D REPATH.
STRATFIELD TURGIS (All SS), *Hants.* R. **D** Win 4 *See* Stratfieldsaye.
STRATFIELDSAYE (St Mary Virg) w Hartley Wespall (St Mary BV) and Stratfield Turgis, *Hants.* R. **D** Win 4 **P** *Duke of Wellington 2 turns, D and C of St Geo Chap Windsor 1 turn* **I** J F W ANDERSON *c-in-c.*
STRATFORD (St Jo Evang w St Steph and Ch Ch and St Jas Forest Gate), *Essex.* V. **D** Chelmsf 5 **P** *V of West Ham* **I** D DRISCOLL *p-in-c,* R J WIGGS *c.*
(St Paul), V. **D** Chelmsf 5 **P** *CPS* **I** R E GROVE.
STRATFORD (St Andr), *Suff.* R. **D** St E 19 *See* Blaxhall.
STRATFORD-LE-BOW (St Mary). **D** Lon 7 *See* Bow (St Mary).
STRATFORD ST MARY (St Mary), *Suff.* R. **D** St E 3 **P** *Duchy of Lanc* **I** C L ROWE.
STRATFORD-ON-AVON (H Trin w St Jas Gt) w Bishopton (St Pet), Shottery (St Andr), Luddington (All SS) and Guild Chap (H Cross), *Warws.* R. **D** Cov 8 **P** *Dioc Bd of Patr* **I** G D SPILLER, D C CAPRON *team v,* K R EVANS *c,* J M LOWEN *c.*
STRATFORD-SUB-CASTLE (St Lawr), *Wilts.* V. **D** Sarum 16 **P** *D and C of Sarum* **I** W G K BAKER *p-in-c.*

STRATFORD-TONY (St Mary Virg), *Wilts.* R. **D** Sarum 19 *See* Bishopstone.
STRATTON (St Pet) w Baunton (St Mary Magd), *Glos.* R. **D** Glouc 13 **P** *R Chester-Master Esq* **I** J H MEAD.
STRATTON (St Mary Virg), *Dorset.*. **D** Sarum 5 *See* Bradford Peverel.
STRATTON (St Andr), *Cornw.* V. **D** Truro 10 **P** *Duchy of Cornw* **I** R W THOMAS.
STRATTON-AUDLEY (St Mary and St Edburga) w Godington (H Trin), *Oxon.* R. **D** Ox 2 **P** *CCC Ox and Ch Ch Ox (alt)* **I** A HICHENS *p-in-c.*
STRATTON, EAST (All SS) w Woodmancote (St Jas) and Popham (St Cath), *Hants.* V. **D** Win 12 *See* Micheldever.
STRATTON, LONG or STRATTON ST MARY (St Mary Virg) w Stratton St Mich (St Mich AA w St Pet) and Wacton Magna (All SS) w Wacton Parva (St Mary), *Norf.* R. **D** Nor 11 **P** *New Coll Ox, G and C Coll Cam, Dioc Bd of Patr in turn* **I** W A V CUMMINGS.
STRATTON-ON-THE-FOSSE (St Vigor), *Somt.* R. **D** B & W *See* Chilcompton.
STRATTON ST MARGARET (St Marg of Antioch) w South Marston and Stanton Fitzwarren, *Wilts.* R. **D** Bris 10 **P** *Patr Bd* **I** M J H HOWELL, T J POTTER *team v.*
STRATTON STRAWLESS (St Marg), *Norf.*. **D** Nor 3 *See* Haynford.
STRATTON, UPPER (St Phil), *Wilts.* V. **D** Bris 10 **P** *Bp* **I** K J I GREENSLADE.
STREAT, or STREET (Dedic unknown), w Westmeston (St Martin), *E Sussex.* R. **D** Chich 14 **P** *W S D Campion Esq and R Fitzhugh Esq* **I** J D MURRAY *p-in-c.*
STREATHAM (St Leon w All SS), *Surrey.* R. **D** S'wark 6 **P** *Bp* **I** E E KEMP *c.*
(Ch Ch), V. **D** S'wark 6 **P** *R of Streatham* **I** B FITZHARRIS *hon c.*
(St Thos Telford Park), V. **D** S'wark 6 **P** *Bp and Trustees* **I** N W A MARLEY.
WEST (Im w St Anselm), V. **D** S'wark 6 **P** *Bp and R of Streatham* alt **I** (Vacant).
(St Jas), V. **D** S'wark 7a **P** *CPAS* **I** G D HAYLES, P R TOWNSEND *c.*
PARK (St Alb), V. **D** S'wark 6 **P** *Ch S Trust* **I** J A RICHARDSON.
(St Paul, Furzedown), V. **D** S'wark 7a **P** *Bp* **I** R J CLOETE, W TURNER *hon c.*
(St Pet), V. **D** S'wark 6 **P** *St Steph Ho Ox* **I** M J WOODGATE.
LOWER (St Andr), V. **D** S'wark 6 **P** *Trustees* **I** (Vacant).
STREATHAM HILL (St Marg the Queen), V. **D** S'wark 6 **P** *Bp* **I** (Vacant).
VALE (H Redeem), V. **D** S'wark 6 **P** *CPAS* **I** B LIPSCOMBE.
STREATLEY (St Mary), *Berks.* V. **D** Ox 18 **P** *Bp* **I** A L THOMAS.
STREATLEY, *Beds.* V. **D** St Alb **P** *Bp* **I** R W WOOD.
STREET or STRETE (St Mich), *Devon.* V. **D** Ex 14 **P** *Bp* **I** R A DURANT.
STREET (H Trin) w Walton (H Trin), *Somt.* R. **D** B & W 7 **P** *Dioc Bd of Patr* **I** D C EVANS, R J COOPER *c.*
STREETLY (All SS), *W Midl.* V. **D** Lich 9 **P** *Bp* **I** R J TAYLOR, R B DORRINGTON *c.*
STRELLEY (All SS), *Notts.*. **D** Southw 8 *See* Bilborough.
STRENSALL (St Mary Virg), *N Yorks.* V. **D** York 5 **P** *Abp* **I** G C GALLEY.
STRENSHAM, *Worcs.*. **D** Worc 5 *See* Earl's Croome.
STRETE (St Mich), *Devon.*. **D** Ex 14 *See* Street.
STRETFORD, *Herefs.* R. **D** Heref 7 *See* Dilwyn.
STRETFORD (St Matt), *Gtr Man.* R. **D** Man 9 **P** *D and C of Man* **I** H R ENTWISTLE.
(All SS), R. **D** Man 9 **P** *Bp* **I** M J R TINKER, R F EFEMEY *c.*
(St Bride), R. **D** Man 9 **P** *Trustees* **I** A PUGMIRE, P J ROGERS *c.*
(St Pet), R. **D** Man 9 **P** *Crown and Bp* alt **I** M J HARDY.
STRETHALL (St Mary), *Essex.* R. **D** Chelmsf *See* Elmdon.
STRETHAM (St Jas Gt) w Thetford (St Geo), *Cambs.* R. **D** Ely 15 **P** *Bp* **I** J S ASKEY.
STRETTON (St Matt), *Chesh.* V. **D** Ches 4 **P** *Mrs P F D B grantham and Dr S P L Du Bois Davidson* **I** E C ROWLANDS.
STRETTON (St Jo Evang), *Staffs.* V. **D** Lich 3 *See* Penkridge.
STRETTON (St Nich), *Leics.* R. **D** Pet 12 *See* Greetham.
STRETTON MAGNA (St Giles), *Leics.* V. **D** Leic 6 *See* Glen Magna.
STRETTON PARVA (St Jo Bapt or St Clem), *Leics.* V. **D** Leic 6 *See* Gaulby.
STRETTON W Claymills (St Mary), *Staffs.* V. **D** Lich **P** *Ld Gretton* **I** A R WAYTE.
STRETTON BASKERVILLE, *Warws.*. **D** Cov 5 *See* Wolvey.
STRETTON-EN-LE-FIELD (St Mich), *Leics.*. **D** Leic *See* Donisthorpe.
STRETTON GRANDISON (St Lawr) w Ashperton (St Bart), Canon Frome (St Jas) and Yarkhill (St Jo Bapt), *Herefs.* V. **D** Heref 6 **P** *Bp and D and C of Heref* **I** (Vacant).
STRETTON-ON-DUNSMORE (All SS) w Princethorpe, *Warws.* V. **D** Cov *See* Bourton-on-Dunsmore.
STRETTON-ON-FOSSE, *Warws.*. **D** Cov 9 *See* Ilmington.
STRETTON-SUGWAS (St Mary Magd), *Herefs.* R. **D** Heref 4 **P** *Dioc Bd of Patr* **I** W L RICHARDS.
STRETTON-UNDER-FOSSE, *Warws.*. **D** Cov 5 *See* Monks Kirby.
STRICKLAND, GT (St Barn) and Strickland, L (St Mary), *Cumb.*. **D** Carl 1 *See* Morland.
STRINGSTON, *Somt.*. **D** B & W *See* Kilve.
STRIXTON (St John), *Northants.* V. **D** Pet 7 *See* Wollaston.
STROOD (St Nich) w (St Mary), *Kent.* V. **D** Roch **P** *Bp and D and C of Roch* **I** G T GRAY.
(St Francis), V. **D** Roch **P** *Bp* **I** A J COX.
STROUD (St Lawr), *Glos.* V. **D** Glouc 4 **P** *Bp* **I** P MINALL, F A G CLARK *c.*
(H Trin), V. **D** Glouc 4 **P** *Bp* **I** R D M GREY.
STROUD GREEN (H Trin), *Lon.* V. **D** Lon 23 **P** *Bp* **I** B KINGSMILL-LUNN.
STROXTON (All SS), *Lincs.* R. **D** Linc *See* Harlaxton.
STRUBBY (St Osw) w Woodthorpe, *Lincs.* V. **D** Linc *See* Withern.
STRUMPSHAW (St Pet), *Norf.*. **D** Nor 1 *See* Buckenham.
STUBBINGS (St Jas L), *Berks.* V. **D** Ox 13 **P** *Dioc Bd of Patr* **I** B A SOLTAU.
STUBBINS (St Phil), *Lancs.* V. **D** Man 12 **P** *Trustees* **I** (Vacant).
STUBTON (St Martin), *Lincs.*. **D** Linc 23 *See* Westborough.
STUCHBURY, *Northants.* R. **D** Pet 1 *See* Helmdon.
STUDHAM (St Mary) w Whipsnade (St Mary Magd), *Beds.* V. **D** St Alb 18 **P** *Ld Chan* **I** J W SHEPHERD.
STUDLAND (St Nich), *Dorset.* R. **D** Sarum 9 **P** *Mrs Pleydell Railston and Mrs Arnold Foster* **I** W D O'HANLON.
STUDLEY (Nativ of BVM), *Warws.* V. **D** Cov 7 **P** *Dioc Bd of Patr* **I** D A G ATCHESON.
STUDLEY, *Oxon.*. **D** Ox *See* Horton.
STUDLEY (St Jo Evang), *Wilts.* V. **D** Sarum 24 **P** *R of Trowbridge* **I** S S VENNER.
STUKELEY, GREAT (St Bart) w Stukeley, Little (St Martin), *Cambs.* V. **D** Ely 10 **P** *S for Maint of Faith and Bp* **I** (Vacant).
STUNTNEY (St Mary), *Cambs.* V. **D** Ely 15 **P** *D and C of Ely* **I** J A OVENDEN *p-in-c.*
STURMER (St Mary), *Essex.* R. **D** Chelmsf 18 *See* Birdbrook.
STURMINSTER-MARSHALL (St Mary), *Dorset.* V. **D** Sarum 11 **P** *Eton Coll* **I** J H RUMENS *p-in-c.*
STURMINSTER-NEWTON (St Mary) w Hinton St Mary (St Pet), *Dorset.* V. **D** Sarum 13 **P** *G Pitt-Rivers Esq 1st 4th and 6th turns, V of Iwerne Minster 3rd turn, Col L L Yeatman 2nd and 5th turns* **I** R JACKSON *c.*
STURRY (St Nich) w Fordwich and Westbere w Hersden, *Kent.* R. **D** Cant 3 **P** *Abp, Ld Chan and St Aug Coll Cant* in turn **I** P J GAUSDEN.
STURSTON, *Norf.*. **D** Nor 19 *See* Tottington.
STURTON (St Hugh), *Humb.*. **D** Linc 2 *See* Stow.
STURTON, GREAT (All SS), *Lincs.* V. **D** Linc 11 *See* Baumber.
STURTON-LE-STEEPLE (St Pet and St Paul) w Littleborough, *Notts.* V. **D** Southw 5 **P** *G M T Foljambe Esq* **I** A BUTT *p-in-c.*
STUSTON (All SS), *Suff.* R. **D** St E 16 *See* Brome.
STUTTON, *Suff.*. **D** St E *See* Brantham.
STYDD (St Sav), *Lancs.*. **D** Blackb 9 *See* Ribchester.
STYVECHALE (St Jas), *W Midl.* V. **D** Cov 3 **P** *Lt-Col A H M Gregory-Hood* **I** L G MORTIMER, R J WORSLEY *c.*
SUCKLEY (St Jo Bapt), *Worcs.* R. **D** Worc 2 *See* Alfrick.
SUDBOROUGH, *Northants.*. **D** Pet *See* Lowick.
SUDBOURNE (All SS), *Suff.*. **D** St E 7 *See* Orford.
SUDBROOKE (St Edw), *Lincs.* R and V. **D** Linc 3 *See* Barlings.
SUDBURY (All SS) w Somersal-Herbert (St Pet), *Derbys.* R. **D** Derby 14 **P** *Bp* **I** F FINCH.
SUDBURY (St Andr), *Gtr Lon.* V. **D** Lon 18 **P** *Bp* **I** A F DAVIS.

SUDBURY (All SS) w Ballingdon and Brundon, *Suff.* V. **D** St E 12 **P** *Simeon Trustees* **I** L F SIMPKINS.
(St Greg w St Pet) and (St Mary Chilton), *Suff.* R. **D** St E **P** *Bp 3 turns, Ch S Trust 1 turn* **I** P HOLLIS.
SUDELEY MANOR (St Mary), *Glos.* R. **D** Glouc 18 *See* Winchcombe.
SUFFIELD (St Marg), *Norf.* R. **D** Nor 8 **P** *Hon Doris Harbord* **I** W M C BESTELINK.
SUGLEY (H Sav), *T & W.* V. **D** Newc T 5b **P** *Bp* **I** M C VINE.
SULGRAVE, *Northants.* V. **D** Pet 1 *See* Culworth.
SULHAM (St Nich), *Berks.* R. **D** Ox 12 *See* Tidmarsh.
SULHAMSTEAD-ABBOTS (St Mary) w Sulhamstead-Bannister (St Mich) and Ufton-Nervet (St Pet), *Berks.* R. **D** Ox 12 **P** *Qu Coll Ox and Or Coll Ox (alt)* **I** M WATTS.
SULLINGTON (St Mary) and Thakeham w Warminghurst, *W Sussex.* R. **D** Chich 7 **P** *Bp and Dioc Bd of Patr (alt)* **I** N E LEMPRIERE.
SUMMERFIELD (Ch Ch), *W Midl.*. **D** Birm 2 *See* Birmingham.
SUMMERSTOWN (St Mary), *Surrey.* V. **D** S'wark 7a **P** *Trustees* **I** F P GOUGH.
SUMMERTOWN (St Mich AA), *Oxon.*. **D** Ox *See* Oxford.
SUNBURY (St Mary), *Surrey.* V. **D** Lon 13 **P** *D and C of St Paul's* **I** J Y R TUCKER, A K TUCKER *c.*
UPPER (St Sav), V. **D** Lon 13 **P** *V of Sunbury* **I** A F P BROWN.
SUNDERLAND (H Trin) w (St Jo Evang), V, *T & W.* R. **D** Dur *See* Hendon.
(St Bede, Town End Farm Conv Distr). **D** Dur 8 **P** *Bp* **I** J W POULTER *c-in-c.*
(St Chad, E Herrington), V. **D** Dur 8 **P** *Bp* **I** J H ADAMS *c.* *See also* BISHOP WEARMOUTH AND MONK WEARMOUTH..
SUNDERLAND, NORTH (St Paul), *Northumb.* V. **D** Newc T 8 **P** *Ld Crewe's Trustees* **I** D G ROGERSON.
SUNDON, *Beds.* V. **D** St Alb **P** *Bp* **I** A R SLADE.
SUNDRIDGE (St Mary) w Ide Hill (St Mary Virg), *Kent.* R. **D** Roch 7 **P** *Abp* **I** R D JOHNSON.
SUNK ISLAND (H Trin), *Humb.* V. **D** York 15 *See* Ottringham.
SUNNINGDALE (H Trin), *Berks.* V. **D** Ox 11a **P** *Bp* **I** D R PRICE.
SUNNINGHILL (St Mich AA), *Berks.* V. **D** Ox 11a **P** *St Jo Coll Cam* **I** T W GUNTER.
SUNNINGWELL (St Leon), *Oxon.* R. **D** Ox 11 **P** *Dioc Bd of Patr* **I** K KINNAIRD.
SUNNYBROW (St Jo Div), *Durham.*. **D** Dur 9 *See* Willington.
SUNNYSIDE (St Mich AA) w Bourne End (St Jo Evang), [Herts]. V. **D** St Alb 3 **P** *Duchy of Cornw* **I** M K M SCOTT.
SURBITON (St Andr and St Mark), *Surrey.* V. **D** S'wark 11 **P** *Bp* **I** D K R GERRARD, C J E MOODY IN C OF ST ANDR, D N HEAD *c,* B E NICHOLS *hon c.*
(St Matt), V. **D** S'wark 11 **P** *Trustees* **I** R E LEWIS, P G RICH *c,* D C WARD *c.*
HILL (Ch Ch), V. **D** S'wark 11 **P** *Trustees* **I** D I FRASER, S TAYLOR *c.*
SURFLEET (St Lawr) and W Pinchbeck, *Lincs.* V. **D** Linc 17 **P** *Bp* **I** J D BROWN.
SURLINGHAM (St Mary w St Sav), *Norf.* V. **D** Nor 14 *See* Bramerton.
SURREY SQUARE (All SS), *Surrey.*. **D** S'wark 6 *See* Newington.
SUSTEAD (St Pet and St Paul), *Norf.* V. **D** Nor 5 *See* Felbrigg w Metton.
SUTCOMBE (St Andr) w Putford (St Steph), *Devon.* V. **D** Ex 9 **P** *Bp* **I** H J ROCHE.
SUTTERBY (St Jo Bapt), *Lincs.* R. **D** Linc 7 *See* Langton-by-Partney.
SUTTERTON (St Mary BV) and Wigtoft (St Pet and St Paul), *Lincs.* V. **D** Linc 21 **P** *Bp and Crown (alt)* **I** J A SKIPPER.
SUTTON (St Geo), *Mer.* V. **D** Ches 13 **P** *Trustees* **I** D S HARRISON.
(St Jas), V. **D** Ches 13 **P** *Trustees* **I** C F EASTWOOD.
SUTTON (St Jo Bapt) w Bignor (St Cross), *W Sussex.* R. **D** Chich 6 **P** *Ld Egremont* **I** R G JOHNSON *p-in-c.*
SUTTON (St Mary) w Duckmanton (St Pet and St Paul), *Derbys.* R. **D** Derby 2 **P** *Simeon Trustees* **I** (Vacant).
SUTTON (St Andr), *Cambs.* V. **D** Ely 15 **P** *D and C of Ely* **I** R W S L GUSSMAN *p-in-c,* T R HOLLAND *hon c.*
SUTTON (St Nich) w (St Mich), *Herefs.* R. **D** Heref 4 **P** *Bp* **I** G D ABELL, E R I CHURCHUS *c.*
SUTTON (St Nich St Mich AA and All SS), *Mer.* R. **D** Liv 10 **P** *Dioc Bd of Patr* **I** M SOULSBY, H J BAKER *team v,* R G MYERS *hon c.*
SUTTON (St Mich), *Norf.* R. **D** Nor 9 *See* Ingham.
SUTTON (St Mich AA) w Upton, *Cambs.*. **D** Pet 14 *See* Castor.
SUTTON, *Beds.* R. **D** St Alb 17 *See* Potton.
SUTTON (All SS), *Suff.* V. **D** St E 7 *See* Shottisham.
SUTTON (St Nich), *Surrey.* R. **D** S'wark 8 **P** *Hertf Coll Ox* **I** F E RUSBY, E M HILL *hon c.*
(Ch Ch), V. **D** S'wark 8 **P** *R of Sutton* **I** J HACKETT, J P WICKENS *c.*
NEW TOWN (St Barn), V. **D** S'wark 8 **P** *Bp* **I** B D RODERICK, H G WOOD *hon c.*
SUTTON (St Bart) w Lound (St Anne), *Notts.* V. **D** Southw 5 **P** *Bp* **I** A G B PARSONS.
SUTTON-AT-HONE (St Jo Bapt), *Kent.* V. **D** Roch 1a **P** *D and C of Roch* **I** L G THOROGOOD.
SUTTON BASSETT, *Northants.*. **D** Pet *See* Ashley.
SUTTON-BENGER (All SS), *Wilts.* R. **D** Bris *See* Christian Malford.
SUTTON-BINGHAM (All SS), *Somt.* R. **D** B & W 12 *See* Coker, East.
SUTTON BONINGTON (St Anne) w (St Mich), *Notts.* R. **D** Southw 11 **P** *Bp* **I** A CLARKE.
SUTTON-BRIDGE (St Matt), *Lincs.* V. **D** Linc **P** *Bp* **I** B PARSONS.
SUTTON-BY-DOVER (SS Pet and Paul), *Kent.* R. **D** Cant *See* Mongeham, Great.
SUTTON CHENEY (St Jas Gt), *Leics.* V. **D** Leic 15 *See* Cadeby.
SUTTON COLDFIELD (H Trin), *W Midl.* R. **D** Birm 12 **P** *Bp* **I** A P ROSE, N B P KING *c,* W A WOOD *hon c.*
(St Chad), V. **D** Birm 12 **P** *Bp* **I** P A W WATTS.
(St Columba), V. **D** Birm 12 **P** *Bp* **I** M GRAHAM.
SUTTON COURT (St Mich). **D** Lon 12 *See* Chiswick.
SUTTON COURTENAY (All SS) w Appleford, *Oxon.* V. **D** Ox 11 **P** *D and C of Windsor* **I** C G CLARKE, F NELSON *hon c.*
SUTTON, GREAT (St Jo Evang), *Chesh.* V. **D** Ches 9 **P** *V of Eastham* **I** C J THOMAS.
SUTTON, GREAT (All SS) w Shopland *Essex.* R. **D** Chelmsf 11 **P** *Rev B M Lambert* **I** G A BISHTON *p-in-c.*
SUTTON-IN-ASHFIELD (St Mary Magd w St Modwen), *Notts.* V. **D** Southw 2 **P** *Bp* **I** J L D HARDY.
(St Mich AA), V. **D** Southw 2 **P** *Bp* **I** P L BOTTING.
SUTTON-IN-CRAVEN (St Thos Ap and Mart), *W Yorks.* V. **D** Bradf 11 **P** *Ch Ch Ox* **I** W G JOHN.
SUTTON-IN-HOLDERNESS (St Jas) w Wawne or Waghen (St Pet), *Humb.* R. **D** York 17 **P** *Dioc Bd of Patr* **I** T W DOHERTY, R A CLEGG *team v,* M R WHITE *c.*
(St Mich AA), V. **D** York 17 **P** *Abp* **I** J F E BORNE.
SUTTON-LE-MARSH (St Clem), *Lincs.* V. **D** Linc 8 **P** *Bp* **I** T P W RUDMAN.
SUTTON, LONG (H Trin) w Long Load (Ch Ch), *Somt.* V. **D** B & W 10 **P** *D and C of Wells and V of Martock* **I** G COWDRY.
SUTTON, LONG (St Mary), *Lincs.* V. **D** Linc 16 **P** *Lady E S McGeoch* **I** J M WARWICK.
(St Edmund), V. **D** Linc 16 *See* Suttons, The.
(St James), V. **D** Linc 16 *See* Suttons, The.
(St Nicholas),. **D** Linc 16 *See* Lutton.
SUTTON, LONG (All SS), *Hants.*. **D** Win *See* Odiham.
SUTTON MADDOCK (St Mary), *Salop.* V. **D** Lich 25 *See* Kemberton.
SUTTON MANDEVILLE (All SS), *Wilts.* R. **D** Sarum 19 *See* Fovant.
SUTTON MONTIS (H Trin), *Somt.* R. **D** B & W 4 **P** *M M Trust* **I** P F L CONNOR *c-in-c.*
SUTTON-ON-DERWENT (St Mich AA), *Humb.* R. **D** York 6 *See* Elvington.
SUTTON-ON-PLYM (St Jo Evang), *Devon.* V. **D** Ex 23 *See* Plymouth.
SUTTON-ON-THE-FOREST, *N Yorks.* V. **D** York 5 **P** *Ld Chan* **I** K BAILES *p-in-c.*
SUTTON-ON-THE-HILL (St Mich), *Derbys.*. **D** Derby 14 *See* Church Broughton.
SUTTON-ON-TRENT (All SS), *Notts.* V. **D** Southw 4 **P** *Bp* **I** D G HATTER.
SUTTON POINTZ, *Dorset.*. **D** Sarum 6 *See* Preston.
SUTTON SCOTNEY, *Hants.*. **D** Win *See* Wonston.
SUTTON-UNDER-BRAILES (St Thos á Becket), *Warws.* V. **D** Cov 9 **P** *Bp* **I** N J MORGAN.
SUTTON VALENCE (St Mary Virg) w Sutton, East (St Pet and St Paul) and Chart Sutton (St Mich), *Kent.* V. **D** Cant 15 **P** *Abp* **I** (Vacant).
SUTTON-VENY (St Jo Evang), *Wilts.*. **D** Sarum 22 *See* Heytesbury.
SUTTON-WALDRON (St Bart), *Dorset.* R. **D** Sarum 13 *See* Iwerne Minster.
SUTTONS, THE (St Jas and St Edm) w Tydd (St Mary), *Lincs.* V. **D** Linc 16 **P** *Ld Chan 1st turn, V of Long Sutton 2nd and 3rd turns* **I** J M WOODS.

SWABY (St Nich) w Thoresby, South (St Andr), *Lincs*. R. **D** Linc *See* Withern.

SWADLINCOTE (Em Ch), *Derbys*. V. **D** Derby 16 **P** *V of Ch Gresley* **I** R M PARSONS.

SWAFFHAM (St Pet and St Paul), *Norf*. V. **D** Nor 19 **P** *Bp* **I** K W REEVES.

SWAFFHAM-BULBECK (St Mary), *Cambs*. V. **D** Ely 3 **P** *Bp* **I** F T DUFTON *p-in-c*.

SWAFFHAM PRIOR (St Mary, St Cyriac and St Julitta) w Reach (St Etheldreda and H Trin), *Cambs*. V. **D** Ely 3 **P** *D and C of Ely* **I** J K BYROM.

SWAFIELD (St Nich), *Norf*.. **D** Nor *See* Trunch.

SWAINSTHORPE, *Norf*.. **D** Nor 13 *See* Newton Flotman.

SWAINSWICK (St Mary Virg) w Langridge (St Mary Magd) and Woolley, *Avon*. R. **D** B & W 13 **P** *Or Coll Ox and Ld Chan* alt **I** G E WOODS.

SWALCLIFFE (St Pet and St Paul), *Oxon*. V. **D** Ox 6 *See* Epwell.

SWALECLIFFE (St Jo Bapt), *Kent*. R. **D** Cant 4 **P** *Abp* **I** (Vacant).

SWALLOW (H Trin) w Cabourn (St Nich), *Lincs*. R. **D** Linc 5 **P** *Ld Chan and Earl of Yarborough* **I** H CLAREY *p-in-c*.

SWALLOWBECK (St Geo), *Lincs*. V. **D** Linc 15 **P** *Bp and V of Skellingthorpe* **I** (Vacant).

SWALLOWCLIFFE (St Pet) w Ansty, *Wilts*. V. **D** Sarum 19 *See* Tisbury.

SWALLOWFIELD (All SS) and Farley Hill (St Jo Evang), *Berks*. V. **D** Ox 15 **P** *D and C of Heref* **I** J G SUMNER.

SWALWELL (H Trin), *T & W*. V. **D** Dur 4a **P** *R of Whickham* **I** J M H GIBSON.

SWAN (Grendon Underwood w Edgcott, Marsh Gibbon, Preston Bissett, Chetwode, Barton Hartshorn and Twyford), *Bucks*. R. **D** Ox 25 **P** *Dioc Bd of Patr* **I** A R DE PURY, C W NEWTON *team v*.

SWANAGE (St Mary Virg) w Herston (St Mark), *Dorset*. R. **D** Sarum 9 **P** *D C Dudley-Ryder Esq* **I** D BAILEY, D J PASKINS *c*, R G H STACEY *c*, C DYMOKE-MARR *hon c*.

SWANBOURNE (St Swith) w Horwood, Little (St Nich), *Bucks*. V. **D** Ox 27 *See* Mursley.

SWANBOROUGH (Wilcot, Huish, Oare, Woodborough w Manningford Bohune, Beechingstoke, Alton Barnes w Alton Priors, Stanton St Bernard, Manningford Bruce, Manningford Abbas and North Newnton), *Wilts*. R. **D** Sarum 27 **P** *Swanborough Patr Bd* **I** J C WHETTEM, M J BEASLEY *team v*.

SWANLEY (St Paul), *Kent*. V. **D** Roch 1a **P** *Merchant Taylor's Co* **I** D J BETTS.

(St Mary Virg), V. **D** Roch 1a **P** *Guild of All S* **I** R L GWYTHER, R H COLLINS *c*.

SWANMORE (St Barn) , *Hants*. V. **D** Portsm 2 **P** *Dioc Bd of Patr* **I** G R PATERSON.

SWANMORE (St Mich AA) w Havenstreet (St Pet), *Isle of Wight*. V. **D** Portsm 6 **P** *S for Maint of Faith* **I** M O H CATON.

SWANNINGTON (St Marg), *Norf*. R. **D** Nor 6 *See* Alderford.

SWANSCOMBE (St Pet and St Paul) w (All SS, Galley Hill), *Kent*. R. **D** Roch 3 **P** *Dioc Bd of Patr* **I** J R HAMBIDGE.

SWANTON-ABBOT (St Mich) w Skeyton (All SS), *Norf*. R. **D** Nor 8 **P** *J T D Shaw Esq* **I** R J TUCK *p-in-c*.

SWANTON MORLEY (All SS) w Worthing (St Marg), R *Norf*.. **D** Nor 20 **P** *G and C Coll Cam* **I** L A WILMAN.

SWANTON NOVERS, *Norf*. R. **D** Nor 24 *See* Melton Constable.

SWANWICK (St Andr) w Pentrich (St Matt), *Derbys*. V. **D** Derby 1 **P** *Wright Trustees and Duke of Devonshire* **I** P A B VESSEY, C C WARNER *c*.

SWANWICK Hants. **D** Portsm 1 *See* Sarisbury.

SWARBY (BVM and All SS), *Lincs*.. **D** Linc 12 *See* Aswarby.

SWARDESTON (St Mary Virg), *Norf*. V. **D** Nor 13 **P** *Bp* **I** P MCFADYEN.

SWARKESTONE (St Jas), *Derbys*.. **D** Derby 15 *See* Stanton-by-Bridge.

SWARRATON, *Hants*.. **D** Win *See* Northington.

SWATON (St Mich) w Spanby (St Nich) *Lincs*. V and R. **D** Linc 22 *See* Helpringham.

SWAVESEY (St Andr), *Cambs*. V. **D** Ely 5 **P** *Jes Coll Cam* **I** H BAMBER.

SWAY (St Luke), *Hants*. V. **D** Win 9 **P** *Bp* **I** D L PAINE.

SWAYFIELD (St Nich), *Lincs*. R. **D** Linc *See* Corby Glen.

SWAYTHLING, *Hants*.. **D** Win 11 *See* Stoneham, South.

SWEFFLING (St Mary Virg), *Suff*. R. **D** St E 19 *See* Rendham.

SWELL, *Somt*.. **D** B & W *See* Fivehead.

SWELL, (NETHER (St Mary) w Upper (St Mary), *Glos*.. **D** Glouc 16 *See* Longborough.

SWEPSTONE (St Pet) w Snarestone, *Leics*. R. **D** Leic 12 **P** *MMT* **I** C G S COX.

SWERFORD w Showell (St Mary), *Oxon*. R. **D** Ox 3 *See* Hook-Norton.

SWETTENHAM (Dedic unknown), *Chesh*. R. **D** Ches 12 *See* Brereton.

SWILLAND (St Mary Virg) w Ash-Bocking (All SS), *Suff*. V. **D** St E 1 *See* Witnesham.

SWILLINGTON (Woodlesford St Mary), *W Yorks*. R. **D** Ripon 7 **P** *Bp* **I** W J HULSE.

SWIMBRIDGE (St Jas Ap) w Gunn and W Buckland, *Devon*. V. **D** Ex 18 **P** *Bp and Trustees of Earl Fortescue* **I** N JACKSON-STEVENS.

SWINBROOK (St Mary BV), *Oxon*. V. **D** Ox *See* Asthall.

SWINDALE, *Cumb*.. **D** Carl *See* Shap.

SWINDERBY (All SS) (Thorpe-on-the-Hill, Eagle and North Scarle), *Lincs*. V. **D** Linc **P** *Bp 1st turn, Ld Chan 2nd turn, Mrs D Kirk 3rd turn, D and C of Linc 4th turn* **I** K J SAUNDERS.

SWINDON (St Lawr) w Uckington and Elmstone Hardwicke (St Mary Magd), *Glos*. R. **D** Glouc 11 **P** *Bp* **I** M E BENNETT.

SWINDON (Ch Ch), *Wilts*. V. **D** Bris 10 **P** *Ld Chan* **I** O C BARRACLOUGH, P M DOWN *c*, P W DYSON *c*.

(All SS), V. **D** Bris 10 **P** *Bp* **I** P A C CADOGAN *p-in-c*.

(St Aug), V. **D** Bris 10 **P** *Bp* **I** C DOBB.

(St Barn), V. **D** Bris 10 **P** *Bp* **I** R J HARRIS.

(St Jo Bapt and St Andr), R. **D** Bris 10 **P** *Bp* **I** H L ORMEROD, S L BESSENT *team v*.

(Dorcan, St Paul), R. **D** Bris 10 **P** *Bp* **I** B E PEARCE, G R M FISON *team v*.

NEW TOWN (St Mark w St Jo Evang St Sav and St Luke), V. **D** Bris 10 **P** *Bp* **I** L R HURRELL, R J COSH *c*, F W T FULLER *c*, M R WEBSTER *c*.

SWINDON (St Jo Evang), *Staffs*. V. **D** Lich 7 **P** *Trustees* **I** R D PAYNE.

SWINE (St Mary), *Humb*. V. **D** York 14 **P** *W J A Wilberforce Esq and another* **I** B P THOMPSON.

SWINEFLEET (St Marg), *Humb*. V. **D** Sheff 9 **P** *V of Whitgift* **I** P S LINDECK *p-in-c*.

SWINESHEAD (St Mary), *Lincs*. V. **D** Linc 21 **P** *Bp* **I** L G STANDLEY.

SWINESHEAD (St Nich), *Beds*. R. **D** St Alb *See* Pertenhall.

SWINETHORPE (All SS), *Notts*.. **D** Southw 3 *See* Harby.

SWINFORD (All SS), *Leics*. V. **D** Leic 14 *See* Stanford.

SWINFORD, OLD, or STOURBRIDGE (St Mary), *Worcs*. R. **D** Worc 11 **P** *Bp* **I** H L DAVIES, P J MARTIN *hon c*.

(St Thos), V. **D** Worc 11 **P** *Bp* **I** D L BARRETT.

SWINGFIELD, *Kent*.. **D** Cant *See* Denton.

SWINHOPE (St Helen) w Thorganby (All SS), *Lincs*. R. **D** Linc 10 **P** *Dioc Bd of Patr* **I** R J CROOKES.

SWINSTEAD (St Mary), *Lincs*. R. **D** Linc *See* Corby Glen.

SWINTON (St Pet), *Gtr Man*. R. **D** Man 3 **P** *Bp, Archd of Man and V of Eccles* **I** T H STOKES *team v*.

(H Rood), V. **D** Man 3 **P** *V of Swinton* **I** D G BARNETT.

SWINTON (St Marg), *S Yorks*. V. **D** Sheff 10 **P** *Earl Fitzwilliam* **I** M R JACKSON, K J BARNARD *c*.

SWITHLAND (St Leon), *Leics*. R. **D** Leic 10 **P** *Ld Chan* **I** F R WALTERS *p-in-c*.

SWYNCOMBE (St Botolph), *Oxon*. R. **D** Ox 1 **P** *Ld Chan* **I** D P MEMBERY *p-in-c*.

SWYNNERTON (St Mary), *Staffs*. R. **D** Lich 19 **P** *Bp* **I** W G H GARDINER *p-in-c*.

SWYNSHED (St Nich), *Beds*.. **D** St Alb *See* Swineshead.

SWYRE (H Trin), *Dorset*. R. **D** Sarum 2 *See* Puncknowle.

SYDE, *Glos*.. **D** Glouc 13 *See* Brimpsfield.

SYDENHAM (St Mary), *Oxon*.. **D** Ox 1 *See* Chinnor.

SYDENHAM (St Bart), *Kent*. V. **D** S'wark 18 **P** *Earl of Dartmouth* **I** B F MOBBS *p-in-c*.

(H Trin), V. **D** S'wark 18 **P** *Simeon Trustees* **I** J M P CALDICOTT *p-in-c*, R W HAYTER *c*.

(St Phil), V. **D** S'wark 18 **P** *V of Sydenham* **I** J M P CALDICOTT.

LOWER (St Mich AA Bell Green), V. **D** S'wark 18 **P** *Bp* **I** R F SHAW, R W POTTIER *c*.

(All SS), V. **D** S'wark 18 **P** *V of Sydenham* **I** J M P CALDICOTT *p-in-c*, K M HODGES *c*.

SYDENHAM DAMEREL (St Mary), *Devon*. R. **D** Ex 22 *See* Lamerton.

SYDERSTONE (St Mary) w Barmer and Bagthorpe, *Norf*. R. **D** Nor **P** *Mrs S C Reed and Capt E H Longsdon (alt)* **I** A W HOLLANDS.

SYDLING ST NICHOLAS (St Nich), *Dorset*.. **D** Sarum 5 *See* Bradford Peverell.

SYDMONTON (St Mary Virg), *Hants.*. **D** Win 5 *See* Ecchinswell.

SYKEHOUSE (H Trin), *S Yorks.* V. **D** Sheff 9 **P** *D and C of Dur* **I** F BICKERTON *p-in-c.*

SYLEHAM (St Mary), *Norf.* V. **D** St E 17 *See* Hoxne.

SYMONDSBURY (St Jo Bapt) w Eype (St Pet) and Broadoak (St Paul). *Dorset.* R. **D** Sarum 2 **P** *Bp* **I** P G BLOOMFIELD *p-in-c.*

SYRESHAM (St Jas) w Whitfield (St Jo Evang), *Northants.* R. **D** Pet 1 **P** *Dioc Bd Patr and Worc Coll Ox* alt **I** R R OSBORN *p-in-c.*

SYSTON (St Pet and St Paul), *Leics.* V. **D** Leic 9 **P** *Univ of Ox* **I** C E WALL, S T W GEARY *c.*

SYSTON (St Mary), *Lincs.* V. **D** Linc 23 *See* Barkston.

SYSTON (St Anne), *Avon.* R. **D** Bris 8 **P** *Bp* **I** J C POARCH.

SYWELL (St Pet and St Paul) w Overstone, *Northants.* R. **D** Pet 7 **P** *Duchy of Cornw* **I** C E HARRIS.

TABLEY, OVER or TABLEY SUPERIOR (St Paul) w High Leigh or Legh, *Chesh.* V. **D** Ches 12 **P** *Bp, T R P Langford-Brook Esq and C L S Cornwall-Legh Esq* **I** C MATTHEWS.

TACKLEY (St Nich), *Oxon.*. **D** Ox *See* Steeple Aston.

TACOLNESTON (All SS), *Norf.* R. **D** Nor 13 *See* Wreningham.

TADCASTER (St Mary), *N Yorks.* V. **D** York 9 **P** *Abp* **I** D BURNETT, A W V MACE *c.*

TADDINGTON (St Mich) w Chelmorton (St Jo Bapt), *Derbys.* V. **D** Derby 10 **P** *V of Bakewell* **I** J F HILDAGE *p-in-c.*

TADLEY (St Pet) w (St Sav), *Hants.* R. **D** Win 3 **P** *Bp* **I** W A CANHAM.
NORTH (St Mary's), V. **D** Win 3 **P** *Bp* **I** J TALBOT.

TADLOW (St Giles), *Cambs.* V (*See Shingay Group*). **D** Ely 8 **P** *Down Coll Cam* **I** (Vacant).

TADMARTON (St Nich), *Oxon.*. **D** Ox 6 *See* Epwell.

TADWORTH (Good Shepherd), *Surrey.* V. **D** S'wark 12 **P** *V of Kingswood* **I** N C GRIFFIN.

TAKELEY (H Trin) w Little Canfield (All SS), *Essex.* R. **D** Chelmsf 23 **P** *Bp* **I** E G GALLON.

TALATON (St Jas Ap and M), *Devon.* R. **D** Ex 7 **P** *Dioc Bd of Patr* **I** O R TENNANT.

TALBOT VILLAGE (St Mark), *Dorset.* V. **D** Sarum 14 **P** *Talbot Village Trustees* **I** C J F RUTLEDGE *p-in-c.*

TALKE (St Martin Bishop and Confessor and St Sav), *Staffs.* R. **D** Lich 17 **P** *V of Audley* **I** R WEAVER.

TALKIN, *Cumb.*. **D** Carl 2 *See* Hayton.

TALLAND (St Tallan), *Cornw.* V. **D** Truro 13 **P** *Mr W G Mills and Dioc Bd of Patr* alt **I** J K P S ROBERTSHAW *p-in-c.*

TALLINGTON (St Lawr), *Lincs.* V. **D** Linc 13 **P** *Lady M Barclay-Harvey* **I** G C SMITH.

TAMERTON FOLIOT (St Mary), *Devon.* V. **D** Ex 23 **P** *Ld Chan* **I** C W H GOODWINS.

TAMERTON, NORTH, w Boyton *Devon.* R. **D** Truro 11 **P** *Duke of Cornwall and MMT (alt)* **I** (Vacant).

TAMWORTH (St Editha) w Glascote (St Geo) and Hopwas (St Chad), *Staffs.* V. **D** Lich 6 **P** *Bp* **I** A EDWARDS, C S MINCHIN *team v*, P A HARDWICKE *c.*

TANDRIDGE (St Pet), *Surrey.* V. **D** S'wark 10 **P** *Trustees of late Mr Turner* **I** D C W LANE.

TANFIELD (St Marg), *Durham.* V. **D** Dur 7 **P** *Bp* **I** A S VASEY *p-in-c.*

TANFIELD, WEST (St Nich) and Well (St Mich) w Snape (St Mary), *N Yorks.* R. **D** Ripon 3 **P** *Mrs Bourne-Arton* **I** D W EYLES *p-in-c.*

TANG HALL (St Hilda Conv Distr), *N Yorks.* V. **D** York 1 *See* York.

TANGLEY (St Thos), *Hants.* V. **D** Win 2 *See* Hatherden.

TANGMERE (St Andr), *W Sussex.* R. **D** Chich 3 **P** *Duke of Richmond and Gordon* **I** B J MARSHALL.

TANKERSLEY (St Pet), *S Yorks.* R. **D** Sheff 7 **P** *Earl Fitzwilliam* **I** S E BRINKMAN.

TANNINGTON, *Suff.*. **D** St E *See* Worlingworth.

TANSLEY (H Trin), *Derbys.* R. **D** Derby 17 **P** *Bp* **I** J B HURST *p-in-c.*

TANSOR (St Mary) w Cotterstock (St Andr) and Fotheringhay (St Mary Virg and All SS), *Northants.* R. **D** Pet 11 **P** *D and C of Linc* **I** A J J REEVES P-IN-C OF TANSOR W FOTHERINGHAY, L R CADDICK P-IN-C OF COTTERSTOCK *p-in-c.*

TANWORTH-IN-ARDEN (St Mary Magd), *Warws.* V. **D** Birm 11 **P** *F D Muntz Esq* **I** M W TUNNICLIFFE.

TAPLOW (St Nich), *Bucks.* R. **D** Ox 24 **P** *Bp* **I** J G E KEMP *p-in-c.*

TARDEBIGGE (St Bart), *Worcs.* V. **D** Worc 7 **P** *Earl of Plymouth* **I** (Vacant).

TARLETON (H Trin w BVM), *Lancs.* R. **D** Blackb 6 **P** *St Pet Coll Ox* **I** W RILEY.

TARPORLEY (St Helen w St John and H Cross, Cotebrook), *Chesh.* R. **D** Ches 5 **P** *Bp and others* **I** C W J SAMUELS.

TARRANT GUNVILLE, *Dorset.* R. **D** Sarum 10 *See* Tarrant Valley.

TARRANT HINTON, *Dorset.* R. **D** Sarum 10 *See* Tarrant Valley.

TARRANT KEYNSTON (All SS) and Tarrant Crawford (St Mary), *Dorset.* R. **D** Sarum 10 *See* Tarrant Valley.

TARRANT MONKTON w Tarrant Launceston, *Dorset.* R. **D** Sarum 10 *See* Tarrant Valley.

TARRANT RUSHTON (St Mary), *Dorset.* R. **D** Sarum 10 *See* Tarrant Valley.

TARRANT VALLEY (Tarrant Gunville, Hinton, Monkton, Launceston, Rushton, Rawston, Keynston and Crawford), *Dorset.* R. **D** Sarum 10 **P** *Pemb Coll Cam 1st turn, Bp 2nd and 4th turns and Univ Coll Ox 3rd turn* **I** M G ST JOHN NICOLLE (FORMERLY NICOLLE).

TARRING-NEVILLE (St Martin), *E Sussex.* R. **D** Chich *See* Denton.

TARRING, WEST (St Andr), *W Sussex.* R. **D** Chich 9 **P** *Abp* **I** K W DENFORD, K G X TINGAY *c.*

TARRINGTON (St Phil and St Jas), w Stoke-Edith (St Mary Virg), Aylton, Pixley, Munsley and Putley, *Herefs.* R. **D** Heref **P** *D & C of Heref, Hon Mrs Hervey-Bathurst, A T Foley Esq, Hopton Trustees and H W Wiggin Esq* **I** R W M SKINNER.

TARVIN (St Andr) w Duddon (St Pet), *Chesh.* V. **D** Ches 2 **P** *Bp* **I** G E RUNDELL.

TASBURGH (St Mary Virg), *Norf.* R. **D** Nor 11 **P** *MMT* **I** (Vacant).

TASLEY (St Pet and St Paul), *Salop.* R. **D** Heref 9 *See* Bridgnorth.

TATENHILL (St Mich AA), *Staffs.* R. **D** Lich **P** *Bp* **I** J A WALSH *p-in-c.*

TATHAM, *Lancs.*. **D** Blackb 13 *See* Melling.

TATHAM FELLS, *Lancs.*. **D** Blackb 13 *See* Wray.

TATHWELL (St Vedast) w Haugham (All SS), *Lincs.* V. **D** Linc *See* Raithby.

TATSFIELD (St Mary), *Surrey.* R. **D** S'wark 10 **P** *Trustees* **I** (Vacant).

TATTENHALL (St Alb) and Handley (All SS), *Chesh.* R. **D** Ches 5 **P** *Bp and D and C of Ches* **I** A W FELL.

TATTENHAM CORNER and BURGH HEATH (St Mark), *Surrey.* V. **D** Guildf 9 **P** *Bp* **I** D J BAKER.

TATTENHOE (St Giles), *Bucks.* R. **D** Ox 27 *See* Whaddon.

TATTERFORD (St Marg), *Norf.* R. **D** Nor 21 **P** *Bp* **I** A W HOLLANDS *p-in-c.*

TATTERSET (St Andr), *Norf.* R. **D** Nor 21 **P** *Rt Rev G D Hand* **I** A W HOLLANDS.

TATTERSHALL (H Trin Colleg Ch) w Tattershall Thorpe, *Lincs.* V. **D** Linc *See* Coningsby.

TATTINGSTONE (St Mary BV), *Suff.* R. **D** St E 5 *See* Bentley.

TATWORTH (St Jo Evang), *Somt.* V. **D** B & W 19 **P** *V of Chard* **I** (Vacant).

TAUNTON (St Mary Magd), *Somt.* V. **D** B & W 23a **P** *CPS* **I** R F ACWORTH *p-in-c.*
(All SS Halcon), V. **D** B & W 23a **P** *Bp* **I** A J WRIGHT.
(St Andr Rowbarton), V. **D** B & W 23 **P** *Bp* **I** R E FLOWER *p-in-c.*
(St Jas), V. **D** B & W 23 **P** *Simeon Trustees* **I** M D BOLE *p-in-c*, J R HAREWOOD *c.*
(St Jo Evang), V. **D** B & W 23a **P** *Bp* **I** R F ACWORTH *p-in-c*, C E B NEATE *hon c.*
(H Trin), V. **D** B & W 23a **P** *Bp* **I** F I SEWARD *c-in-c.*
(St Pet Lyngford), V. **D** B & W 23 **P** *Bp* **I** R M AIRD *c-in-c.*

TAVERHAM (St Edm K and Mart) w Ringland (St Pet), *Norf.* R. **D** Nor 4 **P** *Bp and Maj Mills* alt **I** R J HEWETSON.

TAVISTOCK (St Eustachius) w (St Paul) Gulworthy, *Devon.* V. **D** Ex 22 **P** *Bp* **I** R T GILPIN, J P BIRD *c*, A N WIBBERLEY *c.*

TAVY (St Mary), *Devon.* R. **D** Ex 22 **P** *Guild of All S* **I** C J WARLAND.
(St Pet), R. **D** Ex 22 **P** *Guild of All S* **I** R T GILPIN *c-in-c.*

TAWSTOCK, *Devon.* R. **D** Ex 15 **P** *Trustees of Sir H B Wrey* **I** (Vacant).

TAWTON, NORTH (St Pet) and Bondleigh, *Devon.* R. **D** Ex **P** *MMT and D and C of Ex* **I** B A BAILEY.

TAWTON, SOUTH (St Andr) w Zeal, South and Belstone, *Devon.* V. **D** Ex 12 **P** *D and C of Windsor and Bp* **I** J F A ELLIS.

TAXAL (St Leon now called St Jas) w Fernilee (H Trin), *Derbys.* R. **D** Ches 16 **P** *Bp of Ches and Bp of Derby* alt **I** J A FOSTER.

TAYNTON, *Oxon.*. **D** Ox *See* Burford.

TAYNTON (St Lawr), *Glos*. R. **D** Glouc 6 *See* Tibberton.
TEALBY (All SS), *Lincs*. V. **D** Linc *See* Walesby.
TEAM, LOW (St Paul), *T & W*.. **D** Dur 4 *See* Gateshead.
TEAN, UPPER (Ch Ch), *Staffs*. V. **D** Lich 14 **P** *R of Chickley* **I** J G DODD.
TEBAY (St Jas), *Cumb*.. **D** Carl 1 *See* Orton.
TEDBURN ST MARY (St Mary Virg), *Devon*. R. **D** Ex 6 **P** *Dioc Bd of Patr* **I** D R E WERNER.
TEDDINGTON (St Mary w St Alb Mart), *Gtr Lon*. V. **D** Lon 8 **P** *Bp* **I** R T CARTER.
(SS Pet and Paul), V. **D** Lon 8 **P** *V of Teddington* **I** J G GIBSON.
(St Mark S Teddington), V. **D** Lon 8 **P** *Bp* **I** R S WALLACE.
(St Mich and St Geo Fulwell), V. **D** Lon 8 **P** *Trustees* **I** S D HARRIS *p-in-c*.
TEDDINGTON (St Nich), *Glos*.. **D** Worc 3 *See* Overbury.
TEDSTONE-DELAMERE (St Jas), *Herefs* w Edvin-Loach, *Worcs* and Tedstone Wafer (St Jas), *Herefs*. R. **D** Heref 2 **P** *BNC Ox and Pers Rep of T P Barneby Esq* alt **I** R J COLBY *p-in-c*.
TEETON, *Northants*. V. **D** Pet 5 *See* Ravensthorpe.
TEFFONT-EVIAS (St Mich AA), w Teffont Magna (St Edw), *Wilts*. R. **D** Sarum *See* Fovant.
TEIGH (H Trin) w Whissendine (St Andr) and Market Overton (St Pet and St Paul), *Leics*. R. **D** Pet **P** *Bp and Ld Gretton (alt)* **I** P A PAYNTON.
TEIGNGRACE (St Pet and St Paul), *Devon*.. **D** Ex *See* Highweek.
TEIGNMOUTH, EAST (St Mich), *Devon*. V. **D** Ex 6 **P** *V of Dawlish* **I** P G LUFF, A K SHAW *c*.
TEIGNMOUTH, WEST (St Jas L) w Ch Ch Kingway, *Devon*. V. **D** Ex 6 **P** *Hyndman Trustees* **I** A W ROSE, J CRUSE *c*.
TELFORD, Central (H Trin Dawley, St John Lawley, St Leon Malins Lee), *Salop*. R. **D** Lich 27 **P** *Patr Bd 3 turns, Crown 1 turn* **I** R A J HILL, P H CLAY *team v*, A M GANN *team v*, J B METCALFE *c*.
TELFORD PARK (St Thos), V. **D** S'wark 6 *See* Streatham.
TELLISFORD (All SS), *Wilts*. R. **D** B & W 16a *See* Rode Major.
TELSCOMBE (St Lawr) w Piddinghoe and Southease, V (St Jo Evang), *E Sussex*. R. **D** Chich 15 **P** *Gorham Trustees and Bp* **I** R J G HOLMES.
TEME VALLEY, NORTH. **D** Worc *See* Knighton-on-Teme, Lindridge, Stanford-on-Teme.
TEME VALLEY, SOUTH (Eastham w Rochford, Stoke-Bliss, Kyre Wyard, Hanley William and Hanley Child), *Worcs*. R. **D** Worc **P** *Ld Chan 1st turn, Bp 2nd turn and Mrs V and Mr H M Miles 3rd turn* **I** F W BIDDLECOMBE *p-in-c*.
TEMPLE BALSALL (St Mary), *W Midl*. V. **D** Birm 11 **P** *Govs of Balsall Hosp* **I** K C JARRETT.
TEMPLE BRUER (St Jo Bapt), *Lincs*.. **D** Linc *See* Graffoe.
TEMPLE CLOUD (St Barn), *Avon*.. **D** B & W 15 *See* Cameley.
TEMPLE COMBE and Abbas w Horsington (St Jo Bapt), *Somt*. R. **D** B & W 5 **P** *Bp and Ch Trust Fund* **I** F E WANKLING.
TEMPLE EWELL, or EWELL (St Pet and St Paul) w Lydden (St Mary Virg), *Kent*. V. **D** Cant 5 **P** *Abp* **I** P E BANNISTER.
TEMPLE FORTUNE (St Barn), *Lon*. V. **D** Lon 17 **P** *Bp* **I** C C TAYLOR.
TEMPLE GRAFTON (St Andr) w Binton, *Warws*. V. **D** Cov 7 **P** *Dioc Trustees and Bp* alt **I** C BOWEN.
TEMPLE GUITING (St Mary Virg) w Cutsdean, *Glos*. V. **D** Glouc 16 *See* Guitings, The.
TEMPLE MILLS (St Luke Miss), *Essex*.. **D** Chelmsf 3 *See* Leyton.
TEMPLE-NORMANTON (St Jas Ap and Mart), *Derbys*. V. **D** Derby 3 **P** *Bp* **I** H R O ANDERSON.
TEMPLE-SOWERBY (St Jas), *Cumb*. V. **D** Carl 1a *See* Kirkby Thore.
TEMPLETON (St Marg) *Devon*. R. **D** Ex 8 *See* Washfield.
TEMPSFORD (St Pet) w L Barford (St Denys), *Beds*. R. **D** St Alb 17 *See* Blunham.
TENBURY (St Mich AA), V. **D** Heref 12 **P** *Trustees of St Mich Coll Tenbury* **I** G A H ATKINS *p-in-c*, F M GRAZEBROOK *hon c*.
TENBURY WELLS (St Mary), *Worcs*. R. **D** Heref 12 **P** *Rev F J Evans* **I** R H GARNETT, G H M THOMPSON *team v*.
TENDRING (St Edm K and Mart) and Little Bentley w Beaumont and Moze, *Essex*. R. **D** Chelmsf 28 **P** *Ball Coll Ox and Em Coll Cam* **I** F MILLAR.
TENTERDEN (St Mildred) w Small Hythe, *Kent*. V. **D** Cant 11 **P** *D and C of Cant* **I** T E ROBERTS.
(St Mich AA), V. **D** Cant 11 **P** *Abp* **I** M D J BARROW.
TERLING (All SS), *Essex*. V. **D** Chelmsf 29 *See* Fairsted.
TERRIERS (St Francis), *Bucks*. V. **D** Ox 32 **P** *V of High Wycombe* **I** R A CARTMILL.
TERRINGTON (All SS), *N Yorks*. R. **D** York 21 **P** *Abp* **I** W BESWICK.
TERRINGTON ST CLEMENT, *Norf*. V. **D** Ely 18 **P** *Crown* **I** (Vacant).
TERRINGTON ST JOHN (St Jo Bapt), *Norf*. V. **D** Ely **P** *Crown* **I** R C WRIGHT.
TERWICK (St Pet), *W Sussex*. R. **D** Chich 5 **P** *Ld Chan* **I** (Vacant).
TESTERTON, *Norf*.. **D** Nor *See* Ryburgh, Great.
TESTON (St Pet and St Paul) w West Farleigh (All SS), *Kent*. R. **D** Roch 6 *See* Wateringbury.
TESTWOOD (St Winfrid), *Hants*. R. **D** Win 9 *See* Totton.
TETBURY (St Mary) w Beverston, *Glos*. V. **D** Glouc 17 **P** *Maj J E B Pope and Crown* **I** M C G SHERWOOD, W S LLEWELLYN *c*.
TETCOTT (H Cross) w Luffincott, *Devon*. R. **D** Ex 9 **P** *Sir J St Aubyn Bt* **I** (Vacant).
TETFORD (St Mary) w Salmonby *Lincs*. R. **D** Linc 7 **P** *Reps of Late Sir H Cholmeley Bt and Reps of Late Mrs Booth* **I** P E FLUCK *c-in-c*.
TETNEY (St Pet and St Paul), *Lincs*. V. **D** Linc 10 **P** *Bp* **I** (Vacant).
TETSWORTH (St Giles), Adwell w South Weston, Lewknor and Stoke-Talmage w Wheatfield,. **D** Ox 1 **P** *Peache Trustees, W R A Birch-Reynardson Esq, Earl of Macclesfield and Mrs D C H Mann* **I** N JEFFERYES.
TETTENHALL REGIS (St Mich AA), *Staffs*. R. **D** Lich **P** *Lady Wrottesley & Bp* **I** J D MAKEPEACE, T B FYFFE *team v*, J G HAMMERSLEY *team v*, M J L ANNELY *c*, C R J FOSTER *c*.
TETTENHALL WOOD (Ch Ch), *Staffs*. V. **D** Lich 7 **P** *Ld Wrottesley & Bp* **I** R C W DAMPIER, M G ALEXANDER *c*.
TETWORTH, *Cambs*.. **D** Ely 13 *See* Everton.
TEVERSAL (St Cath), *Notts*. R. **D** Southw 2 **P** *A Herbert Esq* **I** D A JONES.
TEVERSHAM (All SS), *Cambs*. R. **D** Ely 6 **P** *Bp* **I** A R HEAWOOD *p-in-c*.
TEW, GT (St Mich AA) w L Tew (St Jo Evang), *Oxon*. V. **D** Ox 3 **P** *Bp and Maj E Robb* alt **I** H S COLCHESTER *p-in-c*.
TEWIN (St Pet), *Herts*.. **D** St Alb *See* Datchworth.
TEWKESBURY (St Mary Virg Abbey Ch) w Walton Cardiff, *Glos*. V. **D** Glouc 10 **P** *Ld Chan* **I** M A MOXON, G EDMUNDS *c*, C J HARRISON *c*.
(H Trin), V. **D** Glouc 10 **P** *Ch Society Trust* **I** J F HAUGHAN.
TEY, GREAT (St Barn) w Tey, Little (St Jas L), R *Essex*. V. **D** Chelmsf 22 **P** *CPS and E M Scratton Esq* **I** N J COTGROVE *p-in-c*.
TEYNHAM (St Mary w St Andr), *Kent*. V. **D** Cant 7 **P** *Archd of Cant* **I** L E J OWEN.
THAKEHAM (St Mary) w Warminghurst (H Sepulchre), *W Sussex*.. **D** Chich 7 *See* Sullington.
THAME (St Mary Virg) w Towersey (St Cath), *Oxon*. V. **D** Ox 1 **P** *Peache Trustees* **I** R H FAULKNER, J D FRYAR *c*, B S W GREEN *c*, B L STANLEY *c*.
THAMES DITTON (St Nich), *Surrey*. V. **D** Guildf 8 **P** *K Coll Cam* **I** P C N CONDER, S J A RAMSEY *hon c*.
THAMESMEAD Kent. R **D** S'wark 17 **P** *Bp* **I** K S POUND, R M C FRITH *team v*, W B METCALFE *team v*, G C M SMITH *team v*, P G HADDLETON *c*.
THANET, *Kent*.. **D** Cant 8 *See* St Peter-in-Isle of Thanet.
THANINGTON (St Nich) w Milton (St Jo Bapt), *Kent*. V. **D** Cant 3 **P** *Abp* **I** P L BAYCOCK.
THARSTON (St Mary), *Norf*. V. **D** Nor 11 **P** *Bp* **I** (Vacant).
THATCHAM (St Mary), *Berks*. V. **D** Ox 14 **P** *Society of St Mary and St Francis Lancing* **I** T J W BAKER.
THATTO HEATH (St Matt), *Mer*. V. **D** Liv 10 *See* Eccleston.
THAXTED (St Jo Bapt), *Essex*. V. **D** Chelmsf 26 **P** *St Alb and Chelmsf Ch Trust and Bp* **I** P C E ELERS, J F H SHEAD *c*.
THE WYLYE VALLEY GROUP, *Wilts*. **D** Sarum *See* Ashton Gifford and Yarnbury.
THEALBY, *Humb*.. **D** Linc 4 *See* Burton-on-Stather.
THEALE (Ch Ch), *Somt*. V. **D** B & W 1 *See* Wedmore.
THEALE (H Trin) and Englefield, *Berks*. R. **D** Ox 12 **P** *Magd Coll Ox and Benyon Trust* **I** S N H ROBERTS.
THEBERTON (St Pet), *Suff*. R. **D** St E 19 **P** *Crown* **I** C RALPH.
THEDDINGWORTH Leics. V **D** Leic *See* Husbands Bosworth.
THEDDLETHORPE (St Helen), *Lincs*. R. **D** Linc 12 **P** *Bp 2nd turn, Earl of Ancaster 1st and 3rd turn* **I** T D KEIR *c-in-c*.

THELBRIDGE, *Devon*. R. **D** Ex 19 *See* Witheridge.
THELNETHAM (St Nich), *Suff*. R. **D** St E 9 **P** *Bp* **I** (Vacant).
THELVETON w Frenze (St Andr), *Norf*. R. **D** Nor 17 *See* Dickleburgh.
THELWALL (All SS), *Chesh*. V. **D** Ches 4 **P** *Keble Coll Ox* **I** R BIGGIN.
THEMELTHORPE, *Norf*.. **D** Nor *See* Bintry.
THENFORD (St Mary Virg), *Northants*. R. **D** Pet 1 *See* Marston.
THERFIELD (St Mary Virg), *Herts*. R. **D** St Alb 5 **P** *D and C of St Paul's* **I** J G E STONE *p-in-c*.
THETFORD (St Geo), *Cambs*.. **D** Ely 15 *See* Stretham.
THETFORD (St Cuthb w H Trin and St Pet), R. **D** Nor 18 **P** *Bp and CPAS* **I** D W PRICE, P R OLIVER *team v*, F J ROOM *team v*.
THEYDON-BOIS (St Mary), *Essex*. V. **D** Chelmsf 2 **P** *M G E N Buxton Esq* **I** A D JONES.
THEYDON GARNON, *Essex*. R. **D** Chelmsf 2 **P** *Bp* **I** E R PILKINGTON.
THEYDON MOUNT (St Mich), *Essex*.. **D** Chelmsf *See* Stapleford Tawney.
THIMBLEBY (St Marg), *Lincs*. R. **D** Linc 11 **P** *Bp* **I** H R WHALER *c-in-c*.
THIRKLEBY (All SS) w Kilburn (St Mary) and Bagby (St Mary), *N Yorks*. V. **D** York 26 **P** *Abp* **I** J H B DOUGLAS.
THIRSK (St Mary Virg) w South Kilvington (St Wilfrid) and Carlton Miniott w Sand Hutton, Baldersby and Skipton-on-Swale *N Yorks*. R. **D** York 26 **P** *Patr Bd* **I** R LEWIS, G LAMBERT *team v*, W SMITH *team v*.
THISTLETON Leics. R **D** Pet *See* Greetham.
THIXENDALE, *N Yorks*.. **D** York *See* Fridaythorpe.
THOCKRINGTON, *Northumb*. R. **D** Newc T 2 *See* Chollerton.
THORESBY, NORTH (St Helen), *Lincs*. R. **D** Linc 10 **P** *Mrs W B Ashley* **I** G L BIERLEY.
THORESBY, SOUTH (St Andr), *Lincs*. R. **D** Linc 12 *See* Swaby.
THORESTHORPE, *Lincs*.. **D** Linc 8 *See* Saleby.
THORESWAY (St Mary) w Croxby (All SS), *Lincs*. R. **D** Linc 5 **P** *Dioc Bd of Patr* **I** (Vacant).
THORGANBY (All SS), *Lincs*.. **D** Linc 10 *See* Swinhope.
THORGANBY (St Helen) w Skipwith (St Helen) and N Duffield, *N Yorks*. V. **D** York 6 **P** *Lt-Col Sir J Dunnington Jefferson and Ld Chan* alt **I** P RATHBONE.
THORINGTON (St Mary Magd), *Essex*.. **D** Chelmsf 28 *See* Frating.
THORINGTON (St Pet) w Wenhaston (St Pet), *Suff*. V. **D** St E 15 *See* Wenhaston.
THORLEY (St Swith), *Isle of Wight*. V. **D** Portsm 7 **P** *Bp and Ld Chan* **I** J F R RYALL *p-in-c*.
THORLEY (St Jas Gt) w Bishop's Stortford (H Trin), *Herts*. R. **D** St Alb 4 **P** *Bp* **I** A J COLE.
THORMANBY (St Mary Virg), *N Yorks*. R. **D** York 5 **P** *Visc Downe* **I** J D HARRIS-DOUGLAS *p-in-c*.
THORN (St Marg of Antioch), *Somt*. V. **D** B & W 26 *See* Wellington.
THORN-FALCON (H Cross), *Somt*. R. **D** B & W 23a *See* Ruishton.
THORNABY-ON-TEES (St Paul and St Luke), *Cleve*. R. **D** York 22 **P** *Abp* **I** J G O'CONNOR, G W A BACON *team v*, R D G BULLEN *team v*, N JACOBSON *team v*, P A BLIGH *c*.
THORNAGE (All SS) w Brinton (St Andr), Hunworth and Stody, *Norf*. R. **D** Nor 24 **P** *Lady Hastings and Marquess of Lothian* alt **I** J F LORD.
THORNBOROUGH (St Mary Virg), *Bucks*.. **D** Ox 23 *See* Nash.
THORNBURY (St Marg), *W Yorks*. V. **D** Bradf 3 **P** *Vs of Bradford, Laisterdyke, and Calverley* **I** M J REAR, R D A TANKARD *hon c*.
THORNBURY (St Pet), *Devon*. R. **D** Ex 9 *See* Black Torrington.
THORNBURY (St Mary Virg), *Avon*. V. **D** Glouc 8 **P** *Ch Ch Ox* **I** E A NOBES, N C J MULHOLLAND *c*.
THORNBURY, *Herefs*.. **D** Heref *See* Edvin Ralph.
THORNBY (St Helen), *Northants*. R. **D** Pet 6 *See* Cottesbrooke.
THORNCOMBE (St Mary) w Winsham and Cricket (St Thos), *Dorset*. V. **D** B & W **P** *Commdr W J Eyre, RN and Bp of Worc* **I** (Vacant).
THORNDON, *Suff*.. **D** St E *See* Rishangles.
THORNE (St Nich), *S Yorks*. V. **D** Sheff 9 **P** *Mrs A B Coventry* **I** J D BENSON.
THORNE-COFFIN (St Andr), *Somt*.. **D** B & W 11 *See* Tintinhull.
THORNER (St Pet), *W Yorks*. V. **D** Ripon 7 **P** *Earl of Mexborough* **I** B ABELL.
THORNES (St Jas w Ch Ch), *W Yorks*. V. **D** Wakef 12 **P** *Dioc Bd of Patr* **I** G GOOD.
THORNEY (St Helen) w Wigsley and Broadholme, *Notts*. V. **D** Southw *See* Harby.
THORNEY ABBEY (St Mary and St Botolph) w Wrydecroft and Knarr Fen, *Cambs*. V. **D** Ely 20 **P** *Bp* **I** P J SHEPHERD.
THORNEY, WEST (St Nich), *W Sussex*.R. **D** Chich *See* Southbourne.
THORNEYBURN (St Aid) w Greystead (St Luke), *Northumb*. R. **D** Newc T *See* Bellingham-Otterburn.
THORNFORD (St Mary Magd) w Beer Hackett (St Mich), *Dorset*. R. **D** Sarum 7 **P** *Maj K S D Wingfield-Digby and Reps of F J B Wingfield-Digby* **I** D A K GREENE *p-in-c*.
THORNGUMBALD (St Mary), *Humb*.. **D** York 15 *See* Burstwick.
THORNHAM, *Kent*. V. **D** Cant 14 *See* Thurnham.
THORNHAM (St Jo Evang), *Gtr Man*. V. **D** Man 17 **P** *R of Middleton* **I** J D HOLT.
(St Jas), V. **D** Man 15 **P** *Bp* **I** G M IKIN.
THORNHAM (All SS), *Norf*. V. **D** Nor *See* Hunstanton St Mary.
THORNHAM MAGNA (St Mary Magd) w Thornham Parva, *Suff*. R. **D** St E 17 **P** *Ld Henniker* **I** L TRENDER.
THORNHAUGH, *Cambs*.. **D** Pet *See* Wittering.
THORNHILL (St Mich AA), *W Yorks*. R. **D** Wakef 10 **P** *Ld Savile* **I** N D J WEBB.
THORNHILL LEES (H Innoc) w Savile Town (St Mary), *W Yorks*. V. **D** Wakef 10 **P** *Bp* **I** M T A HAYNES.
THORNLEY, *Durham*. V. **D** Dur 3 **P** *Bp* **I** P G MOLD.
THORNLEY (St Bart), *Durham*. V. **D** Dur 3 *See* Wolsingham.
THORNTHWAITE (BVM) cum Braithwaite (St Herbert) and Newlands, *Cumb*. V. **D** Carl 10 **P** *V of Crosthwaite and V of St John, Keswick* **I** T R HARPER.
THORNTHWAITE (St Sav) w Darley (Ch Ch) and Thruscross (H Trin), *N Yorks*. V. **D** Ripon 3 **P** *V of Hampsthwaite 3 turns, V of Fewston 1 turn* **I** S M BURNS *p-in-c*.
THORNTON (St Jas), *W Yorks*. V. **D** Bradf 1 **P** *V of Bradf* **I** I WILSON.
THORNTON (St Mich AA), *Bucks*. R. **D** Ox 23 *See* Nash.
THORNTON (St Pet) w Bagworth (H Rood), *Leics*. V. **D** Leic 17 **P** *MMT* **I** A S COSTERTON.
THORNTON (St Wilfrid) w Martin (St Mich), *Lincs*. R. **D** Linc 11 **P** *Bp and Reps of Ld Mamhead* **I** H R WHALER.
THORNTON (St Mich) w Allerthorpe (St Botolph), Melbourne, Waplington, and Storwood, *Humb*. V. **D** York *See* Seaton Ross Group.
THORNTON-CURTIS (St Lawr), *Humb*. V. **D** Linc 6 **P** *Dioc Bd of Patr* **I** R D GWYNNE *p-in-c*.
THORNTON DALE (All SS) w Ellerburne (St Hilda) and Wilton (St Geo), *N Yorks*. R. **D** York 24 **P** *Mrs E M Morgan and Abp* alt **I** A CLEMENTS.
THORNTON HEATH (St Paul), *Surrey*. V. **D** Cant 16 **P** *Crown* **I** D W TURTON.
(St Jude w St Aidan), V. **D** Cant 16 **P** *Abp* **I** C H A GARRETT.
THORNTON-HOUGH (All SS), *Mer*. V. **D** Ches 9 **P** *Simeon Trustees* **I** D E FATHERS.
THORNTON-IN-CRAVEN (St Mary), *N Yorks*. R. **D** Bradf 10 *See* Marton-in-Craven.
THORNTON-IN-LONSDALE (St Osw) w Burton-in-Lonsdale (All SS), *N Yorks*. V. **D** Bradf 7 **P** *Bp* **I** A L HUGHES.
THORNTON-IN-THE-MOORS (St Mary Virg) w Ince (St Jas) and Elton, *Chesh*. R. **D** Ches 3 **P** *Bp* **I** P M BISHOP.
THORNTON-LE-BEANS, *N Yorks*.. **D** York *See* Thornton-le-Street.
THORNTON-LE-FYLDE (Ch Ch), *Lancs*. V. **D** Blackb 9 **P** *Trustees* **I** E M E FLOOD.
(St John), V. **D** Blackb 9 **P** *Bp* **I** (Vacant).
THORNTON-LE-MOOR, *N Yorks*.. **D** York *See* Thornton-le-Street.
THORNTON-LE-MOOR (All SS), *Lincs*. R. **D** Linc 5 *See* Owersby, North.
THORNTON-LE-STREET (St Leon) w North Otterington (St Barn) Thornton-le-Moor (St Barn), Thornton-le-Beans and South Otterington (St Andr), *N Yorks*. V. **D** York **P** *Ch Ch Ox 1st turn, Linc Coll Ox 2nd turn, Abp 3rd turn* **I** C S M HUNTER.
THORNTON-STEWARD (St Osw), *N Yorks*. V. **D** Ripon 2 *See* Thornton Watlass.
THORNTON-WATLASS (St Mary) w Thornton Steward and East Witton, *N Yorks*. R. **D** Ripon 2 **P** *Bp, Sir J C Smith Dodsworth, Bart, and Maj W V Burden* **I** A N THOMAS.
THOROTON (St Helen), *Notts*. V. **D** Southw 9 *See* Orston.

THURSTASTON (St Bart), *Mer.* R. **D** Ches 8 **P** *D and C of Ches* **I** M B KELLY.
THURSTON (St Pet), *Suff.* V. **D** St E 9 **P** *Bp* **I** J F MAIR.
THURSTONLAND (St Thos), *S Yorks.* V. **D** Wakef 7 **P** *V of Kirkburton* **I** R L WAINWRIGHT.
THURTON (St Ethelbert), *Norf.* R. **D** Nor 14 *See* Ashby.
THUXTON, *Norf.*. **D** Nor *See* Garveston.
THWAITE (All SS), *Norf.* R. **D** Nor 3 *See* Alby.
THWAITE (St Mary), *Norf.* R. **D** Nor 14 **P** *Brig W G Carr* **I** G F WALKER.
THWAITE (St Geo), *Suff.* R. **D** St E 6 *See* Stoke Ash.
THWAITES (St Anne), *Cumb.* V. **D** Carl 9 **P** *Certain Landowners* **I** J HOGARTH.
THWAITES BROW (St Barn), *W Yorks.* V. **D** Bradf 11 **P** *Dioc Bd of Patr* **I** W HOLLIDAY.
THWING (All SS), *Humb.* R. **D** York 12 **P** *Ld Chan* **I** (Vacant).
TIBBERTON (H Trin) w Taynton, *Glos.* R. **D** Glouc 6 **P** *P Price Esq and D and C of Glouc* **I** R GREENSLADE *p-in-c.*
TIBBERTON (All SS) w Kynnersley (St Chad) and Preston Wealdmoors, *Salop.* R. **D** Lich 21 **P** *R of Edgmond, MMT and Trustees of Preston Hosp* **I** J J DAVIES.
TIBBERTON (St Pet-ad-Vincula) w Bredicot (St Jas L), *Worcs.*. **D** Worc 8 *See* Hadzor.
TIBENHAM (All SS), *Norf.* V. **D** Nor *See* Bunwell.
TIBSHELF (St Jo Bapt), *Derbys.* V. **D** Derby 1 **P** *MMT* **I** G S C CAMPBELL.
TICEHURST (St Mary) and Flimwell (St Aug of Cant), *E Sussex.* V. **D** Chich 20 **P** *Bp and Hon Elinor Daphne Courthope* **I** B C WILLIAMS.
TICHBORNE (St Andr), *Hants.*. **D** Win 6 *See* Cheriton.
TICHMARSH (St Mary Virg), *Northants.* R. **D** Pet 9 **P** *S of Merchant Ventures of Bris* **I** H W WILLIAMS.
TICKENCOTE (St Pet), *Leics.* R. **D** Pet 13 *See* Casterton, Great.
TICKENHAM (St Quiricus and St Julietta), *Avon.* R. **D** B & W 16 **P** *Ld Chan* **I** R W I GHEST.
TICKHILL (St Mary Virg) w Stainton (St Winifrid), *S Yorks.* V. **D** Sheff 8 **P** *Bp* **I** J A BOWERING.
TICKNALL (St Geo) w Calke (St Giles), *Derbys.* V. **D** Derby 15 **P** *Exors of Mrs Mosley* **I** R BAGNALL.
TICKTON, *Humb.* V. **D** York 11 *See* Beverley.
TIDCOMBE (St Mich) and Fosbury (Ch Ch), *Wilts.* V. **D** Sarum 27 *See* Grafton, East.
TIDEBROOK (St Jo Bapt), *E Sussex.* V. **D** Chich 20 **P** *V of Wadhurst and V of Mayfield* alt **I** T D M RAVEN.
TIDEFORD (St Luke), *Cornw.* V. **D** Truro 9 **P** *V of St Germans* **I** R E B MAYNARD.
TIDENHAM (St Pet) w Beachley (St Jo Evang) and Lancaut, *Glos.* V. **D** Glouc 7 **P** *Bp* **I** M T GEE.
TIDESWELL (St Jo Bapt), *Derbys.* V. **D** Derby 10 **P** *D and C of Lich* **I** (Vacant).
TIDMARSH (St Lawr) w Sulham (St Nich), *Berks.* R. **D** Ox 12 **P** *Exors of C A Vandervell and Exors of Rev H C Wilder* **I** D M MCDONALD *p-in-c.*
TIDMINGTON, *Warws.*. **D** Cov 9 *See* Shipston-on-Stour.
TIDWORTH (H Trin), *Wilts.* R. **D** Sarum 18 **P** *Ld Chan* **I** D J BURTON.
TIFFIELD (St Jo Bapt), *Northants.* R. **D** Pet 2 *See* Gayton.
TILBROOK (All SS), *Cambs.* R. **D** Ely 11 **P** *S for Maint of Faith* **I** F ANDREW.
TILBURY, *Essex.*. **D** Chelmsf 18 *See* Ovington.
TILBURY, EAST (St Cath) and West (St Jas) and Linford, *Essex.* R. **D** Chelmsf 15 **P** *Ld Chan* **I** J A BRANCH.
TILBURY DOCKS (St Jo Bapt), *Essex.* V. **D** Chelmsf 15 **P** *Bp* **I** F J HICKEY.
TILE CROSS, *W Midl.*. **D** Birm *See* Yardley.
TILE HILL (St Osw), *W Midl.* V. **D** Cov 3 **P** *Bp* **I** S G ELLIOTT.
TILEHURST (St Mich), *Berks.* R and V. **D** Ox 15 **P** *Magd Coll Ox* **I** J S TILSTON, D R R SEYMOUR *c.*
(St Cath), V. **D** Ox 15 **P** *Magd Coll Ox* **I** N J BROWN.
(St Geo), V. **D** Ox 15 **P** *Bp* **I** D F F EVANS.
(St Mary Magd) V. **D** Ox 15 **P** *Bp* **I** K P MELLOR.
TILFORD (All SS), *Surrey.* V. **D** Guildf 3 **P** *Bp* **I** D J INNES *p-in-c.*
TILLINGHAM (St Nich), *Essex.* V. **D** Chelmsf 13 **P** *D and C of St Paul's* **I** S G BROWN.
TILLINGTON (All H), *W Sussex.* R. **D** Chich 6 **P** *Ld Egremont* **I** A BUCKNALL.
TILMANSTONE (St Andr), *Kent.* V. **D** Cant 7 *See* Northbourne.
TILNEY (All SS), *Norf.* V. **D** Ely 18 **P** *Pemb Coll Cam* **I** R C WRIGHT.
(St Lawr).. **D** Ely **P** *Pemb Coll Cam* **I** R C WRIGHT.
TILSHEAD (St Thos à Becket) w Orcheston and Chitterne, *Wilts.* V. **D** Sarum 21 **P** *Bp 3 turns D and C of Sarum 1 turn* **I** (Vacant).
TILSTOCK (Ch Ch), *Salop.* V. **D** Lich 27 **P** *R of Whitchurch* **I** R UPTON *c-in-c.*
TILSTON (St Mary Virg), *Chesh.* R. **D** Ches 5 **P** *Bp* **I** G H GREENHOUGH.
TILSTONE FEARNALL (St Jude) w Wettenhall (St D), *Chesh.* V. **D** Ches 5 **P** *Bp and V of St Chad Over* **I** A REECE.
TILSWORTH (All SS), *Beds.* V. **D** St Alb 18 *See* Stanbridge.
TILTON-ON-THE-HILL (St Pet) and Halstead w Lowesby (All SS) and Cold Newton, *Leics.* V. **D** Leic 8 **P** *MMT* **I** E WILLIAMS.
TILTY (St Mary Virg), *Essex.* V. **D** Chelmsf 23 *See* Broxted.
TIMBERLAND (St Andr), *Lincs.* V. **D** Linc 18 **P** *Bp* **I** J L M LE MARCHAND *p-in-c.*
TIMBERSCOMBE (St Petrock), *Somt.* V. **D** B & W 21 **P** *Bp* **I** E J MILLER.
TIMPERLEY (Ch Ch), *Gtr Man.* V. **D** Ches 10 **P** *Trustees* **I** D PROBETS, M E HEPWORTH *c*, A J JEYNES *c.*
TIMSBURY (St Andr), *Hants.* V. **D** Win 10 *See* Michelmersh.
TIMSBURY (St Mary Virg), *Avon.* R. **D** B & W 13 **P** *Ball Coll Ox* **I** C A JONES *p-in-c.*
TIMWORTH, *Suff.*. **D** St E *See* Fornham (St Martin),.
TINCLETON (St Jo Evang), *Dorset.*. **D** Sarum 5 *See* Woodsford.
TINGEWICK (St Mary Magd) w Water Stratford, Radclive w Chackmore, *Bucks.* R. **D** Ox 23 **P** *New College Ox and Dioc Bd of Patr (alt)* **I** R O N WILLMOTT.
TINGRITH, *Beds.*. **D** St Alb *See* Westoning.
TINSLEY (St Lawr), *S Yorks.* V. **D** Sheff 1 **P** *Earl Fitzwilliam* **I** H W EVEREST.
TINTAGEL (St Materiana), *Cornw.* V. **D** Truro 12 **P** *D and C of Windsor* **I** I H GREGORY.
TINTINHULL (St Marg) w Chilthorne Domer, Yeovil Marsh and Thorne Coffin, *Somt.* V. **D** B & W 11 **P** *Guild of All S* **I** C A BILLINGTON.
TINTWISTLE (Ch Ch), *Derby.* V. **D** Ches 14 **P** *Trustees* **I** M J RUSSELL.
TINWELL (All SS), *Leics.* R. **D** Pet 13 **P** *Marq of Ex* **I** (Vacant).
TIPTON (St Jo Evang) w Venn Ottery, *Devon.* V. **D** Ex 7 **P** *V of Ottery 2 turns, Dioc Bd of Patr 1 turn* **I** A J H POLHILL, J K HANCOCK *c.*
TIPTON (St Martin w St Luke, Gt Bridge), *W Midl.* V. **D** Lich 10 **P** *MMT* **I** J H ALGAR.
(St Mark Evang Ocker Hill), V. **D** Lich 10 **P** *Bp* **I** J S LUNGLEY.
(St Jo Evang), V. **D** Lich 10 **P** *V of St Jas W Bromwich* **I** M J LEADBEATER.
(St Matt), V. **D** Lich 10 **P** *Simeon Trustees* **I** A E MATHERS, A D N FERGUSON *c.*
(St Mich Tividale), V. **D** Lich 10 **P** *Bp* **I** R S P HINGLEY *c.*
(St Paul), V. **D** Lich 10 **P** *V of Tipton* **I** A E MATHERS *p-in-c.*
TIPTREE (St Luke), *Essex.* R. **D** Chelmsf 29 *See* Tolleshunt Knights.
TIRLEY, *Glos.* V. **D** Glouc 10 *See* Hasfield.
TISBURY (St Jo Bapt) and Swallowcliffe with Ansty and Chilmark, *Wilts.* R. **D** Sarum 19 **P** *Patr Bd* **I** R A WILLIS, P M HAND *team v*, C M HUTCHINGS *team v.*
TISSINGTON (St Mary), *Derbys.*. **D** Derby *See* Fenny Bentley.
TISTED, EAST (St Jas Ap) w Colmer (St Pet-ad-Vincula), *Hants.* R. **D** Win *See* Newton Valence.
TISTED, WEST, *Hants.*. **D** Win *See* Ropley.
TITCHFIELD (St Pet), *Hants.* V. **D** Portsm 1 **P** *D & C of Win* **I** T W W PEMBERTON.
TITCHWELL (St Mary Virg), *Norf.* R. **D** Nor *See* Brancaster.
TITHBY, *Notts.*. **D** Southw *See* Tythby.
TITLEY, *Herefs.*. **D** Heref *See* Lyonshall.
TITSEY, *Surrey.*. **D** S'wark *See* Limpsfield.
TITTENSOR (St Luke), *Staffs.* V. **D** Lich 19 **P** *Simeon Trustees* **I** W G H GARDINER *p-in-c.*
TITTLESHALL (St Mary Virg) w Godwick, Wellingham (St Andr) and Weasenham, Norf]. R. **D** Nor 20 **P** *Earl of Leic and Bp (alt)* **I** I K H COOKE.
TIVERTON (St Pet), *Devon.* R. **D** Ex 8 **P** *Peache Trustees* **I** D A E WHITAKER.
(St Andr), V. **D** Ex 8 **P** *Bp* **I** E R BARDSLEY.
(St Geo), V. **D** Ex 8 **P** *MMT* **I** C G H DUNN.
(St Paul, West Exe), V. **D** Ex 8 **P** *Peache Trustees* **I** S HOLBROOKE-JONES.
TIVETSHALL (St Mary w St Marg), *Norf.* R. **D** Nor *See* Winfarthing.
TIVIDALE, *W Midl.*. **D** Lich 10 *See* Tipton (St Michael).
TIXALL (St Jo Bapt), *Staffs.* R. **D** Lich *See* Ingestre.

TIXOVER (St Luke), *Leics.* V. **D** Pet 13 *See* Duddington.
TOCKENHAM (St Giles), *Wilts.* R. **D** Sarum 25 *See* Clyffe-Pypard.
TOCKHOLES (St Steph), *Lancs.* V. **D** Blackb 5 **P** *V of Blackburn* **I** (Vacant).
TOCKWITH (The Epiph) and Bilton w Bickerton, *N Yorks.* V. **D** York 2 **P** *Abp and D & C of York* **I** P J MULLEN.
TODBERE (Dedic unknown), *Dorset.*. **D** Sarum 13 *See* Stower Provost.
TODDINGTON (St Geo of E), *Beds.* R. **D** St Alb 18 **P** *Bp* **I** T A KNOX.
TODDINGTON, *Glos.*. **D** Glouc 18 *See* Dumbleton.
TODENHAM (St Thos of Cant), w Lower Lemington (St Leon), *Glos.* R. **D** Glouc 16 **P** *Bp* **I** S T LAMBERT *p-in-c.*
TODMORDEN (Ch Ch w St Mary and St Aid), *Lancs,* w Harley Wood (All SS), *W Yorks.* V. **D** Wakef 3 **P** *Bp* **I** C DAWSON, T M THORNTON *c.*
TODWICK (St Pet and St Paul), *S Yorks.* R. **D** Sheff 5 **P** *Bp* **I** J FROGGATT.
TOFT (St Andr) w Caldecote (St Mich AA) and Childerley, *Cambs.* R. **D** Ely 1 **P** *Bp and Ch Coll Cam* **I** J S BEER.
TOFT (St Jo Evang), *Chesh.* V. **D** Ches 12 *See* Knutsford.
TOFT (St Pet and St Paul) w Newton (St Mich), *Lincs.* R. **D** Linc 5 **P** *Dioc Bd of Patr* **I** B B HUMPHREYS *p-in-c.*
TOFT MONKS (St Marg), *Norf.* R. **D** Nor 14 *See* Haddiscoe.
TOFTREES (All SS) w Sherford, *Norf.* V. **D** Nor 21 **P** *Marq Townshend* **I** (Vacant).
TOFTS, WEST (St Mary Virg), w Buckenham Parva, *Norf.* R. **D** Nor 18 **P** *Guild of All S* **I** (Vacant).
TOKYNGTON (St Mich), *Gtr Lon.* V. **D** Lon 18 **P** *Bp* **I** R JONES.
TOLLAND, *Somt.*. **D** B & W *See* Lydeard.
TOLLARD-ROYAL (St Pet-ad-Vincula) w Farnham (St Laur), *Dorset.* R. **D** Sarum 10 **P** *Ch S Trust 3 turns, Ld Chan 1 turn* **I** J A P STANDEN MCDOUGAL.
TOLLER FRATRUM (St Basil), *Dorset.*. **D** Sarum 5 *See* Compton Abbas.
TOLLER, GREAT, or TOLLER PORCORUM (St Andr and St Pet) w Hooke, (St Giles), R *Dorset.* V. **D** Sarum *See* Beaminster Area.
TOLLERTON (St Pet), *Notts.* R. **D** Southw 10 **P** *Lady Ball* **I** M H C LUMGAIR.
TOLLESBURY (St Mary) w Salcot Virley, *Essex.* V. **D** Chelmsf 29 **P** *Bp, Mrs C M Wheatley, Ex Coll Ox 2 turns* **I** K M B LOVELL.
TOLLESHUNT D'ARCY (St Nich) w Tolleshunt Major (St Nich), *Essex.* V. **D** Chelmsf 29 **P** *Dr R Comerford and MMT* alt **I** N A THORP.
TOLLESHUNT KNIGHTS (All SS) w Tiptree (St Luke), *Essex.* R. **D** Chelmsf 29 **P** *Ld Chan and Bp* alt **I** A C BICKERSTETH.
TOLLINGTON PARK. **D** Lon 6 *See* Holloway.
TOLPUDDLE (St Jo Evang), *Dorset.*. **D** Sarum 5 *See* Puddletown.
TOMPSON, *Norf.*. **D** Nor 19 *See* Caston.
TONBRIDGE (St Pet and St Paul w St Sav), *Kent.* V. **D** Roch 9 **P** *Mabledon Trust* **I** C SEARLE-BARNES, R M DAVIES *c,* C H OVERTON *c,* J L J YATES-ROUND *c,* P I RUDLAND *hon c.*
(St Steph), V. **D** Roch 9 **P** *CPAS* **I** A E ORMISTON, D B KITLEY *c.*
TONERS PUDDLE or TURNERSPUDDLE (H Trin), *Dorset.* R. **D** Sarum 8 *See* Affpuddle.
TONG (St Jas w St Jo Evang) w Holme Wood (St Chris), *W Yorks.* V. **D** Bradf 3 **P** *Commun of Resurr* **I** A KITCHEN, S NAYLOR *c.*
TONG (St Mary w St Bart), *Salop.* V. **D** Lich 25 **P** *Bp* **I** R M C JEFFERY *p-in-c.*
TONGE, *Kent.* V. **D** Cant 13 *See* Bapchild.
TONGE (St Mich AA) w Alkrington, *Gtr Man.* V. **D** Man 17 **P** *R of Middleton* **I** G N HIGHAM.
TONGE FOLD (St Chad), *Gtr Man.* V. **D** Man 11 **P** *Bp and Trustees* alt **I** D R HARRISON.
TONGE MOOR (St Aug of Cant), *Gtr Man.* V. **D** Man 19 **P** *Trustees* **I** D T HADLEY, R M WATSON *c.*
TONGHAM (St Paul), *Surrey.* V. **D** Guildf 1 **P** *Archd of Surrey* **I** C PAWLEY.
TONGUE END (St Mich), *Lincs.*. **D** Linc *See* Deeping St Nich.
TONWELL (Ch Ch), *Herts.*. **D** St Alb 8 *See* Bengeo.
TOOLEY STREET (St John), *Surrey.*. **D** S'wark 7 *See* Bermondsey.
TOOT BALDON (St Laur), *Oxon.*. **D** Ox *See* Marsh Baldon.
TOOTING (All SS), V. **D** S'wark 7a **P** *Bp* **I** N A FRAYLING, C PULLIN *c.*
(St Aug of Cant), V. **D** S'wark 7a **P** *Bp* **I** S J LOPEZ FERREIRO *c.*
GRAVENEY (St Nich), *Surrey.* R. **D** S'wark 7a **P** *MMT* **I** J B HALL, J F DUNN *c.*
UPPER (H Trin), *Surrey.* V. **D** S'wark 7a **P** *R of Streatham* **I** J B GOULD, S J LOPEZ FERREIRO *c.*
TOPCLIFFE (St Columba) w Dalton (St John) and Dishforth (Ch Ch), *N Yorks.* V. **D** York 26 **P** *D and C of York* **I** W SMITH *p-in-c.*
TOPCROFT (St Marg), *Suff.*. **D** Nor *See* Hempnall.
TOPPESFIELD (St Marg of Antioch) w Stambourne (St Pet and St Thos), *Essex.* R. **D** Chelmsf 24 **P** *Duchy of Lanc* **I** J SPEERS *p-in-c.*
TOPSHAM (St Marg), *Devon.* V. **D** Ex 1 **P** *D and C of Ex* **I** J C STYLER.
TORBRYAN, *Devon.* R. **D** Ex 11 *See* Ipplepen.
TORKSEY (St Pet), *Lincs.* V. **D** Linc 2 **P** *Dioc Bd of Patr* **I** L SALT.
TORMARTON w LITTLETON, WEST, *Avon.* R. **D** Bris 8 **P** *Bp* **I** (Vacant).
TORPENHOW (St Mich AA), *Cumb.* V. **D** Carl 11 **P** *Bp* **I** D V SCOTT.
TORPOINT (St Jas Greater), *Cornw.* V. **D** Truro 9 **P** *V of Antony* **I** J E PROTHERO.
TORQUAY, CENTRAL (St Jo Evang) *Devon.* R. **D** Ex 10 **P** *Centr Torquay Patr Bd* **I** B G BURR, P W IRWIN *team v,* R I MCDOWALL *team v,* J R BURTON *c.*
(St Luke), V. **D** Ex 10 **P** *D and C of Ex* **I** P MILLER.
(St Mary Magd w St Jas Upton), R. **D** Ex 10 **P** *Simeon Trustees and CPS* alt **I** W A STEWART.
(St Matthias, Ilshan w St Mark and H Trin), V. **D** Ex **P** *Bp and Trustees* **I** P J LARKIN.
TORRINGTON, EAST (St Mich) w Torrington, West (St Mary), *Lincs.*. **D** Linc 5 *See* Barkwith Group.
TORRINGTON, GREAT (St Mich), Torrington Little and Frithelstock, *Devon.* V. **D** Ex 20 **P** *D and C of Ox 8 turns, Baron Clinton 1 turn and Mrs B W Stevens-Guille 1 turn* **I** J D HUMMERSTONE.
TORRINGTON, LITTLE (St Giles), *Devon.* R. **D** Ex *See* Torrington, Great.
TORRISHOLME (The Ascen), *Lancs.* V. **D** Blackb 11 **P** *Bp* **I** T J FAWCETT.
TORTINGTON (St Mary Magd), *W Sussex.* V. **D** Chich 1 *See* Arundel.
TORTWORTH, *Avon.* R. **D** Glouc 8 *See* Cromhall.
TORVER (St Luke), *Cumb.* R. **D** Carl 15 **P** *Peache Trustees* **I** M C RIDYARD *p-in-c.*
TORWOOD (St Mark), *Devon.*. **D** Ex 10 *See* Torquay.
TOSELAND (St Mich), *Cambs.*. **D** Ely 13 *See* Yelling.
TOSSIDE, or HOUGHTON (St Bart), *N Yorks.* V. **D** Bradf 6 **P** *V of Gisburn* **I** J G HOYLAND *p-in-c.*
TOSTOCK, *Suff.*. **D** St E 9 *See* Pakenham.
TOTHAM, GREAT (St Pet), *Essex.* V. **D** Chelmsf 29 **P** *Bp* **I** (Vacant).
TOTHAM, LITTLE (All SS), *Essex.*. **D** Chelmsf 14 *See* Goldhanger.
TOTHILL, *Lincs.*. **D** Linc 8 *See* Authorpe.
TOTLAND BAY (Ch Ch), *Isle of Wight.* V. **D** Portsm 7 **P** *CPS* **I** K C WHITE.
TOTLEY (All SS), *S Yorks.* V. **D** Sheff 2 **P** *Bp* **I** A K JOCKEL.
TOTNES (St Mary) w Bridgetown (St John), *Devon.* V. **D** Ex 13 **P** *Bp* **I** R E HARRIS.
TOTON (St Pet), *Notts.*. **D** Southw 8 *See* Attenborough.
TOTTENHAM (All H), *Lon.* V. **D** Lon 22 **P** *D and C of St Paul's* **I** R B PEARSON.
(Ch Ch West Green w St Pet), V. **D** Lon 22 **P** *V of H Trin Tottenham* **I** J T HAMBLIN.
(H Trin), V. **D** Lon 22 **P** *Bp* **I** J N A BRADBURY, H G JAMES *c.*
(St Ann, Stamford Hill), V. **D** Lon 22 **P** *D and C of St Paul's* **I** R C FIELD.
(St Bart, Stamford Hill). V. **D** Lon 22 **P** *Crown* **I** J M PEET *p-in-c,* B M SMITH *c.*
(St Benet Fink), V. **D** Lon 22 **P** *D and C of St Paul's* **I** M A DAVENPORT, R D KNIGHT *c.*
(St Jo Bapt), V. **D** Lon 22 **P** *R of St Jas Piccadilly* **I** R GUNN.
(St Jo Div, Vartry Road, Stamford Hill), V. **D** Lon 22 **P** *V of St Ann, Stamford Hill* **I** B M SMITH *c.*
(St Mary Virg Lansdowne Road), V. **D** Lon 22 **P** *Bp* **I** D F EVANS.
(St Paul, Park Lane), V. **D** Lon 22 **P** *V of Tottenham* **I** A S HOPES, L W S PHILLIPS *c,* J L SALTER *c.*
(St Phil Ap), V. **D** Lon 22 **P** *Bp* **I** J N LUSCOMBE.
TOTTENHILL (St Botolph) w Wormegay (St Mich AA and H Cross), *Norf.* V. **D** Ely 17 **P** *Bp* **I** I R LILLEY *c-in-c.*
TOTTERIDGE (St Andr), *Herts.* V. **D** St Alb 2 **P** *R of Hatfield* **I** J H KNOWLES-BROWN.

TOTTERNHOE (St Giles) w Stanbridge and Tilsworth, *Beds.* V. **D** St Alb **P** *Bp and V of Leighton Buzzard* **I** D E COOK.
TOTTINGTON (St Andr) w Sturston (H Cross), *Norf.* V. **D** Nor **P** *Ld Walsingham* **I** (Vacant).
TOTTINGTON (St Anne), *Gtr Man.* V. **D** Man 12 **P** *R of Bury* **I** G A SUTCLIFFE.
TOTTON (Eling, Testwood and Netley Marsh), *Hants.* R. **D** Win 9 **P** *Bp* **I** C R ARDAGH-WALTER, G R BIGGS *team v,* D W GRIMWOOD *team v.*
TOVIL (St Steph), *Kent.* V. **D** Cant *See* Maidstone.
TOW LAW (St Phil and St Jas), *Durham.* V. **D** Dur 13 **P** *Bp* **I** (Vacant).
TOWCESTER (St Lawr) w Easton Neston, *Northants.* V. **D** Pet 2 **P** *Trustees of Ld Hesketh and Bp* alt **I** J E ATWELL.
TOWEDNACK, ST (St Tewinnock the Confessor), *Cornw.* V. **D** Truro 5 **P** *Bp* **I** J B D COTTER.
TOWERSEY (St Cath) *Oxon.* V. **D** Ox 1 *See* Thame.
TOWNSTAL (St Clem w St Sav), *Devon.*. **D** Ex 13 *See* Dartmouth.
TOWTON, *N Yorks.*. **D** York 9 *See* Saxton.
TOXTETH (St Cypr w Ch Ch), *Mer.* V. **D** Liv 4 **P** *Simeon Trustees* **I** J W H FLAGG, R J G PANTER *c.*
TOXTETH PARK (Ch Ch), *Mer.* V. **D** Liv 2 **P** *Trustees* **I** A THOMAS.
(St Agnes), V. **D** Liv 2 **P** *St Chad's Coll Dur* **I** H N ANNIS.
(St Bede), V. **D** Liv 4 **P** *Simeon Trustees* **I** S M STARKEY *p-in-c.*
(St Clem), V. **D** Liv 4 **P** *Trustees* **I** D A THOMPSON.
(St Cleopas), V. **D** Liv 4 **P** *Can B C Price* **I** J W WHITLEY *p-in-c.*
(St Marg Virg and Mart), V. **D** Liv 4 **P** *St Chad's Coll Dur* **I** C B OXENFORTH.
(St Mich-in-the-Hamlet w St Andr), V. **D** Liv 2 **P** *Simeon Trustees* **I** R CAVAGAN.
(St Philemon w St Gabr), R. **D** Liv 4 **P** *Dioc Bd of Patr* **I** C M BEDFORD, R DERBRIDGE *team v.*
TOYNTON (St Pet w All SS), V *Lincs.* R. **D** Linc 7 **P** *Earl of Ancaster* **I** (Vacant).
TOYNTON, HIGH (St Jo Bapt), *Lincs.* V. **D** Linc 11 **P** *Bp* **I** A A EDE.
TOYNTON, LOW, *Lincs.* R. **D** Linc 11 *See* Horncastle.
TRAFFORD, OLD (St Hilda), *Gtr Man.* R. **D** Man 9 **P** *Crown and Bp* alt **I** V C BROWN.
(St Jo Evang), R. **D** Man 9 **P** *Crown and Bp* alt **I** C S FORD.
PARK (St Cuthb), R. **D** Man 9 **P** *Crown and Bp* alt **I** (Vacant).
See also STRETFORD..
TRANMERE, HIGHER (St Cath of Alex), *Mer.* V. **D** Ches 1 **P** *R of Bebington* **I** S R BECKLEY.
(St Paul) w (St Luke), V. **D** Ches 1 **P** *Bp* **I** E J GORDON.
TRAWDEN (St Mary), *Lancs.* V. **D** Blackb 6a **P** *Bp* **I** P W ALLSOP.
TREALES (Ch Ch), *Lancs.* V. **D** Blackb 9 **P** *V of Kirkham* **I** G I HIRST *p-in-c.*
TREBOROUGH Somt. **D** B & W *See* Cleeve, Old.
TREDINGTON (St Greg) w Darlingscott w Newbold-on-Stour, *Warws.* R. **D** Cov 9 **P** *Jes Coll Ox* **I** C G REDGRAVE, J W ROLFE *c.*
TREDINGTON (St Jo Bapt) w Stoke Orchard, *Glos.* V. **D** Glouc 10 **P** *Bp* **I** C J HARRISON *c-in-c.*
TREETON (St Helen), *S Yorks.* R. **D** Sheff 6 **P** *Ch Trust Fund Trust* **I** G D N SMITH.
TREFONEN (All SS), *Salop.* V. **D** Lich 24 **P** *Bp* **I** M HILL *p-in-c.*
TREGAMINION, *Cornw.*. **D** Truro *See* Tywardreath.
TREGAVETHAN, *Cornw.*. **D** Truro 6 *See* Kenwyn.
TREGONY w St Cuby and Cornelly, *Cornw.* R. **D** Truro 6 **P** *Bp* **I** C F P SHEPHERD *p-in-c.*
TRELEIGH (St Steph), *Cornw.* V. **D** Truro 2 **P** *Bp* **I** M P SIMCOCK.
TRELYSTAN (St Mary Virg), w Leighton (H Trin), *Powys.* V. **D** Heref 13 **P** *Bp* **I** K J F BRADBURY.
TREMAINE, *Cornw.*. **D** Truro 11 **P** *Bp 2 turns, Duchy of Cornw 1 turn* **I** R W P HOWLETT.
TRENEGLOS (St Werburgh), *Cornw.*. **D** Truro 10 *See* Jacobstow.
TRENODE, *Cornw.*. **D** Truro *See* Morval.
TRENT (St Andr), *Sarum.* R. **D** Sarum 7 *See* Compton, Over.
TRENT VALE (St Jo Evang), *Staffs.* V. **D** Lich 18 **P** *R of Stoke-on-Trent* **I** H F HARPER.
TRENTHAM (St Mary and All SS), *Staffs.* V. **D** Lich 19 **P** *Countess of Sutherland* **I** E C HAMLYN, J L ASTON *c.*
TRENTISHOE, *Devon.*. **D** Ex 18 *See* Kentisbury.
TRESCO, *Cornw.*. **D** Truro 6 *See* Scilly, Isles of.
TRESILIAN, *Cornw.*. **D** Truro 6 *See* Lamorran.
TRESLOTHAN (St Jo Evang), *Cornw.* V. **D** Truro 2 **P** *Mrs Warwick-Pendarves* **I** C F H SUTCLIFFE *p-in-c.*
TRESMERE (St Nich), *Cornw.* V. **D** Truro 11 *See* Laneast.
TRESWELL (St Jo Bapt) w Cottam, *Notts.* R. **D** Southw *See* Rampton.
TRETIRE (St Mary) w Michaelchurch (St Mich) and Pencoyd (St Denys), *Herefs.* R. **D** Heref 8 **P** *Bp* **I** J R JACKSON *p-in-c,* G H CODRINGTON *c.*
TREVELGA (St Petrock), *Cornw.* R. **D** Truro 12 *See* Davidstow.
TREVENSON, *Cornw.*. **D** Truro *See* St Illogan.
TREVERBYN (St Pet), *Cornw.* V. **D** Truro 1 **P** *Crown* **I** R L STRANGE *p-in-c.*
TREWEN, *Cornw.*. **D** Truro 11 *See* Petherwyn, South.
TREYFORD (St Pet), *W Sussex.*. **D** Chich 5 *See* Elsted.
TRIMDON (St Mary Magd), *Durham.* V. **D** Dur 3 **P** *Exors of F J L Bury Esq* **I** J D HARGREAVE.
TRIMDON STATION (St Alb and St Paul), *Durham.* V. **D** Dur 12a **P** *Bp* **I** F J HARRIS.
TRIMINGHAM (St Jo Bapt), *Norf.*. **D** Nor 5 *See* Trunch.
TRIMLEY (St Martin w St Mary Virg), *Suff.* R. **D** St E 2 **P** *Ld Chan and Bp (alt)* **I** D B GRAY.
TRING (St Pet and St Paul Tring, St Jo Bapt Albury and Puttenham w Long Marston), *Herts.* R. **D** St Alb **P** *Bp* **I** D L HOWELLS, T C JOHNS *team v,* G R WARREN *team v.*
TRIPLOW or THRIPLOW (St Geo), *Cambs.* V. **D** Ely 9 **P** *Bp* **I** M C DONALD.
TROSTON (St Mary), *Suff.* R. **D** St E 9 *See* Honington.
TROTTISCLIFFE (St Pet and St Paul), *Kent.* R. **D** Roch 6 *See* Addington.
TROTTON (St Geo) w Chithurst (St Mary), *W Sussex.* R. **D** Chich 5 **P** *Can T R Franklin and Dr L M Franklin* **I** O Q HAIGH *p-in-c.*
TROUTBECK (Jesus), *Cumb.* V. **D** Carl 14 **P** *Bp* **I** (Vacant).
TROWBRIDGE (St Jas), *Wilts.* R. **D** Sarum 24 **P** *CPS* **I** H G JACK.
(H Trin), R. **D** Sarum 24 **P** *Bp and R of Trowbridge* **I** B J GARRATT, R M LOWRIE *team v.*
(St Thos Ap), V. **D** Sarum 24 **P** *Trustees and Bp (alt)* **I** J DARLING *c.*
TROWELL (St Helen), *Notts.* R. **D** Southw 8 **P** *Ld Middleton* **I** B C WALKER.
TROWSE (St Andr), *Norf.* V. **D** Nor 14 **P** *D and C of Nor* **I** H R CRESSWELL.
TRULL (All SS) w Angersleigh (St Mich AA), *Somt.* R. **D** B & W 23a **P** *Dioc Bd of Finance and Mrs J H Spurway* **I** J M PRIOR.
TRUMPINGTON (St Mary and St Nich), *Cambs.* V. **D** Ely 2 **P** *Trin Coll Cam* **I** D D M MADDOX.
TRUNCH, Trunch (St Botolph) w Swafield (St Nich), Antingham w Thorpe Market, Bradfield, Gimingham, Southrepps, Mundesley, Paston w Knapton and Trimingham), *Norf.* R. **D** Nor 5 **P** *Duchy of Lanc 3 turns, Patr Bd 1 turn* **I** G NORMAN, J S K FRESTON *team v,* R W GYTON *hon c.*
TRURO (St Mary Cathl and Par Ch), *Cornw.* R. **D** Truro 6 **P** *Crown* **I** VERY REV D J SHEARLOCK.
(St Geo Mart), V. **D** Truro 6 **P** *Crown* **I** K ROGERS *p-in-c.*
(St Jo Evang), V. **D** Truro 6 **P** *V of Kenwyn* **I** B W BUNT *p-in-c.*
(St Paul and St Clem), V. **D** Truro **P** *Bp* **I** P B STAPLES.
TRUSHAM (St Mich), *Devon.* R. **D** Ex 6 *See* Ashton.
TRUSLEY (All SS), *Derbys.* R. **D** Derby 14 *See* Dalbury.
TRUSTHORPE (St Pet), *Lincs.* R. **D** Linc 8 *See* Mablethorpe.
TRYSULL (All SS), *Staffs.* V. **D** Lich 7 **P** *Trustees* **I** A C TAPSFIELD *p-in-c.*
TUBNEY (St Laur), *Oxon.* R. **D** Ox 11 *See* Fyfield.
TUCKHILL (H Innoc), *Salop.* V. **D** Heref 9 **P** *Miss L B Amphlett* **I** (Vacant).
TUCKINGMILL (All SS), *Cornw.* V. **D** Truro 2 **P** *Bp* **I** M L UREN *p-in-c.*
TUCKSWOOD (St Paul), *Norf.* V. **D** Nor 4a **P** *Bp* **I** P E HALLS.
TUDDENHAM (St Mary) w Cavenham, *Suff.* R. **D** St E 11 **P** *Dioc Bd of Patr* **I** W R JESSUP.
TUDDENHAM (St Martin), *Suff.*. **D** St E *See* Westerfield.
TUDDENHAM, EAST, *Norf.*. **D** Nor *See* Honingham.
TUDDENHAM, NORTH (St Mary Virg), *Norf.* R. **D** Nor 12 **P** *Exors of W A Williamson* **I** (Vacant).
TUDELEY (All SS) w Capel (St Thos of Cant), *Kent.* V. **D** Roch 9 **P** *Bp* **I** (Vacant).
TUDHOE (H Innoc), *Durham.* V. **D** Dur 9 **P** *D and C of Dur* **I** P E B WELBY.
TUDHOE GRANGE (St Andr), *Durham.* V. **D** Dur 9 **P** *Bp* **I** N D BAKER, D J KENNEDY *c.*

UFFINGTON (H Trin), Upton Magna and Withington, *Salop*. V. **D** Lich 26 **P** *J R de Quincey Quincey Esq* **I** D H N WELLS.
UFFINGTON (St Mich AA), *Lincs*. R. **D** Linc 13 **P** *Lady M Barclay-Harvey* **I** (Vacant).
UFFINGTON w Woolstone and Baulking or Balking (St Nich), *Berks*. V. **D** Ox 17 **P** *Bp* **I** D B ASHBURNER.
UFFORD (St Andr), *Cambs*. R. **D** Pet 13 *See* Barnack.
UFFORD (The Assump), *Suff*. R. **D** St E 7 **P** *Maj E Blois Brook and Mrs E M Garnett* **I** (Vacant).
UFTON (St Mich AA), *Warws*. R. **D** Cov 10 **P** *Bp* **I** F L MARRIOTT.
UFTON-NERVET (St Pet), *Berks*. R. **D** Ox 12 *See* Sulhampstead Abbots.
UGBOROUGH, *Devon*. V. **D** Ex 21 **P** *Grocers' Co* **I** G F RICKARD.
UGGESHALL (St Mary) w Sotherton (St Andr), Wangford and, Henham, *Suff*. R. **D** St E 15 **P** *Earl of Stradbroke* **I** E M COPLEY.
UGGLEBARNBY, *N Yorks*.. **D** York *See* Eskdaleside.
UGLEY (St Pet), *Essex*. V. **D** Chelmsf 26 **P** *Ch Hosp* **I** R N HUMPHRIES.
UGTHORPE (Ch Ch), *N Yorks*. V. **D** York 27 **P** *Abp* **I** C E FOX *c-in-c*.
ULCEBY (St Nich), *Lincs*. V. **D** Linc 6 **P** *Ld Chan* **I** (Vacant).
ULCEBY (All SS) w Fordington and Dexthorpe, *Humb*. R. **D** Linc 8 **P** *Ball Coll Ox* **I** A G TAYLOR.
ULCOMBE (All SS), *Kent*. R. **D** Cant 15 **P** *Marq of Ormonde* **I** A J H SALMON *p-in-c*.
ULDALE, *Cumb*.. **D** Carl *See* Ireby.
ULEY (St Giles) w Owlpen (H Cross) and Nympsfield (St Bart), *Glos*. R. **D** Glouc 5 **P** *Ld Chan* **I** S J DAVIES.
ULGHAM (St Jo Bapt), *Northumb*. V. **D** Newc T 10 **P** *Bp* **I** J S MATTHEWSON.
ULLENHALL (St Mary Virg) w Aspley, *Warws*. V. **D** Cov *See* Beaudesert.
ULLESKELF, *N Yorks*.. **D** York 9 *See* Kirkby-Wharfe.
ULLEY (H Trin) w Brampton, *S Yorks*. V. **D** Sheff 5 **P** *Exors of Ld Halifax* **I** (Vacant).
ULLINGSWICK, *Herefs*. R. **D** Heref 4 *See* Ocle-Pychard.
ULROME, *Humb*.. **D** York *See* Skipsea.
ULTING (All SS), *Essex*. V. **D** Chelmsf 29 *See* Hatfield Peverel.
ULVERSTON (St Mary Virg w St Jude) w Osmotherly (St Jo Evang), *Cumb*. R. **D** Carl 15 **P** *Peache Trustees* **I** D A SMETHURST, P E P NORTON *c*.
UNDERBARROW (All SS) *Cumb*. V. **D** Carl 17 **P** *V of Kendal* **I** A F J LOFTHOUSE.
UNDERRIVER (St Marg), *Kent*. V. **D** Roch 7 **P** *Bp* **I** D M L LYNCH *p-in-c*.
UNDERWOOD, *Notts*.. **D** Southw *See* Brinsley.
UNSTONE (St Mary), *Derbys*.. **D** Derby 3 *See* Dronfield.
UNSWORTH (St Geo), *Gtr Man*. V. **D** Man 12 **P** *R of Prestwich* **I** R C N CAPEY, G P MITCHELL *hon c*.
UPAVON (St Mary Virg) w Rushall (St Matt), *Wilts*. V. **D** Sarum 18 **P** *Ld Chan and Mert Coll Ox* alt **I** G A RAYMOND.
UPBERRY, *Kent*.. **D** Roch *See* Gillingham.
UPCERNE (Dedic unknown), *Dorset*. R. **D** Sarum 5 *See* Cerne Abbas.
UPCHURCH (St Mary Virg) w Lower Halstow (St Marg), *Kent*. V. **D** Cant 14 **P** *D and C of Cant* **I** F K CHARE.
UPHAM (Blessed Mary), *Hants*. R. **D** Portsm 2 **P** *Ld Chan* **I** J F WILLARD.
UP HATHERLEY (St Phil and St Jas), *Glos*. V. **D** Glouc 11 **P** *Ch U* **I** J H HEIDT, A J HAWKER *c*.
UPHILL (St Nich), *Avon*. R. **D** B & W 3 **P** *Ch S Trust* **I** D N MITCHELL, R JONES *c*.
UP HOLLAND (St Thos Mart), *Lancs*. R. **D** Liv 9 **P** *Dioc Bd of Patr* **I** M M WOLFE, D E EMMOTT *team v*, P D D BRADLEY *c*.
UP-LAMBOURN (St Luke Evang), *Berks*.. **D** Ox 14 *See* Lambourn.
UPLANDS (All SS), *Glos*.. **D** Glouc 4 *See* Slad.
UPLEADON (St Mary Virg), *Glos*.. **D** Glouc *See* Pauntley.
UPLEATHAM (St Andr), *Cleve*. V. **D** York *See* Skelton-in-Cleveland.
UPLOWMAN (St Pet), *Devon*. R. **D** Ex 4 *See* Sampford-Peverell.
UPLYME, *Devon*. R. **D** Ex 5 **P** *Bp* **I** F S WORTH.
UPMINSTER (St Laur), *Essex*. R. **D** Chelmsf 4 **P** *Revd H R Holden* **I** M HARPER, D D J ROSSDALE *c*.
UP NATELY (St Steph), *Hants*. R. **D** Win 4 *See* Newnham.
UPNOR (St Phil and St Jas), *Kent*. V. **D** Roch 5 *See* Frindsbury.
UPOTTERY (St Mary Virg) Luppitt and Monkton, *Devon*. V. **D** Ex 5 **P** *D and C of Ex 2 turns, Bp 1 turn* **I** L LLOYD JONES P-IN-C OF UPOTTERY, J W I TREVELYAN P-IN-C OF MONKTON, N J WALL P-IN-C OF LUPPITT.
UPPER ARLEY (St Pet), *Salop*.. **D** Worc 12 *See* Arley, Upper.
UPPER GORNAL (St Pet), *W Midl*.. **D** Lich 1 *See* Gornal, Upper.
UPPER KENNET *See* Kennet, Upper.
UPPER LANGWITH (St Leon), *Derbys*.. **D** Derby *See* Langwith Upper.
UPPER RYEDALE (Bilsdale Midcable, Hawnby w Old Byland and Scawton w Cold Kirby), *N Yorks*. R. **D** York **P** *Abp, Archd of Cleve, Ld Feversham and Capt V M Wombwell* **I** A G ALDERSON.
UPPER STOUR, w Bourton (St Geo), Zeals (St Martin) and Stourton (St Pet), *Wilts*. R. **D** Sarum 22 **P** *Trustees, Bp and H P R Hoare Esq in turn* **I** R F SEAL *p-in-c*.
UPPERBY (St Jo Bapt), *Cumb*. V. **D** Carl 3 *See* Carlisle.
UPPERTHONG (St Jo Evang), *W Yorks*. V. **D** Wakef 5 **P** *Bp* **I** J P DODSON.
UPPINGHAM (St Pet and St Paul) w Ayston, *Leics*. R. **D** Pet 12 **P** *Bp* **I** J SMITH, M H W ROGERS *c*.
UPPINGTON (H Trin) w Aston, *Salop*. V. **D** Lich 29 **P** *Hon H J N Vane* **I** W S FROST *p-in-c*.
UPSHIRE, *Essex*.. **D** Chelmsf *See* High Beech.
UPTON (St Jas) w Skilgate (St Jo Bapt), *Somt*. R. **D** B & W 21 *See* Brompton-Regis.
UPTON (St Mary), *Mer*.. **D** Ches 8 *See* Overchurch.
UPTON (H Ascen), *Chesh*. V. **D** Ches 2 **P** *Duke of Westmr* **I** F LAPHAM.
UPTON, *Devon*.. **D** Ex 10 *See* Torquay.
UPTON, *Leics*. R. **D** Leic 15 *See* Sibson.
UPTON (All SS) w Kexby, *Lincs*.. **D** Linc 2 **P** *Bp* **I** H J KNIGHT.
UPTON, *Cambs*. V. **D** Pet 14 *See* Sutton.
UPTON (St Pet and St Paul), *Notts*. V. **D** Southw 15 **P** *Ld Chan* **I** N H TODD *p-in-c*.
UPTON (St Mary Virg), *Berks*. R. **D** Ox 18 **P** *Bp* **I** H J PICKLES.
UPTON w Chalvey, *Berks*.. **D** Ox *See* Slough.
UPTON (St Marg) w Copmanford, *Cambs*. R. **D** Ely 11 **P** *Bp* **I** B E CLOSE *p-in-c*.
UPTON (St Marg V and M), *Norf*. V. **D** Nor 1 **P** *Bp* **I** (Vacant).
UPTON BISHOP, *Herefs*. V. **D** Heref *See* Linton.
UPTON CRESSETT, *Salop*. R. **D** Heref 9 *See* Monk Hopton.
UPTON CROSS (St Pet), *Essex*. V. **D** Chelmsf 5 *See* Forest Gate.
UPTON GREY (St Mary), Weston Patrick (St Lawr), Tunworth (All SS), Herriard and Winslade, *Hants*. V. **D** Win 4 **P** *Qu Coll Ox, J L Jervoise Esq and Visc Camrose* **I** D M INCE.
UPTON HELLIONS (St Mary), *Devon*. R. **D** Ex 2 *See* Sandford.
UPTON LOVELL, *Wilts*. R. **D** Sarum 21 *See* Codford.
UPTON MAGNA (St Lucia), *Salop*. R. **D** Lich *See* Uffington.
UPTON NOBLE (St Mary Magd), *Somt*.. **D** B & W 5 *See* Batcombe.
UPTON-ON-SEVERN (St Pet and St Paul), *Worcs*. R. **D** Worc 5 **P** *Bp* **I** A R KING.
UPTON PARK (St Alb), *Essex*. V. **D** Chelmsf 5 *See* Ham East.
UPTON PARVA or UPTON WATERS (St Mich), *Salop*. R. **D** Lich 21 **P** *J B Davies Esq* **I** P ELDRED-EVANS.
UPTON PRIORY **D** Ches *See* Macclesfield.
UPTON PYNE (Ch-of-Our-Lady), *Devon*. R. **D** Ex 2 **P** *Earl of Iddesleigh* **I** G LINDEN.
UPTON ST LEONARDS, *Glos*. R. **D** Glouc 2 **P** *Bp* **I** T P JACKSON.
UPTON SCUDAMORE (St Mary Virg), *Wilts*. R. **D** Sarum 22 **P** *Qu Coll Ox* **I** A T JOHNSON.
UPTON SNODSBURY (St Kenelm), and Broughton Hackett (St Leon) w the Flyfords (St Jo Bapt and St Pet) and North Piddle (St Mich AA), *Worcs*. V. **D** Worc **P** *Ld Chan 1st turn, Bp and Trustees of Croome Estate 2nd turn* **I** J W R MOWLL.
UPTON WARREN, *Worcs*. R. **D** Worc 8 *See* Wychbold.
UP-WALTHAM (St Mary Virg), *W Sussex*. R. **D** Chich 6 **P** *Ld Egremont* **I** (Vacant).
UPWELL (St Pet), *Norf*. R. **D** Ely 20 **P** *C E Townley Esq* **I** R C WALLIS.
UPWELL-CHRISTCHURCH (Ch Ch), *Cambs*. R. **D** Ely 19 **P** *C E Townley Esq* **I** (Vacant).
UPWEY (St Lawr), *Dorset*. R. **D** Sarum *See* Bincombe.
UPWOOD (St Pet) w Gt and L Raveley, *Cambs*. V. **D** Ely 12 **P** *Bp 2 turns, Ld de Ramsey 1 turn* **I** B N JONES.
URCHFONT (St Mich AA) w Stert (St Jas), *Wilts*.. **D** Sarum 23 **P** *D and C of Windsor* **I** D M FIDGIN *p-in-c*.

URMSTON (St Clem of Rome), *Gtr Man.* V. **D** Man 9 **P** *Bp* **I** T H W DUNWOODY, D R OTTLEY *c.*
URSWICK (St Mary Virg), *Cumb.* V. **D** Carl 15 **P** *Miss D M La Touche and Resident Landowners (alt)* **I** B DAWSON.
USHAW MOOR (St Luke), *Durham.* V. **D** Dur 2 **P** *Bp* **I** T J TOWERS.
USSELBY (St Marg), *Lincs.* V. **D** Linc 5 **P** *Bp* **I** F RODGERS *p-in-c.*
USWORTH (H Trin), *T & W.* r. **D** Dur 1 **P** *Dioc Bd of Patr* **I** J W ELLIOTT, R CUTHBERTSON *c*, C P KUUSK *c.*
UTLEY (St Mark), *Lincs.* V. **D** Bradf **P** *Bp and Incumbent of Keighley* **I** W D JAMIESON.
UTTERBY (St Andr), *Lincs.* R. **D** Linc 12 *See* Fotherby.
UTTOXETER (St Mary) w Bramshall (St Lawr), R *Staffs.* V. **D** Lich 20 **P** *D and C of Windsor* **I** W H O MOSS, R K BOUGHEY *c*, P MILN *hon c.*
UXBRIDGE (St Marg), *Gtr Lon.* V. **D** Lon 9 **P** *Bp* **I** RT REV D S ARDEN *p-in-c.*
(St Andr), V. **D** Lon 9 **P** *Bp* **I** M W JARRETT.
UXBRIDGE MOOR (St John), *Gtr Lon.* V. **D** Lon 9 **P** *Bp* **I** A P VENABLES *c-in-c.*
UXBRIDGE ROAD. **D** Lon 7 *See* Hammersmith.

VALLEY END, *Surrey.* **D** Guildf 5a *See* Chobham.
VANGE (All SS), *Essex.* R. **D** Chelmsf 10 **P** *MMT* **I** H J MOORHOUSE.
VAUXHALL (St Pet), *Surrey.* V. **D** S'wark 4 **P** *Trustees* **I** (Vacant).
VENTNOR (St Cath), *Isle of Wight.* V. **D** Portsm 6 **P** *Bp and CPS* alt **I** M PICKERING, A W SWANBOROUGH *c.*
(H Trin), V. **D** Portsm 6 **P** *Bp and CPS* alt **I** M PICKERING, A W SWANBOROUGH *c.*
VERNEY, COMPTON, *Warws..* **D** Cov 9 *See* Combroke.
VERNHAM DEAN (St Mary Virg) w Linkenholt, *Hants.* V. **D** Win *See* Hurstbourne Tarrant.
VERWOOD (St Mich AA), *Dorset.* V. **D** Sarum 11 **P** *Bp* **I** J A D ROBERTS *p-in-c.*
VERYAN (St Symphoriana), *Cornw.* V. **D** Truro 6 **P** *D and C of Truro* **I** B G DORRINGTON *hon c.*
VICTORIA DOCKS (Ascen w St Matt Custom Ho), *Essex.* V. **D** Chelmsf 5 **P** *Bp* **I** N J COPSEY *c.*
(St Luke), V. **D** Chelmsf 5 **P** *Ld Chan* **I** K M ELBOURNE *p-in-c.*
VICTORIA PARK (St Mark). **D** Lon 4 *See* Bow.
VICTORIA PARK (St Chrys), *Gtr Man.* R. **D** Man 5 **P** *Bp* **I** M J G MELROSE.
VINEY HILL (All SS), *Glos.* V. **D** Glouc 7 **P** *Univ Coll Ox* **I** W R J WATTS.
VIRGINIA WATER (Ch Ch), *Surrey.* V. **D** Guildf 7 **P** *Simeon Trustees* **I** J A KIDD.
VIRGINSTOW (St Bridget Virg), *Devon..* **D** Truro 11 *See* Werrington.
VOBSTER (St Edm), *Somt.* V. **D** B & W 16a *See* Mells.
VOWCHURCH (St Bart etc) w Turnastone (St Mary Magd), [Herefs]. V. **D** Heref 1 **P** *Bp of Birm and Bp of Heref 1 turn in 3* **I** J C DE LA T DAVIES P-IN-C OF MOCCAS.

WABERTHWAITE, *Cumb..* **D** Carl *See* Muncaster.
WACTON, *Herefs.* V. **D** Heref 2 *See* Bredenbury.
WACTON MAGNA (All SS) w Wacton Parva (St Mary), *Norf.* R. **D** Nor 11 *See* Stratton, Long.
WADDESDON (St Mich AA) w Over Winchendon (St Mary Magd) and Fleet Marston (St Mary Virg), *Bucks.* R. **D** Ox 21 **P** *Duke of Marlborough* **I** D PEARSON-MILES.
WADDINGTON (St Helen) w W Bradford (St Cath), *Lancs.* V. **D** Bradf 6 **P** *Trustee* **I** C F GOODCHILD.
WADDINGTON (St Mich), *Lincs..* **D** Linc 18 **P** *Linc Coll Ox* **I** J L A JACOB.
WADDINGWORTH, *Lincs.* R. **D** Linc 11 *See* Gautby.
WADEBRIDGE, *Cornw..* **D** Truro *See* St Breocke and Egloshayle.
WADENHOE (St Mich AA), *Northants.* R. **D** Pet 11 *See* Pilton.
WADHURST (St Pet and St Paul), *E Sussex.* V. **D** Chich 20 **P** *Hon Hilda Beryl Courthope and Hon Elinor Daphne Courthope* **I** T D M RAVEN.
WADINGHAM (St Mary and St Pet) w Snitterby, *Lincs.* R. **D** Linc *See* Bishop Norton.
WADSLEY, *S Yorks.* V. **D** Sheff 4 **P** *CPS* **I** H F C COLE.
WADSLEY BRIDGE, *S Yorks.* V. **D** Sheff 4 *See* Hillsborough.
WADWORTH (St Jo Bapt) w Loversall, *S Yorks.* V. **D** Sheff 8 **P** *V of Doncaster and Dioc Bd of Patr (alt)* **I** R M HARVEY.
WAGHEN or WAWNE (St Pet), *Humb..* **D** York 17 *See* Sutton-in-Holderness.
WAINFLEET (All SS), *Lincs.* R. **D** Linc 8 **P** *Ld Chan* **I** D C BAKER.
(St Mary BV), V. **D** Linc 8 **P** *Bp* **I** D C BAKER *p-in-c.*
WAITH (St Martin), *Lincs..* **D** Linc 10 *See* Waythe.
WAKEFIELD (All SS Cathl w H Trin), *W Yorks.* V. **D** Wakef 12 **P** *Bp* **I** (Vacant).
(Ch Ch). **D** Wakef *See* Thornes.
(St Andr w St Mary), V. **D** Wakef 12 **P** *Peache Trustees* **I** B S ELLIS, G C GOALBY *c.*
(St Jo Bapt), V. **D** Wakef 12 **P** *V of Wakef* **I** K UNWIN, I M GASKELL *c.*
(St Mich Arch), V. **D** Wakef 12 **P** *V of Alverthorpe* **I** R J HOWARD.
WAKERING (St Mary Virg), *Essex.* V. **D** Chelmsf 11 *See* Barling.
GREAT (St Nich) w Foulness (St Mary Virg), V. **D** Chelmsf 11 **P** *Bp* **I** K R PLAISTER.
WAKERLEY (St Jo Bapt), *Northants.* R. **D** Pet 17 *See* Barrowden.
WAKES COLNE (All SS) w Chappel or Pontesbright, *Essex.* V. **D** Chelmsf 22 **P** *Chappel PCC and Dioc Bd of Patr* **I** N J COTGROVE *p-in-c.*
WALBERSWICK (St Andr) w Blythburgh (H Trin), *Suff.* V. **D** St E 15 **P** *Sir Gervase Blois Bt* **I** G C SMITH.
WALBERTON (St Mary) w Binsted (St Mary), *W Sussex.* V. **D** Chich 1 **P** *Bp* **I** (Vacant).
WALCOT, *Avon..* **D** B & W 13 *See* Bath.
WALCOT (St Nich), *Lincs.* V. **D** Linc 22 *See* Pickworth.
WALCOT (All SS), *Norf.* V. **D** Nor 9 *See* Happisburgh.
WALCOT (St Osw), *Lincs..* **D** Linc 22 *See* Billinghay.
WALCOT, *Wilts..* **D** Bris *See* Swindon.
WALCOTE, *Leics.* R. **D** Leic 14 *See* Misterton.
WALDERSHARE (All SS), *Kent.* R. **D** Cant *See* Eythorne.
WALDINGFIELD, GREAT (St Lawr), *Suff.* R. **D** St E 12 *See* Acton.
WALDINGFIELD, LITTLE, *Suff..* **D** St E *See* Acton.
WALDITCH (St Mary w Ch Ch), *Dorset.* V. **D** Sarum 2 *See* Bothenhampton.
WALDRINGFIELD (All SS) w Hemley (All SS) and Newbourn (St Mary), *Suff.* R. **D** St E 2 **P** *Sir Joshua Rowley Bt 1st turn, Ld Chan 2nd turn, Canon T Waller and Rev A H Waller 3rd turn* **I** J P WALLER.
WALDRON (All SS and St Bart), *E Sussex.* R. **D** Chich 18 **P** *Ex Coll Ox* **I** (Vacant).
WALES (St Jo Bapt), *S Yorks.* V. **D** Sheff 5 **P** *Bp* **I** H J PATRICK.
WALESBY (Claxby, Normanby-le-Wold, Willingham North, Stainton-le-Vale, Kirmond-le-Mire and Tealby), *Lincs),.* **D** Linc **P** *Bp, Dioc Bd of Patr and W Drakes Esq* **I** F M MASSEY.
WALESBY (St Edm K and Mart), *Notts.* V. **D** Southw 6 **P** *Dioc Bd of Patr* **I** I CLARK.
WALFORD-ON-WYE (St Mich AA), w Bishopswood (All SS), *Herefs.* V. **D** Heref 8 **P** *Ld Chan* **I** M C LAPAGE.
WALGRAVE (St Pet) w Hannington and Wold (St Andr), *Northants.* R. **D** Pet 6 **P** *Bp and BNC Ox* alt **I** F H B ELDRIDGE.
WALHAM GREEN (St Jo Div). **D** Lon 11 *See* Fulham.
WALKDEN (St Paul), *Gtr Man.* V. **D** Man 14 **P** *Bp* **I** A E BALLARD.
WALKER (Ch Ch), *T & W.* V. **D** Newc T 5a **P** *Bp* **I** S H CONNOLLY, G A NEWMAN *c.*
WALKER GATE (St Osw Eccles Distr), *T & W..* **D** Newc T 5a *See* Newcastle upon Tyne.
WALKERINGHAM (St Mary Magd), *Notts.* V. **D** Southw 1 *See* Beckingham.
WALKERITH, *Lincs..* **D** Linc 2 *See* Morton.
WALKERN (St Mary), *Herts.* R. **D** St Alb 12 **P** *K Coll Cam* **I** G E MARSHALL.
WALKHAMPTON, *Devon.* V. **D** Ex 22 **P** *Ld Roborough* **I** C J WARLAND *p-in-c.*
WALKINGTON, *Humb.* r. **D** York 11 *See* Bishop Burton.
WALKLEY (St Mary), *S Yorks..* **D** Sheff 4 *See* Sheffield.
WALL (St Jo Evang), *Staffs.* V. **D** Lich 2 **P** *R of St Mich Lich* **I** W J WEBB *p-in-c.*
WALL, *Northumb..* **D** Newc T 4 *See* St Oswald-in-Lee.
WALLASEY (St Hilary of Poitiers), *Mer.* R. **D** Ches 7 **P** *Bp* **I** W S WALKER, J F SPEAKMAN *c.*
(St Nich), V. **D** Ches 7 **P** *Bp* **I** E J BENTLEY.
(St John, Egremont), V. **D** Ches 7 **P** *Bp* **I** J F MADDOCK-LYON, G J PARKES *hon c.*
(St Chad's Leasowe), V. **D** Ches 7 **P** *Bp* **I** J EARDLEY.
(St Thos, Liscard), V. **D** Ches 7 **P** *Bp* **I** A J CHENNELL.
(Em, New Brighton), V. **D** Ches 7 **P** *Bp* **I** J P MACMILLAN.
(St Jas, New Brighton), V. **D** Ches 7 **P** *Bp* **I** H BAGULEY.
(All SS, New Brighton), V. **D** Ches 7 **P** *Dioc Bd of Patr* **I** E R ROYDEN.

(St Luke, Poulton), V. **D** Ches 7 **P** *Bp* **I** J P EDWARDSON.
(St Paul, Seacombe), V. **D** Ches 7 **P** *Trustees* **I** P L ROBINSON.
WALLINGFORD St Mary-le-More and All H w St Leon and St Pet) w Crowmarsh Gifford (St Mary Magd) and Newnham Murren, *Oxon*. R. **D** Ox **P** *Bp* **I** M J GILLHAM *team v*, H D ETCHES *c*.
WALLINGTON, *Norf*.. **D** Ely *See* Runcton, South.
WALLINGTON (H Trin), *Surrey*. V. **D** S'wark 8 **P** *Ch Soc Trust* **I** N G E ISSBERNER, D HOWES *min*, R F KEY *c*, D G WILLIS *c*, S J PIX *hon c*.
(Roundshaw Conv Distr). **D** S'wark **P** *Bp* **I** (Vacant).
WALLINGTON (St Mary) w Rushden, *Herts*. R. **D** St Alb 5 *See* Sandon.
WALLSEND (St Pet formerly H Cross), *T & W*. R. **D** Newc T 6 **P** *Bp* **I** P R STRANGE.
(St John), V. **D** Newc T 6 **P** *Bp* **I** F WILSON.
(St Luke), V. **D** Newc T 6 **P** *Bp* **I** P HEYWOOD, S P PICKERING *c*.
WALMER (St Mary w St Sav), *Kent*. V. **D** Cant 8 **P** *Abp* **I** P C HAMMOND, J B SHORTT *hon c*.
WALMERSLEY (Ch Ch), *Gtr Man*. V. **D** Man 12 **P** *Five Trustees* **I** R M FREEMAN.
WALMLEY (St Jo Evang), *W Midl*. V. **D** Birm 12 **P** *Trustees* **I** M B HARPER, J P BENSON *c*.
WALMSGATE (St Francis), *Lincs*.. **D** Linc 12 *See* Muckton.
WALMSLEY (Ch Ch), *Gtr Man*. V. **D** Man 19 **P** *V of Bolton* **I** F R COOKE, R E PARKER *c*.
WALNEY, ISLE OF (St Mary Virg), *Cumb*. V. **D** Carl 16 **P** *V of Dalton-in-Furness* **I** R B HILL, J A ARMES *c*, T J HYSLOP *c*.
WALPOLE ST PETER (St Pet and St Paul), *Norf*. R. **D** Ely 18 **P** *Crown and Dioc Bd of Patr (alt)* **I** H R BARKER.
WALPOLE ST ANDREW (St Andr), V. **D** Ely 18 **P** *Crown and Dioc Bd of Patr (alt)* **I** H R BARKER.
WALPOLE, *Suff*.. **D** St E *See* Bramfield.
WALSALL (St Matt w St Luke), *W Midl*. V. **D** Lich 9 **P** *Bp* **I** R F SAINSBURY, W J G HEALE *c*, R A SUTTON *c*.
(Ch Ch). **D** Lich 9 *See* Blakenhall Heath.
(St Andr), V. **D** Lich 9 **P** *Bp* **I** C R MARSHALL.
(St John, The Pleck and Bescot), V. **D** Lich 9 **P** *V of Walsall* **I** F R WALFORD *hon c*.
(St Mary and All SS, Palfrey), V. **D** Lich 9 **P** *Bp* **I** P J BRYAN *p-in-c*.
(St Mich AA, Caldmore), V. **D** Lich 9 **P** *Bp* **I** P G BARNETT *p-in-c*.
(St Paul), V. **D** Lich 9 **P** *Bp* **I** B L GANT.
(St Pet), V. **D** Lich 9 **P** *V of Walsall* **I** J S ARTISS.
(Em Bentley), V. **D** Lich 9 **P** *Bp and Sir A Owen* **I** M F WALKER.
FULLBROOK (St Gabr), V. **D** Lich 9 **P** *Bp* **I** T R H COYNE, B L WILLIAMS *c*.
WALSALL WOOD (St John), *W Midl*. V. **D** Lich 9 **P** *V of Walsall* **I** M A RHODES, M S HATTON *c*.
WALSDEN (St Pet), *W Yorks*. V. **D** Wakef 3 **P** *Bp* **I** C DAWSON *p-in-c*.
WALSGRAVE-ON-SOWE (St Mary), *W Midl*. V. **D** Cov 1 **P** *Ld Chan* **I** A K TUCK.
WALSHAM-LE-WILLOWS (St Mary), *Suff*. V. **D** St E 9 **P** *Wing-Commdr J Martineaux* **I** J A E RUTHERFORD P-IN-C OF HINDERCLAY.
WALSHAM, NORTH (St Nich), w Antingham (St Marg), *Norf*. V. **D** Nor 8 **P** *Bp* **I** W O STEELE, J LEACH *c*.
WALSHAM, SOUTH (St Lawr w St Mary), *Norf*. R. **D** Nor 1 **P** *Qu Coll Cam* **I** (Vacant).
WALSHAW (Ch Ch), *Gtr Man*.. **D** Man 12 **P** *Simeon Trustees* **I** R HOPE, H A HALLETT *c*, R M POWLEY *hon c*.
WALSINGHAM (St Mary and All SS) w (St Pet) and Houghton-in-the-Dale (St Giles), *Norf*. V. **D** Nor 21 **P** *J Gurney Esq* **I** J E BARNES.
WALSOKEN (All SS), *Cambs*. R. **D** Ely 20 **P** *Dioc Bd of Patr* **I** I E D FARROW.
WALTER BELCHAMP (St Mary), *Essex*.. **D** Chelmsf 18 *See* Bulmer.
WALTERSTONE (St Mary Virg), *Herefs*. V. **D** Heref *See* Ewyas Harold.
WALTHAM, *Kent*. V. **D** Cant 2 *See* Petham.
WALTHAM (All SS) w New Waltham (St Matt), *Humb*. R. **D** Linc 10 **P** *Crown* **I** W J A NUNNERLEY.
WALTHAM ABBEY (H Cross and St Laur), *Essex*. V. **D** Chelmsf 2 **P** *Trustees* **I** M J LOWLES *c*, S J WILLIAMS *c*.
WALTHAM CROSS (Ch Ch), *Herts*. V. **D** St Alb 6 **P** *V of Cheshunt* **I** J A FURNESS, C J IVORY *c*.
WALTHAM, GREAT (St Mary and St Lawr) w Ford End, *Essex*. V. **D** Chelmsf **P** *Trin Coll Ox* **I** G L SANDERS.
WALTHAM, LITTLE (St Martin), *Essex*. R. **D** Chelmsf 11 **P** *Ex Coll Ox* **I** D O R PARRY.
WALTHAM, NORTH (St Mich) w Steventon, Ashe (H Trin and St Andr) and Deane (All SS), *Hants*. R. **D** Win 5 **P** *Dioc Bd of Patr* **I** G R TURNER.
WALTHAM ST LAWR (St Lawr w All SS), *Berks*. V. **D** Ox 13 **P** *Ld Braybrooke* **I** P RADLEY.
WALTHAM, WHITE (BVM), *Berks*.. **D** Ox 13 *See* Shottesbrooke.
WALTHAM-ON-THE-WOLDS (St Mary Magd) w Stonesby (St Pet) and Saltby (St Pet), *Leics*. R. **D** Leic 4 **P** *Duke of Rutld* **I** J HICKLING.
WALTHAMSTOW (St Mary w St Steph), *Essex*. V. **D** Chelmsf 8 **P** *Simeon Trustees* **I** K H DRUITT, G B CHARRETT *c*, R G V FOREMAN *c*.
(All SS Highams Park), V. **D** Chelmsf 8 **P** *Bp* **I** (Vacant).
(St Andr), V. **D** Chelmsf 8 **P** *Bp* **I** M R J LAND.
(St Barn w St Jas Gtr), V. **D** Chelmsf 8 **P** *Bp* **I** A D COUCHMAN.
(St Gabr), V. **D** Chelmsf 8 **P** *Simeon Trustees* **I** G P GIBBON, J GUTTERIDGE *hon c*.
(St Luke), V. **D** Chelmsf 8 **P** *Simeon Trustees* **I** P J WOOD.
(St Jo Evang), V. **D** Chelmsf 8 **P** *V of Walthamstow* **I** J S SUTTON.
(St Mich AA), V. **D** Chelmsf 8 **P** *Bp* **I** M BEBBINGTON.
(St Pet), V. **D** Chelmsf 8 **P** *Sir Henry Warner Bt* **I** (Vacant).
(St Sav), V. **D** Chelmsf 8 **P** *Bp* **I** P D D JAMES.
WALTON (H Trin), *Somt*.. **D** B & W *See* Street.
WALTON (St Mary), *Cumb*. V. **D** Carl *See* Lanercost.
WALTON (St Jo Evang), *Chesh*. V. **D** Ches 4 **P** *Trustees of P G Greenall* **I** D W HARRIS.
WALTON, *Leics*. R. **D** Leic 14 *See* Kimcote.
WALTON (St Thos), *Staffs*.. **D** Lich 5 *See* Berkswich.
WALTON (H Trin), *Bucks*. V. **D** Ox 21 *See* Aylesbury.
WALTON (St Mich), *Bucks*. R. **D** Ox 26 *See* Wavendon.
WALTON (St Mary), *Suff*. V. **D** St E 2 **P** *Ch Trust Fund* **I** K E WAKEFIELD, N DAVIS *c*.
WALTON (St Pet), *N Yorks*.. **D** York 9 *See* Thorp-Arch.
WALTON BRECK (H Trin), *Mer*. V. **D** Liv 5 **P** *Simeon Trustees* **I** (Vacant).
WALTON CARDIFF (St Jas), *Glos*. V. **D** Glouc 10 *See* Tewkesbury.
WALTON D'EIVILE (St Jas), *Warws*. R. **D** Cov 8 **P** *Sir R Hamilton, Bt* **I** C C O BENNETT.
WALTON, EAST (St Mary Virg), *Norf*. V. **D** Nor 25 *See* Gayton Thorpe.
WALTON, HIGHER (All SS), *Lancs*. V. **D** Blackb 6 **P** *Bp and V of Blackb* alt **I** F COOPER.
WALTON-IN-GORDANO (St Mary) w (St Paul), *Avon*. R. **D** B & W 16 **P** *Bp* **I** W R T MARRIOTT C-IN-C OF CLAPTON-IN-GORDANO *c-in-c*, N G MARTIN *c*.
WALTON-LE-DALE (St Leon), *Lancs*. V. **D** Blackb 6 **P** *V of Blackb* **I** (Vacant).
WALTON-LE-SOKEN (All SS), *Essex*. V. **D** Chelmsf 28 **P** *Trustees* **I** (Vacant).
WALTON-LE-WOLDS (St Mary), *Leics*. R. **D** Leic 9 *See* Seagrave.
WALTON-ON-THAMES (St Mary), *Surrey*. V. **D** Guildf 8 **P** *Bp* **I** T J SEDGLEY, A P R GREGORY *c*.
WALTON-ON-THE-HILL (St Pet), *Surrey*. R. **D** Guildf 9 **P** *Bp* **I** R D W BEDFORD.
WALTON-ON-THE-HILL (St Mary), *Mer*. R. **D** Liv 5 **P** *Bp* **I** C M SMITH, S W C GOUGH *c*, R C HARDCASTLE *c*, S E YOUNG *c*.
(St Jo Evang), V. **D** Liv 5 **P** *Bp, Archd of Liv and R of Walton* **I** A S CONWAY.
(St Luke Evang), V. **D** Liv 5 **P** *Bp* **I** H E ROSS.
(St Nath Fazakerley), V. **D** Liv 5 **P** *Bp* **I** M B ROBERTS.
WALTON-ON-THE-NAZE (All SS), *Essex*.. **D** Chelmsf 28 *See* Walton-le-Soken.
WALTON-ON-TRENT (St Laur) w Croxall (St Jo Bapt) and Oakley, *Derbys*. R. **D** Derby 16 **P** *Bp and D H W Neilson Esq* **I** G DICKENSON.
WALTON, WEST (St Mary Virg), *Norf*. R. **D** Ely 18 **P** *Ld Chan* **I** D T HURLEY.
WALWORTH (St Pet, Liverpool Grove and St Chris Pemb Coll Cam Miss, Tatum Street), Gtr Lon. R. **D** S'wark 5 **P** *Bp* **I** P JOBSON, G G THOMPSON *team v*, R N ARNOLD *c*, L G URWIN *c*, M M H MOORE *hon c*.
(St Jo Evang), V. **D** S'wark 5 **P** *Bp* **I** V A DAVIES.
(St Pet), R. **D** S'wark 5 **P** *Bp* **I** (Vacant).
WAMBROOK (St Mary Virg), *Dorset*. R. **D** B & W *See* Combe St Nicholas.
WANBOROUGH (St Andr), *Wilts*.. **D** Bris *See* Lyddington.
WANBOROUGH (St Bart), *Surrey*. V. **D** Guildf 5 *See* Puttenham.
WANDSWORTH (All SS w H Trin), *Surrey*. V. **D** S'wark 7 **P** *Ch Soc* **I** A G SIRMAN, E C LAST *c*.
(St Anne), V. **D** S'wark 7 **P** *Bp* **I** G F SMITH.

WARWICK (St Mary w St Nich), *Warws.* R. **D** Cov 11 **P** *Ld Chan and Patr Bd (alt)* **I** J D RUDD, P M FREEMAN *team v*, D R TILLEY *team v*, G BENFIELD *hon c*.
(All SS Emscote), V. **D** Cov 11 **P** *Earl of Warwick* **I** P N SNOW, A G R BRISTOW *c*.
(St Paul), V. **D** Cov 11 **P** *V of Warwick* **I** S GODFREY *p-in-c*.
WARWICK AVENUE (St Sav). **D** Lon 16 *See* Paddington.
WARWICK SQUARE (St Gabr). **D** Lon 19 *See* Westminster.
WASDALE NETHER (Dedic unknown) w Wasdale Head, *Cumb.*. **D** Carl 12 *See* Gosforth.
WASHBOURNE, GREAT (St Mary), *Glos.* V. **D** Glouc 18 *See* Alderton.
WASHBOURNE, LITTLE, *Worcs.*. **D** Worc 3 *See* Overbury.
WASHBROOK (St Mary), *Suff.*. **D** St E 5 *See* Copdock.
WASH COMMON (St Geo), *Berks.*. **D** Ox 14 *See* Newbury.
WASHFIELD (St Mary Virg), Stoodleigh (St Marg), Withleigh (St Cath), Calverleigh (St Mary Virg), Oakford (St Pet), Morebath (St Geo), Templeton (St Marg), Loxbeare Rackenford (All SS), Cruwys-Morchard (H Cross), Chevithorne, Cove (St Jo Bapt), Bickleigh (St Mary) and Cadeleigh (St Bart). *Exe Valley Team Ministry Devon.* R. **D** Ex 8 **P** *Dioc Bd of Patr 1st 2nd and 4th turns, Ld Chan 3rd turn* **I** K H BLYTH, H J ALDRIDGE *team v*, F G GODBER *team v*, H G WHITTY *team v*.
WASHFORD-PYNE (St Pet), *Devon.* R. **D** Ex 8 *See* Woolfardisworthy, East.
WASHINGBOROUGH (St John) w Heighington, *Lincs.* R. **D** Linc 18 **P** *Reps of Late Mrs Lilian Bridge* **I** C W A HUTCHINSON.
WASHINGTON (St Mary), *W Sussex.*. **D** Chich *See* Ashington.
WASHINGTON (H Trin), *T & W.* R. **D** Dur **P** *Bp* **I** D C HAWTIN, J S BAIN *c*.
WASHWOOD HEATH (St Mark), *W Midl.* V. **D** Birm 13 *See* Saltley.
WASING, *Berks.*. **D** Ox *See* Aldermaston.
WASPERTON (St Jo Bapt), *Warws.* V. **D** Cov 8 *See* Barford.
WATCHET (St Decuman), *Somt.* V. **D** B & W *See* St Decuman's.
WATCHFIELD CHAP, *Oxon.*. **D** Ox *See* Shrivenham.
WATER EATON, *Bucks.*. **D** Ox 26 *See* Fenny Stratford.
WATER NEWTON (St Remigius), *Cambs.* R. **D** Ely 14 **P** *Keble Coll Ox* **I** P O POOLEY *p-in-c*.
WATER ORTON (St Pet and St Paul), *Warws.* V. **D** Birm 9 **P** *Trustees* **I** C T DAVIES.
WATER-STRATFORD (St Giles), *Bucks.*. **D** Ox 23 *See* Tingewick.
WATERBEACH (St Jo Evang), *Cambs.* V. **D** Ely 6 **P** *Bp* **I** P S G CAMERON.
WATERDEN, *Norf.*. **D** Nor *See* Holkham.
WATERFALL (St Jas and St Bart), *Staffs.* V. **D** Lich 13 **P** *Bp* **I** W R D ALEXANDER.
WATERFOOT (St Jas), *Lancs.* V. **D** Man 18 **P** *Trustees* **I** R T RICHARDSON.
WATERFORD (St Mich AA), *Herts.* V. **D** St Alb 8 *See* Bramfield w Stapleford.
WATERHEAD (H Trin), *Gtr Man.*. **D** Man 15 *See* Oldham.
WATERHOUSES (St Paul), *Durham.* V. **D** Dur 2 **P** *R of Brancepeth* **I** M J WILKINSON.
WATERINGBURY (St Jo Bapt) w Teston (St Pet and St Paul) and W Farleigh, *Kent.* R. **D** Roch 6 **P** *D and C of Roch and Peache Trustees* **I** D BISH.
WATERLOO (Ch Ch), *Mer.* V. **D** Liv 1 **P** *Trustees* **I** C W PAKENHAM.
(St Jo Div), V. **D** Liv 1 **P** *Trustees* **I** S B SYMONS.
(St Mary Virg), V. **D** Liv 1 **P** *Trustees* **I** C W E PENNELL.
WATERLOOVILLE (St Geo), *Hants.* V. **D** Portsm 3 **P** *Bp* **I** M S R GOVER *c*.
WATERMILLOCK (All SS), *Cumb.* R. **D** Carl 6 **P** *R of Greystoke* **I** A W BROOKSBANK.
WATERMOOR (H Trin), *Glos.*. **D** Glouc 13 *See* Cirencester.
WATERPERRY (St Mary Virg), *Oxon.* R. **D** Ox 5 *See* Holton.
WATERSTOCK (St Leon), *Oxon.* R. **D** Ox 5 *See* Haseley, Great.
WATERS UPTON (St Mich), *Salop.*. **D** Lich 21 *See* Upton Parva.
WATFORD (St Mary w St Jas), *Herts.* V. **D** St Alb 13 **P** *Ch Trust Fund Trust* **I** D C MOORE, D A JOHNSON *c*.
(Ch Ch), V. **D** St Alb 13 **P** *Bp, Patrons and V of St Andr, Watford* **I** R C LEWIS, J FERGUSON *c*, J S QUILL *c*.
(St Andr), V. **D** St Alb 13 **P** *Trustees* **I** N B MOORE.
(St Jas), V. **D** St Alb 13 *See* St Mary.
(St Jo Evang), V. **D** St Alb 13 **P** *Trustees* **I** R SALTER.
(St Luke), V. **D** St Alb 13 **P** *Bp, Archd of St Alb, V of Watford, Ch Trust Fund* **I** G G GUINNESS.
(St Mich AA), V. **D** St Alb 13 **P** *Bp* **I** J B BROWN, R F SIBSON *c*.
(St Pet), V. **D** St Alb 13 **P** *Bp* **I** F W MEAGER.
WATFORD, *Northants.*. **D** Pet 6 *See* Buckby, Long.
WATH (St Mary), *N Yorks.* R. **D** Ripon 2 *See* Kirklington.
WATH-ON-DEARNE (All SS) w Adwick-upon-Dearne (St Jo Bapt), *S Yorks.* V. **D** Sheff 10 **P** *D and C of Ch Ch Ox* **I** J R PACKER, J A MACKINNEY *c*.
WATLINGTON (St Pet and St Paul), *Norf.* R. **D** Ely 17 **P** *Ld Kenyon, Col Fitzhugh* **I** I R LILLEY *c-in-c*.
WATLINGTON (St Leon) w Pyrton and Shirburn, *Oxon.* V. **D** Ox 1 **P** *Bp, Earl of Macclesfield and D and C of Ch Ch Ox* **I** J M MATHER.
WATTISFIELD (St Marg), *Suff.* R. **D** St E 9 *See* Hinderclay.
WATTISHAM, *Suff.*. **D** St E *See* Bildeston.
WATTON (St Mary), *Norf.* V. **D** Nor 19 **P** *Ld Chan* **I** P E JEFFORD.
WATTON-AT-STONE (St Andr and St Mary), *Herts.* R. **D** St Alb 12 **P** *T Abel Smith Esq* **I** R A THOMSON.
WATTON (St Mary), w Beswick (St Marg) and Kilnwick, *Humb.* V. **D** York 13 **P** *Abp* **I** E LANGDON.
WAVENDON (Assump BVM) with Walton (St Mich), *Bucks.* R. **D** Ox 26 **P** *H P R Hoare Esq and Dioc Bd of Patr (alt)* **I** N J COTTON *p-in-c*.
WAVERTON (St Pet), *Chesh.* V. **D** Ches 5 **P** *Bp* **I** D R MARR.
WAVERTON, *Cumb.* V. **D** Carl 3 *See* Bromfield.
WAVERTREE (H Trin), *Mer.* R. **D** Liv 2 **P** *Bp* **I** R L METCALF, L B BRUCE *c*.
(St Bridget), V. **D** Liv 2 **P** *R of Wavertree* **I** G A RIPLEY, P B PRITCHARD *hon c*.
(St Mary), R. **D** Liv 2 **P** *Bp* **I** A J BELL.
(St Thos), V. **D** Liv 2 **P** *Simeon Trustees* **I** W HEWITT.
WAWNE or WAGHEN (St Pet), *Humb.*. **D** York 17 *See* Sutton-in-Holderness.
WAXHAM, GREAT (St John) w Palling (St Marg of Antioch), *Norf.* V. **D** Nor 9 **P** *Bp* **I** (Vacant).
WAYFIELD, *Kent.*. **D** Roch 3 *See* Walderslade.
WAYFORD (St Mich), *Somt.* R. **D** B & W 19 *See* Crewkerne.
WAYTHE, or WAITH (St Martin), *Lincs.* V. **D** Linc 10 **P** *Reps of Late C L Haigh Esq* **I** G L BIERLEY.
WEALD (St Geo), *Kent.* V. **D** Roch 7 **P** *R of Sevenoaks* **I** J E INGHAM.
WEALD, NORTH (St Andr), *Essex.* V. **D** Chelmsf 6 **P** *Bp and CPAS* alt **I** T C THORPE.
WEALD, SOUTH (St Pet), *Essex.* V. **D** Chelmsf 9 **P** *Bp* **I** B D CORNISH.
WEALDSTONE (H Trin), *Gtr Lon.* V. **D** Lon 24 **P** *Dioc Bd of Patr* **I** B T LLOYD, D C RUNCORN *c*. *See also* HARROW WEALD..
WEAR (St Luke), *Devon.*. **D** Ex 3 *See* Countess Wear.
WEARE (St Greg) w Badgworth and Biddisham, *Somt.* R. **D** B & W 2 **P** *Ld Chan and Bp of Lon (alt)* **I** G MILLIER.
WEARE GIFFARD (H Trin) w Landcross, *Devon.* R. **D** Ex 17 **P** *Bp* **I** P V SIMPSON *p-in-c*.
WEASENHAM (All SS w St Pet), *Norf.*. **D** Nor 20 *See* Tittleshall.
WEASTE, *Gtr Man.*. **D** Man 8 *See* Salford.
WEAVERHAM (St Mary Virg), *Chesh.* V. **D** Ches 6 **P** *Bp* **I** G F PARSONS.
WEAVERTHORPE (St Nich, formerly St Andr) w Helperthorpe (St Pet), Luttons Ambo (St Mary Virg) and Kirby Grindalythe (St Andr), *N Yorks.* V. **D** York 3 **P** *Abp 2 turns, D and C of York 1 turn* **I** C I M N SMITH.
WEBHEATH (St Phil), *Worcs.*. **D** Worc *See* The Ridge, Redditch.
WEDDINGTON (St Jas) and Caldecote, *Warws.* R. **D** Cov 5 **P** *G R Hall Esq* **I** G R CORNWALL-JONES.
WEDMORE (St Mary) w Theale (Ch Ch) and Blackford (H Trin), *Somt.* V. **D** B & W 1 **P** *Bp* **I** D R MILLER.
WEDNESBURY (St Bart), *W Midl.* V. **D** Lich 10 **P** *Bp* **I** G OWEN.
(St Jas Gt and St Jo Evang), R. **D** Lich **P** *Bp and Trustees* **I** I B COOK.
(St Paul), V. **D** Lich 10 **P** *Bp* **I** W J BUCKNALL, R B RALPHS *c*.
WEDNESFIELD (St Thos), *W Midl.* V. **D** Lich 12 **P** *Bp* **I** J N CRAIG, D J COOPER *team v*, G JOHNSON *team v*, G D L FREEMAN *c*.
(St Greg Gt), V. **D** Lich 12 **P** *Bp* **I** A W WARNER.

WEDNESFIELD HEATH, *W Midl.*. D Lich 12 *See* Heath Town.
WEEDON-BEC (St Pet and St Paul) w Everdon (St Mary BV), *Northants*. V. D Pet 3 P *Bp* I D W WITCHELL.
WEEDON LOIS (St Mary Virg and St w Plumpton and Moreton Pinkney (St Mary Virg), Virg) and Wappenham, *Northants*. V. D Pet 1 P *Bp, Jes Coll Ox and Or Coll Ox* I R W LEE.
WEEFORD (St Mary Virg), *Staffs*. R. D Lich 2 P *Bp* I P D BROTHWELL *p-in-c*.
WEEK ST MARY (Nativ of St Mary Virg), *Cornw*. R. D Truro 10 P *SS Coll Cam* I J G EDWARDS *p-in-c*.
WEEK or WYKE ST GERMANS, *Devon*. V. D Ex 22 *See* Broadwood Widger.
WEEKE or WYKE (St Matt), *Hants*. R. D Win 12 P *Bp* I J O C ALLEYNE, N W BIRKETT *c*, G F SHERWOOD *c*, R C STONE *c*.
WEEKLEY (St Mary Virg), *Northants*. V. D Pet 8 *See* Geddington.
WEELEY (St Andr) and Little Clacton, *Essex, R*. D Chelmsf 28 P *BNC Ox* I E W NUGENT.
WEETHLEY, *Warws*.. D Cov 7 *See* Alcester.
WEETING (All SS w St Mary), *Norf*. R. D Ely 16 P *G and C Coll Cam* I G H M WEBB.
WEETON (St Mich), *Lancs*. V. D Blackb 9 P *V of Kirkham* I K H GIBBONS *p-in-c*.
WEETON (St Barn), *N Yorks*. V. D Ripon *See* Kirkby Overblow.
WELBECK CHAPEL, *Notts*.. D Southw 7 *See* Norton Cuckney.
WELBORNE (All SS), *Norf*. R. D Nor 12 P *Bp* I P H MOSS *c-in-c*.
WELBOURN (St Chad), *Lincs*. R. D Linc 23 P *Hyndham Trustees and Lt-Col W Reeve* I (Vacant).
WELBURN (St Jo Evang), *N Yorks*. R. D York 4 *See* Bulmer.
WELBURY (St Leon), *N Yorks*. R. D York 23 *See* Rounton, West.
WELBY (St Bart), *Lincs*.. D Linc 19 *See* Heydour.
WELCOMBE, *Devon*.. D Ex *See* Hartland.
WELDON (St Mary Virg) w Deene (St Pet), *Northants*. R. D Pet 10 P *Earl of Winchelsea and Nottm and E Brudenell Esq* I R KIRKPATRICK.
WELFORD (St Mary Virg) w Sibbertoft (St Helen), *Northants*. V. D Pet 6 P *Bp* I M E YOUNG.
WELFORD (St Greg Gt) and Wickham (St Swithun) w Gt Shefford (St Mary), *Berks*. R. D Ox 14 P *Bp and Brasenose Coll Ox alt* I N C SANDS.
WELFORD (St Pet) w Weston (All SS) and Clifford Chambers (St Helen), *Warws*. R. D Glouc 12 P *Ld Sackville* I R FINCH *c*.
WELHAM (St Andr), *Leics*. V. D Leic 5 *See* Bowden, Great.
WELL (St Marg) *Lincs*. R. D Linc 8 P *Mrs S E Rawnsley* I G I GEORGE-JONES.
WELL (St Mich) w Snape (St Mary), *N Yorks*. V. D Ripon 3 *See* Tanfield West.
WELLAND, *Worcs*. V. D Worc 5 *See* Hanley Castle.
WELLESBOURNE MOUNTFORD w Wellesbourne Hastings (St Pet), *Warws*. V. D Cov 8 P *Ld Chan* I C C O BENNETT.
WELL HALL, *Kent*.. D S'wark 21 *See* Eltham.
WELLING (St John), *Kent*. V. D Roch 15 P *Bp* I P L TONG, R P FULLER *c*, R HERBERT *c*.
WELLING (St Mary Virg), *Kent*. V. D S'wark 17 P *Bp* I N WALTER, B O WRIGHT *hon c*.
WELLINGBOROUGH (All H), *Northants*. V. D Pet 7 P *Exors of Maj S Byng Madick* I E BUCHANAN, M HOUGHTON *c*.
(All SS), V. D Pet 7 P *V of Wellingborough* I (Vacant).
(St Andr), V. D Pet 7 P *Bp* I C I PRITCHARD.
(St Barn), V. D Pet 7 P *Bp* I C W RYLAND.
(St Mark), V. D Pet 7 P *Bp* I D A BOWLES.
(St Mary), V. D Pet 7 P *Guild of All S* I T FINCH.
WELLINGHAM (St Andr), *Norf*.. D Nor 20 *See* Tittleshall.
WELLINGORE (All SS) *Lincs*.. D Linc *See* Graffoe.
WELLINGTON and District, Wellington (St Jo Bapt and All SS), West Buckland (BVM and H Trin), Nynehead (All SS), Thorne St Margaret and Sampford Arundel, *Somt*. R. D B & W 22 P *Dioc Bd of Patr* I J T GEORGE, J D FOWLER *team v*, R E PITT *team v*, C E ROLFE *team v*, G R TODD *c*.
WELLINGTON (St Mary) w Moreton-on-Lugg (St Andr) w Pipe and Lyde, *Herefs*. V. D Heref 4 P *Bp 1st turn, S of Faith 2nd turn and D and C of Heref 3rd turn* I W P JOHNS P-IN-C OF FORD.
WELLINGTON, *Staffs*.. D Lich 18 *See* Hanley.
WELLINGTON (All SS) w Eyton (St Cath), *Salop*. V. D Lich 27 P *Ch Trust* I J C DUXBURY.
(Ch Ch), V. D Lich 27 P *V of Wellington* I T C SMYTH.
WELLINGTON HEATH (Ch Ch), *Herefs*. V. D Heref 6 P *Bp* I M H CROSS *p-in-c*.
WELLOW (St Julian), *Avon*. V. D B & W *See* Peasedown St John.
WELLOW (St Swith), *Notts*. V. D Southw 7 P *Bp* I T W SWIFT.
WELLOW, E and W (St Marg), *Hants* V. D Win 10 P *Bp* I D BLAIR-BROWN, C B FIRTH *hon c*.
WELLS (St Cuthb) w Coxley (Ch Ch) and Wookey Hole (St Mary Magd), *Somt*.. D B & W 6 P *D and C of Wells* I K W DAVIS, D RODGERS *c*.
(St Thos) w Horrington, V. D B & W 6 P *D and C of Wells* I C T TOOKEY.
WELLS-NEXT-THE-SEA (St Nich), *Norf*. R (*in Wells Group - See also Holkham, Warham*).. D Nor 21 P *Mrs Beddard and W A Williamson Esq* I D J CHAPMAN.
WELNEY (St Mary), *Norf*.. D Ely 19 P *Bp* I (Vacant).
WELSH BICKNOR (St Marg), *Herefs*. R. D Heref 8 *See* Goodrich.
WELSH FRANKTON (St Andr), *Salop*. V. D Lich 24 P *Bp* I N A FENN.
WELSHAMPTON (St Mich), *Salop*. V. D Lich 22 P *Trustees* I (Vacant).
WELSH NEWTON (St Mary B Virg) w Llanrothal, *Herefs*. R. D Heref 8 P *Bp* I J R JACKSON *p-in-c*.
WELTON (St Jas Chap), *Cumb*.. D Carl 3 *See* Rosley-w-Woodside.
WELTON (St Martin) w Ashby St Ledgers (BVM and St Leodegarius), *Northants*. V. D Pet 3 P *Bp, Visc Wimborne and Exors of W A Coleman* in turn I T P HAMERTON.
WELTON (St Helen) w Melton, *Humb*. V. D York 17 P *Admin of J B Harrison-Broadley Esq* I J A SLATER.
WELTON-LE-MARSH (St Martin), V w Gunby (St Pet), *Lincs*. R. D Linc 8 P *J M Montgomery-Massingberd Esq* I R H IRESON.
WELTON ST MARY (St Mary), *Lincs*. V. D Linc 3 P *Bp* I B J P PRITCHARD.
WELWICK (St Mary) w Holmpton (St Nich), *Humb*. V. D York 15 *See* Hollym.
WELWYN (St Mary Virg) w Ayot St Peter, *Herts*. R. D St Alb 7 P *All S Coll Ox* I J T WENHAM, P C S ABEYWARDENA *c*, W G BRYANT *c*.
WELWYN GARDEN CITY (St Francis of Assisi), *Herts*. V. D St Alb 7 P *Bp* I T L JONES, P H JOHNSON *c*.
WEM (St Pet and St Paul), *Salop*. R. D Lich 27 P *Ld Barnard* I N MACGREGOR, R J RANFORD *c*.
WEMBDON (St Geo), *Somt*. V. D B & W 17 P *Ch S Trust* I A P BANNISTER.
WEMBLEY (St Jo Evang), *Gtr Lon*. V. D Lon 18 P *CPS* I B B MOORE.
(Ascen), V. D Lon 18 P *Bp* I (Vacant).
WEMBLEY, NORTH (St Cuthb), *Gtr Lon*. V. D Lon 18 P *Bp* I T H COMLEY, E L R SMITH *c*.
WEMBLEY PARK (St Aug), *Gtr Lon*. V. D Lon 18 P *Bp* I J C BROADHURST *c-in-c*, M D WAY *hon c*.
WEMBURY (St Werburgh), *Devon*. V. D Ex 21 P *D and C of Windsor* I A K F MACEY.
WEMBWORTHY (St Mich), *Devon*. R. D Ex 16 P *Bp of Ex, Earl of Portsm and G E Cruwys jointly (1) D and C Exon (2) Bp of Ex (3)* I V J R RICHARDS *p-in-c*.
WENDENS AMBO, *Essex*.. D Chelmsf 27 *See* Saffron Walden.
WENDLEBURY, *Oxon*.. D Ox 2 *See* Chesterton, Gt.
WENDLING (St Pet and St Paul), *Norf*. V. D Nor 20 *See* Scarning.
WENDON LOFTS (St Dunstan), *Essex*. R. D Chelmsf *See* Elmdon.
WENDOVER (St Mary Virg), *Bucks*. V. D Ox 30 P *Ld Chan* I A F MEYNELL, P D F HORNER *c*.
WENDRON, ST (St Wendrona), *Cornw*. V. D Truro 4 P *S for Maint of Faith* I W J F GRIGG *p-in-c*.
WENDY (All SS) w Shingay, *Cambs*. V (*in Shingay Group - See also Croydon w Clopton; Guilden Morden; Litlington w Abington Pigotts; Steeple Morden: Tadlow*). D Ely 8 P *CPS* I S BRIDGE *p-in-c*.
WENHAM, GREAT (St Jo Evang), *Suff*. R. D St E 3 *See* Holton St Mary.
WENHAM, LITTLE, *Suff*.. D St E 5 *See* Capel St Mary.
WENHASTON (St Pet) w Thorington and Bramfield w Walpole, *Suff*. V. D St E 15 P *CPS 1 turn, Ld Chan 3 turns* I J E MURRELL.
WENLOCK (Cressage, Shenton, Harley, Kenley, Hughley, Church Preen, Much Wenlock, Bourton, Shipton, and Long Stanton w Easthope), *Salop*. R. D Heref P *Bp, Mary Juliana Motley, D and C of Heref, A Curry Esq, Sir*

J More, Ld Barnard and Mrs E A Bird I M THOMAS, F G R DEACON *team v*, A B GRUNDY *team v*.
WENLOCK, LITTLE (St Lawr), *Salop*. R. D Heref 14 *See* Coalbrookdale.
WENNINGTON (St Mary and St Pet), *Essex*. R. D Chelmsf 4 P *MMT* I P W L RATCLIFFE.
WENSLEY (H Trin), *N Yorks*. R. D Ripon 2 P *Ld Bolton* I (Vacant).
WENTBRIDGE (St Jo Evang), *W Yorks*. V. D Wakef 11 *See* Darrington.
WENTNOR (St Mich AA) and Ratlinghope w Myndtown and Norbury, *Salop*. R. D Heref 10 P *Ch Ch Ox 2 turns Publ Trustees 1 turn* I F J CARLOS.
WENTWORTH, *Cambs*.. D Ely 15 *See* Witchford.
WENTWORTH (H Trin), *S Yorks*. V. D Sheff 10 P *Earl FitzWilliam* I C M A DAWSON.
WEOBLEY (St Pet and St Paul) w Sarnesfield, *Herefs*. V. D Heref 5 P *R A Marshall Esq 1 turn, Bp 2 turns* I S C SNEYD P-IN-C OF NORTON CANON, A LORD *c*.
WEOLEY CASTLE (St Gabr), *W Midl*. V. D Birm 2 P *Bp* I M D CASTLE, D P BYRNE *c*.
WEREHAM, *Norf*.. D Ely 16 *See* Fincham.
WERNETH or COMPSTALL (St Paul), *Gtr Man*. V. D Ches 16 P *Trustees* I G L CROSLAND, H BATTERSBY *c*.
WERNETH, *Gtr Man*.. D Man 15 *See* Oldham.
WERRINGTON (St Phil), *Staffs*. V. D Lich 18 P *V of Caverswall* I T THAKE.
WERRINGTON (St Jo Bapt), *Cambs*. V. D Pet 14 P *Bp* I J R LITTLEWOOD, D H P FOOT *c*.
WERRINGTON (St Martin of Tours) w St Giles in the Heath and Virginstow, *Devon*. V. D Truro 11 P *A M Williams Esq* I V J E BOATRIGHT.
WESHAM (Ch Ch), *Lancs*. V. D Blackb 9 P *V of Kirkham* I C BIRKET.
WESSINGTON (Ch Ch) w Brackenfield (H Trin), *Derbys*. V. D Derby 1 P *V of Crich and Trustees* I J H WATTS P IN C OF WESSINGTON.
WEST BAY, *Dorset*.. D Sarum 2 *See* Bridport St Mary.
WEST BROMWICH (All SS), *W Midl*. V. D Lich 11 P *Bp* I D EDE, R N ARMITAGE *c*, P H MYERS *c*, D J H JONES *hon c*.
(Ch Ch), V. D Lich P *Bp* I D J BELCHER *p-in-c*.
(Ch of Good Shepherd w St Jo Evang), V. D Lich 11 P *Bp* I S BAILEY.
(H Trin), V. D Lich 11 P *Peache Trustees* I J T GLOVER.
(St Andr and St Mich), V. D Lich 11 P *V of W Bromwich* I P A R HAMMERSLEY *p-in-c*.
(St Jas), V. D Lich 11 P *Bp* I M J LEWIS.
(St Paul, Golds Hill), V. D Lich 11 P *V of Tipton* I D M K DURSTON *p-in-c*.
(St Pet), V. D Lich 11 P *Bp* I P LOCKETT *p-in-c*.
(St Phil), V. D Lich 11 P *Bp* I S BAILEY *p-in-c*.
(St Francis, Friar Park), V. D Lich 11 P *Bp* I A J JONES, D I STANDEN *c*.
WEST CLIFFE (St Pet), *Kent*.. D Cant 5 *See* St Margaret-at-Cliffe.
WEST DERBY (St Mary), *Mer*. R. D Liv 6 P *Bp* I A G MYERS, HUMPHREYS *team v*, A ALKER *c*.
(Ch Ch Kensington), V. D Liv 4 *See* Edge Hill.
(Ch of Good Shepherd), V. D Liv 6 P *Bp and R of W Derby* I (Vacant).
(St Jas), V. D Liv 6 P *Trustees* I W N LETHEREN.
(St Luke), V. D Liv 6 P *Bp* I M H HUNT, R J HILL *c*.
(St Paul Ap Croxteth), V. D Liv 6 P *Bp and I of Good Shepherd W Derby* I I G BROOKS *min*.
WEST DRAYTON (St Paul), *Notts*.. D Southw *See* Gamston.
WEST DRAYTON (St Martin), *Gtr Lon*. V. D Lon 19 P *Bp* I P D GOODRIDGE, W G RAINES *c*.
WEST END (H Trin), *Surrey*.. D Guildf 5a *See* Bisley.
WEST END (St Jas), *Hants*. V. D Win 15 P *Bp* I G ROWSTON.
WEST END or THRUSCROSS (H Trin), *N Yorks*.. D Ripon *See* Thruscross.
WEST EXE (St Paul), *Devon*.. D Ex 8 *See* Tiverton.
WEST FELTON (St Mich), *Salop*. R. D Lich 24 P *Bp* I J F G TALBOT.
WEST GREEN (Ch Ch). D Lon 27a *See* Tottenham.
WEST HALLAM (St Wilfrid) w Mapperley (H Trin), *Derbys*. R. D Derby 13 P *Bp* I F SMITH.
WEST HAM, *Essex*.. D Chelmsf 5 *See* Ham, West.
WEST HEATH (St Anne's), *W Midl*. V. D Birm 4 P *Bp* I B GREEN, A H W DOLMAN *c*.
WEST HILL (St Mich AA), *Devon*. V. D Ex 7 P *V of Ottery* I F G DENMAN *p-in-c*.
WEST HOE (St Mich). D Ex 23 *See* Plymouth.
WEST HYTHE, *Kent*. V. D Cant 11 *See* Lympne.
WEST-ITCHENOR (St Nich), *W Sussex*. R. D Chich 3 *See* Birdham.
WEST KIRBY (St Bridget), *Mer*. R. D Ches 8 P *D and C of Ches* I D M FERRIDAY, R G J HERRON *c*, A V MCKINNON *c*, A E D MURDOCH *c*.
(St Andr), V. D Ches 8 P *D and C of Ches* I B L BARNBY.
WEST MARSH (St Paul), *Humb*.. D Linc 29 *See* Grimsby.
WEST MEON (St Jo Evang) w Warnford (Our Lady), *Hants*. R. D Portsm 4 P *Bp and Dioc Bd of Patr* I K C A WILLS.
WEST MOORS (St Mary Virg), *Dorset*. V. D Sarum 11 P *Bp* I N W TAYLOR.
WEST TOWN (St Matt), *W Yorks*. V. D Wakef 5 *See* Dewsbury.
WEST VALE, *W Yorks*. V. D Wakef 2 *See* Greetland.
WEST ROW (St Pet), *Suff*,. D St E *See* Barton-Mills.
WEST WICKHAM Kent. D Cant 11 *See* Wickham West.
WEST WYCOMBE Bucks. D Ox 32 *See* Wycombe, West.
WESTACRE (All SS), *Norf*. V. D Nor 25 P *H Birkbeck Esq* I J P GRANT *p-in-c*.
WESTBERE (All SS) w Hersden (St Alb), *Kent*. R. D Cant 3 *See* Sturry.
WESTBOROUGH (All SS), R 1st Mediety w Dry Doddington (St Jas) V 2nd Mediety, and Stubton R, *Lincs*.. D Linc *See* Claypole.
WESTBOURNE (St Jo Bapt), *W Sussex*. R. D Chich 8 P *Bp* I P M BADEN.
WESTBOURNE, *Dorset*.. D Win 7 *See* Bournemouth.
WESTBOURNE PARK. D Lon 16 *See* Paddington.
WESTBURY (St Mary), *Salop*. V. D Heref 13 P *Bp* I (Vacant).
WESTBURY (St Aug of Cant), w Turweston (St Mary) Shalstone and Biddlesden, *Bucks*. V. D Ox 23 P *Bp, D and C of Westmr, Mrs M L G Purefoy and Execs of Lt Col T R Badger* I J G HARFORD.
WESTBURY (All SS) w Westbury Leigh (Ch of the H Sav) and Dilton (St Mary), *Wilts*. V. D Sarum 22 P *Bp* I M J FLIGHT.
WESTBURY-ON-SEVERN (St Pet and St Paul) w Flaxley (St Mary Virg) and Blaisdon (St Mich), *Glos*. V. D Glouc 6 P *Sir T M Boevey Bt and D and C of Heref* I J W THORPE, J L MAGEE *c*.
WESTBURY-ON-TRYM (H Trin) w Southmead Miss, *Avon*. V. D Bris 6 P *S for Maint of Faith* I P E HAWKINS, C L MACDONNELL *c*.
WESTBURY PARK (St Alb). D Bris 5 *See* Clifton.
WESTBURY-SUB-MENDIP (St Lawr) w Easton (St Paul), *Somt*. V. D B & W 1 P *Bp* I M J WYNES.
WESTBY, *Lincs*.. D Linc 2 *See* Ingoldsby.
WESTCLIFF-ON-SEA (St Alb), *Essex*. V. D Chelmsf 11 P *Bp* I R B WHITE *p-in-c*.
(St Andr), V. D Chelmsf 11 P *Bp* I A CORNISH.
(St Cedd & the Saints of Essex), V. D Chelmsf 11 P *Bp* I D E COOPER.
(St Mich AA), V. D Chelmsf 11 P *Bp* I F C V PRANCE.
(St Paul), V. D Chelmsf 11 *See* Prittlewell.
(St Sav), V. D Chelmsf 11 P *Bp, Archd and Wardens* I C J SLY, S A R BURCH *c*.
WESTCOMBE PARK (St Geo), *Kent*. V. D S'wark 17 P *CPAS* I M C FREEMAN.
WESTCOTE BARTON (St Edw Conf) w Steeple Barton (St Mary) Duns Tew and Sandford St Martin, *Oxon*. R. D Ox 10 P *Bp, Duke of Marlborough, Dioc Bd of Patr, Mrs C M Webb and Mrs S C Rittson-Thomas* I P P DANCE.
WESTCOTE (St Mary BV) w Icomb (St Mary) and Bledington, *Glos*. R. D Glouc 16 P *D and C of Worc 1st turn, D and C of Ch Ch Ox 2nd turn and Bp 3rd turn* I N J LEADBEATER.
WESTCOTT (H Trin), *Surrey*. V. D Guildf 6 P *Mrs N Barclay* I J D H WEYMAN.
WESTERDALE (Ch,Ch), *N Yorks*. V. D York 27 P *Abp* I (Vacant).
WESTERFIELD (St Mary Magd) w Tuddenham (St Martin), *Suff*. R. D St E 4 P *Bp and Dioc Bd of Patr* alt I H LUNNEY *p-in-c*.
WESTERHAM (St Mary), *Kent*. V. D Roch 7 P *Maj J O'B Warde* I A MCCABE.
WESTERLEIGH (St Jas Gt), *Avon*.. D Bris *See* Yate New Town.
WESTFIELD (St Pet), *Somt*. V. D B & W 16b P *Bp* I A V SAUNDERS.
WESTFIELD (St Mary), *Cumb*.. D Carl 8 *See* Workington.
WESTFIELD (St Jo Bapt), *E Sussex*. V. D Chich 22 P *Bp* I E WILKINSON.
WESTFIELD (St Andr), *Norf*. V. D Nor 12 *See* Whinburgh.
WESTGATE-IN-WEARDALE (St Andr), *Durham*. V. D Dur 13 P *Bp* I C SMITH.

WESTWOOD (St Mary Virg), *Wilts.* V. **D** Sarum 24 **P** *D and C of Bris* **I** (Vacant).

WESTWOOD CHAPEL (St Paul), *Devon..* **D** Ex 1 *See* Broad Clyst.

WETHERAL (H Trin) w Warwick (St Leon), *Cumb.* R. **D** Carl 2 **P** *D and C of Carl* **I** (Vacant).

WETHERBY (St Jas), *W Yorks.* V. **D** Ripon 4 **P** *Bp* **I** M GREEN *c.*

WETHERDEN, *Suff..* **D** St E *See* Haughley.

WETHERINGSETT, *Suff..* **D** St E *See* Stoke Ash.

WETHERSFIELD (St Mary Magd and St Mary Virg) w Shalford (St Andr), *Essex.* V. **D** Chelmsf 19 **P** *Bp* **I** A J IRWIN.

WETLEY ROCKS (St Jo Evang), *Staffs.* V. **D** Lich 16 **P** *Bp* **I** D R WHITELEY.

WETMOOR (St Mary), *Staffs..* **D** Lich 8 *See* Stretton.

WETTENHALL (St D), *Chesh..* **D** Ches 5 *See* Tilstone Fearnall.

WETTON (St Marg), *Staffs.* V. **D** Lich 13 **P** *C W W Blackett Esq* **I** J W HAMPTON *p-in-c.*

WETWANG (St Nich now called St Mich), *Humb.* V. **D** York 13 *See* Sledmere.

WEXCOMBE (Burbage, Chute w Chute Forest, The Collingbournes and Everleigh, East Grafton w Tidcombe and Fosbury, Shalbourne and Ham), *Wilts.* R. **D** Sarum **P** *D and C of Sarum, Windsor and Win, MMT and V of Gt Bedwyn* **I** M A WARD, J D ANDERSON *team v,* A BEARDSMORE *team v,* P N RAPSEY *team v.*

WEXHAM (St Mary), *Bucks.* R. **D** Ox 24 **P** *Ld Chan* **I** J E A SMITH, T R BOYLE *c.*

WEYBOURNE (All SS) w U Sheringham (All SS), *Norf.* V. **D** Nor 24 **P** *Bp of Nor, Bp of Liv and Ld Walpole (in turn)* **I** H OLDALE, F N WARD *hon c.*

WEYBREAD (St Andr), *Suff.* V. **D** St E 17 *See* Fressingfield.

WEYBRIDGE (St Jas w St Mich AA), *Surrey.* R. **D** Guildf 8 **P** *Ld Chan* **I** M R BUCKLEY, J P CRESSWELL *c.*

WEYHILL or Penton Grafton (St Mich AA) and Penton Mewsey, *Hants.* R. **D** Win *See* Hatherden.

WEYMOUTH (St Mary, Melcombe Regis), *Dorset..* **D** Sarum 6 *See* Radipole.

(H Trin w St Martin and St Nich), V. **D** Sarum 6 **P** *Bp* **I** G E WALTON, G R TRISTRAM *c,* B WAKELING *c.*

(St Jo Evang), V. **D** Sarum 6 *See* Radipole.

(St Paul), V. **D** Sarum 6 **P** *Bp* **I** D J GREEN, D B FISHER *c.*

(St Edm of Cant), V. **D** Sarum 6 **P** *R of Wyke Regis* **I** J R ADAMS *p-in-c.*

WHADDON (St Mary Virg), *Cambs.* V. **D** Ely 8 **P** *D and C of Windsor and D and C of Westmr* alt **I** J F AITCHISON.

WHADDON (St Marg), *Glos..* **D** Glouc 3 *See* Brookthorpe.

WHADDON (St Mary) w Tattenhoe (St Giles), *Bucks.* V. **D** Ox 27 *See* Newton Longville.

WHADDON, *Wilts..* **D** Sarum 24 *See* Hilperton.

WHALEY THORNS (St Luke), *Notts..* **D** Derby *See* Langwith, Upper.

WHALLEY (St Mary Virg and All SS), *Lancs.* V. **D** Blackb 7 **P** *Hulme Trustees* **I** J M C ACKROYD, G A PARKER *c.*

WHALLEY RANGE (St Marg), *Gtr Man.* R. **D** Man 5 **P** *Trustees* **I** R H HAMILTON.

(St Edm K and Mart), R. **D** Man 5 **P** *Simeon Trustees* **I** D J CASIOT.

WHALTON, *Northumb.* R. **D** Newc T 10 *See* Bolam.

WHAPLODE (St Mary), *Lincs.* V. **D** Linc 16 **P** *Ld Chan* **I** L H N CARTER.

WHAPLODE DROVE (St Jo Bapt), *Lincs.* V. **D** Linc 16 **P** *Feoffees* **I** O G FOLKARD.

WHARRAM, *N Yorks.* V. **D** York 3 *See* Settrington.

WHARTON (Ch Ch), *Chesh.* V. **D** Ches 6 **P** *R of Davenham* **I** J A MINNS.

WHARTON, *Lincs..* **D** Linc 2 *See* Blyton.

WHATCOTE (St Pet), *Warws..* **D** Cov 9 **P** *Dioc Bd of Patr* **I** D R S JEPHSON.

WHATFIELD (St Marg) w Semer, *Suff.* R. **D** St E 3 **P** *Jes Coll Cam 2 turns, H T S Ball Esq and Mrs Morgan 1 turn* **I** B W HAZLEDINE.

WHATLEY w Chantry, *Somt..* **D** B & W *See* Mells.

WHATLINGTON (St Mary Magd), *E Sussex.* R. **D** Chich 17 *See* Sedlescombe.

WHATTON-IN-THE-VALE (St John of Beverley) w Aslockton (St Thos), *Notts.* V. **D** Southw 9 **P** *D and C of Linc and Miss E Player* alt **I** S F RISING.

WHATTON, LONG (All SS) and Diseworth (St Mich AA), *Leics.* R. **D** Leic 10 **P** *Ld Chan 2 turns, Christ's Hosp and Haberdashers' Co 1 turn each* **I** A R H GREAVES.

WHEATACRE (All SS), *Suff.* R. **D** Nor 14 *See* Aldeby.

WHEATACRE-BURGH, *Norf..* **D** Nor *See* Burgh St Peter.

WHEATFIELD, *Oxon..* **D** Ox *See* Stoke Talmage.

WHEATHAMPSTEAD (St Helen), *Herts.* R. **D** St Alb 14 **P** *Bp* **I** T PURCHAS, J J THROSSELL *c.*

WHEATHILL, *Salop.* **D** Heref *See* Aston Botterell.

WHEATLEY (St Mary) w Forest Hill and Stanton St John, *Oxon.* V. **D** Ox **P** *Bp 1st turn, Linc Coll Ox 2nd turn and New Coll Ox 3rd turn* **I** F G SELBY *hon c.*

WHEATLEY HILL (All SS), *Durham.* V. **D** Dur 3 **P** *Bp* **I** T W THUBRON.

WHEATLEY, NORTH w South and West Burton (St Pet and St Paul), *Notts.* R. **D** Southw 5 **P** *Ld Middleton* **I** A BUTT.

WHEATON ASTON (St Mary), *Staffs..* **D** Lich 3 *See* Lapley.

WHEELOCK (Ch Ch), *Chesh.* V. **D** Ches 11 **P** *V of Sandbach* **I** P D BRADBROOK.

WHELDRAKE (St Helen), *N Yorks.* R. **D** York 6 **P** *Abp* **I** J C P COCKERTON.

WHELFORD (St Ann), *Glos..* **D** Glouc 14 *See* Kempsford.

WHELNETHAM, GREAT (St Thos à Becket), w Little Whelnetham (St Mary Magd), *Suff.* R. **D** St E 10 **P** *Bp 2 turns, Marchioness of Bris 1 turn* **I** J M COOK *p-in-c.*

WHENBY (St Martin), *N Yorks.* V. **D** York 21 *See* Dalby.

WHEPSTEAD (St Petronilla) w Brockley (St Andr), *Suff..* **D** St E 13 *See* Chevington.

WHERSTEAD (St Mary), *Suff.* V. **D** St E 5 **P** *MMT* **I** J D YATES *p-in-c.*

WHERWELL (St Pet and H Cross), *Hants.* V. **D** Win 2 *See* Chilbolton.

WHETSTONE (St Pet), *Leics.* V. **D** Leic 13 **P** *Bp* **I** K L ADLINGTON.

WHETSTONE (St Jo Ap), *Gtr Lon.* V. **D** Lon 16 **P** *Bp* **I** S J TERRY.

WHICHAM (St Mary) w Whitbeck, *Cumb.* R. **D** Carl 12 *See* Bootle.

WHICHFORD (St Mich), *Warws.* R. **D** Cov 9 **P** *Ch Ch Ox* **I** E J RAINSBERRY.

WHICKHAM or WICKHAM (St Mary), *T & W.* R. **D** Dur 1 **P** *Crown* **I** A J MEAKIN, M BUTLER *c.*

WHILTON, *Northants.* R. **D** Pet 3 *See* Brington.

WHIMPLE (St Mary), *Devon.* R. **D** Ex 1 **P** *D and C of Ex* **I** H G TUCKER.

WHINBURGH (St Mary) w Westfield (St Andr), *Norf.* R. **D** Nor 12 **P** *Ch S Trust* **I** A G N DAYNES *p-in-c.*

WHIPPINGHAM (St Mildred), *Isle of Wight..* **D** Portsm 7 *See* Cowes, East.

WHIPSNADE (St Mary Magd), *Beds.* R. **D** St Alb 18 *See* Studham.

WHIPTON (St Bonif), *Devon.* V. **D** Ex 3 **P** *Bp* **I** D MCCULLOCH, A G CANNON *hon c.*

WHISBY, *Lincs..* **D** Linc 6 *See* Doddington.

WHISSENDINE (St Andr), *Leics.* V. **D** Pet 12 *See* Teigh.

WHISSONSETT (St Mary) w Horningtoft (St Edm), *Norf.* R. **D** Nor 20 *See* Colkirk.

WHISTON (St Nich), *Mer.* V. **D** Liv 10 **P** *V of Prescot* **I** E MITCHELL.

WHISTON (St Mary Virg), *Northants.* R. **D** Pet 4 **P** *Marq of Northn* **I** J M OULESS.

WHISTON (St Mary Magd or St Jas), *S Yorks.* R. **D** Sheff 6 **P** *Bp* **I** G C M MILLS.

WHITBECK (St Mary), *Cumb.* V. **D** Carl 12 *See* Whicham.

WHITBOURNE (St Jo Bapt), *Herefs.* R. **D** Heref 2 **P** *Bp* **I** R J COLBY *p-in-c.*

WHITBURN (Dedic unknown), *T & W.* R. **D** Dur 8 **P** *Bp* **I** H H S L HALL *c-in-c.*

WHITBY (St Mary w St Mich, St Jo Evang, St Ninian, Baxtergate, and St Hilda), *N Yorks.* R. **D** York 27 **P** *Abp* **I** J C PENNISTON.

WHITCHURCH (St Nich), *Avon.* V. **D** Bris 2 **P** *Bp and Earl Temple* alt **I** R H CRAIG, N D TOOTH *c.*

WHITCHURCH (St Mary BV), *Warws..* **D** Cov 8 *See* Preston-on-Stour.

WHITCHURCH (St Andr), *Devon.* V. **D** Ex 22 **P** *Bp* **I** I F T MORSHEAD.

WHITCHURCH (St Dubricius) w Ganarew (St Swith), *Herefs.* R. **D** Heref 8 **P** *Bp* **I** T F HORSINGTON *p-in-c,* S F D PARRETT *c.*

WHITCHURCH (St Lawr), *Gtr Lon..* **D** Lon 23 *See* Stanmore, Little.

WHITCHURCH (St Mary Virg w St Jo Bapt), *Oxon.* R. **D** Ox 7 **P** *Bp* **I** R M HUGHES.

WHITCHURCH (St Jo Evang) w Creslow, *Bucks.* V. **D** Ox *See* Schorne.

WHITCHURCH (All H) w Tufton and Litchfield (St Jas L), *Hants.* V. **D** Win 5 **P** *Bp 3 turns, T G Harding Esq 1 turn* **I** D L J WARNER.

WHITCHURCH (St Alkmund) w Dodington, *Salop*. R. **D** Lich 27 **P** *Ld Brownlow* **I** R D JENKINS.
WHITCHURCH CANONICORUM (St Candida w H Cross) w Stanton-St-Gabr (St Gabr), Wootton Fitzpaine and Monkton Wyld, *Dorset*. V. **D** Sarum 2 **P** *Bp* **I** J AFFLECK *p-in-c*, L T S SIMS-WILLIAMS *hon c*.
WHITCOMBE (Dedic unknown), *Dorset*. V. **D** Sarum 5 *See* Winterbourne Came.
WHITE CITY ESTATE. **D** Lon *See* Hammersmith.
WHITE COLNE (St Andr), *Essex*. V. **D** Chelmsf 24 **P** *Keble Coll Ox* **I** A S J HOLDEN.
WHITE LADIES ASTON (St Jo Bapt) w Churchill (St Mich) and Spetchley, *Worcs*. V. **D** Worc 3 *See* Peopleton.
WHITE LION STREET (All SS Miss). **D** Lon 6 *See* Islington.
WHITE RODING (St Martin), *Essex*. R. **D** Chelmsf 23 **P** *Sir P Maryon-Wilson* **I** E W C EXELL.
WHITECHAPEL (St Jas), *Lancs*. V. **D** Blackb 10 **P** *Bp* **I** A H BENNETT.
WHITECHAPEL (St Geo-in-the-East w St Paul, Dock Street), *Lon*. R. **D** Lon 4 **P** *Bp* **I** U E E J SCHARF, D R STOKES *c*, M J W COOK *hon c*.
WHITECHAPEL, *W Yorks*.. **D** Wakef 4 *See* Cleckheaton.
WHITEGATE (St Mary Virg) w Little Budworth (St Pet), *Chesh*. V. **D** Ches 6 **P** *Ld Delamere & Bp* **I** D A D SMITH.
WHITEHALL PARK (St Andr).. **D** Lon 6 *See* Holloway, Upper.
WHITEHAVEN (St Jas Gt), *Cumb*. V. **D** Carl 12 **P** *Patr Committee* **I** A J POSTLETHWAITE, C GODDARD *c*.
(St Pet Kells), V. **D** Carl 12 **P** *Bp* **I** M R BRAITHWAITE, P M BROAD *c*.
(St Andr Mirehouse), V. **D** Carl 12 **P** *Bp* **I** E F H GRIMSHAW.
WHITEHAWK (St Cuthman), *W Sussex*. V. **D** Chich 14a **P** *Bp* **I** T B H HALL *p-in-c*.
WHITELACKINGTON (St Mary Virg), *Somt*. V. **D** B & W 20 *See* Ilminster.
WHITEPARISH (All SS), *Wilts*. V. **D** Sarum 17 **P** *Bp* **I** R KEELEY.
WHITESHILL (St Paul), *Glos*. V. **D** Glouc 4 **P** *Bp* **I** L S ROSE.
WHITESTAUNTON (St Andr), *Somt*. R. **D** B & W 19 **P** *Group-Captain N W D Marwood-Elton* **I** (Vacant).
WHITESTONE (St Kath) w Oldridge (St Thomas), *Devon*. R. **D** Ex 6 **P** *Em Coll Cam* **I** R S HAWKINS *p-in-c*.
WHITEWELL (St Mich), *Lancs*. V. **D** Blackb 7 **P** *Hulme Trustees* **I** G R WOOD *p-in-c*.
WHITEWELL (St Mary), *Salop*.. **D** Ches *See* Tushingham.
WHITFIELD or BEAUXFIELD w Guston, *Kent*. V. **D** Cant 5 **P** *Abp and D and C of Cant (alt)* **I** J W PHILPOTT.
WHITFIELD (St Jas Gt), *Derbys*. V. **D** Derby 5 **P** *Bp* **I** A BUCKLEY *p-in-c*.
WHITFIELD, *Northumb*. R. **D** Newc T 4 *See* Allendale.
WHITFIELD (St Jo Evang), *Northants*. R. **D** Pet 1 *See* Syresham.
WHITGIFT (St Mary Magd) w Adlingfleet (All SS) and Eastoft (St Bart), *Humb*. V. **D** Sheff 9 **P** *Ld Chan and Bp* alt **I** P S LINDECK.
WHITINGTON, *Norf*. V. **D** Ely 16 **P** *CPS* **I** F CHADWICK.
WHITKIRK (St Mary), *W Yorks*. V. **D** Ripon 7 **P** *Meynell Trustees* **I** M O HUNTER, J F HAMILTON *c*, J F WALKER *c*.
WHITLEIGH (St Chad), *Devon*. V. **D** Ex 23 **P** *Bp* **I** A V CAMPBELL, T R DEACON *c*.
WHITLEY (St Jas), *W Midl*. V. **D** Cov 1 **P** *Bp* **I** (Vacant).
WHITLEY or HEXHAMSHIRE (St Helen), *Northumb*. V. **D** Newc T 4 **P** *Bp* **I** P MOORE.
WHITLEY (Ch Ch), *Berks*. V. **D** Ox 15 *See* Reading (Ch Ch).
WHITLEY, *Wilts*. V. **D** Sarum 24 *See* Shaw (Ch Ch).
WHITLEY (All SS), *N Yorks*.. **D** Wakef 11 *See* Kellington.
WHITLEY, LOWER (St Mary and St Mich), *S Yorks*. V. **D** Wakef 10 **P** *Ld Savile* **I** N D J WEBB.
WHITLEY, NETHER or LOWER (St Luke), *Chesh*. V. **D** Ches *See* Leigh, Little.
WHITLEY BAY, *T & W*.. **D** Newc T *See* Cullercoats.
WHITLINGHAM, *Norf*.. **D** Nor 14 *See* Kirby Bedon.
WHITMINSTER or WHEATENHURST, *Glos*.. **D** Glouc *See* Frampton-on-Severn.
WHITMORE (St Mary and All SS), *Staffs*. R. **D** Lich 19 **P** *R Cavenagh-Mainwaring Esq* **I** J D D PORTER *p-in-c*.
WHITNASH (St Marg), *Warws*. R. **D** Cov 15 **P** *Ld Leigh* **I** A B GARDNER.
WHITNEY (St Peter and St Paul) w Winforton (St Mich), *Herefs*. R. **D** Heref 5 **P** *Mrs C E Hope 2 turns, Exors of Mrs A M Dew 1 turn, C Hobhouse Esq 1 turn* **I** W R KING *p-in-c*.
WHITSBURY (St Leon), *Hants*. R. **D** Win 8 *See* Rockbourne.
WHITSTABLE (All SS w St Pet), *Kent*. V. **D** Cant 4 **P** *Abp* **I** C G LEWIS, A J ALLAN *c*, R S WALLIS *c*.
WHITSTONE, *Cornw*. R. **D** Truro 10 **P** *Coll of the H Ho of Walsingham* **I** J G EDWARDS *p-in-c*.
WHITTINGHAM, *Lancs*.. **D** Blackb 7 *See* Goosnargh.
WHITTINGHAM (St Bart), *Northumb*. V. **D** Newc T 7 **P** *D and C of Carl* **I** F W CAMP.
WHITTINGTON-IN-LONSDALE (St Mich Arch), *Lancs*. R. **D** Blackb 13 *See* Arkholme.
WHITTINGTON (St Bart), *Derbys*. R. **D** Derby 3 **P** *Bp* **I** D I HAYNES *p-in-c*.
WHITTINGTON, NEW (St Barn), *Derbys*. V. **D** Derby 3 **P** *Bp* **I** (Vacant).
WHITTINGTON (St Bart), *Glos*. R. **D** Glouc 15 *See* Sevenhampton.
WHITTINGTON (St Jo Bapt), *Salop*. R. **D** Lich 24 **P** *A Lloyd Esq* **I** C A BUTLER.
WHITTINGTON (St Giles), *Staffs*. V. **D** Lich 2 **P** *Bp* **I** P D BROTHWELL.
WHITTINGTON, *Worcs*.. **D** Worc 6 *See* Norton.
WHITTLEBURY (St Mary) w Silverstone (St Mich), *Northants*. V. **D** Pet 2 **P** *Crown* **I** F T W SMITH.
WHITTLE-LE-WOODS (St Jo Evang), *Lancs*. V. **D** Blackb 4 **P** *V of Leyland* **I** E LACEY, R CARTMELL *c*.
WHITTLESEY (St Andr and St Mary), *Cambs*. V. **D** Ely 19 **P** *Ld Chan and Executors of J W Childers (alt)* **I** D FLEMING, A T SCHOFIELD *c*.
WHITTLESFORD (St Mary and St Andr), *Cambs*. V. **D** Ely 7 **P** *Jes Coll Cam* **I** C J L JONES.
WHITTON (St Mary Virg), *Salop*.. **D** Heref 12 *See* Burford.
WHITTON (St Jo Bapt), *Humb*.. **D** Linc 4 *See* Alkborough.
WHITTON (St Phil and St Jas), *Gtr Lon*. V. **D** Lon 8 **P** *V of Twickenham* **I** E J BRACK.
(St Aug of Cant), V. **D** Lon 8 **P** *Bp* **I** (Vacant).
WHITTON (St Botolph) and Thurleston w Akenham, *Suff*. R. **D** St E 4 **P** *Bp 2 turns, G R Drury Esq 1 turn* **I** G G BAULCOMB, B D HINES *c*, I J MANN *c*, M J STONE *c*.
WHITTON, Aldbourne (St Mich) w Baydon (St Nich) and Ramsbury (H Cross) w Axford, Chilton Foliat and Froxfield), [Wilts]. R. **D** Sarum 26 **P** *Dioc Bd of Patr* **I** S SWIFT *team v*, E G F SWINNERTON *team v*.
WHITTONSTALL (St Phil and St Jas), *Northumb*. V. **D** Newc T 3 **P** *D and C of Newc T* **I** J ROSS *c-in-c*.
WHITWELL (St Lawr), *Derbys*. R. **D** Derby 2 **P** *Bp* **I** J FEATHERSTONE.
WHITWELL (St Mich AA), *Norf*. V. **D** Nor 6 *See* Reepham.
WHITWELL (St Mich AA), *Leics*. R. **D** Pet 12 *See* Exton.
WHITWELL (St Mary Virg and St Radigund), *Isle of Wight*. V. **D** Portsm 6 **P** *Bp* **I** E E CURTIS *p-in-c*.
WHITWELL (St Jo Evang) w Crambe, Flaxton, Foston and Huttons Ambo, *N Yorks*. V. **D** York **P** *Abp and D and C of Dur* **I** P GREGORY.
WHITWICK (St Jo Bapt), *Leics*. V. **D** Leic 11 **P** *Duchy of Lanc* **I** P S LAWRIE.
(St Andr w Thringstone), V. **D** Leic 11 **P** *Duchy of Lanc* **I** B MATTHEWS.
WHITWICK ST GEORGE (St Geo) w Swannington and Cole Orton, *Leics*. V. **D** Leic 11 **P** *V of Whitwick & Trustees of Sir G Beaumont Bt (alt)* **I** R N PARKINSON.
WHITWOOD (All SS), *W Yorks*. R. **D** Wakef 11 **P** *Bp* **I** S G RIDLEY.
WHITWORTH, *Durham*. V. **D** Dur 9 *See* Spennymoor.
WHITWORTH (St Bart), *Lancs*. V. **D** Man 17 **P** *Keble Coll Ox* **I** A N WILSON, K W STEVENSON *team v*.
Whitworth, Manchester. **D** Man 5 *See* St Ambrose, Manchester.
WHIXALL (St Mary), *Salop*. V. **D** Lich 27 **P** *V of Prees and R of Wem* **I** J MACDONALD.
WHIXLEY (Ascen) w Green Hammerton (St Thos), *N Yorks*. V. **D** Ripon 3 **P** *Dioc Bd of Patr and V of Knaresborough* alt **I** R A NOAKES.
WHORLTON (St Mary Virg), *Durham*. V. **D** Dur 10 **P** *V of Gainford* **I** (Vacant).
WHORLTON (St John) w Newbiggin Hall (St Wilfrid) and Chapel House (H Nativ), *T & W*. R. **D** Newc T 5b **P** *Bp* **I** G K WATERS, P KENNEY *team v*, W D MILLER *team v*, P C LAMBERT *c*, E O WILLIAMS *c*.
WHORLTON (H Cross) w Carlton and Faceby, *N Yorks*. V. **D** York 25 **P** *Mrs H F Steele and Mrs K F L Davies* **I** D L FRANKS.
WHYKE (St Geo) w Rumboldswhyke (St Mary) and Portfield, *W Sussex*. R. **D** Chich 3 **P** *Bp* **I** D J BRECKNELL, W A E JONES *c*.

WHYLE, *Herefs*.. **D** Heref 7 *See* Puddleston.
WHYTELEAFE (St Luke), *Surrey*. V. **D** S'wark 9 **P** *Bp* **I** A R FLETCHER.
WIBTOFT (Assump of Our Lady), *Warws*. V. **D** Leic *See* Claybrooke.
WICHENFORD (St Lawr or St Mich AA), *Worcs*. V. **D** Worc *See* Martley.
WICHNOR (St Leon), *Staffs*. V. **D** Lich 2 **P** *Exors of W H Harrison* **I** J E COLSTON.
WICK (St Lawr), *Avon*.. **D** B & W 3 *See* Kewstoke.
WICK (St Bart) w Doynton (The Blessed Trin) R *Avon*. V. **D** Bris 8 **P** *Simeon Trustees and Ld Chan* alt **I** M P L WALL.
WICK, *All SS), W Sussex*. V. **D** Chich 1 **P** *Bp* **I** D W HEWITT *p-in-c*, L R D RYDER *c*.
WICK (St Mary), *Worcs*. V. **D** Worc 3 *See* Pershore.
WICKEN (St Lawr), *Cambs*. V. **D** Ely 3 **P** *CPS* **I** R F BELOE.
WICKEN (St Jo Evang), *Northants*. R. **D** Pet 2 **P** *S of Merchant Venturers Bris* **I** P TOWNSEND *c-in-c*.
WICKEN-BONHUNT (St Marg), *Essex*.. **D** Chelmsf *See* Quendon.
WICKENBY (St Pet and St Laur) w Friesthorpe (St Pet), *Lincs*. R. **D** Linc 5 **P** *Bp* **I** A G D SHEARWOOD.
WICKERSLEY (St Alban), *S Yorks*. R. **D** Sheff 6 **P** *Dioc Bd of Patr* **I** J METCALFE.
WICKFORD (St Cath) and Runwell (St Mary), *Essex*. R. **D** Chelmsf 10 **P** *Bp* **I** A R THOMAS, R CARTER *team v*, D J S LLOYD *team v*.
WICKHAM (St Mary), *T & W*.. **D** Dur 4a *See* Whickham.
WICKHAM (St Swith), *Berks*.. **D** Ox 14 *See* Welford.
WICKHAM (St Nich), *Hants*. R. **D** Portsm 2 **P** *P Rashleigh Esq* **I** C H GEORGE.
WICKHAM BISHOPS (St Bart), *Essex*. R. **D** Chelmsf 29 **P** *Bp* **I** M J SMITH.
WICKHAM, EAST (St Mich), *Kent*. V. **D** S'wark 17 **P** *Provost and Chapter of S'wark* **I** M H CLARK, B E COOK *c*.
WICKHAM MARKET (All SS), *Suff*. V. **D** St E 18 **P** *Ch Trust Fund* **I** (Vacant).
WICKHAM ST PAUL (All SS) w Twinstead, *Essex*.. **D** Chelmsf 18 *See* Henny, Great.
WICKHAM-SKEITH, *Suff*.. **D** St E *See* Cotton.
WICKHAM, WEST (St Jo Bapt), *Kent*. R. **D** Cant 16 **P** *Abp* **I** J D B POOLE, G W RAYMOND *c*.
(St Francis), V. **D** Cant 16 **P** *Abp* **I** J R C WEBB.
(St Mary of Nazareth), V. **D** Cant 16 **P** *Abp and Crown* alt **I** F S MADGE.
WICKHAM, WEST (St Mary), *Cambs*. V. **D** Ely 4 **P** *Bp and Govs of Charterho (alt)* **I** H S FINKENSTAEDT *p-in-c*, H W NESLING *hon c*.
WICKHAMBREAUX or WICKHAMBROASE w Stodmarsh, *Kent*. R. **D** Cant 1 *See* Ickham.
WICKHAMBROOK (All SS) w Stradishall (St Marg) and Denston (St Nich), *Suff*. V. **D** St E 8 **P** *Ld Chan and Mrs H Leader* alt **I** W H DAVIS.
WICKHAMFORD (St Jo Bapt), *Worcs*. V. **D** Worc 1 **P** *Ch Ch Ox* **I** P D MITCHELL.
WICKHAMPTON (St Andr), *Norf*. R. **D** Nor 1 *See* Freethorpe.
WICKLEWOOD (All SS and St Andr) w Crownthorpe and Deopham (St Andr) w Hackford (St Mary Virg) *Norf*. V. **D** Nor **P** *A C Heber-Percy Esq 2 turns, Ld Kimberley 1 turn* **I** (Vacant).
WICKMERE (St Andr) w L Barningham and Itteringham (St Mary), *Norf*. R. **D** Nor 3 **P** *Ld Walpole* **I** R S OSSELTON.
WICKWAR (H Trin) w Rangeworthy, *Avon*. R. **D** Glouc 8 **P** *Earl of Ducie and V of Thornbury* **I** E A PERRY.
WIDCOMBE, *Avon*.. **D** B & W 13 *See* Bath.
WIDDINGTON (St Mary), *Essex*. R. **D** Chelmsf 26 **P** *Bp* **I** P S GRIMWOOD.
WIDDRINGTON (H Trin), *Northumb*. V. **D** Newc T 10 **P** *Bp* **I** J S MATTHEWSON.
WIDECOMBE-IN-THE-MOOR (St Pancras) w Leusden and Princetown w Postbridge and Huccaby Chaps, *Devon*. R. **D** Ex **P** *Duke of Cornw 2 turns, Dioc Bd of Patr 1 turn* **I** J W E BROWN, R E FARTHING *team v*.
WIDFORD, *Oxon*.. **D** Ox *See* Asthall.
WIDFORD (St Mary), *Essex*. R. **D** Chelmsf 12 **P** *CPAS* **I** J R CARR, I M BLAKE *c*.
WIDFORD (St Jo Bapt), *Herts*. R. **D** St Alb *See* Hunsdon.
WIDLEY (St Mary Magd), *Hants*.. **D** Portsm *See* Wymering.
WIDMERPOOL (St Pet), *Notts*. R. **D** Southw 10 **P** *MMT* **I** J G BOOKLESS *p-in-c*.
WIDNES (St Mary), *Chesh*. V. **D** Liv 7 **P** *Bp* **I** W J T FROST.
(St Ambrose), V. **D** Liv 7 **P** *Trustees* **I** P T JONES.
(St John), V. **D** Liv **P** *Bp and V of Farnworth* **I** D J GAIT.
(St Paul), V. **D** Liv 7 **P** *Bp* **I** W NELSON.
WIDWORTHY (St Cuthb), *Devon*. R. **D** Ex 5 *See* Offwell.
WIELD (St Jas), *Hants*. V. **D** Win 1 *See* Medstead.
WIGAN (All SS), *Gtr Man*. R. **D** Liv 12 **P** *Bp* **I** K M FORREST, A M M CALLON *c*.
(St Andr), V. **D** Liv 12 **P** *R of Wigan* **I** R N ARBERY, J C BAKER *c*.
(St Anne), V. **D** Liv 12 **P** *Bp* **I** D TINSLEY.
(St Barn, Marsh Green),. **D** Liv 12 **P** *Bp and V of St Mark, Newtown, Pemberton* **I** I F GREENHALGH.
(St Cath), V. **D** Liv 12 **P** *R of Wigan* **I** N BOND.
(St Geo), V. **D** Liv 12 **P** *R of Wigan* **I** B C HARRISON.
(St Jas), V. **D** Liv 12 **P** *Bp* **I** A CARRUTHERS.
(St Mich AA), V. **D** Liv 12 **P** *R of Wigan* **I** C WALKER.
(St Steph), V. **D** Liv 12 **P** *Bp* **I** D HALL.
(St Thos), V. **D** Liv 12 **P** *R of Wigan* **I** A CARRUTHERS *c-in-c*.
(St John, New Springs), V. **D** Liv 12 **P** *Bp* **I** (Vacant).
WIGBOROUGH, GREAT (St Steph) w Wigborough, Little (St Nich), *Essex*. R. **D** Chelmsf 21 *See* Peldon.
WIGGENHALL (St Germans w St Mary Virg and Islington), *Norf*. V. **D** Ely 18 **P** *Ld Chan 2 turns, D and C of Nor 1 turn, MMT 1 turn* **I** L C WALDRON.
(St Mary Magd), V. **D** Ely 18 **P** *Ld Chan 2 turns, D and C of Nor 1 turn, MMT 1 turn* **I** L C WALDRON.
WIGGINTON (St Leon), *Staffs*. V. **D** Lich 6 **P** *V of Tamworth* **I** M G C NORTON.
WIGGINTON (St Bart), *Herts*. V. **D** St Alb 3 **P** *Bp* **I** B H JONES.
WIGGINTON, *N Yorks*.. **D** York *See* Haxby.
WIGGLESWORTH, *N Yorks*.. **D** Bradf *See* Rathmell-in-Craven.
WIGGONHOLT (Dedic unknown) w Greatham, *W Sussex*. R. **D** Chich 7 *See* Parham.
WIGHILL (All SS), *N Yorks*. V. **D** York 2 *See* Healaugh.
WIGHTON (All SS), *Norf*.. **D** Nor *See* Warham.
WIGMORE (St Jas Ap) w Leinthall Starkes (St Mary Magd), *Herefs*. V. **D** Heref 7 **P** *Bp* **I** E J BRYANT *c*.
ABBEY, (Brampton Bryan, Downton, Burrington, Aston, Elton, Leintwardine and Adforton), *Salop*. R. **D** Heref 12 **P** *Bd of Trustees* **I** R H SMITH, T R BONIWELL *c*.
WIGMORE (St Matt), *Kent*.. **D** Roch 2 *See* Gillingham, South.
WIGSTON MAGNA (All SS w St Wolstan), *Leics*. V. **D** Leic 6 **P** *Haberdashers' Co and Ch Hosp* alt **I** E J GREEN.
WIGSTON PARVA, *Leics*. V. **D** Leic 16 *See* Sharnford.
WIGSTON, SOUTH *Leics*.. **D** Leic *See* Glen Parva.
WIGTOFT (St Pet and St Paul), *Lincs*.. **D** Linc 21 *See* Sutterton.
WIGTON (St Mary) *Cumb*. V. **D** Carl 3 **P** *Bp* **I** C G JOHNSON.
WILBARSTON (All SS), *Northants*. V. **D** Pet 10 *See* Stoke Albany.
WILBERFOSS (St Jo Bapt), *N Yorks*.. **D** York *See* Kexby.
WILBRAHAM, GREAT (St Nich), *Cambs*. V. **D** Ely 6 **P** *Exors of R S Hicks* **I** D D BOLT.
WILBRAHAM, LITTLE (St Jo Evang), w Six Mile Bottom, *Cambs*. R. **D** Ely 6 **P** *CCC Cam* **I** D D BOLT.
WILBURTON (St Pet), *Cambs*. V. **D** Ely 15 **P** *Archd of Ely* **I** D WEBB.
WILBURY, *Herts*. V. **D** St Alb **P** *Bp* **I** D E DOWLING.
WILBY (All SS) w Hargham, *Norf*.. **D** Nor 18 *See* Quidenham.
WILBY (St Mary Virg), *Northants*. R. **D** Pet 7 **P** *Lt-Col H C M Stockdale* **I** D A BOWLES *p-in-c*.
WILBY (St Mary) w Brundish (St Lawr), *Suff*. R. **D** St E 17 **P** *F W Marriot Esq 1st 3rd and 4th turns, Bp 2nd turn* **I** J G NICHOLLS *p-in-c*.
WILCOT (H Cross) w Huish (St Nich) and Oare (H Trin), *Wilts*. V. **D** Sarum 27 *See* Swanborough.
WILCOTE (St Pet), *Oxon*. R. **D** Ox 3 **P** *A C W Norman Esq* **I** J C S NIAS *c-in-c*.
WILDBOARCLOUGH (St Sav), *Chesh*.. **D** Ches 14 *See* Wincle.
WILDEN (St Nich) w Colmworth (St Denis) and Ravensden (All SS), *Beds*. R. **D** St Alb 21 **P** *Miss F A L Chalk, J W Pullan Esq, and Bp in turn* **I** J L P GRIFFITH.
WILDEN (All SS), *Worcs*. V. **D** Worc 12 **P** *Earl Baldwin* **I** (Vacant).
WILDMORE (St Pet), *Lincs*. V. **D** Linc 21 *See* Brothertoft.
WILDSWORTH (St Jo Bapt), *Humb*.. **D** Linc 2 *See* Laughton.
WILFORD (St Wilfrid), *Notts*. R. **D** Southw 11 **P** *Lt-Col P Clifton* **I** P NEWTON.

I R P APPLETON.
WINCHELSEA (St Thos Ap), *E Sussex*. R. D Chich 22 P *Guild of All S* I C G SCOTT.
WINCHENDON, NETHER (St Nich), *Bucks*.. D Ox 21 *See* Chearsley.
WINCHENDON, OVER (St Mary Magd), *Bucks*. V. D Ox 29 *See* Waddesdon.
WINCHESTER (Ch Ch), *Hants*. V. D Win 12 P *Simeon Trustees* I S A HONES *c*.
(All SS) w Chilcomb (St Andr) and Chesil (St Pet), R. D Win 12 P *Ld Chan and Bp* alt I R P THOMAS.
(H Trin), R. D Win 12 P *Bp* I T G NASH *p-in-c*, R CRAWFORD *hon c*.
(St Bart Hyde), V. D Win 12 P *Ld Chan* I N G SMITH.
(St Cross Hosp w St Faith). D Win 12 P *Bp* I A C B DEEDES *master*.
(St Jo Bapt) w Winnall (St Marton), V. D Win 12 P *Bp* I (Vacant).
(St John's Hosp). D Win 12 I (Vacant).
(St Maurice w St Mary, Kalendre, St Pet Colebrooke, and St Laur w St Swithun-upon-Kingsgate), R. D Win 12 P *Bp and Ld Chan* I T G NASH, N H DE LA MOUETTE *c*.
(St Luke, Stanmore), V. D Win 12 P *Bp* I (Vacant).
WINCHFIELD (St Mary) w Dogmersfield, *Hants*.. D Win *See* Hartley Wintney.
WINCHMORE HILL (St Paul), *Lon*. V. D Lon 21 P *V of Edmonton* I D J NASH, R B WATSON *c*.
(H Trin), V. D Lon 21 P *V of Winchmore Hill* I C M GRAY.
WINCLE (St Mich) w Wildboarclough (St Sav), *Chesh*. V. D Ches 13 P *Earl of Derby and V of Prestbury* alt I J PREECE.
WINCOBANK (St Thos), *S Yorks*. V. D Sheff 3 P *Trustees* I F HERRINGTON.
WINDERMERE (St Martin), *Cumb*. R. D Carl 14 P *Trustees* I C ELLIOTT.
(St Jo Evang), V. D Carl 14 P *Bp* I A H ATTWELL.
(St Mary), V. D Carl 14 P *Bp* I W E BARKER.
WINDERTON, *Warws*.. D Cov 12 *See* Brailes.
WINDHILL (Ch Ch), *W Yorks*. V. D Bradf 1 P *Bp* I (Vacant).
WINDLESHAM (St Jo Bapt w St Alb), *Surrey*. R. D Guildf 5a P *Ld Chan* I J A R PIERSSENE.
WINDLEY, *Derbys*.. D Derby 12 *See* Turnditch.
WINDMILL HILL (St Mich AA), *Avon*.. D Bris *See* Bedminster.
WINDRUSH (St Pet), *Glos*.. D Glouc 15 *See* Sherborne.
WINDRUSH, LOWER, (Stanton Harcourt, Northmoor, Standlake and Yelford), *Oxon*. R. D Ox 9 P *Bp, Dioc Bd of Patr, St Jo Coll Ox and B Babington-Smith Esq* I M T FARTHING.
WINDSOR (St Nath), *Mer*.. D Liv 2 *See* Edge Hill.
WINDSOR, NEW (St Jo Bapt w All SS and H Trin), *Berks*. R. D Ox 13 P *Ld Chan* I D N GRIFFITHS, P N CHALLENGER *team v*.
(H Trin), R. D Ox 13 *See* Windsor, New.
OLD (St Pet), V. D Ox 13 P *Ld Chan* I J W STAPLES.
WINESTEAD (St German), *Humb*. R. D York 15 *See* Patrington.
WINFARTHING (St Mary) w Shelfanger (All SS) w Burston, Gissing and Tivetshall, *Ncrf*. R. D Nor 17 P *Bp, Ld Chan and Hertf Coll Ox* I J H LISTER.
WINFORD (St Mary Virg w St Pet), *Avon*. R. D B & W 15 P *Worc Coll Ox* I R E HICKES.
WINFORTON (St Mich), *Herefs*. R. D Heref 5 *See* Whitney.
WINFRITH NEWBURGH (St Chris) w Chaldon Herring (St Nich). *Dorset*. R. D Sarum *See* Lulworths, the.
WING (All SS), w Grove (St Mich AA), *Bucks*. V. D Ox 27 P *Bp* I D A SMITH.
WING (St Pet and St Paul) w Pilton, *Leics*. R. D Pet 12 *See* Preston.
WINGATE GRANGE (H Trin), *Durham*. V. D Dur 3 P *Bp* I E W TAYLOR.
WINGATES (St Jo Evang), *Gtr Man*. V. D Man 13 P *V of Deane* I G THOMSON.
WINGERWORTH (All SS), *Derbys*. R. D Derby 3 P *Bp* I C H PERRY *c*, F H SHAW *c*.
WINGFIELD (St Andr), *Suff*. V. D St E *See* Fressingfield.
WINGFIELD, NORTH (St Lawr) w Pilsley (St Mary Virg) and Tupton, *Derbys*. R. D Derby 3 P *Bp* I J M ROFF, A F NASH *team v*, R J I PAGET *team v*.
WINGFIELD or WINKFIELD (St Mary), *Wilts*. R. D Sarum 24 P *CPAS* I J DARLING *c*.
WINGHAM (St Mary Virg), *Kent*.. D Cant 1 *See* Preston.
WINGRAVE (St Pet and St Paul), w Rowsham Aston Abbots and Cublington, *Bucks*. V. D Ox 27 P *Bp and Linc Coll Ox* I W J G HEFFER.
WINKBURN (St John of Jer), *Notts*. V. D Southw 15 P *Bp* I W G CALTHROP-OWEN *p-in-c*.
WINKFIELD (St Mary) w Chavey Down (St Martin), *Berks*. V. D Ox 11a P *Bp* I R CROUCH.
WINKLEIGH (All SS), *Devon*. V. D Ex 16 P *D and C of Ex* I A J MACKERACHER.
WINLATON (St Paul) w Rowland's Gill, and High Spen, *T & W*. R. D Dur 4a P *Bp* I E JONES, C COLLINS *team v*.
WINMARLEIGH (St Luke), *Lancs*. V. D Blackb *See* Cockerham.
WINNALL (St Martin), *Hants*. R. D Win 12 *See* Winchester, (St Jo Bapt).
WINNINGTON (St Luke), *Chesh*. V. D Ches 6 *See* Northwich.
WINSCOMBE (St Jas Gt) w Sandford (All SS), *Avon*. V. D B & W 3 P *D and C of Wells* I B B SALMON.
WINSFORD (St Mary Magd), *Somt*.. D B & W 21 *See* Exton.
WINSFORD Chesh. D Ches 6 *See* Over.
WINSHAM (St Steph) w Cricket (St Thos), *Somt*. V. D B & W *See* Thorncombe.
WINSHILL (St Mark), *Staffs*. V. D Derby 16 P *Ld Gretton* I W G POTTS.
WINSLADE, *Hants*.. D Win *See* Herriard.
WINSLEY (St Nich), *Avon*. V. D Sarum 24 P *D and C of Bris* I D C RITCHIE.
WINSLOW (St Laur DM), *Bucks*. V. D Ox 25 P *Ld Chan* I A P A BARNES.
WINSON (St Mich), *Glos*.. D Glouc 14 *See* Bibury.
WINSTER (H Trin), *Cumb*. V. D Carl 17 P *V of Kendal* I K PARTINGTON.
WINSTER (St Jo Bapt), *Derbys*. V. D Derby 17 P *PCC* I K E SERVANTE P-IN-C SOUTH DARLEY *p-in-c*.
WINSTON (St Andr), *Durham*. R. D Dur 10 P *Bp and Trin Coll Cam [alt]* I T J LEE WARNER.
WINSTON, *Suff*.. D St E *See* Pettaugh.
WINSTONE, *Glos*.. D Glouc 13 *See* Daglingworth.
WINTERBOURNE (St Mich), *Avon*. R. D Bris 7 P *St Jo Coll Ox* I E I BAILEY, W CLYNES *c*.
WINTERBOURNE (St Jas), *Berks*.. D Ox 14 *See* Chieveley.
WINTERBOURNE-ABBAS (St Mary) w Steepleton (St Mich), *Dorset*.. D Sarum 5 *See* Winterbournes.
WINTERBOURNE ANDERSON, *Dorset*.. D Sarum *See* Winterbourne Zelstone.
WINTERBOURNE BASSETT (St Kath), *Wilts*. R. D Sarum 26 *See* Kennet, Upper.
WINTERBOURNE CAME (St Pet) w Whitcombe, *Dorset*. R. D Sarum 5 *See* Stinsford.
WINTERBOURNE-CLENSTON, *Dorset*.. D Sarum *See* Winterbourne Whitchurch.
WINTERBOURNE DOWN (All SS), *Avon*. V. D Bris 7 P *S for Maint of Faith* I R J THOMAS *p-in-c*, G CURTIS *c*.
WINTERBOURNE EARLS (St Mich AA) w Winterbourne Dauntsey and Winterbourne Gunner (St Mary), *Wilts*. V. D Sarum 17 *See* Bourne Valley.
WINTERBOURNE-HOUGHTON (St Andr), *Dorset*. R. D Sarum 10 *See* Winterbourne Stickland.
WINTERBOURNE KINGSTON, *Dorset*.. D Sarum *See* Winterbourne Zelstone.
WINTERBOURNE-MONKTON (St Michael and St Jude), *Dorset*. R. D Sarum 5 *See* Stinsford.
WINTERBOURNE-MONKTON (St Mary Magd), *Wilts*. V. D Sarum 26 *See* Avebury.
WINTERBOURNE ST MARTIN (St Martin), V. D Sarum 5 *See* Winterbournes.
WINTERBOURNE STICKLAND (St Mary) and Turnworth, Winterbourne Houghton, Winterbourne Whitechurch and Winterbourne Clenston, *Dorset*. R. D Sarum 10 P *Bp 3 turns, Mrs V P Railston and Mrs D A Forster 1 turn* I A G GILL.
WINTERBOURNE-STOKE, *Wilts*. V. D Sarum 21 P *Bp* I S M W TRICKETT *p-in-c*.
WINTERBOURNE TOMSON, *Dorset*.. D Sarum *See* Winterbourne Zelstone.
WINTERBOURNE WHITECHURCH (St Mary) w Winterbourne Clenston, *Dorset*. R. D Sarum 10 *See* Winterbourne Stickland.
WINTERBOURNE ZELSTONE (St Mary) w Tomson (St Andr), Anderson (St Mich) and Kingston (St Nich), *Dorset*.. D Sarum 10 *See* Red Post.
WINTERBOURNES, THE (St Martin, St Mary and St Mich) and Compton Valence (St Thos of Cant), *Dorset*. R. D Sarum 5 P *Archd of Sherborne, Linc Coll Ox and Sir R P N Williams, Bt, in turn* I D G HOSIE.
WINTERINGHAM (All SS), *Humb*. R. D Linc *See* Alkborough.

WINTERSLOW (All SS and St John), *Wilts.* R. **D** Sarum 17 **P** *St Jo Coll Ox* **I** A G WILLIAMS, W T CLAYTON *hon c.*
WINTERTON (All SS), *Humb.* V. **D** Linc 4 **P** *Bp* **I** A W J BURTON.
WINTERTON (All SS) w East Somerton, *Norf.* R. **D** Nor 2 **P** *S for Maint of Faith* **I** L O HARRIS.
WINTHORPE (St Mary), *Lincs.*. **D** Linc *See* Skegness.
WINTHORPE (All SS and BVM), *Notts.* R. **D** Southw 3 **P** *Keble Coll Ox* **I** H W LANGFORD.
WINTON (St Mary Magd), *Gtr Man.* V. **D** Man 3 **P** *Trustees* **I** F E HARRIS.
WINTRINGHAM (St Pet), *N Yorks.*. **D** York *See* Rillington.
WINWICK (All SS), *Cambs.* V. **D** Ely 11 **P** *Bp* **I** (Vacant).
WINWICK (St Osw), *Chesh.* R. **D** Liv 11 **P** *Earl of Derby* **I** J A LAWTON.
WINWICK, *Northants.*. **D** Pet *See* Haddon, West.
WIRKSWORTH (St Mary) w Carsington (St Marg), *Derbys.* R. **D** Derby 17 **P** *Bp* **I** G BUSBY.
WISBECH (St Pet and St Paul), *Cambs.* V. **D** Ely 20 **P** *Bp* **I** (Vacant).
(St Aug), V. **D** Ely 20 **P** *Bp* **I** D W SPENCER *c.*
WISBECH ST MARY (St Mary), *Cambs.* V. **D** Ely 20 **P** *Bp* **I** W J PATTERSON.
WISBOROUGH GREEN (St Pet-ad-Vincula), *W Sussex.* V. **D** Chich 6 **P** *Bp of Lon* **I** C G F DARE.
WISHAW (St Chad), *Warws.* R. **D** Birm 12 **P** *Bp* **I** R J WILKINS.
WISHFORD MAGNA (St Giles), *Wilts.* R. **D** Sarum 21 **P** *Earl of Pembroke* **I** J W GOODALL *p-in-c.*
WISLEY w Pyrford (St Nich), *Surrey.* R. **D** Guildf 11 **P** *Bp* **I** J P B GARDNER, P M BOND *c.*
WISPINGTON, *Lincs.* V. **D** Linc 11 *See* Edlington.
WISSETT, *Suff.*. **D** St E *See* Spexhall.
WISSINGTON, *Suff.*. **D** St E *See* Nayland.
WISTANSTOW (H Trin), *Salop.* R. **D** Heref 11 **P** *Bp* **I** A H WOODHOUSE, J B METCALFE *c.*
WISTASTON (St Mary Virg), *Chesh.* R. **D** Ches 15 **P** *Trustees* **I** D SIMPSON, HOWELL *c.*
WISTESTON, *Herefs.* V. **D** Heref 4 *See* Marden.
WISTON (St Mary), *W Sussex.*. **D** Chich *See* Ashington.
WISTOW (St Jo Bapt), *Cambs.* R. **D** Ely 12 **P** *Bp* **I** P R CUTTING.
WISTOW (St Wiston) w Newton Harcourt (St Luke), *Leics.* V. **D** Leic 6 **P** *Hon Ann Brooks* **I** (Vacant).
WISTOW (All SS), *N Yorks.* V. **D** York 8 **P** *Abp* **I** D BOND *p-in-c.*
WITCHAM (St Martin), V w Mepal, *Cambs.* R. **D** Ely 15 **P** *D and C of Ely* **I** R W S L GUSSMAN *p-in-c,* T R HOLLAND *hon c.*
WITCHAMPTON (St Mary and Cuthberga and All SS) and Hinton Parva w Crichel, Long (St Mary Virg) and Crichel, Moor (St Mary Virg), *Dorset.* R. **D** Sarum 11 **P** *Hon Mrs M A Marten* **I** C P DE CANDOLE.
WITCHFORD (St Andr) w Wentworth (St Pet), R *Cambs.* V. **D** Ely 15 **P** *D and C of Ely* **I** J A R LISNEY.
WITCHINGHAM, GT and L *Norf.*. **D** Nor *See* Weston Longville.
WITCOMBE, GT (St Mary Virg) w Bentham (St Pet), *Glos.* R. **D** Glouc 2 **P** *Exors of W W Hicks Beach* **I** J THORNTON.
WITHAM (St Nich), *Essex.* V. **D** Chelmsf 29 **P** *Bp* **I** D SHERLOCK, M G HONEYBALL *c,* G R LANE *hon c.*
WITHAM FRIARY (BVM St Jo Bapt and All SS) w Marston Bigot (St Leon) *Somt.* R. **D** B & W 16a **P** *Duke of Somerset and Bp* **I** M M K WARREN.
WITHAM, NORTH (St Mary), *Lincs.* R. **D** Linc 14 **P** *Bp* **I** M J B NUTTALL.
WITHAM-ON-THE-HILL (St Andr), *Lincs.* V. **D** Linc 13 **P** *Bp* **I** (Vacant).
WITHAM, SOUTH (St Jo Bapt), *Lincs.* R. **D** Linc 14 **P** *Sir H T Tollemache Bt* **I** M J B NUTTALL.
WITHCALL (St Martin), *Lincs.* R. **D** Linc *See* Raithby.
WITHCOTE (Dedic unknown), *Leics.*. **D** Leic *See* Owston.
WITHECOMBE-RALEIGH (St Jo Evang), *Devon.*. **D** Ex 1 *See* Withycombe-Raleigh.
WITHERIDGE (St Jo Bapt), Thelbridge (St D), Creacombe (St Mich AA), Meshaw (St Jo Bapt), E and W Worlington (St Mary), *Devon.* V. **D** Ex 19 **P** *Bp, MMT, C M K Bruton Esq, Rt Hon Ld Portsmouth and Sir D Stucley Bt* **I** W R HUDSON.
WITHERLEY (St Pet) w Atterton, *Leics.* R. **D** Leic 16 **P** *Ld O'Neill* **I** R E REYNOLDS *p-in-c.*
WITHERN (Authorpe w Tothill, Belleau w Claythorpe, Aby and Greenfield, Gayton-le-Marsh, Strubby, Swaby and S Thoresby), *Lincs.* R. **D** Linc **P** *Ld Chan 1st turn, D and C of Linc 2nd turn, Earl of Ancaster 3rd turn, Duchy of Lanc 4th turn, Dioc Bd of Patr 5th turn and Bp 6th turn* **I** G PARROTT.
WITHERNSEA (St Mary), *N Humb.* V. **D** York 15 *See* Owthorne.
WITHERNWICK, *Humb.* V. **D** York 14 *See* Aldbrough.
WITHERSDALE, *Suff.*. **D** St E 17 *See* Metfield.
WITHERSFIELD (St Mary Virg), *Suff.* R. **D** St E 8 **P** *Bp* **I** D DUVAL P-IN-C OF GT WRATTING *c-in-c.*
WITHERSLACK (St Paul), *Cumb.* V. **D** Carl 17 **P** *Trustees of Dean Barwick's Charity* **I** K PARTINGTON.
WITHERSTONE, *Dorset.*. **D** Sarum *See* Powerstock.
WITHIEL (St Clem), *Cornw.* R. **D** Truro 1 **P** *Bp* **I** N H TOOGOOD *p-in-c.*
WITHIEL FLOREY (St Mary Magd), *Somt.* V. **D** B & W 21 *See* Brompton Regis.
WITHINGTON (St Mich) and Compton Abdale (St Osw) w Haselton, *Glos.* R. **D** Glouc 15 **P** *Bp 2 turns, Ld Chan 1 turn* **I** W C WORSDELL.
WITHINGTON (St Pet) w Westhide (St Bart), *Herefs.* R. **D** Heref 4 **P** *Bp and D and C of Heref* alt **I** G D ABELL, E R I CHURCHUS *c.*
WITHINGTON (St Jo Bapt), *Salop.* V. **D** Lich *See* Uffington.
WITHINGTON (St Paul), *Gtr Man.* R. **D** Man 10 **P** *Trustees* **I** R J ELFORD *hon c.*
(St Crispin), R. **D** Man 5 **P** *Bp* **I** R CROFT.
WEST (St Chris), R. **D** Man 10 **P** *Crown and Bp* alt **I** C G W PILKINGTON.
WITHINGTON, LOWER, *Chesh.*. **D** Ches *See* Chelford.
WITHLEIGH (St Cath), *Devon.* V. **D** Ex 8 *See* Washfield.
WITHNELL (St Paul), *Lancs.* V. **D** Blackb 4 **P** *V of Leyland* **I** W M NORTHCOTT.
WITHYBROOK (All SS) w Copston Magna (St Jo Bapt), *Warws.* V. **D** Cov 5 **P** *Bp* **I** K R HAGAN *p-in-c.*
WITHYCOMBE (St Nich) w Rodhuish (St Bart), *Somt.* R. **D** B & W 21 **P** *Bp* **I** G M HICKMAN.
WITHYCOMBE RALEIGH (St Jo Evang) w Exmouth (All SS), *Devon.* V. **D** Ex 1 **P** *D and C of Ex* **I** J A BENTON, L M BATE *team v,* R J PERRY *team v.*
WITHYHAM (St Mich AA) w Blackham (All SS), *E Sussex.* R. **D** Chich 20 **P** *Earl de la Warr* **I** P L SCOTT.
(St Jo Evang Crowborough), V. **D** Chich 20 **P** *Guild of All S* **I** J A TAYLOR.
WITHYPOOL (St Andr), *Somt.*. **D** B & W *See* Hawkridge.
WITLEY (All SS), *Surrey.* V. **D** Guildf 4 **P** *Chandler Trustees* **I** P T C CASE.
WITLEY, GT L (St Mich AA) and Hillhampton, *Worcs.*. **D** Worc 12 *See* Shrawley.
WITNESHAM (St Mary) w Swilland (St Mary Virg) and Ashbocking (All SS), *Suff.* R. **D** St E 1 **P** *Ld Chan and Peterho Cam* alt **I** I G DAVIDSON *p-in-c.*
WITNEY (St Mary Virg w H Trin Wood Green and St John, Curbridge), *Oxon.* R. **D** Ox 9 **P** *Bp* **I** R E MEREDITH, A J L BARNETT *c,* J C D COOK *c.*
WITTENHAM, LONG or EARLS (St Mary Virg) w Wittenham, Abbots or Little (St Pet), *Oxon.* V. **D** Ox 11 **P** *Ex Coll Ox and Dioc Bd of Patr* **I** P L DEWEY *p-in-c.*
WITTERING (All SS) w Thornhaugh (St Andr) and Wansford (St Mary Virg), *Cambs.* R. **D** Pet 13 **P** *Marq of Ex 2 turns, Bp 1 turn* **I** G H BRADSHAW.
WITTERING, EAST (St Jo Bapt) w Earnley and Almondington, *W Sussex.* R. **D** Chich 3 *See* Earnley.
WITTERING, WEST (St Pet & St Paul), *W Sussex.* V. **D** Chich 3 **P** *Bp* **I** W GREENFIELD.
WITTERSHAM (St Jo Bapt), *Kent.* R. **D** Cant 13 **P** *Abp* **I** C R DUNCAN.
WITTON (All S), *W Midl.* V. **D** Birm *See* Birchfield.
WITTON (St Mark), *Lancs.* V. **D** Blackb 2 **P** *V of Blackb* **I** D C WOTHERSPOON.
WITTON or NORTHWICH (St Helen), *Chesh.* V. **D** Ches 6 **P** *Bp* **I** P L WILLIAMS.
WITTON (St Marg) w Ridlington (St Pet), *Norf.* V. **D** Nor *See* Bacton.
WITTON (St Marg) w Brundall (St Lawr), and Bradeston (St Mich), *Norf.* R. **D** Nor 1 **P** *Bp and Mrs C L chamberlin* alt **I** R M BAKER.
WITTON, EAST (St Jo Evang), *N Yorks.* V. **D** Ripon 2 *See* Thornton Watlass.
WITTON-GILBERT (St Mich AA), *Durham.* R. **D** Dur 2 **P** *D and C of Dur* **I** I D HOSKINS.
WITTON-LE-WEAR and Fir Tree (St Mary Virg), *Durham.* V. **D** Dur 9 **P** *Bp and Crown* **I** H TAYLOR.
WITTON PARK (St Paul), *Durham.* V. **D** Dur 9 **P** *Bp* **I** N M J W BEDDOW.
WITTON, WEST (St Bart), *N Yorks.* V. **D** Ripon 2 **P** *Ld Bolton* **I** (Vacant).
WIVELISCOMBE (St Andr), *Somt.* V. **D** B & W 22 **P** *Bp* **I** C J B MARSHALL.

WIVELSFIELD (St Jo Bapt), *E Sussex*. V. **D** Chich 11 **P** *Dioc Bd of Patr* **I** E F TAYLOR.
WIVENHOE (St Mary Virg), *Essex*. R. **D** Chelmsf 21 **P** *Bp* **I** S HARDIE.
WIVERTON, *Norf*.. **D** Nor *See* Cley-next-the-Sea.
WIX (St Mary), *Essex*. V. **D** Chelmsf 25 *See* Wrabness.
WIXFORD (St Milburga), *Warws*.. **D** Cov 7 *See* Exhall.
WIXOE (St Leon), *Essex*. R. **D** St E 8 *See* Stoke-by-Clare.
WOBURN (St Mary) w Eversholt, Milton Bryan, Battlesden and Fottesgrove, *Beds*. V. **D** St Alb **P** *Trustees of Duke of Bedford's Settled Estates* **I** P R MILLER.
WOBURN SANDS (St Mich AA), *Bucks*. V. **D** St Alb 15 **P** *Bp* **I** A E PULLIN.
WOBURN SQUARE (Ch Ch). **D** Lon 2 *See* Bloomsbury.
WOKING (St Pet), *Surrey*. V. **D** Guildf 11 **P** *Ch S* **I** J P HEYHOE *c*.
(Ch Ch), V. **D** Guildf 11 **P** *Ridley Hall Cam* **I** C P SEARLE, D F LAMBERT *chap*.
(St Jo Bapt w Brookwood St Sav), V. **D** Guildf 11 **P** *V of Woking* **I** J SONG, J K HAYWARD *c*, G H REID *hon c*.
(St Mary-of-Bethany), V. **D** Guildf 11 **P** *V of Ch Ch Woking* **I** N G NORGATE, J W RICHARDS *c*, A V RASHBROOK *hon c*.
(St Paul), V. **D** Guildf 11 **P** *Ridley Hall, Cam* **I** P A WAINWRIGHT.
WOKINGHAM (All SS), *Berks*. R. **D** Ox 16 **P** *Bp* **I** B C BAILEY, A A CLEMENTS *c*.
(St Paul), R. **D** Ox 16 **P** *Dioc Bd of Patr* **I** A L DAVIES, M J CLAYTON *c*.
(St Sebastian), V. **D** Ox 16 **P** *Bp* **I** C J S JONES.
WOLBOROUGH (St Mary) w Newton Abbot (St Leon w St Paul), *Devon*. R. **D** Ex 11 **P** *Earl of Devon* **I** L P N STOKES.
WOLD (St Andr), *Northants*. R. **D** Pet 6 *See* Walgrave.
WOLD-NEWTON (All SS) w Hawerby and Beesby, *Lincs*. R. **D** Linc 10 **P** *Ld Chan* **I** (Vacant).
WOLD-NEWTON (All SS), *Humb*. V. **D** York 12 **P** *Abp* **I** (Vacant).
WOLDINGHAM (St Paul), *Surrey*. R. **D** S'wark 9 **P** *Bp* **I** D A RHYMES.
WOLFERLOW (St Andr), *Herefs*. V. **D** Heref 2 *See* Sapey, Upper.
WOLFERTON (St Pet) w Babingley, *Norf*. R (*See Sandringham Group*).. **D** Nor 23 **P** *HM the Queen* **I** (Vacant).
WOLFORD (St Mich AA) w Burmington, *Warws*. V. **D** Cov 9 **P** *Mert Coll Ox* **I** J B WOODWARD-COURT.
WOLLASTON (St Mary) w Strixton, *Northants*. V. **D** Pet 7 **P** *Bp* **I** E W C BALE.
WOLLASTON (St Jas), *Worcs*. V. **D** Worc 11 **P** *Bp* **I** F B HONEY.
WOLLASTON, GREAT (All SS w St Jo Bapt), *Salop*. V. **D** Heref 13 **P** *Bp* **I** M BUDGE.
WOLLATON (St Leon), *Notts*. R. **D** Southw 8 **P** *Ld Middleton* **I** J A BANKS, D J DAVIES *c*, A E MCGRATH *c*, S G WARD *hon c*.
WOLLATON PARK (St Mary), *Notts*.. **D** Southw 14 **P** *CPAS* **I** H M KITCHEN.
WOLLESCOTE (St Andr), *W Midl*.. **D** Worc 11 **P** *Bp* **I** A R HAYWARD.
WOLSINGHAM (St Mary w St Steph) w Thornley (St Bart), *Durham*. R. **D** Dur 13 **P** *Bp* **I** J G BATES.
WOLSTANTON (St Marg) w Porthill, *Staffs*. R. **D** Lich 17 **P** *Bp* **I** K H MILLER, G H NEWTON *team v*, D P VALE *team v*.
WOLSTON (St Marg) and Church Lawford w King's Newnham, *Warws* V. **D** Cov **P** *Dioc Bd of Patr 2 turns, Bp 1 turn* **I** F C HENDERSON.
WOLSTON, GT (H Trin) w Wolston, L (H Trin), *Bucks*.. **D** Ox 26 *See* Woolstone.
WOLTERTON, *Norf*. R. **D** Nor 3 *See* Wickmere.
WOLVERCOTE (St Pet), *Oxon*.. **D** Ox 8 *See* Oxford.
WOLVERDINGTON, *Warws*.. **D** Cov 13 *See* Wolverton.
WOLVERHAMPTON (St Pet Colleg Ch w St Mary, All SS, St Chad, St Mark and St Geo), *W Midl*. R. **D** Lich 12 **P** *Bp* **I** J H GINEVER, A M K BRANNAGAN *team v*, I R FORSTER *team v*, J G RIDYARD *team v*, I T SHIELD *team v*, K M JUKES *c*, R A COMMANDER *hon c*.
(St Andr), V. **D** Lich 12 **P** *Bp* **I** G A C BROWN.
(St Jo Evang), V. **D** Lich 12 **P** *Exors of Earl of Stamford and Bp (alt)* **I** W T D ATTOE, L L THOMAS *hon c*.
(St Jude), V. **D** Lich 12 **P** *St Jo Coll Nottm Patr Trust* **I** A W C THOMAS.
(St Luke), V. **D** Lich 12 **P** *Trustees* **I** E MALCOLM.
(St Martin, Rough Hills), V. **D** Lich 12 **P** *Bp* **I** R C KNOWLING.
(St Matt), V. **D** Lich 12 **P** *Baldwin Pugh Trustees* **I** R W JACKSON, G GITTINGS *c*.
(St Paul), V. **D** Lich 12 **P** *Trustees and Bp* alt **I** W T D ATTOE.
(St Steph), V. **D** Lich 12 **P** *Bp* **I** P T RIVERS.
WOLVERLEY (St Jo Bapt), *Worcs*. V. **D** Worc 10 **P** *D and C of Worc* **I** R W CIRCUS *p-in-c*.
WOLVERTON (H Trin) (w St Geo Mart), *Bucks*. R. **D** Ox 26 **P** *Bp* **I** D V JONES, R L STURCH *team v*.
WOLVERTON (St Cath) w Ewhurst and Hannington (All SS), R *Hants*.. **D** Win *See* Baughurst.
WOLVERTON or WOLVERDINGTON w Norton Lindsey (H Trin) and Langley, *Warws*. R. **D** Cov 7 **P** *Bp* **I** A G ERREY.
WOLVEY (St Jo Bapt) w Burton Hastings and Stretton Baskerville, *Warws*. V. **D** Cov 5 **P** *Bp* **I** K R HAGAN *p-in-c*.
WOLVISTON (St Pet), *Cleve*. R. **D** Dur 14 **P** *D and C of Dur* **I** D G BILES.
WOMBOURNE (St Benedict), *Staffs*. V. **D** Lich 7 **P** *Trustees* **I** S HUYTON.
WOMBRIDGE (St Mary and St Leon), *Salop*. V. **D** Lich 27 **P** *Trustees of Apley Estate* **I** C E HART.
WOMBWELL (St Mary w St Geo), *S Yorks*. R. **D** Sheff 10 **P** *Trin Coll Cam* **I** D WARNER, E SCOTT *c*.
WOMENSWOULD (St Marg), *Kent*. V. **D** Cant 1 *See* Wymynswold.
WOMERSLEY (St Martin), *N Yorks*. V. **D** Wakef 11 **P** *Earl of Rosse* **I** E L THACKER.
WONERSH (St Jo Bapt), *Surrey*. V. **D** Guildf 5 **P** *Selw Coll Cam* **I** T S FARRELL *p-in-c*.
WONSTON (H Trin), *Hants*. R. **D** Win 12 **P** *Bp* **I** V W NORRISS.
WOOBURN (St Paul), *Bucks*. V. **D** Ox 32 **P** *Bp* **I** G D STAFF, I RUMALSHAH *c*.
WOOD DALLING (St Andr), *Norf*. V. **D** Nor 6 *See* Thurning.
WOOD DITTON (St Mary Virg) w Saxon Street, *Cambs*. V. **D** Ely 4 **P** *Mrs D A Bowlby and Countess of Ellesmere (alt)* **I** A V DAVIS.
WOOD END (St Mich), *Warws*.. **D** Birm 9 *See* Kingsbury.
WOOD GREEN (St Mark, Noel Park), *Lon*. V. **D** Lon 22 **P** *Bp* **I** J D POINTS *c*, R A SMITH *c*.
(St Cuthb Chitts Hill), V. **D** Lon 22 **P** *CPAS* **I** J H LEDGER.
(St Mich), V. **D** Lon 22 **P** *V of Tottenham* **I** C R TRUSS, M J FOSTER *c*, J F WELLINGTON *c*.
(St Sav), V. **D** Lon 23 **P** *Bp* **I** W E HOWELL.
WOOD NORTON (All SS), *Norf*. R. **D** Nor *See* Twyford.
WOOD WALTON (St Andr), *Cambs*. R. **D** Ely 10 *See* Abbots Ripton.
WOODBASTWICK (St Fabian and St Sebastian), *Norf*. V. **D** Nor *See* Ranworth.
WOODBERRY DOWN (St Olave), *Lon*. V. **D** Lon 2 **P** *Ld Chan* **I** P JAMESON, R J LEWIS *c*.
WOODBOROUGH (St Mary Magd) w Manningford Bohune and Beechingstoke (St Steph), *Wilts*. R. **D** Sarum 27 *See* Swanborough.
WOODBOROUGH (St Swith), *Notts*. V. **D** Southw 13 **P** *Bp* **I** D GARRATT.
WOODBRIDGE (St Mary Virg), *Suff*. R. **D** St E 7 **P** *Rev R B Dand* **I** (Vacant).
(St Jo Evang), V. **D** St E 7 **P** *CPS* **I** R G SPECK, P J PLUMLEY *c*.
WOODBURY, (St Swith) w Exton, (St Andr), *Devon*. V. **D** Ex 1 **P** *D and C of Ex* **I** A E OSMOND.
WOODBURY-SALTERTON (H Trin), *Devon*.. **D** Ex 1 *See* Clyst St Geo.
WOODCHESTER AND BRIMSCOMBE, *Glos*. R. **D** Glouc 9 **P** *Simeon Trustees* **I** D N GREEN.
WOODCHURCH (All SS), *Kent*. R. **D** Cant 10 **P** *Abp* **I** G I L GREENLEES.
WOODCHURCH (H Cross), *Mer*. R. **D** Ches 1 **P** *Miss E M Robin* **I** R E TOSTEVIN, G D BOTTOMS *c*, A H B TAYLOR *c*.
WOODCOTE (St Pet), *Salop*.. **D** Lich 21 *See* Sheriffhales.
WOODCOTE, *Oxon*.. **D** Ox *See* Langtree,.
WOODCOTE (St Mark), *Surrey*.. **D** S'wark 9 *See* Purley (St Mark).
WOODCOTT (St Jas), *Hants*. V. **D** Win 5 *See* St Mary Bourne.
WOODEATON, *Oxon*. R. **D** Ox 2 **P** *Bp* **I** D R WESTCOTT *c-in-c*.
WOODEND, *Northants*. V. **D** Pet 2 *See* Blakesley.
WOODFORD (St Mary Virg) w St Phil and St Jas), *Essex*. R. **D** Chelmsf 7 **P** *Bp* **I** S R BIRCHNALL, D L NEWTON *c*, M J TRODDEN *c*.
(St Barn), V. **D** Chelmsf 7 **P** *Bp* **I** M G W ROGERS, P F COATES *c*.

SOUTH (H Trin, Hermon Hill), *Essex*. V. **D** Chelmsf 7 **P** *Bp* **I** P J BEECH.
WOODFORD (Ch Ch), *Gtr Man*. V. **D** Ches 12 **P** *Lt-Col W Bromley-Davenport* **I** J H HALL.
WOODFORD, *Glos*.. **D** Glouc 5 *See* Stone.
WOODFORD (St Mary Virg) w Twywell (St Nich), *Northants*. R. **D** Pet 9 **P** *Dioc Bd of Patr* **I** M C PRENTICE.
WOODFORD BRIDGE (St Paul), *Essex*. V. **D** Chelmsf 7 **P** *R of Woodford* **I** F L RAYNES.
WOODFORD HALSE (St Mary Virg) w Eydon, *Northants*. R. **D** Pet 1 **P** *Bp and Ld Chan* **I** H C SMART.
WOODFORD VALLEY (All SS, St Mich, St Andr), *Wilts*. V. **D** Sarum 13 **P** *Bp* **I** P R OADES.
WOODFORD WELLS or WOODFORD GREEN (All SS), *Essex*. V. **D** Chelmsf 7 **P** *Trustees* **I** M J COLE, J L HUMPHREYS *c*, H J MORRIS *c*.
WOODHALL (St Jas Gt), *N Yorks*. V. **D** Bradf 3 **P** *Bp* **I** E MURGATROYD.
WOODHALL SPA (St Pet) and Kirkstead (St Leon) [Lincs]. V. **D** Linc 11 **P** *Bp* **I** J W HANSON.
WOODHAM (All SS), *Surrey*. V. **D** Guildf 11 **P** *Bp* **I** W D PLATT, R DODD *c*, T D WATSON *c*.
WOODHAM FERRERS (St Mary Virg), *Essex*. R. **D** Chelmsf 11 **P** *Ld Fitzwalter* **I** J W STONE.
WOODHAM FERRERS, SOUTH (St Mary), *Essex*. V. **D** Chelmsf 11 **P** *Bp* **I** J C ABDY.
WOODHAM MORTIMER (St Marg) w Hazeleigh (St Nich), *Essex*. R. **D** Chelmsf 14 **P** *Lt Col J O Parker* **I** J M HALL *p-in-c*.
WOODHAM WALTER (St Mich), *Essex*. R. **D** Chelmsf 14 **P** *CPAS* **I** J M HALL *p-in-c*.
WOODHAY, EAST (St Martin) w Woolton Hill (St Thos), *Hants*. R. **D** Win 5 **P** *Bp* **I** D J CARTER.
WOODHAY, WEST (St Laur) and Enborne w Hamstead Marshall, Inkpen and Combe, *Berks*. R. **D** Ox 14 **P** *Trustees, D and C of Windsor and Exors of Ld Brocket* **I** R JEANS, W R BIRT *c*.
WOODHEAD, *W Yorks*.. **D** Bradf 5 *See* Menston-in-Wharfedale.
WOODHEAD (St Jas), *Gtr Man*.. **D** Ches 14 *See* Mottram-in-Longdendale.
WOODHORN w Newbiggin (St Bart), *Northumb*. V. **D** Newc T 10 **P** *Bp* **I** J B HAY.
WOODHOUSE (St Mary-in-the-Elms), *Leics*. V. **D** Leic 10 **P** *Dioc Bd of Patr* **I** R P RANKIN *c-in-c*.
WOODHOUSE (St Mark), *W Yorks*. V. **D** Ripon 5 **P** *Trustees* **I** R SIMPSON.
WOODHOUSE (St Jas), *S Yorks*. V. **D** Sheff 1 *See* Handsworth Woodhouse.
WOODHOUSE (Ch Ch), *W Yorks*. V. **D** Wakef 4 **P** *Bp* **I** S K M HENRY.
WOODHOUSE EAVES (St Paul), *Leics*. V. **D** Leic 10 **P** *Dioc Bd of Patr* **I** R P RANKIN.
WOODHOUSE PARK (Wm Temple), *Gtr Man*. V. **D** Man 10 **P** *Bp* **I** C R BOND *c*.
WOODHURST, *Cambs*.. **D** Ely 12 *See* Broughton.
WOODINGDEAN (H Cross), *E Sussex*.. **D** Chich 14a *See* Ovingdean.
WOODKIRK or ARDSLEY, WEST (St Mary), *W Yorks*. V. **D** Wakef 10 **P** *E C S J Brudenell Esq* **I** T R KING.
WOODLAND (St Jo Bapt), *Devon*. V. **D** Ex 11 *See* Broadhempston.
WOODLANDS (St Kath), *Somt*. V. **D** B & W 16a **P** *Dioc Bd of Patr* **I** G J WRAYFORD *p-in-c*, H E ALLEN *c*.
WOODLANDS, *N Yorks*.. **D** Bradf 2 *See* Oakenshaw.
WOODLANDS (St Mary Virg), *Berks*. V. **D** Ox 14 **P** *J Gilbey Esq* **I** M C CLARKE.
WOODLANDS (St Mary), *Kent*. V. **D** Roch 8 *See* Kemsing.
WOODLANDS (The Ascen), *Dorset*. V. **D** Sarum *See* Cranborne.
WOODLANDS (All SS), *S Yorks*. V. **D** Sheff 8 **P** *Bp* **I** J A HAWLEY.
WOODLANDS (St Paul), *Hants*. V. **D** Win 5 *See* Kingsclere Woodlands.
WOODLEIGH (St Mary) w Loddiswell (St Mich AA), *Devon*. R. **D** Ex 14 **P** *D and C of Ex and Mart Mem Trust* **I** R J K LAW.
WOODLESFORD (All SS), *W Yorks*. V. **D** Ripon 7 *See* Oulton.
WOODLEY (St Jo Evang), *Berks*. V. **D** Ox 15 **P** *Dioc Bd of Patr* **I** J EASTGATE, D M FLAGG *c*, F F SIMON *c*.
WOODMANCOTE (St Pet), *W Sussex*. R. **D** Chich 14 *See* Henfield.
WOODMANCOTE (St Mark), *Glos*.. **D** Glouc 5 *See* Dursley.
WOODMANCOTE (St Jas), *Hants*. V. **D** Win 12 *See* Micheldever.
WOODMANSTERNE (St Pet), *Surrey*. R. **D** S'wark 8 **P** *Ld Chan* **I** C C COOPER, S G FRANKLIN *c*.
WOODNESBOROUGH (St Mary B Virg), *Kent*. V. **D** Cant 8 **P** *Abp* **I** E R A ALDER *p-in-c*.
WOODNEWTON (St Mary), *Northants*. V. **D** Pet 11 *See* Apethorpe.
WOODPLUMPTON (St Anne), *Lancs*. V. **D** Blackb 10 **P** *V of St Michael-on-Wyre* **I** R P SPENCER.
WOODRISING (St Nich) w Scoulton, *Norf*. R. **D** Nor 19 *See* Carbrooke.
WOODSETTS (St Geo), *S Yorks*. V. **D** Sheff 5 **P** *Bp* **I** J W A WOODS.
WOODSFORD (St Jo Bapt) w Tincleton (St Jo Evang), *Dorset*.. **D** Sarum *See* Moreton.
WOODSIDE, *Surrey*.. **D** Cant *See* Croydon.
WOODSIDE, *Cumb*.. **D** Carl 3 *See* Rosley.
WOODSIDE (St Jas), *N Yorks*. V. **D** Ripon 5 **P** *Bp* **I** R CHIVERS.
WOODSIDE (St Andr) w Hyde, East (H Trin), *Beds*. V. **D** St Alb 20 **P** *D and C of St Paul's* **I** M J WITHEY.
WOODSIDE PARK (St Barn). **D** Lon 24 *See* Finchley.
WOODSTOCK (St Mary Magd) w Bladon (St Mart), *Oxon*. R. **D** Ox **P** *Duke of Marlborough* **I** E G A W PAGE-TURNER, D C PARKER *c*.
WOODSTON (St Aug of Cant), *Cambs*. R. **D** Ely 11 **P** *Bp* **I** H S JOSEPH.
WOODTHORPE, *Lincs*.. **D** Linc 8 *See* Strubby.
WOODTHORPE (St Cath), *S Yorks*.. **D** Sheff 1 *See* Sheffield.
WOODTON w Bedingham, *Suff*.. **D** Nor *See* Hempnall.
WOODVILLE (St Steph), *Derbys*. and *Leics*. V. **D** Derby 16 **P** *Bp* **I** (Vacant).
WOOKEY (St Matt) w Henton (Ch Ch), *Somt*. V. **D** B & W **P** *Bp* **I** D RODGERS *c-in-c*.
WOOKEY HOLE (St Mary Magd), *Somt*.. **D** B & W 6 *See* Wells.
WOOL (H Rood) w Burton, East and Coombe Keynes and East Stoke, *Dorset*. V. **D** Sarum 9 **P** *Bp 3 turns Keble Coll Ox 1 turn* **I** F SMEDLEY.
WOOLACOMBE (St Sabinus), *Devon*. R. **D** Ex 15 *See* Ilfracombe.
WOOLASTON (St Andr) w Alvington (St Andr), *Glos*. R. **D** Glouc 7 **P** *Dioc Bd of Patr* **I** R A NORMAN.
WOOLAVINGTON (St Mary), *Somt*. V. **D** B & W 17 **P** *D and C of Windsor* **I** M FREDRIKSEN.
WOOLAVINGTON (St Pet), *W Sussex*.. **D** Chich 6 *See* Graffham.
WOOLBEDING (All H), *W Sussex*. R. **D** Chich 5 **P** *Exors of E C Lascelles* **I** A PULLIN.
Woolbrook **D** Ex 7 *See* Sidmouth.
WOOLER (St Mary) w Doddington, Ilderton, Ingram, Kirknewton, Chatton and Chillingham, *Northumb*. R. **D** Newc T 8 **P** *Ld Chan 1 turn Dioc Bd of Patr 4 turns* **I** W J THOMAS, W G CHESHAM *team v*, B COWEN *team v*.
WOOLFARDISWORTHY, EAST (St Mary), Cheriton-Fitzpaine, Kennerleigh, Washford Pyne (St Pet), Puddington (St Thos à Becket), Poughill and Stockleigh English (St Mary Virg) and Morchard Bishop (St Mary), Stockleigh Pomeroy, Down St Mary and Clannaborough *Devon*. R. **D** Ex 2 **P** *Dioc Bd of Patr 2nd, 3rd and 4th turns, Ld Chan 1st turn* **I** J L DAVIDSON, M E HEWLETT *team v*, B SHILLINGFORD *team v*.
WOOLFARDISWORTHY, WEST (H Trin) w Bucks Mills, *Devon*. V. **D** Ex 17 **P** *Bp and S for Maint of Faith* **I** D A BATES.
WOOLFOLD (St Jas), *Gtr Man*. V. **D** Man 12 *See* Bury.
WOOLHAMPTON (St Pet) w Midgham (St Matt) and Beenham Valence, *Berks*. V. **D** Ox **P** *Bp, CPAS and Keble Coll Ox* **I** J L WATSON.
WOOLHOPE (St Geo), *Herefs*. V. **D** Heref 4 **P** *D and C of Heref* **I** W I O MCDONALD.
WOOLLAND (Dedic unknown), *Dorset*. V. **D** Sarum 13 *See* Okeford-Fitzpaine.
WOOLLEY (St Mary), *Cambs*. R. **D** Ely 11 *See* Spaldwick.
WOOLLEY (St Pet), *W Yorks*. V. **D** Wakef 13 **P** *M A Walker, Esq* **I** J S PEARSON.
WOOLLEY (All SS), *Somt*.. **D** B & W 13 *See* Swainswick.
WOOLPIT (St Mary Virg), *Suff*. R. **D** St E 10 **P** *A H Clarke Esq* **I** C G H RODGERS.
WOOLSTASTON (St Mich AA), *Salop*. R. **D** Heref 15 *See* Smethcote.
WOOLSTHORPE (St Jas Gt) w Stainwith, *Lincs*. R. **D** Linc 19 **P** *Duke of Rutland* **I** J M ASHLEY.
WOOLSTON (St Mark), *Hants*. V. **D** Win 11 **P** *Bp* **I** F P MATTHEWS.
WOOLSTONE, *Oxon*.. **D** Ox 17 *See* Uffington.

WOOLSTONE, GREAT w Woolstone, L, *Bucks*. R. **D** Ox 26 *See* Woughton.
WOOLSTONE (St Martin of Tours) w Oxenton and Gotherington, *Glos*. R. **D** Glouc 10 **P** *Sir R Coventry and others* **I** F J WRIGHT.
WOOLTON HILL, *Hants*.. **D** Win *See* Woodhay, East.
WOOLTON, MUCH, *Mer*.. **D** Liv 2 *See* Much Woolton.
WOOLVERSTON (St Mich), *Suff*.. **D** St E 5 *See* Freston.
WOOLVERTON (St Lawr), *Somt*.. **D** B & W 16a *See* Rode Major.
WOOLWICH (St Mary Magd w H Trin w St Mich AA), *Kent*. R. **D** S'wark 17 **P** *Bp and Keble Coll Ox* **I** D E RHYS.
(St Thos), R. **D** S'wark 17 **P** *Bp* **I** L S C HARVEY.
(H Trin Charlton), V. **D** S'wark 17 *See* Charlton, New.
WOOLWICH, NORTH (St Jo Evang) w Silvertown, *Essex*. V. **D** Chelmsf 5 **P** *Corp of City of Lon and Bp alt* **I** J F LOWE.
WOORE (St Leon), *Salop*. V. **D** Lich 23 **P** *Bp and R of Mucklestone* **I** J J HOGAN.
WOOTTON (St Martin), *Kent*. R. **D** Cant 4 *See* Denton.
WOOTTON (St Andr), *Humb*. V. **D** Linc 6 **P** *Bp* **I** (Vacant).
WOOTTON (St Mary), *Oxon*. R. **D** Ox 10 **P** *New Coll Ox* **I** J BIDDLESTONE *p-in-c*.
WOOTTON (St Pet), *Oxon*. V. **D** Ox 11 **P** *Bp* **I** A A D SMITH.
WOOTTON (St Geo Mart) w Quinton (St Jo Bapt) and Preston Deanery, *Northants*. R. **D** Pet 4 **P** *Ex Coll Ox and Bp* alt **I** D SCHOLEY.
WOOTTON (St Edm K and Mart), *Isle of Wight*. R. **D** Portsm 7 **P** *Dioc Bd of Patr* **I** G C RAYNER.
WOOTTON (St Mary Virg), *Beds*. V. **D** St Alb 19 **P** *MMT* **I** J V M KIRKBY, A R PRICE *c*.
WOOTTON (St Lawr), *Hants*.. **D** Win *See* Oakley, Church.
WOOTTON BASSETT (All SS and St Bart), *Wilts*. V. **D** Sarum 25 **P** *Dioc Bd of Patr* **I** R R COOPER.
WOOTTON COURTENAY (All SS), *Somt*. R. **D** B & W 21 **P** *Bp* **I** E J MILLER.
WOOTTON FITZPAINE, *Dorset*.. **D** Sarum 2 *See* Whitechurch Canonicorum.
WOOTTON-GLANVILLE (St Mary Virg) w Holnest (The Assumption), *Dorset*. R. **D** Sarum 7 **P** *Dioc Bd of Patr 2 turns, Mrs C B Ireland-Smith 1 turn* **I** D HOPLEY.
WOOTTON, NORTH, *Dorset*. V. **D** Sarum 7 *See* Folke.
WOOTTON, NORTH (All SS), w Wootton, South (St Mary), *Norf*. R. **D** Nor 25 **P** *Lt-Col H R Howard and Ld Chan* alt **I** M P GREEN.
WOOTTON, NORTH (St Pet), *Somt*. V. **D** B & W 6 *See* Pilton.
WOOTTON RIVERS (St Andr), *Wilts*. R. **D** Sarum 27 **P** *St Jo Coll Cam and BNC Ox* alt **I** J A CRACE.
WOOTTON, SOUTH (St Mary), *Norf*. R. **D** Nor 26 *See* Wootton, North.
WOOTTON-WAWEN (St Pet), *Warws*. V. **D** Cov 7 **P** *K Coll Cam* **I** A G SOUTHEARD.
WORCESTER (All SS w St Andr and St Helen), *Worcs*. R. **D** Worc 6 **P** *Bp 2 turns D and C of Worc 1 turn* **I** T STOUT *c*.
(H Trin w St Matt Ronkswood), V. **D** Worc 6 **P** *Bp* **I** K C MARTIN *p-in-c*.
(St Barn Rainbow Hill w Ch Ch Tolladine), R. **D** Worc 6 **P** *Bp* **I** M R SMITH, E F WILLIAMS *team v*.
(St Clem), R. **D** Worc 2 **P** *D and C of Worc* **I** D O BELL *p-in-c*.
(St Geo w St Mary Magd), V. **D** Worc 6 **P** *V of Claines* **I** S LOWE.
(St Jo Bapt-in-Bedwardine), V. **D** Worc 2 **P** *D and C of Worc* **I** F W H BENTLEY, P J A LEVERTON *c*.
(St Jo Bapt Claines) V. **D** Worc 6 **P** *Bp* **I** W D OWEN, P J WEDGWOOD *c*.
(St Martin-in-the-Cornmarket and St Paul), R. **D** Worc 6 **P** *Bp and D and C of Worc* **I** J P LANKESTER, J R DINGLE *c*.
(St Nich), R. **D** Worc 6 **P** *Bp* **I** G T M NOTT *p-in-c*.
(St Steph Barbourne), V. **D** Worc 6 **P** *Bp* **I** G LYALL.
Worcester South East (St Martin w St Pet, St Mark and Norton w Whittington), R. **D** Worc 6 **P** *Bp and D and C of Worc* **I** G S CROSS *team v*.
WORCESTER PARK, *Surrey*.. **D** Guildf 8 *See* Cuddington and Malden.
WORCESTER PARK, *Surrey*.. **D** S'wark 8 *See* Cheam Common.
WORDSLEY (H Trin), *W Midl*. R. **D** Lich 1 **P** *Bp* **I** A E WILLIAMS, L P AUDEN *team v*, A R H HEARD *team v*, G HODGSON *c*.
WORDWELL, *Suff*.. **D** St E *See* Culford.
WORFIELD (St Pet Ap), *Salop*. V. **D** Heref 9 **P** *J R S Greenshields* **I** S B THOMAS, M TURTLE *c*.
WORKINGTON (St Mich), *Cumb*. R. **D** Carl 11 **P** *E S C Curwen Esq* **I** K HUTCHINSON.
(St John), V. **D** Carl 11 **P** *R of Workington* **I** W F ROAN, W P HEWITT *c*.
(St Mary, Westfield), V. **D** Carl 11 **P** *Bp* **I** A HERBERT.
WORKSOP (Priory Ch of St Mary and St Cuthb) and Carburton, *Notts*. V. **D** Southw 7 **P** *SSJE* **I** P H BOULTON, A N EVANS *c*, D A MINSHALL *c*, A J SNASDELL *c*.
(St Anne), V. **D** Southw 7 **P** *Bp* **I** A H BROWN.
(St Jo Evang), V. **D** Southw 7 **P** *CPAS* **I** B A HUNT, D C BAILEY *c*, F SUDWORTH *c*.
(St Paul, Manton), V. **D** Southw 7 **P** *Bp* **I** (Vacant).
WORLABY (St Clem), *Humb*. V. **D** Linc 6 **P** *Mrs P I Dunn* **I** D G TUCKER.
WORLDHAM, EAST w Worldham, West (St Nich), Hartley Mauditt, Kingsley (All SS w St Nich) and Oakhanger (St Mary Magd), *Hants*. V. **D** Win 1 **P** *Bp and D and C of Win* alt **I** V H EARWAKER.
WORLE (St Martin), *Avon*. V. **D** B & W 3 **P** *Ld Chan* **I** D J RACTLIFFE, M F HERBERT *c*.
WORLESTON, *Chesh*.. **D** Ches 15 *See* Acton.
WORLINGHAM (All SS), *Suff*. R. **D** St E 18 **P** *Ld Chan* **I** G K JOHNSON.
WORLINGTON, *Suff*.. **D** St E *See* Freckenham.
WORLINGTON, WEST, w Worlington, East, *Devon*. R. **D** Ex 19 *See* Witheridge.
WORLINGWORTH (St Mary) w Southolt, Tannington (St Ethelbert) and Bedfield w Monk Soham, *Suff*. R. **D** St E **P** *Sir J Henniker-Major 1st turn, Hon G N Rous 2nd turn, Dioc Bd of Patr 3rd turn and Bp 4th turn* **I** W H DONNAN.
WORMBRIDGE (St Pet), *Herefs*.. **D** Heref 1 *See* St Devereux.
WORMEGAY or WERMEGAY (St Mich AA and H Cross), *Norf*.. **D** Ely 17 *See* Tottenhill.
WORMESLEY (St Mary), *Herefs*. V. **D** Heref 4 *See* Credenhill.
WORMHILL (St Marg) w Peakdale (H Trin) and Peak Forest (Chas K and Mart), *Derbys*. V. **D** Derby 10 **P** *Bp and Duke of Devonshire* **I** R S CANEY *p-in-c*.
WORMINGFORD (St Andr), *Essex*. V. **D** Chelmsf 22 **P** *S J Tufnell Esq* **I** A C COX.
WORMINGHALL (St Pet and St Paul), *Bucks*. V. **D** Ox 21 **P** *Bp and Guild of All S* **I** R H COLLIER.
WORMINGHURST (H Sepulchre), *W Sussex*. V. **D** Chich 7 *See* Thakeham.
WORMINGTON (St Cath), *Glos*. R. **D** Glouc 18 *See* Dumbleton.
WORMLEIGHTON (St Pet), *Warws*.. **D** Cov 8 *See* Priors Hardwick.
WORMLEY, *Herts*.. **D** St Alb 6 *See* Broxbourne.
WORMSHILL (St Giles), *Kent*. R. **D** Cant 13 *See* Frinsted.
WORPLESDON (St Mary), *Surrey*. R. **D** Guildf 5 **P** *Eton Coll* **I** C VALLINS, A S BROWNE *c*.
WORSALL, HIGH (All SS) w Worsall, Low *N Yorks*. V. **D** York 25 **P** *Abp 3 turns, V of Northallerton 1 turn* **I** D MOORE.
WORSBROUGH (St Mary), *S Yorks*. V. **D** Sheff 7 **P** *Dioc Bd of Patr* **I** R THOMSON.
WORSBROUGH COMMON (St Luke), *S Yorks*. V. **D** Sheff 7 **P** *Bp* **I** D J DRYE.
WORSBROUGH (St Thos w St James), *S Yorks*. V. **D** Sheff 7 **P** *Crown and Bp* **I** H ANSELL.
WORSLEY (St Mark) w Ellenbrook (St Mary Virg), *Gtr Man*. V. **D** Man 3 **P** *Bp* **I** J M M DALBY, S D A KILLWICK *c*, V H MARKLAND *c*.
WORSTED (St Mary) w Westwick (St Botolph), and Sloley (St Bart), *Norf*. V. **D** Nor 8 **P** *J F B Petrie Esq Lt-Col Sir J E H Neville and D and C of Nor (in turn)* **I** A M BOWMAN *p-in-c*.
WORSTHORNE (St Jo Evang), *Lancs*. V. **D** Blackb 3 **P** *Hulme Trustees* **I** T F ELLEL.
WORTH (St Pet and St Paul), *Kent*. V. **D** Cant 8 **P** *Abp* **I** E R A ALDER *p-in-c*.
WORTH (St Nich), *W Sussex*. R. **D** Chich 12 **P** *Dioc Bd of Patr* **I** (Vacant).
WORTH MATRAVERS (St Nich) (in St Aldhelm Group), *Dorset*. V. **D** Sarum 9 **P** *R of Swanage* **I** H J LLOYD.
WORTHAM (St Mary), *Suff*. R. **D** St E 16 **P** *K Coll Cam* **I** R M KNOTT *p-in-c*.
WORTHEN (All SS), *Salop*. R. **D** Heref 13 **P** *New Coll Ox* **I** N D MINSHALL.
WORTHING (Ch Ch), *W Sussex*. V. **D** Chich 9 **P** *R of Broadwater* **I** P W WALTON.
(H Trin w St Matt), V. **D** Chich 9 **P** *Trustees* **I** (Vacant).
(St Andr), V. **D** Chich 9 **P** *Keble Coll Ox* **I** E J R CHOWN, E G OGDEN *hon c*.

WYKEHAM (St Helen or All SS) and Hutton Buscel (St Matt), *N Yorks*. V. **D** York 24 **P** *Visc Downe and Earl Fitzwilliam* alt **I** E RICHARDS.
WYKEHAM CHAP (St Nich), *Lincs*.. **D** Linc 5 *See* Spalding.
WYKEHAM, EAST, *Lincs*.. **D** Linc 12 *See* Kelstern.
WYKEN (St Mary Magd), *W Midl*. R. **D** Cov 2 *See* Coventry, Caludon.
WYLAM-ON-TYNE, *Northumb*.. **D** Newc T 3 **P** *Bp* **I** W K BODDY.
WYLDE GREEN (Em Ch), *W Midl*. V. **D** Birm 12 **P** *Bp* **I** H P BURGESS, J S HOLLAND *c*.
WYLYE (St Mary Virg) w Fisherton Delamere and The Langfords, *Wilts*. R. **D** Sarum *See* Yarnbury.
WYMERING (St Pet and St Paul), w Widley (St Mary Magd), *Hants*. V. **D** Portsm 3 **P** *E J Nugee Esq* **I** D C ALLISON.
WYMESWOLD (St Mary) and Prestwold w Hoton, *Leics*. V. **D** Leic 10 **P** *Bp and S J Pack-Drury-Lowe Esq (alt)* **I** K W FARMER.
WYMINGTON (St Lawr) w Podington, *Beds*. R. **D** St Alb 21 **P** *Capt R A B Orlebar 1 turn, Dioc Bd of Patr 3 turns* **I** D J WARDROP.
WYMONDHAM (St Pet) w Edmondthorpe (St Mich), *Leics*. R. **D** Leic 4 **P** *Ld Chan* **I** (Vacant).
WYMONDHAM (St Mary Virg and St Thos à Becket), *Norf*. V. **D** Nor 13 **P** *Bp* **I** G R HALL, P H HARRISON *c*.
WYMONDLEY, GREAT (St Mary) w Little (St Mary Virg) w Graveley and Chivesfield, *Herts*. R. **D** St Alb **P** *Bp and MMT* **I** P J MADDEX.
WYMYNSWOLD (St Mary), *Kent*. V. **D** Cant 1 **P** *Abp* **I** E L W BELL *p-in-c*.
WYNFORD EAGLE (St Laur), *Dorset*.. **D** Sarum 5 *See* Compton Abbas.
WYRARDISBURY (St Andr), *Berks*.. **D** Ox 24 *See* Wraysbury.
WYRE PIDDLE, *Worcs*.. **D** Worc 3 *See* Fladbury.
WYRESDALE (Ch Ch), *Lancs*. V. **D** Blackb 11 **P** *Countess of Sefton* **I** (Vacant).
WYRLEY, GREAT (St Mark), *Staffs*. V. **D** Lich 4 **P** *R of Cannock* **I** G F SMITH.
WYSALL (H Trin), *Notts*.. **D** Southw *See* Willoughby-on-the-Wolds.
WYTHALL (St Mary), *Warws* and *Worcs*. V. **D** Birm **P** *R of King's Norton* **I** D M OSMOND.
WYTHAM (All SS), *Oxon*. R. **D** Ox 8 **P** *Univ of Ox* **I** E S LANDEN.
WYTHBURN, *Cumb*.. **D** Carl *See* St John-on-the-Vale.
WYTHENSHAWE (St Martin, Royal Oak), *Gtr Man*. V. **D** Man 10 **P** *Bp* **I** C BARNES *p-in-c*, D A CATTERALL *c*.
WYTHER (Ven Bede), *W Yorks*.. **D** Ripon 8 *See* Leeds.
WYTHOP (St Marg), *Cumb*.. **D** Carl *See* Embleton.
WYTON, *Cambs*.. **D** Ely 10 *See* Houghton.
WYVERSTONE, *Suff*.. **D** St E *See* Bacton.
WYVILLE (St Cath), *Lincs*. R. **D** Linc 14 *See* Harlaxton.

YAFFORTH, *N Yorks*.. **D** Ripon 2 *See* Ainderby Steeple.
YALDING (St Pet and St Paul) w Collier Street (St Marg), *Kent*. V. **D** Roch 6 **P** *Ld Chan* **I** P F WILKINSON.
YANWORTH (St Mich), *Glos*.. **D** Glouc 15 *See* Chedworth.
YAPHAM, *Humb*.. **D** York *See* Pocklington.
YAPTON (St Mary) w Ford (St Andr), *W Sussex*. R. **D** Chich 1 **P** *Bp* **I** H A HAMNETT.
YARBURGH (St Jo Bapt), *Lincs*. R. **D** Linc *See* Mid Marsh Group.
YARCOMBE (St Jo Bapt) w Membury (St Jo Bapt), *Devon*. V. **D** Ex 5 **P** *Crown* **I** L LLOYD JONES P-IN-C OF UPOTTERY.
YARDLEY (St Lawr), *Herts*.. **D** St Alb 5 *See* Ardeley.
YARDLEY (St Edburgh), V *W Midl*.. **D** Birm 13 **P** *St Pet Coll Ox* **I** E G LONGMAN, A M C DUNN *c*, P N S GIBSON *c*.
(St Pet Tile Cross), V. **D** Birm 9 **P** *Bp* **I** M S ALLEN, M R MCKINNEY *c*.
YARDLEY, SOUTH (St Mich AA), *W Midl*. V. **D** Birm 13 **P** *Bp* **I** D J NEW.
YARDLEY GOBION (St Leon), *Northants*. R. **D** Pet 2 *See* Potterspury.
YARDLEY HASTINGS (St Andr), *Northants*. R. **D** Pet 4 **P** *Marq of Northn* **I** J C DAVIES.
YARDLEY WOOD (Ch Ch), *W Midl*. V. **D** Birm 5 **P** *Bp* **I** R H POSTILL, N E BALL *c*.
YARKHILL (St Jo Bapt), *Herefs*. V. **D** Heref 6 *See* Stretton Grandison.
YARLINGTON (St Mary B Virg), *Somt*. R. **D** B & W 4 *See* Camelot.
YARM (St Mary Magd), *Cleve*. R. **D** York 25 **P** *Abp* **I** G C BIRCH, P W ELLIOTT *c*.
YARMOUTH, GT (St Nich w St Pet, St John, St Andr, St Jas, St Paul and St Luke), *Norf*. V. **D** Nor 2 **P** *D and C of Nor* **I** R ALLINGTON-SMITH (FORMERLY SMITH), I L HOYLE *c*, K J SKIPPON *c*.
YARMOUTH (St Jas Ap and Mart), *Isle of Wight*. R. **D** Portsm 7 **P** *Keble Coll Ox* **I** A H DANIELS.
YARNBURY (Wylye, Fisherton Delamere, The Langfords and Stockton), *Wilts*. R. **D** Sarum **P** *Bp 1st turn, CCC Ox 2nd turn, D and C of Sarum 3rd turn* **I** (Vacant).
YARNSCOMBE, *Devon*. V. **D** Ex 20 *See* Newton Tracey.
YARNTON (St Bart), *Oxon*. V. **D** Ox 10 **P** *St Cath Coll Ox* **I** A C ADCOCK.
YARPOLE (St Leon), *Herefs*.. **D** Heref *See* Croft.
YARWELL (St Mary Magd), *Northants*.. **D** Pet *See* Nassington.
YATE NEW TOWN (Yate St Mary, Wapley w Codrington and Dodington St Pet, Westerleigh St Jas Gt), *Avon*. R. **D** Bris 7 **P** *Bp* **I** G GRANT, P D WINKS *team v*, D T PARKINSON *c*.
YATELEY (St Pet), *Hants*. V. **D** Win 4 **P** *Bp* **I** P E D WARBURTON, A S W CULLIS *c*, F J GREED *c*.
YATESBURY (All SS), *Wilts*. R. **D** Sarum 25 *See* Oldbury.
YATTENDON (St Pet and St Paul) w Frilsham, *Berks*. R. **D** Ox *See* Hermitage.
YATTON (St Mary Virg), *Avon*. V. **D** B & W *See* Yatton Moor.
YATTON, *Herefs*.. **D** Heref 6 *See* Much Marcle.
YATTON KEYNELL (St Marg), *Wilts*. R. **D** Bris 9 **P** *Bp and Win Coll* alt **I** M W DITTMER, J E B MARSH *c*.
YATTON MOOR (Kenn, Kingston Seymour and Yatton), *Avon*. V. **D** B & W **P** *Bp and Dioc Bd of Finance* **I** (Vacant).
YAVERLAND (St Jo Bapt), *Isle of Wight*.. **D** Portsm *See* Brading.
YAXHAM (St Pet), *Norf*. R. **D** Nor 12 **P** *Bp* **I** P H MOSS *c-in-c*.
YAXLEY (St Pet), *Cambs*. V. **D** Ely 14 **P** *Ld Chan* **I** J F WOODLEY.
YAXLEY (St Mary Virg), *Suff*.. **D** St E *See* Eye.
YAZOR (St Mary Virg), *Herefs*. V. **D** Heref 4 *See* Mansel Lacy.
YEADING (St Edm). **D** Lon 18 *See* Hayes.
YEADON (St Jo Evang), *W Yorks*. V. **D** Bradf 5 **P** *R of Guiseley* **I** J F N ROBINSON.
(St Andr), V. **D** Bradf 5 **P** *Bp* **I** K C POTTER.
YEALAND CONYERS (St John), *Lancs*. V. **D** Blackb 13 *See* Warton.
YEALMPTON (St Bart), *Devon*. V. **D** Ex 21 **P** *Bp* **I** M A P COMEAU.
YEARSLEY, *N Yorks*. V. **D** York 5 *See* Crayke.
YEAVELEY, *Derbys*.. **D** Derby *See* Alkmonton.
YEDINGHAM (St Jo Bapt), *N Yorks*. V. **D** York *See* Heslerton.
YELDEN (St Mary) w Melchbourne, *Beds*. R. **D** St Alb *See* Dean.
YELDHAM, Gt (St Andr) w L (St Jo Bapt), *Essex*. R. **D** Chelmsf 18 **P** *Bp and Ld Chan (alt)* **I** (Vacant).
YELFORD (St Nich and St Swith), *Oxon*.. **D** Ox 9 *See* Windrush, Lower.
YELLING (H Cross) w Toseland (St Mich), *Cambs*.. **D** Ely 1 *See* Graveley.
YELVERTOFT (All SS) w Clay Coton (St Andr) and Lilbourne (All SS), *Northants*. R. **D** Pet 6 **P** *MMT* **I** HON J M A KENWORTHY.
YELVERTON, *Devon*. V. **D** Ex 22 **P** *Bp* **I** R G ELLIS.
YELVERTON, *Norf*.. **D** Nor *See* Bergh Apton.
YEOVIL (St Jo Bapt) w Preston Plucknett (St Jas) and Kingston Pitney, Hendford (H Trin), Penn Mill (St Mich AA), Barwick and Closworth, *Somt*. R. **D** B & W 12 **P** *Patr Bd 3 turns, Crown 1 turn* **I** H ANDREWES UTHWATT, M D ELLIS *team v*, A T HUGHES *team v*, T W STOKES *team v*, D C BINDON *c*, D J HUNT *c*, C T JENKINS *c*, D M JONES *c*, A J WEBB *c*.
YEOVIL MARSH (All SS), *somt*.. **D** B & W 11 *See* Tintinhull.
YEOVILTON (St Bart), *Somt*. R. **D** B & W 10 *See* Ilchester.
YETMINSTER (St Andr) w Ryme Intrinseca (St Hippolytus), *Dorset*. V. **D** Sarum 7 **P** *Bp and Duchy of Cornw* alt **I** C D WIDDECOMBE.
YIEWSLEY (St Matt), *Gtr Lon*. V. **D** Lon 9 **P** *V of Hillingdon* **I** J H WEEKS.
YOCKLETON (H Trin), *Salop*. R. **D** Heref 13 **P** *Bp* **I** M BUDGE.
YORK (All SS, Pavement, w St Crux and St Martin w St Helen and St Denys), *N Yorks*. R. **D** York 1 **P** *Abp* **I** J H ARMSTRONG, T L PRESTON *team v*.

(All SS, Huntington), R. **D** York 1 **P** *Patr Bd* **I** H N MACKAY.
(H Redeemer Distr Acomb). **D** York 1 **P** *Crown* **I** A T WILLIS.
(H Trin Heworth). V. **D** York 1 **P** *CTS* **I** R D BARRON *c.*
(H Trin w St Jo Evang, St Martin and St Greg Micklegate), R. **D** York 1 **P** *D and C of York* **I** H FALL.
(St Barn), V. **D** York 1 **P** *CPAS* **I** M T A BULMAN, J G F GRAHAM-BROWN *hon c.*
(St Chad), V. **D** York 1 **P** *Abp* **I** J D HALL.
(St Helen, now St Edw the Confessor, Dringhouses), V. **D** York 1 **P** *Abp* **I** A M GIRLING, G MOUNTAIN *c.*
(St Hilda), V. **D** York 1 **P** *Abp* **I** E J HUDSON.
(St Lawr w St Nich and New Fulford), V. **D** York 1 **P** *D and C of York* **I** A R JONES.
(St Luke), V. **D** York 1 **P** *Abp* **I** G H WEBSTER.
(St Mary, Bishophill Senior w St Clem), R. **D** York 1 **P** *Abp* **I** R L CARBERRY.
(St Mary, Bishophill Junior) w (All SS North Street), V. **D** York 1 **P** *D and C of York* **I** A C M HOWARD, P L BASTOCK *c,* G S HIGGINSON *hon c.*
(St Mary Castlegate w St Mich Spuriergate), R. **D** York 1 **P** *Abp* **I** B C NORRIS.
(St Mich-le-Belfrey w St Cuthb), V. **D** York 1 **P** *Abp* **I** G A CRAY *c,* D K WERNER *c,* J H LAMBERT-SMITH *hon c.*
(St Olave w St Giles), V. **D** York 1 **P** *Abp* **I** J A HESLOP, G A LAW *hon c.*
(St Osw Fulford), V. **D** York 1 **P** *Abp* **I** D H REYNOLDS.
(St Paul, Holgate), R. **D** York 1 **P** *Trustees* **I** D R WOOLDRIDGE.
(St Phil and St Jas Clifton), V. **D** York 1 **P** *Trustees* **I** R G FLETCHER.
(St Steph Acomb), V. **D** York 1 **P** *A H Sampson Esq J P and H Harrison Esq* **I** F L BURNHAM, J HARRISON *c.*
(St Thos w St Maurice), V. **D** York 1 **P** *Abp* **I** J W WALMSLEY.
(St Jas the Deacon Acomb Moor), V. **D** York 1 **P** *Abp* **I** J W HORTON.
YORKTOWN (St Mich), *Surrey.* V. **D** Guildf 5a *See* Camberley.
YOULGREAVE (All SS) w Middleton (St Mich AA), *Derbys.* V. **D** Derby 9 **P** *Duke of Devonshire* **I** D V GIBLING *p-in-c,* D J PRYOR *hon c.*
YOXALL (St Pet), *Staffs.* R. **D** Lich 2 **P** *Bp* **I** B P BROWNLESS.
YOXFORD (St Pet), *Suff.* V. **D** St E 19 **P** *Bp* **I** P R OWENS *p-in-c.*

ZEAL MONACHORUM (St Pet), *Devon.* R. **D** Ex **P** *Dioc Bd of Patr* **I** B H GALES.
ZEAL, SOUTH, *Devon..* **D** Ex 12 *See* Tawton, South.
ZEALS (St Martin), *Wilts.* R. **D** Sarum 22 *See* Upper Stour
ZENNOR, St (St Senner), *Cornw.* V. **D** Truro 5 **P** *Bp* **I** J B D COTTER.

INDEX OF PARISHES—WELSH

ABBEY CWMHIR (St Mary Virg) *Powys*. V **D** Swansea 7 *See* Llandewi Ystradenny.

ABER (St Bodfan), *Gwyn*. R **D** Bangor 2 *See* Llanfairfechan.

ABERAMAN (St Marg w St Barn w Abercwmboi (St Pet), *Mid Glam*. V **D** Llandaff 1 **I** G S PRASADAM.

ABERAVON (St Mary w St Paul and St Teilo), *W Glam*. **D** Llandaff 7 **I** H G B HOPKINS.

(H Trin), V **D** Llandaff 7 **I** E B DOWDING.

ABERAYRON, *Dyfed*. **D** St David's *See* Henfynyw.

ABERBARGOED, *Gwent*. **D** Monmouth *See* Bedwellty.

ABERCANAID (St Pet and St Jas), *Mid Glam*. **D** Llandaff 8 **I** D E PHILLIPS.

ABERCARN (St Luke), *Gwent*. **D** Monmouth 8 **I** (Vacant).

ABERCRAVE (St D) w Callwen (St Jo Bapt), *Powys*. V **D** Swansea 10 **I** J I HOLDSWORTH.

ABERCWMBOI, *Mid Glam*. **D** Llandaff 1 *See* Aberaman.

ABERCYNON (St Donat w St Gwynno), *Mid Glam*. V **D** Llandaff 1 **I** B EVANS.

ABERDARE (St Jo Bapt w St Elvan and St Mary Virg St Jo Evang and St Matt), *Mid Glam*. V **D** Llandaff 1 **I** N A B DAVIES *c*.

ST FAGAN (St Fagan w St Luke, Cwmdare and St Jas Llwydcoed), V **D** Llandaff 1 **I** W T PRICE.

ABERDARON (St Mywyn) and Bodferin (St Mary) w Rhiw and Llanfaelrhys, *Gwyn*. V *Sin*. R **D** Bangor 11 **I** (Vacant).

ABERDOVEY (St Pet), *Gwyn*. R **D** Bangor 12 **I** J J G JAMES, W P W GLADWIN *c*.

ABEREDW (St Cewydd) w Llandilo-Graban (St Teilo) and Llanbadarn-y-Garreg (St Padarn), *Powys*. R **D** Swansea 3 **I** H P JONES *p-in-c*.

ABERERCH (St Cawrdaf), *Gwyn*. V **D** Bangor 11 **I** R F DONALDSON.

ABERFFRAW (St Beuno) w Llangwyfan (St Mary w St Cwyfan), *Gwyn*. R **D** Bangor 4 **I** J E WILLIAMS.

ABERGAVENNY (St Mary w Ch Ch) w Llanwenarth Citra (St Pet), *Gwent*. V and R **D** Monmouth 1 **I** M L CLEMENT, A R TREW *c*.

(H Trin), V **D** Monmouth 1 **I** R DAVIES.

ABERGELE (St Mich), *Clwyd*. V **D** St Asaph 6 **I** M C DONALDSON, D WILLIAMS *c*.

ABERGORLECH, *Dyfed*. **D** St David's *See* Brechfa.

ABERGWILI (St D) w Llanfihangeluwch-Gwili, *Dyfed*. V **D** St David's 11 **I** J H V HUGHES.

ABERGYNOLWYN, *Gwyn*. **D** Bangor *See* Llanfihangel-y-pennant.

ABERHAFESP, *Clwyd*. **D** St Asaph *See* Newtown.

ABERNANT, *Dyfed*. **D** St David's *See* Trelech.

ABERPERGWM (St Cadoc) w Blaengwrach, *W Glam*. V **D** Llandaff 9 **I** (Vacant).

ABERPORTH (St Cynwyl) w Tremain (St Mich), *Dyfed*. R **D** St David's 8 **I** W J G VARNEY.

ABERSYCHAN (St Thos) and Garndiffaith (St John), *Gwent*. V **D** Monmouth 11 **I** C R F CALE.

ABERTILLERY (St Mich), *Gwent*. V **D** Monmouth 9 **I** P A RILEY.

(St John, Six Bells) **D** Monmouth *See* Six Bells.

ABERYSKIR (St Cynidr and St Mary) w Llanfihangel-Nantbran (St Mich), *Powys*. R **D** Swansea 1 **I** B M JONES.

ABERYSTRUTH or BLAINA (St Pet), *Gwent*. R **D** Monmouth 9 **I** B J PARFITT.

ABERYSTWYTH (St Mich AA w St Mary and H Trin), *Dyfed*. R **D** St David's 10 **I** B LEWIS, R M CAPPER *team v*, M L REES *team v*.

AFAN VALE (St Gabr), *W Glam*. V **D** Llandaff 7 *See* Glyncorrwg.

ALLTMAWR, *Powys*. **D** Swansea *See* Builth.

ALLTWEN, *W Glam*. **D** Llandaff *See* Cilybebyll.

AMBLESTON w St Dogwells and Walton East *Dyfed*. **D** St David's *See* Wiston.

AMLWCH (St Eleth) and Rhosybol (Ch Ch) w Llandyfrydog (St Tyfrydog) and Llanwenllwyfo (St Gwenllwyfo) w Llaneilian (St Eilian), w Llangwyllog (St Cwyllog) w Coedana (St Ana) w Llannerchymedd w Rhodogeidio w Gwredog, *Gwynedd*. R **D** Bangor 6 **I** H E GRIFFITH.

AMMANFORD, *Dyfed*. **D** St David's *See* Bettws (St David).

AMROTH (St Elidr), *Dyfed*. V **D** St David's 5 *See* Crunwere.

ANGLE or NANGLE (St Mary), *Dyfed*. R **D** St David's *See* Castlemartin.

ARTHOG (St Cath) w Fairbourne (St Cynon), *Gwyn*. V **D** Bangor 12 **I** G W HEWITT.

BAGILLT (St Mary), *Clwydd*. V **D** St Asaph 4 **I** T A STILLINGS.

BAGLAN (St Cath), *W Glam*. V **D** Llandaff 7 **I** D I LEWIS.

BALA Gwynedd. **D** St Asaph *See* Llancycil.

BANGOR (St Jas), *Gwyn*. V **D** Bangor 1 **I** E T ROBERTS, N E C GAMBLE *c*.

(St Mary), V **D** Bangor 1 **I** (Vacant).

BANGOR-MONACHORUM (St Dunawd), *Clwyd*. R **D** St Asaph 11 **I** L M DANIEL.

BANGOR TEIFI (St D) w Henllan (St D), Llanfair Orllwyn, and Llangynllo (St Cynllo), *Dyfed*. R **D** St David's 6 **I** D PUGH.

BARGOED (St Gwladys) and Deri w Brithdir, *Mid Glam*. V **D** Llandaff 3 **I** J G D OEPPEN, D W W THOMAS *c*, P N THOMPSON *c*.

BARMOUTH, *Gwynedd*. **D** Bangor *See* Llanaber.

BARRY (All SS), *S Glam*. **D** Llandaff 10 **I** W D DAVIES, B J EVANS *c*.

BARRY DOCKS, *S Glam*. **D** Llandaff *See* Penarth.

BARRY, EAST, *S Glam*. **D** Llandaff *See* Merthyr Dyfan.

BASSALEG (St Basil) w Rogerstone, *Gwent*. V **D** Monmouth 7 **I** P W WOODMAN, C J NICKLESS *c*, J H WINSTON *c*.

BATTLE, *Powys*. **D** Swansea *See* Brecon (St Mary).

BAYVIL, *Dyfed*. **D** St David's *See* Nevern.

BEAUFORT (St Jo Evang w St D and St Andr), *Gwent*. V **D** Monmouth 9 *See* Ebbw Vale.

BEAUMARIS, *Gwyn*. **D** Bangor *See* Llandegfan.

BEDDGELERT (St Mary), *Gwyn*. V **D** Bangor 10 **I** K E FRANCIS.

BEDLINOG (St Cadoc and St Mary), *Mid Glam*. V **D** Llandaff 8 **I** J H SCOTT.

BEDWAS (St Barrwg) *Gwent*. V **D** Monmouth 7 **I** W M DAVIES.

BEDWELLTY (St Sennan) w Aberbargoed (St Pet), *Gwent*. R **D** Monmouth 8 **I** R T GREY.

BEGELLY (St Mary) w Kilgetty, *Dyfed*. **D** St David's 4 **I** D G WILLIAMS.

BEGUILDY (St Mich and St Pet) and Heyope (St D), *Powys*. V **D** Swansea 6 **I** M L WISHART.

BERRIEW (St Beuno) w Manafon, *Powys*. V **D** St Asaph 10 **I** O THOMAS.

BERSE DRELINCOURT, *Clwyd*. w Southsea (All SS) V **D** St Asaph 16 **I** G L FRANCIS.

BETTISFIELD (St Jo Bapt), *Clwyd*. V **D** St Asaph *See* Hanmer.

BETTWS (St D) w Ammanford (St Mich AA and All SS), *Dyfed*. V **D** St David's 12 **I** A J R THOMAS, A TEALE *c*.

BETTWS (St D), *Mid Glam*. R **D** Llandaff 2 **I** A D PEGLER.

BETTWS, *Gwent*. **D** Monmouth **I** R P MATTHEWS.

BETTWS-BLEDRWS (St Bledrws) w Llangybi (St Cybi) and Silian, *Dyfed*. R **D** St David's 9 **I** (Vacant).

BETTWS-CEDEWAIN (St Beuno) and Tregynon (St Cynon) w Llanwyddelan (St Gwyddelan), *Powys*. V **D** St Asaph 7 **I** R H FAIRBROTHER.

BETTWS, *Powys*. **D** Swansea *See* Clyro.

BETTWS-DISSERTH, *Powys*. **D** Swansea *See* Llansantffraed-in-Elwel.

BETTWS-EVAN (St John) w Brongwyn (St Mary), *Dyfed*. V **D** St David's 6 **I** T G O JENKINS.

BETTWS-GARMON (St Garmon or Germanus) w Waunfawr (St John), *Gwyn*. V **D** Bangor 1 *See* Llanbeblig.

BETTWS-GWERFYL-GOCH, *Clwyd*. **D** St Asaph *See* Cerrigydrudion.

BETTWS-LEIKI, *Dyfed*. **D** St David's *See* Blaenpennal.

BETTWS-NEWYDD, *Gwent*. **D** Monmouth *See* Trostrey.

BETTWS-PENPONT, *Powys*. **D** Swansea *See* Trallwng.

BETWS-y-COED (St Mich AA w St Mary Virg) w Capel Curig (St Curig), *Gwyn*. V **D** Bangor 2 **I** M O PRITCHARD.

BETWS-YN-RHOS (St Mich), *Clwyd*. V **D** St Asaph 6 *See* Llanelian.

BISHOPSTON (St Teilo), *W Glam*. R **D** Swansea 8 **I** A B EVASON.

BISHTON, *Gwent*. **D** Monmouth *See* Llanwern.

BISTRE (Em), *Clwyd*. V **D** St Asaph 14 **I** G R JONES, M J COMER *c*.

BLACKWOOD (St Marg), *Gwent*. V D Monmouth 8 I R K COURAGE.
BLAENAU FFESTINIOG (St D), *Gwyn*. D Bangor *See* Ffestiniog.
BLAENAVON (St Pet) w Capel Newydd (St Paul w St Jas and St Jo Evang), *Gwent*. V D Monmouth 11 I R G HACKETT.
BLAENGARW, *Mid Glam*. D Llandaff *See* Pontycymmer.
BLAENGWRACH, *W Glam*. D Llandaff *See* Aberpergwm.
BLAENPENNAL (St D) w Llangeitho (St Ceitho) w Bettws-Leiki, [Dyfed]. V D St David's 9 I (Vacant).
BLAENPORTH (St D), *Dyfed*. V D St David's *See* Penbryn.
BLAINA, *Gwent*. D Monmouth *See* Aberystruth.
BLEDDFA, *Powys*. D Swansea *See* Llangynllo.
BLETHERSTON, *Dyfed*. D St David's *See* Llawhaden.
BODEDERN (St Edeyrn) w Llechgynfarwy and Llechylched w Ceirchiog w Llanfihangel-yn-Nhywyn w Caergeiliog, *Gwyn*. R D Bangor 3 I E W ROWLANDS.
BODELWYDDAN (St Marg), *Clwyd*. V D St Asaph 1 I R V BYLES.
BODEWRYD, *Gwyn*. D Bangor *See* Llanfechell.
BODFARI (St Steph), *Clwyd*. R D St Asaph 2 I R J EDWARDS.
BODFEAN (St Buan), *Gwyn*. D Bangor 11 *See* Llannor.
BODWROG, *Gwyn*. D Bangor *See* Llandrygarn.
BONTDDU, *Gwyn*. D Bangor *See* Llanaber.
BONVILSTON (St Mary Virg) w St Nich and St George-super-Ely (St Geo), *S Glam*. R D Llandaff 10 I O G REES.
BORTH (St Matt), *Dyfed*. V D St David's 10 I I T WINTERBURN.
BOSHERSTON (St Mich AA) w St Twynnells (St Gwynog), *Dyfed*. R D St David's 1 I G R BALL.
BOTTWNNOG, *Gwyn*. D Bangor *See* Mellteyrn.
BOUGHROOD, *Powys*. D Swansea *See* Llandefalle.
BOULSTON, *Dyfed*. D St David's *See* Slebech.
BRAWDY (St D) w Hays Castle (St Mary) and Llandeloy (St Teilo), V D St David's 2 I D B REES.
BRECHFA (St Teilo) w Abergorlech and Llanfihangel-Rhos-y-Corn, *Dyfed*. R D St David's 14 I E M GREY.
BRECON (St Jo Evang Cathl w St Mary) w Battle (St Cynog), *Powys*. V D Swansea 1 I VERY REV A R JONES, W J MORRIS *c*.
BRECON or LLANFAES (St D) w Ch Coll *Powys*. V D Swansea 2 I J W C COUTTS.
BRIDELL, *Dyfed*. D St David's *See* Kilgerran.
BRIDGEND, *Mid Glam*. D Llandaff *See* Coity.
BRITHDIR (St Mark) w Bryncoedifor (St Paul), *Dyfed*. D Bangor 12 *See* Dolgellau.
BRITON FERRY (St Clem), *W Glam*. R D Llandaff 9 *See* Llansawel.
(St Mary, Llansawel), V D Llandaff *See* Llansawel.
BRONGWYN, *Dyfed*. D St David's *See* Betws Evan.
BRONINGTON or NEW FENNS, *Clwyd*. D St Asaph *See* Hanmer.
BRONLLYS (St Mary) w Llanvillo (St Bilo) and Llandefaelog Tre'rgraig (St Maelog), *Powys*. R D Swansea 5 I P DIXON.
BROUGHTON, *Clwyd*. D St Asaph *See* Hawarden.
BROUGHTON (St Paul), *Clwyd*. V D St Asaph 16 I B SMITH, G R MATTHIAS *c*.
BRYMBO (St Mary w St John and St Alb) w Bwlch-Gwyn (Ch Ch), *Clwyd*. V D St Asaph 16 I S H GILBERT, C E WILLIAMS *c*.
BRYN, *Mid Glam*. D Llandaff *See* Llangynwyd.
BRYNAMAN (St Cath), *Dyfed*. V D St David's 12 I V P ROBERTS.
BRYNCOEDIFOR, *Gwyn*. D Bangor *See* Brithdir.
BRYNCROES, *Gwyn*. D Bangor *See* Llangwnadl.
BRYNEGLWYS (St Tyssilio) and Llandegla (St Tecla), *Clwyd*. V D St Asaph 12 I G B NEWTON.
BRYNFORD (St Mich) w Ysceifiog (St Mary), *Clwyd*. D St Asaph 4 *See* Gorsedd.
BRYNGWYN (St Mich AA) w Newchurch (St Mary), Llanbedr-Painscastle (St Pet) and Llandewi Fach (St D), *Powys*. R D Swansea 5 I M P RALPH-BOWMAN *c*.
BRYNGWYN, *Gwent*. D Monmouth *See* Llanarth.
BRYNGWYN, *Dyfed*. D St David's *See* Brongwyn.
BRYNMAWR (St Mary), *Gwent*. V D Swansea 4 I D R WILLIAMS.
BRYNYMAEN, *Clwyd*. D St Asaph *See* Trofarth.
BUCKLEY (St Matt), *Clwyd*. V D St Asaph 14 I E G PRICE.
BUILTH (St Mary) w Llanddewi'r Cwm (St D) w Maesmynis, Llanynys and Alltmawr, *Powys*. V D Swansea 3 I E C JOHN.
BURRY PORT (St Mary) w Pwll (H Trin) *Dyfed*. D St David's 13 I T R K GOULSTONE, E J W ROBERTS *hon c*.
BURTON (St Mary in Rhos), *Dyfed*. R D St David's 5 I J HALE.
BUTTINGTON (All SS) and Pool Quay (St Jo Evang), *Powys*. V D St Asaph 10 I P K D EVANS.
BWLCH-GWYN, *Clwyd*. D St Asaph *See* Brymbo.
BWLCH-Y-CIBAU (Ch Ch), *Powys*. V D St Asaph I S F HADLEY.
BYLCHAU, *Clwyd*. D St Asaph *See* Llansannan.

CADOXTON-JUXTA-BARRY (St Cadoc and St Mary), *S Glam*. R D Llandaff 10 I G R STEELE.
CADOXTON-JUXTA-NEATH (St Cattwg), *W Glam*. V D Llandaff 9 I N M COOPER.
CAER RHUN (St Mary) w Llangelynnin (St Celynin), *Gwyn*. V D Bangor 2 I R D WHITE.
CAERAU (St Mary) w Ely (St D), *S Glam*. V D Llandaff 4 I J C BUTTIMORE, C P SUTTON *c*.
CAERAU (St Cynfelin) w Natyffyllon (St Pet), *Mid Glam*. D Llandaff 7 I E G JONES.
CAERDEON, *Gwyn*. D Bangor *See* Llanaber.
CAERFALLWCH or RHOSESMOR (St Paul), *Clwyd*. V D St Asaph 14 I L EDWARDS.
CAERGEILIOG, *Gwyn*. D Bangor *See* Llechylched.
CAERLEON, *Gwent*. D Monmouth *See* Llangattock-juxta-Caerleon.
CAERNARFON, *Gwyn*. D Bangor *See* Llanbeblig.
CAERPHILLY (St Martin, St Cath, Ch Ch and St Andr), *Mid Glam*. R D Llandaff 3 I N W MARTIN *c*.
CAERSWS (St Mary) D Bangor *See* Llanwnnog.
CAERWENT (St Steph) w Dinham and Llanfair Discoed, *Gwent*. V and R D Monmouth 2 I W J PEACOCK.
CAERWYS (St Mich), *Clwyd*. R D St Asaph 2 I R J EDWARDS.
CALDICOT (St Mary Virg), *Gwent*. V D Monmouth 2 I D C VICKERY.
CALLWEN, *Powys*. D Swansea *See* Abercrave.
CAMRHOS or CAMROSE (St Ishmael), *Dyfed*. V D St David's 5 I B JONES.
CANTON (St Jo Evang), *S Glam*. R D Llandaff 4 I D A V FRAYNE.
(St Cath w St Cadoc), V D Llandaff 4 I A D HUNTER.
(St Luke), V D Llandaff 4 I G F HORWOOD.
(St Paul, Grangetown), V D Llandaff 4 I L V DAVIES.
CANTREF, *Powys*. D Swansea *See* Llanfrynach.
CAPEL BANGOR (St Comgall), *Dyfed*. V D St David's 10 I (Vacant).
CAPEL COELBREN, *Powys*. V D Swansea 10 I W A E BEYNON.
CAPEL COLMAN (St Colman) w Llanfihangel-Penbedw (St Mich) and Clydau (St Clydai) w Penrhydd and Castellan, *Dyfed*. D St David's I A W WILLIAMS.
CAPEL CURIG, *Gwyn*. D Bangor 2 *See* Betws-y-Coed.
CAPEL CYNON (St Cynon) w Talgarreg (St D), *Dyfed*. R D St David's 7 I D P D GRIFFITHS *c*.
CAPEL DEWI SANT, *Dyfed*. D St David's 7 *See* Llansantffraed.
CAPEL GARMON (St Garmon or Germanus), *Gwyn*. D St Asaph 5 *See* Llanrwst.
CAPEL NANTDDU, *Powys*. D Swansea *See* Cefn Coed.
CAPEL NEWYDD, *Gwent*. D Monmouth *See* Blaenavon.
CAPEL TAFFECHAN, *Powys*. D Swansea *See* Vaynor.
CAPEL-Y-FFIN, *Powys*. D Swansea *See* Llanigon.
CARDIFF (St Jo Bapt w St Jas Gt St Mich AA and St Alb), *S Glam*. V D Llandaff 4 I E I DAVIES, S C PARE *c*, J H RICHARDS *c*.
(St Mary Virg and St Steph), V D Llandaff 4 I K J JORDAN.
EGLWYS DEWI SANT (Dewi Sant, Welsh Ch), V D Llandaff 4 I D L B EVANS.
ST ANDREW (St Andr w St Teilo and St Illtyd), V D Llandaff 4 I A E ALDER.
ST DYFRIG (St Dyfrig) w U Grangetown (St Samson), V D Llandaff 4 I F W BEGLEY.
ST GERMAN (St German and St Lawr) D Llandaff *See* Roath.
(St Marg, St Anne, St Agnes, and St Edw) D Llandaff *See* Roath.
(St Martin and St Cypr) D Llandaff *See* Roath.
(St Paul, Grangetown) D Llandaff *See* Canton.
(St Sav St Francis and St Columba) D Llandaff *See* Roath.
CARDIGAN (St Mary) w Mount (H Cross) and Verwick (St Pedrog), *Dyfed*. V D St David's 8 I A J DAVIES.
CAREW (St Mary), *Dyfed*. V D St David's 1 I W C BOWEN.

CARMARTHEN (St Pet w St Jo Evang), *Dyfed.* V **D** St David's 11 **I** D H DAVIES, P H B THOMAS *c,* J D WILLIAMS *c.*
(St D w Ch Ch), V **D** St David's 11 **I** R T DAVIES.
CARNHEDRYN, *Dyfed.* **D** St David's *See* Llanrhian.
CARNO (St Jo Bapt), *Powys.* **D** Bangor *See* Llanwnnog.
CASCOB (St Mich), *Powys.* R **D** Swansea 6 **I** R A F PARSONS.
CASTELLAN, *Dyfed.* **D** St David's *See* Capel Colman.
CASTELLDWYRAN, *Dyfed.* **D** St David's *See* Llanfallteg.
CASTLE-BIGH or BYTHE, *Dyfed.* **D** St David's *See* Puncheston.
CASTLE-CAEREINION (St Garmon), *Powys.* R **D** St Asaph 10 *See* Welshpool.
CASTLEMARTIN (St Mich AA) w Warren, Angle (St Mary), Rhoscrowdder (St Decumanus or Dagman) and Pwllcrochan, *Dyfed.* R **D** St David's 1 **I** J H M DAVIES.
CATHEDINE (St Mich), *Powys.* R **D** Swansea 1 *See* Llangorse.
CEFN (St Mary), *Clwyd.* R **D** St Asaph 1 **I** (Vacant).
CEFN COED (St Jo Bapt) w Capel Nantddu (St Mary), *Powys.* V **D** Swansea 2 **I** D T WALTERS.
CEFNLLYS, *Powys.* **D** Swansea *See* Llandrindod.
CEIRCHIOG, *Gwyn.* **D** Bangor *See* Llechylched.
CELLAN (All SS) w Llanfair Clydogau (St Mary), *Dyfed.* R **D** St David's 9 **I** J M MATHIAS.
CEMAIS (St Tydecho), *Gwyn.* R **D** Bangor 9 *See* Mallwyd.
CENARTH (St Llawddog) w Cilrhedyn (St Teilo and St Llawddog), *Dyfed.* V and R **D** St David's *See* Llandygwydd.
CERRIG-Y-DRUDION (St Mary Magd) w Llangwm, Llanfihangel-glynmyfry, Yspytty-Ifan (St Jo Bapt), Pentrefoelas, Betws GG and Dinmael, *Clwyd.* R **D** St Asaph 12 **I** J E HYDE-LINAKER.
CHAPEL HILL, *Gwent.* **D** Monmouth *See* Tintern Parva.
CHEPSTOW (St Mary), *Gwent.* V **D** Monmouth 2 **I** D THOMAS, C J BLANCHARD *c,* P J WILLIAMS *c.*
CHERITON, *Dyfed.* **D** St David's *See* St Petrox.
CHERITON, *W Glam.* **D** Swansea *See* Llanmadoc.
CHIRK (St Mary), *Clwyd.* V **D** St Asaph 13 **I** J D DENNIS.
CHRISTCHURCH (H Trin), *Gwent.* V **D** Monmouth 10 **I** J C WOODWARD, M G HADDOCK *c.*
CILCAIN, or KILKEN (St Mary), *Clwyd.* V **D** St Asaph *See* Nanerch.
CILCENNIN (H Trin), *Dyfed.* **D** St David's *See* Llanfihangel Ystrad.
CILFYNYDD (St Luke), *Mid Glam.* V **D** Llandaff 11 **I** S F MINTY.
CILGERRAN, *Dyfed.* **D** St David's *See* Kilgerran.
CILGWYN, *Dyfed.* **D** St David's *See* Newport.
CILIAU-AERON, *Dyfed.* **D** St David's *See* Llanercheron.
CILRHEDYN, *Dyfed.* **D** St David's *See* Cenarth.
CILYBEBYLL (St Jo Evang) w Alltwen (St Jo Bapt), *W Glam.* R **D** Llandaff 9 **I** E L HOUGH.
CILYCWM (St Mich w Ystradffin (St Barn) and Rhandirmwyn (St Paulinus or Peurlin) and Llanfair-ar-y-Bryn (St Mary), *Dyfed.* V **D** St David's 14 **I** D J LLOYD.
CILMAENLLWYD, *Dyfed.* **D** St David's 18 *See* Llanglydwen.
CLARBESTON, *Dyfed.* **D** St David's *See* Moat, New.
CLOCAENOG (St Foddhyd or St Caenog) w Gyffylliog (St Mary), *Clwyd.* R **D** St Asaph 3 **I** (Vacant).
CLYDACH (St Jo Bapt w St Mary), *Powys.* V **D** Swansea 10 **I** D EVANS, D H E MOSFORD *c.*
CLYDACH VALE (St Thos and St Dyfrig), *Mid Glam.* V **D** Llandaff 12 *See* Llwynypia.
CLYDAU, *Dyfed.* R **D** St David's 9 *See* Capel Colman.
CLYNNOG FAWR (St Beuno), *Gwyn.* V **D** Bangor 1 **I** I THOMAS.
CLYRO (St Mich) w Bettws and Llowes and Glasbury (All SS), *Powys.* V **D** Swansea 5 **I** A L WILLIS.
CLYTHA, *Gwent.* **D** Monmouth *See* Llanarth.
COCKETT, *W Glam.* **D** Swansea *See* Swansea.
COEDANA, *Gwyn.* **D** Bangor *See* Llangwyllog.
COEDKERNEW (All SS) w St Bride, Wentloog, *Gwent.* **D** Monmouth *See* Marshfield.
COED-Y-PAEN, *Gwent.* **D** Monmouth *See* Llangybi.
COELBREN **D** Swansea *See* Capel Coelbren.
COGAN, *S Glam.* **D** Llandaff *See* Llandough.
COITY (St Mary) w Nolton (St Mary), *Mid Glam.* R **D** Llandaff 2 **I** D RICHARDS, R DUBE *c,* A M HIRST *c.*
COLVA, *Powys.* **D** Swansea *See* Gladestry.
COLWINSTON (St Mich) w Llandow (H Trin) and Lisworney (St Tydfil), *S Glam.* R **D** Llandaff 6 **I** D R LEWIS.
COLWYN (St Cath), *Clwyd.* V **D** St Asaph 6 **I** S CLOSS-PARRY.
COLWYN BAY (St Paul), *Clwyd.* V **D** St Asaph 6 **I** T G DAVIES.
CONNAH'S QUAY (St Mark), *Clwyd.* V **D** St Asaph 4 **I** D P MORRIS.
CONWAY or CONWY (St Mary BV and St Mich) w St Agnes and Gyffin (St Benedict), *Gwyn.* V **D** Bangor 2 **I** R D JONES, A J WILLIAMS *c.*
CONWIL ELFED (St Cynwyl), *Dyfed.* V **D** St David's 11 **I** J D JONES.
CONWYL-GAYO or GAIO (St Conwyl) w Llansawel (St Sawyl) and Talley (St Mich AA), *Dyfed.* V **D** St David's 14 **I** C E JONES.
CORRIS (H Trin), *Gwyn.* **D** Bangor 9 *See* Pennal.
CORWEN (St Mael and St Sulien) and Llangar (St Jo Evang), *Clwyd.* R **D** St Asaph 12 **I** I PHILLIPS, L RICHARDS *c.*
COSHESTON (St Mich) w Nash and Upton, *Dyfed.* R **D** St David's 1 **I** W C BOWEN.
COWBRIDGE, *S Glam.* **D** Llandaff *See* Llanblethian.
COYCHURCH (St Crallo) w Llangan and St Mary Hill, *Mid Glam.* R **D** Llandaff 2 **I** D VICARS.
CRAY, *Powys.* **D** Swansea *See* Llanulid.
CRICCIETH (St Cath w St Deiniol) w Treflys (St Mich), *Gwyn.* R **D** Bangor 10 **I** T D WILLIAMS.
CRICKADARN (St Mary) w Gwenddwr (St Dubricius), *Powys.* **D** Swansea 3 **I** (Vacant).
CRICKHOWELL (St Edm K and Mart) w Llanfihangel Cwm Du and Tretower, *Powys.* R **D** Swansea 4 **I** M E GRIFFITHS.
CRIGGION, *Powys.* **D** St Asaph *See* Llandrinio.
CRINDAU, *Gwent.* **D** Monmouth *See* Newport.
CRINOW, *Dyfed.* **D** St David's *See* Narberth.
CROESYCEILIOG (St Mary), *Gwent.* V **D** Monmouth 11 **I** (Vacant).
CRUMLIN (St Marg), *Gwent.* V **D** Monmouth 9 **I** D J YOUNG.
CRUNWERE (St Elidyr) w Amroth, *Dyfed.* R **D** St David's 4 **I** (Vacant).
CRYNANT (St Marg Conv Distr), *W Glam.* **D** Llandaff 9 **I** D C BRYANT.
CWM (St Mael and St Sulien), *Clwyd.* **D** St Asaph 1 *See* Dyserth.
CWM (St Paul), *Gwent.* V **D** Monmouth 9 *See* Ebbw Vale.
CWMAMAN (St Jos), *Mid Glam.* V **D** Llandaff 1 **I** G H BOWEN.
CWMAMMAN (Ch Ch), *Dyfed.* V **D** St David's 12 **I** H L WALTERS.
CWMAVON, *W Glam.* **D** Llandaff *See* Michaelston-super-Avon.
CWMBACH (St Mary Magd), *Mid Glam.* V **D** Llandaff 1 **I** J GAINER, D G JAMES *c.*
CWMBACH-LLECHRYD, *Powys.* **D** Swansea *See* Llanelwedd.
CWMBRAN (St Gabriel), *Gwent.* R **D** Monmouth 11 **I** J T E DAVIES, H J DAVIES *team v,* B R PIPPEN *team v,* J Y W RITCHIE *team v.*
CWMBWRLA, *W Glam.* **D** Swansea *See* Swansea.
CWMCARN (St Jo Evang), *Gwent.* V **D** Monmouth 7 **I** R W A JONES.
CWMCARVAN, *Gwent.* **D** Monmouth *See* Trellech.
CWMDEUDDWR (St Ffraid or St Bride) w Nantgwyllt and St Harmon w Llanwrthwl, *Powys.* V **D** Swansea 7 **I** G J DAVIES.
CWM DU, *Powys.* **D** Swansea 4 *See* Llanfihangel Cwm Du.
CWMFFRWDOER, *Gwent.* **D** Monmouth *See* Pontnewynydd.
CWMLLYNFELL, *W Glam.* V **D** St David's 12 **I** V P ROBERTS.
CWMPARC (St Geo), *Mid Glam.* V **D** Llandaff 12 **I** L MILES.
CWMTILLERY (St Paul), *Gwent.* V **D** Monmouth 9 **I** B J FAVELL.
CWMYOY w Llanthony, *Gwent.* V **D** Monmouth 1 *See* Llanvihangel Crucorney.
CYFARTHFA (Ch Ch), *Mid Glam.* V **D** Llandaff *See* Merthyr Tydfil.
CYMMER (St Jo Evang) w Porth, *Mid Glam.* V **D** Llandaff 12 **I** P G MORRIS.
CYMMER AVAN, *W Glam.* **D** Llandaff 7 *See* Glyncorrwg.

DAFEN (St Mich AA), *Dyfed.* V **D** St David's 13 **I** J B DAVIES.
DALE (St Jas), *Dyfed.* V **D** St David's 5 **I** D A REES.

DAROWEN (St Tudyr), *Powys.* D Bangor 9 *See* Penegoes.
DEGANWY, *Gwyn.* D St Asaph *See* Eglwys Rhos.
DENBIGH (St Marcella w St Mary and St D), *Clwyd.* R D St Asaph 2 I E B WILLIAMS, G HANCOCKS *c.*
DENIO, *Gwyn.* D Bangor *See* Pwllheli.
DERI, *Mid Glam.* D Llandaff 3 *See* Bargoed.
DERWEN (St Mary) w Llanelidan (St Elidan), R *Clwyd.* D St Asaph 3 I J P COOKE.
DEVAUDEN, *Gwent.* D Monmouth *See* Kilgwrrwg.
DEVYNOCK (St Cynog) w Rhydybriw and Llandilo'-r-Fan (St Teilo), *Powys.* V D Swansea 2 I W J M DAVIES.
DIHEWYD (St Vitalis), *Dyfed.* V D St David's *See* Llanerchaeron.
DINAS (St Brynach) w Llanllawer, *Dyfed.* R D St David's 8 I G A DAVIES.
DINAS w Penygraig (St Barn), *Mid Glam.* V D Llandaff 12 I J H S THOMAS.
DINAS ISAF, *Mid Glam.* D Llandaff *See* Williamstown.
DINAS POWIS CHAP OF EASE, *S Glam.* D Llandaff *See* St Andrew.
DINGESTOW (St Dinigat) w Llangovan (St Cofen) and Pen-y-Clawdd (St Martin), *Gwent.* V D Monmouth 3 I K W SHARPE.
DINHAM, *Gwent.* D Monmouth *See* Caerwent.
DINMAEL, *Clwyd.* D St Asaph *See* Llawr-y-Betws.
DISSERTH, *Clwyd.* D St Asaph *See* Dyserth.
DISSERTH (St Cewydd w St D), *Powys.* V D Swansea I (Vacant).
DOLANOG or PONT DOLANOG, *Powys.* D St Asaph *See* Llanfihangel-yng-Nghwynfa.
DOLBENMAEN, *Gwyn.* D Bangor 10 *See* Llanystumdwy.
DOLFOR (St Paul), *Powys.* V D St Asaph 7 I (Vacant).
DOLGARROG, *Gwyn.* D Bangor *See* Llanbedr-y-Cennin.
DOLGELLAU (St Mary Virg) w Llanfachraeth (St Machraeth) and Brithdir (St Mark) w Bryncoedifor (St Paul), w Llanelltud, *Gwyn.* R D Bangor 12 I E E HUGHES, P HUGHES *c.*
DOLWYDDELAN (St Eliz), *Gwyn.* V D Bangor 2 I W R JONES.
DOWLAIS (St Jo Bapt w Ch Ch Pant and St Mich Pengarnddu), *Mid Glam.* R D Llandaff 8 I E B THOMAS.
DUFFRYN, *Mid Glam.* D Llandaff *See* Dyffryn.
DUFFRYN HONDDU, *Powys.* D Swansea *See* Merthyr Cynog.
DWYGYFYLCHI (St Gwynin) w Penmaenmawr (St Seiriol), *Gwyn.* V D Bangor 2 I G B HUGHES, A J HAWKINS *c.*
DYFFRYN (St Matt), *S Glam.* V D Llandaff 9 I D G REES.
DYLIFE, *Powys.* D Bangor *See* Llanbrynmair.
DYSERTH (St Bridget) and Trelawnyd and Cwm, *Clwyd.* V D St Asaph 1 I R W ROWLAND.

EBBW VALE (Ch Ch w St Matt and St Teilo) w Victoria (St Mary) Beaufort and Cwm, *Gwent.* R D Monmouth 9 I A P HAWKINS, D J CARPENTER *team v,* W JONES *team v.*
(St John), V D Monmouth 9 I (Vacant).
EDERN, *Gwyn.* D Bangor *See* Nefyn.
EFENECHTYD, *Clwyd.* D St Asaph *See* Llanfwrog.
EGLWYSBACH (St Martin), *Gwyn.* V D St Asaph 5 *See* Llansantffraid-Glan-Conway.
EGLWYSBREWIS (St Brewis) w St Athan and Flemingston (St Mich) w Gileston (St Giles), *S Glam.* R D Llandaff 6 I J W BINNY.
EGLWYS GYMIN (St Marg Marlos) w Marros, *Dyfed.* R D St David's 15 I R W JAMES.
EGLWYSFACH (St Mich) w Llancynfelin, *Dyfed.* V D St David's 10 I I T WINTERBURN.
EGLWYS-FAIR-A-CHURIG, *Dyfed.* D St David's *See* Llanwinio.
EGLWYSILAN (St Ilan, St Mary, St Jas, St Pet and St Cenydd), *Mid Glam.* R D Llandaff 3 I E J EVANS.
EGLWYSNEWYDD w Yspytty-Ystwyth (St Jo Bapt), *Dyfed.* V D St David's 10 I J O DAVIES.
EGLWYS-OEN-DUW w Llanfihangel-Abergwessin and Llanddewi, *Powys.* V D Swansea 3 *See* Llanwrtyd.
EGLWYS-RHOS or LLANRHOS (St Eleri and St Mary Virg) w St Paul, Llandudno, Deganwy (All SS), St Sannan, and St D Penrhyn, *Gwyn.* D St Asaph 5 I W D JENKINS, D H HUGHES *c.*
EGLWYSWEN, *Dyfed.* D St David's *See* Whitechurch.
EGLWYSWRW (St Cristiolus) w Meline, *Dyfed.* V D St David's 8 I W J JONES.
EGREMONT, *Dyfed.* D St David's *See* Llandyssilio.
ELERCH, *Dyfed.* D St David's *See* Penrhyncoch.
ELY, *S Glam.* D Llandaff *See* Caerau.
ERBISTOCK, *Clwyd.* D St Asaph *See* Overton.
ERRYRYS, *Clwyd.* D St Asaph *See* Treuddyn.
ESCLUSHAM (H Trin), *Clwyd.* V D St Asaph 16 I P C SOUTHERTON.
ESTYN, *Clwyd.* D St Asaph *See* Hope.
EVANCOYD (St Pet), *Powys.* V D Swansea 6 *See* Radnor, New.
EWENNY (St Mich), *Mid Glam.* V D Llandaff 2 I (Vacant).

FAIRBOURNE (St Cynon), *Gwyn.* D Bangor 12 *See* Arthog.
FAIRWATER (St Pet), *S Glam.* V D Llandaff 5 I M M DAVIES, D ALLEN *c.*
FAIRWATER, *Gwent.* V D Monmouth 11 I (Vacant).
FELINFOEL (H Trin), *Dyfed.* V D St David's 13 I D F D JONES.
FENNS, NEW, *Clwyd.* D St Asaph *See* Bronington.
FERNDALE (Ch Ch) w Maerdy (All SS w St Luke) and St Dunstan (Welsh) and St Thos, *Mid Glam.* V D Llandaff 12 I A E MORTON.
FERRYSIDE, *Dyfed.* D St David's *See* St Ishmael.
FFESTINIOG (St Mich) w Blaenau Ffestiniog (St D), *Gwyn.* R D Bangor 7 I I WILLIAMS.
FFYNNON-GROYW (All SS), *Clwyd.* D St Asaph 4 I (Vacant).
FISHGUARD (St Mary) w Llanychaer, *Dyfed.* V D St David's 2 I W C G MORGAN.
FLEMINGSTON or FLIMSTONE (St Mich), w Gileston (St Giles), *S Glam.* D Llandaff 6 *See* Eglwysbrewis.
FLEUR-DE-LYS (St D), *Gwent.* V D Monmouth 8 I D J ELIAS, R J PRICE *c.*
FLINT (St Mary), *Clwyd.* R D St Asaph 4 I E A GREY.
FOCHRIW, *Mid Glam.* D Llandaff *See* Pontlottyn.
FORD, *Dyfed.* D St David's *See* St Lawrence.
FORDEN, *gwent.* D St Asaph *See* Montgomery.
FREYSTROP, *Dyfed.* D St David's I G PENDLETON.
FRONGOCH, *Gwyn.* D St Asaph *See* Llanycil w Bala.

GABALFA or MAENDU (St Mark Evang), *S Glam.* V D Llandaff 5 I J C MEARS, W M DAVIES *c.*
GAIO, *Dyfed.* D St David's *See* Conwyl Gaio.
GARNDIFFAITH (St John) w Varteg, *Gwent.* V D Monmouth 11 *See* Abersychan.
GARTH, *Powys.* D Swansea *See* Llangammarch.
GARTH, *Mid Glam.* D Llandaff *See* Treoedrhiw Garth.
GARTHBEIBIO (St Tydecho) w Llanerfyl and Llangadfan, *Gwent and Powys.* R D St Asaph 8 I (Vacant).
GARTHBRENGY (St D) w Llandefaelog-Fach (St Maelog) and Llanfihangel Fechan (St Mich), *Powys.* V D Swansea 1 I J P H WALTERS.
GARTHELI (St Gartheli), *Dyfed.* V D St David's 9 *See* Nantcwnlle.
GARW VALLEY, *Mid Glam.* D Llandaff *See* Pontycymmer.
GELLIGAER (St Cattwg and St Marg Gilfach), *Mid Glam.* R D Llandaff 3 I C M P JONES.
GILESTON, *S Glam.* D Llandaff *See* Flemingston.
GILFACH GOCH (St Barn) w Llandyfodwg (St Tyfodwg), *Mid Glam.* V D Llandaff 12 I P M FARROW.
GLADESTRY (St Mary) w Colva (St D), *Powys.* R D Swansea 6 I G N REES.
GLAN ELY (Ch of the Resurr), *S Glam.* V D Llan 4 I R H MORGAN, A M REYNOLDS *c.*
GLANADDA (St D) w Penrhosgarnedd (St Pet), *gwyn.* V D Bangor 1 I T E P EDWARDS.
GLANOGWEN (Ch Ch), *Gwyn.* V D Bangor 2 I E ROBERTS, A EDWARDS *c.*
GLANTAWE (St Marg w St Pet), *W Glam.* D Swansea 9 I (Vacant).
GLAN CONWAY D St Asaph *See* Llansantffraid-Glan-Conway.
GLASBURY (St Pet), *Powys.* V D Swansea 5 I E T D LEWIS.
(All SS) D Swansea 5 *See* Clyro.
GLASCOED, *gwent.* D Monmouth *See* Usk.
GLASCOMBE (St D) w Rhulen (St D), *Powys.* V D Swansea 3 I (Vacant).
GLYNCORRWG (St Jo Bapt) w Afan Vale (St Gabr) and Cymer Afan (St Clare), *W Glam.* R D Llandaff 7 I S BARNES.
GLYNDYFRDWY (St Thos), *Clwyd.* V D St Asaph 12 I (Vacant).
GLYNTAFF (St Mary), *Mid Glam.* V D Llandaff 11 I H G CLARKE.
GLYN-TRAIAN, *Clwyd.* D St Asaph *See* Pontfadog.
GOETRE (St Pet), *Gwent.* D Monmouth 5 I H J T RICHARDS, D F ELDERKIN *c.*

D Bangor 7 I D G RICHARDS.
LLANAELHAIARN (St Aelhaiarn) w (St Geo Trevor), *Gwyn.* R D Bangor 1 I I THOMAS.
LLANAFAN FAWR, *Powys.* D Swansea 3 *See* Llanganten.
LLANAFAN-Y-TRAWSCOED (St Afan) w Llanwnnws, *Dyfed.* V D St David's *See* Llanfihangel-y-Creuddyn.
LLANALLGO, *Gwyn.* D Bangor *See* Llaneugrad.
LLANANNO, *Powys.* D Swansea *See* Llanbister.
LLANARMON, *Gwyn.* D Bangor *See* Llangybi.
LLANARMON-DYFFRYN-CEIRIOG (St Garmon) w Llansantffraid-Glyn-Ceirog and Pontfadog, *Clwyd.* V D St Asaph 13 I O L WILLIAMS.
LLANARMON-MYNYDD-MAWR, *Clwyd.* D St Asaph *See* Llanrhaiadr-ym-Mochnant.
LLANARMON-YN-IAL (St Garmon), *Clwyd.* V D St Asaph 3 I G B NEWTON.
LLANARTH (St D) w Llanina (St Ina) and Mydroilyn (H Trin), *Dyfed.* V D St David's 7 I J E WILLIAMS, D P D GRIFFITHS *c.*
LLANARTH (St Teilo) w Clytha w Llansantffraed (St Bridget) and Bryngwyn (St Pet), *Gwent.* R D Monmouth 5 I H TRENCHARD.
LLANARTHNEY (St D) w Llanddarog (St Darog), *Dyfed.* V D St David's 11 I J H REES.
LLANASA (St Asaph and St Cyndeyrn), *Clwyd.* V D St Asaph 4 I J G GRIFFITHS.
LLANBABO, *Gwyn.* D Bangor *See* Llandeusant.
LLANBADARN-FAWR (St Padarn), *Dyfed.* R D St David's 10 I B J H JONES.
LLANBADARN-FAWR (St Padarn), *Dyfed* w Llandegley (St Tegla) and Llanfihangel Rhydithon (St Mich AA), *Powys.* R D Swansea 7 I N D HALL.
LLANBADARN-FYNYDD, *Powys.* D Swansea *See* Llanbister.
LLANBADARN-ODWYN, *Dyfed.* D St David's *See* Llanddewi Brefi.
LLANBADARN-TREFEGLWYS, *Dyfed.* D St David's *See* Llansantffraed.
LLANBADARN-Y-GARREG, *Powys.* D Swansea *See* Aberedw.
LLANBADOC (St Madog) w Llanllowel (St Llywell), *Gwent.* V D Monmouth 6 I A J WAY.
LLANBADRIG (St Patr) w (St Patr) Cemmaes Bay, *Gwyn.* V D Bangor 6 *See* Llanfechell.
LLANBEBLIG (St Peblig) w Caernarfon (Ch Ch, St Mary and St D) and Betws Garmon (St Garmon) w Waunfawr (St Jo Evang), *Gwyn.* R D Bangor 1 I E T JONES *team v,* C S WILLIAMS *c.*
LLANBEDR, *Gwyn.* D Bangor *See* Llandanwg.
LLANBEDR-DYFFRYN-CLWYD (St Pet) w Llangynhafal (St Cynhafal), *Clwyd.* R D St Asaph 3 I D J WILLIAMS P-IN-C OF LLANYCHAN.
LLANBEDR-GOCH, *Gwyn.* D Bangor *See* Llanfairmathafarneithaf.
LLANBEDR-PAINSCASTLE, *Powys.* D Swansea *See* Bryngwyn.
LLANBEDR-PONT-STEPHEN, *Dyfed.* D St David's *See* Lampeter-Pont-Stephen.
LLANBEDR-Y-CENNIN (St Pet) w Dolgarrog (St Mary) w Trefiw w Llanrhychwyn, *Gwyn.* R D Bangor 2 I J B DAVIES.
LLANBEDR-YSTRADYW (St Pet) and Patricio (St Ishow), *Powys.* R D Swansea 4 I A REED.
LLANBEDROG (St Pedrog), *Gwyn.* R D Bangor 11 I F M JONES.
LLANBERIS (St Peris), *Gwyn.* R D Bangor 1 I A JONES.
LLANBEULAN (St Peulan) w Llanfaelog (St Maelog) and Talyllyn, *Gwyn.* R D Bangor 3 I (Vacant).
LLANBISTER (St Cynllo) w Llanbadarn-Fynydd (St Padarn) and Llananno (St Anno), *Powys.* V D Swansea 7 I T EVANS.
LLANBLETHIAN (St Bleddian) w Cowbridge (H Cross), Llandough (St Dochdwy), and St Mary Church (BVM), *S Glam.* V and R D Llandaff 6 I G E WILLIAMS, D A HUNTLEY *c.*
LLANBOIDY, *Dyfed.* D St David's *See* Meidrim.
LLANBRADACH (All SS), *Mid Glam.* V D Llandaff 3 I S J DUNSTAN.
LLAN-BRYNMAIR (St Mary) w Dylife, *Powys.* R D Bangor 9 *See* Penegoes.
LLANCARFAN (St Cadoc) w Llantrithyd (St Illtyd), *S Glam.* V D Llandaff 6 I W J FIELD.
LLANCYNFELIN, *Dyfed.* D St David's *See* Eglwysfach.
LLANDAFF (St Pet and St Paul Cathl Par), *S Glam.* V D Llandaff 5 I VERY REV A R DAVIES, D G BELCHER *c.*
(All SS) D Llandaff 5 I D JENKINS.
LLANDANWG (St Tanwg) w Llanbedr (St Pet), *Gwyn.* R D Bangor 7 I (Vacant).
LLANDAWKE, *Dyfed.* D St David's *See* Laugharne.
LLANDDANIEL-FAB, *Gwyn.* D Bangor *See* Llanidan.
LLANDDAROG, *Dyfed.* D St David's *See* Llanarthney.
LLANDDEINIOL, *Dyfed.* D St David's *See* Llanrhystyd.
LLANDDEINIOLEN (St Deiniolen), *Gwyn.* D Bangor 1 *See* Llanfairisgaer.
LLANDDERFEL, *Gwyn.* D St Asaph *See* Llandrillo-yn-Edeyrnion.
LLANDDEUSANT, *Dyfed.* D St David's *See* Gwynfe.
LLANDDEUSANT (St Marcellus) w Llanbabo (St Pabo), Llantrisant (St Ieuan, St Afran, and St Sanan), and Llanllibio, *Gwyn.* D Bangor 3 *See* Llanfachraeth.
LLANDDEW (St D) w Talachddu (St Mary), *Powys.* V D Swansea 1 I R G EVANS.
LLANDDEWI, *Clwyd.* D St Asaph *See* Llangernyw.
LLANDDEWI, *W Glam.* D Swansea *See* Port Eynon.
LLANDDEWI-ABERARTH (St D), *Dyfed.* V D St David's *See* Henfynw.
LLANDDEWI-ABERGWESSIN, *Powys.* D Swansea *See* Eglwys-Oen-Duw.
LLANDDEWI-BREFI (St D) w Llanbadarn Odwyn (St Padarn), *Dyfed.* V D St David's 9 I (Vacant).
LLANDDEWI-FACH, *Powys.* D Swansea *See* Bryngwyn.
LLANDDEWI-FACH, *Gwent.* D Monmouth *See* Panteg.
LLANDDEWI'R CWM, *Powys.* D Swansea *See* Builth.
LLANDDEWI-RHONDDA (St D), *S Glam.* D Llandaff 11 *See* Pwllgwaun.
LLANDDEWI-RHYDDERCH (St D) w Llanfapley (St Mable) and Llanfihangel-Gobion (St Mich) w Langattock-juxta-Usk (St Cadocus), *Gwent.* V and R D Monmouth 1 I J R ELLIS.
LLANDDEWI-SKIRRID (St D) w Llanvetherine (St Jas the Elder), Llangattock-Lingoed (St Cadoc) and Llanfair Chap (St Mary), *Gwent.* R D Monmouth 1 I D H WILLIAMS.
LLANDDEWI-VELFREY (St D), *Dyfed.* V D St David's *See* Lampeter Velfrey.
LLANDDEWI-YSTRADENNY (St D) and Abbey Cwmhir (St Mary Virg), *Powys.* V D Swansea 7 I N J DAVIS-JONES *p-in-c.*
LLANDDOGET (St Doged), *Gwyn.* R D St Asaph *See* Llanrwst.
LLANDDONA, *Gwyn.* D Bangor *See* Llansadwrn.
LLANDDOWROR (St Teilo), *Dyfed.* D St David's 18 *See* St Clears.
LLANDDULAS (St Cynbryd) and Llysfaen (St Cynfran), *Clwyd.* R D St Asaph 6 I V M GRIFFITHS.
LLANDDWYWE, *Gwyn.* D Bangor *See* Llanenddwyn.
LLANDEBIE (St Tybie), *Dyfed.* V D St David's 12 I T J W RICHARDS.
LLANDECWYN, *Gwyn.* D Bangor *See* Llanfihangel-y-Traethau.
LLANDEFAELOG-FACH, *Powys.* D Swansea *See* Garthbrengy.
LLANDEFAELOG TRE'R-GRAIG, *Powys.* D Swansea *See* Bronllys.
LLANDEFALLE (St Matehlu) w Llyswen (St Gwendoline), Boughrood (St Cynog), and Llanstephan (St Steph), *Powys.* R D Swansea 5 I R M H JONES.
LLANDEFEILOG (St Tyfaelog), *Dyfed.* V D St David's 11 I (Vacant).
LLANDEGAI (St Tegai), *Gwyn.* V D Bangor 2 I J A ROBERTS.
LLANDEGFAN (St Tegfan) w Beaumaris (SS Mary and Nich) and Llanfaes (St Cath) w Penmon (St Seiriol) and Llangoed (St Cawrdaf) w Llanfihangel Dinsylwy (St Mich), *Gwyn.* R D Bangor 5 I M FOULKES, W A JONES *team v,* JONES *team v,* D M OUTRAM *c,* P A G WESTLAKE *c.*
LLANDEGLA (St Tecla), *Clwyd.* D St Asaph *See* Bryneglwys.
LLANDEGLEY, *Powys.* D Swansea *See* Llanbadarn-Fawr.
LLANDEGVETH, *Gwent.* D Monmouth *See* Panteg.
LLANDEGWNNING, *Gwyn.* D Bangor *See* Mellteyrn.
LLANDEILO VAWR (St Teilo) w Llandyfaen and Maesteilo (St John) and Llandyfeisant (St Teifi), *Dyfed.* V D St David's 14 I D PRICE.
LLANDELOY, *Dyfed.* D St David's *See* Brawdy.
LLANDENNY, *Gwent.* D Monmouth *See* Raglan.
LLANDEVAUD, *Gwent.* D Monmouth 4 *See* Penhow.
LLANDILO, *Dyfed.* D St David's *See* Maenclochog.
LLANDEILO-ABERCYWYN (St Teilo) w Llan-y-bri (H Trin), *Dyfed.* V D St David's 11 *See* Llanstephan.
LLANDILO FAWR, *Dyfed.* D St David's *See* Llandeilo Vawr.
LLANDILO-GRABAN, *Powys.* D Swansea 3 *See* Aberedw.
LLANDILO'-R-FAN, *Powys.* D Swansea *See* Devynock.

LLANDILO-TALYBONT (St Teilo w St Mich), *W Glam.* V **D** Swansea 9 **I** A J MEATS.
LLANDINAM (St Llonio) w Trefeglwys and Penstrowed, *Powys.* V **D** Bangor 8 **I** T R BLACKSHAW.
LLANDINGAT or LLANDOVERY (St Dingad) w Llanfair (St Mary) and Myddfai (St Mich), *Dyfed.* V **D** St David's 14 **I** C THOMAS, M A SMITH *c.*
LLANDINORWIG (Ch Ch) w Penisa'r-waun *Gwyn.* V **D** Bangor 1 **I** (Vacant).
(St Mary) **D** Bangor 1 **I** (Vacant).
LLANDOGO (St Odoceus) w Whitebrook (H Trin) and Tintern Parva w Chapel Hall), *Gwent.* R **D** Monmouth 2 **I** W R THOMAS.
LLANDOUGH w St Mary Church, *S Glam.* **D** Llandaff *See* Llanblethian.
LLANDOUGH (St Dochdwy) w Leckwith (St Jas) Cogan (H Nativ), and Old Cogan (St Pet), *S Glam.* R **D** Llandaff 10 **I** F A G MUDGE.
LLANDOVERY, *Dyfed.* **D** St David's *See* Llandingat.
LLANDOW (H Trin) w Lisworney (St Tydfil), *S Glam.* R **D** Llandaff 6 *See* Colwinston.
LLANDRILLO-YN-EDEYRNION (St Trillo) w Llandderfel (St Derfel Gadarn), *Gwyn.* V and R **D** St Asaph 15 **I** G W JONES.
LLANDRILLO-YN-RHOS (St Trillo), *Clwyd.* V **D** St Asaph 6 **I** R ROBERTS.
LLANDRINDOD (H Trin), V w Cefnllys (St Mich AA), *Powys.* R **D** Swansea 7 **I** G M H HUGHES.
LLANDRINIO (St Trinio, St Pet and St Paul) w Criggion, *Powys.* R **D** St Asaph 10 *See* Llandysilio.
LLANDRYGARN (St Tygarn) w Bodwrog (St Twrog) and Hen Eglwys w Trewalchmai (St Llwydian), *Gwyn.* V **D** Bangor 4 **I** J F W JONES.
LLANDUDNO (St Tudno), *Gwyn.* R **D** Bangor 2 **I** E ROBERTS, J N M C MEREDITH *team v.*
(St Paul) **D** St Asaph *See* Eglwys-Rhos.
LLANDUDWEN, *Gwyn.* **D** Bangor *See* Nefyn.
LLANDULAS IN TIR Abad, *Powys.* **D** Swansea *See* Llanwrtyd.
LLANDWROG (St Twrog) w Groeslon (St Thos), *Gwyn.* R **D** Bangor 1 **I** R L EDWARDS *p-in-c.*
LLANDYFAEN, *Dyfed.* **D** St David's *See* Llandeilo Vawr.
LLANDYFEI, *Dyfed.* **D** St David's *See* Lamphey.
LLANDYFEISANT, *Dyfed.* **D** St David's *See* Llandeilo Vawr.
LLANDYFODWG (St Tyfodwg), *Mid Glam.* V **D** Llandaff 2 *See* Gilfach Goch.
LLANDYFRIOG and Troedyraur, *Dyfed.* V **D** St David's 6 *See* Newcastle Emlyn.
LLANDYFRYDOG, *Gwyn.* **D** Bangor *See* Rhosybol.
LLANDYGAI (St Tegai), *Gwyn.* V **D** Bangor 2 *See* Llandegai.
(St Ann w Tregarth), V **D** Bangor 2 **I** A T LEWIS.
LLANDYGWYDD (St Tygwydd) w Cenarth (St Llawddog) and Cilrhedyn, *Dyfed.* V **D** St David's 6 **I** B T RICE.
LLANDYRNOG (St Tyrnog) w Llangwyfan, *Clwyd.* R **D** St Asaph 2 **I** (Vacant).
LLANDYRY, *Dyfed.* **D** St David's *See* Pembrey.
LLANDYSILIO (St Tysilio w St Mary), *Gwyn.* V **D** Bangor 5 **I** R G WILLIAMS.
LLANDYSILIO (St Tyssilio), Penrhos (H Trin), Llandrinio (St Trinio, St Pet and St Paul) and Criggion, *Powys.* R **D** St Asaph 10 **I** R A BIRD.
LLANDYSSIL (St Tyssil), *Powys.* R **D** St Asaph *See* Montgomery.
LLANDYSSILIO-GOGO (St Tyssilio and St Mark), *Dyfed.* V **D** St David's *See* Llangranog.
LLANDYSSILIO-IN-DYFED (St Tyssul) w Egremont (St Mich) and Llanglydwen (St Cledwyn) w Cilmaenllwyd, *Dyfed.* V **D** St David's 15 **I** A G BASSETT.
LLANDYSSUL (St Tyssul), *Dyfed.* R and V **D** St David's 6 **I** I D JOHN.
LLANEDEYRN (St Edeyrn), *Gwent.* V **D** Monmouth 7 **I** O P D REES.
LLANEDWEN, *Gwyn.* **D** Bangor *See* Llanidan.
LLANEDY (St Edith) w Hendy, *Dyfed.* V **D** St David's 12 **I** (Vacant).
LLANEGRYN (St Mary and Egryn) and Talyllyn, *Gwyn.* V **D** Bangor 12 **I** B W THOMAS.
LLANEGWAD (St Egwad) w Llanfynydd (St Egwad) w Maesteilo (St John), *Dyfed.* V **D** St David's 14 **I** R I PROTHEROE.
LLANEILIAN (St Elian), *Gwyn.* R **D** Bangor 6 *See* Amlwch.
LLANELIAN (St Elian Geimiad) and Betws-yn-Rhos (St Mich), *Clwyd.* R **D** St Asaph 6 **I** (Vacant).
LLANELIDAN, *Clwyd.* **D** St Asaph *See* Derwen.
LLANELIEU, *Powys.* **D** Swansea *See* Talgarth.
LLANELLEN or LLANELEN, *Gwent.* **D** Monmouth *See* Llanfoist.
LLANELLTUD (St Illtud), *Gwyn.* **D** Bangor *See* Dolgellau.
LLANELLY (St Elli), *Powys.* R **D** Swansea 7 **I** T A WILLIAMS.
LLANELLY (St Ellyw w All SS and St Alb), *Dyfed.* V **D** St David's 13 **I** H MOSES, F O EVANS *c,* N F GILLMAN *c,* E L THOMAS *c,* R A WILLIAMS *c.*
(Ch Ch w St D), V **D** St David's 13 **I** T G JONES.
(St Paul w St Pet and St Jo Bapt), V **D** St David's 13 **I** J A HOPKINS, R THOMAS *c.*
LLANELWEDD (St Matt) w Llanfaredd (St Mary) and Cwmbach-Llechryd (St Jo Evang), *Powys.* R and V. **D** Swansea 3 **I** P A C PEARCEY.
LLANENDDWYN (or DYFFRYN) (St Enddwyn) w Llanddwywe (St Ddwywe), *Gwyn.* R **D** Bangor 7 **I** R A BEACON.
LLANENGAN (St Engan) w Llangian (St Gian) and Abersoch (St John), *Gwyn.* R **D** Bangor 11 **I** W L JONES.
LLANERCH-AERON, V w Ciliau Aeron (St Mich) and Dihewyd (St Vitalis), R *Dyfed.* **D** St David's 7 **I** S DAVIES.
LLANERCHYMEDD (St Mary) w Rhodogeidio (St Ceidio) and Gwredog (St Mary), *Gwyn.* V **D** Bangor 6 *See* Llangwyllog.
LLANERFYL (St Erfyl), *Clwyd.* **D** St Asaph 8 *See* Garthbeibio.
LLANEUGRAD (St Eugrad) w Llanallgo (St Gallgo) Penrhosllugwy and Llanfihangel Tre'r Beirdd, *Gwyn.* R **D** Bangor 6 **I** H HUGHES.
LLANFABON (St Mabon, St John and St Cynon), *Mid Glam.* R **D** Llandaff 3 **I** D L D CHIVERTON, J H POWELL *c.*
LLANFACHES, *Gwent.* **D** Monmouth *See* Llanvaches.
LLANFACHRAETH (St Machraeth) w Llanynghenedl (St Enghenedl), Llanfigael (St Migael) and Valley (St Mich) w Llanddeusant w Llanbabo, Llantrisant and Llanllibio, *Gwyn.* R **D** Bangor 3 **I** (Vacant).
LLANFACHRETH (St Machreth), *Gwyn.* **D** Bangor 12 *See* Dolgellau.
LLANFAELOG, *Gwyn.* **D** Bangor *See* Llanbeulan.
LLANFAELRHYS, *Gwyn.* **D** Bangor *See* Rhiw.
LLANFAENOR, *Gwent.* **D** Monmouth *See* Llangattock-Vibon-Avel.
LLANFAES (St Cath), *Gwyn.* **D** Bangor *See* Llandegfan.
LLANFAES, *Powys.* **D** Swansea *See* Brecon.
LLANFAETHLU (St Maethlu) w Llanfwrog (St Mwrog), Llanrhuddlad (St Rhuddlad), Llanfair-y-nghornwy (St Mary) and Llanrhwydrus (St Rhwydrus), *Gwyn.* R **D** Bangor 3 **I** W H DAVIES.
LLANFAGLAN, *Dyfed.* **D** Bangor *See* Llanwnda.
LLANFAIR CHAP, *Gwent.* **D** Monmouth *See* Llanddewi-Skirrid.
LLANFAIR-AR-Y-BRYN (St Mary), *Dyfed.* V **D** St David's 14 *See* Cilycwm.
LLANFAIR CAEREINION (St Mary) w Llanllugan (St Mary), *Powys.* V **D** St Asaph 8 **I** J C O EVANS.
LLANFAIR-CLYDOGAU, *Dyfed.* **D** St David's *See* Cellan.
LLANFAIR-DYFFRYN-CLWYD (St Pet), *Clwyd.* V **D** St Asaph 3 **I** R H GRIFFITHS.
LLANFAIR-HARLECH, *Gwyn.* **D** Bangor *See* Harlech.
LLANFAIR-KILGEDDIN, *Gwent.* **D** Monmouth 5 *See* Llanover.
LLANFAIR NANT-gwyn, *Dyfed.* **D** St David's *See* Whitechurch.
LLANFAIR-NANT-Y-GOF, *Dyfed.* **D** St David's *See* Letterston.
LLANFAIR-ORLLWYN (St Mary), *Dyfed.* R **D** St David's *See* Bangor Teifi.
LLANFAIR-PWLL-GWYNGYLL (St Mary) w Penmynydd (St Credifael), *Gwyn.* R **D** Bangor 5 **I** G M HUGHES.
LLANFAIR-TALHAIARN (St Mary), *Clwyd.* R **D** St Asaph 6 **I** D V GRIFFITH.
LLANFAIR-TRELYGEN, *Dyfed.* **D** St David's **I** (Vacant).
LLANFAIR-YN-CWMWD, *Gwyn.* **D** Bangor *See* Llangeinwen.
LLANFAIR-YN-NEUBWLL, *Gwyn.* **D** Bangor *See* Holyhead.
LLANFAIRFECHAN (St Mary w Ch Ch) w Aber (St Bodfan), *Gwyn.* R **D** Bangor 2 **I** J E JONES.
LLANFAIRISGAER (St Mary) w Llanddeiniolen, *Gwyn* **D** Bangor 1 **I** R JONES, P D RODERICK *c.*
LLANFAIRMATHAFARNEITHAF (St Mary) w Llanbedrgoch (St Pet), *Gwyn.* **D** Bangor 5 **I** D N JONES, G D LOVELUCK *hon c.*

LLANFAIR-YNG-NGHORNWY, *Gwyn.* **D** Bangor *See* Llanfaethlu.
LLANFALLTEG w Castell Dwyran, Clynderwen, Henllan-Amgoed and Llangan, *Dyfed.* R **D** St David's 15 **I** J W EVANS.
LLANFAPLEY, *Gwent.* **D** Monmouth *See* Llanddewi Rhydderch.
LLANFAREDD, *Powys.* **D** Swansea *See* Llanelwedd.
LLANFECHAIN (St Garmon), *Powys.* R **D** St Asaph 9 **I** J H EVANS.
LLANFECHAN, *Powys.* **D** Swansea *See* Llangammarch.
LLANFECHELL (St Machulus or Mechell) w Llanfflewin (St Fflewin) Bodewryd (St Mary) Rhosbeirio (St Peirio) and Llanbadrig, *Gwyn.* R **D** Bangor 6 **I** G W EDWARDS.
LLANFERRES (St Berres or Britius), *Clwyd.* R **D** St Asaph 14 **I** J B THELWELL.
LLANFEUGAN (St Meugan) w Llanthetty (St Tetta) and Llansantyffraed-Juxta-Usk (St Ffraed), *Powys.* R **D** Swansea 1 **I** W S P JACKSON.
LLANFFINAN, *Gwyn.* **D** Bangor *See* Llanfihangel-Ysgeifiog.
LLANFFLEWIN, *Gwyn.* **D** Bangor *See* Llanfechell.
LLANFIGAEL, *Gwyn.* **D** Bangor *See* Llanfachraeth.
LLANFIHANGEL-ABERBYTHYC (St Mich), *Dyfed.* V **D** St David's 12 **I** (Vacant).
LLANFIHANGEL-ABERCOWIN (St Clears), *Dyfed.* V **D** St David's 15 **I** D C EVANS.
LLANFIHANGEL-ABERGWESSIN, *Powys.* **D** Swansea *See* Eglwys-Oen-Duw.
LLANFIHANGEL-AR-ARTH (St Mich) w Pencader (St Mary), *Dyfed.* V **D** St David's 11 **I** J O EVANS.
LLANFIHANGEL BACHELLAETH, *Gwyn.* **D** Bangor *See* Llannor.
LLANFIHANGEL-BRYN-PABUAN, *Powys.* **D** Swansea *See* Newbridge-on-Wye.
LLANFIHANGEL CWM DU or CWM DU (St Mich) w Tretower (St Jo Evang), *Powys.* R **D** Swansea 4 *See* Crickhowell.
LLANFIHANGEL DINSYLWY, *Gwyn.* **D** Bangor *See* Llandegfan.
LLANFIHANGEL FECHAN or LOWER CHAPEL (St Mich), *Powys.* **D** Swansea *See* Garthbrengy.
LLANFIHANGEL-GENAU'R-GLYN (St Mich) w Talybont (St D), Rhydmeirionydd, *Dyfed.* V **D** St David's 10 **I** W D M GRIFFITHS.
LLANFIHANGEL-GLYN-MYFYR, *Clwyd.* **D** St Asaph *See* Cerrig-y-Druidion.
LLANFIHANGEL-GOBION, *Gwent.* **D** Monmouth 5 *See* Llanddewi-Rhydderch.
LLANFIHANGEL-HELYGEN, *Powys.* **D** Swansea *See* Llanyre.
LLANFIHANGEL-LLANTARNAM (St Mich), *Gwent.* V **D** Monmouth 11 **I** (Vacant).
LLANFIHANGEL-LLEDROD, *Dyfed.* **D** St David's *See* Llangwyryfon.
LLANFIHANGEL-NANTBRAN, *Powys.* **D** Swansea *See* Aberyskir.
LLANFIHANGEL-NANTMELAN, *Powys.* **D** Swansea *See* Radnor, New.
LLANFIHANGEL-PENBEDW, *Dyfed.* V **D** St David's 8 *See* Capel Colman.
LLANFIHANGEL-RHOS-Y-CORN (St Mich), *Dyfed.* V **D** St David's 10 *See* Brechfa.
LLANFIHANGEL-RHYDITHON, *Powys.* **D** Swansea *See* Llanbadarn-Fawr.
LLANFIHANGEL-TALLYLYN (St Mich AA) w Llanywern (St Mary Virg) and Llangasty-Talyllyn (St Gastayn), R *Powys.* **D** Swansea 1 **I** H G W GARBUTT.
LLANFIHANGEL-TRE'R-BEIRDD, *Gwyn.* **D** Bangor *See* Llaneugrad.
LLANFIHANGEL-UWCH-GWILI, *Dyfed.* **D** St David's *See* Abergwili.
LLANFIHANGEL-Y-CREUDDYN w Llanafan-y-Trawscoed (St Afan) and Llanwnnws, *Dyfed.* V **D** St David's 10 **I** P A CROCKETT.
LLANFIHANGEL-YNG-NGHWYNFA (St Mich) w Llwydiarth (St Mary), *Powys.* **D** St Asaph 9 *See* Llanwyddyn.
LLANFIHANGEL-YN-NHOWYN, *Gwyn.* **D** Bangor *See* Llechylched.
LLANFIHANGEL-Y-PENNANT (or ABERGYNOLWYN) (St Mich), *Gwyn.* R **D** Bangor 10 **I** W JONES.
LLANFIHANGEL-Y-PENNANT w Talyllyn, *Gwyn.* **D** Bangor *See* Llanegryn.
LLANFIHANGEL-YSGEIFIOG (St Mich) w Llanffinan (St Ffinan), *Gwyn.* R **D** Bangor 4 **I** I THOMAS.
LLANFIHANGEL YSTRAD (St Mich) w Cilcennin, *Dyfed.* V **D** St David's 7 **I** D J JONES.
LLANFIHANGEL-Y-TRAETHAU (St Mich) w Llandecwyn (St Tecwyn), *Gwyn.* **D** Bangor 7 *See* Harlech.
LLANFOIST (St Ffwyst) w Llanelen (St Helen), *Gwent.* R **D** Monmouth 1 **I** T A FOSTER.
LLANFOR or LLANFAWR, *Gwyn.* **D** St Asaph *See* Rhos-y-Gwalia.
LLANFRECHFA (All SS), *Gwent.* V **D** Monmouth 11 **I** A V BLAKE.
UPPER, or PONTNEWYDD (H Trin) **D** Monmouth 11 **I** D G BRUNNING.
LLANFROTHEN, *Gwyn.* R **D** Bangor *See* Penrhyn-Deudraeth.
LLANFRYNACH (St Brynach) w Cantref (St Mary) and Llanhamlach, *Powys.* R **D** Swansea 1 **I** P G R SIMS.
LLANFRYNACH, *S Glam.* **D** Llandaff *See* Llansannor.
LLANFWROG, *Gwyn.* **D** Bangor *See* Llanfaethlu.
LLANFWROG (St Mwrog and St Mary Virg) w Efenechtyd (St Mich), *Clwyd.* R **D** St Asaph 3 **I** W L DAVIES.
LLANFYLLIN (St Myllin), *Powys.* R **D** St Asaph 9 **I** S F HADLEY.
LLANFYNYDD, *Dyfed.* **D** St David's 14 *See* Llanegwad.
LLANFYNYDD (Ch Ch), *Clwyd.* R **D** St Asaph 16 **I** C J D PROBERT.
LLANFYRNACH (St Brynach), *Dyfed.* **D** St David's *See* Llanwinio.
LLANGADFAN (St Cadfan), *Powys.* **D** St Asaph *See* Garthbeibio.
LLANGADFARCH, *Powys.* **D** Bangor *See* Penegoes.
LLANGADOG (St Cadog and St D) and Gwynfe w Llanddeussant, *Dyfed.* V **D** St David's 14 **I** J N HUGHES.
LLANGADWALADR (St Cadwaladr), *Gwyn.* R **D** Bangor 4 **I** (Vacant).
LLANGADWALADR, *Clwyd.* **D** St Asaph *See* Llansilin.
LLANGAFFO, *Gwyn.* **D** Bangor *See* Llangeinwen.
LLANGAIN, *Dyfed.* **D** St David's *See* Llangynog.
LLANGAMMARCH (St Cadmarch) w Garth, Llanlleonfel, and Llanfechan (St Avan), *Powys.* R **D** Swansea 3 *See* Llanganten.
LLANGAN, *Dyfed.* **D** St David's *See* Llanfallteg.
LLANGAN (St Canna) and St Mary Hill (St Mary Virg), *S Glam.* **D** Llandaff 2 *See* Coychurch.
LLANGANTEN (St Cannen or St Canten) w Llanafan Fawr (St Avan), Llangammarch, Llanfechan and Llanlleonfel *Powys.* R **D** Swansea 3 **I** A G THOMAS.
LLANGAR (St Jo Evang), *Clwyd.* R **D** St Asaph *See* Corwen.
LLANGASTY-TALYLLYN, *Powys.* **D** Swansea *See* Llanfihangel-Talyllyn.
LLANGATHEN (St Cathen) w Court Henry (St Mary), *Dyfed.* V **D** St David's 14 **I** J E LEWIS.
LLANGATTOCK (St Cattwg) and Llangynidr, *Powys.* R **D** Swansea 4 **I** R M E PATERSON.
LLANGATTOCK-JUXTA-CAERLEON (St Cadoc), *Gwent.* V **D** Monmouth 10 **I** P R S MORGAN, D K POPE *c.*
LLANGATTOCK-JUXTA-USK, *Gwent.* **D** Monmouth 5 *See* Llanddewi-Rhydderch.
LLANGATTOCK-LINGOED **D** Monmouth *See* Llanddewi-Skirrid.
LLANGATTOCK-VIBON-AVEL (St Cadoc) w Llanvaenor and St Maughan (St Meughan), *Gwent.* V **D** Monmouth 3 *See* Rockfield.
LLANGEDWYN, *Clwyd.* **D** St Asaph 9 *See* Llansilin.
LLANGEFNI (St Cyngar) w Tregaean (St Caian) w Llangristiolus (St Cristiolus) w Cerrig-Ceinwen (St Ceinwen), *Gwyn.* R **D** Bangor 4 **I** R L OWEN.
LLANGEINOR (St Ceinor, St D and St John), *Mid Glam.* V **D** Llandaff 2 **I** C I EVANS.
LLANGEINWEN (St Ceinwen) w Llangaffo (St Caffo) and Llanfair yn y Cwmwd (St Mary), *Gwyn.* R **D** Bangor 4 *See* Newborough.
LLANGEITHO, *Dyfed.* **D** St David's *See* Blaenpennal.
LLANGELER (St Geler), *Dyfed.* V **D** St David's 6 **I** L J L WOODLIFFE.
LLANGELYNNIN, *Gwyn.* **D** Bangor *See* Caer Rhun.
LLANGELYNNIN (or Llanwyngwril) (St Celynnin) w Rhoslefain (St Mary), *Gwyn.* R **D** Bangor 12 **I** (Vacant).
LLANGENNECH (St Cennych), *Dyfed.* V **D** St David's 13 **I** G H THOMAS.
LLANGENNITH (St Cennydd), *W Glam.* V **D** Swansea 8 **I** A M BURN-MURDOCH.
LLANGENNY (St Cenea), *Powys.* **D** Swansea 4 **I** A REED.
LLANGERNYW (St Digain) w Llanddewi (St D) and Gwytherin (St Winifred), *Clwyd.* V **D** St Asaph 5 **I** D V GRIFFITH *p-in-c.*
LLANGEVIEW, *Gwent.* **D** Monmouth *See* Llangwm Uchaf.
LLANGIAN, *Gwyn.* **D** Bangor *See* Llanenegan.

LLANSADWRN (St Sadwrn) w Llanwrda (St Cwrda), *Dyfed.* V **D** St David's 14 **I** T H BRACE.
LLANSADWRNEN, *Dyfed.* **D** St David's *See* Laugharne.
LLANSAINT, *Dyfed.* **D** St David's *See* St Ishmael.
LLANSAMLET (St Samlet), *W Glam.* V **D** Swansea 10 **I** B H JONES, W W L HOPKIN *c.*
LLANSANNAN (St Sannan) w Bylchau (St Thos) and Nantglyn (St Jas), *Clwyd.* R **D** St Asaph 2 **I** (Vacant).
LLANSANNOR (St Senwyn) and Llanfrynach w Penllyn and Ystradowen, *S Glam.* R **D** Llandaff 6 **I** B M LODWICK.
LLANSANTFFRAED, *Powys.* **D** Monmouth *See* Llanarth.
LLANSANTFFRAED-IN-ELWELL (St Bridget) w Bettws-Disserth (St Mary) and Cregrina (St D), *Powys.* V **D** Swansea 3 **I** P A C PEARCEY.
LLANSANTFFRAED-JUXTA-USK, *Powys.* **D** Swansea *See* Llanfeugan.
LLANSANTFFRAID-GLAN-CONWAY (St Ffraid) w Eglwysbach, *Clwyd.* R **D** St Asaph 5 **I** (Vacant).
LLANSANTFFRAID-GLYN-CEIROG (St Ffraid), *Clwyd.* V **D** St Asaph 13 *See* Llanarmon.
LLANSANTFFRAID-YM-MECHAIN (St Ffraid or St Bride), *Powys.* V **D** St Asaph 9 **I** L ROGERS.
LLANSANTFFRAID-GLYN-DYFRDWY (St Bride), *Clwyd.* R **D** St Asaph 12 **I** (Vacant).
LLANSANTFFRAED (St Bridget) and Dewi Sant w Llanbadarn Trefeglwys, *Dyfed.* V **D** St David's 7 **I** G I THOMAS.
LLANSAWEL, *Dyfed.* **D** St David's *See* Conwil Gaio.
LLANSAWEL (St Mary) w Briton Ferry, *W Glam.* V **D** Llandaff 9 **I** J P BUTLER.
LLANSILIN (St Silin) w Llangadwaladr (St Cadwaladr) and Llangedwyn (St Cedwyn), *Clwyd.* V **D** St Asaph 9 **I** C F CARTER.
LLANSOY (St Tysoi), *Gwent.* **D** Monmouth *See* Raglan.
LLANSPYDDID (St Cattwg) w Llanilltyd (St Illtyd), *Powys.* V **D** Swansea 2 **I** (Vacant).
LLANSTADWELL (St Tudwall), *Dyfed.* V **D** St David's 5 **I** M K LIKEMAN.
LLANSTEPHAN, *Powys.* **D** Swansea *See* Llandefalle.
LLANSTEPHAN (St Ystyffan) w Llan-y-bri and Llandeilo Abercywyn, *Dyfed.* V **D** St David's **I** T I THOMAS.
LLANSTINAN (St Justinian), *Dyfed.* **D** St David's *See* Llanwnda.
LLANTARNAM, *Gwent.* **D** Monmouth 11 *See* Llanfihangel-Llantarnam.
LLANTHETTY, *Powys.* **D** Swansea *See* Llanfeugan.
LLANTHEWY VACH, *Gwent.* **D** Monmouth 11 *See* Llanddewi-Fach.
LLANTHEWY-SKIRRID, *Gwent.* **D** Monmouth 1 *See* Llanddewi-Skirrid.
LLANTHONY, *Gwent.* **D** Monmouth 1 *See* Llanvihangel Crucorney.
LLANTILIO-CROSSENNY (St Teilo), V w (St Mich AA), Llanvihangel-Ystern-Llewern, and Penrhos, *Gwent.* R and V **D** Monmouth 5 **I** J H SELBY.
LLANTILLIO-PERTHOLEY (St Teilo) w Bettws, *Gwent.* V **D** Monmouth 1 **I** D FRANCIS.
LLANTOOD, *Dyfed.* V **D** St David's 8 *See* St Dogmael's.
LLANTRISANT, *Gwyn.* **D** Bangor *See* Llanddeusant.
LLANTRISANT, *Dyfed.* **D** St David's *See* Yspytty-Cynfyn.
LLANTRISANT (St Illtyd, St Tyfodwg, and St Gwynno), *Mid Glam.* V **D** Llandaff 11 **I** P G LEWIS, V W BEYNON *c.*
LLANTRISSENT, *Gwent.* **D** Monmouth *See* Tredunnoc.
LLANTRITHYD (St Illtyd), *S Glam.* R **D** Llandaff 6 *See* Llancarfan.
LLANTWIT MAJOR (St Illtyd) w St Donats (St Donat), *S Glam.* V **D** Llandaff 6 **I** D M JENKINS, P I REID *c,* A PARRY *hon c.*
LLANTWIT-VARDRE (St Illtyd), *Mid Glam.* V **D** Llandaff 11 **I** A J D WILLIAMS.
LLANTYSILIO (St Tysilio), *Clwyd.* V **D** St Asaph 13 *See* Llangollen.
LLANULID or CRAY ST ILID (St Ilid), *Powys.* V **D** Swansea 2 **I** (Vacant).
LLANUWCHLLYN (St Deiniol) w Llangywair (St Cywair), *Gwyn.* V **D** St Asaph 15 **I** (Vacant).
LLANVACHES, *Gwent.* **D** Monmouth *See* Penhow.
LLANVAETHLU, *Gwyn.* **D** Bangor *See* Llanfaethlu.
LLANVAIR DISCOED (St Mary), *Gwent.* R **D** Monmouth *See* Caerwent.
LLANVERRES, *Clwyd.* **D** St Asaph *See* Llanferres.
LLANVETHERINE, *Gwent.* **D** Monmouth *See* Llanddewi-Skirrid.
LLANVIHANGEL-CRUCORNEY (St Mich) w Oldcastle (St Jo Bapt) R, Cwmyoy (St Martin) and Llanthony (St D), *Gwent.* V **D** Monmouth 1 **I** P C PRICE.
LLANVIHANGEL-PONTYMOILE, *Gwent.* **D** Monmouth *See* Mamhilad.
LLANVIHANGEL ROGGIETT, *Gwent.* **D** Monmouth *See* Roggiett.
LLANVIHANGEL-TOR-Y-MYNYDD, *Gwent.* **D** Monmouth *See* Llanishen.
LLANVIHANGEL-YSTERN-LLEWERN, *Gwent.* **D** Monmouth *See* Llantilio-Crossenny.
LLANVILLO, *Powys.* **D** Swansea *See* Bronllys.
LLANWAPLEY, *Gwent.* **D** Monmouth *See* Llanvapley.
LLANWDDYN (St Wddyn) and Llanfihangel-yng Nghwynfa and Llwydiarth, *Powys.* V **D** St Asaph 9 **I** W R MORTIMER.
LLANWENARTH CITRA (St Pet), *Gwent.* R **D** Monmouth 1 *See* Abergavenny.
LLANWENARTH ULTRA (Ch Ch) w Govilon, *Gwent.* R **D** Monmouth 1 **I** D E STANDISH.
LLANWENLLWYFO (St Gwenllwyfo), *Gwyn.* R **D** Bangor 6 *See* Amlwch.
LLANWENOG (St Gwenog) w Llanwnen, *Dyfed.* V **D** St David's 9 *See* Llanybyther.
LLANWERN (St Mary) w Bishton (St Cadwaladr), *Gwent.* R **D** Monmouth 4 **I** (Vacant).
LLANWINIO (St Gwynio) w Elgwys-Fair-a-Churig (St Mary) and Llanfyrnach (St Brynach), *Dyfed.* V **D** St David's 15 **I** D G BEYNON.
LLANWNDA (St Gwyndaf) w Llanfaglan (St Baglan), *Gwyn.* V **D** Bangor 1 **I** R E WILLIAMS.
LLANWNDA (St Gwyndaf) w Manorowen, Goodwick and Llanstinan, *Dyfed.* V **D** St David's 2 **I** C D L GRIFFITHS.
LLANWNEN, *Dyfed.* **D** St David's *See* Llanwenog.
LLANWNNOG (St Gwynog) and Caersws (St Mary) w Carno, *Powys.* **D** Bangor 8 **I** D J PARRY.
LLANWNNWS, *Dyfed.* **D** St David's *See* Llanafan-y-Trawscoed.
LLANWONNO (St Gwynno) w Ynysybwl (Ch Ch), *Mid Glam.* V **D** Llandaff 11 **I** J M HUGHES.
LLANWRDA, *Dyfed.* **D** St David's 2 *See* Llansadwrn.
LLANWRIN (SS Ust and Dyfnig), w Machynlleth (St Pet w Ch Ch), *Powys.* R **D** Bangor 9 **I** W ROBERTS.
LLANWRTHWL (St Gwrthl), *Powys.* V **D** Swansea *See* Cwmdauddwr.
LLANWRTYD (St Jas) and Llandulas in Tir Abad (St D) and Eglwys Oen Duw and Llanfihangel Abergwessin w Llandewi, *Powys.* V **D** Swansea 3 **I** (Vacant).
LLAN-Y-BRI, *Dyfed.* **D** St David's *See* Llandeilo-Abercywyn.
LLANYBYDDER (St Pet) and Llanwenog w Llanwnnen, *Dyfed.* V **D** St David's 9 **I** E D GRIFFITHS.
LLANYCEFN, *Dyfed.* **D** St David's *See* Maenclochog.
LLANYCHAER, *Dyfed.* **D** St David's *See* Fishguard.
LLANYCHAIARN (St Chaiarn), *Dyfed.* V **D** St David's 10 **I** (Vacant).
LLANYCHAN, *Clwyd.* **D** St Asaph *See* Llanynys.
LLANYCHLLWYDOG, *Dyfed.* **D** St David's *See* Morfil.
LLANYCIL (St Beuno) w Bala (Ch Ch) and Frongoch (St Mark), *Gwyn.* R **D** St Asaph 15 **I** H E JONES.
LLANYCRWYS (St D), *Dyfed.* **D** St David's *See* Pencarreg.
LLANYMAWDDWY, *Gwyn.* **D** Bangor *See* Mallwyd.
LLANYNGHENEDL, *Gwyn.* **D** Bangor *See* Llanfachraeth.
LLANYNYS, *Powys.* **D** Swansea *See* Builth.
LLANYNYS (St Saeran) w Llanychan (St Hychan), *Clwyd.* **D** St Asaph 3 **I** D J WILLIAMS P-IN-C OF LLANYCHAN.
LLANYRE (St Llyr Virg) w Llanfihangel-Helygen (St Mich AA) and Disserth (St D and St Cewydd), *Powys.* R **D** Swansea 7 **I** J W J REES.
LLANYRNEWYDD, *W Glam.* **D** Swansea *See* Penclawdd.
LLANYSTUMDWY (St Jo Bapt) w Llangybi and Llanarmon and Dolbenmaen, *Gwyn.* R **D** Bangor 10 **I** W JONES.
LLANYWERN, *Powys.* **D** Swansea *See* Llanfihangel-Tallylyn.
LLAWHADEN (St Aeddan) w Bletherston (St Mary), *Dyfed.* V **D** St David's 3 **I** G D GWYTHER.
LLAWR-Y-BETWS (St Jas Gt), *Clwyd.* V **D** St Asaph 12 **I** (Vacant).
LLAY (St Martin), *Clwyd.* V **D** St Asaph 16 **I** G L JONES.
LLECHGYNFARWY, *Gwyn.* **D** Bangor *See* Bodedern.
LLECHRYD (St Tydfil), *Dyfed.* **D** St David's *See* Llangoedmor.
LLECHYLCHED w Ceirchiog (H Trin), Llanfihangel-yn-Nhywyn and Caergeiliog, *Gwyn.* V **D** Bangor 3 *See* Bodedern.
LLEDROD, *Dyfed.* **D** St David's *See* Llanfihangel-Ledrod.
LLOWES (St Meilig), *Powys.* V **D** Swansea 5 *See* Clyro.

LLWYNDERW (Ch H Cross), *W Glam.* V **D** Swansea 9 **I** (Vacant).
LLWYDIARTH, *Powys.* **D** St Asaph *See* Llanfihangel-yng-Nghwynfa.
LLWYNDERW (Ch H Cross), *W Glam.* V **D** Swansea 9 **I** A E PIERCE.
LLWYNHENDY, *Dyfed.* V **D** St David's 13 **I** (Vacant).
LLWYNYPIA (St Andr) w Clydach, *Mid Glam.* V **D** Llandaff 12 **I** K J GILLINGHAM.
LLYSFAEN, *Clwyd.* R **D** St Asaph 6 *See* Llanddulas.
LLYSWEN, *Powys.* **D** Swansea *See* Llandefalle.
LLYSWERRY, *Gwent.* **D** Monmouth *See* Newport (St Andr).
LLYSYFRAN, *Dyfed.* **D** St David's *See* Walton, East.
LLYWEL (St D Teilo) w Traeanglas (St Mary), *Powys.* V **D** Swansea 2 **I** J J DAVIES.
LOUGHOR (St Mich AA), *W Glam.* R **D** Swansea 9 **I** J S ROSE.
LOVESTON w Yerbeston (St Lawr), *Dyfed.* R **D** St David's 4 **I** D E FAULKNER.
LUDCHURCH (St Elidyr) w Templeton, *Dyfed.* R **D** St David's 4 **I** J B LEWIS.

MACHEN (St Mich w St John), *Gwent.* R **D** Monmouth 7 **I** C F WARREN.
MACHYNLLETH, *Powys.* **D** Bangor *See* Llanwrin.
MAENCLOCHOG (St Mary), Llanycefn Llandilo (St Teilo) and Henry's Moat (St Bryrach or St Bernard), *Dyfed.* V **D** St David's 3 **I** (Vacant).
MAENTWROG (St Twrog) w Trawsfynydd (St Madyrn), *Gwyn.* **D** Bangor 7 **I** T B HUGHES.
MAERDY (All SS w St Luke), *Mid Glam.* **D** Llandaff 12 *See* Ferndale.
MAESMYNIS, *Powys.* **D** Swansea 3 *See* Builth.
MAESTEG, *Mid Glam.* **D** Llandaff *See* Llangynwyd.
MAESTEILO **D** St David's 14 *See* Llanegwad.
MAGOR (St Mary Virg) w Redwick (St Thos Ap) and Undy (St Mary), *Gwent.* V **D** Monmouth 4 **I** P G COBB.
MAINDEE (St Jo Evang), *Gwent.* V **D** Monmouth 10 **I** C A LONG, J K BEARDMORE *c.*
MALLWYD (St Tydecho) w Cemmaes (St Tydecho), and Llanymawddwy (St Tydecho), *Gwyn.* R **D** Bangor 9 **I** G J VAUGHAN-JONES.
MALPAS (St Mary), *Gwent.* V **D** Monmouth 10 **I** K A E TYTE, D KELLEN *c.*
MAMHILAD ST ILLTUD w Llanvihangel Pontymoile (St Mich), *Gwent.* R and V **D** Monmouth 6 **I** (Vacant).
MANAFON (St Mich), *Powys.* R **D** St Asaph 8 *See* Llanwyddelan.
MANOR-OWEN, *Dyfed.* **D** St David's *See* Llanwnda.
MANORBIER (St Jas), *Dyfed.* V **D** St David's 1 **I** R W C WILLIAMS.
MANORDEIFI (St D), *Dyfed.* R **D** St David's 8 **I** P EVANS.
MANORDEILO (St Paul) w Taliaris, *Dyfed.* V **D** St David's 14 **I** T H BRACE.
MANSELTON, *W Glam.* **D** Swansea *See* Swansea.
MARCHWIEL (St Marcella) *Clwyd.* R **D** St Asaph 11 **I** T O JONES.
MARCROSS (H Trin) w Monknash (St Mary) and Wick (St Jas), *S Glam.* R **D** Llandaff 6 **I** D W LEWIS.
MARGAM (St Mary Virg), *W Glam.* V **D** Llandaff 7 **I** M R ELLIS.
MARLOES, *Dyfed.* **D** St David's *See* St Bride's.
MARROS, *Dyfed.* **D** St David's *See* Eglwys Gymin.
MARSHFIELD (St Mary Virg) w Peterstone Wentloog (St Pet) w Coedkernew and St Bride's Wentloog, *Gwent.* V and R **D** Monmouth 7 **I** A V JONES.
MARTLETWY (St Marcellus) w Lawrenny and Minwear, *Dyfed.* V **D** St David's 4 **I** (Vacant).
MATHERN (St Tewdric) w Mounton and St Pierre, *Gwent.* V **D** Monmouth **I** K M DENISON.
MATHRY (H Martyrs) w St Edrens (St Edeyrn), Grandston (St Cath) and St Nicholas (St Nich) and Jordanston, *Dyfed.* V **D** St David's 2 **I** W G JONES.
MATTHEWSTOWN w Ynysboeth, *Mid Glam.* **D** Llan 7 *See* Penrhiwceiber.
MEIDRIM (St D), w Llanboidy (St Bryach) and Merthyr (St Enfail), *Dyfed.* V **D** St David's **I** (Vacant).
MEIFOD (St Tyssilio and St Mary) w Llangynyw (St Cynyw), *Powys.* V **D** St Asaph 8 **I** W P S DAVIES.
MELANGELL, *Powys.* **D** St Asaph *See* Llangynog.
MELIDEN (St Melydd) and Gwaenysgor, *Clwyd.* V **D** St Asaph 1 **I** R H TEAGUE.
MELINE, *Dyfed.* **D** St David's *See* Eglwyswrw.
MELLTEYRN (St Pet-ad-Vincula) w Bottwnnog (St Beuno), Llandygwnning (St Gwyninin) and Llaniestyn (St Iestyn), *Gwyn.* R **D** Bangor 11 **I** J H VEVAR.
MENAI BRIDGE, *Gwyn.* **D** Bangor *See* Llandysilio.
MERTHYR Dyfed. **D** St David's *See* Meidrim.
MERTHYR CYNOG (St Cynog) w Duffryn Honddu (St Cynog), *Powys.* V **D** Swansea 1 **I** J P H WALTERS.
MERTHYR-DYFAN (St Dyfan and St Teilo) w E Barry (St Paul), *S Glam.* R **D** Llandaff 10 **I** C M DAVID, L W WAY *c.*
MERTHYR-MAWR (St Teilo), *Mid Glam.* R **D** Llandaff 2 **I** (Vacant).
MERTHYR TYDFIL (St Tydfil w St D) and Cyfarthfa (Ch Ch), *Mid Glam.* R **D** Llandaff 8 **I** D S LEE, G G FOSTER *team v,* S S MORGAN *team v,* D T JENKINS *hon c.*
MERTHYR VALE (St Mary Virg), *Mid Glam.* **D** Llandaff 8 **I** M J SHORT.
MICHAELSTON-LE-PIT, *S Glam.* **D** Llandaff *See* St Andrew Major.
MICHAELSTON-SUPER-AVON or CWMAVON (St Mich) w (All SS), *W Glam.* V **D** Llandaff 7 **I** K W CHANT.
MICHAELSTON-Y-FEDW (St Mich) w Rudry (St Jas), *Gwent.* R **D** Monmouth 7 **I** L C BARTLE-JENKINS.
MICHAELSTONE-SUPER-ELY (St Mich), *S Glam.* R **D** Llandaff *See* St Fagans.
MICHEL-TROY (St Mich), *Gwent.* **D** Monmouth 3 *See* Monmouth.
MILFORD HAVEN (St Cath V and M), *Dyfed.* V **D** St David's 5 **I** P S JONES *c.*
MINERA (St Mary w St Tudfil) w Coedpoeth, *Clwyd.* V **D** St Asaph 16 **I** T PIERCE.
MINWEAR, *Dyfed.* **D** St David's *See* Martletwy.
MISKIN (St Jo Bapt and St D), *Mid Glam.* V **D** Llandaff 1 **I** N C H BROWN.
MITCHEL-TROY, *Gwent.* **D** Monmouth *See* Michel-Troy.
MOCHDRE (All SS), *Powys.* V **D** St Asaph 7 **I** C I DAY.
MOLD (St Mary w St D), *Clwyd.* V **D** St Asaph 14 **I** W H WILLIAMS, B TAYLOR *c.*
MONACHLOGDU, *Dyfed.* **D** St David's *See* Mynachlogddu.
MONINGTON, *Dyfed.* **D** St David's *See* Moylgrove.
MONKNASH, *S Glam.* **D** Llandaff *See* Marcross.
MONKSWOOD, *Gwent.* **D** Monmouth *See* Usk.
MONKTON, *Dyfed.* **D** St David's *See* Pembroke.
MONMOUTH (St Mary Virg), *Gwent.* V **D** Monmouth 3 **I** J ROGERS, P B MARTIN *c.*
(St Thos-over-Monnow w St Wonnow, Wonastow and St Mich, Michel Troy), V **D** Monmouth 3 **I** N H PRICE.
MONTGOMERY (St Nich) w Forden (St Mich AA) and Llandyssil (St Tyssil) *Powys.* R and V **D** St Asaph 10 **I** J W M ROBERTS.
MORFIL (St Jo Bapt) w Pontfaen and Llanychllwydog (St D) w Puncheston and Little Newcastle, *Dyfed.* R **D** St David's 2 **I** (Vacant).
MORRISTON (St D), *W Glam.* V **D** Swansea 10 **I** W K PRICE, A J KNIGHT *c,* P MORGAN *c.*
MORVIL, *Dyfed.* **D** St David's *See* Morfil.
MOSTYN (Ch Ch), *Clwyd.* V **D** St Asaph 4 **I** D T RICHARD.
MOTHVEY, *Dyfed.* **D** St David's *See* Myddfai.
MOUNT, *Dyfed.* **D** St David's *See* Verwick.
MOUNTAIN ASH (St Marg w St D), Newtown (St Dyfrig) and Cefnpennar (St Illtyd), *Mid Glam.* V **D** Llandaff 1 **I** (Vacant).
MOUNTON, *Gwent.* **D** Monmouth *See* Mathern.
MOUNTON, *Dyfed.* **D** St David's *See* Narberth.
MOYLGROVE (St Andr) w Monington, *Dyfed.* V **D** St David's *See* St Dogmael's.
MYDDFAI or MOTHVEY, *Dyfed.* **D** St David's 17 *See* Llandingat.
MYDRIM (St D), w Llanboidy (St Bryach), *Dyfed.* V **D** St David's 15 **I** A HOWELLS.
MYDROILYN, *Dyfed.* **D** St David's *See* Llanarth.
MYNACHLOGDDU (St Dogmael) w Llangolman (St Colman), *Dyfed.* V **D** St David's 3 **I** (Vacant).
MYNYDDYSLWYN (St Tudwr), *Gwent.* V **D** Monmouth 8 **I** A B WATERS, R J SUMMERS *c.*

NANGLE, *Dyfed.* **D** St David's *See* Angle.
NANNERCH (St Mich) w Cilcain (St Mary) and Rhydymwyn, *Clwyd.* R **D** St Asaph 14 **I** P R OWEN.
NANTCWNLLE (St Gwynllen?) and Trefilan (St Hilary) w Gartheli, *Dyfed.* V **D** St David's 9 **I** (Vacant).
NANTGLYN, *Clwyd.* **D** St Asaph 2 *See* Llansannan.
NANTGWYLLT, *Powys.* **D** Swansea *See* Cwmdauddwr.
NANTMEL, *Powys.* **D** Swansea 7 *See* Rhayader.
NANTYGLO (H Trin), *Gwent.* V **D** Monmouth 9 **I** (Vacant).

NANTYMOEL (St Pet and St Paul) w Wyndham (St D), *Mid Glam.* V **D** Llandaff 2 **I** (Vacant).
NARBERTH (St Andr) and Mounton w Robeston-Wathen (Dedic unknown) and Crinow, *Dyfed.* R **D** St David's 4 **I** T H THOMAS.
NASH, *Gwent.* **D** Monmouth *See* Goldcliff.
NASH, *Dyfed.* **D** St David's *See* Cosheston.
NEATH (St D w St Thos) w Llantwit (St Illtyd), *W Glam.* R **D** Llandaff 9 **I** T J PRICHARD, F P CROSSLAND *c*, G W A HOLCOMBE *c*, D G MORRIS *c*.
NEFYN or Nevin (St D) w Morfa Nefyn, Pistyll (St Beuno), Edern, Tudweiliog and Llandudwen, *Gwyn.* V **D** Bangor 11 **I** E W THOMAS.
NERCWYS (St Mary), *Clwyd.* V **D** St Asaph *See* Treuddyn.
NETHERWENT, *Gwent.* **D** Monmouth *See* St Bride, Netherwent.
NEVERN (St Bryach) w Bayvil, *Dyfed.* V **D** St David's 8 **I** E T JONES.
NEVIN **D** Bangor 11 *See* Nefyn.
NEW FENNS, *Clwyd.* **D** St Asaph *See* Bronington.
NEW MOAT (St Nich) w Clarbeston (St Martin of Tours) and Llysyfran (St Meilor), *Dyfed.* R **D** St David's 3 **I** L M JONES.
NEWBOROUGH (St Pet) w Llangeinwen, Llangaffo and Llanfair yn y Cwmwd, *Gwyn.* R **D** Bangor 4 **I** R L NEWALL.
NEWBRIDGE (St Paul), *Gwent.* V **D** Monmouth 8 **I** A R WILLIE.
NEWBRIDGE-ON-WYE (All SS) w Llanfihangel-Bryn-Pabuan, *Powys.* V **D** Swansea 3 **I** O W JONES.
NEWCASTLE (St Illtyd), *Mid Glam.* V **D** Llandaff 2 **I** H E MORGAN.
NEWCASTLE EMLYN (H Trin) w Llandyfriog (St Tyfriog) and Troedyraur, *Dyfed.* V **D** St David's 6 **I** E A B HUGHES, R J WILLIAMS *c*.
NEWCASTLE, LITTLE, *Dyfed.* **D** St David's *See* Puncheston.
NEWCHURCH, *Powys.* **D** Swansea *See* Bryngwyn.
NEWCHURCH (St Mich), *Dyfed.* V **D** St David's 11 **I** J D JONES, K A M PAINE *chap.*
NEWCHURCH (St Pet), *Gwent.* V **P** *Monmouth 2* **I** (Vacant).
NEWMARKET, *Clwyd.* **D** St Asaph *See* Trelawnyd.
NEWPORT (St Woolos Cathl w St Luke and St Martin), *Gwent.* V **D** Monmouth 10 **I** VERY REV F G JENKINS.
(All SS Crindau), V **D** Monmouth 10 **I** (Vacant).
(St Andr w St Phil Liswerry) **D** Monmouth 10 **I** R J DENNISS.
(St Jo Bapt), V **D** Monmouth 10 **I** C D WESTBROOK.
(St Jo Evang) **D** Monmouth *See* Maindee.
(St Julius and St Aaron), St Julian, V. **D** Monmouth 10 **I** R G DAVIES, I R GALT *c*, A T EDWARDS *hon c*.
(St Mark), V **D** Monmouth 10 **I** D G LEWIS, J E L WHITE *c*.
(St Matt), V **D** Monmouth 10 **I** D A G HATHAWAY.
(St Paul), V **D** Monmouth 10 **I** J HARRIS, J D TRINDER *c*.
(St Steph w H Trin), V **D** Monmouth 10 **I** B M W STARES.
(St Teilo), V **D** Monmouth 10 **I** R VICKERS.
NEWPORT (St Mary) w Cilgwyn, *Dyfed.* R **D** St David's 8 **I** M M GRIFFITHS.
NEWQUAY, *Dyfed.* **D** St David's *See* Llanllwchaiarn.
NEWTON NORTH, *Dyfed.* **D** St David's *See* Slebech.
NEWTON ST PETER (St Pet), *W Glam.* V **D** Swansea 9 **I** H E WILLIAMS.
NEWTON-NOTTAGE (St Jo Bapt) w Porthcawl (All SS), *Mid Glam.* R **D** Llandaff 7 **I** H W EVANS, C L GEAKE *c*, J H JAMES *c*, T MAINES *hon c*.
NEWTOWN (St D w All S) w Llanllwchaiarn (St Llwchaiarn) and Aberhafesp (St Gwynog), *Powys.* R **D** St Asaph 7 **I** P B JONES.
NICHOLASTON, *W Glam.* **D** Swansea *See* Penmaen.
NOLTON, *Mid Glam.* **D** Llandaff *See* Coity.
NOLTON (St Madog), R w Roch (St Mary Virg), *Dyfed.* V **D** St David's 5 **I** A CRAVEN.
NORTHOP (St Eurgain and St Pet), *Clwyd.* V **D** St Asaph 14 **I** J M R G REES.
NORTON, *Powys.* **D** Swansea *See* Knighton.

OAKWOOD (St John), *W Glam.* V **D** Llandaff 7 **I** R DONKIN.
OLDCASTLE, *Gwent.* **D** Monmouth *See* Llanvihangel-Crucorney.
OVERMONNOW, *Gwent.* **D** Monmouth *See* Monmouth.
OVERTON (St Mary Virg), w Erbistock (St Hilary), *Clwyd.* R **D** St Asaph 11 **I** T P JONES.
OXWICH (St Illtyd), *W Glam.* R **D** Swansea 8 *See* Penmaen.
OYSTERMOUTH (All SS), *W Glam.* V **D** Swansea 9 **I** G H THOMAS, C G LEE *c*.

PANT, *Mid Glam.* **D** Llandaff *See* Dowlais.
PANTEG (St Mary) w Llanddewi-Fach and Llandegfeth, *Gwent.* R **D** Monmouth 11 **I** T C MORGAN.
PATRICIO, *Powys.* **D** Swansea *See* Llanbedr-Ystradyw.
PEMBREY (St Illtyd) w Llandyry, *Dyfed.* V **D** St David's 13 **I** W H RICHARDS.
PEMBROKE (St Mary Virg w St Mich), *Dyfed.* V **D** St David's 1 **I** T H HILL.
(St Nich Monkton), V **D** St David's 1 **I** H G ROBERTS.
PEMBROKE DOCK (St Jo Evang w St Patr), *Dyfed.* V **D** St David's 1 **I** A THOMAS, M BROTHERTON *c*.
PENALLT w Pentwyn, *Gwent.* V **D** Monmouth 3 **I** J RICHARDSON.
PENALLY (St Nich), *Dyfed.* V **D** St David's **I** L I DAVIES.
PENARTH (St Aug) w Lavernock (St Lawr), *S Glam.* R **D** Llandaff 10 **I** N H COLLINS, K ANDREWS *c*.
(All SS), V **D** Llandaff 10 **I** D M THOMAS, P A COX *c*, A R FARR *c*.
PENBOYR (St Llawddog w St Barn), *Dyfed.* R **D** St David's 6 **I** (Vacant).
PENBRYN (St Mich) w Blaenporth, *Dyfed.* V **D** St David's 8 **I** T G O JENKINS.
PENCADER, *Dyfed.* **D** St David's *See* Llanfihangel-ar-Arth.
PENCARREG (St Patr) w Llanycrwys (St D), *Dyfed.* V **D** St David's 9 **I** J A MORGAN.
PENCLAWDD or LLANYRNEWYDD (St Gwynour), *W Glam.* V **D** Swansea 8 **I** T J LEWIS.
PENCOED, *Mid Glam.* **D** Llandaff *See* Llanilid.
PENDERYN (St Cynog), *Powys.* R **D** Swansea 2 **I** R E THOMAS.
PENDINE (St Lawr), *Dyfed.* R **D** St David's 15 **I** R W JAMES.
PENDOYLAN (St Cadoc), *S Glam.* V **D** Llandaff 5 **I** (Vacant).
PENEGOES or LLANGADFACH (St Cadfarch) and Darowen (St Tudyr) w Llanbryn-Mair and Dylife, *Powys.* R **D** Bangor 9 **I** (Vacant).
PENGARNDDU, *Mid Glam.* **D** Llandaff *See* Dowlais.
PENHOW (St Jo Bapt) w St Bride's, Netherwent (St Bridget), Llanvaches (St Dyfrig or Dubritius) and Llandevaud (St Pet), *Gwent.* R **D** Monmouth 4 **I** R K JONES.
PENISA'R-WAUN (St Helen) *Gwyn.* **D** Bangor 1 *See* Llandinorwig.
PENLEY (St Mary Magd), *Clwyd.* V **D** St Asaph *See* Worthenbury.
PENLLECH, *Gwyn.* **D** Bangor *See* Llangwnadl.
PENLLERGAER (St D), *W Glam.* V **D** Swansea 9 **I** D E MORRIS.
PENLLINE, *S Glam.* V **D** Llandaff *See* Llansannor.
PENMACHNO (St Tuddlud), *Gwyn.* V **D** Bangor 2 **I** W R JONES.
PENMAEN (St Jo Bapt) w Nicholaston (St Nich) and Oxwich, *W Glam.* R **D** Swansea 8 **I** I RICHARDS.
PENMAEN (St D), *Gwent.* V **D** Monmouth 8 **I** D J YOUNG.
PENMAENMAWR, *Gwyn.* **D** Bangor *See* Dwygyfylchi.
PENMARK (St Mary) w Porthkerry, *S Glam.* V **D** Llandaff 10 **I** (Vacant).
PENMON (St Seirol) w Llangoed w Llanfihangel-Din-Sylwy, *Gwyn.* **D** Bangor 5 *See* Llandegfan.
PENMORFA, *Gwyn.* **D** Bangor *See* Ynyscynhaiarn.
PENMYNYDD (St Credifael), *Gwyn.* V **D** Bangor 5 *See* Llanfair-Pwyll-Gwyngyll.
PENNAL (St Pet-ad-Vincula) and Corris (H Trin), *Gwyn.* R **D** Bangor 9 **I** G AP IORWERTH.
PENNANT (St Thos) or Penybont-Fawr w Hirnant (St Illog) and Llangynog (St Cynog w St Melangell), *Powys.* V **D** St Asaph 9 **I** (Vacant).
PENNARD, *W Glam.* **D** Swansea *See* Ilston.
PENRHIWCEIBER (St Winefred) w Matthewstown (All SS) and Ynysboeth, *Mid Glam.* V **D** Llandaff 1 **I** G J FRANCIS.
PENRHOS (St Cynvil), *Gwyn.* **D** Bangor **I** (Vacant).
PENRHOS (St Cadoc), *Gwent.* **D** Monmouth 5 *See* Llantilio-Crossenny.
PENRHOS, *Powys.* **D** St Asaph *See* Llandysilio.
PENRHOSLLUGWY (St Mich), *Gwyn.* **D** Bangor 6 *See* Llaneugrad.
PENRHYDD, or PENRIETH, *Dyfed.* **D** St David's *See* Capel Colman.
PENRHYN, *Gwyn.* **D** St Asaph *See* Eglwys-Rhos.

ROBESTON WEST, *Dyfed.* D St David's *See* Walwyn's Castle.
ROCH, *Dyfed.* D St David's *See* Nolton.
ROCKFIELD (St Cenhedlon) and Llangattock-Vibon-Avel w St Maughan, *Gwent.* V D Monmouth 3 I G E LOVITT.
ROGGIETT (St Mary) w Llanvihangel-Roggiett (St Mich) and Portskewett, *Gwent.* R D Monmouth I T H J PALMER.
ROSEMARKET or RHOSMARKET (St Ismael), *Dyfed.* V D St David's 5 I J HALE.
ROSSETT (Ch Ch), *Clwyd.* V D St Asaph 16 I J PUGH.
RUABON (St Mabon and St Mary Virg) w Penylan (All SS), *Clwyd.* V D St Asaph 16 I T W PRITCHARD.
RUDBAXTON (St Mich), *Dyfed.* R D St David's *See* Prendergast.
RUDRY, *Gwent.* D Monmouth *See* Michaelston-y-Fedw.
RUMNEY (St Aug), *Gwent.* V D Monmouth 7 I R HALLETT.
RUTHIN (St Pet) w Llanrhydd (St Meugan), *Clwyd.* R D St Asaph 3 I R E SMART, G C JONES *c.*

ST ANDREW'S MAJOR (St Andr) w Dinas Powys, Eastbrook, and Michaelston-le-Pit (Chap of Ease, St Pet), *S Glam.* R D Llandaff 10 I J G KEANE.
ST ANN, *Gwyn.* D Bangor *See* Llandegai.
ST ARVANS, *Gwent.* D Monmouth *See* Itton.
ST ASAPH (Cathl Ch of St A Par Ch of St A, St Cyndeyrn and St A), *Clwyd.* D St Asaph 1 I B A ORFORD *c,* A J PRICE *c.*
ST ATHAN, *S Glam.* D Llandaff *See* Eglwysbrewis.
ST BRIDE'S (St Ffraid or St Bride), w Marloes (St Pet), *Dyfed.* R D St David's 5 I D A REES.
ST BRIDE'S MAJOR (St Bridget), *Mid Glam.* V D Llandaff 2 I D B BEVAN.
ST BRIDE'S MINOR (St Bride) Bryncethin (St Theodore), *Mid Glam.* R D Llandaff 2 I C R CARE.
ST BRIDE'S NETHERWENT, *Gwent.* D Monmouth *See* Penhow.
ST BRIDE'S, WENTLOOG, *Gwent.* D Monmouth *See* Coedkernew.
ST BRIDE'S-SUPER-ELY (St Bride), *S Glam.* R D Llandaff 5 *See* Peterston-super-Ely.
ST CLEARS (St Mary) w Llanginning (St Cynin) and Llanddowror (St Teilo), *Dyfed.* V D St David's 15 I G A EDWARDS.
ST DAVID'S (St D Cathl), *Dyfed.* D St David's 2 I VERY REV L BOWEN.
ST DOGMAEL'S (St Thos) w Llantood and Molygrove w Monington, *Dyfed.* D St David's 8 I M C DAVIES.
ST DOGWELLS, *Dyfed.* D St David's *See* Ambleston.
ST DONATS (St Donat), *S Glam.* D Llandaff *See* Llantwit Major.
ST EDRENS, *Dyfed.* D St David's *See* Mathry.
ST ELVIS, *Dyfed.* D St David's *See* Whitchurch.
ST FAGAN w St Winifred, *Mid Glam.* D Llandaff *See* Aberdare (St Fagan).
ST FAGAN'S (St Mary) w Michaelstone-super-Ely (St Mich), *S Glam.* R D Llandaff 5 I H L CLARKE.
ST FLORENCE (St Florencius) w Redberth, *Dyfed.* R and V D St David's 1 I L I DAVIES.
ST GEORGE or KEGIDOG, *Clwyd.* R D St Asaph 6 I R V BYLES.
ST GEORGE-SUPER-ELY (St Geo), *S Glam.* D Llandaff *See* Bonvilston.
ST HARMON (St Germanus or Garmon), *Powys.* V D Swansea 7 *See* Cwmdauddwr.
ST HILARY (St Hilary), *S Glam.* V D Llandaff 6 I (Vacant).
ST HILARY GREENWAY, *S Glam.* D Mon 7 I M C WARREN.
ST ISHMAEL (St Ishmael) w Llansaint (All SS) and Ferryside (St Thos), *Dyfed.* V D St David's 13 I (Vacant).
ST ISHMAEL'S, *Dyfed.* D St David's *See* Herbrandston.
ST ISSELLS (St Issell), *Dyfed.* V D St David's 4 I M BUTLER.
ST JOHN-JUXTA-SWANSEA, *W Glam.* D Swansea *See* Swansea.
ST LAWRENCE w Ford, *Dyfed.* R D St David's 2 I B JONES.
ST LYTHAN'S, *S Glam.* D Llandaff *See* Wenvoe.
ST MARY CHURCH, *S Glam.* D Llandaff *See* Llandough.
ST MARY HILL, *S Glam.* D Llandaff *See* Llangan.
ST MAUGHAN, *Gwent.* D Monmouth *See* Llangattock-Vibon-Avel.
ST MELLONS, *S Glam.* V D Monmouth 7 I W D LLEWELLYN.
ST NICHOLAS, *S Glam.* D Llandaff *See* Bonvilston.
ST NICHOLAS (St Nich), *Dyfed.* D St David's *See* Mathry.
ST PETROX (St Petrox) w Stackpole Elidor (or Cheriton) and Cheriton (St Jas and St Elidyr), *Dyfed.* R D St David's 1 I D B G DAVIES.
ST PIERRE, *Gwent.* D Monmouth *See* Mathern.
ST THOMAS-OVER-MONNOW, *Gwent.* D Monmouth *See* Monmouth.
ST TWYNNELLS, *Dyfed.* D St David's *See* Bosherston.
SEVEN SISTERS (St Mary and St D), *W Glam.* V D Llandaff 9 I R I BLACKMORE.
SHIRENEWTON (St Thos à Becket), *Gwent.* R D Monmouth 2 I (Vacant).
SHOTTON (St Ethelwold), *Clwyd.* V D St Asaph 14 I A C ROBERTS.
SILIAN (St Sulien), *Dyfed.* D St David's *See* Bettws-Bledrws.
SIX BELLS (St John), *Gwent.* D Monmouth 9 I B J FAVELL *p-in-c.*
SKENFRITH, *Gwent.* D Monmouth *See* Grosmont.
SKETTY (St Paul), *W Glam.* V D Swansea 9 I I R L THOMAS, G M REED *c.*
SKEWEN (St John, St Mary Virg and All SS), *W Glam.* V D Llandaff 9 I D E LAKE, D A RICHARDS *c.*
SLEBECH (St Jo Bapt) w Uzmaston (St Ismael) and Boulston and Newton North, *Dyfed.* V D St David's 3 I W H WATKINS.
SOLVA Dyfed. D St David's I (Vacant).
SOUTHSEA (All SS), *Clwyd.* V D St Asaph 16 *See* Berse.
SPITTAL w Tregarn, *Dyfed.* D St David's *See* Tregarn.
STACKPOLE ELIDOR or CHERITON, *Dyfed.* D St David's *See* St Petrox.
STEYNTON, *Dyfed.* D St David's *See* Johnston.
STRATA FLORIDA (St Mary), *Dyfed.* V D St David's *See* Ystradmeurig.
SULLY (St Jo Bapt), *S Glam.* R D Llandaff 10 I R HOLTAM.
SWANSEA (St Mary w H Trin and St Mark), *W Glam.* V D Swansea 9 I D E LEWIS, T F L GRIFFITHS *c,* I R LOWELL *c,* D W THOMAS *c.*
(Ch Ch), V D Swansea 9 I E T HUNT.
(St Barn), V D Swansea 9 I D R WILKINSON.
(St Gabr), V D Swansea 9 I E M WASTELL.
(St Jo Bapt-juxta-Swansea), V D Swansea 9 I D W E BRINSON *c-in-c.*
(St Jude), V D Swansea 9 I D W WHITE.
(St Luke, Cwmbwrla), V D Swansea 9 I W R LEWIS.
(St Matt w Greenhill), V D Swansea 9 I I J BROMHAM.
(St Mich AA Manselton), V D Swansea 9 I R NEWBURY.
(St Nich-on-the-Hill), V D Swansea 9 I D J WILKINSON.
(St Pet Cockett), V D Swansea 9 I A G LEE.
(St Teilo Caereithin), V D Swansea I J W G HUGHES.
(St Thos Ap w St Steph w Kilvey (All SS), V D Swansea 9 I D E REES.

TALACHDDU, *Powys.* D Swansea *See* Llanddew.
TALBENNY, *Dyfed.* D St David's *See* Walton, West.
TALGARREG, *Dyfed.* D St David's *See* Capel Cynon.
TALGARTH (St Gwendoline) w Llanelieu (St Ellyw), *Powys.* V D Swansea 1 I N LEA.
TALIARIS, *Dyfed.* D St David's *See* Manordeilo.
TALLARN GREEN, *Clwyd.* D St Asaph *See* Worthenbury.
TALLEY or TAL-Y-LLYCHAM (St Mich AA) w Taliaris, *Dyfed.* V D St David's 17 *See* Conwyl-Gaio.
TALYBONT, *Dyfed.* D St David's *See* Llanfihangel Genaur's Glyn.
TALYGARN (St Ann), *Mid Glam.* V D Llandaff *See* Pontyclun.
TALYLLYN, *Gwyn.* D Bangor *See* Llanbeulan.
TALYLLYN, *Gwyn.* D Bangor *See* Llanegryn.
TALYSARN, *Gwyn.* D Bangor *See* Llanllyfni.
TEMPLETON, *Dyfed.* D St David's *See* Ludchurch.
TENBY (St Mary) w Gumfreston (St Lawr), *Dyfed.* R D St David's 4 I D M BRIDGES, A J SIDEBOTTOM *c.*
TINTERN PARVA (St Mich AA) w Chapel Hill (St Mary), *Gwent.* R D Monmouth 2 *See* Llandogo.
TIR ABAD or LLANDULAS, *Powys.* D Swansea *See* Llanwrtyd.
TONDU (St Jo Div), *Mid Glam.* V D Llandaff 2 *See* Penyfai.
TONGWYNLAIS (St Mich AA), *S Glam.* V D Llandaff 5 I R L BROWN, D I LEWIS *hon c.*
TONNA, *W Glam.* V D Llandaff 9 I C G PITMAN.
TONYREFAIL (St D w St Alb and St John), *Mid Glam.* V D Llandaff 12 I W P THOMAS, P G HATHERLEY *hon c.*
TOWYN (St Mary), *Clwyd.* V D St Asaph 6 I P FOWLES.
TRAEANGLAS, *Powys.* D Swansea *See* Llywel.

YSTRADMEURIG (St Jo Bapt) and Strata Florida, *Dyfed*. V **D** St David's 9 **I** (Vacant).
YSTRAD-MYNACH (H Trin), *Mid Glam*. V **D** Llandaff 3 **I** C H JAMES.
YSTRADOWEN (St Owain), *S Glam*. V **D** Llandaff 6 *See* Llansannor.
YSTRAD-RHONDDA (St Steph), *Mid Glam*. V **D** Llandaff 12 **I** D H RHYDDERCH.
YSTRADYFODWG (St Jo Bapt, St Pet, St D & St Mark), *Mid Glam*. V **D** Llandaff 12 **I** R E YOUNG.

INDEX OF INCUMBENCIES—SCOTTISH

ABERCHIRDER (St Marnan), *Banff.* R D Moray I VERY REV C A BARNES.
ABERDEEN (St Andr Cathl), King Street D Aberdeen I (Vacant).
(St Clem) Ind Miss Prince Regent Street D Aberdeen I (Vacant).
(St Jas), Union Street West D Aberdeen I R E ALLSOPP.
(St Jo Evang), Crown Street, R D Aberdeen I (Vacant).
(St Marg of Scotld), Gallowgate, R D Aberdeen I J ROSS.
(St Mary), Carden Place, R D Aberdeen I J D ALEXANDER.
(St Ninian), Seaton, Dep Miss D Aberdeen I (Vacant).
ABERDOUR (St Columba) Priv Chap, *Fife.* D St Andrews *See* Burntisland.
ABERFOYLE (St Mary), *Perth.* D St Andrews I J M CROOK *p-in-c,* D L REDWOOD *c.*
ABERLOUR (St Marg of Scotld), *Banff.* D Moray I W B LUNN.
ABOYNE (St Thos), *Aberdeen.* D Aberdeen I A C ADAMSON.
AIRDRIE (St Paul), *Lanark.* D Glasgow I (Vacant).
ALEXANDRIA (St Mungo), *Dunbarton.* D Glasgow I J WILDING *p-in-c.*
ALFORD (St Andr), *Aberdeen.* D Aberdeen I D W M GRANT.
ALLAN, BRIDGE OF (St Sav), *Stirling.* D Dunblane *See* Bridge of Allan.
ALLOA (St Jo Evang), *Clackmannan.* D St Andrews I J T SHONE *p-in-c,* A H D KNOCK *c.*
ALYTH (St Ninian) w Meigle (St Marg), *Perth.* D Dunkeld I D ROBERTS.
ANNAN (St Jo Evang), and Eastriggs Dep Miss *Dumfries.* D Glasgow I M LINDSAY-PARKINSON, W T M PIRIE *c.*
ARBROATH (St Mary), *Angus.* D Brechin I W F WARD.
ARDBRECKNISH (Chap) (St Jas), *Argyll.* D Argyll I (Vacant).
ARDCHATTAN (H Spirit) Dep Miss D Argyll *See* Oban.
ARDROSSAN (St Andr), *Ayr.* D Glasgow I D GOLDIE, G WELSH *hon c.*
ARRAN, Dep Miss of *Bute.* D The Isles I C J WOOD.
AUCHINDOIR (St Mary Virg), *Aberdeen.* D Aberdeen I D W M GRANT.
AUCHTERARDER (St Kessog), *Perth.* D St Andrews I J W DUFFY.
AYR (H Trin), w St Jo Bapt Miss, St Osw Miss Maybole, *Ayr.* D Glasgow I VERY REV S S SINGER, B H G COLLIE *hon c.*

BAILLIESTON (St Jo Evang) w Shettleston, *Lanark.* D Glasgow I (Vacant).
BALERNO (St Mungo) Ind Miss *Midlothian.* D Edinburgh I J PELHAM *hon c.*
BALLACHULISH (St John), w St John's Chap, *Argyll.* D Argyll I G M Q WILSON.
BALLATER (St Kentigern), *Aberdeen.* D Aberdeen I A C ADAMSON.
BALLINTUIM Miss Station (St Mich AA), *Perth.* D St Andrews I (Vacant).
BANCHORY TERNAN (St Ternan), *Kincardine.* D Aberdeen I G C MUNGAVIN.
BANFF (St Andr), w Macduff Miss *Banff.* P *Aberdeen* I (Vacant).
BATHGATE (St Columba), *Linlithgow.* D Edinburgh I E M ROBERTSON *p-in-c.*
BEARSDEN (All SS) w Milngavie (St Andr), *Dunbarton.* D Glasgow I M R M WILSON.
BERWICK, NORTH, *East Lothian.* D Edinburgh *See* North Berwick.
BIELDSIDE (St Devenick), *Aberdeen.* R D Aberdeen I K D GORDON.
BISHOPBRIGGS (St Jas-the-Less), *Glasgow,* R. D Glasgow I H G C LEE.
BLAIRGOWRIE (St Cath), *Perth.* D Dunkeld I D ROBERTS.
BO'NESS (St Cath) w Linlithgow Miss, *Linlithgow.* D Edinburgh I J A MEIN P-IN-C OF BO'NESS, E M ROBERTSON P-IN-C OF LINLITHGOW.
BRAEBURN (St Francis) Priv Chap D Edinburgh *See* Edinburgh (St Cuthb).
BRAEMAR (St Marg of Scotld) Miss *Aberdeen.* D Aberdeen I A C ADAMSON.
BRECHIN (St Andr), *Angus.* D Brechin I I G HAY.
BRIDGE OF ALLAN (St Sav), *Stirling.* D Dunblane I J T SHONE, D FINLAYSON *c,* A H D KNOCK *c.*
BRIDGE OF WEIR (St Mary Virg), *Renfrew.* D Glasgow *See* Kilmacolm.
BRORA (St Columba) Miss Station D Caithness I D J EALES-WHITE *p-in-c.*
BROUGHTY FERRY (St Mary), *Angus.* D Brechin I R W BREADEN.
BUCKIE (All SS) w Cullen (St Mary), *Banff.* D Aberdeen I S J G BENNIE.
BUCKSBURN (St Machar), *Aberdeen.* D Aberdeen I (Vacant).
BURNTISLAND (St Serf), w Aberdour Priv Chap (St Columba) and Kinghorn (St Leon), Miss *Fife.* D St Andrews I A J BAYNHAM.
BURRAVOE (St Colman) Miss Charge, I of Yell, *Shetland.* D Orkney I L S SMITH.

CALLANDER (St Andr), *Perth.* D St Andrews I J M CROOK *p-in-c,* D L REDWOOD *c.*
CAMBUSLANG (St Cuthb) w Newton Dep Miss D Glasgow I P D NOBLE, G B STEEL *c.*
CAMPBELTOWN (St Kiaran), *Argyll.* D Argyll I K V PAGAN.
CARNOUSTIE (Holy Rood), *Angus.* D Brechin I D B MACKAY.
CARSEBARRACKS Miss Station, *Forfar.* D Dunkeld *See* Forfar.
CASTLE DOUGLAS (St Ninian), *Kirkcudbright.* D Galloway I (Vacant).
CATTERLINE (St Phil), *Kincardine,* R D Brechin I (Vacant).
CHALLOCH (All SS) w Newton-Stewart (St Andr), *Wigtown.* D Galloway I N J PARKES, W J BRENNAN *c.*
CLARKSTON (St Aid), *Renfrew.* D Glasgow *See* Glasgow.
CLYDEBANK (St Columba), *Dunbarton.* R D Glasgow I G L NICOLL *c.*
COATBRIDGE (St Jo Evang), *Lanark.* D Glasgow I D P M STRACHAN.
COLDSTREAM (St Mary and All S), *Berwick.* D Edinburgh I M D G C RYAN *p-in-c.*
COLINTON (St Cuthb) D Edinburgh *See* Edinburgh.
COMRIE (St Fillan) w St Fillan's Miss (Ch of H Spirit), *Perth.* D St Andrews I G J SIMMONS.
CONNEL FERRY (St Mary) Summer Miss, *Argyll.* D Argyll *See* Oban.
COODHAM (Priv Chap), *Ayr.* D Glasgow *See* Kilmarnock.
CORSTORPHINE Ind Miss D Edinburgh *See* Edinburgh.
CORTACHY CHAPEL, *Forfar.* D Dunkeld *See* Kirriemuir.
COUPAR ANGUS (St Anne), *Perth.* D Dunkeld I D ROBERTS.
COVE (St Mary Virg) Miss Chap Dedic, *Kincardine.* D Brechin *See* Torry.
CRIEFF (St Columba and St Mich), *Perth.* D St Andrews I G J SIMMONS.
CROMARTY (St Regulus) Miss Station, *Cromarty.* D Ross *See* Fortrose.
CROMBIE Dep Miss, *Fife.* D St Andrews *See* Dunfermline.
CROMLIX Priv Chap, *Perth.* D Dunblane *See* Dunblane.
CRUDEN (St Jas), *Aberdeen.* D Aberdeen I G H STRANRAER-MULL.
CULLEN (St Mary), *Banff.* D Aberdeen *See* Buckie.
CULLIPOOL (St Pet) Dep Miss Dedic (Isle of Luing), *Argyll.* D The Isles *See* Oban.
CUMBERNAULD (H Name), *Dunbarton.* D Glasgow I J F C WOODLEY *p-in-c.*
CUMBRAE (H Spirit), Colleg Ch and Cathl of the Isles w Millport (St Andr), *Bute.* D The Isles I (Vacant).
CUMINESTOWN (St Luke), *Aberdeen.* D Aberdeen I (Vacant).
CUPAR FIFE (St Jas) w Ladybank, *Fife.* D St Andrews I W SMURTHWAITE.

DALBEATTIE (Ch Ch), *Kircudbright.* D Galloway I I G STOCKTON.
DALKEITH (St Mary), Ind Miss *Midlothian.* D Edinburgh I P W G BURWELL, T A G B STEWART *hon c,* W M WATT *hon c.*

DALMAHOY (St Mary), *Midlothian.* D Edinburgh
I A B CAMERON.
DALRY Ind Miss (St Pet), *Ayr.* D Glasgow I I BOFFEY *c.*
DAVIDSON'S MAINS (H Cross), *Midlothian.*
D Edinburgh I R T HALLIDAY, H A CURTIS *c,*
J W CHADWIN *hon c.*
DEER (St Drostan) w New Deer Dep Miss, *Aberdeen.*
D Aberdeen I D P BOVEY.
DINGWALL (St Jas Gt) w Strathpeffer (St Anne) Miss, *Ross.* D Ross I S A T MALLIN.
DOLLAR (St Jas Gt), *Clackmannan.* D Dunblane
I J T SHONE *p-in-c,* W L GLAZEBROOK *c,* A H D KNOCK *c.*
DORNOCH (St Finnbarr) Miss, *Sutherland.* D Caithness
I D J EALES-WHITE *p-in-c.*
DOUNE (St Modoc), *Perth.* D St Andrews
I J M CROOK *p-in-c,* D L REDWOOD *c.*
DRUMLITHIE (St Jo Bapt), *Kincardine.* D Brechin
I E HAYES.
DRUMTOCHTY (St Palladius), *Kincardine.* D Brechin *See* Laurencekirk.
DUFFTOWN (St Mich), Ind Miss, *Banff.* D Aberdeen
I (Vacant).
DUMBARTON (St Aug), *Dunbarton.* D Glasgow
I A M Q MACPHERSON.
DUMFRIES (St Jo Evang) w Maxwelltown (St Ninian), Miss Station, *Dumfries.* D Glasgow I J M TAYLOR,
C D LYON *c.*
DUNBAR (St Anne), *East Lothian.* D Edinburgh
I F R STEVENSON *c.*
DUNBLANE (St Mary) w Cromlix Priv Chap, *Perth.*
D St Andrews I J F W SYMON.
DUNDEE CATHL (St Paul), Castlehill w St Roque Miss Station, *Angus.* R D Brechin *See* Cathedral.
(H Trin) Dep Miss Well Road, Hawkhill D Brechin *See* St Mary Magd.
(All SS) Dep Miss Cochrane Street D Brechin *See* St Mary Magd.
(St Jo Bapt), Albert Street, Ind Miss D Brechin
I J WALKER *p-in-c,* G M GREIG *c.*
(St Luke) Ind Miss Downfield D Brechin I G SCOTT.
(St Marg Lochee), (New Ch), w W St Columba Miss
D Brechin I W J MCAUSLAND, D M GREEN *hon c.*
(St Martin), Derby Street Ind Miss D Brechin I (Vacant).
(St Mary Magd), Blinshall Street, w H Trin and All SS Miss
D Brechin I D SHEPHERD, G M GREIG *c.*
(St Ninian) Dep Miss D Brechin I D W DAY *p-in-c.*
(St Salvador), St Salvador Street D Brechin I H P DUFF,
D ELDER *hon c.*
DUNFERMLINE (H Trin), w Masterton (St Marg of Scotld), Crombie, *Fife.* D St Andrews I KAY,
J W MARSHALL *c,* T DENNISON *hon c.*
DUNKELD (St Mary) w Birnam, *Perth.* D Dunkeld
I D H WRIGHT.
DUNOON (H Trin), *Argyll.* D Argyll I A M MACLEAN.
DUNS (Ch Ch), *Berwick.* D Edinburgh I B H C GORDON *c.*
DUROR (St Adamnan) w Portnacrois and Glencreran, *Argyll.* D Argyll I (Vacant).

EARLSFERRY Dep Miss, *Fife.* D St Andrews *See* Elie.
EAST KILBRIDE (St Mark Miss), *Renfrew.* D Glasgow
I G S CAMPBELL.
EASTRIGGS Dep Miss, *Dumfries.* D Glasgow *See* Annan.
EDINBURGH CATHL (St Mary), Palmerstonplace w Water of Leith Dep Miss H Trin Dean Bridge, and St Luke Dep Miss Dalry, *Midlothian.* D Edinburgh *See* Cathedral.
(St Mich and All SS), Brougham Street, D Edinburgh
I W G REID.
(Ch Ch Morningside) D Edinburgh I N G WICKHAM,
R A GILLIES *c,* A G MACINTYRE *hon c.*
(Ch Ch Trinity Road) D Edinburgh *See* Leith.
(Good Shepherd), Murrayfield D Edinburgh I (Vacant).
(H Trin Dean Bridge) D Edinburgh *See* Cathedral.
(St Aid Dep Miss) Niddrie Mains D Edinburgh
I D BOAG *p-in-c.*
(St Andr Holyrood Road), R D Edinburgh I (Vacant).
(St Barn Cathl Miss) Greenside D Edinburgh I (Vacant).
(St Columba), Johnston Terrace D Edinburgh I B A HARDY.
(St Cuthb), Colinton w St Francis Priv Chap Braeburn
D Edinburgh I D COLE.
(St D of Scotld Dep Miss) Pilton D Edinburgh
I R M SINCLAIR *hon c.*
(St Fillan), R D Edinburgh 10 I D M CAMERON,
M A WHATMOUGH *c.*
(St Geo), York Place D Edinburgh *See* St Paul.
(St Hilda, Colinton Mains) D Edinburgh I D M CAMERON,
M A WHATMOUGH *c.*
(Ch Ch and St Jas), Inverleith Row D Edinburgh
I R A GRANT, C CHAPLIN *c.*
(St Jas L) Constitution St, *Edinburgh.* D Edinburgh *See* Leith.
(St Jo Evang), Princes Street w St Kentigern's Miss
D Edinburgh I N CHAMBERLAIN, A S BLACK *team v,*
J F BURDETT *c,* R C FYFFE *c,* L M BROWN *hon c.*
(St Luke Dep Miss) Dalry D Edinburgh *See* Cathedral.
(St Marg) Easter Road D Edinburgh I J N WYNN-EVANS.
(St Mark) Portobello, *Edinburgh.* D Edinburgh *See* Portobello.
(St Martin), Dalry and Gorgie Roads, R D Edinburgh
I W J T BROCKIE, K G FRANZ *c,* D YEOMAN *c.*
(St Ninian Dep Miss), Comely Bank D Edinburgh
I (Vacant).
(St Paul, Old), Carrubbers Close, w St Sav Dep Miss
D Edinburgh I G N R SOWERBY, D W T CROOKS *c,*
G J T FORBES *c,* A B SHEWAN *c.*
(St Paul w St Geo) D Edinburgh I T VEITCH, D G BOND *c.*
(St Pet), Lutton Place D Edinburgh I W F HARRIS,
S L ROBERTSON *c.*
(St Phil Dep Miss) Beaverbank D Edinburgh
I J N WYNN-EVANS *p-in-c.*
(St Salvador, Stenhouse w St Steph) D Edinburgh
I J M DUNCAN.
(St Sav Dep Miss) Canongate D Edinburgh *See* St Paul, Old.
(St Thos, Corstophine), Chap D Edinburgh
I J G WESSON *chap,* E M CULBERTSON *c,* K WHITE *c.*
Water of Leith Dep Miss D Edinburgh *See* Cathedral.
ELGIN (H Trin) w Lossiemouth Miss Station, *Moray.*
D Moray I J D PAUL, S A FALLOWS *hon c.*
ELIE and EARLSFERRY (St Mich AA), *Fife.* R
D St Andrews I R FLATT *c.*
ELLON (St Mary on the Rock), *Aberdeen.* D Aberdeen
I G H STRANRAER-MULL.
EYEMOUTH (St Ebba Dep Miss), *Berwick.* D Edinburgh
I E C POCKLINGTON *p-in-c.*

FALKIRK (Ch Ch), *Stirling.* R D Edinburgh
I J A TRIMBLE.
FASQUE (St Andr), w Fettercairn, *Kincardine.* D Brechin *See* Laurencekirk.
FOCHABERS, Gordon Castle Chap, *Elgin.* D Moray
I W B LUNN.
FOLLA-RULE (St Geo), *Aberdeen.* D Aberdeen
I A B MACGILLIVRAY.
FORFAR (St Jo Evang), w Carsebarracks Miss, *Forfar.*
D Dunkeld I C B R PRESTON-THOMAS.
FORRES (St Jo Evang), *Elgin.* D Moray I R W FORREST,
G W SMITH *hon c.*
FORT GEORGE, Garrison Chap, *Inverness.* D Moray *See* Nairn.
FORTROSE (St Andr), w Cromarty (St Regulus) Miss *Ross.* D Ross I J A HOWARD.
FORT WILLIAM (St Andr), *Inverness.* D Argyll
I J H J MACLEAY.
FRASERBURGH (St Pet) w Lonmay, *Aberdeen.* R
D Aberdeen I R A C GRIEVE.
FURNACE (St Brendan), Miss Station, Lochfyne, *Argyll.*
D Argyll *See* Inveraray.
FYVIE (All SS), *Aberdeen.* D Aberdeen *See* Woodhead.

GALASHIELS (St Pet), *Selkirk.* R D Edinburgh
I D W SMITH.
GARTCOSH Dep Miss (St Andr), *Lanark.* D Glasgow
I (Vacant).
GATEHOUSE OF FLEET Dep Miss, *Kirkcudbright.*
D Galloway *See* Kirkcudbright.
GIRVAN (St John), *Ayr.* D Glasgow I (Vacant).
GLAMIS (St Mich AA), Priv Chap, *Forfar.* D Dunkeld
I W MILNE *chap.*
GLASGOW (All SS), Jordanhill, *Glasgow.* D Glasgow
I (Vacant).
(Ch of Ascen), Mosspark Dep Miss D Glasgow
I R J BURNS.
(Ch Ch), Brook Street D Glasgow I D HUNTER.
(H Cross), Knightswood D Glasgow I W J BROMLEY.
(H Trin), Riddrie D Glasgow I D HUNTER *p-in-c.*
(St Aid), Clarkston D Glasgow I D C GOLDIE.
(St Barn) Craigpark, R D Glasgow I J Y I WARDROP *p-in-c.*
(St Bride) D Glasgow I D MCCUBBIN, M S D BROWN *hon c.*
(St Gabr), Greenfield Street, Govan D Glasgow
I G HARTLEY *c-in-c.*
(St Geo), Maryhill D Glasgow I (Vacant).
(St Jas L), Springburn, R D Glasgow I (Vacant).

(St Marg), Newlands w St D Pollockshaws D Glasgow I J H E B HOPKINS.
(St Martin), Dixon Road, Polmadie D Glasgow I E P PACEY *c.*
(St Mary Virg Cathl Ch), R D Glasgow I M E GRANT, R O DICK *c.*
(St Matt) Ind Miss Possilpark D Glasgow I K L MACAULAY *p-in-c.*
(St Ninian), Pollokshields D Glasgow I D W J REID.
(St Osw), King's Park D Glasgow I K E WIGSTON.
(St Serf) Shettleston. D Glasgow I (Vacant).
(St Silas) D Glasgow I M C EVANS, M CLANCY *hon c,* G E W SCOBIE *hon c.*
(Ch of the Good Shepherd), Hillington D Glasgow I R J BURNS.
GLENALMOND, Trin Coll Chap, *Perth.* D Dunkeld I A M ROFF *chap.*
GLENCARSE (All SS), *Perth.* D Brechin I J B PATERSON *p-in-c.*
GLENCOE (St Mary), *Argyll.* D Argyll I G M Q WILSON.
GLENCRERAN (St Mary), *Argyll.* D Argyll *See* Duror.
GLENROTHES (St Luke), *Fife.* D St Andrews I G MACGREGOR, M LAWRENSON *c,* W LYONS *c.*
GLEN URQUHART (St Ninian), *Inverness.* D Ross I F F LAMING *p-in-c.*
GOUROCK (St Bart), *Renfrew.* D Glasgow I W C DANSKIN *c-in-c.*
GOVAN, *Renfrew.* D Glasgow *See* Glasgow.
GRANGEMOUTH (St Mary), *Stirling.* D Edinburgh I J A MEIN P-IN-C OF BO'NESS.
GRANTOWN (St Columba), *Moray.* D Moray I W D KORNAHRENS.
GREENOCK (St Jo Evang), w St Ninian's Dep Miss and St Stephen's (Cartsdyke) Miss, *Renfrew.* D Glasgow I R G L MCALISTER.
GRETNA (All SS), *Dumfries.* R D Glasgow I G V KENDALL *c-in-c.*
GULLANE (St Adrian), *Haddington.* R D Edinburgh I A MACKINTOSH.

HADDINGTON (H Trin), *East Lothian.* R D Edinburgh I F R STEVENSON *c,* J WOOD *c,* T COUPAR *hon c.*
HAMILTON (St Mary Virg), *Lanark.* R D Glasgow I C M BROUN.
HAWICK (St Cuthb), *Roxburgh.* R D Edinburgh I H M LOPDELL-BRADSHAW.
HELENSBURGH (St Mich AA), *Dunbarton.* D Glasgow I A B LAING.
HUNTER'S QUAY (Ch Ch), *Argyll.* D Argyll *See* Dunoon.
HUNTLY (Ch Ch), *Aberdeen.* R D Moray I VERY REV C A BARNES.

INCHINNAN (All H) Dep Miss, *Refrew.* D Glasgow *See* Paisley.
INNELLAN (St Marg of Scotld), Miss Station, *Argyll.* D Argyll *See* Dunoon.
INNERLEITHEN (St Andr) Ind Miss, *Peebles.* D Edinburgh I E C PARKER *p-in-c.*
INSCH (St Drostan), *Aberdeen.* D Aberdeen I A B MACGILLIVRAY.
INVERARAY (All SS), w Furnace (St Brendan) Miss, *Argyll.* D Argyll I (Vacant).
INVERBERVIE, *Kincardine.* D Brechin *See* Montrose.
INVERGORDON (St Ninian) Ind Miss *Ross.* D Moray I P J S EDWARDS *p-in-c.*
INVERGOWRIE (All S), *Perth.* D Brechin I N PEYTON *p-in-c.*
INVERKEITHING (St Pet) Dep Miss, *Fife.* D St Andrews I J H BAKER *p-in-c.*
INVERNESS (St Andr) Cathl *Inverness.* D Moray *See* Cathedral.
(St Jo Evang) w (St Mich) D Moray I L A BLACK.
INVERURIE (St Mary), *Aberdeen.* D Aberdeen I D W M GRANT.
IONA (St Columba) Priv Chap, *Argyll.* D Argyll I (Vacant).
IRVINE NEW TOWN (Dep Miss), *Ayr.* D Glasgow I D GOLDIE, A T BROWN *hon c.*

JEDBURGH (St Jo Evang), *Roxburgh.* R D Edinburgh I D K MAYBURY, F J L PHELAN *c.*
JOHNSTONE (St Jo Evang), *Renfrew.* D Glasgow I K T ROACH.

KEITH (H Trin), *Banff.* D Moray I VERY REV C A BARNES, J C S ARNAUD *hon c.*
KELSO (St Andr), *Roxburgh.* D Edinburgh I E M PINSENT, T J LENNARD *hon c.*
KEMNAY Miss Station, *Aberdeen.* D Aberdeen I D W M GRANT *p-in-c.*
KENTALLEN Miss D Argyll *See* Duror.
KILLIN (St Fillan), Priv Chap *Perth.* D St Andrews I C E J FRYER *p-in-c.*
KILMACOLM (St Fillan) w Bridge of Weir (St Mary Virg), *Renfrew.* D Glasgow I A W G FLETCHER.
KILMARNOCK (H Trin) w Coodham Chap *Ayr.* D Glasgow I D M MAIN.
KILMARTIN (St Columba), *Argyll.* D Argyll *See* Lochgilphead.
KILMAVEONAIG, MISS STATION, *Perth.* D St Andrews *See* Pitlochry.
KINCARDINE O'NEIL (Ch Ch), *Aberdeen.* D Aberdeen I G C MUNGAVIN.
KINGHORN (St Leon) Miss Station, *Fife.* D St Andrews *See* Burntisland.
KINLOCHLEVEN (St Paul) Miss Station, *Argyll.* D Argyll *See* Nether Lochaber.
KINLOCHMOIDART (St Finan) Station, *Inverness.* D Argyll I (Vacant).
KINLOCH RANNOCH (All SS) Miss Station, *Perth.* D Dunkeld I (Vacant).
KINROSS (St Paul), *Kinross.* D St Andrews I (Vacant).
KIRKCALDY (St Pet), St Mich Pathhead, *Fife.* D St Andrews I J R LEIGH.
KIRKCUDBRIGHT (St Francis of Assisi) w Gatehouse of Fleet, *Kirkcudbright.* R D Glasgow I C A SIMISTER.
KIRKWALL (St Olaf), w Stromness (St Mary), *Orkney.* D Orkney I M J R TURNER.
KIRRIEMUIR (St Mary), w Cortachy, *Forfar.* R D St Andrews I T L FROST.
KISHORN Priv Chap, *Ross.* D Ross I (Vacant).

LADYBANK AND KETTLE Miss Station, *Fife.* D St Andrews *See* Cupar Fife.
LANARK (Ch Ch), *Lanark.* R D Glasgow I H MCINTOSH, W J WALKER *hon c.*
LANGHOLM (All SS) Ind Miss, *Dumfries.* R D Glasgow I G V KENDALL *p-in-c.*
LARGS (St Columba), *Ayr.* D Glasgow I E M LOGUE *hon c.*
LASSWADE (St Leon), *Midlothian.* D Edinburgh I P W G BURWELL, T A G B STEWART *hon c,* W M WATT *hon c.*
LAURENCEKIRK (St Laur) w Drumtochty (St Palladius), Fasque (St Andr) and Fettercairn, *Kincardine.* R D Brechin I A C CRIGHTON.
LEITH (Ch Ch), Trinity Road, *Midlothian.* D Edinburgh *See* Edinburgh Cathl, (Ch Ch and St Jas), Inverleith Row.
(St Jas L) w Miss Chap N Leith, *Midlothian.* R D Edinburgh I T D MORRIS, A SUTHERLAND *c.*
LENZIE (St Cypr) w St Barn Miss Kirkintilloch, *Dunbarton.* D Glasgow I H K TRUDGILL.
LERWICK (St Magnus), *Shetland.* D Orkney I L S SMITH.
LEVEN (St Marg of Scotld), *Fife.* R D St Andrews I L A MOSES, R T EVANS *c.*
LINLITHGOW Miss, *Linlithgow.* D Edinburgh *See* Bo'ness.
LIVINGSTON Dep Miss D Edinburgh I N D MAC CALLUM *team v.*
LOCHALSH (St Donnan) Miss, *Ross.* D Ross *See* Glenurquhart.
LOCHBUIE, MULL (St Kilda), Miss Station, *Argyll.* D The Isles I (Vacant).
LOCHEARNHEAD (St Angus) Miss Station, *Perth.* D St Andrews I C E J FRYER *p-in-c.*
LOCHEE (St Marg), *Angus.* D Brechin *See* Dundee.
LOCHGELLY (St Finnian), *Fife.* R D St Andrews I J H BAKER.
LOCHGILPHEAD (Ch Ch) w Kilmartin (St Columba), *Argyll.* R D Argyll I M S CHERRY.
LOCHLEE (St Drostane), *Angus.* D Brechin I (Vacant).
LOCKERBIE (All SS), *Dumfries.* R D Glasgow I M LINDSAY-PARKINSON.
LONGSIDE (St Jo Evang), *Aberdeen.* D Aberdeen I D P BOVEY.
LONMAY (St Columba), *Aberdeen.* D Aberdeen *See* Fraserburgh.
LOSSIEMOUTH Miss Station, *Moray.* D Moray *See* Elgin.
LUNGA, LOCH SHUNA (St Mary) Priv Chap, *Argyll.* D Argyll *See* Oban.

MACDUFF Mission, *Banff*. D Aberdeen *See* Banff.
MASTERTON (St Marg of Scotld) Miss Station, *Fife*. D St Andrews *See* Dunfermline.
MAXWELLTOWN (St Ninian) Dep Miss, *Dumfries*. D Glasgow *See* Dumfries.
MAYBOLE Dep Miss, *Ayr*. D Glasgow *See* Ayr.
MEIGLE (St Marg), *Perth*. D Dunkeld *See* Alyth.
MELDRUM (St Matt) w All SS Whiterashes Dep Miss, *Aberdeen*. R D Aberdeen I A B MACGILLIVRAY.
MELROSE (H Trin), *Roxburgh*. D Edinburgh I O L S DOVER.
MILLPORT (St Andr), I of Cumbrae, *Bute*. D The Isles *See* Cumbrae.
MILNGAVIE Miss, *Stirling*. D Glasgow *See* Bearsden.
MOFFAT (St Jo Evang), *Dumfries*. D Glasgow I P R PONT.
MONIFIETH (H Trin), *Angus*. D Brechin I R JONES.
MONTROSE (St Mary and St Pet), w Inverbervie, *Angus*. D Brechin I I JONES.
MONYMUSK w Kemnay Miss Aberdeen. D Aberdeen *See* Kemnay.
MOTHERWELL (H Trin), *Lanark*. D Glasgow I K G STEPHEN.
MUCHALLS (St Ternan), *Kincardine*. R D Brechin I S T HUTCHINSON *p-in-c*.
MUSSELBURGH (St Pet), *Midlothian*. D Edinburgh I I A DEIGHTON, P D DIXON *c*, A J BOYD *hon c*.
MUTHILL (St Jas), *Perth*. D St Andrews I G J SIMMONS.

NAIRN (St Columba) w Garrison Chap Fort George, *Nairn*. D Moray I R W FORREST.
NETHER LOCHABER (St Bride), w Kinlochleven (St Paul), *Inverness*. R D Argyll I (Vacant).
NEWBURGH (St Kath) Dep Miss, *Fife*. D St Andrews I (Vacant).
NEW DEER Dep Miss Aberdeen. D Aberdeen *See* Deer.
NEW GALLOWAY (St Marg of Scotld), *Kirkcudbright*. D Galloway I G H YEO *p-in-c*.
NEW PITSLIGO (St Jo Evang), *Aberdeen*. D Aberdeen I R A C GRIEVE.
NEWPORT (St Mary), w Tayport Miss Station, *Fife*. D St Andrews I R M R STONE.
NEWTON (St Columba) Cathl Miss *Lanark*. D Glasgow *See* Cambuslang.
NEWTON-STEWART (St Andr), Dep Miss, *Wigtown*. D Galloway *See* Challoch.
NIDDRIE (St Andr) Dep Miss Charge, *Midlothian*. D Edinburgh *See* Edinburgh.
NORTH BERWICK (St Baldred), *East Lothian*. D Edinburgh I A MACKINTOSH.

OBAN (St Jo Div), (Cathl Ch), w Ardchattan Connel Ferry (Summer Miss), Cullipool Miss and Salen, *Argyll*. D Argyll *See* Cathedral.

PAISLEY (H Trin), and Barrhead (H Spirit), *Renfrew*. D Glasgow I R A HANSON.
(St Barn), R D Glasgow I I E WALTER.
PATHHEAD (St Mich), Dep Miss D St Andrews *See* Kirkcaldy.
PEEBLES (St Pet), *Peebles*. R D Edinburgh I A W M MCCAY *p-in-c*.
PENICUIK (St Jas Less), *Midlothian*. D Edinburgh I A D PALMER, N F SUTTLE *c*.
PERTH CATHL w Thimblebrow Dep Miss, *Perth*. D Dunkeld *See* Cathedral.
(St Jo Bapt), D Dunkeld I T T IRVINE, R H DARROCH *hon c*.
PETERHEAD (St Pet), *Aberdeen*. D Aberdeen I (Vacant).
PILTON (St D of Scotld) Dep Miss, *Midlothian*. D Edinburgh *See* Edinburgh.
PITLOCHRY (H Trin) Kilmaveonaig Miss and Blair Atholl Station, *Perth*. D St Andrews I (Vacant).
PITSLIGO, NEW D Aberdeen *See* New Pitsligo.
PITTENWEEM (St Jo Evang), *Fife*. D St Andrews I R FLATT *c*.
POOLEWE (St Maelrubha) Miss, *Ross*. D Ross I (Vacant).
PORT GLASGOW (St Mary Virg), *Renfrew*. D Glasgow I D G WALLACE.
PORTNACROIS (St Cross), *Argyll*. D Argyll *See* Duror.
PORTOBELLO (St Mark) w St Anne's Miss, *Midlothian*. D Edinburgh I R J DENHOLM, W L F MOUNSEY *c*.
PORTPATRICK Dep Miss, *Wigtown*. D Glasgow *See* Stranraer.
PORTREE, I OF SKYE (St Columba), *Inverness*. R D The Isles I (Vacant).
PORTSOY (St Jo Bapt), *Banff*. D Aberdeen I S J G BENNIE.
PRESTONPANS (St Andr) Dep Miss, *East Lothian*. D Edinburgh I I A DEIGHTON *p-in-c*, P D DIXON *c*.
PRESTWICK (St Ninian), *Ayr*. R D Glasgow I (Vacant).

QUEENSFERRY, SOUTH (St Mary of Mount Carmel, Old Carmelite Priory Ch), Miss, *Linlithgow*. P *Edinburgh* I E W BRADY *p-in-c*.

RENFREW (St Marg), Cathl Miss, *Renfrew*. D Glasgow I S D N BARRETT.
RIDDRIE, *Lanark*. D Glasgow *See* Glasgow.
ROSSLYN (St Matt), formerly a Colleg Ch (15th cent) now a Proprietary Chap, *Midlothian*. D Edinburgh I E N DOWNING *hon c*.
ROSYTH (St Andr and St Geo), *Fife*. D St Andrews I J H BAKER *p-in-c*.
ROTHESAY (St Paul) w Arran Miss, *Bute*. D The Isles I (Vacant).
ROTHIEMURCHUS (St Jo Bapt) Miss Station, *Inverness*. D Moray I W D KORNAHRENS.

ST ANDREWS (St Andr), *Fife*. D St Andrews I F H MAGEE, R FLATT *c*, J S RICHARDSON *c*.
(All SS), Castle Street, *Fife*. D St Andrews I R E INGHAM.
ST FILLAN'S Miss Station, *Perth*. D Dunkeld *See* Comrie.
SALEN, MULL (St Columba), Miss Station, *Argyll*. D Argyll *See* Oban.
SELKIRK (St Jo Evang), *Selkirk*. D Edinburgh I G H GILMOUR.
SHETTLESTON, *Lanark*. D Glasgow *See* Baillieston.
SHOTTS Miss, *Lanark*. D Glasgow *See* Wishaw.
STANLEY (St Columba), *Perth*. D St Andrews I (Vacant).
STIRLING (H Trin), w St Ninian's Miss Station, *Stirling*. D Edinburgh I J W MCINTYRE.
STONEHAVEN (St Jas), *Kincardine*. D Brechin I M C PATERNOSTER.
STORNOWAY (St Pet), w Eorrapaidh Miss Station, *Ross*. R D Argyll I A E NIMMO *p-in-c*.
STRANRAER (St John) w Portpatrick (St Ninian), *Wigtown*. D Galloway I A E KERRIN *p-in-c*.
STRATHMARTINE (St Luke) Ind Miss, *Angus*. D Brechin *See* Dundee.
STRATHNAIRN (St Paul), *Inverness*. D Moray I (Vacant).
STRATHPEFFER (St Anne) Miss Station, *Ross*. D Ross *See* Dingwall.
STRATHTAY (St Andr), *Perth*. D St Andrews I D H WRIGHT.
STRICHEN (All SS), *Aberdeen*. D Aberdeen I D P BOVEY.
STROMNESS (St Mary Virg) Ind Miss, *Orkney*. D Orkney *See* Kirkwall.
STRONTIAN (St Mary) Priv Chap, *Argyll*. D Argyll I (Vacant).

TAIN (St Andr), *Ross*. D Ross I D C SPEEDY.
TAYPORT Miss Station, *Fife*. D St Andrews *See* Newport.
THURSO (St Pet and H Rood) Ind Miss *Caithness*. D Caithness I J C HADFIELD *p-in-c*.
TILLYMORGAN (St Thos), *Aberdeen*. D Aberdeen *See* Folla Rule.
TORRY (St Pet) w Cove (St Mary Virg), *Kincardine*. D Aberdeen I (Vacant).
TROON (St Ninian), *Ayr*. D Glasgow I J MCGILL.
TURIFF (St Congan), *Aberdeen*. D Aberdeen I (Vacant).

UDDINGSTON (St Andr), *Lanark*. D Glasgow I P D NOBLE.
ULLAPOOL Miss, *Ross*. D Ross I (Vacant).

WEST LINTON (St Mungo), *Peebles*. R D Edinburgh I A D PALMER.
WESTER HAILES and Baberton, *Midlothian*. D Edinburgh I W J T BROCKIE *p-in-c*, D YEOMAN *c*.
WHITERASHES (All SS) Dep Miss Station, *Aberdeen*. D Aberdeen *See* Meldrum.
WICK (St Jo Evang), *Caithness*. D Caithness I J C HADFIELD.
WISHAW (St Andr) w Shotts Miss, *Lanark*. D Glasgow I K G STEPHEN.
WOODHEAD, FYVIE (All SS), *Aberdeen*. D Aberdeen I A B MACGILLIVRAY.

INDEX OF PARISHES—IRISH

AASLEAGH (St Jo Bapt), *Mayo.* **D** Tuam
I C G GREGORY *c-in-c.*
ABBEYFEALE, *Kerry.* **D** Ardf *See* Kilnaughtin.
ABBEYLARA, *Longf.* **D** Ard *See* Granard.
ABBEYLEIX w Ballyroan and Dysart Galen (All SS), *Leix.* **D** Leigh 5 **I** H T M HEWITT.
ABBEYMAHON, *Cork.* **D** Ross *See* Timoleague.
ABBEYSTREWRY w Creagh, Tullagh, Clear Island, and Castlehaven, *Cork.* **D** Ross 2 **I** R E B WHITE.
ABINGTON, *Lim.* **D** Killaloe *See* Stradbally.
ACHILL w Dugort, Ballycroy, and Mallaranny, *Mayo.* **D** Tuam 1 *See* Aughaval.
ACHONRY (St Crumnathy) Cathl w Tubbercurry (St Geo) Kilmactigue, *Sligo.* **D** Achon 3 **I** C J ROUNTREE.
ACTON w Drumbanagher (St Mary), *Arm.* **D** Arm 4
I F A NOEL.
ADAMSTOWN (St Mary), *Wexf.* **D** Ferns *See* Killegney.
ADARE w Croom and Kilpeacon, *Lim.* **D** Lim 1
I R WARREN.
AGHABOG w Newbliss, Ematris and Rockcorry, *Monagh.* **D** Clogh 8 **I** (Vacant).
AGHADA, *Cork.* R and V **D** Cloyne *See* Corkberg.
AGHADE (All SS) w Ardoyne (H Trin), *Carlow.* **D** Leigh 1 *See* Fenagh.
AGHADERG (St Mellan) w Donaghmore (St Bart), *Down.* **D** Drom 1 **I** G N LITTLE.
AGHADOWEY (St Tuggens), *Derry.* **D** Derry 3
I J MAYES.
AGHADOWN (St Matt) Cross Church w Kilcoe, *Cork.* **D** Cork **I** J J PERROTT.
AGHADRUMSEE, *Ferman.* **D** Clogh 8 **I** V E KILLE.
AGHALEE, *Arm.* **D** Drom 6 **I** S J BRENNAN.
AGHALURCHER and Tattykeeran, *Ferman.* **D** Clogh 4
I V H FORSTER.
AGHANAGH, *Rosc.* **D** Elph *See* Boyle.
AGHANCON w Kilcolman, *Offaly.* **D** Killaloe 3
I C B CHAMP.
AGHANLOO, *Derry.* **D** Derry *See* Tamlaghtard.
AGHANUNSHIN, *Doneg.* **D** Raph *See* Conwall.
AGHAVEA (St Lasser), *Ferman.* **D** Clogh 4 **I** (Vacant).
AGHAVILLY (St Mary), *Arm.* R **D** Arm 9 **I** (Vacant).
AGHAVOE, *Leix.* **D** Oss *See* Borris-in-Ossory.
AGHER, *Meath.* **D** Meath *See* Rathcore.
AGHERN, *Cork.* **D** Cloyne *See* Rathcormac.
AGHERTON (St John), Portstewart, *Derry.* **D** Connor 8
I T F CALLAN.
AGHNAMEADLE, *Tip.* **D** Killaloe *See* Ballinaclough.
AGHOLD (St Mich) w Mullinacuff, *Carlow.* **D** Leigh *See* Tullow.
AGHOUR w Odagh and Ballinamara, *Kilk.* **D** Oss 7
I (Vacant).
AGLISH, *Kerry.* **D** Ardf *See* Kilcolman.
AGLISHCLOHANE, *Tip.* **D** Killaloe *See* Borrisokane.
AHAMPLISH, *Sligo.* **D** Elph *See* Drumcliffe.
AHASCRAGH (St Cath), *Galw.* **D** Clonf *See* Creagh.
AHOGHILL (St Colmannell) w Portglenone, *Antr.* **D** Connor 2 **I** M E LEEMAN.
ALMORITIA (St Nich), W *Meath.* **D** Meath *See* Ballymore.
ALTAR, *Cork.* **D** Cork *See* Teampol-na-Mbocht.
ALTEDESERT w Pomeroy, *Tyr.* **D** Arm 1 **I** P T REILLY.
ANEY w Galbally (St John), Caherconlish, Ballylanders, and Bruff, *Lim.* **D** Lim *See* Kilmallock.
ANNACLONE (Ch Ch), *Down.* **D** Drom *See* Magherally.
ANNADUFF, EAST, *Leitr.* **D** Ard *See* Mohill.
ANNADUFF, WEST (St Anne), *Leitr.* **D** Ard *See* Kiltoghart.
ANNAGH, *Cav.* **D** Kilm *See* Belturbet.
ANNAGHCLIFFE, *Cav.* **D** Kilm *See* Urney.
ANNAGHMORE (St Francis), *Arm.* **D** Arm 7 **I** R H BOYD.
ANNAHILT, *Down.* **D** Drom 2 **I** E KINGSTON.
ANNALONG or KILHORNE, *Down.* **D** Drom 5
I B T BLACOE.
ANNAMOE, *Wickl.* **D** Glendal *See* Derralossary.
ANTRIM (All SS), *Antr.* **D** Connor 1 **I** J L FORSYTHE, T HASKINS *c.*
ARAN (St Thos), *Galw.* **D** Tuam *See* Galway.
ARBOE, *Tyr* and *Derry.* **D** Arm 8 **I** (Vacant).
ARDAGH (St Pet) w Moydow, Tashinny, Kilcommick and Shrule, *Longf.* **D** Ard 3 **I** J PICKERING.
ARDAGH, *Meath.* **D** Meath *See* Enniskeen.
ARDAMINE (St Jo Evang) w Kiltennel, Killenagh and Glascarrig, *Wexf.* **D** Ferns 6 **I** W A NOBLETT.
ARDARA (St Conall) w Glencolumbkille and Killybegs (St Columb), *Doneg.* **D** Raph 2 **I** M S HARTE.
ARDBRACCAN, *Meath.* **D** Meath *See* Donaghpatrick.
ARDCANNY, *Lim.* **D** Lim *See* Kilcornan.
ARDCARNE, *Rosc.* **D** Elph 2 *See* Boyle.
ARDCLARE, *Rosc.* **D** Elph 1 *See* Elphin.
ARDCLINIS w Tichmacrevan, *Antr.* **D** Connor 7
I R B BANNON.
ARDCOLM w Kilpatrick and Killurin, *Wexf.* **D** Ferns 8
I E F GRANT.
ARDCRONEY, *Tip.* **D** Killaloe *See* Borrisokane.
ARDEE (St Mary), *Louth.* R and V **D** Arm *See* Charlestown.
ARDFERT, *Kerry.* **D** Ardf *See* Tralee.
ARDFIELD, *Cork.* **D** Ross *See* Castleventry.
ARDFINNAN, *Tip.* **D** Lism *See* Cahir.
ARDGLASS (St Nich) w Dunsford (St Mary), *Down.* **D** Down 4 **I** G M DUNN *c.*
ARDKEEN (Ch Ch), *Down.* **D** Down 1 **I** F W A BELL.
ARDMAYLE, *Tip.* **D** Cash *See* Ballintemple.
ARDMORE w Craigavon (St Sav), *Arm.* **D** Drom 6
I M HARVEY.
ARDMORE (St Paul) and Templemichael, *Waterf.* **D** Cloyne 2 **I** MAYES.
ARDNAGEEHY, *Cork.* **D** Cloyne *See* Rathcormac.
ARDNURCHER, *W Meath.* **D** Meath *See* Clara.
ARDOYNE, *Carlow.* **D** Leigh *See* Aghade.
ARDOYNE (Im), *Antr.* **D** Connor 3 **I** (Vacant).
ARDQUIN, *Down.* **D** Down *See* Ballyphilip.
ARDRAGH (St Patr), *Meath.* **D** Clogh *See* Carrickmacross.
ARDRAHAN w Kilcolgan, *Galw.* **D** Kilmac *See* Kilmacduagh.
ARDSTRAW (St Eugenius?) w Baronscourt, *Tyr.* **D** Derry 6 **I** J PIKE.
ARDTREA (St Andr) w Desertcreat, *Tyr.* **D** Arm 8
I R J N PORTEUS.
ARKLOW (St Sav), *Wickl.* **D** Glendal 3 **I** W F H VANSTON.
ARMAGH (St Mark), *Arm.* **D** Arm 9 **I** H S MORTIMER, I M ELLIS *c*, J D G KINGSTON *c.*
ARMAGHBREAGUE, *Arm.* **D** Arm *See* Keady.
ARMOY (St Patr) w Loughguile and Drumtullagh, *Antr.* **D** Connor 6 **I** W E MCCRORY.
ARVAGH w Carrigallen and Gowna, *Cav.* **D** Kilm 3
I (Vacant).
ASHFIELD, *Cav.* **D** Kilm *See* Drumgoon.
ASKEATON w Shanagolden and Loughil, *Lim.* **D** Lim 1
I (Vacant).
ATHASSEL (St Mary), *Tip.* **D** Cash *See* Cashel.
ATHBOY (St Jas) w Kildalkey (St Mary), Girley (St Marg) Ballivor, Killallon and Clonmellon, *Meath.* **D** Meath 13
I (Vacant).
ATHEA, *Kerry.* **D** Ardf *See* Listowel.
ATHENRY w Monivea, *Galw.* **D** Tuam 2 **I** L D A FORREST.
ATHACCA, *Lim.* **D** Lim *See* Kilmallock.
ATHLEAGUE, *Galw.* **D** Elph *See* Roscommon.
ATHLONE (St Mary w St Pet), Kilkenny West (Benowen), Kiltoom, Moydrum and Ballymore w Forgney, *Rosc.* and *Meath.* **D** Meath 3 **I** I J POWER.
ATHNOWEN (St Mary), *Cork.* **D** Cork 7 *See* Carrigrohane.
ATHY (St Mich) w Kilberry, *Kild.* **D** Glendal 5 **I** J PASLEY.
ATTANAGH, *Leix.* **D** Oss *See* Killermogh.
AUGHAVAL or Westport (H Trin) w Ayle (St Patr), Slingan, Kilmina, Burrishoole (St Cath), Achill, Dugort, Ballycray and Mallaranny, *Mayo.* **D** Tuam 1
I M W SEARIGHT.
AUGHER (St Mark) w Newtownsaville, *Tyr.* R **D** Clogh 1
I I R BETTS.
AUGHMACART, *Leix.* **D** Oss *See* Killermogh.
AUGHNAMULLEN (St Patr or Ch Ch), *Monagh.* **D** Clogh *See* Ballybay.
AUGHRIM (H Trin) w Clontuskert, Woodlawn, Loughrea and Kiltormer, *Galw.* **D** Clonf 1 **I** E W TALBOT.
AYLE (St Patr), *Mayo.* **D** Tuam *See* Aughaval.

BADONEY, LOWER (St Patr) w Greenane and Upper Badoney, *Tyr.* **D** Derry 6 **I** K R KINGSTON.
BADONEY, UPPER (St Patr), *Tyr.* **D** Derry *See* Badoney, Lower.
BAGENALSTOWN, *Carlow.* **D** Leigh *See* Dunleckney.

BAILIEBOROUGH w Mullagh, *Cav.* **D** Kilm 1 **I** W E R GARRETT.
BALBRIGGAN (St Geo) w Balrothery (St Pet), *Dub.* **D** Dub *See* Holmpatrick.
BALLA (H Trin), *Mayo.* **D** Tuam *See* Castlebar.
BALLAGHAMEEHAN, *Ferman.* **D** Kilm *See* Manorhamilton.
BALLAGHTOBIN, *Kilk.* **D** Oss *See* Kells.
BALLEE w Bright and Killough, *Down.* **D** Down 5 **I** J I H STAFFORD.
BALLEEK, *Arm.* **D** Arm *See* Ballymoyer.
BALLINA, *Mayo.* **D** Killala *See* Kilmoremoy.
BALLINABOY, *Cork.* **D** Cork *See* Carrigaline.
BALLINACLASH w Macreddin, *Wickl.* **D** Glendal 3 **I** G T BAYNHAM.
BALLINACLOUGH w Templederry and Agnameadle, *Tip.* **D** Killaloe 7 **I** E W STANLEY.
BALLINACOURTY, *Galw.* **D** Tuam *See* Galway.
BALLINADEE, *Cork.* **D** Cork *See* Innishannon.
BALLINAFAGH, *Kild.* **D** Kild 2 **I** (Vacant).
BALLINAHINCH, *Galw.* **D** Tuam *See* Moyrus.
BALLINAKILL (St Thos), *Galw.* **D** Tuam 4 *See* Omey.
BALLINAKILL, *Waterf.* **D** Waterf *See* Waterford.
BALLINALEE, *Longf.* **D** Ard *See* Clonbroney.
BALLINAMARA, *Kilk.* **D** Oss *See* Aghour.
BALLINLASOE, *Galw.* **D** Clonf *See* Creagh.
BALLINDERRY (St Jo Bapt) w Tamlaght, *Derry.* **D** Arm 8 **I** H J W MOORE.
BALLINDERRY (no Dedic), *Antr.* **D** Connor 9 **I** S MCCOMB.
BALLINGARRY, *Lim.* **D** Lim *See* Rathkeale.
BALLINGARRY, *Tip.* **D** Killaloe *See* Cloughjordan.
BALLINROBE (St Mary) w Ballyovie (Ch Ch), Kilcommon U (Kilcolman, Crossboyne and Kilmaine), and Hollymount, *Mayo.* **D** Tuam 5 *See* Cong.
BALLINTEMPLE (St Mary) w Clonoulty, Donohill, Holycross, Ardmayle, and Mealiffe, *Tip.* **D** Cash 1 **I** (Vacant).
BALLINTEMPLE, *Cav.* **D** Kilm *See* Kilmore.
BALLINTEMPLE, *Wickl.* **D** Glendal *See* Castlemacadam.
BALLINTOY, *Antr.* **D** Connor 6 *See* Dunsverick.
BALLINTUBBERT, *Leix.* **D** Leigh *See* Stradbally.
BALLIVOR, *Meath.* **D** Meath *See* Athboy.
BALLYBAY (Ch Ch) w Aughnamullen, Crossduff and Tullycorbet, *Monagh.* **D** Clogh 1 **I** V MCMULLAN.
BALLYBEEN, *Down* **D** Down **I** N JARDINE *c.*
BALLYBOY w Killoughley, *Offaly.* **D** Meath 1 **I** R H BOYLE.
BALLYBUNION, *Kerry.* **D** Ardf *See* Listowel.
BALLYBURLEY, *Offaly.* **D** Kild *See* Monasteroris.
BALLYCANEW (St Edan or St Mogue), *Wexf.* **D** Ferns 2 *See* Leskinfere.
BALLYCARNEY, *Wexf.* **D** Ferns *See* Monart.
BALLYCASTLE (in par of Ramoan), Antr **D** Connor *See* Ramoan.
BALLYCLOG, *Tyr.* **D** Arm *See* Donaghendry.
BALLYCLOUGH, *Cork.* **D** Cloyne *See* Castlemagner.
BALLYCLUG, *Antr.* **D** Connor *See* Ballymena.
BALLYCOMMON, *Offaly.* **D** Kild 3 *See* Geashill.
BALLYCONREE, *Galw.* **D** Tuam *See* Omey.
BALLYCOTTON (St Colman), *Cork.* **D** Cloyne 2 *See* Youghal.
BALLYCROY, *Mayo.* **D** Tuam *See* Achill.
BALLYCULTER (Ch Ch), w Kilclief, *Down.* **D** Down 5 **I** W E KENNEDY.
BALLYCUSHLANE, *Kerry.* **D** Ardf *See* Castleisland.
BALLYDEHOB, *Cork.* **D** Cork 4 **I** J J PERROTT.
BALLYEASTON, *Antr.* **D** Connor *See* Ballynure.
BALLYEGLISH (St Matthias), *Derry.* **D** Arm *See* Desertlyn.
BALLYFIN (extra-par chap St John), *Leix.* **D** Leigh *See* Clonenagh.
BALLYGAWLEY, *Tyr.* **D** Arm *See* Errigal Kerrogue.
BALLYHALBERT (St Andr), *Down.* **D** Down **I** F W A BELL.
BALLYHEA, *Cork.* **D** Cloyne *See* Buttevant.
BALLYHEIGUE, *Kerry.* **D** Ardf *See* Tralee.
BALLYHOLME (St Columbanus), *Down.* **D** Down 2 **I** J J G MERCER, N J W WAUGH *c.*
BALLYHOOLEY (Ch Ch), *Cork.* **D** Cloyne *See* Fermoy.
BALLYHUSKARD, *Wexf.* **D** Ferns *See* Kilnamanagh.
BALLYJAMESDUFF w Castlerahan, *Cav.* **D** Kilm *See* Kildrumferton.
BALLYKEAN, *Offaly.* **D** Kild *See* Portarlington.
BALLYLANDERS, *Lim.* **D** Emly *See* Aney.
BALLYLONGFORD, *Kerry.* **D** Ardf *See* Kilnaughtin.
BALLYLOUGHLOE w Mount Temple, *W Meath.* **D** Meath *See* Kilcleagh.
BALLYMACARRETT (St Patr), *Down.* **D** Down 4 **I** W A MACOURT, W J R LAVERTY *c.*
(St Chris) **D** Down 4 *See* Belfast.
(St Martin Miss Distr) **D** Down 4 *See* Belfast.
BALLYMACASH (St Mark) w Stoneyford, *Antrim.* **D** Connor **I** T W W JONES, F L GRAHAM *c.*
BALLYMACELLIGOTT w Ballyseedy, *Kerry.* **D** Ardf 1 **I** R W P DOHERTY.
BALLYMACHUGH (St Paul), *Cav.* **D** Kilm *See* Kildrumferton.
BALLYMACKEY, *Tip.* **D** Killaloe *See* Nenagh.
BALLYMACORMAC, *Longf.* **D** Ard *See* Killashee.
BALLYMAGLASSON, *Meath.* **D** Meath *See* Dunshaughlin.
BALLYMARTLE w Cullen and Ballinaboy, *Cork.* **D** Cork *See* Kinsale.
BALLYMASCANLAN w Carlingford (Trin) and Omeath (St Andr), *Louth.* **D** Arm 5 **I** S M NOEL.
BALLYMENA (St Patr Kirconriola) w Ballyclug (no Dedic), *Antr.* **D** Connor 2 **I** F J RUSK, C W BELL *c,* F J REILLY *c,* T SCOTT *c.*
BALLYMODAN w Bandon (St Pet), Kilbrogan (Ch Ch) and Rathclaren, *Cork.* **D** Cork 3 **I** G M D WOODWORTH, F C CALLENDER *c.*
BALLYMONEY (Dedic unknown), *Antr.* **D** Connor 8 **I** R S STEWART.
BALLYMONEY (St Paul), *Cork.* **D** Cork *See* Kinneigh.
BALLYMORE w Forgney, *W Meath.* **D** Meath 8 *See* Athlone.
BALLYMORE or TANDRAGEE (St Mark), *Arm.* **D** Arm 7 **I** R M WILKINSON.
BALLYMORE EUSTACE, *Wickl.* **D** Glendal *See* Hollywood.
BALLYMOYER (St Luke) w Balleek, *Arm.* **D** Arm *See* Newtownhamilton.
BALLYNAFEIGH (St Jude), *Down.* R **D** Down 3 **I** W M MOORE.
BALLYNAHINCH, *Down.* **D** Drom *See* Magheradroll.
BALLYNAHINCH, *Galw.* **D** Tuam *See* Moyrus.
BALLYNAKILL (St Thos), *Galw.* **D** Tuam *See* Ballinakill.
BALLYNAKILL (St Mary), *Galw.* **D** Clonf *See* Lickmolassy.
BALLYNASCREEN (St Columba), *Derry.* **D** Derry 4 *See* Kilcronaghan.
BALLYNURE (Dedic unknown), *Wick.* **D** Leigh *See* Baltinglass.
BALLYNURE (Ch Ch) w Ballyeaston (St Jo Evang), *Antr.* **D** Connor 7 **I** J F A BOND.
BALLYOVIE (Ch Ch), *Mayo.* **D** Tuam *See* Ballinrobe.
BALLYPHILIP w Ardquin, *Down.* **D** Down 1 **I** J P O BARRY.
BALLYRASHANE (St Jo Bapt) w Kildollagh, *Antr* and *Derry.* **D** Connor 8 **I** W MCKINNEY.
BALLYROAN, *Leix.* **D** Leigh *See* Abbeyleix.
BALLYSAKEERY, *Mayo.* **D** Killala *See* Killala.
BALLYSAX, *Kild.* **D** Kild *See* Ballysonnon.
BALLYSCULLION, *Antr.* **D** Connor *See* Duneane.
BALLYSCULLION (St Tida), *Derry.* **D** Derry 3 **I** (Vacant).
BALLYSEEDY, *Kerry.* **D** Ardf *See* Ballymacelligott.
BALLYSHEEHAN, *Tip.* **D** Cash *See* Cashel.
BALLYSILLAN, *Antr.* **D** Connor *See* Belfast.
BALLYSODARE w Collooney, *Sligo.* **D** Achon 1 **I** R M STRATFORD.
BALLYSONNON w Balysax, *Kild.* **D** Kild 4 **I** W B HENEY.
BALLYSUMAGHAN w Killery, *Sligo.* **D** Elph 2 *See* Taunagh.
BALLYVOURNEY, *Cork.* **D** Cloyne *See* Macroom.
BALLYWALTER (H Trin), *Down.* **D** Down 1 **I** C R MITCHELL.
BALLYWILLAN w Portrush (H Trin), *Antr.* **D** Connor 8 **I** M ROYCROFT, P W ROOKE *c.*
BALRATHBOYNE (St Baithen), *Meath.* **D** Meath *See* Kells.
BALROTHERY (St Pet) w Balscaddan, *Dub.* **D** Dub *See* Balbriggan.
BALTEAGH (St Canice) w Carrick (Ch Ch), *Derry.* **D** Derry 9 **I** J J HEMPHILL.
BALTINGLASS (St Mary) w Ballynure w Stratford-on-Slaney (St John) and Rathvilly, *Wickl.* **D** Leigh 2 **I** R R WILSON.
BANAGHER, *Derry.* **D** Derry 2 **I** G F ANDERSON.
BANAGHER, *Offaly.* **D** Meath *See* Rynagh.
BANDON, *Cork.* **D** Cork *See* Ballymodan.
BANGOR (St Comgall), *Down.* **D** Down 2 **I** G A MITCHELL.
ABBEY CH **D** Down 2 **I** H LECKEY, W A MCMONAGLE *c.*
BANNOW w Duncormick, *Wexf.* **D** Ferns 1 *See* Horetown.

BAR, *Tyr.* D Clogh *See* Donacavey.
BARNA, *Galw.* D Tuam *See* Galway.
BARNAHASK, *Wexf.* D Ferns *See* Newton Barry.
BARONSCOURT, *Tyr.* D Derry 6 *See* Ardstraw.
BARONSTOWN, *Louth.* D Arm *See* Dundalk.
BEAULIEU (St Brigid), *Louth.* D Arm *See* Termonfeckin.
BECTIVE (St Mary), *Meath.* D Meath *See* Trim.
BELCARRA, *Mayo.* D Tuam *See* Castlevar.
BELFAST (St Anne) Cathl and Old Par Ch of Shankill (St Pet), *Antr.* D Connor 4 I S B CROOKS, G F CRAIG *c.*
(All SS) D Connor 4 I S SMART, P J A COOK *hon c.*
(Ch Ch) D Connor 4 I S N M BAYLY.
(Ch of Epiph U Malone) D Connor 4 I N B JACKSON.
(H Redeemer) D Connor 4 I T P G LEPINE *p-in-c.*
(H Trin) D Connor 3 I J CLYDE, A J GRIMASON *c.*
(St Aid) D Connor 5 I G N SPROULE.
(St Bart Stranmillis) D Connor 5 I E H GOUGH, R E RAYNOR *c.*
(St Barn) D Connor 3 I H D HEATLEY.
(St Brendan) D Down 3 I J R P FERGUSON.
(St Chris Ballymacarrett) D Down 4 I M WITHERS.
(St Clem) D Down 4 I J STEWART, H R GIVEN *c.*
(St Columba, Knock), R D Down 4 I G A MCCAMLEY.
(St Donard) D Down 4 I P J SYNNOTT, G M KINGSTON *c.*
(St Geo) D Connor 4 I R E TURNER.
(St Jas) D Connor 3 I J O ROLSTON.
(St John, Laganbank w Orangefield) D Down 3 I A J DOUGLAS, W T LONG *c*, R B ROUNTREE *c.*
(St John, Malone) D Connor 5 I E F DARLING, R B HAYTHORNTHWAITE *c.*
(St John, Whitehouse) D Connor *See* Whitehouse.
(St Jo Bapt Upper Falls) D Connor 5 I J NOLAN *c.*
(St Kath) D Connor 3 I T E BEACOM.
(St Luke w St Sav Lower Falls) D Connor 4 I N C SHORTT.
(St Mark, Ballysillan), *Antr.* D Connor 3 I R W WILLIAMS, W A LEWIS *c.*
(St Martin Miss Distr Ch of Ireland S Miss) D Down 4 I (Vacant).
(St Mary) D Connor 4 I R FOX, N R CUTLIFFE *c*, G PITT *c.*
(St Mary Magd) D Connor 5 I W H LENDRUM.
(St Matt Shankill) D Connor 4 I J ROONEY.
(St Mich) D Connor 4 I N B DODDS.
(St Molua, Stormont) D Down 4 I E R HAMILTON.
(St Nich), V D Connor 5 I R C STEVENSON.
(St Ninian) D Connor 3 I J P WALKER.
(St Paul) D Connor 3 I J ARBUTHNOT.
(St Pet) D Connor 3 I W E HARRIS.
(St Silas) D Connor 3 I J O ROLSTON.
(St Simon w St Phil Drew Memorial) D Connor 5 I W T HOEY.
(St Steph) D Connor 4 I N C SHORTT.
(St Thos) D Connor 5 I E P M ELLIOTT, G W ODLING-SMEE *hon c.*
See also DUNDELA AND FINAGHY.
BELLEEK, *Ferman.* D Clogh *See* Garrison.
BELTURBET or ANNAGH w Quivvy and St Andrews, *Cav.* D Kilm 3 I CANON J R WHEELOCK IN C OF CLOVERHILL.
BELVOIR (Ch of Transfig), *Down.* D Down 4 I D H HANNA, S D LOGAN *c.*
BEREHAVEN or CASTLETOWN BEREHAVEN w Glengarriff (H Trin), R *Cork.* D Ross 3 I F H GARRETT.
BESSBROOK, *Arm.* D Arm *See* Camlough.
BILBO, *Carlow.* D Leigh *See* Mothel.
BILLIS, *Cavan.* D Kilm 1 I W D JOHNSTON.
BILLY (no Dedic) and Derrykeighan, *Antr.* R D Connor 8 I A A JOHNS.
BIRR or PARSONSTOWN (St Brendan) w Eglish and Dorrha, *Offaly.* D Killaloe 3 I D L KEEGAN.
BLACKROCK (St Mich), *Cork.* D Cork *See* St Michael, Blackrock.
BLACKROCK (All SS), *Dub.* D Dub 3 I M B TAYLOR.
BLESSINGTON (St Mary) w Kilbride, *Wickl.* D Glendal 6 I R S STOKES.
BOHOE, *Ferman.* R D Clogh *See* Devenish.
BOOTERSTOWN (St Phil and St Jas) w Carysfort (Ch Ch), *Dub.* D Dub 3 I D J O BARR.
BORRIS, *Carlow.* D Leigh *See* Clonagoose.
BORRIS-IN-OSSORY w Aghavoe, *Leix.* D Oss 5 *See* Offerlane.
BORRISNAFARNEY, *Offaly.* D Killaloe *See* Templeharry.
BORRISOKANE w Ardcroney and Aglishclohane, *Tip.* R D Killaloe 8 I J CAMIER.
BOURNEY (St Burchin) w Dunkerrin, and Corbally, *Tip.* D Killaloe 4 I J A A CONDELL.
BOVEVAGH (St Eugenius), *Derry.* D Derry *See* Dungiven.
BOYLE w Aghanagh, Kilbryan and Ardcarne, *Rosc.* D Elph 2 I (Vacant).
BRACKAVILLE, *Tyr.* D Arm 6 I J W BEAMISH.
BRANTRY, *Tyr.* D Arm *See* Caledon.
BRAY (Ch Ch w St Paul), *Wickl* and *Dub.* R D Dub 7 I R G LARGE.
BRIGHT, *Down.* D Down *See* Ballee.
BRIGOWN (St Geo) or Mitchelstown, *Cork.* D Cloyne 4 I B R JOHNSON.
BRINNY, *Cork.* D Cork 3 *See* Innishannon.
BROOMFIELD (H Trin), *Monagh.* D Clogh *See* Mucknoe.
BROSNA, *Lim.* D Ardf *See* Kilnaughtin.
BRUFF, *Lim.* D Cash *See* Aney.
BRYANSFORD (Kilcoo), *Down.* D Drom *See* Drumgooland.
BUMLIN (St Jo Bapt), *Rosc.* D Elph *See* Elphin.
BUNCLODY (St Mary) w Kildavin and Barnahask, *Wexf* and *Carlow.* D Ferns 3 I W A M COX.
BUNDORAN, *Doneg.* D Clogh *See* Finner.
BURNCHURCH (St Mary Virg), *Kilk.* D Oss *See* Kells.
BURRISHOOLE (St Cath), *Mayo.* D Tuam *See* Aughavale.
BUTTEVANT (St John) w Ballyhea (Charlville) and Castletownroche, *Cork.* D Cloyne 5 I N M CUMMINS.

CAHERAGH (St Mary), *Cork.* D Cork *See* Drimoleague.
CAHIR, *Kerry.* D Ardf *See* Valentia.
CAHIR (St Paul) w Ardfinnan and Tubrid, Derrygarth and Clogheen, *Tip.* D Lism 1 I I J E KNOX.
CAHIRCONLISH, *Lim.* D Aney *See* Cash.
CAIRNCASTLE, *Antr.* D Connor *See* Kilwaughter.
CALARY, *Wickl.* R D Glendal *See* Derralossary.
CALEDON (St John) w Brantry (H Trin), *Tyr.* R D Arm 1 I F E BEAMISH.
CALLAN (St Mary), *Kilk.* D Oss *See* Kells.
CALRY, *Sligo.* D Elph 2 I T P S WOOD.
CAMLOUGH (Bessbrook) (Ch Ch) w Mullaglass (St Luke), *Arm.* D Arm 4 I R G HOEY, A E CRAWFORD *c.*
CAMUS-JUXTA-BANN (St Mary), *Derry.* D Derry 9 I J I ARMSTRONG.
CAMUS-JUXTA-MOURNE (Ch Ch) w Strabane, *Derry.* D Derry 7 I E W O M LOVELL.
CAPPAGH (St Eugenius), *Tyr.* D Derry 5 I J M C LINNEGAN.
CAPPAMORE or TOUGH (St Jo Evang), *Lim.* D Cash *See* Newport.
CAPPOQUIN (St Ann) w Villierstown and Whitechurch, *Waterf.* D Lism *See* Lismore.
CARBURY, *Kild.* D Kild 1 I S J ALLEN *c-in-c.*
CARLINGFORD (Trin) w Omeath (St Andr), *Louth.* D Arm 5 *See* Ballymascanlan.
CARLOW (St Mary) w Urglin and Staplestown, *Carlow.* D Leigh 3 I F A G WILLIS.
CARNALEA (St Gall), *Down.* D Down 2 I W J SCOTT.
CARNALWAY, *Kild.* D Kild *See* Kilcullen.
CARNDONAGH, *Doneg.* D Derry *See* Donagh.
CARNE (H Trin), *Wexf.* D Ferns *See* Kilscoran.
CARNEW w Kibrush, *Wickl.* D Ferns 2 I F T SHANNON.
CARNMONEY (H Evangelists), *Antr.* D Connor 3 I (Vacant).
CARNTEEL (St Jas) w Crilly, *Tyr.* D Arm 1 I J M BARTON.
CAROGH w Timahoe, *Kild.* D Kild 2 I (Vacant).
CARRAWALLEN, *Leitr.* D Kilm *See* Killdallon.
CARRICK, *Derry.* D Derry *See* Balteach.
CARRICK-ON-SUIR (St Nich), *Tip.* D Lism *See* Killaloan.
CARRICKFERGUS (St Nich), *Antr.* D Connor 7 I D WRIGHT, W P HOUSTON *c*, T R MCKNIGHT *c.*
CARRICKMACROSS (St Finbar) w Killany, Donaghmoine, Inniskeen, Magheracloone, Maghcross, and Ardagh, *Monagh Louth* and *Meath.* D Clogh 2 I (Vacant).
CARRICKMINES, *Dub.* D Dub *See* Tullow, Co Dublin.
CARRIGALINE (St Mary) w Killanully, Ballinaboy and Marmullane, *Cork.* D Cork 2 I B W MCCREA.
CARRIGALLEN, *Leitr.* D Kilm *See* Arvagh.
CARRIGROHANE w Inishkenny and Athnowen, *Cork.* D Cork 2 I (Vacant).
CARRIGTWOHILL (St D), *Cork.* D Cork *See* Rathcooney.
CARROWDORE (Ch Ch) w Millisle, *Down.* D Down 2 I T A MCAULEY.
CARRYDUFF, *Down.* D Down *See* Killaney.
CARYSFORT (Ch Ch) Blackrock, *Dub.* D Dub *See* Booterstown.

CASHEL (St Patr-on-the-Rock, Cathl and Par Ch w St Jo Bapt) w Knockgriffan, Athassel, Mogorban and Ballysheehan, *Tip.* **D** Cash 1 **I** D G A CLARKE.
CASHEL, *Longf.* **D** Ard *See* Kilcommick.
CASTLANE, *Kilk.* **D** Oss *See* Fiddown.
CASTLE ARCHDALE ('The Blindbridge Ch'), *Ferman.* **D** Clogh 7 **I** (Vacant).
CASTLEBAR (Ch Ch) w Belcarra, Turlough, and Balla, *Mayo.* **D** Tuam 5 **I** G R VAUGHAN.
CASTLEBLAKENEY, *Galw.* **D** Elph *See* Roscommon.
CASTLECOMER (St Mary) w Colliery, *Kilk.* **D** Oss 6 **I** H J KEOGH.
CASTLECONNOR, *Sligo.* **D** Killala *See* Kilmoremoy.
CASTLEDAWSON, *Derry.* **D** Derry 4 **I** D S MCLEAN.
CASTLEDERG, *Derry.* **D** Derry *See* Derg.
CASTLEDERMOT (St Jas) w Kinneagh and Kilkea, *Kild.* **D** Glendal 5 **I** H J V PACKHAM *c-in-c.*
CASTLEFLEMING, *Leix.* **D** Oss *See* Rathdowney.
CASTLEHAVEN (St Barrahane), *Cork.* **D** Ross *See* Abbeystrewry.
CASTLEISLAND w Ballycushlane, *Kerry.* **D** Ardf 2 **I** (Vacant).
CASTLEJORDAN, *Offaly* and *Meath.* **D** Meath *See* Killucan.
CASTLEKIRKE, *Galw.* **D** Tuam *See* Cong.
CASTLEKNOCK (St Brigid) w Mulhuddart (St Thos) w Clonsilla, *Dub.* **D** Dub 10 **I** C W BRYAN.
CASTLELOST, *W Meath.* **D** Meath *See* Mullingar.
CASTLELYONS (Aghern), *Cork.* **D** Cloyne 3 **I** G C PAMMENT.
CASTLEMACADAM (H Trin) w Kilmacow or Connonee (St Bart) and Ballintemple, *Wickl.* **D** Glendal 3 **I** G T BAYNHAM.
CASTLEMAGNER w Kilbrin, Ballyclough and Clonmeen w Kanturk and Dromtariffe, *Cork.* **D** Cloyne 5 *See* Mallow.
CASTLEMARTYR w Kilcredan and Dungourney, *Cork.* **D** Cloyne 2 *See* Youghal.
CASTLEPOLLARD w Oldcastle, Mount Nugent, Killeagh, Loughcrew and Drumcree, *W Meath.* **D** Meath 5 **I** J R P FLINN.
CASTLERAHAN, *Cav.* **D** Kilm *See* Billis.
CASTLEREA, *Rosc.* **D** Elph *See* Kilkeevin.
CASTLERICKARD, *Meath.* **D** Meath *See* Rathmolyon.
CASTLEROCK (Ch Ch) w Dunboe (St Paul) and Fermoyle, *Derry.* **D** Derry 9 **I** W B EVANS.
CASTLETERRA, *Cav.* **D** Kilm 1 *See* Drung.
CASTLETOWN (Vastina), *Meath.* **D** Meath *See* Newtown Fertullagh.
CASTLETOWN BEREHAVEN, *Cork.* **D** Ross *See* Berehaven.
CASTLETOWNARRA, *Tip.* **D** Killaloe *See* Killaloe.
CASTLETOWNROCHE, *Cork.* **D** Cloyne 4 *See* Buttevant.
CASTLEVENTRY, *Cork.* **D** Ross 1 *See* Ross.
CASTLEWELLAN (St Paul) w Kilcoo (Bryansford), *Down.* **D** Drom 4 **I** R F GREER.
CELBRIDGE or KILDROUGHT (Ch Ch) w Straffan, *Kild.* **D** Glendal 4 **I** J S C STRONGE.
CHAPELIZOD (St Jude), *Dub.* **D** Dub *See* Dublin.
CHARLEMONT, *Tyr.* **D** Arm *See* Moy.
CHARLESTOWN w Stabannon, Clonkeen, and Ardee, *Louth.* **D** Arm 2 **I** F K JENNINGS.
CHARLEVILLE, *Cork.* **D** Cloyne *See* Ballyhea.
CHRIST CHURCH, Rushbrooke, *Cork.* **D** Cloyne *See* Clonmel w Rushbrooke.
CLABBY (St Marg), *Tyr.* **D** Clogh 4 **I** J A MCMASTER.
CLANABOGAN, *Tyr.* **D** Derry 5 **I** G C CURRY.
CLANE (ST Mich AA) w Donadea, *Kild.* **D** Kild 6 **I** S F GILLMOR.
CLARA or VASTINA (St Brigid) w Ardnurcher, Kilnagarenagh, Kilcleagh (or Moate) and Ballyloughloe, *Offaly.* **D** Meath 1 **I** A E CRAWFORD *c.*
CLARE, *Arm.* **D** Arm *See* Loughgilly.
CLARE ABBEY, *Clare.* **D** Killaloe *See* Drumcliff.
CLASHMORE (St Patr), *Waterf.* **D** Lism *See* Ardmore.
CLAUDY, *Derry.* **D** Derry *See* Cumber, Upper.
CLEAR ISLAND, *Cork.* **D** Ross *See* Abbeystrewry.
CLEENISH, *Ferman.* **D** Clogh 5 **I** R J RIDDEL.
CLIFDEN, *Galw.* **D** Tuam *See* Omey.
CLOGH or CLOUGH (H Trin) w Drumsnatt (St Mollua), *Monagh.* **D** Clogh 8 **I** (Vacant).
CLOGHEEN, *Tip.* **D** Lism *See* Cahir.
CLOGHER (Cathl and Par Ch) w Errigal-Porthclare, *Tyr.* **D** Clogh 4 **I** N O'NEILL.
CLOGHERNY (St Patr), *Tyr.* **D** Arm 1 **I** D B WILSON.
CLOGHRAN, *Dub.* **D** Dub *See* Santry.
CLOMANTAGH, *Kilk.* **D** Oss *See* Fertagh.
CLONAGOOSE, or BORRIS, *Carlow.* **D** Leigh *See* Leighlin.
CLONALLON w Warrenpoint, *Down.* **D** Drom 3 **I** S M J DICKSON.
CLONARD, *Meath.* **D** Meath *See* Killucan.
CLONASLEE w Rosenallis, *Leix.* **D** Kild 5 *See* Mountmellick.
CLONBEG, *Tip.* **D** Cash *See* Tipperary.
CLONBRONEY (St John) w Killoe, *Longf.* **D** Ard 3 **I** R HENDERSON.
CLONBULLOGE (St Kevin), *Offaly.* **D** Kild *See* Clonsast.
CLONCHA (Septem Sancti Episcopi), *Doneg.* **D** Derry *See* Donagh.
CLONDALKIN w Rathcoole, *Dub.* **D** Dub 10 **I** C A FAULL.
CLONDEHORKY, *Doneg.* **D** Raph 3 **I** D STEWART-MAUNDER.
CLONDEVADDOCK (Christ the Redeemer) w Portsalon (All SS), *Doneg.* **D** Raph 4 **I** R MCKEMEY *c-in-c.*
CLONDUFF (St John), *Down.* **D** Drom *See* Drumgath.
CLONE, *Wexf.* **D** Ferns *See* Enniscorthy.
CLONEGAL, *Carl Wickl* and *Wexf.* **D** Ferns 4 **I** W F BENSON.
CLONEGAM (H Trin) w Guilcagh (St Jo Evang), Kilmeaden (St Mary), Killotheran (St Pet) and Mothel, *Waterf.* **D** Lism 2 **I** R J HAZELTON.
CLONENAGH or MOUNTRATH (St Pet) w Roskelton and Ballyfin, *Leix.* **D** Leigh 6 **I** H H J GRAY.
CLONES (St Tighernach), *Ferman.* and *Monagh.* **D** Clogh 8 **I** R W MARSDEN.
CLONEYHURKE, *Offaly.* **D** Kild *See* Portarlington.
CLONFADFORAN, *W Meath.* **D** Meath *See* Newtown Fertullagh.
CLONFEACLE w Derrygortreavy, *Tyr* and *Armagh.* **D** Arm 6 **I** G V HINCHLIFF.
CLONFERT (St Brendan, Cathl and Par Ch) w Donanaughta (St Jo Bapt), Lickmolassy (Ch Ch) and Lawrencetown, *Galw.* **D** Clonf 2 **I** (Vacant).
CLONGISH, *Longf.* **D** Ard *See* Templemichael.
CLONKEEN, *Louth.* **D** Arm *See* Charlestown.
CLONLEA, *Clare.* **D** Killaloe *See* Kilseily.
CLONLEIGH (St Lugadius), *Doneg.* **D** Raph **I** S W REEDE.
CLONMACNOIS (St Kieran and Templeconor), *Offaly.* **D** Meath *See* Rynagh.
CLONMEEN, *Cork.* **D** Cloyne *See* Castle Magner.
CLONMEL w Rushbrooke (Ch Ch), *Cork.* **D** Cloyne 2 **I** B M M KENNEDY.
CLONMEL (St Mary) w Innislonagh, Tullameelan, and Kilronan, *Tip.* **D** Lism 2 **I** I J E KNOX.
CLONMETHAN (St Mary) w Naul, *Dub.* **D** Dub *See* Swords.
CLONMORE (St John), *Carlow.* **D** Leigh *See* Hacketstown.
CLONMORE (St John) w Edermine, *Wexf.* **D** Ferns *See* Enniscorthy.
CLONMULSH, *Carlow.* **D** Leigh *See* Dunleckny.
CLONOE (St Mich), *Tyr.* **D** Arm *See* Tullaniskin.
CLONOULTY w Ardmayle, *Tip.* **D** Cash *See* Ballintemple.
CLONSAST (St Kevin), w Clonbulloge, Rathangan, and Thomastown, *Offaly.* **D** Kild 2 **I** C W FINNEY.
CLONSILLA, *Dub.* **D** Dub *See* Castleknock.
CLONTARF (St Jo Bapt), *Dub.* **D** Dub 9 **I** R G MCCOLLUM.
CLONTIBRET (St Colman), *Monagh.* **D** Clogh 8 *See* Mucknoe.
CLONTUSKERT (St Matt), *Galw.* **D** Clonf *See* Aughrim.
CLONYHURK, *Offaly.* **D** Kild *See* Portarlington.
CLOONCUMBER, *Longf.* **D** Ard *See* Templemichael.
CLOONE (St Jas) w Lough Rynn (Chap), *Leitr.* **D** Ard *See* Mohill.
CLOONEY (All SS), *Derry.* **D** Derry 8 **I** G C WILLOUGHBY, R J STEWART *c.*
CLOUGH, *Monagh.* **D** Clogh *See* Clogh.
CLOUGHFERN (Ch of Ascen), *Down.* **D** Connor 3 **I** J E C PARR, J O MANN *c.*
CLOUGHJORDAN w Modreeny and Ballinbarry, *Tip.* **D** Killaloe 7 **I** S C D ATKINSON.
CLOVERHILL (St Jo Div), *Cav.* **D** Kilm *See* Killoughter.
CLOYDAGH Carlow. **D** Leigh *See* Killeshin.
CLOYNE (St Coleman, Cathl and Par Ch) w Kilmahon, *Cork.* **D** Cloyne 1 **I** J K S R BARKER.
COLAGHTY, *Ferman.* **D** Clough *See* Lack.
COLERAINE (St Patr), *Derry.* **D** Connor 8 **I** J A MONROE, E J HARRIS *c.*
COLLIERY, *Kild.* **D** Oss *See* Castlecomer.
COLLINSTOWN (St Fechin), *W Meath.* **D** Meath 5 *See* Rathgraffe.

COLLON w Tullyallen, *Louth* and *Meath.* R **D** Arm 3 **I** F K JENNINGS.
COLLOONEY, *Sligo.* **D** Achon *See* Ballysodare.
COLPE (St Mary), *Meath.* **D** Meath *See* Julianstown.
COLUMBKILLE, *Longf.* **D** Ard 3 **I** (Vacant).
COMBER (St Mary), *Down.* **D** Down 2 **I** F D SWANN, R D LEE *c.*
CONG (St Mary) w Ballinrobe, Ross (All SS), *Galw* and Castlekirke (St Patr), *Mayo.* **D** Tuam 3 **I** (Vacant).
CONNELL, GREAT w Carnalway and Kilcullen (St John), *Kild.* **D** Kild **I** W B HENEY.
CONNOR (St Sav Cathl) *Antr.* **D** Connor 2 **I** A S HOFMEESTER.
CONVOY (St Ninian) and Donaghmore (St Patr & St Ann) w Monellan, *Doneg.* **D** Raph 5 **I** R C HANNA.
CONWALL and LECK w Aghanunshin and Gartan, *Doneg.* **D** Raph 4 **I** P G CARTWRIGHT.
COOKSTOWN, *Tyr.* **D** Arm *See* Derryloran.
COOLBANAGHER (St Jo Evang), *Leix.* **D** Kild 5 *See* Mountmellick.
COOLOCK (St Jo Evang), *Dub.* **D** Dub *See* Raheny.
COONEEN w Mullaghfad, *Tyr.* **D** Clogh 4 **I** V H FORSTER.
COOTEHILL, *Cav.* **D** Kilm *See* Drumgoon.
CORACLONE, *Leix.* **D** Leigh *See* Stradbally.
CORBALLY (Ch Ch), *Tip.* **D** Killaloe *See* Bourney.
CORK (St Fin Barre Cathl), *Cork.* **D** Cork 1 **I** VERY REV J M G CAREY, E P MILLS *c.*
(St Ann Shandon) **D** Cork *See* St Luke.
(H Trin w St Paul and St Pet Shandon) **D** Cork 1 **I** (Vacant).
(St Luke) w (St Ann and St Mary Shandon) **D** Cork 1 **I** G A SALTER.
CORKBEG (SS Mich AA) w Inch and Aghada, *Cork.* **D** Cloyne 1 **I** J K S R BARKER.
CORRAWALLEN, *Cavan.* **D** Kilm *See* Kildallon.
COURTMACSHERRY, *Cork.* **D** Ross *See* Timoleague.
CRAIGSDOOISH, *Doneg.* **D** Raph *See* Taughoyne.
CRAIGS w Dunaghy (St Jas) and Killigan, *Antr.* **D** Connor 2 **I** E R LAVERY.
CREAGH or Skibbereen, *Cork.* **D** Ross *See* Abbeystrewry.
CREAGH (St Jo Evang) w Ballinasloe (St John), Taughmacconnell and Ahascragh (St Cath) **D** Clonf 1 **I** (Vacant).
CREGAGH (St Finnian), *Down.* **D** Down 3 **I** S G E LLOYD *c.*
CREGGAN w Forkill, Jonesborough and Killeavy, *Arm.* and *Louth.* **D** Arm 4 **I** S M NOEL.
CRILLY, *Tyr.* **D** Arm *See* Carnteel.
CRINKEN BRAY (St Jas), *Wick.* **D** Dub 7 **I** (Vacant).
CROGHAN, *Rosc.* **D** Elph *See* Elphin.
CROHANE Tip. **D** Cash *See* Kilcooley.
CROOM w Bruff, *Lim.* **D** Lim *See* Kilpeacon.
CROSSBOYNE, *Mayo.* **D** Tuam *See* Ballinrobe.
CROSSDUFF (St Pet), *Monagh.* **D** Clogh *See* Ballybay.
CROSSMOLINA (St Mary) w Kilcommon Erris, Kilmore Erris and Poulathomas, *Mayo.* **D** Killala 2 **I** (Vacant).
CROSSPATRICK w Kilcommon Kilpipe and Preban, *Wickl.* **D** Ferns 3 **I** C CHALLENDER.
CRUAGH, *Dub.* **D** Dub *See* Whitechurch (Dub).
CRUMLIN (St Mary), *Dub.* **D** Dub 8 **I** H B WHYTE.
CULDAFF (St Bodonus), *Doneg.* **D** Derry *See* Donagh.
CULFEIGHTRIM, *Antr.* **D** Connor 6 **I** D B E PERRIN *c-in-c.*
CULLEN (Ch Ch), *Cork.* **D** Cork *See* Ballymartle.
CULLEN, *Tip.* **D** Cash *See* Tipperary.
CULMORE (H Trin) w Muff and Belmont (St Pet), *Derry.* **D** Derry 8 **I** C L MACONACHIE.
CUMBER, LOWER, (H Trin), *Derry.* **D** Derry 2 **I** G F ANDERSON.
CUMBER, UPPER or CUMBER CLAUDY (St Eugenius) w Learmount, *Derry.* **D** Derry 2 **I** F W FAWCETT.
CURRIN w Drum and Newbliss, *Monagh.* **D** Clogh **I** (Vacant).
CUSHENDALL, *Antr.* **D** Connor *See* Layde.
CUSHENDUN, *Antr.* **D** Connor *See* Layde.

DALKEY (St Patr), *Dub.* **D** Dub 6 **I** J F O WILLIAMS.
DELGANY (Ch Ch), *Wickl.* **D** Glendal 1 **I** C J PRICE.
DELVIN (St Mary), *W Meath.* **D** Meath 9 **I** (Vacant).
DENN, *Cav.* **D** Kilm *See* Urney.
DERG or CASTLEDERG w Termonamongan (St Bestius), *Derry.* **D** Derry 6 **I** W P QUILL.
DERRALOSSARY w Annamoe and Laragh (St John), *Wickl.* **D** Glendal 3 *See* Rathdrum.
DERRIAGHY (Ch Ch), *Antr.* **D** Connor 9 **I** (Vacant).
DERRY (St Columb's Cathl and Par Ch, Templemore), *Derry.* **D** Derry 8 **I** G F GOOD, P H A LAWRENCE *c.*
(Ch Ch) **D** Derry 8 **I** B D A HANNON.
(St Aug Chap of Ease), V **D** Derry 8 **I** C HOWE.
(St Pet, Belmont), V **D** Derry 8 *See* Culmore.
DERRYBRUSK ('Derryharney Church'), *Ferman.* **D** Clogh *See* Maguiresbridge.
DERRYGORTREAVY, *Tyr.* **D** Arm *See* Clonfeacle.
DERRYGRATH, *Tip.* **D** Lism *See* Cahir.
DERRYHEEN, *Cav.* **D** Kilm *See* Urney.
DERRYKEIGHAN. Antr. **D** Connor 8 *See* Billy.
DERRYLANE, *Cav.* **D** Kilm 3 **I** (Vacant).
DERRYLORAN w Cookstown, *Derry* and *Tyr.* **D** Arm 8 **I** T P R KENNY.
DERRYNOOSE (St John), *Arm.* **D** Arm *See* Keady.
DERRYVOLGIE, *Antr.* **D** Connor 9 **I** J N B WILKINSON.
DERRYVULLAN (St Tighernach), *Ferman.* **D** Clogh 5 **I** W LUMLEY.
NORTH (Irvinestown), *Ferman.* **D** Clogh 6 **I** V E S MCKEON.
DESERTCREAT, *Tyr.* **D** Arm *See* Ardtrea.
DESERTEGNY, *Doneg.* **D** Derry *See* Fahan, Lower.
DESERTLYN (St John) w Ballyeglish, *Derry.* **D** Arm 8 **I** R C C O'CONNOR.
DESERTMARTIN (St Comghall), *Derry.* **D** Derry 4 **I** M E G MOORE.
DESERTOGHILL, *Derry.* **D** Derry *See* Errigal.
DESERTSERGES w Murragh (St Patr) and Killowen (St John), *Cork.* **D** Cork 6 **I** D J P LLEWELLYN.
DEVENISH (St Molaise) w Bohoe, *Ferman.* **D** Clogh 5 **I** W T ALLISTER.
DIAMOND, THE, *Arm.* **D** Arm *See* Kilmore.
DINGLE (St Jas) w Ventry, *Kerry.* **D** Ardf **I** P STEPHENS *p-in-c.*
DONABATE (St Patr) w Lusk, *Dub.* **D** Dub 11 **I** W J MOYNAN.
DONACAVEY (Fintona) w The Bar, *Tyr.* **D** Clogh 7 **I** W E MCGIRR.
DONADEA, *Kild.* **D** Kild *See* Clane.
DONAGH (St Salv) w Tyholland, *Monagh.* **D** Clogh 8 **I** H G JAMIESON.
DONAGH (St Salvator) w Cloncha, Culdaff and Clonmany, *Doneg.* **D** Derry 1 **I** J E HENDERSON.
DONAGHADEE, *Down.* **D** Down 2 **I** J C SWENARTON.
DONAGHCLONEY (H Trin) w Waringstown (St Patr), *Down.* **D** Drom 6 **I** J C MOORE.
DONAGHEADY (St Jas), *Tyr.* **D** Derry 7 **I** E T DUNDAS.
DONAGHENDRY w Ballyclog, *Tyr.* **D** Arm 6 **I** D G BOTHWELL.
DONAGHMOINE (St Patr w H Trin), *Monagh.* **D** Clogh *See* Carrickmacross.
DONAGHMORE (St Bart), *Down.* **D** Drom *See* Aghaderg.
DONAGHMORE (St Mich) w Donaghmore, Upper, *Tyr.* **D** Arm 1 **I** W G H WILLIAMS.
DONAGHMORE (St Patr and St Ann), *Doneg.* **D** Raph *See* Convoy.
DONAGHMORE, *Leix.* **D** Oss *See* Rathodowney.
DONAGHMORE, UPPER *Tyr.* **D** Arm *See* Donaghmore.
DONAGHPATRICK (St Patr) w Kilshine (St Sinche), Drakestown (St Patr), and Ardbraccan (St Ultan), *Meath.* **D** Meath 12 **I** (Vacant).
DONANAUGHTA (St Jo Bapt), *Galw.* **D** Clonf *See* Clonfert.
DONARD, *Wickl.* **D** Glendal *See* Donoughmore.
DONEGAL, w Killymard and Lough Eske (Ch Ch), *Doneg.* **D** Raph 1 **I** A B STEWART.
DONEGORE, *Antr.* **D** Connor *See* Templepatrick.
DONERAILE, *Cork.* **D** Cloyne 4 **I** (Vacant).
DONNYBROOK, *Dub.* **D** Dub *See* Dublin, St Mary.
DONOHILL, *Tip.* **D** Cash *See* Ballintemple.
DONOUGHMORE w Donard, *Wickl.* **D** Glendal 6 **I** N P STYLES.
DOON, *Lim.* and *Tip.* **D** Cash *See* Tipperary.
DORRHA, *Tip.* **D** Killaloe *See* Birr.
DOUGLAS (St Luke) w Frankfield, *Cork.* **D** Cork 2 **I** H G WATTS.
DOWN (H Trin Cathl parish) w Holly Mount, *Down.* **D** Down 6 **I** R S PETERS.
DOWRA (St Thos), *Cav* and *Leitr.* **D** Kilm *See* Killinagh.
DRAKESTOWN (St Patr), *Meath.* **D** Meath *See* Donaghpatrick.
DRIMOLEAGUE (St Matt) w Caheragh (St Mary), *Cork.* R **D** Cork 6 **I** (Vacant).
DRINAGH, *Cork.* **D** Cork *See* Fanlobbus.
DROGHEDA (St Pet) w Ballymakenny and Termonfeckin w Beaulieu (St Brigid), *Louth.* **D** Arm 3 **I** C J G BEVAN.
DROGHEDA (St Mary de Ponte) w Duleek, Slane (St Patr), Paynestown and Stackallan, *Meath.* **D** Meath 4 **I** A J NELSON.
DROMARA (St Matt) w Garvaghy, *Down.* **D** Drom 2 **I** S E LONG.

DROMARD, *Sligo*. **D** Killala *See* Skreen.
DROMCLIFFE, *Sligo*. **D** Elph *See* Drumcliffe.
DROMISKIN, *Louth*. **D** Arm *See* Kilsaran.
DROMOD PRYOR w Valentia and Cahir, *Kerry*. **D** Ardf 3 **I** (Vacant).
DROMORE, *Tyr*. **D** Clogh 7 **I** J S FRAZER.
DROMORE (Christ the Redeemer Cathl and Par Ch), *Down*. **D** Drom 2 **I** C H E CLAYTON.
DROMTARIFF, *Cork*. **D** Cloyne *See* Castlemagner.
DRUM, *Monagh*. **D** Clogh 8 *See* Currin.
DRUMACHOSE (Ch Ch) w Limavady, *Derry*. **D** Derry 9 **I** G W A KNOWLES, P F BARRETT *c*.
DRUMBALLYRONEY, *Down*. **D** Drom *See* Drumgath.
DRUMBANAGHER (St Mary), *Arm*. **D** Arm 4 *See* Acton.
DRUMBEG (St Patr), *Down*. **R D** Down 3 **I** H L UPRICHARD.
DRUMBO (H Trin), *Down*. **D** Down 3 **I** J C BELL.
DRUMCANNON w Dunhill, *Waterf*. **D** Waterf 4 **I** J R H PORTER.
DRUMCAR (St Fintan) w Dunany, *Louth*. **D** Arm 2 **I** (Vacant).
DRUMCLAMPH w Drumquin, *Tyr*. **D** Derry 6 **I** W J JOHNSTON.
DRUMCLIFFE w Ennis, Clare Abbey, and Kildysart, *Clare*. **D** Killaloe 2 **I** M J TALBOT.
DRUMCLIFFE (St Columba) w Lissadell, Munninane, and Ahamplish, *Sligo*. **D** Elph 2 **I** J M G SIRR.
DRUMCONDRA (St Jo Bapt) w N Strand and St Barn Dub, *Dub*. **D** Dub 9 **I** W S BAIRD.
DRUMCONRATH (St Pet) w Drakestown (St Patr) and Siddan (St Mary), *Louth*. **D** Meath 12 *See* Eniskeen.
DRUMCREE (Ch of Ascen), *Arm*. **D** Arm 7 **I** J A FORD.
DRUMCREE (St John), *W. Meath*. **D** Meath 5 *See* Castlepollard.
DRUMGATH or RATHFRILAND w Drumballyroney (St John) and Clonduff, *Down*. **R D** Drom 3 **I** J W MCKEGNEY.
DRUMGLASS (Dungannon) (St Ann), *Tyr*. **D** Arm 6 **I** A S O'CONNOR.
DRUMGOOLAND, *Down*. **D** Drom 2 **I** J W MCKEGNEY.
DRUMGOON (Cootehill) w Ashfield and Killesherdoney (St Mark), *Cav*. **D** Kilm 1 **I** P TARLETON.
DRUMHOLME w Laghey, *Doneg*. **D** Raph **I** (Vacant).
DRUMKEERAN, *Ferman*. **D** Clogh 6 *See* Magheraculmoney.
DRUMLANE, *Cav*. **D** Kilm *See* Tomregan.
DRUMLEASE w Killenumery (St Mich), *Leitr*. **D** Kilm 1 *See* Manorhamilton.
DRUMLUMMON, *Longf*. **D** Ard *See* Granard.
DRUMMAUL (Randalstown), *Antr*. **D** Connor 1 **I** J R WILSON.
DRUMMULLY, *Ferman* and *Monagh*. **D** Clogh *See* Galloon.
DRUMNAKILLY (H Trin), *Tyr*. **D** Arm 1 **I** H W MINCHIN.
DRUMRAGH (Omagh) (St Columba) w Mountfield, *Tyr*. **D** Derry **I** D C ORR, S MCVEIGH *c*.
DRUMREILLY, *Leitr*. **D** Kilm *See* Oughterragh.
DRUMSHAMBO, *Leitr*. **D** Ard 4 *See* Kiltoghart.
DRUMSNATT (St Mollua), *Monagh*. **R D** Clogh *See* Clogh.
DRUMTULLAGH, *Antr*. **D** Connor *See* Armoy.
DRUNG w Castleterra, *Cav*. **D** Kilm 1 **I** J G B ROYCROFT.
DUBLIN (St Patr National Cathl) **D** Dub *See* Cathedral List.
(Ch Ch Dioc Cathl), Dub and Glendal **D** Dub *See* Cathedral List.
(All SS), Grangegorman **D** Dub 4 **I** R G F JENKINS.
Harold's Cross **D** Dub 2 **I** E M NEILL.
King's Hosp Chap **D** Dub **I** G S MAGAHY.
Mission Chap (ICM), Townsend Street **D** Dub **I** (Vacant).
Rathmines (H Trin) **D** Dub 1 **I** E V C WATSON.
Rotunda Hosp Chap, Rutland Square **D** Dub 3 **I** A H KERR *chap*.
(St Andr), St Andr Street **D** Dub 3 **I** (Vacant).
(St Ann), Dawson Street **D** Dub 1 **I** R W M WYNNE, A W U FURLONG *c*, N MCENDOO *c*.
(St Barn) **D** Dub *See* Drumcondra.
(St Bart), Clyde Road w (Ch Ch), Leeson Park **D** Dub 1 **I** J R W NEILL, E G ARDIS *c*.
(St Cath w St Victor's Chap), Thomas Street and (St James), James Street. **D** Dub 2 **I** (Vacant).
(St Geo), Hardwicke Place w Clonliffe (St Aid) and St Aug Free Church. **D** Dub 5 **I** W R J GOURLEY.
(St Jo Evang), Sandymount **D** Dub 2 **I** M A GRAHAM *p-in-c*, G P IRVINE *c*.
(St Jude) Inchicore, Chapelizod **D** Dub 2 **I** M BYRNE *c-in-c*, A H KERR *c*.
(St Kevin), S Circular Road **D** Dub 1 **I** W J SMALLHORNE.
(St Luke w St Nich Within and Without), Coombe **D** Dub 2 **I** G H J BURROWS *c-in-c*.
(St Mary), Donnybrook **D** Dub 3 **I** R H BERTRAM.
(St Matt), Irishtown, **R D** Dub 3 **I** R H BERTRAM.
(St Paul), King Street North w (St Michan), Church Street and (St Mary), Mary Street **D** Dub 3 **I** (Vacant).
(St Pet), Aungier Street w (St Audoen, St Mich and St Matthias) **D** Dub 1 **I** (Vacant).
(St Phil), Milltown **D** Dub 8 **I** J D MURRAY.
(St Steph), Upper Mount Street **D** Dub 1 **I** R W M WYNNE, A W U FURLONG *c*.
(St Thos) Foster Avenue, Mount Merrion **D** Dub 1 **I** T S HIPWELL.
(St Thos), Marlborough Street **D** Dub 5 **I** (Vacant).
(St Werburgh w St John, St Bride, and St Mich-le-Pole), Werburgh Street **D** Dub 2 **I** (Vacant).
Sandford Ch, Ranelagh **D** Dub 1 **I** C T A CARTER.
Zion Ch, Rathgar **D** Dub 8 **I** R A WARKE.
DUGORT, *Mayo*. **D** Tuam *See* Achill.
DULEEK (St Keenan), *Meath*. **D** Meath *See* Drogheda.
DUNAGHY (St Jas) w Killaghan, *Antr*. **D** Connor *See* Craigs.
DUNAMON, *Rosc*. **D** Elph *See* Roscommon.
DUNANY, *Louth*. **D** Arm *See* Drumcar.
DUNBOE, *Derry*. **D** Derry *See* Castlerock.
DUNBOYNE w Moyglare, Raddanstown, Maynooth (St Mary), Kilcock (St Patr), Dunshauglin and Ballymaglasson, *Meath*. **D** Meath 10 **I** J F HAMMOND.
DUNCORMICK, *Wexf*. **D** Ferns *See* Bannow.
DUNDALK (St Nich) w Baronstown, *Louth*. **D** Arm 4 **I** J F MCCARTHY.
DUNDELA (St Mark), *Down*. **D** Down 4 **I** J E MOORE, J W R CRAWFORD *c*, R S HEWITT *c*.
DUNDERROW, *Cork*. **D** Cork *See* Kinsale.
DUNDONALD, *Down*. **D** Down 4 **I** E CROOKS, A F ABERNETHY *c*.
DUNDRUM, *Dub*. **R D** Dub *See* Taney.
DUNDRUM (St Donard), *Down*. **D** Drom *See* Kilmegan.
DUNEANE w Ballyscullion, *Antr*. **D** Connor 1 **I** J R WILSON.
DUNFANAGHY (H Trin) w Raymunterdoney and Tullaghobegley, *Doneg*. **D** Raph 3 **I** (Vacant).
DUNFEENY (St John), *Mayo*. **D** Killala *See* Killala.
DUNGANNON, *Tyr*. **D** Arm *See* Drumglass.
DUNGANSTOWN w Redcross, *Wickl*. **D** Glendal 2 **I** D P R CARMODY.
DUNGARVAN (St Mary) w Ringagoonagh, *Waterf*. **D** Lism 2 **I** MAYES.
DUNGIVEN w Bovevagh, *Derry*. **D** Derry 2 **I** J S DOWNEY.
DUNGOURNEY, *Cork*. **D** Cloyne *See* Castlemartyr.
DUNHILL, *Waterf*. **D** Waterf *See* Drumcannon.
DUNKERRIN, *offaly*. **D** Killaloe *See* Bourney.
DUN LAOGHAIRE, *Dub*. **D** Dub *See* Kingstown.
DUNLAVIN (St Nich) w Hollywood and Ballymore Eustace, *Kild* and *Wickl*. **D** Glendal 6 **I** H C BROOKS.
DUNLECKNEY (Bagenalstown) w Nurney Clonmulsh and Lorum, *Carlow*. **D** Leigh 5 **I** S W ROUNDTREE.
DUNLEER, *Louth*. **D** Arm *See* Kilsaran.
DUNLEWEY, *Doneg*. **D** Raph *See* Gweedore.
DUNLUCE (St Jo Bapt), *Antr*. **D** Connor 8 **I** F G GUY.
DUNMANWAY (St Mary), *Cork*. **D** Cork *See* Fanlobbus.
(St Edm) **D** Cork 6 **I** (Vacant).
DUNMORE, EAST, w Killea (St Nich), *Waterf*. **D** Waterf 4 **I** (Vacant).
DUNMURRY (St Colman), *Antr*. **D** Connor 9 **I** J T R RODGERS.
DUNNALONG (St John), *Tyr*. **D** Derry *See* Leckpatrick.
DUNSVERICK w Ballintoy, *Antr*. **D** Connor 6 **I** J N PATTERSON.
DUNSFORD (St Mary), *Down*. **D** Down *See* Ardglass.
DUNSHAUGHLIN w Ballymaglasson (St Keiran), Ratoath (H Trin), *Meath*. **D** Meath 10 *See* Dunboyne.
DURROW, *Offaly* and *W. Meath*. **D** Meath *See* Newtown Fertullagh.
DURROW-IN-OSSORY, *Kilk*. **D** Oss *See* Killermogh.
DURRUS or KILCROHANE w Rooska (St Jas), *Cork*. **D** Cork 4 **I** J P CLARKE.
DYSART ENOS, *Leix*. **D** Leigh *See* Maryborough.
DYSART GALLEN (All SS), *Leix*. **D** Leigh *See* Abbeyleix.

EASKEY (St Ann) w Kilglass, *Sligo*. **D** Killala 1 **I** J L HAWORTH.
EASKEY, *Arm*. **D** Droom *See* Ardmore.
EDENDERRY, *Tyr*. **D** Derry 5 **I** G C CURRY.
EDENDERRY, *Offaly*. **D** Kild *See* Monasteroris.

EDERMINE, *Wexf.* **D** Ferns *See* Enniscorthy.
EGLANTINE (All SS), *Down.* **D** Connor 9 **I** H N PEDLOW.
EGLISH, *Arm.* **D** Arm 9 **I** J M BATCHELOR.
EGLISH (H Trin), *Offaly.* **D** Killaloe *See* Birr.
EIRKE, *Kilk.* **D** Oss *See* Fertagh.
ELPHIN (St Mary) w Bumlin (St Jo Bapt), Groghan and Ardclare, *Rosc.* **D** Elph 1 **I** W W SLACK.
EMATRIS (St Jo Evang) w Rockcorry, *Monagh.* **D** Clogh *See* Aghabog.
EMLAGHFAD w Killaraght, Castlemore and Killoran, *Sligo.* **D** Achon 3 **I** (Vacant).
ENNIS, *Clare.* **D** Killaloe *See* Drumcliffe.
ENNISCOFFEY, *W Meath.* **D** Meath *See* Mullingar.
ENNISCORTHY (St Mary) w Clone , Clonmore and Edermine *Wexf.* **D** Ferns 4 **I** K S WILKINSON.
ENNISCRONE, *Sligo.* **D** Killala *See* Kilglass.
ENNISKEEN (St Ernon) w Nobber Drumconrath, Siddan, Moybologue and Ardagh, *Cav* and *Meath.* (Ulster and Leinster) **D** Meath 7 **I** T G CORRIGAN.
ENNISKILLEN (St Macartin Cathl), *Ferman.* **D** Clogh 5 **I** T CLEMENTS.
ENNISNAG (St Pet), *Kilk.* **D** Oss 2 **I** (Vacant).
ERRIGAL (Garvagh) (St Paul) w Desertoghill, *Derry.* **D** Derry 3 **I** S SIMPSON
ERRIGAL-KEEROGUE (St Matt) w Ballygawley and Killeshill, *Tyr.* **D** Arm 1 **I** E G C B INGRAM.
ERRIGAL-PORTCLARE (St Mary), *Tyr.* **D** Clogh *See* Clogher.
ERRIGAL-TROUGH (St Muadan) w Errigal-Shanco (St Mary), *Monagh.* **D** Clogh 4 **I** H G JAMIESON.
ERRIGLE-SHANCO (St Mary), *Monagh.* **D** Clogh *See* Errigal-Trough.
ERRISLANNAN, *Galw.* **D** Tuam *See* Omey.
ERRISMORE, *Galw.* **D** Tuam *See* Omey.
ESKEY, *Arm.* **D** Drom *See* Montiaghs.
ETTAGH (St Mark), *Offaly.* **D** Killaloe *See* Shinrone.

FAHAN, LOWER (Ch Ch) w Desertegney, *Doneg.* **D** Derry 1 **I** C THORNTON.
FAHAN, UPPER w Inch, *Doneg.* **D** Derry 1 **I** C THORNTON.
FALLS, LOWER, *Antr.* **D** Connor *See* Belfast.
FALLS, UPPER, *Antr.* **D** Connor *See* Belfast.
FANLOBBUS or DUNMANWAY (St Mary w St Edm) w Drinagh, *Cork.* **R D** Cork 6 **I** G P S J HILLIARD.
FARAHY (St Colman), *Cork.* **D** Cloyne **I** (Vacant).
FAUGHANVALE (St Canice), *Derry.* **D** Derry 2 **I** W B A NEILL.
FEAKE, *Clare.* **D** Killaloe *See* Tulloh.
FEIGHCULLEN, *Kild.* **D** Kild *See* Kildare.
FENAGH (St Cath), *Leitr.* **D** Ard *See* Oughteragh.
FENAGH (All SS) w Myshall, Kiltennel and Aghade w Ardoyne, *Carlow.* **D** Leigh 3 **I** (Vacant).
FERMOY w Kilworth and Ballyhooley, *Cork.* **D** Cloyne 4 **I** G C PAMMENT.
FERMOYLE, *Derry.* **D** Derry *See* Castlerock.
FERNS (St Aid Cathl and Par Ch) w Kilbride (H Trin) and Tombe, *Wexf.* **D** Ferns 4 **I** (Vacant).
FERTAGH (St Mary) w Eirke, Clomantagh and Kilmanagh, *Kilk.* **D** Oss 7 **I** W G NEELY *c-in-c.*
FETHARD (H Trin) w Kilvemnon, Killamery, and Lismalin, *Tip.* **D** Cash 3 **I** I J E KNOX.
FETHARD (St Mogue) w Tintern, Killesk, and Templetown, *Wexf.* **D** Ferns 5 **I** (Vacant).
FIDDOWN w Castlane, *Kilk.* **D** Lism 2 **I** R J HAZELTON.
FINAGHY (St Polycarp), *Down.* **D** Connor 5 **I** J R HALL.
FINGLAS (St Canice), *Dub.* **D** Dub 9 **I** (Vacant).
FINNER, BUNDORAN (Ch Ch) w Rossinver, *Doneg.* **D** Kilm 2 **I** G G WARRINGTON.
FINNOE, *Tip.* **D** Killaloe *See* Kilbarron.
FINTONA, *Tyr* **D** Clogh *See* Donacavey.
FINVOY, *Antr.* **D** Connor *See* Rasharkin.
FIVEMILETOWN, *Tyr.* **D** Clogh 4 **I** B W V HASTIE.
FONTSTOWN (St John), *Kild.* **D** Glendal *See* Narraghmore.
FORGNEY w Ballymore and Almoritia, *Longf.* **D** Meath 8 **I** (Vacant).
FORKILL, *Arm.* **D** Arm *See* Creggan.
FOYRAN, *W Meath.* **D** Meath *See* Rathgraffe.
FRANKFIELD, *Cork.* **D** Cork *See* Douglas.

GALBALLY (St John), *Lim.* **D** Cash *See* Aney.
GALLEN, *Offaly.* **D** Meath *See* Rynagh.
GALLOON (St Comgall) w Drummully, *Ferman.* **D** Clogh 8 **I** J HAY.
GALTRIM (St Mary), *Meath.* **D** Meath *See* Trim.
GALWAY (St Nich) w Inverin, Barna, Moycullen, Ballinacourty, and Aran, *Galw.* **D** Tuam 2 **I** L D A FORREST.
GARRISON w Slavin and Beleek, *Ferman.* **D** Clogh 6 **I** (Vacant).
GARTAN, *Doneg.* **D** Raph *See* Conwall.
GARTREE, *Antr.* **D** Connor *See* Killead.
GARVAGH (St Paul), *Derry.* **D** Derry *See* Errigal.
GARVAGHY, *Down.* **D** Drom *See* Dromara.
GARVARY (H Trin), *Ferman.* **D** Clogh 5 **I** W LUMLEY.
GEASHILL (St Mary) w Killeigh and Ballycommon, *Offaly.* **D** Kild 3 **I** J JACOB.
GILFORD (St Paul), *Down.* **D** Drom 1 **I** E ARMSTRONG.
GILNAHIRK (St Dorothea), *Antr.* **D** Down 4 **I** K J SMYTH.
GIRLEY (St Marg), *Meath.* **D** Meath *See* Athboy.
GLASCARRIG, *Wexf.* **D** Ferns 6 *See* Ardamine.
GLASNEVIN, *Dub.* **D** Dub *See* Santry.
GLENALLA (St Columbkille), *Dongeg.* **D** Raph *See* Mevagh.
GLENAGEARY (St Paul), *Dub.* **D** Dub 6 **I** G C S LINNEY.
GLENARM, *Antr.* **D** Connor *See* Tickmacrevan.
GLENAVY (St Aid), *Antr.* **D** Connor 9 **I** T O THOMPSON.
GLENBEAGH CHAP, *Kerry.* **D** Ardf *See* Killorglin.
GLENCOLUMBKILLE, *Doneg.* **D** Raph *See* Ardara.
GLENCRAIG, *Down.* **D** Down 4 **I** A MACONACHIE.
GLENDERMOTT, *Derry.* **D** Derry 8 **I** R N MOORE.
GLENEALY, *Wickl.* **D** Glendal *See* Rathdrum.
GLENEELY (All SS), *Doneg.* **D** Derry 1 *See* Moville.
GLENGARRIFF (H Trin), *Cork.* **R D** Ross *See* Berehaven.
GLENTIES, *Doneg.* **D** Raph *See* Inniskeel.
GLYNN, Raloo (St Jo Evang) w Templecorran, *Antr.* **D** Connor 7 **I** S H REID *c-in-c.*
GOREY or KILMICHAELGUE (Ch Ch) w Kilnahue (St Jo Div), *Wexf.* **D** Ferns 6 **I** W S PARKER.
GORT, *Galw.* **D** Kilmac *See* Kilmacduagh.
GOWNA, *Cav.* **D** Ard *See* Arvagh.
GOWRAN, *Kilk.* **D** Oss *See* Mothel.
GRAIGUE (St Pet w St Mullins), *Kilk.* **D** Leigh *See* Leighlin.
GRANARD w Mostrim, Kilglass, Abbeylara and Drumlummon, *Longf.* **D** Ard 3 **I** R HENDERSON.
GRANGE, *Arm.* **D** Arm 9 **I** C S LOWRY.
GRANGEGORMAN, *Dub.* **D** Dub *See* Dublin (All Saints).
GRANGE-SYLVAE (St Geo), *Kilk.* **D** Leigh *See* Leighlin.
GREAN, *Lim.* **D** Emly *See* Tipperary.
GREAT CONNELL w Morristownbiller (St Patr), *Kild.* **D** Kild 6 **I** (Vacant).
GREENCASTLE (St Finian), *Doneg.* **D** Derry *See* Moville, Lower.
GREENISLAND(H Name), *Antr.* **D** Connor 7 **I** G R H JOHNSTON.
GREY ABBEY (St Sav), *Down.* **D** Down 1 **I** (Vacant).
GREYSTONES, *Wickl.* **D** Glendal 1 **I** E J SWANN.
GROOMSPORT, *Down.* **D** Down 2 **I** J D TYNEY.
GUILCAGH, *Waterf.* **D** Lism *See* Clonegam.
GWEEDORE w Dunlewey and Templecrone, *Doneg.* **D** Raph 3 **I** (Vacant).

HACKETSTOWN w Clonmore (St John), *Carlow* and *Wickl.* **D** Leigh 1 *See* Kiltegan.
HAROLD'S CROSS, *Dub.* **D** Dub *See* Dublin (Harold's Cross).
HELEN'S BAY (St Jo Bapt), *Down.* **D** Down 4 **I** M W DEWAR.
HEADFORD (St Jo Bapt), *Galw.* **D** Tuam *See* Tuam.
HEYNESTOWN (St Paul) w Louth and Killencoole, *Louth.* **D** Arm 5 **I** J F MCCARTHY.
HILLSBOROUGH (St Malachi w St Jas Chap of Ease), *Down.* **D** Down 3 **I** J BARRY.
(St John) **D** Down *See* Kilwarlin.
HOLLYMOUNT, *Down.* **D** Down *See* Down.
HOLLYMOUNT, *Mayo.* **D** Tuam *See* Ballinrobe.
HOLLYWOOD w Ballymore Eustace, *Wickl.* and *Kild.* **D** Glendal *See* Dunlavin.
HOLMPATRICK (St Patr) w Kenure (Chap) and Balbriggan w Balrothery, *Dub.* **D** Dub 11 **I** H C MILLS.
HOLYCROSS, *Tip.* **D** Cash *See* Ballintemple.
HOLYWOOD (St Phil and St Jas), *Down.* **D** Down 4 **I** E S BARBER, N N LYNAS *c,* C J WILCOCK *c.*
HORETOWN (St Jas) w Taghmon, Bannow and Duncormick, *Wexf.* **R D** Ferns 8 **I** E A BRANDON.
HOWTH (St Mary), *Dub.* **D** Dub 9 **I** T F BLENNERHASSETT.

INCH, *Cork.* **D** Cloyne *See* Corkbeg.

INCH, *Doneg.* **D** Derry *See* Fahan, Upper.
INCH, *Down.* **D** Down *See* Saul.
INCH, *Wexf.* **D** Glendal 3 **I** W F H VANSTON.
INCHICORE, *Dub.* **D** Dub *See* Dublin (St Jude).
INCHIGEELAGH, *Cork.* **D** Cloyne *See* Macroom.
INISHKENNY (St John), *Cork.* **D** Cork *See* Carrigrohane.
INISHMAGRATH Leitr. **D** Kilm 2 *See* Killinagh.
INISTIOGE w The Rower, Kilfane and Knocktopher, *Kilk.* **D** Oss 2 **I** C A EMPEY.
INNISCALTRA, *Clare.* **D** Killaloe 6 **I** (Vacant).
INNISHANNON (Ch Ch) w Leigmoney, Templemichael, Brinny and Ballinadee, *Cork.* **D** Cork 3 **I** G M D WOODWORTH.
INNISHMACSAINT, *Ferman.* **D** Clogh 5 **I** F J L SKUCE.
INNISKEEL w Lettermacaward and Glenties, *Doneg.* **D** Raph 2 **I** W B JOHNSTON.
INNISKEEN (St Daigh), *Monagh.* and *Louth.* **D** Clogh *See* Carrickmacross.
INNISLONAGHT, *Tip.* **D** Lism *See* Clonmel.
INVER w Mountcharles, *Doneg.* **D** Raph 2 **I** J A HILL.
INVER (St Cedma), *Antr.* **D** Connor *See* Larne.
INVERIN, *Galw.* **D** Tuam *See* Galway.
IRISHTOWN, *Dub.* **D** Dub *See* Dublin (St Matthew).
ISLANDMAGEE (St John), *Antr.* **D** Connor *See* Whitehead.

JONESBOROUGH, *Armagh.* **D** Arm *See* Creggan.
JORDANSTOWN (St Patr), *Antr.* **D** Connor 3 **I** E J MOORE, H V N COLLINS *c.*
JULIANSTOWN (St Mary) w Colpe, *Meath.* **D** Meath 4 **I** A J NELSON.

KANTURK (St Pet) w Dromtariffe, *Cork.* **D** Cloyne *See* Castlemagner.
KEADY (St Matt) w Armaghbreague and Derrynoose, *Arm.* **D** Arm 9 **I** J A PICKERING.
KELLS (St Columba) w Balrathboyne (St Baithen), Moynalty (St Mary) and Kilskyre, *Meath.* **D** Meath 6 **I** A R C OLDEN.
KELLS (St Mary) w Burnchurch, Kilmoganny, Ballaghtobin, and Callan, *Kilk.* **D** Oss 3 **I** C A EMPEY.
KENMARE (St Patr) w Templenoe, Kilgarvan (St Pet) and Sneem (Ch of Transfig), *Kerry.* **D** Ardf 2 **I** VERY REV C M GRAY-STACK.
KENSTOWN, *Meath.* **D** Meath *See* Navan.
KENURE (Chap), *Dub.* **D** Dub *See* Holmpatrick.
KILBARRON (St Anne) w Rossnowlagh, *Doneg.* **D** Raph 1 **I** A J ROWE.
KILBARRON w Killodiernan and Finnoe, *Galw.* and *Tip.* **D** Killaloe 8 **I** J CAMIER.
KILBEGGAN, *W Meath.* **D** Meath *See* Newtown Fertullagh.
KILBEHENNY, *Tip.* **D** Cash *See* Templeneiry.
KILBERRY, *Kild.* **D** Glendal *See* Athy.
KILBIXY (St Bigseach) w Leney and Almoritia, *W Meath.* **D** Meath 8 **I** (Vacant).
KILBONANE, *Cork.* **D** Cork *See* Moviddy.
KILBRIDE (St Bride), *Antr.* **D** Connor 1 **I** R R COX.
KILBRIDE (H Trin), *Wexf.* **D** Ferns *See* Ferns.
KILBRIDE, ARKLOW, *Wickl.* **D** Glendal 3 **I** W F H VANSTON.
KILBRIDE, BLESSINGTON, *Wickl.* **D** Glendal *See* Blessington.
KILBRIDE, BRAV, *Wickl.* **D** Glendal *See* Powerscourt.
KILBRIDE (St Cath) (or Tullamore), *Meath.* **D** Meath *See* Tullamore.
KILBRIN, *Cork.* **D** Cloyne *See* Castlemagner.
KILBROGAN (Ch Ch), *Cork.* **D** Cork *See* Ballymodan.
KILBRONEY, ROSTREVOR (St Bronach), *Down.* **D** Drom 3 **I** (Vacant).
KILBRYAN, *Rosc.* **D** Ardf *See* Boyle.
KILCAR, *Doneg.* **D** Raph *See* Killybegs.
KILCLEAGH or MOATE w Ballyloughloe (H Trin), Ferbane, *W Meath.* **D** Meath *See* Clara.
KILCLIEF, *Down.* **D** Down *See* Ballyculter.
KILCLUNEY, *Arm.* **D** Arm 7 *See* Mullabrack.
KILCOCK (St Patr), *Kild.* **D** Meath *See* Dunboyne.
KILCOE, *Cork.* **D** Ross *See* Aghadown.
KILCOLGAN (St John), *Galw.* **D** Kilmac *See* Kilmacduagh.
KILCOLMAN, *Offaly.* **D** Killaloe *See* Aghancon.
KILCOLMAN (St John), *Mayo.* **D** Tuam *See* Ballinrobe.
KILCOLMAN w Aglish, Kiltallagh and Killorglin w Glenbeigh, *Kerry.* **D** Ardf 3 **I** M J D SHANNON.
KILCOMMICK (St Geo) w Cashel and Ruthcline, *Longf.* **D** Ard 5 *See* Ardagh.
KILCOMMON, *Wexf* and *Wickl.* **D** Ferns *See* Crosspatrick.
KILCOMMON (St Mary) w Crossboyne Kilcolman (St John) and Kilmaine, *Mayo.* **D** Tuam *See* Ballinrobe.
KILCOMMON ERRIS w Poulathomas and Kilmore Erris, *Mayo.* **D** Killala *See* Crossmolina.
KILCONDUFF w Killedan, *Mayo.* **D** Achon *See* Straid.
KILCONLA, *Galw.* **D** Tuam *See* Tuam.
KILCOO or BRYANSFORD, *Down.* **D** Drom 4 *See* Castlewellan.
KILCOOLEY w Littleton, Crohane and Killenaule, *Tip.* **D** Cash 4 **I** W G NEELY.
KILCORMACK, *Wexf.* **D** Ferns *See* Kilnamanagh.
KILCORNAN w Kildimo, Ardcanny and Kilkeedy, *Lim.* **D** Lim 1 **I** (Vacant).
KILCREDAN, *Cork.* **D** Cloyne *See* Castlemartyr.
KILCROHANE, *Kerry.* **D** Ardf *See* Kenmare.
KILCROHANE, *Cork.* **D** Cork *See* Durrus.
KILCRONAGHAN w Ballynascreen, *Derry.* **D** Derry 4 **I** (Vacant).
KILCULLEN (St John) w Carnalway (St Patr), *Kild.* **D** Kildare 6 *See* Connell, Great.
KILCUMMIN w Skrebe, *Galw.* **D** Tuam 2 **I** C G GREGORY.
KILDALKEY (St Mary), *Meath.* **D** Meath *See* Athboy.
KILDALLON w Newtowngore and Corrawallen, *Cav.* **D** Kilm 3 **I** B W KINGSTON.
KILDARE (St Brigid's Cathl parish) w Lackagh, Kilmeague and Feighcullen, *Kild.* **D** Kild 4 **I** VERY REV J T F PATERSON.
KILDARTON, *Arm.* **D** Arm 9 **I** M C KENNEDY.
KILDAVIN, *Wexf.* **D** Ferns *See* Newtown Barry.
KILDIMO, *Lim.* **D** Lim *See* Kilcornan.
KILDOLLAGH (St Paul), *Antr* and *Derry.* **D** Connor *See* Ballyrashane.
KILDRESS (St Patr), *Tyr.* **D** Arm 8 **I** J E DAVIDSON.
KILDROUGHT, *Dub.* **D** Glendal *See* Celbridge.
KILDRUMFERTON w Ballymachugh, Ballyjamesduff and Castlerahan, *Cav.* **D** Kilm 1 **I** G N CAVE *c-in-c.*
KILDYSART, *Clare.* **D** Killaloe *See* Drumcliff.
KILEAGH, *Waterf.* **D** Waterf *See* Dunmore, East.
KILFANE, *Kilk.* **D** Oss *See* Inistioge.
KILFARBOY, *Clare.* **D** Killaloe 1 **I** (Vacant).
KILFAUGHNABEG, *Cork.* **D** Ross *See* Ross.
KIFENORA (St Fachan Cathl and Par Ch) w Lisdoonvarns, *Clare.* **D** Kilfen 10 **I** (Vacant).
KILFERGUS (St Paul), *Lim.* **D** Ardf *See* Kilnaughtin.
KILFERAGH w Killard, *Clare.* **D** Killaloe 1 **I** (Vacant).
KILFIANE, *Lim.* **D** Lim *See* Kilflyn.
KILFITHMONE, *Tip.* **D** Cash *See* Templemore.
KILFLYN and Kilfinane, *Lim. See* Kilmallock.
KILFLYNN w Rattoo, *Kerry.* **D** Ardf 4 **I** (Vacant).
KILGARIFFE w Kilnagross and Kilmalooda, *Cork.* **D** Ross 1 *See* Timoleague.
KILGARVAN (St Pet), *Kerry.* **D** Ardf *See* Kenmare.
KILGLASS (St Anne), *Longf.* **D** Ard *See* Granard.
KILGLASS w Enniscrone, *Sligo.* **R D** Killala *See* Easkey.
KILGOBBIN w Killiney (H Trin), *Kerry.* **D** Ardf 1 **I** (Vacant).
KILHORNE, *Down.* **D** Drom *See* Annalong.
KILKEA, *Kild.* **D** Glendal 5 *See* Castledermot.
KILKEEDY, *Clare.* **D** Killaloe *See* Kilnaboy.
KILKEEDY (SS Phil and Jas), *Lim.* **D** Lim *See* Kilcornan.
KILKEEL (Ch Ch), *Down.* **D** Drom 5 **I** J T MCCAMMON.
KILKEEVIN (Trin) w Castlerea, Oran, Longhglynn, Tibonhine, and Kiltullagh, *Rosc.* **D** Elph 1 **I** (Vacant).
KILKENNY (St Canice's Cathl and Par Ch w St Mary), *Kilk.* **D** Oss 6 **I** B HARVEY.
KILKENNY, WEST, *W Meath.* **D** Meath *See* Athlone.
KILL (St John), *Dub.* **D** Dub 6 **I** W S GIBBONS.
KILL (St Jo Evang), *Kild.* **D** Kild *See* Naas.
KILLABBAN, *Leix.* **D** Leigh 4 *See* Killeshin.
KILLADEAS (Priory Ch), *Ferman.* **D** Clogh *See* Trory.
KILLADERRY, PHILIPSTOWN, *Offaly.* **D** Kild *See* Ballycommon.
KILLAGAN, *Antr.* **D** Connor *See* Dunaghy.
KILLAGHTEE, *Doneg.* **D** Raph 2 **I** J A HILL.
KILLALA (St Patr) Cathl w Dunfeeny, Lackan and Ballysakeery, *Mayo.* **D** Killala 4 **I** (Vacant).
KILLALAGHTON, *Galw.* **D** Clonf *See* Aughrim.
KILLALLON, *Meath.* **D** Meath *See* Athboy.
KILLALOAN w Newchapel, Rathronan and Carrick-on-Suir (St Nich), *Tip.* and *Waterf.* **D** Lism 2 **I** (Vacant).
KILLALOE (St Flannan's Cathl) w Ogonelloe (St Mary), Kilmastulla, Castletownarra, and Tomgraney (SS Colman and Cronan), *Clare.* **D** Killaloe 6 **I** VERY REV F. R. BOURKE.
KILLARMERY, *Tip.* **D** Cash *See* Fethard.

KILLANEY w Carryduff, *Down.* D Down 3 I J H R GOOD, H LONG *c*.
KILLANNE w Templeudigan and Templeshambo, *Wexf.* D Ferns 4 I (Vacant).
KILLANULLY (Ch Ch), *Cork.* D Cork *See* Carrigaline.
KILLANY (St Ultan), *Louth.* D Clogh *See* Carrickmacross.
KILLARAGHT, *Mayo* and *Sligo.* D Achon *See* Emlaghford.
KILLARD, *Clare.* D Killaloe *See* Kilfieragh.
KILLARGUE, *Leitr.* D Kilm *See* Killinagh.
KILLARNEY (St Mary) w Muckross (H Trin), *Kerry.* D Ardf 2 I B F B LOUGHEED.
KILLASHEE, *Kild.* D Kild *See* Naas.
KILLASHEE (St Paul) w Ballymacormac, *Longf.* D Ard 5 *See* Templemichael.
KILLASNETT (H Trin), *Kild.* D Kilm *See* Manorhamilton.
KILLEA, *Doneg.* D Raph 5 *See* Taughboyne.
KILLEA (St Nich), *Waterf.* D Waterf *See* Dunmore, East.
KILLEAD (St Cath) w Gartree, *Antr.* D Connor 1 I (Vacant).
KILLEAGH, *Cork.* D Cloyne *See* Youghall.
KILLEAGH, *Meath* D Meath *See* Oldcastle.
KILLEAVY (Ch Ch), *Arm.* D Arm *See* Camlough.
KILLEDAN, *Mayo.* D Achon *See* Straid.
KILLEEVAN (St Laebhan), *Monagh.* D Clogh I R W MARSDEN.
KILLEGAR, *Cav* and *Leitr.* D Kilm *See* Killeshandra.
KILLEGNEY w Rossdroit (St Pet) and Adamstown, *Wexf.* D Ferns 7 I (Vacant).
KILLEHENNY (or Ballybunion), *Kerry.* D Ardf *See* Kilnaughtin.
KILLEIGH, *Offaly.* D Kild *See* Geashill.
KILLELAGH, *Derry.* D Derry *See* Maghera.
KILLENAGH, *Wexf.* D Ferns *See* Ardamine.
KILLENAULE, *Tip.* D Cash 3 *See* Kilcooley.
KILLENCOOLE, *Louth.* D Arm *See* Heynestown.
KILLENUMERY (St Mich) w Killargue, *Leitr.* D Kilm *See* Drumlease.
KILLENVOY, *Rosc.* D Elph *See* Roscommon.
KILLERMOGH w Aughmacart, Durrow, and Attanagh, *Leix.* D Oss 6 I (Vacant).
KILLERY, *Sligo.* D Elph *See* Ballysumaghan.
KILLESHANDRA w Killegar, *Cav.* D Kilm 3 I (Vacant).
KILLESHER (St John), *Ferman.* D Kilm 3 I J R SIDES.
KILLESHERDONEY (St Mark), *Cav.* D Kilm *See* Drumgoon.
KILLESHILL, *Tyr.* D Arm *See* Errigal-Keerogue.
KILLESHIN w Cloydagh (St John), Killabban and Mayo, *Leix.* D Leigh I D W MCKENNA.
KILLESK (All SS), *Wexf.* D Ferns *See* Fethard.
KILLIMOR (H Trin), *Galw.* D Clonf *See* Lickmolassy.
KILLINAGH w Kiltyclogher, Dowra (St Thos) Inishmagrath and Killargue, *Cav.* D Kilm 2 I R S P RICHEY.
KILLINANE, *Galw.* D Kilmac *See* Kilmacduagh.
KILLINCHY w Kilmood and Tullynakill, *Down.* D Down 2 I R R W DEVENNEY.
KILLINEY, *Kerry.* D Ardf *See* Kilgobbin.
KILLINEY (St Matthias), *Dub.* D Dub 7 I V S DUNGAN.
(H Trin) D Dub 7 I E A CARRY.
KILLINICK, *Wexf.* D Ferns *See* Kilscoran.
KILLINKERE, *Cav.* D Kilm 1 I W D JOHNSTON.
KILLISKEY, *Wickl.* D Glendal 2 *See* Wicklow.
KILLODIERNAN, *Tip.* D Killaloe *See* Kilbarron.
KILLOE (St Cath), *Longf.* D Ard *See* Clonbroney.
KILLORAN, *Sligo.* D Achon *See* Emlaghfad.
KILLORGLIN w Glenbeigh, *Kerry.* D Ardf 3 *See* Kilcolman.
KILLOSCULLY, *Tip.* D Killaloe *See* Stradbally.
KILLOTTERAN (St Pet), *Waterf.* D Waterf *See* Clonegam.
KILLOUGH, *Down.* D Down 5 *See* Ballee.
KILLOUGHTER w Cloverhill (St John), *Cav.* D Kilm 3 I CANON J R WHEELOCK IN C OF CLOVERHILL.
KILLOWEN D Cork *See* Desertserges.
KILLOWEN (St Jo Evang), *Derry.* D Derry 9 I H H WOODHEAD.
KILLUCAN or RATHWIRE (St Etchen), Kinnegad (St Jo Bapt), Castlejordan and Clouard, *W Meath.* D Meath 2 I E J R TOBIAS.
KILLURIN, *Wexf.* D Ferns *See* Ardcolm.
KILLYBEGS (St Columb), *Doneg.* D Raph *See* Ardara.
KILLYGAVAN (St Columb), *Doneg.* D Raph 4 *See* Tullyaughnish.
KILLYLEA, *Arm.* D Arm 9 I J M BATCHELOR.
KILLYLEAGH, *Down.* D Down 6 I R E CONN.
KILLYMAN (St Andr), *Arm* and *Tyr.* D Arm 6 I D G W GRIFFITH.
KILLYMARD, *Doneg.* D Raph *See* Donegal.
KILMACABEA, *Cork.* D Ross *See* Ross.
KILMACDUAGH (St Colman's Cathl) w Gort (St Ann), Killinane, and Ardraham, *Galw.* D Kilmac 2 I E W TALBOT.
KILMACOW, *Wickl.* D Glendal *See* Castlemacadam.
KILMACOW, *Kilk.* D Waterf *See* Waterford.
KILMACRENAN, GARTAN, *Doneg.* D Raph *See* Tullyaughnish.
KILMACSHALGAN, *Sligo.* D Killala *See* Skreen.
KILMACTEIGUE, *Sligo.* D Achon *See* Tubbercurry.
KILMACTRANNY, *Sligo* and *Rosc.* D Elph *See* Taunagh.
KILMAHON, *Cork.* D Cloyne *See* Cloyne.
KILMAINE (H Trin), *Mayo.* D Tuam *See* Ballinrobe.
KILMAKEE (St Hilda), *Antr.* D Connor 4 I R S J H MCKELVEY.
KILMALLOCK (St Pet and St Paul) w Athlacca, Kilflynn, Kilfinane, Knockaney, Bruff and Caherconlish, *Lim.* D Lim 3 I B SNOW.
KILMALOODA (All SS), *Cork.* D Ross *See* Kilnagross.
KILMANAGH, *Kilk.* D Oss 3 *See* Fertagh.
KILMANAHEEN w Lahinch, *Clare.* D Kilfen 10 I (Vacant).
KILMASTULLA, *Tip.* D Killaloe *See* Killaloee.
KILMEADEN (St Mary) Carrick, *Waterf.* R D Waterf *See* Clonegam.
KILMEAGUE, *Kild.* D Kild *See* Kildare.
KILMEEN (Ch Ch), *Cork.* D Ross *See* Castleventry.
KILMEGAN, or DUNDRUM (St Donard), w Maghera, *Down.* D Drom 4 I J D CALDWELL.
KILMESSAN (St Mary), *Meath.* D Meath *See* Trim.
KILMICHAEL, *Cork.* D Cloyne *See* Macroom.
KILMINA, *Mayo.* D Tuam *See* Aughaval.
KILMOCOMOGUE, *Cork.* D Cork 4 I J C M CONNER.
KILMOE (St Brendan) w Teampol-na-mbocht (or Altar), *Cork.* D Cork 4 I L A ELLIOTT.
KILMOGANNY, *Kilk.* D Oss *See* Kells.
KILMOOD (St Mary), *Down.* D Down *See* Killingchy.
KILMORE (St Aid) w The Diamond, *Arm.* D Arm 7 I (Vacant).
KILMORE (St Aedhan), *Monagh.* D Clogh 8 *See* Monaghan.
KILMORE (Ch Ch), *Down.* R D Down 6 I A J PARKHILL *c*.
KILMORE, *Rosc.* D Elph 1 *See* Kiltoghart.
KILMORE, *Tip.* D Killaloe *See* Nenagh.
KILMORE (St Fethlimidh's Cathl w New Cathl Bp Bedell and Par Ch) and Ballintemple, *Cav.* D Kilm 2 I R C H TURKINGTON.
KILMORE ERRIS, *Mayo.* D Killala *See* Crossmolina.
KILMOREMOY (St Mich) (Ballina) w Castleconnor Straid and Kilconduff, *Mayo* and *Sligo.* D Killala 2 I C SPENCE, M F GRAHAM *c*.
KILMOYLEY (All SS), *Lim.* D Ardf *See* Tralee.
KILMUCKRIDGE, *Wexf.* D Ferns *See* Kilnamagh.
KILMURRY (St Andr), *Cork.* D Cork *See* Moviddy.
KILMURRY, *Clare.* D Killaloe *See* Kilrush.
KILNABOY (St Cath) w Kilkeedy, New Quay and Rathbourney, *Clare.* D Killaloe 2 I (Vacant).
KILNAGARENAGH, *Offaly.* D Meath *See* Clara.
KILNAGROSS w Kilmalooda, *Cork.* D Ross 1 *See* Kilgariffe.
KILNAHUE (St Jo Div) w Kilpipe, *Wexf.* D Ferns *See* Gorey.
KILNAMANAGH (St John) w Kilcormack, Ballyhuskard and Kilmuckridge, *Wexf.* D Ferns 6 I (Vacant).
KILNASOOLAGH w Quin and Kilfinaghty, *Clare.* D Killaloe 9 I (Vacant).
KILNAUGHTIN w Listowell, Killehenny, Kilfergus (St Paul), Brosna, Abbeyfeale, Duagh, Rattoo, and Ballylongford, *Kerry.* D Ardf 4 I (Vacant).
KILPATRICK, *Wexf.* D Ferns *See* Ardcolm.
KILPEACON w Croom, *Lim.* D Lim 2 *See* Adare.
KILPIPE, *Wickl* and *Wexf.* D Ferns *See* Crosspatrick.
KILREA (St Patr), *Derry.* D Derry 3 I J MAYES.
KILRONAN, *Lim.* D Lim *See* Newcastle, Limerick.
KILRONAN, *Waterf.* D Lism *See* Tullameelan.
KILRONAN (St Thos), *Rosc.* D Ard *See* Kiltoghart.
KILROOT (St Colman), *Antr.* R D Connor I I F R PATTERSON.
KILROSSANTY w Rossmire, Stradbally, and Monksland, *Waterf.* D Lism 3 I H H E PEACOCK, C B WARREN.
KILRUANE, *Tip.* D Killaloe *See* Nenagh.
KILRUSH, *Wexf.* D Ferns *See* Carnew.
KILRUSH w Kilmurry, *Clare.* D Killaloe 1 I (Vacant).
KILSALLAGHAN, *Dub.* D Dub *See* Swords.

KILSARAN (St Mary) w Dromiskin and Dunleer, *Louth.* **D** Arm 2 **I** W S DONALDSON.
KILSCORAN (St Pet) w Killinick, Rosslare, Carne and Mulrankin, *Wexf.* **D** Ferns 1 **I** T A H FOSTER.
KILSHANE, *Tip.* **D** Cash *See* Templeneiry.
KILSHANNIG, *Cork.* **D** Cloyne *See* Mallow.
KILSHINE, *Meath.* **D** Meath *See* Donaghpatrick.
KILSIELY w Clonlea, *Clare.* **D** Killaloe *See* Kilfenaghty.
KILSKEERY w Trillick, *Tyr.* **D** Clough 7 **I** T R MOORE.
KILSKYRE, *Meath.* **D** Meath 6 *See* Kells.
KILTALLAGH, *Kerry.* **D** Ardf *See* Kilcolman.
KILTEEVOGUE (St John), *Doneg.* **D** Raph *See* Stranorlar.
KILTEGAN (St Pet) w Hacketstown, Clonmore and Moyne, *Wickl.* **D** Leigh 2 **I** (Vacant).
KILTENNELL, *Wexf.* **D** Ferns *See* Ardamine.
KILTENNELL, *Carlow.* **D** Leigh *See* Fenagh.
KILTERNAN (St Tiernan), *Dub.* **D** Dub 10 **I** J B FISHER.
KILTINANLEA, *Clare.* **D** Killaloe *See* Stradbally.
KILTOGHART (St Geo) w Annaduff, West (St Ann), Toomna, Kilmore Drumshambo, Kilronan (St Thos) and Kilturbride, *Leitr* and *Rosc.* **D** Ard 5 **I** (Vacant).
KILTOOM, *Rosc.* **D** Elph *See* Athlone.
KILTORMER, *Galw.* **D** Clonf *See* Aughrim.
KILTUBRIDE, *Leitr.* **D** Ard *See* Kiltoghart.
KILTULLAGH, *Rosc.* **D** Tuam *See* Kilkeevin.
KILTURK (St John), *Wexf.* **D** Ferns *See* Mulranken.
KILTYCLOGHER, *Ferman.* **D** Kilm *See* Killinagh.
KILVEMNON, *Tip.* **D** Cash *See* Fethard.
KILWARLIN (St John), *Down.* **D** Down 3 **I** (Vacant).
KILWAUGHTER (St Patr) w Cairncastle, *Antr.* **D** Connor 7 **I** D D CALDWELL.
KILWORTH, *Cork.* **D** Cloyne *See* Fermoy.
KINAWLEY, *Ferman.* **D** Kilm 2 **I** C L B H MEISSNER.
KINGSTOWN (Dun Laoghaire) (Ch Ch), *Dub.* **D** Dub 6 **I** R C ARMSTRONG.
THE MARINERS' CH **D** Dub 6 **I** R C ARMSTRONG.
KINEAGH, *Kild.* **D** Glendal *See* Castledermot.
KINNEGAD (St Jo Bapt), *W Meath.* **D** Meath *See* Killucan.
KINNEIGH (Ch Ch w St Bart) w Ballymoney, *Cork.* **D** Cork 6 **I** D J P LLEWELLYN.
KINNITTY, *Offaly.* **D** Meath *See* Ballyboy.
KINSALE (St Multose) w Dunderrow, Rincurran, Templetrine, Ballymartle w Cullen and Ballinaboy, *Cork.* **D** Cork 5 **I** O A P PEARE.
KIRCONRIOLA, *Antr.* **D** Connor *See* Ballymena.
KIRKCUBBIN (H Trin), *Down.* **D** Down 1 **I** (Vacant).
KNAPPAGH (St Thos) w Louisburgh, *Mayo.* R **D** Tuam 1 **I** (Vacant).
KNOCKANEY, *Lim.* **D** Lim *See* Aney.
KNOCKBREDA, *Down.* **D** Down 4 **I** W R D MCCREERY.
KNOCKBRIDE w Shercock, *Cav.* **D** Kilm 1 **I** W E R GARRETT.
KNOCKGRIFFAN, *Tip.* **D** Cash *See* Cashel.
KNOCKNAGONEY (Ch of Annunc) **D** Down 4 **I** J R L BOWLEY *c.*
KNOCKNAMUCKLEY (St Matthias), *Arm* and *Down.* **D** Drom 6 **I** D WILSON.
KNOCKNAREA (St Ann), *Sligo.* **D** Elph *See* Sligo.
KNOCKTOPHER (St David), *Kilk.* **D** Oss *See* Inistioge.

LACK, or COLAGHTY, *Tyr* and *Ferman.* **D** Clogh 6 **I** R J JOHNSTON.
LACKAGH, *Kild.* **D** Kild *See* Kildare.
LACKAN, *Mayo.* **D** Killala *See* Killala.
LAGHEY, *Doneg.* **D** Raph 1 *See* Drumholm.
LAHINCH, *Clare.* **D** Kilfen *See* Kilmanaheen.
LAMBEG, *Antr.* **D** Connor 9 **I** R H LOWRY.
LANGFIELD, LOWER w Upper, *Tyr.* **D** Derry 5 **I** (Vacant).
LARA, *Cav.* **D** Kilm *See* Lavey.
LARACOR (St Pet), *Meath.* **D** Meath *See* Trim.
LARAGH, *Wickl.* **D** Glendal *See* Derralossary.
LARNE (All SS) w Inver (St Cedma), *Antr.* **D** Connor 7 **I** J A FAIR, M A MCCULLAGH *c.*
LAVALLY, *Galw.* **D** Tuam *See* Tuam.
LAVEY w Lara, *Cav.* **D** Kilm 1 **I** J G B ROYCROFT.
LAWRENCETOWN, *Galw.* **D** Clonf *See* Clonfert.
LAYDE w Cushendun, *Antr.* **D** Connor 6 **I** (Vacant).
LEA, *Leix.* **D** Kild 5 *See* Portarlington.
LEARMOUNT, *Derry* and *Tyr.* **D** Derry *See* Cumber, Upper.
LECK, *Doneg.* **D** Raph *See* Conwall.
LECKPATRICK (St Patr) w Dunnalong (St John), *Tyr.* **D** Derry 7 **I** A E TILSON.
LEIGHLIN (St Lazerain Cathl) w Shankill, Grange Sylvae, Wells, Graigue (St Pet w St Mullins) and Clonagoose, *Carlow.* **D** Leigh 4 **I** F R BOLTON.
LEIGHMONEY, *Cork.* **D** Cork *See* Innishannon.
LEIXLIP (Sancta Maria de Hernie) w Lucan (St Andr), *Dub.* **D** Glendal 4 **I** E H DESPARD.
LENEY and Almoritia (St Nich) w Stonehall, *W Meath.* **D** Meath 8 *See* Kilbixy.
LESKINFERE w Ballycanew (St Edan or St Mogue) and Monamolin (St Molig), *Wexf.* **D** Ferns 2 **I** G N DICKSON.
LETTERKENNY, *Doneg.* **D** Raph *See* Conwall.
LETTERMACAWARD, *Doneg.* **D** Raph *See* Inniskeel.
LICKMOLASSY (Ch Ch) w Tynagh, Ballynakill and Killimor, *Galw.* **D** Clonf 2 *See* Clonfert.
LIMAVADY, *Derry.* **D** Derry *See* Drumachose.
LIMERICK (St Mary Cathl and Par Ch w St Patr), *Lim.* **D** Lim 5 **I** VERY REV G W CHAMBERS.
(St Mich) **D** Lim 5 **I** VERY REV G W CHAMBERS.
LISBELLAW, *Ferman.* **D** Clogh 5 **I** R J ST LEDGER, R J ST LEDGER.
LISBURN, or BLARIS (Ch Ch Cathl and Par Ch), *Antr* and *Down.* **D** Connor 9 **I** VERY REV W N BARR, W M ADAIR *c*, W W RUSSELL *c.*
(Ch Ch) **D** Connor 9 **I** E G GRAHAM *c*, J W STEWART *c.*
(St Paul) **D** Connor 9 **I** K W COCHRANE, W J DAWSON *c*, W G IRWIN *c.*
(St Matt Broomhedge) **D** Connor 9 **I** W J F MOORE.
LISDOONVARNA, *Clare.* **D** Kilfen *See* Kilfenora.
LISLEE, *Cork.* **D** Ross *See* Timoleague.
LISLIMNAGHAN (H Trin), *Tyr.* **D** Derry 5 **I** (Vacant).
LISMALIN, *Tip.* **D** Cash *See* Fethard.
LISMORE (St Carthagh Cathl and Par Ch) w Mocollop Cappoquin (St Ann), Villierstown and Whitechurch, *Waterf.* **D** Lism 5 **I** MAYES.
LISNADIL, *Arm.* **D** Arm 9 **I** M C KENNEDY.
LISNASKEA (H Trin), *Ferman.* **D** Clogh 4 **I** R S JACKSON.
LISSADELL, *Sligo.* **D** Elph *See* Drumcliffe.
LISSAN, *Derry* and *Tyr.* **D** Arm 8 **I** T A B SAWYERS.
LISTOWEL (St John), *Kerry.* **D** Ardf *See* Kilnaughtin.
LITTLETON, *Tip.* **D** Cash *See* Kilcooley.
LOCKEEN, *Tip.* **D** Killaloe *See* Shinrone.
LONDONDERRY, *Derry.* **D** Derry *See* Derry.
LORRHA w Terryglass, *Tip.* **D** Killaloe 7 **I** J CAMIER.
LORUM, *Carlow.* **D** Leith *See* Dunleckney.
LOUGHAN, *Cav.* **D** Kilm *See* Lurgan.
LOUGHCREW (St Kieran) w Killeagh, *Meath.* **D** Meath *See* Oldcastle.
LOUGH ESKE (Ch Ch), *Doneg.* **D** Raph *See* Donegal.
LOUGHGALL (St Luke), *Arm.* **D** Arm 7 **I** C S LOWRY.
LOUGHGILLY (St Patr) w Clare, *Arm.* **D** Arm 4 **I** J L WILSON.
LOUGHGLYNN, *Sligo.* **D** Elph *See* Kilkeevin.
LOUGHGUILE (All SS), *Antr.* **D** Connor *See* Armoy.
LOUGHILL, *Lim.* **D** Lim *See* Askeaton.
LOUGHINISLAND (St John), *Down.* **D** Down 6 **I** W B DRUMMOND *c-in-c.*
LOUGHMOE (St Mich), *Tip.* **D** Cash *See* Thurles.
LOUGHREA (St Brandon) w Killinane, *Galw.* **D** Clonf *See* Kilmacduagh.
LOUGH RYNN, *Leitr.* **D** Ard *See* Cloone.
LOUISBURGH, *Mayo.* **D** Tuam *See* Knappagh.
LOUTH, *Louth.* **D** Arm *See* Heynestown.
LOWER FALLS, *Antr.* **D** Connor *See* Belfast (St Luke).
LUCAN (St Andr), *Dub.* **D** Glendal *See* Leixlip.
LUGGACURREN, *Leix.* **D** Leigh *See* Stradbally.
LURGAN, *Arm.* **D** Drom *See* Shankill.
LURGAN w Munterconnaught and Loughan, *Cav.* **D** Kilm 3 **I** W D JOHNSTON.
LUSK (St MacCullen), *Dub.* **D** Dub *See* Donabate.
LYNALLY (St Bart), *Leix.* **D** Meath *See* Tullamore.

MACREDDIN, *Wickl.* **D** Glendal *See* Ballinaclash.
MACROOM (St Colman of Cloyne) w Inchigeelagh, Kilmichael, Ballyvourney, and Magourney, *Cork.* **D** Cloyne 6 **I** (Vacant).
MAGHERA (St Lourochias) W Killelagh and Termoneeny, *Derry.* **D** Derry 4 **I** I H MCDONALD, J W C TRAILL *c.*
MAGHERA, *Down.* **D** Drom *See* Kilmegan.
MAGHERACLOONE (St Molua), *Monagh.* **D** Clogh *See* Carrickmacross.
MAGHERACROSS, *Ferman.* **D** Clogh 7 **I** J A M MCNUTT.
MAGHERACULMONEY (St Mary) w Drumkeeran, Muckross and Templecarne, *Ferman.* **D** Clogh 6 **I** F A BAILLIE I OF MAGHERACULMONEY, J MCCLOUGHLIN R OF DRUMKEERAN, MUCKROSS AND TEMPLECARNE.
MAGHERADROLL (Ballynahinch), *Down.* **D** Drom 2 **I** C W M COOPER.
MAGHERAFELT (St Swithin), *Derry.* **D** Arm 8 **I** MCGONIGLE.

MAGHERAGALL, *Antr.* D Connor 9 I J R MUSGRAVE.
MAGHERAHAMLET or MAGHERAHAMILTON, *Down.* D Drom 2 I (Vacant).
MAGHERALIN or MARALIN (H and Undiv Trin), *Down.* D Drom 6 I R L HUTCHINSON, R ADAMS *c.*
MAGHERALLY (St Jo Evang) and Annaclone, *Down.* D Drom 1 I W T MCKEE.
MAGHEROSS, *Louth.* D Clogh *See* Carrickmacross.
MAGOURNEY, *Cork.* D Cloyne *See* Macroom.
MAGUIRESBRIDGE (Ch Ch) w Derrybrusk ('Derryharney Church'), *Ferman.* D Clogh 5 I J A DAY.
MALAHIDE (St Andr) w Portmarnock (St Marnock) and St Doulagh's, *Dub.* D Dub 9 I W G P COOPER.
MALARNNY, *Mayo.* D Tuam *See* Achill.
MALLOW (St Jas) w Mourne Abbey, Rahan Kilshannig (St Seanach), Castlemagner, Kilbrin, Ballyclough, Clonmeen, Kanturk and Dromtariffe, *Cork.* D Cloyne 4 I N M CUMMINS.
MALLUSK, *Antr.* D Connor I J S MARTIN.
MALONE, *Antr.* D Connor *See* Belfast (St John).
MANORHAMILTON w Killasnett (H Trin), Ballaghameehan Drumlease and Killenumery (St Mich), *Leitr.* D Kilm 2 I P J KNOWLES.
MARALIN, *Down.* D Drom *See* Magheralin.
MARKET HILL, *Arm.* D Arm *See* Mullabrack.
MARMULLANE (no Dedic), *Cork.* D Cork 2 *See* Carrigaline.
MARYBOROUGH (St Pet) w Dysart Enos *Leix.* D Leigh 6 I R G KINGSTON.
MAYNE, *W Meath.* D Meath *See* Rathgraffe.
MAYNOOTH (St Mary), *Kild.* D Meath *See* Dunboyne.
MAYO, *Leix.* D Leigh *See* Killeshin.
MEENGLASS (St Ann), *Doneg.* D Raph *See* Stranorlar.
MEVAGH (H Trin) w Milford (St Columbkille) and Glenalla (St Columbkille), *Doneg.* D Raph 3 I (Vacant).
MIDDLETOWN (St John), *Arm.* D Arm *See* Tynan.
MIDLETON (St Jo Bapt), *Cork.* D Cloyne 2 I J K S R BARKER.
MILFORD (St Columbkille), *Doneg.* D Raph 4 *See* Mevagh.
MILLISLE, *Down.* D Down *See* Carrowdore.
MILLTOWN (St Andr), *Arm.* D Arm 7 I W R TWADDELL.
MILLTOWN, *Dub.* D Dub *See* Dublin (St Philip).
MOCOLLOP, *Waterf.* D Lism *See* Lismore.
MODREENY, *Tip.* D Killaloe *See* Cloughjordan.
MOGORBAN, *Tip.* D Cash *See* Cashel.
MOHILL (St Mary) w Cloone (St Jas) Laigh Rymm (Chap) and Annaduff E, *Leitr.* D Ard 4 I J A KNOWLES.
MOIRA (St John), *Arm.* D Drom 6 I C R J RUDD.
MONAGHAN w Tydavnet (St Daunet) and Kilmore, *Monagh.* D Clogh 8 I B LIVINGSTON.
MONAMOLIN (St Molig), *Wexf.* D Ferns *See* Leskinfere.
MONART (St Pet) w Templescobin and Ballycarney, *Wexf.* D Ferns 7 I S E A ROWE.
MONASTEREVAN (St Jo Evang) w Nurney, *Kild.* D Kild 4 I T G HUDSON.
MONASTERORIS (Edenderry) and Ballyburley, *Offaly.* D Kild 1 I C W FINNEY.
MONELLAN, *Doneg.* D Derry *See* Convoy.
MONIVEA, *Galw.* D Tuam *See* Athenry.
MONKSLAND, *Waterf.* D Lism *See* Kilrosanty.
MONKSTOWN (St Jo Div), *Cork.* D Cork 1 I (Vacant).
MONKSTOWN (St Mary), *Dub.* D Dub 6 I K DALTON.
(St John), *Dub.* D Dub 6 I A C KENNEDY.
MONSEA, *Tip.* D Killaloe *See* Nenagh.
MORRISTOWNBILLER, St Patrick, *Kild.* D Kild *See* Great Connell.
MOSSLEY (H Spirit), *Antrim.* D Connor 3 I H HOPKINS.
MOSTRIM, *Longf.* D Ard *See* Granard.
MOTHEL, *Waterf.* D Lism *See* Clonegam.
MOTHEL w Bilbo and Gowran (St Mary), *Waterf.* D Oss 4 I (Vacant).
MOUNTCHARLES, *Doneg.* D Raph *See* Inver.
MOUNTFIELD, *Tyr.* D Derry *See* Drumragh.
MOUNTMELLICK w Coolbanagher (St Jo Evang), Clonaslee, and Rosenallis, *Leix.* D Kild 5 I P M DAY.
MOUNT MERRION (Ch of Pentecost), *Antr.* D Down 3 I W B NEILL.
MOUNT NUGENT, *Meath.* D Meath *See* Oldcastle.
MOUNTRATH, *Leix.* D Leigh *See* Clonenagh.
MOUNT TALBOT, *Rosc.* D Elph *See* Roscommon.
MOUNT TEMPLE, *W Meath.* D Meath *See* Kilcleagh.
MOURNE ABBEY, *Cork.* D Cloyne *See* Mallow.
MOVIDDY w Kilmurry, Kilbonane and Templemartin, *Cork.* D Cork 7 I J D HUTCHINSON.
MOVILLE (St Columb), Moville Upper (St Finian), Greencastle (St Finian) w Chap of Ease (St Columb), *Doneg.* D Derry 1 I A E T HARPER.
MOY (St Jas) w Charlemont, *Tyr.* and *Arm.* D Arm 6 I C W M ROLSTON.
MOYBOLOGUE, *Cav.* D Meath *See* Enniskeen.
MOYCULLEN, *Galw.* D Tuam *See* Galway.
MOYDOW, *Longf.* D Ard *See* Ardagh.
MOYDRUM, *W Meath.* D Meath *See* Athlone.
MOYGLARE, *Meath.* D Meath *See* Dunboyne.
MOYLISCAR, *W Meath.* D Meath 9 *See* Mullingar.
MOYLOUGH (H Trin), *Galw.* D Tuam *See* Tuam.
MOYNALTY, *meath.* D Meath 6 *See* Kells.
MOYNTAGHS (or Ardmore), *Arn.* D Drom *See* Ardmore.
MOYRUS (Roundstone) w Ballynahinch, *Galw.* D Tuam *See* Omey.
MUCKAMORE (St Jude), *Antr.* D Connor 1 I E W HASSEN.
MUCKNOE (St Maeldoid) w Broomfield and Clontibret, *Monagh.* D Clogh 2 I V MCMULLAN.
MUCKROSS, *Kerry.* D Ardf *See* Killarney.
MUCKROSS (St John) w Templecarne, *Ferman.* D Clogh 6 *See* Magheraculmoney.
MUFF, *Doneg.* D Derry 8 *See* Culmore.
MULHUDDART (St Thos), *Dub.* D Dub *See* Castleknock.
MULLABRACK w Markethill and Kilchuney, *Arm.* D Arm 7 I C WEST.
MULLAGH, *Cav.* D Kilm *See* Baileborough.
MULLAGHDUN, *Ferman.* D Clogh 5 I R J RIDDEL.
MULLAGHFAD, *Tyr.* D Clogh *See* Cooneen.
MULLAGLASS (St Luke), *Arm.* D Arm 4 *See* Camlough.
MULLAVILLY, *Arm.* D Arm 7 I F W GOWING.
MULLINACUFF, *Wickl.* D Leigh *See* Aghold.
MULLINGAR (All SS) w Portnashangan (St Mary), Moyliscar (St Nich), Enniscoffey, and Castlelost, *W Meath.* D Meath 9 I I W MACDOUGALL.
MULRANKIN (St D) w Tomhaggard or Kilturk (St Jo Bapt) and Rathmacknee (St John), *Wexf.* D Ferns 1 *See* Kilscoran.
MUNTERCONNAUGHT, *Cav.* D Kilm *See* Lurgan.
MURRAGH, *Cork.* D Cork 6 *See* Desertserges.
MYROSS, *Cork.* D Ross 2 *See* Ross.
MYSHALL, *Carlow.* D Leigh *See* Fenagh.

NAAS (St D) w Killashee, Kill (St Jo Evang) and Rathmore, *Kild.* D Kild 6 I J C W BERESFORD.
NANTENAN, *Lim.* D Lim *See* Rathkeale.
NARRAGHMORE (Ch of H Sav) w Fontstown and Timolin, *Kild.* D Glendal 5 I A M JACKSON.
NAUL, *Dub.* D Dub *See* Clonmethan.
NAVAN (St Mary) w Kentstown (St Mary), Skryne (St Columba), and Tara (St Patr), *Meath.* D Meath 11 I J A G BARRETT.
NENAGH (St Mary) w Kilmore, Monsea and Youghalarra, *Tip.* D Killaloe 7 I E W STANLEY.
NEWBLISS, *Monagh.* D Clogh *See* Currin.
NEWCASTLE (St John), *Down.* D Drom 4 I F N WARREN.
NEWCASTLE w Newtownmountkennedy, *Wickl.* D Glendal 1 I T R JENNINGS.
NEWCASTLE LYONS, *Dub.* D Dub *See* Rathcoole.
NEWCHAPEL, *Tip.* D Lism *See* Killaloan.
NEWMARKET, *Cork.* D Cloyne *See* Clonfert.
NEWPORT (St Jo Evang), *Tip.* D Killalloe *See* Stradbally.
NEW QUAY, *Clare.* D Kilfen *See* Kilnaboy.
NEW ROSS (St Mary and St Cath) w Rosbercon, Old Ross, and Whitechurch, *Wexf.* D Ferns 7 I C H LLOYD.
NEWRY (St Mary), *Down.* D Drom 5 I T G D ANDREWS.
(St Patr) D Drom 5 I M R WILSON.
NEWTOWN, *Cav.* D Meath *See* Moynalty.
NEWTOWNARDS (St Mark), *Down.* D Down 2 I R J CHISHOLM.
NEWTOWNCROMMELIN, *Antr.* D Connor *See* Skerry.
NEWTOWN CUNNINGHAM, *Doneg.* D Raph *See* All Saints.
NEWTOWN FERTULLAGH (Ch Ch) w Kilbeggan, Durrow, Clonfadforan (St Sinan), and Castletown, *W Meath.* D Meath 1 I (Vacant).
NEWTOWNGORE, *Leitr.* D Kilm *See* Kildallon.
NEWTOWNHAMILTON w Ballymoyer (St Luke) and Balleek, *Arm.* D Arm 4 I C F MOORE.
NEWTOWNMOUNTKENNEDY, Chap (St Matt), *Wickl.* D Glendal 1 *See* Newcastle.
NEWTOWNPARK (All SS), *Dub.* D Dub *See* Blackrock (All SS).
NEWTOWNSAVILLE, *Tyr.* D Clogh *See* Augher.
NOBBER, *Meath.* D Meath *See* Enniskeen.
NOHOVAL w Tracton, *Cork.* D Cork 5 *See* Templebrady.
NURNEY, *Kild.* D Kild *See* Monasterevan.
NURNEY (St John), *Carlow.* D Leigh *See* Dunleckney.

O'BRIEN'S BRIDGE, *Clare.* **D** Killaloe *See* Stradbally.
ODAGH, *Kilk.* **D** Oss *See* Aghour.
OFFERLANE (Coolrain) w Skirk and Borris-in-Ossory w Aghavoe and Seir Kyran, *Leix.* **D** Oss 5 **I** H H J GRAY.
O'GONNILLOE, *Clare.* **D** Killaloe *See* Killaloe.
OLDCASTLE (St Bride) w Mount Nugent, Killeagh and Loughcrew, *Meath.* **D** Meath 5 *See* Castlepollard.
OLD ROSS, *Wexf.* **D** Ferns *See* New Ross.
OMAGH, *Tyr.* **D** Derry *See* Drumragh.
OMEATH, *Louth.* **D** Arm *See* Carlingford.
OMEY or CLIFDEN (Ch Ch) w Errismore, Errislannan, Ballyconree, Moyrus, Ballinakill and Ballynahinch, *Galw.* **D** Tuam 4 **I** J P LEWIS, D E TINNE *c.*
ORAN, *Rosc.* **D** Elph *See* Kilkeevan.
ORANGEFIELD, *Down.* **D** Down *See* Belfast.
OUGHTERAGH w Fenagh and Drumreilly, *Leitr.* **D** Ard 4 **I** (Vacant).
OUTRAGH, *Tip.* **D** Lism 1 *See* Cahir.

PARSONSTOWN, *Offaly.* **D** Killaloe *See* Birr.
PAYNESTOWN (St Mary) w Stackallan, *Meath.* **D** Meath *See* Drogheda.
PETTIGO, *Doneg.* **D** Clogh *See* Templecarne.
PHIBSBOROUGH, *Dub.* **D** Dub *See* Dublin, All Saints.
PHILIPSTOWN, *Offaly.* **D** Kild *See* Ballycommon.
POMEROY, *Tyr.* **D** Arm *See* Altedesert.
PORTADOWN (St Mark), *Arm.* **D** Arm 7 **I** J C COMBE.
(St Sav) **D** Arm 7 **I** F K LIVINGSTONE.
(St Columba) **D** Arm 7 **I** H CASSIDY.
PORTAFERRY, *Down.* **D** Down *See* Ballyphilip.
PORTARLINGTON (St Mich 'English Ch' w St Paul 'French Ch'), Ballykean, Cloneyhurke, *Leix* and *Offaly.* **D** Kild 5 **I** E C J WOODS.
PORTGLENONE, *Antr.* **D** Connor 2 *See* Ahoghill.
PORTMARNOCK, *Dub.* **D** Dub *See* Malahide.
PORTNASHANGAN, *W Meath.* **D** Meath *See* Mullingar.
PORTRUSH, *Antr.* **D** Connor *See* Ballywillan.
PORTSALON (All SS), *Doneg.* **D** Raph *See* Clondevaddock.
PORTSTEWART, *Derry.* **D** Connor *See* Agherton.
POULATHOMAS, *Mayo.* **D** Killala *See* Crossmolina.
POWERSCOURT (St Patr) w Kilbride, Bray, *Wickl.* **D** Glendal 1 **I** A E STOKES.
PREBAN (St John), *Wickl.* **D** Ferns 3 *See* Crosspatrick.

QUEENSTOWN, *Cork.* **D** Cloyne *See* Clonmel.
QUIN (St Finghin), *Clare.* **D** Killaloe *See* Kilnasoolagh.
QUIVVY, *Cav.* **D** Kilm *See* Belturbet.

RADDANSTOWN, *Meath.* **D** Meath *See* Dunboyne.
RAHAN, *Offaly.* **D** Meath *See* Tullamore.
RAHAN, *Cork.* **D** Cloyne *See* Mallow.
RAHENY (All SS) w Coolock (St Jo Evang), *Dub.* **D** Dub 9 **I** C M WILSON, K A KEARON *c.*
RALOO, *Antr.* **D** Connor *See* Glynne.
RAMOAN (St Jas) w Ballycastle, *Antr.* **D** Connor 6 **I** W A DUNCAN.
RANDALSTOWN, *Antr.* **D** Connor *See* Drummaul.
RAPHOE (St Eunan) w Raymochy, *Doneg.* **D** Raph 5 **I** S W REEDE.
RASHARKIN (St Andr) w Finvoy, *Antr.* **D** Connor 8 **I** S J BLACK.
RATHANGAN, *Kild.* **D** Kild *See* Clonsast.
RATHASPECK, *Wexf.* **D** Ferns *See* Wexford.
RATHASPECK (St Thos) w Russagh and Streete, *W Meath.* **D** Ard 3 **I** R HENDERSON.
RATHBARRY, *Cork.* **D** Ross *See* Ross.
RATHBOURNEY, *Clare.* **D** Kilfen *See* Kilnaboy.
RATHCAVAN, *Antr.* **D** Connor *See* Skerry.
RATHCLAREN, *Cork.* **D** Cork *See* Ballymodan.
RATHCLINE, *Longf.* **D** Ard *See* Kilcommick.
RATHCONNEL, *W Meath.* **D** Meath **I** (Vacant).
RATHCOOLE (St Comgall), *Antr.* **D** Connor 3 **I** G B MOLLER.
RATHCOOLE w Newcastle Lyons, *Dub.* **D** Dub *See* Clondalkin.
RATHCOONEY (St Lappan) w Carrigtwohill (St D), *Cork.* **D** Cork 1 **I** W E M K ALLANDER.
RATHCORE (St Mich) w Agher, *Meath.* **D** Meath 13 **I** (Vacant).
RATHCORMAC w Ardnageehy, Knockmourne and Aghern, *Cork.* **D** Cloyne 3 **I** G C PAMMENT.
RATHDOWNEY w Donaghmore, Castlefleming, and Rathsaran, *Leix.* **D** Oss 5 **I** J G MURRAY.
RATHDRONAN, *Lim.* **D** Lim *See* Newcastle, Lim.
RATHDRUM (Silvae Salvatoris) w Glenealy and Derralossary w Annamoe and Laragh (St John), *Wickl.* **D** Glendal 3 **I** A H V FRAZER.
RATHFARNHAM, *Dub.* **D** Dub 8 **I** A WILSON, M A J WILSON *c.*
RATHFRILAND (St John), *Down.* **D** Drom *See* Drumgath.
RATHGAR, *Dub.* **D** Dub 8 *See* Dublin, Zion Church.
RATHGRAFFE w Mayne, Foyran and Collinstown, *W Meath.* **D** Meath 5 **I** (Vacant).
RATHKEALE (H Trin) w Nantenan, Ballingarry and Rathronan, *Lim.* **D** Lim 4 **I** (Vacant).
RATHLIN (St Thos), *Antr.* **D** Connor 6 **I** (Vacant).
RATHMACKNEE, *Wexf.* **D** Ferns 1 *See* Mulrankin.
RATHMICHAEL, *Dub.* **D** Dub 7 **I** W J MARSHALL.
RATHMINES, *Dub.* **D** Dub 1 *See* Dublin, Rathmines.
RATHMOLYON w Laracor and Castlerickard, *Meath.* **D** Meath 13 **I** E D SLATOR *c.*
RATHMORE, *Kild.* **D** Kild 6 *See* Naas.
RATHMULLAN, *Down.* **D** Down 5 *See* Tyrella.
RATHRAE, *Mayo.* **D** Killala 2 *See* Killala.
RATHRONAN, *Lim.* **D** Lim *See* Rathkeale.
RATHRONAN, *Tip.* **D** Lism 2 *See* Killaloan.
RATHSARAN, *Leix.* **D** Oss 5 *See* Rathdowney.
RATHVILLY (Dedic unknown) *Carlow.* **D** Leigh *See* Baltinglass.
RATHWIRE, *W Meath.* **D** Meath 2 *See* Killucan.
RATOATH, *Meath.* **D** Meath 10 *See* Dunshauglin.
RATOO, *Kerry.* **D** Ardf 4 *See* Kilmaughtin.
RAYMOCHY, *Doneg.* **D** Raph 5 *See* Raphoe.
RAYMUNTERDONEY w Tullaghobegly, *Doneg.* **D** Raph 3 *See* Dunfanaghy.
REDCROSS, *Wickl.* **D** Glendal 2 *See* Dunganstown.
RICHHILL (St Matt), *Arm.* **D** Arm 7 **I** R W R COLTHURST.
RINCURRAN (St Cath), *Cork.* **D** Cork 3 *See* Kinsale.
RINGAGONAGH, *Waterf.* **D** Lism 3 *See* Dungarvan.
RINGRONE (St Jas), *Cork.* **D** Cork 3 *See* Rathclaren.
ROCKCORRY, *Monagh.* **D** Clogh 1 *See* Ematris.
ROOSKA, *Cork* **D** Cork 4 *See* Durrus.
ROSBERCON, *Wexf.* **D** Ferns 7 *See* New Ross.
ROSCOMMON w Dunamon, Castleblakeney, Athleague, Mount Talbot and Killenvoy, *Rosc.* **D** Elph 1 **I** D W GRAHAM.
ROSCREA (St Cronan), *Offaly* and *Tip.* **D** Killaloe 3 **I** J A A CONDELL.
ROSENALLIS (St Jas), *Leix.* **D** Kild 3 *See* Clonaslee.
ROSKELTON, *Galw.* **D** Leigh 6 *See* Clonenagh.
ROSS (All SS), *Galw.* **D** Tuam 3 *See* Cong.
ROSS, NEW, *Wexf.* **D** Ferns 7 *See* New Ross.
ROSS, OLD, *Wexf.* **D** Ferns 7 *See* New Ros.
ROSS (St Faughnan's Cathl and Par Ch) w Rathbury, Kilfanghnabeg, Kilmacabea, Mycross and Castleventry, *Cork.* **D** Ross 1 *See* Cathedral List.
ROSSDROIT, *Wexf.* **D** Ferns 7 *See* Killegny.
ROSSES, THE, *Sligo.* **D** Elph *See* Sligo.
ROSSINVER, *Leitr* and *Sligo.* **D** Kilm 2 *See* Finner.
ROSSLARE, *Wexf.* **D** Ferns 1 *See* Kilscoran.
ROSSMIRE, *Waterf.* **D** Lism 3 *See* Kilrosanty.
ROSSNOWLAGH, *Doneg.* **D** Raph 1 *See* Kilbarron.
ROSSORY (St Fancea), *Ferman.* **D** Clogh 5 **I** C T PRINGLE.
ROSTREVOR, *Down.* **D** Drom 3 *See* Kilbroney.
ROUNDSTONE, *Galw.* **D** Tuam 5 *See* Moyrus.
ROWER, THE, *Kilk.* **D** Oss 2 *See* Inistiogue.
RUSHBROOKE, *Cork.* **D** Cloyne 2 *See* Clonmel.
RUSSAGH, *W Meath.* **D** Ard 3 *See* Rathaspeck.
RYNAGH (St Paul) or Banagher w Gallen, Clonmacnoise (St Keiran), Templeconnor and Kinnitty, *Offaly.* **D** Meath 3 **I** R H BOYLE.

ST ANDREW'S (St Andr), *Cav.* **D** Kilm 3 *See* Belturbet.
ST COLUMBA'S COLL CHAP RATHFARNHAM, *Dub.* **D** Dub 8 **I** (Vacant).
ST DOULAGH'S, *Dub.* **D** Dub 9 *See* Malahide.
ST MICHAEL, BLACKROCK w St Nich and H Trin, *Cork.* **D** Cork 2 **I** M H G MAYES.
SAINTFIELD or TONAGHNIEVE, *Down.* **D** Down 2 **I** N W WOODROW.
SALLAGHY, *Ferman.* **D** Clogh 8 **I** J A O B ROGERS.
SANDFORD, *Dub.* **D** Dub 1 *See* Dublin.
SANDYMOUNT, *Dub.* **D** Dub 3 *See* Dublin, St Jo Evang.
SANTRY (St Pappan) w Glasnevin (St Mobhi), and Cloghran, *Dub.* **D** Dub 9 **I** R D HARMAN.
SAUL (St Patr) w Inch, *Down.* **D** Down 6 **I** J A DONNELLY.
SCARVA (St Matt), *Down* and *Arm.* **D** Drom 1 **I** (Vacant).
SCHULL or SKULL (H Trin), *Cork.* **D** Cork 4 **I** G E M G C B BANNISTER.

SEAGOE (St Gobham), *Arm.* **D** Drom 6 **I** J SHEARER, T KEIGHTLEY *c.*
SEAPATRICK (H Trin) w St Patr Chap of Ease, *Down.* **D** Drom 1 **I** N R HAMILTON, R JONES *c.*
SEIR-KYRAN (St Kieran), *Offaly.* **D** Oss 5 *See* Offerlane.
SHANAGOLDEN, *Lim.* **D** Lim 1 *See* Askeaton.
SHANKILL, LURGAN (Ch Ch), *Arm.* **D** Drom 6 **I** R J N LOCKHART, S G BOURKE *c*, R C NEILL *c.*
(St Jo Evang), *Lurgan.* **D** Drom 6 **I** D COE.
SHANKILL (St Matt), Antr **D** Connor 3 *See* Belfast.
SHANKILL (St John), *Kilk.* **D** Leigh 4 *See* Leighlin.
SHERCOCK (Dedic unknown), *Cav.* **D** Kilm 1 *See* Knockbride.
SHILLELAGH, *Wickl.* **D** Leigh 3 *See* Tullow.
SHINRONE w Ettagh and Lockeen, *Offaly.* **D** Killaloe 4 **I** C B CHAMP.
SHRULE, *Longf.* **D** Ard *See* Ardagh.
SIDDAN, *Louth.* **D** Meath 12 *See* Drumconrath.
SION MILLS, *Doneg.* **D** Derry 8 *See* Urney.
SIXMILECROSS w Termonmaguirke, *Tyr.* **D** Arm 1 **I** T MURPHY.
SKERRY w Rathcavan (St Patr) and Newtowncrommelin, *Antr.* **D** Connor 2 **I** T V STONEY.
SKIBBEREEN, *Cork.* **D** Ross 2 *See* Creagh, Co Cork.
SKIRK, *Leix.* **D** Oss 5 *See* Offerlane.
SKREBE, *Galw.* **D** Tuam 2 *See* Kilcummin.
SKREEN w Dromard and Kilmacshalgan, *Sligo.* **D** Killala 3 **I** C V PASLEY.
SKRYNE, *Meath.* **D** Meath *See* Navan.
SLANE (St Patr) w Paynestown and Stackallan, *Meath.* **D** Meath 4 *See* Drogheda.
SLAVIN, *Ferman.* **D** Clogh *See* Garrison.
SLIGO (Cathl Ch of St Mary Virg and St Jo Bapt) w Knocknarea and the Rosses, *Sligo.* **D** Elph 2 **I** C C W BROWNE.
SLINGAN, *Mayo.* **D** Tuam *See* Aughaval.
STABANNON, *Louth.* **D** Arm *See* Charlestown.
STACKALLAN, *Meath.* **D** Meath *See* Drogheda.
STAPLESTOWN, *Carlow.* **D** Leigh *See* Carlow.
STILLORGAN (St Brigid), *Dub.* **D** Dub 8 **I** M B TAYLOR, R J E F B BLACK *c.*
STONEHALL, *W Meath.* **D** Meath *See* Leney.
STONEYFORD (St Jo Evang), *Antr.* **D** Connor 9 *See* Ballymacash.
STRABANE, *Tyr.* **D** Derry *See* Camus-juxta-Mourne.
STRADBALLY (Ch Ch) w O'Brien's Bridge, Newport (St Jo Evang) Abington, Killoscully, and Kiltinanlea, *Lim.* **D** Killaloe 5 **I** VERY REV F. R. BOURKE.
STRADBALLY (St Patr) w Ballintubbert (St Brigid), Coraclone (St Pet), Timogue (St Mogue) and Luggacurren (Ch of the Resurr), *Leix.* **D** Leigh 7 **I** S P SEMPLE.
STRADBALLY, *Waterf.* **D** Lism *See* Kilrosanty.
STRAFFAN, *Kild.* **D** Glendal *See* Celbridge.
STRAID or TEMPLEMORE w Kilconduff and Killedan, *Mayo.* **D** Achon *See* Kilmoremoy.
STRAND, N, *Dub.* **D** Dub *See* Drumcondra.
STRANORLAR (St Anne) w Meenglass and Kilteevogue, *Doneg.* **D** Raph 5 **I** H GILMORE.
STRATFORD-ON-SLANEY (St John), *Wickl.* R **D** Leigh *See* Baltinglass.
STREETE, *W Meath.* **D** Ard *See* Rathaspeck.
SWANLINBAR w Templeport, *Cav.* **D** Kilm 2 **I** J R T WATSON *c.*
SWORDS (St Columba) w Kilsallaghan (St D) and Clonmethan (St Mary), *Dub.* **D** Dub 11 **I** W J MOYNAN.

TAGHMON (St Munnu), *Wexf.* R **D** Ferns *See* Horetown.
TALLAGHT (St Maelruain) *Dub.* **D** Dub **I** W S LAING.
TALLOW w KILWATERMOY, (St Cath), *Waterf.* **D** Lism 5 **I** MAYES.
TAMLAGHT, *Derry* and *Tyr.* **D** Arm *See* Ballinderry.
TAMLAGHTARD (St Gedanus) w Aghanloo, *Derry.* **D** Derry 9 **I** J BRYANS.
TAMLAGHT FINLAGAN (St Finglaanus), *Derry.* **D** Derry 2 **I** R D MOORE.
TAMLAGHT O'CRILLY, LOWER (St McNossonus) and Upper, *Derry.* **D** Derry 3 **I** J MILLER.
TANDRAGEE, *Arm.* **D** Arm *See* Ballymore.
TANEY (Dundrum) (Ch Ch) (St Thos), *Dub.* **D** Dub 8 **I** W J M BURROWS, E C T PERDUE *c.*
TARA, *Meath.* **D** Meath *See* Navan.
TARTARAGHAN (St Paul), *Arm.* **D** Arm 7 **I** W E C FLEMING.
TASHINNY, *Longf.* **D** Ard 5 *See* Ardagh.
TATTYKEERAN, *Ferman.* **D** Clogh *See* Aghalurcher.
TAUGHBOYNE w Craigadooish and Killea, *Doneg.* **D** Raph 5 **I** A MOORE.
TAUGHMACONNELL, *Galw.* **D** Clonf *See* Creagh.
TAUNAGH w Kilmactranny, Ballysumaghan and Killery, *Sligo.* **D** Elph 2 **I** R A ROBINSON.
TEAMPOL-NA-MBOCHT (or Altar), *Cork.* **D** Cork *See* Kilmoe.
TEMPLEBREEDY (H Trin) w Tracton and Nohoval, *Cork.* **D** Cork 2 **I** D S G GODFREY.
TEMPLECARNE or PETTIGO (no Dedic), *Doneg.* **D** Clogh 6 *See* Muckross.
TEMPLECONOR, *Offaly.* **D** Meath *See* Rynagh.
TEMPLECORRAN (St John), *Antr.* **D** Connor 6 *See* Glynn.
TEMPLECRONE, *Doneg.* **D** Raph *See* Gweedore.
TEMPLEDERRY, *Tip.* **D** Killaloe *See* Ballinaclough.
TEMPLEHARRY w Borrisnafarney, *Tip.* and *Offaly.* **D** Killaloe 4 **I** (Vacant).
TEMPLEMARTIN, *Cork.* **D** Cork *See* Moviddy.
TEMPLEMICHAEL (St John) w Clongish and Clooncumba and Killashee (St Paul) w Ballymacormac, *Longf.* **D** Ard 3 **I** T J BOND.
TEMPLEMICHAEL, *Cork.* **D** Cork *See* Innishannon.
TEMPLEMICHAEL, *Waterf.* **D** Lism *See* Ardmore.
TEMPLEMORE, *Mayo.* **D** Achon *See* Straid.
TEMPLEMORE, *Derry.* **D** Derry *See* Derry.
TEMPLEMORE (St Mary) w Kilfithmone, Thurles (St Mary) and Loughmoe, *Tip.* **D** Cash 4 **I** F S G H JOHNSTONE.
TEMPLENEIRY, *Tip.* **D** Cash 5 *See* Tipperary.
TEMPLENOE, *Kerry.* **D** Ardf *See* Kenmare.
TEMPLEPATRICK (St Patr) w Donegore, *Antr.* **D** Connor 1 **I** J MOORE.
TEMPLEPORT, *Cav.* **D** Kilm *See* Swanlinbar.
TEMPLESCOBIN (St Busk), *Wexf.* **D** Ferns *See* Monart.
TEMPLESHAMBO, *Wexf.* **D** Ferns *See* Killanne.
TEMPLETOWN, *Wexf.* **D** Ferns *See* Fethard.
TEMPLETRINE, *Cork.* **D** Cork *See* Kinsale.
TEMPLEUDIGAN, *Wexf.* **D** Ferns *See* Killaune.
TEMPO, *Ferman.* **D** Clogh 7 **I** J A MCMASTER.
TERMONAMONGAN (St Bestius), *Tyr.* **D** Derry 6 *See* Derg.
TERMONBARRY, *Rosc.* **D** Ard *See* Kilmore, Rosc..
TERMONEENY (St Conlus), *Derry.* **D** Derry *See* Maghera.
TERMONFECKIN w Beaulieu (St Brigid), *Louth.* **D** Arm 3 *See* Drogheda.
TERMONMAGUIRKE (St Columbkill), *Tyr.* **D** Arm 1 *See* Sixmilecross.
TERRYGLASS, *Tip.* **D** Killaloe *See* Lorrha.
THOMASTOWN, *Kild.* **D** Kild *See* Clonsast.
THOMASTOWN, *Kilk.* **D** Oss 3 **I** (Vacant).
THURLES (St Mary) w Loughmoe, *Tip.* **D** Cash *See* Templemore.
TIBOHINE, *Rosc.* **D** Elph *See* Kilkeevan.
TICKMACREVAN or GLENARM (St Patr), *Antr.* **D** Connor *See* Ardclinis.
TIMAHOE, *Kild.* **D** Kild *See* Carogh.
TIMOGUE, *Leix.* **D** Leigh 7 *See* Stradbally.
TIMOLEAGUE (The Ascen) w Lislee, Courtmacsherry, Abbeymahon and Kilgariffe, *Cork.* **D** Ross 1 **I** F R SKUSE.
TIMOLIN, *Kild.* **D** Glendal *See* Narraghmore.
TINTERN, *Wexf.* **D** Ferns *See* Fethard.
TIPPERARY (St Mary Virg) w Templeneiry, Clonbeg and Doon, *Tip.* **D** Cash 5 **I** (Vacant).
TOMBE (St Cath), *Wexf.* **D** Ferns *See* Ferns.
TOMGRANEY (SS Colman and Cronan), *Clare.* **D** Killaloe *See* Killaloe.
TOMHAGGARD or KILTURK, *Wexf.* **D** Ferns *See* Mulrankin.
TOMREGAN w Drumlane, *Cav.* **D** Kilm 3 **I** (Vacant).
TONAGHNIEVE, *Down.* **D** Down *See* Saintfield.
TOOMNA, *Rosc.* **D** Elph *See* Kiltoghart.
TOUGH (or Cappamore), *Lim.* **D** Cash *See* Abington.
TRACTON, *Cork.* **D** Cork *See* Nohoval.
TRALEE (St Jo Evang) w Ardfert, Kilmoyley (All SS) and Ballyheigue, *Kerry.* **D** Ardf 1 **I** R W P DOHERTY.
TRILLICK, *Tyr.* **D** Clogh *See* Kilskerry.
TRIM (St Patr) w Bective, Kilmessan, Galtrim and Laracor, *Meath.* **D** Meath 13 **I** VERY REV T A N BREDIN.
TRINITY CHURCH, *Ferman.* **D** Kilm 3 **I** C L B H MEISSNER.
TRORY (St Mich) w Killadeas, *Ferman.* **D** Clogh 5 **I** O G PIERCE.
TUAM (St Mary Cathl and Par Ch) w Lavally, Moylough, Headford and Kilconla, *Galw.* **D** Tuam 5 **I** VERY REV W J GRANT.
TUBBERCURRY (St Geo) w Kilmactigue, *Sligo.* **D** Achon *See* Achonry.
TUBRID (St John), *Tip.* **D** Lism *See* Cahir.

TULLAGH (Baltimore) (St Matt), *Cork*. **D** Ross *See* Abbeystrewry.
TULLAGHOBEGLY, *Doneg*. **D** Raph *See* Dunfanaghy.
TULLAMEELAN, *Tip*. **D** Lism *See* Clonmel.
TULLAMORE (or Kilbride) (St Cath) and Tyrrellspass w Lynally (St Bart) and Rahan, *Offaly*. **D** Meath 1 **I** A T WATERSTONE.
TULLANISKIN (H Trin) w Clonoe (St Mich), *Tyr*. **D** Arm 6 **I** W FENTON.
TULLOW (St Columba) w Shillelagh, Aghold (St Mich) and Mullinacuff *Carlow*. **D** Leigh 3 **I** N YOUNG.
TULLOW, Carrickmines w Clonoe, *Dub*. **D** Dub 7 **I** C G HYLAND.
TULLYALLEN, *Louth* and *Meath*. **D** Arm *See* Collon.
TULLYAUGHNISH (St Paul) w Kilmacrenan and Killygavan, *Doneg*. **D** Raph 4 **I** W B A SMEATON.
TULLYCORBET, *Monagh*. **D** Clogh *See* Ballybay.
TULLYLISH (All SS), *Down*. **D** Down 1 **I** (Vacant).
TULLYNAKILL, *Down*. **D** Down *See* Killinchy.
TURLOUGH, *Mayo*. **D** Tuam *See* Castlebar.
TYDAVNET (St Daunet), *Monagh*. **D** Clogh *See* Monaghan.
TYHOLLAND (St Cillin), *Monagh*. **D** Clogh *See* Donagh.
TYNAGH, *Galw*. **D** Clonf *See* Lichmolassy.
TYNAN (St Vindic) w Middletown (St John), *Arm*. **D** Arm 7 **I** T R B TAYLOR.
TYRELLA (St John) w Rathmullan, *Down*. **D** Down 5 **I** C H QUINN.

UPPER FALLS, *Antr*. **D** Connor *See* Belfast, Upper Falls.
URGLIN, *Carlow*. **D** Leigh 3 *See* Carlow.
URNEY (Cavan) w Annagalliffe, Denn, and Derryheen, *Cav*. **D** Kilm 2 **I** G C A MILLER.
URNEY (Ch Ch) w Sion Mills (Ch of Good Shepherd), *Tyr* and *Doneg*. **D** Derry 7 **I** G J A CARSON.

VALENTIA w Cahir (St Jo Bapt), *Kerry*. **D** Ardf 3 *See* Dromod.
VASTINA (or Castletown), *Offaly*. **D** Meath *See* Clonfadforan.
VENTRY (no Dedic) w Kildrum, *Kerry*. **D** Ardf *See* Dingle.
VILLIERSTOWN, *Waterf*. **D** Lism *See* Cappoquin.

WARINGSTOWN, *Down*. **D** Drom *See* Donaghcloney.
WARRENPOINT, *Down*. **D** Drom *See* Clonallan.
WATERFORD (Blessed Trin Cathl and Par Ch) w St Olaf, Ballinakill and Kilmacow, *Waterf*. **D** Waterf 4 **I** (Vacant).
WELLS, *Carl*. and *Kilk*. **D** Leigh *See* Leighlin.
WESTPORT, *Mayo*. **D** Tuam *See* Aughaval.
WEXFORD (St Iberius w St Selskare) and Rathaspeck (Union of sixteen other parishes), *Wexf*. **D** Ferns 8 **I** E F GRANT.
WHITECHURCH, *Wexf*. **D** Ferns *See* New Ross.
WHITECHURCH w Cruagh, *Dub*. **D** Dub 8 **I** A H N MCKINLEY.
WHITECHURCH, *Waterf*. **D** Lism *See* Cappoquin.
WHITEHEAD (St Patr) and Islandmagee (St John), *Antr*. **D** Connor 7 **I** K E RUDDOCK.
WHITEHOUSE (St Jo Div), *Antr*. **D** Connor 3 **I** E J H SHEPHERD.
WHITEROCK (St Columba), *Antr*. **D** Connor 4 **I** R S CUNNINGHAM, D P HOEY *c*.
WICKLOW w Killiskey, *Wickl*. **D** Glendal 2 **I** S PETTIGREW.
WILLOWFIELD, *Down*. **D** Down 3 **I** D B HUTCHINSON, B J COURTNEY *c*, S D HAMILTON *c*, J SCOTT *c*.
WILSON'S HOSP, *W Meath*. **D** Meath 3 **I** J E MCKEON *warden*.
WOODSCHAPEL (St John), *Derry*. **D** Arm 8 **I** T S COULSON.
WOODLAWN, *Galw*. **D** Clonf *See* Aughrim.

YOUGHAL (St Mary) and Killeagh w Castlemartyr and Ballycotton, *Cork*. **D** Cloyne 2 **I** SIR H M D M ST G DURAND.
YOUGHALARRA, *Tip*. **D** Killaloe *See* Nenagh.

ABERDEEN CITY LIBRARIES

Oxford University Press

The English Hymnal

Musical Editor: Dr. Ralph Vaughan Williams

'I have used the English Hymnal for more than 30 years and have found that it meets almost all the needs of choirs and congregations in Cathedrals, Parish Churches and schools. The book makes generous provision for all seasons of the Church's year and for special occasions. There are relatively few omissions. The distinguished musical editorship of Ralph Vaughan Williams has led to the inclusion in the book of a number of his own fine tunes including Down Ampney and Sine Nomine, and the harmonizations and arrangements of the tunes are invariably in good taste. Now nearly 80 years old, the book has stood the test of time and is likely to be of service to the Church for many years to come.' Sir David Willcocks.

For details of the Full Music, Melody, and various Words editions, and of the grants available for introductions, please write to the English Hymnal Grants Department, Oxford University Press, Walton Street, Oxford OX2 6DP.

The English Hymnal Service Book

The English Hymnal Service Book was produced in 1962 to help churches where congregational singing and participation in the liturgy are especially fostered. It contains over 290 widely used hymns drawn from the *English Hymnal* (with the E.H. Number also given) and a supplement of further hymns and carols, 37 in number, together with the Canticles and Psalter simply pointed, the Versicles and Responses at Mattins and Evensong set for familiar chants, Marbeeke's setting of the Holy Communion and the words of those parts of the Offices and Communion Service which are said by all.
A separate Full Music edition provides for the needs of choir and clergy. Grants are available for its Introduction as in the case of the *English Hymnal.*

English Praise

A Supplement to *The English Hymnal*

This collection of just over a hundred items includes some comparatively recent hymns, some which have already proved their worth elsewhere, a number of new works, written for *English Praise,* carols for various seasons, and a small section of responsorial psalms. The tunes are at a pitch to suit unison congregational singing. The arrangement follows the pattern of *English Hymnal,* but concludes with three more general sections: Praise and Thanksgiving, Christian Unity, and Social Justice. Generous grant terms will be available to schools and churches on introductory orders.

Oxford University Press

World Christian Encyclopedia

A Comparative Survey of Churches and Religions in the Modern World, AD 1900–2000

Edited by David B. Barrett

This major new reference work is the first survey ever to deal comprehensively with the subject of contemporary Christianity in all its many versions across the modern world, set against both secular and religious backgrounds. It describes systematically the present extent, status, and characteristics of the Christian religion, and covers all the main ecclesiastical traditions and the manifold activities of organized Christianity throughout the world. It gives detailed information on all the various denominations, as well as dioceses, jurisdictions, missions, assemblies, and fellowships. The material is given in an inter-denominational or ecumenical presentation, set in the context of all other faiths and beliefs, including the so-called 'New Religions', as well as atheism, agnosticism, and the secular quasi-religions. 1024 pp, 1500 illustrations, 34 colour maps £65

Christians in Ulster 1968–1980

Eric Gallagher and Stanley Worrall

This book describes and assesses the part played by the Churches in Northern Ireland's recent troubles. After a brief historical introduction it gives a chronological narrative of the events of the last twelve years. There are also chapters devoted to special subjects such as education, the peace movement, and ecumenism. The book ends with a chapter assessing the story and prospects for the future. £10

The Holy Land

An Archaeological Guide from Earliest Times to 1700

Jerome Murphy-O'Connor, OP

'The book will prove to be an indispensable companion for all future visitors to the Holy Land. It provides a brief but excellent guide to almost all the archaeological sites of that country that the visitor is likely to be able to see.' *Church Times.* Illustrated £8.50
Oxford Paperbacks £3.95

The Oxford Dictionary of Saints

D. H. Farmer

'The author of this deceptively slim work manages to achieve the almost impossible. He has tackled the subject with objectivity and thoroughness. . . . He breathes life into his scholarship and has produced a dictionary which makes compulsive reading.' *The Tablet.*
£8.50